AWARDS, HONORS & PRIZES

Highlights

Volume 2 of *Awards, Honors & Prizes (AHP)* is the single most comprehensive source of information on awards offered by organizations in more than 100 countries outside the United States and Canada. These awards recognize achievement in virtually all areas of human endeavor, including:

- Advertising
- Agriculture
- Architecture
- Arts and Humanities
- Business and Finance
- Communications
- Computers
- Conservation
- Education
- Engineering
- Environment
- Fashion
- Films
- Journalism
- Law
- Librarianship
- Literature
- Management
- Medicine
- Music
- Performing Arts
- Photography
- Public Affairs
- Publishing
- Radio and Television
- Religion
- Safety
- Science
- Social Science
- Sports
- Technology
- Transportation
- Women

Volume 2 provides contact information for more than 3,500 organizations worldwide and details on the nature and purpose of the nearly 9,000 awards they bestow. (For information on awards given by organizations in the United States and Canada, consult Volume 1 of *AHP*. For listings of the winners of many of the world's most prominent awards described in both volumes of *AHP*, consult *World of Winners*, also published by Gale Research Inc.)

Features in This Edition

AHP continues to track trends in award giving, which in turn reflect the current values and priorities of society. Volume 2 features listings for some 700 awards new to this edition in such fields as art, literature, education, and science, and covering such contemporary issues as the environment, medical technology, freedom, and international relations.

Starting with this edition, the organization and award indexes list all the entries in both volumes of *AHP*, making it possible for the user to locate the Pulitzer Prizes in Volume 1 and the Nobel Prizes in Volume 2 in a single look-up, for example.

Many Uses for *AHP*

Awards, Honors & Prizes can be used:

- by organizations, associations, and individuals to locate information on awards in a particular field of interest or that are mentioned in the media;
- by organizations and individuals to determine their eligibility for particular awards;
- by organizations to provide guidance in establishing a new award or expanding an existing program; and
- by employers in evaluating the significance of the awards listed on a job applicant's resume.

Available in Other Formats

Diskette and magnetic tape versions of *AHP*, as well as customized mailing labels, are available from Gale Research Inc.

AWARDS, HONORS & PRIZES

An International Directory of Awards and Their Donors Recognizing Achievement in Advertising, Architecture, Arts and Humanities, Business and Finance, Communications, Computers, Consumer Affairs, Ecology, Education, Engineering, Fashion, Films, Journalism, Law, Librarianship, Literature, Medicine, Music, Performing Arts, Photography, Public Affairs, Publishing, Radio and Television, Religion, Science, Social Science, Sports, Technology, and Transportation

VOLUME 2
INTERNATIONAL AND FOREIGN

**11th EDITION
1995-96**

DEBRA M. KIRBY,
EDITOR

 Gale Research Inc. • DETROIT • WASHINGTON, D.C. • LONDON

Debra M. Kirby, *Editor*

Deborah J. Morad, *Assistant Editor*

Ned Burels, Catherine C. DiMercurio, Wendy H. Mason,
Diane M. Sawinski, and Sara Tal Waldorf, *Contributing Associate Editors*

Dawn R. Barry and Scot R. Ferman, *Contributing Assistant Editors*

Linda S. Hubbard, *Senior Editor*

Victoria B. Cariappa, *Research Manager*
Gary J. Oudersluys, *Research Supervisor*
Tracie A. Wade, *Editorial Associate*
Melissa E. Brown, Andreia L. Earley, Charles A. Jewell, Michele L. McRobert,
Michele P. Pica, Amy T. Roy, and Phyllis N. Shepherd, *Editorial Assistants*

Mary Beth Trimper, *Production Director*
Evi Seoud, *Assistant Production Manager*
Catherine Kemp, *Production Assistant*

Cynthia Baldwin, *Art Director*
Mark Howell, *Cover Designer*
C.J. Jonik, *Desktop Publisher*

Benita L. Spight, *Manager Data Entry Services*
Gwendolyn S. Tucker, *Data Entry Supervisor*
Beverly Jendrowski, *Sr. Data Entry Associate*
Edgar C. Jackson, *Data Entry Associate*

Theresa A. Rocklin, *Manager of Systems and Programming*
Ida M. Wright, *Programmer Analyst*

While every effort has been made to ensure the reliability of the information presented in this publication, Gale Research, Inc. does not guarantee the accuracy of the data contained herein. Gale accepts no payment for listing; and inclusion in the publication of any organization, agency, institution, publication, service, or individual does not imply endorsement of the editors or publisher.

Errors brought to the attention of the publisher and verified to the satisfaction of the publisher will be corrected in future editions.

∞™ The paper used in this publication meets the minimum requirements of American National Standard for Information Sciences--Permanence Paper for Printed Library Materials, ANSI Z39.48-1984.

♻ This book is printed on recycled paper that meets Environmental Protection Agency standards.

This publication is a creative work fully protected by all applicable copyright laws, as well as by misappropriation, trade secret, unfair competition, and other applicable laws. The authors and editors of this work have added value to the underlying factual material herein through one or more of the following: unique and original selection, coordination, expression, arrangement, and classification of the information.

All rights to this publication will be vigorously defended.

Copyright © 1994
Gale Research Inc.
835 Penobscot Bldg.
Detroit, MI 48226-4094

Library of Congress Catalog Number 85-070620
ISBN 0-8103-7906-6 (2 volume set)
ISBN 0-8103-7908-2 (volume 2)

Printed in the United States of America

Published simultaneously in the United Kingdom
by Gale Research International Limited
(An affiliated company of Gale Research Inc.)

The trademark **ITP** is used under license.

Contents

Volume 2

International and Foreign

(United States and Canadian awards are covered in Volume 1)

Highlights ii
Preface vii
Introduction ix
User's Guide xi
Awards, Honors & Prizes: Descriptive Listings

Albania	1	France	284
Angola	1	Gabon	376
Argentina	1	Germany	376
Armenia	6	Ghana	415
Australia	6	Greece	416
Austria	44	Grenada	419
Bahamas	57	Guadeloupe	419
Bahrain	57	Guatemala	420
Bangladesh	57	Guyana	420
Barbados	58	Haiti	421
Belgium	58	Honduras	421
Bolivia	84	Hong Kong	421
Bosnia-Hercegovina	84	Hungary	423
Brazil	85	Iceland	433
Bulgaria	90	India	433
Burkina Faso	93	Indonesia	449
Cameroon, United Republic of	93	Iran	449
Chile	93	Iraq	450
China, People's Republic of	95	Ireland	450
Colombia	95	Ireland, Northern	457
Costa Rica	106	Israel	457
Cote d'Ivoire	108	Italy	465
Croatia	108	Jamaica	494
Cuba	109	Japan	494
Czech Republic	110	Jordan	515
Denmark	115	Kenya	515
Dominican Republic	122	Korea, Republic of	516
Ecuador	122	Kuwait	517
Egypt	122	Liberia	518
El Salvador	122	Libyan Arab Jamahiriya	518
England	123	Liechtenstein	518
Finland	278	Lithuania	518

Luxembourg	518	Scotland	613
Macedonia	519	Senegal	623
Madagascar	519	Serbia	623
Malaysia	520	Singapore	625
Mali	521	Slovakia	627
Malta	521	Slovenia	629
Mexico	522	South Africa, Republic of	631
Monaco	543	Spain	649
Morocco	544	Sri Lanka	666
Namibia	544	Sweden	668
Netherlands	545	Switzerland	679
New Caledonia	566	Taiwan	702
New Zealand	566	Tanzania, United Republic of	703
Nigeria	576	Thailand	703
Norway	576	Trinidad and Tobago	704
Pakistan	582	Tunisia	705
Paraguay	584	Turkey	705
Peru	584	Uganda	708
Philippines	585	Uruguay	708
Poland	588	Vatican City	708
Portugal	597	Venezuela	709
Romania	604	Wales	712
Russia	608	Zambia	715
Saudi Arabia	612	Zimbabwe	715

Subject Index of Awards ... 717
Organization Index ... 799
Award Index ... 889

Preface

The greatest of humankind's efforts have long provided occasion for recognition and celebration. From the ancient Greek Olympics to the new Lemelson-MIT Prize for Invention and Innovation, societies worldwide continue to acknowledge extraordinary accomplishment in all fields of human endeavor.

This edition of *Awards, Honor & Prizes*, with its coverage of 1,300 new U.S. and Canadian and 900 international and foreign awards, offers evidence of our desire to honor individuals and groups who foster intellectual growth, set records, stimulate creativity, demonstrate courage, and inspire and encourage humanitarian efforts and international understanding. Following is a representative sampling of newly established awards designed to confer such recognition.

Freedom and Human Rights. The PEN/Newman's Own First Amendment Awards, established by actor Paul Newman and literary biographer A.E. Hotchner, honors those who have fought courageously, despite adversity, to safeguard the First Amendment right to freedom of expression as it applies to the written word. This award carries a $25,000 monetary prize and presentation of a limited-edition work of art.

The NOW Legal Defense and Education Fund has established the Muriel Fox Award for Communications Leadership Toward a Just Society (The Foxy) to recognize leaders in the business or fashion world who advance women's equality in the corporate community.

Science and Technology. The Lemelson-MIT Prize for Invention and Innovation seeks to raise the status and visibility of American inventors and innovators. The annual award carries a $500,000 award for U.S. citizens who have shown excellence in creativity, invention, and/or innovation in the fields of medicine and health care, energy and environment, telecommunications and computing, consumer products, and durable goods and industrial products.

Excellence in the field of aerospace engineering is rewarded by a gold medal and $100,000 by the American Institute of Aeronautics and Astronautics' Walter J. and Angeline H. Crichlow Trust Prize.

The Academie Royale de Belgique recognizes the best work in zoology by researchers from Belgian or Zairian universities with an award of 100,000 Belgian francs.

Important work in applied or industrial physics is honored by the Institut de France, which each year presents the Prix Mesucora, worth 100,000 French francs.

The Prize for Research and Studies of the Repercussions of the Iraqi Invasion of Kuwait, established by the Kuwait Foundation for the Advancement of Sciences, recognizes distinguished accomplishment in the arts, humanities, and sciences.

Education. The Camille and Henry Dreyfus Foundation bestows awards of $60,000 to young faculty members who demonstrate exceptional promise and talent in the research and teaching of the chemical sciences.

The Thomas J. Brennan Award, given by the Astronomical Society of the Pacific, recognizes high school astronomy teachers for excellence in teaching.

Students in the ninth and tenth grades are given monetary awards for excellence in analytical thinking and writing through the Anthem Essay Contest, which is sponsored by the Ayn Rand Institute.

International Relations. A monetary prize of 5,000,000 Japanese yen is awarded annually by the Victor Company of Japan to the person, company, or group that best demonstrates the importance of international contribution and cooperation.

The John D. and Catherine T. MacArthur Foundation awards grants of $10,000 to $15,000 to support intellectual and scientific efforts for research and policy analysis in the countries of the former Soviet Union to scholars, journalists, policy analysts and other citizens residing in the territory of the former Soviet Union.

Individuals or institutions who have used international law to promote peace in Europe and improve cooperation with eastern and southeastern European countries are presented with the Immanuel Kant Prize of 100,000 German marks by Stiftung F.V.S.

The Edouard Saouma Award includes a monetary prize of $25,000 for the regional institution that has managed a particularly efficient project funded by the Food and Agriculture Organization of the United Nations.

Journalism. Great Britain's *Financial Times* established an award in Memory of *Financial Times* photographer Alan Harper, who was killed in Kuwait with fellow journalist David Thomas. The award is given for excellence in journalistic photography and carries a £5,000 grant to support a photographic assignment of the recipient's choice.

The Goldsmith Prize in Investigative Journalism honors journalists whose investigative reporting best promotes more effective and ethical conduct of government, public policy making, or political practice. A monetary award of $25,000 is presented annually.

Reporting and writing that enlightens the general public on the rights of disabled people is recognized by the *Detroit Free Press* through its James Neubacher Award. The $1,000 award was established to honor the memory of James Neubacher, who wrote a regular column dealing with the concerns of the physically handicapped.

The National Lesbian and Gay Journalists Association presents the annual Crossroads Market/NLGJA Prize for excellence in print journalism on issues concerning the gay and lesbian community.

Arts and Entertainment. The Vercorin Manuscript Writing Award recognizes outstanding film treatments and encourages original ideas for the cinema. Prizes include monetary awards of up to 20,000 Swiss francs, equipment, and distribution to European producers.

The Truman Capote Awards for Literary Criticism honor lifetime achievement and the best book of general literary criticism. The lifetime achievement award, administered by Stanford University, is bestowed every four years and carries a $100,000 cash prize. The best book prize of $50,000 is awarded annually by the University of Iowa, Iowa Writer's Workshop.

The Australia Council for the Arts awarded its first Red Ochre Award this year to honor artists who have made a great contribution to the recognition of aboriginal and Torres Strait Island art and culture in the wider community at both the national and international levels. This award, which includes a cash prize of $50,000, was established to mark the International Year for the World's Indigenous People.

Choreographers who have created a substantial body of work are presented with the $20,000 Jean A. Chalmers Award for Distinction in Choreography by the Ontario Arts Council.

In Israel, the Rita Poretsky Prize in Photography is given to honor exceptional talent, determination, ability, and creative expression in the field of photography.

Sports. The ESPY Awards, established by ESPN Inc., honor excellence in 32 categories of sports performance. ESPN also awards the Arthur Ashe Award for Courage.

The United States Olympic Committee recently established the Robert J. Kane Award to recognize athletes who have distinguished themselves in Olympic Festival competition by exemplifying the spirit and ideals of the Olympic movement.

Introduction

News reports, by their very nature, frequently convey information that is less than welcome to world audiences. War, civil unrest, political upheaval, crime, health and environmental concerns, and other issues and events claim a majority of media attention. Perhaps that is why news of awards and their recipients, often featured prominently in local and global print and broadcast media reporting, comes as a welcome change.

Humankind has long celebrated achievement of all kinds and in every field, from art and literature to science and technology. Individuals of all ages and from all walks of life are recognized when they transcend the bounds of the ordinary to provide encouragement and inspiration by establishing new records, exploring new frontiers, demonstrating extraordinary courage, challenging the intellect, establishing new standards of excellence, creating something beautiful, or improving the quality of everyday life.

Awards, Honors & Prizes (AHP), now in its 11th edition, continues to provide perspective on the variety, scale, significance, and number of awards given throughout the world. Volume 2 of *AHP* is the single major source of descriptive information on awards bestowed in all subject areas by organizations, foundations, corporations, universities, and government bodies in more than 100 countries outside the United States and Canada. Volume 1 covers U.S. and Canadian awards.

New in this Edition

Volume 2 describes 9,000 awards and their 3,500 donors and features listings for 700 awards new to this edition, including:

- Annual Prize of the Society of Czech Architects
- Committee on Space Research Zeldovich Medals
- Financial Times Alan Harper Bursary
- Immanuel Kant Prize
- Inaugural Red Ochre Award
- Queen's Awards for Environmental Achievement
- Rita Poretsky Prize in Photography
- The Vercorin Manuscript Writing Award

Content and Arrangement

Volume 2 of *Awards, Honors & Prizes* comprises descriptive listings for awards and their administering organizations, and three indexes.

Descriptive Listings are arranged alphabetically, within country, by administering organization; entries for the awards administered by each organization are listed alphabetically (by their English names) following organization entries.

The **Subject Index of Awards** classifies awards by their principal areas of interest.

The **Organization Index** provides an alphabetical listing of all organizations appearing in both volumes that administer or sponsor awards, including former and foreign names.

The **Award Index** provides an alphabetical listing of all award names, including alternate, former, and popular names listed in both volumes.

Preparation of This Edition

The 11th edition of *Awards, Honors & Prizes* represents the complete revision and updating of the previous edition. Information was obtained via survey mailings and follow-up correspondence and telephone calls. Information on awards not previously covered in *AHP* was obtained from questionnaires sent to administering organizations.

Volume 1 Covers U.S. and Canadian Awards

Information on awards given by organizations in the United States and Canada is available in Volume 1 of *AHP*. It provides descriptive information on approximately 16,000 awards given by some 5,000 organizations, foundations, universities, corporations, and government bodies located in the United States and Canada.

Companion Volume Identifies Award Recipients

World of Winners, also published by Gale Research Inc., provides a historical perspective on a wide range of awards and their winners. It lists more than 100,000 winners of some 2,500 of the world's major awards that are described in both volumes of *AHP*.

AHP Information Offered in Other Formats

Awards, Honors & Prizes is also available for licensing on magnetic tape or diskette in a fielded format. Either the complete database or a custom selection of entries may be ordered. The data base is available for internal data processing and non-publishing purposes only. For more information, phone 800-877-GALE.

Acknowledgments

The editors are grateful to the large number of individuals in organizations throughout the world who generously responded to our requests for updated information. Without their cooperation, this book would not be possible. Additionally, we would like to thank the members of our advisory board, Boyd Childress, Reference Librarian, Auburn University Library; George M.A. Cumming, Jr., Science Reference Librarian, Boston Public Library; Rev. Jovian P. Lang, Professor of Library Science, University of North Texas; and Rebecca Morrison, Head Reference Librarian, Kemp Public Library, for their valuable advice on the scope and content of this edition as well as enhancements to the organization and award indexes.

Suggestions Welcome

We welcome reader suggestions regarding new and previously unlisted organizations and awards. Please send comments or suggestions to:

Editor
Awards, Honors & Prizes
835 Penobscot Bldg.
Detroit, MI 48226-4094

Phone: (313) 961-2242
Toll-free: 800-347-GALE
Fax: (313) 961-6815

Debra M. Kirby

User's Guide

This volume is comprised of the following sections:

- Descriptive listings for awards and their administering organizations
- Subject Index of Awards
- Organization Index
- Award Index

Descriptive Listings

The descriptive listings are arranged alphabetically by administering organization; entries on the awards administered by each organization follow that organization's listings.

The organization and award entries shown below illustrate the kind of information that is or might be included in these entries. Each item of information is preceded by a number and is explained in the paragraph of the same number following the sample entries.

Sample Entries

---

(1) ⬜ 11852
(2) **Canadian Parks/Recreation Association**
(3) **(Association Canadienne des Loisirs/Parcs)**
(4) 333 River Rd.
Vanier City, ON, Canada K1L 8H9
(5) Phone: (613)748-5651
(6) Toll-free: 800-748-5600
(7) Fax: (613)748-5652

(8) Formerly: (1980) Canadian Parks Association

(9) ⬜ 11853
(10) **Award of Merit**
(11) **(Prix de Merite)**
(12) To give national recognition for meritorious achievements at the municipal, regional, or provincial levels that have made significant and distinct contributions to the furtherance of some aspect of local parks/recreation. Canadian individuals or organizations are eligible. The deadline for applications is February 15. (13) A wood plaque is (14) awarded annually. (15) Established in 1965. (16) Sponsored by the Canadian Park Service. (17) (Discontinued in 1985) (18) Formerly: (1982) Canadian Park Service Award.

---

(1) **Organization Entry Number:** Entries for administering organizations are listed alphabetically, each followed by an alphabetical listing of its awards. All entries - organization and award - are numbered in a single sequence. These numbers are used as references in the indexes. Organization entry numbers are preceded by a horizontal rule across the column.

xi

② **Organization Name:** The name of the organization administering the awards that follow.

③ **Organization Name in Alternate Language(s):** The name of the organization is given in up to two additional languages, when provided by the organization.

④ **Mailing Address:** The organization's permanent mailing address for information on awards.

⑤ **Telephone Number:** The telephone number(s) for the administering organization.

⑥ **Toll-free Number:** The toll-free telephone number for the administering organization.

⑦ **Fax Number:** The facsimile number for the administering organization.

⑧ **Former Name of Organization:** The former name of the organization is provided if the name has changed, the organization merged, or the organization absorbed another organization. The year the name change occurred is also provided, when available.

⑨ **Award Entry Number:** Entries on awards are listed alphabetically following the entry for their administering organization. All entries -- organization and award -- are numbered in a single sequence. These numbers are used as references in the indexes.

⑩ **Award Name:** Name of the award, honor, or prize is listed in English whenever possible.

⑪ **Award Name in Alternate Language(s):** The award name is provided in up to two additional languages, when provided by the organization.

⑫ **Purpose of Award and Eligibility Criteria:** The description of the award indicates the purpose for which it is given, the criteria for eligibility, whether one can apply or must be nominated for the award, and the application or nomination deadline.

⑬ **Character:** Identifies the nature of the award, such as a medal, monetary award, certificate, inclusion in a hall of fame, or the presentation of a lecture.

⑭ **Frequency:** Information on the frequency of award presentation and the occasion on which it is presented.

⑮ **Year Established:** The year the award was established and in whose honor or memory it is presented.

⑯ **Sponsor:** The sponsor or co-sponsor of an award, if it is an organization other than the administering organization.

⑰ **Status:** If an award has been discontinued or is currently inactive, the year it was discontinued or last presented may be provided.

⑱ **Former Name:** The former name of an award and the year of the name change, if provided.

Indexes

Subject Index of Awards

The **Subject Index of Awards** classifies all awards described in this volume by their principal areas of interest. The index contains more than 400 subject headings. Identically named awards are followed by an indented alphabetical list of the organizations administering an award by that name. Each award is indexed under all relevant headings. The index also contains numerous cross-references to direct users to related topics. Awards are listed alphabetically under each subject heading, and the number following an award name identifies that award's entry in the descriptive listings portion of this volume.

Organization Index

The alphabetical **Organization Index** provides access to all sponsoring and administering organizations listed in both volumes, as well as to organization acronyms and alternate-language and former names. Index references include the volume in which the organization appears and book entry numbers in the descriptive listing section. In the case of sponsoring organizations, citations are to the specific awards they sponsor.

Award Index

The **Award Index** provides an alphabetical listing of all award names listed in both volumes, as well as alternate-language, former, and popular award names, such as the Oscars and Tonys. In the case of generic award names (e.g., Gold Medal, Achievement Award, Grand Prize), the award name is followed by an alphabetical listing of the organizations administering an award by that name.

References to the volume in which the award may be found followed by the award's entry number in the descriptive listings section follow each award citation.

AWARDS, HONORS & PRIZES

INTERNATIONAL
AND FOREIGN

Volume 2
International and Foreign

Albania

1

Union of Writers and Artists of Albania
(Lidhja e Shkrimtareve dhe Artisteve te Shqiperise)
Konferenca e Pezes St., Nr. 4
Tirana, Albania   Phone: 2691

Formed by merger of: Union of Artists; Union of Writers.

2

Union of Writers and Artists of Albania Competitions
To recognize writers and artists including composers, painters, sculptors, actors, and singers. Competitions are held and awards are given.

Angola

3

Angolan Writers Union
(Uniao dos Escritores Angolanos)
Caixa Postal 2767C
Luanda, Angola   Phone: 322155

4

Premio Nacional de Literatura
(National Literature Award)
To recognize achievement in the field of writing as a contribution to the building of a national literature. A national jury makes the nomination. A monetary prize, a trophy, and a plaque are awarded annually. Established in 1979.

Argentina

5

Academia Nacional de Agronomia y Veterinaria
Av. Alvear 1711, 2 piso
1014 Buenos Aires, Argentina

6

Premio Academia Nacional de Agronomia y Veterinaria
For recognition of individuals or institutions that have contributed to progress in agriculture. Established by the Academy as its highest award.

7

Premio Bayer en Ciencias Veterinarias
For recognition of contributions to veterinary science. Awarded biennially. Established in 1976 by Bayer Argentina.

8

Premio Bolsa de Cereales de Buenos Aires
For recognition of contributions to the production, industrialization, and commercialization of grains. Awarded biennially. Established in 1979 by Bolsa de Cereales de Buenos Aires on the occasion of the 125th anniversary of its founding.

9

Premio Dr. Francisco C. Rosenbusch
For recognition of research concerning the relationship between human health and animal sanitation. Awarded biennially. Established in 1976 by Ines Rosenbusch de DeCamps in memory of her father, Dr. Francisco C. Rosenbusch.

10

Premio Fundacion Celulosa Argentina
For recognition of contributions to the field of forestry. Established in 1987 by the CIEF.

11

Premio Fundacion Manzullo
For recognition of persons who have contributed to the field of public health. Established by Fundacion Manzullo in 1975.

12

Premio Fundacion Rene Baron
For recognition of individuals who have contributed to agriculture or livestock breeding.

13

Premio Jose Maria Bustillo
For recognition of an outstanding contribution in the field of agricultural economics. Awarded biennially. Established in 1975 by Maria Luisa Devoto de Bustillo in memory of her husband, Jose Maria Bustillo.

14

Premio Massey Ferguson
For recognition of individuals or institutions who have contributed to national agriculture. Awarded annually. Established in 1977 by Massey Ferguson.

15

Premio Vilfred Baron
For recognition of scientific research in agronomy and veterinary science. Awards are given biennially, alternating between agronomy and veterinary science. Established in 1983 by the Vilfred Baron Foundation.

Argentina — Awards, Honors & Prizes, 1995-96

16
Academia Nacional de la Historia
Balcarce 139
1064 Buenos Aires, Bs. As., Argentina
Phone: 1 3315147
Phone: 1 3434416
Fax: 1 3314633

17
Premio Academia Nacional de la Historia
For recognition of the best works concerning the history of Argentina from its beginning until 1950. Published or unpublished works are eligible. A monetary prize and a certificate are awarded for first, second, and third place winners. Established in 1964 in honor of the founding of Argentina.

18
Premio Enrique Pena
For recognition of the best historical work on the discovery, conquest, and settlement of the Rio de Plata. University students are eligible. Certificates are awarded annually. Established in 1944 in memory of the scholar, Dr. Enrique Pena.

19
Premio Republica Argentina
For recognition of the best investigative work on General Jose de San Martin's life and personality. A monetary prize, publication of the work, and 100 copies for the author are awarded annually. Established in 1974 in honor of General Don Jose San Martin.

20
Argentina
Ministry of Education and Justice
Eizzurno 935
1020 Buenos Aires, Bs. As., Argentina

21
First Book Prize
To provide recognition for the first literary work written by a young author under 30 years of age. Prose, poetry and essays are considered. Monetary prizes are given in each category of literature. Awarded annually.

22
National Prize for Literature
To provide recognition for the best works of prose and poetry. Monetary prizes are awarded triennially.

23
Regional Production Prizes
To provide recognition for works in the following fields: (1) ethnology, archaeology and history; (2) folklore and literature; and (3) science. Monetary prizes are awarded in all three fields annually. The prizes are given in eight regions of Argentina, with annual rotation.

24
Theatre Production Prize
To provide recognition for the best staged play. Dramas, comedies, and musicals are considered. Awarded triennially.

25
Argentine Book Chamber
(Camara Argentina del Libro)
Av. Belgrano 1580
1093 Buenos Aires, Bs. As., Argentina

26
Carlos Casavalle Prize
For recognition of the best book published in Argentina in the following categories of literature: (1) fiction; (2) poetry and drama; and (3) essay, including scientific writing. The award is presented alternately among the three disciplines of writing. A monetary prize is awarded annually. Established and named for the first Argentinian bookseller, Carlos Casavalle.

27
Argentine Paleontological Association
(Asociacion Paleontologica Argentina)
Maipu 645, 1er piso
1006 Buenos Aires, Bs. As., Argentina
Phone: 1 322 2820

28
Premio Florentino Ameghino
To reward and encourage the publication of original research by young people in the Association's magazine *Ameghiniana*. Members who are 35 years of age or younger may submit manuscripts. A diploma is awarded annually. Established in 1975 in honor of Florentino Ameghino.

29
Argentine Society of Authors
(Sociedad General de Autores de la Argentina)
J. A. Pacheco de Melo 1820
1126 Buenos Aires, Bs. As., Argentina
Phone: 1 42 1227

30
Gran Premio de Honor Argentores
For recognition of achievement in the field and services of value to the institution. Awards are given in different fields each year. The categories awarded are: (1) drama; (2) television; (3) radio; and (4) cinema. Members of the Society who have served the Society as officers are eligible. A plaque is awarded annually. Established in 1974.

31
Premio Argentores
For recognition of the best productions in the different genres for which royalties are collected by the Society. Authors who are members of the Society are considered for works produced during the preceding year. Awards are given in the following categories: (1) drama; (2) radio; (3) television; and (4) cinema. Awarded annually. Established in 1981.

32
Argentinian Association of Dermatology
(Asociacion Argentina de Dermatologia)
Hospital Ramos Mejia
Gral. Urquiza 609
1221 Buenos Aires, Argentina

33
Argentinian Association of Dermatology Awards
To recognize dermatologists in Argentina. Awarded annually.

34
Buenos Aires Municipality
Secretariat of Culture and Social Activities
Av. de Mayo 525
1083 Buenos Aires, Bs. As., Argentina
Phone: 1 34 62 12
Phone: 1 34 58 73

35
Buenos Aires Drama Prize
To recognize an outstanding playwright. A monetary prize is awarded annually.

36
Buenos Aires Literary Prizes
To provide recognition for the best works written or published during the year in Buenos Aires. Awards are given in the following categories: (1)

fiction; (2) essay (including biography and literary criticism); and (3) poetry. Monetary prizes are awarded annually.

37

Buenos Aires Music Prize
For recognition of notable achievement in music. A monetary prize is awarded annually.

38

Ricardo Rojas Prize
For recognition of prose, such as imaginative writing, criticism, and essay. A monetary prize is awarded biennially.

39

Bunge y Born Foundation
(Fundacion Bunge y Born)
25 de Mayo 565, 8 piso
1002 Buenos Aires, Bs. As., Argentina   Phone: 1 32 7311

40

Television Journalism Prize
To stimulate television journalism in Argentina and support its participation in the cultural development of the country.

41

Centre of Art and Communication
(Centro de Arte y Communicacion)
Elpidio Gonzalez 4070
Buenos Aires, Argentina   Phone: 1 5668046

42

Centre of Art and Communication Awards
To recognize and promote experimental and avant-garde art in Argentina and Latin America. Artists, musicians, dramatists, architects, communications experts, and other interested individuals are eligible. Competitions are held.

43

Dentists Association of Argentina
(Asociacion Odontologica Argentina)
Junin 959
1113 Buenos Aires, Bs. As., Argentina   Phone: 1 83 6041 44

44

Premio Prof. Dr. Alejandro Cabanne
To recognize an odontologist for contributions to the profession. A medal, certificate and a scholarship are awarded annually. Established in 1969 in memory of Alejandro Cabanne.

45

Socio Colabrador
For distinguished service in the promotion of odontology. Candidates are nominated by the Assembly. A certificate is awarded every five years. Established in 1985.

46

Emece Editores S.A.
Alsina 2048, piso 2   Phone: 1 9540105
1009 Buenos Aires, Argentina   Fax: 1 9534200

47

Concurso Literario Premio Emece
To recognize the best novel or book of short stories in the Spanish language. Established in 1954.

48

Fundacion Quinquela Martin para la Investigacion y Docencia en Medicina
Pi y Margall 750
1155 Buenos Aires, Bs. As., Argentina   Phone: 1 362 2772

49

Quinquela Martin Foundation Prize
(Premio Fundacion Quinquela Martin)
For recognition of outstanding medical research. The application deadline is October 31 each year. A monetary award, a medal and a certificate are awarded annually on Doctor's Day. Established in 1962 in memory of Dr. Benito Quinquela Martin.

50

Institute for Latin American Integration
(Instituto Para la Integracion de America Latina)
Esmeralda 130, Piso 18   Phone: 1 394 2260
1035 Buenos Aires, Bs. As., Argentina   Fax: 1 394 2293

51

Institute for Latin American Integration Award
To recognize the best original work on Latin American Cooperation and Integration.

52

Institute of Hispanic Culture
(Instituto de Cultura Hispana)
H. Yrigoyen 672
1086 Buenos Aires, Bs. As., Argentina

53

Hispanic Culture Gold Medal
For recognition of a significant contribution to Hispanic culture. A gold medal is awarded annually.

54

Instituto Torcuato di Tella
11 de Septiembre 2139
1428 Buenos Aires, Bs. As., Argentina   Phone: 1 781 5013

55

Premio Trienal Instituto Torcuato di Tella Mozarteum Argentina
For recognition of a contribution to a field of activity in music. A monetary prize is awarded triennially. Established in 1984.

56

Latin American Federation of Thermalism and Climatism
(Federacion Latinoamericana de Termalismo)
Anchorena 1198
Apartado Postal 2
1425 Buenos Aires, Argentina   Phone: 1 9610825

57

Latin American Federation of Thermalism and Climatism Awards
To recognize scientists from varying disciplines interested in hydrothermalogy and climatology. The Federation sponsors competitions and bestows awards.

58

Liga Argentina Contra la Tuberculosis
Avda. Santa Fe 4292   Phone: 1 7749145
1425 Buenos Aires, Bs. As., Argentina   Fax: 1 7774691

[59] Premio Consagracion Rodolfo A. Vaccarezza
For recognition of outstanding activity in the antituberculosis fight. Selection is by nomination. A medal is awarded triennially. Established in 1981 in honor of Dr. Rodolfo A. Vaccarezza.

[60] Premio Profesor Dr. Ricardo Hansen
For recognition of achievements in the antituberculosis fight. The best scientific free work on phthisio-pneumonology is eligible. A medal is awarded biennially. Established in 1966 in honor of Dr. Ricardo L. Hansen.

---

[61]
National Academy of Medicine
(Academia Nacional de Medicina)
Las Heras 3092
1425 Buenos Aires, Bs. As., Argentina   Phone: 1 83 6890

[62] Elena Allemand de Gunche Prize
For recognition of the best original work in dermatology published in Argentina. Awarded annually.

[63] Geronimo H. Alvarez Prize
For recognition of the best work on normal and pathological pre and post-operation behavior. Awarded biennially.

[64] Annual Stimulus Subprize
For recognition of the best original, unpublished work in Argentina by doctors or investigators seeking the causes and cures of *Virosis hemorragica* of Northeast Buenos Aires residents, commonly known as *Mal de Los Rastrojos*. Awarded annually.

[65] Elsa E. Arini de Masnatta Prize
For recognition of outstanding contributions in the following areas: (1) clinical investigation in hematology; and (2) experimental investigation with preference toward the use of radio isotopes in hematology. Awarded annually, in alternating years in each category.

[66] Padre Fermin G. Arnau S.J. - Obra De San Lazaro Prize
For recognition of the most outstanding work on leprosy. Awarded annually.

[67] Alois Bachmann Prize
For recognition of the best experimental or clinical work in microbiology. Awarded triennially.

[68] Juan Bonorino Cuenca Prize
For recognition of a significant achievement in the diagnosis or cure of infectious diseases. Awarded biennially.

[69] Carlos Bonorino Udaondo Prize
For recognition of the best original work or experimental or clinical study on gastroenterology. Works which were already awarded distinctions, honors and prizes cannot compete. Awarded triennially.

[70] Samuel M. Bosch Prize
For recognition of the best experimental, clinical or surgical work in aeronautical medicine. Awarded triennially.

[71] Osvaldo L. Bottaro Prize
For recognition of the best work on virology and virus diseases or on biology applied in medicine. Awarded biennially.

[72] Domingo J. Brachetto Brian Prize
For recognition of the best work in the following areas: (1) bone pathology; and (2) general pathological anatomy. Awarded annually in alternate years in each category.

[73] Rafael A. Bullrich Prize
For recognition of the best experimental or clinical work in cardiology. Awarded biennially.

[74] Eliseo Canton Prize
For recognition of the best work on the biology of gestation written in Argentina. Awarded triennially.

[75] Mariano R. Castex Prize
For recognition of the most outstanding experimental or clinical work in internal medicine carried out in Argentina. Awarded annually.

[76] Baudilio Courtis Prize
For recognition of the best work on the prevention of blindness. Awarded annually.

[77] Pedro I. Elizalde Prize
For recognition of the best investigative work on the theme of pathological biology. A specific theme is selected for each competition. Awarded biennially.

[78] Rosalia Feldblit de Garfunkel Prize
For recognition of outstanding work in experimental, clinical or social investigation of heart diseases. Awarded biennially.

[79] Enrique Finochietto Prize
For recognition of the most significant contributions in the following areas: (1) clinical or experimental investigation in the field of general surgery; and (2) clinical or experimental investigation in the field of general traumatology. Awarded biennially, in alternate years in each category.

[80] Avelino Gutierrez Prize
For recognition of the best work on a theme of surgical anatomy, with the theme to be announced each year. Awarded annually.

[81] Marcellino Herrera Vegas Prize
For recognition of the best work on children's surgery written in Argentina. Awarded triennially.

82
Angela Iglesia de Llano Prize
For recognition of the best experimental or clinical work on non-tubercular diseases of the respiratory system. Awarded biennially.

83
Jewish Colonization in the Argentine Republic Prize
To recognize an individual for the discovery of a specific and effective preventive or curative treatment for *Virosis hemorragica* of Northeast Buenos Aires, commonly known as *Mal de Los Rastrojos*. The prize is open until the disease is vanquished. Awarded annually.

84
Jose M. Jorge Prize
For recognition of the best work on rehabilitation of the handicapped. Docents, the graduates and the students of the Schools of Medicine in Argentina and Uruguay may submit applications. Awarded biennially.

85
Lucio V. Lopez Prize
For recognition of the best work in psychiatry. Awarded biennially.

86
Juan Jose Montes de Oca Prize
For recognition of the best work on infection in the hospital or infirmary situation, written in Argentina. Awarded triennially.

87
National Academy of Medicine Prize
For recognition of the best original, unpublished work written in Argentina on a medical-scientific theme, with the specific theme to be announced each year. Awarded annually.

88
Juan Carlos Navarro Prize
For recognition of the best unpublished work on pediatrics. Professors of Academies of Medical Sciences are excluded from applying for the prize. Awarded triennially.

89
Edgardo Nicholson Prize
For recognition of the most distinguished work on gynecology. Awarded annually.

90
Raul Nicolini Prize
For the recognition of the most outstanding work on immunology in the cancerous diseases. Awarded biennially.

91
Adolfo Noceti and Atilio Tiscornia Prize
For recognition of outstanding achievement on a theme related to ophthalmology. Awarded biennially.

92
Angelica Ocampo Prize
For recognition of the best work in Argentina in clinical, immunological, epidemiological or experimental studies of leukemia. Awarded biennially.

93
Alberto Peralta Ramos Prize
For recognition of the best original work in obstetrics. Authors of works published in Latin American countries are eligible. Awarded biennially.

94
Ignacio Pirovano Prize
For recognition of the best work on a theme of progress in surgery. Awarded triennially.

95
Jorge E. Pons Goldaracena Prize
For recognition of the best work on orthopedics and traumatology. Awarded annually.

96
Marcial V. Quiroga Prize
For recognition of a notable contribution in the investigation, diagnosis, or treatment of connective tissue diseases. Awarded biennially.

97
Alejandro A. Raimondi Prize
For recognition of the best work in phthisiology. Awarded biennially.

98
Bernandino Rivadavia Prize
For recognition of the best original, unpublished work written in Argentina on the treatment of cancer. Awarded triennially.

99
Federico Guillermo Schlottmann Prize
For recognition of the best work on arteriosclerosis or leukemia. Awarded biennially.

100
Enrique Tornu Prize
For recognition of a notable contribution to pulmonary tuberculosis in any of the following areas: clinical, surgical, therapeutic, hygiene, or prophylaxis. Awarded annually.

101
Eufemio Uballes Prize
For recognition of the best effort in experimental, clinical or therapeutic investigation which contributes to knowledge in the fight against cancer. Awarded annually.

102
Leopoldo Uriarte Y Pineiro Prize
For recognition of the best laboratory or clinical work on the pests of the Orient or human microbiology. Awarded every four years.

103
Roberto A. Vacarezza Prize
For recognition of the most important work on diseases acquired from animals or animal parasites in the rural situation carried out in Argentina. Awarded biennially.

104
Pena Fotografica Rosarina
Urquiza 2124
Casilla de Correo 621
2000 Rosario, Argentina   Phone: 41 256180

105
**Rosario International Photographic Salon
(Salon International Fotografico de Rosario)**
To recognize the best entries in the International Salon. Photographs may be submitted in the following categories: Monochrome prints, color prints, color slides, nature slides, photo travel slides, and photojournalism slides. The Medalla Ciudad de Rosario (City of Rosario Medal) is awarded in each category. In addition, the Medal El Gaucho recognizes the best photograph from any of the six categories. The Medal

El Gaucho was established in 1952 in memory of "Gauchos." The Medalla Ciudad de Rosario was established in 1975.

106
La Prensa
Instituto Popular de Conferencias
Avda de Mayo 567
1319 Buenos Aires, Bs. As., Argentina   Phone: 1 33 1001

107
Premio Alberdi - Sarmiento
To recognize a distinguished journalist, writer, or public figure of the Americas for a contribution to Inter-American cooperation and friendship. A monetary award, a plaque and travel to Buenos Aires were awarded annually. Established in 1950 by Dr. Alberto Gainza Paz, publisher of *La Prensa*. The award commemorates Juan Bautista Alberdi (1810-1884), Argentine journalist, writer and essayist, and Domingo Faustino Sarmiento (1811-1888), Argentine journalist, writer, educator and statesman. (Discontinued in 1980)

108
World Federation of Rose Societies
(Federation Mondiale des Societes pour la Culture de la Rose)
Solis 1255
Buenos Aires, Argentina   Phone: 1 665 2070

109
Rose Gold Medal
To recognize exceptional services to the rose and the World Federation of Rose Societies. Candidates must be members of a National Rose Society which belongs to the World Federation. A medal is presented at conventions held every two to four years. Established in 1979.

110
Rose Pin
For recognition of service to the World Federation of Rose Societies. Selection is by nomination. A Rose Pin is awarded at the World Congress held every two or three years. Established in 1985.

Armenia

111
Academy of Sciences, Armenia
Marshal Baghramian av. 24   Phone: 52 07 04
Yerevan, Armenia   Phone: 52 54 32

112
Mesrop Mashtots Award
To recognize an individual for a prominent contribution to a field of Armenian studies. Individuals may submit published material. (The award is not given posthumously.) A monetary award of 1,000 rubles, a certificate and a plaque are awarded triennially. Established in 1969 by the Academy of Sciences of the Armenian SSR and Council of Ministers of the Armenian SSR to honor Mesrop Mashtots, who created the Armenian alphabet in the beginning of the 5th century A.D.

113
Stephan Shaumian Prize
To recognize outstanding scientific works in the field of economics, philosophy, history, and the history of literature. Soviet citizens may be nominated by scientific and educational institutions. A monetary award of 1,000 rubles, a medal, certificate and a badge are awarded triennially. Established in 1978 by the Presidium of the Armenian Academy to honor Stephan Shaumian, the Armenian revolutioner. Sponsored by the Division of Philosophy and Philology.

114
Toros Toramanian Prize
To recognize an individual for scientific works devoted to the history of Armenian architecture. Nominations may be submitted by the scientific societies of the scientific establishments, and the educational institutions. A certificate and a medal are awarded once in four years. Established in 1969 by the Presidium of the Armenian Academy in honor of the great Armenian architect, Toros Toramanian. Sponsored by the Division of Philosophy and Philology.

Australia

115
ACTA Shipping
GPO Box 4006
Sydney, NSW 2001, Australia

116
ACTA Australian Maritime Art Award
To promote and foster interest in maritime art. Works with a theme of commercial shipping and/or port based maritime activities in Australia, past or present, are eligible. Australian citizenship and residency are required. A monetary award is presented annually. Established in 1985. Sponsored by ACTA Shipping, GPO Box 4006, Sydney, NSW 2001, Australia.

117
The Age
Literary Ed.
250 Spencer St.   Phone: 3 600 4211
Melbourne, VIC 3000, Australia   Fax: 3 670 7514

118
***The Age* Book of the Year Awards**
For recognition of Australian books of outstanding literary merit which best express Australia's identity and prevailing concerns. Two prizes are awarded: one to a novel or other work of imaginative writing, and the other to a non-fiction work. One is named *The Age* Book of the Year, and the other the best work in its category. The prize for the work of imaginative writing is awarded to a novel, a collection of short stories, or a collection of poetry. The prize for the non-fiction work is awarded to the book considered the best biography, autobiography, the best history, or the best scholarly work of social, political or topical interest. Works must have been published during the preceding year between November 1 and October 31, and written by Australian citizens. Publishers may submit no more than two works of imaginative writing and/or three works of non-fiction by October 31. Two monetary prizes (one of $3,000, and one of $4,000 for the book named *The Age* Book of the Year) are awarded annually at a literary luncheon. Established in 1974.

119
Allen & Unwin Pty Ltd
PO Box 8500   Phone: 2 9014088
St. Leonards, NSW 2065, Australia   Fax: 2 9062218

120
Australian/Vogel Literary Award
To encourage young Australian writers of fiction or history. Australian residents under 35 years of age may submit manuscripts of a minimum of 30,000 words by May 31. A monetary prize of $15,000 Australian is awarded annually. Established in 1979 by Nils Stevns of Vogel's Australia. Additional information is available from Allen & Unwin.

121

ANZIAM-Australian and New Zealand Industrial and Applied Mathematics
Australian Mathematical Society
Dept. of Mathematics
Univ. of Newcastle Division of Applied
  Mathematics
Newcastle, NSW 2308, Australia

Phone: 49 215530
Fax: 49 216898

Formerly: Australian Mathematical Society - Division of Applied Mathematics.

122

T. M. Cherry Student Prize
For recognition of the best student paper presented at the annual conference of ANZIAM. Any postgraduate student whose higher degree thesis has not been submitted more than three calendar months before the commencement of the annual conference is eligible. A monetary prize is awarded annually at the conference. Established in 1969 and renamed in 1976 in memory of T. M. Cherry, one of Australia's leading applied mathematicians.

123

Art Gallery of New South Wales
Art Gallery Rd.
Domain
Sydney, NSW 2000, Australia

Phone: 2 225 1700

124

Archibald Prize
For recognition of a portrait painting of a distinguished person in art, letters, science, or politics. A monetary prize of $20,000 (Australian) is awarded annually. Established in 1921 by a bequest of J.F. Archibald, in trust of the Perpetual Trustee Company.

125

Sulman Prize
For recognition of a subject or genre painting. A monetary prize of $5,000 (Australian) is awarded annually.

126

Arts Management Pty Limited
180 Goulburn St.
Darlinghurst, NSW 2010, Australia

Phone: 2 2832066
Fax: 2 2648201

127

Miles Franklin Literary Award
To encourage and assist the advancement of Australian literature and for recognition of a novel or play that portrays an aspect of Australian life. Novels published during the preceding year are considered. A monetary prize of $25,000 (Australian) is awarded annually. Established in 1957 in memory of Miles Franklin, an Australian author.

128

Portia Geach Memorial Award
For recognition of the best portraits painted from life of a man or woman distinguished in art, letters, or the sciences. Any female artist, resident in Australia during the preceding twelve months, who was born in Australia or was British born or has become a naturalized Australian and whose place of domicile is Australia is eligible. A monetary prize of $18,000 is awarded annually. Established in 1965 by a bequest of Miss Florence Kate Geach, who died in 1962, in memory of her sister, Portia Geach.

129

Association for the Study of Australian Literature
School of Humanities & General Studies
Univ. of W. Sydney
Macarthur Campus
Campbelltown, ACT 2560, Australia

Phone: 46 20 3151
Fax: 46 28 1298

Absorbed: (1982) Australian Literature Society.

130

Australian Literature Society Gold Medal
For recognition of an outstanding literary work published in Australia during the previous calendar year between January 1 and December 31. Nominations are accepted. A monetary prize and a medal are awarded annually at the annual conference of the Association. Established in 1928. Additional information is available from Monash University, English Dept., Wellington Road, Clayton, VIC 3168, Australia, phone: 3 565 4000. Formerly: (1982) Herbert Crouch Medal.

131

Mary Gilmore Award
For recognition of the best first book of poetry published in Australia in the preceding calendar year. Nominations are accepted. A monetary prize and a gold medal are awarded annually at the Annual conference of the Association. Established in 1985 in honor of Mary Gilmore, an Australian poet.

132

Walter McRae Russell Award
For recognition of a first work of literary scholarship on an Australian subject published in the preceding year between January 1 and December 31. Nominations are accepted. A monetary prize is awarded annually at the Annual Conference of the Association. Established in honor of Walter McRae Russell, last president of the Australian Literature Society.

133

A. A. Phillips Award
To recognize a work of outstanding achievement in the field of Australian literary scholarship. A monetary award of about $500 is presented on occasion. The award has been made only once - to W.H. Wilde, Barry Andrews and Joy Hooton for the *Oxford Companion to Australian Literature* in 1986.

134

Association of Consulting Engineers Australia
75 Miller St.
PO Box 1002
North Sydney, NSW 2060, Australia

Phone: 2 9224711
Fax: 2 9572484

135

ACEA Engineering Awards
To recognize engineers who maintain high ethical and professional standards and work to enhance the status of the engineering profession. Awarded annually.

136

Astronomical Society of Western Australia
Box S 1460
Perth, WA 6001, Australia

137

Arthur Farrant Award
For recognition of the most creditable contribution towards the furtherance of the objectives of the Society or the science of astronomy. Members of the Society are eligible. A trophy is awarded annually when merited.

138 Australia — Awards, Honors & Prizes, 1995-96

138
Australasian Corrosion Association
PO Box 250
Clayton, VIC 3168, Australia
Phone: 3 5440066
Fax: 3 5435905

Formed by merger of: Australian Association for Corrosion Prevention; New Zealand Corrosion Association.

139
Australasian Corrosion Association Awards
To recognize contributions by individuals who work to decrease the cost of damage due to corrosion in Australasia. The Association bestows awards annually.

140
Australasian Political Studies Association
Dept. of Political Science
Univ. College
Australian Defense Force Academy,
 Cambell
Canberra, ACT 2600, Australia
Phone: 6 2688845
Fax: 6 2688852

141
Crisp Medal
For recognition of originality and intellectual contribution of a work in political science published during the preceding three years. Citizens or permanent residents of Australia or New Zealand are eligible for nomination. Individuals who have held a doctorate for ten years or more or whose first appointment to a tenurable post at atertiary institution was ten or more years ago are not eligible. The deadline for submissions is July 15. A monetary prize of $500 (Australian) and a medal are awarded annually at the Annual General Meeting of the Association. Established in 1988 by the Association and the Commonwealth Bank of Australia in memory of Leslie Finlay Crisp, Foundation Professor of Political Science at Canberra University College (later The Australian National University) and Chairman of the Board of the Commonwealth Bank of Australia from 1975 until his death in 1984.

142
Women and Politics Prize
For recognition of the best unpublished work on women and politics and to promote the study of women and politics. Works between 5,000 and 10,000 words may be submitted by September 1. A monetary award of $500 (Australian) and publication in *Australian Journal of Political Science* or the *Australian Quarterly* are awarded biennially. Established in 1981. Co-sponsored by the Women's Caucus and the Royal Australian Institute of Public Administration.

143
Australia
Department of Veterans' Affairs, Public Relations Dept.
Heidelberg Repatriation Hospital
Banksia St.
Heidelberg West, VIC 3081, Australia
Phone: 490 2646
Fax: 499 7427

144
Storywriting and Art Project
To provide therapeutic activity for eligible veterans and war widows. Storywriting awards are given in the following categories: True War Experiences, True Life Experiences, Fiction, and Poetry. Art awards are given in the following categories: Oil Painting - open or experienced, Oil Painting - novice, Other Media, Craft, and Restricted - for entrants who have won First Prize in Oil Painting - Open or Other Media categories. The Sir Edward Herring Memorial Prize is given for the overall outstanding entry. Monetary prizes totaling more than $5,000, trophies, and ribbons are awarded annually. Established in 1962.

145
Australia
New South Wales Ministry for the Arts
1 Francis St.
PO Box 810
Darlinghurst, NSW 2010, Australia
Phone: 361 9111
Fax: 361 9100

146
Fellowships and Scholarships
The New South Wales Government offers each year a number of fellowships and scholarships to writers and artists living in New South Wales. No age restrictions apply to any fellowships or scholarships. The following awards are presented: New South Wales Travelling Art Scholarship - $25,000; New South Wales Writer's Fellowship - $10,000; New South Wales History Fellowship - $10,000; Robert Helpmann Scholarship - alternantes biennially with the Rex Cramphorn Theater Scholarship, $15,000; New South Wales Women and Arts Fellowship - $15,000; David Paul Landa Music Scholarship for Pianists (biennial) - $25,000; New South Wales Government and Frederick May Foundation Scholarship - $5,000; and Paul Lowin Compostition Awards (triennial) - Orchestra Prize of $45,000 and Song Cycle Prize of $20,000.

147
New South Wales State Literary Awards
To honor distinguished achievement by Australian writers in the following categories of writing: fiction, nonfiction, poetry, children's books, and play and scriptwriting. Writers must be residents of Australia. Works may be nominated by writers or publishers. The following prizes are awarded: Christina Stead Prize, for fiction; Douglas Stewart Prize, for nonfiction; Kenneth Slessor Prize, for poetry; Children's Book Award; Play Award; Script Writing Award; Ethnic Affairs Commission Award; and Special Award. Awarded annually. Established in 1979 by the New South Wales Government. Formerly: (1987) New South Wales Premier's Literary Awards.

148
Australia
Victorian Ministry for the Arts
2 Kavanagh St.
South Melbourne, VIC 3205, Australia
Phone: 3 684 8784
Fax: 3 686 6186

149
Premier's Literary Awards
For recognition of achievement in Australian literature in the following categories: fiction; nonfiction; poetry; drama; Australian studies; first fiction; children's literature; and literary translation. Authors must be living, residents of Australia, or Australian citizens to be eligible. Entries must be submitted by May 1. The following monetary prizes are awarded: Vance Palmer Prize for Fiction - $15,000; Nettie Palmer Prize for Nonfiction - $15,000; Louis Esson Prize for Drama - $7,500; C. J. Dennis Prize for Poetry - $7,500; A. A. Philips Prize for Australian Studies - $7,500; Sheaffer Pen Prize for First Fiction - $7,500; Diabetes Australia Alan Marshall Prize for Children's Literature - $7,500; and Dinny O'Hearn/SBS Bookshow Prize for Literary Translation - $7,500. Established in 1985. For further information, contact Lisa O'Donnell, Executive Secretary, at 3 6848784.

150
Australia Council
Community Cultural Development Board
181 Lawson St.
Redfern, NSW 2016, Australia
Phone: 2 9509000
Fax: 2 9509111

151
Ros Bower Memorial Award
To recognize achievements in community arts in Australia. Nominations may be submitted by August each year. A monetary prize of $25,000 is awarded annually. Established by the Ros Bower Memorial Trust in memory of Ros Bower, the first Director of the Community Arts Board.

152
Australia Council
Literature Board

PO Box 788
Strawberry Hills, NSW 2012, Australia

Phone: 2 9509000
Phone: 2 9509056
Fax: 2 9509111

153
Australia-New Zealand Literary Exchange

To promote Australian and New Zealand literature and writers. The Award is not open to application. An expenses-paid four-week promotions visit to either New Zealand or Australia is awarded annually. Established in 1986 by the Australia Council and theQueen Elizabeth II Arts Council of New Zealand.

154
Canada-Australia Literary Award

To promote Australian and Canadian literature and writers. The award is not open to application. A monetary prize of $3250 Canadian and a visit to either Canada or Australia are awarded annually. Established in 1976 by the Australia Council and Canada Council. Additional information is available from the Writing and Publication Section, Canada Council, P.O. Box 1047, Ottawa, ON, Canada K1P 5V8.

155
Category A Fellowships

To assist published Australian writers of substantial achievement to complete a major project or projects. applicants must have had at least three works published or performed by nationally required companies. Awards are granted on the basis of literary merit to writers working in the areas of fiction, poetry, drama, and creative prose. The latter category includes autobiography, biography, essays, history, and literary criticism. Applications must be submitted by May 15. The Board considers the following criteria: literary works listed to the writer's credit; the likelihood of the planned work being retarded or impaired if no grant were available; the likelihood of eventual pub lication of works written under grants; and the contribution of the work to the development of Australian literature and its recognition overseas. Writers awarded full or half Fellowships are expected to give up full time employment for the duration of the grant. The following monetary awards are presented: one year Fellowships valued at $30,000; and four years Fellowships valued at $20,000. Formerly: Writers' Fellowships.

156
Category B Fellowships

To provide living allowances for Australian writers who have recently achieved publication. Applicants must have had at least one work published or performed by a nationally required company. Grants are awarded to writers working in the areas of fiction, poetry, drama, and creative prose. The latter category includes autobiography, biography, essays, histories, and literary criticism. Applications must be submitted by May 15. The Board considers the following criteria: the literary talent and persistence of the writer to produce a work of high standard; the likelihood of the planned work being retarded or impaired if no grant were available; the likelihood of eventual publication of works written under grants. Writers awarded Fellowships are expected to give up full time employment for the duration of the grant. One-year Writers' Fellowships worth $24,000 are awarded annually.

157
Australia Council
Performing Arts Board
PO Box 788
Strawberry Hills, NSW 2012, Australia

Phone: 2 9509000
Fax: 2 9509111

158
Don Banks Composer Fellowship

To recognize the finest Australian composers and to provide them with the means whereby they may devote one year fully to composition. Composers must apply by April 15. A monetary prize of $50,000 (Australian) is awarded annually. Established in 1984 in honor of Don Banks, an Australian composer and the first chairperson of the Music Board.

159
Australia Council for the Arts
Visual Arts/Craft Board

PO Box 788
Strawberry Hills, NSW 2012, Australia

Phone: 2 9509000
Toll-free: 008 226912
Fax: 2 9509111

160
Australian Artists Creative Fellowships

To encourage further outstanding artistic contributions to Australia from the most established, visionary, and innovative artists and to enhance their already renowned talents. Inaugurated in 1988, the fellowships are financed by the federal government and administered by the Australia Council.

161
Australian Visual Arts Board Award for Illustration

For recognition of an outstanding picture book for children. Both the text and illustration are taken into consideration. A monetary prize of $3,000 Australian is awarded annually. Established in 1974. (Discontinued)

162
Don Banks Fellowship

To publicly honor the finest Australian composers and to provide them with an opportunity to devote themselves fully to compostition for the fellowship period. A fellowship of $50,000 is awarded annually by the Performing Arts Board.

163
Ros Bower Memorial Award

To recognize an artsworker or organization with a proven record of high achievement in the area of community arts. A monetary prize of $25,000 is awarded annually. Given by the Community Cultural Development Board with the Ros Bower Memorial Trust.

164
Community, Environment, Art, and Design (CEAD) Award

To recognize innovative approaches to environmental design. Given by the Australia Council's CEAD Committee.

165
Inaugural Red Ochre Award

To honor artists who have made a great contribution to the recognition of Aboriginal and Torres Strait Island art and culture in the wider community at both the national and international level. A monetary award of $50,000 per year for up to three years is presented. First awarded in 1994 to mark the International Year for the World's Indigenous People by the Aboriginal and Torres Strait Islander Arts Committee.

166
Literature Board's Emeritus Fellowship Awards

To honor writers over the age of 65 who have made outstanding and lifelong contributions to Australian literature, and who are seen to be in financial need. A monetary gift of $25,000 and a small income enhancement component for life accompany each award. The Awards grew out of the Commonwealth Literary Fund's Pensions scheme.

167
Visual Arts/Craft Board Emeritus Award

To recognize an eminent and senior Australian visual or craft artist whose contributions continue to inspire and whose life and work merit greater public attention. A monetary prize of $25,000 (Australian) is awarded annually. Established in 1987.

168
Visual Arts/Craft Board Emeritus Medal
To honor the professional achievements of writers, curators, administrators, and advocates who have made major contributions throughout their careers to Australian visual art and craft. Commemorative medals are awarded annually. Established in 1993.

169
Visual Arts/Craft Board's Emeritus Fellowships and Medals
To honor the life and work of eminent visual and craft artists whose contribution to the arts merits greater public recognition, and whose life and work continues to inspire other Australian artists. A monetary gift of $25,000 accompanies the fellowships. Emeritus Medals honor the professional achievements of writers, curators, administrators, and advocates who have made major contributions throughout their careers to visual art and craft in Australia.

170
Australian Academy of Science
PO Box 783
Canberra City, ACT 2600, Australia
Phone: 6 247 5777
Fax: 6 257 4620

171
Burnet Lecture
To recognize the scientist in any discipline most deserving of the honor and recognition. An honorarium of $200 (Australian), a medal, honorary recognition, and an invitation to deliver the Burnet lecture, are awarded every other year, alternating with the Matthew Flinders Lecture. Established in 1971 in honor of Sir Macfarlane Burnet.

172
Matthew Flinders Lecture
To recognize the scientist in any discipline most deserving of the honor and recognition. An honorarium of $200 (Australian), a medal, honorary recognition, and an invitation to present the Matthew Flinders Lecture, are awarded every other year, alternating with the Burnet Lecture. Established in 1956.

173
Geoffrey Frew Fellowship
To recognize distinguished overseas scientists and to enable them to participate in the Australian Spectroscopy Conference and visit scientific centers in Australia. Travel expenses and a daily living allowance are awarded biennially. Established in 1971 by Mrs. G.S.V. Frew.

174
Gottschalk Medal
To recognize a scientist under 36 years of age for distinguished research in the medical or biological sciences. Scientists who are not Fellows of the Academy and who have completed most of the research in Australia are eligible. An honorarium of $100 (Australian), a medal, and honorary recognition are awarded annually. Established in 1976 by Dr. A. Gottschalk.

175
Rudi Lemberg Travelling Fellowship
To recognize overseas or Australian scientists of standing and to enable them to visit scientific centers in Australia and to deliver lectures. Scientists in the field of biology, particularly biochemistry, conservation, and Australian flora, are eligible. Travel expenses and a daily living allowance are awarded. Established in 1979 by Mrs. Hanna Lemberg in memory of Professor M.R. Lemberg. (Suspended in 1991 for two years)

176
Thomas Ranken Lyle Medal
To recognize an outstanding researcher in mathematics or physics. The research must have been completed during the previous five years, largely in Australia. A bronze medal and honorary recognition are awarded biennially. Established in 1931.

177
Mawson Lecture
To recognize an Australian scientist in the field of geology. An honorarium of $200, a bronze medal, and an invitation to deliver the Lecture at the convention of the Geological Society of Australia are awarded annually. Established in 1979 in honor of Sir Douglas Mawson.

178
Pawsey Medal
To recognize a scientist under 36 years of age for distinguished research in experimental physics. The research must be carried out mainly in Australia. Honorary recognition and a medal are awarded annually. Established in 1965 in honor of Dr. Pawsey and his contribution to science in Australia.

179
Selby Fellowship
To recognize distinguished overseas scientists and to enable them to undertake public lectures and visit scientific centers in Australia. Travel expenses and a daily living allowance are awarded annually. Established in 1961.

180
Ian William Wark Medal and Lecture
To recognize a scientist for a contribution to the prosperity of Australia where such prosperity is attained through the advance of scientific knowledge or its application, or both. Also, to focus attention on applications of scientific discoveries that have benefited the community. A medal and lecture are awarded biennially. Established in 1987 in memory of Sir Ian Wark, whose work was at the interface of science and industry.

181
Frederick White Prize
To recognize scientists who are engaged in research of intrinsic scientific merit and which contributes to an understanding of natural laws and new concepts. Younger scientists whose research has been undertaken mainly in Australia, and is in the physical sciences, the terrestrial and planetary sciences, or the biological sciences are eligible. A monetary prize is awarded biennially. Established in 1981 by Sir Frederick White.

182
Australian Academy of the Humanities
GPO Box 93
Canberra, ACT 2601, Australia
Phone: 6 2487744
Fax: 6 2486287

183
Crawford Medal
To recognize the outstanding achievements of scholars in the humanities in Australia. Australian-based scholars who are currently engaged in research and whose publications contribute towards an understanding of their disciplines by the general public are eligible. In making the award, the Council of the Academy shall take into account the actual or potential contributions of the research to the enrichment of cultural life in Australia. The medal is awarded biennially at an annual general meeting. Established in 1992.

184
Australian-American Educational Foundation
GPO Box 1559
Canberra, ACT 2601, Australia
Phone: 6 247 9331
Fax: 2 476 554

185
Fulbright Awards - American Program
To provide the opportunity for senior scholars, postdoctoral fellows, and postgraduate students to spend a period of three to twelve months at an academic or research institution in Australia. These longer term Fulbright Awards are open to any American citizen. Those wishing to be considered for the Senior Scholar/Postdoctoral Fellow category should

apply to the Council for International Exchange of Scholars (CIES), 3400 International Dr. NW, Ste. 500, Washington, DC 20008-3097. Nominations are forwarded to the Foundation in September each year and the Board of Directors makes the final selections. The competition for awards in the Postgraduate Student category is conducted by the Institute of International Education in New York. Final selection of students is made by the Foundation's Board of Directors. Postgraduate Students may apply for either one year of research as part of their advanced degree program at an American institution or for enrollment in a higher degree program at an Australian institution. There is also a Short-Term Senior Scholar Award available to Americans who have been invited to Australia by a university, learned society, or professional association for a significant short-term purpose, such as a keynote speaker at a national or international conference, participant in a program of seminars/workshops or research activities. Selection of Short-Term Senior Scholars is made by the Foundation's Board of Directors at their last meeting in November each year. Benefits of an award for grantees in the longer-term category normally cover a return airfare United States-Australia; a stipend plus loadings for accompanying dependents; and an all-inclusive allowance and health insurance. Short-term Senior Scholars normally receive a return airfare United States-Australia; a fixed allowance toward cost of travel within Australia; a per diem, and health insurance. Established in 1949 by the governments of Australia and the United States to honor former U.S. Senator J. William Fulbright.

186

Fulbright Awards - Australian Program
To provide the opportunity for senior scholars/senior professionals, postdoctoral fellows, and postgraduate students to spend a period of three to twelve months at an academic or research institution in the United States. Postgraduate Student Awards are renewable each year for students undertaking Master's or Doctor's degrees. There is a Scholar-in-Residence Award that is available only when the Foundation calls for applications. With the exception of the Scholar-in-Residence category, all Fulbright awards to Australians are offered only through annual competitions conducted nationally by the Foundation. Final selection is made by the Foundation from lists of recommended candidates put forward by state-based selection panels on the basis of competition results. Senior, Postdoctoral Fellow, and Postgraduate Student competitions are announced in July each year. The Postdoctoral Fellow and Postgraduate Student competitions close in late September; the Senior competition in late November. Benefits of an award for grantees in the Senior Scholar/Senior Professional, Postdoctoral Fellow, and Postgraduate Student categories normally cover a return airfare Australia-United States, an all-inclusive allowance, and health insurance. Established in 1949 by the governments of Australia and the United States to honor former U.S. Senator J. William Fulbright.

187

Australian and New Zealand Association for the Advancement of Science
GPO Box 873 Phone: 2 5521693
Sydney, NSW 2001, Australia Fax: 2 5163220

188

ANZAAS Medal
To recognize an individual for outstanding achievements in science. Individuals who normally reside in Australia or New Zealand may be nominated. A medal is awarded annually. Established in 1965.

189

Mackie Medal
For recognition of the most significant contribution to the study of education. Australian or New Zealand citizens or residents of Australia or New Zealand for the two years immediately prior to the award are eligible. A medal is awarded annually. Established in 1961.

190

Mueller Medal
For recognition of important contributions to anthropological, botanical, geological or zoological science. Preference is given to work having special reference to Australasia. There is no restriction on eligibility for the award. A medal is awarded annually. Established in 1902.

191

Orbit Award of the ANZAAS International Scientific Film Exhibition and Competition
For recognition of the most outstanding scientific 16mm film from the point of view of cinematic value, scientific content and general appeal. Awarded annually when merited.

192

Australian Book Publishers Association
89 Jones St. Phone: 2 281 9788
Ultimo, NSW 2007, Australia Fax: 2 281 1073

193

Book Design Awards
For recognition of excellence in book design in Australia. Entries must be published and designed in Australia, but may be printed anywhere. Entries may be submitted by November 30. Awards are given to designers and certificates are given to publishers. The following prizes are awarded: Joyce Nicholson Award for the best designed book of the year - $1,000; ABPA/Andrew Fabinyi Award for the best book designed for secondary education purposes - $500; Weldon International Award for the best book designed for primary education purposes - $500; Bulletin Award for the best jacket design of the year - $500; Book Printer Award for the best designed paperback - $500; Ashton Scholastic Award for the best designed illustrated children's book - $500; Reader's Digest Young Designer Award for the best book by a designer under 30 years of age by December 31st of the year of the award - $500; Griffin Press Award for the best book with a price above $50 - $500; Penguin Award for the best non-illustrated book - $500; D. W. Thorpe Award for the best designed promotional material - $500; Collins Australian English Dictionaries Award for the best designed popular reference book - $500; University of Queensland Press Award for the best designed undergraduagte, graduate, and professional book - $500; and an award for the best designed calendar or diary. Awarded annually. Established in 1951.

194

Australian Broadcasting Corporation
c/o Concert Music Gen. Mgr.
PO Box 9994
221 Pacific Hwy. Phone: 2 3941662
Sydney, NSW 2001, Australia Fax: 2 3941678

Formerly: (1983) Australian Broadcasting Commission.

195

ABC Sports Award of the Year
For recognition of excellence in individual and team achievement in sport on behalf of Australia, in Australia or overseas. Australian citizens who have gained outstanding achievement representing Australia at major international or national sporting events are eligible. A gold-plated statue is awarded annually. Established in 1951. Additional information is available from Marijke Steffens, Production Co-ordinator TV Sport. Formerly: (1983) ABC Sportsman of the Year.

196

Bicentennial Fiction Award
To recognize an outstanding work of fiction.

197

Young Performers Award
To encourage professional development of young solo musicians. Awards are presented in four categories: vocal, orchestral strings, keyboard, and instrumental. Individuals between 18 and 30 years of age who are citizens or permanent residents of Australia for a minimum of one year are eligible. A monetary prize of $4,000 is presented to the best performer in each category. The overall winner is designated the Young Performer of the Year and receives a monetary award of $7,500 and

concert engagements with ABC orchestras. Awarded annually. Established in 1944. Formerly: (1986) ABC Young Performers' Competition; (1985) Instrumental and Vocal Competition; (1967) ABC Concerts and Vocal Competition.

198
Australian Cinematographers Society
Federal Exec.
PO Box 207
Cammeray, NSW 2062, Australia   Phone: 2 413 8818

199
Milli Award
For recognition of the best achievement in cinematography by an Australian cinematographer. Membership in the Society is necessary for consideration. Awards are given in the following categories: (1) Cinematographer of the Year; (2) Cunningham-Steward Memorial Award; (3) Feature Production Section (Cinema and Television); (4) Television Drama Series; (5) Dramatized Documentary Section (Cinema and Television); (6) Documentary Section (Cinema and Television); (7) Fiction Drama Section (Cinema and Television); and (8) Current Affairs Section. A trophy is awarded annually. Established in 1968.

200
Australian College of Education
42 Geils Ct.   Phone: 62 81 1677
Deakin, ACT 2600, Australia   Fax: 62 285 1262

201
Australian College of Education Medal
For recognition of an outstanding contribution to education in Australia. Australian citizens or long-term residents of Australia may be nominated for the Award. Selection is made by a committee. A medal and framed citation are awarded annually at the College national conference. Established in 1981.

202
Fellowship of the Australian College of Education
For recognition of a distinctive contribution to the advancement of education. College members must be nominated for selection by a committee. A parchment is awarded annually at the College national conference. Established in 1959.

203
Australian Council of National Trusts
c/o Australian Heritage Award Secretariat
PO Box 1002   Phone: 62 476766
Civic Square, ACT 2608, Australia   Fax: 62 491395

204
Australian Heritage Award
For recognition of outstanding achievement in preserving and promoting Australia's heritage. Individuals, associations, government bodies, and companies are eligible for nomination. There is one annual Australian Heritage Award with selection taking place from the following categories: Government, Planning, Private, Publications, Media & Education, Cultural Conservation and Interpretation, Architecture, Nature Conservation, Contemporary, and Individual. A monetary endowment of $10,000 (Australian) is awarded to the overall winner. Finalists in each category are awarded a certificate of merit. Awarded annually. Established in 1986. In 1988, the Australian Bicentennial Heritage Award was also presented. Sponsored by Jones Lang Wootton. (Inactive in 1991)

205
Australian Decorations Advisory Committee
Australian Bravery Decorations
Government House
Canberra, ACT 2600, Australia

206
Antarctic Medal
For recognition of outstanding service by people connected with Australian Antarctic expeditions. Australia's Governor-General, on recommendation of the government minister responsible for the Antarctic territory, approves awards of the Antarctic Medal. The medal is part of the Australian system of honors and awards and is announced each year on Mid-Winter's Day (June 21 in the Southern Hemisphere), which has special significance to members of expeditions to the Antarctic. Established in 1987.

207
Australian Bravery Decorations
Australia Bravery Decorations consist of the following awards for individuals: Cross of Valour - for acts of the most conspicuous courage in circumstances of extreme peril; Star of Courage - for acts of conspicuous courage in circumstances of great peril; Bravery Medal - for acts of bravery in hazardous circumstances; and Commendation for Brave Conduct - for other acts of bravery in hazardous circumstances. Also awarded is the Group Citation for Bravery. Australian citizens are eligible. Non-Australians are also considered for acts of bravery performed in Australia or in Australia's interest. The decorations may be awarded posthumously.

208
National Medal
To recognize members of the Defence Force, or an Australian police force, ambulance service, fire service, protective service, correctional service, or emergency service for 15 years' service. A clasp to the medal is awarded for each further period of 10 years' service. Service for the National Medal may be rendered on a full-time or volunteer (part-time), paid, or unpaid basis. The medal is circular, made of bronze, and displays the Arms of the Commonwealth contained within a wide rim carrying the inscription "The National Medal: For Service." It is suspended by a Crown attached to a ribbon of 15 alternating gold and blue narrow vertical stripes symbolizing 15 years of service.

209
Australian Elizabethan Theatre Trust
139 Regent St.
PO Box 73   Phone: 2 698 1688
Chippendale, NSW 2008, Australia   Fax: 2 699 1618

210
BP Arts Media Awards
For recognition of journalistic contributions to the arts through print, television and radio. Australian residents are eligible. Monetary awards of $3,000 each (Australian) and a crystal trophy are presented annually. Established in 1984. Sponsored by BP Australia.

211
Australian Federation of University Women
PO Box 6620
Upper Mt. Gravatt, QLD 4122, Australia   Phone: 7 345 7141

212
Georgina Sweet Fellowship
To assist women who do not reside habitually in Australia to carry out some advanced study or research in Australia for a period of four to twelve months. Members of the International Federation may apply by July 31 in the year of the offer. A fellowship of $8,000 Australian is awarded biennially. Established in 1965 in honor of Dr. Georgina Sweet, a

foundation member and an active member of the Victorian Branch of the Federation.

[213]

Australian Federation of University Women
Queensland Fellowship Fund
PO Box 586
Kenmore, QLD 4069, Australia   Phone: 7 8572556

[214]

AFUW - QLD Freda Bage Fellowship
To provide for postgraduate research. The deadline is September 30. A fellowship of $31,000 Australian is awarded annually for a maximum period of three years. The Fellowship is tenable at any Australian University or other approved tertiary institute in Australia. If the award is made to an Australian it is also tenable overseas. Established in 1971 in honor of Freda Bage. The AFUW - QLD Commemorative Fellowship is also awarded. Established in 1987.

[215]

Australian Federation of University Women
South Australia Trust Fund
Univ. of Adelaide
Box 634
Adelaide, SA 5001, Australia

Formerly: (1989) Australian Federation of University Women - South Australia.

[216]

AFUW-SA Inc. Trust Fund Bursary
To assist women with study towards a Master's degree by coursework at a recognized higher education institution in Australia. There is no restriction on age or field of study. The deadline is the last day of February. A monetary award of $3,000 Australian is presented annually in June. Established in 1991.

[217]

Thenie Baddams Bursary
To assist women with research towards a Master's by research or Ph.D. degree at a recognized higher education institution in Australia. Applicants must have completed one year of postgraduate research. There is no restriction on age or field of study. The deadline is the last day of February. A monetary award of $6,000 Australian is presented. Established in 1986 to honor Thenie Baddams, President of AFUW from 1982 to 1985.

[218]

Jean Gilmore Bursary
To assist women with research towards a Master's by research or Ph.D. degree at a recognized higher education institution in Australia. Applicants must have completed one year of postgraduate research. There is no restriction on age or field of study. The deadline is the last day of February. A monetary award of $6,000 Australian is presented annually in June. Established in 1969 to honor Jean Gilmore, President of the AFUW from 1965 to 1968.

[219]

Winifred E. Preedy Post-Graduate Bursary
To assist women who are or have been students in the Faculty of Dentistry in The University of Adelaide at the time of application to further their studies at postgraduate level in Dentistry or a related field. Applicants must have completed one year of their postgraduate degree. Applications must be submitted by the last day of February. A monetary award of $5,000 is presented annually. Established in 1992 from the bequest of Winifred E. Preedy BDS (1901-1989), a devoted Life Member of AFUWSA Inc., who graduated in 1927, the second woman to graduate BDS in The University of Adelaide.

[220]

Australian Film Institute
49 Eastern Rd.   Phone: 3 696 1844
South Melbourne, VIC 3205, Australia   Fax: 3 696 7972

[221]

Australian Film Institute Awards
For recognition of achievement and excellence in film and television production. Films must be either produced in Australia using a significant Australian cast (if applicable), key creative production personnel and facilities, or must be an official Australian co-production. The film must be completed or theoretically released between July 1 and June 30 during the preceding year. Feature films are dramatised story films of over 60 minutes in length produced for theatrical release on 16mm, 35mm, or 70mm stock. Feature awards are given in the following categories: Best Film; Best Original Screenplay; Best Screenplay Adapted from Another Source; Best Performance by an Actress in a Leading Role; Best Performance by an Actor in a Leading Role; Best Performance by an Actress in a Supporting Role; Best Performance by an Actor in a Supporting Role; Best Achievement in Cinematography; Best Achievement in Direction; Best Achievement in Editing; Best Original Music Score; Best Score Featuring Adapted Music; Best Achievement in Production Design; Best Achievement in Costume Design; Best Achievement in Sound; and the Young Actors Award (film). Non-feature awards are given in the following categories: Best Documentary; Best Short Fiction Film; Best Animation Film; Best Screenplay in a Short Film; Best Achievement in Cinematography in a Non Feature Film; Best Achievement in Editing in a Non Feature Film; Best Acievement in Sound in a Non Feature Film; and Open Craft Award (for achievement in a craft area other than screenplay, cinematography, editing, or sound). Television awards are presented in the following categories: Best Mini-Series or Telefeature; Best Episode in a TV Drama Series; Best Episode in in a TV Drama Serial; Best Children's TV Drama; Best TV Documentary; Best Achievement in Direction in a TV Drama; Best Screenplay in a TV Drama; Best Performance by an Actress in a Leading Role in a TV Drama; Best Performance by an Actor in a Leading Role in a TV Drama; and Young Actors Award (television). Trophies are presented annually. Established in 1958, with the Television awards being introduced in 1986.

[222]

Byron Kennedy Memorial Prize
To recognize an individual working in any area of the Australian film or television industry, whose quality of work is marked by the pursuit of excellence. A monetary award of $10,000 and a trophy are presented. Established in 1984.

[223]

Raymond Longford Award
For recognition of an individual who has made a significant contribution to Australian filmmaking. A trophy is awarded annually. Established in 1968.

[224]

Australian Institute of Energy
PO Box 230   Phone: 2 4491800
Wahroonga, NSW 2076, Australia   Fax: 2 9839665

[225]

Australian Institute of Energy Medal
For recognition of achievement in the field of energy. Members only may be nominated. A medal is awarded when merited. Established in 1980.

[226]

Australian Institute of Genealogical Studies
PO Box 339, Blackburn   Phone: 3 8773789
Melbourne, VIC 3130, Australia   Fax: 3 8779066

227
Alexander Henderson Award
To recognize the best family history published in Australia, improve the quality of published family histories, and encourage people to write their family history. Any writer is eligible. The deadline is November 30. A trophy is awarded annually. In addition, the President's Award (currently under review), which recognizes the best family history by an individual 18 years of age or younger, is also awarded. Established in 1974 in honor of Alexander Henderson, an Australian pioneer genealogist.

228
Australian Institute of International Affairs
32 Thesige Ct.
Deakin, ACT 2600, Australia
Phone: 62 822133
Phone: 62 822730
Fax: 62 852334

229
Prizes for Excellence in the Study of International Affairs
For recognition of excellence in the study of international relations. Undergraduate students enrolled in their final honors courses at an Australian University or at the University College of the Northern Territory may apply with the submission of a final honors dissertation if it deals with a topic related to Australian foreign policy or to a major theme in international relations. Monetary prizes of $200 (Australian) and plaques are awarded annually. Established in 1986.

230
Australian Institute of Management
10 St. Leonards Ave.
St. Kilda
Melbourne, VIC 3182, Australia
Phone: 3 5348181
Fax: 3 5345050

231
John Storey Medal
For recognition of a distinguished contribution to the development of management in Australia or the development of management by an Australian. The award may be presented to the following individuals: practicing manager for a direct contribution to raising the standards of a management practice in the business, industrial, or commercial scene; practicing manager for contribution in community "management" work (through associations, institutions, charities, other community organizations, etc.); public administrator for contribution to management in the public sector of the community at local, state, or national level; manager, management scholar, or academic for contribution to the advancement of management thinking in his or her institution and/or in the community; statesman for contribution in the field of management towards the development of Australia; and public or other figure for contribution in the field of management to the community in general. Select ion is by nomination by a division of the Institute. A medal is awarded annuall y. Established in 1962 in memory of Sir John Storey.

232
Australian Institute of Physics
National Science Centre
191 Royal Parade
Parkville, VIC 3052, Australia
Phone: 3 3266669
Fax: 3 3282670

233
Walter Boas Medal
For recognition of an achievement by an Australian in physics. A medal is awarded annually. Established in 1984 in honor of Walter Boas.

234
Bragg Gold Medal for Excellence in Physics
To recognize the student who is judged to have completed the most outstanding Ph.D. in physics under the auspices of an Australian university and whose degree has been approved in the previous thirteen months. Established in 1992 to commemorate the work of W. L. and W. H. Bragg.

235
Harrie Massie Medal
To recognize an Australian physicist or a non-Australian physicist working or residing in Australia for contributions to physics or its application. A medal is awarded annually. Established in 1988 in honor of Sir Harrie Massey.

236
Australian Library and Information Association
PO Box E441
Queen Victoria Terrace
Canberra, ACT 2600, Australia
Phone: 6 2851877
Fax: 6 2822249

Formerly: (1988) Library Association of Australia.

237
H. C. L. Anderson Award
To recognize an individual who has rendered outstanding service to librarianship or to the library profession in Australia, or to the theory or practice of librarianship. Professional members of the Association who hold overseas qualifications in librarianship or archives that are recognized as professional qualifications by a Library Association or Archives Association in the country concerned are eligible. Any member of the Association or the Council of a Division may nominate persons for this award. A statuette is awarded irregularly. Established in 1973 to honor Henry Charles Lennox Anderson.

238
Ellinor Archer Award
To recognize an individual who has rendered outstanding service to a library or libraries, the promotion of a library or libraries, to the theory or practice of librarianship, or an associated field such as systems, conservation, management, or bibliography. Individuals who are employed in libraries and who are not eligible for Associateship of the Association are eligible. Any member of the Association or the Council of a Division may nominate persons for this award. A statuette is awarded irregularly. Established in 1984 to honor Mary Ellinor Lucy Archer.

239
Redmond Barry Award
To recognize an individual who has rendered outstanding service to the promotion of a library or of libraries, to the Association, to the theory or practice of librarianship, or to an associated field such as bibliography. Individuals who are not eligible to be professional members of the Association and who are not employed in a library are eligible. Any member of the Association or the Council of a Division may nominate persons for this award. A statuette is awarded irregularly. Established in 1973 to honor Sir Redmond Barry.

240
Fellow
To recognize an Associate (professional) member who, in the opinion of the Board, has made a distinguished contribution to the theory and/or practice of library and information science. Nominees must have at least eight years' standing as a professional member of the Association. Any professional member(s) of the Association or the Council of a Division may nominate a professional member for this distinction. A certificate is awarded irregularly. Established in 1963.

241
Maria Gemenis Award
To recognize an individual for an outstanding contribution to special librarianship. Only members of the ALIA Special Libraries Section NSW Group may be nominated. Awarded annually. Established in 1983 to honor Maria Gemenis.

242
Letter of Recognition
To recognize a person or an institution or organization that has rendered a significant, specific service to a library or libraries, to the Association, or to the promotion or development of libraries or library science, or who has over a period demonstrated significant service above the call of duty in these fields. The Letter of Recognition is not available routinely to people working in or with libraries or with the Association who are retiring or to office bearers of the Association who are finishing their term of office. Any member of the Association or the Council of a Division may nominate persons for this award. A Letter of Recognition is awarded irregularly. Established in 1985.

243
Library Manager of the Year
To recognize and encourage good management practices within Australian libraries and information services, and to encourage the development of an organizational climate within information agencies that promotes innovation and a better working relationship between managers and their staff. Open to any member of the Association responsible for the management of a library service, an individual library or information service, or a significant organizational unit within a larger library or information service. The award is for management rather than supervision, and the nominee is expected to be responsible for the direction of staff, including professional staff. Nominations must be proposed and seconded by two staff members or clients of the organization where the nominee is employed, including at least one person within the managed library or unit. A Perspex Trophy is awarded annually. Established in 1987. Sponsored by Co-op Subscriptions.

244
Library Technician of the Year
To recognize outstanding contributions to the advancement of library technicians and/or the Library Technicians Section of the ALIA. A trophy and a citation are awarded annually. Established in 1989.

245
Metcalfe Medallion
For recognition of the most outstanding essay or other piece of work on any topic of interest to library and information services submitted by a student taking a first award course in library and information science. Entries must be pieces of work of publishable or reproducible standard and up to 5,000 words in length. Winning entries are published by the Association. Entries close on December 15 each year. A medallion is awarded annually. Established in 1984 in memory of John Wallace Metcalfe and his contribution to librarianship and library education.

246
Study Grant Awards
To provide support for practicing librarians/information professionals wishing to undertake a study project. The Association's intention in offering study grants is to provide an opportunity for librarians to undertake projects they would otherwise be unable to do because of the time and costs involved. A practicing librarian in a supervisory or middle management position, with a minimum of three years' experience in library and information work is eligible. Applications must be submitted by August 31 each year. Monetary awards are presented annually. Established in 1984.

247
WA Special Librarian Award
To recognize outstanding contribution to the library profession by a special librarian. Nominees must be members of the ALIA Special Libraries Section, WA Group and have demonstrated a willingness to share professional expertise and to participate in formal and informal networking activities, good management practices, and successful promotion of the library. Awarded annually.

248
Australian Library and Information Association School Libraries Section (W.A. Group)
Address unknown since 1992.

249
West Australian Young Readers' Book Award
To promote reading; to give recognition to those who read and write children's literature; and to provide a focus for the mutual interest of those concerned with children and their literature. Titles are nominated by young readers nine to fifteen years of age, thus allowing children the major say in selecting the prize winning literature. The purpose is to generate enthusiasm for pleasure reading, to enrich children's reading experiences, and to develop their powers of discrimination in comparing quality literature. Nominations must be submitted by the middle of the school year. Thirty primary books and 30 secondary books published during the five years preceding the award are accepted. A trophy is presented annually. Established in 1980.

250
Australian Library Promotion Council
c/o Australian Library & Information
 Association
PO Box E441
Queen Victoria Terr.
Canberra, ACT 2600, Australia

251
Alfred McMicken Award
To recognize an individual who has made a commendable contribution to library promotion in Australia. Established in 1977 in honor of Alfred E. McMicken, a distinguished librarian, whose contribution was wide and varied in the development of library services within Victoria and Australia. (The Council was disbanded in 1989. Library promotion now occurs on an individual basis in most states.)

252
Australian Mathematical Society
Mathematics Dept.
Univ. of Tasmania
GPO Box 252 C
Hobart, TAS 7001, Australia
Phone: 2 202442
Fax: 2 202867

253
Australian Mathematical Society Medal
For recognition of distinguished research in the mathematical sciences. Members who have not reached the age of forty at the beginning of the year in which the Council makes the award are eligible. A medal is awarded annually. Established in 1981.

254
Bernhard H. Neumann Prize
For recognition of the best student talk at the annual meeting. Students (part-time or full-time) who are members of the Society are eligible. A monetary prize of $100 (Australian) and a certificate are awarded each year at the annual meeting. Established in 1985 in honor of Professor Bernhard H. Neumann.

255
Australian National University
PO Box 4
Canberra City, ACT 2604, Australia
Phone: 6 2493780
Fax: 6 2490767

256
J. G. Crawford Award
To recognize the author of a research paper making a substantial and original contribution to scholarship in the field and to understanding

between Australia and Japan. To be eligible for consideration the paper should address some aspect of the operation of the Japanese economy or economic policy, Japan's international relations with Australia, or the political environment affecting these affairs. Authors must be either Australian or Japanese nationals and no more than 35 years of age by December 31 of the award year. Both published and unpublished papers must be nominated by December 31. A monetary prize of $2,000 is awarded. Where possible, the paper selected is published by the Australia-Japan Research Centre as part of its Pacific Economic Papers (PEP) series. Established in 1987. Additional information is available from Executive Officer, Australia-Japan Research Centre, telephone: 6 2493780.

257

Australian Numismatic Society
Box R4
Royal Exchange, NSW 2000, Australia   Phone: 2 419 5790

258

Bronze Medal
For recognition of services to numismatics, but not warranting the gold or silver medal. Mainly members of the Society are eligible. A bronze medal is awarded annually when merited. Established in 1983.

259

Gold Medal
For recognition of long and distinguished service to numismatics or for research on numismatics. Mainly members of the Society are eligible. A gilt medal is awarded annually when merited. Established in 1968.

260

Silver Medal
For recognition of long and distinguished service to numismatics; but not warranting the gold medal. Mainly members of the Society are eligible. A silver medal is awarded annually when merited. Established in 1968.

261

Australian Singing Competition
c/o Music & Opera Singers Trust Unlimited
Gridiger & Company
67 Castlereagh St.   Phone: 2 2314888
Sydney, NSW 2000, Australia   Fax: 2 2218201

262

Mathy & Opera Awards
This, the richest and most prestigious singing competition in Australia is held to encourage professional careers and to recognize exceptional classical singing talent. Entries must be submitted by July 1. Numerous scholarships and awards are presented annually, including the Marianne Mathy Scholarship of $20,000 and travel opportunities for an Australian singer under 26 years of age. Established in 1982. Sponsored by Commonwealth Bank of Australia.

263

Australian Society for Parasitology
ACTS
GPO Box 2200   Phone: 62 498015
Canberra, ACT 2601, Australia   Fax: 62 573256

264

Bancroft - Mackerras Medal of the Australian Society for Parasitology
For recognition of achievements in the science of parasitology. Members of the Society must be nominated by September 30 each year. A medal is awarded each year when merited at the annual general meeting of the Society. Established in 1982 in honor of the Bancroft and Mackerras families.

265

John Frederick Adrian Sprent Prize
For recognition of an outstanding Ph.D. thesis in parasitology published during the preceding three years. Members of the Society may apply. A monetary prize and medal are awarded triennially. Established in 1987.

266

Australian Society of Archivists
PO Box 83   Phone: 6 2093646
O'Connor, ACT 2601, Australia   Fax: 6 2093931

267

Australian Society of Archivists Award
To encourage excellence in archival studies, to stimulate interest in the archival profession, and to increase support for the aims of the Society. A monetary prize of $100 Australian, a certificate, and associate membership for one year are awarded annually. Established in 1988.

268

Honorary Member
To recognize members for service to the Society or the profession of archivists. Life membership is awarded biennially when merited. Established in 1977.

269

Australian Teachers of Media
PO Box 222   Phone: 03 4822393
Carlton South, VIC 3053, Australia   Fax: 03 4825018

270

ATOM Awards
To promote the educational use of film and video; to give recognition to film and videomakers in this field; to assist teachers in selecting new, innovative and quality programs for the classroom; to encourage the pursuit of excellence in the production of educational resources; and to highlight the importance of media education. Awards are given in the following categories: Short Fiction; Animation; General Documentary; Science and Environment; Social Issues; Education Resource; Training/Instruction; Subject Specific; Secondary Student Production; Tertiary Student Production; Children's Television; Television Drama; Television Series/Serial; Television Documentary; and the Australian Multimedia Award. In addition, The Gold Atom is awarded to the best film or video from all finalists, special prizes are presented to two individual film and video makers, and awards are presented for the two best productions in the primary and secondary student categories. Films and videotapes under 60 minutes produced during the twelve months preceding the award are eligible. Awarded annually. Established in 1982.

271

Australian Telecommunications and Electronics Research Board
PO Box 93   Phone: 2 8878221
North Ryde, NSW 2113, Australia   Fax: 2 8872736

Formerly: (1984) Radio Research Board.

272

ATERB Medal Outstanding Young Investigator Telecommunications and Electronics
To recognize outstanding researchers for contributions in the field of telecommunications and electronics. Contributions can be recognized by research papers, patents, commercial success, and benefit to Australia. Research must be done mainly in Australia by an individual under 36 years of age to be eligible. The deadline is January 31. A monetary prize of $2,500 Australian and a medal are awarded annually. Established in 1987.

273
Australian Veterinary Association
PO Box 371
Artarmon, NSW 2064, Australia
Phone: 2 4112733
Fax: 2 4115089

274
AVA Prize for Undergraduates
To recognize outstanding students in veterinary pathology. A $150 check towards the cost of books is awarded annually in each of the Faculties of Veterinary Science at the University of Sydney, the University of Queenland, the University of Melbourne, and Murdoch University. Established in 1955.

275
AVA Student Award
To recognize students who, through their academic work and participation in student affairs, are considered to be an asset to the student body and potentially an asset to the veterinary profession and the Association. A certificate and a two-year membership subscription are awarded at the annual general meeting. Established in 1978.

276
Gilruth Prize
To recognize an individual for meritorious service to veterinary science in Australia. Awarded annually. Established in 1953 to honor Dr. J.A. Gilruth, Dean of the Faculty of Veterinary Science of the University of Melbourne, the first Chief of the Division of Animal Health of the CSIR, and an outstanding veterinary authority.

277
Kendall Oration and Medal
To recognize outstanding Australian veterinarians. A medal is awarded when merited at the annual conference of AVA. Established in 1930 by the five sons of Dr. W.T. Kendall to honor his memory. Dr. William Tyson Kendall migrated to Australia in 1880 and he made a unique contribution to veterinary science in Australia.

278
Kesteven Medal
To recognize Australian veterinarians for distinguished contributions to international veterinary science in the fields of technical and scientific assistance to developing countries. A medal is presented each year at the annual general meeting of the Australian Veterinary Association or the Australian College of Veterinary Scientists at which the recipient may be invited to speak briefly about his or her work. The award was inaugurated by the late Dr. K.V.L. Kesteven, and first awarded in 1980. Sponsored by the Australian College of Veterinary Scientists.

279
Meritorious Service Award
To recognize service by members to the Association, regional divisions, branches, or special interest groups. The award may also be made to persons who are not eligible for membership in the Association but who have provided meritorious service to it. Established in 1978.

280
Australian Widescreen Association
c/-18 Kangerong Rd.
Box Hill, VIC 3128, Australia

281
Australian International Widescreen Festival
To encourage the amateur use of Widescreen in St. 8, Super-8, 16mm, movies, and to encourage slides taken with Widelux/Horizont panoramic cameras, and SLRs with anamorphic lenses. Application, films must be photographed in widescreen format of not less than 2:1 ratio. A trophy for the Best Film at the Festival is awarded annually. Established in 1971. Sponsored by AGFA, Photo Express, and Crawford Productions. Additional information is available from Brian P. Beatty, 6 Menwood Street, Forest Hill, VIC 3131, Australia.

282
Australian Writers Guild
60 Kellett St.
Kings Cross, NSW 2011, Australia
Phone: 2 357 7888
Fax: 2 357 7776

283
Awgie Awards
For recognition of excellence in scriptwriting for stage, film, radio, and television. Members of the Society who are Australian citizens may submit scripts that have been produced during the preceding calendar year. Awgie statuettes are awarded in the following categories: (1) Best Script of the Year; (2) documentary; (3) children's drama; (4) comedy review/sketch material (any medium); (5) television series episode; (6) television serial episode; (7) television comedy; (8) television mini-series (adapted); (9) television mini-series (original); (10) telemovie (adapted); (11) telemovie (original); (12) original work for the stage; (13) feature screenplay; (14) theater-in-education/community theater; (15) radio drama (original); (16) radio drama (adaptation); (17) Dorothy Crawford Award for a member of the industry who has furthered the cause of Australian writing for stage or screen; (18) Monte Miller Memorial Award for the best unproduced script by an Associate Member; (19) Frank Parsons Award for a special contribution to Australian comedy; (20) Richard Lane Award for long-standing service and dedication to the Guild; and (21) Hector Crawford Award for a significant contribution to the craft via a body of script editing work. The Major Awgie Award is presented when merited to an outstanding winner from the category winners. Awarded annually in a presentation ceremony which alternates between Melbourne and Sydney. Established in 1968.

284
Blake Society
PO Box 4484
Sydney, NSW 2001, Australia

285
Blake Prize for Religious Art
To encourage contemporary artists to explore religious themes of all beliefs. Any religious art work such as painting, sculpture, tapestry, or print may be entered by early November. A monetary prize of $10,000 Australian is awarded annually at the Exhibition of Selected Works. The first Blake Prize was awarded in 1951. For further information and entry form, write to Blake Society Box 4484, G.P.O. Sydney 2001, Australia.

286
Braille and Talking Book Library
31-51 Commercial Rd.
South Yarra, VIC 3141, Australia
Phone: 3 867 6022
Fax: 3 820 1335

287
Tilly Aston Award
No further information provided on this braille-related award for this edition.

288
The Bathurst: Narrator of the Year
To encourage the highest standards of excellence in the narration of audio books. Actors who have narrated one of the six titles shortlisted for the Braille Book of the Year Award are considered. A crystal decanter is awarded annually. Established in 1985 in honor of Hector Bathurst, President, Braille & Talking Book Library 1970-1984.

289
Benella Award
No further information available on this audio-related award for this edition.

290

Braille and Talking Book Library Award
To make the best of current Australian literature available to print handicapped readers. Australian works published during the preceding year are considered. An original sculpture is awarded annually. Established in 1974 in memory of Louis Braille. Formerly: (1991) Braille Book of the Year.

291

Brisbane Warana Festival Ltd.
234 Grey St.
PO Box 3611
South Brisbane, QLD 4101, Australia
Phone: 7 8462333
Fax: 7 8461944

292

City of Brisbane Short Story Award
To recognize an outstanding short story and to encourage new and unpublished writers. Stories between 1,000 and 5,000 words by residents of Australia must be submitted by July 31. Stories submitted must not have been previously published nor offered for publication prior to the announcement of the award. A monetary award of $1,000 is presented annually in September. Established in 1987 by the Warana Writers' Week Committee. Sponsored by the Brisbane City Council.

293

Premier's Poetry Award
To recognize the best poem or group of poems up to three hundred lines, and to encourage new and unpublished poets. Residents of Australia may submit poems by July 31. Poems submitted must not have been previously published nor offered for publication prior to the announcement of the Award. A monetary award of $1,000 is presented annually in September. Established in 1987 by the Warana Writers' Week Committee.

294

Steele Rudd Award
To recognize the best collection of short stories. Australian collections published in the preceding twelve months must be submitted by the end of April each year. A monetary award of $10,000 is presented annually at the opening of Warana Writers' Week in Brisbane each September. Sponsored by the Queensland Government.

295

Broken Hill Proprietary Company
GPO Box 86A
Melbourne, VIC 3001, Australia

296

BHP Awards for the Pursuit of Excellence
To identify Australian men and women from a wide range of backgrounds and vocations whose efforts may have gone unrecognized outside their special area of endeavor and whose examples could become an inspiration to others. Awards were given in six categories: commerce, industry and management; community service and welfare; environment; literature and the arts; rural development; and science and technology. A grant of $40,000 Australian and the Pursuit of Excellence Trophy, a specially-commissioned bronze statuette by the sculptor, Meszaros, were awarded to each winner. Established in 1984 by Sir James McNeill, then chairman of the Australian Broken Hill Proprietary Group. (Discontinued)

297

The Bulletin
54 Park St.
Sydney, NSW 2000, Australia
Phone: 2 282 8000
Fax: 2 267 2150

298

***The Bulletin* Black and White Artists' Awards**
For recognition of achievement in black and white (newspaper) art. Awards were given in the following categories: Best Comic Strip; Best Realist Illustration; Best Editorial/Political Cartoon; Best Single Gag Cartoon; Best Adventure Comic; Best Graphic Design; Best Caricature; Artist of the Year; Year's Best Contributor to Black and White Art; Best Symbolic Illustration; Winner of the People's Choice from the Exhibition at the State Library of New South Wales; and Bob Mitchell Award. A trophy was awarded annually. Established in 1985 in memory of Stan Cross. (Discontinued in 1992)

299

***The Bulletin*/Compaq Young Executive of the Year**
For recognition of an outstanding young executive. A trophy was awarded annually. Established in 1986. (Discontinued about 1988)

300

***The Bulletin*/Qantas Business Woman of the Year**
For recognition of an outstanding business woman. A trophy was awarded annually. Established in 1979. (Discontinued in 1992)

301

Canberra Times
PO Box 7156
Canberra Mail Centre
Canberra, ACT 2610, Australia
Phone: 6 280 2105
Fax: 6 280 7531

302

***Canberra Times* and Commonwealth Bank National Short Story of the Year**
For recognition of outstanding short stories by residents of Australia. A monetary prize of $3,000 was awarded annually to the winner, and $1,200 to the runner-up. Established in 1974. (Discontinued in 1991)

303

***Canberra Times* National Art Award**
For recognition of an outstanding painting. A monetary prize of $5,000 is awarded. (Discontinued in 1991)

304

Cardiac Society of Australia and New Zealand
145 Macquarie St.
Sydney, NSW 2000, Australia
Phone: 2 2565452
Fax: 2 2565449

305

R. T. Hall Prize
To recognize an individual investigator or group of investigators for work that advances knowledge of the cardiovascular system and its diseases and is published in a scientific journal or journals during the three-year period preceding the closing date. The work must have originated in Australia or New Zealand but the investigators need not be members of The Society. The deadline for entry is September 30. A monetary prize of $3,000 (Australian) is awarded annually. Established in 1961 by the R.T. Hall Trust Fund in honor of R. T. Hall.

306

Ralph Reader Prize
To recognize the best individual presentation by an investigator aged 35 years or under at the time of the annual Scientific Meeting of the Cardiac Society. The work must have been carried out in Australia or New Zealand and the applicant must have made a significant contribution to the concept and execution of the work. A monetary prize of $1,000 (Australian) is awarded annually. Established in 1981 in honor of Dr. Ralph Reader, CMG., FRACP.

307
Chartered Institute of Transport in Australia
PO Box Q398, Queen Victoria Bldg. Phone: 2 264 6413
Sydney, NSW 2000, Australia Fax: 2 267 1682

308
Australian Transport Industry Award
To recognize an outstanding, innovative contribution to the improvement of Australian transport. Improvements developed within Australia, related to all modes of transport that are not detrimental to the environment may be submitted by July 31 for consideration. An engraved bronze plaque is awarded annually. Established in 1977.

309
Children's Book Council of Australia
PO Box 387 Phone: 3 8579372
Croydon, VIC 3136, Australia Fax: 3 8579372

310
Book of the Year Award: Older Readers
To recognize outstanding books that generally require mature reading ability to appreciate the topics, themes, and the scope of emotional involvement. Only books published in the English language or bilingual books where one language is English may be entered. Books in manuscript form or other nonbook materials are not eligible. Books must have been published in Australia between January 1 and December 31 of the year prior to the awards. The creators must be of Australian nationality or a resident in Australia for at least two years prior to December 31 in the year of publication. A monetary prize and a medal are awarded annually. Established in 1946.

311
Book of the Year Award: Younger Readers
For recognition of books for readers who have developed independent reading skills but are still developing in literary awareness. Only books published in the English language or bilingual books where one language is English may be entered. Books in manuscript form or other nonbook materials are not eligible. Books must have been published in Australia between January 1 and December 31 of the year prior to the awards. The creators must be of Australian nationality or a resident in Australia for at least two years prior to December 31 in the year of publication. A monetary prize and a medal are awarded annually. Established in 1982.

312
Picture Book of the Year Award
To recognize outstanding books in which the author and illustrator achieve artistic and literary unity; or in wordless books, where the story, theme, or concept is unified solely through illustrations. Only books published in the English language or bilingual books where one language is English may be entered. Books in manuscript form or other nonbook materials are not eligible. Books must have been published between January 1 and December 31 of the year prior to the award. The creator must be of Australian nationality or a resident in Australia for at least two years prior to December 31 in the year of publication. A monetary prize and a medal are awarded annually. Established in 1952. The Visual Arts Board Awards have also been given from 1974 to 1976. From 1977 they have been divided amongst the winning illustrators in the Picture Book of the Year Awards. From 1989, the award is presented to the winning illustrator and also to the author who is not the illustrator of a text.

313
Eve Pownall Award: Information Books
To recognize outstanding nonfiction books that present well-authenticated data in combination with imaginative presentation and variation of style. Only books published in the English language or bilingual books where one languge is English may be entered. Books in manuscript form or other nonbook materials are not eligible. Books must have been published between January 1 and December 31 of ther year prior to the award. The creators must be of Australian nationality or a resident of Australia for at least two years prior to December 31 of the year of publication. A monetary prize and a medal are awarded annually. Established in 1993 in honor of Eve Pownwall, the late Australian award-winning children's author.

314
Children's Book Council of Australia
New South Wales Branch
PO Box 765 Phone: 2 8100737
Rozelle, NSW 2039, Australia Fax: 2 8181327

315
Lady Cutler Award
For recognition of distinguished service to children's literature in New South Wales. Service should be well beyond a professional association with children's literature. The contributions should be primarily in New South Wales, and sympathetic to the aims of the Council. A trophy, citation certificate, and gift are awarded annually at the Lady Cutler Dinner. Established in 1981 in honor of the late Lady Cutler, Patron of the Children's Book Council and wife of Sir Roden Cutler, former governor of New South Wales.

316
City of Springvale
397 Springvale Rd. Phone: 3 5491111
Springvale, VIC 3171, Australia Fax: 3 5491196

317
City of Springvale Short Story Awards
For recognition of excellence in Australian writing. Entries from Australian citizens may be submitted by December 1. Stories must be 3000-5000 words. The following prizes are awarded: City of Springvale Open Award - $5,000; City of Springvale 21-26 Award - $3,000; and Westpac Under 21 Award - $1,000. Awarded annually on Australia Day, January 26. Established in 1981. Sponsored by the City of Springvale and Westpac Banking Corporation.

318
City of Sydney Cultural Council
617 Town Hall House
456 Kent St. Phone: 2 261 8366
Sydney, NSW 2000, Australia Fax: 2 261 8161

Formerly: (1975) City of Sydney Eisteddfod.

319
Citibank Choral Awards
No further information was provided for this edition.

320
City of Sydney Ballet Scholarship
To encourage professional development in ballet. Dancers who are amateur or professional, male and female, and between 16 and 20 years of age are eligible. A scholarship of $10,000 and a trophy for first prize are awarded annually. This award is one of several given under the McDonald's City of Sydney Performing Arts Challenge Program. Established in 1974. Formerly: Rothmans Foundation Ballet Scholarship.

321
City of Sydney Piano Scholarship
To encourage professional piano development. Contestants must be between 16 and 24 years of age. Both amateur and professional pianists, men and women (a) born in Australia or New Zealand; or (b) naturalized citizens of Australia who have been domiciled in Australia or New Zealand for at least six years may enter. A scholarship of $5,000 and a trophy are awarded annually. Established in 1982 by Miss B.M. Henderson. Formerly: City of Sydney Eisteddfod Pianoforte Scholarship.

322

Heritage Art Awards
To encourage the work of painters and to recognize a painting which best captures the spirit of Australia, past or present, and embodies a feeling for its man-made or natural environment. The following awards were given: Art Prize - $15,000 for a professional or amateur; and Art Scholarship - $9,000 plus return airfare to Europe for a student or amateur painter. Awarded annually. Established in 1977. (Discontinued)

323

McDonald's Operatic Aria
To encourage professional vocal development. Both amateur and professional singers, men and women (a) born in Australia or New Zealand; or (b) naturalized citizens of Australia who have been domiciled in Australia or New Zealand for at least six years are eligible. The age limit is 32 years of age on September 1. The following prizes are awarded: (1) Grand Prize - a monetary prize of $5,000, a scholarship of $12,000, and return economy air fare to Europe; and (2) Five Finalists - $1,000 each. Awarded annually. Established in 1933. Formerly: Sydney *Sun* Aria Contest.

324

Cladan Cultural Exchange Institute of Australia
PO Box 420
Double Bay
Sydney, NSW 2028, Australia
Phone: 2 326 2405
Fax: 2 326 2604

325

Cladan Award
For recognition of the most significant contribution to Sydney theatre. A monetary prize and a plaque are awarded annually or when considered appropriate. Established in 1989 by Claire Dan, AM OBE.

326

Sydney International Piano Competition of Australia
To encourage the careers of young concert pianists, to promote professional development, and to provide performance opportunities. The Competition is open to artists of any nationality, between 18 and 32 years of age. The deadline for application is usually six months prior to each event. The following monetary prizes are awarded: (1) First prize - The Council of the City of Sydney Prize - $15,000 (Australian); (2) Second prize - $7,000; (3) Third prize - Dr. M. Kennedy Prize - $4,000; (4) Fourth prize - Kawai Prize - $2,500; (5) Fifth prize - $1,500; (6) Sixth prize - $1,000; (7) Seventh to Ninth prizes - $750 each; (8) Tenth to Twelfth prizes - $500 each; (9) Hephzibah Menuhin Memorial Scholarship Prize for the Best Australian Pianist - $5,000; (10) Reisner-Pennycuik Concerto Prize - $4,500; (11) People's Choice Prize Claden Award - $5,000; (12) Edward Sternberg Chamber Music Prize - $2,000; and (13) Mozart Concerto Prize - $1,500. Awarded every four years. Established in 1977. Sponsored by the Cladan Cultural Exchange Institute of Australia, in cooperation with the Sydney Conservatorium of Music.

327

Collins/Angus & Robertson Publishers Pty Ltd.
A Div. of HarperCollins Publishers
 (Australia)
4/31 Waterloo Rd.
PO Box 290
North Ryde, NSW 2113, Australia
Phone: 2 888 4111
Fax: 2 888 9972

328

Angus & Robertson Writers' Fellowship
To encourage creative writing and to recognize a manuscript or book of outstanding originality, preferably by a new author. Awarded annually. Established in 1971. (Discontinued in 1989)

329

Angus & Robertson Writers for the Young Fellowship
For recognition of books by Australian and New Zealand writers for young people. Awarded annually. (Discontinued in 1989)

330

Colophon Society
Civic Sq.
Canberra, ACT 2608, Australia
Phone: 6 2076636

331

Canberra Book of the Year Award
To recognize the best book written, designed, printed, or published in Canberra during the preceding year. Entries must be submitted by May 31. Awarded annually.

332

Commonwealth Council for Educational Administration
Faculty of Education
Univ. of New England
DAHAES Bldg.
Armidale, NSW 2350, Australia
Phone: 67 732543
Fax: 67 733363

333

Fellow
For recognition of achievement in or contributions to the management and administration of education in institutions and systems in the Commonwealth of Nations. Individuals must be nominated by 10 or more members of the CCEA, and chosen by a committee of Fellows. A plaque and citation are awarded biennially at two regional or four yearly conferences. Established in 1978.

334

Council for the Order of Australia
Government House
Canberra, ACT 2600, Australia

335

Australian Fire Service Medal
To recognize distinguished service by members of Australian full-time and volunteer fire services. Recommendations are made by the responsible Minister to the Governor-General for approval. An annual quota exists for each fire service. Established in 1988.

336

Australian Police Medal
To recognize distinguished service by members of Australian police forces. Recommendations are made by the responsible Minister to the Governor-General for approval. An annual quota exists for each police service. Established in 1986.

337

Australian Service Medals
To recognize service in prescribed areas. The Australian Active Service Medal is given to recognize service in a prescribed warlike operation and the Australian Service Medal is given to recognize service in a prescribed peacekeeping, but nonwarlike, operation. The awards are given to denote the prescibed operation and any subsequent award of either Medal to the same person will be made in the form of a further clasp to the Medal. Awards are made by the Governor-General on the recommendation of the Chief of the Defence Force or his/her delegate. Established in 1988.

338

Champion Shots Medal
To honor winners in the annual target shooting contest with standard issue weapons conducted by each arm of the Defence Force. Three medals (one for each Service) are awarded annually. The award is made with a clasp to denote the year of the competition and any subsequent award to the same person is made in the form of another clasp. Awards are made by the Governor-General on the recommendation of the Chief of the Defence Force or his/her delegate. Established in 1988.

339
Conspicuous Service Decorations
To recognize outstanding or meritorious achievement or devotion to duty in nonwarlike situations by members of the Defence Force and certain others. The Conspicuous Service Cross (CSC) is given for outstanding devotion to duty or outstanding achievement in the application of exceptional skills, judgement, or dedication in nonwarlike situations. The Conspicuous Service Medal (CSM) is also given for meritorious achievement or devotion to duty in nonwarlike situations. Each decoration may be awarded posthumously. The awards are made by the Governor-General on the recommendation of the Minister for Defence. Established in 1989.

340
Defence Force Service Awards
To recognize 15 years of diligent service by members of the Defence Force. Three awards are given. The Defence Force Service Medal is awarded to all full-time service personnel. The Reserve Force Decoration (RFD) is awarded to Reserve Force officers. (This is the only long-service award with postnominal entitlement in the Australian system.) The Reserve Force Medal is also given to those with other ranks in the Reserve Force. Recommendations are made by the Chief of the Defence Force or his/her delegate to the Governor-General for approval. Members of the philanthropic organizations serving with the Defence Force are eligible for nomination. A clasp is awarded for each additional five years of qualifying service. Established in 1982.

341
Distinguished Service Decorations
To recognize members of the Defence Force and certain others for distinguished command and leadership in action or distinguished performance of duties in warlike operations. There are three levels of awards. The Distinguished Service Cross (DSC) is given for distinguished command and leadership in action. The Distinguished Service Medal (DSM) is given for distinguished leadership in action. The Commendation for Distinguished Service is given for distinguished performance of duties in warlike operations. Each decoration may be awarded posthumously. The awards are made by the Governor-General on the recommendation of the Minister for Defence. Established in 1991.

342
Gallantry Decorations
To recognize members of the Defence Force and certain others who perform acts of gallantry in action. There are three levels of awards. The Star of Gallantry (SG) is given for acts of great heroism or conspicuous gallantry in action in circumstances of great peril. The Medal for Gallantry (MG) is given for acts of gallantry in action in hazardous circumstances. The Commendation for Gallantry is given for other acts of gallantry that are considered worthy of recognition. Each decoration may be awarded posthumously. The awards are made by the Governor-General on the recommendation of the Minister for Defence. The Governor-General may also delegate his power to make immediate awards to military commanders in the field. Established in 1991.

343
Nursing Service Cross
To recognize outstanding performance of nursing duties in both operational and nonoperational situations by members of the Defence Force and certain others. The decoration may be awarded posthumously. Awards are made by the Governor-General on the recommendation of the Minister for Defence. Established in 1989.

344
Order of Australia
For recognition of achievement and merit in service of Australia. The Order of Australia consists of a General Division and a Military Division. Australian citizens, including members of the Defence Force, are eligible to be appointed to the Order as members in the General Division. Persons other than Australian citizens are eligible to be appointed to the Order as honorary members in the General Division or may be appointed a member if it is desirable that the person be honored by Australia. The Medal of the Order in the General Division may be awarded to Australian citizens and other persons. In the General Division, appointments are made in the following categories: Companions or honorary Companions - for eminent achievement and merit of the highest degree in service to Australia or to humanity at large; Officers or honorary Officers - for distinguished service of a high degree to Australia or to humanity at large; Members or honorary Members - for service in a particular locality or field of activity or to a particular group; and Medal of the Order - for service worthy of particular recognition. Any person or organization may submit to the Secretary of the Order for consideration by the Council a nomination of an Australian citizen for appointment to the Order as a member in the General Division or a nomination of a person for the award of the Medal of the Order in the General Divison. Members of the Defence Force are eligible to be appointed to the Order as members in the Military Division. Members of the armed forces of a country other than Australia are eligible to be appointed to the Order as honorary members in the Military Divison. In any calendar year, the number of appointments (other than honorary appointments) to the Military Division shall not exceed one-tenth of one percent of the average number of persons who were members of the Defence Force on each day of the immediately preceding year. The Medal of the Order in the Military Division may be awarded to members of the Defence Force. In the Military Division, appointments are made in the following categories: Companions or honorary Companions - for eminent service in duties of great responsibility; Officers or honorary Officers - for distinguished service in responsible positions; Members or honorary Members - for exceptional service or performance of duty; and Medal of the Order - for meritorious service or performance of duty. Upon the recommendation of the Minister for Defence, appointments as members or honorary members of the Order in the Military Divison and awards of the Medal of the Order in the Military Divison are made with the approval of the Sovereign, by Instruments signed by the Governor-General. Appointments are made biennially on Australia Day (January 26) and on the celebration of the Queen's Birthday in June. Established in 1975.

345
Police Overseas Service Medal
To recognize service with international peacekeeping organizations by officers of Australian police forces. The award is made with a clasp to denote the area of prescribed service and any subsequent award to the same person is made in the form of a further clasp with the prescribed service appropriately inscribed. Awards are made by the Governor-General on the recommendation of the Chief Officer of an Australian police force.

346
Public Service Medal
To recognize outstanding service by members of Australian public services and other government employees, including those in local government. Recommendations are made by the responsible Minister to the Governor-General for approval. An annual quota exists for each government public service. Established in 1989.

347
Unit Citations
To recognize gallantry in action or outstanding service in warlike operations by units of the Defense Force and/or units of the defense forces of other countries. The Unit Citation for Gallantry is given for extraordinary gallantry in action and the Meritorious Unit Citation is given for sustained outstanding service in warlike operations. Each citation consists of a certificate of citation to the Unit signed by the Governor-General and insignia for each recipient. Insignia may be awarded posthumously. The award is made by the Governor-General on the recommendation of the Minister for Defence. Established in 1991.

348
Victoria Cross for Australia
In recognition of persons who, in the presence of the enemy, perform acts of the most conspicuous gallantry. To honor daring or preeminent acts of valour or self-sacrifice or extreme devotion to duty. Posthumous awards may be presented. Established in 1991.

349
Vietnam Medal
To recognize service in Vietnam between May 29, 1964 and January 27, 1973. Qualifying service includes: 28 days in ships or craft on inland

waters or off the coast of Vietnam; one day or more on the posted strength of a unit or formation on land; one operational sortie over Vietnam or Vietnamese waters by aircrew on the posted strength of a unit; or official visits either continuous or aggregate of 30 days. Established in 1968.

350
Creativity Centre
PO Box 92
Coorparoo, QLD 4151, Australia   Phone: 7 3989370

351
Creativity Centre Inc. Poetry Prize
To recognize outstanding poetry. Submissions must be made by August 31. First, second, and third prizes are awarded annually. Established in 1971 in memory of Harold Kesteven. Formerly: Harold Kesteven Poetry Prize.

352
Dalgety Farmers Limited
38 Bridge St.   Phone: 2 2382000
Sydney, NSW 2000, Australia   Fax: 2 2382850

Formerly: (1983) Dalgety Australia Limited.

353
Dalgety Farmers Limited Awards for Excellence in Rural Journalism
To promote excellence in rural reporting and/or journalism. Awards are given in the following categories: print, television, radio, and journalist writing for a regional or country based medium. All journalists involved in the rural and regional media in Australia are eligible. The major awards are travel awards of $5,000 and a trophy for the winner, and $3,000 and trophies to each of two runners-up. A special travel award of $2,000 and a trophy are awarded for the best entry submitted by a journalist writing for a country newspaper, radio, or television station anywhere in Australia. Awarded annually in October. Established in 1973. Formerly: (1983) Dalgety Study Award.

354
Drummoyne Municipal Art Society
Honorary Sec.
PO Box 178
Drummoyne, NSW 2047, Australia

355
DMAS Annual Art Awards
To promote the visual arts, and to recognize individual excellence in the artist's chosen medium. Awards are presented in the following categories: (1) Traditional Oil or related media; (2) Watercolor; (3) Modern; (4) Prints; (5) Drawing; and (6) Portrait. Monetary awards and certificates are presented annually. Established in 1964.

356
Eaglehawk Dahlia and Arts Festival
99 Victoria St.
Eaglehawk, VIC 3556, Australia   Phone: 5 446 8140

357
Literary Competition
To recognize outstanding literature. Australian citizens are eligible for original, unpublished works on an Australian theme. The following awards are presented: Rolf Boldrewood Award for a short story on any topic. First prize is $200 and a medallion; second prize is $50; Gordon Pittaway Memorial Award for a story suitable for children aged 10-14 years - $150 and a medallion. Sponsored by Dorothy Pittaway in memory of her late husband, Gordon Pittaway, founder and editor of the Australian Writers Professional Service; Apollo Award for a poem up to 20 lines. First prize is $200 and a medallion; second prize is $50; and Allan Llewellyn Award for Bush verse with an Australian theme, written in rhyme and traditional metre. First prize is $150 and a medallion; second prize is $50. Sponsored by Bendigo Advertiser Newspapers. The deadline for applications is January 31. Awarded at the Eaglehawk Dahlia and Arts Festival. For additional information, contact Ms. Ruth Claridge, Literary Committee Chairperson.

358
Economic History Society of Australia and New Zealand
Economic History
La Trobe Univ.   Phone: 3 4792722
Bundoora, VIC 3083, Australia   Fax: 3 4710689

359
S. J. Butlin Prize
For recognition of the best graduate thesis concerned with the economic history of Australia and/or New Zealand. Theses that have been accepted by a university within five years preceding each triennial closing date may be considered. A monetary prize of $500 Australian is awarded triennially. Established in 1982 in memory of Professor S.J. Butlin, Professor of Economic History at the University of Sydney and an eminent scholar.

360
Electronic Media Arts (Australia) Ltd.
PO Box 316   Phone: 2 552 4220
Paddington, NSW 2021, Australia   Fax: 2 552 4229

Formerly: (1989) Australian Video Festival.

361
Australian International Video Festival
For recognition of outstanding videos. The following prizes are awarded: (1) Qantas Student Prize; (2) Video Art Award - Open; (3) Video Art Award - Australian; (4) Computer Graphics & Animation Award; (5) Video Dance Award; (6) Experimental/Low Budget Award; (7) Australia Historical/Social Issues Award; and (8) Political/International Issues Award. Established in 1984. Additional information is also available from 58 Allen Street, Glebe, NSW 2037, Australia.

362
English Association/Sydney Branch
PO Box 667
Chatswood, NSW 2067, Australia

363
H. M. Butterley - F. Earle Hooper Award
To encourage and promote the career of a promising Australian creative writer or literary critic who is not yet established. Previously unpublished writers who have had an article, story or poem published in the Association's literary journal, *Southerly*, during the year of the award are eligible. The writer of the best such article/story/poem is selected by a judge who is appointed by the Association and who is a distinguished writer, critic or academic. A monetary prize is awarded annually at the annual dinner. Established in 1969 in memory of the life and work of two pioneer members of the Association, H.M. Butterley, Honorary Secretary of the Association from 1930 to 1961, and Miss F. Earle Hooper, a Foundation member from 1923 and an active member of the Executive Committee from 1936 to 1945.

364
A. W. Faber-Castell (Aust) Pty. Ltd.
69 O'Connell St., Unit 1
Locked Bag 62 PO   Phone: 2 7255666
Smithfield, NSW 2164, Australia   Fax: 2 7255135

365

Faber-Castell Award for Drawing
To encourage the art of drawing. Awards were given in two separate categories: The Professional Section - for an artist who has had a major solo exhibition. Each competitor may only enter one work; and The Student or Amateur Section - a student or amateur is defined as an artist who has not held a major solo exhibition. A monetary prize of $6,000 was awarded in the professional section; and two monetary prizes of $1,000 each were awarded in the student or amateur section. Established in 1983. (Discontinued)

366

Farrer Memorial Trust
c/o New South Wales Dept. of Agriculture
PO Box K220
Haymarket, NSW 2000, Australia
Phone: 2 3720120
Fax: 2 3720155

367

Farrer Memorial Medal
To provide encouragement and inspiration to those engaged in agricultural science and to recognize an individual who has rendered distinguished service in agricultural science in Australia in the fields of research, education, or administration. The recipient of the medal is invited to deliver an oration on a topical subject of his own choice. Established in 1936 in memory of William James Farrer, plant breeder.

368

Fellowship of Australian Writers
New South Wales
Box 3448 GPO
Sydney, NSW 2001, Australia
Phone: 2 5461814

369

Walter Stone Memorial Award
For recognition of a monograph, biography, or bibliography dealing with some aspect of Australian literature. Submissions are accepted by October 31. A monetary prize of $500 is awarded biennially at the Seminar in October. Established in 1984 in honor of Walter Stone, publisher, and president of City Regional FAW and NSW State Council FAW.

370

Fellowship of Australian Writers
Queensland
PO Box 1871
Brisbane, QLD 4001, Australia

371

Carson Gold Memorial Short Story Competition Awards
For recognition of a short story of not more than 5,000 words with a setting in Australia or the adjacent islands. Australian born authors are eligible. The following prizes are awarded: (1) first prize - $600 (Australian); (2) second prize - $300; and third prize - $100. Awarded annually. Administered by Union Fidelity Trust in association with the Union Fidelity Trustee Company of Australia and the Fellowship of Australian Writers/Queensland.

372

Fellowship of Australian Writers
South Australia
Hindle St.
PO Box 8016
Adelaide, SA 5000, Australia

373

Ian Murdie Memorial Awards
To recognize outstanding poetry and short stories. Awarded annually.

374

Fellowship of Australian Writers
Western Australia
Tom Collins House
9 Servetus St.
Swanbourne, WA 6010, Australia
Phone: 9 3844771
Fax: 9 3844771

375

Tom Collins Poetry Award
To recognize outstanding poetry. Entries must be submitted by December 31. A monetary award of $500 is presented annually. For auditions of entry, send a SASE to the competition secretary, 163 Rannoch Circle, Hamersley, WA 6022, Australia.

376

Lyndall Hadow/Donald Stuart Short Story Award
To recognize an outstanding short story. Entries must be submitted by June 30 each year. A monetary award of $500 is presented annually. For auditions of entry send a SASE to the competition secretary, 163 Rannoch Circle, Hamersley, WA 6022, Australia.

377

Fellowship of Australian Writers (VIC) Inc.
PO Box 528
Camberwell, VIC 3124, Australia
Phone: 3 8175243

378

FAW Adele Shelton-Smith Award for Play, Radio or Other Scripts for Young Writers
To recognize scripts for stage, radio, film, or TV by young writers between 15 and 22 years of age. The deadline for entries is December 31. Monetary prizes of $120, $100, and $50 are awarded annually.

379

FAW Alan Marshall Award
To encourage literature which contains a strong narrative element. A monetary prize of $500 Australian was awarded annually. Established in 1977 in honor of Alan Marshall, an Australian storyteller. (Discontinued)

380

FAW Anne Elder Poetry Award
To recognize a poet for a first published collection of poetry. Books published during the preceding year are eligible. The deadline for entries is December 31. A monetary award of $1,000 Australian and a second prize of $500 Australian are awarded. Established in 1977.

381

FAW Australian Unity Award
For recognition of a book of sustained quality and distinction with an Australian theme. The deadline for entries is December 31. A monetary prize of $1,000 Australian is awarded annually. Established in 1978. Formerly: FAW Australian Native's Association Literature Award.

382

FAW Barbara Ramsden Award
For recognition of a book which demonstrates a superior quality of writing. This book is considered the best "Book of the Year." Plaques, specially designed by Andor Meszaros, were awarded to the author and the publisher's editor. Awarded annually. Established in 1971 to honor Barbara Ramsden, an editor of distinction. (Discontinued)

383

FAW C. J. Dennis Award
To recognize the author of an outstanding book on Australian natural history published in Australia. A monetary prize of $1,000 Australian was awarded annually. Established in 1976. (Discontinued)

384

FAW Caltex-Bendigo Advertiser Award
For recognition of a book-length work. A monetary prize of $1,000 Australian is awarded biannually. (Discontinued)

385

FAW Christina Stead Award
To recognize an outstanding autobiography. A monetary award of $200 Australian is awarded. Established in 1988.

386

FAW Christopher Brennan Award
This, one of Australia's most prestigious poetry awards, is given to recognize a poet in Australia whose work achieves distinction. The deadline for entries is December 31. A bronze plaque is awarded. Established in 1973. Formerly: Robert Frost Award.

387

FAW Di Cranston Awards
To recognize young writers. Monetary awards of $50 and $100 Australian are presented.

388

FAW Fedora Anderson Young Writers Poetry Award
To recognize an unpublished poem by young writers 15 to 22 years of age. The deadline for entries is Deceember 31. Monetary awards of $100, $30, and $20 Australian are presented.

389

FAW Frank Dalby Davison Award
To recognize stories by young writers 15 to 22 years of age. Monetary awards of $50 to 200 Australian were presented. Established in 1969. (Discontinued)

390

FAW Herb Thomas Literary Award
For recognition of a biography, autobiography, or a memoir. The deadline for entries is December 31. A monetary prize of $500 Australian is awarded annually. Established in 1973. Sponsored by Herb Thomas Memorial Trust. Formerly: Con Weickhardt Award.

391

FAW John Morrison Short Story Award
For recognition of the best published and unpublished short stories by Australian writers. Monetary prizes ranging from $50 to at least $1,000 Australian were awarded annually. Established in 1964. (Discontinued) Formerly: (1991) .

392

FAW John Shaw Neilson Award
To recognize an unpublished poem of 14 lines or more. The following prizes were awarded: First prize - $550 Australian; Second prize - $30; Third prize - $20; and Commended. Established in 1971. (Discontinued)

393

FAW Judah Waten Collection of Creative Writing (Young Writers)
To recognize young writers. Monetary awards of $150 Australian were presented. Established in 1969. (Discontinued)

394

FAW K and M Teychenne Short Story Awards
To recognize short story writers of all ages. Awards were presented in the following categories: (1) Open - $500 Australian and a certificate; (2) 18 years and under - plaque; and (3) 12 years and under - plaque. (Discontinued)

395

FAW Kate Tracy Memorial Young Writers Award
To recognize poems and short stories (about 1,200 words) dealing with youth homelessness. Writers must be between 16 and 24 years old. Cash prizes of $50 for winning poems and $150 for winning short stories are awarded. The deadline for entries is December 31. This award honors the memory of Kate Tracy, an inspirational youth worker who died in 1992 at age 31. Sponsored by Malvern & Caufield Youth Accomodation Services, Inc.

396

FAW Local History Award
For recognition of a superior book on local or regional Australian history published during the preceding year. A monetary prize of at least $200 Australian was awarded annually. Established in 1972. (Discontinued)

397

FAW Mary Grant Bruce Award for Children's Literature
For recognition of an outstanding manuscript intended for children between 10 and 15 years of age. The deadline for entries is December 31. Monetary prizes of $600, $250, and $150 Australian are awarded annually. Established in 1981.

398

FAW Patricia Weickhardt Award
To recognize an Aboriginal writer. Entries are not required. A monetary prize of $100 is awarded annually.

399

FAW Warana Writers' Award
For recognition of poetry, feature articles, and short stories. Awarded annually. (Discontinued)

400

Griffin Press Literary Award
For recognition of a book of nonfiction of literary merit, printed in Australia. A monetary prize of $400 Australian was awarded annually. Established in 1977. (Discontinued) Formerly: (1991) FAW Wilke Literary Award.

401

Field Naturalists Club of Victoria
c/o National Herbarium
Birdwood Ave.
South Yarra, VIC 3141, Australia   Phone: 3 6508661

402

Australian Natural History Medallion
For recognition of the most meritorious contribution to the understanding of Australian natural history. A person of any age may be nominated by May 1 of any year for a contribution made in the preceding ten year period. A medal is awarded annually. Established in 1940 by Mr. J.K. Moir.

403

Film and Television Institute (W.A.)
92 Adelaide St.
Fremantle, WA 6160, Australia   Phone: 9 335 1055

404

W. A. Film and Video Festival
For recognition of excellence, innovation and talent in film or video making. The Festival is divided into two categories: the Showcase Section which screens all the films, videos, documentaries, animations, etc. made in Western Australia for the year by the industry; and the Competitive Section which is open to filmmakers 25 years of age and under. The filmmaker must be 25 years of age and under. The Young Filmmaker of the Year is awarded for the most outstanding filmmaker of

the Competitive Section; and receives a certificate plus a study course at the Australian Film Television and Radio School in Sydney, NSW, Australia. Awarded annually in November. Established in 1979. Sponsored by Australian Film Commission, The Western Australian Film Council, Australian Film Television and Radio School, W.A. Department for the Arts, Rural and Industries Bank of Western Australia, and The Screen Producers Association of Western Australia.

405
Foundation for Australian Literary Studies
James Cook Univ. of N. Queensland
Dept. of English Phone: 77 814451
Townsville, QLD 4811, Australia Phone: 77 814077

Formerly: Townsville Foundation for Australian Literary Studies.

406
Collin Roderick Lectures
To foster the study of Australian literature in the University and the wider community. To date, seventeen of these series of lectures have been published in the Foundation's monograph series, and they have made a significant contribution to the critical discussion of Australian literature. Awarded annually. Established in 1966.

407
Townsville Foundation for Australian Literary Studies Award
For recognition of the best book published each year in Australia that deals with any aspect of Australian life. Publications entered may be in any field of Australian writing and may be in verse or prose. Publications considered must be published in Australia, even though they may be printed elsewhere, and deal with some aspect of Australian life. A publication or any number of publications may be entered by any author or publisher by February 28 of the year following the year of publication. A monetary prize of $4,000 Australian is awarded at the annual dinner of the Foundation. Since 1980, the winner has also received the H. T. Priestley Memorial Medal. Established in 1967.

408
Galley Club
Address unknown.

409
Galley Club Award for Excellence
To recognize outstanding book publishing. Books of Australian origin published during the preceding 15 months are eligible. Awarded annually.

410
Governors of Dromkeen
Dromkeen
Main Rd. Phone: 54 286701
Riddells Creek, VIC 3431, Australia Fax: 3 4581120

411
Dromkeen Librarian's Award
To recognize a teacher, teacher/librarian, or a children's librarian currently working within or outside the educational systems for his/her commitment to the furtheration of children's literature. The award is presented each December at the Dromkeen Literary Luncheon.

412
Dromkeen Medal
To recognize an individual for an outstanding contribution to children's literature in Australia. A bronze medal, designed by Robert Ingpen, is awarded annually in February. Established in 1982 in memory of Courtney Thomas Oldmeadow, the founder of Dromkeen.

413
Grenfell Henry Lawson Festival of Arts
PO Box 77 Phone: 63 43 1779
Grenfell, NSW 2810, Australia Phone: 63 43 1548

414
Australian Arts Award
To recognize the individual who has contributed the most to the arts in Australia during the preceding year. Nominations may be submitted by April. The recipient is chosen by the Australian Journalists Association. A statuette is awarded annually during the Festival. Established in the 1970s.

415
Grenfell Henry Lawson Festival of Arts Awards
To encourage interest in Australian culture. Awards are given in the following categories: (1) verse; (2) prose; (3) song; and (4) art. Original, unpublished work on an Australian theme may be submitted to the Secretary. Monetary prizes and bronze statuettes are awarded annually. Established in 1959 in honor of Henry Lawson, an Australian poet.

416
Heidelberg Repatriation Hospital
Department of Veterans' Affairs
Public Relations Department
Building 5 Phone: 03 496 2111
Banksia St. Toll-free: 008 13 4864
Heidelberg West, VIC 3081, Australia Fax: 03 496 2541

417
Storywriting and Art Project
To encourage creative endeavors of ex-servicemen and women in repatriation hospitals in Victoria, and to recognize outstanding entries to the project. Prizes are given in the following categories: storywriting, including true war experiences, true life experiences, fiction, and poetry; and art, including oil paintings (open or experienced, and novice), other media, restricted, and craft. Monetary awards and trophies are presented annually. Major sponsors include Le Pine Funeral Services, Rehabilition Work Group, Australian Legion of Ex-Servicemen and Women, Retuned Services League - Victorian Branch, and T & PI Association. Established in 1962.

418
Institute of Metals and Materials Australasia
191 Royal Parade
Parkville, VIC 3052, Australia Phone: 3 347 2544

Formerly: Australasian Institute of Metals.

419
Silver Medal
For recognition of an outstanding scientific or technological contribution to physical and secondary metallurgy in Australia. The person nominated need not be a member of the Institute, a native-born Australian, or a permanent resident of Australia. A silver medal engraved with a design depicting early metallurgists at work is awarded annually. Established in 1957.

420
Institution of Engineers, Australia
11 National Circuit Phone: 6 270 6555
Barton, ACT 2600, Australia Fax: 6 273 1488

421
Agricultural Engineering Award
For recognition of a project, invention, design, or manufacturing process that represents a significant agricultural engineering achievement and

that has been completed within the previous two years. A monetary award and a plaque are awarded biennially. Established in 1986.

422
G.N. Alexander Medal
To honor the author of the best paper on hydrology and/or water resources published in an IE Aust publication. It is usually awarded every 18 months. The first award was given in 1988, with selection responsibility being with the National Committee on Water Engineering.

423
Australian Geomechanics Award - John Jaeger Memorial Award
To recognize and promote contributions of the highest order in the field of Australian geomechanics. Contributions may take the form of papers published in any publication of the Society, Institution, or Institute or presented at any meeting, conference, or symposium of one of these bodies. Papers may also be the design, construction, or supervision of any project in the field of geomechanics. The award is not restricted to members of the Australian Geomechanics Society. Nominations should be made by at least three persons (not necessarily members), to the Secretary of the National Committee of the Society six months prior to the Conference at which the award is to be presented. A bronze medallion is awarded every four years. Established in 1980 in memory of Professor John Conrad Jaeger, who was Professor of Geophysics and Geochemistry at the Australian National University from 1953 until his death in 1979. Professor Jaeger's work of the greatest importance related to the physics of heat flow and rock mechanics and he published several classic books in this field. He became a Fellow of the Australian Academy of Science in 1954 and a Fellow of the Royal Society in 1970. Sponsored by the Australian Geomechanics Society, a joint organization of The Institution of Engineers, Australia and The Australasian Institute of Mining and Metallurgy.

424
Award for Achievement in Engineering Enterprise
To recognize a corporate member of the Institution who, by personal endeavors, has significantly contributed to an enterprise built around the successful commercialization of innovative engineering endeavor. A memento is presented as a recognition of the award. Established in 1986.

425
Awards for Work Displaying Engineering Excellence
To recognize work that is considered to embrace consideration for users, the human and natural environment, aesthetic standards, and benefits to the community in all engineering disciplines. Works must have been completed within two years prior to judging. The awards are in the form of a commemorative plaque and/or a certificate. The following awards awards are given each year: South Australian Engineering Excellence Awards (est. 1972), Queensland Engineering Excellence Awards (est. 1976), Victorian Division Excellence Awards (est. 1978), Western Australian Engineering Excellence Awards (est. 1978), Newcastle Engineering Excellence Awards (est. 1979), Northern Territory Division Engineering Excellence Awards (est. 1981), Tasmania Division Engineering Excellence Awards (est. 1987), Sydney Division Engineering Excellence Awards (est. 1984), and Canberra Division Engineering Excellence Awards (est. 1985).

426
O. F. Blakey Memorial Prize
For recognition of the best prepared paper of approximately 20 minutes duration delivered on an engineering subject to a meeting of the Western Australian Division by a graduate or student member of that Division. In the event of there being more entries than can be conveniently heard in one evening, pre-selection is carried out. A significant proportion of the points are awarded for the standard of presentation of the paper. The prize consists of the O.F. Blakey Memorial Medal and a monetary award of $250. Awarded annually. Established in 1955 in memory of Professor O.F. Blakey, the first Professor of Civil Engineering at the University of Western Australia, who was a Councillor of the Institution from 1936 to 1951, Chairman of the former Perth Division in 1936 and 1942, and President of the Institution in 1945.

427
John A. Brodie Medal
For recognition of a paper in chemical engineering considered superior by the College of Chemical Engineers. The award is not limited to members of the Institution. A bronze medal is awarded annually. Established in 1963 in honor of J.A. Brodie, a leading industrial innovator.

428
Frederick Brough Memorial Prize
For recognition of the best prepared paper of approximately 20 minutes duration delivered on any engineering subject by a graduate or student member of the Tasmania Division. A monetary prize of $250 and a medal are awarded annually. Established in 1949 in memory of Mr. Frederick Brough who was Honorary Secretary of the Tasmania Division from 1929 until his death in 1948. He was a member of the staff of the Hydro-Electric Commission from 1920 to 1947.

429
Bulk Materials Handling Award
To recognize outstanding contributions in the field of bulk materials handling technology by either: a paper published by the IE Aust; research, design, or development work; or in recognition of an individual's professional contribution. This annual plaque was first presented in 1989, is open to both members and nonmembers of IE Aust, with the National Committee on Bulk Materials Handling having selection responsibility.

430
R. W. Chapman Medal
For recognition of a paper on structural engineering considered the best by the College of Civil Engineers. Members of the Institution are eligible. A bronze medal is awarded annually. Established in 1935 in memory of Sir Robert Chapman, President of the Institution in 1922.

431
Chemeca Medal
This, the most prestigious award in the profession of chemical engineering in Australia, is given for achievement and distinction in the profession. This award is not limited to members of the three sponsoring associations. A medal is awarded annually at the Chemeca Conference. Sponsored by The Institution of Engineers, Australia, Chemical College, The Institution of Chemical Engineers, ANC, and The Royal Australian Chemical Institute, Industrial Chemical Division.

432
Chemeca Student Design Prize
For recognition of the best chemical engineering design project by a student from one of the chemical engineering faculties in Australia. A monetary prize of $1,500 and a medal are awarded annually. Established in 1981. Co-sponsored by the Institution of Engineers, Australia, The Institution of Chemical Engineers, and Davy McKee (Australia) Ltd.

433
College of Electrical Engineers Student Prizes
To raise the profile of the Institution and the Electrical College in electrical engineering schools of tertiary institutions, thereby encouraging students to become members. The college provides funds on the basis of $400 per electrical engineering school, to divisional electrical branches for allocation as appropriate to local circumstances. Established in 1990.

434
L.P. Coombes Medal
To award the speaker who is invited to deliver the Coombes lecture, which is sponsored by the Aviation and Space Branch of the Victoria Division and the Aeronautical Research Laboratories. Given annually, the award consists of a medal and certificate. Established in honor of Lawrence Percival Coombes, who was acclaimed for his use of dynamic models in performance analysis.

435
Jennifer Cox Memorial Prize
To honor second-year students in the engineering course at the University of Canberra for achieving academic excellence. A certificate and a cash award of $100 is awarded annually in honor of Jennifer Cox, a student who would have been the first woman to graduate in engineering at the University, had she not been killed her final year.

436
CRA Award
For recognition of outstanding applied chemical engineering. A monetary prize of $2,500 is awarded. Established in 1990.

437
E. H. Davis Memorial Lecture
To recognize a person selected for a distinguished recent contribution to the theory and practice of geomechanics in Australia. The selected lecturer is presented with a framed certificate. Established in 1985 in honor of E.H. Davis, who achieved eminence in the field of geomechanics.

438
Engineering 2000 Awards
To recognize and to promote the advancement of women in engineering. A broad ranging series of initiatives are considered: an organization's internal promotional program, policies proposed or introduced to create a stimulus to women to enter the profession, and career path development in the engineering profession based on the special needs of women. Established in 1990.

439
Esso Award
For recognition of significant ongoing contributions to chemical engineering through innovations or a series of related publications over a number of years. A monetary prize of $2,500 is awarded. Established in 1990.

440
Ian Henderson Memorial Prize
For recognition of the best of a group of papers, each of approximately 20 minutes duration, on an engineering subject delivered to a single meeting of the Newcastle Division by a graduate or student member of the Division. In the event of there being more than four entries in any one year, pre-selection is carried out. Twenty-five percent of the points are awarded for the standard of presentation of the paper. A monetary prize of $250 and a medal are awarded annually. Established in 1977 in memory of Mr. I.F.G. Henderson who was employed by BHP Company Ltd. for over 45 years, and who was closely associated with the Newcastle Division for many years until his death in 1975.

441
ICI Award
For recognition of distinguished and continuing contributions to chemical engineering education or to the profession. A monetary prize of $2,500 is awarded. Established in 1990.

442
Institution of Engineers, Australia Award
Australian Maritime College
To recognize the best final-year project of the Bachelor of Engineering (Maritime). The award is presented annually and consists of the Norman Selfe Medal and a cash prize of $200. The medal is named in honor of Norman Selfe, who was a great promoter of technical education.

443
Institution of Engineers, Australia Award
Ballarat University College
To recognize final-year engineering students at the Ballarat University College. Based on academic record and involvement in extra-curricular activities and special projects. The award consists of the A.E. Stohr Medal and a cash prize of $200. Selection is made by the Faculty/Ballarat Group Panel. Established in 1977.

444
Institution of Engineers, Australia Award
Curtin University of Technology
To recognize a final year student at Curtin University of Technology on the basis of interest in the Institution, academic record, and qualities of leadership. The award consists of the Digby Leach Medal and a cash prize of $200. Established in 1968.

445
Institution of Engineers, Australia Award
James Cook University of North Queensland
To recognize James Cook University of North Queensland engineering students. The award is based on a final year project and selection is made on appraisal by faculty staff. The award consists of the C.N. Barton Medal and a cash prize of $200. Established in 1972.

446
Institution of Engineers, Australia Award
LaTrobe University College of Northern Victoria
In recognition of final-year engineering students at the LaTrobe University College of Northern Victoria. Awarded on the basis of academic record and involvement in extra-currilcular activities and special projects. Selection is made by the Bendigo and Northern Group and presentation is made at a meeting of the Group by the Group Chairman or his/her nominee. The award consists of a medal and a cash prize of $200. Established in 1977.

447
Institution of Engineers, Australia Award
Monash University
To honor final-year engineering students at Monash University. The award is based on academic record and involvement in extra-curricular activities and special projects. It consists of the Ian Langlands Medal and a cash prize of $200. Established in 1977.

448
Institution of Engineers, Australia Award
Monash University - Caulfield Campus
In recognition of the Monash University, Caulfield Campus student with the best academic record and involvement in extra-curricular activities and special projects. The award consists of a medal and a cash prize of $200 and is presented each March at a meeting of the Institution's Caulfield Campus Chapter. Established in 1977.

449
Institution of Engineers, Australia Award
Monash University Gippsland
To recognize final-year engineering students at the Monash University Gippsland. Awarded on the basis of academic record and involvement in extra-curricular activities and special projects. The award consists of a medal and a cash prize of $200. Presentation is made at a special meeting of the Gippsland Group by the Group Chairman or his/her nominee. Established in 1977.

450
Institution of Engineers, Australia Award
Queensland University of Technology
To recognize Queensland University of Technology engineering students. The award is based on a final year project and selection is made on appraisal by the faculty staff. The award consists of the J.H. Curtis Medal and a cash prize of $200. Established in 1973.

451
Institution of Engineers, Australia Award
Royal Melbourne Institute of Technology
To recognize final-year engineering students at the Royal Melbourne Institute of Technology. The award is granted on the basis of academic record and involvement in extra-curricular activities and special projects. It consists of a medal and a cash prize of $200. Presentation is made at the Annual Awards Presentation of the Royal Melbourne Institute of

Technology by the Division Chairman or his/her nominee. Established in 1977.

452
Institution of Engineers, Australia Award
Swinburne Institute of Technology
To recognize final-year engineering students at the Swinburne College of Technology. Awarded on the basis of academic record and involvement in extra-curricular activities and special projects. The award consists of the W.P. Brown Medal and a cash prize of $200. Selection is made by a Faculty/Campus Chapter Panel. Established in 1977.

453
Institution of Engineers, Australia Award
University College of Southern Queensland
To recognize University College of Southern Queensland engineering students. The award is based on a final year project and selection is made on appraisal by faculty staff. The award consists of the G.R. Wilmoth Medal and a cash prize of $200. Established in 1974.

454
Institution of Engineers, Australia Award
University of Adelaide
To annually recognize a final year engineering student at the University of Adelaide who is selected on the basis of personality and high level of academic attainment. The award consists of the Sir Arvi Parbo Medal and a cash prize of $200. Established in 1977.

455
Institution of Engineers, Australia Award
University of Canberra
To recognize aeronautical engineering students at the University of Canberra. Based on academic record and involvement in extra-curricular activities and special projects. Called the W.E. Sansum Medal after the late Air Commodore "Bill" Sansum, who was elected as a Fellow of the Institution in 1981, was Chairman of the Canberra Branch of the Royal Aeronautical Society in 1987-1988, and Chairman of the Canberra Division of the Institution in 1988. Established in 1988.

456
Institution of Engineers, Australia Award
University of College of Central Queensland
To recognize University College of Central Queensland engineering students. The award is based on a final year project and selection is made on appraisal by faculty staff. The awards consists of the Faldt Guthrie Medal and a cash prize of $200. Established in 1973.

457
Institution of Engineers, Australia Award
University of Melbourne
To honor final-year engineering students at the University of Melbourne. Based on academic record and involvement in extra-curricular activities and special projects. The award consists of the L.R. East Medal and a cash prize of $200. Selection is made by a Faculty/Campus Chapter Panel. Established in 1977.

458
Institution of Engineers, Australia Award
University of New South Wales
To honor a student at the University of New South Whales based on the overall performance in his/her final year full-time course or the last two years of the part-time course. The award consists of a medal and a cash prize of $200. Established in 1977.

459
Institution of Engineers, Australia Award
University of New South Wales - Australian Defence Force Academy
To honor the top student graduating in engineering from the Australian Defence Force Academy. The award consists of the Arthur Corbett Medal and a cash prize of $200. Between 1971 and 1985, the award was made for the best final year engineering student from the Royal Military College Duntroon.

460
Institution of Engineers, Australia Award
University of Newcastle
To annually recognize a final year student who completes the Bachelor of Engineering degree with First Class Honors at the University of Newcastle. The award consists of the J.M.C. Corlette Medal and a cash prize of $200. Established in 1961.

461
Institution of Engineers, Australia Award
University of Queensland
To recognize University of Queensland engineering students. The award is based on a final year project and selection is made on faculty appraisal. The award consists of the W.H.R. Nimmo Medal and a cash prize of $200. Established in 1976.

462
Institution of Engineers, Australia Award
University of South Australia
To annually recognize a final year engineering student at the University of South Australia who is selected on the basis of personality and a high level of academic attainment. The award consists of the K. Johinke Medal and a cash prize of $200. Established in 1977.

463
Institution of Engineers, Australia Award
University of Sydney
To honor, on the recommendation of the Dean of the Faculty of Engineering, the candidate working toward a Bachelor of Engineering degree who shows the greatest proficiency. The award consists of the R.A. Priddle Medal and a cash prize of $200. Established in 1978.

464
Institution of Engineers, Australia Award
University of Tasmania
To honor the engineering student at the University of Tasmania, who on the appraisal of the faculty staff, shows the highest degree of proficiency in the subject of engineering design in the final year of the course. The award consists of the Allen Knight Medal and a cash prize of $200. Established in 1963.

465
Institution of Engineers, Australia Award
University of Technology, Sydney
To recognize a final year student in the Faculty of Engineering for excellence in development as a professional engineer through high-level endeavor academically, maturity in industrial experience, and participation in extra-curricular activities. The award consists of a medal and cash prize of $200. Established in 1977.

466
Institution of Engineers, Australia Award
University of Western Australia
To recognize University of Western Australia engineering students. The award is made annually to the student completing the Bachelor of Engineering degree at the University who, in the opinion of the Board of Examiners in Engineering, has given the best academic performance in the final year of the course. The award consists of the Russell Dumas Medal and a cash prize of $200. Established in 1970.

467
Institution of Engineers, Australia Award
University of Wollongong
To honor the engineering student at the University of Wollongong with the best academic record. The award consists of a medal and a cash prize of $200. Established in 1977.

468
Institution of Engineers, Australia Award
Victoria University of Technology - Footscray Campus
To honor final-year engineering students at the Footscray Institute of Technology/Victoria University of Technology and is awarded on the basis of academic record and involvement in extra-curricular activities and special projects. The award consists of a medal and a cash prize of $200. Presentation is made at the Annual General Meeting of the Institution's Western Region Campus Chapter by the Chapter Chairman or his/her nominee. Established in 1977.

469
Institution of Engineers Medal
To recognize and acknowledge a notable engineering contribution to the economic or social development of Australia. The award may be given to an individual or to an organization. Exceptional performance in one or a number of the following areas is considered: development or application of engineering technology, contributing to Australia's economic performance, implementation of policies leading to industrial development or enhanced quality of life, achievement in the education of young Australians, or contributing toward the development of a technical-literate society. Up to four medals are awarded annually. Established in 1989.

470
George Julius Medal
For recognition of a paper on mechanical engineering considered the best by the College of Mechanical Engineers. Members of the Institution are eligible. A bronze medal is awarded annually. Established in 1955 in memory of George Julius, inventor of the automatic totalizator and President of the Institution in 1925. Formerly: (1976) Mechanical Engineering Prize.

471
Local Government Engineering Medal
To recognize the engineer responsible for the design/project judged to be the best of those completed in the last two years. The award consists of a bronze medal and a certificate. Awarded biennially.

472
John Madsen Medal
For recognition of a paper on electrical engineering considered the best by the College of Electrical Engineers. Members and non-members are eligible. A bronze medal is awarded annually. Established in 1927. Renamed in 1976 to honor Sir John Madsen, one of Australia's great electrical engineers and foundation professor of Electrical Engineering at the University of Sydney.

473
A. G. M. Michell Medal
For recognition of a significant contribution through technical innovation to the science or practice of mechanical engineering, or for notable and sustained leadership pertaining to mechanical engineering. A bronze medal is awarded annually. Established in 1978 in honor of Anthony George Maldon Michell, Australia's outstanding mechanical engineer, and inventor of the tilting-pad thrust bearing and the viscometer. Michell also developed hydraulic power transmissions and designed a series of crankless engines.

474
John Monash Medal
For recognition of the best paper on multi-disciplinary engineering. Members of the Institution are eligible. A bronze medal is awarded annually. Established in 1976 in honor of Sir John Monash, Australia's greatest military commander and an outstanding engineer.

475
C. H. Munro Oration
To recognize a person eminent in the field of water resources in Australia. A gift and a framed certificate are awarded every 18 months. Established in 1978 to honor C.H. Munro for his contributions to hydrology.

476
National Engineering Excellence Awards
To reward achievement, promote better engineering, show the community how good engineering creates wealth and improves living standards, and encourage young people to join the profession. Given biennially, entries comprise the winning entrants from the Divisional competitions over the previous two years. A special issue of *Engineers Australia* gives details of all the entries. An award is given in each of the following categories: building and civil design; engineering products; engineering project management; engineering reports, procedures, and systems; environmental engineering; manufacturing facilities; public works; research; resource development; and the Sir William Hudson Award for the overall winner.

477
National Excellence Awards for Engineering Journalism
To encourage and enhance the reporting of engineering issues to the public. Awards are presented in three categories: the print media, radio and television. A monetary award of $1,000 and a suitably inscribed medal are awarded in each category. Established in 1990.

478
National Professional Young Engineer of the Year
Mirrors the Professional Engineer of the Year Award in its criteria but relates to graduate members of the Institution within six years of graduating.

479
R. W. Parsons Memorial Prize
To recognize a graduate or student member of the South Australian Division for the best prepared paper of approximately 20 minutes duration delivered on an engineering subject. In the event of there being more entries than can be conveniently heard in one evening, pre-selection of the papers is carried out. A significant proportion of the points awarded are for the standard of presentation of the paper. A monetary prize of $250 and a medal are awarded annually. Established in 1962 in memory of Mr. R.W. Parsons, a former Principal of the South Australian School of Mines (1940-1960) and a former Director of the South Australian Institute of Technology (1960-1961). Parsons was a Councillor of the Institution from 1947 to 1961, Chairman of the former Adelaide Division in 1943 and President of the Institution in 1955.

480
President's Prize
To recognize corporate members of the Institution who have made a major effort in promulgating the contribution that the engineering profession makes to the general welfare of the Australian people. A medal and a certificate are awarded annually. Established in 1990.

481
Professional Engineer of the Year
To recognize a corporate member of the Institution for competence and significant achievement in community affairs, a demonstrated understanding of the role and purpose of the engineering profession within society, proficiency in the use of communication and managerial skills in engineering projects, and/or effective communication with the mass media. In addition, the National Professional Young Engineer of the Year Award is presented to members within six years of graduating.

482
Queensland Division Chemical Branch Award
To recognize a chemical engineering student at the University of Queensland. A monetary award of $100 is presented.

483
Railway Engineering Award
For recognition of an outstanding contribution to railway engineering in Australia. A monetary prize of $500 and a plaque are awarded. Established in 1984 by the Institution's National Committee on Railway Engineering.

484
A.W. Roberts Award
To recognize the achievements of a young person in bulk materials handling. Candidates must be under 35 years of age (preferably under 30), must have proven outstanding academic achievement, and must have made notable contributions to bulk materials handling since graduation. An engraved plaque is awarded annually by the National Committee for Bulk Materials Handling in recognition of Professor Alan Roberts. It was first awarded in 1992.

485
Peter Nicol Russell Memorial Medal
This, the most prestigious award of the Institution, is given for notable contributions to the science and practice of engineering in Australia. Fellows of the Institution who are at least 45 years of age are eligible. A bronze medal is awarded annually. Established in 1923 in memory of Peter Nicol Russell, a Sydney industrialist who made major donations to the cause of engineering education in Australia.

486
M. A. Sargent Medal
To recognize the outstanding Australian electrical engineer of the year. Selection of the recipient is based on: a highly significant contribution, through technical innovation to the science or practice of electrical engineering; long-standing eminence in science or practice of electrical engineering; exceptional and sustained management or leadership relating to electrical engineering; or a notable combination of the foregoing qualities. A bronze medal is awarded. Established in 1989.

487
Shedden Pacific Medal and Prize
To recognize the members of The Institution of Chemical Engineers or the College of Chemical Engineers, their practical services to the profession, and the practice of chemical engineering in Australia. Achievments may be in technical, marketing, or management fields and nominations may be made either by individuals themselves or by others. The award is donated by Shedden Pacific and consists of a medal and a cash prize of $1,000.

488
Kevin Stark Memorial Award
To encourage excellence in coastal and ocean engineering. Any author who has a paper published in a forthcoming Australasian Conference on Coastal and Ocean Engineering, sponsored biennially by the National Committee on Coastal and Ocean Engineering, is eligible. The award is in the form of an engraved bronze medal. Established in 1993.

489
Tasmania Division Award of Merit
To recognize meritorious contributions to the engineering profession by members of the Tasmania Division. Candidates must have provided distinguished service to the engineering profession, made outstanding contributions to a specific engineering project of a substantial nature, and sustained high standard involvement in and contribution to a specific field of engineering activity. The award is given annually.

490
Transport Engineering Medal
To promote and recognize a contribution of the highest order in the field of Australian transport engineering. The medal is usually awarded every two years. It is not restricted to IE Australian members and selection responsibility rests with the National Committee on Transport. Established in 1989.

491
D. H. Trollope Medal
For recognition of the best doctoral thesis in the discipline of geomechanics. It is not limited to members of the Institution. A bronze medal is awarded biennially. Established in 1987.

492
University of Tasmania - Launceston Award
To recognize those who have completed their second year at the University of Tasmania - Launceston Department of Engineering and will be transferring to the Hobart Campus of the University for the final two years of their BE course. A $200 award is given to the best performed student completing year two.

493
Warman International Students Design Award Competition
To recognize outstanding third-year Mechanical Engineering Students. All recognized engineering teaching institutions may submit a team for the national award after conducting in-house competitions to ascertain their representations. A separate design problem is set each year. Awarded annually. Sponsored by Warman International.

494
W. H. Warren Medal
For recognition of a paper on civil engineering considered the best by the College of Civil Engineers. Members of the Institution are eligible. A bronze medal is awarded annually. Established in 1929 in honor of W.H. Warren, the First President of the Institution and first professor of Engineering at the University of Sydney.

495
Western Australian School of Mines Award
To recognize final year students completing a Bachelor of Engineering degree at the Western Australia School of Mines on the basis of interest in the Institution, academic achievement, and leadership qualities. The annual award consists of a medal and cash prize of $200. Established in 1993.

496
Young Engineers Speaking Competition
To recognize outstanding young speakers. Division winners are funded to attend the National Engineering Conference. A monetary prize and a certificate are awarded annually. Established in 1989.

497
International Academy of Medicine and Psychology
38 Denistone Rd.
Eastwood, NSW 2122, Australia
Phone: 8 58 4749
Fax: 2 804 7149

498
IAMP Awards
For recognition of contributions in psychological medicine, medical psychology, and research. No further information on awards is available for this edition.

499
International Association of Volcanology and Chemistry of the Earth's Interior
Australian Geological Survey Organization
GPO Box 378
Canberra, ACT 2601, Australia
Phone: 6 2499377
Fax: 6 2499983

500
Thorarinsson Medal
For recognition of excellence in volcanological research. A medal and $2,000 US for travel expenses is awarded every four years at the IAVCEI General Assembly. Established in 1987 in honor of Professor Sigurdur Thorarinsson of Reykjavik University.

501
L. R. Wager Prize
For recognition of outstanding contributions to the study of volcanic rocks. Scientists under 40 years of age on December 31 of the year preceding the award are eligible. A monetary prize of $2,000 US to attend

the IAVCEI General Assembly, where the award is presented, is awarded every four years. Established in 1975 by the Volcanology Subcommittee of the Royal Society (London) to commemorate the work of the late Professor L. R. Wager.

502
International Federation of Netball Associations
99 Awaba St.
Mosman, NSW 2088, Australia
Phone: 2 9601428
Fax: 2 9694347

503
International Federation of Netball Associations Awards
To recognize outstanding ability in netball. The following prizes are awarded: World Championship Awards and World Youth Cup. Medallions are presented every four years to the winners and the runners-up. In addition, a badge is awarded for recognition of outstanding services on the executive committee of the Federation.

504
International Federation of Netball Associations Service Awards
For recognition of service to the game of netball on an international scale. (Netball is played outdoors or indoors using a soccer ball.) Nominations must be submitted by members. A badge is awarded biennially. Established in 1979.

505
International PEN - Sydney Centre
PO Box 153
Woollahra, NSW 2025, Australia
Phone: 2 9183537

506
Sydney PEN Short Story Award
To encourage short story writing. Residents of Australia may submit entries. Monetary prizes are awarded for first and second place annually in December. Established in 1990.

507
International Solar Energy Society
c/o National Science Foundation
PO Box 124
Caulfield E.
Parkville, VIC 3145, Australia
Phone: 3 5717557
Fax: 3 5636860

508
Achievement Through Action Award
To recognize a group of persons or a corporate body such as a university department that has made an important contribution to the harnessing of solar energy for practical use. Members and non-members may be nominated by October 31 in even-numbered years. The prize money may be divided among the recipients or used to pay for some specific research program or equipment. A monetary award and certificate are presented biennially at the International Congress. Established in 1983 in memory of Christopher A. Weeks.

509
Farrington Daniels Award
For recognition of outstanding contributions to science, technology, or engineering of solar energy applications leading toward ameliorating the conditions of humanity, and for furthering this cause through the International Solar Energy Society. Members may be nominated by October 31 in even-numbered years. A certificate is presented biennially at the International Congress. Established in 1974 in memory of Professor Emeritus Farrington Daniels of the University of Wisconsin.

510
Katanning Shire Council
PO Box 130
Katanning, WA, Australia
Phone: 98 214 200
Fax: 98 211 458

511
Katanning Art Prize
To recognize and acquire contemporary art works to add to the Katanning Shire Council's collection of paintings. Applications may be submitted by October 18. Awards are presented in three categories: (1) Oil & Oil Based - $2,000 (Australian); (2) Water Based Media - $1,500 (Australian); and (3) Miniature, any media - $750 (Australian). Awarded biennially on the Friday prior to the first Tuesday in November. Established in 1979.

512
Grace Leven Prize for Poetry Trust
c/o Perpetual Trustee Company
39 Hunter St.
GPO Box 4172
Sydney, NSW 2001, Australia
Phone: 2 2330777
Fax: 2 2210920

513
Grace Leven Prize for Poetry
For recognition of the best volume of poetry published during the twelve months immediately preceding the year the award is made. Writers must be Australian-born and writing as Australians, or naturalized in Australia and resident in Australia for not less than ten years. A monetary prize of $200 (Australian) is awarded annually. Established in 1947 at the bequest of William Baylebridge.

514
Library and Information Service of Western Australia
Stirling St.
PO Box 8232
Perth, WA 6000, Australia
Phone: 9 4273337
Fax: 9 4273336

515
Western Australian Premier's Book Awards
To honor and celebrate the literary achievements of Western Australian writers. Entrants must have been born in Western Australia, usually reside there, or must make Western Australia the primary focus of their work. Awards are presented in the following categories: Poetry, Fiction, Historical and Critical Studies, Children's Books, Special Award (for scripts written for theater, radio, film, or television), and Premier's Prize, for the overall winner selected from the winners of the five categories. Monetary awards of Aus.$5,000 for each of the first five awards and Aus.$20,000 for the Premier's Prize are presented annually during Western Australia Week. Established in 1982 by the Western Australia Week Council. Formerly: Western Australia Week Literary Awards.

516
Paul Lowin Trust
c/o Perpetual Trustee Company
39 Hunter St.
Sydney, NSW 2000, Australia
Phone: 2 2330777
Fax: 2 2210920

517
Paul Lowin Orchestral Prize
To recognize an outstanding musical composition. Applicants must be at least 18 years of age and Australian citizens at the closing date for entries. (The 1994 closing date was June 30.) Compositions must not be completed earlier than three years before the closing date for entries, and must not have been performed in public or broadcast. Orchestral works must be at least 20 minutes in duration, and use orchestral forces (exceeding those of a classical or chamber orchestra) of a size up to the normal complement of a modern symphony orchestra using as a guide the instrumental strengths of the Melbourne Symphony Orchestra or the Sydney Symphony Orchestra. The work may be with or without instru-

mental soloists. The 1994 award was $45,000. Established under the will of Paul Lowin, an Australian businessman who loved music.

518
Paul Lowin Song Cycle Prize
To recognize an outstanding music composition. Applicants must be at least 18 years of age and Australian citizens at the closing date for entries. (The 1994 closing date was June 30.) Compositions must not be completed earlier than three years before the closing date for entries, and must not have been performed in public or broadcast. Entrants may use existing and/or specially composed lyrics and must be in the English language. The composer and lyricist(s) may be different people. The lyrics should have some similarity or unity in thought and feeling. The voice (maximum of two voices) may be accompanied by an instrument or group of instruments (maximum of six instruments) or be unaccompanied. A monetary award of $20,000 is presented triennially. Established under the will of Paul Lowin, an Australian businessman who loved music.

519
Maryborough Golden Wattle Festival Association
PO Box 213
Maryborough, VIC 3465, Australia   Phone: 54 612646

520
Australian Bird Call Championship
To recognize the individual best able to imitate Australian native birds. A monetary award of $200 and a trophy depicting the lyrebird are awarded annually during the Wattle Festival. Established in 1981.

521
Australian Gumleaf Playing Championship
To choose the best Gumleaf player in Australia. To enter the championship, players must use a genuine Australian Gumleaf. A monetary prize of $1,000 Australian, a trophy, and the Golden Gumleaf Award are awarded annually in early October. Established in 1977.

522
Media Entertainment and Arts Alliance
245 Chalmers St.   Phone: 2 3330999
Redfern, NSW 2016, Australia   Fax: 2 3330933

523
AMP W.G. Walkley Awards for Journalism
For recognition of the best examples of Australian journalism. Best Business Report is open to entries from all areas of business journalism. Best Journalism/Gold Award is an award of $3,000 presented annually for the most outstanding newspaper, radio, or television journalism. Bronze Awards in Print are presented for: Best Coverage of Current Story, Best Investigative Writing, Best Three Headings, Best Feature Writing, Best News Photograph, Best Feature Photograph, Best Cartoon, Best Illustration, and Best Application of the Print Medium to Journalism. Bronze Awards in Radio are presented for: Best Coverage of Current Story, Best Investigative Report, and Best Application of the Radio Medium to Journalism. Bronze Awards in Television are presented for: Best Coverage of Current Story, Best Investigative Report, and Best Application of the Television Medium to Journalism. Bronze Awards in All Media are presented for: Best Suburban, Country, or Rural Report; Best International Report; Most Outstanding Contribution to Journalism; and Best Business Report. A monetary award of $1,000 is presented annually in each category. Deadline for entries is October 7. Established in 1956 by Sir William Gaston Walkley, founder of Ampol Petroleum and one of the pioneers of oil exploration in Australia.

524
Melbourne International Film Festival
GPO Box 2760EE   Phone: 3 663 2953
Melbourne, VIC 3001, Australia   Fax: 3 662 1218

525
Melbourne International Film Festival Shorts Awards
To give encouragement, recognition and reward to short film makers. Short films less than 60 minutes in length are eligible. The deadline for entry is March 31. The following prizes are awarded: (1) Erwin Rado Prize: Best Australian Short (Sponsored by Film Victoria) - $1,500 (Australian); (2) The City of Melbourne Award for Best Film (Grand Prize) - $4,000 (Australian); (3) Front Page Management Ltd. Award for Best Fiction Film - $1,500 (Australian); (4) The *Herald and Weekly Times* Award for Best Documentary - $1,500 (Australian); (5) The Schwartz Publishing Award for Best Experimental Film - $1,500 (Australian); (6) The Kino Cinemas Award for the Best Student Film - $500 (Australian); (7) Best Animated Film - $1,500 (Australian); and (8) State Film Centre Award for the Best Children's Film. Awarded annually. Established in 1962.

526
MEMC
437 Murray Rd.
Preston, VIC 3072, Australia   Phone: 3 470 1816

Formerly: (1986) Melbourne 8mm Movie Club.

527
Moomba International Amateur Film Festival
To provide recognition for the ten best 8mm amateur films. Video entries are also accepted. Trophies and certificates of merit are awarded annually. In addition, a Best Student Award is presented. Established in 1946.

528
Mobil Oil Australia Limited
PO Box 4507   Phone: 3 617 3111
South Melbourne, VIC 3205, Australia   Fax: 3 614 4150

529
Mobil Business in the Arts Awards
For recognition of the support given by the private sector for the arts. Any company, foundation, statutory government authority or commercial organization which has been active in supporting any art form is eligible. A certificate is awarded annually. Established in 1978 by A.R.T.S. Limited (now defunct). In addition, a Mobil Fellowship in Arts Administration is awarded. (Currently inactive)

530
Museums Association of Australia
Museum of Victoria
328 Swanston St.
Melbourne, VIC 3000, Australia   Phone: 3 419 7092

531
Fellow
For recognition of achievement in fields related to museums and/or an outstanding contribution to the Association. Members of the Association may be nominated. The honor is announced annually, usually at the convention. Established before 1980.

532
Museum of the Year Awards
To encourage excellence in museums, to promote awareness of high standards, and to increase public awareness of museums and focus attention on the Australian heritage. Member museums of the Association are eligible. Monetary prizes, certificates, and plaques are awarded annually, at a presentation ceremony at the Victorian Branch. Established in 1982 on the occasion of Victoria's 150th anniversary. Sponsored by WESTPAC and IBM Australia Limited.

[533]
National Book Council
21 Drummond Pl., Ste. 3
Carlton, VIC 3053, Australia
Phone: 3 6638655
Fax: 3 6638658

[534]
Banjo Awards
For recognition of a book of high literary merit and to encourage the writing and publishing of high quality Australian literature. Writers who reside in Australia and books that are published in Australia are considered. Two monetary prizes of $20,000 each are awarded to a fiction winner and nonfiction winner as well as a bronze statuette of Andrew Barton "Banjo" Paterson. In addition, the Turnbull Fox Phillips Poetry Prize of $7,500 is awarded. Awarded annually at a dinner in June during the Australian Book Trade Fair at Darling Harbour, Sydney. Established in 1974 in honor of Andrew Barton "Banjo" Paterson. Sponsored by C.U.B..

[535]
National Council on Intellectual Disability
GPO Box 647
Canberra, ACT 2601, Australia
Phone: 6 2476022
Fax: 6 2470729

Formerly: (1988) AAMR.

[536]
Making the Difference
For recognition of achievement in or contributions to the improvement of the quality of life for people with intellectual disabilities in Australia. Nominations must be submitted by July 31. A plaque is awarded annually in September or October. Established in 1989.

[537]
National Health and Medical Research Council
PO Box 9848
Canberra, ACT 2601, Australia
Phone: 62 289 1555
Fax: 62 289 6957

[538]
Australian Applied Health Sciences Fellowships
To provide training in scientific research methods, including those of the social and behavioral sciences, which can be applied to any area of clinical or community medicine. Australian Applied Health Sciences Fellowships are not restricted to medical and dental graduates. In considering applications, the Council places emphasis on the applied value of the proposed research, with preference given to persons who already have some research experience and are seeking further training in scientific research methods. To be eligible to apply, candidates must: hold appropriate qualifications, although it is not essential to hold a doctorate; have demonstrated their interest in and ability to pursue a career in research and/or teaching in the specific fields of applied health sciences and be currently engaged in such activities in Australia, or, under exceptional circumstances, overseas; not have more than three years' post-doctoral experience since the most recent doctoral award at the time of the application; and be Australian citizens or be graduates from overseas, with permanent Australian resident status, not under bond to any foreign government. The deadline for applications is July 31. The fellowships are usually awarded for a maximum of four years.

[539]
Australian Post-Doctoral Fellowships
To provide a vehicle for training in basic research within the biomedical sciences in Australia and to enable fellows to work on research projects under nominated advisers. Their aim is to encourage persons of outstanding ability to make medical research a full-time career. To be eligible to apply, candidates must: hold a doctorate in a medical, dental, or related field of research or have submitted a thesis for such by December of the year of the application. No offer of award is made unless written confirmation of submission is received; be actively engaged in such research in Australia or, under exceptional circumstances, overseas; not have more than three years' post-doctoral experience; be Australian citizens or be graduates from overseas, with permanent Australian resident status, not under bond to any foreign government; not be currently supported at Senior Research Officer level or above, or hold equivalent status; nominate an institution, department, or research group other than that where the applicant's doctorate was obtained, to undertake the fellowship (applies to applicants within Australia only); and incorporate a clear indication of the training component proposed. Candidates enrolled for a doctorate at the time of applying for this fellowship are expected to complete the degree successfully before the award can be taken up. The deadline for applications is July 31. The fellowships are usually awarded for a maximum of four years.

[540]
Neil Hamilton Fairley Fellowships
To provide training in scientific research methods, including those of the social and behavioral sciences, which can be applied to any area of clinical or community medicine. Fellowships are not restricted to medical and dental graduates. In considering applications, the Council places emphasis on the applied value of the proposed research training, with preference given to persons who already have research experience and are seeking advanced study not available in Australia. To be eligible to apply, candidates must: hold appropriate qualifications, although it is not essential to hold a doctorate; have demonstrated their interest in, and ability to pursue, a career in research and/or teaching in the specific fields of applied health science and be currently engaged in such activities in Australia; not have more than three years' postdoctoral experience since the most recent doctoral award at the time of the application; be Australian citizens or be graduates from overseas, with permanent Australian resident status, not under bond to any foreign government; provide a specific study plan within a clearly defined area; organize affiliation with an overseas investigator/institution to carry out the study; and have reasonable prospects of a responsible position in Australia, on completion of the fellowship. The deadline for applications is July 31. The fellowships are usually awarded for a period of four years; the first two years are spent overseas and the remainder in Australia. The fellowships are named after the late Sir Neil Hamilton Fairley, an Australian scientist whose research in areas of preventive and tropical medicine received international acclaim.

[541]
Dora Lush Biomedical Postgraduate Scholarships
To encourage science graduates of outstanding ability to gain full time medical research experience. All candidates must enroll for a higher degree. Scholarships are held within Australia. Those eligible to apply are: Australian citizens who are graduates and graduates from overseas who have permanent resident status and are currently residing in Australia. A stipend is awarded with allowances to spouse and incidentals.

[542]
C. J. Martin Fellowships
To enable fellows to work overseas on specific research projects within the biomedical sciences under nominated advisers. These fellowships are offered to a limited number of young persons of outstanding ability who wish to make medical research a full time career. To be eligible to apply, candidates must: hold a doctorate in a medical, dental, or related field of research or have submitted a thesis for such by December of the year of application. No offer of award is made unless written confirmation of submission is received; be actively engaged in such research in Australia; not have more than three years' post-doctoral experience at the time of the application; and be Australian citizens or be graduates from overseas, with permanent Australian resident status, not under bond to any foreign government. Candidates enrolled for a doctorate at the time of applying for this fellowship are expected to complete the degree successfully before the award can be taken up. The deadline for applications is July 31. The fellowships are usually awarded for a period of four years; two years are spent overseas and the remainder in Australia. The fellowships are named after the late Sir Charles Martin, a British scientist who had a profound influence on medical research and teaching in Australia early this century.

543

Medical Postgraduate Research Scholarships and Dental Postgraduate Research Scholarships
To assist medical or dental graduates to gain full time research experience. All candidates must enroll for a higher degree. The scholarships are held within Australia. Those eligible to apply are: Australian citizens who are graduates; and graduates from overseas who have permanent resident status and are currently residing in Australia. The deadline for applications is June 30. Scholarships and allowances for dependents are awarded for up to three years.

544

Public Health Travelling Fellowships
To enable fellows to make postgraduate study tours abroad, which relate to their work and specialty and which are of benefit to public health in Australia. The fellowships are open to all graduates working in the field of public health, and to qualified paramedical and nursing personnel, provided they have appropriate post-basic qualifications and are employed in the public health field in Australia. Each fellowship is for a period not exceeding twelve months and cannot be taken up prior to January 1 of the year following submission of the application, nor can it be deferred for a period greater than six months. The fellowships are intended to provide assistance toward travel expenses, living allowances, and course enrollment fees.

545

Research Program Grants
To provide guaranteed support over five years for a research team that normally comprises several independent scientists. The application is two-stage with the first stage deadline of August 31.

546

Research Project Grants
To support research in all fields of medicine and dentistry in Australia. In general, medical research is defined as including all research that involves human subjects and all investigations in physiology, biochemistry, pathology, and other medical sciences and disciplines reasonably likely to have close bearing on problems of human health. The closing date for applications is March 12. The grants may provide funding for salaries for research workers and assistants, equipment maintenance, and other specific expenses.

547

National Library of Australia
Parkes Pl.
Canberra, ACT 2600, Australia
Phone: 6 62 1111
Fax: 6 25 71703

548

Australian Audio Book-of-the-Year
To improve the quality of audio books produced in Australia; to give recognition to quality audio books produced in Australia; and to promote the availability of audio books in Australia. Audio books produced in Australia during the preceding year may be submitted by the producers. A trophy is awarded annually. Established in 1988. Co-sponsored by the Commonwealth of Australia Department of Community Services and Health; and the Chief Librarian, Disability Services Section. Formerly: (1990) National Audio Book of the Year Award.

549

Harold White Fellowship
To promote the library as a centre of scholarly activity and research; to encourage scholarly and literary use of the collections and the production of publications based on them; and to publicize the library's collections. Open to established scholars, writers and librarians of any nationality. Grant-in-aid and traveling expenses are awarded annually. Established in 1984 to honor Sir Harold White, former National Librarian.

550

New South Wales Film & TV Office
1 Francis St. Level 6
Darlinghurst, NSW 2010, Australia
Phone: 380 5599
Fax: 360 1090

551

Nevill Wran Award for Excellence
To encourage an outstanding contribution to the Australian Feature Film industry, and to recognize excellence and achievement in a particular feature film or for a standard of excellence attained through a body of work or service to the industry. Australians who work in the feature film industry were eligible. A monetary prize of $10,000 was awarded. (Discontinued in 1988)

552

Northern Territory Literary Awards Committee
Northern Territory Univ.
Myilly Point Campus
PO Box 40146
Casuarina, NT 0811, Australia
Phone: 89 46 6585
Fax: 89 27 0612

553

Arafura Short Story Award
To provide encouragement for writers of short stories. Awards are given in two categories: (1) Open Section - open to anyone; and (2) Northern Territory Section - open to indviduals with a minimum of two years residence in Northern Territory. Unpublished works may be submitted by August 23. Unpublished works may be submitted by August 23. Monetary prizes of $1,200 in the Open section, and $1,000 in the Northern Territory section are awarded annually in October. Established in 1984. Sponsored by the Northern Territory government. Additional information is available from P.O. Box 1774, Darwin, NT 0801, Australia, phone: 897375.

554

Award for Aboriginal and Torres Strait Islander Writers
To recognize Aboriginal or Torres Strait Islander writers for short stories, poems or narratives, including testimony material. Open to Aboriginal or Torres Strait Islander people who have lived in the Northern Territory for at least two years. (In the context of this award, this section is open to those who are of Aboriginal or Torres Strait Islander descent, who identify as Aborigines or Torres Strait Islanders, and who are accepted as such by the communities in which they live.) Unpublished works may be submitted by August 23. A monetary award of $1,000 and a medallion are awarded annually in October.

555

Red Earth Poetry Award
To provide encouragement for writers of poetry. Awards are given in two categories: (1) Open Section - open to anyone; and (2) Northern Territory - minimum of two years residence in Northern Territory. Unpublished works may be submitted by August 23. Monetary prizes of $1,200 in the Open section, and $1,000 in the Northern Territory section are awarded annually in October. Established in 1984. Sponsored by the Northern Territory government. Additional information is available from P.O. Box 1774, Darwin, NT 0801, Australia, phone: 897375.

556

Northern Territory University
PO Box 40146
Casuarina, NT 0811, Australia
Phone: 89 466275
Fax: 89 270612

557

Jessie Litchfield Award
To provide encouragement for new and unknown Australian writers, especially those writing about the Northern Territory. Open to all literary forms including novels, historical works, plays, collections of essays, short stories, or poetry. The deadline for entries is January 31. A monetary prize of $1,200 and a certificate are awarded biennially. Established in 1964 to honor Jessie Sinclair Litchfield (1883-1956), a

prolific writer, newspaper editor, journalist, and the first woman to be appointed justice of the peace in the Northern Territory. Prior to 1990, the award was administered by the Bread and Cheese Club, Melbourne.

558
Oceania Basketball Confederation
PO Box 6170
The Plaza
Coffs Harbour, NSW 2450, Australia
Phone: 66 515767
Fax: 66 515769

559
Competitions
To promote basketball in the Pacific region. Awards are presented.

560
Oceania Weightlifting Federation
395 Camberwell Rd.
Camberwell, VIC 3124, Australia
Fax: 3 7648622

561
Awards
To promote the development of weightlifting in Oceania. Awards are presented.

562
Omega Society
PO Box 5271, Mail Centre
North Rockhampton, QLD 4702, Australia
Phone: 7927 1370

563
Member of the Year Award
For recognition of achievements by members in various fields. Members are individuals whose I.Q. equals or surpasses the 1983 *Guinness Book of World Records* "highest I.Q." of 197. A certificate is awarded when merited. Established in 1987 in honor of Steve Whiting. (Discontinued)

564
Opera Foundation Australia
364-372 Sussex St., Bldg. 2GB
PO Box R483
Royal Exchange, NSW 2000, Australia
Phone: 2 212 7101
Fax: 2 212 7095

565
American Institute of Musical Studies Award
To further the advancement of a young Australian singer's professional career. Applications must be submitted by March 30. A six-week summer course in the American Institute of Musical Studies in Graz, Austria is awarded. Finalists for other Opera Foundation Australia scholarships or other suitable applicants are eligible. Total value of this award approximates $8,000, which includes tuition, accommodation, and transportation to and from Australia. Awarded annually. Sponsored by Swarovski International.

566
Austrian Operatic Award
To enable a young singer to study in Vienna. A monetary award of up to $35,000 is presented, along with round-trip airfare, tuition, and a living allowance.

567
Bayreuth Scholarship
To provide assistance for artists who are professionally engaged in some facet of opera. Singers, conductors, repetiteurs, producers, and designers are eligible. Applications must be submitted by March 30. For a period of approximately two months, the German government, through the German Academic Exchange Service (D.A.A.D.), provides a living allowance and domestic airfares for travel within Germany as well as assistance with any tuition fees. Established in 1973. Airfares are donated by the Wagner Society.

568
Dame Mabel Brookes Memorial Fellowship
To provide a young artist with specialist coaching and on-stage experience for a career in opera. To be eligible for the award, singers must be Australian citizens or have been resident in Australia for a minimum of 12 months and be between 19 and 35 years of age. The deadline is May 31. The coaching and experience received by the young artist is valued at $15,000. The young artist will be one of six outstanding artists taking part in an annual program conducted by the Victoria State Opera. Established in 1983 by the Opera Foundation Australia and Opera Foundation Victoria in honor of Dame Mabel Brookes. Sponsored by Opera Foundation Victoria.

569
Lady Galleghan Encouragement Award
This award is made to a finalist of the Shell, Royal Opera House, Convent Garden Scholarship (see separate entry). A monetary prize of $3,000 is awarded.

570
German Operatic Award
To enable a young singer to become a member of the Opera Studio attached to the Cologne State Opera, West Germany, for its operating year. Austrian citizens or permanent residents between 23 and 33 years of age are eligible. Applicants must have a voice with good operatic potential, musical background, and artistic aptitude. They must be Australian citizens and must have resided in Australia for six months prior to the final auditions. The deadline is in December. The award is valued in excess of $30,000. The winner receives return airfare to Cologne provided by Lufthansa Airlines, a settling in allowance, and a monthly living allowance to supplement the allowance made available by the Cologne State Opera to the Australian Winner. Established in 1988. Sponsored by the German Corporate Community.

571
Metropolitan Opera Auditions - Australian Regional Finals
To recognize Australian Regional winners and help them to advance their musical skills. Applicants must meet the following age limit requirements: sopranos, 19-33; mezzo sopranos and contraltos, 19-33; and tenors, baritones, and basses, 20-33 (these age limits are required for the period between January, 1995 through April, 1995). Applicants must have a voice with operatic potential and have vocal training, musical background, and artistic aptitude. Applicants must have resided in Australia for at least six months. The deadline is mid-May. The following prizes are awarded: Lady Galleghan Prize - First prize - a monetary prize of $5,000, and a $5,000 scholarship; Second prize - $2,000; Third prize - $1,000; and runners-up - $250. The Regional Winner is flown to New York to work with members of the Metropolitan's artistic staff and to compete in the U.S. National Semi-finals on the Metropolitan Opera Stage. If selected to perform at the non-competitive National Finals concert, he or she wins another scholarship of $5,000 and benefits from further coaching. The Metropolitan Opera Education Fund is available to assist former first place regional winners with further financial aid if their progress warrants it. The yearly awards and scholarships of the Metropolitan Opera Auditions program total approximately $100,000. Awarded annually. Established in 1963 by Lady Mary Fairfax in association with the Metropolitan Opera, New York City, New York. Sponsored by the Metropolitan Opera and the Opera Foundation (NSW).

572
Shell, Royal Opera House, Covent Garden Scholarship
To provide a young Australian opera singer with the opportunity to study in London. Applicants must be between 23 and 32 years of age and must have a voice with operatic potential, musical background, and artistic aptitude. Some professional experience is preferred. Applicants must be Australian citizens and have resided in Australia for at least 12 months. The winner is granted a year of study at the National Opera Studio London, or advanced private coaching as recommended by the Royal Opera House. This program is flexible in order to cater to the individual needs of the winner and also carries an appropriate living allowance, in

addition to tuition fees and airfares to the United Kingdom. The total value of this scholarship does not exceed $35,000. In addition, the Lady Galleghan Encouragement Award of $3,000 is presented to a finalist at the discretion of the judges. Awarded annually. Established in 1984. Sponsored by the Shell Company of Australia.

573
Pacific Area Newspaper Publishers Association
80 Alfred St.
Milsons Point, NSW 2061, Australia
Phone: 2 9594396
Fax: 2 9594919

574
Hegarty Prize
To recognize management potential in newspaper executives.

575
PANPA Newspaper Awards
To recognize excellence in design, production, and use of color in member newspapers.

576
Pacific Arts Association
South Australian Museum
North Terrace
Adelaide, SA 5000, Australia

577
Citation of Merit
To recognize the contribution of an individual to the arts of a particular Pacific culture and their preservation. A certificate is given every four years at the International Symposium. Established in 1989.

578
Manu Daula Frigate Bird Award
To recognize an individual for outstanding service and dedication to the arts of the Pacific. A bronze medallion is awarded every four years at the International Symposium. Established in 1985.

579
Geraldine Pascall Foundation
Gridiger & Company
67 Castlereagh St., Level 4
Sydney, NSW 2000, Australia
Phone: 2 2314888
Fax: 2 2218201

580
Pascall Prize
To recognize an Australian critic or reviewer for excellence. The specific field changes annually. Individuals writing regularly for a newspaper or periodical published in Australia or broadcasting regularly on radio or television in Australia are eligible. Nomination deadline is August 31. A monetary award of 15,000 Australian dollars is presented annually. Established in 1988 to honor Geraldine Pascall, a journalist who died in 1983 at the age of 38.

581
Pharmacy Guild of Australia
14 Thesiger Ct.
PO Box 36
Deakin, ACT 2606, Australia
Phone: 62 81 0911
Fax: 62 82 4745

582
Distinguished Service Certificate
For recognition of distinguished service given to the profession of pharmacy by a member of the Guild within a Branch. A membership certificate is awarded when merited. Established in 1988.

583
Distinguished Service Medal
For recognition of outstanding contributions to the pharmacy profession. An engraved medallion is awarded when merited. Established in 1978.

584
Honorary Life Member
For recognition of distinguished service to the pharmacy profession over an extensive period or distinguished service to the community by a pharmacist over an extensive period. A certificate is awarded annually when merited. Established in 1929 by The Federated Pharmaceutical Service Guild of Australia.

585
Honorary Member
For recognition of significant service to the profession of pharmacy in Australia and/or the Guild over a period of years. Honorary Membership is awarded on an annual basis on the recommendation of a Branch Committee to the National Council for approval.

586
Quadrant
PO Box 1495
Collingwood, VIC 3066, Australia
Phone: 3 4176855
Fax: 3 4162980

587
George Watson Essay Award
To recognize the best political essay published during the preceding year. A monetary award of $2,000 was awarded annually. (Discontinued)

588
Royal Australasian College of Dental Surgeons
64 Castlereagh St., 6th Fl.
Sydney, NSW 2000, Australia
Phone: 2 232 3800
Fax: 2 221 8108

589
F. G. Christensen Memorial Prize
For recognition of a candidate who gains the highest marks in the College's Primary Examination. A dentist qualified to practice in the country of qualification, who is enrolled with the College, and has passed the Primary Examination is eligible. A monetary prize and a bronze medallion are awarded annually. Established in 1971 by Dr. F.G. Christensen.

590
Kenneth J. G. Sutherland Prize
For recognition of a candidate who gains the highest marks in General Dentistry by demonstrating eminence in the elective section of the College's General Stream Final Examination. A dentist, qualified to practice in the country of qualification, who is enrolled in the College and is eligible to take the Final Examination held in late January each year is eligible. A monetary prize and the College Medal are awarded annually when merited at Scientific Meetings of the College. Established in 1987 by Emeritus Professor K.J.G. Sutherland, AM.

591
Royal Australasian College of Radiologists
Level 9, 51 Druitt St.
Sydney, NSW 2000, Australia
Phone: 2 2477797
Fax: 2 2514629

592
Thomas Baker Memorial Fellowship for Radiologists
To provide funds for a qualified radiologist to further his or her knowledge by study abroad. Applicants must be citizens of Australia or New Zealand, graduates of a University of Australia, New Zealand or other medical school approved by council, and be members of the Royal Australasian

College of Radiologists. A fellowship of Australian $10,000 maximum is awarded.

[593]

Junior Member and Travel Awards
The following awards are presented: Schering A. G. Berlin Study Grants - to a fellow of not more than five years' standing, an associate member, or a student member to assist travel to the annual meeting; Varian Prize - for the best presentation by a student member of the college on the radiation oncology section of the scientific program of the annual meeting; Du Pont Prize - for the best presentation by a junior member or a student member of the college on the scientific program of the annual meeting.

[594]

Royal Australasian College of Surgeons
Spring St.
Melbourne, VIC 3000, Australia
Phone: 3 6621033
Fax: 3 6634075

[595]

John Mitchell Crouch Fellowship
To recognize an individual who, in the opinion of the Council, is making an outstanding contribution to the advancement of surgery or anaesthesia, or to fundamental scientific research in these fields. The individual must be working actively in his/her field, and the award must be used to assist the continuation of this work. Fellows and fellows of the faculty who are graduates of Australian or New Zealand Medical Schools, resident in Australia or New Zealand, are eligible. Graduates from other countries are eligible if domiciled in Australia or New Zealand for five years or more. A fellowship of approximately $40,000 (Australian) is awarded annually. Established in 1978 by Mrs. Elisabeth Unsworth, in memory of her son, John Mitchell Crouch, a young fellow of the College, who died early in his career.

[596]

Royal Australian Chemical Institute
National Secretariat
1/21 Vale St.
North Melbourne, VIC 3051, Australia
Phone: 3 347 1577
Fax: 3 349 1409

[597]

Applied Research Medal
For recognition of a significant contribution towards the development of innovation in applied research, or in industrial fields. Members of the Institute are eligible. An honorarium of $250 (Australian) and a bronze medal are awarded annually. Established in 1980. Each award of the medal is named for a distinguished chemist.

[598]

Cornforth Medal
To recognize an RACI member for the most outstanding Ph.D. thesis submitted in a branch of chemistry, chemical science, or chemical technology in the previous 13 months. A candidate's degree must have been approved by the governing body of an Australian University, although not necessarily conferred, in the previous 13 months. No candidate may be nominated more than once. Each Australian university may nominate one candidate through the Deputy Vice-Chancellor (Research) or person holding the equivalent office of the University. A bronze relief medal and cash prize are awarded annually. Deadline for nominations is July 31.

[599]

Leighton Memorial Medal
For recognition of eminent services to chemistry in its broadest sense. Nominations must be made by April 28. A medal is awarded annually in May. Established in 1965 in honor of A.E. Leighton.

[600]

C. S. Piper Prize
To recognize a RACI member for the best published original research work carried out mainly in Australia in the fields of either soil chemistry or the mineral nutrition of plants. The successful candidate will deliver a lecture on the occasion of the presentation of the award and may be invited to lecture to other branches of the Institute. A medal, a monetary prize of $8,000, plus $2,000 travel expenses, if required, are awarded biennially when merited.

[601]

Rennie Memorial Medal
For recognition of published research. Members of the Institute who are less than 33 years of age may be nominated by July 28. A medal is awarded annually. Established in 1931 in honor of E.H. Rennie.

[602]

H. G. Smith Medal
To recognize the individual who has contributed the most to the development of some branch of chemical science. The contribution is judged by research work published or accepted for publication during the ten years immediately preceding the award. Most of the work should have been done in Australia while the candidate was an Institute member. An honorarium and a bronze medal are awarded annually. Established in 1929 in memory of H.G. Smith.

[603]

Wolskel Industrial Chemistry Essay Award
To recognize an essay relating industrial chemistry to logic and/or economics. The competition is open to all Australian citizens. Essays should be between 5,000 and 15,000 words and include a synopsis of approximately 100 words. A monetary prize of $750 is awarded.

[604]

Royal Australian College of General Practitioners
c/o F.H. Faulding Memorial Fellowship
  Committee
College House
15 Gover St.
North Adelaide, SA 5006, Australia
Phone: 8 2671249
Fax: 8 2673577

[605]

Francis Hardy Faulding Memorial Fellowship
For recognition of a completed research project relating to general practice. General practitioners who work actively in general practice 50 percent of the time may submit a thesis. A monetary prize of $5,000 is awarded annually. Established by F.H. Faulding and Company, Ltd., in memory of Francis Hardy Faulding, founder of the F.H. Faulding Pharmaceutical Manufacturing Company. Sponsored by F. H. Faulding and Company, Ltd.

[606]

Royal Australian Historical Society
History House
133 Macquarie St.
Sydney, NSW 2000, Australia
Phone: 2 278001
Fax: 2 2477854

Formerly: (1921) Australian Historical Society.

[607]

Royal Australian Historical Society Competitions
To recognize individuals who work to advance the study of Australian history and expand opportunities for historical research and writing. The Society sponsors competitions and bestows awards.

608
Royal Australian Institute of Architects
2A Mugga Way
PO Box 3373
Manuka, ACT 2603, Australia
Phone: 62 731548
Fax: 62 731953

609
National Architecture Awards
To recognize achievement in architecture. The following awards are presented: Commercial Award - to recognize outstanding commercial products; Interior Architecture Award - to recognize interiors completed for commercial or other purposes, new building interiors, or interior refurbishment of existing buildings; International Award - established in 1991 to recognize the overseas work of Australian architects in many parts of the world; Lachlan MacQuarie Award - established in 1982 to recognize conservation and restoration, both domestic and commercial, where the work has led to the restoration or conservation of the building with due consideration for its historic purpose; President Award - established in 1985 to recognize residential and nonresidential renovation projects; Robin Boyd Award - established in 1981 to recognize residential work, including both completed new buildings and extensions (not including such major projects as hotels); Sir Zelman Cowen Award - established in 1981 to recognize nonresidential work including commercial-, institutional-, and recreational-type projects, both new and extensions; and Walter Burley Griffen Award - established in 1989 to recognize excellence in the field of design of civic amenities.

610
RAIA Gold Medal
To recognize architects who have given distinguished service to the architectural profession by designing or executing buildings of high merit, or who have produced work of great distinction resulting in the advancement of architecture. Architects in countries within the Australian sphere of influence are eligible. A gold medal is awarded annually at the general meeting. Established in 1960.

611
Royal Blind Society of New South Wales
c/o Dir. of Library Services
PO Box 176
Burwood, NSW 2134, Australia
Phone: 2 3343333
Fax: 2 7475993

612
3M Talking Book of the Year
To highlight the importance of talking books for readers with print disabilities, to improve the quality of talking books, to recognize significant Australian books, and to recognize the support given by Australian authors and publishers for the production of talking books. Awards are given in two categories: Adult category and Variety Club Young People's category (books for young people over 11 or 12 years of age). Books published in Australia by an Australian author or about Australia during the year preceding the award are eligible. Poetry and unconnected short stories are not eligible. A monetary award and a trophy are presented to the author and narrator at a public dinner. The presentation is followed by discussion with the author and narrator. Awarded annually. Established in 1979. Co-sponsored by the 3M Company and the Royal Blind Society of New South Wales.

613
Royal College of Pathologists of Australasia
Durham Hall
207 Albion St.
Surrey Hills, NSW 2010, Australia
Phone: 2 3324266
Fax: 2 3311431

614
Distinguished Fellow
For recognition in the field of pathology. Established in 1986.

615
Royal Geographical Society of Queensland
112 Brookes St.
Fortitude Valley, QLD 4006, Australia
Phone: 7 2523856
Fax: 7 2524986

616
Fellow
To recognize members who have rendered valuable services to the Society or who have promoted its objectives. A Diploma of Fellowship is awarded.

617
J. P. Thomson Medal
For recognition of scholarship and contribution to the study of geography as exemplified by the life of Dr. J. P. Thompson. The following criteria are considered: research that has advanced knowledge of the discipline of geography or advanced the understanding of the importance of the role of geography in daily life; teaching or writing that has contributed to geographical education, including the development or application of techniques that have promoted the progress or application of geographical studies; and activities in fields not necessarily identified as geography that are clearly influenced by a geographical outlook or knowledge. Established in 1901 to honor James Park Thompson. Formerly: J. P. Thompson Foundation Gold Medal.

618
Royal Melbourne Institute of Technology
GPO Box 2427 V
Melbourne, VIC 3001, Australia
Phone: 52 6603627

619
J. N. McNicol Prize
For recognition of achievement and to encourage professional development in the field of technology. Nominees must have exhibited outstanding academic achievement, leadership potential, initiative, and successful completion of an undergraduate course at the Royal Melbourne Institute of Technology. A monetary award, medal, and certificate are awarded annually. Established in 1976 by E. J. Reilly in memory of J. N. McNicol for his assistance and encouragement to students.

620
Francis Ormond Medal
To recognize a member of the Institute's academic, teaching, or general staff who has served the Institute with distinction or has given meritorious service which has not been recognized by the Institute by any other honorary award. A medal is awarded annually. Established in 1983 in memory of Francis Ormond, founder of the Institute and president of the Council (1882-1889).

621
Royal Society of New South Wales
134 Herring Rd.
North Ryde, POB 1525
Macquarie Centre, NSW 2113, Australia
Phone: 2 8874448

622
Walter Burfitt Medal and Prize
To recognize the worker whose contributions published during the past six years are deemed of the highest scientific merit. Only investigations described for the first time and carried out by the author mainly in Australia and New Zealand are considered. A medal and a monetary prize of $300 (Australian) are awarded triennially when merited. Established in 1929 by Dr. and Mrs. W. F. Burfitt.

623
Clarke Medal
For recognition of distinguished work in the natural sciences done in, or on, the Australian Commonwealth and its territories in one of the follow-

ing three categories: geology, botany, zoology. A medal is awarded annually when merited. Established in 1878 in memory of Reverend William Branwhite Clarke, Vice-President of the society, 1866-1878.

624
Clarke Memorial Lectureship
To recognize an individual for advancement in geology. Awarded biennially.

625
James Cook Medal
For recognition of outstanding contributions to science and human welfare in and for the Southern Hemisphere. A medal is awarded annually when merited. Established in 1947.

626
Edgeworth David Medal
To recognize Australian research workers under the age of 35 for work done mainly in Australia or its territories, or for contributions to the advancement of Australian science. A medal is awarded annually when merited. Established in 1948.

627
Liversidge Memorial Lectureship
To recognize an individual for outstanding research in chemistry. Awarded biennially.

628
Archibald D. Olle Prize
To recognize the member of the society who has submitted the best paper during the year. Awarded biennially. Established in 1956.

629
Poggendorff Memorial Lecture
To recognize an individual for outstanding achievement in agriculture. The recipient is chosen by the council to present a memorial lecture. Established in 1987 to honor Walter Hans Georg Poggendorff.

630
Society Medal
To recognize a member of the society for meritorious contributions to the advancement of science, including administration and organization of scientific endeavour, and for recognition of services to the society. A medal is awarded annually when merited. Established in 1882.

631
Royal Society of South Australia
South Australian Museum, N. Terrace
Adelaide, SA 5000, Australia   Phone: 8 2235360

Formerly: (1880) Adelaide Philosophical Society.

632
Sir Joseph Verco Medal
For recognition of distinguished scientific work published by a member of the Society. The Council of the Society makes the award on the recommendation of the Society's awards committee, which considers members of the Society who have been nominated by fellow members. A medal is awarded annually when merited. Established in 1928 in honor of Sir Joseph Verco (1851-1933).

633
Royal Society of Tasmania
PO Box 1166M   Phone: 2 350777
Hobart, TAS 7001, Australia   Fax: 2 347139

634
R. M. Johnston Memorial Medal
To recognize a lecturer chosen by the Council to deliver the R. M. Johnston Memorial Lecture. A bronze medal is given at the discretion of the Council. Established in 1920 to commemorate Robert Mackenzie Johnston, a statistician and scientist.

635
Clive Lord Memorial Medal
To recognize a lecturer chosen by the Council to deliver the Clive Lord Memorial Lecture. A bronze medal is awarded usually triennially. Established in 1934 in memory of Clive Lord, Director of the Tasmanian Museum.

636
Royal Society of Tasmania Medal
For recognition of research of high merit. Members of the Society are eligible. An oval bronze medal is awarded by a decision of a general meeting of members. Established in 1927.

637
Royal Society of Victoria
9 Victoria St.   Phone: 3 6635259
Melbourne, VIC 3000, Australia   Fax: 3 6632301

638
Royal Society of Victoria Medal
For recognition of scientific research of outstanding merit in one of the following four categories: biological sciences - agriculture, biochemistry, botany, forestry, physiology, zoology, and related sciences; earth sciences - geology, geochemistry, geochronology, geophysics, planetary physics, meteorology, oceanography, physical geography, and related sciences; physical sciences - astronomy, chemistry, engineering, mathematics, physics, and related sciences; and social sciences - anthropology, archaeology, economics, human geography, psychology, sociology, and related sciences. The work must have been carried out in or on Australia with preference given to work done in Victoria or on Victoria. Scientific societies, universities, C.S.I.R.O., and members of the Royal Society may nominate individuals. A silver medal is awarded annually at the Medal Lecture. Established in 1959, the centenary year of the society.

639
Royal Society of Western Australia
Western Australian Museum
Francis St.   Phone: 4272771
Perth, WA 6000, Australia   Fax: 9 3288686

640
Royal Society of Western Australia Medal
To provide recognition for distinguished work in science connected with Western Australia. There are no restrictions on eligibility. A sterling silver medallion is awarded at the discretion of the council of the Society, about every four years. Established in 1924.

641
Royal South Australian Society of Arts
Kintore Gallery
Institute Bldg., North Terr.
Adelaide, SA 5000, Australia   Phone: 223 4704

642
Fellow
For recognition of achievement in the arts. Society members may be nominated by October 1 each year. A scroll is awarded annually. The first recorded fellowships were awarded in 1893.

643
Royal Western Australian Historical Society
Stirling House
49 Broadway
Nedlands, WA 6009, Australia   Phone: 386 3841

644
Lee Steere History Essay Competition
To promote an interest in and recording of Western Australian history. Tertiary students and members of historical societies are eligible. A monetary prize is awarded at the discretion of the RWAHS Council from time to time in order to commemorate a special anniversary. Established in 1948 to commemorate the late Sir Ernest Lee Steere.

645
Royal Zoological Society of New South Wales
PO Box 20
Mosman, NSW 2088, Australia   Phone: 2 9697336

646
Whitley Awards
For recognition of an outstanding book published on Australasian fauna or the history of Australasian zoology during the preceding year. Applications must be submitted by June 30. Awards may be presented in the following categories: best children's book, best field guide, best illustrated book, best reference book, best textbook, best zoological history book, best zoological periodical, and other appropriate categories. A silver medal is awarded to the author of the outstanding book; the publisher receives a certificate and citation. Certificates of commendation are awarded to category winners. Established in 1978 to honor Gilbert Whitley (1903-1975), an Australian zoologist. Additional information is available from Ron Strahan, Australian Photographic Index, Australian Museum, 6-8 College St., 2000 New South Wales, Australia.

647
St. Kilda Film Festival
Private Bag No. 3   Phone: 3 5361397
St. Kilda, VIC 3182, Australia   Fax: 3 5349105

648
St. Kilda Film Festival
For recognition of the best Australian independent film. A monetary prize of $1,000 is awarded annually for the City of St. Kilda Prize. Other monetary prizes are awarded in various categories. Established in 1984. Sponsored by the City of St. Kilda.

649
Sherbrooke Art Society
8 Monbulk Road
Belgrave, VIC 3168, Australia   Phone: 3 754 4264

650
Tom Roberts Award
To recognize individuals for outstanding achievement. A monetary award is presented annually. Established in 1971 to honor Tom Roberts.

651
Sir Arthur Streeton Award
To recognize individuals for outstanding achievement. Citizens of Australia are eligible. A monetary award is presented annually. Established in 1968 to honor Sir Arthur Streeton.

652
Society of Australian Film and Television Arts and Sciences
Ingrid Berg & Associates
85e Wigram Rd.
Glebe, NSW 2037, Australia

653
Sammy Awards
For recognition of outstanding film and television. Awards are given in the following categories: (1) Gold (Man); (2) Gold (Woman); (3) Chips Rafferty Memorial Award; (4) Best Actor in a Single TV Performance; (5) Best Actress in a Single TV Performance; (6) Best Film Actor; (7) Best Film Actress; (8) Best Actor in a TV Series; (9) Best Actress in a TV Series; (10) Best Supporting Film Actor; (11) Best Supporting Film Actress; (12) Best Variety Performer; (13) Best New Talent; (14) Best Drama Series; (15) Best Short Drama Series; (16) Best Comedy Program; (17) Best TV Play; (18) Best Variety Program; (19) Best Film; (20) Best Short Length Film (Factual); (21) Best Short Length Film (Fiction); (22) Best Animated Film; (23) Best Documentary Program; (24) Best News Coverage; (25) Best Current Affairs Program; (26) Best Sports Coverage; (27) Best Children's Series; (28) Best Light Entertainment Series; (29) Best Cinematographer (Film); (30) Best Cinematographer (TV); (31) Best Art Direction (TV); (32) Best Art Direction (Film); (33) Best Writer Feature Film; (34) Best Writer TV Series; (35) Best Writer TV Play; (36) Best Theme Music; (37) Best Editing (Film); (38) Best Editing (TV); (39) Best Special Effects (Film); (40) Best Direction (Film); (41) Best Direction (TV); (42) Best Sound (Film); and (43) Best Costume Design.

654
Society of Automotive Engineers - Australasia
191 Royal Parade   Phone: 3 3472220
Parkville, VIC 3052, Australia   Fax: 3 3470464

655
J. E. Batchelor Award
For recognition of an outstanding paper presented to the Society. Any individual who is a resident of Australia or New Zealand is eligible. Awarded annually.

656
FISITA Travelling Fellowship
Awarded to young engineers so they can attend the biennial FISITA automotive and engineering congress.

657
Gas Turbine Award
For recognition of an outstanding original contribution to gas turbine technology in Australia or New Zealand. Residents of Australia and New Zealand are eligible. Awarded annually.

658
Hartnett Award
For recognition of an outstanding contribution to automotive or aeronautical engineering knowledge or practice, in any branch of the profession, or within the scope of activities or interests of the Society. Residents of Australia or New Zealand are eligible. Awarded annually.

659
O'Shannessy Award
For recognition of an outstanding paper delivered to the Society or published in the journal. Residents of Australia or New Zealand are eligible for nomination. Rodda Award and J.E. Batchelor Award winners are ineligible. Nominees must be less than 30 years of age. Awarded annually.

660
Rodda Award
To recognize a member of the Society who submitted an outstanding written paper concerned with the original work and ideas in the fields of

design, development, research or management relevant to the automotive industry. Awarded annually.

661
Society of Women Writers Australia
20 Prosperity Rd.
Lower Plenty, NSW 3093, Australia					Phone: 2 98 6117

662
Alice Award
For recognition of a distinguished and long-term contribution to literature by an Australian woman. Selection is by nomination. A non-acquisitive statuette (The Alice) designed by Alan Ingham accompanied by a hand-lettered certificate are awarded every two years at the biennial conference. Established in 1978 by the Federal Council to commemorate fifty years of the Society (1925-1975) and the late Alice Booth, a former school teacher and member of the Society in New South Wales.

663
Kitty Archer-Burton Poetry Competition
For recognition of a poem by a high school student resident in Australia and under 19 years of age. A monetary prize is awarded biennially at the delegates' conference. Established in 1977 in honor of Kitty Archer-Burton, a violinist chosen for the orchestra accompanying MELBA and secretary of the Society of Women Writers New South Wales for fourteen years.

664
Dame Alexandra Hasluck Short Story Competition
To recognize an outstanding short story by an Australian woman. Awarded biennially to coincide with the delegates' conference. Established in 1986 to honor Dame Alexandra Hasluck.

665
Hilarie Lindsay Award
To recognize a significant contribution to literature by a member of the Society. A pewter ewer is awarded biennially. Established in 1981 in honor of Hilarie Lindsay.

666
Charles Meeking Award for Poetry
For recognition of outstanding poems submitted for the poetry competition for Australian women. A monetary prize is awarded biennially to coincide with the delegates' conference. Established in 1979 in honor of Charles Meeking, former editor of *The Canberra Times*.

667
Soroptimist International of the South West Pacific
GPO Box 1439									Phone: 2 2350439
Sydney, NSW 2001, Australia							Fax: 2 2350439

668
Soroptimist International of the South West Pacific Awards
To recognize individuals who participate in the struggle for peace and human rights, particularly the rights of women. Awards are given biennially.

669
Sounds Australian
Australian Music Centre Ltd.
PO Box N690
Grosvenor Pl.									Phone: 2 2474677
Sydney, NSW 2000, Australia							Fax: 2 2412873

670
Australian One-Act Opera Project
To provide an opportunity for younger Australian composers and librettists to write operas and have them professionally performed. Australian citizens or permanent residents, 40 years of age or less, may enter by October 30. Commission fees to composers and librettists, and an opportunity to work with first class directors and singers in composition and production of opera are awarded. Established in 1987 by the Australian Music Centre in collaboration with the State Opera and Adelaide Symphony, and funding from the Australia Council. (Discontinued) Formerly: (1991) Australian Composer National Opera Awards.

671
Sounds Australian Awards
To recognize outstanding musicians. There are two divisions of the awards: Sounds Australian Music Awards in which one award is given for composition and one for performance. Nominations are made by a committee in each state; assessment is made by a national committee. The nominating and assessment committees are made up of composers, musicians, critics, and others with expertise in contemporary music; and Sounds Australian Presenter Awards in which National awards to organizations specializing in the presentation of new music; organizations whose activities extend beyond presentation of new music, individuals, broadcasters, radio, or writers appearing in the mass media. (One of the winners of the above six categories is chosen for a special award for the most distinguished contribution from all categories). The State Awards are also given in each state to the person or group making the most distinguished contribution to the presentation of Australian music. All award winners receive a certificate. Additionally, the national Presenter Awards winners each receive the original copy of a short work written for them by a leading Australian composer.

672
South Australia
Ministry for the Arts and Cultural Heritage
Arts Division
GPO Box 2308									Phone: 8 207 7100
Adelaide, SA 5001, Australia							Fax: 8 207 7111

673
Festival Awards for Literature
To recognize distinguished Australian and South Australian writing in the novel and short story form, poetry, children's literature, and non-fiction. The deadline for submissions is November 1. The following awards are presented: National Fiction Award - for a published novel or a collection of short stories, $12,000; the John Bray Award for Poetry (National) - for a published collection of poems or for a single poem of substantial length, $12,000; Non-fiction award - for a published work of nonfiction, $12,000; National Children's Book Award - for a published work of fiction or nonfiction, $12,000; the Jill Blewett Playwright's Award (National) - for a play script performed by a professional theatre company, or a professional production unit, in South Australia, $12,000; Carclew Fellowship - a six-month fellowship - open to South Australian writers for young people, $18,000; and the Barbara Hanrahan Fellowship - a six-month fellowship - open to South Australian writers of poetry and creative prose. Awarded biennially during Writers' Week as part of the Adelaide Festival of Arts. Established in 1976.

674
South Australian Film and Video Centre
Lumiere Lane
Westside Commerce Centre
113 Tapleys Hill Rd.								Phone: 8 3489355
Hendon, SA 5014, Australia							Fax: 8 3454222

675
International Children's Film and Video Festival
For recognition of the best feature film and best short film for children between 4 and 16 years of age. Awards are given for the best feature film, best short film, and best Australian film or video. A Children's Jury Prize

is also awarded. A wooden statuette of a clown, the logo of the Chiff Award is awarded biennially at the Festival for each category. Established in 1986 by the South Australian Council for Children's Films and Television. Sponsored by Foundation South Australia and Australian Film Commission. Formerly: International Film Festival for Young Australians.

676
South Australian Photographic Federation
Interphot Secretary
34 Deepdene Ave.
Bellevue Heights, SA 5050, Australia
Phone: 8 3741840
Fax: 8 3743692

677
Interphot - Adelaide International Exhibition of Photography
For recognition of outstanding photography. Awards are given in the following categories: Monochrome Prints, Contemporary Prints, Pictorial Color Slides, Contemporary Slides, Nature Prints, Wild Life Prints, Wild Life Slides, Nature Slides, and Color Prints. Entries must be submitted by April 4. PSA medals, APS plaques, SAPF plaques, FIAP ribbons, and Kodak awards are presented biennially. Established in 1964.

678
Southdown Press
TV Week
32 Walsh St.
West Melbourne, VIC 3003, Australia
Phone: 3 3207000
Fax: 3 3207409

679
TV Week Logie Awards
To acknowledge and honor Australia's most popular television performers and programs, along with outstanding contributions in all areas - from news and public affairs, to light entertainment and drama. The program or performance must have occurred during the calendar year for which the awards are presented. Awards are given in the following categories: Public Voted Awards - Most Popular Personality on Australian TV, Most Popular Actor and Actress on Australian TV, Most Popular Drama Series, Most Popular Actor and Actress in a Single Drama or Mini-Series, Most Popular Sports Coverage, Most Popular Single Drama or Mini-Series, Most Popular Light Entertainment/Comedy Program, Most Popular Music Video, Most Popular Children's Program, Most Popular Public Affairs Program, and Most Popular New Talent in Australia; and Panel Voted Awards - Hall of Fame, Most Outstanding Actor and Actress, Most Outstanding Achievement in Public Affairs, Most Outstanding Single Documentary or Series, Most Outstanding Achievement in News, and Most Outstanding Achievement by a Regional Channel. Statuettes, including silver TV Week Logie Awards for Australia's most popular actor and actresses, and a gold TV Week Logie Award for Australian television's most popular personality are awarded annually. Established in 1958. The TV Week Logie Award is named after Scottish John Logie Baird, the inventor of television.

680
Sport Australia Hall of Fame
PO Box 1613
Broadbeach, QLD 4218, Australia
Phone: 75 701144
Fax: 75 920703

681
Sport Australia Hall of Fame
For recognition of outstanding achievement in Australian sport (Member), and in functions associated with Australian sporting achievement, such as sports administration, coaching, science, or media (Associate Member). Nominations may be submitted by anyone but must be endorsed by the relevant national sporting association or the Hall of Fame Selection Committee. A medal is awarded to Members; a certificate is awarded to Associate Members. Awarded annually. Established in 1985 by Garry Jeffery Daly. To date, 255 Members and 96 Associate Members have been selected.

682
State Library of New South Wales
Macquarie St.
Sydney, NSW 2000, Australia
Phone: 2 230 1414
Fax: 2 233 2003

683
C. H. Currey Memorial Fellowship
To encourage the writing of Australian history from the original sources. Individuals may apply before October 1 each year. A monetary prize of $10,000, which may be divided between two or more applicants, is awarded annually. Established in 1975 in honor of Charles Herbert Currey, an Australian historian.

684
Sydney Film Festival
PO Box 950
Glebe, NSW 2037, Australia
Phone: 2 6603844
Fax: 2 6928793

685
Dendy Awards for Australian Short Films
To recognize the best films made in Australia during the preceding year. Maximum running time is 59 minutes at 24 frames per second. Films produced by television stations, or made for a television series are not eligible. The deadline for 1994 entries was April 3. The following prizes are awarded: Dendy Award for the Best Film in the Documentary Category - $2,500; Dendy Award for the Best Film in the Fiction Category - $2,500; Dendy Award for the Best Film in the General Category - $2,500; Yoram Gross Animation Award - $2,500 (donated by Yoram Gross Filmstudios Limited) for Best Short Animation Film; and STA Travel Award - return airfare for the filmmaker, awarded by an international jury for a film of special merit. Awarded annually. Established in 1974. Sponsored by Dendy Cinema, Sydney. Formerly: (1988) Greater Union Awards; (1974) Benson and Hedges Awards.

686
Ethnic Affairs Commission of New South Wales Award
To recognize the best film produced in Australia during the preceeding year that reflects the cultural diversity of Australia. Maximum running time is 59 minutes. To qualify, the film must meet one of the following criteria: treat issues arising from the Australian immigration and settlement process; address general issues in one or more cross-cultural settings; or contain material or languages that celebrate the cultural and linguistic diversity of Australia. A monetary award of $2,500 is awarded annually in one of the following catagories: documentary, fiction, and general, for films concerned with exploring the formal possibilities of film as an end in itself or made as a personal response to some area of the film-maker's experience where articulating that response is an end in itself. The award is presented during the opening night ceremony of the festival. Established in 1992. Sponsored by Ethnic Affairs Commission of New South Wales.

687
New South Wales Film and Television Office Rouben Mamoulian Award
To recognize the best short film produced in Australia the preceeding year among the Dendy Award finalists for short film. Maximum running time is 59 minutes. A monetary award of $2,500 award is given annually in one of the following categories: documentary, fiction, and general, for films concerned with exploring the formal possibilities of film as an end in itself or made as a personal response to some area of the film-maker's experience where articulating that response is an end in itself. The award is presented by a panel of international judges during the opening night ceremony at the festival. Established in 1974 in honor of Rouben Mamoulian who presented the Inaugural Award. Sponsored by New South Wales Film and Television Office.

688

Technical Association of the Australian and New Zealand Pulp and Paper Industry
191 Royal Parade
Parkville, VIC 3052, Australia
Phone: 3 3472377
Fax: 3 3481206

689

Technical Association of the Australian and New Zealand Pulp and Paper Industry Awards
To recognize individuals who work to expand the industrial application of the pulp and paper industry. The association awards the L. R. Benjamin Medal and Oertel Nadebaum Distinguished Service Award.

690

Television Society of Australia
630 Warrigal Rd.
Chadstone, VIC 3148, Australia
Phone: 3 569 0229

691

Penguin Awards
For recognition of excellence in television. Awards are given in the following categories: (1) Colin Bednall Award - for outstanding contribution to the television industry; (2) Bruce Gyngell Critics Awards: (3) Program Awards (in 20 categories); (4) Individual Achievement Awards (in 53 categories); (5) Commercial Awards (in 10 categories); (6) Regional Station Program Awards (in 4 categories); (7) Corporate Television; (8) Community Television (in 3 categories); and (9) Educational Television (in 4 categories). Residents of Australia who have produced work for Australian television are eligible. A trophy and a certificate are awarded annually. Established in 1959. The Bednall Award was established in 1978 in honor of Colin Bednall, the first managing director of GTV Channel 9.

692

Tweed River Regional Art Gallery
PO Box 816
Murwillumbah, NSW 2484, Australia
Phone: 66 720 409
Fax: 66 720 409

693

Douglas J. Moran Portraiture Prize
For recognition of portraits by and of Australian citizens or permanent residents. Winners receive $100,000 (Australian) and 30 finalists receive $1,000 (Australian). Finalists tour nationally in Australia. Final jugding is conducted by an international judge. The winning painting becomes part of Tweed River Regional Art Gallery's Portrait Collection. Awarded biennially. Established in 1988.

694

University of Melbourne
Faculty of Arts
Asst. Registrar
Grattan St.
Parkville, VIC 3052, Australia
Phone: 3 3445244
Fax: 3 3470424

695

Wesley Michel Wright Prize for Poetry
For recognition of a composition of original English verse or poetry by an Australian citizen. Poems with a minimum of 50 lines must be submitted by July 31. A monetary prize varying between $1,500 and $2,000 Australian is awarded annually. Established in 1982 by Wesley Michel Wright.

696

University of Melbourne
Faculty of Science
Grattan St.
Parkville, VIC 3052, Australia
Phone: 3 3444000
Fax: 3 3445803

697

David Syme Research Prize
For recognition of the most distinguished contribution to biology, chemistry, geology, or physics. Preference is given to work of value to the industrial and commercial interests of Australia. Candidates must have spent five out of the last seven years in Australia. Professors of Australian universities are not eligible. A monetary prize of $2,500 (Australian) and a bronze medallion are awarded annually. Established in 1904 by David Syme.

698

University of New South Wales
PO Box 1
Kensington, NSW 2033, Australia
Phone: 2 697 3086
Fax: 2 313 7895

699

Dirac Medal
For recognition of contributions to the advancement of theoretical physics. The individual selected to deliver the Dirac Lecture receives a silver medal. Awarded at least biennially. Established in 1979 by the University of New South Wales to commemorate the only visit to Australasia of Professor P.A.M. Dirac, 1975, organized by the University. Co-sponsored by the Australian Institute of Physics (NSW Branch).

700

Francis Patrick Dwyer Memorial Medal
For recognition of distinguished achievement in the field of coordination chemistry. Honorary recognition, an invitation to deliver the Dwyer Memorial Lecture at the University of New South Wales, and a medal were awarded annually by the University of New South Wales Chemical Society. Established in 1962 to commemorate the life and work of Francis Patrick Dwyer, a distinguished Australian inorganic chemist. (Discontinued)

701

David Mellor Lecture in Chemical Education
To promote interest in chemical education. An invitation to deliver the David Mellor Lecture in Chemical Education and a medal were awarded biennially. Established in honor of Emeritus Professor D.P. Mellor, who made contributions in the field of chemical education. (Discontinued)

702

Sir Rupert H. Myers Award in Materials Engineering
For recognition of distinguished contributions to the science of materials engineering. A medal and an invitation to deliver the Rupert H. Myers Lecture were awarded. The Lecture was a key feature of an annual symposium conducted by the Department of Civil Engineering Materials. Established in 1975. (Discontinued)

703

University of Newcastle
Newcastle, NSW 2308, Australia
Phone: 49 685219
Fax: 49 601661

704

Mattara Poetry Prize
For recognition of an outstanding poem. A monetary prize of $6,000 Australian was awarded annually. Established in 1981 by Dr. Paul Kavanagh in honor of the Mattara Festival. (Discontinued)

705

Warringah Shire Council
Civic Centre
Pittwater Rd.
Dee Why, NSW 2099, Australia
Phone: 2 9820333

706 Australia

706

Warringah Art Prize
For recognition of art exhibited at the art competition. Awards are given in the following categories: (1) Warringah Shire Award; (2) Manly Daily Award; (3) Print Prize; (4) Watercolor Prize; (5) Local Painting Prize; (6) Ceramic Prize; (7) Textile Prize; and (8) Local Craft Prize. The competition is open to artists from anywhere (only 3 of the lesser awards are restricted to Shire residents.) Monetary awards totaling $7,000 for purchase of art are available annually at the competition held in late September. Established in 1975.

707

Patrick White Literary Award Trust
c/o Perpetual Trustee Company
39 Hunter St.
GPO Box 4172
Sydney, NSW 2001, Australia
Phone: 2 2330777
Fax: 2 2214885

708

Patrick White Literary Award
For recognition of an Australian writer whose work has not received the recognition it deserves. A monetary prize is awarded annually. Established in 1972 by Patrick White, who donated a Nobel Prize for literature to create this annual literary award for Australian writers.

709

Winton Tourist Promotion Association
PO Box 44
Winton, QLD 4735, Australia
Phone: 76 571502
Fax: 76 571738

710

Bronze Swagman Award
For recognition of outstanding Bush verse. Verse in traditional Australian form that has an Australian Bush theme may be entered from any country, but must be written in English and be less than 1,300 words. Entries must be submitted by May 31. A bronze statuette of a Swagman, designed by Daphne Mayo, and a Winton opal are awarded annually. In addition, verses are selected for publication in the *Bronze Swagman Book of Bush Verse* and contributors receive a complimentary copy of the book. Established in 1972.

711

World Federation for Culture Collections
Dept. of Microbiology
Univ. of Queensland
St. Lucia 4067
Brisbane, QLD, Australia
Phone: 7 3652396
Fax: 7 3651566

712

WFCC Skerman Award for Taxonomy
For recognition of a contribution by a young scientist to taxonomy. Individuals under 35 years of age are eligible. A monetary prize and travel expenses are awarded every four years at the Congress of the Federation. Established in 1988 in honor of Prof. V.B.D. Skerman.

713

World Federation of Personnel Management Associations
Capital Financial Group
9 Castlereagh St.
Sydney, NSW 2001, Australia
Phone: 2 2207293
Fax: 2 2216882

714

Awards for Exemplary Contributions to the Human Resource Management Field
To recognize exemplary contributions to the human resource management field. Awarded annually at a the Federation Congress.

715

World's Woman's Christian Temperance Union
(Ligue des Femmes Abstinentes)
Cloverlea
Branxholm, TAS 7261, Australia
Phone: 3 54 6172

716

Mrs. James Nelson Award
To encourage individuals under the age of 30 to learn more about the organization and become actively involved in temperance work. Individuals between the ages of 16 and 30 with more about the organization and become actively involved in temperance work. Individuals between the ages of 16 and 30 with qualities of abstainance and leadership may apply for the award. A travel grant is awarded triennially. Established in 1976 by the late Mrs. James Nelson of Canada.

717

Ulster Award
To encourage women to learn more about the organization and to become involved in leadership in temperance work. Women members under the age of 50 are eligible for the award. A travel grant is awarded triennially. Established in 1971 by the Ulster Union.

718

Young Australians Best Book Award Council
PO Box 238
Kew, VIC 3101, Australia
Phone: 3 4286324
Fax: 3 8537684

719

Young Australians Best Book Award
To encourage Victorian children to read Australian children's fiction and to give them the chance to choose those which they like best. Australian books nominated may be picture story or fiction for older readers or younger readers. Nominations must be submitted by April 15. Young Victorian readers in grades 1 through 9 may vote. A citation, reading "From YABBA Council and the Children of Victoria," is awarded annually. Established in 1985.

Austria

720

Alpine Countries International Filmmaking and Writing Academy
(Internationale Alpenlandische Film- und Autorenakademie)
Rathaus der Stadt Bludenz
Postfach 158
A-6700 Bludenz, Austria
Phone: 5552 62020

721

International Film Festival Bludenz
To recognize the best films of the festival, and to promote independent filmmakers. Independent movies and productions of all categories may be submitted by June 1. The Golden Unicorn, the heraldic figure of the Alpine town, Bludenz, is awarded in the following categories: (1) Best feature film; (2) Best animated cartoon film; (3) Best experimental film; (4) Best documentary film; and (5) Best amateur film. Special prizes are awarded for the best direction, direction of camera, film editing (golden scissors), best film with a critical theme on social policy, for an unusual film theme, for the best sense of humor in a film, and the best performance. Awarded annually on the occasion of the "alpinale," International Film Festival Bludenz. Established in 1982.

722

Amt der Salzburger Landesregierung
Kulturabteilung
Postfach 527
A-5010 Salzburg, Austria
Phone: 662 80422729
Fax: 662 80422160

723

Rauriser Literaturpreis
To recognize a first book of prose by a German-speaking author. A monetary prize and a certificate are presented annually. Established in 1972. Sponsored by the Salzburg region. Additional information is available from Dr. Brita Steinwendtner, Zwieselweg 7, A-5020 Salzburg, Austria.

724

Georg Trakl Prize for Poetry
(Georg Trakl Preis fur Lyrik)
To recognize an outstanding German-speaking poet. A monetary award and a certificate are presented every few years to commemorate Georg Trakl's (1887-1914) date of birth or death. Established in 1952. Sponsored by the Salzburg region. Additional information is available from Bundesministerium fur Unterricht, Kunst, und Sport, Freyung 1, A-1014 Vienna, Austria.

725

Amt der Tiroler Landesregierung, Kulturabteilung
Neues Landhaus Phone: 512 576377102
A-6020 Innsbruck, Austria Fax: 512 576377200

726

Alpenlandischer Volksmusikwettbewerb
To further the development of folk music among young people. Performers who are between 7 and 24 years of age and who are from Austria, Switzerland, South Tyrol, and Bavaria may apply. A plaque and a document are awarded biennially. Established in 1974. Additional information is available from Dr. Josef Sulz, Hochschule "Mozarteum," Abteilung Musikerziehung, Marktgraben 2, A-6020 Innsbruck, 512/588457.

727

Emil Berlanda Preis
For recognition of a contribution to the promotion and interpretation of contemporary music. Selection is by nomination. A monetary prize is awarded biennially. Established in 1982 by Magdalena Berlanda and the Kulturabteilung in memory of Emil Berlanda (1905-1960), one of Tyrol's most important composers in the first half of the twentieth century.

728

Grosse Literaturstipendien des Landes Tirol
For recognition of achievements in contemporary literature. Individuals from the Tyrol are eligible. Selection is by nomination. Two monetary prizes of 100,000 Austrian schillings are awarded. Established in 1991.

729

Osterreichischer Graphikwettbewerb
To encourage professional development in the graphic arts. Austrian citizens may apply. Monetary prizes and other prizes by various institutions, including the Bundesministerium fur Unterricht und Kunst and the Land Tirol, are awarded biennially. Established in 1952. Additional information is available from Dr. Magdalena Hormann, Kulturabteilung im Amt der Tiroler Landesregierung.

730

Jakob Stainer Preis
For recognition of a contribution to the promotion of old music. Individuals who are active in the field of old music may be nominated. A monetary prize is awarded biennially. Established in 1983 in memory of Jakob Stainer (1617-1683), world-famous violin maker, who was born in Absam near Innsbruck.

731

Tiroler Erfinderpreis Josef Madersperger
To encourage development in the field of technology. Candidates from Tyrol and South Tyrol may apply. A monetary prize is awarded irregularly. Established in 1971 in memory of Josef Madersperger (1768-1850), inventor of a first prototype of the sewing machine.

732

Tiroler Landespreis fur Kunst
For recognition of achievement in the arts. Artists from the Tyrol and South Tyrol may be nominated. A monetary prize of 150,000 Austrian schillings is awarded annually. Established in 1984. Formerly: (1983) Wurdigungspreis des Landes Tirol fur Literatur, Musik etc..

733

Tiroler Landespreis fur Wissenschaft
For recognition of achievement in the fields of humanities or science. Candidates from the Tyrol and South Tyrol may be nominated. A monetary prize of 150,000 Austrian schillings is awarded annually. Established in 1984.

734

Wettbewerb "Jugend musiziert"
To encourage and recognize young, talented musicians. Performers (soloists and groups) between 10 and 21 years of age who are from the Tyrol and South Tyrol may apply to participate in the national competition "Jugend musiziert." Awarded biennially. Established in 1973. Additional information is available from Mag. Walter Meixner, Kulturabteilung, Sillgasse 8 Landhaus, A-6020 Innsbruck, telephone: 512 576377105.

735

Association of Austrian Industrialists
(Vereinigung Osterreichischer Industrieller)
Schwarzenbergplatz 4 Phone: 1 71135
A-1031 Vienna, Austria Fax: 1 7136899

736

Anton Wildgans Prize of Austrian Industry
(Wildgans-Preis)
To recognize authors of the younger or middle generation. Austrian novelists, essayists, dramatists, or lyric poets are eligible. A monetary prize of 100,000 Austrian schillings is awarded annually. Established in 1962.

737

Association of Austrian Librarians
(Vereinigung Osterreichischer Bibliothekarinnen Bibiothekare)
Innrain 50 Phone: 512 5072087
A-6010 Innsbruck, Austria Fax: 512 5072307

738

Dr. Josef Bick Ehrenmedaille
For recognition of special service to librarianship in Austria. Members of the Society are eligible. Gold, silver, and bronze medals are awarded biennially. Established in 1966 in honor of Dr. Josef Bick, former director of the Austrian national library.

739

Austria
Ministry of Economic Affairs
(Austria
Bundesministerium fur Wirtschaftliche Angelegenheiten)
Stubenring 1 Phone: 1 711 00
A-1011 Vienna, Austria Fax: 1 713 79 95

740

Medal for Brave Performance in Mining
(Grubenwehrehrenzeichen)
For recognition of a special lifesaving performance in mining. A medal is awarded at the convention. Established in 1954.

741 Austria — Awards, Honors & Prizes, 1995-96

741

Most Beautiful Books of Austria
(Staatspreis fur die Schonsten Bucher Osterreichs)
For recognition of the best designed books. Austrian publishing houses are eligible. Five monetary prizes of 10,000 Austrian schillings, and honorary recognition are awarded annually. Established in 1953.

742

National Prize for Consulting
(Staatspreis fur Consulting)
For recognition of outstanding consulting. Applications are accepted. Trophies and certificates are awarded annually. Established in 1990.

743

National Prize for Industrial and Commercial Building
(Staatspreis fur gewerbliche und industrielle Bauten)
To recognize the best commercial buildings for their architectural form as well as their effect on the surrounding environment. Firms representing industry, trade, commerce, and crafts are eligible. Gold, silver, and bronze plaques and certificates are awarded annually. Established in 1991. Additional information is available from Mag. Pachner, Bundesministerium fur wirtschaftliche Angelegenheiten.

744

National Prize for Jewelry
(Staatspreis fur Schmuck aus Edelmetall)
To recognize a producer of outstanding jewelery. Diplomas and a trophy are awarded triennially. Established in 1990.

745

Osterreichischer Staatspreis fur den Werbefilm
To recognize film producers for outstanding filmed advertisements. Awarded annually. Established in 1980. Additional information is available from Osterreichische Gesellschaft fur Filmwissenschaft, Rauhensteingasse 5, A-1010 Vienna, Austria, phone: 222 512 99.

746

Public Relations State Emblem
(PR-Staatspreis)
For recognition of special services rendered in the field of public relations. A certificate is awarded annually. Established in 1984. Additional information is available from MR Mag. Pein, Presseabteilung, Ministry of Economic Affairs or Public Relations, Verband Austria, Postfach 56, A-1031 Vienna, Austria, phone: 1 42 5339.

747

Staatspreis fur geprufte Qualitat
For recognition of products of approved quality. Application may be made. Three monetary prizes of 50,000 Austrian schillings each and honorary recognition are awarded. Established in 1987. Additional information is available from Arbeitsgemeinschaft fur Osterreichishe Qualitatsarbeit, Bauernmarkt 18/1, A-1010 Vienna, Austria, phone: 222 53 53 748.

748

Staatspreis fur gestaltendes Handwerk
For recognition of originality in the design of craftman's products. Applications may be submitted. Medals and certificates are awarded annually. Established in 1989.

749

Staatspreis fur Radiowerbung
For recognition of outstanding radio advertising. Awarded annually. Established in 1986.

750

State Emblem for Adequate Packaging
(Staatspreis fur Vorbildliche Verpackung)
To promote good packaging. Austrian firms producing packing materials are eligible. Diplomas and honorable mentions are awarded annually. Established in 1957. Additional information is available from Insitut fur Verpackungswesen, Gumpendorferstrasse 6, A-1060 Vienna, Austria, phone: 222 588 86.

751

State Emblem for Furniture
(Staatspreis fur Mobel)
To recognize originality in the design and construction of furniture. Individuals active in the Austrian wood processing industry were eligible. A diploma and honorary recognition were awarded annually. Established in 1972. (Discontinued in 1982)

752

State Emblem for Innovation
(Osterreichischer Staatspreis fur Innovation)
To promote innovations in Austria. A monetary prize of 100,000 schillings and a trophy are awarded annually. Established in 1979 by Minister Dr. Josef Staribacher. Additional information is available from Min. Rat Dipl. Ing. Hanns Fellner.

753

State Emblem for Outstanding Design
(Staatspreis fur Gutes Design)
To recognize companies producing products of outstanding design. Monetary prizes of 15,000 Austrian schillings, distinctions of 5,000 Austrian schillings, and certificates are awarded annually. Established in 1954. Co-sponsored by the Austrian Design Institute. Formerly: (1987) Staatspreis fur Gute Form.

754

State Emblems for Economic Advertising (Domestic/Foreign) and Advertising for Social Matters
(Staatspreise fur Wirtschaftswerbung (Inland/Export) und Werbung fur gesellschaftliche Anliegen)
For recognition of outstanding advertising. Awards are given in foreign and domestic categories. Certificates are awarded. Established in 1972. Additional information is available from Osterreichische Werbewissenschaftliche Gesellschaft, Augasse 2-6, A- 1090 Vienna, Austria, phone: 222 43 05 26.

755

Austria
Ministry of Education and Arts
(Austria
Bundesministerium fur Unterricht und Kunst)
Section IV, Kunst Angelegenheiten
Freyung 1
A-1010 Vienna, Austria   Phone: 1 53120

756

Austrian Medal of Honor in the Arts and Sciences
(Oesterreichisches Ehrenzeichen fur Wissenschaft und Kunst)
To honor persons of any land in the arts and sciences who have distinguished themselves through accomplishments of superlative quality. Thirty-six members of Austrian citizenship and no more than thirty-six foreign members are honored. Established in 1956 by the Austrian Ministry of Education.

757

Austrian National Book Award for Children's Literature
(Oesterreichischer Kinderund Juyendbuchpreis)
For recognition of outstanding books published in Austria for children and teenagers. Awards are given in the following categories: best children's books in different age groups (up to 8 years, 8 to 11, and 11 to 14); best book for young people; best work of nonfiction; best illustration; and best translation. Monetary prizes of 250,000 Austrian schillings and diplomas are awarded annually. Established in 1955.

758

**Austrian State Encouragement Prizes
(Foerderungspreise des Bundesministeriums fur Unterricht und Kunst)**
To encourage and reward creative work in the field of fine arts, literature, music, film, photography and video. Austrian citizens are eligible. Monetary prizes totaling 190,000 Austrian schillings and a certificate are awarded annually. Established in 1955.

759

**Austrian State Grand Prize
(Grosser Oesterreichischer Staatspreis)**
To recognize the entire contribution of an individual in the field of literature, music, fine arts, and film. Monetary prizes of 300,000 Austrian schillings in each discipline were awarded annually until 1972, and are now given irregularly in alternating categories.

760

**Austrian State Prize for Cultural Publications
(Oesterreichischer Staatspreis fur Kulturpublizistik)**
To recognize journalists, critics, and philosophers for outstanding achievements in the field of literary criticism, cultural philosophy, and essay-writing. A monetary prize of 100,000 Austrian schillings is awarded annually. Established in 1979.

761

**Austrian State Prize for European Composers
(Oesterreichischer Staatspreis fur Europaeische Komponisten)**
To recognize a renowned European composer for the sum of his work. A monetary prize of 200,000 Austrian schillings and a certificate are awarded irregularly. Established in 1985.

762

**Austrian State Prize for European Literature
(Oesterreichischer Staatspreis fur Europaeische Literatur)**
To recognize a renowned European author for the sum of his work. A monetary prize of 200,000 Austrian schillings and a certificate are awarded annually. Established in 1965.

763

**Austrian State Prize for Literary Translators
(Oesterreichischer Staatspreis fur literarische Ubersetzer)**
To recognize the work of a literary translator for translations from a foreign language into German by Austrian citizens only, and for translations of contemporary Austrian writers from German into a foreign language. A monetary prize of up to 100,000 Austrian schillings is awarded annually. Established in 1985.

764

**Austrian State Prize for Poetry for Children
(Oesterreichischer Kinderlyrik-Staatspreis)**
To recognize and outstanding work of an author written in the German language. A monetary prize of 50,000 Austrian shillings is awarded biannually. Established in 1993.

765

**Austrian State Recognition Prizes
(Wuerdigungspreise des BMUK)**
For recognition of outstanding works in the field of art, literature, film, and music. Austrian citizens are eligible. Monetary prizes of 100,000 Austrian schillings in each discipline are awarded annually. Established in 1972.

766

Grillparzerringe
For recognition of scientists, actors, and actresses. A ring was awarded annually. Established in 1965. The Raimundring, which was established in 1980, was also awarded. (Discontinued in 1989)

767

Oesterreichischer Auslandskulturpreis
For recognition of an outstanding contribution to the promotion of the Austrian culture on foreign soil. Established in 1986.

768

Osterreichischer Theaterpreis
For recognition of outstanding new theatrical work. A monetary prize of 100,000 Austrian schillings was awarded annually. Established in 1990. (Discontinued).

769

**Recognition Prize for Children's and Youth's Literature
(Oesterreichischer Wuerdigungspreis fur Kinder-und Jugendliteratur)**
To recognize the lifework of a writer. A monetary prize of 70,000 Austrian schillings is awarded triennially. Established in 1980.

770

Albin Skoda Ring
For recognition of achievement in the theatrical arts. A ring, which is passed on to another artist after five years, is awarded. Established in 1971 in memory of the outstanding elocutionist, Albin Skoda.

771

**Austrian Broadcasting Corporation
Upper Austrian Regional Studios
(Osterreichischer Rundfunk
Landesstudio Oberosterreich)**
Franckstrasse 2a   Phone: 732 6900267
A-4010 Linz, Austria   Fax: 732 6900270

772

Prix Ars Electronica
To recognize compositions of computer music, computer produced graphics, and animations. In 1990, the fourth category of Interactive Art was introduced. This new category is open for interactive art in all its forms, provided the application of the special capabilities of the computer in interaction plays a significant part in its realization or production. Awards are given in the following categories: Computer Animation, Computer Graphics, Computer Music, and Interactive Art. For each category there is one Prix Ars Electronica and two Ars Electronica Honorary Mentions. In the categories of Computer Graphics, Computer Music, and Interactive Art, the Prix Ars Electronica amounts to 150,000 Austrian shillings each, and the Honorary Mentions, 50,000 Austrian shillings each. In the category of Computer Animation, the Prix Ars Electronica is allocated 300,000 Austrian shillings with the Golden Nica, and the Honorary Mentions, 100,000 Austrian shillings each. Awarded annually. Established in 1984. The Prix Ars Electronica is funded by Kapsch AG and supported by the State of Upper Austria and the City of Linz.

773

**Austrian Composers Association
(Osterreichischer Komponistenbund)**
Baumannstrasse 8-10
A-1030 Vienna, Austria   Phone: 1 75 72 33

774

**Vienna International Composition Contest
(Concours International de Composition Vienne)**
For recognition of a composition of symphonic music. Previously unperformed, unpublished works for string quartet may be submitted. All composers regardless of age are eligible. The panel of judges consists of leading figures from the international world of music. The following prizes are awarded: (1) a monetary prize of 30,000 Austrian schillings - first prize; (2) 20,000 Austrian schillings - second prize; (3) 10,000 Austrian schillings - third prize; and (4) AKM special prize of 10,000 Austrian schillings is awarded to the best work by an Austrian composer; the

winners of the three standard prizes will not be considered. The Viennese publishers, Verlag Doblinger, will publish the best Austrian work, if the composer agrees. The Austrian Radio, ORF, has agreed to make studio recordings of the winning work and the best Austrian work. Awarded every four years. Established in 1977. Sponsored by the Austrian Composers Association, with the support of the Federal Ministry of Education and Art, the Cultural Office of the Vienna Municipality, the AKM, Austro Mechana, Jeunesses Musicales of Austria, and the Austrian Radio ORF.

775
Austrian Design Institute
(Osterreichisches Institut fur Formgebung)
St. Ulrichsplatz 4 Phone: 1 5238782
A-1070 Vienna, Austria Fax: 1 5238781

776
State Prize for Arts and Crafts
(Staatspreis fur getaltendes Handwerk)
To recognize Austrian craftsmen for products of excellent craftsmanship and high artistic value with a high degree of functionality. A trophy and a certificate are awarded annually. Established in 1989. Sponsored by the Austrian Ministry of Economic Affairs and the Economic Promotion Institute of the Austrian Federal Economic Chamber.

777
State Prize for Design
(Staatspreis fur Design)
To encourage industry to produce products of good design and for recognition of the best of entries in the categories of: Office Furniture and Supplies; Table and Household Devices; Machinery and Tools; Sport and Leisure; Transport; Lighting; Heating and Plumbing; and Medical Equipment. Products produced in Austria may be submitted. A trophy and a certificate are awarded annually. Established in 1962. Sponsored by the Austrian Ministry of Economic Affairs and the Economic Promotion Institute of the Austrian Federal Economic Chamber. Formerly: (1987) Staatspreis fur gute Form.

778
Austrian Geographical Society
(Osterreichische Geographische Gesellschaft)
Karl Schweighofer-Gasse 3
A-1071 Vienna, Austria Phone: 1 5237974

779
Hans Bobek Preis
To recognize outstanding geographic work by Austrians and foreigners under 40 years of age. The works can be in either German or English. A monetary prize of 20,000 Austrian schillings is awarded annually. Established in memory of Hans Bobek, by his widow.

780
Franz von Hauer Medaille
For recognition of outstanding achievements in the field of geography. Individuals are nominated. A medal is awarded when merited. Established in 1893 by K.u.K. Geographische Gesellschaft Wien in honor of Franz Ritter von Hauer. (From 1893 until 1989, there have been 37 winners.)

781
Austrian Pen Centre
Concordia Haus
A-1010 Vienna, Austria Phone: 222 5334459

782
Annual Literary Festival
To recognize individuals for contributions to promoting mutual understanding among countries and providing for freedom of thought and expression within and between nations. The Centre conducts an annual literary festival and bestows awards.

783
Austrian Society of Film Sciences, Communications and Media Research
(Osterreichische Gesellschaft fur Filmwissenschaft Kommunikations-und Medienforschung)
Rauhensteingasse 5/3 Phone: 1 5129936
A-1010 Vienna 1, Austria Fax: 1 5135330

784
Osterreichischer Staatspreis fur den Werbefilm
To promote the quality of advertising film as an audio-visual medium and for recognition of the production technique so that, in addition to fulfilling the commercial goals, the film establishes the reputation of the film producer. Awards are given in the following categories: cinema advertisement, T.V. advertisement, and business film. Films of two minutes or less in length may be submitted by Austrian producers and advertising agencies. A monetary prize of 35,000 Austrian schillings and a diploma are awarded annually. In addition, the Prize of the Verband der Sparkassen is awarded. Established in 1979 by the Ministry of Trade, Commerce and Industry.

785
Preis fur Film und Fernsehforschung
To encourage scientific studies on problems in film, especially in connection with Austrian developments. Austrian citizens or foreigners whose works are connected with Austrian film or television are eligible. The following awards are presented: a monetary award of 35,000 Austrian schillings - first prize; 12,000 Austrian schillings - second prize; and 10,000 Austrian schillings - third prize. Awarded triennially. Established in 1958. Formerly: Osterreichischer Filmhistorikerpreis.

786
Austrian Statistical Society
(Osterreichische Statistische Gesellschaft)
Hintere Zollamtsstrasse 2b
PO Box 90 Phone: 1 711287712
A-1033 Vienna, Austria Fax: 1 7146252

787
Honorary Member
(Ehrenmitgliedschaft)
For recognition of exceptional merits in the field of statistics. Selection is by nomination by the general assembly. A certificate is awarded when merited. Established in 1951.

788
City of Vienna Magistrate
(Magistrat der Stadt Wien)
Magistratsabteilung 7-Kultur
8, Friedrich-Schmidt-Platz 5 Phone: 1 4000 84767
A-1082 Vienna, Austria Fax: 1 4000 7104

789
City of Vienna Prizes for Art, Science, and Humanities
(Preise der Stadt Wien fur Kunst, Wissenschaft und Volksbildung)
For recognition of outstanding achievements in the fields of literature, journalism, music, painting, sculpture, applied arts, architecture, humanities, the natural and medical sciences, popular education, and technology related to the City of Vienna and emphasizing its importance as a cultural center. Individuals rather than organizations are eligible. Foreign citizens are also considered. Monetary prizes of 75,000 Austrian schillings each, up to a total budgeted possibility of 900,000, and certificates are awarded annually. Established in 1947.

790

City of Vienna Prizes for Books for Children and Young People
(Kinder- und Jugendbuchpreis der Stadt Wien)
To recognize living authors and illustrators of children's books. Awards are given in three categories: authors of children's books, authors of juvenile books, and illustrators. Works published in the preceding year that have not won prizes are eligible. Monetary awards of 30,000 Austrian schillings and diplomas are awarded annually to the authors, and a monetary award of 20,000 Austrian schillings is awarded to the illustrator. Established in 1954.

791

City of Vienna Promotional Prizes
(Forderungspreise der Stadt Wien)
For recognition of outstanding achievement in the fields of literature, music, science, art, and folk art. Austrian citizens under 40 years of age who have lived or worked in Vienna for at least three years are eligible. Monetary prizes of 40,000 Austrian schillings are awarded. Established in 1951.

792

Josef Kainz-Medaille der Stadt Wien
For recognition of outstanding performance by an actor, actress, and producer or, in special cases, stage or costume director. Citizens of Austria or other countries are eligible. Promotional prizes of 30,000 Austrian schillings and certificates are given in these categories. Awarded annually. Established in 1958 in memory of Viennese actor Josef Kainz on the one hundredth anniversary of his birth.

793

Ernst Krenek-Preis der Stadt Wien
For recognition of outstanding musical composers or lyricists. Artists closely connected to the City of Vienna are eligible. A monetary prize of 100,000 Austrian schillings is awarded biennially. Established in 1986 in memory of the honored Viennese citizen, Ernst Krenek, on the eighty-fifth anniversary of his birth.

794

Nestroy-Ring der Stadt Wien
For recognition of an outstanding and unusual creative accomplishment promoting the satirical-critical character of the City of Vienna and its people in the spirit of Nestroy. A unique ring and a certificate are awarded annually. Established in 1976 in memory of author Johann Nestroy on the one hundred seventy-fifth anniversary of his birth.

795

Karl Renner Preis
For recognition of contributions to the settling of disputes in public life, the promotion of peace or progress in cultural, social, or economic fields, the enhancement of Austria and the City of Vienna, or to recognize exemplary achievement in the role of the individual in a democratic society. Individuals or organizations connected with the City of Vienna, even though their contributions may be international in scope, are eligible. A monetary prize of 600,000 Austrian schillings (total) may be divided among no more than six recipients. Awarded triennially when merited. Established in 1951 by the City of Vienna to celebrate Dr. Karl Renner's birthday. Co-sponsored by the Dr. Karl Renner Stiftung.

796

Cultural Department of the Municipality of Spittal and the Singkreis Porcia
(Kulturamt Spittal und Singkreis Porcia)
Burgplatz 1
A-9800 Spittal an der Drau, Austria
Phone: 47 623420
Fax: 47 623237

797

International Competition for Choirs
(Internationaler Chorbewerb)
For recognition of outstanding mixed choirs. Awards are given in the categories of choral works (classical and modern) and folksong. The choir should not have more than 50 singers or less than 16, and they must be amateurs. Qualities considered by the jury are: innovation, general choral sound, dynamic flexibility, and rhythm and style. Deadline for entry is January 31. The following monetary prizes are awarded in Category A (Choral works): 1st prize - 20,000 Austrian schillings, 2nd prize - 12,000 Austrian schillings, 3rd prize - 8,000 Austrian Schillings; and in Category B (folksong): 1st prize - 12,000 Austrian schillings, 2nd prize - 9,000 Austrian schillings, 3rd prize - 6,000 Austrian schillings. Presented once a year at the Competition that is held at the Castle of Porcia. Established in 1964. Sponsored by the Federal Ministry of Education and Arts, the Regional Government of Carinthia, Austrian Radion-Studio Carinthia, Singkreis Porcia-Spittal an der Drau and the Cultural Department of the Municipality of Spittal an der Drau.

798

English American Institute
University of Vienna
(Institut fur Anglistik und Amerikanistik der Universitat Wien)
Universitatsstrasse 7
Luegerring
A-1010 Vienna, Austria
Phone: 1 4300

799

Abraham Woursell Prize
To provide financial support for outstanding literary achievements. Individuals between 22 and 35 years of age who are active writers may apply. Members of the Communist party or citizens of Communist auxiliaries are not eligible. Grants of US $25,000 annually for five years are awarded. Established in 1965 by Abraham Woursell. (Inactive)

800

Federal Board of Austrian Pharmacists
(Osterreichische Apothekerkammer)
Spitalgasse 31
A-1091 Vienna, Austria
Phone: 1 404 14
Fax: 1 48 84 40

801

Franz-Dittrich-Ehrenring
For recognition of achievement and merits in the field of pharmacy. Outstanding pharmacists are considered without consideration of age or membership. A ring is awarded when merited. Established in 1967 in memory of Mag. pharmacist Franz Dittrich (1889-1977), president of the Osterreichische Apothekerkammer.

802

Festival of Nations, Ebensee
(Festival der Nationen)
Gaumbergstrasse 82
A-4060 Linz, Austria
Phone: 732 673693
Fax: 732 673693

803

Festival of Nations
(Festival der Nationen)
For recognition of short non-commercial amateur films and videos. The following formats are eligible: Super-8 and 16mm films and video systems VHS, S-VHS, U-matic LB. The deadline for entry is in May every year. The following awards are presented: The Austrian Education and Art Minister's Prize - 10,000 Austrial shillings; the Ebenseer Bear - Gold, Silver, and Bronze medals; Special Awards for Best Experimental Film; Special Award for Best Film of the Competition - an invitation for free participation in the Festival of Nations the next year; and Cups and Certificates. Awarded annually. Established in 1972 by Franz David. Additional information is available from the Organization Committee, Europaeisches Video Archiv, Erich Riess, Gaumbergstrasse 82, A-4060 Linz, Austria.

804
Graz School of Music and Dramatic Art
(Hochschule fur Musik und Darstellende Kunst, Graz)
Leonhardstr. 15
A-8010 Graz, Austria
Phone: 316 3890
Fax: 316 32504

805
International Competition of Franz Schubert and Twentieth Century Music
(Internationaler Wettbewerb Franz Schubert und Musik des 20 Jahrhundes)

For recognition of an outstanding performance in piano duo, piano and voice duo, and trio for piano, violin, and violoncello. This award is currently under revision and is scheduled to resume in 1997. Established in 1989 in memory of Franz Schubert. (Currently inactive)

806
International Association for Cereal Science and Technology
(Internationale Gesellschaft fur Getreidewissenschaft und technologie)
PO Box 77
Wiener Strasse 22A
A-2320 Schwechat, Austria
Phone: 1 707 72 02
Fax: 1 707 72 04

807
Clyde H. Bailey Medal

To honor an outstanding scientist in the field of cereal science. Individuals may be nominated. A medal is awarded when merited, usually at the Cereal and Bread Congresses. Established in 1970 in memory of Dr. Clyde H. Bailey, a past president of the Association and renowned cereal scientist.

808
Harald Perten Award

For recognition of outstanding achievements in the furtherance of cereal science. A monetary prize of $5,000 US is awarded annually at ICC meetings. Established in 1989 by Ing. Harald Perten. Sponsored by the Harald Perten Foundation.

809
Friedrich Schweitzer Medal

To honor distinguished service in furthering the aims and ideals of the ICC. The Medal is normally awarded annually at ICC meetings. Established in 1989 in memory of one of the founders of the Association, Prof. Dr. Friedrich Schweitzer, who served as President and Secretary General, and was renowned as a cereal scientist worldwide.

810
International Association for Suicide Prevention
c/o Institute for Med. Psychology
Central Admin. Office
Severingasse 9
A-1090 Vienna, Austria
Phone: 1 408 35 68
Fax: 1 408 356 812

811
Stengel Research Award

To recognize an outstanding and active researcher with at least 10 years of scientific activity in the field of suicide prevention, as evidenced by a number of publications in internationally acknowledged journals.

812
Stengel Service Award

For recognition of an outstanding contribution to the field of suicide prevention and crisis intervention. Members and nonmembers who are acknowledged as a national initiator or leader in the field are eligible.

813
International Federation of Accordionists
(Confederation Internationale des Accordeonistes)
Dietrichgasse 51/19
Postbox 323
A-1031 Vienna, Austria
Phone: 1 74367111
Fax: 1 74830320

814
CIA Merit Awards

For recognition of outstanding services to the accordion movement. Applications are accepted. A certificate is awarded annually. Established in 1953.

815
International Federation of Automatic Control
IFAC Secretariat
Schlossplatz 12
A-2361 Laxenburg, Austria
Phone: 2236 71447
Fax: 2236 72859

816
Applications Paper Prize

For recognition of outstanding technical contributions in the area of control applications. Candidate papers are selected by the Congress International Program Committee. A monetary prize of 1,500 Swiss francs and a certificate are awarded triennially at the International World Congress. Established in 1987.

817
Automatica Prize Paper Awards

For recognition of outstanding contributions to the theory and practice of control engineering or control science, documented in a paper published in the IFAC journal *Automatica*. Three prizes of 1,000 Swiss francs are awarded triennially at the International World Congress. Established in 1979. Financed by the publisher of *Automatica*, Pergamon Press Ltd.

818
Control Engineering Textbook Prize

For recognition of author(s) of a control engineering textbook or textbooks in one of the official IFAC languages for which the first edition(s) occurred not later than the Congress just prior to the one at which the award is presented. A monetary award of 1,500 Swiss francs and a certificate are awarded at the Triennial Congress. Established in 1987.

819
Giorgio Quazza Medal

This, the highest award of the Society, is given to recognize distinguished control engineers. A monetary prize of 2,000 Swiss francs and a medal are awarded by the IFAC Council on the recommendation of a selection committee. Awarded triennially at the International World Congress. Established in 1981 as a memorial to Giorgio Quazza, a leading Italian electrical and control engineer who served IFAC in many capacities.

820
Young Author Prize

For recognition of outstanding contributions of young authors (35 years or under) at the Triennial IFAC World Congress. Both written paper and presentation of that paper at the Congress are determining factors for selection of the winner. The criterion are high technical quality and good presentation of results. A monetary prize of 1,500 Swiss francs and a certificate are awarded triennially at the IFAC World Congress. Established in 1987.

821
International Federation of Translators
(Federation Internationale des Traducteurs)
c/o Mrs. L. Katschinka
Dr. Heinrich Maierstrasse 9
A-1180 Vienna, Austria
Phone: 1 443607
Fax: 1 443756

822

Pierre Francois Caille Memorial Medal
(Medaille Pierre Francois Caille)
For recognition of outstanding services to the translating profession. Members of the Society may propose a member for consideration three months before the opening of the FIT Conventions. A medal and a diploma are awarded every three or four years at the FIT Congress. Established in 1981 in honor of Pierre Francois Caille, founder of FIT in 1953 in France, and a long time president.

823

FIT Astrid Lindgren Translation Prize
(Prix FIT de la Traduction Astrid Lindgren)
To promote the translation of a work written for children. Members of the Society may propose a member for consideration six months prior to the opening of a FIT Congress. A monetary prize and a diploma are awarded at the FIT Congress every three or four years. Established in 1981 by Zygm. Stoberski of Poland in honor of Astrid Lindgren, an author of children's books. Sponsored by Astrid Lindgren of Stockholm.

824

FIT - UNESCO Translation Prize
(Prix FIT - UNESCO de la Traduction)
For recognition of a literary and a non-literary translation that demonstrates an outstanding contribution to improving the quality of translation. Members of the Society may propose a member for consideration six months prior to the opening of the FIT Congress. A monetary prize and a diploma are awarded every three or four years at the FIT Congress. Established in 1970 by Zlatko Gorjan, FIT president. Previously sponsored by Carl-Bertil Nathhorst-Stiftelser, Stockholm; now by UNESCO, Paris Formerly: FIT C. B. Nathhorst Translation Prize; FIT C. B. Nathhorst Translation Prize.

825

International Foundation Mozarteum
(Internationale Stiftung Mozarteum)
Postfach 34
Schwartztrasse 26
A-5024 Salzburg, Austria
Phone: 662 88940
Fax: 662 882419

826

Goldene Mozart-Medaille
For recognition of outstanding service in the endeavors of the Mozarteum Foundation. Gold, silver, and bronze medals are awarded annually. Established in 1913.

827

Goldene Mozart-Nadel
For recognition of special service to the Mozart Foundation. A golden stickpin is awarded. Established in 1982.

828

Lilli-Lehmann-Medaille
For recognition in the field of music. Established in 1924.

829

Bernhard-Paumgartner-Medaille
For recognition of the most meaningful and outstanding interpretation of Mozart's work. Students of the Mozarteum Music Academy or those associated with a notable Salzburg musician are eligible. A medal is awarded annually. Established in 1968 in honor of the 80th birthday of Dr. Bernhard Paumgartner, president of the Mozarteum Foundation.

830

Zauberfloten-Medaille
For recognition in the field of music. Established in 1928 and resumed in 1950.

831

International Gustav Mahler Society
(Internationale Gustav Mahler Gesellschaft)
Wiedner Guertel 6/2
A-1040 Vienna, Austria
Phone: 1 6508355

832

Gustav Mahler Medal
(Gustav Mahler Medaille)
For recognition of contributions that promote Gustav Mahler's music. A medal was awarded annually when merited. Established in 1958. (Discontinued in 1988)

833

International Hugo Wolf Society
(Internationale Hugo Wolf-Gesellschaft)
Latschkagasse 4/14
A-1090 Vienna, Austria
Phone: 222 3101388

834

Hugo Wolf-Medaille
To recognize individuals for accomplishments in the field of music. A medal is awarded at the convention. Established in 1968 to honor Hugo Wolf, Austrian composer and music critic.

835

International Institute for Applied Systems Analysis
Information Management and Archives
Schlossplatz 1
A-2361 Laxenburg, Austria
Phone: 2236 71521
Fax: 2236 71313

836

Distinguished Principal Founding Member
For recognition of exemplary dedication to the ideals of the charter and support for the objectives of the institute, as well as distinguished accomplishments in promoting the research of the institute. Established in 1987.

837

Honorary Scholar
For recognition of outstanding contributions made to the development of the Institute and to the advancement of its objectives. Honorary recognition is awarded when merited. Established in 1975.

838

Peccei Scholar
To recognize outstanding contributions of young scientists participating in the IIASA Summer Program. A scholarship of 18,000 Austrian shillings per month for three months and travel expenses are awarded annually. Established in 1984 to commemorate Aurelio Peccei's contributions towards understanding global problems and promoting research through multinational collaboration.

839

International Luge Federation
(Federation Internationale de Luge de Course)
Olympiastrasse 168
A-8786 Rottenmann, Austria
Phone: 3614 2266
Fax: 3614 3831

840

Honour Roll
(Ehrentafel)
For recognition of long and meritorious service to the Federation. The following awards are presented: Honorary Golden Award of the FIL with Distinction, Golden Award of the FIL, Silver Honorary Award of the FIL, Bronze Honorary Award of the FIL, and Honorary Member. Awarded annually at the convention. Established in 1957. Additional information is

available from J. Steler, Secretaire General FIL, 56, Chemin du Vallon de Toulouse, F-13009 Marseille, France, telephone: 9174 2150.

841
International Music Center
(Internationales Musikzentrum Wien)
Lothringerstrasse 20
A-1030 Vienna, Austria
Phone: 1 713 0777
Fax: 1 713 077777

842
Dance Screen Award
To stimulate and disseminate the production of audiovisual dance programs. Awards are given in the following categories: Stage Recording/Studio Adaptation, Camera Re-work, Screen Choreography, and Documentary. The competition is open to dance films, dance videos, and television programs on dance and ballet completed during the previous year. The deadline for entry is February 28. A monetary prize of 100,000 French francs is awarded annually. Established in 1990 by the IMZ in cooperation with the Alte Oper Frankfurt. Additional information is available from Pia Kalinka, IMZ.

843
Innsbruck Radio Prize for Early Music
(Innsbrucker Radiopreis fur Alter Musik)
To stimulate general interest in early music created up to the middle of the 18th century and to pay tribute to radio productions of early music and their radio-specific presentation. The contest is open to all radio organizations, each one being entitled to enter one of its own productions. The application deadline is April 30. The following monetary prizes are awarded: first prize - 100,000 Austrian shillings; second prize - 60,000 Austrian shillings; third prize - 40,000 Austrian shillings; and an encouragement prize of 30,000 Austrian shillings. Awarded triennially. Established in 1981 by the City of Innsbruck and the Vienna International Music Centre in cooperation with the Austrian Broadcasting Service (ORF). Sponsored by the City of Innsbruck. Additional information is available from Monika Gelbmann, IMZ.

844
Opera Screen Award
For recognition in the audiovisual competition of stage recordings, adaptations for video, and video creations. Awards are given for professionalism in the best stage recording/transmission of an opera, the most innovation, and creativity in video musical theater. A monetary prize of 100,000 French francs is awarded biennially in August. Formerly: Video Opera Prize.

845
International Organization of Supreme Audit Institutions
Dampfschiffstrasse 2
A-1033 Vienna, Austria
Phone: 1 71171
Fax: 1 7129425

846
Jorg Kandutsch Preis
To recognize important achievements and contributions in the field of auditing by supreme audit institutions. Nominations may be made for achievements or contributions in the three calendar years preceding the year of INTOSAI's triennial Congress. A wall plaque is awarded triennially. Established in memory of Dr. Jorg Kandutsch, former Secretary General of INTOSAI.

847
Elmer B. Staats International Journal Award
To encourage excellence in the writing of articles for the *International Journal of Government Auditing*. Authors of articles published in the journal in the three calendar years preceding the year of the triennial Congress are eligible for nomination. A sterling silver medallion and a scroll suitable for framing are awarded triennially. Established in 1983 in memory of Dr. Elmer B. Staats, former comptroller general of the United States, and former chairman of the Journal's Board of Editors.

848
International Society for Engineering Education
(Internationale Gesellschaft fur Ingenieurpadagogik)
Universitat Klagenfurt
Universitatsstrasse 65-67
A-9020 Klagenfurt, Austria
Phone: 463 2700371
Fax: 463 2700292

849
IGIP Award
(IGIP-Preis)
To honor outstanding scientific or practical works in the field of engineering education. A monetary award is presented biennially. Established in 1986.

850
International Union of Forestry Research Organizations
(Union Internationale des Instituts de Recherches Forestieres)
Schonbrunn
Tirolergarten
A-1131 Vienna, Austria
Phone: 1 8770151
Fax: 1 8779355

851
Scientific Achievement Award
For recognition of distinguished individual scientific achievement within the forestry field. Selection is based on research results published in scientific journals, proceedings of scientific meetings, appropriate patents, or in books, which clearly demonstrate the importance of the advancement of forestry, forestry research, and forest products. Persons under 45 years of age at the time of presentation whose parent organization is a member of IUFRO are eligible. No Divisional, Deputy Divison Coordinator, or member of the IUFRO Executive Board is eligible while holding such office. Nominations of candidates for the award may be made by a responsible official of the parent organization, by a leader of a subject or project group, or by their deputies. Nominations, accompanied by one other independent testimonial, are sent to the President of IUFRO. Deadline for nominations is April 1. Up to nine awards, each consisting of a cash honorarium, a medal, and a scroll are awarded every five years at the Congress. The Next Conference is in August, 1995. Established in 1971.

852
Jugend musiziert
Max Tendler-Strasse 16
Postfach 14
A-8700 Leoben, Austria
Phone: 3842 45 991
Fax: 3842 44 436

853
Jugend musiziert Preis
To challenge young instrumental and vocal musicians and encourage professional development. Citizens of Austria and South Tyrolia between the ages of 10 and 23 for instrumental musicians, and 16 and 28 for singers, are eligible. A monetary prize, invitations to orchestra concerts, and a certificate are presented biennially to first, second, and third place winners. Established in 1969 by Professor Mag. Friedrich H. Knoppek.

854
Fritz Kreisler International Competition
Liebhartstalstr. 8/19
A-1160 Vienna, Austria
Phone: 1 45 61 70

855
Fritz Kreisler International Competition Prizes
To provide recognition for the best violin and viola performance. Monetary prizes of 130,000, 100,000, and 70,000 Austrian schillings and concert appearances are awarded every four years. Established in memory of Fritz Kreisler, the Austrian violinist and composer, who died in 1962.

856

Linzer Veranstaltungsgesellschaft
Brucknerhaus
Untere Donaulande 7
A-4010 Linz, Austria

Phone: 732 7612
Fax: 732 783745

857

Linz International Anton Bruckner Organ Competition
(Internationaler Anton-Bruckner-Orgelwettbewerb Linz)
To recognize outstanding organists of all nationalities under 35 years of age. Plaques, monetary prizes of 50,000 Austrian schillings for first prize, 40,000 Austrian schillings for second prize, and 30,000 Austrian schillings for third prize are awarded every four years. Established in 1974 in honor of Anton Bruckner. The next competition is planned for 1996.

858

Lower Austria Cultural Department
(Amt der Niederosterreichischen Landesregierung, Kulturabteilung)
Herrengasse 9
A-1014 Vienna 1, Austria

Phone: 1 53110
Fax: 1 53110

859

Lower Austria Prize for the Advancement of Fine Arts and Literature
(Forderungspreis des Landes Niederosterreich)
For recognition of outstanding works in the field of literature, music, fine arts, and science. Austrian citizens residing in Lower Austria and individuals whose works promote Lower Austria's nurturing of the arts and sciences are eligible. Monetary prizes of 25,000 Austrian schillings are awarded annually. Established in 1974.

860

Lower Austria Recognition Prize in Arts and Sciences
(Anerkennungspreis des Landes Niederosterreich)
For recognition of outstanding achievements in the field of music, fine arts, literature, scientific research, and scientific publication. Austrian citizens residing in Lower Austria are eligible as well as individuals whose work promotes Lower Austria. A monetary prize of 12,000 Austrian schillings is awarded annually. Established in 1973.

861

Franz Stangler Memorial Prize for Adult Education
(Franz Stangler Gedachtnispreis fur Erwachsenenbildung)
For recognition of outstanding achievement in one of the areas of adult education, public library work, promotion of tradition, folklore authorship, or the collection of materials for folklore museums. A monetary prize of 50,000 Austrian schillings is awarded annually. Established in 1985 in memory of Franz Stangler, 1910-1983.

862

Wurdigungspreis
(Lower Austria Prize of Honor)
This, the highest recognition of lower Austria, is given for achievement in the sciences, literature, fine arts, and music, and yearly changing special awards. A monetary award of 100,000 Austrian schillings is awarded annually. Established in 1973. Formerly: Kulturpreis.

863

Magistrat der Landeshauptstadt Salzburg
Schloss Mirabell
A-5024 Salzburg, Austria

Phone: 662 8072

864

Honorary Citizen of the City of Salzburg
(Ehrenburgerbrief)
This, the highest award of the city of Salzburg, is given to recognize individuals who have made a special contribution to the city. An artistically designed certificate in the form of a triptych is awarded.

865

Honorary Rings of the City of Salzburg
(Ehrenring der Stadt Salzburg)
For recognition of outstanding achievement. The following prizes are given: Paracelsus Ring - a gold ring with a portrait medallion of the physician, scientist, and philosopher, Paracelsus, is awarded for outstanding scientific achievement; and Heraldic Ring (Wappenring) - a gold ring with the coat of arms of the city of Salzburg is awarded for outstanding artistic achievement. Individuals or organizations are eligible. Only ten living persons may be in possession of these two rings at the same time. Awarded irregularly. Established in 1955.

866

Letter of Citizenship of the City of Salzburg
For recognition of outstanding contributions or service to the city of Salzburg. Austrian citizens with residence in Salzburg are eligible. A certificate is usually awarded to more than one person at a time. Awarded when merited.

867

Medal of the Mozart City of Salzburg
(Medaille der Mozartstadt Salzburg)
For recognition of outstanding achievement in music or for the promotion of such achievement. The following prizes are awarded: grand gold medal (no more than five), gold medal (no more than ten), grand silver medal (no more than 15), and silver medal (no more than 20). Awarded irregularly. Established in 1950.

868

Salzburg Heraldic Medal
(Wappenmedaille)
For recognition of special contributions to the city of Salzburg. A gold or silver medal is awarded several times a year. Established in 1964.

869

Salzburg Prize for the Promotion of the Arts, Science and Literature
To support and encourage the work of artists, scientists and writers, as well as to recognize outstanding achievements in the areas of the plastic and performing arts, science, music, literature, and culture with special relevance to the city of Salzburg. A monetary prize of 50,000 Austrian schillings and a certificate are awarded in each discipline when merited. Established in 1966.

870

Televised Opera Prize of the City of Salzburg
(Fernschopernpreis der Stadt Salzburg)
To recognize an opera created especially for television. The producing television company is eligible. A first prize of 125,000 Austrian schillings and a recognition prize of 12,500 Austrian schillings, each accompanied by a certificate, are awarded triennially. Established in 1956. Additional information is available from IMZ, Lothringerstrasse 20, A-1030 Vienna, Austria, telephone: 222 725795.

871

Mozarteum Academy of Music and Performing Arts in Salzburg
(Hochschule fur Musik und darstellende Kunst Mozarteum, Salzburg)
Mirabellplatz 1
A-5020 Salzburg, Austria

Phone: 662 88908200
Fax: 662 8890851

872
International Mozart Competition
(Internationaler Mozart Wettbewerb)
For recognition of outstanding singers, pianists, and string quartets at the competition. Musicians of all nationalities from 15 to 35 years of age are eligible. The following monetary prizes are awarded: Mozart prize - 120,000 Austrian shillings, Second Prize - 60,000 Austrian shillings, and Third Prize - 30,000 Austrian shillings. The prize winners are also offered engagements by the Salzburg Festival, the International Mozarteum Foundation, the Salzburg Cultural Association and other concert organizers in Austria, Germany, and Japan (Tokyo). Awarded every four years. (Next competition is January 1995.) Established in 1975 in memory of Wolfgang Amadeus Mozart. Sponsored by the Austrian Ministry of Science and Research and private sponsors. Additional information is available from the Austrian Press and Information Service, 31 East 69th St., New York, NY 10021.

873
Osterreichische Film Tage
Columbusgasse 2
A 1100 Vienna, Austria
Phone: 1 6040126
Fax: 1 6020795

874
Award of Austrian Film Days
(Preis der Osterreichischen Film Tage)
To honor the best long feature film of the festival. Films must be produced or coproduced with Austria or be productions of Austrian filmmakers abroad. A monetary award of $13,500 is presented annually at the festival. Established in 1990. Sponsored by the Federal County Government of Upper Austria.

875
Osterreichische Gesellschaft fur Klinische Chemie
Wahringerstr. 10
A-1090 Vienna, Austria
Phone: 1 40400 2428
Fax: 1 42 52 26 40

876
Forderungspreis der Osterreichische Gesellschaft fur Klinische Chemie
For recognition in the field of clinical chemistry and clinical biochemistry. Austrian citizens under 40 years of age may apply by March 31. A monetary award and a certificate are awarded biennially. Established in 1978. Sponsored by Austro-Merck Vienna (Austria).

877
Sandoz Research Institute
(Sandoz Forschungsinstitut)
Brunner Strasse 59
Postfach 80
A-1235 Vienna, Austria
Phone: 1 86 75 11
Fax: 1 86 70 18

878
Sandoz Preis
To recognize and encourage young academic scientists in the fields of chemistry, biology (including biochemistry), medicine, and veterinary medicine, liberal arts, literature, music, and the visual arts. Citizens or residents of Austria under 40 years of age who do not hold a professorship are eligible. Monetary prizes of 75,000 Austrian shillings each and a certificate are awarded annually in four of the different disciplines. Established in 1970.

879
Franz Schmidt Society
Musikverein/Archiv der Gesellschaft der
 Musikfreunde
Bosendorferstrasse 12
A-1010 Vienna, Austria
Phone: 1 65 72 71

880
Honorary Member
To honor scientists (musicology), singers, musicians, directors, etc., for books and essays on Franz Schmidt, or for teaching and performing his musical works. A certificate is awarded at the convention. Established in 1955 to honor Franz Schmidt, composer, teacher, musician and rector of the Vienna Music High School.

881
Schubert Gesellshaft Wien-Lichtental
Marktgasse 40
A-1090 Vienna, Austria
Phone: 1 34 73 01

882
International Franz Schubert Male Choir Contest - Vienna
(Internationaler Mannerchor Wettbewerb Franz Schubert - Wien)
For recognition of outstanding male choirs. Male choirs, with a minimum of 16 singers, compete in a compulsory program and a choice program. The deadline for entry is June 30. The following prizes are awarded: First Prize, 30,000 Austrian schillings; Second Prize, 15,000 Austrian schillings; and Third Prize, 8,000 Austrian schillings. A special prize of 10,000 Austrian schillings for the best interpretation of Schubert is also awarded. Established in 1984.

883
Society of Friends of Music - Vienna
(Gesellschaft der Musikfreunde in Wien)
Boesendorferstrasse 12
A-1010 Vienna, Austria
Phone: 1 505 86 81
Fax: 1 505 94 09

884
International Competition for Composers Mozart
(Internationaler Kompositionswettbewerb Mozart)
To encourage young composers to write orchestra music and/or chamber music for wind instruments. Individuals under 36 years of age may submit compositions by December 5. Compositions must be no more than 20 minutes in duration, unpublished, not yet performed in public, and must not have received a prize in any other competition. Awards are presented in two categories: (1) a work for orchestra with the instrumentation of the usual Mozart orchestra: First prize - 120,000 Austrian schillings; Second prize - 80,000 Austrian schillings; and Third prize - 50,000 Austrian schillings; and (2) a work for wind music instrumentation: First prize - 80,000 Austrian schillings; Second prize - 50,000 Austrian schillings; and Third prize - 30,000 Austrian schillings. Prize winning works receive public performances. Established in 1990. Co-sponsored by Austria - Ministry of Education, Arts and Sports. (Inactive since 1990)

885
International Lieder Competition
(Internationaler Wettbewerb fur Liedgesang)
To encourage young singers to engage themselves in singing German lieder, and for recognition of their achievements and abilities in the field of singing lieder. Singers of all nationalities who are between 21 and 35 years of age are eligible. The following prizes are awarded for men and for women: (1) First prize - 50,000 Austrian schillings; (2) Second prize - 35,000 Austrian schillings; and (3) Third prize - 20,000 Austrian schillings. Further special prizes may be awarded. Established in 1978 in collaboration with the Vienna Festival. (Inactive since 1990)

886
Stadt Villach
Magistrat
Europaplatz
A-9500 Villach, Austria
Phone: 4242 205249
Fax: 4242 2444417

887
Kulturpreis der Stadt Villach
For recognition of cultural and scientific achievements reflecting the cultural life of the city of Villach. A monetary prize of 50,000 Austrian schillings is awarded annually. Established in 1986 by the Magistrat Villach.

888
Paracelsusring der Stadt Villach
For recognition of scientific or artistic achievements in the spirit of Paracelsus, a Swiss-born alchemist and physician of the 16th century. Austrian and foreign scholars are eligible. A golden ring is awarded triennially. Established in 1953 by Stadt Villach in honor of Theophrastus Bombastus von Hohenheim, called Paracelsus; and of his father, Wilhelm Bombast von Hohenheim, who lived and worked in Villach for 32 years. Sponsored by Stadt Villach.

889
Stadtmagistrat Innsbruck
Abteilung II, Kulturamt
Herzog - Friedrichstrasse 21
A-6020 Innsbruck, Austria   Phone: 5222 20 0 23

890
Paul Hofhaimer Prize of the Tyrolian Capital City Innsbruck
(Paul Hofhaimer - Wettbewerb der Landeshauptstadt Innsbruck)
For recognition of an outstanding interpretation of classic organ masterpieces. Participation in the contest is not bound by age, training or nationality. The following prizes are awarded: (1) a monetary prize of 30,000 Austrian schillings and the Paul Hofhaimer medal - first prize; (2) 20,000 Austrian schillings - second prize; and (3) 10,000 Austrian schillings - third prize. Awarded triennially. Established in 1969 in memory of Paul Hofhaimer, organist at the court of Emperor Maximilian I.

891
Preis der Landeshauptstadt Innsbruck fur Kunstlerisches Schaffen
For recognition of outstanding achievement in art, poetry and music. Awards are given in alternate years for: (1) art; (2) poetry; and (3) music. Artists who were born in Innsbruck or who have resided in Tyrol for at least six years are eligible. The following prizes are awarded: (1) a monetary prize of 20,000 Austrian schillings - first place; (2) 15,000 Austrian schillings - second place; and (3) 10,000 Austrian schillings - third place. Awarded biennially. Established in 1974.

892
Otto Stoessl-Stiftung
Semmelweisgasse 9   Phone: 1 438905
A-8010 Graz, Austria   Fax: 1 4085342

893
Otto Stoessl-Preis
For recognition of the best narrative prose. Authors who write in the German language and are unpublished are eligible. A monetary prize of 50,000 Austrian schillings and a certificate are awarded biennially. The prize cannot be divided. Established in 1981 by Professor Dr. Franz Stoessl in memory of his father, Otto Stoessl, an Austrian poet (1875-1936).

894
Hans Swarowsky International Conducting Competition
(Hans Swarowsky Internationale Dirigenten Wettbewerb)
Vienna Master Courses
Goethegasse 1
A-1010 Vienna, Austria   Phone: 1 52 28 85

895
Hans Swarowsky International Conducting Competition
For recognition of an outstanding performance by student or professional conductors not older than 33 years. Monetary prizes of 75,000, 50,000 and 25,000 Austrian schillings are awarded, and the first prize winner has the honor of conducting the Vienna State Opera Orchestra. Awarded every four years. The next competition will be held in 1992. Established in 1977 in honor of Hans Swarowsky.

896
Touristik-Verband Klopeiner See/Turnersee
c/o Gemeinde St. Kanzian
A-9122 St. Kanzian, Austria   Phone: 4239 2222

897
International Amateur Film Festival, Golden Diana
(International Filmfestival des nichtprofessionell en Films, Goldene Diana)
For recognition of outstanding amateur filmmakers. Only films by amateurs (format Super 8 and 16mm and Video VHS and Super VHS with or without sound, black and white or color) are accepted. Producers are permitted to submit several films. A Golden Diana is awarded in the following categories: (1) Best Direction; (2) Best Camera Work; (3) Best Script; (4) Best Cutting and Editing; (5) Best Acoustic Arrangement; (6) Humor; (7) Sport; and (8) Documentation. Sponsored by Filmclub Volkermarkt. Established in 1987.

898
UNESCO
International Book Committee
c/o Dr. Lucia Binder, Gen.Sec.
A-1041 Vienna   Phone: 1 5050359
A-3000 Mayerhofgasse 6, Austria   Fax: 2622 21153

899
International Book Award
For recognition of outstanding services to the cause of books and literacy, including library services, encouragement of reading habits, imaginative bookselling, and promotion of international cooperation. Authors, publishers, translators, book designers, and printers are eligible. Honorary recognition is awarded annually. The selection of the winner is made by the International Book Committee, an interprofessional body representing publishers, authors, librarians, booksellers, and other members of the international book community.

900
Upper Austria State Government
(Amt der o.o. Landesregierung)
Kulturabteilung
Spittelwiese 4   Phone: 732 27205486
A-4010 Linz, Austria   Fax: 732 27207786

901
Upper Austria Culture Prize for Film
(Landeskulturpreis fur Film und Video)
For recognition of achievement in film. Individuals over the age of 35 may apply or be nominated. A monetary award of 100,000 Austrian schillings is presented annually. Established in 1990.

902
Upper Austria Culture Prize for Fine Arts
(Landeskulturpreis fur Bildende Kunst)
For recognition of achievement in the fine arts. Individuals over the age of 35 may apply or be nominated for the award. A monetary award of 100,000 Austrian schillings is presented annually. Established in 1975.

903
**Upper Austria Culture Prize for Literature
(Landeskulturpreis fur Literatur)**
For recognition of achievement in literature. Individuals over the age of 35 may apply or be nominated for the award. A monetary award of 100,000 Austrian schillings is presented annually. Established in 1975.

904
**Upper Austria Culture Prize for Music
(Landeskulturpreis fur Musik)**
For recognition of achievement in music. Individuals over the age of 35 may apply or be nominated for the award. A monetary award of 100,000 Austrian schillings is presented annually. Established in 1975.

905
**Upper Austria Culture Prize for Science
(Landeskulturpreis fur Wissenschaft)**
For recognition of achievement in science. Individuals over the age of 35 may apply or be nominated for the award. A monetary award of 100,000 Austrian schillings is presented annually. Established in 1975. Since 1986, two prizes have been awarded for science, one for natural science and one for the arts.

906
**Upper Austria Prize for Architecture
(Landeskulturpreis fur Architektur)**
For recognition of achievement in architecture. Individuals over the age of 35 may apply or be nominated for the award. A monetary award of 100,000 Austrian schillings is presented annually. Established in 1978.

907
Verein fur Volkskunde
Laudongasse 19　　　　　　　　　　　　　　Phone: 1 438905
A-1080 Vienna, Austria　　　　　　　　　　　Fax: 1 4085342

908
Ehrennadel fur Verdienste um die Osterreichische Volkskunde Huterstern
For recognition of service in the field of folklore, especially in the areas of collection and documentation. A lapel pin of honor is awarded annually when merited. Established in 1982.

909
Michael Haberlandt Medal
For recognition of special contributions to the Society and to studies of Austrian folklore. A silver medal with a portrait of Michael Haberlandt is awarded when merited. Established in 1974 in memory of M. Haberlandt, founder of the Society and the Ethnological Museum of Vienna.

910
**Vienna Chamber Opera
(Wiener Kammeroper)**
Fleischmarkt 24　　　　　　　　　　　　　Phone: 1 5120100
A-1010 Vienna, Austria　　　　　　　　　　Fax: 1 5124448

911
**International Belvedere Competition for Opera Singers
(Internationaler Belvedere Wettbewerb fur Opernsanger Wien)**
To encourage the professional development of opera singers. Women under 33 and men under 35 of any nationality may apply to the Competition office in Vienna by June 20. The following monetary prizes are awarded: first prize - 50,000 Austrian schillings; second prize - 30,000 Austrian schillings; and third prize - 15,000 Austrian schillings. All participants receive certificates, and diplomas are awarded to the finalists. The following special prizes are awarded: Mozart Opera Prize - 25,000 Austrian schillings for the best Mozart interpreter, donated by the Austrian Ministry for Science and Research. This prize-winner is selected by a Jury of professors from the Austrian Music Schools of Vienna, Salzburg, and Graz; *Opernwelt* Prize - consists of an article on one of the participants in the Competition to be published in this opera magazine. The choice of the singer is the decision of the chief editor of *Opernwelt*; *Kurier* Prize - 10,000 Austrian schillings for the winner chosen by the audience after the Opera House Concert. Donated by the Austrian newspaper, *Kurier*; Japan Prize - donated by Mr. Shimkichi Nakajima, Chairman of the "Worldwide Madame Butterfly Competition," Tokyo. A winner of his choice will be invited to several recitals in Japan; Prague Opera Prize - National Opera House Prague offers a guest appearance to one or two finalists. The choice of the singers is the decision of Mr. Tomas Karlicek from PRAGOKONCERT; and Newport Festival Prize - donated by General Manager Mark Malkovich III, Newport Festival, Rhode Island. The winner of the first prize is invited to an appearance at the Festival. Awarded annually. Established in 1982 by Profess or Hans Gabor, General Manager of the Vienna Chamber Opera. Sponsored by OMV.

912
**Vienna Mozart Society
(Mozart Gemeinde Wien)**
Mollardgasse 8
A-1060 Vienna, Austria　　　　　　　　　　Fax: 1 8767201

913
Mozart Medal
For recognition of achievement related to Mozart. Musicians, journalists and organizers of events connected with Mozart are considered. Up to four medals are awarded annually. Established in 1950.

914
**Prize for Mozart Interpretation
(Mozart Interpretation-Preis)**
To recognize an outstanding interpretation of the music of Mozart. Austrian artists up to 35 years of age are eligible. A monetary award and a certificate are presented annually at a concert. Established in 1963.

915
**Prize for Musicology
(Musikwissenschaftspreis)**
To recognize an outstanding work in musicology. Austrian and foreign musicologists of any age are eligible. A monetary award and a certificate are presented annually at a concert.

916
Wiener Flotenuhr
To recognize an outstanding recording of the music of Mozart. Austrian and foreign artists of any age are eligible. A monetary award and a certificate are presented annually at a concert. Established in 1969.

917
**Vienna University of Music and Dramatic Arts
(Hochschule fur Musik und Darstellende Kunst, Wien)**
Lothringertstrasse 18　　　　　　　　　　　Phone: 1 58806
A-1030 Vienna, Austria　　　　　　　　　　Fax: 1 5872897

918
**International Beethoven Piano Competition
(Internationaler Beethoven Klavierwettbewerb)**
To encourage the professional development of young pianists. Musicians between 17 and 32 years of age are eligible. The Competition is exclusively dedicated to the work of Ludwig van Beethoven. The following monetary prizes are awarded: first prize - 80,000 Austrian schillings, a Boesendorfer piano model 200, and concert appearances; second prize - 60,000 schillings; third prize - 50,000 schillings; and three other prizes of 20,000 schillings. Awarded quadrennially. Established in 1961. Sponsored by Fa. Boesendorfer and Austrian Airlines. (The next competition will take place in June 1997.)

[919]

World Academy of Art and Science
Address unknown.

[920]

Clarence James Gamble Award
For recognition of contributions to population problems and their social and international implications. An international jury panel composed of WAAS Fellows and other scholars allocates the award. A monetary prize of $1,000 and a certificate are presented as merited. Established in 1979.

[921]

Rufus Jones Award
For furtherance of knowledge and recognition of contributions to peace and international understanding. An international jury panel, composed of WAAS Fellows and other scholars, allocates the award. A monetary award of $1,000 and a certificate are presented as merited. Established in 1979.

[922]

Harold Dwight Lasswell Award
For recognition of communication in a divided world. An international jury panel, composed of WAAS Fellows and other scholars, allocates the prize. A monetary award of $1,000 and a certificate are presented as merited. Established in 1981.

[923]

Premio Nacional de Educaccion
To recognize a Chilean educator for his or her accomplishments, both morally and intelectually, in support of national education. A monetary prize is awarded biennially in odd-numbered years.

Bahamas

[924]

Bahamas Chamber of Commerce
Shirley St. & Collins Ave.
PO Box N-665
Nassau, Bahamas
Phone: 809322-2145
Fax: 809322-4649

[925]

Businessperson of the Year
For recognition of outstanding and sustained contribution and dedicated service in business to the Commonwealth of the Bahamas and its people. Selection is by nomination, which are invited from the general public. Candidates must have been in business for at least 10 years, participate in community activities, and have a record of exemplary success in the community. A plaque is awarded annually. Established in 1991 for the annual Chamber promotional week. Sponsored by the Chamber Week Coordinating Committee. Formerly: Distinguished Citizens Awards.

[926]

Rookie Businessperson of the Year
For recognition of outstanding and sustained contribution and dedicated service in business to the Commonwealth of the Bahamas and its people. Selection is by nomination. Candidates must have been in business for at least 5 years, participate in community activities, have a record of exemplary success in the community, and have started a business and successfully competed in the market place. A plaque is awarded annually. Established in 1991 for the annual Chamber promotional week. Sponsored by the Chamber Week Co-ordinating Committee.

[927]

Templeton Foundation
PO Box N7776
Nassau, Bahamas
Phone: 809362-4904
Fax: 809362-4914

[928]

Templeton Prize for Progress in Religion
To recognize a living person of any religious tradition or movement. The judges consider a nominee's contribution to progress in religion made either during the year prior to selection or during his or her entire career. The qualities sought in awarding the prize are: freshness, creativity, innovation, and effectiveness. Such contributions may involve new concepts of the spirit, new organizations, new methods of evangelism, new and effective ways of communicating God's wisdom and infinite love, creation of new schools of thought, creation of new structures of understanding the relationship of the Creator to His ongoing creation of the universe, to the physical sciences, the life sciences, and the human sciences, the releasing of new and vital impulses into old religious structures and forms, etc. A monetary prize of £650,000 sterling or its equivalent, is awarded each year at a ceremony in honor of the recipient, where the recipient delivers a lecture. Established in 1972 by Sir John Templeton, the donor of the Templeton Foundation, a U.S. foundation. The award is administered from a Bahamian office.

Bahrain

[929]

Bahrain Contemporary Art Association
PO Box 26232
Manama, Bahrain
Phone: 728046
Fax: 723341

[930]

Gold Medal
To recognize individuals for service to the plastic art in Bahrain, and to acknowledge the artists' efforts in laying down the foundations for the plastic art movements. Plastic artists who have been practicing for a period of at least twenty years are eligible. A gold medal is awarded biennially. Established in 1981.

Bangladesh

[931]

Antarjatik Beshamarik Sheba Sangstha
Zohura Mansion, 1st Fl., Rm. 18
27/1 Mymensingh Rd.
Dacca 1000, Bangladesh
Phone: 2 502071
Fax: 2 863060

[932]

Antarjatik Beshamarik Sheba Sangstha Competitions
To recognize local civic groups, philanthropists, and international organizations that provide disaster relief including food, primary health care, and volunteers. Competitions are held.

[933]

Bangla Academy
Language and Literary Section
Burdwan House
Dhaka 1000, Bangladesh
Phone: 500131 4

[934]

Bangla Academy Literary Award
To encourage and recognize individuals for contributions to the field of literature. Recognized Bangladeshi writers who have published works to their credit are eligible. Two monetary prizes of 25,000 taka each are awarded annually. Established in 1960 to commemorate the Language Movement of 1952.

935
Institution of Engineers, Bangladesh
Headquarters, Ramna　　　　　　　　　　　　Phone: 2 239485
Dhaka, Bangladesh　　　　　　　　　　　　　　Fax: 2 862556

936
Convention Medal and Convention Certificate
To recognize individuals for contributions to engineering science, and to encourage professional development. Individuals are nominated by the Council. A medal and a certificate are awarded at the convention. Established in 1948.

937
Man For Mankind
PO Box 2786　　　　　　　　　　　　　　　　　Phone: 2 415764
Dacca 1000, Bangladesh　　　　　　　　　　　　Fax: 2 411312

938
Man for Mankind Awards
To recognize individuals for contributions to child welfare and the prevention of substance abuse. The Association sponsors competitions. Awards are given annually.

Barbados

939
Caribbean Conference of Churches
PO Box 616　　　　　　　　　　　　　　　　Phone: 809427-2681
Bridgetown, Barbados　　　　　　　　　　　　Fax: 809429-2075

940
Caribbean Prize for Peace Through the Pursuit of Justice
To recognize persons with distinguished records of service in the promotion of peace at the regional level, and/or persons dedicated to the fullness of life. Citizens of a Caribbean country may be nominated. A plaque is awarded every five years at the General Assembly of the Conference. Established in 1986.

941
Regional Ecumenism Award
To recognize persons who have made outstanding contributions to the fostering of ecumenism regionally. Citizens of a Caribbean country may be nominated. A plaque is awarded every five years at the General Assembly of the Conference. Established in 1986.

Belgium

942
Academie Internationale d'Heraldique
57, rue Martin Lindekens
B-1150 Brussels, Belgium

943
Prix Paul Adam-Even
To recognize an individual for a contribution of international worth about medieval rolls of arms. A silver plaque is awarded biennially. Established in 1970 by Mr. & Mrs. Paul Toinet Adam-Even, Paris, France, to honor Paul Adam-Even, French heraldist and past president of the Academie internationale d'heraldique, 1902-1964.

944
Prix Amerlinck
To recognize an individual for a scientific contribution to heraldic bibliography. A silver plaque is awarded biennially. Established in 1975 by Mr. Teodoro Amerlinck y Zirion, Mexico City, Mexico.

945
Prix Arvid Berghman
To recognize an individual for a scientific contribution about commoners' and municipal heraldry. A silver plaque is awarded biennially. Established in 1971 to honor Arvid Berghman, Swedish heraldist, 1897-1961. Sponsored by Arvid Berghman heraldiska Stiftelse, Stockholm, Sweden.

946
Prix Riquer
To recognize an individual for a scientific contribution about general or particular aspects of European medieval heraldry before 1500. A silver plaque is awarded biennially. Established in 1984 by Don Martin de Riquer, Conde de Casa Davalos, Barcelona, Spain.

947
Prix Sao Payo
To recognize an individual for a contribution of international worth about heraldic subjects. A silver plaque is awarded biennially. Established in 1969 by Dom Antonio P. de Sao Payo and Castro Moniz Torres de Lusignan, Marques de Sao Payo, Lisboa, Portugal. (Inactive since 1973)

948
Academie Royale d'Archeologie de Belgique
Musee de Bellevue
7, Place des Palais
B-1000 Brussels, Belgium

949
Prix Simone Bergmans
(Prijs Simone Bergmans)
For recognition of an unpublished study on the art of Belgium and the area around Liege (painting and sculpture). A monetary prize of 40,000 Belgian francs is awarded triennially.

950
Academie Royale de Belgique
Classe des Beaux-Arts
Palais des Academies　　　　　　　　　　　Phone: 2 514 40 64
Rue Ducale 1　　　　　　　　　　　　　　Phone: 2 514 42 56
B-1000 Brussels, Belgium　　　　　　　　　　Fax: 2 502 04 24

951
Prix Arthur De Greef
For recognition of the best musical composition for piano solo conceived in the true tradition of the instrument and not aiming at virtuosity. Belgian composers are eligible. A monetary prize of 50,000 Belgian francs is awarded biennially. Established in 1989.

952
Prix Baron Horta
To recognize the designer of an architectural work that has already been built or studied as a project. The finished work must have been constructed in one of the Common Market countries, or the project must have been planned for construction in Common Market countries. Architects of any nationality are eligible. A monetary prize of 400,000 Belgian francs is awarded every five years. Established in 1966.

953
Prix Charles Caty
To recognize a painter who has studied regularly and successfully at the Academy of Fine Arts at Mons. A monetary prize of 65,000 Belgian francs is awarded triennially. Established in 1956.

954

Prix Constant Montald
For recognition of a large fresco or a mural in oils, leaded glass, or tapestry, portraying human figures. The work must be at least one meter high. A monetary prize of 60,000 Belgian francs is awarded triennially. Established in 1946.

955

Prix E. du Cayla-Martin
To recognize the work of a painter not yet awarded by the Academy. A monetary prize of 100,000 Belgian francs is awarded biennially. Established in 1991.

956

Prix Egide Rombaux
To recognize a sculptor for a work on a subject chosen by the Academy in decorative or monumental art. Belgian sculptors between 30 and 40 years of age are eligible. A monetary prize of 300,000 Belgian francs is awarded triennially. Established in 1952.

957

Prix Emile Sacre
To recognize the painter of the most noteworthy work that was executed and publicly displayed during the preceding six year period. A monetary prize of 60,000 Belgian francs is awarded every six years. Established in 1914.

958

Prix Ernest Acker
For recognition of an architectural project presented to the Academy on a subject chosen by the Classe des Beaux-Arts. Young Belgian architects are eligible. A monetary prize of 180,000 Belgian francs is awarded triennially. Established in 1922.

959

Prix Gustave Camus
To recognize a Belgian painter who has already accomplished a notable work. A monetary prize of 150,000 francs is awarded biennially.

960

Prix Irene Fuerison
For recognition of the best unpublished musical composition in the following categories: chamber music, orchestral music, vocal music, and electronic music. Young Belgian musicians or foreign musicians less than 50 years of age who have been residents of Belgium for three years are eligible. Awards are given in alternate years for chamber music, orchestral music, vocal music, and electronic music. A monetary prize of 140,000 Belgian francs is awarded biennially. Established in 1932.

961

Prix Jos Albert
To encourage the work of a Belgian painter of the representational trend. A monetary prize of 50,000 Belgian francs is awarded annually. Established in 1982.

962

Prix Joseph-Edmond Marchal
To recognize the author of the best work, published or manuscript, on national antiquities or archaeology. A monetary prize of 60,000 Belgian francs is awarded every five years. Established in 1918.

963

Prix Jules Raeymaekers
To encourage an artistic activity that uses color as its form of expression. A monetary prize of 500,000 Belgian francs is awarded triennially. Established in 1981.

964

Prix Lavalleye-Coppens
For recognition of achievements in the fields of archaeology, art history, or restoration of monuments. Awards are given in alternate years to the Belgian author or authors or the foreign author for the best published or unpublished work on archaeology or art history of ancient Southern Netherlands and the ancient ecclesiastic principalities of Liege and Stavelot; and the author of the best work on restoration of monuments or works of art erected or preserved in Belgium. A monetary prize of 120,000 Belgian francs is awarded biennially. Established in 1972.

965

Prix Louise Dehem
To recognize a painter who has been out of a fine arts school or an academy less than ten years and whose works, preferably human figures or still lifes, have been shown publicly and have revealed a truly artistic temperament. A monetary prize of 60,000 Belgian francs is awarded biennially. Established in 1928.

966

Prix Paul Artot
To recognize the painter of a fresco or oil painting. The theme of the painting must be expressed by human figures. Belgian artists under the age of 40 are eligible. A monetary prize of 160,000 Belgian francs is awarded biennially. Established in 1959.

967

Prix Paul Bonduelle
To recognize the originator(s) of a great architectural project. The subject is decided by the Classe des Beaux-Arts. Belgian architects who are not members of the Academy are eligible. A monetary prize of 750,000 Belgian francs is awarded triennially. Established in 1962.

968

Prix Pierre Carsoel
For recognition of the most technically and artistically successful work conceived and executed by an architect during the preceding five year period. Belgian architects are eligible. A monetary prize of 180,000 Belgian francs is awarded every five years. Established in 1928.

969

Prix Rene Janssens
To recognize outstanding Belgian painters. Awards are given in alternate years to a painter who has excelled at portraits and a painter who has excelled at paintings of interiors. An indivudal's entire work is considered. A monetary prize of 60,000 Belgian francs is awarded triennially. Established in 1934.

970

Prix Victor Tourneur
For recognition in the studies of numismatics and sigillography and to encourage the art of the medal. A monetary prize of 60,000 Belgian francs is awarded every ten years. Established in 1948. Awarded in alternate years by the Classe des Lettres.

971

Academie Royale de Belgique
Classe des Lettres et des Sciences Morales et Politiques
Palais des Academies Phone: 2 514 40 64
rue Ducale 1 Phone: 2 514 42 56
B-1000 Brussels, Belgium Fax: 2 502 04 24

972

Fondation Camille Liegeois
To assist scientific research of travel by Belgian researchers under 35 years of age. A monetary prize of 55,000 Belgian francs is awarded triennially. Awarded alternately with the Classe des Sciences. Established in 1936.

973
Fondation Edmond Fagnan
To encourage travel for Muslim and Semitic studies and to facilitate the publication of original work. Belgian and French researchers are eligible to apply by February 1. A monetary prize of 50,000 Belgian francs is awarded annually. Established in 1926.

974
Fondation Emile Waxweiler
For recognition in the field of social science, particularly on the subject of social organization. Travel for study or research requests must be submitted by October 1. Monetary prizes totaling 50,000 Belgian francs are awarded.

975
Fondation Ernest Mahaim
To encourage studies on political economics and international law. Applications may be submitted by October 1. A monetary prize of 60,000 Belgian francs is awarded every five years. Established in 1946.

976
Fondation Henri Pirenne
To assist travel for study or research in Belgium or another country, particularly studies concerning the history of Belgium. A monetary prize of 50,000 Belgian francs is awarded triennially. Established in 1923.

977
Prix Adelson Castiau
For recognition of the best work which has as its object or its effect the promotion of social progress. Belgian authors are eligible. A monetary prize of 55,000 Belgian francs is awarded triennially. Established in 1883.

978
Prix Anton Bergmann
For recognition of a historical work or monograph on a Flemish town or community of any size in Belgium. Authors of any nationality may submit works written in Dutch and edited in Belgium or the Low Countries. A monetary prize of 50,000 Belgian francs is awarded every five years. Established in 1895.

979
Prix Auguste Teirlinck
For recognition of a contribution to Dutch literature. A monetary prize of 55,000 Belgian francs is awarded every five years. Established in 1895.

980
Prix Charles Duvivier
For recognition of the best work on the history of Belgian or foreign law, or on the history of Belgian political, judicial, or administrative institutions. Belgian authors are eligible. A monetary prize of 50,000 Belgian francs is awarded triennially. Established in 1907.

981
Prix de Psychologie
For recognition of the best doctoral thesis on scientific psychology, earned in a Belgian university by a Belgian citizen during the three preceding years. A monetary prize of 35,000 Belgian francs is awarded triennially. Established in 1961.

982
Prix de Saint-Genois
To recognize the author of the best historical or literary work written in Dutch. A monetary prize of 50,000 Belgian francs is awarded every five years. Established in 1890.

983
Prix de Stassart
To recognize a noted Belgian. The award is given in alternate years to: (1) historians; (2) writers; and (3) scientists and artists. A monetary prize of 60,000 Belgian francs is awarded every six years. Established in 1853.

984
Prix de Stassart pour Histoire Nationale
For recognition of an outstanding contribution to national history. A monetary prize of 60,000 Belgian francs is awarded every six years. Established in 1871.

985
Prix Emile de Laveleye
To recognize a scholar whose total work has brought about important progress in political economy and social science, including finance, international and public law, and general or national politics. Living Belgian or foreign scholars are eligible. A monetary prize of 70,000 Belgian francs is awarded every six years. Established in 1895.

986
Prix Ernest Discailles
For recognition of the best work on the history of French literature or on contemporary history. Awards are given in alternate years in the following categories: (1) history of French literature; and (2) contemporary history. Belgians are eligible for the former, and foreigners who are studying or have studied at the University of Ghent are eligible for the latter. A monetary prize of 60,000 Belgian francs is awarded every five years. Established in 1925.

987
Prix Eugene Lameere
For recognition of the best history textbook for Belgian primary and secondary schools and colleges of education, in which illustrations play an important part in making the text understandable. A monetary prize of 55,000 Belgian francs is awarded every five years. Established in 1895.

988
Prix Franz Cumont
For recognition of a work on the ancient history of religion or science in the Mediterranean basin before Mohammed. Belgian or foreign authors are eligible. A monetary prize of 100,000 Belgian francs is awarded triennially. Established in 1970.

989
Prix Goblet d'Alviella
For recognition of the best work of a strictly scientific and objective character on the history of religions. Belgian authors are eligible. A monetary prize of 55,000 Belgian francs is awarded every five years. Established in 1925.

990
Prix Henri Lavachery
For recognition of a written work or filmed commentary on ethnology. Belgian authors may submit works written in French and published in the preceding five years. A monetary prize of 55,000 francs is awarded every five years. Established in 1952.

991
Prix Herman Schoolmeesters
For recognition of a manuscript or printed work useful in promoting small and medium-sized firms. A monetary prize of 60,000 Belgian francs is awarded every five years. Established in 1968.

992
Prix Joseph De Keyn
For recognition of works by Belgian authors on secular instruction and education. Awards are given in alternate years in the following categories: (1) works useful for primary schools; and (2) works on secondary

instruction or education, including industrial art. A monetary prize of 70,000 Belgian francs is awarded annually. Established in 1953.

993
Prix Joseph Gantrelle
For recognition of a work in classical philology. Belgian authors are eligible. A monetary prize of 60,000 Belgian francs is awarded biennially. Established in 1893.

994
Prix Jules Duculot
For recognition of a manuscript or printed work on the history of philosophy. Belgians or foreigners with a degree from a Belgian university may submit works written in French. A monetary prize of 120,000 Belgian francs is awarded every five years. Established in 1966.

995
Prix Leon Leclere
For recognition of the best manuscript or printed work on national or general history. First works by a young historian are eligible. A monetary prize of 55,000 Belgian francs is awarded every five years. Established in 1927.

996
Prix Polydore de Paepe
For recognition of the best account of a spiritualist philosophy founded on pure reason or experience. Preference is given to works which develop the principles stated by Paul Le Monyne in *De l'Idee de Dieu, sa transformation, ses consequences morales et sociales*. Belgian or foreign authors are eligible. A monetary prize of 50,000 Belgian francs is awarded every five years. Established in 1935.

997
Prix Suzanne Tassier
To recognize a woman who has obtained her doctorate at a Belgian university, and who has written an important scientific work in the fields of history, philology, law, or the social sciences. If no worthy work is found in these categories, a work on natural, medical, or mathematical sciences will be considered. A monetary prize of 65,000 Belgian francs is awarded biennially. Established in 1956.

998
Prix Tobie Jonckheere
For recognition of a manuscript or printed work on the science of education. A monetary prize of 55,000 Belgian francs is awarded triennially. Established in 1955.

999
Prix Victor Tourneur
To encourage numismatic and sigillographical studies, and to encourage the art of medal making. A monetary prize of 60,000 Belgian francs is awarded alternately every five years by the Classe des Lettres and the Classe des Beaux Arts. Established in 1918.

1000
Academie Royale de Belgique
Classe des Sciences
Palais des Academies
Rue Ducale 1
B-1000 Brussels, Belgium

Phone: 2 514 40 64
Phone: 2 514 42 56
Fax: 2 502 04 24

1001
Fondation Camille Liegeois
To provide for research or scientific travels by Belgians less than 30 years of age. The award is given alternately by the Classe des Sciences and the Classe des Lettres et des Sciences morales et politiques. A monetary prize of 55,000 French francs is awarded triennially.

1002
Fondation Jean de Meyer
To provide for research in the field of biological physical-chemistry, especially human physiology, cardiology, endocrinology and hormones. Belgian researchers or foreigners studying at Universite Libre de Bruxelles, who are less than 35 years of age are eligible. A monetary prize of 90,000 French francs is awarded triennially.

1003
Fondation Jean Lebrun
For recognition of the best works on biogeography and ecology. Scientists from French-speaking research institutions of Belgium are eligible. A monetary prize of 80,000 Belgian francs is awarded biennially. Established in 1987.

1004
Fondation Marc Poll
For recognition of the best work on zoology (systematic, comparative anatomy, zoo geography, or animal ecology). Reserved for researchers of Belgian french-speaking or Zairian universities. A monetary prize of 100,000 Belgian francs is awarded biennially. Established in 1992.

1005
Fondation Octave Dupont
To recognize projects of fundamental scientific research in the fields of human an animal physiology and physiopathology. Reserved for Belgian french-speaking scientists. A subsidy of 3,200,000 Belgian francs is presented every eight years. Established in 1989.

1006
Prix Adolphe Wetrems
For recognition of the most useful discoveries or inventions made during the preceding year in: (1) the mathematical and physical sciences; and (2) the natural sciences. Belgian scientists are eligible. Two monetary prizes of 50,000 Belgian francs each are awarded annually. Established in 1926.

1007
Prix Agathon De Potter
For recognition of outstanding research work in: (1) astronomy; (2) physics; (3) mathematics; (4) chemistry; (5) mineralogy; (6) animal biology; and (7) plant biology. Belgian researchers are eligible. Monetary prizes of 40,000 Belgian francs each are awarded triennially. Sponsored by Fondation Agathon De Potter. Established in 1918.

1008
Prix Albert Brachet
For recognition of the best work on embryology, preferably causal embryology. Work published during the preceding three-year period in French, Flemish, German, English or Italian, is eligible. A monetary prize of 75,000 Belgian francs is awarded triennially. Established in 1930.

1009
Prix Auguste Sacre
For recognition of an invention bringing about real and important progress in mechanical engineering, in any type of industry, or for any work on mechanical engineering containing new and valuable theories. Belgian researchers are eligible. A monetary prize of 75,000 Belgian francs is awarded every six years. Established in 1906.

1010
Prix Baron Van Ertborn
For recognition of the best published work on geology. Belgian authors who are not members of the Academy are eligible. A monetary prize of 50,000 Belgian francs is awarded biennially. Established in 1939.

1011
Prix Charles Lagrange
For recognition of the best mathematical or experimental work contributing to the progress of mathematical knowledge in the world. Belgian or

foreign researchers are eligible. A monetary prize of 50,000 Belgian francs is awarded every four years. Established in 1904.

1012
Prix Charles Lemaire
For recognition of the best published report on public works related preferably to experiences and practical works on engineering or theoretical research on the resistance of materials, the stability of buildings, or hydraulics. A monetary prize of 50,000 Belgian francs is awarded biennially. Established in 1894.

1013
Prix de Boelpaepe
For recogniton of an important discovery likely to bring about progress in photography. The work can be on the properties of emulsions, and physico-chemical techniques used in photographic processes, or can be used for a new development in photography that may add to scientific progress. Belgian researchers are eligible. A monetary prize of 80,000 Belgian francs is awarded biennially. Established in 1927.

1014
Prix de la Belgica
To recognize a scholar or a group of scholars who have successfully devoted themselves to scientific research inside the Antarctic Polar Circle. Scientists of all nationalities are eligible. Surplus funds of the foundation may be given to subsidize oceanographic work by Belgians. A gold medal is awarded every five years. Established in 1959.

1015
Prix de l'adjudant Hubert Lefebvre
For recognition of the best published work on botany, or to help a scientist undertake research in botany. Belgian researchers are eligible. A monetary prize of 50,000 Belgian francs is awarded triennially. Established in 1883.

1016
Prix Dubois - Debauque
For recognition of the best works relating to the production of electrical currents by living organisms, and the nature of these currents. Belgian or foreign scientists are eligible. A monetary prize of 50,000 Belgian francs is awarded every four years. Established in 1936.

1017
Prix Edmond de Selys Longchamps
For recognition of the best original work on present day Belgian fauna. If no entry on this subject is deemed worthy, works on Belgian fauna in the past or on the fauna of Zaire will be considered. Belgian and foreign researchers are eligible. A monetary prize of 80,000 Belgian francs is awarded every five years. Established in 1904.

1018
Prix Edouard Mailly
To recognize a scientist who has contributed to progress in astronomy or has helped spread interest in and knowledge of this science. Belgian or naturalized Belgian scientists are eligible. A monetary prize of 50,000 Belgian francs is awarded every four years. Established in 1892.

1019
Prix Emile Laurent
For recognition of outstanding work in the field of botany. Awards are given in alternate years for: (1) the best work on the flora or vegetation of Zaire (including works on the anatomy and physiology of plants from Zaire); and (2) the best work on botany including agriculture and horticulture. Belgian researchers are eligible. A monetary prize of 40,000 Belgian francs is awarded every four years. Established in 1910.

1020
Prix Eugene Catalan
To recognize a Belgian or French scholar who has made important progress in pure mathematics. Works must be submitted in French and must have been published during the five preceding years. A monetary prize of 60,000 Belgian francs is awarded every five years. Established in 1964.

1021
Prix Francois Deruyts
To recognize one or more authors who have made progress in synthetic or analytic superior geometry. Belgian researchers are eligible. A monetary prize of 50,000 Belgian francs is awarded every four years. Established in 1906.

1022
Prix Frederic Swarts
To reward the best work, published or in manuscript form, in the field of pure or industrial chemistry. The work has to be written in French or in Flemish and must be the work of a Belgian citizen who holds an engineering degree from one of the Belgian universities of the Ecole des Mines de Mons, and who graduated in the preceding eight years. If the prize is not awarded for two consecutive periods, it may be awarded to a chemist with a doctorate. A monetary prize of 50,000 Belgian francs is awarded biennially. Established in 1938.

1023
Prix Georges Vanderlinden
For recognition of the best discovery or the most noteworthy work in the physical sciences, in particular, radio-electricity. The prize is given alternately for national and international works. For the national competition, the work should be written in French or Dutch. For the international competition, the work should be in English, German, or Italian. A monetary prize of 60,000 Belgian francs is awarded biennially. Established in 1932.

1024
Prix Henri Buttgenbach
For recognition of studies on mineralogy, petrography and paleontology that are based on materials gathered in Belgium. Belgian scientists are preferred. Dutch, French, or English scientists can be considered. A monetary prize of 50,000 Belgian francs is awarded triennially. Established in 1945.

1025
Prix Jacques Deruyts
For recognition of progress in mathematical analysis. Belgian researchers are eligible. A monetary prize of 50,000 Belgian francs is awarded every four years. Established in 1948.

1026
Prix Jean-Servais Stas
To recognize university students who have passed their doctoral examinations in chemical science, with the greatest distinction. Belgian students are eligible. A copy of the book *Florilege des Sciences en Belgique* is awarded annually.

1027
Prix Joseph Schepkens
For recognition of work in the field of botany or agronomical research. Awards are given in alternate years for: (1) the best experimental work on the genetics of plants, particularly highly cultivated plants; (2) the best work on phytopathology and applied entomology; and (3) agronomical research. Monetary prizes of 50,000 Belgian francs each are awarded triennially. Established in 1921.

1028
Prix Lamarck
For recognition of morphological works published in French or Flemish and dealing with a zoological group including humans. All the author's work must have brought to light the greatest number of facts and new explanations on animal evolution or zoological phylogeny. A monetary prize of 55,000 Belgian francs is awarded every five years. Established by Paul Pelseneer. Established in 1914.

1029

Prix Leo Errera
To recognize the author or authors of the best original work on general biology. A monetary prize of 60,000 Belgian francs is awarded triennially. Established in 1909.

1030

Prix Leon et Henri Fredericq
To recognize a scholar who has distinguished himself by original experimental research in physiology or any related science (biochemistry, biophysics, pharmacodynamics, molecular biology, etc.). Belgian and foreign scientists whose research is done in a Belgian laboratory are eligible. Individuals must be under 45 years of age. A monetary prize of 100,000 Belgian francs is awarded biennially. Established in 1968.

1031

Prix Louis Melsens
For recognition of the most noteworthy work on applied chemistry or physics. Belgian or naturalized Belgian researchers are eligible. A monetary prize of 50,000 Belgian francs is awarded every four years. Established in 1904.

1032

Prix P. J. et Edouard Van Beneden
To recognize the author or authors of the best original manuscript or published work on embryology or cytology during the preceding three-year period. Belgian or foreign researchers are eligible. A monetary prize of 75,000 Belgian francs is awarded triennially. Established in 1915 by P. Nolf. Established in 1915.

1033

Prix Paul and Marie Stroobant
To recognize the Belgian or French scientist who has written the best theoretical or observational work on astronomy. A monetary prize of 45,000 Belgian francs is awarded biennially. Established in 1950.

1034

Prix Paul Fourmarier
To recognize a scholar who, during the preceding ten years, has made important discoveries or has brought about considerable progress in theoretical concepts in the geological sciences. Work in geology and its applications, petrography, relations with the creation and evaluation of mineral masses, physical geography, paleontology, or understanding of the general evolution of the earth is eligible. A gold medal is awarded every ten years. Established in 1856.

1035

Prix Pol and Christiane Swings
For recognition of outstanding research in the field of astrophysics. Scientists who are not older than 40 years of age are eligible. The prize is awarded in alternate years to a Belgian and to a foreigner. A monetary prize of 70,000 Belgian francs is awarded every four years. Established in 1976.

1036

Prix Professeur Louis Baes
For recogniton of the best discovery or the most noteworthy studies on elasticity, plasticity, resistance of materials, the stability of buildings and the calculation of machine parts, including theoretical and practical applications. Candidates must be from Common Market countries and papers must be in French. A monetary prize of 45,000 Belgian francs is awarded biennially. Established in 1962.

1037

Prix Theophile de Donder
For recognition of the best original work on mathematical physics. Candidates under 40 years of age are eligible. A monetary prize of 60,000 Belgian francs is awarded triennially. Established in 1957.

1038

Prix Theophile Gluge
For recognition of the best work on physiology. Belgian and foreign researchers are eligible. A monetary prize of 50,000 Belgian francs is awarded biennially. Established in 1906.

1039

Association des Ecrivains Belges de Langue Francaise
Maison des Ecrivains - Maison Camille
  Lemonnier
Chaussee de Wavre 150
B-1050 Brussels, Belgium   Phone: 2 5122968

1040

Prix Alex Pasquier
For recognition of the best unpublished or published historical novel during the preceding five years. All Belgian writers of the French language are eligible. A monetary prize of 25,000 Belgian francs is awarded every five years. Established in 1972 by Madame Alex Pasquier in memory of Alex Pasquier, her husband and president of the Association.

1041

Prix Constant de Horion
For recognition of the best essay of literary history or literary criticism on an established Belgian writer or on an aspect of Belgian literature of French expression. Belgian writers who are at least 40 years of age are eligible. A monetary prize of 50,000 Belgian francs is awarded biennially. Established in 1977 by a bequest of Baron Jean Constant (in literature, Constant de Horion).

1042

Prix Gilles Nelod
To recognize the author of an unpublished story or narrative, not only for children. The text cannot be the result of a collaboration. Belgian writers of French expression who live in Belgium are eligible. A monetary prize of 10,000 Belgian francs is awarded biennially. Established in 1984.

1043

Prix Hubert Krains
For recognition of an unpublished work of poetry or prose. The award is given in alternate years for prose and poetry. Writers who are not older than 40 years of age are eligible. A monetary award of 20,000 Belgian francs is awarded biennially. Established in 1950 in honor of Hubert Krains, president of the Association.

1044

Prix Rene Lyr
For recognition of an unpublished work of poetry written in French. A monetary award of 25,000 Belgian francs is presented triennially. Established in 1959 to honor Rene Lyr.

1045

Association des Ingenieurs Electriciens Sortis de l'Institut Montefiore
rue Saint-Gilles 31   Phone: 41 222946
B-4000 Liege, Belgium   Fax: 41 222388

1046

George Montefiore Foundation Prize
(Prix de la Fondation George Montefiore)
To recognize an individual who has made significant contributions to the advancement of the technology of electricity through scientific or engineering inventions or innovations. Self-nominations will not be accepted. Only recent papers, written or published during the five years preceding the deadline for receipt of papers, are considered for the award. A monetary prize of 800,000 Belgian francs is awarded every five years.

1047
Association Internationale pour L'Etude der Argiles
Katholieke Universiteit Leuven
Kardinaal Mercierlaan 92
B-3001 Leuven, Belgium
Phone: 16 220931
Fax: 16 295126

1048
AIPEA Medals
To recognize eminent senior lay scientists for outstanding contributions to clay science and to the clay community at large. A maximum of 2 medals are awarded quadrennially.

1049
Bradley Award
To encourage young scientists in the field of clay research. Individuals under 35 years of age may submit papers. A monetary prize of $1,000 and a diploma are awarded at the International Clay Conference every four years. Established in 1985 in honor of Bill Bradley, eminent clay scientist.

1050
Association of Belgian Historic Houses
(Association Royale des Demeures Historiques de Belgique)
24, rue Vergote
1200 Brussels, Belgium
Phone: 2 7350965
Fax: 2 7359912

1051
Prix L.-Pierre Descamps
To recognize the author of the best archaeological article, literary or scientific, and to increase public awareness of the threatening architectural situation in the French and German areas of the country. Articles submitted should be devoted to the study of an architectural monument or group in these regions, and if possible, should cover an endangered monument that has not yet been researched extensively. A monetary prize of 50,000 Belgian francs is awarded at the associations' annual General Assemby. The winning article will be published in the quarterly review, "Maisons d'Hier et d'Aujourd'hui."

1052
Prix Master Foods des Demeures Historiques
To recognize a person or institution responsible for the restoration and safeguarding of a historic home or a building, park, or garden that is part of the estate of a historic home. To qualify, homes, buildings, parks, and gardens must be located on Belgian territory and the restoration must have been completed within the preceding three years. The following prizes are awarded each December at an official ceremony that is preceded by a press conference: First Prize - 600,000 Belgian francs; Second Prize - 300,000 Belgian francs; and Third Prize - 100,000 Belgian francs.

1053
Prix Paul de Pessemier
For recognition of studies of historic houses of Belgium or their architects or designers. A monetary prize of 50,000 Belgian francs is awarded annually. Established in 1984 by Paul de Pessemier.

1054
Belgian Centre for Music Documentation
(Centre Belge de Documentation Musicale)
Rue d'Arlon 75-77
B-1040 Brussels, Belgium
Phone: 2 2309437

1055
Prix Quadriennal de Composition Musicale Camille Huysmans
(Vierjaarlijkse prijs voor muziekcompositie Camille Huysmans)
To further the composition of orchestral works by Belgian composers. Symphonic works by a Belgian composer that have not been published or performed are eligible. There are no age limitations. A monetary award is presented quadrennially. Established in 1971 by Camille Huysmans Stichting (Antwerp) in memory of Camille Huysmans, the former Belgian statesman and politician.

1056
Belgian Geological Society
(Societe Geologique de Belgique)
Universite de Liege
7 place du Vingt-Aout
B-4000 Liege, Belgium
Phone: 41 665283
Fax: 41 665700

1057
Andre H. Dumont Medal
For recognition of outstanding contributions to the earth sciences (geology, applied geology, petrography, mineralogy, physical geography, and paleontology) during the last ten years. Scientists of any nationality are eligible. A gilded medal is awarded annually. Established in 1939.

1058
Belgian Institute of Administrative Sciences
(Institut Belge des Sciences Administratives)
Voorlopig Bewindstraat 15
B-1000 Brussels, Belgium

1059
Belgian Institute of Administrative Sciences Prize
For recognition of the best work on some aspect of administrative science. The recipient may not be older than 40 years of age. A monetary prize of 25,000 Belgian francs is awarded annually.

1060
Belgian Municipal Credit Institution
(Credit Communal de Belgique)
Boulevard Pacheco 44
B-1000 Brussels, Belgium
Phone: 2 2221111
Fax: 2 2224038

1061
History Prize
To promote the local and regional history of Belgium. University or amateur historians and history societies are eligible. A monetary prize of 50,000 Belgian francs is awarded annually. Established in 1960 by Credit Communal. Additional information is available from Denis Morsa, Credit Communal Cultural Division.

1062
Journalism Prize
(Prix du Journalism)
To promote a better general knowledge of society, financial, economic, sports, and cultural life. Professional print and broadcast journalists are eligible. A monetary prize of 50,000 Belgian francs is awarded to each winner. Established in 1963. Additional information is available from Credit Communal Press Service.

1063
Law and Economics Prize
To recognize an author from Belgium or elsewhere, who has written on the administrative, juridical, social or economic life of the communities or of the public agencies of the country. A monetary prize of 65,000 Belgian francs is awarded biennially. The prize is awarded in alternate years for a work published in French and in Dutch. (Discontinued)

1064
Belgian National League Against Tuberculosis
56, rue la Concorde
B-1050 Brussels, Belgium
Phone: 2 5125455

1065
Arthur de Falloise Quinquennial Prize
For recognition of an unpublished work or set of published works on the physiology or pathology of the respiratory organs. A Belgian physician, who has been an alumnus of a Belgian university for less than 15 years, is eligible. A monetary prize of 75,000 francs is awarded every five years.

1066
Belgian National Office for the Promotion of Agricultural and Horticultural Products
(Office National des Debouches Agricoles et Horticoles)
Treurenberg 2
B-1000 Brussels, Belgium
Phone: 2 210 17 11
Fax: 2 218 46 67

1067
International Floral Decoration Competition
(Entente Florale)
To recognize municipalities and villages in Europe for excellence in horticultural displays. Trophies are presented annually by tourist boards and horticulture societies of European countries. Established in 1975. Sponsored by the International Association of Horticultural Producers.

1068
Belgian Radio and Television
(Belgische Radio en Televisie)
August Reyerslaan 52
B-1040 Brussels, Belgium
Phone: 2 737 51 28

1069
International Competition, Opera and Bel Canto
To provide opportunities for exposure for opera singers to the public, reviewers and opera directors via radio and television and via co-production with European broadcast, radio and television companies. Promising opera singers 21 to 33 years of age who are delegated by a radio or television organization, opera house or studio, or music institution are eligible. The following prizes are awarded: (1) Grand Prize - 125,000 Belgian francs; (2) Press Prize - 100,000 Belgian francs; (3) Youth Jury Prize - 75,000 Belgian francs; and (4) Encouragement prizes. Awarded annually in August during a televised concert with the Laureates accompanied by an opera orchestra at the Ostend Casino. Established in 1978.

1070
Belgische Vereniging van Auteurs, Componisten en Uitgevers
(Societe Belge des Auteurs, Compositeurs et Editeurs)
c/o Awards Committee
Rue d'Arlon, 75-77
B-1040 Brussels, Belgium
Phone: 2 2302660
Fax: 2 2311800

1071
Troubadour de la SABAM
For recognition of artistic achievement by authors, composers, or editors in many different disciplines. Members of the Society are eligible. Monetary prizes and trophies are awarded annually. Established in 1961 by Conseil d'Administration SABAM.

1072
Belgium
Ministry of Foreign Affairs
(Belgium
Ministere des Affaires Etrangeres)
Service des Ordres
Rue Belliard 65
B-1040 Brussels, Belgium
Phone: 251 51779
Fax: 230 0280

1073
Order of Leopold
(Ordre de Leopold)
For recognition of services rendered to the State. The Order is divided into five classes: First Class - Grand Ribbon (Grand Cordon), Second Class - Grand Officer, Third Class - Commander, Fourth Class - Officer, and Fifth Class - Knight. Each degree can be awarded in three categories: Civil, military, or naval. The nominations to the Order are announced only by the King. The decoration of the Order consists of a white enamel cross carrying a garland of laurel and oak leaves between each of the four limbs and bearing on one side, in the center, a black enameled escutcheon, encircled by red, between two small golden circles with the King's cipher. Awarded when proposed by a governmental Minister or by Royal decree. Established in 1832 and named for King Leopold, Belgium's first king.

1074
Order of the Crown
(Ordre de la Couronne)
To recognize individuals who have distinguished themselves through artistic, literary, or scientific merits, or through outstanding accomplishments in the field of commerce and industry. Artists, scientists, or industrialists of any country who contributed to the development of the Belgian culture in Belgium or abroad are eligible for consideration. The Order is divided into the following classes: Grand Cross, Grand Officer, Commander, Officer, Knight, Golden and Silver Palms, and gold, silver, and bronze classes, to which a medal is presented. Awarded when proposed by a governmental Minister or by Royal decree. Established in 1897.

1075
Ordre de Leopold II
(Orde van Leopold II)
For recognition of service. The Order is divided into the following classes: Grand Cross, Grand Officer, Commander, Officer, Knight, and gold, silver, and bronze classes, to which a medal is presented. Awarded when proposed by a governmental Minister or by Royal decree. Established in 1900 and named for King Leopold II, Belgium's second king.

1076
Belgium
Ministry of the Flemish Community
(Belgium
Ministerie van de Vlaamse Gemeenschap)
Kolonienstraat 29-31
B-1000 Brussels, Belgium
Phone: 2 510 35 93

1077
Best Film Script in the Dutch Language
For recognition of the respective authors of three original Dutch language scripts for a full length feature film. The amount is divided as follows: (1) 150,000 Belgian francs for the winner; (2) 100,000 Belgian francs for the first runner-up; and (3) 50,000 Belgian francs for the second runner-up. Awarded annually.

1078
Koopal Bursary for Literature
To recognize the author of the best Dutch-language translation of one or more works published during the relevant period by Belgian or foreign writers. A monetary prize of 48,000 Belgian francs is awarded biennially.

1079
Prize for a Flemish Short Film
To encourage young Flemish filmmakers. A monetary prize of 100,000 Belgian francs is awarded every year at the Brussels International Film Festival (national non-competitive category).

1080
Staatsprijs ter Bekroning Van een Schrijverscarriere
For recognition of a writer on the basis of his complete works. A monetary prize of 400,000 Belgian francs is awarded triennially. Established in 1851.

1081
Staatsprijs voor Jeugdliteratuur
For recognition in the field of children's literature published in the Flemish language. A monetary prize of 200,000 Belgian francs is awarded triennially. Established in 1971.

1082
Staatsprijs voor Kritiek en Essay
For recognition in the field of criticism and essay published in the Flemish language. A monetary prize of 200,000 Belgian francs is awarded triennially. Established in 1851.

1083
Staatsprijs voor Poezie
For recognition of achievement in the field of poetry published in Flemish. A monetary prize of 200,000 Belgian francs is awarded triennially. Established in 1851.

1084
Staatsprijs voor Romans en Verhalend Proza
For recognition in the field of narrative prose published in the Flemish language. A monetary prize of 200,000 Belgian francs is awarded triennially. Established in 1851.

1085
Staatsprijs voor Toneelletterkunde
For recognition in the field of drama published in the Flemish language. A monetary prize of 200,000 Belgian francs is awarded triennially. Established in 1851.

1086
Staatsprijs Voor Vertaling Van Nederlandse Letterkunde
To encourage translation of literature and to recognize outstanding translations. A monetary prize of 200,000 Belgian francs is awarded triennially. Established in 1983.

1087
State Grand Prize for Literature
(Grand Prix Quinquennal de l'Etat)
To recognize an author for the totality of his work. Belgian authors writing in French may submit works. A monetary prize of 400,000 Belgian francs is awarded every five years jointly by the French community and the Flemish community. Established in 1930.

1088
Benelux Phlebology Society
(Societe Beneluxienne de Phlebologie)
Korte Meer 12 Phone: 91 25 83 49
B-9000 Ghent, Belgium Fax: 91 741508

1089
Prix de Bruxelles
For recognition of contributions in the field of phlebology. Awarded triennially.

1090
Brussels International Fantasy Film Festival
Ave. de la Reine, 144 Phone: 2 2421713
1210 Brussels, Belgium Fax: 2 2162169

1091
Fantasy Film Awards
To recognize excellence in fantasy and science-fiction films. Awards are presented in the following catagories: Grand Prize, Prize of the Audience, and Special Prize of the Jury. Trophies are presented at the annual festival in March. The Grand Prize winner also receives a monetary promotional award. To be eligible, films must be produced within the previous two years before the festival. Established in 1983 by Peymey Diffusion. For more information, contact Guy Delmote.

1092
Bureau International de la Recuperation
24, rue du Lombard, Boite 14 Phone: 2 5142180
B-1000 Brussels, Belgium Fax: 2 5141226

1093
BIR Gold Medal
For recognition of outstanding promotion of the recycling of resources. A medal and a certificate are awarded when merited. Established in 1979.

1094
Camera Club Liegeois
Quai de Rome, 51
Bte. 052
B-4000 Liege, Belgium Phone: 41 52 10 90

1095
Biennale Internationale du Cinema Humain Marcel Mignon
For recognition of outstanding amateur photography in 16mm or super 8mm films. Films must extol some facet of human life. Amateur cameramen, whether a member of a camera club or not, are eligible. The deadline for entries is November 12. The following prizes are awarded: (1) Grand Prix Marcel Mignon; (2) Prix du Camera Club Liegeois; (3) Prix de l'Agence de voyages Wasteels au Premier Film Belge; (4) Prix de la Ville de Liege; (5) Prix de l'E.P.L.I.C.I.N.A. Pour Son Aspect Social; (6) Prix du Ministre Michel Hansenne, minister of employment and labor; (7) Prix du Gouvernement Provincial de Liege; (8) Prix de l'E.C.C.F.B. for the quality of reporting; (9) Prix du President du Jury; (10) Prix du Festival de Wattreloos for the originality of subject; (11) Prix du Ministre-President de l'Executif de la Communaute Francaise de Belgique; (12) Prix du President du Camera Club Liegeois; (13) Prix du President des Affaires Culturelles de la Province de Liege; (14) Prix du Vice-Premier Ministre Jean of Gol, minister of Justice; (15) Prix de l'Echevinat de la Participation et des Relations avec le Quartier, Jeunesse et Sport de la Ville de Liege; (16) Prix de l'Echevinat des Affaires Culturelles de la Ville de Liege; (17) Prix de la Commission Culturelle de l'Union des Anciens Eleves de l'Athenee Royal de Liege; and (18) Le Prix du Public. Certificates and gold coins are awarded biennially. Established in 1980 in memory of Marcel Mignon, President, who died in 1979 and was the author of films which extol some facet of human life. The Belgian government, the Province and the Town Council of Liege are among the sponsors.

1096
Centre Universitaire du Film Scientifique
Universite Libre de Bruxelles
Avenue F.D. Roosevelt, 50 (CP 165) Phone: 2 650 31 10
B-1050 Brussels 5, Belgium Phone: 2 650 28 55

1097
Brussels International Festival of Films on the Engineering Profession
(Festival International du Film Consacre au Metier d'Ingenieur)
For recognition of films and video-tapes with a bearing on civil engineering, public works, mining, the metallurgical industry, electrical engineering, electricity, data-processing (CAD, CAM, CAD/CAM), applied mechanics, industrial chemistry, (advanced) technology, aeronautical engineering, energy production, applied physics, numerical methods, and all the other uses of engineering in industry. Films and video-tapes entered must be recent (post-1980) productions. Films entered may be

16mm or 35mm, silent or with sound, equipped with optical or magnetic (but not double) sound-tracks, black or white, or in color. The deadline for entries is October 15. The following prizes are awarded: (1) the Festival Grand Prix; (2) the Public Prize; and (3) a number of prizes for various disciplines. Established in 1985. (No Festival was held in 1991)

1098
Brussels International Festival of Scientific and Technical Films
(Festival International du Film Scientifique et Technique, Bruxelles)
For recognition of academic and non-clinical scientific films and videotapes which, because of their presentation and content, are attractive from the points of view of research, university teaching and industry. Straight advertising, filmed lessons and recording intended for programmed learning are not eligible. One day has been set aside for films and video-tapes of interest to be used with the 15-18 year age-group in secondary education. The Festival is open to films and video-tapes with a bearing on the exact sciences (biochemistry, biology, botany,chemistry, crystallography, data meteorology, mineralogy, physics, pure mechanics, zoology, etc.), pharmacy, physiology (excluding clinical material) and the arts (archaeology, architecture, education, ethnography, history, the social sciences, town and country planning, etc.). Films entered may be either 8mm, super 8mm, 16mm or 35mm; silent or sound films, in color or black and white, and with optical or magnetic sound track. When possible, French copies are preferred. For secondary school teaching, French copies are compulsory. The following prizes are awarded: (1) for the best film shown - Grand Prix du Festival de Bruxelles; (2) for the best research film - Prix de la Recherche Fondamentale; (3) best didactic film at the university level - Prix de l'Enseignement Universitaire; (4) best didactic film at the secondary level - Prix de l'Enseignment Secondaire; (5) Prix de la Communication Scientifique; (6) Prix du Public; (7) Prix de l'Enseignement Superior des Sciences; and (8) best film in each discipline of science. Silver and bronze medals and diplomas are awarded triennially. Established in 1961. (No Festival was held in 1991)

1099
Cercle d'Etudes Numismatiques
Boulevard de l'Empereur, 4
B-1000 Brussels, Belgium   Phone: 2 519 56 00

1100
Prix Quinquennal de Numismatique
For recognition of a contribution to the field of numismatics. Nominations alternate between a Belgian and non-Belgian for numismatic activities and publications during the preceding five years. A monetary prize and a medal are awarded every five years. Established in 1964.

1101
Cinema Novo
Vaartstraat 32
8000 Bruges, Belgium

1102
Karibu
To foster the distribution of films from Africa, Asia, and Latin America and introduce directors and films from these continents in Belgium. A monetary prize is awarded at the annual festival in March. Established in 1989. For further information, contact George Micholt.

1103
Comite International de l'Organisation Mondiale de la Presse Periodique
Avenue du Roi, 191
B-1060 Brussels, Belgium   Phone: 2 539 03 69

1104
Arthur Desguin International Prize
(Premio Internacional Arthur Desguin)
For recognition of journalists of the international periodical press for a written contribution such as editorial, analysis, report, or essay on an announced theme. Every journalist, aged over 25, regularly collaborating on a publication of the Periodical Press, is eligible for participation in the contest for the Prize of Merit. As for the Prize for Promotion, the competition is open for every trainee-journalist, or journalist, aged not more than 25 years, and currently collaborating on a publication of the Periodical Press. The following monetary prizes are awarded: (1) Prize for Merit - 200,000 Belgian francs; and (2) two Prizes for Promotion - 50,000 Belgian francs each.

1105
Concours International Printemps de la Guitare
Place du Chef-Lieu, 9
B-6040 Charleroi-Jumet, Belgium   Phone: 71 350448
                                            Fax: 71 355320

1106
Concours International Printemps de la Guitare
For recognition of outstanding performances on the guitar. Solo guitarists under 32 years of age are eligible to apply by June 30. The following monetary prizes are awarded: first prize - 200,000 Belgian francs, original works by two Belgian artists, and 30 compact discs; second prize - 150,000 Belgian francs; third prize - 100,000 Belgian francs; fourth prize - 75,000 Belgian francs; fifth prize - 50,000 Belgian francs; sixth prize - 30,000 Belgian francs; seventh prize - 20,000 Belgian francs; eighth prize - 15,000 Belgian francs; ninth prize - 12,000 Belgian francs; tenth prize - 10,000 Belgian francs; Prize of the SABAM (Belgian Society of Authors, Editors and Composers) for the best interpretation of the Belgian works, semifinals - 20,000 Belgian francs, and finals - 25,000 Belgian francs; and the Kiwanis International Award - 10,000 Belgian francs. Awarded biennially. Established in 1988.

1107
Cooperative International de Recherche et d'Action en Matiere de Communication
RTBF-Liege
Palais des Congres
B-4020 Liege, Belgium   Phone: 41 410356

1108
Regional Radio and Television Awards
To recognize and promote cooperation and exchange among broadcasters, media specialists, and academicians. The organization sponsors competitions and bestows awards in conjunction with the Council of Europe and the European Media Institute.

1109
Council of the French Community of Belgium
(Conseil de la Communaute francaise de Belgique)
Rue de la Loi 6
B-1000 Brussels, Belgium   Phone: 2 513 79 80

1110
Prize for Literature of the Council of the French Community of Belgium
(Prix Litteraire du Conseil de la Communaute Francaise de Belgique)
For recognition of a work by a Belgian author writing in the French language. The work must either be an illustration of the sensibility of the Community or it must be about the Community's cultural patrimony. Over each five-year period, the Prize alternates annually between the following types of work: (1) novels, fiction, short stories; (2) poetry; (3) literary essays; (4) plays, including radio or television plays which have been broadcast; and (5) works about the cultural patrimony of the French Community of Belgium. In order to qualify, the work may either be unpublished (in which case the Council may grant a subsidy to allow for,

Belgium

or to facilitate, its publication) or it must have been published within five years prior to the award of the Prize. Additionally, the work must not have won any other (national or international) Prize. The Prize is selected by a jury consisting of members of the Academy of French Language and Literature, the Association of Belgian French-language authors, the French-language section of the Pen Club, and the French-language Youth Council. Works may be submitted to the Secretariat of the jury of the Prize for Literature of the Council of the French Community, by March 1 in the year in which the Prize is awarded. A monetary prize of 100,000 Belgian francs is awarded annually. Established in 1976.

1111
Professor Lucien Dautrebande Physiopathology Foundation
Address unknown.

1112
Dautrebande Physiopathology Foundation Prize
For recognition of a work on human or animal physiopathology with special emphasis on the therapeutic implications of the work. Scientists who have not been granted a very important prize in the five previous years are eligible. A monetary prize of 2,000,000 Belgian francs is awarded triennially. Established in 1959.

1113
Eternit
Kuiermanstraat 1   Phone: 15 71 71 71
B-2920 Kapelle-op-den-Bos, Belgium   Fax: 15 71 71 79

1114
International Prize for Architecture
(Prix International d'Architecture)
To encourage high quality architecture. Awards are given in the following categories: single family dwelling; grouped housing developments, dwellings and/or flats; other type of building; Renovation Award; and Special Eternit Prize - for the use of Eternit materials; and Special Resopal Award. Monetary awards totaling 3,400,000 Belgian francs, trophies, and commemoration symbol for participants were awarded biennially. The Premier Award, established in 1990, was awarded for work which best embodied and exemplified the spiritual aims of the Prize. A gold and silver medallion set with a diamond was awarded. Established in 1970 by Eternit Belgium. (Discontinued)

1115
European Amateur Baseball Confederation
(Confederation Europeenne de Baseball Amateur)
Thonetlaan 52   Phone: 3 2190440
2050 Antwerp, Belgium   Fax: 3 2190440

1116
CEBA Honour List
For recognition of outstanding contributions to baseball in Europe. Gold, silver, and bronze medals are awarded.

1117
European Baseball Championships
(Campionato Europeo Baseball)
For recognition of the national team that wins the European Championship. Awarded annually. Established in 1954. The European Baseball Cup is also awarded to the National Club Champions. This competition was established in 1963. In addition, a Cup of Cups, a CEBA-Cup, Junior European Baseball Champion, European Cadest, and European Juvenile Championships are awarded.

1118
European Aquaculture Society
Secretariat
Coupure Rechts   Phone: 92 237722
B-9000 Ghent, Belgium   Fax: 92 237604

Formerly: (1984) European Mariculture Society.

1119
Honorary Life Members
For recognition of achievement in aquaculture. Awarded irregularly. Established in 1981.

1120
European Association for the Promotion of Poetry
(Association Europeenne pour la Promotion de la Poesie)
Boskantstraat 30
B-3200 Louvain, Belgium   Phone: 16 235351

1121
European Music and Poetry Competitions
To recognize individuals involved in poetry and to promote a widespread knowledge of European languages and ideas. European music and poetry competitions are held triennially.

1122
European Association of Radiology
(Association Europeenne de Radiologie)
Dept. of Radiology
Univ. Hospitals
Herestraat 49   Phone: 16 213770
B-3000 Louvain, Belgium   Fax: 16 213769

1123
Medaille Boris Rajewsky
For recognition of scientific or professional contributions to European radiology. A medal is awarded annually. In addition, the Diplome d'Honneur de l'A.E.R. is awarded.

1124
European Chamber for the Development of Trade, Industry, and Finances
(Chambre Europeenne pour le Developpement du Commerce, de l'Industrie, et des Finances)
Ave. des Arts, 18 boite 2
B-1040 Brussels, Belgium   Phone: 2 2171959

1125
Artiste Europeen Prize
To recognize and improve contact between business people and others who make a professional contribution to European prosperity. The Artiste Europeen prize is awarded along with other medals and plaques.

1126
European Confederation of Agriculture
(Confederation Europeenne de l'Agriculture)
rue de la Science 23125
Boite 23
B-1040 Brussels, Belgium   Phone: 56 413177

1127
Awards
For recognition in the field of agriculture. Competitions are held and awards are presented.

[1128]
European Council of Chemical Manufacturers Federations
(Conseil Europeen des Federations de l'Industrie Chimique)
Avenue Louise 250, Bte 71   Phone: 2 640 20 95
B-1050 Brussels, Belgium   Fax: 2 640 19 81

[1129]
CEFIC Environment Award
To recognize an outstanding innovation that enables the chemical industry to help solve an environmental problem. Entries are accepted from individual persons or groups until the closing date of January 8. A monetary prize of 25,000 ECU is awarded biennially in March. Established in 1987.

[1130]
European Direct Marketing Association
36, rue du Gouvernement Provisoire   Phone: 2 2176309
B-1000 Brussels, Belgium   Fax: 2 2176985

[1131]
Best of Europe - International Direct Marketing Awards
(Concours International de campagnes de Marketing Direct)
For recognition of the best direct marketing campaigns in Europe. Awards are given in the following categories: consumer products, consumer services, business-to-business, non-profit, and multinational campaigns. Gold, silver, and bronze prizes, special awards, and letters of distinction are awarded annually. Established in 1976. Additional information is available from Isabelle Van Durme.

[1132]
European Disposables and Nonwovens Association
51, ave. des Cerisiers   Phone: 2 7349310
B-1040 Brussels, Belgium   Fax: 2 7333518

[1133]
European Disposables and Nonwovens Association Awards
To recognize manufacturers and converters of nonwoven fabrics used in medicine and industry. The Association bestows awards at the triennial congress.

[1134]
European Ophthalmological Society
(Societas Ophthalmologica Europaea)
c/o Professor L. Missotten
U.Z. St. Rafael
Dept. of Ophthalmology
Kapucijnenvoer, 33   Phone: 16 332398
B-3000 Leuven, Belgium   Fax: 16 332367

[1135]
Charamis Medal
To recognize a European ophthalmologist who has most contributed in the field of ophthalmic surgery to the development and the fame of European ophthalmology. A medal is awarded every four years. Established in 1974 in memory of Professor J. Charamis, founder of the Hellenic Ophthalmological Society.

[1136]
Helmholtz Medal
To recognize the European ophthalmologist who has done the most for the Society and for ophthalmology. A gold medal is awarded every four years. Established in 1971 in honor of Helmholtz, a German ophthalmologist known for his scientific work on color vision, and the inventor of the ophthalmoscope.

[1137]
European Society for Comparative Physiology and Biochemistry
Laboratory of Animal Physiology
Univ. of Liege
22, quai van Beneden   Phone: 41 665046
B-4020 Liege, Belgium   Fax: 41 665020

[1138]
ESCPB Young Scientists Awards
To encourage the participation of young scientists at the annual ESCPB Conferences. Scientists who do not hold Ph.D.'s are eligible to submit an application and abstract for an oral presentation or a poster. Applications are examined by a scientific committee. A monetary award, a free one-year Society membership, and free registration at the annual conference are awarded annually to five individuals. Established in 1988.

[1139]
European Society for Therapeutic Radiology and Oncology
Dept. of Radiotherapy
Univ. Hospital St. Rafael
Capucijnenvoer 33   Phone: 16 21 22 13
B-3000 Louvain, Belgium   Fax: 16 21 22 28

[1140]
Awards
For recognition of contributions to improve the standards of cancer treatment.

[1141]
European Society of Regional Anaesthesia
Kempenlaan 12   Phone: 14 422773
B-2300 Turnhout, Belgium   Fax: 14 439284

[1142]
Karl Koller Gold Medal
For recognition of achievement in regional anaesthesia. Individuals who have made outstanding contributions must be nominated. A medal is awarded annually when merited. Established in 1983 in memory of Karl Koller who first applied cocaine in humans for topical anaesthesia.

[1143]
European Sports Press Union
(Union Europeenne de la Presse Sportive)
153, Herdebeek   Phone: 2 5691223
B-1701 Itterbeek-Brussels, Belgium   Fax: 2 7344018

[1144]
European Sportsman and Sportswoman of the Year
(Sportive et Sportif Europeen de l'Annee)
To honor the best male and female European athlete of the year. A trophy is awarded annually. Established in 1983.

[1145]
European Union of Jewish Students
(Union Europeene des Etudiants Juifs)
89 chaussee de Vleurgat   Phone: 2 6477279
B-1050 Brussels, Belgium   Fax: 2 6482431

[1146]
Honorary Life Member
For recognition of a contribution towards improving the environment to enable Jewish students to flourish and for contributions to the Union. Selection is by nomination. A certificate is awarded biennially at the Congress. Established in 1984.

1147
Faculte Polytechnique de Mons
c/o Chef du Service Comptabilite
9, rue de Houdain
B-7000 Mons, Belgium
Phone: 65 37 41 11
Phone: 65 37 40 15
Fax: 65 37 42 00

1148
Maurice Lefranc Scholarships
To provide opportunities for young engineers wishing to perfect their experience in a foreign university. The Directory Council makes the selection. A monetary prize of 300,000 Belgian francs is awarded annually. Established in 1959 by a bequest of Maurice Lefranc.

1149
Federation of European Aerosol Associations
(Federation Europeenne des Associations Aerosols)
49, Square Marie-louise
B-1040 Brussels, Belgium
Phone: 2 2389711
Fax: 2 2308288

1150
Erik Rotheim Medal
For recognition of achievement by Board Members. A medal is awarded at the end of the member's term. Established in 1984 by Robin Hearn in honor of Erik Rotheim, who invented the aerosol.

1151
Flanders Festival Bruges
(Festival van Vlaanderen - Brugge)
Internationale Muziekdagen
Collaert Mansionstraat 30
B-8000 Bruges, Belgium
Phone: 50 332283
Fax: 50 345204

1152
Early Music Festival - Bruges
(Internationale Muziekdagen - Brugge)
To encourage professional development in the field of early music and for recognition of the best musical performance in one of the following musical categories: solo singing; melody instruments, lute and ensembles (Middle Ages and Renaissance); organ; and harpsichord. In 1994, the International Organ Competitions will feature a competition for soloists, "The Baroque in Europe", with a first prize of at least 750,000 Belgian francs and a competition for two chamber organs with a first prize of at least 750,000 Belgian francs. In 1996, the Musica Antiqua Competition Bruges is featured with the following categories: solo singing, melody instruments, lute (first prize 100,000 Belgian francs), and ensembles (Middle Ages, up to 1800). First prize in most categories is 150,000 Belgian francs. In 1995, the Harpsichord and Fortepiano Competitions have first prizes of 150,000 Belgian francs and 100,000 Belgian francs, respectively. Awarded annually. Established in 1964.

1153
Foundation Europalia International
10, Rue Royale
B-1000 Brussels, Belgium
Phone: 2 5078550
Fax: 2 5135488

Formerly: (1991) Europalia.

1154
Europalia Literary Prize of the European Community
To recognize an author for excellence of a life's work. Living authors whose works reflect their national culture while having a universal appeal are eligible. The nominee must be a citizen of the country that is invited by Europalia to show its culture in Belgium. A monetary award of $500 Belgian francs (paid out in European Ecus) is presented biennially in October. Established in 1977.

1155
Francqui Foundation
(Fondation Francqui)
rue d'Egmont, 11
B-1050 Brussels, Belgium
Phone: 2 511 81 00
Fax: 2 513 64 11

1156
Francqui Prize
(Prix Francqui)
To recognize a Belgian scholar who has contributed to the prestige of Belgium. Awards are given in alternate years in the following categories: mathematics, physics, or chemistry; social sciences; and natural and medical sciences. Candidates under 50 years of age may be nominated by a former prize winner or two members of a Belgian Academy. A monetary prize of 3,000,000 Belgian francs is awarded annually. Established in 1932.

1157
Front de l'Independence
14, rue Van Lint
B-01070 Brussels, Belgium
Phone: 2 5224041

1158
Front de l'Independence Awards
To recognize individuals who fight against all racial, political, philosophical and religious discrimination. Awards are presented annually.

1159
Huy - World Festival of Movies of Short Films
(Festival Mondial du Cinema de Court Metrages de Huy)
5, rue Nokin
B-4520 Huy, Belgium
Phone: 85 217829
Fax: 85 231077

1160
Huy - World Festival of Movies of Short Films Awards
For recognition of outstanding short films in the following categories: fiction, documentary, travel, animation, and genre films by amateur film makers; and films by independent film makers. Gold, silver, and bronze medals are awarded to the best films in each of the amateur and independent categories. In addition, the following awards are presented: Le Cwerneu d'Or - for the best amateur film; Le Coq-Joli - for the best independent film; City of Huy Prize - for the best actor; and Prix Radio Bassinia - for the best work of the fantastic. Awarded annually. Established in 1961. Sponsored by the Belgian Government.

1161
Imagin'Art, Brussels International Art and Archaeology Film Festival
(Imagin'Art, Festival International du Film d'Art et d'Archeologie de Bruxelles)
Address unknown.

1162
Brussels International Art and Archeaology Film Festival
(Festival International du Film d'Art et d'Archeologie de Bruxelles)
For recognition of achievement in a film production concerning art and archaeology. Films in all artistic fields - graphic and plastic arts (engraving, drawing, painting, sculpture, comic strips, performances), architecture, music, dance, photography - at all periods and throughout the world; and on all archaeological subjects, from prehistory to the industrial era, throughout the world, are considered. Films of all categories (news, documentary, fiction, animation, research, education), produced by any private or public body, may enter the competition. Formats may be 16/35 mm film, U-Matic 3/4, PL, SECAM, and NTSC Video. A trophy and diploma are awarded for each of the following prizes: (1) Grand Prix; (2) Jury's Special Prize (optional); (3) Prize for the Best Archaeology and Technology Film; (4) Prize for the Best Art Film; (5) Prize for the Best Educational Film; (6) Prize for the Best Commentary; (7) Prize for the Best Soundtrack;

(8) Prize for the Best Picture; and (9) Public's Prize. Awarded triennially. Established in 1980 by Cercle d'Histoire de l'Art et d'Archeologie de l'Universite Libre de Bruxelles.

1163

Interallied Confederation of Reserve Officers
(Confederation Interalliee des Officiers de Reserve)
Bureau de Liaison CIOR
NATO 2055
B-1110 Brussels, Belgium   Phone: 2 7285296

1164

H.R.H. Prince Peter Award
For recognition of a contribution to the aims of the Confederation. A medal is awarded at the convention. Established in 1982 in memory of His Royal Highness Prince Peter of Greece and Denmark, President of CIOR 1962-1964.

1165

International Association for Physical Education in Higher Education
(Association Internationale des Ecoles Superieures d'Education Physique)
Institut Superieur d'Education Physique
Universite de Liege au Sart Tilman, Bat 1   Phone: 41 563890
B-4000 Liege, Belgium   Fax: 41 224108

1166

International Jose Maria Cagigal Award in Physical Education
(Premio Internacional de Educacion Fisica Jose Maria Cagigal)
To encourage professional development and to recognize outstanding essays in the field of physical education. Original papers may be submitted by individuals of any nationality. A monetary prize of approximately $7,000 US is awarded annually. Established in 1985 in memory of Jose Maria Cagigal who was killed in a plane crash in 1983.

1167

International Biennial of Lace-Making - D.B.K. asbl.
Avenue du Domaine 149, bte 8
B-1000 Brussels, Belgium   Phone: 2 344 88 11

1168

Queen Fabiola Prize
To honor lace-makers whose work reflects both complete mastery of the craft and new forms of artistic expression. Individuals exhibiting at the International Biennial of Lace Making are eligible. Her Majesty Queen Fabiola awards the Queen Fabiola Prize of 150,000 Belgian francs at the opening of the exhibition of laces selected for display and awards. The Golden Bobbin, Silver Bobbin, and Bronze Bobbin awards are also awarded at the start of the exhibition. Established in 1983.

1169

International Biennials of Poetry
(Biennales Internationales de Poesie)
SABAM
75-77 rue d'Arlon   Phone: 2 2302660
B-1040 Brussels, Belgium   Fax: 2 2311800

1170

Grand Prix des Biennales Internationales de Poesie
To recognize living poets of any nationality whose works have significantly influenced world poetry. A monetary prize of 100,000 Belgian francs is awarded biennially. Established in 1951 by the International House of Poetry. Sponsored by SABAM (Societe Belge des Auteurs, Compositeurs et Editeurs).

1171

International Catholic Organization for Cinema and Audiovisual
(Organisation Catholique Internationale du Cinema et de l'Audiovisuel)
rue de l'Orme, 8   Phone: 2 734 42 94
B-1040 Brussels, Belgium   Fax: 2 734 32 07

1172

Ecumenical Prize
For recognition of films from any country that promotes human and spiritual values. A bronze medal is awarded at film festivals throughout the world, such as Cannes, Locarno, Montreal, Moscow, San Sebastian, and others. Established in 1974.

1173

OCIC-Prize
To encourage the circulation, promotion, and production of valuable films promoting human and spiritual values. Films presented at film festivals throughout the world where the OCIC has a panel of judges are eligible. A trophy representing a sail craft is awarded at the Festivals such as Berlin, Ouagadougou, Troia, Cartagena, Venice, Carthage, Rio, Havana, and others. Established in 1947.

1174

International Commission for Scientific Religious Psychology
(Commission Internationale de Psychologie Religieuse Scientifique)
186, rue Washington
B-1050 Brussels, Belgium   Phone: 2 343 50 23

1175

Quinquennial Award in the Psychology of Religion
(Prix Quinquennal de Psychologie Religieuse Scientifique)
For recognition of an outstanding contribution to scientific research into the psychology of religion. Books and manuscripts may be nominated by members of the International Commission. A monetary award of $1,000 US and promotion through official reports or other publications are awarded every fifth year. Established in 1965 by Lumen Vitae International Center.

1176

International Commission of Agricultural Engineering
(Commission Internationale du Genie Rural)
Agricultural Engineering Research Sta.
Van Gansberghelaan 115   Phone: 9 2521821
B-9820 Merelbeke, Belgium   Fax: 9 2524234

1177

Armand Blanc Prize
(Prix Armand Blanc)
To recognize the best paper presented at CIGR Congresses by a young student or agricultural engineer. Citizens of CIGR member countries who are not more than 30 years of age may submit papers on a topic dealing with the Congresses' program. A medal and expenses are awarded every five years on the occasion of each CIRG Congress. Established in 1964 to honor Armand Blanc, Honorary General Director of Agricultural Engineering and Hydraulics, founder-member and former President of CIGR.

1178

International Committee for the Defense of the Breton Language
(Comite International pour la Sauveguarde de la Langue Bretonne)
Lenoirstraat 13   Phone: 2 428 5614
B-1090 Brussels, Belgium   Fax: 2 2410452

1179
CISLB Awards
For recognition of efforts to promote the use of the Breton language in schools, radio, television, and civil services. Awarded irregularly.

1180
International Committee of Military Medicine
(Comite International de Medecine Militaire)
Hopital Militaire
rue Saint-Laurent, 79   Phone: 41 222183
B-4000 Liege, Belgium   Fax: 41 222150

Formerly: (1991) International Committee of Military Medicine and Pharmacy.

1181
Prix Jules Voncken
For recognition of the best study paper or report submitted describing work of an innovative nature that has been performed in the medical, legal, or diplomatic fields, and is likely to improve the organization and provision of aid to victims of armed conflicts; contribute to the adoption of humanitarian principles; facilitate the organization and improve the efficiency of humanitarian missions of rescue and relief; and develop the spirit a of professional confraternity between the medical services of the armed forces of different countries at the international level. Members or former members of the medical services of the armed forces are eligible, but any person or organization whose activity is in keeping with the objectives of the committee is considered. A monetary prize of 100,000 Belgian francs is awarded every four years. Established in 1973 in honor of General Jules Voncken, MC, founder and secretary general of the International Committee from 1921 to 1975.

1182
International Diabetes Federation
(Federation Internationale du Diabete)
40, rue Washington   Phone: 2 6474414
B-1050 Brussels, Belgium   Fax: 2 6408565

1183
Educational Foundation Grant
To provide education and training of health care professionals in the field of practical care and management of diabetes mellitus. Applications must be submitted. A monetary award for travel to a training center is awarded annually. The IDF Education Foundation was formally established in 1992.

1184
International Federation of Oto-Rhino-Laryngological Societies
IFOS/MISA/NKO
Oosterveldlaan 24   Phone: 3 4433611
B-2610 Wilrijk, Belgium   Fax: 3 4433611

1185
IFOS Golden Award
For recognition of special services rendered to the Federation. A medal is awarded occasionally. Established in 1985.

1186
IFOS Thanking Award
To recognize individuals who have served as IFOS officers. Awarded every four years at the World Congress. Established in 1985.

1187
World Film Festival of ORL Scientific Films and Videotapes
To recognize outstanding ORL scientific films and videotapes during the World Congress of ORL. Prizes are awarded in the following categories: (1) Scientific - Gold Medal, Silver Medal, and Bronze Medal; (2) Surgical - Gold Medal, Silver Medal, and Bronze Medal; (3) Professional Education - Gold Medal, Silver Medal, and Bronze Medal; (4) Public Education - established by the Founder-Chairman Prof. J. Marquet in 1985; and (5) Otology Politzer Society Award - established in 1985. Awarded every four years. The Festival was established in 1977.

1188
International Federation of Photographic Art - Kodak Award
(Federation Internationale de l'Art Photographique - Prix Kodak)
Heindriesstraat 14
PO Box 3   Phone: 91 223395
B-9052 Ghent, Belgium   Fax: 91 646699

1189
FIAP Kodak Award
For recognition of creativity in art photography. There was a local competition in each participating country. The winning prints or slides from each country were entered for the International FIAP Kodak Award given during the following year. The following prizes were awarded: (1) First prize - $1,000 equivalent of Kodak products, a gold medal and an invitation to attend the FIAP Congress and the International FIAP Kodak Award exhibition in the Netherlands (including travel costs and accommodation for 4 nights); (2) Second prize - $750 equivalent of Kodak products, and a silver medal; (3) Third prize - $500 equivalent of Kodak products, and a silver medal; (4) Fourth prize - $250 equivalent of Kodak products, and a bronze medal; and (5) Fifth prize - $100 equivalent of Kodak products and a bronze medal. Awarded biennially. Established in 1990. Sponsored by Eastman Kodak Company (European Division, London). (Discontinued)

1190
International Festival of Economics and Training Films
(Festival International du Film Economique et de Formation)
48 av. F.D. Roosevelt   Phone: 2 6422502
B-1050 Brussels, Belgium   Fax: 2 6419346

1191
International Festival of Economics and Training Films
To acquaint both business people and lecturers with the audio-visual medium as an aid for training and teaching, particularly inside companies, and to encourage the production and circulation of economics and training films. Any film dealing with business/industry, education, or safety/training is accepted. Categories include: Image & Promotion, Safety, Sales Techniques, and Internal Communication. Formats must be VHS and U-Matic (PAL, SECAM, and NTSC). The Mercure d'Argent trophy is awarded for the Grand Prize, and the Mercure de Bronze for winners in various categories. Awarded biennially in October. Established in 1979. Organized by the students of the Solvay Business School, Free University of Brussels.

1192
International Flanders Film Festival - Ghent
(Internationaal Filmgebeuren van Vlaanderen - Gent)
1104 Kortrijkse Steenweg   Phone: 9 221 89 46
B-9051 Ghent, Belgium   Fax: 9 221 90 74

1193
Impact of Music on Film Competition
(Competitie de Impact van Muziek op Film)
For recognition of achievement in incorporating music into film. Non-musical fiction films are eligible. Awards are given for best film and best music. Selection is by the festival organizing committee. A monetary prize of $20,000 US for first prize is awarded annually. Established in 1985 by the International Film Festival of Flanders - Ghent. Sponsored by the City of Ghent, the Ministry of Flemish Culture, the Ministry of Economic Affairs, and many private sponsors.

1194
Joseph Plateau Prize
(Joseph Plateauprijzen)
For recognition of a Belgian filmmmaker's contributions to the development of national cinema. Awards are given in the following categories: Best Belgian Film; Best Belgian Director; Best Actor in a Belgian Film; Best Actress in a Belgian Film; Best Belgian Television Film; Joseph Plateau Life Achievement Award (International Award); Joseph Plateau Music Award (International Award); and Joseph Plateau Audience Award (Best Box-Office of a Belgian Film). A trophy resembling Plateau's device is awarded annually. Established in 1985 in honor of Joseph Plateau, a Belgian physicist who discovered the principle of the eye's inertia and who invented the phenakistoscope by which the illusion of motion could be created. In 1992, the Ghent and Antwerp Film festivals have joined forces to form a new organization, the International Film Festivals Foundation.

1195
International Jacques Brel Foundation
(Fondation Internationale Jacques Brel)
44, boulevard du Jardin Botanique, boite 12
B-1000 Brussels, Belgium
Phone: 2 218 26 75
Fax: 2 2102613

1196
Awards
To recognize poets, musicians, and stage and screen artists; and to foster appreciation of Brel and his works and to encourage study of his life and art. A Hall of Fame is also maintained.

1197
International Naturist Federation
(Federation Naturiste Internationale)
Sint Hubertusstraat 3
B-2600 Antwerp, Belgium
Phone: 3 2300572
Fax: 3 2812607

1198
INF-Press Prize
(INF-Presse Preis)
To encourage the publication of articles on naturism in the non-naturist press and media. Articles published in a non-naturist daily paper or magazine are considered. A monetary award is presented annually. Established in 1973.

1199
International Pharmaceutical Zambon
Avenue Vandendriessche 18/B-1
B-1150 Brussels, Belgium
Phone: 2 7719936
Fax: 2 7718570

1200
Prix G. Zambon
For recognition of a scientific work that makes an original contribution to human and animal pharmacology. The work may be written in French, Dutch, English, or German. Eligible authors who are 45 years of age or younger must be Belgian citizens or associated with a Belgian university. A monetary prize of 500,000 Belgian francs is awarded biennially. Established in 1975.

1201
International Society for Human and Animal Mycology
Laboratory for Mycology
Institute of Tropical Medicine
Nationalestraat 155
B-2000 Antwerp, Belgium
Phone: 3 2476335
Fax: 3 2161431

1202
ISHAM Lucille K. Georg Award
For recognition of achievement in medical and veterinary mycology. Members of the Society may be nominated by a specially appointed Awards Committee. Monetary awards and a medallion are awarded every three or four years at the Society Congress. Established in 1964 in honor of Dr. Lucille K. Georg, formerly at the Center for Disease Control, in Atlanta, Georgia, U.S.A.

1203
International Society for Military Law and Law of War
(Societe Internationale de Droit Penal Militaire et de Droit de la Guerre)
c/o Auditorat Gen. pres de la Cour
Militaire
Palais de Justice
B-1000 Brussels, Belgium
Phone: 2 5086611
Fax: 2 5086085

1204
Fondazione Professor Giuseppe Ciardi
To recognize a study of military law and law of war. Awarded triennially. Established in 1970.

1205
International Society for Research on Civilization Diseases and Environment
(Societe Internationale pour la Recherche sur les Maladies de Civilisation et l'Environnement)
1, place Luxembourg
BP 19
B-1040 Brussels, Belgium
Phone: 3 230 92 32
Fax: 3 230 16 44

1206
Competitions
The Society sponsors competitions for recognition of research on solving problems connected with the protection of the environment, the ills of modern civilization which threaten the health of humanity, and the harm suffered by man.

1207
International Society of Psychoneuroendocrinology
Neuroendocrinology Section, CHU B 23
University of Liege
Sart Tilman
B-4000 Liege, Belgium
Phone: 41 56 25 37
Fax: 41 30 72 61

1208
Kurt P. Richter Prize
To recognize an outstanding paper on psychoneuroendocrinology. Manuscripts may be submitted by January 31 by authors under 40 years of age. An honorarium of US $1,000 and a travel grant of up to US $1,000 to attend the International Congress are awarded annually. The winning paper is considered for publication in the Journal *Psychoneuroendocrinology*. Established in 1979 to honor Curt Richter. Sponsored by Pergamon Press. Additional information is available from Dr. Robert Rubin, Department of Psychiatry, Harbor UCLA Medical Center, Torrance, CA 90509 U.S.A.

1209
International Union of Radio Science
(Union Radio Scientifique Internationale)
Univ. of Ghent
Sint-Pietersnieuwstraat 41
B-9000 Ghent, Belgium
Phone: 92 643320
Fax: 92 643593

Belgium

1210
Appleton Prize
To recognize contributions to studies in ionospheric physics. Established in 1967 and administered by the Royal Society of London.

1211
John Howard Dellinger Gold Medal
For recognition of outstanding work in radio science, preferably in radio wave propagation. Work must have been carried out during the six-year period preceding the year of the URSI General Assembly at which the medal is presented. A medal is awarded triennialy at the URSI General Assembly. Established in 1966 by the United States Member Committee of URSI in honor of Professor John Howard Dellinger, Honorary President of URSI. Administered by the U.S. Member Committee of URSI, c/o the National Academy of Sciences, Washington, D.C. 20418.

1212
Issac Koga Gold Medal
For recognition of outstanding work in radio science carried out by a young scientist. Candidates must be 35 years of age or younger and the work must have been carried out during the six-year period preceding the year of the URSI General Assembly at which the medal is presented. A medal is awarded triennially at the URSI General Assembly. Established in 1984 by the URSI Member Committee in Japan in honor of Professor Issac Koga, Honorary President of URSI. Administered by the URSI Member Committee in Japan, c/o the Science Council, Tokyo, Japan.

1213
Balthasar van der Pol Gold Medal
For recognition of outstanding work in radio science. Work must have been carried out in the six-year period preceding the year of the General Assembly at which the Medal is awarded. A medal with an effigy of Professor van der Pol is awarded every three years and presented on the occasion of the General Assembly. Established in 1963 in memory of Professor Balthasar van der Pol, Honorary President of the Union, by his widow, Mrs. P. Le Corbeiller-Posthuma.

1214
International Voice Competition of Verviers
(Concours International de Chant de Verviers)
Opera Royal de Wallonie
1, rue des Dominicains
B-4000 Liege, Belgium
Phone: 41 23 59 10
Fax: 41 21 01 01

1215
Concours International de Chant Lyrique de Verviers
For recognition of outstanding lyric artists - opera and comic opera. Lyric artists of all nationalities, women 18-30 years of age, and men 18-35 years of age are eligible. The following prizes are awarded: (1) Grand Prix - 200,000 Belgian francs; (2) First prize for both men and women - 125,000 Belgian francs each; (3) Second prize for both men and women - 75,500 Belgian francs each; (4) Third prize for both men and women - 50,000 Belgian francs each; (5) Four prizes for both men and women - 25,000 Belgian francs; and (6) One Special Prize, the Vocation Award of 200,000 Belgian francs to a finalist who is a member of the Communaute francaise de Belgique to study with a voice professor. Awarded biennially. Established in 1975 by the Opera Royal de Wallonie. Sponsored by A.S.B.L. Concours International de Chant.

1216
King Baudouin Foundation
(Fondation Roi Baudouin)
Rue Brederode 21
B-1000 Brussels, Belgium
Phone: 2 511 18 40
Fax: 2 511 52 21

1217
King Baudouin International Development Prize
To recognize persons or organizations, without regard to national origin, who have made a substantial contribution to the development of the Third World or towards the cooperation and good relations between industrialized and developing countries, and among their peoples. Particular importance is attached to activities having a multiplier effect and those which make it possible for the populations of the Third World to provide for themselves by their own development. Individuals or organizations may be nominated. A monetary prize of 4,000,000 Belgian francs is awarded biennially. Established in 1980.

1218
League of Families
(Ligue des Familles)
127, rue du Trone
B-1050 Brussels, Belgium
Phone: 2 5131960

1219
Prix Bernard Versele
To encourage reading among children and to promote books of high literary, artistic, and educational value, not necessarily those best known on the market. Books are pre-selected by specialists in literature from those written in French and published during the preceding year. About 30,000 children from 3 to 12 years of age vote for the best liked children's books. Awards are given for books for children in the following age categories: 3-5 years, 5-8 years, 8-10 years, 10-12 years, and 12-14 years. Four monetary prizes of 20,000 Belgian francs each are awarded annually at the end of June. Established in 1979 in memory of Bernard Versele, a young psychologist, who dedicated his professional life to children.

1220
Prix Van Der Beeken
To encourage any scientific research or any action program aimed at the revival of the French-speaking community in Belgium. (Discontinued)

1221
Libertarian Center Netherlands
(Libertarisch Centrum)
PO Box 21
Essen, Belgium
Phone: 1654 1695

1222
Benelux Libertarian Award
For recognition of contributions to libertarianism. Selection is by nomination. A plaque is awarded annually. Established in 1982.

1223
Mechelen Festival
(Festival van Mechelen)
c/o Koninklijke Mechelse Fotokring
Auwegemvaart 79
B-2800 Mechelen, Belgium
Phone: 15 202430

1224
International Diaporama Festival
(Festival International de Diaporamas)
For recognition of outstanding audio-visuals (slide series with sound). Diaporamas are works that join to the beauty of the form a valid content, story, song, information, music, illustration, message, etc. The deadline for entries is February 22. A Grand Prize of the City of Mechelen is awarded for the overall winner. Awarded biennially. Established in 1966.

1225
National Housing Institute
(Institut National du Logement)
Address unknown.

1226
Economics Prize
For recognition of outstanding studies, one in French and one in Dutch, about the economic aspects of housing. It is open to Belgian nationals who, when submitting their text, have a University degree. Non-Belgians may also compete, on the same conditions, if they hold a Belgian degree. Two monetary prizes of 75,000 Belgian francs for the best study written in French and 75,000 Belgian francs for the best study written in Dutch are awarded every four years.

1227
International Prize for Architecture of the National Housing Institute
(Prix International Architecture de l'Institut National du Logement)
To recognize a practicing architect of a European Economic Community member country whose design best incorporates progressive ideas of housing. Awards are presented in the following categories: (1) single-family house or an apartment building, taking into consideration the qualities presented by the design and which comply, notably, with present considerations concerning aesthetic appeal, disposition and equipment of the premises, acoustic and thermal insulation, choice and use of materials as well as cost price; and (2) a complex of single-family houses, a complex of apartment buildings, or a mixed complex of single-family houses and apartment buildings, as far as its conception is liable to bring about progress with respect to rational use of land, the layout and aesthetics of the buildings, the layout of roads and pedestrian paths, private or community open spaces, and playgrounds as well as other community facilities. The aforesaid complex must both preserve the intimacy of the inhabitants' private lives and favor the development of social relations among them. Two monetary prizes of 200,000 Belgian francs each and diplomas are awarded annually. Established in 1960.

1228
Law Prize
For recognition of outstanding studies, one in French and one in Dutch, about the legal aspects of housing. It is open to Belgian nationals and to de facto or legal Belgian associations who, when submitting their text, hold a University degree in law. If the study is submitted by an association, one of its members at least must hold the above-mentioned degree. The Prize is open also to non-Belgians and on the same conditions, if they have a Belgian degree. Two monetary prizes of 75,000 Belgian francs for the best study written in French and 75,000 Belgian francs for the best study written in Dutch are awarded every four years.

1229
Sociology Prize
For recognition of outstanding studies, one in French and one in Dutch, about the sociological aspects of housing. It is open to Belgian nationals as well as to de facto or legal Belgian associations who, when submitting their text, have a final diploma in sociology, social studies or political and social sciences. If the study is submitted by an association, at least one of its members must have a degree in one of the above-mentioned fields. The Prize is open also to non-Belgians and on the same conditions, if they have a Belgian diploma. Two monetary prizes of 75,000 Belgian francs for the best study written in French and 75,000 Belgian francs for the best study written in Dutch are awarded every four years.

1230
New Foundation A Blomme
Hortensiastraat 7
B-8800 Roeselare, Belgium   Phone: 51 211989

1231
Grote Prys Alfons Blomme
To recognize and encourage young artists. Painters, as well as other artists are eligible. Individuals who are at least 21 years of age in January of the award year are eligible. A monetary award of 100,000 Belgian francs and a diploma are awarded biennially. Established in 1978 to honor Alfons Blomme, a painter who founded a museum for paintings and granted it in his will to the town of Roeselare.

1232
North Atlantic Treaty Alliance - Brussels
(Organisation du Traite de l'Atlantique Nord - Bruxelles)
B-1110 Brussels, Belgium
Phone: 2 2410040
Fax: 2 7284579

1233
Atlantic Award
(Prix Atlantique)
To recognize a citizen of a NATO member nation who has made an outstanding contribution to the further development of peaceful and friendly international relations by strengthening member nations' free institutions, bringing about a better understanding of the principles upon which these institutions are founded, promoting conditions of stability and well-being, elimination of conflict in member nations' international economic policies, and encouraging economic collaboration between member nations. Candidates are nominated by their governments. Belgium, Canada, Denmark, France, Federal Republic of Germany, Greece, Iceland, Italy, Luxembourg, Netherlands, Norway, Portugal, Spain, Turkey, United Kingdom, and the United States establish their nominating procedures and forward national nominees, ranked in priority order, to the NATO Director of Information by July 1 supported by written material. An international Atlantic Award Selection Committee chooses and notifies the award winner by early October. A monetary award of 300,000 Belgian francs (currently about US $7,500) is presented annually by the Secretary General of the North Atlantic Treaty Organization in November. The grantee is invited to deliver a formal lecture on a theme to be agreed upon with the Organization, both in Brussels at the time of the presentation of the award and in his or her home country. Established in 1984.

1234
Pax Christi International
Plantijnen Moretuslei 174
B-2018 Antwerp, Belgium
Phone: 3 2353640
Fax: 3 2350748

1235
Peace Award
To recognize individuals who: (1) work for peace while bearing witness to the peace of Christ; (2) contribute to a more humane world, with respect for the life of each human being; (3) collaborate with other Christian groups and peace movements; and (4) struggle against sources of injustice such as violence, war, hatred, and economic inequality. The Peace Award is presented at the biennial council.

1236
Pax Mundi, Diplomatic Academy of Peace
(Academie Diplomatique de la Paix, Pax Mundi)
Address unknown.

1237
International Dag Hammarskjold Award
(Prix Internationaux Dag Hammarskjold)
To recognize outstanding contributions in the following fields: (1) peace, cooperation and international solidarity (reserved to Heads of State or of government); (2) literature; (3) science; (4) performing arts; (5) journalism; (6) diplomacy; and (7) human solidarity. A gold medal and plaque are awarded in each category annually. Established in 1963 in collaboration with the World Organization of Diplomatic Correspondents and the World Organization of Diplomatic Cooperation in memory of Dag Hammarskjold, former Secretary-General of the United Nations and Nobel Peace Prize winner in 1961.

1238
Permanent International Association of Navigation Congresses
Gen. Sec.
WTC-Tour 3, 26e etage
30, boulevard Simon Bolivar
B-1210 Brussels, Belgium
Phone: 2 212 52 16
Phone: 2 212 52 18
Fax: 2 212 52 15

1239
Gustave Willems Prize
To encourage young engineers, research workers, and others to pursue studies in the fields of interest to the Association and to submit articles on these subjects suitable for publication in the *PIANC Bulletin*. Members of PIANC or individuals sponsored by a member who are under the age of 35 may submit articles and application forms to the General Secretariat of PIANC before December 31 of the year preceding the awarding of the prize. A monetary award (amount determined each year), a five-year membership, and an invitation to present the paper at the Annual Meeting are awarded annually at the General Assembly. Established in 1984 in memory of Professor Gustave Willems, President of PIANC from 1956 until his death in 1982.

1240
Peymey Diffusion
144 Avenue de la Reine
B-1210 Brussels, Belgium
Phone: 2 2421713
Fax: 2 2162169

1241
Brussels International Festival of Fantasy Thriller and Science-Fiction Films
(Festival International du Film Fantastique, de Science-Fiction, et Thriller de Bruxelles)
For recognition of outstanding fantasy and science fiction films. The following prizes are awarded: LaCorbeau Grand Prix - a monetary prize of $6,000 and a sculpture of Joseph Henrion; Prix des Televisions Europeen (short); Prix du Public du Meilleur Court-Metrage Europeen (short); two Prix Special du Jury Sculptures; and Le Pegase Prize of the Audience- a sculpture of Daniel Monic. Awarded annually. Established in 1984. A Make-up Competition is also held. First, second, and third prizes are given for amateur, semi- professional, and monster categories.

1242
Province of Antwerp/Eugene Baie Foundation
(Provinciebestuur van Antwerpen/Eugene Baiecomite)
Koningin Elisabethlei 22
B-2018 Antwerp, Belgium
Phone: 3 2405011
Fax: 3 2406470

1243
Internationale Eugene Baieprijs
For recognition of published work on Flemish civilization, culture, or art of the past, including works on Flemish influence abroad. Foreign (non-Belgian) authors writing in their own language are eligible. The winner is nominated by a five member jury. A monetary prize of 100,000 Belgian francs, a medal, and a charter are awarded every five years. Established in 1946 by Eugene Baie.

1244
Queen Elisabeth International Music Competition of Belgium
(Concours Musical International Reine Elisabeth de Belgique)
20, rue aux Laines
B-1000 Brussels, Belgium
Phone: 2 5130099
Fax: 2 5143297

1245
Queen Elisabeth International Music Competition of Belgium Prizes
For recognition of the best performances on piano, violin, singing, and occasionally for composition. In 1996, the competition features singing, violin, and compositions and in 1995, piano. Pianists and violinists must be 31 years of age or under to compete. The deadline for application is January 15. Monetary prizes totaling over 3,200,000 Belgian francs and diplomas are awarded for piano, violin, and voice. A monetary award of 200,000 Belgian francs is presented for composition. Award winners are also given the opportunity for concerts, recitals, and recordings. Awarded every four years for each discipline. Established in 1951.

1246
S. A. Rossel & Cie
Journal *Le Soir*
Place de Louvain 21
B-1000 Brussels, Belgium
Phone: 2 217 77 50

1247
Prix Victor Rossel
For recognition of an outstanding novel or collection of short stories written in French by a Belgian citizen. Works published during the preceding twelve months are considered. A monetary prize of 200,000 Belgian francs is awarded annually in November. Established in 1938 by M. Th. Rossel, managing editor of Rossel & Cie; M. Lucien Fuss, director of *Le Soir*; and M. Charles Breisdorff, Chief editor, in memory of Victor Rossel, the son of the founder of *Le Soir*.

1248
Royal Academy for Sciences, Letters and Fine Arts of Belgium
(Koninklijke Academie voor Wetenschappen, Letteren en Schone Kunsten Van Belgie)
Paleis der Academien
Hertogsstraat 1
B-1000 Brussels, Belgium
Phone: 2 5112623
Phone: 2 5112629
Fax: 2 5110143

1249
Antwoorden Prijsvragen, Klasse der Letteren
For recognition in the humanities. Established in 1941.

1250
Antwoorden Prijsvragen, Klasse der Schone Kunsten
For recognition in the field of music and the fine arts. Established in 1942.

1251
Antwoorden Prijsvragen, Klasse der Wetenschappen
For recognition in the field of science. Established in 1941.

1252
Octaaf Callebaut Prize
For recognition of contributions to the relief of food problems in the Third World. Established in 1988.

1253
J. Coppens Prize
For recogntion in the fields of history of Leuven University, history of Bible exegesis, or Old Testament studies.

1254
C. De Clercq Prize
For recognition in the field of religious history of Flanders. Established in 1987.

1255
O. Dupont Prize
To recognize an outstanding contribution to human and animal physiology and physiopathology. Established in 1991.

1256
J. Gillis Prize
For recognition in the fields of history and/or philosophy of post-Renaissance science. Established in 1969.

1257
R. Lenaerts Prize
For recognition in the field of musical science. Established in 1991.

1258
MacLeod prijs
For recognition in the field of biology. Established in 1951.

1259
H. Schoutedenprijs
For recognition in zoology, such as the study of fauna, preferably African, systematics, ecology, ethology, or animal anatomy. Established in 1963.

1260
Floris van der Mueren Prize
For recognition in the field of musicology. Established in 1976.

1261
Paul van Oyeprijs
For recognition in the field of biology, hydro biology, biogeography, and systematics of protista or of invertebrates. Established in 1969.

1262
H. L. Vanderlinden Prize
For recognition in the field of astronomy.

1263
Royal Academy of Dutch Language and Literature
(Koninklijke Academie Voor Nederlandse Taal-en Letterkunde)
Ministerie van de Vlaamse Gemeenschap
Koningstraat 18
B-9000 Ghent, Belgium
Phone: 92 252774
Fax: 92 232718

1264
Lode Baekelmans Prize
For recognition of the best literary work in Dutch, including novels, poetry, plays, radio-plays, and essays dealing with the sea, sailors, navigation, harbors, or a related topic. Belgian nationals are eligible. A monetary prize of 75,000 Belgian francs is awarded triennially. Established in 1940.

1265
Dr. Karel Barbier Prize
For recognition of the best historical novel written in Dutch. Short stories and romanticized biographies are considered. Belgian nationals are eligible. A monetary prize of 20,000 Belgian francs is awarded biennially when merited. Established in 1927.

1266
August Beernaert Prize
For recognition of the best literary work, irrespective of the genre, that is written in Dutch. Published or unpublished works by Belgian nationals are eligible. A monetary prize of 50,000 Belgian francs is awarded biennially. Established in 1912.

1267
Karel Boury Prize
For recognition of the best unpublished Flemish school songs or folk songs (at least two). Belgian nationals are eligible. A monetary prize of 20,000 Belgian francs is awarded every four years. Established in 1909.

1268
Arthur H. Cornette Prize
For recognition of the best essay written in Dutch. Belgian nationals are eligible. A monetary prize of 60,000 Belgian francs is awarded every five years. Established in 1950.

1269
Nestor de Tiere Prize
For recognition of the best unpublished play written in Dutch. Belgian nationals are eligible. A monetary prize of 20,000 Belgian francs is awarded biennially. Established in 1930.

1270
Joris Eeckhout Prize
For recognition of the best literary essay about an author. Works written in Dutch and a minimum 100 pages in length are considered. Belgian national are eligible. A monetary prize of 20,000 Belgian francs is awarded biennially. Established in 1937.

1271
Prof. Leon Elaut Prize
For recognition of the best dissertation in the field of the cultural history of Flanders from 1815 till 1940 in connection with the Flemish movement. A monetary prize of 100,000 Belgian francs is awarded biennially. Established in 1981.

1272
Guido Gezelle Prize
For recognition of the best volume of Dutch poetry that is published or in manuscript form. Belgian nationals are eligible. A monetary prize of 50,000 Belgian francs is awarded every five years. Established in 1941.

1273
Maurice Gilliams Prize
For recognition of the best volume of poetry, essay about poetry, or complete poetical works, written in Dutch, without regard to the nationality of the author. Works may be published or in manuscript form. A monetary prize of 100,000 Belgian francs is awarded every four years. Established in 1985.

1274
Arthur Merghelynck Prize
For recognition of the two best literary works in either prose or poetry form. Works written in Dutch that are published or in manuscript form are considered. Belgian nationals are eligible. Monetary prizes of 50,000 Belgian francs each for prose and for poetry are awarded triennially. Established in 1946.

1275
Noordstarfonds - Dr. Jan Grauls Prize
For recognition of the best essay in the field of Dutch linguistics and folklore. Writings on semantics, onomastics, dialectology, and studies on proverbs and purism are preferred. Essays written in Dutch that are published or in manuscript form are considered. Belgian nationals are eligible. A monetary prize of 50,000 Belgian francs is awarded every five years. Established in 1973.

1276
Ary Sleeks Prize
For recognition of the best novel, volume of short stories, or essay written in Dutch. Candidates must be Belgian nationals and may not have been awarded a prize before. A monetary prize of 25,000 Belgian francs is awarded triennially. Established in 1974.

1277
Karel van de Woestijne Prize
For recognition of an outstanding contribution to the study of the poetry of Karel van de Woestijne. A presentation of the complete works or a publication of exceptional importance is considered. A monetary prize of 100,000 Belgian francs is awarded every five years. Established in 1977.

1278
Jozef Van Ginderachter Prize
For recognition of the best literary, historical, art-historical, linguistic publication, or a work of folklore glorifying the province of Brabant, preferably the cantons of Asse and Vilvoorde. Individuals, periodicals, or

institutions that have published works in the above mentioned fields are eligible. A monetary prize of 20,000 Belgian francs is awarded every four years. Established in 1935.

1279
Jozef Vercoullie Prize
For recognition of the best doctoral dissertation in the field of Dutch philology presented in a Belgian university. A literary and a linguistic study can be alternately considered for the award. Belgian nationals are eligible. A monetary prize of 20,000 Belgian francs is awarded every four years. Established in 1938.

1280
Leonard Willems Prize
For recognition of an outstanding contribution to the Middle Dutch literary studies, either by the presentation of complete works, or by a publication of exceptional importance. Belgian nationals of Flemish background are eligible. A monetary prize of 100,000 Belgian francs is awarded biennially. Established in 1961.

1281
Royal Academy of French Language and Literature
(Academie Royale de Langue et de Litterature Francaise)
Palais des Academies
1 Rue Ducale
B-1000 Brussels, Belgium

1282
Beernhaert Prize
(Prix Auguste Beernaert)
To recognize a Belgian author for an outstanding work written in the French language. A monetary prize is awarded every four years. Established in 1925.

1283
Ernest Bouvier-Parviliez Prize
(Prix Ernest Bouvier-Parviliez)
To recognize a Belgian author for his/her entire work, written in French. A monetary prize is awarded every four years. Established in 1925.

1284
Albert Counson Prize
(Prix Albert Counson)
For recognition of a scholarly work written in French on romance languages. Belgian or foreign authors are eligible. A monetary prize is awarded every five years. Established in 1940.

1285
Felix Denayer Prize
(Prix Felix Denayer)
To recognize a Belgian writer, writing in French, for a single work or for the entire literary work. A monetary prize is awarded annually. Established in 1956.

1286
Camille Engelman Prize
For recognition of the outstanding literary work of the year, published or unpublished, written in French. A monetary prize is awarded annually.

1287
Grand Prix de Litterature Francaise hors de France
To recognize a writer of works written in French that are "French Literature." Writers of French nationality or members of the Royal Academy are not eligible. Established in 1959 by Fondation Nessim Habif.

1288
Malpertuis Prize
(Prix Lucien Malpertuis)
For recognition of an outstanding contribution to Belgian literature in the field of drama, poetry, short story, or essay written in French. A monetary prize is awarded biennially. Established in 1940.

1289
Albert Mockel Grand Prize for Poetry
(Grand Prix de Poesie Albert Mockel)
To recognize the work of a Belgian poet writing in French. A monetary prize is awarded every five years. Established in 1953.

1290
Emil Polak Prize
(Prix Emile Polak)
For recognition of a distinguished literary work written in French, perferably by a poet. A monetary prize is awarded biennially. Established in 1931.

1291
Prix Alix Charlier-Anciaux
To recognize a Belgian writer. Awarded every five years. Established in 1969.

1292
Prix Andre Praga
For recognition of a dramatic script for either stage or television. Awarded biennially. Established in 1984 by Jacqueline Van Praag-Chantraine in honor of Dr. Andre Van Praag who wrote, under the pseudonym, Andre Praga, dramatic work.

1293
Prix Auguste Michot
For recognition of a literary work of prose or verse by a Belgian author which celebrates the beauty of Flanders. Unpublished manuscripts as well as work published during the preceding two years are considered. Awarded biennially. Established in 1924.

1294
Prix Carton de Wiart
To recognize a writer who best describes episodes or aspects of Belgian national life of the past or present in any literary form (historical novel, story or tale, memoirs, or narratives). Awarded every ten years. Established in 1926.

1295
Prix Emmanuel Vossaert
For recognition of a Belgian writer for a work of prose or verse, and especially for an essay about literary character. Awarded biennially. Established in 1952.

1296
Prix Eugene Schmits
For recognition of the best collection of poems or small pieces of prose, published or unpublished, which contributes to the moral perfection of the reader. Awarded triennially. Established in 1924.

1297
Prix Franz de Wever
For recognition alternately of a book of poems and an essay or short stories by a writer under 40 years of age. Awarded annually. Established in 1962.

1298
Prix Gaston et Mariette Heux
To recognize a writer over 40 years of age for an important literary work or for his total work. Established by Raymond Heux in honor of his mother and poet father, Gaston and Mariette Heux.

1299
Prix George Garnir
To recognize a Belgian author for a novel or collection of stories which evoke the sights and morals of the Wallonnes Province in Belgium. Awarded triennially. Established in 1945.

1300
Prix Georges Lockem
To recognize a young Belgian poet who writes in the French language. Individuals 25 years of age and younger are considered for work published during the preceding year or for a manuscript of at least 24 pages. Awarded annually. Established in 1974 by George Lockem.

1301
Prix Henri Davignon
For recognition of a work of religious inspiration. Awarded every five years. Established in 1965.

1302
Prix Jean Kobs
To recognize a Belgian poet over 40 years of age for a collection of poems of spiritual inspiration and classical form. The collection should be less than 80 pages. Awarded triennially. Established in 1984 in memory of Jean Kobs, a priest-poet.

1303
Prix Leopold Rosy
For recognition of an essay. Awarded triennially. Established in 1942.

1304
Prix Nicole Houssa
For recognition of a first volume of verse, either published or unpublished. Individuals originally from Wallonie who are under 30 years of age are eligible. Awarded triennially. Established in 1964.

1305
Prix Robert Duterme
To recognize an author under 30 years of age for a collection of stories which take place in a universe touched by the fantastic. Awarded annually. Established by Robert Duterme.

1306
Prix Sander Pierron
To recognize a Belgian writer for a novel or collection of stories. Awarded biennially. Established in 1972.

1307
Georges Vaxelaire Prize
(Prix Georges Vaxelaire)
To recognize a Belgian playwright for a play set in Belgium. Stage production, radio and television plays are considered. A monetary prize is awarded biennially. Established in 1945.

1308
Royal Academy of Medicine
(Koninklijke Academie Voor Geneeskunde Van Belgie)
Hertogsstraat 1
B-1000 Brussels, Belgium

1309
Doctor Raoul Biltris Prize
For recognition of an original paper dealing with the experimental study of cancer. Manuscripts must be written in Dutch, French, or German by a medical doctor who has practiced at least ten years. A monetary prize is awarded every four years.

1310
Paul De Backer Prize
For recognition of an original paper dealing with radiodiagnosis, radiotherapy, radiobiology, or the clinical applications of nuclear energy. Manuscripts must be written in Dutch, French, or English. A monetary prize is awarded triennially.

1311
Dr. Roland De Ruyck Prize
To recognize an original paper, published or not published, on cancerology or another disesase that is incurable or fatal in humans.

1312
Fund Dr. en Mevr. Schamelhout-Koettlitz
For recognition in the field of medicine. Candidates must be Flemish and manuscripts must be written in Dutch.

1313
Prijs Jan-Frans Heymans
For recognition of an original paper dealing with experimental pharmacy or chemistry. Reports must be written by a medical doctor in Dutch, English, or German. A monetary prize is awarded biennially.

1314
Fund Professor Doctor A. Lacquet
To promote clinical and experimental research in the field of surgery and the diffusion of surgical knowledge. Candidates must be Belgian. An allowance and an invitation to deliver lectures in Belgium on clinical or experimental surgery are awarded to a foreign scientist. Awarded triennially.

1315
Sidmar Prize
To recognize an imporatnt contribution to the fundamental or clinical knowledge of a chronic disease that causes severe disablement and is considered incurable. Research must have been performed, entirely or in the greater part, in the Benelux.

1316
Denis Thienpont Prize
For recognition of an important scientific contribution to the clinical and fundamental knowledge of mycology or parasitology (helminthology, protozoology). Manuscripts must be written in Dutch, French, or English.

1317
Prijs Albert Van Dyck
To recognize an investigator in basic or clinical science who has acquired special merit in the study of leukemia or another disease that is considered incurable or fatal. Unpublished manuscripts as well as published work written in Dutch, French, English, or German are considered. A monetary prize is awarded triennially.

1318
Prijs Franz Van Goidsenhoven
For recognition of an original paper dealing with clinical medicine, particularly, internal medicine. Manuscripts must be written in Dutch, French, English, or German. A monetary prize is awarded triennially.

1319
Prijs J. B. Van Helmont
For recognition of an original paper dealing with general pathology, biophysics, or biochemistry. Reports must be written in Dutch, French, English, or German. A monetary prize is awarded triennially.

1320
Fund Professor Doctor G. Verdonk
For recognition of an original, printed, or written memoir on dietetics or geriatrics written in Dutch, French, English, or German. A monetary prize is awarded triennially. Established in 1986.

1321
Dr. Karel Verleysen Prize
To recognize successful achievements in scientific research in human medicine and the promotion of health and to support and stimulate further research.

1322
Royal Academy of Medicine of Belgium
(Academie Royale de Medecine de Belgique)
Palais des Academies
rue Ducale 1
B-1000 Brussels, Belgium   Phone: 2 511 24 71

1323
Prix Albert-Pierre-Jean Dustin
For recognition of experimental research in cellular pathology. Scientists who are either Belgians or who have done their research in Belgium and are under than 40 years of age are eligible. The work must be written in French or in Flemish. A monetary prize of 50,000 Belgian francs is awarded every five years. Established in 1963.

1324
Prix Alexander Straetmans
To recognize medical doctors who have contributed to the cure of cancer. Only works written in French or in Dutch are considered. A monetary prize of 50,000 Belgian francs is awarded triennially. Established in 1957.

1325
Prix Alvarenga de Piauhy
To recognize the author of the best memoirs or work in any branch of medicine. Works written in either French or Flemish are eligible. A monetary prize of 50,000 Belgian francs is awarded annually. Established in 1888.

1326
Prix Anonyme
To encourage research that would elucidate the pathogenesis and therapy of nervous system illnesses, particularly epilepsy. Authors of unpublished works in either French or Flemish are eligible. A monetary prize of 50,000 Belgian francs is awarded triennially. Established in 1878.

1327
Prix Artois - Baillet Latour de la Sante
This, the most important medical award in Belgium, is given for a contribution in the field of medicine. A monetary prize of 5,000,000 Belgian francs is awarded biennially. Established in 1979.

1328
Prix Cornelis - Lebegue
To encourage the study of cancer cures. Works, published or unpublished, that are written in French, Dutch, German, English, and Italian are eligible. A monetary prize of 50,000 Belgian francs is awarded triennially. Established in 1930.

1329
Prix Denis Thienpont
For recognition of an outstanding contribution in the field of parasitology or mycology. A jury, under the auspices of the Academie Royale de Medicine de Belgique and the Koninklijhe Academie voor Geneeskunde van Belgie, rules on the eligibility of the candidates. Works written in French, Dutch, or English may be submitted if they have been published, at least in part, in the preceding two years. A monetary prize of US$25,000 is awarded biennially. Established in 1982 by the Janssen Research Foundation in Beerse, Belgium.

1330
Prix du Docteur Frans Johnckheere sur l'Historie de la Medecine
For recognition of a work in French or Flemish that contributes to the advancement of medical history. Eligible authors must be Belgian. A monetary prize of 50,000 Belgian francs is awarded every three years. Established about 1957.

1331
Prix du Docteur Jules Deminne et sa femme nee Anne Fabry
For recognition of a work written in French, preferably related to stomatology or general medicine. Medical doctors under 35 years of age who are Belgian citizens are eligible. A monetary prize of 50,000 Belgian francs is awarded biennially. Established in 1956.

1332
Prix du Docteur Louis de Give de Muache
To recognize the author of the best works in the medical field written in French or Flemish. Published or unpublished works are accepted. Citizens of Belgium are eligible. A monetary prize of 100,000 Belgian francs is awarded every ten years. Established about 1928.

1333
Prix Hamoir
To recognize a veterinarian who has written the best work or works, of an original nature, that relate to veterinary sciences such as bovine, ovine, caprine, or porcine. The work must be written in French or in Flemish. A monetary prize of 100,000 Belgian francs is awarded every five years. Established in 1928.

1334
Prix Henriette Simont
For recognition of the best work, published or unpublished, concerning the treatment of asthma. Works can be written in either French or Flemish. A monetary prize of 50,000 Belgian francs is awarded every five years. Established in 1922.

1335
Prix Henry Fauconnier
For recognition of outstanding works written in French or in Flemish on the search for a cure for cancer, tuberculosis, or any other social disease. A monetary prize of 50,000 Belgian francs is awarded every four years. Established in 1935.

1336
Prix Joseph Lepoix
For recognition of the best work in French or Flemish concerning poisoning and, above all, the symptoms that allow a diagnosis. The work must educate the public, parents, doctors, and nurses. A monetary prize of 50,000 Belgian francs is awarded every four years. Established in 1950.

1337
Prix Melsens
For recognition of a remarkable, published or unpublished work on professional hygiene written in French or Flemish. Authors of the Belgian nationality only are eligible. A monetary prize of 50,000 Belgian francs is awarded every four years. Established in 1900.

1338
Prix Pfizer
For recognition of an important contribution in the field of infectious pathology. Awards are given to both a French speaking author and a Dutch speaking author. Belgian writers may submit a published or unpublished original work written in French, Dutch, German, or English. Works that have already received national and international awards are not eligible. The jury consists of members from the two Royal Academies of Medicine. Two monetary prizes of 250,000 Belgian francs each are awarded annually. Established in 1956.

1339
Prix Quinquennal des Sciences Pharmaceutiques et Therapeutiques
For recognition of the best work on pharmaceutical or therapeutic sciences. Awards are given in alternate years in the categories of pharmaceutical science and therapeutic science. Works written in French or in Flemish by an author of Belgian nationality are eligible. A

monetary prize of 50,000 Belgian francs is awarded every five years (in 1988 for pharmaceutical sciences). Established during the war of 1914-1918 by the Comite National de Secours et d'Alimentation.

1340

Prix Quinquennal Docteur Albert Dubois pour la Pathologie tropicale

To encourage clinical or experimental research in the field of tropical pathology in its broadest sense. Authors of any nationality may submit published or unpublished work, written in French, Dutch, or English, completed during the preceding five years. The prize may be awarded to an individual or a team. A monetary award of 500,000 Belgian francs is awarded every five years. Established in 1979.

1341

Prix Quinquennaux des Sciences Medicales du Gouvernement

For recognition of outstanding contributions in the categories of research in the field of basic medical sciences and research in the field of clinical or applied sciences. Works showing genuine scientific progress in either field, written in French, Flemish, English, or German are accepted during the five year period. The author must be Belgian by birth or by naturalization. Two monetary prizes of 150,000 Belgian francs each are awarded every five years.

1342

Prix SmithKline Beecham

For recognition of an important contribution in the field of human or veterinary medicine or pharmaceutical science. Awards are given to both a French speaking researcher and a Dutch speaking researcher. Belgian researchers may submit a published or unpublished original work written in French, Dutch, German, or English. Works that have already received national and international awards are not eligible. The jury consists of members from the two Royal Academies of Medicine. Two monetary prizes of 500,000 Belgian francs each are awarded biennially. Established in 1959 by SmithKline Beecham.

1343

Prix Triennal Professeur Pierre Rijlant pour l'Electrophysiologie Cardiaque

For recognition of a major contribution in one of the following fields: cardiac electrophysiology, Comput hybride in electrocardiography, electrocardiography on the time of Comput, and electrography and vectography and analogous simulation. Individuals or a team of researchers may submit a published or unpublished work written in French, Dutch, English, or German. Works that have already received national or international prizes are not eligible. A monetary prize of 500,000 Belgian francs is awarded triennially. Established in 1985.

1344

Royal Belgian Numismatic Society
(Societe de Numismatique de Belgique)
Avenue de L'observatoire, 9, bte 12
B-1180 Brussels, Belgium

1345

Quadrennial Prize of the Royal Belgian Numismatic Society

For recognition of a scientific work on numismatics or sigillography that is original and unpublished. Authors who are under 35 years of age may submit manuscripts. The work may be written in French, English, German, Dutch, Italian, or Spanish. A monetary prize of 50,000 Belgian francs, and a diploma are awarded every four years. Established in 1976.

1346

Royal Carillon School Jef Denyn
(Koninklijke Beiaardschool Jef Denijn)
Frederik de Merodestraat 63
B-2800 Mechelen, Belgium   Phone: 15 204792

1347

International Contest for Carillon Composition

For recognition of a composition for a four octave carillon (c tot c''''), three pages minimum, lasting a maximum of eight minutes. The composer has free choice of a musical form in Category I. In Category II, the carillon compositions are based on an old folksong or use a folksong as a basic element. Compositions already published, performed, or sent in on the occasion of previous competitions are not allowed, and not more than one work by the same composer may obtain a prize. The following monetary prizes, each of them with a diploma, may be awarded: Category I: first prize - Jef Denyn Prize - 15,000 Belgian francs; second prize - Stad Mechelen Prize - 10,000 Belgian francs; third prize - Carillon School Prize - 7,500 Belgian francs; and Category II: first prize - Staf Nees Prize - 7,500 Belgian francs; and second prize - Tower and Carillon Prize - 6,000 Belgian francs. Awarded annually. Established in 1952. Formerly: Internationale Kompositiewedstrijd voor Beiaard.

1348

Triennial International Carillon Competition - Queen Fabiola (Driejaarlijkse Internationale Beiaardwedstrijd Koningin Fabiola)

For recognition of outstanding performance of original carillon compositions. Carillonneurs from all over the world may participate. All candidates must present nine original carillon compositions, including three baroque, three romantic, and three modern works. All compositions must be of a very high virtuosity level. The following prizes are awarded: first prize - 100,000 Belgian francs, a bronze bell in a frame, diploma, and a concert tour through Belgium; second prize - 75,000 Belgian francs plus a medal and diploma; third prize - 50,000 Belgian francs plus a medal and diploma; fourth prize - 25,000 Belgian francs plus a diploma; fifth prize - 25,000 Belgian francs plus a diploma; and sixth prize - 25,000 Belgian francs plus a diploma. Application forms are due before March 31. Established in 1987 under the patronage of Her Majesty Queen Fabiola.

1349

Royal Entomological Society of Belgium
(Societe Royale Belge d'Entomologie)
Rue Vautier, 29
B-1040 Brussels, Belgium   Phone: 2 648 04 75

1350

Prix Adolphe Crevecoeur

To encourage studies in entomolgy. Members of the Society who have published in the last volume of the Bulletin of the Society are eligible. A monetary prize of 10,000 Belgian francs is awarded annually. Established in 1962 by Adolphe Crevecoeur.

1351

Royal Film Archive of Belgium
(Cinematheque Royale)
Ravenstein 23   Phone: 2 5078370
B-1000 Brussels, Belgium   Fax: 2 5131272

1352

Age d'Or Prijs

To promote the creation and distribution of films that depart from all cinematographic conformities by the originality, the oddity of their substance, and form. Competing films must be longer than 60 minutes and completed in the preceding three years. The films must be presented in their original and uncut version. If not in English, French, or Dutch, the films must be subtitled in one of these languages. A monetary prize of 400,000 Belgian francs is awarded to the winning film. This sum is divided into three parts and are awarded to the producer (125,000 Belgian francs), to the director (125,000 Belgian francs) and to the Belgian distributor (150,000 Belgian francs), who may, within one year, present proof of genuine distribution in Belgium and of possession of a print of the film in its original version, subtitled in French and Dutch. Formerly: Prix de l'Age d'Or.

1353
Belgian Film Archive Prizes for the Distribution of Quality Films
(Premies voor de verspreiding van de betere film in Belgie)
To provide recognition for quality films of any country, longer than 60 minutes, whose innovative nature makes their release problematic; and to recognize the Belgian distributors who may, within one year of the award, present proof of distribution of these films in Belgium in original and uncut versions with French and Dutch subtitles. Seven monetary awards of 150,000 Belgian francs each are awarded annually.

1354
Saint Joan's International Alliance
(Alliance Internationale Jeanne d'Arc)
19, Quai Churchill, boite 061
B-4020 Liege, Belgium
Phone: 41 420471
Fax: 41 237066

1355
Awards
For recognition of contributions to equal rights and opportunities for men and women in church, state, and society.

1356
Sarton Committee of the University of Ghent
(Sarton Comite van de Rijksuniversiteit Gent)
Blandijberg 2
B-9000 Ghent, Belgium
Phone: 9 2643952
Fax: 9 2644197

1357
Sarton Chair
(Sarton Leersoel)
For recognition of achievement in the history or philosophy of science. Individuals proposed by two scientists by January of each year are eligible. A certificate and medal are awarded annually. Established in 1986 by the University of Ghent in honor of George Sarton.

1358
Sarton Medal
(Sarton Medaille)
For recognition of a contribution to a field of activity in the history or philosophy of science and for encouragement in that field. Individuals proposed by two scientists by January of each year are eligible. A certificate and medal are awarded annually. Established in 1986 by the University of Ghent in honor of George Sarton.

1359
Scientific Committee of the Tytgat Prize
Laboratoire de Chimie Physiologique, Tour
 I.C.P.
Avenue Hippocrate 75
B-1200 Brussels, Belgium

1360
Alexandre and Gaston Tytgat Prize
For recognition of research on the causes, origins and therapy for cancer. Only Belgian candidates are considered. A monetary prize of 500,000 Belgian francs is awarded triennially.

1361
SECO Technical Control Bureau for Construction
(Bureau de Controle Technique pour la Construction)
Rue d'Arlon 53
B-1040 Brussels, Belgium
Phone: 2 2382211
Fax: 2 2382261

Formerly: Bureau of Security Control of Construction.

1362
Magnel Prize
For recognition of scientific work in the area of safety control of construction that has practical application for the field. The research results must be written in French, Dutch, German, or English. The author must be attached to a university or a research institute of a member country, and must be no older than 40 years of age. A monetary award of 300,000 Belgian francs is awarded every four years. Established in 1964.

1363
Verdeyen Prize for Soil Mechanics
For recognition of scientific research on soil mechanics, with practical application for control and safety of constructions. The work must be written in French, Dutch, German, or English. Research workers not older than 40 years of age are eligible. A monetary award of 200,000 Belgian francs is awarded every eight years. Established in 1974.

1364
Societe Royale de Chimie
ULB, Campus Plaine
CP 206-4
Boulevard du Triomphe
B-1050 Brussels, Belgium
Phone: 2 6505208
Fax: 2 6505184

Formerly: (1986) Societe Chimique de Belgique.

1365
Prix Paul Janssen
To honor a young French (part Belgian) researcher for his contribution in the field of therapeutical chemistry. To be eligible, a researcher must submit a Ph.D. thesis or a scientific published paper in organic chemistry, biochemistry, chemical biology. The candidate cannot be older than 35 years of age and must be a Society member. A monetary prize of 40,000 Belgian francs is awarded biennially.

1366
Prix Triennal de la Societe Royale de Chimie
To honor a chemist whose work has received international recognition. Members of the Society of any nationality who are living permanently in Belgium or Belgian chemists living abroad are eligible. The candidate cannot be older than 40 years of age, and must have been a Society member for at least five years. A monetary prize of 75,000 Belgian francs is awarded triennially.

1367
Societe Royale des Sciences de Liege
Univ. of Liege
15, avenue des Tilleuls
B-4000 Liege, Belgium

1368
Prix de la Fondation du 150e anniversaire de la Societe royale des Sciences de Liege
To recognize an individual or a group for outstanding contributions in mathematics, physics, chemistry, or biology. Individuals who are 35 years of age at the end of the five-year award period are eligible. French and German-speaking scientists were eligible in 1990; and international in 1995, etc. The following awards are presented every five years on October 1: Prix Edouard Van Beneden - 75,000 Belgian francs for contributions in biology, Prix Lucien Godeaux - 75,000 Belgian francs for mathematics, Prix Louis d'Or - 75,000 Belgian francs for chemistry, and Prix Pol Swings - 75,000 Belgian francs for physics. Established in 1985.

1369
Sovereign Western Order
(Ordre Souverain d'Occident)
24 Bis, Rue des Fripiers
B-1000 Brussels, Belgium
Phone: 2 218 50 25

1370

Sovereign Western Order
(Ordre Souverain d'Occident)
To recognize eminent personalities who have practiced and promoted Western humanism. Individuals can be elected to one of the following five classes of the Order: (1) First Class - Grand Croix; (2) Second Class - Grand-Officier; (3) Third Class - Commandeur; (4) Fourth Class - Officier; and (5) Fifth Class - Chevalier. A five-pointed star enameled white on a metal background with a small metal sun in the center with the inscription "un seul esprit" (only one mind) is awarded when merited.

1371

A. Spinoy Foundation
(Stichting A. Spinoy)
Grote Markt 21
B-2800 Mechelen, Belgium
Phone: 15 297571
Fax: 15 297570

1372

A. Spinoy Award
(Prijs A. Spinoy)
For recognition of contributions to the developing countries. Belgian citizens are eligible. A monetary prize is awarded biennially. Established in 1987 in honor of A. Spinoy, a former mayor who died in 1967.

1373

Stichting de Vlaamse Gids
De Nieuwe Gaet
Leopoldstraat 10
B-2000 Antwerp, Belgium
Phone: 3 231 96 80
Fax: 3 232 64 12

1374

Prijs de Vlaamse Gids
For recognition of the best volume of Dutch poetry in Belgium. Books of poetry written in Flemish that were published during the preceding two years by Belgian poets under 40 years of age are eligible for consideration. A monetary prize of 25,000 francs is awarded biennially. Established in 1970.

1375

Unda International Catholic Association for Radio and Television
(Unda Association Catholique Internationale pour la Radio et la Television)
12, rue de l'Orme
B-1040 Brussels, Belgium
Phone: 2 7349708
Fax: 2 7347018

1376

Unda Dove
(Colombe Unda)
To recognize radio and television programs of high technical quality that convey a spiritual message at the International Television Festival of Monte Carlo. Applications are accepted. Awards are presented for fiction programs and current affairs. A trophy is awarded annually in February. Established in 1962.

1377

University Foundation
(Fondation Universitaire)
Rue d'Egmont 11
B-1050 Brussels, Belgium
Phone: 2 5118100
Fax: 2 5136411

1378

Emile Bernheim European Prizes
(Prix Europeens Emile Bernheim)
To recognize works on European integration. A prize is awarded for a work helping those who are engaged in implementation of European integration, especially in the framework of the Common Market. The applicant must hold a degree for at least three years from a Belgian university or another higher school recognized by the University Foundation. A monetary prize of 300,000 Belgian francs is awarded every four years. Established in 1954. A second prize is awarded for a work on European integration written by a person who is or has been a student of a Belgian university or another higher school recognized by the University Foundation, and who has not received a degree within three years of receiving the award. A monetary prize of 50,000 Belgian francs is awarded every four years. Established in 1955.

1379

Fernand Colin-Prijs
For recognition of an original manuscript or printed work that is an important contribution to science. A Belgian with a degree in law or economics, received from a Belgian university less than 20 years before, may submit a work that must be written in Dutch. A monetary prize of 300,000 Belgian francs and the title, Laureaat van de Fernand Colin Prijs, are awarded biennially. Established in 1962.

1380

Prix Scientifiques Louis Empain
To encourage Belgian students to conduct research works. The title, Laureat du Prix Scientifique Louis Empain, and 100,000 Belgian francs were awarded every five years in the categories of mathematics, physics, chemistry, natural sciences and medicine, and engineering. Established in 1935. (Discontinued in 1989)

1381

Vlaamse Wetenschappeliike Stichting
Oude Baan 305
B-3000 Leuven, Belgium
Phone: 16 25 03 39

1382

Prijs voor wetenschappelijk Werk van de Stad Lier
To recognize a dissertation that contributes to the knowledge of the Town Lier (Stadt Lier). Students in a Flemish university are eligible. A monetary prize is awarded annually. Established in 1975. Sponsored by the Town of Lier.

1383

Women's International Film Festival
(Festival International de Films de Femmes)
71 Avenue Moliere
B-1180 Brussels, Belgium
Phone: 2 347 44 95

1384

Festival International de Films de Femmes
For recognition of recent fiction feature films that were directed by a woman. The following prizes are awarded: (1) Prix Special du Jury - a jury composed of journalists, director, and comedians, makes the selection; (2) Prix Special du Public - for recognition of the film at the Festival that receives the most votes by the public attending the festival; and (3) Prize to the best short film selected by 10 young actresses. A monetary prize or a painting is awarded biennially. Established in 1982. Organized by "La femme dans le cinema" and "Cinelibre," 10 rue des Palais, B-1030 Brussels, Belgium.

1385

World Association of Inventors and Researchers
(Association Mondiale des Inventeurs)
353 Chaussee de St. Job
B-1180 Brussels, Belgium
Phone: 2 375 34 95

1386

World First Postal Automatization Award
(Premier Prix Mondial de l'Automatisation Postale)
For recognition of the most important achievement in the postal field since the invention of the postal stamp. Inventions that have applied for a

Bolivia

1387

Alcaldia Municipal
Oficial Mayor de Cultura
La Paz, Bolivia

1388

Concurso Anual de Literatura Premios Franz Tamayo
(Franz Tamayo Annual Competition for Literature Prizes)
To provide recognition for outstanding achievement in the field of literature, for a novel, poem, drama, or short story. Bolivian authors are eligible. Monetary prizes ranging from 5,000 to 15,000 pesos, publication of the work, and diplomas are awarded annually.

1389

Salon Anual de Artes Plasticas Premios Pedro Domingo Murillo
(Pedro Domingo Murillo Annual Salon of Visual Arts Prizes)
For recognition of outstanding achievement in painting, sculpture, non-traditional techniques, watercolor, engraving and drawing. Bolivian and foreign artists with, at least, five years of residence in the country may submit works. Monetary awards ranging from 5,000 to 10,000 pesos are awarded annually. Established in 1953.

1390

Bolivia
Ministry of Education and Culture
Avda Arce 2408
La Paz, Bolivia   Phone: 2 373260

1391

National Prizes for Culture
(Premios Nacionales de Cultura)
For recognition of outstanding achievements in literature, the arts or science. Bolivian citizens are considered. A monetary prize of 50,000 pesos and a medal are awarded biennially.

1392

Bolivia
Office of the President
Palacio de Gobierno
Place Murillo
La Paz, Bolivia   Phone: 2 371317

1393

Condor of the Andes
This, the highest official decoration of the Bolivian Government, is given for recognition of outstanding contributions to Bolivian culture. Bolivian and foreign citizens are eligible. The award is given for outstanding achievements in six categories: Grand Collar, for premier representatives; Gran Cross, for outstanding ambassadors and generals of the army; Grand Official, for outstanding business strengths of colonels of the army and other high authorities; Commander, for literary and scientific commanders in the general consul; Official, for the first and second Mission Secretaries; and Gentleman, for assistant secretaries, associates, and other citizens. Decorations are awarded when merited.

1394

Centro Impulsor de Educacion Profesional
Casilla No. 1929   Phone: 34 2200
Santa Cruz, Bolivia   Fax: 35 1034

1395

Gold Book
(Libro de Oro)
For recognition of economic contributions and permanent support to the Center's goals and activities. Nominations or applications are accepted. A plaque is awarded annually in January. Established in 1984.

1396

Editorial Los Amigos del Libro
Avda Heroinas E-0311
Casilla 450
Cochabamba, Bolivia   Phone: 42 22920

1397

Concurso Nacional de Biografias Hector Cossio Salinas
For recognition of biographies that emphasize people who have been important for the development of Bolivia. The following prizes were awarded: 300,000 Bolivian pesos, a certificate, 20 copies of the first edition, and 10 per cent of the estimated future royalties - first prize; 150,000 Bolivian pesos, a certificate, 20 copies of the first edition, and 10 per cent of the estimated future royalties - second prize; and 50,000 Bolivian pesos, a certificate, 20 copies of the first edition and 10 per cent of the estimated royalties - third prize. Awarded biennially. Established in 1977 by Werner Guttentag in honor of the Bolivian poet, Hector Cossio Salinas (1929-1972). (Discontinued) Formerly: .

1398

Concurso Nacional de Novela Erich Guttentag
For recognition of outstanding achievement in the field of Bolivian literature, specifically for a novel, and to increase the production and circulation of this literary genre. Bolivian-born authors and foreign authors with at least two years of residence in Bolivia are eligible. A monetary prize is awarded biennially. The deadline for entries is July 1. The following prizes are awarded: first prize - $2,000 US, fifteen copies of the published works, and a certificate; and second prize - $759 US, fifteen copies of the published works, and a certificate. Established in 1966 by Werner Guttentag, owner of "Los Amigos del Libro", in honor of his father, Erich Guttentag.

Bosnia-Hercegovina

1399

Geographical Society of Bosnia and Hercegovina
(Geografsko drustvo Bosne i Hercegovine)
Prirodno-matematicki fakultet
Vojvode Putnika 43A
71000 Sarajevo, Bosnia-Hercegovina   Phone: 71 645 328

1400

Pocasni Clan
(Honorary Member)
To recognize members for contributions to geography. The Honor Diploma was given from 1962-1967; the Memorial Plaque from 1947-1977; and the Honorary Membership from 1982.

1401

Radio Television Sarajevo
(Radio-Televizija Sarajevo)
VI proleterske brigade 4   Phone: 71 455110
71000 Sarajevo, Bosnia-Hercegovina   Fax: 71 455166

1402

Hit of the season
(Slager sezone)
For recognition of achievement in the field of pop music. Applications must be submitted. A monetary prize and a plaque are awarded annually. Established in 1966.

1403

Svjetlost Publishing House
Petra Preradovica 3
71000 Sarajevo, Bosnia-Hercegovina   Phone: 71 512144

1404

Svjetlost Prizes
To recognize the best writers from Bosnia and Herzegovina. Monetary prizes are awarded annually.

Brazil

1405

Academia Deletras Jose Dealencar
Box 7102
80001 Curitiba, Paraiba, Brazil

1406

Festival da Torneira Poetica
To encourage professional development in the field of literature. A medal and trophy are awarded annually. Established in 1967.

1407

Associacao Brasileira de Propaganda
Avenida Rio Branco 14, 17 andar   Phone: 21 233 1197
20090 Rio de Janeiro, RJ, Brazil   Phone: 21 233 1492

1408

Premio Comunicacao
For recognition in the field of advertising in various categories. Nominees must work in Brazil. A plaque is awarded annually. An Outstanding Businessman Award and "Veiculo do Ano" Award are also presented. Established in 1971.

1409

Brazil
Office of the President
Palacio do Planalto
Praca des Tres Poderes
70150 Brasilia, DF, Brazil   Phone: 61 223 2714

1410

Oswaldo Cruz Medal of Merit
To recognize outstanding national or foreign figures for significant performance in the fields of science, education, culture and administration. Gold, silver, and bronze medals were awarded. (Discontinued)

1411

Oswaldo Cruz Prize
To recognize outstanding accomplishments in the field of medicine and biology.

1412

Mobral Journalism Prize
To recognize and encourage programs to teach literacy in the territory of Brazil.

1413

National Cultural Awards
To recognize outstanding intellectual and artistic accomplishments in the fields of literature, theatre, sciences, social studies, music, cinematography and the arts.

1414

National Order of Education
To recognize national or international personalities for outstanding work in the field of education in Brazil. A medal in the form of a cross is awarded in four classes: Grand Cross, Grand Official Cross, Official Cross, and Knight Cross.

1415

National Order of the Southern Cross
To recognize individuals or groups of foreigners for outstanding accomplishments in the fields of education, science, literature, art and culture related to Brazil. The order is conferred in five classes: Grand Collar, Grand Cross, Official, and Knight. Established in 1971.

1416

National Record Award
To recognize the native or naturalized author of the best classical, popular or folkloric record of the year. Awarded annually.

1417

Order of Rio Branco
For recognition of outstanding service to the Brazilian nation by a citizen or a foreigner. The order is conferred in five classes: Grand Cross, Grand Official, Knight Commander, Official, and Knight. Established in 1963.

1418

Roquette Pinto Prize
To provide recognition for the best adaptation from a book to a film scenario by a Brazilian author.

1419

Brazilian Academy of Letters
(Academia Brasileira de Letras)
Avenida Presidente Wilson 203
20030 Rio de Janeiro, RJ, Brazil   Phone: 21 220 5441

1420

Afonso Arinos Prize
For recognition of the best work of fiction published or written during the two years preceding the year of award. A monetary prize is awarded annually.

1421

Arthur Azevedo Prize
For recognition of the best works of drama, history of the theatre, and theatrical criticism. A monetary prize is awarded annually.

1422

Olavo Bilac Prize
For recognition of the best book of poetry. A monetary prize is awarded annually.

1423

Antonio Larragoiti Prize
To recognize the author of the best original work on a Portuguese-Brazilian theme in the field of literature, philology, history, law, politics or the social sciences published during the preceding year. Brazilian or Portuguese authors are eligible. A monetary prize of 12,000 Portuguese escudos is awarded biennially. Presented alternately by the Brazilian Academy of Letters and the Lisbon Academy of Sciences. Established in 1945 by Antonio Larragoiti.

1424
Monteiro Lobato Prize
For recognition of the best works of children's literature. A monetary prize is awarded annually.

1425
Julia Lopes of Ameida Prize
To provide recognition for the best unpublished or published literary work written by a woman, preferably for a novel or collection of short stories. A monetary prize is awarded annually.

1426
Machado de Assis Prize
This, one of Brazil's highest literary awards, is given to recognize an outstanding Brazilian writer for the sum of his work. A monetary prize of 200,000 Brazilian cruzeiros is awarded annually. Established in 1943.

1427
Brazilian Association for the Advancement of Science (Sociedade Brasileira para o Progresso da ciencia)
Avenida Pedroso de Moraes 1512
05420 Pinheiro, Maranhao, Brazil   Phone: 11 2120740

1428
Brazilian Association for the Advancement of Science Awards
To recognize Brazilian scientists, researchers and organizations. Awards are bestowed annually at the annual congress.

1429
Brazilian Institute of Art and Culture (Instituto Brasileiro de Arte e Cultura)
Rua da Imprensa, 16, 5 Andar-Centro   Phone: 21 2976116
20030 Rio de Janeiro, RJ, Brazil   Phone: 21 2624895

1430
Gustavo Capanema Prize
To recognize an artist who has exhibited at the National Salon of Fine Arts (Salao Nacional de Artes Plasticas) for the totality of his work. A monetary prize of 50,000 Brazilian cruzados is awarded annually. Established in 1977.

1431
Cenafor Prize for a Monograph (Premio Cenafor de Monografica)
For recognition of the best unpublished and up-to-date monograph on professional education. Training organizations, teachers, professors, researchers, coordinators or directors of programs in the field of professional education in Brazil are eligible. A monetary prize of 70,000 Brazilian cruzados and publication of the work by Cenafor (National Center for Improvement of Professional Qualifications for the Personnel) are awarded annually. Established in 1978 by Cenafor.

1432
Cross of Merit for Moral and Civic Education
To recognize outstanding accomplishments of national personalities in the field of moral and civic education.

1433
Marc Ferrez Photography Award
To recognize Brazilian artists and researchers for photography documentation, the writing of essays, and the development of technical or theoretical research on photography. Five monetary awards are given. Re-established in 1993.

1434
Mambembe Trophy
For recognition of contributions to theatre - the best children's and adult plays and performances. Awards are given annually in five categories: Author of a Brazilian play; Director; Actor; Actress; and Special category (theatrical groups, outstanding personality, costume designer, scenographer, producer, or impresarios). Established in 1993.

1435
Odorico Mendes Prize
For recognition of the best translation of literature from a foreign language into Portuguese. A monetary prize is awarded annually.

1436
National Annual Exhibition of Fine Arts (Salao Nacional de Artes Plasticas)
To bring attention to the main sources of the Brazilian production in fine arts. A study trip abroad is awarded to the first place winner annually. Other selected participants receive works of art.

1437
National Competition in Teaching of Journalism Prize (Concurso Nacional de Ensino de Redacao)
To recognize the best teachers of the Portuguese language, particularly those who distinguish themselves by teaching their students techniques of creative writing and journalism. Monetary prizes of 90,000, 60,000 and 40,000 Brazilian cruzados are awarded annually. Established in 1977.

1438
National Contest for Opera Singers
To recognize the best opera performances. Monetary prizes are awarded annually as follows: First prize - 800,000 cruzados; Second prize - 600,000 cruzados; Third prize - 400,000 cruzados; and Fourth and fifth prizes - 350,000 cruzados each. Established in 1993.

1439
National Drama Contest
To recognize the best in theater. Prizes are awarded in three categories: Theater for adults (Nelson Rodrugues Prize); Children's Theater (Pedro Veiga Prize); and Marionette Theater (Hermilio Borba Filho Prize). Each category awards three monetary prizes: First place - 1,000,000 cruzados; Second place - 600,000 cruzados; and Third place - 400,000 cruzados and a statuette created by a well-known Brazilian artist, the late Aloisio Magalhaes. There is also an incentive prize for 20 beginners groups.

1440
National Music Award
To recognize the artistic and cultural value of Brazilian musicians in the areas of opera, ballet, symphonic, chamber, theater, electro-acoustic, and multimedia music. The award also recognizes the contributions of musicologists including research, books, catalogs, music scores, or any contribution to Brazilian musicology. Monetary prizes are awarded. Established in 1993.

1441
National Salon of Fine Arts Prizes (Premios de Salao Nacional de Artes Plasticas)
To recognize artists of the best works. All participants receive a certificate of participation. Four foreign travel prizes of 180,000 Brazilian cruzeiros each, four national travel prizes of 70,000 cruzeiros each, and five acquisition prizes of a total value of 70,000 cruzados are awarded annually. Established in 1977.

1442
Premio MEC de Arte (MEC Art Prizes)
For recognition of outstanding achievements in classical music, popular music, fine arts, and folklore. Brazilian artists are eligible. Four monetary awards (one in each discipline) are awarded annually. Established in 1977 and sponsored by the National Art Foundation.

1443
Prize for Research in Education of the National Institute of the Book
(Premio de Pesquisa Estudantil Instituto Nacional do Livro)
For recognition of the best works on a theme chosen by the National Institute of the Book. Monetary prizes are awarded annually. Established in 1977 by the National Institute of the Book and the Ministry of Education and Culture.

1444
Silvio Romero Folklore Prize
For recognition of the best work in Brazilian folklore and popular culture. Monetary prizes are awarded annually. Established in 1960.

1445
Jose Verissimo Prize
For recognition of the best essay and a work of scholarship. A monetary prize is awarded annually.

1446
Brazilian Organization for Agricultural Research
(Empresa Brasileira de Pesquisa Agropecuaria)
Parque Rural
SAIN - Av. W3 Norte (Final)
Cx. Postal 040315   Phone: 61 3484227
70770-901 Brasilia, DF, Brazil   Fax: 61 3474860

1447
Frederico de Menezes Veiga Prize
(Premio Frederico de Menezes Veiga)
To recognize scientists for significant contributions to the development of agricultural research. One researcher from EMBRAPA and one from other Brazilian research institutions are eligible for the prize. Nomination is by scientists or research institutions by January 1. A monetary prize of US $2,000, a gold medal, and a diploma are awarded annually. Established in 1975 in honor of Frederico de Menezes Veiga, a sugarcane breeder who made important contributions to Brazilian agriculture.

1448
Science and Information Prize
(Premio Ciencia e Informacao)
To recognize scientists, institutions or private corporations for significant contribution to the technology transfer from the scientific organization to the farmers. Nominations by individuals or institutions may be submitted by January 31. A golden medal and a diploma are awarded annually on the Organization's anniversary. Established in 1981. (Discontinued)

1449
Brazilian PEN Club
(PEN Clube do Brasil)
Praia do Flamengo 172, 10 andar
2000 Rio de Janeiro, RJ, Brazil   Phone: 21 285 0491

1450
Graca Aranha Prize
To provide recognition of the best Brazilian novel. A monetary prize is awarded.

1451
Luisa Claudio de Sousa Prize
To provide recognition for the best book published in the previous year. Novels, plays, and literary history and criticism works are considered. Awarded annually.

1452
Brazilian Society of Cultural and Artistic Promotions
(Sociedade Brasileira de Realizacoes Artistico-Culturais)
Avenida Franklin Roosevelt, 23 S/310   Phone: 21 551 1468
22021 Rio De Janeiro, RJ, Brazil   Phone: 21 240 1053

1453
Contest for Piano Accompanists
(Concours Pour Pianistes Accompagnateurs)
To recognize outstanding piano accompanists. Candidates of all nationalities are eligible. The following monetary prizes are awarded: first prize - $5,000; second prize - $3,000; third prize - $1,500; and a gold medal. A number of minor prizes are also awarded. Established in 1987.

1454
International Singing Contest of Rio de Janeiro
(Concours International de Chant de Rio de Janeiro)
To recognize the best young singers of the competition. The following prizes were awarded: First prize - $6,000; Second prize - $4,000; Third prize - $3,000; two prizes of $2,000 each; a gold medal - Villa-Lobos Prize; Silver medal - Nayla Jabor Prize; and a number of minor prizes. Engagements for concerts, recitals and the official season of the Opera House were arranged for the first three prize winners. Awarded biennially. Established in 1963 by Helena Oliveira. (Discontinued)

1455
Esso Brasileira de Petroleo S.A.
Departmento de Assuntos Externos
Av. Presidente Wilson 118, 60 Andar
20030 Rio de Janeiro, RJ, Brazil   Phone: 21 277 2000

1456
Premio Esso de Jornalismo
For recognition of outstanding journalistic contributions published in Brazilian newspapers and magazines during the preceding year. Awards are given in the following categories: (1) reporting; (2) photography; (3) sports; (4) economics; (5) technology; (6) regional journalism; (7) politics; (8) culture; and (9) cartoons. Brazilian journalists are eligible for reports written in Portuguese on subjects related to Brazilian subjects and persons or a Brazilian theme. Monetary prizes from $100 to $500 and certificates are awarded annually. Established in 1956. Additional information is available from Equipe de Comunicacao Programada, Travessa Euricles de Matos, 24, Rio de Janeiro, RJ 22240, Brazil, phone: 21 205 8097.

1457
Foto-Cine Clube Bandeirante
Rua Jose Getulio 442
P.O. 8861
01000 Sao Paulo, SP, Brazil   Phone: 11 279 9418

1458
Bandeirante Trophy
To provide recognition for the best photographs presented by a local or a foreign photo-club. The following prizes are awarded: (1) an effigy of an explorer (bandeirante), made of bronze, mounted on Brazilian gems; (2) gold, silver and bronze medals - for the best monochrome prints and color prints by an amateur or professional photographer, Brazilian or foreign; and (3) honorable mentions and certificates to the individual photographers selected by the jury. Awarded biennially. Established in 1955.

1459
Foundation for the Promotion of Science of the State of Sao Paulo
(Fundacao de Amparo a Pesquisa do Estado de S. Paulo)
Rua Pio X1 1500   Phone: 11 8370311
05468-901 Sao Paulo, SP, Brazil   Fax: 11 8313169

1460
Gleb Wataghin Award
(Premio Gleb Wataghin)
For recognition of an outstanding contribution in physics. Brazilian scientists under 30 years of age who are doing research in the state of Sao Paulo are eligible. A monetary prize and diploma are awarded biennially. Established in 1986 in honor of Prof. Glebn Wataghin for his contribution to the development of physics in Brazil. Additional information is available from Prof. Oscar Sala, Department of Physics, University of Sao Paulo, Sao Paulo, Brazil.

1461
Ibero-Latin-American College of Dermatology
(Colegio Ibero-Latino-mericano de Dermatologia)
c/o Divisao de Dermatologia
Hospital das Clinicas da Faculdade
  Medicina, U.S.P.
Caixa Postal 8091
Sao Paulo, SP, Brazil
Phone: 11 852 5069
Fax: 11 2580032

1462
Xavier Vilanova Prize
For recognition of the best original work on clinical dermatology. Members of the College are eligible. A monetary prize of $1,000 is awarded every four years during the Congress of the College.

1463
Indice - O Banco de Dados
Endereco: Rua Alcindo Guanabara, no. 24
  - Centro
2003 Rio de Janeiro, RJ, Brazil
Phone: 21 220 0707

1464
Premio Visconde de Cairu
To recognize outstanding achievement in the development of economic interchange between Brazil and the countries in the international economic community; particularly the development of trade and the flow of capital and technology. Two entrepreneurial leaders are chosen each year, one a Brazilian, the other a citizen of the EEC. A statuette and certificate are awarded annually. Established in 1978 in memory of Visconde de Cairu, the Brazilian politician and man of letters who inspired the opening of Brazilian ports to friendly nations.

1465
Instituto Brasil - Estados Unidos
Avenida N.S. de Copacabana 690, 11
  andar
22050-000 Rio de Janeiro, RJ, Brazil
Phone: 21 255 8332
Fax: 00 55 21 2558332

1466
IBEU Theater Prize
(Premio IBEU de Teatro)
To recognize the best American play staged in Rio de Janeiro in the previous year. Monetary awards and medals were presented annually. Established in 1968 to further cultural exchange between Brazil and the United States in the field of drama. (Discontinued in 1989)

1467
IBEU Visual Arts Award
(Premio IBEU de Artes Plasticas)
For recognition of achievement and to encourage professional development of the artists whose exhibition in this organization's art gallery was considered the best of the year. Money and a round trip from Rio de Janeiro, Brazil to New York City, New York are awarded annually, at the beginning of the year. Established in 1968 as the Premio Viagem, discontinued in 1978, re-established in 1984, discontinued again in 1989, and re-established in 1991.

1468
Instituto Nacional do Livro
SCRN 704/705, B1.C, no. 40, 2 andaer
70730 Brasilia, DF, Brazil
Phone: 61 274 2315

1469
Bibliotheconomy and Documentation National Award
(Premio Nacional de Biblioteconomia e Documentacao)
For recognition of an outstanding contribution to documentation and to encourage professional development on the bibliotheconomy and documentation fields. Works must be unpublished and written in Portuguese. A monetary prize and co-edition of the winning work are awarded biennially in the even-numbered years. Established in 1977. Formerly: (1989) Premio de Biblioteconomia e Documentacao.

1470
Jabuti Prize
(Premio Jabuti)
To recognize the best Brazilian literary and scientific works of the preceding year in the following categories: novels; poetry; short stories; literary studies; childrens' and young peoples' literature; illustration; translations of literary or scientific works; biography/memoirs; literary and journalistic criticism; social, exact, and natural sciences; technological science; and journalism. A statue of a "jabuti" is awarded annually. Established in 1959.

1471
Antonio Maria Special Award
(Premio Especial Antonio Maria)
For recognition of achievement in narrative writing published in a book during the present year. Works must be written in Portuguese. A monetary prize is awarded annually. Established in 1989 in memory of Antonio Maria, a popular song lyrics writer and narrative writer.

1472
National Book Institute Juvenile Literature Award
(Premio Instituto Nacional do Livro de Literatura Infantil)
To encourage professional development in juvenile literature writing and illustrating. Unpublished works written in Portuguese may compete for the best text. The best illustration works are chosen from the winning texts. A monetary prize and co-edition of the winning works in both categories are awarded biennially in the even- numbered years. Established in 1970.

1473
National Translation Award
(Premio Nacional de Traducao)
For recognition of an outstanding contribution to the field of translation and to encourage professional development in this field. Only works published in the preceding two years are eligible. A monetary prize is awarded biennially in the odd-numbered years. Established in 1980.

1474
Premios Literarios Nacionais
For recognition of recently published works, and to encourage publication of works still unpublished. Awards are given in alternate years in the following fields: (1) short story and poetry; (2) novel and biography; and (3) history and literary essay. Works must be written in Portuguese and should be submitted between January 2 and May 31. Winners of the regional awards may compete for the national awards. These winners are in five geographical areas and in each category. A monetary prize and co-edition of works still unpublished are awarded annually. Established in 1975.

1475
Santa Rosa Award
(Premio Santa Rosa)
For recognition of achievement in book design (graphic arts), including cover, diagrams, printing and other technical features. Books published in Portuguese in the prior year are eligible. A monetary prize is awarded annually. Established in 1969 and resumed in 1988 in memory of Thomas

Santa Rosa Jr., whose life was dedicated to the printing art and to other arts in general.

1476

International Bocce Federation
(Federation Internationale de Boules)
Rua Buenos Aires 93, Salas 1208
20070 Rio de Janeiro, RJ, Brazil   Phone: 21 2329008

1477

International Bocce Federation Competitions
To promote the sport of bocce (also bocci or boccie), a game of Italian origin similar to lawn bowling played on a long, narrow, usually dirt court. The Federation sponsors competitions.

1478

International Federation of Sports Medicine
Tres Figuetas 95
91330 Porto Alegre, Rio Grande do Sul,   Phone: 512 348083
   Brazil   Fax: 512 272295

1479

Bronze Medal
To recognize Honorary Members and others who have performed signal services for the organization. Those named as Honorary Members by the Executive Committee, or nominated by it to the Council of Delegates are eligible for the award. A bronze medal is awarded as merited. Established in 1932.

1480

Gold Medal
To recognize outstanding contributions to sports medicine over a period of years in leadership, education, research and practice. Nominations may be made by the Executive Committee to the Council of Delegates. A gold medal is presented biennially when the Council of Delegates meets. Established in 1932.

1481

International Festival of Film, Television and Video of Rio de Janeiro
(Associacao do Festrio, Festival Internacional de Cinema, Televisao e Video do Rio de Janeiro)
Rua Paissandu 362   Phone: 21 285 6642
22210 Rio de Janeiro, RJ, Brazil   Fax: 21 285 7599

1482

Golden Toucan
(Tucano de Ouro)
For recognition of achievement in the fields of film, television, and video. Nominations or applications may be submitted by October 30. Golden Toucans are awarded for the Best Film, Best Television Program, and the Best Video Production. Silver Toucans are awarded for the: (1) Best Director - Glauber Rocha Award; (2) Best Actress; (3) Best Actor; (4) Best Short Film; (5) Best Musical Video; (6) Best Television Entertainment Program; (7) Best Television Journalistic Program; (8) Best Television Fiction Program; (9) Best Experimental Video; and (10) Best Documentary Video. Awarded annually. Established in 1984.

1483

International Seaweed Association
Instituto de Biociemcias
Universidade de Sao Paulo
Caixa Postal 11.461 CEP 05499
01000 Sao Paulo, SP, Brazil   Phone: 7 593320

1484

International Seaweed Association Awards
To recognize scientific and commercial communities for contributions to the management of seaweed resources. Awards are presented triennially. For more information contact Dr. Enrico Oliveira.

1485

International Society of Sugar Cane Technologists
Departmento Tecnico Rural-Esalo
Avenida Padua Dias 11
Caixa Postal 09
13400 Piracicaba, SP, Brazil   Phone: 194 324656

1486

Triennial Challenge Cup
For recognition in the field of sugar cane technology. Members who participate in the Triennial Congress are eligible. A chalice is awarded triennially at post-congress events. Established in 1986 by Ikatan Ahli Gula Indonesia (Association of Indonesian Sugar Technologists).

1487

Nami Jafet Institute for the Advancement of Science and Culture
(Instituto Nami Jafet para o Progreso da Ciencia e Cultura)
Rua Agostinho Gomes 1455
Sao Paulo, SP, Brazil

1488

Nami Jafet Prize
To provide recognition for achievement in science and culture. The award rotates annually and is given in the following disciplines: (1) science; (2) technology; and (3) culture, including music, visual arts, film, and architecture. Two monetary prizes of a total amount of 3,000 Brazilian cruzados, a gold medal, a diploma, and scholarships are awarded. Established in 1961 in memory of Prof. Nami Jafet, an industrialist.

1489

Medical Academy of Sao Paulo
(Academia de Medicina de Sao Paulo)
Rua Teodoro Sampaio, 115 2 piso
05405 Sao Paulo, SP, Brazil   Phone: 11 853-9677

1490

Medical Academy of Sao Paulo Prize
(Premio Academia de Medicina de Sao Paulo)
To encourage medical development and the practice of medicine in the state of Sao Paulo. A medal and diploma are awarded annually. Established in 1918.

1491

Museum of Modern Art of Sao Paulo
(Museu de Arte Moderna de Sao Paulo)
Parque Ibirapuera s/no.   Phone: 11 5499688
04098 Sao Paulo, SP, Brazil   Fax: 11 5492342

1492

Panorama of Actual Brasilian Art
(Panorama de Arte Atual Brasileira)
To provide for acquisition of works of art for the museum and for recognition of outstanding art in the categories of: painting, sculpture and objects, and art on paper. Monetary prizes are awarded annually to two to four artists. Established in 1969.

Brazil

1493

National Bank
c/o O Globo Newspaper
Rua Irineu Marinho 35
POB 1090
Rio de Janeiro, RJ, Brazil   Phone: 21 272 2000

1494

Walmap Prize
To provide recognition for unpublished literary works in the Portuguese language. Authors of any nationality are eligible. Monetary prizes of approximately $13,000 are awarded biennially.

1495

Moinho Santista Foundation
(Fundacao Moinho Santista)
Av. Maria Coelho Aguiar
215, Bloco D, Andar   Phone: 11 5456832
05804-903 Sao Paulo, SP, Brazil   Fax: 11 5451288

1496

Moinho Santista Prizes for Young People
(Premios Moinho Santista Juventude)
To promote recognition for outstanding lifetime service and achievement in any scientific, literary, or artistic field. Individuals under 35 years of age are eligible. Prizes rotate during a six-year cycle in the following disciplines: biological sciences and public health, agricultural sciences, technology and exact sciences, philosophy and education, human and social sciences, art, and literature. Two prizes of approximately $15,000 each, silver medals, and diplomas of recognition are awarded annually. This award is considered to be the Brazilian equivalent of the Nobel Prize. Established in 1980.

1497

Moinho Santista Prizes
(Premio Moinho Santista)
To promote recognition for outstanding lifetime service and achievement in any scientific, literary, or artistic field. Prizes rotate during a six-year cycle in the following disciplines: biological sciences and public health, agricultural sciences, technology and exact sciences, philosophy and education, human and social sciences, art, and literature. Two prizes of approximately $35,000 each, gold medals, and diplomas of recognition are awarded annually. This award is considered to be the Brazilian equivalent of the Nobel Prize. Established in 1955.

1498

Sao Paulo International Film Festival
(Mostra Internacional de Cinema Em Sao Paulo)
Alameda Lorena 937-CJ 302   Phone: 11 883 5137
01424 Sao Paulo, SP, Brazil   Fax: 11 853 7936

1499

Sao Paulo International Film Festival
For recognition of the best film of the festival. Feature films or shorts not previously shown in Brazil must be submitted by September 1. The public selects one film and the jury of critics also selects one. The Bandeira Paulista, a flag of Sao Paulo stylized by the designer, Tomie Ohtake, is awarded annually. Established in 1977 by Leon Cakoff. In addition, a Critics Prize, Best Short Film Prize, and special prizes are awarded.

1500

Villa-Lobos Museum
(Museu Villa-Lobos)
Rua Sorocaba, 200   Phone: 21 266 3894
22271 Rio de Janeiro, RJ, Brazil   Phone: 21 266 3845

1501

International Villa-Lobos Guitar Competition
(Concorso Internacional de Violao Villa-Lobos)
To recognize the best guitarist in the competition, and to encourage the development of Villa-Lobos works and Brazilian works in general. Guitarists of any age may submit entries and tapes by April 20. The following monetary prizes are awarded biennially: (1) First prize - $3,000 US; and (2) Second prize - $2,000 US. Established in 1971 by Museu Villa-Lobos in honor of Heitor Villa-Lobos.

1502

International Villa-Lobos Piano Contest
(Concorso Internacional de Piano Villa-Lobos)
To recognize the best pianist in the competition, and to encourage the development of Villa-Lobos works and Brazilian works in general. Pianists of any age may submit entries and tapes by April 20. The following prizes are awarded: (1) first prize - 200,000,00 Brazilian cruzeiros; (2) second prize - 100,000,00 Brazilian cruzeiros; and (3) third prize - 50,000,00 Brazilian cruzeiros. Semi finalists may be awarded Distinctions. The winner also accepts the commitment to perform a pre-selected work by Villa-Lobos with orchestra. Established in 1974 by Museu Villa-Lobos in honor of Heitor Villa-Lobos.

Bulgaria

1503

Bulgaria
Office of the President
Dondukov Boulevard 2   Phone: 2 881767
BG-1123 Sofia, Bulgaria   Fax: 2 803418

1504

Christo Botev International Prize for Revolutionary Poetry
To recognize foreign authors for their work of a highly artistic lasting value, and for their struggle for social justice. A gold medal, a monetary prize of 2,500 leva, and a diploma were awarded every five years. (Discontinued)

1505

Brothers St. Cyril and Methodius International Prize
To recognize foreign nationals for their scientific published or social work devoted to Bulgarian studies or education. A diploma, a gold badge and a monetary award of 5,000 leva were awarded biennially. (Discontinued)

1506

Madarski Konnik Order
To recognize foreign diplomatic representatives, public figures, private persons, and soldiers who have rendered great services to the establishment, by strengthening and maintaining friendly relations with the People's Republic of Bulgaria. Honorary recognition and the Order are awarded.

1507

Order of the Rose
To recognize prominent foreign political, public, economic, and social figures for great service to the People's Republic of Bulgaria. Honorary recognition and a gold or silver medal are awarded.

1508

Stara Planina Order
To recognize foreign heads of state or government, ministers, diplomats, political, public, cultural and economic figures for their contributions to the establishment, strengthening and maintaining close and friendly relations with the People's Republic of Bulgaria, and for the strengthening of peace between peoples. Bulgarian ambassadors may also be recognized. Honorary recognition and a medal with or without a ribbon are awarded.

1509

Thirteen Centuries of Bulgaria Order
This, Bulgaria's highest Order, is given to recognize outstanding service to Bulgaria. A medal is awarfed when merited. Established in 1981.

1510

N. Vaptsarov International Prize
To recognize foreign authors for their merited artistic and social work which is imbued by the noble principles of the struggle for peace, by the pathos of humanism and social progress. The award included a gold medal and a monetary award of 4,000 leva. Awarded every five years. (Discontinued)

1511

Bulgarian Academy of Sciences
(Academie Bulgare des Sciences)
Central Library
15 Noemvri, 1
BG-1040 Sofia, Bulgaria
Phone: 2 878966
Fax: 2 803127

1512

Bulgarian Academy of Science Honorary Badge - Marin Drinov Medal
To recognize Bulgarian and foreign scientists as well as outstanding cultural workers on the occasion of their jubilees for major scientific achievements and considerable contributions to Bulgarian science. Selection is made by the Bulgarian Academy of Science Presidium or the Presidium Bureau at the proposal of the Scientific Secretariat, the Research Centres or the independent scientific organizations attached to the Presidium. A medal with the relief image of Prof. Marin Drinov, first president of the Academy, a certificate of merit, and an honorary badge are awarded. The medal was established in 1975, and the honorary badge in 1981. (Temporarily suspended)

1513

Bulgarian Academy of Science - Kliment Ohridski University of Sofia Prizes
For recognition of outstanding scientific work. The following accomplishments were considered for the award: published research works that contribute to the development of the respective branch of science or to the country's social and economic development; completed original research and developments acknowledged as discoveries or inventions of major importance; original research and development accomplished through creative application and further development of foreign achievements and experience implemented with considerable economic or social results; exceptional achievements in the field of education and teaching; and other major scientific achievements of outstanding national or international consequence. The following prizes were awarded: Paisiy Hilendarski Prize for Bulgarian studies; Dimiter Blagoev Prize for social and political sciences; Professor Dr. Asen Zlatarov Prize for chemical sciences; Academy Nikola Obreshkov Prize for mathematical sciences; and Professor Vasil Zlatarski Prize for History, Archaeology, and Ethnography; Academician Aleksandar Teodorov-Balan Prize for History of Bulgarian Language and History of Linguistics; Academician Georgi Nadzhakov Prize for Physical Sciences; Academician Doncho Kostov Prize for Biological Sciences; Academician Aleksi Puhlev Prize for Medical and Biological Sciences; Academician George Bonchev Prize for Earth Sciences; Academician Hristo Daskalov Prize for Agrobiological Sciences; Prize for Theory of Literature; Academician Vladimir Georgiev Prize for Research of Contemporary Bulgarian Language and Contemporary Philology; Prize for Science of Art; and Prize for Technical Sciences. A certificate of merit and honorary badge were awarded annually on the day of commemoration of the Bulgarian education and culture, the Slav alphabet and the Bulgarian press, May 24. Established in 1975. (Temporarily suspended)

1514

Cyril and Methodius Prize
For recognition of research representing a considerable original scientific contribution in the field of old Bulgarian writing, literature, and culture. A diploma and honorary recognition were awarded annually on the day of commemoration of Bulgarian education and culture, the Slav alphabet and the Bulgarian press, May 24. Established in 1971. (Temporarily suspended)

1515

Bulgarian Society of Violin Makers
c/o International Competitions
  Management
Tina Kirkova Street 16
BG-1000 Sofia, Bulgaria
Phone: 2 80 18 02
Phone: 2 83 54 10

1516

International Competition for Violin and Viola Makers
(Concours International de Lutherie)
To recognize outstanding violin and viola makers of all nationalities. Competitors of any age may submit not more than two violins and two violas which must have been made during the preceding three years. Applications may be submitted by September 15. The following prizes are awarded for violas and violins: (1) Grand Prix of Kazanluk - 3,500 leva, a gold medal and diploma; (2) First prize - 3,000 leva, gold medal and diploma; (3) Second prize - 2,500 leva, silver medal and diploma; (4) Third prize - 2,000 leva, bronze medal and diploma; and (5) another Third prize of VTD "Hemus" - 2,000 leva, bronze medal and diploma. The competition is held every three years. Established in 1984.

1517

Bulgarian Television and Radio
(Bulgarska Televiziya i Radio)
International Relations Dept.
Dragan Tzankov blvd. 4
BG-1040 Sofia, Bulgaria
Phone: 2 66 11 49
Fax: 2 66 22 15

1518

Golden Chest International Television Festival
(Zlatnata Rakla)
To promote international television cooperation and a better knowledge of achievements in the field of television drama. Productions must be on a contemporary theme and must be based on a literary work of national origin; plays written for television; TV-versions of theatre plays or television dramatizations. The award is given in two categories: (1) Television drama for adults (running time of up to 100 minutes); and (2) Television drama for children and adolescents (70 minutes). The productions must have been released during the preceding two years and must not have been shown at other foreign festivals. Applications must be submitted by August 15. The following prizes are awarded: (1) Golden Chest - Grand Prix of Bulgarian Television and Radio; (2) Silver Chest - Special Prize of Bulgarian Television and Radio; (3) Special Prize of the Interhotels - Balkantourist Chain; and (4) Special Prize for Best Actor's Performance. In the children's category the following prizes are awarded: (1) Golden Chest - Grand Prix of Bulgarian Television and Radio; (2) Silver Chest - Special Prize of the People's Council of the City of Plovdiv; and Special Prize of CIFEJ. Established in 1968 by Bulgarian Television.

1519

House of Humour and Satire
PO Box 104
BG-5300 Gabrovo, Bulgaria
Phone: 66 2 72 29
Phone: 66 2 93 00

1520

Charlie Chaplin Prize
To stimulate humour and satire in the film and television arts and to further humanism and mankind's cultural development. Works may be submitted by March 1. A monetary prize of 2,000 leva, a Charlie Chaplin statuette, and a certificate are awarded biennially in odd-numbered years. Established in 1981. Sponsored by the Bulgarian Film Makers Union, the Committee for Television, the Bulgarian Ministry of Culture, and the Bulgarian Cinematography Corporation.

1521

Golden Aesop Prize
For recognition of outstanding achievements in each one of the fields: Cartoons, Drawing and Illustration, Graphic Works, Painting, and Sculpture. A statuette and honorary recognition are awarded biennially. Sponsored by Gabrovo International Biennial of Humour and Satire in the Arts.

1522

Hitar Petar/Artful Peter/Grand Prize for Humor and Satire in Literature
For recognition of the best work of world literature in the field of humor and satire, and to stimulate the development of humorous and satiric literature in the service of humanism, progress and the moral perfection of mankind. The honored book is translated into Bulgarian and published by Hristo G. Danov Publishing House. A monetary prize of 2,000 levas and a bronze and leather plate are awarded biennially in May. Sponsored by the Bulgarian Ministry of Culture.

1523

Photo-Jokes Competition
For recognition of photographs that show funny situations from everyday life and reveal the richness of the human smile by means of photography. Black and white and color photographs of minimum size 18x24 cm, and of maximum size 30x40 cm may be submitted by March 1. A monetary prize of 1,800 leva is awarded biennially in odd-numbered years. Established in 1975. Sponsored by The Bulgarian Photography Union.

1524

International Competition for Young Opera Singers - Sofia
Dept. of International Competitions
Alabin Street 56
BG-1090 Sofia, Bulgaria   Phone: 2 87 17 72

1525

International Competition for Young Opera Singers - Sofia (Concours International de Jeunes Chanteurs d'Opera)
For recognition of the achievements of young opera singers. Singers of all nationalities can take part in the Competition. Men may not be older than 35, and women not older than 33 years of age. The Competition takes place in three stages; the third one involves singing a principal part in a regular performance of the Sofia National Opera. The Grand Prix of Sofia consists of a monetary prize of 4,000 levas, a gold medal, a gold ring and a diploma. The following prizes are also awarded to both men and women: (1) First prize - 3,500 levas, a gold medal and a diploma; (2) Second prize - 2,500 levas, a silver medal and a diploma; and (3) Third prize 1,500 levas, a bronze medal, and a diploma. The winners are offered invitations for guest performances in Bulgaria and other countries of Europe. Awarded every four years. Established in 1961. (The 10th competition will be held June 19-July 3, 1992.)

1526

Pancho Vladiguerov International Competition for Pianists
For recognition of achievements in piano performance and to encourage professional development. Pianists under 32 years of age of all nationalities may submit applications by November 1. The following prizes are awarded: (1) Grand Prix - a Grand piano "Petrof" PE IV, 1,500 leva and a gold medal; (2) First Prize - 3,500 leva and a gold medal; (3) Second Prize - 3,000 leva and a silver medal; (4) Third Prize - 2,500 leva and a bronze medal; (5) Fourth Prize - 2,000 leva; and (6) Fifth Prize - 1,500 leva. Established in 1986 in honor of Pancho Vladiguerov, an outstanding Bulgarian composer.

1527

International Festival of Red Cross and Health Films
c/o Bulgarian Red Cross Central
  Committee
Festival Directorate
Biruzov Blvd. 1   Phone: 2 44 29 96
BG-1527 Sofia, Bulgaria   Phone: 2 44 17 59

1528

International Festival of Red Cross and Health Films
To recognize the best films on topical Red Cross, health, ecological and humanitarian subjects. Films produced during the preceding two years by the International Institutions and National Red Cross and Red Crescent Societies, by film production companies, television studios and other institutions, are eligible. Films can be entered in the following two categories: (1) Non-fiction Red Cross and Health Films for Cinema and Television (under 60 min.) - (a) Films promoting the ideas of the Red Cross and Red Crescent; (b) Popular-science, documentary, animation films and spots on health and ecological subjects; and (c) Scientific and instructional films; and (2) Feature Films - (a) Feature films for the cinema - 35 mm; and (b) TV dramas and parts of serials. The films judged to be the best in their category and subgroup, are awarded the following prizes: (1) Non-fiction Red Cross and Health Films for Cinema and Television - (a) Golden Ship Grand Prix of the President of the Bulgarian Red Cross for the best film in the category; (b) Grand Prix of the League of Red Cross and Red Crescent Societies for the best Red Cross film; (c) Special Prize for the best health or ecological film; and (d) Special Prize for the best scientific or instructional film. First and Second prizes of Gold and Silver medals are also awarded for each of the subgroups; and (2) Feature Films - (a) Grand Prix for the best feature film for the cinema; (b) Grand Prix for the best TV drama; (c) Prize for the best direction; (d) Prize for the best actress; (e) Prize for the best actor; and (f) Special Prize of the League of Red Cross and Red Crescent Societies for the best film with humanitarian character. A Special Prize is awarded by the World Health Organization for the best film on Communication for Health. In addition, the FIPRESCI (International Federation of Cinema Press) Prize and the CIDALC (International Committee for the Dissemination of Art and Literature through Cinema) Prize are awarded. Participation Diplomas are presented to all films shown in competition during the Festival. Awarded biennially. Established in 1965. Sponsored by The League of Red Cross and Red Crescent Societies, the International Committee of the Red Cross, and the World Health Organization.

1529

Sofia International Film Festival on Organization and Automation of Production and Management
Rakovsky Str. 135-a
BG-1000 Sofia, Bulgaria

1530

Sofia International Film Festival on Organization and Automation of Production and Management Awards
To provide recognition for the best films and videos in the festival. Format requirements are 16/35mm Film, U-Matic, HS, PAL and SECAM Video. Films may be entered in the categories of research, scientific-technical, training, and scientific-popular. First, Second and Third prizes are awarded biennially. Sponsored by the Central Council of Scientific-Technical Unions.

1531

Union of Bulgarian Artists
Shipka Street 6
BG-1040 Sofia, Bulgaria   Phone: 2 45 28 40

1532

International Print Biennal - Varna
To recognize the world's achievements in print art and stimulate an interaction and search for creativity between artists from all over the world. The following prizes are awarded: Grand Prix of the Town of Varna, Young Author Prize, and Union of Bulgarian Artists Prize. A gold, silver, or bronze plaque and a diploma are awarded biennially. In addition, the winner of the Grand Prix is invited to participate in an individual exhibition during the following Biennial. Established in 1981.

1533

Laureate of the Triennial of the Realistic Painting
To unify the efforts of artists who have taken their stand on realistic positions and are fighting through their art for humanism and social

progress, and demonstrate the great force of realism and its place in the development of modern artistic culture in the world. An international jury awards the prize during the exhibition of the Triennal. A monetary prize of 3,000 leva, a plaque, and a diploma are awarded triennially. Established in 1973 by the Committee of Culture and the Union of Bulgarian Artists. Sponsored by the Committee of Culture and the Municipality of Sofia.

1534

Union of Bulgarian Motorists
Sveta Sofiaste 6
Sofia, Bulgaria
Phone: 2 87 88 01
Phone: 2 86 151

1535

Golden Sands Rally
(Albena Zlatni Piassatsi Sliven)
To recognize the race car with the best timing in the Golden Sands Rally. An award of one car type "Lada" 1300 is presented. Awarded annually. Established in 1970. Sponsored by the Bulgarian Association for Recreation and Tourism.

1536

Union of Bulgarian Writers
Angel Kanchev 5
BG-1040 Sofia, Bulgaria
Phone: 2 87 47 11

1537

International Vaptsarov Prize
To provide recognition for outstanding poetry. Poets of any nationality are eligible. A monetary prize of 4,000 leva and a gold medal bearing the likeness of the Bulgarian poet Nicola Vaptsarov (1909-1942) are awarded. Established in 1979.

1538

Varna International Ballet Competition
(Concours International de Ballet, Varna)
Rusky Blvd. 1
BG-1000 Sofia, Bulgaria
Phone: 2 88 33 77
Phone: 2 80 18 02

1539

Varna International Ballet Competition
(Concours International de Ballet, Varna)
For recognition of outstanding ballet dancers. Men and women dancers from all nationalities can take part in the Competition. Awards are presented in two independent classes: (1) Class A (Seniors) - for ballet dancers not older than 26 years of age; and (2) Class B (Juniors) - for boys and girls from 14 to 19 years of age. Competitors under 19 years of age who wish to compete in Class A - Seniors should receive special permission from the international jury. If the candidates decide to dance a pas de deux in one of the three stages of the competition, the ballet couples may be formed from one and the same class or from the two different classes. The candidates have to perform five pieces. The following prizes are awarded in Class A - Seniors: (1) Laureate of the International Ballet Competition and the Grand Prix of Varna - 20,000 leva, a gold medal and a diploma; (2) First Prizes (one for men and one for women) - 15,000 leva each, a gold medal, and a diploma; (3) two Second Prizes - 10,000 leva each, a silver medal, and a diploma; (4) Third Prize - 8,000 leva, a bronze medal, and a diploma; (5) Special Prize Nina Ricci - 12,000 leva, a commemorative medal and a diploma; and (6) Special Prize Repetto - 12,000 leva, a commemorative medal and a diploma. The following prizes are awarded in Class B - Juniors: (1) Excellent Performer of the International Ballet Competition and Special Distinction of the Youth Organization of Varna - 10,000 leva, a diploma, concerts, and a medal; (2) First Class Awards (one for girls and one for boys) - 6,000 leva each, a diploma and a medal; (3) two Second Class Awards - 4,000 leva each, a diploma and a medal; and (4) two Third Class Awards - 2,000 leva each, a diploma and a medal. Special awards, token awards and distinctions are also awarded. Awarded biennially. Established in 1964. Varna is one of four locations for the International Ballet Competition, the others being Moscow, USSR; Jackson, Mississippi, U.S.A.; and Helsinki, Finland.

Burkina Faso

1540

Panafrican Film and Television of Ouagadougou Festival
(Festival Panafricain du Cinema de Ouagadougou)
Sec. Gen. of the Festival
01 BP 2505
Ouagadougou 01, Burkina Faso
Phone: 30 75 38
Fax: 31 25 09

1541

Panafrican Film and Television Festival of Ouagadougou
(Festival Panafrican du Cinema de Ouagadougou)
For recognition of the full-length African film deemed by the jury to be the best account of the African cultural identity or social realities. A monetary award and the Yennenga Stallion Trophy are awarded biennially at the Festival. Established in 1972 by the government of Burkina Faso to honor Princess Yennenga, Mossi's ancestor, who used a horse to fight.

Cameroon

1542

African Insurance Organization
(Organisation des Assurances Africaines)
BP 5860
Douala, Cameroon
Phone: 424162
Fax: 421335

1543

African Insurance Organization Awards
To recognize African insurance, reinsurance, and brokerage companies and insurance supervision authorities in 40 countries, and to encourage cooperation in the insurance industry. The organization bestows awards, and maintains a hall of fame.

Chile

1544

Chile
Ministerio de Educacion
Direccion de Bibliotecas
Archivos y Museos
Ave. Libertador Bernardo O'Higgins No. 651
Santiago 1371, Chile

1545

Premio Nacional de Arte
To recognize a Chilean artist distinguished by outstanding quality of works and achievement in visual arts, music, or performing arts. Awarded biennially in even-numbered years.

1546

Premio Nacional de Ciencias
To recognize Chilean scientists for outstanding work in the field of pure and applied sciences of humanity and the environment. A monetary award is presented biennially in odd-numbered years.

1547

Premio Nacional de Historia
To recognize a Chilean historian for significant contributions to cultural history of historiography. A monetary prize is awarded biennially in even-numbered years.

1548
Premio Nacional de Literatura
To recognize a Chilean author of distinction in any of the literary fields of the novel, poetry, theater, essay, and literary criticism. Chilean writers must be nominated by an accredited academic institution and three or more people associated with the prize. A monetary prize and a certificate are awarded biennially in even-numbered years. Established in 1942 by Por Ley de la Republica.

1549
Premio Nacional de Periodismo
To recognize a Chilean journalist distinguished by his or her method of communication or expression and for significant support of written or audiovisual journalism. A monetary prize is awarded biennially in odd-numbered years.

1550
Chilean Academy of Language
(Academia Chilena de la Lengua)
Almirante Montt 453
Santiago 1349, Chile   Phone: 2 382847

1551
Chilean Academy of Language Prize
(Premio Academia Chilena de la Lengua)
To promote literary excellence and to recognize the best book chosen by the Academy. Books must have been published in Chile during the previous year to be considered. A certificate is awarded annually in September. Established in 1963.

1552
Alonso de Ercilla Award
(Premio Alonso de Ercilla)
For recognition of achievement in literary criticism. Individuals may be nominated. A diploma is awarded annually. Established in 1990 to honor Alonso de Ercilla y Zuniga, author of the epic poem *La Araucana*.

1553
Alejandro Silva de la Fuente Award
(Premio Alejandro Silva de la Fuente)
To promote journalism written in good Castillian Spanish. Chilean journalists are eligible for consideration. A certificate is awarded annually in September. Established in 1953 in honor of Don Alejandro Silva de la Fuente, a former director of the Academy. Formerly: (1960) Premio Periodistico.

1554
Chilean Society of Dermatology and Venereology
(Sociedad Chilena de Dermatologia y Venereologia)
Avenida Presidente Riesco 6007
Santiago, Chile

1555
Chilean Society Awards for Scientific Works
To recognize individuals for contributions to the development of dermatology and venereology, especially the socio-medical aspects of dermatological and venereal diseases. Awards are given at a biennial congress.

1556
Chilean Society of History and Geography
(Sociedad Chilena de Historia y Geografia)
Londres 65
Santiago, Chile   Phone: 2 6382489

1557
Gold Medal
(Medalla de Oro)
To recognize outstanding works specializing in the fields of interest of the Society and to reward members for dedication and service. A medal is awarded at the convention. Established in 1912.

1558
Honorary Member
To recognize members for distinguished contributions. The honorary title is conferred at the convention.

1559
Colegio Medico Veterinario de Chile
Consejo Nacional
Cirujano Guzman 40 - Providencia   Phone: 2 256386
Santiago, Chile   Fax: 2 250136

1560
Premio a la Actividad Cientifica Dr. Alvaro Blanco Blanco
For recognition in the field of veterinary medicine. A medal and a diploma were awarded. (Discontinued in 1989)

1561
Premio a la Actividad Gremial Dr. Roberto Tapia Alarcon
For recognition in the field of veterinary medicine. A medal and a diploma were awarded. (Discontinued in 1989)

1562
Premio a la Actividad Profesional Dr. Hugo K. Sievers Wicke
For recognition in the field of veterinary medicine. A medal and a diploma were awarded. (Discontinued in 1989)

1563
Editorial Andres Bello
Av. Ricardo Lyon 946
Casilla 4256   Phone: 2 2049900
Santiago, Chile   Fax: 2 2253600

1564
Premio Iberoamericano de Primeras Novelas
To encourage the development of Chilean literary works. Chilean citizens may submit unpublished novels. A monetary prize of $300,000 (Chilean), a diploma, and publication of the novel are awarded biennially. Established in 1980. Formerly: Premio de Novela Andres Bello.

1565
Fundacion Pablo Neruda
Calle Fernando Marquez de la Plata 0192
Barrio Bellavista   Phone: 2 7778741
Santiago, Chile   Fax: 2 7378712

1566
Premio Pablo Neruda
To promote literary creativity among authors under 40 years of age. A monetary prize is awarded annually. Established in 1987 in memory of Pablo Neruda, the Chilean author.

1567
Ilustre Municipalidad de Santiago
Santiago, Chile

1568

Premio Municipal de Literatura
To recognize authors of the best novels, short stories, poetry, dramas, and essays. Established in 1934.

1569

International Musical Contest Dr. Luis Sigall Competition
(Concurso Internacional de Ejecucion Musical Dr. Luis Sigall)
Calle Arlegui 683, Casilla 4-d
Vina del Mar, Chile
Phone: 32 883358
Fax: 32 680633

1570

International Musical Contest Dr. Luis Sigall Competition
For recognition of outstanding musical performances. Performers of all nationalities between 17 and 32 years of age are eligible. The deadline for applications is August 30. Individuals who are selected as contestants are reimbursed for air fare and accommodations. Awards are given in the following categories: Song (1994), Violin (1995), and Cello (1996). The following monetary prizes are awarded: first prize - $4,000; second - $2,000; and third prize - $1,000. Winners are also expected to perform with the Regional Symphony Orchestra of Vina del Mar. Established in 1973.

China, People's Republic of

1571

Chinese Chemical Society
Deputy Sec.
PO Box 2709
Beijing 100080, People's Republic of China
Phone: 1 2564020
Fax: 1 2568157

1572

Chinese Chemical Society Awards
To recognize the development of chemical science by Chinese and foreign chemists and government institutions. The Society sponsors competitions and bestows the Young Chemists Award and the Professor Wang Baoren's Award biennially.

1573

National Vaccine and Serum Institute Beijing
c/o Research and Education Div.
Chaoyang District National Vaccine and
  Serum Institute
Beijing, People's Republic of China
Phone: 1 5762911
Fax: 1 5762404

1574

National Vaccine and Serum Institute Award
For recognition of contributions to disease prevention. The award is designed to recognize a study on the etiology and epidemiology of epidemic cerebrospinal meningitis and purification of a meningococcal vaccine. A monetary prize and a trophy or plaque are awarded annually. Established in 1980. Sponsored by the Ministry of Public Health of China.

1575

Organizing Committee of the Shanghai Television Festival
651 Nanjing Rd. W.
Shanghai 200041, People's Republic of
  China
Phone: 21 2537115
Phone: 21 2537214
Fax: 21 2552000

1576

Magnolia Prize
To recognize outstanding television achievement at the Shanghai Television Festival. Awards are presented in the following categories: Best Feature Film or TV Play; Best Actor; Best Actress; Best Director; Best Documentary; Best Short Documentary; and Best Photography. Gold, silver, and copper cups are awarded biennially at the closing ceremony of the Festival. Established in 1988.

Colombia

1577

Academia Colombiana de Ciencias Exactas, Fisicas y Naturales
Carrera 3A, No. 17-34, piso 3
Apartado Aereo 44763
Bogota 1, D.E., Colombia
Phone: 1 241 48 05
Phone: 1 242 41 74

1578

Colombian Academy of Science Prize
(Premio Academia Colombiana de Ciencias)
For recognition of the best research in the sciences, exact, physical, and natural. The second best work receives honorable mention. Scientists under the age of 35 who are Colombian citizens are eligible. Works must be unpublished, unless as a recent thesis, and must be relevant to the varying theme chosen by the administrators. A monetary prize varying in amount up to 500,000 Colombian pesos is awarded annually. Established in 1987.

1579

Colombian Academy of Science Third World Prize
(Premio Academia de Ciencias del Tercer Mundo)
To promote young scientists in the field of scientific investigation. Awards are given in alternate years for biology, physics, chemistry, and mathematics. Original work done in Colombia during the preceding four years by Colombian scientists under 35 years of age is considered. A monetary prize of 500,000 Colombian pesos is awarded annually. Established in 1987.

1580

Ames Foundation for Investigation in the Field of Basic Health Science
(Fundacion Ames Pro Investigacion en Ciencias de la Salud "Fundames")
Calle 71, No. 13-10, Office 302
Apartado Aereo 90144
Santafe de Bogota, D.C., Colombia
Phone: 1 2456066
Fax: 1 2853591

Formerly: (1989) Comision Premio Ames a la Investigacion en el Laboratorio Clinico.

1581

Ames Prize for Investigation in the field of Basic Health Sciences
(Premio Ames a la Investigacion en Ciencias Basicas de la Salud)
To recognize work in clinical laboratories and research in the health sciences field. Unpublished and original works may be submitted. Entries may be from independent authors or groups. Works must be conducted according to the guidelines established by the international norms. The deadline for entry is September 30. A monetary prize of 2,500,000 Colombian pesos and publication of the study are awarded annually. Established in 1982. Formerly: (1989) Premio Ames a la Investigacion en el Laboratorio Clinico.

1582

Alejandro Angel Escobar Foundation
(Fundacion Alejandro Angel Escobar)
Address unknown.

1583

Alejandro Angel Escobar Charity Prizes
(Premios de Beneficencia Alejandro Angel Escobar)
To recognize individuals who have performed outstanding works of public charity which will have lasting results in Colombia, such as work for hospitals, asylums, orphanages, leprosy centers, and schools and

1584 Colombia — Awards, Honors & Prizes, 1995-96

camps for poor children. A monetary prize of 400,000 Colombian pesos, a silver medal, and a diploma are awarded annually. Established in 1954 by Dr. Escobar in his will.

1584
Alejandro Angel Escobar Science Prize
(Premio de Ciencias Alejandro Angel Escobar)
For recognition in the field of applied sciences. One prize is given to recognize living authors of scientific works in the following disciplines: agriculture; livestock; soil improvement; mechanization of human work; and management of communication; and the other prize is given for recognition of scientific work in the fields of: medicine; surgery; chemistry; physics; psychopathology; meteorology; mechanics or other applied sciences. Colombian scientists, university professors, laboratory workers and others involved in scientific research who present to the jury published works, registered inventions or industrial models during the year preceding the prize are eligible. Two monetary prizes of 500,000 Colombian pesos each, a medal and a diploma are awarded annually when merited. Established in 1954.

1585
Antioquia Society of Tourism
(Sociedad de Turismo de Antioquia S.A. Turantioquia)
Carrera 48, No. 58-11
Apartado Aereo 51759
Medellin, Colombia
Phone: 4 254 38 64

1586
Beca Eugenia Gomez Sierra
For recognition of the best students of the Tourist Administration at the Colegio Mayor de Antioquia. Applications are accepted. A monetary prize is awarded annually. Established in 1976 in honor of Beca Eugenia Gomez Sierra, the founder of Colegio Mayor de Antioquia and Oficina de Turismo y Fomento de Medellin.

1587
Gregorio Becerra Duque Trophy
To stimulate the development of the troubadour's art. An individual who has never participated in the national festivals of troubadors may be recognized for authentic poetic inspiration combined with superior vocal and instrumental qualities. A trophy with the Gregorio Becerra Legend is awarded annually. Established in 1979 by Elvira Berrio de Jaramillo, Director of Turantioquia, in memory of the first King of Troubadours, Gregoria Becerra Duque. (Inactive)

1588
Orden Rodrigo Correa Palacio
For recognition of contributions to the cultural and native values of the Antioquenan people. Applications must be submitted. A certificate is awarded annually. Established in 1985 in honor of Rodrigo Correa Palacio, a writer and poet.

1589
Banco de la Republica
Carrera 7A, No. 14-78
Apartado Aereo 3531
Bogota, D.E., Colombia
Phone: 1 831 11 11
Fax: 1 286 60 08

1590
Premio Banco de la Republica
To stimulate and promote research on and the development of the economy of Colombia. Individuals who have contributed to solving problems of the Colombian economy in general or individual enterprises in particular, and who have contributed to the improvment of education in the field of economics are eligible. A monetary prize of 50,000 Colombian pesos and a diploma are awarded annually. Established in 1975. Co-sponsored by the Colombian Society of Economists.

1591
Center of International Studies
(Centro de Estudios Internacionales)
Universidad de Los Andes
Calle 19, 1-46
Apartado Aereo 4976-12340
Bogota, D.E., Colombia
Phone: 1 286 6283

1592
National Essay Contest on Colombian Foreign Policy
(Certamen National de Ensayos Sobre Politica Exterior)
To recognize the best unpublished, original essay on Colombian foreign policy during the period of the National Front (1958 to 1974) by a student or professional. Essays must be in Spanish. Only one essay per author may be submitted. Monetary prizes of 50,000, 30,000, and 20,000 Colombian pesos, a subscription to *Colombia Internacional*, and publication of the essay are awarded. Established in 1989.

1593
Central Hidroelectrica de Betania
Carrera 5, No. 6-28
Edificio Metropolitano, piso 5, Torre B
Apartado Aereo No. 709
Neiva, Colombia
Phone: 72 12 29/49
Fax: 72 67 20

1594
Concurso de Ecologia Cacique Chuira
For recognition and promotion of outstanding contributions to the research, conservation and reclamation of the environment and natural resources. Colombian citizens, scientists, students, and technicians as well as public or private organizations interested in the preservation of the environment are eligible. Monetary prizes totaling 3,500,000 Colombian pesos are awarded. Established in 1990.

1595
Cia de Seguros Bolivar
Secretaria del Premio
Carrera IDA No. 16-39 Oficina 1002
Apartado Aereo 4421
Bogota, Colombia
Phone: 1 242 01 30

1596
Premio Nacional de Television Simon Bolivar
To recognize the best Colombian-produced television programs which have been aired in Colombia during the previous year. Recipients may be of foreign origin, but must have lived in Colombia for at least five years. Registration with Seguros Bolivar is necessary to compete for the prize. A special monetary prize of 500,000 Colombian pesos, the Gran Bolivar de Oro is awarded annually in addition to prizes of 250,000 Colombian pesos in each of nineteen different categories. Established in 1986 in memory of the great liberator Simon Bolivar and to recognize the great successes in Colombian Television.

1597
Colombia
Administrative Department of Civil Aeronautics
(Colombia
Departemento Administrativo de Aeronoutica Civil)
Aeropuerto Internacional Eldorado
Bogota, D.E., Colombia
Phone: 1 413 9500
Fax: 1 413 8091

1598
Civil Aeronautics Cross of Merit
(Orden de la Cruz del Merito Aeronautico Civil)
To honor national and foreign persons for services rendered to civil aviation. Awards are given in the following categories: (1) Extraordinary Cross - to State Chiefs, former State Chiefs, and elected Presidents; (2) Grand Cross - to State Ministers, Ambassadors, Chief of Missions, and

Commandant of Civil Aircrafts and flight instructors, of evident capacity and experience. Individuals whose contribution to the improvement of civil aviation is considered exceptionally important; to legal entitities and persons that are distinguished by their contribution to civil aviation; and to other national and foreign members who are equal in positon to any of the persons mentioned above; (3) Silver Cross - to pilots, navigators and flight engineers who are outstanding in the performance of their profession; to the Executive Board Members of Civil Aviation enterprises; Government Officers up to the Chief of Division level inclusive; Aviation Technical Experts at the University level; legal entities or persons; and any other kind of national and foreign persons who occupy positions equal to those above mentioned; and (4) Knight Cross - to maintenance or administrative technical personnel in the private or public sector; auxiliary ground and flight personnel, who are outstanding in the performance of their profession and any other national or foreign persons, who occupy positions equal to those above mentioned. Crew members who are distinguished by an extraordinary act and, as a consequence, save crew or passenger lives may be awarded the Grand Cross, the Silver Cross or the Knight Cross. Medals are awarded annually. Established in 1973 by the President of the Republic of Colombia.

1599

**Colombia
Ministry of Agriculture
(Colombia
Ministerio de Agricultura)**
Avenida Jimenez, No. 7-65
Bogota, D.E., Colombia

Phone: 1 3419005
Fax: 1 2841775

1600

National Distinction of the Environment
To recognize an individual or institution for their devotion to conservation and sustained use of natural resources, education, and community involvement on environmental issues and research and development of realty activities in the country. The following distinctions are presented: for the life and work on study, protection, and conservation of the environment; for a project on conservation of the natural resources; and of a project that involves the community in improving the use of the natural resources.

1601

**National Prize for Agriculture
(Premio Nacional de Agriculture)**
To provide recognition for outstanding contributions to the improvement and development of agriculture. A monetary prize of 200,000 Colombian pesos was awarded annually in the city of Palmira (Cauca). Established in 1978. Sponsored by the Caja Agraria. (Discontinued in 1991)

1602

**Order of Merit in Agriculture
(Orden del Merito Agricola)**
To stimulate and recognize outstanding service of those whose work and leadership in agricultural businesses and other similar activities have contributed to the development of the country. The following awards are presented: Great Cross, Great Official Cross, Commander Cross, and Knight Cross. Awarded annually. Established in 1969.

1603

**Colombia
Ministry of Communications
(Colombia
Ministerio de Comunicaciones)**
Edificio Murillo Toro, Carreras 7 y 8
Calle 12 y 13
Apartado Aereo 14515
Bogota, D.E., Colombia

Phone: 1 284 90 90
Fax: 1 286 1185

1604

**Medal for Postal Merit
(Medalla al Merito Postal)**
For recognition of outstanding service to the postal system. Public officials in Colombia and abroad who devoted their energy and capabilities to the development of communication networks in the country for the benefit of all citizens are eligible. The following awards are presented: Extraordinary gold medal - to the President or Ex-President of Colombia or to the heads of States from other friendly nations; gold medal, first class-to ministers and other highest officials, Colombian and foreign; silver medal, second class - to heads of departments in the Ministry of Communication in Colombia and abroad; bronze medal, third class - to all other officials not included above. Awarded annually. the best Colombian cinematographers for full-length feature films, film shorts, documentaries, and animations. Established in 1956 in memory of Colombia's president in 1865 when telegraphic messages were first sent.

1605

**Medalla Merito de las Comunicaciones Manuel Murillo Toro
(Manuel Murillo Toro Medal for Postal Merit)**
For recognition of outstanding contributions to the Colombian communication system. Colombian citizens and foreign nationals are eligible. Gold, silver and bronze medals are awarded annually. Established in 1965.

1606

Guillermo Lee Stiles Medal
For recognition of distinguished service to communications. Colombians and foreigners are eligible. Gold, silver and bronze medals are awarded annually. Established in 1965.

1607

**Colombia
Ministry of Economic Development
(Colombia
Ministerio de Economico Desarrollo)**
Carrera 26, No. 13-19, piso 34
Bogota, Colombia

Phone: 1 281 43 60
Fax: 1 281 8803

1608

**Civic Medal of Cartagena
(Medalla Civica de Cartagena)**
To recognize a citizen who has distinguished himself for services to the city of Cartagena. A medal is awarded irregularly. Established in 1861 by the Municipal Council of Cartagena.

1609

**Exporters Medal
(Medalla del Exportador)**
To recognize Colombians or foreigners for contributions to the development of the Colombian export business. Gold, silver and bronze medals are awarded annually. Established in 1969.

1610

**Medal of Merit in Tourism
(Condecoracion al Merito Turistico)**
For recognition of outstanding efforts in the promotion of the Colombian tourist industry. Medals of gold, silver and bronze are awarded. Established in 1974.

1611

**National Prize of Quality
(Premio Nacional de la Calidad)**
To stimulate the technological and industrial development of the country by means of adequate systems of quality control. Industrial or commercial organizations are considered for services and products delivered to the market which in the opinion of the National Council of Standards and Quality are of outstanding quality. A diploma and a gold plated silver medal are awarded annually in the categories of large industry, medium and small industry, and individuals and services. Established in 1975.

1612
Orden Departmental de Bolivar
To recognize those who have rendered outstanding services to the Department of Bolivar in the area of public administration or the armed forces. A green ribbon is given for civil merit. A red ribbon is given for military merit. Awarded irregularly. Established in 1861 and later discontinued. Reconstituted in 1977 by the government of the Department of Bolivar. Additional information is available from Isabel Foreno de Moreno, Jefe Division de Documentacia de COLCIENCIAS, Apartado Aereo 051580, Bogota, Colombia.

1613
Order of Merit in Commerce
(Orden del Merito Comercial)
To stimulate and recognize services on behalf of national commerce. Colombian citizens or foreigners are eligible. The following awards are presented: Great Cross, Great Official, Official and Knight. Established in 1953.

1614
Order of Merit in Industry
(Orden del Merito Industrial)
To stimulate and recognize services on behalf of national industry. The following awards are presented: Great Cross, Great Official Cross, Official Cross and Knight Cross. Awarded annually. Established in 1954.

1615
Pedro Romero Medal
To recognize the citizens of Cartagena who have distinguished themselves by their civic and cultural services or excellence in sports. A medal is awarded irregularly. Established in 1861 by a decree from City Hall of Cartagena.

1616
Tourism Research Prize and Medal of Merit
(Medalla al Merito Turistico en Investigacion)
To stimulate research in the field of tourism. Works on a topic indicated by the Corporation of Tourism may be submitted. Individuals and organizations are eligible. A monetary prize of 50,000 Colombian pesos, a medal, and publication of the work are awarded annually. Established in 1978.

1617
Colombia
Ministry of Foreign Affairs
(Colombia
Ministerio de Asuntos Exteriores)
Palacio de San Carlos
Calle 10, No. 5-51
Bogota, Colombia   Phone: 1 242 15 16

1618
Cruz de Boyaca
This is the highest national award of Colombia. To recognize officers of the Armed Forces, officials of the government, and citizens of Colombia or other friendly countries who distinguish themselves for heroism and a spirit of international brotherhood. The following awards are presented: Great Collar; Great Extraordinary Cross; Great Cross; Great Official Cross; Silver Cross; and Commander, Official and Knight Crosses. Awarded when merited. Established in 1919. These awards were originally created by the liberator, Simon Bolivar in 1828 to honor the efforts and sacrifices of those who aided him, and were re-established on the centenary of the Battle of Boyaca.

1619
Orden Nacional al Merito
To recognize individuals or institutions, both Colombian and foreign, who have distinguished themselves through notable service to the country, including the defense of its values. The following awards are presented: Great Extraordinary Cross, Great Cross, Great Official, Silver Cross, Commander, Official, and Knight.

1620
Order of San Carlos
To recognize citizens of Colombia and foreigners, mostly diplomats (both civilian and military) who have contributed to the improvement of relations between their countries and Colombia. A medal is awarded in seven classes: Collar; Great Cross with Golden Plaque; Great Cross; Great Official; Commander; Official; and Knight. Awarded irregularly. Established in 1954.

1621
Guillermo Valencia Prize for Hispanic Culture
For recognition of outstanding services and contributions to Hispanic culture. Individuals and organizations, Colombian and foreign, are eligible. The following awards are presented: a gold medal with an emerald; a gold medal; a silver medal; and a diploma. Awarded irregularly. Established in 1973. The Colombian Institute of Hispanic Culture administers the Prize.

1622
Colombia
Ministry of Government (Interior)
(Colombia
Ministerio de Interno Asuntos)
Palacio Echeverry
Carrera 8A, No. 8-09
Bogota, D.E., Colombia   Phone: 1 286 2324

1623
National Prize for Anthropology
For recognition of outstanding research on a subject related to the Colombian Indians. Studies of sites inhabited by the indigenous population in order to learn about their culture, customs and problems are eligible for consideration. A monetary prize of 80,000 Colombian pesos and publication of the work are awarded annually. Established in 1975 by Dr. Guillermo Hernandez de Alba.

1624
Colombia
Ministry of Justice
(Colombia
Ministerio de Justicia)
Calle 26, No. 27-48, 2
Bogota, Colombia   Phone: 1 283 9493

1625
Jose Ignacio De Marquez, Santiago Perez, and Antonio Ricaurte Prizes
To stimulate and exalt the judicial function and its performance, and to recognize the integrity, dedication and perseverance of individuals who serve the state in a judicial capacity. Gold, silver or bronze medals are awarded annually. Established in 1970 to honor the memory of three important judges.

1626
Defenders of Justice
(Defensores de la Justicia)
For recognition of exceptional service and personal valor in scientific research as it pertains to the effective administration of justice. Established in 1989.

1627
Distinction for Distinguished Services
(El Distintivo de Servicios Distinguidos)
To recognize the merits and oustanding work of the personnel employed by the prison branch of the Ministry of Justice. A maltese silver cross, a gray plaque and a diploma are awarded annually. Established in 1965.

1628
Distinction for Time of Service
(El Distintivo de Antiguedad)
To recognize employees of the prison branch of the Ministry of Justice for outstanding and long lasting service. A golden plated silver medal for fifteen years, and a bronze medal for ten years of service are awarded, plus a diploma and a blue plaque to be worn with the uniform are awarded annually. Established in 1965.

1629
Medal for Bravery
(Medalla al Valor)
To stimulate professional virtues, recognize merits and distinguish outstanding acts done by personnel in the prisons branch. Employees who, in the performance of their duties, endangered themselves or participated in meritorious acts which temporarily or permanently incapacitated them are eligible. Awarded annually. Established in 1965.

1630
Penitentiary Order of Merit
(Orden del Merito Penitenciario)
To recognize the virtues of the functionaries of the General Division of Prisons who have distinguished themselves for services in both prison security and rehabilitation of the inmates and who have often sacrificed their own peace and life for the betterment of the society and for justice. A star and a diploma are awarded annually. Established in 1965.

1631
Colombia
Ministry of Labor and Social Security
(Colombia
Ministerio de Trabajo y Seguridad Social)
Calle 20, No. 8-18 9
Bogota, D.E., Colombia   Phone: 1 242 2007

1632
Order of Labor
(Orden del Trabajo)
To recognize those who have given special services to the cause of labor, nationally or internationally. Colombians and other nationals are eligible. A medal is awarded annually. Established in 1963.

1633
Colombia
Ministry of National Defence
(Colombia
Ministerio de Defensa Nacional)
Centro Administrativo Nacional
Avda Eldorado, 2
Bogota, Colombia   Phone: 1 288 4184

1634
Condecoracion Servicios Distinguidos en Guerra Exterior
For recognition of members of the Armed Forces for outstanding service in a foreign war. An Iron Cross, Bronze Star, plaque, and a diploma are awarded when merited.

1635
Medalla al Merito Logisgtico y Administrativo Contralmirante Rafael Tono
To recognize members of the Armed Forces for outstanding service.

1636
Medalla Militar Francisco Jose de Caldas
To recognize officials of the military forces who obtained the title of Military Professor, and alumni of the Escuela Superior de Guerra. Gold, silver, and bronze medals and a diploma are awarded annually.

1637
Medalla Militar Soldado Juan Bautista Solarte Obando
To recognize the best soldier or sailor in each contingent of the Armed Forces who has distinguished himself by his excellent conduct, military qualities, ability to learn, and comradeship. A silver medal and a diploma are awarded annually.

1638
Medalla Servicios Distinguidos a la Aviacion Naval
To recognize members of the Armed Forces for outstanding service.

1639
Medalla Servicios Distinguidos en Orden Publico
To recognize members of the Armed Forces who have given their services to maintain public order, and who are outstanding for valor in action, above the normal call of duty. A Teutonic Cross and a diploma are awarded when merited.

1640
Medalla Servicios Distinguidos Infanteria de Marinia
To recognize members of the Armed forces for outstanding service.

1641
Medalla Servicios Distinguidos la Fuerza de Superficie
To recognize members of the Armed Forces for outstanding service.

1642
Medalla Tiempo de Servicio
To give public recognition to military personnel who have given distinguished service for at least 15 years. Gold, antique gold, silver, and bronze medals are awarded annually.

1643
Orden del Merito Aeronautico Antonio Ricaurte
For recognition of members of the Colombian Air Force who have performed outstanding heroic and professional acts and contributed to the greatness of the nation. Awards are given in the following classes: (1) Great Cross; (2) Great Official; (3) Knight; and (4) Companion. A medal and a diploma are awarded annually. Established in 1948.

1644
Orden del Merito Jose Maria Cordoba
To reward excellent services given by the military personnel. Awards are given in the following classes: (1) Commander; (2) Official; (3) Knight; and (4) Companion. A medal and a diploma are awarded annually.

1645
Orden del Merito Militar Antonio Narino
This, the highest award for military virtues, is conferred on the military and civilian personnel of the Colombian Military Forces. Awards are given in the following classes: (1) Great Cross; (2) Great Official; (3) Commander; (4) Official; (5) Knight; and (6) Companion. A medal and a diploma are awarded annually.

1646
Orden del Merito Naval Almirante Padilla
For recognition of members of the Navy for outstanding services to the nation. Awards are given in the following classes: (1) Great Cross; (2) Great Official; (3) Official; and (4) Companion. A cross and a diploma are awarded annually.

1647
Orden del Merito Sanitario Jose Fernandez Madrid
For recognition of personnel of the Health Section of the Armed Forces for extraordinary services in their profession. Awards are given in the following classes: (1) Great Cross; (2) Great Official; (3) Official; (4) Knight; and (5) Commander. A medal and a diploma are awarded annually.

1648
Orden Militar San Mateo
To recognize members of the Armed Forces who have performed historic acts of valor in defense of the nation. Awards are given in the following classes: (1) First Class Cross; (2) Second Class Cross; and (3) Third Class Cross. A cross and a diploma are awarded annually. Established in 1913.

1649
Servicios Distinguidos a la Fuerza Submarina
To recognize members of the Armed Forces for outstanding service.

1650
Colombia
Ministry of National Education
(Colombia
Ministerio de Educacion Nacional)
Centro Administrativo Nacional
Avda Eldorado, Of. 501
Bogota, D.E., Colombia   Phone: 1 2224597

1651
Gerardo Arellano Cultural Merit Medal
(Medalla al Merito Cultural de Gerardo Arellano)
To honor outstanding Colombian persons or institutions in art, music, theater, plastic and visual art, and literature. A medal is awarded annually. Established in 1990 in honor of Gerardo Arellano, a musician, opera singer, and teacher who is well-known internationally. Additional information is available from Universidad Pedagogica Nacional, Bogota, Colombia.

1652
Andres Bello Medal
(Medalla Andres Bello)
To recognize outstanding Colombian professionals. Established in 1991 in memory of Don Andres Bello.

1653
Simon Bolivar Medal
(Medalla Simon Bolivar)
For recognition of outstanding services in education, cooperation, good relations, and professionalism in general. Colombians who have 20 years of service may be nominated. A medal is awarded annually. Established in 1983 in memory of Simon Bolivar, a national hero.

1654
Augustin Nieto Caballero Medal
(Gran Medalla Augustin Nieto Caballero)
To recognize educators who demonstrate dedication and spirit in their vocation and continue to improve the lives of children and youth in Colombia. Established in 1992.

1655
Colombian Composers Competition Prizes
(Concurso de Compositores de Colombia)
To stimulate and create opportunities for composers of serious and popular music, thereby contributing to the spiritual education of the Colombian people and their feelings of national pride. The following awards are presented: Grand National Prize for chamber music - a monetary prize of 250,000 Colombian pesos; Grand National Prize for Symphony - 250,000 pesos; Jose A. Morales First Prize for Popular Music - 120,000 pesos; other monetary prizes, diplomas, and honorary mentions.

1656
Educational Merit Diploma
(Diploma al Merito Educativo)
To honor individuals, educational institutions, and governments that provide services that contribute to the advancement of education, science, culture, and technology. Established in 1992.

1657
Grand National Medal General Francisco de Paula Santander
To recognize persons who have given extensive service to education and the cultural development of the nation. A medal (Official or Commander) was awarded annually. Established in 1974 to honor the memory of General Santander. (Discontinued in 1982)

1658
Magical Folklore of Choco Prize
(Choco Magico Folklorico)
To stimulate and preserve regional folklore. A monetary prize of 10,000 Colombian pesos and publication of the work are awarded irregularly. Established in 1973.

1659
Ministry of National Education Medal
To recognize Colombians who have distinguished themselves for their eminent services in the Ministry or have contributed to the cultural development of the country. A statuette of General Santander and a golden medal are awarded annually. Established in 1939.

1660
National Prize for Arts
(Premio Nacional de Artes)
To provide recognition for an outstanding work of art. Colombian artists are eligible. A monetary prize of 100,000 Colombian pesos and a diploma are awarded annually. Established in 1964.

1661
National Prize for History
(Premio Nacional de Historia)
To recognize an outstanding work on history written by a Colombian author. A monetary prize of 100,000 Colombian pesos and a diploma are awarded annually. Established in 1964.

1662
National Prize for Literature
(Premio Nacional de Literatura)
To recognize an outstanding literary work written by a Colombian writer. A monetary prize of 100,000 Colombian pesos and a diploma are awarded annually. Established in 1964.

1663
National Prize for Sciences
(Premio Nacional de Ciencias)
For recognition of the best scientific work that constitutes the most valuable contribution to Colombian culture. A monetary prize of 100,000 Colombian pesos and a diploma are awarded annually. Established in 1964.

1664
Camilio Torres Civic Medal
To recognize teachers for their eminent service, spirit, and perseverance in the performance of their profession. Gold, silver, or bronze medals, plus a diploma were awarded annually. Established in 1948, to honor the memory of Camilo Torres. (Discontinued in 1982)

1665
Jose Maria Vergara y Vergara Prize
To recognize Colombian authors, in order to promote literary development and to discover native talent. Works that would not otherwise be published for lack of funds are particularly desirable. A monetary award of 10,000 Colombian pesos, publication of the work, and a diploma are awarded annually. Established in 1937.

1666
Colombia
Ministry of Public Health
(Colombia
Ministerio de Salud)
Calle 16, No. 7-39, Of. 701
Bogota, D.E., Colombia   Phone: 1 282 0002

1667
Jorge Bejarano Civic Medal for Health and Welfare Merits
(Medalla Civica del Merito Asistencial y Sanitario Jorge Bejarano)
For recognition of outstanding contributions, support and initiatives on behalf of the public health and welfare program in Colombia. Colombians and foreigners are eligible. The following awards are presented: Gold medal for exceptional merits; silver medal for distinguished acts of efficiency in the exercise of a profession related to the welfare of a community; and bronze medal to professors, physicians, sanitary engineers and nurses who have rendered services in the field of public health and welfare with superior competence, dedication and exemplary conduct. Awarded annually. Established in 1966.

1668
Colombia
Ministry of Public Works and Transportation
(Colombia
Ministerio de Obras Publicas y Transporte)
Consejo Nacional de Obras Publicas
Minobas CAN   Phone: 1 222 3380
Bogota, D.E., Colombia   Fax: 1 222 1647

1669
Orden al Merito Julio Garavito
To recognize the merits of certified Colombian engineers who have rendered distinguished service to the nation. The following orders may be awarded: (1) Gran Cruz con Placa de Oro - the Great Cross with the Plaque of Gold. This may be awarded only to former Colombian presidents; (2) Gran Cruz - the Great Cross is presented to those who have held the offices of the Minister of Dispatch, President of the Society of Colombian Engineers, Rector of the University, and Manager of the Department of Public Decentralization; (3) Gran Oficial - the Plaque of the Great Official is presented to those who have held the offices of Secretary General, Director of the Ministry, president of some society of engineers, of an academic group, or a national servant such as a congressional representative, or those who have merited the title of Professor Emeritus or won some of the prizes conferred by the Colombian Society of Engineers; (4) Cruz de Plata - the silver cross is presented to official organizations or jurists who have distinguished themselves in service to the country; (5) Cruz de Comendador - the Cross of Commendation is presented to those who have served as chief of a branch of the Ministry or the equivalent, a noted public servant or jurist, university professor of engineering, or persons of equivalent status; (6) Cruz Oficial - the Official Cross is presented to those who have served as chiefs of a Division of the Ministry, or its equivalent, members of professional councils of engineering and architecture, or held other public office; and (7) Cruz de Caballero - the Knight's Cross is presented to those who are judged by the Order's council to be deserving of the honor through professional service. Awarded annually. Established in 1963 by the President of the Republic.

1670
Colombia
National Police
(Colombia
Policia Nacional)
Transv. 45, No. 40-11 CAN
Bogota, D.E., Colombia   Phone: 1 269 96 00

1671
Distintivo al Merito Canino
To recognize the value of the police dog in the role of pacification and maintenance of public order in all the national territory. Police or privately owned dogs who in the performance of their duties have risked their physical integrity in protecting the security of members of the police forces or civilians are eligible. A maltese cross that hangs from a ribbon which is tied to the dog's neck is awarded annually. Established in 1966.

1672
Distintivo al Merito Docente Gabriel Gonzales
Meritorious distinction for meritorious service in the national police force is awarded. Established in 1986.

1673
Estrella de la Policia
To recognize members of the National Police for outstanding services rendered, for protection of the people's rights and public peace, for patriotism and courage, and for protection of democratic institutions in Colombia. The Civic Star "Commander," Civic Star "Official," and Civic Star "Companion," are awarded annually. Established in 1953.

1674
Medalla al Valor
To recognize the personnel of the Police Forces who, during the performance of their duties, have endangered their lives in order to defend the life, honor, or property of citizens, or to reward personnel of the Police Forces who during the performance of their duties have participated in meritorious actions or suffered temporary or permanent incapacitating lesions. The first class award is a silver brooch in the form of a cross that is worn only with the parade uniforms. Police in street uniforms wear a silver plaque. The second class award is a bronze brooch that is also worn only with the parade uniforms and is replaced by a green plaque for everyday use. Awarded annually. Established in 1954.

1675
Medallos de los Servicios
To reward members of the Police Force who have distinguished themselves by their loyalty and good service. Officers, subofficers, agents and civil personnel who have completed 15 to 35 years of service are eligible. Gold, silver and bronze medals are awarded annually. Established in 1958 by the President of the Republic.

1676
General Santander Medal
(Medalla General Santander)
To recognize the best students of the General Santander Police School. Students from Colombia and from other Latin American countries are eligible. A medal and a diploma are awarded annually. Established in 1965.

1677
Servicios Distinguidos
Distinctions are awarded in three categories. Established in 1954.

1678
Colombian Academy of Language
(Academia Colombiana de la Lengua)
Carrera 3A, Numero 17-34   Phone: 1 334 11 90
Bogota, D.E., Colombia   Phone: 1 334 88 93

1679
Felix Restrepo Prize for Philology
To recognize the best paper submitted to the philology contest. Papers must focus on linguistics and grammatical studies done in Latin America and the Philippines or must be monographs on some particular aspect of the history or development and progress of philology in Spanish speaking countries. The work selected is considered a fundamental contribution to the study, teaching, enrichment and dissemination of the Spanish language. Works submitted must be written in Spanish and may not have been published before. The authors may be from Colombia or other countries, but they cannot be members of the Colombian Academy of Language. A monetary prize of 300,000 Colombian pesos is awarded annually. Established in 1966 in memory of Felix Restrepo, S.J.

1680

Colombian Association for the Advancement of Science
(Asociacion Colombiana para el Avance de la Ciencia)

PO Box 92581
Bogota, Colombia
Phone: 221 7348
Phone: 221 3313
Fax: 221 6950

1681

Scientific Merit Award
(Premio Al Merito Cientifico)

To recognize previous or current contributions, in three categories, to scientific and technological development, preferably applicable to the solution of Colombian scientific problems. Candidates must be nominated by national and international organizations who promote science and technology; university rectors and deacons; and the administrative council of ACAC. Primary work must have been done in Colombia. The three award categories are: Category I, which has a monetary award of $6,000 (Colombian pesos), and is given to a Colombian scientist whose life and continued research in Colombia represent an important contribution to science and/or technology; Category II, which has a monetary award of $4,000 (Colombian pesos), and is given to a young Colombian scientist whose work represents a meaningful contribution to the advancement of science and/or technology; and Category III, which has a monetary award of $3,000 (Colombian pesos), and is given to an individual or institution that has greatly contributed to the spreading of scientific and/or technological knowledge in Colombia. The Prize is awarded annually. Established in 1989.

1682

Technological Innovation Award
(Premio a la Innovacion Tecnologica)

To recognize enterprises that have made a significant overall contribution to technological innovation. A gold medal, a silver medal, and a diploma/plate are awarded in four categories; large-size enterprises, medium-size enterprises, small-size enterprises, and micro-size enterprises.

1683

Colombian Association of Disabled People
(Asociacion Colombiana de Personas Impedidas)

Calle 16 No. 35-42/48
Apartado Aereo 32259
Bogota, Colombia
Phone: 1 2011829
Fax: 1 2010940

1684

DPI-ACOPIM Journalism Award

To recognize individuals for work for equality on the behalf of mentally and physically handicapped individuals.

1685

Colombian Association of Librarians
(Asociacion Colombiana de Bibliotecarios)

Calle 10, No. 3-16
Apartado Aereo 30883
Bogota, Colombia
Phone: 1 269 42 19

1686

Ruben Perez Ortiz Prize

To provide recognition for outstanding contributions to the profession made during the previous year. National or foreign librarians are eligible. A parchment is awarded annually. Established in 1950 in memory of Ruben Perez Ortiz, a librarian.

1687

Colombian Fund for Scientific Investigation and Special Projects Francisco Jose de Caldas (COLCIENCIAS)
(Fondo Colombiano de Investigaciones Cientificas y Proyectos Especiales Francisco Jose de Caldas)

Tr. 9-A, No. 133-28
PO Box 051580
Bogota, D.E., Colombia
Phone: 1 216 9800
Phone: 1 274 4460

1688

Caldas Science Prize
(Premio Caldas de Ciencias)

To stimulate scientific and technological research based or applied in Colombia and to aid the development of science and technology in the country with reference to national development and the well-being of the people. Scientists may be nominated by a scientific organization for research which has led to the solution of scientific or technological problems, or for a teaching contribution. The highest distinction of COLCIENCIAS is given for outstanding original work in one of the following disciplines: sciences, social sciences, medical and health sciences, agricultural sciences, technological and engineering sciences. The prize can be divided among a team of researchers. A monetary prize of 200,000 Colombian pesos, a gold medal, and a diploma are awarded biennially. Established in 1969 by Capitan Alberto Ospina Tarborda to honor Dr. Ephraim Otero Ruiz.

1689

Colombian Oceanographic Commission
(Comision Colombiana de Oceanografia)

Calle 41, No. 46-20, piso 4
Apartado Aereo 28466
Bogota, D.E., Colombia
Phone: 1 222 04 08
Phone: 1 222 04 49
Fax: 1 222 04 16

1690

National Marine Science Prize
(Premio Nacional de Ciencias del Mar)

For recognition of outstanding contributions by Colombian scientists to marine science and technology. Individual or group work is eligible for consideration. A plaque and publication of the work is awarded. Established in 1990.

1691

Colombian Pediatric Society
(Sociedad Colombiana de Pediatria)

Hospital Militar Central
Entrepiso 1
Bogota, Colombia
Phone: 1 288 3985

1692

Calixto Torres Umana Award
(Premio Calixto Torres Umana)

To encourage pediatric basic and clinical investigation. Members of the Society may submit unpublished research work. A monetary award of $200, a certificate, and publication of the work are awarded annually on the anniversary of the establishment of the Society. Established in 1986 in memory of Professor Calixto Torres Umana, a prominent Colombian pediatrician.

1693

Corporacion Nacional de Turismo

Calle 28, No. 13A-15, piso 16-18
Apartado Aereo 8400
Bogota, D.E., Colombia
Phone: 1 2839466
Fax: 1 2843818

1694

**Golden Bowl
(Poporo de Oro)**
To stimulate the tourist industry in Colombia. Colombian and foreign organizations are eligible. Gold, silver, and bronze medals, and a diploma are awarded annually. Established in 1979.

1695

Medal of Merit for Tourism
To recognize contributions to the creation, promotion, and development of the tourism industry. Colombian citizens or foreign individuals and organizations are eligible. Gold, silver, and bronze medals are eligible. Awarded annually. Established in 1974.

1696

Federacion Nacional de Cultivadores de Cereales
Carrera 14, Numero 97-62
Apartado Aereo 8694   Phone: 1 2181755
Bogota, Colombia   Fax: 1 2189463

1697

Federacion Nacional de Cultivadores de Cereales Competitions
To recognize and promote the interests of wheat, barley, corn, and sorghum producers. The Federation sponsors competitions.

1698

Fundacion Mariano Ospina Perez
Avenida 22, No. 39-32   Phone: 1 2878611
Bogota, D.E., Colombia   Fax: 1 2858162

1699

**Premio Mariano Ospina Perez
(Mariano Ospina Perez Award)**
For recognition of outstanding contributions toward rural development and the well-being of farmers. A monetary prize of 2,000,000 Colombian pesos and a silver plaque are awarded annually. Established in 1977 in honor of Dr. Mariano Ospina Perez, President of the Republic of Colombia. Discontinued in 1981 and re-established in 1987.

1700

FUNDALECTURA - Fundacion para el fomento de la Lectura
Avenida (calle) 40 No. 16-46
Apartado 048902   Phone: 1 2877272
Bogota, Colombia   Fax: 1 2877071

1701

Premio a la Mejor Labor de Promocion de Lectura
To recognize schools, libraries, cultural centers, institutions, or public and private organizations that develop lecture programs. A monetary award of 3,000,000 Colombian pesos and 1,000 titles from FUNDALECTURA's recommended list are presented. Established in 1994.

1702

Premio al Mejor Libro Infantil y Juvenil Colombiano
To promote the creation and publishing of children's books. Awards are given in two categories: children's books and juvenile books. Books published in Colombia, and written or illustrated by a Colombian citizen are eligible. A diploma is awarded biennially. The books are distinguished with a sticker mentioning the award. Established in 1986. (Discontinued in 1992)

1703

Premio FUNDALECTURA de Literatura Infantil y Juvenil Colombiana
To stimulate new talents in the creation of children's literature. Awarded to unpublished Colombian writers. Travel expenses to attend the IBBY Congress will be awarded biennially. Established in 1994.

1704

**Gobernacion
Cartagena-Bolivar**
Jefe Division de Documentacion
  COLCIENCIAS
Establecimiento Publico del Sector
  Educativo
Transversal 9A, No. 133-28
Bogota, D.E., Colombia   Phone: 1 274 00 04

1705

Orden Rafael Nunez
To honor individuals who have contributed to the cultural, social and economic development of the country. The following awards are presented: Gran Cruz Extraordinaria (given only to chiefs of state); Gran Cruz; Gran Oficial; Comendador; and Caballero. Awarded annually. Established in 1974.

1706

Hospital Militar Central
Division de Educacion Medica
Transversal 5a No. 49-00   Phone: 1 2852520
Bogota, Colombia   Fax: 1 2876873

1707

Pablo Elias Gutierrez Award
For recognition of the best research paper done by a resident in internal medicine. Residents at the Hospital Militar Central, Bogota, Colombia, who are Colombian citizens may apply. A monetary prize is awarded annually. Established in 1982 in honor of Pablo Elias Gutierrez.

1708

Coronel Medico Jorge Esguerra Lopez Award
For recognition of the best research paper done by a resident in hospital administration. Established in 1988 in honor of Jorge Esguerra Lopez.

1709

Lope Carvajal Peralta Award
For recognition of the best research paper done by a resident in surgery. Residents at the Hospital Militar Central, Bogota, Colombia, who are Colombian citizens may apply. A monetary prize is awarded annually. Established in 1982 in honor of Lope Carvajal Peralta.

1710

Instituto Caro y Cuervo
Carrera 11 No. 64-37
Apartado Aereo 51502   Phone: 1 2557753
Bogota, Colombia   Fax: 2 170243

1711

**Miguel Antonio Caro and Rufino Jose Cuervo National Order
(Orden Nacional de Miguel Antonio Caro y Rufino Jose Cuervo)**
To recognize Colombians or foreigners who have made outstanding contributions to the national, cultural, and humanistic patrimony. Admission to the Order will be granted to Colombians who have distinguished themselves in scientific investigation, the humanities, and arts and letters, or those who have been of great service to the cultural well-being of the country. Admission will also be granted to foreigners, corporations, associations, or institutions who have been of great service to Colombian culture and language. The following awards are presented: Collar; Great

Cross with a plaque of gold; Great Cross; Grand Official; Commander; Official and Knight Crosses; and a diploma. The insignia for all classes is a maltese cross in varying forms with a medallion in its center. Awarded annually. The number of members in the Order may not exceed 50. Established in 1970.

1712

Instituto Colombiano de Cultura
Carrera 3A, No. 18-24, piso 5 y 7
Bogota, D.E., Colombia   Phone: 1 282 03 36

1713

Medalla Instituto Colombiano de Cultura
To recognize persons or institutions who distinguish themselves in the field of Colombian culture and to promote cultural investigation. A medal is awarded annually. Established in 1968.

1714

National Library of Colombia Prize
To provide recognition for the best effort at compiling a history of the National Library of Colombia to honor the bicentennial of its foundation. A monetary first prize of 100,000 Colombian pesos, second prize of 50,000 pesos, a diploma and publication of the work are awarded. Established in 1974.

1715

Instituto de Investigaciones Technologicas
Avenida 30, No. 52-A-77
Apartado Aereo 7031
Bogota, D.E., Colombia   Phone: 1 221 00 66

Defunct organization.

1716

Medalla de Servicios Distinguidos
To stimulate technological investigation and to recognize individuals who had contributed to the development of the Institute through the quality of their work and through social, economic, technical or scientific programs. A medal was awarded irregularly. Established in 1974. (Discontinued in 1990)

1717

Instituto Geografico Agustin Codazzi
Carrera 30, No. 48-51, Apdo 6721   Phone: 1 2682055
Bogota, D.E., Colombia   Fax: 1 2694401

1718

Agustin Codazzi Medal
To stimulate scientific research and to recognize individuals who have given exceptional support to the Institute. A gold medal is awarded irregularly. Established in 1968 in memory of the scientist and cartographer, Agustin Codazzi.

1719

Belisario Ruiz Wilches Award
For recognition of outstanding service to the Institute. A grand cross and medals of gold and silver are awarded. Established in 1980 in memory of Belisario Ruiz Wilches, founder of the Institute.

1720

International Society of Dermatology: Tropical, Geographic and Ecologic
Apartado Aereo 90123   Phone: 1 2575568
Bogota, Colombia   Fax: 1 2182596

Formerly: (1984) International Society of Tropical Dermatology.

1721

Castellani - Reiss Medal and Award
To recognize the most outstanding work in tropical, geographic ecology of dermatoses, and/or the underlying basic sciences, during the period between World Congresses of the Society. A monetary prize of $1,000, a gold medal, and travel expenses to attend the World Congress are awarded every five years. Established in 1969 in honor of the founders of the Society, Aldo Castellani and Frederick Reiss. Additional information is available from Vincent A. Cipollaro, M.D., Treasurer-General, 1016 Fifth Avenue, New York, NY 10028-0132, U.S.A.

1722

Antonio Machado Foundation
(Fundacion Antonio Machado)
Icetex
Carrera 3a, No. 18-24
Bogota, Colombia   Phone: 1 286 55 66

1723

Antonio Machado Prize for Essay
(Premio International de Ensayo Antonio Machado)
For recognition of the best written work with the theme of education for liberty, international understanding, and peace. A monetary prize of $2 million Spanish pesetas and publication of the winning work are awarded. Established in 1988 in memory of the poet, philosopher and writer, Antonio Machado, fifty years after his death.

1724

National Academy of Medicine
(Academia Nacional de Medicina)
Calle 60A, No. 5-29
Apdo Aereo 23224   Phone: 1 249 31 22
Bogota, Colombia   Phone: 1 212 03 71

1725

Concurso Nacional de Obras Medicas
(National Contest of Medical Research Works)
For recognition of achievements in Colombian medicine. Students and faculty of universities or institutions of higher learning who present original and unpublished works are eligible for awards. A monetary prize of 2,500,000 Colombian pesos, a medal and a diploma are awarded irregularly. Established in 1979. Additional information is available from Salvat Editores Colombiana, Division Medicina, Cra. 10a, No. 19-65, P-5 Bogota, Colombia, phone: 1 284 58 01.

1726

Juan N. Corpas Prize
To recognize the best final year student of the Academy of Medicine at the Universidad Nacional for performance in surgery. A medal and a diploma are awarded annually.

1727

Carlos Esguerra Prize
To recognize the best intern during the previous academic year in the internal medicine service rotation at the Academy of Medicine of the Universidad Nacional. A medal and a diploma are awarded annually.

1728

Manuel Forero Prize
This, the highest award of the National Academy of Medicine to Colombian scientists, is given for recognition of outstanding experimental research. A monetary prize, a trophy and a diploma are awarded irregularly.

1729
Roberto Franco Prize
To recognize the best third year student specializing in internal medicine who has distinguished himself during the previous academic year. A medal and a diploma are awarded annually.

1730
Public Education Prize
To stimulate a spirit of scientific research in the Academy of Medicine and to recognize the best thesis written by a student. A monetary prize of 2,240 Colombian pesos for the best thesis and two gold medals for the best interns are awarded annually. Established in 1928 by the President of the Republic.

1731
National Company of Navigation - NAVENAL
(Compania Nacional de Navegacion - NAVENAL)
Carrera 13 No. 37-43, piso 9
Bogota, D.E., Colombia   Phone: 1 274 00 04

1732
Order for Industrial Merit
(Orden al Merito Industrial)
For recognition of outstanding contributions to the development of the country's industry and commerce through navigation. A Grand Cross, shield, medal, sash, and certificate are awarded annually. Established in 1954 by Doctor Mariano Melendro Serna.

1733
National Federation of Coffee Growers of Colombia
(Federacion Nacional de Cafeteros de Colombia)
Calle 73, Numero 8-13
Apartado Aereo 57534
Bogota 2, D.E., Colombia   Phone: 1 2170600
    Fax: 1 2171021

1734
Manuel Mejia Medal of Merit in the Coffee Industry
(Medalla al Merito Cafetero Manuel Mejia)
To reward and honor individuals who have rendered excellent service to the development of the coffee industry. Ordinary medals are awarded to the outstanding Colombian coffee growers, and a special medal is awarded to foreigners. Awarded annually as decided by the National Coffee Committee. Established in 1963 by the National Committee in memory of Manuel Mejia, General Manager of the Federation.

1735
National Institute of Geosciences, Mining and Chemistry Research (INGEOMINAS)
(Instituto Nacional de Investigaciones en Geociencias-Mineria y Quimica)
Diagonal 53, No. 34-53
Apartado Aereo 4865
Bogota, Colombia   Phone: 1 221 1811
    Fax: 1 222 3597

1736
National Geology Award
(Premio Nacional de Geologia)
To support research activities among geologists. A monetary prize of 50,000 Colombian pesos was awarded annually. Established in 1978. (Discontinued in 1992).

1737
National Prize for Chemistry
(Premio Nacional de Quimica)
For recognition of outstanding chemical research and contributions to national development. Established in 1986. Co-sponsored by the Asociacion Quimica Colombiana.

1738
Scientific Prize
(Premio Cientifico)
To support research activities among members of the Institute. A monetary prize of 25,000 Colombian pesos was awarded annually. Established in 1978. (Discontinued in 1992)

1739
Pontificia Universidad Javeriana
Carrera 7, No. 40-76
Apartado Aereo 56710   Phone: 1 2458981
Bogota, Colombia   Fax: 1 2853348

1740
Distincion Felix Restrepo
For recognition of distinguished service to the university by its employees, graduates, or professors. Gold, silver, and bronze medals are awarded annually. Established in 1990.

1741
Orden Universidad Javeriana
To recognize an individual in the area of academics who has given invaluable services to the university, and thus to the development of university education in the nation as a whole. A cross is awarded for the following grades: Gran Cruz Extraordinaria, Gran Cruz, Cruz de Plata, Comendador, Oficial, and Caballera/Dama. Awards are presented annually. Established in 1952.

1742
Prensa Nueva
Calle 20, No. 7-86
barrio Interlaken o al Apdo. aereo 0012
Apartado Aereo 0012
Ibague, Colombia   Phone: 30604

1743
Concurso Nacional de Cuento Periodico *Prensa Nueva*
To encourage literary creativity. Colombian authors may submit unpublished works on any theme that have won no other prizes. Works of art, books, and records are awarded. Awarded annually. Established in 1986.

1744
Sociedad Colombiana de Ingenieros
Carrera 4, No. 10-41, Apdo 340   Phone: 1 2862200
Bogota, Colombia   Fax: 1 2816229

1745
Lorenzo Codazzi Prize
For recognition of the best works in engineering and science which contribute to a greater understanding of the physical aspects of the national territory. A monetary prize, a gold medal, and a diploma are awarded annually.

1746
Enrique Morales Prize
For recognition of the best original and unpublished work written on electrical energy, or for an electrical engineering work constructed in or planned for Colombia during the year preceding the award. A monetary prize, a gold medal, and a diploma are awarded annually.

1747
National Engineering Prize
(Premio Nacional de Ingenieria)
To recognize a Colombian engineer who has designed or executed a work of outstanding scientific or technical merit during the year preceding the award. A monetary prize of 10,000 Colombian pesos, a medal, and a diploma are awarded annually. Established in 1937.

1748
Manuel Ponce de Leon Prize
To recognize the best graduate of the Department of Engineering of the National University in Bogota. A monetary prize, a gold medal, and a diploma are awarded annually.

1749
Diodoro Sanchez Prize
To recognize a Colombian engineer who published the best book on the technical, economic, or historical aspects of engineering science in Colombia during the preceding year. A monetary prize, a gold medal, and a diploma are awarded annually.

1750
Universidad de Medellin
Carrera 87 No. 30-65
Apartado Aereo 1983
Los Alpeo Belen
Medellin, Antioquia, Colombia   Phone: 4238 38 06

1751
Condecoracion del Merito Universitario
For recognition of distinguished service to the university. Medals are awarded in the categories of Servidor Eminente, Servidor Meritorio, and Servidor Efficiente. Established in 1978.

1752
Medellin University Prize
To stimulate research and the publication of works of an educational nature which contribute to the development of university education in Colombia. Monetary prizes of 10,000 and 6,000 Colombian pesos are awarded irregularly.

1753
Universidad del Valle

Apartado Aereo 2188
Cali, Colombia

Phone: 23 392360
Phone: 23 393041
Fax: 23 398520

1754
Gran Cruz de la Universidad del Valle
For recognition of outstanding services to the University by those serving on the staff, or for outstanding investigations and intellectual contributions by members of the University community. Faculty members who have been retired for over a year, who have been residents of the state of Valle for more than fifteen years, and who hold no public office are eligible. A cross is awarded annually. Established in 1954.

1755
Universidad Externado de Colombia
Apdo Aereo 034141
Calle 12, Nos. 1-17 Este.
Bogota, Colombia   Phone: 1 282 6066

1756
National Photography Competition
(Concurso Nacional de Fotografia)
For recognition of outstanding photography. First, second, and third prizes are awarded. Established in 1990.

1757
National Short Story Competition
(Concurso Nacional del Cuento)
To promote the development of children's literature and an interest in literature by young people. Monetary prizes of 6,000, 2,000, and 1,000 Colombian pesos, and a diploma are awarded annually. Co-sponsored by the Asociacion Colombiana de Universidades ASCUN, Apdo Aereo 012300, Carrera 10, No. 88-45, Bogota, Colombia, phone: 1 2361424.

Costa Rica

1758
Commission for the Defense of Human Rights in Central America (Comision para la Defensa de los Derechos Humanos en Centroamerica)
Paseo de los Estudiantes
Apartado 189   Phone: 213462
San Jose, Costa Rica   Fax: 320484

1759
Commission for the Defense of Human Rights in Central America Awards
To recognize outstanding contributions to the protection of human rights in Central America. The Commission sponsors competitions and bestows awards annually.

1760
Costa Rica
Ministry of Culture, Youth and Sport
(Costa Rica
Ministerio de Cultura, Juventud y Deportes)
Apartado 10227   Phone: 33 14 71
San Jose 1000, Costa Rica   Fax: 33 7066

1761
Aquileo J. Echeverria Prize
To recognize Costa Rican citizens for excellence in the fields of literature (novel, short story, poetry, essay, scientific literature); history; theatre; music; and fine arts. Monetary prizes of 40,000 colones divided amongst the selected works, the total sum of awards not exceeding 8,000,000 Costa Rican colones, and a certificate are awarded annually. Established in 1962.

1762
Joaquin Garcia Monge Prize
To recognize a foreign or Costa Rican journalist for promoting and disseminating literary, scientific and artistic works of Costa Ricans, or for pointing out cultural values of Costa Rica. A monetary prize and honorary recognition are awarded annually.

1763
Magon National Prize of Culture
To recognize a Costa Rican writer, artist or scientist for contributions to literature and research. A monetary prize of 16,000 Costa Rican colones is awarded annually.

1764
Premio Nacional de Ciencias y Tecnologia Clodomiro Picado Twight
For recognition of works in science and technology in the interest of Costa Rican cities. Costa Rican citizens under 36 years of age are eligible. A monetary prize of 50,000 Costa Rican colones is awarded in alternate fields annually. Established in 1976.

1765
Premio Nacional de Periodismo Pio Viquez
To recognize a journalist for outstanding contributions. Awarded annually. Established in 1972.

1766
Premio Nacional de Teatro
For recognition of achievement in the theatre. The following awards are presented: (1) Premio Olga Zuniza - best young actress; (2) Premio

Eugenio Arias - best young actor; (3) best actress; (4) best actor; (5) best supporting actress; (6) best supporting actor; (7) best director; (8) best scenario; and (9) best theatrical group. A plaque is awarded annually. Established in 1972.

1767
Editorial Costa Rica

Apdo 10010
San Jose 1000, Costa Rica

Phone: 23 93 03
Phone: 23 48 75
Fax: 506 22 9303

1768
Concurso Carmen Lyra
(Carmen Lyra Literary Prize)
To encourage the writing of literature intended for children and young people. Awards are given for unpublished works. A monetary award of 75,000 colones and publication are awarded annually. Established in 1974 in honor of the writer, Maria Isabel Carvajal (Pseudonym Carmen Lyra).

1769
Concurso Joven Creacion
(Young Creators Literary Prize)
To stimulate young writers in the fields of poetry and narrative/stories. Awards are given for unpublished works by writers no more than 30 years of age. A monetary prize of 50,000 colones and publication are awarded annually. Established in 1976 in collaboration with the Asociacion de Autores of Costa Rica and the Ministerio de Cultura, Juventud y Deportes.

1770
Premio Editiorial Costa Rica
(Editorial Costa Rica Literary Prize)
To encourage creative writing generally. Awards are given for unpublished works alternately in the following categories: fiction, stories, theatre, essays, short stories, poetry, biography, and history. A monetary award of 125,000 colones and publication are awarded annually. Established in 1972.

1771
Editorial Universitaria Centroamericana
Apartado 64
Ciudad Universitaria Rodrigo Facio
San Jose 2060, Costa Rica

Phone: 25 87 40
Fax: 34 00 71

1772
Premio Poesia y Narrativa
To recognize authors from Latin American countries for the best published works of poetry and narratives. The poetry award is given every year. The narrative award is given in alternating years for a story and a novel. A monetary prize and a medal are awarded annually. Established in 1970. Formerly: Premio del Certamen Literario Latinoamericano.

1773
Inter-American Institute for Cooperation on Agriculture
(Instituto Interamericano de Cooperacion para la Agricultura)
Apartado Postal 55
2200 Coronado
San Jose, Costa Rica

Phone: 29 02 22
Fax: 29 47 41

1774
Inter-American Agricultural Award for Young Professionals
(Premio Agricola Interamericano para Profesionales Jovenes)
To recognize young professionals in the agricultural sciences who have distinguished themselves in any of the areas covered by IICA's programs and who have demonstrated an outstanding willingness to serve, exceptional initiative and dedication in working for the well-being of the rural population, and an ability to program and carry out activities that contribute to improving methods used in agriculture and in social and enterprise systems. Candidates must be under 35 years of age at the time of nomination. A monetary award of $10,000 US and a certificate are presented biennially honoring only one candidate per IICA area. Established in 1976.

1775
Inter-American Agricultural Development Award
(Premio en Desarrollo Agricola Interamericano)
For international recognition of those who distinguished themselves through important and exemplary contributions in the field of agricultural development in their own country and in other countries of the continent. A silver statuette representing the American campesino was presented annually. Established in 1976. (Discontinued in 1989)

1776
Inter-American Agricultural Medal
(Medalla Agricola Interamericano)
For international recognition of those professionals who have distinguished themselves through outstanding contributions to the development of agriculture and the improvement of rural life in the Americas. Professionals who work or have worked in any of the fields covered by the programs of the Inter-American Institute for Cooperation on Agriculture are eligible, regardless of age, sex, profession, occupation, nationality, residence or other factors. A medal is presented biennially. Established in 1957.

1777
Inter-American Award for the Participation of Women in Rural Development
(Premio Interamericano a la Participacion de la Mujer en el Desarrollo Rural)
For international public recognition of those women who have distinguished themselves through important contributions to the rural development process in general, and to improving the quality of life, in particular, in their own countries or in other countries in the Americas. A gold medal and a certificate are presented biennially. Established in 1979.

1778
Inter-American Institute of Human Rights
(Instituto Interamericano de Derechos Humanos)
Apartado Postal 10081
San Jose 1000, Costa Rica

Phone: 34 04 03
Fax: 340955

1779
Inter-American Institute of Human Rights Awards
To promote scientific research, education, and other functions in the area of human rights, with emphasis on the American continent. The Institute sponsors competitions and presents awards. No further information on awards is available for this edition.

1780
Inter-American Scout Committee
(Consejo Interamericano de Escultismo)
PO Box 10297
San Jose 1000, Costa Rica

Phone: 29 2315
Phone: 29 2121
Fax: 29 2396

1781
Youth of the Americas
(Juventud de las Americas)
For recognition of outstanding service to youth and children in the Americas (within or outside the Scout movement). Adults who have demonstrated noteworthy leadership to youth in their own or other countries, through government positions, youth organizations or other positions of influence may be nominated. A medallion to be worn around the neck, an embroidered emblem for the uniform, and a diploma are awarded biennially at each Inter-American Scout Conference. Established in 1972.

1782

International Federation of Business and Professional Women (Federacion de Mujeres Profesionales y de Negocios de Costa Rica)
Apartado 8-4680
San Jose, Costa Rica   Phone: 32 35 91

1783

Honor al Merito
To recognize women who have distinguished themselves through outstanding service to the business and professional women of Costa Rica. Candidates may be Costa Rican citizens or nationals of other lands. A certificate of merit is presented annually at the "Internacional Noche de las Velas." Established in 1982 in honor of Carmen Madrigal de Gennette y Mae, founder of the federation in 1970.

1784

Organization for Tropical Studies (Organizacion para Estudios Tropicales)
Apartado 676-2050
San Pedro de Montes de Oca   Phone: 406696
San Jose, Costa Rica   Fax: 406783

1785

Organization for Tropical Studies Awards
To recognize individuals for outstanding research in tropical biology, agroecology, and forestry. (Discontinued)

Cote d'Ivoire

1786

Cote d'Ivoire
Presidency of the Republic
BP 1354 A
Abidjan 01, Cote d'Ivoire   Phone: 225 320222

1787

Grand Collier
For recognition of outstanding contributions and service to the country. An elaborate chain with medallions and a large decorated cross is awarded. The names of the Presidents of the Republic are engraved on the reverse of the medallions.

1788

Medaille d'Honneur de la Police
For recognition of outstanding service in the Police Department. A medal with a palm leaf and a simple medal are awarded.

1789

Medaille d'Honneur des Douanes
For recognition of outstanding service in the Customs Department. A cross is awarded for First, Second, and Third Class.

1790

Medaille d'Honneur du Travail
For recognition of an outstanding contribution to labor in the Ivory Coast. The following medals are awarded: Grande Medaille d'Or; Medaille d'Or; Medaille de Vermeil; and Medaille d'Argent.

1791

Ordre de la Sante Publique
For recognition of outstanding service in public health. A medal is awarded for Commander, Officer, and Chevalier.

1792

Ordre de l'Education Nationale
For recognition of an outstanding contribution to education in the Ivory Coast. A cross is awarded for Commander, Officer, and Chevalier.

1793

Ordre du Merite Agricole
For recognition of an outstanding contribution to agriculture in the Ivory Coast. An eight pointed star is awarded for Commander, Officer, and Chevalier.

1794

Ordre du Merite des P. et T.
For recognition of service to the country. A seven-pointed star is awarded for Commander, Officer, and Chevalier.

1795

Ordre du Merite Ivoirien
For recognition of outstanding service to the country. The following awards are given: (1) Grand-Croix; (2) Grand Officier; and (3) Commander, Officer, and Chevalier. A star shaped medal is awarded.

1796

Ordre du Merite Sportif
For recognition of outstanding contributions in the field of sport. A medal is awarded for Commander, Officer, and Chevalier.

1797

Ordre National
For recognition of outstanding service to the country. The following awards are given: (1) Grand-Croix; (2) Grand Officier; and (3) Commander, Officer, and Chevalier. A cross on a medallion is awarded.

Croatia

1798

Croatian Library Association (Hrvatsko Bibliotekarsko Drustvo)
National and University Library
Marulicev trg 21   Phone: 41 446322
41000 Zagreb, Croatia   Fax: 41 426676

1799

Kukuljeviceva povelja (Kukuljevic Charter)
For recognition of achievement in librarianship. Society membership is necessary for consideration. A charter is awarded at the convention irregularly. Established in 1968 in honor of Ivan Kukuljevic Sakcinski, the author of the first Croatian retrospective bibliography (1863).

1800

Croatian Music Institute (Hrvatski Glazbeni Zavod)
Gunduliceva 6
41000 Zagreb, Croatia   Phone: 41 424 533

1801

Vaclav Huml International Violin Competition
For recognition of outstanding violin performances. Individuals between 16 and 30 years of age of all nationalities are eligible. Monetary prizes and performances are awarded for first through sixth prizes. In addition, the Institute gives a special monetary prize for the best performance of a composition by a Yugoslav composer, and the Symphony Orchestra of the Zagreb Radio gives an engagement for the competitor who best cooperates with the orchestra. Awarded quadriennally. Established in 1977. The first prize is named in honor of Zlatko Balokovic, a famous

Croatian violinist (1895 Zagreb - 1965 Venice). The competition is named in honor of Vaclav Huml, violin pedagogue and teacher. Formerly: Medunarodno violinisticko natjecanje Vaclav Huml.

1802

Croatian National Theatre Split
(Hrvatsko narodno kazaliste Split)
Trg Gaje Bulata I
Postanski pretinac 195
58000 Split, Croatia   Phone: 58 585 999

1803

Split Summer Festival
(Splitsko Ljeto)
To recognize achievement in opera, drama and ballet programs of the Split Summer Festival, which takes place every year from July 15 to August 15. Bronze sculptures by Vasko Lipovac are awarded annually. Established in 1984 by the journal *Danas*, in memory of Marko Marulic, the first writer on Croatian language. Sponsored by the Zagreb Weekly magazine, *Danas-Vjesnik*.

1804

Croatian Pharmaceutical Society
(Hrvatsko Farmaceutsko drustvo)
Masarykova 2   Phone: 41 427944
41000 Zagreb, Croatia   Fax: 41 431301

Formerly: (1991) Farmaceutsko drustvo Hrvatske.

1805

Julije Domac Medal
(Medalja Julije Domac)
For recognition of a contribution to the development of pharmaceutical science and the profession. Members of the Society are eligible. A medal is awarded annually when merited. Established in 1955 in memory of Julije Domac, the first professor of the pharmaceutical faculty in Zagreb, Institute for Pharmacognosy (1886 to 1924).

1806

Republic of Croatia
Ministry of Science, Technology and Informatics
(Republika Hrvatska)
Amruseva 4
41000 Zagreb, Croatia

Formerly: (1991) Socialist Republic of Croatia; Republic Committee for Science, Technology and Informatics.

1807

Rudjer Boskovic Awards
To recognize scientific work important to the development of natural sciences. A monetary prize and plaque are awarded annually. Established in 1960 in honor of Rudjer Boskovic, physicist, mathematician, astronomer, and philosopher.

1808

Croatian Socialist Republic Prizes
For recognition of the best literary works by authors living in the Croatian Socialist Republic. Authors may submit novels, poetry, drama, literary studies, children's literature, and translations. A monetary prize is awarded annually on the state holiday, May 1.

1809

Ivan Filipovic Awards
To recognize research work in the field of education and teaching, the promotion of pedagogical theory and practice, and the development of educational systems in general. A monetary prize of 5,000 dinars is awarded annually. An additional prize of 20,000 dinars is given annually for life-long contributions to teaching. Awarded by the Republic Committee for Educational System, Culture, Physical and Technical Culture.

1810

Bartol Kasic Award
To recognize scientific work in the field of socio-humanistic sciences. A monetary prize and a plaque are awarded annually on May 30. Established in 1960 in honor of Bozidar Adzija, politician, publicist, national partisan and hero. Renamed in 1991 in honor of Bartol Kasic, a Croatian scholar and Jesuit monk who was author of the first Croatian grammar in the Sixteenth century. Formerly: (1991) Bozidar Adzija Award.

1811

Life Achievement Award
To recognize an individual for his life's work in scientific research. Six monetary awards of 10,000 German marks each are presented annually on May 30 for work in any scientific area. Established in 1960.

1812

Vladimir Nazor Awards
For recognition of contributions to the arts in the following fields: literature, film, theatre, music, and painting. A monetary prize of 15,000 dinars is awarded annually. A monetary prize of 35,000 dinars is also awarded annually to recognize a life-long contribution to one of those arts. Awarded by the Republic Committee for Educational System, Culture, Physical and Technical Culture.

1813

Nikola Tesla Awards
To recognize scientific work in the field of technical and engineering sciences. A monetary prize and plaque are awarded annually on May 30. Established in 1960 in honor of Nikola Tesla, physicist, researcher, and inventor in the field of electrical engineering and radio-technics.

1814

Fran Tucan Award
To recognize a scientist for contributions to the popularization of any field of science. A monetary prize and a plaque are awarded annually on May 30. Established in 1986 in honor of Fran Tucan, mineralogist and petrologist.

1815

Zagreb World Festival of Animated Films
(Svjetski Festival Animiranih Filmova, Zagreb)
Nova Ves 18   Phone: 41 410134
41000 Zagreb, Croatia   Fax: 41 410134

1816

Svjetski Festival Animiranih Filmova, Zagreb
(Zagreb World Festival of Animated Films)
For recognition of the best animated films (cartoons, puppets, collage, paper-cuts, computer films, etc.) that do not exceed 30 minutes. Awards are given in the following categories: 30 second to 5 minute running time - Best Film, 3,000 German marks and two second prizes of 1,000 German marks each; 5 minute to 30 minute running time category - Best Film, 3,000 German marks and two second prizes of 1,000 German marks each; Best First Production Zlatko Grgic Award - 5,000 German marks; two Special Awards; and Best Film Producer at the Festival. Awarded biennially. Established in 1972.

Cuba

1817

Cuban Book Institute
(Instituto Cubano del Libro)
O'Reilly No. 4 esquina a Tacon
Habana Vieja   Phone: 7 628091
Havana, Cuba   Fax: 7 338187

Cuba

1818
Premio a las Mejores Obras Cientificas o Tecnicas Publicadas en el Ano
For recognition of the ten best scientific or technical books published each year. Established in 1989.

1819
Premio de la Critica a los Mejores Libros Publicados
For recognition of the ten best books published each year. Established in 1983.

1820
Premio Nacional de Critica Literaria Mirta Aguirre
For recognition of Cuban literary criticism. Awards are given in three categories: essay, article, and review. Awarded annually. Established in 1983.

1821
Premio Nacional de Literatura
For recognition of Cuban authors for the totality of their outstanding literary work. A monetary prize of 5,000 pesos is awarded annually. Established in 1983. Co-sponsored by the Cuban Ministry of Culture.

1822
Cuban Society of Mathematics and Computer Science
(Sociedad Cubana de Matematica y Computacion)
Universidad de la Habana
Municipio Plaza
Havana 10400, Cuba
Phone: 537 704700
Fax: 537 322757

Formerly: (1988) Cuban Society of Mathematics.

1823
Sociedad Cubana de Matematica y Computacion "Pablo Miguel" Awards
To foster scientific research or the teaching of mathematics and computer science among members. Prizes and medals are awarded triennially.

1824
International Association of Crime Writers
(Asociacion Internacional de Escritores Policiacos)
17 y H
Vedado
Havana, Cuba
Phone: 320491

1825
Hammett Award
To recognize professional crime writers who are involved in the translation of crime story books. The Association organizes festivals on crime literature. Awarded annually.

1826
Alexei Tolstoi Award
To recognize professional crime writers who are involved in the translation of crime story books. Awarded annually.

1827
International Festival of New Latin American Cinema
(Festival Internacional del Nuevo Cine Latinoamericano)
Calle 23
No. 1155 Plaza de la Revolucion
Vedado
Havana 4, Cuba
Phone: 30 5041
Phone: 30 4400

1828
Premio CORAL
For recognition of outstanding Latin American films. Prizes are awarded in the following major categories: (1) Feature Films - (A) First, Second, and Third CORAL prizes; (B) Special jury prize; (C) Special CORAL prize for the best non-Latinoamerican fiction film; (D) Best actress; (E) Best actor; (F) Best scenario; (G) Best photography; (H) Best editing; (I) Best musical score; and (J) Best direction; (2) Documentaries - (A) Best documentary film - First, Second, and Third CORAL prizes; (B) Special jury prize; and (C) Special prize for the best non-Latinoamerican Documentary; and (3) Animated Films - (A) Best animated film - First, Second, and Third CORAL prizes; and (B) Best unedited scenario. Trophies and plaques are awarded annually. Established in 1979. Sponsored by the Cuban Film Institute.

Czech Republic

1829
Bratislova City Hall
Primacialne nam. 1
814 99 Bratislava, Czech Republic
Phone: 7 335405
Fax: 7 356124

1830
Prize of the Capital of Slovakia Bratislava
For recognition of achievements in scientific, technical, artistic, and other socially beneficial activities important for the economic, culture, and social development of the city. An individual or team may be considered for contributions during the preceding year. Awarded in accordance with voting of the deputies of the City Assembly.

1831
Prize of the Mayor of the City of Bratislava
For recognition of achievements in humanitarian, cultural, and socially beneficial activities important for the city's development. An individual or team may be considered for contributions during the preceding year. Awarded by the Mayor and based on the recommendation of the Executive Board.

1832
Chopin Society, Czechoslovakia
(Spolecnost Fryderyka Chopina v CSSR)
Hlavni 47
353 01 Marianske Lazne, Czech Republic
Phone: 165 5330
Phone: 165 2617
Fax: 165 5346

1833
Chopin Piano Competition, Czechoslovakia
(Cena Chopinovy klavirni souteze)
To encourage students of music, between the ages of 15 to 25, who are citizens of the Czech Republic and from any music school, conservatory, or academy. A monetary prize and a plaque are awarded biennially. Established in 1962 by the Chopin Society in memory of Frederik Chopin, a Polish composer who visited Marienbad in 1836. Sponsored by the cultural and social centre in Marianske Lazne/Marienbad.

1834
Clubcentrum Usti-nad-Orlici
(Klubcentrum Usti-nad-Orlici)
Havlickova 621
562 01 Usti nad Orlici, Czech Republic
Phone: 4652245

Formerly: (1991) United Workers' Club Usti-nad-Orlici.

1835
Heran Violoncello Competition
To encourage the professional development of youth and to recognize outstanding performers on the violoncello. Individuals who are 16 years of age and under are eligible. Diplomas and works of art are awarded biennially. Established in 1968 by the Music School of Jaroslav Kocian in honor of Bohus Heran.

1836
Kocian Violin Competition
To encourage the professional development of youth and to recognize outstanding violin performers. Individuals who are 16 years of age and under are eligible. Diplomas and works of art are awarded annually in early May. Established in 1959 by the Music School of Jaroslav Kocian in honor of Jaroslav Kocian.

1837
Czech Radio, Prague
(Cesky Rozhlas, Praga)
Vinohradska 12
120 99 Prague 2, Czech Republic
Phone: 2 4094288
Fax: 2 4218089

1838
Concertino Prague International Radio Competition for Young Musicians
(Mezinarodni rozhlasova soutez Mladych hudebniku Concertino Praga)
To recognize young talented musicians and enable them to compare their skills on an international scale, to acquaint the broad radio audiences with their performances, and to assist in establishing contacts among the youngest artistic generation. The competition is open to soloists in the categoreis of piano, violin, and violoncello. Musicians no older than 16 years of age are eligible. Candidates take part in the competition through tape recordings sent in by radio organizations associated in the International Organization for Radio and Television or in the European Broadcasting Union. Each radio organization can enter one participant in each competition category. In case one of the three instruments is not represented, the second competitor may be admitted for one of the remaining categories. The selection of soloists whose performances have to be judged is made by the participating radio organization itself. The deadline for sending in the application is April 30. The deadline for submitting recordings is August 31. In each competiton category, the jury awards first and second prizes. On consideration, the jury may award an honorary diploma to runners-up whose score comes close to those of the first and second prize winners. The winners, first, and second prize laureates are invited by the organizer to perform at public concerts in Prague and at the South Bohemia Concertino Praga Festival to defend their victory. The concerts are offered to members of the broadcasting unions for live or delayed broadcasts. Expenses for the winners' stay in Prague and at the South Bohemian Concertino Praga Festival, and travel to and from the Festival are paid by Czech Radio. Awarded annually.

1839
Czech Section of the International Board on Books for Young People
Staropramenna 2
150 00 Prague 5, Czech Republic
Phone: 2 549006

1840
Gold Ribbon
To recognize outstanding new writers and illustrators of children's books and to support traditionally first-rate domestic book production for children and young adults. Twice per year, writers, illustrators, and publishers (for editorial work) are chosen to receive the Gold Ribbon award for first edition books published within the past six months.

1841
Marie Majerova Award
For recognition of life-long literary work for children. Awards were given to an author and to an illustrator. A monetary prize and a diploma were awarded biennially. Established in 1966 in memory of Marie Majerova, a well-known author for children. (Discontinued in 1991)

1842
Bohumil Riha Prize
To recognize Czechoslovak or foreign citizens who achieved excellent results in popularization of books for children and youth. A monetary award, a medal, and a diploma were awarded annually on April 4. Established in 1988 by the Czechoslovak Section of IBBY, Circle of Children's Book Friends in Slovakia, and the Association of Friends of Books for Youth in honor of B. Riha (1907-1987), an artist. (Discontinued in 1991)

1843
Czech Television
International Television
Kavci hory
140 70 Prague 4, Czech Republic
Phone: 2 6927027
Fax: 2 6927202

Formerly: Czechoslovak Television, Prague.

1844
International Television Festival Golden Prague
(Mezinarodni Televizni Festival Zlata Praha)
To present television music programs, promote their international exchanges, and initiate production of original programs created for the television medium. The competition is divided into two categories: Dramatic music programs, including operas, operettas, musicals, singspiels, and dance programs presented on television or produced for television; and concert works and other types of music programs, including portraits of musicians, documentary music programs, and other such programs created by television or film techniques. In both categories, programs may be shown which are parts of serials but form separate artistic wholes, and can be judged separately. Recommended footage is 10 minutes minimum and 90 minutes maximum for dramatic music programs, and 60 minutes for concert works and other types of music programs. Applicants may enter programs in both categories. Any television organization (broadcasting television programs) can take part in the festival as well as producer companies, provided that they submit applications in keeping with the rules of the competition. The Golden Prague trophy and a monetary prize of 10,000 DM are awarded. In each category, the "Czech Crystal" is awarded to the best program. In each category, three honorable mentions can be awarded. Deadline for entries is March 15.

1845
Czechoslovak Association of Liberty and Anti-Fascist Fighters
(Ceskoslovensky Svaz Bojovniku za Svobodu a Proti Fasismu)
Legerova 22
120 49 Prague 2, Czech Republic
Phone: 2 295541

Formerly: (1990) Czechoslovak Association of Anti-fascist Fighters.

1846
Czechoslovak Association of Liberty and Anti-Fascist Fighters Awards
To recognize members of the resistance movement during the Nazi occupation of Czechoslovakia, 1939-45 and family members of resistance veterans. Awards are presented.

1847
Czechoslovak Radio, Brno
(Ceskoslovensky Rozhlas, Brno)
Beethovenova 4
657 42 Brno, Czech Republic
Phone: 5 26111
Fax: 5 26007

1848
Prix Musical de Radio Brno
For recognition of the best radio musical programs of serious music accompanied by the spoken word; to encourage professional development; and to support cooperation among broadcasting organizations. Any broadcasting studio of any country may submit one competition program in any of the following categories: (1) Thematic - music programs accompanied by the spoken word, 40-60 minutes long in the sphere of symphonic, vocal, and chamber music; and (2) Non-thematic - music features up to 20 minutes long. A theme is announced each year. The verbal part must be recorded in the language normally used by the sponsoring broadcasting station. A jury awards in the first category a first, second, and third Prix Musical de Radio Brno Prizes and special prizes. In the second category, first, second and third prizes are awarded. Monetary prizes, trophies, plaques, travel expenses for foreigners, and diplomas are awarded. Established in 1967. Co-sponsored by the Czech and Slovak Music Fund.

1849
Czechoslovak Violin Makers Competitions
(Ceskoslovenske houslarske souteze)
Skroupova ul. 9 Phone: 49 658
501 97 Hradec Kralove 1, Czech Republic Fax: 49 614555

1850
Oskar Nedbal Award
(Cena Oskara Nedbala)
For recognition of the best made viola. A medal is awarded every four years. Established in 1985 in honor of Oskar Nedbal, a well-known Czech composer of the 20th century. Sponsored by Czechoslovak Musical Instruments - Industrial Group.

1851
Czechoslovakia
Ministry of Commerce and Tourism
(Czechoslovakia
Ministerstvo obchodu a cestovniho ruchu)
Publicity Mgr.
Staromestske Namesti 6 Phone: 2 2897
110 01 Prague 1, Czech Republic Fax: 2 326815

1852
International Festival of Tourist Films - Tourfilm
(Mezinarodni Festival Filmu Cestovniho Ruchu - Tourfilm)
To recognize films and video-recordings which by content and artistic level help to develop tourist travel on the national and international plane in the spirit of the festival motto and, at the same time, to promote a wide international dissemination of such films and recordings. The competition is held in two categories: (1) 35mm and 16mm films that promote popularization of tourism or support its commercial aims. Documentary, publicist and popular science films related to tourism and leisure time are included; and (2) video-recordings - films shot by video technique that promote tourism or support its commercial aims. Documentary, publicist and popular science video-recordings related to tourism and leisure time are included. The following prizes are awarded: (1) The Golden Flower Award (Zlaty kvet) - Tourfilm Grand Prix; (2) The Silver Flower; (3) The Bronze Flower; and (4) Spectator Prize. Trophies and diplomas are awarded annually. Established in 1968 by the Government Committee and the Regional Committees for Tourism in East Bohemia. Additional information is available from Merkur, Tourfilm Sekretariat, PO Box 818, Vaclavske nam. 28, 112 13 Prague 1, Czechoslovakia.

1853
Czechoslovakia
Ministry of Culture, Czech
Valdstejnska 10 Phone: 5132248
116 75 Prague 1, Czech Republic Fax: 24510346

1854
Annual Prize of the Czech Musical Fund
For recognition of outstanding musical interpretation. Concert artists, chamber ensembles, singers, and conductors are eligible. Monetary prizes are awarded annually.

1855
Czechoslovakia
Office of the President
Urad predsednistzavlady Phone: 2 2101
Nabr. Kpt. Jarose 4 Phone: 2 534 541
125 09 Prague 1, Czech Republic Fax: 2 298 496

1856
Czechoslovak National Artist
To recognize Czech and Slovak writers for a lifetime's work which has contributed to the cultural development of the nation.

1857
Hradec nad Moravici Castles Administration
(Sprava zamku Hradce nad Moravici a Radune)
Mestecko C. 2
747 41 Hradec nad Moravici, Czech
 Republic Phone: 653 91185

Formerly: (1991) Kulturni stredisko zamek Hradec.

1858
Beethoven's Hradec Music Competition
(Cena Beethovenova Hradce)
For recognition of achievement, and to encourage professional development in the field of music. Awards are given in two repertoires—violin and viola—that are broken into two age categories—category I, not older than 19 years; category II, not older than 30 years. Monetary prizes are given annually for first, second, and third place in each category of each repertoire. Established in 1962. Sponsored by Czech Music Fund Prague.

1859
International Federation of Social Science Organizations
(Federation Internationale des Organisations de Sciences Sociales)
Inst. of State & Law
Narohni 18 Phone: 2 205889
116 91 Prague 1, Czech Republic Fax: 2 2320878

1860
Administrative Visitors Fellowship Programme
To support and develop the social sciences and encourage international cooperation in the field, contribute to the development of social sciences, especially in developing countries, and further active participation of the social sciences in discussions on problems of modern society and in efforts to find solutions. Administrative officers of research councils are eligible. One Fellowship is awarded per year to enable the awardee to undertake a study trip of two to four weeks.

1861
International Festival of Films and Television Programs on Environmental Problems - Ekofilm
(Mezinarodni festival filmu a televiznich poradu o zivotnim prostredi - Ekofilm)
 Phone: 2 2360620
PO Box 668 Phone: 2 2350947
113 57 Prague 1, Czech Republic Fax: 2 2359788

1862
Ekofilm Awards
For recognition of the best films and television programs dealing with the most urgent aspects of environmental conservation. Every year, a different central subject is proclaimed. The Festival intends to present and honor films which promote, by their contents and artistic composition, the dissemination of current information on environmental problems, important from a political, scientific and generally human point of view; point out unconventional approaches to various problems; and stress the ecological aspects of the forming and protection of the environment. The subject of films and television programs entered should pertain to problems of the human environment. The program of the Festival includes both competitive and informative films and television showings. International and national organizations, institutions, enterprises, and individual persons who are sponsors, producers, distributors, owners, or authors of films may enter. The deadline for submissions is March 15. Only films and television programs produced during the preceding two years are accepted. The International Jury awards the Ekofilm Grand Prix and five Main Awards. It may also award a Special Award and Honorable Mentions. It further awards prizes of the Ostrava Lord Mayor and of the Ekofilm Director. Other awards are awarded by the co-organizers. Trophies and plaques are awarded annually. Established in 1974. Sponsored by the Federal Committee for Environment.

1863
International Organization of Journalists
(Mezinarodni organizace novinaru)
Celetna 2   Phone: 2 2364496
110 01 Prague 1, Czech Republic   Phone: 2 2320426

1864
Julius Fucik Honorary Medal
To recognize outstanding personalities and organizations (first of all, to journalists) for their exceptional merits in strengthening peace, and in promoting international cooperation and mutual understanding among nations. The Honorary Medal can be awarded to each holder only once. Established in 1974.

1865
International Journalism Prize
For recognition of outstanding achievement in the scientific theory of journalism and professional activity which has given, in the spirit of the UNO Charter, a valuable contribution to the maintaining of peace in the world, the strengthening of friendly relations among peoples and the promotion of unity among journalists. Candidates may be of any nationality. Two prizes are conferred every year by the Presidium of Executive Committee of the International Organization of Journalists on individual journalists or editorial staffs. A monetary prize of $2,000 and a diploma are awarded annually to each of two winners. Established in 1958.

1866
International Radio and Television Organization
(Organisation Internationale de Radiodiffusion et Television)
Skokanska 1
169 56 Prague 6, Czech Republic   Phone: 2 322587

1867
International Radio and Television Festivals and Competitions
To recognize outstanding broadcasting and television programming. The Organization holds festivals and competitions.

1868
International Union of Students
(Union Internationale des Etudiants)
17th November St.
PO Box 58   Phone: 2 2312812
110 01 Prague 1, Czech Republic   Fax: 2 2316100

1869
November 17th Medal
To recognize outstanding contributions made to the student movement in the following fields: education and literacy, culture, press and information, and peace and solidarity. Nominations of organizations/individuals submitted by IUS member organizations are accepted. Medals are presented irregularly. Established in 1976 to commemorate the date of the anti-fascist student uprising in Czechoslovakia, whose participants were brutally oppressed by Nazi occupation authorities on November 17, 1939.

1870
Interpretation Competition
Vrsovcu 1
Chomutov, Czech Republic

1871
Interpreters Competition of Slovak Republic
To provide for the selection of the Czechoslovak concert artists for Slovkoncert in alternating categories. Individuals under 30 years of age with professional education, and Czechoslovak citizenship are eligible. A monetary prize and registration in the category of concert artists are awarded annually in November. Established in 1977.

1872
KF Ltd. - Agrofilm
Jindrisska str.34   Phone: 2 4212456
112 07 Prague 1, Czech Republic   Fax: 2 4212053

1873
Agrofilm International Short Film Festival
For recognition of outstanding agricultural films and videorecordings. Awards are given for films under 30 minutes in length that respond to the most urgent problems of human nutrition by documenting the latest scientific and technological achievements aimed at a substantial and effective expansion of agricultural production and food processing; as well as films and videorecordings dealing with forestry and water conservancy, ecology of rural regions, and optimization of living and working conditions in the agrosphere. Awards are given in the following categories: science and research; popular science; educational and instructive; documentaries; and informative. Entries may be submitted by May 15 and are judged by an international jury. A Grand Prize and an Agrofilm prize are awarded in each category. Established in 1984.

1874
Techfilm International Film Festival
For recognition of short films that are under 30 minutes. Awards are given for science and research, popular science, instruction and teaching, documentary, and publicity/informative. Films may be entered by producers, sponsors, distributors, authors, and organizations. The Techfilm Grand Prize and prizes in each category are awarded. Established in 1962.

1875
Mozart Association of Czechoslovakia
Kriva 8
130 00 Prague 3, Czech Republic

1876
Dusek Competition of Musical Youth
(Duskova Soutez Hudebni Mla'deze)
For recognition of the best interpretation of Czech classical music and works of W.A. Mozart. Between 1971 and 1985, awards were given in the following categories: (1) piano - ages 13-21 years; (2) string instruments - ages 13-21 years; (3) chamber music - ages 13-21 years; and (4) wind instruments. Since 1986, the only category for competition is Chamber music. Awards may be given to foreigners. Awarded annually.

1877

**Our Army Publishing House
(Nase Vojsko, nakladatelstvi)**
Na Dekance 3
128 12 Prague 2, Czech Republic
Phone: 2 291700
Fax: 2 294274

1878

**Nase Vojsko Prizes
(Vyrocni cena nakladatelstvi Nase vojsko)**
For recognition of the best books in the following categories: politics; military theory; and fiction. A monetary prize was divided among the winners in each category. Established in 1975. (Discontinued in 1992)

1879

**Prague Spring International Music Competition
(Mezinarodni hudebni festival Prazske jaro)**
Hellichova 18
118 00 Prague 1, Czech Republic
Phone: 2 533474
Phone: 2 24510422
Fax: 2 536040

1880

**Prague Spring International Music Competition
(Mezinarodni hudebni soutez Prazske jaro)**
For recognition of an outstanding performance in the field of music by young talent. Categories change annually, and there may be more than one category within any given competition. The competition in 1992 features violin, French horn, trumpet, and trombone; in 1993, piano, string quartet; in 1994, violon cello, organ, harpsichord; and in 1995, conducting. Musicians of all nationalities are eligible. The age limit varies according to category (30 or 35 years). The following awards are presented: (1) a monetary award of 15,000 to 50,000 Czechoslovak crowns and a gold plaque - first prize; (2) 12,000 to 20,000 Czechoslovak crowns and a silver plaque - second prize; and (3) 9,000 to 15,000 Czechoslovak crowns and a bronze plaque - third prize. Prize-winners also receive the title of Laureate of the Competition and the opportunity to appear at a concert of laureates. Awarded annually. Established in 1948. Sponsored by the Ministry of Culture.

1881

**Society of Czech Architects
(Obec architektu)**
Letenska 5
118 45 Prague 1, Czech Republic
Phone: 2 24511294
Fax: 2 3114926

Formerly: (1990) Union of Czech Architects.

1882

**Annual Prize of the Society of Czech Architects
(Cena Obce Architektu za Realizaci Roku)**
For recognition of contemporary national architecture in the fields of new buildings, reconstructions, interior design, town planning, landscape architecture, and garden design. The competition is open to projects designed by Czech architects and created in the territory of the Czech Republic. Established in 1993.

1883

**Josef Havlicek Prize
(Cena Josefa Havlicka)**
For recognition of outstanding contributions to architecture in the fields of urban design, town and country planning, and theoretical, historical or pedagogical achievement in architecture. A maximum of three monetary prizes and plaques were awarded annually. Established in 1976 in honor of Josef Havlicek, a Czech architect, an outstanding representative of the avant-garde movement in the 1930s, and the founder of the socialist project - institutions after World War II. (Discontinued)

1884

**Union of Czech Architects - Annual Prize
(Cena Svazu ceskych architektu)**
For recognition of long-term activity within the Union of Czech Architects. A maximum of three monetary prizes and honorary diplomas were awarded annually. Established in 1976. Sponsored by the Czech Fine Arts Fund. (Discontinued in 1990) Formerly: .

1885

**Union of Czech Writers
(Svaz ceskychspisovatelu)**
Narodni trida 11
11 147 Prague 1, Czech Republic

1886

Brno Literary Prize
For recognition of the best book written and published in Brno. A monetary prize is awarded annually.

1887

Mlada Fronta Award
For recognition of literary works of prose, poetry, journalism, popular science and translations published by Mlada Fronta during the preceding year. A monetary prize is awarded annually. Additional information is available from Mlada Fronta Publishing House, Panska 8, 112 22 Prague, Czechoslovakia.

1888

Prague Literary Prize
For recognition of the best creative work which has enriched human knowledge, contributed to the construction of socialism and furthered the development of culture in the city of Prague. A monetary prize is awarded annually.

1889

Ustredni Reditelstvi Ceskoslovenskeho Filmu
Jindrisska 34
112 06 Prague, Czech Republic
Phone: 226 34 38
Phone: 223 65 385
Fax: 222 0325

1890

**Gottwaldov Festival of Children's Films
(Festival Filmu pro Deti Gottwaldov)**
For recognition of the best children's films that contribute to intellectual and emotional development in the spirit of progress and peaceful coexistence. Three juries award prizes: (1) Jury for full-feature; (2) Jury for animated films; and (3) Children's Jury. Films produced in Czechoslovakia during the preceding year are eligible. The following prizes are awarded annually in May: Full-length Feature Films - (1) Prize of Czechoslovak Film - The Festival Figure; (2) Prize of Czechoslovak Film - The Little Silver Whistle; (3) Best actor; (4) Best actress; and (5) Special Prize; Animated Films - (1) Prize of Jiri Trnka; (2) Prize of Czechoslovak Film - The Little Weathercock; and (3) Special Prize; and Children's Jury Prize - selected by an audience of children. Established in 1961 by Czechoslovak film Gottwaldov Municipal National Council, Central Committee of the Union of Czech Dramatic Artists.

1891

Karlovy Vary International Film Festival
To introduce and evaluate outstanding films that, by their artistic contents and form, contribute to the development of cinematography. An international jury comprised of prominent representatives of the art of film, film production, and film theory and criticism selects the films. Every invited country may enter one full-length feature film in the competition. Films must have been produced within the preceding year and must not have been entered in competitions at other international film festivals. The following prizes are awarded by jury: (1) The Grand Prix - a Crystal Globe; (2) Main Prize - Rose of Lidice Prize; (3) Best Director Prize; (4) The Best Actress Prize; (5) The Best Actor Prize; and (6) Special Prizes. In addition,

the following prizes are awarded in the Debut competition: (1) A.M. Brousil's Prize; and (2) Honorable Mentions. Awarded biennially in July. Established in 1948.

1892

Zerotin Singing Choir
(Pevecko - hudebni spolek Zerotin)
Hrncirska 24
772 00 Olomouc, Czech Republic
Phone: 68 259049
Fax: 68 259049

Formerly: Park kultury a oddechu, Olomouc.

1893

Iuventus Mundi Cantat Competition
For recognition of achievement in the singing competition, Iuventus Mundi Cantat. Members of a children's choir up to the age of 17 are eligible. Gold, silver, and bronze medals are awarded biennially at the Festival "Holidays of Songs." Established in 1987 by the Ministry of Culture. Sponsored by the Ministry of Culture and the Czechoslovakia Music Fund.

1894

Smetana Piano Competition
(Smetanovska klavirni souteze)
To recognize an outstanding artistic performance by a pianist. The categories awarded are international and national. The contestants may not be over the age of 25 in the first category or over the age of 19 in the second. A monetary prize and a piano are presented to the Laureates biennially when merited in Hradec Kralove. Established in 1963 in memory of the 19th century Czech composer, Bedrich Smetana.

Denmark

1895

Academy of Fine Arts
(Akademiet for de skonne Kunster)
Akademiraadet
Charlottenborg
Kongens Nytorv 1
DK-1050 Copenhagen K, Denmark
Phone: 33 126860

1896

Thorvald Bindesboll Medal
To recognize an individual for an achievement of high value within the fields of applied art and industrial graphic art. Individuals who are not members of the Council of the Academy are eligible. A bronze medal designed by the sculptor and painter, Poul Gernes, is awarded when merited. Established in 1979 in commemoration of the 75th anniversary of the printing of Thorvald Bindesboll's label for "Carlsberg Pilsner."

1897

Eckersberg Medal
To recognize an individual for an achievement of high artistic value within the fine arts or the architectural arts. Individuals who are not members of the Council of the Academy are eligible. A bronze medal, designed by the medallist Harald Conradsen, is awarded when merited. Established in 1883 in memory of C. V. Eckersberg, a painter, on the occasion of the centenary of his birth.

1898

Gold Medal Conanti Award
For recognition of work in architecture, painting, or sculpture. A monetary prize of 150,000 Danish kroner and a gold medal with the inscription "Conati" by Jacques Saly (first awarded in 1759) are awarded triennially. Established in 1993.

1899

C. F. Hansen Medal
This, the highest honor that the Academy awards an architect, is given for distinguished achievement in the architectural arts. Individuals who are not members of the Council of the Academy at the time are eligible. A silver medal is awarded when merited. Established in 1830.

1900

N. L. Hoyen Medal
To recognize an individual for an achievement of high value within research, interpretation, or procurement of the fine arts. Individuals who are not members of the Council of the Academy are eligible. A medal is awarded when merited. Established in 1979 in memory of N. L. Hoyen, a professor at the Royal Academy of Fine Arts 150 years ago (in the 1830s).

1901

Neuhausen Foundation Award
For recognition of the best work, executed individually or jointly, by architects, painters or sculptors, for the competition announced by the Academy. A monetary prize of about 50,000 Danish kroner, which was divided into three parts at the most, was awarded triennially. Established in 1838. (Discontinued in 1988)

1902

Thorvaldsen Medal
This, the highest honor that the Academy awards a sculptor and a painter, is given for distinguished achievement in the fine arts. Individuals who are not members of the Council of the Academy are eligible. A silver medal, designed by the medallist Chr. Christensen and cast in 1838, is awarded when merited. Established in 1838 in honor of the sculptor, Bertel Thorvaldsen, on the occasion of the receipt of his works from Rome.

1903

Carlsberg Laboratory
(Carlsberg Laboratorium)
Dept. of Physiology
Gamle Carlsbergvej 10
DK-2500 Copenhagen Valby, Denmark
Phone: 31 221022
Fax: 33 274766

1904

Emil Christian Hansen Foundation for Microbiological Research Award
(Emil Christian Hansen Fondets Pris for Mikrobiologisk Forskning)
For recognition of outstanding contributions to microbiology. A monetary prize of 30,000 Danish kroner and a gold medal are awarded every two to four years. Established in 1914 by Professor and Mrs. Emil Christian Hansen.

1905

Council of Nordic Academies of Music
(Nordisk orkesterdirigentkonkurrence)
Fuglesangs Alle 26
DK-8210 Aarhus, Denmark
Phone: 86 155388
Fax: 86 158476

1906

Nordic Biennial for Young Soloists
To provide an opportunity for young Nordic soloists and ensembles to get to know each other in an atmosphere that is completely different from that prevailing in musical competitions, and to concentrate on a program of new Scandinavian music. The young performers present themselves to a wide audience, to concert organizers, TV and radio companies, and to music critics.

1907
Nordic Competition for Young Orchestra Conductors
For recognition of the best performance of young conductors under 35 years of age and not yet artistically established. Engagement and monetary awards are presented every four years. Established in 1987.

1908
**Danish Academy
(Danske Akademi)**
7 Vognmagergade
DK-1120 Copenhagen K, Denmark
Phone: 33 13 11 12
Fax: 33 32 80 45

1909
Danish Academy Prize for Literature
For recognition of an outstanding work of literature. A monetary prize of 200,000 Danish kroner is awarded biennially. Established in 1960. The Academy also awards the following smaller prizes: (1) Otto Gelsted pris - established in 1976; (2) Kjeld Abell Pris - established in 1976; (3) Selskabets pris - established in 1976; (4) Beatrice Pris - established in 1984; and (5) Klaus Rifbjerg Pris - established in 1984; and (6) Overstterprisen - established in 1988 for translation.

1910
**Danish Academy of Technical Sciences
(Akademiet for de Tekniske Videnskaber)**
266 Lundtoftevej
DK-2800 Lyngby, Denmark
Phone: 42 881311
Fax: 45 931377

1911
Valdemar Poulsen Gold Medal
For recognition of outstanding achievement in the field of magnetic recording or the communication technique that is based on electromagnetic waves. A gold medal was awarded every three years. Established in 1939 on the occasion of Dr. Valdemar Poulsen's 70th birthday and awarded to him for contributions to radio and magnetic recording. (Discontinued in 1993)

1912
**Danish Jazz Center
(Danske Jazzcenter)**
Borupvej 66 B
DK-4683 Ronnede, Denmark
Phone: 53 711327
Fax: 53 711749

1913
Jazzpar Prize
To recognize an internationally known and fully active jazz artist who especially deserves further recognition. A monetary prize of 200,000 Danish kroner, a statuette, a prize concert tour, and recordings are awarded annually. Established in 1988. Sponsored by the Scandinavian Tobacco Company.

1914
**Danish Library Association
(Danmarks Biblioteksforening)**
Telegrafrej 5 II
DK-2750 Ballerup, Denmark
Phone: 4468 1466
Fax: 4468 1103

1915
R. Lysholt Hansens Bibliotekspris
To recognize special achievement in library or cultural work. Nominations must be submitted. A monetary award is presented annually when merited. Established in 1983 to honor R. Lysholt Hansen.

1916
Edvard Pedersens Biblioteksfonds Forfatterpris
To recognize outstanding authors. A monetary award is presented annually. Established in 1986 to honor Edvard Pedersen.

1917
**Danish Publishers Association
((Danske Forlaeggerforening))**
Kobmagergade 11
DK-1150 Copenhagen, Denmark

1918
Publishers Prize
For recognition of efforts for better books, design, and dissemination. A monetary prize of 25,000 Danish kroner was awarded occasionally. (Discontinued)

1919
**Danish School Librarian Association
(Danmarks Skolebibliotekarforening)**
Gogevet 2
DK-4130 Viby, Denmark
Phone: 42 393440
Fax: 42 394349

1920
Danmarks Skolebibliotekarforenings Bornebogspris
To support writers of outstanding literature for children. Only Danish writers are eligible. A monetary award of 8,000 Danish kroner and a diploma are awarded annually in October. Established in 1978. Additional information is available from Bert Rasmussen, Boelskilde 44, Bredalle, DK-7120 Vejle, Denmark.

1921
**Danish Timber Information Council
(Traebranchens Oplysningsraad)**
Lyngby Kirkestraede 14
DK-2800 Lyngby, Denmark
Phone: 873833
Fax: 880833

1922
Wood Prize
To recognize Danish architects for works that demonstrate special artistic qualities and technical skill. A monetary prize of 50,000 Danish kroner is awarded annually when merited. Established in 1958.

1923
**Danish Writers' Association
(Dansk Forfatterforening)**
Strandgade 6
DK-1401 Copenhagen K, Denmark
Phone: 33 95 51 00
Fax: 31 54 01 15

1924
Emil Aarestrup Prize
To recognize a poet. A monetary prize of 4,000 Danish kroner and a medal are awarded annually. Established in 1950 in commemoration of the Danish lyric poet, Carl Ludwig Emil Aarestrup.

1925
Danish Authors Lyric Prize
To provide recognition for outstanding poetry. A monetary prize of 5,000 Danish kroner was awarded annually. (Discontinued)

1926
Dansk Oversaetterforbunds Aerespris
For recognition of an outstanding translation of foreign literature into Danish. A monetary prize of 20,000 Danish kroner and a diploma are

awarded annually. Established in 1954. Sponsored by Denmark - Ministry of Cultural Affairs.

1927
Johannes Ewald Prize
To provide recognition for prose, poetry, and dramatic works. A monetary prize of 5,000 Danish kroner is awarded annually.

1928
Holberg Medal
To provide recognition for outstanding contributions to Danish literature. A monetary prize of 25,000 Danish kroner and a medal are awarded annually.

1929
Martin Andersen Nex Prize
To recognize the author of an outstanding work of literature. A monetary prize of 5,000 Danish kroner is awarded annually. Established in 1956 to commemorate the Danish socialist writer, Nex, who spent the last years of his life in Dresden.

1930
Adam Oehlenschlager Prize
To recognize outstanding Danish writers. A monetary prize of 5,000 Danish kroner is awarded annually. Established in 1955.

1931
Dansk Husflidsselskab
c/o Sekretariatet
Tyrebakken 11
DK-5300 Kerteminde, Denmark
Phone: 65 322096
Fax: 65 325611

1932
N. C. Roms Guldmedalje
For recognition of achievement in promoting the art of handicraft. Individuals may be nominated. A monetary prize and a medal are awarded annually. Established about 1900 in memory of N.C. Rom, founder of Dansk Husflidsselskab.

1933
**Dansk Teknologisk Institut
(Emballage & Transportinstituttet)**
Gregersensvej, Postboks 141
DK-2630 Taastrup, Denmark
Phone: 43 504465
Fax: 43 507283

Formerly: Danish Packaging Research Institute.

1934
Danstar
To recognize outstanding achievement in packaging. Awarded biennially. Established in 1987. (Discontinued)

1935
**Denmark
Ministry of Cultural Affairs**
Nybrogade 2
DK-1203 Copenhagen K, Denmark
Phone: 33 923370
Fax: 33 913388

1936
**Danish Prize for Children's Literature
(Kulturministeriets Bornebogspris)**
For recognition of the best Danish books for children and teenagers. A monetary prize of 30,000 Danish kroner is awarded annually. Established in 1954.

1937
Dansk Oversaetterforbunds Aerespris
For recognition of an outstanding translation of foreign literature into Danish. A monetary prize of 30,000 Danish kroner and a diploma are awarded annually. Established in 1954. Co-sponsored by the Danish Writers' Union.

1938
Illustratorprisen
To recognize an illustrator who has contributed to raising the artistic quality within the art of book illustration through his/her production and, possibly, with reference to a specific work. A monetary prize of 30,000 Danish Kroner is awarded annually. Established in 1979.

1939
Order Ingenio et Arti
A special reward for Danish scientists and artists. It can also be bestowed upon foreigners. The order has one class, gold. A medal is presented irregularly when merited. On the obverse, the Order carries the portrait of the reigning monarch, currently Queen Margrethe II; on the reverse, a winged genius in relief, designed by the famous Danish sculptor, Berthel Thorvaldsen, with the inscription "Ingenio et Arti." The name of the recipient is engraved along the edge of the Order. Instituted in 1841 by King Christian VIII.

1940
**Denmark
Ordenskapitlet**
Chr. VIII s Palae, Amalienborg
DK-1257 Copenhagen K, Denmark
Phone: 33 143628

1941
Order of the Dannebrog
For recognition of public service. The order is bestowed on any subject, in one of the following classes: Grand Commander Class and three Classes of the Order; the second and third Classes are each divided into two grades: Grand Commander, Grand Cross, Commander First Degree, Commander, Knight First Degree, and Knight. The decoration consists of a white-enamelled gold Latin cross (a silver cross in case of knights) with a red border, surmounted by a royal crown over the reigning sovereign's monogram. The obverse bears the crowned monogram of Christian V and the device Gud og Kongen (God and the King). On the reverse are the crowned monograms of Valdemar II and Frederik VI, together with the dates 1219, 1671, and 1808. In the angles of the cross are royal crowns. The decoration of Grand Commander has 14 table-cut diamonds instead of white enamel on the obverse, as well as diamonds in the other embellishments of the cross. The reverse bears the crowned monograms of Valdemar II, Christian V, and Frederik VI, together with Gud og Kongen on white enamel. The statutes of the Order were proclaimed on October 12, 1671, and imposed a maximum membership of 50, plus the king and his sons.

1942
Order of the Elephant
To recognize foreign heads of state and members of royalty, though a few exceptionally meritorious commoners have been awarded the decoration. Women have an equal right with men to receive the award. The decoration of the Order consists of a white-enamelled gold elephant with a blue cover, bearing on the obverse a cross of diamonds, and on the reverse the monogram of the reigning sovereign. On the elephant's back is a watchtower, and on its neck a Moor holding a spear. Rules of the Order first occur in the statutes proclaimed by Christian V on December 1, 1693, which fixed the maximum number of knights at 30, excluding the king and his sons. The Order has always been bestowed on sovereigns, Danish and foreign, as well as on prominent men of the Danish nobility.

1943

EURALEX - European Association for Lexicography
c/o O. Norlig - Christensen
The Danish Dictionary
University of Copenhagen
Njalsgade 80
DK-2300 Copenhagen 5, Denmark
Phone: 3 5328995
Fax: 3 1542595

1944

Verbatim Award
To support research, training, or work of any kind associated with lexicography. Members must submit applications by July 1. A monetary prize of £250 to £1,500 is awarded annually. Established by 1990 *Verbatim, The Language Quarterly*.

1945

Federation of Danish Architects
(Danske Arkitekters Landsforbund/Akademisk Arkitektforening)
Bredgade 66
Postbox 1163
DK-1010 Copenhagen K, Denmark
Phone: 33 13 12 90
Fax: 33 93 12 03

1946

Kaleidoscope of Honor
(Ereskalejdoskop)
For recognition of achievement in architecture. Public authorities, institutions or private persons who have set or solved architectural tasks in an inspiring way within one or more of the fields of architecture are eligible for nomination. A trophy is awarded annually. Established in 1979.

1947

Medal of Honor
For recognition of an important contribution to architecture. Members, honorary members of the Federation, and institutions and individuals worthy of special attention are considered for the award. Selection is by nomination. A gold and silver medal and a plaque are awarded when merited. Established in 1932.

1948

Prize of Architecture
(Arkitekturprisen)
For recognition of achievement in architecture. Selection is by nomination. A monetary prize is awarded when merited. Established in 1981.

1949

Geological Society of Denmark
(Dansk Geologisk Forening)
Oster Voldgade 5-7
DK-1350 Copenhagen K, Denmark
Phone: 3 5322354
Fax: 3 5322325

1950

Steno Medal
(Steno Medaljen)
To recognize contributions within the field of geological sciences. The medal is awarded to foreigners and, in special cases, also to Danes. A gold medal is awarded at least every fifth year. Established in 1969 in the memory of Niels Stensen (Nicolai Stenonis) on the tercentary of the publication of his "De solido intra solidum naturaliter contento dissertationis prodromus."

1951

Greenland Society
(Gronlandske Selskab)
Kraemer Hus
L.E. Brunnsvej 10
DK-2920 Charlottenlund, Denmark
Phone: 31 63 57 33

1952

Rink Medal
(Rink Medaillen)
To recognize individuals who have contributed to the exploration of Greenland or have made unselfish and commendable contributions to benefit the people of Greenland. A silver medal is awarded irregularly. Established in 1961 in memory of Hinrich J. Rink (1819-1893).

1953

Gyldendalske Boghandel
Nordisk Forlag A/S
Klareboderne 3
DK-1001 Copenhagen K, Denmark
Phone: 33 110775
Fax: 33 110323

1954

Soren Gyldendal Prisen
To recognize authors of fiction or of scientific or educational work. A writer in the middle of his or her creative process is eligible. A monetary prize of 100,000 Danish kroner is awarded annually. Established in 1958 in memory of Soren Gyldendal, founder of Gyldendal, in connection with his birthday, April 12 (1742).

1955

International Association for the Study of Lung Cancer
The Finsen Inst./Rigshospitalet
Dept. of Oncology
Blegsdamsvej 9
DK-2100 Copenhagen, Denmark
Phone: 31 386633
Fax: 31 356906

1956

International Association for the Study of Lung Cancer Awards
To recognize oncologists for outstanding service in research and the treatment of lung cancer. Awards are presented.

1957

International Association of Sedimentologists
(Association Internationale de Sedimentologistes)
Oster Voldgade 10
Geologisk Centralinstitut
DK-1350 Copenhagen K, Denmark

1958

Awards and Grants
To promote the study of sedimentology and the interchange of research, particularly where international cooperation is desirable.

1959

International Committee of Sports for the Deaf
(Comite International des Sports des Sourds)
Langaavej 41
DK-2650 Hvidovre, Denmark
Phone: 35 361588
Fax: 35 360155

1960

CISS Medallions of Honor
For recognition of meritorious services to those who distinguished themselves in working for the International Committee of Sports for the Deaf. Gold, silver, and bronze medals are given during the congress held in connection with the Summer Games every four years. Established in 1949.

1961

Rubens-Alcais Challenge
To recognize countries that have promoted exceptionally well sports for the deaf. Member countries of the CISS are eligible. Awarded biennially. Established in 1967.

1962
International Odense Film Festival
(Odense kommune)
Scotsgade 5
DK-5000 Odense C, Denmark
Phone: 6 6131372
Fax: 6 5914318

1963
International Odense Film Festival
For recognition of outstanding films in the following categories: Fairy tale films, including live or animated films of 60 minutes maximum running time and experimental/imaginative films. The following awards are presented: Best film - 35,000 Danish kroner and a statuette; Most Imaginative Film - 20,000 Danish kroner and a statuette; Most Surprising Film - 15,000 Danish kroner and a statuette; Personal prizes of each member of the jury - a statuette; and Best Films for Children selected by a jury consisting of children - first prize is 5,000 Danish kroner and a statuette and second and third prizes are 2,000 Danish kroner each. Awarded biennially. Established in 1975. Next festival to be held August 1-6, 1995.

1964
International Organ Competition, Odense
Laessoegade 74
DK-5230 Odense M, Denmark
Fax: 6613 6363

1965
International Organ Competition, Odense
For recognition of young organists of all nationalities. The deadline for application is April 1. The following prizes are awarded: first prize - 20,000 Danish kroner; second prize - 15,000 Danish kroner; and third prize - 10,000 Danish kroner. Organ pipes with inscription are also awarded. The fourth, and fifth, best receive an inscribed organ pipe and 5,000 Danish kroner. The organ pipes are donated by the organ-builder, Marcussen and Son, Aabenraa. Established in 1987 under the patronage of His Royal Highness, Prince Henrik of Denmark.

1966
International Society for Neurochemistry
(Societe Internationale de Neurochimie)
The Protein Laboratory
Univ. of Copenhagen, Panum Institute
3C, Blegdamsvej, Bldg. 6.2
DK-2200 Copenhagen, Denmark
Phone: 31 357900
Fax: 35 360116

1967
Raven Lecturer
For recognition of outstanding contributions in the field of neurochemistry. A medal and monetary award to attend a biennial meeting to deliver a lecture are awarded from time to time. Established in 1988. Formerly: ISN Medal.

1968
Young Scientist Award
To recognize individuals for outstanding contributions to neuroscience. Scientists who are less than 35 years of age may be nominated. A travel award is presented biennially. Established in 1989.

1969
International Society of Hypertension
Medical Dept. C.
Glostrup Hospital
DK-2600 Glostrup, Denmark
Phone: 42 96 43 33
Fax: 43 43 75 55

1970
Astra Award
To recognize outstanding work in clinical pharmacology and therapy of arterial hypertension. A monetary prize is awarded biennially. Established in 1974.

1971
Merck, Sharp and Dohme International Award
For recognition of distinguished work relating to the etiology, epidemiology, pathology or treatment of hypertension. A monetary prize is awarded biennially. Established in 1974.

1972
Pfizer Award Fellowship
To recognize an investigator for an outstanding research project on calcium and transport mechanisms. Established in 1990.

1973
Schering Plough International Award Fellowship
To recognize an investigator for an outstanding research project on basic or clinical aspects of hypertension. Established in 1990.

1974
SmithKline Beecham Pharmaceuticals Young Investigator
To recognize an outstanding young investigator. Persons under the age of 40 are eligible. A monetary award plus funding for research are presented biennially.

1975
Franz Volhard Award
For recognition of a person who has initiated a concept in the field of hypertension which remains of current interest. A monetary prize and the opportunity to present the Franz Volhard Lecture is conferred biennially. Established in 1972 to commemorate the centenary birth of Franz Volhard, a pioneer in high blood pressure research.

1976
Young Investigator Awards of the Dr. C. and F. Demuth Medical Foundation
To recognize three investigators, under the age of 35, whose work has been accepted for presentation at the scientific meeting. Travel expenses for the presentations at the meeting are awarded. Established in 1980.

1977
Jutland Archaeological Society
(Jysk Arkaeologisk Selskab)
Moesgaard
DK-8270 Hojbjerg, Denmark
Phone: 86 272433
Fax: 86 272378

1978
J.J.A. Worsaae Medal
For recognition of research in the field of Nordic archaeology. Individuals may be nominated. A monetary award and a medal are awarded at the convention. Established in 1956 in honor of J.J.A. Worsaae, the founder of scholarly Danish archaeology.

1979
Legatbestyrelsen for Ellen og Niels Bjerrum's Kemikerpris
Bldg. 207
Technical Univ. of Denmark
DK-2800 Lyngby C, Denmark
Phone: 41 883111
Fax: 42 883136

1980
Ellen and Niels Bjerrum Award for Chemists
(Ellen og Niels Bjerrum's Kemikerpris)
For recognition of achievement in chemistry. Danish citizenship is required for consideration. A monetary prize and a gold medal are awarded biennially. Established in 1959 by Elisabeth and Jorgen Dreyer in honor of Niels and Ellen Bjerrum.

1981
Nicolai Malko International Competition for Young Conductors
Radio Denmark, Radiohuset
Rosenorns Alle 22
DK-1999 Frederiksberg C, Denmark
Phone: 35206371
Fax: 35206121

1982
Nicolai Malko International Competition for Young Conductors
For recognition of the best performance of young conductors between 20 and 31 years of age. The following monetary awards are presented: first prize - $10,000 U.S.; second prize - 40,000 Danish kroner; third prize - 30,000 Danish kroner; fourth prize - 20,000 Danish kroner; fifth prize - 15,000 Danish kroner; and sixth prize - 10,000 Danish kroner. Awarded triennially. Established in 1965. Sponsored by Danmarks Radio and the Nicolai Malko Foundation. The next competition is scheduled for 1995.

1983
Carl Nielsen International Violin Competition
(Internationale Carl Nielsen Violin Konkurrence)
Odense Koncerthus
Claus Bergs Gade 9
DK-5000 Odense C, Denmark
Phone: 66 129357
Fax: 65 910047

1984
Carl Nielsen International Violin Competition
(Internationale Carl Nielsen Violin Konkurrence)
To recognize violinists under 30 years of age of all nationalities. Monetary prizes totaling a minimum of 250,000 Danish kroner, plaques, and certificates are awarded. In addition, the Professor Karol Stryja Special Memorial Prize for the best interpretation of Carl Nielsen's works, the Audience's Prize, and the Orchestra Prize are awarded. Prize winners are offered concert engagements. The competition is held every four years (next in 1996). Application deadline is November 15. Established in 1980 to honor the Danish composer Carl Nielsen, whose violin concerto is played in the competition's finals.

1985
Novo Nordisk Foundation
Krogshoejvej 55
DK-2880 Bagsvaerd, Denmark

1986
August Krogh Lecture and Award
For recognition of outstanding research in medical sciences. Any Danish doctor is eligible. A monetary award of 50,000 Danish kroner is awarded annually. Established in 1972.

1987
Novo Nordisk Prize
To recognize a considerable contribution in the field of medical science. A monetary award of 100,000 Danish kroner to be used for research is presented annually to a scientist working in a Danish university or institution.

1988
Politiken
Radhuspladsen 37
DK-1585 Copenhagen V, Denmark
Phone: 33 11 85 11
Fax: 33 15 41 17

1989
Frihedspris
(Freedom Prize)
To recognize and pay respect to an individual who personally has been involved in fighting for human rights or in the protection of civil liberties. The chief editors of two daily papers - *Politiken*, Copenhagen, Denmark, and *Dagens Nyheter*, Stockholm, Sweden - select the individual to receive the award. A monetary award of US $10,000 is presented annually at a ceremony that is held alternately in Stockholm and Copenhagen. Co-sponsored by *Dagens Nyheter*. Additional information is available from Mr. Arne Ruth, Chief Editor, *Dagens Nyheter*, 105 15 Stockholm, Sweden; phone: 8 738 10 10, and fax: 8 51 86 11.

1990
Radio Denmark
(Danmarks Radio)
TV-Centre
DK-2860 Soeborg, Denmark
Phone: 35 203040
Fax: 35 204015

1991
Danmarks Radio TV Award
To recognize creative effort in television. A monetary award of 15,000 Danish kroner is presented annually in April. Established in 1994. Additional information is available from the Director of Television.

1992
Kryger Prize
(Krygerprisen)
To recognize special efforts in broadcasting. A monetary award of 15,000 Danish kroner is presented annually on December 19. Established in 1973 to honor radio producer Christian Kryger. Additional information is available from the Managing Director, Radio.

1993
P1-Prize
(P1-prisen)
To recognize the development of programs other than daily news broadcasts that bring a new informational perspective into the Society. A monetary prize of 50,000 Danish kroner is awarded annually in April. Established in 1991 by the Danish painter, Harry Lovenskjold to honor dentist Ruth Else Klara-Brossel Nielsen. Additional information is available from the Managing Director, Radio.

1994
Radio Denmark Language Award
(Sprogprisen)
To recognize staff members who speak beautiful and understandable Danish. A diploma and a silver or gold microphone are awarded annually in October. Established in 1987. Additional information is available from the Managing Director, Radio.

1995
Rosenkjaer Prize
(Rosenkjaerprisen)
To recognize scientists or cultural personalities who have been able to make a difficult subject understandable to people in general in Danish by way of lectures. A monetary award of 25,000 Danish kroner is presented annually on November 22. Established in 1963 to honor Jens Rosenkjaer. Additional information is available from the Managing Director, Radio.

1996
Royal Danish Geographical Society
(Kongelige Danske Geografiske Selskab)
Oster Voldgade 10
DK-1350 Copenhagen K, Denmark
Phone: 33 13 21 05
Fax: 33 14 81 05

1997
Vitus Bering Medal
(Vitus Bering Medaillen)
For recognition of outstanding performance in the geographical sciences. Geographers of any nation are eligible. A medal is awarded when merited. Established in 1941.

1998
Egede Medal
(Egede Medaillen)
For recognition of geographical investigations and research in the Arctic areas. Geographers and Arctic scientists are eligible. A medal is awarded when merited. Established in 1916.

1999
Galathea Medal
(Galathea Medaillen)
For recognition of geographical investigations and research outside the Arctic areas. Geographers of any nation are eligible. A medal is awarded when merited. Established in 1916.

2000
Honorary Member
(Aeresmedlem)
For recognition of outstanding performance in the geographical sciences. Geographers of any nation are eligible. A certificate is awarded when merited. Established in 1982.

2001
Niels Nielsen Award
(Niels Nielsen Prisen)
To recognize young geographers for outstanding and promising work in the field of geography. Receivers of the award also get a diploma. Established in 1993.

2002
Royal Danish Theatre
(Kongelige Teater og Kapel)
Tordenkjoldsgade 8
Postboks 2185
DK-1017 Copenhagen K, Denmark
Phone: 33 322020
Fax: 33 144606

2003
H. C. Andersen Ballet Award
(H. C. Andersen Balletprisen)
For recognition of the most outstanding ballet performances during the previous season. An award is presented to a female dancer, a male dancer, and a choreographer. An Honorary Award of Merit is awarded to a person who has made an outstanding contribution to ballet. Leading ballet companies from all over the world may nominate candidates. The awards consist of a Royal Copenhagen statuette of Hans Christian Andersen, the famous Danish fairy teller, with a congratulatory bouquet in his hand. Established in 1988.

2004
Scandinavian Packaging Association
OTI/ETI
Box 141
Gregersensuij
DK-2630 Taasdrup, Denmark
Phone: 43 504484
Fax: 43 507283

2005
Scanstar Packaging Competiton
For recognition in the field of packaging. Awarded annually. Established in 1968.

2006
Society for the Dissemination of Natural Science
(Selskabet for Naturlarens Udbredelse)
c/o UNI-C
Vermundsgade 5
DK-2100 Copenhagen, Denmark
Phone: 31 681744
Fax: 31 681788

2007
H. C. Orsted Medal
(H. C. Orsted Medaljen)
For recognition of achievements in the exact sciences, primarily physics, and chemistry; and for substantial contributions to the dissemination of natural sciences. Danish citizens must be nominated. Applications are not invited. A gold medal is awarded irregularly. Established in 1908 to honor Hans Christian Orsted, the Danish physicist who discovered electromagnetism and founded the Society. In 1960, a Silver Medal was established for substantial contributions to the dissemination of natural sciences not necessarily done in connection with personal scientific achievements.

2008
Leonie Sonning Music Foundation
(Leonie Sonnings Musikfond)
H. C. Andersens Boulevard 37
DK-1553 Copenhagen V, Denmark
Phone: 3 3114600
Fax: 3 3930306

2009
Leonie Sonning Music Award
(Leonie Sonnings Musikpris)
For recognition of outstanding achievement in music. Composers, conductors, musicians, and singers are eligible for consideration. A monetary award of 250,000 Danish kroner and a diploma are awarded annually. Established in 1959 by Mrs. Leonie Sonning.

2010
University of Copenhagen
(Kobenhavns Universitet)
The Sonning Foundation
Frue Plads Port A - Norregade 10
DK-1017 Copenhagen K, Denmark
Phone: 33 91 08 28
Fax: 33 91 18 28

2011
Sonning Prize
To recognize a man or woman who has made an outstanding contribution toward the advancement of European civilization. Recommendations for candidates are invited from European universities. A monetary prize of 500,000 Danish kroner is awarded biennially on April 19, Mr. Sonning's birthday. The prize was first given as a special award to Winston Churchill in 1950. It has been presented biennially since 1959. Established in 1949 in memory of C.J. Sonning, a writer and editor.

2012
Erik Westerby Foundation
(Erik Westerby-fondet)
Rigsantikvaren Nationalmuseet
Frederiksholms Kanal 12
DK-1220 Copenhagen K, Denmark
Phone: 33 134411
Fax: 33 321811

2013
Erik Westerby Prize
(Erik Westerby-prisen)
For recognition of achievement in the field of Danish prehistoric archaeology. A monetary award of 100,000 Danish kroner is awarded annually. Established in 1982 by Mrs. Hjordis Hurwood, in honor of her brother Erik Westerby, the prominent amateur archaeologist.

Dominican Republic

2014
Council of American Development Foundations, Solidarios
(Consejo de Fundaciones Americanas de Desarrollo, Solidarios)
Apartado Postal 620
Calla 6, 10 Paraiso
Santo Domingo, Dominican Republic
Phone: 809544-2121
Fax: 809544-0550

2015
Solidarios Award to Latinoamerican and Caribbean Development
(Premio Solidarios con el Desarrollo de America Latina y del Caribe)
For recognition of contributions to the social and economic development of people in Latin America, through philanthropic and voluntary service and professional achievements in the development sciences field. A citizen from a Latin or Caribbean country may be proposed by a National Development Foundation member of the council by June 1. A trophy, a plaque, and expenses to attend the Solidarios General Assembly to receive the award are awarded biennially. Established in 1986.

Ecuador

2016
Ecuador
Department of Culture
(Ecuador
Casa de la Cultura Ecuatoriana)
Avenida 6 Diciembre 794
Casilla Postal 67
Quito, Ecuador
Phone: 565 808
Phone: 566 070

2017
Eugenio Espejo National Prize for Culture
(Premio Nacional de Cultura de Ecuador Eugenio Espejo)
For recognition of an outstanding work of literature, artistry or scientific achievement. Ecuadorian writers are eligible. Awarded annually by the President of the Republic.

Egypt

2018
African Farmers Association
PO Box 14
Gizah 12211, Egypt
Phone: 2 3607403

2019
Knight of African Agriculture
For recognition of a contribution to any field activity that develops agriculture. Selection is by nomination of the national farmers unions. A plaque is awarded annually. Established in 1985.

2020
Egyptian Red Crescent Society
29 El Galaa St.
Cairo, Egypt
Phone: 2 750558

2021
Egyptian Red Crescent Society Competitions
To recognize individuals who provide health services in Egypt, particularly for children, and work to improve the welfare of society and young people. The Society sponsors competitions.

2022
Ophthalmological Society of Egypt
42 Sharia Kasr El-Aini
Dar El Hekma
Cairo, Egypt
Phone: 2 3541538

2023
Gold Medal
For recognition of major services and activities in the Society and ophthalmology. Members of the Society who are over 50 years of age are considered for services and activities other than scientific activities. A gold medal is awarded when merited. Established in 1943.

El Salvador

2024
El Salvador
Ministerio de Salud Publica y Asistencia Social
Public Relations
Calle Arce 827
San Salvador, El Salvador
Phone: 21 1001

2025
Premio Nacional de Medicina, Dr. Luis Edmundo Vasquez
To encourage professional development and achievement in medical science in El Salvador. Applications may be submitted for the annual contest. A monetary prize, a gold medal, and a diploma are awarded annually on August 26, the birthday of Dr. Luis Edmundo Vasquez, one of the most famous Salvadorean physicians. Established in 1984 by Dr. Napoleon E. Cardenas, Minister of Public Health and Social Assistance.

2026
National Nuclear Energy Commission
(Comissao Nacional de Energia Nuclear)
c/o Ministerio de Economia
1A Calle Poniente y 73 Auda Norte
San Salvador, El Salvador
Phone: 21 295 1194

2027
Octacilio Cunha Award
(Premio Octacilio Cunha)
For recognition of achievements in the technological or scientific study of the peaceful use and development of nuclear energy. Associations, Brazilian citizens, or individuals who have lived in Brazil for more than five years and have contributed to nuclear energy development are eligible. A monetary prize and a certificate are awarded annually. Established in 1981 in memory of Admiral Octacilio Cunha.

2028
Carneiro Fellipe Medal
(Medalha Carneiro Fellipe)
For recognition of achievements in the technological or scientific study of the peaceful use and development of nuclear energy. Associations, Brazilian citizens, or individuals who have lived in Brazil for more than five years and have contributed to nuclear energy development are eligible. A monetary prize and a medal are awarded annually. Established in 1972 in memory of Professor Jose Carneiro Fellipe.

England

2029

ABSA/Arthur Andersen Awards in Association with *The Times*
Nutmeg House
60 Gainsford St.
Butlers Wharf
London SE1 2NY, England
Phone: 71 3788143
Fax: 71 4077527

2030

ABSA Business Awards
To recognize and encourage imaginative and effective support of the arts by commercial organizations. Awards are given in the following categories: British Art Overseas, Commission of New Art In Any Medium, Corporate Programme, First Time Sponsor, Increasing Access to the Arts, Long Term Commitment, Single Project, Sponsorship by a Small Business, and Youth Sponsorship. The Awards are open to all companies sponsoring arts events, projects, or organizations in the United Kingdom, and all companies sponsoring British arts events overseas. Nominations should be submitted on the nomination form and the major part of the sponsorship should have taken place in the 12 months prior to the closing date (always in September). The Awards are presented by a member of the Royal Family at the Royal National Theatre of Great Britain in November or December. The Awards themselves are commissioned from an artist by Arthur Andersen.

2031

The Arthur Andersen Award for the Business in the Arts Advisor of the Year
To celebrate and commend the work of business managers who have volunteered their time and skills to an arts organization through the Business in the Arts Placement Scheme. There are separate nomination forms for this Award.

2032

BP Arts Award
To recognize the nominating arts organization making the best use of sponsorship to develop and maintain the quality of its activities. A monetary prize of £5,000 and a work of art are awarded annually. Sponsored by British Petroleum.

2033

***The Daily Telegraph* Award**
To recognize the individual who has made the most inspiring contribution to a sponsored activity. A monetary prize of £5,000 and a work of art are awarded.

2034

Elf Arts Award
To recognize the arts organization that has made the best use of sponsorship to maintain and develop its activities. The award consists of a work of art commissioned from an artist by Elf Petroleum UK and a check for £6,000.

2035

***The Times* Critics' Award**
To recognize an arts organization whose work through the year has been outstanding. The organization must have had commercial sponsorship in order to qualify. The award given at the discretion of the arts critics of The Times newspaper.

2036

Action Research
Vincent House
North Parade
Horsham, W. Sussex RH12 2DP, England
Phone: 403 210406
Fax: 403 210541

Formerly: (1991) Action Research for the Crippled Child.

2037

Harding Award
For recognition of outstanding work of immediate or future benefit to the disabled. The award can be presented for developments in research or in the general field of care for the disabled. A sculptured trophy is awarded annually at the Annual Meeting of AR. Awarded alternately by Action Research and the Royal Association for Disability and Rehabilitation. Established in 1971 in honor of Field Marshall Lord Harding of Petherton, Chairman of Action Research for the Crippled Child from 1960 to 1973.

2038

African Book Publishing Record
Noma Award for Publishing in Africa
Hans Zell Assocs.
PO Box 56
Oxford OX1 3EL, England
Phone: 865 511428
Fax: 865 793298

2039

Noma Award for Publishing in Africa
To encourage publication of works by African writers and scholars whose work is published in Africa. Outstanding new books by authors who are indigenous to Africa are considered in any of the following three categories: scholarly or academic; books for children; and literature and creative writing (including fiction, drama, and poetry, as well as essays on African literature). Works published during the previous year (regardless of the place of manufacture) by a publisher domiciled on the African continent or its offshore islands may be submitted by publishers by February 28. Any original work written in any of the indigenous or official languages of Africa is eligible for consideration. Translations, anthologies, edited collections, and similar compilations are not eligible. Quality of content is the overriding criterion. Books should be a minimum of 48 pages but, in certain categories of creative writing and children's literature, books of shorter length may be considered. A monetary prize of $5,000 and a plaque are awarded annually. Established in 1979 by the late Shoichi Noma, founder of Kodansha Limited, Tokyo, Japan.

2040

Air-Britain (Historians) Ltd.
Witham-on-the-Hill
Bourne, Lincs. PE10 OJP, England
Phone: 77 833677

2041

AAHS Trophy (American Aviation Historical Society)
To recognize the author of the best article or publication in *Air Britain* with a North American biased content during a given year. Originality of research and content and literary merit are the criteria considered for the award. A DC-3 trophy is presented each year at the Annual General Meeting in April. Established in 1973 by the chairman of AAHS in California to celebrate the 25th Anniversary of Air-Britain and to recognize the cooperation between the two aviation historical societies. Additional information is available from Mr. P.J. Marson, Chairman of the Awards Committee 18, King George VI Drive, Hove, Sussex, BN3 6XF, United Kingdom.

2042

Writer's Trophy
To recognize the author of the best article or series of articles in *Digest* magazine during a given year. Articles by members are judged for originality of content, depth of research, and literary merit. A monetary award and a pen trophy are presented annually at the Annual General Meeting in April. Established in 1952 by C.W. Cain, the founder of the International Association of Aviation Historians. Additional information is available from Mr. P.J. Marson, Chairman, Awards Committee, 18, King George VI Drive, Hove, Sussex, BN3 6XF, United Kingdom.

2043

Air League
4 Hamilton Pl.
London W1V 0BQ, England
Phone: 71 4910470
Fax: 71 4996230

2044
Air League Challenge Trophy
Awarded through annual competition among the Voluntary Gliding Schools of the (RAF) Air Cadets organization. A silver Challenge Cup is awarded annually. Established in 1921 by Major General Sir Sefton Brancker KCB AFC and Philip Foster Esq.

2045
Air League Founders' Medal
For recognition of the most meritorious achievement in the field of British aviation during the year. British nationals and, exceptionally, foreign nationals are eligibe. A medal is awarded annually when merited. Established in 1960 by a gift of the late Stephen Marples to commemorate the Founders of the Air League in 1909.

2046
Air Public Relations Association
Address unknown since 1992.

2047
C. P. Robertson Memorial Trophy
To honor the best interpretation of the Royal Air Force to the public in the past year or the continuous effort over a number of years. Nominations are accepted. A trophy, with a silver miniature for retention, is awarded annually. Established in 1954 in memory of C.P. Robertson.

2048
Aircraft Owners and Pilots Association
British Light Aviation Centre
50a Cambridge St.
London SW1V 4QQ, England
Phone: 71 834 5631
Fax: 71 834 8623

2049
AOPA Awards for Achievement & Endeavor in Light Aviation
To recognize individuals who, in striving for success, bring together all sections of the private flying community. Candidates may be nominated for awards in the following categories; Student Award - a person who has overcome specific obstacles in learning to fly; Aerodrome Award - a good place to visit, offering value for money and helpful service; Customer Care Award - a flying school or club recommended by private or student pilots; Individual Merit Award - a pilot who has made an outstanding achievement or attempt at an achievement; Controller of the Year - a controller or AFISO who has provided especially good service to private pilots; Instructor of the Year - an instructor who has made a special contribution to the training of student pilots for the PPL, or private pilots for added qualifications; *Flyer* Contribution to the Community Award - presented by *Flyer* magazine, in conjunction with AOPA, for a flying organization that works to make friends outside the aviation world, by forging links with its local community; and Lennox Boyd Trophy - the premier award in the field of light aviation, established in 1953 by the Rt Hon. Alan Lennox Boyd (subsequently Viscount Boyd of Merton). Awarded annually to individual(s), Club, Group or Center, or other light aviation organization who have contributed to the development or improvement of flying training, Club flying or piloting standards in the previous year or years. Awards are presented when merited.

2050
Aldeburgh Poetry Trust
Goldings
Goldings Lane
Leiston, Suffolk 1P16 4EB, England
Phone: 728 830631
Fax: 728 452715

2051
Aldeburgh Poetry Festival Prize
For recognition of promise and achievement in a first full collection (at least 40 pages) of poetry published in the United Kingdom and Eire in the twelve months preceding the November Aldeburgh Poetry Festival. A monetary prize of £500 with an invitation to take part in the following year's festival is awarded annually. Established in 1989. Sponsored jointly by Waterstone and Company and the Aldeburgh Bookshop.

2052
All England Lawn Tennis and Croquet Club Wimbledon
Church Rd.
Wimbledon
London SW19 5AE, England
Phone: 81 944 1066
Fax: 81 947 8752

2053
The Championships, Wimbledon
To recognize the winners of the following tennis events: men's singles, men's doubles, women's singles, women's doubles, and mixed doubles. Trophies are awarded annually after the final of each event. Established in 1877 by the All England Croquet and Lawn Tennis Club.

2054
Lady Allen of Hurtwood Trust
Thomas Coram Foundation for Children
40 Brunswick Sq.
London WCIN 1AU, England
Phone: 81 9409660

2055
Lady Allen of Hurtwood Trust Award
To enable individuals working with children to travel in order to extend their knowledge or experience for the benefit of their work. The fund does not support research or courses leading to qualification. A monetary prize is awarded annually. Established in 1977.

2056
Alpine Garden Society
AGS Centre
Avon Bank
Pershore, Hereford and Worcs. WR10 3JP, England
Phone: 386 554790
Fax: 386 554801

2057
Certificate of Honour
For recognition of work within the society. Established in 1985.

2058
Lyttel Trophy
For recognition of members of the society for outstanding contributions to a profession or field of activity. A trophy is presented annually. Established in the 1930s to honor Professor Lyttel, a former president of the society.

2059
Alvis Owner Club
Vallis
Tintells Ln.
West Horsley, Surrey KT24 6JD, England
Phone: 4865 3541

2060
Ruth and Jim Hulbert Memorial Trophy
To recognize the Alvis owner club member, or 12/50 register member who gains the most points in vintage sports car club race meetings or speed events throughout the season. A trophy is awarded annually. Established in 1984 in honor of Ruth and Jim Hulbert.

2061
Amateur Athletic Association of England
225A Bristol Rd.
Edgbaston
Birmingham B5 7UB, England
Phone: 21 4405000
Fax: 21 4400555

2062

C. N. Jackson Memorial Cup
To recognize the outstanding athlete of the year. Athletes who are members of the Amateur Athletic Associaton are eligible. Selection is made by the AAA Championships Committee. The AAA also makes the following awards: Harvey Cup - to recognize the best AAA champion of the year; Pepsi-Cola Award - to recognize the United Kingdom champion; John Thornton Award - for recognition of the best performance in the high hurdles in the United Kingdom; Carborundum Golden Jubilee Trophy - for recognition of the best track performance in the championships; W. J. Pepper Trophy - for recognition of the best field performance in the championships; Philips Trophy - for recognition of the best performance in the AAA indoor championships; George Hogsflesh Trophy - to recognize the best junior athlete; Joe Turner Trophy - for recognition in the junior championships; and Jack Crump Trophy - to recognize the best youth athlete. Awarded annually.

2063

Amateur Swimming Association
Harold Fern House
Derby Sq.
Loughborough LE11 0AL, England
Phone: 509 230431
Fax: 509 610720

2064

Henry Benjamin National Memorial Trophy
For recognition of the club with the most points in the following National Championships and the National Winter Championships for Men, viz: 50, 100, 200, 400, 1,500 metres Freestyle; Long Distance; 100 and 200 metres Backstroke, Breaststroke and Butterfly; and 200 and 400 metres Individual Medley, Club Medley Team, and Club Freestyle Team. The total number of points obtained by the clubs either through their team or individual entries are added together on completion of the championships and the club obtaining the highest aggregate is declared the winner.

2065

G. Melville Clark National Memorial Trophy
For recognition of the club with the highest points in the Diving Championships. The competition for the G. Melville Clark National Memorial Trophy is open to all men's clubs or men's sections of clubs affiliated to the ASA. The competitions are confined to the following championships: All ASA Summer and Winter Diving Championships and the two principal District Diving Championships other than plain diving, which are declared by each District Association no later than June 1 in each year. The trophy is awarded annually.

2066

Dawdon Trophy
For recognition of the winning club of the ASA Age Group Diving Competitions. The total number of points obtained by each club are added together on December 31 each year, and the club obtaining the highest total is declared the winner. The winning club is entitled to hold the trophy. Awarded annually.

2067

Harold Fern Award
To recognize the most outstanding contribution to swimming on the national or international level through education or instructional achievement, for architectural design of swimming facilities, for writing or development of original material, or for competitive performance. Clubs, individuals, or associations (amateur and professional) may be nominated by District Associations by September 1. A monetary award of £50 and a framed certificate are presented each year in February at the annual council meeting. Established in 1961 in honor of Harold E. Fern C.B.E. J.P., Secretary to the ASA from 1921 to 1969.

2068

Harold Fern National Trophy
For recognition of the club with the most points in the National Championships and the National Winter Championships for Women 50, 100, 200, 400, 800 metres Freestyle; Long Distance; 100 and 200 metres Backstroke, Breaststroke and Butterfly; and 200 and 400 metres Individual Medley, Club Medley Team, and Club Freestyle Team. The total number of points obtained by the clubs either through their team or individual entries, are added together on completion of the Championships, and the club obtaining the highest aggregate is declared the winner. The winning club is entitled to hold the Harold Fern National Trophy. Awarded annually.

2069

George Hearn Cup
To recognize the diver who is a member of a club affiliated with the ASA whose performance is adjudged by the ASA Diving Committee to be the best for the year. Awarded annually. Established to honor George Hearn, Present of the ASA in 1908.

2070

Alan Hime Memorial Trophies
To recognize the male and the female swimmers who are members of a club affiliated to the ASA and whose performance is adjudged by the ASA Swimming Committee to be the best at the ASA National Winter Championships. A memento is awarded to each annually.

2071

Swimming Enterprises Trophy for Synchronised Swimmer of the Year
To recognize a synchronised swimmer who is a member of a club affiliated to the ASA, and whose performance is adjudged by the ASA Synchronised Swimming Committee to be the best for the year. Awarded annually.

2072

***The Swimming Times* Water Polo Award**
To recognize the outstanding water polo player of the year. A member of a club affiliated with the ASA is eligible for the award. Presented annually. Established in 1979.

2073

Norma Thomas National Memorial Trophy
To recognize a junior diver who is a member of a club affiliated to the ASA and whose performance is adjudged by the ASA Diving Committee to be the best for the year. Awarded annually. Established to honor Norma Thomas.

2074

Alfred H. Turner Award
For recognition of outstanding contributions to swimming on the national or international level, through educational or instructional achievement, for architectural design of swimming facilities, for writing or development of original material, or for competitive performance. This award is given to a female if the Harold Fern trophy is given to a male, and vice versa. Nominations may be made by district associations, clubs, individuals, and associations, both amateur and professional by September 1. A monetary award of £50 and a framed certificate are awarded each year at the annual council meeting held in February. Established in 1982 to honor Alfred H. Turner, O.B.E., A.I.B., the Honorary Treasurer from 1968 to 1985, and the President in 1982.

2075

Belle White National Memorial Trophy
For recognition of the club with the highest points in the Diving Championships. All women's clubs or women's sections of clubs affiliated to the ASA are eligible. The competitions are confined to the following championships: All ASA summer and winter Championships and the two principal District Diving Championships other than plain diving, which are declared by each District Association not later than June 1 in each year. A trophy is awarded annually.

2076

T. M. Yeadon Memorial Trophy
To recognize the swimmer whose performance is the best for the year as judged by the Amateur Swimming Association Committee. A trophy is

presented annually. Established in 1970 in memory of T. M. Yeadon, an ASA officer and President in 1924.

2077
American Express Bank Ltd.
PO Box 766
60 Buckingham Palace Rd.   Phone: 71 5836666
London SW1W ORU, England   Fax: 71 7305980

2078
Amex Bank Review Awards
For recognition of the best 3000-4000 word essays in international economics of relevance to today's financial markets written exclusively for the competition. Only unpublished essays may be submitted. Essays may be on any subject in international economics of current relevance to financial markets. Papers may address a narrow or a broad subject matter within the above stated field as authors desire. Where a narrow subject matter is chosen, the relevance of the analysis to a wide international audience should be drawn out in the essay. The competition is open to all except employees and immediate family of the American Express Company. All entries must be received on or before June 1. The following awards are given to the best essays as judged by the *Review Editors* and the Award Committee: First Prize - US $25,000; two Silver Awards - US $10,000 each; and five Bronze Awards - US $5,000. All essays are published in an Oxford University Press book and summarized in the *The Amex Bank Review*. Presented annually at an awards ceremony. Established in 1987 in memory of Robert Marjolin, the distinguished French economist, who played a central role in rebuilding the economy of Europe after 1945.

2079
Angel Hotel
Angel Hill
Bury St. Edmunds, Suffolk IP33 1LT,   Phone: 284 753926
   England   Fax: 284 750092

2080
Angel Literary Award
To encourage East Anglian writers. Awards are given in two categories: nonfiction book - documentary, travel, topography, natural history, or local history; and fiction - novel, short story, poetry, or play. Writers living and working in East Anglia (Suffolk, Norfolk, Essex, and Cambridgeshire) are eligible. Books published during the preceding year between October and October must be submitted by August 31. A monetary prize of £1,000 for first place, and £500 for second place are awarded annually. Established in 1982 by Mr. S. C. Gough. (Temporarily discontinued)

2081
Anglo-Austrian Music Society
c/o Richard Tauber Prize Committee
46 Queen Anne's Gate
Westminster
London SW1H 9AU, England   Phone: 71 2220366

2082
Richard Tauber Prize
For recognition of an outstanding British or Austrian singer. Men and women ordinarily resident in Great Britain or Austria over 21 years of age and preferably under 30 in the case of women, and 32 in the case of men, are eligible. Applications must be submitted by January 29. The prize consists of a travel bursary to enable the winner to spend a minimum of two months in Austria or England, and a study grant to enable the winner to prepare for a public recital in London under the auspices of the Anglo-Austrian Music Society. Established in 1950.

2083
Animal Health Trust
PO Box 5   Phone: 638 661111
Newmarket, Suffolk CB8 7DW, England   Fax: 638 665789

2084
A. D. and P. A. Allen Memorial Fellowship
To provide for research into methods for the improvement of farm animal welfare. Veterinarians or scientists with postgraduate research experience may apply. Research must take place at an approved United Kingdom institution. Up to three awards are presented annually. Applications must be submitted between October and April each year. Established in 1973 by Mrs. A. M. Allen in honor of Mr. A. D. Allen and Mr. P. A. Allen.

2085
Blount Memorial Scholarship
To provide for facilities for education or research in agriculture, poultry science, and animal behavior. Candidates may be research workers, but must hold at minimum a good Second Class Honors Degree in science or veterinary medicine. Research must take place at an approved institution in the United Kingdom for one to three years. Applications must be submitted between October and Apil each year. A scholarship is awarded annually. Established in 1969 by Lord Nugent of Guildford, Mr. A. S. Alexander, Mr. A. C. A. Keevil, and Mr. C. J. Rutter in honor of Dr. Percy Blount.

2086
Livesey Research Fellowship
To provide for research in veterinary medicine and allied sciences. Recently qualified veterinary surgeons may apply. A fellowship is awarded triennially. Research must take place at an approved institution in the United Kingdom. Established in 1943 in honor of Geoffrey Herbert Livesey.

2087
Wooldridge Farm Livestock Research Fellowship
To provide for veterinary research into major factors influencing health and productivity of cattle, sheep, or pigs in the United Kingdom. Veterinarians or scientists with post-graduate research experience may apply. A fellowship is awarded annually. Study must be at an approved institution in the United Kingdom. Established in 1973 in honor of Dr. W. R. Wooldridge, founder of the Animal Health Trust.

2088
Arboricultural Association
Ampfield House
Ampfield   Phone: 794 368717
Romsey, Hants. S051 9PA, England   Fax: 794 368978

2089
Arboricultural Association Award
For recognition of achievement and service to arboriculture. Nominations are accepted by the end of June. A plaque is presented annually. Established in 1982. Sponsored by the Arboricultural Association Trust Fund.

2090
Beeching Award for Arboricultural Contracts
To promote the Arboricultural Association and its approved consultants and contractors by honoring the production of appropriate tender documents. Nominations must be submitted by June 30. A monetary award, a certificate, and travel expenses to the Association's annual conference are presented annually. Established in 1987 by I. J. Keen, Past Chairman and Managing Director of Beeching of Ash Ltd. (Discontinued)

2091

Architectural Association
34-36 Bedford Sq.
London WC1B 3ES, England   Phone: 71 636 0974

2092

Anthony Pott Memorial Award
To assist studies or the publication of studies related to the field of architecture. Architects and students of architecture and related subjects may apply. Candidates wishing to use the award for research rather than the publication of studies will, in their application, either have to demonstrate some pre-knowledge of the proposed field of study or satisfy the Award Committee that they are sufficiently competent to undertake new work. Projects are to be related to the subject of architecture and design, taken in its widest sense. A monetary award of £800 is presented biennially. Established in memory of Anthony Pott who was a student at the Architectural Association, a distinguished member of the staff of the Building Research Station, and Chief Architect of the Ministry of Education.

2093

Michael Ventris Memorial Award
To promote the study of architecture and the study of Mycenaean civilization. Awards for the two fields of study are made in alternate years. It is intended that the award should support a specific project rather than a continuing program of study. Architects or students of not less than RIBA Intermediate status or other comparable level of achievement from all countries may apply. A monetary award of £700 is awarded annually. Established in 1957 in memory of Michael Ventris, in appreciation of his work in the fields of architecture and Mycenaean civilization.

2094

Bernard Webb Studentship
For the encouragement of the study of architecture or archaeology. Students of post graduate standing, 32 years of age and under, who are citizens of the British Commonwealth and have been members of the Architectural Association for not less than two years may apply. Awards are given in the following categories: (1) architecture; and (2) archaeology. A stipend of £1,500 and travel expenses are awarded biennially for a three month architecture or archeology study visit, based on the British School at Rome.

2095

Stephen Arlen Memorial Fund
London Coliseum
St. Martin's Ln.   Phone: 71 8360111
London WC2N 4ES, England   Fax: 71 8368379

2096

Stephen Arlen Memorial Fund Award
To encourage further artistic development following a career in any branch of music, drama, or ballet. Only residents of the United Kingdom are eligible. There are no age limits. The annual deadline is February 28. A monetary prize is presented annually in the autumn. Established in 1970 by Mrs. Stephen Arlen in memory of her husband, Stephen Arlen, former managing director of English National Opera.

2097

Armstrong Siddeley Sapphire Owners Club
9 Crawshaw Rd.
Poole, Dorset BH14 8Q2, England   Phone: 202 722363

2098

Armstrong Siddeley Car Rally Prizes
For recognition of leading places in Armstrong Siddeley car rallies. Members of the Club are eligible. Cups, plaques, trophies, and badges are awarded annually. Established in 1962.

2099

Arts Council of Great Britain
14 Great Peter St.   Phone: 71 3330100
London SW1P 3NQ, England   Fax: 71 9736590

2100

Arts Council of Great Britain Schemes
The Arts Council has an annual program of awards and schemes to assist the arts. In the area of writers awards, awards are given to writers of outstanding literary achievement for the research and writing of their next book. British and non-British subjects resident in England are eligible. Fifteen bursaries are awarded annually in the field of fiction, poetry, biography, and autobiography.

2101

John Whiting Award
For recognition of the best original play of the year. The award is intended to help further the careers and enhance the reputations of younger British playwrights, and to draw public attention to the importance of writers in contemporary theater. The following criteria are considered in judging a play: writing of special quality, relevance and importance to contemporary life, and potential value to the British theater. The judges shall not have regard to whether or not the play has received a production, or is likely to receive a production or publication. To be considered, British playwrights must, over the previous two years, have had either an offer of an award under the Arts Council Theatre Writing Schemes, a commission from one of those theater companies in receipt of annual subsidy from either the Arts Council or a Regional Arts Board, or a premiere production by a theater company in receipt of annual subsidy from either the Arts Council or a Regional Arts Board. No writer who has previously won the award may reapply, and no play that has previously been submitted for the award is eligible. The entry deadline is early January. A monetary prize of £6,000 is awarded annually. Established in 1965 in memory of John Whiting for his contribution to post-war British theater.

2102

Arvon Foundation
Kilnhurst, Kilnhurst Rd.   Phone: 706 816582
Todmorden, Lancs. OL14 6AX, England   Fax: 706 816359

2103

Arvon Foundation International Poetry Competition
For recognition of outstanding poetry submitted by individuals from Great Britain and abroad. Each entry must be written in English. The following prizes are awarded biennially: (1) First prize - £5,000; (2) Runners-up for first prize - five prizes of £500 each; and (3) ten prizes of £250 each. Established in 1980. Co-sponsored by *The Observer* and Duncan Lawrie Limited.

2104

Association for Industrial Archaeology
The Wharfage   Phone: 952 453522
Ironbridge, Salop TF8 7AW, England Fax: 952 452204

2105

AIA Award for Fieldwork
To recognize contributions to field work in the preservation of historic industrial sites. Awarded annually.

2106

AIA Conference Award
To recognize contributions to the study and preservation of historic industrial sites. Awarded annually.

2107

Dorothea Award for Conservation
To recognize contributions to the study and preservation of historic industrial sites. Awarded annually.

Association of Building Engineers
Jubilee House
Billing Brook Rd.
Northampton, Northhants. NN3 8NW,
England

Phone: 604 404121
Fax: 604 784220

2109
Fire Safety Award
To recognize a person, company, or organization that through invention, research, publicity, education, training, or any other related activity has made significant contribution to the advancement of fire protection or fire engineering. An engraved hand-cut crystal bowl and a commemorative certificate are awarded annually.

2110
Peter Stone Award
For recognition of outstanding service and contribution in the field of building surveying in the United Kingdom. Mature candidates of senior standing in the UK construction industry are eligible. An engraved silver salver is awarded annually. Established in 1982 in memory of Peter Stone, President, 1981-82.

2111
Association of Chief Police Officers of England, Wales and Northern Ireland
Wellington House, Rm. 311
67-73 Buckingham Gate
London SW1E 6BE, England

Phone: 71 230 7184
Fax: 71 230 7212

2112
Provincial Police Award
For recognition of an act of bravery in support of law and order performed by a member of the public anywhere in England or Wales outside the area controlled by the Metropolitan Police and City of London Police. Individuals may be nominated. A gold medal is awarded annually. Established in 1965.

2113
Association of Clinical Biochemists
Clinical Chemistry Dept.
Children's Hospital
Ladywood Middleway
Birmingham B16 8ET, England

Phone: 21 4544851
Fax: 21 4542956

2114
ACB Foundation Award
To recognize a member of the Association, normally a resident in the British Isles, who is acknowledged as having made an outstanding contribution to clinical biochemistry. The subject matter of the Foundation Award Lecture should reflect the interests of the award recipient, and should be of a scientific nature, reflecting the state of the art in one area of clinical biochemistry. Nominations for the award may be made by any three members of the Association. The award, which is presented by the President or Chairman of the Association, comprises a suitable memento and an honorarium. Prior to the presentation, the recipient delivers the ACB Foundation Award Lecture. Awarded annually. Established in 1990 by the ACB Foundation. For more information contact Dr. D. J. Worthington, National Meetings Secretary.

2115
Ames Medal and Award
To recognize a junior member of the Association who has presented the best scientific paper at a national meeting. Members of the Association under 35 years of age are eligible to participate in the competition. A monetary award and a silver medal are awarded annually. Established in 1971 by Miles Laboratories Ltd., Ames Division.

2116
Boehringer Mannheim Award
To finance the visit of an international scientist to lecture at the national meeting of the Association. Individuals must be nominated. A monetary award for travel is presented annually. Established in 1985. Formerly: BCL Award Lecture.

2117
Corning Award
To finance a visiting international lecturer who will give the Corning lecture at a regional meeting. Individuals must be nominated. A monetary award for travel is presented annually. Established in 1984 by CIBA Corning Medical.

2118
Kone Award
To honor a medical scientist whose work has been of major importance to clinical biochemistry. Medical students whose work in practice, research, or education has led to improved international cooperation particularly in Europe may be nominated. A monetary award for travel to present the lecture is awarded annually. Established in 1981 by Kone Instruments.

2119
Vickers Award
To recognize a clinical biochemist for contributions to the application of analytical chemistry or related sciences to the development of clinical biochemistry in the investigation of disease. Awarded annually. Established in 1974. (Discontinued in 1984)

2120
Wellcome Prize
To recognize a person who made an outstanding contribution to the quality of clinical biochemistry as practiced in the U.K. A monetary prize and a piece of engraved glass were awarded annually. Established in 1972. Sponsored by Wellcome Diagnostics (Wellcome Reagents Ltd.). (Discontinued in 1990)

2121
Association of Cricket Umpires
5 The Glade
Enfield EN2 7QH, England

Phone: 81 363 9397

2122
John Budgen Award
To recognize individuals who have gained the highest level of competence in the techniques of scoring in cricket. Candidates over the age of 14 who take a qualifying written examination and complete a full score sheet are eligible. Books are presented at the time of selection and commemorative plaques are awarded annually at a general meeting at Lords. Established in 1986 by John Budgen.

2123
Arthur Sims Award
To recognize individuals who have gained the highest possible knowledge of cricket law, demonstrated by achievement in both written and oral examinations in the field. Candidates of all ages are eligible. Cricket books and a commemorative plaque are awarded annually at a general meeting at Lords. Established in 1970 in memory of Arthur Sims.

2124
Association of European Atomic Forums (Forum Atomique Europeen)
22 Buckingham Gate
London SW1E 6LB, England

Phone: 71 8280116
Fax: 71 8280110

2125

FORATOM Award
To recognize companies and research institutions that further the economic development of peaceful uses of nuclear energy. Awarded annually.

2126

Association of Free Newspapers
27 Brunswick Sq.
Gloucester GL1 1UN, England
Phone: 452 308100
Fax: 452 300912

2127

AFN - AGFA Awards
For recognition in the field of journalism. The following prizes are awarded: (1) AFN - AGFA Award for the Free Newspaper of the Year - for recognition in design, editorial and advertisement content, photographic and artistic illustration, impact and typography; (2) Compugraphic Trophy - for the best designed free local newspaper with average pagination in excess of 36; (3) Adverkit Trophy - for the best designed free local newspaper with average pagination of 36 and under; (4) DPS Award - for the best advertisement designed in-house; (5) Bridgewater Trophy - for the best advertisement feature (with editorial); (6) C Text Award - for the best composite advertisement feature (without editorial); (7) Media Sales Bureau Trophy - for the best campaign to promote the image of a free local newspaper to agencies and national advertiser; (8) Cotsworld Travel Trophy - for community involvement; (9) Goss Award - for editorial excellence in a free local newspaper with average pagination in excess of 36; (10) G.B. Techniques Award - for editorial excellence in a free local newspaper with average pagination of 36 and under; (11) UK Press Gazette Award - for the Free Newspaper Journalist of the Year; (12) Free Media Digest Award - for the Free Newspaper Photographer of the Year; and (13) Free Media Sales Trophy - for the most unusual or successful revenue producing idea in a free local newspaper during the year.

2128

Association of Golf Writers
17 Cheniston Ct., Ridgemount Rd.
Sunningdale, Berks. SL5 9SF, England
Phone: 71 9227118
Fax: 71 34424977

2129

Golfer of the Year
To recognize achievement in European golf. European professional and amateur golfers (male and female) are considered. The Golf Writers' Trophy and a permanent memento are awarded annually in December. Established in 1951.

2130

Association of Photographers
9-10 Domingo St.
London EC1Y 0TA, England
Phone: 71 608 1441
Fax: 71 253 3007

Formerly: Association of Fashion Advertising and Editorial Photographers.

2131

Association Awards
To increase the awareness of the general public and the creative world of photography produced by members. Members are eligible. Trophies and certificates (Gold, Silver, Merit) are awarded annually in the commissioned, non-commissioned, and series categories. Established in 1983. Formerly: (1990) AFAEP Awards.

2132

Association of Photographers/Kodak Student Competition
To encourage the development of students training to succeed in fashion, advertising, and editorial photography and to creatively and technically satisfy briefs devised and judged by major photographers and art directors in fashion, advertising, and editorial photography. A monetary award and a certificate are awarded annually. Established in 1985. Sponsored by Kodak UK Professional Photography Division. Formerly: (1990) AFAEP/Kodak Student Competition.

2133

Association of Track and Field Statisticians
15 Crossway
South Shields, Tyne and Wear NE34 6PK, England
Phone: 91 4546625

2134

Association of Track and Field Statisticians Honorary Member
For recognition of service to the Association in particular or to track and field athletics in general. The Executive Committee nominates individuals who are voted upon at the convention. Winners are not subject to payment of dues. Awarded biennially in even-numbered years. Established in 1958.

2135

Jan Popper Memorial Prize
To recognize the author of the publication which, having appeared in the previous four years, was adjudged by the Executive Committee to contribute most to the statistical history of women's track and field. Established in 1987.

2136

Astrological Association
396 Caledonian Rd.
London N1 1DN, England
Phone: 602 265473

2137

Astrological Association Awards
For recognition of contributions to the field of astrology.

2138

AT&T Global Information Solutions Ltd.
206 Marylebone Rd.
London NW1 6LY, England
Phone: 71 723 7070
Phone: 71 725 8244
Fax: 71 724 6519

Formerly: NCR Ltd..

2139

NCR Book Award
To stimulate interest in nonfiction writing, publishing and reading in the UK. Books from within the following categories are considered: the arts, autobiography, biography, business and commerce, criticism, current affairs, history, natural history, popular science, religion, sport and travel. Books written in English by writers from the British Commonwealth and the Republic of Ireland, that were published in the UK by a British publisher during the preceding year may be submitted by publishers. Authors should be living at the time of entry of their books. Entries may be submitted by November 21. A short list of four books is selected by the judges. From these they choose the winning book, the author of which receives £25,000. Authors of the three other shortlisted books each receive £1,500. All four books are promoted. Awarded annually. Established in 1987.

2140

Athena Poster and Print Company International
Pentos Group
165 Victoria St.
London SW1 E5NA, England
Phone: 71 828 5433

2141

Athena Arts Prize
For recognition of outstanding art. A monetary prize of £25,000 is awarded. Three supplementary prizes of £2,000 each are also awarded. The best works entered are presented in a special exhibition. Established in 1984.

2142

Austin Seven Clubs Association
Lorien
Newbury, Bucks., England

2143

Ken Warren Memorial Trophy
For recognition of outstanding contributions to the Association's quarterly magazine. Membership in an Associated Club (36 world-wide) is necessary for consideration. A trophy is awarded annually at the General Meeting. Established in 1985 in memory of Ken Warren.

2144

Austin Ten Drivers Club Ltd.
53 Oxted Green
Milford
Godalming, Surrey, England

2145

Driver of the Year
For recognition of an outstanding driver of the Club who scores the most points in driving attendance events during the preceding year; and to encourage participation in vintage driving events. Members must use a Club eligible car (1931-39 Austin). A trophy is awarded annually.

2146

Australian Musical Foundation in London
1, Puddle Dock
Blackfriars
London EC4V 3PD, England
Phone: 71 236 8000
Fax: 71 236 7503

2147

Australian Musical Foundation in London Award
To recognize an unusually talented young Australian musician whose career and training would specially benefit from such help. Normally the award is intended for advanced musical study in Europe. Entry is open to singers and instrumentalists. Applicants must be Australian by birth or naturalization, regardless of present residence. They must be over 18 years of age. The deadline for application is April 22. A monetary prize of £8,000 is awarded over two years at £4,000 per annum. Awarded annually. Established in 1975.

2148

Authors' Club
40 Dover St.
London W1X 3RB, England
Phone: 71 4998581
Fax: 71 4090913

2149

Authors' Club First Novel Award
To recognize the author of the most promising first novel published in the United Kingdom during the preceding year. A monetary prize of £750 is awarded annually. Established in 1954. Women writers first became eligible in 1967.

2150

Sir Banister Fletcher Prize Trust
For recognition of the best book on architecture or the fine arts published in the United Kingdom during the preceding year. A monetary prize of £500 is awarded annually by the Committee at a dinner held in the Club. Established in 1954 by Sir Banister Fletcher, President of the Club for many years.

2151

Nelson Hurst & Marsh Biography Award
To recognize the most significant biography published by a British publisher in the preceding two years. A monetary award of £3,000 is presented biennially.

2152

Badminton Association of England
National Badminton Centre
Bradwell Rd.
Loughton Lodge
Milton Keynes, Bucks. MK8 9LA, England
Phone: 908 568822
Fax: 908 566922

2153

English Badminton Award
To recognize long-standing exceptional service to badminton in England.

2154

Herbert Scheele Medal
To recognize outstanding contributions to the development and administration of the sport of badminton. Consideration is given to a member of the Association or its other national governing bodies. A silver medal is presented as merited at All-England Championships. Established in 1981. The award commemorates Herbert Scheele, a one-time secretary of the Association and of the International Badminton Federation.

2155

Balint Society
Tollgate Health Centre
220 Tollgate Rd.
London E6 4JS, England
Phone: 71 474 5656

2156

Balint Society Prize Essay
To encourage understanding of doctor-patient relationships. Unpublished essays based on personal experience on an announced subject may be submitted by April 1. Medical or paramedical employment is required. A monetary prize of £250 and publication in the Journal of the Society are awarded annually in June. Established in honor of Dr. Michael Balint, a psychoanalyst of London and Budapest.

2157

Ballroom Dancers Federation
151, Brudenell Rd.
London SW17 8DF, England
Phone: 81 672 876

2158

BDF Awards
For recognition of outstanding services to ballroom dancing. Awards are given in the following categories: Outstanding Amateur Modern Couple, Outstanding Professional Modern Couple, Outstanding Amateur Latin Couple, Outstanding Professional Latin Couple, Overseas Award, Promoter's Award, and Services to Dancing. A medal or trophy is awarded annually.

2159

BBC Magazines
35 Marylebone High St.
London W1M 4AA, England
Phone: 71 580 5577
Fax: 71 486 7764

| 2160 |

***Radio Times* Drama & Comedy Awards**
To recognize original works for either radio or television not previously performed in public. Each entry must be supported by a sponsor experienced in production. Details of awards are announced in *Radio Times* in March. Monetary awards of £5,000 are presented in each category. Awarded annually. The drama category was established in 1973; the comedy category was added in 1985.

| 2161 |

BBC Wildlife Magazine
Broadcasting House
Whiteladies Rd.
Bristol BS8 2LR, England
Phone: 272 238166
Fax: 272 467075

| 2162 |

Wildlife Photographer of the Year Competition
To find the best wildlife pictures taken by photographers worldwide, and to emphasize through the work of such photographers the beauty, wonder, and importance of the natural world. Emphasis is placed on photographs taken in wild and free conditions. Open to all amateur and professional photographers. Up to three photographs can be entered in each category. Color slide transparencies may be submitted by the end of June in the following categories: Animal Behavior: Mammals, Animal Behavior: Birds, Animal Behavior: Insects, Animal Behavior: All Other Animals, The World in Our Hands, Endangered Wildlife, In Praise of Plants, The Underwater World, From Dusk to Dawn, Urban Wildlife, Composition and Form, Wild Places, and Animal Portraits. Monetary awards totaling £12,000 are presented, composed of a first prize of £500 and a second prize of £250 in each category. The Wildlife Photographer of the Year title is awarded to the photographer who submits the best single image. The prize consists of a bronze trophy of a scarlet ibis and £2,000. The Eric Hosking Award, a natural history holiday for two to an exotic location, and an owl sculpture was introduced in 1991 in memory of the famous wildlife photographer and is given for the best portfolio submitted by a photographer under 27 years of age. All winning and commended photographs are displayed in a special exhibition at the Natural History Museum and are published in a book. The exhibition also tours the United States, Germany, France, Holland, and Japan. Awarded annually. Established in 1984. Organized by *BBC Wildlife Magazine* and the Natural History Museum, London. Sponsored by British Gas. For additional information regarding U.S. tours and entry forms, contact Ann Jacobson, 14 New Hampshire Ave., Bradford, MA 01835; telephone: (508) 521-1674.

| 2163 |

Young Wildlife Photographer of the Year Competition
To recognize the best wildlife pictures taken by young photographers aged 17 years and under. Prints or slides of wild animals or plants or natural landscapes may be submitted by June 21. Awards are presented in the following categories: Photographer aged 10 years and under, Photographer aged 11-14 years, and Photographer aged 15-17 years. A first prize of £200 and a runner-up prize of £100 are presented in each category. The title "Young Wildlife Photographer of the Year" is awarded to the person (of any age) whose picture is judged to be the best in the competition. The award includes £300, a day on location with wildlife photographer Heather Angel, and the British Gas Award - a bronze statue of an ibis. Winning pictures are published in *BBC Wildlife Magazine* and form part of a major exhibition in the Natural History Museum, London and on tour in the United Kingdom and overseas. For additional information regarding U.S. tours and entry forms, contact Ann Jacobson, 14 New Hampshire Ave., Bradford, MA 01835; telephone: (508) 521-1674.

| 2164 |

Berkeley Enthusiasts Club
St. John's
41 Gorsewood Rd.
Woking, Surrey GU21 1UZ, England
Phone: 483 475330

| 2165 |

Excelsior Endurance Award
To recognize those who have driven an excelsior powered car for everyday use during the past year. Members of the Club must be nominated. A plaque and a retained cup are awarded annually. Established in 1981.

| 2166 |

Bibliographical Society
British Library
Great Russell St.
London WC1B 3DG, England
Phone: 71 3237567
Fax: 71 3237566

| 2167 |

Medal for Services to Bibliography
For recognition of achievement in the field of bibliographical studies. Individuals are elected. A medal is awarded irregularly. Established in 1929. Formerly: Silver-gilt Medal for Bibliography.

| 2168 |

Biochemical Society
59 Portland Pl.
London W1N 3AJ, England
Phone: 71 580 5530
Fax: 71 637 7626

| 2169 |

BDH Award In Analytical Biochemistry
For recognition of outstanding work carried out in a laboratory situated in the United Kingdom or Irish Republic leading to advances in biochemistry related to the development and application of a new reagent or method. A monetary award of £500, a medal, and an invitation to deliver a lecture were awarded triennially. The Lecture was published in *Biochemical Society Transactions*. Established in 1969. Established and sponsored by BDH Chemicals Ltd. (Discontinued)

| 2170 |

CIBA Medal and Prize
For recognition of outstanding research in any branch of biochemistry. Candidates of any nationality who carry out their work in the United Kingdom may be nominated by January 1. A monetary award of £500, a medal, and travel expenses are awarded annually. The recipient is expected to deliver a lecture. The lecture is published in *Biochemical Society Transactions*. Established in 1964 by CIBA Laboratories. Sponsored by CIBA-GEIGY Corporation, Pharmaceuticals Division.

| 2171 |

Colworth Medal
For recognition of work of an outstanding nature by a British biochemist. British citizens under the age of 35 at the end of the year that the award is made may be nominated by January 1. A medal is awarded annually. The recipient is expected to deliver a lecture. The lecture is published in *Biochemical Society Transactions*. Established in 1963 by Unilever Research Laboratory.

| 2172 |

Honorary Member
To recognize individuals for outstanding contributions to the field of biochemistry. Awarded when merited. Established in 1969.

| 2173 |

Sir Frederick Gowland Hopkins Memorial Lecture
To recognize an individual in the field of biochemistry. The lecturer is required to assess the impact of recent advances in his chosen field upon progress in biochemistry. Biochemists of any nationality may be nominated by January 1. A bronze medal and an honorarium are awarded every two or three years. Established in 1958 in memory of Sir Frederic Gowland Hopkins.

2174
Jubilee Lecture and Harden Medal
To recognize a biochemist of distinction from any part of the world. Nominations are invited by the awards committee. Travel expenses for two lectures, one in London and one repeated outside London, are awarded. The lecture is published in *Biochemical Society Transactions*. Since 1978, the lecturer has also received the Harden Medal. Awarded every two to three years when the Hopkins Lecture is not presented. Established in 1961 to commemorate the 50th anniversary of the society.

2175
Keilin Memorial Lecture
For recognition of work in the field of biochemistry and biology. Biochemists of any nationality may be nominated by January 1. Travel expenses, a medal, and the invitation to deliver the lecture are awarded biennially. The lecture is published in *Biochemical Society Transactions*. Established in 1964 in memory of David Keilin.

2176
Krebs Memorial Scholarship
To provide for a post-graduate scholarship, tenable at any British University. Candidates who wish to proceed to a higher degree in biochemistry or in an allied biomedical science, but whose careers have been interrupted for non-academic reasons beyond their own control and/or who are unlikely to qualify for an award from public funds are eligible. It will cover a personal maintenance grant at an appropriate level and all necessary fees. Applications may be made at any time. Although the scholarship is primarily aimed at graduate students, the award of a post-doctoral fellowship might be considered for a candidate whose circumstances merit such consideration. Established in 1982 to commemorate the life and work of Sir Hans Krebs, F.R.S.

2177
Morton Lecture
For recognition of outstanding contributions to lipid biochemistry. Individuals may be nominated by January 1. An honorarium, an invitation to deliver the lecture, and full travel expenses are awarded biennially. The lecture is published in *Biochemical Society Transactions*. Established in 1978 to honor R.A. Morton.

2178
Travel Fund
To enable younger scientists to attend scientific meetings or to make short visits to laboratories. Available only to members of the Biochemical Society.

2179
Wellcome Trust Award for Research in Biochemistry Related to Medicine
For recognition of distinguished research leading to new advances in medical science. Biochemists in a field of biochemistry related to medicine who are under 45 years of age may be nominated by January 1. The work of the nominee must have been carried out within the preceding seven years in the United Kingdom or Irish Republic. A monetary award of £500 and a medal are awarded biennially. The lecture is published in *Biochemical Society Transactions*. Established in 1978 by Wellcome Trust.

2180
Biodeterioration Society
International Mycological Institute
Balceham Ln.
Egham, Surrey TW20 9TY, England
Phone: 78 4470111
Fax: 78 4470909

2181
Biodeterioration Society Awards
To recognize academics, representatives of the biocide industry, and research scientists from industry and government organizations. The Society conducts the Bunker Memorial Lecture and bestows awards.

2182
Biological Council
Institute of Biology
20 Queensberry Pl.
London SW7 2DZ, England
Phone: 71 581 8333

2183
Biological Council Awards
To provide funds for student expeditions overseas. Support is considered for expeditions being undertaken by undergraduate students in biological sciences. The expeditions should have a specific biological aim, or, in multidisciplinary expeditions, there should be a clearly defined biological component. Awarded annually.

2184
Biological Engineering Society
Royal College of Surgeons of England
Lincoln's Inn Fields
London WC2A 3PN, England
Phone: 71 2427750

2185
Butterworth Hrinemann Prize
For recognition of the best paper in medical engineering and physics. A monetary award is given annually.

2186
Nightingale Prize
To encourage medical and biological engineering by recognizing the best paper in the preceding two years in the journal, *Medical and Biological Engineering and Computing*. Individuals of any nationality are eligible. A monetary prize and a citation are awarded biennially. Established in 1964. Co-sponsored by the International Federation for Medical and Biological Engineering. (Discontinued)

2187
BirdLife International
Wellbrook Ct.
Girton Rd.
Cambridge CB3 0NA, England
Phone: 223 277318
Fax: 223 277200

Formerly: International Council for Bird Preservation.

2188
Birdlife International/FFPS Conservation Expedition Competition
To encourage university or other teams to adopt a wildlife conservation objective for their expeditions from Europe to the developing world. A project proposal for an expedition outside Europe and North America should be submitted by December 31. In selecting the prize-winning projects, attention is paid to conservation content and likely impact, feasibility, and relationship to the BirdLife International/Fauna and Flora Preservation Society conservation priorities. Monetary awards of £3,000 each are awarded to the winners in the following categories: Tropical Forests, Oceanic Islands and Marine, Wetlands, and Threatened Species. Eight runners-up received £1,000 each. There is a follow-up fund of £7,500 available to the most successful of these expeditions. Established in 1985.

2189
Birkenhead Photographic Association
29 Fairview Rd.
Oxton, Birkenhead L43 5SD, England
Phone: 51 6524773

2190
Birkenhead International Colour Salon
For recognition of achievement in traditional (general) contemporary and nature photography. Four slides in each section may be submitted by

January. Gold, silver, and bronze medals and certificates are awarded annually. Established in 1970.

2191

Boardman Tasker Memorial Trust
14 Pine Lodge
Dairyground Rd.
Bramhall
Stockport, Cheshire SK7 2HS, England   Phone: 61 439 4624

2192

Boardman Tasker Memorial Award for Mountain Literature
For recognition of an original literary work. The central theme must be concerned with the mountain environment. Fiction, nonfiction, drama, or poetry written (whether initially or in translation) in the English language may be nominated by publishers only. Books must have been published or distributed in the United Kingdom for the first time between November of the preceding year or October 31 of the year the prize is awarded. Entries must be submitted by August 1. A monetary award of £2,000 is awarded annually in October/November. Established in 1983 in memory of Peter Boardman and Joe Tasker, authors of mountain literature who disappeared on Mt. Everest in 1982.

2193

Book Trust (England)
Book House
45 East Hill   Phone: 81 8709055
London SW18 2QZ, England   Fax: 81 8744790

Formerly: (1986) National Book League (England).

2194

Anglo-Hellenic League's Runciman Award
For recognition of the best literary work about Greece published in the United Kingdom during the current year. A monetary award of £1,000 was presented at the annual meeting of the Anglo-Hellenic League. Established in 1985 by the Anglo Hellenic League in memory of Sir Steven Runciman. (Discontinued)

2195

Booker Prize
This, Britain's major literary prize for fiction, is given for recognition of a full-length novel. Publishers may submit up to three books which are written in English and have been published for the first time in the United Kingdom. Citizens of Britain or the British Commonwealth, the Republic of Ireland, and South Africa are eligible. A monetary prize of £20,000 is awarded annually. Established in 1968 by Booker PLC, an international food company in cooperation with the Book Trust and Publishers' Association. Formerly: Booker McConnell Prize.

2196

Booker Russian Novel Prize
To stimulate wider knowledge of modern Russian fiction in the Western world, to encourage translations, and to increase sales of the books. The winner is chosen by an international panel of five judges. Established in 1991. For further information, contact Anne Riddoch, 40 York Rd., Woking, Surrey, England GU22 7XN

2197

Constable Trophy
For recognition of the best unpublished novel a writer from the North of England (Cumbria, the Isle of Man, the North East, North and South Humberside, Lincolnshire, Yorkshire, Lancashire, Greater Manchester, Merseyside, Cheshire and the High Peak District of Derbyshire). Entries must be sent by September 30. A monetary prize of £1,000 and the Constable Trophy are awarded biennially. On acceptance for publication by Constable, a further advance of £1,000 against royalties is made. Sponsored by Constable & Co. Ltd., 3 The Lanchesters, 162 Fulham Palace Rd., London W6 9ER.

2198

Deo Gloria Award
To promote fiction for adults which portrays something of the uniqueness of the Christian revelation in whole or in part. The author must be a citizen of the United Kingdom or the Commonwealth. A monetary prize of £5,000 is awarded annually. Established in 1990 by the Deo Gloria Trust. Sponsored by the Deo Gloria Trust. Contact the Trust, Selson House 212-220 Addington Rd., South Croydon, Surrey CR2 8LD for further information.

2199

David Higham Prize for Fiction
For recognition of a first novel or book of short stories published in the United Kingdom in the year of the award. Novels must be written in English and should show promise for the author's future. Citizens of Britain or the British Commonwealth, the Republic of Ireland, and South Africa are eligible. A monetary prize of £1,000 is awarded annually. Established in 1975.

2200

Sir Peter Kent Conservation Book Prize
To recognize the best book on environmental issues published in the United Kingdom during the previous two years. A monetary award of £5,000 is awarded. In addition, £2,000 is awarded for a work written for children aged 8 to 14. Established in 1977.

2201

The Mail on Sunday **- John Llewellyn Rhys Prize**
For recognition of a memorable literary work of fiction, nonfiction, poetry, or drama written in English and published in the UK during the current year. British or Commonwealth writers who are under 35 years of age at the time of publication are eligible. The deadline is October 31. A monetary prize of £5000 is awarded annually. Established in 1941 by the widow of John Llewellyn Rhys, an airman killed while on active duty. Sponsored by *The Mail on Sunday*. Formerly: (1989) John Llewellyn Rhys Memorial Prize.

2202

Kurt Maschler Award
For recognition of a children's book that diplays excellent and perfectly harmoniuos text and illustration. Books published in English in the United Kingdom by a citizen or resident of Britain for more than ten years are considered. A monetary prize of £1,000 and a bronze figure of Emil are awarded annually in the autumn. Established in 1982 by Kurt Maschler in honor of Erich Kaestner and Walter Trier. Formerly: Emil Kurt Maschler Award.

2203

Francis Minns Award
To recognize a designer who, in the opinion of the Selectors for the Book Trust British Book Design and Production Exhibition, earned special recognition. (Discontinued)

2204

Odd Fellows Book Award
For recognition of a book, or pamphlet of not less than 10,000 words, that provides the most stimulating impetus for the improvement of living conditions within fields of social concern (specified each year). A monetary prize of £2,000 was awarded annually. Established in 1977. (Discontinued) Formerly: .

2205

Parents Magazine Best Book for Babies Award
To recognize the best book for babies and toddlers under four years of age published in Britain in the year ending May 31. A monetary award of £1,000 was presented annually. Established in 1985. (Discontinued)

2206

Smarties Book Prize
To encourage high standards and stimulate interest in books for children in three categories: 5 years and under, 6 to 8 years, and 9 to 11 years.

133

Books published in Britain and written in English by citizens or residents of the United Kingdom are eligible. A monetary prize of £2,000 is awarded for each category and an overall winner receives an additional £6,000. Awarded annually in the autumn. Established in 1985 by Rowntree Mackintosh, now known as Nestle Rowntree. Formerly: Smarties Prize fro Children's Books.

2207
H. H. Wingate Awards
or recognition of a work of fiction and nonfiction that best stimulated an interest in Jewish themes. Two prizes of £2,000 each were awarded annually. Established in 1977. (Discontinued) Formerly: .

2208
Books for Children
Whiteway Court
The Whiteway
Cirencester, Glos. GL7 7BA, England
Phone: 285 657081
Fax: 285 657086

2209
Mother Goose Award
To recognize the most exciting newcomer to the field of illustration of children's books in Great Britain. The submitted work must be the first major children's book produced by the illustrator, and must have been produced between March 1st and February 28th/29th of the preceding year. The deadline is March 1. A monetary award of £1,000 and a bronze goose egg are presented. The runners-up receive a scroll and a bottle of champagne. Awarded annually during the first week of May. Established in 1979. Sponsored by the Books for Children Book Club.

2210
Booksellers Association of Great Britain & Ireland
Minister House
272 Vauxhall Bridge Rd.
London SW1V 1BA, England
Phone: 71 8345477
Fax: 71 8348812

2211
Whitbread Literary Awards
To encourage and promote good English literature. Books are considered in the following categories: biography or autobiography, children's novel, novel, first novel, and poetry. Authors who have been living in Great Britain or Ireland for three or more years are eligible. Selection is made from books first published in the United Kingdom or Ireland within the previous year. Works must be submitted by publishers only. The deadline is July 29. The following monetary awards are presented: £2,000 each for the winner in each category, and an additional £20,500 to the overall winner, Whitbread Book of the Year, chosen from the five category winners. Awarded annually in January. Established in 1971. Additional information is available from Alice Kennelly, Kallaway Limited, 2 Portland Rd., Holland Park, London W11 4LA, England; telephone: 71 2217883.

2212
BP Peter Pears Award
43 St. Dunstan's Rd.
London W6 8RE, England

2213
BP Peter Pears Award
To recognize young professional singers and their accompanists. A monetary prize of £5,000 and a London recital were awarded annually. Established in 1989 to honor Sir Peter Pears. (Discontinued)

2214
Brick Development Association
Woodside House
Winkfield
Windsor, Berks. SL4 2DX, England
Phone: 344 885651
Fax: 344 890129

2215
Brick Design Awards
To recognize and promote excellence in design using brickwork. Awards are presented in the following categories: housing, paving and hard landscaping, structural brickwork, design in context, commercial and industrial, and public building. One winner is presented with the award for Best Overall Design. Co-sponsored by the *Architect's Journal*. Formerly: Architectural Award.

2216
Quality Brickwork Award
To recognize the quality of craftsmanship in brick buildings throughout the United Kingdom. Entries must be submitted by January 15. Personal recognition is given to the individual responsible for the brickwork; a ceramic plaque is presented to the building owner. Awarded annually. Established in 1986.

2217
Bridport Arts Centre
South St.
Bridport, Dorset DT6 3NR, England
Phone: 308 27183

2218
The Bridport Prize
To encourage people to write. Awards are given for poetry and short stories. Entries should be written in English, of the length specified in the current conditions of entry. A monetary first prize of £1,000, a second prize of £500, and a third prize of £250 are awarded in each category annually. Established in 1980. Formerly: Creative Writing Competition.

2219
Creative Writing Junior Competition
To encourage children to write. Awards are given for poetry and short stories in two age categories: 8 to 11 years and 12 to 17 years. Works in English must be submitted by April 5. Monetary awards are presented annually. Established in 1990. Additional information is available from the Junior Competition Secretary.

2220
British Academy
20-21 Cornwall Terrace
London NW1 4QP, England
Phone: 71 4875966
Fax: 71 2243807

2221
Derek Allen Prize
To recognize an individual for contributions to musicology.

2222
British Academy Research Awards
The British Academy awards annual research awards to British Scholars for advanced academic research in the humanities.

2223
Burkitt Medal for Biblical Studies
For recognition of contributions to Biblical studies. Awarded annually. Established in 1925.

2224
Grahame Clark Medal
No further information was available for this edition.

2225
Rose Mary Crawshay Prize for English Literature
To recognize a woman of any nationality who, in the judgement of the British Academy, has written or published during the preceding three years an outstanding historical or critical work on any subject connected with English literature. Preference is given to works on Byron, Shelley or

Keats. Monetary prizes totaling £600 are awarded annually. Established in 1888 by Rose Mary Crawshay and first awarded in 1916.

2226
Cromer Greek Awards
No further information on this award was available for this edition.

2227
Fellow
To recognize an individual for outstanding contributions to English literature. (Discontinued)

2228
Sir Israel Gouancz Prize
No further information was available for this edition.

2229
Kenyon Medal for Classical Studies
To recognize an individual for contributions to classical studies.

2230
Serena Medal for Italian Studies
To recognize an individual for an outstanding contribution to Italian studies.

2231
British Academy of Film and Television Arts
195 Piccadilly　　　　　　　　　　Phone: 71 7340022
London W1V 9LG, England　　　　Fax: 71 7341792

Formerly: (1976) Society of Film and Television Arts.

2232
BAFTA Scholarship
To encourage new talent into the film industry and to enable a talented student to study at The National Film and Television School. A scholarship is awarded jointly with The Post Office. Established in 1991.

2233
British Academy of Film and Television Arts Awards - Film
For recognition of outstanding films in the areas of performance, and craft and production. The voting lists are compiled from suggestions received from academy members throughout the year. The nominations for the Production, Direction, and Craft Awards are determined by vote. Juries decide the winner in each category. The Best Film and Performance Awards are decided by membership vote. Awards are given in the following categories: Film, David Lean Award for Best Achievement in Direction, Original Screenplay, Adapted Screenplay, Actress, Actor, Supporting Actress, Supporting Actor, Achievement in Film Music, Film Not in the English Language, Cinematography, Production Design, Costume Design, Editing, Sound, Best Achievement in Special Effects, Make-Up Artist, Short Film, Michael Balcon Award for Outstanding British Contribution to Cinema, Short Animated Film Award, and BAFTA Fellowship. Trophies are awarded annually. Awards related to the Academy go back as far as 1947. Sponsored by Lloyds Bank UK.

2234
British Academy of Film and Television Arts Awards - Television
For recognition of outstanding television programs in the areas of performance, and craft and production. The voting lists are compiled from suggestions received from academy members throughout the year. The nominations for the Production, Direction, and Craft Awards are determined by vote. Juries decide the winner in each category. The Best Television Performance Awards are decided by membership vote. Awards are given in the following categories: Single Drama, Drama Series/Seria, Factual Series, Light Entertainment Program or Series, Comedy Program or Series, Hu. Wheldon Award for Best Arts Program, Actuality Coverage, Actress, Actor, Light Entertainment Performance, Flaherty Documentary Award, Original Television Music, Children's Program - Fiction, Children's Program - Factual, Video Lighting, Make-up, Film or Video Photography - Factual and Fiction, Costume Design, Graphics, Film Sound - Factual and Fiction, Film Editor - Factual and Fiction, Design, Writer's Award, Foreign Television Program Award, Television Award for Originality, Alan Clarke Award for Outstanding Creative Contribution to Television and Richard Dimbleby Award for the Most Important Personal contribution on the screen in factual television. Trophies are awarded annually. Awards related to the Academy go back as far as 1947. Sponsored by Lloyds Bank.

2235
British Actors' Equity Association
Guild House　　　　　　　　　　　Phone: 71 3796000
Upper St. Martin's Ln.　　　　　　Phone: 71 637 9311
London WC2H 9EG, England　　　Fax: 71 3767001

2236
Clarence Derwent Award (British)
To provide recognition for the actor and actress giving the best supporting stage performance during the previous year. A monetary award of £100 is awarded annually. Established in 1948 by a grant from Clarence Derwent, an American actor and former president of Actors' Equity.

2237
British Agricultural and Garden Machinery Association
14-16 Church St.　　　　　　　　　Phone: 923 720241
Rickmansworth, Herts. WD3 1RQ, England　　Fax: 923 896063

2238
Garden Machinery Annual Awards
For recognition of supplier support for the specialist garden machinery trade. Manufacturers/importers are invited to nominate one machine in each of the following classes: Best Machine - grass cutting; Best Machine - other than grass cutting; New Product of the Year; Best Commercial Machine; Most Supportive Manufacturer; and Bob Falder Award for individuals or companies who have given most to the industry. Members vote for the final selection. Trophies are awarded annually. Established in 1979. Formerly: (1985) BAGMA Annual Awards.

2239
British Appaloosa Society
Address unknown.

2240
British Appaloosa Society National Champions
For recognition of the best of the breed. Members of the Society may enter horses in the competition. Awards are presented in the following classes: (1) Yearlings - the Rogers Cup; (2) two and three year old Fillies and Geldings - the Chapman Trophy; (3) Junior Stallions (licensed) - the Ivy and John Williams Award; (4) Senior Stallions (licensed) - the Kingswood Cup; (5) Registered Male Progeny of Two Registered Appaloosas - the Ben Barrett Trophy; (6) Brood Mares - the Dorian Williams Cup; (7) Foals - the Blythwind Cup; (8) Mares - the Hart Shield; (9) Geldings - the White Trophy; (10) Registered Female Progeny of Two Registered Appaloosas - the Tibertich Cup; (11) In-Hand Championships - the Linda McCartney Cup for the Male Champion and the David Hart Cup for the Female Champion; (12) Western Pleasure Riding - the Box Mayhew Trophy; (13) Riding Horse 15 Hands and Under - the Riding Magazine Cup; (14) Riding Horse Over 15 Hands - the Vallei Bowl; (15) Family Horse - the Harmsworth Bowl; and (16) Working Hunter - the Gobions Plate; Awarded annually. Established in 1976.

2241
National Champion Challenge Cup
For recognition of the best appaloosa. Registered appaloosas are eligible. A perpetual Challenge Cup is awarded annually. Established in 1976.

2242
British Archaeological Association
c/o The Hon. Editor
Institute of Archaeology
36 Beaumont St.
Oxford, Oxon. OX1 2PG, England

2243
Reginald Taylor Essay Prize
To recognize the best unpublished essay submitted to the *Journal of the British Archaeological Association* during the year. The essay, not exceeding 7,500 words in length, should show original research on a subject of archaeological, art-historical or antiquarian interest within the period from the Roman era to A.D. 1830. Essays may be submitted by October 31, 1994. A monetary award of £100 and possible publication of the essay are awarded biennially. Established to honor E. Reginald Taylor, an active and valuable member of the British Archaeological Association for many years, and its Secretary from 1924 until his death in 1932.

2244
British Archaeological Awards
56 Penn Rd.
Beaconsfield, Bucks. HP9 2LS, England

2245
Archaeological Book Award
For recognition of the best book on British archaeology (broadly defined) published in the last two years. All books published in this period (for national distribution) are automatically considered. Sponsored by the Ancient & Medieval History Book Club.

2246
BP Award
For recognition of the best non-archaeologist who, in the course of his/her normal, non-archaeological employment, finds archaeological artifacts/remains and causes them to be reported to the appropriate authorities. The deadline for entries is June 30. Awarded biennially. Sponsored by BP Exploration.

2247
Heritage in Britain Award
For recognition of the best project that secures the long term preservation of a site or monument. The project may range from field monuments, ruined structures, roofed and used buildings, and gardens. Industrial monuments may include the machinery related to the structure. The deadline for entries is June 30. Awarded biennially. Sponsored by English Heritage, Historic - Scotland, and CADW - Wales.

2248
Ironbridge Award
For recognition of the best project involving the adaptive re-use of any historic or industrial building or structure, especially where this permits the continued commercially-viable existence of those previously thought impossible to preserve. Museums and publicly-displayed sites are excluded. The deadline for entries is June 30. Awarded biennially. Sponsored by the Ironbridge Gorge Museum Trust, Ironbridge, Shropshire.

2249
Nationwide Silver Trowel Award
For recognition of the greatest initiative and originality in archaeology. All entrants for other awards are considered automatically for this award, but additional direct entries are acceptable. The deadline for entries is June 30. Awarded biennially. Sponsored by Nationwide Building Society. Formerly: Legal & General Silver Trowel Award.

2250
Pitt-Rivers Award
For recognition of the best project undertaken by a voluntary body or individual. Professional technical help is permitted. The deadline for entries is June 30. Awarded biennially. Sponsored by the Robert Kiln Trust.

2251
Sponsorship Award
For recognition of the best sponsorship of archaeology based upon imagination, value for money, and the overall benefits to archaeology from the sponsorship. The deadline for entries is June 30. Awarded biennially. Sponsored by the Wedgewood Group. Formerly: Thames Television Award.

2252
Virgin Group Award
For recognition of the best presentation of an archaeological project to the public, thus stimulating awareness of, and curiosity about, Britain's national heritage. The deadline for entries is June 30. Awarded biennially. Sponsored by the Virgin Group.

2253
British Association for the Advancement of Science
23 Savile Row   Phone: 71 494 3326
London W1X 1AB, England   Fax: 71 734 1658

2254
British Association Film and Television Awards
To recognize and encourage high quality productions which contribute most to an awareness of science and technology or their effects on society and to the science and technology education of young people. Awards were given for both films and television in the following categories: (1) Science; (2) Technology; and (3) Education. British films, videos and TV programs were eligible. A trophy was awarded annually. Established in 1969. The Technology Awards and the Education Awards were jointly sponsored by the Fellowship of Engineering and the Association for Science Education. (Discontinued in 1992)

2255
Science and Technology Media Fellowships
To improve the communication of science and technology to the general public by giving scientists an opportunity to learn something of the workings of the media. Scientists and technologists working full time in industry, academia, or government service in the United Kingdom are eligible. Fellows spend from four to eight weeks working on a newspaper, magazine, television or radio station. Established in 1987 by the British Association on behalf of COPUS, the Committee on the Public Understanding of Science.

2256
Special Lectures
No further information was available for this edition.

2257
British Association of Aesthetic Plastic Surgeons
Royal College of Surgeons
35-43 Lincoln's Inn Fields   Phone: 71 4052234
London WC2A 3PN, England   Fax: 71 8314041

2258
BAAPS Senior Registrar's Prize
To encourage professional development and to select an individual to give a paper to the instructional meeting of the BAAPS in September. FRCS Senior Registrars in plastic surgery must apply in June/July. A cut glass silver necked decanter valued at £100 is awarded annually. Established in 1989.

2259

Hackett Memorial Prize
To recognize trainees in plastic surgery. The deadline for applications is in February/March. Four crystal champagne glasses are awarded annually.

2260

British Association of Barbershop Singers
Geoff Howe P.R.O.
Manor Rd.
Claybrooke Magna, Leics. LE17 5AY, Phone: 455 209555
 England Fax: 455 202198

2261

Crawley Plaque
To recognize the winner of the British Barbershop Chorus contest. The plaque is bestowed annually at the convention. Established in 1975 in honor of the first recipients of the plaque, the Crawley Barbershop Club.

2262

Tyneside Trophy
To recognize the winners of the British Barbershop Quartet contest. A trophy and individual medals are bestowed annually at the convention. Established in 1974 and named in honor of the hosts of the first British Barbershop Convention, the Tyneside Club.

2263

British Association of Dermatologists
3 St. Andrews Pl.
Regent's Park Phone: 71 9358576
London NW1 4LB, England Fax: 71 2240321

2264

British Association of Dermatologists Awards
To recognize individuals for outstanding contributions to the knowledge and teaching of dermatology.

2265

British Association of Industrial Editors
3 Locks Yard, High St.
Sevenoaks, Kent TN13 1LT, England Phone: 732 459331
 Fax: 732 461757

2266

BAIE Editing for Industry Awards
For recognition of achievement in corporate communication journalism. Internal and external magazines, newspapers, newsletters, and other publications published during the preceding year are eligible. All entries must be printed in English, but house journals from across the world are welcome. Awards are given in the following categories: (1) Internal Employee Newspapers; (2) Internal Employee Newsletters and News Magazines; (3) Internal Employee Magazines; (4) External publications; (5) Solo Award; (6) Corporate Videos; (7) Humor in Print; (8) Specials; (9) Financial; (10) New Editors; (11) New Journals; (12) News Story; (13) Feature Articles and Profiles; (14) Headlines; (15) Photography; (16) Picture Handling; (17) Design; (18) Printing; and (19) Multilingual Publications. Trophies and certificates are awarded annually at the spring convention. Established in 1954. Formerly: (1982) BAIE National House Journal Competition.

2267

Communicator of the Year
For recognition of achievement in organizational communication. Nominations may be submitted by December 31. An electronic sculpture is awarded annually in the spring. Established in 1976.

2268

British Association of Landscape Industries
Landscape House
9 Henry St. Phone: 535 606139
Keighley, W. Yorks. BD21 3DR, England Fax: 535 610269

2269

BALI National Landscape Awards
To draw attention to the landscape industry's participation in creating an improved environment, and for recognition of the best contributions by BALI Members made to this aim. Landscape construction must have been undertaken by a BALI Member and completed within two years of the entry date to be eligible. Plaques are awarded annually at BALI's National Landscape Awards Luncheon in London. The awards given are The Grand Award, Principal Awards, and Awards of Merit. Established in 1977.

2270

British Association of Urological Surgeons
c/o Royal College of Surgeons of England Phone: 71 4053474
35-43 Lincoln's Inn Fields Phone: 71 4051390
London WC2A 3PN, England Fax: 71 4045048

2271

Bard Award
For recognition of the best essay submitted specifically for consideration for the award by members of the Association (non-members must be sponsored by a full member). Essays should be based on original work on any topic connected with urological surgery, either clinical or experimental. The essay shall be given a specified time in the program of the annual meeting when a paper not exceeding 20 minutes duration shall be given. The presentation of the award will then be made by the President. Submission must be made by March 1. A monetary prize of £1,500 and the Bard Silver Medal are awarded annually when merited. Established in 1979. Sponsored by C. R. Bard International Limited.

2272

BAUS Travelling Fellowship
For recognition of any article(s) of outstanding merit in each volume of the *British Journal of Urology*. Candidates for the prize must be Fellows of one of the Royal Colleges of Surgeons in the British Isles, Canada, Australia, or South Africa; they must be undergoing urological training or have obtained a consultant post not more than ten years before the date of submission of the paper. In the case of multiple authorships, the authors would have to decide which of them should receive the prize. The successful prize winner must submit a program of visits to the urological centres outside Britain for consideration by the Council. The adjudicators shall be the Officers of the Association and the Editor of the *British Journal of Urology*. A travelling fellowship of £2,000 is awarded annually when merited. Established in 1972.

2273

***British Journal of Urology* Travelling Fellowship**
To recognize an outstanding paper and to enable a senior registrar or numbered career/research registrar to attend the American Urological Association Meeting. Papers must be new work not previously published and not resulting from a thesis. A fellowships of £1,500 is awarded annually in April at the Annual Scientific Meeting of the Senior Urological Registrar Group (SURG).

2274

William Cook Travelling Fellowship
To enable members of the British Association of Urological Surgeons to visit surgeons/hospitals and further their education. Applications must be submitted by February 1. Monetary awards of £3,000 to finance a minimum of three travelling fellowships are awarded annually. Successful applicants are required to submit a report on the experience gained in the center visited. Sponsored by William Cook Europe Ltd.

2275

Lewis Medical Travelling Scholarship
To recognize the outstanding paper presented at the annual meeting of the Senior Urological Registrars group. The scholarship is available to any person appointed to a numbered urological training post. The scholarship covers travel, accommodation, and registration expenses associated with attending the annual meeting of the American Urological Association. Established in 1990. Sponsored by Lewis Medical Limited.

2276

Shackman Travelling Fellowship
To provide sufficient support to enable the holder to undertake a period of study, either in the United Kingdom or abroad, for a period of not less than six weeks. The subject to be studied must be related either to urology or to renal transplantation and may be either a laboratory or a clinical investigation. Applications are invited from medical practitioners registered in the United Kingdom who are senior registrars in an accredited training program in urology or consultant urological surgeons within five years of appointment. Applicants of equivalent university status will also be considered. One or two awards of up to £1,500 may be made each year. Established by Mrs. Ralph Shackman in memory of the contribution to urology and renal transplantation made by her husband, Ralph Shackman, at the Royal Postgraduate Medical School, Hammersmith Hospital, London, during the period 1946 to 1974. Additional information is available from Messrs. Taylor Vinters, Solicitors, Lushington House, 119 High St., Newmarket CB8 9AG, England.

2277

Simpla Research Prize
To support a basic clinical research project. A monetary award of £1,000 was presented annually. (Discontinued)

2278

Surgitek Prize
To recognize the paper that makes the most significant contribution to urology. The prize consisted of a full-sponsored visit to the American Urological Association's Annual Meeting, and a tour of Surgitek's manufacturing facility in Racine, Wisconsin. (Discontinued)

2279

British Association of Women Entrepreneurs
29, Bedford St.
London WC2E 9RT, England   Phone: 71 836 1157

Formerly: (1985) British Association of Women Executives.

2280

BAWE Businesswomen's Enterprise Award
To recognize professionalism and entrepreneurial flair in a female executive within industry or commerce, and to stimulate the active participation of women in industry or commerce. A monetary award of £250 to be spent within the business, and a further £250 for travel and visit to a similar company in a member country were awarded biennially. A trophy and a certificate were also awarded. Established in 1984 by Nicky Joyce, president of the Association (1980-1985). (Discontinued in 1989)

2281

European Businesswoman of the Year
To recognize achievement in business. A candidate should be in full-time employment in a business established in a European country as a proprietor and/or a company director with a financial stake in the company she is operating. The candidate's business should have a turnover of not less than £500,000 and be trading in two or more European countries. Members of BAWE or of any of its European counterparts are eligible. Candidates are evaluated in the following areas: entrepreneurial flair, business acumen, initiative in regard to new opportunities and exploitation thereof, administrative ability, and ecological awareness. Entries may be submitted by March 1, 1991. A monetary award of £750, a trophy and other prizes are awarded. Established in 1989, and to be presented for the first time in 1992. The frequency is to be decided after 1992.

2282

Joyce Award
To recognize the member who has done the most for the Association during the year, or who has made contributions to improve the position of women in business. Members of the Association are eligible to be chosen by the current president and committee. A trophy is awarded annually. Established in 1982 by Nicky Joyce, president of the Association (1980-1985). Additional information is available from Nicky Joyce, The Mission House, Royal Pier Road, Gravesend, Kent DA12 2BD, England, phone: 474 356545.

2283

Rising Star Award
To recognize achievement in business. A candidate should be in full-time employment in a business established in a European country as a proprietor and/or a company director with a financial stake in the company she is operating. Candidates should have built a business from scratch to a turnover in excess of £100,000 in no more than three years. Members of BAWE or of any of its European counterparts are eligible. Candidates are evaluated in the following areas: entrepreneurial flair, business acumen, initiative in regard to new opportunities and exploitation thereof, administrative ability, and ecological awareness. A monetary award of £250, a certificate and other prizes are awarded. Established in 1989. The first award was presented in 1992.

2284

British Astronomical Association
Burlington House, Piccadilly
London W1V 9AG, England   Phone: 71 734 4145

2285

Lydia Brown Award for Meritorious Service
For recognition of prolonged and valuable service to the BAA in an honorary capacity. Members of the BAA are eligible. A monetary prize and a silver-gilt medal are usually awarded biennially. Established in 1972.

2286

Walter Goodacre Medal and Gift
For recognition of prolonged and outstanding contribution to the progress of astronomy. Members of the BAA are eligible. A monetary prize and a gold medal are awarded biennially. Established in 1930.

2287

Merlin Medal and Gift
For recognition of an outstanding discovery and contribution to astronomy. Members of the BAA are eligible. A monetary prize and a silver medal are awarded biennially. Established in 1961.

2288

Steavenson Memorial Award
For recognition of diligence and excellence as an astronomical observer. Members of the BAA are eligible. A book chosen by the recipient is awarded annually. Established in 1975.

2289

British Birds
Fountains
Park Lane   Phone: 767 40025
Blunham, Beds. MK44 3NJ, England   Fax: 767 40025

2290

Best Annual Bird Report
To provide public acknowledgment of the high quality of local, county and regional bird reports, and to encourage and promote high standards of content and production of annual publications in Britain and Ireland. Established in 1991.

2291
Best Bird Book of the Year
To recognize the best bird book reviewed during the previous 12 months. The winning book may, in one year, be an important erudite scientific treatise and, in another, a lighter, less academic book, but must always be reliable, well-produced, and thoroughly worthy of inclusion in any library. Books submitted for review to the journal *British Birds* are eligible. Parchments are awarded to the publisher, the author(s), and artist(s) annually. Established in 1980.

2292
Bird Illustrator of the Year
To recognize an artist for the best bird illustration. Amateur and professional artists are invited to submit four line-drawings of specific dimensions suitable for reproduction in the jounal *British Birds*. The subjects should be birds recorded in West Palearctic (Europe, North Africa, and the Middle East). The winner receives £100 and an inscribed salver, the two runners-up receive £40 and £25, and all three receive Kowa telescopes (value over £1,000) at a Press Reception at the Mall Galleries in London. Established in 1979. Sponsored by Kowa Telescopes. Two additional awards are presented: Richard Richardson Award - to recognize the best work submitted by an artist under 21 years of age. A monetary award and a book to the total value of £60 are awarded. Established in 1979 to honor Richard Richardson, the East Anglian ornithologist and artist; and PJC Award for Individual Merit - to recognize a bird-illustrator for a single work of merit. Established in 1987 by David Cook in memory of his wife, Pauline.

2293
Bird Photograph of the Year
To recognize the best bird photograph in the competition. Up to three color transparencies, each taken during the previous year, may be submitted by each photographer. Preference is given to photographs taken in the West Palearctic, but those of species on the West Palearctic list taken anywhere in the world are also eligible. The deadline is January 30. The following awards are presented: First prize - £100 and an engraved salver; Second prize - £40 and Christopher Helm and Collins books valued at £25; Third prize - £25 and Christopher Helm and Collins books valued at £25. The best recent black-and-white bird photographs are also selected. Established in 1977. Sponsored by Christopher Helm Publishers Ltd. and Harper Collins Publishers Ltd. Established in 1960.

2294
British Broadcasting Corporation
Broadcasting House
London W1A 1AA, England   Phone: 71 580 4468

2295
Mastermind Award
To recognize the winner of a television program quiz. A Caithness (engraved) Glass Trophy is awarded annually. Established in 1972.

2296
British Broadcasting Corporation Television
Young Musician of the Year
BBC Kensington House   Phone: 81 8956144
Richmond Way   Phone: 81 8956145
London W14 OAX, England   Fax: 81 8956974

2297
BBC Television Young Musician of the Year
For recognition of achievement in the field of music performance and composition (includes musicality, technique, stage presentation, etc.). The performers competition is held for piano/organ, strings, wind, brass, and percussion. Performers 19 or under on January 1 of a competition year, who are grade 8 standard and British citizens are eligible. Composers in two groups, one 19 and under, one 24 and under are eligible. The following monetary awards are presented biennially in even-numbered years: for performers - 500 prizes ranging from £50 - £2,000, and for composers - 12 prizes ranging from £500-£2,000. In addition, the Walter Todds Bursary of £500 is given to the competitor who shows the most potential. Established in 1978 by Walter Todds and Humphrey Burton. Sponsored by Lloyds Bank.

2298
British Canoe Union
Adbolton Lane
W. Bridgford   Phone: 602 821100
Nottingham, Notts. NG2 5AS, England   Fax: 602 821797

2299
Award for Valour
For recognition of a canoeist whose gallantry or devotion in bringing assistance to others in an aquatic situation is considered to be of outstanding merit. The award may be made posthumously. Nominations may be submitted by a witness and, if possible, supported by a recognized agency. A citation is presented as merited. Established in 1981.

2300
Award of Honour
For recognition of outstanding service to canoeing over a number of years, either nationally or internationally, in any branch of the sport. Nominations are accepted by organizations associated with the Union. An engraved plaque or medal, accompanied by a citation, are presented to the winner. Established in 1962.

2301
Award of Merit
For recognition of those who have given distinguished service to canoeing, normally over a number of years. Nominations are accepted from organizations associated with the Union. A citation is presented to the winner. Established in 1969.

2302
Presidential Commendation
For recognition of those who have undertaken a particular or specific outstanding service for the Union. Nominations are accepted from organizations associated with the Union. A citation is presented to the winner. Established in 1982. A Letter of Commendation is also awarded.

2303
British Cartographic Society
c/o Bartholomew
Unit 4, Manchester Park   Phone: 256 20123
Tewkesbury Rd.   Phone: 256 491518
Cheltenham, Glos. GL51 9EJ, England   Fax: 256 22575

2304
John Bartholomew Award
For recognition of excellence in small scale thematic cartography. Submissions are accepted from any individual or organization by May 1 each year. A certificate and a plaque are awarded annually at the September symposium. Established in 1980. Sponsored by John Bartholomew and Sons Ltd.

2305
British Cartographic Society Design Award
For recognition of the most outstanding map produced by a member. Members of the Society may apply by May 1 each year. A medal and a trophy are awarded annually at the September symposium. Established in 1978.

2306
Keuffel and Esser Awards
For recognition of meritorious work by cartography students. United Kingdom students who are at Ordinary BTEC Level and Higher Level Tec. by July 20 are eligible. A certificate and drawing instruments are awarded annually at the September symposium. Established in 1978. Sponsored by Keuffel and Esser Ltd.

2307
Laser Scan Award in Digital Cartography
For recognition of meritorious work by students in the field of digital cartography. United Kingdom students in digital cartography who will hold the equivalent of a first year degree or diploma by April 15 are eligible. A certificate and a micro-computer are awarded annually at the September symposium. Established in 1985 and sponsored by Laser Scan Laboratories of Cambridge Ltd.

2308
National Geographic Society Award
To recognize students who have demonstrated outstanding achievement in cartography and to encourage the completion of a first degree course or the pursuit of a post-graduate course. A £500 scholarship is awarded. Established in 1993. Sponsored by National Geographic Society.

2309
Pyser-SGI Award
For recognition of the most outstanding article published in *The Cartographic Journal*. A monetary prize and a medal are awarded annually at the September symposium. Established in 1975. Formerly: Survey and General Instrument Company Award.

2310
British Chess Federation
9a Grand Parade
St. Leonards-on-Sea, E. Sussex TN38 0DD,
  England
Phone: 424 442500
Fax: 424 718372

2311
BCF Player of the Year
For recognition of the best annual performance in chess-play. The winner is chosen by a poll of chess writers and direct members. A monetary award and a plaque are presented annually. Established in 1984.

2312
Club of the Year
To encourage activity in chess clubs. Nominations are accepted for the award. A monetary award and a trophy are presented annually. Established in 1984.

2313
President's Award for Services to Chess
For recognition of outstanding contributions to the game of chess. Nominations are accepted. A monetary award and a plaque are presented annually. Established in 1983.

2314
British Coatings Federation
Alembic House
93 Albert Embankment
London SE1 7TY, England
Phone: 71 582 1185
Fax: 71 735 0616

Formerly: Paintmakers Association of Great Britain Limited.

2315
Silver Medal
For recognition of meritorious services to the industry of paint making. There are no restrictions to the award, although the prize is not normally given simply on retirement from high office. A special ex officio jury makes the awards. A medal is awarded annually at the conference. Established in 1981 in honor of Leslie Silver OBE.

2316
Venables Award
For recognition of the best original papers on practical aspects of the manufacture or use of thermoset powder coatings. Two monetary prizes of £400 and £200 and certificates were awarded annually at the luncheon of PA Powder Coatings group. Established in 1984 in honor of Gilbert Venables, a pioneer of Powder Coatings in Britain. (Discontinued)

2317
British Comparative Literature Association
St. John's College
Oxford OX1 3JP, England
Phone: 865 277381
Fax: 865 277435

2318
BCLA Translation Competition (EC Languages)
To encourage literary translation from any language of the European community into English. Literary translation includes poetry, fiction, or literary prose from any period. The deadline for submissions is December 15. A monetary prize of £350 for First Prize and £150 for Second Prize are awarded as well as publication in *Comparative Criticism*. Awarded annually in June or July. Established in 1983.

2319
BCLA Translation Competition (Non-EC Languages)
For recognition of literary translations from non-EC Languages into English. Literary translation includes poetry, fiction, or literary prose from any period. Awards are given in the following languages: Swedish - monetary prizes of £350 for First prize and £150 for Second prize are awarded biennially. Established by the Anglo-Swedish Literary Fund, SELTA, and the Swedish Embassy; Hebrew, Yiddish, and other languages on a Jewish theme - translations may be from Hebrew, Yiddish, or from any other language providing the material is on a Jewish theme. Monetary prizes of £350 for First prize and £150 for Second prize are awarded annually. Established by the Spiro Institute in memory of Hannah and Jacob Lieberman; Persian - monetary prizes of £350 for First prize and £150 for Second prize are awarded biennially. Established by the Foundation for Iranian Studies. The deadline for all entries is December 15. The prize-winning entries are published in the annual journal *Comparative Criticism* (Cambridge University Press). Bursaries may also be available for entrants at the British Centre for Translation of the University of East Anglia, Norwich, for those wishing to take up residence for a specific period up to a year. Established in 1991.

2320
British Computer Society
PO Box 1454
Station Rd.
Swindon SN1 1TG, England
Phone: 793 480269
Fax: 793 480270

2321
BCS Awards
This, the most prestigious form of acknowledgement in the computer industry, is given to encourage the very best in UK information technology and its applications. Awards are presented to projects demonstrating excellence and the relevance or significance of computing. The BCS Awards scheme is open to anyone working in the fields of computing and information technology in the United Kingdom. Nominations for the awards should refer to projects which either have come to fruition or, in the case of continuous or long-term projects, have demonstrated measureable achievement in the twelve months up to the closing date. Medalists are expected to demonstrate their project to an invited audience held in London at the end of the year. It is on this occasion that the winners are announced. Three awards are normally presented each year. Established in 1972.

2322
Alan Taylor Award
To recognize the organization judged to have run the most effective professional development scheme program during the year. Submissions are welcome from both established users and from companies preparing to introduce PDS. Entries must be limited to 1500 words and submitted by September 18. The presentation of the award to the winning organization is towards the end of the year at the House of Commons as part of the Computer Weekly Training Awards.

2323
Wilkes Award
To recognize the most outstanding paper in *The Computer Journal*. Authors under 30 years of age are eligible. Awarded annually.

2324
British Cycle Speedway Council
Central Office
57 Rectory Lane
Poringland
Norwich NR14 7SW, England Phone: 508 493880
 Fax: 508 493880

Formed by merger of: (1972) British Cycle Speedway Federation; National Amateur Cycle Speedway Association.

2325
Wilkinson Sword Award of Merit
To recognize an individual(s) who has made the greatest contribution to the sport of Cycle Speedway. Individuals may be nominated by representatives of the BCSC. A sword trophy mounted on a plaque is awarded annually in November at the general meeting of the Council. Established in 1979. Co-sponsored by Wilkinson Sword.

2326
British Cycling Federation
36 Rockingham Rd.
Kettering, Northhants. NN16 8HG, England Phone: 536 412211
 Fax: 536 412142

Formerly: (1959) National Cyclists Union.

2327
Gold Badge of Honour
For recognition of service to the federation. Members of the federation who have given outstanding service over a number of years are eligible and must be passed by a two-thirds majority of the National Council. A gold brooch badge is awarded when merited. Established in 1959.

2328
British Deaf Association
38 Victoria Pl.
Carlisle CA1 1HU, England Phone: 228 48844
 Fax: 338 41420

2329
Medal of Honour
For recognition of services to the British deaf community. Individuals who are British or foreign, deaf or hearing, members or nonmembers may be nominated. A medal is awarded at the Congress or occasionally at a conference. Established in 1959.

2330
British Direct Marketing Association Ltd.
Haymarket House
London SW1Y 4EE, England Phone: 71 6307322
 Fax: 71 3212525

2331
DMA/Royal Mail Direct Marketing Awards
To recognize outstanding work in direct marketing in each of 27 categories such as mail order, direct mail, fund raising, and multimedia. The material needs to fulfill the criteria requirements for its particular category and to have appeared between September and August of the previous year. A gold award is presented for the most outstanding work in any category, and a trophy is presented to the winner in each of the 27 categories. Awarded annually. Established in 1980 and sponsored by Royal Mail Streamline. Formerly: BDMA/Post Office Direct Marketing Awards.

2332
British Ecological Society
Burlington House
Piccadilly
London W1V 0LQ, England Phone: 71 4342641

2333
BES Fellowships and Grants
To provide funds for research. Awards presented include: BES Expedition Grants - up to £1,000 to groups or societies organizing overseas expeditions with objectives to widen the ecological experience of the participants as well as to produce publishable data; BES Travelling Fellowships; and Small Ecological Grants Scheme. Awarded annually.

2334
President's Medal
To recognize individuals in mid-career for exceptional achievement in ecology. Awarded biennially when merited.

2335
British Fantasy Society
15 Stanley Rd.
Morden, Surrey SM4 5DE, England Phone: 1 540 9443

2336
British Fantasy Awards
To recognize the best novel, anthology or collection, short story, artist, newcomer and small press magazine published/released in the science fiction, fantasy and horror genre. Material published in the calendar year prior to the award may be submitted. A trophy (statuette) is awarded annually at the British Fantasy Convention (FANTASYCON). The August Derleth Award is given in the Best Novel category, and the Icarus Award, sponsored by the Icarus SF Group in Birmingham, for the Best Newcomer. Established in 1971 in memory of August Derleth, author, editor and publisher, for his contribution to the fantasy field. Formerly: (1977) August Derleth Fantasy Award.

2337
British Fashion Council
British Apparel & Textile Centre
7 Swallow Pl.
London W1R 7AA, England Phone: 71 4080020
 Fax: 71 4936276

2338
Lloyds Bank British Fashion Awards
To recognize British designers for achievement in fashion. Awards are given in the following categories: best designer, British Glamour (or evening wear), innovative designer (or young designer), knitwear, British Classics, couture and accessories, and Design led Retailer. Trophies are awarded annually. A Hall of Fame Award is also given. Established in 1984. Formerly: British Fashion Council Awards; British Fashion Council Awards.

2339
British Federation of Film Societies
FSU
21 Stephen St.
London W1P 1PL, England Phone: 71 2551444
 Fax: 71 4367950

2340
Film Society of the Year Award
For recognition of outstanding achievement and/or development of an individual society. Societies registered with the British Federation of Film Societies may apply or be nominated. The Basil Engholm Trophy is awarded annually at the national spring event held in London. Additional awards are presented for: School Film Society, Program of Films, Student Film Society, Program Notes, New Film Society, Publicity, Film of the

Year, and Roebuck Cup. Established in 1969 by Sir Basil Engholm in honor of the past chairman of the British Film Institute. Sponsored by the British Film Institute.

2341
Kodak Community Award
For recognition of a member film society that has achieved outstanding or innovative work within its community for the benefit of all. A monetary award of £450 and a certificate were awarded annually. Established in 1972. (Discontinued in 1986)

2342
British Film Institute
21 Stephen St.
London W1P 1PL, England
Phone: 71 2551444
Fax: 71 4367950

2343
Anthony Asquith Award
For recognition of outstanding achievement in film music. Awards are given in two categories: Young Composer Award - for the composition of music for television or film; and Film Music Award. Established in memory of Anthony Asquith, a film director. (Discontinued)

2344
BFI Fellowships
To provide recognition for outstanding achievements in film and television. A trophy is awarded annually at a gala evening. Established in 1983.

2345
BFI Film Award
For recognition of outstanding achievement in the fields of film and television. Established in 1958 in honor of the Duke of Sutherland, a former chairman of the Institute. Formerly: (1973) Sutherland Trophy.

2346
BFI Special Awards
To provide recognition for outstanding contributions to film amd television culture in originality and imaginativeness. The following awards are given: Archival Achievement, Career in the Industry, and BFI Award for Innovation. Nominations must be submitted by May. A trophy is awarded annually at a gala evening.

2347
Grierson Award
To provide recognition for the outstanding documentary film of the year. A trophy is awarded annually at a gala evening. Established in 1983.

2348
Mari Kuttna Award
For recognition of the best animated film produced by a new animator. Established in 1983.

2349
Michael Powell Book Award
For recognition of a book that advances the moving image culture. Established in 1983.

2350
British Fire Services Association
86 London Rd.
Leicester, Leics. 2 0QR, England
Phone: 533 542879

2351
Gallantry Medal
For recognition of gallantry. Members of the fire service engaged in operations are eligible. A medal and citation are awarded when merited. Established in 1949.

2352
Meritorious Service Decoration
For recognition of outstanding service to the Association. Members of the Association are eligible. A medal and citation are awarded when merited. Established in 1949.

2353
British Glass Manufacturers Confederation
Northumberland Rd.
Sheffield, S. Yorks. S1O 2UA, England
Phone: 742 686201
Fax: 742 681073

Formed by merger of: Formed by merger of: British Glass Industry Research Association; Glass Manufacturers Federation..

2354
British Glass Manufacturers Confederation Awards
To recognize manufacturers of glass and glass products in the British Isles for glass container design. (Currently inactive)

2355
British Government
Central Chancery of the Orders of
 Knighthood
St. James' Palace
London SW1A 1BG, England

2356
Air Force Cross
To recognize officers and warrant officers of the Royal Air Force for outstanding services in flying operations not against the enemy. It can also be awarded to equivalent ranks of the Royal Navy and the Army for similar services. Instituted in 1919.

2357
Air Force Medal
To recognize non-commissioned ranks of the Royal Air Force for outstanding services in flying operations not against the enemy. It can also be awarded to equivalent ranks of the Royal Navy and the Army for similar services. Instituted in 1919.

2358
Albert Medal
For gallantry in saving life at sea or on land. A medal and a £100 tax free annuity are awarded.

2359
British Empire Medal
To recognize men and women who do not qualify by rank for the higher awards in the Order of the British Empire.

2360
Conspicuous Gallantry Medal
To recognize petty officers and seamen of the Royal Navy, non-commissioned officers and men of the Royal Marines and equivalent ranks in the other armed forces, or to men of the Merchant navy, for acts of conspicuous gallantry in the face of the enemy at sea. Instituted in 1874.

2361
Distinguished Conduct Medal
To recognize non-commissioned officers and men of the Army for gallantry and leadership in action. Instituted in 1854.

2362
Distinguished Flying Cross
To recognize officers and warrant officers for bravery in air operations against the enemy. It can also be awarded to equivalent ranks of the Royal Navy and the Army for similar services. Instituted in 1918.

2363
Distinguished Flying Medal
To recognize non-commissioned ranks of the Royal Air Force for bravery in air operations against the enemy. It can also be awarded to equivalent ranks of the Royal Navy and the Army for similar services. Instituted in 1918.

2364
Distinguished Service Cross
To recognize officers and warrant officers of the fighting services for distinguished services at sea in the presence of the enemy. It may also be awarded to officers of the Merchant Navy. Instituted in 1914.

2365
Distinguished Service Medal
To recognize petty officers and men of the Royal Navy; non-commissioned officers and men of the Royal Marines; equivalent ranks in the other armed forces; and men of the Mercantile Marine for gallantry in the face of the enemy at sea which is not sufficient to merit the Conspicuous Gallantry Medal. Instituted in 1914.

2366
Distinguished Service Order
To honor gallantry and leadership in action displayed by officers of the armed forces of the Crown. It can be awarded to officers of the Merchant Navy. It is now the only gallantry award which cannot be given posthumously. Instituted in 1886.

2367
Edward Medal
For recognition of heroic acts by miners and quarrymen, or by others who have endangered their lives in rescuing those so employed. A medal and a £100 tax free annuity are awarded.

2368
George Cross
To honor great heroism or conspicuous courage. It was intended primarily for civilians but is not limited to them; in practice more servicemen and women have received it than civilians. A tax-free annuity of £100 a year is payable to holders of the Cross. Instituted in 1940.

2369
George Medal
For recognition of an act of bravery that has not been sufficiently outstanding to merit the Cross. It can be awarded to foreigners. Instituted in 1940.

2370
Imperial Service Order
To honor civil servants for their work throughout the British Empire. The only rank is that of Companion. Founded in 1902.

2371
Military Cross
To recognize ranks between Major and Warrant Officer inclusive for gallant and distinguished services in the presence of the enemy on land. Instituted in 1914.

2372
Military Medal
To recognize non-commissioned members of the Army for bravery under fire. Instituted in 1916.

2373
Most Ancient and Most Noble Order of the Thistle
The Order consists of the Sovereign and 16 Knights. They include the former Prime Minister Lord Home of the Hirsel. Royal Knights and Extra Knights are admitted by special statutes. The Order is conferred on the personal decision of the Sovereign. Created in 787 and revived in 1687 by James II.

2374
Most Distinguished Order of St. Michael and St. George
For recognition of service overseas or in connection with foreign or Commonwealth affairs. The Grand Master is the Duke of Kent. Ranks in the Order, and their customary abbreviations, are: (1) Knight or Dame Grand Cross G.C.M.G.; (2) Knight or Dame Commander - K.C.M.G. or D.C.M.G.; and (3) Companion - C.M.G. Founded in 1818.

2375
Most Excellent Order of the British Empire
To recognize civilians or service personnel for public services or other distinctions. The Grand Master is the Duke of Edinburgh. There are two divisions, military and civil. Ranks in the Order, which is open to both sexes, and the customary abbreviations, are: (1) Knight or Dame Grand Cross - G.B.E.; (2) Knight or Dame Commander - K.B.E. or D.B.E.; (3) Commander - C.B.E.; (4) Officer - O.B.E.; and (5) Member - M.B.E. Founded in 1917.

2376
Most Honourable Order of the Bath
For recognition of conspicuous services to the Crown. This Order is open to both sexes. The Great Master and First or Principal Knight Grand Cross is the Prince of Wales. There are two divisions, military and civil. Ranks in the order, and their customary abbreviations, are: (1) Knight or Dame Grand Cross: G.C.B.; (2) Knight or Dame Commander: K.C.B. or D.C.B.; and (3) Companion: C.B. Established as a separate order in 1725 but with medieval origins.

2377
Most Noble Order of the Garter
The Order consists of the Sovereign, the Duke of Edinburgh, the Prince of Wales, certain lineal descendants of King George I, if selected, and 24 other members (excluding other sons of the Sovereign and Ladies of the Garter). Foreigners, normally sovereigns, can be admitted as Extra Knights or Ladies. The Order is conferred on the personal decision of the Sovereign. Established in 1348.

2378
Order of Merit
For recognition of eminent services rendered in the armed services, or towards the advancement of art, literature and science. It is open to both sexes. The Order is limited to 24 members, plus foreign honorary members. The insignia is awarded in either a military or a civil form. Founded in 1902.

2379
Order of the Companions of Honour
For recognition of service of conspicuous national importance. The Order is open to both sexes and is limited to 65 persons. The only rank is that of Companion and the award carries no title. Founded in 1917.

2380
Polar Medal
To recognize individuals who have made notable contributions to the exploration and/or knowledge of the Polar Regions and who, in so doing, have undergone the hazards and rigors imposed by a Polar environment to life and movement. Expeditioners to Polar Regions who have spent not less than twelve months in a Polar climate (usually including a winter) are eligible. A silver, octagonal medal is awarded by Her Majesty the Queen. Established in 1857 by Queen Victoria and authorized by King Edward VII in 1904.

2381
Queen's Fire Service Medal for Gallantry
For recognition posthumously. There is also the Queen's Fire Service Medal for Distinguished Service. Instituted in 1954.

2382
Queen's Gallantry Medal
To recognize acts of exemplary bravery. The medal is intended primarily for civilians but may be awarded to military personnel for actions for which purely military honors are not granted. Instituted in 1974.

2383
Queen's Police Medal for Gallantry
For recognition posthumously. There is also The Queen's Police Medal for Distinguished Service. Instituted in 1954.

2384
Royal Red Cross
To recognize exceptional services by nurses rendered in any of the fighting services. There is also a second class of award known as "Associate." Instituted in 1883.

2385
Royal Victorian Order
To reward services to the Royal Family. The Grand Master is Queen Elizabeth The Queen Mother. Ranks in the Order, which is open to both sexes, and the customary abbreviations, are: (1) Knight or Dame Grand Cross - G.C.V.O.; (2) Knight or Dame Commander - K.C.V.O. or D.C.V.O.; (3) Commander - C.V.O.; (4) Member 4th Class - M.V.O.; and (5) Member 5th Class - M.V.O. Instituted in 1896 by Queen Victoria.

2386
Sea Gallantry Medal
For recognition of gallantry at sea. A silver bronze medal is awarded. Instituted by an Act of Parliament in 1854. Formerly: Board of Trade Medal for Life Saving at Sea.

2387
Victoria Cross
This, the most esteemed of all British gallantry medals, is given to honor outstanding valor in the presence of the enemy. Normally intended for servicemen but it may be conferred on civilians serving under military command. A tax-free annuity of £100 a year is payable to holders of the Cross. Instituted in 1856.

2388
British Grassland Society
No. 1 Earley Gate
Univ. of Reading
Reading, Berks. RG6 2AT, England
Phone: 734 318189
Fax: 734 666941

2389
British Grassland Society Award
To acknowledge those who have made an outstanding contribution to the understanding or application of grassland and forage crop husbandry and technology. A member of the Society may be nominated by any one member supported by two others. A trophy is awarded annually at the Winter Meeting in December. Established in 1979.

2390
British Herdsmens' Club
9, Kings Meadow
Gt. Cornard
Sudbury, Suffolk CO10 OHP, England
Phone: 787 73137

2391
Herdsman of the Year
To recognize an outstanding herdsman. The competition includes dairy and beef cattle, pig and sheep raising and technical knowledge. Members are eligible. A trophy is awarded annually. The Club was established in 1894.

2392
British Holstein Society
Foley House
28 Worcester Rd.
Malvern, Hereford and Worcs. WR14 4QW, England
Phone: 68 45 65477
Fax: 68 48 93290

Formerly: British Canadian Holstein Society.

2393
Herds Competition
For recognition of contributions in cow productivity based on the production of herds of cows. Members of the Society are eligible. Trophies are awarded in the following categories: small herds; medium herds - the Jim Jackson C.B.E. Cup; intermediate herds; and large herds. Trophies are awarded annually at the summer meeting in October. Additional awards include the Philip Outhwaite Trophy, Newby Trophy, Crab Apple Cup, and Iron Grandma Award. Established in 1974.

2394
British Institute of Architectural Technicians
397 City Rd.
London EC1V 1NE, England
Phone: 71 278 2206
Fax: 71 837 3194

Formerly: (1986) Society of Architectural and Associated Technicians.

2395
Architectural Technician of the Year Award
To recognize excellence and innovation in the construction industry. Open to all. Awards are presented in two categories: housing and non-housing. Each category winner receives a monetary and a plaque. One of the category winners is named Architectural Technician of the Year. The overall winner receives an additional prize and an engraved commemorative trophy. Established in 1990. Sponsored by Building Design & New Barbicon Motel.

2396
BIAT/Pugh Award
To encourage professional development and communication within the construction industry. Papers may be submitted on specified subjects by July 31. A monetary prize and a plaque are awarded biennially. Established in 1982 in honor of Pugh, who donated a sum of money to SAAT (now BIAT) for the award. Additional information is available from the Secretary of National Technical Committee, BIAT.

2397
BIAT Student Award
For recognition of achievements of students in courses leading to architectural technician qualifications and their college. The judging takes place at regional and national levels. Groups undertaking project work in a recognized course may be nominated by the college by June 30. Plaques and certificates are awarded to students as well as one year's free associate membership of the institute. A trophy and monetary prize are awarded to the college. Awarded annually at a special awards ceremony. Established in 1983. Additional information is available from the Education and Membership Offices. Formerly: BIAT National Student Award.

2398
British Institute of Non-Destructive Testing
1 Spencer Parade
Northampton NN1 5AA, England
Phone: 604 30124
Fax: 604 231489

2399
John Grimwade Medal
To recognize the best paper written in the *British Journal of Non-Destructive Testing*. Works by any member of the institute are automatically eligible for consideration. A medal is presented at the Annual

British Conference on NDT. Established in 1981 in memory of John G. Grimwade, an Honorary Fellow of the institute.

2400
Hugh MacColl Award
For recognition of practical innovation in non-destructive testing condition monitoring. Nominations must be submitted by December 31. A certificate is awarded and £300 is held in credit for the recipient to spend in improving his technical education. Awarded annually at the institute's conference. Established in 1988 in memory of Hugh MacColl, a founder member of the NDT Society of Great Britain and a pioneer of NDT education.

2401
Nemet Award
To recognize examples of outstandingly effective use of NDT, especially those that might encourage small firms to apply NDT methods for the first time. Nominations must be submitted by December 31. A certificate is awarded to the company operating the successful scheme, and a monetary prize of £500 to the person or persons nominated by the company as responsible for the innovation. Awarded annually at the institute's conference. Established in 1989 by the generosity of Dr. A. Nemet.

2402
Roy Sharpe Prize
To recognize a significant contribution through research and development in any branch of NDT to the benefit of industry or society. Nominations must be submitted by December 31. A certificate plus a monetary prize to the winner are presented by the sponsoring company. Awarded annually at the institute's conference. Established in 1989 in honor of Roy Sharpe.

2403
British Institute of Radiology
36 Portland Pl.
London W1N 4AT, England
Phone: 71 5804085
Fax: 71 2553209

2404
3M Mayneord Memorial Lecture
To recognize an individual or group of collaborators for recent or current contributions to radiology. Nominations must be submitted by March 31 of each year. An honorarium of £250, a plaque, and expenses are awarded each year at the annual conference. Established in 1984 in memory of Professor W. V. Mayneord CBE FRS, past president and honorary member of the Institute.

2405
Barclay Medal
To recognize an individual whose contribution to the *British Journal of Radiology* over a period of years has been of special merit, contributing materially to the science and practice of radiology. Members and nonmembers of the Institute are eligible. A medal is awarded annually in January or February at the BIR Conversazione. Established in 1952 in memory of Dr. Alfred Ernest Barclay, who by his will bequeathed to the Institute a legacy for the general purposes of the *British Journal of Radiology*.

2406
Barclay Prize
To recognize a member whose contribution to the *British Journal of Radiology* is of special merit. The subject of the contribution must be diagnostic radiology, which includes the clinical or experimental aspects or physics relating to this field. A certificate is awarded annually in January or February at the BIR Conversazione. Established in 1952 in memory of Dr. Alfred Ernest Barclay.

2407
BIR Travel Bursaries
To enable younger members of the Institute to present a paper at a national or international meeting. All members age 35 or under who have been members of the Institute for one year prior to their application are eligible. Applications must be sent to the Chief Executive by the end of July. A monetary award of £500 is awarded annually. Established in 1991.

2408
Clinical MRI Prize
To recognize the best proffered paper on magnetic resonance imaging and to promote the study and dissemination of information in this field. Individuals under 40 years of age are eligible. The presentation is judged on both scientific and potential clinical value. A monetary prize of £50 and a commemorative statuette are awarded at the BIR Annual Congress.

2409
Mackenzie Davidson Lecture
To provide support for a lecture on radiology by a member of the medical profession. Nominations must be sent to the Chief Executive by the end of May. A monetary award of £50, a medal, and expenses to attend and deliver the lecture at the BIR Annual Congress are awarded each year. Established in 1920 in memory of Sir James Mackenzie Davidson, a pioneer in British radiology.

2410
Flude Memorial Prize
To recognize a member who has conducted research that has significantly advanced the science and practice of radiology. All members of the Institute are eligible. A monetary award of £125 is awarded. Established in 1992 by Royston Flude, a member of the Institute, in memory of his late father, Arthur Charles Edwin Flude.

2411
Leonard Levy Memorial Prize
To recognize the best paper submitted to the BIR Congress by a younger member. Members of the Institute who are under 30 years of age are eligible. In the case of multiple authorship, the prize is awarded to the leading author. A monetary award or a book up to the value of £125 is awarded. Established in 1992 by Bennett-Levy and Levy Hill Laboratories in memory of the late Dr. Leonard Levy.

2412
Nic McNally Memorial Prize
To enable an individual to travel to either a scientific meeting or another laboratory. Young scientists under 35 years of age at the date of application, both members and nonmembers, and employed in a scientific post are eligible. A travel busary is awarded annually. Established by the friends, collegues, and BIR staff in memory of Dr. Nic McNally, a long-serving honorary editor of the *British Journal of Radiology* and President-elect of the BIR before his untimely death in 1991.

2413
Stanley Melville Award
To enable members of the Institute to visit clinics and institutions abroad. Members who are 35 years of age or under are eligible. The deadline for applications is the end of December. A grant for traveling expenses is awarded triennially. Established in 1946 in honor of Dr. Stanley Melville.

2414
Nycomed Scandinavian Scholarships
To enable members to visit clinics in Scandinavia for up to two months to study diagnostic and interventional radiological procedures. Open to radiologists of Senior Registrar or Junior Consultant status with an interest in diagnostic or interventional procedures concerned with intravascular contrast media. The deadline for applications is the end of August. Established in 1985 through the financial assistance of Nycomed (UK) Ltd.

2415
***RAD Magazine* Best Poster Prize**
To encourage and maintain a high standard of visual and scientific presentation for posters submitted to the BIR Annual Congress. Individuals presenting a poster at the Congress are considered. Three prizes are awarded: first prize - £100; second prize - £50; and third prize - £25.

Established in 1992 by Kingsmoor Publications Ltd., publishers of *RAD Magazine*.

2416

Rontgen Prize
To recognize a member, or a team of workers including a member, whose contribution to the *British Journal of Radiology* has been of special merit. The subject of the contribution must have been radiotherapy, radiobiology, or physics relating to these fields. A certificate is awarded at the BIR Conversazione or other BIR event. Established in 1924 in memory of W. C. Rontgen.

2417

Silvanus Thompson Memorial Lecture
To provide support for a lecture on radiology by an individual who is not a member of the medical profession. Nominations must be sent to the Chief Executive by the end of May. A monetary award of £50, a medal, and paid expenses to attend and deliver the lecture at the BIR Annual Congress are awarded each year. Established in 1918 in memory of Professor Silvanus P. Thompson, the first president of the Rontgen Society.

2418

Tubiana Award
To enable a member of the Institute to visit radiotherapy centers in Paris, France. A monetary award of £200 towards travel and subsistence costs associated with the visit is awarded annually.

2419

British International Print Exhibition
Asst. Keeper of Exhibitions
Cartwright Hall, Lister Park
Bradford, W. Yorks. BD9 4NS, England
Phone: 274 493313
Fax: 274 481045

2420

British International Print Exhibition
For recognition of the best contemporary prints in an international exhibition that was held every three years. (Discontinued)

2421

British Interplanetary Society
27/29 S. Lambeth Rd.
London SW8 1SZ, England
Phone: 71 7353161
Fax: 71 8201501

2422

Honorary Fellow
To recognize individuals for exceptional contributions to astronautics and to the work of the Society. Honorary Fellowship is awarded as merited. The total is limited to 10 at any one time. Established in 1946.

2423

Silver Plaque
For recognition of outstanding achievements in astronautics. Organizations are eligible. A silver trophy is awarded as merited. Established in 1954.

2424

Space Achievement Medal
To recognize an individual for contributions of outstanding merit to astronautics. A gold or bronze medal is awarded as merited. Established in 1954.

2425

British Lichen Society
Dept. of Plant Sciences
Univ. of Bath
Bath, Avon BA2 7AY, England
Phone: 225 826826
Fax: 225 826779

2426

British Lichen Society Awards
To recognize professional, academic, and amateur lichenologists involved in research. Awards are bestowed annually at the convention in January.

2427

British Medical Association
Board of Science and Education
BMA House
Tavistock Sq.
London WC1H 9JP, England
Phone: 71 383-6240
Fax: 71 383 6233

2428

BLITHE Video Seal of Educational Value
To stimulate the production of a greater number of videos that contributed to effective learning in medical and health education. Established in 1984. (Discontinued in 1988) Formerly: BLAT Video Seal of Educational Value.

2429

BMA Film and Video Competition
To encourage the production of films which are effective in medical and health education. This is an open competition. Gold, silver and bronze medals, and certificates of educational merit are presented annually. Established in 1957.

2430

BMA Medicine in the Media Award
For recognition of films of outstanding educational merit in the fields of medicine and health education at the BMA Film and Video Competition. Films originally produced for broadcast television are eligible. Established in 1968 and restructured in 1991. Formerly: ABI/BMA Trophy.

2431

Brackenbury Award
For recognition of research of immediate practical importance to public health, to a medico-political or medico-sociological problem, or to an educational question whether general medical or postgraduate. Candidates must be members of the Association. A monetary prize is awarded triennially.

2432

John William Clark Award
For recognition of research into the causes of blindness. Candidates must be members of the Association. A monetary prize is awarded annually.

2433

Annie Clegg Award
For recognition of research in the field of medicine. Each year the research is defined by the Board of Science and Education. Candidates must be registered medical practitioners. A monetary prize is awarded annually.

2434

Vera Down Award
For recognition of research into disseminated sclerosis, muscular dystrophy and neurological disorders. Candidates must be registered medical practitioners. A monetary prize is awarded annually.

2435

Charlotte Eyck Award
For recognition of outstanding work in the field of medicine. Each year, the research is defined by the Board of Science and Education. Candidates must be registered medical practitioners. A monetary prize is awarded annually.

[2436]

Gold Medal for Distinguished Merit
To recognize individuals who have conspicuously raised the character of the medical profession by scientific work, by extra-ordinary professional services, or by special services rendered to the British Medical Association. A gold medal is awarded when merited. Established in 1877.

[2437]

T. P. Gunton Award
For recognition of research into health education with special regard to the early diagnosis and treatment of cancer. Both medical and non-medical researchers are eligible. A monetary prize is awarded annually.

[2438]

Katherine Bishop Harman Award
To assist research into the diminution and avoidance of risks to health and life in pregnancy and child-bearing. Candidates must be medical practitioners registered in the United Kingdom or any country at any time forming part of the British Empire. A monetary prize is awarded biennially.

[2439]

Nathaniel Bishop Harman Award
For recognition of research in regard to the outcome of treatment in hospital practice. Candidates must be registered medical practitioners on the staff of a hospital in Great Britain or Northern Ireland and not members of the staff of a recognized undergraduate or post-graduate medical school. A monetary prize is awarded biennially.

[2440]

Sir Charles Hastings Award
For recognition of observation, research and record keeping in general practice. Candidates must be members of the Association and engaged in general practice. A monetary prize is awarded biennially.

[2441]

Charles Oliver Hawthorne Award
For recognition of observation, research and record keeping in general practice. Candidates must be members of the Association and engaged in general practice. A monetary prize is awarded biennially.

[2442]

Doris Hillier Award
For recognition of research into rheumatism, arthritis and/or Parkinson's Disease. Candidates must be registered medical practitioners. A monetary prize is awarded annually.

[2443]

Geoffrey Holt Award
For recognition of research into cardiovascular and respiratory disease. Candidates must be members of the Association. A monetary prize is awarded annually.

[2444]

Insole Award
For recognition of research into the causation, prevention or treatment of disease. Candidates must be members of the Association. A monetary prize is awarded biennially.

[2445]

T. V. James Fellowship
For recognition of and to assist research into the nature, causation, prevention or treatment of bronchial asthma. Members of the Association are eligible. A monetary prize is awarded annually.

[2446]

Harold E. Lewis Award for Research
To encourage the development of film techniques in the service of medical researchers. (Discontinued)

[2447]

Albert McMaster Award
For recognition of cancer research. Candidates must be members of the Association. A monetary prize is awarded annually.

[2448]

Middlemore Award
For recognition of research in any branch of ophthalmic medicine or surgery. Any registered medical practitioner is eligible. A monetary prize is awarded triennially.

[2449]

C. H. Milburn Award
For recognition of research in medical jurisprudence and/or forensic medicine. Candidates must be registered medical practitioners. A monetary prize is awarded biennially.

[2450]

Doris Odlum Award
For recognition of research in the field of mental health. Candidates must be medical practitioners registered in the British Commonwealth or the Republic of Ireland. A monetary prize is awarded biennially.

[2451]

H. C. Roscoe Fellowship
To promote research into the elimination of the common cold and/or diseases of the human respiratory system. Candidates must be members of the Association or non-medical scientists working in association with a member. A monetary prize is awarded annually.

[2452]

Helen Tomkinson Award
For recognition of cancer research. Candidates must be members of the Association. A monetary prize is awarded annually.

[2453]

E. Townsend Award
For recognition of research in the field of medicine. Each year the research is defined by the Board of Science and Education. Candidates must be registered medical practitioners. A monetary prize is awarded annually.

[2454]

Edith Walsh Award
For recognition of research in cardiovascular and respiratory disease. Candidates must be members of the Association. A monetary prize is awarded annually.

[2455]

Elizabeth Wherry Award
For recognition of research into kidney disease. Candidates must be registered medical practitioners. A monetary prize is awarded annually.

[2456]

British Mexican Society
60 Ellerby St.
London SW6 6EZ, England   Phone: 71 731 0556

[2457]

British Mexican Society Postgraduate Prize
For recognition of the best Ph.D. thesis on a topic relating to Mexico. The prize is open to students of any nationality and in any academic discipline. The thesis must be produced at a British university (or other institute of higher education). A monetary prize of £250 is awarded annually. Established in 1984.

2458
British Music Society
7 Tudor Gardens
Upminster, Essex RM14 3DE, England

2459
British Music Society Awards
To encourage the performance of neglected British music (especially by dead composers 1850-1950) through a contest for young performers. Students of a British music college may be nominated by the college. A certificate and recital are awarded biennially at the Society's annual general meeting. Established in 1988.

2460
British Nuclear Energy Society
The Institution of Civil Engineers
1-7 Great George St., Westminster
London SW1P 3AA, England   Phone: 71 630 0726

2461
British Nuclear Energy Society Travelling Scholarships
To provide an opportunity for members of any age to make a contribution to nuclear science or engineering in fields beyond their normal employment or course of education. One or more Travelling Scholarships were awarded annually. Established in 1982. (Discontinued)

2462
Plowden Prize
For recognition of the best paper contributed by a person under 35 years of age to *Nuclear Energy*, the journal of the Society. Papers that have not been published elsewhere are eligible. A monetary award of £250 and the opportunity to apply for a travel sponsorship of up to £1,000 are awarded annually when merited. Established in 1984 in honor of Lord Plowden.

2463
British Ornithologists' Union
c/o The Natural History Museum
Ornithology   Phone: 442 890 080
Tring, Herts. HP23 6AP, England   Fax: 442 890 693

2464
Godman-Salvin Medal
To recognize an individual for a diverse and substantial contribution to the development of ornithology. Awarded periodically when merited. Established in 1922.

2465
David Lack Studentship
To provide funds for a student to do research on a British Ornithologists' Union expedition. Applications are invited from graduate students working toward a Ph.D. degree. In addition, other research grants are awarded annually.

2466
Union Medal
To recognize individuals for eminent services to ornithology and to the Union. Established in 1912.

2467
British Paper and Board Industry Federation
Dir. Gen.
Papermakers House
Rivenhall Rd.
Westlea   Phone: 793 886086
Swindon SN5 7BD, England   Fax: 793 886182

Formerly: British Paper and Board Makers' Association.

2468
Paper Industry Gold Medal
To recognize an individual who has made an outstanding contribution to the affairs of the British paper and board industry. Individuals must be nominated by a special industry committee by November. A gold medal is awarded annually in the spring. Established in 1967 by Benn Brothers plc, and now sponsored by the Paper Industry. Formerly: *World's Paper Trade Review* Medal.

2469
British Pelargonium and Geranium Society
134 Montrose Ave.
Welling, Kent DA16 2QY, England   Phone: 81 8566137

Formerly: (1960) Geranium Society.

2470
Lady Astor Presidents Cup
For recognition of services to the Society and to the development of the plant. Members of the Society are eligible. A trophy is awarded annually. Established in 1960 by Lady Astor.

2471
British Philatelic Federation
British Philatelic Centre
107 Charterhouse St.   Phone: 71 251 5040
London EC1M 6PT, England   Fax: 71 490 4253

2472
Award of Merit
To recognize those stamp collectors who have performed outstanding volunteer work to advance the interest of philately at the local or regional level. Nominations are accepted. Certificates confirming that awardees' names have been entered in the Book of Merit are presented annually. Established in 1978. Additional information is available from Mrs. Lesley Hampton, Chairman BPF Awards Committee, Westcroft, 188 Exeter Road, Exmouth EX8 3DZ, England.

2473
Congress Medal
To recognize those stamp collectors whose outstanding activities to advance the interest of philately have been conducted on a national level. Nominations for the award may be made by a member or by any regional Federation Association, Society or other body affiliated with BPF. A medal is awarded annually. Established in 1959. Additional information is available from Mrs. Lesley Hampton, Chairman BPF Awards Committee, Westcroft, 188 Exeter Road, Exmouth EX8 3DZ, England.

2474
Distinguished Philatelist
To recognize a philatelist who is distinguished by having served philately either by research work made available to others or in some public or other capacity. Nominations may be made by former honorees or those associated with the Federation. The awardee is invited to sign the Roll of Distinguished Philatelists. Awarded annually. Established in 1921. Additional information is available from Mrs. Lesley Hampton, Chairman BPF Awards Committee, Westcroft, 188 Exeter Road, Exmouth EX8 3DZ, England.

2475
Honorary Member
To recognize individuals for outstanding service.

2476
Melville Junior Stamp Competition
To recognize outstanding junior stamp collections. There are four classes of competition for the following age groups: (1) 19-21 years of age; (2) 16-18 years of age; (3) 14-15 years of age; (4) 12-13 years of age;

and (5) up to 11 years of age. The competition is open to young stamp collectors in the United Kingdom and Eire. All entries must be submitted through societies affiliated with the British Philatelic Federation. Silver, Silver-Bronze, Bronze Medals, and Certificates may be awarded in each class. In addition, a silver trophy will be held for one year by the winner in each class. Awarded annually since 1949 by The Philatelic Congress of Great Britain. Additional information is available from Mrs. Lesley Hampton, Chairman BPF Awards Committee, Westcroft, 188 Exeter Road, Exmouth EX8 3DZ, England.

2477
British Phonographic Industry
25 Savile Row
London W1X 1AA, England
Phone: 71 287 4422
Fax: 71 287 2252

2478
BRIT Awards
For recognition of achievement in music. Awards are presented in the following categories: Best British Male Solo Artist, Best British Female Solo Artist, Best British Group, Best British Dance Act, Best Album by a British Artist, Best British Producer, Best British Newcomer, Best International Male Solo Artist, Best International Female Solo Artist, Best International Group, Best International Newcomer, Best Soundtrack/Cast Recording, Best Video by a British Artist, Best Single by a British Artist, and Outstanding Contribution to the British Music Industry. A silver Britannia statuette is awarded annually. Established in 1982.

2479
British Poultry Meat Federation
High Holborn House
52-54 High Holborn
London WC1V 6SX, England
Phone: 71 2424683
Fax: 71 8310624

2480
Tom Newman International Memorial Award
To recognize the author of a research work considered the most important contribution to poultry husbandry. A monetary award of £200 and a silver gilt medal are awarded annually.

2481
British Printing Industries Federation
11 Bedford Row
London WC1R 4DX, England
Phone: 71 2426904
Fax: 71 4057784

2482
British Book Design and Production Awards
To recognize outstanding book design and production.

2483
National Business Calendar Awards
To recognize outstanding printed calendars, to extend the use of printed business calendars, and to encourage high standards in their design and production. Awards are given in the following categories: Pictorial Bespoke Calendars; Typographic/Novelty Calendars; Stock Calendars; Robert Horne Student Calendar Awards; and Kodak Excellence in Colour Reproduction Award. Calendars must be for the forthcoming year, must have been produced for advertising or publicity purposes (not retail), and have been printed in Great Britain. A trophy is awarded to the publisher of the winning entry in each of the categories. Printers and designers of prize-winning calendars each receive a certificate. Publishers, printers, and designers of other entries that the judges consider to reach a high standard also receive certificates of merit. Additionally, the Kodak photographic trophy(ies) is awarded to the photographer(s) of the best commissioned photography in a calendar selected by the judges from the trophy and certificate winners in any category. Special certificates and £100 of book tokens are also awarded at the discretion of the judges to the winning student. Trophy winners have the right to reproduce the Awards motif for the year to publicize their success. Awarded annually in January. Established in 1968 by the London College of Printing. Co-sponsored by BPIF, Kodak Ltd, Robert Thorne, the British Advertising Calendar Association, Petrushkin, and the London College of Printing.

2484
Safety Awards
To promote high safety standards in the printing industry.

2485
British Psychological Society
St. Andrews House
48 Princess Rd. E.
Leicester LE1 7DR, England
Phone: 533 549568
Fax: 533 470787

2486
Book Award
To recognize the authors of recently published books that have made significant contributions to the advancement of psychology in one or more ways and are likely to achieve a noteworthy place in the literature of psychology. Candidates must be residents of the United Kingdom and must not have published their book prior to 1991. The deadline for nominations is June 17. A monetary award of £500 and a certificate are presented at the annual conference each year.

2487
British Psychological Society Prize for "A" Level Psychology
To recognize a student who has achieved the best results on the Associated Board "A" Level Psychology examination. A £150 bursary to the student for the purchase of study materials, £100 to the school or college attended by the winning candidate for the purchase of books and supplies concerned with psychology, and a certificate are awarded each year at the annual conference. In the event of a tie, prize money will be divided among the winners. Established in 1989.

2488
Honorary Fellow
To recognize an individual for an entire career in the field of psychology.

2489
Honorary Life Member
To recognize the major contribution individuals make to the development of the Society. The award consists of a commemorative certificate, free life membership of the Society, and free registration at a Society Conference each year. On occasions the award may be made to non-psychologists who have similarly made outstanding services to psychology through their involvement with the activities of the Society.

2490
Presidents' Award
For recognition of achievement in the field of scientific research that contributes to psychological knowledge. This mid-career award is intended as a timely acknowledgement of the achievements of those currently engaged in research of outstanding quality. Candidates who are normally residents of the United Kingdom are eligible. Honorary Life Membership in the Society, a certificate, and the opportunity to present a paper at a plenary session at the Society's annual conference are awarded each year. Established in 1981.

2491
Spearman Medal
For recognition of a published work of outstanding merit in psychology. Individuals with degrees in psychology obtained not longer than ten years ago are eligible. A medal is awarded annually. Established in 1965.

2492
British Quarter Horse Association
4th St., N.AC.
National Agricultural Center
Stoneleigh
Kenilworth, Warks. CV8 2LG, England
Phone: 203 696549
Fax: 203 696729

2493

Annual Awards
For recognition of outstanding quarter horses competing in open competition. The following prizes are awarded: (1) Manar Trophy for English ridden events; (2) Maccstone Trophy for western ridden events; (3) Earldoms Trophy for inhand events; (4) Duster Sport Trophy for Most Versatile Purebred; (5) Duster Sport Trophy for Most Versatile Partbred; (6) Oberleigh Trophy for junior riders; and (7) Channel Four Trophy for BQHA ridden events.

2494

Perpetual Trophy Awards
For recognition of outstanding Quarter Horses competing at the Annual Breed Show. The following named trophies are awarded: (1) Diablo - two trophies for purebred colt/filly foal; (2) Mountain Cash - partbred foal; (3) Earldoms - five separate trophies for purebred mares and geldings; (4) Duster's Sport Memorial - aged purebred stallion; (5) Grand Champion Trophies - Sterling Trophy for purebred mare, the Skipchipadee Trophy for purebred stallion, and the Zero Cassia Bay Trophy for a partbred mare; (6) Supreme Champion trophies - the Harley Trophy for purebred, and the Cara Mia Trophy for partbred; (7) Hollywood Challenge Trophy; (8) Snaffle-Bit Association Trophy; (9) Brynlow Gay Dusters Perpetual Trophy; (10) Showmanship awards - Steve Ward Shield for a purebred, Eventer for partbred, and Mister Brody for junior; (11) High point awards - Rowley for British bred, Holden British Equestrian, Waccabe for dressage, Champion Hyline Gentry for all round pure, and Tengate for all round partbred.

2495

British Science Fiction Association
60 Bournemouth Rd.
Folkestone, Kent CT19 5AZ, England   Phone: 303 252939

2496

British Science Fiction Association Awards
To recognize achievement in science fiction. Awards are presented in the following categories: novel, short fiction, and art. Awards are presented annually at the British National Science Fiction Convention, the Eastercon. Established in 1966 and reorganized in 1979.

2497

British Short Film Institute
BBC Threshold House, Rm. 313
65-69 Shepherds Bush Green
London W12 7RJ, England   Phone: 81 7438000
                                 Fax: 81 7408540

2498

British Short Film Festival
To recognize the best in British and International short films produced in the preceding two years. Short films of 40 minutes or less are eligible. The deadline for submissions is June 3.

2499

British Show Pony Society
124 Green End Rd.
Sawtry
Huntingdon, Cambs. PE17 5XA, England   Phone: 487 831376
                                              Fax: 487 832779

2500

British Show Pony Society Rosettes
To recognize a mare or gelding as the best pony of the year. Rosettes are awarded at all affiliated shows to the Champion and Reserve Show Pony, Working Horse Pony, and Show Hunter Pony.

2501

Show Hunter Ponies Awards
To recognize the best ponies of the year in the following areas: (1) Novice Show Hunter Pony; and (2) Open Show Hunter Pony. A mare or gelding, four years of age or over, that has not won a first prize of £5.00 prior to October 1, and that is registered with the Society is eligible for novice classes. Awards are presented at shows of the Society, and are awarded by a panel of judges.

2502

Show Ponies Awards
To provide recognition for the best show ponies of the year. The following general awards are given: (1) British show pony cups and trophies - to recognize members of the Society with ponies registered with the Society. A cup or trophy is presented annually, to be held for one year, and returned to the Society. Show ponies that are registered with the Society are eligible in the following categories: (1) Novice Show Pony - to a pony four years of age or older; (2) Three year old pony; and (3) Open Show Pony - to a pony four years of age or older. Ponies must not have won a first prize of £5.00 or over prior to October 1 to be eligible for novice classes. Cups and trophies are presented at shows of the Society, and are awarded by a panel of judges.

2503

Working Hunter Ponies Awards
To recognize the best ponies of the year in the following areas: (1) Novice Working Hunter Pony; and (2) Open Working Hunter Pony. A mare or gelding four years of age or over, that has not won a first prize of £5.00 or over prior to October 1, and that is registered with the Society is eligible for novice classes. Awards are presented at shows of the Society, and are awarded by a panel of judges.

2504

British Slot Car Racing Association
48 Wiltshire Gardens
Bransgore
Christchurch, Dorset BH23 8BJ, England   Phone: 425 672060

Formerly: (1983) Electric Car Racing Association.

2505

National Model Car Racing Champion
For recognition of model car racing champions in 3 classes: Grand Prix, Sports/GT, and Saloon. Members of the Association who have competed in the races are eligible. Trophies are awarded annually. Established in 1964.

2506

British Small Animal Veterinary Association
Church Ln.
Shurdington
Cheltenham, Glos. GLS1 5TQ, England   Phone: 242 862994
                                             Phone: 242 863009

2507

Amoroso Award
For recognition of outstanding contributions to small animal studies. Any non-clinical member of a University staff is eligible.

2508

Blaine Award
For recognition of outstanding contributions to the advancement of small animal medicine or surgery. Veterinarians and non-veterinarians are eligible for nomination.

2509

Bourgelat Award
For recognition of really outstanding contributions to the field of small animal practice. Anyone is eligible.

2510
Dunkin Award
For recognition of the most valuable article published in the JSAP by a small animal practitioner during the 12 months ending on October 31. Any small animal practitioner is eligible.

2511
Melton Award
For recognition of meritorious contributions by veterinary surgeons to small animal practice. Veterinary surgeons in general practice are eligible.

2512
Simon Award
For recognition of outstanding contributions in the field of veterinary surgery. Members of the Association are eligible.

2513
Woodrow Award
For recognition of outstanding contributions to the field of small animal veterinary medicine. Members of the Association are eligible.

2514
British Society for Antimicrobial Chemotherapy
Dept. of Infection and Tropical Medicine
Birmingham Heartlands Hospital
Birmingham B9 5ST, England
Phone: 21 7731740
Fax: 21 7668752

2515
Garrod Medal
For recognition of achievement in the field of antimicrobial chemotherapy. Nominations are made by the Council of the Society. A medal and an invitation to present the Garrod Memorial Lecture are awarded annually. Established in 1982 in honor of Paul Garrod.

2516
British Society for Research on Ageing
Univ. of Manchester
School of Biological Sciences
1.124 Stopford Bldg.
Oxford Rd.
Manchester M13 9PT, England
Phone: 61 2755252
Fax: 61 2755363

2517
Lord Cohen of Birkenhead Medal
For recognition of services to gerontology. Individuals who have made a considerable contribution to ageing research either through original research or in the promotion of the subject of gerontology in its broadest aspects are eligible for consideration. A medal is awarded annually when merited. The recipient delivers a lecture, if appropriate. Established in 1979 by Professor John Phillips FRS in honor of Lord Cohen of Birkenhead.

2518
British Society for Rheumatology
3 St. Andrew's Pl.
Regent's Park
London NW1 4LB, England
Phone: 71 224 3739
Fax: 71 224 0156

Formed by merger of: (1983) Heberden Society; British Association of Rheumatology and Rehabilitation.

2519
Margaret Holroyd Prize
To recognize excellence in the field of clinical rheumatology. Submissions of an essay on a topic of clinical interest that would not normally be laboratory-based from both senior and junior members are accepted. Relevant laboratory investigations are also accepted. A medal and L250 are presented at the Annual General Meeting. Established in 1993. For further information, contact Anne Mansfield, deputy executive secretary.

2520
Michael Mason Prize
For recognition of excellence in clinical or scientific research in the field of rheumatology. Members of the Society 40 years of age or younger may submit scientific papers based on their own research by October 28. A monetary prize of £500 and a medal are awarded annually at the annual general meeting. Established in 1986. Additional information is available from Anne Mansfield, deputy executive secretary.

2521
Non-Clinical Bursary
To encourage exchange of scientific data and development of scientific techniques. A discretionary award of L1,000 is available to postdoctoral scientists who wish to visit other units involved in rheumatology. Application deadline is September 16. For further information, contact Anne Mansfield, deputy executive secretary.

2522
British Society for the History of Science
Southide
31 High St.
Stanford-in-the-Vale
Faringdon, Oxon. SN7 8LH, England
Phone: 227 764000
Fax: 227 475423

2523
Singer Prize
For recognition of the best unpublished essay on any aspect of the history of science, including medicine and mathematics. Individuals who are under 35 years of age, or within five years of first registering for an appropriate postgraduate degree are eligible. A monetary prize of £250 is awarded biennially. Established in 1978 in honor of Professor Charles Singer.

2524
British Society for the Study of Orthodontics
BSSO Office, Eastman Dental Hospital
256 Grays Inn Rd.
London WC1X 8LD, England
Phone: 71 8372193
Fax: 71 8372193

2525
Chapman Prize Essay
To encourage professional development in the field of orthodontics. Individuals who have been qualified no more than 15 years may submit an essay on original work. A monetary prize and a certificate are awarded annually when merited. Established in 1960 in honor of Harold Chapman.

2526
Northcroft Memorial Lecture
For recognition of a contribution to orthodontics on an international basis. International reputation and original work are considered. A certificate is awarded annually when merited. Established in 1947 in honor of George Northcroft.

2527
British Society of Rheology
27 Alexander Rd.
Stotfold, Hitchin, Hereford and Worcs. SG5 4NA, England
Phone: 763 244280
Fax: 763 244298

2528
Annual Award
To recognize a significant or promising contribution and/or services to the advancement of rheology in any of its many aspects. Individuals, groups, or institutions are eligible. A certificate or monetary prize

appropriate to the nature and significance of the contribution is awarded annually. Established in 1978.

Scott Blair Scholarship
To encourage excellence in research in rheology and to enable the recipient (Ph.D. students or equivalent in their first years of research) to undertake research activities not normally possible without such a grant. Established in 1988 to commemorate the work and example of Dr. G.W. Scott Blair.

Gold Medal
To recognize distinguished work in the theory and application of rheology. Individual scientists are eligible. A gold medal is awarded irregularly. Established in 1966.

Pergamon Scott Blair Biorheology Scholarship
The award is similar to the BSR Scott Blair Scholarship, but the recipient must work in the field of biorheology. Established in 1989 to commemorate the work of the late Dr. G.W. Scott Blair, who was the first print editor of *Biorheology Journal*.

British Society of Scientific Glassblowers
Society Office
21 Grebe Ave., Eccleston Park
St. Helens, Merseyside WA10 3QL,
England
Phone: 51 709 1438
Fax: 51 707 0631

Bibby Cup
To encourage excellence in scientific borosilicate glassworking. Members of the society who have less than five years experience are eligible. A cup to be held for one year and a replica for the winner to keep are awarded annually at the symposium. Established in 1966 by James A. Jobling Ltd. Sponsored by J. Bibby Scientific Products. Formerly: (1983) Corning Cup.

Norman Collins Memorial Award
To provide an opportunity for experienced scientific glassblowers to demonstrate their outstanding skills in scientific glassware. All members of the society are eligible. Winners of the Bibby Cup and A.D. Wood Cup are automatically considered. A trophy to be held for one year is awarded annually at the symposium. Established in 1980 in memory of Norman Collins.

David Flack Memorial Trophy
To provide an opportunity for scientific glassblowers to express their artistic talent in the medium of glass. Members of the society are eligible. A trophy to be held for one year and a pewter tankard for the winner to keep are awarded annually at the symposium. Established in 1972 in memory of David Flack, by his parents.

Literary Prizes
For recognition of contributions to the society journal. Monetary awards and certificates of achievement are awarded annually. Established in 1981.

Lucy Oldfield Cup (Premier Award)
For recognition of contributions to the society journal. A trophy and certificates of achievement are awarded annually. Established in 1982 by Dr. Lucy Oldfield.

Thames Valley Award
To recognize a member who has contributed most to the society. A trophy to be held for one year is awarded annually at the annual symposium. Established in 1970 by members of the Thames Valley Section of the society.

TSL Trophy
To encourage excellence in scientific vitreous silica glassworking. All members of the society are eligible. A trophy to be held for one year and a pewter tankard for the winner to keep are awarded annually at the symposium. Established in 1969 by Thermal Syndicate, Ltd.

A. D. Wood Cup
To encourage excellence in scientific borosilicate glassworking. Members of the society who have less than three years experience are eligible. A cup to be held for one year and a replica for the winner to keep are awarded annually at the symposium. Established in 1966 by Mr. A.D. Wood of A.D. Wood Ltd.

British Society of Soil Science
Dept. of Soil Science
Univ. of Reading
Reading RG1 5AQ, England
Phone: 734 753 884
Fax: 734 869 858

Jubilee Prize
For recognition of the best paper published by a young scientist in the *European Journal of Soil Science*. Members of the Society who are under 35 years of age are eligible. A monetary prize of £25 and a medal are awarded annually. Established in 1975. Formerly: Silver Jubilee Award.

British Spotted Pony Society
Broomells Farm
Beare Green
North Dorking, Surrey RH5 4QQ, England
Phone: 935 89 14 66

Formerly: (1976) British Horse and Pony Society.

Breed Horse Show Awards
To encourage those people who study the difficult genetics of this rare and beautiful animal and attempt to keep a high standard of produce but seldom get enough credit for their work. British citizens who are present members of the British Spotted Pony Society are eligible.

Supreme Champion Awards
To encourage preservation of this rare breed. The following awards are presented: Supreme Champion - Gosling Trophy, Reserve Supreme Champion, Driving Champion, and Performance Championship - Adrian Walsh Trophy. Trophies are awarded annually. Established in 1985.

British Theatre Association
Cranbourn Mansions
Cranbourn St.
London WC2 H7AG, England
Phone: 71 935 2571

Defunct organization.

2547
***Drama* Magazine Awards**
For recognition of achievements in British theatre and to promote the art of the theater. Awards are given in the following categories: (1) Best New Play; (2) Best Director; (3) Best Designer; (4) Best Actor; (5) Best Actress; (6) Best Supporting Actor; (7) Best Supporting Actress; (8) Best Musical Production; (9) Best Young People's Theatre Award - 7 to 13 year old age category; (10) Best Young People's Theatre Award - 13 years and over age category; (11) Amateur Theatre Award; (12) *Drama* Special Award; and (13) Special sponsor's awards. Certificates are awarded annually. Established in 1979. Sponsors vary from year to year.

2548
British Tourist Authority
Thames Tower
Black's Rd.
Hammersmith   Phone: 81 846 9000
London W6 9EL, England   Fax: 81 563 0302

2549
Come to Britain Trophy
For recognition of the most outstanding new tourist service, facility, or amenity within the United Kingdom providing an additional attraction for visitors, and introduced for the first time in the previous year. Established in 1956. (Discontinued)

2550
British Trust for Ornithology
The National Center for Ornithology
The Nunnery   Phone: 842 750050
Thetford, Norfolk IP24 2PU, England Fax: 842 750030

2551
Jubilee Medal
For recognition of services to the trust that are not scientific. Members of the trust are eligible. A medal is awarded annually. Established in 1985 to commemorate 50 years of the BTO.

2552
Bernard Tucker Medal
For recognition of scientific services. Members of the trust are eligible. A medal is awarded annually. Established in 1954 in honor of Bernard Tucker.

2553
British Veterinary Association
7 Mansfield St.   Phone: 71 6366541
London W1M 0AT, England   Fax: 71 4362970

2554
Harry Steele-Bodger Memorial Scholarship
A traveling scholarship or contribution to a tour of study abroad is awarded at least once every four years. Eligible candidates include graduates of the Veterinary Schools in the United Kingdom and Ireland who have been qualified not more than three years and those who are in the year before their final year or their final year of school. The deadline for applications is April 6. Travel scholarships of £1,100 are awarded to assist a visit to a veterinary or agricultural school or research institute in Europe or some other course of study approved by the governing committee. Established in 1953 in memory of Henry W. Steele-Bodger, President of the Association from 1939 to 1941 and Chairman of the Survey Committee from 1939 to 1946, in recognition of his services to the veterinary profession and agriculture.

2555
Britten-Pears Foundation
The Red House
Golf Lane   Phone: 728 452615
Aldeburgh, Suffolk IP15 5PZ, England Fax: 728 453076

2556
Benjamin Britten Composers' Competition
To encourage young composers. Composers of all nationalities who are under 35 years of age may submit unpublished works for a specified instrumentation written during the previous three years. A monetary commission to write a work to be performed during the Aldeburgh Festival is awarded triennially. The deadline for submissions is March 31. Established in 1983 to mark the seventieth anniversary of Benjamin Britten's birth.

2557
Bromsgrove Festival Young Musicians' Platform
PVA Management Limited
Hallow Park   Phone: 905 640663
Worcester WR2 6PG, England   Fax: 905 640633

2558
Bromsgrove Festival Young Musicians' Platform
To provide a platform for young musicians. Individuals between 17 and 25 years of age, who have attained at least a Grade VIII Distinction or Honors by one of the recognized examining boards are eligible. Monetary awards of £500 for First Prize, £300 for Second Prize and £100 for finalists are awarded annually. Established in 1981.

2559
Building Employers Confederation
National Contractors Group
82 New Cavendish St.
London W1M 8AD, England   Phone: 71 580 5588

Formerly: National Federation of Building Trades Employers.

2560
National Contractors Travelling Scholarship
To recognize students in England and Wales, not over 26 years of age, who achieve above average results in building subjects in HNC or HND of the Business and Technician Education Council, and who have obtained building degrees. Candidates must have had at least one year's practical experience with a bona fide building contractor and be employed by a firm within membership of the Building Employers Confederation, or have fulfilled his/her one year's experience within a sandwich course with one member firm, or more of the BEC. Colleges in England and Wales may nominate students for the award. A monetary prize of £2,000 is awarded for visiting construction sites abroad in order to broaden his/her experience of building techniques and management. A further £150 is presented to the college from which the successful candidate comes. Awarded annually. Formerly: (1984) Cartwright Group Travelling Scholarship.

2561
Business and Industry Commitment to the Environment
227A City Rd.
London EC1V 1LX, England   Phone: 71 253 3716

2562
Business and Industry Commitment to the Environment Awards
To recognize outstanding commitment to the environment. Any industry or business, local authority, corporation working with business, or professional working with a business client is eligible. Five Premier Awards and ten major commendations are presented. Plaques and certificates are awarded annually. Established in 1973. Sponsored by British Gas plc.

2563
Business Archives Council
The Clove Building
4 Maguire St.
Butler's Wharf
London SE1 2NQ, England   Phone: 71 4076110

2564
Wadsworth Prize for Business History
For recognition of an outstanding contribution to British business history in any one calendar year. Books or articles on British business history published during the year are eligible. A monetary prize of £200 is awarded annually. Established in 1978 upon the retirement from the Council of Professor J. E. Wadsworth after 50 years continuous association.

2565
Cambridge Philosophical Society
Scientific Periodicals Library
Bene't St.   Phone: 223 334743
Cambridge CB2 3PY, England   Fax: 223 334748

2566
William Bate Hardy Prize
For recognition of the best memoir, investigation, or discovery by a member of the University of Cambridge in the field of biological science. Work published during the previous three years by members of Cambridge University is eligible. Three Fellows of the Society, nominated by the Council of the Society for each occasion, judge the work. A monetary prize is awarded triennially. Established in 1964 in memory of Sir William Bate Hardy (1864-1934).

2567
William Hopkins Prize
For recognition of the best original memoir, invention, or discovery in the field of mathematico-physical science or mathematico-experimental science that may have been published during the three preceding years. Members of Cambridge University are judged by three Fellows of the Society who are nominated by the Council of the Society. A monetary prize is awarded triennially. Established in 1866 in memory of William Hopkins (1793-1866).

2568
Jonathan Cape
Address unknown since 1992.

2569
***The Times*/Jonathan Cape Young Writers Prize**
For recognition of first novels. A monetary prize of £5,000 and publication by Jonathan Cape Ltd. of the work were awarded annually in August. Established in 1984. Co-sponsored by *The Times* of London. (Discontinued)

2570
Caterer Hotelkeeper
Reed Business Publishing Group
Quadrant House
The Quadrant   Phone: 81 661 3500
Sutton, Surrey SM2 5AS, England   Fax: 81 661 8973

2571
Acorn Awards
To recognize individuals in the catering and hotel industry for outstanding work achievement. Individuals under 30 years of age are eligible. Awarded annually.

2572
Catey Awards
To recognize outstanding achievement in the catering and hotel industry. Awards are presented annually in the following categories: (1) Housekeeper of the Year; (2) Wine Award; (3) Function Menu of the Year; (4) Best Independent Marketing Campaign; (5) Best Group Marketing Campaign; (6) Newcomer of the Year; (7) Tourism Award; (8) Hotel of the Year; (9) Industrial Caterer of the Year; (10) Restaurateur of the Year; (11) Food Service Award; (12) Chef Award; and (13) Special Award - for outstanding contribution to the industry. In addition, the Lifetime Achievement Award is presented every three years. Established in 1984.

2573
Hotelier of the Year Award
To recognize the top hotelier in the UK. Awarded annually.

2574
National Hotel Receptionist Award
To recognize an outstanding hotel receptionist. Awarded annually.

2575
Challenger Society for Marine Science
IOS Deacon Laboratory
Wormley   Phone: 51 6538633
Godalming, Surrey GU8 5UB, England   Phone: 51 653 6269

Formerly: (1988) Challenger Society.

2576
Cath Allen Prize
To encourage good poster presentations at the biennial UK Oceanography meeting. A monetary prize and a certificate are awarded biennially at the UK Oceanography meeting. Established in 1988 in honor of Dr. Catherine M. Allen. Formerly: (1991) Poster Prize.

2577
Norman Heaps Prize
To encourage good presentations by young oceanographers. Individuals who are 35 years of age or younger are considered. A monetary prize and a certificate are awarded at the biennial UK Oceanography meeting. Established in 1988 in honor of Dr. Norman S. Heaps. Formerly: World Development Awards for Business.

2578
Chartered Association of Certified Accountants
29 Lincoln's Inn Fields
London WC2A 3EE, England   Phone: 71 242 6855

Formerly: (1974) Association of Certified Accountants.

2579
Accountancy Journalist of the Year
For recognition of achievement in reporting accounting matters. Applications are accepted from journalists active in the reporting of accountancy. A monetary prize and a trophy are awarded annually. Established in 1988.

2580
Chartered Institute of Building
Englemere, Kings Ride   Phone: 990 23355
Ascot, Berks. SL5 8BJ, England   Fax: 990 23467

2581
Building Manager of the Year Awards
To recognize outstanding performance in the management of building projects. Nominations are accepted by March 11 for projects carried out in the United Kingdom. Awards and medals are bestowed annually. Established in 1979 in honor of Queen Elizabeth II's Silver Jubilee.

2582

Ian Murray Leslie Awards
To encourage the development of the communication skills of members and to facilitate the exchange of knowledge in matters relating to building. Papers that are of an academic or theoretical nature or have a practical theme and relate to building technology, building economics, building management, or education and training for building may be submitted. The papers must not have been previously published. Dissertations may also be considered. All applicants must register with the Institute before September 30 of the year of the award. The following prizes are awarded: a monetary prize and a silver medal - first place; a monetary prize and a silver medal - second place to a member of the Institute; a monetary prize and a bronze medal - third place to a member under 30 years of age; a monetary prize and a bronze medal - fourth place to a non-corporate member; and a further monetary award and a silver medal to a non-member for the best paper when the open competition is won by a member of the Institute. Awarded annually. Established in 1974 in honor of Ian Murray Leslie, former editor of the journal *Building*.

2583

Chartered Institute of Journalists
2 Dock Offices
Surrey Quays Rd.
London SE16 2XL, England
Phone: 71 2528871
Fax: 71 2322302

Formerly: Institute of Journalists.

2584

Chartered Institute of Journalists Gold Medal
For recognition of outstanding service to journalism and the fundamental freedom of the press. Journalists and others of any nationality are eligible. A gold medal with the Institute emblem on the reverse and the name of the recipient, wreathed on the obverse, is awarded when merited. Established in 1963 by the Chartered Institute of Journalists.

2585

Chartered Institute of Transport
80 Portland Pl.
London W1N 4DP, England
Phone: 71 6369952
Fax: 71 6370511

2586

Henry Spurrier Memorial Lecture
To promote knowledge of road transport from the commercial point of view. The Council of the Institute invites an individual to deliver the Lecture. In addition, sums of money are available for study in road transport. Established in 1945 in memory of Henry Spurrier (1868-1942), pioneer of road transport.

2587

Transport Journalist of the Year
To recognize the best article on transport. Articles published in the United Kingdom are eligible. A monetary award and a silver medal are presented annually. Established in 1991 by Alan Jones. Sponsored by TNT (UK) Ltd.

2588

Transport Photographer of the Year
To recognize the best transport photograph. Photographers from the United Kingdom are eligible. A monetary award and a silver medal are presented annually. Established in 1991 by Alan Jones. Sponsored by TNT (UK) Ltd.

2589

Chartered Institution of Building Services Engineers
Delta House
222 Balham High Rd.
London SW12 9BS, England
Phone: 81 6755211
Fax: 81 6755449

2590

Barker Silver Medal
For recognition of papers contributing substantially to heating, ventilating, and air conditioning associated with the built environment. Papers that describe the author's experience in the application of engineering/scientific knowledge may be submitted. A silver medal is awarded annually when merited. Established in 1958 in honor of Mr. A. H. Barker.

2591

Carter Bronze Medal
For recognition of the best paper presented to the Institution on the application and development of heating, ventilating, and air conditioning. A bronze medal and a certificate are awarded annually when merited. Established in 1977.

2592

Dufton Silver Medal Award
For recognition of a paper that advances the science of building services through original research that leads to new development. A silver medal is awarded annually when merited. Established in 1958 in honor of Mr. A. F. Dufton.

2593

Leon Gaster Bronze Medal
For recognition of the best paper presented to the Institution dealing with the research or theory of lighting and/or vision. A bronze medal and a certificate are awarded annually. Established in 1931 in honor of Mr. Leon Gaster.

2594

Lighting Award
To recognize contributions to the lighting profession. A certificate and a trophy are awarded annually.

2595

Napier - Shaw Bronze Medal
For recognition of the best paper presented to the institution dealing with the research or theory of heating, ventilating, and air conditioning. A bronze medal and a certificate are awarded annually when merited. Established before 1948.

2596

President's Prize
For recognition of the most outstanding final-year student pursuing a bachelor's in engineering who is enrolled in a building services engineering course accredited by CIBSE. A monetary prize, a medal, and a certificate are awarded annually. Established in 1994.

2597

Tanner Award
To recognize and reward imaginative, responsible design in the field of heating, ventilating, and air conditioning. Individuals or a team of individuals may enter by October. A monetary prize is awarded annually. Established in 1985 in honor of Mr. Tanner. Sponsored by the Design Council, CIBSE, and MYSON Group.

2598

Walsh - Weston Bronze Award
For recognition of the best paper presented to the Institution dealing with the development of light sources or lighting application. A bronze medal and a certificate are awarded annually. Established in 1963 in memory of Dr. J. W. T. Walsh and Mr. H. C. Weston.

2599

Young Lighters of the Year
For recognition of the best papers on lighting by individuals under 30 years of age. Monetary awards and certificates are awarded annually. Established in 1989. Formerly: Millar Award; Millar Award.

2600
Chartered Insurance Institute
The Hall, 20 Aldermanbury
London EC2V 7HY, England
Phone: 71 606 3835
Fax: 71 726 0131

2601
Ellis Carson Award
To recognize the most meritorious student attending one of the full-time diploma courses run by the CII College of Insurance. Established in 1972 by Ellis H. Carson, FCII, to recognize an essay or research in the field of insurance, and changed in 1988 to recognize a student.

2602
Paul Golmick Scholarship
To enable an individual to spend not less than twelve months with an insurance office in a European country other than his country of origin in order to perfect his or her knowledge of the language of that country and to become acquainted with the conduct of insurance business in that country. The scholarship is offered in alternate years to an applicant from the U.K. and to an applicant from one of a group of nominated European countries. Applicants must be under 28 years of age and employed in insurance. The closing date for applications is December 1. A scholarship of £4,000 is awarded annually.

2603
Walter T. Greig Scholarship
To enable an individual to travel for a period of not less than three months in a country other than his or her country of origin. The candidate is expected to make an intensive study of an approved aspect of insurance or reinsurance, and to submit a written thesis on completion of the research. Preference is given to reinsurance subjects, though not to the exclusion of other fields of insurance study. The scholarship is offered in alternate years to an applicant from the U.K. and to an applicant from Australia or New Zealand or a third country. Applicants should be diploma-holders of the Institute or of an affiliated institute, or graduates with two years' service in insurance, though other candidates with a minimum of five years' service in insurance will also be considered. Individuals who are 21 to 35 years of age are eligible. The closing date is December 1 in the year preceding the award.

2604
Morgan Owen Medal
To recognize a notable essay or work of research by an individual in the field of insurance. The entry must be written in English, a minimum of 5,000 words, and unpublished prior to the competition. Fellows or associates of the Chartered Insurance Institute are eligible. A monetary award of £2,000 and a medal are awarded annually. Established in 1933 by a bequest of O. Morgan Owen, FCII, president of the Institute in 1911.

2605
Rutter Gold Medal and Prize
To recognize the individual with the highest score on completing the qualifying examination for fellowship of the Chartered Insurance Institute. Members of the Institute are eligible. A monetary award of £500 and a gold medal are presented annually. Established in 1914 by Sir Frederick Pascoe Rutter, FCII, President of the Institute from 1910-1911.

2606
Chartered Society of Designers
29 Bedford Sq.
London WC1B 3EG, England
Phone: 71 6311510
Fax: 71 5802338

Formerly: (1987) Society of Industrial Artists and Designers.

2607
CSD Medal
For recognition of outstanding achievement in design. Awarded annually for a single design, a group of related designs, or as recognition of work of exemplary standard over a number of years. Professional designers from any country are eligible. Nominations must be made by September 30 to the Council only by fellows and members of the Society. Established in 1957. Formerly: (1987) SIAD Medal.

2608
Honorary Fellow
To recognize an individual for achievement in professional design.

2609
Minerva Awards
To recognize outstanding creative and professional design work. Practicing designers and consultancies may submit applications. Awards are presented in the following categories: environmental, graphic, product, fashion and textile, and design management. A plaque is presented annually in the late spring. Established in 1991.

2610
Chefs & Cooks Circle
Hotelympia Competition
13 Underne Ave.
Southgate
London N14 7ND, England

2611
Hotelympia Competition
To recognize outstanding culinary ability. The competition is built around research and development and establishing food trends for the future. Medals are awarded. Winners participate in the Culinary Olympics held every four years in Frankfurt, Germany, with the winners of the other international regional competitions: Culinary World Cup (Luxembourg); Salon Culinaire Mondial (Basel, Switzerland); Food & Hotel Asia Competition (Singapore); Culinary Arts Salon (USA); Chef Ireland (Ireland); and Culinary Masters (Canada). Established in 1900.

2612
Cheltenham Festival of Literature
Town Hall, Imperial Sq.
Cheltenham, Glos. GL50 1QA, England
Phone: 242 521621
Fax: 242 573902

2613
TLS/Cheltenham Literature Festival Poetry Competition
To encourage professional development in the field of poetry writing. Monetary prizes were awarded. Awarded annually. Established in 1976. Sponsored by the *Times Literary Supplement*. (Discontinued in 1989)

2614
Children's Book Bulletin
94 Cranworth Gardens
London SW9 ONT, England

Formerly: (1979) Children's Rights Workshop.

2615
The Other Award
To recognize progressive books of literary merit; to draw attention to important new writing and illustration for children; and to give recognition to those writers and illustrators who are widening the literary experience of young readers. Awarded annually. Established in 1975 by Rosemary Stones and Andrew Mann, editors of *Children's Book Bulletin*. (Discontinued in 1987)

2616
Children's Book Foundation
c/o Book Trust (England)
Book House
45 East Hill
London SW18 2QZ, England
Phone: 81 870 9055

2617
Eleanor Farjeon Award
To recognize an individual for distinguished services to children and books. Anyone working with or for children through books, both in the United Kingdom and overseas, is eligible. A monetary prize of £500 is awarded annually. Established in 1965 in memory of Eleanor Farjeon, a children's writer. Sponsored by Books for Children Book Club.

2618
Church Commissioners for England
1 Millbank
London SW1P 3JZ, England   Phone: 71 222 7010

2619
Parsonage Design Award
To encourage, reward and give public recognition to designers who, while complying with recommendations for accommodation and layout, display skill and sensitivity in designing a parsonage which is sympathetic to its surroundings, is of high visual merit and has been built within reasonable cost constraints. Both newly built parsonage houses and major alteration/conversion schemes of existing houses are eligible. A monetary prize and a plaque are awarded from time to time. Established in 1988 by Church Commissioners and the Ecclesiastical Architects and Surveyors Organisation.

2620
City and Guilds of London Institute
76 Portland Pl.   Phone: 71 580 3050
London W1N 4AA, England   Fax: 71 436 7630

2621
The Associateship of the City and Guilds of London Institute
Conferred exclusively on the engineering graduates of the City and Guilds College, Imperial College of Science, Technology and Medicine, London University. It denotes the ability to demonstrate, to the level equivalent to that of a degree of Bachelor of Science (Engineering), Bachelor of Engineering, or Master of Engineering, the understanding and application of the principles of a branch of Engineering or of Computing Science approved by the Institute. This ability is to be demonstrated through the satisfactory completion of an approved course of full-time study of three or four years duration and through success in the associated examinations at the City and Guilds College. A diploma is awarded that specifies the subject area of the award. Holders are entitled to use the letters ACGI after their names and to wear the approved gown, hood, and mortar board. Established in 1887.

2622
Fellowship of the City and Guilds of London Institute
The Fellowship is the highest distinction that can be conferred by the Institute. It denotes the ability to manage people, information, and operations in complex professional or technical situations and to formulate and implement strategies at the highest levels of responsibility. This achievement is to be demonstrated over a number of years in demanding appointments. The Fellowship may be conferred *Honoris Causa* (HonFCGI) on individuals whose professional achievement and advancement have been of outstanding significance over a period of years and/or who have made an outstanding contribution to the Institute's affairs. It was, until 1990, exclusive to former students of the City and Guilds College. Since 1990, applicants for the Fellowship may come from any profession or industry. Fellows of the Institute may be of any nationality and either sex. There is no restriction on the number of Fellowships which may be conferred annually. Applicants are normally not less than 40, with 10 years in positions of the highest responsibility. They must have made an outstanding contribution to the promotion and practice of their profession and be personally sponsored by two existing Fellows or Members of the Council of the Institute. A diploma and designatory letters FGGI are conferred. Established in 1892.

2623
Gold Medal for Craft Excellence
To encourage individuals who had reached the highest standard of craftsmanship in their chosen field. It was awarded annually to the person who produced a piece of work which attained excellence in its own right. The medal represented outstanding achievement and recognized the winners' artistic and technical mastery. Established in 1988. (Discontinued)

2624
Graduateship of the City and Guilds of London Institute
To recognize achievements in industry, commerce, and the public services. The Graduateship denotes the ability to understand and apply the principles of a technical subject or professional activity. This ability is to be demonstrated in an employment-based context through the design, development, improvement, or critical assessment of an artefact, process, system, or service. The level of competence required is that which could be expected of a graduate of a recognized European university, with several subsequent years of relevant experience. A diploma is awarded that specifies the subject area of the award. Holders are entitled to use the letters GCGI after their names and to wear the approved gown, hood, and mortar board. Established in 1990.

2625
Licentiateship of the City and Guilds of London Institute
To recognize achievement in industry, commerce, and the public services. The Licentiateship denotes the ability to understand and practice the principles of a technical subject or professional activity. This ability must be demonstrated in the context of advanced education and training and/or of employment. A diploma is awarded that specifies the employment sector of the award. Holders are entitled to use the letters LCGI after their names and to wear the approved gown and mortar board. Established in 1979.

2626
Medals for Excellence
To recognize the candidates who have demonstrated outstanding ability in their particular subjects. Three types of medals are awarded: Bronze - to candidates gaining a City and Guilds qualification at Level 1 or 2; Silver - to candidates gaining a City and Guilds qualification at Level 3 or 4; and Gold - to candidates gaining a City and Guilds qualification at National Vocational Qualification (NVQ) Level 5 or gaining Graduateship (GCGI), Associateship (ACGI), or Membership (MCGI) of the Institute. Medals are awarded to recognize excellence and a determined commitment to a high quality of work. To support an application, examples of work may be submitted which show: highly developed skills, outstanding knowledge of a subject directly related to the City and Guilds assessment undertaken, innovation and originality, enterprise, and versatility and adaptability. Also of relevance to an application would be examples that show a candidate has: made a significant contribution to his or her place of work, made a significant contribution to a special project, and overcome significant hardship or disability. Nominations will be accepted from any center in the UK and EC that is registered with City and Guilds. Medals will also be awarded to overseas candidates.

2627
Membership of the City and Guilds of London Institute
To recognize achievement in industry, commerce, and the public services. The Membership denotes the ability to exercise personal, professional responsibility for the design, development, or improvement of an artefact, process, system, or service. The emphasis is on individual competence and application of knowledge. The level of competence required is that which could be expected of a holder of a master's degree, with subsequent years of supervisory management or advanced technical experience, similar to that required for full membership of a major professional body. A diploma is awarded that specifies the subject area of the award. Holders are entitled to use the letters MCGI after their names and to wear the approved gown, hood, and mortar board. Established 1990.

2628

Prince Philip Medal
This, the most important award of the Institute, is given for recognition of exceptional achievement in industry, science, or technology. An individual whose career began with direct entry to employment as an apprentice or trainee and whose progress to an appointment of senior management responsibility has been by way of the ladder of opportunity provided by the City and Guilds system of progressive technological qualifications is eligible for consideration. The award is normally made sufficiently early in life for it to be a mark of personal success as well as an augury for further achievement. Nominations must be submitted by December 31. The Medal is presented annually at a special ceremony at Buckingham Palace. Established in 1962 by Prince Philip, Duke of Edinburgh, President of the City and Guilds of London Institute. Sponsored by Prince Philip.

2629

City of London Carl Flesch International Violin Competition
City Arts Trust
Bishopsgate Hall
230 Bishopsgate
London EC2M 4QD, England
Phone: 71 377 0540
Fax: 71 377 1972

2630

City of London Carl Flesch International Violin Competition
For recognition of excellence in violin playing. Violin performers of any nationality who are under the age of 28 are eligible. The deadline for applications is February 28. A monetary award of £6,000, the Carl Flesch Medal, a Garner Wilson gold-mounted bow, a certificate, and engagements are awarded for first prize. Additional monetary awards of £4,000, £3,000, £1,750, £1,250 and £750, as well as other special prizes, are awarded biennially (next in 1994). The second prize (Emily Anderson Prize for Violin) is given in association with the Royal Philharmonic Society. The medal was first awarded in 1945 to honor Carl Flesch, the violinist and teacher. The Competition was established in 1968.

2631

City of London Walther Gruner International Lieder Competition
City Arts Trust
Bishopsgate Hall
230 Bishopsgate
London EC2M 4QD, England
Phone: 71 3770540
Fax: 71 3771972

2632

City of London Walther Gruner International Lieder Competition
To discover major talent in the field of Lieder singing and to help further a professional career. The competition is open to singers of all nationalities. The age limit is 28 for singers and 35 for accompanists. The application deadline is February 4. The following prizes are awarded: (1) First Prize - £3,500 and London debut; (2) Second Prize - £2,250; (3) Third Prize - £1,250; (4) Fourth Prize - £750; and (5) Accompanist's Prize - £1,250. Awarded biennially. Established in 1983 by a bequest of Walther Gruner. Formerly: (1989) Walther Gruner International Lieder Competition.

2633

City of Westminster Arts Council
Marylebone Library
Marylebone Rd.
London NW1 5PS, England
Phone: 71 798 1018

2634

Menuhin Prize for Young Composers
To encourage young composers and to promote the composition of music for orchestra. A monetary award and a public performance of the winning are conferred. Awarded triennially. Established in 1974. (Discontinued in present form)

2635

Civic Trust
17 Carlton House Terr.
London SW1Y 5AW, England
Phone: 71 930 0914
Fax: 71 321 0180

2636

Civic Trust Awards
To stimulate interest in the appearance of British cities, towns, villages, and countryside; to create a greater awareness of the importance of environmental design in all its aspects, including architecture, planning, civic, and landscape design; and to draw attention to the best contributions now being made in these fields. Any scheme, completed within two years of submission, which has contributed to the quality of townscape or landscape is eligible. The awards are run on a two-year cycle - alternating each year between metropolitan and non-metropolitan areas of Britain. A bronze plaque is awarded for award-winning schemes, and certificates for the owners, designers, and contractors of award-winning and commended schemes. Awarded annually. An illustrated report on all the successful schemes is published each year. Established in 1959.

2637

Cleveland (UK) International Drawing Biennale
PO Box 41
Middlesbrough, Cleveland TS3 OYZ, England
Phone: 642 327583

2638

Cleveland International Drawing Biennale Prize
For recognition of the best drawings in the competition. Artists who use the drawing medium may submit entries. Monetary prizes totaling £12,000 for purchases are awarded biennially. Established in 1973. Sponsored by Northern Arts.

2639

Collins Publishers
8 Grafton St.
London W1X 3LA, England
Phone: 71 493 7070

2640

Collins Religious Book Award
For recognition of the book which has made the most distinguished contribution to the relevance of Christianity in the modern world in one of the following fields: science, ethics, sociology, philosophy, or comparative religion. Citizens of Great Britain, the Commonwealth, the Republic of Ireland and the Republic of South Africa are eligible. A monetary prize of £2,000 is awarded biennially. Established in 1969. Additional information is available from Lesley Walmsley.

2641

Crossword Champion
For recognition of individuals who are outstanding at solving crossword puzzles. The regional champions who become finalists are asked to attempt four London *Times* Crossword puzzles with half an hour allowed for each. The national champion receives an engraved Waterford crystal trophy and a £500 Harrods gift voucher. The second, third and fourth prizes are Harrods gift vouchers with the value of £300, £200, and £100, respectively. Four other prizes are awarded. Established in 1970 by *The Times*. Additional information is available from D.J. Swarbrick. Formerly: Collins Dictionaries/*The Times* Crossword Championship.

2642

Ian St. James Literary Award
For recognition of an outstanding short story. The competition is open to individuals who have not already had fiction published in book form. The following monetary prizes are awarded: (1) First prize - £12,000; (2) Second prize - £5,000; (3) Third prize - £2,000; and (4) Nine finalists - £1,000 each. The 12 stories are published by Collins. Established in 1989.

2643
Commonwealth Association of Architects
66 Portland Pl.
London W1N 4AD, England
Phone: 71 6368276
Fax: 71 2551541

2644
Robert Matthew Award
For recognition of specific buildings which, in the opinion of member institutes (33 in the Commonwealth), show a significant response to the cultural, physical, and climatic context of the country. Deadline for nomination is October 14. A scroll is awarded biennially at the CAA General Assembly. Established in 1983 in honor of Sir Robert Matthew, founder and first President of the Association. Formerly: (1983) CAA National Awards.

2645
Commonwealth Association of Science, Technology and Mathematics Educators
Education Dept.
Marlborough House, Pall Mall
London SW1Y 5HX, England
Phone: 71 7476279
Fax: 71 9300827

Formerly: (1982) Commonwealth Association of Science and Mathematics Educators.

2646
CASTME Awards
To encourage teaching of the social significance of science, technology and mathematics in Commonwealth countries. The scope of the awards is interpreted broadly, and social aspects includes the relevance of science, technology and mathematics curricula to local needs and conditions and to the impact of technology, industry and agriculture on the local community. Teachers and officials (advisors, inspectors, etc.) working in primary, secondary and tertiary education in Commonwealth countries are eligible to enter. Individuals or syndicates may enter. Judging is based on the following criteria: evidence of originality and creativity; evidence of use practicability and cost effectiveness. (Entries based on ideas, proposals or general arguments which have not been tried out are not acceptable); evidence of evaluation of the idea or material in use; evidence of the social relevance of the project; and standards of presentation of the report. In addition to a small money prize donated by CASTME, a few travelling fellowships may be awarded at the discretion of the Judges. These fellowships, the gift of the Commonwealth Foundation, enable the prize-winners to follow a short program of professional visits in a Commonwealth country. Awarded annually. Established in 1974. Sponsored by the Commonwealth Foundation. Formerly: (1982) CASME Award.

2647
Commonwealth Association of Surveying and Land Economy
15 Greycoat Pl.
London SWIP 1SB, England
Phone: 71 222 8961
Fax: 71 976 8304

2648
Aubrey Barker Awards
To enable young qualified surveyors to widen their training and experience in a country other than their own. Candidates must be 35 years of age or less and a citizen of and resident in a developing Commonwealth country. A monetary award is presented annually when merited. Established in 1972 in honor of B. Aubrey Barker, OBE of Guyana.

2649
Commonwealth Forestry Association
Oxford Forestry Institute
OFI South Parks Rd.
Oxford OX1 3RB, England
Phone: 865 275072
Fax: 865 275074

2650
Tom Gill Memorial Award
To encourage literary achievement in forestry related subjects. Essays may be submitted. A monetary award and a medal with a Tom Gill head and CFA logo are presented annually at the CFA meeting. Bequeathed in 1972 by Tom Gill through his will.

2651
Queen's Award for Forestry
To recognize an individual for mid-career forestry achievement with the potential to benefit and communicate to others in the land-based disciplines. Members of the Commonwealth between 30 and 55 years of age are eligible. A travel fellowship worth £3,000 approximately and a scroll signed by Her Majesty are awarded every 2 years. Established in 1988 by Her Majesty E.R.

2652
Schlich Memorial Trust Award
To recognize services to forestry around the world. Any entrant considered by the trustees as suitable is eligible. A monetary award is presented annually. Established in 1928 in memory of Sir William Schlich.

2653
Commonwealth Foundation
Marlborough House, Pall Mall
London SW1Y 5HY, England
Phone: 71 930 3783
Fax: 71 839 8157

2654
Commonwealth Writers Prize
To reward and encourage writing in all parts of the Commonwealth. A major prize of £10,000 for the best entry and an award of £3,000 for the best newly published book are awarded annually for works of fiction. These are selected from eight regional winners, who each receive prizes of £1,000. Administered by the Association for Commonwealth Literature and Language Studies.

2655
Fellowship Scheme to Promote Commonwealth Understanding
To encourage professionals of influence to undertake a one-month program on Commonwealth affairs. Twelve fellowships are awarded annually. Fellowships are not available on personal application. Commonwealth institutions are invited to nominate suitable candidates for consideration by a selection committee made up of members of the Board of Governors.

2656
Fellowships and Training Programmes
Two programs are administered: The Commonwealth Secretariat's Fellowships and Training Programme to help Commonwealth developing countries increase their pool of skilled manpower in areas important to national development. Each year, some 2000 people, most of them middle-level technologists, managers, or officials, pursue courses or work attachments on training awards made under the Programme; and The Commonwealth Industrial Training and Experience Programme (CITEP) - a training scheme, started in 1986, to help Commonwealth countries improve their industrial performance by providing practical training and experience in industry for technologists, technicians and others. CITEP offers them opportunities for skills development and familiarization with advanced technologies and new manufacturing processes that are not available in their countries.

2657
Fellowships in Arts and Crafts
To promote excellence in arts and crafts and to foster Commonwealth cooperation. Ten fellowships are offered biennially. Administered by the Commonwealth Institute of London.

2658
Medical Electives Bursaries
To encourage medical students to undertake their elective period of work/study in a Commonwealth country other than their own. Approximately 45 bursaries of up to £1,000 each are offered annually. Administered by the Association of Commonwealth Universities.

2659
Special Awards
Ten Special Awards, advertised and administered through the appropriate Commonwealth Professional Associations, are offered from time to time in a field of priority need in the developing Commonwealth. Awards have been made in areas including schools links, nursing, surveying, broadcasting, and disaster preparedness. The Foundation also provides assistance for participation in regional training programs in collaboration with the appropriate regional bodies. Subject areas in which such programs have been organized include primary health care, trade union education, archives management, biological control of pests and fisheries.

2660
Commonwealth Games Federation
(Federation des Jeux du Commonwealth)
Walkden House
3-10 Melton St.   Phone: 71 3835596
London NW1 2EB, England   Fax: 71 3835506

2661
Commonwealth Games Federation
To promote quadrennial Commonwealth games for amateur sport. Competitors representing constituent parts of the Commonwealth are eligible. Medals are awarded at victory ceremonies to three competitors in each sport.

2662
Commonwealth Institute
The Arts Librarian
Kensington High St.
London W8 6NQ, England   Phone: 71 603 4535

2663
Commonwealth Poetry Prize
For recognition of poetry in the following categories: (1) best published edition by any author; (2) best published edition by a first-time published poet; and (3) individual world area awards for Africa, Americas (Canada/Caribbean), Asia, Australasia/Pacific and UK/Europe. World area winners were submitted to the International Jury in London, with the world area recommendations for the separate category "best first-time published poet." World area winners and the "best first-time published poet" winner were required to attend the London Prize Ceremony in November and to be available in the UK for a specified time for paid reading engagements. Monetary prizes were awarded annually in the following categories: (1) £2,500 - best published edition by any author; (2) £2,000 - best published edition by a first-time published poet; and (3) £1,000 - individual world area awards for Africa, Americas (Canada/Caribbean), Asia, Australasia/Pacific and UK/Europe. The overall British Airways Commonwealth Poetry Prize winner was announced in London in November. The winner, in receiving the first prize of £5,000, retained the individual world area title as well, but did not receive the £1,000 award. Established in 1972. Administered jointly with the Book Trust, London. (The last award presented was in 1988) (Discontinued)

2664
Standard Chartered Commonwealth Photography Award
To recognize outstanding photography. Regional winners were selected from Europe, the Caribbean, Africa, Asia and the Pacific. A first prize winner was selected from the regional winners and received a monetary award of £5,000. Sponsored by Standard Chartered Bank, 10 Clements Lane, London EC4, England. (Discontinued)

2665
Commonwealth Magistrates' and Judges' Association
28 Fitzroy Sq.   Phone: 71 387 4889
London W1P 6DD, England   Fax: 71 383 0757

Formerly: Commonwealth Magistrates' Association.

2666
Commonwealth Magistrates' Hall of Fame
For recognition of contributions to the following: (1) the advancement of the administration of the law by the promotion of judiciary independence; (2) fostering of education in the law, administration of justice, treatment of offenders, and prevention of crime within the Commonwealth; and (3) dissemination of information concerning the legal process within Commonwealth countries.

2667
Commonwealth Press Union
Studio House
Hen and Chickens Ct.
184 Fleet St.   Phone: 71 2421056
London EC4A 2DU, England   Fax: 71 8314923

2668
Astor Award
To recognize an individual for an outstanding contribution to Commonwealth understanding. Established by the late Lord Astor of Hever to mark his family's association with the Union.

2669
Commonwealth Press Union Scholarships
To promote high standards of journalistic ethics and literacy, and to uphold the principles of press freedom and free expression. Working journalists employed by newspapers and news agencies in membership in the Commonwealth Press Union are eligible. Fellowships and scholarships are awarded.

2670
Commonwealth Youth Programme
Commonwealth Secretariat
Marlborough House, Pall Mall   Phone: 71 839 3411
London SW1Y 5HX, England   Fax: 71 930 1647

2671
Commonwealth Youth Service Awards
To recognize and reward the contribution made by young people in working collectively to develop their societies and to foster cooperation and exchange of ideas and experience among young people of the Commonwealth. Awards are made to projects nominated by governments that: are examples of effective teamwork by young people, preferably aged 15 to 25; are devised, set up and maintained by young people themselves; respond to and meet a local need; show potential for long-term effectiveness; and provide a model or inspiration to other localities both nationally and Commonwealth-wide. Applications must be passed through appropriate government departments and then to the relevant CYP Regional Center. A monetary award of £1,000 toward further development of the project and a certificate are awarded annually. In addition, personal mementos such as medallions for each member of the award-winning project teams are presented. Established in 1985.

2672
Concrete Society
Framewood Rd.
Wexham   Phone: 753 66 2226
Slough SL3 6PJ, England   Fax: 753 66 2126

2673
Concrete Society Award
For recognition of excellence in the use of concrete in building and civil engineering. The criteria include excellence in the functional use of the material coupled with its harmony and appearance in the context of its surroundings, as well as workmanship and cost effectiveness. A plaque is awarded annually. Established in 1968.

2674
Confederation of British Industry
Centre Point
103 New Oxford St.
London WC1A 1DU, England
Phone: 71 3797400
Fax: 71 2401578

2675
Toshiba Year of Invention Awards
To foster the spirit of British inventiveness by identifying and promoting innovative ideas not yet in production. Established in 1989. (Discontinued)

2676
Conservation Foundation (UK)
1 Kensington Gore
London SW7 2AR, England
Phone: 71 8238842
Fax: 71 8238791

2677
Ford European Conservation Awards
To provide recognition for conservation projects in progress or recently completed in the following categories: natural environment, heritage, and conservation engineering. The awards run in 22 countries, each with its own national program which makes awards to three category winners, one of which is chosen as the national prize winner to go forward into the European competition. Applications may be submitted by September 1. The following prizes are awarded: European Winner - $50,000 U.S.; second prize - $25,000; third prize - $10,000; and a $2,000 prize for the best project in each participating European country. Awarded annually. Established in 1982. Sponsored by the Ford Motor Company Limited. Awards are held in Austria, Belgium, Denmark, France, Germany, Greece, Holland, Ireland, Italy, Luxembourg, Norway, Portugal, Poland, Spain, Russia, Slovakia, Switzerland, United Kingdom, Hungary, and the Czech Republic.

2678
Young Scientists for Rainforests
To enable young scientists to develop their ethno-medical research work. A grant of up to £10,000 is awarded throughout the year.

2679
Constable & Co. Ltd.
3 The Lanchesters
162 Fulham Palace Rd.
London W6 9ER, England
Phone: 81 7413663

2680
Constable Trophy
To recognize an author in the North of England for the best unpublished novel of the year. A monetary award of £2,000 and a minimum of £1,000 in advance on acceptance for publication by Constable and Company is presented annually. Established in 1984. Co-sponsored by Constable and Company, Northern Arts, North West Arts and Yorkshire and Humberside Arts. Additional information is available from Constable and Company, 10 Orange Street, London WC2H 7EG, England.

2681
Construction Industry Computing Association
Guildhall Pl.
Cambridge CB2 3QQ, England
Phone: 223 311246
Fax: 223 62865

Formerly: (1980) Design Office Consortium.

2682
Construction Industry Computing Association Awards
To recognize and promote the appropriate use of computers in the construction industry.

2683
Thomas Cook Travel
45 Berkley St.
London W1A 1EB, England
Phone: 71 499 4000

2684
Thomas Cook Travel and Guide Book Awards
To encourage the art of travel writing. Awards are offered in three categories: for recognition of the best travel book, for recognition of the best factual guide book, and for recognition of the best illustrated guide book. Books written in English and published during the preceding year may be submitted by October 31. A monetary prize of £7,500 is awarded for the best travel book, a monetary prize of £2,500 for the best factual guide book, and a monetary prize of £1,000 for the best illustrated guide book. Awarded annually. Established in 1980 by Thomas Cook.

2685
Duff Cooper Prize
54 St. Maur Rd.
London SW6 4DP, England
Phone: 71 736 3729
Fax: 71 731 7638

Formerly: Duff Cooper Memorial Prize Fund.

2686
Duff Cooper Prize
To recognize work written in English on the subjects of history and biography published within the last year. A monetary award and a presentation copy of Duff Cooper's autobiography *Old Men Forget* are awarded annually. The Prize was founded by Duff Cooper's friends after his death in 1954. Formerly: Duff Cooper Memorial Prize.

2687
Dr. M. Aylwin Cotton Foundation
Albany Trustee Company
PO Box 232, Pollet House, The Pollet
St. Peter Port, Guernsey, England
Phone: 481 24136

2688
Dr. M. Aylwin Cotton Foundation Fellowship Awards
To provide fellowships for studies in the archaeology, architecture, history, language and arts of the Mediterranean. Persons engaged in academic research, normally of postdoctoral standard (although no formal academic qualifications are necessary) may apply by February 28. Fellowships are normally of one year's duration and may exceptionally be renewable. Up to £7,500 is awarded to cover the costs of accommodation, travel, photography, photocopying and all other expenses relating to the work for which the Fellowship is awarded. Fellows are expected to arrange for the publication of their research. Awarded annually. Established in 1971 by Dr. M. Aylwin Cotton.

2689
Dr. M. Aylwin Cotton Foundation Publication Grants
To provide publication grants for studies in the archaeology, architecture, history, language, and art of the Mediterranean. Applicants, who should be either the author or the editor of the work, should supply a brief

account of the proposed publication, the name of the publisher, and an estimate of the likely cost of publication. The grants are open to men and women of all nationalities. The deadline for application is February 28. The costs of publication of academic research already completed or imminently available for publication are awarded annually. Established in 1971 by Dr. M. Aylwin Cotton.

2690
Council for Awards of Royal Agricultural Societies
Little Folly, Edneys Hill
Wokingham, Berks. RG11 4DR, England
Phone: 734 781214
Fax: 734 781214

2691
Fellows and Associates of Royal Agricultural Societies
For recognition of achievement in practical farming and the development of new husbandry practices, as well as technological, economic, educational, and administrative achievement contributing to the efficiency and well-being of agriculture in the United Kingdom. The Associateship (A.R.Ag.S.) is available to those over 25 years of age domiciled in England, Northern Ireland, Scotland, or Wales who can demonstrate the required level of achievement in any of the fields of activity set out above. The Fellowship (F.R.Ag.S.) is conferred on an Associate, normally not less than five years after qualification for Associateship. It is intended for those who are making a mark in the profession and is not usually awarded before a person has reached 35 years of age. Under certain circumstances, there is the provision for individuals who have made or are making an outstanding contribution to the profession of agriculture to be elected directly to Fellowship. Certificates are awarded. Established in 1970. Sponsored by the Royal Agriculture Society of England, Royal Highland and Agricultural Society of Scotland, the Royal Ulster Agricultural Society and the Royal Welsh Agricultural Society.

2692
Council for British Archaeology/BUFVC AV Media Working Party
55 Greek St.
London W1V 5LR, England
Phone: 71 734 3687
Fax: 71 287 3914

2693
Channel 4 Film Awards
For recognition of the best film on an archaeological subject by British filmmakers. Entries must be British-produced and released during the preceding two years in the the following categories: programs made for television, nonbroadcast educational films or videos, nonbroadcast single-site or site-specific films or videos, nonbroadcast archaeological science and conservation films or videos, and nonbroadcast promotional films or videos. Two cash prizes and a British Archaeological Awards Certificate are awarded biennially to coincide with the BAA Awards. Established in 1988. Sponsored by Channel Four Television Corporation, UK. For further information, contact John Gorton, Hon. Sec. of the BAA, 56 Penn Rd., Beaconsfield, Bucks HP9 2LS.

2694
Council for Education in World Citizenship
Seymour Mews House
Seymour Mews
London W1H 9PE, England
Phone: 71 9351752
Fax: 71 9355741

2695
Dobinson Award
For outstanding work in education for international understanding. Individuals, schools, and colleges that have membership in CEWC are eligible for considerati on. Entries must be submitted by June 1 each year. Monetary prizes of approximately £150 are awarded annually. Established in 1983 by Professor C.H. Dobinson, CMG.

2696
Council for National Academic Awards
344-354 Gray's Inn Rd.
London WC1X 8BP, England
Phone: 71 278 4411
Fax: 71 833 1012

Defunct organization.

2697
British Sociological Association/Council for National Academic Awards Annual Undergraduate Essay Prize in Sociology
To encourage standards of excellence in the field of sociology, and to encourage contributions which integrate conceptual or theoretical ideas with the use of empircal evidence. A first prize of L100 and Second prize of L50 were awarded annually. (Discontinued)

2698
Sir Michael Clapham Prize in International Business
For recognition of a written work in the area of international business, not more than 6000 words in length, either prepared as part of the course or written especially for the competition. Monetary prizes of L300 for First prize and L200 for Second prize were awarded annually. (Discontinued)

2699
CNAA/RIPA Prize in Public Administration
For recognition of the best essay by a student enrolled i the United Kingdom for a CNAA degree course, which includes the study of public administration. A monetary prize of L100 was awarded annually. Sponsored by the Royal Institute of Public Administration. (Discontinued)

2700
Lord Kings Norton Prize in Economics
For recognition of a written work in economics not more than 5000 words in length, either prepared as part of the course, or written especially for the prize. Monetary prizes of L300 for First prize and L200 for Second prize wre awarded annually. (Discontinued)

2701
Social Policy Association Essay Prize
To encourage standards of excellence in the field of social policy and administration and to encourage contributions which integrate conceptual or theoretical ideas with the use of empirical evidence. A First prize of L100 and a Second prize of L50 were awarded annually. Sponsored by the Social Policy Association. (Discontinued)

2702
Council of European Industrial Federations
c/o International Visual Communications
  Association
Bolsover House
5/6 Clipstone St.
London W1P 7EB, England
Phone: 71 580 0962
Fax: 71 436 2606

2703
International Industrial Film and Video Awards
For recognition of the most outstanding business and industrial films in the following categories: (1) Industrial Activities; (2) Products and Materials; (3) Services; (4) Society; (5) Safety and Health; (6) Education; (7) Technology and Research; and (8) Training. The festival is organized each year by one of the Industrial Federation members of CEIF in different European cities. The following prizes are awarded: (1) CEIF Grand Prix; (2) First, Second and Third prizes in each category; and (3) Enterprise Information Group Special Prize - to the production best explaining the role of business and industry in society as well as fundamental economic relationships of the free market system. Established in 1961. Formerly: International Industrial Film Festival Awards.

2704
Country Landowners Association
Press Office
16 Belgrave Sq.
London SW1X 8PQ, England
Phone: 71 2350511
Fax: 71 2354696

2705
Farm Buildings Award Scheme
For recognition of new farm buildings that are functionally sound, good value for money, and aesthetically satisfying in the countryside. The award scheme covers farm houses, cottages, farm buildings, silos, fixed equipment, and extensions completed within seven years of the entry closing date. To qualify, conversions must remain within the ownership of the farm or estate. Awards are presented in four regions. A monetary award, a plaque, and a certificate are awarded biennially. Established in 1969.

2706
Coventry General Charities
Old Bablake, Hill St.
Coventry CV1 4AN, England
Phone: 203 222769

Formerly: (1986) Coventry Centre for the Performing Arts.

2707
Sir Thomas White's Music Scholarship
To provide opportunities for young persons to extend their musical aptitude in all kinds of music, instrumental, vocal and composition. Persons who have an association with the City of Coventry by birth or by upbringing may apply. A monetary prize is awarded annually. Established in 1970. Formerly: Sir Thomas White's Educational Foundation Music Scholarship.

2708
Crime Writers' Association
PO Box 172
Tring, Herts. HP23 5LP, England

2709
CWA '92 Award
For recognition of a crime novel set mainly in continental Europe. A monetary prize of L200 was awarded. (Discontinued)

2710
CWA/Cartier Diamond Dagger Award
To recognize an author, rather than a book, for outstanding contribution to the genre of crime writing. A diamond dagger and a memento are awarded annually. The winner's name is engraved on the dagger, and a personal memento is given in the form of a diamond brooch or cufflinks. Established in 1986.

2711
CWA Gold Dagger Award
For recognition of the best crime novel published in the United Kingdom during the year. Books are submitted by publishers. An independent panel of reviewers from leading London and provincial newspapers make the selection. A monetary prize and an engraved gold-plated dagger are awarded annually. A monetary prize and a silver-plated dagger are awarded to the second place winner. Established in 1955.

2712
CWA Gold Dagger Award for Non-Fiction
For recognition of the best nonfiction writing on crime. An independent panel of doctors, policemen, and other experts make the selection. A monetary prize and an engraved gold-plated dagger are awarded annually. Established in 1978.

2713
CWA John Creasey Memorial Award
For recognition of the best crime novel of the year by a previously unpublished author. A monetary prize and an engraved magnifying glass are awarded annually. Established in 1973 in memory of John Creasey, founder of Crime Writers' Association.

2714
CWA Last Laugh Award
For recognition of the most amusing crime novel of the year. Books are submitted by publishers and the winner chosen by an independent panel of reviewers from leading London and provincial newspapers. The prize is a gold-plated fountain pen in an inscribed presentation case. Established in 1989.

2715
CWA Rumpole Award
For recognition of the crime novel which, in the opinion of the editor of the *New Law Journal*, best portrays legal procedure. Submissions must be by publishers on publication of a novel written during the two preceding years. A monetary prize is awarded. Sponsored by the *New Law Journal*.

2716
CWA Short Story Competition
For recognition of an outstanding crime story. Among the prizes were publication of the winning story in the 'Sunday Times' and an invitation to the Crime Writers' Association Awards Dinner in December. (Discontinued)

2717
Police Review Board
To recognize a crime novel set in Britian that best portrays police work and procedure. A monetary prize was awarded annually. Established in 1986. (Discontinued in 1989)

2718
***Sunday Express Magazine* - Veuve Clicquot Short Story Competition**
For recognition of outstanding short stories. Previously unpublished works were considered. A monetary prize and a birthday bottle of champagne for life were awarded annually. Sponsored by Veuve Clicquot and 'Sunday Express Magazine'. (Discontinued in 1989)

2719
Cromwell Association
Cosswell Cottage
Northedge, Tupton
Chesterfield, Derbyshire S42 6AY, England
Phone: 1 4352391

2720
Cromwell Association Award
For recognition of the best essay on the period of Oliver Cromwell and the history of the Commonwealth and Protectorate. Students are eligible. Awarded annually.

2721
Crossword Club
Hilberry Farm
Awbridge Hill
Romsey, Hants. S051 OHF, England
Phone: 794 524346

2722
Crossword Club Competitions
To promote the art of crossword puzzling and composing. The Club sponsors competitions. No further information on awards is available for this edition.

2723

Cystic Fibrosis Research Trust
Alexandra House,
5 Blyth Rd.
Bromley, Kent BR1 3RS, England
Phone: 81 464 7211
Fax: 81 313 0472

2724

John Panchaud Medallions
For recognition of valuable service in the fight against cystic fibrosis and the Cystic Fibrosis Research Trust since its formation in 1964. Selection is by nomination. Medals and certificates are awarded occasionally. Established in 1983 with the agreement of the Panchaud family in honor of John Panchaud.

2725

Daily Mail
2 Derry St.
Kensington
London W8 5TT, England
Phone: 895 677677
Fax: 895 676027

2726

British National Carnation Society Award
For recognition of the best British scented carnation. The *Daily Mail* gold cup is awarded annually.

2727

The *Daily Mail* Awards of Excellence
For recognition of the best new ideas for the home in terms of new products shown at the exhibition by British and foreign manufacturers. As many as ten blue ribbons are awarded annually.

2728

Gladiolia Society Award
For recognition of the best bloom cultivated and produced in the United Kingdom.

2729

Daiwa Anglo-Japanese Foundation
Dir. General
Condor House
14 St. Paul's Churchyard
London EC4M 8BD, England
Phone: 71 548 8302
Fax: 71 334 9314

2730

Daiwa Scholarships
To enable outstanding young UK graduates of any discipline to acquire a lasting knowledge of Japanese life and culture and of spoken and written Japanese. Individuals must be 21 to 28 years of age and citizens of the United Kingdom. The deadline is December 20, 1994. Two-year scholarships, including grants, tuition fees, and travel expenses are awarded annually. Established in 1991.

2731

Deaf Accord
Charity Base, The Chandlery
50 Westminster Bridge Rd.
London SE1 7QY, England
Phone: 721 7689
Fax: 721 7409

2732

Young Deaf Achiever
To recognize achievement of young, deaf, deaf-blind or hard of hearing individuals in employment, education, recreation, or personal development. Individuals between 16 and 29 years of age may be nominated by August 30. A monetary award, a certificate, and an engraved glass trophy are awarded annually at a luncheon in December. Established in 1988. Currently sponsored by IBM.

2733

Deloitte Haskins & Sells
Media Group
128 Queen Victoria St.
London EC4P 4JX, England

2734

Coopers Deloitte Bookcover Award
To recognize the best bookcover design. Any book published in the UK in the previous year is eligible. A monetary prize is awarded annually. Established in 1987. Sponsored by Cooper *Deloitte* and *Bookseller* Magazine. (Discontinued in 1990)

2735

Delphinium Society
Takakkaw
Ice House Wood
Oxted, Surrey RH8 9DW, England

2736

Delphinium Society Awards
To encourage the culture of delphiniums and the production of new and improved varieties by sponsoring competitions. Cups, medals, and certificates of merit are awarded. No further information on awards is available for this edition.

2737

Design Council
28 Haymarket
London SW1Y 4SU, England
Phone: 71 839 8000
Fax: 71 925 2130

2738

British Design Awards
To promote the importance of good design by identifying and publicizing outstanding examples of British design within the areas of medical equipment, automotive, computer software, consumer and contract goods, and engineering products and components. Products that have been in production and service for some time and were designed by a British designer working in the U.K. or abroad, or by a designer resident in the U.K. are eligible. Certificates are awarded and publicity and the use of the British Design Award logo are also provided. Established in 1957. Formerly: Design Council Awards.

2739

Design Council British Aerospace Engineering Design Prizes
To encourage interest in the principles and practice of good engineering design. Students following first degree courses in engineering in the United Kingdom are eligible. Two entries from each university engineering course may be submitted by the end of July. Monetary awards totaling £4,100 and certificates are awarded annually. Five equal prizes of £500, together with four prizes of £150 for Special Commendations are presented. Two additional awards of £500 each are awarded: *The Times Higher* Educational Supplement Award for the best presented report chosen from the prize-winning and special commendation entries and the Desmond Molins Award, sponsored by Molins plc, which honors the best development of an original idea from concept into product. Established in 1972 by the Design Council and Molins plc. Sponsored by British Aerospace until March 1994. Formerly: Design Council Molins Design Prize.

2740

Design Council GKN Production Engineer's Design Prize
To find and reward successful production engineering ideas in the manufacturing industry, to improve the status and reputation of production engineering designers, and to encourage new ideas in manufacture. A monetary award, a certificate, and a visit to a GKN European plant and the Hanover Fair were awarded annually, usually in April. (Discontinued in 1986)

2741

Mobil Design Award for Small Firms
To help small firms achieve success from well-designed products. A monetary award of £10,000, a certificate, and advice from Mobil on marketing, advertising, and promoting sales were awarded biannually. Established in 1982. (Discontinued in 1986)

2742

Prince Philip Prize for the Designer of the Year
To recognize the designer who has made the greatest contribution to design. A certificate is presented to the winner at a ceremony at Buckingham Palace by Prince Philip. Awarded annually. Established in 1958 in honor of Prince Philip. Additional information is available from the Design Council's Award Office. Formerly: Duke of Edinburgh's Designer's Prize.

2743

Isaac Deutscher Memorial Prize
c/o Lloyds Bank Ltd.
71 Lombard St.
London EC3 P3BS, England

2744

Isaac Deutscher Memorial Prize
To recognize and encourage outstanding research and writing in the field of Marxist thought. Essays or full-scale works written in any of the main European languages are eligible. Material must be submitted by May 1. The award consists of a monetary prize of £100 and the presentation of the Isaac Deutscher Memorial Lecture. Awarded annually. Established in 1968 by a group of European and American scholars to further the aims to which Isaac Deutscher was dedicated.

2745

Digital Equipment Company
PO Box 110
Reading, Bucks. RG2 0TR, England
Phone: 734 868711
Fax: 734 575027

2746

Digital Dance Awards
To encourage cross fertilization of new choreography/dance within the United Kingdom to enable new dance works to be produced. All dance companies of professional status promoters and choreographers with a proven record are eligible. A grant to pay for the commission of new choreography and a trophy are awarded annually in June. Established in 1987. Also, since 1989, the Digital Premier Award of £30,000 has been given to recognize an individual making an outstanding contribution to British dance. Additional information is available from Julie Cork, Crowcroft Gourley, 62 Britton Street, London EC1M 5PJ, England, phone: 71 251 1191.

2747

Digital Schneider Trophy
To recognize the winner of the Digital Schneider Trophy Race, Europe's largest air race. A monetary prize and a trophy were awarded annually. Established in 1984 and named after the Schneider Seaplane Contests held from 1913-1931. (Discontinued in 1991)

2748

Dorset Natural History and Archaeological Society
Dorset County Museum
High West St.
Dorchester, Dorset DT1 1XA, England
Phone: 305 262735

Formed by merger of: (1928) Dorset Natural History; Antiquarian Field Club.

2749

Mansel-Pleydell and Cecil Trusts
To encourage papers on Dorset archaeology, geology, local and natural history, containing original research and material hitherto unpublished. Papers must be submitted by persons living in Dorset or having past or present connections with the county by December 31 in any year. A monetary prize is awarded annually on the last Tuesday in June. Established about 1905 in honor of J.C. Mansel-Pleydell Esq and Lord Eustace Cecil.

2750

Charles Douglas-Home Memorial Trust
57 Thorpebank Rd.
London W12 0PG, England
Phone: 81 740 8705

2751

Charles Douglas-Home Memorial Award
To provide an annual scholarship for a writer, researcher, scholar or journalist for research on a specific subject which will commemorate the ideals and perpetuate the work of the late Charles Douglas-Home. Anyone may apply, following the subject announcement. A grant for one year, plus expenses as agreed by the Trustees, are awarded annually. Established in 1987 in memory of Charles Douglas-Home, former editor of *The Times* Newspaper.

2752

Dracula Society
(Societe du Comte Dracula)
36 Elliston House
100 Wellington St.
London SE18 6QF, England
Phone: 81 317 9007

2753

Hamilton Deane Award
For recognition of the most significant contribution to the gothic genre in the performing arts. Any performance or technical contribution to a production in a given year is eligible. The winner is voted upon by the members of the Society. A framed scroll is awarded annually. Established in 1974 in memory of Hamilton Deane, the dramatizer of "Dracula". Formerly: (1977) Actor of the Year Award.

2754

Dudley International Piano Competition
Holcombe
59 Wrottesley Rd.
Tettenhall
Wolverhampton WV6 8SG, England
Phone: 902 744926

Formerly: Dudley National Piano Competition.

2755

Dudley International Piano Competition
For recognition of outstanding performance by pianists under 30 years of age. The following prizes are awarded: First Prize - £3,000, a London debut recital, and a series of public engagements including performances with orchestras during the next two years; Second Prize - £2,000; Third Prize - £1,000; and Recital Prize - £500 for the best performance in the Jury's opinion of a 20th Century Work offered in the Recital Stage of the Competition. Formerly: Dudley National Piano Competition.

2756

Education
21-27 Lambs Conduit St.
London WC1N 3NJ, England
Phone: 71 2422548
Fax: 71 8312855

2757

***Education* School Design Award**
For recognition of the best designed school or extensions to a school during the preceding three years. Submissions may be from local authorities, voluntary bodies, or architects in the U.K. only. A plaque is awarded biennially. Established in 1976.

2758

Schools Curriculum Award
For recognition of schools that made a significant contribution to school curriculum in their area taking into account the needs of the community. The award was based on two principles. First, it sought to identify schools which, in the opinion of the assessment panel, used the resources of their community and their environment to fulfill the educational philosophy of the school and to assist the pupils in their learning. Second, the award took into account the community's understanding of the work at the school, and its appreciation of the contributions that the school made to the community. Schools received award certificates. Established in 1982. Sponsored by the Society of Education Officers, the Association of Directors of Education in Scotland, and *Education*. (Discontinued)

2759

Educational Television Association
The King's Manor
Exhibition Sq.
York YO1 2EP, England
Phone: 904 433929
Fax: 904 433929

2760

Educational Television Awards Scheme
To recognize the production of creative and effective video material. To give wider recognition to those producers and technicians whose work deserves acknowledgment; to publicize the successful use of production creativity and techniques in meeting educational objectives; and to encourage video producers to make critical evaluations of their own work. Any type of video material is acceptable provided that it is in the form in which it will be presented to the intended users. Open to members and non-members. The following awards are presented: Premier Award - a plaque is awarded for the video material that has most effectively exploited the resources available to its producers to meet a specific educational need (sponsored by Panasonic Broadcast Europe); Educational Video Resource Award - for use of video as an education resource, especially in higher education, for worldwide use as part of a video print package (sponsored by Carafax Publishing Company); Broadcast Award (sponsored by McMillan (UK) Ltd.); Peter Turner Award - a plaque is awarded to the best video production produced by pupils or students (8-16 years old) under the guidance of a teacher (Held in conjunction with BBC Education with certain winning entries being broadcast on the BBC); Student Production Award - for the outstanding production by students over 16 years old as part of a media course or in connection with a media-related society (sponsored by BBC Television Training); Small Unit Award - for an outstanding videotape produced by a small video production unit (sponsored by 3M (UK) Ltd.); and Craft Awards - for lighting, camerawork, sound, editing, and graphics. Awards and plaques are presented. Awarded annually.

2761

Egypt Exploration Society
3 Doughty Mews
London WC1N 2PG, England
Phone: 71 2421880

2762

Egypt Exploration Society Centenary Studentship
To encourage projects relating to the aims of the Society, which are to undertake Egyptological researches, whether in Egypt or abroad, and publish the results. Applications must be submitted by February of each year. A monetary award is presented annually in September. Established in 1984 to honor the Centenary of the Egypt Exploration Society in 1982.

2763

Emphemera Society
84 Marylebone High St.
London W1M 3DE, England
Phone: 71 9357305
Fax: 71 9357305

2764

Samuel Pepys Medal
For recognition of outstanding contributions to ephemera studies. Ephemera are defined by the Society as the "transient minor documents of everyday life." A medal is awarded approximately every two years at a special ceremony in November. The medal is a gold-plated replica of a seventeenth century ivory medallion preserved at Magdalene College, Cambridge. Established in 1980 in memory of Samuel Pepys, the British diarist and early collector of ephemera.

2765

Employment Department: National Training Awards Office
Rm. W823, Moorfoot
Sheffield S1 4PQ, England
Phone: 742 593419
Fax: 742 593593

Formerly: (1988) Manpower Services Commission.

2766

National Training Award for Individual Achievement
To recognize individuals who have made exceptional achievements at work or in the community as a result of training, education, and personal development. Individuals should show enterprise, initiative, and personal commitment to their development above and beyond their employer's expectations. Approximately 20 awards consisting of a trophy and a monetary prize of £1,000 each are awarded. Regional winners receive £200 each and a certificate. Established in 1991.

2767

National Training Awards
To recognize and reward examples of exceptionally effective training. Any company or organization in the United Kingdom which undertakes training or is involved in its provision is eligible. A trophy, plaque, and use of the logo on stationery are awarded. About 80 awards are presented annually. Established in 1987 to provide a training equivalent to the Queen's Awards for Export and Technology.

2768

Engineering Council
10 Maltravers St.
London WC2R 3ER, England
Phone: 71 240 7891
Fax: 71 240 7517

2769

The Environment Award for Engineers
No further information on this award was provided for this edition.

2770

Prince of Wales Award for Industrial Innovation and Production
To encourage industrial innovation by identifying new products and ways of hastening their production and marketing. A monetary award of £10,000 was awarded annually. Established in 1980 by the Department of Trade and Industry. (Discontinued)

2771

Young Engineers for Britain
To encourage young people under the age of 19 to undertake engineering project work and to strengthen links between education and industry. Projects may be based on any branch of engineering. The following awards are presented: (1) Michael Faraday Prize - £600 and trophy presented by the Institution of Electrical Engineers for the project which exhibits the best use of electrical and electronic engineering principles and techniques; (2) Department of Education and Science Prize - £600 for the school entering the competition for the first time with the most imaginative project; (3) Wise Award (Womem Into Science and Engineer-

ing Award) - £500 for the best project by a girl or team of girls; (4) Comino Foundation Grant - £5,000 for the project which possesses the most potential and which has made the most commercial progress during the year following the national final; and (5) Young Engineer for Britain - £250. Established in 1977 by the Department of Trade and Industry.

2772
Engineering Industries Association
16 Dartmouth St., Westminster
London SW1H 9BL, England Phone: 71 2222367

2773
NatWest Bank Engineering Marketing Award
For recognition of marketing and innovation by an engineering business. Awards were given in three different categories based on employee numbers: up to 50, 50-250, and 250 plus. Due to reorganization of the National Westminster Bank, the award has been temporarily abandoned. Established in 1984.

2774
English Basket Ball Association
48 Bradford Rd.
Stanningley
Leeds LS28 6DF, England Phone: 532 361166
  Fax: 532 361022

2775
Coach of the Year
To recognize outstanding basketball coaches. Awarded annually. Established in 1976.

2776
Fair Play Award
To recognize the player registered in National Competitions whose attitude and approach to basketball is the most sportsmanlike. Awarded annually. Established in 1973.

2777
National Championship Cup Finals
To recognize the championship team from the men's and women's finals held among the National League Divisions. The George Williams Trophy is awarded annually. The Men's National Championship Cup Finals were established in 1936. The Women's National Championship Cup Finals were established in 1965. In the 1980-81 season the Women's Competition was reorganized, and two separate competitions were held - the National Cup, which is an open competition for all clubs, and the National Championship, which is a play off between the top teams in the National League.

2778
National League Player of the Year
To recognize basketball achievement in National competitions. Any player registered for National Competitions is eligible. A memento is presented annually. Established in 1976/1977.

2779
National Trophy (Men and Women)
To recognize the winners of the men's competition and the women's competition. Each competition is open to clubs except those in membership of the National League Division One.

2780
Player of the Year (Men and Women)
To recognize basketball achievement in the National Competitions. English players registered for National Competitions are eligible for the award. Trophies are presented annually. Established in 1971.

2781
English Centre of International PEN
7 Dilke St., Chelsea
London SW3 4JE, England Phone: 71 3526303
  Fax: 71 3510220

2782
J. R. Ackerley Prize
For recognition of outstanding literary achievement. Members of the English PEN Executive Committee submit the best unofficial autobiographies published during the previous calendar year. A monetary prize of £2,000 is awarded annually at the PEN Writers' Day in March. Established in 1982.

2783
Macmillan Silver Pen Award for Fiction
To recognize an outstanding collection of short stories written in English by an author of British nationality and published in the United Kingdom during the previous calendar year. A monetary prize of £500 and a silver pen are awarded annually at PEN Writers' Day in March. Established in 1985. Sponsored by Macmillan. Formerly: Silver Pen Award.

2784
Time-Life Silver Pen Award for Non-Fiction
To recognize an outstanding work of non-fiction, written in English, by an author of British nationality and published in the United Kingdom during the previous calendar year. A monetary prize of £1,000 and a silver pen are awarded annually at PEN Writers' Day in March. Sponsored by Time-Life. Formerly: Silver Pen Award.

2785
English Draughts Association
54, Mayfield Rd.
Ryde, Isle of Wight PO33 3PR, England Phone: 983 565484

2786
Alexander Shield
To recognize an individual as the English Amateur Draughts Champion. The candidate for the award must have been the winner of the annual amateur competition. A shield is presented annually. Established in 1910 to honor A. Alexander, the English Draughts Association president in 1910.

2787
Gelsthorpe Cup
To recognize an individual as the English Open Draughts Champion. The candidate for the award must have been the winner of the biannual Open Tournament Cup. The award is presented biennially. Established in 1885 to honor G. Gelsthorpe, who became the English Draughts Association president in 1909.

2788
English Folk Dance and Song Society
Cecil Sharp House
2, Regent's Park Rd.
London NW1 7AY, England Phone: 71 4852206
  Fax: 71 2840523

2789
Gold Badge
For recognition of an outstanding contribution to folk music and dance. A medal/badge is awarded annually. Established in 1922 by the English Folk Dance Society.

2790
English Speaking Board (International)
26a Princes St.
Southport, Merseyside PR8 1EQ, England Phone: 704 501730

2791

Speaker of the Year
For recognition of clarity, originality and vitality in the spoken language and for recognition of achievement. An engraved glass and inscription were awarded annually. Established in 1984. (Discontinued in 1988)

2792

Young Speaker of the Year
To encourage professional development. A trophy and a certificate were awarded annually. Established in 1985 in honor of Elizabeth Henry. (Discontinued in 1988)

2793

English Stage Company at Royal Court Theatre
Sloane Sq.
London SW1, England   Phone: 71 7305174

2794

George Devine Award
To recognize creative artists in the theater, typically young playwrights. The deadline for entry is in March. A monetary prize of £3,500 is occasionally shared. Awarded annually. Established in memory of the founder of the English stage company, George Devine.

2795

English Vineyards Association
38 West Park   Phone: 81 8570452
London SE9 4RH, England   Fax: 81 8514864

2796

English Wine of the Year Competition
To recognize the wine adjudged the best English Wine of the Year (previous vintage). A panel of judges make the selection by tasting following chemical analyses. The following awards are given in the two sections: Gore-Browne Trophy for the best wine in Section A; Jack Ward Memorial Salver for the best wine of the previous vintage; Wine Guild of the U.K. Trophy for the best wine of any other year's vintage; Brenard Theobald Trophy for best red wide in all competition; President's Cup for the best wine in Section B; and gold, silver, and bronze medals. Established in 1974 in honor of the pioneering work of Colonel Gore Browne in establishing modern viticulture in England.

2797

Ergonomics Society
3 Randolph Close
Knaphill
Woking, Surrey GU21 2NF, England   Phone: 509 234904

2798

Ulf Aberg Post Graduate Award
To recognize the best postgraduate student project in ergonomics. The postgraduate project should be in an area of ergonomics; however, the postgraduate course need not be one recognized by the Society. Entries may be submitted by the student's supervisor or head of department by July 1. Winners receive a monetary award of £50. (If the subject is in the field of consumer ergonomics, then this may be supplemented by a further £25 from the Institute of Consumer Ergonomics.) In addition, a certificate and expenses to attend the Annual Dinner are awarded. Established in 1977. Formerly: (1985) Student Award - Postgraduate Division.

2799

Applications Award
To recognize the most significant application of ergonomics put into practice during the previous five years by a member or group of members of the Society. Awarded annually when merited. Established in 1979. (Discontinued in 1988. The Award is covered by the Otto Edholm Award.)

2800

Sir Frederic Bartlett Medal
To honor an individual(s) who has made significant contributions to original research, the development of methodology, or application of knowledge within the field of ergonomics. Entries may be submitted by July 1. A medal, a certificate and expenses to attend the Annual Dinner are awarded annually when merited. Established in 1971. Submissions for all of the Society's awards should be sent to: Ergonomics Society Honours, The Ergonomics Society Office, Department of Human Sciences, University of Technology, Loughborough, Leics. LE11 3TU, United Kingdom.

2801

Otto Edholm Award
To honor an individual or individuals who have made significant contributions to basic or applied research in ergonomics. Entries may be submitted by July 1. A certificate and expenses to attend the Annual Dinner are awarded.

2802

Ergonomics Society Special Award
To recognize an individual, individuals, institutes or groups for service or accomplishments inappropriate for other categories of award or honor. Entries may be submitted by July 1. A certificate and expenses to attend the Annual Dinner are awarded when merited. Established in 1985.

2803

Ergonomics Society's Meritorious Service Award
To recognize an individual for unstinting and altruistic service to the Society over many years. Entries may be submitted by July 1. A certificate and expenses to attend the Annual Dinner are awarded annually when merited. Established in 1984.

2804

Honorary Fellow
To recognize an individual who has made a significant contribution to ergonomics over a long period of time and is recognized as a senior member of the ergonomics community. A certificate is awarded.

2805

Hywel Murrell Award
To recognize the best undergraduate student project in ergonomics. The undergraduate project should be in an area of ergonomics; however, the undergraduate course need not be one recognized by the Society. Entries may be submitted by the student's supervisor or head of department by July 1. Winners receive a monetary award of £50. (If the subject is in the field of consumer ergonomics, then this may be supplemented by a further £25 from the Institute of Consumer Ergonomics.) In addition, a certificate and expenses to attend the Annual Dinner are awarded. Established in 1977. Formerly: (1984) Student Award - Undergraduate Division.

2806

President's Medal
To honor institutes or organizational groups whose work has made a significant contribution to original research, the development of methodology, or application of knowledge within the field of Ergonomics. Entries may be submitted by July 1. A medal, a certificate and expenses to attend the Annual Dinner are awarded.

2807

Research Award
To recognize a number of significant contributions that represented a comprehensive program contribution to an extension of knowledge in an area of ergonomics. Awarded annually when merited. Established in 1983. (Discontinued in 1988. The award is covered by other awards.)

2808

Society Lecturer
A member of the Ergonomics Community is honored by giving a lecture to the Society. Quality of work and presentation ability are considered. The

topic varies from year to year and when possible, takes account of contemporary issues. A plaque and travel expenses incurred within the United Kingdom are awarded annually.

2809
Essex Salon Office
Southend-on-Sea Borough Council
Cliffs Pavilion
Station Rd.
Westcliff-on-Sea, Essex SSO 7RA, England   Phone: 0702 331852

2810
Essex International Salon of Photography
For recognition of outstanding photography in the following categories: (1) Portraiture/Full Figure; (2) Photo-Journalism/Action, Documentary; (3) Landscape and Seascape; (4) Record; Scientific; Technical and Architectural; (5) Natural History including domestic animals; and (6) Any subject not classified above. These may be in both monochrome and color. Monochrome prints must be the unaided work of the exhibitor, and color prints must be produced by a genuine photographic process. The maximum number of prints per entrant is ten. Any print previously shown in the Salon or any print so similar as to be taken for a previous entry is not eligible. The following prizes are awarded: (1) Best Print in Salon - Southend-on-Sea Borough Council Trophy; (2) Runner up to Best Print in Salon - Syd Ingram Trophy; (3) Best Print by an Essex Author - Arthur Gayner Perpetual Trophy; (4) First, Highly Commended, Commended in each section - Certificate of Award; and (5) Each print displayed in the Salon - Certificate of Acceptance and Shown.

2811
Euromoney Publications Limited
Nestor House, Playhouse Yard
London EC4V 5EX, England   Phone: 71 236 3288

2812
Banker of the Year
To recognize the investment banker of the year.

2813
Borrower of the Year
To recognize the biggest corporate borrower in the world.

2814
Central Banker of the Year
For recognition of a central banker who has done an outstanding job.

2815
Finance Minister of the Year
For recognition of a finance minister of a country who has done an outstanding job.

2816
Global Equity Awards
For recognition of stockbrokers throughout the world for speed of execution, prices, and professionalism. Winners are determined by a poll of more than 200 brokers from the top 12 equities markets, both in their home market and in foreign markets.

2817
Worst Finance Minister of the Year
For recognition of a finance minister of a country who has done the most to harm his country's economy. (Also known as the Wooden Spoon Award).

2818
European Association for Cancer Research
Cancer Research Laboratory
University of Nottingham   Phone: 602 513418
Nottingham NG7 2RD, England   Fax: 602 515115

2819
EACR Italian Fellowship Program
To support scientists and clinicians, specifically in Europe, to undertake cancer research projects in Italy. Fellowships range from three months to one year in Italian research institutions. The deadlines for applications are April 1 and October 1. Sponsored by the Italian Association for Cancer Research. For further information, contact the Secretariat of the EACR.

2820
EACR Travel Fellowships
To enable cancer researchers, preferably under 35 years of age, to undertake further research in another location. Researchers must be sponsored by members of the Association. Fellowships of up to $2,000 are awarded.

2821
European Association for the Science of Air Pollution
Mechanical Engineering Dept.
Imperial College
London SW7 2A2, England

2822
Young Scientist Award
For recognition of the best scientific paper submitted by a young scientist related to scientific aspects of air pollution. Individuals under 33 years of age are eligible. A monetary prize of £200 and a certificate are awarded biennially. Established in 1989.

2823
European Chemical Marketing Research Association
FEMRA Secretariat
Studio 38
Wimbledon Business Centre
Riverside Rd.   Phone: 81 8790709
London SW17 0BA, England   Fax: 81 9472637

2824
Lawrie Waddams Award
To recognize an individual for service to the Association. A trophy and a plaque are awarded annually when merited at the annual conference. Established in 1985 to honor A. L. Waddams. Additional information is available from Carl Plunger, Chairman, Awards Committee, ECMRA Hoechst AG, D-Frankfort, Federal Republic of Germany.

2825
European Council of International Schools
21 Lavant St.   Phone: 730 268244
Petersfield, Hants. GU32 3EL, England   Fax: 730 267914

2826
ECIS Award For International Understanding
To recognize students who are good representatives of their countries, display a positive attitude towards the life and culture of others, have the ability to converse in at least two languages, are contributing forces in the life of the school, and have an ability to bring different people together in a sense of community, thus furthering the cause of international understanding. Nominees are selected by the student's school faculty. Awarded annually to a student in each participating member school.

2827
ECIS Awards
For recognition in the field of education.

2828
European Federation of Societies for Ultrasound in Medicine and Biology
The Studio
43 Bond St.
London W5 5AS, England   Phone: 81 567 9307

2829
EUROSON Young Persons Award
To recognize and encourage new work in the fields of clinical and/or basic research. Members under 35 years of age are eligible. A monetary prize is awarded triennially at the Federation Congress. Established in 1990.

2830
European General Galvanizers Association
(Association Europeenne des Industries de la Galvanisation d'Articles divers)
London House
68 Upper Richmond Rd.
Putney
London SW15 2RP, England   Phone: 81 874 2122
                              Fax: 81 874 3251

2831
Bablik Medal
For recognition of outstanding activities of direct benefit to the galvanizing industry. The award is normally made for an extended series of activities. Individuals who have retired or who are within three years of retirement age are eligible. Current members of the Bablik Awards Committee or of the Secretariat are not eligible. Nomination of an individual for receipt of a Bablik Medal may be made at any time by letter to the Secretariat from a member of the Board. Nominations must be signed by at least three people from different countries. The inaugural Bablik Medal in gold was presented to Professor Bablik and to Mr. Sendzimir who had each made unique contributions to the industry. A silver medal is awarded at International Galvanizing Conferences but may be presented at other times such as Annual Meetings of EGGA.

2832
EGGA Pin
To recognize practitioners of galvanizing and others who have made valuable contributions to international development of galvanizing and to the development of the Association. A tie pin and a certificate are awarded annually at general assemblies or international conferences.

2833
Honorary Member
To recognize an individual for outstanding contributions and service to the galvanizing industry. Awarded when merited.

2834
European Organization for Caries Research
(Organisation Recherche de la Carie)
School of Dentistry
Dept. of Oral Biology, Clarendon Way
Univ. of Leeds
Leeds LS2 9LU, England   Phone: 532 336159

2835
ORCA Rolex Prize
For recognition of merit in any aspect of caries research. The field of scientific investigation from which a recipient is selected should be as broad as possible. A Rolex watch is awarded annually. Established in 1964.

2836
European Orthodontic Society
Flat 31
49 Hallam St.
London W1N 5LL, England   Phone: 71 9352795
                            Fax: 71 9352795

2837
Ernest Sheldon Friel Memorial Lecture
For recognition of work in the field of orthodontics. The award is associated with a named lecture known specifically as the Friel Memorial Lecture, which is presented at an annual congress and published in the Society's journal. Established in 1973 by the family of the late Professor Ernest Sheldon Friel to commemorate his services to orthodontics and to the European Orthodontic Society of which he was a president and honorary member.

2838
W. J. B. Houston Research Awards
To recognize outstanding presentations at the annual congress. Awards are presented for the best research paper and the best poster presenting the results of original research on a topic of orthodontic interest. Papers and posters must be presented in English by a member under the age of 35. A scroll and monetary award of £1,000 is presented in each category. Established in 1993 in memory of W. J. B. Houston, honorary editor and post president and secretary of the Society.

2839
European Parliament
c/o Information Office
2 Queen Anne's Gate
London SW1H 9AA, England   Phone: 71 222 0411

2840
Europa Prize
For recognition of contributions to the European economic and financial field. Awarded annually. Established in 1967. Sponsored by the financial publications *Handelsblatt*, *La Vie Francaise*, *La Metropole*, *Elseviers*, and *Il Sole/24ore*, with the Union of European Economic and Financial Press. (Discontinued in 1971)

2841
European Parliament Sakharov Prize for Freedom of Thought
To provide for study or work on one of the following topics: (1) the development of East-West relations in the light of the Helsinki Final Act, in particular the third basket on cooperation in humanitarian and other fields; (2) safeguarding the freedom of scientific inquiry; (3) the defense of human rights and respect for international law; and (4) government practice as compared with the letter of constitutional provisions. A monetary prize is awarded annually. Established in 1986. Additional information is available from European Parliament, Centre European, Kirchburg, Luxembourg.

2842
European Piano Teachers Association
28 Emperor's Gate
London SW7 4HS, England   Phone: 71 3737307

2843
Young Pianists Yearly Award
To recognize piano teachers and their students. The Association sponsors competitions, awards travel grants for teachers to attend meetings, and presents a Young Pianists Yearly Award to a junior pianist and his/her teacher.

2844
European Society for Microcirculation
Diabetes Research Laboratories
  (Microvascular Studies)
Noy Scott House, Postgraduate Med.
  School
Haldon View Terr.
Exeter EX2 5EQ, England

Phone: 392 403064
Fax: 392 403027

2845
ESM Career Development Award
To support young scientists who are committed to a career in microvascular research. A monetary award of up to £2,000 is presented at the Programme and Awards Committee Meeting in March. Deadline is the end of February.

2846
Malpighi Prize
To recognize an eminent scientist for a notable contribution to the field of microcirculation. Before 1984, the Prize was given for the best film on microcirculation presented at the biennial conference. Members of the Society may make nominations to the Commission about 15 months before the award. A medal and travel and expenses to attend the meeting are awarded biennially. The awardee is expected to give a Malpighi Lecture describing his research work at the biennial meeting of the Society. Established in honor of Marcello Malpighi, an Italian who discovered microcirculation (capillaries, etc.) in 1661.

2847
Travel Awards
Funded by the society to meet registration and travel costs of the biennial meetings. Awarded on the basis of submitted abstracts for the meeting. A minimum of five awards are made.

2848
European Table Tennis Union
43 Knowsley Rd.
Bolton, Lancs. BL1 6JH, England

Phone: 204 42223
Fax: 204 495129

2849
European Competitions
To recognize the winners of the biennial tournament for senior citizens and the annual European Youth Championship.

2850
Ewart-Biggs Memorial Award
33a Brondesbury Rd.
London NW6, England

2851
Christopher Ewart-Biggs Memorial Prize
For recognition of the published work which contributes the most to peace and understanding in Ireland, to closer ties between the peoples of Britain and Ireland, or to cooperation between the partners of the European Community. Writers of any nationality are eligible. Works written in English or French and published during the award year are considered. A monetary prize of £4,000 is awarded biennially. Established in 1977 in memory of Christopher Ewart-Biggs, the British Ambassador to Ireland, who was assassinated in 1976 while in Dublin.

2852
Executive Travel
6 Chesterfield Gardens
London W1Y 8DN, England

Phone: 71 3551600
Fax: 71 3559630

2853
Airline of the Year
For recognition of excellence in air travel. Awards are given in a variety of categories based on survey responses of readers of *Executive Travel* magazine. A golden 747 trophy and certificates are awarded annually in January. Established in 1982. Sponsored by Wagonlit Travel.

2854
Hotel of the Year Awards
For recognition of the most outstanding hotels in the world. *Executive Travel* magazine and Utell International select the winners in a variety of categories based on popularity and written comments. Established in 1982. Co-sponsored by Utell International.

2855
Experimental Psychology Society
Dept. of Psychology
Royal Holloway
University of London
Egham, Surrey TW20 0EX, England

Phone: 784 443710
Fax: 784 434347

2856
Bartlett Lecture
For recognition of contributions to experimental psychology or cognate subjects. An honorarium, expenses for travel, and the opportunity to present a lecture are awarded annually. Established in 1971 in honor of Sir Frederic Bartlett, a British psychologist.

2857
Experimental Psychology Society Prize
For recognition of distinguished work in experimental psychology or a cognate discipline by an individual in an early stage of his or her career. An honorarium and the opportunity to present a lecture are awarded annually. Established in 1994.

2858
Faber and Faber Limited
3 Queen Sq.
London WC1N 3AU, England

Phone: 71 4650045
Fax: 71 4650034

2859
Samuel Beckett Award
To give support and encouragement to new playwrights at a crucial stage in their careers. A monetary award of £1,000 in each category plus possible publication were awarded annually. Jointly sponsored by Channel 4, the Royal Court Theatre and Faber & Faber. Additional information is available from Frank Pike, Drama Editor. (Discontinued)

2860
Geoffrey Faber Memorial Prize
For recognition of a volume of verse or a volume of prose fiction of great literary merit that was first published in the United Kingdom during the preceding two years. Awards are given in alternate years for verse and prose fiction. The authors must not be older than 40 years of age and must be either British citizens or citizens of any other Commonwealth state, the Republic of Ireland, or the Republic of South Africa. Submissions for the prize may not be made. The three judges are regular reviewers of poetry or of fiction, as the case may be and are nominated each year by editors or literary editors of newspapers and magazines that regularly publish such reviews. A monetary prize of £1,000 is awarded annually. Established in 1963 in memory of Geoffrey Faber, founder of Faber and Faber Ltd.

2861

Faculty of Building
Central Office
35 Hayworth Rd.
Sandiacre, Notts. NG10 5LL, England
Phone: 602 490641
Fax: 602 491664

2862

Edwin Williams Memorial Award
For recognition of significant advancement in urban design. The competition is limited to the planning authorities in the Greater London area at the discretion of the Faculty. An engraved plaque and citation are awarded annually. Established in 1979 in memory of Edwin Williams, who contributed to architecture and town planning in the Greater London area.

2863

Fan Circle International
Cronk-Y-Voddy
Rectory Rd.
Coltishall NR12 7HF, England

2864

FCI Competition Essay
To recognize essays which contribute to the knowledge and appreciation of fans. Society members must submit essays by December 1. A monetary award and publication in *Fans* is awarded biennially in May. Established in 1989.

2865

Fauna and Flora Preservation Society
(Sociedad para la Preservacion de la Fauna y Flora)
1 Kensington Gore
London SW7 2AR, England
Phone: 71 8238899
Fax: 71 8239690

2866

Fauna and Flora Preservation Society Grants
To provide for research pertaining to the prevention of extinction of wild animals and plants by promoting the conservation of wildlife, the establishment of new national parks, the enactment and enforcement of laws to protect wildlife, and the education of governments and individuals in the value of world wildlife as a non-renewable natural resource. Applications are considered quarterly. Projects and programs relating to endangered species of fauna and flora are considered. Grants up to $2,000 are awarded.

2867

Fawcett Society
46 Harleyford Rd.
London SE11 5AY, England
Phone: 71 587 1287

Formerly: London Women's Suffrage Society.

2868

Fawcett Book Prize
For recognition of the book which best illuminates women's position in society. Awards are given in alternate years for fiction and nonfiction. Books of 50,000 words first published in English in Britain, Ireland, and the Commonwealth during the previous two years are eligible. A monetary prize of £500 is awarded annually. Established in 1982.

2869

Federation of British Artists
17 Carlton House Terr.
London SW1Y 5BD, England
Phone: 71 930 6844
Fax: 71 839 7830

2870

Federation of British Artists Prizes and Awards
To recognize outstanding artists. The FBA has become the leading national center for prizes and awards through the major competitions it has set up. All the FBA Society exhibitions are open to submission by non-members. More than 7,000 artists submit work to be judged throughout the year. Further prizes are given through the Societies' own exhibitions for works of excellence. Awards include the Carroll Foundation Award, which was established in 1988 to recognize and encourage young portrait painters, and which presents a monetary award of £3,000 and a medal.

2871

Federation of British Tape Recordists
Woodend
31 West Field
Little Abington
Cambridge, Cambs. CB1 6BE, England

2872

Class Prizes in British Amateur Tape Recording Contest
To encourage the development of all aspects of sound and video recording by amateurs: speech and drama, reportage, documentary, music (live and electronic), technical experiment, and sounds from nature. Candidates must be citizens of the United Kingdom (there is an international amateur tape recording contest, CIMES, open to all individuals). The award consists of a trophy or cup and prizes donated by the audio industry. Awarded annually at a prize presentation evening in November. Established in 1957 by Mr. D. Brown, editor and publisher of *Tape Recording Magazine*. Sponsored by companies in the audio industry.

2873

Federation of Children's Book Groups
30 Senneleys Park Rd.
Northfield
Birmingham, W. Midlands B31 1AL,
  England
Phone: 274 575301

2874

Children's Book Award
To recognize the achievement of authors and illustrators who give children so much pleasure, and to foster an interest in children's books among children and parents. Works of fiction suitable for children that were published for the first time in the United Kingdom in the previous year, are eligible for consideration. Entries must be submitted by December 31. A silver and oak prize valued at over £7,000 and a presentation book filled with letters, pictures, reviews, and comments from the children who are the judges are awarded to celebrate the winning book. Shortlisted authors and illustrators also receive presentation books. The "Pick of the Year" booklist is produced annually in the spring. Established in 1980. Sponsored by Save and Prosper Educational Trust.

2875

Federation of Old Cornwall Societies
Tremarsh
Launceston, Cornwall, England
Phone: 566 773509

2876

Kernow Goth Trophy
For recognition of an essay on a subject of Cornish historical interest. Society members only are eligible to submit entries. A trophy consisting of a piece of Cornish quartz mounted on mahogany is awarded annually. Established in 1985.

2877
Federation of Small Businesses
140 Lower Marsh, Westminster Bridge
London SE1 7AE, England
Phone: 71 928 9272
Fax: 71 401 2544

Formerly: (1991) National Federation of Self Employed and Small Business.

2878
Guildhall Helping Hand Awards
To recognize individuals or organizations for outstanding help and support to the small business sector and the self-employed. Awards are presented in the following categories: Politician's Award - open to all MP's and MEP's who have vigorously promoted small business issues in Parliament and their constituencies; National Press Award - open to individuals, and teams of journalists who have consistently highlighted the concerns of small businesses in national newspapers and magazines; Regional Press Award - open to press working on regional newspaper, whether daily, weekly, or free-sheets. Journalists who have proved particularly caring and helpful on local small business campaigns are eligible; and Broadcasting Award - for the television or radio program station or presenter who has most effectively voiced the feelings of Britain's small business sector. The award is open to both the national and regional broadcasting media. A bronze statue is awarded annually. Established in 1988. Sponsored by Tollit & Harvey Ltd. (currently inactive)

2879
Film and Video Press Group
81 Dean St.
London W1V 6AA, England
Phone: 71 437 4355

2880
Clifford Wheeler Award
For recognition of the greatest enterprise and imagination in use and distribution of a commissioned film or video program. Applications may be submitted. A silver ingot is awarded annually. Established in 1967 in honor of Clifford Wheeler, one of the great proponents of sponsored film distribution by the Central Office of Information. Sponsored by Kodak (UK) Ltd.

2881
Filtration Society
48 Springfield Rd.
Horsham, W. Sussex RH12 2PD, England
Phone: 403 259419
Fax: 403 265005

2882
Gold Medal
To recognize the most meritorious original paper on filtration and separation technology. A medal and a certificate are awarded biennially.

2883
H. K. Suttle Award
To encourage and recognize the achievements of younger workers in the field of filtration and separation technology. Authors under 35 years of age may submit papers in English. A monetary prize of £500 and a certificate are awarded biennially. The award is named after the Founder-Chairman of the Society, Harold K. Suttle.

2884
Travel and Study Abroad
To enable workers in the field of filtration to visit analogous centers of study, both academic and industrial, in other countries. Applications must be submitted. A monetary award of £500 to assist in defraying the cost of travel is awarded.

2885
Financial Times
c/o Press Office
1 Southwark Bridge
London SE1 9HL, England
Phone: 71 873 3000
Fax: 71 873 3072

2886
Architecture Award
To encourage higher standards in architectural and environmental design for industrial and commercial buildings and to recognize new buildings that enhance the urban or rural landscape and the lives of the people who work in them. Awarded biennially. Established in 1967. Jointly administered by the Royal Institute of British Architects.

2887
Financial Times/**London Business School Design Management Award**
To recognize organizations that have established comprehensive policies for the management of design and the provision of a consistently high quality of product, service, environment and communication, and were seen to be effective in carrying them out. The award was not given for individual products, services, buildings, and communications. The biennial award carried considerable prestige for the recipient and provided valuable opportunities for promotion and publicity. Established in 1965. (Discontinued in 1991)

2888
Alan Harper Bursary
To recognize excellence in journalistic photography. Winners of the award are eligible to receive a £5,000 grant from British Telecom Inc. (BTI) to do a photographic assignment of their choice. Entrants must submit a portfolio of work and a project proposal. They must also be under 26 years of age on December 31st of the year prior to the award. Sponsored by the Guild of Picture Editors. Established in 1992 in memory of *Financial Times* photographer Alan Harper, who was killed in Kuwait with fellow journalist David Thomas.

2889
Industrial Photographer of the Year
For recognition of the best portfolio of four photographs taken by a professional photographer. A trophy and £250 were awarded annually. (Discontinued)

2890
Young Business Writer
To recognize excellence in business journalism among undergraduate and other young writers. Winners are invited to a presentation ceremony and given the opportunity to accompany *Financial Times* journalists for a day and visit the *Financial Times* printing site. Entrants are required to write an essay on a given title. Two levels of competition are held: Undergraduate and Sixth Form. Sponsored by the Clifford Chance Solicitors and the City University Business School.

2891
Fingerprint Society
Fingerprint Bureau
c/o The Chairman
LLoyd House, Colmore Circus
Birmingham, England
Phone: 707 33 11 77

Formerly: (1976) National Society of Fingerprint Officers.

2892
Lewis Minshall Award
For recognition of outstanding contributions to the science of fingerprints, identification, or research, world-wide. Members or non-members of the Society are eligible. A trophy is presented annually when merited at the general meeting. Established in 1980 by the widow of Detective Superintendent Lewis Minshall, Queen's Police Medal, in memory of her husband, the first president of the Fingerprint Society.

2893
Fireball International
Pendennis
Parsonage St.
Bradninch
Exeter, Devon EX5 4NW, England   Phone: 392 881972

2894
International Fireball Worlds Trophy
For recognition of achievement in the field of competitive sailing. A trophy is awarded annually to the world champion helmsman. Established in 1966 by Bill Kempner, D.S.C.

2895
Fish Farmers' Specialist Branch
c/o National Farmers' Union
Agriculture House
Knightsbridge
London SW1X 7NJ, England   Phone: 71 235 5077

Formerly: British Trout and Salmon Marketing Union.

2896
Peter Jones Memorial Award
To recognize outstanding contributions to fish farming or fisheries industries. Individuals from the United Kingdom may be nominated. A bronze salmon is awarded when merited. Established in 1984 in memory of Peter Jones, Secretary of Fish Farmers' Specialist Branch, for his work in establishing the industry in the United Kingdom.

2897
Flying Fifteen International
29 Stamford Rd.   Phone: 509 843896
Oakham, Leics., England   Fax: 509 843629

2898
Flying Fifteen World Championship
For recognition of the winners of the Flying Fifteen World Championships. The International Flying Fifteen Class is a one design racing keelboat. Members of FFL affiliated associations are eligible. The following Perpetual World Championship Trophies are presented biennially: (1) UFFA Fox Trophy - for the World Champion; (2) Armada Dish (Biffa Trophy) a silver dish with historic hallmarks - for the Crew of the 1st placed boat in the Open-Champion crew; (3) Tom Ratcliff Trophy (crystal and silver swans) - 2nd overall; (4) WAFFA Salver - 3rd overall; (5) NZNFFA Trophy (kauriwood) - 4th overall; (6) Kellett Island Trophy (silver dragon) - leading overseas helm; (7) Dixon Trophy - (silver rose bowl) - winner 1st race; (8) Kinsale Yacht Club Trophy (waterford crystal) - winner 2nd race; (9) Napier Sailing Club Trophy (Maori War Canoe) - winner 3rd race; and (10) Hayling Island SC Trophy (silver wire Fifteen) - winner 7th race. Established in 1979. Additional information is available from International Yacht Racing Union 8840, c/o J. Michael Evans, Exec. Dir., 60 Knightsbridge, London SW1X 7JX, England, phone: 71 235 6221.

2899
Folkestone Menuhin International Violin Competition
c/o Callaway Ltd
2 Portland Rd., Holland Park   Phone: 71 221 7883
London W11 4LA, England   Fax: 71 229 4595

2900
Folkestone Menuhin International Violin Competition
For recognition of outstanding violin performances by violinists under 22 years of age. Monetary prizes totaling £15,400 are awarded biennially. Established in 1983.

2901
Folklore Society
Univ. College London
Gower St.
London WC1E 6BT, England   Phone: 71 3875894

2902
Katharine Briggs Folklore Award
To encourage a high standard of publication and scholarship in folklore. Books published for the first time in English in the United Kingdom between June 1 and May 31 are eligible. Included are scholarly revised editions of previously published texts, but excluded are reprints or folktales retold for children. A monetary prize and an engraved goblet are awarded annually. Established in 1982 in honor of Dr. Katharine Briggs, a distinguished English folktale and literary scholar, and a past president of the Society.

2903
Coote-Lake Medal for Folklore Research
For recognition of research in the field of folklore studies and for service to the Folklore Society. Individuals must be nominated by a committee of the Society. A medal is awarded when merited. Established in 1941 by Mrs. H. A. Lake-Barnett, a treasurer and secretary of the Folklore Society, in memory of Harold Coote-Lake, the founder's brother and a treasurer and secretary of the Folklore Society.

2904
Forensic Science Society
Clarke House
18 A Mount Parade   Phone: 423 506068
Harrogate, N. Yorks. HG1 1BX, England   Fax: 423 530948

2905
Forensic Science Society Awards
To recognize forensic scientists, lawyers, pathologists, police officers, odontologists and police surgeons and to promote the study and application of forensic science. Awards are presented.

2906
Franco-British Society
Linen Hall, Rm. 623
162-168 Regent St.
London W1R 5TB, England   Phone: 71 7340815

2907
Franco-British Landscape Gardening Award
To draw attention to an outstanding horticultural achievement each year, either in Britain or France, thus encouraging and developing further contacts between the two countries in the areas of garden history and landscape design. Established in 1988.

2908
Enid McLeod Literary Prize
To recognize the author of the work of literature that has contributed the most to Franco-British understanding. Any full length work of literature written in English by a citizen of the United Kingdom, British Commonwealth, Republic of Ireland, Pakistan, Bangladesh, or South Africa, and first published in the United Kingdom is eligible. A monetary prize and a copy of Miss McLeod's memoirs are awarded annually. Established in 1983 in honor of Miss Enid McLeod.

2909
Vlado Perlemuter Piano Scholarship
To select from auditions the British piano student, between 17 and 25 years old, whose career would benefit most from an international summer school course in France. The annual winner of the scholarship receives tuition and expenses to study at the Academie Internationale de Musique Maurice Ravel, St. Jean-de-Luz, near Biarritz. Established in

1983 in honor of the distinguished pianist, Vlado Perlemuter, pupil of Ravel.

2910
Friends of Sadler's Wells
Sadler's Wells
Rosebery Ave.
London EC1R 4TN, England
Phone: 71 2786563
Fax: 71 8370965

2911
John Newson Award
To recognize the member of a presentation at Sadler's Wells who is considered to have made the most outstanding creative contribution to the life of the theatre. A trophy and certificate are awarded annually, at a performance at Sadler's Wells. Established in 1986 in honor of John Newson, former chairman of the Friends of Sadler's Wells.

2912
Friends of the Earth
26-28 Underwood St.
London N1 7JQ, England
Phone: 71 490 2380

2913
EARTHWORM Children's Book Award
To promote and reward environmental awareness and sensitivity in literature for children of all ages. Books must be submitted by publishing houses by April 30. A monetary prize of £2,500 is awarded for First prize and three runners-up receive £500 and a bronze bookmark each. Awarded annually. Established in 1987. Sponsored by Save and Prosper Educational Trust.

2914
Galpin Society
2 Quinton Rise
Oadby, Leics. LE2 5PN, England
Phone: 533 855136

2915
Research Grant
To assist in original research in anticipation of an article suitable for inclusion in the Society's journal. Members of the Society may apply by April 1, except officers and committee members. A monetary prize is awarded annually. Established in 1966.

2916
Gemmological Association and Gem Testing Laboratory of Great Britain
27 Greville St.
(Saffron Hill Entrance)
London EC1N 8SU, England
Phone: 71 404 3334
Fax: 71 404 8843

Formerly: Gemmological Association of Great Britain.

2917
Tully Medal
To recognize an individual who submits the best set of answers in the Gemmology Diploma Examination. The answers must be, in the opinion of the examiners, of sufficiently high standard to merit the award. Trade or non-trade candidates are eligible. A silver medal is awarded by the examiners when merited. Established in 1930 in memory of Tully, the inventor of a substantially-sized table model refractometer for jewellers. In addition, the following awards are presented: Anderson Bank Prize - to the best non-trade candidate; Diploma Trade Prize - to the best candidate of the year who derives his or her income from activities essentially connected with the jewelery trade; Anderson Medal - to the best candidate of the year in the Preliminary Examination; and Preliminary Trade Prize - to the best candidate, under the age of 21 years on June 1 of the year of examination, who derives his or her main income from activities essentially connected with the jewelry trade.

2918
Geological Society
Senior Admin. Sec.
Burlington House
Piccadilly
London W1V OJU, England
Phone: 71 4349944
Fax: 71 4398975

2919
Aberconway Medal
For recognition of distinguished contributions to the advancement of the profession and practice of geology. Individuals may be nominated. A medal is awarded annually at the general meeting in March. Established in 1980 by Lord Aberconway of Bodnant. Sponsored by English China Clays Ltd.

2920
Major John Sacheverell A'Deane Coke Medal
To recognize scientists for their contributions to geology, and for recognition of significant service to geology, for example through administrative, organizational, or promotional activities resulting in benefits to the community. Also the field may be extended to include scientists whose training and interests are outside the main fields of geology but whose contributions are of great significance to our science. A medal is awarded annually.

2921
Bigsby Medal
To recognize an individual under 45 years of age for eminent services in any department of geology. A medal is awarded biennially.

2922
Major Edward D'Ewes Fitzgerald Coke Medal
To recognize scientists for their contributions to geology, and for recognition of significant service to geology through administrative, organizational, or promotional activities resulting in benefits to the community. Also the field may be extended to include scientists whose training and interests are outside the main fields of geology but whose contributions are of great significance to our science. A medal is awarded annually.

2923
Sue Tyler Friedman Medal
To recognize an individual for distinguished contributions to the recording of the history of geology. Established in 1987 by a gift from a Northeastern Science Foundation of Troy, New York.

2924
Lyell Medal
To recognize an individual who has made a significant contribution to the science by means of a substantial body of research. Workers in both pure and applied aspects of the geological sciences are eligible. A medal is awarded annually. The Lyell Fund is awarded to contributors to the earth sciences on the basis of noteworthy published research.

2925
Murchison Medal
To recognize authors of memoirs or persons actually employed in any enquiries bearing upon the science of geology. A monetary prize and a medal are awarded annually. Established in 1873 through the will of Sir Roderick Impey Murchison (1792-1871). The Murchison Fund is also awarded to contributors to the earth sciences on the basis of noteworthy published research.

2926
President's Awards
To recognize geologists who are under the age of 30 and who made a notably early contribution to the science. Established in 1980 by Professor Perce Allen.

2927
Prestwich Medal
To recognize scientists who have undertaken special research bearing on stratigraphical or physical geology. A medal is awarded annually.

2928
William Smith Medal
For recognition of excellence in contributions to applied and economic aspects of the science. Candidates must have initiated significant contributions, which will normally take the form of published papers. Although in view of the confidential nature of the work in the case of some candidates, other criteria may be used as the basis of the award. A medal is awarded annually. Established in 1977. A William Smith Fund is also awarded to scientists under 40 years of age.

2929
Wollaston Medal
This, the highest award of the Society, is normally given to geologists who have had a significant influence by means of a substantial body of excellent research in either or both pure and applied aspects of the science. A medal is awarded annually. The Wollaston Fund is awarded to contributors to the earth sciences on the basis of noteworthy published research.

2930
R. H. Worth Prize
For recognition of meritorious geological research carried out by amateur geologists, or for the encouragement of geological research by amateurs.

2931
Girls' Brigade International Council
The Old Bridewell
3 Burgh Rd.
Aylsham, Norfolk NR11 6AJ, England
Phone: 263 734917
Fax: 263 734917

2932
International Award
To recognize girls between the ages of 18 and 25 for achievement. A scholarship is awarded. Established in 1968.

2933
Margaret O'Rourke Scholarship
To provide financial assistance for further education in youth work. Established in 1978 in memory of the late Margaret O'Rourke, past president of the Council.

2934
Queen's Award
To recognize girls between the ages of 18 and 25 for achievement. A scholarship is awarded. Established in 1968.

2935
Glaxo/Association of British Science Writers
Glaxo House
Berkeley Ave.
Greenford, Greater London UB6 ONN, England
Phone: 71 4934060
Fax: 81 9668827

2936
Glaxo Science Writers Awards
To recognize individuals who have done the most in the opinion of the judges, to enhance the quality of science journalism. Awards are given in six categories: best article or series of articles in a national or regional newspaper on a science subject; best article or series of articles in a specialist journal on a science subject; best radio program or contribution to a series of programs on a science subject; best television program or contribution to a series of programs on a science subject; best entry from any medium on the theme, "Improving Human Health in the 1990s"; and the best communication of science in a non-science context. Nominations or applications are accepted from specialist writers, newspaper reporters, freelance journalists, and television and radio producers, directors, and writers. Work must have been published or broadcast during the preceding year. Six monetary awards of £2,000 each and certificates are awarded annually in the summer. Established in 1966.

2937
Glyndebourne Festival Opera
Glyndebourne
Lewes, E. Sussex BN8 5UU, England
Phone: 273 812321
Fax: 273 812783

2938
John Christie Award
To enable a young and promising singer from the Glyndebourne company to further studies and to travel abroad to do so if necessary. A scholarship is awarded annually. Established in 1965. Sponsored by the Worshipful Company of Musicians.

2939
Carl Ebert Award
To assist younger members of the Glyndebourne production staff to pursue their studies. Selection is by nomination. A monetary award is presented when merited. Established in 1981 by the Leche Trustees in memory of Carl Ebert, Artistic Director, Glyndebourne 1934 - 1959. Sponsored by Leche Trustees.

2940
Esso - Glyndebourne Touring Opera Singers' Award
To recognize a young singer engaged by Glyndebourne. A monetary prize is awarded. Established in 1977 through the generosity of an anonymous private donor. Sponsored since 1983 by Esso Exploration and Production UK Limited.

2941
Glyndebourne Peter Stuyvesant Award
To recognize a young singer engaged by Glyndebourne. Established in 1984 by the Peter Stuyvesant Foundation to mark the 50th anniversary of the Glyndebourne Festival Opera. Awarded in 1986 to mark the Silver Jubilee of the Peter Stuyvesant Foundation.

2942
Jani Strasser Award
To assist a young member of the staff on the musical side of Glyndebourne's operation in the furtherance of his or her career. Established in 1983 in memory of Jani Strasser, former head of the music staff.

2943
Erich Vietheer Memorial Award
To recognize a promising young Glyndebourne singer. Selection is by nomination. A monetary prize is awarded annually. Established in 1990 by the Erich Vietheer Memorial Trust in memory of Erich Vietheer. Sponsored by Erich Vietheer Memorial Trust.

2944
Goldsmiths' Company
Goldsmiths' Hall
Foster Ln.
London EC2V 6BN, England
Phone: 71 6067010
Fax: 71 6061511

2945
Binney Memorial Award
For recognition of bravery in support of law and order within the metropolitan and city police areas of London. Individuals must be nominated by the police. A medal and certificates of merit are awarded annually. Established in 1947 by friends of Captain Ralph Binney R.N., who was killed in an attempt to prevent a robbery in the City of London.

2946
Granada Television Limited
Television Centre
Manchester M60 9EA, England   Phone: 61 832 7211

2947
***What the Papers Say* Award**
For recognition of special achievement in the field of journalism. Awards are given in varying categories such as: Newspaper of the Year; Journalist of the Year; Columnist of the Year; Sports Writer of the Year; Scoop of the Year; and the Gerald Barry Award for excellence in journalism. A panel of program editors and producers makes the selections based on nominations from all the presenters of the *What the Papers Say* program during the preceding year. A flong - a small physical reproduction of publishing room equipment - is awarded annually.

2948
William Grant & Sons
Independence House
84 Lower Mortlake Rd.   Phone: 1 332 1188
Richmond, Surrey TW9 2HS, England   Fax: 1 332 1695

2949
Glenfiddich Awards
To recognize writers and broadcasters who have contributed most to raising the standard, and our knowledge, of what is eaten and drunk in Britain today. Awards are given in the following categories: (1) Food Book of the Year - for the best book relating to food; (2) Drink Book of the Year - for the best book relating to drink; (3) Food Writer of the Year - for outstanding work covering any area of food (prose rather than recipe-led work); (4) Drink Writer of the Year - for outstanding work covering any area of drink; (5) Cookery Writer of the Year - specifically for recipe-led work which inspires the reader to cook; (6) Restaurant Writer of the Year - for restaurant writing which encourages eating out; (7) Whisky Writer of the Year - for the writer contributing to the appreciation of Scotch Whisky and in particular Malt Whisky; (8) Trade Writer of the Year - for excellence in writing in any sector of the trade press relating to food and drink; (9) Radio/Television Programme of the Year - for the best work relating to food and drink broadcast in the preceding year; (10) Visual Category - for visual work relating to food and drink, including photography, illustration, editing and any area of production; and (11) The Special Award - awarded at the discretion of the judges, to a particularly outstanding entry which does not fit into any of the above categories. In addition, the judges may choose to recognize any event or work, such as a campaign, lecture or personality seen to have made a special contribution to the subjects of food and drink in the relevant year. An independent panel of judges selects 11 category winners from material published and broadcast in the United Kingdom during the preceding year. A monetary prize of £800, a case of Glenfiddich Pure Malt Whisky, and an engraved commemorative Scottish quaich are awarded to each of the category winners. From these category winners the Judges choose who is to receive the overall Glenfiddich Trophy, which is held for a year, and a further check for £3,000. Awarded annually. Established in 1970. Additional information is available from Conal Walsh, The Glenfiddich Awards, 186 Drury Lane, London, WC2B 2PE, England, phone: 71 405 8638; fax: 71 405 6328.

2950
Great Grimsby International Competition for Singers
23 Enfield Ave.
New Waltham
Great Grimsby, Humberside DN36 5RD,
   England   Phone: 472 812113

2951
Alec Redshaw Memorial Award
To encourage development in a singing career. Individuals between 20 and 30 years of age of any nationality who are in the fourth or final year at a music college/university or who are singing professionally may apply by March 31. Awards are presented in the following voice categories: soprano, mezzo-soprano/contralto/counter tenor, tenor, and baritone/bass. The following awards are presented in each voice category: First prize - £2,000, a medal, and a concert engagement; Second prize - £1,000 and a medal; and Third prize - £450. In addition, an Accompanist's Prize of £600 is awarded to a pianist between the ages of 20 and 27. A monetary prize of £250 is also awarded for the best performance of an English song, a French melody, a German lied, and an Italian aria. Established in 1980 by Anne Holmes and Frank Tondeur in honor of Alec Redshaw.

2952
The Guardian
119 Farringdon Rd.
London EC1R 3ER, England   Phone: 71 278 2332

2953
Business in the Future Award
To recognize an outstanding essay concerning the social and economic implications of automated offices and computer networking to the business community. Travel expenses for a ten-day trip to Silicon Valley, California, as guests of Dictaphone Company Ltd. were awarded. (Discontinued in 1986)

2954
***The Guardian* Children's Fiction Award**
For recognition of the best novel for children published in Britain by a British or Commonwealth author. Books published during the previous calendar year may be submitted by December 31. A monetary prize of £500 is awarded annually. Established in 1967. Additional information is available from Stephanie Nettell, *The Guardian* Children's Books Editor, 24 Weymouth Street, London W1N 3FA, England.

2955
***The Guardian* Fiction Prize**
For recognition of a novel published by a British or Commonwealth writer. A monetary prize of £1,000 is awarded annually by the literary editor and fiction reviewers of the *Guardian* newspaper. Established in 1965.

2956
Student Media Awards
To recognize students for journalistic achievement. Awards are given in the following categories: (1) Best Magazine; (2) Best Newspaper; (3) Best Student Journalist; (4) Best Use of Graphics; (5) Best Campus Radio Program: and (6) a Special Award for the most improved student publication. Winners are selected by a panel of journalists, not all of whom are from *The Guardian*. Monetary awards of £1,200 are awarded annually with NUS (National Union of Students).

2957
Young Businessman of the Year Award
To recognize publicly and highlight the contributions made by successful young businessmen under the age of 45. Those who have made significant contributions to business at a personal level and also in the national context are considered for the award. A silver trophy is bestowed at the Mansion House, London, at an annual luncheon. Established in 1970.

2958
Guild of Agricultural Journalists of Great Britain
c/o Pharo Committee
41-75 Brighton Rd.
Redhill RH1 6YS, England

2959
Netherthorpe Award
To recognize a guild member who has made an outstanding and sustained contribution to the dissemination of knowledge and understanding about agriculture. A trophy and a certificate are bestowed annually. Established in 1977. The award honors the late Lord Netherthorpe. Additional information is available from Don Gomery, Hon. Gen. Secre-

tary, Phono Communications, Forum House, 41-51 Brighton Road, Redhill, Surrey, England, phone: 737 67631.

Guild of British Butlers
c/o Awards Committee
12 Little Bornes Dulwich
London SE21 8SE, England
Phone: 81 6708424
Fax: 81 6700055

Ivor Spencer Top Butler of the Year Award
To recognize the top butler of the year. Individuals who pass the examination at the Guild of British Butlers with top marks are eligible. A trophy is awarded annually. Established in 1985 by Ivor Spencer, principal of the Ivor Spencer International School for Butler Administrators, Personal Assistants.

Guild of Hairdressers
Address unknown.

Formerly: Incorporated Guild of Hairdressers, Wigmakers and Perfumers.

Guild-CAT National Open Presentation Trophy
To test hairdressers with a view to finding new talented hairworkers for future national and international events. There is no age limit. Established in 1988.

Guild College Fantasy Championship
To recognize achievement by a team of three college students. A trophy and certificate are awarded annually. Two additional awards are presented: College Fantasy Theme Prize; and College Fantasy Individual Award. Established in 1984.

Guild under "18" Styling Award
To recognize achievement by YTS trainees. A trophy and a certificate are awarded annually. Established in 1986. Formerly: (1989) Guild Blowstyling Award.

Men's National Young Hairstyling Championship
For recognition of achievement in men's hairdressing. Men's hairdressers or trainee men's hairdressers are eligible. A trophy is awarded annually. Established in 1982.

National Young Hairstyling Championship
For recognition of achievement in hairdressing. Hairdressers or trainee hairdressers under 20 years of age are eligible. A trophy is awarded annually. Established in 1957.

Guild of Incorporated Surveyors
1 Alexandra St.
Queens Rd.
Oldham, Lancs. OL8 2AU, England
Phone: 61 6272389
Fax: 61 6273336

Formerly: (1990) Guild of Surveyors.

Guild Silver Medal
For recognition of outstanding services to the Guild. Individuals must be nominated by a Guild member. A silver medal is awarded when merited. Established in 1950.

Guild of Motoring Writers
2 Pembrok Villas
The Green
Richmond, Surrey TW9 1QF, England
Phone: 81 940 6974

Driver of the Year Award
To recognize a driver for his skill, courage and endurance. Awarded annually.

Sir William Lyons Award
To encourage young writers in automotive journalism, and to foster interest in the motoring industry. British citizens resident in the United Kingdom between 17 and 23 years of age may submit essays. A monetary award of £500 is presented annually.

Pemberton Trophy
To recognize a Guild member for achievements in the field of motoring journalism.

Guild of Professional Toastmasters
c/o Awards Committee
12 Little Bornes, Dulwich
London SE21 8SE, England
Phone: 81 6705585
Fax: 81 6700055

Guild of Professional Toastmasters Best After Dinner Speaker of the Year
To recognize the best after dinner speaker of the year. Selection is by members of the Guild. A trophy is awarded annually. Established in 1967 by Ivor Spencer.

Guild of Television Cameramen
Whiteacres
1 Churchill Rd.
Whitchurch
Tavistock, Devon PL19 9BU, England

Annual Awards
To recognize an outstanding contribution to the art of a cameraman. Awards are presented annually.

Guildhall School of Music and Drama
Barbican
London EC2Y 8DT, England
Phone: 71 6282571

Gold Medal
For recognition of outstanding performance in the fields of music and drama. In the field of music, awards are given alternately to: instrumentalists and singers. An award is given annually in drama. Individuals with a minimum of three years and a maximum of five years attendance

as full-time students at the Guildhall School are eligible. Gold medals are awarded annually. Established in 1915 by Sir H. Dixon Kimber Bt., MA.

2980
Calouste Gulbenkian Foundation (Lisbon)
United Kingdom Branch
98 Portland Pl.
London W1N 4ET, England
Phone: 71 6365313
Fax: 71 6362948

2981
Calouste Gulbenkian Foundation Grants
To encourage and to provide support for programs in the arts, education, and social welfare. There is also a special program for Anglo-Portuguese Cultural Relations. Grant applications for projects in the United Kingdom and the Republic of Ireland whose principal beneficiaries are people in these countries are accepted. Preference is given to original new developments, not yet a part of the regular running costs of an organization; to developments which are either strategic, such as practical initiatives directed to helping tackle the underlying causes of problems, or which provide facilities in an area deficient in them, or seminal, because they seem likely to influence policy and practice elsewhere; or to projects which are of more than local significance. The majority of grants are for less than £5,000.

2982
Thomas Hardy Society
21 Abbot's Walk
Cerne Abbas, Dorches. DT2 7JN, England
Phone: 300 341434

2983
Thomas Hardy Society Book Prize
For recognition of the best book on Thomas Hardy's work and/or life. The award is open to any publication without restriction provided the book has been published during the preceding two years. A monetary prize of £200 and a medal are awarded biennially at the summer conference. Established in 1984 in memory of Thomas Hardy.

2984
Harkness Fellowships of the Commonwealth Fund of New York
28 Bedford Sq.
London WC1B 3EG, England

2985
Harkness Fellowships
To promote international understanding by enabling individuals to study, travel, and gain practical experience in the continental United States. The Fellowships are open to married or single men and women who are citizens of the United Kingdom (up to 12 awards annually); citizens of Australia (4 awards annually); and New Zealand citizens (2 awards annually). There are no formal age limits. In the United Kingdom, preference is given to those between their late 20s and early 40s; in Australia to those between 21 and 36; and in New Zealand to those between 25 and 35. For the United Kingdom awards, study is restricted to the fields of Promoting Good Health, Human Resources in the 21st Century, and People in Cities. In Australia and New Zealand, there are no restrictions on field of study, but candidates must have a degree or equivalent professional qualification, or an outstanding record of achievement in the creative arts, journalism, or other comparable career. MBA candidates, in addition, must have had substantial full-time postgraduate administrative experience. Candidacy is not open to anyone who is already in the United States or holding another award. The deadline for applications is variable but normally in October of the year preceding award in the United Kingdom, and early August for Australia and New Zealand. Between 7 to 12 months' study is offered to United Kingdom candidates and between 12 and 21 months to those from Australia and New Zealand. Financial support includes travel to and from the United States. Established in 1925 by Anna M. Harkness and Mr. and Mrs. Edward S. Harkness. For more information, write to the appropriate address in the country of award. Australia: Mr. R.D.B. Beale, c/o Department of Prime Minister and Cabinet, Locked Bag 14, Queen Victoria Terrace, Parkes, ACT 2600, Australia. New Zealand: Professor R.L.M. Faull, Department of Anatomy, University of Auckland, Privat Bag, Auckland, New Zealand. United Kingdom: Harkness Fellowships, 28 Bedford Square, London WC1B 3EG, England. Formerly: (1959) Commonwealth Fund Fellowships.

2986
Harrogate International Festival
Festival Office, Royal Baths
Harrogate, N. Yorks. HG1 2RR, England
Phone: 423 562303
Fax: 423 521264

2987
Dorothy Parkinson Award for Young British Musicians
To provide an opportunity for a young performer at the start of his professional career to perform a concert at a major British Festival. British musicians under 26 years of age are nominated by a selection panel. A monetary prize of £400 is awarded annually in August. Established in 1982 in honor of Lady Dorothy Parkinson. Sponsored by Dorothy Parkinson Memorial Trust.

2988
Clive Wilson Award for Young Musicians
To encourage young performers at the start of their professional careers. Individuals under 28 years of age who are nominated by the Harrogate International Festival are eligible. A monetary prize is awarded annually. Established in 1990 in memory of Clive Wilson, founder of the Festival.

2989
Harveian Society
Lettsom House
11 Chandos St.
London W1M OEB, England
Phone: 71 580 1043

2990
Lister Boyd Beaver Award
To recognize a medical student for electives.

2991
Buckston Browne Prize Medal
To recognize an individual for a meritorious contribution to medical science. Individuals under 40 years of age are eligible. A monetary prize and a medal are awarded triennially. Established in 1927 by Sir Buckston Browne.

2992
Harvey Essay Prize
To recognize an individual for an original essay on a topic of medical history. Pupils of the Harvey Grammar School, The Folkstone Grammar School for Girls and King's School Canterbury are eligible. A monetary prize is awarded annually. Established in 1954 in honor of William Harvey.

2993
Harveys Leeds International Pianoforte Competition
The Univ. of Leeds
Leeds LS2 9JT, England
Phone: 532 502004
Phone: 532 446586
Fax: 532 391066

Formerly: (1985) Leeds International Pianoforte Competition.

2994
Harveys Leeds International Pianoforte Competition
To recognize and encourage the professional development of talented young pianists. The competition is open to professional pianists of all nationalities who are under 30 years of age. Applications must be received by March 15. The total prize money is in excess of £50,000. The first prize winner receives the Edward Boyle Prize of £10,000 and the Princess Mary Gold Medal. Prizes include a substantial number of

engagements worldwide. The competition is held triennially. Established in 1963 by Fanny Waterman and Marion Thorpe.

2995

Hastings Writer's Group
81 All Saints St.
Hastings, E. Sussex TN 34 3BH, England   Phone: Hastings 424640

2996

Catherine Cookson Cup
To encourage short story writing. Members of the Hastings Writers' Group are eligible. A monetary award and a cup are presented annually. Established in 1980 to honor Catherine Cookson.

2997

David Gemell Cup
To encourage short story writing and to bring writers and writers' groups in southeast England together. Writers living in southeast England are eligible. A monetary award and a cup are presented annually. Established in 1989 to honor David Gemell.

2998

Helicopter Club of Great Britain
Ryelands House
AYNHO   Phone: 86 9810646
Banbury, Oxon. 17 3AT, England   Fax: 86 9810755

2999

Airtour Sword
To recognize the winner of the navigation event in Club Championships. Members are eligible and must hold a private pilot's license (helicopters). A trophy is awarded annually. Established in 1969. Sponsored by Airtour International.

3000

Auto-Alloys Precision Trophy
To recognize the winner of the slalom event in Club Championships. Members are eligible and must hold a private pilot's license (helicopters). A trophy is awarded annually. Established in 1978. Sponsored by Auto-Alloys Ltd.

3001

Babcock and Wilcox Trophy
To recognize the winner of precision events in British Helicopter Championships from 1974-79; thereafter, to recognize the winner of slalom events in British Helicopter Championships. The entrant must hold a pilot's license (helicopters) and a UK passport. A trophy is awarded annually (except in the year of World Championships). Established in 1974. Sponsored by Babcock and Wilcox Company (Spanish Branch).

3002

British Helicopter Advisory Board (BHAB) Trophy
To recognize the winner of navigation events in British Helicopter Championships. The entrant must hold a pilot's license (helicopters) and a UK passport. A trophy is awarded annually (except in the year of World Championships). Established in 1972. Sponsored by the British Helicopter Advisory Board.

3003

Everard Trophy
To recognize an individual for achievement as a champion helicopter crewman in Great Britain. The entrant must hold a UK passport. A trophy is awarded annually (except in the year of World Championships). Established in 1974 in memory of P.A.W.B. Everard, founder of the Helicopter Club of Great Britain.

3004

Famous Grouse Trophy
To recognize the winner of rescue events in British Helicopter Championships. The entrant must hold a pilot's license (helicopters) and a UK passport. A trophy is awarded annually (except in the year of World Championships). Established in 1980. Sponsored by Matthew Gloag and Son Ltd.

3005

Helicopter Club of Great Britain Championship Trophy
To recognize the achievement of the overall winner of the Club Championship. Members are eligible and must hold a private pilot's license (helicopters). A trophy is awarded annually. Established in 1967.

3006

Imperial Tobacco Trophy
To recognize an individual for achievement as a champion helicopter pilot in Great Britain. The entrant must hold a pilot's license (helicopters) and a UK passport. A trophy is awarded annually (except in the year of World Championships). Established in 1972. Sponsored by the Imperial Tobacco Company.

3007

Livingston and Doughty Trophy
To recognize the winner of precision/rescue events in Club Championships. Members are eligible and must hold a private pilot's license (helicopters). A trophy is awarded annually. Established in 1969. Sponsored by Livingston and Doughty Company Ltd.

3008

Precision Timing Trophy
To recognize the winner of timed arrival events in Club Championships. Members are eligible and must hold a private pilot's license (helicopters). A trophy is awarded annually. Established in 1983.

3009

William Hill Organization
Greenside House
50 Station Rd., Wood Green   Phone: 81 3657211
London N22 4TP, England   Fax: 81 8890472

3010

William Hill Sports Book of the Year
To honor the best sports book of the year in the United Kingdom. Books published in the United Kingdom during the previous calendar year are eligible. A monetary prize, free bet and free day at the races, and a leather bound book are awarded annually. Established in 1989. Additional information is available from Tim Moss, telephone: 71 8371475.

3011

Hippopotamus Press
22, Whitewell Rd.
Frome, Somerset BA11 4EL, England   Phone: 373 466653

3012

Outpost's Poetry Competition
To recognize outstanding poetry. The first prize varies but is not less than £400, with prizes for second and third place winners. Awarded annually.

3013

Howard Sergeant Memorial Award
For recognition of an outstanding contribution to poetry. A monetary prize of £1,000 is awarded annually. Established in 1988 in memory of Howard Sergeant, founder of Outposts *Poetry Quarterly*. Additional information is available from Jean Sergeant, 72 Burwood Road, Walton-on-Thames, Surrey KT12 4AL, England.

3014
Historic Churches Preservation Trust and Incorporated Church Building Society
Fulham Palace
London SW6 6EA, England   Phone: 71 7363054

3015
King of Prussia's Gold Medal
For recognition of achievement in the repair of churches. Architects are eligible. A medal is awarded annually. Established in 1985 in memory of Friedrich Willhelm IV Koenig von Preussen.

3016
Historical Association
59a Kennington Park Rd.   Phone: 71 7353901
London SE11 4JH, England   Fax: 71 5824989

3017
Norton Medlicott Medal
For recognition of an outstanding major contribution to the field of history. Nominations may be submitted. A medal is awarded annually. Established in 1984 in honor of Professor W. Norton Medlicott, past president of the Association.

3018
Hodder and Stoughton Ltd.
Sec. to the Judges of the Stanford Prize
47 Bedford Sq.
London WC1B 3DP, England   Phone: 71 6369851

3019
Winifred Mary Stanford Prize
For recognition of a book published in the United Kingdom in the English language that has been inspired in some way by the Christian faith and written by a man or woman 50 years of age or under at the date of publication. The book must be readable by the general public and not require specialist theological, philosophical, or linguistic expertise for its understanding. Poetry, fiction, biography, autobiography, biblical exposition, religious experience, and witness are considered. Literary merit is a prime factor in selection. Publishers may submit books during the preceding year by January 15. A monetary prize of £1,000 is awarded biennially in even-numbered years at Easter. Established in 1978 by Mr. Leonard Cutts in memory of Winifred Mary Stanford, his wife.

3020
Hong Kong Study Circle
37 Hart Ct.
Newcastle-under-Lyme, Staffs ST5 2AL,
  England   Phone: 782 627901

3021
Wilde Cup and Webb Cup
To promote the study of stamps and postal history of Hong Kong and the treaty ports of China and Japan, and to recognize the best discovery of the year. No further information on awards is available for this edition.

3022
Honourable Society of Cymmrodorion (Anrhydeddus Gymdeithas y Cymmrodorion)
30 Eastcastle St.
London W1N 7PD, England   Phone: 71 6310502

3023
Cymmrodorion Medal
For recognition of outstanding services to Wales in the fields of literature, science, and the arts. Individuals are selected by the council of the Society. A bronze medal designed by Joseph Edwards is awarded infrequently. Established in 1877 and first awarded in 1883.

3024
Horsley Marketing and Communications
5 Langley St.   Phone: 71 379 3404
London WC2H 9JA, England   Fax: 71 240 8311

3025
UK Technology Press Awards
To recognize and promote standards of excellence in the field of technology publications. Awards were given in the following categories: Technology Journal of the Year; Technology Journalist of the Year (News); Technology Journalist of the Year (Features); Technology Columnist of the Year; Technology Photographer of the Year; Best Designed Technology Journal of the Year; Technology Programme of the Year for TV or Radio; and Technology Press Personality of the Year. Established in 1984. Supported by *The Times* newspaper. (Discontinued) Formerly: UK Computer Press Awards.

3026
House & Garden
Vogue House
Hanover Sq.
London W1R 0AD, England   Phone: 71 435 4348

3027
New Designers
To find the best of Britain's graduating design talent in industrial design, furniture, lighting, furnishing fabrics, wall coverings, floor coverings, tableware - china, glass, silver and cutlery, interior design and domestic product design. Final year students at the level accepted by the Chartered Society of Designers for Diploma Membership and selected by their college and Chartered Society of Designers to exhibit in The New Designers exhibition are eligible. Eighteen monetary awards totaling £18,200 are awarded annually in July. Established in 1983 by Peta Levi, Design Correspondent of *House & Garden,* who was invited to set up and launch the Award Scheme, to bridge the gap between graduates and industry. Additional information is available from Peta Levi, 9 Burgess Hill, London NW2 2BY, England, phone: 71 435 4348 and fax: 71 435 5487. Formerly: (1988) *House & Garden*/IDDA Decorex Young Designer of the Year.

3028
Huddersfield Contemporary Music Festival
Huddersfield University
Queensgate   Phone: 484 425082
Huddersfield HD1 3DH, England   Fax: 484 425082

3029
Yorkshire & Humberside Arts Young Composers Awards
To give experience to active young composers, during the Huddersfield Contemporary Music Festival held in November each year. Applications are accepted by early October. The opportunity to work with professional ensembles and composers during the Huddersfield Contemporary Music Festival is awarded annually together with cash prizes. Established in 1984 by Yorkshire Arts. Formerly: (1990) Yorkshire Arts Young Composers Competition.

3030
Humane Slaughter Association
c/o The Secretary
34 Blanche Ln.
South Mimms
Potters Bar, Herts. EN6 3PA, England
Phone: 707 659040
Fax: 707 649279

3031
Dorothy Sidley Memorial Award
To encourage young people to take an interest in the Association's specialist area of food animal welfare, thereby improving welfare conditions for food animals and birds in livestock markets, during transit or in slaughterhouses. Students in agricultural, veterinary, or meat sciences, and trainees in the livestock and meat industries are eligible. Proposals for research programs may be submitted by February 28. A monetary award of £500 is presented annually. Established in 1986 in memory of Dorothy Sidley MBE, who was General Secretary of the Association for forty-eight years.

3032
Hunterian Society
Edgware General
London HA8 0AD, England

3033
Hunterian Medal
To stimulate an original contribution in essay form on a medical scientific topic chosen by the Society. Registered Medical Practitioners in Great Britain are eligible. A medal is awarded annually. Established in 1984 in honor of John Hunter.

3034
Hydrographic Society
University of East London
Longbridge Rd.
Dagenham, Essex RM8 2AS, England
Phone: 81 5971946
Fax: 81 5909730

3035
President's Prize
For recognition of outstanding contributions to the science or practice of hydrography. A monetary prize is awarded when merited. Established in 1984.

3036
Society Awards for Journal Articles
For recognition of outstanding articles in the field of hydrography. Articles that were published in the Society Journal during the preceding year are eligible. Monetary awards are given annually for the best article and the best first article. Established in 1974.

3037
The Illustrated London News
91-93 Southwark St.
London SE1 0HX, England
Phone: 71 928 2111
Fax: 71 620 1594

3038
London Awards
For recognition in the work of improving London. Awards are given in the following categories: (1) Development; (2) Environment; (3) Innovation; (4) Entertainment; and (5) Londoner of the Year. Formerly: Festival Awards.

3039
Museum of the Year Award
For recognition of new features completed in British museums and for new museum services or facilities introduced during the year. A monetary prize of £2,000 and a porcelain sculpture by Henry Moore, to be held by the winning museum for one year, were awarded annually. Established in 1973 in conjunction with the National Heritage Organization. (Discontinued in 1989)

3040
Incorporated Society of Musicians
10 Stratford Pl.
London W1N 9AE, England
Phone: 71 6294413
Fax: 71 408538

3041
Distinguished Musician Award
To recognize the outstanding contribution of a colleague to British musical life. A silver gilt medallion bearing the ISM logo is awarded annually when merited. Established in 1976. Formerly: (1980) Musician of the Year.

3042
Honorary Member
To recognize an individual who has given public service to the art of music or to kindred arts and sciences.

3043
The Independent
40 City Rd.
London EC1Y 2DB, England
Phone: 71 2531222
Fax: 71 9620016

3044
***The Independent* Foreign Fiction Award**
To recognize and promote the best foreign fiction published in the United Kingdom. Any full-length novel or collection of short stories translated into English from another language and published in the United Kingdom for the first time in the year preceding the award is eligible. The book must have been published in its original langauge no more than 15 years before entry. The prize operates on a bimonthly schedule. Every two months, starting in June, the judges select a book that forms the shortlist. At the end of the year, the overall winner is chosen from this shortlist of 6. A monetary prize of £10,000 is divided equally between the author and translator. No financial prize is attached to the bi-monthly award. Established in 1990.

3045
Independent Retailer Organisation
Anbrian House
St. Mary's St.
Worcester, Hereford and Worcs. WR1 1HA,
  England
Phone: 905 612238

3046
Independent Retailer Organisation Awards
To recognize independent retailers. The Organisation sponsors competitions and presents awards.

3047
Institute for Complementary Medicine
21 Portland Pl.
London W1N 3AF, England
Phone: 71 636 9543

3048
Dower Prize
To encourage professional development of individual students of the natural therapies. Dissertations by final year students in any of the natural therapies may be submitted. A monetary award of £100 and a scroll are awarded annually. Established in 1987 by Mrs. Lavender Dower.

3049
Institute for Social Inventions
20 Heber Rd.
London NW2 6AA, England
Phone: 81 2082853
Fax: 81 4526434

3050
Social Inventions Prizes
For recognition of social inventiveness. A social invention is defined as a new and imaginative solution to a social problem, or way of meeting an unmet social need - for instance, a new social service, a new way for people to relate to each other, a new organizational structure, or a new combination of existing ideas. New products, technological inventions, or patentable devices are excluded. Entries must be submitted by June 1. Awards are given in the following categories: ideas; projects already underway; projects underway abroad that could with advantage be tried in the United Kingdom (or that are being tried); and ideas and projects suggested by youngsters under 18 (that may be accompanied with drawings, A4 size). Monetary prizes totaling £1,000 and certificates are awarded annually. Established in 1985.

3051
Institute of Acoustics
Agriculture House
5 Holywell Hill
St. Albans, Herts. AL1 1EU, England
Phone: 727 848195
Fax: 727 850553

3052
Simon Alport Memorial Prize
For recognition of the best published paper describing work involving the use of computers in acoustics. Residents in the United Kingdom who are under 28 years of age in the year of publication are eligible. Awarded annually. Established in 1987 by Cirrus Research Limited in memory of Simon Alport.

3053
Rayleigh Medal
For recognition of outstanding contributions to acoustics by a United Kingdom and a foreign acoustician, alternately. A medal and a citation are awarded annually. Established in 1975 by the British Acoustical Society in memory of John William Strutt, Third Baron Rayleigh, a physicist and physician who won a Nobel Prize for physics in 1904.

3054
Stephens Lecture
To honor distinguished acousticians. The lecture is held annually at the spring conference and is intended to be an important occasion at an IOA Meeting, marked by the presentation of a scroll to the lecturer. Established in 1984 in honor of Dr. Stephens, a graduate of Imperial College, London where he subsequently created his Acoustics Research group, and also the first President of the Institute of Acoustics, which he was instrumental in creating. The Stephens Lecture was set up in honor of his eightieth birthday.

3055
Tyndall Medal
For recognition of achievement and service in the field of acoustics. Citizens of the United Kingdom, preferably under the age of 40, are eligible. A medal and a citation are awarded biennially in even-numbered years. Established in 1975 by the British Acoustical Society in memory of John Tyndall (1820-1893), an experimental physicist and one of the world's most brilliant scientific lecturers.

3056
A. B. Wood Medal and Prize
For recognition of distinguished contributions in the application of acoustics, with preference given to candidates whose work is associated with the sea. The prize is awarded alternately to a person domiciled in the United Kingdom, and in the United States or Canada. The Acoustical Society of America selects recipients from the United States or Canada. Individuals, preferably under 35 years of age in the year of the award, are considered. A silver-gilt medal, a parchment scroll, and a monetary prize are awarded annually. Established in 1968 by the Institute of Physics, London, in memory of Albert Beaumont Wood, a research scientist for the Admiralty on anti-submarine problems.

3057
Institute of Actuaries
Staple Inn Hall
High Holborn
London WC1V 7QJ, England
Phone: 71 2420106
Fax: 71 4052482

3058
Finlaison Medal
For recognition of services to the actuarial profession in furthering one or more of the various objectives set out in the Royal Charter. Awarded when merited. Established in 1966. Formerly: (1985) Silver Medal.

3059
Gold Medal
For recognition of work of pre-eminent importance either in originality, content, or consequence in the actuarial field. Awarded when merited. Established in 1919.

3060
Messenger and Brown Prize
For recognition of meritorious contributions to actuarial science. A monetary prize is awarded when merited.

3061
Institute of Administrative Management
(Union Internationale des Entrepreneurs de Peinture)
40 Chatsworth Parade
Petts Wood
Orpington, Kent BR5 1RW, England
Phone: 689 75555
Fax: 689 70891

3062
Institute of Administrative Management Competitions
To recognize professional managers and students and to promote and develop the science of administrative management and the latest techniques in administration and personnel management. The Institute sponsors competitions and bestows awards at the annual convention.

3063
Institute of Advanced Legal Studies
c/o Univ. of London
Charles Clore House
17 Russell Sq.
London WC1B 5DR, England
Phone: 71 637 1731
Fax: 71 580 9613

3064
Howard Drake Memorial Award
To encourage collaboration and exchanges between legal scholars and law librarians, especially between those of different countries, and to promote the study of law librarianship and the training of law librarians. Established in 1978 in memory of Howard Drake, the first librarian of the Institute.

3065
Georg Schwarzenberger Prize in International Law
To recognize a student in the Faculty of Laws in the University of London considered to be outstanding in the field of Public International Law. Nomination is by the heads of the five London University Law Schools. A monetary prize is awarded annually. Established in 1981 by friends and former students of Professor Georg Schwarzenberger.

3066

Institute of Amateur Cinematographers
PO Box 618
Ealing
London W5 1SX, England
Phone: 81 9986748

3067

IAC International Film and Video Competition
To recognize outstanding films and videos entered in the Competition. The deadline for entry is January 31. The following awards are presented: *Daily Mail* Trophy - for the very best entry of the IAC International Film and Video Competition. Only bona fide amateur moviemakers may compete. Established in 1934; IAC American Cup - for the best entry from North America. Only bona fide amateur moviemakers may compete. Established in 1966; International Awards - for the best films in the IAC International Film and Video Competition. Established in 1965; Student/Semi-Pro Awards. Those competing for this award may not win the IAC American Cup. Established in 1984; and various Craft Awards (Best Editing, Best Sound, etc.) and various Category Awards (Best Animation, Best Documentary). Established in 1965 (amateur) and in 1987 (student/semi-pro). A medallion or a framed certificate is given as a permanent memento to all the winners. The winners become part of a circulating program of winning entries for hire from the IAC Film and Video Library. The competition is held annually. Established in 1932.

3068

Institute of British Foundrymen
Bordesley Hall
The Holloway, Alvechurch
Birmingham B48 7QA, England
Phone: 527 596100
Fax: 527 596102

3069

British Foundry Medal and Prize
For recognition of achievement in the development of the cast metals industry and for imparting knowledge to fellow members of the Institute. A medal is awarded annually. Established in 1944.

3070

Foundry Industry Award
To recognize contributions to the foundry industry. Established in 1977.

3071

E. J. Fox Gold Medal
For recognition of achievement in the development of the cast metals industry and for imparting knowledge to fellow members of the Institute. A gold medal is awarded annually. Established in 1937.

3072

Honorary Member
To recognize an individual for outstanding contributions to the cast metals industry.

3073

Voya Kondic Medal
For recognition in the field of foundry education and training. Established in 1991.

3074

Meritorious Services Medal
For recognition of achievement in the development of the cast metals industry and for imparting knowledge to fellow members of the Institute. A medal is awarded annually. Established in 1933.

3075

Oliver Stubbs Gold Medal
For recognition of achievement in the development of the cast metals industry and for imparting knowledge to fellow members of the Institute. Institute members are eligible. A gold medal is awarded annually. Established in 1922 by Oliver Stubbs, past president of the Institute.

3076

Worshipful Company of Ironmongers Jubilee Award
To recognize an individual who has either: conducted the best piece of practical investigation relating to the production of properties of iron or steel castings; or made the best personal contribution to any practical development of value to the ferrous foundry industries. Individuals under 33 years of age are eligible. A medal and all expenses to attend the International Foundry Congress are awarded annually. Established by The Worshipful Company of Ironmongers to commemorate the Queen of England's Jubilee. Additional information is available from G.A. Schofield, Secretary.

3077

Institute of Ceramics
Shelton House
Stoke Rd.
Stoke-on-Trent, Staffs ST4 2DR, England
Phone: 782 202116

3078

Institute of Ceramics Awards
For recognition of contributions to the materials science of ceramics, which includes pottery, glass, refractories, vitreous enamel, heavy clayware, cement, concrete, electro-ceramics, abrasives, special ceramics, and glass-ceramics.

3079

Institute of Chartered Accountants in England and Wales
PO Box 433
Moorgate Pl.
London EC2P 2BJ, England
Phone: 71 628 7060

3080

Awards for Published Accounts
To encourage excellence in financial reporting in the U.K. Judged by senior representatives from the investment community, accountancy, and law. Annual reports from all of the U.K. and Irish companies currently quoted at the London Stock Exchange are eligible. Judging is done in two categories: companies with more than £50 million balance sheet net assets; and companies with less than £50 million balance sheet net assets. Trophies are awarded. Jointly sponsored by the Institute of Chartered Accountants in England and Wales, the Institute of Chartered Accountants of Scotland, the Institute of Chartered Accountants in Ireland, and the London Stock Exchange.

3081

Charity Accounts Award
To encourage charities to produce better reports and accounts. Registered charities are considered. The deadline for entries is July 31. A monetary award of £1,000 is given in three categories: those receiving annual income over £1,000,000; annual income over £100,000; and income under £100,000. In addition, a discretionary prize of £500 may be awarded. Awards are presented annually in November. Established in 1983. Sponsored by Institute of Chartered Accountants in England and Wales, the Charities Aid Foundation, and the Charity Forum.

3082

Founding Societies' Centenary Award
To recognize outstanding achievement in any field of endeavor. Members of the Institute are eligible. A trophy and citation are awarded annually, at a special dinner, usually in April. Established in 1979 by District Societies of Chartered Accountants in Liverpool, London, Manchester and Sheffield to mark the centenary of the Institute of Chartered Accountants in England and Wales (founded in 1880).

3083
Institute of Civil Defence and Disaster Studies
Bell Court House
11 Blomfield St.
London EC2M 7AY, England
Phone: 71 5883700
Fax: 262 488518

3084
Institute of Civil Defence and Disaster Studies Competitions
For recognition of service to civil defense and emergency planning. Members and honorary members are eligible. Gold, silver, and bronze medals are awarded. The following competitions are sponsored by the Institute: Sir John Hodsoll Open Theses, Sir John Hodsoll Published Works, and Gerald Drewitt Award (restricted thesis competition), and DML/ICDDS Annual Award for Academic Research into Disaster Management.

3085
Institute of Contemporary History and Wiener Library
4 Devonshire St.
London W1N 2BH, England
Phone: 71 6367247
Fax: 71 4366428

3086
Fraenkel Prize in Contemporary History
To recognize outstanding work in the field of contemporary history. Finished but unpublished work written in either English, French, German, or Russian that covers one of the traditional fields of interest to the Wiener Library, such as 20th Century history of Central Europe, recent Jewish history, World War II, fascism and totalitarianism, political violence, and racialism is eligible. Studies must be between 10,000 and 100,000 words. The deadline is May 2. Two distinct Fraenkel Prize awards are made: US $5,000, open to all entrants, and US $3,000, open only to those under 30. The Wiener Library may invite the winner of the award to give a public lecture in London. The Wiener Library will have the option to publish part of the award-winning work in the *Journal of Contemporary History*. Awarded annually in late summer. Established in 1989 by Ernst Fraenkel, chairman of the Institute.

3087
Institute of Energy
18 Devonshire St.
London W1N 2AU, England
Phone: 71 5807124
Fax: 71 5804420

3088
Institute of Energy Award
To recognize individuals for contributions to energy issues and programs. Awarded annually.

3089
Institute of Engineers and Technicians
100 Grove Vale
East Dulwich
London SE22 8DR, England
Phone: 81 6931255
Fax: 81 2990862

3090
Castrol Award
For recognition of an outstanding paper in the field of engineering. A monetary prize of £200 and a silver medal are awarded annually. Established in 1948. Formerly: Burmah-Castrol Silver Medal.

3091
Certificates of Merit
To recognize individuals or companies for outstanding contributions to industry. Recommendations may be made for consideration of the Council.

3092
Frank Haskell Silver Medal
For recognition of the best article in the field of engineering appearing in the Institute's *Journal*. A silver medal and a certificate of merit are awarded annually. Established in 1948 in honor of F. H. Haskell, council member and editor of the *Journal*.

3093
IET Woman's Engineer Award
To recognize a woman engineer for excellence of leadership, example, or effort. Nominations may be made by employers, senior colleagues, or lecturers. A monetary award is presented annually. Established by Bernard Brook-Partridge HonFiet.

3094
Jackson Silver Medal
For recognition of the best paper read before any local branch in the field of engineering. A silver medal and a certificate of merit are awarded annually. Established in 1948 in honor of A. L. Jackson, founder, past president, and Honorary Secretary of the Institute.

3095
John E. Morgan Silver Cup
For recognition in the field of engineering. Winners are nominated by the previous cup holder. A silver cup is awarded annually. Established in 1948.

3096
Tipping Bronze Apprentice Medal
For recognition in the field of engineering. A medal and a certificate of merit are awarded annually. Established in 1948 in honor of W. V. Tipping, a past president and former council member.

3097
Institute of Export
Export House
64 Clifton St.
London EC2A 4HB, England
Phone: 71 2479812
Fax: 71 3775343

3098
Institute of Export Prizes
For recognition of achievement in the Institute's professional examinations. Registered students are eligible. The following awards Professional Examination Part II in Export Management - Midland Bank Travel Award, Department of Trade and Industry Prizes, Ariel Maritime UK Ltd. Prize, UPS Ltd. Prize, and Midland Bank Prize (Export Distribution); and Professional Examination Part I - Clive Schmitthoff Commercial Law Prize (Sweet and Maxwell), Maerskline UK Prize, T & R (Insurance Services) Limited Prize, Alex Lawrie Factor Ltd. Prize, Clive and Twinkie Schmitthoff Prize (Principles of Law Relating to Overseas Trade), National Westminster Bank Prize (International Trade and Payments), SITPRO Prize (International Physical Distribution), Society of Shipping Executives Education Trust Prize, and P & O Containers Prize. The best student in either part one or part two is awarded the Company of World Traders Silver Salver. Monetary prizes and, in a few cases, a trophy are awarded annually.

3099
Institute of Financial Accountants
Burford House
44 London Rd.
Sevenoaks, Kent TN13 1AS, England
Phone: 732 458080
Fax: 732 455848

Formerly: (1987) Institute of Administrative Accountants.

3100
Institute of Financial Accountants Awards
To recognize individuals for: (1) excellence of achievement in the examinations for the awards of Licentiate and Associate of the Institute; (2) outstanding contributions to the theory of accountancy; and (3) high levels of performance in the practice of the profession. Examination prizes are awarded twice a year in June and December. The prizes for Professional Qualification are book tokens. Formerly: Institute of Administrative Accountants Awards.

3101
Institute of Food Science and Technology (UK)
5 Cambridge Court
210 Shepherd's Bush Rd.
London W6 7NL, England Phone: 71 603 6316

3102
Honorary Fellow
For recognition of outstanding achievement at the national or international level in the profession of food science and/or technology. Members may be nominated. Benefits of membership and an honorary certificate are awarded when merited. Established in 1966.

3103
Institute of Heraldic and Genealogical Studies
 Phone: 227 462618
79-82 Northgate Phone: 227 768664
Canterbury, Kent CT1 1BA, England Fax: 227 765617

3104
Julian Bickersteth Memorial Medal
To honor individuals who have made significant contributions to family history studies. The Trustees of the Institute may nominate individuals. A gold medal is awarded annually when merited at the annual luncheon. Established in 1962 by Cecil R.J. Humphery-Smith in memory of Kenneth Julian Faithfull Bickersteth (1885-1962), an educator and canon of Canterbury Cathedral. The Institute also presents other awards: Fellowship; Frank Higenbottam Memorial Prize - for library work; and Dr. Peter Wren Prize - for best student.

3105
Institute of Information Scientists
44-45 Museum St. Phone: 71 8318003
London WC1A 1LY, England Fax: 71 4301270

3106
Annual Award for Outstanding Achievement in the Field of Information Science
To recognize information scientists and information managers who promote the advancement of information science. Awarded annually.

3107
Institute of Management
2 Savoy Ct.
Strand
London WC2R 0EZ, England Phone: 71 4970580
 Fax: 71 4970463

3108
Bowie Medal
To recognize a member of the Institute for significant contributions to management and for services in the field of management education. Awarded annually. (Discontinued in 1979)

3109
Burnham Medal
To recognize a person who made an outstanding contribution to management training techniques. Awarded annually. (Discontinued in 1979)

3110
Gold Medal
For recognition of outstanding achievement in the art, science, or practice of management. Awarded annually. Established in 1980.

3111
Verulam Medal
For recognition of outstanding service to the Institute. A gold medal is awarded occasionally. Established in 1962 in memory of the Earl of Verulam, former Chairman of the Council.

3112
Institute of Manufacturing
56 Calrendon Ave.
Leamington, Warks. CV32 4SA, England Phone: 926 55498

3113
Institute of Manufacturing Awards
To recognize individuals involved in manufacturing for new developments, techniques, processes, and methods in the field of manufacturing.

3114
Institute of Marine Engineers
76 Mark Ln. Phone: 71 4818493
London EC3R 7JN, England Fax: 71 4881854

3115
BMEC Donald Maxwell Award
For recognition of the best paper read at the Institute by a member or nonmember of any nationality on the research and/or development of some aspect of marine equipment and its market potential. Joint authors are also eligible. Papers are to be assessed by the IMarE Technical Papers and Conferences Committee, whose recommendations are passed to the Donald Maxwell Fund Trustees for approval. A monetary prize of £500 is awarded annually.

3116
Denny Gold Medal
For recognition of the most worthy paper read to the Institute by a member during the year. Joint authors are eligible providing the first named is a member. A gold medal and certificate are awarded annually.

3117
Stanley Gray Award
To recognize the most worthy papers read to the Institute by a member or nonmember. Awards are given in the following categories: marine technology, offshore technology, and marine electrical technology. A monetary prize of £500 and a certificate are awarded annually in each category. In addition, £500 and a certificate are awarded to the most worthy paper read by a member or nonmember at each conference organized by the Institute and branch meeting on any aspect of marine technology, offshore technology, or marine electrical technology.

3118
Stanley Gray Fellowships
To enable post-graduate students to undertake research in approved maritime subjects. Applicants must have obtained an approved engineering degree or the DTp Extra First Class Certificate of Competency and be members of the Institute. The deadline for applications is July 31. A monetary award of £2,000 per year (for a maximum of three years) is presented annually.

3119

Institute Silver Medal
For recognition of the best paper read to the Institute by a nonmember. Joint authors are eligible providing the first named is a nonmember. A silver medal and certificate are awarded annually.

3120

Percy Jackson Award
To recognize the author(s) of the best paper on the use and application of new technology in the development of marine propulsion systems. A monetary prize of £300 and a certificate are awarded biennially. Formerly: Percy Jackson Diesel Engine Award.

3121

Herbert Akroyd Stuart Award
To recognize the author(s) of the best paper read to the Institute on the origin and development of heavy oil engines. Open to members and nonmembers. A monetary prize of £50 and a certificate are awarded biennially.

3122

Institute of Marketing
Moor Hall
Cookham
Maidenhead, Berks. SL6 9QH, England
Phone: 6285 24922
Fax: 6285 31382

3123

Institute of Marketing Awards
To recognize marketing executives and students. Awards are presented annually at the annual conference.

3124

Institute of Materials
1 Carlton House Terrace
London SW1Y 5DB, England
Phone: 71 839 4071
Fax: 71 839 1702

3125

Ablett Prize
To recognize a paper of particular merit published by the Institute during the preceding two years associated with engineering in a metals works. A monetary award of £200 is presented. Established in 1939.

3126

Guy Bengough Medal and Prize
To recognize a paper that most clearly indicates promise that the research described or the review of practice or literature made in it could lead to an economic improvement in the control of metallic corrosion. Papers published by the Institute during the preceding two years are eligible. Selection of the recipient is the responsibility of the *British Corrosion Journal* Editorial Panel. A monetary award of £200 is presented. Established in 1979.

3127

Bessemer Gold Medal
For recognition of contributions to the iron and steel industry. Awards are given in the following areas: to the inventor or introducer of any important invention, either in the mechanical or the chemical processes employed in the manufacture of iron or steel; for a paper of special merit to manufacturing of steel and iron; for a contribution to the journal of the Institute, being an original contribution with valuable practical implications to iron and steel trades; and at the President's discretion for contributions to the iron and steel trades. A gold medal is awarded annually. Established in 1874 by the Iron and Steel Institute.

3128

Andrew Carnegie Research Fund
Grants totaling £2,400 are made to younger members principally to assist them in attending conferences.

3129

Tom Colclough Medal and Prize
To recognize an individual for distinguished achievement in production or engineering connected with the metals industries. A monetary award of £300 is presented. Established in 1963.

3130

Cook Prize
To recognize a paper of particular merit and of practical character published by the Institute during the preceding two years concerned with the manufacture and use of nonferrous metals. A monetary award of £200 is presented. Established in 1975.

3131

Dowding Medal and Prize
For recognition of a major contribution to the invention, development, or design of a metallurgical plant leading to improved economy, yield, or quality in metal production. A monetary award of £300 is presented. Established in 1980.

3132

Elegant Work Prize
To recognize a paper published by the Institute during the preceding two years that illustrates particularly elegant work on research or on the development of industrial processes. A monetary award of £200 is presented. Established in 1971.

3133

Edward Emley Award
For recognition in the field of metallurgy. A monetary award of £200 was presented for first prize and £100 for second prize. (Discontinued)

3134

A. A. Griffith Medal and Prize
For recognition of achievement in materials science. Individuals may be nominated by the end of the calendar year. A monetary award of £300 and a medal are awarded annually. Established in 1965 by the Materials Science Club and Rolls Royce Ltd. in honor of A.A. Griffith.

3135

Dr. Paul Grunfeld Memorial Award and Medal
For recognition of original and/or progressive work on the production and use of alloys in the metallurgical industries. Individuals in early to mid career are eligible. A monetary award of £750 to further the recipient's career is presented. Established in 1986.

3136

Sir Robert Hadfield Medal and Prize
To recognize distinguished achievement in relation to metallurgical practice, process development, corrosion, or design engineering. A monetary award of £300 is presented. Established in 1947.

3137

Charles Hatchett Award
To recognize the author of a paper on materials research. A monetary award of £200 is presented. Sponsored by CBMM, Brazil.

3138

Leslie Holliday Prize
To recognize the development of new materials of outstanding technological and therefore commercial importance or the development of new experimental techniques of outstanding importance. The work should be recent or continuing, and preference is given to younger candidates. Selection is the responsibility of the Materials Science Committee. A monetary award of £50 is presented. Established in 1968.

3139
Hume-Rothery Prize
To recognize distinguished achievements concerned with phase relationshps in metallic materials or nonmetallic materials of metallurgical interest. A monetary award of £300 is presented. Established in 1979.

3140
Kroll Medal and Prize
To recognize distinguished achievements in chemical metallurgy. A monetary award of £300 is presented. Established in 1972.

3141
T.B. Marsden Professional Award
To recognize an individual for services to the profession over a period of 20 years or more. A monetary award of £500 is presented. Established in 1982.

3142
Metaserv Awards
For excellence in the field of metallography. Various prizes valued between £500 and £100 are awarded in conjunction with Bueller UK Ltd. Established in 1976.

3143
National Lecture Competition
To recognize the best lecturers from 12 heats held around the country. Awards are presented in the categories of those 23 years of age and under and those 24 to 28. First prizes of £200 and second prizes of £100 are awarded.

3144
Pfeil Medal and Prize
To recognize a paper of particular merit, published by the Institute during the previous two years, concerned with physical metallurgy. A monetary award of £200 is presented. Established in 1971.

3145
Platinum Medal
For recognition of outstanding services to the nonferrous metal industries regardless of race or nationality. A medal is awarded annually. Established in 1938 by the Institute of Metals.

3146
Poster Presentation Competition
To recognize individuals for industrial and academic presentations. A monetary award of £100 for first prize and £50 for second prize were awarded. (Discontinued)

3147
Prain Medal and Prize
To recognize an individual for distinguished achievement in the development, manufacture, application, or promotion of copper or copper alloys. The aim is to encourage and recognize advances in copper technology. Individuals of either sex, without restriction on age or nationality may be nominated. A monetary prize of £300 is awarded annually at the annual general meeting. Established in 1981 by the Copper Development Association to honor Sir Ronald L. Prain's long service to the copper industry. Sponsored by the Copper Development Association.

3148
Rosenhain Medal and Prize
For recognition of outstanding contributions to the field of physical metallurgy and materials science. Individuals under 45 years of age, regardless of nationality, sex, or membership of the Institute are eligible. A monetary award of £300 and a medal are awarded annually. Established in 1951.

3149
Royal Charter Prize
To recognize an individual for overall performance and achievement in an accredited undergraduate course. A monetary award of £250 is presented. Established in 1976.

3150
Stokowiec Medal and Prize
To recognize distinguished work related to the technical, manufacturing, or processing aspects of high-alloy steels. A monetary award of £300 is presented. Established in 1977.

3151
Technician of the Year Award
To recognize an individual for achievement and promise as a technician in the field of metallurgy or materials. A monetary award of £150 is presented. Established in 1980.

3152
Sidney Gilchrist Thomas Medal and Prize
To recognize an individual for personal achievement expressed through a body of literature. A monetary award of £200 is presented. Established in 1963.

3153
Urethane Medal
For service in the urethane industry.

3154
Verulam Medal and Prize
To recognize distinguished contributions to economic production in the processing or fabricating of metals. A monetary award of £300 is presented. Established in 1975. Sponsored by VANITEC.

3155
Williams Prize
To recognize a paper of particular merit and of practical character, published by the Institute during the preceding two years, concerned with the manufacture and use of iron and steel. A monetary award of £200 is presented. Established in 1927.

3156
Institute of Measurement and Control
87 Gower St.
London WC1E 6AA, England   Phone: 71 3874949

3157
Bimcam Ardley Prize
For recognition of the best paper by a member of the institute read to a local section. The paper may be on any aspect of the design and use of instruments in industry.

3158
Callendar Medal
To recognize an engineer or scientist for a considerable contribution to the art of instruments or measurement. A silver medal is awarded annually. Established in 1969 in honor of Professor Callandar.

3159
Sir Harold Hartley Medal
For recognition of a contribution of outstanding merit to the technology of measurement and control. There are no eligibility restrictions. A silver medal is awarded annually. Established in 1969 to honor Sir Harold Hartley, a past president of the institute.

3160
Honeywell International Medal
For recognition of distinguished work on control in any sphere. Chartered measurement and control technologists or the equivalent are eligible. A medal is awarded annually. Established in 1975 by Honeywell International to commemorate the granting of a Royal Charter to the institute.

3161
Honeywell Prize
To recognize the best article for publication in *Measurement and Control*, the institute journal. The criteria for the assessment of these articles is as follows: general interest to the institute's members, importance of the subject to the institute, and lucidity and originality. Awarded annually.

3162
Alec Hough-Grassby Memorial Award
To recognize an individual for a significant contribution to the research, development, evaluation or application of process analyzers in industrial development. Established in memory of Alec Hough-Grassby.

3163
ICI Prize
For recognition of the best paper in the *Transactions* of the institute or the author(s) of the outstanding paper to appear in the proceedings of an institute symposium.

3164
Sir George Thomson Gold Medal
For recognition of a contribution to measurement science which has resulted in fundamental improvements in the understanding of the physical world. There are no restrictions on eligibility. A gold medal is awarded every five years. Established in 1975 to honor Sir George Thomson, the first President of the institute.

3165
Institute of Medical Laboratory Sciences
12 Queen Anne St.
London W1M 0AU, England   Phone: 71 636 8192

3166
Bacteriology Prize of the IMLS
For recognition of an original work in bacteriology. Fellowship or Associateship of IMLS is necessary for consideration. A monetary prize of £250 is awarded triennially. Established in 1974. Sponsored by Difco Laboratories. Formerly: Microbiology Prize.

3167
Malcolm Breach Award
To recognize a candidate for the highest marks in bacteriology in the special examination for Fellowship of the Institute. Fellows or Associates of the IMLS are eligible. A monetary award of £130-£150 is presented annually. Established in 1982 in memory of Mr. M.R. Breach.

3168
Cellular Pathology Prize
For recognition of a paper on original work in cellular pathology. Fellowship or Associateship of IMLS is necessary for consideration. A monetary prize of £250 is awarded triennially. Established in 1974. Sponsored by Difco Laboratories.

3169
Honorary Fellow
For recognition in the field of medical laboratory science. The Council of the Institute elects the honoree. Established in 1945.

3170
Earl King Prize
For recognition of a paper on an original work in clinical chemistry. Fellowship or Associateship of IMLS is necessary for consideration. A monetary prize of £1,000 is awarded triennially. Established in 1965 in honor of Professor E.J. King. Sponsored by Boehringer Corporation Limited.

3171
R. J. Lavington Prize
To recognize the candidate who at first attempt receives the highest marks in the four written papers of the special examination for Fellowship of the Institute. Fellowship or Associateship of the IMLS is necessary for consideration. A fellowship of £300 and a medal are awarded annually. Established in 1977 in honor of Mr. R.J. Lavington, General Secretary of IMLS from 1948 to 1970.

3172
Life Membership of IMLS
For recognition of long and valuable service in the interests of the Institute in the field of medical laboratory science. The Council of the Institute elects the honoree. A life membership is awarded.

3173
Membership in Retirement
To recognize members who have retired from active professional life after long and valuable service in the interests of the Institute and the field of medical laboratory science. A membership is awarded.

3174
R. R. Race Prize
For recognition of a paper on original work on haematology and blood transfusion. Fellowship or Associateship of the IMLS is necessary for consideration. A monetary prize of £500 is awarded triennially. Established in 1974 in honor of Dr. R.R. Race. Sponsored by Ortho Diagnostic Systems Limited.

3175
Sims Woodhead Medal
For recognition of services to the Institute and the profession of medical laboratory scientist. A medal is awarded when merited. Established in 1924 in honor of Professor German Sims Woodhead.

3176
Institute of Motor Industry
Fanshaws   Phone: 992 511521
Brickendon, Herts. SG13 8PQ, England   Fax: 992 511548

3177
Castrol Gold Medal
To recognize an individual or individuals, company, or organization for the greatest contribution to the advancement of road transport made during the review year. A gold medal is awarded annually. Established in 1929 by Viscount Wakefield of Hythe, founder of the Castrol Company. Additional information is available from Burman-Castrol (UK) Ltd., Burma House, Pipers Way, Swindon, Wilts. SN3 1RE, England; telephone: 793 30151.

3178
Institute of Patentees and Investors
207-208 Abbey House
Victoria St.
London SW1, England   Phone: 71 ABBEY 1616

3179
Richardson Gold Medal
To recognize the best invention patented in the United Kingdom of Great Britain and Northern Ireland and the Isle of Man. The patented invention

may be the subject of either a patent application or a complete patent, but no patent is eligible for consideration if taken out more than five calendar years before the year of the competition. The best invention is interpreted as the invention which in the opinion of the Judges: (1) best anticipates some future need of common society; or (2) best meets a known demand of common society by some improved method. A gold medal is awarded annually. Established in 1965. Sponsored by the Richardson Gold Medal Trust.

3180
Institute of Petroleum
61 New Cavendish St. Phone: 71 6361004
London W1M 8AR, England Fax: 71 2551472

3181
Cadman Memorial Medal
For recognition of services to the international petroleum industry. A medal is awarded when merited. Established in 1946.

3182
Redwood Medal
To recognize an outstanding petroleum technologist who is known internationally. A medal is awarded when merited. Established in 1919.

3183
Institute of Physics
47 Belgrave Sq. Phone: 71 2356111
London SW1X 8QX, England Fax: 71 2596002

3184
Max Born Medal and Prize
For recognition of outstanding contributions to physics. A monetary prize of £750, a silver medal, and a certificate are awarded annually in even-numbered years to a German physicist and presented in England, and in odd-numbered years to a British physicist and presented in Germany. Established in 1972 by the Institute of Physics and the German Physical Society in memory of Max Born, a physicist.

3185
Charles Vernon Boys Medal and Prize
For recognition of distinguished research in experimental physics. A monetary prize of £750 and a silver medal are awarded annually. Established in 1944 by a bequest of Sir Charles Vernon Boys, former president of the Physical Society.

3186
Bragg Medal and Prize
For distinguished contributions to the teaching of physics. A monetary prize of £500 and a bronze medal are awarded annually. Established in 1965 in honor of Sir Lawrence Bragg, teacher and popularizer of physics.

3187
Charles Chree Medal and Prize
For distinguished research in terrestrial magnetism, atmospheric electricity, and/or other aspects of geophysics comprising the earth, oceans, atmosphere, and solar-terrestrial problems. A monetary prize of £500, a silver medal, and a certificate are awarded in odd-numbered years. Established in 1939 in memory of Dr. Chree, past president of the Physical Society.

3188
Paul Dirac Medal and Prize
For outstanding contributions to theoretical (including mathematical) physics. A monetary prize of £750 and a silver medal are awarded annually. Established in 1987 in memory of P. A. M. Dirac, an honorary fellow of the Institute of Physics.

3189
Duddell Medal and Prize
To recognize a person who has made outstanding contributions to the application of physics or who has contributed to the advancement of knowledge by the invention or design of scientific instruments or the discovery of materials used in the construction of scientific instrument. A monetary prize of £500 and a bronze medal are awarded annually. Established in 1923 by the Physical Society in memory of William du Bois Duddell, inventor of the electromagnetic oscillograph.

3190
Glazebrook Medal and Prize
In recognition of outstanding contributions in the organization, utilization, or application of science. A monetary prize of £1,000 and a silver gilt medal are awarded annually. Established in 1965 by the Institute of Physics and the Physical Society in honor of Glazebrook, the first director of the National Physical Laboratory.

3191
Guthrie Medal and Prize
To recognize a physicist of international reputation for contributions to physics. A monetary prize of £1,000 and a silver gilt medal are awarded annually. Established in 1914 in memory of Professor Frederick Guthrie, founder of the Physical Society.

3192
Holweck Medal and Prize
For distinguished work in experimental physics, or theoretical physics if closely related to experimental work in progress or completed within the preceding 10 years. A monetary prize of £750, a gold medal, and a scroll are awarded in odd-numbered years to a French physicist and presented in England, and in even-numbered years to a British physicist and presented in France. Established in 1945 and administered jointly by the French and British Physical Societies in memory of Fernand Holweck, director of the Curie Laboratory of the Radium Institute of Paris.

3193
Harrie Massie Medal and Prize
To recognize contributions to physics or its applications. Individuals who have had association with Australia or physics in Australia are eligible. A monetary prize of £750, a silver medal, and a certificate are awarded in even-numbered years by the Institute of Physics and in odd-numbered years by the Australian Institute of Physics. Established in 1988 to mark the 25th anniversary of the founding of the Australian Institute of Physics. The first award was made in 1990.

3194
Maxwell Medal and Prize
For contributions made to theoretical physics during the preceding 10 years. Candidates must be under 35 years of age. A monetary prize of £500 and a bronze medal are awarded annually. Established in 1961.

3195
Paterson Medal and Prize
For outstanding contributions to the development, invention, or discovery of new systems, processes, or devices that demonstrate the successful exploitation of physics. Candidates must under 40 years of age. A monetary prize of £500 and a bronze medal are awarded annually. Established in 1981 in honor of Sir Clifford Paterson, founder of GEC Research Laboratories and a past president of the Institute.

3196
Rutherford Medal and Prize
In recognition of contributions to nuclear physics, elementary particle physics, or nuclear technology. A monetary prize of £500 and a bronze medal are awarded annually in even-numbered years. Established in 1939 in memory of Lord Rutherford of Nelson. Formerly: Rutherford Memorial Lecture.

3197
Simon Memorial Prize
In recognition of distinguished work in experimental or theoretical low-temperature physics. A monetary prize of £300, a bronze plaque, and a certificate are awarded every three years. Established in 1958 in memory of Sir Francis Simon.

3198
Thomas Young Medal and Prize
For distinguished work in optics, including the optical principles existing in branches of physics other than that concerned with the visible region of the spectrum. Work relating to infrared rays, ultraviolet rays, x-rays, radio-physics, or some aspects of electron physics is considered. A monetary prize of £500 and a bronze medal are awarded in odd-numbered years. Established in 1907 as the Thomas Young Oration by the Optical Society, taken over by the Physical Society of London in 1932, and changed to its present state in 1961 by the amalgamated Institute of Physics and Physical Society. Formerly: Thomas Young Oration.

3199
Institute of Practitioners in Advertising
44 Belgrave Sq.
London SW1X 8QS, England
Phone: 71 2357020
Fax: 71 2459904

3200
IPA Advertising Effectiveness Awards
To provide a bank of case history material to demonstrate the contribution that advertising can make to successful marketing. The main objectives are to improve understanding of the crucial role advertising plays in marketing; to provide documented analyses of advertising effectiveness and to encourage use of methods of evaluation; and to generate objective case studies about how advertising works, which could then be used in connection with marketing training. Awards are given in the following categories: products or services that are new or have no significant history of advertising; new campaigns from previously advertised brands that resulted in significant short term effects on sales or behavior; and advertising campaigns that benefited a business by maintaining or strengthening a brand over a longer period. The overall best paper wins £3,000 and the Grand Prix trophy. In each category the judges aim to award one gold, two silver, and three bronze awards. The prize money for these categories is £2,000 (Gold), £1,000 (Silver), and £500 (Bronze). Special prizes are awarded for the paper best demonstrating the integration of advertising with other marketing tools, the best case featuring direct response advertising, the best case about a campaign that ran in more than one European country, the paper that demonstrates the most ingenious response to limited advertising or research funds, the case involving the best use of a media planning, and the best example of innovative strategic or executional thinking. The winning case studies and a selection from the commended papers are published in a book, *Advertising Works*. Presented biennially. Established in 1980.

3201
Institute of Professional Investigators
31 A Wellington St.
St. John's
Blackburn, Lancs. BB1 8AF, England
Phone: 254 680072
Fax: 254 59276

3202
Institute of Professional Investigators Awards
To recognize criminal, police, and civil investigators, handwriting experts, pathologists, and others in 28 countries working in the investigative field. The institute bestows awards.

3203
Institute of Public Relations
The Old Trading House
15 Northburgh St.
London EC1V 0PR, England
Phone: 71 2535151
Fax: 71 4900588

3204
Sword of Excellence Awards
To recognize outstanding work in public relations. Awards are presented in the following categories: City, Financial, and Investor Relations; Internal Communication; Public Affairs; Consumer Products; Industry and Commerce; Community Relations; and Special Programs. Three special awards may be made, at the discretion of the judges, to entries from any category in recognition of excellence in: long-term public relations programs, international practice of public relations, and the use of visual communication in a public relations program. A miniature knight's sword, a certificate, and champagne are awarded annually. Established in 1984. Sponsored by PIMS International, PLC.

3205
Institute of Quarrying
7 Regent St.
Nottingham NG1 5BS, England
Phone: 602 411315
Fax: 602 484035

3206
Institute of Quarrying Awards
To recognize individuals employed in the quarrying and related industries and to promote education and training in all aspects of quarry operation and business management. Awards are bestowed annually.

3207
Institute of Road Transport Engineers
1 Cromwell Pl.
London SW7 2JF, England
Phone: 71 5893744
Fax: 71 2250494

3208
Mackenzie Junner Rose-Bowl Trophy
To recognize a contribution in the field of road transport engineering. A monetary award and a trophy are presented annually. Established in memory of the Institute founder.

3209
Institute of Statisticians
43 St. Peters Sq.
Preston, Lancs. PR1 7BX, England
Phone: 772 20437
Fax: 772 204476

3210
C. Oswald George Prize
To provide recognition for the best article published in the magazine *Teaching Statistics*. Articles may be nominated by the Editorial Board of *Teaching Statistics*. A monetary award is presented annually. Established in 1980 by the Institute of Statisticians in honor of C. Oswald George. Additional information is available from Dr. D.R. Green, Editor, *Teaching Statistics*, Department of Mathematical Sciences, Loughborough University, Loughborough LE11 3TU, England.

3211
Institute of the Furniture Warehousing and Removing Industry
277 Gray's Inn Rd.
London WC1X 8SY, England
Phone: 71 8323088

3212
Institute of the Furniture Warehousing and Removing Industry Awards
To recognize employees in furniture removal and associated industries. Awards are presented.

3213

Institution of Chemical Engineers
Geo. E. Davis Bldg.
165-171 Railway Terr.
Rugby, Warks. CV21 3HQ, England

Phone: 788 578214
Fax: 788 560833

3214

Brennan Medal
To recognize the best book published by the institution each year. Awarded annually. Established in 1988 to honor Basil Brennan, the Institution's first General Secretary.

3215

Council Medal
To recognize a member or non-member who has given exceptional service on a special project. Awarded annually. Established in 1967.

3216

George E. Davis Medal
For recognition of a contribution in the field of chemical engineering. Awarded every four or five years. Established in 1965 in honor of George E. Davis, the father of the discipline.

3217

Donald Medal
To recognize an individual for outstanding services to biochemical engineering. Established in 1988 to honor Prof. Donald, a long-serving Honorary Secretary and former Ramsay Professor at University College London where biochemical engineering was first established in the United Kingdom.

3218

Ned Franklin Medal
To recognize an individual for outstanding service in the fields of occupational health, safety, loss prevention, and care for the environment. Awarded annually. Established in 1988 to honor Ned Franklin, a past president of the institution and a major personality in the development of the nuclear power industry.

3219

Arnold Greene Medal
For recognition of the most meritorious contribution to the progress of the institution. Awarded annually. Established in 1928 in honor of F. A. Greene, a founder member and honorable treasurer for 33 years. Formerly: (1964) Osborne Reynolds Medal.

3220

Hanson Medal
For recognition of the best article contributed to the institution's monthly publication, *The Chemical Engineer*. A medal is awarded annually. Established in 1987.

3221

John William Hinchley Medal
To recognize the best student in the graduating class at Imperial College London. Awarded annually. Established in 1988 to honor John William Hinchley, the driving force behind the founding of the institution in 1922.

3222

Hutchison Medal
To recognize the author of the best paper that is either philosophical in nature or deals with practical matters. Awarded annually. Established in 1991 to honor Sir Kenneth Hutchison, former president (1959-1960) of the institution.

3223

Junior Moulton Medal
For recognition of the best paper published by the institution during the year. Papers written by members under 30 years of age are considered. Awarded annually. Established in 1929.

3224

Macnab Medal
For recognition of the best answer to the institution's Design Project in any year. A medal is awarded annually. Established in 1935.

3225

Senior Moulton Medal
For recognition of the best paper published by the institution during the year. Awarded annually. Established in 1929.

3226

Institution of Civil Engineers
1-7 Great George St.
Westminster
London SW19 3AA, England

Phone: 71 2227722
Fax: 71 7991325

3227

Russell Allin Prize
To recognize an associate member or a student for a paper dealing with soil mechanics and foundations, either general or in any of their aspects, such as theory, research, design, construction, testing, or with a particular form of foundation. A monetary prize of £100 and a certificate are awarded annually. Established in 1958 in memory of Russell Allin (1881-1957), a pioneer in soil mechanics.

3228

Baker Medal
For recognition of services in the development of engineering practice or investigation into problems that Sir Benjamin Baker was especially identified with. Preference is given to individuals primarily responsible for the development, investigation, and writing of a paper accepted by the Institution A medal is awarded triennially. Established in 1934 in memory of Sir Benjamin Baker (1849-1907), past president.

3229

Brunel Medal
For recognition of services to civil engineering. Individuals must be nominated by December 31 each year. A medal is awarded when merited. Established in 1982 in honor of I. Brunel, a founding engineer.

3230

Build a Building Competition
To provide a competition for young professionals in the construction industry. Open to multidisciplinary teams of four to six members, all of whom must be 30 years of age or younger. The competition is held at the Institution over a two-day period. A monetary prize of £1,000 and certificates are awarded to the winning team. Established in 1993 by the Institution and the Junior Liason Organization under the umbrella of the Construction Industry Council. Sponsored by the Worshipful Company of Constructors.

3231

Robert Alfred Carr Premium
To recognize the author of the best paper on dock, railway, and gas engineering subjects published by the Institution during the past year. A monetary prize of £50 and a certificate are awarded annually. Established in 1963 by Robert Alfred Carr (1864-1942) in memory of his father Robert Carr and his brother Harold Oswald Carr.

3232

Civil Engineering Prizes for Students
For recognition of achievement in course work, examination performance, and ability in civil engineering design. Students in final years of an

engineering degree course are eligible. Certificates and a monetary award of £100 are awarded.

3233

Coopers Hill War Memorial Prize
For recognition of a paper by a corporate member published by the Institution. The award is made irrespective of the age of the author and of any other award made for the same paper. A monetary prize, medal, and certificate are awarded. Established in 1921 by the Coopers Hill Society in memory of its members and relatives of its members who fell in the First World War.

3234

Crampton Prize
For recognition of the best paper, preferably on the construction, ventilation, and working of tunnels of considerable length, or on any other subject that may be selected. A monetary prize of £50 and a certificate are awarded every four years. Established in 1890.

3235

Bill Curtin Medal
To recognize the best paper presented to the Institution on innovative design in civil engineering. A medal is awarded annually. Established by Curtins Consulting Engineers to commemorate W. G. Curtin's contribution to engineering.

3236

James Alfred Ewing Medal
For recognition of contributions to the science of engineering in the field of research. Members or nonmembers of the Institution are eligible. Recommendations are made by the Institute of Civil Engineers, the Institute of Mechanical Engineers, the Royal Institution of Naval Architects, and the Institution of Electrical Engineers. A gold medal with a bronze replica is awarded annually jointly with the Royal Society. Established in 1936 in memory of Sir Alfred Ewing (1855-1935), Honorary Member.

3237

James Forrest Medal
To recognize the writer of the best student or associate member's paper presented to the Institution. A monetary award of £150 and a medal are awarded annually. Established in 1897 in honor of James Forrest, secretary of the Institution (1860-1896).

3238

Geotechnical Research Medal
To recognize the author(s) of the best contribution in the field of research in geotechnical engineering published by the Institution in the previous year. A medal is awarded annually. Established in 1989 following a bequest by the late A. W. Bishop.

3239

Halcrow Premium
For recognition of the best paper published by the Institution on harbours, tunnels, and hydroelectric projects. Corporate members are eligible. A monetary prize of £50 is awarded annually. Established in 1960 by a bequest of Sir William Halcrow, president of the Institution in 1946-1947.

3240

David Hislop Award
For recognition of the best paper published in the *Proceedings* or in an Institution conference volume on heavy marine design and construction, with particular reference to offshore engineering. A monetary prize of £500 is awarded triennially. Established in 1975 in memory of David Hislop (1928-1973).

3241

Howard Medal
For recognition of a paper on any of the uses or properties of iron. Corporate, associate, or student members of the Institution may submit papers. A medal is awarded every four years. Established in 1872 by Thomas Howard who carried out investigations in connection with steam and wrought iron. Formerly known as the Howard Quinquennial Prize, it was presented in the form of a medal and premium from 1877 until 1937, and was renamed in 1955. Formerly: Howard Quinquennial Prize.

3242

T. K. Hsieh Award
To recognize the author of the best paper published by the institution in the field of structural and soil vibration caused by mechanical plant, winds, waves, or seismic effects. A monetary prize of £50 is awarded annually. Established in 1979 in memory of Dr. Tso Kung Hsieh.

3243

Renee Redfern Hunt Memorial Prize
For recognition of the best essays written in the spring, autumn, and overseas sessions of the professional examination for corporate membership of the Institution. A monetary prize and a certificate are awarded. Established in 1982 in memory of Miss Renee Redfern Hunt, MBE, Professional Examination Officer at the Institution from 1945 until within a few months of her death in 1981.

3244

Institution Gold Medal
To recognize an individual whose contribution to a major world-recognized civil engineering or construction project is of sufficient magnitude and stature to merit an Institution premier award outside those given for papers. The contribution may be in design, research development or investigation, construction, management, and education and training. A gold medal is awarded. Established in 1993.

3245

Institution Medal and Premium (Local Associations) Competition
For recognition of a paper on engineering design, research, or practice that has been presented at a local association meeting. Nominations may be submitted by the committees of the local associations. Associate members, graduates, and students may be nominated. A monetary prize of £150 and a medal are awarded annually. From October 1985, a shield bearing the Institution's crest has been awarded to the winner to be retained by the author's local association for one year. Since 1969, there has been a special prize of £25 for the best paper entered in the competition by undergraduate students, provided that they are not winners of the competition. Awarded annually. Established in 1951.

3246

Institution Medal and Premium (Universities) Competition
For recognition of a paper on engineering design, research, or practice. Undergraduates of universities and polytechnics in the United Kingdom may be nominated by the heads of the engineering colleges. A monetary prize of £150 and a medal are awarded annually. All authors presenting papers in the final and not awarded the medal receive a check and a certificate. Established in 1946. Formerly: (1987) Institution Medal and Premium (London Universities) Competition.

3247

James Prescott Joule Medal
For recognition of the best paper presented on an engineering subject, preferably one dealing with the transformation of energy. Associate members under 27 years of age or students of the Institution may submit papers. A medal is awarded triennially.

3248

Kelvin Medal
For recognition of distinguished service in the application of science to engineering rather than to the development of physical science itself. A medal is awarded triennially. Established in 1914 in memory of Lord Kelvin, a British physicist.

3249

Lindapter Award
To recognize the author of the best paper submitted to the Institution's Medal and Premium (Local Associations and Universities) Competitions. Students pursuing a course of study approved by the Institution are

eligible. A monetary prize of £200 is awarded. The winner's name and that of the university/college is recorded on a trophy and displayed by that university/college for the following eight months. Sponsored by Lindapter International Ltd.

3250

Manby Premium

For recognition of papers read at meetings of the Institution. A monetary prize of £25 and a certificate are awarded every four years. Instituted in 1857 by Charles Manby (M), secretary of the Institution from 1839 to 1859.

3251

MERIT Competition

MERIT (Managing Engineering Resources Involves Teamwork) is a construction management simulation run by the Institution and sponsored by Balfour Beatty Ltd. It is open to teams of 4 to 6 members, all of whom must be 30 years of age or under. The competition is played by post, with the top six teams after five rounds competing against each other at a two-day final. The competition first took place in 1988. The winning team receives a prize from Balfour Beatty and is presented with an engraved salver to be retained for one year. Each team member also receives a certificate. Formerly: MERIT Game.

3252

Miller Prizes

For recognition of the best papers or series of papers by associate members, graduates, or students. Certificates and 10 prizes of £100 each are awarded annually. Established by a bequest of Joseph Miller (1797-1860), who was associated with marine engine design.

3253

Overseas Premium

For recognition of the best papers received during the year on a subject connected with works carried out outside the British Isles. Corporate members of the Institution are eligible. Two monetary prizes of £50 each and certificates are awarded annually.

3254

Frederick Palmer Prize

For recognition of a paper published by the Institution. Preference is given to papers of merit dealing with the economic and financial aspects of civil engineering. A monetary prize of £60 and a certificate are awarded annually. Established in 1960 by a bequest made by John Palmer to mark the centenary of the birth of his father, Sir Frederick Palmer (1862-1934), president of the Institution in 1926-1927.

3255

Parkman Medal

For recognition of the best paper published by the Institution in the previous year on the practical aspects of the control or management of the design and/or construction of a specific scheme. A medal is awarded. Established in 1988 by the Parkman Group to commemorate their centenary.

3256

Reed and Mallik Medal

To recognize the author of the best paper published in the previous year covering the construction aspects of a civil engineering project. A monetary prize and a medal are awarded annually. Established in 1983 following a donation by the Rush & Tompkins Group to commemorate the achievements of their civil engineering contracting subsidiary Reed and Mallik Ltd.

3257

Safety in Construction Medal

To recognize the author of a paper published by the Institution in the previous year that discusses a project or feature within a project that best describes the measures taken to safeguard the health and safety of the construction team, the user, and the public. A medal is awarded annually. Established in 1984 by John Derrington, CBE, FEng, president of the Institution in 1984-1985, to foster actively improved health and safety in construction works.

3258

George Stephenson Medal

For recognition in the field of civil engineering. Established in 1881.

3259

Telford Medal

This, the highest award of the Institution for a paper, is given to recognize a paper or series of papers presented to the Institution, irrespective of any previous recognition. Medals and monetary prizes are awarded annually when merited. Established in 1835 by a bequest made to the Institution by Thomas Telford (1757-1834), first president of the Institution. First awarded in 1837.

3260

Telford Premium

For recognition of a paper presented to the Institution. The income from the Telford endowment fund, after provision has been made for the Telford Medal, is used to provide up to four premiums in the amount of £50 each. Premiums and certificates are awarded annually. Established in 1835.

3261

Trevithick Premium

For recognition of a paper presented to the Institution. A monetary prize of £50 is awarded triennially. Established in 1890 in memory of Richard Trevithick (1771-1833) and augmented in 1932 by a gift from Mrs. H. K. Trevithick.

3262

Garth Watson Medal

To recognize dedicated and valuable service to the Institution related to any field of its activities or for a contribution to a specific Institution project by a member or a member of staff. Established in 1993 in honor of Garth Watson, a respected past secretary of the Institution.

3263

James Watt Medal

For recognition of papers on mechanical engineering subjects. A medal is awarded annually. Established in 1858 to honor James Watt, Scottish mechanical engineer and inventor.

3264

Webb Prize

For recognition of papers on railway engineering and transportation in general. Two prizes of £65 each and certificates are awarded annually. Established in 1908 by a bequest of Francis William Webb (1838-1906), vice president.

3265

Institution of Diagnostic Engineers
3 Wycliffe St.   Phone: 533 392552
Leicester LE1 5LR, England   Fax: 533 592444

3266

Collacott Prize

To encourage members to submit information of diagnostic interest and of value to increasing a member's store of knowledge and events that can or may occur, and of techniques of deduction. Entries should be brief and factual, preferably illustrated by line sketches. A monetary prize is awarded annually. Established in 1985.

3267

Institution of Electrical Engineers
The Council Office
Savoy Pl.   Phone: 71 2401871
London WC2R OBL, England   Fax: 71 3797707

Formed by merger of:.

3268
Charles Babbage Premium
For recognition of a paper published in the *Software Engineering Journal*. A monetary prize of £150 and a certificate are awarded annually in October. Established in 1959 by the Institution of Electronic and Radio Engineers in honor of Charles Babbage.

3269
Blumlein-Brown-Willans Premium Award
For recognition of papers on the science and art of television or pulse and wideband techniques. Papers published in IEE publications are eligible. A monetary prize of £150 and a certificate are awarded annually in October.

3270
Bridgeport Prize
To recognize the best project on quality management in an accredited engineering degree course. The following prizes are awarded annually: first prize - £250 and a certificate; second prize - £100 and a certificate; and third prize - £50 and a certificate.

3271
Centres Premium
For recognition of the best paper presented by a younger member at a Short Papers Evening. Centre regulations permit each Younger Member Section in the United Kingdom and each International Centre to award one Premium. A monetary award of £100 and a certificate plus a second award of £50 when four or more papers are presented are awarded annually when merited.

3272
Coopers Hill War Memorial Prize and Medal
For recognition of the best paper on a professional subject by a corporate member under 35 years of age. A monetary prize, a bronze medal, and a certificate are awarded annually by the Institution of Civil Engineers and triennially jointly with the IEE, the School of Military Engineering (Chatham) and the School of Forestry (Oxford). Established by the members of the Royal Indian Engineering College (Coopers Hill) in commemoration of members of the College who fell in the 1914-1918 War.

3273
Divisional Premium
For recognition of papers published in IEE publications from October to September. Awards are given in the following divisions: Electronics Division (Mountbatten Premium), Computing and Control Division (F. C. Williams Premium), Management and Design Division, Power Division, Manufacturing Division, and Science, Education, and Technology Division. Six monetary awards of £500 each and a certificate are awarded annually. In addition to the Divisional Premiums, each Division may award the following Premiums of £150 each and a certificate annually: Electronics Division - Ambrose Fleming Premium, Oliver Lodge Premium, Marconi Premium, and J. J. Thomson Premium; Computing and Control Division - Hartree Premium, Heaviside Premium, Kelvin Premium, and Mather Premium; Management and Design Division - Lord Hirst Premium; Power Division - Crompton Premium, Sebastian Z. de Ferranti Premium, John Hopkinson Premium, and Swan Premium; and Science, Education, and Technology Division - Ayrton Premium, Duddell Premium, Maxwell Premium, and Snell Premium.

3274
***Electronics and Communication Engineering Journal* Premium**
For recognition of a paper published in the *Electronics and Communication Engineering Journal*. A monetary prize of £150 is awarded annually in October. Established in 1988.

3275
***Electronics Education* Premium**
For recognition of the best article in *Electronic Systems News*. A monetary prize of £150 is awarded annually in October. Established in 1988. Formerly: *Electronic Systems News* Premium.

3276
***Electronics Letters* Premium Awards**
For recognition of papers published in *Electronics Letters* from October to September. Three monetary prizes of £150 each and a certificate are awarded annually in October.

3277
Engineering Journals Premia
To recognize outstanding papers published in the following journals: *Power Engineering Journal*, *Computing and Control Engineering Journal*, *Intelligent Systems Engineering Journal*, *Engineering Management*, *Engineering Science and Education Journal*, and *Manufacturing Engineering*. A monetary prize of £150 and a certificate are awarded annually for one paper in each journal.

3278
Faraday House Commemorative Prize
For recognition of the best lecture presentation by a younger member. Presentations made by members under 30 years of age at an IEE meeting are considered. The deadline for entries is May 31. A monetary prize of £150 and a certificate are awarded annually in October.

3279
Faraday Medal
For recognition of notable scientific or industrial achievement in electrical engineering, or for conspicuous service rendered to the advancement of electrical science. There are no restrictions as regards nationality, country of residence, or membership in the institution. A bronze medal and vellum certificate are awarded annually in March.

3280
Tony Goldsmith Cup
To recognize a member of the Institution active in the work of the Manufacturing Division for a meritorious contribution to the progress of the division. A cup, held for one year by the recipient, is presented annually in October.

3281
Harry Henniker Premium
For recognition of a paper by a younger member of the Institution. Sponsored by the Scottish Centre.

3282
IEE Achievement Medal
For recognition of achievement in the following categories: computing and control; power electrical engineering; science, education, and technology; electrical engineer in engineering management, engineering design, or an area within the scope of the Management Group M2 (Engineering and Society). A person or group of persons without restriction as regards nationality, country of residence, or membership of the Institution may be considered. A maximum of four awards (one for each category) are made annually. A bronze medal engraved with the recipient's name and year of award is presented in October.

3283
IEE Benefactors Prize
To recognize meritorious students who have satisfied the Institute's educational requirements in the preceding year. Members of IEE are eligible. The deadline is March 31. A monetary prize of £200 and a certificate are awarded annually in October.

3284
IEE Measurement Prize
For recognition of a contribution to the science, art, and practice of electrical measurement. A monetary prize of £500 is awarded annually at the Science Education and Technology Divisional Lecture in October. Established in 1987.

3285
IEE Prize
To recognize outstanding students in IEE accredited courses. The deadlines for nominations are September 30 for the Northern Hemisphere and January 31 for the Southern Hemisphere. A monetary award, a certificate, and free membership in IEE for two years following graduation may be awarded by each establishment that runs courses accredited by the IEE or by a National Institution with which the IEE has a mutual recognition agreement.

3286
IEE Prize for Helping Disabled People
For recognition of the best application of electronic or electrical techniques for helping disabled people. Devices that in any way improve the quality of life of disabled people are awarded only after the invention is in use and is seen to be successful in helping disabled people. Devices that have been developed or improved since the previous award are eligible. While applicants may work for companies or organizations, the award is given to the individuals who have contributed to the idea. If more than one individual contributed to the project, the prize may be shared. Applicants need not be members of the Institution. Applications are considered from any part of the world. The deadline for entries is May 31. A monetary award of £6,000 and a certificate are awarded triennially in November.

3287
IEE Prize for Innovation
For recognition of ideas for innovative products. There are no restrictions on the ideas for products, but all submissions must be original, of sound design, and have clear commercial potential. The submission of concepts, where no hardware is yet available, is acceptable. Products designed for employers are not eligible, nor are products already commissioned by clients from consultant members of the IEE and the IMechE residing in the United Kingdom. The deadline is November 30. The following monetary prizes are awarded: first prize - £500; second prize - £200; and third prize - £100. Medals are also awarded to recipients. Awarded annually. Awarded in association with the IMechE and the Design Council.

3288
IEE Rayleigh Book Award
To recognize an outstanding book published by the IEE. A monetary award of £500 and a certificate are presented annually.

3289
IEE Scotland North Premium
For recognition of the best two papers presented by the Younger Members of the Sub-Centre. Two monetary awards of £25 each are awarded annually. Formerly: North of Scotland Sub Centre Premium.

3290
IERE Benefactors Premium
For recognition of a paper on the application of broadcast and communication technology, including papers on applications for educational purposes. A monetary prize of £50 is awarded annually in October when merited. Established in 1988.

3291
Institution Premium
For recognition of papers published in IEE publications (including books and conference publications) over the period of October to September each year. The prize may not be awarded more than once to any one author. A monetary prize of £1,500 and a certificate are awarded annually when merited in October.

3292
International Premium Awards
To recognize papers published in IEE publications from October through September. For single author papers, the author must be an IEE member; for multi-author papers, one author must be an IEE member. All authors must be resident outside the United Kingdom. Awards of £150 are presented both to a senior member and to student and associate members under 30 years of age. Two prizes are awarded annually when merited in June or July.

3293
Oliver Lucas Automotive Electronic Engineering Award
For recognition of an outstanding contribution to the field of automotive electronic engineering. In years when the International Conference on Automotive Electronics is held, proposals for the award should be made to the Computing and Control Divisional Board by the Conference Organizing Committee, for the most significant contribution to the Conference. In years when there is no International Conference on Automotive Electronics, the award is presented either for the paper making the greatest contribution to automotive electronics and published in a recognized British technical or scientific publication within the two years prior to March 31 in the year of award (but excluding all papers published at the previous International Conference on automotive electronics); or for the most outstanding contribution to automotive electronics by an individual working in the United Kingdom within the same period. A monetary award of £200, a trophy, and a certificate are awarded annually in October when merited. Established by Lucas Industries and named after Oliver Lucas, the grandson of the founder of the company who was responsible for many significant developments in automotive electrical equipment during the formative years of the 1920s.

3294
Manufacturing Prize
To recognize the best project by a student in an accredited undergraduate degree course. Seven awards are presented annually: Jones & Shipman Prize, - £500; Sir Walter Puckey Prize - £100; Lord Austin Prize - £100; Sir Robert Telford Prize - £100; Sir Alan Veale Prize - £100; IBM MEng Project Prize - £100; and Professor J. Cherry Prize - £100. Certificates are also awarded.

3295
Eric Megaw Memorial Prize
To recognize the best lecture presentation and paper by a final year student of the Electrical and Electronic Engineering Department of the Queen's University of Belfast. A monetary prize of £100 and a certificate are awarded annually in March. The four best lectures and papers will be delivered at a Centre evening meeting of the Northern Ireland Centre.

3296
Mensforth International Gold Medal
To recognize outstanding contributions to the advancement of manufacturing engineering technology or manufacturing management. A gold medal is awarded annually in October.

3297
Henry Nimmo Premium
For recognition of the best paper by a student on a subject within the field of electricity supply. A monetary award of £50 is given annually. Established in memory of Henry Nimmo, former chairman of the Southern Electricity Board by its members.

3298
Nuffield Silver Medal
To recognize a member of the Institution for meritorious contribution to the progress of the manufacturing profession. A silver medal is awarded annually in October.

3299
Overseas Student Medallion
For recognition of a papers published in IEE publications from October to the following September. For single author papers, the author must be an IEE member For multi-author papers, one author must be an IEE member. All authors must be resident overseas. Two monetary prizes of £150 each are awarded to: Senior Members; and Students and Associate Members under 30. Awarded annually in June or July.

3300
RAF Apprentice Engineering Technician Prize
To recognize apprentice engineering technicians in each entry at No. 2 School of Technical Training Royal Air Force (Cosford) who have earned the highest aggregate marks in all subjects. Two to three book tokens up to a £25 value are awarded annually in April and October.

3301
A. H. Reeves Premium
To recognize the best paper published in any Institution publication on digital coding. A monetary prize of £150 and a certificate are presented annually. Established in honor of Alec Harley Reeves for his work on PCM at the laboratories of STC (1902-1971).

3302
Rolls Royce Jubilee Award
To recognize individuals in two categories: those under 30 years of age who demonstrate high levels of achievement, consistent career progression, and developing professionalism; and those who demonstrate technical innovation in the field of manufacturing engineering or manufacturing systems engineering. A monetary prize of £250 and a medal are awarded to the winner in each category annually in October.

3303
Sir Henry Royce Award
To recognize the best industrial-based project, paper, or achievement submitted by a younger member. The deadline for entries is in April. A monetary prize of £250, a medal, and a certificate are awarded annually in October. Sponsored by the Sir Henry Royce Memorial Foundation.

3304
J. D. Scaife Award
To recognize the best paper published in the *International Journal of Production Research*. A monetary award of £100 and a certificate are presented annually in October.

3305
Student Medallion Award
For recognition of a paper presented outside the United Kingdom at a meeting sponsored by the IEE or co-sponsored with the National Institution. The recipient need not be an IEE member but should be a member of the National Institution. An inscribed medallion is awarded when merited. Formerly: Overseas Student Medallion.

3306
J. Langham Thompson Premium
To recognize a paper published in the *Electronics & Communication Engineering Journal*. A monetary prize of £150 and a certificate are awarded annually. Established in 1962.

3307
J. J. Thomson Medal
For recognition of outstanding work by a person or group of persons in electronics theory, practice, development, or manufacture. There are no restrictions regarding nationality, country of residence, or membership of the Institution. A bronze medal is awarded annually.

3308
Willans Premium
For recognition of the best paper read or published dealing with the utilization or transformation of energy treated especially from the point of view of efficiency or economy. The award is given in alternate years by IEE and IMechE. A monetary prize or medal is awarded triennially in October.

3309
Young Engineer of the Year
To recognize competitors in the Engineering Council's Young Engineers of the Year competition. A monetary prize of £500 is awarded annually.

3310
Young Enterprise Award
For recognition of the best answer to the "Manufacturing Engineering" question in the Young Enterprise examination paper set by the University of Oxford Delegacy of Local Examinations. Winners receive a salver and industrial tour and finalists receive institution publication and an industrial tour. Five awards are presented annually in July.

3311
Younger Members' Premiums Awards
For recognition of the best lecture presentations and papers by younger members over the year. Papers and lectures by members who are under 30 years of age are considered. Lectures must be given at IEE meetings. The deadline is May 31. The following monetary prizes are presented annually in July: for a lecture - one prize of £300, two of £300, two of £150, and a certificate; and for a paper - one of £300, two of £150, and a certificate.

3312
Dr. V. K. Zworykin Premium
For recognition of papers published by the IEE on medical and biological electronics. A monetary prize of £150 is awarded annually in October. Established in 1961 by the Institution of Electronic and Radio Engineers in honor of Dr. V. K. Zworykin.

3313
Institution of Environmental Sciences
14 Princess Gate
Hyde Park
London SW7 1PU, England   Phone: 71 252 515511

3314
Institution of Environmental Sciences Awards
To recognize the best essays on environmental issues by a university or college student in the United Kingdom and to promote public interest, awareness, and involvement in the problems of world environment and environmental sciences. A monetary prize of £30, membership in the Institution, and publication of the paper are awarded annually. Established in 1986.

3315
Institution of Gas Engineers
17 Grosvenor Crescent   Phone: 71 245 9811
London SW1X 7ES, England   Fax: 71 245 1229

3316
W. H. Bennett Travelling Fellowship
To enable the holder to study, either in England or overseas, technical developments of interest to the gas industry. Qualified engineers or technologists within the age group 25 to 35 years who are members of the Institution or any of its affiliated organizations are eligible. Established in 1963 by Mrs. V.J. Bennett in memory of her husband, William Henry Bennett who died in 1960, after a long and distinguished career in the gas industry.

3317
Birmingham Medal
To encourage the extension of the uses of coal gas. It is bestowed for originality in connection with the manufacture and application of gas, such qualification to be interpreted in its widest possible sense. Members may submit names of individuals who are members of the Institution or any of its affiliated organizations for the consideration of the Council. A medal is awarded biennially when merited. Established in 1881.

3318
Celette Prize
To further the education of any non-Corporate Member of the Institution. The recipient should not be older than 35 years during the year of the

award. The award may include benefits or activities such as grant aid for academic study, travelling fellowships, or research projects. Established in 1991 by Celette (Industrial Housings) Ltd..

3319

Clark Travelling Fellowship
To enable the holder to study technical developments overseas in areas of interest to the gas industry. Members of the Institution, not more than 35 years of age, who are qualified academically in an engineering or technical subject are eligible. Established in 1984 to honor Joseph George Clark (1879-1953), who instigated research and training in the field of gas utilization which led to the establishment of Watson House.

3320

Dempster Travelling Fellowship
To enable the holder to study, either in England or overseas, the technical developments of interest to the gas industry. Candidates must not be more than 30 years of age and must be individuals who are members of the Institution or any of its affiliated organizations. Established in 1951 by Mr. Charles Dempster in memory of the late Robert Dempster, senior and junior, and John Dempster.

3321

Dieterichs/Maclay Memorial Prize
For recognition of students who have obtained the Scottish Technical Education Council and the Technician Education Council certificates in gas subjects with a view to becoming Associate Members (Technician Grade) of the Institution. Two awards are available annually, one for candidates specializing in gas distribution and one for candidates specializing in gas utilization. No candidate is eligible for more than one award. Candidates are eligible for the award in the sessional year in which they successfully complete the certificate course. Moderators appointed by the Education and Training Committee may submit nominations from the training colleges offering the SCOTEC and BTEC national certificate courses in gas subjects. Candidates are assessed on their overall record in the certificate examinations. Established in 1983 as the Dieterichs/Maclay Memorial Prize which replaces the William Dieterichs Memorial and the James Archibald Maclay Memorial prizes, which were originally endowed in 1951 and 1964, respectively. Formerly: William Dieterichs Memorial Prize; James Archibald Maclay Memorial Prize.

3322

Arthur Duckham Research Award
For recognition of distinguished service to industry in general and to the gas industry in particular. Established in 1934 in memory of Sir Arthur Duckham. (Discontinued)

3323

T. V. Garrud Fellowship
To enable the holder to develop his/her experience in matters relating to the gas industry. Candidates should be under 30 years of age and members of a Gas Association for at least twelve months. Awarded triennially. Established in 1980 in memory of T.V. Garrud by his widow.

3324

Charles Hunt Memorial Medal
For recognition of gas engineering students. Candidates must have attained a standard sufficient to justify the award and must have successfully completed one of the following: (1) B.Sc. degree course in Civil Engineering for gas engineers of Heriot-Watt University, Edinburgh; or (2) B.Sc. degree course in Gas Engineering of the University of Salford. An award is given for candidates specializing in gas distribution and one for candidates specializing in gas utilization. No candidate is eligible for more than one award. Candidates are eligible for an award in the sessional year (September 1 to August 31) in which they successfully complete the degree course. Candidates will be assessed on their overall record as gas engineering students. Awarded annually. Established in 1930.

3325

Institution Bronze Medal
For recognition of a paper accepted for presentation to and read at a General Meeting of a Gas Association in the calendar year preceding the year of the award. A Presidential Address is not eligible for the award and the author of a paper must be a member of the Gas Association before which the paper is read. A bronze medal is awarded annually. Established in 1905.

3326

Institution Gold Medal
For recognition of a paper on any subject, accepted for presentation to and read at a General Meeting of the Institution in the calendar year preceding the year of the award. Individuals who are members of the Institution or any of its affiliated organizations are eligible. A gold medal is awarded annually. Established in 1912.

3327

Institution Silver Medal
For recognition of a paper accepted for presentation to and read at a General Meeting of a District Section of the Institution or of an Affiliated District Association in the calendar year preceding the year of the award. A Chairman's or a Presidential Address is not eligible for the award and the author of a paper must be a member in any class of the Institution. A silver medal is awarded annually. Established in 1905.

3328

H. E. Jones London Medal
For recognition of a paper accepted for presentation to and read at a General Meeting of the Institution in the calendar year preceding the year of the award. The paper must deal with the principles involved in the construction of works or plants for the manufacture or distribution of gas and/or the points of good management of a gas undertaking considered in relation to the management of labor, the facilitating and popularizing the use of gas for general purposes, or improvement in carbonizing and purifying processes, or in the development of residuals. Individuals who are members of the Institution or any of its affiliated organizations are eligible. A medal is awarded annually. Established in 1905.

3329

James Ransom Memorial Medals
For recognition of gas engineering student technicians. Candidates must have attained a standard sufficient to justify the award and must have successfully completed the Scottish Technician Education Council (SCOTEC) or the Business Technician Education Council (BTEC) Higher National Certificate courses in gas subjects. Two medals are available annually, one for candidates specializing in gas distribution and one for candidates specializing in gas utilization. No candidate is eligible for more than one award. Candidates are eligible for the award in the sessional year in which they successfully complete the Certificate course. Established in 1979 to honor James Ransom for his work in the field of education and training in the gas industry.

3330

Sugg Heritage Award
For recognition of a paper judged to contribute most to the understanding of the history, traditions or aspirations and achievements of the gas industry (as defined by By-Law 1 of the Institution of Gas Engineers) as to a particular activity or period of either engineering, scientific or social import. Individuals who are members of the Institution or any of its affiliated organizations are eligible. The paper is to be selected by a Panel comprising the Chairman and two members or nominees of the Panel for the History of the Industry from those accepted for presentation to a General Meeting of a District Section or Gas Association of Great Britain or a paper accepted for presentation to a General Meeting of the Institution in the calendar year preceding the award. A trophy is presented at the Institution Annual General Meeting. Established in 1981.

3331
Corbet and Henry Woodall, and William Cartwright Holmes Postgraduate Award
To encourage postgraduate education or research in the University of Leeds. The Corbet Woodall Scholarship was endowed in 1915 by the late Sir Corbet Woodall to celebrate the Jubilee in 1913 of the Institution of Gas Engineers. To perpetuate the memory of Mr. Henry Woodall (Sir Corbet's son), the Scholarship was more than doubled and its name changed to the Corbet and Henry Woodall Scholarship. The Scholarship in Gas Engineering was tenable at the University of Leeds. The William Cartwright Holmes Scholarship, in Gas Engineering and tenable at the University of Leeds, was endowed in 1929 by Mr. P.F. Holmes and Mr. D.M. Henshaw as a memorial to William Cartwright Holmes, of Huddersfield. In 1968, the families of the donors agreed to combine the assets of the two endowments into one fund. Formerly: (1966) Corbet and Henry Woodall Scholarship; (1966) William Cartwright Holmes Scholars.

3332
Institution of Mechanical Engineers
Northgate Ave.
Bury St. Edmonds
Suffolk IP32 6BN, England
Phone: 0284 763277
Fax: 0284 704006

3333
Institution of Mechanical Engineers Awards
To support and encourage research and training for members. The following awards are offered to corporate and non-corporate members of the Institution: Raymond Coleman Prescott Scholarship, Clayton Grants, Bramah Scholarship, Clayton Grants for Postgraduate Studies, Bryan Donkin Awards, Labrow Grant, Neil Watson Grants, Thomas Andrew Common Grants, Overseas Study Bursaries and Flatman Grants, Students Aid Fund, and undergraduate scholarships. Monetary awards are presented annually.

3334
James Watt International Medal
To recognize an individual for work as a mechanical engineer and the ability to apply science to the progress of mechanical engineering. Engineering institutions and societies of any nationality may nominate engineers who have attained international recognition. A gold medal is presented biennially. Established in 1937 in memory of James Watt, the inventor of the steam engine.

3335
Institution of Mining and Metallurgy
44 Portland Pl.
London W1N 4BR, England
Phone: 71 5803802
Fax: 71 4365388

3336
Arthur Claudet Student's Prize
For recognition of a paper written by a student in the field of mining and metallurgy.

3337
Consolidated Gold Fields Gold Medal
For recognition of outstanding papers in the field of mining and metallurgy. A gold and silver medal are awarded.

3338
Stanley Elmore Fellowships
To provide for research into all branches of extractive metallurgy and mineral processing at United Kingdom universities. Applications are accepted until March 16. Fellowships to the value of £1,500-£6,000 per annum are awarded.

3339
G. Vernon Hobson Bequest
To provide for the advancement of teaching and practice of geology as applied to mining. The application deadline is March 16. Approximately £1,500 is available for one or more awards for travel, research, or other objectives.

3340
IMM Gold Medal
For recognition of dedicated service to the mining industry, the Institution, and the education of mining engineers. A gold medal is awarded.

3341
IMM Honorary Fellow
For recognition of distinguished services to the Institution and to the minerals industry internationally.

3342
Edgar Pam Fellowship
To provide for postgraduate study in subjects within the Institution's fields of interest, which range from exploration geology to extractive metallurgy. Those eligible for the award are young graduates, domiciled in Australia, Canada, New Zealand, South Africa, and the United Kingdom, who wish to undertake advanced study or research in the United Kindgom. The application deadline is March 16. The value of the fellowship, which is tenable for one year, is approximately £3,500.

3343
Bosworth Smith Trust Fund
To provide assistance for postgraduate research in metal mining, non-ferrous extraction metallurgy, or mineral dressing. Applications are considered for grants towards working expenses, the cost of visits to mines and plants in connection with such research, and purchase of apparatus. The application deadline is March 16. Approximately £3,000 is available for grants.

3344
Institution of Nuclear Engineers
Allan House
1 Penerley Rd.
London SE6 2LQ, England
Phone: 81 698 1500
Phone: 81 698 4750
Fax: 81 695 6409

3345
Graduate Award
For recognition of a verbal presentation at the Universities Nuclear Technical Forum. Post graduate researchers for an M.Sc. or Ph.D. degree or those who have recently completed the same are eligible. A monetary prize of £80,000 and a commemorative certificate are awarded annually. The winner is invited, without obligation, to publish in the Institution's journal. Established in 1970. Financed by the Educational Trust Fund.

3346
Hinton Medal
For recognition of demonstrated achievement in the nuclear field by an individual considered to be an outstanding engineer early in his or her career. Nominations are sought from the leaders of the industry. A monetary prize of £250, a silver gilt medal, and a commemorative certificate are awarded triennially. The recipient is invited to give a public lecture (without obligation). Established in 1978.

3347
HMS Sultan Prize
To recognize the best student on the operators course, as determined by recommendation of the commanding officer. Five awards of £30 and commemorative certificates are given each year. Established in 1979.

3348
Honorary Fellowship
For recognition of distinguished service to the Institution, to the UK profession, and to the international profession. A commemorative certificate and free membership in the Institution are awarded. One or two awards are presented annually. Established in 1984, the Silver Jubilee Year of the Institution.

3349
Pinkerton Award
For recognition of an article or articles of outstanding merit that appeared in the Institution's journal *The Nuclear Engineer*. Non-members as well as members of the Institution are eligible. A monetary prize of £100 and a certificate are awarded annually when merited. Established in 1960 and named after the founder of the Institution.

3350
Royal Naval College, Greenwich Prize
Awarded on the recommendation of the head of the Nuclear Science and Technology Department for work on the Nuclear Reactor Course, which is recognized for the award of the post-graduate diploma in nuclear reactor technology by the Council for National Academic Awards. Two awards of £50 each and commemorative certificates are awarded each year. Established in 1972.

3351
Gilbert Tomes Award
Given to meritorious undergraduates in financial need. An annual award of £250 and a commemorative certificate are bestowed on the recommendation of the Membership Education & Training Committee. Established in 1987.

3352
University of Cambridge Arthur Shercliff Prize
To recognize the candidate performing best in the nuclear engineering option. The prize is given on the recommendation of the examiners and includes a cash award of £50 and a commemorative certificate.

3353
University of Manchester Prize
To recognize the best final-year undergraduate in nuclear engineering. This annual award includes a cash prize of £80 and a commemorative certificate and is given on the recommendation of the University's engineering professors. Established in 1979.

3354
Bruce Youngman Award
To recognize an individual for meritorious services to the Institution. A monetary award of £100 (or gifts to the value of) and a commemorative certificate are awarded at the discretion of the Council. Established in 1991 to honor Bruce Youngman, the late former Secretary of the Institution.

3355
Institution of Plant Engineers
77 Great Peter St.
London SW1P 2EZ, England
Phone: 71 233 2855
Fax: 71 233 2604

3356
BP Oil Award
For recognition of a contribution to the advancement of plant engineering. A monetary prize of £1,000 was awarded by BP Oil Ltd. (Discontinued)

3357
Members Prize
For recognition of two papers that contribute most to the advancement of plant engineering. Papers eligible for submission may have been presented either at a Branch or a general meeting of the Institution, or may be prepared especially for the prizes. Papers must not have been previously published. Members other than students are eligible to submit papers by the end of February. Monetary prizes of £400 for first place, and £250 for second place are awarded annually. Established in 1984.

3358
Institution of Structural Engineers
11 Upper Belgrave St.
London SW1X 8BH, England
Phone: 71 2354535
Fax: 71 2354294

3359
Gold Medal
For recognition of outstanding personal contributions to the advancement of structural engineering. Individuals from anywhere in the world are eligible. A gold medal is awarded when merited. Established in 1922.

3360
Special Awards
For recognition of structural engineering excellence, as expressed in a physical form in an existing building or structure. Organizations from anywhere in the world are eligible. An appropriate award and a plaque are awarded when merited. Established in 1968.

3361
International Advertising Festival
Woolverstone House
61/62 Berners Street
London W1P 3AE, England
Phone: 71 6366122
Fax: 71 6366086

3362
Euro Best Awards
For recognition of advertising excellence for campaigns presented in Europe across a range of media categories: Print, TV/Cinema, Outdoors/Billboards, Packaging, Logo, and Corporate Reports. Applications are accepted. Trophies are awarded annually at the awards ceremony. Established in 1988.

3363
International Advertising Festival, Cannes
To recognize the best in world audio/visual advertising in 28 consumer products categories in the Festival. The Festival is open to advertising agencies and production houses throughout the world. All films submitted must have been produced during the preceding year. Entries must advertise consumer or capital goods or consumer services (with the exception of those entered in Category 26 - Public Service & Social Welfare - Political advertising). All work submitted must be designed for and exhibited in public cinemas or on television networks. The following prizes are awarded: Grand Prix du Festival - to entrant company for the best commercial in the Festival; Palme d'Or - offered by the city of Cannes to the production company obtaining the highest number of marks for its ten best commercials in the Festival, irrespective of whether these have been entered by the production company or the advertising agency; and Category prizes - the Jury will award one Gold Lion, one Silver Lion, and one Bronze Lion. Awarded annually. The festival is held in the 3rd week of June in Cannes, France. Established in 1953.

3364
International Advertising Press & Poster Festival
For recognition of outstanding advertising entries in the Press and Poster Festival. Established in 1992.

3365

International Agency for the Prevention of Blindness (Organization Mondiale Contre Le Cecite)
c/o Sight Savers
Grosvenor Hall, Bolnore Rd.
Haywards Heath, W. Sussex RH16 4BX,
England
Phone: 444 412424
Fax: 444 415866

Formerly: (1975) International Association for the Prevention of Blindness.

3366

IAPB Awards
For recognition of contributions to coordinate international research into the causes of impaired vision or blindness, to promote measures calculated to eliminate such causes, and to disseminate knowledge worldwide on preventing blindness and on matters pertaining to the care and use of the eyes. Awards are presented at the General Assembly. Established in 1982.

3367

International Association for Religious Freedom
2 Market St.
Oxford OX1 3EF, England
Phone: 865 202744
Fax: 865 202746

3368

Albert Schweitzer Award
For recognition of distinguished service to the cause of international liberal religion. Members of the Association may nominate individuals who have exhibited exemplary commitment to the cause of international liberal religion. A plaque is awarded triennially, at each triennial IARF World Congress. Established in 1975 in memory of Albert Schweitzer.

3369

International Association of Paediatric Dentistry
Dept. of Child Dental Health
The London Hospital Medical College
Turner St.
London E1 2AD, England
Phone: 71 3777000
Fax: 71 3777058

Formerly: (1989) International Association of Dentistry for Children.

3370

Bengt Magnusson Memorial Prize
To recognize a supporting member for the most outstanding essay on a subject in the field of child dental health. Awarded at the biennial congress.

3371

International Association on Water Quality
1 Queen Anne's Gate
London SW1H 9BT, England
Phone: 71 222 3848
Fax: 71 233 1197

Formerly: International Association on Water Pollution Research and Control.

3372

Honorary Member
To recognize an individual who has made an outstanding contribution both to the association and to water pollution, research, and control. Selection is by nomination. A decorative scroll is awarded at the biennial international conferences. Established in 1966.

3373

IAWQ Pergamon Publications Medal
To recognize an IAWQ individual member who is an author or a co-author of the best paper of those presented in general sessions or seminars at the previous biennial conference. The award, donated by Pergamon Press, is in the form of a gold medal on a wooden plaque with brass plates indicating the recipients. The awardee(s) receives a silver replica medal engraved with the name of the recipient and year. Awarded biennially. Established in 1988. Formerly: IAWPRC Pergamon Publications Medal.

3374

Karl Imhoff - Pierre Koch Medal
To recognize achievements on the practical side of water pollution control. Members of the association responsible for a contribution of international impact relating to facilities involved in water quality control are eligible. Any member of IAWQ can prepare a nomination and submit it to a national committee for endorsement. A bronze medal is awarded biennially. Established in 1988.

3375

Samuel H. Jenkins Medal
For recognition of meritorious service to the association. Any member of the association is eligible. Nominations for this award may be made by national committees and corporate and individual members with the endorsement of their national committee. A silver medal is awarded biennially. Established in 1983 in memory of Dr. Samuel Harry Jenkins, an outstanding contributor both to the development of IAWQ and to water pollution research and control.

3376

International Badminton Federation
4 Manor Park
Mackenzie Way
Cheltenham, Greater London GL51 9TX,
England
Phone: 242 234904
Fax: 242 221030

3377

Distinguished Service Award
For recognition of long and/or distinguished service to badminton throughout the world. Long service means at least fifteen years in international play and/or administration. Distinguished service, where less than fifteen years involvement is not fulfilled, means a service which is clearly distinguished in an international sense. All nominations must be presented to the Council which approves the award to each person. The decision must be unanimous in every case. A certificate and a lapel badge are awarded biannually. Established in 1985.

3378

Honorary Life Vice-Presidents
For recognition of services rendered in the past. Honorary Life Vice-Presidents are entitled to attend general meetings, but have no vote. Such nominations may be made by the Council or by any national organization, subject to the approval of the Council.

3379

Meritorious Service Award
For recognition of long and meritorious service to badminton. Long service means at least fifteen years. Nominations should preferably be received from the nominee's National Organization but the Council may dispense with the requirement. A certificate and a lapel badge are awarded biannually. Established in 1985.

3380

Herbert Scheele Trophy
For recognition of outstandingly exceptional services to badminton. A trophy and certificate are awarded when merited. Established in 1986 in memory of Herbert Scheele, past honorable secretary of the Federation (1937-1976).

3381

International Bar Association
2 Harewood Pl., Hanover Sq.
London W1R 9HB, England
Phone: 71 629 1206
Fax: 71 409 0456

3382
International Legal Aid Award
For recognition of outstanding services to the community in the field of legal aid. A plaque and a gift are awarded annually. Established in 1984.

3383
International Broadcasting Convention
Institution of Electrical Engineers
Savoy Pl.   Phone: 71 2403839
London WC2R OBL, England   Fax: 71 3445405

Formerly: IBC Award.

3384
IBC John Tucker Award
To recognize an internationlly significant contribution over any period by an individual or a group of persons, to any aspect of broadcasting, including research, design, development, manufacture, operational practice, or management without restriction as to nationality or country. The award may not be made to a company or organization, but only to individuals. Projects or inventions and achievements or contributions that have been recognized by another major award are not considered. A monetary prize of £5,000 and a specially commissioned sculpture in glass are awarded biennially at the convention. Established in 1984 to mark the 10th International Broadcasting Convention. Renamed for John Tucker in recognition for the past chairman's many years of service to the IBC. Formerly: IBC Award.

3385
International Carbohydrate Organization
Laboratory of Lipid and General Chemistry
National Institute for Medical Research
Mill Hill, London NW7 1AA, England   Phone: 81 959 3666

3386
Roy L. Whistler Award
To recognize outstanding younger scientists active in carbohydrate research. Younger, active scientists (less than 40 years of age) may be nominated by June 1 in odd-numbered years. A monetary award of $10,000 is presented biennially at the convention. Established in 1984 to honor Professor Roy L. Whistler, Purdue University. For more information contact R. H. Gigg, Secretary.

3387
International Confederation for Thermal Analysis
(Confedertion Internationale d'Analyse Thermique)
c/o British Geological Survey   Phone: 6077 6111
Keyworth, Notts. NG12 5GG, England   Fax: 6077 6602

3388
ICTA DuPont Award
For recognition of an outstanding contribution to the science of thermal analysis and/or leadership in the profession of thermal analysis. Selection is by nomination. An honorarium of $1,000 US, a plaque, and expenses to attend the International Conference on Thermal Analysis are awarded every four years. Established in 1977.

3389
ICTA Young Scientist Award
To encourage young scientists early in their careers to consider and utilize thermoanalytical methods. Scientists under 35 years of age are eligible. All necessary financial support to attend the ICTA Congress is awarded every four years. Established in 1985.

3390
International Confederation of Art Dealers
(Confederation Internationale des Negociants en Oeuvres d'Art)
PO Box 4   Phone: 844 274584
Aylesbury, Bucks. HP17 9UB, England   Fax: 844 274585

3391
CINOA Award
To encourage the study of art history. Candidates must be residents of one of the 13 member nations where CINOA is represented. A monetary award of $5,000 is presented annually. Established in 1976. Formerly: Prix CINOA.

3392
International Congress of Americanists
c/o Dept. of Geography
Univ. of Manchester   Phone: 61 2753636
Manchester M13 9PL, England   Fax: 61 2734407

3393
Congress Prizes
To recognize the high quality of contributions by younger participants in Congress meetings. Individuals who are 35 years of age or under are eligible. Monetary prizes of $1,000 each are awarded every three years. Three to five prizes may be awarded. Established in 1982.

3394
International Council of Graphic Design Associations
PO Box 398   Phone: 71 6038494
London W11 4UG, England   Fax: 71 3716040

3395
Excellence Awards
For recognition of achievement in the field of graphic design. Professional graphic designers are eligible for nomination by the proposal of member societies. Also, individuals, institutions, and companies who have made outstanding contributions to graphic design may be recommended by the board of the association. A trophy and diploma are awarded. Established in 1983.

3396
President's Trophy
For recognition of contributions to the work and aims of the association in the field of graphic design. Professional graphic designers or design administrators are eligible. A trophy and diploma are awarded biennially at the general assembly. Established in 1970.

3397
International Dance Teachers' Association
76 Bennett Rd.   Phone: 273 685652
Brighton BN2 5JL, England   Fax: 273 674388

Formerly: (1967) International Dancing Masters Association.

3398
Miss Dance of Great Britain
To recognize theatrical dance ability and to encourage the winners to continue a career in dance. Candidates over the age of 16 are eligible for the competition. Monetary awards of over £1,700 are presented annually. Established in 1973.

3399
International Dental Federation
(Federation Dentaire Internationale)
64 Wimpole St.
London W1M 8AL, England

Phone: 71 935 7852
Fax: 71 486 0183

3400
International Miller Prize
To recognize one or at most three persons who have rendered the most eminent services to dentistry in the areas of dental research, clinical dentistry, or academic dentistry. Individuals must be nominated by a Member Association of the FDI. A medal and diploma are awarded every five years. Established in 1910.

3401
Jessen Fellowship in Children's Dentistry
To assist developing countries to improve their dental health services for children by allowing a young dentist to visit another country to study its dental health services for children. The candidate must be nominated by a Member Association of the FDI. A monetary prize of US $2,000 is awarded every five years at the Annual World Dental Congress. Established in 1967. (The Fellowship Program has been under review in 1992.)

3402
Johnson & Johnson Preventive Dentistry Awards
For recognition in the field of preventive dentistry. Awards are given in two categories: (1) Dental Research; and (2) Community Programs. Any person working in the dental health field except employees of Johnson & Johnson Dental Care Company and Federation Dentaire Internationale is eligible. The deadline is September 1. A monetary prize totaling US $8,000 is awarded equally in the two categories. Awarded annually at the Federation Dentaire Internationale Annual World Dental Congress. Established in 1977 by Johnson & Johnson. Sponsored by Johnson & Johnson.

3403
Georges Villain Prize
For recognition of outstanding contributions in the field of orthodontics or prosthodontics. Individuals must be nominated by a Member Association of the FDI. A bronze medal is awarded every five years at the Annual World Dental Congress. Established in 1947.

3404
International Egg Commission
Agriculture House
25/31 Knightsbridge
London SW1X 7NJ, England

Phone: 71 235 5077
Fax: 71 259 6252

3405
IEC Promotion and Marketing Award
For recognition of outstanding efforts in the fields of promotion and marketing of eggs. The IEC nominates a country which then selects an award winner. A trophy is presented annually. Established in 1970. Formerly: (1991) International Egg Marketing Award.

3406
International Federation for Theatre Research
(Federation Internationale pour la Recherche Theatrale)
Darwin College
The University
Canterbury, Kent CT2 7NY, England

Phone: 227 764000
Fax: 227 475470

3407
Bellonci Scholarship
To provide opportunities for students in theatre research to attend international courses from the Venice Institute. A scholarship is awarded annually under the auspices of the Universities Commission. Established in 1958 by Professor C. Bellonci, Venice.

3408
International Federation of Air Line Pilots Associations
Interpilot House
Gogmore Ln.
Chertsey, Surrey KT16 9AP, England

Phone: 932 571711
Fax: 932 570920

3409
IFALPA Scroll of Merit
For recognition of the sustained efforts of individuals who have served IFALPA with loyalty, honor, and distinction. Established in 1969.

3410
Polaris Award
For recognition of acts of heroism and/or exceptional airmanship in civil aviation. Selection is by nomination. A medal is awarded annually at the Conference. Established in 1983.

3411
Clarence N. Sayen Award
To honor a person whose personal contribution towards the achievement of the Federation's aims and objectives has been outstanding. Established in 1965.

3412
International Federation of Airworthiness
IFA Secretariat
58 Whiteheath Ave.
Ruislip
Middlesex HA4 7PW, England

Phone: 895 672504
Fax: 895 676656

Formerly: IFA International Aviation Scholarship.

3413
IFA Len Gore Scholarship
To encourage professional development, particularly in third world countries. Young persons who are employed by member organizations must be nominated by their companies by August 1. The award consists of one year of training by an aerospace manufacturer or airline in the United States or the United Kingdom, temporary employment by the host company, and a settling in grant of $1,500 from IFA. Awarded annually. Established in 1980. Additional information is available from R.D. Hammond, IFA Award Administrator, 10 Graham Ave, Te Atatu, Auckland 1008, New Zealand. Formerly: IFA International Aviation Scholarship.

3414
International Federation of Essential Oils and Aroma Trades
Kemp House, 3rd Fl.
152-160 City Rd.
London EC1V 2NP, England

Phone: 71 253 9421
Fax: 71 487 5436

3415
IFEAT Distinguished Service Medal
For recognition of distinguished service in the field of essential oils and aroma chemicals. Individuals are nominated and selected by the 15 nations represented on the IFEAT Executive Committee. A medal is awarded annually. Established in 1984.

3416
International Federation of Multiple Sclerosis Societies
10 Heddon St.
London W1R 7LJ, England

Phone: 71 7349120
Fax: 71 2872587

3417
Jean-Martin Charcot Award
For recognition of pioneering research in multiple sclerosis. Nominations are accepted. A monetary grant of $1,000 and a plaque are pre-

sented biennially at the Multiple Sclerosis World Conference. Established in 1969 in honor of Professor Jean-Martin Charcot.

3418
Jacqueline du Pre Award
To enable a promising research worker to further his or her experiments under the supervision of an established research institution. A monetary award of U.S. $37,000 is awarded annually. Established in 1985 in honor of Jacqueline du Pre, a famed cellist.

3419
James D. Wolfensohn Award
For recognition of an outstanding person with multiple sclerosis who has overcome his or her handicapp. Individuals must be recommended by national MS Societies and reviewed by an awards committee. A monetary prize and a plaque are awarded annually. Established in 1984.

3420
International Federation of Societies of Cosmetic Chemists
(Federation Internationale des Societes des Chimistes Cosmeticiens)
G. T. House
24/26 Rothesay Rd.
Luton, Beds. LU1 1QX, England
Phone: 582 26661
Fax: 582 405217

3421
IFSCC Award and IFSCC Honorary Mention
For recognition of the most meritorious paper presented at an IFSCC Congress. Papers that are original and that have important scientific content and relevance to the cosmetic and toiletry industry may be submitted nine months before a Congress meets. The IFSCC Award includes a monetary prize of 4,000 Swiss francs. Also awarded is an Honorable Mention prize of 1,000 Swiss francs plus illuminated scrolls commending the achievment. Awarded biennially. Established in 1970.

3422
IFSCC Poster Prize
For recognition of the most meritorious paper presented at an IFSCC Congress. Posters that are original and that have important scientific content and relevance to the cosmetic and toiletry industry may be submitted nine months before a Congress meets. The IFSCC Award includes a monetary prize of 1,000 Swiss francs and a scroll. Awarded biennially. Established in 1970.

3423
International Filariasis Association
(Societe Internationale des Filarioses)
Commonwealth Institute of Parasitology
395A Hatfield Rd.
St. Albans, Herts. AL4 0XU, England
Phone: 727 833151

3424
O'Connor Award
For recognition of exceptional scientific work in any aspect of filariasis. Awarded every four years. No further information on awards is available for this edition.

3425
International Glaciological Society
Lensfield Rd.
Cambridge CB2 1ER, England
Phone: 223 355974
Fax: 233 836543

3426
Seligman Crystal
For recognition of unique contributions to snow and ice studies that enrich the subject significantly. A hexagonal 5 1/2 inch column of crystal glass that is engraved with an ice crystal on a sloping top surface is awarded when merited. Established in 1963.

3427
International Guild of Artists
Ralston House
41 Lister St.
Riverside Gardens
Ilkley, W. Yorks. LS29 9ET, England
Phone: 943 609075
Fax: 943 603753

3428
Old Masters Award
For recognition of achievement of the highest calibre in the field of fine art. A replica of an artist's pallette colored and signed by David Shepherd OBE, Terence Cuneo OBE, and Rowland Hilder OBE, is awarded annually. Established in 1987 in memory of the late Italian Master, Pietro Annigoni.

3429
International Hydrofoil Society
(Societe Internationale Pour les Hydroglisseurs)
51 Welbeck St.
London W1M 7HE, England
Phone: 71 935 9274

3430
Mark Thornton Gold Challenge Award
To recognize an individual under 40 years of age who has advanced the science and technology of hydrofoils.

3431
International Institute of Welding
(Institut International de la Soudure)
Abington Hall
Abington
Cambridge CB1 6AL, England
Phone: 223 891162
Fax: 223 894180

3432
Arata Award
To recognize outstanding contributions to research and development in welding and associated technologies. Winners are selected by recommendations of member societies of IIW.

3433
Edstrom Medal
To recognize a person for outstanding service. Not open to competition.

3434
Goldschmidt-Clermont Prize
For recognition of an outstanding film or video system communicating relevant scientific and/or technical information concerning the welding processes or allied processes. Entries must be submitted by the national delegation. A medal is awarded quadrennially at the annual assembly. Established in 1969 by Professor P. Goldschmidt-Clermont. Sponsored by the Belgian Delegation to IIW.

3435
Granjon Prize
To recognize papers resulting from research in welding and associated technologies leading to the award of an M.Sc., Ph.D., or equivalent professional qualification. Entries must be submitted through the national IIW Member Society. Awards are presented in each of three subject areas. The competition is held at least biennially. Established in 1991 to honor Henri Granjon of Institut de Soudure, Paris.

3436
Andre Leroy Prize
For recognition of outstanding audio-visual material intended for use in teaching or professional training in any aspect of welding and allied processes. Entries must be submitted by the national delegation. A commemorative medal donated by the French delegation is awarded quadrennially. Established in 1980 in honor of Andre Leroy.

3437
International Intra-ocular Implant Club
(Club International d'Implants Oculaires)
10 St. John St.
Sydenham
Manchester M3 4DY, England

3438
Ridley Medal
For recognition of outstanding achievement in, and contribution to, the development of intra-ocular lens implanatation. Nominations to the Medal Committee of the Club are accepted. A gold medal is awarded quadrennially. Established in 1977 in honor of Ridley, the originator of practical intra-ocular lens implantation.

3439
International Map Collectors' Society
29 Mount Ephraim Rd.
Streatham
London SW16 1NQ, England
Phone: 81 769 5041
Fax: 81 677 5417

3440
Awards
To promote map collecting and the study of cartography and its history. Awards are presented.

3441
International Martial Arts Federation
Address unknown since 1990.

3442
Budo Koro Sho
(Spirit of Fighting Awards)
For recognition of achievements in the field of martial arts. The following awards are given: a monetary award, a gold badge, and shield to those who render distinguished service to propagate and promote Budo internationally; a silver badge and shield to those who continuously dedicate themselves to improve Budo techniques, exercise, leadership, and propagate Budo; and a copper badge and shield to those who work hard to propagate and develop Budo. Awarded annually. Established in 1952 by Prince Higashikuni, former Prime Minister of Japan.

3443
International Optometric and Optical League
10 Knaresborough Pl.
London SW5 OTG, England
Phone: 71 3704765
Fax: 71 3731143

3444
International Optometrist of the Year
For recognition of achievement in the field of international optometry. Nomination is made by the executive committee of the League. A plaque is awarded annually. Established in 1988.

3445
IOOL Emeritus
To recognize past delegates and officers who have served the League and world optometry with distinction. Holders of the title are eligible to attend meetings of the League. The title of Emeritus (e.g., Delegate Emeritus, President Emeritus, etc.) is awarded. Established in 1978.

3446
IOOL Medal
For recognition of service to the League and to international optometry. Contributions by optometrists, ophthalmologists, and others to the advancement of the science or profession of optometry or ophthalmic optics are considered. A medal is awarded when merited. Established in 1965.

3447
International Organ Festival Society
PO Box 80
St. Albans, Herts. AL3 4HR, England
Phone: 727 865133
Fax: 727 844765

3448
Interpretation Competition
For recognition of the outstanding organ performance during the International Organ Festival interpretation competition. Individuals under the age of 31 may compete. There are three elimination rounds. A monetary prize of £3,500, and recitals in St. Bavo, Haarlem, St. Paul's Cathedral (London), ThomasKirche, Leipzig, and Notre Dame des Champs (Paris) are awarded for first prize; £2,500 and recital engagements at King's College (Cambridge), St. Albans Cathedral, and St. Giles (Cripplegate, London) for second prize; and £1,250 for third prize. Awarded biennially. Established in 1963 by Dr. Peter Hurford. Co-sponsored by several commercial companies.

3449
Jury's Special Award
For recognition of the best performance on the IOFS organ of any competition piece in the second elimination and semi-final rounds of the Interpretation Competition and the Tournemire Prize for Improvisation. Given to a competitor who is not a recipient of any other prize. A monetary prize of £400 is presented.

3450
Tournemire Prize
For recognition of outstanding organ improvisation during the International Organ Festival. Individuals under the age of 31 may compete. There are two elimination rounds. A monetary prize of £1,250, a medal, and a recital at Ste Clotilde (Paris) and St. Alban's Cathedral, are presented biennially. Established in 1973 by Madame Tournemire in honor of Charles Tournemire.

3451
International Organization for Succulent Plant Study
The Herbarium
Royal Botanic Gardens
Kew
Richmond, Surrey TW9 3AE, England
Phone: 81 3325250
Fax: 81 3225278

3452
Cactus d'Or
(Golden Cactus)
For recognition of contributions to the scientific knowledge of succulent plants by exploration in the field. Nomination is by the Executive Board of the organization. A trophy is awarded biennially at the congress. Established in 1978 by HRH Princess Grace of Monaco. Sponsored by Jardin Exotique, Monaco.

3453
International Phycological Society
Dept. of Marine Biology
Port Erin, Isle of Man PL1 2PB, England
Phone: 624 832027
Fax: 624 835788

3454
George F. Papentuss Poster Award
To recognize the best poster presented at the International Phycological Congress. A monetary award and a plaque are presented triennially at the Congress. Established in 1982 to honor Prof. G.F. Papentuss.

3455

**International Police Association
(Association Internationale de Police)**
International Administration Centre
National Headquarters
1 Fox Rd.
W. Bridgford, Notts. NG2 6AJ, England
Phone: 602 813638
Fax: 602 810489

3456

Diploma of Honour and Medal
For recognition of services to the association and the police service by a member. A gold medal and diploma, silver medal with diploma, or bronze medal and diploma are awarded when merited. Established in 1984.

3457

International Primary Aluminum Institute
Trafalgar Pl.
2-4 Cockspur St.
London SW1Y 5BQ, England
Phone: 71 930 0528
Fax: 71 321 0183

3458

Honorary Member
To recognize a person who has made a significant contribution to the work of the Institute, the furtherance of the objects of the Institute, or the furtherance of the interests of primary aluminum producers. Individuals may be recommended by the Board of Directors. Honorary membership and its rights are awarded when merited. Established in 1976.

3459

International Professional Security Association
IPSA House
3 Dendy Road
Paignton, Devon TQ4 5DB, England
Phone: 803 554849
Fax: 803 529203

3460

Roll of Honor
To recognize individuals for loyal and outstanding service to the association in furtherance of professionalism within the industrial/commercial security industry. A medal and a parchment are awarded annually. Established in 1985.

3461

International Science Policy Foundation
12 Whitehall
London SW1A 2DY, England
Phone: 71 839 4985

3462

Swraj Paul Award for the Promotion of Science & Technology Policy
To recognize an individual for the promotion of science and technology policy. A monetary prize of £2,000, a certificate, and travel to the presentation ceremony are awarded annually. Established in 1991 in honor of Dr. Swraj Paul.

3463

International Sheep Dog Society
Chesham House
47 Bromham Rd.
Bedford MK40 2AA, England
Phone: 234 52672
Fax: 234 327065

3464

Supreme Champion
For recognition of the achievements of the outstanding handler of a working border collie. Individuals must be members of the International Sheep Dog Society to be eligible. A monetary prize of £500 and numerous trophies are awarded annually. Established in 1930.

3465

Young Handler Award
To recognize an outstanding young handler of sheep dogs.

3466

**International Society for Education Through Art
(Societe Internationale pour l'Education Artistique)**
7A High St.
Corsham, Wilts. SN13 OES, England
Phone: 249 714825

3467

Awards
To promote the exchange of information in the field of art and design education through publications, papers, and conferences.

3468

International Society for Heart Research
Cardiovascular Research
The Rayne Institute
St. Thomas Hospital
London SE1 7EH, England
Phone: 71 9289292
Fax: 71 9280658

3469

Richard J. Bing Award
To encourage young investigators in the field of heart research. Investigators 35 years of age or younger are eligible. Certificates and travel expenses to the International Heart Congress are awarded every three years. Established in 1976.

3470

Peter Harris Award
To recognize distinguished scientists in the field of cardiovascular research. Individuals who have made significant contributions in clinical or experimental cardiology and are established leaders in cardiovascular sciences are eligible. A monetary prize of $3,000, certificates, and expenses to attend the World Heart Research Congress are awarded every three years. Established in 1984.

3471

Outstanding Research Awards
To recognize outstanding research papers in cardiology. A monetary prize of $1,000 and a medal were awarded annually to each of the six successful candidates. Established in 1984. (Discontinued in 1989)

3472

International Society for Soil Mechanics and Foundation Engineering
Univ. Engineering Dept.
Trumpington St.
Cambridge CR2 1PZ, England
Phone: 223 355020
Fax: 223 359675

3473

Kevin Nash Gold Medal
For recognition of outstanding contributions to practice, research, and teaching in the field of geotechnical engineering. Members of the Society are eligible. A medal is awarded every four years. Established in 1985 in honor of Kevin Nash, former secretary general of ISSMFE.

3474

International Society for the Study of European Ideas
Pergamon Press plc
Headington Hill Hall, Oxon. OX3 0BW,
England
Phone: 865 64881
Fax: 865 60285

3475
Maxwell Prizes
To recognize original essays of interest to the general reader. The themes for 1988-89 were: (1) Europe's Babylon: Towards One European Language; and (2) The Politics of Culture. Monetary awards of $1,000 each are presented.

3476
International Society of Blood Transfusion
(Societe Internationale de Transfusion Sanguine)
National Directorate of NBTS
NWRHA
Gateway House, Piccadilly South
Manchester M60 7LP, England
Phone: 61 236 2263
Fax: 61 236 0519

3477
Jean Julliard Prize
For recognition of recently completed scientific work on blood transfusion and related subjects. In general, the prize is awarded to one individual; in special cases, the prize may be shared by more than one scientist. Scientists under 40 years of age may submit manuscripts. A monetary prize of 3,000 Swiss francs and a certificate are awarded biennially. Established in 1964 in memory of Jean Julliard, the first secretary general of the Society.

3478
International Society of Literature
20 Skipton Rd.
Ilkey, W. Yorks., England
Phone: 9435 863081

3479
Annual Competition Awards
To recognize the works of writers and poets and encourage international understanding through their works. The Society sponsors an annual competition and literary dinner and presents awards for the best short story and poem.

3480
International Stoke Mandeville Wheelchair Sports Federation
(Federation Internationale des Jeux en Fauteuil Roulant)
Guttmann Sports Centre
Harvey Rd.
Aylesbury, Bucks. HP21 9PP, England
Phone: 296 436179
Fax: 296 436484

Formerly: (1990) International Stoke Mandeville Games Federation.

3481
Pursuit Trophy
To recognize a sportsman or sportswoman who has been outstanding in his or her sport over a number of years and has exemplified the ideals of the ISMWSF: "Friendship, Unity and Sportsmanship." A trophy is awarded biennially. Administrators are eligible for a similar award. A monetary prize and a trophy are awarded biennially. Established in 1984 in honor of Sir Ludwig Guttmann.

3482
International Tennis Federation
(Federation Internationale de Tennis)
Palliser Rd.
Barons Ct.
Wimbledon
London W14 9EN, England
Phone: 71 3818060
Fax: 71 3813839

3483
Grand Slam of Tennis
To recognize the male or female tennis player who wins all the following championships in a calendar year: Wimbledon, the French Open, the Australian Open, and the United States Open. The first Grand Slam Champion was Don Budge, recognized in 1938.

3484
ITF Award for Services to the Game
For recognition of long service or special service to tennis, or to recognize individuals working closely with the ITF. Individuals may be nominated at any time. A medal is awarded and presented when possible at the annual general meeting. Established in 1979.

3485
Tennis World Champions
To recognize the outstanding male and female tennis player of the year.

3486
International Tube Association
(Internationaler Rohrverband)
PO Box 84
Leamington Spa, Warks. CV32 5FX, England
Phone: 926 34137
Fax: 926 314755

3487
President's Trophy - Papers Award
For recognition of technical quality of papers that further tube technology and are presented at the Association's International Conference. A trophy is awarded annually. Established in 1982.

3488
International Union for Quaternary Research
Centre for Loess Research
Dept. of Geography
Univ. of Leicester
Leicester, Leics. LE1 7RH, England
Phone: 533 523821
Fax: 533 523918

3489
Honorary Member
To recognize individuals for contributions to Quaternary Research. Honorary Membership is awarded.

3490
International Union for Surface Finishing
17 Alexandra Grove
Finchley
London N12 8HE, England
Phone: 81 4456881

3491
International Union for Surface Finishing Awards
To recognize contributions to the surface finishing industry. Awards are presented.

3492
International Union for Vacuum Science, Technique, and Applications
(Union Internationale pour la Science, la Technique et les Applications)
Centre for Thin Film & Surface Research
EE Dept.
Univ. of Salford
Salford M5 4WT, England
Phone: 61 745 5247
Fax: 61 745 5999

3493
Welch Foundation Scholarship
To recognize a promising scholar who wishes to contribute to the study of vacuum science techniques or their application in any field and to provide an opportunity to work for one year in a country in which he or she has not previously studied. Individuals must apply by April 15. A scholarship of $10,000 is awarded annually. Established in 1967 by Dr. M.W. Welch. Additional information is available from Dr. W.D. Westwood, Department 5C20, Bell Northern Research, Box 3511, Station C, Ottawa, Ontario, Canada K1Y 4H7.

3494
International Union of Air Pollution Prevention Associations (Union Internationale des Association de Prevention de la Pollution Atmospherique)
136 North St.
Brighton, E. Sussex BN1 1RG, England
Phone: 273 326313
Fax: 273 735802

3495
Christopher E. Barthel, Jr. Award
For recognition of outstanding service to the cause of clean air throughout the world over many years. Contributions of a civic, administrative, legislative, or judicial nature are considered. Nomination is by a member or contributing associate without further restriction. An illuminated parchment is awarded triennially at the World Clean Air Congress. Established in 1981 in honor of Christopher E. Barthel, Jr., a founding member of IUAPPA.

3496
World Clean Air Congress Award
To recognize an individual (or group of individuals) who has made a contribution of outstanding significance internationally to the progress of science or technology pertaining to air pollution. An illuminated parchment is awarded triennially at the World Clean Air Congress. Established in 1990.

3497
International Union of Crystallography
5 Abbey Sq.
Chester CH1 2HU, England
Phone: 244 345431
Fax: 244 344843

3498
Ewald Prize
For recognition of outstanding contributions to the science of crystallography. Selection is by nomination. The deadline is in August of the year preceding an award year. A monetary award, a medal, and a certificate are awarded triennially at the International Congresses of Crystallography. (The next award will be presented in 1996.) Established in 1986 in honor of Professor Paul Peter Ewald, who made significant contributions to the foundations of crystallography and to the founding of the International Union of Crystallography.

3499
International Union of Pure and Applied Chemistry
Bank Court Chambers
2-3 Pound Way
Templars Sq., Cowley
Oxford OX4 3YF, England
Phone: 865 747744

3500
Porter Medal
To recognize the individual(s) who has made the most important recent contribution to photochemistry. Application must be made on behalf of a candidate or by a candidate him-or herself. Awarded periodically when merited. Established in 1986 to honor Sir George Porter for his contribution to chemistry, both in teaching and in research. Additional information is available from Prof. F. Wilkinson, Department of Chemistry, Loughborough University of Technology, Loughborough, Leics., LE11 3TU, England.

3501
International Visual Communications Association
Bolsover House
5/6 Clipstone St.
London W1P 7EB, England
Phone: 71 580 0962
Fax: 71 436 2606

Formed by merger of: International Television Association.

3502
International Visual Communications Association Awards
For recognition of effective and excellent business communications in film, video, and live events. There are three types of awards: those defined by a particular category of use, those recognized craft skills, and several special awards. Programs are judged by panels of experts who bestow gold, silver, and bronze awards in subject categories, gold awards in the craft categories, and the Grand Prix Award to the best of the festival. Category awards are given in the following categories: Attitudinal and Motivational Training, Practical Training, Generic Training, Corporate Health and Safety, Education, Recruitment, Sales Products, Sales Services, Public Display, Corporate Image, Public Relations, Internal Communications, Regular Employee Communications, Medical, Public Welfare and Safety, Video Publishing, Business Events, Business Television, and Multimedia. Craft awards are given in the following categories: Best Music, Best Animation/Graphics, Best Performance, Best Film Photography, Best Editing, Best Script, Best Direction, Best Drama, and the Post Office Best Documentary Award. Several special awards are also presented: the CBI Award for Effective Communication is given to the project that demonstrates the most positive effect on its client's business; and the the Bill Stewart Award is given to an individual who has made an outstanding creative contribution to the industry. Awarded annually. Entry deadline is November 10. Established in 1968 by the British Industrial and Scientific Association.

3503
International Water Supply Association
1 Queen Anne's Gate
London SW1 H9BT, England
Phone: 71 9574567
Fax: 71 2227243

3504
Maarten Schalekamp Award
To recognize the best scientific paper in any field of water supply. A monetary award of £1,000 and a plaque are presented biennially. Established in 1988 by IWSA to honor Maarten Schalekamp, director of the Zurich water supply.

3505
International Wine and Food Society
9 Fitzmaurice Pl.
Berkeley Sq.
London W1X 6JD, England
Phone: 71 4954191
Fax: 71 4954172

3506
Andre Simon Medal
To recognize individuals for contributions to gastronomy. Society members are eligible. Gold, silver, and bronze medals are awarded at the discretion of the Council. Established in 1960 to honor Andre Louis Simon, CBE, the first president and founder of the Society.

3507
International Wire and Machinery Association (Internationaler Draht-und Maschinenverband)
PO Box 84
Leamington Spa, Warks. CV32 5FX, England
Phone: 926 334137
Fax: 926 314755

3508

Presidents Paper Trophy Award
For recognition of the best technical paper given at the International Conferences of the Association and to encourage technical education and progress. Papers accepted for the conference are considered. A silver trophy depicting the original wire drawing method is awarded annually when merited. Established in 1978 in honor of Harry Bennett, first president of the Association.

3509

International Youth Hostel Federation
(Federation Internationale des Auberges de la Jeunesse)
9 Guessens Rd.
Welwyn Garden City, Herts. AL8 6QW, England
Phone: 707 324170
Fax: 707 323980

3510

IYHF Certificate of Merit
For recognition of service at the international level that contributes to the development of the system, and the promotion of international understanding and outdoor education. A parchment certificate with gift and an insignia plaque are awarded at the international conference or at national meetings. Established in 1981.

3511

IYHF Roll of Honour
To recognize individuals who contribute to projects, commissions, task groups, etc., in either a volunteer or professional capacity. A parchment certificate with gift and insignia plaque are awarded at the international conference or at national meetings. Established in 1981.

3512

Jerwood Award
34 John St.
London WC1N 2EU, England
Phone: 71 430 9653
Fax: 71 405 3280

3513

Jerwood Award
To recognize and encourage achievement and excellence in education with results extending beyond the influence of an individual school, to stimulate the individual teacher, and to encourage the teaching profession. A monetary award of £150,000, a commemorative diploma, and a silver trophy were awarded annually. Established in 1989 by John Jerwood. Sponsored by the Jerwood Foundation. (Discontinued)

3514

Jewish Historical Society of England
33 Seymour Pl.
London W1H 5AP, England
Phone: 71 7234404

3515

A. S. Diamond Memorial Prize
To encourage research into the history of Anglo-Jewry and its roots and connections in other countries. A monetary award of £300 is presented biennially. Established in 1979 by the West London Synagogue with the Jewish Historical Society of England. The award honors Arthur Sigismund Diamond (1897-1978) MM, LLD., Master of the Supreme Court of England, President of the Jewish Historical Society of England, and President of the West London Synagogue of British Jews. Sponsored by the West London Synagogue.

3516

Journal of Industrial Economics
c/o Basil Blackwell Ltd.
108 Cowley Rd.
Oxford OX4 1JF, England
Phone: 865 791 100
Fax: 865 791 347

3517

P. W. S. Andrews Memorial Essay Prize
For recognition of an essay by a young scholar in the field of industrial economics and the theory of the firm, broadly interpreted. The essay (in English and not exceeding 10,000 words) should be a work of original research by the candidate only, not previously published or awarded any other prize. Entry to the Competition is open to anyone under 30 years of age (or over 30 but not more than eight years may have elapsed since taking a first degree). The deadline for entries is December 31. A monetary prize of £300 is awarded. The winning essay is normally published in *The Journal of Industrial Economics*. Additional information is available from B. Cox, University House, The University of Lancaster, Bailrigg, Lancaster, LA1 4YW, England, or The North American Editor, *Journal of Industrial Economics*, Graduate School of Business Administration, New York University, 90 Trinity Place, New York, NY 10006, U.S.A.

3518

Jowett Car Club
626 Huddersfield Rd., Wyke
Bradford, W. Yorks. BD12 8JR, England
Phone: Bradford 677324

3519

Horace Grimley Award
For recognition of outstanding service to the marque and the Club. Members are eligible. A monetary prize is awarded annually at the general meeting. Established in 1985 to honor Horace Grimley, a relative of the founders of Jowett Car Ltd, who worked for the company for 33 years and was responsible for engineering development.

3520

King George's Fund for Sailors
8 Hatherley St.
London SW1P 2YY, England
Phone: 71 4320000
Fax: 71 4320095

3521

Book of the Sea Award
For recognition of the book that contributes most to the knowledge and/or enjoyment of those who love the sea. The book should be relevant to ships or those who have sailed in them. Nonfiction books that have been published or first put on sale in the United Kingdom in the year of the award are eligible. A monetary prize is awarded. Established in 1970.

3522

Martin Luther King Memorial Prize
Nat West Bank Ltd.
7 Fore St.
Chard, Somerset TA20 1PJ, England

3523

Martin Luther King Memorial Prize
For recognition of a literary work reflecting the ideals to which Dr. King dedicated his life. Fiction, nonfiction, scripts for radio, television, films or stage plays and poems or collections of poems of substantial length (exceeding 500 lines) that have been first published or performed in the United Kingdom during the preceding year are considered. Entries must be submitted by January 15. A monetary prize of £100 is awarded annually when merited on April 4, the anniversary of Dr. King's death. Established in 1969 in memory of Dr. Martin Luther King, a civil rights leader in the United States. (Discontinued)

3524

King's School
Canterbury, Kent CT1 2ES, England
Phone: 227 475501
Fax: 227 457380

3525

Calvin and Rose G. Hoffman Prize for Distinguished Publication on Christopher Marlowe
For recognition of the essay that most informatively examines and discusses in depth the life and works of Christopher Marlowe and the authorship of the plays and poems now commonly attributed to William Shakespeare. The deadline for entry is September 1. A monetary prize of not less than £8250 is awarded annually. Established in 1988 by a bequest of Calvin Hoffman in memory of Calvin and Rose G. Hoffman.

3526

Kraszna-Krausz Foundation
5 Beechwood Dr.
Marlow, Bucks. 2L7 2DH, England
Phone: 0628 477577
Fax: 0628 477577

3527

Kraszna-Krausz Award
To recognize outstanding achievements in the publishing and writing of books on the art, practice and technology of photography and the moving image. A monetary prize of £33,000 is awarded annually. Established in 1985.

3528

Labologists Society
c/o Dale C. Adams
48 Moss Lane
Pinner HA5 3AX, England
Phone: 81 8662645

3529

Label of the Year Competition
To recognize excellence in label design for beer labels. Awards are given in the following categories: Best Individual Label, Best Set of Labels, and Best Commemorative. Labels produced during the preceding year may be submitted by August 20. Winners receive a society shield, which is held for one year, and a Certificate of Merit. Certificates are also awarded to runners-up and third-placed entrants in each category. Awarded annually. Established in 1983.

3530

John Laing PLC
Studio House
Borehamwood, Herts. WD6 1SD, England
Phone: 81 905 1091
Fax: 81 207 2264

3531

Laing Collection Art Competition
To encourage and recognize artists from the United Kingdom and to give them an opportunity to have work hung in a London gallery. All United Kingdom resident artists are eligible. A monetary prize of £5,000 is awarded for first prize, and the next five highly commended receive £1,000 each. Awarded annually. Established in 1972.

3532

Lancia Motor Club Limited
Rubyville
26 B Mopley Close
Blackfield
Southhampton, Hants. SO4 1YL, England
Phone: 703 898848

3533

Awards at the AGM and the Concours
The following awards are given at the AGM (annual general meeting) and the Concours: (1) Yves Ketterer Picture - for the best pre-War Lancia (excluding the Aprilia) in the Concours; (2) Reuben Lovell Memorial Aprilia Trophy - for the best Aprilia in the Concours; (3) Appia Trophy - for concourse mileage; (4) Gerrish Flavia/2000 Trophy - for the best Flavia/2000 in the Concours, but if there is no suitable recipient then to the owner of a Flavia/2000, who the Board considers has completed the most original journey; (5) Gerrish Fulvia Consortium Trophy - for the best Fulvia (not necessarily standard) in the Concours, but if no suitable recipient, then to the Fulvia best placed in a race or rally; (6) Frank Barkway Plaque - for the best Beta or later model in the Concours; (7) Rudler Zagato Trophy - for the best Zagato bodied Lancia in the Concours; (8) Beta Silver Trophy - for the best example of a restoration in the Concours; (9) Nevile Buckle Cup - for the best car overall in the Concours; (10) Win Buckle Trophy - for the runner-up in the Concours; (11) Stewart Master Shield - for the best of those cars that have previously won the Nevile Buckle Cup; (12) Neil Freedman Trophy U.K. - for the member travelling furthest from their permanent home in the U.K. to the AGM; and (13) Neil Freedman Trophy Overseas - for the member travelling furthest from their permanent home abroad to the AGM.

3534

Lancia Motor Club Trophies
The Lancia Club awards the following trophies when merited on an annual basis: (1) John Maltby Trophy - for the greatest contribution to the Club by an ordinary member before the AGM (annual general meeting); (2) Torino Award - for the best performance in a pre-War car at the Club Driving Tests, before the AGM; (3) Lancia Challenge Trophy - for the best performance in a post-War car at the Club Driving Tests, before the AGM; (4) Ladies Rosebowl - for the best performance by a lady in the Club Driving Tests before the AGM; (5) John Borthwick Trophy - for the best performance in a Lancia in an event other than the Club Driving Tests before the AGM; (6) Hugo Boyd Memorial Trophy - for the best performance in an overseas event in a Lambda before the AGM. Established by the Lancia Motor Club and the Italian Lancia Club in memory of Hugo Boyd, a club member who was killed in an accident in Italy with his Lambda while on his way to a rally; (7) Lancia Plaque - for the best performance in an overseas event in a Lancia other than a Lambda at the AGM. Established in 1974 by Yves Ketterer, a member of the Lancia Motor Club who lives in France. The Award commemorates the Lancia Rally to Monte Carlo in 1974; (8) Farnham Aprilia Trophy - for the member having the greatest daily use of an Aprilia before the AGM; (9) Aurelia Mille Miglia Trophy - for the member having the greatest daily use of an Aurelia before the AGM; (10) Theta Pot Award - for the best Journal article before the AGM; (11) Toyo Tyre Trophy - for the person who has made the greatest achievement in racing in a Lancia during the past year; (12) Chairman's Trophy - for the person who has given the Chairman the most help during the past year; and (13) Swedish Fulvia Trophy - for the best Fulvia Berlina Restoration of the Year.

3535

Land-Rover Register 1947-1951
10 Rowan Mount
Wheatley Hills
Doncaster, S. Yorks. DN2 5PJ, England

3536

Land-Rover Register Shield
For recognition of the best rebuilt early land-rover carried out in the preceding year. Outstanding workmanship by registered members is eligible. A perpetual shield with replica is awarded annually when merited. Established in 1980 by Tony Hutchings, A.R.I.B.A. Additional information is available from Tony Hutchings, Willowdale, North Stroud Lane, Stroud, Petersfield GU32 3PL, England.

3537

Sascha Lasserson Memorial Trust
Flat 2
81 Shepherds Hill
London N6 RG, England

3538

Sascha Lasserson Memorial Trust Prize
To encourage professional development in the field of music. British residents anywhere and foreign born residents in the United Kingdom for two years at the time of competition are eligible. A monetary prize, a bow,

and London Debut Recital are awarded biennially. Established in 1979 by N.E. Hill & Sons and others in honor of Sascha Lasserson.

3539
Lawn Tennis Association
Barons Ct,, W. Kensington
London W14 9EG, England
Phone: 71 385 2366
Fax: 71 381 5965

3540
Lawn Tennis Association National Awards
For recognition of performance, standards and achievements in the field of lawn tennis. Awards are given in the following categories: (1) Player of the Year; (2) Official of the Year; (3) County Team of the Year; (4) Tournament of the Year; (5) National Event of the Year; (6) Meritorious Service Award; (7) National Team Award; (8) Special Award; (9) Grand Prix/Virginia Slims Tournament of the Year (excluding Wimbledon); (10) National Tournament of the Year; (11) Media Person of the Year; and (12) Carl Aarvold Award for International Achievement. British citizenship is required. Engraved decanters are presented to the winners annually at the LTA Awards Dinner. Established in 1982. (Inactive since 1987)

3541
LTA International Award
To recognize outstanding lawn tennis players. Players nominated to represent Great Britain in the International Team Championships (Davis Cup, Federation Cup and European Team Championships) may qualify for this award. Established in 1937. Formerly: (1984) LTA Colours and Badges.

3542
League Against Cruel Sports
83-87 Union St.
London SE1 1SG, England
Phone: 71 403 6155
Phone: 71 407 0979
Fax: 71 403 4532

3543
Gwen Barter Award
In recognition of courageous action in the fight against animal cruelty. The award is in the form of an animal statuette. This award has replaced the League's Silver Medal award. Established in 1948.

3544
Houghton Award
For recognition of outstanding services to animal welfare. Nominations are accepted. An engraved glass plaque set in solid brass is presented annually at a general meeting of one of four groups. Established in 1980 by four animal welfare groups in honor of Lord Houghton of Sowerby, who pioneered the campaign to "put animals into politics." Co-sponsored by the Scottish Society for the Prevention of Vivisection and the British Union for the Abolition of Vivisection. Additional information is available from S.S.P.V. 10 Queensferry St., Edinburgh, Scotland.

3545
Lord Soper Award
For recognition of outstanding fundraising in conjunction with the promotion of the League's aims. Those with the highest income raised during one year through publicity and promotion of the League are eligible. A bronze statuette of an otter on a plinth is awarded annually at the May annual general meeting. Established in 1987 in honor of Lord Soper, President of the League Against Cruel Sports.

3546
Peter Wilson Award
To recognize journalistic services to the campaign against cruel sports. Nominations are accepted. A Silver Fox on Plinth is presented annually. Established in 1982 in memory of Peter Wilson, a leading sports writer of the *Daily Mirror*, who attacked cruelty to animals in sports.

3547
Leeds Philosophical and Literary Society
Central Museum
Leeds WY LS1, England
Phone: 532 452894

3548
Leeds Philosophical and Literary Society Medal
For recognition of a contribution to science and the arts. Individuals may be nominated. A silver medal is awarded when merited. Established in 1820. (Inactive since 1984)

3549
Leek Arts Festival
44 Rudyard Rd.
Biddulph Moor
Stoke-On-Trent, Staffs ST8 7JN, England
Phone: 782 517892

3550
Leek Arts Festival International Poetry Competition
For recognition of an unpublished poem no longer than 40 lines on any subject and in any style. The deadline for submissions is April 30. Monetary prizes totaling $2,500 are awarded annually on the last Friday in May. Established in 1983. (Discontinued)

3551
LEPRA
Fairfax House, Causton Rd.
Colchester, Essex CO1 1PU, England
Phone: 206 562286
Fax: 206 762151

3552
LEPRA Essay Competition
To bring leprosy to the attention of medical students. Any UK medical student may submit an essay on a subject proposed by the panel. A monetary prize is awarded annually in June. Established in 1982.

3553
Leverhulme Trust
15-19 New Fetter Ln.
London EC4A 1NR, England
Phone: 71 8226938

3554
Leverhulme Memorial Lecture
To invite a person of some distinction to deliver the triennial lecture. Designed to reflect the wide range of the Founder's interests, the Lecture can be on any subject concerned with the economic and social problems of the day and the welfare of society at home and abroad, widely interpreted. The Trustees meet the cost of the Lecture and its publication. Established in 1968 in memory of the First Lord Leverhulme and organized by the University of Liverpool, where it is held in concert with the Universities of Keele, Lancaster, Manchester and Salford, and the University of Manchester Institute of Science and Technology.

3555
Leverhulme Tercentenary Medal
To recognize outstanding contributions to science and its application. A gold medal is awarded triennially. Established in 1960 by the Leverhulme Trust to commemorate the Tercentenary of the Royal Society. Sponsored by the Royal Society.

3556
Liberal International
1 Whitehall Pl.
London SW1A 2HE, England
Phone: 71 839 5905
Fax: 71 925 2685

3557

Prize for Freedom
For recognition of contributions in the service of the fundamental liberal value of freedom. Selection is by nomination. A plaque is awarded annually. Established in 1985.

3558

Libertarian Alliance
1 Russell Chambers
The Piazza
Covent Garden
London WC2E 8AA, England   Phone: 71 8215502

Formerly: (1979) Radical Libertarian Alliance.

3559

Libertarian Alliance Awards
To recognize individuals who promote libertarian ideas. Awarded annually at a conference.

3560

Library and Information Research Group
Lancashire Polytechnic Library   Phone: 772 201201
Preston, Lancs. PR1 2TQ, England   Fax: 772 52095

3561

Daphne Clark Award
To recognize individuals who promote awareness of the need for library and information research and work to bridge the gap between library research and practice. The Award is given to fund research.

3562

Library Association
Service Provision Dept.
7 Ridgmount St.
London WC1E 7AE, England   Phone: 71 636 7543

3563

Alan Ball Local History Awards
To encourage the publishing of local history material. Awards are made annually to public libraries in the U.K. A separate leaflet is available, details are sent to all public libraries, and a notice appears in the *Library Association Record*.

3564

Besterman Medal
For recognition of an outstanding bibliography or guide to the literature first published in the United Kingdom during the preceding year. The following criteria are taken into consideration in making an award: the authority of the work and the quality and kind of articles or entries, the accessibility and arrangement of the information, the scope and coverage, the quality of the indexing, the adequacy of the references, the up-to-dateness of the information, the physical presentation, and the originality of the work. A medal is awarded annually. Established in 1970 in honor of Dr. Theodore Besterman, an internationally known bibliographer.

3565

J. D. Stewart Bursary Award
To recognize a research project or a study tour in the U.K. or overseas aimed at collecting information that will be of practical use to the library community in the U.K. A monetary award of L4,000 is given annually to Association members with at least three years of post-Charter experience. Details are advertised in the *Library Association Record*.

3566

Carnegie Medal
For recognition of an outstanding book for children written in English and first published in the United Kingdom during the preceding year. Books published simultaneously in the United Kingdom and abroad are also eligible for consideration. Recommendations are invited from members of the Association. The following criteria for fiction and information books may act as a general guide: for fiction, the choice is based upon consideration of plot, style, and characterization; for information books, the choice is based upon consideration of accuracy, method of presentation, style, and format. A medal is awarded annually. Established in 1936 in honor of Andrew Carnegie. Sponsored by Peters Library Service Ltd.

3567

T. C. Farries Public Relations and Publicity Awards
To recognize libraries for outstanding public relations work. Awards are present in five categories: Public Relations/Total PR Program, Promotions, PPRG Media Awards (Posters, Handout Publicity, Publications for Sale, and Audio Visual), LA Branches and Groups Awards, and Special Awards (Public Libraries and Academic Libraries). All members of the Library Association are eligible. An engraved cut glass trophy is awarded annually. Established in 1983. Additional information is available from T. C. Farries and Co., Ltd., Irongray Rd., Lochside, Dumfries DE2 OLH, Scotland.

3568

Kate Greenaway Medal
To recognize an outstanding book, in terms of illustration for children, first published in the United Kingdom during the preceding year or published simultaneously in the United Kingdom and abroad. A medal is awarded annually. Established in 1955 in memory of Kate Greenaway, the 19th century illustrator. Sponsored by Peters Library Service Ltd.

3569

International Librarian of the Year
To recognize the librarian who has made the most significant contribution to the development of good relations between British librarians and those in other countries in the preceding two years. Awarded biennially.

3570

Holt Jackson Community Initiative Award
To honor a library-based community initiative or project that encourages the use of libraries and information services. The winning initiative should be an example of good practice, should have started within the past three years, and be ongoing. Applicants or nominators should be able to demonstrate that the initiative is achieving defined objectives and that it has had a measurable impact on the community it serves. Open to initiatives in the U.K. only. A trophy, certificate, and L5,000 to be used to further the winning initiative is presented each November, and up to two runners-up receive certificates of commendation. The award is given as a result of an agreement between the Holt Jackson Book Company Ltd., the Library Associatin, and the Community Services Group. For further information, contact The Holt Jackson Community Initiative Award, c/o The Holt Jackson Book Company Ltd., Library Booksellers, Preston Rd., Lytham St. Annes, Lancs FY8 5AX.

3571

McColvin Medal
For recognition of an outstanding reference book first published in the United Kingdom during the preceding year. Books of the following types are considered for the award: encyclopedias (general and special); dictionaries (general and special); biographical dictionaries; annuals, yearbooks, and directories; handbooks and compendia of data; and atlases. The following criteria are taken into consideration in making an award: the authority of the work and the quality and kind of articles or entries; the accessibility and arrangement of the information; the scope and coverage; the style; the relevance and quality of the illustrations; the quality of the indexing; the adequacy of the bibliographies and references; the up-to-dateness of the information; the physical presentation; and the originality of the work. Members of the Association may submit nominations. A medal is awarded annually. Established in 1970 in honor of Lionel McColvin, former City Librarian of Westminster and President of the Association.

3572
Meckler Award for Innovation Through Information Technology
To recognize organizations in the library and information science community in the United Kingdom and the Republic of Ireland. An annual trophy and cash prize are given to the project selected as the most effective in meeting the following criteria: promoting the use of information technology in an innovative manner; having a measurable impact on either the quality or efficiency of service delivery in the organization that instituted the project; providing an example of good practice capable of being applied in other settings and environments. Presented at the annual Computers in Libraries International conference and exhibition. Application deadline is August 1. For further information, contact Meckler, Artillery House, Artillery Row, London SW1 1RT.

3573
Ulverscroft Munford Research Fellowship
To give librarians and other information specialists the opportunity to produce and publish a piece of research on the supply of books, other reading material, or information in other media to the disadvantaged. An award of L5,000 is awarded biennially.

3574
Wheatley Medal
For recognition of an outstanding index published in the United Kingdom during the preceding three years. Printed indexes to any type of publication may be submitted for consideration provided that the whole work, including the index, or the index alone, has originated in the United Kingdom. Recommendations for the award are invited from members of the Library Association, and the Society of Indexers, publishers, and others. A medal is awarded annually. Established in 1962 in honor of Henry B. Wheatley, sometimes referred to as "the father of British indexing". Administered with the cooperation of the Society of Indexers.

3575
Lichfield District Council
Donegal House, Bore St.
Lichfield, Staffs WS13 6NE, England
Phone: 543 252109
Fax: 543 250673

3576
Lichfield Prize
To help publicize Lichfield City and District, and for recognition of an unpublished novel. Submissions are accepted. A monetary prize of £5,000 and the possibility of having the novel published are awarded biennially. Established in 1989 to commemorate Lichfield's attachment to literary figures. Sponsored by booksellers James Redshaw Ltd. and Orion Publishing Group.

3577
Lighting Association
Stafford Park 7
Telford TF3 3BQ, England
Phone: 952 290905
Fax: 952 290906

Formerly: Decorative Lighting Association.

3578
Student Lighting Design Awards
To recognize student designers at the start of their careers in the lighting industry. Students of industrial design at educational institutions in the United Kingdom are eligible. The following monetary awards are presented: £1,500 - first prize, £750 - second prize, and £250 - third prize. In addition, commendations and minor cash awards are presented. The award is given annually. Established in 1985.

3579
Lighting Industry Federation
Swan House
207 Balham High Rd.
London SW17 7BQ, England
Phone: 81 675 5432
Fax: 81 673 5880

3580
Energy Management in Lighting Awards Scheme
To recognize a high standard of efficiency in the use of energy for lighting industrial and commercial-type premises and associated areas. A trophy and four certificates were awarded in each of the following sections: Industrial, Commercial, and New Lighting Schemes. Established in 1975 by the Electricity Association and Lighting Industry Federation. (Discontinued. Merged with the Na tional Lighting Awards to form the Lighting Design Awards in 1993.)

3581
Lighting Design Awards
To promote excellence and innovation in all aspects of lighting design. Formed by the merger of the National Lighting Awards and the Energy Management in Lighting Awards Scheme in 1993.

3582
National Lighting Awards
To promote an awareness of the unique role that good lighting plays in our everyday lives and to commend and reward the design skills and technical expertise of lighting designers. A trophy and two certificates were awarded in each of the following sections: Industrial, Civic, Commercial, and Leisure. Established in 1986. (Discontinued. Merged with the Energy Management in Light ing Awards in 1993 to form the Lighting Design Awards.)

3583
Linnean Society of London
Burlington House
Piccadilly
London W1V 0LQ, England
Phone: 71 434 4479

3584
Bicentenary Medal
To recognize work done by a biologist under the age of 40. Any biologist, who is not at the time a member of the Council, is eligible. A silver medal is awarded annually. Established in 1978 to commemorate the two hundredth anniversary of the death of Linneaus.

3585
H. H. Bloomer Award
To recognize an amateur naturalist who has made an important contribution to biological knowledge. The award may be given to any person not at the time a member of the Council. Presented alternately to a botanist and a zoologist. A silver medal is awarded annually. Established in 1963 from a legacy by the late Harry Howard Bloomer.

3586
Darwin - Wallace Medals
Gold and silver medals were struck in 1908 and 1958 to commemorate the fiftieth and one hundredth anniversaries of the reading of the joint paper by Charles Darwin and Alfred Russel Wallace, "On the Tendency of Species to form Varieties; and the Perpetuation of Varieties and Species by Natural Means of Selection," which was read on July 1, 1858.

3587
Linnean Medal
To recognize a botanist and/or a zoologist for service to science. Any biologist, who is not at the time a member of the Council, is eligible. A medal is awarded at the Anniversary Meeting. Established in 1988 in connection with the Centenary of the Society.

3588
Irene Manton Prize
To recognize the best thesis in botany examined for a doctorate of philosophy during the year beginning in September and ending in August. It is open to candidates whose research has been carried out while registered at any institution in the United Kingdom. Theses on the full range of plant sciences are eligible. A monetary prize of £1,000, and a

piece of sculpture or other work of fine art are awarded. A letter of recommendation and an abstract of the thesis must be submitted by September 30.

3589

Jill Smythies Award
To recognize published illustrations, such as drawings or paintings, in aid of plant identification, with the emphasis on botanical accuracy and the accurate portrayal of diagnostic characteristics. Although the work may have been published at any date, preference is given to recently completed items and to those by the younger worker. Illustrations of cultivars of garden origin are not eligible. Individuals who are not at the time members of the Council are eligible. A silver medal and a purse are awarded, usually annually. Established in 1986 by Mr. B.E. Smythies, FLS, in honor of his wife Florence Mary Smythies ("Jill"), whose career as a botanical artist was cut short by an accident to her right hand.

3590

Trail - Crisp Award
To recognize an outstanding contribution to biological microscopy published in the United Kingdom. Preference is given to the younger worker. Individuals who are not at the time members of the Council are eligible. A bronze medal is awarded every two or three years. Established in 1910 as the Trail Award and the Crisp Award. The awards were combined in 1966.

3591

Liszt Society
23 Vineyard Hill Rd.　　　　　　　　　　　　　　Phone: 81 9467486
London SW19 7JL, England　　　　　　　　　　Fax: 81 9467486

3592

Liszt Society Prize
To recognize the best performance of a work by Liszt in the Royal Overseas Music Competition in London. Young musicians from the United Kingdom, Commonwealth, and former Commonwealth countries are eligible. A monetary prize of £200 is awarded annually.

3593

Liverpool School of Tropical Medicine
Pembroke Pl.　　　　　　　　　　　　　　　　Phone: 51 708 9393
Liverpool L3 5QA, England　　　　　　　　　　Fax: 51 707 0155

3594

Mary Kingsley Medal
For recognition of distinguished achievement in the field of tropical medicine. Scientists who have given distinguished service in this field are eligible. Awarded from time to time when merited. Established in 1903 to commemorate the work of the late Mary Kingsley in West Africa.

3595

Livewire UK
Hawthorne House
Forth Banks　　　　　　　　　　　　　　　　Phone: 91 2615584
Newcastle Upon Tyne NE1 3SG, England　　　Fax: 91 2611910

3596

Livewire Start-up Awards
To provide assistance and encouragement to young persons who come forward with a reasonable idea for creating their own business. Individuals between 16 and 25 years of age who have produced a business plan or who have started a business during the preceding year are eligible. Monetary awards of more than £175,000 are presented annually at the awards ceremony. Established in 1982. Sponsored by Shell UK Ltd. Formerly: Livewire UK Awards.

3597

Lloyd's of London Press
1 Singer St.
London EC2A 4LQ, England　　　　　　　　　Phone: 206 772277

3598

BIMCO/Lloyd's List Maritime Book Prize
For recognition of the best manuscript on a maritime subject actively aiding the shipping industry. A monetary prize of 15,000 Swiss francs plus guaranteed publication and travel expenses are awarded biennially at the BIMCO Annual General meeting. Established in 1987. Sponsored by BIMCO and Lloyd's List. Additional information is available from BIMCO Publications A/S, Peter Thornton, Editor, Kristianiagade 19, DK-2100, Copenhagen, Denmark.

3599

The London Evening Standard
PO Box 136
118 Fleet St.
London EC4P 4DD, England　　　　　　　　　Phone: 71 353 8000

3600

***The London Evening Standard* Ballet and Opera Awards**
For recognition of the most outstanding achievements in ballet and opera. A bronze statuette is awarded annually. Established in 1973. Formerly: *Evening Standard* Ballet Award.

3601

***The London Evening Standard* Drama Awards**
To recognize the best actor, best actress, best director, best play, best comedy, best musical, and most promising playwright. Bronze statuettes are awarded annually. Established in 1955. Formerly: *Evening Standard* Drama Awards.

3602

Catherine Pakenham Memorial Award
To recognize published and unpublished articles written by women between 18 and 30 years of age. Women involved in or intending to take up a career in journalism are eligible. A monetary award of £500 is presented for first prize and £25 to five runners-up. Awarded annually. Established in memory of Catherine Pakenham, youngest daughter of Lord and Lady Longford.

3603

London International Piano Competition
National Power World Piano Competition
　London
28 Wallace Rd.　　　　　　　　　　　　　　Phone: 71 3541087
London N1 2PG, England　　　　　　　　　　Fax: 71 7041053

3604

National Power World Piano Competition London
For recognition of outstanding piano performance. Pianists of all nationalities who are 29 years of age and under are eligible. Monetary prizes are awarded every three years. Established in 1991 by the National Power World Piano Competition. Sponsored by National Power PLC.

3605

London International String Quartet Competition
62 High St.
Fareham, Hants. PO16 7BG, England　　　　　Phone: 329 283603

3606
London International String Quartet Competition
For recognition of achievement in standard of musical performance. String quartets of all nationalities, with an aggregate age of the members not to exceed 120 years, are eligible. The following monetary prizes are awarded: First Prize - £8,000, The Amadeus Trophy and Restall and Boyle "Quartet of Bows"; Second Prize - £4,800; Third Prize - £3,200; Fourth Prize - £2,400; Fifth Prize - £1,600; Menuhin Prize - £750; and Audience Prize - £500. Professional engagements are also arranged. Awarded triennially. Established in 1979 by Yehudi Menuhin. The next competitions will be held in April, 1994 and 1997.

3607
London Mathematical Society
Burlington House, Piccadilly
London W1V ONL, England
Phone: 71 437 5377
Fax: 71 439 4629

3608
Berwick Prize
For recognition of a work actually published by the Society in any of its publications during the preceding four years. Members of the Society on January 1 of the year of the award are eligible. A monetary prize and a certificate are awarded biennially. Established in 1946 by Mrs. Berwick in memory of Professor William Edward Hodgson Berwick, ScD, member of the Society (1914-1944), Council (1925-1929), and Vice President (1929).

3609
De Morgan Medal
For recognition of contributions to mathematics. Mathematicians who are normally resident in the United Kingdom are eligible. A gold medal and a certificate are awarded triennially. Established in 1884 in honor of Professor A. De Morgan, first president of the Society.

3610
Forder Lectureship
For recognition of contributions to, influence on, and general service to mathematics. Members of the Society who on January 1 of the year of the award are normally resident in the United Kingdom are eligible. A four to six week lecturing tour of most New Zealand universities is awarded biennially. Established in 1986 to honor Professor H.G. Forder, formerly of the University of Auckland and a benefactor of the London Mathematical Society.

3611
Hardy Lectureship
For recognition of contributions to, influence on, and general service to mathematics. Mathematicians who on January 1 of the year of the award are not normally resident in the United Kingdom are eligible. A lecture tour of about ten universities in the United Kingdom and Ireland, also incorporating the Hardy Lecture to the Society, is awarded biennially. Established in 1966 to honor Professor G.H. Hardy, LMS President (1926-28 and 1939-41), and De Morgan Medallist (1929).

3612
Junior Berwick Prize
For recognition of a work actually published by the Society in any of its publications during the preceding four years. Members whose age on January 1 in the year of the award does not exceed 40 years and who have not at that date gained the distinction of being elected as a Fellow of the Royal Society are eligible. A monetary prize and a certificate are awarded biennially. Established in 1947 by Mrs. Berwick in memory of Professor W.E.H. Berwick, ScD, Member of the Society (1914-44), Council (1925-29), and Vice President (1929).

3613
Junior Whitehead Prize
For recognition of contributions to and influence on mathematics. Mathematicians, who on January 1 of the year of the award are either normally resident in the United Kingdom or members of the Society mainly educated in the United Kingdom, are eligible. A monetary prize and a certificate are awarded annually. Established in 1978 by Professor Whitehead's friends and a donation from Mrs. Whitehead in memory of Professor J.H.C. Whitehead, LMS President (1953-55).

3614
Naylor Prize in Applied Mathematics
For recognition of contributions to applied mathematics and/or the applications of mathematics. Mathematicians who are normally resident in the United Kingdom and Northern Ireland are eligible. A monetary prize and a certificate are awarded biennially. Established in 1977 in memory of Vernon Dalrymple Naylor, by his sons.

3615
Polya Prize
For recognition of outstanding creativity in, imaginative exposition of, or distinguished contribution to, mathematics within the United Kingdom. A monetary prize and a certificate are awarded in those years not numbered by a multiple of three. Established in 1986 by a donation from Mrs. Polya in memory of Professor G. Polya, member of the Society (1925-1985), and Honorary Member (1956-1985).

3616
Senior Whitehead Prize
For recognition of contributions and service to mathematics, and lecturing gifts. Mathematicians who are normally resident in the United Kingdom on January 1 of the year of the award are eligible. A monetary prize and a certificate are awarded biennially. Established in 1973 by Professor Whitehead's friends and a donation from Mrs. Whitehead in memory of Professor J.H.C. Whitehead, LMS President (1953-55).

3617
London Symphony Orchestra
Barbican Centre
London EC2Y 8DS, England
Phone: 71 5881116
Fax: 71 3740127

3618
Shell - LSO Music Scholarship
To discover and encourage outstanding young musical talent, to give participants first hand experience of highest standards among contemporaries and thereby stimulate musical achievement, and to provide the winner with a scholarship to be used for musical development. The scholarship is awarded in alternate years for woodwind, strings, brass, and percussion. Individuals who are 15 to 22 years of age and are British citizens or normally resident in the United Kingdom for at least the previous three years may apply in November. A scholarship of £6,000 and gold medal are awarded for first place, £3,000 and a silver medal for second place, £1,500 and a bronze medal for third place, and £750 for fourth place. In addition, the Gerald McDonald Award of £750 is awarded to the most promising candidate under 18 years of age. Awarded annually. Sponsored by Shell UK Ltd.

3619
Malacological Society of London
Hon. Sec. Dr. G. B. J. Dussart
c/o Ecology Research Group
Canterbury Christ Church College
Canterbury, Kent CT1 1QU, England
Phone: 929 462314
Fax: 929 462180

3620
Annual Award
To honor and encourage an exceptionally promising initial contribution in the study of molluscs. Nominations should be made by a member of the Society by October 31 of each year. A monetary prize of £100 is presented annually. Established in 1976.

3621
Sir Charles Maurice Yonge Award
To recognize the best bivalve paper of the year to be published in the *Journal of Molluscan Studies*. A committee appointed by the Council of the society selects the winners.

3622
Mallinson-Denny
Address unknown.

3623
Carpenters Award
To encourage high general standards in hardwood and softwood joinery and for an outstanding example of joinery in terms of its suitability of design in relation to its location and purpose, the choice of timber, its manufacture, installation and finish. Any joinery work in or associated with any building in the United Kingdom which has been put to its intended use (i.e. occupied) in the two years immediately prior to January 1 of the year of the award is eligible. Nominations may be made by the architect or by the construction or joinery companies responsible for the work, but nominations may also be submitted by anyone provided permission of the owner has been obtained. The deadline is February 16. The Award is a specially designed engraved plaque, crafted in wood. Certificates are also presented to those responsible for the design and execution of the work. Awarded biennially. In addition, five regional awards each with a Highly Commended runner-up are awarded. For purposes of the Regional Awards, the country has been divided up as follows: England, Greater London, Scotland, Wales and Northern Ireland. The Carpenters Award winner is chosen from the five Regional Award winners. Established in 1971. Co-sponsored by The Worshipful Company of Carpenters and Mallinson-Denny Ltd.

3624
Maltsters Association of Great Britain
31B Castle Gate
Newark on Trent, Notts. NG24 1AZ,
England
Phone: 636 700781
Fax: 636 701836

3625
MAGB Malting Diploma
To recognize individuals who demonstrate extensive understanding of and experience in all practical aspects of the malting process and related operations. Candidates are expected to possess a basic understanding of the scientific and engineering principles of the malting process and must have a minimum of three years experience in the malting industry in work closely related to technical matters. A diploma and a tankard are awarded to the winner of the Walter Hyde Trophy for distinction. Established in 1981.

3626
Mananan Festival Trust
Mananan Festival Office
Port Erin, Isle of Man IM9 6JB, England
Phone: 624 83 3836
Phone: 624 83 2870

3627
Lionel Tertis International Viola Competition and Workshop (Internationaler Wettbewerb und Seminar fur Bratsche)
To recognize outstanding viola players. Individuals of any nationality not over 30 years of age may submit applications by March 1. The following prizes are awarded at the triennial competition: First prize - Ruth Fermoy Memorial Prize of £2,500 and a viola; Second prize - Arthur Rubinstein Memorial Prize of £1,500; Third prize - Lillian Tertis Award of £1,000; Finalists - the Ealing Strings Prize of a viola bow; Man Sing Prize - a silver mounted bow to be awarded at the discretion of the Jury; and the Peter Schidlof Prize - a viola bow awarded to the finalist with the most beautiful sound. Also awarded are five publishers prizes and 10 special prizes. Established in 1980 by John Bethell in memory of Lionel Tertis (1876-1975). In addition to the competition, a viola workshop is held.

3628
Manpower Society
39 Appletree Walk
Climping
Littlehampton, W. Sussex BN17 5QN,
England
Phone: 903 731728
Fax: 903 731728

3629
Manpower Society Essay Competition
For recognition of the best paper submitted on human resource management. Entry is not restricted to members of the Society. Monetary prizes are awarded annually. A prize for the best paper by a student is also awarded.

3630
Marine Biological Association of the United Kingdom
The Laboratory
Citadel Hill
Plymouth, Devon PL1 2PB, England
Phone: 752 222772
Fax: 752 226865

3631
Ray Lankester Investigatorship
To advance knowledge on marine animals and plants. An honorarium is awarded and winners may use laboratory facilities at MBA Plymouth. Awarded annually. Established in 1911 by Dr. G.P. Bidder in honor of Sir Ray Lankester, president of the MBA for 40 years.

3632
The Maritime Trust
2 Greenwich Church St.
London SE10 9BG, England
Phone: 81 8582698
Fax: 81 8586976

Formerly: (1991) Cutty Sark Maritime Trust.

3633
Cutty Sark Medal
To recognize an individual for an outstanding contribution to the conservation of a historic British vessel or vessels; to the display or interpretation of Britain's maritime heritage; to the knowledge of Britain's maritime past, contained in published research, whether through book, learned paper, article or on video or film; and that follows the spirit of *Cutty Sark* in sail, navigation, or furtherance of man's understanding of the sea and ships - large and small. A medal may be awarded annually or less frequently. Established in 1990.

3634
Massey-Ferguson (UK) Ltd.
Stareton
Kenilworth, Warks. CV8 2LJ, England
Phone: 203 531500
Fax: 203 531229

3635
Massey Ferguson National Agricultural Award
For recognition of outstanding contributions to the advancement of agriculture in the United Kingdom. Farmers and others engaged in non-commercial support to agriculture are eligible. A monetary prize of £5,000, a bronze medallion, and a silver trophy are awarded annually at the presentation ceremony, where the awardee delivers the Massey Ferguson Agricultural Lecture. Established in 1964. Formerly: Massey-Ferguson National Award for Services to United Kingdom Agriculture.

3636
Medical Society of London
Lettsom House
Cavendish Sq.
11 Chandos St.
London W1M OEB, England
Phone: 71 580 1043
Fax: 11 580 5793

3637

Fothergillian Medal
For recognition of the best essay on some branch of practical medicine or practical surgery, or for a literary work published during the preceding five years. British subjects are eligible. A medal is awarded triennially. Established in 1787 in memory of Dr. John Fothergill. Formerly: (1989) Fothergillian Gold Medal.

3638

Lettsomian Medal
To recognize a Fellow of the Society who is selected to give a lecture to the Society. A medal is awarded annually.

3639

Mensa International
15 The Ivories
6-8 Northampton St.
London N1 2HY, England

Phone: 71 2266891
Fax: 71 2267059

3640

Mensa International Competitions
To recognize individuals from 100 countries whose intelligence, as measured by standardized tests, is within the top 2 percent of the general population, and to promote social contact among intelligent people. Competitions are sponsored periodically and awards are given.

3641

Mercury Books
Gold Arrow Publications Ltd.
862 Garratt Lane
London SW17 DNB, England

Phone: 81 682 3858
Fax: 81 682 3859

3642

Mercury Business Book Award
To recognize a previously unpublished work that makes a readable and practical contribution to the solution of problems facing management. The deadline for submission is December 31. A monetary award of £2,000 and publication are awarded annually. Established in 1990.

3643

Meteoritical Society
Dept. of Mineralogy
Cromwell Rd.
London SW7 5BD, England

Phone: 71 938 8800
Fax: 71 938 9268

3644

Barringer Medal
For recognition of outstanding work in the field of terrestrial impact cratering or work that has led to a better understanding of impact phenomena. Any scientist, regardless of race, nationality, creed or sex is eligible for nomination. A monetary stipend of $1,000 and a medal are awarded annually. Established in 1982 by the Meteoritical Society and the Barringer Crater Company in memory of D.M. Barringer.

3645

Leonard Medal
To recognize outstanding, original contributions to the science of meteoritics and closely allied fields of research. Any scientist, regardless of race, nationality, creed or sex, is eligible for nomination. The deadline is March 31. A medal is awarded annually. Established in 1962 in memory of Professor Frederick C. Leonard, the Society's first president.

3646

Metropolitan Owners' Club
South Cottage
School Lane
Washington, W. Sussex RH20 4AP,
England

Phone: 903 893264
Fax: 903 893264

3647

MOC Cup
To preserve surviving marques (Metropolitan automobiles) which were originally produced by the Austin Motor Company of Longbridge, Birmingham, England until 1961. The MOC Cup is awarded annually.

3648

Midland Bank
International Trade and Export Finance
  Dept.
110 Cannon St.
London EC4N 6AA, England

Phone: 71 260 5647
Phone: 71 260 5552

3649

Export Awards for Small Businesses
To recognize independent small British companies which can demonstrate an increase in export earnings over the past two years. These earning must have exceeded £100,000 in the last year and entrants must employ fewer than 200 people. The deadline for entries is March 16. Five monetary prizes totaling £35,000 are awarded. Runners-up receive certificates of merit. Sponsored by British Overseas Trade Board, Thomas Cook, Price Waterhouse, and Kelly's UK Exports.

3650

MIND (National Association for Mental Health)
Granta House, 15-17 Broadway
London E15 4BQ, England

Phone: 71 6370741
Fax: 81 5221725

3651

MIND Book of the Year - Allen Lane Award
For recognition of the book which makes the greatest contribution to public understanding of the experience, nature, cause, treatment, or consequences of mental health problems. Books published in the United Kingdom must be submitted on or before December 31 each year. A monetary prize of £1,000 is awarded annually. Established in 1981 in honor of Allen Lane. Sponsored by The Allen Lane Foundation.

3652

Minerals Engineering Society
2 Ryton Close, Blyth
Worksop, Notts. 381 8DN, England

Phone: 909 591787

Formerly: Coal Preparation Society.

3653

Lessing Memorial Medal
For recognition of persons whose contributions to the field of mineral processing engineering have made them eminent in this sphere. Nominations are made in council, but may be initiated by a section committee or any group of ten members. Awarded from time to time in memory of Rudolph Lessing who, in the 1920's and 30's, was a determined advocate of the economic benefits to be obtained from coal cleaning and a pioneer in the introduction and establishment of coal preparation techniques.

3654

Papers and Publications Committee Prizes
To recognize the author of the best paper submitted in two categories: scientific/technical and practical/operational. The deadline is June 30. A prize is presented in each category at the annual meeting.

3655

Travel Award
To subsidize an individual visit or attendance at a relevant conference or some other activity. Open to any person who is training or engaged in minerals engineering. Applications to the National Secretary are accepted. Awarded annually.

3656

Minit/*European Management Journal*
c/o Basil Blackwell Ltd.
108 Cowley Rd.
Oxford, Oxon. OX4 1JF, England
Phone: 865 791100
Fax: 865 791347

3657

Minit/EMJ Trophy
For recognition of the best management essay of the year. Any full-time student studying in a European Business School or European students attending business schools anywhere are eligible. The deadline for entry is June 30. The following prizes are awarded: (1) First prize - 5,000 ECU and a trophy; (2) Second prize - 3,000 ECU and a certificate; and (3) Third Prize - 1,000 ECU and a certificate. Awarded annually between June and September usually. Established in 1988 by Dr. Ryan of the Minit Corporation.

3658

Mirror Group Newspapers
Holborn Circus
London EC1P 1DO, England
Phone: 71 822 3917

3659

Sunday People Tattersall Trophy
For recognition of the best design of current Resort/Tourist Board posters. The competition is open to members of the British Resorts Association only. A silver engraved trophy is awarded annually at the Association's conference. Established in 1932 by Lord Tattersall. Formerly: (1984) Tattersall Trophy.

3660

Morgan Sports Car Club, Ltd.
41 Cordwell Close
Castle Donington
Derby DE7 2JL, England
Phone: 332 811644
Fax: 332 853412

Formerly: (1975) Morgan 4/4 Club.

3661

Challenge Shield
To recognize the best overall performance in the Club Championship in any car. The deadline is December 31 each year. A shield is presented annually at the club dinner dance. Established in 1966.

3662

East Anglian Trophy
To recognize the best performance in the Club Championship in any Morgan. In addition, the club awards 34 other awards for performance and contributions to the Club.

3663

Mushroom Growers Association
2 St. Paul St.
Stamford, Lincs. PE9 2BE, England
Phone: 780 66888
Fax: 780 66558

3664

Sinden Award
For recognition of the most outstanding practical contribution to the mushroom industry in research, development, or advisory work. Individuals engaged in research, development, or advisory work on mushrooms in research institutes, universities, advisory services, and in the industry may be nominated by January 31. The Sinden Award Sub-Committee reviews the nominations and puts forward one recommendation for the Award to the Executive Committee for ratification. A framed scroll and an engraved piece of glass are awarded annually. Established in 1975 in honor of Dr. James Sinden, whose work has benefited the mushroom industry.

3665

Young Scientist or Grower of the Year Award
To recognize an individual for contributions to the mushroom industry. Open to those training or working in the industry. Candidates are expected to have either studied or pursued research, with distinction in the field of mushroom science, engineering, production, management, or marketing. Performance in the industry, course work, project work, or postgraduate studies are considered. Awarded annually. Established in 1991.

3666

Music Teacher
Rhinegold Publishing Ltd.
241 Shaftesbury Ave.
London WC2H 8EH, England
Phone: 71 836 2384
Fax: 71 528 7991

3667

***Music Teacher* Awards**
For recognition of outstanding contributions to music teaching and education in the following categories: private music teacher of the year; school music teacher of the year; pupil of the year; and music education. A trophy was presented annually. Established in 1981. (Discontinued in 1986)

3668

Musicians Benevolent Fund
16 Ogle St.
London W1P 7LG, England

3669

Musicians Benevolent Fund Awards
To recognize excellence in the field of music. Awards include the Henry and Lily Davis Fund Awards, the H.A. Thew Fund Awards, the Miriam Licette Scholarship, and the Guilhermina Suggia Gift for the Cello.

3670

National Art Collections Fund
Millais House
7 Cromwell Pl.
London SW7 2JN, England
Phone: 071 2254800
Fax: 071 2254848

3671

National Art Collections Awards
For outstanding achievement on the part of curators, educators, and administrators in the presentation and interpretation of the visual arts. Selection is by nomination. Entries must be received by January 31. Cash awards in the amounts of £5,000 for winners and £1,000 for runners-up are presented annually. Recipients are selected in each of four categories: Exhibitions, Education, Art Outside the Gallery, and New Projects. Established in 1987. Sponsored by The Jerwood Foundation.

3672
National Association of Public Golf Courses
948 Castle Lane East
Bournemouth BH7 6SP, England   Phone: 202 483017

3673
Peter Alliss and Roy Beckett Crystal Rose Bowl
For recognition of achievement as the best female golfer from public course clubs in England and Wales. Members of a public course club in England and Wales are eligible. A crystal rose bowl is awarded annually. Established in 1967.

3674
Championship Silver Challenge Trophy
For recognition of achievement as the best male golfer from public course clubs in England and Wales. Members of a public course club in England and Wales are eligible. A silver trophy is awarded annually. Established in 1927.

3675
National Association of Shopfitters
NAS House, 411 Limpsfield Rd.
The Green   Phone: 883 624961
Warlingham, Surrey CR6 9HA, England   Fax: 883 626841

3676
NAS Design Prize
To encourage and recognize good design associated with the type of work undertaken by shopfitters. The competition is open to architects and designers practicing in the United Kingdom. Entries may be submitted either in the name of the designer or the practice. The design project should be one for which the contract works have been completed and carried out in the United Kingdom by a member of the Association. Employees of NAS Member firms are not eligible to enter. Entries are required in three classes: Retail Outlets, Hotels and Restaurants, and Banks, Offices, and Public Buildings. The judges take into consideration the following: suitability of the design for the location and purpose of the project, choice of materials with particular reference to the needs of both design and cost effectiveness laid down in the design brief, creativity and originality in interpreting the design brief and to overcome problems inherent in the site or premises, and special design features of functional or decorative relevance. The winning entry in each class receives a certificate. The entry adjudged the Best of Competition receives the overall Design Prize - £1,000 and a plaque. Awarded biennially. Established in 1978.

3677
National Back Pain Association
16 Elmtree Rd.
Teddington, Greater London TW11 8ST,   Phone: 81 9775474
  England   Fax: 81 9435318

Formerly: (1987) Back Pain Association.

3678
National Back Pain Association Medal
For recognition of the most outstanding scientific research paper on the subject of back pain published during the year in one or more scientific journals in the English language. The paper must have come to the attention of the awarding committee of the Society for Back Pain Research. A monetary prize of £200, a medal, and a certificate are awarded annually. Established in 1978. Formerly: (1990) Back Pain Association Medal.

3679
National Backgammon Players Society (of Great Britain)
27 Moorfield Rd.
Manchester M20 8UZ, England   Phone: 61 946 0828

3680
UK Cup
To recognize the winner of the National Championship Tournament. This annual competition aims to find the top classical backgammon player of the year. The tournament is run as an "OPEN" for all to take part. There are no entry restrictions.

3681
National Deaf Children's Society
NDCS Family Services Centre
24 Wakefield Rd.
Rothwell Haigh   Phone: 32 823458
Leeds, W. Yorks. LS26 0SF, England   Fax: 32 824113

3682
NDCS Scholarship
To enable an outstanding and experienced teacher to train as a teacher of deaf children. Teaching qualifications and experience are considered. A grant towards living expenses and full course fees for training in the United Kingdom are awarded annually in May. Established in 1984.

3683
National Federation of Music Societies
Francis House, Francis St.   Phone: 71 8287320
London SW1P 1DE, England   Fax: 71 8285504

3684
NFMS/ESSO Young Concert Artists
To assist young solo performers in obtaining concert engagements at the beginning of their professional careers. Professional musicians under the age of 28 (30 for singers) who hold British passports and are normally residents of Great Britain are eligible. The award consists of 70 concert engagements with music clubs and societies. Finalists are awarded engagements and are included in a publicity brochure circulated to 1,300 affiliated societies. The competition is held annually on a four year cycle for voice, piano, strings, wind, and brass (1992 - Piano; 1993 - Women's Voices; 1994 - Strings, Winds, and Brass; 1995 - Men's Voices). Established in 1961.

3685
National Federation of Plastering Contractors
82 New Cavendish St.
London W1M 8AD, England   Phone: 71 580 5588

3686
Plaisterers Trophy Competition
To uphold the image of the plastering craft in all its diverse skills and to demonstrate the high level of craftsmanship that the plastering industry can still offer to the building industry; and for recognition of the best plastering contract executed during the entry period having regard to excellence of workmanship and service. Entries are accepted from any firm or company carrying out a plastering contract. Entries may comprise solid plastering only, fibrous plastering only, or a combination of both in any proportion; and may comprise either in total or in part traditional aspects of the craft, e.g. granolithic paving, external finishes, etc., or more recently introduced processes such as spray finishes, dry-lining etc. Contracts must be of a value of £10,000 and upwards. A trophy is awarded annually. Organized in association with Royal Institute of British Architects and Worshipful Company of Plaisterers.

3687
National Federation of Women's Institutes
39 Eccleston St.
London SW1W 9NT, England   Phone: 71 730 7212

3688
Denman Cup
To recognize outstanding creative writing. Topics may include a short play; poetry; a carol for Christmas; an essay, etc. Open to all members of the Women's Institutes in England and Wales. Awarded annually.

3689
NFWI Design Award
To encourage all members of the Women's Institutes in England and Wales to show their ability and flair in design. A different area of work is chosen each year, such as crafts, garden, or photography. Members submit works by the deadline in October/November each year. A trophy and certificate are awarded annually and certificates only for those whose work shows excellence.

3690
National Library for the Handicapped Child
Reach Resource Centre
Ash Ct.
Rose St.
Wokingham, Berks. RG11 1XS, England
Phone: 734 891101
Fax: 734 790989

3691
Apple Tree Award
To recognize creative writing by children with disabilities that affect their use of language. Applicants must be British citizens between the ages of 5 and 16 years. Entries may be submitted in print, braille, sign language, video, sound cassette, or handwriting by the end of the Easter Term. Monetary prizes totaling £200 plus a carved wooden apple are awarded annually. Established in 1990 by Ruth Craft in memory of Geoffrey Alley, lecturer, NZ National Librarian.

3692
National Maritime Museum
Greenwich
London SE10 9NF, England
Phone: 81 858 4422

3693
National Maritime Museum Ship Model Competition
To encourage ship model making of the highest standard. The competition was divided into several classes according to ship type. Gold, silver and bronze medals and commendations were awarded occasionally at the exhibition of entries at the Museum. Established in 1976. (Discontinued in 1991)

3694
National Operatic and Dramatic Association
Noda House
1 Crestfield St.
London WC1H 8AU, England
Phone: 71 8375655
Fax: 71 8330609

3695
National Operatic and Dramatic Association Awards
To recognize opera and drama societies and individuals who are involved in amateur stage performances. Competitions are held and awards are given annually at a general assembly.

3696
National Poetry Foundation
27 Mill Rd.
Fareham, Hants. P016 OTH, England
Phone: 329 822218

3697
Rosemary Arthur Award
For recognition of a first book of poetry by a resident of the UK who has not previously had a book published. Full cost of publishing a book, £100, and an engraved clock are awarded annually on February 3. Established in 1981 by Rosemary Arthur.

3698
National Poetry Foundation
To provide encouragement for the promotion of the work of little-known good poets. Residents of the UK are eligible. A book of poetry is published at no charge for each poet. Established in 1981 by Johnathan Clifford.

3699
Dorothy Tutin Award
To recognize the person who has done the most to encourage the love of and interest in poetry throughout the United Kingdom. Residents of the UK are eligible. A glass and brass carriage clock is awarded occasionally in September. Established in 1979 by Johnathon Clifford.

3700
National Pony Society
Willingdon House
102 High St.
Alton, Hants. GU34 1EN, England
Phone: 420 88333
Fax: 420 80599

3701
NPS Medal of Honour
To recognize individuals who have given outstanding service to the Society. A medal is awarded when merited. Established in 1990.

3702
NPS Stud Assistant's Certificate
To encourage professional development. Certificates are awarded annually. Established in 1976. A NPS Diploma is also awarded.

3703
National Portrait Gallery - London
St. Martins Pl.
London WC2H OHE, England
Phone: 71 306 0055
Fax: 71 306 0056

3704
BP Portrait Award
To encourage young painters to specialize in portraiture, to foster new talent, and to help sustain Britain's long tradition of portraiture. British and Commonwealth citizens resident in the United Kingdom for at least five years, and older than 18 years of age but not over 40 years of age, are eligible. A monetary award of £10,000 and a commission for painting a subject to be agreed upon between the National Portrait Gallery and the artist that will be accepted as part of the Gallery's contemporary portrait collection are awarded. A cash award is made to the second and third place artists. Up to five additional entries may be specially commended at the discretion of the judges and the artists presented with a cash award and commemorative certificate. Awarded annually in June. Established in 1980, in association with the National Portrait Gallery where selected portraits competing for the award are exhibited. Sponsored by British Petroleum. Formerly: (1990) John Player Portrait Award; (1983) Imperial Tobacco Portrait Award.

3705
National Rifle Association
Bisley Camp
Brookwood, Surrey GU24 OPB, England
Phone: 483 797777
Fax: 483 797285

3706

Queen's Prize NRA Gold Medal
To recognize an individual who has achieved the highest aggregate score in a course of rifle fire over distances of 300, 500, 600, 900, and 1,000 yards. Subjects of H.M. The Queen are eligible. A monetary prize of £250, a gold medal, and a badge are awarded annually on the fourth Saturday in July. Established in 1860 by H.M. Queen Victoria. The award was given as the King's Prize from 1901 through 1951. Formerly: (1951) King's Prize.

3707

National Sheep Association
The Sheep Centre
Malvern, Hereford and Worcs. WR13 6PH, England
Phone: 684 892661
Fax: 684 892663

3708

George Hedley Award
For recognition of outstanding service to the sheep industry. Selection is by nomination. Nomination deadline is the end of September. A trophy is awarded annually. Established in 1961 in memory of George Hedley.

3709

National Small-Bore Rifle Association
Lord Roberts House
Bisley Camp, Brookwood
Woking, Surrey GU24 0NP, England
Phone: 48 3476969
Fax: 48 3476392

3710

Special Service Awards
To recognize exceptional services to small-bore and air gun shooting. There are four classes of awards: Gold Award, Silver Award, Bronze Award, and Diploma. Recommendations for the issue of Special Service Awards are considered by the Awards Sub-Committee, who in turn determines the class of award for the final approval of the Chairman of Council. The Committee regards the four awards in the following light: Gold Award - for outstanding work on behalf of shooting at club, county, regional, and national levels; Silver Award - for distinguished service to shooting at club, county, regional, and national levels; and Bronze Award - for long and faithful service to the sport at club, county, and possibly regional levels. Established in 1974.

3711

National Society for Education in Art and Design
The Gatehouse, Corsham Court
Corsham, Wilts. SN13 0B2, England
Phone: 249 714825
Fax: 249 716138

Formerly: (1984) National Society for Art Education.

3712

NSEAD/Berol Curriculum Development Award for Art and Design Teachers
To encourage research among first time researchers who are directly involved principally as teachers and lecturers, in art, craft, and design education. Practicing teachers or lecturers (including those qualified to do so but not currently in employment) interested in conducting their own independent studies into any aspect of art and design education are eligible to apply. A monetary award is bestowed of up to £2,000 over an agreed thirteen-month period beginning at the end of the summer term of the year award is made. Awarded annually in April. Established in 1977. Sponsored by Berol Ltd.

3713

Natural World
20 Upper Ground
London SE1 9PF, England
Phone: 71 9282111
Fax: 71 6201594

3714

***Natural World* Book of the Year Award**
To promote the publication of high quality, original natural history books. Books primarily concerning United Kingdom wildlife or the countryside are eligible. A monetary prize of £500 is awarded annually. Established in 1987.

3715

Nautical Institute
202 Lambeth Rd.
London SE1 7LQ, England
Phone: 71 928 1351

3716

Nautical Institute Competitions
To encourage and promote high standards of knowledge and competence among those operating sea-going vessels. Competitions are sponsored by the Institute including an annual essay competition on a maritime subject restricted to members of the Institution. Scholarships are also awarded by the Institute.

3717

Airey Neave Trust
House of Commons
London SW1A 0AA, England
Phone: 71 4950554
Fax: 71 4911118

3718

Airey Neave Research Award
To advance education by promoting research into freedom under the law of any nation in the world and the dissemination of the useful results of such research. Research topics may include: Extradition and Human Freedom, Rights of Child Civilians in War, and Human freedom to enter and leave any country. Fellowships for one or two years are presented annually. Established in 1979 to honor Airey Neave, a Member of Parliament for Abingdon from 1953 until his assassination in 1979. The program was re-activated in 1988. Formerly: (1988) Airey Neave Scholarship.

3719

New Statesman
Foundation House
Perseverance Works
38 Kingsland Rd.
London E2 8DQ, England
Phone: 71 739 3211
Fax: 71 739 9307

3720

Prudence Farmer Award
For recognition of the best poem published in the *New Statesman* during the previous year. A monetary award of £100 is awarded annually. Established in 1974 by a donation from Prudence Farmer.

3721

Northampton Borough Council
Leisure and Recreation Dept.
Guildhall
Northampton, England
Phone: 604 34734

3722

H. E. Bates Short Story Competition
To encourage use of language. Anyone may submit short stories of 2,000 words maximum by September 1. Awards are presented in various categories, including under 16 and under 11 years of age. A monetary prize of £100 and other prizes are awarded annually. Established in 1975 in honor of H.E. Bates.

3723

Anne Tibble Poetry Competition
To encourage use of language. Residents of Northampton may submit poems by September 1. Winning poems are published and circulated locally. Established in 1975 in honor of Anne Tibble. Additional information is available from Tourist Information Centre, 21 St. Giles St., Northampton NN1 1JA, England, phone: 604 22677.

3724

Northern Arts
9-10 Osborne Terrace, Jesmond
Newcastle Upon Tyne NE2 1NZ, England
Phone: 91 2816334
Fax: 91 2813276

3725

Northern Arts Literary Fellowship
To provide a fellowship for a period of two academic years at the Universities of Durham and Newcastle upon Tyne to allow the writer time to concentrate on new work and to encourage creative writing in each university. The Northern Arts Literary Fellow must come to the Northern Arts Region to live and work. A Fellowship is awarded biennially. Established in 1967.

3726

Northern Arts Writers' Awards
To recognize established authors resident in the Northern Arts area on the basis of literary merit and financial need. Monetary awards are presented annually. In addition, Northern Arts awards a month at the Tyrone Gutherie Center in Ireland and Travel Exchange Award.

3727

The Observer
Chelsea Bridge House
Queenstown Rd.
London SW8 4NN, England
Phone: 71 627 0700

3728

Young Observer Teenage Fiction Prize
For recognition of the best new fiction work for teenagers. A monetary prize of £600 was awarded annually in November. Established in 1981. (Discontinued in 1987) Formerly: (1984) Young Observer Fiction Prize.

3729

Oil and Color Chemists' Association
Priory House
967 Harrow Rd.
Wembley, Middlesex, Greater London HA0 2SF, England
Phone: 1 9081086
Fax: 1 9081219

3730

Ellinger-Gardonyi Award
To recognize the best paper presented at the Association technical meetings. Established in 1989 in memory of Dr. M. Ellinger.

3731

Jordan Award
To recognize the best contribution to the science or technology of surface coatings published in the Association's journal. Members of the Association under 35 years of age of any nationality are eligible. A monetary award of £200 and a scroll are awarded biennially. Established in 1970.

3732

Old Bottle Club of Great Britain/B.B.R. Publishing
2 Strafford Ave.
Elsecar, Nr. Barnsley, S. Yorks. S74 8AA, England
Phone: 226 745156
Fax: 226 745156

3733

National Bottle Show Champion
To encourage the collecting and appreciation of antique bottles and related artifacts. Awards are given in various categories such as Ginger Beers, Coloured top/transfer g.b.'s, Cream Pots/jugs, Old Stoneware, Whisky jugs, and Advertising water jugs. Applications are accepted for the show. A trophy is awarded for each category winner. Monetary prizes from £50 to £10 are awarded for the overall four winners. Awarded biennially at the U.K. National Bottle Show. Established in 1985. Sponsored by B.B.R. Publishing.

3734

Ongar Music Club
Chipping Ongar, Essex, England
Phone: Ongar 0824750303
Phone: 277 362545
Fax: 0824750303

3735

The Essex Chronicle Awards for the Essex Schools Musician of the Year
To encourage young musicians up to the age of 18 who are still at school. Entry is limited to those attending schools in Essex, England. Two prizes are presented: first prize - £100, an award of £100 to the school's music department, the James Dace Prize of vouchers valued at £100, the Ongar Music Club Trophy to be retained for one year, and a place in the semifinal of the competition for the Essex Young Musician of the Year; second prize - £75 and an award of £75 to the school's music department, and the Alison Baker Trophy to be retained for one year. Sponsored by the *Essex Chronicle* Newspaper Group. Formerly: John Lill Awards for the Essex Schools Musician of the Year.

3736

John Lill Awards for Essex Young Musician of the Year
To recognize instrumentalists and singers born or living in Essex, England. Individuals not over 25 years of age on the day of the contest are eligible. Five prizes are presented annually in July: first prize - a monetary award of £500, the Essex Chronicle Trophy to retain for one year, an offer of engagements with Ongar Music Club and Chelmsford Music Society during next season at fees of £200, and an invitation to give a short recital at the Wigmore Hall, London; second prize - £300 and the Musgrave Trophy to retain for one year; third prize - £200; fourth prize - £100; and Hugh Terry Prize - £100 for the most outstanding performance given by a candidate, not already a prizewinner, aged 18 or below. The award honors John Lill, an Essex-born international pianist. Established in 1984. Sponsored by the *Essex Chronicle* Newspaper Group.

3737

Oppenheim John Downes Memorial Trust
36 Whitefriars St.
London EC4Y 8BH, England

3738

Oppenheim John Downes Memorial Trust
To enable deserving artists of any kind to pursue their vocation. Artists unable to pursue their vocation by reason of their poverty are eligible to apply by November 30. The following qualifications are mandatory: Individuals must be over 30 years of age and natural born British subjects born within Great Britain, Northern Ireland, The Channel Islands, or The Isle of Man; their parents must be British subjects born within the British Isles and neither of whose parent being of colonial or overseas origin after 1900. Monetary awards of £50 to £1,500 are presented annually in December. Established in 1969 by Mrs. G.E. Downes in honor of her father, E. Phillips Oppenheim and his grandson, John Downes.

3739

Orchid Society of Great Britain
Athelney
145 Binscombe Village
Godalming, Surrey GU7 3QL, England
Phone: 689 829777

3740
Eric Young Trophy
For recognition of the best grown plant shown at a Society meeting in any one year. Society members may show plants owned for at least one year. A trophy is awarded annually. Established in 1973 in honor of Eric Young, President of the Society.

3741
Order of St. John/St. John Ambulance
1 Grosvenor Crescent
London SW1X 7EF, England
Phone: 71 235 5231
Fax: 71 235 0796

3742
Grand Prior's Trophies
To recognize the U.K. Champions at First Aid. Holders of adult first aid certificates issued by St. John compete in various eliminating rounds, regionally and nationally. Trophies and medallions are awarded annually, with the Grand Prior's trophy awarded to the winning team following a knock-out competition.

3743
Life-Saving Medal of the Order
To recognize outstanding life-saving efforts. Gold, silver, and bronze medals are awarded. A Certificate of Honor is given when the rescuer's life is not at risk. The Brigade and Association also award Certificates for Meritorious First Aid and the Commissioner-in-Chief and Director-General issue Letters of Commendation for First Aid.

3744
Order of St. John
Membership of this, the oldest Order of Chivalry in the world, is principally accorded for good service in the humanitarian and charitable relief of sickness, distress, suffering, and danger. The Order has the following six different grades: Esquires, Serving Brothers/Sisters, Officers, Commanders, Knights/Dames, and Bailiffs Grand Cross. Additional information is available from the Order of St. John, St. John's Gate, London EC1M 4DA, England, telephone: 71 2536644; fax: 71 2538826.

3745
Service Medal of the Order
To recognize a minimum of ten years' satisfactory service to the Order/Ambulance.

3746
Organisation of Commonwealth Associations
Commonwealth Trust
18 Northumberland Ave.
London WC2, England
Phone: 71 242 1222

3747
Commonwealth Professional Associations Awards for Innovation
To recognize Commonwealth nationals, who were members of Commonwealth professional associations, for innovative activities that contributed to sustainable development in Third World Commonwealth countries and had application in other such countries. Established in 1985. (Discontinued in 1989)

3748
Oriental Ceramic Society
31B Torrington Sq.
London WC1E 7JL, England
Phone: 71 6367985

3749
George de Menasce Memorial Trust
To provide a bursary for research in some aspect of oriental art. Individuals may apply by September 30. A fellowship of £1,500 is awarded about every four years. Established in 1972 by Pierre de Menasce in memory of his father, George de Menasce OBE.

3750
George Orwell Memorial Fund
Birkbeck College
Univ. of London
Malet St.
London WC1E 7HX, England
Phone: 71 631 6542

3751
George Orwell Memorial Fund Prize
To assist a young writer on some project that Orwell might have liked had he lived. A monetary award of £2,000 was presented annually. Established in 1981 by Bernard Crick, in memory of George Orwell. (Discontinued in 1987)

3752
Overseas Press and Media Association
c/o Eric Wolfensohn Associates
Grafton House, 2nd Fl., Ste. 14
2-3 Golden Sq.
London W1R 3AD, England
Phone: 71 323 0886

3753
International Advertising Award
For recognition of the most impressive international campaign. The advertiser may be foreign, but the campaign must take place in the United Kingdom. Two plaques are awarded annually.

3754
Oxford Preservation Trust
10 Turn Again Ln.
Oxford OX1 1QL, England
Phone: 865 242918
Fax: 865 794312

3755
Annual Environmental Awards
To encourage a high standard of design and workmanship in architectural and landscaping projects in Oxford and its Green Belt. Projects large or small that have been completed within the preceding two years are eligible. Plaques and certificates are awarded annually at the October awards ceremony. Established in 1977.

3756
Pan Macmillan Children's Books
18-21 Cavaye Pl.
London SW10 9PG, England
Phone: 71 3736070
Fax: 71 3700746

Formerly: (1991) Macmillan Children's Books.

3757
Macmillan Prize for a Children's Picture Book
To stimulate new work from young illustrators in British art schools and to help them start their professional lives. The competition is open to all students in British art schools who have not published a book. Monetary prizes of £1,000, £500, and £250 are awarded respectively. Pan Macmillan Children's Books reserves the option to publish any of the prize winners. Awarded annually. Established in 1985.

3758
Pan Macmillan School Library Award
To recognize the school making the best use of its book resources across the curriculum. Open to all infant, primary, junior, middle and lower secondary schools. The first prize is £5,000 worth of Pan Macmillan books, with £500 worth of books for each category winner. Awarded biennially. Established in 1989. (Discontinued)

3759
Parker Harris and Company
30 Trigon Rd.
London SW8 1NH, England
Phone: 71 7930373
Fax: 71 7357433

3760
Hunting/*Observer* Art Prizes
Annual open exhibition open to all artists resident in the U.K. Monetary prizes totaling £20,500 are awarded annually. Established in 1980. Sponsored by Hunting Group Plc. Formerly: (1990) Hunting Group Art Prizes.

3761
Partitioning & Interiors Association
Jago House
692 Warwick Rd.
Solihull, W. Midlands B91 3DX, England
Phone: 21 705 9270
Fax: 21 711 2892

Formerly: Partitioning Industry Association.

3762
Contractors' Award
To encourage professional and first-class workmanship by contractors. Association members may apply by submitting descriptions of jobs completed between May 31 of the previous year and June 1 of the current year. Plaques are awarded in four categories: (1) for projects above £20,000; (2) for projects below £20,000; (3) sliding/folding and operable wall systems; and (4) office interiors (including partitioning, suspended ceilings, etc.). Presentations are made annually at the weekend conference. Established in 1980.

3763
Patrons of New Art
Friends of The Tate Gallery
Tate Gallery
Millbank
London SW1P 4RG, England
Phone: 887 8000

3764
Turner Prize
To recognize a British artist under 50 years of age for an outstanding exhibition or other presentation of work in the previous twelve months. Individuals may be nominated by a designated date in June of each year to the Director of the Tate Gallery. A monetary prize of £20,000 is awarded annually by the Turner Prize Jury (who vary each year). The award, given under the auspices of the Patrons of New Art, a group within the Tate Gallery Foundation, is made at a special reception each November. Established in 1984 and supported by an anonymous benefactor and member of the Patrons of New Art for the first three years, it was sponsored by Drexel Burnham Lambert from 1987-89, suspended in 1990, and resumed in 1991 with sponsorship from Channel 4 Television who doubled the prize money from £10,000 to £20,000.

3765
J. W. Pearce - Kirklees Trust
Mrs. Sunderland Musical Competition
23 Station Rd., Shepley
Huddersfield HD8 8DG, England
Phone: 484 602334

3766
J. W. Pearce - Kirklees Prize
To assist and recognize young people planning professional careers in music, in any area. A monetary prize of £600, a trophy, and concert engagements were awarded annually in February. The winner was known as the Kirklees Young Musician of the Year. Established in 1948 by Mr. J.W. Pearce, a resident and musician of Huddersfield. Sponsored by the Mrs. Sunderland Musical Competition, the competitive music festival in Huddersfield. (Discontinued in 1992)

3767
Performing Right Society
Administrator
29/33 Berners St.
London W1P 4AA, England
Phone: 71 580 5544
Fax: 71 927 8296

3768
Leslie Boosey Award
To recognize an individual - not primarily a composer, conductor or solist - who has made an outstanding contribution to the furtherance of contemporary music and, in particular, British music. A bronze trophy specially commissioned from the distinguished sculptress Dame Elisabeth Frink is held for two years by the recipient, who also receives a medallion to keep. Awarded biennially. Established in 1980 to honor Leslie Boosey, President of Honour who died in 1979 at the age of 92. Additional information is available from Miss Terri Anderson, PRS Public Affairs Controllers, telephone: 71 927 8272.

3769
Vivian Ellis Prize
To encourage young writers for the musical stage. Writers under 35 years of age who are normally resident in the United Kingdom and the Republic of Ireland for the past three years are eligible. A monetary prize of £1,000 and exposure to leading figures in the world of the musical theatre are awarded annually. Established in 1985 on the occasion of the 80th birthday of Vivian Ellis, CBE President of the Society. Additional information is available from: The Administrator of the Vivian Ellis Prize, telephone: 71 927 8286.

3770
PRS Enterprise Awards
To recognize choirs, orchestral, and concert societies that demonstrate enterprise in their programming of copyright music throughout their concert programs. Entries are judged by a joint panel of PRS and the National Federation of Music Societies. Programs that contain a good amount of contemporary and twentieth century music, particularly works still in copyright (i.e., by living composers or by composers whose death occurred not more than fifty years ago) are considered. The number and size of the Awards are determined in light of the applications received. Established in 1985. Additional information is available from: Miss Terri Anderson, PRS Public Affairs Controller, telephone: 71 927 8272. Formerly: PRS Awards for Choral Enterprise.

3771
Periodical Publishers Association
Imperial House
15-19 Kingsway
London WC2B 6UN, England
Phone: 71 3796268
Fax: 71 3795661

3772
British Society of Magazine Editors Awards
To honor those who have shown outstanding editing skills during the year. Any editor of a British magazine that is published at least four times per year is eligible. Awards are presented annually for Editors of the Year and Editor's Editor of the Year in the following categories: women's magazines (weekly), women's magazines (monthly), business-to-business magazines, contract magazines, special interest magazines (weekly), special interest magazines (nonweekly), general interest magazines (weekly), general interest magazines (nonweekly), and supplements. The Mark Boxer Award for editorial excellence is awarded annually to a journalist or designer who has made an outstanding contribution to the magazine industry. The deadline for entries is September 22.

3773
Innovation Writer of the Year
To highlight, reward, and encourage coverage by business press titles of the best of British innovation. Awards will be made to the writer or writers of articles that have successfully highlighted ideas, concepts, or discoveries whose commercial exploitation has added value to an institution or company and enhanced prospects for UK enterprise as a whole. The

Writer of the Year will be awarded a check for £3,000 and the editor of the winning title will be awarded a check for £2,000. The deadline for entry is October 15. Co-sponsored by the British Business Press and the Department of Trade and Industry.

3774

PPA Magazines Awards for Editorial and Publishing Excellence
To recognize outstanding achievement through editorial and publishing excellence over the last year. Awards are presented in the following categories: Designer of the Year (Consumer Magazines), Designer of the Year (Business and Professional Magazines), Columnist of the Year (Consumer Magazines), Columnist of the Year (Business and Professional Magazines), Writer of the Year (Consumer Magazines), Writer of the Year (Business and Professional Magazines), Publisher of the Year (Companies with less than 25 employees), Publisher of the Year (Consumer Magazines), Publisher of the Year (Business and Professional Magazines), Editor of the Year (Consumer Magazines), Editor of the Year (Business and Professional Magazines), Editorial Campaign of the Year, International Magazine of the Year (Business and Professional Magazines), International Magazine of the Year (Consumer Magazines), Customer Magazine of the Year, Consumer Specialist Magazine of the Year, Business and Professional Magazine of the Year, and Consumer Magazine of the Year. Trophies are awarded to the winner in each category and certificates are awarded to runners up. Established in 1979.

3775

PPA Subscription Awards
To recognize the increasing importance of subscriptions in the sales of UK magazines and to recognize those companies actively participating in subscription promotion campaigns. Awards are given for work originally published for and addressing the UK market, regardless of where the publication originated. The following awards are presented: Direct Mail Package - Consumer, Direct Mail Package - Business, International Direct Mail Package, In-Magazine Promotion, Renewal Series, and New Launch Promotion. The deadline for entries is September 10. Co-sponsored by Royal Mail Streamline and Royal Mail International. Established in 1993.

3776

Perkins Engines Limited
Frank Perkins Way, Eastfield
Peterborough, Cambs., England
Phone: 733 67474
Fax: 733 582240

3777

Perkins Power Award
For recognition of the best articles by members of the Guild of Agricultural Journalists based in the United Kingdom on the subject of power in agriculture. Monetary prizes of £1,100 are awarded annually. Established in 1972. The award is organized by the Guild of Agricultural Journalists of the United Kingdom.

3778

Pfizer Limited
Ramsgate Rd.
Sandwich, Kent, England
Phone: 304 616161

3779

Pfizer Academic Awards
To support young scientists who have carried out meritorious research at British universities or equivalent institutions. The research should have potential application in the search for human or animal health medicines. Awards are presented in the following categories: Chemistry, Pharmaceutical Sciences, Biology, and Animal Health Research. Individuals are selected on the merit of their work published in the previous two years or, in the case of a second consecutive award, in the previous twelve months. Applications are not accepted. Monetary awards of £6,000 each are presented for the personal use of the recipients to further their research. Established in 1983.

3780

Philatelic Traders' Society
c/o Stampex Limited
107 Charterhouse St.
London EC1M 6PT, England
Phone: 71 4901005
Fax: 71 2530414

3781

Stampex Exhibition Awards
To recognize outstanding philatelic exhibits at the annual Stampex Exhibition. Two main classes of awards are presented: International Class: Prix d'Honneur - Harmers Diamond Jubilee Trophy and R.A.G. Lee International Award; and National Classes: Silver Mailcoach, National Philatelic Society Queen Elizabeth II Silver Jubilee Trophy, Post Office Trophy, National Postal Museum Medal, Phillips Trophy, P.T.S. Trophy, Urch Harris Trophy, Stanley Gibbons Cup, Ebby Gerrish Trophy, Argyll Postal History Salver, Postal History Award, Cinderella Stamp Club Trophy, Link House Thematic Trophy, Aerophilatelic Class Award, British Aerophilatelic Federation Award, Albert H. Harris Literature Award, Francis Webb Memorial Trophy, B.P.E. Inter-Federation Award, William Ferris Bowl, British Caribbean Philatelic Study Group Award, H.L. Katcher Helvetia Trophy, and Jack Grumbridge Pacific Island Trophy.

3782

Photogrammetric Society
Dept. of Photogrammetry and Surveying
Univ. College London
Gower St.
London WC1E 6BT, England
Phone: 71 387 7050
Fax: 71 380 0453

3783

President's Medal
For recognition of services to photogrammetry in the United Kingdom and to the Society. A medal and an inscription of the winner's name on the Honors Board are awarded biennially at the annual general meeting in November. Established in 1954.

3784

President's Prize
To recognize the originality of the content and value to photogrammetry of a paper published in The Photogrammetric Record in the preceding two-year period up to and including April of the year in which the award is to be made. Contributors to The Photogrammetric Record (except previous winners, winners of the President's Medal, members of council, editor and assistant editor, and invited contributors from overseas) are eligible. A monetary prize and a certificate are awarded biennially at the annual general meeting in November. Established in 1954.

3785

Plain English Campaign
New Mills
PO Box 3
Stockport SK12 4QP, England
Phone: 663 744409
Fax: 663 747038

3786

Plain English Award
To promote the use of plain English and clear layout in forms, leaflets, and consumer agreements, and to recognize the worst and the best in official writing. Awards are presented to the three senders of the worst gobbledegook. Recognition is also given in the following categories to the examples of good plain English: money, public utilities, government departments, and health and health education.

3787

Player Piano Group
93 Evelyn Ave
Ruislip HA4 8AN, England
Phone: 89 5634288

3788
Honorary Member and Honorary Associate
To recognize individuals who have contributed to the group. An honorary membership or associateship is awarded irregularly. Established in 1960.

3789
The Poetry Society
22 Betterton Street
London WC2H 9BU, England
Phone: 71 2404810
Fax: 71 2404818

3790
Alice Hunt Bartlett Prize
To recognize a young or emerging poet for a volume of poetry comprising not less than 20 poems or 400 lines. If the poems were translated into the English language, the prize was then equally divided between the poet and the translator. A monetary prize of £500 was awarded annually. Established in 1966 by Alice Hunt Bartlett. (Temporarily discontinued)

3791
European Poetry Translation Prize
For recognition of a book of poems in translation of poetry from any European language into English. Works nominated must have been published within one year prior to the award. A monetary prize of £750 is awarded biennially. Established in 1983 by Mihail Popescu of Romania in memory of his son, Corneliu M. Popescu, a young poet and translator who died in the 1977 Romanian earthquake at the age of 17. (Temporarily discontinued)

3792
National Poetry Competition
For recognition of an outstanding unpublished poem. Individuals over 16 years of age who live anywhere are eligible. Entries must be submitted October/November. A monetary prize of £3,000 (1st), £500 (2nd), £250 (3rd), £100 (ten additional awards), ten special commendations, and publication of prizewinning poems in an anthology are awarded annually. Established in 1978. (Temporarily discontinued)

3793
Dylan Thomas Award
To honor the contribution made to English literature by Dylan Thomas and to encourage writers working in the two literary genres of poetry and the short story for which Dylan Thomas' work is celebrated. Awards were given in alternate years in the categories of poetry and short story. A monetary award of £1,000 was presented on October 27, the anniversary of Dylan Thomas' birth. Established in 1983. Sponsored by the Dylan Thomas Memorial Plaque Committee, Harlech Television, the Arts Council of Great Britain, and the Dylan Thomas Society of Wales. (Temporarily Discontinued)

3794
Polish Institute and Sikorski Museum
11 Leopold Rd.
London W5 3PB, England

3795
Awards
For recognition of contributions to the study of the Polish Underground Movement during World War II. Established by the Polish Underground Movement 1939-1945 Study Trust.

3796
Pony Club of Great Britain
British Equestrian Centre,
Stoneleigh
Kenilworth, Warks. CV8 2LR, England
Phone: 203 696697
Fax: 203 692351

3797
Cubitt Award
To recognize individuals for long, devoted, and distinguished service in a voluntary capacity to the Pony Club of Great Britain. Individuals who have served over 15 years, and preferably over 20 years, are eligible. A certificate and a badge are awarded annually at Council meetings. Established in 1988 to honor Colonel C. G. Cubitt, past chairman and president of the Club.

3798
Prehistoric Society
Institute of Archaeology
Univ. College London
31-34 Gordon Sq.
London WC1H OPY, England

Formerly: (1935) Prehistoric Society of East Anglia.

3799
R. M. Baguley Award
For recognition of an archaeological publication. Papers published in the proceedings of the Society are considered. A trophy, donated by R.M. Baguley, is awarded annually. Established in 1979.

3800
Bob Smith Award
To fund research in the field of prehistory. Members must submit applications to the Society's research fund. A monetary award is presented annually in February. Established in 1987 by Dr. G.J. Wainwright in memory of Dr. Bob Smith.

3801
PRO Dogs National Charity
Rocky Bank
4 New Rd.
Ditton, Kent ME20 6AD, England
Phone: 732 848499

3802
PRO Dogs National Charity Open Creative Writing & Photographic Competition
To recognize the Charity, to show the general public that dogs are necessary and useful in our modern stressed society, and to focus attention on the desirability of being a responsible dog owner. Unpublished works may be submitted by October 1. Poem up to 32 lines, stories up to 1,000 words, and black and white or color photographs on any subject are eligible. Monetary prizes totaling £250 are awarded biennially. Special prizes are awarded to the best story or poem about a dog and/or photograph including a dog(s); and for the best story or poem in the under 16-year-old category. Established in 1988 by Michaela Edridge of PRO Dogs.

3803
Professional Cycling Association
30 Windermere Rd.
Wolverhampton, W. Midlands WV6 9DL,
   England
Phone: 902 751831
Fax: 902 756989

3804
Newcomers Award
To recognize the rider acknowledged to be the most consistently placed newcomer (first season) as a new professional. A trophy is awarded. Established in 1984.

3805
Professional of the Year
To recognize the individual with the highest number of cycle race points (top ten placings) as a professional in Great Britain. Members of the

Society are eligible. A monetary award and a trophy are awarded annually. Established in 1984.

3806

Team Champions
To recognize the three members of a professional team aggregating the highest number of points in old domestic professional events only. A trophy is awarded. Established in 1984.

3807

Professional Golfers' Association
National Headquarters
Apollo House
The Belfry
Sutton Coldfield, W. Midlands B76 9PT,
England
Phone: 675 470333
Fax: 675 470674

3808

Lord Derby's Knowsley Safari Park Tournament
To recognize the winner of the annual tournament. Awarded annually. Established in 1985.

3809

National Pro-Am Championship
To recognize the winning team in the National Pro-Am Championship. Established in 1979.

3810

PGA Club Professional Championship
To recognize the winner of the annual PGA Club Professional Championship. Established in 1973.

3811

PGA Cup
To recognize the team winning the biennial competition between the United States and Europe. Established in 1973.

3812

PGA Fourball Championship
To recognize the winner of the Fourball Championship. Established in 1984.

3813

PGA Junior Championship
To recognize the boys' and girls' winners of the Junior Championship. Established in 1979.

3814

PGA National Assistants' Championship
To recognize the winner of the National Assistants' Championship. Awarded annually. Established in 1930.

3815

PGA Pro-Am Matchplay Championship
To recognize the winners of the Pro-Am Matchplay Championship. Teams consist of a professional and amateur golfer. Established in 1988.

3816

PGA Pro-Captain Challenge
To recognize the winning team in the PGA Pro-Captain Challenge. Established in 1993.

3817

PGA Regional Team Championship
To recognize the winner of the PGA Regional Team Championship. Established in 1989.

3818

PGA Seniors' Championship
To recognize the winner of the annual Seniors' Championship. Established in 1957. Sponsored by Forte.

3819

Ryder Cup
To recognize the winner of a biennial professional golf team competition between the United States and Europe. Established in 1927. The cup was donated by Samuel Ryder, a patron of professional golf in England.

3820

Ryle Memorial Medal
To recognize the winner of the British Open Golf Championship. Members of the Professional Golfers' Association are eligible. Awarded annually. Established in 1901.

3821

Braid Taylor Memorial Medal
To recognize the member of the Professional Golfer's Association, born in the United Kingdom or Republic of Ireland or who has one or both parents born in the United Kingdom or Republic of Ireland, who finishes highest in the British Open Golf Championship. Awarded annually. Established in 1966.

3822

Tooting Bec Cup
To recognize the member of the Professional Golfer's Association, born in the United Kingdom or Republic of Ireland or who has one or both parents born in the United Kingdom or Republic of Ireland, who returns the lowest single round score in the British Open Golf Championship. Awarded annually. Established in 1901. From 1901-1922, the Tooting Bec Trophy was contested over 36 holes, prior to its association with the British Open Championship.

3823

Harry Vardon Trophy
To recognize the leader of the Order of Merit. Awarded annually. Established in 1939 to honor Harry Vardon, an internationally famous British golfer.

3824

Whitcombe-Cox Trophy
To recognize the PGA Trainee of the Year who is considered by the examiners to be the best overall candidate in the final examinations. The award was introduced in 1974 and the trophy was commissioned in 1991.

3825

Prudential Awards for the Arts
Kallaway Ltd.
2 Portland Rd., Holland Park
London W11 4LA, England
Phone: 71 221 7883
Fax: 71 229 4595

3826

Prudential Awards for the Arts
To recognize innovation and creativity, coupled with excellence and accessibility by arts organizations in the five fields of dance, music, opera, theatre, and visual arts. Nonprofit UK-based arts organizations may apply by January 31 for these awards, the richest ever annual Awards for the Arts. A monetary award of £25,000 is presented to a winner in each category. An additional grand award of £75,000 is presented to one of the category winners. Award money must be used on the company's artistic program. Established in 1988. Sponsored by Prudential Corporation PLC and presented in association with the Arts Council of Great Britain.

3827
Public Relations Consultants Association
Willow House
Willow Pl., Victoria
London SW1P 1JH, England   Phone: 71 2336026

3828
Awards for Outstanding Consultancy Practice
For recognition of achievement in the field of public relations. Members and associates of the Association are eligible. A certificate is awarded annually. Established in 1987.

3829
Queen's Awards Office
c/o The Secretary
Dean Bradley House
52 Horseferry Rd.   Phone: 71 2222277
London SW1P 2AG, England   Fax: 71 2224707

3830
Queen's Awards for Environmental Achievement
For recognition of a significant advance by British industry in the development of products, technology, or processes that offer major environmental benefits. An award is only made when a product, technology, or process has achieved commercial success. The deadline for applications is October 31 of each year. Winners are formally announced in a supplement to the *London Gazette* on April 21 of the following year. A Grant of Appointment in scroll form and a stainless steel emblem of the award set in an acrylic block are presented at a ceremony by a Lord-Lieutenant on behalf of the Queen. Holders of the award, which is valid for five years from the date of the announcement, are entitled to fly the award flag and display the emblem. Established in 1992.

3831
Queen's Awards for Export Achievement
To recognize a substantial and sustained increase in export earnings to a level that is outstanding for the products or services concerned and for the size of the applicant unit's operations. Figures are required over three consecutive 12-month periods with the last year ending between prescribed dates (December 31, 1993 and October 31, 1994 for the 1995 Awards, for example). The goods must have been shipped or the services supplied. Unfulfilled orders and payments received in advance of shipment must be omitted. Estimated figures are not accepted. Applicants are expected to explain the basis of the achievement, such as improved export sales/marketing organization or new market initiative. Export earnings considered include receipts by the applicant unit in the United Kingdom from the export of goods produced in the United Kingdom, the provision of services to non-residents, merchant profit on re-export of foreign goods and/or on trade arranged between overseas countries, royalties and fees from abroad, and income from direct investments in overseas branches, subsidiaries or associates in the same line of business as the applicant (but not income derived from other overseas investment or interest received on overseas loans or credits). The closing date for receipt of completed applications is October 31 each year. The award winners are formally announced in a supplement to the *London Gazette* on April 21 in the following year. A Grant of Appointment in scroll form and a stainless steel emblem of the award set in an acrylic block are presented at a ceremony by a Lord-Lieutenant on behalf of the Queen. Holders of the award, valid for five years from the date of announcement, are entitled to fly the award flag and display the emblem. Established in 1965.

3832
Queen's Awards for Technological Achievement
For recognition of a significant advance leading to increased efficiency in the application of technology to a production or development process in British industry or the production for sale of goods that incorporates new and advanced technological qualities. An award is made only when there is evidence that an innovation has achieved commercial success. The closing date for receipt of completed applications is October 31 of each year. The award winners are formally announced in a supplement to the *London Gazette* on April 21 in the following year. A Grant of Appointment in scroll form and a stainless steel emblem of the award set in an acrylic block are presented at a ceremony by a Lord-Lieutenant on behalf of the Queen. Holders of the award, which is valid for five years from the date of announcement, are entitled to fly the award flag and display the emblem. Established in 1965.

3833
Racegoers Club
Seddon House
Gas Lane, Station Rd.   Phone: 734 341666
Twyford, Berks. RG10 9LX, England   Fax: 734 343795

3834
National Hunt Champion Award
For recognition of the most outstanding steeplechaser or hurdler of the year. A panel of journalists selects the winner. A bronze statuette sculpted by Jean Walwyn is awarded annually. Established in 1965 by the Racecourse Association which invited The Racegoers Club to take over the award in 1978.

3835
Racehorse of the Year Award
For recognition of the outstanding racehorse of the year. The award originated as a publicity idea designed to stimulate public interest in horseracing. Any horse that has raced on a British racecourse during the year is eligible. A panel of journalists selects the winner. A twelve inch bronze statuette sculpted by Jean Walwyn and entitled "The Winner" is awarded annually. Established in 1965 by the Racecourse Association which invited The Racegoers Club to take over the award in 1978.

3836
Ramsay Memorial Fellowships Trust
Univ. College London
Gower St.   Phone: 71 387 7050
London WC1E 6BT, England   Fax: 71 380 7380

3837
Ramsay Memorial Fellowship for Chemical Research
To enable the holder to devote himself or herself full-time to postdoctoral research in chemistry. Individuals preferably born within the British Commonwealth who graduated with honors in chemistry from a commonwealth university may apply by November 15. A Fellowship, tenable for two years in the United Kingdom, is awarded annually. Established in 1920 in memory of Sir William Ramsay, KCB FRS (1852-1916).

3838
Redditch Music Society
227 Birchfield Rd.
Redditch, Hereford and Worcs. B97 4LX,
    England   Phone: 527 546056

3839
AT&T Istel Young Musicians Awards
To recognize and encourage young people to become professional musicians. The deadline is June 30. A monetary prize and a concert engagement are awarded annually in October. Established in 1988. Sponsored by AT&T and Istel Ltd.

3840
Redland Roof Tiles
Redland House   Phone: 737 242488
Reigate, Surrey RH2 OSJ, England   Fax: 737 240247

3841
Redland Pitched Roof Awards
To recognize and encourage excellence in design and craftmanship in roofing of new and refurbished buildings. The competition is open to architects and roofing contractors who have completed buildings in the preceding two years before the year of the competition. The deadline is June 30. First prize winners receive £2,000, a certificate, and a trophy. Certificates and trophies may be presented in the following areas for commendations: concrete tiles, plain or profiled; clay tiles, plain or profiled; and slate appearance. Craftsman's medals and certificates may be awarded for outstanding worksmanship. Established in 1987.

3842
Remote Sensing Society
Dept. of Geography
Univ. of Nottingham
Nottingham NG7 2RD, England
Phone: 602 587611
Fax: 602 420825

3843
Leonard Curtis European Award
For recognition of distinguished science articles in the field of remote sensing. Awarded annually. Formerly: (1991) Eurosense Award.

3844
Poster Paper Prize
For recognition of the best poster paper presented at the society's annual conference.

3845
President's Award
For recognition of the best oral presentation on a selected theme presented at the society's annual conference.

3846
Remote Sensing Society Medal
This, the highest award of the society, is given for recognition of an outstanding contribution in the field of remote sensing. Awarded annually.

3847
Remote Sensing Society Student Awards
For recognition of the best student dissertation or thesis (one M.S. and one Ph.D.) on a remote-sensing topic. Awarded annually.

3848
Taylor and Francis Best Letter Award
For recognition of the best letter to be published in the *International Journal of Remote Sensing*. Awarded annually.

3849
Reuter Foundation
85 Fleet St.
London EC4P 4AJ, England
Phone: 71 324 7015
Fax: 71 510 8599

3850
Reuter Foundation Fellowship
To aid the media of developing countries by providing opportunities for journalists to study at universities in Europe and the United States. Six or more Reuter Fellowships are offered annually for print and broadcast journalists - three at Oxford University, England; two at Stanford University, California, United States; and one at Bordeaux University, France. Applications may be submitted by January 31 by practicing journalists from countries outside Europe, North America, Japan, Australia and New Zealand. To be eligible, applicants must: (1) be full time journalists employed by newspapers, news agencies, general circulation magazines, radio or television; (2) have had a minimum of five years full time experience with such organizations; (3) be between the ages of 25 and 40; (4) be proficient in English if applying for Oxford or Stanford, or in French, if applying for Bordeaux; and (5) be committed to a career in journalism in the country in which they work. The Reuter Foundation pays the costs of the return fare between the Fellow's home and the University, tuition fees and living expenses. Each Fellowship is tenable for one/two or three academic terms. Fellowship Certificates by the Reuter Foundation are awarded. Established in 1982 by the Reuter Foundation. One of the three fellowships at Oxford is in memory of Najmul Hasan, a Reuter correspondent from India who was killed while covering the Iran/Iraq War in 1983.

3851
Willie Vicoy Reuter Fellowship
To aid photo-journalists and picture editors. Applications may be made by practicing photo-journalists and photographers from countries outside Europe, North America, Japan, Australia and New Zealand. To be eligible, applicants must be: (1) full time photo-journalists/picture editors employed by newspapers, news agencies other than world agencies, general circulation magazines or freelancers who can demonstrate by cuttings regular publication of their work; (2) be proficient in English; (3) have had a minimum of three years professional experience; and (4) be under the age of 35. Entries may be submitted by January 31. One four-month fellowship is awarded annually at the University of Missouri School of Journalism, United States. Established in 1987 in memory of Willie Vicoy, a Reuter photographer from the Philippines who was fatally injured in an ambush in the northern Philippines in 1986.

3852
The Review of Income and Wealth
c/o J. W. Arrowsmith Ltd.
Winterstoke Road
Bristol BS3 2NT, England

3853
John W. Kendrick Prize
For recognition of an outstanding article in the field of economics published in the *Review*. All articles published in the *Review* during the year are eligible. Established by John W. Kendrick, a long-standing member of the IARIW.

3854
Rolls-Royce Enthusiasts Club
The Hunt House
Pulerspiery, Notts. NNI2 7NA, England
Phone: 32 733489
Fax: 32 733797

3855
Rolls-Royce Enthusiasts Awards
To recognize winners of rallies and meets. Twenty separate classes are judged. Rolls-Royce motor cars from 1904 to the present day and Bentleys from 1933 to the present are eligible. Trophies are awarded annually.

3856
Romantic Novelists' Association
Cobble Cottage
129 New St.
Baddesley Ensor
North Atherstone, Warks. CV9 2DL, England
Phone: 827 714776

3857
Netta Muskett Award
To recognize new romance writers for an unpublished full length novel. Probationary members of the RNA who submit full length manuscripts of romantic novels between September 1 and September 30 are eligible. A silver salver to be held for one year is awarded annually in April. Established in 1965 to honor Netta Muskett, a romantic novelist from the 1930s to the 1960s.

3858
Romantic Novel of the Year
For recognition of the best romantic novel, modern or historical, published in English in the United Kingdom during the year. Entries may be submitted from September 1 through November 30. A monetary award is presented annually. Established in 1960. Formerly: (1988) Boots Romantic Novel of the Year.

3859
Routledge
11 New Fetter Ln.
London EC4P 4EE, England
Phone: 71 583 9855
Fax: 71 583 0701

3860
Croom Helm Nursing Prize
To encourage members of the nursing profession to contribute to nursing literature. A monetary prize of £500 was awarded annually for three years. Established in 1987. (Discontinued in 1989)

3861
Routledge Ancient History Prize
For recognition of the best contribution in English to the understanding of the history of the classical world. The prize is intended to attract high quality work from scholars regardless of seniority or standing. The deadline for submissions is August 31. A monetary prize of £500 and publication of the book are awarded annually in November. Established in 1986 by Croom Helm.

3862
Royal Academy of Arts
Burlington House
Piccadilly
London W1V 0DS, England
Phone: 71 4397438
Fax: 71 4340837

3863
Jack Goldhill Award for Sculpture
For recognition of outstanding sculpture in each year's Royal Academy Summer Exhibition. A monetary award of £5,000 is presented. Established by the Jack and Grete Goldhill Charitable Trust.

3864
Royal Academy Summer Exhibition
For recognition of different categories of work exhibited in the Royal Academy's annual Summer Exhibition: an open competition of works featuring painting, sculpture, architecture and engraving, print-making and draftsmanship. A total of £54,000 is awarded in prizes.

3865
Charles Wollaston Award
For recognition of the most distinguished exhibit in the annual Royal Academy Summer Exhibition: an open competition of works featuring painting, sculpture, architecture and engraving, print-making, and draftsmanship. A monetary award of £25,000 is awarded for the most distinguished work in the exhibition. Established in 1977 by Charles Wollaston, Esquire.

3866
Royal Academy of Dancing
36 Battersea Sq.
London SW11 3RA, England
Phone: 71 2230091
Fax: 71 9243129

3867
The Phyllis Bedells Bursary
Available to students worldwide who have completed their Intermediate Executant Examination with either Highly Commended or above. A monetary prize is given. Similar prizes are also given in Australia, New Zealand, and South Africa. Contact local Academy offices in these countries for further details.

3868
The Grace Busustow Award
To recognize a retired teacher of repute and to provide monetary help for retirement. Candidates may be nominated. Established by Dame Margot Fonteyn de Arias after her first teacher.

3869
Adeline Genee Award
This award, the Academy's top student award, is available to students who have gained either their Advanced Executant Examination with Highly Commended or gained the Solo Seal Examination. Following one week of coaching by top teachers at Academy headquarters, students must then pass a semi-final to take part in public finals, which are held at a London theatre. A monetary prize is awarded to help students continue their dance education.

3870
The President's Award
To honor any individual from anywhere throughout the world who has given dedicated service to the Academy. Nominations should be sent to the Development Committee. Established in 1992 by the Academy's President, Antoinette Sibley.

3871
Queen Elizabeth II Coronation Award
To recognize an individual who has made a significant contribution to British ballet. A plaque is awarded annually. Established in 1954 by Dame Adeline Genee, founding president of the Royal Academy of Dancing in honor of Her Majesty, Queen Elizabeth II, who succeeded her grandmother, Queen Mary, as Patron of the Academy.

3872
Royal Academy of Dramatic Art
62-64 Gower St.
London WC1E 6ED, England
Phone: 71 636 7076
Fax: 71 323 3865

3873
Bancroft Gold Medal
For recognition of outstanding acting talent. A gold medal with an effigy of Shakespeare was awarded annually. Established in 1904 by Sir Squire Bancroft, actor and manager. (Discontinued in 1988)

3874
Royal Academy of Engineering
MacRobert Award Admin.
29 Great Peter St.
London SW1P 3LW, England
Phone: 71 222 2688
Fax: 71 233 0054

Formerly: Fellowship of Engineering.

3875
MacRobert Award
For recognition of an outstanding contribution by way of innovation in engineering or the physical technologies, or in the application of the physical sciences which is or will be for the benefit of the community. Entries should be submitted by March 31. A monetary prize of £50,000 and a gold medal are awarded annually. Established in 1968 by the MacRobert Trusts which were founded by Lady MacRobert of Douneside and Cromar, wife of Sir Alexander MacRobert, head of the British India Corporation.

3876
Royal Academy of Music
Marylebone Rd.
London NW1 5HT, England
Phone: 71 9355461
Fax: 71 4873342

3877

Honorary Member

To recognize an individual for outstanding contributions to the Academy and to music.

3878

Queen's Commendation for Excellence

This, the highest award of the Academy, is given to recognize the best all-around student of the year at the Royal Academy of Music. Awarded annually as a gift of Her Majesty the Queen, Patron of the Royal Academy of Music. In addition, numerous other awards are presented by the Academy at the annual graduation ceremony.

3879

Royal Aeronautical Society
4 Hamilton Pl.
London W1V 0BQ, England

Phone: 71 4993515
Fax: 71 4996230

3880

Peter Allard Silver Medal

To recognize practical achievement leading to the use of composite materials in aerospace. Established in 1992. Sponsored by the Pete Allard Charitable Foundation and presented by Ricardo Graph, plc.

3881

R. P. Alston Medal

For recognition of practical achievement associated with the flight testing of aircraft. A medal is awarded annually. Established in 1940 by Mrs. H. G. Alston in memory of her husband, Peter Alston, who was killed in a flying accident in 1939. The award was originally intended for work aiming at the improvement of the safety of aircraft, particularly in stability and control.

3882

Buchanan Barbour Award

To recognize outstanding achievement in civil or military aerospace medicine.

3883

British Bronze Medal

For recognition of a practical contribution to the professsion of aerospace. Established in 1989.

3884

British Gold Medal

For recognition of outstanding practical achievement leading to advancement in aeronautics. A gold medal is awarded annually. Established in 1933. The medal commemorates Sir George Cayley and his first model aeroplane of 1804.

3885

British Silver Medal

For recognition of practical achievement leading to advancement in aeronautics. A silver medal is awarded annually. Established in 1933. The medal commemorates the Henson machine of 1842 and the Stringfellow model of 1848.

3886

John Britten Prize

To recognize the best paper on light aviation published by the Society.

3887

Sir Vernon Brown Prize

To recognize the best paper on aircraft maintenance published by the Society.

3888

Busk Prize

For recognition of the best paper on aerodynamics (including flight testing) published by the Royal Aeronautical Society. Awarded annually.

3889

J. R. Cooper Prize

To assist young people with interests in future aerospace technologies with the extension, in the broadest sense, of their education and experience. Individuals between 18 and 40 years of age are eligible.

3890

Sir Roy Fedden Award

For recognition of a paper that has been written or innovative work carried out in the field of aerospace propulsion. Younger persons who are not yet recognized authorities in the subject are eligible, with the object of encouraging them in their career. Topical subjects of importance such as noise attenuation and fuel economy are considered suitable. An honorarium is awarded irregularly.

3891

Flight Simulation Silver Medal

To recognize an individual for achievement in the field of flight simulation. A medal is awarded annually. Established in 1991.

3892

Hafner VTOL Prize

To recognize the best paper on VTOL Technology by an individual under 30 years old.

3893

Hodgson Prize

For recognition of the best paper on general subjects, such as policy, law, operations, management, education, and history, published by the Society.

3894

Herbert Le Sueur Award

To assist a student or graduate member where studies or experience will be enhanced by attending the European Rotorcraft Forum or similar event.

3895

Alan Marsh Award

To recognize technical promise in the rotary winds field. Established in in memory of Squadron Leader Henry Alan Marsh, AFC.

3896

Alan Marsh Medal

For recognition of outstanding helicopter pilotage achievement. British pilots are eligible. A medal is awarded annually. Established by the Helicopter Association of Great Britain (now the Rotorcraft Section of the Society) in 1955 to commemorate the work of Henry Alan Marsh, the outstanding test pilot who was killed in 1950 while flying the Cierva Air Horse, at that time the largest helicopter to be built in the United Kingdom.

3897

Handley Page Award

For recognition of original work leading to advancement and progress in the art and science of aeronautics, with special reference to the practical application of a device, or the long-term implications of a new concept, directed towards the safety of those who work with aircraft or travel in aircraft. Only citizens of the British Commonwealth who are engaged in work preferably within the Commonwealth are eligible. A monetary prize that may be used to finance the proposed work through the provision of facilities, equipment, travel expenses, and any such means of furthering the proposal is awarded. Established in memory of the late Sir Frederick Handley Page, in recognition of his contributions to aviation.

3898
Pardoe Space Award
To recognize a significant contribution to space.

3899
Pilcher-Usborne
To recognize papers that have been either read to the graduates, young technicians and students sections or sub-sections or at branches by graduates, young technicians, students, or associate members under the age of 30. Publications are considered if no spoken papers are submitted.

3900
Presidential Sword
To recognize a member for outstanding services to the Society.

3901
R38 Memorial Prize
To recognize a paper or work on airships.

3902
Frank Radcliffe Travelling Fellowship
The Travelling Fellowship in Reliability and Quality Assurance in aerospace enables lecturer to give a presentation at all 16 universities and polytechnics in the United Kingdom with aeronautical engineering courses.

3903
N. E. Rowe Medals
For recognition of the best lecture given before any branch of the Society by a young member of a branch, or of the graduate, young technician, and students section or its sub-sections. The award was instituted to encourage the younger members of the branches. Awards are given to individuals in two age categories: between 23 and 27 years of age and under 23 years of age. Medals are awarded annually. Established in 1956.

3904
Royal Aeronautical Society Bronze Medal
For recognition of a work leading to an advance in aerospace. A bronze medal is awarded annually. Established in 1908.

3905
Royal Aeronautical Society Companion
This, the Society's highest award to members and nonmembers, is given for recognition of continued service to the profession of aerospace. Awarded when merited to not more than two individuals. Established in 1950. Formerly: (1975) Honorary Companion.

3906
Royal Aeronautical Society Gold Medal
To recognize an individual for work of an outstanding nature in aerospace. A gold medal is awarded annually. Established in 1909.

3907
Royal Aeronautical Society Honorary Fellow
This, the greatest distinction of the Society, is given for long and distinguished contributions to aerospace. Awarded annually to not more than three individuals. In addition, the council may invite two individuals who have rendered important service to the profession of aeronautics to become Companions. Established in 1920.

3908
Royal Aeronautical Society Silver Medal
To recognize work contributing to major advances in aerospace. A silver medal is awarded annually. Established in 1909.

3909
Silver Turnbuckle
To recognize long and valued service in the field of aircraft maintenance.

3910
Simms Prize
For recognition of the best paper on electrical, electronic, and other systems (including the ground environment) published by the Royal Aeronautical Society.

3911
Akroyd Stuart Prize
For recognition of the best paper on propulsion published by the Society.

3912
George Taylor (of Australia) Prize
For recognition of the best paper on design, construction, production, and fabrication (including structures and materials) published by the Society. Awarded annually.

3913
B. W. O. Townshend Award
To recognize a paper or device contributing to escape, survival from an aircraft and search, and rescue at sea.

3914
Wakefield Gold Medal
For recognition of contributions towards safety in aerospace. A gold medal is awarded irregularly. Established in 1926 by Castrol Limited in memory of the company's founder, Viscount Wakefield of Hythe.

3915
Wilbur and Orville Wright Memorial Lecture
For recognition of distinguished contributions to the field of aeronautics. The lecture has become one of the most important in aviation and has been given by men distinguished in aeronautics in both Great Britain and the United States. An invitation to deliver the Wright Memorial Lecture is awarded annually. Established in 1912.

3916
Royal Agricultural Society of England
National Agricultural Centre
Stoneleigh
Kenilworth, Warks. CV8 2LZ, England
Phone: 203 696969
Fax: 203 696900

3917
Bledisloe Gold Medal for Landowners
For recognition of distinguished service in encouraging the application of science and technology to some branch of British animal husbandry. Landowners are eligible. A gold medal is awarded, usually annually, at the Royal International Agricultural Show. Established in 1957 by the First Viscount Bledisloe.

3918
Bledisloe Veterinary Award
For recognition of an effective contribution to animal health. The selection of candidates is made by a Committee comprised of representatives of the Royal Veterinary College, the Royal College of Veterinary Surgeons and the Royal Agricultural Society of England. A silver medal is awarded, usually annually, at the Royal Show. Established in 1946.

3919
Sir Roland Burke Trophy
To recognize a British manufacturer of agricultural implements or machines that has made an outstanding impact on farming generally or on a particular branch of agriculture or horticulture. British manufacturers are eligible. A trophy is awarded annually at the Royal Show. Established in 1970. Formerly: (1981) Burke Perpetual Challenge Trophy.

3920
Gold Medal for Distinguished Services to Agriculture
For distinguished services to agriculture either in practice or in science. A gold medal and honorary membership in the Society are awarded annually when merited. Established in 1933.

3921
Honorary Fellow
To recognize individuals for outstanding contributions to the agricultural industry.

3922
Machinery Award Scheme
To assist potential users of equipment by identifying machines that meet the judging criteria as soon as can safely be done. The secondary aim is to assist manufacturers to develop and make widely known that good new equipment has been independently assessed in field conditions. Entries for the Society's Machinery Awards must be complete machines, appliances, or important ancillary equipment which significantly contributes to performance or economy. The equipment should have a definite application to agriculture, horticulture, forestry or estate services. The equipment must be commercially available. The following criteria are considered: (1) fulfillment of some purpose of value for which no other machine or appliance has been available heretofore; (2) embodiment, with consequent advantage, of some new or substantially improved principle of working; (3) a method of construction and/or use of material or component which gives an improved technical performance; and (4) performance which shows a significant advance over current practice in productivity of labor or overall economics of use. A very high standard is maintained for the Award of a Silver Medal. Entries of high merit which in the opinion of the Judging Panel do not quite attain that standard may be given the RASE Award of Merit. The Society's Gold Medal (Machinery) may be awarded to a Silver Medal winner whose entry, in the opinion of the Judges, is of outstanding merit. Eligible entries include medal winners from both the November and May lists immediately proceeding each Royal Show. Established in 1840.

3923
Research Medal for Research Work of Benefit to Agriculture
For recognition of outstanding research work, carried out in the United Kingdom, which has proved, or was likely to be of benefit to agriculture. Workers actually engaged in active research are eligible. A monetary award of 300 guineas and a medal are awarded annually when merited at the Royal Show. Established in 1954.

3924
Technology Award
For recognition of technological innovation now proven in the field in the areas of livestock production, crop production and agricultural mechanization in the commercial sector. Awards are given in alternate years in the following categories: (1) Livestock; (2) Crop Production; and (3) Agricultural Engineering. Any United Kingdom company is eligible. A monetary prize of 300 guineas and a medal are awarded annually at the Royal Show. Established in 1985.

3925
Royal Anthropological Institute of Great Britain and Ireland
50 Fitzroy St.
London W1P 5HS, England
Phone: 71 387 0455
Fax: 71 383 4235

3926
Curl Bequest Prize
For recognition of the best essay not exceeding 10,000 words relating to the results or analysis of anthropological work. Anthropologists of any nationality may submit applications by September 30. A monetary prize of £1,100 is awarded annually. Established in 1951.

3927
J. B. Donne Essay Prize on the Anthropology of Art
To recognize an essay on any aspect of the anthropology of art, including the visual and performing arts. The essay must be unpublished, 10,000 words or less, and available for publication by the institute. A monetary prize of approximately £500 is awarded biennially.

3928
Arthur Maurice Hocart Prize
For recognition of an unpublished essay not exceeding 10,000 words on an anthropological subject. Students of any nationality studying at a university of higher education in the British Isles are eligible. A monetary prize of £150 is awarded triennially. Established in 1948 by Mrs. E.G. Hocart in memory of her husband, Arthur Maurice Hocart.

3929
Huxley Memorial Medal and Lecture
This, the highest honor awarded by the Institute, is given for recognition of outstanding contributions to anthropology. Scientists of any nationality are eligible. A medal and lectureship are awarded annually. Established in 1900 in memory of Thomas Henry Huxley.

3930
Amaury Talbot Prize for African Anthropology
For recognition of the most valuable work of anthropological research published during the preceding calendar year. Preference is given to first works relating to Nigeria, and then to any other part of West Africa or West Africa in general, although works relating to other regions of Africa may also be considered. A monetary prize of approximately £400 is awarded annually. Additional information is available from Barclay's Bank Ltd, Trustee Department, Radbroke Hall, Knutsford, Cheshire WA16 9EU, England.

3931
Wellcome Medal for Anthropological Research as applied to Medical Problems
To encourage the development of medical anthropology through recognition of an outstanding published work. Nominations or applications are accepted. Candidates in the early part of their careers are considered more favorably. A bronze medal and £600 are awarded biennially. Established in 1931 by Sir Henry Wellcome. Sponsored by the Wellcome Trust.

3932
Royal Asiatic Society
60 Queen's Gardens
London W2 3AF, England
Phone: 71 724 4742

3933
Burton Memorial Medal
To encourage Oriental studies through travel. Individuals who have travelled in the interests of Oriental scholarship are considered. A medal is presented at intervals of at least three years at the convention. Established in 1923 in memory of Sir Richard Burton, the explorer.

3934
Gold Medal
To recognize outstanding research that is considered to have contributed the most to the advancement of Oriental learning. The research must be published either in books or articles, in English or as Oriental texts with editorial matter in English. A medal is presented at intervals of at least three-years at the convention. An additional special medal was created in 1973 to mark the sesquicentenary year. Established in 1897. The award commemorates the Diamond Jubilee of the Society.

3935
Honorary Fellow
To recognize individuals for outstanding contributions to Oriental scholarship. Awarded when merited. Established in 1954. In addition, Foreign Extraordinary Fellows and Fellows Honoris Causa may be selected.

3936
Royal Astronomical Society
Burlington House
Piccadilly
London W1V ONL, England
Phone: 71 734 4582
Fax: 71 494 0166

3937
Chapman Medal
For recognition of specific investigations of outstanding merit in the fields of geophysics and planetary science. A medal is awarded at intervals of not less than three years. Established in 1973 to honor Professor Sidney Chapman.

3938
Eddington Medal
To recognize specific investigations of outstanding merit in the field of theoretical astronomy, especially those branches in which Eddington worked. A medal is awarded at intervals of not less than three years. Established in 1953 to honor Sir Arthur Stanley Eddington.

3939
Gold Medal
To recognize outstanding contributions to astronomy and geophysics. A medal is presented annually. Not more than one medal in the field of astronomy (excluding planetary science), and one in the field of geophysics and planetary science may be awarded in one year. Established in 1824.

3940
Herschel Medal
To recognize specific investigations of outstanding merit in those branches of astronomy not included in the fields of interest of the Eddington and Chapman medals. A medal is awarded at intervals of not less than three years. Established in 1974 to honor Sir William Herschel.

3941
Hannah Jackson (nee Gwilt) Gift and Medal
For recognition of the invention or improvement of any astronomical instrument, of outstanding observational work, or of the promotion in any other way of the science of astronomy. A monetary award and a bronze medal are presented at intervals of not less than three, nor more than seven, years. Established in 1897 to honor Mrs. Hannah Gwilt Jackson.

3942
Price Medal
To recognize specific work in the fields of geomagnetism and aeronomy. Awarded triennially. Established in 1993 to honor Professor Albert Thomas Price.

3943
Royal Automobile Club
89, Pall Mall
London SW1Y 5HS, England
Phone: 71 930 2345
Fax: 71 976 1086

3944
Segrave Trophy
To recognize the British subject who accomplishes the most outstanding demonstration of the possibilities of transport by land, sea or air. A trophy is awarded annually. Established in 1930 by Segrave Trustees in memory of Sir Henry Segrave, a racing driver. Sponsored by Ford Motor Company.

3945
Royal Bath and West of England Society
The Showground
Shepton Mallet, Somerset BA4 6QN,
England
Phone: 749 823211
Fax: 749 823169

3946
Art Scholarship
To recognize professional artists in the United Kingdom. Individuals between 22 and 35 years of age are eligible. A monetary award of £2,000 is presented biennially.

3947
Royal Bath and West Scholarship Awards (World and European)
To provide funds for travel overseas that enable young people to study their chosen subjects in another country. Projects must be concerned with agriculture, horticulture, forestry, or any form of food production. Individuals between 20 and 35 years of age are preferred for consideration. Financial assistance of £2,500 for World and £1,200 for European is awarded annually. The Wilfrid Cave Scholarship also awards up to £1,200 to enable individuals to make a short visit either in this country or overseas to study a particular system or technique with the broad objective of identifying a low-cost approach to farm production. Established in 1977.

3948
Royal College of Obstetricians and Gynaecologists
27 Sussex Pl.
Regent's Park
London NW1 4RG, England
Phone: 71 2625425
Phone: 71 402 2317

3949
Bernhard Baron Travelling Scholarship in Obstetrics and Gynaecology
To provide funds for short-term travel to expand the applicant's experience in areas where he or she already has experience. Fellows and members of the college may apply. Funds for travel up to £5,000 are awarded biennially. Established in 1953.

3950
Malcolm Black Travel Fellowship
To enable a college member or fellow of up to five years' standing to travel, either to the British Isles or from the British Isles abroad, for a period of time to attend postgraduate training courses or to visit centers of research or particular expertise within the specialty of obstetrics and gynaecology. The fellowship is awarded every three years commencing in 1990. The deadline for application is September 1. Travel and subsistence costs up to a maximum of £1,000 are awarded triennially. Established in 1987 by Mrs. Mattie Black in memory of her husband, Malcolm Duncan Black, a member of the college in 1935 who was elevated to the fellowship in 1947.

3951
Florence and William Blair-Bell Memorial Fellowship
To support research workers. Members and fellows may apply. The salary of the award holder or qualified technical assistant is awarded annually. Established in 1970 in memory of Florence and William Blair-Bell.

3952
William Blair-Bell Memorial Lectureship in Obstetrics and Gynaecology
To honor members of the Royal College of Obstetricians and Gynaecologists or fellows of not more than two years' standing. Two individuals are selected annually to present lectures on either obstetrics or gynaecology, or closely related subjects. Preference is given to lectures based on original work, particularly in regard to the morphology, physiology, and pathology of the female reproductive organs, but this need not be considered an absolute condition of the appointment, particularly if the alternative be a problem connected with malignant neoplastic disease.

Entries may be submitted by September 1. An honorarium of £200 is awarded for each lecture.

3953

Eden Travelling Fellowship in Obstetrics and Gynaecology
To enable the fellowship holder to visit, for a specified period of time, another department or departments of obstetrics and gynaecology or of closely related disciplines, to gain knowledge and experience in the pursuit of a specific research project. Medical graduates of approved British or Commonwealth Universities of not less than two years' standing are eligible. The deadline is September 1. A monetary award of up to £5,000, according to the project undertaken and the travel expenses involved, is awarded annually. Established in 1967 in honor of Dr. Thomas Watts Eden.

3954

Edgar Research Fellowship
To support research into obstetric and gynaecological conditions, particularly research into chorion carcinoma or other forms of malignant disease. Individuals with high academic standing may apply by January 7. Up to £18,500, depending on the project undertaken, is awarded. Funds for research are usually available annually. Established in 1976.

3955

Edgar Gentilli Prize
For recognition of original work on the cause, nature, recognition, and treatment of any form of cancer of the female genital tract. Every fifth year the award is restricted to chorion carcinoma (next time in 1991). All medical practitioners are eligible. The deadline is September 1. A monetary prize of £400 and a medical book of a value not exceeding £100 are awarded annually. Established in 1960 by the late Mr. and Mrs. Gilbert Edgar.

3956

Green-Armytage and Spackman Travelling Scholarship
To enable scholarship holders to visit centers where similar work to their own is being conducted on some particular aspect of obstetrical or gynaecological practice. Fellows and members of the college may apply. Funds for travel up to £4,000 are awarded triennially. Established in 1969 in honor of Mr. V. B. Green-Armytage and Colonel W. C. Spackman.

3957

Harold Malkin Prize
For recognition of the best original work of an individual while holding a registrar or senior registrar post in a hospital in the United Kingdom or the Republic of Ireland. Candidates for or holders of membership in the Royal College of Obstetricians and Gynaecologists are eligible. The deadline is September 1. A monetary prize of £200 is awarded annually. Established in 1971 by the late Harold Malkin.

3958

Royal College of Psychiatrists
17 Belgrave Sq. Phone: 71 235 2351
London SW1X 8PG, England Fax: 71 245 1231

3959

Natalie Cobbing Travelling Fellowship (Psychiatry of Mental Handicap)
To further the training of specialists in the branch of psychiatry of mental handicap by enabling them to extend their experience with travel to appropriate centers overseas. All applicants must possess the MRCPsych; must be working in the United Kingdom or Republic of Ireland; and must be under the age of 40. Entries may be submitted by May 31. A fellowship of £2,000 is awarded biennially.

3960

Philip Davis Prize in Old Age Psychiatry
For recognition of an essay, between 4,000 and 6,000 words, on a broadly-based clinical topic relating to the care of the elderly mentally ill. Only members or inceptors of the college below the rank of consultant psychiatrist or the equivalent are eligible. A monetary prize of £300 is awarded annually. The deadline is April 30. Established in 1991 in honor of the late Dr. Philip R. H. Davis.

3961

Gaskell Medal and Prize
To recognize individuals who have been qualified medical officers in one or more mental hospitals or clinics in psychiatry in the United Kingdom or elsewhere in the British Commonwealth for at least two years, and have passed the MRCPsych examination or possess any other degree or diploma in psychological medicine. This prize is considered to be one of the most prestigious in the field of clinical psychiatry. Candidates must be over 23 and under 35 years of age on January 1 of the year of the examination. Entries may be submitted by March 31. The examination includes a written paper, a clinical and an oral. A monetary prize of £500 and a medal are awarded annually. Established in 1886 in honor of Samuel Gaskell, Medical Superintendent of the County Asylum, Lancaster.

3962

Laughlin Prize
To recognize the candidate who obtains the highest marks and the best recommendation from the examiners in the MRCPsych Examinations. A monetary prize of £250 is awarded twice a year after the spring and autumn examinations. Established in 1979.

3963

Lilly Travelling Fellowships
To enable members of the College working in the United Kingdom or the Republic of Ireland to travel abroad, to one or two centers, for a period of not less than three months, in pursuit of further study, research or clinical training relevant to the applicant's current interests. Individuals who are of Senior Registrar or Lecturer grade or equivalent, or Consultants within three years of their first Consultant appointment are eligible. Applications may be submitted by April 30. A fellowship of £7,750 is awarded.

3964

Morris Markowe Public Education Prize
For recognition of an article on a psychiatric topic of approximately 1,000 words, suitable for publication in a regional newspaper, lay journal, the paramedical press, or a general practitioners' magazine. The article must not have been previously published at the time of submission. Only members or inceptors of the college below the rank of consultant of equivalent are eligible. A monetary prize of £200 is awarded annually. Entries should be submitted to Professor B. Pitt, Public Education Officer, by May 1 of each year. Established in 1989 in memory of Dr. Morris Markowe, Honorary Fellow and Registrar of the Royal College of Psychiatrists from 1972-78.

3965

Brian Oliver Prize in the Psychiatry of Learning Disabilities
Recognition for research in the psychiatry of learning disabilities. Applicants may be trainees or consultants in psychiatry. Submissions may take the form of an original piece of work or a literature review and may be presented in the form of an essay or dissertation. The application deadline is March 31. A monetary prize of £500 is awarded annually. Established in 1991 in memory of the late Dr. Brian Oliver, who was Honorary Secretary of the Mental Handicap Psychiatry Specialist Advisory Committee.

3966

Gillian Page Prize in Adolescent Psychiatry
To recognize an original piece of work in the field of adolescent psychiatry. A monetary prize of £500 was awarded. Established in 1986. (Discontinued in 1994).

3967

President's Essay Prize
To recognize the winner of this essay contest. Applicants may submit a 2,000-3,000 word essay on the designated topic, which changes each year. Open to all members or associates of the college without restrictions as to age or seniority. The deadline is March 31. A monetary prize of

£200 is awarded annually. Entries will be assessed for publication in the *British Journal of Psychiatry*.

3968
Research Prize and Bronze Medal
For recognition of research. Members or inceptors of the College below the rank of consultant psychiatrist or equivalent at the time the research is submitted to the Royal College are eligible. Research involving collaboration between workers, whether psychiatrists or in other disciplines, may be submitted, but the prize may be shared between no more than two eligible psychiatrists. The research should be presented in the form of an essay or dissertation with accompanying tables or figures. Entries may be submitted to the Dean by March 31 of each year. A monetary prize of £500 and a bronze medal are awarded annually. Established in 1882.

3969
Peter Scott Memorial Scholarship
To encourage young doctors or medical students to further their studies in the field of forensic psychiatry or delinquency by enabling them to carry out research, to travel, to write, to complete a research project or to suggest any other relevant activity. Any member of the medical profession or a medical student may apply by March 31. A scholarship of up to £1,000 is awarded biennially. Established in memory of Dr. Peter Scott, CBE.

3970
Woodford-Williams Prize
To recognize research in the prevention of dementia. Research involving collaboration may be submitted, but the award may be shared by no more than two eligible applicants. Submissions of recently published essays or dissertations should be between 10,000 and 30,000 words. The deadline is January 31. A monetary award of £300 is presented every three years. Established in 1984 to honor Dr. Eluned Woodford-Williams, CBE, a pioneer of British geriatrics and former Director of the Health Advisory Service. This prize derives from the bequest she made to the College.

3971
Royal College of Radiologists
38 Portland Pl.
London W1N 3DG, England
Phone: 71 6364432
Fax: 71 3233100

3972
Royal College of Radiologists Award
To recognize and advance the science and practice of radiological technology. Awards are advertised annually in July and October.

3973
Royal College of Surgeons of England
35-43 Lincoln's Inn Fields
London WC2A 3PN, England
Phone: 71 4053474
Fax: 71 8319438

3974
Cartwright Prize
For recognition of the best essay written in English on a proposed subject. Candidates must hold dental qualifications capable of registration under the Dental Acts of the Kingdom. An honorarium of £1,000 and a bronze medal are awarded every five years. Established in 1884 by the Association of Surgeons Practising Dental Surgery to commemorate the services of Samuel Cartwright, F.R.C.S., to dentistry.

3975
Colyer Gold Medal
For recognition of liberal acts or distinguished labors, researches, and discoveries eminently conducive to the improvement of natural knowledge and to dental surgery. Established in 1951 by the Faculty of Dental Surgery.

3976
John Hunter Medal and Triennial Prize
For recognition of exceptional work in anatomy, physiology, histology, embryology, or pathological anatomy. Fellows or members of the College are eligible for work accomplished within the preceding ten years. Council members are not eligible. A bronze medal and a certificate are awarded triennially. Established in 1820.

3977
Hunterian Oration
To recognize an individual who will express the merits of the contributions of John Hunter and others to surgical science through their works in the areas of comparative anatomy, physiology, and surgery. Members of the council may be the orators. A medal is awarded biennially. Established in 1813. Formerly: Hunterian Oration and Festival.

3978
Jacksonian Prize
To recognize the author of the best dissertation related to a practical subject in surgery. Candidates must be fellows or members of the College or Fellows in Dental Surgery of the College. Members of the council are not eligible. A monetary prize of £250 and a bronze medal are awarded annually. Established in 1800 by Samuel Jackson, F.R.S., M.R.C.S.

3979
Lister Memorial Medal
For recognition of distinguished contributions to surgical science. Individuals of any nationality are eligible. A bronze medal and £1,000 are awarded every three years. The recipient is required to give an address in London under the auspices of the Royal College of Surgeons. Established by public subscription in memory of the Right Honorable Lord Lister, OM, FRS, FRSC. In 1920, the Lister Memorial Fund was transferred to the College. (This award is currently under review.)

3980
Royal College of Surgeons of England Honorary Medal
For recognition of liberal acts or distinguished labors, researches, and discoveries eminently conducive to the improvement of natural knowledge and of the healing art. Members of the council are not eligible. A gold medal and a record of the award are awarded irregularly. Established in 1802.

3981
Walker Prize
For recognition of the best work during the preceding five years that advances the knowledge of the pathology and therapeutics of cancer. Individuals of any nationality are eligible. Members of the council are not eligible. A monetary prize of £750 and a document declaratory of the award are awarded every five years. Established in 1894 under a trust set up by the late Charles Clement Walker. (This award is currently under review.)

3982
Royal College of Veterinary Surgeons
32 Belgrave Sq.
London SW1X 8QP, England
Phone: 71 235 4971
Fax: 71 245 6100

3983
Robert Daubney Research Fellowship in Virology and Helminthology
To enable the holder to undertake a period of research in the fields of virology and helminthology. The Fellowship is open to any Fellow or member who shows evidence of postgraduate experience in an appropriate field of veterinary science. The value of the fellowship is £10,000 a year and is tenable for a maximum of three years.

3984
DUPHAR Award
To enable research to be undertaken or continued into the nature and/or prevention of disease in domestic animals in the United Kingdom. Any fellow or member of the Royal College of Veterinary Surgeons is eligible. The award consists of a payment of £5,000 per annum payable quarterly in advance. The award is made initially for a period of one year only, but may be renewed for a further year at a time, provided that no person or group of persons receive the award for more than three successive years. Any such renewal is subject to the submission to the Selection SubCommittee of a satisfactory progress report. Established in 1984.

3985
J. T. Edwards Memorial Medal
For recognition of outstanding work in the fields of pathology, bacteriology and virology or, as an alternative, veterinary history. A monetary prize and a medal are awarded at least triennially. Established in 1961 in memory of James Thomas Edwards (1889-1952).

3986
G. Norman Hall Medal for Research into Animal Diseases
To recognize veterinary surgeons for outstanding work. The maximum age of entry for competitors is 45 by July 12 in the year of presentation. A gold medal is awarded triennially. Established in 1969 by a bequest of Dr. George Norman Alfred Hall (1885-1965).

3987
R. W. Hall of Barry, Glamorgan, Prize
To recognize graduate members or fellows of the Royal College of Veterinary Surgeons judged by the council to have made an outstanding contribution in the field of clinical observation and practice among farm animals. A monetary prize is awarded biennially. Established in 1959 by a bequest of Reginald William Hall (1874-1956).

3988
Francis Hogg Prize
To recognize an individual who has done the most serviceable work towards the advancement of small-animal practice. A monetary prize is awarded annually. Established in 1956 by a bequest of Major Francis Hogg.

3989
Livesey Medal
To recognize the individual who has done the most serviceable work towards the prevention and/or alleviation of pain and/or fear in animals. A medal is awarded triennially. Established in 1950 by a bequest of Geoffrey Herbert Livesey (1874-1943).

3990
MacKellar Award
To enable a veterinary surgeon in general practice to pursue a research project or attend a course of further education (or postgraduate training), whether or not it leads to a further qualification. The subject matter of the project of study must be related to general veterinary practice and may be a of a clinical or managerial nature. Awarded annually. Established in 1979 in memory of John Campbell MacKellar.

3991
D. R. Melrose Memorial Trust
To enable graduates to carry out research work into aspects of animal health, production and/or preventative veterinary medicine in cattle, sheep and pigs. Scholarships are normally awarded for a period of up to one year and applications are considered by Trustees after May 31 for the following academic year. Established in 1984 in memory of David Richard Melrose.

3992
Prof. W. M. Mitchell Memorial Fund
To promote, encourage and advance the study and practice of the art and science of veterinary surgery and medicine. Awarded when merited. Established in 1972 in memory of Emeritus Professor William McGregor Mitchell (1903-1971), who was, at the time of his retirement, Director of Education in the Royal (Dick) School of Veterinary Studies of the University of Edinburgh.

3993
Share-Jones Lectureship in Veterinary Anatomy
To invite an individual to lecture on some subject(s) associated with veterinary anatomy in its widest sense. The appointment of the lecturer shall be made by invitations and shall be made every second year by the Council of the college on the recommendation of the Education Committee. The lecturer shall be invited because of his or her special eminence in the subject, or in some aspect of the subject. Awarded biennially. Established in 1956 by a bequest of Prof. John T. Share-Jones (1877-1950).

3994
Sir Frederick Smith and Miss Aleen Cust Research Fellowships of the RCVS
To enable the holder to pursue original research or to prepare for such research in any branch of veterinary science at such place or places as may be approved by the Council. The "Miss Aleen Cust Research Fellowship" is awarded only to a member of the Royal College of Veterinary Surgeons who is a natural born English, Scottish, Welsh or Irish man or woman and, in deciding between such candidates of equal merit, the Council shall give preference to women. Applicants must be nominated by a Professor, Reader or Lecturer of a University or College, or by a Director of a Research Institute, preferably the person who will supervise their work. The Fellowships are £1,000 per annum with up to £200 per annum available for equipment or other expenses arising from the research, including such payment, if any, as may be required in respect of the facilities provided by the university, research institute or other centre where the work is being carried out. Established in 1955.

3995
John Henry Steel Memorial Medal
For recognition of a scientific or literary work of merit connected with the profession. Fellows and members of the Royal College of Veterinary Surgeons are alone eligible for the award. A medal is awarded when merited. Established in 1892 in memory of John Henry Steel (1855-1891), Army Veterinary Department, Principal of the Bombay Veterinary College.

3996
Royal Commonwealth Society
18 Northumberland Ave. Phone: 71 930 6733
London WC2N 5BJ, England Fax: 71 930 9705

3997
Commonwealth Essay Competition
To give young people an opportunity to exercise their intellect and imagination in English, the working language of the Commonwealth. Essay topics are tailored to suit different interests and the four age-groups, and cover social, economic, literary, and development issues in the Commonwealth. Educational trips, cash awards and books are awarded annually. Special prizes are awarded in each age group for handicapped entrants. Established in 1913.

3998
Walter Frewen Lord Prize
To recognize an essay on any aspect of Commonwealth or British Empire history or the history of an individual Commonwealth country. Essays between 15,000 and 40,000 words may be submitted by September 30. A monetary award of at least £300 is presented. Established in 1930 in memory of Walter Frewen Lord, Professor of Modern History at Britain's Durham University and author of several books on the history of the British Empire.

3999
Royal Economic Society
Univ. of York
York YO1 5DD, England
Phone: 71 904433575
Fax: 71 8237685

4000
Royal Economic Society Prize
To recognize the best article published in *The Economic Journal*. Members of the Society may make submissions. A monetary prize of £1,000 is awarded biennially. Established in 1984 and revised in 1989.

4001
Royal Entomological Society of London
41 Queen's Gate
London SW7 5HU, England
Phone: 71 5848361
Fax: 71 5818505

4002
Wigglesworth Medal
For recognition of outstanding contributions to the field of entomology at the international level. Society members make the selection. A silver medal is awarded every five years. Established in 1980 in honor of Professor Sir Vincent Wigglesworth FRS, the first recipient.

4003
Royal Exchange Theatre Company Manchester
St. Ann's Sq.
Manchester M2 7DH, England
Phone: 61 833 9333
Fax: 61 832 0881

4004
Mobil Playwriting Competition for the Royal Exchange Theatre, Manchester
To encourage the writing of new plays by both new and established writers. The competition is open to any author regardless of nationality (or country of residence) for an original full-length play (estimated playing time 100 minutes or longer) written in English and not previously produced or offered for production in any medium. Any play offered elsewhere before the announcement of the results is disqualified. The following monetary prizes are awarded: First Prize - £15,000; Second Prize - £8,000; Third Prize - £3,000; and four special prizes - £1,000 each. The winning play or plays are performed by the Royal Exchange Theatre Company. A Bursary of £10,000 is provided to fund a writer-in-residence for one year at the Royal Exchange Theatre. The Bursary is awarded to one of the winners or to any entrant who shows potential through fresh and vivid writing. Awarded every two to three years. Established in 1984 by the Mobil Oil Company Limited.

4005
Royal Geographical Society
1 Kensington Gore
London SW7 2AR, England
Phone: 71 5895466
Fax: 71 5844447

4006
Back Award
To recognize individuals for scientific geography and discovery. Awarded annually when merited. Established by Admiral Sir George Back.

4007
Busk Medal
To recognize an individual for fieldwork abroad in geography or in a geographical aspect of an allied science. The Medal is granted irrespective of age or nationality. Individuals cannot apply for this medal. A silver medal is awarded annually or at such intervals as the Council may decide.

4008
Founder's Medal
To encourage and promote geographical science and discovery. Individuals cannot apply for this medal. Two gold medals are awarded annually. Established by H. M. King William IV at the foundation of the Society.

4009
Geographical Award
To recognize a company that has provided help for expeditions.

4010
Gill Memorial
For encouragement of geographical research. Awarded annually. Established in 1886 by the gift of Miss Gill.

4011
Edward Heath Award
To recognize contributions to the geography of Europe or the developing world.

4012
Cherry Kearton Medal and Award
To recognize an explorer concerned with the study or practice of natural history, with a preference for those with an interest in nature photography or cinematography. A monetary award and a bronze medal are awarded when merited. Established in 1958 by a bequest of Mrs. Cherry Kearton to honor her late husband, Cherry Kearton.

4013
Murchison Award
To recognize an individual for contributions to geographical science. Monetary awards for individuals to do fieldwork or for authors of memoirs are presented annually. Established by a bequest of Sir Roderick Murchison.

4014
Mrs. Patrick Ness Award
To recognize explorers who have successfully carried out their plans, or to encourage those who wish to pursue or follow up investigations that have been partially completed. Awarded annually. Established in 1953 by Mrs. Patrick Ness.

4015
Patron's Medal
To encourage and promote geographical science and discovery. Individuals cannot apply for this medal. Two gold medals are awarded annually. Established by H. M. King William I on the accession of Queen Victoria.

4016
Cuthbert Peek Award
To assist individuals who are intending to explore a region with the object of extending geographical knowledge. Individuals must have a complete knowledge of field astronomy, exploratory survey, and geology or economic botany. Awarded annually. The award may be given to the same explorer for more than one year.

4017
Victoria Medal
To recognize an individual for conspicuous merit in scientific research in geography. Individuals cannot apply for this medal. Awarded when merited. Established in 1901 to honor Queen Victoria.

4018
Royal Historical Society
Univ. College London
Gower St.
London WC1E 6BT, England
Phone: 71 387 7532
Fax: 71 387 7532

4019
Alexander Prize
To recognize an individual for an essay on any historical subject approved by the Literary Director of the society. The essay must be by an author normally under 35 years of age. Subject to certain exceptions, the essay must be an unpublished work of original research not exceeding 8,000 words including footnotes. Works must be submitted by November 1. A monetary award of £100, a silver medal, and publication of the paper in the society's *Transactions* are awarded annually. Established in 1897 by L.C. Alexander.

4020
David Berry Prize
To recognize an individual for an essay on any subject inclusively dealing with Scottish history within the reigns of James I to James VI. Subjects must be submitted to and approved by the society's council. The essay must be an unpublished work of original research. It should be between 6,000 and 10,000 words in length, and must be submitted by October 31. A monetary prize of £100 is currently awarded triennially. Established in 1929 by David Anderson Berry in memory of his father, the Reverend David Berry.

4021
Whitfield Prize
To provide recognition for the best work within a field of British history. It must be the author's first solely written history book, and be an original and scholarly work of historical research. Books published in the United Kingdom during the preceding year must be submitted to the society by December 31. A monetary prize of £1,000 is awarded annually. Established in 1976 out of the bequest of the late Professor Archibald Stenton Whitfield.

4022
Royal Horticultural Society
Office of the Secretariat
80 Vincent Sq.
London SW1P 2PE, England
Phone: 71 8344333
Fax: 71 6306060

4023
Affiliated Societies' Cup
For recognition of a collection of fruit shown by an affiliated society. Awarded annually. Established in 1908.

4024
Associates of Honour
To recognize an individual for service to the field of horticulture. Individuals of British nationality employed in the field of horticulture are eligible. The number of Associates of Honour may not exceed 100 at any given time. Established in 1930.

4025
Peter Barr Memorial Cup
To recognize an individual who has done good work of some kind in connection with daffodils. Awarded annually. Established in 1912 by the Trustees of the Peter Barr Memorial Fund in commemoration of Peter Barr.

4026
Bowles Cup
For recognition of daffodils shown by amateurs. Three stems of each of fifteen cultivars of daffodils representing not fewer than four Divisions may be shown by an amateur. Awarded annually at the Daffodil Show. Established in 1949 by the late J.L. Richardson.

4027
Stephenson R. Clarke Cup
To recognize an exhibitor in one of the Ornamental Tree and Shrub Competitions. Awarded annually. Established by the late R.N. Stephenson Clarke in 1978 in memory of his grandfather, Stephenson R. Clarke.

4028
Reginald Cory Memorial Cup
To encourage the production of new hardy hybrids of garden origin. A plant which is raised and fulfills the following conditions is eligible: it must be either the result of a deliberate cross which, as far as is known, has not been made before or a new and distinct cultivar resulting from the deliberate repetition of a previously made cross; parent A must be a species or a subspecies; parent B must be either a different species, a subspecies of a different species, a different subspecies of the same species or a hybrid into the parentage of which has entered a species or subspecies different from parent A. The terms species and subspecies include varieties and cultivars of the species and subspecies concerned; it must be a herbaceous perennial, a shrub or a tree, grown for ornament (i.e., excluding fruits and vegetables), and be hardy in the climate of Kew; and it must have received an award at one of the Society's Shows during the current year. A cup is awarded annually. Established in 1962. Formerly: Cory Cup.

4029
Crosfield Cup
For recognition of the best exhibit of one truss of each of six Rhododendron hybrids raised by or in the garden of the exhibitor and shown at the Rhododendron Show. Awarded annually. Established in 1964 by J.J. Crosfield.

4030
Lionel de Rothschild Cup
For recognition of the best exhibit of one truss of each of eight species of Rhododendron. Awarded annually at the Rhododendron Show. Established in 1946.

4031
Devonshire Trophy
For recognition of the best exhibit of twelve daffodil cultivars representing at least three Divisions, one stem of each. Awarded annually at the Daffodil Competition. Established in 1958 by Mary, Duchess of Devonshire in memory of the 10th Duke of Devonshire, a keen daffodil grower.

4032
E. H. Trophy
For recognition of the best exhibit in which carnations or pinks predominate, shown to the Society during the year. Awarded annually. Established in 1961 by the late W.J.M. Hawkey in memory of his grandmother, mother and wife, Mrs. Elizabeth, Mrs. Ellen and Mrs. Emma Hawkey.

4033
Engleheart Cup
For recognition of the best exhibit of one stem daffodils of each twelve cultivars raised by the exhibitor. Awarded annually at the Daffodil Show in April. Established in 1913.

4034
Farrer Trophy
For recognition of the best exhibit of plants suitable for the rock garden or alpine house staged during the year at one of the Society's Shows other than the Chelsea Show. Awarded annually. Established in 1959 in memory of Reginald Farrer (1880-1920), the plant collector and authority on alpine plants.

4035
Foremarke Cup
For recognition of the best exhibit of one spike of each of twelve cultivars of gladioli. The competition is open to trade and amateur growers at the Show in August. Awarded annually. Established by the late Sir Francis Burdett Bt, in 1919.

4036
Gordon-Lennox Cup
For recognition of the best exhibit of fruit or vegetables staged during the year at one of the Society's Shows other than the Chelsea Show. Awarded annually. Established in 1913 by the late Lady Algernon Gordon-Lennox. Up to 1944 usually awarded for the best exhibit of fruit shown by an amateur at the Autumn Fruit and Vegetable Show. From 1945 to 1949 it was not offered. From 1950 to 1971, it was awarded for the best exhibit of fruit shown by an amateur during the year.

4037
Holford Medal
For recognition of the best exhibit of plants and/or flowers (fruit and vegetables excluded) staged during the year by an amateur at one of the Society's Shows other than the Chelsea Show. Awarded annually. Established in 1928 in memory of the late Sir George Holford.

4038
Honorary Fellow
This, the highest honor of the Society, is given for recognition in the field of horticulture. Awarded when merited.

4039
Jones-Bateman Cup
For recognition of original research in fruit culture that has added to our knowledge of cultivation, genetics, or other relative matters. The work should have been mainly carried out by the candidate in the United Kingdom, and mostly during the preceding five years. A cup is awarded triennially. The cup is held for three years by the successful candidate, who must give a bond for its safe return. The holder is eligible to compete on the next or any succeeding occasion. When the cup is relinquished the holder receives a Hogg Medal. Established in 1920 by Miss. Jones-Bateman, of Cae Glas, Abergele.

4040
Lawrence Medal
For recognition of the best exhibit shown to the Society during the year. Awarded annually. No exhibitor may receive this medal more than once in three years. Established in 1906 to celebrate Sir Trevor Lawrence's twenty-one years' tenure of office as President of the Society.

4041
Leonardslee Bowl
For recognition of the best exhibit of one bloom of each of twelve camellias. Awarded annually at the Camellia Show in April. Established by Sir Giles Loder Bt, in 1965.

4042
Loder Cup
For recognition of the best exhibit of one truss of a Rhododendron hybrid. Awarded annually at the Rhododendron Show. Established by the late Gerald Loder (Lord Wakehurst) and transferred to the Society in 1946.

4043
Loder Rhododendron Cup
For recognition of work in the field of horticulture. The judges consider not merely the floral display, but the value to horticulture of the work of the recipient whether such work shall include the production of flowers or not. The cup is awarded annually, but not more than once in seven years to the same individual. Established in 1921 by Gerald Loder (Lord Wakehurst) in memory of his brother, Sir Edmund Loder, Bt.

4044
Long-Service Medal
To recognize any man or woman of British nationality, resident in the United Kingdom, who has completed forty years' continuous satisfactory employment as a gardener or in some other horticultural capacity in a private, commercial, public or botanical garden, nursery, market garden, fruit plantation or seed trial-ground with one employer or family, or in one place. A form of application for a medal may be obtained from the Secretary. Bars are awarded for fifty and sixty years' service. Established in 1958.

4045
Lyttel Lily Cup
To recognize an individual who has done good work of some kind in connection with Lilium, Nomocharis or Firtillaria. Awarded annually. Established in 1939 by the Rev. Professor E.S. Lyttel.

4046
McLaren Cup
For recognition of the best exhibit of one truss of a species of Rhododendron shown at the Rhododendron Show. Awarded annually at the Rhododendron Show in April. Established by the Honorable Henry McLaren (the Late Lord Aberconway) and transferred to the Society in 1946.

4047
George Monro Memorial Cup
For recognition of the best collection of vegetables shown by an affiliated society or an individual in the special class at the Vegetable Show in October. Awarded annually when merited. Established in 1921 by Mr. George Monro and his brothers in memory of their father. Up to 1938, awarded for the best exhibit of grapes shown by an amateur at the Fruit and Vegetable Show. From 1939 to 1949 it was not offered. From 1950 to 1970 it was offered for award for the best exhibit of vegetables shown by an amateur during the year.

4048
George Moore Medal
To recognize the exhibitor of the new hybrid Paphiopedilum, Selenipedium, Phragmipedium, or intergeneric hybrid between these genera that shows the greatest improvement on those of the same or similar parentage and that was submitted to the Society during the year. Awarded annually. Established in 1926 by the late G.F. Moore.

4049
RHS Vegetable Cup
To recognize the competitor who secures the greatest number of prize-points for exhibits of vegetables of the Vegetable Show. Awarded annually. Established in 1910.

4050
Richardson Trophy
For recognition of the best exhibit of twelve cultivars of daffodils, representing not fewer than three Divisions, to be selected from Division 1 to 4, one stem of each, shown by an amateur at the Daffodil Show. Awarded annually. Established in 1976.

4051
Riddell Trophy for Vegetables
For recognition of a class of vegetables at the Fruit and Vegetable Show. Awarded annually. Established in 1931 by Lord Riddell.

4052
Mrs. F. E. Rivis Prize
To encourage excellence in cultivation and to recognize the gardener or other employee responsible for the cultivation of the exhibit for which the Williams Memorial Medal is awarded. Awarded annually. Established in 1960 by Miss A.K. Hincks in commemoration of her sister, Mrs. F.E. Rivis.

4053
Rosse Cup
To recognize the winner of Class 8, Conifers shown for their foliage. Awarded annually at the November Ornamental Plant Competition. Established by Anne Countess of Rosse in 1980 in memory of the 6th Earl of Rosse.

4054
Rothschild Challenge Cup
For recognition of the best non-competitive group of rhododendrons and azaleas staged by a trade grower at the Rhododendron Show. Awarded annually. Established by the late Lionel de Rothschild and transferred to the Society in 1946.

4055
Sewell Medal
For recognition of exhibits of plants suitable for the rock garden or alpine house. Awarded in alternate years for the finest trade exhibit at the Show in mid-April and the finest amateur exhibit of six pans of alpine plants specifically entered for the competition in the mid-April Show. Awarded annually. Established in 1929 by the late A.J. Sewell.

4056
Simmonds Medal
For recognition of the Society's Daffodil Competitions. Bronze, silver and silver-gilt medals are awarded annually. Established in 1968 in commemoration of Arthur Simmonds, Secretary of the Society.

4057
Roza Stevenson Cup
For recognition of the best exhibit of one spray of a species of rhododendron. Awarded annually. Established in 1922 by Major-General E.G.W.W. Harrison in memory of his wife.

4058
Veitch Memorial Medal
For recognition of contributions to the advancement of the science and practice of horticulture, and for special exhibits. Medals and prizes are awarded annually. Established in 1870 in memory of James Veitch of Chelsea.

4059
Victoria Medal of Honour in Horticulture - V.M.H.
To recognize an individual for contributions in the field of horticulture. Horticulturists who are residents of the United Kingdom are eligible. Sixty-three medals are awarded, symbolic of the 63 year reign of Her Majesty Queen Victoria. Established in 1897.

4060
A. J. Waley Medal
To recognize a working gardener who has helped the cultivation of rhododendrons. Awarded annually. Established in 1937 by the late Alfred J. Waley.

4061
Westonbirt Orchid Medal
For recognition in the field of orchid cultivation in the following categories: to the exhibitor of the best cultivar of an orchid species or of a hybrid grex that has been shown to the Society for the first time and received an award during the year or which, having received an award during the previous five years, has had the award raised during the year; for the most meritorious group of orchids staged in the Society's Halls during the year; for the most finely grown specimen orchid shown to the Society during the year; or for any scientific, literary, or any other outstanding personal achievement in connection with orchids. Awarded annually. Established in 1960 by Mr. H.G. Alexander, in commemoration of the collection of orchids made at Westonbirt.

4062
Wigan Cup
For recognition of the best exhibit shown to the Society during the year by a local authority. Awarded annually. Established in 1911 and offered as an award for an exhibit of roses.

4063
Williams Memorial Medal
For recognition of a group of plants and/or cut blooms of one genus (fruit and vegetables excepted) that show excellence in cultivation, staged at one of the Society's Shows during the year. Awarded annually. Established in 1896 by the Trustees of the Williams Memorial Fund in commemoration of B.S. Williams.

4064
Guy Wilson Memorial Vase
For recognition of the best exhibit of six cultivars of white daffodils representing any or all of Divisions 1 to 3, three stems of each, at the Daffodil Show. Awarded annually. Established in 1982.

4065
Royal Humane Society
Brettenham House
Lancaster Pl.
London WC2E 7EP, England   Phone: 71 836 8155

4066
Royal Humane Society Awards
To recognize individuals who, at personal risk, save or endeavor to save lives by rescues from the following dangers: drowning, accidents in ships or aircraft; cliffs or other heights; asphyxia in confined spaces, such as wells, sewers, blast furnaces and fallen earth works; electrocution; or other circumstances where risks are run and awards from other sources are not available. Life-saving is not in itself sufficient to merit a bravery award. The degree of risk is the paramount factor in awards for bravery and the skill exhibited by the rescuer is taken into consideration. Duplication of awards from other sources is avoided as far as possible. Awards are only made in exceptional circumstances when a close relationship exists between the rescued and the rescuer. British nationals, nationals of the Commonwealth, and foreign citizens where British lives are involved are eligible. Professional persons in the exercise of their calling, on or off duty, are not normally awarded. Gold, silver, and bronze medals are awarded depending on the degree of bravery. The Stanhope Gold Medal awarded, for the most meritorious case reported to the society during the current year, is open to the Commonwealth societies of Australia, Canada, New Zealand and New South Wales. It was established in 1962. Additional awards include the Testimonial on Vellum, "In Memoriam" Testimonial, Testimonial on Parchment, Certificate of Commendation, and Resuscitation Certificate.

4067
Royal Institute of British Architects
Birmingham and Midland Institute
Margaret St.
Birmingham B3 3SP, England   Phone: 21 2332321

4068
Housing Design Awards
To encourage high standards of design and layout in both public and private sector housing schemes; the planning of schemes which relate well to the environment; and the provision of dwellings which are suited to the needs of people who live in them. Housing schemes must have been occupied to be eligible. Awards are given in the following categories: National Awards and Regional Awards-General Housing (City, Town, Suburban, and Village); Housing for Retired and Elderly People; and Housing for Frail Elderly People. Applications must be submitted by March 15. Diplomas are presented to the architect or designer, builder, and client or developer of award-winning and highly commended schemes. Award-winning schemes also receive a building plaque to record the award on site. Awards are presented biennially. Co-sponsored jointly by the Department of the Environment, the National House-Building Council and the Royal Institute of British Architects.

4069
RIBA Architecture Awards
For recognition of an outstanding building or group of buildings in the United Kingdom completed up to two years and three months preceding the award. The architect responsible for the project must be a member of the RIBA, RIAS, or RSUA. For the purposes of these awards, the country is divided into 14 regions, and national/regional awards are given in each region at the discretion of the jury. Plaques are presented to the award winning buildings. Diplomas are given to the architect or firm of architects, the owner of the building, and the building contractor. Award winning buildings receive a plaque. Awarded annually. Established in 1966.

4070
RIBA Student Competition
To recognize outstanding design by students. (Discontinued)

4071
Royal Gold Medal for Architecture
This, the architectural world's most prestigious individual award, is given to recognize an architect, or group of architects, for work of high merit; or to recognize another distinguished person or group whose work has promoted either directly or indirectly the advancement of architecture. The award is conferred by Her Majesty, the Queen on the recommendation of RIBA. A gold medal is awarded annually. Established in 1848.

4072
Royal Institute of British Architects and *The Times*
Community Enterprise Scheme
66 Portland Pl.
London W1N 4AD, England   Phone: 71 580 5533

4073
Community Enterprise Scheme
To recognize the most imaginative, viable and need fulfilling community projects in the built environment in the United Kingdom and to encourage community initiatives of all kinds where local enthusiasm and drive has been advanced with the support and assistance of community architects or other relevant environmental professions. Awards are given in the following categories: (1) The Housing Associations Charitable Trust Award for Housing - sponsored by the Housing Associations Charitable Trust for tackling the needs of badly housed or homeless people through self-help, self-build, tenant or resident action, or by community or neighborhood groups; (2) *The Times* Environment Award - sponsored by Shell UK Ltd for general environmental improvements, particularly those involving a partnership between the public, private and voluntary sectors; (3) The Gulbenkian Award for Workplaces - sponsored by the Calouste Gulbenkian Foundation for managed and small business workshops, community offices, shops and factories, built or improved through community initiative; (4) The Gulbenkian Award for Community Centres - sponsored by the Calouste Gulbenkian Foundation for any type of new or refurbished community facilities, particularly in areas where no other facilities already exist; (5) The Community Projects Foundation Award for Partnership - sponsored by Barclays Bank plc for any type of partnership which has brought benefits to a local community through a built environment project; (6) The National Children's Play Award - sponsored by the National Children's Play and Recreation Unit for community initiated play projects, particularly those involving children, at the planning stage; (7) The Community Architecture Award - sponsored by the Calouste Gulbenkian Foundation for any type of building project, new build or refurbishment, in which the design process has involved local community or user groups, the success of the project in meeting their needs and aspirations and the quality of the overall design; (8) The Community Enterprise Award for Training - sponsored by Marks & Spencer plc to community organizations undertaking built environment regeneration projects, which as a result assists local people to obtain skills and employment opportunities; and (9) The Community Enterprise Award for New Business - sponsored by the Post Office for community organizations who, through a built environment regeneration project, have promoted successful new businesses to meet a community need. Any community-initiated building project is eligible including new build, self-help/self-build, refurbishment and renovation projects, housing, community and arts centres, adventure playgrounds, training centres, business premises, workshops, urban farms, environmental improvements and facilities and improvements for the disabled. Entries are invited from England, Scotland, Wales and Northern Ireland. Projects must be able to prove their viability at the time of entry and are eligible for an Honorable Mention or Commendation if they are still in the process of being developed or built. Schemes completed during the preceding two years are eligible for an Award or Commendation. For the Community Architecture category, only completed schemes are eligible and they must have become operational during the preceding four years. Any individual or organization may enter, whether from the community, business, local authority or any other sector. Award winning schemes receive prize money, a plaque to be erected on site to record the award and a certificate. Commendations and Honorable Mentions receive a certificate and representatives of all winning schemes are invited to attend the Awards Presentation. Established in 1985. Sponsored by *The Times* and the Royal Institute of British Architects.

4074
Royal Institute of Navigation
1 Kensington Gore   Phone: 71 5895021
London SW7 2AT, England   Fax: 71 8238671

Formerly: (1972) Institute of Navigation.

4075
Bronze Medal
To recognize the contributor of the most notable paper published in the Institute's journal in a given year. Nominations are made by the Technical Committee. Criteria considered are the significance of the work in relation to the subject, the importance of the subject, the presentation of the paper, and the originality of the approach to the subject, of the work, and of the publication. A bronze medal and certificate are awarded annually. Established in 1950.

4076
Fellow
To recognize individuals who fall into one of the following categories: those who achieve distinction as professional navigators; those who contribute to navigation by invention, research, literature, or in other ways, or who achieve distinction in the field of training; or those who perform exceptional feats of navigation. Fellows of the institute may submit nominations by January 15.

4077
Gold Medal
This, the Institute's highest award, is given to recognize a particular contribution or a series of contributions made progressively over a number of years in the field of navigation. Nominations, accompanied by a statement of the candidate's claims, may be made by any member of the Institute. The deadline is January 15. A Gold Medal and certificate are awarded annually. Established in 1951.

4078
Honorary Member
To recognize distinguished persons in the field of navigation. The Council of the Institute makes the selection.

4079
Silver Medal
To recognize an outstanding contribution to the affairs of the Institute. A Silver Medal is awarded annually.

4080
Royal Institute of Public Administration
3 Birdcage Walk   Phone: 71 222 2248
London SW1H 9JH, England   Fax: 71 222 2249

4081
Haldane Essay Competition Medal
For recognition of significant and original essays in English relevant to the understanding of public administration. Entry is open to all persons irrespective of present profession or country of residence. A monetary prize of £350 and the Haldane Silver Medal are awarded annually. Established in 1924 in honor of Lord Haldane, a British civil servant.

4082
Royal Institute of Public Health and Hygiene
28 Portland Pl.
London W1N 4DE, England   Phone: 71 5802731

Formed by merger of: Institute of Hygiene; Royal Institute of Public Health.

4083
Royal Institute of Public Health and Hygiene Awards
To recognize individuals who work to advance domestic, industrial, and personal health and hygiene, and to encourage the study of hygiene, preventive medicine, and public health. Prizes are presented for achievement in RIPHH examinations.

4084
Royal Institution of Chartered Surveyors
12 Great George St.
Parliament Sq.   Phone: 71 222 7000
London SW1P 3AD, England   Fax: 71 222 9430

4085
RICS Awards
To recognize a wide variety of professional disciplines which show support for the need to conserve the rural and the urban environment. Open to any company, individual or project which demonstrates outstanding development, design and management of land, property and construction. Entries may be submitted by January 31. Awards are presented in seven categories: (1) RICS Award for Building Conservation; (2) RICS Award for Techniques in Building Conservation; (3) RICS Award for Conservation of the Environment; (4) RICS Award for Urban Renewal; (5) RICS Award for Building Efficiency; and (6) RICS Theme Award - a category of Award for which the theme will change every year. In 1991, the theme was diversification of agricultural land; and (7) RICS Media Award - open to journalists in the fields of land, property or construction. A plaque and trophy are awarded annually. Established in 1990.

4086
Royal Institution of Great Britain
21 Albemarle St.   Phone: 71 4092992
London W1X 4BS, England   Fax: 71 6293569

4087
Actonian Prize
To recognize the author of the best essay illustrative of the wisdom and beneficence of the Almighty, in some department of science, selected by the Council of the Royal Institution of Great Britain. A monetary prize of £105 is awarded every seven years. Established in 1838 by Mrs. Hannah Acton in memory of her husband, Samuel Acton.

4088
Royal Institution of Naval Architects
10 Upper Belgrave St.   Phone: 71 235 4622
London SW1X 8BQ, England   Fax: 71 245 6959

4089
Samuel Baxter Prize
For recognition of the best contribution during the year towards the safety and/or efficiency of sea-going vessels. The Council considers nominations after October 31. A monetary prize of up to £200 is awarded annually.

4090
Calder Bequest
For recognition of the best essay on some aspect of the design or development of small craft by a person under 25 years of age, preferably engaged in boat design or boat building or on a recognized course of study in yacht and boat building. The essay may also be considered for publication in *The Naval Architect*. Submissions are accepted until September 1. A monetary prize of £40 is awarded annually.

4091
William Froude Medal
To recognize a person of any nationality who, in the judgement of the Council of the Institution, has made some conspicuous contribution to naval architecture and/or shipbuilding and whose outstanding services and personal achievements in this direction merit special consideration. Nominations may be made by November. A gold medal is awarded when merited. Established in 1955.

4092
Froude Research Scholarship in Naval Architecture
To provide a post graduate scholarship in naval architecture. British subjects and citizens of EEC countries under the age of 30 who are members of the Institution may submit applications. Awarded annually as funds permit. Established in 1948.

4093
RINA Gold, Silver and Bronze Medals
To recognize any person who presents a paper which is accepted for publication by the Institution and which paper, in the judgement of the Council, merits such a distinction. Gold, silver and bronze medals are awarded.

4094
RINA Small Craft Group Medal
For recognition of contributions to the design of small fast craft.

4095
Trusler Prize
To recognize undergraduates at the completion of their penultimate year of study in an Honors degree course, who at the time of their examinations are Junior Members of the RINA and who, in the opinion of their Professor of Naval Architecture or Ship Science, have shown high academic ability and have also contributed to maritime activities. The awards are made in succession to students at the Universities of Glasgow, London, Newcastle, Southampton, and Strathclyde. Two prizes of £50 are awarded annually.

4096
Wakeham Prize
For recognition of the best paper written by a Junior Member of the Institution and accepted for publication. Books, instruments, and computer hardware or software to the value of £100 are awarded.

4097
Watts Prize
To recognize a member of the Institution for proposals to improve crew or passenger accommodation in merchant ships or for improvement of life-saving apparatus. Submissions should be made by July 31. A monetary prize of up to £100 is awarded annually.

4098
Sir William White Post-Graduate Scholarship in Naval Architecture
To enable British and EEC students of naval architecture or marine engineering under the age of 30, who have at some time been employed in shipbuilding or marine engineering, and who have passed with merit through an approved course of study in a university or college, to carry out research work into problems connected with the design and construction of ships and their machinery, or to follow a post-graduate advanced course of study relevant to ship technology. A scholarship of £1,250 per annum plus fees is awarded and is tenable for two years subject to a satisfactory report at the end of the first year. Established in 1915 in memory of Sir William H. White, K.C.B., LL.D. (1845-1913), who was a distinguished Director of Naval Construction and an Honorary Vice-President of The Institution of Naval Architects.

4099
Royal Life Saving Society U.K.
4 Windsor Ct.
Green Hill St.
Stratford upon Avon, Warks. CV36 6GG,
  England   Phone: 789 295222

4100
Certificate of Commendation
To recognize those people who have received RLSS lifesaving training, which is used to perform a rescue. Awarded quarterly.

4101
Mountbatten Medal
To recognize the most gallant rescue attempt by a Royal Life Saving Society award holder in the British Commonwealth in each calendar year. Consideration for the award is given to holders of an RLSS Award. A medal and a citation are bestowed at a specially arranged presentation ceremony. Awarded annually. Established by the late Earl Mountbatten of Burma, Grand President of the RLSS.

4102
Royal Meteorological Society
James Glaisher House
Greenville Pl.
Bracknell, Berks. RG12 1BX, England   Phone: 344 422 957

4103
Aircraft Safety Prize
For recognition of an outstanding contribution made during the preceding year toward the safety of aircraft and flying personnel. Awarded annually.

4104
Meteorology Prize
For recognition of a distinguished contribution to the science of meteorology or the application of meteorology to aviation.

4105
Symons Memorial Medal
For recognition of distinguished work in the field of meteorology. Meteorologists of any nationality are eligible. An inscribed silver gilt medal is awarded biennially. Established in 1902 in memory of George J. Symons, F.R.S.

4106
Royal Musical Association
c/o Faculty of Music   Phone: 865 276125
St. Aldares, Oxon. OX1 1DB, England   Fax: 865 276128

4107
Dent Medal
For recognition of an outstanding contribution and important original research in the field of musicology. Musicologists of any country are eligible. Candidates, who are normally under 40 years of age, are nominated by the Directorium of the International Musicological Society and the Council of the Royal Musical Association. A bronze medal is awarded annually by the Council of the Royal Musical Association. Established in 1961.

4108
Royal National Rose Society
Chiswell Green   Phone: 727 850461
St. Albans, Herts. AL2 3NR, England   Fax: 727 850360

4109
President's International Trophy
To provide recognition for the best new seedling rose of the year. To be eligible, the rose must be proven an outstanding garden rose over a three year trial period (and also must have received a gold medal). A trophy is presented annually when merited. Established in 1952.

4110
Royal Northern College of Music
124 Oxford Rd.   Phone: 61 273 6283
Manchester M13 9RD, England   Fax: 61 273 7611

4111
Companion
To recognize individuals who have rendered service of outstanding distinction to the college. A certificate is presented at the congregation of awards. Established in 1974.

4112
Fellow
To recognize musicians for their service to the art of music. A certificate is presented at the annual congregation of awards. Established in 1974.

4113
Honorary Member
To recognize individuals who are not professional musicians, but have in various lay capacities brought substantial benefits to music or the arts, to the quality of life in general in the north of England in particular, or to the work of the college. A certificate is presented at the annual congregation of awards. Established in 1979.

4114
Royal Orchestral Society for Amateur Musicians
100 Shakespeare Crescent
Manor Park
London E12 6LB, England   Phone: 71 588 6488

Formerly: (1986) Royal Amateur Orchestral Society.

4115
Royal Orchestral Society Medal
To encourage young musicians in their career. Amateur musicians under 25 years of age are eligible. A silver medal and a bronze medal are awarded annually. Established in 1957 by Arthur Davison, CBE. M.Mus.

4116
Royal Over-Seas League
Over-Seas House
Park Pl.
St. James's St.
London SW1A 1LR, England
Phone: 71 4080214
Fax: 71 4996738

4117
Royal Over-Seas League Music Competition
Instrumentalists who 28 years of age or younger, and singers and composers who 30 years of age or younger may submit applications by February 8. The competition is open to Commonwealth citizens, including the United Kingdom and also citizens of former Commonwealth countries. The deadline is February 18. The following awards are presented: (1) Solo Awards: Gold Medal and First Prize - £3,000; Eagle Star Award for Keyboard - £1,000; Eagle Star Award for Strings - £1,000; Ernst & Young Award for Singers - £1,000; Worshipful Company of Dyers Awards for Woodwind/Brass - £1,000; (2) Ensemble Prize: RTZ Ensemble Prize and Miller Trophy - £1,000; (3) Composition Award: Bernard Shore Composition Award - (This award alternates with the Bernard Shore Memorial Scholarship - $2,500 for an outstanding viola player), and Performing Right Society Award - $2,500 awarded biennially in odd-numbered years; (4) Publishers & Musical Instrument Manufacturers' Awards - the winner of each of the Main Solo Awards and the Ensemble Prize receive tokens for £100 from one of the following firms: Boosey & Hawkes, Chester Music, Oxford University Press, Novello, and Schott; (5) Overseas Awards: Overseas Prize and Overseas Trophy - £1,000; Philip Crawshaw Memorial Prize for a musician of promise from overseas - £500; Australian Musical Assoc. Prize - £500; Stella Murray Prize for a musician from New Zealand - £300; New Zealand Society Prize for a New Zealand pianist or wind player of promise - £500; New Zealand Society Prize for a New Zealand singer of promise - £500; and Irene Brown Memorial Prize for a New Zealand string player of promise - £500; and (6) Other Awards: Society of Women Musicians Prize for an outstanding woman musician - £500; Marisa Robles Harp Prize - £300; Joan Davies Memorial Prize - £150; Ivor Walsworth Memorial Prize for a string player of promise - £100; The Yorke Trust Prize for a double bass player - £100; Daphne Boden Prize for a harpist of promise - £100; Sir Ernest Cassel Prize for a brass player - £100; Eric Rice Memorial Prize for an accompanist - £100; and Lisa Fuchsova Prize for a chamber music pianist - £150. Awarded annually. Established in 1952.

4118
Royal Philatelic Society, London
41 Devonshire Pl.
London W1N 1PE, England
Phone: 71 4861044
Fax: 71 4860803

4119
Crawford Medal
For recognition of the most valuable and original contribution to the study and knowledge of philately published during the two years preceding the award. The award is open to worldwide competition. A medal is awarded annually. Established in 1920 in honor of the 26th Earl of Crawford KT, president of the society (1910-1913).

4120
Royal Philatelic Society, London Exhibition Medal
For recognition at the London Exhibition. A medal was awarded annually. Established in 1948. (Discontinued in 1968)

4121
Royal Philatelic Society, London Medal
For recognition of outstanding service rendered to the society by a fellow member or associate other than in the course of duty as an officer of the society. A medal is awarded annually. Established in 1968.

4122
Tapling Medal
For recognition of the best paper that is written by a fellow, member or associate and read before the society or published in the society's journal during the two years preceding the date of the award. A medal is awarded annually. Established in 1920 in honor of Thomas Keay Tapling MP, Vice President of the society (1881-1891).

4123
Tilleard Medal
For recognition of the best display of stamps, essays, proofs, reprints, or postal stationery given at a meeting of the society by a fellow, member or associate during the two years preceding the date of the award. A medal is awarded annually. Established in 1920 in honor of John Alexander Tilleard M.V.O., Honorary Secretary of the society, (1894-1913).

4124
Royal Philharmonic Society
10 Stratford Pl.
London W1N 9AE, England
Phone: 71 491 8110
Fax: 71 493 7463

4125
Composition Prize
For recognition of a composition by past or present students of the Royal Academy of Music, Royal College of Music, Guildhall School of Music and Drama, Trinity College of Music, Royal Northern College of Music, London College of Music, Birmingham Conservatorie, Welsh College of Music and Drama, and the Royal Scottish Academy of Music and Drama. Composers of any nationality under 26 years of age may enter through the above colleges. Monetary awards are presented annually.

4126
Gold Medal
To recognize artists of eminence for their services to the Society and to the art of music. A gold medal, designed by the sculptor and numismatist, Leonard C. Wyon, to commemorate the centenary of Beethoven's birth is awarded when merited. Established in 1870.

4127
Julius Isserlis Scholarship
To enable music students in all performing categories and of any nationality (but normally a resident of the United Kingdom) and between the ages of 15 and 25 to study outside the British Isles for two years. A scholarship of £20,000 (£10,000 per year for two years) is awarded every two or three years.

4128
RPS Music Awards
For recognition of outstanding accomplishments in the field of music. Awards are given in 12 categories of music making, judged by experts and by the public to be the best of their kind in the UK in the preceding calendar year. The categories include awards for the best large and small scale compositions; for large and small ensemble playing; for conductor, singer, and instrumentalist; for opera; for a concert series; a debut; radio, TV, and video work; and for music writing. Winners receive a silver trophy. Established in 1989. Formerly: RPS Charles Heidseick Award.

4129
Royal Photographic Society of Great Britain
The Octagon, Milsom St.
Bath BA1 1DN, England
Phone: 225 462841
Fax: 225 448688

4130
Centenary Medal
To recognize sustained and significant contributions to the art of photography. A gold medal and Honorary Fellowship in the Society are awarded annually. Established in 1994.

4131
Bertram Cox Bequest
To enable an illustrated paper on the subject of the aestetics of creative photography or an allied subject to be prepared and presented in the form of a lecture. The paper must have an attractive balance between research

and illustrations. A monetary prize that covers the cost of presentation and illustration of the paper is awarded.

4132
Fenton Medal
To recognize an individual for outstanding contributions to the work of the Society. Both members and non-members of the Society are eligible for nomination. Established in 1980 to honor Roger Fenton, a Society founder who, for several years after its foundation, filled the post of Honorary Secretary.

4133
Honorary Fellowship
To recognize distinguished individuals having, from their position or attainments, an intimate connection with the science or fine art of photography. Both members and non-members of the Society are eligible for nomination. Not more than five Honorary Fellowships may be awarded in any one year.

4134
Honorary Membership
To recognize individuals who have rendered distinguished service to the Society or to photography. Both members and non-members of the Society are eligible for nomination.

4135
Hood Medal
To recognize an individual for meritorious performance in some branch of photography, with particular emphasis on any work that reveals the most outstanding advance in photography for public service. Both members and non-members of the Society are eligible for nomination. A medal is awarded annually. Established in 1933 by Harold Hood, a Fellow of the Society.

4136
Progress Medal
This, the Society's premier award, recognizes an individual for an invention, research, publication, or exhibition which, in the opinion of the Council, has resulted in an important advance in the development of photography. Both members and non-members of the Society are eligible for nominations. A silver medal is awarded annually. Established in 1878.

4137
Rodman Medal
To recognize an individual for outstanding work in the field of medical imaging. Both members and non-members of the Society are eligible for nomination. Awarded annually. Established in 1935 under the terms of the will of Dr. George Hook Rodman, President of the Society from 1920-1922.

4138
Royal School of Church Music
Addington Palace Phone: 81 654 7676
Croydon CR9 5AD, England Fax: 81 655 2542

4139
Harold Smart Anthem Competition
To recognize composers for works tailored to the technical resources of choirs with limited ability. A monetary award and possible publication of the winning composition are awarded annually. Established in 1988 to honor Dr. Harold Smart.

4140
Royal Society
Press and Information Office
6 Carlton House Terr. Phone: 71 839 5561
London SW1Y 5AG, England Fax: 71 930 2170

4141
Appleton Prize
In recognition of distinguished contributions to ionospheric physics. Work must have been carried out during the six year period preceding the year of the General Assembly of the Union Radio Scientifique Internationale (URSI) at which the prize is awarded. Candidates may be nominated by National Member Committees of URSI. A monetary award of £250 is awarded triennially. Established in 1969 by the Royal Society in honor of Sir Edward Appleton, President of URSI (1934-1952).

4142
Armourers & Brasiers' Award
For recognition of excellence in materials science and materials technology. There is no restriction on the nationality of the recipient, but the work must be done in the United Kingdom. Nominations are invited from Fellows of the Society in the appropriate areas and from such other sources as the Committee may decide. A monetary prize of £1,000 and a silver medal are awarded triennially. Established in 1984 by agreement with the Armourers & Brasiers' Company.

4143
S. G. Brown Award and Medal
For recognition of contributions to the promotion and development of mechanical inventions. Established in 1963. (Discontinued)

4144
Buchanan Medal
For recognition of distinguished original research in the broad area of medical sciences without limit of nationality or sex. A monetary award of £1,000 and a silver gilt medal are awarded every five years. Established in 1897.

4145
Copley Medal
This, the premier award of the Society, is presented for outstanding achievements in research in any branch of science. Customarily, the award alternates between the physical sciences and the biological sciences. A monetary award of £2,500 and a silver gilt medal are awarded annually. Established in 1731.

4146
Darwin Medal
For recognition of work of acknowledged distinction in the broad area of biology in which Charles Darwin worked, notably in evolution, population, biology, organismal biology, and biological diversity. The award may be made either to a British subject or a foreigner, without distinction of sex. A monetary award of £1,000 and a silver medal are awarded biennially. Established in 1890.

4147
Davy Medal
For recognition of an outstandingly important recent discovery in any branch of chemistry made in Europe or North America. A monetary award of £1,000 and a bronze medal are awarded annually. Established in 1877.

4148
Esso Energy Award and Medal
For recognition of an outstanding contribution to the advancement of science, engineering or technology leading to the more efficient mobilization, use, or conservation of energy resources. A monetary award of £1,000 and a gold medal are awarded annually. Established in 1974 by the Society and Esso UK plc.

4149
Michael Faraday Award
To recognize the scientist or scientists who have done the most to promote the public understanding of science in the United Kingdom. The Council of the Society makes the selection. A monetary award of £1,000 and a silver gilt medal are awarded annually. Established in 1986.

4150
Gabor Medal
To recognize an individual for acknowledged distinction of work in the life sciences, particularly in the fields of genetic engineering and molecular biology. A monetary award of £1,000, and a medal are awarded biennially. Established in 1988 in memory of Dennis Gabor, F.R.S., by his brother, Andre Gabor.

4151
Hughes Medal
For recognition of an original discovery in the physical sciences, particularly electricity and magnetism or their applications. There are no restrictions on the sex or nationality of the recipient. A monetary award of £1,000 and a silver gilt medal are awarded annually. Established in 1902.

4152
Leverhulme Medal
For recognition of an outstandingly significant contribution in the field of pure or applied chemistry or engineering, including chemical engineering. A monetary award of £500 and a gold medal are awarded triennially. Established in 1960 on the tercentenary anniversary of the Society. Sponsored by Leverhulme Trust, 15-19 New Fetter Lane, London EC4A 1NR, England.

4153
Mullard Award and Medal
For recognition of an outstanding contribution to the advancement of science, engineering or technology directly promoting national prosperity in the United Kingdom of Great Britain and Northern Ireland. A monetary award of £2,000 and a silver gilt medal are awarded annually. Established in 1967.

4154
Royal Medals
For recognition of the most important contributions to the advancement of physical and biological sciences and for distinguished contributions in the applied sciences, published originally in the British Commonwealth. Monetary awards of £1,000 for each discipline and three medals, one in each discipline, are awarded annually by the Sovereign upon the recommendation of the Council of the Royal Society.

4155
Royal Society Grants
The Royal Society administers grants and fellowships in most areas of science. Information about application procedures is available from the Secretary of the Royal Society. The following programs are administered by the Society: (1) Research Professorships - to those with not only a past record of excellence in research, but also an undoubted future potential for continuing long-term achievement in research of the highest quality. In making appointments, Council seeks evidence that the candidate cannot achieve full research capability, for reasons that would be removed if he or she were appointed to a Royal Society research professorship. Privately-funded professorships are also available; (2) Senior Research Fellowships - five Senior Research Fellowships, four funded from private sources and one from the Grant-in-aid; (3) Research Fellowships - currently over 30 research fellowships - three funded from the Grant-in-aid and the others funded from private sources; (4) University Research Fellowships - for outstanding young scientists aged between 26 and 33, to work for up to ten years in departments of science, mathematics, engineering and technology in universities or polytechnics in the UK; (5) Guest Research Fellowships - to assist outstanding leaders in research in the UK to invite, as guests, scientists of proven ability, normally resident overseas, to come and work with them for periods ranging from four months to one year. The aim is to provide for research needs which can best be met by such international collaboration; and (6) Royal Society/Science and Engineering Research Council Industrial Fellowships - to help scientists, engineers and mathematicians to move, for between six months to two years, either from an academic institution into industry, or vice versa, to undertake a project of importance both to the academic institution and the UK company concerned. Applicants, who must be ordinarily resident in the UK and preferably in the age range of 30 to 45 years, must be of Ph.D. or equivalent status, and be normally holding a tenured post in a university or polytechnic or employed as a scientist, mathematician or engineer in industry or in an industrial research organization.

4156
Rumford Medal
For recognition of an outstandingly important recent discovery in the field of thermal or optical properties of matter made by a scientist working in Europe. A monetary award of £1,000 and a silver gilt medal are awarded biennially. Established in 1800.

4157
Science Book Prizes
To recognize popular non-fiction science and technology books which contribute to the public understanding of science. Two prizes are awarded annually: for a book intended for general readership and a book written for young people. A monetary award of £1,000 is awarded in each category. An additional prize of £500 for an outstanding book for the under eight-year-old age group is awarded at the judge's discretion. Sponsored by the Science Museum, London.

4158
Sylvester Medal
To encourage mathematical research irrespective of nationality. A monetary award of £1,000 and a bronze medal are awarded triennially. Established in 1901.

4159
Wellcome Foundation Prize and Lecture
For recognition of original contributions to medicine and veterinary science published within ten years from the date of the award. A monetary prize of £2,500 and a medal are awarded biennially. The recipient is called upon to give an evening lecture. Established in 1980 by the Wellcome Foundation Ltd. to commemorate the centenary year of the Wellcome Foundation.

4160
Royal Society for Nature Conservation
The Green, Witham Park   Phone: 522 544400
Lincoln LN5 7JR, England   Fax: 522 511616

4161
Christopher Cadbury Medal
For recognition of services to the advancement of nature conservation in the British Islands. Ordinary members of the Society or members of its corporate member bodies may apply by June 30. A silver medal is awarded annually. Established in 1990 in honor of Christopher Cadbury, former president of the Royal Society for Nature Conservation, who retired in 1988.

4162
Royal Society for the Mentally Handicapped Children and Adults
MENCAP National Centre
123 Golden Ln.   Phone: 71 2501536
London EC1Y ORT, England   Fax: 71 4549193

4163
Business Enterprise Awards
To recognize and publicize the contributions made by business enterprise to British society through the creation of wealth and employment. The award is open to any UK company or UK subsidiary of an overseas company with an annual turnover of at least £5 million. Companies are judged on their economic contribution to British society in terms of wealth created, employment generated, and on the degree of enterprise they have shown in the design, manufacture, and marketing of their products and services. In addition, the following criteria are considered: achievements must be shown in the company's reported profits; attention is paid primarily to the company's most recent achievements, but account is also

taken of both past and likely future performance; the achievements must be attributable to the company's own enterprise. A company that has created profits through courageous risk-taking, commercial flair, or effort and skill in exploiting opportunities is preferred to a company that has gained its profits in the form of an unforeseen windfall or has bought them through a takeover; and wealth and employment generation are evaluated on the basis of: real pre-tax profitability, UK employment, and productivity (value added). Nominations or applications are accepted by August 31. A plaque and publicity are awarded annually in November to the Company of the Year. Established in 1980. Sponsored by *Sunday Telegraph*, Midland Bank, and Henley - Management College and supported by the Confederation of British Industry, in aid of MENCAP, the Royal Society for Mentally Handicapped Children and Adults.

4164
Royal Society for the Prevention of Accidents
Cannon House, The Priory Queensway
Birmingham, W. Midlands B4 6BS,
  England
Phone: 21 200 2461
Fax: 21 200 1254

4165
Distinguished Service Awards
To recognize an individual for an outstanding contribution to health and safety at work beyond one's own workplace. A Certificate and special tie are awarded.

4166
Eagle Star Training Award
To recognize achievement in the area of health and safety training at work. Awarded to the company or organization with the most effectively managed health and safety training program over the past year. Applications may be made by the last day of February each year. A trophy and a commemorative plaque are awarded annually, at a special ceremony. Established in 1976 by William A. Nicol, then Chairman of Midland Assurance, Ltd. Formerly: (1990) Midland Assurance Trophy; (1984) William A. Nicol Trophy.

4167
Sir George Earle Trophy
To recognize outstanding achievement in the field of occupational health and safety. Applications may be made by the last day of February each year. A trophy and a commemorative plaque are awarded annually, at a special ceremony. Established in 1956 in honor of Sir George Earle, former President of the Portland Cement Company who donated the trophy.

4168
Gold, Silver, Bronze and Merit Awards
To recognize and celebrate the achievement of a very high standard of health and safety at work. The gold award is for three years; silver for two years; and bronze and merit awards are for one year. In addition, the Gold Medal is awarded to winners of five consecutive Gold Awards, and the President's Award to winners of ten consecutive Gold Awards.

4169
Kearton Award
To recognize an individual, organization, or company that has made a significant contribution to the safety of young people. Awarded to mark Lord Kearton's seven years' distinguished service as President of RoSPA. A monetary prize of £1,000 was awarded annually. (Discontinued)

4170
Kimberly-Clark Special Award
To recognize the best performance by a new entry to the award scheme. A trophy is awarded annually. Established in 1990. Sponsored by Kimberly-Clark Ltd.

4171
Safety Officer of the Year
To recognize the most outstanding contribution to occupational safety and health during the preceding year. An all-expense paid two weeks travel scholarship to the USA that included a one week course at the International Loss Control Institute in Atlanta, Georgia, together with a work pack containing approximately £1,000 worth of equipment was awarded. There are also five runner-up prizes of the work pack containing approximately £1,000 worth of equipment. Established in 1986 by RoSPA and Crown Paints. (Discontinued)

4172
Sector Awards
To recognize the most outstanding performance in health and safety by a company or organization within a particular industry sector. Entrants must demonstrate four years consistently excellent or continuously improving health and safety performance with a high standard of safety policy and commitment. An engraved trophy is awarded annually.

4173
Sun Alliance Trophy
To recognize outstanding achievement in the field of hazard reduction at work. The Award consisted of the Sun Alliance Trophy to be held for one year, a miniature of the Trophy to be held permanently as a record of the achievement, and entitlement to use the trophy emblem on letterheadings, etc. Established in 1988 by the Sun Alliance Insurance Group. (Discontinued)

4174
Royal Society for the Protection of Birds
The Lodge
Sandy, Beds. SG19 2DL, England
Phone: 767 680551
Fax: 767 692365

4175
RSPB Medal
For recognition of loyal service to bird conservation and protection. Two sponsors are required for nomination. A silver medal is awarded at the discretion of the Society at the annual general meeting. Established in 1907.

4176
Royal Society of British Artists
17 Carlton House Terr.
London SW1Y 5BD, England
Phone: 71 930 6844
Fax: 71 839 7830

4177
De Laszlo Medal
For recognition of the best painting or sculpture at the Society's annual open exhibition. A medal is awarded annually. Established in 1910.

4178
Higgs and Hill Bursary
A monetary award of £2,500 is presented annually.

4179
Royal Society of British Sculptors
108 Old Brompton Rd.
London SW7 3RA, England
Phone: 71 373 5554

4180
Otto Beit Award
To recognize the best work of sculpture exhibited during the year in the Commonwealth and United Kingdom outside London. A bronze medal is awarded annually.

4181

Silver Medal
To recognize the best work of sculpture of the year exhibited in London. Awarded annually.

4182

Royal Society of Chemistry
Burlington House
Piccadilly
London W1V 0BN, England

Phone: 71 4378656
Fax: 71 7341227

Formerly: Chemical Society.

4183

Adrien Albert Lectureship
To promote interest in the study of the laws connecting chemical structure with biological activity. A lectureship is awarded biennially. Established from a bequest from the late Adrien Albert, professor of chemistry at the Australian National University, Canberrra and long-standing member of the Society.

4184

Analar Lectureship
To recognize the analytical scientist who has made the most outstanding contributions to the development, innovation, and application of analytical techniques on the basis of published work. There are no restrictions on nationality or place of residence. A gold medal and an honorarium of £1,000 are awarded triennially. Established in 1984 by BDH Chemicals Ltd. to mark the Golden Jubilee of the publication of *Analar Standards*. Administration of the award was transferred to the Society in 1990.

4185

Bader Award
To recognize an individual for eminence in organic chemistry. There is no restriction on age, but nominees must not hold or have held professorships in the British Isles. The major part of the nominee's work must have been carried out in an academic institution in the United Kingdom or Republic of Ireland and the person must currently work in such an institution. The deadline is April 1. A monetary award of £2,000 is presented annually. The winner may be asked to write an article on his or her research for *Aldrichimica Acta*. Established in 1989 by an endowment from Dr. Alfred Bader.

4186

Barrer Award
To recognize the most meritorious recent work in the field of pure or applied molecular sieve zeolites. Candidates under the age of 37 who are born in the United Kingdom or the Republic of Ireland, or persons of any nationality whose work is being carried out in an institution or company in the United Kingdom or Republic of Ireland are considered for the award. Applications must be submitted by December 1. An honorarium of £500 and a scroll are awarded triennially. Established in 1983. Jointly administered by the Society of Chemical Industry.

4187

Beilby Medal and Prize
To recognize scientists or engineers for original work of exceptional merit that has led to advances of practical significance in the fields of chemical engineering, materials science and engineering, or energy efficiency. A monetary prize of £1,000 and a silver gilt medal are awarded annually. Established in 1924 in memory of Sir George Beilby, and administered jointly by The Royal Society of Chemistry, the Society of Chemical Industry, and the Institute of Materials, of which Sir Beilby was President.

4188

Ronald Belcher Memorial Lectureship
To encourage students to make a positive contribution to, and to take an active interest in, the profession of analytical chemistry. Candidates may be nominated by any supervisor of postgraduate students registered with a higher educational establishment within the British Isles. Nominations must be accompanied by a paper or manuscript co-authored by the student. A monetary award of £300 to assist the student to attend a national or international conference and a scroll are presented annually. The winner is given the opportunity to present his or her work at the Research Topics Meeting. Established in 1983 in memory of Professor Ronald Belcher.

4189

Bourke Lectureship
To enable distinguished scientists from overseas to lecture in the United Kingdom in the field of physical chemistry and chemical physics. An honorarium of £500, a silver medal, and a lectureship are awarded annually. Established in 1954 by the Faraday Society in memory of Lieutenant Colonel Bourke, a benefactor of the Society.

4190

Robert Boyle Medal in Analytical Chemistry
To enhance the image of analytical chemistry, particularly in the eyes of scientists in other disciplines. Candidates must be recommended by a member of the Council of the Analytical Division of the Society and supported by a statement of outstanding contributions in all aspects of analytical chemistry (research, practice, teaching, etc). Consideration will be given to the full impact of the recommended work, which must be recognized internationally. A gold medal is awarded biennially when merited. Established in 1981.

4191

S. F. Boys - A Rahman Lectureship
To recognize an individual for outstanding innovatory research in the area of computational chemistry, including both quantum chemistry and molecular simulations. Open to individuals of any age and nationality. Membership in the Society is not a requirement. The deadline is May 31. A monetary award of £500 and a silver medal are presented biennially. Established through funds derived from the 1987 International Conference on the Impact of Supercomputers on Chemistry.

4192

Carbohydrate Chemistry Award
For recognition of the most meritorious contribution to the knowledge of any aspect of carbohydrate chemistry. Members of the Royal Society of Chemists whose work was published during the year in question and the five preceding years and who are citizens of the United Kingdom or the Commonwealth are eligible. Applications must be submitted by October 31. A lecture is usually delivered at the spring meeting of the Carbohydrate Chemistry Discussion Group. A monetary prize of £500 and a silver medal are awarded biennially. Established in 1970. Sponsored by Tate and Lyle.

4193

Centenary Lectureship
To promote the interchange of chemists between Britain and overseas countries. Any scientist normally working outside of Britain is eligible. Three Centenary Lectureships with medals and the opportunity to visit a number of scientific centers in the United Kingdom are awarded annually. Established in 1949 by the British Chemical Industry to commemorate the centenary of the Chemical Society in 1941.

4194

Corday-Morgan Medal and Prize
To recognize chemists who have published during the preceding six years the most meritorious contributions to experimental chemistry. British chemists under 37 years of age are eligible. Applications must be submitted by December 31. Up to three awards, each consisting of a monetary prize of £500 and a silver medal, are presented annually for work in different branches of chemistry. Established in 1949.

4195

Faraday Medal and Lectureship
To recognize a physical/theoretical chemist. A bronze medal and an invitation to present the lecture are awarded. The Faraday Lecture is

usually delivered every three years. Established in 1867 in memory of Michael Faraday, a Fellow of the Society from 1842 to 1867.

4196
Flintoff Medal and Prize
For recognition of an outstanding contribution to the knowledge of the relationship between chemistry and botany. Members of the Society are eligible. A monetary prize of £500 and a medal are awarded triennially. Established in 1954 from a bequest to the Society by the late Robert Flintoff.

4197
Sir Edward Frankland Fellowship
For the encouragement of research in organometallic chemistry or co-ordination chemistry of transition metals. In considering persons for the award, particular attention is paid to evidence of independent creativity in: experimental studies on organometallic chemistry, the latter defined by compounds containing metal-to-carbon bonds excluding those of boron, silicon, germanium, or phosphorus; and experimental studies in the complex compounds of transition metals, including biomimetic chemistry of metals or mechanistic studies and homogeneous catalysis by transition metal complexes. Candidates must be under 36 years of age, be members of the Royal Society of Chemistry, British citizens, and working for the period of the award in a chemistry department in a university, college, or polytechnic in the United Kingdom. Awarded biennially. Established in 1984.

4198
Sir Edward Frankland Prize Lectureship
For recognition of meritorious contributions to pure and applied research in the field of organometallic chemistry as defined by compounds containing metal to carbon bonds, excluding those of boron, silicon, germanium, and phosphorus. There are no restrictions with regard to nationality or membership in the Society. Applications must be submitted by December 31. A monetary prize of £1,000 is presented biennially and the honoree delivers an award lecture. Established in 1982.

4199
Harrison Memorial Prize
To recognize a chemist who has conducted during the previous five years the most meritorious and promising investigations in chemistry, and published the results in scientific periodicals. British chemists under 30 years of age are eligible. Applications must be submitted by December 31. A monetary prize of £500 and a bronze plaque are awarded annually. Established in 1922 in memory of Colonel Edward Frank Harrison, deputy comptroller of the Chemical Warfare Department. Administered jointly by the Society of Chemical Industry, the Royal Pharmaceutical Society, and the Royal Society of Chemistry.

4200
Haworth Memorial Lectureship and Medal
To recognize an eminent chemist. The lecture deals with the advances in any subject of carbohydrate chemistry including contributions that further the better understanding of other branches of chemical science. A monetary prize of £500, a bronze medal, and a lectureship are awarded biennially. Established in 1969 in memory of Sir Norman Haworth, a President of the Society.

4201
Hickinbottom Fellowship
For recognition of research in organic chemistry. Persons holding a Ph.D. degree or equivalent in chemistry and working for the period of the award in a chemistry department in a university, polytechnic, or college in the United Kingdom or Republic of Ireland are eligible. Candidates must not be more than 36 years of age as of October 31 of the year of the nomination and must normally be domiciled in the British Isles. Awarded annually for a two-year period. Established in 1981.

4202
Industrial Lectureship
For recognition of major contributions to and innovations in chemical discovery and chemical-based industry. There are no eligibility restrictions. Awarded biennially. Established in 1981.

4203
Ingold Lectureship
For recognition of exceptional contributions to the field of chemistry. The lecture deals with the relationship between structure and reactivity in chemistry, or any aspect of this theme associated with Sir Christopher Ingold. A monetary prize of £500, a silver medal, and a lectureship are awarded biennially. Established in 1973 in memory of Sir Christopher Ingold, a President of the Society from 1952 to 1954. Formerly: Ingold-Albert Lectureship.

4204
John Jeyes Lectureship
To recognize the individual who has made the most meritorious contributions to the general theme of "Advances in Chemistry Relating to a Better Environment." A monetary prize of £500, a silver medal, and a lectureship are awarded biennially. Established in 1976 by the Jeyes Group in memory of John Jeyes.

4205
Liversidge Lectureship
For recognition of significant accomplishments in chemistry. The lecture deals with the description of new knowledge, and points out the directions in which further research in general, physical, and inorganic chemistry is desirable. A monetary prize of £500, a silver medal, and a lectureship are awarded biennially. Established in 1927 in memory of Professor Archibald Liversidge, a benefactor of the Society.

4206
Longstaff Medal
To recognize a member of the Society who has done the most to promote the science of chemistry by research. A medal is awarded triennially. Established in 1881 in memory of Dr. George Dixon Longstaff, an original member and benefactor of the Society.

4207
Josepf Loschimidt Prize
For recognition of excellence in physical organic chemistry, broadly construed to embrace organic structures, reactivity, and reaction mechanisms. The major part of the work must have been conducted in an academic institution in the United Kingdom or the Republic of Ireland and the nominee must currently work in such an institution. Nominees must not hold or have held professorships in the British Isles. A monetary prize of £2,000 is awarded biennially. Established by Dr. A. Bader.

4208
Marlow Medal and Prize
For recognition of outstanding articles on physical chemistry or chemical physics subjects covered by the Faraday Division's *Transactions*. The award is made on the basis of publications in *Transactions* or elsewhere. Members of the Faraday Division who are under 34 years of age are eligible. Applications must be submitted by January 1. A monetary prize of £500 and a medal are awarded annually. Established in 1957.

4209
Meldola Medal and Prize
To recognize British chemists for showing the most promise as indicated by published chemical work that may have been conducted anywhere in the world. British chemists under 30 years of age on December 31 of the year of the award are eligible. Applications must be submitted by December 31. A monetary prize of £500 and a bronze medal are awarded annually. Established in 1921 by the Society of Maccabaeans in memory of Raphael Meldola, former President of the Society and the former Institute of Chemistry.

4210
Ludwig Mond Lectureship
To recognize accomplishments in the general area of inorganic chemistry. The lectureship is open to chemists of any nationality working in the United Kingdom or overseas. Awarded biennially. Established in 1981 by Imperial Chemical Industries.

4211
Hugo Muller Lectureship
For recognition of valuable scientific endeavors. The subject of the lecture deals with the relationship between chemistry and either botany or mineralogy. A monetary prize of £500, a silver medal, and a lectureship are awarded triennially. Established in 1918 in memory of Dr. Hugo Muller, a President of the Society.

4212
Nyholm Lectureship
To enable a scientist to present a lecture that deals with subjects of interest to either the Dalton Division or the Education Division, and has regard to the wide international interests of Sir Ronald Nyholm. A monetary prize of £500, a silver medal, and a lectureship are awarded annually. Established in 1973 in memory of Sir Ronald Nyholm, a President of the Society.

4213
Pedler Lectureship and Medal
To commend an outstanding chemist and allow him or her to present a lecture that deals with the description of new knowledge and the directions that further research in any branch of organic chemistry. A monetary prize of £500, a silver medal, and a lectureship are awarded biennially. Established in 1927 in memory of Sir Alexander Pedler, a benefactor of the Society. Sponsored by Pfizer Ltd.

4214
Theophilus Redwood Lectureship
To recognize a leading analytical chemist. A monetary prize of £500, an inscribed scroll, and a lectureship are awarded. The lecture is given each year at the annual chemical conference. Established in 1972 to commemorate the 1874 formation of the Society of Public Analysts (now the Analytical Division of the Royal Society of Chemistry).

4215
Rhone - Poulenc Lectureship
For recognition of notable contributions to organic chemistry. There are no restrictions in regard to the nationality or age of the recipient, and membership in the Society is not a requirement. A monetary prize of £500, a silver medal, and a lectureship are awarded biennially. Established in 1984 to mark the sesquicentenary of May and Baker Ltd. Formerly: May and Baker Lectureship.

4216
Robert Robinson Lectureship
To honor a distinguished scientist. The lecture reviews progress in any branch of chemistry and is presented at the Society's annual congress. A monetary prize of £500, a silver medal, and a lectureship are awarded biennially. Established in 1962 in honor of Sir Robert Robinson on his seventieth birthday.

4217
R. A. Robinson Memorial Lectureship
For recognition of contributions in the field of the physical chemistry of solutions. At least one in three of the lectures will be given by a United Kingdom lecturer visiting Singapore and Malaysia, or by a lecturer from one of these countries visiting the United Kingdom. A monetary prize of £500, a silver medal, and a lectureship are awarded annually. Established in 1981 by Professor R. H. Stokes in memory of Professor R. A. Robinson.

4218
RSC Interdisciplinary Awards
To draw attention to the importance of interdisciplinary studies, particularly those of public interest, involving chemistry and one or more other sciences, and to the Society's interest in the willingness to encourage such work that reaches across traditional boundaries; and to enable work that involves chemists working with scientists from different disciplines to be appropriately rewarded and publicized. There are neither age nor nationality restrictions for the awards, but nominees are expected to be domiciled in the United Kingdom or Republic of Ireland. The individual awards consist of an inscribed memento and an honorarium of £500, while the presentation of the award is associated with a lecture by the successful candidate forming the center place of a one-day scientific meeting. Up to three interdisciplinary awards may be made each year. Established in 1986.

4219
RSC Sponsored Awards
To recognize individuals who have made fundamental contributions to their respective fields of chemistry and whose work has been directed to its application. Men and women of British nationality, including Commonwealth citizens or those normally domiciled in the British Isles, are considered for the awards. Each award consists of a monetary prize of £500 and a silver medal. Awarded at varying intervals. These prizes are made possible by the assistance of a number of industrial companies. The sponsoring bodies and the dates established are shown after the names of the individual awards: Analytical Reactions and Analytical Reagents - Merck Ltd. (1980); Analytical Separation Methods - Roche Products Ltd. (1981); Analytical Spectroscopy - Unicam Ltd. (1980); Chemical Dynamics - B. P. Chemicals Ltd. (1993); Chemical Analysis and Instrumentation - Perkin-Elmer Ltd. (1971); Chemical Education - Beecham Pharmaceuticals (1972); Chemistry and Electrochemistry of Transition Metals - Inco Europe Ltd. (1980); Chemistry of the Noble Metals and Their Compounds - Engelhard (1981); Chromatography and Separation Chemistry - Whatman Scientific Ltd. (1980); Combustion and Hydrocarbon Oxidation Chemistry - Esso Petroleum Company Ltd. (1993); Electroanalytical Chemistry - ABB Kent Taylor Ltd. (1981); Electrochemistry - Chapman E. Hall Journals Division (1991); Enzyme Chemistry - the Charmian Medal - Lilly Research Centre Ltd. (1980); Health, Safety, or Environmental Chemistry - Shell UK Ltd. (1981); Hetherocyclic Chemistry - Fisons plc Pharmaceutical Division (1980); Industrial Analysis - Tioxide Group Ltd. (1980); Industrial Chemistry - Harcros Chemical Group (1970); Inorganic Biochemistry - Chapman & Hall Scientific Data Division (1992); Inorganic Reaction Mechanisms - ICI plc (1993); Macromolecules and Polymers - Courtaulds plc. (1971); Main Group Element Chemistry - Albright & Wilson Ltd. (1970); Materials Science - ICI plc. (1991); Medicinal Chemistry - Boots Pharmaceuticals (1971); Natural Product Chemistry - Roche Products Ltd. (1970); Organic Reaction Mechanisms - BP Research (1980); Organometallic Chemistry - Monsanto (1970); Photochemistry - Cookson Group plc. (1993); Reaction Kinetics - Shell Research Ltd. (1980); Solid State Chemistry - Johnson Matthey plc, Materials Technology Division (1975); Stereochemistry - Glaxo Group Research Ltd. (1992); Spectroscopy - Varian NMR Division (1980); Structural Chemistry - Kratos Group plc. (1970); Surface and Colloid Chemistry - Unilever Research (1971); Synthetic Organic Chemistry - CIBA (1971); Theoretical and Computational Chemistry - Pergamon Press Ltd. (1992); Tertiary Education - ICI plc (1991); and Thermodynamics and Statistical Mechanics Unileve Research and Engineering (1994).

4220
SAC Gold Medal
To enhance the image of analytical chemistry in the United Kingdom, particularly in the eyes of scientists in other disciplines. Candidates must be British subjects. Consideration is given to the full impact of the candidate's work in research, practice, and teaching. The candidate's work must also be internationally recognized. A gold medal is awarded when merited by the Analytical Division of the Society. Established in 1964.

4221
SAC Silver Medal
To encourage young scientists working in any field covering the practices and teaching of analytical chemistry. Consideration is given to those who, in the opinion of the Analytical Division of the Society, have made the

greatest contributions and whose work has made the most significant impact on any branch of analytical chemistry. A monetary prize of £500, a silver medal, and an opportunity to deliver a lecture to the Analytical Division are awarded when merited. Established in 1973.

4222
Simonsen Lectureship
To provide the opportunity for younger workers of all nationalities in the field of the chemistry of natural products to present a lecture. A monetary prize of £500, a silver medal, and a lectureship are awarded triennially. Established in 1957 in memory of Sir John Simonsen, Vice President of the Society, by his wife, Lady Simonsen.

4223
Spiers Memorial Lectureship
To enable a respected chemist from the United Kingdom or overseas to present a lecture that serves as the Introduction to a General Discussion. An honorarium of £500, a silver medal, and a lectureship are awarded triennially. Established in 1928 by the Faraday Society in memory of F. S. Spiers, the first Secretary of the Society.

4224
Tilden Lectureship
To encourage work in chemistry. The lecture deals with the progress in some branch of chemistry. Younger members of the Society are eligible. Three appointments as Tilden Lecturers are named annually. Established in 1939 in memory of Sir William Agustus Tilden, a President of the Society.

4225
Royal Society of Health
RSH House
38A St. George's Dr.
London SW1V 4BH, England   Phone: 71 630 0121

4226
Lord Cohen Award
For recognition of outstanding work in the field of health. A gold medal is awarded triennially.

4227
Gold Medal
To recognize an outstanding worker in any of the professions and disciplines identified with health. Awarded triennially. Established in 1966.

4228
John William Starkey Award
To recognize a person of any nationality for the best research paper in the English language on mental health.

4229
John Edward Worth Prize
For recognition of the best essay related to an aspect of health. A monetary prize is awarded annually.

4230
Royal Society of Literature
1 Hyde Park Gardens   Phone: 71 7235104
London W2 2LT, England   Fax: 71 4020199

4231
Benson Medal
To recognize outstanding works of poetry, fiction, biography, or belles-lettres. A silver medal is awarded periodically when merited. Established in 1916 by Dr. A. C. Benson.

4232
Winifred Holtby Memorial Prize
For recognition of the best regional work of fiction written in the English language. Writers of British or Irish nationality, or citizens of the Commonwealth are eligible. If in any year it is considered that no regional novel is of sufficient merit, the prize may be awarded to an author, qualified as aforesaid, of a literary work of nonfiction or poetry, concerning a regional subject. Entries must be submitted by October 31. A monetary prize of £800 awarded annually. Established in 1966 by Vera Brittain to honor Winifred Holtby, who died at the age of thirty-seven.

4233
Royal Society of Literature Award
For recognition of literary works published during the preceding year, and to encourage genuine contributions to literature. Preference is given to those publications which are less likely to command big sales, e.g., poetry, biography, criticism, philosophy, and history. Special interest is taken in younger authors who are not yet well recognized. Publishers, not authors, must submit books written in English to the committee for consideration. Entries must be submitted by October 31. As many as three prizes totaling £5000 may be awarded annually. Established in 1944 to honor W. H. Heinemann.

4234
Royal Society of Medicine
1 Wimpole St.
London W1M 8AE, England   Phone: 71 4082119

4235
John Arderne Medal and Prize
To recognize a recipient selected by the Council of the Section of Colonproctology for the quality of presentation and the content of a paper delivered at a meeting of the Section. The recipient must be a person who has not yet reached consultant status; exceptionally, the award may be made to a person who is not medically qualified. The successful candidate need not be a Fellow of the Royal Society of Medicine. The award consists of a medal struck in silver-gilt and an honorarium of £100. The medal and prize are presented annually to the recipient by the President of the Section at the annual dinner.

4236
Blair-Bell Medal
For recognition of outstanding work in the science of gynecology and obstetrics. The Council of the Section of Obstetrics and Gynaecology nominates a recipient. A gold medal is awarded every five years. Established in 1955 in memory of Professor William Blair-Bell.

4237
Colyer Prize
For recognition of the best original work in dental science completed during the previous five years by a dental surgeon educated at any duly recognized dental school in Great Britain or Northern Ireland, and who has not been qualified to practice more than 10 years at the date of the award. Applications from candidates, together with a general account of their projects, must be submitted to the Prize Committee not later than March 31 preceding the date of the award. A monetary prize is awarded triennially. Established in 1926 to commemorate the twenty-five years' service of Sir Frank Colyer as Honorary Curator of the Odontological Museum.

4238
A. C. Comfort Memorial Award
For recognition of a paper on some aspects of clinical research in geriatric medicine, written by a practitioner of not more than five years' standing from qualification, or by a student or intern approaching the medical degree. A monetary prize of £200 and the cost of publishing the award-winning paper are presented annually. Established by Dr. Alex Comfort in 1981 as a memorial to his late father, A. C. Comfort.

4239
Dalby Prize
To encourage the science and art of otology. Persons of British nationality recommended to the Council of the Society by the President and Vice-Presidents of the Section of Otology as having published or done the best original work in otology during the previous five years are considered. The prize may be shared if, in the opinion of the Council of the Society, there are at any time two people whose work is considered to be of equal merit. A monetary prize is awarded every five years. Established in 1928 by Lady Hyacinthe Dalby, widow of William Dalby.

4240
W. E. Dixon Lecture
To provide for lectures on therapeutic and pharmacological subjects. Fellows, members of Sections, and persons invited by the Section with the Council's approval are considered. An honorarium of 50 guineas is awarded triennially. Established in 1934.

4241
Doubleday Lectureship
To provide for a lecture in the field of odontology. Individuals who are of British nationality and who hold a higher qualification in dentistry or in medicine or the Honors degree in science of a University are eligible for consideration. The lecturer is appointed by the Council of the Society upon the nomination of a committee consisting of three members of the Section of Odontology. An honorarium of £105 is awarded every five years. Established in 1977 in the will of Dr. F.N. Doubleday.

4242
Dowling Lecturerships
To provide for a lecture in the field of dermatology and to encourage the production of, and the dissemination of, information about original work in dermatology and the constructive inter-change of knowledge both at home and abroad. Lecturers are appointed by the Council of the Society on the recommendation of the Council of the Section of Dermatology. An honorarium of £50 and travelling expenses are awarded annually. Established in 1971.

4243
Downs Travelling Scholarship
To support travel to centers of laryngology or rhinology overseas, and for recognition of a paper on a subject within the field of laryngology and rhinology submitted each year by an author of senior registrar status or by a consultant within two years of his appointment. All papers to be considered must be submitted on the understanding that the author may be required to read his or her paper at a meeting of the Section, that the decision of the judges shall be final, and that the winning paper will be offered for publication to the Editor of the Journal or the Royal Society of Medicine. A monetary prize of £1,000 is awarded annually. Established in 1980.

4244
Alan Edwards Prize
To advance the study of clinical medical science. Individuals who have not yet gained consultant status are eligible for the case presentation in each session adjudged most likely to advance the study of clinical medical science. A monetary prize of £25 is awarded annually. Established in 1979 in memory of Alan Edwards.

4245
Ellison-Cliffe Medal and Lecture
To provide for a lecture by a medically qualified person of eminence in his or her field at the Society's House on a subject connected with the contribution of fundamental science to advances in medicine. Invitations to the Lecture are not restricted to members of the Society and special care is taken to invite scientists working in areas that could become related to medicine. A medal and expenses for the lecturer are awarded annually. Established by Percy Cliffe and his wife, Carice Ellison.

4246
Ernest Fletcher Memorial Lecture
To provide for a lecture upon a rheumatological subject. An honorarium of £50 is awarded triennially. Established in 1964.

4247
Norman Gamble Research Prize
For recognition of the best original work in otology completed during the four years prior to the month of October in the year of the award. The competition for this prize is open to any British subject, whether lay or medical. A monetary prize of £50 is awarded every four years. Established in 1930 by Mr. Norman Gamble.

4248
William Gibson Research Scholarship for Medical Women
To recognize a woman who is a British subject and possesses a registrable medical qualification. No qualifying examination is necessary, but the Committee in their choice of the scholar takes into consideration research work either already done or contemplated by her. The scholar must be free to travel for the purposes of the research she has undertaken. A scholarship is awarded biennially. Established in 1919.

4249
Gold Medal of the Royal Society of Medicine
To recognize scientists who, in the opinion of the Council of the Society, have made valuable contributions towards the progress of the art and science of medicine, preventive medicine, or surgery either by original discoveries or by the practical application of the results of previous investigations of other scientists. A small selection committee chooses up to three names to be submitted to the Council of the Society with whom the final selection rests. A gold medal is awarded triennially. The recipient may be invited to give an address dealing with the special branch of medical science in which he has obtained eminence. Established in 1920.

4250
Alexander Haddow Lecture
To advance the study of oncology and to provide for a lecture on some subject related to cancer. Individuals must be nominated by a subcommittee of the Council of the Section of Oncology. The lecturer is appointed by the Council of the Society. An honorarium of £100 is awarded biennially. Established in 1977.

4251
W. J. Harrison Prize (Laryngological Section)
To recognize a member of the Section of Laryngology who, in the two preceding years, has made the greatest contribution towards advancement of knowledge in the Section. A monetary prize is awarded biennially. Established in 1928 by a bequest of William John Harrison.

4252
Richard Hewitt Award
To recognize a person who has made a notable and recognized contribution to the improvement of human health. A monetary prize of $10,000 and commemorative award are presented by the Royal Society of Medicine, London, and the Royal Society of Medicine Foundation, Inc., New York. Awarded annually. Established in 1982 by SmithKline Beckman Corporation in honor of Richard Hewitt, former secretary of the Society.

4253
Henry Hill Hickman Medal
For recognition of an original work of outstanding merit in anaesthesia or in a subject directly connected with anaesthesia. Open to any person of any nationality and not necessarily to medical men or women. A bronze medal bearing on one side a portrait of Henry Hill Hickman and on the other a design symbolizing the triumph of anaesthesia over pain is awarded triennially.

4254
Samuel Hyde Memorial Lecture
To provide for a lecture in the field of rheumatology and rehabilitation. A lecturer is appointed by the Council of the Society on the nomination of the Council of the Section of Rheumatology and Rehabilitation. An honorarium of £30 is awarded triennially. Established in 1910 in memory of Dr. Samuel Hyde of Buxton, founder of the British Balneological and Climatological Society. Sponsored by the British Balneological and Climatological Society.

4255
Hughlings Jackson Lecture and Medal
To advance the science of neurology by providing a lecture. The Council of the Section of Neurology submits to the Council of the Society the names of three people to be invited to deliver the next lecture. A gold medal and an honorarium of not more than 100 guineas is awarded triennially. Established in 1897 in memory of Hughlings Jackson.

4256
Jenner Medal
For recognition of distinguished work in epidemiological research or for pre-eminence in the prevention and control of epidemic disease. The Council of the Society on the recommendation of the Council of the Section of Epidemiology and Public Health makes the selection. The selection is restricted to British subjects. A bronze medal is awarded when merited. Established in 1898 by the Epidemiological Society in memory of Edward Jenner.

4257
Jephcott Lectures
To provide for lectures in the field of medicine. An honorarium is awarded annually. Established in 1959.

4258
Richard Kovacs Prize
For recognition of distinguished work in physical medicine during the previous three years. The Council of the Society, on the recommendation of the Council of the Section of Rheumatology and Rehabilitation, makes the selection. A monetary prize of £100 is awarded triennially. The person to whom the prize is awarded may, at the discretion of the Council of the Section, be invited to deliver a lecture to a meeting of the Section. Established in 1961.

4259
Leah Lederman Memorial Lectures
To provide for the delivery of a lecture in the Society's House on a subject connected with some aspect of cancer of the breast or of the female genital tract. The lecturer is appointed by the Council of the Society upon the recommendation of a nominating committee. An honorarium of £100 is awarded biennially. Established in 1973 by Dr. M. Lederman.

4260
Nichols Fellowship
For recognition of the most valuable contribution by a British subject towards the discovery of the cause and the prevention of death in childbirth from septicaemia. To provide for research to advance knowledge in obstetrics and gynaecology. The work must be conducted in an approved institution providing suitable facilities. Candidates for the Fellowship are allowed as wide a choice as possible within the terms of the bequest, but the line and character of the research intended must be stated in the candidates's application. An honorarium of £200 per annum and a grant of £25 per annum for expenses is awarded triennially. Established in 1938 by a bequest of Dr. Thomas Nichols to the Society.

4261
Nuffield Lecture
To provide for a lecture to be delivered from time to time as decided upon by the Council of the Society (but not more than once in any calendar year) on October 10, or on the nearest suitable day in honor of Lord Nuffield and to advance the science and art of medicine. Lecturers are appointed by the Council of the Society on the recommendation of a Committee consisting of the President of the Society for the time being, all living past presidents of the Society willing to serve, and, during the lifetime of Lord Nuffield, three other members nominated by him. A gold medal and an honorarium of 100 guineas are awarded every three to four years. Established in 1959 by Lord Nuffield.

4262
Odontological Commemorative Lecture
To provide for a lecture in the field of odontology. The Council of the Society on the recommendation of the Council of the Section of Odontology makes the selection. Such persons are preferably drawn from overseas. An honorarium of £100 is awarded every five years. Established in 1972.

4263
Ophthalmology Fund Prizes and Lectures
To recognize the ophthalmologist judged to have done, in the British Isles, the best piece of original work published during the previous twelve months. To be eligible for the award, the candidate, who may be of any nationality, must not have attained an official consultant appointment, nor have undertaken professional clinical work of equivalent responsibility for any substantial period before or during the execution of the original work. The following prizes are awarded: £50, awarded annually and established in 1963; Lecture and Lang Medal - £150 and a medal, awarded triennially and established in 1964; and Travelling Fellows - £200, awarded annually and established in 1964.

4264
Lloyds Roberts Lecture
To provide for a lecture in the field of medicine. Established in 1910 by a bequest of the late Dr. David Lloyd Roberts of Manchester.

4265
RSM May and Baker Pharmaceuticals Prizes
For recognition of a paper on the subject of anaesthesia. To be eligible, a practitioner must, at the submission date, be a junior in training at any grade from House Officer to Senior Registrar in the National Health Service (or its equivalent). The training appointment must be in a field related to, and designed as part of training for, a career in anaesthesia. It must be in a department or hospital in, or in the armed forces of, a country of the Commonwealth, the Republics of South Africa, or Eire. The applicant need not be a native of the country of appointment nor need be a member of the Royal Society of Medicine. Although the anaesthetist must be of the above grade at the time the paper is submitted, he or she may change in grade before the declaration of the result. An author may submit only one paper in any one year's competition. Two prizes each for £150 are awarded annually. Established in 1961. Formerly: (1984) Registrar's Prize.

4266
Sherrington Memorial Lecture
To provide for a lecture to be delivered in April or May devoted to the advancement of the sciences of neurology and of physiology. A gold medal and an honorarium of 100 guineas are awarded every five years. Established in 1957 in memory of Sir Charles Scott Sherrington.

4267
Joseph Toynbee Memorial Lectureship
To provide for a lecture in otology. The Lectureship is open, without restriction of nationality, to any person who is, in the opinion of the Selection Committee, qualified to contribute to the advancement of the science and practice of otology. An honorarium of £100 and an illuminated certificate are awarded biennially. Established jointly by the Royal College of Surgeons of England and the Royal Society of Medicine.

4268
Hugh Wallace Essay Prize
For recognition of a review article written in English and not exceeding 3,500 words on a clinical subject or an essay of a speculative or philosophical nature on any aspect of dermatology. A monetary prize and publication in the Journal of the Society are awarded. Established by a bequest of Dr. Hugh Wallace.

4269
Hugh Wallace's Registrars' Prize
To recognize a dermatologist of registrar or senior registrar grade (or of equivalent academic status) considered to have made the most outstanding contribution at Section Meetings during the session preceding the year of award. A Selection Committee is established annually to submit a recommendation to the Council of the Society. A monetary prize of £50 is awarded annually. Established in honor of Hugh Wallace, a former president of the Section.

4270
C. E. Wallis Lecture
To provide for a lecture on the history of dentistry. The lecturer is appointed by the Council on the recommendation of a Committee of Selection nominated by the Council of the Section of Odontology and of the Council of the Section of the History of Medicine. An honorarium is awarded every five years. Established in 1932 by Mr. Ferdinand Wallis in memory of his brother, Mr. C. E. Wallis.

4271
Albert Wander Lecture
To provide for a lecture in the field of general practice of medicine. An honorarium is awarded annually. Established in 1963.

4272
Edith Whetnall Lectureship
To provide for a lecture on a subject connected with the diagnosis, causation, prevention, and management of deafness in children, preference being given to a lecture dealing with the auditory approach. The lecturer is appointed by the Council of the Society upon the nomination of a committee. An honorarium of £100 and a bronze medal are awarded biennially. Established in 1971.

4273
Michael Williams Lecture
To provide for a lecture on the subject of the causes or prevention of cancer. Lecturers are chosen by the Council or, at the discretion of the Council, by the Council of any Section under whose auspices the lecture is to be delivered. An honorarium of not less than £150 is awarded biennially. Established in 1963 in memory of Michael Williams.

4274
Winsbury-White Lecture
To provide for a lecture upon a medical subject to be delivered in the Society's House from time to time. The lecturer is chosen by the Council of the Society upon the recommendation of the Council of the Section of Urology. An honorarium of £100 is awarded biennially. Established in 1964 by a bequest of Horace Powell Winsbury-White.

4275
Royal Society of Tropical Medicine and Hygiene
Manson House
26 Portland Pl.
London W1N 4EY, England
Phone: 71 580 2127
Fax: 71 436 1389

4276
Chalmers Memorial Medal
For recognition of research of outstanding merit contributing to knowledge of tropical hygiene. Individuals under 45 years of age are eligible. A silver-gilt medal is awarded biennially. Established in 1923 in memory of Dr. Albert John Chalmers, who was known for his work in tropical medicine.

4277
Sir Rickard Christophers Medal
For recognition of work in tropical medicine and hygiene in its broadest sense with particular consideration given to practical and field applications. Fellows of the Society may nominate a candidate by October 31. A bronze medal is awarded triennially. Established in 1979 in memory of Sir Rickard Christophers, for a lifetime spent in the relentless and inspired pursuit of knowledge.

4278
Honorary Fellow
To recognize an individual for an outstanding contribution to the field of tropical medicine and hygiene. Established in 1967.

4279
George Macdonald Medal
For recognition of outstanding research leading to improvement of health in tropical countries. The London School Council and the Council of the Society propose the names of the candidates. A medal is awarded by the Dean of the School at a meeting decided by the Council of the Society. Awarded triennially. Established in 1968 in memory of Dr. George Macdonald, Professor of Tropical Hygiene at the London School of Hygiene and Tropical Medicine, and Director of the Ross Institute. Co-sponsored by the London School of Hygiene and Tropical Medicine.

4280
Donald Mackay Medal
For recognition of outstanding work in tropical health, especially relating to improvements in the health of rural or urban workers in the tropics. There are no restrictions as to the nationality or sex of the candidates. Preference will be given to suitable medically qualified candidates, but those in other disciplines are eligible. Any Member or Fellow of either Society is entitled to nominate a candidate, not later than October 31 of the year preceding the award. The Medal is awarded annually; in years of even date by the Royal Society of Tropical Medicine and Hygiene and in years of odd date by the American Society of Tropical Medicine and Hygiene. Established in 1990 in memory of Dr. Donald Mackay, who was Deputy Director of the Ross Institute at the London School of Hygiene and Tropical Medicine, who died in 1981 after many years of outstanding work in tropical occupational health, especially on the tea plantations of South Asia.

4281
Manson Medal
This, the Society's highest mark of distinction, is given for original work in any branch of tropical medicine or tropical hygiene. Fellows of the Society may nominate a candidate by October 31. A bronze medal is awarded triennially. Established in 1922 in memory of Sir Patrick Manson, first president of the Society.

4282
Royal Television Society
Tavistock House E.
Tavistock Sq.
London WC1H 9HR, England
Phone: 71 387 1970
Fax: 71 387 0358

4283
Royal Television Society Gold Medal
This, the highest award of the Society, is given for outstanding services in the field of television. A gift of the Chairman is awarded annually. Established in 1969.

4284
Royal Television Society Programme Awards
For recognition of the best television programs. Awards are given annually in the following categories: (1) Single Drama; (2) Drama Series; (3) Drama Serial; (4) Single Documentary; (5) Documentary Series; (6) Situation Comedy; (7) Light Entertainment; (8) Arts; (9) Outside Broadcasts - this category is for coverage of a live event - sports, or a major public event which would have taken place anyway; (10) Technique - open to anyone specializing in electronic effects, lighting, videotape or film editing, sound or camerawork; (11) Regional - open to any program made by an ITV company or by a BBC region and must have been shown first within a region; (12) Childrens' Awards: (a) Drama and Light Entertainment Award; and (b) Factual Award; (13) Performance Awards - made at the discretion of the jury; (14) Cyril Bennett Award - presented annually by London Weekend Television in recognition of an outstanding contribution

to television programming over a number of years by an individual or a group; (15) Judges' Award - to recognize other outstanding achievements which do not fit neatly into any other category; and (16) Performance Awards. Awarded annually.

4285
Royal Television Society Silver Medal
For recognition of outstanding creative achievement behind the camera. Awarded annually by the Program Awards Committee. (Discontinued)

4286
Royal Television Society Student Director Award
To encourage young people studying television with a view to entering the program side of the industry. Each college may select an entry that is the work of a single undergraduate or a group of undergraduates taking a first degree course which includes television. The entry should be a single subject television program of an entertainment or educational nature. Entries must be electronically made and have a maximum duration of 30 minutes. The choice of program content is limited to a particular area. In 1985 it is in the documentary/current affairs areas, in 1986 drama, and in 1987 music and art - performance or documentary, and in 1990 drama. A monetary prize of £250 and a certificate are awarded annually. Established in 1983.

4287
Royal Television Society Technology Awards in Memory of Geoffrey Parr
To recognize engineering and operational developments in television broadcasting. The following awards are presented: (1) Operational Systems Award - to an individual or team for outstanding developments or innovation in engineering or operational systems, as applied to the television broadcasting chain, or in program production use in television studios/location areas of work. (2) Research and Development Award - to an individual or team for research or development which has led to a significant advance in the technology of television; and (3) Communications Innovation Award - for an outstanding innovation to the technique or equipment for communications used in connection with broadcasting. In addition, a Judge's Award may be presented. Awarded annually. Established in 1983. Formerly: Geoffrey Parr Award.

4288
Royal Television Society Television Journalism Awards
To recognize and encourage the highest professional standards in news and current affairs television programs. Awards are given in the following categories: (1) Current Affairs Awards (Home and International) - to recognize an original approach to contextual news reporting rather than factual news gathering. Investigations into matters of public concern are included in this category and of particular importance are items not previously reported. One award is given for Home and one for International; (2) News Awards - for the best news item in each category, however covered. The Home section is for any UK news story covered by UK broadcasting organizations or agencies and transmitted as soon as possible after the event either regionally or on the networks. The International section is for any news story from abroad covered by UK broadcasting organizations or agencies. The Topical Feature is for one item up to 15 minutes in length, as broadcast; (3) Regional Awards - for the best regional news magazine program. The judges take into account the editorial approach, studio presentation including direction, design, lighting, sound, graphics, newsreaders and anchor men, etc., in short the style and professionalism of the complete program. (4) Television Journalist of the Year - for the best presentation by a broadcast journalist on sound or camera of a news story either on location or in the studio. A portfolio of two or three items is required. The style and clarity of the report and the extent to which the journalist uses his specialist knowledge of the subject is taken into account by the judges; (5) Television News Cameraman/Woman of the Year - portfolio of two or three items, mute or with sound, ENG or film taken by one cameraman/woman to demonstrate the range of skills is required, including: (a) working under difficult conditions; (b) telling a story in pictures; (c) opportunism; and (6) Judges' Award - a special award to an individual or production team for an outstanding contribution to the advancement of television journalism. Awarded annually.

4289
Royal Town Planning Institute
26 Portland Pl.
London W1N 4BE, England

Phone: 71 6369107
Fax: 71 3231582

4290
Annual Award for Planning Achievement
For recognition of an achievement of significant environmental improvement of lasting community benefit, or some other outstanding achievement judged to have significantly advanced the science and art of town planning for the benefit of the public. Citizens of the United Kingdom are eligible. The following criteria are considered: the enhancement of the physical environment with recognizable social and economic benefit resulting from the achievement in terms of human happiness, greater safety, greater efficiency; the originality and innovation of the achievement or approach; the quality of the professional work involved in design, development of planning concepts, and application of planning techniques; the extent that the scheme serves as a model for other work elsewhere or as a base for the development of further related schemes; and the role played by the planner as an enabler and coordinator. The size of a project is not necessarily relevant to the evaluation of an achievement. The award is for group and not individual achievement and may be presented to a planning team, planning firm, community group, or local authority judged to merit such recognition for the winning achievement. A Silver Jubilee Cup and certificates are awarded annually. Established in 1977 on the occasion of the 25th anniversary of the Queen's accession to the throne.

4291
Gold Medal
For recognition of outstanding achievement in the field of town and country planning. Candidates must be citizens of the United Kingdom. A gold medal is awarded irregularly at the discretion of the Council of the Royal Town Planning Institute. Established in 1953.

4292
George Pepler International Award
To enable individuals of any country to visit Britain for a short time to study an aspect of town and country planning or a related subject. Individuals under 30 years of age are eligible. A monetary prize of £750 or its equivalent is awarded annually. Established in 1963 by Lady Pepler in memory of Sir George Pepler.

4293
Royal United Services Institute for Defence Studies
Whitehall
London SW1A 2ET, England

Phone: 71 9305854
Fax: 71 3210943

4294
Chesney Memorial Gold Medal
To recognize the author who has made, over time, a major contribution to advance military science or knowledge. Individuals may be nominated. A gold medal is awarded when merited. Established in 1900 in memory of General Sir George Chesney, military author, reformer, and engineer.

4295
Trench Gascoigne Prize Essay Competition
To recognize an essayist for originality in military thinking. Candidates, particularly officers and individuals under 30 years of age, may submit essays by December 15 of the year preceding the award. Authors may be of any nationality but must present their work in English. They need not be members of the Institute. The subject is to be in the broad field of defense and international security, ideally with emphasis upon the military sciences and it should be related to contemporary problems. Work originated in UK or other Commonwealth Staff College schemes is eligible and is particularly encouraged. The winning essay may be published in the the RUSI journal. A monetary award is presented annually . Established in 1897 by Colonel F. C. Trench Gascoigne.

4296
Royal Watercolour Society
Bankside Gallery
48 Hopton St., Blackfriars
London SE1 9JH, England
Phone: 71 9287521
Fax: 71 9282820

4297
Royal Watercolour Society Award
To encourage professional development in the field of watercolor painting. Students in their final year at art college, or who have graduated within the last two years are eligible. A monetary prize of £1,000 is awarded annually. Established in 1989.

4298
Royal Yachting Association
Sec. Gen.
RYA House, Romsey Rd.
Eastleigh, Hants. SO5 4YA, England
Phone: 703 629962
Fax: 703 629924

4299
RYA Award
To recognize an individual for services to the sport of yachting. A medal, a scroll, and a gold anchor pin are awarded each year at the annual general meeting. Established in 1971.

4300
Sir Henry Royce Memorial Foundation
92 Kimberley Rd.
Solihull B92 8PX, England
Phone: 21 743 2966

4301
British Petroleum Build A Car Competition
To provide a competition to design and build a car. Members of the team are to be under 20 years on October 1st of the year of opening of the competition. Each vehicle must be supported by a log of the design and development and include the research and its sources. The Foundation provides judges and, until 1984, provided a £100 prize but this has been temporarily suspended and it is hoped that it can be restored possibly in 1996. The competition takes place in even-numbered years.

4302
Engineering Council Young Engineer for Britain Competition
To encourage young engineers of 12 to 19 to undertake engineering projects and to strengthen the links between education and industry. The award is coupled with a day at the Hunt House. Awarded when merited.

4303
Foundation Award to the Technician of the Year in the Rolls-Royce Dealer Network Chosen by a Craft Competition
To recognize the Technician of the Year. A monetary award of £100, gold medal, and certificate of merit are presented when merited.

4304
Foundation Prestige Lectures
To discuss issues ranging from highly technological to historical; or to recall personal memories or periods or events associated with the pursuit of excellence or with Sir Henry and his successors. Speakers are presented with a certificate of merit. Lectures are presented annually.

4305
Ministry of Defence Medal
To recognize the Ministry of Defence apprentice with the most appropriate project. A monetary prize of £100, a medal and a certificate of merit are awarded annually. Established in 1983 by Nigel Hughes.

4306
Queen's Silver Jubilee Competition
To encourage better communication by engineers. The competition is held each year with a trophy to the overall winner and a £1,000 check. There are cash prizes totaling approximately £5,000 to the losing finalists and to the winners in the fourteen regions. The Foundation awards a certificate of merit to the winner, which is presented at an appropriate occasion at the Hunt House. Organized by the Qualifications and Educational Board of the Institution of Mechanical Engineers and partially funded by the Foundation.

4307
Rover Midlander Open Design Award
To recognize the teacher or school contributing the most towards encouraging engineering design in secondary education. A certificate and up to £250 is awarded to the winner. Administered by the midland Branch of the Institute of Mechanical Engineering.

4308
IIE Sir Henry Royce Award for Achievement
To recognize the best electrical project. A monetary award of £250, a medal, and a certificate are presented when merited.

4309
Sir Henry Royce Initiative Award
To recognize a member of the Institution of Mechanical Engineers for the best innovation of the year. A monetary prize of £75, a medal and a certificate are awarded. Established in 1989.

4310
Sir Henry Royce Memorial Award of the Worshipful Company of Carmen
To recognize outstanding work in extending the frontiers of achievement in pursuit of excellence in the field of transportation. A trophy, certificate of merit, and gold medal are presented annually. Administered by the Worshipful Company of Carmen and partially funded by the Foundation.

4311
Sir Henry Royce Memorial Award
For recognition of outstanding work in extending the frontiers of achievement in the pursuit of excellence in the field of transport. A monetary prize of £250, a gold medal, illuminated citation, and certificate of merit are awarded annually. Administered by the Worshipful Company of Carmen and partially funded by the Foundation.

4312
Sir Henry Royce Memorial Lecture
To recognize excellence in mechanical engineering. A trophy and a certificate of merit from the Foundation are awarded when merited. Organized by the Automobile Division of the Institute of Mechanical Engineers and partially funded by the Foundation.

4313
Sir Henry Royce Memorial Lecture
To provide for a lecture on the subject of the pursuit of excellence. A trophy which is retained by the lecturer consisting of a "Spirit of ecstacy" mounted on a pedestal in the form of a Rolls-Royce radiator is awarded. The lecturer is also presented with a Foundation certificate of merit. Awarded annually in alternate years with the FISITA lecture. Established in 1980.

4314
Sir Henry Royce Prestige Lecture on the Institution of Incorporated Engineers
To recognize the speaker at this event. A medal is presented when merited. Jointly organized by IMechE and SHRMF and partially funded by the Foundation.

4315

Sir Henry Royce Pupil Prize

To recognize the best submitted paper or project resulting from a school pupil request for information to the Foundation, R-REC or any Rolls-Royce company or plant. The deadline for submissions is December 31. A monetary award of £100, a medal, and a certificate of merit are presented when merited.

4316

Sir Henry Royce Trophy for the Pursuit of Excellence

To recognize the highest performance in the pursuit of excellence in the field of transport engineering, mechanical or coachwork. The projects may range from model making, through manufacturing devices to fully operational equipment and units associated with any form of transport. The criterion is the best work demonstrating the skills and dedication necessary for the perfection required to satisfy the true meaning of the pursuit of excellence in a practical product having an end product. The Trophy (to be held for one year) is accompanied by a medal, a certificate of merit and a cash award of between £250 and £500 at the discretion of the award committee. Established in 1985.

4317

RSA
Royal Society for the Encouragement of
Arts, Manufactures & Commerce
8 John Adam St.
London WC2N 6EZ, England
Phone: 71 9305115
Fax: 71 8395805

4318

Albert Medal

For recognition of outstanding contributions to the promotion of arts, manufactures, and commerce. Individuals may be nominated by the Fellows of the Society. A gold medal is awarded annually. Established in 1863 in memory of Prince Albert (1819-61), a former president of the Society.

4319

R. B. Bennett Commonwealth Prize

To recognize the Commonwealth citizen who has made the most outstanding contribution to the promotion of arts, agriculture, industries or commerce. A monetary prize is awarded triennially. Established in 1945.

4320

Bicentenary Medal

To recognize a person who, in a manner other than as an industrial designer, has exerted an exceptional influence in promoting art and design in British Industry. Candidates may be nominated. A medal is awarded annually. Established in 1954 to commemorate the founding of RSA two hundred years earlier.

4321

Environmental Management Awards

To recognize significant initiatives in the pursuit of sustainability that seek to eliminate the negative impacts of business on the environment while still maintaining the long-term viability of the business. The Award was established in 1993 with the assistance of Nuclear Electric and the Department of the Environment and support of CBI. For further information, contact Myra Henderson, Project Manager, RSA Environment Programme. Formerly: Better Environment Awards for Industry.

4322

Benjamin Franklin Medal

To recognize a citizen of Britain or the United States who has made a notable contribution to Anglo-American understanding in the arts, industry or commerce. Nominations may be made by Fellows in the United Kingdom. A medal is awarded alternately to citizens of the United Kingdom and the United States. Established in 1956.

4323

Royal Designers for Industry

To enhance the status of designers in industry and encourage a high standard of industrial design. Citizens of the United Kingdom who have attained eminence, efficiency, and visual excellence in creative design for industry are considered. The number of persons who may hold the distinction at any one time is limited to 100, and it is regarded as the highest honor to be obtained in the United Kingdom in the field of industrial design. In addition, the Society confers on a limited number of distinguished international industrial designers the award of Honorary Royal Designer for Industry (HonRDI). Established in 1936.

4324

RSA Music Scholarships

To enable young professional singers to undertake advanced studies overseas. A monetary award was presented annually to finance a course, purchase an instrument or help fund a concert. (Discontinued)

4325

Swiney Prize for a Work on Jurisprudence

For recognition of the best published work on medical and general jurisprudence. A monetary prize of £100 and a silver cup are awarded alternately in the two fields. Awarded every five years.

4326

RTZ Corporation
6 St. James's Sq.
London SW1Y 4LD, England
Phone: 71 9302399
Fax: 71 9303249

4327

David Watt Memorial Prize

To recognize a writer for an outstanding contribution towards the clarification of international and political issues and the promotion of greater understanding of such issues. Entries in the English language must be submitted by March 20. A monetary award of £5,000 is presented. Established in 1988 by RTZ to honor David Watt, a man widely regarded as one of the outstanding writers, thinkers, and political commentators of our generation.

4328

St. John's College
Master's Lodge
Cambridge CB2 1TP, England
Phone: 223 338600

4329

Kenneth Craik Award

For recognition of distinguished work in physiological psychology. The award is made by invitation only and is not open to application. A monetary prize of £450 and the opportunity to spend a few days in Cambridge to meet those interested in his work and to give a lecture are awarded annually. Established in 1946 in memory of Kenneth Craik, a research Fellow of St. John's College and first Director of a Unit for Applied Psychology of the Medical Research Council.

4330

Linacre Lecture and Award

To recognize a distinguished scientist for work in the life sciences. The award is made by invitation only and is not open to application. A monetary prize of £450 and a lectureship are awarded annually. The award was endowed by Thomas Linacre, first president of the Royal College of Physicians, and physician to Henry VIII; it was reconstituted on an annual basis in 1908.

4331
Salters' Institute of Industrial Chemistry
c/o The Salters' Company
Salters' Hall
Fore St.
London EC2Y 5DE, England
Phone: 71 5885216
Fax: 71 6383679

4332
Graduate Prizes
In recognition of academic merit in chemistry or chemical engineering at British universities and of potential to occupy a leading position in the United Kingdom chemical industry. Final year undergraduates who must be nominated by the head of the department, and who expect to graduate with honors in chemistry or chemical engineering and have the intention of taking a post in a United Kingdom chemical industry may apply by late January each year. A monetary award and certificates are awarded annually in November or December. Established in 1979.

4333
School of Oriental and African Studies
Thornhaugh St., Russell Sq.
London WC1H 0XG, England
Phone: 71 6372388
Fax: 71 6377355

4334
Edgar Graham Book Prize
For recognition of a work of original scholarship, published in English, on agricultural and/or industrial development in Asia and/or Africa. Works published during the preceding two years may be submitted by the publisher or author. A monetary prize of £1,000 is awarded twice a year at the end of the second year. Established in 1985 in honor of Edgar Graham. (Discontinued) Formerly: Edgar Graham Memorial Prize.

4335
Sir Peter Parker Awards for Spoken Business Japanese
For recognition of outstanding spoken business Japanese. Established in 1990. Sponsored by the Japan External Trade Organisation, the International Business Communications Council of Japan, and the School of Oriental and African Studies, University of London.

4336
Science Fiction Foundation
University of Liverpool Library
PO Box 123
Liverpool L69 3DA, England
Phone: 051 7942696
Fax: 051 7942681

4337
Arthur C. Clarke Award
For recognition of the best science fiction novel published for the first time in the United Kingdom in the previous year. A monetary prize of £1,000 and a plaque are awarded annually. Established in 1986 by Arthur C. Clarke. Administered by the Science Fiction Foundation in collaboration with the British Science Fiction Association and the International Science Policy Foundation. Established in 1987. Further information is available from David V. Barrett, 23 Oakfield Rd., Croydon, Surrey, CR0 2UD, England.

4338
Sempervivum Society
11 Wingle Tye Rd.
Burgess Hill, W. Sussex RH15 9HR,
England
Phone: 444 236848

4339
Award of Merit Scheme
To recognize new cultivars, not available commercially, grown by the Society for a period of twelve months. While under trial they are assessed for their distinctiveness from other cultivars already in cultivation. In this way it is hoped to regulate the introduction of new cultivars. New cultivars of the genus sempervivum and jovibarba are considered. Established in 1973.

4340
Rosette Awards
To recognize outstanding cultivars of the genus sempervivum and jovibarba that are generally commercially available and to a certain extent reflect the popularity of the plants that receive awards. There are three awards of differing standards - "Gold Rosette" (GR), "Silver Rosette" (SR) and "Bronze Rosette" (BR). Established in 1975.

4341
Andre Simon Memorial Fund
5 Siou Hill Pl.
Bath, Avon BA1 5SJ, England
Phone: 0225 336 305

4342
Andre Simon Fund Book Awards
To recognize the authors of the best books published during the year in the categories of food and drink. Books published in England on food or drink may be submitted by December 31. A monetary award of £2,000 to the winner in each category and £200 to any book short-listed for the award are presented annually. Established in 1978 to honor Andre Simon.

4343
W. H. Smith and Son
Strand House
7 Holbein Pl.
London SW1W 8NR, England
Phone: 71 7301200
Fax: 71 7300195

4344
W. H. Smith Illustration Awards
To recognize illustrators who have made outstanding contributions to the art of illustration. Established in 1987 as part of the W.H. Smith Arts Programme. Organized jointly by Book Trust and the National Art Library of the Victoria and Albert Museum.

4345
W. H. Smith Literary Award
To recognize the author of a book that has made an outstanding contribution to literature. Books published in the United Kingdom during the preceding year that are written in English by citizens of the United Kingdom or the Commonwealth are eligible. Submissions are not accepted. Three independent judges select the winner. A monetary prize of £10,000 is awarded annually. Established in 1959.

4346
W. H. Smith Young Writers' Competition
To recognize young writers in the following age categories: 8 years and under, 9-12 years, and 13-16 years. Monetary awards totaling over £7,000 are presented to individual young writers and schools of consistent merit. Established in 1959 and taken on by W.H. Smith in 1977.

4347
Society for Applied Bacteriology
Exec. Sec.
PO Box 510
Harrold, Beds. MK43 7YU, England
Phone: 234 720047
Fax: 234 720048

4348
W. H. Pierce Memorial Prize
For recognition of a substantial contribution to bacteriology, such as publication in the *Journal of Applied Bacteriology* or a presentation at the Symposium held at the summer conference of the Society. Younger members of the Society are eligible for nomination by other members. A monetary award of £1,750 and a scroll are awarded annually. Established

in 1984 by Oxoid Ltd. in honor of W. H. (Bill) Pierce, former chief bacteriologist. Sponsored by Unipath, Wade Road, Basingstroke, Hants RG24 OPW, United Kingdom.

4349
Society for Army Historical Research
c/o National Army Museum
Royal Hospital Rd.
London SW3 4HT, England

4350
Templer Medal
For recognition of the book making the most notable contribution to the history of the British or Commonwealth Land Forces. The award committee makes the selection from books published during the preceding calendar year that have been nominated. The medal is presented at the annual general meeting. Established in 1981 in memory of Field Marshal Sir Gerald Templer KG, President of the Society.

4351
Society for Co-operation in Russian and Soviet Studies
320 Brixton Rd.
London SW9 6AB, England
Phone: 71 2742282
Fax: 71 4890391

Formerly: Society for Cultural Relations with the USSR.

4352
Pushkin Institute Scholarship, Moscow
To improve the speaking and teaching of Russian in the United Kingdom. Individuals between the ages of 18-60 years who are members of the Society and residents in Britain may submit applications. Subsidised places for five and ten months at the Pushkin Institute for Foreign Language Students, Moscow, are awarded to successful applicants in competition. Two subsidised places are awarded annually. Established in 1969 by the Union of Soviet Friendship Societies, 14 Kalinin Prospect, Moscow, USSR, to honor Alexander Pushkin, a Russian poet. Sponsored by Russian Association in International Co-operation and Development, 14 Vozdvizhenka Street, Moscow.

4353
Society for General Microbiology
Marlborough House
Basingstoke Rd.
Spencers Wood
Reading RG7 1AE, England
Phone: 734 885577
Fax: 734 885656

4354
Colworth Prize Lecture
To recognize an individual for an outstanding contribution in an area of applied microbiology. Individuals must be nominated by two members of the Society. A monetary award of £1,000 is awarded biennially. Established in 1987. Sponsored by Colworth Laboratory (Unilever Research).

4355
Fleming Award
For recognition of outstanding research by a young microbiologist. Nominations by two members of the Society are accepted, with a deadline in January. Nominees must be under 36 years of age on June 1 of the year of the award and a majority of the work taken into consideration must have been done in the United Kingdom or the Republic of Ireland. A monetary award of £500 and a lectureship are awarded. The lecture is published in *Microbiology* or the *Journal of General Virology*. Awarded annually. Established in 1976 in memory of Sir Alexander Fleming, the discoverer of penicillin and first president of the Society.

4356
Marjory Stephenson Prize Lecture
To recognize an individual for an outstanding contribution of current importance in any area of microbiology. Individuals must be nominated by two members of the Society. A monetary award of £1,000 is awarded biennially. Established in 1987 to honor Marjory Stephenson, one of the founders of the Society. Formerly: (1987) Marjory Stephenson Memorial Lecture.

4357
Society for Italic Handwriting
Highfields, Nightingale Rd.
Guildford, Surrey GU1 1ER, England
Phone: 483 68443

4358
Society for Italic Handwriting Award
To encourage the use of italic hand, and specifically the formation of a good italic style. Members of the Society are eligible to enter in July of each year. Awards are given in three categories: (1) over 16 years of age; (2) 12 to 16 years of age; and (3) under 12 years of age. Monetary prizes and certificates are awarded annually. Established in 1970.

4359
Society for Medicines Research
Inst. of Biology
20 Queensberry Pl.
London SW7 2DZ, England
Phone: 71 5818333
Fax: 71 8239409

Formerly: Society for Drug Research.

4360
Award for Drug Discovery
To recognize researchers in academic institutions and the pharmaceutical industry as well as other concerned individuals. Awarded biennially.

4361
Society for Medieval Archaeology
c/o Dr. Paul Stamper
Archaeology Unit of Shropshire
Winston Churchill Bldg., Radbrook Centre
Radbrook Rd.
Shrewsbury SY3 9BJ, England
Phone: 743 254009
Fax: 743 254047

4362
Eric Fletcher Award
For recognition of projects relating to the Society's interest in archaeological research of the European Middle Ages. Society members may apply before mid-February each year. Several monetary awards of between £50 and £250 are presented annually. Established in 1984 by the late Lord Fletcher, honorary vice-president of the Society. Formerly: (1983) Colt Fund.

4363
Medieval Archaeology Research Fund
To encourage research in medieval archaelogy. A cash award of up to £2,000 to be used for research is presented annually.

4364
Sudrey's Fund
To encourage research into the Viking Age. Awardees will receive up to £500 for research.

4365
Society for Nautical Research
c/o National Maritime Museum
Greenwich
London SE10 9NF, England   Phone: 71 8732737

4366
Anderson Prize Essay
To encourage research relating to seafaring, shipbuilding, and other language and customs of the sea. Manuscripts must not have been published or accepted for publication elsewhere in order to be considered. A monetary prize of £250 is awarded biennially. Established in 1985 in memory of Dr. R. C. Anderson, distinguished historian and founding member of the Society.

4367
Society for Research into Higher Education
Univ. of Surrey   Phone: 483 39003
Guildford, Surrey GI2 5XH, England   Fax: 483 300803

4368
Society for Research into Higher Education Awards
To recognize individuals involved in higher education research and to conduct educational programs. The Society bestows awards at its annual conference.

4369
Society for Research into Hydrocephalus and Spina Bifida
Institute of Child Health
30 Guilford St.
London WC1N 1EM, England   Phone: 71 242 9789

4370
Casey Holter Memorial Prize
For recognition of an essay reporting original work bearing on the pathogenesis or treatment of hydrocephalus or spina bifida. Any professional worker in a field concerned with hydrocephalus and/or spina bifida may submit an essay in a form suitable for publication. Essays should include personal observations and experiences collected by the candidate in the course of his work and must not have been previously published. Entries may be submitted by February 28 every three years (next in 1995). A monetary prize of £250 is awarded triennially when merited. Established in 1966 by Mr. J. W. Holter, Pennsylvania, U.S.A., in memory of Casey Holter.

4371
Society for the Advancement of Anaesthesia in Dentistry
59 Summerlands Ave., ACTON   Phone: 81 993 6844
London W3 6EW, England   Fax: 81 993 6844

4372
Drummond-Jackson Prize
For recognition of the most meritorious essay on any subject related to dental anaesthesia, analgesia or sedation in out-patient or office dentistry. All dental and medical graduates in the United Kingdom and throughout the world are eligible. A monetary prize of £1,000 is awarded triennially. Established in 1976 in memory of S.L. Drummond-Jackson, founder of SAAD, who died in 1975.

4373
Society for the History of Alchemy and Chemistry
c/o Mr. J.A. Hudson, Hon. Sec.
Anglia Polytechnic University
East Rd.
Cambridge, Cambs. CB1 1PT, England   Phone: 223 63271
                                       Fax: 223 352979

4374
Partington Prize
To encourage young scholars in the history of chemistry. Essays may be submitted on any aspect of the history of alchemy and chemistry by writers under 30 years of age. Essays must not have been previously published and must not exceed 5,000 words. A monetary prize of £100 and a certificate are awarded triennially. Established in 1975 in memory of Professor J. R. Partington.

4375
Society for the Promotion of New Music
Francis House
Francis St.   Phone: 71 8289696
London SW1P 1DE, England   Fax: 71 9319928

4376
Composition Competitions
To recognize and promote new music by bringing composers' works to the attention of publishers, concert promoters, and the public. The Society sponsors the annual Composers' Weekend seminar, forums, workshops, and composition competitions.

4377
Society for the Study of Inborn Errors of Metabolism
Willinic Biochemical Genetics Unit
Royal Manchester Children's Hospital
Pendlebury   Phone: 61 7944696
Manchester M27 1HA, England   Fax: 61 7283898

4378
SSIEM Award
To encourage and improve the quality of scientific contributions at the annual symposium. Members of the Society are eligible. A monetary prize and a certificate are awarded annually at the Society Symposium. Established in 1981 in memory of Dr. D. Noel Raine, a former member of the Society. Formerly: (1987) Noel Raine Award.

4379
Society for Theatre Research
c/o The Theatre Museum
1e Tavistock St.
London WC2E 7PA, England

4380
William Poel Memorial Festival
To encourage good stage speech, especially in sixteenth/seventeenth century drama. Entry is restricted to nominees from invited professional theatre schools in Great Britain. The festival currently takes place annually at the National Theatre, normally in May. Small prizes may be awarded at the Society's discretion. Established in 1952 by Dame Edith Evans in memory of William Poel (1852-1934), an innovative theatre director.

4381
Research Awards
To provide for research on the history and practice of the British theatre. Private scholars, theatre professionals, academic staff, and students, unrestricted as to status or nationality, may apply for grants. Applications must be submitted by February 1. The following grants are awarded: The Anthony Denning Award of the Society for Theatre Research, and The Kathleen Barker Award of the Society for Theatre Research - each up to £2,000; and the Stephen Joseph Award of the Society for Theatre Research, and Research Awards of the Society for Theatre Research - £100 to £500. Awarded annually.

4382

Society of Antiquaries of London
Burlington House, Piccadilly
London W1V OHS, England
Phone: 71 734 0193
Fax: 71 287 6967

4383
Frend Medal
For recognition of a contribution to the archaeology of the Christian Church. A bronze medal and £50 for books are awarded annually. Established in 1981 by Professor William Frend, TD, MA, D.Phil., DD.

4384
Gold Medal
For recognition of an outstanding contribution to the field of archaeology. Individuals may be nominated. A gold medal is awarded usually twice in three years. Established in 1934.

4385

Society of Authors
84 Drayton Gardens
London SW10 9SB, England
Phone: 71 3736642
Fax: 71 3735768

4386
K. Blundell Trust
To assist young published authors working on their next book. British subjects under 40 years of age whose work contributes to the greater understanding of existing social and economic organization are eligible. The deadline is April 30. Monetary awards are presented annually. Established in 1987 by Miss K. Blundell.

4387
BUPA Prizes for Medical Writing and Illustration
To recognize an author(s) or editor(s) of a medical textbook, an illustrated textbook, or a medical atlas which, in the opinion of the judges, made the greatest contribution to understanding in any particular field. Any medical or dental textbook written in English, or any illustrated book published in the United Kingdom during the preceding calendar year is eligible. A monetary award of £3,000 is awarded annually. Established in 1983. Sponsored by BUPA. Formerly: (1985) Abbott Prize; Glaxo Prize for Medical Writing.

4388
Cholmondeley Award for Poets
To recognize and encourage poets of any age, sex, or nationality. The complete work of the poet is considered, rather than a specific book of poetry. Submissions are not required. Monetary prizes totaling £4,000 are awarded annually. Established in 1966 by the Marchioness of Cholmondeley.

4389
Eric Gregory Awards
To encourage young poets. Candidates who are British subjects by birth, residents of the United Kingdom, and under 30 years of age may submit a published or unpublished volume of belles-lettres, poetry, or drama. Monetary awards totaling over £20,000 are awarded annually. Established by Eric Gregory.

4390
Somerset Maugham Awards
To recognize a promising British author for a published work in the field of poetry, fiction, criticism, biography, history, philosophy, belles-lettres, or travel. Authors must be under 35 years of age. The award is designed to encourage writers to travel and acquaint themselves with the customs of other countries, and to extend the basis and influence of British literature. Monetary awards of £3,000 to £4,000 are awarded annually. A candidate who wins an award must spend more than three months outside Great Britain. Established in 1946 by Somerset Maugham.

4391
Margaret Rhondda Award
To assist and support a woman journalist with a particular project. A monetary award of £500 is presented. Established by friends of Lady Rhondda. Awarded triennially.

4392
Tom-Gallon Trust
To recognize fiction writers of limited means who have had at least one short story accepted. Awarded biennially. Established in 1946.

4393
Betty Trask Award
To recognize authors under the age of 35 for a first novel, published or unpublished, of a romantic or traditional nature. British/Commonwealth citizens are eligible. Monetary awards totaling £25,000, which must be used for travel abroad, are presented annually. Established in 1983 by Margaret Elizabeth Trask, an author of romantic novels.

4394
Travelling Scholarships
To enable British writers to travel abroad. Monetary awards of varying amounts are presented annually. Established in 1944.

4395

Society of Authors Translators Association
84 Drayton Gardens
London SW10 9SB, England
Phone: 71 373 6642

4396
John Florio Prize
For recognition of the best translation from Italian into English of a twentieth century Italian work of literary merit and general interest. Works published in the United Kingdom by a British publisher during the award year and the preceding year must be submitted by December 31. A monetary prize of £1,000 is awarded biennially. Established in 1963 under the auspices of the Italian Institute of Culture for the United Kingdom, the British Italian Society, and the Society of Authors.

4397
Scott Moncrieff Prize
For recognition of the best translation from French to English of a twentieth century French work of literary merit and general interest. Works published in the United Kingdom by a British publisher during the award year may be submitted by the publisher. A monetary prize of £1,000 is awarded annually under the auspices of the Society of Authors. Established in 1964.

4398
Schlegel - Tieck Prize
For recognition of the best translation from German to English of a twentieth century German work of literary merit and general interest. Works published in the United Kingdom by a British publisher during the award year may be submitted by the publisher. A monetary prize of £2,000 is awarded annually under the auspices of the Society of Authors. Established in 1964.

4399

Society of Chemical Industry
14/15 Belgrave Sq.
London SW1X 8PS, England
Phone: 71 235 3681
Fax: 71 823 1698

4400
Armstrong Lecture
A lecture is delivered at intervals in memory of Professor H.E. Armstrong (1848-1937), regarded as one of the fathers of chemical engineering in the

United Kingdom; it was his life's work to teach chemistry as part of an education in engineering. Established in 1943.

4401
Baekeland Lecture
A lecture on the subject of synthetic resins and related matters is delivered at approximately four-year intervals. Established to commemorate the work of Dr. Leo H. Baekeland (1863-1944) of the USA on synthetic resins. Established in 1943.

4402
Canada International Lecture
To recognize an individual for outstanding service to chemical industry in the international sphere. Awarded biennially. Established in 1976. Formerly: Canadian International Medal Lecture.

4403
Canada Lecture and Medal
For recognition of outstanding service to chemical industry in Canada. A medal is awarded biennially. Established in 1939 by the Canadian Section of the Society.

4404
Castner Lecture and Medal
A lecture on applied electrochemistry is delivered by a person of authority. The award honors Hamilton Young Castner (1858-1898), a pioneer in the field of industrial electrochemistry. Established in 1946.

4405
Centenary Medal and Lecture
To recognize men or women of high distinction in industry or of recognized authority on chemistry as applied in industry. Awarded annually. The Centenary Medal was struck to commemorate the 100th anniversary of the Society in 1981.

4406
Chemical Industry Medal
To recognize a person who has rendered conspicuous service to applied chemistry as an active, guiding force in the management of his or her company during periods of maximum growth or in the development of new chemical or allied fields. A medal is awarded annually. Established in 1933 by the American Section of the Society.

4407
Environment Medal
Awarded annually to a member fo the society for contributions to environmental science and/or its application. Established in 1992.

4408
Carl Hanson Medal
To recognize an individual for achievements in solvent extraction science and technology. A medal is awarded jointly by SCI and DECHEMA. Established in 1986 in memory of Carl Hanson, renowned for his work on all aspects of solvent extraction.

4409
Hilditch Lecture
A lecture delivered at intervals on a topic connected with oil and fats or applied chemistry. The lecture was endowed in memory of Professor T.P. Hilditch (1888-1965), the first holder of the Campbell Brown Chair of Industrial Chemistry in the University of Liverpool, who made outstanding contributions to the knowledge of oils and fats.

4410
Robert Horne Lecture
A lecture delivered at intervals in Bristol or in South Wales. Established in memory of Viscount Horne, the first Chairman of the Imperial Smelting Corporation. Sponsored by the Bristol and the South Wales Sections of the society.

4411
Hurter Lecture
A lecture delivered at intervals on applied chemistry. Established in 1898 by the Liverpool Section of the society as a memorial to Dr. Ferdinand Hurter (1844-1898), an authority on the Leblanc system for soda production, in recognition of his services to applied chemistry and his contribution to the society.

4412
Lampitt Medal
For recognition of outstanding service to the society through the groups and sections. Awarded biennially. Established in 1958 to commemorate Dr. Leslie H. Lampitt, who played a major role in the society's affairs for 37 years.

4413
Le Sueur Lecture
A lecture delivered every two years at a meeting of the Canadian Section. Established to honor Ernest A. Le Sueur who made many outstanding contributions to early industrial chemistry in Canada, including the first successful commercial electrolytic cell for the manufacture of chlorine and caustic soda.

4414
Leverhulme Lecture
To promote research and education in connection with the chemical industry. The lecture is delivered at three-yearly intervals. Established in 1943 by the Leverhulme Trust in memory of the first Viscount Leverhulme (1851-1925), the founder of Port Sunlight.

4415
Ivan Levinstein Memorial Lecture
A lecture delivered before the Manchester Section of the Society. Endowed in 1946 in memory of Ivan Levinstein (1845-1916), a pioneer in the manufacture of synthetic dyestuffs.

4416
Julius Lewkowitsch Memorial Lecture
A lecture delivered on any technical aspect of the natural oils and fats. Awarded every two or three years in London. Endowed in 1980 to commemorate the work of Julius Lewkowitsch in the oils and fats field.

4417
Listar Memorial Lecture
Awarded to an authority on chemistry and medical science. Established in 1944.

4418
Messel Medal and Lecture
This award is given to recognize a person who has achieved meritorious distinction in science, literature, industry, or public affairs. Awarded biennially at the annual meeting of the society. Established in 1921 by a fund bequeathed to the society by Dr. Rudolph Messel, an eminent international chemist and a founder of the society.

4419
Oils and Fats Group International Lecture
A lecture delivered periodically before the Oils and Fats Group of the Society. Established in 1964.

4420
Perkin Medal
To recognize the United States resident who is active in the chemical profession, for successful applied chemistry resulting in outstanding commercial development. An individual or a leader of a group effort is eligible. A medal is awarded annually. Established in 1906 by the American Section of the Society to commemorate the 50th anniversary of the coal tar industry.

4421
President's Medal
Awarded when merited by the President of the Society as a mark of distinction to persons whom he selects as worthy of honor. Established in 1962.

4422
Arthur B. Purvis Lecture
A lecture delivered biennially at a meeting of the Canadian Section. Established in 1947 to honor the memory of the late Rt. Hon. Arthur B. Purvis who, as president of Canadian Industries Ltd., played a leading role in shaping the pattern of Canada's chemical industry and who was killed in 1941 while serving as Chairman of the British Supply Council in North America.

4423
Rideal Memorial Lecture
A lecture given by a person distinguished in colloid or interface science. The Rideal Memorial Trust was set up jointly in 1976 between the society and the Chemical Society to commemorate the life and work of the late Sir Eric Rideal MBE FRS (1890-1974).

4424
SCI International Medal
To recognize a person who has contributed to international cooperation in the sphere of the Society's interest. A medal is awarded irregularly. Established in 1947.

4425
Richard Seligman Lecture
A lecture delivered every two or three years on any aspect of engineering or processing in the food or beverage industries in order to advance the education of the public in such matters. Endowed in 1973 by APV Holdings Ltd. in memory of Dr. Richard Seligman, the founder of the company who had been a member of the society for over 50 years.

4426
Society's Medal and Lecture
For recognition of conspicuous services to applied chemistry by research, discovery, and invention, or for improvements to the society in the furtherance of its objectives. Scientists of any nationality are eligible. A medal is awarded biennially, normally at the annual meeting of the society. Established in 1896.

4427
Charles Tennant Memorial Lecture
A lecture delivered before the Glasgow Section of the Society on some subject of chemical research and knowledge. Endowed in 1943 by Charles Tennant & Co. Ltd. in memory of Charles Tennant (1768-1838), a pioneer chemical industrialist who patented various methods of making bleaches of importance to the growing textile industry.

4428
Society of Designer-Craftsmen
24 Rivington St.
London EC2A 3DU, England   Phone: 71 7393663

Formerly: Arts & Crafts Exhibition Society.

4429
Marlowe Award
To encourage young designers in their professional development. New entrants to the Society after leaving college are eligible for all crafts. A monetary award of £250 is presented annually.

4430
TSB Award
To encourage young designers in their professional development. New entrants to the Society after leaving college are eligible. A monetary award of £250 is presented annually. Formerly: Constance West Award.

4431
Society of Dyers and Colourists
Perkin House
PO Box 244
82 Grattan Rd.   Phone: 274 725138
Bradford, W. Yorks. BD1 2JB, England   Fax: 274 392888

4432
George Douglas Lecture
To provide a lecture on some subject connected with the coloring or finishing of textiles. A monetary award is presented with an invitation to lecture. Alternatively, the fund may be utilized for other educational purposes. Established in 1949.

4433
Honorary Fellow
To recognize individuals who have contributed to the field of dyeing and coloring. Awarded when merited. Established in 1969.

4434
Honorary Member
To recognize individuals who have contributed to the field of dyeing and coloring. Awarded when merited. Established in 1884.

4435
Medals of the Society of Dyers and Colourists
For recognition of exceptional services to the Society or in the interests of the tinctorial and allied industries. Gold, Silver, Bronze, and Centenary Medals are awarded annually. Established in 1908.

4436
Perkin Medal
For recognition of exceptional services in the interests of the tinctorial and allied industries. A gold medal is awarded when merited. Established in 1908 in memory of Sir William Henry Perkin, the founder of the coal-tar dye industry, and President of the Society in 1907.

4437
Turner - Scholefield Award
To recognize an Associate or Graduate Diplomate under the age of 33 who has made notable and meritorious contributions to the science or technology of coloring matters or their application, or has demonstrated the ability to apply his or her knowledge and skills in an appropriate field of color science or technology. Awarded annually or when merited. Established in 1970 under the will of the late Mr. H. A. Turner in memory of Fred Scholefield.

4438
Worshipful Company of Dyers Research Medal
To recognize the authors of papers embodying the results of scientific research or technical investigation connected with the tinctorial arts published in the *Journal* of the Society. A gold or silver medal was awarded annually. Established in 1908. (Discontinued)

4439
Worshipful Company of Feltmakers Research Medal
To recognize authors of papers published in the *Journal* (or other Society publication) which are related to any of the following subjects: the properties of wool, fur and other felting fibres which have relevance to the phenomenon of felting; the felting process; feltmaking and the coloration of felts; the process of cloth milling; the use of felts, e.g., in papermaking; anti-felting or shrink-resist processes; non-woven fabrics made from fibres other than the traditional felting fibres; and the manufacture,

coloration and use of carpets. A medal is awarded biennially. Established in 1963.

```
4440
```
Society of Engineers
Guinea Wiggs
Wazland
Colchester, Essex CO6 4NF, England
Phone: 71 435 5600
Fax: 71 435 5600

```
4441
```
Churchill Medal
To recognize individuals for an important contribution to contemporary engineering; an original engineering project or development solely conceived by the nominees and executed under their supervision; or a project or development to which the nominees have made the major engineering contribution. Engineers from the United Kingdom or Commonwealth are eligible. Nominations may be made by major engineering institutes and institutions in the United Kingdom or by two or more corporate members of the Society of Engineers. A silver gilt medal is awarded biennially. Established in 1946 in honor of Sir Winston Churchill, honorary fellow of the Society. The medal was first awarded in 1952.

```
4442
```
Gairn E.E.C. Medal
To recognize important contributions to contemporary engineering, science, or technology. Contributions make take the form of an original engineering project or development solely conceived by the nominees and executed under their supervison, or a project or development to which the nominees have made a major engineering contribution. Engineers from the European Economic Community are eligible. Nominations may be made by the Ambassadors or major engineering institutes and institutions of the European Economic Community, or by two or more corporate members of the Society of Engineers. A silver gilt medal is awarded biennially. Established in 1972 by Stanley Nash Bruce Gairn when he was president of the Society of Engineers. It is intended as a counterpart within the European Economic Community of the Society's Churchill Medal.

```
4443
```
President's Medal
For recognition of the best paper delivered to an ordinary meeting during the current session and published in the *Journal*. The Council judges the papers. A medal is awarded annually. Established as a President's Premium in 1887 and changed to a medal in 1893.

```
4444
```
Simms Medal
To recognize the author of a paper submitted to the editor and published in the *Journal* relating to new discoveries or innovative research in the field of engineering. A medal is awarded annually. Established in 1944 by Frederick Richard Simms.

```
4445
```
Society's Prizes
For recognition of a meritorious paper delivered during the calendar year and published in *Engineering World*, the journal of the Society of Engineers. The council awards prizes, formerly called Premiums, which usually take the form of technical books or instruments. The awards are named successively the Bessemer Prize, the Nursey Prize, and the Bernays Prize. They commemorate Sir Henry Bessemer, former president and secretary of the founding society Perry F. Nursery and former president Joseph Bernays, and were established in 1887, 1907, and 1908, respectively.

```
4446
```
Society of Indexers
38 Rochester Rd.
London, Surrey NW1 9JJ, England
Phone: 71 9167809

```
4447
```
Carey Award
For recognition of services to indexing. Individuals are nominated by the Council of the Society. A framed parchment is awarded when merited. Established in 1977 in honor of Gordon V. Carey, the first President of the Society.

```
4448
```
Wheatley Medal
For recognition of an outstanding index first published in the United Kingdom during the preceding three years. Recommendations for the award are invited from anyone, but especially publishers and members of The Library Association and the Society of Indexers. A joint panel of The Library Association and the Society of Indexers make the selection. Printed indexes to any type of publication must be submitted by February 28 provided that the whole work (including the index) or the index alone, has originated in the United Kingdom. A medal is awarded annually. Established in 1962 in honor of Henry B. Wheatley, sometimes referred to as "the father of British indexing."

```
4449
```
Society of Metaphysicians
Archers' Ct.
Stonestile Ln.
The Ridge
Hastings, E. Sussex TN35 4PG, England
Phone: 424 751577
Fax: 424 722387

```
4450
```
Neometaphysical Merit Award
To encourage the study and application of fundamental laws and to establish neometaphysical standards on an international level. Members of the Society or other qualified persons are eligible to apply by June 30. A monetary prize of £100 and a certificate are awarded annually. Established in 1956 by Dr. John J. Williamson, D.Sc. Formerly: Williamson Neometaphysical Award.

```
4451
```
Society of Ornamental Turners
17 Chichester Dr. E.
Saltdean, E. Sussex BN2 8LD, England
Phone: 273 301031

```
4452
```
Cattell Cup
To encourage the design and making of suitable apparatus for ornamental turning. Society members are eligible. A silver cup is awarded annually. Established in 1989 by Mr. S.N. Cattell.

```
4453
```
Friendship Cup
For recognition of high practical and artistic skills. Members of the Society who are resident in the United States are eligible. A silver cup is awarded annually. Established in 1990.

```
4454
```
Haythorntwaite Cup
For recognition of high practical and artistic skills in the art of both plain and ornamental turning. Members of the Society are eligible. A cup is awarded annually.

```
4455
```
Howe Cup
For recognition of high practical and artistic skills in the art of both plain and ornamental turning. Members of the Society are eligible. A cup is awarded annually.

4456

Jowett Medal
For recognition of high practical and artistic skills in the art of both plain and ornamental turning. Members of the Society are eligible. A medal is awarded biennially.

4457

President's Cup
To encourage the display of work at the meeting. Society members are eligible. A silver cup is awarded annually. Established in 1989.

4458

Tweddle Medal
For recognition of high practical and artistic skills in the art of both plain and ornamental turning. Members of the Society are eligible. A medal is awarded biennially.

4459

Society of Public Health
28 Portland Pl.
London W1M 4DE, England

Formerly: (1989) Society of Community Medicine.

4460

John Kershaw Award
For recognition of notable service to the cause of public health. Such service may have been given by original research, published in medical journals or elsewhere, by notable work in any part of the services mentioned over a substantial period, or by the publication of books or other work making a notable contribution to the practice, theory, or philosophy of public health. Any medically qualified man or woman who holds a full-time or part-time appointment in the National Health Service is eligible. A monetary award of £300 is awarded biennially. Additional information is available from Dr. P. A. Gardner, Honorary Secretary, 31 Battye Ave., Huddersfield HD4 5PW, England.

4461

Maddison Prize
For recognition of the most meritorious piece of original research carried out by a member of the public health service. The application must be made within 3 years of the complete research and the material submitted must not have been previously awarded a prize by this or any other Society. A monetary award of £400 is awarded triennially. Additional information is available from Dr. P. A. Gardner, Honorary Secretary, 31 Battye Ave., Huddersfield HD4 5PW, England.

4462

Neech Prize
For recognition of the most meritorious paper on public health matters published or presented by a member to a meeting of the Society during the year. A monetary prize of £75 is awarded annually. Additional information is available from Dr. P. A. Gardner, Honorary Secretary, 31 Battye Ave., Huddersfield HD4 5PW, England.

4463

Arthur Newth Memorial Prize
For recognition of the most meritorious work, usually published, by a medical officer engaged full-time or part-time in school health service work. To be eligible for consideration a paper must have been presented to a meeting of the Society, including its Symposia, or have been published in *Public Health* or another professional journal between October 1 and September 30 in the relevant period. A monetary prize of £75 is awarded annually. Additional information is available from Dr. P. A. Gardner , Honorary Secretary, 31 Battye Ave., Huddersfield HD4 5PW, England.

4464

Public Health Award
To recognize distinguished significant contributions to the health of the public. Individuals, who need not be medical practitioners, are eligible. A monetary prize of £300 is awarded biennially. Established in 1987. Additional information is available from Dr. P. A. Gardner, Honorary Secretary, 31 Battye Ave., Huddersfield HD4 5PW, England.

4465

Society of West End Theatre
Bedford Chambers, The Piazza   Phone: 71 836 3193
Covent Garden   Phone: 71 379 0559
London WC2E 8HQ, England   Fax: 71 497 2543

4466

Laurence Olivier Awards
To recognize distinguished artistic achievement in the West End Theatre. Awards are given in the following categories: Best Set Designer, Best Lighting Designer, Best Costume Designer, Best Director of a Play, Best Director of a Musical, Best Choreographer in Theatre, Best Comedy Performance, Best Actor, Best Actress, Best Actor in a Supporting Role, Best Actress in a Supporting Role, Best Actor in a Musical, Best Actress in a Musical, Best Supporting Performance in a Musical, Best Comedy, BBC Award for Best Play, Best Revival, American Express Award for Best Musical, Best Musical Revival, Best Entertainment, Outstanding Achievement in Opera, Best New Opera Production, Outstanding Achievement in Dance, Best New Dance Production, and the Observer Award for Outstanding Achievement (in memory of Kenneth Tynan). The awards are decided upon by members of the profession and members of the theatre-going public. The annual presentation has become the highlight of London's theatrical year. Sponsored by American Express. Established in 1976.

4467

Society of Wildlife Artists
17 Carlton House Terr.
London SW1Y 5AH, England

4468

Member
To recognize outstanding wildlife artists. Awarded when merited.

4469

Soho Poly Theatre
16 Riding House St.
London W1O 7PD, England   Phone: 71 580 6982

4470

Verity Bargate Award
To encourage new writing in the theatre. Unperformed plays may be submitted. A monetary prize of £1,000, publication by Methuen Books Ltd. and possible production at Soho Poly are awarded annually in the spring. Established in 1983 by Barrie Keeffe in memory of Verity Bargate, founder of Soho Poly Theatre.

4471

Soil Association
86 Colston St.   Phone: 272 290661
Bristol BS1 5BB, England   Fax: 272 252504

4472

Loraine Award for Nature Conservation
For recognition of an organically managed farm of up to 400 acres where profitable husbandry, the production of healthy foods, and the conservation of native wildlife work together.

4473
Soil Association Awards for Organic Food Products
To recognize, celebrate, and promote the best organic foods on the market.

4474
Sonic Arts Network
West Heath Studios
174 Mill Lane
London NN6 1TB, England
Phone: 71 794 5638
Fax: 71 431 3750

4475
EMAS/Performing Right Society Prize
For recognition of an electro-acoustic composition. A monetary prize and a performance in London were awarded at irregular intervals. Established in 1979. (Discontinued in 1990)

4476
Sony Broadcast
Jays Close
Viables
Basingstoke, Hants. RG22 4SB, England

4477
Sony Radio Awards
For recognition of outstanding radio programs and performances. Awards are given in 25 categories including: (1) Community Service Program; (2) Documentary and Features; (3) Drama Script; (4) Best Actress; (5) Best Actor; and (6) Classical Music. Awarded annually. Formerly: Imperial Tobacco Awards.

4478
South Publications (UK)
Rex House, 1st Fl.
4/12 Lower Regent St.
London SW1 4PE, England
Phone: 71 930 8411
Fax: 71 930 0980

4479
Asian Advertising Award
For recognition of outstanding advertising in Asia. Awarded biennially. Established in 1984.

4480
Southern Arts Board
13 St. Clement St.
Winchester, Hants. SO23 9DQ, England
Phone: 962 855099
Fax: 962 861186

Formerly: (1988) Southern Arts Association.

4481
Southern Arts Literature Prize
For recognition of the finest literary achievement by a published author living in the Southern Arts' region (Hampshire, Berkshire, Wiltshire, Oxfordshire, Isle of Wight, Southeast Dorset, and Buckinghamshire). Books written during the previous three year period are eligible. The author must be living at the time of the award. A monetary award of £1,000 and a commissioned piece of craftwork are presented annually on a three year cycle for works of fiction, poetry, and nonfiction. Established in 1977.

4482
The Spectator
56 Doughty St.
London WC1N 2LL, England
Phone: 71 4051706
Fax: 71 2420603

4483
Adam and Company/Spectator Art Award
To recognize the most outstanding art works that best reflect a particular theme decided upon by the sponsors. Artists under 40 years of age are eligible. Up to three framed artworks may be submitted by each artist. The following awards are presented: first prize - £2,000 and purchase of the art work by Adam and Company or a commission given to the artist; second prize - £1,000; and third prize - £500. Sponsored by Adam and Company, which associates the award with support for the Renton Foundation, a charity that helps to fund the arts and leisure opportunities for individuals with learning disabilities through Mencap's Gateway Clubs. Additional information is available from Parker Harris and Company, PO Box 1390, London SW8 1QZ; telephone: 71 7930373.

4484
Shiva Naipaul Memorial Prize
To recognize the writer best able to describe a visit to a foreign country or with a foreign group of people. The award is not for travel writing in the conventional sense, but for the most acute and profound observation of cultures and/or scenes evidently alien to the writer. Such scenes and/or cultures might be found as easily within the writer's native country as outside it. English language writers of any nationality under the age of 35 are eligible. The deadline for entries is December 1. Submissions must not be more than 4,000 words and must not have been previously published. A monetary prize of £1,000 is awarded annually. Established in 1986 by *The Spectator* in memory of Shiva Naipaul, a gifted writer who died at the age of 40 in 1985.

4485
Spectator/Highland Park Parliamentarian of the Year Awards
For recognition of parliamentary contributions. The following awards are presented: Member to Watch, Backbencher of the Year, Parliamentarian of the Year, and other awards that vary each year. Awarded annually.

4486
Spero Communications
Grampian House, Unit D8
Meridian Gate, Marsh Wall
Docklands
London E14 9XT, England
Phone: 71 538 9946
Fax: 71 538 4747

4487
Mercury Communications Award for the Prince's Trust
To recognize achievement by individuals in personal development, and by groups in contributing to the community. Individuals who have received a grant from the Prince's Trust between 1988 and 1991 are eligible. A monetary prize and a trophy were awarded. Established in 1991 and first awarded in 1991. The prize may become annual. Sponsored by Mercury Communications.

4488
Northern Telecom Arts Europe
To promote multi-lateral collaborative initiatives between European artists and arts organizations. Awards of up to £300,000 are given.

4489
Teachers Scramble
To recognize the winning amateur golf team in the United Kingdom and in Europe after 1992. A trophy and a gift are awarded annually. Established in 1990. Sponsored by William Teacher & Sons Limited.

4490
Times - Shell Museums Year Award
To find the most innovative museum, the best community museum and the best curator. The winner received The Shell Sponsorship Award to the value of £20,000 and the Museums Year Trophy. In addition, a prize was awarded for the Community Museum of the Year, a local museum which provided the best service in the eyes of users. The prize was a Shell Sponsorship Award to the value of £10,000 and a trophy. A third part of the competition, run by the Museums Association, the organizers of

Museums Year, was to find the museum professional who undertook the most innovative work for the benefit of visitors. The winners were announced at an awards ceremony in December. Established in 1989. (Discontinued in 1991)

4491
Stand Magazine
179 Wingrove Rd., Fenham
Newcastle on Tyne, Tyne and Wear NE4
 9DA, England   Phone: 91 2812614

4492
Stand International Short Story Competition
To encourage writers of the short story. Entries in the English language and not published, broadcast, or under consideration elsewhere must be submitted by March 31. A monetary prize and publication are awarded biennially. Additional monetary awards totaling £1,000 and one-year subscriptions are awarded. Established in 1983.

4493
Strategic Planning Society
17 Portland Pl.   Phone: 71 6367737
London W1N 3AF, England   Fax: 71 3231692

4494
Bruce Kyle Prize
For recognition of an article published in Long Range Planning describing innovative applications of strategy within an organization. A monetary prize and a commemorative memento were awarded annually. Established in 1985. (Discontinued)

4495
The Long Range Planning Award
To recognize the best article appearing in The Long Range Planning Journal. £5,000 is awarded.

4496
Stroud and District Festival
Highmead, Field Rd.
Stroud, Glos. GL5 2JQA, England

4497
Stroud and District Festival
To provide recognition to area arts and artists. Music, plays and choral works are commissioned. There are poetry and literary competitions for children. Established in 1947. Formerly: Stroud Festival International Composers Competition; Stroud Festival International Poetry Competition.

4498
Sun Life Assurance Society
Amateur Photographer
Reed Business Publishing Ltd
Prospect House
9-13 Ewill Rd.
Cheam, Surrey SM1 4QQ, England   Phone: 1 661 4300

4499
Sun Life/Amateur Photographer Monochrome Awards
To encourage amateur photography throughout the United Kingdom. The subject is open. Amateur photographers may enter. A monetary prize is awarded annually at the award presentation. Established in 1981.

4500
Sunday Express
245 Blackfriars Rd.   Phone: 71 922 7330
London SE1 9UX, England   Fax: 71 922 7964

4501
Sunday Express Book of the Year Award
This, Britain's richest fiction prize, is given for recognition of the most stylish but also compulsively readable work of fiction first published in Britain each year. Selection is by nomination by a special panel. A monetary prize of £20,000, a silver trophy, and a specially bound copy of the winning book are awarded annually. Four or five runners-up each receive £1,000. Established in 1987.

4502
Sunday Times
1 Pennington St.
London E1, England   Phone: 71 7825000

4503
The Sunday Times
1 Pennington St.   Phone: 71 782 5718
London E1 9XW, England   Fax: 71 782 5658

4504
Sunday Times Small Publishers Award
For recognition of the best small publisher producing between 5 and 40 titles p er year. A monetary prize of £1,000 is awarded annually. Sponsored by the Sunday Times.

4505
The Sunday Times Sportswomen of the Year Award
To recognize the achievements of women in sport. Awards are given for International Sportswoman, Team, Sportswoman, Student, Schoolgirl and Administrator. Awarded annually. Established in 1988. Sponsored by the CCPP, Moet & Chandon, and British Airways.

4506
Television and Radio Industries Club
Corbetts House
Norwood End
Fyfield
Chipping Ongar, Essex CM5 ORW,
 England   Phone: 27 785 337

Formerly: (1981) Radio Industries Club.

4507
Product of the Year
To highlight the enormous technological advance made by brown goods manufacturers in recent years, and to recognize the product(s) that underlines that technological advance and which creates awareness in the High Street. A panel of judges representing all aspects of the industry chooses the Product of the Year annually and makes recommendations in respect of other products. The Serviscope Trophy is presented to the manufacturer submitting the winning product and Certificates of Commendation are presented to runners-up at the Serviscope-sponsored TRIC luncheon in June.

4508
TRIC Annual Celebrity Awards
For recognition of the best in contributions in radio and television in the previous twelve months. Awards are given in the following categories: (1) Television Newscaster/Presenter of the Year; (2) Television Personality of the Year (IBA); (3) Television Personality of the Year (BBC); (4) Television Programme of the Year (IBA); (5) Television Programme of the Year (BBC); (6) Television Situation Comedy of the Year; (7) Television

Theme Music of the Year; (8) Radio Personality of the Year; (9) Radio Programme of the Year; (10) Science Based Programme of the Year; (11) Sports Presenter of the Year; (12) Children's Programme of the Year; and (13) New TV Talent. Monetary prizes, trophies and certificates are awarded annually. Established in 1969.

4509
TRIC/*Electrical Retailing* Advertising Awards
To acknowledge the advantages and the need for good advertising. Both the manufacturer and the retailer submitted advertisements in the following categories: Best Trade Press Advertisements, Best Consumer Magazine Advertisement, and Best Television Commercial. *Electrical Retailing* and TRIC also acknowledged The Best Advertisement Campaign each year. Awarded annually. Established by *Electrical Retailing* and TRIC. (Discontinued)

4510
Young Technician of the Year
To recognize the young employee who demonstrated an all-embracing knowledge of the electronics industry. The Young Technician of the Year also indicated a desire to remain in the industry and show an ability for leadership in either the retail trade or in manufacturing. A certificate and a cash prize were presented. Sponsored by Pye. (Discontinued)

4511
Test and Cricket Board
Lord's Cricket Ground
St. John's Wood Rd.
St. John's Wood
London NW8 8QZ, England
Phone: 71 2864405
Fax: 71 2895619

4512
National Westminster Bank Trophy
For recognition of the undefeated cricket team in the nationwide competition. The Cricket Competition is organized for major and minor counties, plus Scottish and Irish Cricket Unions. The games are played on a "Knock Out" basis. Monetary awards, a trophy, medals, and ties are awarded annually. Established in 1963 as the Gillette Cup. Renamed in 1981. Sponsored by the National Westminster Bank plc. Additional information is available from Mrs. Barbara Quinn, Special Events, National Westminster Bank plc, 1st Floor, 2 Broadgate, London EC3V 3NN, England. Formerly: (1981) Gillette Cup.

4513
Textile Institute
10 Blackfriars St.
Manchester M3 5DR, England
Phone: 61 8348457
Fax: 61 8353087

Formed by merger of: Clothing and Footwear Institute.

4514
Carothers Medal
For recognition of creativity in the production or use of fibers. Established in 1992 in memory of Wallace H. Carothers who discovered nylon.

4515
Companion Membership
To recognize individuals for substantially advancing the general interests of all the industries based on fibres. Institute members over 40 years of age are eligible. The status of Companion Member and an illuminated parchment are awarded annually. Established in 1956 and limited to 50 living members worldwide.

4516
Holden Medal
For recognition of an outstanding contribution to education for, or the technology of, the clothing industry. A medal is awarded annually. Established in 1981.

4517
Honorary Fellow
This, the highest honor within the Institute, is given for recognition of major advances in knowledge achieved by an individual as a result of ingenuity and application over many years. Members of the Institute worldwide are eligible. An illuminated parchment is awarded irregularly. Established in 1928.

4518
Honorary Life Member
This, the highest award granted for service to the Institute, is given to recognize exceptional and sustained service to the Institute in the furtherance of its Charter objectives and to textiles, including clothing and footwear, in general. Institute members worldwide are eligible. An illuminated parchment is awarded irregularly. Established in 1979.

4519
Institute Medal
For recognition of distinguished services to textiles, including clothing and footwear in general, and to the Institute. Institute members worldwide are eligible. One to three medals are awarded annually. Established in 1921.

4520
Lemkin Medal
For recognition of exceptional service to the Institute. A medal is awarded annually. Established in 1960.

4521
Section Awards
For recognition of distinguished service to one of the 60 Sections or National Committees of the Institute. Members of the Institute worldwide are eligible. Certificates are awarded annually. Established in 1980.

4522
Service Medal
For recognition of valuable services rendered to the Institute. The award is normally presented to members of the Institute, but it may also be awarded to others who have rendered some particularly valuable service to the Institute. One to three medals are awarded annually. Established in 1940.

4523
S. G. Smith Memorial Medal
To recognize individuals for contributions to the furtherance of scientific knowledge concerned with the physical and structural properties of fibres, whether such work has been published or not. There are no restrictions as to nationality. A medal is normally awarded annually. Established in 1964 by the Cotton, Silk, and Man-made Fibres Research Association in memory of Stuart Grayson Smith.

4524
Textile Institute Design Medal
To recognize professional designers or groups of designers worldwide for contributions to the field of textile design and design management. Contributions are assessed not only for aesthetic appeal, but also for commercial success. A medal is normally awarded annually. Established in 1971.

4525
Textile Institute Development Award
To recognize individuals, groups, or organizations for outstanding achievements in enhancing international textile (including clothing and footwear) interests through commerce or marketing or economic development. Established in 1990.

4526
Textile Institute Jubilee Award
For recognition of successful research and invention by teams or groups of researchers working within any appropriate organization worldwide.

An illuminated parchment is usually awarded annually. Established in 1960 to commemorate the Institute's Golden Jubilee Year.

4527

Warner Memorial Medal
To recognize outstanding work in textile science and technology, the results of which have been published. Special consideration is given to work published in the *Journal of the Textile Institute*. Awarded annually. Established in 1930.

4528

Weaver's Company Medal and Prize
To recognize outstanding contributions to the weaving sector of the United Kingdom textile industry. Awarded annually. Established in 1979 by Weavers' Company, the oldest of the Livery Companies of the City of London.

4529

Maggie Teyte Prize Fund
2 Keats Grove
London NW3 2RT, England
Phone: 71 4355861
Fax: 71 4355861

4530

Maggie Teyte Prize Competition
To recognize a young female singer with a particular gift for the interpretation of French song. A classical aria and recitation by Gluck, Handel, or Mozart are also required at audition. Females 30 years of age or younger must apply one month before the competition. A monetary prize of £1,000 plus a recital in the Royal Opera House Crush Bar (Young Singers at the R.O.H. Series) is presented. The Megan Foster Accompanist's Prize of £100 is also awarded at the discretion of the judges. Awarded annually. Established in 1968 by Dame Maggie Teyte's (1888-1976), renowned in particular for her interpretation of the French song repertoire. The competition is now held in her memory.

4531

Sir George Thalben-Ball Memorial Trust
St. Michael's Vestry, Cornhill
c/o Jonathan Rennert
London EC3V 9DS, England
Phone: 71 602 7483

4532

Sir George Thalben-Ball Memorial Scholarships
To recognize and assist young organists and church musicians in their studies. Monetary prizes and training assistance are awarded annually. Established in 1989 to commemorate the life and work of Sir George Thalben-Ball (1896-1987).

4533

Thames Television Limited
c/o Television House
306-316 Euston Rd.
London NW1 3BB, England
Phone: 71 387 9494

4534

Color Television Advertising Award
For recognition of the best color television commercial. A monetary prize of £1,000 is awarded annually.

4535

Thames Television Playwright Scheme
To recognize a promising writer. A monetary award of £1,000 is presented to the playwright as well as to the theatre which produced the play.

4536

Thimble Press
Lockwood, Station Rd.
South Woodchester
Stroud, Glos. GL5 5EQ, England
Phone: 453 873716
Phone: 453 872208
Fax: 453 878599

4537

***Signal* Poetry Award**
For recognition of excellence in poetry published for children, and for work done to promote poetry with children. The award is designed to sharpen response to the poetry published for children. The award selectors' are given space in the May issue of *Signal* to discuss their views on the winner and on other poetry books published during the year. Books published during the preceding year by British trade publishers are eligible, no matter what the country of origin. A monetary prize of £100 plus a lengthy citation in each May issue of *Signal* are awarded annually. Established in 1979.

4538

Third World Foundation for Social and Economic Studies
Rex House, 1st Fl.
4/12 Lower Regent St.
London SW1Y 4PE, England
Phone: 81 930 8411
Fax: 71 930 0980

4539

Third World Prize
To recognize an individual(s) or institution(s) for outstanding contributions to Third World development, particularly in the economic, social, political, and scientific fields. The principal qualities which the prize aims to honor are originality, inspiration, enterprise, creativity, innovation and service to the general good of the peoples of the Third World. All persons regardless of race, nationality, creed or sex are eligible for nomination. The prize may be jointly conferred when the recipients have worked together or are otherwise considered equally deserving of recognition. A monetary prize of $100,000, a medallion, and a scroll are awarded annually. Established in 1979 by the Bank of Credit and Commerce International S.A.

4540

Tidy Britain Group
The Pier
Wigan WN3 4EX, England
Phone: 942 824620

4541

Britain in Bloom Awards
To recognize cities, towns and villages for improvements in overall appearance through the planting of trees, shrubs, and flowers, increasing local pride in the environment, and attracting more business and tourism. Nominations may be submitted by the Tourist Boards of England, Scotland, Wales, Northern Ireland and the Isle of Man. The awards program was taken over in 1983 from the British Tourist Authority after 18 successful years.

4542

Queen Mother's Birthday Awards
To recognize voluntary organizations, companies, local authorities, statutory and other bodies, youth, and individuals for outstanding effort in promoting environmental improvement, particularly through litter abatement and involvement in the Beautiful Britain campaign. A trophy and certificates were awarded. (Discontinued)

4543

***Time Out* Group Ltd.**
Universal House
251 Tottenham Court Rd.
London W1P 0AB, England
Phone: 71 8133000
Fax: 71 8136001

4544
Time Out Eating and Drinking Awards
No further information was provided for this edition.

4545
Time Out Theatre, Dance and Comedy Awards
For recognition of achievement in the London theatre, dance, and comedy scene. Awards are given for performance, direction, choreography, design, and writing. Individuals who have been associated with dance, theatre or comedy during the past year from June to June are eligible. Plaques are awarded annually. Established in 1986. Formerly: Time Out/01 - for London Awards.

4546
Time Out Travel Writer and Photographer of the Year
No further information was provided for this edition.

4547
The Times Educational Supplement
Priory House
St. John's Ln.
London EC1M 4BX, England
Phone: 71 253 3000
Fax: 71 608 1599

4548
TES Information Book Awards
To provide recognition for contributions to information books for children. Awards are given in the following categories: (1) Junior category - for books appropriate to children nine years of age or under; and (2) Senior category - for books appropriate to children between ten and 16 years of age. Books originating in Great Britain or the Commonwealth during the 12 months prior to the closing date of August 31 are eligible. A monetary prize of £500 is awarded to the authors of the two selected books, and the judges reserve the right to make a further award of £250 to the illustrator in each case. Awarded annually. Established in 1972. Additional information is available from the Children's Book Foundation, Book House, 45 East Hill, London S18 2QZ, England, phone: 81 870 9055.

4549
TES Schoolbook Award
To recognize the author (or if appropriate, the author, editor and illustrator) of the most outstanding textbook to be published in the category specified for the year. The Award may be won either with a single book for use in class, or with a representative book from a graded series; entries are normally non-net. No more than five books may be entered by any one publisher and no book may be entered simultaneously for the TES Schoolbook Award and for The TES Information Book Award. To be eligible, books must have originated in Great Britain or in the Commonwealth between September 1 and August 31 or over a longer period if specified in any given year. Awards are given annually with a particular subject area and age range being specified each year. A monetary prize of £500 is awarded annually to the author or divided if necessary among the author, editor, and illustrator. Established in 1986. Administered jointly by The Times Educational Supplement and the Educational Publishers Council.

4550
The Times/PM Environment Award
PO Box 486
1 Pennington St.
London E1 9XN, England

4551
The Times/PM Environment Award
To recognize local individuals, groups, or communities, who have made the most significant contribution to improving their environment or the environment in general in the past year. Judges develop a short list of five entries to be featured in the newspaper and on the radio program. Readers and listeners are the final judges, choosing the winner from the shortlist. Entry is restricted to projects or schemes within the United Kingdom. Neither professionals nor local authorities are barred, but the judges expect to see work and initiative which extends beyond a regular job. A monetary prize of £5,000 to be spent on the furthering of the winning project, a commemorative trophy, and extensive national publicity are awarded. Established in 1988. Co-sponsored by BBC Radio Four's PM.

4552
Town and Country Planning Association
17 Carlton House Terr.
London SW1Y 5AS, England
Phone: 71 930 8903
Fax: 71 930 3280

4553
Ebenezer Howard Memorial Medal
For recognition of those who have made consistent and distinguished contributions to the advancement of ideas on town and country planning, and garden cities and new towns, as originally articulated by Sir Ebenezer Howard. A medal is awarded irregularly. Established in 1938 in memory of Sir Ebenezer Howard, founder of the Garden Cities Movement (now called New Towns Movement).

4554
Treasurer to the Queen
Buckingham Palace
London SW1A 1AA, England

4555
Queen's Gold Medal for Poetry
For recognition of a book of verse that is written in the English language. A gold medal is awarded when merited. Established in 1933 by King George V at the suggestion of John Masefield, poet laureate.

4556
Tunbridge Wells International Young Concert Artists Competition
Crowborough, E. Sussex TN6 2QP,
England
Phone: 892 654384

4557
Tunbridge Wells International Young Concert Artist Competition
To assist young professional instrumental and vocal soloists at the outset of their careers. Instrumentalists and vocalists not over 28 years of age of any nationality are eligible. Monetary prizes totaling £9,000 were presented in 1992: Four class winners (piano, strings, wind, vocal) each received £1,500; runners-up received £500; and an additional award of £1,000 and a crystal goblet was presented to the overall winner. Awarded biennially in June of even-numbered years. Established in 1980.

4558
UK
Department of Trade & Industry
151 Buckingham Palace Rd.
London SW1W O9SS, England
Phone: 71 2151691
Fax: 71 2152909

4559
SMART (Small Firms Merit Awards for Research & Technology)
To provide small firms with the necessary funding to develop innovative ideas that could lead to new products or processes. Individuals or businesses with fewer than 50 employees, located in the United Kingdom are eligible. The competition is divided into two stages. In Stage 1, winners receive 75 percent of the first £60,000 of project costs (maximum award £45,000). The selection criteria include the quality and novelty of the project; the qualifications and experience of the people involved, the significance of the project and its potential commercial benefit to the UK, the means proposed for turning the idea into a commercially successful product or process, and the financial need of the applicant in relation to the project ("Additionality"). Stage 2 is a separate competition open to winners who make satisfactory progress in Stage 1. The Stage 2 competition opens about seven months into Stage 1 and is designed to run on

from a 9-15 month project. A Stage 2 Award provides 50 percent of the first £120,000 of project costs (maximum award £60,000). Awarded annually at several presentation ceremonies. Established in 1986.

4560
UK Press Gazette
Mitre House
44 Fleet St.
London EC4Y, England

4561
British Press Awards
For recognition of outstanding work by British professional journalists, photographers, or graphic artists. Entries must have been published during the preceding year in any morning, evening, Sunday or weekly newspaper in England, Scotland, Wales or Northern Ireland and may be submitted by editors, newspaper proprietors, individual journalists or interested members of the public. Cuttings of the published photographs must be provided. The photographer/artist must be professional and employed by a newspaper or by an agency regularly supplying work to newspapers. Qualified freelancers are also eligible. Prizes are awarded in the following categories: (1) Journalist of the Year; (2) Reporter of the Year; (3) International Reporter of the Year; (4) Provincial Journalist of the Year; (5) Young Journalist of the Year - to any journalist not more than 25 years of age; (6) General Feature Writer of the Year; (7) Specialist Writer of the Year; (8) Sports Journalist of the Year; (9) Columnist of the Year; (10) Critic of the Year; (11) Campaigning Journalist of the Year; (12) The David Holden Award - to any British correspondent resident abroad; (13) Color Magazine Writer of the Year; (14) News Photographer of the Year; (15) Graphic Artist of the Year; and (16) Arthur Sandles Award - for travel writing. Awarded annually. Established in 1962 as the Hannen Swaffer National Press Awards by the International Publishing Corporation (IPC). The Awards are organized by UK Press Gazette in collaboration with Express Newspapers, *The Financial Times*, Guardian Newspapers, *The Observer*, The Press Association, Thomson Regional Newspapers, Times Newspapers, Mail Newspapers, Mirror Group Newspapers, *Daily Telegraph* and Westminster Press.

4562
Union for the International Language IDO
(Uniono por la Linguo Internaciona IDO)
24 Nunn St.
Leek, Staffs ST13 8EA, England   Phone: 538 381491

4563
Certificate of Merit
(Atesto di Merito)
For recognition of many years' work for the international language IDO. Members of the Union for the International Language IDO may be nominated. Certificates may be awarded at conferences. Established in 1981.

4564
United Nations Association - UK
3 Whitehall Ct.   Phone: 71 9302931
London SW1A 2EL, England   Fax: 71 9305893

4565
Media Peace Prize
To recognize a journalist for a contribution in the United Kingdom media to the understanding and the enhancement of peace. Journalists whose work appears during the relevant year on radio, television, or newspapers/journals in the United Kingdom are eligible. A monetary prize of £1,000 and a cut glass bowl are awarded annually. Established in 1980. (Temporarily discontinued)

4566
Universities Athletic Union
28 Woburne Sq.
London WC1H 0LU, England   Phone: 71 637 4828

4567
Divisional Team Championships
To recognize the winning university in the following sports: Association Football; Badminton; Basketball; Cricket; Fencing; Golf; Hockey; Lacrosse (Women); Lawn Tennis; Netball; Rugby League Football; Rugby Union Football; Squash Rackets; Table Tennis; Volleyball; and Water Polo. Athletes must be full-time registered students at a university in England or Wales. The following awards are given: Trophy for first team; Plaque for first individual; Silver medal for second individual; and Bronze medal for third individual. Awarded annually. Established at various times.

4568
Individual Championships
To recognize individual champions in the following sports: Archery; Athletics; Badminton; Canoeing; Cross Country; Cycling; Decathlon; Dry Skiing; Fencing; Golf; Orienteering; Rifle Shooting; Squash Rackets; Swimming and Diving; Table Tennis; Tenpin Bowling; and Weight Lifting. In certain sports, individual members of non-affiliated universities are permitted to compete. Athletes must be full-time university students. Challenge cups or trophies are held for one year only. Awarded annually. Established at various times.

4569
Team Championships (non-divisional)
To recognize achievement in inter-university sports in the following categories: Archery; Assocation Football; Athletics; Canoeing; Cricket; Cross Country; Cycling; Dry Skiing; Orienteering; Rifle Shooting; Rowing VIII's; Rugby Union Football; Swimming and Diving; Swimming Short Course; Tenpin Bowling; and Weight Lifting. Regional competitions in hockey, indoor hockey, lacrosse and netball are also considered. The athletes must be full-time registered students at a university in England or Wales. The following awards are given: Trophy for first team; Plaque for first individual; Silver medal for second individual; and Bronze medal (only in some cases) for third individual. Awarded annually. Established at various times.

4570
Universities Federation for Animal Welfare
The Secretary
8 Hamilton Close
South Mimms   Phone: 707 58 202
Potters Bar, Herts. EN6 3QD, England   Fax: 707 49 279

4571
Small Project Grants
To improve the welfare of farm, laboratory, companion, wild or zoo animals through small-scale research, educational or investigatory projects. Monetary awards are presented annually.

4572
Zoo Animal Welfare Award
To recognize individuals for improving conditions for animals in zoos. Established in 1986.

4573
University of Liverpool
12 Abercromby Sq.
PO Box 147   Phone: 51 7942458
Liverpool L69 3BX, England   Fax: 51 7086502

4574
John Buchanan Prize in Esperanto
To encourage knowledge and use of Esperanto. Students or graduates of the University of Liverpool or any approved university and teachers in United Kingdom schools may submit an original composition in Esperanto and a translation from English into Esperanto on an announced subject by May 1 each year. A monetary prize of £150 is awarded annually. Established in honor of John Buchanan. Additional information is available from Mr. D.S. Lord, lecturer in Esperanto, Faculty of Arts, University of Liverpool, P.O. Box 147, Liverpool L69 3BX, England.

4575
Felicia Hemans Prize for Lyrical Poetry
For recognition of outstanding lyrical poetry. Past and present members and students of the University of Liverpool may submit not more than one published or unpublished poem by May 1. A monetary award of £20 and a commemorative certificate are awarded annually. Established in 1971 in memory of Felicia Hemans, a poet from Liverpool.

4576
Thomas Eric Peet Travelling Prize
To encourage study of egyptology and prehistory of the Mediterranean lands and the Near East. Graduates of any British university are eligible. A travel prize of approximately £300 is awarded every five years. Established in memory of Thomas Eric Peet, Brunner Professor of Egyptology, 1920-1933.

4577
University of London
Senate House
London WC1E 7HU, England   Phone: 71 636 8000

4578
Norman Hepburn Baynes Prize
For recognition of an essay on some aspect of the history, including the art, religion, and thought of the Mediterranean lands within the period 400 B.C. and A.D. 1453. The essay may take the form of one or more completed chapters of an intended thesis. The prize is open to all persons who have taken a degree in the University and/or persons who are pursuing a course in the University in preparation for a higher degree provided that not more than eight years have elapsed since their first registration for a first degree in the University or that not more than six years have elapsed since their registration for a higher degree of the University. A monetary prize of £3,000 is awarded biennially.

4579
Rogers Prize
For recognition of an essay or dissertation on alternately a medical or surgical subject to be decided by the University on the advice of the relevant Board of Studies at least twelve months before the last date of entry for the Prize. A thesis prepared for the degree of Doctor of Medicine or of Master of Surgery may be submitted as an entry for the prize. Essays and dissertations must be in English and must be the work of one individual. The deadline is June 30. A monetary prize of £250 is awarded annually.

4580
University of London
Institute of Commonwealth Studies
28 Russell Sq.   Phone: 71 580 5876
London WC1B 5DS, England   Fax: 71 255 2160

4581
Trevor Reese Memorial Prize
To recognize the best scholarly work by a single author the field of Imperial and Commonwealth history. Works published in the previous two years are eligible. A monetary prize of £1,000 is awarded biennially. Established in 1979 to honor Dr. Trevor Reese, a distinguished scholar of imperial history, who was Reader in Imperial Studies at the Institute up to his death in 1976, and was founder and first editor of the *Journal of Imperial and Commonwealth History*. Deadline for submissions is in March.

4582
University of Oxford
Board of the Faculty of Music
Univ. Offices
Wellington Sq.   Phone: 865 270200
Oxford OX1 2JD, England   Fax: 865 270708

4583
Donald Tovey Memorial Prize
To provide assistance for research in the philosophy, history, or understanding of music. Men or women without regard to nationality, age, or membership of a university are eligible. A monetary prize usually to the value of £1,000 is awarded every three to five years. Additional information is available from the Heather Professor of Music, Faculty of Music, St. Aldate's, Oxford OX1 1DB, England.

4584
University of Sheffield
The Registrar and Sec.   Phone: 742 768555
Sheffield S10 2TN, England   Fax: 742 720845

4585
Arthur Markham Memorial Prize
For recognition of the best short story, essay in prose, poem, group of six poems, first chapter of a novel, and one act play written for the competition. Candidates must be, or have been, manual workers at a coal mine in England, Scotland, or Wales. There is no age limit. A monetary prize of approximately £350 is available biennially.

4586
University of Sussex Library
     Phone: 273 678158
Brighton, E. Sussex BN1 9QL, England   Fax: 273 678441

4587
Ralph Lewis Award
To support an approved three-year program of publishing new writing. A monetary prize is awarded triennially. Established in 1984 by a bequest of Ralph Henry Lewis, author and art dealer of Brighton, East Sussex, England.

4588
Uranium Institute
Bowater House, 12th Fl.
68 Knightsbridge   Phone: 71 2250303
London SW1X 7LT, England   Fax: 71 2250308

4589
Gold Medal
To honor outstanding contributions which have facilitated the deployment of nuclear energy for peaceful purposes. A gold medal was awarded biennially. Established in 1985. (Discontinued)

4590
T. E. Utley Memorial Fund
60 St. Mary's Mansions
St. Mary's Terr.
London W2 1SX, England   Phone: 71 723 1149

4591

T. E. Utley Memorial Award
To encourage young political commentators of promise. Individuals under 35 years of age may submit work that has appeared in any English language medium in the past year. A monetary award of £5,000 is presented. The winner must deliver a lecture on a subject of his choice. Established in 1988 to honor T.E. Utley, a journalist.

4592

VER Poets
Haycroft
61/63 Chiswell Green Ln.
St. Albans, Herts. AL2 3AL, England   Phone: 727 867005

4593

VER Poets Open Competition
For recognition of achievement in poetry. Members of VER Poets and non-members may make submissions by April 30 each year. Monetary prizes of £500 for first place, £300 for second place, and £100 each for two third prizes are awarded annually in July. Established in 1944 by May Badman. Formerly: (1984) Michael Johnson Memorial.

4594

Victoria and Albert Museum
c/o Jacqueline Barber
Press Office
Cromwell Rd.
London SW7 2RL, England   Phone: 71 9388363

4595

W. H. Smith Illustration Award
For recognition of an outstanding contemporary illustration. Awards are presented for book illustration and magazine illustration. The following awards are presented: a monetary award of £3,000 to the best overall illustration regardless of category; two second prizes of £1,000 each are awarded, one for book illustration and the other for magazine illustration; and commended awards of £500 each the discretion of the judges. Awarded annually. Established in 1987 by the National Art Library at the Victoria and Albert Museum in association with W.H. Smith and Son, LTD. Organized jointly by the Book Trust, the National Art Library of the Victoria and Albert Museum and W. H. Smith and Son, Ltd. Formerly: Francis Williams Prize.

4596

Victorian Military Society
3 Franks Rd.
Guildford, Surrey GU2 6NT, England   Phone: 483 60931

4597

Browne Medal for Original Research
To encourage original research in the Victorian military and its presentation for publication in the Society's journal *Soldiers of the Queen*. Researcher and presenter must be a member of the Society. The material must be based on original sources, and must have been published in the journal to be considered for the award. A medal is awarded annually at the Victorian Military Fair in March. Established in 1988 by Dr. Howard Browne, Newport, Rhode Island, who has a deep interest in the Society, and the service of two of his forebears in Queen Victoria's Army.

4598

Viking Society for Northern Research
Gower St.
Univ. College
London WCIE 6BT, England   Phone: 71 3807176

4599

Viking Society for Northern Research Awards
For recognition of contributions that promote interest in the literature and antiquities of the Scandinavian North. The Gabriel Turville-Petre Prize and J.A.B. Townsend Prize are awarded to students at the Department of Scandinavian Studies, U.C.L. for excellence. The Margaret Orme Prize is awarded to students in any university in the United Kingdom participating in the essay competition.

4600

Vincent Owners Club
15 Priory St.
Farnborough, Hants. GU14 7HX, England   Phone: 252 543938

4601

Vincent Owners Club Awards
To recognize the winners of the Concours d'Elegance and for recognition of sporting achievements that feature the Vincent motorcycle, manufactured between 1928 and 1955.

4602

W. V. Publications
57-59 Rochester Place   Phone: 71 4850011
London NW1 9JN, England   Fax: 71 2842145

4603

British Amateur Video Awards
To encourage the amateur in the art of movie making. The movie must be shot on video tape and entered on "PAL" video tape. Trophies plus monetary prizes of £2,000, £1,000, £500 for first, second and third prizes, respectively, and trophies for the top twelve winners are awarded annually. Established in 1989. Co-sponsored by W. V. Publications, *WHAT Video* and *Camcorder User* magazines.

4604

Whitechapel Art Gallery
80-82 Whitechapel High St.
London E1 7QX, England   Phone: 71 377 5015

4605

Open Exhibition
To recognize outstanding work by East London artists. In 1989, the following awards were presented: a monetary award of £1,000 for the most outstanding sculpture, sponsored by Conder Group; £1,000 for the most outstanding work by an artist under 35, sponsored by Coopers & Lybrand; £1,000 for the most outstanding painting, donated by Save & Prosper Educational Trust; and £2,000 for the most outstanding work in any medium, sponsored by Unilever. Awarded annually. (Discontinued)

4606

Whitechapel Artists Award
To recognize and support promising young artists living in Britain. Two monetary awards of £3,000 each and the opportunity to exhibit work in the Gallery in the year following the award were presented annually. Established in 1987. (Discontinued)

4607

Wolfson Foundation
18-22 The Haymarket   Phone: 71 9301057
London SW1Y 4DQ, England   Fax: 71 9301036

4608

Wolfson Foundation Literary Awards for History
To promote and encourage standards of excellence in the writing of history whereby public taste, discernment, and knowledge in the field

may be advanced and increased. Books published in the preceding year are eligible. A monetary prize of £25,000 is awarded annually (the prize may be split between two winners). Established in 1971.

4609
Woman's Journal
King's Reach Tower
Stamford St.
London SE1 9LS, England   Phone: 71 261 6131

4610
Woman's Journal British Fashion Award
For recognition of British High Street fashion in the following categories: (1) coats; (2) co-ordinates; (3) dresses; (4) suits; (5) sportswear - the topical category changes each year; (6) early evening wear; (7) ballgowns; and (8) designer of the year. Garments must be designed and manufactured in the United Kingdom and intended for the following autumn and winter seasons. Trophies are awarded annually.

4611
Women's Campaign for Soviet Jewry
Pannell House   Phone: 81 458 7148
779/781 Finchley Rd.   Phone: 81 458 7149
London NW11 8DN, England   Fax: 81 458 9971

4612
All Party Parliamentary Award for Soviet Jewry
No further information was available for this edition.

4613
Ross McWhirter Foundation Awards
For recognition of activity in the human rights field. An All Party Parliamentary Award is presented.

4614
President's Award (Israel)
No further information was provided for this edition.

4615
World Association for Celebrating Year 2000 - WAYSEE 2000 (Association Mondiale pour la Celebration de l'An 2000)
Environmental Consulting Office
31 Clerkenwell Close   Phone: 71 2514818
London EC1R 0AT, England   Fax: 71 4900063

Formerly: (1963) World Millennial Association.

4616
World Association for Celebrating Year 2000 Awards
To organize town and city corporations around the world in order to mark the year 2000 and plan a decade of celebrations. Awards will be presented and a hall of fame established.

4617
World Association of Christian Radio Amateurs and Listeners (Association Mondiale des Radio-Amateurs et des Radioclubs Chretiens)
Micasa
13 Ferry Rd.
Wawne
Hull, Humberside HU7 5XU, England   Phone: Hull 822276

4618
WACRAL Award Certificate
For recognition of individuals achieving contacts over the air with WACRAL members. Proof of contact is required. The following awards are presented: basic award - for contact with 10 members; bronze award - for contact with 25 members; silver award - for contact with 35 members; gold award - for contact with 70 members; and Heavenly Pilots - for contact with five Ministers. Plaques are presented. Established in 1968 in memory of the founder, Rev. Arthur W. Shepherd, C3NGF. Additional information is available from Alan Nixon, GIEFU, Award Manager, 14 Carlton Road, Lowten St. Lukes, Warrington WA3 2EP, England.

4619
World Association of Sarcoidosis & Other Granulomatous Disorders
149 Harley St.
London W1N 1HG, England   Phone: 71 9354444

4620
Best Research Lectures on Sarcoidosis
For recognition of the best lectures on sarcoidosis. A monetary award of $1,000 US is presented. Established in 1987.

4621
World Confederation for Physical Therapy
4A Abbots Pl.   Phone: 71 328 5448
London NW6 4NP, England   Fax: 71 624 7579

4622
Mildred Elson Award for International Achievement in Physical Therapy
For recognition of a contribution to international physical therapy. National associations which are members of the Confederation make nominations. A trophy or a plaque is awarded every four years at the International Congress. Established in 1987 by the American Physical Therapy Association in honor of Mildred Elson, first president of the Confederation.

4623
World Dance & Dance Sport Council
87 Parkhurst Rd.
Holloway
London N7 0LP, England   Phone: 71 6091386

Formerly: International Council of Ballroom Dancing.

4624
World Championships in Ballroom and Latin Dancing
For recognition of outstanding ballroom and Latin dancing.

4625
World Ploughing Organisation
29 Parkside Ave.   Phone: 900 823079
Corkermouth, Cumbria CA13 0DR, England   Fax: 900 68736

4626
World Ploughing Championship Awards (Weltmeister im Pflugen)
To encourage improved skills of ploughing the land, and to recognize the highest standards of soil tillage. Individuals qualify through local, regional, and national matches to enter the world championship. The following prizes are awarded: Golden Plough Trophy for the champion; Silver Rose Bowl for the runner-up; and Friendship Trophy for the third place winner. Awarded annually. Established in 1952.

4627
World Ship Trust
202 Lambeth Rd.   Phone: 71 2619535
London SE1 7JW, England   Fax: 71 4012537

4628
Maritime Heritage Award Medal
To recognize and encourage specially meritorious ship preservation achievements on a world-wide basis. A medal is awarded at the discretion of the Trustees when merited. Established in 1980.

4629
World Small Animal Veterinary Association
Royal Veterinary College
Hawkshead Ln., N. Mymms
Hatfield, Herts. AL9 7TA, England
Phone: 707 55486
Fax: 707 52090

4630
WSAVA International Prize for Scientific Achievement
For recognition of outstanding contributions by a veterinarian which have had a significant impact on the advancement of knowledge concerning the cause, detection, cure and/or control of disorders of companion animals. The recipient is chosen on the basis of contributions published in scientific journals or books, and/or information presented at veterinary congresses. Veterinarians with outstanding records of achievement must be nominated by February. A monetary award of £1,000 and a plaque are awarded annually. Established in 1984. Sponsored by Mars, Inc., United States of America.

4631
WSAVA International Prize for Service to the Profession
For recognition of exemplary service by any individual that has fostered and enhanced the exchange of scientific and cultural ideas throughout the world. The recipient is chosen on the basis of service to local, state, national, and international organizations that have catalyzed scientific meetings, exchange of information, and international good will. Veterinarians with outstanding records of service must be nominated by February. A monetary award of £1,000 and a plaque are awarded annually. Established in 1984. Sponsored by Mars, Inc., United States of America.

4632
World Society for the Protection of Animals
Park Pl.
10 Lawn Ln.
London SW8 1UD, England
Phone: 71 793 0540

4633
Marchig Animal Welfare Award
To further the replacement of laboratory animals by alternative methods in scientific, commercial or educational fields and to recognize a person who made an outstanding contribution to this specific scientific subject. Applications may be submitted by September 30. A monetary prize of 40,000 Swiss francs is awarded for research work, teaching practice or the implementation of a new idea or technique or of an existing but previously not implemented procedure that will directly reduce the numbers of animals used. Established in 1986.

4634
Worldaware
1 Catton St.
London WC1R 4AB, England
Phone: 71 8313844
Fax: 71 8311746

Formerly: Centre for World Development Education.

4635
Worldaware Business Awards
To encourage British business, by recognizing its achievement, to play an expanding role in supporting economic and social progress in the developing countries of Asia, Africa, and Latin America. The deadline for entry is June 15. Five trophies are awarded annually: Tate and Lyle Award for Sustainable Development - for commercial activity that has moved a community towards developing its own sustainable resources; The RTZ Award for Long-term Commitment - for a company whose operational commitment to the sustainable development process is proven over time; The Williamson Tea Award for Social Progress - for a commercial activity that has made an important contribution to social progress; and The Worldaware Award for Effective Communication - for publicity material that demonstrates how a company's operations contribute to progress in developing countries; and The BookerTate Award for Small Businesses - for a company with less than 100 employees whose activity has contributed to sustainable development. Established in 1989. Formerly: World Development Awards for Business; World Development Awards for Business..

4636
Worshipful Society of Apothecaries of London
Apothecaries Hall
Black Friars Ln.
London EC4V 6EJ, England
Phone: 71 2361180
Fax: 71 3293272

4637
Galen Medal
This, the Society's highest honor, is given for recognition of outstanding contributions in the field of therapeutics. Individuals may be nominated by members of the Society's governing body. A medal is awarded annually. Established in 1925.

4638
Rogers Prize
To recognize an individual who has written the best or only good essay on the treatment of the sick poor of England, and/or the preservation of the health of the poor in England. A monetary award is given every 10 years. The next award will be 1996. Established in 1925 by an Order of the Charity Commissioners, and with money from the bequest of the will of Dr. Joseph Rogers, who died in 1889.

4639
Yachting Journalists' Association
Spinneys
Woodham Mortimer
Maldon, Essex CM9 6SX, England
Phone: 245 223189
Fax: 245 223189

Formerly: Guild of Yachting Writers.

4640
Yachtsman of the Year Award
For recognition of achievement in the field of boating by a British citizen during the previous year. Nomination is by journalists belonging to the Association. The entire association votes for the final winner. The trophy, a silver navigation buoy on a sea of crystal, is awarded annually. Established in 1955 by Sir Max Aitken Bt. Sponsored by BT plc, formerly British Telecommunications.

4641
Young Sailor of the Year Award
To recognize endeavor and achievement by young sailors. Open to young sailors who are under 21 years of age before December 31 of the award year and who have a British passport or are immediately eligible to receive a British passport. Nominations may be submitted by members of a Royal Yachting Association-affiliated organization, an RYA recognized teaching establishment, or members of the Yachting Journalists Association. A trophy, held for one year by the recipient, and cash prizes are awarded for the final three competitors. Cash prizes are held in trust by the RYA for the winners to use for approved sailing-related expenses. Sponsored by BT (British Telecom). Established in 1993.

4642
Yeats Club
PO Box 30
Thame, Oxon. 0X9 3AD, England
Phone: 84421 6870
Fax: 84421 6677

4643
Yeats Club Open Poetry Competition
For recognition of original poetry and poetry in translation. The deadline for entry is May 1. The following prizes are awarded for original poetry: (1) Grand Prize - £250; (2) First Prize - £150; (3) Second Prize - £75; (4) Third Prize - £50; and (5) Certificates of Distinction. The following prizes are awarded for poetry in translation: (1) DuQuesne Award - an original sculpture for the best poem in translation from a modern language; (2) Catullus Prize - an original sculpture for the best poem in translation from an ancient language; (3) Certificate of Exceptional Merit; and (4) Certificate of Distinction. Awarded annually. Established in 1983.

4644
Yorkshire Post
PO Box 168
Wellington St.
Leeds LS1 1RF, England   Phone: 0532 432701

4645
***Yorkshire Post* Art and Music Award**
To recognize literary works that contribute to the understanding and appreciation of music and art. Books published during the preceding year in the U.K. are eligible. Nominations from publishers must be submitted by January 15. Monetary awards of £1,000 each are awarded annually.

4646
***Yorkshire Post* Best First Work Award**
To recognize and encourage new authors. Original first works published during the preceding year by new authors are eligible. Nominations must be made by publishers. A monetary prize of £1,000 and a scroll are awarded annually. Established in 1964.

4647
***Yorkshire Post* Book of the Year Award**
To encourage literary work of a higher standard and for recognition of the best work of fiction or nonfiction published each year in the U.K. The author need not be British. A monetary award of £1,200 and a scroll are awarded annually. Established in 1965.

4648
Young Concert Artists Trust
14 Ogle St.
London W1P 7LG, England   Phone: 71 637 8743
                                  Fax: 71 323 6985

4649
Young Concert Artists Trust Award
To recognize outstanding young musicians (instrumentalists and singers), and to promote their careers until they are established with a recognized commercial agent. The applicants must be under 28 years for instrumentalists; under 32 for singers; and be British citizens or resident in the United Kingdom. Auditions are held. The deadline for applications is in early February. Management services and promotion of career are awarded annually. Established in 1983 by W. H. Smith and Son, the founding sponsor. Supported by numerous trusts and foundations.

4650
Young Ornithologists' Club
Royal Society for the Protection of Birds
The Lodge   Phone: 767 680551
Sandy, Beds. SG19 2DL, England   Fax: 767 692365

4651
Wild Places
To recognize outstanding field naturalists and conservationists who adopt and record the species and habitats at a local site, and suggest improvements that will aid the wildlife there. Books and optical equipment are awarded to winners in three age categories - under 9, 10-12, and 13 and over. The overall winner wins a trip to the Highlands of Scotland. Formerly: Young Ornithologist of the Year.

4652
Wildlife Action Award
For recognition of action for conservation of birds and other wildlife. Individuals under 19 years of age are eligible. A certificate and a gold, silver, or bronze badge are awarded when an individual reaches the set number of credit points. Established in 1993. Formerly: (1993) Action for Birds Award.

4653
Zinc Development Association
(Association pour le Developpement du Marche du Zinc)
42 Weymouth St.
London WlN 3LQ, England   Phone: 71 499 6636

4654
Zinc Castings 86
To encourage outstanding or innovative use of zinc alloy die castings. United Kingdom designers or producers of castings are eligible. Awards are given in two categories: (1) Engineering design - sponsored by Kenrick Hardware, Ltd.; and (2) Innovation - sponsored by Dynacast International, Ltd. A monetary prize, trophy, and certificate are awarded annually. Established in 1986.

4655
Zoological Society of London
Regent's Park   Phone: 71 722 3333
London NW1 4RY, England   Fax: 71 483 4436

4656
Frink Medal for British Zoologists
To recognize professional zoologists who have made substantial and original contributions to the advancement of zoology. British citizens who are residents of the United Kingdom and whose work is based there may be nominated. A bronze medal designed by Elisabeth Frink is awarded annually when merited. Established in 1973.

4657
Thomas Henry Huxley Award
To recognize postgraduate research students for original work in zoology. Postgraduate students who are attending a university in Great Britain and Northern Ireland and were awarded the Doctor of Philosophy degree during the preceding year may be nominated. A bronze medal is awarded annually when merited. Established in 1961.

4658
Prince Philip Prize
To recognize students for an account of practical work involving some aspect of animal biology. Pupils of schools in Great Britain, Northern Ireland, the Channel Isles, and the Isle of Man who are under 19 years of age are eligible. A bronze medal and a certificate are awarded annually when merited. The winner's school will also receive an award of money to be used in promoting the teaching of animal biology. Prizes of books or a certificate may also be awarded as honorable mentions. Entry deadline is October 1. Established in 1961.

4659
Stamford Raffles Award
To recognize amateur zoologists who have made distinguished contributions to zoology or to recognize professional zoologists who have made contributions outside the scope of their professional activities and principal specialization. Nominations are accepted. A bronze sculpture by Anita Mandl is awarded annually when merited. Established in 1961.

4660
Scientific Medal
For recognition of distinguished work in zoology. Men and women under 40 years of age may be nominated. Up to three silver medals may be awarded each year. Established in 1938.

4661
Silver Medal
To recognize persons who have contributed to the understanding and appreciation of zoology. Selection is based on such activities as public education in natural history and conservation. A silver medal is awarded periodically when merited. Nominations are requested annually. Established in 1837 and first awarded in 1847.

Finland

4662
Archival Association
(Arkistoyhdistys r.y.)
c/o Valtionarkisto
PO Box 258
SF-00171 Helsinki, Finland
Phone: 0 176 911

4663
Honorary Member
For recognition of contributions to the Association.

4664
Artists Association of Finland
(Suomen Taiteilijaseura/Konstnarsgiller i Finland)
Yrjonkatu 11
SF-00120 Helsinki, Finland
Phone: 0 943919
Fax: 0 607561

4665
Artists Association of Finland Award
(Suomen Taiteilijaseuran tunnustusapuaraha)
To encourage professional development of artists in Finland. Participants in the annual exhibition of Suomen Taiteilijain Nayttely (Exhibition of Finnish Artists) are eligible. A monetary prize is awarded annually. Established in 1981.

4666
Association of Finnish Writers for Children and Youth
(Suomen Nuorisokirjailijatry)
Aurorastreet 5A 8
SF-00100 Helsinki, Finland
Phone: 0 713558

4667
Lydecken - palkinto
(Lydecken prize)
For recognition of the best children's book of the year. A monetary prize of 10,000 Finnish marks is awarded.

4668
Paaskynen palkinto
(Swallow Prize)
To promote outstanding children's literature in the press, on television, on radio and in books. A monetary prize of 9,000 Finnish marks and a plaque are awarded biennially.

4669
Suomalainen kuvakirja palkinto
(Finnish picturebook prize)
For recognition of the best picture book of the year. A monetary prize of 6,000 Finnish marks is awarded.

4670
Biochemical, Biophysical and Microbiological Society of Finland
(Societas Biochemica, Biophysica Microbiologica Fenniae)
Univ. of Helsinki
Dept. of Genetics
17 (Arkadiankatu 7)
FIN-00014 Helsinki, Finland
Phone: 0 1917378
Fax: 0 1917382

4671
A. I. Virtanen - Award
For recognition of achievements in the field of chemistry, biochemistry, microbiology, or nutrition research. A monetary prize and a medal are awarded biennially. Established in 1981 in memory of A. I. Virtanen, the Finnish Nobel Prize winner in chemistry in 1945. Co-sponsored by the Foundation for Nutrition Research and Finnish Chemical Society.

4672
Cancer Society of Finland
Liisankatu 21B
SF-00170 Helsinki, Finland
Phone: 0 135331
Fax: 0 1351093

4673
Cancer Campaign Medals of Merit
To recognize individuals for outstanding work for the cancer campaign, and to show public gratitude. A gold or silver medal is awarded to persons outside of the cancer organizations. A bronze medal is awarded to the employees of cancer organizations. Awarded annually. Established in 1956.

4674
Erkki Saxen Medal
To recognize a Finnish citizen or a foreigner for a cancer campaign, epidemiological cancer research or cancer registration, or to recognize a foreigner who collaborated with the Finnish cancer researchers or the Finnish Cancer Registry. Nomination is necessary. A medal is awarded annually by the Finnish Foundation for Cancer Research. Established in honor of Professor Erkki Saxen, former Director of the Finnish Cancer Registry.

4675
Fine Arts Association of Finland
(Suomen Taideyhdistys-Finska Konstforeningen)
Helsingin Taidehalli
Nervanderinkatu 3
FIN-00100 Helsinki, Finland
Phone: 0 494656

4676
Fine Arts Association of Finland Awards
To provide recognition in the field of fine arts. The following awards are presented: Awards for Artists, Dukaatti Prizes, Richter Awards for Art Critics, and Art Literature Prize. Monetary awards of 6,500 - 30,000 Finnish marks are presented annually. Established in 1880 by Suomen Taideyhdistys.

4677
Finland
Ministry of Defense
ET. Makasiininkatu 8A
SF-00130 Helsinki, Finland
Phone: 0 1613941
Fax: 0 1613993

4678
Order of the Cross of Liberty
To recognize during war or peace, members of the Armed Forces of Finland for military merit; to recognize civilians who work for the Armed Forces or who work in favor of the Armed Forces for services rendered to the Armed Forces; to recognize "in time of war" units of the Armed Forces as well as organizations and establishments of Finland; and to

recognize foreigners for service to Finland. The Grand Cross of the Order of Freedom, the Cross of Freedom, first, second, third, and fourth class and the Medal of Freedom are awarded to military persons. The Medal of Merit is awarded to civilians. In addition, the following special decorations of the Order are awarded: Cross of Mannerheim, first class, to members of the Armed Forces for extraordinary courage during military operations; Cross of Mannerheim, second class, to members of the Armed Forces for extraordinary courage during military operations. An individual may receive this cross more than once; Medal of Freedom with a rosette, to a superior commander of a unit composed of different armies for recognition of the execution of a military operation selected by the Grand Master; Medal of Merit in gold, for recognition of particularly remarkable merit chosen by the Grand Master of the Order; Cross of Mourning, to a parent of a combatant killed in action; and Medal of Mourning, to a parent of a person who dies during wartime while serving the National Defense. The Cross of the Order with a two edged sword is white enamel cross-bordered with gold. A rose herald is in the center. The medal is silver with a lion in the center. Established in 1918 by Baron Gustaf Mannerheim, former President of the Republic, and formed into a permanent military order in 1940.

4679
Order of the Lion of Finland
For recognition of civilians and military of outstanding merit. Foreigners may also be recognized by this order. The President of the Republic confers the Order. The Order consists of the following classes: Commanders of the Grand Cross; Commanders of the first class; Commanders; Chevaliers of the first class; Chevaliers; Medal for Finland of the Order of the Lion, given to artists and writers; and Cross of Merit. The cross of the order is white enamel bordered with gold and has a lion in gold in the center. The medal is silver and has a gold lion in the center. Established in 1942 by Resto Ryti, President of the Republic.

4680
Order of the White Rose of Finland
To recognize citizens of Finland and foreigners for special service to the country. The Chief of State of Finland has the right to confer the decoration. The Order consists of the following classes: Commanders Grand Cross; Commanders, first class and second class; Chevaliers, first class and second class; Insigne of Merit; Medal, first class with a cross of gold; and Medals, first and second class. The cross of the order is white enamel bordered with gold and has a rose heraldry in the center. The Medal is silver with a rose in the center. Established in 1919 by the Baron Gustaf Mannerheim, former President of the Republic.

4681
Finnish Academy of Technology
Kansakoulukatu 10A Phone: 0 6944260
SF-00100 Helsinki, Finland Fax: 0 6945041

4682
Walter Ahlstrom Prize
(Walter Ahlstromin palkinto)
To recognize significant technological achievements which enable, or will enable, widely applicable industrial advances in the use of energy, the utilization of raw materials, or in minimizing environmental impact. A monetary award is presented annually in October at a Jubilee Meeting. Established in 1990 to honor Walter Ahlstrom. Sponsored by the Walter Ahlstrom Foundation.

4683
Craftsman's Award
For recognition of meritorious achievement connected with technical research and development in which manual dexterity is required. Mechanics and other technical assistants, inventors and developers are eligible. A diploma and a stipend are awarded annually. Established in 1972.

4684
Medal of Merit
For recognition of outstanding achievements in the fields of technoscientific research, creative technical work or the general development of technology, or for meritorious support of the activities and/or the goals of the Academy. An individual or an organization is eligible. A silver medal designed by the sculptor, Terho Sakki, is generally awarded annually. Established in 1962 as a gold medal; the award has been a silver medal since 1976.

4685
Finnish Board of Literature
(Suomen Kirjasaatio)
Merimiehenkatu 12 A 6
SF-00150 Helsinki, Finland Phone: 0 179185

4686
Finlandia Prize
(Finlandia-palkinto)
To provide recognition for the best novel of the year written by a Finnish citizen. A monetary prize of 100,000 Finnish marks is awarded annually. Established in 1984.

4687
Rudolf Koivu Prize
(Rudolf Koivu - palkinto)
For recognition of the best illustration of juvenile books of the year. Books written in Finnish or Swedish and published in Finland are eligible. A monetary prize of 30,000 Finnish marks and a plaque are awarded biennially. Established in 1949 by the Finnish Board of Juvenile Books and the Grafia in memory of Rudolf Koivu (1890-1946), a juvenile and fairy tale illustrator.

4688
Tieto-Finlandia Prize
(Tieto-Finlandia-palkinto)
To provide recognition for the best nonfiction book of the year written by a Finnish citizen. A monetary prize of 100,000 Finnish marks is awarded annually. Established in 1989.

4689
Topelius Prize
(Topelius-palkinto)
For recognition of the best Finnish children and youth fiction book of the year. Books published in Finland that are written in Finnish or Swedish are eligible. A monetary prize and a plaque are awarded annually. Established in 1946 by the Finnish Board of Juvenile Books and the Association of Children's Books Authors in memory of Zacharias Topelius (1818-1898), a juvenile and fairy tale writer, scholar, historian, and Finnish patriot of 19th century romanticism. Additional information is available from Mr. Kari Vaijarvi, Porvoonkatu 9A, SF-00510 Helsinki, Finland.

4690
Finnish Broadcasting Company
(Oy. Yleisradio Ab.)
Music Dept.
PO Box 10 Phone: 0 14801
SF-00241 Helsinki, Finland Fax: 0 14802089

4691
Record of the Year Prize
To promote and encourage the production of Finnish records. Awards are given for classical music. A diploma is awarded annually. Established in 1971. An award for light music was given from 1971 to 1981.

4692
Finnish Cultural Foundation
(Suomen Kulttuurirahasto)
PO Box 203 Phone: 0 602144
FIN-00121 Helsinki, Finland Fax: 0 640474

4693
Finnish Cultural Foundation's Prize
To recognize creative work contributing to Finnish culture. Three prizes are awarded annually. Established in 1939.

4694
Mirjam Helin International Singing Competition
(Kansainvalinen Mirjam Helin laulukilpailu)
To recognize the winners of the international singing competition and to provide grants for promising young singers. The competition is open to women 31 years of age or under and to men 33 years of age or under regardless of nationality. The deadline for applications is March 15. The following prizes are awarded to men and women: first prize - 90,000 Finnish marks; second prize - 65,000 Finnish marks; third prize - 40,000 Finnish marks; fourth prize - 25,000 Finnish marks; Special Prize for Young Talent to both a man and a woman; and the Martti Talvela Prize for the best performance of a Finnish song. Awarded every five years. Established in 1981 by Mrs. Mirjam Helin who endowed the Finnish Cultural Foundation with the special Mirjam and Hans Helin Fund.

4695
Finnish Dramatists' Society
(Suomen Naytelmakirjailijaliitto)
Vironkatu 12 B   Phone: 0 1356191
SF-00170 Helsinki 17, Finland   Fax: 0 1356171

4696
LEA Award
(LEA-palkinto)
For recognition of an outstanding theater play or a dramatist's whole work. Finnish citizens are eligible. A monetary prize is awarded annually at the convention. Established in 1984 and named for the first performed Finnish play by Aleksis Kivi, *LEA*.

4697
Finnish Historical Society
(Suomen Historiallinen Seura)
Arkadiankatu 16 B 28   Phone: 0 440 369
SF-00100 Helsinki 10, Finland   Fax: 0 441 468

4698
Correspondent Membership
(Kirjeenvaihtajajasenyys)
To promote historical research and to recognize achievements in the field of Finnish history. Awarded annually. Established in 1975.

4699
Finnish Library Association
((Suomen Kirjastoseura))
Museokatu 18 A 5   Phone: 80 441984
SF-00100 Helsinki 10, Finland   Fax: 80 441345

4700
Finnish Library Association Awards
To encourage the dissemination of library information to policymakers in Finland and to influence national library policy. The Association grants scholarships and bestows awards annually.

4701
Finnish Museums Association
(Suomen museoliitto ry)
Annankatu 16 B 50   Phone: 0 649001
SF-00120 Helsinki, Finland   Fax: 0 608330

4702
Finnish Museums Association 50th Anniversary Medal
(Suomen museoliiton 50-vuotisjuhlamitali)
For recognition of activity in the field of museums. Individuals, societies, or towns are eligible. Five to ten medals are awarded annually. Established in 1973.

4703
Finnish Section of the International Board on Books for Young People
(Suomen Nuortenkirjaneuvosto)
Pohjolankatu 3
SF-00610 Helsinki, Finland   Phone: 0 790464

4704
Anni Swan Prize
(Anni Swanin Mitali)
For recognition of the best children's book written in Finnish or Swedish by a Finnish writer, and published during the preceding three years. A silver medal is awarded triennially. Established in 1961 in honor of the writer, Anni Swan.

4705
Finnish Society of Philosophy of Law
(Suomen Oikeusfilosofinen yhdistys)
Ruusulantatu 11 B 39
SF-00260 Helsinki, Finland   Phone: 0 18 25 365

4706
Otto Brusiin Award
(Otto Brusiin palkinto)
For recognition of the best Finnish article in the field of legal theory. Younger scholars, who write in the Finnish language, may be nominated. A monetary prize is awarded biennially. Established in 1986 in honor of Otto Brusiin. Sponsored by the Otto Brusiin Foundation.

4707
Finnish Society of Sciences and Letters
(Finska Vetenskaps-Societeten)
Mariankatu 5   Phone: 0 633005
FIN-00170 Helsinki, Finland   Fax: 0 661065

4708
Professor E. J. Nystroms Prize
(Professor E. J. Nystroms pris)
To recognize outstanding scientific contributions. Members of the Society may submit nominations. A monetary award is presented annually. Established in 1962 to honor Professor E. J. Nystrom, former president of the Society, who died in 1960.

4709
Foundation for the Promotion of Finnish Music
(Luovan Saveltaiteen edistamissaatio)
Lauttasaarentie 1   Phone: 0 68101252
FIN-00200 Helsinki, Finland   Fax: 0 6820770

4710
Grant or Prize
(Apuraha tai Palkinto)
For recognition of teachers of music, representatives of the science of music, composers, performers of music, and persons who have in other ways meritoriously promoted music in Finland. Only Finnish citizens are eligible. Monetary awards are presented every year on the birthday of Jean Sibelius, the famous Finnish composer. Established in 1955 by the Finnish Parliament which donated the basic capital for the establishment

of the Foundation on the occasion of the 90th birthday of Professor Jean Sibelius, who died in 1957.

4711

Geographical Society of Finland
(Suomen Maantieteellinen Seura)
Hallituskatu 11
SF-00014 Helsinki 10, Finland
Phone: 0 1912434
Fax: 0 1912641

4712

Fennia Gold Medal
(Kultainen Fennia-mitali)
This, the highest medal of the Society, is given for recognition of scientific expeditions of exceptional value and for studies that are of great importance from the point of view of Finnish geographical research. Finnish and foreign explorers or scientists active in the field of geographical and regional studies are eligible. A gold medal is awarded irregularly. Established in 1941.

4713

Fennia Silver Medal
(Hopeinen Fennia-mitali)
To provide recognition for meritorious studies within the scope of the Society's interests or for creditable work for the aims of the Geographical Society of Finland. Finnish and foreign scientists may be nominated. A medal is awarded irregularly. Established in 1962.

4714

Ragnar Hult Medal
(Ragnar Hult-mitali)
For recognition in the field of geography. Selection is by nomination. A medal is awarded irregularly. Established in 1987 in memory of Docent Ragnar Hult (1857-1899), the founder of Finnish scientific geography.

4715

Geological Society of Finland
(Suomen Geologinen Seura-Geologiska Sallskapet i Finland)
Kivimiehentie 1
SF-02150 Espoo, Finland
Phone: 0 46931

4716

Eskola Medal
(Eskola-Mitali)
To recognize a scientist in the field of geology or mineralogy who has made Finland known to the world or to recognize a scientist for achievements in research on the Finnish bedrock. A gold medal is awarded every five years. Established in 1963 in honor of Professor Pentti Eskola, a metamorphic petrologist. Sponsored by the Outokumpu Company. Additional information is available from Hilkka Leino, phone: 0 4561; fax: 0 456 6390.

4717

GRAFIA - Association of Finnish Graphic Design
(Grafia - Graafisen Suunnittelun Jarjesto)
Uudenmaankatu 11 B 9
SF-00120 Helsinki, Finland
Phone: 0 601941
Fax: 0 601942

4718

Association of Finnish Graphic Design Awards
To recognize creative designers working in graphic design, illustration, layout and book jacket and package design. The Association sponsors education seminars and presents scholarships and awards.

4719

Helsinki Festival
(Helsingin Juhlaviikot)
Unioninkatu 28
SF-00100 Helsinki 10, Finland
Phone: 0 174142
Fax: 0 656715

Formerly: Sibelius Viikot (Sibelius Weeks).

4720

Artist of the Year, Helsinki Festival
(Helsingin Juhlaviikkojen Vuoden taiteilija)
For recognition of achievement and to encourage professional development in the field of art. The Fine Arts Exhibition Committee of the Helsinki Festival selects one Finnish artist who meets the criteria of long-term high-level artistic work. The Board of the Festival confirms the winner. The award consists of an exhibition in Helsinki during the Festival. Awarded annually. Established in 1971.

4721

International Council of Sport Science and Physical Education
Univ. of Jyvaskyla
PL 35
SF-40351 Jyvaskyla, Finland
Phone: 41 603160
Fax: 41 603161

Formerly: (1983) International Council of Sport and Physical Education.

4722

Philip Noel Baker Research Award
To recognize an individual for both scientific work and personal contribution to the Council's activities. A diploma is awarded annually. Established in 1969 to honor Lord Philip Noel Baker, first president of ICSSPE and Laureat of the Nobel Prize for Peace. Additional information is available from Dr. Ernst Jokl, 340 Kingsway, Lexington, KY 40502 U.S.A.

4723

Sport Science Award of the IOC President
To recognize outstanding scientific achievements in the field of sport and physical education. Awarded in alternative years in two areas: biomedical sciences, and social sciences. Accomplishments in the following areas are considered which: (1) study the development of the Olympic movement and world sport and their impact upon peace and international understanding; (2) substantially contribute to the knowledge of sport and physical education in general and in their various branches; (3) study the implications of life-long participation in sport on personality development and health; or (4) contribute to the further development of sport science and its disciplines. A monetary award of US $7,500, a commemorative medal, and a diploma are awarded annually. Established in 1989 to honor the President of the International Olympic Committee. Sponsored by the International Olympic Committee.

4724

International Federation of Bowlers
(Federation Internationale des Quillieurs)
Linnustajantie 6 I 49
SF-02940 Espoo 94, Finland
Phone: 0 594 541

4725

International Federation of Bowlers Awards
To foster worldwide interest in amateur ten pin and nine pin bowling and international friendship through world and zone tournaments and bowling competitions between bowlers of different countries. The Federation sponsors world amateur championships.

4726

International Federation of Psychoanalytic Societies
Lansitie 9
SF-02160 Espoo, Finland
Phone: 0 426425
Fax: 0 424614

4727

Werner Schwidder Award
For recognition of distinguished work in the field of psychoanalysis. Individuals who make contributions to the Society are considered. An inscribed medal and diploma are awarded at the convention. Established in 1970 in memory of Werner Schwidder, M.D., cofounder of the Society.

4728

International Jean Sibelius Violin Competition
PO Box 31
SF-00101 Helsinki, Finland   Phone: 0 405441

4729

International Jean Sibelius Violin Competition
To recognize the best violinists of the Competition. Violinists of any nationality born in 1965 or later are eligible. Monetary prizes totaling $42,000 are awarded every five years. In addition, the Finnish Broadcasting Company awards $2,000 for the best performance of the Sibelius Violin Concerto. Established in 1965 to commemorate one hundred years after the birth of Jean Sibelius by the Sibelius Society of Finland.

4730

International Mathematical Union
Dept. of Mathematics
Univ. of Helsinki
Hallituskatu 15   Phone: 0 90 1911
SF-00100 Helsinki, Finland   Fax: 0 65 6591

4731

Fields Medal
This, the highest honor bestowed on mathematicians, is given for recognition of outstanding achievements in mathematics. Young mathematicians are eligible. A monetary prize and a medal are awarded every four years at the International Congress of Mathematicians. At least two and no more than four medals are awarded. Established by Professor Fields and first awarded in 1936.

4732

Rolf Nevanlinna Prize
For recognition of outstanding achievements in the mathematical aspects of information science. Young mathematicians are eligible. A monetary prize and a medal are awarded every four years at the International Congress of Mathematicians. Established in 1982 with funds provided by the University of Helsinki.

4733

ITI International Ballet Competition, Helsinki
c/o Finnish Centre of the
International Theatre Institute   Phone: 0 135 7887
Meritullinkatu 33   Phone: 0 335 7861
SF-00170 Helsinki, Finland   Fax: 0 135 5522

4734

Helsinki International Ballet Competition
For recognition of outstanding ballet performances. The Competition is open to dancers of all nationalities. All participants must be qualified by the selection committee. Qualifications are based on recommendations from their directors/teachers or ITI Centres. The competitors are judged individually and in two divisions: (1) Junior Division - age 15 to 18; and (2) Senior Division - age 19 to 26 at the time of the Competition. The following prizes are awarded for both Senior division, women and Senior division, men: (1) First prize - 40,000 Finnish marks; (2) Second prize - 25,000 Finnish marks; (3) Third prize - 15,000 Finnish marks; (4) Fourth prize - 10,000 Finnish marks; (5) Fifth prize - 5,000 Finnish marks; and for both Junior division, girls and Junior division, boys: (1) First prize - 15,000 Finnish marks; (2) Second prize - 10,000 Finnish marks; and (3) Third prize - 5,000 Finnish marks; and Choreography awards: (1) Special prize - 40,000 Finnish marks; and (2) Other awards - 25,000 Finnish marks, 15,000 Finnish marks, and 10,000 Finnish marks. Helsinki is one of the four locations for the International Ballet Competition, the others being Moscow, USSR; Jackson, Mississippi, U.S.A.; and Varna, Bulgaria.

4735

Yrjo Jahnsson Foundation
(Yrjo Jahnssonin Saatio)
Ludviginkatu 3-5A   Phone: 0 649636
SF-00130 Helsinki, Finland   Fax: 0 605002

4736

Dissertation Prize in Economics
To recognize from one to five persons who have written outstanding master's theses in economics. The choice is made by the heads of economics departments of Finnish universities. Monetary prizes of 9,000 Finnish marks are awarded annually.

4737

Yrjo Jahnsson Award in Economics
To honor a European economist younger than 45 years of age for a significant contribution in economics. A monetary prize of 12,000 Finnish marks is given biannually.

4738

Sigrid Juselius Foundation
Aleksanterinkatu 48 B
SF-00100 Helsinki, Finland   Phone: 0 634 461

4739

Medical Research Grants
To enable Finnish researchers to conduct medical research. Resources are allocated only to Senior and Advanced Researchers and for work of established staff of universities. Established in 1930 by Fritz Arthur Juselius.

4740

Kaustinen Folk Music Festival
(Kaustisen Kansanmusiikkijuhlat)
PO Box 24   Phone: 968 8611252
SF-69601 Kaustinen, Finland   Fax: 968 8611977

4741

Folk Music Festival - Plaketti
For recognition of contributions in the field of Finnish folk music or folk dance. A plaque is awarded annually. Established in 1968.

4742

Mestaripelimanni, Mestarikansanlaulaja
For recognition of meritorious Finnish folk musicians and folk singers. A trophy is awarded annually. Established in 1970.

4743

Kordelin Foundation
Hallituskatu 1
SF-00170 Helsinki, Finland

4744

Kordelin Prize
For recognition of outstanding contributions to Finnish culture and literature. A number of monetary prizes and an honorary prize are awarded annually.

4745
Lahti Organ Festival
Kirkkokatu 5
FIN-15110 Lahti, Finland
Phone: 18 7823184
Fax: 18 7832190

4746
Lahti International Organ Competition
(Lahden Kansainvalinen Urkukilpailu)
To recognize outstanding organists. Competitors must be under 30 years of age. The following awards are presented: First prize - 25,000 Finnish marks; Second prize - 15,000 Finnish marks; and Third prize - 10,000 Finnish marks. The jury may distribute the prizes differently and present special awards. The next competition will be held in 1997.

4747
Lappeenranta City
(Lappeenrannan Kaupunki)
Valtakatu 37B
SF-53100 Lappeenranta, Finland
Phone: 953 4531061
Fax: 953 518309

4748
Lapeenranta National Singing Competition Awards
(Lappeenrannan Valtakunnalliset Laulukilpailut)
To recognize the best male and female singers in Finland. Female Finnish singers under 30 years of age and male Finnish singers under 32 years of age may apply. The following monetary awards are presented triennially: First Prize - 30,000 Finnish marks, Second Prize - 20,000 Finnish marks, and Third Prize - 15,000 Finnish marks. In addition, special prizes are available. Established in 1969 by Lappeenranta City. The next competition is scheduled for January 1995.

4749
Naantali Music Festival
(Naantalin Musiikkijuhlat)
Paulo Cello Competition
PO Box 46
SF-21101 Naantali, Finland
Phone: 21 755363
Fax: 21 755425

4750
International Paulo Cello Competition
(Kansainvalinen Paulon Sellokilpailu)
For recognition of outstanding cello performances. The competition is open to cellists of all nationalities who are between 16 and 33 years of age. The following monetary prizes are awarded: first prize - $20,000; second prize - $12,000; third prize - $8,000; fourth prize - $2,000 plus travel fund; fifth prize - $2,000 plus travel fund; and sixth prize - $2,000 plus travel fund. Awarded every five years. Established in 1991. Sponsored by the Paulo Foundation.

4751
National Federation of Business and Professional Women in Finland
(Suomen Liike- ja Virkanaisten Liitto - Finlands Yrkeskvinnors Forbund)
Liisankatu 27 B 2
SF-00170 Helsinki, Finland
Phone: 0 1352483
Fax: 0 1355122

4752
Woman of the Year in Finland
(Vuoden Nainen)
To recognize a woman in Finland who is especially distinguished in science, professional, business, or civil life. The nomination is made by the Board of the Federation on the basis of proposals made by 35 Finnish business and professional women's clubs. A plaque is awarded each year at the annual meeting in April. Established in 1955.

4753
Oulu International Children's Film Festival
Torikatu 8
SF-90100 Oulu, Finland

4754
Star Boy Award
To recognize the director of the best children's film at the festival. A monetary award of 3,000 ecus and a statuette are awarded annually. Established in 1992 by Kaleva Newspaper.

4755
Society of the Friends of History
(Historian Ystavain Liitto)
Kaupinkatu 22 A5
SF-33500 Tampere, Finland
Phone: 931 556282

4756
Society of the Friends of History Award
(Historian Ystavain Liiton Palkinto)
To recognize a work which has promoted the widening of historical knowledge in Finland. A silver medal of Yrjo Koskinen is awarded annually. Established in 1972 in honor of Yrjo Koskinen, (1830-1903), a prominent Finnish historian and statesman.

4757
Tampere Film Festival
(Tampereen elokuvajuhlat)
PO Box 305
SF-33101 Tampere 10, Finland
Phone: 31 2235681
Fax: 31 2230121

Formerly: (1980) Society for Film Art in Tampere.

4758
Tampere International Short Film Festival
(Tampereen Kansainvaliset lyhytelokuvajuhlat Grand Prix)
For recognition of short films in a national and international competition of a high standard that have a human theme and seek new forms of cinematic expression. Films screened publicly for the first time during the preceding year by January 1 may be entered in the following categories: animated films, documentary films, and fiction films. The deadline is January 15. The running time for international films may not exceed 35 minutes. An international jury awards the following prizes: Grand Prix - a monetary award of 25,000 Finnish marks and a "Kiss" statuette; Category Prizes - a monetary prize and a "Kiss Statuette"; One Special Prize - a monetary prize; and Diplomas of Merit. Awarded annually in March. Established in 1970.

4759
Union of Finnish Critics
(Suomen Arvostelijain Liitto Finlands Kritikerforbund ry)
Runeberginkatu 49 A 1
SF-00260 Helsinki, Finland
Phone: 0 441 641
Fax: 0 441 641

4760
Spurs of Criticism
(Kritiikin kannukset)
To recognize a Finnish creative or performing artist or group for a meritorious achievement in the field of visual arts, literature, music, theatre, or cinema or for a worthy inter-art achievement. The prize is intended primarily for young artists. The best artistic breakthrough or comparable achievement of the year is considered. A trophy of silver spurs with a plaque is awarded annually in April. Established in 1962.

Finland

4761
Wihuri Foundation for International Prizes
(Wihuri kansainvalisten palkintojen rahasto)
Arkadiankatu 21 A 14
SF-00100 Helsinki 10, Finland   Phone: 0 444 145

4762
Wihuri International Prize
(Wihurin kansainvalinen palkinto)
To provide recognition for creative work that has specially furthered and developed the cultural and economic progress of mankind. Individuals or collective bodies regardless of race, religion, nationality, or language are eligible. All recipients have been scientists representing a vast range of fields. A monetary prize of $50,000 is awarded for the International Prize or the Sibelius Prize at least every third year. Established in 1953 by Antti Wihuri, a sea captain and industrialist.

4763
Wihuri Sibelius Prize
(Wihurin Sibelius palkinto)
To recognize prominent composers who have become internationally known and acknowledged. Individuals or collective bodies regardless of race, religion, nationality, or language are eligible. A monetary prize of $50,000 is awarded for the Sibelius Prize or the International Prize at least every third year. Established in 1953 by Antti Wihuri, a sea captain and industrialist.

4764
World Federation of the Deaf
(Federation Mondiale des Sourds)
Ilkantie 4
Postilokero 65
SF-00401 Helsinki, Finland

4765
Prix Federation Mondiale des Sourds
For recognition of special achievement in education and social rehabilitation of the deaf. Awards are presented.

4766
World Peace Council
(Conseil Mondial de la Paix)
Lonnrotinkatu 25 A 5   Phone: 0 6931044
SF-00180 Helsinki 10, Finland   Fax: 0 6933703

4767
World Peace Council Awards
For outstanding services to the cause of peace, development, and understanding among peoples. The Joliet-Curie Gold Medal for Peace and other awards are presented.

France

4768
Academie d'Agriculture de France
18, rue de Bellechasse   Phone: 1 47051037
F-75007 Paris, France   Fax: 1 45550978

4769
Diplomes de Medailles
To recognize students graduating first in their classes from the National Agronomy Institute Paris-Grignon and the National School of Agriculture at Montpellier or Rennes. The following medals are awarded annually: Medaille Tisserand, Medaille d'Or, Medaille de Vermeil, and Medaille d'Argent.

4770
Prix de la Fondation Xavier - Bernard
To recognize the authors of the best work in applied research in the fields of vegetable and animal production. Works should contribute to the advancement of agriculture, to better quantity and quality yields, or to the struggle against pests and diseases. Studies of rural economics of agricultural production (administration of agricultural production as well as the professional sectors) and the economics of agricultural product distribution (patterns of consumption, research to open up new avenues of trade, conditions of production, etc.) are considered. One or two prizes totaling 20,000 French francs are awarded annually. Jointly administered by the Fondation Xavier-Bernard and the Bureau d'Academie d'Agriculture de France. Established in 1955.

4771
Prix Jean Dufrenoy
For recognition of researchers active in a sensitive, agronomic field that is emerging with practical applications in agriculture and French farm production. French researchers under 40 years of age are eligible. One or two prizes totaling 30,000 French francs and a medal are awarded annually at Seance Solennelle. Established in 1973 by Marie-Louise Dufrenoy in memory of her brother, Jean Dufrenoy, a member of the Academy. Sponsored by Legs Dufrenoy.

4772
Academie d'Architecture
Hotel de Chaulnes
9, Place des Vosges   Phone: 1 48878310
F-75004 Paris, France   Fax: 1 48874442

Formerly: Association reconnue d'utilite publique.

4773
Medaille d'Archeologie
To recognize an architect who through work or services has contributed to the field of archaeology. A silver medal is awarded annually. Established in 1875.

4774
Medaille d'Architecture Fondation le Soufache
To recognize an architect for an outstanding work. Government buildings are excluded. A silver medal is awarded annually. Established in 1874 by Fondation le Soufache.

4775
Medaille d'Architecture Prix Dejean ou Prix Delarue
To recognize a young architect. The following two prizes are awarded in alternate years: Prix Dejean - to assist a young French architect in his or her studies, research, or work on some technical point of architecture. Established in 1902 by the Societe Centrale; Prix Delarue - to recognize an exceptionally talented architect who is less than 40 years of age. Established in 1905 by Societe Centrale. A monetary prize of 1,000 French francs is awarded annually.

4776
Medaille de la Jurisprudence
To recognize a lawyer or architect who has contributed to the special laws regarding building codes. A silver medal is awarded annually. Established in 1874.

4777
Medaille de la Recherche et de la Technique
To recognize an engineer or researcher who has contributed to the construction techniques necessary for architectural expression. A silver medal is awarded annually. Established in 1970.

4778
Medaille de la Restauration
For recognition of contributions to the field of conservation or restoration of ancient buildings. A silver medal is awarded annually. Established in 1965.

4779
Medaille de l'Academie d'Architecture
To recognize an individual who has made an outstanding contribution to the understanding and appreciation of architecture. A silver medal is awarded annually. Established in 1972.

4780
Medaille de l'Analyse Architecturale
To recognize an architect or other individual who has contributed through writing or other means of communication to the broadening of the architectural debate. A silver medal is awarded. Established in 1985.

4781
Medaille de l'Architecture d'Accompagnement
To recognize artists for an outstanding contribution to the creation of architectural spaces. A silver medal is awarded.

4782
Medaille de l'Histoire de l'Art
To recognize an art historian for an important and exceptional work. French or foreign historians are eligible. A vermeil medal is awarded annually. Established in 1971.

4783
Medaille de l'Urbanisme
For recognition of a design or completed regional or urban project that is well adapted to its site. A silver medal is awarded annually. Established in 1965.

4784
Medaille des Arts Plastiques
To recognize a painter, sculptor, ceramicist, glass worker, etc. for a collection of work or a single work that contributes to the completion of an architecture or town plan. A silver medal is awarded annually. Established in 1972.

4785
Medaille des Publications
To recognize a writer, editor, journalist, or filmmaker who through articles, publications, or films has contributed to the field of architecture. A silver medal is awarded annually. Established in 1965.

4786
Medaille d'Honneur de l'Academie d'Architecture
To recognize a French architect of talent and distinction. A vermeil medal is awarded annually. Established in 1895 by Fondation Guerinot.

4787
Medaille d'Or de l'Academie d'Architecture
This, the highest honor of the Academy, is given for recognition of an outstanding contribution to the field of architecture. French and foreign architects are eligible. A gold medal is awarded annually. Established in 1965.

4788
Prix Fondation Bernard Hamburger
To assist a young French architect to travel in the United States for three months. A grant of 30,000 French francs is awarded. Established in 1985.

4789
Prix Fondation Richard Lounsbery
To provide the opportunity for a young French architect to study in an American university. A grant of $16,000 is awarded. Established in 1984.

4790
Academie de Gastronomie Brillat-Savarin
c/o Gaston L. Panuel
7, rue d'Aumale
F-75009 Paris, France   Phone: 1 4281 30 12

4791
Prix Litteraires
(Literary Awards)
To recognize the best books of the year involved in the gastronomic field, or in regional or special cooking. Books have to be submitted to the lecturer committee at least six months in advance. A diploma of the Academy is awarded annually for the Prix Brillat-Savarin. Established in 1984 in honor of Brillat-Savarin, well-known gastronome and writer in France.

4792
Academie des Arts et Techniques du Cinema
19, av. du President Wilson
F-75116 Paris, France   Phone: 1 4723 72 33

4793
Cesar Awards
For recognition of outstanding contributions in the field of film. Awards are given in the following categories: (1) Best Film; (2) Best Actor; (3) Best Actress; (4) Best Supporting Actor; (5) Best Supporting Actress; (6) Most Promising Actress; (7) Most Promising Actor; (8) Best First Film; (9) Best Director; (10) Best Screenplay, Dialogue or Adaptation; (11) Best Original Screenplay and Dialogue; (12) Best Adaptation and Dialogue; (13) Best Original Screenplay or Adaptation; (14) Best Photography; (15) Best Scenery; (16) Best Foreign Film; (17) Best Musical; (18) Best Editing; (19) Best Sound; (20) Best Costume; (21) Best Film Publicity; (22) Best French Film outside of France; (23) Best Poster; (24) Best Short Film - Animation; (25) Best Short Documentary; and (26) Best Short Feature. Trophies are awarded annually. Established in 1975 by Georges Cravenne.

4794
Academie des Sciences, Arts et Belles-Lettres de Dijon
Bibliotheque Municipale de Dijon
5, rue de l'Ecole-de-Droit   Phone: 80 30 36 39
F-21000 Dijon, France   Fax: 80 49 99 68

4795
Prix de l'Academie des Sciences, Arts et Belles Lettres de Dijon
For recognition of outstanding works in the fields of science, art, or literature. Manuscripts of 50 typewritten pages or published books written in French on a subject chosen by the Commission du Prix are considered. Works of a religious or political character are excluded. A single work or the complete work of an author or artist may be considered. A monetary prize of 10,000 francs and a gold medal are awarded annually. Established in 1740 and revived in 1971.

4796
Academie Goncourt
Place Gaillon
75002 Paris, France   Phone: 1 42651516

4797
Concourt Fellowship
(Bourse Goncourt de la Nouvelle)
To provide recognition for the best written news accounts, reports short stories published during the year. A monetary prize of 10,000 French francs is awarded annually by the Goncourt Academy during the International Book Festival in Nice.

4798
**Goncourt Prize
(Prix Goncourt)**
This, one of the most prestigious literary prizes in France, is given to recognize an author for an outstanding prose work, preferably a novel, published during the preceding year. Younger writers may submit works. Honorary recognition and a monetary award of 50 French francs are awarded annually in the fall. Established in 1914 by a bequest of Edmond de Goncourt.

4799
Academie Mallarme
Hotel de Massa
38, rue du Faubourg St. Jacques
F-75014 Paris, France   Phone: 1 4707 25 99

4800
Prix de l'Academie Mallarme
To recognize an outstanding poet. A monetary prize of 20,000 francs is awarded annually. Established in 1937 and reactivated in 1975. Sponsored by Fondation Yves Rocher.

4801
Academie Nationale de Medecine
Bibliotheque de l'Academie Nationale de
  Medecine
16, rue Bonaparte
F-75006 Paris Cedex 06, France   Phone: 4 634 60 70

4802
Bourse Gonzague Mulliez
To encourage research into and prevention of breast cancer. A monetary grant of 5,000 French francs is awarded. Established in 1986. (Inactive)

4803
Bourse Veronique Dejouany
To provide assistance to researchers in the field of digestive cancer, especially colon cancer. Research in the epidemiology, prevention, or treatment is considered. A grant of 60,000 French francs is awarded. (Inactive)

4804
Prix a l'Etudiant Medaille d'Or de l'Internat
To recognize a student in medical school. Awards are given in alternate years to a student of internal medicine and a student of surgery. A medal is awarded annually. (Inactive)

4805
Prix a un Etudiant de l'Ecole Dentaire
To recognize a student in a dental school. A medal is awarded annually. (Inactive)

4806
Prix a un Etudiant en Chirurgie
To recognize a student in the field of surgery. A medal is awarded every four years. Established in 1986. (Inactive)

4807
Prix Aimee et Raymond Mande
To encourage research and treatment of Parkinson's disease or chronic leukemia. A monetary prize of 150,000 is awarded annually. Established in 1987.

4808
Prix Amelie Marcel
For recognition of a work on the treatment of leukemias. A monetary prize of 1,500 French francs is awarded annually. Established in 1975.

4809
Prix Andre Batel-Rouvier
For recognition of research in the fight against tuberculosis. A monetary prize of 2,000 French francs is awarded annually. Established in 1956. (Inactive)

4810
Prix Antoine et Claude Beclere
To recognize the author of a published work on cancer therapy in the field of radioimmunology and molecular and carcinogenic research. A monetary prize of 7,000 French francs is awarded biennially in even-numbered years. The award may not be shared. Established in 1982.

4811
Prix Auguste Secretan
To recognize a student of medicine, either internal or external, whose work gives relief to pain. A monetary prize of 1,500 French francs is awarded annually when merited. Established in 1975.

4812
Prix Bernard Ladougne
For recognition of a thesis on mental illness caused by loneliness, particularly among young people or the unemployed, and that causes illness or suicides. A monetary prize of 50,000 francs was awarded one time. Established in 1982. (Inactive)

4813
Prix Berthe Pean
To recognize a doctor or scholar for work that contributes to the discovery of a cure for cancer or tuberculosis. A monetary prize of 3,000 French francs is awarded biennially in even-numbered years. Established in 1933.

4814
Prix Cancer
For recognition of research in the field of cancer. A monetary prize of 12,000 French francs is awarded biennially in odd-numbered years.

4815
Prix Charles Achard
To encourage work or research judged worthy by the Academy. A monetary prize of 500 French francs is awarded biennially in even-numbered years. Established in 1946.

4816
Prix Chimie
For recognition of research in the field of chemistry. A monetary prize of 500 French francs is awarded annually. (Inactive)

4817
Prix CIBA-GEIGY
To recognize a French doctor, known for his original work within the scope of public health. This prize can also be awarded in recognition of work in the areas of public health, preventative medicine, the environment, administrative health management, or socio-economics. A monetary prize of 20,000 French francs is awarded annually. The award may not be shared. Established in 1981.

4818
Prix Cordier
For recognition of the best work on cancer of the bladder. A monetary prize of 16,000 French francs is awarded annually. Established in 1949. (Inactive)

4819
Prix de la Mutualite Interprofessionnelle
To encourage young French researchers who have contributed to progress in the field of surgery and to permit the continuation of research. A

monetary prize of 30,000 French francs is awarded annually. Established in 1953. (Inactive)

4820
Prix de la Societe des Eaux Minerales d'Evian-des-Bains
To encourage scientific research. A monetary prize of 5,000 French francs is awarded annually. Established in 1960.

4821
Prix de la Ville de Paris
To recognize and encourage work in the field of medicine that the Academy judges worthy. A monetary prize of 11,300 French francs is awarded annually. Established in 1948.

4822
Prix de l'Academie Nationale de Medecine
To encourage work or research judged worthy by the Academy. A monetary prize of 1,000 French francs is awarded annually.

4823
Prix de l'Union Nationale des Caisses Chirurgicales Mutualistes
To encourage young French researchers who have completed works that contribute to progress in the field of surgery. A monetary prize of 30,000 French francs is awarded annually. The award may be shared. Established in 1953. (Inactive)

4824
Prix Dermatologie Immunologie
To encourage and provide for work in immunology aiming at therapeutic and eventually dermatologic orientation. A monetary prize of 7,000 French francs is awarded annually. Established in 1987. (Inactive)

4825
Prix Dermatologie Syphiligraphie
For recognition of research in the field of dermatology and the study of syphilis. A monetary prize of 1,700 French francs is awarded annually. (Inactive)

4826
Prix des Fondations Oulmont, Zaval, Dreyfous
For recognition of students in the field of surgery. A medal is awarded annually. (Inactive)

4827
Prix Deschiens
For recognition of outstanding works on infectious illnesses or parasites. A monetary prize of 13,000 French francs is awarded biennially in odd-numbered years. The award may not be shared. Established in 1980.

4828
Prix Devouement
For recognition in the field of medicine. A medal is awarded annually. (Inactive)

4829
Prix Docteur Albert Belgrand
To recognize a young French surgeon dedicated to research and to permit him to continue scientific activity. A monetary prize of 8,000 French francs is awarded biennially in even-numbered years. The award may not be shared. Established in 1967.

4830
Prix Docteur Darolles
To provide aid for researchers of a center of scientific research of particular interest to the Academy. A monetary prize of 12,000 French francs is awarded annually. Established in 1970.

4831
Prix Drieu-Cholet
To encourage and assist researchers in the fields of cancer, vascular disease or some other of use to the Academy. A monetary prize of 80,000 French francis is awarded biennially in even-numbered years. Established in 1986.

4832
Prix du Centre de Recherches Cliniques et Biologiques sur la Nutritiotion de l'Homme
For recognition of an original study dedicated to the digestion or nutrition of humans or animals. A monetary prize of 2,000 French francs is awarded biennially in even-numbered years. Established in 1972.

4833
Prix du Docteur Robert Netter
To recognize or encourage a French or foreign researcher in the field of ophthalmology. A monetary prize of 20,000 French francs is awarded annually when merited. Established in 1983. (Inactive)

4834
Prix du Ministere de la Jeunesse et des Sports
For recognition the best work concerning biology applied to physical activities and sports. A monetary prize of 10,000 French francs is awarded annually. Established in 1954.

4835
Prix d'Urologie
To recognize a surgeon for work in the field of urology. A monetary prize of 13,000 francs is awarded biennially in odd-numbered years.

4836
Prix Electrotherapie
For recognition of a work concerning electrotherapy. A monetary prize of 300 French francs is awarded annually. (Inactive)

4837
Prix Emile Delannoy-Robbe
To recognize a young surgeon for work in clinical or experimental surgery. A monetary prize of 200,000 French francs is awarded annually. Established in 1991.

4838
Prix Etienne Chabrol
For recognition the best work on infant hepatitis during the preceding two years. A monetary prize of 1,000 French francs is awarded biennially in odd-numbered years. Established in 1971.

4839
Prix Fauconnier
To provide for research in the cure for cancer, tuberculosis, or other social calamity. A monetary prize of 2,400 French francs is awarded triennially. Established in 1936. (Inactive)

4840
Prix Gallet et Breton
For recognition of cancer research in the area of treatment technique or therapy. The award may not be shared. A monetary prize of 172,500 French francs is awarded annually. Established in 1985.

4841
Prix Gustave Roussy
For recognition of research on malignant tumors. A monetary prize of 5,000 French francs is awarded biennially in odd-numbered years. The award may be shared. Established in 1969. (Inactive)

4842
Prix Helene Rubillard
For recognition of students in the field of dentistry. (Inactive)

4843
Prix Henri Baruk
For recognition of the best research concerning difficulties in articulation of language. A monetary prize of 4,000 French francs is awarded biennially in even-numbered years. Established in 1981.

4844
Prix Henri Mondor
For recognition of a scientific work on surgical emergencies. A monetary prize of 7,000 French francs is awarded biennially in even-numbered years. The award may be shared. Established in 1970.

4845
Prix Henry et Mary Jane Mitjavile
To recognize a French scholar or researcher for a work in the fight against cancer. If cancer is arrested, then the prize will be given for another terrible disease. A monetary prize of 250,000 French francs is awarded annually. The award may not be shared. Established in 1983.

4846
Prix Jansen
For recognition of outstanding work in the field of medicine. The selection is made by the administrative council in consultation with experts on the subjects treated by the candidates. A monetary prize of 2,500 French francs is awarded annually. Established in 1938.

4847
Prix Jean Escalle
For recognition of a work or thesis in the field of cardiology. A monetary prize of 2,500 French francs is awarded biennially in even-numbered years. Established in 1989.

4848
Prix Jean-Etienne Marcel
To recognize a young surgeon for work in urology. A monetary prize of 2,500 French francs is awarded annually. Established in 1975. (Inactive)

4849
Prix Jean-Francois Coste
For recognition of a work on the history of medicine. A monetary prize of 3,000 French francs is awarded annually. Established in 1982 by the city of Versailles.

4850
Prix Jean-Francois Ginestie
To recognize a young doctor for a work in the field of radiology or medical imagery of the vascular system or joints. A monetary prize of 20,000 French francs is awarded biennially in even-numbered years. Established in 1982.

4851
Prix Jeanne et Maurice Chevassu
For recognition of an original surgical work that provides the basis for research in the pathologic anatomy. A monetary prize of 3,500 French francs is awarded biennially in odd-numbered years. Established in 1973.

4852
Prix Jocelyn Chedoudi
To recognize a researcher or team of researchers who has found a predetermined factor (causes, manifestation or consequences) in different forms of depression of adults or adolescents. A monetary prize of 35,000 French francs is awarded. The award may not be shared. Established in 1984. (Inactive)

4853
Prix Joseph-Antoine Maury
To recognize an individual who finds a way to relieve the suffering of the human body. A monetary prize of 15,000 French francs is awarded biennially in even-numbered years. The award may not be shared. Established in 1977.

4854
Prix Jules Perreau
For recognition of outstanding research in the treatment of hyperchlorhydry and of the duodenum ulcer. A monetary prize of 3,500 French francs is awarded biennially in odd-numbered years. Established in 1947. (Inactive)

4855
Prix Leon Baratz
For recognition of work or research in the struggle against dangerous diseases, including cancer, polio, tuberculosis, rheumatism, etc. A monetary prize of 8,000 French francs is awarded biennially in even-numbered years. The award may be shared. Established in 1965.

4856
Prix Leon Launoy
To recognize the author of a work on pharmacology or of exotic pathology. A monetary prize of 3,500 French francs is awarded biennially in odd-numbered years. Established in 1975.

4857
Prix Lian
To recognize the author of an outstanding work in the field of heart or blood vessel disease. A monetary prize of 2,500 French francs is awarded biennially in odd-numbered years. Established in 1971.

4858
Prix Lutte Contre L'Alcoolisme
To recognize research on the preventative and curative aspects of alcoholism or disorders induced by alcohol abuse. A monetary prize of 10,000 French francs is awarded annually. Established in 1991.

4859
Prix Lutte Contre le Tabagisme
For recognition of a work completed on the preventative and curative aspects of nicotine addiction.

4860
Prix Maladies Mentales
For recognition of research in the field of mental illness. A monetary prize of 2,000 French francs is awarded annually. (Inactive)

4861
Prix Maurice-Louis Girard
To recognize a researcher of medicine, pharmacy, veterinary science or some other science who has presented an outstanding project in biochemistry or clinical immunology. Work should have been completed in the two preceding years. A monetary prize of 16,000 French francs is awarded annually. Established in 1988.

4862
Prix Medecin General Inspecteur Raymond Debenedetti
For recognition of a work, published or unpublished, on some aspect of medicine in the armed services. Reserve or active, doctors, pharmacists, veterinarians, dentists, and administrative officers of the Health Services or the Veterinarian Corps are eligible. A monetary prize of 500 French francs is awarded biennially in odd-numbered years. Established in 1963. (Inactive)

4863
Prix Medecine
For recognition in the field of medicine. A monetary prize of 9,000 French francs is awarded annually.

4864
Prix Medecine Veterinaire
For recognition of research in veterinary medicine. A monetary prize of 1,000 French francs is awarded annually. (Inactive)

4865
Prix Michel Noury
To recognize a researcher (a doctor, veterinarian, biologist) or a team of researchers whose work has resulted in the discovery and improvement of the treatment of rabies. A monetary prize of 100,000 French francs is to be awarded one time only. The award may not be shared. Established in 1980.

4866
Prix Neurologie
For recognition in the field of neurology. A monetary prize of 1,000 French francs is awarded annually. (Inactive)

4867
Prix Obstetrique
For recognition of research in the field of obstetrics. A monetary prize of 600 French francs is awarded annually. (Inactive)

4868
Prix O.R.L.
For recognition of medical research. A medal is awarded annually. (Inactive)

4869
Prix Paul Mathieu
For recognition of research with the purpose of fighting malignant tumors. A monetary prize of 50,000 French francs is awarded biennially in odd-numbered years. The award may be shared. Established in 1972.

4870
Prix Pharmacie
For recognition of research in the field of pharmacy. A medal is awarded annually. (Inactive)

4871
Prix Pierre et Celine Lhermite
For recognition of an original study on digestion or nutrition of humans or animals. A monetary prize of 3,500 French francs is awarded biennially in odd-numbered years. Established in 1981.

4872
Prix Prince Albert Ier de Monaco
For recognition of a work that meets requirements established by the Academy. A monetary award of 15,000 French francs is awarded biennially in odd-numbered years. The award may not be shared. Established in 1923.

4873
Prix Prosper Veil
To assist a student in ophthalmology or medicine or a medical researcher in a field of interest and merit. A monetary prize of 10,000 French francs is awarded annually. Established in 1990.

4874
Prix Specia
To recognize a research team under the direction of a doctor or French doctor for a work in clinical chemotherapy. A monetary prize of 12,000 French francs is awarded annually.

4875
Prix Specialities Chirurgicales
For recognition of research in the field of surgery. A monetary prize of 1,700 French francs is awarded annually. (Inactive)

4876
Prix Tuberculose
For recognition of research in the field of tuberculosis. A monetary prize of 1,000 French francs is awarded annually. (Inactive)

4877
Prix Victor et Clara Soriano
For recognition of an unpublished work in the field of neurology. A monetary prize of 10,000 French francs is awarded annually. Established in 1988.

4878
Prix Yvonne Foulley
For recognition of research in the field of cancer. A monetary prize of 7,000 French francs is awarded biennially in odd-numbered years. Established in 1972. (Inactive)

4879
Subvention de l'Academie Nationale de Medecine
For recognition in the field of medicine. A monetary prize of 85,000 French francs is awarded annually. Established in 1974.

4880
Academie Nationale de Reims
7, rue des Ecoles
F-51100 Reims, France   Phone: 25 472075

4881
Grand Prix d'Histoire Nationale Maurice Payard
To recognize a book of national or provincial history of considerable length that treats a sensitive subject. The work must be previously unpublished in large part. An independent researcher is eligible. A monetary prize of 15,000 French francs is awarded biennially in December. Established in 1976 by Maurice Payard.

4882
Agence de Cooperation Culturelle et Technique
13, quai Andre-Citroen
F-75015 Paris, France   Phone: 1 4575 62 41

4883
Prix de la Meilleure Nouvelle Francophone
For recognition of the best novel by a French speaking author. A monetary prize of 18,000 French francs and a grant for one year in France are awarded. Sponsored by Alliance Francaise, and Le Monde.

4884
Prix Litteraire International Charles-Helou
For recognition of an outstanding literary work on an announced theme, usually in the field of the French language and its universality. Residents of the member countries of the Agency are eligible. A monetary prize of 100,000 French francs and publication of the work are awarded. Established in 1985. Three prizes are also awarded to young people 15 to 21 years of age.

4885
Ales Film Festival
(Festival Cinema d'Ales)
Mas Bringer - 30100 ALES   Phone: 66302426
F 30100 Ales en Cevennes, France   Fax: 66568724

4886
Ales Film Festival
To recognize and encourage young filmmakers of short feature films. Films must be in French and have a maximum length of 30 minutes. The

following awards are given annually: Grand Prize of the Jury, Public Award, and Special Jury Award. Established in 1985.

4887

Amateurs Photographes et Cineastes d'Auvergne
10, rue Riquet
F-63000 Clermont-Ferrand, France   Phone: 73 93 36 32

4888

Salon International diapositives d'Auvergne
For recognition of outstanding photographs. Photographs of any subject which are 2x5x5 may be submitted. Awards are given in two categories: (1) General; and (2) Stereo (3D). The following prizes are awarded: General - (1) Best of Show - Medaille d'or of the Photographic Society of America; and (2) Medaille d'or, Medaille d'argent, and Medaille de bronze - of the Federation Internationale de l'art Photographique; and Stereo - (1) Best of Show - Medaille d'or of the Photographic Society of America; and (2) Medaille de la Ville de Clermont-Ferrand. Awarded annually.

4889

Amiens International Film Festival
(Festival International du Film d'Amiens)
36, rue de Noyon   Phone: 2291 0144
F-80000 Amiens, France   Fax: 2292 5182

4890

Amiens International Film Festival
(Festival International du Film d'Amiens)
For recognition of the best quality film produced during the previous year. A Golden Unicorn trophy is awarded for the Best Feature Film, the Best Short Film, the Best Actor and Actress, and the Best Documentary Film. Awarded annually. Established in 1980.

4891

Amis de la Reliure d'Art
34, rue de Metz   Phone: 61 526826
F-31000 Toulouse, France   Fax: 61 536923

4892

Trophee International de la Reliure D'Art
To recognize an outstanding contribution in the field of bookbinding. Awarded at the annual exposition. Established in 1988 in honor of Antoine Grandmaison, member of the original Committee of Patrons of the Amis de la Reliure d'Art. Formerly: Prix Antoine Grandmaison.

4893

Amities Acadiennes
17, quai de Grenelle   Phone: 1 45750999
F-75015 Paris, France   Fax: 1 45753677

4894

Prix France-Acadie
To recognize outstanding work by French speaking Acadians. Awards are given in two categories: literature (including theater, poetry, and drama); and social sciences (including history and sociology). Authors writing in French who were born in the territory of maritime Canada or claiming Acadian descent are eligible. Two monetary prizes of 8,500 French francs each and a week in Paris are awarded annually in each category. Established in 1979.

4895

Anthropology Society of Paris
(Societe d'Anthropologie de Paris)
Musee d'Homme
Place du Trocadero   Phone: 1 4405 7265
F-75116 Paris, France   Fax: 1 4405 7261

4896

Bertillon Prize
To provide recognition for the best work concerning anthropology and demography. Anthropologists and demographers without regard to sex or nationality are eligible. Awarded triennially. Established in 1885 by the Brothers Bertillon conforming to their father, Adolphe Bertillon's will.

4897

Broca Prize
To provide recognition for the best thesis on a subject of human anatomy, comparative anatomy, or physiology linked to anthropology. Anthropologists worldwide are eligible. Awarded biennially. Established in 1881 by Mrs. Broca.

4898

Vallois Prize
To provide recognition for a work dealing with physical anthropology *sensu stricto*. French anthropologists up to 40 years of age are eligible. Established in 1976 in the bequest of H.V. Vallois.

4899

Aspects Artistiques, Litteraires et Photographiques de la region Hazebrouckoise
9, Ave. Pierre-Curie
F-59190 Hazebrouck, France   Phone: 2841 0744

4900

Prix ALPHA de la Nouvelle
To recognize a novelist for a work that has not been published. A monetary prize of 5,000 French francs, a medal, and publication in *Annales de l'Association* are awarded annually, usually in June. Established in 1983 by Bruno Dewaele. Sponsored by Ville d'Hazebrouck.

4901

Association Aeronautique et Astronautique de France
6, rue Galilee   Phone: 1 47230749
F-75782 Paris Cedex 16, France   Fax: 1 47230748

4902

Grand Prix
To recognize a person who has gained distinction through his or her works or services rendered to aeronautics or astronautics. Citizens of France or other countries are eligible. A medal and a diploma are awarded annually. Established in 1973.

4903

Prix d'Aeronautique
To recognize an individual who has gained distinction through his or her work in the field of aeronautics. French citizens are eligible. A medal and a diploma are awarded annually. Established in 1974.

4904

Prix d'Astronautique
To recognize an individual for outstanding work in the field of astronautics. A medal and a diploma are awarded annually. Established in 1974.

4905

Prix des Jeunes
To recognize an individual who has distinguished himself through scientific work, originality of writings, or an enterprising spirit. Individuals

under 30 years of age are eligible. A monetary prize of 5,000 francs and a diploma are awarded annually. Established in 1973.

4906
Association de Presse France - Japon
14, Rue Cimarosa
F-75116 Paris, France
Phone: 1 4727 3090
Fax: 1 4727 5832

4907
Concoulrs Reportage Seer le Japon
To provide young French journalists less than 35 years of age who have never visited Japan with the opportunity to visit Japan. Applications must be submitted by June 2. The prize consists of round-trip travel from Paris to Tokyo, a railway ticket with unlimited miles for 21 days, spending money, and a one week stay with a Japanese family in Osakas. Formerly: Prix Decouverte du Japon.

4908
Association de Soutien et de Diffusion d'Art
170, boulevard Haussmann
F-75008 Paris, France
Phone: 1 4289 18 28
Fax: 1 4225 39 72

4909
ASDA Prize
To recognize a modestly sized or particularly innovative exhibition catalogue judged to have made an outstanding contribution to art-historical studies. A monetary prize of $10,000 is awarded when merited. Established in 1990.

4910
Prix Minda de Gunzburg
(Minda de Gunzburg Prize)
To encourage and give special recognition to the research of art historians who are authors of exhibition catalogues on Western art from the Middle Ages to the twentieth century. Temporary exhibition catalogues published during the preceding year may be submitted by sending three copies by January 20. Authors of all nationalities can apply. The jury's decision is based on the scholarly qualities of rigor and insight. A monetary prize of $25,000 is awarded annually. Established in 1987 by Alain de Gunzburg and his sons, John and Charles, in honor of Minda de Gunzburg, their wife/mother who first created ASDA and did a lot for Art History.

4911
Association des Amis d'Alfred-Georges Regner
30, rue de Dr. Michel
F-14400 Bayeux, France
Phone: 1637 92 26 48

4912
Prix Regner de gravure
For recognition of achievement in the field of engraving. Engravers from any country are eligible. A monetary prize, a plaque, and exhibitions in Paris and France are awarded. Established in 1989 in memory of A.G. Regner, painter-engraver (1902-1987). Additional information is available from Groupe Corot 139, av. St. Ouen, F-75017 Paris, France.

4913
Association des Amis de Jacques Gautier et Andree Gautier
c/o Galerie Jacques Gautier
36, rue Jacob
F-75006 Paris, France
Phone: 1 4260 84 33

4914
Prix Jacque Gautier
To recognize young designers of contemporary jewelry. The deadline for entry is in June. Two prizes are awarded annually.

4915
Association des Anciens Eleves de Marcel Mercier
57 rue Chambiere
F-57000 Metz, France
Phone: 87 30 57 57

4916
European Piano Competition
(Concours Europeen de Piano)
For recognition of outstanding piano performances by artists who are less than 30 years old and originally from a member country of the Common Market. The following monetary prizes are awarded: (1) First prize - 10,000 ECUs; (2) Second prize - 7,000 ECUs; (3) Third prize - 6,000 ECUs; and (4) Fourth prize - 4,500 ECUs. The competition is held biennially. Established in 1987.

4917
Association des Ecrivains de Langue francaise
14, rue Broussais
F-75014 Paris, France
Phone: 1 43219599
Fax: 1 43201222

4918
Grand Prix de la Mer
For recognition of a novel, short story, a volume of or essays, poems, or drama on a theme related to the sea. Works written in French and published during the preceding two years are eligible. A monetary prize of 2,000 francs is awarded annually. Established in 1971.

4919
Grand Prix Litteraire de l'Afrique Noire
For recognition of an outstanding literary work written in French by a writer from a state of black Africa and published during the preceding year. An author may be recognized for a single work or his complete work. A monetary prize of 2,000 French francs is awarded annually. Established in 1960.

4920
Grand Prix Litteraire de l'Oceanie
For recognition of a work written in French concerning Oceania (the South Sea Islands). Poetic works, works of pure imagination (novels and short stories), historical essays, and reports, published during the preceeding two years, are considered. A monetary prize of 2,000 French francs is awarded biennially. Established in 1978.

4921
Grand Prix Litteraire de Madagascar
For recognition of a literary work or the total work of a writer from Madagascar or a French writer on the subject concerning Madagascar. Novels, poems, drama, essays, historical or geographical studies, and reports written in French and published during the preceding two years are eligible. A monetary prize of 2,000 French francs is awarded biennially. Established in 1951.

4922
Prix de l'Afrique Mediterraneenne/Maghreb
For recognition of a literary work or the total work written in French by an author from the Mediterranean Africa and published during the preceeding year. A monetary prize of 2,000 French francs is awarded annually. Established in 1972.

4923
Prix de Litterature des Alpes et du Jura
For recognition of literary works written in French by authors from the Swiss Confederation or from the Swiss or French Alps. Literary work such as novels, essays, short stories, poetry, drama, history, biography, and reports published during the preceding year are considered. A monetary prize of 2,000 French francs is awarded annually. Established in 1972.

4924
Prix Europeen de l'ADELF
For recognition of original writing by authors from European countries not covered by other Association prizes (Luxembourg, Belgium, Quebec, and Switzerland). Novels, short stories, biographies, histories, reports, drama, and poems written in French during the preceeding year are considered. A monetary prize of 2,000 French francs is awarded annually. Established in 1982.

4925
Prix France - Belgique
For recognition of a literary work by a French or Belgian writer. The award is given in alternate years to a French writer and to a Belgian writer. Works written in French and published in the preceding two years are eligible. A monetary prize of 2,000 French francs is awarded annually. Established in 1956.

4926
Prix France - Liban
For recognition of an outstanding literary work including history and reports. Works written in French on Lebanon or by Lebanese authors published during the preceeding year are eligible. A monetary prize of 2,000 French francs is awarded annually. Established in 1981.

4927
Prix Litteraire de l'Asie
For recognition of a literary work, history, or report written in French by an author originally from Asia or on a subject concerning Asia and published during the preceeding year A monetary prize of 2,000 French francs is awarded annually. Established in 1972.

4928
Prix Litteraire des Caraibes
For recognition of a literary work written in French by an author from Haiti, Antilles, or Guyana and published during the preceeding two years. A monetary prize of 2,000 French francs is awarded biennially. Established in 1964.

4929
Prix Litteraire des Mascareignes, des Seychelles et des Comores
For recognition of a writer of French expression originally from Mascareignes, Seychelles, or Comores. Literary works including novels, short stories, essays, histories, or poems published during the preceeding two years are considered. A monetary prize of 2,000 French francs is awarded biennially. Established in 1964.

4930
Prix Litteraire France - Quebec/Jean Hamelin
For recognition of an outstanding literary work written in French by a writer originally from Quebec. The work must have been published during the preceeding year. An author may be recognized for a single work or his complete work. A monetary prize of 5,000 French francs is awarded annually. Established in 1964.

4931
Association des Ecrivains du Rouergue
7, rue de Saunhac
F-12000 Rodez, France   Phone: 6542 55 13

4932
Prix Antonin Artaud
For recognition of a collection of French poems published in the preceding two years. Poets who write in the French language are eligible. A monetary prize of 10,000 francs is awarded annually at the Journees Poesis de Rodez. Established in 1951.

4933
Prix Claude Sernet
For recognition of poetry written in French by foreigners. Poems published in the preceding two years are eligible for consideration. A monetary prize of 3,000 francs is awarded annually. Established in 1969.

4934
Prix Ilarie Voronca
For recognition of a manuscript of poems, 42 pages maximum length. Poets who write in French are eligible. Publication of the manuscript is awarded annually. Established in 1952.

4935
Association des Grandes Orgues de Chartres
75, rue de Grenelle
F-75007 Paris, France   Phone: 1 4548 31 74

4936
Chartres International Organ Competition
(Concours International d'Orgue de Chartres)
To recognize the best organ performers under 35 years of age. The deadline for entry is April 30. A monetary prize of 30,000 French francs is awarded for First prize in the interpretation category and the improvisation category, and 10,000 French francs is awarded for Second prize in each of the categories. The Competition is held biennially. The finals of the Competition are held in the Chartres Cathedral. Established in 1971 by Pierre Firmin-Didot, president and founder.

4937
Association des Inventeurs et Fabricants Francais
79, rue Temple
F-75003 Paris, France   Phone: 1 4887 83 98

4938
Concours Lepine
For recognition of outstanding inventions that are displayed at the exhibition, Concours Lepine, at the Salon International de l'Invention de Paris. The following prizes are awarded: (1) Coupe du Marche Commun - a trophy; (2) Coupe du Prefet du Police - a medal; (3) Coupe Internationale - a trophy; (4) Prix du President de la Republique - a Sevres crystal vase; (5) Grand Prix AIFF and gold, silver and bronze medals of the Association; (6) Prix du Ministere de la Recherche et de la Technologie - a medal; (7) Prix de l'ANVAR - 5,000 francs; (8) Prix de la Chambre de Commerce et d'Industrie de Paris - a medal; (9) Assemblee Permanente des Chambres de Commerce et d'Industrie - 1,500 francs; (10) Prix du Ministere de l'Agriculture - a medal; (11) Prix du Ministere de l'Environnement - a medal; (12) Chambre syndicale de Metallerie de la Region Parisienne - 1,000 francs; (13) Prix de la Foire de Paris - 2,500 francs; (14) Prix de la MAAF - 5,000 francs and 3,000 francs; (15) Prix de la Ville de Paris - silver and bronze medals; (16) Prix de la Banque Populaire Industrielle et Commerciale de la Region Sud de Paris - 1,500 francs; and (17) Prix de M. El Baz - 1,000 francs. Awarded annually. Established in 1902.

4939
Association du Prix Albert Londres
c/o Hotel de Massa
38, rue du Faubourg Saint - Jacques
F-75014 Paris, France   Phone: 1 4354 18 66

4940
Prix Albert Londres
To recognize outstanding young, French speaking reporters under 40 years of age. Two monetary prizes of 10,000 French francs each are awarded annually for journalism and for an audiovisual film. Established in 1933 by Florise Martinet-Londres in memory of her father, the journalist who disappeared during the fire of the ship, *Georges Philippar*, in the Red Sea in 1932.

4941
Association for the Development of Research on Cancer (Association pour la Recherche sur le Cancer)
16, avenue Paul Vaillant Couturier
BP 3
F-94801 Villejuif Cedex, France
Phone: 1 4559 59 59
Fax: 1 4726 04 75

4942
Prix Griffuel
For recognition of outstanding achievement in the treatment of cancer. Scientists or physicians of any nationality are eligible. A monetary prize of 300,000 French francs and a medal are awarded annually in the spring. Established in 1970 in memory of Leopold Griffuel.

4943
Association for the Promotion of Humor in International Affairs
5, rue de la Manutention
F-75116 Paris, France
Phone: 1 4723 51 68

4944
Booby Prize
To recognize public figures who try to be serious and fail. A prize is chosen to fit the remarks of the winner. Established in 1973 by Alfred E. Davidson, John E. Fobes, and Richard H. Moore. Information is available in the U.S.A. from P.O. Box 18418, Asheville, NC, 28804, U.S.A.

4945
Noble Prize
To recognize a humorist author of world stature and to respond to the world's great and growing need for humor in the face of violence, wars, assassinations, and the threat of global system collapse. The founders of the Association make the selection. An appropriate recognition is awarded annually. Established in 1973 by Alfred E. Davidson, John E. Fobes, and Richard H. Moore. Information is available in the U.S.A. from P.O. Box 18418, Asheville, NC 28804, U.S.A.

4946
Association Francaise des Observateurs d'Etoiles Variables
Observatoire de Strasbourg
11, rue de l'Universite
F-67000 Strasbourg, France

4947
Medaille Abbott
To encourage cooperative observations of variable stars. Members of the Association were eligible. A silver medal was awarded biennially. Established in 1926 by Mr. W.N. Abbott. Sponsored by the Conseil de l'Universite de Lyon. (Last awarded in 1935)

4948
Association Francaise du Froid
12, rue La Boetie
F-75008 Paris, France
Phone: 1 4742 30 60

4949
Prix de la Fondation Jean-Bernard Verlot
For recognition of works in the refrigeration and air-conditioning fields. A monetary prize is awarded annually. Established in 1982 in memory of Jean-Bernard Verlot who died in 1980.

4950
Association Francaise pour l'Etude du Sol
4, rue Redon
F-78370 Plaisir, France
Phone: 3054 4510

4951
Membre d'honneur
For recognition of service to French educational methods. French or foreign individuals may be nominated. Awarded annually.

4952
Prix du Troisieme Cycle
To encourage the best work of students. The author is awarded publication of the article in *Science du Sol*. Awarded annually.

4953
Association Guy Levis Mano
6, rue Huyghens
F-75014 Paris, France
Phone: 1 4322 45 49

4954
Prix GLM
To recognize and to encourage young artists or artisans whose professional and creative talents serve poetry by writing, editing, typography or any other means. Awards are presented in the following categories: (1) Poetry; (2) Typography; and (3) Illustration. A monetary prize of 10,000 French francs is awarded in each category annually. Established in 1982. Formerly: Bourses Guy Levis Mano.

4955
Association Internationale des Critiques Litteraires
Hotel de Massa
38, rue de Faubourg St. Jacques
F-75014 Paris, France
Phone: 1 40513300
Fax: 1 43370750

4956
Grand Prix de la Critique Litteraire
For recognition of the best work of literary criticism. Authors who have published an outstanding book of criticism since the date of the previous prize are eligible. A monetary prize of 10,000 francs is awarded annually. Established in 1949 by Yves Gandon.

4957
Association Notre-Dame et la Mer
36, Cours d'Estienne d'Orves
F-13001 Marseille, France
Phone: 9154 39 32

4958
Grand Prix International d'Arts et Lettres Notre-Dame et la Mer
For recognition of contemporary creative work in the fields of art and literature inspired by the sea and water, especially in respect to Our Lady and the Sea as an appeal for friendship among people and civilizations. Awards are given in the following categories: (1) poetry; (2) prose; (3) sculpture; (4) dance; (5) painting; (6) photography; and (7) theater. Amateurs, semi-professionals, and students may submit works to the festival. Monetary prizes, trophies, medals, travel, and different works are awarded at two festivals in May and July or August. Established in 1986 by Elise Bertrand, artist, and Magali Berck (pen name of Elise Roman), poet.

4959
Association of National Olympic Committees
21, rue d'Artois
F-75008 Paris, France
Phone: 1 42562171
Fax: 1 42561857

4960
A.C.N.O. Merit Award
No further information was available for this edition.

4961

**Association of the Friends of Georges de Beauregard
(Association les Amis de Georges de Beauregard)**
17 bis, rue Erlanger
F-75016 Paris, France   Phone: 1 4520 9359

4962

**Georges de Beauregard Prize
(Prix Georges de Beauregard)**
For recognition of the best French direction of a French film in all areas of cinema creation without regard to the age or fame of the director. The following prizes are awarded: Best French Director of the Year; Revelation Prize - a special discovery prize to recognize the best direction of a full length film with quality, originality, and impact; Prix Court-Metrage - to recognize the best direction of a short fiction film that is no longer than 15 minutes; Best European Producer of the Year; Best French Producer of the Year; Young Producer Prize - to recognize someone new in the film industry and in need of support; and Miss Beauregard Prize - to recognize a young French actress with talent and beauty. Monetary prizes and trophies are awarded annually in October. Established in January, 1985, by Chantal de Beauregard, daughter of Georges de Beauregard, film producer who promoted "the New Wave."

4963

Association pour le Prix Scientifique Philip Morris
5 rue Greffulhe   Phone: 1 47425300
75008 Paris, France   Fax: 1 47422411

4964

Prix Scientifique Philip Morris
To recognize French researchers or establishments in France that have completed a project in applied research. Awards are given in three fields, changing each year (i.e. in 1994, laser technology, ethnology, and biogeochemistry), and one special award is presented for food-related research. Monetary prizes totaling 700,000 French francs are awarded.

4965

Association pour l'Etude et la Recherche en Radiologie
Service de Radiologie
Hopital Pellegrin
F-33076 Bordeaux, France   Phone: 5696 8383

4966

Prix de l'APERR
For recognition of research programs in the field of medical imagery that have not been published. The deadline for submissions is July 15. The following monetary prizes are awarded: 80,000 French francs for first prize and four prizes of 20,000 French francs. Awarded annually.

4967

Association pour l'Organisation de Festivals a Biarritz
Comite de Tourisme et des Fetes -
  Javalquinto
F-64200 Biarritz, France   Phone: 5924 20 24

4968

Festival de Biarritz du Film Iberique et Latino-Americain
For recognition of outstanding documentary films and fiction films produced for television. The following awards are given: (1) Makhila d'Or - Grand Prize; (2) Makhila d'Argent - Special jury prize for fiction and film; (3) two Makhilas d'Honneur - one for interpretation, and one for the Art et Essai prize; and (4) Makhila d'Honneur - awarded by a jury of the public for films of fiction. Trophies in the form of a Makhila, a traditional Basque baton or stick for walking, are awarded annually. Established in 1979. Sponsored by Air France and Air Inter, Philip Morris Club Espace Cinema, Fondation Cointreau and SNC Esplanade.

4969

Association Professionnelle et Artistique du Theatre
19, avenue du President Wilson
F-75116 Paris, France   Phone: 4723 72 33

4970

Les Molieres
For recognition of outstanding contributions to the theatre in France. Awards are given in the following categories: (1) Best Comedian, Male; (2) Best Comedian, Female; (3) Best Supporting Comedian, Male; (4) Best Supporting Comedian, Female; (5) Best Musical; (6) Best Comedy; (7) Best Theatrical Discovery; (8) Best One Man Show; (9) Best Off Center Show; (10) Best Writer; (11) Best Adaptation of a Foreign Work; (12) Best Director; (13) Best Stage Designer; (14) Best Costume Designer; (15) Best Show of the Year (Subsidized Theater); and (16) Best Show of the Year (Private Theater).

4971

Association Zino Francescatti
31, cours Mirabeau   Phone: 4238 36 38
F-13100 Aix en Provence, France   Phone: 4238 42 22

4972

International Violin Competition Zino Francescatti
To recognize outstanding violinists. Prizes are given for the best interpreter of French music, and for playing Bach. Monetary awards and medals are presented biennially. Established in 1985 by Mrs. Marie-Paule Soulier.

4973

L'Atelier Imaginaire
BP 2
F-65290 Juillan, France

4974

Concours Max-Pol Fouchet
To recognize a French poet who is unknown or unrecognized. Publication of the first manuscript is awarded. Established in 1981.

4975

Concours Promethee
To recognize a French novelist who has never been published. Publication of the novel is awarded. Established in 1977.

4976

Atelier Musique de Ville d'Avray
10, rue de Marnes   Phone: 47 50 44 28
F-92410 Ville d'Avray, France   Fax: 47 50 53 90

4977

**Concours International de Composition Musicale, Avray
(International Composition Prize)**
For recognition of a musical composition. (In 1992, the composition was for harp, flute, clarinet, and string quartet. The score also included a double bass part, but the composition should be playable without it.) Composers of all ages and nationalities are eligible to submit unpublished and unperformed works by November 30. The Grand Prix de Composition de Ville d'Avray of 10,000 French francs and a public performance is awarded. Established in 1985.

4978

Automobile Club de l'Ouest
PO Box 19X   Phone: 1 43402424
F-72040 Le Mans Cedex, France   Fax: 1 43726983

4979
Le Mans 24-hour Grand Prix d'Endurance
To recognize the winning team in a 24 hour endurance race on the famous Sarthe track located 3 miles south of Le Mans, France. The track, which is part raceway and part roadway, is 13.535 km (8 miles) long. In 1993, the winning Peugeot completed 5200 km at an average speed exceeding 137 mph. The race is held annually in June. Established in 1923.

4980
Auvergne Lyric Center
(Centre Lyrique d'Auvergne)
19, rue Bardoux
F-63000 Clermont-Ferrand, France   Phone: 7392 30 91

4981
International Oratorio and Lied Competition
(Concours International d'Oratorio et de Lied)
To encourage professional development, and for recognition of outstanding performance of oratorio and lied. The competition is open to all singers, professional or nonprofessional, without age limit. Monetary prizes and trophies are awarded annually. Established in 1985. Sponsored by the City of Clermont-Ferrand and France Telecom.

4982
Avoriaz International Festival of Fantasy and Science-Fiction Films
(Festival International du Film Fantastique d'Avoriaz)
c/o Promo 2000 Secretariat and Press Service
33, avenue MacMahon
F-75017 Paris, France   Phone: 1 4267 71 40

4983
Avoriaz Film Awards
To provide recognition for the best film fantasy and science fiction films. The following prizes are awarded: (1) Grand Prize; (2) Special Jury Prize; (3) Critics Prize; (4) Prix TF1 for short films; and (5) varying special prizes. Paintings or prints by famous artists are awarded annually in January. Established in 1973.

4984
Bibliotheque des Arts
3, place de l'Odeon   Phone: 1 4633 18 18
F-85006 Paris, France   Phone: 1 4046 95 56

4985
Prix Elie Faure
For recognition of works on painting presenting an exceptionally interesting methodology. The following prizes are awarded: (1) Prix des Ecrits de Peintres; (2) Prix de la Monographie; (3) Prix de la Reproduction; and (4) Prix du Catalogue Picturologique. Monetary prizes totaling 80,000 French francs are awarded. Established in 1980.

4986
Bibliotheque Municipale Valery Larbaud
106/110, rue du Marechal Lyautey
BP 67
F-03203 Vichy Cedex, France   Phone: 7032 11 22

4987
Prix Valery Larbaud
To provide recognition for a work of fiction or nonfiction or for the totality of a writer's work. A monetary prize of 20,000 French francs is awarded annually.

4988
Bibliotheque Nationale
58, rue Richelieu   Phone: 1 4703 81 26
F-75084 Paris Cedex 02, France   Fax: 1 4296 84 47

4989
Grand Prix de la Bibliotheque Nationale
To recognize an individual in the fields of literature and the human sciences for his complete work. Living authors were considered for works written in French. A monetary prize of 100,000 French francs was awarded. Established in 1989. (Awarded one time only in 1991)

4990
Bibliotheque Saint-John Perse Jeunesse
2, rue E. Poisson
F-93300 Aubervilliers, France   Phone: 834 11 72

4991
Prix de Traduction de Litterature Enfantine
To encourage the development of translations into French from the following nine languages: Arabic, Bambara (Africa), Berbere, Creole, Spanish, Italian, Yugoslavian, and Turkish. Adults and young people who are bilingual may submit translations of children's literature of 2,500 to 3,000 words. Nine monetary awards (one per language) of 1,000 French francs are awarded. In addition, a monetary prize of 500 French francs is awarded for the best translation for the theme of "the child and the city." All participants receive a lithograph by a young painter from the town of Aubervilliers. Awarded biennially. Established in 1983. Sponsored by the town of Aubervilliers, and two local children's associations, the Agence pour le developpement des Relations Interculturelles, and Direction du Livre.

4992
Botanical Society of France
(Societe Botanique de France)
16 rue Buffon
F-75005 Paris, France   Phone: 1 4683 55 20

4993
Prix de Coincy
For recognition of achievement or to encourage young botanists. Botanical works by members of the Society are considered. A medal is awarded annually. Established about 1920.

4994
Prix du Conseil de la Societe
For recognition of outstanding work in botany in France. Botanical works by members of the Society are considered. A medal is awarded annually. Established in 1957.

4995
Prix Gandoger
For recognition of achievement or to encourage young botanists. Botanical works by members of the Society are considered. A medal is awarded annually. Established in 1920.

4996
Boucheron Joaillier
26, place Vendome
F-75001 Paris Cedex 01, France   Phone: 1 42615816

4997
Grand Prix Litteraire de la Femme
To recognize a novel, an essay, or history by a woman in the French language. The winner receives original jewelry valued at about 70,000 French francs, designed by Alain Boucheron. Awarded annually. Established in 1989. (Discontinued)

4998
Bourges Experimental Music Group
(Groupe de Musique Experimentale de Bourges)
BP 39
Place Andre Malraux
F-18001 Bourges Cedex, France
Phone: 48 204187
Fax: 48 204551

4999
International Electroacoustic Music Competition Bourges
(Concours International de Musique Electroacoustique Bourges)
To recognize composers of electroacoustic music and to promote electroacoustic music. The Competition is held in three sections: the Residences - open to all composers 25 years of age or younger, and all students in composition. The entries are anonymous. Six visits of approximately three weeks to study and work in an electroacoustic center are awarded. The object of these prizes is to further contact and professional training among young composers; the Prizes - open to all composers 25 years of age and older. The entries are anonymous. The object of these prizes is to promote the creativity of established composers; and the Magisterium - open to any composers having at least 20 years of professional experience in electroacoustic music. The composers may enter individually or may have their entries made by a professional organization. The purpose of this section is to define works of reference in electroacoustic music with evident intellectual and musical qualities. For the Prizes and the Magisteres, monetary prizes and recordings on CD are awarded. Also, diffusion of the winning works on 33 radios, festivals of new music, and invitation of the Laureates by 18 centers of electroacoustic music are awarded annually. Established in 1973.

5000
Puy of Electroacoustic Music Competition
To recognize composers of electroacoustic music. Awards are presented in four categories: Electroacoustic Music and Humor, Occasional Electroacoustic Music, Electroacoustic Music for Young People, and Electroacoustic Music and Dance. Monetary prizes, recordings on CD, and the diffusion of winning works on radio are awarded.

5001
Cafe des Deux Magots
6 Place Saint Germain des Pres
F-75006 Paris, France
Phone: 1 4548 55 25
Phone: 1 4326 73 52
Fax: 1 4633 16 16

5002
Deux Magots Prize
(Prix des Deux-Magots)
For recognition of an avant-garde book by a young writer. The selection is made by a jury of 10 judges, as was the first prize in 1933. A monetary prize of 10,000 French francs is awarded annually in January at the Cafe des Deux Magots. Established in 1933 by Henri Philippon. Writers, painters, and sculptors who frequented the cafe each contributed 100 francs for the prize. Additional information is available from 5, rue de Conde, F-75006 Paris, France.

5003
Cannes International Film Festival
(Festival International du Film, Cannes)
Documentation - Regie des Films
71, rue du Faubourg Saint-Honore
F-75008 Paris, France
Phone: 1 42669220
Fax: 1 42666885

5004
Cannes International Film Festival
(Festival International du Film, Cannes)
To recognize feature films and shorts. The Festival aims to focus attention on works of quality in order to contribute to the progress of the motion picture arts and to encourage the development of the film industry throughout the world. Films must have been produced during the year prior to entry in the Festival. Short films must not exeed 15 minutes in length. The deadline for applications is March 1. A print or a cassette of the films proposed to the selection committee must reach the Festival before March 15, accompanied by a synopsis in French and the technical list relative to the film. The following awards are presented for feature-length films: Palme d'Or - for the best feature; Grand Prix du Jury - for the film that shows the most originality; Best Performance by an Actress; Best Performance by an Actor; Best Director; and Jury Prize - which is determined each year. The Jury may award two prizes, one for best original screenplay, and a second for best artistic contribution. The following awards are presented for short subjects: The Palme d'Or - for the best picture and awards to the best short films (possibly two), the nature of which is determined by the jury. Each film chosen by the Board of Directors for presentation at the Festival receives a Certificate of Participation. In addition, the Camera d'Or for the best first film and Grand Prix Technique for the best technical quality are awarded by two different juries. The Festival is held annually in May. Established in 1946.

5005
Cefilm
15, bis rue de Marignan
F-75008 Paris, France
Phone: 1 4359 69 40

5006
European Grand Prize of Corporate Image
(Festival Europeen de l'Image de l'Entreprise)
For recognition of the best European presentation of corporate image. Corporate films and videos during the preceding year are eligible. First prize and Dauphin Trophies are awarded in both the General Public category and the Specific Audience category. Awarded annually. In addition, a Special Prize of the Jury for the International Aspect is awarded. Established in 1990.

5007
Festival National de l'Audiovisuel d'Entreprise
For recognition of outstanding audiovisual productions of business firms. Awards are given in various categories for films, videos, and interactive informative programs. A Grand Prix du Festival is awarded as well as special awards. Dauphin trophies are awarded annually. Established in 1957.

5008
Center for Science and Industry
(Cite des Sciences et de l'Industrie (La Villette))
30, avenue Corentin Cariou
F-75019 Paris, France
Phone: 1 4005 70 00

5009
Oscar la Villette du Jeu et Jouet a Caractere Scientifique et Technique
To encourage creativity in developing scientific toys and to promote the toy industry. French designers and manufacturers are eligible to enter the competition. Three trophies are awarded annually in November. Established in 1983.

5010
Centre d'Etudes et des Recherches sur l'Orient Chretien
BP 761
F-75123 Paris Cedex 03, France
Phone: 1 4272 69 22

5011
Prix Chretiente d'Orient
To encourage publication on the history, culture, and dialogue between communities of Christians in the Middle East. A monetary prize of 5,000 French francs is awarded annually in June. Established in 1984.

5012
Centre for Political and Society Studies
(Centre d'etudes politique et Social)
80, rue Grenelle
F-75007 Paris, France

5013
Louis Michel Prize
To recognize an individual for contributions to European unity and a spirit of dialogue and tolerance.

5014
Centre International Humanae Vitae
9, avenue Niel
F-75017 Paris, France   Phone: 1 4572 28 62

5015
Prix de Centre International Humanae Vitae
For recognition of efforts to protect and improve human life and to defend the environment. Society members are eligible for nomination. A medal, plaque and trophy are awarded annually at conventions. Established in 1968. Additional information is available from the Academie Sciences Morales et Politiques.

5016
Centre National de la Recherche Scientifique
Mission de la Communication et de
 l'information Scientifique
et Technique
3, Rue Michel-Ange   Phone: 1 4496 40 00
F-75794 Paris Cedex 16, France   Fax: 1 4496 50 00

5017
Le Cristal du CNRS
To honor members of the CNRS support staff (engineers, technicians, and administrators) who have made a significant contribution to the advancement of science. Awarded annually. Established in 1992.

5018
Medaille d'Argent du CNRS
To recognize researchers in mid-career whose works are nationally and internationally renowned for their orignality, quality, and importance. A silver medal is awarded annually to approximately 15 scientists. Established in 1954.

5019
Medaille de Bronze du CNRS
To encourage young researchers to continue their work, and to recognize them for their first work which shows promise and which has made them specialists in their fields. Usually this first work is a thesis. A bronze medal is awarded annually. Established in 1954.

5020
Medaille d'Or du CNRS
To recognize an internationally renowned scientist who has made an outstanding contribution to the advancement and worldwide impact of French research. Research fields cover all disciplines. A gold medal is awarded annually. Established in 1954.

5021
Cercle Interallie
33 rue du Fg. St. Honore
F-75008 Paris, France   Phone: 1 4265 96 00

5022
Prix Interallie
To provide recognition for a superior novel preferably written by a journalist. Honorary recognition is awarded annually at the Restaurant Lasserre by a jury of ten writers. Established in 1930.

5023
Chaine des Rotisseurs
7, rue d'Aumale   Phone: 1 4281 30 12
F-75009 Paris, France   Fax: 1 4016 81 85

Formerly: (1948) Maitrise des Rotisseurs.

5024
Concours du Meilleure Jeune Commis Rotisseur
To encourage young chefs or young professional cooks to preserve cooking as a traditional art. Chefs are brought together to learn to execute recipes that will make their jobs easier. Young chefs under 25 years of age must be presented by employers or by members of the Chaine to be considered. Gold, silver, or bronze medals and diplomas are awarded annually. The gold medal is awarded at the International Challenge. Established in 1977. Additional information is available from Gaston L. Panuel.

5025
Chaine des Rotisseurs
Ordre Mondial des Gourmets Degustateurs
7, rue d'Aumale   Phone: 1 4281 30 12
F-75009 Paris, France   Fax: 1 4016 81 85

5026
Prix Litteraires
(Literary Awards)
To recognize serious and interesting books on the subject of wines, liquors, vineyards, alcohol, and brandies. Books must be submitted to the lecturer committee six months in advance. A diploma is awarded annually. Established in 1965. Additional information is available from Gaston L. Panuel.

5027
Chamrousse International Festival of Comedy Film
(Festival International du film d'Humour de Chamrousse)
MC4
2, rue de Belgrade   Phone: 7656 24 14
F-38000 Grenoble, France   Fax: 7656 99 82

5028
Chamrousse International Festival of Comedy Films
(Festival International du Film d'Humour de Chamrousse)
For recognition of outstanding comedy films. The following prizes are awarded: (1) Grand Prize of the Festival; (2) Critics' Prize; (3) Prize of the Public; (4) Special Jury Prize; and (5) Prize for a Short Film. Awarded annually in March. Established in 1977.

5029
Chretiens-Medias
108, rue Saint-Maur
F-75011 Paris, France   Phone: 1 4357 93 52

5030
Grand Prix des Treize
To recognize a work of literary and artistic quality in the field of children's literature that has a Christian understanding of man and the world. A jury composed of thirteen individuals from various fields makes the selection. Travel is awarded. Established in 1966 by the Association des Parents

d'Eleves de l'Enseignement Libre. Co-sponsored by UNAPEL and Chretiens Medias.

5031

Cinema du Reel
c/o Bibliotheque Publique d'Information
Centre G. Pompidou
19, rue Beaubourg
F-75197 Paris Cedex 04, France
Phone: 1 44784430
Fax: 1 44781224

5032

International Film Festival of Visual Anthropology and Social Documentation
(Festival International du Film Ethnographique et Sociologique Cinema du Reel)
For recognition of the best ethnological or sociological documentary. Films produced during the preceding year are eligible. The following prizes are awarded: Prix Cinema du Reel - 50,000 French francs; Prix du Court Metrage for the best short film - 15,000 French francs; Prix des Bibliotheques - 30,000 French francs; Prix du Patrimoine - 15,000 French francs; Prix Louis Marcorelles by the Ministere des Affaires Etrangeres; Prix Joris Ivens - 15,000 French francs; and Prix de la Scam - 30,000 French francs. Established in 1979. Sponsored by Bibliotheque Publique d'Information.

5033

City of Paris International Competitions
(Concours Internationaux de la Ville de Paris)
5, rue Bellart
F-75015 Paris, France
Phone: 1 47833358
Fax: 1 43066879

5034

Grand Prix de la Ville de Paris
(City of Paris Grand Prize)
To recognize and encourage professional development and outstanding musical performances. The Grand Prix is awarded at the following competitions: Concours International de Flute Jean-Pierre Rampal - for outstanding flute performances; Concours International de Lutherie et d'Archeterie de la Ville de Paris - for outstanding lute performances; Concours International de Piano Jazz Martial Solal - for outstanding jazz performances; and Concours International de Trompette Maurice Andre - for outstanding trumpet performances. Monetary prizes and medals are awarded every five years. Established in 1984.

5035

Club Europeen de la Sante
9, boulevard des Capucines
F-75002 Paris, France
Phone: 1 4265 51 23

5036

Prix Sante et Entreprise
For recognition of efforts to inform business firms of health and hygiene problems and of drug, alcohol, and tobacco problems by using films, slides, or brochures; to encourage early detection of problems; or to develop an apparatus or device for early detection of health problems. Five prizes totaling 200,000 French francs are awarded.

5037

Club Partir
21, rue Patou
F-59800 Lille, France
Phone: 2030 05 00

5038

Lille Sport Film Festival
(Festival du Film Sportif Lille)
To encourage professional sport films development and to recognize outstanding films that feature sports. Film producers may submit films by October 25. A trophy is awarded for the Grand Prix of the Festival annually at the closing ceremony. In addition, a Prize of the Press, Prize of the Public, and other special prizes are awarded. Established in 1982 by Paul Zouari.

5039

COGEDIM
21, rue d'Astorg
F-75008 Paris, France

5040

Prix COGEDIM
To recognize young architects who have not had a contract for a major real estate development during the preceding year. The deadline for entry is October 7. The first prize is the development of apartments in Paris.

5041

Colmar International Competition for Chamber Music Ensembles
(Concours International d'Ensembles de Musique de Chambre de Colmar)
Service des Activities Culturelles
Hotel de Ville
F-68000 Colmar, France
Phone: 8923 99 68

5042

Concours International d'Ensembles de Musique de Chambre de Colmar
(Colmar International Competition for Chamber-Music Ensemble)
For recognition of outstanding music ensembles. Awards are given in alternate years for: (1) piano trios; (2) quartets of strings; and (3) quintets of wind instruments (flute, oboe, clarinet, bassoon, and horn). The average age of the competitors may be no older than 35 years. Only one of the members from the ensemble may be 40 years old. The following prizes are awarded annually: (1) First Prize - Prix of Marie-Joseph Erb of 30,000 French francs and 20,000 French francs by the Johann Wolfgang von Goethe-Stiftung; (2) Second Prize - 15,000 francs; and (3) Third Prize - 10,000 francs. Prix Frederic Liebstoeckl of 1,000 Swiss francs, Prix Joseph Rey of 4,000 French francs, and Prix Charles Zwickert of 3,000 French francs for the best interpretation of Brahms are also awarded. Established in 1967. The Competition is organized by the Association Culture et Loisirs of the City of Colmar.

5043

Comite d'Action de la Resistance
45, rue Lacepede
F-75005 Paris, France
Phone: 1 4707 02 95

5044

Prix de la Resistance
(Literary Prize of the Resistance)
To provide recognition for a work contributing to the history, and honoring the spirit of the Resistance. A monetary prize of 10,000 French francs is awarded annually.

5045

Comite d'action pour le solaire
45, rue de Richelieu
F-75001 Paris, France
Phone: 1 42962477
Fax: 1 42962643

5046

Maisons solaires, maisons d'aujourd'hui
For recognition of individuals who have constructed or occupied housing heated successfully by solar energy for at least one heating season. Awards are given for individual houses and apartment housing. Co-sponsored by the Agence de l'environnement et pour la maitrise de l'energie.

5047
Comite du Rayonnement Francais
11, rue Nicolo
F-75116 Paris, France
Phone: 1 45274617
Fax: 1 42248058

5048
Prix Chateaubriand
To recognize an author for a complete work in the year of publication of one of his or her books. The award takes into account the influence of the French culture achieved by the book. A monetary prize of 50,000 French francs is awarded annually. Established in 1975.

5049
Prix de l'Illustration des Arts
To recognize an artist, a group, or a company for contributions to the international reputation of French arts. Any discipline of the arts is eligible. An award of 50,000 French francs is granted annually. Established in 1981. (Inactive)

5050
Prix des Sciences Biologiques et Medicales
To recognize one or several researchers or practitioners whose work or results have acquired international recognition. An award of 50,000 French francs is granted annually. Established in 1981.

5051
Prix des Sciences Economiques et Sociales
To recognize a team of collaborators that has played a major part in extending a national undertaking to an international project. An award of 50,000 French francs is granted annually. Established in 1981.

5052
Prix des Sciences Physiques et Mathematiques
To recognize one or several researchers whose work or its results have acquired international significance. An award of 50,000 French francs is granted annually. Established in 1981.

5053
Prix Exceptionnel du Centenaire Leon Dubois du Rayonnement Francais
To recognize a company or an individual who has contributed to the reputation of France in the field of engineering or public works. A monetary award of 50,000 French francs was awarded by Madame Leon Dubois. Established in 1990. (Discontinued)

5054
Prix Total du Rayonnement Francais dans le Tiers Monde
To recognize one or several individuals whose action, research, and results contributed to affirming the role of France in the development of countries of the Third World. A monetary prize of 50,000 French francs was awarded annually. Sponsored by Total, Compagnie Francaise des Petroles. (Discontinued)

5055
Comite Francais de l'Association Mondiale Veterinaire
Ecole National Veterinaire d'Alfont
7, avenue du General de Gaulle
F-94704 Maisons Alfort, France
Phone: 43759211

5056
Medaille d'Honneur du Comite Francais de l'AMV
For recognition of contributions to the veterinary profession. Works that contribute to scientific research or to national or international activity in the field of breeding or public health are eligible. Non-French individuals may be nominated by members of the Administrative Council. A medal and a diploma are awarded biennially. Established in 1974.

5057
Comite Francais d'Histoire de l'Art
Musee du Louvre
34-36, quai du Louvre
F-75041 Paris Cedex 01, France
Phone: 1 40205080
Fax: 1 40205347

5058
Prix Paul Cailleux
To help the publication of a doctoral dissertation in the field of French 18th century art. The manuscript must be submitted to a jury of members of the Comite Francais and representatives from Galerie Cailleux. A monetary award of 20,000 French francs for publication of the dissertation is awarded annually. Established in 1965 by Jean and Denise Cailleux in memory of Paul Cailleux (1884-1964), their father. Sponsored by Galerie Cailleux, Paris. Additional information is available from Marianne Roland Michel, Galerie Cailleux, Paris. Formerly: Prix de la Fondation Paul Cailleux.

5059
Committee of European Foundry Associations
(Comite des Associations Europeennes de Fonderie)
2, rue de Bassano
F-75783 Paris Cedex 16, France
Phone: 1 4723 55 50
Fax: 1 4720 44 15

5060
Best Apprentice Competition
For recognition of an outstanding apprentice.

5061
Committee on Space Research
(Comite Mondial pour la Recherche Spatiale)
51, boulevard de Montmorency
F-75016 Paris, France
Phone: 1 4525 06 79
Fax: 1 4050 98 27

5062
COSPAR Award
To honor a scientist who has made outstanding contributions to space science. All scientists working in fields covered by COSPAR are eligible. Awarded biennially at the COSPAR Plenary Meetings. Established in 1984.

5063
COSPAR Distinguished Service Medal
To recognize extraordinary services rendered to COSPAR over many years.

5064
International Cooperation Medal
Given for significant contributions, by an individual or a group, to the promotion of international scientific cooperation.

5065
Massey Award
In recognition of outstanding contributions to the development of space research, interpreted in the widest sense, in which a leadership role is of particular importance. Awarded jointly with the Royal Society, London.

5066
Nordberg Medal
To honor distinguished contributions to the application of space science in a field covered by COSPAR.

5067
Vikram Sarabhai Medal
To recognize exceptional contributions to space research in developing countries. Awarded jointly with the Indian Space Research Organization.

5068

Zeldovich Medals
To acknowlege excellence and achievements of young scientists. One medal is awarded for each COSPAR Scientific Commission. Awarded jointly with the Space Research Institute, Moscow.

5069

Communaute des Radios Publiques de Langue Francaise
Maison de Radio France
116, avenue du President Kennedy   Phone: 1 42302741
F-75786 Paris Cedex 16, France   Fax: 1 42304453

Formerly: (1983) Communaute Radiophonique des Programmes de Langue Francaise.

5070

CRPLF Awards
To promote the international community of French-speaking countries and to ensure cooperation among members through the exchange of radio programs, by the creation of radio productions in all fields, and by the organization of several competitions. The following prizes are awarded: Grand Prix du Journalisme Radiophonique - 5,000 Swiss francs to recognize the best journalistic treatment of an actual event or the best piece of investigative journalism or a report on an event of society; Bourse Rene-Payot - 10,000 Swiss francs to permit a young journalist to broadcast a news radio program that promotes the French language and to be welcomed during one or two months in each of four societie's newsroom; Grands Prix Paul-Gilson - 5,000 Swiss francs annually to both a dramatic work and a cultural documentary; Grand Prix Paul-Gilson Musique - 10,000 Swiss francs biennially to recognize a new musical work with a French text; Concours de Jazz - 5,000 Swiss francs to a jazz ensemble that submits a work of 8 to 15 minutes on a theme inspired by one of the creators of jazz from one of the four member countries of CRPLF - Canada, France, Belgium, and Switzerland; Trojkee de la Chaufon Francophone - Truffe de Perigueux - 20,000 French francs to a young singer from one of the four members countries to permit him or her to perform in the three other countries.

5071

Concours International de Chant Offenbach
79, rue Jouffroy   Phone: 1 4704 76 38
F-75016 Paris, France   Fax: 1 4727 35 03

5072

Concours International de Chant Offenbach
(International Offenbach Singing Competition)
To discover and present talented singers capable of singing the Offenbach and the French "Opera-Comique" repertoire. Singers of any nationality who are between 18 and 45 years of age are eligible. Laureates are invited to sing the following season in the Festival International de Carpentras, and in different theaters, such as Lausanne. Monetary prizes totaling 120,000 French francs re awarded biennially. Established in 1985. Sponsored by the France - Ministry of Culture and Communication.

5073

Concours International de Piano d'Epinal
4, Quai des Bons-Enfants
F-88000 Epinal, France   Phone: 29 82 53 48

5074

Concours International de Piano, Epinal
For recognition of outstanding pianists under 30 years of age. A first prize of 20,000 French francs is awarded to the winner. The second prize is 7,000 French francs, the third prize 5,000 French francs and the fourth 3,000 French francs. Medals are also awarded. The first prize winner is also given a contract for a recital during the following season organized by the Association of Classical Concerts of Epinal. The jury awards a special prize of 3,000 French francs for the best interpretation of this work. A prize of 30,000 French francs - Prix du Comite Albert Roussel - is awarded for the best interpretation of an A. Roussel work. Awarded biennially. Established in 1965.

5075

Concours International du Festival de Musique de Toulon
Palais de la Bourse, Av. Marechal Leclerc   Phone: 9493 5284
F-83000 Toulon, France   Fax: 9424 1610

5076

Concours International du Festival de Musique de Toulon
To discover new talent and to encourage young artists. Individuals from 18 to 30 years of age are eligible. Awards are given in alternate years in the following categories: horn, 1992; trumpet, 1993; bassoon, 1994; trombone, 1995; and clarinet, 1996. The following prizes are awarded: First prize - 20,000 French francs; Second prize - 12,000 French francs; and Third prize - 8,000 French francs. Silver or bronze medals are also awarded annually. Established in 1976.

5077

Concours Seymour Cray France
L'informatique scientifique
18, rue de Tilsitt
F-75017 Paris, France   Phone: 1 47660155

5078

Concours Seymour Cray France
To recognize and encourage individuals who have demonstrated outstanding creativity and quality in their research, and to encourage research of quality for the benefit of humanity in the 21st century. For the 1994 Competition, the following themes are considered: micro-electronics, architecture systems, numeric simulation, parallel algorithms, and industrial applications. The deadline for submissions is June 15. The following monetary prizes are awarded annually in March: first prize - 150,000 French francs, second prize - 75,000 French francs, and third prize - 50,000 French francs. Also awarded is the Prix Special Jeunes Chercheurs to researchers under 30 years of age. Established in 1986 by Cray Research France.

5079

Conservation Foundation (France)
(Fondation Nature et Patrimoine Prix Ford France)
7, rue Emile Cossonneau   Phone: 1 4300 12 80
F-93360 Neuilly - Plaisance, France   Fax: 1 4300 61 34

5080

Prix Nature et Patrimoine
For recognition of conservation projects that are in progress or have been recently completed. Individuals, groups, or organizations are eligible. A monetary prize of 30,000 French francs and a trophy are awarded. Categories include: Urbanisme - for projects that safeguard or renovate an urban zone; Zones Rurales - for projects that safeguard or renovate a rural area; Patrimoine Architectural - for projects concerned with protection, renovation, maintenance, and the repair of buildings, the means of transportation, or other objects or symbols of the French heritage; Economies d'Energie - for projects that reduce the rate of consumption of energy resources such as coal, iron, minerals, gas, or petroleum. Anti-pollution projects are also eligible; Jeunes - for a project by a person who is under 18 years of age or a group; Industrie - for the protection or the development of an environmental enterprise for society; and Patrimoine Culturel. To be eligible, an industry must sponsor the project and actively participate. The winner is awarded a trophy and enters an international competition for the Grand Prix Europeen. A monetary prize of 40,000 French francs is awarded to the grand prize winner. Awarded every year. Established in 1984.

5081
Cooperation Center for Scientific Research Relative to Tobacco (CORESTA)
(Centre de Cooperation pour les Recherches Scientifiques relatives au Tabac (CORESTA))
53, quai d'Orsay
F-75347 Paris Cedex 07, France
Phone: 1 4556 60 19
Fax: 1 4556 62 30

5082
CORESTA Prize
(Prix CORESTA)
For recognition of achievement in tobacco science or technology. The nominee must be older than 40 years of age. Members may apply by March 15, the year of award. A monetary prize of about US $5,000, a diploma, and travel are presented biennially at a Congress or Symposium. Established in 1972. Formerly: (1978) Philip Morris International Prize.

5083
Art Manzelli Prize
(Prix Art Manzelli)
To provide for individuals to attend the presentation of papers. Sponsored by ZOE-CON Corporation.

5084
Coordinating Committee for International Voluntary Service
c/o UNESCO
1, rue Miollis
F-75015 Paris, France
Phone: 1 4568 27 31
Fax: 1 4273 05 21

5085
Certificate of Outstanding Work in the Field of Voluntary Service
For recognition of work done by volunteers in the activities of member organizations of CCIVS. Member organizations may make nominations. A diploma is awarded annually on May 27, the day of international voluntary service. Established in 1985.

5086
Council of Europe
(Conseil de l'Europe)
Publications and Documents Division
BP 431 R6
F-67075 Strasbourg Cedex, France
Phone: 8841 2000
Fax: 8841 2781

5087
Citizens Europe Prize
To encourage personal commitment among journalists and to promote a European dimension in the work of the media. A The following prizes were awarded: editorials - first prize of 6,000 French francs and a silver medal; and feature articles and reports - first prize of 6,000 French francs and a silver medal. Established in 1982. (Discontinued in 1989)

5088
Council of Europe Museum Prize
To honor a museum judged to have made an original contribution to the preservation of the European heritage. The prize comprises a bronze statuette donated by the Spanish Artist Joan Miro and a sum of roughly 30,000 French francs. The winning museum is selected by the Parliamentary Assembly's Committee on Culture and Education from among the museums shortlisted by the independent European Museum of the Year Award Committee. Awarded annually. Established in 1977.

5089
Europe Prize
To recognize the municipalities that have made an outstanding effort to propagate the idea of European unity. The committee on environment, regional planning, and local authorities of the parliamentary assembly designates the winning municipality or municipalities from those that have submitted their candidature or whose candidature has been submitted by one of the international organizations of local authorities with consultative status. A trophy in the form of a shield, made of wood with a bronze plaque decorated with allegorical figures and with a Latin inscription is awarded annually. The trophy is retained until the next winning municipality is determined. The shield bears the name of each municipality that has won the prize. A bronze medal, to be retained permanently by the winning municipality, a parchment, and a scholarship of 40,000 French francs to be spent on travel in Europe for one or more young persons from the winning municipality are also awarded. Established in 1955.

5090
Europe Prize - Flag of Honor
For recognition of work in promoting the idea of European unity. Municipalities are eligible. A number of European flags are awarded each year in ceremonial presentation to approximately 30 municipalities. Established in 1955.

5091
Europe Prize - Plaque of Honor
To recognize certain municipalities or other territorial authorities that have already held the Flag of Honor for several years and whose efforts to propagate the idea of European unity are considered worthy of this distinction. The plaque, rectangular in shape, engraved with the name of the winning town and year of the award, is decorated with the European symbol similar to that on the Europe Prize Medal. It is presented by a member of the committee on environment, regional planning and local authorities or by another member of the parliamentary assembly, at a ceremony organized by the municipality and which the public is invited to attend. Established in 1988.

5092
European Human Rights Competition (Rene Cassin Competition)
To make the European Convention on Human Rights better known in European universities. The event was organized by the Juris Lundi Association (comprised of students from the University of Strasbourg), with the assistance of the Council of Europe and the International Institute of Human Rights. The participants in the competition, students of law and politics of the signatory countries of the European Convention on Human Rights, took part of a fictitious case presented to an ad hoc "Court of Human Rights" so that the different aspects of the case could be defended. (Discontinued in 1991)

5093
European Human Rights Prize
To recognize a person, group of persons, institution or non-governmental organization that has been active in promoting or protecting human rights in accordance with the principles of individual freedom, political liberty, and the rule of law. An exceptional contribution to the cause of human rights is necessary for consideration. A medal and a certificate are awarded triennially. Established in 1980.

5094
European Nature Conservation Diploma
To recognize particularly fine examples of protected landscapes or conservation schemes of international importance. It is awarded to natural parks, reserves, or sites that comply with certain criteria relating to the safeguarding of the natural heritage and that takes their scientific, cultural, and/or recreational value into account. An area so selected is placed under the sponsorship of the Council of Europe for a five-year period that may be renewed for further five-year periods after strict on-the-spot appraisal by specialists. Established in 1965.

5095
European Theatre Prize
To discover new talent, and to introduce theatrical productions worthy of interest to the European public. Its aim is to arouse the curiosity of critics and audiences, to draw their attention to an intense and original source of artistic activity, and to encourage the latter to persevere. A monetary prize of 50,000 French francs is awarded. Established in 1985. A new version of this prize is under study.

5096
Prix Europa
For recognition of the most original and creative fiction and nonfiction (whether local, regional, or national) European television programs. Four monetary prizes are awarded: Prix Europa for fiction - 40,000 French francs; Prix Europa for non-fiction - 40,000 French francs; and two special prizes of 40,000 French francs each to local or regional stations. Each year, the prize-giving ceremony takes place in a different European city (1987 Amsterdam; 1988 Berlin; 1989 Strasbourg; 1990 Barcelona; and 1991 Reykjavik). Established in 1987. Organized and financed by the Council of Europe, the European Parliament (PE), the Commission of the European Communities, the Berlin Senate, the European Cultural Foundation (based in Amsterdam), the Sender Freies Berlin-ARD, and the Senate of Berlin. Additional information is available from the European Cultural Foundation, Jan van Goyenkade 5, NL-1075 HN Amsterdam, Netherlands, phone: 2076 02 22.

5097
Courage Quotidien
Address unknown.

5098
Prix Courage Quotidien
To recognize individuals who have overcome great personal difficulties and become useful to others by their benevolent acts. Individuals may be nominated. Monetary awards of 10,000 French francs are presented annually in May. Established in 1983.

5099
Prix d'Honneur Courage Quotidien
To recognize an individual of great courage. An individual who has demonstrated courage throughout his life is chosen to receive Prix d'Honneur. Monetary awards of 25,000 French francs are presented annually in May. Established in 1983.

5100
Georges Cravenne Conseil
19, avenue du President Wilson
F-75116 Paris, France   Phone: 1 4723 72 33

5101
Prix de la Fondation Mumm pour la Presse Ecrite
For recognition of the best report, article, column, or drawing written in the French newspapers. A monetary prize of 100,000 francs is awarded annually. Established in 1985 by Georges Cravenne. Sponsored by Fondation Mumm.

5102
Prix Mumm Kleber-Haedens
To recognize the author of a work which reflects an optimistic view of life. A monetary prize of 100,000 French francs is awarded annually. Established in 1980.

5103
Credit Cooperatif
Parc de la Defense
33, rue des Trois-Fontanot
BP 211
F-92002 Nanterre, France

5104
Trophees de l'Initiative
For recognition of the most innovative initiatives of social economy in cities and towns by science and industry. Three prizes totaling 600,000 French francs are awarded. Established and awarded for the first time in 1988 on the occasion of the fiftieth anniversary of Credit Cooperatif.

5105
Demeure Historique
57, quai de la Tournelle
F-75005 Paris, France   Phone: 1 42390286

5106
Annual Prize for Best Restoration Program
For recognition of the best restoration program. Awarded annually. The organization also sponsors competitions.

5107
D'Orgue Europeen de Beauvais
70, rue de Rivoli
F-75004 Paris, France   Phone: 1 42786023

Formerly: Amie de l'Orgue.

5108
Concours D'Orgue Europeen de Beauvais
To recognize outstanding organists for both execution and improvisation. The competitions are held in alternate years. The Grand Prize winner receives 22,000 French francs, and each finalist receives 2,200 French francs. Awarded in odd-numbered years.

5109
Elle
6, rue Ancelle
F-92525 Neuilly-sur-Seine Cedex, France   Phone: 1 4088 60 81

5110
***Elle* Literary Prize**
(Grand Prix des Lectrices de *Elle*)
To provide recognition for a novel and an informative book. The winners are selected by readers of *Elle*. Established in 1970.

5111
Encyclopaedia Universalis
10, rue Vercingetorix
F-75014 Paris, France   Phone: 1 4321 41 10
                                         Fax: 1 4321 62 89

5112
Prix Diderot Universalis
For recognition of an achievement in disseminating the French culture. A book, movie, exhibition, or any wider subject may be selected by the jury. A monetary prize of 50,000 French francs is awarded annually. Established in 1984 by Peter F. Baumberger, Chairman of Encyclopaedia Universalis.

5113
European and Mediterranean Plant Protection Organization
(Organisation Europeenne et Mediterraneenne pour la Protection des Plantes)
1, rue Le Notre
F-75016 Paris, France   Phone: 1 4520 77 94
                                         Fax: 1 4224 89 43

5114
Medaille d'Or
(Gold Medal)
For recognition of special service and merit in promoting international cooperation and research in plant protection. A gold medal is awarded when merited. Established in 1973.

5115
European Centre for Environmental Communication
(Centre Europeen pour la Communication sur l'Environment)
55, rue de Varenne   Phone: 1 4544 40 60
F-75341 Paris Cedex 7, France   Fax: 1 4222 65 54

5116
European Environmental Film Festival
(Biennale Europeenne du Film Sur l'Environnement)
For recognition of the best films or television programs concerning environmental issues. The theme varies at each festival. Films of all categories (reportage, documentary, fiction, animation, education, and research) and produced by any private or public body of all countries in Europe can be admitted for the competition. Films made with the purpose of advertising are excluded. The following prizes are awarded: (1) Grand Prix television - 30,000 French francs for the director; (2) Grand Prix independent production - 30,000 French francs; (3) Best short film - 20,000 French francs; (4) Best documentary film television - 15,000 French francs for the director; (5) Best documentary film independent production - 15,000 French francs and 10,000 French francs for distribution; (6) Best fiction film - 15,000 French francs for the director; (7) special prize of the jury - 15,000 French francs; (8) Special Institutional Awards by the Council of Europe and the European Parliament; and (9) European Business Awards - for the best film on the environment. Awarded biennially. Established in 1981 by the European Cultural Council.

5117
European Committee for Rink Hockey
(Comite Europeen de Rink Hockey)
62, rue Edgar Quinet   Phone: 40676648
F-44100 Nantes, France   Fax: 40469763

5118
Championnats d'Europe de Rink-Hockey
For recognition at European championships and cup competitions. Champions in the following categories are awarded: (1) Seniors; (2) Juniors; and (3) Clubs. A trophy is awarded. Established in 1976 by the Confederation Europeenne de Roller Skating.

5119
European Committee of the International Ozone Association
9, rue de Phalsbourg
F-75854 Paris Cedex 17, France   Phone: 1 4227 38 91

5120
Prize
For recognition of an original paper on the utilization of ozone technologies in industry. Awarded biennially.

5121
European Confederation of Public Relations
(Confederation Europeenne des Relations Publiques)
35/41, rue de l'Oasis   Phone: 1 450 6 53 43
F-92800 Puteau, France   Fax: 1 450 6 53 43

5122
Michel Linon Prize
For recognition in the field of public relations. In addition, the following awards are also presented: (1) Columns of CERP; (2) Code of Athens; and (3) Michel Linon Prize.

5123
European Council of Jewish Community Services
(Conseil Europeen des Services Communautaires Juifs)
4 bis, rue de Lota
F-75116 Paris, France   Phone: 1 4453 31 26

5124
Prix de l'Education Alfred Weichselbaum
(Alfred Weichselbaum Education Prize)
For recognition of the best educational program for vacation centers. A monetary prize is awarded annually at the Statutory meeting. Established in 1983 in memory of Alfred Weichselbaum, the late president of the European Association of Community Centers, and champion of the youth cause, who died in 1984.

5125
European Festival of Corporate Image
(Festival Europeen de l'Image de l'entreprise)
15, bis rue de Marignan
F-75008 Paris, France   Phone: 1 4359 69 90

5126
Grand Prix of the European Festival
(Grand Prix du Festival Europeen)
For recognition of the best European productions in films and videos concerning industries and services. All European, private or public companies are eligible. A trophy in the shape of a dolphin is awarded annually. Established in 1990 by Cefilm. Sponsored by the Confederation of French Industries and Services.

5127
European Society for Cardiovascular Surgery
(Societe Europeenne de Chirurgie Cardiovasculaire)
Hopital Broussais
96, rue Didot   Phone: 1 5419305
F-75675 Paris Cedex 14, France   Fax: 1 5424057

5128
Dos Santos Prize
To recognize cardiac and vascular surgeons who are involved in the study of cardiovascular diseases. Young researchers are eligible. Awarded biennially.

5129
European Society of Paediatric Radiology
(Societe Europeene de Radiologie-Pediatrie)
Service Radiologie
Hopital Saint-Vincent-de-Paul
74, Ave. Denfert Rochereau
F-75674 Paris Cedex 14, France   Phone: 1 4048 81 11

5130
Jacques Lefebvre Memorial Award
To encourage professional development in the field of pediatric radiology. Members of the Society under 34 years of age may submit papers. A monetary prize is awarded annually at the Congress. Established in 1976 in memory of Dr. Lefebvre. Formerly: Prix Jacques Lefebvre.

5131
European Union of Geosciences
c/o European Science Foundation
1, quai Lezay-Marnesia
F-67000 Strasbourg, France   Phone: 8835 30 63

5132
Foreign Honorary Fellow
For recognition of merit and their achievements in the field of the earth and planetary sciences. Citizens of countries outside the Council of Europe are considered. Six certificates are awarded to the designated Fellows biennially. The Foreign Honorary Fellows are exempted from paying annual dues to the Union.

5133
Arthur-Holmes Medal
For recognition of scientific achievements in terrestrial or extraterrestrial materials sciences and, in particular, successful efforts in using physicochemical methods in establishing relationships between earth's materials genesis and terrestrial dynamics, and in understanding the historical evolution of the main geological cycles in the spirit of A. Holmes. The recipients may be citizens of any country in the world. The medal may be jointly awarded to two scientists or more, whether they have worked together or not in the case of simultaneous and identical or complementary discoveries. The medal, bearing a likeness of Arthur Holmes and the recipient's name, both engraved, is awarded either for a specific major discovery or for the achievement of a life-time career.

5134
Outstanding Young Scientist Award
To recognize scientific achievements in any field made by a scientist who is under 35 years of age. The award may be made jointly to two scientists. A certificate and an invitation to make a presentation of the scientific work at the EUG biennial meeting is award every other year.

5135
Alfred-Wegener Medal
For recognition of scientific achievements in the earth sciences and, in particular, successful efforts at bridging together various fields of the earth sciences in order to solve geodynamic problems, as demonstrated in the work A. Wegener. Exceptional achievements within a single field of the earth sciences may also be considered. The recipients may be citizens of any country in the world. The medal may be jointly awarded to two scientists or more, whether they have worked together or not in the case of simultaneous and identical or complementary discoveries. The medal, bearing a likness of Alfred Wegener and the recipient's name, both engraved, is awarded either for a specific major discovery or for the achievement of a life-time career.

5136
Federation Aeronautique Internationale
93, Boulevard du Montparnasse
F-75006 Paris, France
Phone: 1 4954 38 92
Fax: 1 4954 38 88

5137
Antonov Aeromodelling Diploma
To recognize technical innovations in aeromodelling. Each year an active member of the FAI may submit the name of one candidate by November 15. The Antonov Diploma can be granted more than once to the same person for different technical innovations made in different years. Only one Diploma is awarded annually. This Diploma is donated by the National Aeroclub of Russia to the FAI. Established in 1987.

5138
Leon Biancotto Diploma
To recognize individuals or organizations that have contributed significantly to the sport of aerobatics. Awarded annually. Established in 1993.

5139
Louis Bleriot Medal
To recognize the holders of the highest records for speed, altitude, and distance in a straight line attained in the previous year by light aircraft. Three medals are awarded annually (unless the records of the preceding year have not been broken). Established in 1936 in memory of Louis Bleriot, an aviation pioneer and vice president of FAI.

5140
Colibri Diploma
To recognize outstanding contributions to the development of microlight aircraft by action, work, achievements, initiative, or devotion. Each active member of the FAI may submit the name of a candidate. Only one Diploma is awarded annually. Established in 1983.

5141
Leonardo Da Vinci Diploma
To recognize a parachutist. Eligible candidates include those who have: obtained at least three times consecutively the title of National Parachuting Champion; obtained at least once the title of World Absolute Parachuting Champion and at least twice the title of Combined Champion at an international parachuting competition; successfully fulfilled the function of Chief Judge at least twice at an international competition and at least once at a World Parachuting Championship; fulfilled at least three times consecutively the function of International Judge at a World Parachuting Championship; established at least three World Parachuting records; fulfilled at least twice the function of Competition Director at an International Parachuting Contest and at least once at a World Parachuting Championship; been nominated Honorary President of the FAI Parachuting Commission; or been for at least 10 consecutive years, and still are a national delegate to the FAI Parachuting Commission. Each year, an active member of the FAI may submit the name of one candidate of his country. A diploma is awarded annually. Established in 1970.

5142
De La Vaulx Medal
To recognize the holders of absolute world records achieved during the previous year. A medal is awarded annually. Established in 1933 in memory of Comte de La Vaulx, a founder-member and president of FAI.

5143
Diploma for Outstanding Airmanship
For recognition of a pilot or flight crew on an aircraft in sub-orbital flight for a feat of outstanding airmanship having occurred during one of the previous two years and that resulted in the saving of life, or that was carried out with that objective. Eligible nominees include pilots, flight crew, or any person being temporarily in charge of an aircraft in the air. A pilot or crew engaged in a routine search and rescue mission is not eligible. A diploma is awarded annually. Established in 1985.

5144
FAI Aeromodelling Gold Medal
To recognize aeromodellers of an FAI member for outstanding merit in organization activities. Recipients must have: fulfilled at least twice the function of Competition Director or a similar function at World or European Championships; fulfilled at least three times the function of an FAI jury member at World or European Championships; fulfilled at least five times the function of a judge or a similar function at World or Continental Championships; served at least three years as a delegate to the FAI Aeromodelling Commission, or served another function therein; or shown outstanding merits in developing aeromodelling by organizational activities. Each year active members of the FAI may submit the name of one candidate of their country by November 15. One medal is awarded annually by the FAI Council on recommendation of the FAI Aeromodelling Commission. Established in 1987.

5145
FAI Airsport Medal
To recognize individuals or groups for outstanding services in connection with air sport activities. Any number of medals may be given annually for work in FAI Commissions and Committees; organizing World and Continental championships; training and education of new pilots, parachutists, or aeromodellers; or promoting aviation in general and especially with young people. Applications must be submitted by FAI Members, FAI Commissions and Committees, and the FAI President on uniform application form to FAI Secretariat. Applications are subject to the approval of the FAI president or secretary general. Established in 1991, the 100th anniversary of Lilienthal's first flights.

5146
FAI Bronze Medal
To recognize individuals who have rendered eminent services to the FAI in administrative work, in commissions or committees, or in organizations of international sporting competitions. The award is decided by the Council by a simple majority vote. A medal is awarded annually upon proposal by the Director General of FAI. Established in 1962.

5147
FAI Gold Air Medal
This medal, one of FAI's two highest awards, is given for recognition of outstanding contributions to the development of aeronautics through activities, work, achievements, initiative, or devotion to the cause of aviation. Active members may submit one candidate who is of the same nationality. The medal may be awarded posthumously. A gold medal is awarded annually. Established in 1924.

5148
FAI Gold Parachuting Medal
For recognition of an outstanding accomplishment in parachuting. Contributions in the realm of sport, safety, or, at the option of the Commission, an invention are considered. Each year, an active member of the FAI may submit the name of one candidate who is not a member of the FAI Parachute Commission. A medal is awarded annually. Established in 1968.

5149
FAI Gold Rotorcraft Medal
To reward a particularly remarkable achievement in rotorcraft, including the use of a sporting vehicle or eminent services to the development of rotorcraft over an extended period of time. Established in 1993.

5150
Yuri A. Gagarin Gold Medal
To recognize the astronaut who, in the previous year, has accomplished the highest achievement in the conquest of space. An active member may submit one candidate of the same nationality. The medal may be awarded posthumously. A gold medal is awarded annually. Established in 1968 in memory of Astronaut Yuri A. Gagarin, who performed the first human space flight in 1961 and who lost his life in an aircraft accident while carrying out a training flight.

5151
Gold Space Medal
This medal, one of FAI's two highest awards, is awarded to individuals who have contributed greatly to the development of astronautics by their activities, work, achievements, initiative, or devotion to the cause of space. An active member may submit one candidate of the same nationality. The medal may be awarded posthumously. A gold medal is awarded annually. Established in 1963.

5152
Hang Gliding Diploma
To recognize an individual who has made an outstanding contribution to the development of hang gliding by initiative, work, or leadership in flight achievements. Nominations are accepted by the FAI Hang Gliding Commission. A diploma is awarded annually. Established in 1979.

5153
Honorary Group Diploma
To recognize a group of people who has made notable contributions to the progress of aeronautics or astronautics during the previous year or years. Each year, an active member of the FAI may submit the names of two candidates, one for aeronautics and one for astronautics. A diploma is awarded annually. Established in 1965.

5154
V. M. Komarov Diploma
To recognize astronauts and members of multi-seater crews for outstanding achievements in the exploration of outer space during the previous year. Each year, an active member of the FAI may submit the name of two astronauts (multi-spaceship crews) from his country. A diploma is awarded annually. Established in 1970 in memory of V. M. Komarov, the cosmonaut who participated in the World Space record flight of Voskhod 1 in 1964 and who lost his life while on duty on a cosmic flight.

5155
Korolev Diploma
To recognize technicians or engineers who, having worked in orbit or on a celestial body in building structures and/or equipment or in a non-planned restoration or repair of a broken device to make possible the continuation of a mission, have shown human work in space. Only one Diploma is awarded each year. Established in 1988.

5156
Lilienthal Medal
For recognition of a particularly remarkable performance in gliding or for eminent services to gliding over a long period of time. A glider pilot who has broken an international record during the past year, made a pioneer flight during the past year, or has given eminent services to gliding over a long period of time and is still an active glider pilot is eligible. Each year, an active member of the FAI may submit the name of one candidate. A medal is awarded annually. Established in 1938.

5157
Charles Lindberg Diploma
For recognition of a significant contribution for more than 10 years to the progress and success of general aviation in either its sporting or transportation manifestations or in the work of international bodies; or to recognize technical breakthroughs in the field of General Aviation as an incentive toward general progress and for the purpose of stimulating research and development of new concepts and equipment contributing to operational efficiency and flight safety. No more than one candidate shall be proposed by any FAI member each year. One diploma is awarded annually when merited. Established in 1983.

5158
Pepe Lopes Medal
To recognize outstanding contributions to sportsmanship or international understanding in the sport of hang gliding. Awarded annually on the recommendation of the FAI Hang Gliding Commission for significant acts or services. Established in 1993 in memory of Pedro Paulo ("Pepe") Lopes, World Hang Gliding Champion in 1981.

5159
Pelagia Majewska Medal
To recognize a female glider pilot for a particularly remarkable performance in gliding during the past year, or eminent services to gliding over a long period of time. Each year any FAI member may submit the name of one candidate to be considered and acted upon by the FAI Gliding Commission and the Council. A medal is awarded annually. Established in 1989 following a proposal by the Aero Club of Poland in memory of Madame Pelagia Majewska, eminent Polish glider pilot who was awarded the Lilienthal Medal in 1960, holds 17 world gliding records, and lost her life in an air accident in 1988.

5160
Henry Mignet Diploma
To recognize the amateur aircraft builder who has constructed an aircraft of a new design with notable improvements. A candidate is proposed by the FAI Amateur Built Aircraft Committee. A diploma is awarded annually. Established in 1984.

5161
Montgolfier Diploma
To recognize each of the following: the best sporting performance in the previous Montgolfier year of a gas balloonist; the best sporting performance in the previous Montgolfier year of a hot air balloonist; and a major contribution to the development of the sport of ballooning in general. Sporting performances, including: records for distance, altitude, duration, and precision of landing: number of ascents; hours of flying; or any other performance that might be judged by the FAI Ballooning Commission to be most meritorious may be submitted for consideration. A diploma may also be awarded for a series of performances that together represent a remarkable achievement and, therefore, a contribution to the development of the sport of ballooning in general. Each year, active members of the FAI may submit the names of three candidates from their

country (one for each diploma). Three diplomas are awarded annually if merited. Established in 1960.

5162
Nile Gold Medal
For recognition of distinguished work in the field of aerospace education, particularly during the preceding year. A person, group of persons, or organization is eligible. Each active member of the FAI may propose one candidate each year. A gold medal is presented annually by the Aero Club of Egypt to the FAI. Established in 1972.

5163
Odyssey Diploma
To recognize a person or a group of persons whose actions, achievements, or works on earth, in space, or on a celestial body have safeguarded or may safeguard human life in space. Each year, an FAI member may submit the name of one candidate before the end of January. Awarded annually. Established in 1988 upon proposal by the FAI Astronautic Records Commission.

5164
Alphonse Penaud Diploma
To recognize an aeromodeller of FAI members who have: obtained at least three times consecutively the title of National Champion or at least once obtained the title of World Champion; established at least three world records; been at least twice Competition Director or a similar function at world and/or continental championships; been at least three times an FAI jury member at world and/or continental Championships; been at least three times an FAI judge at world and/or continental championships; been at least for three years Delegate of their NAC to CIAM; or shown outstanding merits in developing aeromodelling as a sport, technique, or organization. Active members of the FAI may submit the name of a candidate of their country. A diploma is awarded annually. Established in 1979.

5165
Phoenix Diploma
For recognition of the best reconstruction or restoration of a vintage (more than 30 years old) aircraft achieved by an amateur. Each active member may submit the name of one candidate. A diploma is awarded annually. Established in 1978.

5166
Paul Tissandier Diploma
For recognition of distinguished service to the cause of aviation in general and sporting aviation in particular. Each active member of the FAI may submit the name of a candidate. A diploma is awarded annually. Established in 1952 in memory of Paul Tissandier, secretary general of FAI from 1919 to 1945.

5167
Andrei Tupolev Diploma
For recognition of an outstanding record performance in aeromodelling. Each year an active member of the FAI may submit the name of one candidate. Only one Diploma is awarded annually. Donated annually by the FAS of the USSR to the FAI. Established in 1989.

5168
Andrei Tupolev Medal
To recognize aeromodellers who, in the same year, win the World and National Aeromodelling Championships in the same class of models. Donated annually by the National Aeroclub of Russia to the FAI. One medal is awarded each year. Established in 1989.

5169
Young FAI Artists Contest
To make the children of FAI-member countries more familiar with aeronautics and astronautics. Winners are chosen from three age classes: 5-8, 9-12, and 13-15. Gold, silver, and bronze FAI medals and a diploma are awarded to three winners in each age class at the Annual General Conference. Established in 1986. Sponsored by the FAI Aerospace Education Committee (CIEA) with the help of national and regional aero clubs.

5170
Federation francaise de vol a voile
29, rue de Sevres
F-75006 Paris, France   Phone: 1 4544 04 78

5171
Grand Prix de Vitesse en Planeur a Luchon
For recognition of the best performance by gliders with 25 meter wingspans. The courses are 200 to 500 kilometers. Established in 1986.

5172
Festival du Court Metrage en Plein Air
4, rue Hector Berlioz   Phone: 7654 4351
F-38000 Grenoble, France   Fax: 7651 2443

5173
Festival du Court-Metrage en Plein Air
For recognition of short films. The following prizes are awarded: Prix de la Ville de Grenoble - 10,000 French francs; Prix du Conseil General Isere - 5,000 French francs; Prix Aaton - loan of material; Prix Canal - purchase of the next film valued at 25,000 French francs; Prix d'Aide a la Creation; Prix Les Affiches de Grenoble et du Dauphine - 3,000 French francs; Prix Fuji - for quality film technique - 10,000 French francs; Coupe Juliet Berto; Prix de la Presse; and Prix Public. Awarded annually. Established in 1977.

5174
Festival du Film Court de Villeurbanne
117 Cours Emile Zola   Phone: 78 934265
F-69100 Villeurbanne, France   Fax: 72 430962

5175
Festival du Film Court de Villeurbanne
To recognize the best French short film made during the preceding year. The following prizes are awarded: Grand Prix de la Ville de Villeurbanne, Prix FR3, Prix Cites T.V., Prix SACEM, Prix de la Caisse d'Epargne, Prix Fuji, Prix Pyral, Prix Public, Prix des Producteurs de Cinema Francais, Prix Jacquard, and Prix Canal. Awarded annually. Established in 1980. Sponsored by the City of Villeurbanne, France - Ministry of Culture and Communication, Centre National de la Cinematographie, SACEM, Caisse d'Epargne Rhone-Alpes Lyon, and Groupement Regional d'Action Cinematographique.

5176
Festival Estival de Paris
20, rue Geoffroy l'Asnier
F-75004 Paris, France   Phone: 1 4804 98 01

5177
Concours International de Clavecin de Paris
For recognition of an outstanding harpsichord interpretation. Harpsichord performers of any nationality under the age of 32 are eligible. There is a special competition for basso continuo performance. The following awards are presented: (1) a monetary prize of 30,000 francs - first prize; (2) 18,000 francs - second prize; (3) 10,000 francs - third prize; (4) 12,000 francs - special prize for basso continuo; and (5) 12,000 francs - contemporary music prize. Awarded biennially. Established in 1973 by Bernard Bonaldi. Sponsored by the Municipality of Paris and the Ministry of Culture and Communication, Radio France and l'Association Francaise d'Action Artistique.

5178

Festival International de Danse de Paris
36, rue de Laborde
F-75008 Paris, France
Phone: 1 45222874
Fax: 1 45226024

5179

Concours International de Danse de Paris
To recognize the best dancers, classical and contemporary, in the competition. Co-sponsored by the City of Paris.

5180

Festival International de Musique de Besancon et de Franche-Comte
2d, rue Isenbart
F-25000 Besancon, France
Phone: 81 807326
Fax: 81 804636

5181

Besancon International Competition for Young Conductors
(Concours International de Jeunes Chefs d'Orchestre Besancon)
To recognize the aptitudes of young artists for conducting, rather than to check their technical knowledge. Individuals who are less than 32 years of age are eligible. A monetary prize and opportunities to conduct various orchestras are awarded annually. Established in 1951.

5182

International Competition of Music Composition
(Concours International de Composition Musicale)
To recognize an outstanding music composition for an orchestra. The contest is open to composers of any nationality who are under 35 years of age. Recipients are awarded Prize of the Festival of Besancon and 25,000 French francs. The piece that wins first place is played at the final session of the Young Conductors Contest of the Music Festival of Bensancon the following year. Awarded annually. Established in 1988.

5183

Festival International du Film de Vol Libre
Office du tourisme
F-38720 St. Hilaire du Touvet, France
Phone: 7608 3399
Fax: 7697 2056

5184

Festival International du Film de Vol Libre
For the promotion of hang-gliding films. The following prizes are awarded: Grand Prix du Festival, Prix du Public, Prix de la Critique, Mention Special du Jury, Mention Reportage, Prize for the Best Film Script, Prize for the Best Artistic Film, Prize for the Best Documentary or News Film, and Prize for the Best Advertising Film. Trophies are awarded annually in September. Established in 1983.

5185

Festival International du Film Historique
Hotel de Ville
13 Bd. Foch
F-92500 Rueil-Malmaison, France
Phone: 47 32 65 44

5186

Festival International du Film d'Histoire
(International Festival of Historic Films, Rueil-Malmaison)
To recognize outstanding historic films made for television and cinema. Gold and Silver Eagles (Aigle d'Or) are awarded in both categories. Established in 1983 by the town of Rueil.

5187

Festival La Plaine-Atlantique
7, quai de Versailles
F-44000 Nantes, France
Phone: 4035 46 46
Fax: 4042 09 10

5188

International Voice Competition la Plaine-Atlantique
(Concours International de Chant la Plaine-Atlantique)
For recognition of outstanding vocal performances. The competition is open to singers of all nationalities, who are more than 18 years and less than 33 years of age in the year of the Competition. The following prizes are awarded: (1) Grand Prize - a Sevres Vase presented by H.E. The Ministry of the Culture, and 40,000 French francs, a Medal, and engagements presented by the Europe Council; (2) Second Prize Men's Voices - a medal and 20,000 French francs; (3) Second Prize Prize Women's Voices - a medal and 20,000 French francs presented by the Department of Loire-Atlantique; (4) Third Prize Men's Voices - a medal and 5,000 French francs presented by the Credit Industriel de l'Ouest; (5) Third Prize Women's Voices - a medal and 5,000 French francs presented by the Credit Industriel de l'Ouest; (6) Special Prize: Prix Comite Albert Roussel - 15,000 French francs for the Man's Prize-Winner and 15,000 French francs for the Woman's Prize-Winner; (7) Special Prize - 3,000 French francs, presented by the Societe des Auteurs, Compositeurs et Editeurs de Musique, is awarded to a finalist man or woman, for the best interpretation of a twentieth century French composer's melody sung in one of the three rounds of the competition; (8) Special Prize: Prix Mady Mesple - 3,000 French francs presented by the prima donna Mady Mesple is awarded the best vocalist; (9) Special Prize - a medal and one engagement in the Nantes' Opera presented by the City of Nantes; and (10) Special Prize: Prix Helena Oliveira - three engagements in Rio de Janeiro presented by Helena Oliveira. Established in 1984. Sponsored by the Secretariat of the Conseil de l'Europe and France Ministry of Culture and Communication.

5189

Les Films de L'Atalante
43, rue du Faubourg
Montmartre
F-75009 Paris, France
Phone: 1 4770 34 43

5190

Prix Jean Vigo
To recognize the author of a full-length film and the author of a short film produced in France. Films should be by authors who are still unrecognized in their field. Two prizes are awarded annually. Established in 1951 in memory of Jean Vigo. Sponsored by Telcipro, Kodak, FIAJI and Encyclopaedia Universalis.

5191

Florilege Vocal de Tours
Hotel de Ville
BP 1452
F-37014 Tours Cedex, France
Phone: 47 216526
Fax: 47 216936

Formerly: Rencontres Internationales de Chant Choral de Tours.

5192

Composition Competition, Tours
(Concours de Composition, Tours)
For recognition of a choral composition "a capella." The competition is open for all composers. The 1994 competition is for "equal voices" and "mixed voices" in the French language. The work presented must either last three to five minutes or be in cyclic form with several sequences, lasting five to ten minutes overall. At the composer's request, each sequence of a cycle may be judged separately as an independent work. The subject is left to the discretion of the composer. The piece must be original music. Harmonizations of traditional melodies, songs, etc., are excluded. The work, easy or of average difficulty, must be accessible to performance by amateur choirs, be unpublished, and have a title. Each composer may enter a maximum of three works by March 31. The following monetary prizes are awarded: first prize - 10,000 French francs; second prize - 5,000 French francs; and third prize - 3,000 French francs. In 1994 a special prize will be awarded to a piece written on a text by Francois RABELAIS (1494-1553). Awarded annually. Established in 1973.

5193
International Choral Competition, Tours
(Concours International de Chant Choral de Tours)
For recognition of outstanding choral music sung "a cappella" by the following categories of singing groups: mixed choirs; men's choir and women's choir; mixed voice ensembles; and free program. Competition in each category consists of performing a program of the contestant's own choice within the required time periods. The deadline for entry is December 6. The following monetary prizes are awarded for the first category, mixed choirs: 10,000 French francs - first place; 6,000 French francs - second place; and 4,000 French francs - third place. The following monetary prizes are awarded in second and third categories: 8,000 French francs - first place; 4,800 French francs - second place; and 3,200 French francs - third place. The following monetary prizes are awarded for the fourth category: 5,000 French francs - first place; 3,000 French francs - second place; and 2,000 French francs - third place. The best choirs of each category present a closing concert. At the close of the concert the following prizes are awarded: Prix du Public - 3,000 French francs; Grand Prix de la Ville de Tours - 20,000 French francs to recognize the chorus that is most outstanding during the competition and the closing concert; Prix Special du concours de composition - 4,000 French francs to a choir giving the best interpretation during the "Rencontres" of a work that has received a Composition Competition award; and Prix du Ministre de la Culture et de la Communication - 10,000 French francs to the choir giving the best interpretation of a French work. Awarded annually at Pentecost. Established in 1972 by Claude Panterne.

5194
Fondation Amon Ra
Le Verger
F-01210 Ornex-Maconnex, France   Phone: 5041 44 87

5195
Grand Prix Amon Ra
To recognize writers of the French or Creole language originally from Haiti. Candidates must have command of the French and Creole languages. Preference is given to individuals who speak more than the two languages including also English, Spanish or Portuguese. Awards are given for works in the following categories: (1) poetry, drama or prose; (2) industrial design; and (3) photography or painting. Works may be submitted between September 1 and December 1. A monetary prize of 1,000 gourdes is awarded annually Established by Michel R. Doret in memory of the Haitian writer Frederic Doret.

5196
Fondation de France
40, avenue Hoche   Phone: 1 44213100
F-75008 Paris, France   Fax: 1 44213101

5197
Prix International Arthur Honegger de Composition Musicale
To recognize a composer of a published or unpublished oratorio with solo, choir, and orchestra of a minimum length of 20 minutes. Composers of any age or nationality who are living at the opening of the competition are eligible. The object of the Arthur Honegger prize is to honor composers or musicians whose work or activity is within the realm of the ideal as illustrated by the composer, Arthur Honegger. A monetary prize of 50,000 French francs is awarded biennially. Established in 1971 by Mrs. Arthur Honegger in memory of her husband, composer Arthur Honegger. Formerly: (1986) Prix de Musique International Arthur Honegger.

5198
Prix de Gravure Lacouriere
To recognize a young line engraver for an outstanding print. Engravers under 40 years of age who are French citizens or have been residents for five years are eligible. Prints must not have been produced with any technique or photo technique foreign to line engraving. A monetary prize of 50,000 French francs is awarded annually. Established in 1979 by Madeleine Lacouriere in honor of Roger Lacouriere, an engraver and master printer. Additional information is available from the Bibliotheque Nationale - Dep. Estampes Prix Lacouriere, 58, rue de Richelieu, F-75084 Paris Cedex 02, France.

5199
Prix de Peinture Andre et Berthe Noufflard
For recognition of a young figurative painter for oil works painted during the preceding five years. French nationals or other nationals who have been residents of France for at least three years and are under 40 years of age are eligible. A monetary prize of 15,000 French francs is awarded annually. Established in 1985 by Fondation Andre et Berthe Noufflard in honor of French figurative painters, Andre and Berthe Noufflard. Sponsored by Fondation Andre et Berthe Noufflard.

5200
Fondation de la Maison de la Chimie
Maison de la Chimie
28, rue St. Dominique   Phone: 1 47051073
F-75007 Paris, France   Fax: 1 45559862

5201
Prix de la Fondation de la Maison de la Chimie
For recognition of a work in the field of chemistry that benefits humanity, life, or nature. Candidates must be nominated by a learned society or a national or international scientific organization. A monetary prize of 150,000 French francs is awarded. Established in 1988.

5202
Fondation Feneon
Cabinet du Recteur de l'Academie de
  Paris
47, rue des Ecoles   Phone: 1 40462015
F-75005 Paris, France   Fax: 1 40462010

5203
Prix Felix Feneon
To assist young writers, painters, or sculptors to pursue their literary or artistic education. Candidates must be younger than 35 years of age. Painters and sculptors must already have exhibited works and writers must have one published work written in French to be considered. Two awards of 25,000 French francs each are awarded to a writer and an artist. Awarded annually in June. Established in 1949 by Rectorat de l'Academie de Paris in memory of Felix Feneon, chronicler and critic of art.

5204
Prix Henri Hertz
For recognition of literary, historical, or artistic works that make better known or understood the civic and ethical preoccupations of Henri Hertz. A monetary prize of 27,000 French francs is awarded annually. Established in 1986 by the Chancellerie des Universites de Paris in memory of Henri Hertz (1875-1966).

5205
Fondation France-Libertes
1, place Trocadero 11 Novembre   Phone: 1 4755 81 81
F-75007 Paris, France   Fax: 1 4755 81 88

5206
Prix de la Memoire
For recognition of an important public event carried by different media. The subject may be a book, film, pictoral or musical work, a collective action, etc., showing a remembered or forgotten victory which was spontaneous or systematically organized. Established by Eva Weil and Jean-Claude Gasewitch.

5207
Fondation Franco-Americaine
38, avenue Hoche
F-75008 Paris, France
Phone: 1 4563 28 30
Fax: 1 4256 09 75

5208
Prix de la Meilleure Initiative Franco-Americaine
For recognition of the best French-American initiative. A monetary prize of 50,000 French francs was awarded biennially in the spring. Established in 1985. (Discontinued in 1989)

5209
Fondation Louise Charpentier
Residence Jean Moulin
F-07400 Le Teil d'Ardeche, France
Phone: 7552 15 30

5210
Concours International de Harpe Louise Charpentier
To encourage the use of the harp as an instrument of recital. Harpists who are 30 years of age or younger are eligible to enter the competition by March 5. A monetary prize of 50,000 French francs is awarded biennially. Established in 1984 in honor of Louise Charpentier, harpist.

5211
Fondation Marcel Bleustein-Blanchet pour la Vocation
60, avenue Victor Hugo
F-75116 Paris, France
Phone: 1 4501 29 28

Formerly: Fondation de la Vocation.

5212
Bourses de la Vocation
To encourage and facilitate vocations. French citizens between the ages of 18 and 30 who have begun to achieve success in their chosen field are eligible for consideration. The judges consider their level of study, their development, and the character of their vocation. While over 250 different vocations have been recognized, a young French author and a young French poet annually receive the Prix Litteraire de la Vocation and the Prix de Poesie, respectively. A monetary award of 30,000 francs is presented, and permanent moral or financial support as well as contacts are available to the winners. Awarded annually in December. Established in 1960 by Marcel Bleustein-Blanchet, President of Publicis SA. The award honors a different personality every year. Many French and foreign companies support the Foundation.

5213
Fondation Napoleon
82, rue de Monceau
F-75008 Paris, France
Phone: 1 45222457

5214
Grands Prix de la Fondation Napoleon
For recognition of the best work written concerning the First Empire (Napoleon I) or the Second Empire (Napoleon III). Works written during the preceding year November 1 to October 31 are eligible. A monetary prize is awarded annually on December 2. Established in 1978 in memory of Napoleon I and Napoleon III. Formerly: (1990) Grand Prix du Souvenir Napoleonien.

5215
Fondation pour la Liberte de la Presse
23, rue Jean Giraudoux
F-75116 Paris, France
Phone: 1 4723 67 47

5216
Prix de la Meilleure une Journalistique - Les Libertes d'Or
For recognition of the best edition of a newspaper published in the French language. A trophy is awarded annually. Established in 1985.

5217
Prix de la Presse Libre - Les Libertes d'Or
To recognize a journalist who has not given in to pressure. A trophy is awarded annually. Established in 1982.

5218
Prix du Journalisme d'Investigation - Les Libertes d'Or
For recognition of the best investigative reporting published in French by a French speaking reporter. A trophy is awarded annually. Established in 1985.

5219
Prix du Livre Historique d'Investigation - Les Libertes d'Or
To recognize a book that investigates an historical subject in order to resolve contradictory evidence. Books published before December 31 each year are eligible. A trophy is awarded annually. Established in 1985.

5220
Prix du Livre Media ou du Livre d'Investigation - Les Libertes d'Or
To recognize a book of investigative journalism on some subject that the press has not covered. Books published in the French language by December 31 are eligible. A trophy is awarded annually. Established in 1985.

5221
Fondation pour l'Enfance Anne-Aymone Giscard d'Estaing
8, rue des Jardins Saint-Paul
F-75004 Paris, France
Phone: 1 42745303
Fax: 1 42726719

5222
Prix Scientifique/Prix Innovante/Prix Media
To encourage the study, research, and original initiatives in the field of child abuse. Three monetary prizes are awarded annually. Established in 1985. Formerly: Prix Scientifique/Prix Encouragements/Prix Artistique.

5223
Fondation Simone et Cino del Duca
10, rue Alfred de Vigny
F-75008 Paris, France
Phone: 1 4766 01 21

5224
Prix Mondial Cino del Duca
To reward and promote a writer whose work is, in a scientific or literary form, a message of modern humanism. Nominees are selected by a jury and applications are not solicited. A monetary award of 200,000 French francs is awarded annually in October. Established in 1969 by Madame Simone del Duca in memory of her husband. The Foundation also offers maintenance and traveling grants.

5225
Fondation Singer-Polignac
43, avenue Georges-Mandel
F-75116 Paris, France
Phone: 1 47273866
Fax: 1 53709960

5226
Singer-Polignac Grants
For recognition of outstanding work in the field of science, art, literature, or music. French citizens are eligible. Established in 1945 in memory of Princess Edmond de Polignac (1865-1943).

5227
Food and Wines from France/SOPEXA
43/45, rue de Naples
F-75008 Paris, France   Phone: 1 4294 41 00

5228
Grand Prix SOPEXA du Sommelier
To recognize the winner of the French Wine and Spirits Sommelier Competition. National-title-winning sommeliers from around the world in 18 regional competitions compete in the promotion and serving of French wines and spirits. An international panel of judges assess each candidate's professionalism in service and the harmony of food and wine, and test each on both practical and theoretical knowledge of French wine and spirits. Fine glassware, magnums of wine, and trips are awarded biennially. Established in 1986. Additional information is available from Food and Wines from France, c/o Amy Albert, Director of Public Relations, 24 East 21st Street, New York, NY 10010, phone: (212) 477-9800, fax: (212) 473-4315.

5229
**Foundation for National Defense Studies
(Fondation pour les Etudes de Defense Nationale)**
Hotel National des Invalides   Phone: 1 4705 12 07
F-75007 Paris, France   Fax: 1 4555 39 29

5230
Prix Amiral Castex
To recognize a work written in French contributing to the development of defense strategy or the understanding of contemporary strategic problems. Works published during the preceding year are eligible. Noninations and applications may be submitted by late February or early March. A monetary prize and medal are awarded annually in October. Established in 1987 in memory of Admiral Raoul Castex, a French military theorist known for his writing.

5231
**Four Juries Prize
(Prix Meridien des Quatres Jurys)**
Address unknown.

5232
Hassan II des Quatre Jurys
To recognize a young author of a novel who was a candidate for one of the important French literary prizes such as the Goncourt Prize, the Renaudot Prize, the Femina Prize, or the Interallie Prize, but who failed to become a winner. A monetary prize of 30,000 French francs and a week in Morocco are awarded annually. Established in 1952 by Jean-Pierre Dorian.

5233
J. M. Fournier Productions
45, rue La Boetie
F-75008 Paris, France   Phone: 1 4562 69 71

5234
World Music Masters
For recognition of outstanding pianists. The competition is open exclusively to finalists of other international music competitions. Applications are accepted from individuals under 35 years of age. The deadline is March 15. A monetary prize of $30,000 and a trophy are awarded as well as engagements in London, Paris, Munich, Vienna, and other large cities and festivals. Awarded annually. Established in 1989 by Jean-Marie Fournier. Sponsored by Philip Morris France S.A.

5235
**France
Grande Chancellerie de la Legion d'Honneur**
1, rue de Solferino
F-75700 Paris, France   Phone: 1 45559516

5236
**National Order of Merit
(Ordre Merite)**
For recognition of distinguished merit either in public office, civil or military, or for special services rendered in private enterprises. The Order of Merit is composed of chevaliers, officers, and commanders. The dignitaries of the order are the Grand Officers and the Grand Cross. The insignia of the Order of Merit is a star with six double branches in blue enamel crowned by a ring of interwoven oak leaves. The center of the star is encircled by interlaced laurel leaves; the obverse bears the effigy of the Republic with "Republique Francaise" engraved on the exergue; the reverse bears two tricolor flags with the inscription: "Ordre National du Merite" and the date" Decembre 1963." The insignia of chevalier is in silver, is worn on the left side of the breast and is attached by a French blue moire ribbon. The Grand Master determines by decree, for a three-year period, the number of proposals of nomination or of promotion which the ministers and the chancellor of the order are authorized to present to him. Nominations and promotions are enacted by decree of the President of the Republic. Foreigners may be recognized by this Order. Established in 1963.

5237
**National Order of the Legion of Honor
(Ordre de Legion d'Honneur)**
This, the highest Order of France, is given for recognition of eminent service to France. The national Order of the Legion of Honor comprises five grades: chevalier or knight, officer, commander, grand officer, and grand cross. Nominations and promotions are made by decree signed by the President of the Republic. A twenty-year period of distinguished service in the public office or 25 years of prominence in a professional activity is required to be named chevalier. A person cannot be promoted to a higher rank in the order unless he or she has been the holder of a lower rank for a specified number of years. Nomination of foreigners is through the sponsorship of the French Ministry of Foreign Affairs. A five-double-pointed star surmounted by a laurel leaf is awarded. Established in 1802 by Napoleon Bonaparte.

5238
**National Order of the Liberation
(Ordre de la Liberation)**
To recognize individuals or military and civilian groups for acts of heroism or distinguished service at great personal cost and in the face of great danger during the liberation of France and her overseas territories. The order has only one class, namely, companion of the liberation, and its grand master was General de Gaulle. The unique badge of the Order of Liberation consists of an ecu (oblong plaque) surmounted by a broadsword overlaid with the Lorraine Cross, and on the reverse side the inscription, "Patriam Servando, Victoriam Tulit." The black and green ribbon of moire silk is a symbol of the mother country's mourning and hope. Established in 1940 by General de Gaulle in Brazzaville. The Cross of the Liberation, worn immediately below the Legion of Honor, was not awarded after January 23, 1946.

5239
**France
Ministry of Agriculture and Forestry
(France
Ministere de l'Agriculture et Foret)**
78, rue de Varenne   Phone: 1 4955 49 55
F-75700 Paris, France   Fax: 1 4555 95 50

5240
Ordre du Merite Agricole
For recognition of an outstanding contribution in the field of agriculture.

5241

Prix Sully-Olivier-de-Serres
To recognize a farmer or a member of a farmer's family for a work of unpublished fiction. The deadline for entry is October 16. Publication of the manuscript is awarded at the Salon du Livre in Paris. Established in 1990. Sponsored by the Societe Shering. The following additional prizes are also given: Prix Eugene-Le-Roy, Prix Michel-Auge-Laribe for a work on rural life concerning the farm economy or other social aspect, Prix Lecouteaux for the best monograph, and Prix de Theses.

5242

France
Ministry of Defense
(France
Ministere de la Defense)
14, rue Saint Dominique
F-75700 Paris, France					Phone: 1 4555 95 20

5243

Croix de Guerre
To recognize fighting units for feats of arms and acts of devotion. Civilians, men or women, towns, various institutions, in combat areas, and foreigners mentioned in Army orders as having rendered distinguished services in the front line are eligible. The holders of the Croix de Guerre do not constitute an order and have no degrees of rank, the number of clasps attached to the ribbon being the only token of special distinction. The names of recipients are listed only on the military records. The medal, Florentine bronze, 35 millimeters in diameter, consists of a cross with four branches supported on two crossed swords. On the obverse, there is an effigy of the Republic wearing a Phrygian (Liberty) cap, a wreath of laurel, and the inscription "Republicque Francaise." On the reverse, there is the date. Established in 1915; confirmed in 1921 for Theaters of Overseas Operations (T.O.E.) and again in September 1939.

5244

Medaille Militaire
To reward acts of bravery and distinguished military service. Noncommissioned officers and soldiers are eligible. The award is by decree of the President of the Republic. Established in 1852.

5245

Medal of the French Resistance
To recognize and reward the "resistance of the French people against the enemy and his accomplices since June 18, 1940." An insignia, consisting of a bronze medal with the Lorraine cross, suspended from a black ribbon with red horizontal stripes is awarded. Established in 1943 by the National Committee for Free France.

5246

Prix Science et Defense
For recognition of outstanding research work or studies which advance the science and technology in fields pertaining to national defense. The deadline for nominations is April 15. A monetary prize of 120,000 French francs is awarded annually. Established in 1983. Additional information is available from Mission Recherche, Delegation General pour l'Armement, 14 rue Saint Dominique, F-75997 Paris, France.

5247

France
Ministry of Youth and Sports
(France
Ministere de la Jeunesse et des Sports)
78, rue Olivier de Serres					Phone: 1 4828 40 00
F-75739 Paris Cedex 15, France				Phone: 1 4651 39 26

5248

International Festival of Sport Films
(Festival International du Film Sportif)
To recognize outstanding professional films and videos on sports themes. Productions may be submitted in the following categories: (1) Animation; (2) Documentary; (3) Fiction; (4) Report; (5) Edited; and (6) Sport and Health. The Commission chooses four films (only one of which is full-length) to represent each country in the competition. The following prizes are awarded: (1) Prix du President de la Republic; (2) Prix du Comite International Olympique; (3) Prix du Ministere de la Jeunesse et des Sports; (4) Prix de la Ville de Rennes; and (5) Prix CIDALC Nicolas Pillat, a special jury prize. Trophies and certificates are awarded biennially. Established in 1965 by Comite International pour la Diffusion des Arts et Lettres par le Cinema. Additional information is available from Mairie de Rennes, B.P. 26A, F-35031 Rennes Cedex, France, phone: 9928 55 55. Sponsored by Ville de Rennes, Centre National de la Cinematographie, Maison de la Culture de Rennes, and Comite International pour la Diffusion des Arts et des Lettres par le Cinema - CIDALC.

5249

Youth Award
To recognize a film at the Festival de Cannes. A jury of seven young people from 18 to 25 years of age chosen by the Ministry of Youth and Sports selects the film of the festival. A trophy is awarded annually in May, during the Cannes International Film Festival. Established in 1982 by the Ministry of Youth and Sports. Formerly: Prix de la Jeunesse.

5250

France
Office of the Prime Minister
57, rue de Varenne
F-75700 Paris, France					Phone: 1 4275 80 00

5251

Prix des droits de l'homme
To recognize an individual for a contribution to human rights. A monetary prize of 200,000 French francs is awarded. Established in 1987.

5252

La France
7, rue de Molitg
F-66500 Prades, France

5253

Prix de la Nouvelle de la France
To encourage the development of the novel as a literary form. Subscribers to the La France review are eligible. The following monetary prizes are awarded annually: (1) First prize - 2,500 French francs; and (2) Second prize - 1,000 French francs. Established in 1982. Sponsored by the City of Perpignan.

5254

French Center of Comparative Law
(Centre Francais de Droit Compare)
28, rue Saint-Guillaume					Phone: 1 44398614
F-75007 Paris, France					Fax: 1 44398628

5255

Dissertation Prize
For recognition of the best thesis on foreign or comparative law. Dissertations completed in the preceding twelve months may be submitted. A monetary prize of 2,000 French francs is awarded annually. Established in 1951. Formerly: Prix de These.

5256
French Federation of Booksellers
(Federation francaise des syndicats de libraires)
259, rue St. Honore
F-75001 Paris, France

5257
French Booksellers Prize
(Prix des Libraires)
To recognize the author of the best novel in the French language. Generally, only French novelists are considered. Honorary recognition is awarded annually. Special promotions are carried out featuring the prize announcement. Established in 1955.

5258
French Federation of Tennis
(Federation Francaise de Tennis)
2, avenue Gordon-Bennett
Stade Roland-Garros
F-75016 Paris, France
Phone: 1 47434800
Fax: 1 46516724

5259
French Open
(Championnats Internationaux de France)
To recognize tennis players in nine different events. Five senior events are held: Men's Singles - Coupe des Mousquetaires; Ladies' Singles - Coupe Suzanne Lenglen; Men's Doubles - Coupe Jacques Brugnon; Ladies' Doubles; and Mixed Doubles. Four junior events are also held: Junior Singles (Boys and Girls); and Junior Doubles (Boys and Girls). Players and teams are accepted based on their rankings. Trophies and monetary prizes totaling 50,000,000 French francs are awarded at the Roland Garros Stadium. Established in 1891.

5260
Paris Open
(Open de la Ville de Paris)
To recognize tennis players in two different events: men's singles and men's doubles. Players are nominated according to their rankings. A trophy is awarded in each event annually, at the end of October. Established in 1986 by Jacques Chirac, Mayor of Paris, and Philippe Chatrier, president of the French Tennis Federation. Formerly: Trophee Poirier.

5261
French Foundation for Medical Research
(Fondation pour la Recherche Medicale)
54, rue de Varenne
F-75007 Paris, France
Phone: 1 44397575
Fax: 1 44397599

5262
Grand Prix de la Fondation pour la Recherche Medicale
To recognize outstanding research of an individual, a team, or several researchers. A monetary award of 300,000 French francs is awarded biennially. Established in 1981.

5263
Prix de la Fondation pour la Recherche Medicale
To provide prizes for young researchers in several medical disciplines which are announced each year.

5264
Prix Delahautemaison
To recognize an individual for outstanding contributions to laboratory research. French laboratory researchers are eligible. The award is presented in alternate years in the following categories: nephrology research and cancer research. A monetary award of up to 100,000 French francs is presented biennially. Established in 1977.

5265
Prix Rosen de Cancerologie
For recognition of outstanding research in cancer. Well-known French researchers are eligible. A monetary prize of up to 200,000 French francs is awarded annually. Established in 1969.

5266
French-Language Cultural and Technical Union
(Union Culturelle et Technique de Langue Francaise)
7, boulevard Lannes
F-75116 Paris, France
Phone: 1 4504 56 79

5267
Prix Jean Mermoz
For recognition of the contribution of a French national, living abroad, to the promotion of the French language and culture. A medal and a trip to the offical reception at the Senate in Paris is awarded biennially. Established in 1976. Co-sponsored by the Ministere des Relations Exterieures, and the Ministere de la Culture.

5268
Prix Leopold Sedar Senghor
To encourage foreign individuals who are not officials for a work in favor of French cultural values.

5269
UCTF Awards
To facilitate contacts between peoples and national groups of French thought, language and culture. Awards are presented annually.

5270
French League for Animal Rights
(Ligue Francaise des Droits de l'Animal)
61, rue du Cherche-Midi
F-75006 Paris, France
Phone: 1 4222 25 91

5271
Prix de Biologie Alfred Kastler
To encourage research and experimental methods that are not traumatic for animals. French-speaking researchers in the fields of biology, medicine, and pharmacy, are eligible. A monetary prize of 25,000 French francs is awarded annually in January. Established in 1985 in memory of Professor Alfred Kastler, French winner of the 1966 Nobel Prize of Physics and president of the League from 1979 to 1984. Formerly: Prix Alfred Kastler.

5272
French Ministry of Culture and Communication
(France
Ministere de la Culture et de la Communication)
DIC
3, rue de Valois
F-75042 Paris Cedex 01, France
Phone: 1 4015 87 78
Fax: 1 4286 97 36

5273
Grand Prix National de la Chanson
For recognition of an outstanding contribution to song by a composer, author, or singer. A monetary prize of 50,000 French francs is awarded annually. Established in 1979.

5274
Grand Prix National de la Creation Audiovisuelle
To recognize a writer, director, actor, personality, or organization for a work or a career that has served French television. A monetary prize of 50,000 French francs is awarded annually at the Festival International des Programmes Audiovisuels in Cannes during January. Established in 1990.

5275
Grand Prix National de la Creation Industrielle
For recognition of an outstanding work in industrial design. A monetary prize of 50,000 French francs is awarded annually. Established in 1985.

5276
Grand Prix National de la Danse
For recognition of an outstanding contribution in the field of dance. A monetary prize of 50,000 French francs is awarded annually. Established in 1979. Additional information is available from Direction de la musique et de la danse, 53, rue Saint Dominique, F-75007 Paris, France.

5277
Grand Prix National de la Museographie
For recognition in the field of museum studies. A monetary prize of 50,000 French francs is awarded. Established in 1986.

5278
Grand Prix National de la Musique
For recognition of an outstanding contribution to music. A monetary prize of 50,000 French francs is awarded annually. Established in 1967. Additional information is available from Direction de la musique et de la danse, 53, rue Saint Dominique, F-75007 Paris, France.

5279
Grand Prix National de la Peinture
To recognize French painters for the quality of their complete bodies of work. A monetary prize of 50,000 French francs is awarded annually. Established in 1952 as the Grand Prix National des Arts. In 1979, three separate grand prizes in painting, sculpture, and graphic arts began to be awarded. Additional information is available from Delegation aux arts plastiques, 27, avenue d'l'Opera, F-75001 Paris, France. Formerly: Grand Prix National des Arts.

5280
Grand Prix National de la Photographie
To recognize a photographer for outstanding quality in a collection of works. A monetary prize of 50,000 French francs is awarded annually. Established in 1978.

5281
Grand Prix National de la Poesie
To recognize poets whose entire works have contributed to French literature. Poets who write in French are eligible. A monetary prize of 50,000 French francs is awarded annually. Established in 1981.

5282
Grand Prix National de la Sculpture
To recognize sculptors for outstanding quality in a collection of their work. A monetary prize of 50,000 French francs is awarded annually. Established in 1952 as the Grand Prix National des Arts. In 1979, three separate grand prizes in Painting, Sculpture and Graphic Arts began to be awarded. Additional information is available from Delegation aux arts plastiques, 27, avenue de l'Opera, F-75001 Paris, France. Formerly: Grand Prix National des Arts.

5283
Grand Prix National de la Traduction
To recognize an individual for an outstanding translation of a literary work into French. A monetary prize of 50,000 French francs is awarded annually. Established in 1985.

5284
Grand Prix National de l'Archeologie
For recognition of an outstanding achievement in the field of French archeology. A monetary prize of 50,000 French francs is awarded biennially. Established in 1977.

5285
Grand Prix National de l'Architecture
For recognition of an outstanding contribution to architecture. A monetary prize of 50,000 French francs is awarded annually. Established in 1976. Additional information is available from Division du Patrimoine, 3, rue de Valois, F-75001 Paris, France.

5286
Grand Prix National de l'Entreprise Culturelle
For recognition of an outstanding cultural undertaking. A monetary prize of 50,000 French francs is awarded annually. Established in 1988.

5287
Grand Prix National des Arts Graphique
To recognize French graphic designers or artists for the quality of their body of work. A monetary prize of 50,000 French francs is awarded annually. Established in 1952 as the Grand Prix National des Arts. In 1979, three separate grand prizes in painting, sculpture and graphic arts began to be awarded. Additional information is available from Delegation aux Arts plastiques, 27, avenue de l'Opera, F-75001 Paris, France. Formerly: Grand Prix National des Arts.

5288
Grand Prix National des Lettres
To recognize a man or a woman writer whose literary work illustrates particularly good French literature. Individuals who write in French are eligible. A monetary prize of 50,000 French francs is awarded annually. Established in 1950.

5289
Grand Prix National des Metiers d'Art
For recognition in the field of art. A monetary prize of 50,000 French francs is awarded annually. Established in 1981.

5290
Grand Prix National d'Histoire
To recognize writers for their outstanding contributions to the knowledge of French history. A monetary prize of 50,000 French francs is awarded annually. Established in 1977.

5291
Grand Prix National du Cinema
To recognize authors, directors, or actors for their contributions to French filmmaking. A monetary prize of 50,000 French francs is awarded annually. Established in 1974.

5292
Grand Prix National du Cirque
For recognition of outstanding contributions to the circus. A monetary prize of 50,000 French francs is awarded annually. Established in 1979. Additional information is available from Direction du theatre et des spectacles, 53, rue Saint Dominique, F-75007 Paris, France.

5293
Grand Prix National du Patrimoine
For recognition of contributions in the field of French heritage and culture. A monetary prize of 50,000 French francs is awarded annually. Established in 1978. Additional information is available from Direction du Patrimoine, 3, rue de Valois, F-75001 Paris, France.

5294
Grand Prix National du Theatre
For recognition of an exceptional theatrical personality (author, director, staff manager, or actor) for the whole of his or her work. A monetary prize of 50,000 French francs is awarded annually. Established in 1969. Additional information is available from Direction du Theatre et des Spectacles, 53 rue Saint Dominique, F-75007 Paris, France.

5295
Order of the Academic Palms
(Palmes Academiques)
To reward distinguished service in public education. The Order consists of the grades of Chevalier, Officer, and Commander. Nominees should have rendered at least 15 years of service in public education to be nominated for the grade of Chevalier and at least five years for the grades of Officer and Commander. The deadlines for nomination are January 1 and July 14. The Order was established on October 4, 1955 to replace the honorary distinctions of the Academic Palms, which had been founded in 1808.

5296
French Society for Medical Hydrology and Climatology
1, rue Monticelli
F-75014 Paris, France   Phone: 1 45406330

5297
French Society for Medical Hydrology and Climatology Prize
For recognition of research or clinical work in the field of thermal therapeutics or climatology. Scientists without regard to nationality are eligible. A monetary prize is awarded biennially. Established in 1968.

5298
Fusion/Biennale Internationale de Limoges - Arts Du Feu
7, boulevard de Fleurus   Phone: 5534 5827
F-87000 Limoges, France   Fax: 5532 6822

5299
Biennale Internationale de Limoges
To recognize outstanding worldwide creations in the field of contemporary enameling and porcelain. Honorary awards are presented biennially. Established in 1971 to honor Georges Magadoux, founder of the biennale.

5300
Fyssen Foundation
194, rue de Rivoli   Phone: 1 42975316
F-75001 Paris, France   Fax: 1 42601795

5301
International Prize
(Prix de la Fondation Fyssen)
To recognize an individual for a major contribution to the progress of knowledge in the fields of research supported by the Foundation such as ethology-psychology, neurobiology, anthropology-ethnology, and human paleontology. The 1994 topic is "Developmental Psychology in Humans." The deadline for nominations is September 1. A monetary award of 200,000 French francs and a diploma are awarded annually. Established in 1980.

5302
Geological Society of France
(Societe Geologique de France)
77, rue Claude-Bernard   Phone: 1 4331 77 35
F-75005 Paris, France   Fax: 1 4535 79 10

5303
Prix Barbier
For recognition in the field of civil engineering, hydrogeology, metallurgy, and mineral substances. A medal is awarded biennially. Established in 1987 by a gift of R. Barbier.

5304
Prix Barrabe
For recognition of methods in the fields of physics, chemistry, numerics, geophysics, and planetology. A medal is awarded biennially. Established in 1962 by Madame Barrabe.

5305
Prix de Lamothe
For recognition in the fields of geology, micropaleontology, and biostratigraphy. A medal is awarded biennially. Established in 1935 by a bequest of L.J. de Lamothe.

5306
Prix Fondation Pierre Pruvost
For recognition in the field of structural geology. A medal is awarded biennially. Established in 1960 by Pierre Pruvost.

5307
Prix Fontannes
To recognize the French author of the best stratigraphic work published during the last five years. A medal is awarded biennially. Established in 1888 by a bequest of F. Fontannes.

5308
Prix Gaudry
This, the greatest distinction of the Society, is given to recognize a French or foreign geologist or paleontologist. A diploma is awarded. Established in 1910 by a bequest of A. Gaudry.

5309
Prix Georges Millot
To recognize individuals for distinguished scientific or technical work, particularly in the earth sciences. Individuals who have developed applications of earth sciences, given service to the Academy, or demonstrated scientific research in laboratories, institutes, or French offices are eligible. A medal is awarded alternately with the Prix Prestwich. Established in 1979 by George Millot.

5310
Prix Gosselet
For recognition of a work of applied geology. A medal is awarded biennially. Established in 1910 by Jules Gosselet.

5311
Prix Jacques Bourcart
For recognition in the fields of geology concerning sediment and the oceans. A medal is awarded biennially. Established in 1976.

5312
Prix Leon Bertrand
To recognize a geologist for work in the field of applied geology. Members of the Society are eligible. Awarded biennially. Established in 1949 by Leon Bertrand.

5313
Prix Prestwich
To encourage new research and to recognize one or several geologists, men or women from a country other than France, who have displayed a zeal for the progress of the science of geology. A medal is awarded biennially. Established in 1902 by a bequest of Sir J. Prestwich.

5314
Prix Raymond et Madeleine Furon
For recognition in the field of endogenous geology. A medal is awarded biennially. Established in 1977 by Raymond Furon.

5315

Prix Viquesnel

To encourage geological studies and to recognize the author of a work published in the *Bulletin* or the *Memoires*. Members of the Society of any nationality are eligible. Awarded biennially. Established in 1875 by Madame Viquesnel.

5316

Prix Wegmann

For recognition of a work concerning the history of geology. Established in 1984 by a bequest of E. Wegmann.

5317

Prix van Straelen

The Society awards 15,000 FF annually. Established in 1993 in memory of Professor Victor Van Straelen.

5318

Grand Prix de la Publicite
c/o Ecole Superieure de Commerce de
  Paris
79, avenue de la Republique
F-75007 Paris, France   Phone: 1 4355 53 33

5319

Advertising Grand Prize
(Grand Prix de la Publicite)

For recognition of achievement in the advertising field. Advertisements broadcast in Paris and its suburbs are eligible. Selection is based on questionnaires completed by residents of Paris. A medal and certificate are awarded annually in May. Established in 1959.

5320

Les Grandes Compagnies de l'Est Parisien
79, avenue de Saint-Mande
F-75012 Paris, France   Phone: 1 4338 37 38

5321

European Cup of Wargame
(Coupe d'Europe de Jeux d'Histoire)

For recognition of achievement in a wargame competition. Members of an official team of wargame are eligible. A bowl and medal are awarded annually at the European convention. Established in 1985. Sponsored by the Mayor of the City of Paris. Additional information is available from Mr. Claussmann Laurent, 11, rue Emile Level, F-75017 Paris, France, phone: 4627 91 87.

5322

Tournoi de Paris de Jeux d'Histoire Antico - medieval

For recognition of achievement in a wargame competition of the ancient and medieval periods. Members of the French Club of Wargames are eligible. A cup is awarded. Established in 1986. Additional information is available from Claussmann Laurent, 11, rue Emile Level, F-75017 Paris, France, phone: 4627 91 87.

5323

Group for Advanced Analytical Methods
(Groupe pour l'Avancement des Science Analytiques)
88, boulevard Malesherbes   Phone: 1 4563 93 04
F-75008 Paris, France   Fax: 1 4953 04 34

Formerly: (1989) Groupement pour l'Avancement des Methodes Spectroscofiques et Physico-chimiques d'Anolyte.

5324

GAMS Prize
(Prix du GAMS)

For recognition of contributions to analytical chemistry. Individuals who have at least one French publication in the field of analytical chemistry are eligible. A monetary prize is awarded annually. Established in 1956.

5325

Groupe Consultatif International de Recherche sur le Colza
174, avenue Victor Hugo   Phone: 1 44347246
F-75116 Paris, France   Fax: 1 47559409

5326

Superior Scientist Award

To recognize superior scientific innovations that have played a major role in rapeseed research. A medal is awarded every four years at the International Rapeseed Conference. Established in 1985. The next award is scheduled for 1995.

5327

Guilde Europeenne du Raid
11, rue de Vaugirard   Phone: 1 4326 97 52
F-75006 Paris, France   Fax: 1 4634 75 45

5328

Les Ecrans De L'Aventure International Festival of Adventure Documentaries

For recognition of documentary 16mm or 35mm films or videos about any kind of adventure, such as mountain expeditions, arctic travels, sailing races around the the world, ballooning, underwater diving, speleology, outstanding sport performances, and any dramatic events that are milestones in adverturism. Within this framework, the festival attempts to bring together the best of recently produced or non-released films from all parts of the world. The following prizes are awarded: Grand Prix du Festival, Prix Special du Jury, seven gold medals, Prix de la Presse, and honorary mentions by the jury. Any number of films may be submitted by an entrant. Awarded annually. Established in 1977. Sponsored by La Plagne, a ski resort located in Dijon - Bourgogne. Formerly: Festival Internationl du Film d'Aventure de la Plagne (La Plagne International Real Life Adventure Film Festival).

5329

IBM France
Direction Scientifique
36, ave. Raymond Poincare
F-85116 Paris, France

5330

Prix Scientifique IBM France

For recognition in the fields of mathematics, computer science, physics, and materials science. French researchers under 33 years of age in mathematics and computer science and 38 years of age in physics and materials science are eligible. Four monetary prizes, one in each discipline, of 100,000 French francs each are awarded. Established in 1987.

5331

Institut de Biologie Physicochimique
13, rue Pierre et Marie Curie
F-75005 Paris, France

5332

Prix Nine Choucroun

To recognize a young researcher for work in the field of physio-chemical biology. Researchers under 30 years of age are eligible. A monetary prize of 1,400 French francs is awarded. Established in 1986.

5333

Institut de France
23, quai de Conti
F-75006 Paris, France   Phone: 1 4329 55 10

5334

Fondation Jaffe
To encourage students and teachers of science to undertake experiments destined to aid humanity. A monetary prize of 50,000 French francs is awarded by the Institut on the recommendation of the Academie des Sciences.

5335

Fondation Memain-Pelletier
To recognize a scholar or physician who, by his works or discoveries, has contributed the most to relieve humanity of the many maladies that afflict it. A monetary prize of 10,000 French francs is awarded by the Institut on the recommendation of the Academie des Sciences.

5336

Prix Alfred Verdaguer
For recognition of outstanding work in the arts, literature, or science. Recommendations are offered alternately by the Academie francaise and Academie des Sciences.

5337

Prix Andre Lequeux
To recognize a French researcher for work in the field of science or literature that is unselfish or useful. Established in 1982.

5338

Prix Balleroy
For recognition of a poet and a painter. The prize is awarded alternately to a poet by the Academie francaise and to a painter by the Academie des Beaux-Arts. Unknown or little known artists who have talent are eligible. Awarded every five years.

5339

Prix Botiaux-Dulac
For recognition of persons or institutions that contribute to the protection of animals and an increase in understanding between man and animals.

5340

Prix d'Aschen-Presles
For recognition of acts of unselfishness. Awarded by the Academie francaise.

5341

Prix d'Aumale
For recognition of outstanding intellectual works or for recognition of first efforts that deserve encouragement. The prize may be awarded posthumously to assist the family. The prize is divided among the five academies of the Institut for awarding.

5342

Prix Georges Bizet
For recognition of a music composer. Awarded by the Academie des Beaux-Arts.

5343

Prix Hercule Catenacci
To encourage the publication of beautifully illustrated books of poetry, literature, history, archaeology, or music. Each of the five Academies awards this prize annually.

5344

Prix Injalbert
To recognize a young sculptor. Awarded by the Academie des Beaux-Arts.

5345

Prix Jeanne Burdy
To recognize a painter. Awarded biennially on the recommendation of the Academie des Beaux-Arts by the Institut. Established in 1983.

5346

Prix Jules et Louis Jeanbernat et Barthelemy de Ferrari Doria
To recognize a young French author for a book of literature, science, or art. The prize is awarded alternately by each of the five Academies. The prize should not be divided. Established by Emmanuel Jeanbernat in memory of her two sons who died for France.

5347

Prix Osiris
For recognition of a discovery or outstanding work in the field of science, literature, art, industry, or generally any field that affects the public. Awarded every three years by a special commission whose members are from each of the five Academies.

5348

Prix Paul Belmondo
For recognition of a work of art that embodies the values, morals and humanity of the sculptor, Paul Belmondo. A monetary prize of 60,000 French francs is awarded annually. Established by Jean-Paul Belmondo.

5349

Prix Volney
For recognition of a work of comparative philology. Awarded by the Institut on the recommendation of the Academie des Inscriptions et Belles Lettres.

5350

Institut de France
Academie des Beaux Arts
Institut de France
23, Quai de Conti
F-75006 Paris Cedex 06, France   Phone: 1 44414320

5351

Fondation Dulac
For the restoration of Catholic churches of France of artistic value. A monetary prize is awarded annually.

5352

Grand Prix d'Architecture de l'Academie des Beaux-Arts
To recognize architects or architectural students under 30 years of age for outstanding work. The competition consists of three phases: candidates submit a draft on the subject proposed by the Academy, 20 candidates who have the most interesting drafts submit a sketch, and 10 candidates who have the best sketches submit an architectural project. The architect of the best project is the grand prize winner. The following awards are presented: grand prize - a monetary prize of 50,000 francs and Prix Charles Abella; second prize - 25,000 francs and Prix Andre Arfvidson; and thrid prize - 10,000 francs and Prix Paul Arfvidson. Awarded annually.

5353

Prix Achille Fould-Stirbey
For recognition of a painting of excellent design and color in the grand French humanist tradition. An artist may receive the prize only one time. Three monetary prizes of 25,000, 15,000, and 10,000 French francs are awarded annually at the Salon des Artistes francais.

5354

Prix Achille Leclere
For recognition of the best architectural project on a specific subject assigned by the Academy. Architects under 31 years of age are eligible. Collaboration in the execution of the projects is not permitted. The prize

may not be awarded to the same person more than once. A monetary prize is awarded annually.

5355

Prix Alfred Verdaguer

For recognition of works of art. Prizes are awarded in alternate years by one of the three academies: the Academie francaise, Academie des Sciences, and Academie des Beaux Arts. A monetary prize is awarded triennially.

5356

Prix Alphonse Cellier

To recognize a painter who is a student of l'Ecole des Beaux-Arts and is less than 30 years of age. Awarded annually.

5357

Prix Alphonse de Neuville et Sanford Saltus

For recognition of a military painting exhibited at the expositions of the Salon des Artistes Francais. A monetary prize is awarded triennially.

5358

Prix Andre Caplet

To recognize a music composer for the remarkable quality of his work. Composers of less than 40 years of age are eligible. A monetary prize is awarded biennially.

5359

Prix Antoine-Nicolas Bailly

For recognition of an architectural work or a publication on architecture. For two consecutive times, the prize is awarded to a French architect; then on the third time, to a French author. A monetary prize is awarded every four years.

5360

Prix Ary Scheffer

For recognition of the best copperplate engraving exhibited at the Salon des Artistes Francais. A monetary prize is awarded biennially.

5361

Prix Auguste Durand et Edouard Ordonneau

For recognition of a copper-plate engraving exhibited at the Salon des Artistes Francais. A monetary prize is awarded every four years.

5362

Prix Balleroy

To recognize an unknown or little known painter. This prize of the Institut is awarded by the Academie des Beaux-Arts every four years.

5363

Prix Bastien-Lepage

To recognize a French painter who has an exhibition at the Salon des Artistes Francais. A monetary prize is awarded annually.

5364

Prix Bordin

For recognition of the best book on painting, sculpture, engraving, architecture, or music. Awards are given in alternate years in the categories of painting, sculpture, engraving, architecture, and music. A monetary prize is awarded annually.

5365

Prix Breaute

For recognition of a painting, a sculpture, or an engraving exhibited at the Salon de la Societe des Artistes francais. Awards are given in alternate years in the of painting, sculpture, and engraving. Awarded annually.

5366

Prix Brizard

To recognize an exhibitor of an oil painting at the Salon des Artistes Francais who is under 28 years of age. To be eligible, a painter must be French or a naturalized citizen. Awards are given in alternate years in landscape and seascape genres. Paintings that place third and above at the Exposition are eligible. A monetary prize is awarded triennially.

5367

Prix Catenacci

For recognition of outstanding contributions in the categories of interior or exterior ornamentation of a building, garden, or public square and publication of deluxe illustrated books. Two equal monetary prizes are awarded annually.

5368

Prix Ch. M. Tornov-Loeffler

For recognition of the best musical composition of the past two or four years. Composers who are descended from at least four French generations are eligible. A monetary prize is awarded every two or four years.

5369

Prix Chartier

For recognition of a chamber music composition. French composers are eligible. A monetary prize is awarded biennially.

5370

Prix Chaudesaigues

To recognize a young architect. French architects who are under 32 years of age may submit sketches on the assigned subject. The 12 candidates who have the best sketches are invited to present a project based on their sketch. A monetary prize is awarded biennially.

5371

Prix Claude Berthault

To recognize painters, sculptors, or architects who have created a beautiful work of art or decoration in the best French spirit. Artists born in France are eligible. A monetary prize is awarded annually. Awarded by the Fondation de Madame Claude Berthault.

5372

Prix Claude Raphael-Leygues

To recognize a sculptor. A monetary prize of 20,000 francs was awarded. Established in 1981. (Discontinued)

5373

Prix Colmont

To recognize a painter, sculptor or an engraver exhibiting a work at the Salon de la Societe des Artistes francais. Awards are given in alternate years to a painter, a sculptor, and an engraver. A monetary prize of 5,000 francs is awarded annually.

5374

Prix Dagnan-Bouveret

For recognition of a painting, a nude, a portrait, or a simple head, shown at the Salon des Artistes Francais. Members of the Institut de France are not eligible. A monetary prize of 15,000 French francs is awarded annually.

5375

Prix de Dessin Pierre David - Weill

For recognition of excellence in drawing competitions. Artists must be under 30 years of age and, if foreigners, must have lived at least one year in France. All drawing techniques are allowed with the exception of water color, gouache and pastel. Each candidate presents at least ten drawings. Monetary prizes of 20,000 francs, 15,000 francs and 10,000 francs are awarded annually. At least the 50 best entries are publicly exhibited. Sponsored by the Pierre David - Weill Foundation.

5376
Prix de la Fondation Florence Gould
To recognize engravers working in copper plate, wood or lithography, or medals, and to recognize a composer of music. Two monetary prizes of 10,000 francs are awarded annually. Established by Florence Gould, a corresponding member of the Academie des Beaux Arts.

5377
Prix de la Societe Francaise de Gravure
For recognition of copper-plate engravings exhibited at the Salon des Artistes Francais. A monetary prize is awarded biennially.

5378
Prix de Portrait Paul-Louis Weiller
For recognition of a painted portrait or a sculpted bust. Awards are given in an international contest in alternate years in the categories of portrait painting and sculpture. A monetary prize of 30,000 francs is awarded to an artist of any age; and two monetary prizes of 10,000 francs, to an artist under 35 years of age. All works which pass the first selection are exhibited publicly. Awarded annually. Established by Paul Louis Weiller, a member of the l'Academie des Beaux Arts.

5379
Prix de Soussay
For recognition of a libretto, in verse or prose, that has not been presented. A monetary prize is awarded.

5380
Prix des Cathedrales
For recognition of a religious sculpture. French sculptors under 30 years of age are eligible. A monetary prize is awarded biennially. Established by J.B. Dampt, a member of the Institute de France.

5381
Prix Desprez
For recognition of a work by a sculptor. French artists under 35 years of age may submit work completed in France during the preceding two years. A monetary prize is awarded triennially.

5382
Prix Doublemard
To recognize a young sculptor who is preparing for the Rome competition.

5383
Prix du Baron de Joest
For recognition of a discovery or work in the field of art history that is most useful to the public good. A monetary prize is awarded annually by one of the five Academies of the Institut.

5384
Prix Duc
To encourage advanced study of architecture. A monetary prize is awarded every four years.

5385
Prix Dulac
To recognize painters of landscapes exhibited at the Salon des Artistes Francais. A monetary prize is awarded biennially. Established by Pierre-Francois-Simon Dulac.

5386
Prix Dumas-Millier
To recognize a painter or a sculptor. French artists over 45 years of age whose work is inspired by the traditions of the l'Ecole francaise are eligible. Awards are given in alternate years to a painter and a sculptor. A monetary prize is awarded annually.

5387
Prix Estrade-Delcros
For recognition of either a work of fine art, including painting, sculpture, architecture, line engraving or medal engraving, or a work of musical composition. Members of the Academie des Beaux Arts are not eligible. A monetary prize is awarded every five years.

5388
Prix et Fondations Concernant l'Academie de France a Rome
To recognize painters, sculptors, architects, and engravers. Prizes awarded and Foundations awarding prizes are as follows: Fondation Pinette; Fondation Chedanne; Prix Injalbert; Fondation Jean-Paul Alaux; Fondation Daumet; Fondation Redon; Fondation de Mme. Veuve Beule; Fondation Gustave Clausse; Fondation Gustave Germain; Fondation de Caen; and Fondation Marmottan. Monetary awards are for study at the Academie de France in Rome. Awarded annually. Established in 1666.

5389
Prix Eugene Piot
For recognition of a sculpture or painting of a nude child. Awards are given in alternate years in the categories of sculpture and painting. A monetary prize is awarded biennially.

5390
Prix Florent Schmitt
For recognition of distinguished composers. French composers who are over 45 years of age are eligible. Three monetary prizes are awarded biennially.

5391
Prix Francoise Abella
To provide financial assistance to a student of architecture. Awarded annually.

5392
Prix Frederic et Jean de Vernon
To recognize French sculptors and engravers under 40 years of age. Awards are given in alternate years to a sculptor and an engraver. A monetary prize of 8,000 francs is awarded annually.

5393
Prix Gabriel Ferrier
For recognition of a painting exhibited at the Salon de la Societe des Artistes francais. Paintings of figures or history are considered. An artist may be awarded the prize for several years. A monetary prize is awarded biennially.

5394
Prix Georges Bizet
To recognize a composer who has produced a notable work during the preceding five years. Men under 41 years of age are eligible. A monetary prize is awarded biennially.

5395
Prix Georges Wildenstein
To recognize the artists, including painters, sculptors, architects, engravers, musicians and filmmakers, who were granted a fellowship by the French government and a residence in the Casa de Velasquez in Madrid. A monetary prize of 5,000 francs is awarded annually.

5396
Prix Gustave Courtois
For recognition of a painting, a nude, or a portrait, accepted by the Salon des Artistes francais or the Societe Nationale. A monetary prize is awarded biennially.

5397
Prix Gustave-Francois Redon
To enable a French painter who is less than 35 years of age to pursue a career in the arts. A monetary prize of 10,000 French francs is awarded annually.

5398
Prix Haumont
For recognition of a painting of a landscape with figures. French artists under 30 years of age are eligible. A monetary prize is awarded triennially.

5399
Prix Hector Lefuel
For recognition of a painting, sculpture, work of architecture, or musical composition. Awards are given in alternate years in the categories of painting, sculpture, architecture, and musical composition. A monetary prize is awarded annually.

5400
Prix Henri Dauberville
To recognize superior architects or musicians. Prizes are awarded in alternate years to architects and musicians. A monetary prize of 10,000 francs is awarded annually. Established by Henri Dauberville, a corresponding member of the Academie des Beaux Arts.

5401
Prix Henri Lehmann
To recognize a painter who has completed a work that protests the most eloquently against the degradation of art. Paintings or cartoons by artists under 25 years of age are considered. A monetary prize is awarded triennially.

5402
Prix Henriette Renie
For recognition of a composition for harp. Composers of all ages and nationalities are eligible. A monetary prize is awarded triennially.

5403
Prix Houllevigue
For recognition of a remarkable work of painting, sculpture, architecture, engraving, or musical composition; or, for a book on art or art history. A monetary prize is awarded biennially.

5404
Prix J. J. Berger
For recognition of the most oustanding work of art concerning the city of Paris or serving as a decoration in Paris. A monetary prize is awarded every five years by the Academie des Beaux Arts. Awarded annually by one of the five Academies of the Institut.

5405
Prix Jacques Durand
For recognition of a symphonic work or a work of chamber music. French authors may submit published or unpublished compositions. A monetary prize is awarded biennially.

5406
Prix Jean Reynaud
For recognition of the most noteworthy and original work of art produced during the preceding five years. Members of the Institute are not eligible. A monetary prize is awarded every five years.

5407
Prix Jules et Louis Jeanbernat et Barthelemy de Ferrari Doria
For recognition of a work on art by a young French author. A monetary prize is awarded every five years by the Academie des Beaux Arts. Awarded annually by one of the five Academies of the Institut. Established by Emmanuel Jeanbernat, in memory of his two sons who died for France.

5408
Prix Karl Beule
To recognize a painter for a remarkable Oriental style. Painters who exhibited at the Salon des Artistes Francais and have received no other awards are considered. A monetary prize is awarded biennially.

5409
Prix Kastner-Boursault
For recognition of the best book on the history of music published during the preceding three years. A monetary prize is awarded triennially.

5410
Prix Le Guay-Lebrun
To recognize an artist under 40 years of age for a painting, sculpture, or drawing exhibited at the Salon des Artistes Francais. Prizes are awarded in alternate years in the categories of painting, sculpture, and drawing. A monetary prize is awarded annually.

5411
Prix Leclerc - Maria Bouland
To recognize a painter who has received a mark of distinction at the Salon des Artistes Francais. French painters, under 30 years of age, without fortune, are eligible. A monetary prize is awarded annually.

5412
Prix Maurice R... D...
To recognize an artist exhibiting at the Salon des Artistes francais who is noted for the seriousness and the conscience of his work. A monetary prize is awarded biennially.

5413
Prix Maxime David
For recognition of the best portrait miniature shown at the Salon des Artistes Francais. A monetary prize is awarded triennially.

5414
Prix Meurand
To recognize a young landscape or historical painter whose talent has been recognized at the Salon des Artistes Francais. A monetary prize is awarded every four years.

5415
Prix Monbinne
To recognize the composer of a comic opera performed for the first time during the past two years, or a symphonic work if a worthy comic opera has not been written. The symphony may be purely instrumental or with a chant, preferably a religious composition. A monetary prize is awarded triennially.

5416
Prix Nicolo
For recognition of the best melodic composition. A monetary prize is awarded every five years.

5417
Prix Paul Chabas
To recognize a painter whose work is marked by interesting, imaginative qualities. A monetary prize is awarded annually at the Salon de la Societe des Artistes francais.

5418
Prix Paul-Louis Weiller
To recognize painters, sculptors, engravers, and musical composers for overcoming a handicap and accomplishing outstanding work. Awards are given in alternate years to painters or sculptors and engravers or musical composers. Two monetary prizes of 10,000 francs each are awarded annually.

5419
Prix Paul Marmottan
For recognition of a book on art. A monetary prize is awarded annually.

5420
Prix Pinet
For recognition of an original engraving exhibited at the Salon des Artistes Francais. A monetary prize is awarded biennially.

5421
Prix Rene Dumesnil
To recognize composers or writers of works on music. Awards are given in alternate years to the author of a work of music criticism or musicology and the author of a musical composition. A monetary prize of 20,000 French francs is awarded annually.

5422
Prix Richtenberger
For recognition of the best book on the history of 14th, 15th, or 16th century painting. A monetary prize is awarded biennially.

5423
Prix Rossini
For recognition of a composition of lyric or religious music; and for recognition of a poetic work of less than two hundred lines of verse, destined to be set to music. Two monetary prizes are awarded.

5424
Prix Rouyer
For recognition of a survey of French architecture. A monetary prize is awarded every five years.

5425
Prix Ruhlman
To recognize a student architect for the best project in interior design.

5426
Prix Samuel - Rousseau
For recognition of a lyric work that has one or several acts. The competition is open to all French composers who are at least 50 years of age. If the jury feels that no work merits the prize, it is reserved and two are awarded the following session. French musicians are eligible. A monetary prize of 30,000 French francs is awarded triennially.

5427
Prix Susse Freres
To recognize a sculptor for a work in high relief of which the gestures and faces reflect a human sentiment. Sculptors born in France, between the ages of 27 and 35 who are exhibited at the Salon des Artistes Francais are eligible. A monetary prize is awarded annually.

5428
Prix Thorlet
To encourage scholarly works on the history of art, in particular on painting. A monetary prize is awarded annually.

5429
Prix Troyon et Edouard Lemaitre
For recognition of a landscape painting. Artists under 30 years of age who are exhibited at the Salon des Artistes Francais are eligible. A monetary prize is awarded every four years.

5430
Institut de France
Academie des Inscriptions et Belle-Lettres
23, quai de Conti
F-75270 Paris Cedex 06, France   Phone: 1 4326 92 82

5431
Concours des Antiquites de la France
For recognition of the best works (manuscripts or publications within the preceding two years) on French antiquities. Works on numismatics are not accepted. Three medals with a value of 3,000 francs, 2,000 francs and 1,000 francs are awarded annually.

5432
Medaille Georges Perrot
For recognition of the best work on the history of ancient art or Greek archeology. A medal is awarded biennially.

5433
Prix Adolphe Noel-des-Vergers
For recognition of archeological studies or excavations. A monetary prize is awarded every six years.

5434
Prix Alfred Croiset
For recognition of a work or collection of printed works studying Greek language and literature (excluding modern Greek literature or works on epigraphy). A monetary prize is awarded every five years. Established by the Duke of Loubat.

5435
Prix Alfred Dutens
For recognition of the most useful work on linguistics. A monetary prize is awarded every ten years.

5436
Prix Allier de Hauteroche
For recognition of the best work on ancient numismatics appearing during the preceding two years. A monetary prize is awarded biennially.

5437
Prix Ambatielos
For recognition of a work on the history or archaeology of Greece appearing during the preceding year. A monetary prize is awarded annually.

5438
Prix Antoine Meillet
For recognition of an original work on comparative grammar or general linguistics. The author need not be French. A monetary prize is awarded every five years. Established in 1979.

5439
Prix Bordin
For recognition of studies in the following categories: (1) Classical antiquity; (2) Oriental; and (3) Medieval and Renaissance civilization. A monetary prize is awarded alternately in the three categories. Awarded annually.

5440
Prix Brunet
For recognition of the best scholarly bibliographic works published in the preceding three years. A monetary prize is awarded triennially.

5441
Prix Charles and Marguerite Diehl
For recognition of a published work on Byzantine history or the history of Byzantine art. The work must be written in French. A monetary prize is awarded biennially.

5442
Prix Charles Clermont-Ganneau
For recognition of a work or collection of studies on the epigraphy of semitic people (from Syria, Phoenicia, Palestine, Cyprus, Carthage and other Punic colonies) or on the ancient history of these regions (studies

on Syrian history may only go up to the Crusades). A monetary prize is awarded every five years. Established by the Duke of Loubat.

5443
Prix de Chenier
To recognize the author of the best method for teaching Greek or for the work that seems the most useful for studying Greek language and literature. A monetary prize is awarded every five years.

5444
Prix de la Fondation Emile Benveniste
For recognition of a work in comparative grammar of Indo-European languages and Iranian linguistics.

5445
Prix de la Fondation Emile Senart
For recognition of a study of ancient India.

5446
Prix de la Fondation Louis de Clercq
For recognition of a work in Oriental archaeology.

5447
Prix de La Fons-Melicocq
For recognition of the best work on the history and the antiquities of Picardy and Ile-de-France (except Paris). A monetary prize is awarded biennially.

5448
Prix de La Grange
For recognition of the publication of a previously unpublished poem of an early poet of France. If no unpublished work is submitted, the prize may go to the best work on a published poem of the early poets. A monetary prize is awarded annually.

5449
Prix Delalande-Guerineau
For recognition of work on the Orient published during the two years preceding the award. A monetary prize is awarded biennially.

5450
Prix du Baron de Courcel
For recognition of a work of literature that attracts public interest to the first centuries of the history of France (the Merovingian and Carolingian), or which popularizes some episode of French history from the earliest time to 1,000 A.D. A monetary prize is awarded every nine years.

5451
Prix du Baron de Joest
To recognize an individual who has made a discovery or written a book best serving the public interest during the preceding year. A monetary prize is awarded annually and is given alternately by one of the five Academies of the Institut.

5452
Prix du Budget
For recognition of studies in the following categories: (1) Classical; (2) Oriental; and (3) Middle Ages and Renaissance antiquity. A manuscript or published work may be submitted on the theme which is chosen by the Academie. A monetary prize is awarded alternately in the three categories. Awarded annually.

5453
Prix du Duc de Loubat
For recognition of the best work on the history, geography, and archaeology of the New World. A monetary prize is awarded triennially.

5454
Prix Duchalais
For recognition of the best work on the numismatics of the Middle Ages appearing in the preceding two years. A monetary prize is awarded biennially.

5455
Prix Edmond Drouin
For recognition of a manuscript or published work on Oriental numismatics. Authors without regard to nationality are eligible. A monetary prize is awarded every four years.

5456
Prix Emile Le Senne
To encourage historical, archaeological, artistic or iconographic studies on Paris and the Seine department. A monetary prize is awarded biennially.

5457
Prix Estrade-Delcros
For recognition of a work re-examining the arrangement of studies by the Academy. The award is not to be divided. A monetary prize is awarded every five years.

5458
Prix Gabriel-Auguste Prost
To recognize the author of the best historical work on Metz or neighboring areas. A monetary prize is awarded annually.

5459
Prix Gaston Maspero
For recognition of a work or collection of works on Ancient Egypt. A monetary prize is awarded every five years. Established by the Duke of Loubat.

5460
Prix Gobert
For recognition of the most profound and knowledgeable work on French history and for other studies that closely fit this description. A monetary prize is awarded annually.

5461
Prix Gustave Mendel
For recognition of a detailed scientific catalogue, written in French, of part of or of a whole collection of Ancient Greek monuments or objects. If no such catalogue is submitted, a scientific work on Greek archaeology is considered. A monetary prize is awarded annually. Established by Louis Gaillet-Billotteau.

5462
Prix Gustave Schlumberger
For recognition of studies in the following categories: (1) Byzantine History; (2) Byzantine Archeology; and (3) the history and archaeology of the Latin Orient. A monetary prize is awarded alternately in the three categories. Awarded annually.

5463
Prix Herbert Allen Giles
For recognition of a work on China, Japan or the Far East. A monetary prize is awarded biennially.

5464
Prix Honore Chavee
To encourage work in linguistics and, in particular, research on Romance languages. A monetary prize is awarded biennially.

5465

Prix Jean Jacques Berger
For recognition of works of the most merit concerning the city of Paris. A monetary prize is awarded every five years.

5466

Prix Jean Reynaud
To recognize the author of the most meritorious work produced during the preceding five years. A monetary prize is awarded every five years.

5467

Prix Jules et Louis Jeanbernat et Barthelemy de Ferrari Doria
To recognize a young French author. The award is not to be divided. A monetary prize is awarded every five years.

5468

Prix Le Fevre-Deumier (de Pons)
For recognition of the most noteworthy work in the fields of comparative mythology, philosophy or religion. A monetary prize is awarded every ten years.

5469

Prix Louis Fould
For recognition of the best work on the history of drawing up to the end of the 16th century. A monetary prize is awarded biennially.

5470

Prix Raoul Duseigneur
For recognition of work on Spanish art and archaeology from the beginning of history to the end of the 16th century, or on the artistic, archaeological treasures of these epochs in the public or private Spanish collections. A monetary prize is awarded triennially. Established by the Marquise Arconati-Visconti.

5471

Prix Roman et Tania Ghirshman
For recognition of the best publication on pre-Islamic Iran. Works may be written on the history of civilization, the history of religion or art, numismatics, or the epigraphy or philology of Elamit, old-Persian, Armenian, Greek or Pahlavi writings. French or foreign authors are eligible. A monetary prize is awarded annually.

5472

Prix Saintour
For recognition of studies published in the preceding three years in the following categories: (1) Classical; (2) Oriental; and (3) Medieval and Renaissance antiquity. A monetary prize is awarded alternately in the three categories. Awarded annually.

5473

Prix Stanislas Julien
For recognition of the best work related to China. A monetary prize is awarded annually.

5474

Prix Toutain-Blanchet
For recognition of work either on the history of Ancient Gaul, before the advent of Clovis (485 A.D.), or on the history of Northern Africa before the end of the Byzantine domination (715 A.D.). A monetary prize is awarded triennially.

5475

Prix Volney
For recognition of a work in linguistics.

5476

Institut de France
Academie des Sciences
23, quai de Conti
F-75270 Paris, France
Phone: 44 414395
Fax: 44 414363

5477

Fondation Aime Berthe
For recognition of outstanding work in mathematics and physical sciences and their applications. Awards are given in alternate years in the following categories: mathematics and physical sciences, chemical and natural sciences, and biological and medical sciences. Young scientists who merit the encouragement of the Academie are eligible. A monetary prize of 4,000 francs is awarded every six years. Established in 1895.

5478

Fondation Aime Laussedat
For recognition of an outstanding work in topography or metrophotography. The prize alternates between a French recipient and a foreign recipient. A monetary prize of 4,000 francs is awarded every 10 years. Established in 1913.

5479

Fondation Albert I de Monaco
For recognition of a work that the Academy deems worthy. The prize is awarded without regard to nationality. A monetary prize of 25,000 francs is awarded every five years. Established in 1921.

5480

Fondation Alexandre Darracq
For recognition of the most remarkable discovery in science, automotives, aviation, chemistry, or mechanics that contributes to national defense. French citizens who are not wealthy are eligible. A monetary prize of 10,000 francs is awarded every six years. Established in 1928.

5481

Fondation Alexandre Joannides
For recognition of scientific, medical, or other research useful to the public good. The prize is awarded alternately by the division of chemistry and natural sciences and the division of mathematics and physics. A monetary prize of 50,000 francs is awarded annually. Established in 1958.

5482

Fondation Alfred Durand-Claye
For recognition of the best treatise on the hygiene of cities and dwellings. A monetary prize of 4,000 francs is awarded every 10 years. Established in 1917.

5483

Fondation Alfred Dutens
For recognition of a book or treatise published during the previous 10 years on electrotherapy. A monetary prize of 4,000 francs is awarded every 10 years. Established in 1914.

5484

Fondation Alhumbert
For recognition of the progress of the sciences and the arts. The prize is awarded alternately by the department of mathematics and physics and their applications or the department of chemistry, biology, medicine, and natural science and their applications. A monetary prize of 4,000 francs is awarded every 10 years. Established in 1817.

5485

Fondation Alphonse Laveran
To recognize French doctors who have made the most progress in exotic pathology. A monetary prize of 4,000 francs is awarded every 10 years. Established in 1946.

5486
Fondation Anatole et Suzanne Abragam
For recognition of a researcher under 40 years of age in the field of physics. A monetary prize of 10,000 francs is awarded biennially. Established in 1987.

5487
Fondation Ancel
For recognition of works of physical astronomy, particularly solar studies. A monetary prize of 4,000 francs is awarded every 10 years. Established in 1908.

5488
Fondation Andre C. Bonnet
For recognition of an outstanding treatise on paleontology or anthropology. A monetary prize of 5,000 francs is awarded biennially. Established in 1910.

5489
Fondation Andre Lallemand
For recognition of outstanding work in the different fields of astronomy. Preference is given to works that have application in some other field. Individuals or teams are eligible. A monetary prize of 50,000 French francs is awarded biennially. Established in 1990 and awarded for the first time in 1992.

5490
Fondation Andre Policard-Lacassagne
To recognize a young French or foreign scientist who has accomplished distinguished work in biochemistry, biophysics, or physical chemistry conducting research in France in these fields. Scientists under the age of 40 who do not belong to the Academie des Sciences are eligible. A monetary prize of 4,000 francs is awarded triennially. Established in 1958.

5491
Fondation Andre-Romain Prevot
To recognize a French bacteriologist whose research has increased our knowledge of bacteria. The Louis Pasteur Medal is awarded annually when merited. Established in 1978.

5492
Fondation Aniuta Winter-Klein
To recognize young researchers whose work contributes to the knowledge or application of the physical chemistry of the solid noncrystalline vitreous state. Individuals of any nationality and residence are eligible. The winner gives one or two lectures in memory of Aniuta Winter Klein. A monetary prize of 18,000 francs is awarded annually. Established in 1982.

5493
Fondation Antoine d'Abbadie
For recognition of work in astronomy or geophysics. An award is given in alternate years in the categories of astronomy and geophysics. A monetary prize of 10,000 francs is awarded biennially. Established in 1899 as an astronomy prize and changed in 1976, when the l'Observatoire d'Abbadie closed.

5494
Fondation Antoinette Janssen
To assist needy young men who plan to study astronomy, particularly astrophysics. A monetary award is granted for five years to the individual chosen. Awarded annually. Established in 1921.

5495
Fondation Arago
For recognition of work in astronomy. A monetary prize of 4,000 francs is awarded every 10 years. Established in 1887.

5496
Fondation Argut
To recognize scientists who have advanced medical knowledge by making a medical discovery permitting the cure of a disease that was previously only curable by surgery. A monetary prize of 4,000 francs is awarded every 10 years. Established in 1902.

5497
Fondation Arthur du Fay
For recognition of work on the movement of solid bodies. A monetary prize of 4,000 francs is awarded every 10 years. Established in 1912.

5498
Fondation Auguste Chevalier
To recognize the author of one or more works relating to plants (systems, biology, and geography) of tropical and subtropical French-speaking countries, in particular to plants from West Africa. A monetary prize of 4,000 francs is awarded biennially. Established in 1955.

5499
Fondation Ayme Poirson
For recognition of work on the applications of science to industry. A monetary prize of 50,000 francs is awarded triennially. Established in 1965.

5500
Fondation Barbier
For recognition of a valuable discovery dealing with the art of healing in the areas of surgery, medicine, pharmacology, or botany. A monetary prize of 4,000 francs is awarded every four years. Established in 1832.

5501
Fondation Bariot-Faynot
For recognition of a scientific discovery contributing to the cure of tuberculosis or cancer. A monetary award of 4,000 francs is awarded triennially. Established in 1923.

5502
Fondation Berthelot
To recognize a scientist who has received a prize for chemistry during the preceding year. The Berthelot Medal is awarded annually. Established in 1902.

5503
Fondation Bigot de Morogues
To recognize the author of the work that has contributed the most to agricultural progress in France. A monetary prize of 4,000 francs is awarded every 10 years. Established in 1834.

5504
Fondation Binoux
For recognition of outstanding work in geography, navigation, or the history or philosophy of science. Awards are given in alternate years. A monetary prize of 4,000 francs is awarded biennially. Established in 1889.

5505
Fondation Boileau
For recognition of research concerning fluid dynamics that has contributed to the progress of hydraulics and has not yet been honored by a prize. Theories should be verified by experiments or observations. A monetary prize of 4,000 francs is awarded every 10 years. Established in 1882.

5506
Fondation Bordin
For recogniton of treatises on subjects touching the public interest, the good of humanity, the progress of science, and national honor. The prize is awarded alternately by the division of mathematical sciences and the

division of chemical science, natural science, biology, and medicine. A monetary prize of 4,000 francs is awarded biennially. Established in 1835.

5507

Fondation Breant

For recognition of advances in the study of cholera and all other epidemic illnesses. A monetary prize of 7,000 francs is awarded biennially. Established in 1849 as a prize to a scientist who could find the causes of cholera and the way to cure it.

5508

Fondation Cahours, Houzeau

To recognize a young deserving chemist for outstanding research. A monetary prize of 5,000 francs is awarded every three years. The Prix Houzeau was established in 1904, the Prix Cahours in 1886. The two prizes were combined in 1979.

5509

Fondation Camere

To recognize a French mining or civil engineer who has conceived and completed a work constituting an advancement in the art of construction. A monetary prize of 6,000 francs is awarded every eight years. Established in 1904.

5510

Fondation Carre-Bessault

For recognition of works by French scientists contributing to progress in the cure or relief of human diseases. A monetary award of 4,000 francs is awarded every 10 years. Established in 1951.

5511

Fondation Carriere de Mathematiques

For recognition of work in mathematics. A monetary prize of 4,500 francs is awarded annually. Established in 1932.

5512

Fondation Carriere de Mineralogie

For recognition of work in mineralogy. A monetary prize of 4,000 francs is awarded every four years. Established in 1932.

5513

Fondation Charles-Adam Girard

For recognition of research or discoveries in chemistry useful to science and in the interest of humanity. A monetary prize of 4,000 francs is awarded every eight years. Established in 1926.

5514

Fondation Charles Dhere

For recogniton of work in biochemistry. A monetary prize of 10,000 francs is awarded biennially. Established in 1955.

5515

Fondation Charles Eugene Guye

For recognition of the work stating most clearly and objectively the progress and tendencies of the philosophy of science during the last 10 years. The selection committee is composed of six members from the Academie des Sciences and three from the Academie des Sciences Morales et Politiques. The Prix Henri Poincare, consisting of a monetary award of 8,000 francs is awarded every 10 years. Established in 1914.

5516

Fondation Charles Fremont

To encourage scientists, engineers, artists, or craftsmen who, through their work, make a useful and glorious contribution for France. A monetary prize of 4,000 francs is awarded every five years. Established in 1931.

5517

Fondation Charles Jacob

For recognition of a work, theoretical or applied, in the field of earth sciences. French or foreign scientists are eligible. A monetary prize of 4,000 francs is awarded every three years. Established in 1965.

5518

Fondation Charles-Leopold Mayer

To encourage and support fundamental research, particularly in the fields of biology, biochemistry, and biophysics. The prize, awarded without regard to country or nationality, may not be given to the same nationality two years in a row. Research that may lead to a discovery or invention to synthesize nucleoproteins, similar to the living cell, or to reveal the fundamental workings of cellular life is considered. Candidates must be 65 years of age or younger. A monetary prize of 250,000 francs is awarded annually. Established in 1960.

5519

Fondation Charles-Louis de Saulses de Freycinet

To aid scientists whose resources are insufficient to permit them to pursue their scientific research, or to encourage research or work profitable to health or progress. A monetary prize of 20,000 francs is awarded annually. Established in 1925.

5520

Fondation Chaussier

To recognize the author of the best publication on practical or forensic medicine. A monetary prize of 6,000 francs is awarded every eight years. Established in 1863.

5521

Fondation Claude Lallemand

For recognition of studies of the nervous system. A monetary prize of 4,000 francs is awarded every five years. Established in 1852.

5522

Fondation Clavel

For recognition of work in organic chemistry. The Prix Lespiau, a monetary prize of 10,000 francs, is awarded biennially. Established in 1979.

5523

Fondation Clement Felix

To enable established French scientists to continue research in the field of electricity. The award is not to be divided. A monetary prize of 4,000 francs is awarded every nine years. Established in 1917.

5524

Fondation Coron-Thevenet

To recognize works on geothermic, solar, or other forms of energy that benefits humanity. A monetary award of 6,000 francs is given triennially. Established in 1991.

5525

Fondation Costantino Gorini

For recognition of work in microbiology. The following prizes are awarded in alternate years: Prix Lac - for studies in the microbiology of milk; and Prix Enzymologia - for work on microbiological fermentation. A monetary prize of 4,000 francs is awarded every 10 years. The Prix Lac was established in 1939 and the Prix Enzymologia in 1940.

5526

Fondation Cuvier

For recognition of the best work in natural history, either in zoology or geology. The Academy awards the prize for two consecutive terms on the advice of the commission on the zoology prize and on the third term on the advice of the commisssion on the geology prize. A monetary prize of 4,000 francs is awarded triennially. Established in 1839.

5527
Fondation Da Gama Machado
For recogniton of treatises written on the coloration of animal coats (including man) and on fertilization in the animal kingdom. A monetary prize of 4,000 francs is awarded every 10 years. Established in 1852.

5528
Fondation Damoiseau
To recognize the author of a theoretical paper, followed by numeric applications, judged the most useful to the progress of astronomy. Individuals of any nationality are eligible. A monetary prize of 4,000 francs is awarded every five years. Established in 1863.

5529
Fondation Dandrimont-Benicourt
For recognition of research in the field of cancer. A monetary prize of 10,000 French francs is awarded annually. Established in 1990.

5530
Fondation Danton
To encourage research in radiant phenomena. A monetary prize of 4,000 francs is awarded every 10 years. Established in 1903.

5531
Fondation de Coincy
To recognize the author of a work on phanerogamy. A monetary prize of 4,000 francs is awarded every 10 years. Established in 1903.

5532
Fondation de la Fons-Melicocq
For recogniton of the best work in botany from the Northern France Departments that include Pas-de-Calais, Ardennes, Somme, Oise, and Aisne. A monetary prize of 4,000 francs is awarded every 10 years. Established in 1864.

5533
Fondation de Madame Albert Demolon
To recognize young researchers in the field of agronomy, particularly in the study of soil. A monetary prize of 8,000 francs is awarded every six years. Established in 1950.

5534
Fondation de Madame Edmond Hamel
To recognize hydrography engineers for distinguished work in their field. The Prix Alexandre Givry of 4,000 francs is awarded every 10 years. Established in 1928.

5535
Fondation de Madame Victor Noury
To encourage the development of scientific culture in its most diverse forms. French citizens under the age of 45 are eligible. A monetary prize of 4,000 francs is awarded every five years. Established in 1917.

5536
Fondation Delalande-Guerineau
To recognize the scholar or traveler who has rendered the most service to science or France. French citizens are eligible. A monetary prize of 4,000 francs is awarded every 10 years. Established in 1872.

5537
Fondation Delesse
For recognition of a work in geology or mineralogy. French or foreign scientists are eligible. A monetary prize of 4,000 francs is awarded every 10 years. Established in 1883.

5538
Fondation Demolombe
For recognition of outstanding work in geology or agriculture. Awards are given in alternate years in the two categories. A monetary prize of 4,000 francs is awarded every 10 years. Established in 1908.

5539
Fondation Deslandres
For recognition of the best work in spectral analysis and its applications. French or foreign scientists are eligible. A monetary prize of 25,000 francs is awarded biennially. Established in 1946.

5540
Fondation Desmazieres
For recognition of the best or most useful work on cryptogamy. French or foreign writers are eligible to submit work published during the preceding year. A monetary prize of 4,000 francs is awarded every six years. Established in 1855.

5541
Fondation du Baron de Joest
To recognize an individual who has made a discovery or written a book best serving the public interest. The award is given in alternate years in the following fields: chemical, natural, biological and medical sciences and their applications; and mathematics and physics and their applications. A monetary prize of 4,000 francs is awarded every 10 years. Established in 1880.

5542
Fondation du Baron Larrey
To recognize surgeons or doctors of the armed forces for the best work on the subject of medicine, surgery, or military hygiene. A monetary prize of 4,000 francs is awarded every 10 years. Established in 1896.

5543
Fondation du Docteur et de Madame Henri Labbe
For recognition of scientific work in biochemistry and nutrition. Monetary prize of 6,000 francs for each achievement in biochemistry and 10,000 francs for work in nutrition are awarded annually. Established in 1948.

5544
Fondation du Docteur et de Madame Peyre
For recognition of outstanding work in medicine or physiology, particularly those works studying the beneficial or harmful effects of certain waves on living organisms, as in the case of cancer or agricultural cultivation. Awards are given in alternate years in the categories of medicine and physiology. A monetary prize of 4,500 francs is awarded every three years. Established in 1945.

5545
Fondation du Docteur Jean Toy
For recognition of the most remarkable discovery or work in medical science. French or foreign authors are eligible. A monetary prize of 30,000 francs is awarded every 10 years. Established in 1932.

5546
Fondation du General Ferrie
To recognize the scientist or inventor who has completed the most interesting work in radio-electricity. A monetary prize of 4,000 francs is awarded every four years. Established in 1936.

5547
Fondation du General Muteau
To recognize organizations, societies, or individuals who, either through support of peace or through their work aimed at the improvement of the system of national defense, have contributed to the greatness of France. Inventions, writings, actions, or heroic conduct by French citizens during the preceding year are eligible. A monetary prize of 4,000 francs is awarded biennially. The prize is awarded alternately by the division of

mathematical and physical sciences and the division of chemical and natural sciences. Established in 1927.

5548

Fondation Dusgate

To recognize the author of the best work on the diagnostic signs of death and on the means of preventing premature interments; or for recognition of important works on medicine or surgery. A monetary prize of 4,500 francs is awarded every 10 years. Established in 1872.

5549

Fondation Edmond Brun

For recognition of work in the mechanics of fluids, thermics, or astronautics. Awards are given in alternate years. A monetary prize of 10,000 francs is awarded annually. Established in 1980.

5550

Fondation Elie Cartan

To recognize a mathematician who has introduced new ideas or solved a difficult problem. Individuals over 45 years of age of any nationality are eligible. A monetary prize of 25,000 francs is awarded triennially. Established in 1980.

5551

Fondation Emil Picard

To recognize a mathematician. A medal is awarded every six years. Established in 1942.

5552

Fondation Emile Jungfleisch

To recognize a Frenchman for important work or discoveries in organic chemistry. A monetary prize of 10,000 francs is awarded biennially. Established in 1923.

5553

Fondation Ernest Dechelle

For recognition of the work of a French scientist in the field of mathematics, physics, astronomy, and natural science. Awards are given in alternate years by the division of mathematics and physics; and the division of chemistry, natural science, biology, and medicine. A monetary prize of 10,000 francs is awarded biennially. Established in 1943.

5554

Fondation Eugene et Amelie Dupuis

To recognize or encourage doctors, pharmacists, chemists, and scientists for research in fighting cancer and tuberculosis. A monetary award of 4,000 francs is awarded every four years. Established in 1930.

5555

Fondation Fanny Emden

For recognition of the best work on psychological influences on animals. If no work on this subject merits the prize, it is awarded for recognition of original research in physiology. A monetary prize of 4,000 francs is awarded every eight years. Established in 1910.

5556

Fondation Fernand Holweck

For recognition of outstanding research in physics. Awards are given in alternate years in the categories of radiation physics and physics of the globe. A monetary prize of 4,000 francs is awarded triennially. Established in 1946.

5557

Fondation Fontannes

To recognize the author of the best publication on paleontology. A monetary prize of 4,000 francs is awarded every eight years. Established in 1883.

5558

Fondation Foulon

For recognition of outstanding work in the fields of botany, rural economics, and zoology. Awards are given in the following categories: botany - an annual monetary prize of 8,000 francs; rural economics - 8,000 francs awarded annually; and zoology - 10,000 francs awarded biennially. Established in 1940.

5559

Fondation Fourneyron

For recognition of work in the field of applied mechanics. A monetary prize of 4,000 francs is awarded every five years. Established in 1867.

5560

Fondation Francoeur

To recognize the author of works useful to the progress of pure and applied mathematics. Preference is given to young scholars or to geometricians not yet established. A monetary prize of 4,000 francs is awarded every five years. Established in 1882.

5561

Fondation Frederic Forthuny

To recognize a young man working in the Observatoire, in whom the Academy has seen a particularly remarkable attitude and whom they judge worthy of encouragement. An allowance of 4,000 francs is granted every five years. Established in 1943 in memory of Frederic Forthuny (1895-1919).

5562

Fondation G. de Pontecoulant

To encourage research in the mechanics of celestial bodies. A monetary prize of 4,000 francs is awarded every 10 years. Established in 1901.

5563

Fondation Gabrielle Sand

For recognition of discoveries useful to humanity. Awards are given in alternate years in the following categories: mathematics and physics; and chemistry and natural sciences. A monetary prize of 4,000 francs is awarded every four years. Established in 1908.

5564

Fondation Gaston Rousseau

To provide recognition for scientific research leading toward an improvement in human welfare, and especially toward the cure of diseases, such as cancer. A scientist or a team of scientists working in the same field (without respect to nationality) are eligible. A monetary prize of 5,000 francs is awarded biennially. Established in 1970 and first awarded in 1978.

5565

Fondation Gay

For recognition of the best work in physical geography. A monetary prize of 4,000 francs is awarded every four years. Established in 1873.

5566

Fondation Gegner

To recognize a needy scientist who indicates by his seriousness that the continuation of the work will be fruitful for the positive progress of science. A monetary prize of 4,000 francs is awarded triennially. Established in 1868.

5567

Fondation Georges Deflandre et Marthe Deflandre-Rigaud

For recognition of a work in micro-paleontology, concerning in particular: evolution, phylogenesis, ontogenesis, ecology, paleobiology, or morphology. Scientists without regard to nationality or age are eligible. A monetary prize of 4,000 francs is awarded triennially. Established in 1970

5568
Fondation Georges Millot
To recognize the author of a work in the field of geochemistry in one of the many areas of earth science, including geology, sedimentology, oceanology, pedology, metallurgy, and ecology. The Prix de Geochimie is awarded triennially. Established in 1979.

5569
Fondation Godard
For recognition of the best treatise on the anatomy, physiology, and pathology of the genitourinary organs. A monetary prize of 4,000 francs is awarded every 10 years. Established in 1862.

5570
Fondation Grammaticakis-Neuman
For recognition of the best work in organic chemistry concerning photochemistry or spectrochemistry, experimental chemistry, mathematical applications in biology, or the philosophy of science. Awards are given alternately in the categories of organic chemistry, mathematical applications in biology (preferably human physiology), and the philosophy of science (preferably the pragmatic approach). A monetary prize of 15,000 francs is awarded annually. In addition, in the area of organic chemistry concerning photochemistry or spectrochemistry, a monetary prize of 7,000 francs is awarded annually. Established in 1982.

5571
Fondation Gustave Ribaud
For recognition of work in the area of thermal exchanges or high frequency. Awards are given in alternate years in the fields of applied physics or theoretical physics. A monetary prize of 10,000 francs is awarded biennially. Established in 1965.

5572
Fondation Gustave Roussy
For recogntion and encouragement of cancer research. A monetary prize of 15,000 francs is awarded triennially. Established in 1967.

5573
Fondation Gustave Roux
To recognize outstanding work by young French scientists. A monetary prize of 5,000 francs is awarded every seven years. Established in 1911.

5574
Fondation Helene Helbronner-Fould
To recognize the widow of a French scientist who, by collaboration or publication, has aided his career or prolonged his fame. A monetary prize of 4,000 francs is awarded every 10 years. Established in 1927.

5575
Fondation Henri Becquerel
To encourage scientific progress. A monetary prize of 4,000 francs is awarded triennially. Established in 1905 by Jean Becquerel in memory of Henri Becquerel, his father and secretary of the Academie des Sciences.

5576
Fondation Henri de Parville
For recognition of outstanding work in the fields of mechanics or physics. Awards are given in alternate years in the two categories. A monetary prize of 4,000 francs is awarded biennially. Established in 1891.

5577
Fondation Henri Mondor
For recognition of a scientific work relating to surgical emergencies. A monetary prize of 12,000 francs is awarded every four years. Established in 1962.

5578
Fondation Henri Poincare
For recognition of an eminent mathematician. A gold medal is awarded when merited. Established in 1914.

5579
Fondation Henriette Regnier
For recognition of works on the cure of cancer and tuberculosis. A monetary prize of 4,000 francs is awarded every eight years. Established in 1932.

5580
Fondation Henry Bazin
For recognition of experimental research in hydraulics. The prize is awarded without regard to nationality. A monetary prize of 4,000 francs is awarded every 10 years. Established in 1923.

5581
Fondation Henry Giffard
For recognition of work in the field of industrial engineering. A monetary prize of 4,000 francs is awarded every four years. Established in 1881.

5582
Fondation Henry Le Chatelier
To recognize the author of scientific research consisting of precise measurements of a nature immediately applicable to industry. A monetary prize of 5,000 francs is awarded every 10 years. Established in 1922.

5583
Fondation Henry Wilde
For recognition of the most outstanding work in astronomy, physics, chemistry, mineralogy, geology, or experimental mechanics. A scientist of any country is eligible. A monetary prize of 4,000 francs is awarded triennially. Established in 1897.

5584
Fondation Hirn
To recognize a scientist for encouraging experimental work, scientific research or travel, or new ideas, and for recognition of work already accomplished. A monetary prize of 4,000 francs is awarded every four years. Established in 1889.

5585
Fondation Hughes
For recognition of an original discovery in physics, especially in electricity and magnetism or their applications. A monetary prize of 4,000 francs is awarded triennially. Established in 1893.

5586
Fondation Ivan Peyches
For recognition of work that studies the condition and usefulness of solar energy or similar applied science fields. A monetary prize of 20,000 francs is awarded annually. Established in 1978.

5587
Fondation Jacques Bourcart
To recognize students of oceanography or physical geography who are distinguished in both academic success and preliminary work. A scholarship of 4,000 francs, intended for travel abroad and not for study expenses or field site expenses, is awarded every three years. Established in 1962.

5588
Fondation Jaffe
To encourage students or masters of science to do experiments leading to progress and the good of humanity. A monetary prize of 50,000 francs is awarded annually. Established in 1930.

5589
Fondation James Hall
For recognition of the best doctoral thesis in geology written during the 10-year period preceding the award. A monetary prize of 4,000 francs is awarded every 10 years. Established in 1911.

5590
Fondation Janine Courrier
To encourage research in the endocrinology of vertebrates and invertebrates. French researchers 40 years of age or younger are eligible. The prize is not to be divided, but a team of two or three researchers may be considered if they publish together. A monetary prize of 20,000 francs is awarded biennially. Established in 1978.

5591
Fondation Janssen
For recognition of work or discoveries in the area of physical astronomy. French or foreign scientists are eligible. Members of the Institut de France are not eligible. A medal is awarded biennially. Established in 1886.

5592
Fondation Jean-Baptiste Dumas
For recognition of work in chemistry. A monetary prize of 4,000 francs is awarded every 10 years. Established in 1943.

5593
Fondation Jean Cuvillier
For recognition of the best work of a young micro-paleontologist of any nationality. A monetary prize of 7,000 francs is awarded triennially. Established in 1970.

5594
Fondation Jean Dagnan-Bouveret
To encourage medical studies. A monetary prize of 7,000 francs is awarded biennially. Established in 1924.

5595
Fondation Jean de Rufz de La Vison
For recognition of works on plant physiology. French citizens are not eligible. A monetary prize of 4,000 francs is awarded every 10 years. Established in 1912.

5596
Fondation Jean du Hamel de Breuil
To recognize the author of an in-depth work on advanced geometry, mechanics, or maritime navigation. The Prix Charles Dupin of 4,000 francs is awarded every 10 years. Established in 1920.

5597
Fondation Jean-Jacques Berger
To recognize outstanding contributions concerning the city of Paris. The award is given in alternate years by the Academie des Sciences, Academie francaise, Academies des Inscriptions et Belles-Lettres, Academie des Beaux-Arts, and Academie des Sciences Morales et Politiques. The prize is not to be divided. If there is not a work that merits the prize, the value of the prize is used to encourage the best works nominated. A monetary prize of 4,000 francs is awarded. Established in 1881.

5598
Fondation Jean-Marie Le Goff
To encourage research in biological chemistry, in particular the study of red blood cells in diabetics and the physiological and therapeutic properties of cobalt and its derivatives. A monetary prize of 4,500 francs is awarded every eight years. Established in 1950.

5599
Fondation Jean Reynaud
For recognition of original scientific work. Awards are given in alternate years in the following categories: mathematics and physics; and chemistry and natural sciences. A monetary prize of 4,000 francs is awarded every five years. Established in 1878.

5600
Fondation Jean Thore
For recognition of the most outstanding treatise on the habits or anatomy of a species of insects, algae, mosses, lichens, or mushrooms. Awards are given in alternate years in the following categories: habits or anatomy of a species of insects of Europe; and algae, mosses, lichens, or mushrooms. A monetary prize of 4,000 francs is awarded every 10 years. Established in 1863.

5601
Fondation Jecker
To recognize the author of the most useful work in organic chemistry or for recognition of works that make progress in organic chemistry. A monetary prize of 6,500 francs is awarded biennially. Established in 1851.

5602
Fondation Jerome Ponti
To encourage the progress of science. Awards are given in alternate years in the following categories: mathematics and physics; and chemistry and natural sciences. A monetary prize of 4,000 francs is awarded every five years. Established in 1879.

5603
Fondation Joseph Labbe
To recognize the author of a work of geology or research improving the mineral resources of France. A monetary prize of 4,000 francs is awarded every eight years. Established in 1908 by the Societe des acieries de Longwy and the Societe anonyme mettallurgique de Gorcy.

5604
Fondation Jules et Louis Jeanbernat et Barthelemy de Ferrari Doria
For recognition of a work of science by a young French author. The prize is not to be divided. A monetary prize of 4,000 francs is awarded every 10 years. Established in 1922.

5605
Fondation Kastner-Boursault
To recognize the author of the best work on the applications of electricity to art, industry, and commerce. A monetary prize of 4,000 francs is awarded every 10 years. Established in 1880.

5606
Fondation Kodak-Pathe-Landucci
For recognition of the best research in the areas of photochemistry, solid physics, physics of surfaces, or thin films. French researchers are eligible. A monetary prize of 40,000 francs is awarded biennially. Established in 1971.

5607
Fondation L. La Caze
For recognition of oustanding work in the field of physics, chemistry, or physiology. All nationalities are eligible. A monetary prize of 5,000 francs is awarded annually. Awarded alternately by the Commission for physics, chemistry, and physiology. Established in 1865.

5608
Fondation La Caille
For recognition of original research that carries on the works of the Abbe La Caille, a member of the old Academy of Science, or for general works of astronomy, particularly those of long duration. All scientists are eligible. A monetary prize of 4,000 francs is awarded every 10 years. Established in 1921.

5609
Fondation Lamb
For recognition of the best studies on the national defense of France. A monetary prize of 40,000 francs is awarded biennially. Established in 1938.

5610
Fondation Langevin
For recognition of outstanding work by a mathematician, chemist, physicist, or biologist. A monetary prize of 7,500 francs is awarded annually. Established through the initiative of Paul Langevin in 1945 in memory of the French scholars killed by the Germans from 1940 to 1945, and to reward works in the disciplines to which those scholars contributed.

5611
Fondation Lannelongue
To aid those who have been negatively impacted by the scientific world, particularly the scientific medical field. A monetary prize of 4,000 francs is awarded triennially. Established in 1903.

5612
Fondation Laplace
To recognize the student graduating with the highest rank from the School of Polytechnic Sciences. A silver-gilt medal with the likeness of M. de Laplace is awarded annually by the President of the Academie des Sciences. Established in 1836.

5613
Fondation Laura Mounier de Saridakis
For recognition of a work of pure science. The applications of the work should contribute to the progress of medicine, biology, physics, and biological or medical chemistry. A monetary prize of 4,000 francs is awarded biennially. Established in 1933-1938.

5614
Fondation Lavoisier
To recognize a scientist who has made distinguished contributions to chemistry. Scientists of all nationalities are eligible. A gold medal is awarded when merited. Established in 1900.

5615
Fondation Le Conte
For recognition of discoveries and of new applications in mathematics, physics, chemistry, natural history, and medical science. A monetary prize of 30,000 francs is awarded triennially. Established in 1876.

5616
Fondation Leon-Alexandre Etancelin
To encourage or recognize discoveries valuable to humanity, primarily in the fight against cancer and other incurable diseases. French citizens or research work done by a French institute or laboratory are eligible. A monetary award of 40,000 francs is awarded every five years. Established in 1945.

5617
Fondation Leon Grelaud
To recognize the author of a work most significant in the study of the upper atmosphere, either by stratospheric devices or other means. A monetary prize of 4,000 francs is awarded every eight years. Established in 1947.

5618
Fondation Leon Lutaud
For recognition of work that makes progress in a discipline of geology. A monetary prize of 40,000 francs is awarded biennially. Established in 1982 on the occasion of the election of Jean Aubouin to l'Academie des Sciences. Sponsored by Comite National Francais de Geologie.

5619
Fondation Leon Velluz
For recognition of a discovery in chemistry or organic biochemistry leading to human therapy. The prize is not to be divided, but may be awarded to a team for a discovery. A monetary prize of 120,000 francs is awarded biennially. Established in 1982.

5620
Fondation Lonchampt
For recognition of the best treatise on the subject of plant, animal, and human diseases caused by excess minerals. A monetary prize of 4,000 francs is awarded triennially. Established in 1896.

5621
Fondation Louis Armand
For recognition of a young researcher (30 years of age or older) for an outstanding work in the field of applied mathematics, mechanical engineering, physics, chemistry, biology, or earth science. A monetary prize of 7,000 francs is awarded annually. Established in 1987 by the Association des Amis de Louis Armand.

5622
Fondation Louis-Daniel Beauperthuy
For recognition of work in epidemiology that contributes to the amelioration of the human condition. A monetary prize of 20,000 French francs is awarded biennially. Established in 1982.

5623
Fondation Louise Darracq
To recognize individuals who discover a cure for cancer or for recognition of works advancing the study of cures for cancer. A monetary award of 4,000 francs is awarded every six years. Established in 1928.

5624
Fondation Lucien Cayeux
To recognize a young geologist pursuing research of sedimentary lithology, at the site or in a laboratory. A scholarship is granted every four years. Established in 1944.

5625
Fondation Marie Guido Triossi
To recognize a scientist for an invention for the good of mankind. Awards are given in alternate years in the categories of mathematics, physics, and chemistry and natural sciences. A monetary prize of 16,000 francs is awarded every four years. Established in 1939.

5626
Fondation Marie Leon-Houry
To recognize the doctor, chemist, or scientist who contributes the most to the conquest of cancer and tuberculosis. A monetary prize of 4,000 francs is awarded every 10 years. Established in 1942.

5627
Fondation Marquet
For recognition of the most worthy scientific discovery. The prize is awarded alternately by the division of mathematics and physics, and the division of chemistry and natural sciences. A monetary prize of 4,000 francs is awarded every five years. Established in 1923.

5628
Fondation Martin-Damourette
To provide recognition for the best work in therapeutic physiology. A monetary prize of 4,000 francs is awarded every eight years. Established in 1883.

5629
Fondation Maujean
For recognition of the best work, discovery, or invention that improved public health or the conditions of workers in dangerous professions, or

found a cure or relief for epidemic and contagious diseases or ailments considered incurable. French citizens are eligible. A monetary prize of 4,000 francs is awarded every 10 years. Established in 1873.

Fondation Max-Fernand Jayle
For recognition of original research in the biochemistry or the physiology of sexual hormones, in particular, research on the function of reproduction of mammals, primates, and humans. French citizens who are at least 45 years of age are eligible. The prize is not be divided. A monetary prize of 20,000 francs is awarded biennially. Established in 1981.

Fondation Mege
This prize is offered once to recognize the writer who completes the essay by Doctor Mege on the factors that have retarded or advanced the progress of medicine from its earliest history to the present. Until the Academie des Science decides to award this prize, it will bestow a prize in medicine of 4,000 francs every 10 years. Established in 1868.

Fondation Memain-Pelletier
To recognize scientists or doctors who, through their work or discoveries, have contributed to finding cures for diseases. The prize is awarded by the Institute on the advice of the Academie des Sciences. A monetary prize is awarded triennially. Established in 1976.

Fondation Mergier-Bourdeix
For recognition in the field of science. Awarded alternately in the fields of mathematics and physics or natural biology, chemistry, and medicine. A monetary award of 300,000 French francs is awarded. Established in 1987.

Fondation Millet-Ronssin
For recognition of research in the natural sciences. A monetary prize of 4,000 francs is awarded triennially. Established in 1825.

Fondation Montagne
For recognition of important works on cellular plants. A monetary prize of 4,000 francs is awarded every three years. Established in 1862.

Fondation Montyon de Medicine et Chirugie
For recognition of an outstanding contribution to surgery and medicine. A monetary prize of 6,000 francs is awarded biennially. Established in 1819.

Fondation Montyon de Physiologie
For recognition of the most useful work on experimental physiology. A monetary prize of 6,000 francs is awarded biennially. Established in 1818.

Fondation Montyon des Arts Insalubres
To recognize an individual who discovers a method to make any mechanical art less unhealthy. A monetary prize of 6,000 francs is awarded biennially. Established in 1819.

Fondation Montyon des Statistiques
To recognize statistical researchers working in all disciplines. A monetary prize of 6,000 francs is awarded biennially. Established in 1817.

Fondation Nicolas Zvorikine
For recognition of a scientific or practical study on ameliorating the economic condition of the small farmer. Consideration is given particularly to studies on developing market gardening and breeding, on using winter leisure time for handicrafts, or on spreading electric power. The work should be sufficiently developed to be used as a model. French or Russian citizens are eligible. A monetary prize of 4,000 francs and a book are awarded every seven years. Established in 1937.

Fondation Odette Lemenon
For recognition of a continuing research work on the causes or cure of cancer or tuberculosis or any other disease that decimates humanity. A monetary prize of 4,000 francs is awarded triennially. Established in 1955.

Fondation Parkin
To provide recognition for the best work in French, German, or Italian on the curative effects of carbon in such various forms as a gas or carbonic acid; on cholera as well as fevers and other maladies; or on the effects of volcanic action in producing epidemics in the plant and animal world and its effects on hurricanes and other atmospheric conditions. A monetary prize of 4,000 francs is awarded every five years. Established in 1885.

Fondation Paul Bertrand
For recognition of outstanding work in paleobotany or stratigraphic geology dedicated to coal-bearing formations. Awards are given in alternate years in the two categories. If there are no candidates in these disciplines, the award goes to a work of anatomy or descriptive botany. A monetary prize of 4,000 francs is awarded triennially. Established in 1960.

Fondation Paul Doistau - Emile Blutet
The purpose of the prize is decided during the year preceding its award by the Academie. A monetary prize of 40,000 francs is awarded biennially. Established in 1954.

Fondation Paul Fallot-Jeremine
To aid young geologists at the beginning of their research; principally, to permit them to accomplish geological studies at a site. Candidates of any nationality or sex should present a recommendation from a professor or researcher familiar with their work. A scholarship of 6,000 francs is awarded when merited. Established in 1953.

Fondation Paul Gallet
To recognize a French Catholic who has contributed best to increasing the prosperity of France and the French people. The prize is awarded alternately by the division of mathematics and physics; or by the division of chemistry, natural sciences, biology and medicine. A monetary prize of 4,000 francs is awarded triennially. Established in 1941.

Fondation Paul Marguerite de la Charlonie
For recognition of original research in chemistry, agriculture, and physics. Awards are given in alternate years in the following categories: chemistry - the research should be in the study of ferrous and aluminum salts, the effect of iron salts on blood, the composition of chlorophyll, or the effect of heat on various dissolved salts; agriculture - the research should be in the effects of ferrous salts on vegetation, the effects of substances other than nitrogren, phosphoric acid, and potassium on vegetation, or the destruction of nauseous plants; and physics - the research should be in the precipitation of a dissolved substance when its solvent evaporates, the variation in amount of heat required to evaporate liquids containing various types of dissolved matter, the effect of pressure on liquids containing various types of matter in suspension, or slow crystallization of matter through controlled evaporation. Individuals of French parentage are eligible. Members of the Academie, their parents, or relatives by blood or marriage are excluded from the competiton. A monetary prize of 5,000 francs is awarded annually. Established in 1902.

| 5648 |

Fondation Paul Pascal
For recognition of research work in physical chemistry, particularly in magnetochemistry and its eventual extensions. Young or middle-aged researchers are eligible. A monetary prize of 10,000 francs is awarded annually. Established in 1972.

| 5649 |

Fondation Petit d'Ormoy
For recognition of works of theory and application of science to medicine, mechanics, and industry. Awards are given in alternate years in the following categories: mathematics and physics; and chemistry and natural sciences. A monetary prize of 8,000 francs is awarded annually. Established in 1875.

| 5650 |

Fondation Philipeaux
For recognition of an outstanding work in experimental physiology. A monetary prize of 4,000 francs is awarded every 10 years. Established in 1888.

| 5651 |

Fondation Philippe A. Guye
For recognition of work in the field of physical chemistry. A monetary prize of 4,000 francs is awarded every six years. Established in 1941.

| 5652 |

Fondation Pierre Desnuelle
To recognize works by biological chemists. A monetary award of 10,000 francs is given biennially. Established in 1991.

| 5653 |

Fondation Pierre Lafitte
For recognition or encouragement of research on electromagnetic waves, in particular, on telephone and telegraph systems. A monetary prize of 4,000 francs is awarded every 10 years. Established in 1924.

| 5654 |

Fondation Pierson-Perrin
For recognition of the best discovery in physics. French citizens are eligible. The prize is awarded alternately by the Commission of the Mechanics Prize or by the Commission of the Physics Prize. A monetary prize of 4,000 francs is awarded every four years. Established in 1898.

| 5655 |

Fondation Plumey
To recognize an individual who perfects steam engines or other devices that contribute to the progress of navigation. A monetary prize of 5,000 francs is awarded annually. Established in 1859.

| 5656 |

Fondation Poncelet
To recognize the author of the work most useful to the progress of pure or applied mathematics. French or foreign authors are eligible. The prize is alternately awarded by the Commission on Mathematics and the Commission on the Mechanical Prize. A monetary prize of 4,000 francs is awarded triennally. Established in 1868.

| 5657 |

Fondation Pouchard
For recognition of outstanding work in the field of zoology. A monetary prize of 4,000 francs is awarded triennially. Established in 1924.

| 5658 |

Fondation Pourat
For recognition of outstanding work on the current issues in physiology. A monetary prize of 4,000 francs is awarded every four years. Established in 1876.

| 5659 |

Fondation Rene Dujarric de la Riviere
For recognition of work in biology with application to rural economics and veterinary medicine. A monetary prize of 7,000 francs is awarded biennially. Established in 1970.

| 5660 |

Fondation Roberge
To recognize the individual who has obtained the best results in curing tuberculosis, syphilis, or cancer. A monetary prize of 4,000 francs is awarded triennially. Established in 1918.

| 5661 |

Fondation Rochat-Juliard
For recognition of outstanding work in physics, mineral chemistry, or medicine. A monetary prize of 4,500 francs is awarded alternately every six years. Established in 1944.

| 5662 |

Fondation Rogissart-Sarazin-Vandevyere
To provide prizes, grants, and assistance to scientific researchers from Ardennais. Established in 1985.

| 5663 |

Fondation Roy-Vaucouloux
To encourage and assist research in the field of biology, preferably on the nature of cancer or its treatment. French scientists or a French laboratory is eligible, however, the prize is not to be divided. A monetary prize of 10,000 francs is awarded annually. Established in 1926.

| 5664 |

Fondation Salman A. Waksman
For recogniton of research in microbiology, preferably on antibiotics. A gold medal is awarded when merited. Established in 1967 for the development of studies of microbiology.

| 5665 |

Fondation Savigny
To recognize young zoologists for outstanding studies of invertebrates of Egypt and Syria. A monetary prize of 4,000 francs is awarded triennially. Established in 1856.

| 5666 |

Fondation Schutzenberger
For recognition of outstanding research in chemistry. Awards are given in alternate years in the categories of mineral chemistry and organic chemistry. A monetary prize of 4,000 francs is awarded every six years. Established in 1948.

| 5667 |

Fondation Serres
For recognition of work on general embryology that can be applied to physiology and medicine. A monetary prize of 4,000 francs is awarded every four years. Established in 1868.

| 5668 |

Fondation Servant
For recognition of outstanding works in mathematics and physics. Awards are given in alternate years. A monetary prize of 10,000 francs is awarded annually. Established in 1952.

| 5669 |

Fondation Tchihatchef
To recognize naturalists from any country for work in lesser-known Asian countries or surrounding islands (except India, Syria, Asia Minor, and Siberia). Explorations must deal with the physical and mathematical sciences and should result from observations made at the site rather than from erudition of the scientists. A monetary prize of 4,000 francs is awarded biennially. Established in 1875.

5670

Fondation Theurlot

To recognize an individual who constructs a precision instrument that, by the ingeniousness of the invention, gives great service to scientists. A monetary prize of 12,000 francs is awarded not more often than every 25 years. Established in 1868.

5671

Fondation Thorlet

For recognition of outstanding scientific work. A monetary prize of 4,000 francs is awarded triennially. Established in 1912.

5672

Fondation Tregouboff

To recognize the authors of particularly distinguished studies on Mediterranean plankton. A monetary prize of 7,000 francs is awarded annually. Established in 1971.

5673

Fondation Tremont

To encourage a scientist, engineer, artist, or craftsman who will make a useful and glorious contribution for France. A monetary prize of 4,000 francs is awarded every six years. Established in 1847.

5674

Fondation Vaillant

For recognition of outstanding research in mathematics, physics, chemistry, and natural science. Awards are given in alternate years in the following categories: mathematics and physics; and chemistry and natural science. A monetary prize of 4,000 francs is awarded every four years. Established in 1872.

5675

Fondation Valentine Allorge

To honor authors of works on cryptograms. The Prix Pierre Allorge, a monetary award of 8,000 francs is given triennially. Established in 1990.

5676

Fondation Victor Raulin

To encourage the publication of works in natural sciences. Awards are given alternately in the following categories: geology and paleontology; mineralogy and petrography; and meteorology and physics of the globe. French citizens are eligible. A monetary prize of 4,000 francs is awarded every seven years. Established in 1905.

5677

Fondation Victor Thebault

To recognize the author of an original study or interesting work in arithmetic or geometry. Preference is given to primary or secondary school teachers. A monetary prize of 4,500 francs is awarded every nine years. Established in 1943.

5678

Fondations Bellion - Charles Bouchard

For recognition of works on human health or the amelioration of the human condition, especially in medicine or surgery. A monetary prize of 5,000 francs is awarded every six years. The Prix Bellion was established in 1881. The Prix Charles Bouchard, established in 1917, was combined with the Prix Bellion in 1979.

5679

Fondations Estrade Delcros, Houllevigue, Saintour, Jules Mahyer

For recognition of outstanding works in the division of mathematics and physics or the division of chemistry and natural sciences. A monetary prize of 5,000 francs is awarded biennially. The Prix Estrade Delcros, Prix Houllevigue, Prix Saintour, and Prix Jules Mahyer were established in 1876, 1880, 1887, 1892, respectively. The four prizes were regrouped as one in 1979.

5680

Fondations Gaston Plante, Francois Hebert-Paul Jousselin

To recognize the author of the most important discovery, invention, or treatise in the field of electricity. A monetary prize of 5,000 francs is awarded every 10 years. The Prix Francois Hebert-Paul Jousselin was established in 1891, and the Prix Gaston Plante, in 1889. The two prizes were combined in 1979.

5681

Fondations Lalande - Benjamin Valz

To recognize an individual in France or elsewhere who has made the most interesting observation or most useful paper in the field of astronomy; or, to encourage a promising student of astronomy. Members of the Institut de France are not eligible. A monetary prize of 5,000 francs or a medal is awarded every eight years. The Prix Lalande was established in 1802. The Prix Benjamin Valz, established in 1874, was combined with the Prix Lalande in 1979.

5682

Prix Adrien Constantin de Magny

To recognize a craftsman or scientist whose practical works are considered remarkable by the Academie. Individuals are not required to have a diploma to be eligible. A monetary prize of 10,000 francs is awarded biennially. Established in 1963 by the Fondation Rheims.

5683

Prix Alfred Verdaguer

For recognition of a remarkable work in art, literature, or science. A monetary prize of 6,000 francs is awarded annually in one of the three fields. Established in 1948 by a large bequest of Alfred Verdaguer.

5684

Prix Ampere d'Electricite de France

To recognize one or several French scientists for remarkable research work in the field of mathematics or physics, fundamental or applied. A monetary prize of 200,000 francs is awarded annually. Established in 1974 by Electricite de France in memory of the scientist, Ampere, whose 200th birthday was celebrated in 1975.

5685

Prix Blaise Pascal du GAMNI-SMAI

To recognize one or several researchers for a remarkable work done in France using the applied numerical methods of the Science of Engineering. A monetary prize of 10,000 francs is awarded annually. Established in 1984 by le Groupement pour l'Avancement des Methodes Numerique de l'Ingenieur (GAMNI) and by la Societe de Mathematiques appliques et Industrielles (SMAI).

5686

Prix d'Aumale

To encourage individuals interested in a career in science. A monetary prize of 3,000 francs is awarded annually. Established in 1886.

5687

Prix de la Fondation Athena

To recognize a team of French medical or biomedical researchers for work they have completed or will complete in the near future that gives promise of prevention or cure of illnesses. Foreign researchers whose accomplishment has affected France or who are part of a French team may be considered. A monetary prize for laboratory equipment or improvement is awarded annually. Established in 1984 by Groupes des Populaires d'Assurances (G.P.A.).

5688

Prix de l'Ecole Centrale

To recognize the first place graduate at l'Ecole Centrale des Arts et Manufactures. A monetary prize of 3,000 francs is awarded annually. Established in 1964.

5689
Prix de l'Information Scientifique
For recognition of a writer, journalist, or science author for an informative work, written or audiovisual, on the progress of science. The work should be of high quality and scientific reliability but accessible to the public or nonspecialist. A monetary prize of 10,000 francs is awarded annually. Established in 1987.

5690
Prix de l'Institut Francais du Petrole
To recognize a French or foreign researcher or research team for a scientific work that contributes to progress in understanding techniques directly or indirectly of interest to the hydrocarbon industry. Techniques concerning action that satisfies the needs of humanity for energy and its products and materials while respecting the environment are eligible. A monetary prize of 200,000 French francs is awarded annually. Established in 1990 and awarded for the first time in 1994.

5691
Prix de Madame Claude Berthault
For recognition of a scientific work that increases the influence of the French nation. French citizens are eligible. A monetary prize of 3,000 francs is awarded annually. Established in 1921.

5692
Prix des Sciences de la Mer
To recognize research works in physical oceanography, marine ecology, chemistry, and biology. A monetary award of 55,000 francs is given biennially. Established in 1992.

5693
Prix du Commisariat a l'Energie Atomique
To recognize one or several Frenchmen for an important scientific or technical discovery in the following fields: physics, mechanics, astronomy, and their applications; and chemistry, biology, human biology, and medical sciences, as well as their applications. The Academie awards an equal number of prizes in each of the two fields. A monetary prize of 200,000 francs is awarded annually for a period of 10 years. Established in 1977 by the Commissioner of Atomic Energy.

5694
Prix du Gaz de France
For recognition of French researchers or researchers from the European Community in the fields of engineering, chemistry, materials, energy, or first matter that contributes to an increase in knowledge of interest to the gas industry. A monetary prize of 200,000 francs is awarded annually. Established in 1987.

5695
Prix Fonde par l'Etat
For recognition of outstanding works in mathematics and physics and their applications; or for works in the chemical, natural, biological, and medical sciences and their applications. The following prizes are awarded in alternate years: Grand Prix des Sciences Mathematiques et Physiques; and Grand Prix des Sciences Chimiques et Naturelles. A monetary prize of 50,000 francs is awarded annually. Established in 1975 by the National Convention and included in the state budget.

5696
Prix France Telecom
To award one or more researchers or engineers for research work in telecommunications. A monetary award of 200,000 francs is given annually.

5697
Prix Franco-Britannique de l'Academie des Sciences
To provide the opportunity for a French researcher to visit in Great Britain for a month at a university or research institute in order to develop collaboration between it and a French center working on the same subject. The Ambassador from Great Britain and the President of the Academy make the selection. Awarded annually.

5698
Prix L. E. Rivot
To recognize the four students who graduate from l'Ecole polytechnique in first and second place in the department of mines and the department of bridges and highways. Monetary prizes of 2,000 francs for each first place and 1,500 francs for each second place are awarded annually. The prize is to be used to buy science books, and for travel expenses for study. Established in 1890.

5699
Prix Lazare Carnot
To recognize excellent research works. A monetary award of 200,000 francs is given biennially. Established in 1992. Given by the Ministry of Defense.

5700
Prix Mesucora
To recognize important works in applied or industrial physics. A monetary award of 100,000 francs is awarded annually. Established in 1992.

5701
Prix Michel Monpetit
To recognize a French researcher or engineer in the field of computer sciences or automation. The judges are guided by such factors as the originality of basic ideas and the serious nature of the work, the confirmation of the results obtained, and the possibility of its practial application in the French computer sciences and automation industries. A monetary prize of 33,000 francs is awarded annually. Established in 1977 by the Institut National de Recherche en Informatique et en Automatique and le Club de la Peri-Informatique.

5702
Prix Montyon de Mecanique
To recognize individuals who design either by inventing or perfecting useful instruments for agriculture, mechanical arts, and theoretical and practical science. A monetary prize of 6,000 francs is awarded biennially. Established in 1819.

5703
Prix Osiris
For recognition of a discovery or a remarkable work in science, literature, art, industry, or anything that enhances the public good, particularly discoveries pertaining to surgery or medicine. A monetary prize of 10,000 francs is awarded triennially. Established in 1899.

5704
Prix Pechiney
To recognize young researchers with doctorates, whose work has contributed to progress in the aluminum industry or, more broadly, the field of metallurgy. The selection is made by a commission composed of members of the Academy or members of CADAS. A monetary prize of 100,000 francs is awarded annually. Established in 1986.

5705
Prix Richard Lounsbery
For recogniton of research in medicine and biology. Scientists under 40 years of age are eligible. A monetary prize of $50,000 is awarded annually. The prize is awarded alternately by the National Academy of Sciences in Washington, D.C., U.S.A., and by the Academie des Sciences in Paris. Established in 1978 and first awarded in 1979 in Washington.

5706
Institut de France
Academie des Sciences Morales et Politiques
23, quai de Conti Phone: 1 4326 3135
F-75270 Paris Cedex 06, France Fax: 1 4329 5510

5707
Prix Robert Blanche
For recognition of a work of philosophy on the subject of logic or epistemology. Awarded every four years.

5708
Bourse Marcelle Blum
To provide the opportunity for studies in female psychology. Awarded annually.

5709
Prix Dagnan-Bouveret
To encourage the study of psychology and for recognition of a work in psychology. A monetary prize is awarded annually. Established by the parents of M. Dagnan-Bouveret, who died for France.

5710
Fondation Thorlet
For recognition of virtue, social work, or scholarship in the field of history or art. Preference is given to a painter. A monetary prize is awarded annually.

5711
Grand Prix de l'Academie des Sciences Morales et Politiques
To recognize an individual for an outstanding career and work in the field of philosophy, law, economics, or history. A monetary prize is awarded. Established in 1984.

5712
Prix Docteur Rene-Joseph Laufer
For recognition of the best work on social prophylaxis. A monetary prize is awarded biennially.

5713
Prix Adrien Duvand
For recognition of the best work on civic and moral education in a democracy. A monetary prize is awarded biennially.

5714
Prix Andre Lequeux
To recognize a French researcher working on a scientific or literary subject. Awarded annually.

5715
Prix Audiffred
For recognition of a published work that inspires love of ethics and virtue, spurns egoism and envy, and instills patriotism; and for recogniton of the greatest and most beautiful self-sacrifice or devotion to any field. A monetary prize is awarded annually.

5716
Prix Auguste Gerard
For recognition of a work on the diplomatic history of France, England, Russia, Italy, Japan, Belgium, the United States, or the Balkan States that were allied with France during World War I. Works written in French are considered. A monetary prize is awarded every five years.

5717
Prix Berriat Saint-Prix
For recognition of the best work on divorce legislation in France by its merit to restrict the number of divorces and keep the family whole. A monetary prize is awarded every five years.

5718
Prix Bigot de Morogues
For recognition of the best work on poverty in France and remedies for that poverty. A monetary prize is awarded every ten years.

5719
Prix Blaise des Vosges
For recognition of the best treatise, manuscript, or book published in French having as its object the moral and material improvement of industrial and agricultural workers through instruction, unionization, or any other means. Individuals are eligible without regard to nationality. A monetary prize is awarded triennially.

5720
Prix Bordin
For recognition of papers on subjects touching the public interest, the good of humanity, the progress of science, and national honor. Awards are given in alternate years by the following sections of the academy: philosophy, morals, legislation, political economy, and history. A monetary prize is awarded biennially.

5721
Prix Carlier
For recognition of the best treatise on new methods to improve moral and material conditions of the largest social class in Paris. A monetary prize is awarded annually.

5722
Prix Charles Dupin
For recognition of the best treatise or work on statistics or political economics. A monetary prize is awarded every six years.

5723
Prix Charles Lambert
To recognize the author of the best published study or manuscript on the future of spiritualism. A monetary prize is awarded triennially.

5724
Prix Charles Leveque
For recognition of a work on methaphysics published during the preceding four years. A monetary prize is awarded every four years.

5725
Prix Charles Lyon-Caen
To recognize the author of a work on philosophy, moral sciences, law, political economics, or history. Prizes are awarded in alternate years in the following categories: philosophy, moral sciences, law, political economics, and history. A monetary prize is awarded triennially. Established by friends and associates of M. Charles-Lyon Caen on the occasion of the 40th anniversary of his election to the academy.

5726
Prix Claude Berthault
For recognition of an artistic or scientific work that increases the reputation of the French nation. Families of farmers or sailors of the coast of the Marche on the ocean, with preference given to veterans of World War I are eligible.

5727
Prix Corbay
For recognition of a useful contribution in the fields of science, art, law, agriculture, industry, or business.

5728
Prix Crouzet
For recognition of the best treatise on philosophical or religious questions exclusively from the point of view of natural religion without any diversion into the area of the supernatural. A monetary prize is awarded every five years.

5729
Prix d'Aumale
To recognize worthy scholars, to recognize those whose initial efforts seem worthy of encouragement, or to provide for the relatives left without

support by the death of such a scholar. A monetary prize is awarded annually by each of the five academies of the institut.

5730
Prix de Joest
For recognition of a discovery or written work that is most useful for the public good. A monetary prize is awarded every five years.

5731
Prix Demolombe
To recognize an author whose works are within the scope of the academie. Awards are given in alternate years in the following categories: philosophy, morality, law, political economy, and history and geography. Monetary awards are presented by one of the five sections of the academie. Awarded every four years.

5732
Prix Drouyn de Lhuys
For recognition of a published or unpublished work on history. A monetary prize is awarded annually.

5733
Prix du Baron de Courcel
For recognition of a work of literature on history that draws the attention of the public to the first centuries of French history, or that popularizes an episode of French history from the earliest time to 1000 A.D. A monetary prize is awarded every nine years.

5734
Prix du Budget
For recognition of works of philosophy, morality, law, political economy, or history and geography. Monetary awards are given in alternate years by one of the five sections of the academie. Awarded biennially.

5735
Prix du Chanoine Delpeuch
For recognition of a contribution to the moral, intellectual, and religious development of France.

5736
Prix Dulac
For recognition of acts of courage or devotion. Members of the police or military are eligible. A monetary prize is awarded annually.

5737
Prix Dupin Aine
For recognition of the best work on civil law, Roman law, criminal law, corporate law, customary law, history of law, the laws of nations, or statute law. The prize can be divided between two winners. A monetary prize is awarded triennially.

5738
Prix Edmond Freville
For recognition of the best original work, book, or article that discusses the organization, function, or work of the ministries of defense, Army or Navy. The work may deal with topics such as central administration, commanding, officers, troops, and different services. Works written in French and published in the preceding two years are considered. A monetary prize is awarded biennially.

5739
Prix Emile Girardeau
For recognition of a work or treatise on the subject of economics or sociology. A monetary prize is awarded annually.

5740
Prix Ernest Lemonon
For recognition of a work concerning contemporary foreign politics or contemporary French or foreign economics and social questions. A monetary prize is awarded annually.

5741
Prix Ernest Thorel
For recognition of the best work designed to educate the people. Pamphlets or books of current reading, other than textbooks are considered. A monetary prize is awarded biennially.

5742
Prix Estrade-Delcros
For recognition of a work completed at the request of the academie. A monetary prize is awarded every five years.

5743
Prix Eugene Salvan
For recognition of an act of courage or self-sacrifice. A monetary prize is awarded every five years.

5744
Prix Fanny et Maurice Baumont
For recognition of contributions to social work.

5745
Prix Felix de Beaujour
To recognize the author of the best treatise that contributes to the solution of the plight of the poor in different countries, particularly France. A monetary prize is awarded every five years.

5746
Prix Gabriel Monod
For recognition of a published work on the sources of the national history of France, or on any subjects favored by Gabriel Monod. A monetary prize is awarded triennially.

5747
Prix Gallet
To recognize the Catholic person or group having contributed the most to the improvement of French law and organization as it relates to the Catholic point of view. French citizens are eligible. A monetary prize is awarded annually.

5748
Prix Gegner
To recognize a philosopher-writer whose works contribute to the progress of positive science. A monetary prize is awarded triennially.

5749
Prix General Muteau
To recognize individuals or institutions who have contributed to the glory of France by their heroism, actions, or writings. A monetary prize is given annually.

5750
Prix Georges Mauguin
For recognition of a scholarly work on Napoleon Bonaparte or his era. A monetary prize is awarded biennially.

5751
Prix Georges Picot
For recognition of distinguished service to one of the causes dear to M. Georges Picot. A monetary prize is awarded every five years. Established by friends and colleagues of Georges Picot.

5752
Prix Grammaticakis-Neuman
For recognition of an outstanding work of pragmatic philosophy. Awards are given in alternate years by the following sections of the academy: philosophy, morals, and political economy. A monetary prize is awarded. Established in 1985.

5753
Prix Gustave Chaix d'Est Ange
For recognition of a work of documentary history about the Chartists movement. A monetary prize is awarded annually.

5754
Prix Halphen
For recognition of the literary work that contributes most to the progress of primary education, or to recognize the person having made such a contribution through his or her actions. A monetary prize is awarded triennially.

5755
Prix Henri Texier
To recognize the author of a treatise on individual freedom and in support of actions directed toward the defense of individual liberty. A monetary prize is awarded annually.

5756
Prix Henri Texier II
For recognition of a work to preserve the beauty of France. Awarded annually.

5757
Prix Hercule Catenacci
To encourage the publication of deluxe illustrated history books. A monetary prize is awarded annually.

5758
Prix Jacques Flach
For recognition of a work on the history of Alsace before 1648. A monetary prize is awarded every four years. Established by Madame Jacques Flach in memory of her husband.

5759
Prix Jean-Baptiste Chevallier
For recognition of the best work on the defense of private property and the laws pertaining to it in the French Civil Code. French writers are eligible. A monetary prize is awarded triennially.

5760
Prix Jean Finot
For recognition of a work with profoundly humanitarian social tendencies. A monetary prize is awarded biennially.

5761
Prix Jean Jacques Berger
For recognition of works of merit in the field of morality and politics concerning the city of Paris. Awards are given in alternate years by one of the five academies: Academie francaise, Academie des Inscriptions et Belle-Lettres, Academie des Sciences, Academie des Beaux-Arts, and Academie des Sciences Morales et Politiques. A monetary prize is awarded annually.

5762
Prix Jean Reynaud
For recognition of a work of great merit produced during the preceding five years. Members of the Institut are not eligible. If no work is judged worthy of the prize, its value may be delivered to a writer in misfortune. A monetary prize is awarded every five years.

5763
Prix Joseph du Teil
For recognition of a work on diplomatic history. A monetary prize is awarded annually.

5764
Prix Joseph Dutens
For recognition of the best book or treatise related to political economics, or its history and applications. A monetary prize is awarded every five years.

5765
Prix Joseph Hamel
For recognition of a work on commercial financial law. A monetary prize is awarded biennially.

5766
Prix Joseph Saillet
For recognition of the best work on a subject of rationalist moral philosophy or scientific morality, independent of any religious ideas. Published or unpublished works written in French may be submitted. All nationalities are eligible. A monetary prize is awarded annually.

5767
Prix Jules Andeoud
For recognition of printed works or to recognize public or private institutions that have contributed to the improvement of the conditions of the poor and working classes. A monetary prize is awarded every four years.

5768
Prix Jules et Louis Jeanbernat et Barthelemy de Ferrari Doria
For recognition of a work of literature, art, or science by a young French author. Monetary awards are given in alternate years by one of the five academies: Academie francaise, Academie des Inscriptions et Belle-Lettres, Academie des Sciences, Academie des Beaux-Arts, and Academie des Sciences Morales et Politiques. Awarded every five years by the Academie des Sciences Morales et Politiques.

5769
Prix Jules Lefort
To recognize the author or authors of working manuscripts on private and social insurance for the common classes, and on mutuality and future planning among the common social classes. A monetary prize is awarded every ten years. Established by M. and Mme. Lefort in memory of their son, Jules Lefort.

5770
Prix Koenigswarter
For recognition of the best book on the history of law published during the preceding five years. A monetary prize is awarded every five years.

5771
Prix Le Dissez de Penanrun
For recognition of works published during the preceding six years on a topic proposed by one of the five sections of the academie. Monetary prizes are awarded in alternate years by one of the five sections of the academie. Awarded annually.

5772
Prix Lefevre-Deumier de Pons
For recognition of a remarkable work on mythology, philosophy, or comparative religion. A monetary prize is awarded every ten years.

5773
Prix Leon Faucher
For recognition of a treatise on a question of political economics or on the life of a famous economist. A monetary prize is awarded triennially.

5774
Prix Limantour
For recognition of the best work on law, history, or political economy. Prizes are awarded in alternate years in the following categories: law by the Legislative Section, history by the History Section, and political

economics by the Political Economics Section. Work published in the past three years is eligible. A monetary prize is awarded biennially.

5775

Prix Louis Liard

For recognition of a work on education, philosophy, or the history of philosophy, using rational or experimental methods and marked by precision results. A monetary prize is awarded triennially.

5776

Prix Louis Marin

For recognition of a work on human sciences. A monetary prize is awarded annually.

5777

Prix Lucien de Reinach

For recognition of a work on the overseas territories written in French during the preceding two years. A monetary prize is awarded biennially.

5778

Prix Lucien Dupont

To recognize an individual who by some action has contributed to the elimination of legal and administrative procedures and formalities that complicate the life of a citizen. A monetary prize is awarded annually.

5779

Prix Maisondieu

To recognize the author or founder of a work that contributes to the improvement of the conditions of the working classes. A monetary prize is awarded biennially.

5780

Prix Malouet

To recognize a secondary school teacher in France with at least four children of whose professional merits and devotion to family deserve public recogniton. A monetary prize is awarded annually.

5781

Prix Marcel Flach

For recognition of a work on the history of Alsace after 1648. A monetary prize is awarded biennially. Established by Madame Jacques Flach at the bequest of her husband, a member of the academie.

5782

Prix Marie Laurent

To recognize the most worthy person for the accomplishment of acts of virtue or self-sacrifice. A monetary prize is awarded annually.

5783

Prix Maurice Travers

For recognition of works relative to international public or private law, or comparative law; or for works on diplomatic history. Prizes are awarded in alternate years in international public or private law or comparative law and diplomatic history. A monetary prize is awarded biennially.

5784

Prix Odilon Barrot

For recognition of the best work on juries, both criminal and civil and for recognition of the most practical and liberal work on decentralization of government. A monetary prize is awarded triennially.

5785

Prix Paul Leroy-Beaulieu

To recognize and encourage effective publicity in favor of increasing the French birth rate and defending the rights and interests of large and average families. A monetary prize is awarded triennially.

5786

Prix Paul-Michel Perret

For recognition of a book on history. Books published during the preceding three years are eligible. A monetary prize is awarded annually. Established by Madame Dupont de Latuillerie in memory of her son.

5787

Prix Paul Vigne d'Octon

To recognize the author, preferably a physician, who has demonstrated through his writings his professional behavior and life, an authentic and tangible devotion to the cause of progress of human relationships or of relationships between groups of human beings. A monetary prize is awarded biennially.

5788

Prix Rene Cassin

For recognition of a legal work of value or to recognize the author of an action or work of civic merit. A monetary prize is awarded triennially.

5789

Prix Rossi

For recognition of the best treatise on a question of social and political economics. A monetary prize is awarded annually.

5790

Prix Saintour

For recognition of works of philosophy, morality, law, political economy, or history and geography. Monetary awards are given in alternate years by one of the five sections of the academie. Awarded biennially.

5791

Prix Stassart

For recognition of the best oration of a moralist or for recognition of a work on a question of morality. A monetary prize is awarded every six years.

5792

Prix Tanesse

To recognize an individual who contributed the most to improving the condition of women during the preceding three years. A monetary prize is awarded triennially.

5793

Prix Ugo Papi - Gaston Leduc

For recognition of an outstanding work on economy. A monetary prize is awarded. Established in 1985.

5794

Prix Victor Cousin

To recognize the author of a treatise on the history of ancient philosophy. A monetary prize is awarded triennially.

5795

Prix Victor Delbos

For recognition of publications that promote spiritual life and religious philosophy in the past and future. A monetary prize is awarded biennially.

5796

Prix Wolowski

For recognition of a work of law or political economy published during the preceding eight years. Awards are given in alternate years in law and political economy. A monetary prize is awarded every four years.

5797

Prix Zerilli Marimo

To recognize an outstanding liberal economist. A monetary prize is awarded. Established in 1984.

5798

Institut de France
Academie Francaise
23, quai de Conti
F-75006 Paris, France   Phone: 1 4329 55 10

5799

Fondation General Muteau
To recognize societies or individuals who, in the preceding year, have best contributed to the glory of France in affirming peace and perfecting national defense capacities through their writings, deeds, heroic conduct, and influence. French citizens are eligible. Monetary prizes are awarded annually by the Academie Francaise, Academie des Sciences, and the Academie des Sciences Morales et Politiques. Established in 1927.

5800

Grand Prix de la Francophonie
To recognize the work of a French-speaking person who in his own country or in the international world has contributed in an eminent way to the presentation and illustration of the French language. Literary or philosophical works that assure the presence or renewal of the French language in the fields of science, technology, and information are eligible. A monetary prize of 400,000 French francs is awarded annually. Established in 1986. Sponsored by Fondation International.

5801

Grand Prix de Litterature
To recognize a writer of prose or a poet for one or more works showing great inspiration and noteworthy style. A monetary prize of 300,000 French francs is awarded biennially. Established in 1912. Sponsored by Fondation le Metais-Larlviere Fils.

5802

Grand Prix de Litterature Paul Morand
To recognize the author of one or several works that are remarkable for qualities of thought, style, and spirit of independence and freedom. Works written in French are considered. Older authors are preferred. A monetary prize of 300,000 French francs is awarded biennially. Established in 1980. Sponsored by Fondation Paul Morand.

5803

Grand Prix de Philosophie
For recognition of an outstanding work in the field of philosophy. A monetary prize of 50,000 French francs is awarded annually. Sponsored by Fondation Broquette-Gonin.

5804

Grand Prix de Poesie
To recognize a poet for his complete work. A monetary prize of 100,000 French francs is awarded annually. Established in 1957. Sponsored by Fondation Roucoules.

5805

Grand Prix du Rayonnement de la Langue Francaise
To recognize French or foreign writers for work contributing to the dissemination of the French language. Medals are awarded annually.

5806

Grand Prix du Roman
To recognize a young writer of prose for an inspirational imaginative work. Monetary prizes of 100,000 French francs are awarded annually. Established in 1912. Sponsored by Fondation Broquette-Gonin.

5807

Prix Alberic Rocheron
For recognition of a work in history or literary criticism which best demonstrates the connections between the literature and the character of an age. A monetary prize of 5,000 French francs is awarded. Established by the Rocheron Foundation.

5808

Prix Alfred Nee
For recognition of a work showing originality of thought and style. A medal is awarded annually.

5809

Prix Alfred Verdaguer
For recognition of a remarkable work of literature. A monetary prize is awarded triennially by the Academie Francaise. Awards are presented alternately by one of the three Academies: the Academie Francaise, Academie des Sciences, and Academie des Beaux-Arts. Awarded annually.

5810

Prix Alice Louis Barthou
To recognize a woman of French letters for one work or her entire work. Medals are awarded annually.

5811

Prix Anais Segalas
For recognition of the work of a talented woman. A medal is awarded annually.

5812

Prix Andre Barre
For recognition of the work with the most original thinking and clearest style. French citizens other than members of the clergy of any religion are eligible. A monetary prize is awarded biennially.

5813

Prix Andre Jullien du Breuil
To recognize a young writer for a work on the resistance, or an imaginative or critical work, preferably in the field of the novel, theatre, cinema or journalism. A monetary prize is awarded every five years.

5814

Prix Annuel de Poesie
For recognition of a work of poetry. A medal is awarded annually.

5815

Prix Antoine Girard
To recognize an individual who has honored France through his scientific, literary or artistic work. French citizens, preferably born of Savoyard parents, are eligible. A monetary prize is awarded every six years.

5816

Prix Antony Valabregue
To recognize a young poet who has published one volume of verse, and to encourage him in his literary work. A monetary prize is awarded biennially.

5817

Prix Auguste Capdeville (De Beziers)
To recognize the three prize-winners of a poetry competition. Poems of 100 lines or less, about the love of a son for his mother, are eligible. A monetary prize is awarded annually.

5818

Prix Balleroy
To recognize a talented poet, even if he is unknown or little known. A monetary prize is awarded every ten years.

5819

Prix Biguet
For recognition in the field of literature. Awards are given for literature, literary criticism, and translation. Monetary prizes are awarded annually in each category.

5820
Prix Bordin
To encourage superior literature. A silver medal is awarded annually.

5821
Prix Botta
For recognition of outstanding achievement in literature. A monetary prize is awarded every five years.

5822
Prix Boudenoot
To recognize the author of a work that best inspires a love of France and maintains the sacred fire of patriotism. Works published during the preceding five years are eligible. A monetary prize is awarded every five years.

5823
Prix Brieux
For recognition of a play of at least three acts, with social or moral implications. Plays presented in France during the preceding two years, or published or unpublished manuscripts chosen by the Academy are eligible. The plays may present any political opinion, but may not be lampoons. The writer must be French. A medal is awarded biennially.

5824
Prix Broquette-Gonin
To recognize the author of a philosophical, political or literary work that inspires the love of truth, beauty, and virtue. A monetary prize of 5,000 French francs is awarded annually.

5825
Prix Calmann-Levy
For recognition of a recently published literary work or for all the literary pieces of a man of letters. Medals are awarded triennially.

5826
Prix Capuran
For recognition of the best poem on a moral or religious subject or for any play with a message for young people. A silver medal is awarded triennially.

5827
Prix Cardinal Grente
For recognition of the entire work of a member of the Catholic clergy, secular or regular. The Academie designates the winner after accepting nominations by Catholic clergy and laity, or agrees to candidates posed directly by the clergy. A monetary prize of 30,000 French francs is awarded biennially. Established by Cardinal Georges Grente.

5828
Prix Charles Blanc
For recognition of a written work in art history. A medal is awarded annually.

5829
Prix Claire Virenque
To recognize young authors of a collection of poems, or a novel or biography demonstrating Christian inspiration. Prizes are awarded in alternate years in the following categories: (1) poetry; and (2) novels or biography. Books published during the preceding year are eligible. A monetary prize is awarded annually.

5830
Prix Constant Dauguet
To recognize the author of the best work on morals, particularly from the Catholic point of view. A silver medal is awarded annually.

5831
Prix de Joest
To recognize the author of a work most useful for the public good. A medal is awarded every five years.

5832
Prix de Jouy
For recognition of an empirical, imaginative or critical work studying current customs. Published works of the preceding two years are considered. Medals are awarded biennially.

5833
Prix de la Biographie
For recogntion of an outstanding biography. A monetary prize of 50,000 French francs is awarded annually. Sponsored by Fondation Broquette-Gonin.

5834
Prix de la Critique
For recognition of outstanding literary criticism. A monetary prize of 50,000 French francs is awarded annually.

5835
Prix de la Nouvelle
For recognition of the best book of short stories. A monetary prize of 100,000 French francs is awarded annually.

5836
Prix de l'Essai
For recognition of the best essay or nonfiction writing. A monetary prize of 50,000 French francs is awarded annually.

5837
Prix de M. et Mme. Louis Marin
For recognition of a work of literature or history. A monetary prize of 5,000 French francs is awarded triennially.

5838
Prix de Soussay
For recognition of an operatic libretto in verse or prose that has not yet been produced. The librettos can be in printed or manuscript form. Selection is made by a committee whose members are divided equally between the Academie Francaise and Academie des Beaux Arts. A monetary prize is awarded triennially.

5839
Prix Diane Potier-Boes
For recognition of a work on the history of Egypt or a Mediterranean country. A monetary prize of 10,000 French francs is awarded annually.

5840
Prix Docteur Binet-Sangle
To recognize the writer whose work expresses the most daring and courageous ideas or to recognize a poet. A monetary prize of 5,000 French francs is awarded annually.

5841
Prix Dodo
For recognition of acts of virtue or bravery, or for works on political economy or practical socialism that benefit religion, morality and good moral character. A silver medal is awarded annually.

5842
Prix du Baron de Courcel
For recognition of a literary work that draws public interest to the first centuries of French history (Merovingian and Carolingian ages), or popularizes the period of history from the beginnings of the French tribes to about 1000 A.D. A medal is awarded every nine years.

5843
Prix du Cinema - Prix Jean Leduc
To honor literary talents which have found expression in French cinematography. A monetary prize of 50,000 French francs is awarded.

5844
Prix du Theatre
To recognize the author of one or several dramatic works created during the preceding year; to recognize the author of a dramatic work which has not been produced but has been published; or to recognize the author of an adaptation that is equal in the French language to an original work. A monetary prize of 50,000 French francs is awarded annually.

5845
Prix Dumas-Millier
To recognize a writer whose work is an honor to the French language and contributes to the dissemination of French thought. French writers who are at least 45 years of age are eligible. A monetary prize of 5,000 French francs is awarded annually.

5846
Prix Durchon-Louvet
For recognition of contributions in any area that the Academie chooses to bestow. A monetary prize of 5,000 French francs is awarded annually.

5847
Prix Emile Augier
To recognize the author of the best prose or verse play of three or more acts shown during the past three years, at the Theatre Francais or the Theatre de l'Odeon. Members of the Academy are eligible. A monetary prize is awarded triennially.

5848
Prix Emile Faguet
For recognition of outstanding literary criticism. A monetary prize is awarded triennially.

5849
Prix Emile Hinzelin
For recognition of a volume of verse or a play in verse. The author must follow the rules of French prosody, and show his love for France. A medal is awarded annually.

5850
Prix Eugene Carriere
For recognition of a work of art history. A medal is awarded annually.

5851
Prix Eugene Colas
For recognition of a work of history. A monetary prize of 10,000 French francs is awarded annually.

5852
Prix Eugene Piccard
For recognition of the best work on Europe or a work on contemporary or modern history. A monetary prize of 10,000 French francs is awarded annually.

5853
Prix Eve Delacroix
For recognition of an essay or a novel which combines literary qualities with a sense of the dignity of man and the responsibility of the writer. A monetary prize of 5,000 French francs is awarded annually.

5854
Prix Fabien
To recognize the author who has proposed the most just, efficient, and practical methods for improving the moral and material position of the largest class. A silver medal is awarded annually.

5855
Prix Feydau de Brou
For recognition of a work on the 16th, 17th, and 18th centuries in French history. The work should distinguish itself by its scholarship and perfection of form. A medal is awarded biennially.

5856
Prix Francois Coppee
For recognition of the work of a poet, preferably a poet who is just beginning his career. A silver medal is awarded biennially.

5857
Prix Furtado (de Bayonne)
To recognize the author of a useful book of literature. A silver medal is awarded.

5858
Prix Georges Dupau
For recognition of outstanding contributions to literature. A monetary prize of 5,000 French francs is awarded annually.

5859
Prix Georges Goyau
For recognition of a historical work on the Catholic missions of the 13th through 18th centuries, or on particular episodes of these missions. If such a work cannot be found, the prize can be given in the interest of historical studies. A silver medal is awarded biennially.

5860
Prix Gobert
For recognition of the most eloquent excerpt of a history of France. A grand prize and a second prize are awarded annually.

5861
Prix Guizot
For recognition of the best work published in the past three years on one of the great epochs of French literature or on the life and works of great French prose or poetry writers, philosophers, historians, orators or critics. A medal is awarded triennially.

5862
Prix Gustave Le Metais Lariviere Fils (Prix d'Academie)
For recognition of a work of literature. A monetary prize and silver medals are awarded annually.

5863
Prix Halphen
For recognition of the work judged by the Academy to be the most noteworthy from a literary, historical, and moral viewpoint. A monetary prize is awarded triennially.

5864
Prix Helene Porges
For recognition of a book that will instill in French school children a love for their country. A monetary prize is awarded every four years.

5865
Prix Henri Jousselin
For recognition of a work of light verse. Poetry which is short and fluent like a song is considered. A medal is awarded biennially.

5866
Prix Henri Mondor
To recognize a poet writing in the style of Stephane Mallarme or a writer of studies on Mallarme. French poets and writers are eligible. A monetary prize of 10,000 French francs is awarded.

5867
Prix Hercule Catenacci
To encourage the publication of deluxe illustrated books on poetry, literature, history, archaeology or music. Monetary prizes are awarded annually by L'Academie Francaise, L'Academie Inscriptions, l'Academie des Beaux-Arts, and L'Academie des Science Morales.

5868
Prix Heredia
To recognize authors of works of poetry or prose. Awards are given in alternate years to: (1) a Latin American writer for a work of prose or poetry written in French; and (2) the author of a printed collection of sonnets. Medals are awarded annually.

5869
Prix J. J. Weiss
For recognition of a prose work in the purest classical style on travel, literature, literary or dramatic criticism or politics. A silver medal is awarded biennially.

5870
Prix Jean Bouscatel
For recognition of an outstanding volume of verse. If no qualifying volume is submitted, a book on poetry, or a poet or poets is considered. A silver medal is awarded triennially.

5871
Prix Jean-Jacques Berger
For recognition of the most outstanding works concerning the city of Paris. Candidates must justify their French qualities. A monetary prize is awarded annually by a different Academy of the Institut de France each year. Awarded every five years by the Academie Francaise.

5872
Prix Jean Reynaud
For recognition of an original work of outstanding style with an inventive and original character, produced in the preceding five years. If no entry is judged worthy of the prize, the money will be given to a literary person who has fallen into misfortune. Members of the Institut de France are not eligible. A monetary prize is awarded every five years.

5873
Prix Jeanne Scialtel
For recognition of the best translation. A monetary prize of 5,000 French francs is awarded triennially.

5874
Prix Jules et Louis Jeanbernat et Barthelemy de Ferrari Doria
For recognition of an outstanding work on literature, science or art. Young French authors are eligible. A monetary prize is awarded annually by each of the five academies: Academie Francaise; Academie des Inscriptions et Belle Lettres; Academie des Sciences; Academie des Beaux Arts; and Academie des Sciences Morales et Politiques. Established by Emmanuel Jeanbernat as a memorial to his two sons who were killed fighting for the freedom of France.

5875
Prix Jules Favre
For recognition of a literary work in the form of poetry or prose that treats moral, educational, philological, or historical questions. Women are eligible. A monetary prize is awarded biennially.

5876
Prix Jules Janin
For recognition of the best translation of a Latin or Greek work published in the preceding three years. A medal is awarded triennially.

5877
Prix Juteau-Duvigneaux
For recognition of works on morality, especially from the Catholic point of view. A silver medal is awarded annually.

5878
Prix Kastner-Boursault
For recognition of one of the works submitted to the various competitions of the Academie. A monetary prize is awarded triennially.

5879
Prix Lafontaine
For recognition of a moral literary work that can be read by all. A bronze medal is awarded biennially.

5880
Prix Lambert
To recognize men of letters or their widows if they deserve public recognition. A monetary prize is awarded annually.

5881
Prix Lange
To recognize individuals of French nationality. Monetary prizes are awarded annually.

5882
Prix Langlois
For recognition of the best translation of verse or prose of a Greek, Latin or other foreign work into the French language. A silver medal is awarded annually.

5883
Prix Le Fevre-Deumier (de Pons)
For recognition of the best poetic work. Epic poems, dramatic poems or single poems published during the preceding five years are considered. A monetary prize is awarded evey five years.

5884
Prix Louis Barthou
To recognize a writer whose work or life has glorified and served the reputation and best interests of France. French writers who are members of the Institute are eligible. A medal is awarded annually.

5885
Prix Louis Castex
For recognition of non-fiction literary works such as reminiscences of important voyages or explorations (excluding adventures in aviation). Efforts which treat discoveries in archaeology and ethnology are also considered. A monetary prize of 10,000 French francs is awarded annually.

5886
Prix Louis P. Miller
For recognition of works contributing to the love of morality and virtue, in particular, remembrance and gratitude. A silver medal is awarded annually.

5887
Prix Lucien Tisserand
To recognize a novelist between 40 and 50 years of age who has proven his talent and has a long future ahead of him. A medal is awarded annually.

5888
Prix Maille-Latour-Landry
To recognize a young writer whose talent has proven that he should be encouraged to follow a literary career. A monetary prize is awarded biennially.

5889
Prix Maise Ploquin-Caunan et Docteur Jacques Perdrizet
To recognize the author of a work of romantic poetry in classical or free verse. The author should be unrecognized previously. A monetary prize of 5,000 French francs is awarded biennially.

5890
Prix Marcelin Guerin
For recognition of works in history, oratory, and all kinds of literature which seem to best honor France, advance French ideas, customs, and character, and lead society toward the most beneficial principles for the future. A silver medal is awarded annually.

5891
Prix Marcelle Millier
To recognize a female writer whose work will be an honor to French literature. French writers who are at least 45 years old are eligible. A monetary prize of 5,000 French francs is awarded.

5892
Prix Marechal Foch
For recognition of a work on the future of the nation's defense. French officers, engineers, scholars, and philosophers are eligible. Books that are not a purely technical work and are readable by a general audience or that favor the progress of military science and art are considered. Medals are awarded biennially.

5893
Prix Marie-Eugene Simon Henri Martin
For recognition of a historical work. A monetary prize of 5,000 French francs is awarded.

5894
Prix Marie Havez-Planque
For recognition of a collection of stories, news stories, or poetry. Awards are given in alternate years in the following categories: (1) a collection of stories or news stories or for a psychological novel, written in poetic prose of "pure" French; and (2) a collection of classical poetry. Preference is given to authors who have not yet been published. A monetary prize is awarded annually.

5895
Prix Maujean
For recognition of a literary, philosophical, historical or political work that benefits the public good. Works by French authors recently published in France are considered. Medals are awarded every four years.

5896
Prix Maurice Trubert
For recognition of a literary work in prose or verse that tends toward the classical traditions and presents morality from a Catholic point of view. Authors born in France who are 30 years of age or less are eligible. A monetary prize is awarded annually.

5897
Prix Max Barthou
To recognize a writer whose highly inspirational talent has been proven or has shown great promise. French writers under 30 years of age are eligible. A silver medal is awarded annually.

5898
Prix Monseigneur Marcel
To recognize the author of a work on the philosophical, literary or artistic history of the Renaissance. A monetary prize is awarded annually or biennially.

5899
Prix Montyon
For recognition of literary works of high moral character. French authors are eligible. A monetary prize of 5,000 French francs is awarded annually.

5900
Prix Mottart
For recognition of a literary work. Monetary prizes of 20,000 French francs and 10,000 French francs are awarded annually.

5901
Prix Narcisse Michaut
For recognition of the best work of French literature. A medal is awarded biennially.

5902
Prix Nicolas Missarel
For recognition of a work on scientific discoveries, relevant to all disciplines, which contributes to the benefit of mankind. A silver medal is awarded annually.

5903
Prix Pascal Fortuny
To recognize the author of a poem of 200 lines or less, preferably written in classical form. A medal is awarded annually.

5904
Prix Paul Flat
For recognition of the best critical work and the best novel published by a young writer. Writers between 30 and 40 years of age are eligible. A silver medal is awarded annually.

5905
Prix Paul Hervieu
To recognize the author of a play of superior and tasteful style, shown in other than regular commercial theatres. A medal is awarded biennially.

5906
Prix Paul Labbe-Vauquelin
For recognition of a collection of verse inspired preferably by regionalism or by intimate feelings. A silver medal is awarded biennially.

5907
Prix Paul Teissonniere
For recognition of the best published liberal work on a moral, philosophical, or religious subject. A silver medal is awarded.

5908
Prix Paul Verlaine
For recognition of poetry of any kind except dramatic poetry. Medals are awarded biennially.

5909
Prix Pierre Benoit
To recognize the author of a work on the life or work of Pierre Benoit. A monetary prize of 40,000 French francs is awarded annually. Sponsored by Fondation Cousin de Mandet.

5910
Prix Pierre de Regnier
For recognition of a literary work. Monetary prizes of 10,000 French francs and 5,000 French francs are awarded annually.

5911
Prix Pierre Villey
To encourage the blind to overcome their disability through intellectual work. Awarded every five years.

5912
Prix Pol Comiant
For recognition of a work on the correct usage of the French language. A medal is awarded triennially.

5913
Prix Raoul Follereau
To recognize a doctor or a missionary who by his work or example played an important part in the "Battle Against Leprosy". Doctors and missionaries are eligible regardless of sex, religion, or nationality. A monetary prize is awarded biennially.

5914
Prix Rene Bardet
For recognition of a poetic work. A silver medal is awarded biennially.

5915
Prix Rene Petiet
For recognition of a writer of history of a Western province (Argoumois, Poitou, Aunis, Saintonage and Bretagne). A medal is awarded.

5916
Prix Roberge
To recognize an author of novels or verse. Awards are given in alternate years to: (1) a young poet who has published no more than two volumes of verse; and (2) a young author who has published no more than two novels. A medal is awarded annually.

5917
Prix Roland de Jouvenal
For recognition of a literary work. A monetary prize of 10,000 French francs is awarded biennially.

5918
Prix Saint-Cricq-Theis
For recognition of a poetic work with a spiritualistic, moral, patriotic, dramatic or other theme. A silver medal is awarded triennially.

5919
Prix Saintour
For recognition of various types of works including lexicons, grammar books, editions of criticism, commentaries and others that are a study of the French language, in particular, from the 16th century to the present. A medal is awarded annually.

5920
Prix Sivet
To recognize a writer not living in Paris. A poet of the land is eligible with preference given to a poet from the Forez region. A monetary prize of 5,000 French francs is awarded every five years.

5921
Prix Sobrier-Arnould
To recognize the two authors of the best works in moral literature which are instructive to youth. French citizens are eligible. Monetary prizes are awarded annually.

5922
Prix Therouanne
For recognition of the best historical work published during the preceding year. A medal is awarded annually.

5923
Prix Thiers
For recognition of the best historical work published during the preceding three years, and to encourage literary and historical writers. A medal is awarded every three years.

5924
Prix Toirac
For recognition of the best comedy in verse or prose that played at the Theatre Francais during the preceding year. A monetary prize is awarded annually.

5925
Prix Toutain
For recognition of a work of local history or a work of regional literature. A medal is awarded triennially.

5926
Prix Valentine Abraham Verlain
To recognize a woman of letters or a needy female artist. A monetary prize is awarded annually.

5927
Prix Valentine de Wolmar
For recognition of the most beautiful novel or collection of poetry published during the preceding year. A monetary award of 5,000 French francs and pieces from the founder's jewelry collection are awarded annually.

5928
Prix Vega et Lods de Wegmann
For recognition of literary works, in prose or verse, of Christian inspiration and true literary merit. Works on patriotism, general sentiment, pure beauty or high morals are considered, if they are of good literary value and are not libertine, as in the 17th century. If no such works are submitted, the prizes may go to aged or ill writers recommended by their talent and dignified life. A monetary prize of 5,000 French francs is awarded when merited.

5929
Prix Vitet
For recognition of contributions in any area that the Academie chooses to bestow. Medals are awarded annually.

5930
Prix Xavier Marmier
To recognize a writer, man or woman, in a difficult situation. A monetary prize is awarded annually.

5931
Prix Yvan Loiseau
For recognition in the field of history. A monetary prize of 5,000 French francs is awarded annually.

5932
Institut de la Vie
Tour C.I.T.
3, rue de l'Arrivee
BP 244
F-75749 Paris Cedex 17, France   Phone: 1 4538 99 09

5933
Prix Moet-Hennessy Louis-Vuitton
For recognition of a discovery in pure or applied science in the field of biotechnology. A monetary prize of 500,000 French francs is awarded. The prize has been given only one time in 1988.

5934
Institut de Paleontologie Humaine
Museum National d'Histoire Naturelle
1, rue Rene Panhard
F-75013 Paris, France   Phone: 1 43316291

5935

Bourse Prince Rainier III de Monaco
To assist a young researcher of any nationality in the fields of prehistory, human paleontology, or quaternary geology. Researchers must apply by December 15. A monetary prize of 20,000 francs to finance research in the field or laboratory is awarded biennially. Established in 1975 in honor of Prince Rainier III of Monaco by the Principality.

5936

Institut des Sciences de la Sante
86, rue Bac
F-75007 Paris, France
Phone: 1 45446810
Fax: 1 42840313

5937

Prix Europe et Medecine
For recognition in the field of medicine at the European level. A monetary prize of 20,000 ECUS is awarded.

5938

Prix Medecine et Culture
For recognition in the field of medicine and culture. A monetary prize of 30,000 French francs is awarded.

5939

Prix Recherche et Medecine
For recognition in the field of research and medicine. A monetary prize of 150,000 French francs is awarded. Established in 1980.

5940

Prix Sante Publique
For recognition of research in the field of health and socio-economics. A monetary prize of 50,000 French francs is awarded. Formerly: (1989) Prix Socio-economie de la Sante.

5941

Institut National de la Sante et de la Recherche Medicale
2 ter, rue Alesia
F-75014 Paris, France
Phone: 1 4581 62 58

5942

Prix Andre Lichtwitz
For recognition of outstanding research on calcium and phosphorus metabolism, either in the field of clinical or experimental biology, or in the field of basic science. French or foreign research workers are eligible for work done during the preceding year. A monetary prize of 11,000 French francs is awarded annually. Established in 1968 by Mme. Antonia Lichtwitz, widow of Dr. Andre Lichtwitz.

5943

International Academy of Astronautics
6, rue Galilee
BP 126816
F-75766 Paris Cedex 16, France
Phone: 1 4723 82 15

5944

Daniel and Florence Guggenheim International Astronautics Award
To recognize individuals who have made outstanding contributions to the advancement of space science and technology. Established in 1961.

5945

International Academy of Astronautics Book Awards
To recognize individuals who have made contributions over a lifetime to the advancement of space science and technology and the peaceful uses of outer space. Nominations are made by the Awards Committee of the International Academy of Astronautics. Established in 1986.

5946

International Academy of Astronautics Section Awards
To recognize individuals who have made contributions over a lifetime to the advancement of space science and technology and the peaceful uses of outer space. Nominations are made by the Awards Committee of the International Academy of Astronautics. A certificate is awarded annually at the honor luncheon of the IAA. Established in 1985.

5947

Von Karman Award
To recognize individuals who have made contributions over a lifetime to the advancement of space science and technology and the peaceful uses of outer space. Nominations are made by the Awards Committee of the International Academy of Astronautics. A certificate is awarded annually at the honor luncheon of the IAA. Established in 1983 in honor of the birth of Theodore von Karman (1881-1963).

5948

International Academy of the History of Science
(Academie Internationale d'Histoire des Sciences)
Secretaire Perpetuel
12, rue Colbert
F-75002 Paris, France

5949

Alexander Koyre Medal
For recognition of an outstanding work of research in the history of science. The Council of the Academy makes the nomination. A silver medal is awarded biennially at the Academy's convention. Established in 1968 to commemorate the work of Alexander Koyre (1892-1964), an historian of science.

5950

Prize for Young Historians of Science
To recognize an outstanding contribution to scholarship in the history of science by a young scholar. Awarded occasionally when merited. Established in 1968.

5951

International Amateur Rugby Federation
(Federation Internationale de Rugby Amateur)
7, Cite d'Antin
F-75009 Paris, France
Phone: 1 4874 84 75
Fax: 1 4526 19 19

5952

FIRA Championship Awards
For recognition of winners at the junior international tournament and FIRA championships.

5953

Medailles de la FIRA
For recognition of outstanding contributions by the directors or various commissions to the sport of rugby. Three classes of Honor Medals are awarded: gold, silver, and bronze. Awarded annually.

5954

Medailles du Merite
For recognition of outstanding contributions by the director, commissions, players or referees to the sport of rugby. Medals of Honor of gold, silver, or bronze are awarded annually.

5955

Rugby World Juniors Championship Awards
No further information was available for this edition.

5956
International Animated Film Centre
(Festival International du Cinema d'Animation - Annecy)
Festival d'Annecy
2, boulevard du Lycee
BP 399
F-74013 Annecy, France
Phone: 5057 41 72
Fax: 5067 81 95

5957
Annecy International Animated Film Festival
(Festival International du Cinema d'Animation Annecy)
For recognition of outstanding feature and short animated films. The jury may award the following official prizes: Grand Prize of the Animated Film, Prize for Best First Film -to a first work made for public presentation, Prize for a Short Film, Best Feature Film Prize, two Special Distinctions -to script or music or quality of animation or backgrounds at the jury's discretion, one Special Distinction -to a computer generated animated film, Prize for Commissioned Film (educational, scientific, for firms, etc.), Prize for Best Commercial, Prize for Best Credits or Trailer or Interlude or Animated Sequence, Prize for T.V. Series (up to 13 feets), Prize for T.V. Series (more than 13 feets), Best Poster, Youth Prize, Audio-Visual Prize from the Ministry of Agriculture and Forestry, Special ASIFA Prize, International Film Critics Prize, Don Quixote Prize awarded by the International Federation of Film Societies, Press Prize, and Audience Prize. The Festival is held biennially. Established in 1956.

5958
International Association for the Exchange of Students for Technical Experience
Boite Postale 3672
54096 Nancy Cedex, France
Phone: 83 376441
Fax: 83 579794

5959
IAESTE Award Certificate
To recognize an individual and/or organization for support and cooperation which over the years has helped promote the aims of IAESTE. Nominations by any IAESTE National Committee may be submitted at any time. A certificate is awarded when merited. Established in 1984.

5960
International Association for the Scientific Study of Mental Deficiency
(Association Internationale Pour l'Etude Scientifique de l'Arrieration Mentale)
c/o Dr. N. Ross
Association de Villepinte
27 rue Maubeuge
F-75009 Paris, France

5961
Awards
To encourage research in the field of mental retardation, including causes, prevention, diagnosis, evaluation, therapy, rehabilitation, management, education, and social habilitation. Awards are presented.

5962
International Association of Cancer Registries
c/o International Agency for Research on
  Cancer
150, cours Albert Thomas
F-69372 Lyon Cedex 08, France
Phone: 7273 8485
Fax: 7273 8575

5963
Honorary Member
For recognition of achievement in the field of cancer registration. Nominations must be made by a member or members of the Association. A certificate is awarded awarded annually at scientific meetings of the Association. Established in 1980. The International Agency for Research on Cancer also grants research training fellowships and a Visiting Scientist Award annually.

5964
International Association of Engineering Geology
(Association Internationale de Geologie de l'Ingenieur)
Laboratoire Central des Ponts et
  Chaussees
58, boulevard Lefebvre
F-75732 Paris Cedex, France
Phone: 1 40435243

5965
International Association of Engineering Geology Awards
To recognize individuals for research and study in various engineering-geological problems. Awards are presented.

5966
International Association of Geodesy
(Association Internationale de Geodesie)
2, avenue Pasteur
F-94160 Saint-Mande, France
Phone: 1 4398 83 27
Fax: 1 4398 80 31

5967
Guy Bomford Prize
For recognition of outstanding individual contributions to geodetic studies. Individuals under 40 years of age are eligible. A monetary prize is awarded every four years at the General Assembly. Established in 1975 by the Royal Society's British National Committee for Geodesy and Geophysics, and the International Association of Geodesy in honor of Brigadier Guy Bomford, formerly President of the International Association of Geodesy, and Chairman of the British National Committee.

5968
International Association of Penal Law
(Association Internationale de Droit Penal)
19 avenue Montebello
F-64000 Pau, France

5969
Honorary Member
To recognize distinguished persons who have served the Association in a particularly important manner.

5970
International Astronautical Federation
3-5, rue Mario-Nikis
F-75015 Paris, France
Phone: 1 4567 42 60

5971
Charles Stark Draper Award
To recognize an outstanding scientific or technical achievement in astronautics with international significance. A monetary award of $1,000 (US) and a diploma were awarded annually during the IAF Congress. Established in 1987 in memory of Charles Stark Draper. (Discontinued in 1989)

5972
Allan D. Emil Memorial Award
For recognition of an outstanding contribution in space science, space technology, space medicine, or space law which involved the participation of more than one nation and/or which furthered the possibility of greater international cooperation in astronautics. An IAF member society may make nominations. A monetary award of $1,000 US and a diploma are awarded annually during the IAF Congress. Established in 1977 in memory of Allan D. Emil.

5973
**International Automobile Federation
(Federation Internationale de l'Automobile)**
8, place de la Concorde
F-75008 Paris, France
Phone: 1 4265 9951
Fax: 1 4924 9800

5974
Challenge for Road Safety
For recognition of the motoring organization that has made the most worthwhile contribution to road safety in the previous three years.

5975
FIA F3000 International Champion
To recognize the winner of the F3000 International Series.

5976
FIA Formula 1 World Champion
To recognize the winner of the Series of Formula 1 races. A prize is also given to the manufacturers. Established in 1950.

5977
FIA World Rally Champion
To recognize the winner of the World Rally and the manufacturer of the winning automobile.

5978
FIA World Sports Prototype Champion
To recognize the winner of the World Sports Prototype Series and the manufacturer of the winning automobile. (Discontinued)

5979
**International Brain Research Organization
(Organisation Internationale de Recherche sur le Cerveau)**
51, boulevard de Montmorency
F-75016 Paris, France
Phone: 1 45206006

5980
IBRO/UNESCO Fellowship Programme
To stimulate and facilitate international and interdisciplinary advanced training and research in the basic sciences of importance to brain research. Two types of fellowships are awarded: IBRO/UNESCO Research Fellowships and IBRO/UNESCO Travel Fellowships. The research fellowships are designed to fulfill the specific interdisciplinary objectives of IBRO and in this way not to duplicate other fellowship programs. Particularly, IBRO fellowships are given to carefully selected basic scientists in one of the various specialties brought together in IBRO. To be eligible, a candidate has to: be already engaged in the field of brain research; apply for a stay in a laboratory in a country specified on the list of fellowships placed at the disposal of IBRO; return to the country of origin (i.e., where the candidate works at the time the application is made) upon termination of the fellowship so that the candidate's home country may benefit from her/his broadened knowledge; produce evidence that the theoretical and practical knowledge to be acquired during a stay in a foreign laboratory will be beneficial to her/his scientific development; and apply, preferably, to visit an institute that employs a multidisciplinary approach to the candidate's own field of research. Applications should be submitted before March 31 or September 30. Fellowship duration is six months to one year, depending on the donor country. Established in 1963 in collaboration with United Nations Educational, Scientific and Cultural Organization (UNESCO).

5981
**International Children's Centre
(Centre International de l'Enfance)**
Chateau de Longchamp
Bois de Boulogne
F-75016 Paris, France
Phone: 1 4520 79 92
Fax: 1 4525 73 67

5982
**International Nathalie Masse Prize
(Prix International Nathalie Masse)**
To recognize an individual who has carried out, either alone or leading a team, a work for deprived children, preferably in a developing country, whatever the field of his activities may be. Individuals who are under 50 years of age may apply by December 31. A monetary prize of 50,000 French francs and travel expenses to Paris for the awarding of the prize are presented annually. Established in 1979 in memory of Dr. Nathalie Masse who died in 1975. She was in charge of the training activities of the ICC for 18 years and made an invaluable contribution to improving the condition of children in the world. Sponsored by ICC Friends Association.

5983
International Commission for Optics
Secretariat
BP 147
F91403 Orsay Cedex, France
Fax: 1 6943192

5984
ICO Galileo Galilei Medal
For recognition of outstanding contributions to the field of optics that are achieved under comparatively unfavorable circumstances. The Galileo Galilei Medal, funding of registration and approved local expenses at the next ICO General Meeting, and special attention and appropriate measures of ICO to support the future activities of the award winner will be presented annually.

5985
ICO Prize
To recognize an individual for outstanding achievement in the field of optics. Individuals under 40 years of age are eligible. A monetary award of $1,000 and a medal are presented annually. Established in 1982.

5986
International Committee for Amateur-Built Aircraft
10/12 rue du Capitaine Menard
F-75015 Paris, France
Phone: 1 4579 24 77
Fax: 1 4579 73 15

5987
Awards
For recognition of achievement in amateur aircraft construction and antique aircraft restoration. Awards are presented.

5988
**International Committee for Fair Play
(Comite International pour le Fair Play)**
c/o ACNO
21, rue d'Artois
F-75008 Paris, France
Phone: 1 4256 21 71
Fax: 1 4256 18 57

5989
**Trophee International du Fair Play Pierre de Coubertin
(Pierre de Coubertin International Trophy for Fair Play)**
For recognition of fair play attitudes and careers that demonstrate fair play in sports. The following criteria are considered for the award: (1) an act of fair play which "costed" or "may have costed" the victory to the sportsman who sacrificed or compromised his or her chances of winning, either by complying to a written or an unwritten rule, or by following a humanitarian feeling. Also considered are audiences that displayed exceptional sporting spirit; (2) a sports career, ended recently or for some time, and remarkable for constant sportsmanship during competition; or (3) the career of a manager (umpire, journalist, trainer, sports administrator, educator, journalist, doctor, etc.) who has encouraged an attitude of fair play among the athletes, the public, and the parents of young competitors. The deadline for nominations is April 15. A trophy is awarded annually at the UNESCO House in Paris. Established in 1964.

5990
International Committee for the Diffusion of Arts and Literature Through the Cinema
(Comite International pour la Diffision des Arts et des Lettres par le Cinema - CIDALC)
24 boulevard Poissoniere
F-75009 Paris, France　　　　　　　　　　Phone: 1 4246 13 60

5991
Leonide Moguy CIDALC Prize
To promote the creation, diffusion, and exchange of educational, cultural, and documentary films to acquaint people with philosophical, legal, social, economic, cultural, and geographical circumstances different than their own, and to improve international relations. Awarded annually.

5992
International Committee for the Support of Charter 77 in Czechoslovakia
(Comite International pour le Soutien de la Charte 77 en Tchecoslovaquie)
5, rue de Medicis
F-75006 Paris, France　　　　　　　　　　Phone: 1 4326 52 23

5993
Jan Palach Prize
To recognize an individual or group for outstanding work in art, literature, humanities, or science. A monetary prize of 50,000 French francs is awarded. Named for Jan Palach, a Czech student who set himself on fire in 1968 as a protest against destruction of basic human freedoms in his country.

5994
International Confederation of Societies of Authors and Composers
(Confederation Internationale des Societes d'Auteurs et Compositeurs)
11, rue Keppler
F-75116 Paris, France　　　　　　　　　　Phone: 1 4553 59 37

5995
CISAC Prize
To provide recognition for the best work dealing with research in the copyright field, preferably the problems of international copyright. A monetary prize is awarded triennially.

5996
International Council for Game and Wildlife Conservation
(Conseil International de la Chasse et de la Conservation du Gibier)
15, rue de Teheran　　　　　　　　　　　Phone: 1 4563 51 33
F-75008 Paris, France　　　　　　　　　　Fax: 1 4563 32 94

5997
International Council for Game and Wildlife Conservation Awards
To recognize national and international agencies, organizations, and individuals including hunters and land users concerned with hunting and wildlife conservation. The Council sponsors competitions and symposia and bestows awards annually.

5998
International Council of the French Language
(Conseil International de la Langue Francaise)
103, rue de Lille
F-75007 Paris, France　　　　　　　　　　Phone: 1 47050793

5999
International Council of the French Language Competitions
To recognize individuals for contributions in understanding problems concerning the usage of the French language, its relationship with other languages, and the education aspects of the language. Competitions are held.

6000
International Council on Monuments and Sites
Hotel Saint-Aignan
75, rue du Temple　　　　　　　　　　　　Phone: 1 4277 35 76
F-75003 Paris, France　　　　　　　　　　Fax: 1 4277 57 42

6001
Gazzola Prize
To recognize a person or group of persons whose life's work has furthered the aims and objectives of ICOMOS, and the defense of conservation and restoration of historic monuments and sites. Members of ICOMOS may be nominated. A monetary prize of US $10,000, a commemorative medal, and a diploma are awarded triennially on the occasion of the General Assembly of ICOMOS. Established in 1979 in honor of Piero Gazzola, one of the founders of ICOMOS and its first President. Formerly: Prix Gazzola.

6002
International Federation for the Rights of Man
(Federation Internationale des Droits de l'Homme)
27, rue Jean Dolent　　　　　　　　　　　Phone: 1 4331 94 95
F-75014 Paris, France　　　　　　　　　　Fax: 1 4336 35 43

6003
Journalism Prize
To recognize a journalist who fights for the right to be informed. Established in 1983 in honor of Valadimir Danchev, a Moscow radio broadcaster who referred on the air to the Soviet "occupation" of Afghanistan. He was fired because of his remarks and interned in a psychiatric hospital. Sponsored by the Committee for the Liberation of Vladimir Danchev.

6004
International Federation of Landscape Architects
(Federation Internationale des Architectes Paysagistes)
4, rue Hardy　　　　　　　　　　　　　　　Phone: 1 30211315
F-78009 Versailles Cedex, France　　　　Fax: 1 39535316

6005
IFLA Competitions
To recognize contributions to the landscape architecture profession and achievement in design, planning, development, and conservation.

6006
International Federation of Newspaper Publishers
(Federation Internationale des Editeurs de Journaux)
25, rue d'Astorg　　　　　　　　　　　　　Phone: 1 4742 85 00
F-75008 Paris, France　　　　　　　　　　Fax: 1 4742 49 48

6007
Plume d'Or de la Liberte
(Golden Pen of Freedom)
For recognition of outstanding efforts on behalf of freedom of the press. Individuals, groups, or institutions, regardless of nationality, are eligible. An engraved plaque and a gold pen are awarded annually. Established in 1961.

6008
Prix Stendhal

For recognition of journalism and communication in Europe. The award recompenses editorial staff and journalists who have best contributed to the growth of a positive European climate with openmindedness and a concrete vision of European integration. A trophy and, in addition, a grant of 15,000 ECU to enable a young journalist to work on the editorial staff or TV network of another country are awarded annually. Established in 1989 by FIEJ/European Community Commission. The award commemorates the 19th century French author, Stendhal, "A Great Traveller with a universal mind, whose works are part of the European tradition." Sponsored by the European Community Commission. Additional information is available from Fondation Adelphi, Registered Office, 84 Rue du Rhone, CH-1211 Geneva 3, Switzerland.

6009
International Federation of Operational Research Societies
(Federation Internationale des Societes de Recherche Operationnelle)
Universite Paris VI & INRIA
Domaine de Volucenu
BP 105
F-78153 Le Chesnay Cedex, France

6010
EURO Golden Medal

To recognize a prominent person or institution, either for a remarkable role played in the promotion of operational research in Europe, or for an outstanding contribution to the operational research science. A medal is awarded. Established by the Association of European Operational Research Societies within IFORS.

6011
International Fencing Federation
(Federation Internationale d'Escrime)
32, rue la Boetie   Phone: 1 4561 14 72
F-75008 Paris, France   Fax: 1 4563 46 85

6012
International Fencing Federation Awards

To recognize the winners of the World Championship Fencing Contest. Awards are given in the following categories: (1) Championnat de Fleuret, Men, team; (2) Championnat Individuel de Fleuret, Men; (3) Championnat de Fleuret, Women, Team; (4) Championnat Individuel de Fleuret, Women; (5) Championnat d'Epee, Team; (6) Championnat Individuel d'Epee; (7) Championnat de Sabre, Team; (8) Championnat Individuel de Sabre; (9) champions under 20 years and champions under 17 years of age in the individual categories; and (10) Grand Prix des Nations. Awarded annually.

6013
International Festival of Maritime and Exploration Films
(Festival International du Film Maritime et d'Exploration)
14, rue Peiresc   Phone: 9492 99 22
F-83000 Toulon, France   Fax: 9491 35 65

6014
International Festival of Maritime and Exploration Films
(Festival International du Film Maritime et d'Exploration)

For recognition of outstanding films on the theme of the sea or exploration that were produced during the preceding three years. Films are divided in the following categories: scientific, exploration, fiction, sports, and advertising. A jury selects the films. The Gold Anchor (Ancres d'or), Silver Anchor and Bronze Anchor with monetary prizes are awarded annually. In addition, the following prizes are awarded: (1) the Special Rolex Prize for Underwater Nature Preservation; (2) the Young Director's Award offered by the French Underwater Sports and Studies Federation; (3) the French Institute of the Sea Award; (4) the Angenieux Award for Best Photography; (5) the Press Prize; (6) the Public Prize; and (7) the World Underwater Activities Confederation Award. Established in 1954 by Dr. Jacques-Henri Baixe, Toulon City French Navy.

6015
International Festival of the Image
(Festival International de l'Image)
BP 418
F-88010 Epinal Cedex, France   Phone: 2982 00 00

6016
International Festival of the Image
(Festival International de l'Image)

To recognize photographers, regardless of nationality, for the best slide shows with recorded sound (Diaporama is an audio-visual show). Photographers may submit slide sequences, designed for dual or multi projection on one screen with dissolve accompanied by sound on magnetic tape. The choice of the subject is free, but the sequence of slides must be entered under one of the following headings: (1) tourism; (2) documentary; (3) poetry, music, song; (4) humor; (5) theme - with a scenario; (6) analysis - personal works; (7) our century - life, human relationships, economic factor, the future of Europe; and (8) professional slide shows. Duration of the projection should not exceed twelve minutes. Overall quality, picture, sound, text, and ideas are judged by an international jury. The following awards are presented: (1) A crystal trophy - the European Cup for Diaporama Epinal to the best sequence presented at the Festival; (2) 3,500 francs - Grand Prize of the City of Epinal to the second best sequence; (3) 2,500 francs - Vosges Prize established by Vosges County Council for third best entry; (4) Grand Prizes, Special Prizes and Prizes for each category; (5) Young Producers Prizes; (6) Three FIAP Medals; and (7) Six Honors. Awarded annually. Established in 1961 by Noir and Couleur. Sponsored by the City of Epinal where the Festival takes place annually.

6017
International Festival of Urban Architecture, Town Planning and Urban Environment Films of Bordeaux
(Festival International du Film d'Architecture d'Urbanisme et d'Environnement Urbain de Bordeaux)
5 Place Dauphine   Phone: 57 221685
F-33200 Bordeaux, France   Fax: 56 423052

6018
Festival International du Film d'Architecture d'Urbanisme et d'Environement Urbain de Bordeaux

For recognition of the best film or videotape on urban architecture, town planning or the urban environment. The following prizes are awarded: Grand Prix du Festival - 50,000 francs; Prix Special du Ministere de l'Equipement, du logement, des Transports et de la Mer - 40,000 French francs; Honorable mentions by the jury; Prix de la Ville de Bordeaux - a medal of the city of Bordeaux; Prix du Ministere de l'Environnement - 10,000 French francs; Prix Special du Conseil Regional de l'Ordre des Architectes d'Aquitaine - 20,000 French francs; Prix de l'Institut Francais d'Architecture - 10,000 French francs; and Prix Ciments Lafarge "L'Art du Beton" - a lithograph by Le Corbusier. Awarded biennially in November. Established in 1981. (Temporarily inactive)

6019
International Film and Student Directors Festival
BP 7144   Phone: 6621 80 63
F-30913 Nimes Cedex, France   Fax: 7202 20 36

6020
International Film and Student Directors Festival
(Festival International du Film et des Realisateurs des Ecoles de Cinema)

To recognize the work of cinema school students. Films are accepted for competition in the following categories: (1) Fiction; (2) Reporting/Documentary; and (3) Animation/Cartoon. For official selection without preselection and entry fee, each school may present an official selection of a maximum of three films made during the preceding year. To compete for the best film school selection, each school must enter three films. For open selection with pre-selection and entry fee, any young director who has completed training at a film school during the year preceding the festival and who is not yet working professionally can submit one film to the Pre-selection Committee in one of the three categories. Films must be no more than 40 minutes long. The Crocodile d'Or (Golden Crocodile) is awarded for: (1) Best Overall Film at FIFREC; (2) Best Fiction Film; (3) Best Reporting/Documentary Film; (4) Best Animation/Cartoon Film; (5) Best Screenplay; (6) Best Actress; (7) Best Actor; (8) Best Photography; (9) Best Soundtrack; (10) Best Editing; (11) Best Original Film Music; and (12) Best Film School Selection. Established in 1989.

6021
International Health Centre of Socio-Economics Researches and Studies
(Centre International d'Etudes et de Recherches en Socio-Economie de la Sante)
Chateau de Fontpertuis
F-45190 Lailly en Val, France   Phone: 3962 97 97

6022
CIERSES Awards
For recognition of efforts to examine the results that current change has on individuals and groups, to organize interdisciplinary research into various socio-economic factors, and to conduct interdisciplinary training in the health fields.

6023
International Henri Langlois Encounters
(Rencontres Internationales Henri Langlois)
1, place de la Cathedrale
F-86000 Poitiers, France   Phone: 4941 8000
                            Fax: 4941 7601

6024
Festival du Film de Fin d'Etudes Cinematographiques
For recognition of the best thesis film. The film must have been made in a film school or workshop. The following awards are presented: Grand Prize, Special Jury Prize, Best Directing Prize, Public Prize, and TV Channel Canalt Prize. Monetary prizes and trophies are awarded annually in December. Established in 1977.

6025
International Institute of Human Rights
1 quai Lazay-Marnesia
F-67000 Strasbourg, France   Phone: 88 350550
                              Fax: 88 363855

6026
Human Rights Medal
To recognize individuals who receive the Institute's diploma. A medal is awarded.

6027
International Institute of Refrigeration
(Institut International du Froid)
177, Boulevard Malesherbes
F-75017 Paris, France   Phone: 1 4227 32 35
                         Fax: 1 4763 17 98

6028
International Institute of Refrigeration Prize
For recognition of outstanding studies presented in the form of papers or reports at either a preceding congress or during inter-congress scientific meetings organized by the institute. The paper must be an original work written in one of the official languages (English or French) of the institute. In order to make a better assessment of the quality of the study, the jury takes into consideration previous contributions that are related to the same topic and that illustrate the originality, value, or scope of the study proposed for the award. Papers must be submitted to the President of the Scientific Council at least nine months prior to the opening date of the Congress in question and must be accompanied by a brief biography of the author(s). A monetary award of about 5,000 French francs, a medal, and a diploma are awarded. Established in 1961.

6029
Prizes to Young Graduates
(Prix pour jeunes diplomes)
For recognition of personal and original work on subjects within the domain of competence of the IIR. Individuals under 30 years of age on the date that the awarded work is published (or defended, in the case of a thesis) are eligible. The following six awards may be given every four years at the International Congress of Refrigeration: Peter Kapitza Prize - for outstanding work in the field of cryophysics; Carl von Linde Prize - for outstanding work in the field of cryogenics; Sadi Carnot Prize - for outstanding work in the field of thermodynamics and heat and mass transfer; James Joule Prize - for outstanding work in the field of refrigerating, air conditioning, and heat pumps systems and machines; Alexis Carrel Prize - for outstanding work in the field of cryobiology, cryomedicine, cryosurgery, and biotechnologies; and Clarence Birdseye Prize - for outstanding work in the field of the refrigerated treatment of foodstuffs and the cold chain. A monetary prize of 5,000 French francs, a medal, a diploma, and registration at the congress are awarded for each prize. Established in 1991.

6030
International Institute of Space Law
c/o International Astronautical Federation
3-5, rue Mario-Nikis
F-75015 Paris, France   Phone: 1 4567 42 60
                         Fax: 1 4273 21 20

6031
Certificate of Honor
To recognize members who have distinguished themselves in the creation and development of space law. A certificate of honor is awarded when merited. Established in 1977.

6032
Lifetime Achievement Award
For recognition of lifetime achievement in the field of astronautics. Established in 1990.

6033
International Movement of Catholic Lawyers
(Mouvement International Juristes Catholiques)
4, square La Bruyere
F-75009 Paris, France   Phone: 1 4280 4954
                         Fax: 1 4874 1500

6034
UNESCO Human Rights Prize
(Prix UNESCO Droits de l'Homme)
In recognition of human rights activities. A gold medal is awarded biennially. Established in 1977 by UNESCO.

6035
International Organization Against Trachoma
(Organisation Internationale Contre le Trachome)
Hopital de Creteil
Universite Paris XII
40, avenue de Verdun
F-94010 Creteil, France   Phone: 4898 77 81
                           Fax: 4898 77 87

6036
Trachoma Gold Medal
(Medaille d'Or du Trachome)
For recognition of achievement in trachoma control. The deadline for nomination or application is March 1. Individuals of any age and citizenship are eligible. A monetary prize of 10,000 French francs and a medal

are awarded annually. Established in 1953. Sponsored by Chibret Laboratories, France.

6037
**International Pediatric Association
(Association Internationale de Pediatrie)**
Chateau de Longchamp
Bois de Boulogne
F-75016 Paris, France
Phone: 1 4527 15 90
Fax: 1 4525 73 67

6038
IPA Medal
To recognize pediatricians for distinguished service to child health at the international level. Pediatricians may be nominated by members of the IPA Administrative Committee. A bronze medal, designed by the Finnish artist, Terno Sakki, is awarded triennially at the convention. Established in 1974.

6039
International Piano Composition Contest
BP 156-20
F-75963 Paris Cedex, France

6040
**International Piano Composition Contest
(Concours International de Composition)**
To recognize outstanding musical compositions for the piano. Individuals of any age or nationality are eligible. Compositions should be 7 to 12 minutes duration. The Voya Toncitch Prize, a monetary award of 3,000 French francs and performances of the composition, is awarded. Established in 1986 by Voya Toncitch, a French pianist.

6041
International Prize for the First Novel
c/o Julliard Publishing
8, rue Garanciere
F-75008 Paris, France
Phone: 1 4634 12 80

6042
International Prize for the First Novel
For recognition of a novel considered the best by readers. Every year, five books written in French, and three books that are translated into French, compete for the first prize. A monetary prize and publication of the book by the Julliard Publishing House are awarded annually.

6043
**International Sailing Film Festival in La Rochelle
(Festival International du Film de Voile de La Rochelle)**
Capitainerie, Port des Minimes
F-17026 La Rochelle Cedex, France
Phone: 4645 14 03
Phone: 4644 41 20

6044
**International Sailing Film Festival in La Rochelle
(Festival International du Film de Voile de La Rochelle)**
For recognition of the best films, videos, and photographs on sailing, and to encourage the production of sailing films and videos. All aspects of sailing may be presented. Films of 16 mm and 35 mm may be entered in three categories: (1) Offshore; (2) Waves and wind; and (3) Unusual sails. Videos are judged in three categories: (1) Documentaries; (2) Sailing techniques - teaching; and (3) Fiction. The photography competition is reserved for worldwide professional photographers who present three prints cibachrome or similar on sailing mounted on an aluminum plate. The following monetary prizes are awarded with a Bronze Trophy: (1) Grand Prix du Festival - 20,000 French francs; (2) Prix Special Margy SRL - 20,000 French francs; (3) Prix Special du Jury - 10,000 French francs; (4) Prize for the Best Sport work - 5,000 French francs; (5) Prize for the Best Historical Work - 5,000 French francs; (6) Prize for the Best Teaching Work - 5,000 French francs; (7) Prix Publicite; (8) Prix A.M.A.P. des Journalistes; (9) Prix du Public; and (10) Mention Speciale. Awarded biennially. Established in 1977. Sponsored by France Challenges Grundig.

6045
**International Sericultural Commission
(Commission Sericicole Internationale)**
25, quai Jean-Jacques Rousseau
F-69350 La Mulatiere, France
Phone: 78504198
Fax: 78860957

6046
**Louis Pasteur Prize
(Prix Louis Pasteur)**
For recognition of achievement in sericulture or bacology. Scientific, technical, or economical sericultural activities that have led to an improvement in the knowledge of silk growing insects in general or in launching or increasing silk production are considered. All works having an international impact or actual possibility of application in various countries are eligible. Candidates must have a minimum of 10 years of professional activity and belong to a member-state of the Commission. A medal is awarded triennially at the ISC Congress. Established in 1974 by Mr. Schenk, secretary general of ISC in memory of Louis Pasteur and his work on the pathology of the silkworm.

6047
**International Singing Competition of Toulouse
(Concours International de Chant de la Ville de Toulouse)**
Theatre du Capitole
F-31000 Toulouse, France
Phone: 6123 2135
Fax: 6122 2434

6048
**International Singing Competition of Toulouse
(Concours International de Chant de Toulouse)**
For recognition of outstanding singers. Young singers (women and men), from 18 to 33 years of age are eligible. A candidate is required to have in his repertoire: six pieces representing a cantata, or oratorio, or melody-lied, with at least one by a French composer; and six pieces representing an opera, comic opera, or opera bouffe, with at least one by a French composer. The deadline for entry is September 1. The following prizes are awarded: First Grand Prize (for a man and a woman) - a Sevres vase presented by H.E. the President of the French Republic and 30,000 French francs presented by the City of Toulouse; Second Grand Prize (for a man and a woman) - a cup presented by the City of Toulouse and 15,000 French francs presented by the Conseil General; Third Prize (for a man and a woman) - a medal presented by the Chambre Syndicale des Directeurs de Theatre de France and 10,000 French francs; and a special prize of 10,000 French francs presented by the Societe Auteurs Compositeurs et Editeurs de Musique is awarded to a finalist, male or female, for the best interpretation of a French composer's melody sung in one of the three rounds of the competition. Awarded annually in September. Established in 1954 by the City of Toulouse.

6049
**International Social Science Council
(Conseil International des Sciences Sociales)**
UNESCO
1, rue Miollis
F-75015 Paris, France
Phone: 1 4568 25 58

6050
Stein Rokkan Prize in Comparative Research
For recognition of a contribution in comparative social science research in either manuscript or book form; and to encourage younger scholars. Individuals under 40 years of age at the time of the award may be considered for works published during the preceding two years. A monetary prize of $2,000 is awarded biennially at the ISSC General Assembly. Established in 1979 by ISSC and Conjunto Universitario Candido Mendes (Rio de Janeiro) in honor of Professor Stein Rokkan, former president of the International Social Science Council (1973-77); and President of the International Political Science Association (1970-73).

| 6051 |

International Society for Plant Pathology
Bacteria Section
INRA-Sta. de Pathologie Vegetale
F-78026 Versailles Cedex, France

| 6052 |

Bacteria Section Awards
To recognize scientists interested in the study of plant pathogenic bacteria.

| 6053 |

International Tar Conference
(Conference Internationale du Goudron)
c/o SPIGED
Tour Aurore
F-92080 Paris La Defense Cedex 5, France   Phone: 1 4778 51 51

| 6054 |

Franck Award
To recognize achievement in the use of coal tar products and derivatives, the standardization of practices and procedures, and the dissemination of scientific information pertaining to these products. A medal, certificate, and prize are awarded.

| 6055 |

International Tourist Film and Video Festival of Tarbes/Pyrenees
(Festival International du Film et des Medias de Tourisme de Tarbes/Pyrenees)
2, Place Ferre
F-65000 Tarbes, France   Phone: 6293 00 78

| 6056 |

Festival International du Film et des Medias de Tourisme
To promote the graphic and audiovisual techniques that awaken in the public the desire to know more about and to visit a particular region or country. Films and video recordings may be submitted. Gold, silver, and bronze Pyrene awards and certificates are presented annually. Established in 1967.

| 6057 |

International Union of Architects
(Union Internationale des Architectes)
51, rue Raynouard   Phone: 1 4524 36 88
F-75016 Paris, France   Fax: 1 4524 02 78

| 6058 |

Sir Patrick Abercrombie Prize
For recognition of outstanding work in the field of town planning or territorial development. A diploma is conferred triennially at the Congress of the Union. Established in 1961 in memory of Sir Patrick Abercrombie, first president of the UIA.

| 6059 |

Gold Medal for Outstanding Architectural Achievement
This, the highest individual award of the UIA, is bestowed upon an architect or group of architects for outstanding contributions to architecture and design excellence over an extended period of time. A jury of international renown selects the Gold Medallist from nominations submitted by UIA National Sections. A gold medal is awarded triennially. Established in 1984.

| 6060 |

Sir Robert Matthew Prize
For recognition of an outstanding improvement in the quality of human settlements. Awarded triennially at the Congress of the Union. Established in 1978 in memory of Sir Robert Matthew, a past president of the UIA.

| 6061 |

Auguste Perret Prize
For recognition of a project which is particularly remarkable for applied technology in architecture. A diploma is conferred triennially at the Congress of the Union. Established in 1961 in memory of Auguste Perret, a past honorary president of the UIA.

| 6062 |

Jean Tschumi Prize
For recognition of architectural criticism, or architectural education. Awarded triennially at the Congress of the Union. Established in 1967 in memory of John Tschumi, a past president of the UIA.

| 6063 |

International Union of Microbiological Societies
IBMC
15 rue Descartes   Phone: 88 417022
F-67084 Strasbourg, France   Fax: 88 610680

| 6064 |

Arima Award
To recognize an individual for contributions to applied microbiology. A monetary award, a plaque, and travel expenses to present a lecture are awarded every four years at the International Congress. Established in 1989 to honor Professor Kli Arima, former president of IUMS.

| 6065 |

Stuart Mudd Award
To recognize an individual for contributions to microbiology. A monetary award, a plaque, and travel expenses to present a lecture are awarded every four years at the International Congress. Established in 1978 to honor Professor Stuart Mudd. Sponsored by the World Academy of Arts and Sciences until 1988.

| 6066 |

Van Niel Prize
To recognize an individual for contributions to bacterial taxonomy. A monetary award is presented every four years at the International Congress. Established by Dr. Vic Skerman to honor Professor Van Niel. Sponsored by the International Committee on Systematic Bacteriology. Additional information is available from Dr. M. Goodfellow.

| 6067 |

International Union of Testing and Research Laboratories for Materials and Structures
(Reunion Internationale des Laboratoires d'Essais et de Recherches sur les Materiaux et les Constructions)
Pavillon du Crous
61, avenue du Pt. Wilson   Phone: 1 4740 23 97
F-94235 Cachan Cedex, France   Fax: 1 4740 01 13

| 6068 |

RILEM Award
To recognize distinguished authors in written exposition in the field of materials of construction and structures. Individuals under 40 years of age may be nominated. A medal is awarded annually at the meeting of the RILEM General Council. Established in 1970 to honor Robert L'Hermite, founder of RILEM.

| 6069 |

International Video Creation Center, Montbeliard
(Centre International de Creation Video, Montbeliard)
Chateau Eugene Peugeot
BP 5   Phone: 8130 90 30
F-25310 Herimoncourt Cedex, France   Fax: 8130 95 25

6070
International Competition of Video Works
(Competition Internationale d'Oeuvres Video)
To encourage independent video creation. All categories are accepted in all languages. The following monetary awards and trophies are presented: (1) First prize - 100,000 French francs; (2) Second prize - 50,000 French francs; (3) Third prize - 30,000 French francs; and (4) Special Mentions of the Jury. Awarded biennially in even-numbered years in June at the Manifestation Internationale de Video et de Television de Montbeliard. Established in 1982.

6071
International Women's Film Festival, Creteil
(Festival International de Films de Femmes de Creteil et du Val de Marne)
Maison des Arts
Place Salvador Allende
F-94000 Creteil, France
Phone: 1 49803898
Fax: 1 43990410

6072
International Women's Film Festival, Creteil
(Festival International de Films de Femmes de Creteil et du Val de Marne)
For recognition of films directed by one or several women and to encourage distribution of films in France. Films are entered in three categories: Full-length fiction films; full-length documentary films; and short length fiction and documentary films. The entry deadline is December 30. The following monetary prizes are awarded: Grand Prix du Jury for a full-length film; Prix de l'Association des Femmes Journaliste for the full-length documentary films; and Prix du Public in all three categories. Awarded annually. Established in 1978.

6073
David Kupfermann Foundation
(Fondation David Kupfermann)
3, rue de l'Harmonie
F-75015 Paris, France
Phone: 1 4533 87 96

6074
Premier Prix
For recognition of an unpublished novel or collection of short stories. Publication of the winning book was awarded annually. Established in 1983. (Discontinued in 1991)

6075
Rutebeuf Poetry Prize
(Prix de poesie Rutebeuf)
For recognition of an unpublished collection of poems written in French. The Foundation published the prize winner's collection of poems in a deluxe edition. Awarded annually in October. Established in 1984. The prize was awarded in the name of writer Daniel Zimmerman's imaginary and unfortunate hero, David Kupfermann. (Discontinued in 1991)

6076
Latin and Mediterranean Group for Sport Medicine
(Groupement Latin et Mediterraneen de Medecine du Sport)
23, boulevard Carabacel
F-06000 Nice, France
Phone: 9385 3377
Fax: 9313 0762

6077
Joachim Cabot and Louis Delezenne/Prize of the LMGMS
(Prix Joachim Cabot et Louis Delezenne/Prix du GLMMS)
For recognition of the best study on practical sports medicine, clinical or biological research. The study or work must be in connection with an arranged topic in the Congress of the LMGSM, which takes place in this same year. A monetary prize of 10,000 French francs is awarded biennially. Established in 1977 in honor of Joachim Cabot and Louis Delezenne.

6078
Librairie Cosmos 2000
17, rue de l'Arc de Triomphe
F-75017 Paris, France
Phone: 1 43803074

6079
Prix Cosmos 2000
For recognition of the novel selected by readers as the best science fiction or fantasy book of the previous year (French edition). Readers vote for the French Edition that they like best. A trophy is awarded annually at Easter time. Established in 1981 by Annick Beguin of Librairie Cosmos 2000.

6080
Librairie le Pont Traverse
17, rue Vanneau
F-75007 Paris, France
Phone: 1 4555 68 30

6081
Max Jacob Poetry Prize
(Prix Max Jacob de Poesie)
For recognition of poetry published during the preceding year, preferably by a relatively unknown poet. A monetary prize of 20,000 French francs is awarded annually. Established in 1951 by a donation of Mme. Marie-France Azar.

6082
Ligue Francaise de l'Enseignement et de l'Education Permanente
3, rue Recamier
F-75341 Paris Cedex 07, France
Phone: 1 4358 97 48

6083
Prix Jean Mace
For recognition of a manuscript submitted by an author or editor. Works on social sciences or essays on themes important to the Ligue, such as culture, education, peace, cooperation, and democratic values are considered. A monetary prize of 5,000 French francs is awarded. Established in 1958 in honor of Jean Mace, founder of the Ligue.

6084
Marguerite Long and Jacques Thibaud International Competition
(Concours International Marguerite Long - Jacques Thibaud)
32, avenue Matignon
F-75008 Paris, France
Phone: 1 42 666680
Fax: 1 42 660643

6085
Marguerite Long and Jacques Thibaud International Competition
(Concours International Marguerite Long et Jacques Thibaud)
To recognize the best piano or violin performer in the Competition in alternate years. The Competition is open to young pianists or violinists of all nationalities between 16 and 30 years of age. The deadline is September 1, 1995 for piano, and 1996 for violin. The following awards are presented: a monetary prize of 150,000 francs and concert engagements - First Grand Prize; 60,000 francs - Second Grand Prize; 40,000 francs - Third Grand Prize; 25,000 francs - Fourth Prize; 15,000 francs - Fifth Prize; 10,000 francs - Sixth Prize; and Special Prizes. Awarded twice over a three year period (one year for piano; and the next year for violin). During the third year in November, a gala concert for the young winners is presented by the older winners. Established in 1943 by Marguerite Long and Jacques Thibaud. Co-sponsored by the France - Ministry of Culture and Communication, Banque Nationale de Paris, and Fujisankei Communications International, Tokyo, Japan.

6086
Mairie de Palaiseau
Service culturel de la mairie
F-91120 Palaiseau, France   Phone: 6014 39 60

6087
Concours de Nouvelles
For recognition of the best short stories. Awarded annually. Established in 1986. Sponsored by Gallimard, Bordes, Desidor, Nouvelles-Nouvelles, and Carrefour.

6088
Mairie de Paris
Direction des Affaires Culturelles
8-10 rue Barbette
F-75003 Paris, France   Phone: 1 4274 22 02

6089
Grand Prix de la Photographie de la Ville de Paris
To recognize a photograher for his complete work, or a person who has contributed to the field of photography. A monetary prize of 40,000 francs is awarded biennially. Established in 1981.

6090
Grand Prix de la Technique de la Ville de Paris
To recognize a French scientist for his complete work in a field of technology, or a team composed completely or partially of French scientists for their work. A monetary prize of 40,000 francs is awarded annually. Established in 1964.

6091
Grand Prix de l'Architecture de la Ville de Paris
To recognize an outstanding French architect or one who has completed the major part of his work in France. A monetary prize of 40,000 francs is awarded every four years. Established in 1982.

6092
Grand Prix des Arts de la Ville de Paris
For recognition of an outstanding contribution in the field of painting, sculpture, or engraving and lithograph drawing. Awards are given in alternate years in the following categories: (1) painting; (2) sculpture; and (3) engraving or lithograph drawing. French artists or artists who have completed a major part of their work in France are eligible. A monetary prize of 40,000 francs is awarded annually. Established in 1951.

6093
Grand Prix Musical de la Ville de Paris
For recognition of an outstanding musical composition. French composers or composers who have done most of their work in France are eligible. A monetary prize of 40,000 francs is awarded annually. Established in 1952.

6094
Grand Prix Scientifique de la Ville de Paris
To recognize an outstanding French scientist or a team composed of all or partially French scientists. A monetary prize of 40,000 francs is awarded annually. Established in 1957.

6095
Grands Prix Litteraire de la Ville de Paris
For recognition of outstanding literature in the following genres: novel, poetry, criticism, essay, history, drama and children's literature. French writers or works written in French are eligible. A monetary prize of 50,000 francs is awarded annually for a novel; and a prize of 50,000 francs is awarded biennially for each of the following: poetry; criticism or essay; history; and drama. Established in 1946. A monetary prize of 25,000 francs is awarded biennially for children's literature. Established in 1979.

6096
Prix Gerard Philipe de la Ville de Paris
To honor and encourage a dramatic performer under 35 years of age. Actors of French nationality are eligible. A monetary prize of 40,000 francs is awarded annually. Established in 1962.

6097
Prix Sola-Cabiati
To recognize a French author for an outstanding historical novel or for a scholarly work that is accessible to the general public. French authors, or works written in French are eligible. A monetry prize of 50,000 francs is awarded annually. Established in 1972. Formerly: Grand Prix Litteraire Sola-Cabiati.

6098
Mairies de France
c/o Concours des Mariannes d'Or
7 bis, Place du Palais Boubon
F-75007 Paris, France

6099
Marianne d'Or
For recognition of individuals who have made outstanding contributions as public servants. Individuals from cities and towns throughout France are eligible. A trophy, the Marianne d'Or, is given in October at the Mairie Expo to several winners. Established in 1983.

6100
Prix Territoria
For recognition of proposals to promote the quality of public service at lower cost, and to encourage innovation in local management. Ideas may be submitted by departmental teams, regions, and large and small cities. A monetary prize of 30,000 French francs is awarded for first prize; 15,000 French francs for second prize; and 15,000 French francs for third prize. Established in 1987. Sponsored by the Minister of Interior Affairs. The additional information is available from TERRITORIA, c/o Richard Sintes, Hotel de Ville, F-92300 Levallois-Perret, France.

6101
Maison de Chateaubriand
87, rue Chateaubriand   Phone: 1 4702 58 61
F-92290 Chatenay-Malabry, France   Fax: 1 4702 05 57

6102
Prix d'Histoire de la Vallee aux Loups
For recognition of an exceptional historical study. Grand Prix d'Histoire is awarded for a work of historical research without limitation on the period or subject (works of fiction may be considered if they are found to be based on serious historical documentation). Grand Prix du Romantisme is awarded for a work about Chateaubriand and the period in which he lived. Literary works must be written in French. A monetary award of 100,000 French francs each is presented annually. Established in 1987 by the Conseil General des Hauts de Seine. Formerly: (1991) Grand Prix d'Histoire de la Vallee aux Loups.

6103
Maison de Poesie
Fondation Emile Blemont
11 bis, rue Ballu
F-75009 Paris, France   Phone: 1 4023 45 99

6104
Grand Prix de la Maison de Poesie
For recognition of a collection of poems or for a whole poetic work by an outstanding poet. A monetary prize is awarded annually. Established in 1930 in memory of Emile Blemont, founder of the Maison de Poesie. In addition, the Maison de Poesie awards a Young Poets Prize and the

Arthur Rimbaud Prize of 30,000 French francs each, sponsored by the French Ministry of Youth and Sports.

6105
Maisons de la Presse
17, rue Meaux
Laval Cedex 19, France   Phone: 4208 55 63

6106
Prix des Maisons de la Presse Prize
To provide recognition for a book of fiction and nonfiction of outstanding quality. Two prizes are awarded annually. Established in 1969.

6107
Mandat des Poetes
60, rue Monsieur-le-Prince
F-75006 Paris, France   Phone: 1 4326 22 73

Formerly: Fondation Pierre Bearn Mandat des Poetes.

6108
Mandat des Poetes
To provide recognition for poetry, and to assist a French poet, young or old, in difficulty. A monetary prize of 50,000 French francs and the title, Poet's Poet, are awarded annually. Established in 1950 by Pierre Bearn, a poet and literary critic.

6109
Marquis de Amodio
93, rue de l'Universite
F-75007 Paris, France   Phone: 1 4551 7904

6110
Prix Anne de Amodio
(Anne de Amodio Prize)
To encourage young people to be interested in the active preservation of historic homes. Persons from any country under the age of 40 years who restored or revitalized an historic house, large or small, inherited or acquired, with a view to residing therein are eligible. A monetary prize of £3,000 Sterling and a hand decorated diploma are awarded biennially at the meeting of the I.B.I. (World Organisation of Historic Castles). Established in 1981 by the Marquis de Amodio, O.B.E., founder-president of the Vieilles Maisons Francaises. (Discontinued)

6111
Mauriac International Medical Film Festival
(Festival International du Film Medical de Mauriac)
14, place Georges Pompidou   Phone: 7167 37 37
F-15200 Mauriac, France   Fax: 7168 10 00

6112
Mauriac International Medical Film Festival
(Festival International du Film Medical de Mauriac)
For recognition of outstanding films in health education, health and environment, and scientific medicine. Prizes are awarded in several categories, including environment and health jury awards, public awards, health education awards, and scientific medical film jury awards. Established in 1987. Co-sponsored by World Health Organization, Regional Council of Auvergne, City of Mauriac, and France - Ministry of Health.

6113
Mateo Maximoff
61, boulevard Edouard Branly
F-93230 Romainville, France   Phone: 1 4857 39 45

6114
Prix Romanes International
To promote knowledge of Gypsy people and their culture. Books written in French or in Romani (Gypsies' language) on Gypsies are considered. A trophy is awarded annually. Established in 1983 by Mateo Maximoff. Additional information is available from Les Etudes Tsiganes 2 rue d'Hautpoul, F-75019 Paris, France.

6115
Media Messages
23, rue Jean-Giraudoux   Phone: 1 4553 50 41
F-75116 Paris, France   Fax: 1 4720 43 23

6116
Lauriers de la FM
To encourage development of FM radio in France and advertising in this field. Advertising jingles and advertising spots are eligible. A trophy and a gift from the sponsor are awarded annually. Established in 1986 in honor of Marcel Bleustein-Blanchet, Head Manager of Publicity and the first advertising agency in France.

6117
Pierre Mendes France Institute
(Institut Pierre Mendes France)
52, rue du Cardinal Lemoine   Phone: 1 44271880
F-75005 Paris, France   Fax: 1 44271882

6118
Pierre Mendes France Prize
(Prix Pierre Mendes France)
To recognize achievement and development in a field of activity related to Pierre Mendes France. A monetary prize is awarded annually. Established in 1985 in honor of Pierre Mendes France's work field and ideas.

6119
Moet & Chandon
41, avenue Hoche   Phone: 1 4563 01 01
F-75008 Paris, France   Fax: 1 4227 72 57

6120
Grand Prix de l'Histoire - Moet-Hennessy
To recognize the best historical book of the preceding year. Important historical writers in France make the selection. To be considered, a work must meet the following criteria: (1) the writers should be from France or a French speaking country; (2) books of fiction are not automatically rejected, and the award is for a book rather than a work; and (3) it should be historical research of literary quality which is accessible to the public. A monetary prize of 100,000 French francs is awarded annually. Established in 1985.

6121
Prix Roger Nimier
For recognition of a novel or an essay written in the style and spirit of Roger Nimier. French writers or editors are considered for novels or essays published during the preceding year. A monetary prize is awarded annually. Established in 1963 by Phillipe Huisman in memory of Roger Nimier, a French writer who died in 1963. Sponsored by Moet & Chandon.

6122
Prix Science pour l'Art - Moet-Hennessy - Louis Vuitton
To reward remarkable scientific or technological initiatives in fields where interactions between art, science and industry may occur. The jury made up of international scientists and personalities of the art world is organized in three groups: Asia, America, and the main jury in Europe. Monetary prizes totaling 200,000 French francs are awarded annually.

6123
**Movement Against Racism and for Friendship Between Peoples
(Mouvement Contre le Racisme et pour l'Amitie Entre les Peuples)**
89, rue Oberkampf
F-75011 Paris Cedex 11, France
Phone: 1 4806 88 00
Fax: 1 4806 88 01

6124
Prix Fraternite Gaby Archenbaud
For recognition of an act, work, or literary, artistic, scientific or philosophical creation that has contributed in France to the ideal of equality and fraternity among men without distinction of origin, race, or religion. A monetary prize of 2,000 French francs and a trophy were awarded annually in November. Established in 1956. Sponsored by Fondation Gaby Archenbaud. (Discontinued in 1974) Formerly: (1987) Prix de la Fraternite.

6125
Municipality of Rueil-Malmaison
Hotel de Ville
13, boulevard Marichal Foch
F-92500 Rueil-Malmaison, France

6126
Prix Richelieu
To recognize an historian for a work on the period before World War II. A monetary prize of 20,000 French francs is awarded. Established in 1988 on the occasion of the fourth centennial of the birth of Richelieu.

6127
Claude-Adolphe Nativelle Foundation for Art and Medicine
Address unknown.

6128
Claude-Adolphe Nativelle Prize for Medicine
To provide recognition for basic clinical or therapeutic research on cardiovascular illnesses. Original work written by French scientists or other nationals of international reputation is eligible. A monetary prize of 500,000 French francs is awarded triennially. Established in 1972 by Francis Langlume.

6129
Nouveau Prix Populiste
1, place de la Gare
F-77500 Chelles, France
Phone: 6008 25 36

6130
Nouveau Prix Populiste
For recognition of a work that best represents the populist movement. This movement is one that rejects romanticism and emphasizes realism in style. The movement was started in 1929. The prize was established in 1929 and was awarded annually until 1978. Re-established in 1984.

6131
Office Municipal du Tourisme d'Anglet
1, avenue de la Chambre d'Amour
F-64600 Anglet, France
Phone: 5903 7701
Fax: 5903 5591

6132
Festival International du Dessin Humoristique
For recognition of humorous designs or drawings by amateur artists who are at least 18 years of age. The 1994 deadline for submissions was May 20. A monetary prize of 7,500 French francs, a trophy and travel expenses are awarded for the Grand Prix d'Honneur winner. In addition, the following prizes are awarded: Prix du Gag - 3,000 French francs and travel expenses; Prix du Graphisme - 3,000 French francs and travel expenses; Prix de la Caricature - 4,000 French francs; Prix Gerard Bouvier - 3,000 French francs for a special theme topic offered by the office de Tourisme; and Young French Hopefuls - 2,000 French francs (for artists 18 to 25 years old) offered by the Club UNESCO de Richelieu. Established in 1979 by Jacques Faizant, President. Drawings or designs by professionals are exhibited at the festival.

6133
**Overseas Academy of Sciences
(Academie des Sciences d'Outre-Mer)**
15, rue Laperouse
F-75116 Paris, France
Phone: 1 47208793
Fax: 1 47208972

Formerly: (1957) Academie des Sciences Coloniales.

6134
Prix Albert Bernard
To recognize a sociological, historical, scientific, or artistic study or work on the "Horn of Africa." The prize may be awarded to an individual or to a group. A monetary prize of 20,000 French francs is awarded when merited. Established in 1992.

6135
Prix Georges Bruel
For recognition of outstanding works in the field of geography, history, meteorology, ethnography or economics of Central Africa. A monetary prize of 500 French francs is awarded annually. Established in 1951.

6136
Prix Pierre Chauleur
To recognize the author of a work concerning the economy of the Third World. A monetary prize of 3,000 French francs is awarded. Established in 1987.

6137
Prix Robert Cornevin
To recognize an author for a work concerning Africa. A monetary prize of 3,500 French francs is awarded. Established in 1989.

6138
Prix Robert Delavignette
To recognize the author of a work concerning the social and cultural study of the Third World and Black Africa in general. A monetary prize of 500 French francs is awarded. Established in 1987.

6139
Prix Eugene Etienne
To recognize an individual or group for a work of a social or scientific nature in the field of health. Special attention is given to the scientists working in Africa. A monetary prize of 500 French francs is awarded annually. Established in 1934.

6140
Prix Marechal Lyautey
To recognize an author for a work of intellectual, scientific, social or moral character that helped to implement the French overseas programs, particularly in Africa, and contributed to the development of mutual understanding between the West and the Orient. A monetary prize of 500 French francs is awarded annually. Established in 1934.

6141
Prix de Monsieur et Madame Louis Marin
To recognize an author for the best work in the social sciences, particularly in the fields of ethnography, anthropology and mutual relations between different peoples of the world. A monetary prize of 1,000 French francs is awarded annually. Established in 1976.

6142
Prix Auguste Pavie
To recognize an author for a work concerning Asia in general, and Indo-China in particular. A monetary award of 500 French francs is presented annually. Established in 1982.

6143
Prix Paul Rivet
To recognize an author for a work on the subject of the Americas. A monetary prize of 500 francs is presented annually. Established in 1984.

6144
Prix Emmanuel-Andre You
To recognize an individual for outstanding service or works on social progress or moral conditions of overseas populations. Individuals originally from France or the overseas French countries are eligible. A monetary prize of 500 French francs is awarded annually. Established in 1953.

6145
Paris Audiovisuel
35, rue la Boetie
F-75008 Paris, France
Phone: 1 43594178
Fax: 1 42254205

6146
Prix Air France/Ville de Paris
(Air France/City of Paris Photography Award)
To encourage young photojournalists to work in a foreign country. Individuals under the age of 40, who are French or members of a participating country through the auspices of Air France are eligible. The deadline for the deposit of a portfolio is March. Travel to a participating country is awarded biennially to 10 French photographers and to 10 foreign photographers. Established in 1980. (Discontinued)

6147
Prix du Mois de la Photo
(Month of Photography Awards)
For recognition of photographs shown during the Paris Month of Photography which are included in the Festival's special competition. Awards are given for: (1) best overall photographer; (2) best overall exhibition; and (3) best newcomer. Monetary prizes totaling 100,000 French francs and trophies are awarded biennially. Established in 1986. (Discontinued)

6148
Paris International Science-Fiction and Fantasy Films Festival
(Festival International de Paris du Film Fantastique et de Science-Fiction)
33, avenue MacMahon
F-75017 Paris, France
Phone: 1 4222 88 51

6149
Festival International de Paris du Film Fantastique et de Science-Fiction
For recognition of outstanding fantasy and science fiction films. Films that have not been released may be entered from any country. The following prizes are awarded: (1) Licorne d'Or (Golden Unicorn) Award; (2) Best Performance (Male); (3) Best Performance (Female); (4) Special Jury Prize; (5) Special Effects Prize; (6) Best Screenplay; (7) Great Humor (Comedy) Prize; (8) Critic Prize; (9) Best Musical Score; and (10) Grand Prix Award - voted by a poll of the public. Established in 1972.

6150
Paris Transport Authority
(Regie Autonome des Transports Parisiens)
53, ter Quai des Grands Augustins
BP 70-06
F-75271 Paris Cedex 06, France
Phone: 1 4046 41 41

6151
Prix les Transports, l'Homme et la Ville
(Transport, Man and Town)
For recognition of a work of in-depth research using human and social sciences. The work should be at the level of a university thesis and must have been carried out in France by a French or foreign researcher during the preceding three years. A monetary prize of 5,000 French francs and, if applicable, assistance for publication of the work are awarded annually. Established in 1986.

6152
Pays Protestante
7, rue du 4 Septembre
F-92170 Vanves, France
Phone: 4642 66 01

6153
Prix de Pays Protestants
For recognition of a literary work on the subject of French Protestantism. A history, novel, commentary, play or poem may be considered. A monetary prize is awarded annually. Established in 1956.

6154
PEN Club Francais
6, rue Francois-Miron
F-75004 Paris, France
Phone: 1 42773787
Fax: 1 42786487

6155
Prix de la Liberte
To recognize a writer from a country other than France who has defended freedom of thought and expression in his or her country in spite of difficulties that such a defense entails. The writer, by his or her life and work should reveal these liberties where they are limited or suppressed, especially in a totalitarian country. Awarded annually. Established in 1980.

6156
Prix du PEN Club
To recognize a writer of the French language for work in defense of the French language and understanding French culture or some foreign cultures. Awarded annually. Established in 1986.

6157
Permanent International Association of Road Congresses
(Association Internationale Permanente des Congres de la Route)
27, rue Guenegaud
F-75006 Paris, France
Phone: 1 4633 71 90
Fax: 1 4633 72 74

6158
Prix de la Belgique
(Belgium Prize)
To recognize the author of the best paper on a problem related to roads. Members of the Association may submit papers. A monetary prize is awarded every four years at the World Road Congress. Established in 1913 by the Government of Belgium. Sponsored by Federation nationale des Entrepreneurs routiers and Association des Congres Belges de la Route.

6159
Prix Adolf Bentinck
33, rue Poissonniere
F-75002 Paris, France
Phone: 1 42331511

6160
Prix Adolf Bentinck
To provide recognition for contributions in the field of international relations or history, that promote European unity and peace, or fight against fanaticism or terrorism. The prize is awarded without regard to nationality. A monetary award of $5,000 is presented annually. Established in 1973 by Baroness Bentinck, in memory of Adolf Bentinck, the Dutch diplomat.

6161
Prix Aujourd'hui
(Aujourd'hui Prize)
12, rue du Quatre-Septembre
F-75002 Paris, France
Phone: 1 42968607
Fax: 1 42968807

6162
Prix Aujourd'hui
For recognition of a work on contemporary history or politics. A jury of journalists selects the winner. Works of a general character, such as memories, biographies, studies, etc. are eligible. Novels are excluded. French work or French translations written in the preceding year and published in France are considered. A monetary prize of 5,000 French francs is awarded annually. Established in 1962.

6163
Prix Cazes
Brasserie Lipp
151, boulevard Saint Germain
F-75006 Paris, France
Phone: 1 45 485391
Fax: 1 45 443320

6164
Prix Cazes-Brasserie Lipp
For recognition of a novel, an essay, a biography, a historical documentary, or an anthology of short stories of excellent literary quality. The work must be written in French and must not have won a major literary prize before. A monetary prize of 20,000 French francs is awarded annually in March. Established in 1935 by Marcellin Cazes, owner of the Brasserie Lipp, a restaurant frequented by writers and artists. Sponsored by the Brasserie Lipp.

6165
Prix du Palais Litteraire
70, boulevard de Port-Royal
F-75005 Paris, France
Phone: 1 4337 92 99

6166
Prix du Palais Litteraire
For recognition of a work published during the year on any subject by an author who works in the judiciary world or by an author on a subject concerning the judiciary life.

6167
Prix *Femina*
16 boulevard Flandrin
F-70016 Paris, France
Phone: 1 4503 17 59

6168
Prix *Femina*
To provide recognition for a novel written by a woman or a man, and to strengthen the bonds between women of letters. The jury consists of all women. A monetary prize of 5,000 French francs is awarded annually in November. Established in 1904 by the reviews *Femina* and *Vie Heureuse*. as an equivalent to the Goncourt Prize which women were unlikely to win. The Prix Femina Vacaresco for a work of nonfiction, established in 1937 by Helene Vacaresco, and the Prix Femina Etranger for a foreign work are also awarded.

6169
Prix Georges Sadoul
3, rue Bretonvilliers
F-75004 Paris, France
Phone: 1 43546574

6170
Prix Georges Sadoul
For recognition of an outstanding first or second feature film by an unknown or little known French and foreign director. A jury composed of film critics, directors, and actors presided over by Ruta Sadoul, widow of Georges Sadoul, selects the winning films. A photo of Georges Sadoul by Henri Cartier-Bresson is awarded annually to a French film and to a foreign film. Established in 1968 in collaboration with the Film and Television Critics Association.

6171
Prix Guillaume Apollinaire
22, rue des Felibres
F-91600 Savigny-S/Orge, France
Phone: 69963524

6172
Prix Guillaume Apollinaire
To recognize a poet for the totality of his work or for a book of poetry published during the year preceding the award. A monetary prize of 10,000 francs is awarded annually in June. Established in 1941 by Henri de Lescoet.

6173
Prix Medicis
25, rue Dombasle
75015 Paris, France
Phone: 1 48287690

6174
Prix Medicis
For recognition of a novel published during the preceding year, with a unique style or form. Authors who write in French and whose talent exceeds their fame are eligible. The prize is awarded annually by the jury during the special luncheon at the Circle Interallie in November. Established in 1958.

6175
Prix Medicis de l'Essai
For recognition of an outstanding essay. The prize is awarded annually by the jury during the special luncheon at the Circle Interallie in November. Established in 1985.

6176
Prix Medicis Etranger
For recognition of a novel or an essay written in any language and translated into French. Any writer in the world whose work was translated into French during the year preceding the prize is eligible. The prize is awarded annually at the luncheon at the Circle Interallie in November. Established in 1970.

6177
Prix Theophraste Renaudot
Tour Eve
3610 La Defense
F-92800 Puteaux, France

6178
Prix Renaudot
To provide recognition for a novelist showing talent and originality. Novels published during the preceding year are considered by a jury of 10 members. A luncheon in the winner's honor and honorary recognition are awarded annually at the Restaurant Drouan at the same time as the Prix Goncourt. Established in 1925.

6179

Prize for the Best Foreign Book
(Prix du Meilleur Livre Etranger)
20, rue Oudinot
F-75007 Paris, France   Phone: 1 45671898

6180

Prize for the Best Foreign Book
(Prix du Meilleur Livre Etranger)
To encourage the translation and publication of foreign literature. Novels or essays published during the year may be submitted to the jury. Awarded annually in March at a reception for the author, the publisher, and the press. Established in 1948. Additional information is available from M. Andre Bay, 28 rue A. Briand, F-95530 La Frette sur Seine, France.

6181

Marcel Proust Prize
Mairie de Cabourg
Cabourg, France

6182

Marcel Proust Prize
To provide recognition for a work of literature written in the style, spirit and tradition of Marcel Proust. A monetary prize of 250,000 French francs is awarded annually. Established in 1971 by the municipality of Cabourg, and sponsored by the Secretariat of the Mayor of Cabourg Calvador, France.

6183

Radio France and the City of Tarbes
Societe Nationale de Radiodiffusion
116, avenue du President Kennedy   Phone: 1 4230 3845
F-75786 Paris Cedex 16, France   Fax: 1 4230 1488

6184

International Guitar Competition
(Concours International de Guitare)
For recognition of outstanding guitar performances in the Concours d'Interpretation and outstanding compositions for the classical guitar in the Concours de Composition. The following awards were presented annually to the guitar performers in the Concours dInterpretation: a monetary prize of 15,000 francs, a silver gift medal, and invitations to 50 recitals in 17 countries - first prize; 8,000 francs and a silver medal - second prize; and 3,000 francs and a bronze medal - third prize. The Cordes Francaises Savarez also offered a first prize of 3,000 francs and several smaller prizes. In the Concours de Composition, monetary prizes of 14,000 francs and medals were awarded to composers. The jury decided what part of this sum went to the first and to the second place winner, if any. The Composer's Competition was held every two years. Established in 1958 by Robert J. Vidal. (Discontinued)

6185

International Guitar Makers Competition
(Rencontres Internationales des Maitres Guitariers)
To recognize outstanding classic guitar makers. This competition was organized by the town of Tarbes as part of the International Guitar Encounters. Classic guitar makers of all nationalities are eligible. There is no age limit. Each maker may exhibit a maximum of two instruments but only one guitar may be entered for the competition. The competition is carried out in two separate stages, aesthetics competition and acoustic competition. The following prizes are awarded: first prize (undivided) - 25,000 French francs; first prize in aesthetics - 5,000 French francs; first prize in acoustics - 5,000 French francs; and Prix du Public - 5,000 French francs. In addition, the following prizes are awarded by diploma: prize for the best quality of sound, prize for the best general appearance, prize for the head, prize for the color of varnish, prize for the most beautiful rosette, prize for the best table, and prize for the choice of material. The instrument gaining the first prize is purchased by the town of Tarbes and offered to Radio-France. Established in 1984. Additional information is available from International Guitar Makers, c/o Robert J. Vidal, 4 rue Demarquay, F-75010 Paris, France, phone: 1 40357574. (Temporarily Inactive)

6186

Region Languedoc Roussilon
Hotel de la Region
201, Avenue de la Pompignane
F-34064 Montpellier Cedex 2, France   Phone: 67 22 80 00

6187

Prix Mediterranee
To reconize a work written in French prose on the subject of the Mediterranean. A monetary prize of 50,000 French francs is awarded annually. Established in 1985 by the Centre Mediterranean de Litterature. Sponsored by Ville de Perpignan, le Conseil General des Pyrenees-Orientales, la Chambre de Commerce et d'Industrie de Perpignan, la Caisse d'Epargne du Roussillon et le Conseil Regional du Languedoc-Roussillon.

6188

Rencontres Internationales de la Photographie
10 Rond Point des Arenes
BP 96   Phone: 90 967606
F-13200 Arles, France   Fax: 90 499439

6189

La Galerie d'Essai
(Research Gallery)
This gallery is open to every photographer, amateur or professional. It gives the opportunity to young photographers to present their work and confront their researches. From July 5 to July 13, a jury of personalities chooses a laureate everyday among a selection of portfolios. The selected photos are then exhibited in the research gallery and the photographer receives a prize of 1,500 francs. His photos are shown to the public the same evening, before the slide-show, in the Antique Theater. Established in 1984, this idea has permitted many photographers to have their photos published in magazines or exhibited in galleries in France or abroad.

6190

Prix du Livre de Photographies
(Prize of the Photo Book)
To recognize the publisher of the best photography book of the year. The prize aims to promote the quality of photography publishing and to encourage production. French publishers and photographers as well as those from abroad are eligible. It can also reward an exhibition catalog. A monetary prize of 30,000 French francs is awarded in July. Established in 1974.

6191

Rencontres Musicales d'Evian
15, rue de Teheran   Phone: 1 4435 26 90
F-75008 Paris, France   Fax: 1 4289 26 50

6192

Evian International String Quartet Competition
(Concours International de Quatuor a Cordes d'Evian)
To recognize the winners of an international string quartet competition. The competition is open to ensembles of all nationalities whose members' average age is not over 30 years. The following prizes are awarded: Premier Grand Prix - 120,000 French francs; Second prize - 60,000 French francs; Special Prize of the International Jury of the Press - 60,000 French francs; Prix de le Ministere de la Culture - 40,000 French francs; Prix de la Ville d'Evian - 60,000 French francs; Prix de la SACEM - 50,000 French francs; Prix du Departement de la Haute-Savoie for the best interpretation of a contemporary work - 30,000 French francs; and other prizes. Following tradition, the prize winners perform before an audience in concerts or radio and television recordings. The final concert may be

recorded and broadcast. The Competition is held biennially in May (next in May, 1995) in Evian, France. Established in 1977.

6193
Ringier France SA
5, quai Voltaire
F-75007 Paris, France   Phone: 1 4260 34 61

6194
Prix Ringier
(Ringier Prize)
For recognition of the best article or radio or television coverage of Switzerland by a French-speaking journalist. A monetary prize of 10,000 Swiss francs is awarded. Established in 1988. Additional information is available from Ringier Switzerland, Dufour Str. 23, CH-8008 Zurich, Switzerland, phone: 1 259 61 11.

6195
Risc - Sauve Qui Peut le Court Metrage
26, rue des Jacobins   Phone: 7391 6573
F-63000 Clermont-Ferrand, France   Fax: 7392 1193

6196
Clermont-Ferrand International Short Film Festival
(Festival International du Court Metrage de Clermont-Ferrand)
To recognize short films in the international competition. The following prizes are awarded: Grand Prix - 20,000 French francs; Prix Special du Jury - 20,000 French francs; Prix du Public - 20,000 French francs; Prix de la Recherche for the most innovative script and technique - 10,000 French francs; Prix de la Jeunesse - 10,000 French francs; Prix Canal - purchase of rights to distribute the film; Prix de la Presse; and Special Mentions of the Jury. Established in 1988.

6197
Clermont-Ferrand National Short Film Festival
(Festival National et International du Court Metrage de Clermont-Ferrand)
To recognize short films in the national competition. The following prizes are awarded: Grand Prix - 20,000 French francs; Prix Special du Jury - 20,000 French francs; Prix du Public - 20,000 French francs; Prix de la Recherche for the most innovative script and technique - 10,000 French francs; Prix SACD for the best first film - 10,000 French francs; Prix de la Jeunesse - 10,000 French francs; Prix Canal - 35,000 French francs for the next film of the director chosen; Prix de la Presse; and Special Mentions of the Jury. Established in 1978.

6198
Ritz Hotel
15, place Vendome
F-75001 Paris, France   Phone: 1 4260 38 30

6199
Ritz Paris Hemingway Award
To recognize the year's best novel published in English. Writers of any nationality are eligible for novels that exemplify the Hemingway tradition of excellence. Nominations are solicited from authors and critics. A monetary award of $50,000 is presented annually when merited. The second part of the award is a $100,000 grant program. Established in 1985 by Pierre Salinger, White House Press Secretary under President John Kennedy; Jack Hemingway, the eldest son of Ernest Hemingway; and Mohamed Al-Fayed, owner of the Hotel Ritz in Paris. The award honors Ernest Hemingway, long associated in the public mind with the Ritz Hotel.

6200
Rostropovitch International Cello Competition
(Concours International de Violoncelle Rostropovitch)
Association Acanthes
146, rue de Rennes
F-75006 Paris, France   Phone: 1 4544 56 50

6201
Rostropovitch International Cello Competition
(Concours International de Violoncelle Rostropovitch)
For recognition of outstanding cello performances. The competition is open to cellists of all nationalities who are 33 years of age or under. The following prizes are awarded: (1) Grand Prix de la Ville de Paris - 60,000 French francs, a concert-appearance with the National Symphony Orchestra (Washington, DC), an appearance in Radio France, a concert-appearance with the Orchestre National Bordeaux-Aquitaine, a recital at the Theatre des Champs-Elysees, a recording engagement offered by "Disques Erato," an appearance on French Television, and an appearance in the Festival d'Evian; (2) Second Grand Prize - 40,000 French francs, and a concert appearance offered by Radio France; (3) Third Prize 20,000 French francs; (4) Fourth Prize - 15,000 French francs; (5) Special Prize for the best execution of the commissioned work by Rodion Shchedrin - 10,000 French francs; and (6) Prize for the most promising candidate, the Pierre Fournier Prize - 10,000 French francs. Awarded every five years. Established in 1978.

6202
Rouen Festival of Books for the Young
(Festival de Rouen du Livre Enfants-Jeunesse)
3, rue de l'Hopital
F-76000 Rouen, France   Phone: 35 98 60 94

6203
Fox of Poster for Books for the Young
(Renards de l'affiche du livre de jeunesse)
For recognition of the importance of posters in promoting reading books for young people. Selection is by nomination. Awards are given in two categories: (1) editors; and (2) exhibitions. A diploma and a trophy are awarded annually. Established in 1991.

6204
Roussel-Uclaf
35, boulevard des Invalides
F-75007 Paris, France   Phone: 4555 91 55

6205
Prix Roussel
For recognition of research that advances understanding in the field of steroids. Individuals of any nationality who work in a laboratory are eligible. A monetary prize of $20,000 is awarded biennially. Established in 1968.

6206
RTL/Poesie 1
87, rue de Sevres
BP 223   Phone: 1 4222 71 20
F-75264 Paris Cedex 06, France   Fax: 1 4544 08 38

6207
Grand Prix RTL/Poesie 1
To recognize an outstanding poet and to attract media attention to poetry, a genre which is ignored in this age. Poets writing in French are eligible for a book published during the preceding year. A monetary prize of 150,000 French francs is awarded publicly on the television network RTL. Established in 1982.

6208
Salon du Laboratoire
10, ave. Hoche
F-75382 Paris Cedex 08, France

6209
Prix du Salon du Laboratoire
To recognize outstanding contributions by researchers in industrial laboratories or universities. Works published in the French language are preferred. A monetary prize of 30,000 French francs is awarded. Established in 1987.

6210
SEPIA
123 rue Crimie
F-75019 Paris, France
Phone: 1 4245 85 90
Fax: 1 4202 34 46

6211
Prix de Poesie *SEPIA*
For recognition of an unpublished collection of poems in the classical or modern style. A minimum of 30 poems and a maximum of 50 poems must be submitted. Two monetary prizes of 500 French francs each and publication are awarded to a male poet and a female poet. Established in 1982.

6212
S.I.N.U.S. Association
(Association S.I.N.U.S.)
390, ave. du general Leclerc
F-77190 Dammarie Les Lys, France
Phone: 6439 96 84

6213
S.I.N.U.S. Association Prize
(Prix S.I.N.U.S.)
For recognition of an outstanding contribution in the field of rhinology and sinusology. E.N.T. specialists who are less than 40 years of age are eligible. A monetary prize and a diploma are awarded annually. Established in 1989.

6214
SIRP
BP 102
F-17206 Royan Cedex, France
Phone: 4638 5857

Formerly: Centre Culturel de Royan.

6215
Salon International de la Recherche Photographique
(International Photographic Research Show)
To promote photography through artistic and technical research by recognizing an outstanding series of photographs. Amateurs and professionals from all over the world may enter. Black and white or color series of photographs must not have been published or exhibited at all. A series of 8 (minimum) to 12 (maximum) photographs or a series of 8 (minimum) to 12 (maximum) photo-panels, all taken by one photographer able to express himself with total freedom, are accepted. The number of photographs on each panel is not restricted. These photographs or panels may present a thematic unity from the point of view of thought or perception and show the photographer's personality, originality, and sense of inquiry into the contemporary world. Each candidate may produce several series. Prize winners among previous exhibitors may take part in the competition. Two monetary prizes of 15,000 and 10,000 French francs are awarded for the Grand Prix International de la Recherche Photographique. Awarded annually. Established in 1970 by the Royan Photo Club.

6216
Societe Astronomique de France
3, rue Beethoven
F-75016 Paris, France
Phone: 1 42241374

6217
Medaille des Anciens Presidents
For recognition of past presidents of the Society when they leave office. A silver medal is awarded every three years.

6218
Medaille des Soixante Ans et Fondation Manley-Bendall
To recognize individuals who have been members of the Society for sixty years. A bronze medal is awarded annually. Established in 1957.

6219
Plaquette du Centenaire de Camille Flammarion
For recognition of long and continuous service to the Society. A silver plaque is awarded annually. Established in 1956.

6220
Prix des Dames
To recognize women for service to the Society. A silver medal is awarded annually. Established in 1897 by three women.

6221
Prix Dorothea Klumpke - Isaac Roberts
To encourage the study of the wide and diffuse nebulae of William Herschel, the obscure objects of Barnard, or the cosmic clouds of R.P. Hagen. A silver medal is awarded biennially. Established in 1931.

6222
Prix Edmond Girard
To encourage a beginning vocation in astronomy or scientific exploration of the sky above the Observatoire de Juvisy. A medal is awarded. Established in 1974.

6223
Prix G. Bidault de l'Isle
To encourage young people who show a special talent for astronomy or meteorology. Individuals are chosen from participants at courses and conferences, collaboration at the Observatory, or through communications in the bulletin during the preceding year. A bronze medal is awarded annually. Established in 1925.

6224
Prix Gabrielle et Camille Flammarion
For recognition of an important discovery and marked progress in astronomy or in a sister science, to aid an independent researcher, or to assist a young researcher to begin work in astronomy. A silver medal is awarded annually. Established in 1930.

6225
Prix Henri Rey
For recognition of an important work in astronomy. A silver medal is awarded annually. Established in 1926.

6226
Prix Janssen
This, the highest award of the Society, is given for recognition of outstanding work in the field of astronomy. The award is given alternately to a professional French astronomer and a foreign one. A medal is awarded. Established in 1897.

6227
Prix Julien Saget
To recognize an amateur for his or her remarkable astronomical photography. A bronze medal is awarded annually. Established in 1969.

6228
Prix Marcel Moye
To recognize a young member of the Society for his or her observations. Individuals must be 25 years of age or less. A silver medal is awarded annually. Established in 1946.

6229
Prix Marius Jacquemetton
For recognition of a work or research by a member of the Society, a student, or a young astronomer. A silver medal is awarded annually.

6230
Prix Viennet-Damien
For recognition of a beautiful piece of optics or for some work in this branch of astronomy. A silver medal is awarded in alternate years with the Prix Dorothea Klumpke - Isaac Roberts.

6231
Societe Celine
38, avenue Montaigne
F-75008 Paris, France   Phone: 1 4723 05 39

6232
Prix Celine
To provide opportunities for medical research. A grant of 300,000 French francs is awarded.

6233
Societe de Chimie Biologique
Secretariat
Tour D4, 1er Etage 115
5, rue J.B. Clement
F-92296 Chatenay-Malabry Cedex, France

6234
Prix Dina Surdin
For recognition of an outstanding doctoral thesis. A monetary prize of 6,000 French francs is awarded.

6235
Prix du Groupe d'Etudes et de Recherches sur les Lipides et les Lipoproteines
For recognition of a young researcher in the field of lipids and lipoproteins. A monetary prize of 3,000 French francs is awarded.

6236
Prix Maurice Nicloux
To recognize an individual for a work published in the journal *Biochimie*. Members of the Society are eligible. A monetary prize of 8,000 French francs is awarded.

6237
Societe de Chimie Therapeutique
Secretariat Gen.
Faculte de Pharmacie
5, rue J.B. Clement
F-92290 Chatenay-Malabry, France

6238
Prix d'Encouragement a la recherche en Chimie Therapeutique
To provide encouragement for a young researcher in therapeutic chemistry to create new medicines. A monetary prize of 15,000 French francs is awarded annually. Established in 1985. Co-sponsored by Laboratoires DEBAT.

6239
Prix Mentzer des Rencontres de Chemie Therapeutique
To recognize a researcher or a team of researchers for work in the field of therapeutic chemistry. Members of the Society may submit nominations. A monetary prize of 5,000 French francs is awarded biennially. Established in 1974 in honor of Charles Mentzer, a researcher in therapeutic chemistry.

6240
Societe de Pathologie Exotique
Institut Pasteur
25, rue du Docteur Roux
F-75015 Paris, France   Phone: 1 45668869

6241
Medaille d'Or Laveran
For recognition of exceptional merit in the field of exotic pathology. A medal is awarded at the convention of the Society. Established in 1908.

6242
Prix Noury-Lemarie
To encourage a young researcher in the field of pathology. A monetary prize of 10,000 French francs is awarded annually. Established in 1980.

6243
Societe des Amis d'Alexandre Dumas
Chateau de Monte Cristo
1 avenue Kennedy
F-78560 Le Port Marly, France   Phone: 1 39165550

6244
Prix Alexandre Dumas Deauville - Trouville
For recognition of an outstanding historical novel or play. Published works were eligible. A monetary prize of 10,000 French francs was awarded annually. Established in 1917 in memory of Alexandre Dumas, a French novelist and dramatist. Since 1986, the award was co-sponsored by the cities of Deauville and Trouville. (Discontinued in 1988) Formerly: (1986) .

6245
Societe des Amis de Maurice Edgar Coindreau
Address unknown.

6246
Prix Maurice Edgar Coindreau
For recognition of the best translation into French of a book written in English by an American author. Translations published between January 1 and December 31 of the preceding year are considered. Members of the jury and former recipients are excluded. A monetary prize of 15,000 French francs is awarded annually. Established in 1981 in honor of Maurice Edgar Coindreau, the greatest French translator of American literature from the 1930's to the 1960's. Co-sponsored by the Societe des Gens de Lettres de France.

6247
Societe des Amis d'Honore de Balzac
45, rue de l'Abbe Gregoire   Phone: 1 4548 25 31
F-75006 Paris, France   Fax: 1 4548 92 67

6248
Prix Balzac
To recognize an individual, an organization, or a work that best illustrates the human comedy of our time. A jury of thirteen members selects the winner. A prize is awarded annually. Established in 1971 to honor the French novelist, Honore de Balzac (1799-1850).

6249

Societe des Auteurs, Compositeurs, Editeurs de Musique
225, av. Charles de Gaulle
F-92521 Neuilly-sur-Seine Cedex, France
Phone: 1 47154715
Fax: 1 47154785

6250

Grand Prix de la Chanson Francaise
For recognition of the best French songwriter. A monetary prize of 15,000 French francs and a medal are awarded annually in December. Established in 1982.

6251

Grand Prix de la Musique Symphonique
For recognition in the field of symphonic music. A monetary prize of 15,000 French francs and a medal are awarded annually in December. Established in 1982.

6252

Grand Prix de l'Edition Musicale
To recognize a French music publisher. A medal is awarded annually in December. Established in 1984.

6253

Grand Prix de l'Humour
For recognition in the field of comedy. A monetary prize of 15,000 French francs and a medal are awarded annually in December. Established in 1983.

6254

Grand Prix de l'Oeuvre Musicale Audiovisuelle
For recognition of the best audiovisual music score. Awarded annually in December. Established in 1983. Formerly: Grand Prix de l'Audiovisuel.

6255

Grand Prix des Poetes
For recognition in the field of poetry. A monetary prize of 15,000 French francs and a medal are awarded annually in December. Established in 1982. Formerly: Grand Prix de la Poesie.

6256

Grand Prix d'Interpretation de la Musique Francaise d'Aujourd'hui
For recognition in the field of French contemporary music interpretation. A monetary prize of 15,000 French francs and a medal are awarded annually in December. Established in 1982. Formerly: Grand Prix de la Musique Francaise d'Aujourd'hui.

6257

Grand Prix du Jazz
To recognize an outstanding jazz composer. A monetary prize of 15,000 French francs and a medal are awarded annually in December. Established in 1982.

6258

Medaille d'Or de la Communication Musicale
No descriptive information available for this edition.

6259

Societe des Gens de Lettres de France
Hotel de Massa
38, rue du Faubourg Saint-Jacques
F-75014 Paris, France
Phone: 1 4354 18 66

6260

Grand Prix de la Litterature
For recognition of an author's complete literary works. A monetary prize of 50,000 francs is awarded. Established in 1984.

6261

Grand Prix de la Poesie
For recognition of the complete work of a poet. A monetary prize of 50,000 francs is awarded annually. Established in 1983.

6262

Grand Prix de la Societe des Gens de Lettres
For recognition of work in two categories: the total works of a writer; and a novel published in the preceding two years. Two monetary prizes of 20,000 francs each were awarded annually. Established in 1947. (Discontinued)

6263

Grand Prix Magdeleine Cluzel
For recognition of a book on the subject of art history or the history of the theater, a travel book, preferably on places around the world, or a piece on the theater. A monetary prize of 40,000 francs was awarded annually. Established in 1982. (Discontinued)

6264

Grand Prix Paul Feval de Litterature Populaire de la Societe des Gens de Lettres
For recognition of the literary work of a popular writer. The complete work of a writer is considered. A monetary prize of 20,000 francs is awarded. Established in 1984.

6265

Grand Prix Poncetton de la Societe des Gens de Lettres
For recognition of the total works of a writer whose value has not been recognized and whose situation has been seriously affected. A monetary prize of 20,000 francs is awarded annually. Established in 1970.

6266

Grand Prix Thyde Monnier
For recognition of a cycle of novels or for a separate work (novel, essay, or collection of poems) published during the preceding two years. Writers whose talents have not brought them material success are eligible. A monetary prize of 20,000 francs is awarded annually. Established in 1975.

6267

Le Prix de Poesie Charles Vildrac
To recognize a writer of a collection of poems published during the year preceding the award. Writers under 40 years of age are eligible. A monetary prize of 10,000 francs is awarded biennially. Established in 1973.

6268

Prix Albert Hennequin
To recognize a poet. A monetary prize of 2,000 francs was awarded annually. (Discontinued)

6269

Prix Alfred Droin
To recognize a poet. A monetary prize of 10,000 francs was awarded annually. (Discontinued)

6270

Prix Andre Barre
For recognition of a work whose author could not be a priest, a minister, or a rabbi. A monetary prize of 1,000 francs was awarded. (Discontinued)

6271

Prix Aram Sayabalian
For recognition of a previously unrecognized work by a non-political, Christian writer. A monetary prize of 2,000 francs was awarded annually. (Discontinued)

6272
Prix Baudelaire
For recognition of the best French translation of a work of prose or verse by a citizen of the Royal Kingdom or a country of the Commonwealth. The translation should be of a 20th century English work published or reprinted by a French editor during the preceding year. A monetary prize of 11,000 francs is awarded annually. Established in 1980.

6273
Prix biennal Marcel Thiebaut
For recognition of a work of literary criticism or an essay related to the literary life. A monetary prize of 10,000 francs is awarded biennially. Established in 1962.

6274
Prix Blanche Bendahan
To recognize the author of a work of poetry of about 300 classical or free verses, published during the preceding year. A monetary prize of 2,000 francs was awarded. (Discontinued)

6275
Prix Campion - Guillaumet
For recognition of an outstanding literary work. Established in 1988. (Disconti nued)

6276
Prix de Litterature Regionaliste Henri Baehelin
To recognize a writer living outside of Paris, who wrote one or several works on his region. A monetary prize of 5,000 francs was awarded annually when merited. Established in 1926. (Discontinued)

6277
Prix de Poesie Louis Montalte
For recognition of the complete works of a known poet. A monetary prize of 20,000 francs is awarded.

6278
Prix de Traduction Pierre-Francois Caille
For recognition of outstanding translations of a literary work and a scientific work, either technical or popular, published during the preceding two years. A monetary prize of 10,000 francs is awarded to a young translator or a translator whose value has not yet been recognized. Co-sponsored by the Societe Francaise des Traducteurs. Established in memory of Pierre-Francois Caille, Honorary President of the SFT.

6279
Prix du Roman Emil Zola - Raoul Gain
For recognition of the best French novel exposing the follies of human stupidity. A monetary prize of 10,000 francs was awarded annually. (Discontinued)

6280
Prix Foulon de Vaulx
To recognize a poet for his complete works. A monetary prize of 10,000 francs was awarded annually. (Discontinued)

6281
Prix Gerard de Nerval
For recognition of an outstanding translation of a German work. A monetary prize of 20,000 is awarded. Established in 1989.

6282
Prix Halperine-Kaminsky/Societe de Gens de Lettres de France
For recognition of the best translation of the year. A monetary prize of 20,000 francs is awarded annually. Also presents an award to the best translation of the year by a young translator. A monetary prize of 10,000 francs is awarded annually. Established in 1937.

6283
Prix Henry Franz
To recognize a woman for a collection of unpublished poems, approximately 4,000 verses, in the classic form and of spiritual inspiration. A monetary prize of 1,000 francs was awarded annually. (Discontinued)

6284
Prix Hubert Gildas
To recognize the work of an author who has satisfied his military obligations and served his time in combat. A monetary prize of 1,000 francs was awarded when merited. Established in 1971. (Discontinued)

6285
Prix Jacques Normand
To recognize the poet of a work of at least 1500 verses. Unpublished works were eligible. A monetary prize of 1,000 francs was awarded. Established in 1979. (Discontinued)

6286
Prix Jeanne Boujassy
To recognize a female novelist for a religious or historical work. A monetary prize of 2,000 francs was awarded annually. (Discontinued)

6287
Prix Lise Lamare
For recognition of novels, short stories, philosophical works or essays, or poems. Awards are given in alternate years in the following categories: a collection of stories, novels, or a romance; a work of philosophy or essay; and a collection of classical poems. A monetary prize of 2,000 francs was awarded. (Discontinued)

6288
Prix Maise Ploquin-Caunan et Docteur Jacques Perdrizet
To recognize the author of a collection of poems written in classical verse on the theme of despair. A monetary prize of 5,000 francs was awarded annually. (Discontinued)

6289
Prix Maria Star. Adrienne Cambry
For recognition of a literary work of moral character. A monetary prize of 1,000 francs was awarded. Established in 1978. (Discontinued)

6290
Prix Maurice-Edgar Coindreau
To support the work of an American author. A monetary prize of 15,000 francs is awarded. Named for Maurice-Edgar Coindreau, a translator responsible for introducing France to the major American writers of the 20th century.

6291
Prix Max du Veuzit
To recognize the author of the novel most reproduced in the press during the preceding four years. A monetary prize of 500 francs was awarded annually. (Discontinued)

6292
Prix SGDL de la Nouvelle
For recognition of an outstanding short story published in the past year. A monetary prize of 20,000 francs is awarded.

6293
Prix SGDL de l'Essai
For recognition of an outstanding essay. A monetary prize of 20,000 francs is awarded. Established in 1984.

6294
Prix SGDL des Arts
For recognition of outstanding works completed in the past year. A monetary prize of 20,000 francs is awarded.

6295
Prix SGDL du Livre d'Histoire
To recognize the author of an historical work. A monetary prize of 20,000 francs is awarded.

6296
Prix SGDL du Livre Jeunesse
For recognition of a book intended for young people by its qualities of invention, writing and presentation. Works written in French and published before March of the preceding year may be submitted by the author or the editor. A monetary prize of 20,000 francs is awarded annually. Established in 1982.

6297
Prix SGDL du Roman
For recognition of an outstanding novel. Works published within the preceding year may be submitted. A monetary prize of 20,000 francs is awarded.

6298
Prix Thyde Monnier
To recognize authors in difficulty. Four prizes of 10,000 French francs each are awarded.

6299
Prix Tristan Tzara de Traduction (Franco-Hongrois)
For recognition of the Hungarian translation of a French work. Established in 1986.

6300
Prix Yvonne Lenoir
For recognition of a collection of poems in free verse. A monetary prize of 2,000 francs was awarded annually. (Discontinued)

6301
Societe des Poetes et Artistes de France
36, rue G. Peri
F-38000 Grenoble, France   Phone: 76 47 54 83

6302
Grand Prix International de Poesie de la Ville de Grenoble
To recognize poets of the French language. Individuals who are 18 years of age, write in French, and have not won a prize in five years are eligible. Awards are given in three categories: (1) Fixed form; (2) Neo-Classical; and (3) Free Verse. Poems may be submitted between May 1 and October 31. First, Second and Third Prizes are awarded in each category as well as a Prix de L'Office du Tourisme, Prix de la Banque Populaire, and Prix du Dauphine Libre. A monetary prize of 1,500 French francs, the title Prix de Grenoble and a diploma are awarded annually to the most outstanding author in the various categories. Established in 1983 by Jean Jacques Bloch. Sponsored by the city of Grenoble.

6303
Societe des Poetes Francais
Hotel de Massa
38, rue du Faubourg Saint Jacques
F-75014 Paris, France   Phone: 1 4622 71 25

6304
Joseph Autran Prize
To recognize a poet for the whole of his work. Awarded annually.

6305
Pascal Bonetti Grand Prize
For recognition of the entire work of a poet. A monetary prize of 1,000 French francs is awarded annually.

6306
Chateauneuf-du-Pape Grand Prize
For recognition of a poetic work (unpublished, or published in the previous five years) which, irrespective of subject, appears most deserving for its formal purity and lofty sentiments. A monetary prize of 1,000 French francs is awarded biennially preferably to a young poet.

6307
Albert Dauzat Prize
For recognition of a poetic work in praise of animals. Awarded annually.

6308
Deldebat de Gonzalya Foundation Prize
For recognition of a small body of poems classical in form and noble in inspiration. A medal is awarded every two years. Established in 1941.

6309
De Pimodan Foundation Prize
To recognize a regional poet celebrting his land. A medal is awarded every five years. Established in 1926.

6310
Erlanger Foundation Prize
(Prix de Fondation Erlanger)
For recognition of a poem, 150 lines maximum, written by someone who has served in the front line of combat. A medal is awarded every five years. Established in 1921.

6311
Ernest Fleury Prize
For recognition of the whole of a poet's work (classical poetry, published or not). Awarded annually. Established by Marthe-Claire Fleury in memory of her father, the poet Ernest Fleury.

6312
Fouraignan Foundation Prize
(Prix de Fondation Fouraignan)
For recognition of a collection of poems in 18th century French style, inspired by current events. A medal is awarded every five years. Established in 1914.

6313
Grand Prize of French Poets
For recognition of the whole body of a poet's work, as decided by the Committee of the Societe des Poetes. No applications are allowed. Awarded annually. Established in 1936.

6314
Edmond Haraucourt Prize
To recognize a member of the Societe des Poetes for the whole body of his work. No applications are allowed. Awarded annually. Formerly: J-M Renaitour Prize.

6315
Clovis Hugues Prize
To recognize a poet whose work is inspired by the same sentiments of social brotherhood as moved Clovis Hugues. Awarded annually.

6316
Jean-Christophe Prizes
To recognize two young poets for a manuscript of a minimum of ten poems, one in classical form, the other in free verse. Awarded every two years. Established by Mrs. Alice Cluchier in memory of the young tragedian, her son.

6317
Georges Lafenestre Foundation Prize
(Prix de Fondation Georges Lafenestre)
For recognition of an unpublished poem of high inspiration and classical form. A medal is awarded every five years. Established in 1938 by the family of Georges Lafenestre on the occasion of the poet's centenary.

6318
Eugene Le Mouel Foundation Prize
(Prix de Fondation Eugene Le Mouel)
For recognition of a poem in any genre, but preferably inspired by Eugene Le Mouel. A medal is awarded every five years. Established in 1936.

6319
Sebastien-Charles Leconte Foundation Prize
For recognition of a volume of classical poetry published in the preceding two years. Awarded biennially. Established in 1935.

6320
Paul Lofler Foundation Prize
For recognition of the best sonnet submitted for competition to the Societe des Poetes. Awarded biennially.

6321
Charles Pitou Foundation Prize
(Prix de Fondation Charles Pitou)
For recognition of a poem in strictly classical form celebrating a French province, preferably Normandy. A medal is awarded every five years. Established in 1928.

6322
Poetic Prose Prize
(Prix de la Prose Poetique)
For recognition of a work of poetry which ignores classical prosody but is essentially poetic in spirit. Awarded every five years or biennially at discretion of the Committee of Societe des Poetes.

6323
Prix Anick Campion-Guillaumet et Bernard Guillaumet
To recognize a poet of great humanist ideas for a work inspired by the sentiments of fraternity and social peace or to recognize a poet devoted to the causes of the less fortunate or to recognize a handicapped poet. The poetry should be classical in form. Awarded annually. Established by Anick Campion-Guillaumet.

6324
Prix de Fondation Duchesse de Rohan
To recognize a young poet for an unpublished manuscript of at least 200 verses. Awarded every five years.

6325
Prix de Fondation Labbe-Vauquelin
For recognition of a collection of intimate and regionally inspired poems. Awarded every five years. Established in 1924.

6326
Prix de la Critique Poetique
To recognize a work or a collection of works of poetry criticism or exegesis. Awarded biennially alternating with Prix des Amities Francaises. Established in 1965.

6327
Prix de la Press Poetique
For recognition of a newspaper or poetry revue devoted to poetry and the exegesis of poetry. Awarded biennially. Established in 1973.

6328
Prix de la Promotion Cinematographique
For recognition of a director or actor for the promotion of French poetry through cinema. Established in 1990.

6329
Prix de la Promotion Poetique
For recognition of a librarian, editor, or educator who has contributed to the promotion of French poetry. The Prix du Libraire is awarded to an editor or librarian, and the Prix de l'enseignement is awarded to an enthusiastic educator. Established in 1990.

6330
Prix de la Promotion Radiophonique de la Poesie
For recognition of an individual who has contributed to the radio promotion of the French language particularly in the form of poetry. Established in 1989.

6331
Prix de la Promotion Televisuelle de la Poesie
For recognition of an individual who has contributed to the television promotion of the French language particularly in the form of poetry. Established in 1989.

6332
Prix des Chants Perdus
To recognize a collection of poems in memory of Ernest Fleury, a poet. The works may be published or unpublished. Awarded annually.

6333
Prix Helene Seguin
To recognize an outstanding poet preferably from the provinces or a poet whose work is a song of the tasks and work of women in the spirit of the poetry of Helene Seguin. Awarded biennially.

6334
Prix International des Amities Francaises
For recognition of contributions to the field of French poetry. Professors or writers studying French poetry, or foreign poets who write French poetry are eligible. A monetary prize of 1,000 French francs and a medal are awarded biennially. Established in 1955 by the Societe des Poetes Francais, founded by President Pascal-Bonetti.

6335
Prix Jacqueline Mompezat
For recognition of a biography. Awarded annually. Established in 1990 by a bequest of Jacqueline Mompezat.

6336
Prix Jacques Raphael-Leygues
To encourage the spread of French poetry worldwide. Awarded annually. Established in 1987.

6337
Prix Marc Chesneau
To recognize a work of poetry of great spirituality, particularly by a poet speaking about fine arts. Preference is given to a struggling poet. Awarded annually. Established in 1981 by Madame Marc Chesneau and her daughter.

6338
Prix Marcel Mompezat
To recognize a poet of quality. Awarded annually. Established in 1990.

6339
Prix Marceline Desbordes-Valmore
To recognize an outstanding female poet whose talent has already been recognized. Awarded annually. Established in 1937.

6340
Prix Marthe Ripert-Sarrut
To recognize a poet who extends the poetic spirit by the charm of the rhythm on subjects that evoke the spiritual life, the magic of love, and images of nature. Awarded annually. Established in 1990 by Madame Ripert-Sarrut.

6341
Prix Mounet-Sully
For recognition of an interpreter of poetry for talent and devotion to the Societe. Awarded biennially.

6342
Prix Sabine Sicaud
To recognize a young poet. Awarded annually. Established in 1988 in memory of Sabine Sicaud, a young poet who died at age 30 and whose work although brief is remarkable.

6343
Prix Victor Bernard
To recognize a classical poem or a collection of poems in a fixed form. Established by Madam Victor Bernard and the Sauvan-Bernard family.

6344
Rose of French Poets Prize
(Rose des Poetes)
To recognize a foreign poet who has celebrated France in his verse. A medal is awarded annually.

6345
Societe d'Etude du XVII Siecle
c/o College de France
11, place Marcelin-Berthelot
F-75231 Paris Cedex 05, France

6346
Prix XVII Siecle
For recognition of a work on the seventeenth century. Anyone is eligible. A monetary prize of 10,000 French francs is awarded annually in December. Established in 1984. Sponsored by the Mayor of Paris.

6347
Societe du Tour de France Ltd.
4, rue Rouget de Lisle   Phone: 1 40932199
92137 Issy les Moulineaux, France   Fax: 1 40932479

6348
Tour de France
This, the world's most prestigious bicycle endurance race is open to the world's top 20 men's professional cycling teams, the Tour is a 22-day cycling race th at covers approximately 4,000 kilometers during the month of July. The overall winner receives a monetary award of 2 million French francs. Established in 1903.

6349
Societe Francaise D'Acoustique
33, Rue Croulebarbe   Phone: 1 45355600
F-75013 Paris, France   Fax: 1 43317426

6350
Medailles d'Argent de la SFA
To recoginze scientific researchers of international fame in the field of acoustics. Individuals need not be members to be eligible for consideration. Two medals, one to a Frenchman and one to a citizen of another country, are awarded annually. Established in 1948 by Professor Chavasse, the founder of GALF.

6351
Prix Chavasse de la SFA
To recognize young scientific researchers in the field of acoustics. Members of SFA are eligible for consideration. Awarded annually. Established in 1948 by Professor Chavasse, the founder of GALF. Formerly: Prix Chavasse - GALF.

6352
Prix Jeune Chercheur
To recognize a young scientific worker in the general field of acoustics. Individuals around 30 years of age and at the doctorate level are eligible.

6353
Prix Philips - France
To recognize young scientific researchers in the field of acoustics. Members of SFA are eligible for consideration. Awarded annually. Established in 1948 by Professor Chavasse, the founder of GALF. Formerly: Prix Philips.

6354
Prix Thomson Sintra
For recognition of scientific work in the field of submarine acoustics. Individuals around 30 years of age and at the doctorate level are eligible.

6355
Societe Francaise de Chimie
250, rue Saint Jacques   Phone: 1 43252078
F-75005 Paris, France   Fax: 1 43258763

6356
Grand Prix Chimie Industrielle
To recognize an industrial researcher for an important contribution in the field of industrial chemistry. Applications should be submitted to the President of the Organic Chemistry Division of the Societe. A monetary prize of 20,000 French francs is awarded. Established in 1988. Co-sponsored by the Societe de Chimie Industrielle. Formerly: Grand Prix de la Societe de Chimie.

6357
Prix Le Bel
For recognition of research contributions in the field of stereo chemistry or on a subject of particular interest to Le Bel. A monetary prize of 20,000 French francs is awarded. Established in 1942 in memory of Le Bel, a benefactor of the Societe.

6358
Prix Pierre Sue
For recognition in the field of chemistry. A prize of 20,000 French francs is awarded. Established in 1964 in memory of Pierre Sue, Secretary General of the Society from 1962 to 1967.

6359
Prix Raymond Berr Atochem
For recognition in the fields of pure and applied chemistry. French researchers under 50 years of age are eligible. Established in the memory of Raymond Berr, chief of industry and scholar. Sponsored by Association Raymond Berr Atochem.

6360
Societe Francaise de Numismatique
Cabinet des Medailles de la Bibliotheque
  Nationale
58, rue de Richelieu
F-75084 Paris Cedex 02, France   Phone: 1 47038334

6361
Prix Babut
For recognition of a book or a paper about ancient, medieval, or modern French numismatics. French members of the Society are eligible. A monetary prize is awarded biennially. Established in 1936 in honor of Commandant A. Babut.

6362
Jeton de Vermeil
For recognition of a contribution in the field of numismatics. Non-French numismatists may be nominated. A medal is awarded annually. Established in 1934.

6363
Societe Francaise de Physique
33, rue Croulebarbe
F-75013 Paris, France
Phone: 1 47073298
Fax: 1 43317426

6364
Grand Prix de Physique Jean Ricard
(Jean Ricard Grand Prize for Physics)
For recognition of an outstanding contribution to the field of physics by a French physicist. A monetary prize of 60,000 francs is awarded annually.

6365
Medaille Rammal
To recognize a physicist for outstanding work that promotes scientific development and exchange, particularly in the Mediterranean area. Awarded annually. Established in 1993 in memory of Lebanese physicist Rammal RAMMAL, who died at the age of 39.

6366
Prix Aime Cotton
For recognition of distinguished research in atomic and molecular physics. Any physicist working in France is eligible. A monetary prize is awarded annually. Established in 1953.

6367
Prix Daniel Guinier
To recognize a student for outstanding work resulting in a degree or in completion of a thesis in his/her third year of study. Established in 1959.

6368
Prix Esclangon
For recognition of distinguished work in the area of electricity. Any physicist working in France is eligible. A monetary prize is awarded biennially. Established in 1956.

6369
Prix Felix Robin
To recognize a French physicist working in France on the basis of his entire work. A medal prize is awarded annually.

6370
Prix Foucault
For recognition of outstanding work in the field of applied physics. A monetary prize is awarded annually. Established in 1971.

6371
Prix Gentner-Kastler
To recognize an outstanding contribution in physics. Awarded alternatively to a French or German physicist. A diploma and a silver medal are presented annually. Established in 1984.

6372
Prix Holweck
To maintain amicable ties between English and French physicists. Awarded alternatively to a French physicist by the Institute of Physics or to an English physicist by the Societe Francaise de Physique. A vermillion medal is presented annually. Established in 1945 by the Physical Society de Londres in memory of Fernand Holweck, an eminent French physicist, who was assassinated by the Gestapo for resisting Nazi occupation.

6373
Prix IBM
To recognize a young physicist under the age of 38. Awarded annually. Sponsored by IBM.

6374
Prix Jean Perrin
For recognition of work contributing to science. Any person whose work can make physics more attractive or understandable to the public is eligible. A monetary prize is awarded annually.

6375
Prix Jean Ricard
To recognize and encourge a French author for outstanding and original work in theoretical or experimental physics. Awarded annually.

6376
Prix Jeune Chercheur IBM
To recognize a young physicist who has completed a doctoral thesis in the preceding year. Awarded annually. Sponsored by IBM.

6377
Prix Joliot-Curie
For recognition of outstanding work in the field of nuclear and particle physics. A monetary prize is awarded annually. Established in 1956.

6378
Prix Langevin
For recognition of outstanding work in the field of theoretical physics. A monetary prize is awarded annually.

6379
Prix Louis Ancel
For recognition of the best work on condensed matter. A medal prize is awarded annually. Established in 1922.

6380
Prix Plasma
To recognize an original work in theoretical or experimental physics. Awarded biennially. Established in 1982.

6381
Prix Yves Rocard
To recognize the successful transfer of technology from the research laboratory to business. Awarded annually. Established in 1992.

6382
Societe Generale
2 Square de l'Opera Louis Jouvet
F-75009 Paris, France
Phone: 1 4298 43 63

6383
Energy Prize
To recognize the best initiatives in the field of energy that improve the French position. A monetary prize of 250,000 French francs is awarded.

6384

Prix 2000 SG
To recognize an individual who is responsible for transforming a technological innovation into a concrete reality in response to the evolution of the market needs. Awards are given in four categories: (1) Print and Visual electronics; (2) Health and Security; (3) Culture; and (4) Individuals under 30 years of age. A monetary prize of 750,000 French francs is awarded in each category.

6385

Societe Protex
BP 177
F-92305 Levallois Perret, France   Phone: 4757 74 00

6386

Prix Protex
For recognition in the fields of applied chemistry and applied biotechnology. Research applicable to human or animal health or the production of energy is particularly considered. Awards are given in alternate years for chemistry and biotechnology. A monetary prize of 30,000 French francs is awarded annually.

6387

Societes de Statistique de Paris et de France
18, boulevard A. Pinard
F-75675 Paris Cedex 14, France

6388

Medaille Bourdin
To recognize the author of the most interesting work published in the journal of the Society during the preceding three years. A gold medal is awarded every three years. Established in 1889.

6389

Prix Coste
To provide for the periodic publication of a detailed evaluation of private and public wealth in France. Awarded infrequently. Established in 1902.

6390

Prix du Statisticien d'Expression Francaise
For recognition of outstanding statistical work in the French language. Awards are given in alternate years to: (1) a well-known foreign statistician; (2) a young French or foreign statistician; and (3) an established French statistician. A medal is awarded annually. Established in 1975.

6391

Prix Edmond Michel
For recognition of the best communication of the Society on the question of property values in cities, the country, and on the question of natural regions. Works concerning the values from a statistical point of view are considered. Awarded irregularly. Established in 1947.

6392

Prix Emile Mercet
For recognition in the field of statistics. A monetary prize of 3,000 French francs and a gold medal are awarded infrequently. Established in 1909.

6393

Prix Michel Huber
For recognition of the best work by a member of the Society. Works in a field of interest to the Society are considered. Awarded irregularly. Established in 1946.

6394

Society of Dramatic Authors and Composers
(Societe des Auteurs et Compositeurs Dramatiques)
11 bis, Rue Ballu
F-75442 Paris Cedex 9, France   Phone: 1 4023 44 44

6395

Grand Prix SACD
To recognize the most outstanding playwright or a composer on the basis of his entire dramatic work. A monetary prize of 10,000 francs is awarded annually. In addition, five Prix SACD are awarded in the following categories: (1) theater; (2) music; (3) dance; (4) film; and (5) radio. Monetary prizes of 5,000 francs are awarded annually. Talent Nouveau (new talent) prizes are given in the above categories. Another prize, the Medaille Beaumarchais is also awarded.

6396

Prix Andre Barde
To recognize the author of the best libretto for an opera. A monetary prize of 1,500 francs was awarded. (Discontinued in 1985)

6397

Prix Andre Mouezy-Eon
To honor a member of the Society of more than 60 years of age, who once was a favorite of the public but who then lived only from his royalties that were no longer adequate. (Discontinued in 1985)

6398

Prix Lugne Poe
To recognize a playwright who had not been a success but whose play demonstrated originality and poetic spirit. The prize could go to an unpublished play if an appropriate published work was not found among new plays. A monetary prize of 1,500 francs was awarded. (Discontinued in 1985)

6399

Prix Talents Nouveau
To recognize new talent in theatre, music, cinema, radio, and dance. Monetary prizes of 1,500 francs are awarded annually.

6400

Prix Tristan Bernard
For recognition of a play, preferably presented on stage during the past years, that was as close as possible to the spirit of the works of Tristan Bernard. A monetary prize of 1,500 francs was awarded. (Discontinued in 1985)

6401

Strat X S.A.
Address unknown.

6402

European Markstrat Competition
For recognition of top performance in the Markstrat strategic marketing business simulation competition. The highest cumulative net marketing contribution generated in the simulation is the winner. Microcomputer/educational materials are awarded annually. Established in 1985.

6403

International Markstrat Competition
To allow management teams to learn about marketing strategy in an international environment without leaving their offices. The competition is based on the leading marketing simulation, Markstrat. An overall winner as well as winners in various categories are selected. Established in 1985. Sponsored by Alcatel, Dec, Hewlett Packard, and Olivetti.

6404
Syndicate of Professional Drama and Music Critics
(Syndicate Professionnel de la Critique Dramatique et Musicale)
H 6 rue de Braque
F-750031 Paris, France   Phone: 1 42741378

6405
Drama Critics Prizes
(Prix du Syndicat de la Critique Dramatique et Musicale)
For recognition of outstanding accomplishments in theater. Awards are given in the following categories: Grand Prize for Best Show, Best Regional Production, Best French Production, Best Foreign Production, Best Set Designer, Best Male Comedian, and Best Book on Theater, Best Female Comedian, Best Stagae Music, and Relevation of the Season. Honorary recognition is awarded in each category annually.

6406
Music Critics Prizes
For recognition of outstanding accomplishments in music. Awards are given in the following categories: Grand Prize; Prix Claude - Rostand, for the best lyric show in the country, Best French Musical Creation, Best Musical Personality of the Year, Best New Talent of the Year, Best Books on Music, and Relevation of the Season. Honorary recognition is awarded in each category annually.

6407
Le Triptyque
11, rue Conseiller - Collignon
F-75116 Paris, France   Phone: 1 45201940

6408
Grand Prix de la Melodie Francaise
For recognition of French melody and to encourage the repertoire of French melodies. Individuals in any country are eligible. A monetary prize is awarded annually. Established in 1984 by Pierre d'Arquennes.

6409
UNESCO
7, place de Fontenoy   Phone: 1 4568 16 82
F-75352 Paris, France   Fax: 1 4065 00 29

6410
Baghdad Prize for Arab Culture
(Prix Bagdad de la Culture Arabe)
To recognize one national of an Arab country and one national of any other country who has contributed to, through artistic and intellectual work, the development and dissemination of Arab culture throughout the world. Candidates may be writers, researchers, practitioners of the plastic arts, musicians, or actors or creative artists in the audio-visual media who have made a significant contribution to the development of Arab culture or its further dissemination throughout the world. Candidates may be nominated by the government of Member States in consultation with their National Commissions and by nongovernmental organizations in consultative status with UNESCO. A monetary prize of $10,000 (US) is awarded biennially and is shared, in equal parts, between the prize-winner from an Arab country and the prize-winner from another country. Established in 1983.

6411
Carlos J. Finlay Prize
To promote research and development in microbiology by rewarding a person or group of persons for an outstanding contribution in that field. Member states of UNESCO make the nominations. A monetary prize of $5,000 and a plaque are awarded biennially coinciding with the year of UNESCO's General Conference. Established in 1977 in memory of Carlos J. Finlay, a Cuban scientist whose discoveries led to the conquest of yellow fever. Sponsored by the Cuban Government.

6412
Nessim Habif Prize
To recognize the authors of outstanding textbooks for use in developing countries and to encourage the production in developing countries of good textbooks that are objective, balanced, and up-to-date in content and pedagogically sound in presentation. Awards are made in successive years to authors of textbooks published in member states of UNESCO in Asia, Africa, Arab States, and Latin America. The awards are open only to authors who have prepared textbooks for use in one of the countries in the regions to be selected annually. There is no limitation of eligibility based on sex, race, color, religion, nationality, or place of domicile. Prizes may be awarded either to a single textbook or to several textbooks that constitute a series. Textbooks are eligible only if published for use in the schools of one of the eligible countries by a publishing house duly registered as such and operating in one of the countries. A monetary prize is awarded annually. Established in 1964 by a bequest of Nessim Habif who died at St. Maurice, Switzerland in 1960. Additional information is available from Mrs. M. Sauliere, ED/SCM, UNESCO.

6413
Felix Houphouet-Boigny Peace Prize
To honor individuals, bodies, or institutions that have made a significant contribution to promoting, seeking, safeguarding, or maintaining peace through education, science, and culture. Nominations may be made by Member States and nongovernmental organizations as well as other specified groups. A monetary prize of 800,000 French francs, a gold medal, and a certificate are awarded annually. Established in 1989.

6414
Javed Husain Prize for Young Scientists
For recognition of outstanding pure or applied research carried out by young scientists. Eligible applicants include individuals who, in the opinion of the jury, have done the most to advance the progress of scientific research as judged by the quality of their publications and/or patents; or individuals whose age does not exceed 35 years at the time of announcement of the Prize. Research specifically aimed at the development of weapons or other military devices shall not be considered for the Prize, and members of the jury cannot be considered for the Prize. Nominations are made by governments of Member States, intergovernmental organizations, or international nongovernmental organizations having formal relations with UNESCO. A monetary prize representing half the biennial interest earned from the Fund, a medal, and a certificate are awarded biennially. Established in 1984 by a donation made by Dr. Javed Husain, an Indian physicist who has held university professional posts in Saudi Arabia and the United States.

6415
International Simon Bolivar Prize
For recognition of activity of outstanding merit that, in accordance with the ideals of Simon Bolivar, has contributed to the freedom, independence, and dignity of peoples and to the strengthening of solidarity among nations; and has fostered their development or facilitated the establishment of a new international economic, social, and cultural order. Such activity may take the form of intellectual or artistic creation, a social achievement, or the mobilization of public opinion. Individuals or institutions may be nominated by the government of a Member State or Associate Member of UNESCO, by an intergovernmental organization, or by a nongovernmental organization having consultative and associate relations or information and consultative relations with UNESCO. A monetary prize of $25,000 is awarded biennially. Established in 1983. Sponsored by the Government of Venezuela.

6416
IPDC - UNESCO Prize for Rural Communication
For recognition of meritorious and innovative activity in improving communication in rural communities, chiefly in the developing countries. Nationals of UNESCO Member States or institutions or organizations that have their headquarters in those States are eligible. They must have adopted one or more particularly outstanding measure to promote rural communication in the spirit of UNESCO's ideals by such means as: furthering the use of local newspapers, films, radio, television, and/or multi-media programmes; furthering the use of traditional forms of communication; and implementing new plans with a view to the full use or

improvement of communication and its techniques and methods in ways adapted to the rural environment. The activity must have occured within a period of two years preceding the submission of nominations. Nominations may be submitted to the Chairman of the Intergovernmental Council the IPDC, by the governments of Member States of UNESCO in consultation with their National Commissions, and by the appropriate non-governmental organizations having consultative status with UNESCO. A monetary prize of $20,000 (US) is awarded biennially. Established in 1985.

6417
Kalinga Prize
For recognition of outstanding interpretation of science to the general public. Persons actively involved in the promotion of public understanding of science and technology are eligible. National Commissions for UNESCO make the nominations. A monetary prize of £1,000, a medal, and a plaque are awarded annually. Established in 1951 by Mr. B. Patnaik, an Indian industrialist of Orissa, India. The prize is named after the ancient Indian emperor who in the second century BC renounced war and devoted his power to the development of science, culture, and education.

6418
Sultan Oaboos Prize for Environmental Preservation
For recognition of outstanding contributions by individuals, groups of individuals, institutes, or organizations in the management or preservation of the environment, consistent with the policies, aims, and objectives of UNESCO, and in relation to the organization's programs in this field (i.e., environmental and natural resources research, environmental education and training, creation of environmental awareness through the preparation of environmental information materials, and activities aimed at establishing and managing protected areas such as Biosphere Reserves and Natural World Heritage Sites). Candidates for the prize are proposed to the Director-General of UNESCO by governments of Member States, in consultation with their National Commissions, by intergovernmental organizations, or by appropriate nongovernmental organizations that have consultative status with UNESCO, each of which may make one nomination in any biennium. A monetary prize of $20,000 US is awarded biennially. Established in 1989.

6419
Official UNESCO Award for Distinguished Services to Physical Education and Sport
For recognition of distinguished services to physical education and sport in accordance with the principles of the International Charter of Physical Education and Sport adopted by the General Conference of UNESCO at its twentieth session. The award is given in two different categories: to an institution or body that has made an outstanding contribution to the development of physical education and sport for all; and to a person who, by his or her active participation, has made a significant contribution to the development of physical education and sport for all. Candidates are selected by the Member States of UNESCO. A diploma of honor and medal are awarded biennially. Established in 1985.

6420
UNESCO Crafts Prize
For recognition of the efforts of craftworkers who, by trying out different forms and techniques, have contributed to the creation of original models in their respective trades. The purpose of the Prize is to stimulate creativity among craftworkers and to encourage new initiatives in creative work in the crafts. Nominations are submitted to the Director-General of UNESCO by the appropriate bodies of Member States responsible for national participation in the regional crafts exhibition. The Prizewinner must have produced a particularly conspicuous and original work in one of the creative crafts trades. A monetary prize of $10,000 is awarded annually on the occasion of a regional crafts exhibition. Established in 1989.

6421
UNESCO - International Music Council Music Prize
To recognize musicians or musical institutions whose works or activities have contributed to the enrichment and development of music, and have served peace, understanding between peoples, international cooperation, and the other purposes proclaimed by the United Nations Charter and UNESCO's Constitution. Nationals of, or institutions having their headquarters in Member States of UNESCO are eligible. The winners shall be selected from among: composers, for their work as a whole; individual performers and ensembles, for their performances as a whole; musicologists and music critics, for their research or criticism as a whole; teachers, for their teaching as a whole; and public figures and musical institutions, for their activities in the service of music as a whole. A diploma is awarded biennially during World Music Week. Established in 1975. Additional information is available from the International Music Council, 1 rue Miollis, 75015 Paris, France, phone: 1 4568 23 50. Formerly: (1978) International Music Council Prize.

6422
UNESCO Literacy Prizes
For recognition of the services of institutions, organizations, or individuals displaying outstanding merit and achieving particularly effective results in contributing to the fight for literacy. The following prizes are awarded: International Reading Association Prize; Noma Prize; and King Sejong Literacy Prize. Institutions, organizations, or individuals displaying outstanding merit and achieving particularly effective results in literacy and post-literacy activities and their integration in basic education programs may be submitted as candidates. Institutions, organizations or individuals must have carried out literacy and post-literacy activities in one of the following ways: by direct teaching; by organizing literacy programs at the national or local level; by promoting support from the public; by producing teaching materials or special media for literacy programs; by carrying out research in fields related to literacy (methods, languages, evaluation, social sciences, etc.); by carrying out special surveys of primary importance for literacy planning; by offering youth the possibility of taking part in literacy activities; or by carrying out non-formal education activities of a social, cultural, economic or political nature, in which literacy and related literacy activities (such as radio and television programs, publications and press, etc.) are integrated. In addition, the following criteria will be considered: the duration of the activity, which must be sufficient to permit an assessment of results and proof of success obtained; the contribution to the basic objectives of the educational system of the country; the contribution to local and national development; the value of the activities as an example to stimulate further similar action; the impact of the action carried out with a view to mobilizing new resources for literacy programs; the contribution to the understanding and development of the national society and culture; and the contribution to the appreciation of other cultures and to international understanding. Monetary prizes are awarded annually. The International Reading Association Literacy Award and the Noma Prize were established in 1979 and 1980 respectively, through the generosity of the International Reading Association and Mr. Shoichi Noma.

6423
UNESCO Prize for Architecture
(Prix UNESCO d'Architecture)
To recognize an architecture student or faculty member in a UNESCO member country for a meritorious architectural project inspired specifically by the aims of the organization. Those students or faculty members who contribute to improving the average standard of dwellings or town planning and reflect interest in environmental problems are eligible. A monetary prize and a certificate are awarded on the occasion of the triennial congress of the International Union of Architects (IUA). Established in 1969.

6424
UNESCO Prize for Landscape Architecture
To recognize a student in landscape architecture, who is the author of a work inspired specifically by the aims of UNESCO. The winner is selected by the Director General, on the recommendation of the jury, from the winners of the international competition in landscape architecture organized by the International Federation of Landscape Architects (IFLA), in accordance with the rules laid down by the Federation in this matter. The prize-winner must be a national of a Member State of UNESCO. A monetary prize of $3,500 is awarded annually. Established in 1989.

6425
UNESCO Prize for Peace Education
For recognition of a particularly outstanding example of activity designed to alert public opinion and mobilize the conscience of mankind in the cause of peace. The following criteria are considered: the mobilization of the consciences in the cause of peace; the implementation, at interna-

tional or regional level, of programs of activity designed to strengthen peace education by enlisting the support of public opinion; the launching of important activities contributing to the strengthening of peace; education action to promote human rights and international understanding; the promotion of public awareness of the problems of peace through the media and other effective channels; and any other activity recognized as essential to the construction of the defences of peace in the minds of men. Member states of UNESCO, intergovernmental organizations, non-governmental organizations granted consultative status with UNESCO and persons whom the Director-General deems qualified in the field of peace may nominate an individual, a group of individuals, or an organization considered to merit the distinction of this Prize by virtue of their activities. The closing date for the submission of nominations is March 31. A monetary prize of approximately $60,000 is awarded annually. Established in 1979 by the Japan Shipbuilding Industry Foundation.

6426

UNESCO Prize for the Teaching of Human Rights
For recognition of activity aimed at developing the teaching of human rights. Nationals of, or institutions or organizations having their headquarters in member states of UNESCO are eligible. They are required to have taken one or more particularly noteworthy initiatives for the development of the teaching of human rights. In addition, the following criteria will be taken into consideration: the duration of the activity must be sufficient to permit its results to be assessed and its effectiveness to be proved; it should make a notable contribution to the basic objectives of the United Nations and of UNESCO in the field of human rights; the work accomplished should serve as an example and be such as to stimulate further similar initiatives; it should have proved effective in mobilizing new resources, intellectual and physical, for the teaching of human rights; it should contribute to the understanding and solution of international or national problems of human rights; and it should contribute to the improvement of understanding among nations, peoples, and individuals, to the promotion of peace, relaxation of international tensions and international understanding and to action to combat racism, racial discrimination and apartheid. Nominations shall be made to the Director-General of UNESCO by governments of Members States by May 31. A monetary prize of $10,000 is awarded biennially. Established in 1978 on the occasion of the 30th anniversary of the Universal Declaration of Human Rights.

6427

UNESCO Science Prize
To recognize a person or group of persons for an outstanding contribution, through the application of science and technology, to the development of a developing member state or region, especially in the fields of scientific and technological research and education, or in the fields of engineering and industrial development. Nomination is by governments of UNESCO member states and non-governmental organizations having consultative status with UNESCO. A monetary prize of $15,000, a medal, and a plaque are awarded biennially. Established in 1967.

6428

Union des Annonceurs
53, Ave. Victor Hugo
75116 Paris, France
Phone: 1 45007910
Fax: 1 45005579

6429

Phenix - U.D.A.
For recognition of the actions of the most highly skilled sponsors of enterprises for their undertakings, and to promote new techniques of communication and new talents among those who daily witness the increasing integration of enterprises into the life of the city. Awards are given in the following categories: culture, heritage, humanitarian causes, audiovisual programs, adventure, sport, education, and environment. A trophy is awarded in each category as well as honorable mention and Special Jury Prizes.

6430

Union des Femmes Artistes et Musiciennes
10, rue du Dome
F-75116 Paris, France
Phone: 1 4704 76 38
Fax: 1 4727 35 03

6431

Concours International de Chant de Paris
To encourage young singers and enable them to begin a career. Men under 35 years of age and women under 32 years of age are eligible. The following monetary prizes are awarded: (1) Grand Prix - 50,000 French francs and performances to a man or a woman; (2) First Prizes - 15,000 French francs each to a man and a woman; (3) Second Prizes - 5,000 French francs each to a man and a woman; (4) Prize for a French Melody - 50,000 French francs to a man or a woman; (5) French Opera Prize - 1,000 French francs each to a man and a woman for the best interpretation of an aria from a French opera. Special engagements for performances are awarded. Awarded biennially with the Chamber Music Competition of Paris. Established in 1967 by Madame Roullet in memory of Pierrre Bernac. Sponsored by France - Ministry of Culture and Communication, the City of Paris, and the Ministry of Foreign Relations.

6432

Concours International de Musique de Chambre de Paris
For recognition of outstanding chamber music groups. Music groups with wind instruments, with or without piano, may enter. A required program is presented that includes one work out of the classical or romantic period; the work of a French composer still living or deceased within the last 10 years; and two works freely chosen. Groups who are under 35 years of age are eligible to apply by September 15. The following monetary prizes are awarded: (1) Grand Prix - 20,000 French francs; (2) Second prize for all categories - 8,500 French francs each; (3) Third prize for all categories - 2,000 French francs each; (4) Prix Special - 5,000 French francs each; and (5) Prix Special Albert Roussel - 10,000 French francs; sponsored by the Comite Albert Roussel on the 50th anniversary of his death. In addition, prize winners are invited to perform at special engagements. Awarded biennially. Established in 1981.

6433

Union des Journaux et Journalistes d'Entreprise de France
63, avenue la Bourdonnais
F-75007 Paris, France
Phone: 1 4555 05 92

6434

Grand Prix du Journal d'Entreprise
For recognition of outstanding business communications in the written, sound, video, or telematic forums. The following awards are given: (1) Grand Prix; (2) external newspapers; (3) newsletters; (4) local collectives; (5) news video; and (6) telematic newspaper.

6435

Union Internationale des Associations Techniques Cinematographiques
11, rue Galilee
F-75116 Paris, France
Phone: 1 4720 55 69

6436

Concours Technique International du Film de l'UNIATEC
For recognition of outstanding film technique. The following prizes are awarded: (1) Grand Prix UNIATEC - for exceptional control of special effects; (2) Prix d'Excellence; and (3) Prix d'Honneur. Established in 1971.

6437

Union Laique de Muret
6, route de Labarthe
F-31600 Muret, France
Phone: 61 56 13 15
Fax: 61 51 02 92

6438

Prix du Jeune Ecrivain "BNP" avec Le Monde
For recognition of outstanding writing by a young French writer or French-speaking writer between 15 and 23 years of age. Unpublished works of prose, such as short stories, drama, or fiction are eligible. Publication of the work is awarded annually in May and edited by Le Monde-Editions. Established in 1985.

6439

Prix du Jeune Ecrivain Francophone
For recognition of outstanding writing by a young, French-speaking writer under 20 years of age who lives outside France. Unpublished works such as short stories, drama, or fiction are eligible. Publication of the work is awarded annually in May. Established in 1985.

6440

Union Litteraire et Artistique de France
35, rue Gayet
F-42000 Saint-Etienne, France   Phone: 7733 2729

Defunct organization.

6441

Concours de l'Union Litteraire et Artistique de France
For recognition of the best works in classical poems and songs, poetry (free verse), short stories and novellas, essays (historical, scientific, critical, philosophical), and other published works. In each section, a maximum of three grand prizes is awarded. Honorary titles, and diplomas are awarded. (Discontinued)

6442

Prix Auvergne
For recognition of the best poem on the subject of Auvergne. Twenty-five lines of verse was the maximum considered. A monetary prize of 30 French francs was awarded. (Discontinued)

6443

Prix de la Nouvelle
For recognition of the best unpublished short story. Five typewritten pages is the maximum considered. A monetary prize of 100 French francs is awarded. (Discontinued)

6444

Prix de Poesie Max d'Arthez
For recognition of an unpublished work of poetry not exceeding 100 verses. A monetary prize of 100 French francs is awarded annually. (Discontinued)

6445

Prix du Conte de Noel
For recognition of the best unpublished story about Christmas in the present time. A monetary prize of 100 French francs is awarded. (Discontinued)

6446

Prix du Jeune Conteur ou Nouvelliste
For recognition of the best tale or short story by an author under 25 years of age. A monetary prize of 50 French francs is awarded. (Discontinued)

6447

Prix du Poeme Breton
For recognition of the best poem about Brittany. Poems may be no more than 30 verses. A monetary prize of 40 French francs is awarded. (Discontinued)

6448

Prix du Poeme Regionaliste
For recognition of a poem on a region or province of France. Poems not exceeding 30 verses were considered. A monetary prize of 30 French francs was awarded. (Discontinued)

6449

Prix du Reportage Touristique
To recognize the author of the best unpublished reporting on a site, a curiosity, or a custom of interest to tourists in a French province or a French town. A monetary prize of 100 French francs is awarded annually. Established in 1958. (Discontinued)

6450

Prix du Sonnet de la Pensee Francaise
For recognition of the best sonnet conforming strictly to the rules of the genre. Each poet may submit up to five different pieces. A monetary prize of 100 French francs is awarded. (Discontinued)

6451

Prix Futuriste
For recognition of the best work on the future. A monetary prize of 50 French francs is awarded. (Discontinued)

6452

Prix Humoristique Max d'Arthez
For recognition of an unpublished work, in verse or in prose, representing original humor, not exceeding 100 lines. A monetary prize of 100 French francs is awarded annually. (Discontinued)

6453

Prix Poetique Francais
For recognition of the best manuscript of twelve unpublished poems (maximum 24 verses each) on any topic selected by the author. A monetary prize of 100 French francs is awarded annually. (Discontinued)

6454

Prix Stephania de Poesie
For recognition of the best poem on a selected theme. Poems may be no more than 30 verses. A monetary prize of 100 French francs is awarded. (Discontinued)

6455

Prix Yves-Le-Kervadec
To recognize the author of the best work or unpublished manuscript of philosophical, moral or patriotic inspiration in prose or in verse. The work should not exceed twenty pages of typewritten manuscript or 100 verses. A monetary prize of 50 French francs is awarded. (Discontinued)

6456

Union of International Fairs
(Union des Foires Internationales)
35 bis, rue Jouffroy-d'Abbans   Phone: 1 42679912
F-75017 Paris, France   Fax: 1 42271929

6457

Union of International Fairs Awards
To recognize international organizers of trade fairs and exhibitions. The Union presents awards at an annual congress.

6458

Union Rationaliste
14, rue de l'Ecole Polytechnique
F-75005 Paris, France   Phone: 1 46330350

| 6459 |

Prix du l'Union Rationaliste
For recognition of work expressing the spirit of rationalism. Honorary recognition is awarded annually. Established in 1967 by Monsieur Darnaud.

| 6460 |

University of Technology of Compiegne
(Universite de technologie de Compiegne)
Industrial Design Div.
BP 649　　　　　　　　　　　　　　　　Phone: 44 23 45 59
F-60206 Compiegne, France　　　　　　Fax: 44 23 44 93

| 6461 |

ICSID/Compiegne Industrial Design Award
To promote design and to favor its link with present and future technologies to improve the quality of everyday life. This international award is open to all designers, engineers, industrialists, professionals, research institutes or students. A monetary prize of 50,000 French francs is awarded triennially. Established in 1988 by Prof. Danielle Quarante, University of Compiegne, with the endorsement of ICSID International Council of Societies of Industrial Design. Additional information is available from the International Council of Societies of Industrial Design, Kluuvikatu 1D, 00 100 Helsinki, Finland.

| 6462 |

Jean Pierre Verlanger
24, rue du Coteau
F-92370 Chaville, France　　　　　　Phone: 4750 77 63

| 6463 |

Prix Julia Verlanger
To recognize a novel of science fiction or heroic fantasy selected by readers as the best of the year. The French editions are eligible. A monetary prize of 10,000 French francs is awarded annually. Established in 1986 by Jean Pierre Verlanger in memory of his wife, Julia Verlanger, also known under the pseudonym of Gilles Thomas, one of the first women authors of science fiction and fantastic novels in France.

| 6464 |

Video Danse
c/o Conseil International de la Danse
45, rue Lamarck　　　　　　　　　　　Phone: 1 4223 40 27
F-75018 Paris, France　　　　　　　　　Fax: 1 4223 60 21

| 6465 |

International Video Dance Grand Prix
(Grand Prix International Video Danse)
To promote the production and broadcasting of dance programs on international television in order to popularize this artistic genre with the help of an adequate visualization; to encourage the development of new choreographic concepts particularly adapted for the audiovisual media; and to create a permanent international forum for people professionally concerned with dance and the audiovisual media. The competition is open to all public and private television organizations and video producers. The following awards are presented: (1) Grand Prix - 100,000 French francs and a trophy; (2) Press Prize - 30,000 French francs and a trophy; and (3) Prize for Musical Creation - 300,000 French francs and a trophy. Awarded annually. Established in Nimes in 1988, on the Region Languedoc-Rousillon initiative.

| 6466 |

Vieilles Maisons Francaises
93, rue de l'Universite　　　　　　　　Phone: 1 4551 78 96
F-75007 Paris, France　　　　　　　　Fax: 1 4551 12 26

| 6467 |

Concours de Sauvegarde Vieilles Maisons Francaises
For recognition of outstanding contributions to the safeguarding of old French houses. The following prizes are awarded: (1) Prix des Delegues - 40,000 French francs; (2) Prix Christie's - 50,000 French francs; (3) Prix de la Caisse Nationale des Monuments Historiques - 20,000 French francs; (4) Prix Demeures et Chateaux du Soleil - 20,000 French francs; (5) Coupe Sazerac - 3,000 French francs; (6) Prix de l'American Women's Group in Paris - 20,000 French francs; (7) Prix Vieilles Maisons Francaises - 80,000 French francs; (8) Prix Friends of VMF - $10,000; and (9) Prix Paris Chapter Friends of VMF - $15,000. Awarded annually.

| 6468 |

Maurice Vieux International Alto Competition
(Concours International d'Alto Maurice Vieux)
c/o S.A.N. de Senart Ville Nouvelle
100 rue de Paris
BP 6　　　　　　　　　　　　　　　　Phone: 1 6060 32 32
F-77567 Lieusaint Cedex, France　　　　Fax: 1 6488 69 69

| 6469 |

Maurice Vieux International Alto Competition
(Concours International d'Alto Maurice Vieux)
For recognition of outstanding performances by alto players. Players, 32 years of age and under, are eligible to enter by January 31. Monetary prizes totaling 100,000 French francs are awarded biennially. Established in 1985. Co-sponsored by Syndicat d'Agglomeration Nouvelle de Melun-Senart, Association Internationale les Amis d'Alto, Orchestre de Melun-Senart, Delegation Regionale a la Musique en Ile-de-France, and France - Ministry of Culture and Communication. Additional information is available from Les Amis d'Alto, c/o Paul Hadjaje, 11 bis, rue Neuve-Saint-Germain, F-92100, Boulogne, France, phone: 4620 44 05.

| 6470 |

Ville de Grenoble
11, boulevard Jean Pain
F-38100 Grenoble, France　　　　　　Phone: 7642 81 42

| 6471 |

Prix Stendhal de la Nouvelle
To recognize an outstanding writer of short stories and to promote new talent and the creation of outstanding literature. Unpublished manuscripts of short stories written in French may be submitted. A writer may enter each year if he has not won first place, but a new manuscript must be presented each year. The most outstanding manuscript is published professionally. Awarded annually. Established in 1984 by the Mayor of Grenoble in memory of Henry Bayle Stendhal, a writer born in Grenoble.

| 6472 |

Ville de Lyon
c/o Division des Affaires Culturelles
BP 1065
F-69205 Lyon Cedex 01, France　　　　Phone: 78 27 71 31

| 6473 |

Grand Prix des Metiers d'Art
For recognition of an outstanding artisan or craftsman from Lyon. An individual is considered for an entire career. A monetary prize of 50,000 French francs is awarded annually. Established in 1985.

| 6474 |

Grand Prix Litteraire de la Ville de Lyon
For recognition of an outstanding literary work. A monetary prize of 30,000 French francs was awarded annually. Established in 1978. A Bourse a la Creation of 7,000 French francs was awarded annually after 1984. (Discontinued)

6475
Prix de Poesie Roger Kowalski
For recognition of an outstanding work of poetry. A monetary prize of 15,000 French francs is awarded annually. Established in 1984.

6476
Wattrelos Short Film and Video Festival
(Festival International du Court Metrage et de la Video)
140, rue Faidherbe
F-59150 Wattrelos, France
Phone: 2075 8646
Fax: 2081 6400

6477
Wattrelos Short Film and Video Festival
(Festival International du Court Metrage et de la Video)
For recognition of outstanding films and videos by amateurs and semi-professionals. The Grand Prix de la Ville de Wattrelos and Grand Prix Special du Festival are awarded in both the amateur and semi-professional film and video categories. Gold, silver, and bronze medals are awarded for animation, fiction, reality, and genre films and videos, both amateur and semi-professional. Established in 1971. Sponsored by Ville de Wattrelos, Conseil general du Nord.

6478
World Federation of Travel Journalists and Writers
(Federation Internationale des Journalistes et Ecrivains du Tourisme)
2, rue Cyrano-de-Bergerac
F-75018 Paris, France
Phone: 1 4252 97 34

6479
Golden Apple
(Pomme d'Or)
For recognition of a meritorious contribution to the development of tourism and quality of service that causes peace and friendship among people. Regions, cities, businesses and individuals are eligible. Applications may be submitted by July 31 through the national association which is a member of FIJET. A trophy representing a golden apple is awarded annually. Established in 1970 by the Federation and *Vue Touristique*.

6480
World Festival of Mountain Pictures
(Festival Mondial de l'Image de Montagne)
62, ave. des Pins du Cap
F-06600 Antibes, France
Phone: 9361 45 45
Fax: 9367 34 93

6481
World Festival of Mountain Pictures
(Festival Mondial de l'Image de Montagne)
For recognition of the best mountain film or video of the year. Awards are given in the following categories: (1) Full-length film or video; (2) Short film or video; (3) Color and black and white photographs; (4) Slides; (5) Slide shows; and (6) Sound series - sequence of images on the same theme accompanied by a musical tape. The Grand Prize of the City of Antibes is awarded to the winner in each category annually. Monetary prizes totaling 110,000 French francs are awarded. In addition, the following prizes are awarded at the Festival: (1) World Book Prize of Mountain Pictures for the best book of pictures of the year - a trophy and 20,000 French francs; and (2) News Prize, Fiction Prize, and Documentary Prize for mountain television productions. Established in 1986. Sponsored by La Ville d'Antibes.

6482
World Festival of Underwater Pictures
(Festival Mondial de l'Image Sous-Marine)
62, ave. des Pins du Cap
F-06600 Antibes, France
Phone: 93 614545
Fax: 93 673493

6483
World Festival of Underwater Pictures
(Festival Mondial de l'Image Sous-Marine)
For recognition of the best underwater film or video of the year. At least 40 percent of the film or video must be underwater shots. Films may be entered in the full-length or short categories. Gold, silver, and bronze Flipper trophies are awarded in each cagegory. Monetary prizes totaling 60,000 French francs are awarded. In addition, a slide competition, a black and white and color photography competition, and a slide-show competition are held. Gold, silver, and bronze Diver trophies are awarded in each category. The Monde de la Mer prize of 5,000 French francs is also awarded to the gold Diver winner in the slide competition. The French Association of Conchology Prize is awarded to the best slide print that, while presenting strong aesthetic qualities, serves to increase knowledge of the world of mollusks. Each year the festival also awards: World Book Prize of Underwater Pictures for the best book of pictures of the year - a gold Flipper and 10,000 French francs; Prix Corail du Livre (French language production); La Musique et la Mer - for music; Apnea Sub-Aqua Documentary Prize - 7,000 French francs; and Underwater Television Productions - News Prize, Fiction Prize, Documentary Prize. Awarded annually. Established in 1974. Sponsored by the Spondyle Club and La Ville d'Antibes.

6484
World Health Organization
International Agency for Research on Cancer
(Organisation Mondiale de la Sante
Centre International de Recherche sur le Cancer)
Education and Training Programme
150, cours Albert Thomas
F-69372 Lyon Cedex 08, France
Phone: 72 738485
Fax: 72 738575

6485
Research Training Fellowship
To provide for training in cancer research. Junior scientists who are actively engaged in research in medical or allied sciences, and wish to pursue a career in cancer research are eligible. Candidates may be accepted in the following fields: environmental carcinogenesis including biostatistics and epidemiology of cancer, all aspects of chemical and viral carcinogenesis, and mechanisms of carcinogenesis. Applications are encouraged from epidemiologists and laboratory scientists for interdisciplinary training that will facilitate the conduct of genetic and molecular epidemiological research. Applicants requiring basic training in cancer epidemiology are also considered. An applicant should provide reasonable assurance that he or she will return to a post in his or her own country at the end of the fellowship. Fellows are, in general, selected from applicants with some post-doctoral experience in medicine or natural sciences. They must have an adequate knowledge, both written and spoken, of the language of the country in which their fellowship is tenable and not be already in their proposed host institute prior to the selection. The selection committee is composed of scientists of international reputation in the field of cancer research who are not members of the IARC Staff, together with scientists working at the IARC. The deadline is December 31. The number of awards is determined by the available funds. A one-year fellowship that is tenable at the Agency in Lyon or in any country and institution abroad where suitable research facilities and material exist, a stipend, and travel costs for the fellow and in certain circumstances for one dependent are awarded annually. Established in 1966 by the World Health Organization.

6486
Visiting Scientist Award
To enable a senior scientist to spend one year at IARC working on the implementation of a collaborative research project related to the Agency's own programs: epidemiology, biostatistics, environmental and viral carcinogenesis, and mechanisms of carcinogenes. Established cancer research workers with a minimum of five years postdoctoral experience may submit their applications after consultation with an IARG scientific staff member. The deadline is December 31 of each year. Applicants must belong to the staff of a university or research institution and have a position to return to at the end of the award period. There is an annual remuneration and the cost of travel is covered. Established in 1982.

6487

**World Organisation of Systems and Cybernetics
(Organisation Mondiale pour la Systemique et la Cybernetique)**
2, rue de Vouille
F-75015 Paris, France   Phone: 1 45336246

Formerly: (1987) World Organisation of General Systems and Cybernetics.

6488

Norbert Wiener Memorial Gold Medal
For recognition of an achievement in, or a contribution to, the field of cybernetics and systems. Nomination is by the Council of the Organisation. A gold medal and a certificate are awarded triennially. Established in 1978 in memory of Dr. Norbert Wiener, the father of cybernetics.

6489

World Packaging Organisation
42, avenue de Versailles   Phone: 1 42882974
F-75016 Paris, France   Fax: 1 45250273

6490

Worldstars for Packaging
To recognize a fully integrated pack that has already received national or international recognition and that scores highly across a wide range of criteria, which include: protection and presentation of contents; ease of handling; filling, closing, opening, and reclosing; sales appeal; graphic design; adequacy of information; quality of production; economy of material, cost reduction, and recyclability; ingenuity of construction; suitability for local conditions; and technical innovations. The World Packaging Competition is open to any package or packaging material that has won any type of domestic or international award related directly or indirectly to packaging, provided it has not been submitted at a previous WPO contest. A trophy and a diploma are awarded annually. Established in 1970. Since 1984, the competition has been held annually.

6491

World SF
1, rue Maitre-Albert
F-75005 Paris, France   Phone: 1 4329 87 03

6492

Harry Harrison Award
For recognition of a contribution toward improving the status of science fiction internationally. Awarded annually. Established in 1983.

6493

Karel Award
For recognition of continuous excellence in the field of translation. Individuals who are citizens of countries that hold a membership in World SF are eligible for nomination. A glass symbolic ornament is awarded annually. Established in 1980 by Frederick Pohl, President WSF, in honor of Karel Capek, the internationalist Czech writer. Additional information is available from Secretary WSF, Patrizia Thiella, Via Novara 3, Rozzano (MI), Italy.

6494

Special President's Award
For recognition of dedicated service in the field of science fiction. Awarded annually when merited. Established in 1983.

6495

World SF President's Award
For recognition of independence of thought in the field of science fiction. Awarded annually when merited. Established in 1983.

6496

World Union of Karate-do Organizations
122, rue de la Tombe-Issoire   Phone: 1 4395 42 00
F-75014 Paris, France   Fax: 1 4543 89 84

6497

World Union of Karatedo Organizations Championships
To promote the international development of karate, its access to continental Olympic Games and to the Olympics, by sponsoring world championships biennially.

6498

World Veterans Federation
17, rue Nicolo   Phone: 1 40726100
F-75116 Paris, France   Fax: 1 40728058

6499

WVF Rehabilitation Prize
To recognize an individual or an organization for services of international value rendered in the field of rehabilitation. Selection is by nomination. The deadline depends on the dates of the General Assembly. A trophy is awarded triennially at the WVF General Assembly. Established in 1953.

6500

**Writing Doctors Association
(Groupement des Ecrivains Medecins)**
7, avenue Curie
F-92370 Chaville, France   Phone: 1 47504210

6501

**Littre Prize
(Prix Littre)**
To encourage contributions to a field of cultural medical activity through a novel or an ethical essay. The novel or essay may be written by a doctor, a medical student, or a layperson, but must be concerned with the subject of medical ethics. Translations are not allowed. A monetary prize of 5,000 French francs is awarded annually in February. Established in 1974 in memory of Littre, a nineteenth century writer. Sponsored by *Impact Medicine*, a medical journal.

6502

Prix Clement Marot de Poesie
For recognition of a poem or a book of poems written by doctors or medical students in French. The following monetary prizes are awarded annually: 1,000 French francs for a poem and 2,000 French francs for a book of poems. Established in 1989 by the medical journal, *Le Quotidien du Medecin*.

6503

Prix de l'Histoire Vecue
For recognition of an autobiographical account by a doctor or a medical student that is written in French. The story must not have been published previously. A monetary prize of 3,000 French francs is awarded annually. Established in 1985 by *Gazaette Medicale*, a medical magazine.

6504

Prix Fernand Mery-Prix Animalier
To encourage veterinarians and veterinary medical students to write. Submissions must be written in French. A monetary prize of 5,000 French francs is awarded annually. Established in 1988 by Mrs. Mery in memory of Dr. Fernand Mery, a veterinarian.

6505

**Short Story Award
(Prix de la Nouvelle)**
To encourage doctors and future doctors to write short stories. Doctors who are active in the field of medicine or studying medicine may submit unpublished short stories of a maximum of 12 pages typewritten in

French. A monetary prize of 2,000 French francs is awarded annually in February. Established in 1974. Sponsored by *Tout Prevoir*, a medical magazine.

Gabon

6506

**International Bantu Civilization Centre
(Centre International des Civilisations Bantu)**
BP 770
Libreville, Gabon
Phone: 739650
Fax: 739650

6507

Biennial of Bantu Contemporary Art
For recognition of outstanding talent among Bantu artists, and to exhibit works showing the sculptural creativity of present-day Bantu artists. The following prizes are awarded: CICIBA Grand Prix - 1,000,000 CFA; CEC Grand Prix - 800,000 FCFA; ACCT Grand Prix - 10,000 French francs; Painting First prize - 400,000 FCFA; Painting Second prize - 400,000 FCFA; Sculpture First prize - 300,000 FCFA; and Sculpture Second prize - 300,000 FCFA. Awarded biennially. Established in 1985.

Germany

6508

**Academy of Arts, Berlin
(Akademie der Kunste, Berlin)**
Hanseatenweg 10
W-1000 Berlin 21, Germany
Phone: 30 391 1031

6509

Berlin Art Prizes
For recognition of outstanding achievements in fine arts, architecture, music, literature, performing arts, film, radio and television. Awards are given in alternate years in the following categories: (1) art; (2) architecture; (3) music; (4) literature - the Fontane Prize; (5) performing arts; (6) film; (7) radio; and (8) television. A monetary prize of 30,000 German marks and honorary recognition are awarded annually. Established in 1948.

6510

Alfred Doblin Prize
For recognition of literary munuscripts which have an epic character, and for remarkable translations, film-scripts, and long poems.

6511

Will Grohmann Prize
To recognize young artists for contributions in art. A monetary prize of 12,500 German marks and honorary recognition are awarded annually. The prize is funded by Dr. Grohmann's family.

6512

Scholarship Prizes
For recognition of the achievements of young artists in the field of fine arts, architecture, music, literature, performing arts, film, radio and television. A monetary prize of 10,000 German marks is awarded annually in each discipline.

6513

**Academy of Sciences and Literature, Mainz
Section of Literature
(Akademie der Wissenschaften und der Literatur zu Mainz Klasse der Literatur)**
Geschwister-Scholl-Strasse 2
W-6500 Mainz, Germany
Phone: 6131 577 22
Fax: 6131 577 40

6514

Wilhelm-Heinse-Medaille
For recognition of literary essays, which usually reflect a life's work. German as well as foreign authors may be nominated. Members of the Academy are not eligible. A medal created by sculptor Toni Stadler is awarded biennially when merited. This award will be given 20 times only. Established in 1978 in memory of Wilhelm Heinse (1746-1803), a German poet and writer, who influenced the writing of later authors, lived for several years in Mainz and was sponsored by the Elector and Archbishop.

6515

**Nossack Academy Writers Award
(Nossack-Akademiepreises fur Dichter und ihre Ubersetzer)**
To recognize creative and excellent translations. A monetary prize of up to 20,000 DM is awarded biennially to nonmember authors. Established in 1977 in memory of Hans Erich Nossack, member of the Academy's Literature Section.

6516

**Academy of Sciences and Technology in Berlin
(Akademie der Wissenschaften zu Berlin)**
Griegstrasse 5-7
W-1000 Berlin 33, Germany
Phone: 30 820905

6517

**Prize for Junior Scientists
(Preis fur Nachwuchswissenschaftler)**
To recognize outstanding young scientists for work in one of the fields of interest of the Academy. The work should address novel questions relevant to more than one discipline. Scientists from any country who are 40 years of age or younger may submit applications by June 30. A monetary award of 25,000 German marks (which may be shared) is awarded at the convention. Established in 1989.

6518

**AMK Berlin, Company for Exhibitions, Fairs and Congresses
(AMK Berlin, Ausstellungs - Messe - Kongress)**
Messedamm 22
D-14055 Berlin 19, Germany
Phone: 30 30380
Fax: 30 30382325

6519

**International Film Competition at the Green Week Berlin
(Internationaler Filmwettbewerb zur Grunen Woche Berlin)**
To improve the quality of agricultural films by international comparison; to provide a survey of pertinent film and television productions, thereby serving advisory and explanatory work; and to promote international cooperation. Cinema films and TV productions on the following subjects were accepted for presentation: Films about: (1) agriculture and rural development - all the various facets of agriculture; agriculture, horticulture, viticulture, fisheries, forestry and the timber industry, rural home economics; (2) agriculture and the environment - the preservation of the basic natural requirements for survival and production: the soil, water, air; (3) agriculture and human nutrition - nutritional sciences, food industry, consumer protection; and films, containing information and advice for agriculture. Feature films as such and films with a commercial message were excluded from the Competition. Gold, silver, and bronze Ear of Wheat Trophies were presented in each of the four subject groups. One Golden Ear was awarded for the developing country which best presents one of its problems. Awarded biennially. Established in 1960 by the Federal Ministry of Food, Agriculture and Forestry, Bonn, and the Senator for Economics, Berlin. (Discontinued) Formerly: .

6520
Anatomical Society
(Anatomische Gesellschaft)
Medizinische Universitat zu Lubeck
Institut fur Anatomie
Ratzeburger Allee 160   Phone: 451 5004030
D-23538 Lubeck, Germany   Fax: 451 5004034

6521
Sobotta Preis
To recognize outstanding scientific achievement. Papers in all fields of anatomy may be submitted by scientists under 40 years of age. Manuscripts must be submitted in either English or German. Scientists may not be awarded the Sobotta Prize more than once. A monetary award of $10,000 US, a medal, and travel to the next international congress of the Society are presented every five years. Established in 1985 by Urban and Schwarzenberg, publishers in Munich, in honor of J. Sobotta, a professor of anatomy in Bonn.

6522
Art Society
(Kunstlergilde)
Hafenmarkt 2
W-73728 Esslingen/Neckar, Germany   Phone: 711 35 91 29

6523
Lovis-Corinth-Preis
For recognition of East German fine arts. Works may be submitted for consideration. A monetary prize of 15,000 German marks for first prize, and two prizes of 7,000 German marks each are awarded annually. Established in 1974 in memory of Lovis Corinth (1858-1925). Sponsored by the Bundesministerium des Innern.

6524
Georg-Dehio-Preis
For recognition of an outstanding contribution to East German cultural and intellectual history. Applications may be submitted. A monetary prize of 15,000 German marks for first prize, and two prizes of 7,000 German marks each are awarded annually. Established in 1964 in memory of Georg Dehio (1850-1932). Sponsored by the Bundesministerium des Innern.

6525
Andreas-Gryphius-Preis
For recognition of the best essay, novel, or poem that deals with the particular problems of the German culture in East Europe. Works may be submitted for consideration. A monetary prize of 15,000 German marks for first prize, and three monetary prizes of 7,000 German marks each are presented. Awarded annually at the "Haus des Deutschen Ostens," Dusseldorf. Established in 1957 in memory of Andreas Gryphius (1616-1664). Sponsored by the Bundesministerium des Innern.

6526
Johann-Wenzel-Stamitz-Preis
For recognition of East German music. Works may be submitted for consideration. A monetary prize of 15,000 German marks for first prize, and two prizes of 7,000 German marks each are awarded annually. Established in 1960 in memory of Johann Wenzel Stamitz (1717-1757). Sponsored by the Bundesministerium des Innern.

6527
Association of German Electrical Engineers
(Verband Deutscher Elektrotechniker)
Stresemannallee 15   Phone: 69 6308 217
W-6000 Frankfurt/Main 70, Germany   Fax: 69 6312 925

6528
Honorary Ring
(Verband Ehrenring)
For recognition of outstanding scientific or technical achievement in electrical engineering. Individuals except members of the board of directors, their professional associations, or members of the selection committee are eligible. An honorary golden ring and a certificate of award are awarded biennially. Established in 1958.

6529
Association of German Electrical Engineers
Information Technology Society
(Informationstechnische Gesellschaft im Verband Deutscher Elektrotechn iker)
Stresemannallee 15   Phone: 69 6308360
60596 Frankfurt am Maim 70, Germany   Fax: 69 6312925

6530
Forderpreis der ITG
For recognition of excellent scientific dissertations in the field of telecommunication. Members of the Society under 30 years of age are eligible. A monetary prize of 1,000 German marks and a certificate of award are presented up to three times per year. Established in 1993.

6531
Karl Kupfmuller Prize
(Karl-Kupfmuller-Preis der ITG)
For recognition of outstanding significant technical or scientific achievements or contributions in the field of telecommunications engineering. Individuals may be nominated. A monetary prize of 10,000 German marks and a certificate of award are presented every four years. Established in 1984 in memory of Karl Kuepfmueller, Professor of Engineering.

6532
Association of Palaeontology
(Palaontologische Gesellschaft)
Senckenberganlage 25   Phone: 251 833951
D-60325 Frankfurt, Germany   Fax: 251 833968

6533
Ehrenmitglied
For recognition of exceptional merits in paleontological science and the Paleontologische Gesellschaft. Society membership is necessary. A certificate is awarded annually at the convention of the Society. Established in 1912.

6534
Korrespondierendes Mitglied
For recognition of exceptional merits in paleontological science and intensive exchange with members of the Society. A certificate is awarded annually at the convention of the Society. Established in 1963.

6535
Karl Alfred von Zittel Medaille
For recognition of exceptional merits in paleontology by amateurs. A certificate and a medal are awarded annually at the convention of the Society. Established in 1984 in honor of Professor Dr. Karl Alfred von Zittel (1839-1904) of Munich, a famous paleontologist and author of an internationally known handbook.

6536
Association of Pulp and Paper Chemists and Engineers
(Verein der Zellstoff- und Papier-Chemiker und -Ingenieure)
Berliner Allee 56   Phone: 6151 33264/65
W-6100 Darmstadt, Germany   Fax: 6151 311076

6537
Walter-Brecht-Denkmunze
For recognition of outstanding technical and scientific contributions to the paper industry. Scientists without regard to nationality are eligible. A medal with a portrait of Walter Brecht, and, on the reverse, the name of the association and the inscription "for outstanding technical and scientific achievement in the field of the paper industry" is awarded irregularly. Established in 1977.

6538
Hans-Clemm-Denkmunze
For recognition of achievements in the field of pulp and paper technology or for special contributions to the Association. Scientists without regard to nationality are eligible. A monetary prize and a medal showing the bust of Hans Clemm, and on the reverse a narrow oak-leaf wreath, the name of the Association, and the inscription "in recogniton of outstanding service" are awarded irregularly. Established in 1936.

6539
Ehrenring der ehemaligen Forschungsstelle Papiergeschichte
For recognition of outstanding, investigative work in the area of the history of paper. Scientists without regard to nationality are eligible. A gold ring with a reproduction of the old watermark "P" is awarded irregularly. Established in 1954.

6540
Goldene Vereinsnadel
For recognition of long years of outstanding service to the Association. Members without regard to nationality are eligible. A gold pin with the insignia of the Association is awarded irregularly. Established in 1970.

6541
Honorary Member
To recognize individuals who distinguish themselves in the sciences of pulp and paper manufacture and contributions to the Association.

6542
Valentin-Hottenroth-Denkmunze
For recognition of successful research in the field of cellulose and its further development. Scientists without regard to nationality are eligible. A medal showing the profile of Valentin Hottenroth and the inscription "in memory of V.H., the most distinguished scientist in the field of cellulose and synthetic fiber technology" is awarded irregularly. Established in 1955.

6543
Eugen-Lendholt-Denkmunze
For recognition of outstanding technical or scientific work which promotes the sodium pulp and sulphate pulp and paper industry. Scientists without regard to nationality are eligible. A medal is awarded irregularly. Established in 1957.

6544
Alexander-Mitscherlich-Denkmunze
For recognition of outstanding scientific or technical achievements which further the pulp and paper industry. Scientists without regard to nationality are eligible. A medal showing the bust of Alexander Mitscherlich, and on the reverse a narrow wreath of oak-leaves, the name of the organization, and the inscription "in recogniton of outstanding contributions" is awarded irregularly. Established in 1936 in memory of Alexander Mitscherlich, founder of the Sulfite-cellulose industry.

6545
Dr. Edmund-Thiele-Denkmunze
For recognition of outstanding achievement in the fields of synthetic fibers, rayons or film production. The award is usually given for a significant publication of the preceding year but can be given in special cases for a scientist's entire body of research. Scientists without regard to nationality are eligible. A medal showing the bust of Edmund Thiele, and on the reverse a narrow oak-leaf wreath, the name of the Association, and the inscription "in recognition of outstanding service" is awarded irregularly. Established in 1937.

6546
**Atlantic Bridge
(Atlantik-Brucke)**
Adenauerallee 131
W-53113 Bonn 1, Germany
Phone: 228 214160
Fax: 228 214659

6547
**Eric M. Warburg Prize of Atlantic Bridge
(Eric-M. Warburg-Preis der Atlantik-Brucke)**
For recognition of an outstanding contribution to German-American friendship. Citizens of Germany or America are eligible. A monetary prize is awarded biennially. Established in 1988 in honor of Eric M. Warburg.

6548
Automobilclub Von Deutschland
Lyoner Strasse 16
Postfach 710153
W-6008 Frankfurt, Germany
Phone: 69 66060
Fax: 69 6606210

6549
Automobilclub Von Deutschland Awards
To recognize and promote driving safety through club sponsorored competitions.

6550
**Bavarian Academy of Fine Arts
(Bayerische Akademie der Schonen Kunste)**
Max Joseph-Platz 3
W-80539 Munich 22, Germany
Phone: 89 294622
Fax: 89 2285885

6551
Horst Bienek Preis fur Lyrik
To recognize outstanding poetry. A monetary award of 30,000 German marks is presented annually. Established in 1991 to honor Horst Bienek. Sponsored by the Horst Bienek Stiftung.

6552
Grosser Literaturpreis der Bayerische Akademie der Schonen Kunste
To recognize an author for his or her literary work. A monetary prize of 30,000 German marks is awarded annually in May, June, or July. Established in 1950. Formerly: (1986) Literaturpreis der Bayerische Akademie der Schonen Kunste.

6553
Adelbert-von-Chamisso-Preis
To recognize outstanding contributions to German literature from foreign authors. A monetary award of 15,000 German marks is presented annually. Established in 1985 to honor Adelbert von Chamisso. Sponsored by the Robert Bosch Stiftung. Awarded in cooperation with the Institut fur Deutsch als Fremdsprache der Universitat Munchen.

6554
Friedrich Ludwig von Sckell Ehrenring
To recognize extraordinary achievements in landscape architecture. A golden ring designed by Franz Rickert is awarded biennially. Established in 1967 to honor Friedrich Ludwig von Sckell, landscape architect, who planned the "English Garden" in Munich.

6555
Karl Wolfskehl Preis fur Exilliteratur
(Karl Wolfskehl Preis fur Exilliteratur)
To recognize authors in exile and to direct attention to the fact of exile as a mental destiny. A monetary award of 25,000 German marks is presented annually. Established in 1988 to honor Karl Wolfskehl, a poet and translator, who died in exile. Formerly: (1991) Internationaler Exil-Preis.

6556
Bavarian Academy of Science
(Bayerische Akademie der Wissenschaften)
Marstallplatz 8
80539 Munich 22, Germany
Phone: 89 23031139
Fax: 89 23031100

6557
Bavarian Academy of Science Competition Prize
For recognition of the best solutions to the scientific problem posed by the Academy to the participants of the competition. A monetary prize of 8,000 German marks is awarded triennially. Established in 1759 by Max III Joseph Kurfurst von Bayern.

6558
Bavarian Academy of Science Prize
For recognition of an outstanding achievement in science. A monetary prize of 10,000 German marks is awarded irregularly when merited. Established in 1956 by the Foundation for the Advancement of Science in Bavaria.

6559
Benemerenti Medals
For recognition of outstanding work for the Academy. Gold, silver, and bronze medals are awarded irregularly; the gold is seldom awarded, while the silver is awarded most years. Established in 1759.

6560
Berlin City Hall
Senatsverwaltung fur Kulturelle
 Agnelegeheiten
Europa Center
W-1000 Berlin 30, Germany
Phone: 30 21231
Fax: 302123 3288

6561
Brothers Grimm Prize
To recognize outstanding achievements by the authors, performing groups and sponsors of modern children's and young people's drama and puppet theatre. A monetary prize of 10,000 German marks is divided among as many as three people or ensembles. Awarded biennially. Established in 1961.

6562
Peter Joseph Lenne Prize
(Peter Joseph Lenne-Preis des Landes Berlin)
For recognition of outstanding planning, or for scientific or artistic achievement in the use of open space and landscape development. Architects or engineers/planners under 40 years of age are eligible. Three monetary prizes of 6,000 German marks each are awarded annually. Established in 1964. Additional information is available from Prof. F. Trillitzsch, Institut fur Landschafts-und Freiraumplanung der Technischen Universitat Berlin, Franklinstrasse, Germany, phone: 30 314 49 75, or from Senator fur Wissenschaft und Forschung, Ref. II aB3, Bredtschneiderstrasse 5, D-1000 Berlin 19, phone: 30 30 32.

6563
Berlin International Film Festival
(Internationale Filmfestspiele Berlin)
Budapester Strasse 50
W-1000 Berlin 30, Germany
Phone: 30 254 89 0
Fax: 30 254 89 20

6564
Berlin International Film Festival
(Internationale Filmfestspiele Berlin)
To recognize the best feature and short films which are not only of interest to selected and expert audiences, but also films of quality that reach a wide public. The competition is limited to feature films and short films (less than 15 minutes) produced during the year preceding the Festival and not released outside their countries of origin. Priority is given to films not yet released. The following prizes are awarded for feature films: (1) Golden Berlin Bear - Grand Prize; (2) Silver Berlin Bear - Special Jury prize; (3) Silver Berlin Bear - for the best director; (4) Silver Berlin Bear - for the best actress; (5) Silver Berlin Bear - for the best actor; (6) Silver Berlin Bear - for an outstanding single achievement; (7) Silver Berlin Bear - for a special category determined each year; and (8) Special Mention. The following prizes are awarded for short films: (1) Golden Berlin Bear for the best short film; and (2) Silver Berlin Bear for the best screenplay or for the best director among the short films. Other prizes of various organizations also awarded at the Berlin International Film Festival are: International Protestant Film Jury Prize; OCIC-Prize (International Catholic Organization for Cinema and Audiovisual Media); FIPRESCI-Prizes; Readers Prize of the *Berliner Morgenpost*; Prize of the German Art Film Theatre Association; CICAE Prize (International Confederation of Art Cinemas); Prize of UNICEF; CIFEJ Prize (International Centre of Films for Children and Young People); Prize of the Berlin Children's Jury; and Gay Teddy Bear (International Gay & Lesbian Film Festival Association). Awarded annually in February. Established in 1951.

6565
Bertelsmann Foundation
(Bertelsmann Stiftung)
Postfach 5555
Carl-Bertelsmann-Strasse 256
W-4830 Gutersloh 100, Germany
Phone: 5241 74060
Fax: 5241 73882

6566
Carl Bertelsmann Prize
(Carl Bertelsmann-Preis)
To honor innovative thought and promising initiatives designed to offer a significant contribution to shaping the evolution of Germany's democratically constituted society, especially of institutions and structures in the fields of industry and communications. Achievements must promote the development of society in Germany and beyond its border. Applications are not accepted. A monetary award of 300,000 German marks is awarded each fall. Established in 1988 to honor Carl Bertelsmann, founder of the Bertelsmann Corporation. Additional information is available from Martin Spilker, Program Director.

6567
New Voices - European Singing Contest
(Neue Stimmen - Europaischer Sangerwettstreit)
For recognition of young opera singers. Female and male singers who are 32 years of age or younger may submit applications. The following monetary awards are presented biennially: first prize - 10,000 German marks; second prize - 6,000 German marks; third prize - 3,000 German marks; and a Special Prize for operetta singers - 5,000 German marks. Established in 1987. Additional information is available from Martin Spilker, Press Officer.

6568
Bioelectrochemical Society
(Institut fur Chemische Pflanzen Physiologie der Universitat Tubingen)
Corrensstrasse 41
Tubingen, Germany

6569
Luigi Galvani Prize
To recognize biochemists, electrophysiologists, and biophysicists and to promote research.

6570

Black Panel World Foundation
Micro Hall Art Center
PO Box 1206
W-2905 Edewecht, Germany   Phone: 44 86 26 97

6571

Black Panel World Foundation Awards
To recognize individuals for outstanding service in promotion of the Foundation. The following awards are presented: (1) Orbitalorden - 200 to 800 German marks; (2) Ikarusmedaille - 1,000 to 2,000 German marks; and (3) Black Panel Malewitsch Medaille - 3,000 German marks. In addition, the title "Docent of Orbital Arts" is conferred for extraordinary service to the Foundation.

6572

**Braunschweig City Cultural Office
(Stadt Braunschweig-Kulturamt)**
Steintorwall 3   Phone: 531 4702445
38100 Braunschweig, Germany   Fax: 531 4703401

6573

Friedrich-Gerstaecker-Preis
To recognize living authors of young peoples' books which convey adventures in the wide world with captivating style, as did world traveller/author Friedrich Gerstaecker, a citizen of Braunschweig. The book, written in German, must have been published within the preceding three years. A monetary prize of 6,000 German marks is awarded biennially. Established in 1947.

6574

Wilhelm-Raabe-Preis
For recognition of an outstanding work of fiction. A monetary prize of 15,000 German marks is awarded triennially. Established in 1944.

6575

Ludwig-Spohr-Preis
To recognize a living composer of chamber music or a musical artist for exceptional service to the musical life of the city of Braunschweig. A monetary award of 10,000 German marks is awarded triennially. Established in 1953 in memory of Ludwig Spohr, a violin virtuoso and composer.

6576

Rudolf-Wilke-Preis
To recognize outstanding young artists and to promote their development in the fine arts. Residents of Braunschweig are eligible. A monetary award of 8,000 German marks is awarded biennially. Established in 1953 in memory of the artist, Rudolf Wilke.

6577

Bremen City Council
Senator fur Bildung Wissenschaft und
   Kunst
Freie Hansestadt Bremen
Rembertiring 9-11
W-2800 Bremen, Germany   Phone: 421 361 4289

6578

**Bremen Literary Prize
(Literaturpreis der Freien Hansestadt Bremen)**
For recognition of an outstanding literary work by a German writer. Books published during the preceding year are eligible. A monetary prize of 30,000 German marks and an additional promotion/advancement award of 10,000 German marks (awarded since 1978) are presented annually. Established in 1954 in memory of Rudolf Alexander Shroder, a poet, translator, and architect (1878-1962).

6579

Bremer Forderpreis fur Bildende Kunst
For recognition in the field of painting, graphic arts, sculpture, carving, film, video, photography, or a performing art. Young artists under 40 years of age who live in the Bremen area are eligible. A monetary prize of 10,000 German marks is awarded annually. Established in 1977.

6580

Bremer Forderpreis fur Kunsthandwerk
For recognition in the field of arts and crafts. Young artists under 40 years of age who live in the Bremen area are eligible to enter up to three works. A monetary prize of 5,000 German marks is awarded biennially. Established in 1977.

6581

Kunstpreis des Landes Bremen
For recognition of outstanding achievement in the art of the region. Monetary assistance of 24,000 German marks and an independent exhibition are awarded quadrennially. Established in 1989.

6582

Rolandpreis fur Kunst im offentlichen Raum
To recognize exceptional creativity in the art of sculpture. Sculptors of all ages and nationalities are eligible. A monetary award of 20,000 German marks is awarded triennially. Established in 1979. Formerly: Bremer Bildhauerpreis.

6583

Stipendien an Autoren/Autorinnen
To provide stipends for regional authors who write in German. Two stipends of 5,000 German marks are awarded annually.

6584

Bundesvereinigung Deutscher Apothekerverbande
Deutsches Apothekerhaus
Postfach 5722
Ginnheimer Str. 26   Phone: 6196 9280
65732 Eschborn, Germany   Fax: 6196 928556

6585

Ehrennadel der Deutschen Apotheker
To recognize an outstanding German pharmacist. A lapel pin and a certificate are awarded annually. Established in 1975.

6586

Fluckiger Medaille
For recognition of outstanding scholarship or service in pharmacology. Scientists of any nationality are eligible. A rectangular plaque is awarded at infrequent intervals. Established in 1893 by the Fluckiger Foundation. Sponsored by the Swiss Pharmaceutical Association, the Association of German Pharmacists, the Pharmaceutical Institute of the University of Bern, and the Pharmaceutical Institute of the University of Strasburg.

6587

Lesmuller-Medaille
For recognition of special service to the German pharmaceutical profession. German pharmacists are eligible. A bronze medal is awarded annually. Established in 1949 by the Federal Chamber of Pharmacists.

6588

Hans Meyer Medaille
For recognition of service to the German pharmaceutical profession and pharmaceutical medicine. A gold or silver medal and a certificate are awarded annually. Established in 1971 by the executive councils of the Professional Association of German Pharmacists, and the Federal Chamber of Pharmacists.

6589

Scheele Plakette
For recognition of outstanding service to the profession of pharmacy. German or non-German pharmacists are eligible. A rectangular plaque is awarded irregularly. Established in 1942, and re-established in 1958.

6590

Center for Children's and Young People's Film (Kinder-und Jugendfilmzentrum in der Bundesrepublik Deutschland)
Kuppelstein 34
W-42857 Remscheid, Germany
Phone: 2191 794235
Fax: 2191 794230

6591

Deutscher Jugend-Video-Preis
To promote qualified videos for children and young people among the commercial video programs. Awards are given in two categories: Videos for Children and Videos for Young People. Videos are suggested to a jury when they are in distribution or on sale during the current award year. The following monetary prizes and an honorable mention are awarded in each category: first prize - 5,000 German marks; second prize - 3,000 German marks; and third prize - 1,000 German marks. Awarded annually. Established in 1985 and announced by Bundesministerium fer Frauen und Jugend (Federal Minister for Family and Youth).

6592

Frankfurter Guckkastenmennchen
For recognition of the best film program of the International Children's Film Festival in Frankfurt. Films that are entered and selected for the International Children's Film Festival are eligible. The deadline for entry is June 20. Two trophies are given as awards annually. Established in 1984 by Deutsches Filmmuseum Frankfurt am Main.

6593

Chopin-Gesellschaft in der Bundesrepublik Deutschland Darmstadt
Kasinostrasse 3
John F.-Kennedy-Haus
64293 Darmstadt, Germany
Phone: 6151 2 59 57
Phone: 6151 5 58 97

6594

European Chopin Piano Competition (Europaischer Chopin-Klavierwettbewerb)
To promote outstanding Chopin interpretation and to prepare artists for the Warsaw Chopin Competition. The Competition is open to pianists studying or having studied in a European country for at least two semesters or one year, and who are not older than 30 years of age. Monetary prizes of 9,000 German marks, 6,000 German marks, and 3,000 German marks are awarded triennially. The next competition is scheduled for 1996. Established in 1983.

6595

City of Cologne (Stadt Koln)
Rathaus
W-5000 Cologne 1, Germany
Phone: 221 2210
Fax: 221 2212211

6596

Jabach Medal (Jabach Medaille)
For recognition of support for the museums of Cologne. Promoters, donors, or collectors are eligible. A medal and certificate are awarded. Established in 1966 by the City Council in memory of Everhard Jabach III, Cologne collector (1618-1695). Additional information is available from Kulturamt der Stadt Cologne, Richartzstraase 2-4, D-50667 Cologne, Germany.

6597

Stephan Lochner Medal (Stephan Lochner Medaille)
For recognition of an outstanding work in the field of contemporary painting or sculpture. Living artists are eligible. A medal and certificate are awarded. Established in 1949 by the City Council in memory of Stephan Lochner, a painter who lived in Cologne around 1410-1451. Additional information if available from Kulturamt der Stadt Cologne, Richartzstraase 2-4, D-50667 Cologne, Germany.

6598

City of Darmstadt (Stadt Darmstadt)
c/o Bormet, Magistrat
Postfach 11 07 80
Luisenplatz 5
W-6100 Darmstadt 11, Germany
Phone: 6151 13 20 23

6599

Ricarda-Huch-Preis
For recognition of outstanding literary works that support German culture and freedom. A monetary prize of 10,000 German marks is awarded triennially. Established in 1978 in memory of the uprising June 17, 1953 and the poetess Ricarda Huch who stood up against the Nazi oppression and for cultural freedom. Additional information is available from phone: 6151 13 3335.

6600

Kunstpreis der Stadt Darmstadt
To recognize outstanding artists of the city. Individuals, under 50 years of age, who enter the art exhibition and who have not previously won prizes, are eligible. A monetary prize of 10,000 German marks, a certificate, and travel costs are awarded annually. The prize may be divided. Established in 1955. Additional information is available from Institut Mathildenhohe, Europaplatz 1, 6100 Darmstadt, Federal Republic of Germany, phone: 6151 13 2778.

6601

Literarischer Marz
For recognition of the most outstanding young lyric authors of the biennial lyric festival, "The Last Week in March." German speaking lyricists, under 35 years of age, who have won no previous prizes are eligible. The following prizes are awarded: (1) Leonce-und Lena-Preis - 12,000 German marks; and (2) two Forderpreise - 6,000 German marks each. Awarded biennially. Established in 1978.

6602

Johann-Heinrich-Merck Ehrung
To recognize individuals for contributions in various fields such as science, art, economics, and architecture. Awarded several times annually. Established in 1955. Additional information is available from phone: 6151 13 3335.

6603

Preis der Neuen Darmstadter Sezession fur Junge Kunstler
For the promotion of young artists in the fields of painting and sculpture. Individuals, under 40 years of age, who are unexhibited and have not previously won prizes are eligible. Prizes are given in alternate years for sculpture and painting. A monetary prize of 4,000 German marks, a certificate, and travel costs are awarded annually. Established in 1975. Additional information is available from Neue Darmstadter Sezession, Geschaftsfuhrung Liane Palesch, Kranichsteiner Strasse 107, 6100 Darmstadt, Federal Republic of Germany, phone: 6151 71 5031.

6604

Club Daguerre
Postfach 1620
W-5030 Hurth, Germany
Phone: 2233 78383

6605
Daguerre-Preis
For recognition of the best scientific work dealing with the historical aspects of photography. Unpublished, scientifically valid works are considered. A monetary prize of 3,000 German marks is awarded. The prize can be divided.

6606
Cologne International Pianoforte Competition - Foundation Tomassoni
Dagobertstrasse 38
D-50668 Cologne, Germany
Phone: 221 912818
Fax: 221 131204

Formerly: (1983) Premio Tomassoni Internationaler Klavier-Wettbewerb of Musikhochschule Koln.

6607
Cologne International Pianoforte Competition
(Internationalen Klavierwettbewerb Koln)
To recognize and promote young piano performers. Pianists of all nationalities between 18 and 29 years of age are eligible. Monetary prizes of 15,000, 10,000, and 5,000 German marks are awarded every three years. Established in 1980 by Caterina Tomassoni in memory of her sister. (Inactive in 1994)

6608
Cologne International Violin Competition
(Internationaler Violinwettbewerb Koln)
Hochschule fur Musik Koln Foundation/
Shiflung Georg Kulenkampff
Dagoberstrasse 38
D-50668 Cologne, Germany
Phone: 221 97278441
Fax: 221 13 1204

6609
Cologne International Violin Competition/Foundation/Shiflung Georg Kulenkampff
(Internationaler Violinwettbewerb Koln)
To recognize outstanding violin performance and to encourage professional development. All violinists up to 29 years of age may submit applications by January 15. A monetary prize is awarded triennially. Established in 1982 by Prof. Dr. Caspar and Dr. Angela Kulenkampff in memory of Georg Kulenkampff.

6610
Council of the City of Frankfurt
(Magistrat der Stadt Frankfurt am Main)
Romerberg 23
W-6000 Frankfurt am Main 1, Germany
Phone: 69 2 12 3 60 91
Fax: 69 2 12 3 78 59

6611
Theodor W. Adorno Award
(Theodor-W.-Adorno-Preis)
For recognition of outstanding achievements in philosophy, music, drama and film. A monetary award of 50,000 German marks and a certificate are presented triennially. Established in 1977 to honor Theodor W. Adorno.

6612
Goethepreis
For recognition of outstanding literary, scientific or artistic achievement. An individual whose work demonstrates the value of or respect for Goethe's ideals and thoughts is eligible. The winner is selected by the Magistrate of Frankfurt am Main. A monetary prize of 50,000 German marks and a certificate are awarded triennially. Established in 1927.

6613
DECHEMA, Deutsche Gesellschaft fur Chemisches Apparatewesen, Chemische Technik und Biotechnologie e.V.
Theodor-Heuss-Allee 25
D-60486 Frankfurt am Main, Germany
Phone: 69 756400
Fax: 69 7564201

6614
ACHEMA Plaque in Titanium
(ACHEMA-Plakette in Titan)
For recognition of outstanding service to DECHEMA, in particular to the ACHEMA Exhibition-Congresses, and to the DECHEMA's non-profit scientific activities. The plaque is awarded triennially. The ACHEMA Plaque was founded by DECHEMA in 1970 to commemorate the 50th Jubilee of the ACHEMA Exhibtion-Congress and was first awarded during the ACHEMA of 1973.

6615
DECHEMA Honorary Membership
(DECHEMA Ehrenmitgliedschaft)
For recognition of outstanding promotion of the field of chemical apparatus, chemical technology, biotechnology, or the advancement of the goals of the Society. Honorary members have all the privileges of full members without the prescribed responsibilities. Chosen by the administrators.

6616
DECHEMA Medal
(DECHEMA-Medaille)
For recognition of outstanding achievement in the field of chemical apparatus. The DECHEMA Medal is traditionally awarded triennially during ACHEMA International Meeting on Chemical Engineering and Biotechnology to one outstanding scientist each in the fields of engineering, chemistry, and biotechnology.

6617
DECHEMA Preis der Max Buchner Forschungsstiftung
For recognition of an outstanding and already published research and development work in the field of chemical apparatus, and its fundamentals in technical chemistry, the materials sciences, measurement and control technology, process engineering, and biotechnology on chemical apparatus or plant development. Preference is given to the works of younger scientists of demonstrated merit from whom further development and application in chemical engineering can be expected. A monetary prize of 30,000 German marks, a gold medal, and a certificate are awarded annually. Established in 1950.

6618
Hellmuth Fischer-Medaille
To recognize primarily younger scientists whose works have advanced the science of electrochemistry, corrosion, or corrosion protection or works that have led to its exemplary application in industrial practice. A medal is given triennially. Established in 1988.

6619
Alwin Mittasch-Medaille
For recognition of scientific works that broaden the fundamentals of catalysis, or their exemplary application in industry. The work must have been conducted in a European country. A medal is awarded triennially. Established in 1988. Co-sponsored by the BASF Aktiengesellschaft.

6620
Deutsche Akademie der Naturforscher Leopoldina
Archiv fur Geschichte der Naturforschung
u. Medizin
August-Bebel Strasse 50a
O-4010 Halle/Saale, Germany
Phone: 345 25014
Fax: 345 21727

6621
Carus Medal
(Carus-Medaille)
To recognize outstanding research in the field of natural sciences or medicine. Scientists, without regard to nationality or membership in the Academy, are eligible. A bronze medal bearing a relief profile of Carl Gustav Carus (1789-1869) and on the reverse the figure of Psyche is awarded twice every two years. Established in 1864, and renewed in 1937. Since 1961, the Carus Medal has been given with the Carus Prize of the City of Schweinfurt in the Federal Republic of Germany where the Academy was founded.

6622
Cothenius Medal
(Cothenius-Medaille)
To recognize prominent research scientists, without regard to nationality, for an important scientific or medical life's work (since 1954). A gold medal bearing a relief profile of Christian Andreas von Cothenius (1708-1789) is awarded twice every two years. Originally established in 1789 as a premium given to the winner of a competition, and since 1863 to a German author of any significant contribution to science or medicine recently published.

6623
Darwin Plaque
(Darwin-Plakette)
To provide recognition for an outstanding contribution that develops the Darwinian ideas and throws light on the main problems of evolution. Scientists without regard to nationality or membership of the Academy are eligible. A medal (plaquette) bearing a relief profile of Charles Darwin (1809-1882) was awarded one time only in 1959 to 18 scientists. Established in 1959 by Academy Leopoldina in memory of Charles Darwin (1809-1882), founder of the theory of evolution by selection, on the occasion of the 100th anniversary of *On the Origin of Species* (1959).

6624
Medal of Merit
(Verdienstmedaille)
For recognition of service in relation to the idea and the welfare of the Academy Leopoldina. Members of the Leopoldina are eligible. A medal bearing a relief profile of the honored personality is awarded when merited. Established in 1961.

6625
Mendel Medal
(Mendel-Medaille)
To provide recognition for an outstanding contribution to biological science. Scientists from any country, members or nonmembers, are eligible. A bronze medal bearing a relief profile of Gregor Mendel is awarded biennially. Established in 1965 in memory of Gregor Mendel (1822-1884), founder of genetics.

6626
Schleiden Medal
(Schleiden-Medaille)
To provide recognition for outstanding contributions to knowledge of the cell. Botanists or zoologists are eligible in alternate years, without regard to nationality or membership in the Academy. A bronze medal bearing a relief profile of Matthias Jacob Schleiden is awarded biennially. Established in 1955 in memory of Matthias Jacob Schleiden (1804-1881), co-founder of the cell theory.

6627
Deutsche Bunsen-Gesellschaft fur Physikalische Chemie
Varrentrappstrasse 40-42
Carl-Bosch-Haus
W-6000 Frankfurt am Main 90, Germany   Phone: 69 7917 201

Formerly: Deutsche Elektrochemische Gesellschaft.

6628
Bunsen-Denkmunze
(Bunsen Medal)
For recognition of outstanding work, scientific or practical, in the field of physical chemistry. A medal is awarded triennially. Established in 1907 by Henry von Bottinger in memory of Robert Wilhelm Bunsen.

6629
Theodor Forster Memorial Lecture
For recognition of outstanding work in the area of photochemistry. A lecture and travel expenses are awarded. Established to honor Theodor Forster. Awarded jointly with the Gesellschaft Deutscher Chemiker.

6630
Honorary Member
To recognize members of extremely outstanding reputation. Members may be nominated. A document is awarded when merited at the convention. Established in 1894.

6631
Nernst - Haber - Bodenstein-Preis
For recognition of achievement in physical chemistry. Younger scientists who are less than 40 years of age are eligible. A monetary award is presented annually. Established in 1953 by German industry.

6632
Deutsche Gesellschaft fur Moor-und Torfkunde
Stilleweg 2   Phone: 511 6432241
D-30655 Hannover, Germany   Fax: 511 6432304

6633
Honorary Member
For recognition of outstanding contributions to the Society with honarary lifetime membership.

6634
C. A. Weber Medaille
For recognition of contributions in bog and peat science. Scientists from any nation may be nominated by a member. A silver medal and honorary lifetime membership are awarded biennially. Established in 1970.

6635
Deutsche Gesellschaft fur Parasitologie
c/o Dr. B. Enders, Secretary   Phone: 6427 392606
D-35001 Marburg 1, Germany   Fax: 6421 394757

6636
Carl Asmund Rudolphi Medal
(Carl-Asmund-Rudolphi-Medaille)
For recognition of outstanding scientific achievement in the area of parasitological research and its application. Scientists who are involved in parasitological research and its application in the field of biology and medical science are eligible. Medals and diplomas are awarded annually. Established in 1986 in memory of Carl Asmund Rudolphi (1771-1832), a scientist in the area of parasitological research and its application.

6637
Deutsche Glastechnische Gesellschaft
Mendelssohnstrasse 75-77   Phone: 69 74 90 88
D-60325 Frankfurt 1, Germany   Fax: 69 74 97 19

6638
Goldene Gehlhoff-Ring
To recognize people who have contributed significantly to the development of the Society and those who have tried to improve deficiencies in

glass manufacturing, science, and technology. A gold ring is awarded when merited. Established in 1950.

6639
Industriepreis fur technisch-wissenschaftliche Arbeiten
For recognition of valuable work in the committees of the Society and to provide an incentive for younger glass workers. A monetary prize of 1,000 German marks and a silver box are awarded biennially. Established in 1952.

6640
Otto Schott Denkmunze
For recognition of special scientific or practical achievement in glass technology or glass research. An engraved commemorative medal is awarded every two or three years. Established in 1927 by the Carl Zeiss Foundation.

6641
Deutsche Meteorologische Gesellschaft
Postfach 340
Mount Royal
W-5580 Traben-Trarbach, Germany   Phone: 6541 18401

6642
Albert Defant-Medaille
For recognition of outstanding scientific achievement in physical oceanography. Awarded triennially. Established in 1985 in honor of Albert Defant.

6643
Deutsche Meteorologische Gesellschaft Ehrenmitgliedschaft
To honor members of the meteorological society for special service to meteorology or to the organization. A certificate is awarded when merited. Established in 1966.

6644
Deutsche Meteorologische Gesellschaft e.V. Forderpreis
To recognize young meteorologists for outstanding achievement in the field. Works that are completed by individuals under 35 years of age and that have been published are considered. There may be no more than three years between publication and awarding of the prize. A monetary prize is awarded annually. Established in 1966. Formerly: Deutsche Meteorologische Gesellschaft e.V. Jugendpreis.

6645
Alfred Wegener-Medaille
To recognize persons for exemplary service and contributions to meteorological science. A medal is awarded triennially. Established in 1966 in honor of Alfred Wegener.

6646
Deutsche Mineralogische Gesellschaft
Institut fur Mineralogie
Westf. Wilhelms-Universitat
Corrensstrasse 24   Phone: 251 833455
D-48149 Munster, Germany   Fax: 251 838397

6647
Georg-Agricola-Medaille
For recognition of outstanding contributions in the field of applied (industrial) mineralogy. Individuals must be nominated. A bronze medal is awarded at the convention. Established in 1974 in honor of Georg Argricola.

6648
Viktor-Moritz-Goldschmidt Preis
For recognition of important scientific contributions of younger scientists. Members of the Society, generally younger than 40 years of age, must be nominated. A monetary prize is awarded at the convention. Established in 1957 in honor of Victor Moritz Goldschmidt.

6649
Abraham-Gottlob-Werner Medaille
For recognition of outstanding scientific contributions to mineralogy. Individuals must be nominated. Gold and silver medals are awarded at the convention. Established in 1950 in honor of Abraham Gottlob Werner.

6650
Deutsche Ornithologen-Gesellschaft
Zoologisches Institut, JWG-Universitat
Frankfurt
SiesmayerstraBe 70   Phone: 69 7984749
D-60323 Frankfurt, Germany   Fax: 69 7984820

6651
Foederpreis Vogelschutz
For recognition of a scientific contribution to bird protection. Unpublished manuscripts may be nominated or submitted. A monetary prize of 3,000 German marks, and a diploma are awarded annually. Established in 1987 by AULA-Verlag.

6652
Ornithologen-Preis
For recognition of important accomplishments in ornithological research. Selection is by nomination. A monetary prize of 3,000 German marks, a medal, and a diploma are awarded annually or biennially. Established in 1985 by an anonymous donor whose name is to be released in 1998.

6653
Erwin-Stresemann-Preis
For recognition of an important ornithological publication. The author may be of any nationality and under 40 years of age at the date of publication. The publication must be written in German and must have been published less than four years before the prize was last awarded. Teamwork is not permitted. A monetary prize of 3,000 German marks, a medal, and a diploma are awarded annually or biennially. Established in 1969.

6654
Werner Sunkel Stiftung
To support work on bird migration and bird banding. Residents of West Germany may be nominated. A monetary prize of 5,000 German marks is awarded biennially. Established in 1985 by Mrs. Sunkel in honor of Werner Sunkel.

6655
Deutsche Physikalische Gesellschaft
Hauptstrasse 5   Phone: 2224 71061
D-53604 Bad Honnef, Germany   Fax: 2224 71063

6656
Max-Born-Preis
For recognition of outstanding scientific contributions to physics. Awards are given in alternate years to German and British physicists by the combined British Institute of Physics and the Deutsche Physikalische Gesellschaft. A monetary prize, a silver medal bearing the likeness of Mr. Born (designed by his daughter, Mrs. Margaret Pryce) on one side and a formula on the other, and a certificate are awarded annually. Established in 1972.

6657
Stern-Gerlach-Medaille
For recognition of outstanding contributions to experimental physics. A gold medal bearing the likeness of Mr. Sterne and Gerlach on one side and a certificate are awarded annually. Established in 1986. Formerly: Stern-Gerlach-Preis fur Physik.

6658

Otto-Hahn-Preis fur Chemie und Physik
To recognize German individuals who have performed a unique service to the development of chemistry, physics, or applied research. A monetary prize, a gold medal bearing the likeness of Mr. Hahn on one side, and a certificate are awarded by the Deutscher Zentralausschuss fur Chemie and the Deutsche Physikalishe Gesellschaft when merited. Established in 1955.

6659

Gustav-Hertz-Preis (Physik-Preis)
To recognize a recently completed, outstanding publication by a younger physicist. A prize is awarded in both experimental and theoretical physics when merited. A monetary prize and a certificate are awarded annually. Established in 1941. Formerly: Preis der Deutschen Physikalische Gesellschaft.

6660

Gentner-Kastler-Prize
To recognize alternately French and German physicists for outstanding contributions to physics. A monetary prize, a silver medal bearing the likeness of Mr. Gentner and Mr. Kastler on one side, and a certificate are awarded annually by the Societe Francaise de Physique and the Deutsche Physikalische Gesellschaft. Established in 1984.

6661

Medaille fur Naturwissenschaftliche Publizistik
For recognition of journalistic achievement contributing to the expansion of natural scientific physical thought in the German-speaking realm. A silver medal and a certificate are awarded when merited. Established in 1984.

6662

Max-Planck-Medaille
For recognition of outstanding theoretical work in quantum theory. A gold medal bearing the likeness of Mr. Planck on one side and a certificate are awarded annually. Established in 1928.

6663

Robert-Wichard-Pohl-Preis
For recognition of outstanding acheivements in physics, especially radiation and other disciplines of science and technology and the dissemination of scientific knowledge through the teaching of physics. A monetary prize and a certificate are awarded annually when merited. Established in 1979.

6664

Karl-Scheel-Preis
For recognition of published works in the field of physics. Young physicists in Berlin are eligible. A monetary prize, a bronze plaque, and a certificate are awarded annually. Established in 1946 by the Physical Society of Berlin.

6665

Walter-Schottky-Preis fur Festkorperforschung
For recognition of outstanding publications and research in solid state physics by a younger scientist. A monetary prize and a certificate are awarded annually. Established in 1972. Sponsored by Siemens A.G.

6666

Deutsche Phytomedizinische Gesellschaft
Essenheimer Strasse 144   Phone: 6131 993047
W-6500 Mainz-Bretzenheim, Germany   Fax: 6131 993080

6667

Otto-Appel-Denkmunze
To honor extraordinary scientific and organistic work in plant pathology. A medal is awarded annually. Established in 1959 in memory of Otto Appel, past master in plant pathology in Germany.

6668

Anton-de-Bary-Medaille
To promote international research in phytopathology. A medal is awarded annually. Established in 1989 in memory of Anton de Bary (who died in 1888), mycologist and one of the founders of plant pathology.

6669

Julius-Kuhn-Preis
To promote research in phytopathology. Scientists who are under 40 years of age are eligible. A monetary prize of 3,000 German marks is awarded biennially. Established in 1978 in memory of Julius Kuhn (1825-1910), founder of the German plant pathology.

6670

Deutscher Literaturfonds
Alexandraweg 23   Phone: 6151 440930
64287 Darmstadt, Germany   Fax: 6151 409299

6671

Paul Celan-Preis
For recognition of French-German translations. A monetary award of 20,000 German marks is presented. Established in 1988.

6672

Literaturpreis des Kranichs mit dem Stein
To recognize the winners of the annual literary competition. Participants are individuals who have held one of the fund's scholarships. Works that can be read in 20 minutes are considered. A monetary prize of 20,000 German marks and a statue are awarded annually. The prize may be divided. Established in 1983.

6673

Deutsches Institut fur Puppenspiel
Hattinger Strasse 467
W-4630 Bochum 1, Germany   Phone: 234 4 77 78

6674

Bochumer Textpreis fur Figurentheater
To encourage authors to write in German for Figurentheater. A monetary prize of 5,000 German marks is awarded biennially during the international festival, Figurentheater der Nationen, in October. Established in 1986. Sponsored by the Bochum Lions Club.

6675

Internationaler Plakatpreis fur Figurentheater
To encourage the production of outstanding posters for the international festival, Figurentheater der Nationen. Graphic designers and free artists from the countries of Austria, Switzerland, and the Federal Republic of Germany are eligible. A monetary prize of 5,000 German marks is awarded irregularly. Established in 1990. Sponsored by Stiftung der Sparkasse Bochum zur Forderung von Kultur und Wissenschaft.

6676

Fritz Wortelmann Preis of the City of Bochum for Amateur Puppetry
(Fritz Wortelmann-Preis der Stadt Bochum fur das Amateur-Figurentheater)
To recognize the best groups of amateur puppeteers. Monetary prizes of 7,500 German marks are awarded annually in May. Established in 1959.

6677

Deutsches Rontgen-Museum
Schwelmer Str. 47   Phone: 02191
D-42897 Remscheid 11, Germany Fax: 11 432737

6678

Rontgen Plakette
For recognition of outstanding merit in the advancement and diffusion of x-ray science and practice. German and foreign radiologists are eligible. A bronze plaque is awarded annually when merited. Established in 1951 by the City of Remscheid.

6679

Deutsches Zentralkomitee zur Bekampfung der Tuberkulose
Address unknown.

6680

Franz Redeker Preis
For recognition of the best publication in the field of prevention and control of tuberculosis. A monetary prize and a certificate are awarded annually when merited. Established in 1956.

6681

**Dusseldorf City Cultural Office
(Landeshauptstadt Dusseldorf)**
Stadtverwaltung Kulturamt
Postfach 1120
Ehrenhof 3
W-4000 Dusseldorf, Germany   Phone: 211 899 6132

6682

Forderpreis fur bildende Kunst der Landeshauptstadt Dusseldorf
For recognition of an outstanding achievement in the field of visual arts, or to honor the entire work of a young artist. Painters, sculptors, graphic artists, architects, stage designers, photographers, cameramen or ceramicists under the age of 35 who have ties with the city of Dusseldorf are eligible. Two monetary prizes of 6,000 German marks and certificates each are awarded annually. Established in 1971.

6683

Forderpreis fur Literatur der Landeshauptstadt Dusseldorf
For recognition of an outstanding artistic achievement or the entire work of a young writer whose development shows promise. Poets, writers, critics, actors, dramatists, translators, and directors should not be older than 35 years of age and have ties with the city of Dusseldorf are eligible. Two monetary prizes of 6,000 German marks and certificates are awarded annually. Established in 1948. Formerly: (1971) Immermann Preis.

6684

Forderpreis fur Musik der Landeshauptstadt Dusseldorf
For recognition of an outstanding contribution to music or dance by a young artist. Composers, conductors, singers, instrumentalists, dancers, choreographers, and music teachers under the age of 35 who have ties with the city of Dusseldorf are eligible. Two monetary prizes of 6,000 German marks and certificates are given annually. Established in 1971.

6685

Forderpreis fur Wissenschaften
For recognition of an outstanding achievement in the field of science. Scientists not older than 35 years of age, whose development shows promise and who work in Nordsheim-Westfalen are eligible for nomination. A monetary prize of 6,000 German marks and a certificate are awarded biennially. Established in 1972.

6686

Heinrich Heine Prize
To recognize achievements in the spirit of Heinrich Heine in basic human rights, political and social progress, and international understanding. A monetary prize of 25,000 German marks and a certificate of award are awarded biennially. Established in 1972.

6687

Ecology Institute
Nordbunte 23   Phone: 4132 7127
D-21383 Oldendorf/Luhe, Germany   Fax: 4132 8883

6688

Ecology Institute Prize
To recognize ecologists for outstanding scientific achievements who are able and willing to provide a critical synthesis and evaluation of their field of expertise, addressing an audience beyond narrow professional borderlines. In an annually rotating pattern, awards are presented in the fields of marine, terrestrial, and limnetic ecology. All ecologists engaged in scientific research are eligible. Nominations must be submitted by September 30. A $5,000 stipend is awarded annually. In addition, the winner of the prize is requested to author a 200 to 300 printed-page book, to be published by ECI in the series *Excellence in Ecology* and to be made available world-wide at cost price. The Ecology Institute Prize is considered unique for two reasons: it was established and is financed by research ecologists, and the prize gives and takes, by both honoring the recipient and requiring him or her to serve science. Established in 1984 by Prof. Otto Kinne.

6689

IRPE Prize (International Recognition of Professional Excellence)
To recognize a young ecologist under the age of 40 who has conducted and published uniquely independent, original, and/or challenging research efforts representing an important scientific breakthrough. Nominations must be submitted by September 30. A $750 stipend is awarded when merited.

6690

Paul Ehrlich Foundation
c/o Vereinigung von Freunden und
    Federern der
Johann Wolfgang Goethe-Universitat
Senckenberganlage 37
60325 Frankfurt, Germany   Fax: 69 7988530

6691

Paul Ehrlich - und Ludwig Darmstaedter Preis
For recognition of outstanding work in the fields of immunology, microbiology, or chemotherapy. A monetary prize of $90,000 German marks and a gold medal are awarded annually. Established in 1929 in honor of Nobel laureate Paul Ehrlich, a pioneer in modern immunology.

6692

Eichendorff-Institut
Bahnhofstrasse 71
W-4030 Ratingen 6 - Hoesel, Germany   Phone: 21 02 63741

6693

Eichendorff Medal
For recognition of outstanding research on Joseph von Eichendorff, a German romantic poet (1788-1857), or for a work on German romanticism. Researchers and sponsors of research work are eligible. A bronze medal is awarded biennially during the meeting of the Society. Established in 1935 according to the project of Theodor von Gosen. In 1982 a new medal was designed by Walter Kalot.

6694

Oskar Seidlin Preis
For recognition of research on German romanticism. Young researchers who have published outstanding research work during the preceding two years are eligible. A monetary prize of 6-7,000 German marks is awarded biennially at the convention of the Society. Established in 1982 in honor of Oskar Seidlin, a researcher from the United States. Formerly: (1985) Forderpreis der Eichendorff - Gesellschaft.

6695
Electric Power Society of the German Association of Electrical Engineers
(Energietechnische Gesellschaft im VDE)
Stresemannallee 15, VDE-Haus
D-60596 Frankfurt am Main, Germany
Phone: 69 6308217
Fax: 69 6312925

6696
Herbert-Kind-Preis der ETG
For recognition of outstanding academic achievement. Students of electrical engineering may be nominated. A monetary prize of up to 15,000 German marks and a certificate of award are presented annually. Established in 1982 in memory of Dr. Herbert Kind.

6697
Literaturpreis der ETG
For recognition of excellence in scientific publications in the field of electric power. Members of the Society under the age of 40 are eligible. A monetary prize of 3,000 German marks and a certificate are awarded several times a year. Established in 1975.

6698
Ludwig-Erhard-Stiftung
Johanniterstrasse 8
W-5300 Bonn 1, Germany
Phone: 228 231343
Fax: 228 231766

6699
Ludwig-Erhard-Preis fur Wirtschaftspublizistik
For recognition of outstanding economic journalism. Authors of articles or radio and television programs that describe or comment on themes dealing with the economy or economic politics or forecasts are eligible. A monetary award of 10,000 German marks and a certificate are awarded annually. Established in 1975 by Dr. Ludwig Erhard. In addition, a prize to promote articles on social market economy by young journalists was added in 1991.

6700
European Academy of Anaesthesiology
c/o Prof. H. K. Van Aken
Dept. of Anaesthesia
UZ Leuven - Herestraat 49
B-3000 Leuven, Germany
Phone: 6131 177117
Fax: 6131 236028

6701
ICI Research Scholarship
To encourage young researchers within the European Academy to spend at least six months for research purposes in other than their home research facilities. Individuals under 40 years of age who apply for Associate membership, have scientific recognition, and are nominated by the Board of Trustees, are eligible. A monetary award is presented biennially at the annual meeting of the EAA. Established in 1987 by ICI Germany. Additional information is available from Prof. H. Stoeckel, Institut fur Anasthesiologie, Sigmund Freud Strasse 25, W-5300 Bonn 1, Germany.

6702
European Association for the Study of Diabetes
Auf'm Hennekamp 32
D-40225 Dusseldorf, Germany
Phone: 211 316738
Fax: 211 3190987

6703
Claude Bernard Lecturer
For recognition of distinguished work in the field of diabetes mellitus. Members may submit nominations by April 15. Travel expenses to the annual meeting of EASD and the Claude Bernard Medal are awarded annually. Established in 1969 by the Paul Neumann Laboratory, in Paris, France.

6704
Eli Lilly/EASD Research Fellowship in Diabetes & Metabolism
To encourage research in the field of diabetes and metabolism and to promote excellence in medical education in Europe. Applications may be made by European members of the EASD under the age of 40 who hold an M.D. degree or European equivalent. The deadline is February 15. A fellowship of $35,000 US is awarded. Established in 1991.

6705
Minkowski Prize
For recognition of outstanding publications that increase knowledge concerning diabetes mellitus. Research must be carried out in Europe by a person normally a resident in Europe, who is under the age of 40 on January 1 of the year of the award. Nominations may be submitted by February 15. A monetary prize of 20,000 German marks, a certificate, and travel expenses to the annual meeting of EASD are awarded annually. Established in 1966 by Farbwerke Hoechst AG.

6706
Mollegaard BB RAT Travel Fellowship
To assist young researchers in the field of diabetes mellitus. Members under the age of 40 may submit applications by February 15. A fellowship, not to exceed £ 800, is awarded annually. Established in 1990 by K.E. Mollegaard of the Mollegaard Breeding Center at Lille Skensved, Denmark in consultation with EASD.

6707
Castelli Pedroli Prize
For recognition of work concerned with the histopathology, pathogenesis, prevention, and treatment of the complications of diabetes mellitus during the preceding five years. Works published in internationally recognized scientific journals during the previous five-year period are considered. Members of the Association who are residents in Europe may be nominated by members only by February 15. A monetary prize of 15 million lire is awarded each year at the annual meeting. In addition, the winner is named the Golgi Lecturer and presents a lecture. Established in 1986 by the family of the late Maria Carla Castelli Pedroli in honor of Camillo Golgi.

6708
Albert Renold Fellowship
To encourage young European investigators to visit another laboratory or laboratories to gain experience in new techniques and methodology, to receive postdoctoral training or to carry out collaborative research. Members under 40 years of age may apply by February 15. One Fellowship of £ 10,000 is awarded annually. Established in memory of Professor Albert Ernst Renold (1923-1988), the founding Secretary of the European Association for the Study of Diabetes.

6709
European Federation of Corrosion
(Federation Europeenne de la Corrosion)
c/o DECHEMA
Gen. Secretariat - Frankfurt Office
Theodor-Heuss-Allee 25
D-60486 Frankfurt, Germany
Phone: 69 7564209
Fax: 69 7564201

6710
Cavallaro Medal
For recognition of outstanding achievement in basic research in the field of corrosion and corrosion protection. Awarded biennially. Established in 1965 by the Universite de Ferrara in memory of Professor Leo Cavallaro, founder of the Center for the Study of Corrosion.

6711
European Federation of Corrosion Medal
For recognition of achievements by a scientist, or group of scientists in the application of corrosion science in the chemical, petroleum, and nuclear industries. The recipients must be of a nationality(ies) corresponding to one, or more, of the member Societies of the EFC and the

work must be conducted within a European country. Proposals for recipients may be submitted mainly by the EFC member Societies; selection is by a Jury. A medal, diploma, and travel expenses are awarded biennially when merited. Established in 1985 by DECHEMA.

6712
European Film Awards
(Europaischer Filmpreis)

Munchener Str. 6
W-1000 Berlin 30, Germany

Phone: 30 261 18 88
Phone: 30 261 18 89
Fax: 30 24 35 45

6713
European Film Awards (Felix Awards)
(Prix du Cinema Europeen)
To recognize outstanding European films. Films premiered in a commercial theatre during the previous year are eligible. Felix Awards are presented in the following categories: (1) European Film of the Year; (2) Young European Film of the Year; (3) European Documentary Film of the Year; (4) European Actor of the Year; (5) European Actress of the Year; (6) European Supporting Actor of the Year; (7) European Supporting Actress of the Year; (8) European Screen-writer of the Year; (9) European Cinematographer of the Year; (10) European Film Composer of the Year; (11) European Production Designer of the Year; (12) European Film Editor of the Year; (13) European Cinema Society Lifetime Achievement Award; and (14) European Cinema Society Award of Merit. Trophies are awarded. In addition, the awards for Young Film and Documentary Film are accompanied by a financial endowment. Awarded annually. Established in 1988 by the Senate of Berlin (West) and organized by the European Cinema Society.

6714
European Geophysical Society
EGS Office
Postfach 49
37189 Katlenburg-Lindau, Germany

Phone: 49 55561440
Fax: 49 55564709

6715
Sir David Bates Medal
To recognize scientists for their exceptional contributions to planetary and solar system sciences.

6716
East European Support Award
To enable scientists from the non-convertible currency countries to attend international meetings.

6717
EGS Badge Award
To recognize individuals for their outstanding service and efforts in the promotion, growth, and running of the Society.

6718
European Geophysical Society Honorary Membership
To recognize scientists who have achieved international standing in geophysics, or who have served the Society in an outstanding way. Honorary membership is awarded when merited.

6719
Milutin Milankovitch Medal
To recognize scientists for their outstanding achievements in climatological sciences.

6720
Young Scientists Publication Awards
To recognize young scientists for outstanding papers on geophysics.

6721
Young Scientists Travel Awards
To enable young scientists to participate in cooperative research projects in geophysics on an intra-European basis.

6722
European Group of Artists of the Ardennes and the Eifel
(Europaische Vereinigung Bildender Kunstler aus Eifel und Ardennen)
Verkehrsamt Prumer Land
Haus des Gastes
Hahnplatz-1
D-54595 Luftkurort Prum, Germany

Phone: 6551 943207
Fax: 6551 7640

6723
Altmeier-Medaille Europamunze der EVBK
For recognition of outstanding artists. Established in 1979.

6724
Kunst-und Kulturpreis des Groupement
For recognition of outstanding artists. Established in 1961.

6725
Kaiser-Lothar-Preis
For recognition of an outstanding artist. A monetary prize of 5,000 German marks and a medal are awarded annually. Established in 1958 by the City of Prum in honor of the emperor Lothar, who has given the name Lothringen-Lorraine.

6726
European Molecular Biology Organization
Postfach 1022.40
D-69012 Heidelberg, Germany

Phone: 6221 383031
Fax: 6221 384879

6727
EMBO Medal
For recognition of contributions in Western Europe to the development of molecular biology. European citizens under the age of 40 are eligible. A monetary prize of 15,000 German marks and a medal are awarded annually. Established in 1986.

6728
European Society of Biomechanics
Arbeitsbereich Biomechanik
Techn. Univ. Hamburg-Harburg
Denickestr. 15
W-2100 Hamburg 90, Germany

Phone: 40 77183253
Fax: 40 77182996

6729
ESB Clinical Biomechanics Award
To encourage the application of biomechanics to clinical problems. Research papers are evaluated at the World Congress. A monetary prize of 300 ECU and a certificate are awarded at the biannual congress of the ESB.

6730
ESB Poster Award
To stimulate the quality of the poster presentations on biomechanics. Winning posters are selected based on clarity of presentation and scientific quality. A monetary prize of 300 ECU and a certificate are awarded at each biannual congress of the ESB.

6731
ESB Research Award in Biomechanics
To promote biomechanics research. Original research papers may be submitted to the chairman of the selection committee before the biennial

conference. The deadline for entry is November 1. A monetary prize of 1,000 ECU, a certificate, and publication of the manuscript in the *Journal of Biomechanics* are awarded at the biannual congress of the ESB. Established in 1986.

6732
European Water Pollution Control Association (Europaische Vereinigung fur Gewasserreinhaltung)
Theodor-Heuss-Allee 17
53773 Hennef
W-5205 St. Augustin 1, Germany
Phone: 22 428720
Fax: 22 42872135

6733
Dunbar Award
To recognize applied technology development in the field of sewage and waste treatment and disposal. Awarded triennially.

6734
European Weed Research Society
Bayer AG
PF-E-BR
W-5090 Leverkusen, Bayerwerk, Germany

6735
Best Paper Award
For recognition of papers published in the Society's journal, *Weed Research*. A monetary prize of 2,000 Swiss francs is awarded biennially. Established in 1987.

6736
Federal Republic of Germany Ministry of Defence
Hardthohe
Postfach 1328
W-5300 Bonn, Germany
Phone: 228 121
Fax: 228 12 5357

6737
Ehrenzeichen der Bundeswehr
For recognition of outstanding long military service or performance of special deeds. Soldiers in the German military or, in exceptional cases, civilians, and even foreigners are eligible. The medal has four classes of honor: (1) Medal of Honor; (2) Cross of Honor, gold; (3) Cross of Honor, silver; and (4) Cross of Honor, bronze. Awarded when merited. Established in 1980 to commemorate the 25th anniversary of the German army.

6738
Federal Republic of Germany Ministry of Foreign Affairs
Adenauerallee 99-103
W-53113 Bonn, Germany
Phone: 228 170
Fax: 228 173402

6739
Verdienstorden der Bundesrepublik Deutschland (Service Orders of West Germany)
For recognition of non-military service to the country. The medal has four classes: Grand Cross, Large Service Cross, Service Cross, and Medals of Service. Established in 1951.

6740
Federal Republic of Germany Ministry of Interior (lundesrepublik Deutschland Bundesminister des Innern)
Graurheindorfer Strasse 198
Postfach 17 02 90
53708 Bonn, Germany
Phone: 228 6811
Fax: 228 681 4665

6741
Deutscher Filmpreis
To promote the cultural status of German films and to recognize outstanding films. Producers of German film projects are considered. Awards are given in the following categories: best full-length film - 1,000,000 German marks and a golden bowl; 900,000 German marks and a golden strip of film, first prize; up to 700,000 German marks and a silver strip pof film, second prize; and 400,000 German marks for up to ten films, third prize; best short film - up to 50,000 German marks and a golden strip of film, first prize; up to 30,000 German marks and a silver strip of film, second prize; 20,000 German marks for up to ten films for third prize; best single achievement, such as a screenplay, performance, camera, or musical score - a golden strip of film; and long-standing influence on the German film industry - a golden strip of film. Awarded annually.

6742
Eichendorff Plakette
For recognition of mountain conservation and hiking associations which, through longstanding efforts, have promoted hiking, patriotism and environmental consciousness. Associations must have existed for 100 years to be eligible. A wall plaque with the likeness of Joseph Freiherr von Eichendorff on the front side, and the national emblem and the motto, "For service to hiking, homeland, and environment," on the reverse side is awarded.

6743
Order of Merit in the Sciences and Arts (Orden Pour le merite fur Wissenschaften und Kunste)
For recognition of a life's achievement in a field of natural or social sciences or the arts. Individuals who have acquired an outstanding reputation by widespread recognition of merits in the sciences or the arts are eligible. A medal is awarded at the election of a new member by a majority of the votes at the convention following the event of a previous member's death. Membership is limited to 30 Germans and 30 foreigners. Established in 1842 by King Friedrich Wilhelm IV of Prussia, and re-established in 1952 after years of inactivity by Federal President Theodor Heuss.

6744
Pro Musica Medal
To recognize societies of amateur musicians. Music societies upon the 100th anniversary of their founding may be awarded a bronze medal by the President of the Federal Republic of Germany. Established in 1968.

6745
Sportplakete des Bundespraesidenten
To recognize the gymnastic and sports clubs as well as sports associations which have distinguished themselves through long standing efforts in the fostering and development of sports. A plaque is awarded on the hundredth anniversary of such clubs upon proof of their founding date. The wall plaque is embellished with the national eagle on the President's insignia, surrounded by the words, "President's Sport Award," and on the reverse side the numeral "100" partially wreathed with laurel leaves.

6746
Zelter Medal
To recognize the contribution of a choral society to the cultivation of choral music. Choral societies may be awarded an oval bronze medal with a portrait of Zelter, and on the reverse, the Federal eagle and the inscription, "For contributions to choral music and folk song." Awarded by the President of the Federal Republic of Germany on the 100th aniversary of the founding of a choral society. Established in 1956.

6747 Federal Republic of Germany
Ministry of Posts and Telecommunications
(Bundesrepublik Deutschland
Bundesminister fur das Post- und Fernmeldewesen)
Heinrich-von-Stephan-Strasse 1 Phone: 228 14 31 15
W-5300 Bonn 2, Germany Fax: 228 14 8872

6748
Philipp Reis Medal
For recognition of exceptional merit in the field of telecommunications. A medal cast in iron, bearing the portrait of Philipp Reis, and on the reverse side Archangel Gabriel, is awarded annually. Established in 1952.

6749
Heinrich von Stephan Medal
For recognition of exceptional merit in the field of postal service. A medal in cast iron bearing the portrait of Heinrich von Stephan is awarded annually. Established in 1952.

6750 Federation Internationale de Sauvetage Aquatique
Holunderweg 5 Phone: 41 31188800
W-21365 Adendorf, Germany Fax: 41 31188840

6751
FIS Medal of Merit
For recognition of an outstanding contribution in the area of water safety. Candidates must have worked in the Committee of Direction or the FIS Commissions for a minimum of eight years. As many as three medals and certificates are awarded each year. Established in 1980.

6752
Inspecteur Honoraire de la Federation Internationale de Sauvetage Aquatique
To recognize persons who have promoted the development of international water life saving in an excellent way. An FIS member (federation) and/or of the President of FIS selects the honoree.

6753 Forderkreis Deutscher Schriftsteller in Baden-Wurttemberg
Rosenbergstrasse 96
70176 Stuttgart, Germany Fax: 471 16365364

6754
Thaddaus-Troll-Preis
For recognition of German writers in the field of literature. Baden-Wurttemberg authors are eligible. A fellowship of 7,000 German marks and a certificate are awarded annually. Established in 1981 in memory of Thaddaus-Troll who was dedicated to promoting young literary talent. Co-sponsored by Ministerium fur Familie, Frauen, Weiterbildung und Kunst Baden-Wurttemberg and Forderkreises Deutscher Schriftsteller.

6755 Fotogruppe Burghausen
c/o Franz Ramgraber
Gluckstrasse 7
D-84489 Burghausen, Germany Phone: 49 86771714

6756
Internationaler Fotosalon
For recognition of the best photographs from the areas of music and dance. The photographs should encompass not only artists and audience but also the atmosphere of the event. Photographs may be entered in two divisions: Monochrome Prints; and Color Prints. The following awards are presented: three FIAP medals; three DVF medals; 10 honorary prizes and 20 certificates. Awarded triennially. Established in 1977. Sponsored by the Federation Internationale de l'Art Photographique, the Photographic Society of America, Deutscher Verband fur Fotografie DVF, and the International Jazz Federation.

6757 Foundation of Lower Saxony
(Stiftung Niedersachsen)
Ferdinandstrasse 4 Phone: 511 315083
D-30175 Hanover, Germany Fax: 511 314499

6758
Hanover International Violin Competition
(Internationaler Violin-Wettbewerb Hannover)
To encourage professional development of young violinists and to recognize their achievements. The competition is open to violinists of all nationalities between 16 and 30 years of age. The following prizes are awarded: first prize - 50,000 German marks; second prize - 30,000 German marks; third prize - 20,000 German marks; fourth prize - 15,000 German marks; fifth prize - 10,000 German marks; and sixth prize - 5,000 German marks. Recording contracts and concert debuts are also awarded. Awarded triennially. Established in 1991 and dedicated to Joseph Joachim.

6759 Freundeskreis zur internationalen Forderung literarischer und wissenschaflicher Ubersetzungen
Im Asemwald 32/18/54
W-7000 Stuttgart 70, Germany Phone: 711 724325

6760
Helmut M. Braem-Preis
For recognition of outstanding quality. A monetary award of 15,000 German marks is presented biennially. Established in 1978 in memory of Helmut M. Braem, journalist and translator (1923-1977).

6761
Christoph-Martin-Wieland-Preis
For recognition in the field of literary translation. A monetary award of 15,000 German marks is presented biennially. Established in 1979 in memory of Christoph-Martin-Wieland, German poet and translator (1733-1813). Co-sponsored by the Ministerium fur Wissenschaft und Kunst Baden-Wurttemberg.

6762 Gemmological Association of Germany
(Deutsche Gemmologische Gesellschaft)
PO Box 12 22 60 Phone: 6781 43011
55714 Idar-Oberstein, Germany Fax: 6781 41616

6763
Hermann Bank Senior Silver Medal
To recognize members for superior gemological appraisals and examinations. Student members of the Association are eligible. An engraved silver medal is awarded annually. Established in 1970.

6764 German Academy of Language and Poetry
(Deutsche Akademie fur Sprache und Dichtung)
Alexandraweg 23 Phone: 6151 40920
D-64287 Darmstadt, Germany Fax: 6151 409299

6765
Georg-Buchner-Preis
To recognize writers and poets whose works further the cultural heritage of Germany. A monetary prize of 60,000 German marks is awarded

annually. Established in 1923 for the arts and literature, and changed to a literature prize in 1951.

6766
Sigmund-Freud-Preis
For recognition of a scientific work which constitutes an effective piece of prose. A monetary prize of 20,000 German marks is awarded annually. Established in 1964.

6767
Friedrich-Gundolf-Preis fur die Vermittlung deutscher Kultur im Ausland
To recognize persons who have rendered outstanding service to the promulgation of German culture on foreign soil. A monetary prize of 20,000 German marks is awarded annually. Established in 1964.

6768
Johann-Heinrich-Merck Preis
For recognition of works of literary criticism and essays. A monetary prize of 20,000 German marks is awarded annually. Established in 1964.

6769
Pramie fur die Beantwortung einer Literarischen oder Philologischen Frage
(Prizes for Answering a Literary or Philogical Question)
For recognition of outstanding works dealing with traditional literary questions and their answers. Works of 40-80 pages are considered. A monetary prize of 5,000 German marks and publication of the work are awarded annually when merited. Established in 1964.

6770
Johann-Heinrich-Voss-Preis fur Ubersetzung
For recognition of excellence in translation of a life's work and also individual works of poetry, drama, or essays. A monetary prize of 20,000 German marks is awarded annually. Established in 1958.

6771
German Aerospace Research Establishment
(Deutsche Forschungs fur Luft - und Raumfahrt E.V.)
Linder Hohe　　　　　　　　　　　　　　Phone: 220 36010
D-51147 Cologne, Germany　　　　　　　Fax: 220 36010

6772
Preise fur herausragende wissenschaftliche Leistungen
For recognition of distinctive contributions to aerospace research. Consideration for the award is given to employees of DLR. A monetary prize and a certificate are awarded each year at the annual meeting. The DLR-Wissenschaftspreis, which is subdivided into three individual prizes, is also awarded. Established in 1964 by Deutsche Gesellschaft for Flugwissenschaften.

6773
German Agricultural Society
(Deutsche Landwirtschafts-Gesellschaft)
Zimmerweg 16　　　　　　　　　　　　　Phone: 69 716 80
W-6000 Frankfurt am Main 1, Germany　　Fax: 69 724 1554

6774
International DLG Prize
(Internationaler DLG-Preis)
For recognition of exceptional professional and honorary achievement in agriculture and its related industry and to provide further and supplementary training. Individuals who are 18 to 36 years of age may be nominated by August 15. The following grants for training are awarded: (1) Junior-Prize, for individuals 18-24 years of age - 5,000 German marks; (2) Supplemental Training Prize, for individuals 24-36 years of age - 7,500 German marks; and (3) Study-Prize, for individuals 24-36 years of age - 25,000 German marks. Awarded annually. Established in 1986 by Deutsche Landwirtschafts-Gesellschaft on the occasion of its 100-year anniversary.

6775
German Booksellers and Publishers Association
Grosser Hirschgraben 17-21
Postfach 10 04 42　　　　　　　　　　　　Phone: 69 1306228
60004 Frankfurt am Main, Germany　　　　Fax: 69 1306382

Formerly: German Booksellers Association.

6776
Peace Prize of the German Book Trade
(Friedenpreis des Deutschen Buchhandels)
To recognize people of any nationality or religion who have made noteworthy contributions to literature, science, and art in the service of peace. A monetary prize of 25,000 German marks is awarded annually during the Frankfurt Book Fair. Established in 1950 by a group of publishers.

6777
German Chemical Society
(Gesellschaft Deutscher Chemiker)
Varrentrappstrasse 40-42　　　　　　　　Phone: 69 7917320
D-60486 Frankfurt am Main, Germany　　　Fax: 69 7917322

6778
Gmelin-Beilstein-Denkmunze
For special recognition of contributions to chemical literature or the history of chemistry, hence also the goals of the German Chemical Society. German and non-German chemists are eligible. A monetary award and a silver medal are awarded every few years. Established in 1954 by Hoechst AG.

6779
Carl-Duisberg-Gedachtnispreis
For recognition of research in chemistry. Younger scientists are eligible. Monetary awards are given annually. First established in 1935 by I. G. Farbenindustrie, and re-established by Bayer A. G. in 1969.

6780
Carl-Duisberg-Plakette
For recognition of special contributions to the advancement of chemistry and the goals of the society. A gold medal is awarded every few years. Established in 1953 by Bayer AG.

6781
Emil-Fischer-Medaille
For recognition of the best work in the field of organic chemistry, especially on experimental color or pharmaceutical chemistry, or to honor those who have made outstanding contributions to the German chemical industry through the discovery of organic and pharmaceutical preparations, dyes, and other products. German chemists are eligible. A monetary award (Bayer AG) and a gold medal are awarded every few years. Established in 1912 by Carl Duisberg.

6782
Fresenius-Preis
For recognition of special contributions to the scientific development of analytical chemistry. A monetary award (Hoechst AG) and a gold medal are awarded every few years. Established in 1961.

6783
Otto-Hahn-Preis fur Chemie und Physik
This, one of the highest German scientific honors, is given for recognition of unique scientific achivement in chemistry or physics in either pure or applied research. German scientists are eligible. A monetary award and a gold medal are awarded when merited. Established in 1955.

6784
Wilhelm-Klemm-Preis
For recognition of outstanding work in the field of inorganic chemistry. German and non-German scientists are eligible. A monetary award and a gold medal are awarded not more frequently than annually. Established in 1984 by Degussa AG.

6785
Joseph-Konig-Gedenkmunze
For recognition of special contributions to the scientific development of food chemistry and for the advancement and recognition of food chemistry. German and non-German scientists are eligible. A monetary award and a bronze medal are awarded every few years. Established in 1934 by the Verein Deutscher Lebensmittelchemiker (Association of German Food Chemists); re-established in 1951 by the Gesellschaft Deutscher Chemiker.

6786
Richard-Kuhn-Medaille
For recognition of special contributions in the area of biochemistry. German and non-German scientists are eligible. A monetary award and a gold medal are awarded biennially. Established in 1968 by BASF AG.

6787
Liebig-Denkmunze
For recognition of outstanding achievements by German chemists. A monetary award (BASF AG) and a silver medal are given at one-, two-, or three-year intervals. Established in 1903 and continued through 1940; re-established in 1950.

6788
Preis der Gesellschaft Deutscher Chemiker fur Journalisten und Schriftsteller
(German Chemical Society Prize for Journalists and Authors)
For recognition of outstanding publications that inform the public about problems of chemistry and their solutions. Journalists and authors are eligible. A monetary award is presented. Established in 1980.

6789
Hermann-Staudinger-Preis
For recognition of contributions in the field of macromolecular chemistry. German and foreign scientists are eligible. A monetary award and a gold medal are awarded biennially. Established in 1970 by BASF AG.

6790
Alfred-Stock-Gedachtnispreis
For recognition of an outstanding independent scientific experimental investigation in the field of inorganic chemistry. A monetary award and a gold medal are awarded biennially when merited. Established in 1950.

6791
Adolf-von-Baeyer-Denkmunze
For recognition of the best published work of the preceding year in the area of organic chemistry, especially on experimental dye or pharmaceutical chemistry, or for contributions to the German chemical industry through the discovery of organic preparations, important dyes or pharmaceutical preparations, perfumes or other products. German chemists are eligible. A monetary prize (Bayer AG) and a gold medal are awarded every few years. Established in 1910 by Carl Duisberg.

6792
August-Wilhelm-von-Hofmann-Denkmunze
For recognition of outstanding achievements in the field of experimental chemistry and to promote experimental chemical research. Non-German chemists and German scientists who are not chemists but who have made special contributions to chemistry are eligible. A gold medal is awarded irregularly every two or three years. Established in 1902 by the Deutsche Chemische Gesellschaft (German Chemical Society), a predecessor of the present sponsor; re-established in 1951 by the Gesellschaft Deutscher Chemiker.

6793
Otto-Wallach-Plakette
For recognition of special achievement in the field of volatile oils, terpenes, and polyterpenes or in the area of biochemical attractants and deterrents. Younger European scientists are eligible. A monetary award and a gold medal are awarded irregularly. Established in 1964 by DRAGOCO, Gerberding & Company.

6794
Karl-Ziegler-Preis
For recognition of outstanding research in the area of organo-metallic chemistry, especially catalysis. German and non-German scientists are eligible. A monetary award and a gold medal are awarded at intervals of several years. Established in 1974 by Hoechst A G and Huels A G.

6795
German Dental Association
(Bundeszahnarzte-kammer)
Universitatsstrasse 71 Phone: 221 40010
D-50931 Cologne 41, Germany Fax: 221 404035

6796
Honorary Gold Pin
For recognition of extraordinary contributions to national or international dentistry. German dentists or other individuals are eligible. A gold chain and a medal are awarded when merited. Established in 1971.

6797
Honorary Member
To recognize dentists who have contributed significantly to international cooperation through service. Foreign dentists are eligible. Honorary membership in the German Dental Association is awarded. The number of honorary memberships cannot exceed 12. Established in 1962.

6798
Honorary Plaque
For recognition of a special service to the science of dentistry and of support of the German Dental Association. Foreign dentists and other individuals, as well as German dentists, in special cases, are eligible. A silver chain and plaque are awarded when merited. Established in 1962.

6799
Fritz Linnert Honorary Award
To recognize a dentist whose work has furthered the goals and aims of the profession. Individuals outside the profession are eligible under special circumstances. A gold decoration is awarded.

6800
Merit Award
For recognition of contributions to the dental profession at the national and international levels. German dentists and non-dentists are eligible to apply to the Distinctions Committee. Established in 1984.

6801
Dr. Erich Muller Prize
For recognition of the best work or report published in the daily press, illustrated papers, or the medical press on the prevention and control of oral diseases. Journalists not working in the dental profession are eligible. A monetary prize of 5,000 German marks is awarded annually. Established in 1971.

6802
German Design Council
(Rat fur Formgebung)
Ludwig-Erhard-Anlage 1 (Messegelande)
PO Box 150311 Phone: 69 747919
W-60063 Frankfurt/Main, Germany Fax: 69 7410911

6803

European Community Design Prize
(Europaischer Designpreis)
To stimulate the use of good design throughout the European industry by recognition of small and medium-sized companies that have shown consistent application of design concepts and therefore project an image of quality worth emulating by other firms. Established in 1988 as a joint initiative between the design promotion organizations of the Member States and the Commission of the European Communities and a part of the Commission's Strategic Programme for Innovation and Technology Transfer.

6804

German Design Prize
(Bundespreis Produktdesign)
To recognize 24 of the best German products. To be considered, products must have received a regional design award and be selected by the regional governments for submission. Each region may nominate up to ten products. A document and a label are given to the winners and the products, and are presented in a traveling exposition. Awarded biennially. Established in 1991 by the German Ministry of Economic Affairs. Formerly: (1990) Bundespreis Gute Form.

6805

German Prize for Design Promoters
(Bundespreis fur Forderer des Designs)
To recognize an individual who has made an outstanding contribution to the development of German design and the enhancement of design quality. Candidates may include designers, industrialists, design managers, teachers, journalists, and other professionals. Nominations are selected by the regional governments and by the Board of the German Design Council. A published monograph on the life and work of the winner is awarded biennially. Established in 1993 by the German Ministry of Economic Affairs.

6806

German Institute of Standards
(Deutsches Institut fur Normung)
Burggrafenstrasse 6
W-1000 Berlin 30, Germany
Phone: 30 2601 1
Fax: 30 2601231

6807

Carl-Walther-Preis
For recognition of an outstanding contribution to the Universal Decimal Classification (UDC). A monetary prize of 5,000 German marks and a certificate are awarded every five years. Established in 1962 in memory of Carl Walther, library administrator and chairman of the Committee of Classification.

6808

German Interior Architects Association
(Bund Deutscher Innenarchitekten)
Konigswinterer Strasse 675
W-53227 Bonn, Germany
Phone: 228 442414
Fax: 228 444387

6809

BDIA-Preis
For recognition of outstanding interior architecture. Members of BDIA and, as interior architects, members of the chamber of architects are eligible. A monetary prize is awarded triennially at the convention. Established in 1981.

6810

Forderpreis fur hervorragende Diplomarbeiten auf dem Gebiet der Innenarchitektur
For recognition of outstanding work in interior design by students in the field. A monetary prize is awarded biennially. Established in 1981.

6811

German Iron and Steel Institute
(Verein Deutscher Eisenhuttenleute)
Sohnstrasse 65
W-4000 Dusseldorf 1, Germany
Phone: 211 67070
Fax: 211 6707310

6812

Carl Lueg Commemoration Medal
(Carl-Lueg-Denkmunze)
To recognize individuals who have distinguished themselves through an invention or introduction of innovations, or through important advancements in the science of iron metallurgy. A gold medal is awarded annually when merited. Established in 1903 in memory of Carl Lueg, chief of the Gutehoffnungshutte, and president of the Society for 25 years.

6813

German Medical Association
(Bundesarztekammer)
Postfach 41 02 20
Herbert-Lewin-strasse 1
D-50862 Cologne, Germany
Phone: 221 4004209
Fax: 221 4004388

6814

Filmpreis der Bundesarztekammer
For recognition of outstanding films promoting the continued development of the medical profession. Films in 16mm size that have not previously been entered in this contest are eligible. Awarded annually. Established in 1980.

6815

Honorable Mention
(Ehrenzeichen der deutschen Arzteschaft)
For recognition of service to medical science, public health, and the medical profession. Non-Germans and German laymen in the profession are eligible. A stickpin is awarded annually. Established in 1958.

6816

Literaturpreis der Bundesarztekammer
For recognition of up to three outstanding German fictional works of poetry or prose in by doctors. A monetary prize of 15,000 German marks is awarded annually. Established in 1982.

6817

Paracelsus Medaille
This, the highest honor of the Assembly, is given for recognition of outstanding medical achievement, contributions to the medical profession, and notable advances in the science of medicine. German doctors are eligible. A medal and a certificate are awarded annually. Established in 1952.

6818

Ernst von Bergmann Plakette
For recognition of outstanding contributions to the medical profession. Individuals of all lands are eligible. A medal and certificate are awarded annually. Established in 1962.

6819

German Pediatric Association
(Deutsche Gesellschaft fur Kinderheilkunde)
Univ.-Kinderklinik
Moorenstr.5
D-40225 Dusseldorf, Germany
Phone: 211 3117642
Fax: 211 9348777

6820

Adalbert Czerny Preis
To stimulate research in pediatrics. Pediatricians from German speaking countries are eligible. A monetary prize of 10,000 German marks and a medal are awarded annually. Established in 1961.

6821
Otto Heubner Preis
For recognition of scientific achievements of the members of the German Pediatric Association. A gold medal is awarded triennially. Established before the First World War and renewed in 1953.

6822
German Pharmaceutical Society
(Deutsche Pharmazeutische Gesellschaft)
Generalsekretariat
Ginnheimer Strasse 26   Phone: 6196 928274
65760 Eschborn, Germany   Fax: 6196 928275

6823
Carl Mannich Medal
For recognition of outstanding achievement in pharmaceutical science. German and international scholars are eligible. A silver medal is awarded irregularly. Established in 1959.

6824
Ferdinand Schlemmer Medal
To recognize members for outstanding services to the Society, including the organization of instructional centers, lectures, or publicity. A silver medal is awarded annually. Established in 1974.

6825
Serturner Medal
For recognition of a scientific publication in the field of pharmacy written by a German scientist. A silver medal is awarded annually. Established in 1928.

6826
Hermann Thoms Medal
For recognition of outstanding contributions to the entire field of pharmacy. German or foreign pharmacists are eligible. A silver medal is awarded when merited. Established in 1961.

6827
German Rontgen Society
(Deutsche Rontgengesellschaft)
Postfach 1204
D-63232 Neu-Isenburg, Germany   Phone: 6102 6668

6828
Heinrich-E.-Albers-Schonberg Medaille
For recognition of outstanding work in radiology. Elder radiologists are eligible. A gold-plated medal is awarded biennially on the occasion of the German Radiological Congress.

6829
Hermann-Holthusen-Ring
To encourage scientific work in radiology. Radiologists under 45 years of age are eligible. A ring is awarded annually.

6830
Hermann-Rieder-Medaille
To recognize a distinguished elder radiologist. A gold-plated medal is awarded biennially on the occasion of the German Radiological Congress.

6831
Wilhelm Conrad Rontgen-Preis
For recognition of outstanding scientific papers that contribute to progress in radiology. A monetary prize of 60,000 German marks is awarded annually on the occasion of the German Radiological Congress. Established in memory of W.C. Rontgen.

6832
German Section of the International Board on Books for Young People
(Arbeitskreis fur Jugendliteratur)
Schlorstrasse 10   Phone: 89 168 4052
W-80634 Munich 19, Germany   Fax: 89 168 4066

6833
German Youth Literature Prize
(Deutscher Jugendliteratur Preis)
For recognition of outstanding books from German-speaking publishing houses in the following areas: picture books, children's books, books for young people, and nonfiction books for children and young people. Books of living authors, written in German, and German translations of books are eligible. Nominations may be made by any resident of Germany. Winners are selected by a panel of 13 judges. Monetary awards of 15,000 German marks are awarded in each category annually. In addition, a special prize is awarded when merited. Established first in 1956 by the Federal Ministry of the Interior; offered at present by the Federal Ministry for Women and Youth.

6834
Sonderpreis
To recognize the best translation of a children's book or a book for young people. Nomination deadline is Novemeber 30. A winner is selected by a panel of three judges. A monetary prize of 20,000 German marks is awarded annually.

6835
German Society for Documentation
(Deutsche Gesellschaft fur Dokumentation)
Hanauer Landstrasse 126-128   Phone: 69 430313
W-6000 Frankfurt/Main 1, Germany Fax: 69 490 9096

6836
Erich Pietsch Preis
For recognition of outstanding publications in the German language in the fields of information science, documentation and communications. A monetary prize and a certificate are awarded at irregular intervals. Established in 1979 in honor of Professor Erich Pietsch, former director of the Gmelin Institute for Non-Organic Chemistry in Frankfurt, and President of DGD from 1955-1961.

6837
German Society for Fat Science
(Deutsche Gesellschaft fur Fettwissenschaft)
Soeste• Strasse 13
D-48155 Munster, Germany   Phone: 251 64745

6838
Kaufmann Memorial Lecture
For outstanding research in the fat science field. The honoree presents a lecture at the convention. Established in 1972 in memory of H. P. Kaufmann, the society's founder.

6839
H. P. Kaufmann-Preis
For recognition of outstanding work in the field of fat and fat product chemistry and technology. Included are studies of fatty acids and their derivatives, as well as related materials and their uses. Members of related sciences are eligible, particularly chemists, biologists, medical and pharmaceutical scientists, and engineers under age 35. A maximum of two candidates may win. A monetary prize of 3,000 German marks, a plaque and a certificate, or a bound series of the society's journal are awarded annually. Established in 1972 in memory of the society's founder and president, H. P. Kaufmann.

[6840]
W. Normann-Medaille
To recognize superior research on fats and fat products in science and technology or to recognize an individual considered worthy by the society for his or her contributions to the advancement of the science of lipids. Scientists of any nationality are eligible. Two medals and certificates may be awarded annually. Established in 1940 in memory of Dr. Wilhelm Normann, a pioneer in the research of fat hardening.

[6841]
German Society for Non-Destructive Testing
(Deutsche Gesellschaft fur Zerstorungsfreie Prufung e.V.)
Unter den Eichen 87   Phone: 30 8114001
D-12205 Berlin, Germany   Fax: 30 8114003

[6842]
Berthold-Preis
For recognition of achievement in non-destructive testing and of the promotion of this field. Individuals under 40 years of age may submit an application. A monetary prize of 8,000 German marks is awarded annually at the convention. Established in 1973 in honor of Professor Dr. Rudolf Berthold, founder of the Society.

[6843]
German Society of Endocrinology
(Deutsche Gesellschaft fur Endokrinologie)
c/o Schering AG   Phone: 30 468 5802
13342 Berlin, Germany   Fax: 30 4691 8056

[6844]
Schoeller-Junkmann-Preis
To recognize young European scientists under 40 years of age for outstanding papers in the field of endocrinology. Both clinical and experimental papers from the various fields of endocrinology are considered, with the exception of papers on diabetes mellitus and on the thyroid gland, since these particular fields are covered by other awards. A monetary prize of 15,000 german marks is awarded. In exceptional cases, the Jury may decide to share the award. Awarded annually. Established in 1967 by Schering AG Berlin and Bergkamen.

[6845]
Marius-Tausk-Preis
For recognition of works on the advancement of clinical endocrinology. Clinical and clinical-experimental work from the various fields of endocrinology, with the exception of work concerning diabetes mellitus and the thyroid gland, since there are already other awards for this subject, are considered. Experimental work that does not show any relation to clinical endocrinology is also excluded. Scientists residing in Europe who are 33 years of age or younger are eligible. A monetary prize of 15,000 German marks is awarded annually. Established in 1971 by ORGANON GmbH Oberschleissheim for a period of 10 years.

[6846]
Von Basedow Prize for Research into the Thyroid Gland
For recognition of outstanding work on the thyroid. Scientists-residents of the Federal Republic of Germany, Austria, or Switzerland who are not employed by industrial or commercial plants and who are 40 years of age or younger are eligible. Monetary prizes of 10,000 German marks for first prize and 5,000 German marks for second prize are awarded annually. Established in 1977 by the E. Merck Company in Darmstadt.

[6847]
Von-Recklinghausen-Preis
For recognition of outstanding work in the field of clinical and experimental research on osteopathy and ca-metabolism. Scientists residing in Europe who are 40 years of age or older are eligible. A monetary prize of 15,000 German marks is awarded annually. Established in 1987 by Henning/Merrell Dow, Berlin.

[6848]
German Society of Metallurgical and Mining Engineers
(LGesellschaft Deutscher Metallhutten und Bergleute)
Paul Ernst Strasse 10   Phone: 5323 3438
HD-38678 Clausthal-Zellerfeld, Germany Fax: 5323 78804

[6849]
Georg Agricola Denkmunze
To recognize outstanding achievement in the area of metallurgy and mining engineering whereby substantial advancement in the scientific, practical, or economic aspects of this field has been reached. Mature, experienced scientists or industrial workers of any nationality are eligible. A silver medal with a portrait of Georg Agricola on a chain is awarded biennially. Established in 1924.

[6850]
Paul Grunfeld Prize
(Paul Grunfeld-Preis)
To recognize young engineers and scientists in the field of special metals in Europe. Individuals from Europe who are under 35 years of age may be nominated by the GDMB Committee for Special Metals. A monetary prize of approximately 3,000 German marks and a plaque are awarded biennially at the general assembly of GDMB. Established in 1986 by Ernst Grunfeld, London (Metallurgy) in memory of his father, Paul Grunfeld. The Metals Society (UK) awards the same prize.

[6851]
Reden Plakette
To recognize students of metallurgy and mining at German technical universities who have passed their examinations with honors. A brass plaque is awarded. Established in 1935; and re-established in 1948.

[6852]
German Society of Military Medicine and Military Pharmacology
(Deutsche Gesellschaft fur Wehrmedizin und Wehrpharmazie e.V.)
Baumschulallee 25
W-5300 Bonn 1, Germany   Phone: 228 632420

[6853]
Paul Schurmann-Medaille
For recognition of recipients of the Paul Schurmann Preis and others who have made exemplary contributions to the military health service. A medal is awarded biennially. Established in 1972.

[6854]
Paul Schurmann-Preis
For recognition of outstanding work and original research in military medicine and pharmacology. Health and medical officers of the armed forces and members of the Association are eligible. A monetary prize of 10,000 German marks and a gilded medal are awarded biennially in memory of Dr. Paul Schurmann. Established in 1966.

[6855]
German Society of Nutrition
(Deutsche Gesellschaft fur Ernahrung)
Feldbergstrasse 28   Phone: 69 9714060
D-60323 Frankfurt, Germany   Fax: 69 97140699

[6856]
German Nutrition Foundation Travel Scholarship
To promote international scientific contact in the field of nutrition and food sciences. A scholarship is awarded annually. Sponsored by the Stiftung zur Forderung der DGE (German Nutrition Foundation) since 1987.

6857

**Journalist Prize of the DGE
(Journalistenpreis of the DGE)**
For recognition of journalists, reporters, and authors of press, radio, and television for contributions in the field of nutrition. The jury consists of members of the German Nutrition Foundation. Monetary prizes of 5,000 German marks each are awarded in four categories: daily newspapers, journals, radio, and television. Established in 1989. Sponsored by Kellogg (Germany).

6858

Hans Adolf Krebs-Preis
To encourage young scientists in the field of nutrition and food sciences. A monetary prize of 10,000 German marks is awarded biennially. The next prize is presented in 1995. Sponsored by the Stiftung zur Forderung der DGE (German Nutrition Foundation) since 1981.

6859

Max Rubner-Preis
For recognition and promotion of research that contributes to the development of preventive and practical dietetics for physicians. A monetary prize of 10,000 German marks is awarded biennially. The next prize is presented in 1997. Sponsored by the German Nutrition Foundation since 1988.

6860

**German Society of Petroleum Sciences and Coal Chemistry
(Deutsche Gesellschaft fur Mineralolwissenschaft und Kohlechemie eV)**
Nordkanalstrasse 28
W-2000 Hamburg 1, Germany   Phone: 40 232450

6861

Carl Engler Medal
For recognition of outstanding contributions in petroleum science and coal chemistry, and related fields such as drilling technology, geology and geophysics. A medal and a certificate are awarded annually. Established in 1935.

6862

Carl Zerbe Prize
For recognition of an outstanding, independent and original work by a young scientist, under 35 years of age, in the fields within the Society's spheres of interest. A monetary prize, determined each year, and a certificate are awarded irregularly, but not more often than once a year. Established in 1973.

6863

**German Society of Physical Medicine and Rehabilitation
(Deutsche Gesellschaft fur Physikalische Medizin und Rehabilitation)**
Klinik der Johann-Wolfgang-Goethe-
   Universitat
Theodor-Stern-Kai 7
W-6000 Frankfurt, Germany   Phone: 069 63011

6864

Boehm Medal
For recognition of scientific research in physical medicine and rehabilitation and to encourage scientific cooperation and contact between members of the society and members of related foreign societies. A medal is awarded infrequently. Established in honor of Professor Boehm, a distinguished promoter of physical medicine in Germany in the forties and fifties.

6865

Corresponding Members
For recognition of scientific research in physical medicine and rehabilitation and to encourage scientific cooperation and contact between members of the society and members of related foreign societies. A certificate is awarded infrequently.

6866

Honorary Member
For recognition of scientific research in physical medicine and rehabilitation and to encourage scientific cooperation and contact between members of the society and members of related foreign societies. A certificate is awarded infrequently.

6867

**German Society of Plastic and Reconstructive Surgery
(Deutsche Gesellschaft fur Plastische und Wiederherstellungschirurgie)**
2. Chirurg. Klinik Diakoniekrankenhaus
   Rotenburg   Phone: 4261 772376
W-27342 Rotenburg, Germany   Phone: 4261 772377

6868

Hans von Seemen Preis
To encourage professional development in the field of plastic and reconstructive surgery. Work published during the preceding two years and submitted to the Society is eligible. A monetary prize and a diploma are awarded biennially. Established in 1984 in honor of Hans von Seemen, founder of the Society.

6869

**German Society of School Music Educators
(Verband Deutscher Schulmusiker)**
Bundesgeschaeftsstelle
Weihergarten 5   Phone: 6131 234049
D-55116 Mainz, Germany   Fax: 6131 246211

6870

Leo Kestenberg Medal
To recognize individuals for their personal commitment to furthering the development of music education in schools. Music teachers and university lecturers in music education are not eligible. Awarded biennially at the congress.

6871

**German-Speaking Mycological Society
(Deutschsprachige Mykologische Gesellschaft)**
Institut fur Medizinisches Mykologie
Postfach 820   Phone: 761 2032176
W-7800 Freiburg, Germany   Fax: 761 2032187

6872

Schoenlein-Plakette
For recognition of achievements in mycology. A medal is awarded when merited. Established in 1981.

6873

**German Surgical Society
(Deutsche Gesellschaft fur Chirurgie)**
Venusberg 1
W-5300 Bonn, Germany

6874
Karl Heinrich Bauer Prize for Surgical Tumor Research
(Karl Heinrich Bauer Preis fur Chirurgische Tumorforschung)
For recognition of the best work on surgical, experimental or pathomorphological tumor research relevant to the oncological theme chosen by the Society, with the goal of promoting scientific surgical research of cancer. Members or groups of members of the Society are eligible, if not related to or working with members of the jury. The work may not have won any other prizes. A monetary prize of 8,000 German marks, which may be divided, is awarded triennially. Established in 1981.

6875
Filmpreis
For recognition of short scientific films concerned with the field of surgery which disseminate new knowledge of operation techniques or which serve as scientifically-based educational aids. Members of the Society are eligible. A monetary prize of 3,000 German marks and a certificate are awarded annually. Established in 1970.

6876
E. K. Frey Preis
For recognition of scientific research in the field of enzyme inhibition in therapy or through innovative research. A monetary prize of 10,000 German marks and a medal were awarded annually alternately by the German Society for Surgery, the German Society for Internal Medicine and the German Society for Gynecology. Established in 1968 by Farbenfabrik Bayer AG. (Discontinued in 1972)

6877
Jubilaumspreis
To recognize those persons or groups who have made special contributions to the development of clinical surgery. A doctor or scientist or a group of such persons in Germany or Austria is eligible. Members of the Society or managers of BRAUN Melsungen may nominate candidates. Self-nominations are not accepted. A monetary prize of 10,000 German marks and a medal are awarded annually. Established in 1972 by B. Braun Melsungen A.G.

6878
Werner Korte Medaille
To recognize persons who have given long years of service to the Society or who have made essential contributions toward the goals of the Society. Doctors and non-doctors are eligible. Gold and silver medals with certificates are awarded when merited. Established in 1971.

6879
Erich Lexer Preis
To encourage reconstructive surgery, including temporary and permanent organ substitution. German and non-German surgeons are eligible and may be nominated by members of the Society. Self-nominations are not accepted. The award can be divided among more than one person. A monetary prize of 10,000 German marks and a silver medal, with a relief of Erich Lexer, are awarded annually alternately by the German Society of Surgery and the German Society for Orthopedics. Established in 1972 by Ethicon GmbH.

6880
Theodor Naegeli Prize
(Theodor-Naegeli-Preis)
For recognition of the best experimental or clinical work in surgery, with the purpose of furthering research in thrombo-embolism, gerontology or geriatrics. A monetary prize of 20,000 Swiss francs is awarded triennially. Established in 1971 in memory of Dr. Naegeli, surgeon and clinical director.

6881
Preis fur Poster - Ausstellungen
To recognize members at the annual convention for poster exhibits which best present the newest surgical advancements. A monetary prize of 3,000 German marks and a certificate are awarded annually. Established in 1980.

6882
Preis fur Wissenschaftliche Ausstellungen
To encourage and recognize the best scientific exhibits at the annual convention showing scientific results and innovative operation techniques. Members of the Society or associated societies are eligible. A monetary prize of 3,000 German marks is awarded annually. Established in 1970.

6883
Seal of the German Surgical Society
(Siegel der Deutschen Gesellschaft fur Chirurgie)
To recognize non-members of the Society, associated societies, or other associations who gave exceptional support to the promotion and development of German surgery. The seal of the Society in coin form and a certificate are awarded annually when merited. Established in 1979.

6884
Ernst Von Bergmann Gedenkmunze
For recognition of special contributions to German surgery. Surgeons in the German language area are eligible. Society members may apply. A medal and certificate are awarded irregularly when merited. Established in 1957.

6885
Von Langenbeck Preis
To encourage the work of younger surgeons by recognizing the best published work in clinical and experimental surgery and their related areas. Members or groups of members of the Society are eligible if their work has not previously appeared before the Von Langenbeck-Preis jury. A monetary prize of 10,000 German marks and a certificate are awarded annually. Established in 1952.

6886
German Veterinary Medical Association
(Deutsche Veterinarmedizinische Gesellschaft)
Frankfurter Strasse 89   Phone: 641 24466
D-35392 Giessen, Germany   Fax: 641 25375

6887
Martin Lerche Forschungspreis
To recognize scientists for outstanding veterinary research. Scientists of veterinary medicine or a closely related field whose work has been published in a scientific journal are eligible. A monetary award of 10,000 German marks is awarded and can be shared. Awarded at conventions of the Veterinary Association. Established in 1983.

6888
Preis der DVG zur Forderung von Nachwuchswissenschaftlern
For recognition of published works of outstanding quality in the field of veterinary medicine. Works by scientists under the age of 40 are considered. A monetary prize is awarded annually. Established in 1989.

6889
Gesellschaft Deutscher Naturforscher und Arzte
Hauptstrasse 5   Phone: 2224 923237
D-53604 Bad Honnef 12, Germany Fax: 2224 923250

6890
Lorenz Oken Medaille
For recognition of the writing and/or editing of publications for the promotion of the general understanding, general knowledge, and the image of the natural sciences and medicine, and for contributions that promote the image of the organization. Selection is by nomination. A gold medal and a document are awarded biennially. Established in 1984 in memory of Lorenz Oken, who founded the Association by initiating the first meeting of German natural scientists and physicians in Leipzig in 1822.

6891

Gesellschaft fur Biologische Chemie
Bahnhofstrasse 9-15
J-82324 Tutzing, Germany
Phone: 8158 224297
Fax: 8158 224119

6892

Otto-Warburg-Medaille
For recognition in the field of biochemistry. Individuals must be nominated. A medal and document are awarded annually. Established in 1963.

6893

Gesellschaft fur deutsche Sprache
Taunusstrasse 11
Postfach 2669
D-65016 Wiesbaden 1, Germany
Phone: 611 52 00 31
Fax: 611 5 13 13

6894

Medienpreis fur Sprachkultur
For the promotion of media communications, journalism, radio, and television, and for recognition of outstanding endeavors in promoting the German language. A certificate and a gift are awarded biennially. Established in 1985.

6895

Alexander Rhomberg Preis
For the encouragement of young journalists, and for the cultivation and promotion of the German language. Established in 1994 as an extension of the Medienpreis fur Sprachkultur.

6896

Gesellschaft fur Naturkunde in Wurttemberg
Rosenstein 1
D-70191 Stuttgart, Germany
Phone: 711 8936

6897

Walter Schall-Preis
For recognition of achievements in or significant contributions to natural sciences concerning the area of the Society (South-West Germany). Applications must be submitted by April 30 every year. Three monetary prizes and documents are awarded annually. Established in 1984 in honor of Dr. Walter Schall, a geologist who is the contributor of the prize.

6898

Gesellschaft Karl-Richter-Orgelwettbewerb
Johannisberger Strasse 15a
W-1000 Berlin 33, Germany
Phone: 30 8213111
Fax: 30 8229757

6899

International Karl Richter Organ Competition
(Internationaler Karl Richter Orgelwettbewerb)
To encourage the professional development of young organists. Organists of any nationality who are under 31 years of age and are recommended by an organ teacher or examination of a music school are eligible. The deadline is April 30. The following monetary prizes are awarded: first prize - 10,000 German marks; second prize - 5,000 German marks; and third prize - 3,000 German marks. In addition, concerts and recordings at Radio of Berlin are awarded. The competition is held triennially. Established in 1988 to honor Karl Richter, the famous organist and conductor.

6900

Goethe Institute
(Goethe Institut)
Zentral Einschreibung
Helene-Weber-Allee 1
Postfach 190419
D-80604 Munich, Germany
Phone: 89 159210
Fax: 89 15921450

6901

Goethe Medaille
For recognition of outstanding service in the promotion of the German language in foreign countries by cultural exchange. Special literary, scientific, pedagogical, or organizational achievement that promotes interaction between the cultures of Germany and the host country are considered. Individuals of any nationality are eligible, but Germans are eligible only when especially merited. A maximum of five medals, Rolf Syzmanski plaques, and certificates are awarded annually on March 22. Established in 1954.

6902

Gottingen Academy of Sciences
(Akademie der Wissenschaften in Gottingen)
Theaterstrasse 7
37073 Gottingen, Germany
Phone: 551 395362
Fax: 551 395365

6903

Gottingen Academy of Sciences Prize
For recognition of outstanding work in the field of philosophy, philology, or historical investigation. A monetary prize of 7,000 German marks is awarded biennially. Sponsored by the Foundation for German Science in Essen.

6904

Gottingen Academy of Sciences Prize for Biology
For recognition of outstanding work in the field of biology. A monetary prize of 6,000 German marks is awarded annually. Sponsored by natural scientific publishers.

6905

Gottingen Academy of Sciences Prize for Chemistry
For recognition of notable scientific work in the area of chemistry. A monetary prize of 5,000 German marks is awarded annually. Sponsored by members of the chemical industry.

6906

Gottingen Academy of Sciences Prize for German History
For recognition of an outstanding contribution in the field of medieval or more recent German history. A monetary prize of 5,000 German marks is awarded irregularly. Sponsored by the Wedekind Foundation.

6907

Gottingen Academy of Sciences Prize for Physics
For recognition of notable work in the area of physics. A monetary prize of 5,000 German marks is awarded annually. Sponsored by members of the chemical industry.

6908

Dannie Heineman Prize
For recognition of distinguished scientific achievements in natural science by an outstanding international scholar. A monetary prize of 50,000 German marks is awarded biennially. Established in 1961 by Minna James Heineman Stiftung in honor of Dannie Heineman, founder. Sponsored by Minna-James-Heineman-Stiftung, c/o Stifterverband fur die Deutsche Wissenschaft, Barkhovenallee 1, 45239 Essen, Germany.

6909

Hans Janssen Prize
For recognition of outstanding scientific work in the area of modern European history of art, with special regard to Italy. A monetary prize of

15,000 German marks is awarded biennially. Sponsored by Hans Janssen Foundation.

6910
Hanns Lilje Prize
For recognition of outstanding research in the fields of biblical literature or church history. A monetary prize of 20,000 German marks is awarded biennially. Sponsored by the Calenberg-Grubenhagenschen-Landschaft.

6911
**Gutenberg Society
(Gutenberg-Gesellschaft)**
Internationale Vereinigung fur Geschichte
    und Gegenwart
der Druckkunst e.v.
Liebfrauenplatz 5   Phone: 6131 226 420
D-55116 Mainz, Germany   Fax: 6131 123 488

6912
**Gutenberg Award
(Gutenberg-Preis)**
To recognize exceptional achievements relating to Gutenberg's inventions in artistic, technical, and scholarly fields. Individuals in the fields of typeface design, typography, printing, and printing technology and scholars in bibliographic studies from all over the world may be nominated. A monetary award of 20,000 German marks and a diploma are presented triennially. Established in 1968 by the Gutenberg Society and the City of Mainz on the Rhine in memory of Johannes Gutenberg, master printer and inventor of moveable type in Mainz, 500 years after his death in 1468 A.D. As of 1994, the Gutenberg Preis will be awarded biennially in Mainz.

6913
Helmholtz Fonds
Physikalisch-Technische Bundesanstalt
Bundesallee 100
Postfach 3345   Phone: 531 5921000
D-38023 Braunschweig, Germany   Fax: 531 5929292

6914
**Helmholtz Prizes
(Helmholtz-Preise)**
For recognition of outstanding research in the fields of: precision measuring technology, metrology in medicine and environment protection, and safety engineering in chemistry and physics. Physicists and engineers, either working or cooperating with scientists in the Federal Republic of Germany are eligible. A monetary prize of 10,000 German marks and certificates are awarded in each category every three years. Established in 1973, and named after the first president of the Physikalisch-Technische Reichsanstalt, Dr. Herrman von Helmholtz (1821-1894).

6915
Hippokrates Verlag
Ruedigerstrasse 14   Phone: 711 8931 0
D-70469 Stuttgart, Germany   Fax: 711 8931 453

6916
Hippocrates Medal
To recognize medical doctors for special achievement in general practice. A medal is awarded annually.

6917
Wissenschaftlicher Wettbewerb der ZFA
For recognition of papers in Zeitschrift fur Allgemeinmedizin contributing to the enhancement of knowledge in general practice. Papers must be submitted in the German language by June 30 of each year and must be no more than 10 pages including figures and tables. The following monetary prizes are awarded: First prize - 4,000 German marks; Second prize - 2,000 German marks; Third prize - 1,000 German marks; and seven book prizes. Awarded annually in November. Established in 1973.

6918
Hochschule fur Musik
Hofstallstrasse 6-8   Phone: 931 50641
W-8700 Wurzburg, Germany   Fax: 931 14408

6919
**Mozart Festival Competition for Young Artists
(Mozartfest-Wettbewerb Wurzburg fur Gesang/Oper)**
To encourage the professional development of young German singers. Singers of German nationality who are under 30 years of age and who possess evidence of previous musical studies are eligible. A monetary prize and certificate are awarded biennially. Established in 1975 in memory of Wolfgang Amadeus Mozart. Formerly: (1977) Mozartfest Wettbewerb.

6920
Hochschule fur Musik Carl Maria von Weber
Blochmannstrasse 2/4
O-8010 Dresden, Germany

6921
**International Carl Maria von Weber Competition, Dresden
(Internationalen Carl-Maria-von-Weber-Wettbewerb, Dresden)**
To promote young composers who began their professional life just a few years ago or who will finish their studies in the near future, and to introduce them to the international public. Only composers under 36 years of age on April 30 are eligible to compete. Contestants are required to submit a complete and easily legible score for a string quartet (2 violins, viola, violoncello) which has not yet been performed, printed, broadcast or published elsewhere. The duration of this piece, which may consist of one or several movements, should not exceed 30 minutes. The following prizes are awarded: (1) First Prize - 4,000 German marks; (2) Second Prize - 2,000 German marks; and (3) Third Prize - 1,000 German marks. The prizewinners are announced at the Dresden Music Festival. Awarded biennially. Established in 1976. Sponsored by the City Council of Dresden.

6922
**Initiative LiBeraturpreis im Okumenischen Zentrum
Christuskirche**
Gottfried-Keller-Strasse 22
W-6000 Frankfurt M 50, Germany   Phone: 69 519161

6923
**LiBerature Prize
(LiBeraturpreis)**
To recognize women authors from the Third World and to raise the consciousness of German readers concerning literary creativity and problems of the Third World countries and women. Third World female authors may be nominated. The book must be translated into German prior to the award and must have been published during the preceding 18 months. A monetary prize of 1,000 German marks and an invitation to give a reading tour in Germany are awarded annually at a ceremony on the Sunday before the Frankfurt Book Fair. Established in 1988. Additional information is available from Peter Ripken, Society for the Promotion of African, Asian and Latin American Literature, Reineckstrasse 3, Postfach 100116, D-6000 Frankfurt 1, Federal Republic of Germany.

6924
Instituut voor Epilepsiebestrijding
Hermannstrasse 9   Phone: 228 462859
W-5300 Bonn 3, Germany   Fax: 228 476826

6925
Michael Award
(Michael Preis)
To recognize the best scientific work in the field of epileptology. Individuals under the age of 40 may submit manuscripts or publications in German or English from the previous two-year period by December 31. A monetary award of 20,000 German marks is presented biennially. Established in 1963. Sponsored by CIBA-GEIGY Corporation.

6926
Inter Nationes
Kennedyallee 91-103 Phone: 228 880 0
D-53175 Bonn, Germany Fax: 228 880 457

6927
Inter Nations Culture Prize
(Inter Nationes - Kulturpreis)
To recognize publishers, historians, writers, translators, etc., who have made a valuable contribution to international understanding in cultural fields. This prize is awarded to foreign nationals only. A monetary prize of 10,000 German marks and a personally dedicated booklet are awarded biennially. Established in 1968. Formerly: (1988) Inter Nationes - Preis fur Werke der Literatur und bildenden Kunst.

6928
International Academy of Cytology
Dept. of Obstetrics & Gynecology
Univ. of Freiburg
Hugstetterstrasse 55
W-7800 Freiburg, Germany Phone: 761 2703012

6929
Maurice Goldblatt Cytology Award
To recognize an individual(s) for outstanding contributions to the advancement of cytologic science and research in applied cellular studies. A medal is awarded annually at the International Congress of Cytology where the honoree delivers the Golodblatt Lecture of the Congress. Established in 1960 to honor Maurice Goldblatt, the Chairman of the Board of the Cancer Research Foundation of the University of Chicago, for his dedication to career research.

6930
International Cytotechnology Award of the IAC
To recognize outstanding achievement and contribution by persons who have distinguished themselves as cytotechnologists. Technologists, educators, researchers and administrators are eligible. Nominations are accepted from members (MIAC, PMIC or CMIAC) or fellows (FIAC or CFIAC) of IAC. A medal, a diploma and an honorarium are awarded at the triennial International Congress of Cytology. Awardees also present a special lecture during the meeting at which they are honored. Established in 1975 through a gift from the Tutorials of Cytology, Chicago, Illinois.

6931
International Association for Plant Taxonomy
Botanischer Garten und Botanisches
  Museum Berben-Dahlem
Konigin-Luise-Strasse 6-8 Phone: 30 8316010
D-14191 Berlin, Germany Fax: 30 83006218

6932
Engler Gold Medal
For recognition of an outstanding contribution to plant taxonomy. Members of the prize committee are not eligible and applications are not accepted. A gold medal is awarded every six years at the International Botanical Congresses. Established in 1987 in honor of Adolf Engler. A silver medal was established in 1990 and is given every three years alternately at the International Congress of Systematic Botany and International Botanical Congresses.

6933
International Association for the Protection of Monuments and Restoration of Buildings
(Wissenschaftlich-Technischer Arbeitskreis fur Denkmalpflege und Bauwerksanierung)
Isardamm 113
W-8192 Geretsried 1, Germany Phone: 81 716428

6934
International Association for the Protection of Monuments and Restoration of Buildings Awards
To recognize scientists, architects, and civil engineers involved in building restoration. Awards are presented.

6935
International Bach Competition
(Internationaler Johann-Sebastien-Bach-Wettbewerb)
Thomaskirchhof 16
PSF 1301
O-7010 Leipzig, Germany Phone: 41 7866

6936
International J. S. Bach Competition
To recognize the best performers of the Competition in the following categories: piano, organ, voice, violin, and cello. Soloists of all nations who are under 32 years of age are eligible. Twenty prizes for a total of 126,000 German marks are given for instrumentalists, and 14 prizes for 63,000 German marks for vocalists. Gold, silver, and bronze medals, certificates, and honorary diplomas are also awarded. The Festival is held every four years. Established in 1956 by the Leipzig City Council.

6937
International Council of Christians and Jews
c/o Martin Buber House
Werlestrasse 2 Phone: 6252 5041
64646 Heppenheim, Germany Fax: 6252 68331

6938
ICCJ - Sternberg Award
For recognition of sustained intellectual contribution to the furtherance of interreligious understanding, particularly, but not exclusively, in the field of Jewish-Christian relations. One or more individuals, institutions, or organizations may be recognized for achievements of international significance with impact beyond the recipient's own country. A monetary prize of £2,000 is awarded annually when merited. Established in 1985 by Sir Sigmund Sternberg, J. P.

6939
International Council of Environmental Law
(Conseil International du Droit de l'Environnement)
Adenauerallee 214 Phone: 228 2692240
53113 Bonn, Germany Fax: 228 2692252

6940
Elizabeth Haub Prize
For recognition of accomplishments in the field of environmental law. No restrictions exist as to membership or citizenship. A jury composed of representatives of ICEL and of the Universite Libre de Bruxelles makes the selection. A monetary prize to be used for specified purposes associated with environmental law and a gold medal are awarded annually. Established in 1974 by the ICEL and the Universite Libre de Bruxelles in honor of Elizabeth Haub.

6941
International Cryogenic Engineering Committee
FUB - Fachbereich Physik
Tieftemperaturlaboratorium
Arnimalle 14
W-1000 Berlin 33, Germany   Phone: 30 8386092

6942
Mendelssohn Award
For recognition in the field of cryogenic engineering. A medal is awarded.

6943
International Federation of Cinematographic Press
(Federation Internationale de la Presse Cinematographique (FIPRESCI))
Schleissheimerstrasse 83   Phone: 89 182303
D-80797 Munich, Germany   Fax: 89 184766

6944
FIPRESCI Prize
(Prix de la Critique Internationale)
To provide recognition for an outstanding achievement in film. Prizes and Special Mentions are awarded annually or biennially in several international film festivals: Cannes, Cracow, Leipzig, Locarno, Mannheim, Moscow, Oberhausen, San Sebastian, Venice, Berlin, Havana, Karlovy-Vary, Montreal, Stockholm, Torino, and Toronto. Established in 1930.

6945
International Federation of Disabled Workers and Civilian Handicapped
(Federation Internationale des Mutiles des Invalides du Travail et des Invalides Civils)
Beethovenallee 56-58   Phone: 228 363071
D-53173 Bonn, Germany   Fax: 228 361550

6946
Decorations
(Ehrenzeichen)
For recognition of an outstanding contribution on a national and international level to the rehabilitation of the disabled. Gold plaques, gold, silver, bronze, and blue medals, and stickpins are awarded when merited upon special occasions. Established in 1985.

6947
International Federation of Popular Sports
(Internationaler Volkssportverband)
Leharstrasse 18   Phone: 8407 760
W-85098 Grossmehring, Germany   Fax: 8407 929410

6948
International Popular Sports Achievement Award
(Internationales Volkssportabzeichen)
For recognition of repeated participation in Volkssport, such as wandering, cycling, swimming, or skiing. All are eligible who participate. Small pins, cloth patches, and certificates are awarded after repeated participation (10, 30, 50. . . Km). Awarded throughout the year. Established in 1968 by four countries: West Germany, Switzerland, Austria, and Liechtenstein. Currently, there are 16 member countries in Western Europe, the United States, and Canada.

6949
International Federation of Roofing Contractors
(Internationale Foderation des Dachdeckerchandwerks)
Fritz Reuter Strasse 1
Postfach 51 10 67   Phone: 221 372058
W-50946 Cologne, Germany   Fax: 221 384336

6950
Pin of Honour
To recognize individuals for contributions to the roofing trade. Members are eligible. A Pin of Honour is awarded at the convention or congress. Established in 1983.

6951
International Federation of Shorthand and Typewriting
(Federation Internationale de Stenographie et de Dactylographie-INTERSTENO)
Postfach 120269   Phone: 228 251509
W-5300 Bonn, Germany   Fax: 228 251509

6952
International Federation of Shorthand and Typewriting Competitions
To recognize stenographers and typists worldwide. The Federation organizes international competitions in shorthand, typewriting, and PC-use in the framework of congresses about shorthand, typewriting, and office technology.

6953
International Film Festival Mannheim
(Internationale Filmwoche Mannheim)
Collini-Center-Galerie   Phone: 621 102943
W-6800 Mannheim 1, Germany   Fax: 621 291564

6954
International Filmfestival Mannheim/Heidelberg
(Internationale Filmwoche Mannheim)
To recognize outstanding films. This small but well-known film festival is one of the oldest in the Federal Republic of Germany. From 1994 on, its venues will be in the cities of Mannheim and Heidelberg. Films must be German premiers unawarded in other European Festivals such as Cannes (all sections), Berlin (all sections), Locarno (competition), and Venice (competition). New first through third fiction features form the backbone of the competitive festival, which prides itself on making artistic discoveries and supporting independent filmmaking. Films in 35mm and 16mm must be submitted by August 15. The festival awards 30,000 German marks, Grand Prix of the Film Festival Mannheim to the first through third fiction films at least 60 minutes long. All others compete in other categories for the following prizes: 10,000 German marks, Special Prize of Mannheim In Memoriam of Rainer-Werner Fassbinder for the most original film; 10,000 German marks, Documentary Prize of the South German Broadcasting Company; the International Short Film Prize; and Special Awards. Awarded annually. Formerly: Mannheim International Filmweek.

6955
International Filmwochenende Wurzburg
Filminitiative Wurzburg e.V.
Gosbertsteige 2   Phone: 931 72845
D-8700 Wurzburg, Germany   Fax: 931 884969

6956
Prize of the Audience
To recognize and honor the best film as chosen by the audience. A monetary prize of 5,000 DM is awarded at the annual festival. Only films by invited directors are eligible for the award. Established in 1989. Contact Berthold Kremmler for further information.

6957

**International Geographical Union
(Union Geographique Internationale)**
Dept. of Geography
Univ. of Bonn
Meckenheimer Allee 166   Phone: 228 739287
53115 Bonn, Germany   Fax: 228 739272

6958

Laureat d'Honneur of the International Geographical Union
To recognize individuals who have made outstanding contributions to international understanding or cooperation or in the application of geography to worldwide problems. Individuals must be nominated by member countries prior to the International Geographical Congress held every four years. A diploma is awarded every four years at the congress. Established in 1976.

6959

**International Geographical Union
Commission Geographical Education**
Research Dept.
Paedagogische Hoshschule   Phone: 761 682426
W-7800 Freiburg, Germany   Fax: 761 1682402

Formerly: Commission Geographical Education.

6960

Commission Geographical Education Awards
For recognition of service to geographical education. Individuals from any country are eligible.

6961

**International Joseph A. Schumpeter Society
(Internationale Joseph A. Schumpeter Gesellschaft)**
Universitat Augsburg
Memminger Strasse 14   Phone: 821 598425
W-8900 Augsburg, Germany   Fax: 821 598305

6962

**Schumpeter Prize
(Schumpeter-Preis)**
For recognition of a recent scholarly contribution in economics on a designated topic related to Schumpeter's work. Applications are accepted. A monetary prize of 10,000 ECU is awarded biennially at the convention. Established in 1986 in honor of Joseph Alois Schumpeter. Sponsored by *Wirtschaftswoche*, a German economic weekly. Additional information is available from Horst Hanusch, Secretary General, Universitat Augsburg, Wiso-Fakultat, Memminger Str. 14, 86135 Augsburg, Germany.

6963

**International Judo Federation
(Federation Internationale de Judo)**
Leipziger Strasse 48
Postfach 380
O-1060 Berlin, Germany   Phone: 22 91633
                             Fax: 22 99392

6964

International Judo Federation
To promote the spread and development of the spirit and techniques of judo by sponsoring world championships.

6965

**International Kuhlau Competition for Flautists
(Internationaler Kuhlau-Wettbewerb fur Flotisten)**
Postfach 2061
Herzogenplatz 5   Phone: 581 800227
D-29525 Uelzen, Germany   Fax: 581 800108

6966

**International Kuhlau Competition for Flautists
(Internationaler Kuhlau-Wettbewerb fur Flotisten)**
To recognize and promote outstanding young flutists and pianists under the age of 32. Awards are given in three categories: flute solo and flute/piano ensembles, flute duets and duets with piano, and flute trios and flute quartets. Monetary prizes totaling 22,000 German marks are awarded triennially. The next competition is scheduled for November 6-10, 1995. Established in 1970 in memory of Friedrich Kuhlau, the composer who was born in Uelzen in 1786. Sponsored by the city of Uelzen.

6967

International League Against Epilepsy
c/o Secretary-General P. Wolf
Klinik Mara I
Epilepsie-Zentrum Bethel
Maraweg 21   Phone: 521 1444897
22617 Bielefeld, Germany   Fax: 521 1444637

6968

CIBA-GEIGY Award for Best Controlled Clinical Trial
To recognize outstanding achievement in the field of epilepsy. A monetary award of 20,000 Swiss francs is presented at the biennial congress of ILAE and IBE. Sponsored by CIBA-GEIGY Corporation.

6969

**International League of Antiquarian Booksellers
(Ligue Internationale de la Librairie Ancienne)**
Rathenaustrasse 21   Phone: 711 2568402
D-70191 Stuttgart 1, Germany Fax: 711 2576174

6970

**Triennial Prize of Bibliography
(Prix triennal de Bibliographie)**
To recognize the author of the best work of learned bibliography or of research into the history of books or of typography, and books of general interest on the subject. Authors of any nationality may submit a published or unpublished work in a language which is universally used. A monetary prize of $10,000 US is awarded triennially. Established in 1963.

6971

**International Ludwig Spohr Violin Competition
(Internationaler Violinwettbewerb Ludwig Spohr)**
Burgunderstrasse 4   Phone: 761 23380
W-7800 Freiburg, Germany   Fax: 761 554862

6972

**International Ludwig Spohr Violin Competition
(Internationaler Violinwettbewerb Ludwig Spohr)**
To recognize young violinists and to encourage the violin tradition that flourished in Germany under Ludwig Spohr. Violinists under 32 years of age must apply by the June preceding the competition. The following monetary prizes are awarded: first prize - 12,000 German marks, second prize - 9,000 German marks, third prize - 7,000 German marks, fourth prize - 5,000 German marks, fifth prize - 4,000 German marks, and sixth prize - 3,000 German marks. In addition, the following special prizes are awarded: prize for the best interpretation of Spohr's work; Prize for the best interpretation of a sonata; prize of the Spohr Society Freiburg; Preis of the Pfluger-Stiftung Freiburg - for the best young musical candidate; and Pianisten-Preise - for the best pianists. Awarded triennially (next in 1994). Established in 1979 by Wolfgang Marschner in memory of Ludwig

Spohr, the founder of a great violin tradition in Germany. Sponsored by the county of Baden-Wurttemberg and the city of Freiburg.

6973

International Music Competition of the Broadcasting Stations of the Federal Republic of Germany
(Internationaler Musikwettbewerb der Rundfunkanstalten der Bundesrepublik Deutschland)
Bayerischer Rundfunk
Rundfunkplatz 1　　　　　　　　　　　Phone: 89 5900 2471
W-8000 Munich 2, Germany　　　　　　Fax: 89 5900 3091

6974

Internationaler Musikwettbewerb der ARD
(Munich International Music Competition of the Broadcasting Stations of the Federal Republic of Germany (ARD))
For recognition of the best perfomers of the musical competition. Awards are given in various categories. Soloists must be between 17 and 30 years of age; singers (female) between 20 and 30 years of age; singers (male) between 20 and 32 years; duos and trios between 17 and 32 years of age; windquintets between 17 and 35 years of age (two members of the ensemble can be 35 years); and the string quartet between 17 and 35 years of age, with the total of the four musicians' ages no more than 120. The competitors are judged for technique, musicality, and artistic personality. Musicians of all nationalities are eligible. Monetary prizes of 10,000 to 35,000 German marks are awarded and invitations are extended to give concerts and make recordings and television performances. Awarded annually. Established in 1952.

6975

International Music Institute of the City of Darmstadt
(Internationales Musikinstitut Darmstadt)
Nieder-Ramstadter Strasse 190　　　　Phone: 6151 132416
W-64285 Darmstadt, Germany　　　　　Fax: 6151 132405

6976

Kranichsteiner Musikpreis
To recognize special achievement in the composition and interpretation of new music. Individuals under the age of 35 of any nationality who participate in the international "Ferienkurse" program are eligible. A monetary prize of 10,000 German marks is awarded biennially. Established in 1952.

6977

International Robert Schumann Competition
(Internationalen Robert-Schumann-Wettbewerbes)
Stadt Zwickau
Kulturburo
Munzstrasse 12　　　　　　　　　　　Phone: 74 22636
D-08056 Zwickau, Germany　　　　　　Fax: 74 23216

6978

International Robert Schumann Choir Competition
For recognition of the best music performance of Schumann's work and contemporary compositions. Amateur male, female, and mixed choirs are eligible. The following prizes are awarded: first place - 10,000 German marks and a gold medal, second place - 5,000 marks and a silver medal, and third place - 3,500 marks and a bronze medal.

6979

International Robert Schumann Competition
(Internationalen Robert-Schumann-Wettbewerbes)
For recognition of the best piano performances of Schumann's work and research into his life and music. The following prizes are awarded: first place - 10,000 German marks and a gold medal, second place - 5,000 marks and a silver medal, and third place - 3,500 marks and a bronze medal. Awarded annually on June 8 in memory of composer Robert Schumann. Established in 1956.

6980

International Scientific and Technical Gliding Organisation
(Organisation Scientifique et Technique Internationale du Vol a Voile)
Institut fur Physik der Atmosphare
Oberpfaffenhofen 8031　　　　　　　　Phone: 8153 28507
W-8031 Wessling, Germany　　　　　　Fax: 8153 28243

6981

International Scientific and Technical Gliding Organisation Awards
To recognize and encourage research on soaring science and technology and on the development and use of the sailplane. Awards for technical achievement, diplomas for valuable papers, and prizes for improvements in sailplane technology are awarded biennially.

6982

International Short Film Festival, Oberhausen
(Internationale Kurzfilmtage Oberhausen)
Christian-Steger-Str. 10　　　　　　　Phone: 208 807008
D-46042 Oberhausen, Germany　　　　Fax: 208 852591

6983

Filmotheque of the Youth
For recognition of documentaries, short feature films, student films, animated films and experimental films by youth, giving them a glimpse of international short filmmaking. Discussions, retrospectives, and information screenings are held as part of the Internationl Short Film Festival. Films must not be longer than 35 minutes and must have been produced during the two years preceding the Festival for films from outside Germany, and during the past year for films from Germany. Videos are accepted. The deadline for entries is February 15. The following awards are presented: Youth Film Prize of the Town of Oberhausen - 3,000 German marks awarded by the Federal Ministry for Youth, Family Affairs, Women and Health; Prize of the Filmotheque Forum - a promotion prize of 1,000 German marks for a film particularly adapted for a juvenile audience; prize for the best video production - 300 German marks; and certificates to the first five competition films chosen by the audience. Awarded annually in April. Foreign contributions will be selected in the producing countries.

6984

International Short Film Festival, Oberhausen
(Internationale Kurtzfilmtage Oberhausen)
For recognition of documentaries, short feature films, student films, animated films and experimental films. Discussions, retrospectives, and information screenings are held as part of the Festival. A special emphasis is on young filmmakers and their first films, and on films from the developing countries. Films must not be longer than 35 minutes and must have been produced during the two years preceding the Festival for films from outside Germany, and during the past year for films from Germany. Videos are accepted. The deadline for entries is February 15. The following awards are presented: Grand Prize of the City of Oberhausen - 10,000 German marks; four monetary prizes of 2,000 marks each; prize for a contribution showing the possibility of living in harmony with animals, plants, and technical science - 5,000 German marks; Owlglass Prize for the most humorous film - 1,000 German marks and an Owlglass figure; best film in the field of educational politics - 5,000 German marks; Alexander S. Scotti Prize for the best film on the subject of old age and death - 2,000 German marks; Prize of the FIPRESCI - 2,000 German marks; Prize of the Catholic Film Association - 2,000 German marks; (9) Prize of INTERFILM - 2,000 German marks; and DGB Prize - 3,000 German marks. Awarded annually in April. Foreign contributions are selected in the producing countries. Established in 1954. Formerly: (1991) International West German Short Film Festival, Oberhausen.

6985

International Society for the History of Pharmacy
Graf Moltke Strasse 46
W-2800 Bremen, Germany

6986
Schelenz Plaque
For recognition of an outstanding contribution to the history of pharmacy. Scholars from any country are eligible. A bronze plaque is awarded not more often than once a year. Established in 1929.

6987
Ludwig Winkler Plaque
To recognize persons or organizations for special contributions to the organization. A plaque with the profile of Ludwig Winkler is awarded.

6988
International Society on Toxinology
c/o Dr. Dietrich Mebs
Zentrum der Rechtsmedezin
Kennedyallee 104
6000 Frankfurt 70, Germany   Fax: 69 63015882

6989
Redi Award
For recognition of outstanding contributions to the knowledge of natural-occurring poisons and venoms. Individuals without regard to nationality may be nominated and voted upon by present and past officers of the Society and past awardees. A monetary award, a plaque, a leather bound illuminated manuscript noting the accomplishments of the awardee, and travel expenses are awarded every three years at the International Congress. Established in 1967 in honor of Francisco Redi, an Italian anatomist of the 17th century who showed it was venom, not spirits that were transferred from snake to victim.

6990
International Union for the Modern Pentathalon and Biathlon
(Union Internationale de Pentathlon Moderne et Biathlon)
Douglasstrasse 11
W-1000 Berlin 33, Germany   Phone: 8 26 48 58

6991
Medal of Honour
(Medaille d'honneur)
To recognize an individual who has contributed to a remarkable degree to the international development of a UIPMB sport. However, the national development of these sports may also be considered as a merit for being awarded the medal. No more than two medals are awarded in one year. Established in 1949.

6992
International Union of Master Painters
(Union Internationale des Entrepreneurs de Peinture)
Maler- und Lackierer-Innung Hamburg
Holstenwall 12   Phone: 40 343887
20355 Hamburg 36, Germany   Fax: 40 3480625

6993
International Union of Master Painters Competitions
To recognize and publicize interests specific to master painters and to promote the establishment of minimum standards in interior design education.

6994
International Youth Library
(Internationale Jugendbibliothek)
Schloss Blutenburg   Phone: 89 8112028
D-81247 Munich 60, Germany   Fax: 89 8117553

6995
White Ravens
(Die Weissen Raben)
To promote high quality children's books of international interest. About 200 children's books, by authors and illustrators from all over the world are given recognition. Children's books submitted during the year prior to the award are considered. White Ravens books are listed in the annual international selected bibliography and exhibited during the Children's Book Fair in Bologna, Italy. Awarded annually. Established in 1963.

6996
Justus-Liebig-Universitat-Giessen
Ludwigstrasse 23   Phone: 41 7022018
D-35390 Giessen, Germany   Fax: 41 7022039

Formerly: Academia Ludoviciana Gissensis.

6997
Award for Historical Works Pertaining to Justus-Liebig University
(Auszeichnung fur wissenschaftliche Arbeiten zu der Geschichte der Justus-Liebig-Universitat)
To promote the research or printing of works concerned with the history of Justus-Liebig University in Giessen. A monetary prize of 4,000 German marks is awarded. Awarded annually. Established in 1982.

6998
Dissertation Honors
To recognize outstanding dissertations in philosophy, social science, natural science, political science, law, agriculture, and the medical sciences. Students at Justus Liebig University are eligible. Self nomination is accepted. Awarded annually. Established in 1979.

6999
Entwicklungslanderpreises der Justus-Liebig-Universitat Giessen
In recognition of outstanding achievement in the acquisition of scientific knowledge about developing countries and the application thereof. Individuals, teams, or institutions are eligible. A variable monetary prize is awarded to individuals or groups biennially. Established in 1982. Co-sponsored by the Kreditanstalt fur Wiederaufbau in Frankfurt am Main.

7000
Preis der Justus-Liebig-Universitat Giessen
To recognize young scientific scholars at the University and to further their work and its printing. Scientific work from the preceding four years and work undertaken earlier by others at the University and now being continued is considered. An award is given in alternate years in the following fields: natural science, medical science, jurisprudence and social science, and culture and linguistics. A monetary prize of 10,000 German marks is awarded annually. Established in 1982.

7001
Roentgen-Preis
For recognition of outstanding scientific work and achievements in fundamental radio-physics and radio-biology research. Younger scientists are eligible. A monetary prize of 10,000 German marks is awarded annually. Established in 1974 by Arthur Pfeiffer Company at Wetzlar and Schunk GmbH of Heuchelheim-Giessen.

7002
Schunk-Preis fur Wirtschaftswissenschaften
In recognition of an outstanding scientific work in economics, particularly by young talent, concerning the "future-oriented" concepts of business ventures and their administration. Both German residents and non-resident university assistants are considered for the prize. A monetary prize of 10,000 German marks is awarded triennially. Established in 1986 by the Schunk-Gruppe.

7003
Ludwig Schunk Prize for Medicine
(Ludwig Schunk-Preis fur Medizin)
To recognize outstanding scientific achievement in medicine and to promote young medical researchers. Awarded in alternate years to non-resident Germans or foreign citizens and university scientists or resident Germans. A monetary prize of 10,000 German marks is awarded annually. Established in 1982 by Firma Schunk & Ebe GmbH.

7004
Ludwig Schunk Prize for Veterinary Medicine
(Ludwig Schunk-Preis fur Veterinarmedizin)
For outstanding scientific achievement in the field of veterinary medicine and its application to human well-being. A monetary prize of 10,000 German marks and a certificate are awarded biennially. Established in 1961 by Firma Schunk & Ebe GmbH.

7005
Franz Vogt-Preise
For recognition of outstanding scientific achievement by young scientists from the University of Giessen in the fields of the humanities and the natural sciences. Self nomination is not accepted. Two monetary prizes of 10,000 German marks and travel costs are awarded annually on an alternating basis. Established in 1986. Sponsored by the Franz-Vogt Foundation.

7006
Kiel Institute of World Economics
(Institut fur Weltwirtschaft an der Universitat Kiel)
Dusternbrooker Weg 120   Phone: 431 8814228
W-2300 Kiel 1, Germany   Fax: 431 8814526

7007
Bernhard-Harms-Preis
For recognition of special research achievements in the field of international economics. Professors who have distinguished themselves through extraordinary achievement in the field of international economics or individuals in the business world who have made significant contributions to the improvement of world economic relations are eligible. Individuals are nominated by a nomination committee. A monetary award of 25,000 German marks and a medal are presented biennially at Kieler Woche. Established in 1964 in memory of Bernhard Harms, professor of economics and the founder of the Kiel Institute of World Economics. Sponsored by Gesellschaft zur Forderung des Instituts fur Weltwirtschaft. In addition, the Bernhard-Harms-Medaille, established in 1980, is awarded at irregular intervals.

7008
Karl Klingler-Stiftung
Intl. Wettbewerb fur Streichquartett
Sudliche Auffahrtsallee 49
W-8000 Munich 19, Germany   Phone: 89 174297

7009
Internationaler Wettbewerb fur Streichquartett Karl Klinger Preis
To recognize an outstanding string quartet, to promote and preserve the great tradition of quartet-playing, in particular the Classic compositions. A high standard of both technical and artistic expertise is demanded in the competition. The competition is open to entrants of all nations who are not over 37 years of age. Three monetary prizes are awarded every three years: (1) First Prize - 25,000 German marks and a medal; (2) Second Prize - 15,000 German marks; and (3) Third Prize - 10,000 German marks. An additional monetary prize of 8,000 German marks is awarded for the best Haydn performance. Established in 1979 by Marianne Klingler, daughter of Karl Klingler. Organized by the Foundation in conjunction with the Hochschule fur Musik and the Richard Strauss Konservatorium in Munich.

7010
Konzertagentur Fahrenholtz
Oberweg 51
W-6000 Frankfurt/Main 1, Germany   Phone: 69 597 14 79

7011
Trio basso International Competition for Composers
(Trio basso Internationaler Kompositions-Wettbewerb)
This one-time competition was held to recognize compositions for the trio combination viola, violoncello and double-bass by composers of all nations and ages. Four monetary prizes of 2,000 German marks, diplomas, a concert with radio recording, and one premiered work published by Breitkopf & Hartel, Wiesbaden, Federal Republic of Germany, were awarded at the convention. Established in 1988 by Trio basso. (Discontinued in 1991)

7012
Korber-Stiftung
Kampchaussee 10   Phone: 40 7250 2439
W-2050 Hamburg 80, Germany   Fax: 40 7250 3789

7013
Herbert Weichmann-Preis
To recognize outstanding scholars, to encourage the historical-political consciousness of young people, and to improve engagement for democracy and friendship among nations. Former winners of the German History Prize up to 25 years of age can apply. A monetary prize of 5,000 German marks and a medal are awarded annually. Established in 1984 by Dr. Kurt A. Korber in memory of Dr. Herbert Weichmann, first mayor of Hamburg (1965-1971).

7014
Kulturamt der Stadt Monchengladbach
Albertusstrasse 44 a   Phone: 2161 256310
W-4050 Monchengladbach 1, Germany   Fax: 2161 256339

7015
Competition for Composers
(Kompositionswettbewerb)
To encourage composers in the field of contemporary music. There is no age limit. Each competitor may submit two compositions for 3 to 10 musicians, based upon the instruments of the classical symphony orchestra. Up to three of these musicians may have other instruments or come from other branches of the arts. The length of performance may not exceed 20 minutes. Only works that have been composed in the last three years and have not yet been performed or published are allowed. Winners are nominated by the prize committee. Monetary prizes totaling 15,000 German marks are distributed among the prize winners, and all prize-winning works are broadcast by West-German-Radio. Established in 1980.

7016
Kuratorium fur die Verleihung des Heinrich-Wieland Preises
Friesenweg 1   Phone: 40 882091
22763 Hamburg, Germany   Fax: 40 882093

7017
Heinrich-Wieland Preis
For recognition of outstanding research on the chemistry, biochemistry, and physiology of fats and lipids, as well as on their clinical importance and their significance in the physiology of nutrition. Authors of unpublished scientific treatises or treatises published during the year preceding the award are eligible. Papers must be written in German, English, or French. All papers must be accompanied by a summary of about three pages. Treatises that have already been awarded some other prize for scientific work are not eligible. A monetary prize of 30,000 German marks and a Heinrich-Wieland plaque are awarded annually. Established in

1964. Sponsored by The Margarine Institute for Health Nutrition in Hamburg.

7018

Landeshauptstadt Munchen
Kulturreferat
Rindermarkt 3-4
80313 Munich, Germany

Phone: 89 2336991
Phone: 89 2335153
Fax: 89 2338622

7019

City of Munich Prizes
(Landeshaupstadt Munchen Preise)
For recognition of lifetime achievement in the arts by authors and artists of Munich. Monetary prizes of 15,000 German marks are awarded biennially in each of the following categories: Literature - to honor an outstanding literary collection, established in 1991; Film - to honor special achievements in film, established in 1992; Journalism - to honor an outstanding journalistic work in print, radio, or television, established in 1992; Art - for special achievements in the field of fine arts, established in 1991; Architecture - for an outstanding exceptional project designed and constructed in Munich, established in 1977; Design - for an outstanding design achievement, established in 1992; Music - for deserving musicians and musical groups in all fields and all genres of music, established in 1992; Theater, established in 1992; and Dance (triennial), established in 1993.

7020

Kultureller Ehrenpreis
To recognize a person of international prominence for their cultural or scientific achievements. A monetary prize of 20,000 German marks is awarded annually. Established in 1958.

7021

Literavision Preis
To recognize an outstanding television program or movie on books or writers. German-speaking individuals and programs are eligible. Two monetary awards totaling 20,000 German marks are presented annually. Established in 1991.

7022

Promotional Prizes
To honor outstanding contributions to German culture in various fields of the arts. Monetary prizes of 12,000 German marks are awarded in film, art, music, and dance.

7023

Scholarships of the City of Munich
To honor outstanding contributions to Germna culture in the fields of literature, fine arts, music, theater, and dance. Scholarships in the amount of 12,000 German marks are awarded annually. Established in 1991.

7024

Geschwister-Scholl-Preis
To honor a book that presents intellectually important insights on civic freedom, morality, and aesthetics. A monetary prize of 20,000 German marks is awarded annually. Established in 1980. Co-sponsored with the Bavarian Publishers and Booksellers Association.

7025

Landesregierung Nordrhein-Westfalen
Mannesmannufer 1a
Postfach 1103
W-4000 Dusseldorf, Germany

Phone: 211 83701
Fax: 211 8371150

7026

Forderpreis des Landes Nordrhein-Westfalen fur junge Kunstlerinnen und Kunstler
(Nordrhein-Westfalen Prize for the Advancement of Young Artists)
To enable young artists to develop their talents and publicize their works with greater ease. Promising artists under 35 years of age who have outstanding talent and have produced works of substantially above average quality are eligible. Competitors must be natives or residents of Nordrhein-Westfalen. Monetary prizes of 10,000 German marks each are awarded annually to two artists in each of the following categories: painting, graphics, sculpture; poets, authors; composers, conductors, instrumentalists; theatrical directors, actors, singers, dancers, scenery designers; film directors, scene designers, cameramen; and architects, interior designers, landscape designers, city planners, and designers of fashion. Prizes may also be awarded to groups or associations of three or more artists who receive 20,000 or 30,000 German marks, respectively. Established in 1972.

7027

Landschaftsverband Westfalen - Lippe Kulturpflegeabteilung
Warendorfer Strasse 24
W-48145 Munster, Germany

Phone: 251 5913856
Fax: 251 5913268

Formerly: (1953) Provinzialverband Westfalen.

7028

Annette-von-Droste-Hulshoff-Preis
For recognition of special achievement in poetry written in either high or low German. Every third time it can be awarded for creative musical achievement. Recipients must be natives or residents of the Westfalian - Lippe region of Germany. A monetary prize of 25,000 German marks and a certificate are awarded biennially. Established in 1946 by the Provinzialverband Westfalen in memory of the German and Westfalian poetess, Annette von Droste-Hulshoff (1797-1848).

7029

Konrad-von-Soest-Preis
For recognition of special achievement in the field of fine and graphic arts. Recipients must be natives or residents of the Westfalian - Lippe region of Germany. A monetary prize of 25,000 German marks and a certificate are awarded biennially. Established in 1952 by the Provinzialverband Westfalen in memory of the great Westfalian medieval artist, Konrad von Soest (about 1400).

7030

Wilhelm-Lehmbruck-Museum Duisburg
Friedrich-Wilhelm-Strasse 40
47049 Duisburg, Germany

Phone: 203 2832630
Fax: 203 2833892

7031

Wilhelm Lehmbruck Prize
To encourage living artists and to promote cultural relations between Germany and other countries. A living German or non-German sculptor whose entire work displays significant artistic achievement is eligible. A monetary award of 20,000 German marks, a certificate of award, and an exhibition of the artist's work in the Wilhelm-Lehmbruck-Museum are awarded every five years. Established in 1966 in memory of the sculptor Wilhelm Lehmbruck, who was born in Duisburg-Meiderich in 1881 and died in 1919.

7032

Leipzig College of Graphic Arts and Book Design
(Hochschule fur Grafik und Buchkunst Leipzig)
Wachterstrasse 11
04107 Leipzig, Germany

Phone: 41 2135123
Fax: 41 312401

7033
Walter Tiemann Award
To recognize independent publishers, small publishers, and printing-presses. One to three different titles published within the preceding two years may be submitted. A small sculpture and a monetary prize of 5,000 German marks for the first prize, 3,000 German marks for the second prize, and 2,000 German marks for a promotion prize are awarded. Established in honor of Walter Tiemann, a teacher and the rector from 1920 to 1945 at the former Leipzig Academie for Graphic Arts and Book Production, now College of Graphic Arts and Book Design, Leipzig.

7034
Leipziger Dok-Filmwoche GmbH
Box 940
04009 Leipzig, Germany
Phone: 41 29 46 60
Fax: 41 29 46 60

7035
International Leipzig Documentary and Animation Film Festival (Internationale Leipziger Dokumetar- und Kurzfilmwoche fur Kino und Fernsehen)
For recognition of cinema and television films in the following categories: documentary films, television reports, and documentations; reconstructed documentations (documentaries using staged reconstructions); and animation films. The competing films are shown at the Festival in their original versions, with simultaneous translations into German and English. An international jury selects the winners. The deadline for entry is September 10. In the category of film and television production under 45 minutes, 5,000 marks and a Golden Dove are awarded for first place, and 3,000 marks and a Silver Dove are awarded for both second and third places. In the category of film and television production over 45 minutes, 5,000 marks and a Golden Dove are awarded for first place, and 3,000 marks and a Silver Dove are awarded for both second and third places. A first prize of 2,500 marks and a Golden Dove are awarded for the best animated film for television or cinema, and 1,500 marks and a Silver Dove, are awarded for second place. Awarded annually. Established in 1957.

7036
Lubeck Hanseatic City Cultural Office (Senat der Hansestadt Lubeck)
Amt fur Kultur
Buddenbrookhaus, Mengstr. 4
D-23539 Lubeck 1, Germany
Phone: 451 1224102
Fax: 451 1224106

7037
Dietrich Buxtehude Prize
For recognition of artistic achievement in the field of church music, and for scientific research and interpretation of music written by Buxtehude, a composer and organist of St. Mary's Church in Lubeck (1668-1707). Musicians and scholars are eligible. A monetary prize of 10,000 German marks is awarded triennially. Established in 1951.

7038
Thomas Mann Prize
For recognition of a work of literature or a work on the history of literature. Writers whose distinguished literary and scholarly work demonstrates the humanitarian concern that has characterized the works of Thomas Mann are eligible. A monetary prize of 15,000 German marks and a certificate are awarded triennially. Established in 1975 on the occasion of the 100th birthday of Thomas Mann.

7039
Magistrat der Universitatsstadt Giessen
Oberburgermeister Manfred Mutz
Berliner Platz 1
D-35390 Giessen, Germany
Phone: 49 3062007

7040
Hedwig-Burgheim Medaille
To recognize an individual who has demonstrated outstanding ability to communicate and foster understanding between people for the betterment of humanity. Awarded annually by the city of Giessen. Established in 1981 in memory of the pedagogue Hedwig Burgheim who was murdered in the concentration camp of Auschwitz.

7041
Walter Meckauer Kreis
Lortzingplatz 7
D-50931 Cologne, Germany
Phone: 221 402350

7042
Walter-Meckauer-Plakette
To recognize outstanding efforts to promote the works of persecuted or forgotten authors. A medal, plaque, certificate, and publicity are awarded annually. Established in 1983 to commemorate the 50th anniversary of the bookburning of Jewish books, and named to honor Walter MecKauer (1889-1966), the German playwright and novelist who was forced to emigrate from 1933-1952 because of his Jewish background.

7043
Medical Women's International Association
Herbert-Lewin-Strasse 1
W-50931 Cologne, Germany
Phone: 221 4004557
Fax: 221 4004557

7044
Honorary Member
To recognize a member of a National Association or individual member who has rendered to the Association or the medical profession any outstanding services. A gilded MWIA brooch and a certificate of Honorary Membership in the organization are conferred at each Congress, about every two to three years. Established in 1929.

7045
Member of Honour
To recognize an individual who is not a member of the Association and who has rendered to the Association or the medical profession outstanding services. A gilded MWIA brooch and a certificate of Member of Honour in the organization are conferred at each congress, about every two to three years. Established in 1987.

7046
Micro Hall Art Center
LITERATURIUM
Heidedamm 6
PO Box 1206
D-26182 Edewecht-Klein Scharrel,
  Germany
Phone: 44 862697
Fax: 44 866485

Formerly: (1986) Dada Research Center.

7047
Black Curtain Award
To recognize outstanding performances given by the LITERATURIUM Stage. Established in 1990.

7048
Golden Award of the Micro Hall Art Center
For recognition of contributions to international correspondence between artists for a better world.

7049
Golden Poet-Tree Award
To recognize excellent works in visual and concrete poetry. Works connected with an exhibition in the Micro Hall Art Center are eligible. Established in 1989.

7050
Ikarus Medaille
For recognition of contributions to international cultural exchange among artists.

7051
**LITERATURIUMS Kabarett Award
(LITERATURIUMS Kabarett-Preis)**
To recognize new ways in culture, including satire, cabaret, and experimental music. Awarded biannually. Established in 1991 to honor Ammerlander Kabarett- und Kleinkunsttage. Sponsored by different banking institutions.

7052
Moon Fish Award
For recognition of activities in Dada connections and artists' world communication. A diploma and medal are awarded at the convention. Established in 1972 by Dr. Klaus Groh.

7053
Ministerium fur Familie, Frauen, Weiterbildung und Kunst Baden-Wurttemberg
Hauptstatterstrasse 67
Postfach 10 34 38   Phone: 711 6442660
W-70029 Stuttgart 10, Germany   Fax: 711 6442659

7054
Johann-Peter-Hebel-Preis
For recognition of literary work. German-speaking authors from the Alemannian regions or whose works give them a special connection there, and authors who have distinguished themselves in the cultivation of Hebel's legacy or German literature in general are eligible for consideration. A monetary prize of 20,000 German marks is awarded biennially on May 10 (Hebel's birthday). Established in 1936 by Land Baden in memory of the German poet Johann Peter Hebel (1760-1826).

7055
**Schiller-Gedachtnispreis des Land Baden-Wurttemberg
(Baden-Wurttemberg Schiller Memorial Prize)**
To recognize individuals who have produced outstanding work of exemplary linguistic form in the field of literature or the humanities, and to encourage young dramatists. A monetary prize of 40,000 German marks and two prizes of 15,000 German marks are awarded triennially on November 10. Established in 1955 by Land Baden - Wurttemberg in memory of the German poet, Friedrich Schiller (1759-1805).

7056
**Anna-Monika Foundation
(Anna-Monika Stiftung)**
c/o Prof. Dr. H. Helmchen, Chairman,
   Committee of Judges
Psychiatrische Klinik und Poliklinik
Freie Universitat Berlin
Eschenallee 3   Phone: 30 3003 700
D-14050 Berlin, Germany   Fax: 30 3003 726

7057
**Anna Monika Foundation Prize
(Anna-Monika Stiftung Preis)**
For recognition of the best reports of investigations of the physical substrate and functional disturbances of depression. Studies of biochemical, histological, neurophysiological, neuropathological, psychopharmacological, psychiatric or psychosomatic nature are given preference. The studies should be carried out in close cooperation with a psychiatric clinic, a university or an equivalent scientific institute. The papers should give information about recent advances in knowledge that should be helpful in promoting treatment and would open up new paths of progress. The papers may be written in German, French or English. Unpublished studies, as well as papers published in the past two years in an international professional journal may also be submitted by September 30. Monetary prizes of $15,000, $10,000 and $5,000 are awarded biennially in odd-numbered years. Established in 1967 by Peter Rehme to honor his wife Anna and his daughter Monika. Additional information is available from Dr. Benno Hess, Am Kaiserhain 19, 44139 Dortmund, Germany, phone: 0231 129054; fax: 0231 129058.

7058
**Munich International Filmschool Festival
(Internationales Festival der Filmhochschulen Munchen)**
c/o Internationale Munchner Filmwochen
Kaiserstrasse 39   Phone: 89 3819040
D-80801 Munich, Germany   Fax: 89 38190426

7059
**Munich International Filmschool Festival
(Internationales Festival der Filmhochschulen Munchen)**
To encourage the professional development of young filmmakers. Film by film students must be entered by the respective film schools for consideration. Film equipment and filmstock are awarded for the various prizes and special prizes. Awarded annually. Established in 1981. Sponsored by private companies, television stations, etc.

7060
Musikschule der Stadt Ettlingen
Pforzheimer Strasse 25a   Phone: 7243 101311
D-76275 Ettlingen, Germany   Fax: 7243 101436

7061
**Ettlingen International Competition for Young Pianists
(Internationaler Wettbewerb fur Junge Pianisten Ettlingen)**
To recognize outstanding young pianists. Pianists of all nationalities are eligible. Awards are given in two categories: those up to 15 years of age and those up to 20 years of age. A monetary award of 1,500 German marks is given to the first place winner in the younger age group, and 3,000 German marks is given in the older age group. Special prizes are also given. Awarded biennially. Established in 1988. Sponsored by Sparkasse Ettlingen.

7062
OKOMEDIA Institut
Habsburgerstrasse 9a   Phone: 761 52024
79104 Freiburg, Germany   Fax: 761 555724

7063
**OKOMEDIA International Ecological Film Festival
(OKOMEDIA Internationale Tage des Okologischen Films)**
For recognition of outstanding contemporary ecological films. In addition, there are film productions on specialized issues: nature films, films on conservation and environmental issues, animation, and experimental films. Each festival highlights a topic, such as ecological films from Eastern Europe or from the U.S.A. or the Third World and ecology, which gives special insight into the ecological situation in the respective regions. The deadline for entry is July 31. The following prizes are awarded: Development Prize of the City of Freiburg - 10,000 German marks: Special Prize of the Federal Minister of the Environment - 5,000 German marks; OKOMEDIA Prize for the Best Artistic Achievement; OKOMEDIA Award for the Best Journalistic Achievement; OKOMEDIA Prize for the Best Nature Film; Hoimar von Ditfurth Prize for the Best Portrayal of Ecological Problems for Children and Young People - 5,000 German marks; and OKOMEDIA Award for the Best Children's/Youth Film. Awarded annually. Established in 1984. Formerly: Freiburg Ecological Film Festival.

7064
Organization for the Phyto-Taxonomic Investigation of the Mediterranean Area
Botanischer Garten und Botanisches
  Museum
Konigin-Luise-Strasse 6-8
D-14191 Berlin, Germany
Phone: 30 83006132
Fax: 30 83006218

7065
OPTIMA Gold Medal
For recognition of an outstanding contribution to the phytotaxonomy of the Mediterranean area. Individuals must not be members of the OPTIMA Prize Commission to be eligible for the award. A medal is awarded triennially, at the OPTIMA meetings. Established in 1977.

7066
OPTIMA Silver Medal
For recognition of the authors of the best papers or books on the phytotaxonomy of the Mediterranean area, published in the three years preceding the award. Individuals must not be current members of the OPTIMA Prize Commission or the OPTIMA International Board to be eligible for the award. Medals are awarded triennially at the OPTIMA meetings. Established in 1977.

7067
Karl Ernst Osthaus-Museum
Hochstrasse 73
W-58042 Hagen 1, Germany
Phone: 2331 207 3131
Fax: 2331 16149

7068
Karl Ernst Osthaus Prize
(Karl Ernst Osthaus-Preis)
For recognition of outstanding artistic achievement. Artists who were born or live in Northrhine-Westfalia are eligible. A monetary prize of 10,000 German marks is awarded biennially. In addition, a monetary prize of 5,000 German Marks is awarded biennially to "young talents." Prizewinners are exhibited. Established in 1947. Sponsored by the City of Hagen.

7069
Paneuropean Union
(Paneuropa-Union)
Karlstrasse 57
D-80333 Munich, Germany
Phone: 89 554683
Fax: 89 594768

7070
Coudenhove-Kalergi Award
To recognize outstanding efforts to unite all European peoples into a nonpartisan political and economic union based on principles of liberty, self-determination, and Christian values. Awarded annually.

7071
Die Pharmazeutische Industrie
Postfach 1255
88322 Aulendorf, Germany
Phone: 7525 20620
Fax: 7525 20627

7072
Preis fur Pharma-Technik
For recognition of qualified scientific work in the area of pharmaceutical technique. Authors of articles from the journal *Die Pharmazeutische Industrie* are eligible. A monetary prize of 4,000 German marks for first prize, and 3,000 German marks for second prize are awarded annually. Established in 1963.

7073
Prix Futura Berlin/SFB
(Sender Freies Berlin)
D-14046 Berlin, Germany
Phone: 30 311610
Phone: 3031 1620
Fax: 30 311619

7074
Prix Futura Berlin
To recognize radio and television productions, which by the quality of their content and form, best identify and reflect the changes that are happening around us and within us, and extend our understanding of them. The competition is open to all broadcasting organizations authorized by national or international law to provide a broadcasting service. Awards are given for both daytime and nighttime programs in the following categories: Radio Drama, Radio Documentary, Television Fiction, and Television Documentary. Daytime awards are presented to the best from all countries, and nighttime awards are for newcomers. The Ake Blomstrom Memorial Prize and the BBC Newcomers Award are presented to nighttime radio programs. Each organization may submit one production in each of the categories and is required to state the category entered. Productions must have been broadcast for the first time between April 1 and April 1 of the preceding two years. They may not include any commercial advertising. Two monetary prizes of 10,000 German marks each and a certificate of honor are awarded biennially in each category. In addition, the Transtel-Jury Prize for outstanding television productions from the countries of Africa, Asia, and Latin America is also awarded. The prize is valued at 10,000 German marks. Co-sponsored by Zweites Deutsches Fernseh, Sender Freies Berlin, and EBU/UER.

7075
Prix Jeunesse Foundation
Bayerischer Rundfunk
80300 Munich, Germany
Phone: 89 59002058
Fax: 89 59003053

7076
Prix Jeunesse International Munchen
To stimulate production of more and better children's and youth programs, to develop internationally applicable standards for such programs, to awaken and deepen understanding among young people of all nations, and to intensify international program exchange. Television programs for children and young people, including fiction (animation, drama, story-telling, light entertainment) and nonfiction (documentary, magazines, mixed forms, natural history, etc.) are considered in the following categories: up to 7 years of age, 7 to 12 years of age, and 12 to 17 years of age. Telecasters authorized under national and international law to operate broadcasting services may enter programs and send experts to the contest. All programs must have been produced and broadcast within the two years preceding the contest. A nomination committee chooses the finalists from among the nominees. All programs not selected for the contest are passed on to the Video-Bar. The prize winning programs at the Prix Jeunesse International contest are not chosen by a jury; rather, all participants accredited by the Contest Management are invited to join in the vote for the prize winning programs. Six prizes and three special prizes are awarded biennially. A trophy, a "kinetic object" created out of stainless steel and acrylic, by Professor Friedrich Becker of Dusseldorf, and a certificate are awarded in each category. UNICEF and the German UNESCO Commission award Special Prizes at the Prix Jeunesse International contest. The Special Prize of the International Advisory Board is awarded to an outstanding program produced by a television organization with restricted production means. Awarded biennially. Established in 1964 by the Free State of Bavaria, City of Munich, Bayerischer Rundfunk; in 1971 Zweites Deutsches Fernsehen joined the foundation; and in 1991 Bayerische Landeszentrale fur Neue Medien.

7077

**Rationalisation Group Packaging within the German Management and Productivity Centre
(Rationalisierungs-Gemeinschaft Verpackung im RKW)**
Dusseldorfer Strasse 40
Postfach 5867　　　　　　　　　　　　　Phone: 6196 495298
65733 Eschborn, Germany　　　　　　　　Fax: 6196 495303

7078

Deutscher Verpackungs-Wettbewerb
To encourage development in the field of packaging. The competition is open to manufacturers, users, and designers of all kinds of packages. A trophy and diploma are awarded every third year in connection with the International Packaging Fair, INTERPACK, at Dusseldorf. Established in 1963.

7079

Seliger-Gemeinde
Bundesverband
Schloss Strasse 92
W-7000 Stuttgart 1, Germany　　　　　　Phone: 711 61 60 10

7080

Wenzel-Jaksch-Gedachtnis-Preis
For recognition of a contribution to the preservation of the heritage of the Sudeten-German labor movement. A monetary prize of 5,000 German marks is awarded annually. Established in 1968 by Ernst Paul, former President of Seliger-Gemeinde, in memory of Wenzel Jaksch, last leader of the Sudeten-German Social Democratic Party (1938-1939). Sponsored by the Bundesministerium des Innern.

7081

**Society for Medicinal Plant Research
(Gesellschaft fur Arzneipflanzenforschung)**
Dr. B. Frank
AM Grundbach 5　　　　　　　　　　　　Phone: 931 8002271
D-97271 Kleinrinderfeld 1, Germany　　　Fax: 931 8002275

Formerly: German Society for Medicinal Plant Research.

7082

**Egon Stahl Award
(Egon Stahl Preis)**
To honor and encourage younger scientists in the field of pharmacognosy (pharmaceutical biology) and analytical phytochemistry. A monetary award of 4,000 German marks and a silver medal are presented to scientists not older than 40 years of age, and 3,000 German marks and a bronze medal are presented to scientists not older than 30 years of age. Awarded annually. Established in 1955 to honor Egon Stahl, founder of the Society, on his 60th birthday.

7083

**Society for Spinal Research
(Gesellschaft fur Wirbelsaulenforschung)**
Orthopadische Universitatsklinik
　Friedrichsheim
Marienburgstrasse 2
6000 Frankfurt am Main 71, Germany

7084

Georg-Schmorl-Preis
To recognize physicians for outstanding publications in the field of spinal column research. A monetary prize of 5,000 German marks is awarded biennially. Established in 1963 to honor pathologist Georg Schmorl.

7085

**Society for the Promotion of Art and the City of Karlsruhe
(Gemeinschaft zur Forderung der Kunst)**
Postfach 2406
D-76012 Karlsruhe, Germany　　　　　　Phone: 721 387454

7086

Hermann Hesse Prize
To promote talented authors, particularly young persons, who write in the German language. Works of fiction (prose, lyric, essay) written in German are considered for the prize. A monetary prize of 15,000 German marks is awarded triennially. Established in 1956 in memory of Hermann Hesse, the German author.

7087

**Society of Applied Botany
(Vereinigung fur Angewandte Botanik)**
Grisebachstrasse 6
W-3400 Gottingen, Germany　　　　　　Phone: 551 393748

7088

Honorary Member
For recognition of excellent scientific work in the discipline of economic botany. Scientific work is nominated and elected by the Society. A document of honour and free membership in the Society are awarded regularly. Established in 1926. Additional information is available from Professor Dr. W. Franke, Meckenheimer Allee 176, D-5300 Bonn 1, Federal Republic of Germany.

7089

**Society of German Cooks
(Verbandder Koche Deutschlands)**
Steinlestrasse 32
60596 Main, Frankfurt, Germany

7090

Culinary Olympics
To recognize outstanding culinary ability. The competition is built around research and development and the establishment of food trends for the future. Medals are awarded. The Culinary Olympics are held every four years. Winners of the other international regional competitions participate: Culinary World Cup (Luxembourg), Salon Culinaire Mondial (Basel, Switzerland), Food & Hotel Asia Competition (Singapore), Culinary Arts Salon (USA), Hotelympia (London), Chef Ireland (Ireland), and Culinary Masters (Canada). Established in 1900.

7091

Stadt Aachen
Direktorium der Gesellschaft fur die
　Verleihung
des Internationalen Karlspreises
Postfach 1210　　　　　　　　　　　　　Phone: 241 432 7306
52058 Aachen, Germany　　　　　　　　Fax: 241 432 8000

7092

**International Charlemagne Prize of Aachen
(Internationaler Karlspreis zu Aachen)**
For recognition of the most notable achievement in encouraging international understanding and cooperation in the European sphere through political, economic, and literary endeavors. Individuals without respect to nationality, religion, or race who further the idea of the creation of the United States of Europe are eligible. A monetary prize of 5,000 German marks, an illuminated document, and a medallion, one side of which is embossed with the ancient Aachen City seal dating from the 12th century, and the reverse side, which contains an inscription concerning the winner of the prize, are awarded annually. Established in 1949 by a number of public-minded Aachen citizens. Formerly: (1988) Internationalen Karlpreis der Stadt Aachen.

7093

Stadt Buxtehude
Postfach 15 55
21605 Buxtehude, Germany
Phone: 4161 501 0
Fax: 4161 501 318

Formerly: (1981) Buchhandlung Ziemann & Ziemann, Buxtehude.

7094

Buxtehuder Bulle
For recognition of the best book of the year for young people. Books written in German, and published during the preceding year are considered. A monetary prize of 10,000 German marks and a plaque are awarded annually. Established in 1971 by Winfried Ziemann in honor of Ferdinand, the peace-loving bull in a famous children's story.

7095

Stadt Dortmund
Kulturburo
Kleppingstrasse 21-23
W-44122 Dortmund, Germany
Phone: 231 50 25177
Fax: 231 50 22497

7096

Kulturpreis der Stadt Dortmund - Nelly-Sachs-Preis
For recognition of personal achievement that has promoted the cultural relationship between people by stressing the ideals of tolerance and reconciliation. A monetary prize of 30,000 German marks is awarded biennially. Established in 1961.

7097

Stadt Mannheim
Brand, Verwaltungsrat
Oberburgermeister/Repr.
Postfach 2203
W-6800 Mannheim 1, Germany
Phone: 621 2931
Fax: 621 101452

7098

Konrad Duden Preis der Stadt Mannheim
For recognition of an outstanding contribution to the German language. The prize is non-competitive. A monetary prize of 15,000 German marks is awarded biennially. Established in 1960 in memory of Konrad Duden (1829-1911), a linguist and authority on German orthography. Co-sponsored by the Bibliographic Institute of Mannheim.

7099

Preis der Stadt Mannheim fur junge Kunstler
To recognize young artists who show promise of further positive development. Artists in all fields, under the age of 35, are eligible. A monetary prize of 10,000 German marks is awarded biennially.

7100

Schiller Preis der Stadt Mannheim
To recognize individuals who have contributed significantly to cultural development or whose previous work shows promise. The prize is non-competitive. A monetary prize of 25,000 German marks is awarded every four years. Established in 1954 in memory of Friedrich Schiller (1759-1805) who lived and worked in Mannheim as a dramatist from July 27, 1783 to April 9, 1785.

7101

Stadt Pforzheim, Kulturamt
Neues Rathaus
Marktplatz 1
D-75158 Pforzheim, Germany
Phone: 392334
Fax: 392105

7102

Reuchlinpreis der Stadt Pforzheim
For recognition of a work in the humanities that represents an advancement. Works in German are nominated by the Heidelberg Academy of Sciences and the Lord Mayor of Pforzheim. A monetary award of 15,000 German marks is awarded biennially when merited. Established in 1955. Sponsored by the City Council of Pforzheim.

7103

Stadt Schweinfurt
Stadtarchiv und Stadtbibliothek
Friedrich-Ruckert Bau
Martin Luther Platz 20
97421 Schweinfurt, Germany
Phone: 9721 51382
Fax: 9721 51265

7104

Carus Preis
To recognize distinguished scientists of any nationality for research in the field of natural sciences and medicine. A monetary prize of 20,000 German marks and a certificate are awarded biennially. Established in 1961. Given jointly with the Carus Medal of the Leopoldina Academy of Researchers in Natural Sciences.

7105

Friedrich Ruckert Preis
To recognize individuals who, through a single cultural or scientific work, have advanced Ruckert's philosophy of the unity of man and have contributed to the cultural life of the German speaking nations. The award is also intended to honor those who have promoted the works of the poet Friedrich Ruckert. A monetary prize of 10,000 German marks and a plaque or medal in bronze are awarded triennially. Established in 1963.

7106

Stiftung F.V.S.
Postfach 10 60 25
D-20041 Hamburg 1, Germany
Phone: 040 33 04 00
Fax: 040 33 58 60

7107

Joseph Bech Prize
For recognition of exemplary services and personal engagement in the cause of European unity by an individual active in the political or intellectual sphere. A monetary prize of 50,000 German marks is awarded annually. Established in 1977 in memory of the Luxembourg statesman.

7108

Hamburg Max Brauer Prize
For recognition of achievements that benefit the Hanseatic City of Hamburg. A monetary prize of 25,000 German marks is awarded annually. First awarded in 1993.

7109

European Prize for Statesmanship
For recognition of achievements in the field of governmental leadership contributing to European unity. A monetary prize of 300,000 German marks is awarded irregularly. Established in 1969.

7110

European Prize for the Preservation of Historic Monuments (Europa Preis fur Denkmalpflege)
To honor extraordinary contributions to the preservation of Europe's architectural heritage. Individuals and organizations are eligible. A monetary prize of 30,000 German marks is awarded annually, as is a gold medal awarded primarily to communities. Established in 1973.

7111

European Prizes for Folk Art
To reward groups or individuals who have made extraordinary contributions to the preservation and development of European folk traditions in

the area of music or the performing arts. Two monetary prizes of 15,000 German marks each are awarded annually. Established in 1973.

7112
Hanseatic Goethe Prize
To provide recognition for humanitarian achievements in the spirit of Johann Wolfgang von Goethe. A monetary prize of 50,000 German marks is awarded once every two to three years. Established in 1949.

7113
Franz Grillparzer Prize
For recognition of exemplary achievements in the field of Austrian literature. A monetary prize of 30,000 German marks is awarded annually. First awarded in 1991 to mark the 200th anniversary of Grillparzer's birth.

7114
Immanuel Kant Prize
To honor individuals or institutions who have used international law to promote peace in Europe and to improve cooperation with eastern and southeastern European countries. A monetary prize of 100,000 German marks is awarded at irregular intervals. Established in 1991.

7115
Alexander Petrowitsch Karpinskij Prizes
The Karpinskij Prize I recognizes outstanding accomplishments by Russian academics in the field of science, including the social sciences. A monetary prize of 30,000 German marks is awarded annually through the Russian Academy of Sciences. Established in 1977. The Karpinskij Prize II recognizes achievements by Russian academics in the field of environmental science and technology. A monetary prize of 30,000 German marks is awarded annually. Established in 1985.

7116
Hans Klose Prize
To reward exceptional merit in the field of nature conservation in former East Germany.

7117
Montaigne Prize
To recognize eminent Europeans from Romance-language speaking countries who further European humanitarian values in the sphere of literature, the arts, or the humanities. A monetary prize of 40,000 German marks is awarded annually through the University of Tubingen. Established in 1966.

7118
Ossian Prize
To recognize creative contributions to the preservation of smaller, independent linguistic and cultural communities belonging to the European tradition. A monetary award and a medal, with representations of the torch of knowledge and an Irish harp, were awarded annually. Established in 1973. (Discontinued)

7119
Wilhelm Leopold Pfeil Prize
To provide recognition for exemplary forestry practice in Europe. A monetary prize of 30,000 German marks is awarded annually. Established in 1963.

7120
Alexander Puschkin Prize
To recognize extraordinary works in modern Russian literature. A monetary prize of 40,000 German marks is awarded annually in cooperation with the Russian PEN Club. Established in 1989.

7121
Fritz Reuter Prize
To recognize outstanding achievements in the preservation and renewal of traditional Low German language and culture. A monetary prize of 10,000 German marks is awarded annually. Established in 1984 after the amalgamation of five Low German prizes.

7122
Fritz Schumacher Prizes
To provide recognition for outstanding work in the preservation of monuments, architecture, urban areas, and the management of land areas. Established in 1949. Two monetary prizes of 30,000 German marks each are awarded annually (since 1960 through the Technical University of Hanover), as is a Henirich Tessenow Gold Medal (established in 1963), which is presented to an individual whose work corresponds with the ideals of the architect Heinrich Tessenow.

7123
Robert Schumann Prize
To recognize Europeans who, through academic or political works, have contributed to the advocacy of European unity in the political or intellectual domain. A monetary prize of 50,000 German marks is awarded biennially through the Friedrich Wilhelms University in Bonn. Established in 1966.

7124
Shakespeare Prize
To recognize individuals in Great Britain who have rendered distinguished services in the field of literature, the humanities, and the visual arts. A monetary prize of 40,000 German marks is awarded annually. Established in 1937 and re-established in 1967.

7125
Henrik Steffens Prize
To recognize achievements by prominent Scandinavians in the preservation of the European cultural heritage and the promotion of humanitarian values. A monetary prize of 40,000 German marks is awarded annually through the Christian Albrechts University, Kiel. Established in 1935-36 and re-established in 1965.

7126
Strasbourg Prizes and Gold Medal
To reward achievements by French and German school students and postgraduates who have produced pieces of written work displaying in-depth understanding of the other country (France for German candidates; Germany for French candidates). Up to 46 monetary prizes and travel scholarships are awarded annually. Established in 1963 and, since 1975, accompanied by a Strasbourg Gold Medal that recognizes achievements by prominent individuals in the field of Franco-German relations.

7127
Johann Heinrich von Thunen Gold Medal
To recognize significant and innovative operational achievements in European agriculture. The medal is awarded biennially (in alteration with the Justus von Liebig Prizes) through the Agricultural Faculty of the University of Kiel. Established in 1966.

7128
Van Tienhoven Prize
To recognize contributions to the preservation and conservation of natural beauty. A monetary prize of 10,000 German marks was awarded annually. (Discontinued)

7129
Gottfried Von Herder Prizes
To provide recognition for outstanding work by individuals from Albania, Belarus, Bulgaria, Croatia, the Czech Republic, Estonia, Greece, Hungary, Latvia, Lithuania, Poland, Romania, Slovakia, Slovenia, Ukraine, and the remains of Yugoslavia, who have contributed to the preservation and renewal of the European cultural heritage. Seven monetary prizes of 30,000 German marks each are awarded annually. Established in 1963.

7130
Alexander Von Humboldt Medal
To provide recognition for insight and imaginative conceptions introduced in the fields of the conservation of nature and landscaping. A gold medal is awarded annually.

7131
Justus Von Liebig Prize
To provide recognition for outstanding achievements in practical agriculture or in scientific or technical work in the field. Two monetary prizes of 30,000 German marks each are awarded biennially (in alternation with the Johann Heinrich von Thunen Gold Medal) through the Agricultural Faculty of the University of Kiel. Established in 1949.

7132
Freiherr Von Stein Prize
To recognize exemplary or innovative contributions to the common good achieved by individuals, groups, or institutions, notably through the solution of economic, social, and cultural problems resulting from the reunification of Germany. A monetary prize of 50,000 German marks is awarded annually through the Humboldt University, Berlin. Established in 1954 and reoriented in 1993.

7133
Joost van den Vondel Prizes
To recognize exemplary achievements in the field of literature, theatre, music, the fine arts, architecture, and academia by individuals or institutions from the Dutch, Flemish, and Low German cultural areas. Two monetary prizes of 40,000 German marks each are awarded annually through the University of Munster. Established in 1960.

7134
Stuttgart City Council
(Landeshauptstadt Stuttgart)
Kulturamt
Postfach 10 60 34
W-70049 Stuttgart, Germany
Phone: 711 2167673
Fax: 711 2167628

7135
Paul Bonatz Preis
For recognition of exceptional merit in the field of architecture that contributed to the development of the city of Stuttgart. Architects, landscape and garden designers, and engineers are eligible. A certificate and a plaque are awarded every four years. Established in 1959.

7136
Hegel-Preis der Landeshauptstadt Stuttgart
For recognition of an outstanding contribution to the advancement of human sciences. A monetary prize of 20,000 German marks and a certificate are awarded triennially. Established in 1967.

7137
Hans-Molfenter-Preis der Landeshauptstadt Stuttgart/Galerie
For recognition of artistic achievement in fine arts in the Baden-Wurttemberg region. A monetary prize of 30,000 German marks is awarded biennially. Established in 1983 in memory of the Stuttgart artist, Hans Molfenter (1884-1979).

7138
Stuttgart City Prize for Young Composers
(Kompositionspreis der Landeshauptstadt Stuttgart)
To encourage young composers and to introduce them to the public. Composers under the age of 35 whose residence is in Germany are eligible. A monetary prize of 20,000 German marks is awarded annually. Established in 1955.

7139
Stuttgart Literary Prize
(Literaturpreis der Landeshauptstadt Stuttgart)
For recognition of achievement in literature or for translation. Writers and translators from Baden-Wurttemberg are eligible. Three monetary prizes of 10,000 German marks each are awarded biennially to two writers and a translator. Established in 1978.

7140
Umweltpreis der Landeshauptstadt Stuttgart
For recognition of outstanding contributions to the retention of the natural environment of Stuttgart or the improvement of environmental conditions. Candidates must be residents, employees in, or businessmen of the city. Monetary prizes totaling 15,000 German marks and certificates are awarded annually. Established in 1985.

7141
Stuttgart International Animation Film Festival
(Internationales Trickfilm Festival Stuttgart)
Teckstrasse 56
(Kulturepark Berg)
D-70190 Stuttgart 1, Germany
Phone: 711 2622699
Fax: 711 2624980

7142
Stuttgart International Festival of Animated Film
(Internationales Trickfilm Festival Stuttgart)
For recognition of the best animated film of the Stuttgart Festival. The following prizes are awarded: State of Baden-Wurttemberg Award (Preis der Landes Baden-Wurttemberg) - 15,000 German marks; State Capital Stuttgart Award (Preis der Landeshauptstadt Stuttgart) - 10,000 German marks; Suddeutscher Rundfunk Award (Preis des Suddeutschen Rundfunks) - 10,000 German marks; TC-Studios Fred Oed GmbH Award for the Film and Media Exchange (Preis der TC-Gruppe Fred Oed GmbH fur die Film-und Medienborse) - 8,000 German marks; Landeskreditbank Baden-Wurttemberg (L-Bank) Award - 5,000 German marks; Landesgirokasse Stuttgart Award for the best student film - 3,000 German marks; Hellthaler International GmbH Award for the most humorous film - 2,000 German marks; Jury Award - 1,000 German marks; Audience Award (Publikumpreis) - 1,000 German marks; and International Mercedes-Benz Sponsorship Award for the Animated Film (Internationaler Mercedes-Benz Forderpreis fur the Animaionsfilm) - 35,000 German marks, a one-year scholarship to the Baden-Wurttemburg Filmakademie, and the making of a free production. Established in 1990.

7143
Sudwestfunk
Landes Studio Freiburg
Schauinslandstrasse 136
W-7800 Freiburg 1, Germany
Phone: 7221 2762784

7144
Peter-Huchel-Preis fur Lyrik
To promote the development of the contemporary German lyric genre. Works published during the preceding year are considered. A monetary prize of 15,000 German marks is awarded annually. Established in 1983 in memory of Peter Huchel, a poet and editor (1903-1982). Co-sponsored by Land Baden-Wurttemberg.

7145
Uberlingen City Cultural Office
(Kulturamt der Stadt Uberlingen)
Postfach 101 863
Landungsplatz 14
W-88662 Uberlingen, Baden-Wurttemberg,
Germany
Phone: 7551 87215
Fax: 7551 66874

7146
Bodensee-Literaturpreis der Stadt Uberlingen
For recognition of a distinguished literary work or for the entire literary work of a German writer. A monetary prize of 10,000 German marks and a certificate are awarded biennially. Established in 1954. Formerly: Lake Constance Literary Prize.

7147
Universitat Karlsruhe (Technische Hochschule)
Kaiserstrasse 12
W-75 Karlsruhe, Germany   Phone: 721 6080

7148
Heinrich Hertz Preis
For recognition of an outstanding scientific and technological achievement in the field of energy technology. Contributions may be of a technological or technical economic character, or relate to work in experimental or theoretical physics. They should have led to important new findings and developments or be conducive to new developments. A monetary prize of 30,000 German marks and a medal are awarded. Established in 1975 to commemorate the 150th anniversary of the University of Karlsruhe.

7149
Verein von Altertumsfreunden im Regierungs-Bezirk Darmstadt
Schoss/Glockenbau
W-6100 Darmstadt, Germany   Phone: 6151 12 56 45

7150
Eduard-Anthes-Preis fur Archaologische Forschungen
For the promotion of young archaeologists and improvement of archaeological science in Hessen. A dissertation and other works are considered. A monetary prize of 5,000 German marks, a certificate, and travel expenses are awarded. Established in 1984 in honor of Eduard Anthes (1859-1922), an archaeologist.

7151
Verlag Junge Welt
Buchredaktion
Postfach 43
O-1026 Berlin, Germany   Phone: 2 2330

7152
Verlagspreis zur Forderung popularwissenschaftlicher Literatur fur das jungere Lesealter
For recognition of achievement in the field of popular scientific literature for children. Books for children from 3 to 10 years of age in nearly all fields of society, nature, sciences and technology in different literary forms are considered. A monetary prize and certificate are awarded to the illustrator and the author. Awarded annually on the occasion of the Leipzig Book Fair. Established in 1978. Additional information is also available from Mauerstrasse 39-40, O-1080 Berlin, Germany.

7153
Alexander von Humboldt-Stiftung
Jean-Paul-Strasse 12   Phone: 228 833109
D-5300 Bonn 2, Germany   Fax: 228 833199

7154
**Konrad Adenauer Research Award
(Konrad-Adenauer-Forschungs-preis)**
To recognize highly qualified Canadian humanities or social science scholars. Nominations are initiated jointly by the University of Toronto and the Royal Society of Canada. Awardees spend a research period of up to one year in the Federal Republic of Germany and receive a monetary award of between 20,000 and 120,000 German marks. Awarded annually. Established in 1989.

7155
Humboldt Research Awards to Foreign Scholars
To recognize outstanding scientists who have gained an international reputation for accomplishments in research and teaching in natural sciences, engineering, medicine, or the humanities (including arts, law, and social sciences). Full/Associate professors of any age may be nominated by eminent German scholars. Applications are not accepted. Monetary prizes ranging from 20,000 to 120,000 German marks for an extended residence at research institutes in Germany to carry out research of the awardee's own choice are awarded. Up to 200 awards are given annually, 80 of which are granted to natural scientists from the U.S. This part of the award program was donated by the Federal Republic of Germany in 1972 in memory of the 25th inauguration anniversary of the aid program initiated by George Marshall. More than 1,800 Humboldt research awards have been granted since 1972.

7156
Humboldt Research Fellowships
To enable highly qualified foreign scholars holding doctorate degrees to carry out a research project in the Federal Republic of Germany. Individuals under the age of 40 from any discipline may submit applications at any time during the year. Scholars from all nations are eligible. Application requirements include: an examination equivalent to the doctorate degree (Ph.D., C.Sc., or equivalent); high academic qualifications; academic publications; a detailed research plan; command of the German language (humanities scholars); and at least command of the English language for science scholars (including medicine and engineering). Up to 600 fellowships for six to twenty-four months are awarded annually. Family allowance, travel expenses, grants for language classes and 3,200 to 4,000 German marks net monthly are awarded.

7157
Japan Society for the Promotion of Science Research Fellowships Science and Technology
To enable highly qualified German scholars holding doctorate degrees to conduct research in Japan for a period of 12 to 24 months. Open to all disciplines. Applications are coordinated by the Alexander von Humboldt Foundation on behalf of the Japan Society for the Promotion of Science. The following assistance is provided: basic fellowship, housing allowance, health insurance, travel expenses, and special Japanese language courses in Japan. Up to 30 fellowships are awarded annually.

7158
Feodor Lynen Research Fellowships
To enable German scholars, not over age 38, to conduct research abroad in cooperation with a former Humboldt Fellow or Awardee. Open to all disciplines. Application requirements include a doctorate degree, high academic qualifications, a detailed research proposal approved by the host, and a good knowledge of English or the respective country's language. Fellowships are for a period of one to four years. A monthly stipend of up to 2,200 German marks, all travel expenses, and assistance upon return are awarded. Up to 200 fellowships are given annually.

7159
Max Planck Research Awards
To recognize outstanding achievements of internationally renowned foreign and German scientists of any academic discipline and to promote intensive cooperation between foreign and German scientists. One German and one foreign scholar (generally full/associate professors) of any age may be nominated by eminent German scholars (in special cases more than one German and/or foreign scholar may be nominated). Applications are not accepted. Awards are worth up to 200,000 German Marks. They are granted for a period of up to three years to cover short-term research stays at the partner institute, travel expenses, expenses for conferences and workshops, and additional expenses for materials, equipment, and research assistance.

7160
Alexander von Humboldt Award for Scientific Cooperation
To encourage scientific cooperation between Germany and other countries. World-renowned researchers of any age specially engaged in bilateral scientific cooperation in any discipline are eligible. Nominations of foreign scholars are directed by German researchers to the Alexander von Humboldt Foundation, which is entrusted with the selection and administration. The selection of the German scholars is coordinated by partner organizations in other countries. Agreements with counterparts exist in Australia, Belgium, Canada, Denmark, Finland, Israel, France, India, Japan, Korea, Netherlands, South Africa, Spain, and Sweden. Negotiations with counterparts in other countries are being conducted. The award consists of a prize and invitation for a period of several months to do research work in the partner's country.

7161
Philipp Franz von Seibold Award
To recognize a Japanese scholar who has played an important part in promoting understanding between Japan and the Federal Republic of Germany. Awardees spend a lengthy research period in Germany and receive a monetary prize of between 20,000 and 120,000 German marks. Awarded annually. Established in 1978.

7162
Ernst Von Siemens Foundation
(Ernst Von Siemens-Stiftung)
Wittelsbacherplatz 2
W-8000 Munich 2, Germany   Phone: 89 234 2201

7163
Ernst Von Siemens Music Prize
(Ernst Von Siemens-Musikpreis)
For recognition of an outstanding achievement in music. Composers, conductors or performers from anywhere in the world are eligible. A monetary prize of 250,000 German marks is awarded. Awarded annually. Established in 1972.

7164
WACC/Europe and Unda/Europe
c/o European Regional Association of
  WACC
Lachnerstrasse 20
W-8000 Munich, Germany   Phone: 89 13 24 92

7165
International Christian Television Week
(Semaine Internationale de Television Chretienne)
For recognition of achievement in Christian programming. A trophy is awarded triennally. Established in 1969 by Unda and WACB. Additional information is available from Prof. Dr. P. Dusterfeld, Kaiserstrasse 163, D-5300 Bonn, Federal Republic of Germany.

7166
World Organization of Gastroenterology
Technische Universitat Munchen
Medizinischen Klinik und Poliklinik
Ismaningerstrasse 22   Phone: 89 41402250
W-8000 Munich, Germany   Fax: 89 41402456

7167
H. L. Bockus Medal
To recognize an outstanding gastroenterologist for life long dedication to gastroenterology, clinical practice, research and teaching. Individuals may be nominated. A medal is awarded every four years at the time of a World Congress. Established in 1982 in memory of Dr. Henry L. Bockus, the founder of the World Organization of Gastroenterology, and prominent American teacher and clinician.

7168
Brohee Medal
For recognition of outstanding achievement in the field of gastroenterology. Gastroenterologists from either the host country or from countries adjoining or close to the meeting place of the World Congress of Gastroenterology are eligible. An honorarium of $100, a medal, and the opportunity to present a lecture are awarded once every four years. Established in 1966 in memory of Dr. Charles Brohee, the founder of the first International Association of Gastroenterologists, and a prominent Belgian gastroenterologist.

7169
Young Investigator Award
For recognition of original research in gastroenterology. Unpublished works based on clinical or laboratory studies by researchers under 35 years of age are considered. A monetary prize and travel expenses to the World Congress of Gastroenterology are awarded every four years at the time of the World Congress. Established in 1982.

7170
World Veterinary Poultry Association
Institute fur Geflugelkrankheiten
Justus Liebig Universitat
Frankfurter Strasse 87   Phone: 641 7024865
D-35392 Giessen, Germany   Fax: 641 201548

7171
Dr. Bart Rispens Research Award
For recognition of achievements in the field of avian diseases. The authors of the best papers published in *Avian Pathology* during the preceding two calendar years are eligible. A monetary award, medallion, and a certificate are awarded biennially. Established in 1975 in honor of Dr. Bart Rispens. Sponsored by Bart Rispens Trustees and the World Veterinary Poultry Association.

7172
World's Poultry Science Association
Klaus-Groth-Weg 11   Phone: 5141 34251
29229 Celle, Germany   Fax: 5141 34251

7173
Macdougall Medal
To recognize individuals for outstanding services to the Association. Any member of the WPSA is eligible. A gold medal is awarded intermittently by a decision of the Council of WPSA. Established in 1962 in memory of Major I. Macdougall.

Ghana

7174
Ghana Institution of Engineers
PO Box 7042
Accra North, Ghana   Phone: 772005

7175
Charles Deakin Award
To recognize the best final year student in all disciplines of engineering at the Faculty of Engineering, University of Science and Technology, Kumasi. A monetary prize and a certificate are awarded annually. Established in 1972 in honor of Charles S. Deakin, a pioneer in engineering training in Ghana.

7176

Institute of African Studies
Univ. of Ghana
PO Box 73
Legon
Accra, Ghana

Phone: 775512
Fax: 23321

7177

Kwame Nkruma Prize in African Studies
To recognize individuals for contributions in the field of African Studies. Awarded annually.

7178

Pharmaceutical Society of Ghana
PO Box 2133
Accra, Ghana

7179

Fellow
For recognition of contributions in the field of pharmacology. Society members may be nominated by regional branches of the Society, and are voted on at the annual general meeting. A certificate is awarded biennially at the national conference. Established in 1973.

Greece

7180

Academy of Athens
(Akadimie Athinon)
Odos Panepistimiou 28
Athens, Greece

Phone: 1 361 45 52

7181

Academy of Athens Medal
To provide recognition for outstanding services to the Greek nation or to mankind. Gold, silver or copper medals are awarded annually.

7182

Academy of Athens Prize
To provide recognition for a work of scientific or literary importance. Honorary recognition and, if possible, a monetary grant are awarded annually.

7183

National Science, Literature and Art Prize
To provide recognition for the advancement of Greek science, Greek literature, Greek social and historical science, and Greek art. Honorary recognition and, if possible, a monetary prize are awarded annually in alternating years to the different disciplines.

7184

Athenaeum International Cultural Center
8, Amerikis Str.
GR-106 71 Athens, Greece

Phone: 1 3633701
Fax: 1 3635957

7185

Maria Callas Grand Prix for Pianists
To recognize outstanding pianists. Pianists of all nationalities up to 30 years of age are eligible. Entries must be submitted by January 30. One Grand Prix of 3,000,000 drachmas, the Maria Callas Gold Medal (instituted by the Municipality of Athens), and a diploma are awarded. In addition, concert appearances are arranged for Grand Prix winner. The Maria Callas International Music Competitions were established in 1975. Formerly: (1994) Maria Callas International Piano Competition.

7186

Maria Callas Grand Prix, Opera, Oratorio-Lied
To recognize outstanding singers. Male singers not older than 32 years of age and female singers not older than 30 years of age are eligible. Awards are presented in three categories: Opera Singers - female; Opera Singers - male; and Oratorio-Lied. Prizes for each category are as follows: Opera Singers - female, one Grand Prix of 1,500,000 drachmas, a gold medal instituted by the Municipality of Athens, and a diploma; Opera Singers - male, one Grand Prix of 1,500,000 drachmas, a silver medal, and a diploma; Oratorio-Lied, the Alexandra Trianti Grand Prix, a silver medal, and a diploma. In addition, concert appearances are arranged for prize winners. Awarded biannually. The Maria Callas International Music Competitions were established in 1975. Formerly: (1994) Maria Callas International Opera, Oratorio-Lied Competition.

7187

Circle of the Greek Children's Book
Greek Section of IBBY
7, Zalongou Str.
GR-106 78 Athens, Greece

Phone: 1 3602990

7188

Award of the Circle of the Greek Children's Book
(Vravio tou Kyklou tou Ellinikou Paidikou Vivliou)
To encourage professional development and to recognize the winners of the national competition for the writing of various types of children's literature. Greek citizens must submit unpublished works in manuscript form by November 30. Monetary prizes are awarded annually on April 2, the International Children's Book Day. Established in 1970.

7189

Book Prizes of the Circle of the Greek Children's Book
To recognize the writer and illustrator of the best Greek children's book of the previous year. Greek citizens must submit books published in the previous calendar year by November 30. Monetary prizes are awarded annually on April 2, the International Children's Book Day. Established in 1988.

7190

Penelope Delta
To recognize a distinguished writer of Greek children's books for the entire body of his or her work. Greek citizens must be nominated. A diploma is awarded annually. Established in 1988 in memory of Penelope Delta (1874-1941), a famous Greek writer for children.

7191

Greek Ministry of Culture
Section for Theatre and Dance
Odos Aristidou 14
GR-101 86 Athens, Greece

Phone: 1 3230149

7192

Literary Prizes
For recognition in the field of literature. The following are awarded: two prizes each for novels, short stories, poetry, essays or criticism; and one prize each for travel impressions and biographical novels. Each prize includes a monetary award that is determined by the Ministry of Culture each year. Awarded annually.

7193

Prizes for Theatrical Works
Three state prizes for playwrights are awarded every year by the Ministry of Culture for the following: best play, best young playwright, and best children's play. Plays submitted for an award may be in any category of theatrical work; must not have been previously published or performed on stage, TV, or radio; nor have been submitted previously to the judging committee or to any other state committee for theatrical awards. Any playwright may submit a theatrical work for the first of the two state awards; however, consideration for the award to new playwrights is

given to works by authors who have never had a play published or performed in a theater, on radio or TV, or by any amateur or professional theatrical group. Three prizes are given for the best theatrical work: first prize - 1,000,000 drachmas; second prize - 500,000 drachmas; and third prize - 250,000 drachmas. In addition to the monetary award, the first prize-winning play will be performed by one of the state theaters of Greece in the season following that in which the award is made. Three new playwrights are selected for awards as follows: first prize - 500,000 drachmas; second prize - 300,000 drachmas; and third prize - 200,000 drachmas. In addition to naming the prize-winners, the committee may single out other entries for special mention for outstanding qualities of writing, structure, or plot. For children's plays, the prizes are: first prize - 500,000 drachmas; second prize - 300,000 drachmas; and third prize - 200,000 drachmas. Awarded annually.

7194
Greek National Bank Foundation
Odos Aeolou 86
Cotzia Sq.
GR-102 32 Athens, Greece   Phone: 1 321 0411

7195
George Stavros Gold Medal
To provide recognition for scientific research and publication in the fields of science, philology, theology, mathematics, philosophy, law, political and social sciences. The award is given for the general appeal and prestige of the work with regard to contemporary Greek Society. A monetary prize of 500,000 drachmas, a gold medal and a diploma for high distinction are awarded triennially.

7196
George Stavros Silver Medal
To provide recognition for scientific research and publication in the fields of science, philology, theology, mathematics, philosophy, law, and political and social sciences during the preceding five years. A monetary prize of 100,000 drachmas, a silver medal and a diploma for distinction are awarded every five years.

7197
Greek National Tourist Organization
(Office National Hellenique du Tourisme)
2, rue Amerikis
PO Box 1017   Phone: 1 3223111
GR-101 10 Athens, Greece   Fax: 1 3224148

7198
Greek National Tourist Organization Awards
Awards are presented in the following areas related to tourism: prizes for the best photographs presented in the Exhibition of Tourism - FILOXENIA; awards to private individuals and legal entities for contributions to the development of tourism; and awards for literature on tourism in conjunction with the Union of Tourism Writers.

7199
Greek Radio Corporation
(Helliniki Radiophonia)
Messogion 432
Aghia Paraskevi   Phone: 1 639 5204
GR-15342 Athens, Greece   Fax: 1 639 6012

7200
Olympia International Composition Prize
(Thiethnis Diagonismos Moussikis Synthessis)
To recognize and promote the composition of new music. Composers of any nationality who are 40 years of age or younger are eligible. Works must be unpublished and submitted by the end of Feburary. The following monetary awards are presented: First prize - $3,000; Second prize - $2,000; and Third prize - $1,000. Awarded annually in May. Established in 1989 by the Greek Radio Corporation.

7201
Historical and Ethnological Society of Greece
Old Parliament Bldg.
Stadiou St.
Athens, Greece   Phone: 1 3237 617

7202
Gold Medal of the Academy of Greece
For recognition of achievements during the last hundred years to a field of national activities. A gold medal is awarded. Established in 1882.

7203
Near East/South Asia Council of Overseas Schools
American Colleges of Greece
PO Box 60018
GR-15310 Aghia Paraskevi, Greece   Phone: 639 6521

7204
Awards
To promote cooperation among international English language schools in the Near East and in southern Asia. Awards are presented.

7205
Alexander S. Onassis Public Benefit Foundation
Athens Office
56, Amalias Ave.   Phone: 1 3310900902
GR-105 58 Athens, Greece   Fax: 1 3310114

7206
Gold Medal
To recognize the Heads of State whose personalities and efforts on behalf of Society have gained international acclaim. A gold medal designed by Ioannis Pappas is awarded when merited. Established in 1981.

7207
Onassis Competition for the Letters, the Sciences and the Arts
To honor individuals for significant and outstanding contributions to society judged as worthy by the Foundation. The theme of the competition varies, and is decided upon by the Jury of International Prizes. Nominations and applications to the International Committee for the Onassis Prizes are accepted from individuals and institutions. A monetary prize, a silver medal, and a scroll are presented biennially in Athens, Greece. Established in 1979 by the Board of Directors of the Foundation, according to the will of Aristotle Onassis. The award is given in honor of Alexander S. Onassis, son of the late Aristotle Onassis. Formerly: Onassis Prize for Man and Mankind - Athinai; Onassis Prize for Man and Society - Aristotelis.

7208
Onassis Prize for Culture, Arts and Humanities
For recognition of individuals or institutions who have made a notable contribution to cultural values and to the safeguarding of our cultural inheritance, or to scientific progress associated therewith. Nominations and applications to the International Committee for the Onassis Prizes are accepted by individuals and institutions. A monetary award of $250,000, a silver medal, and a scroll are awarded biennially in Athens, Greece. Established in 1979 by the Board of Directors of the Foundation according to the will of Aristotle Onassis. The award is given in honor of Alexander S. Onassis, son of the late Aristotle Onassis. Formerly: Onassis Prize for Man and Culture - Olympia.

7209
Onassis Prize for International Understanding and for Social Achievement
To recognize individuals for their cultural, professional, and social contributions to international understanding. Nominees must actively participate in their relevant activities and must not be in the course of retirement. Nominations are accepted from individuals as well as institu-

tions. A monetary prize of $250,000 is awarded biennially. Established in 1979.

7210
Onassis Prize for the Environment
To recognize individuals or organizations for a notable contribution in the field of the protection of the natural environment, political actions, theoretical or scientific achievements, and other cultural, educational, or philosophical works of high political significance. Nominations and applications to the International Committee for the Onassis Prizes are accepted from individuals and organizations. A monetary prize of $250,000, a silver medal, and a scroll are awarded biennially in Athens, Greece. Established in 1988 by the Board of Directors of the Foundation. Formerly: Onassis Prize for Man and His Environment - Delphi.

7211
Parnassos Society
8 Karytsi Pl.
GR-105 61 Athens, Greece
Phone: 1 3221917
Fax: 1 3249398

7212
Kalokerinos Foundation Prize
To provide recognition for the best play of the year. A monetary award and honorary recognition are awarded annually. Established in 1920.

7213
Parnassos Foundation Prize
To recognize the best poems and novellas. A monetary prize and honorary recognition are awarded annually. Established in 1980.

7214
Scientific Group for Space Research
43 Ellanikou St.
GR-116 35 Athens, Greece
Phone: 1 7219 893

7215
Gold Medal
For recognition of an outstanding contribution to the Scientific Group for Space Research in such areas as the promotion of astronomical, radio-astronomical, and space researchers in Greece, or the establishment of an institute or space research center in Greece. Individuals of any nationality are eligible. A plaque with the sign-mark of the group only and the name of the winner and a diploma in parchment are awarded when merited. Established in 1974.

7216
Thessaloniki Film Festival
(Centre du Cinema Grec)
9 Valaoritou Str.
GR-106 71 Athens, Greece
Phone: 1 3646553
Phone: 1 3646544

7217
Thessaloniki Film Festival
To encourage the production of films and to recognize short and feature length documentary films. Greek citizens may submit applications. The Ministry of Culture awards three monetary prizes for the best film in each category. The awards are given to the directors and producers. In addition, a prize is given for: (1) Best first feature film; (2) Best Screenplay; (3) Best Actor; (4) Best Supporting Actor; (5) Best Actress; (6) Best Supporting Actress; (7) Best Music; (8) Best Sound; (9) Best Makeup; (10) Best Costumes; (11) Best Technical Contribution; and (12) Best Editing. The Jury of the Festival presents honorary awards in the following categories: (1) Grand Prize for the best feature film; (2) Grand Prize for the best documentary; (3) Best Director; (4) Best Director for a first feature film; (5) Best Photography; (6) Best Actress; (7) Best Actor; (8) Best Screenplay; and (9) prizes for music, costumes, editing, decoration, sound, makeup, special effects and supporting roles. Awarded annually in October. Established in 1959 by the International Fair of Thessaloniki.

7218
Women's Literary Society
Evrou 4
GR-115 28 Athens, Greece
Phone: 1 7770 374

7219
Excursions and Journeys in Greece Award
To provide encouragement for the young children of Greece to know and love their country. Unpublished works that have an optimistic spirit and belief in life are considered. A monetary prize is awarded biennially. Established in 1965 by the International Bookshop, Eleftheroudakis, in memory of Kostas Eleftheroudakis, founder of the bookshop.

7220
Historic Novel Award
To provide encouragement for young children to know Greek history from ancient times until today. Unpublished works with an optimistic spirit and belief in life are eligible for consideration. A monetary prize and an edition of the work are awarded annually. Established in 1965 by the publishing organization, HESTIA, in memory of Ioannis Kollards, founder of HESTIA.

7221
Myrto's Book Award
To provide small children with well-written poems. Unpublished works with an optimistic spirit and belief in life are eligible for consideration. A monetary prize is awarded annually. Established in 1974 by Nikos Adamandiadis in memory of his father, Christos Adamandiadis.

7222
Short Stories for Small Children Award
To provide children of pre-school age with well-written short stories. Unpublished works with an optimistic spirit and belief in life are eligible for consideration. A monetary prize is awarded annually. Established in 1971.

7223
World Chess Federation
(Federation Internationale des Echecs (FIDE))
PO Box 70080
GR-166 10 Athens, Greece
Phone: 30 18958251
Fax: 30 19657202

7224
Chess World Champions
For recognition of the winner of the Individual World Championship. Champions have been recognized since 1886.

7225
FIDE Master
For recognition of achievement in the game of chess. The title FIDE Master is awarded for any of the following: a rating of at least 2300 based on the completion of at least 24 related games (the national federation is responsible for the payment of the fee established in the financial regulations); first place in the IBCA World Junior Championship with a rating of 2205; first place in the World Championships, Continental Championships, or the Arab Championships in specific age groups (in the event of a tie in either the Continental or Arab Championships, each of the tied players shall be awarded the title of FIDE Master - subject to a maxium of three players); a score of 50 percent or better on the Zonal Tournament of at least nine games; and runners-up of the IBCA World Championship with a rating of 2205. A title, a medal, and a diploma are awarded annually. Established in 1946.

7226
Gold Diploma of Honor
To recognize an exceptional contribution to international chess over a period of years. A plaque is awarded annually by the FIDE Congress. Established in 1980.

7227

Grandmaster
For recognition of achievement in the game of chess. The title Grandmaster is given for any of the following: two or more Grandmaster results in events covering at least 24 games and a rating of at least 2500 in the current FIDE Rating List, or within seven years of the first title result; qualification for the Candidates Competiton for the World Championship; one Grandmaster result in a FIDE Internzonal tournament; first place in the Women's World Championship or World Junior Championship; first place in the Continental Junior Championship or the Women's Candidates Tournament is equivalent to one nine-game Grandmaster result; a tie for first place in the World Junior Championship (equivalent to one nine-game Grandmaster result); and one 13-game Grandmaster result in the Olympiad, which leads to the award of a full title. A title, a medal, and a diploma are awarded annually. Established in 1946.

7228

International Arbiter
To recognize individuals knowledgeable of the Laws of Chess and the FIDE Regulations for chess competitions. The title of International Arbiter is awarded for all of the following: knowledge of the laws of chess and FIDE Regulations; knowledge of at least one official FIDE language; objectivity; and experience as chief or deputy arbiter in at least four FIDE rated events, such as the following: the final of the National Individual Adult Championship (not more than two), all official FIDE tournaments and matches, international title tournaments and matches, and international chess festivals with at least 100 contestants. For applicants from federations who are unable to organize any tournaments listed in the FIDE rated events listed above, the four events may not be FIDE rated provided the applicant has taken and passed an examination set by the Arbiters Commission.

7229

International Master
For recognition of achievement in the game of chess. The title International Master is given for any of the following: two or more International Master results in events covering at least 24 games, and a rating of at least 2400 in the current FIDE Rating List, or within seven years of the first title result; first place in one of the following events: Women's Candidates Tournament, Zonal Tournament, Continental Individual Championship, Continental Individual Junior Championship, Arab Individual and Junior Championships, Centroamerican-Caribbean Junior Championship, World Under-18 Championship, International Braille Chess Association World (IBCA) Championship (champion is given a rating of 2205), and International Committee of Silent Chess World Championship (in the event of a tie for first place in any of the above listed events, each of the tied players shall be awarded the title - subject to a maximum of three players); the top three medalist in the World Junior Championship; qualification for the Interzonal Tournament of the World Championship cycle; one International Master result in the cycle of the Individual World Championship, of at least 13 games; a score of 66 2/3 percent or better in a Zonal Tournament of at least nine games; first place in the World Under-16 Championship and the Continental Under-18 and Under-16 Championships (equivalent to one nine-game International Master result); and one 13-game International Master result in the Olympiad, which leads to the award of the full title. A title, a medal, and a diploma are awarded annually. Established in 1946.

7230

Woman FIDE Master
To recognize the achievements of a female in the game of chess. The title of Woman FIDE Master is given for any of the following: a rating of at least 2100 after the completion of at least 24 games (the national federation is responsible for the payment of the fee established by the financial regulations); first place in any of the following events: World Girls' Championships in specific age groups, Continental Women's Championship, Arab Women's Championship, Continental Girls Championship in specific age groups, and IBCA Women's World Championship with a rating of at least 2005 (in the event of a tie for first place in any of the above events, each of the tied players will receive the title of WFM - subject to a maximum of three players); and a score of 50 percent or better in a Woman's Zonal tournament of at least nine games. A title, a medal, and a diploma are awarded annually.

7231

Woman Grandmaster
To recognize the achievement of a female in the game of chess. The title of Woman Grandmaster is given for any of the following: two or more Woman Grandmaster results in events covering at least 24 games and a rating of at least 2300 in the FIDE Rating List, or within seven years of the first title result; qualification for the Candidates Competition for the Women's World Championship; one Woman Grandmaster result in the cycle of the Individual Women's World Championship, of at least 13 games; first place in the World Girls Championship (equivalent to one nine-game Woman Grandmaster result); first place in the Continental Girls Championship (equivalent to one nine-game WGM result); and one 13-game Woman Grandmaster result in the Olympaid, which leads to a full title. A title, a medal, and diploma are awarded annually.

7232

Woman International Master
To recognize the achievement of a female in the game of chess. The title of Woman International Master is given for any of the following: two or more WIM results in events covering at least 24 games and a rating of at least 2200 in the FIDE Rating List, within seven years of the first title result; qualification for the Interzonal Tournament for the Women's World Championship; first place in any of the following events: Continental Women's Championship, Arab Women's Championship, World Girls Under-18 Championship, Continental Girls Under-20 Championship. In the event of a tie in any of the above events, each of the tied players will be awarded the title of WIM (subject to a maximum of three players); top three medalists in the World Girl Under-20 Championship; one WIM result in the cycle of the Individual Women's World Championship, of not less than 13 games; a score of 66 2/3 percent or better in a Women's World Championship Zonal Tournament of at least 9 games; first place in the World Girls Under-16 Championship and the Continental Girls Under-18 and Under-16 Championships is equivalent to one 9-game WIM result; or one 13-game WIM result in the Olympiad will result in th award of a full title. A title, medal, and diploma are awarded annually.

Grenada

7233

Foundation for Field Research
PO Box 771
St. George's, Grenada

Phone: 809440-8854
Fax: 809440-2330

7234

Grants for Field Research
To fund natural and social science field research in disciplines that use volunteers from the public. The foundation will consider proposals for field research projects concerning (but not limited to) anthropology, archaeology (prehistoric, historic, classic, or marine), astronomy, botany, ecology, entomology, ethnobotany, ethnology, folklore, folk medicine, herpetology, historic architecture, marine biology, ornithology, paleontology, primatology, and zoology in the countries of Grenada and Liberia only. Researchers in the field in which they are applying for the grant are eligible. A two- to three- page letter must be submitted at least 14 months prior to the project's entering the field. Grants to researchers range from $1,000 to $25,000 for field logistic support, transportation, lodging, food, necessary equipment, and a small stipend. Awards are presented three- to four- times per year. Established in 1982.

Guadeloupe

7235

Association for Cooperation in Banana Research in the Caribbean and Tropical America
c/o IRFA
9, Chateau Sainte Marie
97130 Capesterre, Guadeloupe

Guadeloupe

7236

Awards

For recognition of contributions to research, and surveys on banana production in the Caribbean and tropical America. Awards are presented.

Guatemala

7237

Academia de Geografia e Historia de Guatemala
3a. Avenida 8-35, Zona 1
01001 Guatemala City, Guatemala
Phone: 2 23544
Fax: 2 23544

7238

Academico Honorario

For recognition of achievements or contributions in history, geography, and similar sciences. Members may submit nominations. A diploma is awarded at the convention. Established in 1923.

7239

Instituto Guatemalteco Americano
Comite OPUS
Apdo Postal 691
Ruta 1, 4-05 Zona 4
Guatemala City, Guatemala
Phone: 2 344393
Fax: 2 310022

7240

OPUS Prizes

For recognition of accomplishments in the theater by actors, actresses and playwrights. Awards are given in the following categories: (1) Best theatrical work; (2) Best theatrical work for children; (3) Best direction; (4) Best editing; (5) Best set designer; (6) Best musical score; (7) Best wardrobe; (8) Best lighting effects; (9) Best actress; (10) Best actor; (11) Best supporting actress; (12) Best supporting actor; (13) New actor of the year; (14) New actress of the year; (15) Best make-up; (16) Best monologue interpretation; (17) Best theatrical criticism; and (18) Special Opus category - for the most dedication in the theatrical sphere. A jury makes the nomination. Trophies are awarded annually. Established in 1974.

7241

Premio Norma Padilla

For recognition of the best groups in the annual theatrical exhibition. Established in 1984 in honor of Norma Padilla, a supporter of the theater.

Guyana

7242

Guyana
Office of the President
New Garden St.
Georgetown, Guyana
Phone: 2 51330
Fax: 2 63395

7243

Cacique's Crown of Honor

For recognition of service of an exceptionally high quality beyond the normal call of duty in the public service, local government services, social and voluntary services, industry or trade unions or in any other area of public service. Any citizen of Guyana who has achieved excellence of national or international standing and recognition in the arts, professions, sciences or sport or in any other area of activity; or any institution, organization, or group of persons deserving of official recognition for its contribution to the national economy is eligible. Holders are permitted to use the letters "C.C.H." after their names and to wear as a decoration the insignia and the ribbon. Both individuals and organizations hold Membership of the Order of Service of Guyana. Awarded to two citizens of Guyana annually, or to more if a vacancy exists (limited to 75 living citizens).

7244

Cacique's Crown of Valor

For recognition of the highest acts of bravery in circumstances of great danger involving serious risk to life. Members are permitted to have the suffix "C.C.V." placed after their name and to wear the insignia and the ribbon, and are also appointed as a Member of the Order of Service of Guyana. Awarded when merited.

7245

Disciplined Services Medal for Long Service and Good Conduct

To recognize an individual for 15 years continuous whole-time service in the Police Force, the Prisons Service or the Fire Service. The person recommended shall have no entry in his defaulters' record for a period of twelve years and not more than two bars shall be awarded and each bar shall be awarded after an interval of five years.

7246

Disciplined Services Medal for Meritorious Service

For recognition of sustained and dedicated service of a high order in the Police Force, the Prisons Service or the Fire Service. The holder is entitled to have the suffix "D.S.M." placed after his name and wear the insignia and the ribbon on special occasions. He is also appointed a Member of the Order of Service of Guyana. Awarded annually.

7247

Disciplined Services Star for Distinguished Service

For recognition of distinguished service beyond the normal call of duty in the Police Force, the Prisons Service or the Fire Brigade. A person to whom the Star has been awarded is entitled to have the suffix "D.S.S." placed after his name and wear as a decoration the insignia and ribbon. He is also appointed a Member of the Order of Service of Guyana. Awarded annually.

7248

Efficiency Medal

To recognize an individual for ten years of efficient service. Officers and other ranks of the Guyana Defense Force, the Guyana People's Militia and the Guyana National Service are eligible. A medal is awarded.

7249

Golden Arrow of Achievement

For recognition of outstanding service, an achievement of exceptional nature, or long and dedicated service of a consistently high standard in responsible offices, local government services, social and voluntary services, industry or trade unions, or in any other area of public service. Citizens of Guyana or organizations deserving of recognition for their contribution to the national development are eligible. Individuals are entitled to have the suffix "A.A." placed after their name and to wear the insignia and the ribbon. Both individuals and institutions hold Membership of the Order of Service of Guyana. Awarded to a maximum of five citizens of Guyana annually, or to more if vacancies exist (limited to 200 living citizens).

7250

Golden Arrow of Courage

To provide recognition for an act of bravery. A bronze bar to be worn on the ribbon, the insignia and the right to have the suffix "A.C." placed after the name of the recipient of the Golden Arrow of Courage and appointment as a Member of the Order of Service to Guyana are awarded when merited.

7251

Medal of Service

To recognize any citizen who has given service of a special quality deserving of official recognition, or has given not less than ten years' service with exceptional dedication in the public service, in local government services, in industry or the trade unions, or in any other area of service to the community; or to recognize any institution, organization, or group of persons for its contribution to the national economy. Individual holders of the Medal are entitled to have the suffix "M.S." placed after their names and to wear as a decoration the insignia and the ribbon presented for recipients. Both individuals and institutions hold Membership of the Order of Service of Guyana. Awarded to a maximum of ten citizens of Guyana annually, or more if vacancies exist (limited to 350 living citizens).

7252
Military Service Medal
For recognition of gallantry in action or other distinguished service beyond the normal call of duty. A person to whom the Military Service Medal has been awarded is entitled to have the suffix "M.S.M." placed after his name, and to wear the insignia and ribbon as a decoration on appropriate occasions prescribed in the rules of the Order. He is also appointed a Member of the Order of Service of Guyana.

7253
Military Service Star
For recognition of gallantry in action or service of exceptionally high quality beyond the normal call of duty. This is the highest award of the State for military service by officers of the Guyana Defense Force, the Guyana People's Militia and the Guyana National Service. A person to whom the Military Service Star has been awarded is entitled to have the suffix "M.S.S." placed after his name, and to wear the insignia and ribbon as a decoration on appropriate occasions prescribed in the rules of the Order. He is also appointed a Member of the Order of the Service of Guyana.

7254
Order of Excellence of Guyana
This, the highest award of the State, is given to recognize citizens of distinction and eminence in the field of human endeavor of either national or international significance and importance. Appointment as a Member of the Order of Excellence of Guyana entitles the holder to have the suffix "O.E." placed after his name and to wear the insignia and the ribbon of the Order on special occasions. Membership is limited to 25 citizens of Guyana. Any distinguished citizen of another country who has rendered valuable service to Guyana or whom the State wishes to honor may also be appointed as an Honorary Member of the Order of Excellence. Awarded annually to one citizen.

7255
Order of Roraima of Guyana
To recognize any citizen of Guyana who has rendered outstanding service. Appointment as a Member of the Order of Roraima entitles the holder to use the suffix "O.R." after his name and to wear the insignia and the ribbon of the Order on special occasions. Awarded to one citizen annually. Established in 1976. Foreigners may also be appointed as Honorary Members of the Order of Roraima. (Limited to 35 living citizens.)

7256
President's Commendation for Brave Conduct
For recognition of lesser acts of bravery deserving official recognition of the state. A leaf in gold in miniature, a citation signed by the President over the seal of Guyana, and appointment as an Honorary Member of the Order of Service of Guyana are awarded.

Haiti

7257
Maison Henri Deschamps
Les Enterprises Deschamps - Frisch SA
No. 318 Blvd. J.J. Dessalines   Phone: 2 32215
PO Box 164   Phone: 2 32216
Port-au-Prince, Haiti   Fax: 2 34975

7258
Henri Deschamps Literary Prize
(Prix Litteraire Henri Deschamps)
To promote Haitian literature and encourage new Haitian writers in the field of literary creativity. Haitian citizens may submit previously unpublished manuscripts. The deadline is February 28. A monetary prize of $1,000 plus the publication of 1000 copies of the manuscript are awarded annually at the end of May. Established in 1975 in memory of Henri Deschamps who died in 1958 after having contributed to the progress of literature and education in Haiti for fifteen years. Additional information is available from Roger Gaillard, General Secretary of the Jury.

Honduras

7259
Colegio de Arquitectos de Honduras
Barrio La Guadalupe 3A3, CLL 25
Tegucigalpa, Honduras   Phone: 32 7571

7260
Merit Plaque Award
(Placa de Honor al Merito)
For recognition of achievement and leadership in the field of architecture. Individuals are proposed for recognition in a general assembly. A plaque is awarded when merited. Established in 1979 in honor of Arg. Antonio Bendana A.

Hong Kong

7261
Asiaweek Limited
16F Caxton House
1 Duddell St.
Central District
Hong Kong, Hong Kong   Phone: 5 214555

7262
Asiaweek Short Story Competition
To discover and showcase new literary talent in Asia. The Competition is open to all persons over the age of 18 who were born in Asia, or have been resident in Asia for not less than five years or whose roots are in this region (e.g., Asians living in Europe or North America). Each entry must be in English, wholly original, previously unpublished, and submitted by the author. In evaluating each story, the judges look for the hallmark of true short-story fiction: subtle unity of characterization, theme, and effect. Engraved trophies and the following monetary prizes are awarded: (1) $1,500 - first prize; (2) $750 - second prize; and (3) $500 - third prize. Awarded annually. Established in 1981. Additional information is available from Dr. Isabella Wai, Literary Editor.

7263
Hong Kong Film Awards Association Ltd.
13/F, Tung Wui Commercial Bldg.
27 Prat Ave.   Phone: 852 3677888
Tsimshatsui Kowloon, Hong Kong   Fax: 852 7239597

Formerly: (1994) Hong Kong International Film Festival.

7264
Hong Kong Film Awards
To promote Hong Kong films in Hong Kong and abroad; to recognize local film professionals, to encourage professional development, and to promote film culture. Awards are given in the following categories: Ten Best Chinese Films, Ten Best Foreign Films, Best Film, Best Director, Best Actor, Best Actress, Best Supporting Actor, Best Supporting Actress, Best New Performer, Best Screenplay, Best Cinematography, Best Film

Editing, Best Art Direction, Best Costume and Makeup Design, Best Action Choreography, Best Film Music Score, and Best Film Song. All films with a general release in the preceding year are considered. Trophies are awarded annually at the award ceremony. Established in 1982. Formerly: Hong Kong International Film Festival.

7265

Hong Kong Independent Short Film Competition/Urban Council Short Film Awards
To promote quality non-commercial short films and encourage creature independent production in Hong Kong. Films must be directed by Hong Kong residents with Hong Kong identity cards and must be no longer than 60 minutes in length. Films that have already received awards in a competitive film festival or that have previously been submitted to the competition are not eligible. Films must have been produced on or after April 1, 1991. Awards are presented for fiction, animation, documentary, and experimental. The following awards are presented: Gold Award - $30,000 prize and a trophy for the best film; Silver Award - $20,000 prize and a trophy; and merit awards. Winning and selected films are shown at the Hong Kong International Film Festival. Application deadline is October 20. Awarded annually in spring. Established in 1992. Sponsored by Agfa-Gevaert (HK) Ltd., Cinerent Ltd., Kodak Ltd. (Far East), Salon Films (HK) Ltd., Tai Fung & Co., Union Film Laboratory Ltd., and Universal Laboratory Ltd.

7266

Photographic Salon Exhibitors Association
GPO Box 5099　　　　　　　　　　　Phone: 5 8657222
Hong Kong, Hong Kong　　　　　　　Fax: 5 8657880

7267

Associate of the Photographic Salon Exhibitors Association
For recognition of photographic achievement. Any life member who has, by his participation in the monochrome print, color slide and/or color print divisions of international photographic salons in any year or years, acquired - (1) a Red Seal Award (i.e., with not less than 400 acceptances in international photographic salons); (2) a placement within the top ten on the annual Who's Who List of the Photographic Society of America in any division for any one year; (3) placements from the 11th to the 30th position on the List in the same division for any two years; (4) placements from the 11th to the 25th position on the List in the same division for any three years; and (5) placements from the 11th to the 25th position on the List in the same division for any two years, and has made valuable contributions and rendered useful services to the Association may apply for the Fellowship of this Association. Fellows have the right to the personal use of the letter FPSEA. Application must be made by August 31 each year. A certificate is awarded. Established in 1964.

7268

Association Award
To recognize the ten most prolific exhibitors in international salons in the pictorial monochrome, color print and color slide nature and stereo slide sections. On attaining the top ten position on the Who's Who List of the Photographic Society of America each year, each individual member is entitled to the award of one certificate.

7269

Association Seal
To recognize members for accumulative acceptances in international salons in pictorial monochrome, color print, color slide, nature and stereo sections. The following are awarded: (1) Green Seal - for 100 accumulative acceptances; (2) Blue Seal - for 200 accumulative acceptances; (3) Red Seal - for 400 accumulative acceptances; (4) Bronze Seal - for 600 accumulative acceptances; (5) Silver Seal - for 800 accumulative acceptances; and (6) Gold Seal - for 1,000 accumulative acceptances. The closing date for application is on August 31 each year. Applicant must list total acceptances as well as type of association seal applied for. The computation of acceptances is based on the Who's Who list of the Photographic Society of America.

7270

Awards of E.A. International Salon of Photography
To recognize exhibitors of the Salon presented by the Association in June each year in the City Hall, Hong Kong. Awards are given in two divisions: pictorial color and pictorial monochrome prints. Closing date for entries is April each year. All entries are selected and awarded by nine world-renowned judges in photography in each division. One PSA gold medal, FIAP gold, silver and bronze medals (one each), gold, silver and bronze trophies (one each), one trophy/cup for the best set of Hong Kong and Macau exhibitors and twelve bronze medals are awarded in each division. Established in 1968.

7271

Fellow of the Photographic Salon Exhibitors Association
For recognition of photographic achievement. Any life member who has, by his participation in any division of international photographic salons in any year or years, acquired: (1) a Gold Seal Award or a Silver Seal Award (i.e., with not less than 800 acceptances in the photographic salons); (2) acquired first place on the said List in any division for any one year; (3) placements within the top ten on the said List in the same division for any two years; (4) a placement within the top ten on the said List in any division for one year and placements from the 11th to 25th position in the said List in the same division for any two other years; and (5) a placement within the top ten on the said List in any division for one year and has made valuable contributions and rendered useful services to the Association for two years may apply for the Fellowship of this Association. Fellows have the right to the personal use of the letter FPSEA. Application must be made by August 31 each year. A certificate is awarded. Established in 1964.

7272

Honorary Fellow
To recognize members for outstanding photographic achievement, and for outstanding contributions and services to the Association. Honorary Fellows have the right to the personal use of the letters Hon. FPSEA. A certificate is awarded. Established in 1964.

7273

Honorary Member
To recognize members for photographic achievement, valuable contributions, and useful services to the Association. Honorary Members have the right to the personal use of the letters Hon. PSEA. A certificate is awarded. Established in 1964.

7274

Photographic Society HKUSU
Univ. of Hong Kong, Student Union　　Phone: 8583567
HKUSU, Pokfulam Road　　　　　　　Phone: 5479567
Hong Kong, Hong Kong　　　　　　　Fax: 8586440

7275

International Student Salon of Photography
To promote the art of photography and to encourage friendship among photography students all over the world. Awards are given in two categories: (1) monochrome and color prints; and (2) color slides. Students may submit entries before October 15. The following prizes are awarded in each category: (1) Gold trophy; (2) Silver trophy; (3) Bronze trophy; and (4) Bronze medal. Awarded annually. Established in 1960. Sponsored by Jebsen & Company Ltd.

7276

Urban Council Public Libraries Office
City Hall High Block, 6th Fl.
Edinburgh Pl.　　　　　　　　　　　　Phone: 5 92212688
Hong Kong, Hong Kong　　　　　　　Fax: 5 8772641

7277
Awards for the Best Produced Books in Hong Kong
To recognize the outstanding achievements by local publishers and printers, and to encourage an even higher standard of excellence in book production. Books published or printed for the first time in Hong Kong during the preceding calendar year and deposited under the Books Registration Ordinance will be considered. Awards are presented in the following categories: art book, children's book, general book - color, and general book - black and white. A trophy and certificate of merit will be presented to the winning publisher and printer in each category. The deadline for nominations is May 16.

7278
Hong Kong Biennial Awards for Chinese Literature
To recognize the outstanding achievements of established Hong Kong writers and to encourage them to write quality literary work. Awards are presented in the following categories: fiction, prose, poetry, and children's literature. Entries must have been published in Hong Kong within the preceding two years and written in Chinese. A monetary prize of HK$50,000 for each adult work and HK$30,000 for each children's work is awarded biennially. The deadline for nominations is February 29.

7279
Urban Council Awards for Creative Writing in Chinese
To cultivate interest in creative writing in Chinese. Awarded to residents of Hong Kong aged 16 and older in the following categories: prose, poetry, fiction, literary appreciation, children's story book, and children's picture book. A monetary prize of HK$10,000 for each adult category and HK$8,000 for each chldren's category is awarded biennially. The deadline for entries is August 31. Established in 1979.

7280
World Organization of National Colleges, Academies and Academic Associations of General Practitioners/Family Physicians
PO Box 790
Shatin Central   Phone: 852 6036902
New Territories, Hong Kong   Fax: 852 6036926

7281
Fellow
For recognition of outstanding service to the Organization. Active members of WONCA are eligible. Winners are announced at world meetings when merited. Established in 1976.

7282
Honorary Life Direct Member
To recognize individuals for achievements within the organization. Past Presidents and Fellows may be nominated. A certificate is awarded triennially at the World Conference. Established in 1989.

7283
WONCA Foundation Award
To foster and maintain high standards of care in general practice/family medicine by enabling physicians to travel to appropriate countries to instruct in general practice/family medicine, and appropriate physicians from developing countries to spend time in areas where they may develop special skills and knowledge in general practice/family medicine. Established by a donation from the Royal College of General Practitioners.

Hungary

7284
Association of Hungarian Geophysicists
(Magyar Geofizikusok Egyesulete)
Fo utca 68
PO Box 433   Phone: 361 201 9815
H-1027 Budapest 2, Hungary   Fax: 361 201 9815

7285
Best First Presentation
To recognize the best first presentation by a junior member at the biannual meeting of young geophysicists. Awarded at the annual General Meeting.

7286
Best Papers of the Year
To recognize the two best papers of the year published by members of the association in one of the Hungarian geophysical journals (*Magyar Geofizika, Geophysical Transactions, Acta Geodaetica, Geophysica et Montanistica*). Awards are presented for the best theoretical paper and for best case history at the annual General Meeting.

7287
Laszlo Egyed Memorial Award
(Egyed Laszlo emlekerem)
For recognition of research achievements in geophysics and of activity in technical publication and teaching. Society members are eligible. A medal is awarded biennially. Established in 1986 in memory of Laszlo Egyed, former professor of geophysics at the Eotvos Lorand (Budapest) University and founder of the Association.

7288
Lorand Eotvos Memorial Medal
For recognition of achievements in research, in both theoretical and practical geophysics, during the past six years. Hungarian geophysicists are eligible. A medal with the figure of R. Eotvos on one side is awarded triennially. Established in 1957.

7289
Honorary Membership
For recognition of outstanding achievements in geophysics and related sciences, or in attainment of the association's purposes. Both Hungarian and foreign citizens are eligible. Honorary memberships are awarded triennially. Established in 1954.

7290
J. Renner Memorial Award
To recognize Association members of at least 10 years for performing voluntary activities in organizing and developing the Association life or educational works. Two medals are awarded annually. Established in 1986.

7291
Association of Hungarian Journalists
(Magyar Ujsagirok Orszagos Szovetsege)
Andrassy utca. 101   Phone: 1 221 699
H-1062 Budapest, Hungary   Fax: 1 221 881

7292
Aranytoll
(Golden Pen)
For recognition of outstanding journalistic activities. Retired individuals are eligible. A medal is awarded annually. Established in 1978.

7293
Association of Hungarian Librarians
(Magyar Konyvtarosok Egyesulete)
Szabo Ervin ter 1   Phone: 1 1182050
H-1088 Budapest, Hungary   Fax: 1 1182050

7294
Medal for Serving the Association of Hungarian Librarians
(Magyar Konyvtarosok Egyesuleteert Emlekerem)
For recognition of outstanding contributions to the activities of the Association and to Hungarian librarianship and information science. Outstanding achievements in the field of library and information science

and archivism are considered. Nominations must be submitted by May 1. Five plaques are awarded annually. Established in 1985.

7295

Bela Bartok Nemzetkozi Korusverseny Irodaja
Pf 67
H-4001 Debrecen, Hungary
Phone: 52 313977
Fax: 52 316040

7296

Bela Bartok International Choir Contest
To present twentieth century, especially contemporary, choral works in an understandable and convincing way; to popularize high-level collective singing; to assist in creating possibilities for meetings of composers and choral artists of different nationalities; and to widen the relationship between modern music and the public. Only amateur choirs may participate, however conductors, piano accompanists, or choir soloists may be professional artists. Singers who are members of several different choirs are allowed to appear only in one ensemble in the contest. Choirs may compete in several categories. If a mixed choir enters other categories, their number must be decreased according to the staff limit of the given category. Choirs may enter the following categories: children's choir (maximum age 15 years), youth choirs (youth mixed choirs and youth ladies') maximum age 21 years, equal voices (ladies' and male choirs), chamber choirs, and mixed choirs. In all categories except mixed choirs, first place prize is 75,000 forints, second place prize is 60,000 forints, and third place prize is 45,000 forints. The mixed choir category first place prize is 100,000 forints, second place prize is 75,000 forints, and third place prize is 50,000 forints. Choirs scoring 85 points or more and placed first or second in their own categories may compete for the Grand Prize of 150,000 forints. The conductor of the choir winning the Grand Prize receives 30,000 forints. Folklore works are included in the program to give the contest the character of a song festival. The most successful choirs in this area are awarded festival diplomas. Special prizes consisting of monetary awards, diplomas, and plaquettes are also available for certain categories. The contest is held biennially the first whole week of the month of July.

7297

Budapest City Council
V. Varoshaz utca 9-11
H-1840 Budapest V, Hungary

7298

Artistic Award
For recognition of major artistic achievement or cultural organizational activity in theater, film, dance, music, photography, literature, and fine and industrial arts. A monetary prize of 7,000 forints and a medal were awarded annually on April 4, National Commemoration Day. (Discontinued)

7299

Ferenc Foldes Award
In recognition of outstanding work in the education of Budapest youth. A monetary prize of 7,000 forints and a medal were awarded annually on Educators' Day. (Discontinued)

7300

For Budapest Award
In recognition of outstanding achievement in any field. Up to 26 prizes of 60,000 forints and a medal are awarded annually on national holidays, jubilees, or in connection with events in the Capital.

7301

"Honorary Citizen" Title
In recognition of outstanding activity in the development, prosperity, and good fame of the city of Budapest. A gold medal, and a honorary citizen's diploma is awarded annually on November 17, Budapest Day, which commemorates Budapest's unification in 1873.

7302

Jozsef Madzsar Award
In recognition of outstanding achievements in health, preventive medicine, maternal and infant care, and public health organization. A monetary prize of 7,000 forints and a medal were awarded annually on April 4, National Commemoration Day. (Discontinued)

7303

Outstanding Service to Budapest Award
In recognition of outstanding work in public service, production, and public administration. A monetary prize of 7,000 forints and a medal were awarded annually on April 4, National Commemoration Day. (Discontinued)

7304

Pro Urbe Budapest Award
To recognize the achievement of outstanding results, lasting value, and respect. Up to six prizes of 150,000 forints and a medal are awarded annually on November 17, Budapest Day.

7305

Pro Urbe Prize
In recognition of an outstanding achievement in the development of the city of Budapest. A monetary award of 15,000 forints and a medal were awarded annually on February 13, the anniversary of Budapest's liberation. (Discontinued)

7306

Ferenc Reitter Award
In recognition of outstanding work in the capital city architecture, historic preservation, and public transportation. A monetary prize of 7,000 forints and a medal were awarded annually on April 4, National Commemoration Day. (Discontinued)

7307

Federation of Hungarian Medical Societies
(Magyar Orvostudomanyi Tarsasagok es Egyesuletek Szovetsege)
Phone: 112 3807
Columbus utca 11
H-1145 Budapest, Hungary
Phone: 111 6687
Fax: 183 7918

7308

MOTESZ Prize
(MOTESZ-Dij)
For recognition of professional work and knowledge. Hungarian citizens who have been members of one of the Federation societies for at least five years may be nominated. A monetary prize of 50,000 forints, a plaque, and a certificate are awarded annually. Established in 1985.

7309

Geodetic and Cartographic Society
(Geodeziai es Kartografiai Egyesulet)
Alsoerdosor 12
H-1074 Budapest, Hungary
Phone: 1 1420 624

7310

Deak Lazar Memorial Medal
(Lazar Deak Emlekerem)
To recognize Society members for expert work in geodesy, photogammetry, topography and cartography. Hungarian citizens who are members of the Society may be nominted. Two bronze medals are awarded biennially. Established in 1958, in memory of Lazar-Deak, the first known Hungarian map-maker in the 16th century. Additional information is available from Hungary National Office of Lands and Mapping, Kossuth ter 11, H- 1860 Budapest 55, Hungary, phone: 1 1313 736.

7311
Hungarian Academy of Sciences
(Magyar Tudomanyos Akademia)
Roosevelt-ter 9 Phone: 1 382 344
H-1051 Budapest V, Hungary Fax: 1 328 943

7312
Hungarian Academy of Sciences Gold Medal
For recognition of outstanding achievements in science, science policy and science organization. A medal is awarded annually.

7313
Hungarian Association of Non-professional Film and Videomakers
(Magyar Amatorfilm es Video Szovetseg)
Matyas Kiraly utca 7
H-1121 Budapest, Hungary Phone: 1 559 349

7314
Golden Deer
(Arany Szarvas)
For recognition of a personal contribution to the field of amateur filmmaking. Individuals may be nominated for personal activity. A medal and plaque are awarded annually. Established in 1984.

7315
Grand Prize of the National Festival of Hungarian Non-professional Film and Videomakers
(Orszagos Amatorfilm Fesztival Nagydija)
For recognition of achievement in the quality of amateur films. Films may be nominated for the festival. A monetary prize and an artistic object are awarded annually. Established in 1961. From 1935 to 1943, the award was presented as the St. Stephen's Cup in memory of St. Stephen, the first king of Hungary and founder of the Hungarian State.

7316
Prize of the Best National Collection
(Legjobb nemzeti kollekcio dija)
For recognition of the best collection of amateur films at the International Festival of Prize-Winning Films at Gyor, Hungary. Films may be nominated. An artistic object is awarded irregularly when the festival is held. Established in 1972.

7317
UNICA Prize for the Best National Collection
(UNICA - MAFSZ Nemzetek dija)
For recognition of the best national collection of films presented at the UNICA World Festival of non-professional films. Films may be nominated. A cup is awarded annually. Established in 1975.

7318
Hungarian Astronautical Society
(Magyar Asztronautikai Tarsasag)
Fo utca 68
H-1027 Budapest, Hungary Phone: 1 159813

Formerly: Kozponti Asztronautikai Szakosztaly.

7319
Fono Award
(Fono Albert Erem)
For recognition of achievements in astronautics or space research. Members of the society may be nominated. A plaque is awarded annually. Established in 1980 in honor of Prof. Albert Fono, engineer, first president of the Society and a pioneer of jet-propulsion.

7320
Nagy Award
(Nagy Erno Erem)
For recognition of achievements in astronautics or space research. Members of the society under 35 years of age may be nominated. A plaque is awarded annually. Established in 1980 in honor of Erno Nagy, engineer, first secretary of the Society, and a specialist of space technlogy.

7321
Hungarian Chemical Society
(Magyar Kemikusok Egyesulete)
Fo utca 68 Phone: 1 2016883
H-1027 Budapest, Hungary Fax: 1 2018056

7322
Ignac Pfeifer Medal
To recognize members of the Society who have worked 20 to 25 years in the chemical industry with excellent results. A bronze medal is awarded annually. Established in 1968.

7323
Karoly Than Medal
To recognize members of the Society for outstanding work in the Society. A bronze medal is awarded annually. Established in 1955 in memory of Karoly Than, professor at the University of Sciences in Budapest.

7324
Vince Wartha Medal
To recognize members of the Society for outstanding work in the field of chemistry. A bronze medal is awarded annually. Established in 1955 in memory of Vince Wartha, professor at the Technical University of Budapest.

7325
Hungarian Electrotechnical Association
(Magyar Elektrotechnikai Egyesulet)
  Phone: 1 530 117
Kossuth Lajos ter 6-8 Phone: 1 120 662
H-1055 Budapest, Hungary Fax: 1 534 069

7326
Blathy Award
(Blathy Dij)
To recognize Association members for outstanding activity for the Association. A medal with the portrait of Otto Blathy in relief is awarded biennually. Established in 1957 in honor of Otto Blathy, a Hungarian engineer and inventor of the transformer.

7327
Csaki Award
(Csaki Dij)
For recognition in the field of electrical engineering. Established in 1987.

7328
Deri Award
(Deri Dij)
To recognize the authors of papers describing their outstanding practical creative work and its results in the field of heavy-current electrical engineering. Papers published in one of the periodicals of the Association are eligible. A medal, with the portrait of Miksa Deri in relief, is awarded annually. Established in 1959 in honor of Miksa Deri, a Hungarian engineer and inventor of the transformer.

7329

Electrotechnical Award
(Electrotechnical Dij)
To recognize an Association member's lifework or outstanding activity in the Association. A medal is awarded annually. Established in 1968.

7330

Epitoipar Kivalo Munkaert
For recognition in the field of electrical engineering. Established in 1985.

7331

Ipar Kivalo Munkaert
For recognition in the field of electrical engineering. Established in 1984.

7332

Kalman Kando Award
(Kando Kalman Dijasok)
To recognize Association members for continuous outstanding activity in regional groups of the Association. Members of the Association for five years are eligible. A medal with the portrait of Kalman Kando is awarded annually. Established in 1979 in honor of Kalman Kando, a Hungarian engineer in the field of electrical railway engines.

7333

Kisz KB Aranykoszorus Kisz Jelveny
For recognition in the field of electrical engineering. Established in 1987.

7334

Jozsef Liska Award
(Liska Jozsef Dijasok)
To recognize Association members for outstanding theoretical, practical, and educational activity. Membership in the Association for 10 years is necessary for consideration. A medal with the portrait of Jozsef Liska is awarded annually. Established in 1983 in honor of Jozsef Liska, former professor of the Polytechnical University of Budapest, and honorary president of the Association.

7335

Magyar Elektrotechnikai Egyesulet Mtezs
For recognition in the field of electrical engineering. Established in 1970.

7336

MEE Award
(MEE Kivalo Dij)
Awarded annually. Established in 1988.

7337

Nivo Award
(Nivo Dij)
For recognition in the field of electrical engineering. Established in 1987.

7338

Sandor Straub Award
(Straub Sandor Dijasok)
To recognize Association members for outstanding activity in the field of electrical household appliances. A medal is awarded annually. Established in 1985 in honor of Sandor Straub, a Hungarian engineer.

7339

Szocialista Kulturaert
For recognition in the field of electrical engineering. Established in 1987.

7340

Janos Urbanek Award
(Urbanek Janos Dijasok)
To recognize Association members for outstanding activitiy in the field of electrical lighting. A medal is awarded annually. Established in 1984 in honor of Janos Urbanek, a Hungarian engineer.

7341

Laslo Verebely Award
(Verebely Laszlo Dijasok)
To recognize members of the Association for outstanding theoretical, practical and educational activity in the field of electrical networks, traction and defense against lightning. Membership in the Association for 10 years is necessary for consideration. A medal with the portrait of Laszlo Verebely is awarded annually. Established in 1983 in memory of Laszlo Verebely, former professor of the Polytechnical University of Budapest, and chairman of the Association in 1938-41.

7342

Zipernowsky Prize
(Zipernowsky Dij)
To recognize authors of papers read at scientific sessions and published in one of the periodicals of the Association; and to honor members for their long, successful activity in the Association. A medal, with a portrait of Karoly Zipernowsky in relief, is awarded annually. Established in 1913 by the private foundation of Karoly Zipernowsky, President of the Association from 1905 to 1938.

7343

Hungarian Forestry Association
(Orszagos Erdeszeti Egyesulet)
Fo-utca 68
H-1027 Budapest, Hungary   Phone: 1 201 6293

7344

Albert Bedo Award
(Bedo Albert emlekerem)
For recognition of achievements in the science, profession or social activities concerning forest production. Members of the Association are eligible. A monetary prize and a plaque are awarded annually by the General Assembly. Established in 1957 in honor of Albert Bedo, sylviculturist and legislator, prominent in the development of independent branch forestry.

7345

Clusius Carolus Award
(Carolus Clusius emlekerem)
For recognition of scientific, practical and social achievements in the field of mycology in Hungary. Members of the Association and exceptional persons from abroad are eligible. A plaque is awarded annually by the General Assembly. Established in 1966 in honor of Clusius Carolus, author of the scientific work, "Carolus Clusius codex" in mycology and botany.

7346

Karoly Kaan Award
(Kaan Karoly emlekerem)
For recognition of outstanding achievements over a long period of time promoting forestry. Selection is by nomination. A monetary prize and a plaque are awarded annually by the General Assembly. Established in 1984 in honor of Karoly Kaan, former state secretary, reorganizer of the Hungarian forestry politics, and founder of the Hungarian nature protection.

7347

Hungarian Hydrological Society
(Magyar Hidrologiai Tarsasag)
PO Box 433   Phone: 1 2017655
H-1371 Budapest, Hungary   Fax: 1 15612125

7348

Odon Bogdanfy Medal
(Bogdanfy Odon Emlekerem)
For recognition of scientific activities of high quality. Only original research by members or honorary members of the Society involving new results is accepted for nomination. A medal is awarded annually. Estab-

lished in 1951 in memory of Odon Bogdanfy, a prominent Hungarian hydraulic engineer (1863-1941).

7349
Jeno Kvassay Prize
(Kvassay Jeno dij)
For recognition of an exceptional contribution to any aspect of water management by members or honorary members of the Society. A monetary prize and a medal are awarded annually at the convention. Established in 1970 in memory of Jeno Kvassay, eminent Hungarian water engineer (1850-1919). Formerly: Pal Vasarhelyi Prize.

7350
Hugo Lampl Prize
(Lampl Hugo Dij)
To recognize outstanding contribution to the development of new water works and framers. Three to five medals are awarded. Estblished in 1993.

7351
Ferenc Schafarzik Medal
(Schafarzik Ferenc Emlekerem)
For recognition of members of the Society. A medal is awarded annually. Established in 1942 in memory of Dr. Schafarzik, the founding president of the Society (1854-1927) on the 25th anniversary of the formation of the Hungarian Geological Society, which was the legal predecessor of the Hungarian Hydrological Society.

7352
Hungarian Mining and Metallurgical Society
(Orszagos Magyar Banyaszati Es Kohaszati Egyesulet)
Foutca 68
H-1027 Budapest, Hungary   Phone: 1 423943

7353
Marton Debreczeni Medal
For recognition of the design, initiation, and operation of a mining and metallurgy project. Members of the society are eligible. Two medals are awarded annually. Established in 1972 in memory of Marton Debreczeni, inventor of the auger.

7354
Christoph Traugott Delius Medal
To recognize authors of outstanding technical books on mining and metallurgy. Members of the society are eligible. A medal is awarded annually. Established in 1972 in memory of Christoph T. Delius, first professor of mining at the Academy of Mining in 1770.

7355
International Committee for Studies of Bauxites and Aluminum-Oxides-Hydroxides Medal
For recognition of outstanding achievements in the study of bauxites or aluminum-oxides-hydroxides, and for the advancement of international scientific cooperation. Hungarian or foreign ICSOBA members are eligible. A maximum of three silver medals is awarded on the occasion of ICSOBA's General Assembly. Established in 1973.

7356
Antal Kerpely Medal
For recognition of the development of new production technology, and for the introduction of new products in the field of metallurgy. Members of the society are eligible. A medal is awarded annually. Established in 1967 in memory of Antal Kerpely, a technical writer of renown in Europe.

7357
Samuel Mikoviny Medal
For recognition of noteworthy accomplishments in research, science, and education. Members of the society are eligible. Two medals are awarded annually. Established in 1950 in memory of Samuel Mikoviny, first professor of the Mining Officers Training School.

7358
Antal Pech Medal
For recognition of exceptional scientific and technical articles published in the society's periodicals. Members of the society are eligible. Three medals are awarded annually. Established in 1963 in memory of Antal Pech, creator of the Hungarian technical language of mining.

7359
Vilmos Soltz Medal
For recognition of contributions to the society. Members of the society are eligible. A medal is awarded annually. Established in 1967 in memory of Vilmos Soltz, a founder of the society.

7360
Zsigmond Szentkiralyi Medal
For recognition of significant results in theoretical and practical mining development. Members of the society are eligible. A medal is awarded annually. Established in 1972 in memory of Zsigmond Szentkiralyi, a pioneer of the Hungarian language mining literature.

7361
Aladar Wahlner Medal
For recognition of achievement in lowering production costs, and for publishing activities in the field of mining and metallurgy. Members of the society are eligible. A monetary prize and a medal are awarded annually. Established in 1926 in memory of Aladar Wahlner, head of the Mine Authority Department.

7362
Samu Z. Zorkoczy Medal
For recognition of valuable contributions to the development of the society, and for publishing activities. Members of the society are eligible. Two medals are awarded annually. Established in 1936 in memory of Samu Z. Zorkoczy, President of the society.

7363
Vilmos Zsigmondy Medal
For recognition of contributions to the development of deep drilling technology, and for the improvement of water supplies. Members of the society are eligible. A medal is awarded annually. Established in 1967 in memory of Vilmos Zsigmondy, a pioneer of Hungarian artesian and thermal water prospecting.

7364
Hungarian Music Council
PO Box 47
V. Vorosmarty ter 1   Phone: 1 184243
H-1364 Budapest, Hungary   Fax: 1 1178267

7365
Budapest International Composers' Competition
To promote contemporary music and to encourage young composers. Awards are given for compositions in a variety of categories in different years as the occasion arises, such as the commemoration of the anniversary of a composer. Some of the past categories have been: piano solo, piano trio, wind quintet, and string quartet. Composers of all nationalities under 40 years of age may enter by February 28 each year. Monetary prizes are awarded. The prize-winning works are broadcast by the Hungarian Radio; prize-winning scores are published by Editio Musica, Budapest; and prize-winning composers are guests of the Budapest Spring Festival. Awarded annually. Established in 1982 by the Association of Hungarian Musicians, the Budapest Spring Festival, Editio Musica, and the Budapest and Interconcert Festival Office. (Temporarily suspended)

7366

Hungarian PEN Centre
(Magyar PEN Centre)
Vorosmarty ter 1
H-1051 Budapest, Hungary　　　　　　　Phone: 1 184143

7367

Hungarian PEN Club Medal
(PEN Emlekerem)
For recognition of a translation of a Hungarian literary work into foreign languages. A medal is awarded when merited. Established in 1948.

7368

Hungarian Pharmaceutical Society
(Magyar Gyogyszereszeti Tarsasag)
Zrinyi-u 3
H-1051 Budapest, Hungary　　　　　　　Phone: 1 181573

7369

Societas Pharmaceutica Hungarica, and Kazay Endre Award
For recognition of achievement in the field of pharmacology. A plaque is awarded at the convention.

7370

Hungarian Publishers and Booksellers Association
(Magyar Konyvkiadokes Konyvterjesztok Egyesulese)
PO Box 130
Vorosmarty ter 1　　　　　　　Phone: 1 1184758
H-1051 Budapest, Hungary　　　　　　　Fax: 1 1184581

7371

Book of the Year
For recognition of the best published book of the year in all categories of literature. Co-sponsored by Artisjus, Hungarian Organization for Defence of Copyright.

7372

Hungarian Scientific Society for Food Industry
(Magyar Elelmezesipari Tudomanyos Egyesulet)
PO Box 5
Akademia utca 1-3　　　　　　　Phone: 1 1122859
H-1361 Budapest, Hungary　　　　　　　Fax: 1 1310288

Formerly: Hungarian Society for Food Industry.

7373

Louis de Saint Rat Award
For recognition of contributions in the food industry. Authors, publishers, and editors are eligible. A monetary prize and a medal are awarded annually. Established in 1987 by Mrs. Magda de Saint Rat in memory of her husband, Louis de Saint Rat, who contributed theoretical work to the field of the food industry.

7374

Tamas Kosutany Memorial Medal
To recognize Society members for many years of prominent activity in the Society. Two or three medals are awarded annually. Established in 1957.

7375

Elek Sigmond Memorial Medal
For recognition of scientific work and activity. Two memorial plaques are awarded annually. Established in 1956.

7376

Gabor Torok Memorial Medal
For recognition of technical development within the food industry field. Members of the Society are eligible. Two plaques are awarded annually. Established in 1969.

7377

Hungarian Scientific Society of Energetics
(Energiagazdelkodasi Tudomanyos Egyesulet)
Kossuth Lajos-ter 6-8　　　　　　　Phone: 1 532751
H-1055 Budapest, Hungary　　　　　　　Fax: 1 533894

7378

Laszlo Dobo Prize
For recognition of outstanding work in the technical, scientific, and managerial aspects of energy conservation. Hungarian citizens are eligible. Copper medals with the Society's emblem in gold, silver, or bronze are awarded annually. Established in 1964.

7379

Eminent Activist Medal
For recognition of outstanding service to the Society and to the Hungarian economy. Hungarian citizens who have been members of the Society for at least three years are eligible. A copper medal with the Society's emblem in bronze relief is awarded annually. Established in 1970.

7380

Janos Andras Segner Prize
For recognition of outstanding technical, scientific, economic, or publishing activity in the field of energy conservation. Hungarian citizens who have been members of the Society for at least five years are eligible. Bronze medals with gold plating are awarded annually. Established in 1964.

7381

Geza Szikla Prize
For recognition of outstanding achievements in energy conservation, especially in technology, economics, management, work safety, education, and design; and for valuable service to the Society. Hungarian citizens who have been members of the Society for at least five years are eligible. Copper medals with a gold emblem of the Society are awarded annually. Established in 1964.

7382

Hungarian Society for Human Settlements
(Magyar Urbanisztikai Tarsasag)
Gellerthepy u. 30-32　　　　　　　Phone: 568 294
H-1016 Budapest, Hungary　　　　　　　Fax: 568 294

7383

Janos Hild Medal
(Hild Janos Emlekerem)
To recognize a designer for an outstanding contribution to human settlement development. A plaque was awarded annually. Established in 1972 by the Ministry of Construction and Settlement Development. (Discontinued in 1991)

7384

Hungarian Society of Textile Technology and Science
(Textilipari Muszaki es Tudomanyos Egyesulet)
Fo utca 68　　　　　　　Phone: 1 2018 782
H-1027 Budapest, Hungary　　　　　　　Fax: 1 561 215

7385

Kivalo Egyesuleti Munkaert Erem
For recognition of outstanding social activity in the work of the Society. Members of the Society who have been active, and have done successful

work for a long time are eligible. A monetary award and a medal are awarded annually at the general assembly. Established in 1968.

7386
Lehr Ferenc Textilipari Ifjusagi Erem
For recognition of excellent results in scientific, practical, publishing or educational activities. Members of the Society who are under 35 years of age and who do active work in the Society are eligible. A monetary award and a medal are awarded annually at the professional conference. Established in 1985 in memory of Lehr Ferenc, an outstanding personality in the Hungarian textile industry.

7387
A Textilipar Fejleszteseert Erem
For recognition of outstanding official work in an area of the textile industry. Members of the Society are considered for outstanding results, practical or theoretical, in the textile industry. A monetary award and a medal are presented annually at the general assembly. Established in 1957.

7388
Hungarian Writers' Union
(Magyar Iroszovetseg)
Bajza utca 18
H-1062 Budapest, Hungary
Phone: 1 429568
Fax: 1 213419

7389
"Forintos"-Prize
For recognition of the best translation of the year.

7390
Robert Graves Prize
For recognition of the best poem of the year.

7391
Hungary
Council of Ministers
Committee for the Ybl Miklos Prize
Kossuth Lajos ter 1/3
H-1055 Budapest, Hungary
Phone: 1 112 0600
Fax: 1 153 3622

7392
Miklos Ybl Prize for Architecture
(Ybl Miklos Dij)
For recognition of high-level creative and scientific activity in the field of architectural art. Architects who create an architectural work or urban plan are eligible. The deadline for consideration is January 31. A monetary prize, a medal, and a diploma are awarded annually on April 4. Established in 1953 by the Hungarian Council of Ministers in memory of Miklos Ybl (1814-1891), a Hungarian architect in the 19th century.

7393
Hungary
Ministry of Agriculture
(Magyarorszag
Foldugyi es Terkepeszeti Foosztaly)
Dept. of Lands & Mapping
H-1860 Budapest 55, Hungary
Phone: 1 1313736
Fax: 1 1112021

7394
Anthony Fasching Commemorative Plaque
(Fasching Antal Emlekplakett)
For recognition of long-term activity in the field of geodesy and cartography. Two plaques were awarded annually. Established in 1969 in honor of Anthony Fasching, former director. (Discontinued)

7395
Diaconus Lazarus Commemorative Medal
(Lazar Deak Emlekerem)
For recognition of a contribution to an activity in the field of geodesy and cartography. Selection is by nomination. Two medals are awarded biennially at the convention. Established in 1958 in memory of Diaconus Lazarus, a medieval geographer who first mapped Hungary in a 79 x 55 cm map that was published in 1528. Additional information is available from the Hungarian Society for Surveying, Mapping and Remote Sensing, Fo utca 68, Budapest, H-1027 Hungary, telephone: 1 2018642.

7396
Hungary
Ministry of Culture and Education
Szalay utca 10/14
H-1055 Budapest V, Hungary
Phone: 1 153 0600

7397
Janos Csere Apaczai Prize
(Apaczai Janos Csere Dij)
To recognize excellent teachers, and research implementation in the area of education. A monetary prize of 30,000 forints and honorary recognition are awarded.

7398
Jozsef Attila Prize
For recognition of significant work in prose or poetry. Writers, poets, critics and historians of literature are eligible. A monetary prize, a medal and a diploma are awarded annually. Established in 1950. Additional information is available from Muvelodesi Miniszterium, Postafiok 1, H-1884 Budapest, Hungary.

7399
Bela Balanzs Prize for Cinematography
To recognize prominent filmmakers and television productions. A monetary prize, a medal and honorary recognition are awarded annually. Established in 1959.

7400
Ferenc Erkel Prize for Musical Composition
To recognize excellent composers, musical directors, choreographers, and musicologists. A monetary prize, a medallion, a diploma and honorary recognition are awarded annually. Established in 1952.

7401
Mari Jaszai Prize
To recognize distinguished actors and actresses. Monetary prizes and honorary recognition are awarded annually. Established in 1953.

7402
Life-Saving Honorary Medal
For recognition of heroic behavior in the act of saving a human being. A monetary prize of 25,000 forints, a medal and a diploma are awarded when merited. Established in 1965.

7403
Franz Liszt Prize
To recognize superlative musical and dance performers. Monetary awards and honorary recognition are awarded annually. Established in 1952.

7404
Literary Awards
The following literary prizes are presented: (1) Fust Milan Prize; (2) Robert Graves Prize; (3) Andor Gabor Prize; (4) Prize of the Hungarian Trade Union; (5) Laszlo Wessely Prize; and (6) Budapest Pro Urbe Prize. Awarded annually.

7405

Ferenc Mora Memorial Medal
To recognize excellent museologists. A monetary award of 15,000 forints, honorary recognition, and a medal are awarded annually by the Minister of Culture in conjunction with the secretary of the Workers Trade Union.

7406

Michaly Munkacsy Prize for Visual and Applied Arts
To recognize prominent painters, sculptors, goldsmiths and silversmiths, and art historians. Monetary prizes, diplomas and honorary recognition are awarded annually. Established in 1950 by the Hungarian Council of Ministers.

7407

Ferenc Rozsa Prize
To recognize editors and journalists whose work is judged to be superior. Honorary recognition is awarded annually on December 7, Hungarian Press Day. Established in 1959.

7408

Ervin Szabo Medal
For recognition of significant contributions to librarianship. A monetary prize of 6,000 forints, a medallion and honorary recognition are awarded annually by the Minister of Culture in conjunction with the secretary of the Workers Trade Union.

7409

Hungary
Office of the Prime Minister
Kossuth Lajos ter 1-3
H-1055 Budapest V, Hungary
Phone: 1 112 0600
Fax: 1 530 124

7410

Kossuth Prize
In recognition of outstanding artistic creations and contributions to Hungarian culture. The prize is given for achievements in four disciplines: (1) arts and literature; (2) humanities; (3) natural sciences; and (4) social reconstruction. Monetary prizes, a medal, and a diploma are awarded twice in every five-year period. Established in 1948. Additional information is available from Muvelodesi Mintszterium, Postafiok 1, H-1884 Budapest, Hungary.

7411

Outstanding Artist of Hungary
To recognize artists for outstanding accomplishments in spreading socialist culture. A monthly pension, a diploma and honorary recognition are awarded annually. Established in 1950.

7412

State Prize
For recognition of outstanding achievements in the sciences, technology, national economy, medicine and education. Monetary prizes, diplomas and honorary recognition are awarded twice in every five-year period. Established in 1963 by the Presidential Council. Formerly: (1992) Scechenyi Prize.

7413

Interart Festivalcenter
(Interart Festivalkozpont)
PO Box 80
Vorosmarty ter 1
H-1366 Budapest, Hungary
Phone: 1 179910
Fax: 1 179910

Formerly: (1989) Interconcert Festival Bureau.

7414

Budapest International Music Competition
To recognize the best performer of the Competition. Awards are given alternately in the following categories: the Pablo Casals Violoncello Competition; the Leo Weiner String Quartet Competition; Liszt - Bartok Piano Competition; an Organ Competition "in memoriam Franz Liszt"; and Erkel - Kodaly Singing Competition. Individuals under 35 years of age must apply to the competition by March 31. More than one prize is awarded to recognize different instruments. Established in 1933. Sponsored by the Municipal Council of Budapest and the Ministry for Culture and Education.

7415

International Conductors Competition of the Hungarian Television
(Magyar Televizio Nemzetkozi Karmesterversenye)
To recognize an outstanding conductor. The competition is open to conductors of all nationalities who are 35 years of age or younger. The closing date for applications is January 15. Monetary prizes, medals, and concerts are awarded triennially. Established in 1974 in memory of Janos Ferencsik. Additional information is available from Magyar Televizio Zenei Foosztaly, Szabadsag ter 17, H-1810 Budapest, Hungary. The next competition will be held in 1995.

7416

Philip Jones International Brass Chamber Music Competition, Barcs
For recognition of the best performing ensemble of the International Brass Chamber Music Competition in Barcs, South Hungary. Brass chamber ensembles, quartets, and quintets are eligible. The average age of participants should be under 32 years of age and none of the members may be over 35 years. A monetary prize, a diploma, and concert engagements are awarded triennially. Established in 1982 by Jeunesses Musicales Hungary and "Bela Vikar" Music School of Barcs. Sponsored by Hungarian Radio and the Soros Foundation. Formerly: Barcs International Brass Chamber Music Competition.

7417

International Association of Gerontology
Gerontology Center, Medical University
Rokk Szilard u. 13
1085 Budapest, Hungary
Phone: 1 2699158
Fax: 1 1141830

7418

Sandoz Prize for Gerontological Research
To encourage research in all areas of gerontology and geriatric medicine including biological, medical, psychological, social and other relevant aspects with special emphasis on multidisciplinary research programs. Entries are accepted from individuals and groups directly engaged in research in some area of gerontology or geriatrics. Candidates can also be nominated by third parties. Published or unpublished work, documented as normally required for scientific publications, may be submitted. A monetary prize of 50,000 Swiss francs is awarded biennially at an international or regional congress. Established in 1983. Sponsored by Sandoz Ltd., Basel, Switzerland. Additional information is available from Dr. John L. C. Dall, M.D., Coordinator for the Sandoz Prize for Gerontological Research, Consulting Physician, Department of Geriatric Medicine, The Victoria Infirmary, Glasgow.

7419

International Association of Hungarian Studies
(Nemzetkozi Magyar Filologiai Tarsasag)
Orszaghaz utca 30., I/41
H-1014 Budapest, Hungary
Phone: 1 559930
Fax: 1 559930

7420

John Lotz Commemorative Medal
(Lotz Janos Emlekerem)
To recognize scholars living outside of Hungary for an outstanding contribution to the teaching of Hungarian Studies in the fields of Hungarian language, literature, and ethnography. A special award committee

makes the nomination. A medal is awarded every five years on the occasion of the general meetings of IAHS. Established in 1981 in memory of John Lotz (1913-1973), a Hungarian philologist, linguist, and educator.

7421

Endre Szirmai Prize
(Szirmai Endre dij)
For recognition of a discovery or publication of any unknown or unfound relic or source of Hungarian cultural or historical interest, and for any published scholarly work in Hungarian studies written in any international language of scholarship. Nomination is necessary. A monetary prize is awarded triennially. Established in 1987 by Endre Szirmai.

7422

International Kodaly Society
(Nemzetkozi Kodaly Tarsasag)
Karinthy Frigyes utca 17   Phone: 1 653899
H-1117 Budapest, Hungary   Fax: 1 653899

7423

Singing Youth International, Zoltan Kodaly Choral Competition
(Nemzetkozi Eneklo Ifjusag, Kodaly Zoltan Korusverseny)
To assist in achieving Kodaly's desire to encourage the development of musical culture and taste in young people. Amateur choruses where only the conductor may be a professional musician are eligible. Awards are given in the following categories: children's choir - age limit 16 years; youth choir - age limit 21 years; and mixed choir - age limit 30 years. Membership in each category is limited to 60 people. Monetary prizes of 150,000 yen and an invitation to participate in the International Choral Symposium are awarded triennially in each category. Established in 1982 in honor of Zoltan Kodaly, composer, scholar, and educator. Sponsored by the Kodaly Society of Japan. For additional information contact: The Organization Committee of Singing Youth International Choral Competition 1994, 1-27-7 Seijo Setagaya Tokyo 157 Japan.

7424

International League of Esperantist Radioamateurs
(Internacia Ligo de Esperantistaj Radioamatoroj)
Gyozelem 2
H-2730 Albertirsa, Hungary

7425

Esperanto Diploma
To promote the Esperanto movement and the ILERA organization among radioamateurs. A diploma with 8 stamps for the classes is awarded. Established in 1989 to commemorate the founding of ILERA in 1970 in Vienna.

7426

HG 100 EJ Esperanto Radio Amateur Station Award
To recognize individuals in the Esperanto radio competition. A diploma was awarded. Established in 1987 to commemorate the 100th anniversary of the birth of the Esperanto language and the Hungarian Esperantist Group. (Discontinued in 1988)

7427

International Measurement Confederation
(Internationale Messtechnische Konfoderation)
PO Box 457   Phone: 1 531 562
H-1371 Budapest 5, Hungary   Fax: 1 561 215

7428

Distinguished Service Award
For recognition of outstanding services to the Confederation by individuals active for many years and well-known as specialists in the field of measurement. Individuals may be nominated during the year preceding a triennial World Congress. A diploma is awarded at the closing session of the World Congress. Established in 1982.

7429

Gyorgy Striker Junior Paper Award
To recognize a junior university staff member under the age of 35 who presents a paper reflecting a deep understanding of the scope of a World Congress. A diploma and $1,000 is awarded at the Closing Session of the World Congress. Sponsored by the founding secretary general of IMEKO. Established in 1992.

7430

International Sports Film Festival of Hungary
(Magyar Nemzetkozi Sportfilm Fesztival)
Rosenberg Hp. utca 1   Phone: 1 316 936
H-1054 Budapest, Hungary   Fax: 1 322 577

7431

International Sports Film Festival in Budapest
(Budapest Nemzetkozi Sportfilm Fesztival)
For recognition of noteworthy sports films. Sports films can be entered that: (1) make sports popular on an artistic level; (2) arrest either international or national sports events; (3) put on the screen methodological, educational or scientific subjects; (4) deal with the development of the sports movement or of one single sport; (5) propagate hiking, children's and young people's sports as well as their prophylactic effects; and (6) promote regular physical exercise for health preservation. Countries, studios or individuals may enter as many films as they wish provided they were produced during the preceding two years. The following prizes are awarded: (1) Prize of the International Olympic Committee; (2) Prize of the Hungarian Television; (3) Grand Prize of the National Sports Office; (4) Prize of the Hungarian Olympic Committee; (5) CIDALC Prize; (6) Prize of the Hungarian University of Physical Education; (7) Prize of the Italian Olympic Committee; (8) Prize of the International Sporting Cinema and Video Association; (9) Prize of the National Institute of Health Education; and (10) Special prizes. Trophies and diplomas are awarded biennielly. Established in 1971. Sponsored by the National Sports Office, the Hungarian Olympic Committee, and Allami Biztosito/Assurance National.

7432

International Weightlifting Federation
PO Box 614   Phone: 1 131 8153
H-1374 Budapest, Hungary   Fax: 1 153 0199

7433

Award of Merit
To recognize individuals for outstanding service to the development of the sport of weightlifting. Porposals to confer the award must be submitted by the national or continental federations or executive board members.

7434

IWF International Awards
To recognize individuals for outstanding service to the development of the sport of weightlifting over a long period of time. Recipients may be: national federations, officers, coaches, referees, doctors and researchers, IWF and Continental-Federation Executive Board and Committee members, IOC or other sport organizations' representatives, or representatives of companies or persons who have rendered outstanding service to international weightlifting. The Award has three grades: Gold, Silver, and Bronze.

7435

IWF National Awarwd
To recognize members of the national federations. Gold, Silver, and Bronze Awards are awarded for 25, 15, and 10 years, respectively, of continuous membership and work.

7436

President's Diploma of Honour
To recognize those official who have served as a jury member, doctor, competition secretary, technical controller, or technical delegate, at the

Olympic Games, World Championships, Continental Championships, Continental Games, or Regional Games on 10 separate occasions. Following approval by the president, applicants' Diplomas are presented at the IWF Congress.

7437
Ferenc Liszt Society
(Liszt Ferenc Tarsasag)
Vorosmarty utca 35
H-1064 Budapest, Hungary   Phone: 1 421573

7438
International Grand Prix for Liszt Records
(Nemzetkozi Liszt Hanglemez Nagydij)
To provide recognition for outstanding artistic and technical contributions in the field of recording, compact discs and video tapes containing Liszt's works that are produced by record companies throughout the world. Recordings of Liszt records released in the previous year must be submitted to the Liszt Society for evaluation by April 30. A bronze Liszt plaque in a case and a diploma are awarded annually on October 22, Liszt's birthday. Established in 1974 in memory of Ferenc Liszt (1811-1886).

7439
Magyar Amatorfilm Szovetseg
Doktor Sandor utca 45
H-1158 Budapest, Hungary   Phone: 1 361 1633 336

7440
International Festival on General Health, the Red Cross and Environmental Protection Amateur Films
For recognition of an outstanding artistic quality of a film shown at the International Festival. Films may be nominated. An artistic object is awarded biennially for the Grand Prize of the International Red Cross League. The Grand Prize of the Hungarian Red Cross is also awarded. Established in 1980.

7441
National Confederation of Hungarian Trade Unions
(Magyar Szakszervezetek Orszagos Szovetsege)
Dozsa Gyorgy ut 84/B   Phone: 1 532900
H-1415 Budapest, Hungary   Fax: 1 1421924

Formerly: (1990) Magyar Szakszervezetek Orszagos Tanacsa/SZOT.

7442
Trade Union's Art and Cultural Prize
(Szakszervezeti Muveszeti Kulturalis Dij)
To provide recognition for accomplishments in professional or public activity in such fields as literature, the press, radio, television, fine arts, applied arts, social sciences, public education, threatrical art, cinematic arts, and performing arts. Monetary prizes and medals are awarded annually. Established in 1960. Formerly: SZOT Prize.

7443
Optical, Acoustical and Filmtechnical Society
(Optikai, Akusztikai Es Filmtechnikai Egyesulet)
Fo utca 68   Phone: 1 2018964
H-1027 Budapest, Hungary   Fax: 1 2018964

7444
Nandor Barany Medal
For recognition of contributions in the fields of optics, precision mechanics, microtechnics, and particular filmtechnics. Society members are eligible. A monetary award and a medal are awarded annually. Established in 1985.

7445
Bekesy Prize
For recognition of work in acoustics. Society members are eligible. A monetary prize of 8,000 forints is awarded biennially. Established in 1976.

7446
Jozsef Petzval Medal
To recognize Hungarians for significant contributions to optics, acoustics, film and video technology, and photochemistry. Two monetary prizes and two medals are awarded annually. Established in 1962.

7447
Pro Silentio
For recognition of achievements in the field of noise and vibration control. Society members are eligible. A monetary award and a medal are awarded annually. Established in 1978.

7448
Scientific Society for Building
(Epitestudomanyi Egyesulet)
                                  Phone: 1 2018416
Fo utca 68   Phone: 1 201 7137
H-1027 Budapest, Hungary   Fax: 1 561215

7449
Alpar Medal
(Alpar Erem)
For recognition of excellent technical, economic, and scientific work in the field of building engineering and activity in the social work of the Society. Seven monetary prizes of 10,000 forints each and medals are awarded annually. Established in 1958.

7450
ETE Merit Medal
(ETE Erdemerem)
For recognition of an activity in the social and scientific work of the Society. Individuals who are members of the Society for at least two years are eligible. Twenty monetary prizes of 5,000 forints each and medals are awarded annually. Established in 1982.

7451
Scientific Society for Telecommunications
(Hiradastechnikai Tudomanyos Egyesulet)
Kossuth Lajos ter 6-8
PO Box 451   Phone: 1 1531027
H-1372 Budapest 5, Hungary   Fax: 1 1530451

7452
Pollak-Virag Award
To provide recognition for the best article of the year published in the Society's periodical *Hiradastechnika*. A diploma is awarded annually. Established in 1960.

7453
Puskas Tivadar Award
To recognize an individual for successful activity in telecommunications, especially research and development, production, education, and theoretical investigations. Society members are eligible. A plaque is awarded annually. Established in 1957.

7454
Scientific Society of Mechanical Engineers
(Gepipari Tudomanyos Egyesulet)
u. 68
PO Box 433   Phone: 1 2020582
1371 Budapest, Hungary   Fax: 1 2020252

7455
Donat Banki Award
(Banki Donat Dij)
To provide recognition for eminent scientific social work. Members of the Society are eligible. A monetary prize and a bronze medal are awarded annually. Established in 1955 in honor of Prof. Donat Banki, who pioneered new methods of combustion engineering.

7456
Abraham Geza Pattantyus Award
(Pattantyus Abraham Geza Dij)
To provide recognition for eminent scientific, organizational, and educational work. Members of the Society are eligible. A monetary prize and a bronze medal are awarded annually. Established in 1957 in honor of Prof. Abraham Geza Pattantyus, a professor of engineering.

7457
Albert Szent-Gyorgyi Medical University
(Szent-Gyorgyi Albert Orvostudomanyi Egyetem Szeged)
Dugonics ter 13   Phone: 62 312729
H-6721 Szeged, Hungary   Fax: 62 312729

7458
Istvan Apathy Commemorative Medal
(Apathy Istvan Emlekerem)
To inspire students in their scientific endeavors. A maximum of three students may receive the award. Monetary prizes of 2,000 forints each and bronze medals are awarded annually on November 7. Established in 1968 in honor of Istvan Apathy.

7459
Miklos Jancso Commemorative Medal
(Jancso Miklos emlekerem es jutalomdij)
For recognition of scientific activity of outstanding value. Any scientist distinguished in the field of medical science is eligible for nomination. A monetary prize of 50,000 forints and a bronze medal are awarded annually on April 4. The recipient is invited to deliver a lecture about his scientific activity to commemorate Dr. Jancso Miklos. Established in 1968.

7460
Outstanding Instructor
(Kivalo Nevelo)
To recognize two instructors who have educated the students of the university with outstanding results for a considerable length of time. Selection is by nomination. A monetary prize of 10,000 forints is awarded annually. Established in 1972.

7461
Albert Szent-Gyorgyi Commemorative Medal
(Szent-Gyorgyi Albert Emlekerem)
To recognize Hungarian and foreign citizens who have achieved prominent results in medical research for protecting health and have encouraged better human relationships. Selection is by nomination. A medal is awarded biennially. Established in 1987 in honor of Albert Szent-Gyorgyi.

7462
University Commemorative Medal
(Pro Universitate Emlekerem)
To recognize an individual whose human and moral attitude is exemplary and who has performed outstanding work for the benefit of the university for decades. Selection is by nomination. A commemorative medal is awarded at the convention. Established in 1983.

Iceland

7463
Iceland
Office of the President
IS-101 Reykjavik, Iceland

7464
Order of the Falcon
(Falkaordan)
For recognition of foreign as well as Icelandic subjects, men and women. The President of Iceland is the Grand Master of the Order. There is an Order Council which submits recommendations to the Grand Master for awarding the Order, but under special circumstances the President can award the order on the advice of the chairmen of the Order Council alone. When the order is conferred on an Icelandic citizen, it must always be publicly stated, what special merits made him deserving of this honor. The Order of the Falcon has the following four classes: Grand Cross, Grand Knight with a Star, Grand Knight and Knight. Established by King Christian X in 1921.

7465
National Research Council
(Rannsoknarad Rikisins)
Laugaveg 13   Phone: 1 621320
IS-101 Reykjavik, Iceland   Fax: 1 29814

7466
National Research Council Stimulation Prize
(Hvatningarverdlaun Rannsoknarads)
To recognize talented young scientists, 40 years or younger, who are working in applied science and engineering, and to encourage excellence in research and development and draw public attention to the importance of science and technology for social and economic development. Icelandic scientists engaged in applied research and development must be nominated by peers. A monetary prize equivalent to the annual salary of a scientific worker is awarded annually at the annual meeting. Established in 1987.

7467
Asa Wright Honorary Award
To provide recognition for valuable scientific work performed in Iceland or on behalf of Iceland. Citizens of Iceland are eligible. A silver coin, a document and a financial grant are awarded annually. Established in 1968 by Mrs. Asa Gudmundsdottir Wright.

India

7468
Advanced Centre of Cryogenic Research - Calcutta
PO Box 17005
Jadavpur Univ.
Calcutta 700 032, India

7469
A. N. Chatterjee Memorial Medal
For recognition of the best research in the field of cryogenic instrumentation with useful application. Applications or proposals may be submitted. A silver medal is awarded annually. Established in 1977 in memory of A. N. Chatterjee who had a firm conviction in the future of Cryogenic Research in India, out of the interest of an endowment fund donated by Prof. A. Bose, founder President of the Indian Cryogenics Council, Calcutta. Mr. Chatterjee encouraged Prof. Bose in his pioneer cryogenic research during 1933-1942. Co-sponsored by the Indian Cryogenics Council.

7470
K. L. Garg Memorial Award
To promote research and development that is original and contributes to the design of cryogenic hardware/process. Individuals, organizations and institutions must submit applications by October 15. A monetary prize of 10,000 rupees, a silver medal, and a certificate of merit are awarded annually. Established in 1987 in memory of Sri K. L. Garg, one of the Senior founding fellows of the Indian Cryogenics Council. Co-sponsored by the Indian Cryogenics Council.

7471
Indradipta Memorial Medal
For recognition of the best research work leading to useful applications in the field of cryogenic medical or life science with a preference for work on a portable medical oxygen supply assembly for rural health centres. Proposals are invited from fellows. A silver medal is awarded annually. Established in 1976 by an endowment fund donated by Prof. and Mrs. P. K. Bose to commemorate their son Indradipta. Co-sponsored by the Indian Cryogenics Council.

7472
Kini Family Award
For recognition of the development of outstanding cryogenic material. Applications are accepted. A monetary prize of 400 rupees is awarded biennially. Established in memory of Dr. K.A. Kini, formerly director, CFRI, Dhanbad. Co-sponsored by the Indian Cryogenics Council.

7473
Aeronautical Society of India
13-B, Indraprastha Estate
Mahatma Gandhi Rd.
New Delhi 110 002, India   Phone: 11 3317516

7474
Excellence in Aerospace Education
To recognize an outstanding contribution in the field of aerospace education. Individuals actively engaged in the teaching profession in the aeronautical field are eligible. A monetary award of 5,000 rupees is presented biennially at the annual meeting. Established in 1991.

7475
Dr. V. M. Ghatage Award
For recognition of an outstanding contribution in the field of design, development, manufacture, operation, training, maintenance and allied areas in aviation and space. Scientific and technical institutions are invited to make recommendations to an Awards Committee, upon whose recommendation the Council makes the final decision. A monetary prize of 5,000 rupees is awarded annually. Established in 1984 in honor of Dr. V.M. Ghatage, on the occasion of his 75th birthday, by his students and colleagues.

7476
National Aeronautical Prize
For recognition of an outstanding fundamental and applied work in aeronautical science and technology. Established in 1988 by the Aeronautics Research & Development Board, Ministry of Defence of the Government of India, New Delhi.

7477
Dr. Biren Roy Space Science and Design Award
To encourage Indian space scientists and to recognize an outstanding contribution in space science. The Awards Committee selects the nominees, in consultation with ISRO, and makes recommendations to the Council for a final decision. A monetary prize of 20,000 rupees is awarded annually. Established in 1985 by Dr. Biren Roy (Charitable) Trust, Roy Mansions, Behala, Calcutta - 34, well known for its grants for medical relief and scientific progress.

7478
Dr. Biren Roy Trust Award
For recognition of an outstanding contribution in the field of design, development, manufacture, operation, training, maintenance and allied areas in aviation and space. Scientific and technical institutions are invited to make recommendations to an Awards Committee, upon whose recommendation the Council makes the final decision. A monetary prize of 6,000 rupees is awarded annually. Established in 1983 by Dr. Biren Roy (Charitable) Trust, Calcutta.

7479
All India Radio
(Akashvani)
Akashvani Bhavan
Parliament St.
New Delhi 110 001, India   Phone: 11 382021

7480
Akashvani Annual Awards
To encourage producers to develop first rate programs and to explore new areas in broadcasting. All stations of All India Radio and staff working at various radio stations are entitled to participate. Outstanding plays, documentaries, musical productions and innovative programs as well as topical documentaries, Yuv Vani and family welfare programs are considered. A choral singing competition is also held as part of the Akashvani Awards Scheme. The competition is open to two age groups of 5 to 12 years and 12 to 17 years. In each category, two prizes are given: (1) the first prize - 5,000 rupees for producer, and 3,000 rupees for the production team; and (2) the second prize - 3,000 rupees for the producer and 2,400 rupees for the production team. For a play, the authors/adaptors also get a first prize of 3,500 rupees and second prize receives 2,000 rupees. Similarly, for music the author and composers also win a first prize of 2,000 rupees each, and second prize of 1,000 rupees each; (3) The Special Prize for Yuv Vani is 3,000 rupees for the producer and 2,400 rupees for the production team; (4) The Special Prizes for Special Topic Documentary and Family Welfare Program are 5,000 rupees for the producer and 3,000 rupees for the production team in each category; (5) the prize-winning Choral Singing Children's groups are awarded a first prize of 5,000 rupees and second prize of 3,000 rupees for each age group; and (6) Akashvan Annual Award for the Best Commercial Broadcasting Service Centre - a running trophy, established in 1987. Under this scheme, running trophies are given every year to stations for the first prize winning entries in each category of the program. Awarded annually. Established in 1974.

7481
Akashvani Annual Awards for Technical Excellence
To encourage competition and recognize merit in both technology and techniques of broadcasting. The following awards are presented: (1) Best Maintained Station - one in each of the four zones; one shield and one trophy for each zone; (2) Best Installed Project - one in each of the four zones; one shield and one trophy for each zone; (3) Best Designed and Constructed Building - one shield and one trophy each to the architectural and engineering divisions; (4) Best Technical Innovation/Import Substitution - a monetary award of 3,000 rupees and two commendation awards of 1,000 rupees each; (5) Best Technical Paper - a monetary award of 3,000 rupees; (6) Best Research Work - a monetary award of 3,000 rupees; (7) Best Maintained Station amid difficult stations - one shield and trophy; and (8) Best Import Substitution - a monetary award of 3,000 rupees and two commendation awards of 1,000 rupees each. Awarded annually. Established in 1979.

7482
All India Competition for Radio Playwrights
To encourage talented playwrights to write for radio, to discover fresh talent all over the country, and to infuse new life into radio plays. Open to 19 prominent languages of India. The following awards are presented: (1) First prize - 10,000 rupees; (2) Second prize - 5,000 rupees; (3) Third prize - 3,000 rupees; and (4) an additional prize of 10,000 rupees for the best humorous play in each language. The award-winning plays are broadcast by the relevant language regions. Thereafter, these plays are translated into Hindi for national broadcast. Established in 1987.

7483
Anuvrat Global Organization
(Anuvrat Vishva Bharati (Anuvibha))
B-94 Saraswati Marg
Bajaj Nagar
Jaipur 302 015, India
Phone: 141 510347
Fax: 141 510118

7484
Anuvrat Award for International Peace
To promote world peace by honoring people who work for it. An international committee, consisting of eminent people committed to nonviolence, selects a man who has made a significant contribution to world peace by means of nonviolence through his writings, speeches, and dialogues. The people who endeavor to reduce conflict by removing the causes that promote it are also considered for this award. A medal, plaque, and citation are awarded annually. Established in 1987.

7485
Bharatiya Jnanpith
18 Institutional Area
Lodi Road
New Delhi 110 003, India
Phone: 11 698417
Phone: 11 4626467

7486
Jnanpith Award
For recognition of outstanding literary creativity in one of the 15 Indian languages. Living authors of Indian nationality are eligible. A monetary award of 200,000 rupees, a citation plaque and a statue of Vagdevi, the goddess of learning, which has been adopted as a symbol of the award, are awarded annually. Established in 1965 by Shri Shanti Prasad Jain, and his wife, Shrimati Rama Jain.

7487
Moortidevi Sahitya Puraskar
For recognition of outstanding literary work in any of the Indian languages propounding the basic values such as ahimsa, anekanta, aparigraha, peace, sacrifice, compassion, and human-welfare. Authors of Indian nationality are eligible. A monetary award of 51,000 rupees, a Saraswati statue, and a citation plaque are awarded annually. Established in 1983 in memory of the mother of Shri Shriyans Prasad Jain and the late Shri Sahu Shanti Prasad Jain.

7488
Bombay Creative Photographers Association
24 Shalimar S.V. Road
Dahisar (East)
Bombay 400 068, India
Phone: 22 651430

7489
BCPA International Salon of Colour Slides
To recognize the best color slides in the exhibition. Entries may be submitted in the following categories: general; nature; photojournalism; and photo travel. Awards presented include: (1) PSA Gold Medal - for the Best of Show; (2) PSA Gold Medal - for the Best Contemporary Slide; (3) PSA Silver Medal - for Best of Show in the nature section; (4) PSA Silver Medal - for the Best Wild Life in nature section; (5) FIAP Gold Medal - for securing the highest points in general section; (6) FIAP Silver Medal - for securing the second the highest points in the general section; (7) FIAP Silver Medal - for securing the highest points in the nature section; (8) BCPA Gold Medal - for the best slide in the general section; (9) BCPA Gold Medal - for the best slide in the nature section; and (10) Alfred Jendrosezek Gold Medal - awarded in the photojournalism and photo travel sections. Established in 1989.

7490
Delhi Management Association
1/21, Asaf Ali Rd.
New Delhi 110 002, India
Phone: 11 731476
Phone: 11 733396

7491
Escorts Book Award
To encourage original writing on management by Indian writers. Books may be submitted by December 31. Monetary prizes of 5,000 rupees for first prize and 3,000 rupees for second prize are awarded. In cases of joint authors, the prizes are divided equally between them. Awarded annually at the general meeting of the Association. Established in 1965. Sponsored by Escorts Limited.

7492
Documentation Research and Training Centre
8th Mile
Mysore Road
PO R.V. College of Engineering
Bangalore 560 059, India
Phone: 812 604648

7493
Ranganathan Award for Classification Research
To provide recognition for an outstanding contribution in the field of classification in recent years. Work done, published or unpublished, may be submitted or nominated for consideration. Candidates chosen by the International Federation for Documentation, Committee on Classification Research (FID/CR), with no restriction as to nationality, sex or age are eligible. A certificate of merit is awarded biennially. Established in 1976.

7494
Electrochemical Society of India
c/o Indian Institute of Science
Bangalore 560 012, India
Phone: 344 411
Fax: 812 341 683

7495
Ferroguard Award in Electrochemical Technology
For recognition of the two best papers in the field of electrochemical technology published in the journal of the Society. A monetary award of 1,000 rupees for first prize, and 500 rupees and a certificate for second prize are awarded annually. Established in 1977. Sponsored by M/s Guardian Anti Corrosives (PVT) Ltd., 8, Rajaji 2nd Street, West Lake Area, Nungambakkam, Madras, 600 034, India.

7496
Mascot National Award
For recognition of a notable and outstanding contribution in the field of corrosion. An application or nomination may be submitted to the Society. A monetary award of 5,000 rupees and a certificate of merit are awarded annually. Established in 1980. Sponsored by M/s Mascot Chemical Works, B-81, Industrial Estate, Peenya, Bangalore - 560 058, India.

7497
Ramachar Award in Electrochemical Science
For recognition of the two best papers in the field of electrochemical science published in the journal of the Society. A monetary award of 500 rupees and a certificate are awarded for first place and a certificate only for second place. Awarded annually. Established in 1973 in memory of Professor T.L. Ramachar, the founder-President of the Society.

7498
Fertiliser Association of India
10 Shaheed Jit Singm Marg
New Delhi 110 067, India
Phone: 11 667144
Phone: 11 667305
Fax: 11 668001

7499
FAI Silver Jubilee Award
To recognize individuals for outstanding work in the field of fertilizer use in India. Awards are presented in two categories: Outstanding Doctoral Research in Fertiliser Usage in India, and Excellence in Fertiliser Use

Research in India. A monetary award of 7,500 rupees and a gold medal are awarded annually in both categories.

7500
Sulphur Institute Award
To recognize an individual for outstanding work done in India on plant nutrient sulphur. A monetary award of 13,000 rupees is presented. Sponsored by the Sulphur Institute U.S.A.

7501
Indira Gandhi Memorial Trust
1 Akbar Rd.
New Delhi 110 011, India
Phone: 11 3011358
Fax: 11 3011102

7502
Indira Gandhi Prize for Peace, Disarmament and Development
To recognize an individual or organization for creative efforts towards: promoting international peace and disarmament, racial equality, and goodwill and harmony among nations; securing economic cooperation and promoting a new international economic order; accelerating the all-around advancement of developing nations; ensuring that the discoveries of science and modern knowledge are used for the larger good of the human race; and enlarging the scope of freedom and enriching the human spirit. Individuals and organizations without any distinction of nationality, race, or religion are considered. Nominations must be submitted by August 15. A monetary award of 2.5 million rupees (about $79,491) and a trophy made from banded haematite jasper with a citation are awarded annually. Established in 1985 by the Government of India to honor the memory of Indira Gandhi, former Prime Minister, who was assassinated by two of her Sikh guards in 1984.

7503
Geographical Society of India
c/o Dept. of Geography
Calcutta Univ.
35 Ballygunge Circular Rd.
Calcutta 700 019, India
Phone: 33 4753681

7504
Tapati Ghosh Memorial Award
For recognition of the best article in photogrammetry published in the *Geographical Review of India*. Articles submitted for publication are eligible. A medal is awarded annually. Established by Professor Sanjib Kumar Ghosh in memory of Tapati Ghosh. (Discontinued)

7505
Global Futures Network
73 A Mittal Tower
Nariman Point
Bombay 400 021, India
Phone: 22 2045758

7506
Awards
To recognize individuals for futures research and international development. Awards are presented.

7507
Gujarat Vidyapith
Ashram Road
Ahmedabad 380014, India
Phone: 272 429392
Fax: 272 429547

7508
Junior Research Fellowship
To encourage Gandhian studies and peace studies. Individuals who are 21 years of age and have a postgraduate degree may apply. Two fellowships of 600 rupees are awarded annually. Established in 1986.

7509
Haryana Sahitya Akademi
1563/18-D
Chandigarh 160 018, India
Phone: 27739

7510
Geeta Award
To recognize Haryana writers for their contribution to Sanskrit language and literature. Selection is by nomination. A monetary prize of 5,100 rupees, a Robe of Honor, and a replica of the Goddess Saraswati are awarded annually. Established in 1979 in honor of Geeta, a holy book containing sermons delivered by Lord Krishana to Arjuna at Kurukshetra in Haryana.

7511
Hali Award
To recognize writers for their contribution to Urdu language and literature. Selection is by nomination. A monetary prize of 3,100 rupees, a Robe of Honor, and a replica of Goddess Saraswati are awarded annually. Established in 1979 in honor of Altaf Hussain Hali, a renowned Urdu poet of Panipat in Haryana.

7512
Haryana Sahitya Award
To recognize writers for their contribution to the art, culture, history and folk literature of Haryana. Citizens of India are eligible. Selection is by nomination. A monetary prize of 5,100 rupees, a Robe of Honor, and a replica of Goddess Saraswati are awarded annually. Established in 1979.

7513
Bhai Santokh Singh Award
To recognize Haryana writers for their contribution to Panjabi language and literature. Selection is by nomination. A monetary prize of 5,100 rupees, a Robe of Honor, and a replica of the Goddess Saraswati are awarded annually. Established in 1979 in honor of Bhai Santokh Singh, a renowned Panjabi poet of Kaithal in Haryana.

7514
Sur Award
To recognize Haryana writers for their contribution to Hindi language and literature. Selection is by nomination. A monetary prize of 5,100 rupees, a Robe of Honor and a replica of Goddess Saraswati are awarded annually. Established in 1979 in honor of Surdas, a renowned Hindi poet of Sehi in Haryana.

7515
India
Indian Law Institute
Opp. Supreme Court
Bhagwandas Rd.
New Delhi 110 001, India
Phone: 11 389429

7516
Law Books in Hindu Prize
To recognize law books and manuscripts in Hindi. Monetary awards totaling 100,000 rupees may be awarded. The first prize is 10,000 rupees. Awarded annually.

7517
India
Ministry of Human Resource Development, Dept. of Youth Affairs & Sports
Shastri Bhavan
New Delhi 110 001, India
Phone: 11 381298

7518

Arjuna Awards
To recognize outstanding individuals who have turned in a brilliant and outstanding sports performance during the three preceding years and who have achieved excellence during the year for which the Award is given. A monetary prize of 20,000 rupees, a bronze statuette of Arjuna, the most favored and talented student of archery and martial arts in the days of the Mahabharata, and a scroll are awarded.

7519

Billiards and Snookers Awards
To recognize the billiards and snookers World Champion and Runner-up. Monetary prizes of Rs. 2.00 lakhs and Rs. 1.00 lakh are awarded respectively. Winners of Commonwealth and Asian Championships are also eligible for the awards under the scheme of special awards to winners of international sports events.

7520

Cash Prizes to Universities
To recognize universities winning first, second and third positions in 13 specific disciplines of sports in inter-university tournaments. Monetary prizes of 50,000 rupees, 30,000 rupees, and 20,000 rupees are awarded to first, second, and third place.

7521

Chess Awards
To recognize the individuals who obtain the title of International Grand Master and International Master. Monetary prizes of Rs. 2.00 lakhs and 50,000 rupees are awarded respectively. An Indian who becomes a world chess champion is given a special ad-hoc award of Rs. 5.00 lakhs, and an Indian who becomes a losing finalist in the world chess championship is given an award of Rs. 3.00 lakhs. Winners of medals in Asian Chess Championships, Commonwealth Chess Championships and Chess Olympiad are also recognized.

7522

Dronacharya Award
To honor and convey the recognition of the nation to coaches of eminence in the country. Individuals who have coached sportspersons or teams achieving outstanding results in international events during the three years preceding the year of the award are eligible. A monetary prize of 40,000 rupees, a plaque, and a scroll are awarded.

7523

Maulana Abul Kalam Azad Trophy
To recognize the university having the best all-around performance in sports. A trophy is awarded to the first-place university and monetary award of 50,000 rupees, 25,000 rupees, and 10,000 rupees are given to the universities winning over-all first, second and third places in sports.

7524

National Youth Awards
To recognize youth who have excelled in youth work in different fields of development activities and social service, and to recognize a youth organization. In the case of individuals, the award consists of a medal, a scroll and 5,000 rupees; a trophy, a scroll and Rs. 1.00 lakh are awarded to an organization.

7525

Special Awards to Winners of International Sports Events
To recognize individuals of outstanding merit in the field of sports. The following special awards and incentives are presented: (1) to individuals winning medals in Olympic Games or World Championships in any of the sports disciplines included in the Olympic Games, Rs. 5.00 lakhs for a gold medal; Rs. 3.00 lakhs for a silver medal; and Rs. 2.00 lakhs for a bronze medal; (2) to individuals winning medals in Commonwealth Games/Commonwealth Championships in any sports disciplines included in the Commonwealth Games or Asian Games/Asian Championships in sports disciplines included in Asian Games, Rs. 1.50 lakhs for a Gold Medal (by breaking the National record in a measurable discipline); Rs. 1.00 lakh for a Gold Medal (without breaking the National record); 75,000 rupees for a Silver Medal; and 50,000 rupees for a Bronze Medal; and (3) to individuals participating in team events that win medals, with the amounts of the awards being dependent upon the size of the team.

7526

India
Ministry of Human Resource Development, Directorate of Adult Education
Shastri Bhavan
New Delhi 110 001, India   Phone: 11 381298

7527

National Prize Competition for Literature for Neo-Literates
To recognize authors/writers for outstanding literary accomplishment. Awards are given in the following regional languages: Hindi, Tamil, Telugu, Urdu, Kashmiri, Sindhi, Assamese, Punjabi, Gujarati, Bengali, Oriya, Malayalam, Kannada, and Marathi. Established in 1960.

7528

India
Ministry of Information and Broadcasting
Films Division
24 - Dr. Gopalrao Deshmukh Marg   Phone: 22 364633
Bombay 400 026, India   Fax: 22 4949751

7529

Bombay International Film Festival
For recognition of outstanding documentary, short, and animation films produced in India during the past three years. Directors of the award winning films are awarded the following prizes: (1) Best film of 40 minutes duration or less in the non-fiction category - 250,000 Indian rupees; (2) Best film of above 40 minutes duration in the non-fiction category - 250,000 Indian rupees; (3) Best film of 60 minutes or less in the fiction category - 250,000 Indian rupees; (4) Best Animation Film - 250,000 rupees; and (5) Certificates of Participation for films screened in Competition and Information Sections. A Gold Conch and Silver Conch is also awarded in each category. In addition, the following prizes are awarded: (1) International Jury Award - 100,000 rupees; (2) Indian Documentary Producers Association Award - a trophy for the best first film of a director; (3) Critics Award; (4) one minute Animation Contest - 100,000 rupees; and (5) Theme Award - 500,000 rupees for a short film in fiction or nonfiction on an announced theme. Established in 1990.

7530

Bharatendu Harishchandra Award
To encourage original and creative writings in Hindi on various disciplines of mass communication. Radio and television broadcasts and the print media are eligible. Three monetary awards of 15,000 rupees for First prize, 10,000 rupees for Second prize, and 5,000 rupees for Third prize are awarded annually. Established in 1983.

7531

India
Ministry of Science and Technology
CSIR Bldg.
Rafi Marg
New Delhi 110 001, India   Phone: 11 3711744

7532

Bhatnagar Award
To recognize an Indian National for outstanding work in the following scientific disciplines: (1) physical sciences; (2) biological sciences; (3) engineering sciences; (4) medical sciences; (5) mathematical sciences; and (6) earth sciences. Scientists under the age of 45 are eligible. A monetary prize of 20,000 rupees is awarded annually. Established in 1967.

7533
India
National Academy of Art
(India
Lalit Kala Akademi)
Rabindra Bhavan
New Delhi 110 001, India
Phone: 11 38 72 41
Phone: 11 38 72 42

7534
National Akademi Award
For recognition of outstanding achievement in painting, sculpture, drawing, and graphics. Indian citizens are eligible for selection from the National Exhibit of art conducted annually by the Akademi on the merit of each exhibit. Ten monetary awards of 10,000 rupees each and certificates are awarded annually. Established in 1955.

7535
Triennale-India Award of Lalit Kala Akademi
For recognition of outstanding achievement in contemporary art in the field of paintings, sculptures and graphics. The Lalit Kala Akademi invites countries for participation in Triennale-India. The participating countries are responsible for the selection of their exhibits. Ten monetary awards of 50,000 rupees each with a gold medal and a certificate are awarded triennially. Established in 1968.

7536
India
National Academy of Letters
(India
Sahitya Akademi)
Rabindra Bhavan
35 Ferozeshah Rd.
New Delhi 110 001, India
Phone: 11 387064
Fax: 11 382428

7537
Sahitya Akademi Awards
To recognize outstanding writers for books of high literary merit written in each of the 22 languages of India that are recognized by the Academy. Indian nationals only are eligible. A monetary prize of 25,000 rupees and an inscribed copper plaque are awarded annually by the President of the Sahitya Akademi.

7538
Sahitya Akademi Fellowship
This, the highest literary honor in India, is conferred on persons of undisputed eminence in literature. The highest standard of Fellowship is ensured by limiting the number of living Fellows to 21 at any one time.

7539
Sahitya Akademi Prize for Translation
To encourage translation activity in India. This award is given for the best translated creative and critical works in the 22 languages recognized by the Academy. Both the translator and the original author should be Indian nationals. A monetary prize of 10,000 rupees and a certificate are presented annually by the President of the Sahitya Akademi. Established in 1989.

7540
India
National Academy of Music, Dance and Drama
(India
Sangeet Natak Akademi)
Rabindra Bhavan Feroze Shah Rd.
New Delhi 110 001, India
Phone: 11 387246

7541
Bharta Kala Prapoorna in Dance
To recognize a performing artist for distinguished service to dance. Winners are selected by the General Council of the Akademi. A purse of 25,000 rupees and a woolen shawl with a gold lace border are awarded annually. Established in 1960.

7542
Nataka Kala Prapoorna in Drama
To recognize a performing artist for outstanding service and achievement in drama. Winners are selected by the General Council of the Akademi. A purse of 25,000 rupees and a woolen shawl with a gold lace border are awarded annually. Established in 1960.

7543
Gana Kala Prapoorna in Music
To recognize performing musicians for outstanding achievement in music. Winners are selected by the General Council of the Akademi. A purse of 25,000 rupees and a woolen shawl with a gold lace border are awarded annually. Established in 1960.

7544
Kala Praveena Award
To recognize artists who may not be eligible for the honors of Kala Propoorna or Fellowship. Those who have rendered commendable service to music, dance, drama, and folk arts are eligible and are selected by the General Council of the Akademi. A purse of 25,000 rupees and a woolen shawl are awarded annually. Established in 1979.

7545
Sargeet Natak Akademi Fellowships
To recognize the services and achievements of eminent artists in the performing arts. Winners are selected by the General Council of the Akademi. A purse of 25,000 rupees and a woolen shawl are awarded on special occasions such as the 10th Anniversary, 20th Anniversary, Silver Jubilee, etc. A maximum of 30 fellowships may be awarded to living recipients, past and present. Established in 1960.

7546
India
Office of the Prime Minister
South Block
New Delhi 110 011, India
Phone: 11 3012312

7547
Ashok Chakra
For the recognition of the most conspicuous bravery or some daring or preeminent act of valor or self-sacrifice on land, at sea or in the air. Members of the military are eligible.

7548
Ati Vishisht Seva Medal
To recognize personnel of all three Services for distinguished service of the most exceptional order.

7549
Bharat Ratna
For recognition of exceptional service in the advancement of art, literature and science, and for recognition of public service of the highest order. Individuals without distinction of race, occupation, position or sex are eligible. A decoration made of bronze, and worn around the neck is awarded. The award may be given posthumously. The names of the persons upon whom the decoration is confered are published in the Gazette of India, and a register of all such recipients is maintained by the Office of the President. Awarded annually by the President on the Republic Day.

7550
Certificate of Honor
To recognize scholars for outstanding contributions to Arabic, Persian and Sanscrit studies. A monetary prize and a robe of honor are awarded annually by the President.

7551
Jeevan Raksha Padak
To recognize courage and decisive action under circumstances of grave bodily danger to the rescuer, displayed in an act or series of acts of a humane nature in saving human beings from drowning, fire, or rescue operations in mines. A bronze medal, circular in shape, is awarded annually.

7552
Kirti Chakra
For recognition of conspicuous gallantry. Members of the military are eligible.

7553
Maha Vir Chakra
This, the second highest decoration for valor, is given for acts of conspicuous gallantry in the presence of the enemy, whether on land, at sea, or in the air. Members of the military are eligible.

7554
Padma Bhushan
(Lotus Decoration)
For recognition of distinguished service of a high order in any field, including service rendered by government servants. Any person without distinction of race, occupation, position or sex shall be eligible for the award which may be awarded posthumously. The names of the persons, upon whom the decoration is conferred, is published in the Gazette of India and a register of all such recipients of the award is maintained under the direction of the President. A decoration of bronze with gold embossing is awarded annually by the President.

7555
Padma Shri
For recognition of distinguished service in any field, including service rendered by government servants. Any person without distinction of race, occupation, position or sex shall be eligible for the award which may be awarded posthumously. The names of the persons, upon whom the decoration is conferred, is published in the Gazette of India and a register of all such recipients of the award is maintained under the direction of the President. A decoration made of bronze with stainless steel embossing is awarded annually by the President.

7556
Padma Vibhushan
For recognition of exceptional and distinguished service in any field, including service rendered by Government servants. Any person without distinction of race, occupation, position or sex is eligible for the award which may be awarded posthumously. The names of the persons, upon whom the decoration is conferred, is published in the Gazette of India and a register of all recipients is maintained under the direction of the President. A decoration of toned bronze with embossing in white gold is awarded annually by the President.

7557
Param Vir Chakra
This, the highest decoration for valor, is given for the most conspicuous bravery of some daring or pre-eminent act of valor or self-sacrifice in the presence of the enemy, whether on land, at sea or in the air. Members of the military are eligible.

7558
Param Vishisht Seva Medal
To recognize personnel of all three Services for distinguished service of the most exceptional order.

7559
President's Gold Medal
To recognize the best feature film made in India. The following prizes are awarded: a monetary prize of 50,000 Indian rupees and a gold medal to the producer; and 20,000 rupees and a plaque to the director. Monetary prizes and medals are also given for the best feature film on national integration, best information film, best social documentary film, and best animation film. Monetary prizes and plaques are given for excellence in direction, excellence in black and white and in color cinematography, best screenplay, best female and male singers, and best lyric song writer on national integration. The best actor receives a figurine of Bharat, and the best actress receives a figurine of Urvashi. Awards are also given for the best feature film in different regional Indian languages. The awards are presented annually.

7560
Sarvotten Jeevan Raksha Padak
To recognize conspicuous courage, under circumstances of great danger to the life of the rescuer, displayed in an act or a series of acts of a humane nature in saving human beings from drowning, fire, or rescue operations in mines. A gold medal, circular in shape, is awarded annually by the President.

7561
Shaurya Chakra
For recognition of an act of gallantry. Members of the military are eligible.

7562
Uttam Jeevan Raksha Padak
For recognition of courage and swift action under circumstances of great danger to the life of the rescuer, displayed in an act or a series of acts of a humane nature in saving human beings from drowning, fire, or rescue operations in mines. A silver medal, circular in shape, is awarded annually.

7563
Vir Chakra
This, the third in the order of valor awards, is given for acts of gallantry in the presence of the enemy, whether on land, at sea or in the air. Members of the military are eligible.

7564
Vishisht Seva Medal
To recognize personnel of all three Services for recognition of distinguished service.

7565
Indian Adult Education Association
17-B Indraprastha Estate   Phone: 11 3319282
New Delhi 110 002, India   Fax: 11 3315460

7566
Nehru Literacy Award
For recognition of an outstanding contribution to the promotion of literacy and adult education in India. Individuals or institutions are eligible. A monetary award of 5,000 rupees, a plaque, a citation, and a shawl are awarded annually. Established in 1968.

7567
Tagore Literacy Award
For recognition of an outstanding contribution to the promotion of women's literacy and adult education in India. A monetary award of 5,000 rupees, a plaque, a citation, and a shawl are awarded annually. Established in 1987 to honor Gurudev Rabinder Nath Tagore.

7568
Indian Association for the Advancement of Science
55 Kaka Nagar
New Delhi 110 003, India   Phone: 11 697301

7569
World Food Day Award
To encourage professional development and for recognition of outstanding contributions to agriculture by individuals through the mass media. A plaque and a certificate are awarded annually on October 16. Established in 1982 to commemorate World Food Day. Co-sponsored by the Food and Agriculture Organization of the United Nations.

7570
Indian Books Centre
40/5 Shakti Nagar   Phone: 11 7126497
New Delhi 110 007, India   Fax: 11 7227336

7571
Indian Books Centre Oriental Studies Award
To encourage Indological and Buddhist studies in all parts of the world. Books published anywhere in the world during the preceding two years are considered. A monetary prize, a citation, and a shawl are awarded at the All India Oriental Conference. Established in 1981. Additional information is available from the All India Oriental Conference, Bhandarkar Oriental Research Institute, Pune 411 004, India.

7572
Indian Council for Cultural Relations
Azad Bhavan
Indraprastha Estate   Phone: 11 3722079
New Delhi 110 002, India   Fax: 11 3712639

7573
Jawaharlal Nehru Award for International Understanding
To recognize a person who has contributed to the promotion of international understanding, goodwill, and friendship among peoples of the world. Individuals may be nominated regardless of nationality, race, creed, or sex. Work achieved within the five years preceding nomination is considered. A monetary prize of about rupees 15 lakhs and a citation are awarded annually. Established in 1965 by the Government of India as a tribute to the memory of Jawaharlal Nehru, independent India's first Prime Minister and his life long dedication to the cause of world peace and international understanding. Sponsored by the Government of India.

7574
Indian Council of Agricultural Research
Krishi Anusandhan Bhavan
Dr. Rajendra Prasad Rd.
New Delhi 110 001, India   Phone: 11 388991

7575
Dr. Rajendra Prasad Award
To provide recognition for the best book in the agricultural sciences. Awarded annually.

7576
Indian Council of Medical Research
Medical Enclave
Ansari Nagar
PO Box 4508   Phone: 11 667136
New Delhi 110 029, India   Phone: 11 653980

7577
Professor B. K. Aikat Oration Award
To recognize an eminent scientist for outstanding work carried out in the field of tropical diseases. The criteria for award of the prize are the significance and value of the addition to existing knowledge contributed by a worker in the field of tropical diseases in which he has been actively engaged over a number of years and has shown sustained activity in research. A monetary prize of 3,000 rupees is awarded biennially.

7578
Basanti Devi Amir Chand Prize
For recognition of work of outstanding merit in any subject in the field of biomedical science, including clinical research. Senior research workers of more than 10 years are eligible. The criteria for award of the prize are the significance and value of the addition to existing knowledge contributed by a worker in a particular field in which he has been actively engaged over a number of years and has shown sustained activity in research. A monetary prize of 5,000 rupees is awarded annually.

7579
Shakuntala Amir Chand Prizes
For recognition of the best published research on any subject in the field of biomedical sciences, including clinical research. Clinical research covers research into the mechanism and causation of diseases and its prevention and cure, and includes work on patients in hospitals, field studies in epidemiology and social medicine, and observations in general practice. Both medical and non-medical graduates are eligible. Prizes aarded to Indian nationals for work done in any institution in India. Work started in India but completed abroad will not be acceptable. Papers published both in Indian and foreign journals in the previous two years are considered for the award. Four monetary prizes of 1,500 rupees each are awarded annually.

7580
BGRC Silver Jubilee Oration Award
To recognize an eminent scientist for outstanding work carried out in the field of haematology and immunohaematology. The criteria for award of the prize are the significance and value of the addition to existing knowledge contributed by a worker in this specialty in which he has been actively engaged over a number of years and has shown sustained activity in research. A monetary prize of 5,000 rupees is awarded biennially.

7581
Dr. P. V. Cherian Memorial Award
To recognize an eminent scientist for outstanding contributions in the field of nephrology. A monetary prize of 10,000 rupees was awarded. (Discontinued in 1991)

7582
Chaturvedi Ghanshyam Das Jaigopal Memorial Award
To recognize an eminent scientist for outstanding work carried out in the field of immunology. The criteria for award of the prize are the significance and value of the addition to existing knowledge contributed by a worker on a subject in which he has been actively engaged over a number of years and has shown sustained activity in research. A monetary prize of 3,000 rupees is awarded biennially.

7583
Chaturvedi Kalawati Jagmohan Das Memorial Award
For recognition of research in the field of cardiovascular diseases. Eminent scientists, preferably medical persons, are eligible. The criteria include the significance and value of addition to existing knowledge contributed by a worker in cardiovascular diseases in which he or she has been actively engaged over a number of years and has shown sustained activity in research. A monetary prize of 2,000 rupees and a gold medal are awarded triennially.

7584
Dr. Dharamvir Datta Memorial Oration Award
To recognize a scientist (medical or non-medical) below 40 years of age for work carried out in the last five years in India in the field of liver diseases. The criteria include significance and value of addition to existing knowledge contributed by a worker in this speciality, with special reference to application of findings to clinical hepatology. A monetary prize of 3,000 rupees is awarded biennially.

7585
Dr. H. B. Dingley Memorial Award
To recognize individuals for outstanding contribution to research in the field of Paediatrics by Indian scientists below the age of 40 years. The work to be assessed would be research work carried out in India and published in scientific journals during the 3 years preceding the year for which the award is to be given.

7586
Smt. Swaran Kanta Dingley Oration Award
To recognize an eminent scientist for outstanding contribution in the field of reproductive biology. The criteria for award of the prize are the significance and value of the addition to existing knowledge contributed by a worker in the field of reproductive biology in which he has been actively engaged over a number of years and has shown sustained activity in research. A monetary prize of 10,000 rupees is awarded biennially.

7587
ICMR Prize for Biomedical Research Conducted in Underdeveloped Areas
To recognize an eminent scientist for outstanding contributions in any field of biomedical sciences. The criteria for award of the prize are the significance and value of biomedical research carried out by a worker based in under-developed parts of the country, or for work carried out in under-developed parts of the country over a period of five years preceding the year for which the award is to be given. A monetary prize of 5,000 rupees is awarded annually.

7588
ICMR Prize for Biomedical Research for Scientists belonging to Under-privileged Communities
To recognize an eminent scientist for outstanding contributions in any field of the biomedical sciences. The criterion for award of the prize is the significance and value of addition to existing knowledge contributed by a worker in the particular field in which he has been actively engaged over a number of years and has shown sustained activity in research. Scientists belonging to under privileged communities are eligible. A monetary prize of 5,000 rupees is awarded annually.

7589
Dr. M. O. T. Iyengar Memorial Award
To recognize an eminent scientist for an outstanding contribution in the fields of malaria, filariasis, plague or medical entomology. The criteria for award of the prize are the significance and value of the addition to existing knowledge contributed by a worker in any of the fields of malaria, filariasis, plague or medical entomology in which he has been actively engaged over a number of years and has shown sustained activity in research. A monetary prize of 4,000 rupees is awarded annually.

7590
Dr. C. G. S. Iyer Oration Award
To recognize a scientist under the age of 40 for an outstanding contribution in the field of leprosy. The criterion for award of the prize is the significance and value of the addition to existing knowledge contributed by a worker in this speciality in which he/she has been actively engaged over a number of years and has shown sustained activity in research. A monetary prize of 1,500 rupees is awarded biennially.

7591
JALMA Trust Fund Oration Award In The Field Of Leprosy
For recognition of outstanding work carried out in the field of leprosy. The criterion for award of the prize is the significance and value of addition to existing knowledge contributed by a worker on any aspect of leprosy in which he or she has been actively engaged over a number of years and has shown sustained activity in research. A monetary prize of 5,000 rupees and a medal are awarded annually.

7592
Lala Ram Chand Kandhari Award
To recognize an eminent scientist for new outstanding research in the fields of dermatology and sexually transmitted diseases. The criteria for the award are the significance and value of the addition to existing knowledge contributed by the worker on a subject in which he has been actively engaged over a number of years and has shown sustained activity in research. A monetary prize of 5,000 rupees is awarded biennially.

7593
Kshanika Oration Award to a Woman Scientist for Research in the Field of Biomedical Sciences
To recognize an eminent woman scientist for outstanding work carried out in any branch of biomedical science, contributing to the alleviation of human suffering. The criteria for award of this prize are the significance and value of the addition to existing knowledge contributed by her in any field of biomedical sciences in which she has been actively engaged over a number of years and has shown sustained activity in research. A monetary prize of 5,000 rupees is awarded annually.

7594
Prof. Surindar Mohan Marwah Award
To recognize an Indian scientist for significant contribution to the field of geriatrics, through sustained research in India on the problems of the aged as evidenced by research papers in science publications. The subject matter could be biomedical or psychosocial research on problems of the aged, both basic and applied. A monetary prize of 25,000 rupees is awarded triennially.

7595
Dr. Kamala Menon Medical Research Award
To recognize an eminent scientist, preferably a medical person for outstanding contributions to the field of internal medicine and pediatrics. Awards are given in alternate years in the following categories: internal medicine, and pediatrics. The criterion for award of the prize is the significance and value of addition to existing knowledge contributed by a worker on a subject in which he or she has been actively engaged over a number of years and has shown sustained activity in research. A monetary prize of 5,000 rupees is awarded annually.

7596
Amrut Mody-Unichem Prize for Research in Cardiology, Neurology and Gastroenterology
To recognize an eminent scientist for outstanding work carried out in the fields of cardiology and neurology, and gastroenterology. Awards are given in alternate years in the following categories: cardiology and neurology; and gastroenterology. The criteria for award of the prize are the significance and value of the addition to existing knowledge contributed by a worker on a subject in which he has been actively engaged over a number of years and has shown sustained activity in research. A monetary prize of 10,000 rupees is awarded annually.

7597
Amrut Mody-Unichem Prize for Research in Maternal and Child Health and Chest Diseases
To recognize eminent scientists for outstanding work carried out in the fields of maternal and child health, and chest diseases. Awards are given in alternate years in the following categories: maternal and child health, and chest diseases. The criteria for award of the prize are the significance and value of the addition to existing knowledge contributed by a worker on a subject in which he has been actively engaged over a number

7598
Dr. V. N. Patwardhan Prize in Nutritional Sciences
For recognition of outstanding work carried out in India on fundamental, clinical or field studies in nutritional sciences. Eminent scientists, not older than 40 years of age, are eligible. The criteria for the award of the prize are the contribution of a worker to nutritional sciences in which he or she has been activley engaged over a number of years and has shown sustained activity in research. A monetary prize of 7,000 rupees is awarded biennially.

7599
Dr. D. N. Praad Memorial Oration Award
To recognize an Indian scientist for significant contribution to research in the field of pharmacology, carried out in India, as evidenced by research papers and innovations. The criteria for the award will be the significance and value of addition to existing knowledge in research in pharmacology. A monetary prize of 20,000 rupees and a medal are awarded biennially.

7600
Dr. P. N. Raju Oration Award
For recognition of outstanding work of national importance in the field of medicine or public health. Eminent scientists, preferably medical specialists, are eligible. A monetary prize of 5,000 rupees and an invitation to deliver a lecture are awarded biennially.

7601
Dr. T. Ramachandra Rao Award
To recognize a young scientist under the age of 40 for an outstanding contribution in the field of medical entomology. The criterion for award of the prize is the significance and value of the addition to existing knowledge contributed by a worker in this specialty in which he/she has been actively engaged over a number of years and has shown sustained activity in research. A monetary prize of 3,000 rupees is awarded biennially.

7602
Tilak Venkoba Rao Award
To recognize an eminent scientist for research in the field of psychological medicine and reproductive physiology. Awards are given in alternate years in the following categories: psychological medicine and reproductive physiology. The criterion for the award is the significance of contribution to existing knowledge by a worker who has been actively engaged in research on the subject over a number of years. A monetary prize of 5,000 rupees is awarded annually.

7603
Dr. Y. S. Narayana Rao Oration Award in Microbiology
For recognition of outstanding work in the field of microbiology. The criteria for the award of the prize are the significance and value of the addition to existing knowledge contributed by a worker in the field of microbiology in which he has been actively engaged over a number of years and has shown sustained activity in research. Eminent scientists are eligible. A monetary prize of 4,000 rupees is awarded biennially.

7604
Dr. Vidya Sagar Award
To recognize an eminent scientist for outstanding contributions made in the field of mental health. The criteria for award of the prize are the significance and value of the addition to existing knowledge contributed by a worker in the field of mental health in which he has been actively engaged over a number of years and has shown sustained activity in research. A monetary prize of 5,000 rupees is awarded biennially.

7605
Sandoz Oration Award for Research in Cancer
For recognition of an outstanding contribution toward the control, prevention and cure of cancer that is recognized nationally and internationally. Eminent scientists are eligible. A monetary prize of 2,500 rupees is awarded biennially.

7606
Smt. Kamal Satbir Award
To recognize individuals for outstanding contribution to research on non-tuberculous chest diseases, especially respiratory allergy and and chronic obstructive lung diseases, pertaining to mechanism and causation of diseases, their prevention and/or management. The work to be assessed would be the research carried out in India and published in scientific journals during the three years preceding the year for which the award is to be given. A monetary prize of 5,000 rupees is awarded anually.

7607
M. N. Sen Oration Award for Practice of Medicine
For recognition of outstanding work in medical practice medical practice (clinical, laboratory or therapeutic). Eminent scientists are eligible. The criterion for award of the prize is the significance and value of addition to existing knowledge contributed by a worker to the practice of medicine in which he or she has been actively engaged over a number of years and has shown sustained activity in research. A monetary prize of 5,000 rupees is awarded biennially.

7608
Dr. M. K. Seshadri Prize in the Field of Practice of Community Medicine
To recognize an eminent scientist or institution whose original work has led to useful inventions in, or otherwise significantly contributed to, the practice of community medicine. A monetary prize of 10,000 rupees and a gold medal are awarded biennially.

7609
Raja Ravi Sher Singh of Kalsia Memorial Cancer Research Award
For recognition of outstanding work in the experimental or clinical aspects of cancer, or in the organization of any service or research program in cancer prevention and treatment. Young physicians under 40 years of age are eligible for work done in the preceding year. A monetary prize of 2,000 rupees is awarded biennially.

7610
Maj. Gen. Saheb Singh Sokhey Award
To recognize a scientist below the age of 40 years for his or her outstanding contribution to the field of communicable diseases depending upon its significance and value in terms of addition to existing knowledge contributed by the worker in that field. The facets of work to be considered could be basic or applied research which add to the knowledge on the mechanism and causation of communicable diseases, their prevention and/or their management. The work to be assessed would be the research carried out in India and published in scientific journals, during the 3 years preceding the year for which the award is to be given.

7611
Smt. Pushpa Sriramachari Award
To recognize individuals for outstanding contribution to research on pathology and pathophysiology - clinical or experimental. The individual should be an established scientist above the age of 45 years and should have made a comprehensive and significant original contribution in unravelling the understanding and the nature, evolution, or prevention of any human disease entity. A monetary prize of 5,000 rupees and a silver medal are awarded biennially.

7612
Dr. J. B. Srivastav Award in the Field of Virology
To recognize an eminent scientist for outstanding work in virology. The criterion for award of the prize is the significance and value of addition to existing knowledge contributed by a worker in virology in which he or she has been actively engaged over a number of years and has shown sustained activity in research. A monetary prize of 10,000 rupees is awarded biennially.

7613
Prof. B. C. Srivastava Foundation Award
To recognize a scientist under 40 years of age for work in the field of community medicine in medical colleges/recognized institutions. The criterion for the award is the significance of research contributions to the practice of community medicine by a worker. A monetary prize of 5,000 rupees is awarded biennially.

7614
Dr. Prem Nath Wahi Award for Cytology and Preventive Oncology
To recognize and eminent scientist for outstanding contribution in the field of basic and/or clinical cytology, and/or preventive oncology. The criterion for the award is the significance and value of addition to existing knowledge contributed by a worker on the subject in which he or she has been actively engaged over a number of years and has shown sustained activity in research. A monetary prize of 30,000 rupees is awarded bienially.

7615
Indian Dairy Association
IDA House, Sector IV, R.K. Puram
New Delhi 110 022, India
Phone: 11 67 0781
Phone: 11 67 4719

7616
Best Paper Award
To encourage the dissemination of scientific information. Papers published in the IDA-periodicals, such as *Indian Dairyman* and *Indian Journal of Dairy Science*, are considered. A monetary award and a certificate are presented annually in September. Established in 1991.

7617
Dr. Kurien Award
To recognize the achievement of dedicated individuals and institutions and to provide impetus for further progress in every field associated with Indian dairying. A monetary prize of 100,000 rupees and a citation are awarded biennially at the time of the Dairy Industry Conference. Established in 1989 to honor Dr. Verghese Kurien, who pioneered the White Revolution in India.

7618
Patrons and Fellows
For recognition of outstanding achievements in the field of dairy science and the dairy industry. Nomination is required. A plaque and citation are awarded annually to Patrons and Fellows at the general body meeting or any other important function. Established in 1978.

7619
Indian Hospital Association
B-401, Saria Vihar
New Delhi 110044, India
Phone: 11 6835648

7620
Essay Competition
For recognition of an essay on a subject announced by the Scientific Committee of the Association. The best essay is presented during the National Hospital Convention in November. Awarded annually. In addition, the Dr. B. L. Kapur Oration and Dr. James S. Tong Oration are selected every year. The Tong Oration is co-sponsored by the Voluntary Health Association of India.

7621
Indian Institute of Metals
A-1 Flat, 15th Fl.
33A Chowringhee Rd.
Calcutta 700 071, India
Phone: 33 294648
Fax: 33 2472763

7622
Vidy Bharati Prize
To recognize four students who secure highest marks in order of merit in the final B. Tech. B.E./B.Sc. Eng. in Metallurgy.

7623
Bhoruka Gold Medal
For recognition of significant contributions to process control and development systems in the field of metallurgical industry. A gold medal is awarded. Established by the House of Bhoruka Steel, Bangalore, in memory of P. D. Agarwal's efforts on the industrial front.

7624
Binani Gold Medal
To recognize the contributions made in the non-ferrous group through their reference work and published in the Transactions of the Institute. A gold medal is awarded. Established in 1959 by the House of Binanis.

7625
G. D. Birla Memorial Gold Medal
To recognize a distinguished research worker for continuing and outstanding research work in the field of materials sciences and technology. A medal is awarded. Established in memory of the industrialist, G. D. Birla.

7626
Bralco Gold Medal
To recognize contributions made to the development of the non-ferrous metal industry. A medal is awarded. Established in 1972 by Bralco Metal Industries, Bombay.

7627
Sir Padamji Ginwala Gold Medal
To recognize a candidate securing the highest marks in the Associate Membership Examination (Part-I) of the Institute. A gold medal is awarded. Established in 1963 in memory of Sir Padamji Ginwala, Ex-President of IIM.

7628
Honorary Member
To recognize distinguished service to the metallurgical profession and to the IIM.

7629
IIM Platinum Medal
To recognize an eminent metallurgist for his outstanding contributions to the metallurgical profession and to create an incentive by the recognition of such a contribution. A medal is awarded.

7630
IIM Rolling Trophy
To recognize chapters for overall performance and for enrolling the maximum number of new members.

7631
MECON Award
To recognize outstanding contributions in the development of process engineering and equipment. Established in 1984 by Metallurgical and Engineering Consultants (India) Limited (MECON).

7632
Sail Gold Medal
To recognize the best paper published in the Transactions of the Institute during the preceding year. A medal is awarded. Established in 1933 by Steel Authority of India, Ltd., New Delhi. Formerly: Kamani Gold Medal.

7633
Steel Eighties Award
For recognition of a significant contribution to the steel making technology. A monetary prize is awarded.

7634
Tata Gold Medal
To recognize a distinguished personality actively connected with the metallurgical industry. A medal is awarded. Established in 1980 in honor of Mr. J. R. D. Tata.

7635
Indian National Science Academy
Bahadur Shah Zafar Marg
New Delhi 110 002, India   Phone: 11 331 2450

7636
Dr. Nitya Anand Endowment Lecture
To recognize a scientist under 50 years of age who has done outstanding work in any area of biomedical research including new drug development. The award is based on work done in India during the previous 10 years. Nominations for consideration for the award are invited from the Fellowship. The lecture is delivered in any institution involved in work in this area but not in the award winner's own institution. The lecturer is paid 25,000 rupees including funds for journeys performed to deliver the lecture. Awarded biennially. Established in 1986 out of an endowment of 130,000 rupees by the Organizing Committee to celebrate the 60th birthday of Dr. Nitya Anand, an eminent chemist and a Fellow of the Academy. The funds came from Dr. Nitya Anand's friends, students and admirers in academic institutions and the pharmaceutical industry.

7637
Aryabhata Medal
For recognition of achievement in any branch of science. A bronze medal is awarded triennially. Established in 1977.

7638
Prof. R. K. Asundi Memorial Lecture
To recognize persons who have made outstanding contributions in the field of spectroscopy. The lecturer is paid an honorarium and travel expenses for journeys performed to deliver the lecture. Awarded biennially. Established in 1983 from an endowment of 21,000 rupees by the Asundi Endowment Fund to commemorate Professor R.K. Asundi, a Fellow of the Academy, distinguished for research in spectroscopy.

7639
Homi J. Bhabha Medal
For recognition of work in the field of experimental physics. A bronze medal is awarded triennially. Established in 1976.

7640
Satyendranath Bose Medal
For recognition of achievement in the field of theoretical physics. A bronze medal is awarded triennially. Established in 1976.

7641
Anil Kumar Bose Memorial Award
For recognition of the best research paper published in a reputable journal by a recipient of the INSA Medal for Young Scientists on work done in India within five years from the date of receipt of the INSA Medal. Monetary prizes of 1,000 rupees each are awarded in physical sciences and biology.

7642
Jagdish Chandra Bose Medal
For recognition of contributions to biophysics, molecular biology, biochemistry, and related fields. A bronze medal is awarded triennially. Established in 1976.

7643
Dr. G. P. Chatterjee Memorial Lecture
For recognition of outstanding contributions in any field of science. The lecture is to be given biennially. The lecturer is paid an honorarium depending upon the income besides travel expenses for journeys performed to deliver the lecture. Established in 1979 from an endowment of 15,000 rupees by Dr. G.P. Chatterjee and Mrs. Suniti Chatterjee to commemorate Dr. Guru Prasad Chatterjee, an eminent metallurgist and Fellow of the Academy.

7644
Bashambar Nath Chopra Lecture
For recognition of a distinctive contribution in the field of biological sciences. A lectureship and an honorarium of 1,500 rupees are awarded triennially. Established in 1968 from an endowment of 10,000 rupees in memory of Dr. B.N. Chopra by his family.

7645
Indira Gandhi Prize for Popularization of Science
To encourage and recognize popularization of science in any Indian language including English. The nominee must have had a distinguished career as a writer, editor, journalist, lecturer, radio or television program director, film producer, science photographer or as an illustrator, which has enabled him/her to interpret science (including medicine), research and technology to the public. He/she should have a knowledge of the role of science, technology and research in the enrichment of cultural heritage and in the solution of problems of humanity. The prize is open to any Indian national residing in the country. A monetary prize of 10,000 rupees and a bronze medal are awarded. Established in 1986.

7646
Golden Jubilee Commemoration Medal for Biology
For recognition in the field of biological sciences. A bronze medal is awarded triennially. Established in 1986.

7647
Golden Jubilee Commemoration Medal for Chemistry
For recognition in the field of chemical sciences. A bronze medal is awarded triennially. Established in 1986.

7648
Bires Chandra Guha Memorial Lecture
To recognize a scientist who has made an outstanding contribution in the field of biochemistry, nutrition, food and allied sciences. A lectureship and an honorarium of 1,500 rupees are awarded triennially. Established in 1965 from an endowment of 10,000 rupees by Dr. (Mrs.) Phulrenu Guha in memory of her husband, Professor Bires Chandra Guha.

7649
Chandrakala Hora Medal
To recognize an eminent scientist who has done outstanding work in the development of fisheries, aquatic biology, and related areas in India. A bronze medal is awarded every five years. Established in 1945 from an endowment of Dr. and Mrs. S.L. Hora.

7650
INSA Medal for Young Scientists
For recognition of outstanding work in the field of science and technology. Any citizen of India below the age of 32 is eligible for nomination. Bronze medals and a cash prize of 5,000 rupees (maximum 15 awards per year) are awarded annually. In addition, the recipients are considered for a research grant not exceeding 20,000 rupees per year for a period of three years. Established in 1974.

7651
INSA Prize for Material Sciences
For recognition of outstanding contributions in material science. Any citizen of India is eligible for consideration for the prize for outstanding work done in India. Nominations are invited from the Fellowship in the first two weeks of October preceding the year of the award. A monetary prize of 10,000 rupees will be awarded for the first time in 1987 and will be

awarded biennially in the future. Established in 1986 from an endowment of 50,000 rupees by the Organizing Committee of the International Conference on the Application of Mossbauer Effect, held in 1981.

7652

INSA - T. S. Tirumurti Memorial Lecture
To recognize persons who have made outstanding contributions in the field of medical sciences. The lecturer is paid an honorarium depending upon the income besides travel expenses for journeys peformed to deliver the lecture. Awarded biennially. Established in 1985 from an endowment of 25,000 rupees by Mrs. Janaki Ramachandran, daughter of the late Dr. T.S. Tirumurti, who made notable contributions to pathology and medicine and was a Foundation Fellow of the Academy.

7653

INSA - Vainu Bappu Memorial Award
To recognize an astronomer/astrophysicist of international recognition. A monetary award of 25,000 rupees and a bronze medal are awarded. Established in 1985 from an endowment by Mrs. Suwanna Bappu, mother of the late Dr. M.K.V. Bappu, an eminent astronomer and Fellow of the Academy.

7654

K. S. Krishnan Memorial Lecture
To recognize a scientist who has made an outstanding contribution to any branch of the natural sciences. A lectureship and an honorarium of 1,000 rupees are awarded triennially. Established in 1965 in memory of Professor Kariamanikkam Srinivasa Krishman, a Fellow of the Academy.

7655

Prof. L. S. S. Kumar Memorial Award
To recognize a recipient of INSA Medal for Young Scientists for the year in the discipline of Plant Sciences, Animal Sciences and Agriculture in alternate years. In case of more than one person being recommended by the Sectional Committee for the award of the INSA Medal for Young Scientists, the person who is first in order of merit in the list is given the award. A monetary award of 1,000 rupees is awarded annually. Established in 1986.

7656

P. C. Mahalanobis Medal
For recognition of an outstanding contribution to the advancement of engineering and technology. A bronze medal is awarded triennially. Established in 1976.

7657

Prof. Panchanan Maheshwari Memorial Lecture Award
To recognize persons who have made oustanding contributions in any area of plant sciences. The lecture is to be given biennially and is held in alternate years with the T.S. Sadasivan Lecture. The lecturer is paid an honorarium depending upon the income besides travel expenses for journeys performed to deliver the lecture. Established in 1984 from an endowment of 26,200 rupees by the colleagues and friends of the late Professor Panchanan Maheshwari, a distinguished botanist and a Foundation Fellow of the Academy.

7658

Meghnad Saha Medal
For recognition of a distinguished contribution to science. A bronze medal is awarded triennially. Established in 1957.

7659

Sisir Kumar Mitra Memorial Lecture
For recognition of a distinguished contribution to any branch of the natural sciences. A lectureship and an honorarium of 1,000 rupees are awarded triennially. Established in 1963 in memory of Professor Sisir Kumar Mitra, a Fellow of the Academy.

7660

Jawaharlal Nehru Birth Centenary Lectures
To recognize an Indian scientist. Up to two lecturers receive an honorarium of 5,000 rupees each, and travel expenses for delivering the lectures.

7661

Jawaharlal Nehru Birth Centenary Medal
For recognition of international cooperation in science and technology. Scientists of all nations are eligible. A medal, citation and travel expenses are awarded triennially. Established in 1989.

7662

Jawaharlal Nehru Birth Centenary Visiting Fellowship
To select scientists to visit scientific institutions in other countries for a period of up to 4 weeks. Travel and per diem expenses are awarded.

7663

Prof. M. R. N. Prasad Memorial Lecture Award
To recognize an individual who has made an outstanding contribution in the field of animal physiology in its widest sense. The lecture is to be given once in three years. An honorarium of 10,000 rupees and travel expenses are awarded triennially. Established in 1992.

7664

Prof. G. N. Ramachandran 60th Birthday Commemoration Medal Award
To recognize an individual who has made outstanding contributions in the field of molecular biology, biophysics and crystallography. The lecture is to be given once in three years. The lecturer is awarded a Bronze Medal, a monetary prize of 25,000 rupees, and travel expenses. Established in 1991.

7665

Chandrasekhara Venkata Raman Medal
For recognition of contributions to the promotion of science. Scholars who have done outstanding work in any branch of science are eligible. A bronze medal is awarded triennially. Established in 1976.

7666

K. R. Ramanathan Medal
For recognition in the field of atmospheric sciences and meteorology. A bronze medal is awarded triennially. Established in 1986.

7667

Prof. K. Rangadhama Rao Memorial Lecture
To recognize a person who has done exemplary work in the field of spectroscopy. A lectureship and an honorarium are awarded triennially. Established in 1979 from the endowment of 10,000 rupees in memory of Dr. K. Rangadhama Rao by his students.

7668

Prof. T. S. Sadasivan Lecture Award
To recognize persons who have made outstanding contributions in any field of botany. The lecturer is paid an honorarium depending upon the income besides travel expenses for journeys performed to deliver the lecture. Awarded biennially. Established in 1982 from an endowment of 25,000 rupees by the Professor T.S. Sadasivan Endowment Committee to commemorate Professor T.S. Sadasivan, a Fellow of the Academy distinguished for research in physiological plant pathology.

7669

Professor T. R. Seshadri Seventieth Birthday Commemoration Medal
For recognition of meritorious work in any branch of chemistry and chemical technology. Eminent chemists of Indian nationality are eligible. A monetary prize of 1,500 rupees and a bronze medal are awarded triennially. Established in 1971 by an endowment of 10,000 rupees by the students of Professor T. R. Seshadri, an eminent organic chemist and a Fellow of the Academy.

7670
Shanti Swarup Bhatnagar Medal
For recognition of an outstanding contribution to engineering and technology. A bronze medal is awarded triennially. Established in 1957.

7671
Shri Dhanwantari Prize
To recognize an eminent scientist who has done outstanding work in the field of medical sciences including research in drugs and methodology of Ayurveda. This shall include research in medical as well as chemical, physical and biological sciences aimed at the amelioration of human suffering. In fact, its scope shall include any outstanding discovery in drug or modes of treatment or inventions established as a landmark in medical sciences in its widest sense. A monetary prize of 5,000 rupees and a bronze medal are awarded every five years. Established in 1969 by an endowment of 18,500 rupees by Shri A.K. Asundi in memory of his youngest daughter, Shrimati Akkadevi.

7672
Silver Jubilee Commemoration Medal
For recognition of an outstanding contribution to the agricultural sciences and applied sciences. A bronze medal is awarded triennially. Established in 1962.

7673
Srinivasa Ramanujan Medal
For recognition of outstanding work in the field of mathematics or a related subject. A bronze medal is awarded triennially. Established in 1961.

7674
Sunder Lal Hora Medal
To recognize a scientist who has distinguished himself in plant and animal sciences. A bronze medal is awarded triennially. Established in 1957.

7675
Dr. Har Swarup Memorial Lecture
For recognition of outstanding contributions in the field of zoology. The lecture is to be given once in three years. The lecturer is paid an honorarium depending upon the income besides travel expenses for journeys performed to deliver the lecture. Established in 1981 from an endowment of 10,000 rupees by Dr. (Mrs.) Savitri Swarup to commemorate Dr. Har Swarup, a Fellow of the Academy distinguished for his research on endocrinology, physiology and developmental biology.

7676
Prof. B. D. Tilak Lecture Award
To recognize persons who have made outstanding contributions to rural economy and life through innovative and effective application of science and technology. The lecturer is paid an honorarium depending upon the income besides travel expenses for journeys performed to deliver the lecture. Awarded annually. Established in 1982 from an endowment of 100,000 rupees by Professor B.D. Tilak Scientific Research and Education Trust, c/o National Chemical Laboratory, Pune, to commemorate Professor B.D. Tilak, a Fellow of the Academy, distinguished for research in the field of dyestuffs chemistry and organic chemical technology.

7677
Vishwakarma Medal
To recognize eminent scientists who have done outstanding work or whose discovery or invention has led to the start of a new industry in India or to a significant improvement of an existing process resulting in a cheaper or better product. A monetary prize of 7,500 rupees and a bronze medal are awarded triennially. Established in 1976 from an endowment of 33,000 rupees by Dr. P.B. Sarkar, FNA.

7678
D. N. Wadia Medal
To recognize an individual who has done outstanding work in the field of earth sciences (geology, geophysics, geography). A bronze medal is awarded triennially. Established in 1976.

7679
S. H. Zaheer Medal
To recognize an individual who has made outstanding contributions in the field of engineering and technology. A bronze medal is awarded triennially. Established in 1977.

7680
Indian Physics Association
I.I.T., Powai
Bombay 400 076, India

7681
R. D. Birla Award
To provide recognition for achievement in the field of physics. The Sarbadhikari Gold Medal is awarded. Established in 1980.

7682
Indian Science Congress Association
14, Dr. Biresh Guha St.   Phone: 33 47 4530
Calcutta 700 017. India   Phone: 33 40 2551

7683
Prof. Hira Lal Chakravarty Awards
To recognize talented young scientists doing significant research in the field of botany within the country. Candidates must be under 40 years of age on December 31 of the preceding year for the Award and must have a Ph.D. degree in any branch of botany, either pure or applied. The awards are given for original, independent, published work carried out in India within three years prior to the award. Applications must be submitted by July 15. A monetary prize of 4,000 rupees and a certificate are awarded annually during the Inaugural Function of the Congress. Two awards are presented. Established in 1984 from a donation received from Professor Hira Lal Chakravarty and Smt. Toru Chakravarty in honor of Professor Hira Lal Chakravarty.

7684
ISCA Young Scientists' Awards
To encourage young scientists. Candidates must be under 30 years of age. The papers submitted for consideration must be under single authorship and the work must have been carried out in India. Preference is given to independent work. Papers may be submitted by September 30. A monetary prize of 3,000 rupees and a Certificate of Merit are awarded annually during the concluding session of the Congress. Established in 1981.

7685
Pran Vohra Award
To recognize an individual for contributions to science. Established in 1990.

7686
Indian Society for Afro-Asian Studies
297 Sarswati Kunj
Patpargani   Phone: 11 2248246
New Delhi 110 092, India   Fax: 11 3329273

7687
International Youth Award
For recognition of endeavors that contribute to cooperation. A young person between 25 and 40 years of age from any country who contributes by his or her activities either in public life, executive functions, or literary

works to the promotion of understanding, goodwill, and friendship is eligible. A monetary prize of 25,000 rupees and a citation are awarded annually. Established in 1985 to commemorate International Youth Year.

7688
International Film Festival of India
Lok Nayak Bhawan
Khan Market
New Delhi 110 003, India
Phone: 11 61 59 53

7689
International Film Festival of India
To provide a common platform for the cinematographies of the world to project the excellence of their film art, contribute to the understanding and appreciation of the film cultures of different nations in the context of their social and cultural ethos, and promote friendship and cooperation among the different people of the world. The Festival is non-competitive and no awards will be given. Entry forms should be submitted by November 15. Established in 1952. Sponsored by India - Ministry of Information and Broadcasting.

7690
International Society of Tropical Ecology
Dept. of Botany
Banaras Hindu Univ.
Varanasi 5, India

7691
Medal for Distinguished Service to Tropical Ecology
To recognize individuals who make special contributions to tropical ecology. Members of the Society are eligible. A medal is awarded when merited. Established in 1976.

7692
Jamnalal Bajaj Foundation
Bajaj Bhawan, 2nd Fl.
Jamnalal Bajaj Marg
226 Nariman Point
Bombay 400 021, India
Phone: 22 202 3626
Fax: 22 202 2877

7693
Jamnalal Bajaj Foundation Awards
To recognize individuals in India for outstanding contribution in the fields of constructive work, application of science and technology for rural development and uplift, and welfare of women and children. Established in memory of Jamnalal Bajaj, a close associate of Mahatma Gandhi. Three awards of Rs. 200,00 0 each are given annually.

7694
Jamnalal Bajaj International Award for Promoting Gandhian Values Outside India
To recognize an outstanding contribution, made outside India, to any of the following: promotion of peace and harmony among people and friendliness among nations through application of the Gandhian philosophy of truth and non-violence; ending exploitation in any form and seeking solutions to social, cultural, economic, and political problems through Gandhian principles and constructive programs; and innovative work in social organizations with intention to promote Gandhian values of purity of means and ends by awakening moral conscience, fostering community self-reliance, and bringing about harmony of human life with nature. Individuals must be nominated, in writing, by persons belonging to any of the following catagories: former members of the Selection Committee for the Award; persons who have received the Award in the past; members of National Parliaments; recipients of the Nobel Peace Prize; the Secretary General of the United Nations and other leaders or officials of international organizations whose aims are consistent with the objects of the Award; Presidents and Vice-Chancellors of universities and professors of political science, philosophy, religion, economics, sociology, education, rural development, natural sciences, environment, and ecology; heads of Indian embassies and missions in India and abroad and India's permanent representatives to the UNO and similar world organizations; heads of academic institutions and social work organizations; and any other person whom the Trustees may wish to invite to submit proposals for the Award. Self-nominations are not accepted. A monetary award equivalent of Rs. 2 lakhs in foreign currency, a trophy, and a citation are given annually. The award is presented November 4 at the Foundation. Established in 1988 to commemorate the Birth Centenary of Jamnalal Bajaj, a close associate of Mahatma Gandhi.

7695
Kairali Childrens Book Trust
PO Box 624
Kottayam 686 001, Kerala, India
Phone: 563114
Phone: 568214

7696
Bala Sahitya Award
To recognize outstanding contributions to the field of children's literature. Published work may be submitted by November 1. A monetary award and a certificate are presented annually. Established in 1981 to honor Bala Saahitya.

7697
Professor Kaula Endowment for Library and Information Science
Address unknown.

7698
Professor Kaula Gold Medal
For recognition of service in the field of library and information science. Individuals may be nominated. A gold medal is awarded annually. Established in 1975 in honor of Professor P.N. Kaula by the Professor Kaula Festschrift Volume Committee.

7699
Kaula - Ranganathan Gold Medal
To recognize an Indian professional who has made significant contributions in the field of libraries and information services in India. A gold medal is awarded. Established in 1980.

7700
Kerala Sahitya Akademi
PO Box 501
Town Hall Rd.
Thrissur 680 020, Kerala, India
Phone: 331069

7701
I. C. Chacko Award
For recognition of achievement in Shastram, Bhashashastram. A committee selects the best work. A monetary prize of 2,000 rupees and a certificate are awarded annually. Established in 1976 by M.P. Thomas in memory of the late I.C. Chacko, his father.

7702
Kanakasree Award
For recognition of achievement in poetry. A monetary award of 2,000 rupees is awarded annually. Established in 1990.

7703
Kerala Sahitya Akademi Awards
For recognition of achievement in the literary field. Awards are given in the following categories: novel, drama, poetry, short story, essays, biography, criticism, travalogue or humor, translation, and total library contribution. A committee selects the best work. Monetary prizes of 5,000 rupees and certificates are awarded annually. Established in 1958. The categories of poetry, short stories, essays, biography, travelogue/humor, and total library contribution were established in 1959, 1966, 1966, 1969, and 1992 respectively.

7704
C. B. Kumar Award
For recognition of achievement in essays. A committee selects the best work. A monetary prize of 1,500 rupees and a certificate are awarded annually. Established in 1976 by Smt. Sarada Kumar in memory of C.B. Kumar, her husband.

7705
Kuttippuzha Award
For recognition of achievement in Sahitya Vimarsam. A committee selects the best work. A monetary prize of 2,000 rupees and a certificate are awarded biennially. Established in 1982 by the Kuttippuzha Memorial Committee in memory of Kuttippuzha Krishna Pillai.

7706
K. R. Namboodiri Award
For recognition of achievement in Vaidika Sahityam. A committee selects the best work. A monetary prize of 2,000 rupees and a certificate are awarded annually. Established in 1977 by Shri Kandangatha Raman Nambudiri in memory of K.R. Nambudiri.

7707
Natakavedi (Bombay) Award
For recognition of achievement in drama. A monetary prize of 2,500 rupees is awarded annually. Established in 1989.

7708
Sree Padmanabha Swari Prize
For recognition of achievement in children's literature (Bala Sahityam). A committee selects the best work. A monetary prize of 2,500 rupees and a certificate are awarded annually. Established in 1959 by His Highness, the Maharaja of Travancore.

7709
Management Professionals Association
PO Box 1445
25 Krishna St.
T Nagar
Madras 600 017, India
Phone: 44 440677
Fax: 44 441514

7710
Hall of Fame
To recognize outstanding management professionals. Individuals are elected annually. Established in 1981.

7711
Management Expert
To promote professionalism in management and to recognize management professionals. Members of the Association may be nominated. A plaque is awarded at a special award ceremony. Established in 1981.

7712
Mythic Society
2 Nrupathunga Road
Bangalore 560 002, Karnataka, India
Phone: 215034

7713
Mythic Society Scholar
To recognize individuals who have contributed in a significant way in the fields of epigraphy, literature, history, archaeology, and education. The total contribution of the person in his field is considered. A citation and honor at a public gathering arranged by the Society are awarded on special occasions. Established in 1973.

7714
National Centre of Films for Children and Young People
Films Div. Complex
24 G. Deshmukh Marg
Bombay 400 026, India
Phone: 22 3870875
Fax: 22 3875610

7715
International Children's Film Festival of India
For recognition of outstanding films for children. The objects of the festival are to promote and encourage the Children's Film Movement, to foster a closer relationship among the international fraternity of children's film makers and organizations and to afford them an opportunity to exchange their films, and to exhibit the best of the children's films from different countries of the world with a view to promote international understanding and brotherhood among the children of the world. There are three sections at the festival: competitive, information, and market. The festival is open to films suitable for children up to 15 years of age. A film produced during the previous two years may be entered in the competitive section either by the producer or any individual or organization authorized by the producer. A film that has already won an award in any recognized international film festival is also eligible for entry in the Competitive section. No more than one feature film and one short film or two short films are accepted as entries from one country in the section. However, the host country is eligible to enter up to two feature and two short films. If the language of a film is other than English, it should be accompanied by a detailed synopsis and dialogue scripts in English. The following awards are presented: Golden Elephant Award for the Best Live-Action Feature Length Film - 1,000,000 rupees; Silver Elephant Award for the Best Short Film - 50,000 rupees; Silver Elephant Award for the Second Best Live-Action Feature-Length Film - 50,000 rupees; Silver Elephant Award for the Best Animation Film - 50,000 rupees; Silver Elephant Award for the Best Puppet Film; Silver Elephant Award for the Best Director - 50,000 rupees; Silver Elephant Award for the Best Child Artist; Silver Elephant Award for the Best Cinematographer; Silver Elephant Award for the Special Jury Prize - 50,000 rupees; Golden Plaque Award for the Most Popular Children's Film determined by a jury of 15 children; Silver Plaque with a Certificacte of a Merit to the best film in the Interantional Competition Section; Bronze Elephant Award for the Best Child Artist or Technician - 25,000 rupees; Bronze Elephant Award for a film selected by the International Jury - 25,000 rupees; CIFEJ Jury Medal for the Best Feature-Length Film; and Certificates of Merit. Trophies and plaques are awarded biennially. Established in 1979.

7716
Palynological Society of India
Environmental Resources Research Centre
Poomalliyoor Konam
PB 1230
Peroorkada
Thiruvananthapuram 695005, Kerala, India
Phone: 432159

7717
Sir Charles Darwin International Medal for Science and Environment
To recognize the scientific achievements.

7718
Professor Gunnar Erdtman International Award for Palynology
For recognition of contributions that accelerate knowledge, teaching, and research in palynology and allied sciences, and to promote international goodwill and understanding among palynological scientists. Individuals over 40 years of age may be nominated by a committee appointed by the Society. Membership is not required, and there is no restriction on citizenship. A plaque and certificate of merit are awarded every five years starting in 1994. Established in 1968 in honor of Professor Gunnar Erdtman of the Palynology Laboratory, Stockholm, Sweden. Formerly: (1981) Gunnar Erdtman International Medal.

| 7719 |

Poets International Organization
No. 10(4), 1st Cross
Arcot Srinivasachar St.
Bangalore 560 053, India   Phone: 812 70130

| 7720 |

Poets International Organization Awards
For recognition of individuals who make valuable contributions in the field of poetry. The Organization sponsors writing competitions.

| 7721 |

Soviet Land
25 Barakhamba Rd.   Phone: 11 3315370
New Delhi 1, India   Phone: 11 3312722

| 7722 |

Soviet Land **Nehru Award**
To recognize leading figures in the fields of art, literature and journalism, and the child winners (10-13 years of age) in the painting competition. Works and translations of Russian classics and Soviet works in Indian languages and also meritorious work done in creative and cultural fields calculated to promote the cause which Jawaharlal Nehru held dear to his heart are eligible. The following prizes are awarded: (1) three prizes of 20,000 rupees and a two-week visit to the U.S.S.R.; (2) three prizes of 10,000 rupees and a two-week visit to the U.S.S.R.; (3) two prizes of 8,000 rupees and a two-week visit to the U.S.S.R.; (4) ten prizes of 5,000 rupees and a Certificate of Merit; and (5) five prizes to children of 10-13 age group for a free one month's holiday at the Artek Young Pioneers' Camp in Crimea on the Black Sea Coast. Awarded annually. Established in 1964 in memory of Pandit Jawaharlal Nehru, a champion of world peace and friendship among nations.

| 7723 |

World Assembly of Small and Medium Enterprises
                                            Phone: 11 6411417
27, Nehru Place   Phone: 11 6414058
New Delhi 110 019, India   Fax: 11 6852170

| 7724 |

Legion of Honour Award
For recognition of outstanding achievement in the field of small and medium enterprises. Individuals who have at least 15 years of uninterrupted service to the small and medium enterprises sector in any part of the world either at national, regional, or global level irrespective of age, religion, or citizenship are eligible. A gold medal and a citation are awarded biennially. Established in 1980.

| 7725 |

Special Recognition Award
For recognition of special contributions to the promotion and development of small and medium enterprises. A gold plated medal and a certificate are awarded when merited. Established in 1980.

Indonesia

| 7726 |

Indonesian Medical Association
(Ikatan Dokter Indonesia)
Jalan Dr. Samratulangie 29   Phone: 21 3150679
Jakarta 10350, Indonesia   Fax: 21 3900473

| 7727 |

Wahidin Sudiro Husodo Award
To recognize an individual for achievement in professional activities for community welfare. Medical doctors, who are members or non-members of the Association, are eligible. A medal and a certificate are awarded annually. Established in 1986 to honor Dr. Wahidin Sudiro Husodo.

| 7728 |

M. Kodiat Award
To recognize an individual for achievement in medical science development. Medical doctors, who are members or non-members of the Association, are eligible. A medal is awarded annually. Established in 1986 by the Idonesian Medical Association to honor Dr. M. Kodiat, who developed a mass eradication system for frambusia. Additional information is available from the Ministry of Health R.I., Director General for Communicable Disease Center.

| 7729 |

Sudjono Djuned Poesponegoro Award
To recognize the best article in the Indonesian Medical Association Journal. A medal is awarded annually. Established in 1988 to honor Prof. Dr. Sudjono.

| 7730 |

Sutomo Tjokronegoro Award
To recognize a community leader for initiative and leadership in health/medical development in the country. A medal is awarded annually. Established in 1986 to honor Prof. Dr. Sutomo Tjokronegoro. Additional information is available from Mrs. Sutomo Tjokronegoro, Universitas Indonesia.

| 7731 |

R. Wasito Award
To recognize an individual for achievement in the development of self-reliance in family planning practices. Medical doctors who are members of the Association are eligible. A medal is awarded annually. Established in 1988 to honor Dr. R. Wasito. Sponsored by the National Coordinating Board of Family Planning.

| 7732 |

National Film Council of Indonesia
(Dewan Film Nasional Indonesia)
                                            Phone: 21 336106
Menteng Raya 62 A   Phone: 21 320773
Jakarta, Indonesia   Fax: 21 3103560

| 7733 |

Indonesian Film Festival
(Festival Film Indonesia)
To recognize achievements in film. The following awards are presented: (1) Citra Award - for the Best Picture; (2) Widya Awards - for the Best Documentary Film; (3) Kartini Award - for the Best Child Actor/Actress; (4) Bing Slamet Award - for the Best Comedy Film; (5) Ki Mohammad Said Award - for the Best Children's Film; (6) Ismail Marzuki Award - for the Best Musical Theme; (7) Syamsul Bahri Award - for the Best Musical Film; (8) S. Tutur Award - for the Best Film Poster; (9) Chaidir Rahman Award - for the Best Film Critic; (10) Thropy of Malidar Hadiyuwono - for one of the nominated films in the previous Indonesian Film Festival which becomes the box office favorite; and (11) Thropy of H. Antemas - for the cinema which screened the greatest number of Indonesian films during the year. Monetary awards and trophies are presented annually in November. Established in 1975.

Iran

| 7734 |

Children's Book Council of Iran
(Shoraye Ketabe Koudak)
Enghelab Sezavar 69
PO Box 13145 - 133   Phone: 21 6408074
Tehran, Iran   Fax: 21 632360

7735
Children's Book Council Award
(Jayezeye Shoraye Ketabe Koudak)
For recognition of a contribution in the field of children's literature. Iranian writers, illustrators, and translators, as well as outstanding works by Iranian young adults, are eligible. A plaque and diploma are awarded annually. Established in 1963 by A. Yamini Sharif.

7736
Iranian Research Organization for Science and Technology
No. 71 Forsat St. Enghelab Ave.
PO Box 15815-3538
Tehran 15819, Iran
Phone: 21 8280517
Fax: 21 4408340

7737
The Kharazmi Prize
To recognize outstanding research in the fields of engineering, agriculture, basic sciences, medical sciences, or human sciences, and to encourage any scientific work that the IROST scientific board deems worthy. Up to three persons receive a monetary prize of $5,000 and a gift annually. Selection is based on the quality of the research project. Prizes are presented by the president of the Islamic Republic of Iran at an official meeting held during the Islamic Revolution Celebration in February. Established in 1982 in memory of Mohammad Bn Moussa Kharazmi, an Indian mathmatician and astronomer.

7738
Isfahan International Festival of Films for Children and Young Adults
Farhang Cinema
Dr. Shariati Ave.
Gholbak
Tehran 19139, Iran
Phone: 21 265086
Phone: 21 2002088
Fax: 21 267082

7739
Golden Butterfly
To promote outstanding films from all over the world whose main purpose is to entertain and educate children and young adults and to help them acquire a more critical appreciation of film art. The award, a golden butterfly perched on a silver film frame and mounted on a base of marquetry, is presented annually in October. Established in 1985 by the Fajr International Film Festival. Sponsored by Isfahan Mayorality, and the Farabi Cinema Foundation.

7740
Islamic Republic of Iran
Ministry of Education
The Office of Art Tasks - Research and
 Model Making
No. 8, Semnan Lane, Behar Avenue
Tehran, Iran
Phone: 21 762280
Phone: 21 752966
Fax: 21 827787

7741
Roshd International Educational Film Festival
(Jashnvare Beynolmelale e Filmhaye Amouzeshi Tarbeyati Roshd)
To encourage the new abilities and talents to produce educational - pedagogical items and to encourage the young film innovators through presenting their educational-artistic work; and to provide the proper opportunity to exchange ideas through moving pictures and recognition of international experiences in the field of educational films and to develop the utilization of educational films. Awards are given in the following categories: (1) Pre-School; (2) Primary school; (3) Guidance Cycle (Junior High); (4) Secondary School Film group; (5) Teachers' Film group; and (6) Exceptional Children. Films on experimental sciences, and on methodology and teachers training techniques are encouraged. The deadline for entry is September 15. Golden, silver, and bronze books are awarded for first, second and third prize in each category. Merit Certificates are awarded to films for exceptional qualities. The Diploma of Participation is presented to all the screened films. Established in 1963 by the Ministry of Education.

7742
Roshd International Film Festival
8 Semnan Ln.
Bahar Ave.
Tehran 15617, Iran
Phone: 21 7502966
Fax: 21 76228

7743
Roshd International Film Festival Awards
To recognize outstanding films. Golden Book Trophies are presented in the following categories: Best Preschool Film, Best Primary School Film, Best High School Film, Best Teaching Film, Best Exceptional Children and Handicapped Film, and Best Adult Education and Literacy Film. Golden Book Trophies are also presented in the general film category for: Best Film, Best Direction, Best Photography, and Best Screenplay. Merit certificates are also presented.

Iraq

7744
Arab Federation for Food Industries
Jadriah Near Karma Hotel
PO Box 13025
Baghdad, Iraq
Phone: 1 7760472

7745
Certificate of Appreciation
For recognition of a contribution to the dairy, bread, and the date palm industries. A certificate is awarded annually. Established in 1980 by Dr. Falah S. Jabr.

7746
Federation of Arab Scientific Councils
PO Box 13027
Baghdad, Iraq
Phone: 1 5381090

7747
Arabization Prizes
To encourage Arabization and standardization of scientific terms. Selection is by nomination. A monetary prize is awarded biennially. Established in 1982.

7748
General Arab Women Federation
Hay Al-Maghreb
Mahaela 304
Baghdad, Iraq
Phone: 1 4227117

7749
Medal of Distinction
For recognition of distinguished efforts in support of the Arab Women Movement. A medal is awarded annually at the General Conference of the Federation. Established in 1985.

Ireland

7750
Advertising Press Club of Ireland
53 Ragland Road
Dublin 4, Ireland

7751
Mc Connell Award
For recognition of achievement in the field of advertising. Individuals involved in the advertising or print industries may be nominated. A specially commissioned Silver Casket is awarded when merited. Established in 1943 in honor of John Mc Connell of Mc Connell's Advertising.

7752
Apothecaries Hall of Dublin
95 Merrion Sq.
Dublin 2, Ireland

7753
John Sheppard Memorial Lecture
To encourage research and discussion into and about medical general practice. General practitioners or other doctors interested in general practice are eligible. A monetary prize and a lectureship are awarded annually. Established in 1979.

7754
Arts Council An Chomhairle Ealaion
(Chomhairle Ealaion)
70 Merrion Square
Dublin 2, Ireland
Phone: 1 6611840
Fax: 1 6761302

7755
Bursaries, Scholarships, and Travel Awards
To assist individuals in the pursuit of their art. Applicants must be of Irish birth or residence. Visual artists, creative writers, musicians, opera singers, filmmakers, and dancers may apply.

7756
George Campbell Memorial Travel Award
The Arts Council is associated with the Spanish Cultural Institute and the Arts Council of Northern Ireland in awarding the George Campbell Memorial Travel Award. This annual award of approximately £1,500 Irish has been instituted to celebrate George Campbell's special relationship with both parts of Ireland and the strong cultural contact he developed with Spain. In 1994 the award is open to artists from the Republic of Ireland and applications should be made to The Arts Council/An Chomhairle Ealaion.

7757
Denis Devlin Memorial Award for Poetry
For recognition of the best book of poetry in the English language written by an Irish citizen. Works published during the preceding three years are eligible. A monetary prize of £1,500 Irish is awarded triennially. Established in 1959.

7758
Dublin Corporation Arts Scholarship
To provide for studies at an advanced level in music, dance, and the visual arts. Applicants for these scholarships must live in the Dublin Corporation area. Applicants in music and dance are assessed by audition and applicants in visual arts on the basis of portfolios of work. Candidates for a music scholarship may be requested to present a programme in contrasting styles of 20 minutes duration. Applicants for Scholarships in Dance are expected to offer one classical solo and one solo in a contrasting style. Established in 1981. In addition, the Council offers many different scholarships and grants to assist individuals in music, dance, visual arts, and literature. Artists with a disability may apply for the Dublin Corporation Biennial Christy Brown Award.

7759
Douglas Hyde Gold Medal
(Duais Bhonn De Hide)
To encourage painting of Irish historical subjects. Paintings exhibited at the annual Oireachtas Art Exhibition in Dublin are eligible for consideration. A gold medal and £100 Irish are awarded annually. Established in 1947.

7760
Macaulay Fellowship
To further the liberal education of young creative artists. Awards are given in alternate years in the following categories: visual arts, music composition, and literature. Artists born in Ireland who are under 30 years of age on June 30 or under 35 in exceptional circumstances are eligible. A monetary award of £3,500 Irish is awarded annually. The Macaulay fellowship is offered in Visual Arts in 1994 and in music in 1995. Established in 1958 by W.B. Macaulay in honor of President Sean T. O'Kelly.

7761
Prize for Poetry in Irish
(An Duais don bhFiliocht i nGaelige)
To promote the writing of poetry in the Irish language and for recognition of the best book of poetry in the Irish language published during the preceding three years. A monetary prize of £1,500 Irish is awarded triennially. Established in 1962.

7762
Marten Toonder Award
For recognition of works by an artist of established reputation in the fields of literature, music composition, or visual arts. Awards are given in alternate years in the three categories. Applications may be submitted by April 15 by Irish citizens or residents. A monetary prize of £3,500 Irish is awarded triennially. The award is offered in music in 1994. Established in 1977 by Marten Toonder, a Dutch author.

7763
Castelbar International Song Contest
Address unknown.

7764
Berger Trophy
To recognize the composer of the winning song of the contest. Composers worldwide were eligible. A monetary prize of £10,000 Irish and a trophy were awarded annually. Established in 1966 by Castelbar Chamber of Commerce. Sponsored by Berger Paints. (Discontinued in 1988)

7765
Cork International Choral Festival
PO Box 68
Cork, Ireland
Phone: 21 308308
Fax: 21 300685

7766
Cork International Choral Festival
To recognize outstanding choirs. Choirs must be organized for at least one calendar year prior to the festival. All members, except the conductor, must be amateurs. Awards are presented in the following categories: International Trophy Competition - open to any choir of international standing with at least 20 voices. Monetary awards - first prize £3,000 Irish and a trophy, second prize £2,000 Irish, Third prize £1,000 Irish; National Competitions for Adults - Mixed-voice Choirs - open or confined, Chamber Choirs, Equal-voice Choirs - open or confined, Youth Choirs - equal-voice or mixed voice, and Plainchant. Monetary awards, trophies, and certificates for first prize, and certificates for second prize are awarded; National Competitions for Schools - Primary School Choirs, Equal-voice Post-primary School Choirs, and Mixed-voice Post-primary School Choirs. Monetary awards, trophies (first prize), and certificates are awarded for First and Second prize, Certificates of Excellence, Distinction, Commendation, Merit, and Participation are also awarded; and Special Festival Awards-Lady Dorothy Mayer Memorial Trophy - for the best performance of a part-song in the international competitions of the festival, Trofai Cuimhneachain Philib Ui Laoghaire (The Pilib O'Laoghaire Memorial Trophy) - for the best performance of a part-song in Irish in the national adult competitions of the festival, Trofai Chumann Naisiunta nag Cor (the Association of Irish Choirs Trophy) - for the best

performance of a part-song in the school competitions section of the festival, Irish Federation of Musicians & Associated Professions Trophy - for the best performance of a part-song in Irish in the school competitions of the festival, (e) Schutz Perpetual Trophy - for the best performance of a work by Heinrich Schutz, (f) PEACE Trophy - to the choir that, in the opinion of the audience, gives the most enjoyable performance of the festival; and Sean O. Riada Memorial Trophy Competition - established in 1976 to enable up to four Irish choirs to commission a composer born in or resident in Ireland to make an *a capella* setting of an Irish text. Each of the choirs accepted receives the sum of £100 Irish to be given to the composer as a commissioning fee. Each work is performed during the festival by the choir which commissioned it. Two prizes are awarded: First prize £150 Irish, Second prize £75 Irish; the choir whose commissioned work is awarded first place receives the additional sum of £100 Irish. Awarded annually. Established in 1954. Formerly: Cork International Choral and Folk Dance Festival.

7767
International Trophy Competition
This competition is held as part of the Cork International Choral Festival. It is open to any choir of international standing, with a minimum of twenty voices. A maximum of 10 choirs will be accepted for this competition. Awarded annually. Established in 1989.

7768
Cork International Film Festival
Hatfield House
Tobin St.   Phone: 21 271711
Cork, Ireland   Fax: 21 275945

7769
Cork International Film Festival
To recognize and reward excellence in the making of films within the European communities. To be eligible, films must originate in a member state of the European Economic Community and must have been recent productions. The deadline for submissions is July 20. The following awards are presented: European Short Film Award - 10,000 ECU's; Gus Healy Award - £1,000 Irish for the best Irish Short-Film in the competition; and Black & White Film Awards, including Best Black and White Short Film, Best Black & White Feature, and Best Black & White Cinematography. Awarded annually. Established in 1956. Sponsored by the European Commission, Dublin Office.

7770
EOLAS/Irish Science and Technology Agency
Glasnevin   Phone: 1 370 101
Dublin 9, Ireland   Fax: 1 379 620

Formerly: (1987) National Board for Science and Technology.

7771
Awards for Innovation
To recognize innovative achievement in Irish commercial and industrial life. The following awards are given: (1) The NBST New Product Development Award - to a firm which has recently developed and commercialized a major new product; (2) NBST Excellence in Technology Award - for general excellence in the development, performance or application of technology in the industrial context; and (3) NBST Scientist of the Year Award - to an Irish based scientist or technologist for work in applied science and/or technology. A monetary prize of £1,000 Irish and a specially commissioned sculpture are awarded annually for each award.

7772
European Football Commentators Association Television
9 Lakelands Lawn
Upper Kilmacud Rd.
Stillorgan
Dublin, Ireland   Phone: 1 886217

7773
Awards
For recognition in the sport of soccer and in sports broadcasting. Awards are presented.

7774
European Healthcare Management Association
Vergemount Hall, Clonskeagh   Phone: 1 2839299
Dublin 6, Ireland   Fax: 1 2838653

Formerly: (1987) European Association of Programmes in Health Services Studies.

7775
Baxter Award for Healthcare Management in Europe
To recognize an outstanding publication and/or practical contribution to excellence in healthcare management in Europe. Contributions can be in any of the following fields: management development initiatives, health services research, or innovations in management practice. Books, articles, or papers submitted must have been published within the last two years. The deadline is February 28. A monetary award of $5,000 is presented at the Annual Conference of the EHMA. Established in 1986 to honor Jan Blanpain's contributions to the EHMA. Sponsored by Baxter Healthcare.

7776
GPA Book Award
Award Admin.
GPA House   Phone: 61 360000
Shannon, Clare, Ireland   Fax: 61 360888

7777
GPA Book Award
To identify and celebrate the best in contemporary Irish writing. Authors born on the island of Ireland or, if born elsewhere, resident on the island of Ireland for the preceding three years, are eligible for consideration. Books by eligible authors in the categories of fiction, poetry, and general (autobiography, biography, history, essays, belles lettres, and works of criticism) are eligible for consideration for the award if first published during the preceding three years. Reprints, new and revised editions are not eligible. A monetary prize of £50,000 Irish is awarded triennially. Established in 1989.

7778
GPA Dublin International Piano Competition
City Hall   Phone: 1 8727666
Dublin 2, Ireland   Fax: 1 8731835

7779
GPA Dublin International Piano Competition
For recognition of outstanding piano performances. Professional pianists between 17 and 30 years of age are eligible. The following prizes are awarded: first prize - £10,000 Irish; second prize - £7,500 Irish; third prize - £5,000 Irish; fourth prize - £4,000 Irish; fifth prize - £3,000 Irish; sixth prize - £2,000 Irish; Europa Medal - to the best placed competitor from a member state of the European Community; £1,000 Irish to the best placed Irish competitor; GPA Dublin International Piano Competition Trophies to each finalist; six prizes of £750 Irish to the semi-finalists; and eight prizes of £400 Irish each to those eliminated after the second round. A Kawai piano, debut recitals in London, New York, and Vienna and a substantial list of engagements are also awarded to the first prize winner. Awarded triennially. Established in 1988. Sponsored by GPA Group.

7780
Hill and Knowlton Ireland
3 Mount St. Crescent
Dublin 2, Ireland   Phone: 1 616077

| 7781 |

Benson and Hedges Media Awards
For recognition of outstanding work in Irish journalism. The following awards are presented: (1) Young Journalist Award; (2) Outstanding Work in Press Photography; (3) Outstanding Work in Sports Journalism; (4) Outstanding Work in Provincial Journalism; (5) Outstanding Work in Irish Journalism Television; (6) Outstanding Work in Irish Journalism Radio; and (7) Outstanding Work in Irish Journalism Print. Monetary prizes totaling £5,000 and plaques are awarded annually. Established in 1967.

| 7782 |

Honorable Society of King's Inns
Henrietta St. Phone: 8 744840
Dublin 1, Ireland Fax: 8 726048

| 7783 |

John Brooke Scholarship
For recognition of outstanding scholarship in the field of law. Individuals who attain the highest marks on the final law examination of the Barrister-at-Law degree course are eligible. A monetary prize is awarded annually. In addition, the Society's Exhibition Prize and the James Murnaghan Memorial Prize are awarded. Previously, the Victoria Prize was awarded until discontinued in 1971.

| 7784 |

International Advertising Festival of Ireland
35 Upper Fitzwilliam St. Phone: 1 6765991
Dublin 2, Ireland Fax: 1 6614589

| 7785 |

International Advertising Festival of Ireland
For recognition of the best commercials produced for television, cinema, and radio. Entries must advertise consumer or capital goods, consumer services, or public services and social welfare. Entries are accepted from advertising agencies, production companies, advertisers, and recording studios. The following awards are presented: Worldwinner Prize - confined to entries that have already won major awards at other festivals (presented by Saatchi & Saatchi Advertising); Grand Prix Television - for the best television commercial entered in any television section (presented by Radio Telefis Eireann); Grand Prix Cinema - for the best cinema the best commercial entered within the Cinema Group (presented by RSA Advertising); Grand Prix Radio - for the best radio commercial entered in any radio section (presented by Brian Halford Productions Ltd.); Irish Grand Prix - for the best television commercial in the Irish Television Section specially produced for use on Radio Telefis Eirann or Ulster Television (presented by the Film and Video Producers Association); National Awards - for the best entry from each country from which 20 or more television commercials are entered; Palme d'Or - to the production company that attains the highest average marking on a minimum of six commercials entered in the Television and Cinema Sections, except for Worldwinner (presented by the Institute of Advertising Practitioners in Ireland); Premier Gold Award - for television, cinema, and radio commercials within various sections; Delegate Prize - for the best commercial as voted by the delegates of the Festival; and Special Awards - to honor individuals for various aspects of production, including editing, art direction, direction, camera work, humor, writing, post production, animation, special effects, artist performance, music, soundtrack, lighting, and others. The Festival is held annually in September. Established in 1962. Formerly: (1988) Irish Advertising Awards Festival.

| 7786 |

International Songwriters' Association
(Association Internationale des Cordeliers)
22 Sullane Cresent
Raheen Heights, Limerick, Ireland Phone: 61 28837

| 7787 |

International Songwriters' Association Awards
To recognize songwriters, music publishers, and recording executives. The Association organizes competitions and bestows awards.

| 7788 |

Ireland
Department of Defence
Parkgate Phone: 1 718211
Dublin 8, Ireland Fax: 1 6798834

| 7789 |

Distinguished Service Medal
(An Bonn Seirbhise Dearscna)
For recognition of individual or associated acts of bravery, courage, leadership, resource or devotion to duty (other than any such acts or duty performed while on war service) arising out of, or associated with, service in the Defense Forces. The medal may be awarded in three classes: with honor, with distinction, and with merit. Established in 1964.

| 7790 |

Military Medal for Gallantry
(An Bonn Mileata Calmachta)
This, the highest military honor in the State, is given in recognition of the performance of any act of exceptional bravery or gallantry (other than one performed while on war service) arising out of, or associated with military service, and involving risk to life or limb above and beyond the call of duty. The medal may be awarded in three classes: with honor, with distinction, and with merit. Established in 1944.

| 7791 |

Irish Academy of Letters
School of Irish Studies
Thomas Prior House
Merrion Rd.
Dublin 4, Ireland

| 7792 |

Eric Gregory Medal
To recognize individuals for distinction in letters or an outstanding literary work written in the Irish language. A medal is awarded periodically.

| 7793 |

Prize for Novel
To provide recognition for the best novel written in the Irish language. Awarded annually.

| 7794 |

Irish Farm Centre
(Macra na Feirme)
Blue Bell Phone: 508000
Dublin 12, Ireland Fax: 514908

| 7795 |

ESB Community Enterprise Award
To encourage communities to plan economic regeneration of their areas. Promoters of plans must be voluntary community groups to be considered. A monetary prize and an aerial photo of the area are awarded annually in September. Established in 1989. Co-sponsored by Macra na Feirme, Royal Dublin Society and ESB Electricity Supply Board. Additional information is available from Pat Collier, ESB Community Enterprise Awards Committee at the above address. (Discontinued)

7796

National Leadership Award
To recognize outstanding leadership given by active members thus promoting the ideals of self-reliance and leadership. Nomination is by local county/region. A trophy is awarded annually. Established in 1987. Sponsored by Bank of Ireland.

7797

Irish Hotels Federation
13 Northbrook Rd.
Dublin 6, Ireland
Phone: 1 4976459
Fax: 1 4974613

7798

Billy Kelly Award of Excellence
To recognize a hotel manager or an owner/manager for outstanding all-round performance of the hotel. Qualified hoteliers of any age who have at least 15 years service in the hotel industry and have completed a management/development program are eligible. Individuals in good personal standing within the industry, having worked for the good of the industry on a voluntary basis, and been active in professional bodies are considered. An inscribed sterling silver plate and a citation are awarded triennially. Established in 1984 to honor Billy Kelly, owner/manager of Kelly's Strand Hotel, Rosslare, County Wexford.

7799

Irish Lawn Tennis Association
(Cumann Leadoige na h-Eireann)
Address unknown.

7800

Raymond Egan Memorial Trophy
To recognize an individual for a contribution to tennis. Players, officials, and administrators at any level may be nominated by a club or a representative body before December 31. A perpetual trophy is awarded annually. Established in 1985 to honor Raymond Egan.

7801

Irish Life Assurance
Irish Life Centre
Lower Abbey St.
Dublin 1, Ireland
Phone: 1 7042000
Fax: 1 7041900

7802

CERT/Irish Life Souvenir of Ireland Challenge
To recognize new souvenir designs for Ireland by students. Individuals or teams are eligible. The following awards are presented: first place - a commemorative plaque, a gift voucher of £600, and £1,000 worth of equipment for the winner's school; second place - £600 to be split between the school (for equipment) and the winning student; and third place - £300 to be split between the school (for equipment) and the winning student. Each finalist receives a certificate, and supervising teachers receive dinner for two. Established in 1993.

7803

Irish Life Business Awareness Awards
To develop post-primary students' awareness of the role of business in the provision of employment, production of goods and services, the creation of wealth, and the improvement of general living standards. Studies based on firms in the local community with at least 10 employees were considered. The following awards were presented annually: a prize of £1,500 Irish to the overall winning study, eight additional prizes of £500 Irish each, plaques to groups for studies of special merit, and a special scroll to individuals in recognition of their participation and achievement. All prize money was given to the school for use on some aspect of school activities. Established in 1988. (Discontinued)

7804

Irish Life Drama Award
To encourage new writing for the theatre in Ireland. A monetary prize of £1,000 Irish was awarded annually. (Discontinued).

7805

Irish Life Festival Choice Awards
To recognize outstanding theater productions of the Irish Life Dublin Theatre Festival. Awards are presented in the following categories: Best Foreign Production, Best New Irish Play, and Best Irish Production. An inscribed statue is awarded to winners in each category. Established in 1992.

7806

Irish Life Manager of the Year
To recognize the outstanding sports manager for the year. Irish Life Manager of the Month awards were also presented to individuals involved with the following sports: Soccer, Gaelic Football, Hurling, Athletics, Golf, Hockey, Rugby, and Showjumping. Awarded annually. Established in 1982. (Discontinued in 1991)

7807

Irish Life Pensioner of the Year Awards
To encourage individuals over 60 years of age to remain active, and to recognize individuals who are successfully participating in local and community activities. Individuals or organizations may nominate candidates. It is not necessary that a nominee should have formally retired, but the nomination must be for an activity that is not directly related to the nominee's previous or current occupation. Monetary awards of £250 Irish are awarded to six preliminary winners, and monetary awards of £500 Irish are awarded to charities selected by each winner. A monetary award of £250 Irish is presented annually to the overall winner at a presentation luncheon in May, and a monetary award of £2,000 Irish is presented to the winner's selected organization or activity. Established in 1984.

7808

***Sunday Independent*/Irish Life Arts Awards**
To recognize individuals for excellence in the arts in Ireland. Awards were presented in the following categories: visual arts, music, theatre, television, cinema, literature, television film, poetry, architecture, photography; and special awards. Awarded annually. Established in 1981. Sponsored by Irish Life plc. (Discontinued in 1991)

7809

The Irish Times
10-16 D'Olier St.
Dublin 2, Ireland
Phone: 6 792022
Fax: 6 773282

7810

The *Irish Times* Literature Prizes
For recognition of a work of fiction, written in the English or Irish language and published in the United States, Ireland, or Britain during the preceding year. Judges are from each of the three countries. A monetary prize of £22,000 Irish is awarded annually. Established in 1988. Sponsored by *The Irish Times*.

7811

Irish Youth Film & Arts Company
Croppy Boy House
Fairhill, Cork, Ireland
Phone: 21 306019
Phone: 21 504633

7812

Cork Youth International Video and Film Festival
For recognition of achievement in the art of filmmaking. Individuals over 25 years of age are eligible to submit films and videos. The Blarney Trophy (Cuchulainn Trophy), a bronze replica of the famous Cuchulainn Statue in the G.P.O. in Dublin, is awarded annually at the Irish Youth Film

& Arts Week. Established in 1978. In addition, a Best Overall Film Award is given in the category of films by individuals under 18 years of age.

7813
Library Association of Ireland
(Cumann Leabharlann na hEireann)
53 Upper Mount St. Phone: 1 6619000
Dublin 2, Ireland Fax: 1 6761628

7814
Honorary Fellow
To recognize distinguished persons of national or international reputation in librarianship. A scroll is awarded. No more than four honorary members are allowed at any one time.

7815
President's Award
For recognition of achievement in the field of public relations. Members of the Association are eligible. A trophy and a plaque are awarded annually at the annual conference in April. Established in 1990 to honor F. J. E. Hurst.

7816
Panel of Chefs of Ireland
10 Gracepark Gardens
Drumcondra
Dublin 9, Ireland

7817
Chef Ireland
To recognize outstanding culinary ability. The competition is built around research and development and establishing food trends for the future. Medals are awarded. Winners participate in the Culinary Olympics held every four years in Frankfurt, Germany, with the winners of the other international regional competitions: Culinary World Cup (Luxembourg); Salon Culinaire Mondial (Basel, Switzerland); Food & Hotel Asia Competition (Singapore); Culinary Arts Salon (USA); Hotelympia (London); and Culinary Masters (Canada). Established in 1900.

7818
Photographic Society of Ireland
PO Box 830
Parnell Square
Dublin, Ireland

7819
PSI Gold Medals
To provide recognition for the best monochrome print, best color print, and best color slide entered in the Irish Salon of International Photography. Photographers without regard to nationality are eligible. A gold medal is awarded for a monochrome print, a color print, and a color slide. Established in 1970.

7820
PSI Medals
To provide recognition for the best monochrome print, best color print, and best color slide entered in the Irish Salon of International Photography. Photographers residing in Ireland are eligible. Gold, silver, and bronze medals are awarded biennially. Established in 1966.

7821
Physical Education Association of Ireland
Univ. of Limerick Phone: 61 330442
Limerick, Limerick, Ireland Fax: 61 331304

7822
Honorary Member
To recognize an individual for outstanding contributions to the development of physical education in Ireland. Present members of the Association must be nominated by the Awards Committee and approved by the annual general meeting. A plaque is awarded when merited. Established in 1985.

7823
Radio Telefis Eireann
Donnybrook 4, Dublin, Ireland Phone: 1 693111

7824
Golden Harp Television Festival
(Festival de la Harpe d'Or)
To provide recognition for the best 12 to 60 minute television programs which reveal the cultural heritage of the competing country as exemplified in its folk music, folklore, or other traditional elements. Broadcasting companies which are members or associates of the International Telecommunications Union are eligible. Gold, silver and bronze harp trophies are awarded annually. Established in 1966.

7825
Rose of Tralee International Festival
5 Lower Castle St. Phone: 66 21322
Tralee, Kerry, Ireland Fax: 66 22654

7826
Order of the Golden Rose
For recognition of services rendered to organizing the Rose of Tralee selections, a personality contest for young women of Irish descent; and for promoting the Rose of Tralee International Festival, a festival of popular entertainment, concerned with the portrayal of Irish culture, Irish folk art, folk theater, and folk dance. Members of various voluntary committees throughout the world are eligible. Gold cuff links and gold pins bearing the rose emblem are awarded annually. The Festival was initiated in 1959, and the Order of the Golden Rose was established in 1967. Sponsored by the Festival of Kerry, Ltd.

7827
Rose of Tralee
To select a young lady to act as Ambassadress throughout each year, and to promote liaison and goodwill among peoples. Contestants are selected in various centers throughout the world. A monetary prize of £2,000 Irish and a Waterford Glass Trophy, specially designed each year, are awarded annually. Established in 1959. Sponsored by the Festival of Kerry, Ltd.

7828
Royal Academy of Medicine in Ireland
6 Kildare Street Phone: 1 6767650
Dublin 2, Ireland Fax: 1 6611684

7829
Donal Burke Memorial Lecture
An invitation lecture organized by the Section of General Practice of the Royal Academy of Medicine in Ireland. A monetary award and a silver medal are awarded annually. The first lecture was given in 1984.

7830
Conway Lecture
To encourage research in the biological sciences. Workers in the biological sciences who are nominated by two Fellows of the Academy are eligible. A monetary award and a silver medal are awarded. Established in 1977 by the Biological Sciences Section of the Academy in memory of Edward J. Conway, FRS.

7831

Graves Lecture
To encourage clinical research in Ireland. Doctors under 40 years of age who are nominated by two Fellows of the Academy and whose research has been carried out wholly or partly in Ireland are eligible. A monetary award and a silver medal are awarded annually. Established in 1960 by the Royal Academy of Medicine Medical Research Council of Ireland in memory of Robert Graves. Sponsored by the Royal Academy of Medicine - Health Research Board.

7832

Saint Luke's Lecture
To encourage research in the field of oncology. Doctors who are nominated by two Fellows of the Academy and whose research has been carried out wholly or partly in Ireland are eligible. A monetary award of £500 Irish and a silver medal are awarded annually. Established in 1975 by Saint Luke's Hospital.

7833

Royal Dublin Society
Ballsbridge
Dublin 4, Ireland
Phone: 1 6680866
Fax: 1 6604014

7834

Dublin Horse Show
For recognition of outstanding exhibits, horses, and riders entered in horse show competition in the following areas: Farriery Competitions - organized by the Irish Master Farriers Association; Cheese Hunt Chase - sponsored by Irish Dairy Board; Ladies' Day Competition - Best Dressed Woman; Irish Pony Club Mounted Games; Ford/Farmer's Journal Riding Club Jumping Chase; All-Ireland Horseshoe Pitching Championship; Royal Horticultural Society of Ireland Flower Show; Aga Khan Trophy - to the winning team in the Nation's Cup Competition; Irish Trophy - to the winner of the International Grand Prix of Ireland; and Challenge Cups and special prizes - for horses eligible for and exhibited in their appropriate show classes.

7835

Royal Dublin Society Crafts Competition
For recognition of original crafts of outstanding merit in the following categories: ceramics; glass; gold, silver, and other metals; blacksmithing; wood; rod, rush, and straw; leather; jewellery; weaving; musical instruments; furniture; knitting; embroidery; calligraphy and lettering; printed textiles; patchwork and quilting; and lace. The Competition is open to all craftworkers and designers in Ireland including students and apprentices. The following special awards are presented: Muriel Gahan Scholarship or Development Grant - L1,000, sponsored by the Irish American Cultural Institute; California Gold Medal - a gold medal awarded to the winner of a Class award whose work is considered by the judges to be of outstanding merit; Crafts Council of Ireland Purchase Award; Medal for Traditional Country Craft - sponsored by Country Markets Ltd.; and Lillias Mitchell Prize - for a weaver enlarging his or her vision by research into spinning, weaving, or dyeing (must submit both written and practical work). Royal Dublin Society certificates are given to prizewinners in all categories. The present Crafts Competition was established in 1967 as a replacement for the National Arts Competition, which was held from 1923 until 1967. Sponsored by the Educational Building Society.

7836

Royal Hibernian Academy of Arts
15 Ely Pl.
Dublin 2, Ireland
Phone: 1 612558

7837

Royal Hibernian Academy of Arts Awards
For recognition of outstanding works of art at the annual exhibition. The following monetary prizes are awarded: (1) £300 - by the Criel Gallery for a meritorious example of Irish landscape; (2) £300 - by M. Kennedy and Sons for a meritorious example of portraiture; (3) £250 - by O'Sullivan Graphics for a print in any medium; (4) £300 - by the Cambridge Gallery for a watercolor of merit; (5) £400 - by Guinness Peat Aviation for an example of figure work in painting or sculpture; (6) £500 - by the President, Council of the Royal Hibernian Academy for the most popular work as adjudged by ballot at the exhibition; and (7) £1,000 - by the Electricity Supply Board as the Keating-McLoughlin Medal for an outstanding work in any medium. Established in 1985.

7838

Royal Irish Academy
Exec. Sec.
Academy House
19 Dawson St.
Dublin 2, Ireland
Phone: 1 6762570
Fax: 1 6762346

7839

Bicentennial Fellowship
For recognition of an original research project in any field of scholarship. The successful candidate must be based in Ireland and demonstrate a capacity for original research. Awarded every two to three years. Established in 1985 to commemorate the Bicentenary of the Royal Irish Academy.

7840

British Academy Fellowship
To promote academic exchanges in the humanities between Ireland and the United Kingdom. Senior academic researchers working in Ireland must apply by December 1. A monetary award and travel expenses are awarded annually in February.

7841

Edmund Curtis Memorial Prize
For recognition of an essay on Irish history, based on original research or a work of original interpretation. Applications are accepted from candidates under 30 years of age who are or have been a student of a university. A monetary prize of £100 Irish is awarded occasionally. Established in 1952 in memory of Edmund Curtis (1881-1943), once Lecky professor of modern history at the University of Dublin.

7842

Exchange Fellowships
To promote scientific and academic exchange between Ireland and Austria, Hungary, Poland, and the USSR. Researchers working in Ireland must apply by December 1 each year. A monetary award and travel expenses are awarded annually in February. Established in 1981 with Austria and Poland, and in 1985 with Hungary and the USSR.

7843

National Committee for Biochemistry Award
For recognition of outstanding research in biochemistry by a scientist working in Ireland. Nomination must be by two independent scientists. The deadline is April 30. A silver medallion is awarded annually. Established in 1985.

7844

Eoin O'Mahony Bursary
To assist Irish scholars undertaking overseas research on historical subjects of Irish interest. The work must be likely to constitute a scholarly contribution to an historical or educational subject. Preference is given to family or military history. Applications are accepted. A travel bursary of £500 Irish is awarded annually. Established in 1978 by friends of the late Eoin O'Mahony, Barrister-at-Law, Knight of Malta, and genealogist who died in 1970.

7845

Royal Society Fellowship/Study Visit
To promote scientific exchange between Ireland and the United Kingdom. Senior scientific researchers working in Ireland must apply by December 1. A monetary award and travel expenses are awarded annually in February. Established by the Royal Society and the Royal Irish Academy.

7846

Senior Visiting Fellowship
To enable a new scientific research technique or development to be introduced into Ireland. Senior scientific researchers, working in Ireland, must apply by December 1 each year. Travel expenses are awarded annually in February. Established in 1965.

7847

Strathin Enterprises Ltd.
Strathin, Templecarrig
Delgany, Wicklow, Ireland
Phone: 1 2874769
Fax: 1 2874769

7848

Rooney Prize for Irish Literature
To encourage a young Irish writer to develop professionally. Irish writers under 40 years of age who have been published in either Irish or English are eligible for consideration. No entry form or application procedure is required. A monetary award of £5,000 Irish is awarded annually. Established in 1976 by Daniel M. Rooney, Pittsburgh, PA, U.S.A.

7849

**Traditional Irish Singing and Dancing Society
(Comhaltas Ceoltoiri Eireann)**
32/33 Belgrave Sq.
Monkstown, Dublin, Ireland
Phone: 1 800295

7850

Traditional Irish Singing and Dancing Society Awards
To recognize Irish musicians, singers, dancers, and those who wish to promote the Irish tradition of music. The Society sponsors music competitions and bestows awards.

Ireland, Northern

7851

Agricultural Economics Society
Dept. of Agricultural and Food Economics
The Queen's Univ. of Belfast
Newforge Ln.
Belfast BT9 5PX, Northern Ireland
Phone: 232 661166
Fax: 232 668384

7852

Honorary Member
To recognize an individual for outstanding achievement and/or service to the profession or Society. Society members must be nominated. A free Society membership and registration at Society conferences for life are awarded when merited at the annual general meeting. Established in 1926.

7853

Arts Council of Northern Ireland
185 Stranmillis Rd.
Belfast BT9 5DU, Northern Ireland
Phone: 232 381591
Fax: 232 681795

7854

Arts Council of Northern Ireland Bursaries and Awards
To provide support for creative and performing artists active in the fields of drama and dance, music and jazz, literature, traditional arts, community arts, visual arts and those engaged in the direction and presentation of artistic events. Artists who are residents in Northern Ireland for at least one year, contribute regularly to the artistic activity of the community, and who were previous award holders are eligible. Monetary awards of up to £5,000 each are awarded periodically to enable the recipients to concentrate on their work for a lengthy period. A bursary of £1,000 is also available in the field of jazz. In addition, the Council awards the British School at Rome Fellowship, the New York Fellowship, and the Printmaker in Residence Fellowship to encourage professional development in the arts.

7855

Bass Arts Award
To recognize aspiring, creative individuals or groups in all branches of the arts. Individuals who were born in Northern Ireland or who have resided there for at least three years may apply by August 30. Two awards are presented: the Main Bass Ireland Arts Award - £3,000 to individuals or groups in all branches of the arts and the Bass Ireland Arts Award for a nominated discipline - £1,500 to individuals or groups in an announced field of the arts. Awarded annually. Established in 1971. Formerly: Bass Ireland Arts Award.

7856

George Campbell Memorial Travel Grant
To enable an artist to work in Spain. The award is given in alternate years to an artist from the Republic of Ireland and an artist from Northern Ireland. Applicants must be of Irish birth and must apply by April 30. A monetary prize of £1,000 is awarded annually. Jointly sponsored by the Spanish Cultural Institute, the Arts Council of the Republic of Ireland, and the Arts Council of Northern Ireland.

7857

Alice Berger Hammerschlag Trust Award
To enable an artist to travel abroad. Irish artists of any age living anywhere in Northern Ireland or in the Republic of Ireland may apply by April 30. A monetary award of £1,000 is awarded in May. Co-sponsored by the Arts Council of the Republic of Ireland, 70 Merrion Sq., Dublin 2, Ireland and the Arts Council of Northern Ireland.

7858

Gallaher Business Challenge
Freepost BE 1727
Belfast BT15 1BR, Northern Ireland
Phone: 232 328000

7859

Gallaher Business Challenge
For recognition of the company which demonstrates the best example of small business enterprise. Any Northern Ireland-based enterprise employing up to 75 people is eligible. An award is presented in each of the following categories: (1) overall winner; (2) business less than three years old; (3) innovative business; and (4) business which has made use of a local enterprise center. The deadline for entries is May 31. Monetary prizes totaling £23,500 are awarded annually. Established in 1985.

7860

Political Studies Association of the United Kingdom
Dept. of Politics
Queen's University
Belfast BT7 1NN, Northern Ireland
Phone: 232 245133
Fax: 232 235373

7861

W. J. M. MacKenzie Book Prize
For recognition of publications in political science. Nominations by publishers are accepted. A monetary prize of £100 and a plaque are awarded annually. Established in 1987 in honor of W.J.M. MacKenzie.

Israel

7862

**Association for Civil Rights in Israel
(Haagudah Lezechuyot Haezrach Beyisrael)**
29B Keren Hayesod St.
PO Box 8273
91082 Jerusalem, Israel
Phone: 2 638385
Fax: 2 248910

7863
Association for Civil Rights in Israel Awards
To recognize individuals for educational campaigns and research on civil rights issues in Israel. Awards are presented.

7864
Association of Engineers and Architects in Israel
200 Dizengoff St.
PO Box 3082 Phone: 3 5240274
61030 Tel Aviv, Israel Fax: 3 5235993

7865
Pelles Prize
To encourage the public activity of engineers and architects and the advancement of the profession. Members of the Association and members of the Union of Engineers in Israel are eligible. A plaque and an honorary award are presented annually. Established in 1980 in memory of Elhanan Pelles, past chairman of the Association.

7866
Zeev Rechter Award
To encourage the advancement of architecture in Israel and to increase public awareness of architectural achievements. Planners, architects, or members of AEAI may be nominated. A monetary prize and a plaque are awarded biennially. Established in 1962 by the AEAI, the Ministry of Housing, the Technion Faculty of Architecture, and the Rechter family in memory of Zeev Rechter, an Israeli architect in the early 1930s.

7867
Bank of Israel
Kiryat Ben Gurion
PO Box 780
91007 Jerusalem, Israel Phone: 2 552 211

7868
David Horowitz Memorial Prize
For recognition of an outstanding work, theoretical or empirical, on a subject related to the role of the central bank in the domestic and international economy. Works previously unpublished and written in Hebrew or English may be submitted. A monetary prize of $5,000 is awarded in December. Established in 1980 in memory of David Horowitz, the founder and first governor of the Bank of Israel. (Inactive since 1982)

7869
Mordechai Bernstein Literary Prizes Association
(Aguda l'Haanakat Prasim Sifrutiim Al Shem Mordechai Bernstein)
Book Publishers Association of Israel
29 Carlebach St. Phone: 3 5614121
67132 Tel Aviv, Israel Fax: 3 5611996

7870
Award for Book Review in the Daily Press
(Pras l'Bikoret Sifrutit)
To recognize an outstanding newspaper book review of an original Hebrew novel, play, poetry, or short story. A monetary prize is awarded annually. Established in 1979 to honor Mordechai Bernstein, an Israeli author.

7871
Award for Children's Literature
(Pras l'Sifrut Yeladim)
For recognition of an outstanding children's book published in the year prior to the award. A monetary award was presented annually. The prize was given in honor of Mordechai Bernstein, an Israeli author. Established in 1980. (Discontinued)

7872
Award for Original Hebrew Novel
(Pras l'Roman Ivri Mekori)
To encourage authors under the age of 50 who write Hebrew novels. A monetary award is presented biennially. Established in 1977 to honor Mordechai Bernstein, an Israeli author.

7873
Award for Original Hebrew Poetry
(Pras l'Sefer Shira Ivri Mekori)
To encourage Hebrew poets under the age of 50. A monetary award is presented biennially. Established in 1981 to honor of Mordechai Bernstein, an Israeli author.

7874
European Bridge League
(Ligue Europeenne de Bridge)
PO Box 29703 Phone: 3 395 947
61296 Tel Aviv, Israel Fax: 3 204 287

7875
European Bridge Champion
To recognize the country whose bridge team wins the European Bridge Championships. The Championships are held biennially. Medals are awarded. Established in 1940.

7876
Haifa Municipality
Cultural Dept.
20 Rechov Y.L. Peretz Phone: 4 662 044
Haifa, Israel Phone: 4 640 775

7877
Ya'acov Dori Prize
For recognition of a composition, book or a technological invention (patent).

7878
Haifa Prize
For recognition of an outstanding composition on the city of Haifa in the following spheres: the city's history and ethnology, industrial development, society (co-existence), Haifa - past, present, future and city sites.

7879
Yehoshua Kaniel Prize
For recognition of an outstanding composition in the fields of Bible exegesis and Jewish thought.

7880
Marc Lavry Prize
For recognition of a musical work (instrumental - vocal), with original Hebrew libretto, of 12-15 minutes' duration.

7881
Outstanding Sportsman Award
For recognition of achievements in the spheres of body culture or sport contests, including Israeli representation in the international arena or for one's life's work in the sport spheres.

7882
Outstanding Young Citizen Award
For recognition of a young Haifa resident, according to the following criteria: an act of heroism, volunteering, helping others, self sacrifice and other praiseworthy acts.

7883
Frank Peleg Prize
For recognition of an outstanding composition in the field of musicology, or for a life's work in musical education.

7884
David Pinski Prize
For recognition of an original Hebrew play or work in the sphere of Yiddish belles-lettres (novel, poetry anthology, play).

7885
Dr. Arthur Ruppin Prize
For recognition of an outstanding composition on the social sciences, economics, agronomy, political science, Jewish history and ethnology.

7886
Prof. Hermann Struck Prize
For recognition of an outstanding work in the plastic arts, distinguished for its excellence at the annual exhibition of the Artists and Sculptors Association - Haifa and the North.

7887
Hebrew University
Hadassah Medical School
Lautenberg Center for General and Tumor
  Immunology
Jerusalem, Israel
Phone: 2 428725
Fax: 2 424653

7888
Rabbi Shai Shacknai Memorial Prize and Lectureship
For recognition of outstanding contributions to the science of immunology and/or cancer research. Selection is by nomination. A monetary prize of $7,500, travel expenses, and a scroll of honor are awarded annually. Established in 1973 by Senator Frank Lautenberg, NJ, in memory of Rabbi Shai Shacknai of Wayne, New Jersey.

7889
Hebrew Writers Association in Israel
PO Box 7111
Tel Aviv, Israel
Phone: 3 253 256

7890
Brenner Prize
To provide recognition for outstanding literary works. A monetary prize is awarded annually.

7891
Institute for Productivity of Labor and Production
4 Rechov Henrietta Szold
PO Box 33010
61330 Tel Aviv, Israel
Phone: 3 216 889
Phone: 3 430 245

7892
Kaplan Prize
For recognition of achievements in raising efficiency and productivity in industry, agriculture, and services. Developments in advanced technology, improvements in productivity, and new processes which save energy and labor and cut costs are considered. Monetary prizes and medals are awarded annually. Established in 1952.

7893
International Center for Peace in the Middle East
PO Box 29335
61292 Tel Aviv, Israel
Phone: 3 660337
Fax: 3 660340

7894
International Center for Peace in the Middle East Awards
To recognize scholars, educators, political leaders, and other individuals who strive for a comprehensive peace settlement in the Middle East, a solution to the Israeli-Palestinian conflict, and an end to superpower intervention in the Middle East. Awards are presented annually.

7895
International Federation of Clinical Chemistry
Dept. of Clinical Biochemistry
Rambam Medical Center
31096 Haifa, Israel
Phone: 4 528628
Fax: 4 542409

7896
Distinguished Clinical Chemist Award
To recognize an individual who has made outstanding contributions to the science of clinical chemistry or the application of clinical chemistry to the understanding or solution of medical problems. Nominations are made by an award committee. A monetary award and a medal are presented triennially at the International Congress. Established in 1969. For more information, contact Prof. Oren Zinder, Secretary.

7897
Distinguished International Services Award
To recognize an individual who has made unique contributions to the promotion and understanding of clinical chemistry throughout the world. Nominations are made by an award committee. A monetary award and a medal are awarded triennially at the International Congress. Established in 1981. Sponsored by Ames Division of Miles Laboratories, Inc.

7898
International Harp Contest in Israel
(Concours International de Harpe en Israel)
4, Aharonowitz Street
63 566 Tel Aviv, Israel
Phone: 3 5280233
Fax: 3 299524

7899
International Harp Contest in Israel
(Concours International de Harpe en Israel)
To encourage and recognize excellence in playing the harp. Harpists of all nationalities under 35 years of age are eligible. The following prizes are awarded: first prize - Lyon and Healy Concert and Grand Harp; second prize - Rosenbloom Prize of $5,000; third prize - Rosalind G. Weindling Prize of $3,000; Calouste Gulbenkian Prize of $2,500 for a contemporary work; and Aharon Tzvi & Mara Propes Prize of $1,500 for an Israeli work. Established in 1959 by Aharon Zvi Propes and the Israel Festival.

7900
International Pharmaceutical Students' Federation
4 Hachartzit St.
Kiryat Rishon
75143 Rishon Le-Zion, Israel
Fax: 3 233613

7901
Honorary Life Member
For recognition of outstanding service to the Federation. Individuals with two years of service to the Federation are considered. A plaque is awarded at the annual Congress. Established in 1949.

7902
International Student Film Festival
Dept. of Film and Television
Tel Aviv Univ., Ramat Aviv
69978 Tel Aviv, Israel
Phone: 3 420527
Fax: 3 6409935

7903

International Student Film Festival
To encourage professional development in the creative cinematic art. Awards are given in the following categories: Best Fiction Film, Best Documentary Film, Best Animation Film, Best Experimental Film, and Best School Program. Films must be entered by the Film Department of a participating school. A monetary prize and production facilities are awarded biennially. Established in 1986 by Laurance Price. Sponsored by Tel Aviv University and Cinemateque.

7904

Israel
Ministry of Education and Culture
Rechov Shivtei Yisrael 34
91911 Jerusalem, Israel   Phone: 2 278 211

7905

Bialik Prize for Research
To encourage research in Israel. A monetary prize is awarded annually.

7906

Israel Prize
To recognize Israeli citizens, individuals, groups or associations for distinguished contributions in a variety of disciplines. Areas in which awards are given are: (1) Jewish Studies and Humanities (in four areas which alternate on a four year cycle); (2) Social Science and Humanities (in three areas which alternate on a three year cycle); (3) Natural Science and Technology (in two areas which alternate on a two year cycle); (4) Culture, Art, Communications and Sports (in five areas which alternate on a five year cycle); and (5) Lifetime Achievement Award, which is given for a special contribution to society and the state of Israel. Israeli citizens or permanent residents may be nominated. The winners are chosen by a professional and public committee of judges. A monetary award is presented on Israel's Independence Day by the Prime Minister, with the President in attendance. Established in 1953.

7907

Prime Minister's Prize
To encourage creativity in the literary field. A monetary prize is awarded annually.

7908

Prime Minister's Prize for Composition
For recognition of an outstanding music composition.

7909

Prize for Performance of Israeli Works
To recognize artists and ensembles for the performance of music by Israeli composers. Awards are presented by the music department of the National Council of Culture and Art in the Ministry of Education and Culture.

7910

Israel
Ministry of Labour and Social Affairs, Unit for Volunteer Services
2 Rehov Kaplan
Kiryat Ben-Gurion   Phone: 2 694 211
91008 Jerusalem, Israel   Fax: 2 699 427

7911

Shield of the Minister of Labour and Social Affairs
(Magen Ha'sar)
To honor and encourage volunteers in the social services. Individuals who have excellent recommendations, meaningful periods of volunteering, perserverance, and devotion are considered. A plaque of the Minister is awarded annually at a special ceremony to which the public is invited. Established in 1983.

7912

Israel Archives Association
Haifa City Archives
PO Box 4811   Phone: 4 526587
31047 Haifa, Israel   Fax: 4 669958

7913

Israel Archives Association Awards
To recognize archival institutions and archivists in Israel. Awards are given annually.

7914

Israel Biochemical Society
(Aguda Ha'Biochimit Ha'Israelit)
c/o Dept. of Immunological Chemistry
Weizmann Institute of Science   Phone: 8 343974
76000 Rehovot, Israel   Fax: 8 344141

7915

Hestrin Prize
(Pras Hestrin)
For recognition of achievement in the field of biochemistry. Israeli citizens under 35 years of age may be nominated. A monetary prize and a plaque are awarded biennially. Established in 1964 in memory of Professor Shlomo Hestrin.

7916

Israel Broadcasting Authority - The Voice of Israel - Jerusalem
(Rashut Hashidur - Kol Yisrael - Yerushalayim)
21 Helenei Hamalka St.
PO Box 1082   Phone: 2 302 222
91010 Jerusalem, Israel   Fax: 2 248 392

7917

Hebrew Radio Play Prize
For recognition of three outstanding original Hebrew plays written for the radio. There are no eligibility requirement restrictions. Monetary prizes are awarded every four years.

7918

Young Artists' Competition of Kol Israel
To promote young artists and Israeli music. The Competition is open to artists between 17 and 25 years of age and singers between 17 and 30 years of age. Every competition has a piano section and one other instrument: violin/viola, cello, winds or voice in alternate years. The prize-winners in each of the sections receive the Abraham Klein Award and a monetary prize, and are invited to play as soloist with the Jerusalem Symphony Orchestra of the IBA. Second and third monetary prizes may be awarded. Competitors specially interested in Israeli music may compete for the Ben Haim Award. Awarded biennially. Established in 1985 by Kol Israel - The Voice of Jerusalem in cooperation with the Municipality of Jerusalem, the Jerusalem Foundation, and the Israeli League of Composers. Formerly: Paul Ben-Haim Competition.

7919

Israel Museum
Public Affairs Dept.
PO Box 71117
Hakiryah   Phone: 2 708811
91710 Jerusalem, Israel   Fax: 2 631833

7920

Crate and Barrel Israeli Product Design Award for the Home and its Surroundings
To encourage local Israeli professionals working in design fields by enabling them to continue development of their prototypes (in advanced stages) or recently introduced products. Product designers working in

Israel on the home and its surroundings are eligible for prototypes or products designed or produced within the year preceding the award. A monetary award is presented annually. Established in 1990 by Crate and Barrel, Chicago, Illinois. Additional information is available from Gordon Segal, President, Crate and Barrel.

7921
Joseph H. Hazen Art Essay Award for 20th Century Art Literature
To recognize an Israeli resident for an essay on 20th century art history. Israeli residents may submit essays or articles. A monetary award or $1,000 and a certificate are presented annually at the International Council. Established in 1978 by Cynthia Polsky in honor of her father, Joseph H. Hazen. (Temporarily discontinued)

7922
Honorary Fellow
To recognize individuals for outstanding contributions to art and the Israel Museum. Awarded when merited.

7923
International Art Book Prize
To recognize publishers and designers for the best books on any aspect of art, design, photography, architecture, and archaeology. Awards are given for: limited editions and collectors' books, large scale table albums, and general and popular books. Medals are awarded biennially. Established in 1969/70. (Temporarily discontinued)

7924
Israel Discount Bank Prize
To recognize a young established Israeli artist who is a resident in Israel. Works must be submitted by February 28. A monetary prize of $2,500 is awarded annually. Established in 1983.

7925
Jesselson Prize for Contemporary Judaica Design
To recognize and encourage the design of modern Jewish ceremonial objects, using various materials. Established in 1986 by Ludwig and Erica Jesselson.

7926
Enrique Kavlin Photography Grant
To provide recognition for the most outstanding contributions in the field of photography. Photographers who are residents in Israel must apply by February 28. A monetary prize of $1,000 is awarded annually.

7927
Beatrice S. Kolliner Award for a Young Israeli Artist
To recognize and encourage the professional development of a resident young Israeli artist. Works of art must be submitted by February 28. A monetary award of $3,000 and a certificate are presented annually at the International Council. Established in 1978 in memory of Beatrice Kolliner.

7928
Gerard Levy Prize for a Young Photographer
For recognition of achievement by a young Israeli photographer. Non-established photographers who reside in Israel must apply by February 28. A monetary award of $1,000 and a certificate are presented annually. Established in 1982 by Gerard Levy of France.

7929
Sandberg Grant for Research and/or Development
To provide recognition for the most outstanding contributions in design. Artists who are residents in Israel must apply by February 28. A monetary award is presented annually.

7930
Sandberg Prize for Israeli Art
For recognition of outstanding art by a resident of Israel. Works of art must be submitted by February 28. Residency in Israel is required. A monetary prize and a certificate are presented annually. Established in 1978 by Dr. Willem Sandberg.

7931
Percia Schimmel Award for Distinguished Contribution to Archaelogy in Israel
For recognition of achievement in the field of archaelogy in Israel and the lands of the Bible. Nominations are accepted and works must be submitted by February 28. Residency in Israel is not required. A monetary award, a certificate, and a gold-plated engraved medal are presented annually. Established in 1979 by Norbert Schimmel (U.S.A.) in memory of his mother, Percia Schimmel. Additional information is available from the Bronfman Archaeological Museum at the Israel Museum, Jerusalem.

7932
Jerusalem International Book Fair
Municipality of Jerusalem
1 Safra Sq.
PO Box 775
91007 Jerusalem, Israel
Phone: 2 240663
Fax: 2 243144

7933
Editorial Fellowship Program
To enable selected editors with at least six to 12 years of experience from the United States and Europe to attend the fair to get to know the Israeli publishing scene and to meet colleagues from different countries. Established in 1985.

7934
Jerusalem Prize for the Freedom of the Individual in Society
To recognize a world-renowned author who has contributed to the world's understanding of the freedom of the individual in society. Any author regardless of race or religion is eligible. A monetary prize of $5,000, a citation from the City of Jerusalem, and travel expenses are awarded biennially by the Mayor of Jerusalem at the Jerusalem International Book Fair. The Fair, held every two years, is open to the public for browsing and purchasing. Established in 1963 by the Jerusalem Municipality.

7935
Jerusalem Municipality
City Hall
Rechov Yafo 22
94142 Jerusalem, Israel
Phone: 2 232 251

7936
Jerusalem Municipality Awards
The Jerusalem Municipality awards the following prizes: (1) Agnon Prize for Literature; (2) Jerusalem Prize for Literature; (3) Rav Uziel Prize for Religious Literature; (4) Rav Kook Prize for Torah literature; (5) Rav Israel Goldstein Prize to an Outstanding Citizen; (6) Jerusalem Prize for Architecture; (7) Art Prize; (8) Honorary Citizen for Heads of State; (9) Yakir Yerushalayim Prize for Residents who have contributed to the city; (10) Yedid Prize; (11) Prize for Writers on the subject of human freedom in society; (12) Friend of Jerusalem Prize; and (13) Keeps the Faith Prize (Neeman Prize).

7937
Arthur Rubinstein International Music Society
Secretariat: Shalom Tower
PO Box 29404
61293 Tel Aviv, Israel
Phone: 3 651 604
Fax: 3 291 974

7938
Arthur Rubinstein International Piano Master Competition
To foster young pianists with outstanding musicianship and a talent for persuasive, versatile rendering and creative interpretation of works, ranging from the pre-classical to the contemporary. The competiton also

aims to establish a world forum for fostering talented and aspiring young interpreters and promoting their future artistic careers. The International Jury's task is to select pianists with more than average concert standard, who have attained a mature intellectual and emotional response to music. The Competition is open to pianists of all nationalities between 18 and 32 years of age. The Screening Committee prefers candidates who have either won top prizes at other important international competitions or who have been recommended specifically by world renowned artists. Six monetary prizes and medals are awarded at the discretion of the Jury: (1) The Arthur Rubinstein Award - $10,000 and a gold medal - first prize; (2) $5,000 and a silver medal - second prize; (3) $3,000 and a bronze medal - third prize; and (4) $1,000 each and silver medals - fourth, fifth, and sixth prizes. The Competition's Secretariat undertakes to help promote the artistic careers of the prize winners by recommending them for engagements with leading orchestras, concert managements and recording companies. Prizes are awarded triennially by the President of the State of Israel at the Laureates Gala Concert in Jerusalem. Established in 1973. The next competition will take place in April, 1995.

7939
Zalman Shazar Center for Jewish History
Historical Society of Israel
(Merkaz Zalman Shazar Le'Historia Yehudit/Ha'Hevra Ha'Historit Ha 'Israelit)
22 Rashba St.
PO Box 4179
91041 Jerusalem, Israel
Phone: 2 669464
Fax: 2 662135

7940
Zalman Shazar Award for Research in Jewish History
(Pras Zalman Shazar Le'heker Toldot Am Israel)
For recognition of achievement in research on Jewish history. A research work of at least 320 pages in Hebrew, in the form of a manuscript or book that has been printed no later than two years before the application, is eligible for consideration. A monetary prize of $1,500 is awarded annually in October on the memorial date of the late Zalman Shazar in October. Established in 1983 in memory of Zalman Shazar, former president of Israel.

7941
Society of Authors, Composers and Music Publishers in Israel
PO Box 14220
61140 Tel Aviv, Israel
Phone: 3 5620 11 5
Fax: 3 5620 11 9

7942
ACUM Medal for Performing and Distribution of Israeli Works, Music and Literature
(Ot ACUM Baad Bizua Vehafaza Shel Hayezira Ha Israelit)
To encourage the performance and distribution of Israeli works in the fields of music and literature. A medal is awarded. Established in 1987.

7943
ACUM Prizes for Literature and Music
(Prasey ACUM Lesifruth Vemusika)
To encourage creative work in the fields of literature and music. Israeli citizens are eligible. Monetary prizes are awarded annually. Established in 1957.

7944
Technion - Israel Institute of Technology
(Technion - Machon Technologi le'Israel)
Office of the Vice-President for
  Development
Senate House
Technion City
32000 Haifa, Israel
Phone: 4 235 177
Phone: 4 292 543
Fax: 4 221 581

7945
Pras Harvey
(Harvey Prize)
To recognize individuals who have made truly outstanding contributions to the progress of humanity, to make known throughout the world the singular achievement of the prize winners in their respective fields, and to enable the Technion and other institutions of higher learning in Israel to enjoy their presence and inspiration. Prizes are awarded in two of the following fields: science, technology, human health, and outstanding contribution to peace in the Middle East. Individuals without regard to race, religion, nationality, or sex may be nominated by May 31. Two monetary prizes of $35,000 each are awarded annually. Each winner receives a one-month visit to Israel to meet with Israeli scientists and leaders for a free exchange of views and ideas. Established in 1972 by Leo M. Harvey of California. Co-sponsored by the Lena P. Harvey Foundation of Los Angeles and the American Society for Technion. Additional information is available from American Society for Technion - Israel Institute of Technology, 810 Seventh Ave., New York, NY 10019-5818, USA, and the Office of the Harvey Prize, Senate Bldg Room 515, Technion City, Haifa 32000 Israel.

7946
Tel Aviv Municipality
Dept. of Municipal Prizes
Tel Aviv, Israel

7947
Arts Prize - Meir Dizengoff Prize
To recognize artists for painting and sculpture. Two monetary prizes of 1,500 shekels each are awarded every three years.

7948
Arts Prize - Moshe Halevi Prize
To recognize contributions in the dramatic arts. Two monetary prizes of 1,500 shekels each are awarded every three years.

7949
Arts Prize - Yoel Engel Prize
To recognize an original musical composition and research in the field of music. Two monetary prizes of 1,500 shekels each are awarded every three years.

7950
Engineering Prize - Avraham Cravenne Prize
To recognize contributions in garden landscape architecture. Two monetary prizes of 1,500 shekels each are awarded every three years.

7951
Engineering Prize - Dov Hoz Prize
To recognize contributions in sport and aviation. Two monetary prizes of 1,500 shekels each are awarded every three years.

7952
Engineering Prize - Israel Rokach Prize
To recognize engineering projects in the Tel Aviv-Jaffa area. Two monetary prizes of 1,500 shekels each are awarded every three years.

7953
Literary Prize - Bialik Prize for Literature
This, the highest literary award in Israel, is given for recognition of an outstanding contribution to literature and Jewish thought. Four monetary prizes of 4,000 shekels each are awarded annually. The award is named for the famous poet, Chaim Nahman Bialik.

7954
Literary Prize - Education and Instruction Prize
To recognize contributions in education. Two monetary prizes of 1,500 each are awarded bienially.

7955
Literary Prize - Mendele Prize
To recognize outstanding literature in the Yiddish language. Two monetary prizes of 1,500 shekels each are awarded every three years.

7956
Literary Prize - Nachum Sokolov Prize
To recognize outstanding contributions in print and electronic journalism. Four monetary prizes of 1,500 shekels each are awarded every three years.

7957
Literary Prize - Rav Kook Prize
To recognize contributions of original literature and research on Torah subjects. Four monetary prizes of 4,000 shekels each are awarded annually.

7958
Literary Prize - Tchernichowsky Prize
To recognize outstanding translations of literature, Jewish thought and science into Hebrew. Four monetary prizes of 1,500 shekels each are awarded every three years.

7959
Science Prize - Dr. Chaim Weizman Prize
To recognize contributions in the exact sciences. Two monetary prizes of 1,500 shekels each are awarded every three years.

7960
Science Prize - Dr. Moshe Einhorn Prize
To recognize contributions in language research and for the study of Hebrew medical literature. Two monetary prizes of 1,500 shekels each are awarded every three years.

7961
Science Prize - Henrietta Szold Prize
To recognize contributions in medicine and public health. Two monetary prizes of 1,500 shekels each are awarded every three years.

7962
Science Prize - Peretz Naftali Prize
To recognize contributions in the social sciences and economics. Two monetary prizes of 1,500 shekels each are awarded every three years.

7963
Theatre Prize
To encourage writers of original Hebrew plays and to recognize the best theatrical artists in Israel. A monetary prize is awarded biennially.

7964
Tel Aviv Museum of Art
27-29 Shaul Hamelech Blvd.
64239 Tel Aviv, Israel
Phone: 3 6957361
Fax: 3 6958099

7965
Dr. Haim Gamzu Prize
For recognition in the field of the arts. Awarded annually. Established in 1984.

7966
Israeli Discount Bank Prize
For recognition of an Israeli artist. Awarded annually. Established in 1983.

7967
Eugene Kolb Prize
For recognition of a work of Israeli graphic art. Awarded annually. Established in 1983.

7968
Jacques and Eugenie O'Hana Prize
To recognize a young Israeli artist. Awarded annually. Established in 1983.

7969
Rita Poretsky Prize in Photography
To recognize an Israeli photographer/artist or group of artists with exceptional talent, determination, ability, and creative expression in the field of photography. Awarded annually. Established in 1992.

7970
Mendel Pundik Fund
To provide for the acquisition of Israeli art. Awarded annually. Established in 1984.

7971
Francois Shapira Prize
For recognition in the field of music. Awarded annually. Established in 1983.

7972
United Israel Appeal - Keren Hayesod
PO Box 7583
91004 Jerusalem, Israel
Phone: 2 701811
Fax: 2 231597

7973
Leib Yaffe Prize
(Pras Leib Yaffe)
For recognition of literary achievement in the research and writing of Jewish history and culture, and the history and culture of Zionism and Israel. Books published in the previous year in the Hebrew language are eligible for consideration. A monetary award of $500 is presented annually at an awards ceremony. Established in 1957 in memory of Leib Yaffe, the Director of Keren Hayesod, who was killed in an Arab terrorist attack in March 1948.

7974
U.S. - Israel Binational Science Foundation
2 Alharizi St.
PO Box 7677
91076 Jerusalem, Israel
Phone: 2 617314
Fax: 2 633287

7975
Prof. E. D. Bergmann Memorial Award
To encourage and assist young scientists. Any U.S. or Israeli BSF grantee under 35 years of age who received his or her doctoral degree within the previous five years is eligible. An addition to the grantee's grant is awarded annually at a special ceremony. Established in 1977 in honor of Prof. E. D. Bergmann.

7976
Prof. Henry Neufeld Memorial Research Grant
To encourage and assist young Israeli scientists in the life or health sciences. The Foundation grantee proposing the most original and novel project in the health or life sciences is selected. An addition to the grantee's grant is awarded annually at an appropriate scientific meeting. Established in 1987 in memory of Professor Henry Neufeld.

7977 Weizmann Institute of Science
Academic Secretary's Office
76100 Rehovot, Israel
Phone: 8 343491
Phone: 8 343479
Fax: 8 471667

7978 Ernst David Bergmann Prize
For recognition of outstanding work in chemistry. Any member of the scientific staff of the Institute below the rank of professor is eligible. A monetary prize is awarded annually. Established in 1976 by Mrs. Chani Bergmann.

7979 Sir Charles Clore Prize for Distinguished Service of Science to the Society
To promote an activity not part of the regular research program and distinguished by its originality and service to science and the community. Awarded annually.

7980 Mordechai (Momma) Glickson Annual Research Prize
For recognition of research. Awarded annually. Established in 1980 in memory of Mordechai Glickson by his parents, Jacob and Yesha. (Discontinued)

7981 Armando Kaminitz Research Awards
For recognition of research related to energy, health, nutrition, agriculture, and electronics. A prize in each category may be awarded annually. Established in 1982 by Mr. Armando Kaminitz of Sao Paulo.

7982 Morris L. Levinson Prizes
For recognition of outstanding work in the fields of biology, physics, and mathematics. A prize is awarded in each field annually. Established in 1982 by Mr. Morris L. Levinson.

7983 Jeannette and Samuel L. Lubell Memorial Award
For recognition of achievement in science and technology research. Institute scientists under 40 years of age are eligible. A monetary prize is awarded biennially. Established in 1970 by the Lubell family.

7984 Gerhard M. J. Schmidt Memorial Prize
For recognition of an outstanding Ph.D. thesis in chemistry. Awarded annually. Established in 1980.

7985 Somach - Sachs Memorial Award
For recognition of outstanding work in chemistry. A monetary prize is awarded biennially. Established in 1976.

7986 Wolf Foundation
(Keren Wolf)
56 Kidushei Ha'shoa St.
PO Box 398
46103 Herzlia Bet, Israel
Phone: 9 557120
Fax: 9 541253

7987 Wolf Foundation Prizes
To recognize outstanding scientists and artists, and to promote science and art in the interest of mankind. Individuals, regardless of nationality, race, color, religion, sex, or political views may be nominated by universities, academies of science, and former recipients by August 31. The recipients are selected by international prize committees. The Prize in each area consists of a diploma and $100,000 (U.S). equally divided among co-recipients. Awards are given in the fields of agriculture, physics, chemistry, medicine, and mathematics. There may be a sixth prize for the arts (music, painting, sculpture, architecture), or one of the five science prizes may be awarded for art rather than science. Official presentation of the prizes takes place at the Knesset (Israel's Parliament) and the winners are presented their awards by the President of the State in a special ceremony. The Wolf Foundation was established in 1976 by the Israeli chemist, Dr. Ricardo Wolf.

7988 Women's International Zionist Organization
(Organisation Internationale des Femmes Sionistes)
PO Box 33159
38 David Hamelech Blvd.
Tel Aviv, Israel
Phone: 3 257 321

7989 Awards
For recognition of contributions that provide constructive social welfare and educational facilities for women, senior citizens, and children in Israel. Awards are presented.

7990 World Federation of Jewish Fighters, Partisans and Camp Inmates
(Federation Mondiale des Combattants, des Resistants et des Deportes Juifs)
15 Javne St.
PO Box 2660
Tel Aviv, Israel
Phone: 3 613 296

7991 World Federation of Jewish Fighters, Partisans, and Camp Inmates Award
To recognize the author of a research book on the Holocaust. Awarded annually.

7992 World Organization of Jewish Deaf
c/o Association of tbe Deaf in Israel
PO Box 9001
61090 Tel Aviv, Israel
Phone: 3 303355
Fax: 3 396419

7993 World Organization of Jewish Deaf Competitions
To provide for Jewish cultural development among the deaf, promote and defend the rights of Jewish deaf, and organize and coordinate activities for the prevention of discrimination. Competitions are held.

7994 Yad Vashem
PO Box 3477
91034 Jerusalem, Israel
Phone: 2 531202
Fax: 2 433511

7995 Righteous Among the Nations
To honor gentiles who risked their lives to hide, transport, and otherwise save Jews from being killed during World War II.

7996 Yediot Ahronot
138 Petach Tikva Rd.
67012 Tel Aviv, Israel
Phone: 3 257172

7997
Kinor David
(Harp of King David)
To recognize individuals in the areas of entertainment and the performing arts such as, theater, film, music, and television. The winners were selected by the readers of *Yediot Ahronot*, an Israeli evening newspaper, and an academy of experts. A trophy was presented annually. Established in 1963. (Discontinued)

Italy

7998
M. Abbado International Competition for Violinists
(Concorso Internazionale Michelangelo Abbado per Violinisti)
Provincia di Sondrio
Assesserorato Cultura
Via XXV Aprile
I-23100 Sondrio, Italy
Phone: 342 53 11 11
Fax: 342 53 12 77

7999
International Competition M. Abbado for Violinists
(Concorso Internazionale Michelangelo Abbado per Violinisti)
To encourage violinists. Violinists of all nationalities who are under 30 years of age are eligible. A monetary prize, a medal, a trophy, and a plaque are awarded annually on September 22-24. Established in 1981 by Maria Cappetti in memory of the violinist, Michelangelo Abbado (born September 22, and died on September 23, 1979). Sponsored by the town of Abbado, Piazzetta Bossi 1, Milano, Italy. Additional information is available from Conservatorio di Musica "Giseppe Verdi," via Conservatorio 12, I-20100 Milan, Italy.

8000
Academy of Costume and Fashion
(Accademia di Costume e di Moda)
Libero Istituto di Studi Superiori di Belle Arti
Piazza Farnese 44
I-00186 Rome, Italy
Phone: 68 68 169
Phone: 68 64 132

8001
Premio Elio Costanzi
To recognize the best student in costume/fashion of the year. A trophy is awarded annually. Established in memory of Elio Costanzi, the eminent scenographer, costume-painter, fashion expert, and authority in fashion/costume.

8002
Premio Francesco Compagna
To recognize an outstanding student of the third year. A scholarship for the remaining two years is awarded annually. Established in memory of Francesco Compagna, a great man of culture, a man of government and a promoter of Italian culture.

8003
Premio Francesco Pistolese
To recognize the best student of the third year in costume/fashion. A scholarship for the remaining two years is awarded annually. Established in memory of Francesco Pistolese, the noted journalist and science commentator.

8004
Premio Irene Brin
To recognize the best fashion costume designer. Past students starting promising careers are considered. A medal is awarded. Established in memory of Irene Brin, the famous fashion journalist.

8005
Premio Mondo e Cultura
To provide for a scholarship to be granted every four years to a foreign student, recommended by his country for outstanding merits. The scholarship is for the four-year course of the Academy. Established in memory of Giampiero Nitti, a noted internationalist and a man of culture.

8006
Accademia Agraria
Via Mazza 9
I-61100 Pesaro, Italy
Phone: 721 64232

8007
Concorso Esercitazioni agrarie
To provide for the study of agriculture.

8008
Premio Carlotta Strampelli
For recognition of a researcher of plant genetics.

8009
Accademia Biella Cultura
Via Malta 3
I-13051 Biella, Italy
Phone: 15 29195

8010
Premio Biella
For recognition in the field of Italian and European poetry and for a first opera.

8011
Accademia Culturale d'Europa
Villa Silvera
Viale IV Novembre 1
I-01030 Bassano Romano, Italy
Phone: 761 634115

8012
Premi Concorsi Letterari
For recognition in the field of literature.

8013
Accademia d'Arte Leonetto Cappiello per le Nuove Professioni e la Pubblicita
Via della Fornace 33
I-50125 Florence, Italy
Phone: 55 681 3211
Fax: 55 681 3211

8014
Primo Scolastico di Raccordo
For recognition in the field of advertising and publicity.

8015
Accademia del Frignano Lo Scoltenna
Palazzo del Credito
Via Cesare Costa 27
I-41027 Pievepelago, Modena, Italy
Phone: 536 71470

8016
Premio Letterario del Frignano Riccio d'Oro
For recognition in the field of literature.

8017
Accademia della Chitarra Classica, Milan
CP 10673
I-20100 Milan, Italy   Phone: 2 68 00 76

8018
Conquest of the Classical Guitar International Competition
(Concorso Internazionale per la Conquista della Chitarra Classica)
For recognition of outstanding performers on the classical guitar. The competition is open to all amateurs and lovers of the classical guitar. The competition is divided into five categories: Category A - maximum age of 9; Category B - 10 to 13 years old; Category C - 14 to 17 years old; Category D - 18 years old and up; and Category Extra - for players who want to become professionals, no age limits. The jury consists of eminent musicologists and guitarists. Competitors who have already gained a first prize in a category cannot compete in the same category, but must enroll in the following one or in the category Extra. First prize winners of the category Extra cannot participate in future competitions. The following prizes are awarded: first prize Category A - 100,000 Italian lire and the gold medal of the City of Milan; first prize Category B - 150,000 Italian lire and the gold medal of the City of Milan; Category C - 250,000 Italian lire 000 and the gold medal of the City of Milan; first prize Category D - 500,000 Italian lire and the gold medal of the City of Milan; first prize Category Extra - 2,000,000 Italian lire and the gold medal of the City of Milan. A guitar is awarded to the second placed competitors. Presented annually. Established in 1965 in honor of Hector Villa Lobos, the noted Brazilian composer. Sponsored by the City of Milan, Italy.

8019
Accademia delle Scienze Dell'Istituto di Bologna
Palazzo dell'Universita
Via Zamboni 31   Phone: 51 222596
I-40126 Bologna, Italy   Phone: 51 225540

8020
Premi Anita Vecchi
For recognition in the field of bee keeping. Awarded annually.

8021
Premio Maria Teresa e Allessandro Ghigi
For recognition of research in zoology. Awarded triennially.

8022
Accademia delle Scienze di Torino
Via Maria Vittoria 3
I-10123 Turin, Italy   Phone: 11 510 047

8023
Premio Internazionale Amedeo e Frances Herlitzka per la Fisiologia
For recognition of outstanding work in physiology during the preceding ten academic years. Proposals are admitted only upon invitation by the Academy. A monetary prize of 35,000,000 lire is awarded every four years. Established in 1988.

8024
Premio Internazionale con Medaglia d'oro, Professor Modesto Panetti
(Professor Modesto Panetti International Prize with Gold Medal)
To honor a scientist who has particularly distinguished himself in work in applied mechanics during the ten years preceding the prize. Scientists who are not national or foreign members of the Academy are eligible to be proposed by national and foreign members of the Classe di Scienze Fisiche, Matematiche e Naturali of the Accademia delle Scienze di Torino as well as presidents of scientific Italian and foreign academies are invited to propose names of worthy scientists. Proposals are admitted only upon invitation by the Academy. A monetary award and a gold medal are awarded usually every three or four years. Established in 1958.

8025
Accademia di Medicina di Torino
Via Po 18   Phone: 11 8397414
I-10123 Turin, Italy   Fax: 11 8397414

8026
Premi
For recognition of research in the field of medicine.

8027
Accademia di Paestum - Eremo Italico
Palazzo de Santis
Via Trieste 9
I-84085 Mercato San Severino, Italy   Phone: 89 879191

8028
Premi Nazionali Paestum
For recognition of Italian literature.

8029
Accademia di Scienze, Lettere e Arti di Palermo
Palazzo de Simone
Piazza Indipendenza 17
I-90129 Palermo, Italy   Phone: 91 420862

8030
Premi
For recognition in the fields of science, literature, and art.

8031
Accademia di Studi Storici Aldo Moro
Via Carlo Poma 4
I-00195 Rome, Italy   Phone: 6 384093

8032
Premi
For recognition in the fields of science and culture of particular interest to Aldo Moro.

8033
Accademia il Tetradramma
                                                        Phone: 6 6784964
Via IV Novembre 152   Phone: 6 6784994
I-00187 Rome, Italy   Fax: 6 6782994

8034
Premio Tetradramma d'oro
For recognition in the fields of art, science, and culture.

8035
Accademia Internazionale della Tavola Rotonda
Via Zante 21
I-20138 Milan, Italy   Phone: 2 7490506

8036
Premi
For recognition in the field of literature.

8037
Accademia Internazionale Medicea
Via della Scala 4
I-50123 Florence, Italy   Phone: 55 295094

8038
Premi culturali
For recognition in the field of culture.

8039
Accademia Internazionale per l'Unita della Cultura
Piazza San Salvatore in Lauro 13
I-00186 Rome, Italy   Phone: 6 659737

8040
Premio Luigi Prete
For recognition in the fields of science and culture. A gold medal is awarded annually.

8041
Accademia Italiana della Vite e del Vino
Via Roma 2   Phone: 577 220035
I-53100 Siena, Italy   Fax: 577 220325

8042
Premio A. Marescalchi
For recognition in the field of viticulture and enology. Italian or foreign members or other individuals who have studied viticulture and enology are eligible. A monetary award, a silver medal and a plaque are awarded biennially. Established to honor A. Marescalchi, a past president of the Academy.

8043
Premio Internazionale di Viticoltura G. Dalmasso
For recognition in the field of viticulture and enology. Italian or foreign members or other individuals who have studied viticulture and enology are eligible. A monetary award, a silver medal and a plaque are awarded biennially. Established to honor G. Dalmasso, a past president of the Academy.

8044
Premio P. G. Garoglio
For recognition in the field of viticulture and enology. Italian or foreign members or other individuals who have studied viticulture and enology are eligible. A monetary award, a silver medal and a plaque are awarded biennially. Established to honor P. G. Garoglio, a past president of the Academy.

8045
Accademia Musicale Chigiana
Via di Citta 89   Phone: 577 46152
53100 Siena, Italy   Fax: 577 288124

8046
Premio Internazionale Accademia Musicale Chigiana Siena
For recognition of achievement in music. The award is presented in alternate years to violinists and pianists. Musicians under the age of 35 may be nominated. A monetary prize of 15 million lire and a sculpture by Fritz Konig are awarded annually in the summer. Established in 1982 by a private German donor.

8047
Accademia Musicale Napoletana
Via del Parco Margherita 49, pal. 5   Phone: 81 401313
I-80121 Naples, Italy   Fax: 81 401313

8048
Alfredo Casella International Piano Competition (Concorso Pianistico Internazionale Alfredo Casella)
To recognize the best piano performers. Individuals of any nationality who are between 18 and 32 years of age are eligible. The following awards are presented: Grand Prize Alfredo Casella - 10,000,000 lire and 15 solo and orchestral concerts; second prize - 5,000,000 lire and five concerts; third prize - 3,000,000 lire and two concerts. In addition, the Vincenzo Vitali Prize, a monetary award of 2,000,000 lire is given by the Association Thalberg for the best performance of a romantic piece. Awarded biennially in the field. Established in 1952. Discontinued in 1976. Re-established in 1987 by the Banco di Napoli.

8049
Accademia Nazionale dei Lincei
Palazzo Corsini
Via della Lungara 10
I-00165 Rome, Italy   Phone: 6 650831

8050
Fondazione Contessa Caterina Pasolini Dall'Onda Borghese Prize
For recognition of studies on the history of the Italian unification in the 19th century. Italian or foreign authors may submit works. Members of the Academy are not eligible. The work must have been written within four years of the award date. A monetary prize is awarded every four years. Established in 1965.

8051
Fondazione Angiolo Silvio e Jacopo Novaro
For recognition of the best work of poetry, prose, literary criticism, or philology. Italian authors living in Italy or abroad are eligible. A monetary prize is awarded every five years. Sponsored by the Angiolo Silvio and Jacopo Novaro Foundation. (Inactive)

8052
Fondazione Ettore Bora
To provide recognition for the study of biological science and its practical application. Italians or foreigners, except members of the Academy, are eligible. A monetary prize of 500,000 Italian lire is awarded every four years. Established in 1931. (Inactive)

8053
Fondazione Eugenio Morelli
For recognition of work in the field of respiratory studies. A monetary prize of 8,000,000 Italian lire is awarded biennially. Established in 1964.

8054
Fondazione Francesco Sarerio Nitti Prize
For recognition of an outstanding work in economics, finance, or statistics. A monetary prize of 5,000,000 Italian lire is awarded biennially. Established in 1956.

8055
Fondazione Giorgio Maria Sangiorgi
For recognition of original research on the history and ethnology of Africa. A monetary prize of 1,000,000 lire is awarded biennially. Established in 1972.

8056
Fondazione Giovanna Jucci
For recognition of the best work on genetics. A monetary prize is awarded every five years. Established in 1956. (Inactive)

8057
Fondazione Giovanni Di Guglielmo
To recognize studies pertaining to illness. Italian or foreign authors may submit work on red and white blood cell illness, unpublished or published, within eight years of the announcement of the competition. Members of the Academy are not eligible. A monetary prize of 10,000,000

Italian lire is awarded biennially in June. Established in 1969 by Adriana Di Guglielmo.

8058
Fondazione Giuseppe Lugli
For recognition of the best unpublished account of an archaeological dig. A monetary prize of 300,000 lire is awarded. Established in 1972. (Inactive)

8059
Fondazione Guido Donegani
To recognize Italian scientists and technologists for achievement in solving chemical problems of great importance to Italy. A monetary prize, medal, and certificate are awarded.

8060
Fondazione Guido Lenghi e Flaviano Magrassi
For recognition of outstanding work in biological and clinical virology. A monetary prize of 5,000,000 Italian lire is awarded. Established in 1965.

8061
Fondazione Luigi D'Amato
To recognize the author of the best monograph on internal medicine published in Italy within two years of the announcement of the competition. Any Italian citizen who at the announcement of the competition has not yet finished the eight years of the Laurea (Italian equivalent of a B.A. or B.S.) is eligible. Authors must not present their papers for other awards at any time prior to the announcement of the winner. A monetary prize is awarded biennially. Established in 1956 by Teresa Tommassi, widow of Luigi D'Amato. (Inactive)

8062
Fondazione Premio Battista Grassi
For recognition of an outstanding work in zoology, parasitology and biological talassography. A monetary prize of 800,000 Italian lire is awarded annually. (Inactive)

8063
Fondazione Premio Dotte Giuseppe Borgia
For recognition of outstanding contributions to the physical sciences, natural sciences, and mathematics or to the historical and moral sciences. Research, scientific inventions, or literary work may be submitted. Italians under the age of 35 are eligible. A monetary prize of 20,000,000 Italian lire is awarded annually on a rotating basis between scientific and literary works, with every fifth year devoted to research or scientific inventions. Established in 1955.

8064
Fondazione Premio Stanislao Cannizzaro
For recognition of a work on chemistry published abroad or in Italy within five years of the award date. A gold medal is awarded every five years. Established in 1955. (Inactive)

8065
Fondazione Valeria Vincenzo Landi
For recognition of achievement in agrarian genetics. Prizes and scholarships are awarded.

8066
Fondazione Wilhelm Conrad Rontgen
For recognition of work in the field of oncology. A monetary prize of 20,000,000 Italian lire is awarded.

8067
National Institute of Insurance International Prizes
(Premio Internazionali dell' Instituto Nazionale delle Assicurazioni)
To recognize a person of renown in the insurance field. A monetary prize of 50,000,000 lire is awarded annually on a rotating basis in four categories: law; economics, finance, and statistics; mathematics and technique; and in a different area from the other three. (If none is available, then one of the three categories is used.) The emphasis is upon private insurance. Established in 1962.

8068
National Prize of the President of the Republic
(Premio Nazionale del Presidente della Repubblica)
For recognition of research and publications. The award is given in alternate years in the following fields: physics, mathematics, and natural sciences; and moral sciences, history, and philology. Italian scientists are nominated by Academy members, who themselves may not be considered for an award. A monetary prize of 50,000,000 lire is awarded annually. Established in 1949.

8069
Premi Antonio Feltrinelli
To recognize persons distinguishing themselves in various branches of science, the humanities, and literature. The prizes are international, given to both Italians and foreigners. They are awarded annually in rotation of subjects in the following order: moral and historical sciences; physical, mathematical, and natural sciences; literature; fine arts; and medicine. The following prizes are awarded: International Prize - 200,000,000 Italian lire and Italians Prizes - 50,000,000 Italian lire. Established in 1950 in memory of Antonio Feltrinelli, an Italian businessman.

8070
Premi del Ministro per i Beni Culturali e Ambientali
For recognition in the field of physical science or mathematics and alternately for moral science, literature, or philosophy. A monetary prize of 10,000,000 Italian lire is awarded annually.

8071
Premi Ministeriali
To recognize university professors for research and publication in the following fields: philosophy; economics, political, and social science; archaeology, history, and ancient geography; medieval and modern history, related science and geography; philology and linguistics of the ancient world; and history and literary criticism of art and poetry. A monetary prize of 250,000 lire is awarded in each category. (Inactive)

8072
Premio Camillo Golgi
To increase and advance the study of anatomy and physiology of the nervous system by rewarding Italian scholars who distinguish themselves in those fields of investigation. A monetary award from interest on proceeds of subscriptions, approximately 1,500,000 lire, is awarded. (Inactive)

8073
Premio Carmelo Colamonico
For recognition in the field of geography. A monetary prize of 800,000 Italian lire is awarded. (Inactive)

8074
Premio di Laurea Luigi Casati in Discipline Scientifiche
To recognize a young scholar for an outstanding thesis in a scientific discipline. Three monetary prizes of 8,000,000 Italian lire are awarded.

8075
Premio di Laurea Luigi Casati in Discipline Uranistiche
To recognize a young scholar for an outstanding thesis in humanistic discipline. A monetary prize of 8,000,000 Italian lire is awarded.

8076
Premio Internazionale Paolo Gatto
For recognition of works regarding the historic preservation of Venice. A monetary prize of 12,000,000 Italian lire is awarded.

8077
Premio Maria Teresa Messori Roncaglia and Eugenio Mari
To honor, in alternate years, a scientist or a person of letters. Members of the Academy are not eligible. A monetary prize of 15,000,000 lire is awarded annually. Established in 1971.

8078
Premio Mario di Nola
For recognition of literary, philosophical, or historical works. A monetary prize of 8,000,000 Italian lire is awarded.

8079
Premio Santoro
For recognition of discoveries or inventions by Italian engineers, at home or abroad, in physics, chemistry, mechanics, biology, geology, mineralogy, geography, astronomy, agronomy, and all those sciences which are of benefit to agriculture, industry, commerce, and the public's well-being. Italian scientists are eligible. A monetary prize of 5,000,000 lire and a gold medal are awarded every four years. Established in 1954. (Inactive)

8080
Science Prize (Premio Linceo)
For recognition of outstanding contributions in any of the sciences. Academy members are ineligible. Italian citizens may be nominated by Academy members. A monetary prize of 20,000,000 lire is awarded annually. Established in 1971.

8081
Accademia Nazionale di Santa Cecilia
Via Vittoria 6
I-00187 Rome, Italy   Phone: 679 0389

8082
Santa Cecilia Academy Competition for Orchestral Conductors Prize
To recognize the best conductor. A monetary prize of 2,000,000 lire and an invitation to conduct a subscription concert at the Academy were awarded every three years. (Discontinued)

8083
Accademia Pistoiese del Ceppo
Via Porta San Marco 2
I-51100 Pistoia, Italy   Phone: 573 401221

8084
Premio Ceppo Proposte Nicola Lisi
To recognize writers for outstanding narratives and poetry. Monetary prizes of 2,000,000 Italian lire each for prose and poetry, and a gold medal are awarded annually. Established in 1975 in memory of the Catholic author, Nicola Lisi.

8085
Premio Il Ceppo
To recognize authors of outstanding narratives and poetry associated with the province of Pistoia. Works must have been published during the preceding year and may not have won previous prizes. Monetary prizes of 3,000,000 Italian lire each for prose and poetry, and a gold or silver medal are awarded annually. Established in 1956.

8086
Accademia Pontaniana
Via Mezzocannone 8
I-80134 Naples, Italy   Phone: 81 207075

8087
Premio Cavolini - De Mellis
For recognition in the fields of science, literature, and fine arts. A monetary prize of 50,000 lire is awarded annually.

8088
Premio Tenore
For recognition in the fields of science, literature, and fine arts. A monetary prize of 50,000 lire is awarded annually.

8089
Accademia Romana di Scienze Mediche e Biologiche
Via IV Novembre 152   Phone: 6 6784964
I-00187 Rome, Italy   Fax: 6 6782994

8090
Premio Atomo D'oro
For recognition of an outstanding scientist. Awarded annually. Formerly: Premio Cesare Augusto; Premio Cesare Augusto.

8091
Accademia Vitivinicola Daunia
Viale del Lido, 24
Lido di Ostia
I-00122 Rome, Italy   Phone: 6 5625289

8092
Premi internazionali vitivinicoli
For recognition in the field of viniculture.

8093
Ambiente-Incontri
c/o Odessa-Steps
Casella Postale 286
Piazza Maestri del Lavoro, 3   Phone: 434 520404
I-33170 Pordenone, Italy   Fax: 434 522603

8094
City of Sacile Prize
To recognize the best cinema-television and multimedia project not yet completed. A monetary prize of 15,000,000 lire is awarded upon completion of the project with the work presented within two years after the initial competition. Established in 1991. For further information, contact Andrea Croholi, Director.

8095
Grand Prize
To recognize outstanding artistic work, based on the artistic qualities and conformity to the values and purposes of the festival. A monetary prize of 15,000,000 lire is awarded annually in July in Sacile, Italy. Established in 1991. For further information, contact Andrea Croholi, Director.

8096
Jury Award
To recognize an outstanding film based on conformity to the special theme of the festival (i.e. nature and the environment). A plaque is awarded annually in July in Sacile, Italy. Established in 1991. For further information, contact Andrea Croholi, Director.

8097
Arte in Piazza
c/o Sire S.p.A.   Phone: 172 471255
I-12060 Roreto di Cherasco, (CN), Italy Fax: 172 474139

8098
Arte in Piazza International Competition
For recognition of the best piece of work with Klinker Sire tiles for any type of building environment. The contest awards prizes for creativity and excellence. The theme can be created using any of the following categories: interior flooring (horizontal tile design), exterior flooring (horizontal tile design), interior or exterior wall tiles (vertical tile design), sport centers or swimming pool complexes, public malls and parks, and industrial floorings. Any of the above may be selected provided Klinker-Sire tiles are used substantially, creatively, and with an accent on quality. Participants are judged more for the quality of their presentation than for the size of their work. Participants who are enrolled in their professional registers may enter either as individuals or groups. Open to architects, architectural groups or studios, draftsmen, public and private technical studios, engineers, engineering studios, designers, and professional interior decorating studios. The deadline for entry is December 31. A work of art created by a famous artist exclusively for the competition is awarded for First Prize in each of the six categories.

8099
Asolo International Animation Festival
Amministrazione Provinciale
I-31100 Treviso, Italy   Phone: 422 548327

8100
Asolo International Animation Festival
For recognition of outstanding animated films. Monetary awards are presented for: Grand Prize; Best Animation; and Best Script. Awarded annually. Established in 1973.

8101
Association for Competition and Musical Review
(Associazione Concorsi e Rassegne Musicali)
Borgo Albizi 15
I-50122 Florence, Italy   Phone: 55 240672

8102
International Competition for Chamber Music Ensembles
(Concorso Internazionale per Complessi da Camera, Citta di Firenze)
For recognition of outstanding chamber music performances in the following categories: duos - violin and piano; duos - viola and piano; duos - violoncello and piano; Trios and string quartets; and piano and strings trio, quartet, and quintet. Performers must be younger than 32 years of age. For the quartets and quintets the average age can be 32 years. Diplomas and the following monetary prizes are awarded: Premio Vittorio Gui - 12,000,000 Italian lire; Second prize - 5,000,000 Italian lire; Third prize - 4,000,000 Italian lire; Fourth prize - 3,000,000 Italian lire; and Fifth prize - 3,000,000 Italian lire to the best quintet or quartet among those admitted to the final session. Also awarded is the "Special Prize of the Public" - 1,000,000 Italian lire. The winners are invited to perform in concerts held in Italy or in foreign countries. Awarded annually in October. Established in 1977 by Mr. Sergio Mealli in memory of Vittorio Gui, a conductor. Sponsored by Ministerio Turismo e Spettacolo, Azieda Aut. Turismo, Comune di Fi, Cassa di Risparmio di Firenze, Regione Toscana.

8103
Association for the Study of the World Refugee Problem
(Forschungsgesellschaft fur das Weltfluchtlingsproblem)
P. le di Porta Pia, 121
00198 Rome, Italy

8104
Competitions
For recognition of contributions to scholarly research on refugee problems. Awards are presented.

8105
Association of Musical Culture
(Associazione di Cultura Musica)
Vico Ferri, 1   Phone: 19 692135
I-17024 Finale Ligure, (SV), Italy   Fax: 19 680052

8106
Finale Ligure International Chamber Music Competition
(Concorso Internazionale di Musica da Camera di Finale Ligure)
For recognition of outstanding chamber music performance. Awards are given in the following categories: (1) Piano; (2) Piano Duo; (3) Piano/Violin Duo; (4) Piano/Violoncello Duo; (5) Lieder; and (6) Guitar. The age limit is 35 years for competitors for the Piano Section; 45 years for competitors for the Duo Section for Two Pianos, the Duo Section Piano/Violin, and for the Duo Section for Piano/Violoncello; 45 years for the Lieder Section; and 40 years for the Guitar Section. Winners of First Prizes in preceding years are not admitted. The deadline is March 8. The following prizes are awarded in the Piano Section: (1) First prize - Golden Palm, an artistic work finely executed and 2,500,000 Italian lire; (2) Second prize - 1,250,000 Italian lire; (3) Third prize - 625,000 Italian lire; (4) Special Prize for the best performance of the obligatory piece - 625,000 Italian lire; (5) A gold medal for the youngest candidate admitted to the final round (maximum age 18 years); (6) Diploma on parchment with silver medal to the finalists not rewarded; (7) Merit diploma on parchment to the finalists especially distinguished; and (8) C. Augusto Tallone Prize - 5,000,000 Italian lire and a gold medal to the finalist who has achieved an average of not under eight points. The following prizes are awarded in the Lieder Section, Duo Sections, and Guitar Section: (1) First prize - 2,000,000 Italian lire; (2) Second prize - 1,000,000 Italian lire; (3) Third prize - 500,000 Italian lire; (4) Special Prize for the best performance of the obligatory piece - 500,000 Italian lire; (5) Diploma on parchment and silver medal to the finalists not rewarded; and (6) Merit diploma on parchment for each non finalist especially distinguished. Awarded annually in August. Established in 1974. Additional information is available from Secretary, A.A.S.T., Via San Pietro 14, I-17024, Finale Ligure (SV), Italy, phone: 19 692581.

8107
Associazione Amici Della Musica Di Caltanissetta
                                                            Phone: 934 592025
Viale Trieste 308   Phone: 337 954995
I-93100 Caltanissetta, Italy   Fax: 934 592025

Formerly: Commune di Caltanissetta.

8108
Concorso Internazionale Vincenzo Bellini per Pianisti e Cantanti Lirici
To encourage professional development of pianists and singers. A monetary award and a medal are presented annually. Established in 1965 to honor Vincenzo Bellini.

8109
Associazione Compagnia Jazz Ballet
Largo Francia 113   Phone: 11 6690668
I-10138 Turin, Italy   Fax: 11 4366515

8110
Concorso Coreografico Internazionale di Modern Jazz Dance
To encourage young choreographers. The competition is open to Italian and foreign choreographers 18 years of age. The deadline for entry is December 21. The following monetary prizes are awarded: first prize - 4,000,000 Italian lire; second prize - 2,000,000 Italian lire; and third prize - 1,000,000 Italian lire. Trophies and plaques are also awarded annually. Established in 1982 by Adriana Cava. Additional information is available from Jazz Ballet, Teatro Nuovo Torino, M. D'Azeglio 17, I-10126 Torino, Italy.

[8111]

Associazione Culturale Antonio Pedrotti
Via Oriola 12　　　　　　　　　　　　　　Phone: 461 23 12 23
I-38100 Trento, Italy　　　　　　　　　　　Fax: 461 23 12 23

[8112]

Antonio Pedrotti International Competition for Orchestra Conductors
(Premio Internazionale di Direzione d'Orchestra Antonio Pedrotti)
To encourage professional activity of young orchestra conductors. Applicants must be between 18 and 33 years of age. The following monetary prizes are awarded: (1) First prize - 8,000,000 Italian lire; (2) Second prize - 5,000,000 Italian lire; and (3) Third prize - 3,000,000 Italian lire. The first prize includes concerts with many orchestras. Awarded biennially. Established in 1989 by Andrea Mascagni in memory of Antonio Pedrotti, an orchestra conductor, who died in 1975. Additional information is available from Centro S. Chiara, Via S. Croce 67, I-38100 Trento, Italy, phone: 461 98 64 88.

[8113]

Associazione Culturale Ennio Flaiano e *Oggi E Domani*
Via S. Tommasi 5　　　　　　　　　　　　Phone: 85 4517898
65126 Pescara, Italy　　　　　　　　　　　Fax: 85 4517909

[8114]

Premio Internazionale Enno Flaiano
To provide recognition for outstanding works in the following fields: literature, theater, film, and television. Applications must be submitted for the theater award. Nominations must be submitted for the other areas. A monetary award of approximately 60,000,000 lire and a silver trophy designed by Giuseppe di Prinzio are awarded annually. Established in 1974 by Dr. Edoardo Tiboni, editor of *Oggi E Domani*, to honor Ennio Flaiano.

[8115]

Associazione Culturale Relazioni Inernazionali
Cas Post. 288
I-55049 Viareggio, Italy

[8116]

Premio Letterario Racconti di Carnevale
For recognition of Italian prose and poetry.

[8117]

Associazione di Cultura Lao Silesu
Piazza Quintino Sella 34
I-09016 Iglesias, Italy　　　　　　　　　　Phone: 781 41902

[8118]

Premio Iglesias
For recognition in the field of literature, art, and music.

[8119]

Associazione di Cultural Musicale
via San Pietro 14
I-17024 Finale Ligure, Italy　　　　　　　Phone: 19 692581

[8120]

Concorso Internationale di Musica da Camera "Palma d'Oro" di Citta di Finale Lingure
For recognition of accomplishments in chamber music. Three rounds of competition are completed for piano duos, piano and violin, piano and violoncello, guitar, and vocal music. Competiton is open to all nationalities. Winners are selected by a jury panel. Monetary awards for piano soloist include the following: first place - 2,500,000 Italian lire, second place - 1,250,000 lire, third place - 625,000 lire, and special prize for best performance of an obligatory piece - 625,000 lire. A gold medal is also presented to the youngest candidate. Qualifiers in the "Lieder Section" (vocal music), Duo Section (piano and violin, two pianos, piano and violoncello), or Guitar Section each receive the following: first place - 2,000,000 Italian lire, second place - 1,000,000 lire, third place - 500,000 lire, and special prize for best performance of an obligatory piece - 500,000 lire.

[8121]

Associazione Fra i Romani
Via di Porta San Sebastiano 2
I-00179 Rome, Italy　　　　　　　　　　　Phone: 6 775161

[8122]

Premio Anna Magnani
For recognition in the field of film, theater, and television.

[8123]

Associazione Italiana Amici del Cinema d'Essai
V. Carlo Alberto 27　　　　　　　　　　　Phone: 11 5622607
10123 Torino, Italy　　　　　　　　　　　Fax: 11 5622607

[8124]

Premio Cinema d'Essai - Targa AIACE
For recognition in the field of films.

[8125]

Associazione Italiana di Metallurgia
　　　　　　　　　　　　　　　　　　　　Phone: 2 76020551
Piazzale R. Morandi 2　　　　　　　　　　Phone: 2 76021132
I-20121 Milan, Italy　　　　　　　　　　　Fax: 2 784236

[8126]

Aldo Dacco Award
To recognize the best paper dealing with the various techniques used in ferrous and nonferrous foundries.

[8127]

Felice de Carli Award
To recognize outstanding students in metallurgy. New graduates in the last year of study are eligible.

[8128]

Federico Giolitti Steel Medal
(Medaglia d'Acciaio Federico Giolitte)
To recognize a major contribution to the steel plants industry. A steel medal with the portrait of the metallurgist, Federico Giolitti, is awarded triennially. Established in 1958 in memory of Federico Giolitti, a metallurgist and first professor of metallurgy at the Politechnical School of Turin.

[8129]

Luigi Losana Gold Medal
(Medaglia d'oro Luigi Losana)
To recognize an Italian or foreign researcher for an outstanding contribution to the knowledge of metals. During the year preceding the award, the Board designates the country whose researcher shall be chosen. The Gold Medal Luigi Losana is awarded at least every three years. Established in 1950.

[8130]

Eugenio Lubatti Award
To recognize the best paper dealing with electrothermic processes.

8131

Medaglia d'Oro Aim ai Soci Fondtori
To recognize outstanding contributions to the field of metallurgy.

8132

Associazione Italiana par la Musica Contemporanea
c/o Associazione Nuovi Spazi Sonori
Casella postale 196
I-25100 Brescia, Italy
Phone: 30 43237
Fax: 30 3771844

8133

Camillo Togni International Composers Competition
(Concours international de composition Camillo Togni)
To promote the musical production of young composers of all nationalities and develop their activity and professional level. Only compositions written for 1 to 16 instruments from among the following instruments can be submitted, with or without recorded tape: flute (also piccolo or G flute, 1 performer), oboe (also cor anglais, 1 performer), clarinet (B late, also bass clarinet and piccolo, 1 performer), bassoon, horn, trumpet, trombone, 2 violins, viola, cello, double bass, harp, guitar, percussions (1 perfomer), piano (1 performer). The deadline is May 30. The competition is open to musicians under 40 years of age from any country. A monetary award of 10,000,000 lire, publication of the score by RICORDI (Milan), and a concert of the work by CARME, an Italian Chamber Music Organization, are awarded for First Prize. A Second Prize of 5,000,000 lire is also presented by SIAE, the Italian Society of Authors and Publishers. Awarded biennially. Established in 1988.

8134

Associazione Mineraria Subalpina
Dip. georisorse e territorio
Politecnico - Corso Duca degli Abruzzi 14
I-10129 Turin, Italy
Phone: 11 5567681

8135

Premio di laurea
To provide for visits and travel in the field of technology. Awarded biennially.

8136

Premio scientifico-technico
For recognition in the fields of science and technology. Awarded every five years.

8137

Associazione Musicale Alfonso Rendano
Via Principe Aimone, 1
I-00185 Rome, Italy
Phone: 6 70497372

8138

Concorso nazionale pianistico Premio Rendano
For recognition of excellence in piano playing. This piano competition for a young Italian pianist or foreign resident is judged on the basis of memorization, musical selection, interpretation, and clarity of the program. Photocopy of birth certificate or certificate of residency, picture identification, and postal order must be submitted along with application. Finalists receive a diploma of merit. The following prizes are awarded: first prize - 2,500,000 Italian lira, plus five concert appearances; second prize - 1,500,000 Italian lira; third prize - 1,000,000 Italian lira; best musical interpretation - 500,000 Italian lira; and finalist (non-prizewinner) - 300,000 Italian lira.

8139

Associazione Musicale di Monza
Via Frisi 23
I-20052 Monza, (MI), Italy
Phone: 39 382278

8140

Rina Sala Gallo International Piano Competition
(Concorso Pianistico Internazionale Rina Sala Gallo)
For recognition of outstanding piano performances. The competition is open to pianists of all nationalities who are between 15 and 31 years of age, provided they have not won the first prize in any of the previous Rina Sala Gallo competitions. The deadline for entry is May 31. The following prizes are awarded: First Prize - 20,000,000 Italian lire, Citta di Monza Prize, and Concerts; Second Prize - 10,000,000 Italian lire and Elva Bonzagni Prize; Third Prize - 8,000,000 Italian lire and Sporting Club Monza Prize; Fourth Prize - 5,000,000 Italian lire and Credito Artigiano Monza Prize; Fifth Prize - 3,000,000 Italian lire and Rotary Club Monza Est Prize; and Sixth Prize - 2,000,000 Italian lire and Amalia Sala Caprotti Prize. Awarded biennially. Established in 1970.

8141

Associazione Napoletana Amici di Malta
Via Nuova Ponte di Tappia 82
I-80133 Naples, Italy
Phone: 81 327236

8142

Premi
For recognition of contributions to Italian culture.

8143

Associazione Nazionale Enrico Fermi
Via Firenze 21
I-80142 Naples, Italy
Phone: 81 224228

8144

Premio Nazionale di Narrativa
For recognition of Italian literature.

8145

Premio Nazionale di Poesie
For recognition of Italian poetry. The Premio Enrico Fermi is also awarded.

8146

Associazione per il Disegno Industriale
C. Venezia 38
I-20121 Milan, Italy
Phone: 2 406991

8147

Premi e Concorsi il Compasso d'oro
For recognition in the field of industrial design. Awarded biennially. Established in 1954.

8148

Associazione per Il Premio Internazionale di Meridionalistica Guido Dorso
Centro studi per la valorizzazione
delle risorse del Mezzogiorno
Corso Umberto I, 22
I-80138 Naples, Italy
Phone: 81 5527744
Fax: 81 5526959

Formerly: (1990) Centro Studi Nuovo Mezzogiorno.

8149

Premio Internazionale di Meridionalistica Guido Dorso
For recognition of achievement in, or contribution to, political, economic, managerial, scientific, cultural, educational, and publishing activities, specifically focused on southern Italy's growth. Applications must be submitted for the "ordinaria" section, and for the other sections nomination is necessary. Monetary prizes and trophies are awarded annually in

the autumn. Established in 1970 by Dott. Nicola Squitieri in honor of Guido Dorso.

8150
Associazione Premio Internazionale per la Zootecnia Uovo d'Oro
Via Mameli 24
Casatenovo, (CO), Italy					Phone: 31 59131

8151
Premio Internazionale per la Zootecnia Uovo d'Oro
For recognition of a contribution to scientific and practical progress in the field of animal husbandry. Foreign and Italian scientists who are outstanding in the field of animal husbandry are eligible. Trophies are awarded annually. Established in 1964 by Francesco Vismara S.p.A. Additional monetary awards are given occasionally (each ten years) for the best theses in the animal and agricultural sciences.

8152
Associazone Italiana Biblioteche
CP 2461
I-00100 Rome, Italy					Phone: 64463532

8153
Libraries Prize
To provide recognition for literary works on various aspects or problems in the field of arts and letters. A monetary prize of 5,000,000 lire is presented to the publisher, and 1,000,000 lire to the author. Awarded occasionally.

8154
Library Contest Awards
To provide recognition for the library best serving the community, and the best monographs. Awards are presented: (1) for the library best serving the community - a monetary prize of 1,000,000 lire and a print; and (2) for the best monographs on various themes - a monetary prize of 1,000,000 lire and a print. Awarded annually.

8155
Azienda Autonoma di Soggiorno e Turismo
Via del Saracino 4					Phone: 89 875067
I-84017 Positano, Italy					Fax: 89 875760

8156
Leonida Massine Prize for the Art of the Dance
(Premio Positano Leonida Massine per l'Arte della Danza)
To encourage professional development. Young dancers, choreographers, and musicians are eligible for nomination. Medals and plaques are awarded annually. Established to honor Leonida Massina. Formerly: (1964) Scarpette d'Argente.

8157
Azienda di Promozione Turistica Novara
Via Dominioni 4					Phone: 321 623398
I-28100 Novara, Italy					Fax: 321 393291

8158
Guido Cantelli International Competition for Young Conductors
(Concorso Internazionale per giovani Direttori d'orchestgra Premio Guido Cantelli)
To recognize the best young conductors under the age of 35. A monetary prize of 5,000,000 lire, a gold medal, a diploma, and the opportunity to conduct a concert at the Teatro alla Scala with the participation of the pianist winner in the Dino Ciani International Competition for Young Pianists are awarded biennially. Established in 1961 in honor of Maestro Guido Cantelli who was born in Novara. (Inactive since 1983)

8159
Bagutta Restaurant
Via Bagutta 14					Phone: 270 27 67
I-20121 Milan, Italy					Fax: 279 96 13

8160
Bagutta Prize
This, one of Italy's oldest and most prestigious literary awards, is given for recognition of the best book of the year in several categories. Established and young distinguished authors of many literary forms, including the novel, poetry, and journalism are eligible. Submissions are not accepted. A monetary award of 1,000,000 lire and honorary recognition are awarded annually in a small restaurant at Via Baguttain, Milan. Established in 1927.

8161
Bancarella Prize
(Premio Bancarella)
Via Sismondo 5
I-54027 Pontremoli, Italy					Phone: 55 2387 438

8162
Bancarella Sport Prize
For recognition of books on sport, with the aim of encouraging literature focusing on problems of sport in general. To be eligible, books must have been published or translated in the year preceding that in which the prize is awarded, and must be presented to the prize's secretary by January 31. The Jury, composed of 18 members, selects a short-list of finalists (from four to ten books), which are then put to the vote of the Grand Jury. Awarded annually. Established in 1964 by the Citta del Libro Foundation, the Panathlon International and the Panathlon Club of Carrara and Massa, in collaboration with the Union of Booksellers from Pontremoli and the National Bookstall Association.

8163
Bancarellino Prize
To recognize children's books that are outstanding for their quality and sales appeal, preferably written by an Italian author. Awarded annually.

8164
Premio Bancarella
For recognition of efforts to write popular books in Italy. Sales promotion of the book by Librai is awarded annually. Established in 1953 to celebrate the Association's endeavor to promote literary culture.

8165
Bergamo Film Meeting
Via Pascoli 3					Phone: 35 234011
24121 Bergamo, Italy					Fax: 35 233129

8166
Rosa Camuna
To recognize and honor films of high quality and art for sale and distribution in Italy. Participating films are included by invitation of the organizers. Films must not have been previously released in Italy nor have been shown in any other Italian film festival. The deadline is June 15. Three plaques are awarded annually in July at the end of the Bergamo Film Meeting Festival - a gold, silver, and bronze Rosa Camuna, the symbol of Regione Lombardia. Established in 1987. Sponsored by Regione Lombardia.

8167
A. Boito Conservatory of Music Parma
(Conservatorio di Musica A. Boito di Parma)
					Phone: 521 207268
Via del Conservatorio 27				Phone: 521 282320
I-43100 Parma, Italy					Fax: 521 200398

8168

International Double Bass Competition Giovanni Bottesini
(Concorso Internazionale per Contrabbasso Giovanni Bottesini)
To recognize outstanding double bass players. Open to young double-bass players of every nationality from the ages of 16 to 32 as of the first day of the competition. The deadline is May 31. The following monetary prizes are awarded: (1) First prize - the Bruno Manenti Prize, 10,000,000 lire; (2) Second prize - 6,000,000 lire; and (3) Third prize - 4,000,000 lire. Awarded triennially. Established in 1989. The Bruno Manenti Prize honors B. Manenti, an industrialist of Crema. Sponsored by the Conservatory of Runic Parma - Sant'Agostino Cultural Centre Crema.

8169

International Piano Competition Liszt - Mario Zanfi Prize
(Concorso Internazionale Pianistico Liszt - Premio Mario Zanfi)
To recognize young pianists in a competition that is dedicated entirely to Liszt. Pianists who are 16 to 32 years of age as of the first day of the competition may apply by May 31. Three monetary prizes are awarded: (1) First Prize - the Mario Zanfi Prize, 10,000,000 lire; (2) Second Prize - 6,000,000 lire; and (3) Third Prize - 4,000,000 lire. Award winners participate in the final concert and must be available for a 15 day period after the end of the Competition for several concerts with the Emilia-Romagna Symphony Orchestra "Arturo Toscanini." The Mario Zanfi Prize is awarded triennially. Established in 1981 by a bequest from the pianist, Mario Zanfi, to establish a competition dedicated entirely to Liszt. Sponsored by Cassa di Risparmio di Parma.

8170

Bologna Children's Book Fair
(Fiera del Libro per Ragazzi Bologna)
Ente Autonomo Fiere Internazionali di
  Bologna
Piazza Costituzione 6   Phone: 51 28 21 11
I-40128 Bologna, Italy   Fax: 51 28 23 32

8171

Critici in Erba Prize
(Premio Critici in Erba)
For recognition of the best illustrated book for children. A jury of nine children between six and nine years of age selects the winner. Any publisher of children's books exhibiting at the Children's Book Fair in Bologna may submit books published during the preceding two years. The deadline is January 31. A gold plaque is awarded annually to the publisher. Established in 1966.

8172

Graphics Prize Fiera di Bologna for Children and Young Adults
(Premio grafico Fiera di Bologna per l'infanzia e la gioventu)
For recognition of the best typographical and artistic design of books in two categories: Books for children - up to 8-years of age; and Books for young adults - 9 to 15 years of age. Any publisher of children's books exhibiting at the Children's Book Fair in Bologna may submit books published during the preceding two years. The deadline is January 31. The publisher, not the author or illustrator of the prize-winning books, receives an award. Gold plaques are awarded annually at the international Children's Book Fair in Bologna. Established in 1966.

8173

Bologna University
(Universita degli Studi di Bologna)
Via Zamboni 33
I-40100 Bologna, Italy   Phone: 51 228621

8174

Giosue Carducci Prize
(Premi Giosue Carducci)
To recognize a researcher who has published a work on the life and work of the poet, Giosue Carducci. A monetary prize of 1,500,000 lire is awarded every five years. Established in 1957 in memory of the poet, Giosue Carducci, who won the Nobel Prize in 1906. Additional information on awards and scholarships is available from Officio Premi e Borse di Studio - Sez. II, Via Zamboni 33, Bologna, Italy.

8175

British School at Rome
Piazza Winston Churchill 6
Via Gramsci 61
I-00197 Rome, Italy   Phone: 6 8870294

8176

Archaeological Fieldwork Grants
To support archaeological excavation, post-excavation, and research projects in Italy.

8177

Balsdon Fellowship
To provide assistance for work in any field in which the school has an active interest, particularly the fields of archaeology; and the history and letters of Italy in all periods. Three months of free room and board at the School of Rome is provided annually. Established in 1979 in honor of Dr. J. P. V. D. Balsdon, sometime Fellow of Exeter College, Oxford. Additional information is available from the Registrar, BSR, Via Gramsci 61, 00197 Rome, Italy.

8178

Hugh Last Award
To encourage established individual scholars in their collection of research material concerning classical antiquity. Grants are awarded for the collection of such material or for the expenses of visits to Italy for the collection of material, excluding excavations or surveys and any work on Roman Britain.

8179

Research Grants
To enable persons engaged in research, for a higher degree or at the early postdoctoral level, to spend a period of one to four months in Italy to further their studies. Value of the grant will vary but will not be less than £1,080 for one month, £1,850 for two, £2,700 for three, or £3,500 for four months.

8180

Busoni International Piano Competition
(Concorso Pianistico Internazionale F. Busoni)
Segreteria del Concorso Busoni
Conservatorio Statale di Musica C.
  Monteverdi
Piazza Domenicani 19   Phone: 471 976568
I-39100 Bolzano, Italy   Fax: 471 973579

8181

F. Busoni Prize
(Premio F. Busoni)
To recognize the best pianists of the competition. Pianists of all nationalities between 15 and 32 years of age are eligible to apply by May 31. The following prizes are awarded: Bosoni Prize - a monetary prize of 15,000,000 lire and contracts for 60 concerts with symphony orchestras and organizations; second prize - 9,000,000 lire; third prize - 6,000,000 lire; fourth prize - 5,000,000 lire; fifth prize - 4,500,000 lire; sixth prize - 4,000,000 lire; seventh prize - and 3,000,000 lire. Diplomas and certificates are also presented to the finalists. Awarded annually. Established in 1949. Sponsored by Italy - the President of the Council of Ministers, Italy - Ministry of Education, and the Municipality of Bolzano.

8182

Camerata Musicale Barese
Via Sparano 141   Phone: 80 5211908
I-70121 Bari, (BA), Italy   Fax: 80 5237154

8183
Concorso Internazionale Mauro Giuliani Duo di Chitarre
To encourage professional development of guitarists. Applications are accepted. Monetary prizes, guitars, diplomas of merit, and concerts in Italian society are awarded annually. Established in 1980 in memory of Mauro Giuliani. Sponsored by the Ministers of Spettacols, Provincia Bari.

8184
Campiello Foundation
(Fondazione Il Campiello)
Calle Due Portoni n. 6   Phone: 41 983 463
I-30172 Mestre, (VE), Italy   Fax: 41 985 395

8185
Campiello Prize
(Premio Campiello)
To provide recognition for the best Italian prose works of the year. Books of fiction by Italian citizens published during the preceding 12 months are considered. Five monetary prizes of 5,000,000 lire and plaques are awarded with additional money for the super prize winner. A monetary prize of 5,000,000 lire is awarded annually for the super prize. Established in 1963 by Mario Valeri Manera, Associazioni Industriali del Veneto.

8186
Grinzane Cavour Prize Association
(Associazione Premio Grinzane Cavour)
    Phone: 11 83 27 43
Via Montebello 21   Phone: 11 812 68 47
I-10124 Turin, Italy   Fax: 11 83 25 84

8187
Grinzane Cavour Prize
(Premio Grinzane Cavour)
To encourage the diffusion of reading in the Italian school, especially of books of contemporary fiction. Literary critics, scholars, writers, journalists, and people in the world of Italian culture judge the books. Monetary prizes are awarded annually in five categories: (1) contemporary Italian fiction - 5,000,000 lire; (2) contemporary foreign fiction translated into Italian - 5,000,000 lire; (3) translation into Italian; (4) an international prize for the complete works of a foreign writer - 10,000,000 lire; and (5) an award for a young beginning author, aged less than 40 - 5,000,000 lire. Established in 1982 by Prof. Giuliano Soria. Sponsored by Cassa di Risparmio di Torino, Regione Piemonte, SEAT (a division of STET), Provincia di Torino, and Societa Editrice Internazionale.

8188
Dino Ciani Teatro alla Scala International Competition for Young Pianists
(Premio Dino Ciani Teatro alla Scala)
Teatro alla Scala
Via Filodrammatici 2   Phone: 2 88791
I-20121 Milan, Italy   Fax: 2 8879

8189
Dino Ciani International Competition for Young Pianists
(Premio Dino Ciani)
For recognition of the best piano performance by a pianist not older than 30 years of age. The following prizes are presented: First prize - 20,000,000 Italian lire, Second prize - 8,000,000 Italian lire, and Third prize - 3,000,000 Italian lire. Awarded triennially. Established in 1975.

8190
City of Ancona
(Comune di Ancona)
Premio Ancona
Assessorato alla Cultura   Phone: 71 200634
I-60100 Ancona, Italy   Phone: 71 29066

8191
Ancona International Music Composition Competition for Wind Instruments
(Concorso Internazionale di Composizione Musicale per Strumenti a Fiato, Ancona)
To increase the output of contemporary music for wind instruments with no limits as to the style, writing, difficulty or composition trends. The competition is divided into three categories: (1) composition for solo wind instrument (flute, oboe, clarinet, saxophone, bassoon, horn, trumpet, trombone) with keyboard or magnetic tape accompaniment or other types of accompaniment, recorded on tape or video tape; (2) composition for solo wind instrument without accompaniment (flute, oboe, clarinet, saxophone, bassoon, horn, trumpet, trombone); and (3) composition for chamber group consisting of wind instruments with not more than 13 performers and not less than two. Non-wind instruments may be used within the following limits: (a) up to five performers, in Category 1; (b) up to eight performers, in Category 2; and (c) up to 13 performers in Category 3. Applications must be made by April 30. A monetary prize of 2,000,000 Italian lire is awarded to the first prize winner, and the Domenico Guaccero Prize of 500,000 Italian lire is awarded to the youngest winner.

8192
Club Tenco
Via Meridiana 7
I-18038 San Remo, Italy   Phone: 184 505011

8193
Premio Tenco
For recognition of musical artists who have always worked in the musical world with cultural, poetic and social aims. Musical performers may be nominated. A trophy is awarded annually in October. Established in 1974 in honor of Luigi Tenco. Sponsored by the San Remo Municipality.

8194
Collegium Internationale Chirurgiae Digestivae
c/o VI Clinica Chirurgica
Universita deghi Studi di Roma La
    Sapienza
Viale del Policlinico
I-00161 Rome, Italy   Phone: 6 495 3912

8195
Grassi Prize
For recognition of achievement in the field of surgery. Society Members under 35 years of age are eligible. A monetary prize of $1,000 US is awarded biennially at the CICD World Congress. Established in 1982 in honor of Giuseppe Grassi.

8196
Comune di Sanguinetto
Interno Castello 2
I-37058 Sanguinetto, (VR), Italy   Phone: 442 81066

8197
Castello-Sanguinetto Prize
(Premio Castello)
To encourage the development of novels for young readers between 11 and 14 years of age. The novel must be published in Italy before July 15 of the current year. A monetary prize of 3,000,000 lire and a gold medal from the President of the Republic are awarded for first prize annually. The second prize is 1,500 lire. Established in 1951 by Professor Giulietto Accordi. Sponsored by Cassa di Risparmio di Verona - Vicenza e Belluno.

8198
Concorso Ettore Pozzoli
Piazza Risorgimento 34
I-20038 Seregno, Italy   Phone: 362 222914

8199

Ettore Pozzoli International Piano Competition
(Concorso Pianistico Internazionale Ettore Pozzoli)
For recognition of outstanding pianists. Pianists of any nationality who are 32 years of age or younger may participate in the competition. The deadline for entry is August 10. The following prizes are awarded: (1) Pozzoli Prize - 15,000,000 lire and concerts; (2) Second Prize - 8,000,000 lire; (3) Third Prize - 5,000,000 lire; (4) Fourth Prize - 3,000,000 lire; (5) Fifth Prize - 2,000,000 lire; (6) Sixth Prize - 1,000,000 lire in memory of Luigi Pontiggia, tenor from Seregno (1919-1987); (7) Guiulio Confalonieri Special Prize - 1,000,000 lire and a silver medal to the youngest finalist not included in the previous list of prizes; and (8) Mons. Giuseppe Biella Special Prize - 1,000,000 lire for the best performer of Pozzoli's Studies; and (9) an honor diploma with a silver medal to each candidate admitted to the finals and semifinals. Awarded biennially. Established in 1957 in memory of Ettore Pozzoli, illustrious composer and teacher. Information is also available from Jean Micault, Halbergstrasse 68, D-6600 Saarbrucken, Federal Republic of Germany, phone: 681 66793.

8200

Concorso Internazionale di Chitarra Classica Citta di Alessandria
Piazza Garibaldi 16
I-15100 Alessandria, Italy   Phone: 131 53107

8201

City of Alessandria International Competition in Classical Guitar
(Concorso Internazionale di Chitarra Classica Citta' di Alessandria)
For recognition of outstanding performance on the classical guitar. Soloists of any nationality between 20 and 30 years of age are eligible. The following monetary prizes are awarded: (1) 3,000,000 Italian lire - first prize; (2) 1,500,000 Italian lire - second prize; and (3) 500,000 Italian lire - third prize. Awarded annually. Established in 1968.

8202

Concorso Internazionale di Composizione Organistica Oliver Messiaen
c/o Amministrazione provinciale di
  Bergamo
Assessorato alla Spettacolo
Via Fratelli Calvi, 10/A
I-24100 Bergamo, Italy   Phone: 35 243 00 00

8203

Concorso Internazionale di Composizione Organistica Oliver Messiaen
To recognize compositions for organ. Compositions must be entered in the following categories: (1) works for solo organ; and (2) works for organ and one or two voices, employing sacred writings. The compositions must be conceived for the execution with a mechanical organ, one or two manuals, of the Serassian tradition. Published works are eligible, provided publication has occurred within the previous two-year period. Works that have already been given a prize at other contests may not be submitted. The following monetary awards are presented in each category: First prize - 1,200,000 lire; and Second prize - 800,000 lire. Winning scores are performed with the historic organs of the Bergamasca. Established in 1987. (Inactive in 1990)

8204

Concorso Internazionale Musicale Francesco Paolo Neglia
Assessorato alla P. I. del Commune di
  Enna   Phone: 935 40433
I-94100 Enna, Italy   Phone: 935 40447

8205

Concorso Internazionale Musicale Francesco Paolo Neglia
For recognition of outstanding musical performances by pianists and opera singers. Pianists must be under 32 years of age, and opera singers, 35 years of age. The deadline for entry is June 23. The following prizes are awarded in both categories, piano and opera: (1) First prize - 6,000,000 lire; (2) Second prize - 4,000,000 lire; (3) Third prize - 3,000,000 lire; (4) Fourth prize - 2,000,000 lire; and (5) Fifth prize - 1,000,000 lire.

8206

Concorso Pianistico Internazionale Alessandro Casagrande
c/o Commune di Terni   Phone: 744 549 722
Vico San Lorenzo 1   Phone: 744 549 713
I-05100 Terni, Italy   Fax: 744 549 542

8207

Alessandro Casagrande International Piano Competition
(Concorso Pianistico Internazionale Alessandro Casagrande)
To recognize and encourage young pianists. Pianists of any nationality under 30 years of age are eligible. Concert engagements and the following monetary awards are presented: 12,000,000 Italian lire - first prize; 8,000,000 Italian lire - second prize; and 500,000 Italian lire - third prize. Awarded biennially. Established in 1966 by the Municipality of Terni.

8208

Cultural Association Rodolfo Lipizer
(Associazione Culturale Rodolfo Lipizer)
Via don Giovanni Bosco 91   Phone: 481 34775
I-34170 Gorizia, Italy   Fax: 481 536710

8209

International Violin Competition Rodolfo Lipizer Prize
(Concorso Internazionale di Violino Premio Rodolfo Lipizer)
To promote Rodolfo Lipizer's work and help the debut of young concert artists. The Competition is open to violinists of all nationalities who are under 35 years of age. The deadline is April 15. Monetary prizes totaling 37,000,000 lire, plaques, Special Prizes, a total of 70 concert engagements for the first three prize winners, and some travel expenses are awarded annually. Established in 1982 by Professor Lorenzo Qualli, an ex-pupil of Rodolfo Lipizer's teacher in honor of Rodolfo Lipizer.

8210

Alberto Curci Foundation
(Fondazione Alberto Curci)
Via Nardones 8   Phone: 81 417 244
I-80132 Naples, Italy   Fax: 81 415 370

8211

Alberto Curci International Violin Competition
(Concorso Internazionale di Violino Alberto Curci)
To provide recognition for the best violin performance. Musicians under 32 years of age are eligible. The deadline for application is June 30. Three monetary prizes totaling 15,000,000 Italian lire are awarded biennially. Established in 1966.

8212

Gabriele d'Annunzio Provincial Library
(Biblioteca Provinciale G. D'Annunzio)
I-65100 Pescara, Italy   Phone: 85 3724277

8213

Premio G. d'Annunzio
For recognition of biographical or critical work on Gabriele D'Annunzio, for remarkable prose or poetry, or for young peoples' books. Italian writers were eligible. Monetary prizes were awarded annually when merited. Established in 1957 in honor of Gabriele D'Annunzio, an Italian author and soldier (1863-1938). Sponsored by Amministrazione Provinciale di Pescara. (Discontinued in 1982)

8214
Guido d'Arezzo Foundation
(Fondazione Guido d'Arezzo)

Corso Italia 102
I-52100 Arezzo, Italy

Phone: 575 356203
Phone: 575 23835
Fax: 575 34735

8215
International Composition Contest Guido d'Arezzo
(Concorso Internazionale di Composizione Guido d'Arezzo)
For recognition of compositions of polyvocal music with the possibility of adding instruments for a maximum of three players in the following categories: mixed choirs, male choirs, female choirs, and soloist ensembles, in any formation, up to a maximum of 16 voices. The composition must be unpublished and never performed; it may be of sacred or secular character; and it must have a performance time of at least five minutes. Monetary awards totaling 15,000,000 lire are awarded annually at the Concorso Polifonico Internazionale. Established in 1974.

8216
International Polyphonic Contest Guido d'Arezzo
(Concorso Polifonico Internazionale Guido d'Arezzo)
For recognition of outstanding amateur choirs in the following categories: Mixed Choirs, Equal Voice Choirs (male and female), Vocal Ensembles, Children's Choirs, and Gregorian Chant and other Liturgical Monodic Chant. The contest also includes the Internation Choral Folksong Festival. The deadline for application is February 28. Trophies and monetary prizes of 3,000,000 lire for first prize; 1,500,000 lire for second prize; and 750,000 lire for third prize are awarded annually in each category. Additional special prizes are awarded. The Grand Prize "Citta di Arezzo," including 4,000,000 lire and a bronze sculpture, is awarded to the polyphonic institution presenting the choir or vocal ensemble that offers the best performance among all competitors. The winner is designated at the end of the Final Concert on the basis of the evaluation of the Contest Jury in full assembly. The winner of the Grand Premio Citta di Arezzo may be invited to perform and has the right to compete in the European Grand Prize of Choral Chant. Awarded annually. Established in 1952.

8217
Ente David di Donatello
Via di Villa Patrizi 10
I-00161 Rome, Italy

Phone: 6 4402766
Fax: 6 8411746

8218
David Film Awards
(Premi David di Donatello per la Cinematografia Internazionale)
For recognition of outstanding Italian and foreign films; and to stimulate, with the collaboration of authors, critics, technicians, and personalities of industry, culture, and the arts, an adequate form of competition in the sphere of the world's cinematographic production. The Premi David di Donatello are awarded for Italian films and for foreign films. A reproduction of the famous David statue by Donatello is awarded annually in a variety of categories. In addition, the following other awards are given: Premio Luchino Visconti, and Premi David Speciali. Established in 1954/55 by ANICA and AGIS Organizations under the sponsorship of the President of the Italian Republic.

8219
Ente Musicale Novarese Carlo Coccia
Via Prina 3
Casella Postale 43
I-28100 Novara, Italy

Phone: 321 29063

8220
Carlo Coccia International Singing Competition
(Concorso Internazionale di Canto Carlo Coccia)
For recognition of outstanding vocal performances. All young singers, Italian and foreign, can take part in the contest, provided that they are 18 years old and not over 40. The following monetary prizes are awarded: (1) First Prize - 2,000,000 lire; (2) Second Prize - 1,500,000 lire; (3) Third Prize - 1,200,000 lire; (4) Fourth Prize - 800,000 lire; (5) Fifth Prize - 500,000 lire; (6) Special Prize in Honour of Guido Cantelli - 1,000,000 lire to the best interpreter of a piece of music from "Cosi fan tutte" by W.A. Mozart, the last opera conducted by Guido Cantelli; and (7) Special Prize in honor of Alfredo Simonetto - 1,000,000 lire to the best interpreter of a piece of music by Carlo Coccia or Francesco Saverio Mercadante. Some of the winners and other chosen candidates are given parts in the Lyric Season at the Coccia Theater year by year in accordance with the repertory and with the artistic qualities of the interpreters.

8221
Ente Teatro Comunale Treviso
Corso del Popolo 31
Via Armando Diaz 7
I-31100 Treviso, Italy

Phone: 422 410130
Phone: 422 56467
Fax: 422 52285

8222
Toti Dal Monte International Singing Competition
(Concorso Internazionale per Cantanti Toti Dal Monte)
To encourage professional development and to cast Italian and foreign singers for the principal roles in an opera that is announced annually. Contestants of any nationality may submit applications by June 11. Age limits are at least 32 or 35 years, depending on the role sought. Contestants must take part in an audition relevant to the opera and/or present two arias. Competition is divided into preliminaries, quarter-finals, semi-finals, and finals. Winners will be called to play their respective roles in a number of recitals and take part in the "BOTTEGA", a workshop for the production of the opera. Winners will receive monetary awards of either 3,500,000 lire or 2,500,000 lire depending on the role. Certificates of merit may also be awarded to particularly deserving singers who have been admitted to the semi-finals. Also, up to a maximum of 5 study grants for a total of 6,500,000 lire and 2 study grants of 1,500,000 lire each have been set up. A sum of 100,000 lire will be given as a reimbursement of expenses to those contestants admitted to the semi-finals and a further sum of 100,000 lire will be given as travel reimbursement to those contestants who reach the finals.

8223
Treviso Lyric Prize
To provide recognition for the best interpretation by a performer in an opera. A monetary prize of 1,000,000 lire is awarded to the prima donna annually.

8224
Carlo Erba Foundation
(Fondazione Carlo Erba)

Via Giacomo Puccini 3
I-20121 Milan, Italy

Phone: 2 863442
Phone: 2 861820
Fax: 2 874050

8225
Cecilia Cioffrese Prizes for Health Care
(Premi Cecilia Cioffrese Nel Settore Della Cura Della Salute)
For recognition of the most outstanding research on cancer and viral diseases by young research workers. Italian citizens under 31 years of age with a degree in medicine or other disciplines may apply. A monetary prize is awarded annually. Established in 1988 by a bequest of Mrs. Cecilia Cioffrese, benefactrice of the Foundation.

8226
Eta Verde
PO Box 443
I-00100 Rome, Italy

Phone: 6 738668

8227
Aurelio Peccei Prize
(Premio Aurelio Peccei)
To encourage scientific research about macro problems. A plaque is awarded annually. Established in 1986 in honor of Aurelio Peccei, President of the Club of Rome.

8228
European Association for Animal Production
(Federation Europeenne de Zootechnie)
Via A. Torlonia 15A
I-00161 Rome, Italy
Phone: 6 8840785
Fax: 6 44241466

8229
Distinguished Service Award
To recognize outstanding contributions in the service of European and Mediterranean animal production and science. Individuals retired from active service may be nominated. A silver medal and diploma are awarded a maximum of three times in one year when merited. Established in 1989.

8230
EAAP Annual Meeting Awards
For recognition of the best scientific/technical paper in the field of animal production presented at the annual meeting of each one of the seven commissions of the organization. Individuals under 30 years of age are chosen by the Commission Boards. Scientific/technical papers are considered. A trophy and diploma are awarded annually. Established in 1983.

8231
A. M. Leroy Fellowship
To recognize an individual for significant contributions to research or development in the animal sector in Europe and the Mediterranean Basin. By nomination only. A silver plaque and diploma are awarded annually when merited. Established in 1989 by E.A.A.P. to honor Prof. A. M. Leroy, I.N.A., Paris, France.

8232
European Society of Culture
(Societe Europeenne de Culture)
Dorsoduro 909
I-30123 Venice, Italy
Phone: 41 523 02 10
Fax: 41 523 10 33

8233
Prix International de la Societe Europeenne de Culture
For recognition of a work that promotes the solidarity of people. To be eligible, the work is considered as a whole together with the moral authority as "homme de culture" of the author. A medal, diploma, and an original painting, design or engraving offered by a member of the Societe is awarded annually on the occasion of the General Assembly of the Societe. Established in 1977.

8234
European Union of Public Relations
Via del Ronco I3/c
PO Box 306
I-39100 Bolzano-Bozen, Italy
Phone: 661 992272
Fax: 471 200612

8235
Fashion Awards
To recognize individuals for publicity in the field of fashion. Established in 1972.

8236
Federazione Ordini Farmacisti Italiani
Via Palestro 75
I-00185 Rome, Italy
Phone: 6 4450363
Fax: 6 4941093

8237
Medaglia d'Oro Icilio Guareschi
For recognition of a contribution to the pharmaceutical sciences. Individuals may be nominated. A gold medal is awarded periodically. Established in 1957.

8238
Festival dei Popoli - International Review of Social Documentary Film
(Festival dei Popoli - Rassegna Internazionale del Film di Documentazione Sociale)
Via dei Castellani 8
I-50122 Florence, Italy
Phone: 55 294353
Fax: 55 213698

8239
Festival dei Popoli
For recognition of outstanding social documentary films dealing with social anthropological, political, and historical topics, as well as art, music, and cinema. Films must be completed in the previous year. The following awards are presented: Best Documentary - 15,000,000 lire, Best Research - 5,000,000 lire, and Best Anthropological Film - a silver plaque. Awarded annually. Established in 1959. Formerly: (1987) Marzocco d'Ora.

8240
Fondazione Anna Pane
Via Vincenzo Brunacci 15
I-00146 Rome, Italy
Phone: 6 5676604
Phone: 6 5576098

8241
Awards
For recognition in the fields of literature, art, and culture. The following prizes are awarded: (1) Premio Citta Eterna; (2) Premio di Natale piccolo formato; (3) Premio Aldo Palazzeschi; (4) Premio Beato Egidio da Taranto; and (5) Premio Teofilo Patni - Castel di Sangro.

8242
Fondazione Francesco Somaini
Tempio Voltiano
Viale Marconi
I-22100 Como, Italy
Phone: 31 579705

8243
Premio Triennale per la Fisica Francesco Somaini
For recognition in the field of physics. A monetary prize of 12,000,000 lire is awarded triennially.

8244
Fondazione Franco Michele Napolitano
Via Tarsia 23
I-80135 Naples, Italy
Phone: 81 313429

8245
Premio Nazionale Composizione
For recognition of a music composition.

8246
Fondazione Giovanni Agnelli
Via Giacosa 38　　　　　　　　　　　　　Phone: 11 658666
I-10125 Turin, Italy　　　　　　　　　　　Fax: 11 6502777

8247
Senator Giovanni Agnelli International Prize
To promote the need of the cultural world to reflect on the themes of the cohesion between changes in the Western world and fundamental ethical principles. Selection is by nomination by the Turin-based Giovanni Agnelli Foundation. A monetary award of $200,000 is presented biennially. Established in 1987 to honor Senator Giovanni Agnelli, founder of FIAT. Sponsored by FIAT.

8248
Fondazione Pietro Caliceti
Via Zamboni 33
I-40100 Bologna, Italy　　　　　　　　　　Phone: 951 228621

8249
Pietro Caliceti International Prize
(Premio Internazionale Pietro Caliceti)
To recognize an Italian or foreign graduate in medicine and surgery, who during the preceding four years published a scientific work of unquestionable value and of recognized originality in the field of otolaryngology. A monetary prize of 3,000,000 lire, a gold medal, minted from the original mold used by Mrs. Ines Misley, the widow of Professor Caliceti, and a diploma are awarded every four years. Established in 1956 in memory of Professor Pietro Caliceti, a former distinguished professor of clinical otolaryngology of Bologna University.

8250
Fondazione Premio Laura Orvieto
Archivio Contemporaneo del Gabinetto
　G.P. Vieusseux
Via Maggio 42
I-50125 Florence, Italy

8251
Laura Orvieto Prize
(Premio Laura Orvieto)
To provide recognition for the manuscript of a book of fiction or a book of poetry for children from 8 to 11 years of age. Italian authors are eligible. Monetary prizes are awarded biennially. Established in 1954 by Adriana Guasconi Orvieto in memory of Laura Orvieto.

8252
Fondazione Premio Napoli
Palazzo Reale - Piazza Plebiscito　　　　　Phone: 81 403187
I-80132 Naples, Italy　　　　　　　　　　Fax: 81 403187

8253
Naples Prize for Literature
(Premio Napoli di Narrativa)
For recognition of an outstanding work of literature in Italian. Italian and non-Italian authors are eligible. A monetary prize of 10,000,000 Italian lire and a plaque are awarded annually. Established in 1954.

8254
Naples Prize for the Study of Southern and Northern Countries in the World
(Premio Napoli di Saggistica - Il Rapporto Nord-Sud nel Mondo)
For recognition of research on the northern and southern countries in the world, especially those monographs relevant to contemporary, social, and economic issues, and the politics and political instruments, national and local, useful and related to the development of this geographic region. Unpublished literary works, as well as multifaceted activities that have done much to contribute to the study of the northern and southern countries in the world are eligible. A monetary prize of 5,000,000 Italian lire is awarded annually in the spring. Established in 1972.

8255
Premio Napoli di Giornalismo
To recognize three journalists, Italian or non-Italians, for contributions to journalism. A monetary prize of 30,000,000 Italain lire is awarded annually. Established in 1986 by the brothers Amedeo and Elio Matacena.

8256
Premio Napoli - Mezzogiorno
For recognition of a written work in Italian concerning the Mezzogiorno region of Italy. The work may cover its history, culture, politics, economics, social conditions, and the safeguarding of the environment. A monetary prize of 5,000,000 Italian lire is awarded annually.

8257
Premio Napolitain Illustri
To recognize an outstanding contribution by an individual in the fields of art, research, or science who has honored the name of Naples in the world with extraordinary success. Established in 1988 by Ente Provinciale per il Turismo di Napoli.

8258
Fondazione Prof. Domenico Ganassini
Via Boncompagni 63
I-20139 Milan, Italy　　　　　　　　　　Phone: 2 5696946

8259
Premio Europeo Prof. D. Ganassini
For recognition of an unpublished experiment in the fields of biology and biochemistry pertaining to medicine.

8260
Fondazione Russolo-Pratella
Via Bagaini 6　　　　　　　　　　　　　Phone: 332 237245
I-21100 Varese, Italy　　　　　　　　　　Fax: 332 280331

8261
Concorso Internazionale Luigi Russolo
To recognize outstanding young composers and programmers of electroacoustic music. Participants in the International Competition of electroacoustic, analogic, and digital music who are under 35 years of age are eligible. Each competitor can participate with one or more compositions in the following cartegories: analogic or digital electroacoustic music; electroacoustic music with instruments or voice; electroacoustic music for the radio and electroacoustic music for dance. Certificates and CDs (recorded from the competition) are awarded, and one individual receives a scholarship for one month to work in the G.M.E.M. of Marsiglia Research Center. Awarded annually. Established in 1979 in honor of the futuristic composer, Luigi Russolo (1845-1947).

8262
Fondazione Valentino Bucchi
　　　　　　　　　　　　　　　　　　　Phone: 6 817 5687
Via Ubaldino Peruzzi, 20　　　　　　　　Phone: 6 882 1527
I-00139 Rome, Italy　　　　　　　　　　Fax: 6 882 1527

8263
Valentino Bucchi Prize of Rome Capital City
(Premio Valentino Bucchi di Roma Capitale)
To encourage young musicians, and to recognize contributions to the spread of musical culture. The competition is held for different categories each year as follows: (1) piano and two pianos in 20th century (performance and composition) (1991); (2) clarinet (performance and composition), music and poetry in 20th century, music and tradition for childhood (composition) (1992); (3) contrabass (performance and composition),

music and nature for childhood (performance and competition) (1993); and (4) flute and piccolo (performance and composition), wind instruments for childhood (competition) (1994); violin quartet and strings in 20th century (performance and competition) (1995); vocal music in 20th century (performance and competition), music and poetry in 20th century (competition), and music and fairy tales for childhood (competition) (1996); and cello, quartet and strings (performance and competition) (1997). Performers between 32 and 35 years of age and composers under 40 years of age are eligible to apply by September 15 and 30, respectively. Monetary prizes totaling 100,200,000 lire are awarded and all the winners are published by the Periodical Premio Valentino Bucchi. Concerts of the performance competition winners and performance of the winning pieces of the composition competition are given. Awarded annually in November. Established in 1978 in collaboration with Conservatorio di Musica "Santa Cecilia" in Rome in memory of Valentino Bucchi, a composer who died in 1976. Sponsored by Italian Ministries "Beni Culturali" and "Turismo e Spettacolo."

8264

Fondazione Venezia Nostra
Via Luigi Porro Lambertenghi 34
I-20159 Milan, Italy   Phone: 2 6888333

8265

Premio Internazionale per un Articolo o Studio Scientifico o Tecnico
For recognition in the fields of science and technology.

8266

Food and Agriculture Organization of the United Nations
(Organisation des Nations Unies pour l'alimentation et l'agriculture)
Via delle Terme di Caracalla   Phone: 6 52251
I-00100 Rome, Italy   Fax: 6 5225 3152

8267

A. H. Boerma Award
To recognize journalists who have helped to focus public attention on important aspects of the world food problem and have stimulated interest in and support for measures leading to their solutions. An article, articles, and productions in television and radio may be submitted by nationals of any member country of FAO. A monetary prize of $10,000 US and a scroll describing the recipient's achievements are awarded biennially during the FAO conference year. Established in 1975 in honor of Mr. Addeke H. Boerma, Director-General of FAO from 1968 to 1975.

8268

FAO Technical Assistance Fellowship
To provide for study in the fields of agriculture, fisheries, forestry, nutrition, agricultural economics and statistics, rural institutions, and services, etc., to prepare suitably qualified personnel to assist in economic and technical development of own country. Applications are open to nationals of countries where FAO carries out technical assistance projects provided they are working or are destined to work on these projects and have been selected to undertake further studies abroad. Candidates must have adequate basic and technical education and practical experience in the field of study. A fellowship that covers maintenance, tuition, return fares, and other allowances is awarded.

8269

Andre Mayer Research Fellowship
To provide for research in the fields of animal production and health, land and water development, plant production and protection, human resources and institutions, fisheries, forestry, food policy and nutrition, and agricultural economics (commodities, statistics, economic policy analysis). Highly qualified and experienced research workers from FAO member countries may be nominated. Four to six fellowships of $800 to $1,200 per month plus transportation, fees and report allowance are awarded biennially. Named after Andre Mayer (1875-1956), a French scientist and one of the chief architects of FAO.

8270

Osiris Award
To recognize films that contribute to raising public awareness about problems of rural development in agriculture, forestry or fisheries. The prize is awarded at the International Agricultural Film Competition (Berlin - biennially); the International Film Festival in Nitra (Czechoslavakia - annually); and the International Agricultural Film Competition in Zaragoza (Spain - biennially). The Osiris is a bronze replica of a statue of the Egyptian God of Agriculture and Fertility. Established in the late 1960s.

8271

Edouard Saouma Award
To recognize a regional institution that managed a particularly efficient project funded under FAO's Technical Cooperation Programme. A monetary prize of $25,000 is awarded biennially. Established in 1993 to honor Mr. Edouard Saouma, who served as Director General of FAO from 1976 to 1993.

8272

B. R. Sen Award
To recognize FAO field officers who have made outstanding contributions to the advancement of the country or countries to which he/she was assigned. Candidates must have served in the year for which the Award is granted and must have at least two years' continuous service in the field. All FAO field officers are eligible. The Award consists of a medal bearing the recipient's name, a scroll describing achievements, a cash prize of US $5,000 and round-trip airfare to FAO headquarters in Rome for the recipient and spouse. Awarded annually.

8273

Ing. Castaldi Illuminazione
Via Carlo Goldoni 18
Trezzano Sul Naviglio
I-20090 Milan, Italy   Phone: 2 4454374
                                                       Fax: 2 4456946

8274

Design & Light Competition
(Progetto & Luce)
To encourage professional development and to recognize designers who submit the most significant lighting installations, created with units produced by the company. Projects submitted by all designers, both Italian and non-Italian, as well as governments and organizations in the person of engineers designated by them, are eligible. The deadline for entry is the end of February. The following prizes are awarded: first prize - a certificate and 10,000,000 Italian lire; second prize - a certificate and 5,000,000 Italian lire; and third prize - a certificate and 2,500,000 Italian lire. Awarded biennially. Established in 1990.

8275

Institute for University Cooperation
(Istituto per la Cooperazione Universitaria)
Viale G. Rossini 26   Phone: 6 85300722
I-00198 Rome, Italy   Fax: 6 8554646

8276

Institute for University Cooperation Awards
To recognize and further Third World development through the international cooperation of universities and institutions of scientific research. The Institute bestows awards, grants, and scholarships.

8277

International Association of Biblicists and Orientalists
(Internacia Asocio de Bibliistoj kaj Orientalistoj)
Piazza Duomo 4
I-48100 Ravenna, Italy

8278
IABO Awards
For recognition of contributions that explore biblical themes of Oriental cultures, work toward the union of biblical and Oriental studies, and study the ecumenical aspects of the Bible shared by all religions. No further information on awards is available for this edition.

8279
International Balzan Foundation
(Fondazione Internazionale Balzan)
Piazzetta U. Giordano 4
I-20122 Milan, Italy
Phone: 2 76002212
Fax: 2 76009457

8280
Eugenio Balzan Prize
(Premio Balzan)
To promote the most deserving humanitarian and cultural works throughout the world, regardless of nationality, race, or religion. Prizes are awarded for literature, moral sciences, and the arts; physical, mathematical, and natural sciences and medicine; and a special prize for humanity, peace, and brotherhood among peoples. These are Italy's most prestigious academic awards. Up to three monetary prizes of about 350,000 Swiss francs each may be awarded annually. Established in 1961 by Eugenio Balzan. The Balzan Foundation office at Claridenstrasse 35, 8002 Zurich, Switzerland, manages the fund.

8281
International Biennial Exhibition of Humour in Art, Tolentino
(Biennale Internazionale dell'Umorismo Nell'Arte di Tolentino)
c/o Azienda Autonoma Soggiorno Cura
 Turismo
Piazza della Liberta 18
I-62029 Tolentino, Italy
Phone: 733 973049

8282
International Biennial Exhibition of Humour in Art
To recognize outstanding humour in art. Two awards are presented: Cesare Marcorelli Prize - humorous art in its various expressions either graphic or pictorial. First Prize - Gold Tower; Second Prize - Silver Tower; and Third Prize - Bronze Tower. The winner of the first prize will automatically be entitled to a personal show in the following Biennial Exhibition where he/she will be allowed to exhibit up to thirty works; and (2) Luigi Mari Prize - for personal caricature, either in a picture or in sculpture. A plaque is awarded. The works which are awarded the Towers or the Plaque remain the property of the Biennial Exhibition and are kept in the International Museum of Caricature situated in the Palace Parisani-Bezzi of Tolentino. Other prizes, including purchases, may be offered by public and private organizations. The Exhibition is held biennially. The Premio Cesare Marcorelli was established in 1961; and Premio Luigi Mari in 1975.

8283
International Canoe Federation
(Federation Internationale de Canoe)
G. Massaia 59
Florence, Italy

8284
Federation Internationale de Canoe
To promote canoeing and its related activities including racing, slalom, marathons, canoe-polo, and sailing. The Federation sponsors world championships.

8285
International Center for the Study of the Preservation and the Restoration of Cultural Property
Via di San Michele 13
I-00153 Rome, Italy
Phone: 6 587901
Fax: 6 5884265

8286
ICCROM Award
For recognition of a person with exceptional talent in the field of preservation, protection, and restoration of cultural property. The ICCROM Council makes nominations. A bronze sculpture by Peter Rockwell and a citation are awarded biennially at the General Assembly in May. Established in 1979.

8287
International Centre for Theoretical Physics
PO Box 586
Miramare
Strada Costiera 11
34100 Trieste, Italy
Phone: 40 22401
Fax: 40 224163

8288
Dirac Medal
For recognition of contributions in the field of theoretical physics and mathematics. Selection is by nomination. The Dirac Medals are not awarded to Nobel laureates or Wolf Foundation Prize winners. Awarded annually. The winners are announced on August 8, Dirac's birthday. Established in 1985 in honor of Paul Adrian Maurice Dirac (United Kingdom), Nobel Laureate for physics.

8289
ICTP Prize
To recognize an outstanding contribution made by a scientist from a developing country in a particular field of physics and mathematics. Individuals under 40 years of age are eligible. A monetary award of US $1,000, a medal, and a certificate are awarded annually. Established in 1982. The Kastler Prize was awarded in 1983 and 1986 in honor of Professor Alfred Kastler (France), Nobel Laureate for Physics in 1966. The Vallarta Prize was awarded in 1984 in honor of Professor Manuel Sandoval Vallarta (Mexico), second chairman of the ICTP Scientific Council. The Eklund Prize was awarded in 1985 in honor of Professor Sigvard Eklund, Director General Emeritus of the International Atomic Energy Agency. The Bogolubov Prize was awarded in 1987 in honor of Prof. Nikolaj N. Bogolubov. The Heisenberg Prize was awarded in 1988 in honor of Prof. Werner Heisenberg. The Yukawa Prize was awarded in 1989 in honor of Prof. Hideki Yukawa. The Raman Prize was awarded in 1990 in honor of Prof. C. V. Raman. The Majorana Prize was awarded in 1991 in honor of Prof. E. Majorana (Italy). The V.F. Weisskopf Prize was awarded in 1992 in honor of V. F. Weisskopf (United States) for contributions to the field of high energy physics. The J. Robert Schrieffer Prize was awarded in 1993 in honor of Prof. J. Robert Schrieffer (United States)in the fields of solid state, atomic, and molecular physics. The Atiyah Prize will be awarded in 1994 in honor of Sir Michael Atiyah (United Kingdom) in the fields of mathematics, nuclear physics, plasma physics, and other fields of physics. The Weinberg Prize will also be awarded in 1995 in honor of Prof. Steven Weinberg (United States) in the field of high energy physics.

8290
International Cinema Week
Via S. Giacomo
37121 Verona, Italy
Phone: 45 8006778
Fax: 45 590624

8291
Stefano Reggiani Prize
To recognize the best film of the Cinema Week festival. Films are judged by five leading film critics. A trophy is presented at the end of International Cinema Week in April. Awarded annually. Established in 1991 in memory of Stefano Reggiani, a Veronese writer and film critic. Sponsored by La Stampa Publishing Group.

8292

International Competition for Verdian Voices
(Concorso Internazionale per Voci Verdiane)

Piazza G. Verdi 1
I-43011 Busseto, Italy
Phone: 524 92487
Phone: 524 92403
Fax: 524 92360

8293

International Competition for Verdian Voices
(Concorso Internazionale per Voci Verdiane)

For recognition of outstanding performers of Verdi operas and to help young singers in their career. Both male and female singers from any country are eligible to enter. Sopranos and tenors must be 35 years of age or younger, and mezzosopranos, baritones, and basses must be 37 years of age or younger. Monetary prizes totaling 13,000,000 lire are awarded annually in June. Singers are chosen from the finalists to take part in an opera which will be performed in Busseto and later in other theatres of the region Emilia-Romagna. Established in 1961 in honor of Alessandro and Maria Ziliani. Sponsored by the Town Council of Busseto, Emilia-Romagna Region, Ministero Cultura e Spettacolo, and Fondazione Maria Mezzanzana. Formerly: Concorso Internazionale per Voci Verdiane Alessandro e Maria Ziliani.

8294

International Competition of Maritime Film-TV
(Italia Sul Mare - Rassegna Internazionale dei Documentari Cine - TV Marinari)

Via Messina 31
I-00198 Rome, Italy
Phone: 6 84 43 151
Fax: 6 85 75 95

8295

Rassegna Internazionale dei Documentari Cine-TV Marinari
(Milan International Competition on Maritime Film - TV Documentaries)

For recognition of the best films running a maximum of 30 minutes on maritime subjects: navy, merchant fleet, sports, teaching, tourism, research and industry. The following prizes are awarded: (1) Italia Sul Mare Prize; (2) Trophy of the Ministry of Industry; (3) Trophy of the Ministry of Public Works; (4) Trophy of the Italian Boating Association; and (5) many others. Established in 1960.

8296

International Exhibition of Author Films
(Mostra Internazionale del Film d'Autore - Sanremo)

Rotonda dei Mille 1
I-24100 Bergamo, Italy
Phone: 35 243162

8297

Mostra Internazionale del Film d'Autore Gran Premio

For recognition of contributions to the promotion and the development of quality film production and to encourage the wide distribution of such films. Full length feature films written and directed by the same person and produced within the preceding year by Italian or foreign filmmakers, which are presented at any other international festival are eligible. A monetary prize of 5,000,000 lire is to be divided between the author and producer. Special prizes are given for best music score, best actor, and best actress. Awarded annually in San Remo every March. Established in 1958 by Nino Zucchelli, who is still the Festival Director.

8298

International Federation of Beekeepers' Associations
(Federation Internationale des Associations d'Apiculture)

Corso Vittorio Emanuele 101
I-00186 Rome, Italy
Phone: 6 6852286
Fax: 6 6852286

8299

International Federation of Beekeepers' Associations Awards

To recognize national beekeepers associations, and to encourage the dissemination of information regarding new techniques, the results of scientific research, and economic developments in beekeeping. The Federation sponsors competitions, conducts symposia, and bestows awards.

8300

International Film Festival Rassegna - Nature, Man and His Environment
(Mostra Cinematografica Internazionale - La Natura, l'Uomo e il suo Ambiente)

Via di Villa Patrizi 10
I-00161 Rome, Italy
Phone: 6 88473218
Fax: 6 4402718

8301

International Film Festival - Nature, Man and His Environment
(Mostra Cinematografica Internazionale - La Natura, l'Uomo e il suo Ambiente)

To recognize organizations or individuals responsible for significant contributions to the safeguarding of man's environment. The International Film Festival: Nature, Man and His Environment, gives recognition to the producers, directors and technicians who, with significant results, have created films aimed at establishing an awareness of the most dramatic ecological problems. The Film Festival is open to the participation of recent films of short, medium or long footage, in black and white or color, and 35 or 16 mm gauge. The films may be animated and produced for normal or panoramic screens by anyone of any nationality including the film industry, industry in general, television companies, cultural organizations, research institutes, scientific museums, film libraries, film clubs, film enthusiasts, etc. Films must refer to one of the following subjects: basic ecological information; the problems of making people aware of nature and natural resources with the aim of preserving them; chemical, physical and noise pollution of soil, water and air; preservation of flora and natural landscape; preservation of fauna; national parks and reserves; the problems of parks and green belts; man-made landscapes (related to the values of natural landscape); the defense of the historic character of towns and of their ancient buildings; the organization and use of the territory; the safeguard and restoration of works of art and of the cultural heritage; public health, environmental hygiene; various aspects of the quality of life; or environmental education. The deadline is September 10. Three Targhe d'Oro per l'Ecologia (Gold Awards) are awarded annually. In addition, special prizes, the Premi Speciali and the Premi Speciali Comunita' Europee, are awarded when merited. Established in 1971.

8302

International Galileo Galilei Prize Foundation of the Rotary Club of Italy
(Fondazione Premio Internazionale Galileo Galilei dei Rotary Italiani)

Via S. Maria 26
I-56100 Pisa, Italy
Phone: 1 500670
Fax: 1 501901

8303

Galileo Galilei International Prize of the Rotary Club of Italy
(Premio Internazionale Galileo Galilei dei Rotary italiani)

To recognize eminent non-Italian contributors to Italian studies. A selection committee of Italian scholars makes the nomination. A statuette by a prominent Italian sculptor and a gold plaque are awarded annually. Established in 1962 by Tristano Bolelli, Professor of Linguistics in Pisa University.

8304

Premio Maria Cianci

To recognize non-Italian students under 35 years of age who are doing research in Italian civilization and history in different fields. Nomination is by a committee of former winners of the Galileo Galilei Prizes and

Italian specialists. Established in 1991 by Professor Ernesto Cianci in honor of his wife, Maria Cianci.

8305
Nicoletta Quinto Prize
(Premio Nicoletta Quinto)
To recognize non-Italian students under 30 years of age who are doing research in Italian civilization and history in different fields. Nomination is by a committee of former winners of the Galileo Galilei Prizes and Italian specialists. A monetary prize of 10,000,000 lire is awarded annually. Established in 1984 by Professor Pietro Quinto in honor of his daughter, Nicoletta Quinto.

8306
International Institute of Humanitarian Law
(Institut Internazionale di Diritto Umanitario)
Villa Ormond
Corso Cavallotti 115　　　　　　　　　　　Phone: 184 541848
I-18038 San Remo, Italy　　　　　　　　　Fax: 184 541600

8307
International Institute of Humanitarian Law Prize
For recognition of the promotion, dissemination, and teaching of international humanitarian law. Any person or institution whose activities have contributed to the promotion, dissemination, or teaching of international humanitarian law may be nominated. A medal and diploma are awarded annually. Established in 1980.

8308
International Manifestations of Ceramic Arts
(Manifestazioni Internazionali della Ceramica)
Competition Headquarters
Palazzo Delle Esposizioni
Corso Mazzini 92　　　　　　　　　　　　Phone: 546 621111
I-48018 Faenza, (RA), Italy　　　　　　　Phone: 546 28664
　　　　　　　　　　　　　　　　　　　　Fax: 546 621554

8309
International Ceramic Art Competition
(Concorso Internazionale della Ceramica d'Arte)
To encourage the search for new creative expression, new techniques, and new materials, involving artists and ceramists worldwide in the renewal of creative forms and modes. The Competition is open to single artists or teams of artists. Countries, ministries, cultural organizations, category associations etc., may arrange the participation of national groups. The works must not have been shown in other exhibitions. Cash prizes and medals are awarded biennially. Established in 1938. Sponsored by the City of Faenza.

8310
International Society for Medical and Psychological Hypnosis
Corso XII Marzo 57　　　　　　　　　　　Phone: 2 70126489
I-20129 Milan, Italy　　　　　　　　　　　Fax: 2 7491051

8311
International Society for Medical and Psychological Hypnosis Awards
To recognize health care professionals involved with medical and psychological hypnosis in 30 countries, and to support clinical research through fellowships, advanced training, and certification for hypnotherapists. Awards are presented annually.

8312
International Sport Film Festival of Palermo
(Rassegna di Palermo/International Sportfilmfestiva)
CONI
via Notarbartolo 1/G　　　　　　　　　　Phone: 91 6251858
I-90141 Palermo, Italy　　　　　　　　　　Fax: 91 6256256

8313
International Prize Paladino D'Oro
(Premio Internazionale Paladino D'Oro)
To encourage a deeper comparison between films and video works on the subject of sports. Feature films, short films (of no more than 30 minutes in length), and videos produced within the last three years are eligible. Nominations are determined by a selection committee and winners by the International Jury. Film and video submission deadline is July 31. A summary of the plot (either in Italian, French, or English) and at least five photographs must accompany submission. A Golden Paladino trophy is awarded for film, and a Silver Paladino trophy is awarded for short films and video. A participation diploma is given to all nominees. Established in 1981 by Dr. Vito Maggio in honor of Nino Santamarina.

8314
International Sport Press Association
(Association Internationale de la Presse Sportive)
Via Paolo da Cannobio 9　　　　　　　　Phone: 2 877785
I-20122 Milan, Italy　　　　　　　　　　　Fax: 2 877786

8315
Association Internationale de la Presse Sportive Awards
For recognition of worldwide achievement in sports. Awards are given in the following categories: Best Male Athlete, Best Female Athlete, Best Sports Team, Best Press Facilities, and Best Sports Photos in black and white and color. Selection is by nomination. Trophies are awarded annually during the AIPS Congress. Established in 1977.

8316
International Sports Film Festival
(Festival Internazionale di Cinema Sportivo)
Via di Villa Patrizi 10　　　　　　　　　　Phone: 6 88473245
I-00161 Rome, Italy　　　　　　　　　　　Fax: 6 8848079

8317
International Sports Film Festival
(Festival Internazionale di Cinema Sportivo)
To provide a venue for the international motion picture and audiovisual media and a forum for sports-related professionals from all countries to meet, exchange ideas and popularize sports as a form of cultural expression in modern society. Works dealing with any sport activity produced in the past two years may be presented, particularly: (1) narrative feature length, medium and short films; (2) documentary-features educational and promotional films; (3) documentary and advertising spots; and (4) national and international records and sport telecasts. Works in 35 or 16mm., or video cassettes with U-matic, VHS, 625 PAL, SECAM, and NTSC can participate. The following prizes are awarded: (1) City of Turin Prizes - for the best, next best and third best entries reflecting aim of the Festival; (a) for best work on formative values of sports; (b) for the best technical-educational documentary; (3) AGIS Prizes - for the best film feature; (4) Province of Turin Prize - for the most informative work; (5) Chiesa Prize - for the best sports telecast or TV sports news program; (6) a prize for the best TV sports commercial; and (7) AGISscuola Prizes for work with best youth education values assigned by the AGISscuola Presidency. Plaques and trophies are awarded annually. Established in 1945.

8318
International Tourist Film Festival
(Festival Internazionale del Film Turistico)
　　　　　　　　　　　　　　　　　　　　Phone: 6 4741390
Via Sistina, 27　　　　　　　　　　　　　Phone: 6 4826692
I-00187 Rome, Italy　　　　　　　　　　　Fax: 6 4741132

8319
Airone
For recognition of the best tourist film. A gold medal is awarded annually. Established in 1982 by Antonio Conte. Sponsored by Azienda di Promozione Turistica di Montecatini Terme.

8320

International Triennial of Stringed Instruments
(Ente Triennale Internazionalele Degli Strumenti ad Arco)
Via Gioconda 3
I-26100 Cremona, Italy
Phone: 372 21454
Fax: 372 21454

8321

International Triennial of Stringed Instruments
(Triennale Internazionale le Degli Strumenti ad Arco)
To recognize excellence in an international exhibition of stringed instruments. Medals and purchase prizes for the best instruments are awarded triennially. Established in 1976. Sponsored by the City Council, Provincial Council, Camera di Commercio, Fondazione W. Stauffer, and Azienda di Promozione Turistica.

8322

Isle of Elba - Raffaello Brignetti Literary Award
(Premio Letterario Isola d'Elba - Raffaello Brignetti)
c/o Azienda di Promozione Turistica
Calata Italia 26
I-57037 Portoferraio, Italy
Phone: 565 914671
Fax: 565 916350

8323

Isle of Elba - Raffaello Brignetti Literary Award
(Premio Letterario Isola d'Elba - Raffaello Brignetti)
For recognition of outstanding works of prose, poetry, or literary essays. Works by European authors published in Italy or translated into Italian during the previous year are eligible. Monetary prizes totalling 14,000,000 Italian lire are awarded annually in September. A super prize of 5,000,000 Italian lire is awarded to the winner, and 3,000,000 Italian lire is awarded to each of the three finalists. The award cannot be divided. Established in 1962. Renamed in 1984 to honor Raffaello Brignetti. Formerly: (1984) Premio Letterario Isola d'Elba.

8324

Istituto Internazionale delle Comunicazioni
Via Pertinace
Villa Piaggio
I-16125 Genoa, Italy
Phone: 10 294683
Phone: 10 294684

8325

Columbus Prize
To provide recognition for important research in the communications field (sea, land, air space, mail and telecommunications). Monetary prizes are awarded annually.

8326

Premio Innovazione Elettronica
(Electronics Innovation Award)
To recognize Italian citizens working in the Italian electronics industry who have shown high innovative capabilities in the application of scientific discoveries to industrial problems in the field of electronic systems and apparatus. Work performed or published in recent years whose validity may run through the years following the award are eligible. Monetary prizes of 4,000,000 lire to the winner, and 1,000,000 lire to the other four selected candidates are awarded every three years. Established in 1976 by SELENIA - Industrie Elettroniche Associate S.p.A. - Roma.

8327

Istituto Italo-Latino Americano
Piazza G. Marconi 26
I-00144 Rome, Italy
Phone: 6 59091

8328

Premio Istituto Italo-Latino Americano
To promote Latin American literature translated into Italian. Authors who are of Latin American citizenship are eligible for consideration. A monetary prize is awarded biennially. Established in 1970.

8329

Istituto Nazionale di Studi Romani
Piazza dei Cavalieri di Malta 2
I-00153 Rome, Italy
Phone: 6 5743442
Phone: 6 5743445

8330

Certamen Capitolinum
To provide recognition for the best works on the Latin language and literature. Teachers, scholars, and students are eligible. The following prizes are awarded: (1) a monetary prize of 600,000 lire and a silver sculpture of a she-wolf - First prize; (2) 300,000 lire and a silver medallion - Second prize; (3) 100,000 lire and a diploma (to students); and (4) honorable mentions. Awarded annually. Established in 1950.

8331

Istituto Papirologico Girolamo Vitelli
Universita degli Studi
Via degli Alfani 46/48
I-50121 Florence, Italy
Phone: 55 2478969
Fax: 55 2480722

8332

G. Vitelli Prize
(Premio G. Vitelli)
To encourage professional development in the study of Greek and Latin papyri. Selection is by nomination. A monetary prize is awarded.

8333

Italian Association for Metallurgy
(Associazione Italiana di Metallurgia)
Piazzale R. Morandi 2
I-20121 Milan, Italy
Phone: 2 791132
Fax: 2 784236

8334

Italian Association for Metallurgy Awards
To recognize individuals for contributions to materials science and technology that promote progress in traditional and advanced metallurgy. Awards are given biennially.

8335

Italian Chemical Society
(Società Chimica Italiana)
Viale Liegi 48
I-00198 Rome, Italy
Phone: 6 8549691
Fax: 6 8548734

8336

Medagila Domenico Marotta
No further information was provided for this edition.

8337

Medaglia Emanuele Paterno
For recognition of outstanding achievement in chemistry. A medal is awarded triennially. Established in 1923.

8338

Medaglia Giulio Natta
No further information was provided for this edition.

| 8339 |

Medaglia Raffaele Piria
For recognition in the field of chemistry. A medal was awarded every four years. Established in 1958. (Discontinued)

| 8340 |

Medaglia Stanislao Cannizzaro
For recognition in the field of chemistry. A medal is awarded every four years. Established in 1956.

| 8341 |

Italian Council of Ministers
(Presidenza del Consiglio dei Ministri)
Dipartimento per l'Informazione e
  l'Editoria
Via Po 14-16A   Phone: 6 8598 1
I-00187 Rome, Italy   Fax: 6 783998

| 8342 |

Golden Book Prize
(Premio Libro d'Oro)
To recognize the publisher who culturally influenced the public the most. A golden object is awarded annually. Established in 1957 by the Presidency of the Council.

| 8343 |

Golden Pen Prize
(Premio Penna d'Oro)
To recognize the author who has made an important contribution to Italian culture. A monetary prize of 20,000,000 Italian lire is awarded annually. Established in 1957 by the Presidency of the Council.

| 8344 |

Italian Electrical and Electronics Association
(Associazione Elettrotecnica ed Elettronica Italiana)
Ufficio Centrale
Viale Monza 259   Phone: 2 257791
I-20126 Milan, Italy   Fax: 2 2570 512

| 8345 |

Premio A. Barbagelata
For recognition of articles that attempted to summarize and illustrate, in a manner accessible to the majority of readers, the developments within recent years in electronics and electrical engineering. A monetary award of 500,000 lire and a diploma were awarded annually. (Discontinued)

| 8346 |

Premio ABB
For recognition of the most original paper in electrical engineering presented at the AEI's annual meeting of the preceding year. Priority will be given to papers dealing with communication, protection, and control systems for the transmission and distribution networks. A monetary award of 6,000,000 lire will be awarded annually. Established in 1970. Formerly: (1993) ABB Transformatori and Telettra.

| 8347 |

Premio AEI Galileo Ferraris
For recognition of scientific and technical activity in electrical engineering achieved within the last decade. Members of the Association are eligible. A gold medal and a diploma are awarded annually. Established in 1919.

| 8348 |

Premio AEI Guglielmo Marconi
For recognition of scientific and technical activitiy in electronics achieved within the last decade. Members of the Association are eligible. A gold medal and a diploma are awarded annually. Established in 1932. Formerly: (1988) Premio AEI Ricerche.

| 8349 |

Premio AEI - Milano Section
For recognition of the best scientific paper in power, electronics or computer science, originated or developed in the Milano Section area and published in an international journal in the last two years. A monetary award of 10,000,000 lire and a certificate are presented annually. Established in 1987.

| 8350 |

Premio Bonazzi
For recognition of the best work published in an AEI periodical, dealing with electronics, especially experimental electronics. Work published by a member of the Association under 40 years of age within two years preceding the award is eligible. A monetary award of 500,000 lire and a diploma are awarded annually.

| 8351 |

Premio Bottani
For recognition of the best three graduate theses supported in the last year and relating to three selected topics of electrical engineering and information theory. A monetary prize of 3,000,000 lire and a diploma are awarded annually to each of the three winners.

| 8352 |

Premio F. Cameli
For recognition of the best work in electronics concerning radio communications, aids to navigation, and naval automation published in 1993 or presented at the AEI's annual meeting or international meetings. Graduate or doctoratal theses are accepted. A monetary prize of 3,000,000 lire is awarded annually.

| 8353 |

Premio F. Malusardi
For recognition of the best doctorate thesis supported in the years 1992 and 1993 at an Italian university concerning the electrical systems for the constrained steering transports. A monetary prize of 3,000,000 lire will be awarded biennially.

| 8354 |

Premio Maria Faletti-Nosari
For recognition of the best work published in the periodicals of the AEI or in the Acts of the Annual Meeting. AEI members are eligible. Ten awards, each consisting of a diploma and a gold medal, are awarded biennially in odd-numbered years. Established in 1979.

| 8355 |

Italian Institute of Welding
(Istituto Italiano della Saldatura)
Lungobisagno Istria 15   Phone: 10 83411
I-16141 Genoa, Italy   Fax: 10 8367780

| 8356 |

Angela Cevenini Prize
(Premio Angela Cevenini)
To encourage professional development in the field of nondestructive testing. Individuals who have the higher examination graduation of the Courses of Specialization in Welding or of the Courses of NDT Specialization are eligible. A monetary prize is awarded annually at the opening of the course of the following year. Established in 1978 in honor of Mrs. Angela Cevenini, who contributed to the development of nondestructive testing in Italy. Sponsored by the NDT Cevenini Company. Additional information is available from Mr. Maurizio Cevenini, Piazza Diaz 1, 20052 Monza (MI).

8357
Italian Mathematical Union
(Unione Matematica Italiana)
Piazza Porta San Donato 5　　　　　　　　　Phone: 51 243190
I-40127 Bologna, Italy　　　　　　　　　　　Fax: 51 354490

8358
Premio Bartolozzi
For recognition of achievement in the field of mathematics. Italian citizens under 33 years of age must apply or be nominated. A monetary prize is awarded biennially. Established in 1969 in honor of the Giuseppe Bartolozzi family.

8359
Premio Caccioppoli
For recognition of achievement in the field of mathematics. Italian citizens under 36 years of age must apply or be nominated. A monetary prize is awarded every four years. Established in 1960 in honor of Renato Caccioppoli's brother.

8360
Italian Nostra-National Association for the Preservation of the Historical, Artistic and Natural Heritage of the Nation
(Italia Nostra-Association Nazionale per la Tutela del Patrimonio Storico Artistico e Naturale della Nazione)
Via Nicolo Porpora 22
I-00198 Rome, Italy　　　　　　　　　　　　Phone: 6 856 765

8361
Premio Umberto Zanotti Bianco
For recognition of achievement in the field of historic preservation of the artistic and natural heritage of the nation. Nominations or applications are accepted. A gold medal and diploma are awarded annually. Established in 1964.

8362
Italian PEN Club
Via Mangili 2　　　　　　　　　　　　　　　Phone: 2 654421
I-20121 Milan, Italy　　　　　　　　　　　　Fax: 2 654421

Formerly: PEN Club Italiano.

8363
Italian PEN Prize
To recognize the poem, novel, or essay voted by italian PEN members as most outstanding. A monetary prize of 10,000,000 lire is awarded in the medieval village of Campiano (Parma) in September. Established in 1991.

8364
Italy
Ministry for Culture and the Environment
(Italy
Ministero per i beni culturali e ambientali)
Piazza Venezia 11
I-00187 Rome, Italy　　　　　　　　　　　　Phone: 6 797124

8365
Italian Minister for Culture and the Environment Prizes
For recognition of research and contributions in the following fields: (1) physics, mathematics and natural sciences; and (2) moral sciences, history and philology. Two monetary prizes of 4,000,000 lire each are awarded annually. Academy members are not eligible, but may nominate candidates. Established in 1960 by the Italian Ministry of Public Education. Since 1974, the prize has been under the auspices of the Ministry for Culture and the Environment.

8366
Italy
Ministry of Education
(Italy
Ministero della pubblica istruzione)
Viale Trastevere 76A　　　　　　　　　　　Phone: 6 58491
I-00153 Rome, Italy　　　　　　　　　　　　Fax: 6 580 68 92

8367
Personal Recognition Awards in Education
To recognize an individual for distinctive achievement in the field of education. A gold medal is awarded annually.

8368
Italy
Ministry of the Interior
(Italy)
Directorate of General Affairs & Personnel
Commission of Civil Value and Merit
Piazzale del Viminale　　　　　　　　　　　Phone: 6 4667104
I-00184 Rome, Italy　　　　　　　　　　　　Fax: 6 4747185

8369
Medals for Acts of Distinction
(Ricompense al Valor Civile e Merito Civile)
For recognition of bravery, heroism, humanitarianism, and meritorious behavior. The award is given to citizens and foreigners on the proposal of local authorities. Gold, silver, and bronze medals, and certificates are awarded two or three times a year by the President of the Republic. Established in 1956 and 1958.

8370
Italy
Ministry of Tourism and Performing Arts
(Italy
Ministero del turismo e dello spettacolo)
Via della Ferratella in Laterano 51
I-00184 Rome, Italy　　　　　　　　　　　　Phone: 6 77321

8371
Golden Echo Prize
To recognize the best dancer. A plaque is awarded annually.

8372
Italy
Office of the President of the Council of Ministers
(Italy
Presidenza del consiglio dei ministri)
Palazzo del Quirinale
p. Colonna 370　　　　　　　　　　　　　　Phone: 6 4699
I-00187 Rome, Italy　　　　　　　　　　　　Fax: 6 6796894

8373
Cavaliere of the Order Star of Italian Solidarity
This, the highest honor of the Italian government, is given for recognition of outstanding public service to the country. Italians living abroad are also eligible.

8374
Medikinale International Parma
Via Farini 7　　　　　　　　　　　　　　　Phone: 521 237792
I-43100 Parma, Italy　　　　　　　　　　　Fax: 521 237973

8375
International Multimedia Science Film Festival
(Prix Leonardo)
For recognition of the best scientific films and videos in the Festival. Awards are given in the categories of Medical and Scientific Research and Updating, Health and Education, and Ecology and Health. Universities, hospitals, public and private institutions, television networks, independent authors and producers, pharmaceutical industries, and professional schools are invited to participate. The following prizes are awarded: Best Film on Medicine; Best Film on Ecology; Best Film on Science; and Best Film on Technology. Special mentions are also made for excellence in script writing, direction, photography, editing, animation, special effects, and music. A gold medal and certificates are also awarded for special category awards. The festival is held biennially. Established in 1983. Formerly: International Medical Scientific Film Festival.

8376
National Academy of Sciences known as the Forty
(Accademia Nazionale Delle Scienze detta dei XL)
Palazzo della Civilta Italians
Quadrato della Concordia   Phone: 6 5925557
I-00144 Rome, Italy   Fax: 6 5912624

Formerly: (1961) Societa Italiana delle Scienze.

8377
Matteucci Medal
(Medaglia Matteucci)
For recognition of a significant achievement in the field of physics. A medal is awarded annually. Established in 1870 in memory of President Matteucci, the founder of modern electrophysiology.

8378
Medaglia Amedeo Avogadro
For recognition in the field of chemistry. A medal is awarded when merited. Established in 1956. Co-sponsored by the Italian Chemical Society.

8379
Medals of the National Academy of Science
(Medaglia dell'Accademia Nazionale dei XL)
For recognition of achievement in mathematics and the physical and natural science fields. Nomination is by a special commission elected by the Academy. Two medals are awarded annually. Established in 1866 by the Italian Government.

8380
Premio Anton Mario Lorgna
Awarded every five years. Established in 1981.

8381
Premio Domenico Marotta
For recognition of outstanding work in the health sciences. A monetary prize is awarded annually. Established in 1980.

8382
Premio Federico Nitti
For recognition of outstanding achievement in the natural sciences, medicine, biological science, or chemistry. A monetary prize is awarded every three to five years. Established about 1978.

8383
National Association of Nuclear Engineering
(Associazione Nazionale di Ingegneria Nucleare)
Piazza Sallustio 24
I-00187 Rome, Italy   Phone: 6 486415

8384
Gold Plate of ANDIN
(Targa d'Oro ANDIN)
For recognition of achievement in the field of nuclear activities. Nomination is open to individuals of all nationalities. A gold plaque is awarded annually. Established in 1985.

8385
National Institute of Verdi Studies - Rotary Club of Parma
(Istituto Nazionale di Studi Verdiani - Rotary Club di Parma)
Strada della Repubblica 56   Phone: 521 286044
I-43100 Parma, Italy   Fax: 521 287949

8386
Parma Rotary Club International Prize "Giuseppe Verdi"
((Premio internazionale Rotary Club di Parma "Giuseppe Verdi"))
To encourage development of research in the field of Verdi studies. The competition is open to Italian or foreign scholars intending to undertake research on a Verdian topic at the Institute. Proposals must be submitted to the Istituto nazionale di studi verdiani by September 30. A monetary prize of 12 million lire is awarded biennially. Established in 1983 by the Rotary Club, Parma, and the National Institute of Verdi Studies. Formerly: Rotary Club of Palma Giuseppe Verdi Prize.

8387
Noir International Festival
Via Dei Coronari 44   Phone: 6 6833844
I-00186 Rome, Italy   Fax: 6 6867902

Formed by merger of: Mystfest; International Mystery Film Festival.

8388
Mystery Prize
To recognize outstanding achievement in film. Awards may be presented in the following categories: Best Film, Best Leading Actress, Best Leading Actor, Best Original Story, and Special Mention. The application deadline is the end of May. A trophy is awarded annually. Established in 1980 by Mr. Felice Laudadio.

8389
Olivetti Society
(Societa Olivetti)
Via Nuova 21
I-10010 Burolo, Italy   Phone: 0125 57578

8390
Viareggio Prize
To provide recognition for an outstanding research work in sociology. Monetary prizes are awarded annually.

8391
Orchestra Sinfonica dell'Emilia-Romagna Arturo Toscanini
Via Lombardi, 6   Phone: 521 271033
I-43100 Parma, Italy   Fax: 521 75257

8392
Goffredo Petrassi International Competition for Composers
(Concorso Internazionale di Composizione Goffredo Petrassi)
To encourage professional development and to recognize outstanding composers. Musicians of all nationalities without age limit may apply by January 31. Three monetary prizes of 100,000, 7,000,000, and 4,000,000 lire, diplomas of merit, publication of the compositions by Ricordi Publishers, and performances are awarded biennially. Established in 1986 to honor Goffredo Petrassi. Sponsored by Italy - Ministry for Tourism and Performing Arts and the Regional Government of Emilia-Romagana.

8393

**Arturo Toscanini International Competition for Conductors
(Concorso Internazionale di Direzione d'Orchestra Arturo Toscanini)**
To encourage professional development and to recognize outstanding conductors of orchestras. Conductors of all nationalities under the age of 33 may apply by January 31. Three monetary prizes totaling 25,000,000 lire, diplomas of merit, and engagements are awarded biennially. Established in 1985 in memory of Arturo Toscanini who was born in Parma. Sponsored by Italy - Ministry for Tourism and Performing Arts and the Regional Government of Emilia-Romagna.

8394

**Nicolo Paganini International Violin Competition
(Concorso Internazionale di Violino Nicolo Paganini)**
Palazzo Tursi
Via Garibaldi 9, piano terra
I-16124 Genoa, Italy

Phone: 10 20981
Fax: 10 206235

8395

**Nicolo Paganini International Violin Competition
(Concorso Internazionale di Violino Nicolo Paganini)**
To recognize the best violinists in the competition. Violinists of any nationality, who are under 33 years of age must apply by June 20. Previous winners are not eligible. The competition consists of three tests or elimination rounds. Six competitors are admitted to the finals. Prizes are awarded in the following categories: Paganini Prize - first place - a monetary prize of 15,000,000 lire (indivisible) to the winner, who will play Paganini's violin during the closing ceremony of the Columbus Celebrations, and be engaged by the Teatro Comunale dell'Opera di Genova for a concert during the Symphony Season in Genoa, where the winner is allowed to play Paganini's violin on at least two occasions and is given the opportunity to perform several public concerts; second place - 10,000,000 lire; third place - 6,000,000 lire; fourth place - 4,000,000 lire; fifth place - 3,000,000 lire; and sixth place - 2,000,000 lire. Awarded annually in late September/early October. Established in 1954.

8396

**Pezcoller Foundation
(Fondazione Pezcoller)**
Galleria Tirrena, 10
I-38100 Trento, Italy

Phone: 461 980250
Fax: 461 980350

8397

**Pezcoller Prize
(Premio Pezcoller)**
To recognize an outstanding contribution in the various fields of medicine. The prize will be awarded for new therapeutic procedures (surgical or medical) that have made steps toward curing a disease or made fundamental discoveries in the aetiology, pathogenesis, and natural history of some specific disease that resulted in improved treatment and control. A monetary prize of about 100,000 ECU is awarded biennially. The deadline for nominations is April 15. Established in 1979 by Prof. Alessio Pezcoller.

8398

Pezcoller Recognition for Dedication to Oncology
To recognize a single health worker (medical doctor, biologist, nurse, etc.) for a contribution to the development of oncology and the dedication of his/her professional life to the fight against cancer. A monetary prize of 20,000 ECU is awarded biennially. Established in 1987.

8399

**Pordenone Silent Film Festival
(Le Giornate del Cinema Muto)**
c/o Cineteca del Friuli
Via Osoppo, 26
I-33013 Gemona, Italy

Phone: 432 980458
Fax: 432 970542

8400

**Jean Mitry Award
(Premio Jean Mitry)**
For recognition of activities in safeguarding and prizing the cinematographic patrimony. Selection is by nomination. A monetary prize, a plaque, and travel are awarded annually. Established in 1986 in memory of Jean Mitry. Sponsored by the Provincia di Pordenone.

8401

Premio Musicale Citta di Trieste
Palazzo Municipale
Piazza dell'Unita d'Italia 4
I-34121 Trieste, Italy

Phone: 40 368312
Phone: 40 366030
Fax: 40 6754303

8402

**International Competition for Symphonic Composition, Trieste
(Concorso Internazionale di Composizione Sinfonica, Trieste)**
For recognition of a composition for chamber music or a full orchestra. Themes are announced for each competition. The 1995 competition is for full orchestra. The Competition is open to composers of any nationality or age, excluding composers who have won the first prize in previous competitions. The deadline for entry is April 15. The following awards are presented: first prize - a monetary prize of 5,000,000 Italian lire plus a performance of the music during the course of the symphonic season of the "G. Verdi" Municipal Theatre of Trieste; second prize - 2,500,000 Italian lire; and third prize - 1,500,000 Italian lire. A special Alpe Adria Prize of 1,000,000 Italian lire may be awarded to a composer born or resident in a communita di lavoro Alpe Adria region. Established in 1950 by the City of Trieste. Sponsored by the City of Trieste and the Regione Friuli-Venezia Giulia.

8403

Premio Riccione Ater
P. Le Ceccarini 11
47036 Riccione, Italy

Phone: 541 693384
Phone: 541 692124

8404

Premio Riccione - ATER: per un teatro d'autore
To recognize the author of a play that is a distinctive contribution to the Italian theater and to the development of contemporary playwriting. Plays by an Italian author that have never been performed may be submitted by June 30. Previous winners as well as works that have won other awards are not eligible. A monetary prize of 10,000,000 lire and production of the play are awarded biennially. The prize may be divided in case of a tie. If there is no work deserving a prize, the jury may award other prizes, among which is the Paolo Bignami.

8405

Riccione TTVV - Teatro Televisione Video
To recognize the best television productions in theatre and dance. An artistic object is awarded annually.

8406

Premio Viareggio
Via Francesco Borgatti 25
I-00191 Rome, Italy

Phone: 6 328 37 36

8407

Premio Litterario Viareggio
To recognize Italian writers for the best novel, poetry, essay, best first work, and, occasionally, for drama and journalism, published within the preceding year. Two special awards, the Viareggio - Versilia International Prize, and the Leonida Repaci Prize (president of the jury), are often given to foreign writers, theatre directors and poets. Monetary prizes of 10,000,000 Italian lire are awarded annually. Established in 1929.

8408
Pro Loco Tourist Association of Corciano
(Associazione Turistica Pro Loco di Corciano)
Via Laudati 4
I-06073 Corciano, Italy
Phone: 75 697 82 09
Phone: 75 697 86 60

8409
International Competition for Original Composition for Band
(Concorso Internazionale di Composizione Originale per Banda)
To promote band music repertory, hoping to improve its quality and to respond to the requests of modern society. The compositions may be based freely on any theme and musical form, with or without instrumental or vocal soloists (excluding a choir). Musical instruments not normally used in bands may be included (with the exception of electronic instruments). Performed compositions between five and twelve minutes in length may be submitted by July 20. The following prizes are awarded annually: (1) First prize - 4,000,000 Italian lire; and (2) Second prize - 2,000,000 Italian lire; Established in 1980. Sponsored by Cassa di Risparmio di Perugia, Ministero del Tourismo e dello Spettacolo, and Assessorato alla Cultura della Regione dell'Umbria.

8410
Giacomo Puccini Foundation
(Fondazione Giacomo Puccini)
Via di Poggio
Corte San Lorenzo 9
I-55100 Lucca, Italy
Phone: 583 584028

8411
Giacomo Puccini Prize
For recognition of the best vocal interpretation of Puccini's music. Men and women singers under 35 years of age from any country are eligible. Three monetary prizes of 800,000 lire each are awarded annually. Established in 1974 by the Sindaco and the Consiglio Comunale to commemorate Puccini and other musicians of Lucca. Sponsored by the City of Lucca.

8412
RAI - Radiotelevisione Italiana
Viale Mazzini 14
I-00195 Rome, Italy
Phone: 6 312782
Fax: 6 3225270

8413
Prix Italia
For recognition of the best programs from the whole field of radio and television broadcasting. All kinds of radio and television programs may be entered, except television light entertainment. Member organizations may submit programs in the following fields of radio and television: music programs; drama programs; and documentary programs. Italia Prizes and Special Prizes of 15,000,000 lire are awarded in the following categories: (1) Radio - (a) music - Prix Italia and Special Prize; (b) fiction - Prix Italia and Special Prize; and (c) documentary - Prix Italia and Special Prize; and (2) Televison - (a) music - Prix Italia and Special Prize; (b) drama - Prix Italia and Special Prize; and (c) documentary - Prix Italia and Prize of the Town or the Region where the session takes place. In addition, a special prize for title sequences is awarded for both radio and television. Established in 1948 for radio programs. The television competition was added in 1957. Additional information is available from Prix Italia, c/o RAI - Radiotelevisione Italiana, Via Del Babuino 9, I-00187 Rome, Italy.

8414
Riminicinema International Film Festival
(Riminicinema Mostra Internazionale)
Cineteca Comunale
Via Gambalunga 27
I-47037 Rimini (Forli), Italy
Phone: 541 26399
Fax: 541 24227

8415
Golden R
(R D'Oro)
For recognition of achievement at the film festival. Applications must be submitted by June 30. A Gold Brooch and 15 million lire are awarded for first prize, a Silver Brooch for second prize, and a Bronze Brooch for third prize. Awarded annually. Established in 1988 by Cineteca Comunale.

8416
Salerno International Film Festival
(Festival Internationale del Cinema di Salerno)
Casella Postale 137
I-84100 Salerno, Italy
Phone: 89 231953

8417
Gulf of Salerno Grand Trophy
(Gran Trofeo Golfo di Salerno)
For recognition of the best feature, documentary, scientific, educational and television films in reduced formats. Professionals, amateurs, associations, study centers and state organizations may submit films in the following formats: (1) 16mm and super 8 mm; (2) 35 mm; and (3) videotapes. Films must be produced in Italy. Awards are presented in the following categories: (1) The most outstanding film of the Festival - Gulf of Salerno Trophy; (2) Features - trophy and diplomas; (3) Documentary - trophy and diplomas; (4) Scientific - trophy and diplomas; (5) Educational - trophy and diplomas; and (6) Television - trophy and diplomas. Awarded annually in October. Established in 1946. Formerly: Artistiche Sculture del noto Maestro Enzo Assenza Rappresentante la X musa.

8418
Senigallia International Competition for Pianists
(Concorso Pianistico Internazionale Citta di Senigallia)
Palazzetto Comunale Baviera
Piazza del Duca
I-60019 Senigallia, Italy
Phone: 71 65568
Phone: 71 6629350
Fax: 71 6629349

8419
Senigallia International Meeting of Young Pianists
(Incontro Internazionale Giovani Pianisti Citta di Senigallia)
For recognition of outstanding piano students. Open to piano students from all over the world in two categories: candidates under 16 years of age and candidates under 20. The deadline is June 30. The following prizes are awarded in the first category: first prize - a Night and Day (upright) piano and a certificate; second prize - 800,000 lire and a certificate; third prize - 700,000 lire and a certificate; fourth prize - 600,000 lire and a certificate; fifth prize - 500,000 lire and a certificate. The following prizes are awarded in the second category: first prize - a Night and Day (upright) piano and a certificate; second prize - 800,000 lire and a certificate; third prize - 700,000 lire and a certificate; fourth prize - 600,000 lire and a certificate; and fifth prize - 500,000 lire and a certificate. The winner of the two categories with the highest mark will also be offered a concert at Bossi Concert Hall in Bologna. Established in 1972.

8420
Senigallia International Piano Competition
(Concorso Pianistico Internazionale Citta di Senigallia)
For recognition of outstanding piano performance. The contest is open to pianists between 15 and 36 years of age from all over the world. The following prizes are awarded: first prize - 20,000,000 lire, a certificate, and several concerts; second prize - 7,500,000 lire and certificate; third prize - 3,000,000 lire and a certificate; fourth prize - 2,000,000 lire and a certificate; and fifth prize - 1,000,000 lire and a certificate. The best accompanist of Airs and Lieder will be awarded the AnnaMaria Castiglioni Prize of 600,000 lire. The best performer of the chamber music round will be awarded a prize of 1,000,000 lire. The winner of the competition will also be awarded the Antonino Mostacci Prize of 900,000 lire for a concert in Senigallia. All competitors who are graded with points not below 8/10 in the second trial are awarded a certificate of classification. Established in 1972.

8421

Sestri Levante Municipality
Piazza Matteotti 50
Sestri Levante, (GE), Italy   Phone: 185 47251

8422

Andersen Prize
To recognize the year's best fairy tale for children. Professional or amateur writers are eligible. A monetary prize of 1,500,000 Italian lire is awarded annually.

8423

Pilade Queirolo Prize
To recognize the best graduation thesis of the year on the subject of the economy, tourism and social problems of Sestri Levante. A monetary prize of 1,000,000 Italian lire was awarded annually. Established in 1977 by the widow of Pilade Queirolo in memory of her husband. (Discontinued in 1987)

8424

Societa del Quartetto
Via Monte di Pieta 22
Casella Postale 127   Phone: 161 50 15 48
I-13100 Vercelli, Italy   Fax: 161 50 15 48

8425

G. B. Viotti International Music and Dance Competition
(Concorso Internazionale di Musica e Danza G. B. Viotti)
To provide recognition for the best music performances in the following categories: (1) Vocal; (2) Piano; and (3) Violin. Singers and instrumentalists must be under 32 years of age, but there are no age restrictions for composers. The categories vary each year. Monetary prizes totaling 72,000,000 lire, medals and concert performance opportunities are awarded annually. Established in 1950 by Joseph Robbone.

8426

Societa Geologica Italiana
c/o Dipartimento di Scienze della Terra
Universita La Sapienza
Piazzale Aldo Moro 5
I-00185 Rome, Italy   Phone: 6 4959390

8427

Premio Giorgio Dal Piaz
For recognition in the field of geology.

8428

Societa Incremento Toristico Alberghiero Valdostano
                                                Phone: 166 5221
I-11027 Saint Vincent, (AO), Italy   Fax: 166 511616

8429

Saint-Vincent International Prize for Journalism
To provide recognition for outstanding journalism. Prizes were given in the following categories: professional journalism of exceptional quality; investigative writing or articles of special interest; the best radio or television broadcasting of the year; the most interesting special column; writing on the improvement of the Aosta valley region; the best journalism in the Valley of Aosta newspaper; and contributions to the knowledge of the Valley of Aosta. Monetary prizes were awarded annually. (Discontinued in 1990)

8430

Societa Italiana di Nipiologia
c/o Istituto di Clinica Pediatrica II
Viale Regina Elena 324   Phone: 6 4951738
I-00161 Rome, Italy   Phone: 6 490962

8431

Premio Nipiol-Buitoni
For recognition in the field of medicine.

8432

Sondrio Town Council International Festival of Documentary Films on Parks
(Comune di Sondrio Mostra Internazionale dei Documentari sui Parchi)
c/o Comune di Sondrio
Centro Documentazione Aree Protette
Villa Quadrio   Phone: 342 526260
Via IV Novembre, 20   Phone: 342 526261
I-23100 Sondrio, Italy   Fax: 342 513001

8433

Sondrio Town Council International Festival of Documentary Films on Parks
(Comune di Sondrio Mostra Internazionale dei Documentari sui Parchi)
For recogntion of achievement in documentary films in the field of parks and protected areas. The City of Sondrio Gold Plaque (Targa d'Oro Citta di Sondrio) and the City of Sondrio Invitational Award (Premio Ospitalita Citta di Sondrio) are presented annually. Both winners receive a plaque and the winner of the Invitational Award also receives a week's stay in Sondrio for two, a guided tour of Stelvio National Park, and return tickets to Sondrio. Applications must be submitted by June 30. Established in 1987. Sponsored by Comune di Sondrio (Sondrio Town Council), Regione Lombardia, Comunita' Montane, Parco Nazionale dello Stelvio, Provincia di Sondrio, Chamber of Commerce of Sondrio, APT (Tourist Board) Valtellina, and B.I.M.

8434

Southern Center for Environmental Education
(Centro Meridionale di Educazione Ambientale)
PO Box 29
Via S. Maria delle Grazie 7   Phone: 81 878 43 33
I-80067 Sorrento, Italy   Fax: 81 877 19 80

8435

Ermanno Acanfora International Prize
(Premio Internazionale Ermanno Acanfora)
For recognition of unpublished audiovisual works on environmental education. Works are not restricted to formal school materials. The deadline for entry is December 31. Three monetary prizes of 1,000,000 lire each are awarded biennially at the International Review of the Educational Audiovisual.

8436

City of Sorrento Prize
(Premio Internazionale Citta di Sorrento)
For recognition of outstanding audiovisual materials for environmental education. The prize is only for the school and for the works made in it. The authors can enter one of the following five sections: (1) Nursery and Primary school; (2) Secondary school; (3) High school; (4) Art school; and (5) Vocational training. The works of these sections are divided further into three groups: (1) works by teachers; (2) works by pupils; (3) works made outside the school that can be used as supports for teaching. Each work can be entered in only one section. The deadline for entry is December 31. Three prizes and a medal, "Citta di Sorrento," are awarded in each category. Three silver medals "Citta di Sorrento" are awarded to the worthiest authors belonging to the three groups. Awarded biennially at the International Review of the Educational Audiovisual.

8437
Aldo Merola International Prize
(Premio Internazionale Aldo Merola)
For recognition of audiovisual works dealing with the theme, "Environment: knowledge and protection." The deadline for entry is December 31. Three prizes of 2,000,000 lire each are awarded biennially at the International Review of the Educational Audiovisual.

8438
Strega Alberti Benevento
Corso Rinascimento 41 Phone: 6 540 346
I-00186 Rome, Italy Fax: 6 892 919

8439
Strega Prize
To recognize an Italian novel published during the preceding year. The winner is selected by a grand jury of approximately 400 persons. A monetary prize of 1,000,000 Italian lire is awarded annually at the Villa Giulia, one of the most fascinating buildings of the Rome Renaissance. Established in 1947 by the Strega liquor producer, Guido Alberti, and the Italian writers, Goffredo and Maria Bellonci.

8440
Teatro Comunale di Firenze
Via Solferino 15 Phone: 55 27791
I-50123 Florence, Italy Fax: 55 296954

8441
Concorso Internazionale di Direzione d'Orchestra Vittorio Gui
To recognize outstanding orchestra conductors. Orchestra conductors who have not reached the age of 33 years are eligible. A monetary prize and at least one concert with the Orchestra of the Maggio Musicale Fiorentino are awarded to the winner. Established in 1978.

8442
Concorso Internazionale di violoncello Gaspar Cassado
For recognition of outstanding violoncello performances. Violoncellists under 30 years of age from all countries may participate in the competition. The following monetary prizes are presented: (1) First Prize - 10,000,000 lire and a concert with the Orchestra of the Maggio Musicale Fiorentino; (2) Second Prize - 6,000,000 lire; and (3) Third Prize - 4,000,000 lire. Awarded biennially. Established in 1969.

8443
Teatro Municipale Valli
Piazza Martiri 7 Luglio Phone: 522 434244
I-42100 Reggio Emilia, Italy Fax: 522 46605

8444
International String Quartet Competition
(Concorso Internazionale per Quartetto d'Archi)
To recognize outstanding string quartets of any nationality. Individual members must be 35 years of age or younger; the total age of the ensemble must not exceed 120 years. Applications may be submitted by March 31. The following prizes are awarded: (1) First prize - Premio Paolo Borciani - 30,000,000 Italian lire (indivisible); (2) Second prize - 20,000,000 Italian lire; and (3) Third prize - 10,000,000 Italian lire. Established in 1988.

8445
Teleconfronto - International TV Drama Series Festival
(Teleconfronto - Mostra Internazionale del Telefilm)
Address unknown.

8446
Teleconfronto
To encourage international exchange of information on TV drama series production, and to recognize outstanding TV drama series. Single episodes of European co-productions which have the following characteristics are eligible: (1) they should have been shown for the first time in the country of origin during the preceding year or not yet have been shown; (2) they should not have been shown by any Italian television network prior to Teleconfronto; and (3) they should not have been previously shown at any other international or Italian festival or meeting. A trophy representing a peacock is awarded in each of the following categories: (1) Best mini-series episode; (2) Best series episode; (3) Best serial episode; (4) Best actress; (5) Best actor; and (6) Special prize, to be awarded at the discretion of the Jury. The Teleconfronto Executive committee awards the Vittorio Boni Prize to the person or organization making the greatest contribution to the development of television in Europe. A panel of viewers evaluates the programs submitted to the competition using a points system. The Associazione per Chianciano awards a prize to the program with the highest total points. Awarded annually. Established in 1983 by the Comune di Chianciano Terme (town council). Sponsored by Associazione per Chianciano.

8447
Il Tempo
Piazza Colonna 366
I-00187 Rome, Italy

8448
Antonina Colonna Prize
To provide recognition for the best advertising campaign. A golden palm is awarded annually.

8449
Third World Academy of Sciences
Office of the Exec. Sec.
International Centre for Theoretical
  Physics
PO Box 586
Strada Costiera 11, Miramare Phone: 40 22401
I-34100 Trieste, Italy Fax: 40 224559

8450
TWAS Award in Basic Medical Sciences
To recognize scientists from developing countries who have made outstanding contributions to the advancement of basic medical sciences. Candidates for the awards must be nationals of developing countries and, as a rule, working and living in those countries. Fellows of the Third World Academy of Sciences are not eligible. Nominations must be submitted by March 1. A monetary award of $10,000 and a medal are presented annually. Established in 1988.

8451
TWAS Award in Biology
To recognize scientists from developing countries who have made outstanding contributions to the advancement of science in biology. Candidates for the awards must be nationals of developing countries and, as a rule, working and living in those countries. Fellows of the Third World Academy of Sciences are not eligible. Nominations must be submitted by March 1. A monetary award of $10,000 and a medal are presented annually. Established in 1986.

8452
TWAS Award in Chemistry
To recognize scientists from developing countries who have made outstanding contributions to the advancement of science in chemistry. Candidates for the awards must be nationals of developing countries and, as a rule, working and living in those countries. Fellows of the Third World Academy of Sciences are not eligible. Nominations must be submitted by March 1. A monetary award of $10,000 and a medal are presented annually. Established in 1986.

8453
TWAS Award in Mathematics
To recognize scientists from developing countries who have made outstanding contributions to the advancement of science in mathematics. Candidates for the awards must be nationals of developing countries and, as a rule, working and living in those countries. Fellows of the Third World Academy of Sciences are not eligible. Nominations must be submitted by March 1. A monetary award of $10,000 and a medal are presented annually. Established in 1985.

8454
TWAS Award in Physics
To recognize scientists from developing countries who have made outstanding contributions to the advancement of science in physics. Candidates for the awards must be nationals of developing countries and, as a rule, working and living in those countries. Fellows of the Third World Academy of Sciences are not eligible. Nominations must be submitted by March 1. A monetary award of $10,000 and a medal are presented annually. Established in 1985.

8455
TWAS History of Science Prize
To recognize the best research essay highlighting the work of a scientist from a country of the Third World whose achievements had not been previously recognized. The research essays should summarize the major achievements of a Third World Scientist prior to the 20th Century, whose work has not been hitherto clearly recognized. It should indicate the impact of the scientist's contributions on his or her community and, where relevant, establish their influence on modern scientific thought. Essays must be written in English. The length of the essay should be between 20,000 and 50,000 words, but these limits are not binding. The competition is open to scholars both from the Third World and elsewhere. The deadline is March 1. A monetary award of $10,000 US and a medal are awarded biennially. The Third World Academy of Sciences will arrange for the prize-winning essay to be published in book form. Established in 1987.

8456
Third World Network of Scientific Organizations
c/o International Centre for Theoretical
  Physics
PO Box 586   Phone: 40 2240328
I-34100 Trieste, Italy   Fax: 40 2240559

8457
TWNSO Award in Agriculture
To encourage and support scientific research in major Third World problems related to agriculture. Living individuals or institutions from developing or developed countries whose scientific and technical innovations have provided significant and sustainable solutions to some important economic and social problems in the Third World and have brought, or will bring, substantial benefits to the well-being of the people are eligible. Fellows and Associate Fellows of the Third World Academy of Sciences (TWAS) are not eligible for these prizes. Nominations are invited from all members of TWNSO and Third World Academy of Sciences as well as from science academies, national research councils, universities, and research institutions in developing and developed countries. The deadline is March 1. A monetary award of $10,000 US and a medal are awarded annually at a general meeting of the Network. Established in 1990.

8458
TWNSO Award in Technology
To encourage and support scientific research in major Third World problems related to technology. Living individuals or institutions from developing or developed countries whose scientific and technical innovations have provided significant and sustainable solutions to some important economic and social problems in the Third World and have brought, or will bring, substantial benefits to the well-being of the people are eligible. Fellows and Associate Fellows of the Third World Academy of Sciences (TWAS) are not eligible for these prizes. Nominations are invited from all members of TWNSO and Third World Academy of Sciences as well as from science academies, national research councils, universities, and research institutions in developing and developed countries. The deadline is March 1. A monetary award of $10,000 US and a medal are awarded annually at a general meeting of the Network. Established in 1990.

8459
Trento International Film Festival of Mountains and Exploration (Trento Filmfestival Internazionale Montagna Esplorazione)
Centro S. Chiara   Phone: 461 238 178
Via S. Croce 67   Phone: 461 986 120
I-38100 Trento, Italy   Fax: 461 237 832

8460
Trento International Film Festival of Mountain and Exploration (Trento Filmfestival Internazionale Montagna Esplorazione)
To provide recognition for the best 35 and 16mm feature or documentary films or video tapes on mountains or exploration. Films about mountains must contribute to the spreading of knowledge, protection and exploitation of all aspects of the mountains: environmental, social, cultural, alpinistic, excursion and sport. Films on exploration or environmental protection must document little known or completely unknown places, including the universe outside the Earth; or document scientific research on anthropological, ecological, physical, archeological, naturalistic or faunistic subjects. Adventure and sport films must illustrate the skill and daring in adventure and the peaceful message of sport activities in the natural environment. Films may be submitted by March 20. Accepted films compete for the following awards: (1) Gran Premio Citta di Trento - Gold Gentian and 10,000,000 lire - for the film with high artistic qualities, that best reflects the aims and values which inspire the Festival. The Gran Premio does not exclude the winner from the other awards; (2) Silver Gentian - and 3,000,000 lire - for the best feature film (fiction); (3) Silver Gentian - and 3,000,000 lire - for the best film on mountaineering; (4) Silver Gentian and 3,000,000 lire - for the best mountain film; (5) Silver Gentian and 3,000,000 lire - for the best exploration and/or environmental conservation film; (6) Silver Gentian and 3,000,000 lire - for the best adventure and sport film; (7) RAI Award - Italian Radio and Television - Trento Regional Branch - for the best electronically created film; (8) Special Jury Prize - for the best film by an Italian director; and (9) Special Prize - for the best photography. The following awards are given by the specific organizations with their own juries: (1) U.I.A.A. Prize of the International Union of Alpinistic Associations - for the best film portraying an important, modern and genuine mountaineering venture on any mountain in the world; (2) CONI Prize - the Italian National Olympic Committee Cup for the best film portraying the free climbing discipline; (3) F.I.S.I. Prize - the Italian Federation of Winter Sports - 2,000,000 lire - for the best film portraying the educational and competitive spirit of the Olympic Winter Sports disciplines; (4) Carlo Mauri Memorial Trophy - for the best film on adventurous exploration; (5) Mario Bello Prize - 3,000,000 lire to the best mountaineering film; and (6) Antonio Pascatti Rotary Prize - 2,000,000 lire to a film that acknowledges solidarity in the mountains. Awarded annually. Established in 1952.

8461
Turin International Film Festival (Festival Internazionale Cinema Giovani)
Piazza San Carlo 161   Phone: 11 5623309
I-10123 Turin, Italy   Fax: 11 5629796

8462
Turin International Festival of Young Cinema (Festival Internazionale Cinema Giovani)
For recognition of outstanding films submitted to the Festival in the following competitions: full-length films, short film, and Italian films. Awards are given for the Best Film in all competitions, for the best script, for the FIPRESCI Prize, and for the Achille Valdata Prize. Plaques are awarded annually. Established in 1982.

8463
Universita di Ferrara - Centro di Studi sulla Corrosione
Dipartimento di Chemica
Via L. Borsari 46
I-44100 Ferrara, Italy
Phone: 532 291134
Fax: 532 40709

8464
Cavallaro Medal
(Medaille Cavallaro)
For recognition of a researcher who is particularly distinguished by his activity and publications in the field of corrosion research. A medal is awarded biennially by the European Federation of Corrosion. Established in 1965 by the Universita di Ferrara in memory of Professor Leo Cavallaro, founder of the Center for the Study of Corrosion.

8465
University of Padua
P. P. Vergerio European Prize for Children's Literature
(Universita di Padova
Premio Europeo di Letteratura Giovanile P. P. Vergerio)
c/o Settore di Ricerca Sulla Letteura e la
 Letteratura
Via Marsala 59
I-35139 Padua, Italy
Phone: 49 8758855
Fax: 49 8284546

Formerly: (1982) Provincia di Trento.

8466
Pier Paolo Vergerio European Prize for Children's Literature
(Premio Europeo di Letteratura Giovanile "Pier Paolo Vergerio")
To provide recognition for the best literary works for young people. Works must have been published in any official language of the European countries, in the two-year period preceding its announcement and, if unpublished, provided that they have not already participated in other national or international competitions. The European Prize for Children's Literature of 4 million lire is awarded to the author of the best published work. A Special Prize of 1 million lire is awarded to the best unpublished work. In addition a European Prize for Illustrated Albums - 1 million lire may be awarded to recognize the work among those presented, published or unpublished, which achieves the best synthesis between iconic and verbal communication, for children or young people; a European Prize for Poetry - 1 million lire to the best poetic work (or collection) produced by or for young people; a European Prize for Educational Literature - 1 million lire to the best divulgative work aimed at young European readers; and a European Prize for History - 1 million lire for the best historical novel, or the best monographic work on a historical or topical subject. Also a "mention" may be granted to all meritorious works, and a compilation of "list of honor" of works believed to be of particular significance for possible translation into the various European languages. The Prize is held biennially in December. Established in 1962 by Citta di Caorle. The award is in memory of Pier Paolo Vergerio, a writer, literary critic, and tutor to the son of one of Padova's most famous Medieval seigneurs. Co-sponsored by the University and the Municipality and Province of Padua and the Veneto Region.

8467
Vallecorsa Choral Group
(Gruppo Corale Vallecorsa)
Via Virgilio 5
I-03020 Vallecorsa, (FR), Italy
Phone: 39 077567004

8468
Sacred Choral Chant National Competition
(Concorso Nazionale di Canto Corale Sacro)
To maintain the tradition and to save the heritage of polyphonic classical music from neglect, as a result of reformation by the Vatican II Council. Polyphonic choirs are eligible to participate. Monetary prizes, trophies and diplomas are awarded annually in May. Established in 1980 by Alfredo Antonetti. Sponsored by Vallecorsa Ministry of Tourism and Spectacle.

8469
Venice International Film Festival
(Biennale di Venezia - Mostra Internazionale del Cinema)
Ca' Giustinian, San Marco
I-30124 Venice, Italy
Phone: 41 5218711
Phone: 41 5207983

8470
Venice International Film Festival
(Biennale di Venezia - Mostra Internazionale del Cinema)
For recognition of outstanding films, to bring cinema to the attention of the public, to encourage its creative vitality, and to promote its development and growth, in the context of a rapidly-changing society, by means of comparison and study. Films are organized in five different sections: (1) Venice Competition which presents the most interesting films of the year; (2) Venice TV, which presents the most interesting films made for television, with particular emphasis on new experimental technology; (3) Venice Special, which draws out of competition the attention of the public on the new trends and on the most interesting moments of the contemporary cinema in the field of a style-research, study, civil engagement and of experimental films; (4) Venice Youth, which presents out of competition and at midnight, the cinema of today's young people, with the possibility of critic comparison; and (5) Venice de Sica, a sector organized by film makers and producers, which presents the first or second work of young Italian authors. The following awards are given to films entered in the Venice Competition: (1) a Gold Lion (Leone d'Oro) - the best film; (2) a Special Award of the Jury; (3) Volpi Cup for the best actress; (4) Volpi Cup for the best actor; (5) a Silver Lion (Leone d'Argento) - for the best direction; and (6) three Oselle for three films distinguished by outstanding professional contributions. Awarded annually. Established in 1932. From 1934 to 1942 the prizes were called Coppa Mussolini. The Leone d'Oro (Golden Lion) was created in 1949, and from 1949 to 1979 the prize was cancelled. It was restored in 1980. Additional information is available from Donato Mendolia, Ca'Corner della Regina S. Croce 2214, I-30125 Venice, Italy, phone: 41 5242062, fax: 41 5240817.

8471
The Vercorin Manuscript
(Le Manuscript de Vercorin)
Clivo de Cinna 227
I-00136 Rome, Italy

8472
The Vercorin Manuscript Writing Award
To recognize outstanding film treatments and encourage original ideas for the cinema. Awards are intended to assist in the production of the chosen films. Four monetary and technical equipment awards are presented each year in July in Vercorin, Switzerland. First prize is 20,000 swiss francs, his/her treatment sent to 15 European producers, a PANAVISION camera, grip and electrical equipment valued at 65,000 Swiss francs, and a digital Nagra valued at 10,000 Swiss francs. Second prize is 10,000. Third and fourth prize are 5,000 Swiss francs each. The competition is open to anyone. The deadline is February 15. Sponsored by the European Council Panavision, Kudelski, S.S.A., Suissimage, and others. Established in 1992 by Gerald Morin.

8473
Villa I Tatti
Harvard University Center for Italian Renaissance Studies
Via di Vincigliata 26
I-50135 Florence, Italy
Phone: 55603251
Fax: 55603383

8474
Villa I Tatti Fellowships
To provide fellowships for post-doctoral scholars doing advanced research in any aspect of the Italian Renaissance. These are normally reserved for scholars in the early stages of their career. Candidates of any nationality are eligible to apply by October 15. Each Fellow is offered a place to study, use of the Biblioteca and Fototeca Berenson, lunches on weekdays, various other privileges of membership in the I Tatti community, and an opportunity to meet scholars from various countries working

Italy

8475
World Organization of Former Pupils of Catholic Education
(Organisation Mondiale des Anciens et Anciennes Eleves de l'Enseignement Catholique)
Via Vergerio 19
I-35126 Padua, Italy
Phone: 49 757619

8476
Pro Ecelesia et Pontifice
For recognition of achievement and contributions to the realization of the aims of the organization. The following prizes are awarded: (1) Commandeur de l'Ordre de Saint Gregoire le Grand; (2) CChevalier de l'Ordre de la Saint Croix de Jerusalem; and (3) Membership in the Knightly Association of Saint George the Martyr. Medals are awarded annually. Established in 1983.

8477
Worthington Pump International
Via Pirelli 19
I-20124 Milan, Italy
Phone: 2 312098

8478
Henry R. Worthington Technical Award
For recognition of original work dealing with the progress of hydraulic or thermal machinery, or systems of energy conversion. A monetary prize of $10,000 was awarded annually. Established in 1967. (Discontinued in 1979)

8479
Zonta International, Naples Area - Italy
(Zonta Club di Napoli - Italia)
Via Madonna della Salute 4
I-80052 Bellavista, (NA), Italy
Phone: 81 7752805

8480
Concurso Internazionale per Cantanti Lirici Citta di Ercolano
To recognize outstanding opera singers. The competition is open to singers of both sexes and any nationality under 36 years of age. The following prizes are awarded: (1) Premio Zonta - 3,000,000 Italian lire; (2) Premio Citta di Ercolano - 2,000,000 Italian lire; and (3) Premio F. Alfano - 1,000,000 Italian lire. The winners participate in concerts and all finalists receive certificates of participation. Awarded annually in April. Established in 1983.

Jamaica

8481
Institute of Jamaica
12-16 East St.
Kingston, Jamaica
Phone: 809922-0620
Fax: 809922-1147

8482
Musgrave Medal
This, Jamaica's highest cultural honor, is given for recognition of achievement in art, science, and literature. Outstanding individuals in the fields of art, science, and literature may be nominated. Gold, silver, and bronze medals are awarded annually. Established in 1889 in memory of Sir Anthony Musgrave, former Governor of Jamaica who founded the Institute of Jamaica in 1879.

8483
Jamaica
Chancery of the Orders of the Societies of Honour
Jamaica House, Hope Rd.
Kingston, Jamaica
Phone: 809927-7909

8484
Order of National Hero
This, the highest award presented by the Jamaican Government, recognizes individuals for monumental contributions to the development of the country. Established in 1964. Awarded to seven individuals since 1964. In addition, Order of the Nation, Order of Merit, Order of Jamaica, and Order of Distinction (Commander and Officer Classes), are awarded. Additional information is available from Office of the Prime Minister, 1 Devon Rd., P.O. Box 272, Kingston 6, Jamaica.

Japan

8485
Asahi Glass Foundation
Bank of Tokyo Bldg.
Marunouchi 1-4-2
Chiyoda-ku
Tokyo 100, Japan
Phone: 33 285 0591
Fax: 33 285 0592

8486
Blue Planet Prize
To recognize outstanding environmental contributions by institutions or individuals of any nationality. The award is offered in two categories, Academic and Development & Implementation, to spur research and activity in global environmental issues. The deadline each year for nomination is October. Two monetary awards of 50 million yen each are presented annually. Established in 1991.

8487
Asahi Shimbun Publishing Company
5-3-2 Tsukiji, Chuo-ku
Tokyo 104-11, Japan
Phone: 3 35450131

8488
Asahi Fellowship
(Asahi Kokusai Shorei Kin)
To provide scholars, artists, journalists, and others of foreign nationality with the opportunity for a one-year stay in Japan to develop academic or professional expertise and knowledge of Japan, while at the same time contributing to international understanding and cooperation. Non-Japanese who have earned a university degree or the equivalent, are eligible to apply. Applicants who have been living in Japan for an extended period are not eligible. Two to four fellowships of 15,000,000 yen each are awarded annually. Established in 1988 to commemorate the hundredth anniversary of the Asahi's Tokyo head office.

8489
Asahi Forestry Culture Prize
(Asahi Shinrin Bunka Sho)
To recognize groups or individuals who have made outstanding contributions in the field of nature protection, forestry, etc. Applications are accepted. A monetary prize of 1,000,000 yen is awarded to each of the distinguished groups; a monetary prize of 300,000 yen is awarded to each of the encouraged groups. Awarded annually. Established in 1983.

8490
Asahi Nogyo Sho
To recognize groups that have made outstanding contributions to the promotion of farming or the development of modern agriculture. A monetary prize of 1,000,000 yen and honorary recognition are awarded annually. Established in 1963.

8491
Asahi Shakai Fukushi Sho
For recognition of achievement in improving the welfare of the underprivileged. A monetary prize of 2,000,000 yen is awarded annually. Established in 1975.

8492
Asahi Sho
To recognize groups or persons that contribute much to the improvement or advancement of Japanese society or culture. A monetary prize of 2,000,000 yen, a trophy, and honorary recognition are awarded annually. Established in 1929.

8493
Asahi Sports Prize
(Asahi Sports Sho)
To recognize the amateur and professional players who attain an excellent record. A diploma and a monetary prize of 500,000 yen are awarded annually. Established in 1929. Formerly: Asahi Physical Culture Prize.

8494
IBBY-Asahi Reading Promotion Award
(Asahi Kokusai Jido Tosho Fukyu Sho)
To recognize a group or institution in the world that contributes much to the promotion of books for children or for youth. Groups or institutions of any country are eligible. Nominations are made by each IBBY National Section. A diploma and a monetary prize of 1,000,000 yen are awarded annually. Established in 1986 to commemorate the 20th IBBY Congress in Tokyo. Sponsored by Asahi Shimbun Publishing Company. Formerly: (1989) Rising Sun Prize.

8495
Kenko Yuryo Gakko Hyosho
To recognize elementary schools for outstanding achievement in educating children and carrying out original health teaching activities. Elementary schools all over the country may be nominated. A diploma and a trophy are awarded annually. Established in 1951.

8496
Osaragi Jiro Prize
For recognition of outstanding work in the field of literature. A monetary prize of 2,000,000 yen is awarded annually. Established in 1974 in memory of Jiro Osaragi, one of the most popular novelists in Japan.

8497
Asia/Pacific Cultural Centre for UNESCO
Nihon Shuppan Kaikan
6 Funkuromachi
Shinjuku-ku
Tokyo 162, Japan
Phone: 3 3269 4435
Fax: 3 3269 4510

Formerly: Asian Cultural Centre for UNESCO.

8498
ACCU Prizes for Fully-Illustrated Literacy Follow-up Materials
No further information was provided on this biennial program open to nationals of UNESCO member states.

8499
Asia and the Pacific Photography Contest
No further information was provided on this annual award for this edition.

8500
Noma Concours for Picture Book Illustrations
To recognize illustrators of children's picture books in Africa, the Arab states, Latin America and the Caribbean, and the Asia/Pacific countries. Awarded biennially.

8501
Asian Parasite Control Organization
Japan Association of Parasite Control
1-2 Sadohara-cho, Ichigaya
Shinjuku-ku
Tokyo 162, Japan
Phone: 3 3268 1800
Fax: 3 3266 8767

8502
Morishita Prize
(Morishita Sho)
For recognition of a contribution in the field activities in the Integrated Project of family planning, nutrition and parasite control in APCO Member countries. The Steering Committee for the IP project in APCO member countries makes nominations. A monetary award of up to US $1,000 to be used for health education equipment, etc., is awarded annually. Established in 1978 by the Japan Association of Parasite Control to honor Prof. Kaoru Morishita, former Chairman of the Japan Association of Parasite Control. Sponsored by the Hoken Kaikan Foundation.

8503
Asian Productivity Organization
8-4-14 Akasaka
Minato-Ku
Tokyo 107, Japan
Phone: 3 34087221
Fax: 3 34087220

8504
APO National Award
To recognize individuals who have made outstanding contributions to the cause of increasing productivity in their country. Individuals who have made outstanding contributions, with significant impact or achievements in the Asian and Pacific region, or in any one or more of the following fields, are eligible for nomination: original thinking, research, or development in devising new concepts and technology appropriate to the Asian and Pacific region or to the member countries for increasing productivity; application of techniques in special fields of activity for increasing productivity in the Asian and Pacific region or in the member countries; institution building for improving productivity in member countries or the Asian and Pacific region; and propagation of the concepts and techniques of productivity improvement relevant to the Asian and Pacific region or to the member countries through publications, training activities, or other means. A gold medal, a certificate, and a rosette are awarded every five years. Last awareded in 1991. Established in 1985. Formerly: (1986) APO Special National Award.

8505
APO Regional Award
To recognize individuals who have made outstanding contributions to the cause of increasing productivity in the Asian region, thereby giving further impetus to the promotion of the productivity movement throughout the region. Individuals who have made outstanding contributions, with significant impact or achievements in the Asian and Pacific region or in any one or more of the following fields, are eligible for nomination: original thinking, research, or development in devising new concepts and technology appropriate to the Asian and Pacific region or to the member countries for increasing productivity; application of techniques in special fields of activity for increasing productivity in the Asian and Pacific region or in the member countries; institution building for improving productivity in member countries or the Asian and Pacific region; and propagation of the concepts and techniques of productivity improvement relevant to the Asian and Pacific region or to the member countries through publications, training activities, or other means. A gold medal, a certificate, and a rosette are awarded every five years. Last awarded in 1991. Established in 1978. Formerly: (1986) APO Award.

8506

Astronomical Society of Japan
(Nihon Tenmon Gakkai)
National Astronomical Observatory
2-21-1 Osawa, Mitaka
Tokyo 181, Japan
Phone: 422 343648
Fax: 422 311359

8507

Discovery of New Celestial Bodies Award
(Tentai Hakkensho)
For recognition of achievement in discovering new celestial bodies (comets, novae, supernovae). Japanese citizens may be nominated. A medal is presented to the first discoverer who reports finding to the authorized institutes. In addition, the second and third discoverers are recognized. Established in 1936.

8508

Research Award
(Nihon Tenmon Gakki Kenkyu Soreisho)
For recognition of achievement in astronomical research by young researchers under 35 years of age. Members may be nominated by members of the Society. A monetary prize, a medal, and certificate are awarded annually. Established in 1988.

8509

Research Award for Amateurs
To promote investigations of astronomy by amateur members. Japanese members may apply. A monetary award for research activities is presented annually. Established in 1961. Sponsored by Goto Optics Mfg. Co., Mr. Kanji Otsuka and Mr. Akitatsu Sato.

8510

Research Award for Junior Astronomers
To promote investigations of astronomy by junior researchers abroad. Japanese members may apply. A monetary award for research activities is presented annually. Established in 1992. Sponsored by the late Professor S. Hayakawa.

8511

Chemical Society of Japan
(Nippon Kagakukai)
1-5, Kanda-Surugadai
Chiyoda-ku
Tokyo 101, Japan
Phone: 3 32926161
Fax: 3 32926318

8512

Chemical Society of Japan Award
For recognition of a distinguished contribution in the field of pure and applied chemistry. Society members are eligible. A monetary prize, a medal, and a certificate are awarded annually. Established in 1948.

8513

Chemical Society of Japan Award for Chemical Education
For recognition of a distinguished contribution in the field of chemical education. Society members are eligible. A monetary prize, a medal, and a certificate are presented annually. Established in 1976.

8514

Chemical Society of Japan Award for Distinguished Technical Achievements
To recognize individuals who have supported research and development works by their distinguished technical achievements. A monetary prize, a medal, and a certificate are presented annually. Established in 1981.

8515

Chemical Society of Japan Award for Technological Development
For recognition of a distinguished contribution to technological development in the chemical industry. Industries in Japan are eligible. A medal and a certificate are awarded annually. Established in 1951.

8516

Chemical Society of Japan Award for Young Chemists
To recognize chemists under 35 years of age who have made distinguished contributions in the field of pure and applied chemistry. Society members are eligible. A monetary prize, a medal, and a certificate are awarded annually. Established in 1951.

8517

Chemical Society of Japan Award of Merits for Chemical Education
To recognize teachers who have made a distinguished contribution in the practice of chemical education. Society members and members of the Division of Chemical Education are eligible. A monetary prize, a medal, and a certificate are presented annually. Established in 1983.

8518

Divisional Award of the Chemical Society of Japan
To recognize chemists who have achieved a distinguished breakthrough in their research works in the field of pure and applied chemistry. A monetary prize, a medal, and a certificate are awarded annually. Established in 1983.

8519

Chuokoron-sha, Inc.
2-8-7 Kyobashi
Chuo-ku
Tokyo 104, Japan
Phone: 3 3563 1261
Fax: 3 3561 5920

8520

Female Writers Literary Award
(Joryu Bungaku Award)
For recognition of an outstanding literary work by a female writer. A monetary prize of 1,000,000 yen and a trophy are awarded annually. Established in 1962.

8521

Junichiro Tanizaki Award
For recognition of an outstanding literary work. A monetary prize of 1,000,000 yen and a trophy are awarded annually. Established in 1965 to honor Junichiro Tanizaki, the master writer representing Japan.

8522

Sakuzo Yoshino Award
For recognition of an outstanding social science criticism. A monetary prize of 1,000,000 yen and a trophy are awarded annually. Established in 1965 to honor Sakuzo Yoshino, a forerunner of liberalism.

8523

Dentsu
(Kabushiki Kaisha Dentsu)
1-11 Tsukiji
Chuo-ku
Tokyo 104, Japan
Phone: 3 35445104
Fax: 3 35468110

8524

Dentsu Advertising Awards
(Kokoku Dentus Sho)
To raise the standard of advertising creativity in Japan in the Japanese language only. Awards are given for excellence in ad planning and technique in the following divisions: newspaper, magazine, poster, radio, television, and sales promotion. Ads that appeared in Japan during the year from April 1 to March 31 may be submitted by advertisers. Monetary awards, including 1 million yen for the "Grand Prix", are awarded annually in July. Established in 1948.

8525

Suntory Awards for Mystery Fiction
To recognize an outstanding mystery, suspense, detective, or espionage novel. Unpublished manuscripts must be in English or Japanese. Entries

in English should be 40,000 to 80,000 words long. Entries written in English must be postmarked by January 31. The following awards are presented: Grand Prix - 5,000,000 yen (around $33,000 US), publication in Japanese by Bungei Shunju, and a nationwide television special on the novel by Asahi Broadcasting; and Reader's Choice Award - 1,000,000 yen (approximately $6,600 US), and consideration for publication and television. Established in 1983. Sponsored by Suntory Limited of Japan, Bungei Shunju Ltd. publishers and the Asahi Broadcasting Corporation.

8526

Fujihara Foundation of Science
Oji Bldg.
Ginza 3-7-12
Chuo-ku
Tokyo 104, Japan
Phone: 3 5617736
Fax: 3 5617736

8527

Fujihara Award
To recognize Japanese scientists who have contributed most to the advancement of science in the fields of mathematics, physics, engineering, chemistry, biology, agriculture, or medicine. Nominations may be submitted by February 28. Two monetary prizes of 10,000,000 yen each and gold medals are awarded annually. Established in 1959 in honor of Ginjro Fujihara, former President of Oji Paper Manufacturing Company.

8528

Genetics Society of Japan
(Nihon Iden Gakkai)
c/o National Institute of Genetics
Yata 1, 111
Mishima
Shizuoka-Ken 411, Japan
Phone: 559 750771
Fax: 559 713651

8529

Kihara Award
(Kihara Sho)
For recognition of a contribution to genetics. The deadline for applications is May 31. A monetary prize and a medal are awarded annually. Established in 1983 in honor of Dr. Hitoshi Kihara. Sponsored by Kihara Memorial Yokohama Foundation for the Advancement of Life Sciences.

8530

Hiroshima Festival Office
4-17 Kako-Machi
Naka-ku
Hiroshima 730, Japan
Phone: 82 245 0245
Fax: 82 245 0246

8531

International Animation Festival in Japan, Hiroshima
To promote the development and international exchange of animation art, and to promote world peace through animation. Entry works must be on either film or videotape (including computer animation). The running time must be within 30 minutes and works must be completed during the preceding two years. Films should be on 16mm or 35mm format, and be an optical soundtrack system. Videotapes must be on standard 3/4-inch cassette (either NTSC, PAL, or SECAM) or on Betacam (only NTSC acceptable). The deadline for entry forms is March, and the deadline for submitting films/videos is in April. Entrants are requested to specify one of the following categories: promotional works such as commercials or opening titles, etc.; debut works; works for children; works for educational purpose; shorter than 5 minutes: longer than 5 minutes and within 15 minutes; longer than 15 minutes and within 30 minutes. The following prizes are awarded biennially in August: Grand Prize - 1,000,000 yen; Hiroshima Prize - 1,000,000 yen; Debut Prize - 500,000 yen; First and Second Prizes for the best entries in each category; and Special Jury Prizes for some outstanding works. Also, the Organizing Committee welcomes any organization wishing to present its own special awards. Established in 1985 by Hiroshima City, The Hiroshima City Foundation for Promotion of Cultural Activities, and ASIFA (Association Internationale du Film d' Animation)-Japan.

8532

Hiroshima International Amateur Film and Video Festival
(Festival International de Films et Video Amateurs a Hiroshima)
Chugoku Broadcasting Co.
Dept. of Business Promotion
21-3 Motomachi, Nakaku
Hiroshima 730, Japan
Phone: 82 222 1133
Fax: 82 222 1187

8533

Hiroshima International Amateur Film and Video Festival
For recognition of the best films and videos by amateurs that manifest an effort toward "Peace and Reverence for Life," such as a tribute to humanity, or the relation between nature and man. Films in 16mm or 8mm (super-eight or single eight) and video may be silent or sound, black and white, or in color. Documentary, feature, animation, and art films not exceeding 30 minutes may be submitted by January 31. The following awards are presented: (1) Grand Prize: Hiroshima City Mayor's Prize - 500,000 yen, a statuette and a citation; (2) President of Chugoku Broadcasting Company Prize - 250,000 yen, a statuette and a citation; (3) Prizes of Excellence: (a) Prime Minister's Prize; (b) Foreign Minister's Prize; (c) Education Minister's Prize; (d) Hiroshima Prefecture Governor's Prize; (e) Nagasaki City Mayor's Prize; (f) Hiroshima City Board of Education Prize for works by students of high schools, college, universities, and various kinds of academic institutes; (g) President of the National Federation of UNESCO Association in Japan Prize; (h) President of the Japan Foundation Prize; (i) Chugoku Shimbun Company Prize; (j) Asahi Shimbun Company Prize; (k) Mainichi Shimbun Company Prize; (4) Asia Prize and Fuji Film Prize; and (5) Ten Honorable Mention prizes consisting of a statuette or plaque and citation. The Festival is held biennially. Established in 1975 to commemorate the 30th anniversary of the atomic boming of Hiroshima in 1945. The next festival will be held in June 1993.

8534

Honda Foundation
2-6-20 Yaesu
Chuo-ku
Tokyo 104, Japan
Phone: 3 32745125
Fax: 3 32745103

8535

Honda Prize
To recognize a distinguished contribution in the field of "Eco-technology," a new concept of technology which does not pursue efficiency and profits alone, but is geared toward harmony with the environment surrounding human activities. The award was established to spread this concept of eco-technology. Individuals and organizations, regardless of nationality, are eligible. Nominations must be submitted by March 31. A monetary award of 10,000,000 yen, a medal, and a certificate are awarded annually on November 17. Established in 1980 to honor Soichiro Honda, the founder of Honda Motor Company.

8536

Hosei University
International Center
(Hosei Daigaku Kokusaikouryu Center)
2-17-1 Fujimi
Chiyoda-ku
Tokyo 102, Japan
Phone: 3 3264 9662
Fax: 3 3238 9873

8537

Hosei International Fund Foreign Scholars Fellowship
To assist young scholars to carry out non-degree research programs in the areas of humanities, social and natural sciences, and engineering. Positions are not available in medical or veterinary sciences, pharmacology, nursing, agriculture, marine sciences, home economics, fine arts, or crafts. To be eligible, an individual must be under 35 years of age and non-Japanese nationality, must have an advanced academic degree (Master's or Doctorate), and be proficient in Japanese or English. The application deadline is May 31. A monthly allowance of 210,000 yen (in 1994-95) and a travel allowance are awarded to three scholars annually.

Established in 1982 on the occasion of the 100th year anniversary of Hosei University.

8538

Inamori Foundation
87 Kankoboko-cho Shijo-dori
Muromachi, Higashi-iru
Shimogyo-ku
Kyoto 600, Japan
Phone: 75 2552688
Fax: 75 2553360

8539

Kyoto Prizes
For recognition of outstanding contributions in the following categories: advanced technology, basic sciences, and creative arts and moral sciences. Nominations are requested by the Foundation from individuals selected from: representatives of learned societies, presidents, deans, and professors at leading universities; directors of leading research institutions and academies; members and associate members of scientific and cultural academies; former recipients of the Kyoto Prizes and other international prizes; and other individuals of equivalent stature. A monetary prize of 45,000,000 Japanese yen for each category, a gold medal, and a certificate are awarded annually in November. Established in 1985.

8540

Information Science and Technology Association, Japan
Sasaki Bldg.
2-5-7 Koisikawa
Bunkyo-ku
Tokyo 112, Japan
Phone: 3 3813 3791
Fax: 3 3813 3793

Formerly: (1987) UDC Society of Japan, Japan Documentation Society.

8541

INFOSTA Award
For recognition of distinguished service. The following prizes may be awarded: (1) Award for distinguished services in information activities - to those who are in charge of information in their organizations and have rendered services there through the years; (2) Award for distinguished activities in education of documentation and training - to those who have done excellent work in education and training of documentation in Japan; (3) Award for continuous service - to reward members of the staff who have worked for a long time at the INFOSTA office; (4) Award for an excellent organization in documentation activities - for sustaining organization members of INFOSTA that have done remarkable work in documentation activities; and (5) Award for an excellent paper - for comparatively young members who have presented an excellent paper in periodicals, reports, or at the gatherings and events held by INFOSTA. Members are eligible. A souvenir is awarded annually. Established in 1976. Formerly: (1987) NIPDOK Award.

8542

International Association for Structural Mechanics in Reactor Technology
Institute of Industrial Science
University of Tokyo
7-22-1 Roppongi, Minato-ku
Tokyo 106, Japan

8543

Thomas A. Jaeger Prize
To encourage and stimulate basic research by young researchers in structural mechanics applied to reactor technology. The competition is open to those who are 45 years of age or younger. The work presented must be wholly original, related to the topics of the SMiRT 11 Conference and not have been published elsewhere. The prize consists of a certificate, a cash stipend of $2,000 (to be divided equally among multiple authors), and the formal presentation of the paper during the SMiRT Conference. Awarded biennially. Established in 1981.

8544

International Association of Ports and Harbors
Kotohira-Kaikan Bldg.
1-2-8 Toranomon
Minato-ku
Tokyo 105, Japan
Phone: 3 3591 4261
Fax: 3 3580 0364

8545

IAPH Essay Contest
To contribute to the efficiency of ports in developing countries by conducting an essay contest for personnel from IAPH member ports in the forementioned areas. Essays in English, French, or Spanish may be submitted by September 1 of each even-numbered year. Applicants should be those personnel from developing ports that are IAPH members. The first prize winner receives the Akiyama Prize, consisting of US $1,000, a silver medal, a certificate, and an invitation to the Association's conference with airfare and hotel accommodation provided. A second prize of US $500, third prize of US $400, and fourth prize of US $300 are also awarded. Additional prizes of US $100 each are also awarded to any other entries judged by the panel to be of high standard. Awarded biennially. Established in 1979 in honor of Mr. Toru Akiyama, one of the founders and Secretary General Emeritus.

8546

International Association of Traffic and Safety Sciences
2-6-20 Yaesu
Chuo-ku
Tokyo 104, Japan
Phone: 3 32737884
Fax: 3 32727054

8547

Awards
For recognition of research on traffic and traffic safety. No further information about the awards is available for this edition.

8548

International Esperantist League for Go
(Esperantista Go-Ligo Internacia)
2-26-2 Kojima
Chofu
Tokyo 182, Japan
Phone: 424 823776

8549

Esperantista Go-Ligo Internacia Competitions
To promote the Esperanto language through the game of Go and to popularize the Go game through Esperanto. (Go is a Japanese game played on a board with black and white stones; the object is to capture the opponent's stones and possess a larger part of the board.) The League sponsors competitions.

8550

International Organization of Plant Biosystematists
(Organisation Internationale de Biosystematiciens Vege taux)
Dept. of Botany
Faculty of Science
Kyoto 606, Japan
Phone: 75 753 4131
Fax: 75 753 4131

8551

Life Membership
To recognize an individual for contributions in promoting the field of biosystematics and developing the International Organization of Plant Biosystematics. A scroll is awarded triennially at the Symposium. Established in 1989. In addition, the triennial IOPB Award is also presented.

| 8552 |

International Society for Photogrammetry and Remote Sensing
Institute of Industrial Science
Univ. of Tokyo
7-22-1 Roppongi
Minatao-Ku
Tokyo 106, Japan
Phone: 3 3402 6231
Fax: 3 3479 9276

| 8553 |

Brock Gold Medal Award
For recognition of an outstanding contribution to the evolution of photogrammetric theory, instrumentation, or practice. Nomination by two member societies to which the nominee does not belong is required. A gold medal is awarded every four years at the Quadrennial Congress. Established in 1956 by the American Society for Photogrammetry and Remote Sensing in honor of Dr. G.C. Brock.

| 8554 |

Sam G. Gamble Award
For recognition of personal contributions to the administration of the Society or to the organization of activities of the Society's Commissions. Individuals irrespective of nationality are eligible. A gold pin and a certificate are awarded every four years at the Quadrennial Congress. Established in 1985 in honor of Dr. Sam G. Gamble. Sponsored by the Canadian Institute of Surveying.

| 8555 |

Schermerhorn Award
To recognize a Working Group member(s) who, through commitment, has achieved successful scientific meetings of a very high level during the four year Congress period. Established in 1988. Sponsored by the Netherlands Society of Photogrammetry.

| 8556 |

Schwidefsky Medal
To recognize individuals who have made significant contributions to photogrammetry and remote sensing, either through the medium of publication as author or editor, or in another form. A medal is awarded at each Congress of the International Society for Photogrammetry and Remote Sensing. Established in 1988 in memory of Prof. Dr. rer. techn. Dr.-Ing. E.h. Kurt Schwidefsky, honorary member of the Society. Sponsored by the Deutsche Gesselschaft fur Photogrammetrie und Fernerkundung.

| 8557 |

Otto von Gruber Award
For recognition of a significant paper on photogrammetry or an allied subject, written in the four year period preceding the Congress. A monetary award and a gold medal are awarded evey four years at the Quadrennial Congress. Established in 1964 by the ITC-Foundation (International Institute for Aerial Survey Sciences, the Netherlands) in honor of Otto von Gruber.

| 8558 |

Irino Prize Foundation
JML Seminar, Yoshiro Irino Institute of
  Music
5-22-2 Matsubara
Setagaya-Ku
Tokyo 156, Japan
Phone: 3 3323 0646
Phone: 3 3325 5468
Fax: 3 3325 5468

| 8559 |

Irino Prize
To recognize and provide incentive for young composers. Individuals of any nationality who are less than 40 years of age may submit Chamber compositions that had their first performance during the preceding year. Orchestral compositions must be 10 minutes or less in duration, unpublished, not yet performed, and must not have received any prize. The deadline is April 30. Chamber music compositions should be scored for not more than six players and should be 15 minutes or less in duration. The competition rotates annually for an orchestral work and a chamber work. A monetary award of 650,000 yen is presented for the Prize for Orchestral Work (1994); and 200,000 yen for the Prize for Chamber Orchestra (1995). The winning orchestral composition is performed by the New Japan Philharmonic Orchestra. The International Composers Competition was established in 1980 to honor Yoshiro Irino, the greatly celebrated composer.

| 8560 |

Iron and Steel Institute of Japan
(Nippon Tekko Kyokai)
Keidanren Kaikan, 3rd Fl.
1-9-4 Otemachi
Chiyoda-ku
Tokyo 100, Japan
Phone: 3 32796021
Fax: 3 32451355

| 8561 |

Hattori Prize
For recognition of contributions to the steel industry. Awarded annually.

| 8562 |

Honorary Member
To recognize individuals who have contributed to the steel industry of Japan and have honorable fame in the industry. Honorary members are nominated by the council. Awarded annually.

| 8563 |

Iron and Steel Development Award
To recognize a member who has rendered a special contribution to the improvement and development of the steel industry of Japan and to the research and development of science and technology during the past decade. Certificates of merit and medals are awarded.

| 8564 |

Komura Prize
For recognition of contributions to the steel industry. Awarded annually.

| 8565 |

Nishiyama Medal
For recognition of contributions to the steel industry. Awarded annually.

| 8566 |

Noro Prize
To recognize a person who has especially contributed to the development of the activities of ISIJ. Certificates of merit and medals are awarded. Renamed after the first ISIJ President, Dr. Kageyoshi Noro. Formerly: ISIJ Award for Service.

| 8567 |

Tawara Gold Medal
To recognize a member who has rendered outstanding contributions, regardless of nationality, to the development of the steel industry or to the research and development of science and technology, and has an internationally established fame. A certificate of merit and a gold medal are awarded.

| 8568 |

G. Watanabe Medal
For recognition of contributions to the steel industry. Awarded annually.

| 8569 |

Italian Institute of Culture
(Istituto Italiano di Cultura di Tokyo)
2-1-30 Kudan Minami
Chiyoda-ku
Tokyo 102, Japan
Phone: 3 32646011
Fax: 3 32620853

8570
Pico della Mirandola Prize
(Premio Pico della Mirandola)
To promote translation from Italian into Japanese. A monetary award of 1,000,000 yen and a plaque were awarded annually. Established in 1987. Sponsored by Banca Nazionale dell'Agricoltura. (Discontinued)

8571
Marco Polo Prize
(Premio Marco Polo)
To encourage the promotion of Italian culture in Japan. A monetary prize of 1,000,000 yen and a plaque were awarded annually. Established in 1977. (Discontinued)

8572
Iwatani Naoji Foundation
(Iwatani Naoji Kinen Zaidan)
TBR Bldg.
2-10-2 Nagata-cho
Chiyoda-ku
Tokyo 100, Japan   Phone: 3 3580 2251

8573
Iwatani Naoji Memorial Prize
To provide recognition for outstanding achievements in research and development in the fields of gas and energy in Japan. Individuals or groups are eligible. A monetary prize of 1,000,000 yen and a medal are awarded annually in March. Established in 1973.

8574
Japan
Ministry of Education, Science and Culture
3-2-2 Kasumigaseki
Chiyoda-ku
Tokyo, Japan

8575
Arts Achievement Award
(Geijutsu Sensho)
To recognize persons who have in that year achieved excellent results or innovation in the respective fields of the arts. Conferring of the Arts Achievement Awards and New Talent Awards of the Minister of Education, Science and Culture has continued since 1950. In addition, the Dramatic Arts Creativity Special Encouragement Award for outstanding musical or dramatic composition has been presented annually since its institution in 1978. The Outstanding Media Arts Productions Award (movies, broadcasts, records) is also awarded since 1985.

8576
Arts Festival Award
(Geijutsusai Sho)
To recognize superior contributions to dance, theatre, film, radio, television, and recording. The Arts Festival is held to allow wide access to and appreciation of exemplary works of art and to provide artists with the opportunity to give public performance. Individuals or groups are eligible. Honorary recognition is awarded annually. Established in 1946.

8577
Award for Distinguished Cultural Service
(Bunka Korosha)
To recognize persons who have rendered particularly valuable service in the advancement of culture. Awardees are selected by the Minister of Education, Science and Culture from among the individuals nominated by the Committee for Selection of Cultural Awardees. This award is conferred for eminent contribution in the same fields of cultural activity as pertain to the Order of Cultural Merit. Established in 1951.

8578
Decorations and Medals
(Jokun Hosho)
For recognition in the field of culture, decorations are awarded for service in fine arts, literary arts, music, dramatic arts, dance, films, popular entertainment, hobbies and amusements, religion, Japanese language, traditional amusements, traditional entertainments and crafts, as well as in information and reporting, publishing, and protection of cultural properties. Award of decorations is also carried out upon the death of individuals who have in their lifetime distinguished themselves in these areas. Normally awarded to persons of 70 or older. Ranking of these decorations is as follows: sixth rank or above for meritorious service, fourth rank or above for distinguished meritorious service, and second rank or above for particularly distinguished meritorious service. At present, in addition to decorations, medals are also awarded, with six types - brown, green, yellow, purple, indigo, and navy blue - of which the following are awarded in relation to culture: yellow, for assiduity in performing one's duties, serving as a model for the citizens; purple, for outstanding achievement in scientific or artistic invention, reform, creativity; and indigo, for distinguished achievement profiting the people, or diligence in effectively handling the affairs of the people. Awarded twice annually in spring on April 29, and in autumn on November 3. Resumed in 1964 after having been discontinued since the war years.

8579
Order of Cultural Merit
(Bunka-Kunsho)
To recognize persons of outstanding achievement in the advancement of culture. Recipients are selected by the Cabinet of the Japanese government following their nomination by the Minister of Education, Science and Culture in consultation with the Committee For Selection of Cultural Awardees, specially convened once annually. Recipients of the Order of Cultural Merit are normally chosen from among those who had been awarded the Award for Distinguished Cultural Service in previous years. The Order of Cultural Merit is awarded for distinctiuon in any of a wide range of cultural endeavors, including visual arts (Japanese-style painting or drawing, Western-style painting or drawing, the plastic arts, applied fine arts, architecture), literary arts (fiction, poetry, critical essay, translation) and performing arts (Western music, Japanese traditional music, dramatic arts). Established in 1937.

8580
Regional Cultural Commendation
To recognize approximately 100 individuals and groups in the various regions of Japan for efforts made in the promotion of culture or the protection of cultural properties in the respective regions. Awarded annually. Established in 1983.

8581
Japan
Office of the Prime Minister
Decoration Bureau
1-6 Nagata-cho
Chiyoda-ku
Tokyo 100, Japan   Phone: 3 3581 2361

8582
Collar of the Supreme Order of the Chrysanthemum
For recognition of great service to the country. The Collar ranks highest in the line of Japanese honors, and is followed by Grand Cordon of the Supreme Order of the Chrysanthemum; First Class Order of the Rising Sun with Paulownia Flowers; First Class Order of the Rising Sun; First Class Order of the Precious Crown; First Class Order of the Sacred Treasure; Order of Culture; and Medal of Honor with Red Ribbon. Established in 1888.

8583
First Class Order of the Rising Sun Paulownia Flowers
To recognize men of Japanese or foreign origin for great service to Japan. Established in 1888 as an Order ranking higher than the First Class of the Order of the Rising Sun.

8584
Grand Cordon of the Supreme Order of the Chrysanthemum
To recognize individuals who have rendered illustrious service to the country. Foreign heads of state and statesmen as well as Japanese statesmen are eligible. The Collar or the Grand Cordon of the Order is awarded twice a year. Established in 1877 by Emperor Meiji.

8585
Medals of Honor
To recognize Japanese or foreign citizens who have saved human lives, set an example to the people by industrious diligence to their duties, or rendered valuable services in fields of culture and education. Medals with red, green, yellow, purple, blue, and dark blue ribbons are presented.

8586
Order of Culture
To recognize Japanese citizens who have rendered outstanding contributions in the fields of science, literature, painting, sculpture, architecture, music, and drama. There is no class distinction, since it is believed that there should be no distinctions made for cultural services. The orange flower design of the Order symbolizes culture and in the center of the petals of a white cloisonne finish with gold edges there are crescent jades surrounded by 20 tiny gold balls, symbolizing a stamen. Established in 1937.

8587
Orders of the Precious Crown
To recognize Japanese or foreign women for distinguished service. The Order is divided into eight classes. A badge and a star are awarded. The Order is awarded twice a year when merited. Established in 1888 by Emperor Meiji.

8588
Orders of the Rising Sun
For recognition of meritorious service to the country. Only men of Japanese or foreign origin are eligible. This Order is divided into eight classes. A badge and a star are awarded. The Order is awarded twice a year when merited. Established in 1875 by Emperor Meiji.

8589
Orders of the Sacred Treasure
To recognize men and women of Japanese or foreign origin who have rendered distinguished services to Japan. This Order is divided into eight classes. A badge and a star are awarded. The design of the Order features the sacred mirror of the Grand Shrine of Ise, surrounded by profuse shafts of light. Established in 1888 by Emperor Meiji.

8590
Japan
Science and Technology Agency
2-2-1 Kasumigaseki
Chiyoda-ku
Tokyo, Japan

8591
Commendation by the Minister of State for Science and Technology
For recognition of contributions to the development of science and technology. Accomplished individuals and those who supported them both personally and socially are eligible. Honorary recognition is awarded annually. Established in 1959.

8592
Japan Academy
(Nippon Gakushiin)
7-32 Ueno Park
Taito-ku
Tokyo 110, Japan

Phone: 3 3822 2101
Fax: 3 3822 2105

8593
Duke of Edinburgh Prize for the Japan Academy
(Nippon Gakushiin Ejinbara-ko Sho)
For recognition of outstanding scientific achievement in connection with the protection of wildlife and preservation of species. The prize is awarded on the recommendation of the members of the Academy. A monetary award of 500,000 yen and a memorial medal (the Duke of Edinburgh Prize) provided by His Royal Highness Prince Philip, Duke of Edinburgh, Honorary Member of the Academy, are awarded biennially. Established in 1987.

8594
Imperial Prize
(Onshi Sho)
For recognition of outstanding papers, books, treatises, and other scientific achievements. Two Imperial Prizes, one in the field of humanities and social sciences and another in the field of pure and applied sciences are awarded to those already nominated for the Japan Academy Prize for that year. Members of the Japan Academy may recommend Japanese scientists for the award. Two memorial vases are given by the Emperor in addition to the Japan Academy Prize. Awarded annually. Established in 1910.

8595
Japan Academy Prize
(Nippon Gakushiin Sho)
This, the highest award of the Academy, is given to recognize outstanding papers, books, treatises, and other scientific achievements. No more than nine prizes may be awarded on the recommendation of the members of the Academy. Usually four prizes are given for distinguished works in the humanities and social sciences, and five for works in pure and applied sciences. Members of the Academy may not be nominated. Members of the Japan Academy may recommend Japanese scientists for the award. A monetary prize of 500,000 yen and a medal are awarded to each winner annually. Established in 1911.

8596
Japan Art Academy
(Geijutsu-in)
c/o Cultural Affairs Div.
Japanese Ministry of Education
1-30 Ueno-koen
Taito-ku
Tokyo, Japan

8597
Japan Art Academy Prize
(Geijutsu-in Sho)
To recognize individuals for works of art and distinguished services to the development of the fine arts. Monetary prizes are awarded annually. Established in 1949. The Imperial Prize is also awarded.

8598
Japan Art Association
c/o Fuji Television Network, Inc.
3-1 Kawada-cho
Skinjuku-ku
Tokyo 162, Japan

Phone: 3 33513206
Fax: 3 33575808

8599
Praemium Imperiale
To honor artistic values and contributions of surpassing importance in the arts beyond the boundaries of nations and races. These international awards are given to anyone in the world in the following areas: sculpture, painting, music, architecture, and theatre and film. Recipients are selected on the basis of recommendations of an appointed panel of advisors. A monetary prize of 15,000,000 yen and a medal are awarded in each category annually. Established in 1988 in memory of His Imperial Highness Prince Takamatsu. The prize reflects Japan's growing global commitment to support of the arts, and is a reminder that a nation's cultural heritage is as precious as its economic accomplishments could ever be. (First awarded in the autumn of 1989.)

8600
Japan Broadcasting Corporation
(Nippon Hoso Kyokai)
Japan Prize Secretariat
Broadcasting Centre, NHK Hoso Centre
2-2-1 Jinnan
Shibuya-ku
Tokyo 150-01, Japan
Phone: 3 34651111
Fax: 3 34811800

8601
NHK Broadcast Cultural Award
To recognize individuals who have contributed to the development of the broadcasting field or to its cultural standards. Awarded annually. Formerly: NHK Broadcasting Culture Prize.

8602
NHK Japan Prize Contest
(Prix Japon - Concours International de Programmes Educatifs)
To recognize the best educational broadcast program that is judged to have the highest educational value and demonstrates the important role and potential in broadcasting. Broadcasting organizations, or unions or associations of such organizations that provide coverage nationwide, from any country or territory with membership in the International Telecommunications Union (ITU), and authorized by the competent authority to operate a broadcasting service are eligible to participate. In addition, cable TV enterprises or equivalent organizations transmitting programs, educational institutions, or educational research bodies producing educational programs for the purpose of broadcasting, as well as independent producers operating with the same objective, are eligible to participate. There are four categories for television program entries: preschool education - programs intended for children up to six years old; primary education - programs intended for children 6-12 years old; secondary education - programs intended for those 12-17 years old; and adult education - intended for those 18 or older. Programs must have been broadcast during the period from September 1 of the preceding year to August 31 of the year that the contest is held. Each program must not exceed 60 minutes in duration. The major prizes in the Japan Prize Contest are: Japan Prize - awarded to the program of outstanding excellence that is judged to have high educational value and to demonstrate the important role and potential of broadcasting in the field of education; Prizes for Programs of Outstanding Excellence in Each Category include: The Minister for Foreign Affairs Prize, The Minister of Education Prize, The Minister of Posts and Telecommunications Prize, and the Governor of Tokyo Prize; Prizes Awarded to Programs of Merit in Each Category include: The Hoso Bunka Foundation Prize (preschool education), The Japan Association for Education Broadcasting Prize (primary education), The Maeda Prize (secondary education), and the Abe Prize (adult education); The UNICEF Prize - for a program that best presents the life and environment of children in developing countries; The Japan Foundation's President's Prize - for a program that is judged to best contribute to international cultural exchange and cooperative spirit; and the Award of Special Commendation - for two programs that have made significant contributions to the educational demands of the participating countries. The Contest has been held annually since 1991. Established in 1965.

8603
Otaka Prize
To recognize a composer of classical music. Monetary prizes of 300,000 yen were awarded annually. (Discontinued) Formerly: Odaka Prize.

8604
Japan Design Foundation
3-1-800 Umeda 1-chome
Kita-ku
Osaka 530, Japan
Phone: 6 3462611
Fax: 6 3462615

8605
International Design Award, Osaka
To honor individuals, groups and organizations (companies, governmental bodies, research institutes, educational organizations, etc.) from around the world who have made outstanding contributions to the advancement and development of culture and human society through design activities. The award aims to deepen understanding of and interest in design and to show the world truly valuable design activities. Winners are chosen from among candidates nominated by internationally prominent designers, journalists, design educators, and those well-informed and experienced in design and design-related fields. Nominations may be submitted. A diploma, an invitation to the Citation Ceremony where ther award is presented, and an exhibition of the work are awarded biennially. Established in 1981. Sponsored by the Ministry of International Trade and Industry, the Osaka Prefectural Government, the Osaka Municipal Government and the Osaka Chamber of Commerce and Industry.

8606
International Design Competition, Osaka
To provide a competition for designers worldwide, including industrial, graphic, interior, craft, package, and environmental designers, to compete under one theme, using all their talent, either on an individual or group basis. The competition serves to redefine the role played by design while presenting a concrete vision of a better future for humanity as the 21st century nears. All works entered must be recent and previously unpublished. Designers, engineers, and students in every field may submit designs as individuals or as members of a team. The following monetary prizes totaling $80,000 are awarded biennially: Prime Minister's Prize - a grand prize of $35,000; Minister of International Trade and Industry Prize; Chairman of Japan Design Foundation Prize; Governor of Osaka Prefecture Prize; Mayor of Osaka City Prize; Silver Prize; and Copper Prize. In addition, some Honorable Mention awards may be presented. Established in 1981. Sponsored by the Ministry of International Trade and Industry, the Osaka Prefectural Government, the Osaka Municipal Government, and the Osaka Chamber of Commerce and Industry.

8607
Japan Federation of Musicians
(Nihon Enso Renmei)
Secretariat
West Park Bldg, 4F
1-10-16 Ebisunishi
Shibuya-ku
Tokyo 150, Japan
Phone: 3 3462 0601
Fax: 3 3462 0603

8608
International Music Competition of Japan
(Nihon Kokusai Ongaku Konkuru)
To recognize pianists and violinists of all nationalities. Individuals between the ages of 17 and 32 are eligible. The following awards are presented for piano and violin: (1) First prize - 2 million yen and a medal; (2) Second prize - 1.2 million yen and a medal; (3) Third prize - 800,000 yen and a medal; (4) Fourth prize - 500,000 yen; (5) Fifth prize - 400,000 yen; and (6) Sixth prize - 300,000 yen. Three additional awards are presented: (1) the Motonari Iguchi Award of 1 million yen to the best pianist. Motonari Iguchi was the first chairman of the board of the Japan Federation of Musicians; (2) the Prince Takamado Award of a crystal trophy to the first

prize winner of each section. Prince Takamado is Honorary President of the Competition; and (3) the Best Performer of a Japanese Work Prize. The Competition is held triennially. Established in 1980.

8609
Japan Federation of Printing Industries
(Nihon Insatsu Sangyo Rengokai)
1-16-8 Shintomi
Chuo-ku
Tokyo, Japan
Phone: 3 3553 6051
Phone: 3 3553 6079

Formerly: (1992) Japan Printers' Association.

8610
Printing Culture Prize
To provide recognition in the field of printing for a work that is artistically, historically and academically valuable. A monetary award and a plaque are awarded every four years. Established in 1987. Formerly: Insatsu Bunka Sho.

8611
Japan Foundation
(Kokusai Koryu Kikin)
Park Building
3-6, Kioi-cho
Chiyoda-ku
Tokyo 102, Japan
Phone: 3 326344919
Fax: 3 32347884

8612
Japan Foundation Award
(Kokusai Koryu Kikin Sho)
To recognize individuals and organizations at home and abroad who have made outstanding contributions to cultural exchange and mutual understanding between Japan and other countries. The awards are made in recognition of these achievements, and to encourage the recipients in future endeavors. Individuals and companies who are considered to have made especially remarkable contributions and who continue to exert a strong influence in these directions are eligible. A monetary prize of 5,000,000 yen for each winner is awarded annually. Established in 1974.

8613
Japan Foundation Grant Programs
The Japan Foundation administers the following twelve programs: Fellowship Programs, Institutional Support Programs for Japanese Studies, Library Support Program, Study-in-Japan Grant Program, Salary Assistance Program for Full-Time Japanese-Language Teachers, Training Programs for Teachers of the Japanese Language, Japanese-Language Study Program for Librarians, Japanese-Language Teaching Materials Donation Program, Assistance Program for the Development of Japanese-Language Printed Teaching Resources, Publication Assistance Program, Translation Assistance Program, Japanese Language Education Fellowship Program, Exhibitions Abroad Support Program, Film Production Support Program. Completed applications must be submitted by December 1. Awarded annually.

8614
Japan Foundation Prize for the Promotion of Community-Based Cultural Exchange
(Chiiki Koryu Shinko Sho)
To recognize contributions by domestic private organizations engaged in regionally-based international exchange activities. The award is designed to encourage such initiatives and thus, on a national level, to promote a greater diversification of international activities overall. The deadline is in September. A monetary prize of 1,500,000 yen for each winner is awarded annually. Established in 1985.

8615
Japan Foundation Special Prizes
(Kokusai Koryu Shorei Sho)
To recognize individuals and organizations at home and abroad who have made outstanding contributions to cultural exchange and mutual understanding between Japan and other countries. The awards are made in recognition of these achievements, and to encourage the recipients in future endeavors. Individuals and companies who are recognized to have achieved remarkable accomplishments and who are expected to make significant contributions in the same direction in the future are eligible. A monetary award of 3,000,000 yen for each winner is awarded annually. Established in 1974.

8616
Japan Golf Association
Palace Bldg., Ste. 606
1-1-1 Marunouchi
Chiyoda-Ku
Tokyo 100, Japan
Phone: 3 3215 0003
Fax: 3 3214 2831

8617
Japan Golf Championships
For recognition of the winners of various golf championships. The Association sponsors the following tournaments: Dunlop Open Golf Championship, Japan Women's Open Golf Championship, Japan Amateur Golf Championship, Japan Junior Golf Championship, Japan Collegiate Golf Championship, Japan Women's Collegiate Golf Championship, Japan Women's Amateur Golf Championship, Japan Open Golf Championship, Japan Senior Golf Championship, Japan Mid-Senior Golf Championship, Japan Grand Senior Golf Championship, Japan Women's Senior Golf Championship, Japan Amateur Match Play Golf Championship (men and women), and Japan Senior Open Golf Championship.

8618
Jack Nicklaus Best Junior Golfer
For the promotion and development of junior golfers. Winners of the Japan Junior Golf Championship and other junior competitions are considered. A plaque and a set of golf clubs are awarded annually. Established in 1981 by Jack Nicklaus. Sponsored by MacGregor Golf Japan.

8619
Japan Information Center of Science and Technology
(Nihon Kagaku-Gijutsu Joho Sentah)
PO Box 1478
2-5-2 Nagatacho
Chiyoda-ku
Tokyo 100, Japan
Phone: 3 35816790
Fax: 3 35933980

8620
Niwa Prize
To recognize individuals who have made a significant contribution to the development of scientific and technical information in Japan. Individuals may apply or be nominated for an excellent presentation of research in the field of science and technical information. A testimonial and presentation are awarded annually. Established in 1964 in honor of Yasuziro Niwa, the former President of JICST.

8621
Japan International Film - Video Festival of Adventure and Sports in Hakuba
Hakuba Village Office
7025 Hakuba-Mura
Kitaazumi-Gun
Nagano 399-93, Japan
Phone: 261 725000
Fax: 261 726311

8622
Japan International Film - Video Festival of Adventure and Sports in Hakuba
To recognize outstanding film and video at the Festival. The following awards are presented: JIFAS Grand Prix, JIFAS Hakuba Prize, Prizes for Excellence, and Special Mention by the Jury. Awarded biennially at the convention. Established in 1986.

8623
Japan International League of Artists
(Kokusai Gejutsu Renmei)
2-3-16-607 Shinjuku
Shinjuku-ku
Tokyo 160, Japan
Phone: 3 33564033
Fax: 3 33565780

8624
Tokyo International Competition for Chamber Music
For recognition of an outstanding chamber music composition. Composers of all ages and nationalities are eligible to enter. The following monetary prizes are awarded: first prize - 300,000 yen; second prize - 150,000 yen; and third prize - 100,000 yen. Awarded biennially. Established in 1986. Formerly: Tokyo Interntional Competition for Guitar COmpositions; Tokyo International Competition for Guitar Composition.

8625
Japan Newspaper Publishers and Editors Association
(Nihon Shinbun Kyokai)
Nippon Press Center Bldg.
2-2-1 Uchisaiwai-cho
Chiyoda-ku
Tokyo 100, Japan
Phone: 3 35914401
Fax: 3 35916149

8626
Newspaper Advertising Prize
(Shimbun Kokoku Sho)
To honor advertising activities for the year that point the way to new possibilities of newspaper advertising and of contributing to the development of newspapers and advertising. Prizes are given in the Advertiser Planning Division and the Newspaper Company Planning Division, and are awarded to the advertising staff of advertisers and newspapers for newspaper advertising campaigns of distinction.

8627
Newspaper Culture Award
(Shimbun Bunka Sho)
To recognize personalities who have made great contributions over an extended period to the cause of newspaper culture in the country. Eighteen individuals have received this award since its establishment in 1951.

8628
Nihon Shinbun Kyokai Awards
(Shinbum Kyokai Sho)
For recognition of distinguished contributions towards promoting the credibility and authority of newspapers, news agencies, and broadcasting organizations in the eyes of the general public. Members of the Association are eligible. Certificates and medals are given in the following categories: editorial field, management and business field, and technical field. Awarded annually. Established in 1957.

8629
Vaughn - Ueda Prize
(Vaughn - Ueda Sho)
To recognize a journalist who has contributed to the cause of promoting international understanding through international reporting activities. The awardee is chosen among journalists working for newspapers, news agencies, and broadcasting organizations belonging to Nihon Shinbun Kyokai. A monetary prize, a certificate, and bronze bookends are awarded annually in March. Established in 1950 in memory of Mr. Miles W. Vaughn, Vice President of the United Press, and Mr. Teizo Ueda, President of Dentsu, the foremost advertising agency in Japan, who met their untimely deaths in 1949 while duck hunting on a boat on Tokyo Bay. The original funds for the prize were contributed by the U.P.I. and Dentsu. In 1985, the prize was revitalized financially with contributions from six big daily newspapers and two news agencies in Japan. Formerly: (1978) Vaughn Prize.

8630
Japan Poets' Association
322 Temjin-cho Kamimaruko
Nakahara-ku
Kawasaki 211, Japan
Phone: 44 722 7961

8631
Modern Poet Prize
For recognition of achievement in the field of poetry. A monetary prize of 500,000 yen is awarded annually. Established in 1983. Additional information is available from Yutaka Akiya, 3-2-10 Motomachi, Urawa 336, Japan.

8632
Mr. H's Prize
To encourage the professional development of a new poet. A monetary prize of 500,000 yen is awarded annually. Established in 1951. Additional information is available from Yutaka Akiya, 3-2-10 Motomachi, Urawa 336, Japan.

8633
Japan Society for Analytical Chemistry
(Nihon Bunsekikagaku-Kai)
Gotanda Sanhaitsu
1-26-2 Nishigotanda
Shinagawa-ku
Tokyo 141, Japan
Phone: 3 3490 3351

8634
Japan Society for Analytical Chemistry Award
To recognize either members of the Society who have done distinguished work in analytical chemistry or outstanding persons who have published their work in the Society's proceedings and other scientific journals. Nominations may come from local chapters of the Society and members directly, but are not confined to these sources. A monetary prize and a medal are awarded. The following prizes may be awarded: (1) Analytical Chemistry Awards; (2) Analytical Chemistry Award for Technical Achievement; and (3) Analytical Chemistry Award for Younger Researchers. Established in 1952.

8635
Japan Society for the Promotion of Science
(Nihon Gakujutsu Shinko-Kai)
Committee on the International Prize for
  Biology
General Affairs Section
5-3-1, Kojimachi
Chiyoda-Ku
Tokyo 102, Japan
Phone: 3 3263 1721
Fax: 3 3237 8238

8636
International Prize for Biology
(Kokusai Seibutsugaku-sho)
To recognize an individual for an outstanding contribution to the advancement of research in fundamental biology. The specialty within the field of biology for which the Prize is awarded is decided upon annually. There are no restrictions on the nationality of the recipient. Nominations must be submitted by relevant organizations and authoritative individuals by June 30. A monetary award of 10,000,000 yen, a medal, and an Imperial gift are awarded annually in Tokyo in the autumn. The Prize is normally made to one individual. In the event of a Prize being shared by two or more individuals, each receives a medal and an equal share of the

monetary prize. Established in 1985 to celebrate the sixty-year reign of His Majesty the Emperor Showa of Japan and to commemorate the Emperor's longtime devotion to research in biology.

8637
Japan Society for Translators
(Nihon Hon'yakukka Kyokai)
c/o Orion Press
1-55 Kanda-Jimbocho
Chiyoda-ku
Tokyo, Japan
Phone: 3 3294 3936

8638
Japan Translation Culture Prize
(Nihon Honyaku Bunkasho)
To encourage translation from and into the Japanese language without discrimination of nationality and to recognize the most outstanding translation of the year. Subject fields are not restricted. A monetary prize, a plaque and a citation are awarded annually. Established in 1964.

8639
Japan Translation Prize for Publishers
(Nihon Honyaku Shuppan Bunkasho)
To recognize a publisher who has planned and published, along with the translator or translators, valuable works which the selection committee deems will contribute to the enhancement of international understanding. A plaque and citation are awarded annually. Established in 1965.

8640
Japan Society of Human Genetics
(Nihon Jinrui Iden Gakkai)
Dept. of Human Genetics
Tokyo Medical and Dental Univ.
1-5-45 Yushima
Bunkyo-ku
Tokyo, Japan
Phone: 3 3813 6111

8641
Japan Society of Human Genetics Award
(Nihon Jinrui Iden Gakkai Sho)
To recognize individuals who have made a great contribution to the development of human genetics in Japan. Individuals who are recommended by counselors or honorary members of the Society are considered by the award committee. A monetary prize, a medal, and a certificate are awarded annually at the general assembly of the Society. Established in 1959 by Tenamoto Furuhata, M.D., first president of the Society.

8642
Japan Society of Mechanical Engineers
(Nihon Kikai Gakkai)
Shinjuku Sanshin Bldg.
2-4-9, Yoyogi
Shibuya-Ku
Tokyo 151, Japan
Phone: 3 33796781
Fax: 3 33790934

8643
JSME Medal
For recognition of outstanding technical papers and for recognition of achievement in developing new techniques in the field of mechanical engineering. Members are eligible. A medal and certificate of merit are awarded annually at the Plenary Meeting. Established in 1958.

8644
Japan Welding Society
(Yosetsu Gakkai)
1-11 Sakumacho, Kanda
Chiyoda-ku
Tokyo 101, Japan
Phone: 3 32530488
Fax: 3 32533059

8645
Japan Welding Society Award
To provide recognition for distinguished contributions to the advancement of welding engineering and technology and for major contributions to the activities of the Society. Members of the Society are eligible. A monetary prize and a certificate are awarded annually. Established in 1944.

8646
JWS Citation Award for Papers of the Year
To recognize the author of a published work that has made a major contribution to the advancement of welding engineering and technology. A certificate and a medal are awarded annually. Established in 1950.

8647
Kikundo Tanaka Memorial Award
To encourage the advancement of welding technology, and to honor distinguished contributions to the development and improvement of welding technology. Members of the Society are eligible. A monetary prize and a certificate are awarded annually. Established in 1967.

8648
Sasaki Memorial Award
To recognize a member of the Society for major services to the development and dissemination of welding technology and to the education of welding technicians. A certificate and a medal are awarded annually. Established in 1955.

8649
Japanese Biochemical Society
Ishikawa Bldg., Ste. 3f
5-25-16 Hongo
Bunkyo-ku
Tokyo 113, Japan
Phone: 3 3815 1913

8650
Japanese Biochemical Society's Shorei-Sho Awards
To encourage the professional development of young biochemists. Members who are under 40 years of age are eligible. A monetary prize of 100,000 yen and a plaque are awarded annually in October. Established in 1955 by Professor Soda Tokuro.

8651
Japanese Society for Tuberculosis
(Nippon Kekkaku-byo Gakkai)
c/o Research Institute of Tuberculosis, JATA
3-1-24 Matsuyama
Kiyose-Shi
Tokyo 204, Japan
Phone: 424 92 2091
Fax: 424 91 8315

8652
Imamura Memorial Prize
To encourage studies on tuberculosis, with special emphasis on research by young scientists. A monetary prize of 200,000 yen and a certificate are awarded annually. Established in 1969.

8653
Japanese Society of Applied Entomology and Zoology
(Nippon Oyo Dobutsu Konchu Gakkai)
c/o Japan Plant Protection Association
Komagome 1-43-11
Toshima-ku
Tokyo 170, Japan

Phone: 3 39436021
Fax: 3 39436021

8654
Nippon Oyo Dobutsu Konchu Gakkai Sho
For recognition of achievement in the field of applied entomology and zoology. Society members must be nominated by a member of the board. A monetary prize, a medal, and a diploma are awarded annually at the convention. Established in 1957.

8655
Japanese Society of Hematology
(Nippon Ketsueki Gakkai)
Dept. of Internal Medicine
Medical Faculty, Kyoto Univ.
54 Shogoin Kawaharacho
Sakyo-ku
Kyoto 606, Japan

Phone: 75 7518982
Fax: 75 7520761

8656
Usui Foundation for Hematological Research
(Usui Ketsuekigaku Kenkyu-Kikin)
To promote investigations in hematological study. Members of the Society who are under 45 years of age may apply. A monetary award for travel to present one's work at the International Society of Hematology meeting is presented biennially. Established in 1981 by Akira Usui.

8657
Young Investigator Award
(Nihon Ketsueki Gakkai Shorei Sho)
To encourage further studies in hematology. Winners are selected from papers presented by young investigators under 40 years of age at the annual meeting. A monetary award of 200,000 yen and a certificate are presented annually. Established in 1991.

8658
Japanese Society of Sericultural Science
(Nihon Sanshi Gakkai)
c/o Nat.Inst. of Sericultural and
 Entomological Science
Owashi 1-2, Tsukuba
Ibaraki 305, Japan

8659
Japanese Society of Sericultural Science Award
(Sanshigaku Sho)
To recognize individuals who have made distinguished contributions in the sericultural science. Society members may apply. A monetary award, a medal and a certificate are awarded annually. Established in 1931.

8660
Sericultural Science Advancement Award
(Sanshigaku Shinpo Sho)
To praise and encourage individuals for original research in sericultural science. Society members who are under 40 years of age are eligible. Awarded annually in April. Established in 1965.

8661
Japanese Society of Snow and Ice
(Nihon Seppyo Gakkai)
Belvedere-Kudan (Rm. 607)
Fujimi 2-15-5
Tokyo 102, Japan

Phone: 3 3261 2339
Fax: 3 3262 1923

8662
Dr. Hirata Award
(Hirata-sho)
To encourage young scientists. Members who are under 35 years of age may be nominated by any member. Selection is by an Ad Hoc Nomination Committee. A monetary prize, a medal, and a certificate are awarded annually when merited. Established in 1969 in memory of Dr. Tokutaro Hirata (1880-1960), the first president of the Society from 1939 to 1960.

8663
Science Award
(Gakujutsu-sho)
For recognition of scientific achievement in glaciology. Members may be nominated by any member. Selection is by an Ad Hoc Nomination Committee. A monetary prize, a medal, and a certificate are awarded annually when merited. Established in 1966.

8664
Service Award
(Koseki-sho)
For recognition of scientific activities and contributions to the Society's development. Members may be nominated by any member. Selection is by an Ad Hoc Nomination Committee. A certificate and medal are awarded annually when merited. Established in 1966.

8665
Japanese Society of Soil Science and Plant Nutrition
(Nippon Dojohiryo Gakkai)
6-26-10-202 Hongo
Bunkyo-ku
Tokyo 113, Japan

Phone: 3 38152085
Fax: 3 38156018

8666
Japanese Society of Soil Science and Plant Nutrition Award
(Nippon Dojohiryo Gakkai Sho)
For recognition of contributions in the field of soil science and plant nutrition. Society membership is necessary for consideration. A plaque is awarded each year at the annual meeting. Established in 1955.

8667
Progress Award of Japanese Society of Soil Science and Plant Nutrition
(Nippon Dojohiryo Gakkai Shorei Sho)
For recognition of progressive contributions in the field of soil science and plant nutrition. Members under 38 years of age are eligible. A plaque is awarded annually. Established in 1982.

8668
Japanese Society of Tribologists
(Nihon Junkatsu Gakkai)
Kikai Shinko Kaikan 407-2
3-5-8 Shiba Koen
Minato-ku
Tokyo 105, Japan

Phone: 3 3434 1926
Fax: 3 3434 3556

Formerly: (1989) Japan Society of Lubrication Engineers.

8669
JSLE Best Paper Award
For recognition of excellence in papers in the field of lubrication engineering. Members of the Society who have presented papers in the

Journal of JSLE during the preceding three years are eligible. A medal is awarded annually at the convention. Established in 1976.

8670

Japanese Society of Veterinary Science
(Nihon Ju-i Gakkai)
Rakuno-Kaikan Bldg.
1-37-20 Yoyogi
Shibuya-ku
Bunkyo-ku
Tokyo 151, Japan
Phone: 3 3379 0636
Fax: 3 3379 0636

8671

Japanese Society of Veterinary Science Award
To recognize and encourage distinctive contributions to veterinary medicine and science. Members of the Society are eligible. Three awards are presented annually, each consisting of 100,000 yen, a medal, and a certificate.

8672

Japanese Society of Zootechnical Science
(Nippon Chikusan Gakkai)
201 Nagatani Cooporas
2-9-4 Ikenohata
Taito-ku
Tokyo 110, Japan
Phone: 3 3828 8409
Fax: 3 3828 7649

8673

Japanese Society of Zootechnical Science Award
(Nippon Chikusan Gakkai Sho)
For recognition of a contribution in the field of animal science and encouragement of further research development. Members of the Society who are under 50 years of age are eligible. A monetary prize of 100,000 yen and a medal are awarded annually. Established in 1957. The award is sponsored by two companies for animal food and dairy production.

8674

Kadokawa Culture Promotion Foundation
(Kadokawa Bunka Shinko Zaidan)
Kadokawa Hongo Bldg.
5-24-5 Hongo
Bunkyo-ku
Tokyo 113, Japan
Phone: 3 3817 8581

8675

All Japan Description Contest from A Pocket Book Reading
To promote and develop the reading ability of junior high school and high school students, and the citizens, and to recognize their studies. Awards are given for a description of a book, within two thousand words, written by a junior high school student, a high school student, and a citizen. Honorable mention, a plaque, and a camera are awarded annually. Established in 1979. Sponsored by the Japan P.T.A. Association, Cannon Seller Inc., and Kadokawa Shoten, Inc.

8676

Choku Prize
For recognition of an excellent collection of Tanka, Japanese verse of thirty-one syllables. Published collections of Tanka are considered for selection by a special committee. A monetary prize of 500,000 yen and a gold watch are awarded annually. Established in 1967 in honor of Shinobu Origuchi, a scholar of Japanese literature and folklore and a poet of Tanka, whose pen name was Choku.

8677

Dakotsu Prize
For recognition of a collection of Haiku, Japanese verse of seventeen syllables. Published collections of Haiku are considered for selection by a special committee. A monetary award of 500,000 yen and a gold watch are awarded annually. Established in 1967 in honor of Dakotsu Iida, a famous poet of Haiku, whose pen name was Dakotsu.

8678

Japanese Non-Fiction Prize
To provide recognition for the best work of nonfiction by a Japanese writer. Books, magazine articles, and manuscripts are eligible for selection by a special committee. Translations are not accepted. A monetary prize of 500,000 yen and a bronze trophy are awarded annually. In addition, a New Writer Prize of 300,000 yen and a gold watch are also awarded annually. Established in 1974.

8679

Genyoshi Kadokawa Prize
To provide recognition for a distinguished work on Japanese literature and history. A monetary award of 1,000,000 yen and a gold watch are awarded annually. Established in 1979 in memory of Genyoshi Kadokawa, a poet of Haiku and president of Kadokawa Shoten, Inc.

8680

Kinokuniya Company
3-17-7 Shinjuku
Shinjuku-ku
Tokyo 163-91, Japan
Phone: 3 33540141
Fax: 3 33540405

8681

Kinokuniya Theatre Awards
For recognition of achievement in theater. Actors, playwrights, stage designers, directors of outstanding performances, plays, and theatrical productions may be honored. A monetary prize of 2,000,000 yen is awarded to a company, and prizes of 500,000 yen and remembrances are awarded to individuals. Awarded annually. Established in 1966.

8682

Kobe International Flute Competition
c/o Citizen's Cultural Section
Kobe City, 6-5-1
Kano-cho, Chuo-ku
Kobe-shi 650, Japan
Phone: 78 331 8181
Fax: 78 322 6031

8683

Kobe International Flute Competition
For recognition of outstanding performance on the flute. Individuals between 16 and 32 years of age are eligible to apply by January 31, 1993. The following monetary prizes are awarded: first prize - 1,200,000 yen; second prize - 600,000 yen; third prize - 300,000 yen; fourth, fifth, and sixth prizes - 100,000 yen each; diplomas of merit; and special awards. Awarded quadrenially. Established in 1985.

8684

Kodansha Ltd.
Otowa Daini Bldg.
2-12-21 Otowa
Bunkyo-ku
Tokyo 112, Japan
Phone: 3 944 6491

8685

Gunzo Fiction Prize
To provide recognition for an outstanding work of fiction by a new writer. A monetary prize of 300,000 yen is awarded. Established in 1979.

8686

Kamei Katsuichiro Prize
To provide recognition for the best literary review published during the year by an aspiring younger critic. A monetary prize of 200,000 yen and honorary recognition are awarded annually. Established in 1969.

8687
Kodansha Prize
To recognize a publisher whose books are distinguished for outstanding achievement in the following areas: illustration, photographs, nonfiction, and book design. A monetary award of 300,000 yen, a clock, and honorary recognition are awarded annually. Established in 1970.

8688
Kodansha Prize for Cartoon Book
To provide recognition for the best cartoon book of the year. A monetary prize of 500,000 yen and a clock are awarded annually. Established in 1977.

8689
Noma Illustration Prizes
To provide recognition for the best illustrations of books for children. Artists from Asia, Oceania, Arab States, Africa, Latin America and the Caribbean are eligible. A first prize of $1,000 and second prizes of quartz watches are awarded biennially. Established in 1979 by Shoichi Noma, chairman of Kodansha Publishing Company.

8690
Noma Prize for Juvenile Novel
To provide recognition for the best juvenile novel published during the year. A monetary award of 1,000,000 yen and a medal are awarded annually. Established in 1962.

8691
Noma Prize for Literature
To provide recognition for the best novel published during the year. A monetary award of 2,000,000 yen and a medal are awarded annually. Established in 1941.

8692
Noma Prize for Translation
For recognition of outstanding translations of modern Japanese literature. A monetary prize of $10,000 is awarded annually. Established in 1990.

8693
Yoshikawa Eiji Literary Prize
(Yoshikawa Eiji Bungaku Sho)
To provide recognition for the most popular novel published during the year. A monetary prize of 2,000,000 yen and a medal are awarded annually. Established in 1967.

8694
Yoshikawa Elji Prize
To recognize individuals or groups who have limited opportunities to receive awards in spite of their distinguished contributions to the culture of Japan. A monetary award of 500,000 yen and a statuette are awarded annually. Established in 1961.

8695
Mathematical Society of Japan
(Nihon Sugakukai)
4-25-9-203 Hongo
Bunkyo-ku
Tokyo 113, Japan   Phone: 3 3816 5961

8696
Nihon Sugakukai Iyanaga Sho
To encourage and recognize young mathematicians who contributed significantly to the development of mathematics. Members under 40 years of age may be nominated. A monetary prize of 100,000 yen, a Certificate of Merit and an invitation to a plenary address at the annual meeting are awarded in April at the annual meeting. Established in 1973 by the Mathematical Society of Japan with a donation from Professor Shokichi Iyanaga. The award is named for Professor Shokichi Iyanaga.

8697
Meiji Shrine Treasure Museum
(Meiji Jingu Homotsuden)
1-1 Yoyogi, Shibuya-ku
Tokyo, Japan   Phone: 3 379 5511

8698
Meijimura Prize
For recognition of a contribution to research on the scholarship and art of the Meiji period. A monetary prize of 500,000 yen is awarded annually. Established in 1975.

8699
Mita Society for Library and Information Science
(Mita Toshakan Joho Gakkai)
c/o School of Library and Information
   Science
Keio University
2-15-45 Mita
Minato-ku   Phone: 3 34533920
Tokyo 108, Japan   Fax: 3 37987480

8700
Mita Society for Library and Information Science Prize
(Mita Toshokan Joho Gakkai-Sho)
For recognition of achievement in the field of library and information science. Papers published in the *Library and Information Science* are eligible for consideration. A monetary prize is awarded annually at the Society convention. Established in 1977.

8701
Mobil Sekiyu Kabushiki Kaisha
PO Box 5010
Tokyo Int.   Phone: 3 3244 4496
Tokyo 10031, Japan   Fax: 3 3244 4078

8702
Mobil Children's Culture Award
For recognition of a contribution to children's culture in Japan. Candidates are recommended in questionnaire returns from authorities in the fields of education, culture, and the press. A monetary prize of 2,000,000 yen and the Pegasus Trophy are presented annually. Established in 1966.

8703
Mobil Music Award
To recognize an individual or a group for a conspicuous contribution to the development of musical art in Japan. Awards are given in two divisions, Western Classical Music, and Japanese Traditional Music. A monetary prize of 2,000,000 yen and the Pegasus Trophy are awarded to the Japanese and Western music award winners. Awarded annually. Established in 1971.

8704
Naito Foundation
3-42-6, Hongo
Bunkyo-ku   Phone: 3 38133005
Tokyo 113, Japan   Fax: 3 38112917

8705
Naito Foundation Research Prize
(Naito Kinen Kagaku Shinko Sho)
For recognition of outstanding contributions to the advancement of the life sciences. Directors and trustees of the Foundation, and societies in the field of life science may submit recommendations by November 20. A monetary prize of 3,000,000 yen and a gold medal are awarded annually. Established in 1969 by Toyoji Naito.

8706

Nikkei Economic Journal
(Nihon Keizai Shimbun)
1-9-5 Otemachi
Chiyoda-ku
Tokyo 100, Japan   Phone: 3 3270 0251

8707

Nikkei Advertising Awards
To encourage creativity in producing advertisements which have contributed to the success of individual companies and organizations, to reward effective advertisements, and to elevate advertising design techniques. Advertising agents, designers, and copywriters whose advertisements run in the *Nihon Keizai Shimbun*, the *Nikkei Sangyo Shimbun*, the *Nikkei Ryutsu Shimbun* newspapers, and shopping and science magazines are eligible. Trophies, certificates of merit, and monetary prizes are awarded annually.

8708

Niwano Peace Foundation
(Niwano Heiwa Zaidan)
Shamville Catherina 5F
1-16-9 Shinjuku
Shinjuku-ku   Phone: 3 32264371
Tokyo 160, Japan   Fax: 3 32261835

8709

Niwano Peace Prize
To recognize an individual or organization that is making a significant contribution to world peace through promoting inter-religious cooperation. The Foundation solicits nominations from people of recognized intellectual stature around the world. A prize of 20 million yen, a medal, and a certificate are awarded annually. Established in 1983.

8710

Oita International Wheelchair Marathon
3-1-1 Ohte Machi   Phone: 975 36 1111
Oita City 870, Japan   Phone: 975 33 0332

8711

Oita International Wheelchair Marathon
For recognition of achievement in wheelchair racing, and to encourage each individual to have a fighting spirit beyond handicaps. Disabled persons over 16 years of age using a wheelchair may apply by August 31. Trophies are awarded to the top 10 runners, cups to the male and female winners of the total marathon, medals to the top runners of the five classes and certificates are awarded to all who complete the course. Awarded annually. Established in 1981 by Hiramatsu Morihiko, Oita Prefectural Governor. Sponsored by Oita City, Oita Godo Newspaper Company, OMRON Co., SONY, HONDA, etc. Additional information is available from Hirakawa Matsuko, c/o Japan Sun Industries, Kamegawa Beppu, Oita 874-01, Japan, phone: 977 66 0277, fax: 977 67 0453.

8712

Organizing Committee for the Winter Universiade
Sapporo MN-Bldg.
North 1, West 3, Chuo-Ku   Phone: 11 211 3111
Sapporo 060, Japan   Fax: 11 241 0700

8713

Asian Winter Games, Sapporo
For recognition of outstanding sports performance in the following events: (1) Biathlon; (2) Alpine Skiing; (3) Short Track Speed Skating; (4) Cross Country Skiing; (5) Ice Hockey; and (6) Speed Skating. Established in 1989.

8714

Pharmaceutical Society of Japan
(Nihon Yakugakkai)
2-12-15 501 Shibuya
Shibuya-ku
Tokyo 150, Japan   Phone: 3 3406 3321

8715

PSJ Award
(Nihon Yakugakkai Gakkaisho)
For recognition of achievement in the field of pharmaceutical sciences. Society members are eligible. A monetary prize and a medal are awarded annually. Established in 1921. Sponsored by the Research Foundation for Pharmaceutical Sciences.

8716

PSJ Award for Distinguished Service
(Nihon Yakugakkai Korosho)
For recognition of a contribution to the Society. Society members are eligible. A monetary prize and a medal are awarded annually. Established in 1963. Sponsored by the Research Foundation for Pharmaceutical Sciences.

8717

PSJ Award for Divisional Scientific Contributions
(Nihon Yakugakkai Gakujutsukokensho)
To recognize a contribution to a divisional field of the pharmaceutical sciences. Society members are eligible. A monetary prize and a medal are awarded annually. Established in 1994.

8718

PSJ Award for Drug Research and Development
(Nihon Yakugakkai Gijutsusho)
For recognition of achievement in the field of research and development of a new drug (including intermediates of a new drug, diagnostic reagent, etc.). Society members and non-members are eligible. A monetary prize and a medal are awarded annually. Established in 1987.

8719

PSJ Award for Educational Services
(Nihon Yakugakkai Kyoikusho)
For recognition of a contribution to education in the pharmaceutical sciences. Society members are eligible. A monetary prize and a medal are awarded annually. Established in 1963. Sponsored by the Research Foundation for Pharmaceutical Sciences.

8720

PSJ Award for Young Scientists
(Nihon Yakugakkai Shoreisho)
To encourage research development. Society members under 40 years of age are eligible. A monetary prize and a medal are awarded annually. Established in 1955. Sponsored by the Research Foundation for Pharmaceutical Sciences.

8721

Photographic Society of Japan
JCII Bldg., 1st Fl.
25 Ichiban-cho
Chiyoda-ku   Phone: 3 5276 3585
Tokyo 102, Japan   Fax: 3 5276 3586

8722

Photographic Society of Japan Awards
To recognize individuals or groups of any nationality for contributions to the field of photography. Honorary recognition and a medal are awarded annually.

8723

**Phytopathological Society of Japan
(Nippon Shokubutsu-Byori Gakkai)**
Shokubo Bldg.
1-43-11 Komagome
Toshima-Ku
Tokyo 170, Japan
Phone: 3 39436021
Fax: 3 39436021

8724

Phytopathological Society of Japan Prize
For recognition of achievement in phytopathology, or for contributions to the Society. A monetary award of 50,000 yen, a certificate, and a watch are awarded annually. Established in 1953.

8725

Phytopathological Society of Japan Scientific Research Promotion Award
To encourage professional development in the field of phytopathology. A monetary award of 30,000 yen, a certificate, and a medal are awarded annually. Established in 1953.

8726

**Publishers Association for Cultural Exchange
(Shuppan Bunka Kokusai Koryukai)**
1-2-1 Sarugaku-cho
Chiyoda-ku
Tokyo 101, Japan
Phone: 3 3291 5685
Fax: 3 3233 3645

8727

International Publications Cultural Award
For recognition of books or periodicals published in a European language in Japan that contribute to raising the level of world culture or to increasing understanding of Japan. The Grand Prix is awarded by the Foreign Minister. Special Prizes are awarded by the Japan Foundation, the Mainichi Newspaper, the Japan Broadcasting Corporation, and the Publishers Association for Cultural Exchange. The following Special Prizes are awarded biennially: Japan Foundation Prize; Mainichi Newspaper Prize; and NHK Prize (Japan Broadcasting Corporation Prize). Awarded biennially. Established in 1966. (Temporarily inactive)

8728

**Sankei Shimbun
(Sankei Shinbun-Sha)**
1-7-2 Ohtemachi
Chiyoda-ku
Tokyo 100-77, Japan
Phone: 3 3231 7111

8729

Sankei Jidoh Bunka Shuppan Shoh
For recognition of outstanding books for children and for illustrators of children's books. Books published during the preceding year for children are eligible. A Grand Award, Award for Art, and other awards are presented annually on March 5. Established in 1954. Additional information is available from Fuji TV Broadcast, and Nippon Houson Radio Broadcast.

8730

Sapporo Sports Promotion Corporation
Board of Education of Sapporo
Nishi 14 - chome
Minami 1 Chuo-ku
Sapporo 060, Japan
Phone: 11 2144666
Fax: 11 2144668

8731

Sapporo International Ski Marathon
For promotion of cross-country skiing, and to recognize the winners of a 50 km cross country marathon race. Open to both men and women over 19 years of age. The deadline for entry is the end of December. Certificates, plaques, and some extra prizes are awarded annually. Established in 1981.

8732

SBA Consulting Group
Daini Toranomon Denki Bldg.
3-1-10 Toranomon
Minato-Ku
Tokyo 105, Japan
Phone: 3 34319731
Fax: 3 34343820

8733

Prize Mission Special Japan
To provide European students with the opportunity to spend three months in Japan gaining professional exposure through a "personal mission" project. Eligible candidates must be second-year or recently graduated university students of business, engineering, law, design, fashion, or architecture and must be proficient in English. A monetary award and round-trip ticket to Tokyo are awarded.

8734

Prize Objective Japan
To enable European managers to have a deeper knowledge of their Japanese partners, and to contribute to the improvement of relations between European professionals and their Japanese counterparts. SBA is offering young professionals interested in Japan the unique opportunity of "true immersion" into the Japanese business world. Open to graduates from top European universities, business and engineering schools, and fashion, design and architecture schools who have professional experience and are especially interested in Japan. Applications must be submitted by June 1. The winner is awarded a one-year contract as junior consultant in the SBA Consulting Group, which includes a six-month intensive program studying the Japanese language. In addition, Prize Objective Japan - Students is open to students of the same schools who have not graduated yet. The winner is awarded a 2,800 Ecu scholarship to pursue a project study in Japan during the following year. Awarded annually. Established in 1983. Formerly: (1991) Prix Vocation Japon.

8735

Science and Technology Foundation of Japan (JSTF)
Shisei-Kaikan 5F
Hibiya-koen 1-3
Chiyoda-ku
Tokyo 100, Japan
Phone: 3 3508 7691
Fax: 3 3508 7691

Formerly: (1983) Japan Prize Preparatory Foundation.

8736

Japan Prize
This, the most prestigious and honored scientific prize in Japan, is given to recognize scientists and technologists from all parts of the world. It is awarded to persons recognized as having served the cause of peace and prosperity for mankind through original and outstanding achievements in science and technology which have advanced the frontiers of knowledge in these fields. No distinctions are made as to nationality, occupation, race or sex, but only living persons may be named Japan Prize Laureates. Award categories change annually. Awards have been presented in the following areas: biological functions; materials science and technology; information and communications; energy technology; preventive medicine; technology integration; and applied mathematics. The award categories for 1989 are environmental science and technology, and medicinal science. Two laureates are selected each year. A monetary award of 50 million yen (about $360,000), a medal and a certificate are awarded in April during Japan Prize Week. Established in 1982. The first awards were presented in 1985.

| 8737 |

Shibusawa Foundation for Ethnological Studies
3-1-17 Higashicho
Hoya-Shi
Tokyo 202, Japan
Phone: 3 424215003
Fax: 3 424219679

Formerly: (1991) K. Shibusawa Memorial Foundation for Ethnology.

| 8738 |

Shibusawa Memorial Prize
To encourage development in the field of ethnological studies. Members of the Japanese Society of Ethnology under 39 years of age are eligible. A monetary prize, a medal, and a certificate of merit are awarded biennially. Established in 1964 by the Foundation in memory of Keizo Shibusawa.

| 8739 |

Shin Jinbutsu Oraisha Company
Shin Tokyo Bldg.
3-3-1 Marunouchi
Chiyoda-ku
Tokyo 100, Japan
Phone: 3 32123931
Fax: 3 32147355

| 8740 |

Historical Literature Award
(Rekishi Bungaku Sho)
To recognize the best literary work on a historical theme (not only the history of Japan but also Western or Oriental history). Unpublished work may be submitted. The deadline is June 30. A monetary award of 1,000,000 yen and a memorial are awarded annually in January. Established in 1975 to commemorate the 20th anniversary of the founding of Rekishi Dokuhon, the monthly magazine of history.

| 8741 |

Shincho-Sha Publishing Company
71 Yarai-cho
Shinjuku-ku
Tokyo 162, Japan
Phone: 3 3266 5151
Fax: 3 3266 5112

| 8742 |

Japan Art Award
To recognize the best work of art in any medium during the preceding year. A monetary prize of 1,000,000 yen is awarded annually in May. Established in 1987 by Shincho-Bungei-Shinkokai.

| 8743 |

Yukio Mishima Award
To recogznize cultural achievements. A monetary prize of 1,000,000 yen is awarded annually in May. Established in 1987 by Shincho-Bungei-Shinkokai. The award honors the memory of Yukio Mishima.

| 8744 |

Shincho Art and Science Award
To recognize contributions in art and science. A monetary prize of 1,000,000 yen is awarded annually in May. Established in 1987 by Shincho-Bungei-Shinkokai. Established in 1987.

| 8745 |

Shugoro Yamamoto Award
To recognize cultural achievements. A monetary prize of 1,000,000 yen is awarded annually in May. Established in 1987 by Shincho Society for the Promotion of Literature.

| 8746 |

Shogakukan
2-3-1 Hitotsubashi
Chiyoda-Ku
Tokyo 101-01, Japan
Phone: 3 32305658
Fax: 3 32889653

| 8747 |

Shogakukan Bungaku-Sho
For recognition in the field of children's literature. Literature, poems, and stage-plays originally written and published in books, magazines, and newspapers during the preceding year, April through March, are eligible. A monetary prize of 1,000,000 yen and a bronze statue titled "Wakaba" (verdure) by Chizuko Sasdo are awarded annually in early November at the public presentation. Established in 1952 in celebration of the publishing house Shogakukan's 30th anniversary. Formerly: Shogakukan Jido-Bunka-Sho.

| 8748 |

Shogakukan Kaiga-Sho
To recognize an illustration, originally written for children and published in books, magazines, and newspapers during the preceding year, between April and March. A monetary prize of 1,000,000 yen and a bronze statue titled "Wakaba" (verdure) by Chizuko Sasado are awarded annually in early November at the public presentation. Established in 1952 in celebration of the publishing house Shogakukan's 30th Anniversary. Formerly: Shogakukan Jido-Bunka-Sho.

| 8749 |

Society for the Promotion of Japanese Literature
Bungei Shunju Publishing Company
3-23 Kioi-cho
Chiyoda-ku
Tokyo 102, Japan
Phone: 3 32651211
Fax: 3 32652624

| 8750 |

Akutagawa Prize
This, one of the most important literary prizes in Japan, is given to excellent up-and-coming novelists in the field of belles-lettres. A monetary prize of 1,000,000 yen and a watch are awarded twice a year. Established in 1935 by Kan Kikuchi in memory of the novelist, Ryunosuke Akutagawa. Sponsored by Bungei Shunju Ltd.

| 8751 |

Bungakukai Shinjin Sho
(Bungakukai Prize for New Writers)
To recognize the most promising new Japanese writers. A monetary prize of 500,000 yen is awarded twice a year. Established in 1955.

| 8752 |

Kikuchi Prize
To provide recognition for significant achievement in Japanese literature, drama, cinema, newspapers, broadcasting, or magazine publication, and for distinguished service in introducing Japanese literature to America and to Europe. A monetary prize of 1,000,000 yen and a watch is awarded annually. Established in memory of the playwright and novelist who founded Bungei Shunju Sha, Kan Kikuchi.

| 8753 |

Naoki Prize
To recognize excellent novelists in the field of popular literature. A monetary prize of 1,000,000 yen and a watch are awarded twice a year. Established in 1935 by Kan Kikuchi in memory of the novelist, Sanjugo Naoki. Sponsored by Bungei Shunju Ltd.

| 8754 |

Oya Soichi Non-Fiction Prize
To encourage new nonfiction writers and to introduce outstanding works to the world of literature. A monetary award of $3,000 and an around-the-

world airplane ticket from Japan Air Lines are awarded annually. Established in 1968.

8755
Society of Exploration Geophysicists of Japan (Butsuri-Tansa Gakkai)
San-es Bldg.
2-2-18 Nakamagome
Ota-ku
Tokyo, Japan   Phone: 3 3343 0871

8756
Butsuri-Tansa Gakkai-sho (Society of Exploration Geophysicists of Japan Award)
For recognition of achievement in and/or contributions to the geophysical exploration field. The awards committee annually makes nominations from the contributors to the Society journal for the preceding three years or those who are recommended by Society members. An honorary certificate and plaque are awarded annually. Established in 1960.

8757
Sony Foundation of Science Education
4-17-26 Mita
Minato-ku
Tokyo 108, Japan   Phone: 3 456 5811

8758
Sony Science Education Promotion Fund
To promote science education in elementary and junior high schools in Japan. Teachers may submit papers written in Japanese in accordance with application requirement on the subject of how they develop students' abilities in nature study. Monetary awards and certificates are presented annually. Established in 1959 by Masaru Ibuka, founder of Sony Corporation, who is chairman of the Foundation. Sponsored by Sony Corporation, Ltd.

8759
Spirit of Place - Sendai Planning Committee
EST (Environmental Style and Trend)
1-33 Hasekura-Machi, Aoba-Ku   Phone: 22 263 2006
Sendai City 980, Japan   Fax: 22 263 2009

8760
Sendai International Design Competition
To recognize contributions to the emergent need of new concepts in terms of city design/urban planning which encourage an ecologically sustainable society. Entry is open to anyone. The following monetary prizes are awarded: (1) First Prize - 500,000 yen; (2) Second Prize - 300,000 yen; (3) Third Prize - 100,000 yen; and (4) five Recognitions - 50,000 yen each. Established in 1991. Sponsored by the Society of Architects, Miyagi Chapter and major general contractors in the Sendai area. Additional information is available from YSK, 25-25 Tachimachi, Kimura Bldg., Aoba-Ku, Sendai 980, Japan.

8761
Suntory Foundation
Suntory Annex
1-5, Dojima Zchome
Kite-Ku   Phone: 6 3426221
Osaka 530, Japan   Fax: 6 3426220

8762
Takeshi Kaiko Award
To recognize creative observations of human nature, rich in adventure and humor. Fiction is welcome, but entries may also be nonfiction, reveiws, or reports. Unpublished works only are accepted. English manuscripts must be between 8,250 and 82,500 words in length. Manuscripts in Japanese must be between 50 to 500 pages of Japanese 400-character sheets. In addition, a three-page synopsis (in English or Japanese) must be attached. (Submissions in languages other than Japanese or English must be accompanied by a Japanese or English translation which is equivalent to the original in length.) All entries must be postmarked by October 31. A monetary award of 3,000,000 yen and a grand prize trophy are awarded. In addition, a special memento is presented by the Kaiko family. Established in 1990 in memory of Takeshi Kaiko, one of Japan's best loved writers. For over four decades until his death in 1989, Takeshi Kaiko made many outstanding contributions to modern Japanese literature. Additional information is available from Takeshi Kaiko Award Secretariat, c/o TBS Britannica Company Ltd., Shuwa Sanbancho Bldg., 28-1, Sanbancho, Chiyoda-ku, Tokyo 102, Japan, phone: 03-3238-5956.

8763
Suntory Prize for Community Cultural Activities
To recognize individuals and organizations for outstanding contributions to the cultural life of their communities. Wide-ranging activities intended for the creation or furtherance of local cultures are eligible for this prize, such as arts, literature, publication, succession of traditions, beautification of environment, and even food, shelter, and clothing, as well as international exchange and community activities. Awarded annually. Established in 1979.

8764
Suntory Prize for Social Sciences and Humanities
To recognize pioneering achievements by rising critics and researchers in the following four fields: political science and economics, literary and art criticism, life and society, and history and civilization. The work must have been published in Japanese during the preceding year. Awarded annually. Established in 1979.

8765
Tokyo Geographical Society
12-2 Nibancho
Chiyoda-ku   Phone: 3 32610809
Tokyo 102, Japan   Fax: 3 32630257

8766
Medal of the Tokyo Geographical Society
For recognition of a contribution to a field of geoscience and to the society. Selection is by nomination. A medal is awarded at the convention. Established in 1879.

8767
Tokyo International Film Festival
Asano Bldg. 3
2-4-19 Ginza
Chuo-Ku   Phone: 3 563 6305
Tokyo 104, Japan   Fax: 3 563 6310

8768
Tokyo International Film Festival
To promote cultural exchange, friendship, mutual understanding and cooperation among the nations of the world through films, as well as to raise the motion picture arts and sciences and develop the international film industry. The Festival consists of the following competitive sections: (1) The International Competition; and (2) Young Cinema. Films produced in 35mm or 70mm during the 18 months preceding the Festival that have not won an award at other competitive events may be entered by June 10 in the International Competition. The following prizes are awarded: (1) Tokyo Grand Prix - a statuette sculpted by the late Sebo Kitamura; (2) Special Jury Prize; (3) Best Director; (4) Best Actress; (5) Best Actor; (6) Best Artistic Contribution; and (7) Best Screenplay. Each winner receives a trophy and a diploma. The Young Cinema Festival section is designed to encourage the development of world cinema arts by providing promising young international filmmakers, upon whose cinematic talents the film industries of tomorrow depend, with venues for interchange and competition. Film directors satisfying either one of the following categories are eligible: (a) under 35 years of age and directed no more than five

commercially exploited films; or (b) made debut as a film director with this entry film. Films must be submitted by June 5. The international jury of Young Cinema will then judge the winners to receive two awards from those four film candidates: (1) Sakura Gold - for one film, with the prize money of 20,000,000 yen to the director; and (2) Sakura Silver - for one film, with the prize money of 10,000,000 yen to the director. Established in 1985. The festival is held biennially.

8769
Tokyo International Music Competition
1-32-13 Kita-Shinjuku
Shinjuku-ku
Tokyo 160, Japan
Phone: 3 3371 5103
Fax: 3 3361 9477

8770
Tokyo International Music Competition
(Internationaler Musikwettbewerb Tokyo)
For recognition of outstanding work in the field of music. Awards are given in alternate years in the following categories: (1) vocal music; (2) conducting; and (3) chamber music. Individuals of any age or nationality may enter, except in the vocalist competition where they must be between 20 and 36 years of age. The following awards are presented: (1) a monetary award of 800,000 yen, a certificate and medal - first place; (2) 600,000 yen, a certificate, and a medal - second place; (3) 400,000 yen, a certificate and a medal - third place; (4) 200,000 yen, a certificate and a medal - honorable mention; (5) 600,000 yen - Hideo Saito Award to a contestant whom the Organizing Committee deems superior; and (6) 500,000 yen and a Lufthansa round-trip ticket - Japan-Europe-Overseas Scholarship Grant to a finalist of Japanese citizenship. The Asahi Breweries awards the following supplementary prizes: (1) 500,000 yen and a certificate to the first place winner; (2) 300,000 yen and a certificate to the second place winner; and (3) 200,000 yen and a certificate to the third place winner. Awarded annually. Established in 1966. Mr. Hideo Saito was instrumental in the establishment of the contest.

8771
Tokyo Music Festival Foundation
(Zaidan-hojin Tokyo Ongakusai Kyokai)
Tokyo Broadcasting System, Inc.
5-3-6 Akasaka
Minato-Ku
Tokyo 107, Japan
Phone: 3 3586 2406
Fax: 3 3586 2406

Formerly: Tokyo Popular Music Promotion Association.

8772
Tokyo Music Festival
To encourage the songs and artists with international appeal, musical quality, prospective popularity and performances on the stage for possibly breaking the market worldwide. Professionals may apply, possibly through a Japanese contact such as a record company, music publisher, or promoter. The following monetary prizes are awarded: (1) Grand Prize - 3,000,000 yen and a trophy; (2) Most Outstanding Vocal Performance - 2,000,000 yen and a trophy; (3) two Gold prizes - 1,000,000 yen each and trophies; and (4) three Silver Prizes - 500,000 yen each and trophies. In addition, a Best Arrangers Award, Foreign Judge's Award, Best Composer Award, T.B.S. Award, and Festival Award are presented. Established in 1972 to commemorate the 20th Anniversary of Tokyo Broadcasting System. Sponsored by the Tokyo Broadcasting System, Inc.

8773
UniJapan Film
c/o Assoc. for the Diffusion of Japanese
 Films Abroad
5-5-13 Ginza
Chuo-ku
Tokyo 104, Japan
Phone: 3 3572 5106

8774
Competition for Films and Videos on Japan
To stimulate the production of films on Japan and to recognize films which best introduce Japan abroad. The Competition consists of three categories: (1) films dealing with Japan in general; (2) films dealing with Japanese culture and arts; and (3) films dealing with Japanese science and technology. The Competition is open to all film producing companies and individual producers, both professional and amateur. Films must have been produced during the preceding two years and the format may be 16/35mm film, U-Matic, NTSC, PAL, and SECAM Video. The deadline is February 28. The following prizes are awarded: (1) a Gold Prize and a citation for the best film in each category; (2) a Silver Prize, citations, and special prizes for films meriting special recognition; and (3) *The Japan Times* Prize and the *Asahi Evening News* Prize to the companies producing the films awarded the Gold Prizes. Awarded annually. Established in 1957. Co-sponsored by the Association for the Diffusion of Japanese Films Abroad, the Japan Association of Cultural Film Producers, the Ministry of Foreign Affairs, and *Asahi Shimbun*.

8775
Union of Japanese Scientists and Engineers
(Nihon Kagaku Gijyutsu Renmi)
5-10-11 Sendagaya
Shibuya-Ku
Tokyo 151, Japan
Phone: 3 5379 1227
Fax: 3 3225 1813

8776
Deming Prize
(Demingu Sho)
This, the most prestigious industrial award in Japan, is given to recognize companies that demonstrate their commitment to quality control. Until recently the Deming Prize was restricted to Japanese companies, as its initial purpose was to encourage the development of quality control in Japan. In recent years, however, strong interest in the Deming Application Prize has been shown by non-Japanese companies. Basic regulations have been revised to allow the acceptance of overseas companies as candidates since 1987. The following awards are presented: (1) The Deming Prize for Individual Person: (a) to a person who shows excellent achievement in the theory or application of statistical quality control; or (b) to a person who makes an outstanding contribution to the dissemination of statistical quality control; (2) The Deming Application Prizes: (a) The Deming Application Prize is awarded to the enterprise (or public institution) which achieves in the designated year the most distinctive improvement of performance through the application of statistical quality control; (b) The Deming Application Prize for Small Enterprise is awarded to a small-or medium-sized enterprise which achieves in the designated year the most distinctive improvement of performance through the application of statistical quality control; (c) The Deming Application Prize for Divisions is awarded to a division of an enterprise (or a public institution) which achieves in the designated year the most distinctive improvement of performance through the application of statistical quality control; and (3) Quality Control Award for Factory. A monetary award of 500,000 yen and a medal are awarded annually for the Deming Prize for Individual Person. Established in 1951 to recognize Dr. W. Edwards Deming, an American statistician and proponent of quality control techniques who presented a series of lectures in Japan in 1950.

8777
Universal Medical Esperanto Association
(Universala Medicina Esperanto Asocio)
4-8-9 Iwagami-machi
Maebashi-shi 371, Japan
Phone: 0272 31 7839

Formerly: (1961) Tutmonda Esperantista Kuracista Asocio.

8778
UMEA-Shinoda-Premio
For recognition of achievement in the medical field by an excellent Esperanto article or for a contribution to the Esperanto movement in the medical field. Original articles written in Esperanto are considered. A monetary prize of 500 guilders and a silver medal with a low relief of Dr.

Zamenhof, the initiator of Esperanto, are awarded when merited at the Universal Congress of Esperanto. Established in 1973 by the late Dr. Hideo Shinoda, honorary president of UMEA. Additional information is available from Dr. Imre Ferenczy, Pf. 143, H-9002 Gyor, Hungary. Formerly: (1988) UMEA-Premio (Esperanto).

8779

Victor Company of Japan
3-2-4 Kasumigaseki, Kazan Bldg. 3F
Chiyoda-ku
Tokyo 100, Japan
Phone: 3 3581 5715
Fax: 3 3580 8962

8780

Tokyo Video Festival
For recognition of outstanding achievement in making video compositions. Compositions produced with a video camera may be entered in: (1) Division I (No limitation) - Compositions in any style or any theme are acceptable, in two categories: (a) art-inspired type; and (b) general type; and (2) Division II (Video Letter Exchange) - Compositions that explore the possibilities of video as a means of two-way communication. Any style and any method of video production are accepted. Amateurs, professionals, individuals, and groups of any age or nationality may apply by September 10. No 8mm video tape will be accepted. The following prizes are awarded: (1) Video Grand Prix - $3,500, 10-day round-trip to Japan, a trophy and a citation; (2) JVC President Award - $3,500, 10-day round-trip to Japan, a trophy and a citation; (3) Works of Excellence - $1,500 and $2,000 equivalent in JVC video equipment, a trophy and a citation; (4) Works of Special Distinction - $800 and a citation; and (5) Special Merit Awards - $300 and a citation. Awarded annually, usually in November. Established in 1978. Additional information for United States entrants is available from JVC Company of America, c/o Mr. George Meyer, 41 Slater Drive, Elmwood Park, New Jersey 07407, U.S.A., phone: (201) 794-3900.

8781

Yomiuri International Cooperation Prize
(Yomiuri Kokusai Kyoryoku Sho)
To recognize the person, company, or group which best showed the importance of contribution and cooperation to the international society. A monetary prize of 5,000,000 Japanese yen is awarded annually. Established in 1994 to commemorate the 120th anniversary of the Yomiuri Shimbun.

8782

Waseda University
(Waseda Daigaku)
International Center
1-6-1 Nishiwaseda
Shinjuku-ku
Tokyo 169-05, Japan
Phone: 3 32034141
Fax: 3 32038217

8783

Award for Distinguished Service to Sport
(Sports Korosha)
To honor alumni who have made a distinguished contribution to the promotion of sport. Individuals must be over 70 to be eligible. A gold medal and honorable mention are awarded when merited. Established in 1982.

8784

Award for Distinguished Services to Art
(Geihutsu Korosha)
To honor alumni who have made a distinguished contribution to the promotion of art. Individuals must be over 70 to be eligible. A gold medal and honorable mention are awarded when merited. Established in 1984.

8785

Okuma Academic Commemorative Prize
(Okuma Gakujutsu Kinensho)
To recognize a faculty member(s) whose research achievements have been recognized as distinguished, and who has greatly contributed to the progress in the field of study. A monetary award of 1,000,000 yen and honorable mention are presented annually. Established in 1958 in memory of Marquis Shigenobu Okuma, founder of the University.

8786

Okuma Academic Encouragement Prize
(Okuma Gakujutsu Shoreisho)
To recognize a faculty member(s) who has obtained distinguished research results. A monetary award of 500,000 yen plus honorable mention are presented annually. Established in 1958 in memory of Marquis Shigenobu Okuma, founder of the University.

8787

World Association of Societies of Pathology (Anatomic and Clinical)
Dept. of Clinical Pathology
Jichi Medical School
Minami-Kawachi
Tochigi 320-04, Japan
Phone: 285 442111
Fax: 285 448249

8788

Gold Headed Cane
For recognition of a special contribution to the World Association. The former president of the World Association is ordinarily nominated for this award by the Awards Committee. A gold headed cane and a certificate are awarded when merited at the convention. Established in 1969.

8789

Gordon Signy Foreign Fellowship
To foster cooperation between members, sponsor congresses and conventions, and improve standards in anatomic and clinical pathology. Bestows the Gordon Signy Foreign Fellowship for further training of a pathologist from a developing country.

8790

Yomiuri Shimbun
c/o Office of International Affairs
1-7-1 Otemachi
Chiyoda-ku
Tokyo 100-55, Japan
Phone: 3 3242 1111
Fax: 3 3246 0888

8791

Japan Sports Prize
To recognize the best amateur player or a team. Awarded annually.

8792

Yomiuri Education Prize
To recognize important educators who have made distinguished contributions to their field. Awarded annually.

8793

Yomiuri Human Document Prize
(Yomiuri Human Document Taisho)
To provide recognition for an outstanding work of nonfiction. A monetary prize of 10,000,000 yen is awarded.

8794

Yomiuri International Cartoon Contest
(Yomiuri Kokusai Manga Taisho)
To recognize outstanding works of cartoon and to raise the standard in the field. Individuals, both professionals and amateurs, from any country in the world are eligible. The following monetary prizes are awarded: Grand Prize - 1,000,000 Japanese yen; Hidezo Kondo - 500,000 Japanese

yen; Gold prize - 300,000 Japanese yen; and Special prize of the Selection Committee - 200,000 Japanese yen. Medals are also awarded. Announced annually January 1. Established in 1979.

8795

Yomiuri Literature Prize
(Yomiuri Bungaku Sho)
To provide recognition for the best work of literature in six categories: fiction, essays and travelogues, reviews and biography, poetry and haiku, research and translations, and drama. A monetary prize of 1,000,000 yen is awarded to each winner. Awarded annually. Established in 1948.

8796

Zoological Society of Japan
(Nippon Dobutsu Gakkai)
Toshin Bldg.
Hongo 2-27-2
Bunkyo-Ku
Tokyo 113, Japan
Phone: 3 3814 5675
Phone: 3 3814 5461

8797

Zoological Science Award
To recognize the best original papers published in *Zoological Science* during the preceding year, and to encourage contributions to the Journal. All original papers published in the Journal are considered. A monetary award of 500,000 yen is presented annually at the Society's annual meeting. Established in 1985. Sponsored by Narishige Scientific Instrument Laboratory, Tokyo.

Jordan

8798

Jordan
Ministry of Education
(Jordan
Wizarat-At-Tarbiya Wat Ta'lim)
c/o Awards Committee
PO Box 1646
Amman, Jordan
Phone: 6 07181
Fax: 6 66019

8799

Education Medal
(Wisam Al-Muallim (Al-Tarbiya))
For recognition of an achievement or contribution to a field of education, to encourage professional development, or for recognition of long service. Nominations are made by a special committee formed by the Minister. A monetary prize and a medal are awarded annually. Established in 1968.

Kenya

8800

Disabled Peoples' Finance Trust of Kenya
PO Box 67641
Nairobi, Kenya
Phone: 561530
Fax: 333448

8801

Disability Award
For recognition of social, economic, and political involvement in the disability movement. Selection is by nomination. A monetary prize and travel expenses are awarded at the convention. Established in 1982 by Geoffrey P. Muindi, founder of the Trust.

8802

International Centre of Insect Physiology and Ecology
PO Box 30772
Nairobi, Kenya
Phone: 2 802501
Fax: 2 803360

8803

International Centre of Insect Physiology and Ecology Awards
To recognize individuals for contributions to advanced insect biology research and knowledge and to provide research training to doctoral and postdoctoral fellows. Bestows awards annually.

8804

Kenya National Academy of Sciences
Ministry of Research, Science & Technology
PO Box 39450
Nairobi, Kenya
Phone: 2 721138
Phone: 2 721345

8805

Distinguished Professional Contribution Award
To recognize individuals who have made significant contribution through their profession in promoting culture and technology, e.g., an architect who has designed a building of unique character, an engineer who invents a product, or an artist of outstanding quality. Awarded annually. Established in 1983 by the Government of Kenya. Co-sponsored by the Third World Academy of Sciences.

8806

General Award
To recognize individuals identified from the general public for their distinguished record in the service of Kenya's development. Awarded annually. Established in 1983 by the Government of Kenya. Co-sponsored by the Third World Academy of Sciences.

8807

Honorary Fellow
To recognize an individual for an outstanding contribution to science and technology.

8808

Scholastic Award
To recognize Kenyan scientists who have made distinguished contributions to learning in any of the following areas: biological sciences; physical sciences; social sciences; and humanities and technology. Awarded annually. Established in 1983 by the Government of Kenya. Co-sponsored by the Third World Academy of Sciences.

8809

Kenya Publishers Association
PO Box 72532
Oxford Univ. Press
East and Central Africa
Nairobi, Kenya
Phone: 2 336377

8810

Jomo Kenyatta Prize for Literature
To provide recognition for an outstanding literary work written in the English or Swahili languages. Authors from Kenya, Uganda, or Tanzania were eligible. A monetary prize of 10,000 Kenya shillings, divided between a work in English and a work in Swahili, was awarded annually. (Discontinued in 1981)

8811

United Nations Environment Program
(Programme des Nations Unies pour l'Environnement)
PO Box 30552
Nairobi, Kenya
Phone: 2 621234
Fax: 2 226831

8812

UNEP Sasakawa Environment Prize
For recognition of achievement or contribution in the field of the environment. A monetary prize of $200,000 is awarded annually. Established in 1983 by a $1,000,000 endowment from the Japanese Shipbuilding Industry Foundation.

8813

United Nations Environment Program Awards - Global 500 Roll of Honour
To recognize individuals and organizations prominent in the preservation and improvement of the natural environment. More than five hundred people all over the world have been recognized.

Korea, Republic of

8814

Institute for International Economics
King Sejong Univ.
Seongdong-Ku, Gunja-Dong 98   Phone: 2 4600338
Seoul 133-747, Republic of Korea   Fax: 2 4600200

8815

Daeyang Prize in Economics
To support and encourage research in the area of international trade, international finance, and other related economic issues that include general professional interest in international economic affairs. Both theoretical and empirical analysis in international economics, particularly on issues of international economic cooperation, may be submitted by anyone, without restrictions. From papers selected for publication, the prize committee chooses the best manuscript(s) to receive the prize. A monetary prize of $10,000 is awarded annually and announced in the spring issue of the *Journal of International Economic Integration*. Established in 1986 by Myung-gun Choo.

8816

Korea Design and Packaging Center
128-8, Yunkun-dong
Chongro-ku   Phone: 2 744 0226
Seoul 110, Republic of Korea   Fax: 2 745 5519

8817

Good Design Selection
To protect consumers by creating a deeper understanding and interest in design among consumers as well as manufacturers and distributors, and to promote the quality of products by improving the design methods. A monetary prize and the GD MARK, symbol of good design, are awarded annually to the winning designs. Established in 1985.

8818

Korea Good-Packaging Exhibition
To recognize the importance of packaging; to promote good design; to encourage reasonable physical distribution by inducing proper packaging; and to contribute to the up-grading of the quality of products. A monetary prize is awarded annually. Established in 1987. Sponsored by The Minister of Trade & Industry and the Korea Broadcasting System.

8819

Korea Polio Association
(Chung Nip Hwe Gwan)
16-3 Gueui-Dong
Seongdong-Gu   Phone: 2 4461237
Seoul, Republic of Korea   Fax: 2 4542144

8820

Korea Polio Association Awards
To recognize individuals who foster the physical and mental development of the disabled and increase awareness of the needs of the handicapped. The Foundation bestows awards and scholarships.

8821

Korean Culture and Arts Foundation
31 Dong Soong-Dong
Chongro-Ku
PO Box Kwang Hwa Moon 947
Seoul 110, Republic of Korea   Phone: 2 736046

8822

Korean Composition Award
To encourage and contribute to professional development in the field of Korean music. Applicants must be Korean. Works composed and performed within five years, including the year the award is given, that are more than 10 minutes duration may be submitted by late September. The following awards are presented: (1) The Most Outstanding Award - 3,000,000 won for one, plus a concert; (2) The Outstanding Award - 2,000,000 won, plus a concert engagement, for six in the categories of Korean Classical Music and Western Music. Awarded annually from 1977 to 1982, and biennially since 1982. Established in 1977 by the Korean Ministry of Culture and Information (former host organization). Since 1979, the Award has been conducted by the KCAF.

8823

Korean National Literary Award
For recognition of achievement in the literary field and to encourage men of letters. Awards may be given in the following categories: (1) fiction; (2) poetry; and (3) literary criticism. A monetary award is presented annually in December. Established in 1976.

8824

Korean PEN Centre
238 Sinmunro 19A, Jong-ro gu
Seoul 110-061, Republic of Korea   Phone: 2 7208897

8825

Huh Kyun Literary Award
To recognize the work of an unknown young writer. A monetary award of 3,000,000 won is awarded annually. Established in 1979 in coordination with Kirim Publishing Company. Additional information is available from Korean PEN Center, c/o Mrs. Sook Hee Chun, 186-210 Janchung-dong 2-ga, Jung-gu, Seoul 100, Republic of Korea.

8826

Korea Translation Award
To encourage translators to translate foreign works into Korean for the Korean public. A monetary prize of 500,000 won, and a trophy or citation are awarded annually. Established in 1959.

8827

PEN Literary Award
For recognition of creativity and to encourage writers. Members of the Korean PEN Centre are eligible. A monetary award of 1,000,000 won, a trophy, and a citation are awarded annually. Established in 1978.

8828

National Academy of Arts
1 Sejongro, Jongro-gu
Kangnam gu
Seoul, Republic of Korea   Phone: 2 703 901

8829

Fine Arts Prize

For recognition of an outstanding contribution to the fine arts. Painters or sculptors whose artistic activity in a given year is judged particularly worthy to the Korean culture are eligible. A monetary prize of $6,000, a gold medal and a diploma are awarded annually. Established in 1955.

8830

Literary Prize

To recognize the author of an outstanding literary work written during the preceding year, or an outstanding contribution to the development of Korean literature. A monetary prize of $6,000, a gold medal and a diploma are awarded annually. Established in 1955.

8831

Music Prize

For recognition of a significant achievement in music, such as a performance or composition. A monetary prize of $6,000, a gold medal and a diploma are awarded annually. Established in 1955.

8832

Prize for Theatre or Cinema

For recognition of a contribution to the development of the Korean theatre or cinema. Outstanding theatrical or film artists are eligible. A monetary prize of $6,000, a gold medal and a diploma are awarded annually. Established in 1955.

8833

National Classical Music Institute
(Kungnip Kugagwon)
San 14-67 Chang Chung-Dong 2-Ka
Chung-Ku
Seoul, Republic of Korea   Phone: 2 274 1179

8834

National Classical Music Contest
(Chon'guk Kugak Kyongyon Tachoe)

For recognition of achievement in the field of performance of Korean traditional music. The award is given in three divisions for instrumentalists, vocalists, and dancers. Korean citizens over 20 years of age may submit applications. The following monetary prizes are awarded: (1) First Prize - 500,000 won; (2) Second Prize - 300,000 won; and (3) Third Prize - 200,000 won. A citation or plaque is awarded to winners in each section. In addition, a grand prize of 1,000,000 won is awarded to the best performer of the first prize awardees. Awarded annually. Established in 1981. Sponsored by the Ministry of Culture and Information, the Republic of South Korea. Information may be available from the Music Association of Korea, 1-117 Dongsoong-dong, Chongru-ku, Seoul, Korea.

8835

World League for Freedom and Democracy
CPO Box 7173   Phone: 2 2350823
Seoul, Republic of Korea   Fax: 2 2367059

Formerly: (1990) World Anti-Communist League.

8836

Awards

For recognition of contributions.

8837

World Taekwondo Federation
635 Yuksamdong   Phone: 2 5662505
Kangnam-ku   Phone: 2 5575446
Seoul 135, Republic of Korea   Fax: 2 5534728

8838

Competitions

To promote taekwondo internationally. World and Continental Taekwondo Championships are held, including the Asian, European, Pan American, African, a nd CISM (World Military) championships.

Kuwait

8839

Arab Towns Organization
(Monadhamat Al-Modon Al-Arabiyah)
PO Box 4954
Safat 13050, Kuwait   Phone: 2435540

8840

Architectural Awards

To encourage preservation, development, and application of Arab Islamic architecture, to motivate Arab engineers to adhere to its principles and to get inspiration from its heritage, and to promote adaptation of modern technologies for its requirements. Applications must be submitted by March 15 of alternate years. The following three prizes are awarded: Architectural Project Award, Architectural Heritage Award, and Architect Award. A monetary prize, Golden Shield trophy, and certificate of honor are awarded biennially. Established in 1980. Additional information is available from the Municipality of Doha, The Permanent Bureau of ATO's Awards, P.O. Box 820, Doha, Qatar.

8841

Kuwait Foundation for the Advancement of Sciences
                                      Phone: 2429780
PO Box 25263   Phone: 2425898
Safat 13113, Kuwait   Fax: 2403891

8842

Arab Book Fair Prize

To encourage Arabic authors, publishers, and translators in various disciplines to continue and increase publication and translation. Nominated works should employ proper arabic language, should be exhibited at the Arab Book Fair, and should not have won any other award. A cash prize of $16,500 (5,000 KD), a KFAS Shield, and a certificate of recognition are awarded every November at the Arab Book Fair in Kuwait. Established in 1974, the award is sponsored by the Kuwait National Council for Arts, Letters, and Humanities. Contact Dr. Ali Al-Shamlan, Director General, for further information.

8843

The Islamic Organization for Medical Sciences Prizes

To support and promote scientific research in the field of Islamic medicine. One award is given for outstanding documentation of Islamic medical heritage, including medical Islamic jurisprudence, and the second for the premier medical practice addressing professional and well-documented clinical and laboratory experiments. Monetary prizes of $20,000 (6,000 KD) in addition to the Kuwait Foundation for the Advancement of Science Shield and a certificate of recognition are awarded. The awards are presented every two years at the Foundation conference. Established in 1982. Contact Dr. Ali Al-Shamlan, Director General, for further information.

8844

Kuwait Prize

To provide recognition of distinguished research, studies, and accomplishments in the arts, sciences, and humanities. Two prizes are awarded annually in the following fields: basic sciences, applied sciences, economic and social sciences, arts and letters, and Arabic and Islamic scientific heritage. Nominations are accepted from individuals, academic and scientific centres, past recipients, and peers of the nominee. No nominations are accepted from political entities. The scientific research submitted must have been published during the past 10 years. A cash prize of $100,000 (30,000 KD), a gold medal, a KFAS shield, and a certificate of recognition are presented every November in Kuwait. Established in 1979. Contact Dr. Ali Al-Shamlan, Director General, for further information.

8845
Prize for Research and Studies of the Repercussions of the Iraqi Invasion of Kuwait
To provide recognition of distinguished accomplishments in the Arts, Humanities, and Sciences. Awards cover the following fields: environmental research, historical research, psychological and social research, and story and novel. Nominees should be specialists in one of the prize categories, their submission should not have won a previous prize, and it should have been published during the previous year. Political nominations are not accepted. A cash prize of $35,000 and a certificate of recognition are presented every November in Kuwait. Established in 1991.

8846
Organization of Arab Petroleum Exporting Countries
c/o Technical Affairs Dept.
PO Box 20501
Safat 13066, Kuwait   Phone: 2448200

8847
OAPEC Award for Scientific Research
To promote and encourage scientific research by recognizing the outstanding research paper on a specified topic. Papers may be submitted by May 31 each year. A monetary award and certificate are presented annually at the end of the year. Established in 1985.

Liberia

8848
Liberian Association of Writers
PO Box 10-2124
Monrovia, Liberia

8849
Annual Literary Award
To recognize writers who promote and develop Liberian literature. The Association also sponsors competitions.

Libyan Arab Jamahiriya

8850
African Centre for Applied Research and Training in Social Development
(Centre Africain de Recherche Appliquee et de Formation en Matiere de Developpement Social)
PO Box 80606   Phone: 21 833640
Tripoli, Libyan Arab Jamahiriya   Fax: 21 832357

8851
African Centre for Applied Research and Training in Social Development Awards
To recognize individuals for outstanding research on social development in Africa.

Liechtenstein

8852
PEN Club Liechtenstein
PO Box 416   Phone: 75 27271
FL-9490 Vaduz, Liechtenstein   Fax: 75 28071

8853
Liechtenstein-Preis zur Forderung junger Lyriker
To encourage young people to write poems. German-speaking young people up to 35 years of age are eligible. A monetary award of 12,000 Swiss francs, a medal, and a certificate are awarded triennially. Established in 1978.

Lithuania

8854
Academy of Sciences, Lithuania
(Mokslu Akademija)
Gedimino pr.3
232600 Vilnius, Lithuania   Phone: 61 40 07

8855
Tadas Ivanausko premija
For recognition of achievements in biology and environmental protection. Applications are accepted. A monetary prize of 500 rubles is awarded triennially. Established in 1982 in honor of Tadas Ivanausko, a well-known Lithuanian naturalist academician. Sponsored by the State Committee for Protection of Nature.

8856
P. Sivickio premija
For recognition of achievements in experimental zoology. Applications are accepted. A monetary prize of 500 rubles is awarded triennially. Established in 1982 in honor of P. Sivickio, a famous scientist and organizer of investigations in experimental zoology.

Luxembourg

8857
European Information Industry Association
BP 262   Phone: 34981420
L-2012 Luxembourg, Luxembourg   Fax: 34981234

8858
Annual Promotional Activity Award
For recognition of the best sales literature and for the best exhibit at the International Online Information Meeting. Exhibitors at the IOLIM are eligible. Awarded annually. Established in 1989.

8859
European Investment Bank
Information Div.
Boulevard Konrad Adenauer 100
L-2950 Luxembourg, Luxembourg   Phone: 4379 3223

8860
EIB Prize
To recognize a doctoral thesis on a topic related to investment and financing in all its various aspects. A thesis that has been successfully presented as a doctoral dissertation to a university or equivalent academic institution in a member country of the European Community, may be submitted by any person having the nationality of one of the member countries of the European Community, and who is under 40 years of age

on the date the thesis is sent to the EIB. Doctoral - granting theses must have been obtained during the four calendar years prior to the year the prize is to be awarded. A monetary prize of 12,000 ECUs and a diploma signed by the Chairman of the Prize Jury and the President of the European Investment Bank are awarded biennially. Established in 1983 on the occasion of the bank's 25th anniversary.

8861
European Merit Foundation
(Fondation du Merite Europeen)
80 Boulevard de la Petrusse
L-2320 Luxembourg, Luxembourg   Phone: 40 0689

8862
European Merit Award
(Medaille d'Honneur du Merite Europeen)
For recognition of efforts to foster a sense of European identity in all types of activities. Nominations for the award of bronze, silver, and gold European Merit medals may be submitted by the President to the Board for approval. Only natural persons having rendered at least five years of noteworthy service to the cause of European unity are eligible for the Bronze European Merit Medal. Only natural persons having held the Bronze Medal for at least five years and having pursued their efforts on behalf of Europe are eligible for the Silver Medal. Notwithstanding this condition, the medal may be awarded in exceptional cases to persons whose activities render a sigificant contribution to the European cause (for instance, members of the European Parliament). Only prominent persons having held the Silver Medal for at least ten years and having continued to render significant service to Europe shall be eligible for the Gold Medal of European Merit. Notwithstanding this condition, the Medal may be awarded in exceptional cases to top-ranking dignitaries rendering, or having rendered, outstanding service to the European cause (for instance, presidents of the European Parliament). Five to seven gold, 12 to 17 silver, and 15 bronze medals and certificates are awarded annually. Established in 1969 by Francois Visine.

8863
European Showmen's Union
(Europaische Schausteller Union)
Allee Scheffer 23   Phone: 47 31 25
L-2520 Luxembourg, Luxembourg   Fax: 49 23 89

8864
European Showmen's Union Awards
For recognition in the performing arts. Awards are presented.

8865
Federation Internationale de l'Art Photographique
32, rue du Baumbusch   Phone: 310863
L-8213 Mamer, Luxembourg   Fax: 312299

8866
FIAP Awards
For recognition of photographic achievements based on participation in international photographic salons all over the world. Photographers nominated by national photographic associations are eligible. The titles "Artist FIAP" (AFIAP), "Excellence FIAP" (EFIAP), and "Masterphotographer of FIAP" (MFIAP) may be appended to the name and diplomas and badges are awarded as often as requested. AFIAP and EFIAP were established in 1950; MFIAP in 1979.

8867
FIAP Medals
For recognition of outstanding photographic work. Photographers from any country are eligible. Gold, silver, and bronze medals are awarded in about 100 photographic salons under FIAP patronage annually. At least three medals (gold, silver, and bronze) are given in each international salon. Established in 1950.

8868
FIAP Service Awards
For recognition of outstanding contributions to the international photographic movement. Titles "Excellence for Service rendered to FIAP" (ESFIAP) and "Honorary Excellence FIAP" (Hon EFIAP) may be appended to the name and diplomas and badges are awarded when merited. Established in 1960.

8869
FIAP World Cups
For recognition of outstanding photography in the following categories: monochrome prints, color prints, and color slides. National Societies affiliated with FIAP may enter biennial international photographic contests between national photographic societies. Three world cups are awarded biennially in each category. Established in 1960.

8870
International League for Animal Rights
(Ligue Internationale des Droits de l'Animal)
BP 785
Luxembourg, Luxembourg

8871
Order of Nature Award
To recognize individuals who advance the welfare and rights of animals through legislation and public education. Awarded annually.

8872
Vatel-Club Luxembourg
47, route de Mondorf   Phone: 69 525
L-5552 Remich, Luxembourg   Fax: 69 9568

8873
Culinary Military Cup
No further information was available for this edition.

8874
Culinary World Cup
To recognize outstanding culinary ability. The competition is built around research and development and establishing food trends for the future. Medals are awarded at the EXPOGAST trade show held quadrennially in Luxembourg. Established in 1900.

Macedonia

8875
Society of Writers of Macedonia
(Drustvo na Pisatelite na SR Makedonija)
Maksim Gorki 18
91000 Skopje, Macedonia   Phone: 91 236205

8876
Society of Writers of Macedonia Awards
For recognition of the best literary works by Macedonian authors. Monetary prizes are awarded annually.

Madagascar

8877
Grande Chancellerie
c/o Office of the Prime Minister
Mahazoarivo
Antananrivo 101, Madagascar   Phone: 25258

8878
Ordre de Merit de Madagascar
To recognize special achievement in a specific field.

8879
Ordre Nacional de Madagascar
For recognition of distinguished service to the country in the ranks of: Knight, Officer, Commander, Great Officer, and Great Badge. Selection is by the President of the Republic, the Great Master of the Order. Individuals who are at least 40 years of age with 15 years of service are eligible. A medal is awarded annually. Established in 1960.

8880
Malagasy
Ministry of Revolutionary Culture and Art
Antsahovola, BP 305
Antananarivo, Madagascar   Phone: 27092

8881
Prize for Fabrication of Traditional Musical Instrument
For recognition of contributions to the fabrication of musical instruments. Five monetary prizes ranging from 100,000 to 300,000 Malagasy francs are awarded annually.

8882
Prize for Revolutionary Song
For recognition of the best revolutionary song, and for the promotion of popular art. Three monetary prizes of 400,000, 250,000 and 150,000 Malagasy francs are awarded annually.

8883
Prizes for a Theatrical Play
To recognize the best theatrical play. The following monetary prizes are awarded: 300,000 Malagasy francs - first prize; 200,000 Malagasy francs - second prize; and 100,000 Malagasy francs - third prize. Awarded annually.

8884
Prizes for Literature
To recognize an outstanding novel. Monetary prizes of 300,000 and 200,000 Malagasy francs are awarded annually.

8885
Malagasy Academy
(Academie Malgache)
Tsimbazaza
Antananarivo 101, Madagascar   Phone: 210 84

8886
Prize for Better Work
For recognition of superior achievements in literature or science. Anyone is eligible. A monetary prize of 50,000 francs Malgache is awarded at the convention. Established in 1977.

Malaysia

8887
Asia-Pacific Broadcasting Union
PO Box 1164
Pejabat Pos
Jalan Pantai Baru   Phone: 3 274 3592
59700 Kuala Lumpur, Malaysia   Fax: 3 230 5292

8888
ABU Engineering Award
To encourage technical writing in developing countries in broadcast engineering. ABU members in developing countries are eligible. A monetary prize of $400 US and a certificate for the Best Paper and two prizes of $300 each and certificates for the commended papers are awarded annually. Established in 1973.

8889
ABU Prize Competitions for Radio and Television Programmes
For recognition of the high standard of a production in the field of radio and television programs. Member organizations may submit one program per category. The following prizes are awarded for radio: ABU Prize for Information Programs, HBF-ABU Prize for Entertainment Programs, ABU Prize for Children's Programs, and ABU Prize for External Broadcasts. The following prizes are awarded for television: ABU Prize for Information Programs, HBF-ABU Prize for Entertainment Programs, and ABU Prize for Children's Programs. Awarded annually. Established in 1964 and restructured in 1994.

8890
FES Award
For recognition of outstanding contributions to the development of the Asiavision (AVN) news exchange. Awarded annually by the Friedrich-Ebert-Stiftung (FES). Established in 1984.

8891
Asian Football Confederation
Wisma Olympic Council of Malaysia, 1st
   Fl.   Phone: 3 2384860
Jalan Hang Jebat   Phone: 3 2385742
50510 Kuala Lumpur, Malaysia   Fax: 3 2384862

8892
Afro-Asia Club Championship
To recognize matches between the Champion Clubs of both Africa and Asia. The first Championship was inaugurated in 1987.

8893
Afro-Asia Nations Cup
To provide for a competition in football between champion nations of Africa and Asia. A pewter football trophy sculpture with a map of Africa and Asia is awarded. Established in 1978 by Afro Asia Consultative Committee. After the initial competition in 1978, there was no competition until 1985.

8894
Asian Club Championship
To provide for an Asian Club Championship Tournament in line with the European Champion Club Tournament. Starting in 1993, monetary prizes have been awarded. Established in 1967 as Asian Champion Club Tournament for Champion Clubs of Asia. Subsequently, the tournament was centralized in one country with no tournaments in 1969, 1972, 1973, and 1974, and then revived in 1984/85 with the new name Asian Club Championship. Formerly: (1984) Asian Champion Club Tournament.

8895
Asian Cup
To honor the winners of the Football Championship of Asian Nations. Affiliation with the Confederation is necessary for consideration. A trophy is awarded every four years. Established in 1956.

8896
Asian Cup Winners Championship
To recognize the winner of the Championship. Open to all Clubs in their respective countries for the current or previous season. The Championship is organized on a home and away knock-out system. Monetary prizes are awarded annually. Established in 1990.

8897

Asian Cup Women's Football Championship
To recognize the winner of the Asian Cup Women's Football Championship. The Tournament is held every two years. Established in 1975 when teams from Australia and New Zealand also participated.

8898

Asian Youth Football Championship (Under 16)
To honor the Champion Youth U16 Football Team. Players must be under 16 years of age. The Cleland Cup, given in memory of Mr. John Cleland (Philippines) who was responsible for drawing up the AFC Constitution, is awarded every two years. Established in 1984.

8899

Asian Youth Football Championship (Under 19)
To honor the champion football team. Players must be under 19 years of age. The Rahman Gold Cup trophy is awarded biennially. Established in 1959. The award commemorates Tunku Abdul Rahman, the former Prime Minister of Malaysia.

8900

Government of Malaysia
Language and Literary Agency
(Kerajaan Malaysia
Dewan Bahasa dan Pustaka)
PO Box 10803   Phone: 3 2481011
50926 Kuala Lumpur, Malaysia   Fax: 3 2482726

8901

Anugerah Sastera Negara
For recognition of achievement in literature. Selection is by nomination. A monetary prize, a plaque, free medical facilities, etc., are awarded annually. Established in 1981 by the Prime Minister.

8902

Children's Novel Writing Competition
To encourage professional writing in children's literature. Residents of Malaysia are eligible. Monetary prizes are awarded irregularly. Established in 1987.

8903

Hadiah Cerpen Maybank - DBP
To encourage professional development in creative writing, especially among non-Malay writers to write in the national language. A monetary prize is awarded irregularly. Established in 1987. Sponsored by Malayan Banking Berhad. Formerly: Hadia Cerpen Malayan Banking - DBP.

8904

Malaysian Literary Prize
(Hadiah Sastera Malaysia)
For recognition of achievement in literature. Awards are given in the following categories: poetry, short story, drama, novel, and essay and research works. Monetary prizes are awarded biennially. Established in 1971 by the late Prime Minister Tun Abdul Razak.

8905

International Council on Management of Population Programmes
141 Jalan Dahlia
Taman Uda Jaya   Phone: 3 4573234
68000 Kuala Lumpur, Malaysia   Fax: 3 4560029

8906

ICOMP Population Programmes Management Award
To recognize managerial excellence in the solution of population problems. Population management experts, population or management institutes, and program managers may be nominated. A monetary award of US $1,000, a certificate, and a citation are awarded triennially at the ICOMP Conference and General Assembly. Established in 1984. Formerly: ICOMP Population Award; ICOMP Population Award.

8907

World Council of Management (CIOS)
(Conseil Mondiale de Management)
c/o Malaysian Institute of Management
227 Jalan Ampang
16-003 Kuala Lumpur, Malaysia   Phone: 3 425 255

8908

CIOS Gold Medal
To provide recognition for distinguished contributions to scientific and professional management and to improve the standards of living of all nations. A gold medal is awarded triennially at the World Congress.

Mali

8909

Centre national de la Recherche Scientifique et Technologique
BP 5052
Bamako, Mali   Phone: 22 90 85

8910

Third World Academy of Science Prize
(Prix de l'Academie des Sciences du Tiers Monde)
To increase the scientific level of work in countries of the Third World. Citizens of the Third World countries are eligible. A monetary prize is awarded annually. Established in 1986 by the Third World Academy of Sciences.

Malta

8911

Malta Amateur Cine Circle
                                          Phone: 222345
PO Box 450   Phone: 236173
Valletta, Malta   Fax: 225047

8912

Golden Knight International Amateur Film and Video Festival
To encourage professional development of the short film and video. Any number of films and videos which are preferably not longer than 30 minutes may be submitted. Productions entered in past Golden Knight Festivals are not accepted. Entries may be on Super 8mm, Single-8, 16mm or VHS videotape, in color or black/white, and on any subject. The deadline for submission of films/videos is September 30. The Festival is divided into three classes: Class A - Amateur productions by individuals, groups or clubs made for pleasure with no commercial purpose in mind; Class B - Productions made by film-school students during their studies; and Class C - Any production which does not qualify under Class A or Class B may be entered in Class C. The following awards are presented: Golden Knight, which is retainable, and a Certificate of Merit - for the Best Productions in Class A, B and C; Silver Knight, which is retainable, and a Certificate of Merit - for the second place entry in Class A and B; Bronze Knight which is retainable and a Certificate of Merit in Class A and B; Malta Amateur Cine Circle Trophy, retainable for one year, and a Certificate of Merit - for the Best Entry (film or video) in Class A from a resident of Malta; Sultana Cup, retainable for one year, and a Certificate of Merit - to the entry which best extols the merits of Malta from some particular aspect, applicable to one entry from any class; and Highly Commended Certificates - to entries of outstanding merit. Awarded annually in November. Established in 1961. The President of Malta is a patron. Formerly: Golden Knight International Amateur Film Festival.

8913

Repubblika ta' Malta
The Palace
Valletta, Malta   Phone: 228156

8914

Gieh ir-Repubblika Honor Society
This honor society, referred to as Ix-Xirka, recognizes distinguished persons. Maltese citizens may be appointed members of the Society and others may be appointed honorary members by the President of the Republic of Malta on the advice of the Cabinet. The total membership is limited to 20 persons. New appointments are made only when a vacancy occurs. Established in 1975.

8915

Medal for Courage
(Midalja ghall-Qlubija)
To recognize a Maltese citizen for exceptional bravery. A medal is awarded by the President of the Republic of Malta when merited and may be awarded posthumously. Established in 1975 by the Government of Malta.

8916

Medal for Service to the Republic
(Midalja ghall-Qadi tar-Repubblika)
To recognize distinguished service to Malta. Maltese citizens are eligible, and citizens of other countries are eligible on an honorary basis. A medal is awarded by the President of the Republic of Malta when merited. No more than 30 medals may be held at one time. Established in 1975 by the Government of Malta.

Mexico

8917

Academy of Scientific Research
(Academia de la Investigacion Cientifica)
Avenida San Jeronimo 260   Phone: 5 550 6278
San Angel   Phone: 5 550 3906
04500 Mexico City, DF, Mexico   Fax: 5 550 1143

8918

Premio TWAS (Third World Academy of Sciences)
For recognition of an outstanding research project by a young Mexican scientist done in collaboration with a researcher of another developing country. A monetary prize of $2,000US is awarded annually alternating in the areas of biology, chemistry, mathematics and physics. Established in 1987. Co-sponsored by the Third World Academy of Sciences.

8919

Scientific Research Prizes
(Premios de Investigacion Cientifica)
For recognition of contributions to scientific research in the following areas: (1) natural sciences; (2) social sciences; (3) exact sciences; (4) technological innovation; and (5) promotion of science. Mexican scientists and researchers under 40 years of age are eligible. For the promotion of science category there is no age limit. The awards are given for a complete career rather than for a single publication or research paper. A monetary prize of 8,000,000 Mexican pesos and a diploma are awarded in each field annually, except technological innovation which is a biennial prize. Established in 1961.

8920

Weizmann Prizes of the Academy of Scientific Research
(Premios Weizmann de la Academia de la Investigacion Cientifica)
For recognition of the best doctoral thesis in the field of: (1) natural sciences and (2) exact sciences. Originality and scientific importance are considered. Individuals under 35 years of age are eligible for thesis research done in Mexico and the degree must be conferred by a Mexican institution. A monetary prize of 8,000,000 Mexican pesos is awarded for each thesis annually. Established in 1986 by the Mexican Association of Friends of the Weizmann Institute of Sciences.

8921

Asociacion de Periodistas Universitarias
Sinaloa 84-24
Col. Roma
06700 Mexico City, DF, Mexico   Phone: 5 525 5052

8922

Magdalena Mondragon Medal
For recognition of promising women journalists residing in Mexico. Gold and silver medals and certificates are awarded annually to those over fifty years of age and those between thirty and forty years. Established in 1979.

8923

Asociacion de Reporteros Graficos de los Diarios de Mexico
Bucareli 51-2
Col. Juarez
06600 Mexico City, DF, Mexico   Phone: 5 546 8136

8924

Premios Asociacion de Reporteros Graficos
To recognize the best photography that promotes the image of Mexico. Monetary prizes of 500,000 and 250,000 Mexican pesos are awarded annually.

8925

Asociacion Mexicana de Periodistas de Radio y Television
Enrico Martinez 38, 1er piso
Col. Centro
06440 Mexico City, DF, Mexico   Phone: 5 709 0472

8926

Golden Aztec Calendar Prize
(Calendario Azteca de Oro)
To recognize Mexican artists for contributions to the radio and television industries. Nominations must be made by members of the organization. A trophy representing the Aztec calendar is awarded annually. Established in 1953. Formerly: (1954) Macuilxochitl Prize.

8927

Asociacion Mundial de Mujeres Periodistas y Escritoras-Capitulo Mexico
Apartado Postal 41-555
Mexico City, DF, Mexico

8928

Premio de Periodismo Rosario Castellanos
To recognize outstanding women journalists of Mexico and their daily contributions to recording of history as it happens and attending to Mexico's progress into the modern age. Prizes are awarded for reporting, chronicle reporting, information, essay and interview. Monetary prizes of 2,000,000, 1,500,000 and 1,000,000 Mexican pesos are awarded annually.

8929

Asociacion Nacional de Actores
Altamarino 128, 2 piso
06470 Mexico City, DF, Mexico   Phone: 5 705 0624

8930
Magda Donato Prize
(Premio Magda Donato)
For recognition of outstanding contributions of a primarily humanistic nature, through exacting and beautiful language, to the knowledge and proper valuation of the great cultures. A monetary prize of 2,000,000 Mexican pesos and a certificate are awarded annually Established in 1977.

8931
Asociacion Nacional de la Publicidad
Jalapa 147-1
06700 Mexico City, DF, Mexico   Phone: 5 584 2873

8932
Premio Nacional Teponaxtli de Malinalco
To recognize the most outstanding marketers of media publicity with the theme of popular consumption or representatives of industrial products or services. A gold statue is awarded annually in the categories of radio, television, the press, or audiovisual media in general. Established in 1950.

8933
Banca Serfin
Calz. de Tlalpan 3016
04870 Mexico City, DF, Mexico   Phone: 5 689 9522

8934
Premio Nacional de Integracion Latinoamericana
To recognize outstanding masters' theses which promote awareness of the importance of Latin American integration as a formula for regional development. A monetary prize and a certificate are awarded annually. Established in 1984.

8935
Premio Nacional Serfin, sobre Medio Ambiente
For recognition of outstanding masters' theses or investigatory projects contributing to the search for solutions to national problems affecting the quality of life. Awarded annually. Established in 1984 to commemorate the 120th anniversary of the bank's founding.

8936
Camara Nacional de la Ciudad de Mexico
Paseo de la Reforma 51, 4 piso
Edificio Anahuac
06020 Mexico City, DF, Mexico   Phone: 5 592 0460

8937
Concurso Anual de Tesis Profesionales
For recognition of the best theses written by professionals of higher learning in Mexico City in the following categories: public administration, international relations, international trade, tourism, economics, human rights, accounting, and journalism. A monetary prize of 1,250,000 pesos and a certificate are awarded in each category annually. Established in 1976.

8938
Camara Nacional de la Industria Quimico Farmaceutica
Av. Cuauhtemoc 1481
Col. Santa Cruz Atoyac
03310 Mexico City, DF, Mexico   Phone: 5 5243402

8939
Premios CANIFARMA
To recognize outstanding research in pharmaceuticals for human and veterinary uses and the use of medical devices or materials, and to promote the union between scientific and technological research and its industrial application, thereby stimulating its development in Mexico. A monetary prize of 25,000 Mexican pesos for each category is awarded annually. The veterinary category is also known as Premio Dr. Alfredo Tellez-Giron.

8940
Celanese Mexicana S.A.
Direccion de Relaciones Publicas
Avenida Revolucion 1425
01040 Mexico City, DF, Mexico   Phone: 5 548 6960

8941
Chemical Technology Award
(Premio de Tecnologia Quimica)
For recognition of outstanding achievement in chemical technology. Engineers, students and professors are eligible. The following monetary prizes are awarded: (1) 200,000 pesos - first place; and (2) 100,000 pesos - second place. Awarded annually. Established in 1971.

8942
Textile Technology Award
(Premio de Tecnologia Textil)
For recognition of research in the field of textile technology and to promote interest among teachers, students, professionals and technicians of textile technology in teaching and research, in order to introduce innovations to the existing technology and equipment. The research subject must bring new knowledge to the textile industry, especially in the following areas: fibers, machines, apparatus and equipment for textile processes. Any Mexican citizen is eligible. The following monetary prizes are awarded: (1) 200,000 pesos - first place; and (2) 100,000 pesos - second prize. Awarded annually. Established in 1971.

8943
Centre for Latin American Monetary Studies
(Centro de Estudios Monetarios Latinoamericanos (CEMLA))
Durango 54
Col. Roma
06700 Mexico City, DF, Mexico   Phone: 5 5330300

8944
Rodrigo Gomez Prize
(Premio Rodrigo Gomez)
For recognition of achievement and to encourage professional development in monetary, financial, and central banking subjects of interest to the Latin American central banks. Citizens of Latin American and Caribbean countries may submit papers of not more than 100 pages, written in Spanish, Portuguese, English, or French, by January 15. A monetary prize of $5,000 US is awarded to the author of the winning paper. In the case of a tie between two papers, the sum is split. In addition, the paper is published. Awarded annually in July. Established in 1971 by the Governors of Latin American central banks in memory of Mr. Rodrigo Gomez, the Director General of the Bank of Mexico from 1952 to 1970 (year of his death), a distinguished central banker, promoter of economic regional integration and financial cooperation among central banks, and an international figure among central banks.

8945
Centro Mexicano para los Derechos de la Infancia
Apartado Postal 22-319
22 Mexico City, DF, Mexico

8946
National Prize for Journalism for Young People
(Premio Nacional Periodismo porla Infancia)
For recognition of outstanding contributions to the research, development, and promotion of the quality of life for Mexican youth. Open to Mexican journalists and foreign residents in Mexico excluding members of the center. Works should cover the following national problems of Mexican youth: malnutrition, health, education and school, drug addiction and alcoholism, adoption and trafficking of children, prostitution, children's rights, child labor and protective institutions. Monetary prizes of 3,000,000, 2,000,000, and 1,500,000 Mexican pesos and certificates are awarded annually.

8947
Chemical Society of Mexico
(Sociedad Quimica de Mexico)
Mar del Norte, No. 5
Col. San Alvaro, Deleg. Azcapotzalco   Phone: 5 3862905
CP 02090 Mexico City, Mexico   Fax: 5 3860255

8948
Andres Manuel del Rio National Prize in Chemistry
(Premio Nacional de Quimica Andres Manuel del Rio)
For recognition of the best achievement in industrial chemistry, chemical research, technological development, and chemistry education. Members of the Society must make nominations by March 30. Medals and diplomas are awarded annually. Established in 1964 in memory of Andres Manuel del Rio (1764-1849), the discoverer of the element Vanadium, atomic number 23, in 1801.

8949
Cigarrera la Moderna
Relaciones Publicas
Madero Pte. 2750
64000 Monterrey, Nuevo Leon, Mexico   Phone: 918 333 4646

8950
National Technology Competition
(Concurso Nacional de Tecnologie)
For recognition of Mexican university students who demonstrate creativity and inventiveness. Monetary prizes are awarded to the first three places when merited. Judging is assisted by CONACYT. Established in 1970.

8951
Cineteca Nacional
av. Mexico-Coyoacan 389   Phone: 5 6041449
03300 Mexico City, DF, Mexico   Fax: 5 6884211

8952
Salvador Toscano Medal
(Medalla Ing. Salvador Toscano)
For recognition of outstanding contributions to cinematography in industry. Awarded annually. Established in 1982.

8953
Colegio de Contadores Publicos de Mexico
Av. Bosque de Tabachines 44
Frac. Bosques de las Lomas
11700 Mexico City, DF, Mexico   Phone: 5 596 3964

8954
Premio Carlos Perez del Toro
To recognize an outstanding thesis in accounting. Monetary prizes of 2,500,000, 1,000,000, and 500,000 Mexican pesos are awarded annually.

8955
Colegio de Posgraduados
Km. 38.5, Carretera Mexico Texcoco
56230 Chapingo, Mexico   Phone: 595 42200

8956
Premio Efraim Hernandez Xolocotzi
To recognize and promote outstanding contribution to scientific knowledge and the study of botany and to support the development of young Mexican scientists. Monetary prizes of 1,000,000 and 500,000 Mexican pesos and a certificate are awarded biennially. Established in 1988.

8957
Comision Nacional Bancaria
Coordinacion de Investigacion y
   Desarrollo
Rep. de El Salvador 47
Col. Centro
06080 Mexico City, Mexico   Phone: 5 709 6855

8958
National Banking Commission Prize
(Premio Comision Nacional Bancaria)
For recognition of an outstanding contribution to the development of research in the Mexican financial system. A monetary award of 10,000,000 Mexican pesos in bonds and certificates are awarded to the first three places annually. Prize-winning works become the property of the Comision Nacional Bancaria. Established in 1991.

8959
Consejo Consultivo de la Ciudad de Mexico
Plaza de la Constitucion 1, 1er piso
Edificio Antiguo del Departamento del
   Distrito Federal
Col. Centro   Phone: 5 521 0292
06060 Mexico City, DF, Mexico   Phone: 5 512 2498

8960
Gem of Mexico City
For recognition of outstanding contributions by groups or individuals to the welfare of Mexico City's inhabitants. A gold medal is awarded annually. Established in 1989.

8961
Mexico City Medal of Civic Merit
(Medalla al Marito Civico de la Ciudad de Mexico)
For recognition of any Mexican or foreign citizen who has distinguished himself through honorable deeds of prestige, heroism, or altruism to the citizens of Mexico City. A medal is awarded when merited. Established in 1941.

8962
Consejo Consultivo del Programa de Solidaridad
Tamaulipas 150-20
Col. Condesa
06140 Mexico City, DF, Mexico

8963
Solidarity Prize
(Premio Solidaridad)
For recognition of contributions to the war on poverty and to promote research of the living conditions of the most needy. There are two categories, one to commemorate worthy contributions to the cause, and the other to support researchers. Awarded annually. Established in 1989.

8964
Consejo Nacional de Ciencia y Tecnologia
Centro Cultural Universitaria
04510 Mexico City, DF, Mexico   Phone: 5 655 9077

8965
Premio Nacional de Ciencia y Tecnologia de Alimentos
To recognize outstanding work and stimulate research in the field of nutrition. Awards are given in the following categories: (1) Premio Nacional al Merito; (2) Professional; and (3) Student. Awarded annually.

8966
Consejo Nacional de la Cultura y las Artes
Cracovia 90
Col. Guadalupe Inn
01020 Mexico City, DF, Mexico

8967
Bienal de Fotografia
To recognize outstanding photographic talent of Mexico. Monetary production assistance of 8,000,000 Mexican pesos is awarded in four categories.

8968
Consejo Nacional de Poblacion
Angel Urraza 1137, 5 piso
Col. del Valle
03100 Mexico City, DF, Mexico   Phone: 5 559 7318

8969
Premio dos Culturas en Origen
To recognize outstanding artistic works which embody the cultural, political, and social aspects of the Mexican-North American culture. A monetary prize of 1,500,000 Mexican pesos, a week-long study trip, and a certificate are awarded.

8970
Consejo Nacional para la Ensenanza y la Investigacion de las Ciencias de la Comunicacion
Cordobanes 24
Col. San Jose Insurgentes
03900 Mexico City, DF, Mexico   Phone: 5 651 9056

8971
Premio Nacional de Trabajos Recepcionales escritos en Comunicacion
To recognize achievement in the science of communication, to promote research in the field, and to encourage professional reception of young graduates in the discipline. Three monetary prizes are awarded annually: first prize - 2,000,000 Mexican pesos and publication of the work; second prize - 1,000,000 Mexican pesos and recommendation for publication; and third prize - 750,000 Mexican pesos, recommendation for publication, and a certificate. Monetary prizes of 750,000 Mexican pesos, certificates, and publication are also awarded for three special prizes; Premio Communicacion y Frontera; Premio Frontero Norte; and Premio Frontera Sur. Established in 1987.

8972
Ediciones Castillo
Calle Morelos Ote. 451
Apartado Postal 1759
Monterrey, Nuevo Leon, Mexico

8973
Premio Internacional de Novela, Nuevo Leon
To recognize outstanding authors of books in the Spanish language. A monetary prize of 20,000,000 Mexican pesos is awarded annually. Established in 1988.

8974
Editorial Diana
Calle Roberto Gayol 1219
Colonia del Valle
Delegacion Benito Juarez
03100 Mexico City, DF, Mexico   Phone: 5 575 0711

8975
Premio Literario Internacional *Novedades* y Diana
For recognition of the best unpublished novel in the Spanish language. Authors of any nationality or residence are eligible. More than one novel may be submitted. The deadline usually falls in the early part of the year. A monetary prize of 45,000,000 Mexican pesos and publication are awarded annually. Established in 1987. Co-sponsored by *Novedades*.

8976
Editorial *El Porvenir*
Apartado Postal 218
Monterrey, Nuevo Leon, Mexico

8977
Certamen Nacional de Literatura *El Porvenir*
To recognize outstanding Mexican authors. A monetary prize of 4,000,000 Mexican pesos and publication are awarded annually. Established in 1983.

8978
Certamen Nacional de Periodismo Rogelio Cantu Gomez
To recognize outstanding Mexican journalists. A monetary prize of 4,000,000 Mexican pesos and publication are awarded annually.

8979
Editorial Planeta Mexicana, B.A. de C.V.
Insurgentes Sur 1162
Col. Del Valle
03100 Mexico City, DF, Mexico

8980
Editorial Planeta - Joaquin Mortiz International Prize for Novel (Premio Internacional para Novela Planeta - Joaquin Mortiz)
For recognition of an outstanding Latin-American novel. Unpublished novels written in Castillian are eligible. A monetary prize of 150,000,000 Mexican pesos is awarded annually. Established in 1991.

8981
Agustin Yanez First Novel Prize (Premio Agustin Yanez para Primera Novela)
For recognition of outstanding new novelists in Mexico regardless of nationality. They may never have had works published. A monetary prize of 30,000,000 Mexican pesos and publication are awarded annually. Established in 1990. Co-sponsored by the state of Jalisco.

8982
Ericsson
Apartado Postal 1062
06000 Mexico City, DF, Mexico   Phone: 5 7262070

8983
Ericsson National Science and Technology Prize
(Premio Nacional de Ciencia y Technologia Ericsson)
For recognition of outstanding contributions to the strengthening of the infrastructure of the country's telecommunications by a Mexican. (Discontinued)

8984
Festival Bach
Valentin Gomez Farias 12
03730 Mexico City, DF, Mexico   Phone: 5 598 3767

8985
Bach Festival
For recognition of outstanding young Mexican or foreign musicians under the age of 24. Monetary prizes are awarded annually to the first three place winners. The first place winner also merits a guest appearance with the Mexico City Philharmonic Orchestra. The festival alternatively features competitions for violin (1990) and violincello (1991). Established in 1989 by Luis Herrera de la Fuente, Bozena Slavinska (violincello), and Mini Caire, Co.

8986
Fundacion Jorge Sanchez Cordero
Instituto de Investigaciones Juridicas
Centro Cultural Universitaria   Phone: 5 6061086
04510 Mexico City, DF, Mexico   Fax: 5 6652193

8987
Premio Juridico Mtro. Jorge Sanchez Cordero
To recognize a distinguished Mexican jurist of national or international acclaim for his writings in the field and to support jurists who dedicate themselves to the development of Mexican cultural jurisprudence. A monetary prize of 40,000 Mexican new pesos is awarded annually. Established in 1981.

8988
Fundacion Luis Elizondo
Inst.Technologico y de Estudios
  Superiores de Monterrey
Patronato Premio Luis Elizondo
Av. Eugenio Garza Sada 2501 Sur   Phone: 8 3597039
64849 Monterrey, Nuevo Leon, Mexico   Fax: 8 3585608

8989
Premio Luis Elizondo - Premio Cientifico y Technologico
To recognize Mexican scientists who have contributed to the advancement of scientific research in the areas of education, preservation and environment improvement, engineering and technology, medicine, cattle and food technology, economic science, management, and social and natural science. Candidates may be nominated. A monetary prize of N$50,000 Mexican pesos, a gold medal, and a certificate are awarded annually. Established in 1967 in memory of Mr. Elizondo, a great educator and humanitarian.

8990
Premio Luis Elizondo - Premio Humanitario
To recognize those Mexican persons or institutions who have distinguished themselves for heroic accomplishment, philanthropy, charity, or other deeds that save or improve human lives. Candidates may be nominated. A monetary prize of N$50,000 Mexican pesos, a gold medal, and a certificate are awarded annually. Established in 1967 in memory of Mr. Elizondo, a great educator and humanitarian.

8991
Fundacion Miguel Aleman
Ruben Dario 187
Del Miguel Hidalgo   Phone: 5 5317065
11570 Mexico City, DF, Mexico   Fax: 5 2501043

8992
Premio Miguel Aleman Valdes
To recognize and stimulate young researchers and to promote research in the knowledge, prevention, and control of the principal maladies affecting the country's health. Mexican citizens under 40 year of age who are registered researchers in the biological, biomedical, and technological sciences are eligible. A monetary prize of 20,000 Mexican pesos is awarded annually. Established in 1985.

8993
Fundacion nexos
Mazatlan 19
Col. Condesa
06140 Mexico City, DF, Mexico

8994
Carlos Pereyra Prize
For recognition of outstanding accomplishment in the study of contemporaneous Mexican social and political questions. Recipients must be under 35 years of age. An indivisible monetary prize of 15,000,000 Mexican pesos and publication in the magazine nexos is awarded annually. Established in 1991.

8995
Gobierno del Estado de Baja California Sur
Casa de la Cultura del Estado
Francisco I. Madero esq.
Juan Ma. Salvatierra
23000 La Paz, Baja California Sur, Mexico

8996
Premio Nacional de Poesia Ciudad de la Paz
To recognize poets in the Spanish language for outstanding works of unpublished, free-form poetry. Works must be at least 30 pages long. A monetary prize of 2,000,000 Mexican pesos is awarded annually.

8997
Gobierno del Estado de Morelos
Cuernavaca, Morelos, Mexico

8998
Gilberto Figueroa Nogueron Prize
(Premio Gilberto Figueroa Nogueron)
To recognize the most outstanding journalist. A monetary prize is awarded annually by the state of Morelos. Established in 1989.

8999
Gobierno del Estado de Puebla
Reforma 711
72000 Puebla, Puebla, Mexico   Phone: 22 32 14 23

9000
Gabino Barreda
(Medalla Gabin Barreda)
For recognition of more than forty years of teaching by professors. A monetary prize is awarded annually.

9001
Carmen and Aguiles Serdan Prize
(Medalla Carmen y Aguiles Serdan)
For recognition of outstanding contributions to the social development of the state of Puebla. A gold medal is awarded.

9002
Ignacio Zaragosa Jewel
(Presea Ignacio Zaragosa)
For recognition of distinguished service by a citizen of Puebla.

9003
Gobierno del Estado de Tlaxcala
Juarez 62
Tlaxcala 90000
Tlaxcala, Mexico
Fax: 246 21177

9004
Miguel N. Lira Poetry Prize
(Premio de Poesia Miguel N. Lira)
For recognition of outstanding unpublished poetry by Mexican residents under the age of forty years who speak Castillian Spanish. An indivisible monetary prize, publication, and a miniature replica of "La Caprichosa" are awarded. Also, honorable mention and a monetary prize are given for the best opera. Awarded in October.

9005
Gobierno del Estado de Veracruz-Llave
Instituto Veracruzano de Cultura
Francisco Canal, s/n esq.
91700 Veracruz, Veracruz, Mexico

9006
Jorge Cuesta National Poetry Prize
(Premio Nacional de Poesia Jorge Cuesta)
For recognition of outstanding poetry by residents under 30 years of age. An indivisible monetary prize is awarded annually. Cosponsored by Ayuntamiento de Cordova, Veracruz; Secretaria de Educacion y Cultural; and Instituto Veracruzano de Cultural.

9007
Government of the State of Mexico
(Gobierno del Estado de Mexico)
Lerdo de Tejada 300
50000 Toluca, Mexico
Phone: 72 147388
Fax: 72 130634

9008
Galardon Estado de Mexico
To recognize distinguished persons in the diverse areas of civil service, humanistic deeds, art, culture, science, and technology. The Jose Maria Luis Mora Distinction is awarded to non-natives and residents of Mexico. The Jose Maria Alzate Distinction is awarded in the sciences. A monetary prize of 600,000 Mexican pesos and a gold medal are awarded annually. Established in 1983.

9009
International Sculpture Competition in Madera
(Concurso Internacional de la Escultura en Madera)
For recognition of outstanding sculpture in Madera by residents or those living nearby, citizen or foreigner. Four gold medals are awarded annually. Established in 1989. Additional information is available from Instituto Mexiquense de Cultura, Pedro Ascencio Norte 103, Col. Centro, Toluca, Edo. de Mexico, 05000.

9010
National Aquarell Contest
(Concurso Nacional de Acuarela acera de Temas Turisticos del Estado de Mexico)
For recognition of the best works in Aquarelle using tourism as the theme. Monetary prizes and certificates are awarded annually to the first three places. Additional information is available from Direccion General de Turismo, Av. 5, Lerdo de Tejada Poniente 10, Edificio Plaza Toluca, 1er piso, 50000, Toluca, Estado de Mexico, Mexico.

9011
Government of the State of Sinaloa
(Gobierno del Estado de Sinaloa)
Unidad Administrativa s/n
82000 Mazatlan, Sinaloa, Mexico
Phone: 678 244 88

9012
Competition for Children's Theater or Stories
(Concurso de cuento y de Teatro Infantil)
For recognition of the best children's plays or stories by Mexican citizens or residents. Monetary prizes of 2,500,000, 1,750,000, and 1,250,000 Mexican pesos and certificates are awarded annually. Established in 1987. Additional information is available from: Gobierno del Estado de Sinaloa, DIF Sinaloa, Ignacio Ramirez y Riva Palacio, 80200, Culiacan, Sinaloa, Mexico, phone: 671 32969.

9013
Condecoracion al Merito Social
To recognize meritorious persons. The following medals are given annually: (1) Medalla Bernardo Balbuena for persons of artistic, scientific or literary distinction; (2) Medalla Antonio Rosales for recognition of civic merit; and (3) Medalla Agustin Ramirez as recompense for acts of heroism. Established in 1961.

9014
Gilbert Owen National Prize for Literature
(Premio Nacional de Literatura Gilberto Owen)
To recognize radical Mexican writers and poets for unpublished works of outstanding character. Monetary prizes of 10,000,000 Mexican pesos and publication are awarded to first place winners in both poetry and short story. Second and third places receive honorable mentions. Awarded annually. Additional information is available from: Direccion de Investigacion y Fomento de Cultura Regional, Ruperto L. Paliza y Malecon Ninos Heroes, 80000, Culiacan, Sinaloa, Mexico.

9015
Premio Sinaloa de Ciencias y Artes
To recognize distinguished Sinaloans in the sciences and arts for work accomplished within or outside Sinaloa. A monetary prize of 10,000,000 Mexican pesos, a gold medal, and a certificate are awarded annually.

9016
Premio Sinaloa de Periodismo
To recognize outstanding professional journalists with the following distinctions: (1) Premio Genaro Estrada - for columns; (2) Premio Pablo Villavicencio - for interviewing; (3) Premio Julio G. Arce - for news; (4) Premio Alejandro Zazuete - for photography; (5) Premio Gustavo D. Canedo - for sport reporting; and (6) Premio Jose Cayetano Valdez - for reporting; and (7) Premio Carlos Mateo Sanchez - for caricature, cartooning. A monetary prize is awarded annually. Established in 1974.

9017
Grupo Aluminio, S.A. de C.V.
Bosques de Ciruelos 130, 4 piso
Col. Bosques de las Lomas
11700 Mexico City, DF, Mexico
Phone: 5 596 7389
Phone: 5 596 7661

9018

**National Design Competition for the Use of Aluminum
(Concurso Nacional de Diseno para Uso y aplicacon del Aluminio)**
For recognition of the best designs for aluminum usage in industry. Monetary prizes are awarded to the first three place winners.

9019

El Heraldo de Mexico
Carmona y Valle 150
Col. Doctores
06720 Mexico City, DF, Mexico   Phone: 5 578 3632

9020

El Heraldo Music Prizes
For recognition of accomplishments in music. Awards are given in the following categories: best conductor; best record; best composer; best song; best interpretation of music by an unknown performer; and best Mexican folklore songs. Bronze statuettes are awarded annually. Established in 1966.

9021

El Heraldo Prizes
For recognition of accomplishments in film, theatre and television. Awards are given in the following categories: best film, theater and television directors; best actors and actresses of film, theater and television; best supporting male and female actors of film, theater and television; outstanding performance by an unknown artist; and best script written for film and television. Bronze statuettes are awarded annually. Established in 1966.

9022

El Heraldo Sport Prizes
For recognition of outstanding achievements in boxing, cycling, gymnastics, tennis and bull-fighting. Bronze statuettes are awarded annually. Established in 1966.

9023

Hospital General Dr. Manuel Gea Gonzalez
Subdireccion de Ingestigacion y
   Ensenanza
Calz. Tlalpn 4800
Col. Tlalpan
14000 Mexico City, DF, Mexico   Phone: 5 573 2511

9024

Premio Gea Gonzalez - PUIC
To recognize promising young medical scientists and to encourage their participation in medical research. A monetary prize is awarded annually to the three top places, as well as a silver medal to the first and second places, and a certificate to the third. Co-sponsored by the Programa Universitario de Investigacion Clinica de la UNAM.

9025

**Institute of Technology and Higher Studies of Monterrey
(Instituto Technologico y de Estudios Superiores de Monterrey)**
Sucursal de Correos ''J''   Phone: 83 58 2000
64849 Monterrey, Nuevo Leon, Mexico   Phone: 83 58 6000

9026

Premio Romulo Garza para Investigacion
To recognize professors of ITESM for scientific and technical research. Monetary prizes and certificates are awarded annually. Established in 1974 in memory of the Institute's co-founder Romulo Garza.

9027

Premio Romulo Garza para Publicaciones
To recogizde professors of ITESM for scientific, literary and educational publications. Monetary prizes and certificates are awarded biennially. Established in 1974 in memory of the Institute's co-founder, Romulo Garza.

9028

Instituto Cultural Domecq, A.C.
Viena 161 Esq. Mina
Col. del Carmen Covoacan   Phone: 5 6592796
04100 Mexico City, DF, Mexico   Fax: 5 6590695

9029

Bienal de Iberoamericana de Arte
To honor and promote the visual arts as a great manifestation of the culture and foundation of Iberoamerica and to recognize Iberian Americans for outstanding works of art, and thereby promote greater bonds of Ibero-American solidarity. The following prizes are awarded: first prize - 6,500,000 Mexican pesos; second prize - 5,500,000 Mexican pesos; and third prize - 4,500,000 Mexican pesos. Prizes are awarded in two categories, artistic skill and appearance. Established in 1978.

9030

Mozart Medal
To recognize young musicians for their talent in music composition, direction, and interpretation. Mexican composers who are under 35 years of age are eligible. A monetary prize of 3,000,000 Mexican pesos is awarded. Established in 1991 to commemorate the bicentenniel of the death of Mozart.

9031

Premio Literario Netzahualcoyotl
To recognize outstanding authors in Spanish or Portuguese for works on the theme, ''Forgers of the Collective Soul.'' Monetary prizes of 3,000,000, 2,000,000 and 1,000,000 Mexican pesos for first, second, and third place, and 500,000 Mexican pesos for five honorable mentions were awarded annually. Established in 1981. (Discontinued)

9032

Instituto de Investigaciones Electricas
Leibnitz 14-3
Col. Anzures
11590 Mexico City, DF, Mexico   Phone: 5 531 0033

9033

Certamen Anual Nacional de Tesis de Ingenieria
For recognition of outstanding engineering theses in the following fields: (1) electrical systems; (2) mechanical systems; (3) control systems; and (4) power systems. Monetary prizes of up to 5,000,000 Mexican pesos are awarded annually. Established in 1978. Co-sponsored by Comision Federal de Electricidad, and Consejo Nacional de Ciencia y Tecnologia.

9034

Instituto Mexicano de Contadores Publicos
Av. Bosque de Tabachines 44
Col. Bosques de las Lomas
11700 Mexico City, DF, Mexico   Phone: 5 596 6819

9035

Premio el Professor Distinguido
For recognition of achievement in the educational field. A CPA degree and outstanding development as a teacher in a public accounting school are required for consideration. A medal is awarded annually. Established in 1981.

9036
Premio Nacional de la Contaduria Publica
For recognition of the best original and unpublished work on public accounting. The following monetary prizes are awarded: (1) first prize - 10,000,000 pesos; (2) second prize - 600,000 pesos; and (3) third prize - 400,000 pesos. Certificates are also awarded biennially. Established in 1970.

9037
Instituto Mexicano de Ejecutivos de Finanzas
Patricio Sanz 1516
Col. Del Valle
03100 Mexico City, DF, Mexico   Phone: 5 559 8366

9038
IMEF National Prize for Financial Research
(Premio Nacional de Investigacion Financiera IMEE)
For recognition of outstanding financial research, or analysis of related themes, by Mexican citizens or residents. Works may be completed by individuals or teams. Monetary prizes up to 22,000,000 Mexican pesos are awarded in three categories: research projects, theses and published articles. Awarded annually. Established in 1984.

9039
Instituto Mexicano de Recursos Naturales Renovables
Avda. Dr. Vertiz 724
03020 Mexico City, DF, Mexico   Phone: 5 519 1633

9040
Medalla Alfonso L. Herrera al Merito en Ecologia y Conservacion
For recognition of outstanding achievement in the fields of ecology, environment, or conservation. Any Mexican citizen may be nominated or may apply. A medal and a diploma are awarded annually. Established in 1983 in memory of Alfonso L. Herrera, a Mexican biologist.

9041
Instituto Mexicano del Mercado de Capitales
Paseo de la Reforma 295-12
06500 Mexico City, DF, Mexico   Phone: 5 525 7082

9042
Premio Nacional del Mercado de Valores
To recognize outstanding efforts which stimulate and contribute to the development of the stock market, as well as generate interest in the subject. Monetary prizes of 1,500,000, 1,000,000, and 500,000 Mexican pesos as well as certificates and fellowships to fourth and fifth place winners are awarded annually. Co-sponsored by the Bolsa de Valores S.A. de C.V.

9043
Instituto Mexicano del Seguro Social
Oficina de Relaciones Publicas
Paseo de la Reforma 506, piso 13
06600 Mexico City, DF, Mexico   Phone: 5 553 4222

9044
Premios a la Investigacion Medica
For recognition of outstanding medical research in the areas of basic research, clinical research, and public health. A certificate is awarded annually.

9045
Instituto Mexiquense de Cultura
Casa de Cultura de Toluca
Jardin del Arte
Pedro Ascencio 103 Nte.   Phone: 721 473 88
50000 Toluca, Mexico, Mexico   Phone: 721 459 98

9046
Ignacio Manuel Altamirano Prize for Novel
(Premio de Novela Ignacio Manuel Altamirano)
To recognize the region's best author for a work concerning or taking place in the state of Mexico. Monetary prizes are awarded annually to the first three place winners.

9047
Children's Story Prize
(Premio de Cuento para Ninos)
For recognition of the best children's story. Monetary prizes are awarded to the first three place winners annually.

9048
Angel Maria Garibay Kintana Prize for Literary Essay
(Premio de Ensayo Literario Angel Maria Garibay Kintana)
To recognize Mexican authors interested in the lives and works of Mexican authors of other epochs, including those interested in Mexican or foreign authors whose works concern the total body of the state of Mexico's literature. Monetary prizes are awarded annually to the first three place winners.

9049
Josue Mirlo Poetry Prize
(Premio de Poesia Josue Mirlo)
To recognize authors from the state of Mexico for outstanding works of poetry. Monetary prizes are awarded to the first three place winners annually.

9050
Instituto Nacional de Administracion Publica
Km. 14.5, Carretera Mexico-Toluca 2151   Phone: 5 5706945
11910 Mexico City, DF, Mexico   Fax: 5 5700532

9051
Premio del Instituto Nacional de Administracion Publica
For recognition of outstanding contributions to and the promotion of scientific research in the field of public administration. Monetary prizes of 30,000 and 10,000 new Mexican pesos and publication of the work are awarded annually. Established in 1976.

9052
Instituto Nacional de Antropologia e Historia
Cordova 45-1
Col. Roma
06700 Mexico City, DF, Mexico

9053
Premio Alfonso Caso
For recognition of outstanding achievement in the field of archaeology. Monetary prizes of 1,000,000, 800,000 and 700,000 Mexican pesos and Honorable Mentions are awarded annually when merited.

9054
Premio Francisco de la Maza
For recognition of outstanding achievement in the fields of redemption, restoration, and conservation of historic cities and the native culture in the urban scene. Monetary prizes of 1,000,000, 800,000 and 700,000 Mexican pesos and Honorable Mentions are awarded annually when merited.

9055
Premio Francisco Javier Clavijero
For recognition of outstanding achievement in the field of history. Monetary prizes of 1,000,000, 800,000 and 700,000 Mexican pesos and Honorable Mentions are awarded annually when merited.

9056
Premio Fray Bernardino de Sahagun
For recognition of outstanding achievement in the fields of ethnography, ethnology, and ethnohistory. Monetary prizes of 1,000,000, 800,000 and 700,000 Mexican pesos and Honorable Mentions are awarded annually when merited.

9057
Premio Juan Comas
For recognition of outstanding achievement in the field of physical anthropology. Monetary prizes of 1,000,000, 800,000 and 700,000 Mexican pesos and Honorable Mentions are awarded annually when merited.

9058
Premio Manuel Toussaint
For recognition of outstanding achievement in the fields of redemption, restoration, conservation, and protection of the native architure. Monetary prizes of 1,000,000, 800,000 and 700,000 Mexican pesos and Honorable Mentions are awarded annually when merited.

9059
Premio Miguel Covarrubias
For recognition of outstanding achievement in the field of museum design and research. Monetary prizes of 1,000,000, 800,000 and 700,000 Mexican pesos and Honorable Mentions are awarded annually when merited.

9060
Premio Miguel Othon de Mendizabal
For recognition of outstanding achievement in the field of social anthropology. Monetary prizes of 1,000,000, 800,000 and 700,000 Mexican pesos and Honorable Mentions are awarded annually when merited.

9061
Premio Nicolas Leon
For recognition of outstanding achievement in the field of linguistic anthropology. Monetary prizes of 1,000,000, 800,000 and 700,000 Mexican pesos and Honorable Mentions are awarded annually when merited.

9062
Premio Paul Coremans
For recognition of outstanding achievement in the fields of redemption, and conservation of personal property. Monetary prizes of 1,000,000, 800,000 and 700,000 Mexican pesos and Honorable Mentions are awarded annually when merited.

9063
Premio Vicente T. Mendoza
For recognition of outstanding achievement in the field of folklore. Monetary prizes of 1,000,000, 800,000 and 700,000 Mexican pesos and Honorable Mentions are awarded annually when merited.

9064
Instituto Nacional de Neurologia y Neurocirugia
Programa Prioritario de Epilepsia
Insurgentes Sur 3877
14410 Mexico City, DF, Mexico   Phone: 5 573 3822

9065
Premio Anual de Investigacion en Epilpsia
For recognition of outstanding research in the field of epilepsy and to promote new research in the medical-social problem. Prizes are awarded annually in the areas of basic, clinical, and social research. Co-sponsored by the Programa Universitario de Investigacion en Salud.

9066
Instituto Nacional Indigenista
Av. Revolucion 1279-1
01010 Mexico, DF, Mexico   Phone: 5 6513030

9067
Premios INI
For recognition of outstanding contributions to the cultural knowledge of and the betterment of the native Indian population of Mexico. Monetary prizes of up to 10,000,000 Mexican pesos are awarded annually in the categories of native medicine, native technology and the raditional use thereof, promotion of native artisans, written development and recovery of native traditions, justice for the Indians, and native radio broadcasts. Established in 1990. (Discontinued)

9068
Instituto Politecnico Nacional
Unidad Profesional Zacatenco
07738 Mexico City, DF, Mexico   Phone: 5 754 4591

9069
Medalla Juan de Dios Batiz
For recognition of 30 years of teaching technology. A medal is awarded annually.

9070
Instituto Syntex
Paseo de la Reforma 2822
Apartadpo Postal 10-821
11910 Mexico City, DF, Mexico

9071
Premio Anual de Investigacion Medica Dr. Jorge Rosenkranz
For recognition of outstanding Mexican medical research. A monetary prize of 25,000,000 Mexican pesos and a certificate are awarded annually to each of two winners, one residing in Mexico City, the other residing elsewhere in the country.

9072
Interamerican Society of Cardiology
(Sociedad Interamericana de Cardiologia)
Juan Badiano 1
Tlalpan
14080 Mexico City, DF, Mexico   Phone: 5 573 2911

9073
Professor Ignacio Chavez Young Investigator Award
(Premio Joven Investigador Profesor Ignacio Chavez)
To recognize the best cardiological work presented at the Interamerican Congress of Cardiology. The Congress is held every two years in a city of the continent (America). The 1988 Congress was held in Panama. Established in 1981.

9074
International Good Neighbor Council
(Consejo Internacional de Buena Vecindad)
Edificio Latino, Desp. 513
Juan I. Ramon 506 Ote.
64000 Monterrey, Nuevo Leon, Mexico   Phone: 83 42 7633

9075
Good Neighbor Award
To recognize individuals who promote goodwill and understanding among nations of the Western Hemisphere and facilitate communication and cooperation among countries, agencies, and official and private groups with common interests. Nominations are accepted. A medal and plaque are awarded annually. The award commemorates good neighborliness among the nations, through this Organization, founded by Mr. Glenn A. Garrett, former Governor of Texas, and Mr. Jose A. Muguerza, former Governor of Nuevo Leon.

9076
International Organization for Chemical Sciences in Development (Organisation Internationale des Sciences Chimiques pour la Developpement)
Apartado Postal 70-172
Edificio de Coordinacion Cientifica
Coyoacan
04510 Mexico City, DF, Mexico   Phone: 5 5481603

9077
International Organization for Chemical Sciences in Development Awards
To recognize chemists and institutions around the world for collaborative programs aimed at strengthening the chemical sciences in developing countries. Fellowships and awards are presented.

9078
Journalists' Club
(Club de Periodistas)
Filomeno Mata 8, 3 piso
Col. Centro
06000 Mexico City, DF, Mexico   Phone: 5 512 8661

9079
Jose Antonio Alzate Prize
To provide recognition for the best reporting. A first prize of 20,000 pesos, a gold medal, and diplomas are awarded.

9080
Emilio Azcarraga Vidaurreta Prize
To provide recognition for the most timely news transmitted by television. A monetary prize of 20,000 pesos, a gold medal, and diplomas are awarded.

9081
Augustin Casasola Prize
To provide recognition for the best and most timely photography. A monetary prize of 20,000 pesos, a gold medal, and diplomas are awarded.

9082
Juan Ignacio Castorena y Urzua
For recognition of the best survey. A monetary prize of 20,000 pesos, a gold medal, and diplomas are awarded.

9083
Bernal Diaz del Castillo Prize
To recognize the best columnist. A monetary prize of 20,000 pesos, a gold medal, and diplomas are awarded.

9084
Jose F. Elizondo Prize
To provide recognition for the best humorous writing in prose or in verse. A monetary prize of 20,000 pesos, a gold medal, and diplomas are awarded.

9085
Constantino Escalante Prize
To provide recognition for the best caricature. A monetary prize of 20,000 pesos, a gold medal, and diplomas are awarded.

9086
Jose Joaquin Fernandez de Lizaldi Prize
For recognition of the best editorial. A monetary prize of 20,000 pesos, a gold medal, and diplomas are awarded.

9087
Guillermo Gonzalez Camarena
To provide recognition for the best news broadcast transmitted by any television station in Mexico. A monetary prize of 20,000 pesos, a gold medal, and diplomas are awarded.

9088
Jose Guadelupe Posada Prize
To provide recognition for the best graphic report. A first prize of 20,000 pesos, a gold medal, and diplomas are awarded.

9089
Carlos Noria de Bustamente Prize
To provide recognition for the most timely information article. A monetary prize of 20,000 pesos, a gold medal, and diplomas are awarded.

9090
Alfonso Sordo Noriega Prize
To provide recognition for the best radio newsbroadcast. A monetary prize of 20,000 pesos, a gold medal, and diplomas are awarded.

9091
Ignacio Ramirez Prize
To provide recognition for the best interview. A first prize of 20,000 pesos, a gold medal, and diplomas are awarded.

9092
Ing. Salvador Toscano Prize
To provide recognition for the best information in cinematographic press. A monetary prize of 20,000 pesos, a gold medal, and diplomas are awarded. Established in 1982.

9093
Francisco Zarco Prize
To provide recognition for the best article of the greatest national interest. A monetary prize of 20,000 pesos, a gold medal, and diplomas are awarded.

9094
Liga de Economistas Revolucionarios
Paseo del Rio 118
Col. Chimalistac
01070 Mexico City, DF, Mexico   Phone: 5 550 0837

9095
National Economics Prize
(Premio Nacional de Economia)
For recognition of outstanding works by economists on the national level in the following academic areas: (1) the industrial sector versus the opening of commerce and the free trade agreement; (2) the modernization of the agrarian sector; (3) the services sector versus open commerce; and (4) education and economic modernization. The LER reserves the right to publish the winning work. A monetary prize of 20,000,000 Mexican pesos is awarded. Established in 1991.

9096
Mexican Academy of Cinematographic Arts and Sciences
(Academia Mexicana de Ciencias y Artes)
Av. Mexico Coyoacan 340
03340 Mexico City, DF, Mexico   Phone: 5 688 8963

9097
Premio Ariel de Cinematografia
(Ariel Prizes for Cinematography)
To recognize the best films of the year. The following prizes are awarded: Gold Ariel - best film of the year; and Silver Ariels - best directing; best acting; best scenario; best photography; best film editing (documentary and fiction); and best musical score. Awarded annually. Established in 1958.

9098
Mexican Academy of Dermatology
(Academia Mexicana de Dermatologia)
Eucken 15, 1st Fl.   Phone: 5 5311893
11590 Mexico City, DF, Mexico   Fax: 5 2509161

9099
Dr. Antonio Gonzalez Ochoa Award
To recognize a dermatology resident for the best paper in clinical or basic research. Awarded annually in March in Mexico City.

9100
Mexican Academy of Surgery
(Academia Mexicana de Cirugia)
Av. Cuauhtemoc esq. Dr. Marquez, 1er
   piso
Hospital de Oftalmologia
Col. Doctores
06725 Mexico City, DF, Mexico   Phone: 5 519 4687

9101
Premio Dr. Gonzalo Castaneda
For recognition of the best work written by a member of the Mexican Academy of Surgery. Gold, silver, and bronze medals are awarded.

9102
Premio Dr. Jose Aguilar Alvarez Prize
For recognition of the best paper on surgical research. A monetary prize was awarded annually. (Discontinued in 1982)

9103
Premio Dr. Manuel J. Castillejos
For recognition of the best film on surgery used for the training of surgeons or paramedical personnel. Films dealing with surgical techniques can also be submitted to the contest. Films must be in color, last at least 25 minutes and cannot be sponsored by any commercial institution. A monetary prize of 500,000 Mexican pesos and a diploma for first prize; 250,000 Mexican pesos and a diploma for second prize; and 100,000 Mexican pesos for third prize are awarded annually.

9104
Mexican Institute of Chemical Engineers
(Instituto Mexicano de Ingeneiros Quimicos)
Horacio 124
Col. Polanco
11560 Mexico City, DF, Mexico   Phone: 5 545 5817

9105
Mencion IMIQ
For recognition of works presented at the national convention. A plaque and certificate are awarded annually.

9106
Premio IMIQ
To recognize the best work presented at the national convention of IMIQ.

9107
Premio IMIQ-CONACYT
For recognition of the outstanding licentiate's thesis in chemical engineering.

9108
Premio IMIQ, ING. Estanislao Ramirez
For recognition of excellence in the teaching of chemical engineering.

9109
Premio IMIQ, Victor Marquez Dominguez
For recognition of outstanding professional progress in the field of chemical engineering.

9110
Premio para el Estimulo de Docencia e Investigacion en Ingenieria Quimica
(Prize to Stimulate Teaching and Research in Chemical Engineering)
For recognition of original, published or unpublished works presented in the form of an essay or special research project which are considered an important contribution to analysis and planning of further development in Mexico, particularly in the field of chemical engineering. Members of the Institute residing in any part of the world who are authors of works, with the exception of student members or members younger than 30 years of age, are eligible. A diploma and honorary mention are awarded annually.

9111
Mexican National Academy of Medicine
(Academia Nacional de Medicina de Mexico)
Av. Cuauhtemoc 330
Unidad de Congressos del IMSS
06725 Mexico City, DF, Mexico   Phone: 5 578 4271

9112
Dr. Francisco Javier Balmis Prize
To recognize the best paper on public health published during the three years prior to the closing date of the contest. A monetary prize, a medal, and a diploma were awarded annually. (Discontinued)

9113
Hoechst Prize para Investigacion Medica
For recognition of outstanding research in experimental or clinical medicine. A monetary prize was awarded annually. (Discontinued)

9114
Premio Dr. Eduardo Liceaga
For recognition of contributions to biomedical research. Mexican scientists may submit papers that have been published during the three year period prior to July 30 of each year. A monetary prize and a diploma are awarded annually.

9115
Premio Dr. Fernando Ocaranza
To recognize the best paper on experimental surgery published during the three years preceding the closing date of the contest. A monetary prize, a medal, and a diploma were awarded annually. Co-sponsored by the Lepetit Laboratories. (Discontinued)

9116
Premio Fundacion Eli Lilly
To encourage the development of specific research projects in the field of clinical medicine. A monetary prize was awarded annually. (Discontinued)

9117
Mexican Pharmaceutical Association
(Asociacion Farmaceutica Mexicana)
Adolfo Prieto 1649-402
03100 Mexico City, DF, Mexico
Phone: 5 140993
Fax: 5 34098

9118
Dr. Rio de La Loza Prize
To recognize an outstanding contribution to pharmaceutical sciences. A gold medal and a diploma are awarded annually.

9119
Mexican Section of the International Board on Books for Young People
(Asociacion Mexicana para el Fomento del Libro Infantil y Juvenil)
Parque Espana 13
Col. Condesa
06140 Mexico City, DF, Mexico
Phone: 5 2110492
Fax: 5 2110492

9120
Premio Antoniorrobles
(Antoniorrobles Award)
To encourage new writers and illustrators in the field of books for children and young people. Awards are given in three categories: text, illustration, and text and illustration. Original unpublished work must be submitted by December 31. There are no restrictions on age, citizenship, or length of work. Diplomas and promotion of the winners among publishers are awarded annually. Established in 1981 in memory of the Spanish writer, Antoniorrobles, for his contribution to children's literature in Mexico.

9121
Mexican Society for the History of Science and Technology
(Sociedad Mexicana de Historia de La Ciencia y de La Tecnologia)
Apdo. Postal 21-873
04000 Mexico City, DF, Mexico
Phone: 5 6221864
Fax: 5 6596406

9122
Dr. Enrique Beltran Prize of the History of Science and Technology
(Premio Dr. Enrique Beltran de Historia de La Ciencia y La Tecnologia)
To recognize the best essay on any aspect of the history of Mexican science and/or technology (including exact and natural sciences, social sciences, and technology). Essays written in Spanish or translated into Spanish that are at least 150 pages long must be submitted by June 30. A monetary award of 10,000 nuevos pesos and publication of the essay are awarded biennially. Established in 1990 to honor Dr. Enrique Beltran, founder of the Sociedad Mexicana de Historia de La Ciencia y de La Tecnologia in 1964. Sponsored by the Universidad Nacional Autonoma de Mexico, the Universidad Autonoma Metropolitana, and the National Council of Science and Technology.

9123
Mexico
Chamber of Deputies
(Mexico
Camara de Diputados)
Palacio Legislativo
Av. Congreso de la Union s/n
06600 Mexico City, DF, Mexico
Phone: 5 6221864
Fax: 5 6596406

9124
Medalla Eduardo Neri
For recognition of outstanding service to the Mexican nation by a Mexican citizen, in either social, artistic, scientific, or political fields. A gold medal is awarded triennially. Established in 1969 in memory of Mr. Neri's valiant parliamentary participation.

9125
Mexico
Council of General Health
(Mexico
Consejo de Salubridad General)
Ocaso 101, 4 piso
Col. Insurgentes Cuicuilco
04530 Mexico City, DF, Mexico
Phone: 5 655 4354

9126
Auxiliar de Enfermera Lucia Salcido
For recognition of achievement and contribution in the auxiliary nurse field, including outstanding services, research or study, carried out in Mexico. Nominations or applications are accepted by January 15 each year. A monetary prize of 350,000 Mexican pesos is awarded annually. Established in 1981 in memory of auxiliary nurse, Lucia Salcido, who was murdered in 1946, while she was working in a smallpox vaccination campaign.

9127
Condecoracion Dr. Eduardo Liceaga
For recognition of an outstanding contribution in the public health field. Institutions may nominate individuals by January 15 each year. A monetary prize of 750,000 Mexican pesos is awarded annually. Established in 1940 in memory of Dr. Eduardo Liceaga, a Mexican physician (1839-1920), who was one of the first public health workers in Mexico.

9128
Premio al Merito Nacional Enfermera Isabel Cendala Gomez
For recognition of achievement and contribution in the nursing field, including outstanding services, research or study, carried out in Mexico. Nominations or applications are accepted by January 15 each year. A monetary prize of 350,000 Mexican pesos is awarded annually. Established in 1975 in honor of Enfermera Isabel Cendala y Gomez, who brought to Mexico children immunized against smallpox, in order to perform exchange transfusions, arm to arm, with Mexican children.

9129
Premio Gerardo Varela
For recognition of achievement in public health research carried out in Mexico. Nominations or applications may be submitted by January 15 each year. A monetary prize of 350,000 Mexican pesos and a gold medal are awarded annually. Established in 1964 in honor of Dr. Gerardo Varela, a Mexican physician (1899-1977), who made contributions in the epidemiological and microbiological field.

9130
Premio Martin de la Cruz
For recognition of achievement in pharmaceutical research. Nominations or applications are accepted by January 15 each year. A monetary prize of 600,000 Mexican pesos is awarded annually. Established in 1984 in honor of Dr. Martin de la Cruz, a Mexican physician, who lived in the 16th century and was the author of the first herbal medicine treatise published in the local language (Nahuatl).

9131
Premio Miguel Otero
For recognition of achievement in clinical or biomedical research carried out in Mexico. Nominations or applications are accepted by January 15 each year. A monetary prize of 350,000 Mexican pesos and a gold medal are awarded annually. Established in 1974 in memory of Dr. Miguel Otero Arce, a Mexican physician (1855-1915), for typhus research including epidemiological and microbiological facts.

9132

Mexico
Ministry of Foreign Affairs
(Mexico
Secretaria de Relaciones Exteriores)
Ricardo Flores Magon s/n
06995 Mexico City, DF, Mexico   Phone: 5 597 5280

9133

Mexican Order of the Aztec Eagle
(Orden Mexicana del Aguila Azteca)
For recognition of outstanding services to Mexico and humanity by persons of foreign nationality. The following awards are presented in military and civil classes: (1) a chain with an insignia of honor (el collar) - to chiefs of states; (2) a cross - to heads of governments or prime ministers; (3) a sash - to ministers, secretaries of state and ambassadors; (4) a medal - to under secretaries, special envoys and ministers plenipotenciary; (5) a plaque - to charge d'affairs; (6) a badge (la venera) - to public officials in foreign chanceries and members of diplomatic missions; and (7) an insignia - to others the Award Council wants to honor. Awarded when merited. No more than 415 may be awarded. Established in 1933.

9134

Mexico
Ministry of Health and Welfare
(Mexico
Secretaria de Salud)
Lieja 7, 1er piso
06956 Mexico City, DF, Mexico   Phone: 5 553 6888

9135

National Community Service Prize
(Premio Nacional de Servicios a la Comunidad)
To recognize individuals for outstanding volunteer services to the community. An insignia of honor and other prizes are awarded.

9136

Mexico
Ministry of Labor and Social Security
(Mexico
Secretaria de Trabajo y Prevision Social)
Anillo Periferico Sur 4271
Edificio A, Nivel 9   Phone: 5 6455591
14140 Mexico City, DF, Mexico   Fax: 5 6452962

9137

National Labor Prize
(Premio Nacional de Trabajo)
To recognize individuals who, through organizational ability, efficiency, and enthusiasm in their daily work, improved their field and whose example stimulated other workers. A plaque is awarded.

9138

Mexico
Ministry of the Interior
(Mexico
Secretaria de Gobernacion Internal)
Secretaria del Consejo de Premiacion
Direccion General de Comunicacion Social
Bucareli 99, 1er piso
06699 Mexico City 1, DF, Mexico   Phone: 5 566 8188

9139

National Prize for Civic Merit
(Premio Nacional de Merito Civico)
For recognition of outstanding civic aservice. Individuals who have distinguished themselves by their concern for public institutions, rights of individuals and public welfare, and respect for the law are eligible. A badge (la venera) is awarded when merited.

9140

National Prize for Journalism and Information
(Premio Nacional de Periodismo y de Informacion)
To recognize individuals who have distinguished themselves in the following fields: news; photography or film; reporting or interviews; editorials or commentaries; caricatures or cartoons; and publications or programs of a cultural nature. The correct use of the medium, truthfulness and objectivity, plus interest which these works arouse is taken into consideration. Individuals and organizations are eligible. A monetary prize of 10,000,000 Mexican pesos, a medal, and certificates are awarded annually.

9141

Premio Miguel Hidalgo
This, the oldest Order of Mexico, is given for recognition of services to the country or to humanity, or for heroism and exemplary conduct. The following awards are presented: a badge (la venera); a cross; a sash; or a plaque. Awarded when merited.

9142

Mexico
Senate of the Republic
(Mexico
Camara de Senadores)
c/o Comision Medalla Belisario
  Dominguez
Xicotencatl 9
06018 Mexico City, DF, Mexico

9143

Belisario Dominguez Medal of Honor
(Medalla de Honor Belisario Dominguez)
To recognize the Mexican who has distinguished himself as a man of knowledge or for outstanding service to the country or humanity. A gold medal and a certificate are awarded annually on October 7. Established in 1953 to commemorate the sacrifice of Senator Belisario Dominguez.

9144

Mexico Ministry of Public Education
(Secretaria de Education Publica)
Consejo del Premio Nacional de Ciencias
  y Artes
Argentina 28, Oficina 124
06029 Mexico City, DF, Mexico   Phone: 5 5844662

9145

Ignacio Manuel Altamarino Medal
(Medalla Ignacio Manuel Altamarino)
To recognize individuals for more than 50 years of service in education. A monetary prize is awarded annually.

9146

National Prize for Fine Arts
(Premio Nacional de Bellas Artes)
To stimulate creativity and to recognize achievements of Mexican artists. A monetary prize, honorable mention, and a badge are awarded annually.

9147

National Prize for History, Social Sciences and Philosophy
(Premio Nacional de Historia, Ciencias Sociales y Filosofia)
For recognition of outstanding contributions to history, social sciences, or philosophy. Mexican scholars are eligible. A monetary prize, honorable mention, and a badge are awarded annually.

9148
National Prize for Linguistics and Literature
(Premio Nacional de Linguistica y Literatura)
To stimulate the development of Mexican literature and linguistics and to reward the best novels, poetry, essay, biography, drama, motion picture scriptwriting, and works on linguistics. A monetary prize, honorable mention, and a badge are awarded annually.

9149
National Prize for Physics, Mathematics and Natural Sciences
(Premio Nacional de Ciencias Fisico - Matematicas y Naturales)
For recognition of outstanding achievements in the fields of physics, mathematics, and natural sciences and to stimulate research in Mexico. A monetary prize, honorable mention, and a badge are awarded annually.

9150
National Prize for Sports
(Premio Nacional de Deportes)
To recognize outstanding performance in any discipline of sports and to encourage the promotion of sports. Individuals or groups that practice sports as amateurs are eligible. The prize is not awarded to professional or commercial promoters. A medal is awarded. If the prize is awarded to a group or team of athletes, the group receives a certificate and each member of the group receives a medal. Awarded annually.

9151
National Prize for Technology and Design
(Premio Nacional de Tecnologia y Diseno)
For recognition of original works, research, or publications that have contributed to the technological advancement of Mexico. A monetary prize, honorable mention, and a badge are awarded annually.

9152
National Prize in Science and Art
(Premio nacional de Ciencias y Artes)
For recognition of outstanding Mexican contribution to the sciences and the arts. Monetary prizes and certificates are awarded annually in the categories of fine arts; history; social sciences and philosophy; linguistics and literature; physical, mathematical, and natural sciences; and technological and artistic design.

9153
National Youth Prize
(Premio Nacional de la Juventud)
To recognize citizens under 25 years of age whose behavior and dedication to society, work, or academic studies inspired their contemporaries and serve as examples of personal achievement. Individuals or groups are eligible. The award is also given for contributions to community progress. Monetary prizes and medals are awarded in each of five fields. The committee may also choose to award a special prize for honorable mention.

9154
Juan Pablos Editorial Merit Prize
(Premio Juan Pablos al Merito Editorial)
To recognize a national editor. Awarded annually.

9155
Rafael Ramirez Medal
(Medalla Rafael Ramirez)
To recognize individuals for more than 30 years of uninterrupted service. A monetary prize and medal are awarded annually.

9156
Alfonso Reyes Prize
To recognize the best foreign actor whose work relates to that of Alfonso Reyes and to Mexico. A monetary prize is awarded by the Alfonsina (Alfonso Reyes Library) International Society.

9157
Mexinox, S. A. de C. V.
Cracovia 54
01000 Mexico City, DF, Mexico
Phone: 5 6800113
Fax: 5 6511507

9158
Mexinox Prize
(Premio Mexinox)
For recognition of the best ideas in industrial design for the use of stainless steel. Monetary prizes are awarded to the first four place winners. All latin american countries can participate.

9159
Municipality of Monterrey
(Ayuntamiento de Monterrey)
c/o Direccion de Cultura
Palacio Municipal de Monterrey
Monterrey, Nuevo Leon, Mexico
Phone: 83 44 3330

9160
Certamen Nacional de Poesia, Alfonso Reyes
To recognize outstanding national or international poets who have lived in Mexico for at least five years. Monetary prizes of 10,000,000, 8,000,000 and 4,000,000 Mexican pesos are awarded annually.

9161
Municipality of San Juan del Rio
(Ayuntamiento de San Juan del Rio)
San Juan del Rio, Mexico

9162
Juegos Florales Prize of San Juan del Rio, Queretaro
(Premio Juegos Florales de San Juan del Rio, Queretaro)
For recognition of an outstanding unpublished poem or collection of poems by a resident of Mexico. Poems must be at least ten stanzas long. A monetary prize of 2,000,000 Mexican pesos is awarded annually. Established in 1970.

9163
Municipality of Tampico
Direccion de Asuntos Culturales y
 Sociales
Tampico, Mexico

9164
Efrain Huerta National Prize for Short Story and Poetry
For recognition and encouragement of Mexican authors residing in the Republic. Awards are presented for poetry and short stories. A monetary prize of 10,000,000 Mexican pesos is awarded for first place in each category and honorable mentions for second and third place.

9165
Premio Regional de Pintura
To recognize outstanding merit in painting. Up to two works may be submitted by an artist in one of the following categories: oil, acrylic, pastel, watercolor, gouache, tempera, inks, or mixed media. The deadline for submissions is January 1. The following prizes are awarded: first prize - 5,000,000 Mexican pesos; second prize - 3,000,000 Mexican pesos; third prize - 2,000,000 Mexican pesos; and 1,000,000 Mexican pesos for fourth, fifth, and sixth prizes. Awarded annually.

9166
El Nacional
Ignacio Mariscal 24-3
Col. Tabacalera
06030 Mexico City, DF, Mexico   Phone: 5 535 3079

9167
Newspaper Cartoon Competition
(Concurso de Caricatura Periodistica)
For recognition of outstanding young Mexican journalists. Recipients must be under thirty years of age. A monetary prize of 1,000,000 Mexican pesos and publication of the work are awarded.

9168
National Autonomous University of Mexico
(Universidad Nacional Autonoma de Mexico)
Ciudad Universitaria
Delegacion - Coyoacan
04510 Mexico City, DF, Mexico   Phone: 5 550 5215

9169
Concurso de anto Beca Francsco Araiza
For recognition of outstanding talent in vocal music. Monetary prizes are awarded annually. Established in 1987.

9170
Concurso de Cuento de Ciencia Ficcion
For recognition of the best science fiction stories written by students of the college of sciences and humanities. Monetary prizes are awarded annually. Established in 1987.

9171
Concurso de Jovenes Solistas
To recognize and promote young musical talent in piano, flute, and violin. Monetary prizes of 1,000,000, 750,000 and 500,000 Mexican pesos are awarded annually as well as concerts for the top three in each category. Established in 1987.

9172
Concurso de Resena Teatral
For recognition of the best review articles written by students or professors. Monetary prizes and publication in the university's magazine and newspaper are awarded annually. Established in 1990.

9173
Concurso la Mejor Tesis sobre la Mujer in la UNAM
For recogntion of the best theses about women in various fields provided by their university education. Monetary prizes are awarded annually. Established in 1989.

9174
Concurso Nacional de Cuartetos de Cuerdas
For recognition of musical quartets, whose total age is under one hundred, for outstanding performance and to encourage cultural growth in the field of music. Monetary prizes and concert opportunities are awarded biennially. Established in 1991.

9175
Concurso Nacional de Fotografia Cientifica
For recognition of the best works in scientific photography, intending to promote the application of scientific photography in research and teaching. Works in black and white or color, either in print or slide form are eligible. Medals and certificates are awarded annually. Additional information is available from Centro Universitario de Comunicacion de la Ciencia, Ciudad Universitaria, Circuito Escolar, Edificio de Posgrado, 1er piso, 04510, Mexico, DF, phone: 550 5215.

9176
Concurso Nacional de Violin
To recognize musical accomplishment by persons under 20 years of age. Monetary prizes and concert opportunities are awarded biennially. Established in 1987. Additional information is available from UNAM-Escuela Nacional de Musica, Xicotencatl 126, Col. Carmen-Coyoacan, 04100 Mexico, DF, phone: 688 9783.

9177
Concurso Univeritario de Cuento
For recognition of accomplishment in the written word by students of UNAM. Monetary prizes are awarded annually. Established in 1988. Co-sponsored by *El Cuento* magazine.

9178
Concurso Universitario de Artes Plasticas
For recognition of accomplishment in the plastic arts by students of UNAM. Monetary prizes are awarded annually. Established in 1988.

9179
Concurso Universitario de Fotografia
For recognition of outstanding photography by university students and to promote young talent. Photographic equipment and certificates are awarded annually. Established in 1988. Prizes are supplied by Kodak Mexicana.

9180
Diploma al Merito Universitario
For recognition of years of service by professors and researchers at the university. Medals are awarded annually for fifty, thirty-five, and twenty-five years.

9181
Distincion Universidad Nacional para Jovenes Academicos
For recognition of outstanding academic achievement and constant superlative work in fourteen areas. Monetary prizes of 7,000,000 Mexican pesos are awarded in 14 categories annually. Established in 1989.

9182
Premio Lola e Igo Flisser
For recognition of outstanding work in parasitology. A monetary award of 3,000,000 Mexican pesos is awarded annually. Established in 1987. Funded by the Flisser family and awarded under the auspices of the UNAM Dept. of Biomedical Research.

9183
Premio al Deportista Universitario
For recognition of athletic achievement. A monetary prize of 250,000 Mexican pesos is awarded annually. Established in 1987.

9184
Premio Anual de Investigacion Economica Jesus Silva Herzog
For recognition of achievement in economic studies and to promote the development of solutions to economic problems in Mexico. Monetary prizes of 1,000,000, 600,000, and 400,000 Mexican pesos and certificates are awarded. Established in 1983.

9185
Premio Anual de Servicio Social Gustavo Baz Prada
For recognition of outstanding works of social service in the area of public administration, support of research, community development, technological development, public health, and cultural extension. Medals and certificates are awarded.

9186
Premio Beca Nacional de Diseno Industrial Clara Porset
For recognition of outstanding works in industrial design with the intention of promoting a relationship between students of design and the creation of products for which there is great need. A monetary sum of

8,000,000 Mexican pesos is awarded annually. For the best project in nutrition and daily life, Health and education, or industry, 2,000,000 Mexican pesos is awarded. Established in 1987. Additional information is available from Insurgentes Sur, Ciudad Universitaria, Circuito Escolar, 04510, Mexico, DF, phone: 548 4839.

9187
Premio Condumex
For recognition of outstanding contributions by members of the academic community in the areas of: polymers, non-ferrous metallurgy, telecommunications, artificial intelligence and robotics, industrial engineering and mechanical design. Three monetary prizes of 5,000,000 Mexican pesos are awarded. Established in 1988.

9188
Premio de Ciencas Morfologicas Dr. Enrique Acosta Vidrio
For recognition of achievement in the morphological sciences. A monetary prize of 1,500,000 Mexican pesos, a silver medal, and a certificate are awarded annually. Established in 1989. Co-sponsored by Masson Editores.

9189
Premio de Composicion Arquitectonica Alberto J. Pani
For recognition of young architectural achievement. Those under 25 years of age attending any Mexican institution of architecture are eligible. Monetary prizes are awarded annually to the top five winners. Established in 1985.

9190
Premio del Seminario de Economia Agricola del Tercer Mundo
For recognition of outstanding work on the theme of agricultural development and nutrition in the Third World. Publication of the winning essays is awarded.

9191
Premio Derechos Humanos
For recognition in the field of human rights, public service, and teaching. A monetary prize is awarded annually. Established in 1986.

9192
Premio Facultad de Derecho a la Mejor Tesis
For recognition of the best master's thesis in human rights. Monetary prizes of 750,000, 500,000, and 250,000 Mexican pesos are awarded annually. Established in 1987.

9193
Premio Felipe Tena Ramirez
For recognition of the best essays or theses on constitutional rights, preferably related to human rights. Monetary prizes of 2,000,000 and 1,000,000 Mexican pesos are awarded annually. Established in 1987.

9194
Premio Marcos y Celia Mauss
For recognition of the best master's or doctoral thesis in history. A monetary prize is awarded annually. Established in 1987.

9195
Premio Norman Sverdlin
For recognition of the best master's or doctoral thesis in philosophy. A monetary award and publication of the thesis are awarded annually. Established in 1986.

9196
Premio Omeyocan
For recognition of outstanding works in ecology and to promote research by persons in institutions of higher learning, research, or public or private health. Monetary prizes up to 5,000,000 Mexican pesos and certificates are awarded annually. Established in 1990. Additional information is available from Unam-Escuela Nacional de Estudios Profesionales Iztacala, Av. de los Barrios s/n, Col. Los Reyes Iztacala, Tlanepantla, Edo. de Mexico, 54090, Apartado Postal 314.

9197
Premio Puma
For recognition of outstanding athletic coaching at the university. A monetary prize of 1,000,000 Mexican pesos and a trophy are awarded annually. Established in 1987.

9198
Premio Revista Punto de Partida
To recognize outstanding Mexican literature. Monetary prizes of 800,000, and 500,000 Mexican pesos are awarded annually. Established in 1967.

9199
Premio Universidad Nacional
For recognition of university personnel who have distinguished themselves in teaching, research, or cultural contribtion. works of research or teaching in the following fields are eligible: exact sciences; natural sciences; social sciences; economic administration; humanities; higher education; design; and artistic expression. A monetary sum of 25,000,000 Mexican pesos and a certificate are awarded annually. Established in 1985.

9200
Premio Aida Weiss
For recognition of the best original work in oncology. Monetary awards of 4,000,000 and 2,000,000 Mexican pesos and certificates are awarded annually. Established in 1984.

9201
National Bank of Mexico
(Banco Nacional de Mexico, S.N.C. (BANAMEX))
Madero 17, 2 piso
Col. Centro
06000 Mexico City, DF, Mexico   Phone: 5 521 8990

9202
BANAMEX Economics Prize
(Premio BANAMEX de Economia)
To promote research and writing on the economic development of Mexico. Nominations may be submitted by April 30. The following prizes are presented for research: (1) a monetary prize of 30,000,000 pesos - first prize; and (2) 22,000,000 pesos - second prize. The following prizes are presented for the best licentiate thesis in economics: (1) a monetary award of 16,000,000 pesos - first prize; and (2) 8,000,000 pesos - second prize. Certificates are also awarded. Awarded annually in November. Established in 1953.

9203
BANAMEX Science and Technology Prize
(Premio BANAMEX de Ciencia y Tecnologia)
To promote research on cattle raising and the industrial applications of science. A monetary prize of 150,000 pesos was presented in each area. Awarded annually. Established in 1962. (Discontinued)

9204
Premio BANAMEX Atanasio G. Saravia de Historia Regional Mexicana
To promote research on the local history of Mexico from the sixteenth to twentieth centuries. The following prizes are awarded: (1) a monetary prize of 4,000,000 pesos - for research; (2) 2,000,000 pesos - for the best master's thesis; and (3) 1,000,000 pesos - for the best licenciate thesis. Awarded biennially. Established in 1984.

9205
**National Institute of Fine Arts
(Instituto Nacional de Bellas Artes)**
Auditorio Nacional
Bosque de Chapultepec
Miguel Hidalgo
11580 Mexico City, DF, Mexico

Phone: 5 520 7241
Phone: 5 520 2724

9206
Bienal de Pintores Rufino Tomayo
To recognize Mexican artists over age 30. Entries may not have won previous prizes. Prizewinning entries become the property of the Museo de Arte Contemporaneo de Oaxaca. Three "acquisition" prizes of 3,000,000, 2,000,000 and 1,000,000 Mexican pesos are awarded. Established in 1892. Co-sponsored by the state of Oaxaca.

9207
Bienal Iberoamericana de Arte
To recognize outstanding artists for works created during the previous two years. Works by Spanish or Portuguese speaking residents of Mexico for at least five years are eligible. Monetary prizes of 5,000,000, 4,000,000, and and 3,000,000 Mexican pesos and five honorable mentions of 500,000 Mexican pesos each are awarded biennially. Prizewinning works become the property of the Institute. Established in 1976. Co-sponsored by Instituto Cultural Domecq, A.C. Viena No. 161 Coyoacan, 04100 DF Mexico City, DF 04100 Mexico.

9208
Bienal Nacional Diego Rivera for Drawings and Prints
To recognize outstanding sketch artists and engravers who have resided in Mexico for at least five years. Six prizes of acquisition are distributed as follows: In the drawing category, prizes of 3,000,000, 2,000,000 and 1,000,000 Mexican pesos are offered. In the engraving category, prizes of 2,000,000, 1,000,000, and 500,000 Mexican pesos are awarded. Prizewinning entries become the property of the Museo del Pueblo. Established in 1984. Co-sponsored by the state of Guanajuato.

9209
Concurso Latinoamericano de Cuento
To recognize an author in the Spanish language for the best unpublished short story 5-15 pages in length. Mexican residents are eligible. An indivisible monetary prize of 1,500,000 Mexican pesos and a certificate are awarded annually. Established in 1971. Co-sponsored by the state of Puebla.

9210
Concurso Nacional de Artes Plasticas - Grafica (Mini Estampa)
To recognize contributions to the fine arts in the category of small scale graphic arts. Mexican artists and residents of the country for the previous five years are eligible. Three prizes of 250,000 pesos each are awarded annually. Established in 1988. Sponsored by Gilmart, S.A. de C.V.

9211
Concurso Nacional para Estudiantes de Artes Plasticas en Aguascalientes
To recognize contributions to the fine arts in the following categories: (1) painting - first prize of 30,000 Mexican pesos, second prize of 15,000 Mexican pesos, and third prize of 10,000 Mexican pesos; (2) sculpture - first prize of 30,000 Mexican pesos, second prize of 15,000 Mexican pesos, and third prize of 10,000 Mexican pesos; (3) drawing - first prize of 15,000 Mexican pesos, second prize of 7,000 Mexican pesos, and third prize of 5,000 Mexican pesos; (4) graphic arts - first prize of 15,000 Mexican pesos, second prize of 7,500 Mexican pesos, and third prize of 5,000 Mexican pesos. Awarded annually. Co-sponsored by the Patronato de la Feria de San Marcos, the Cigarrera la Moderna, S.A. de C.V. and Casa de Cultura de Aguascalientes.

9212
Encuentro Nacional de Arte Joven
To recognize plastic artists under the age of 30 who reside in Mexico. Only works which have won no previous prizes are eligible. Five monetary prizes of acquisition of 5,000,000 Mexican pesos each are awarded. Prizewinning works become the property of the Museo de Arte Moderno de Aguascalientes. Established in 1980. Co-sponsored by the Patronato de la Feria Nacional de San Marcos and the Instituto Cultural de Aguascalientes.

9213
Instituto de Bellas Artes Concurso de Becas Literarias
To promote the work of young authors under 30 years who reside in Mexico. Scholarships are awarded annually. Established in 1974.

9214
Premio Alfonso X de Traduccion Literaria
To recognize outstanding translators of literary works published in Mexico in general fields, history, or the humanities. Self-nominations are accepted as well as those from publishers, or institutions of cultural education or translation. The deadline is August 31. An indivisible monetary prize of 5,000,000 Mexican pesos and a certificate are awarded annually. Established in 1982 in memory of Spanish King Alfonso X, noted for his initiatives in translating key texts.

9215
Premio de Biografia
In recognition of the best unpublished biography or autobiography by a Spanish-speaking Mexican resident. Works submitted be 120-300 pages in length. An indivisible monetary prize of 10,000,000 Mexican pesos and a certificate are awarded annually. Established in 1987. Co-sponsored by the Universidad de Colima.

9216
Premio de Critica de Arte Luis Cardoza y Aragon
In recognition of an outstanding critical art essay centering on the figure and/or work of Gerardo Murillo or on the principles of plastic movement in force during the period in which he lived. Students, researchers, and other interested parties analyzing the plastic arts in Mexico are eligible. An indivisible monetary prize of 10,000,000 Mexican pesos and a certificate are awarded annually. Established in 1987. Co-sponsored by the state of Nuevo Leon.

9217
Premio de Narrativa Jorge Ibarguengoitia
For recognition of the best unpublished work of narrative, in Spanish, of a parodic, satiric, ironic or humorous character. Residents of Mexico are eligible. The deadline is July 31. A monetary award of 10 million pesos (indivisible) and a plaque are awarded annually during the Festival Internacional Cervantino. Established in 1990 in memory of Mexican author, Jorge Ibarguengoitia.

9218
Premio de Novela Jose Ruben Romero
To recognize unpublished novels of outstanding literary quality by authors in the Spanish language who are residents of Mexico. Works to be considered should be 120-300 pages in length. An indivisible monetary prize of 20,000,000 Mexican pesos and a certificate are awarded annually. Established in 1978 in memory of the Mexican author. Co-sponsored by the state of Michoacan.

9219
Premio de Obra de Teatro
To recognize playwrights in the Spanish language who are residents of Mexico for the best unpublished, unperformed play at least 50 minutes in length. An indivisible monetary prize of 20,000,000 Mexican pesos and a certificate are awarded annually. Established in 1978. Co-sponsored by the city of Baja, California.

9220
Premio de Obra de Teatro para Ninos
To recognize Spanish-speaking playwrights residing in Mexico for the best children's play at least 30 minutes in length. The plays must be unpublished and unperformed. An indivisible monetary prize of 10,000,000 Mexican pesos and a certificate are awarded annually. Established in 1981. Co-sponsored by the state of Coahuila.

9221

Premio de Periodismo Cultural
In recognition of outstanding works of cultural journalism by authors in the Spanish language who are residents of Mexico. Unpublished works of cultural character, 50-150 pages in length, and in the form of feature story, interview, report or review are eligible. An indivisible monetary prize of 10,000,000 Mexican pesos and a certificate are awarded annually. Established in 1983. Co-sponsored by the Sociedad General de Escritores de Mexico.

9222

Premio de Poesia Carlos Pellicer
To recognize Spanish-speaking poets residing in Mexico for the best poetic work published in Mexico in the preceding year. Works must be at least 24 pages in length. The competition is open to all Mexican publishing houses. An indivisible monetary prize of 5,000,000 Mexican pesos is awarded annually. Established in 1978. Co-sponsored by the state of Tabasco in memory of the Mexican poet.

9223

Premio de Poesia Joven de Mexico Elias Nandino
To recognize the best collection of unpublished poems written in Spanish by a resident of Mexico under the age of 30. A monetary prize of 10,000,000 Mexican pesos and a certificate are awarded annually. Established in 1975. Co-sponsored by the Jalisco Departmento de Bellas Artes.

9224

Premio de Testimonio
To recognize an outstanding literary work in testimonial form. Works to be considered should be at least 60 pages long. Authors in the Spanish language who are Mexican residents are eligible. An indivisible monetary prize of 5,000,000 Mexican pesos and a certificate are awarded annually. Established in 1982. Co-sponsored by the state of Chihuahua.

9225

Premio de Traduccion de Poesia
For recognition of the best unpublished collection of poems translated into Spanish from the English, French, Italian or Portuguese. Residents of Mexico and Mexican-Americans residing in the U.S. are eligible. A monetary award of 10,000,000 Mexican pesos (indivisible) and a plaque of recognition are awarded annually. Established in 1990.

9226

Premio Internacional de Ensayo Literario Malcolm Lowry
To recognize the best literary essay written in Spanish. Authors of any country may submit unpublished essays about the work of foreign authors who refer to Mexico. The works must be at least 60 pages in length. The deadline is August 31. An indivisible monetary prize of 10,000,000 Mexican pesos and a certificate are awarded annually. Established in 1987. Co-sponsored by the Instituto Regional de Bellas Artes de Cuernavaca, Morelos.

9227

Premio Josefina Vicens para Novela Breve
For recognition of an outstanding short novel by Mexicans or foreign residents of Mexico. Works must be unpublished and in Spanish. A monetary prize of 10,000,000 Mexican pesos is awarded. Established in 1990.

9228

Premio Juan Rulfo Para Primera Novela
To recognize the best first novel by an author in the Spanish language residing in Mexico. Works to be considered should be 120-300 pages in length. An indivisible monetary prize of 10,000,000 Mexican pesos and a certificate are awarded annually. Established in 1980 in memory of the Mexican author. Co-sponsored by the state of Guerrero.

9229

Premio Latinoamericano de Cuento
For recognition of an unpublished volume of short stories on any subject that is at least 80 pages in length. Spanish speaking writers who reside in Latin America are eligible. An indivisible monetary prize of 5,000,000 Mexican pesos and a diploma are awarded annually. Established in 1972.

9230

Premio Latinoamericano de Narrativa, Colima
To recognize an outstanding book of a narrative nature in the Spanish language. Works submitted must have been published in Latin America in the preceding year. Residents of Latin American countries are eligible. Self-nomination is allowed. An indivisible monetary prize of 5,000,000 Mexican pesos is awarded annually. Established in 1980. Co-sponsored by the Universidad de Colima.

9231

Premio Nacional de Cuento
To recognize the best unpublished book of short stories on any theme that is a minimum of 80 pages in length. Spanish speaking writers who reside in Mexico are eligible. An indivisible monetary prize of 20,000,000 Mexican pesos is awarded annually. Established in 1974. Co-sponsored by the Casa de Cultura in San Luis Potosi.

9232

Premio Nacional de Cuento para Ninos Juan de la Cabada
To recognize an unpublished volume of stories in Spanish for children, no shorter than 50 pages. Authors residing in Mexico are eligible. An indivisible monetary prize of 15,000,000 Mexican pesos and a diploma are awarded annually. Established in 1977. Co-sponsored by the Casa de Cultura in Campeche.

9233

Premio Nacional de Danza INBA-Sinaloa Jose Limon
For recognition of a lifetime of outstanding artistry in the field of dance by Mexican dancers or those residing in Mexico. An indivisible monetary prize of 15,000,000 Mexican pesos is awarded annually. Established in 1988. Co-sponsored by la Direccion de Investigacion y Fomento de Cultura Regional del Gobierno del Edo. de Sinaloa.

9234

Premio Nacional de Ensayo Literario Jose Revueltas
To recognize the best unpublished essay written in Spanish on a Latin American theme or about an outstanding, contemporary, Latin American writer and his literary output. Writers residing in the Republic of Mexico or Mexican citizens studying in the United States are eligible. An indivisible monetary prize of 20,000,000 Mexican pesos and a diploma are awarded annually. Established in 1976. Co-sponsored by the House of Culture of Gomez Palacio in the state of Durango.

9235

Premio Nacional de Novela
To recognize the best unpublished novel on any subject that is at least 160 pages long. Spanish speaking writers who reside in the Republic of Mexico are eligible. A monetary prize of 50,000 Mexican pesos and a diploma are awarded annually. Co-sponsored by the Queretaro State Government.

9236

Premio Nacional de Poesia
To recognize the best unpublished book of poetry by a Spanish speaking poet who is a resident of Mexico. There are no restrictions regarding the subject form and length of the poems. An indivisible monetary prize of 20,000,000 Mexican pesos and a diploma are awarded annually. Established in 1973. Co-sponsored by the House of Culture of Aguascalientes, and the Fair of San Marcos.

9237

Premio Nacional de Poesia Joven Francisco Gonzalez de Leon
To recognize a unpublished collection of poems of at least ten pages in length. Poets residing in Mexico are eligible. The following prizes are awarded: first prize - 25,000 Mexican pesos and a diploma; second prize - 15,000 Mexican pesos and a diploma; and third prize - 10,000 Mexican pesos and a diploma. Awarded annually.

9238
Premio Periodismo Cultural
For recognition of outstanding works by Mexican citizens or residents. Works must be in Spanish, and in the form of interviews, reports, chronicles, or reports on cultural themes. A monetary prize of 15,000,000 Mexican pesos is awarded annually.

9239
Salon Nacional de Artes Plasticas - Ceramica
To recognize outstanding artists in Mexico in the ceramic art category. Mexican artists and residents in the country for the previous three years are eligible. Three prizes of 3,000,000 pesos each are awarded biennially. Established in 1990.

9240
Salon Nacional de Artes Plasticas - Dibujo
To recognize the most outstanding artists in the category of drawing. There are no restrictions regarding the drawing technique. Mexican artists and residents in the country for the previous three years are eligible. Five prizes of 3,000,000 pesos each are awarded annually. Established in 1983.

9241
Salon Nacional de Artes Plasticas - Escultura
To recognize the most outstanding artists in the technique of sculpture. Mexican artists and residents in the country for the previous three years are eligible. Two prizes of 5,000,000 pesos each are awarded triennially. Established in 1979.

9242
Salon Nacional de Artes Plasticas - Espacios Alternativos
To recognize contributions to the fine arts in the category of experimentation: montage, assemblage, found objects, video, audio, multimedia, conceptual art, ready made, etc. Mexican artists and residents in the country for the previous three years are eligible. Three prizes of 2,000,000 pesos each are awarded when merited. Established in 1979.

9243
Salon Nacional de Artes Plasticas - Fotografia
In recognition of outstanding artists in the category of photography. Applicants must be Mexican or residents in Mexico for the previous five years. Five prizes of 1,200,000 pesos each are awarded biennially. Established in 1980. Co-sponsored by the Consejo Mexicano de Fotografia.

9244
Salon Nacional de Artes Plasticas - Graphic Art
To recognize outstanding artists in the category of the graphic arts. There are no restrictions regarding the graphic technique. Mexican artists and residents in the country for the previous five years are eligible. Three prizes of one million pesos each and three more of five hundred thousand pesos each are awarded biennially. Established in 1977.

9245
Salon Nacional de Artes Plasticas - Graphica (Interpretation del Quijote de la Mancha)
To recognize the artistic view of outstanding artists on the theme "Don Quijote de la Mancha" by the Spanish writer, Miguel de Cervantes Saavedra. Mexican artists or residents in Mexico for the previous five years are eligible. Three prizes of 1,500,000 pesos each are awarded annually. Established in 1988 by Eulalio Ferrer, Fundacion Cervantina.

9246
Salon Nacional de Artes Plasticas - Pintura
To recognize the works of outstanding artists in the technique of painting. Mexican artists and residents in the country for the previous three years are eligible. Five prizes of 15,000,000 pesos each are awarded annually. Established in 1970.

9247
Salon Nacional de Artes Plasticas - Tapiz y Arte Textil
To recognize the artistic view of outstanding artists in the category of tapestry. Mexican artists and residents of Mexico for the previous three years are eligible. Five prizes of 5,000,000 pesos each are awarded biennially. Established in 1978.

9248
National Library of Mexico
(Biblioteca Nacional de Mexico)
Insurgentes Sur 3000
Centro Cultural Universitaria   Phone: 5 6226801
04510 Mexico City, DF, Mexico   Fax: 5 6550951

9249
Premio Rafael Heliodoro Valle
For recognition of Spanish American writers. Awards are given in alternate years in the fields of history and literature. Writers and historians who are over 50 years of age may be nominated by universities, academies, or societies of Spanish American countries. A monetary prize of 20,000,000 Mexican pesos, a diploma, and a gold medal are awarded annually. Established in 1976 in honor of Rafael Heliodoro Valle, writer and diplomat. Sponsored by Fideicomiso. Additional information is available from Comite Tecnico, c/o Luis G. Inclan, num. 2709, Col. Villa de Cortes, 03530, Mexico City, DF, Mexico.

9250
Novedades
Morelos 16, 4 piso
06040 Mexico City, DF, Mexico   Phone: 5 512 4228

9251
Certamen Nacional la Letra Impresa
To recognize the best publicity agencies of the competition for creative publicity which generates a positive and promising concept of the future as well as promotes the upholding of traditional moral values and the spirit of work, the only way to promote the advancement of the country. A trophy, a certificate, and publication are awarded annually to the first five places.

9252
Concurso Nacional Carta a mi Hijo
For the most effective "Letter to my Son" promoting a supportive attitude for future generations. Monetary prizes of 300,000, 250,000, and 200,000 Mexican pesos and airplane tickets are awarded annually.

9253
Premio Literario Internacional *Novedades* y Diana
For recognition of the best unpublished novel in the Spanish language. Authors of any nationality or residence are eligible. More than one novel may be submitted. The deadline usually falls in the early part of the year. Monetary prizes of 45,000,000 Mexican pesos and publication are awarded annually. Established in 1987. Co-sponsored by Editorial Diana.

9254
Organizacion Estereo Mundo
Radiodifusora de Morelos
Col. Tlaltenango
Emiliano Zapata 601   Phone: 73 17 38 66
62170 Cuernavaca, Morelos, Mexico   Phone: 73 17 36 17

9255
Premio Mixcoatl
To recognize individuals for work representing a spirit of peace and fraternity and serving as an example for young people and society. Prizes are given in the following areas: literature and journalism; social work; arts and crafts; tourism; sports; industry; administration; and public

service. Honorary recognition is awarded annually at the ceremony held in Cuernavaca. Established in 1978 by Linea Caliente.

9256
Periodistas Cinematograficos de Mexico
Av. Universidad 1195
Col. del Valle
03100 Mexico City, DF, Mexico   Phone: 5 534 6080

9257
Premios Diosa de Plata
For recognition of the most outstanding industrial cinematographer of the year. A silver statuette is awarded annually.

9258
Juan Rulfo Latin American and Caribbean Prize for Literature
Avenida Juarez 975
44280 Guadalajara, Jalisco, Mexico

9259
Juan Rulfo Latin American and Caribbean Prize for Literature
For recognition of an outstanding writer who has produced noteworthy creative work in any literary genre (poetry, novel, drama, short story and essay) and who meets one of the following conditions: (1) is a native of Latin America or the Caribbean and whose language of artistic expression is Spanish, Portuguese, French or English; (2) is a native of any other region of the Americas and whose language of artistic expression is Spanish; or (3) is a native of Spain or Portugal and whose language of artistic expression is Spanish or Portuguese. Nominations may be made by any cultural or educational institution, association or group of persons interested in literature. The Prize may be given as well to a writer who, in the judgement of the members of the Jury, merits the award even if that writer's name has not been put forward by any institution. The deadline for nominations is April 30. A monetary prize of $100,000 is awarded during the last week of November at the Guadalajara International Book Fair (FIL). Established in 1991. Sponsored by Consejo Nacional para la Cultura y las Artes, Universidad de Guadalajara, Gobierno del Estado de Jalisco, Fondo de Cultura Economica, Petroleos Mexicanos, Productoras e Importadoras de Papel, Banco Nacional de Mexico, Banco de Comercio, Banco Nacional de Comercio Exterior, Banca Promex, Ayuntamiento de Guadalajara, and Loteria Nacional para las Asistencia Publica.

9260
Secretaria de Comercio y Fomento Industrial
Direccion General de Normas
Av. Puente de Tecamachalco 6-1
Seccion Fuentes de Tecamachalco
Naucalpan de Juarez
53950 Edo. de Mexico, Mexico

9261
National Prize for Quality
(Premio Nacional de Calidad)
For recognition of the outstanding established enterprises in the country. Eligible enterprises are divided into three categories: those with more than 500 employees, those with fewer than 500 employees, and service oriented enterprises. Awarded annually. Established in 1989.

9262
Secretaria de Desarrollo Urbano y Ecologia
Instituto SEDUE
Boulevard Pipila 1
Tecamachalco, Edo. de Mexico
53950 Mexico City, DF, Mexico   Phone: 5 294 5386

9263
Premio de Ecologia
To recognize deeds carried out by institutions of higher research and communities in the area of conservation, especially environmental protection. A monetary prize of 5,000,000 Mexican pesos and a medal are awarded annually to the best in each category; research institutes, institutions of higher learning, and communities. Established in 1987.

9264
Sindicato de Trabajadores de Produccion Cinematografica
Plateros 109
Col. San Jose Insurgentes   Phone: 5 593 5990
03900 Mexico City, DF, Mexico   Phone: 5 680 6299

9265
Film Competition
(Concurso de Cine)
For recognition of outstanding fiction and documentary films. Monetary prizes of 500,000,000 Mexican pesos are awarded in each of the themes in the categories of: (1) Mexico City; (2) Mexican classics; (3) Open theme. Awarded annually. Established in 1987. Co-sponsored by Departamento del Distrito Federal e Instituto Mexicano de Cinematografia.

9266
Sociedad Alfonsina Internacional
Transmisiones 42
01790 Mexico City, DF, Mexico   Phone: 5 683 1217

9267
Premio Hispanoamericano Xavier Villaurrutia
For recognition of the best work by a young or new author published in Mexico during the preceding year. This prize is from authors for authors. Awards are given in the following categories: (1) prose; (2) poetry; (3) drama; and (4) essay. Monetary prizes totaling 4,000,000 pesos are awarded annually or when merited by the trust managing Alfonsina Chapel (Alfonso Reyes Library). Established in 1955.

9268
Premio Internacional Alfonso Reyes
For recognition of the best works about Mexico written in the spirit of Alfonso Reyes, and promoting the Mexican culture on an international level. A monetary prize of 10,000,000 Mexican pesos is awarded annually through the Mexican government. Established in 1972.

9269
Sociedad de Autores y Compositores de Musica
Calle san Felipe 143
03030 Mexico City, DF, Mexico   Phone: 5 660 2285

9270
Premio Corazon de Oro
To recognize humanitarian actions. A solid gold piece is awarded annually. Established in 1987.

9271
Sociedad de Cosmetologos de Mexico
Napoleon 31
Col. Moderna   Phone: 5 6965347
13510 Mexico City, DF, Mexico   Fax: 5 6965347

9272
Premio Nacional de Desarrollo Quimico Cosmetico
For recognition of outstanding contributions to the development of the chemical cosmetic industry and cosmetic research. Awarded to professionals and students of sciences related to cosmetic science. Monetary

awards of 2,000, 1,000, and 500 Mexican new pesos are awarded biannually.

9273
Sociedad General de Escritores de Mexico
Jose Maria Velasco 59
03900 Mexico City, DF, Mexico
Phone: 5 5933566
Fax: 5 5936017

9274
Concurso Nacional de Escritores de Teatro
To encourage Mexican writers. The prize is awarded irregularly and consists of the performance of the work. Established in 1984.

9275
Sociedad Mexicana de Cardiologia
Juan Badiano 1
Tlalpan
14080 Mexico City, DF, Mexico
Phone: 5 573 0480

9276
Premio Maestro Arturo Rosenblueth
To recognize a young research scientist for the best work in basic science. A monetary prize of 5,000 new pesos is awarded biennially at the National Congress of Cardiology. Established in 1979.

9277
Premio Maestro Ignacio Chavez
For recognition of research efforts and educational contributions to the field of cardiology. The award is presented alternately to a medical researcher and a medical clinician. A monetary prize of 1,000 new pesos is awarded annually. Established in 1970 on the occasion of the jubilee of Doctor Chavez.

9278
Premio Maestro Manuel Vaquero
To recognize an outstanding young clinical researcher. A monetary prize of 5,000 new pesos is awarded. Established in 1983.

9279
Premio Maestro Salvador Aceves
To recognize a distinguished master cardiologist. A silver medal and certificate are awarded annually at the convention. Established in 1979.

9280
Premio Sor Maria del Roble
To recognize a young cardiological nurse for the best work in his/her field. A monetary prize of 1,000 new pesos is awarded biennially during the National Congress of Cardiology.

9281
Sociedad Mexicana de Matematicas
Instituto de Matematicas
Ciudad Universitaria
Circuito Exterior
04510 Mexico City, DF, Mexico
Phone: 5 6224520
Fax: 5 5489499

9282
Olimpiada de Matematicas Mexicana
To recognize outstanding young Mexican mathematicians and promote their entry in the worlds of science and mathematics as qualified Mexican representatives. A certificate is awarded annually. Established in 1987.

9283
Premio Sotero Prieto a la Mejor Tesis de Licenciatura en Matematicas
To recognize outstanding thesis work by young mathematicians.

9284
Trama Visual
Fuente de la Vida 30
Fuentes del Pedregal
14140 Mexico City, DF, Mexico
Phone: 5 652 4939
Fax: 5 655 6165

9285
Bienal Internacional del Cartel en Mexico
To recognize outstanding graphic designers, plastic artists, photographers, and producers of graphic arts in general and to stimulate their creativity. Participants in the poster contest may be individuals or groups of any age and any nationality. Posters are judged in four categories: cultural character, political, ideological, or social character, commercial or publicity, and unpublished entries on the theme of "posters against violence." The following prizes are awarded biennially: first prize - $3,500 and a diploma; second prize - a silver medal and a diploma; and third prize - a bronze medal and a diploma. Established in 1989. Co-sponsored by the Secretaria de Relaciones Exteriores, Consejo Nacional de la Cultura y las Artes e Instituto Nacional de Bellas Artes.

9286
El Trimestre Economico
Av. Universidad 1195
Col. del Valle
03100 Mexico City, DF, Mexico

9287
Premio Internacional Daniel Cosio Villegas
For recognition of outstanding original, unpublished investigative essays on the Latin American economy. Recipients must be under 40 years of age. Monetary prizes of $4,000 US, $2,000 US and $500 US are awarded biennially. Established in 1989.

9288
Union Geofisica Mexicana
Apartado Postal 142024
16100 Mexico City, DF, Mexico

9289
Premio Ricardo Monge Lopez
For recognition of outstanding research and teaching in geophysics. A monetary award of 800,000 Mexican pesos and a certificate are awarded annually. Established in 1987.

9290
Premio Union Geofisca Mexicana
For recognition of outstanding theses in geophysics. A monetary award of 800,000 Mexican pesos is awarded at irregular intervals. Established in 1987.

9291
Universidad Autonoma de Ciudad Juarez
Av. Lopez Mateos No. 20
Apartado Postal 1594-D
Ciudad Juarez, Chihuahua, Mexico

9292
Premio Nacional de Literatura Jose Fuentes Mares
To recognize authors for outstanding literary contributions to the renovation and diffusion of native literature. The prize is awarded in two categories: (1) Letras Nacionales, for Mexican citizens; and (2) Letras Chicanas, for Mexican-Americans. Two indivisible monetary awards of 10,000,000 Mexican pesos are awarded annually. Established in 1986.

9293

Universidad Autonoma de Queretaro
Centro Universitario
76000 Queretaro, Queretaro, Mexico   Phone: 463 25363

9294

Premio Manuel Buendia
For recognition of outstanding contributions to Mexican journalism of high quality and moral strength in honor of Manuel Buendia's strength of character. Individuals, groups, associations or institutions are eligible. Prizes vary according to the participating universities at the annual convention. Established in 1985. Co-sponsored by the Fundacion Manuel Buendia and 30 universities.

9295

Premio Nacional de Literatura Paula Allende
For recognition of outstanding literary contributions by Spanish-speaking Mexican residents. A monetary award of 1,000,000 Mexican pesos is awarded annually. Co-sponsored with the Secretaria de Cultura y Bienestar social del Gobierno del Estado de Queretaro.

9296

Universidad Autonoma Metropolitana
c/o Direccion General de Difusion Cultural
Medellin 28
Col. Roma
06700 Mexico City, DF, Mexico   Phone: 5 511 0717

9297

Premio Nacional de Danza Clasica Contemporanea
For recognition of outstanding choreographical creativity and the promotion of Mexican dance. A monetary prize of 3,000,000 Mexican pesos and a certificate are awarded annually. Established in 1979.

9298

Premio Nacional de Danza Etnocoreografica
For recognition of outstanding creativity in ethnochoreography and the promotion of Mexican dance. A monetary prize of 2,000,000 Mexican pesos is awarded annually.

9299

Universidad de Colima, Rectoria
Av. Universidad 333
28000 Colima, Colima, Mexico

9300

Medalla Lazaro Cardenas del Rio
For recognition of outstanding contributions by Mexican citizens or institutions who best represent the ideals of Mexico. Established in 1983.

9301

Vitromex
Boulevard Isidro Lopez Zertucheno 4103
Apartado Postal 385
25230 Saltillo, Coahuila, Mexico

9302

Premio La Ceramica n la Arquitectura
For recognition of outstanding creativity in the use of ceramics in architecture and to promote the search for new designs acceptable in the world market. Prizes are awarded for exterior design, bath design, and surface design. A monetary prize of 20,000,000 Mexican pesos is awarded in each of the categories. Co-sponsored by Federacion de Colegios de Arquitectos.

9303

World Boxing Council
(Consejo Mundial de Boxeo)
Genova 33, Oficina 503
Colonia Juarez
Cuauhtemoc
06600 Mexico City, DF, Mexico   Phone: 5 578 7143

9304

World Boxing Council Awards
To recognize the winners of world boxing title fights.

9305

World Cultural Council
(Consejo Cultural Mundial)
Address unknown.

9306

Leonardo Da Vinci World Award of Arts
To recognize artists, avant gardists, or art authorities whose works constitute a significant contribution to the artistic legacy of the world. A monetry prize of $10,000 US, a medal, and a diploma are awarded annually in November.

9307

Albert Einstein World Award of Science
To recognize individuals for scientific and technological achievements that have brought progress to science and benefit to mankind. Candidates must be nominated. A monetary prize of $10,000, a medal, and diploma are awarded annually in November.

9308

Jose Vasconcelos World Award of Education
To recognize an educator, an authority in the field of teaching, or a legislator of education policies who has had a significant influence on the advancement of human culture. Candidates must be nominated. A monetary prize of $10,000 US, a medal, and a diploma are awarded annually in November.

Monaco

9309

Fondation Prince Pierre de Monaco
Direction des Affaires Culturelles
8, Rue Louis - Notari   Phone: 93 158303
MC-98000 Monte Carlo, Monaco   Fax: 93 506694

9310

Monte Carlo International Prize of Contemporary Art
To recognize talented artists of any trend or technique. Selection is made by the jury. Candidatures are not admitted. The following prizes are awarded: Grand Prix de S. A. S. Le Prince Rainier III - a monetary prize of 50,000 French francs, a medal with the effigy of S. A. S. The Sovereign Prince of Monaco, and a Diploma of Honor; and Prix Fondation Princesse Grace - a monetary prize of 25,000 French francs and a diploma. An exhibition of the whole selected works is held in Monte Carlo. Awarded annually. Established in 1966.

9311

Prix de Composition Musicale
To recognize a contemporary music work created during the last year. Composers of any nationality are eligible. Candidatures are not admitted. A monetary prize of 50,000 French francs and a medal bearing the effigy of H. S. H. Prince Pierre de Monaco are awarded in the spring of each year. Established in 1960.

9312

Prix Litteraire Prince Pierre-de-Monaco
To recognize an author who writes in the French language and who is already internationally known for the whole of his or her works. A monetary prize of 50,000 French francs and a medal bearing the effigy of H. S. H. Prince Pierre de Monaco are awarded in the spring of each year. Established in 1951.

9313

International Amateur Athletic Federation
(Federation Internationale d'Athletisme Amateur)
17 Rue Princesse Florestine
BP 359
MC-98007 Monte Carlo 98007, Monaco
Phone: 93 307070
Fax: 93 159515

9314

IAAF World Athletic Series
The following competitions are scheduled for 1994 and 1995: IAAF/Snickers World Cross Country Championships, IAAF World Road Relay Championships, IAAF World Junior Championships, IAAF/Mobil Grand Prix Final, IAAF World Cup in Athletics, IAAF World Half Marathon Championships, IAAF World Indoor Championships, IAAF World Marathon Cup, and IAAF/Reebok World Cup of Race Walking. Gold, silver, and bronze medals are awarded for every event in every competition.

9315

IAAF World Championships
To recognize men and women for accomplishments in track and field. Competition is held in the following events: 100 meters, 200 meters, 400 meters, 800 meters, 1,500 meters, 5,000 meters, 10,000 meters, marathon, decathlon (men), heptathlon (women), 3,000-meter steeplechase (men), 10 km walk (women), 20 km walk (men), hurdles, relays, high jump, pole vault (men), long jump, triple jump, shot, discus, hammer (men), and javelin. Medals are awarded every four years. The World Marathon Cup is also awarded.

9316

International Association for Non-Violent Sport
(Association Internationale pour un Sport sans Violence)
Stade Louis II
7 Ave. des Castelans
MC-98000 Monaco, Monaco
Phone: 92 166030
Fax: 93 303649

9317

Per Ludos Fraternitas
To recognize individuals or representatives of sports organizations for preservation of any aspect of sports ethics: fair-play, conviviality, respect for the referee and abidance by the rules, reception etc. Athletes, teams, public officials, sports administrators and journalists, etc. are eligible. A trophy (three different sizes) is awarded when merited. Established in 1974 by Mr. Charles Drago, founder of IANVS.

9318

International Hydrographic Organization
7, avenue President Kennedy
BP 445
MC-98011 Monte Carlo, Monaco
Phone: 93 506587
Fax: 93 252003

9319

Commodore A. H. Cooper Medal
To recognize the best original paper directly related to objectives of the International Hydrographic Organization. Original papers published in the "International Hydrographic Review" during the past year are eligible. A medal is awarded annually. Established in 1988 to honor Commodore Anthony H. Cooper, former hydrographer of Australia and former professional assistant of hydrography at the International Hydrographic Bureau. Sponsored by the Commodore Cooper Trust.

9320

Monte Carlo Television Festival
(Festival de Television de Monte Carlo)
Centre de Congres Auditorium
Boulevard Louis II
MC-98000 Monte Carlo, Monaco
Phone: 93 304944
Phone: 93 509300
Fax: 93 250600

Formerly: International Television Festival of Monte Carlo.

9321

Monte Carlo International Forum for New Images Imagina
For recognition of outstanding techniques of animation. Eight Pixel-INA prizes (symbolized by a teapot created by competition among sculptors) are awarded by the audience in the following categories: realism, animation, scientific, fiction, advertisement, micro-computer graphics, television credit titles, schools and universities. A Grand Prize is given to the best film, and a cash prize for creativity is offered to a young European creator.

9322

Mounte Carlo Television Festival
(Festival International de Television de Monte Carlo)
For recognition of the best television programs. The competition is held in four categories: news reportage, current affairs, television films, and mini series. The following Nymph Awards are presented: Gold Nymphs in each of the four categories; a Silver Nymph in both the news reportage and current affairs on magazine categories; four Silver Nymphs in the television film category for best script, best direction, best performance by an actor, and best performance by an actress; two Silver Nymphs in the mini-series category for outstanding contribution in the fields of scriptwriting, direction, performance, or any other professional aspect of production; Special Mention in each category; Prix AMADE-UNESCO to a film that deals with an issue of human relations and whose plot and treatment neither feature violence nor excite to it. (established in 1973) and other special prizes. Awarded annually in February. Established in 1961. Formerly: International Television Festival of Monte Carlo.

Morocco

9323

World Phosphate Institute
(Institut Mondial du Phosphate)
Angle Rte. d'el Jadida et Blvd. de la
 Grande Ceinture
BP Maarif 5196
Casablanca, Morocco
Phone: 2300025
Fax: 230640

Formerly: World Phosphate Rock Institute.

9324

World Phosphate Institute Awards
To recognize achievements in phosphate fertilizer use and manufacture. Also recognizes phosphate mining companies operating in Algeria, Jordan, Morocco, Senegal, Togo, and Tunisia. The Institute organizes competitions and bestows awards.

Namibia

9325

National Art Gallery of Namibia
Leutwein Streets
PO Box 994
Windhoek 9000, Namibia
Phone: 61 231160
Fax: 61 216561

Formerly: Namibian Arts Association.

9326

Standard Bank Namibia Biennale
For recognition of achievement in the field of fine arts and crafts, and to encourage development and individual quality of fine arts and crafts. Awards are given in the following categories: paintings, young artist, graphics, sculpture, photography, pottery/ceramics, carving/woodwork, textile art, and basketry. Monetary prizes and certificates are awarded biennially. Established in 1981 by the Standard Bank of Namibia. Additional information is available from Annaleen Eins, curator of the Namibian Arts Association. Formerly: (1991) Stanswa Biennale.

Netherlands

9327

Akademie voor Expressie door Woord en Gebaar
c/o Faculteit Theater en Drama
Hogeschool van de Kunsten
Janskerkhof 8
NL-3512 BM Utrecht, Netherlands   Phone: 30 31 26 90

9328

Wanda Reumer Prijs
To recognize a person, group, or organization for a contribution to the development of drama in the Netherlands. A monetary prize of 5,000 guilders is awarded biennially. Established in 1987 on the occasion of the 30th anniversary of the Akademie.

9329

Algemeen Nederlands Verbond
Jan van Nassaustraat 109   Phone: 70 3245514
NL-2596 BS The Hague, Netherlands   Fax: 70 3246186

9330

Visser-Nederlandia dramaprijzen
To encourage playwriting in the Netherlands. A monetary prize of 12,000 Dutch guilders is awarded biennially.

9331

Visser-Neerlandiaprijs
To encourage writing in the Netherlands. A monetary prize of 5,500 Dutch guilders is awarded biennially.

9332

Art and Education Foundation
(Stichting Fonds Kunst en Educatie)
Cicerostraat 7
NL-5216 CC 's-Hertogenbosch, Netherlands   Phone: 73 14 53 23

9333

Art and Education Prize
(Prijs Kunst en Educatie)
For recognition in the fields of art and education. The prize is a piece of art and a trophy. Established in 1988. Sponsored by Netherlands - Ministry of Culture.

9334

Arts Encouragement Foundation
(Stichting Aanmoedigingsfonds voor de Kunsten)
v. Breestraat 186   Phone: 20 6760285
NL-1071 ZZ Amsterdam, Netherlands   Fax: 20 6737053

9335

Perspektiefprys
To encourage young, creative theatre and musical artists. Artists are recognized in the year the work was done. A monetary prize of 7,500 Dutch guilders and travel expenses are provided by KLM. KLM also awards two additional prizes for young artists. Awarded annually. Established in 1985 by Wim Bary, a former theatre manager.

9336

Oskar Back Scholarship Foundation
(Stichting Studiefonds Oskar Back)
Het Concertgebouw N.V.
Concertgebouwplein 2-6   Phone: 20 5730593
NL-1071 LN Amsterdam, Netherlands   Fax: 20 5730560

9337

Composition Prize for Young European Composers
To recognize a composition by a European composer under 30 years of age for a violin and piano composition lasting about seven minutes. The composition will be performed for the first time during the National Violin Competition for young Dutch violinists. A monetary prize of 10,000 guilders and a trip to Amsterdam for the award ceremony are awarded. Sponsored by the European Options Exchange in Amsterdam.

9338

National Violin Competition
To provide a scholarship for violin study outside the Netherlands. Dutch nationals from age 17 through 26 may be recommended by a pedagogue, or by the final exam of one of the Dutch conservatories. 3 monetary prizes are awarded biennially. The main prize was established by H. M. Alvares Correa, in honor of his wife, Etiennette Alvares Correa. Sponsored by the European Options Exchange Amsterdam. Formerly: Etiennette Avares Correa Competition.

9339

Anna Bijns-Stichting
Keizersgracht 486
NL-1017 EH Amsterdam, Netherlands

9340

Anna Bijnsprijs
To recognize a Dutch woman author for works of prose, poetry, or essay. Awarded biennially. Established in 1986.

9341

Buhrmann-Ubbens Papierprijs
Pollaan 1
NL-7202 BV Zutphen, Netherlands

9342

Buhrmann-Ubbens Papierprijs
To recognize an individual or group in the field of sculpture. A stipend of 10,000 Dutch guilders for a project is awarded annually.

9343

Johan and Titia Buning-Brongers Organization
(Johan en Titia Buning-Brongers Stichting)
Leidse Gracht 110
NL-1016 CT Amsterdam, Netherlands   Phone: 20 26 45 17

Formerly: (1985) Titia Buning-Brongers Stichting.

9344

Johan en Titia Buning-Brongers prys
To encourage professional development of Dutch watercolor artists. Individuals under 30 years of age are eligible. A monetary award is presented annually when merited. As many as three awards may be presented. Established in 1965 by Johan Buning and Jeannette Brongers in memory of Titia Buning-Brongers, their sister. Formerly: (1985) Titia Buning-Brongers Award.

9345

Jan Campert Foundation
(Jan-Campertstichting)
Letterkundig Museum
Prinses Irenepad 10
NL-2595 BG The Hague, Netherlands   Phone: 70 347 1114

9346

F. Bordewijk Prize
To recognize the author of the best novel written in the Dutch language published during the preceding year. Flemish authors may also be recognized. A monetary prize of 5,000 guilders is awarded annually. Established in 1978 as successor to the Vijverbey Prijs which was establshed in 1948. Formerly: Vijverberg Prize.

9347

Jan Campert Prize
To recognize the author(s) of the most outstanding poetry written in the Dutch language published during the preceding year. Flemish authors may also be recognized. A monetary prize of 5,000 guilders is awarded annually. Established in 1948.

9348

G. H.'s - Gravesande Prize
For recognition of outstanding merit in the field of literature. A monetary prize of 5,000 guilders is awarded irregularly. This prize is the successor to the Bijzondere Prijs which was established in 1951.

9349

J. Greshoff Prize
For recognition of the best essay or a selection of essays written in the Dutch language. Flemish authors may also be recognized. A monetary prize of 5,000 guilders is awarded biennially in alternate years with the Nienke van Hichtum Prize. Established in 1978 as a successor to the Bijzondere Prijz.

9350

Constantijn Huygens Prize
To recognize a distinguished Dutch author for his complete works. flemish authors may also be recognized. A monetary prize of 10,000 guilders is awarded annually. Established in 1948.

9351

Nienke van Hichtum Prize
For recognition of the best book for children written in the Dutch language. Flemish authors may also be recognized. A monetary prize of 5,000 guilders is awarded biennially in alternate years with the Greshoff Prize.

9352

Carnegie Foundation
(Carnegie Stichting)
Carnegieplein 2   Phone: 70 3024242
NL-2517 KJ The Hague, Netherlands   Fax: 70 3024132

9353

Wateler Peace Prize
(Wateler-Vredesprijs)
To recognize an individual or institution having rendered the most valuable service in the cause of world peace, or having contributed to finding a means of combating war. A monetary prize of 40,000 Dutch guilders is awarded annually in alternate years to a Dutch and a foreign person or organization. Established in 1927 by a bequest to the Carnegie Foundation from J. G. D. Wateler, a Dutch citizen who died in 1927.

9354

Chancery of Netherlands Orders
(Kanselarij der Nederlandse Orden)
PO Box 30436
NL-2500 GK The Hague, Netherlands   Phone: 70 360 68 16

9355

Military Order of William
(Militaire Willems-Orde)
To recognize Netherlanders for conspicuous gallantry in the presence of the enemy. Awarded in four classes. Dutch citizens have to start as Knights 4th class, but can be promoted for further acts of bravery to Knight 3rd Class, Knight 2nd Class and Knight Commander. Such promotions are relatively rare. Established in 1815. (The ranking of the Orders of Knighthood is: (1) Military Order of William; (2) Order of the Netherlands Lion and (3) Order of Orange-Nassau).

9356

Order of Orange-Nassau
(Orde van Oranje-Nassau)
To recognize Dutch citizens or foreigners who have made themselves particularly deserving towards the Dutch people and the State, or towards society. This Order has five classes and affiliated medals of honor. Awarded in two divisions: with swords, for military recipients; and a general division for others. Established in 1892.

9357

Order of the Golden Ark
To recognize outstanding service to the conservation of wildlife and the natural environment. Established in 1972 by H.R.H. Prince Bernhard of the Netherlands, founder-President of the World Wildlife Fund. (The Order of the Golden Ark is a private award of H.R.H. Prince Bernhard of the Netherlands and does not belong to the Netherlands' Orders of Knighthood).

9358

Order of the Netherlands Lion
To recognize Netherlanders who have displayed tested patriotism, unusual dedication and loyalty in the carrying out of their civil duties, or extraordinary skill and performance in the sciences and arts. This Order can also be given to foreigners. The Grand Master of the Order is vested in the Crown of the Netherlands, and consists of three classes: Grand Cross; Commander; and Knight.

9359

Circle of Dutch Theatre Critics
(Kring van Nederlandse Theatercritici)
Postbus 1697
NL-8901 BZ Leeuwarden, Netherlands   Phone: 58 12 99 34

9360

Prijs van de Kritiek
To recognize a theatre production that was an outstanding presentation of the previous season. Judging is by a jury. A trophy can be given for the entire production, or for just a part of it. Awarded annually.

9361
City Council of Groningen
(Gemeente Groningen)
Trompsingel 27 Phone: 50 680111
NL-9724 DA Groningen, Netherlands Fax: 50 680220

9362
Hendrik de Vries Award
(Hendrik de Vries prijs)
To recognize achievement in or contribution to literature and the visual arts. The entry must, in some way, be related to Groningen or to the work of Hendrik de Vries. A monetary prize of 10,000 Dutch guilders is awarded biennially in even-numbered years, alternately for literature and visual arts. Established in 1986 to honor Hendrik de Vries (1896-1989), a poet and painter.

9363
Hendrik de Vries Stipend
(Hendrik de Vries Stipendium)
To encourage development in literature and the visual arts. The entry must, in some way, be related to Groningen or to the work of Hendrik de Vries. A stipend of 5,000 Dutch guilders is awarded biennially in odd-numbered years alternately for literature and visual arts. Established in 1986 by Hendrik de Vries (1896-1989), a poet and painter.

9364
Collective Promotion of the Netherlands Book
(Stichting Collectieve Propaganda van het Nederlandse Boek)
Postbus 10576 Phone: 20 6264971
NL-1001 EN Amsterdam, Netherlands Fax: 20 6231696

9365
Gold Paintbrush
(Gouden Penseel)
For recognition of outstanding illustrations created for a children's book. Dutch and foreign illustrators are eligible for books published during the preceding year. A monetary prize of 3,000 guilders and a Gold Paintbrush are awarded annually to a Dutch illustrator. In addition, a maximum of two Silver Paintbrushes are awarded for the best illustrations by a Dutch or foreign artist. Established in 1973.

9366
Gold Pencil
(Gouden Griffel)
For recognition of the best books written for children that were published during the preceding year in the Netherlands. Three monetary awards of 3,000 guilders and a Gold Pencil are given. In addition, a maximum of eight Silver Pencils are awarded for the best Dutch or translated children's books. Awarded annually during Children's Book Week in the Netherlands. Established in 1971.

9367
Prijs van de Nederlandse Kinderjury
To recognize the best children's books that were published during the preceding year in three age categories. Three diplomas are awarded annually. Established in 1988.

9368
Publieksprijs voor het Nederlandse Boek
To recognize a Dutch author, poet, or illustrator who, based on the results of a nationwide opinion poll, is considered to be the most popular. The author/poet/illustrator must be alive and write in the Dutch language. A monetary award of 15,000 guilders and a trophy are awarded annually in a five-year cycle. Established in 1987.

9369
Venz Kinder Boeken Prijs
To recognize the best sold children's books that was published during the preceding year. A trophy is awarded annually. Established in 1994.

9370
Conamus Foundation
(Stichting Conamus)
PO Box 929 Phone: 35 218748
1218 AC Hilversum, Netherlands Fax: 35 212750

9371
Export Prize
To recognize performers based on the figures of records-sales abroad. These figures are obtained from records companies, music publishers, and personal or business managers of qualifying artists. A trophy is awarded annually.

9372
Golden Harp
This, the highest award in light music in Holland, recognizes individuals who have contributed to national light music in exceptional ways. A trophy is awarded annually.

9373
Annie M. G. Schmidt Prize
To recognize the best theater/cabaret song staged in the previous year.

9374
Silver Harp
To encourage young artists in the field of entertainment who are expected to develop into credits of their trade. A trophy is awarded annually.

9375
Documentary Film Festival - Amsterdam
Postbus 515 Phone: 35 217645
NL-1200 AM Hilversum, Netherlands Fax: 35 235906

Formerly: (1989) Netherlands Film Institute.

9376
Documentary Film Festival - Amsterdam
To encourage the making of professional documentaries. Documentaries of any length, in 35mm or 16mm with combined optical or magnetic sound-track, may be submitted. Films must have been produced during the 15 months preceding the festival. Participating films must not have been screened in the Netherlands before. Films should be submitted in their original version with English subtitles. The Joris Ivens Film Prize, a monetary award of $15,000 US is presented. Established in 1988.

9377
Gouden Eekhoorn
(Golden Squirrel)
To encourage the use of film in the educational field. A trophy and certificate were awarded annually. Established in 1974 by the Netherlands Film Institute. (Discontinued)

9378
Dutch Centre of IAIA
(Nederlandse Vereniging Voor Amateurtheater)
Muurhuizen 30
Postbus 566 Phone: 33 61 57 43
NL-3800 Amersfoort, Netherlands Fax: 33 61 18 67

9379
CVB Amateur Theatre Award
(CVB Amateurtheater Prijs)
To recognize the best amateur theatre performance of the past season. Selection is by nomination. A monetary prize is awarded biennially after the Festival. Established in 1990. Sponsored by Centrale Volksbank.

9380

Dutch Copyright Association
(Vereniging voor Auteursrecht)
Postbus 725　　　　　　　　　　　　　　　Phone: 20 5407416
NL-1180 Amstelveen, Netherlands　　　　　　Fax: 20 5407496

9381

Copyright Prize
(Auteursrechtprijs)
To recognize individuals or organizations for publications that contribute to a better understanding of the field of copyright. A sculpture is awarded biennially at a congress about copyright. Established in 1986.

9382

Dutch Film Days Foundation
(Stichting Nederlandse Filmdagen)
Hoogt 4　　　　　　　　　　　　　　　　Phone: 30 322684
NL-3512 GW Utrecht, Netherlands　　　　　　Fax: 30 313200

9383

Grand Prix of the Dutch Film Golden Calf
(Grote Prijs van de Nederlandse Film Gouden Kalf)
For recognition of achievements in or contributions to Dutch film. Awards may be given in the following categories: best Dutch feature film; best Dutch short film; best documentary short; best male acting performance; best female acting performance; best director; best documentary feature; best television-play; best sound; and exceptional contribution to the Dutch film culture. Monetary prizes and trophies in the form of a Golden Calf are awarded annually at the Dutch Film Days in Utrecht. Founded in 1981.

9384

Dutch Online Users Organization
(Vogin - Nederlandse Vereniging van Gebruikers van Online Informatie Systerem)
SWIDOC
Herengracht 410-412　　　　　　　　　　Phone: 20 6225061
NL-1017 BX Amsterdam, Netherlands　　　　Fax: 20 6238374

9385

Molster Fonds Prijs
(Prize of the Molster Foundation)
For recognition of contributions in the field of online literature research, and information/documentation systems. Applicants must be Dutch citizens or individuals working in the Netherlands. A monetary prize of 1,000 Dutch guilders and a plaque or medal are awarded annually. Established in 1986 by Vogin to honor Mr. Molster, former president of Vogin.

9386

Dutch Section of the International Board on Books for Young People
Secr. A.W.M. Duijx
PO Box 17162　　　　　　　　　　　　　Phone: 20 6363708
NL-1001 JD Amsterdam, Netherlands　　　　Fax: 20 6363708

9387

Jenny Smelik/IBBY Prize
To recognize alternately an author and an illustrator of children's books who contribute to a better understanding of minorities. Selection is by nomination and application. Applications must be made before February 1 of each year. A monetary prize of 8,000 Dutch guilders is awarded triennially by the Dutch section of IBBY. Established in 1983 by Klasina Smelik in honor of the children's book author, Jenny Smelik-Kriggen. Sponsored by Klasina Smelik Stichting. Formerly: Jenny Smelik-Kiggenprijs.

9388

Dutch Society of Sciences
(Hollandsche Maatschappij der Wetenschappen)
Spaarne 17
Postbus 9698
NL-2003 LR Haarlem, Netherlands　　　　　Phone: 2 3321773

9389

Akzo prijs
For recognition of significant scientific research, especially in the fields of chemistry and pharmacy, science and technology, biology and agriculture, medicine and veterinary science, and physics and the geo-sciences. The scientific research must have been performed in the Netherlands. A monetary prize of 25,000 guilders is awarded annually. Sponsored by Akzo Company. Established in 1969.

9390

Prince Bernhard Fund Prize
(Prins Bernhard Fonds-Prijs)
For recognition of significant scientific research in the fields of linguistics, literature, history, philosophy, and theology. The scientific research must have been performed in the Netherlands. A monetary prize of 15,000 guilders is awarded annually. Established in 1980. Sponsored by the Prince Bernhard Fund. (Discontinued)

9391

Pieter Langerhuizen Prize
(Pieter Langerhuizen Bate)
For recognition of significant scientific research in the field of natural sciences. The scientific research must have been performed in the Netherlands. A monetary prize of 30,000 guilders is awarded annually. Established in 1919 in memory of Pieter Langerhuizen Lambertuszoon. Sponsored by Pieter Langerhuizen Lambertuszoon-fonds.

9392

Royal Dutch Shell Prize
(Koninklijke/Shell prijs)
To recognize an outstanding scholar for already performed scientific research in the field of the exact sciences, social sciences, or natural sciences. The scientific research must have been performed in the Netherlands. A monetary prize of 50,000 guilders is awarded annually. Established in 1959. Sponsored by the Royal Dutch Shell Company.

9393

Johannes Cornelis Ruigrok-Prijs
For recognition of significant scientific research in the field of social sciences. The scientific research must have been performed in the Netherlands. A monetary prize of 25,000 guilders is awarded annually. Established in 1983. Sponsored by the J. C. Ruigrok Foundation.

9394

Dirk Jacob Veegens-Prijs
For recognition of research on modern history. The scientific research must have been performed in the Netherlands. A monetary prize of 25,000 guilders is awarded biannually. Established in 1981 in memory of Dirk Jacob Veegens. Sponsored by the Stichting Fonds voor de Geld - en Effectenhandel.

9395

Erasmus Prize Foundation
(Stichting Praemium Erasmianum)
Jan van Goyenkade 5　　　　　　　　　　Phone: 20 6752753
NL-1075 HN Amsterdam, Netherlands　　　　Fax: 20 6752231

9396
Erasmus Prize
(Praemium Erasmianum)
To honor persons or institutions that have made an exceptionally important contribution to European culture or the social science field. Nominations are made by the Board. A monetary prize of 300,000 Dutch guilders is awarded annually when possible. Established in 1958 by H. R. H. Prince Bernhard of the Netherlands.

9397
Esperanto Writers' Association
(Esperantlingva Verkista Asocio)
Volkerakstraat 38 I
NL-1078 XT Amsterdam, Netherlands   Phone: 20 6712664

9398
Theatre Award
(Teatro-Konkurso)
To encourage writing for theatre in Esperanto. Members of EVA are eligible. A monetary award is presented. Established in 1988 to honor Antoni Grabowski, a Polish writer in Esperanto. Sponsored by Mr. Adam Goralski, Tenerife, Canarian Island, Spain. (Inactive since 1989)

9399
Euroavia - Association of European Aeronautical and Astronautical Students
Kluyverweg 1   Phone: 15 785366
NL-2629 HS Delft, Netherlands   Fax: 15 623096

9400
Contact Vamp Trophee
To stimulate activity of all local groups in order to maintain and further good cooperation and contacts in the fields of aeronautics. A trophy is awarded annually. Established in 1990 by Euroavia.

9401
Europa Nostra
35 Lange Voorhout   Phone: 70 3560333
NL-2514 EC The Hague, Netherlands   Fax: 70 3617865

9402
Europa Nostra Awards
For recognition of projects that make an outstanding contribution to the conservation and enhancement of Europe's architectural and natural heritage. Entries must be submitted under one of the five categories of client organizations responsible for commissioning the work: private owners, civic or amenity societies, commercial owners, regional or local government, and national government. The following types of projects may be entered: restoration of old buildings; adaptation of old buildings to new uses, preserving their original character; new construction in conservation areas harmonizing with the older environment, or that pays due respect to the environment in areas of outstanding natural beauty; and conservation of natural or landscaped beauty. Projects must have been completed within the last ten years and must be accompanied by photographs, a summary, and the history and description of the work carried out. About 35 awards are presented annually. All the awards are commemorated by a wall plaque and a certificate. In addition, the most outstanding entries are presented with a medal. Established in 1978 by Europa Nostra, after the success of the European Architectural Heritage Year, 1975, to commemorate the whole conservation movement in Europe. Sponsored by American Express.

9403
Europa Nostra/IBI
Lange Voorhout 35   Phone: 70 3560333
NL-2514 EC The Hague, Netherlands   Fax: 70 3617865

Formerly: (1991) International Castles Institute.

9404
Medals of Honour
(Medailles D'Honneur)
To recognize persons who have performed exemplary work in the restoration of an ancient fortified work or building, castle, ruins, associated park or garden, or dwelling having historic character. Proposals must be written in English or French, in the form of a dossier, and be submitted by November 1. Three medals and diplomas are presented annually by the President or a Representative at a ceremony of the Association. Established by International Castles Institute in 1975.

9405
European Association of Exploration Geophysicists
PO Box 298   Phone: 3404 62655
NL-3700 AG Zeist, Netherlands   Fax: 3404 62640

9406
Hagedoorn Award
To recognize a member for the best technical paper or papers published in *Geophysical Prospecting* or *First Break*. A plaque and a bound copy of the volume of *Geophysical Prospecting* or *First Break* containing the citation are awarded. Established in 1988.

9407
Conrad Schlumberger Award
To recognize a member who has made an outstanding contribution over a period of time to the scientific and technical advancement of geophysics or other service to the geophysical community. A certificate and an appropriately bound copy of the volume of *Geophysical Prospecting* containing the citation of the award are awarded annually. Established in 1955.

9408
Van Weelden Award
For recognition of the best paper read at an Association meeting or published in *Geophysical Prospecting* or *First Break*, by anyone who is under 30 years of age by December 31 of the year the paper is read or published. A certificate and a bound copy of the volume of *Geophysical Prospecting* or *First Break* containing the citation are awarded annually. Established in 1955 in honor of Mr. Arie van Weelden, founder of the Association.

9409
European Institute of Public Administration
(Institut Europeen d'Administration Publique)
O.L. Vrouweplein 22
PO Box 1229   Phone: 43 296222
NL-6201 BE Maastricht, Netherlands   Fax: 43 296296

9410
Alexis de Tocqueville Prize
To recognize one or more persons, or a group of people, whose work and commitment have made a considerable contribution to improving public administration in Europe. Awarded biennially. Established in 1987.

9411

European Packaging Federation
(Federation Europeenne de l'Emballage)
c/o Netherlands Packaging Centre
Postbus 164
NL-2800 AD Gouda, Netherlands
Phone: 1820 12411
Fax: 1820 12769

9412

Eurostar Awards for Packaging
For recognition in the field of packaging at the European Packaging Competition. The competition is open only to packages that have gained an award recognized by the national packaging institutes. Diplomas and Certificates of Merit are awarded annually. Established in 1958.

9413

European Rhinologic Society
Dept. of O.R.L.
Univ. Hospital Utrecht
PO Box 85500
3508 GA Utrecht, Netherlands
Phone: 30 508360
Fax: 30 561922

9414

European Rhinologic Society Prizes
To recognize individuals for clinical or basic research in rhinology. Three monetary and travel prizes are awarded biennially. Established in 1986.

9415

European Society for Clinical Investigation
Central Office
Postbus 332
NL-4130 EH Vianen, Netherlands

9416

Awards
For recognition in the field of biomedical research.

9417

European Society for Opinion and Marketing Research
c/o Esomar Central Secretariat
J. J. Viottastraat 29
NL-1071 JP Amsterdam, Netherlands
Phone: 20 6642141
Fax: 20 6642922

9418

ESOMAR Awards
For recognition of the best papers presented at the annual congress. Original, unpublished papers may be submitted. Awards are presented in three categories: best application paper, best methodology paper, and best overall paper. A monetary award of 3,000 Swiss francs is presented for the best overall paper and 1,500 Swiss francs for each of the winners in the other two categories. Established in 1978.

9419

Experimental Natural Philosophy Society
(Bataafsch Genootschap der Proefondervindelijke Wijsbegeerte)
PO Box 597
NL-3000 AN Rotterdam, Netherlands

9420

Steven Hoogendijk Prijs
To encourage professional development in the field of scientific medical-biological work in Rotterdam and of scientific work under the auspices of the Technical University Delft. Promising young Dutch scientists are eligible for nomination by January of even-numbered years. A monetary prize, a medal, and a diploma are awarded biennially at the general meeting of the Society. Established in 1972 in memory of Steven Hoogendijk, founder of the Society in 1769.

9421

Federatie Cultureel Jongeren Paspoort
Willemsparkweg 52
Postbus 5049
NL-1007 AA Amsterdam, Netherlands
Phone: 20 76 93 46

9422

Zilveren CJP
To recognize a performer or theatre group for a contribution to a cultural presentation that is popular with youth. The award is given in alternate years in Belgium and the Netherlands. A monetary prize of 2,000 guilders is awarded annually.

9423

Federation of European Societies of Plant Physiology
Dept. of Plant Physiology
Agricultural University
Arboretumlaan 4
NL-6703 BD Wageningen, Netherlands
Phone: 8370 83645

9424

FESPP Award
For recognition of outstanding scientific work in recent years. Members who are under 35 years of age may be nominated by January 31 of even-numbered years. A diploma, plenary lecture, and travel and participation expenses are awarded biennially to two individuals at the FESPP Congress. Established in 1986. Sponsored by Georg Thieme Publishers, Stuttgart, Germany. Additional information is available from J.P. Verbelen, Biology Department UIA, Universiteitsplein 1, B-2610 Wilrijk, Belgium.

9425

Feminist Monthly
(Opzy/Feministisch Maanblad)
Postbus 1311
NL-1000 Amsterdam, Netherlands
Phone: 20 551 85 25
Fax: 20 625 12 88

9426

Annie Romein Prys
To recognize a female artist/writer who has assisted in the emancipation of women. The prize is given for a whole body of work; literary quality is considered. A monetary award of 5,000 Dutch guilders is presented biennially. Established in 1979 by Opzy.

9427

Fleuroselect
Parallel Boulevard 214 D
NL-2202 HT Noordwijk, Netherlands
Phone: 1719 49101
Fax: 1719 49102

Formerly: European Organization for Testing New Flower Seeds.

9428

Fleuroselect Gold Medal
To recognize the best new flower seeds. Society members are eligible. A medal is awarded annually at the convention. Established in 1970.

9429

Foundation for Cultural Cooperation - Sticusa
(Stichting voor Culturele Samenwerking - Sticusa)
PO Box 5492
NL-1007 AL Amsterdam, Netherlands
Phone: 20 71 99 44

9430
Sticusa Literature Prize
(Litteraire Prijs Sticusa)
For recognition of a work of literature. Belles-lettres, poetry, plays and literary essays, written in Sranan Tongo, Hindi or Papiamentu were considered. A monetary prize was awarded annually. Established in 1973. (Discontinued in 1976).

9431
Cesar Franck Organ Competition Committee
(Comite Cesar Franck Orgel Concours)
Leeghwaterstraat 14
NL-2012 GD Haarlem, Netherlands   Phone: 23 327070

9432
Cesar Franck Organ Competition
(Cesar Franck Orgelconcours)
For recognition of outstanding organists. The deadline is June 1. The first prize winner receives a monetary prize of 3,000 dutch guilders, the second prize winner receives 2,000 dutch guilders, and the third prize winner receives 1,000 dutch guilders. Three finalists receive an invitation to play at St. Bavo's Cathedral, and the first prize winner is awarded a recording for Dutch radio. In addition, the best Tournemire-player of the finalists receive a prize of 500 dutch guilders. Awarded triennially. Established in 1976. The next competition is scheduled for October 1994.

9433
French Embassy
Cultural Department
Smidsplein 1
NL-2514 BT The Hague, Netherlands

9434
Prix des Ambassadeurs
To recognize a Dutch author under the age of 40 for a novel, essay, poetry or play. A monetary prize of 30,000 Dutch guilders is awarded. Established in 1983.

9435
Friends of the Dutch National Ballet
(Stichting Vrienden van het Nationale Ballet)
PO Box 15387   Phone: 20 551 8226
NL-1001 MJ Amsterdam, Netherlands   Fax: 20 551 8070

9436
Alexandra Radius Prize
(Alexandra Radius-Prijs)
To recognize one dancer a year for his or her outstanding achievements. Selection is by nomination. A monetary prize and a plaque are awarded annually on New Year's Day. Established in 1988 in honor of the Dutch prima ballerina, Alexandra Radius (1942).

9437
Gaudeamus Foundation
(Stichting Gaudeamus)
Swammerdamstraat 38   Phone: 20 6947349
NL-1091 RV Amsterdam, Netherlands   Fax: 20 6947258

9438
International Gaudeamus Interpreters Competition
To stimulate young musicians to play contemporary music. Ensembles and soloists who are 35 years of age or less perform a program of contemporary music (after 1940) including two Dutch works. Four monetary prizes are awarded biennially in the spring. Established in 1963 in cooperation with the Rotterdam Arts Foundation.

9439
International Gaudeamus Musicweek for Young Composers Award
To stimulate the writing of new compositions. Individuals 30 years of age or less may submit compositions by January 31. The Gaudeamus Prize of 10,000 Dutch guilders is awarded as a commission to write a new composition for an opera and musical. Awarded annually at the end of the Musicweek in September. Established in 1948.

9440
Genootschap van Nederlandstalige Misdaadauteuurs
Weesperzijde 95
NL-1091 EL Amsterdam, Netherlands   Phone: 20 94 18 16

9441
Gouden Strop
To recognize an author for a criminal novel published during the preceding year. A monetary prize of 10,000 Dutch guilders is awarded annually. Established in 1986.

9442
Haarlem Boekenstad
Nieuwe Gracht 53
Haarlem, Netherlands

9443
Laurens Janszoon Coster Prize
To recognize individuals or institutions who have served the world of the book. Authors, publishers, booksellers, illustrators, periodicals, and those working in radio and television are eligible. A monetary prize of 5,000 Dutch guilders and a statue of L.J. Coster, made by Kees Verkade, are awarded annually. Established in 1976 by L.J. Veen Jr. and R.H.C. de Vries. The award is named for the inventor of printing in the Netherlands, Laurens Janszoon Coster (1436-83).

9444
Hague Academy of International Law
Peace Palace
Carnegieplein 2
NL-2517 KJ The Hague, Netherlands   Phone: 31 70 302 4242

9445
Hague Academy of International Law Scholarships
To provide scholarships for study at the Academy. Candidates must apply by March 1. No more than two scholarships can be granted to students from each country during the same year. Four residential scholarships are also awarded to doctoral candidates whose theses are in an advanced stage of preparation. Candidates from developing countries who reside in their home country and who do not have access to scientific sources are eligible.

9446
Frans Halsmuseum
Groot Heiligland 62
NL-2011 ES Haarlem, Netherlands

9447
Frans Halsprijs voor Tentoonstellingsvormgeving
To promote the advancement of expertise in exhibition design. A monetary prize of 7,500 Dutch guilders, a publication on the exhibition, and an exhibition in the Frans Hals Museum area awarded every four years. Established in 1988.

9448
Judith Leysterprijs
To recognize women artists working in the Netherlands. A monetary prize of 10,000 Dutch guilders, a publication on the exhibition, and an exhibition in the Frans Hals Museum are awarded biennially. Established in 1989.

9449
Jacobus van Looyprijs
To recognize a sculptor. A monetary prize of 5,000 Dutch guilders and an exhibition in the Frans Hals Museum are awarded every five years. Established in 1985.

9450
Heineken Foundation
(Heineken Stichting)
21 Tweede Weteringplantsoen
NL-1017 ZD Amsterdam, Netherlands
Phone: 20 5239239
Fax: 20 6263503

9451
Amsterdam Prize
To recognize outstanding achievement in the fields of history, art, medicine, and environmental science. Four awards are presented at a special public meeting of the Royal Netherlands Academy of Arts and Sciences. The Amsterdam Prize for Art was first awarded in 1988, the Amsterdam Prize for Medicine was established in 1989, and the Amsterdam Prizes for History and the Environment were added in 1990.

9452
Dr. H. P. Heineken Prize
(Dr. H. P. Heineken Prijs)
For recognition of exceptional discoveries in the fields of biochemistry and biophysics, including microbiology and the physiology of seed germination. The Royal Netherlands Academy of Arts and Sciences established the selection criteria and appoints the selection committee. A monetary prize of 250,000 Dutch guilders and a crystal trophy bearing a miniature of the microscope of Antonie van Leeuwenhoeck are awarded biennially at a special session of the Royal Netherlands Academy of Arts and Sciences. Established in 1963 by Heineken N. V. in memory of Dr. H. P. Heineken, past president of Heineken Brewery.

9453
Holland Animation Film Festival
Hoogt 4
NL-3512 Utrecht, Netherlands
Phone: 30 312216
Fax: 30 312940

9454
Holland Animation Film Festival Awards
To promote commissioned animated film and the individual talent of the animation filmmaker. The Joop Geesink Prize is presented for applied animation, which includes announcements, titles, education and information films, clips, use of tricks in films, and commercials effected by a technique other than live action. Prizes are presented biennially in the following categories: publicity and promotional films; pop promos; educational and information films; and station calls and film leaders. One Grand Prix award is presented to the best film or video selected from the above categories. Entered films must have premiered after June 1, 1989. Established in 1905.

9455
Interfilm - The International Interchurch Film Centre
Postbus 515
NL-1200 AM Hilversum, Netherlands
Phone: 35 17645

Formerly: (1989) Netherlands Film Institute.

9456
Interfilm Award
For recognition of films of high artistic quality at international film festivals. Selection is based on films which express and discuss social and spiritual values. All films which are officially entered in international film festivals are eligible. A medal with a diploma, and frequently a monetary prize are awarded ten times a year. Established in 1957.

9457
International Association for Hydraulic Research
PO Box 177
NL-2600 MH Delft, Netherlands
Phone: 15 569353
Fax: 15 619674

9458
Honorary Member
For recognition of individuals who have made outstanding contributions to hydraulic research. Awarded biennially during IAHR Biennial Congresses.

9459
IAHR-APD Award
To encourage the presentation of research results on hydraulics and water resources at the biennial regional congresses of the Asian and Pacific Regional Division (APD) of IAHR. The awards are conferred to the authors of the two papers judged as the most outstanding presented during the APD Congress. One award is given to the author of the best paper from the host country and the other to the author from outside the host country. A bronze plaque and certificate are awarded biennially. Established in 1983.

9460
IAHR Lecturer Award
To provide an institute of research or higher learning with an IAHR lecturer. The lecturer is appointed by the Secretary-General. Individuals may apply by August 31. The award consists of a maximum of US $2,500 travel allowance, an honorarium of US $2,500, and a certificate. Awarded annually. Established in 1987.

9461
Arthur Thomas Ippen Award
To recognize a member of IAHR who has developed an outstanding record of accomplishment as demonstrated by research, publications, and/or conception and design of signficiant engineering hydraulic works; and who holds great promise for a continuing level of productivity in the field of basic hydraulic research and/or applied hydraulic engineering. IAHR members may submit nominations. Preference is given to members under 40 years of age. An honorarium of $1,000 is awarded biennially at the IAHR Biennial Congress. The recipient delivers the Arthur Thomas Ippen Lecture. Established in 1977 to honor Professor Ippen, IAHR President (1959-1963), IAHR Honorary Member (1963-1974), and for many decades an inspirational leader in fluids research, hydraulic engineering, and international cooperation and understanding.

9462
John F. Kennedy Student Paper Competition
To recognize outstanding student papers. Selection is based on written and oral presentations. A monetary award and a plaque are awarded at the Congress closing ceremony. Additional monetary awards and certificates are presented to runners-up. Established in 1992 in memory of Professor John F. Kennedy, IAHR President (1979-1983) and honorary member (1989-1991), remembered particularly for his efforts to foster younger-member membership and participation.

9463
Harold Jan Schoemaker Award
To recognize the most outstanding paper that was published in the IAHR Bulletin during the preceding two-year period. IAHR members may submit candidates for nomination by January 1. A bronze medal and a certificate are awarded biennially. Established in 1980 in memory of Prof.

Schoemaker, Secretary (1960-1979) who guided the *Journal of Hydraulic Research* in its formative years.

9464
International Association for the Evaluation of Educational Achievement
S.V.O.
Sweelinckplein 14   Phone: 70 346 9679
NL-2517 GK The Hague, Netherlands   Fax: 70 360 9951

9465
IEA - Bruce H. Choppin Memorial Award
For recognition of achievement in empirical research using data from studies conducted by the Association. The competition is open to persons from any nation who have completed a master's or doctoral thesis within the preceding three years that used data collected in connection with any IEA study, and that used statistical methods to analyze the data. Applications are accepted by March 31 of each year. A certificate is awarded annually. Established in 1983 in honor of Bruce H. Choppin. Additional information is available from Prof. Richard M. Wolf, Box 165, Teachers College, Columbia University, New York, NY 10027, U.S.A., phone: (212) 678- 3355; fax: (212) 678-4048.

9466
International Association of Horticultural Producers
(Association Internationale des Producteurs de l'Horticulture)
Bezuidenhoutseweg 153   Phone: 70 3814631
NL-2594 AB The Hague, Netherlands   Fax: 70 3477176

9467
Grand Prize of AIPM/Grand Prize of Excellence
(Grand Prix de l'AIPH and Grand Prix d'Excellence)
To recognize improvement of attractiveness of villages and towns by way of flowers and plants in public and private gardens. A trophy is awarded annually. Established in 1974.

9468
International Association of Hydrological Sciences
TNO Committee on Hydrological Research
Postbus 6067   Phone: 70 15 69 7262
NL-2501 JA Delft, Netherlands   Fax: 70 15 56 4801

9469
International Hydrology Prize
To recognize an individual who has made an outstanding contribution to hydrology such as confers on the candidate universal recognition of his international stature. The contribution should have an identifiable international dimension extending beyond both the country of normal work and the specific field of interest of the candidate. The contribution may have been made through scientific work, as evidenced by the publication in international journals of scientific literature of a high standard, and/or through practical work, as evidenced by reports of the projects concerned. Preference should be given to candidates who have contributed through both scientific and practical work. The Prize may be awarded to hydrologists of long international standing or to those who, while having gained such standing only recently, exhibit the qualities of international leadership in the science and practice of hydrology. An active involvement in the work of IAHS and other international organizations in the field of hydrology should be counted as an advantage. A silver medal is presented annually. Established in 1981. Sponsored by UNESCO and World Meteorological Organization.

9470
Tison Award
To promote excellence in research by young hydrologists. Outstanding papers published by IAHS in a period of two years previous to the deadline for nominations are eligible. Candidates for the award must be under 41 years of age at the time their paper was published. A monetary prize of $750 and a citation are awarded annually during either an IUGG/IAHS General Assembly or an IAHS Scientific Assembly.

9471
International Association on the Political Use of Psychiatry
Postbus 3754   Phone: 20 627 94 91
NL-1001 AN Amsterdam, Netherlands   Fax: 20 620 81 16

9472
Anatoly Koryagin Award
For recognition of outstanding work in the fight against political abuse of psychiatry and in defense of medical ethics. A medal and a certificate are awarded annually. Established in 1987 in honor of Dr. Anatoly Koryagin, the Soviet psychiatrist who spent six years in prison and a camp for his fight against political abuse of psychiatry.

9473
International Bridge Academy
c/o Nederlandse Bridge Bond
W. Dreeslaan 55   Phone: 30 71 26 44
NL-3515 GB Utrecht, Netherlands   Fax: 30 71 14 82

9474
Best Original Article
To recognize an individual for an outstanding original article using the scientific approach to bridge. A monetary award was presented biennially. Established in 1983. (Discontinued)

9475
International Bidding Contest
For recognition of all bridge pairs that finished first in their own country in the bidding contest. Medals were awarded to overall winners and individuals on the world ranking list. Established in 1966. Re-established in 1982. (Discontinued)

9476
International Choir Festival
(International Koorfestival)
Plompetorengracht 3   Phone: 30 31 31 74
NL-3512 CA Utrecht, Netherlands   Fax: 30 31 81 37

9477
AGEC-Preis
To encourage a composer to write musical compositions for amateur choirs. A plaque is awarded annually. Established in 1987.

9478
International Choir Festival
For recognition of outstanding choirs from all over the world participating in the festival. Awards are given in the following five categories: mixed choirs, female choirs, male choirs, youth choirs, and children's choirs. First, second, and third prizes are awarded.

9479
International Colour Association
(Association Internationale de la Couleur)
Philips Lighting
PO Box 80020   Phone: 40 756287
NL-5600 JM Eindhoven, Netherlands   Fax: 40 755861

9480
Judd AIC Award
For recognition of research in color in all aspects, and its application to science, art, and industry. A plaque is awarded biennially. Established in 1973 by Mrs. Judd in honor of Dr. Deane B. Judd, internationally acclaimed authority on color and one of the founders of the Association.

9481

International Council for Building Research, Studies and Documentation
(Conseil International du Batiment)
Postbox 1837　　　　　　　　　　　　Phone: 10 411 02 40
NL-3000 BV Rotterdam, Netherlands　　Fax: 10 433 43 72

9482

CIB Developing Countries Fellowships
To assist CIB members in developing countries to participate in congresses, symposia and other meetings of professional interest. Members are eligible. A monetary grant is awarded occasionally. Established in 1983.

9483

International Council of Ophthalmology
Inst. of Ophthalmology
Philips van Leydenlaan 15　　　　　　Phone: 80 513138
NL-6525 EX Nijmegen, Netherlands　　Fax: 80 540522

9484

International Council of Ophthalmology Awards
To recognize outstanding international research projects and educational programs in the field of ophthalmology. The following awards are presented: Gonin Medal, Duke Elder Intenational Medal, and the Jules Francois Medal. Awarded every four years at the International Congress of Opthalmology.

9485

International Federation for Housing and Planning
(Federation Internationale pour l'Habitation, l'Urbanisme et l'Amernagement des Territoires)
43 Wassenaarseweg
NL-2596 CG The Hague, Netherlands　　Phone: 70 24 45 57

9486

IFHP International Film/Video Competition
For recognition of the best film/video made during the preceding four years in the fields of housing and/or planning. The Competition is open to anyone. The Vienna Challenge Trophy for the best film and the Malmo Challenge Trophy for the best video are awarded every four years. Established in 1954 in Vienna.

9487

IFHP International Student Competition
To encourage the development of innovative and useful ideas, applicable at different times and in different places which must be feasible, at least in some regions of the world, from the economic, technological and institutional point of view. They must also be acceptable to the future society in general, with regard to overall human habits and human needs. University students or groups of students at institutes for urban and/or regional planning, or at other faculties where biophysical, social and/or economic aspects of urban and regional development, or aspects of urban form and institutional organization are being studied are eligible to enter. The competition is organized every two years in two stages. The National Competitions select a maximum of ten best entries to be sent to the International Competition. The Competition's theme usually corresponds to the theme of that year's IFHP International Congress. Two monetary travel awards and study visit grants are usually presented biennially. In addition, the International Jury selects the 10 most innovative, but viable proposals for special mention and world-wide publication.

9488

International Federation of Interior Architects/Interior Designers
(Federation Internationale des Architectes d'Interieur)
Waterlooplein 219
Postbox 19126　　　　　　　　　　　Phone: 20 6276820
NL-1000 GC Amsterdam, Netherlands　Fax: 20 6237146

9489

IFI Award
To recognize a person or an institution for a contribution to the advancement of the profession of interior architecture/interior design, education, (interior) architecture, or philosophy. Citizens of, or institutions established in the country where a biennial IFI Congress is being held, are eligible. Nominations are made by the host member of IFI. Established in 1985. IFI also endorses international design competitions that comply with its guidelines. For more information, please contact the IFI Secretariat in Amsterdam.

9490

International Federation of Library Associations and Institutions
(Federation Internationale des Associations de Bibliothecaires et des Bibliotheques)
PO Box 95312　　　　　　　　　　　Phone: 70 3140884
NL-2509 CH The Hague, Netherlands　Fax: 70 3834827

9491

Honorary Fellow
For recognition of outstanding contributions to librarianship. Awarded when merited.

9492

Honorary President
For recognition of outstanding service. Awarded when merited.

9493

IFLA Medal
For recognition of outstanding service in the field of librarianship. There are no age, society, or citizenship restrictions. A medal and scroll are awarded in odd-numbered years at the conference. IFLA's Council may also confer the title of Honorary Fellow of IFLA. Established in the 1930s.

9494

Martinus Nijhoff Study Grant
To enable a teacher of library science, to study specific subject matter in library science in one or more Western European countries. A monetary award of 10,000 Dutch guilders was awarded annually to cover the costs of study, board, and lodging and any surface study travel within Western Europe. Additionally, economy-class, round-trip, air transportation from the grantee's country to The Netherlands was provided. Established in 1977. (Discontinued)

9495

T. P. Sevensma Prize
To recognize the author of the best unpublished paper devoted to questions of libraries in their relation to current problems. A monetary prize of 1,500 Swiss francs was awarded every three years. Established in 1939. (Discontinued)

9496

Robert Vosper IFLA Fellows Program
To recognize outstanding librarians with an interest in and a commitment to the international aspects of library service, and to enable each Fellow who has potential for leadership and international involvement to develop this potential by working on an activity linked with the development and operation of one of IFLA's Core Programs. Fellows carry out activities mainly in their own institution in close cooperation with and under the supervision of IFLA's Core Program Directors. Four fellows per year for three years (1989/1990/1991) are selected by IFLA's Executive Board. Each Fellow is awarded US $10,000. Established in 1989 in honor of Robert Vosper, Honorary Fellow of IFLA. Sponsored by the Council on Library Resources.

【9497】
International Federation of Manufacturers and Converters of Pressure-Sensitive and Heatseals on Paper and Other Base Materials (Federation Internationale des Fabricants et Transformateurs d'Adhesifs et Thermocollants sur Papiers et Autres Supports)
Laan Copes van Cattenburch 79
NL-2585 EW The Hague, Netherlands
Phone: 70 360 38 37
Fax: 70 363 63 48

【9498】
Self-Adhesive Labelling Awards
For recognition of research to improve the quality and utilization of pressure-sensitive and heatseal materials. The organization holds competitions and presents awards.

【9499】
International Federation of Ophthalmological Societies
Institute of Ophthalmology
15 Philips van Leydenlaan
Nijmegen, Netherlands
Phone: 80 613138
Fax: 80 540522

【9500】
Sir Stewart Duke Elder International Medal
To recognize an ophthalmologist who, by his distinction, leadership, and teaching, has contributed most to the development of international relations and friendship among ophthalmologists. Contributions in writing and organization in ophthalmology are considered. A medal is awarded every four years at the International Congress. Established in 1982.

【9501】
Jules Francois Medal
For recognition of important scientific work in the field of ophthalmology and for international leadership. A medal is awarded every four years at the International Congress. Established in 1986.

【9502】
Gonin Medal
This, the highest award in ophthalmology, is given for recognition of the best ophthalmological works in the world. Prestigious ophthalmologists with important scientific contributions are eligible. A gold medal is awarded every four years on the occasion of the International Congress of Ophthalmology. Established in 1941.

【9503】
International Federation of Purchasing and Materials Management (Federation Internationale de l'Approvisionnement et l'Achat)
F.J. Dekraker, Dir. Gen.
PO Box 289
NL-1860 AG Bergen, Netherlands
Phone: 2208 99197
Fax: 2208 99684

【9504】
Garner-Themoin Medal
To recognize an individual for an outstanding contribution to international purchasing and materials management. A medal and a plaque are presented annually. Established in 1976 to commemorate two outstanding personalities, Mr. Garner from the United Kingdom, and Mr. Themoin from France.

【9505】
Maple Leaf Award
To increase the availability of written communication world wide. A technical paper is selected in the competition. A monetary prize of 1,000 Swiss francs, a plaque, and a diploma are presented annually. Established in 1977. The winning paper is normally published. Sponsored by Purchasing Management Association of Canada-(PMAC).

【9506】
International Finn Association
Josje Dominicus
Kalverstraat 7
NL-8713 KV Hindeloopen, Netherlands
Phone: 416 5362805
Fax: 416 5434567

【9507】
European Finn Seniors Championship
To recognize an individual for achievement in sailing. The Richard Sarby Trophy is awarded annually. Established in 1950 to honor Richard Sarby, designer of the Finn for the winner of the European Finn Seniors Championship.

【9508】
European Junior Finn Championship
To recognize an individual for achievement in sailing. A silver cup is awarded annually. Established in 1967.

【9509】
World Championship
To recognize an individual for achievement in sailing. The Finn Gold Cup is awarded annually. Established in 1956 by Tony Mitchell.

【9510】
International Fiscal Association
Gen. Secretariat
PO Box 30215
NL-3001 DE Rotterdam, Netherlands
Phone: 10 4052990
Fax: 10 4055031

【9511】
Mitchell B. Carroll Prize
For recognition of the work of young individuals under 35 years of age working or studying in the field of international fiscal law. Papers written in English, French, or German devoted to international fiscal law, comparative tax law, or national tax law having an important relationship with fiscal law in foreign countries are accepted. A monetary prize and a medal are awarded annually. Established in 1947 in memory of Dr. Mitchell B. Carroll.

【9512】
International Korfball Federation (Federation Internationale de Korfbal)
Runnenburg 12
PO Box 1000
NL-3980 DA Bunnik, Netherlands
Phone: 3405 70655
Fax: 3405 67025

【9513】
Badge of Honour
For recognition of a contribution to a field of activity over a period of time. Individuals may apply. A badge of honor is awarded at the annual general meeting. Established in 1946.

【9514】
Honorary Member
For recognition of a contribution to a field of activity over a period of time. Individuals may apply. Honorary membership is awarded at the annual general meeting. Established in 1946.

【9515】
International Pharmaceutical Federation (Federation Internationale Pharmaceutique)
Andries Bickerweg 5
NL-2517 JP The Hague, Netherlands
Phone: 70 3631925
Fax: 70 3633914

9516
Awards in Recognition of Excellence
To recognize outstanding achievements in the fields of pharmaceutical practice and pharmaceutical sciences. The following awards are presented by the Federation: FIP Practitioner of the Year Award - presented to an individual or group who has made an outstanding contribution to pharmaceutical practice during the previous year; FIP Lifetime Achievement in the Practice of Pharmacy Award - presented to an individual who has, over many years, contributed to the development of pharmaceutical practice; FIP Pharmaceutical Scientist of the Year Award - presented to a pharmaceutical scientist, or a group of scientists, who have made an outstanding contribution to the pharmaceutical sciences during the previous year; and FIP Lifetime Achievement in the Pharmaceutical Sciences Award - presented to an individual who has, over many years, contributed to the development of the pharmaceutical sciences. Deadline for nomination is January 31. A monetary prize of 2,000 guilders, a commemorative gift, and travel expenses to the FIP Congress are presented annually to the winners of the awards.

9517
Andre Bedat Award
To recognize a pharmacist who is an outstanding practitioner and has made significant contributions to pharmacy at the international level. Candidates may be nominated by January 21. A winner is determined by the Board of Pharmaceutical Practice. A steel plaque is awarded biennially at an FIP Congress. Established in 1986 to honor Andre Bedat, president of FIP from 1978 to 1986.

9518
Development Grants
To provide help to pharmacists in developing countries with funding for a project that will be of benefit to the recipients and their country. Application deadlines are July 31 or December 31.

9519
FIP Fellowships
To permit the recipient to perform research and/or be trained outside his/her own home country. The subject of research or training must be in line with the objectives of the Foundation. Anyone employed in either the practice of pharmacy or the pharmaceutical sciences may apply. Selection is based on: originality/ novelty and creativity; relevance to the Foundation's objectives and current priorities; conciseness and clarity of presentation; application's qualifications and background; demonstration that the project is innovative and needed; the international character of the project; appropriateness of the project design to the stated goals; methods of evalation, including both the monitoring of project developments and the achievement of project goals; specificity and practicality of the project schedule; specificity and practicality of the budget; and documentation of the institutional commitments (funds, materials, facilities, and/or personnel provided). Application deadline is November 30. The amount of the requested fellowship must not exceed 20,000 guilders to cover travel and living expenses.

9520
FIP International Travel Scholarships
To assist pharmacists or pharmaceutical scientists to travel abroad in order to develop, or to help others to develop, skills and/or know- how. Scholarships are also awarded to contribute to travel expenses for speakers at congresses, seminars, or courses in line with the objectives of the Foundation. Anyone employed in either the practice of pharmacy or the pharmaceutical sciences is eligible. Selection is based on the international nature of the travel plan, the applicant's qualifications and background, and relevance to the Foundation's objectives and current priorities. Deadlines for application are January 31 and July 31. Proposed scholarship amounts are not to exceed 5,000 guilders. Awarded semiannually in March and September.

9521
Host-Madsen Medal
To recognize a pharmacist who has particularly distinguished himself by his work and to encourage scientific research by pharmacists. Scientists from any country are eligible. Nominations may be submitted by members of the Federation and the Board of Pharmaceutical Sciences makes the selection. A bronze medal is awarded biennially and there may be more than one medal given. Established in 1955, and awarded for the first time to Dr. Host-Madsen to honor his services to the Federation.

9522
Publisher's Prizes
To recognize the author of the best article or series of articles published in the *International Pharmacy Journal*. Awarded biennially.

9523
International Radiation Protection Association
PO Box 662
NL-5600 AR Eindhoven, Netherlands
Phone: 40 473355
Fax: 40 435020

9524
Sievert Award
For recognition of contributions to radiological protection. A monetary prize and a certificate are awarded at the Association International Congress, which is held every three or four years. Established in 1973 in honor of Rolf Sievert. Additional information is available from Dr. R. V. Osborne, Chairman of the Sievert Award Committee, AECL Research, Chalk River Laboratories, Health Sciences and Services Division, Chalk River, Ontario K0J 1J0 Canada.

9525
International Society for Contemporary Music
Gaudeamus
Swammerdamstraat 38
NL-1091 Amsterdam, Netherlands
Phone: 20 6947349
Fax: 20 6947258

9526
Honorary Member
For recognition of outstanding accomplishment in the field of contemporary music.

9527
International Society of Paediatric Oncology
(Societe Internationale d'Oncologie Pediatrique)
c/o Prof. A. W. Craft, Secretary
PO Box 3283
5203 D6S Hertogenbosch, Netherlands
Phone: 73 429285
Fax: 73 414766

9528
Nycomed Prize
To stimulate the research and development of pediatric oncology by rewarding the quality of either an oral or poster presentation during annual SIOP meetings. A shortlist is drawn up by the scientific committee from abstracts submitted for the annual meeting by February 28. A group prize of $5,000 US to be shared equally by the named authors is awarded annually. Established in 1991, initially for five years.

9529
Schweisguth Prize
For recognition of the best scientific article prepared by a trainee in pediatric oncology. Trainees who are physicians, nurses, social workers, psychologists, etc., are eligible. Judgement is based on a written article describing work done by the trainee him/herself, and considers originality, completeness, scientific accuracy, and contribution to science. The deadline is usually February 28. All entries must be sponsored by the trainee's head of department (usually a SIOP member). An all expenses paid trip to the annual conference and presentation/publication of the winning article are awarded each year at the annual conference. Established in 1986 in honor of Dr. Odile Schweisguth, founding member and first president of the Society.

9530

International Society of Violin and Bow Makers
Maliebaan 105
NL-3581 CH Utrecht, Netherlands
Phone: 30 315669
Fax: 30 315880

9531

International Society of Violin and Bow Makers Competitions
To recognize and promote the art of violin and bow making. Master violin and bow makers over the age 35 are eligible. The Society sponsors competitions and meets biennially.

9532

International Sound Hunters Federation
(Federation Internationale des Chasseurs de Son)
Weteringlaan 7
NL-2243 GJ Wassenaar, Netherlands
Phone: 1751 79438

9533

Jean Thevenot Medal
(Medaille Jean Thevenot)
To encourage sound and video recording. Entries for the international contest are considered. A monetary prize, medal, trophy, and equipment are awarded annually. The Jean Thevenot Medal is awarded when merited. The contest was established in 1951 and the medal in 1984 in honor of Jean Thevenot, founder of FICS. Additional information is available from Mr. Aebi, Mottastrasse 10, CH-3005 Bern, Switzerland.

9534

International Statistical Institute
Prinses Beatrixlaan 428
Postbus 950
NL-2270 AZ Voorburg, Netherlands
Phone: 70 3375737
Fax: 70 3860025

9535

Competition for Young Statisticians from Developing Countries
To encourage the professional development of statisticians. Individuals under the age of 32 who are residents of developing countries are eligible to submit a paper on any topic within the broad field of statistics. Travel expenses to attend the ISI Biennial Session and to present the winning paper are awarded biennially. Established in 1981.

9536

International Union of Amateur Cinema
(Union Internationale du Cinema Non Professionel - UNICA)
Ansinghlaan 34
NL-3431 GT Nieuwegein, Netherlands
Phone: 340 23 54 34

9537

UNICA Awards
To encourage development of cinematographic taste and art among amateurs, and to promote growth in film culture, technique, and critical judgment. The Union sponsors competitions and bestows awards.

9538

International Vocal Competition 's-Hertogenbosch
(Internationaal Vocalisten Concours 's-Hertogenbosch)
Postbus 1225
NL-5200 BG 's-Hertogenbosch,
Netherlands
Phone: 73 136569
Fax: 73 126517

9539

International Vocal Competition 's-Hertogenbosch
(Internationaal Vocalisten Concours 's-Hertogenbosch)
For recognition of oratorio, opera and lied singers of any nationality under the age of 35 who enter the competition in one of the following voices: soprano, mezzosoprano/contralto, tenor, and baritone/bass. The deadline for entries is May 21, 1996. A First Prize of 10,000 guilders, and a Second Prize of 5,000 guilders are offered in each category. Other prizes, varying from 3,000 to 5,000 guilders are offered for outstanding interpretations of arias and lieder. The Grand Prix award (the Prize of the City of 's-Hertogenbosch) is awarded to the singer who merits a special distinction for her/his artistic and technical qualities and is the highest distinction for the best vocalist of the competition. Since the competition began, this special distinction has been given to 23 singers. The Competition was established in 1954 and was held annually. Beginning in 1996, the competition will be held biennially in even-numbered years. Sponsored by the Municipality of 's-Hertogenbosch and other private sponsors.

9540

International World Games Association
Hazeveld 24
NL-2761 Zevenhuizen, Netherlands
Phone: 1802 3363
Fax: 1802 3792

9541

World Games Competitions
International Sports Federations organize annual World Games Competitions.

9542

Judith Leyster Stichting
Postbus 16532
NL-1001 RA Amsterdam, Netherlands
Phone: 20 25 95 97

9543

Judith Leysterprijs
To recognize a woman artist for her complete works. A monetary prize of 10,000 Dutch guilders is awarded biennially. Established in 1987.

9544

Maatschappij Arti et Amicitiae
Rokin 112
NL-1012 LB Amsterdam, Netherlands
Phone: 20 6233508

9545

Willink Van Collen Prize
To recognize and encourage young Dutch painters. Dutch artists under 30 years of age are eligible. The following awards are presented: first prize, a monetary award of 2,000 guilders, second prize, 1,500 guilders; and third prize, 1,000 guilders. Awarded biennially. Established in 1878.

9546

Paul Tetar Van Elven Fund Prize
To recognize and encourage young painters. Painters under 30 years of age are eligible. A stipend for a maximum of four years is awarded triennially. Established in 1928.

9547

Mathematical Programming Society
c/o International Statistical Institute
Prinses Beatrixlaan 428
Postbus 950
NL-2270 AZ Voorburg, Netherlands
Phone: 70 3375737

9548

Dantzig Prize
For recognition of original work in mathematical programming. Prizes are awarded triennially. Established in 1981 by the MPS and the Society of Industrial and Applied Mathematics (SIAM) in honor of George B. Dantzig.

9549
Fulkerson Prize
For recognition of outstanding papers in the field of discrete mathematics. Up to three monetary awards of $750 each are presented. Established in 1981 by MPS and the American Mathematical Society in honor of Ray Fulkerson.

9550
Orchard-Hays Prize
For recognition of achievement in the field of computation. Established in 1984.

9551
Nederlandse Taalunie
Stadhoudersplantsoen 2
NL-2517 JL The Hague, Netherlands   Phone: 70 46 95 48

9552
Prijs der Nederlandse Letteren
For recognition of contributions to poetry and prose. A monetary award of 18,000 Dutch guilders is awarded every three years. Established by the ministries of culture of Belgium and the Netherlands.

9553
Nederlandse Vereniging voor Internationaal Recht
Nederlandse Groep van de International
  Law Association
Alexanderstraat 20-22   Phone: 70 3420300
NL-2514 JM The Hague, Netherlands   Fax: 70 3420359

9554
Francoisprijs
To encourage law students in the field of international law. Law students who are under 30 years of age may submit papers dealing with a subject of private or public international law by July 1 in the year of the award. A monetary award of 4,000 Dutch guilders and a diploma are awarded biennially at the Dutch branch of the International Law Association's meeting. Established in 1974 in memory of J. P. A. Francois, professor of public international law at Rotterdam University and an advisor of the Netherlands Ministry of Foreign Affairs.

9555
Netherlands Association for the Advancement of Natural, Medical and Surgical Sciences
(Genootschap Ter Bevordering van Natuur-genees-en Heelkunde)
Plantage Muidergracht 12
Amsterdam, Netherlands   Phone: 20 525 5125

9556
Reynier De Graaff Medal
To provide recognition for the advancement of medical sciences. Anyone who has made an important contribution to the field of medicine is eligible. A gold medal is awarded every nine years. Established in 1950.

9557
Genootschapsmedaille
To provide recognition for the advancement of science in general. Any Dutch or foreign scientist is eligible. A gold medal is awarded irregularly on special occasions. Established in 1790.

9558
Snellius Medal
To provide recognition for the advancement of physics. Anyone who has made an important contribution to the field of physics is eligible. A gold medal is awarded once every nine years. Established in 1950.

9559
Jan Swammerdam Medal
For recognition of contributions to the advancement of the biological sciences. Scientists of any nationality are eligible. A gold medal is awarded once every nine years. Established in 1880.

9560
Tilanus Medal
To provide recognition for the advancement of surgery in the Netherlands. Young Dutch surgeons are eligible. A gold medal is awarded irregularly. Established in 1895.

9561
Netherlands Psychiatric Association
(Nederlandse Vereniging voor Psychiatrie)
PO Box 20062   Phone: 30 823 303
NL-3502 LB Utrecht, Netherlands   Fax: 03 888 400

9562
Ramaermedaille
To recognize a citizen of the Netherlands who has produced the most meritorious contribution to psychiatric science, in particular to clinical psychiatry. A specially appointed committee makes the selection. A medal is awarded biennially. Established in 1918 by the Nederlandse Vereniging voor Psychiatrie en Neurologie in honor of Dr. J. N. Ramaer, founder of the Netherlands Psychiatric Association.

9563
Charles Nypels Stichting
c/o MTC - M.Th. Cillekens
Hogerweide 14
NL-6002 BV Weert, Netherlands   Phone: 4950 24749

9564
Charles Nypels Prijs
To recognize a contribution to printing. A monetary prize of 25,000 Dutch guilders is awarded. Established in 1985.

9565
Pall Mall Export Stichting
Drentestraat 21
Postbus 7400
NL-1007 JK Amsterdam, Netherlands   Phone: 20 540 69 11

9566
Pall Mall Export Swing Award
To recognize a talented and beloved theatre artist for light entertainment, such as cabaret or music. A monetary prize of 10,000 Dutch guilders, to be used for further study, is awarded annually. Formerly: Kortweg Pall Mallprijs.

9567
Poetry International Foundation
(Stichting Poetry International)
De Doelen, Kruisstraat 2   Phone: 10 4134330
NL-3012 CT Rotterdam, Netherlands   Fax: 10 4334211

9568
Poetry International Award
To recognize persecuted poets. Individuals who are in severe political difficulties due to their literary work are eligible. A monetary prize of 10,000 Dutch guilders and an invitation to the Poetry International Festival are awarded annually. Established in 1979. Formerly: Poetry International Eregeld.

9569
Poetry International/Poetry on the Road Festival
To recognize outstanding poets. The 1992 festival emphasized Chinese poetry. Alongside the nightly international series of readings, the festival offers a variety of related activities: poetry and music projects, exhibitions, and a series of lectures on famous poets. The Poetry International Award and the C. Buddingh Prize for New Dutch Poetry are presented. The Festival is held annually. Established in 1970.

9570
Prince Bernhard Foundation
(Prins Bernhard Fonds)
Herengracht 476
Postbus 19750
NL-1000 GT Amsterdam, Netherlands
Phone: 20 6230951
Fax: 20 6238499

9571
Charlotte Kohler Prijs
To recognize and encourage young Dutch artists in the field of fine arts, architecture, applied arts, and theatre design. Dutch citizens under 40 years of age are eligible. A monetary award of 7,500 guilders is presented annually. Established in 1987 by Charlotte Kohler.

9572
Martinus Nijhoff Prijs voor Vertalingen
For recognition of the work of translators as a literary skill, and to encourage the introduction of important prose, poetry, and drama of other countries into the Netherlands, and vice versa. Individuals who have translated extensively may be nominated. A monetary prize of 20,000 guilders is awarded in January. Established in 1953 in memory of Martinus Nijhoff, a Dutch poet who was an outstanding translator of poetry and drama.

9573
Prins Bernhard Fonds Monumenten Prijs
For recognition of outstanding achievements by a person or organization in the field of preservation of monuments in the Netherlands. A monetary prize of 100,000 guilders, of which at least 90 per cent should be spent on the preservation of monuments, is awarded biennially. Established in 1984 by the Board of the Prince Bernhard Foundation in honor of R. Hotke, on his leaving the Board of the foundation as an advisor.

9574
Prins Bernhard Fonds Museum Prijs
To recognize a museum in the Netherlands that has distinguished itself by means of new or renewed activities especially directed to the public. A monetary prize of 100,000 Dutch guilders is awarded annually. Established in 1990 on the occasion of the fifty years jubilee of the Prins Bernhard Fonds.

9575
David Roell Prijs
To recognize the works of a Dutch artist in the field of fine arts, applied arts, or architecture. Only artists of Dutch nationality are eligible. A monetary award of 20,000 guilders is awarded annually. Established in 1963 in memory of Dr. Roell, former Director of the Rijksmuseum in Amsterdam.

9576
Silver Carnation
(Zilveren Anjers)
To recognize persons for distinguished cultural activities. Dutch nationals are eligible. Honorary recognition and a silver carnation (no more than five a year) are awarded by His Royal Highness Prince Bernhard on the occasion of his birthday, June 29. Established in 1950.

9577
Rijksakademie van Beeldende Kunsten
Sarphatistraat 112
NL-1018 GW Amsterdam, Netherlands
Phone: 20 5270300
Fax: 20 5270301

9578
Prix de Rome
This, the largest prize for young artists and architects in the Netherlands, is presented to recognize and encourage artists under 35 years of age. Individuals of Dutch nationality or those who have lived and worked in Holland for a minimum of two years are eligible. The Prix de Rome is awarded in ten areas of art and architecture. In a five-year cycle two fields are covered annually: (1992) Sculpture and Art in Public Spaces; (1993) Drawing and Printmaking; (1994) Painting and Art & Theatre; (1995) Architecture and Town Planning & Landscape Architecture; and (1996) Photography and Film & Video. A first prize of 40,000 Dutch guilders, second prize of 20,000 Dutch guilders, and two prizes of 10,000 Dutch guilders are awarded annually. Established in 1870 by King William III of the Netherlands and based on the French example at the Academie de Beaux Arts. Reorganized in 1985.

9579
Rotterdam Arts Council
(Rotterdamse Kunststichting)
Mauritsweg 35
NL-3012 JT Rotterdam, Netherlands
Phone: 10 41 41 666
Fax: 10 41 35 195

9580
Pierre Bayle Prijs
For recognition of outstanding and constructive (written) criticism in the arts and literature. Awards are given in alternating years in the following categories: (1) Architecture; (2) Film; (3) Music; (4) Theater; (5) Fine Arts; (6) Dance; and (7) Literature. One monetary prize of 3,000 guilders is awarded annually. Established in 1955 in memory of Pierre Bayle, a French philosopher and critic.

9581
Phenixprijs
To recognize a poet for selections or his whole body of work in poetry in the Dutch language. Awarded irregularly. Established in 1970.

9582
Rotterdam Maaskant Foundation
(Stichting Rotterdam-Maaskant)
Stadsontwikkeling Gemeente Rotterdam
Postbus 6574
NL-3002 AN Rotterdam, Netherlands
Phone: 10 4095761
Fax: 10 4095217

9583
Rotterdam-Maaskant Award
(Rotterdam-Maaskantprijs)
To recognize a group or an individual for promoting the field of architecture by publishing, teaching, and/or research; to demonstrate, clarify, and strengthen the role that the built-up environment and organized landscape plays in cultural and social life; and to promote a better and more intensive experience of architecture, urban planning, and organized landscape of the present and the past, both in general and pertaining to Rotterdam specifically, among a large group of users and observers. A monetary prize of 50,000 Dutch guilders, a plaque and a publication on the prize winner are awarded biennially in even-numbered years. Established in 1976 by Architect Hugh A. Maaskant.

9584
Rotterdam Maaskant Award for Young Architects
(Rotterdam-Maaskantprijs voor Yonge Architekten)
To recognize an individual for distinguished accomplishment in the field of architecture and/or urban planning design. Individuals must not be older than 35 years of age to be considered. A monetary prize of 10,000 Dutch guilders, a plaque, and publication are awarded biennially in odd-

numbered years. Established in 1984 by the foundation committee in honor of the architect, Hugh A. Maaskant.

9585
Royal Dutch Geographical Society
(Koninklijk Nederlands Aardrijkskundig Genootschap)
Weteringschans 12
NL-1017 SG Amsterdam, Netherlands   Phone: 20 277716

9586
Glazen Globe
(Glass Globe)
To recognize authors of youth literature for contributions to the understanding of the world in which children live. Books that help children understand other cultures are considered. A specially designed globe of glass is awarded annually. Established in 1987.

9587
Royal Geological and Mining Society of the Netherlands
(Koninklijk Nederlands Geologisch Mijnbouwkundig Genootschap)
PO Box 157   Phone: 23 300291
NL-2000 AD Haarlem, Netherlands   Fax: 23 352184

9588
Van Waterschoot van der Gracht Plaque
(Van Waterschoot van der Gracht-Penning)
To recognize individuals who have excelled in earth sciences and/or mining technology. Although open to persons of any nationality, only those maintaining relations with the study of earth sciences and/or mining in the Netherlands are eligible. A bronze plaque is awarded irregularly. Established in 1950 to honor Dr. W.A.J.M. van Waterschoot van der Gracht, the first president of the Society.

9589
Royal Institute of Dutch Architects
(BNA)
Keizersgracht 321   Phone: 20 5553666
NL-1016 EE Amsterdam, Netherlands   Fax: 20 5553699

9590
BNA - Kubus
(BNA - Cube)
To recognize and encourage architects for their professional work, or other individuals and organizations for the advancement of building and architecture. Any architect, organization, or non-architect, whether their work is completed or not, is eligible. A trophy is awarded annually. Established in 1965.

9591
A. J. Van Eck Prize
(A. J. Van Eck Prijs)
To recognize an example of architectural integration in construction during the last five years. A monetary prize and a medal are awarded once every five years. Established in 1964 by Mrs. Van Eck in memory of her husband.

9592
Royal Netherlands Academy of Arts and Sciences
(Koninklijke Nederlandse Akademie van Wetenschappen)
29 Kloveniersburgwal   Phone: 20 5510700
NL-1011 JV Amsterdam, Netherlands   Fax: 20 6204941

9593
Amsterdam Prize for Art
For recognition of promising and established artists working in the Netherlands. A monetary prize of 50,000 Dutch guilders is awarded biennially. Established in 1988.

9594
Amsterdam Prize for History
For recognition of work in the field of European history from antiquity to the present day. Preference is given to work which makes a significant contribution to an understanding of Europe generally. A monetary prize of 100,000 Dutch guilders is awarded biennially. Established in 1990. Sponsored by Amsterdam Foundation for History.

9595
Amsterdam Prize for Medicine
For recognition of outstanding scientific research in the field of medicine. A monetary prize of 250,000 Dutch guilders is awarded biennially. Established in 1989. Sponsored by the Amsterdam Foundation for Medicine.

9596
Amsterdam Prize for the Environment
To recognize scientists or institutions for significant contributions to a better relation between man and his natural environment in one of the following fields: the natural sciences, engineering sciences, or the social sciences. A monetary prize of 250,000 Dutch guilders is awarded biennially. Established in 1990. Sponsored by the Amsterdam Foundation for the Environment.

9597
Buys Ballot Medal
To recognize a scientist for outstanding work in the field of meteorology. A gold medal is awarded every ten years. Established in 1888 in memory of Professor C.H.D. Buys Ballot (1817-90). (Discountined)

9598
M. W. Beijerinck Virology Medal
For recognition of outstanding work in the field of virology. A gold medal is awarded triennially. Established in 1965.

9599
De la Court Prize
For conspicuous achievements by non-salaried researchers in the fields of humanities and social sciences. Awarded biennially.

9600
Dr. H. P. Heineken Prize
For recognition of exceptional discoveries in the fields of biochemistry and biophysics, including microbiology and the physiology of seed germination. A monetary prize of 250,000 Dutch guilders and a crystal trophy bearing a miniature of the microscope of Antonie van Leeuwenbeck are awarded biennially at a special session of the Royal Netherlands Academy of Arts and Sciences. Established in 1963 by Heineken N.V. in memory of Dr. H.P. Heineken, past president of Heineken Brewery. Sponsored by the Heineken Foundation.

9601
Gilles Holst Medal
For recognition of outstanding contributions to applied chemistry and applied physics. A gold medal is awarded every four or five years. Established in 1939.

9602
Lorentz Medal
To recognize a scientist for contributions to the field of physics. A gold medal is awarded every four years. Established in 1926 in memory of Professor H.A. Lorentz (1853-1928).

9603
Netherlands Fund for Chemistry Prize
To recognize a Dutch researcher for a project completed during the previous five years in the field of scientific and technical chemistry. Established in 1952 by Professor Dr. A.F. Holleman. (Discontinued)

9604
Bakhuis Roozeboom Medal
To recognize a scientist for outstanding contributions to the field of chemistry, particularly phase theory. A gold medal is awarded every four/five years. Established in 1911 in memory of Professor H.W. Bakhuis Roozeboom (1854-1907).

9605
Van Leeuwenhoek Medal
To recognize a scientist for outstanding work in the field of microscopic organisms. A gold medal is awarded every ten years. Established in 1877 in memory of the Dutch microbiologist, Antonie van Leeuwenhoek (1632-1723).

9606
Royal Netherlands Association of Musicians
(Koninklijke Nederlandse Toonkunstenoors-vereniging)
Keizersgracht 480
NL-1017 EG Amsterdam, Netherlands   Phone: 20 238202

9607
Defresne Prize
For recognition of the best musical composition for a theatrical play. A monetary prize of 2,000 Dutch guilders is awarded.

9608
Royal Netherlands Chemical Society
(Koninklijke Nederlandse Chemische Vereniging)
Burnierstraat 1
NL-2596 HV The Hague, Netherlands   Phone: 70 46 94 06

9609
KNCV Gold Medal
To recognize outstanding young chemists working in the field of chemistry or chemical technology. Chemists under the age of forty are eligible. A gold medal is awarded annually. Established in 1965.

9610
Van Marum Medal
(Van Marum Medaille)
For recognition of achievement in improving public understanding of chemistry. Outstanding scientific journalists, authors or historians are eligible. A medal is awarded annually. Established in 1987 in memory of Martinus Van Marum of Haarlem (1750-1837), who introduced modern chemistry in the Netherlands (1787) and was an assistant of Lavoisier.

9611
Royal Palace Foundation, Amsterdam
(Stichting Koninklijk Paleis te Amsterdam)
Educatieve Dienst
Nieuwezijds Voorburgwal 147   Phone: 20 6248698
NL-1012 RJ Amsterdam, Netherlands   Fax: 20 6233819

9612
Royal Subsidy for Modern Painting
(Koninklijke Subsidie voor de Vrije Schilderkunst)
To recognize and encourage young, modern, and innovative professional painters. Candidates must be 35 years of age or younger, of Dutch nationality, or residents of Amsterdam for at least two years. Monetary prizes are awarded annually. Established in 1947 by HRH the Queen of the Netherlands. Sponsored by the Queen Juliana Foundation.

9613
Scheveningen International Music Competition
(Scheveningen Internationaal Muziek Concours)
Gevers Deynootweg 970 Z   Phone: 70 3525100
NL-2586 BW The Hague, Netherlands   Fax: 70 3522197

9614
Scheveningen International Music Competition
To encourage professional development in the field of music. The competition features different musical instruments each year. Performers must be 28 years of age or under. Applications are accepted. Five monetary prizes and certificates are awarded annually. Established in 1987 by the Adama Zijlstra Foundation.

9615
School for Cabaret Music and Contemporary Music Theater
(Akademie voor Kleinkunst)
Keizersgracht 418
NL-1016 GC Amsterdam, Netherlands   Phone: 70 6230617

9616
Pisuisse Prize
(Pisuisse Prijs)
To encourage professional development in cabaret music and contemporary music theater. Graduate students from the Dutch Theatre Institute are eligible. A monetary prize and a plaque are awarded. Established in 1975 by the Dutch Theatre Institute.

9617
Aleida Schot Foundation
(Aleida Schot Stichting)
PO Box 75265   Phone: 20 6789123
NL-1070 AG Amsterdam, Netherlands   Fax: 20 6789589

9618
Aleida Schot Award
(Aleida Schot-Prijs)
For recognition of the best translation into Dutch of a literary work written in a Slavic language. Nomination is by a jury. A monetary prize of 5,000 Dutch guilders is awarded biennially at a special session. Established in 1969 by Aleida G. Schot.

9619
Sikkens Foundation
(Stichting Sikkens)
c/o Awards Committee
Rijksstraatweg 31
Postbus 3   Phone: 1711 83399
NL-2170 BA Sassenheim, Netherlands   Fax: 1711 83995

9620
Piet Mondriaan Lecture
To recognize an artist who raised and articulated, at an early stage, the problems of modern art through his or her work and writings. The focus is on the visual arts, either independently or in relation to other fields of study. Established in 1979.

9621
Sikkensprijs
For recognition of individuals who have done pioneering work in the use of color. Prizes are not restricted to the fields of visual art and architecture. Awarded annually. Established in 1959 by A. M. Mees, director of Sikkens Sassenheim. Formerly: Stichting Sikkensprijs.

9622
Singermuseum
Oude Drift 1
NL-1251 BS Laren, Netherlands
Phone: 21 5315656
Fax: 21 5317751

9623
Nederlandse Grafiekprijs
To recognize a graphic artist under the age of 40 for design. Three prizes of 5,000 Dutch guilders are awarded biennially. Established in 1986.

9624
Society of Netherlands Literature (Maatschappij der Nederlandse Letterkunde)
Universiteitsbibliotheek Leiden
Witte Singel 27
PO Box 9501
NL-2300 RA Leiden, Netherlands
Phone: 71 27 23 27
Fax: 71 27 26 15

9625
Henriette de Beaufort-prijs
To recognize the author of a biographical work. A monetary prize of 3,000 guilders is awarded every three years, alternately, to a Dutch and a Flemish author. Established in 1986.

9626
Dr. Wijnaendts Francken-prijs
For recognition of a literary work in the following categories: essays in literary criticism, and cultural history. A monetary prize of 3,000 guilders is awarded in each of the two categories alternately. The prize is awarded triennially. The work must have been published during the preceding six years. Established in 1935.

9627
Henriette Roland Holst-prijs
To recognize a literary work that appeared in Dutch prose, poetry or drama, reflecting social concerns. The work must have been published within the preceding six years. A monetary prize of 3,000 guilders is awarded triennially.

9628
Frans Kellendonk-prijs
To recognize an author, preferably 40 years of age or younger, of literary works (prose, essay, theater, or poetry) reflecting intellectual independency and an original view on social or existential questions. A monetary prize of 10,000 guilders is awarded triennially. Established in 1993.

9629
Kruyskamp-prijs
To recognize an author in the field of lexicography, lexicology, or edition and annotation of old Dutch texts. A monetary prize of 5,000 guilders is awarded triennially. Established in 1992.

9630
Prijs voor Meesterschap
To recognize authors in the fields of creative writing, philology, and literature and history. A gold medal is awarded every five years.

9631
Lucy B. and C. W. Van der Hoogt-prijs
To encourage poets or writers of literary works written in the Dutch or South Africaans languages. The work must not have been published more than two years before the award is given. A monetary prize of 5,000 guilders is awarded annually. Established in 1925.

9632
Stichting AKO Literatuur Prijs
Sparrenlaan 37
NL-3742 WD Baarn, Netherlands
Phone: 2154 20820

9633
AKO Literatuur Prijs
To recognize a literary work of nonfiction. A monetary prize of 50,000 Dutch guilders is awarded annually. Established in 1986.

9634
Stichting Amsterdams Fonds voor de Kunst
Stadhuis-Kamer 2280
Amstel 1
Postbus 202
NL-1000 AE Amsterdam, Netherlands
Phone: 20 552 24 16

9635
Aanmoedigingsprijzen
Encouragement prizes are given in the fields of design, indexes trial and typo graphic, architecture, sculpture, photography, music, film/video, and theater (also choreography, mime, and puppet theater). Dutch residents with less than five years of experience in the field are eligible. Monetary awards of 7,500 guilders each are awarded annually. Established in 1986.

9636
Maria Austriaprijs
For recognition of work in photography. A monetary award of 10,000 guilders is presented biennially. In addition, a special encouragement prize of 5,000 guilders (Aanmoedigingsprijs) is given annually to a young person in the field. Awarded alternately with the Professor Pi-Prijs.

9637
Sonia Gaskellprijs
To recognize a recent work of choreography. A monetary award of 15,000 guilders is presented biennially. In addition, a special encouragement prize of 7,500 guilders is given to a young person in the field. Established in 1985.

9638
Herman Gorterprijs
For recognition of a volume of Dutch poetry published during the preceding year. A monetary prize of 15,000 Dutch guilders is awarded annually. Established in 1972 in memory of Herman Gorter, a Dutch poet (1864-1927).

9639
Busken Huetprijs
For recognition of a volume of Dutch essays or a biography published during the preceding year. A monetary prize of 15,000 guilders is awarded biennially in odd-numbered years. Established in memory of Conrad Busken Huet (1826-1886), an essayist and novelist.

9640
L. J. Jordaanprijs
For recognition of an outstanding film or video. A monetary award of 15,000 guilders is presented. In addition, a special encouragement prize of 7,500 guilders is given to a young person in the field. Awarded annually. Established in 1985.

9641
Kho Liang Ie-prijs
For recognition of a work of industrial design. Dutch industrial designers are eligible for work done during the previous year. A monetary prize of 15,000 Dutch guilders is awarded annually. In addition, a special encouragement prize of 7,500 guilders is given to a young person in the field. Established in 1972 in memory of Kho Liang Ie (1927-1975), an industrial designer.

9642
Merkelbachprijs
For recognition for a work of architecture in Amsterdam completed during the preceding three years. A monetary prize of 15,000 guilders is awarded triennially. In addition, a special encouragement prize of 7,500 guilders is given to a young person in the field. Established in 1973 in memory of Ben Merkelbach (1901-1961), an architect. Awarded alternately with the Stanprijs and the Wibautprijs.

9643
Mimografieprijs Amsterdam
For recognition of work in mime art. A monetary award of 15,000 guilders is presented. In addition, a special encouragement prize of 7,500 guilders is given to a young person in the field. Awarded every four years. Established in 1986.

9644
Multatuliprijs
For recognition of a volume of Dutch prose published during the preceding year. A monetary prize of 15,000 Dutch guilders is awarded annually. Established in 1972 in memory of Edward Douwes Dekker (1820-1887), who wrote prose under the pseudonym of Multatuli.

9645
Jan Nelissenprijs
To recognize a recent project of puppet theater. Awarded every four years. Established in 1988.

9646
Professor Pi-Prijs
For recognition of work in illustration. A monetary award of 15,000 guilders is presented biennially. In addition, a special encouragement prize of 7,500 guilders is given annually to a young person in the field. Awarded alternately with the Maria Austria prijs.

9647
Sandbergprijs
For recognition of a work of plastic arts (sculpture, painting, etc.) A monetary award of 15,000 guilders is presented. In addition, five special encouragement prizes of 7,500 guilders each are awarded to young persons in the field. Awarded annually. Established in 1985.

9648
Mark Stamprijs
For recognition of work in interior design. A monetary award of 15,000 guilders is presented. In addition, a special encouragement prize of 7,500 guilders is given to a young person in the field. Awarded triennially. Awarded alternately with the Wibautprijs and the Merkelbachprijs.

9649
Albert Van Dalsumprijs
To recognize a person or group of persons for a Dutch theater production of the previous season. A monetary prize of 15,000 Dutch guilders is awarded annually. In addition, a special encouragement prize of 7,500 guilders is given to a young person in the field. Established in 1972 in memory of Albert Van Dalsum (1889-1971).

9650
Emmy Van Leersumprijs
For recognition of design work in textiles, glass, fashion, ornaments, and ceramics. A monetary award of 15,000 guilders is presented. In addition, a special encouragement prize of 7,500 guilders is given to a young person in the field. Awarded annually. Established in 1985.

9651
Matthijs Vermeulenprijs
For recognition of a musical composition or project performed or composed during the preceding year. A monetary prize of 15,000 Dutch guilders is awarded annually. In addition, a special encouragement prize of 7,500 guilders is given to a young person in the field. Established in 1972 in memory of Matthijs Vermeulen (1888-1967), an essayist and critic.

9652
H. N. Werkmanprijs
For recognition of outstanding typographic work issued in the preceding calendar year. A monetary prize of 15,000 Dutch guilders is awarded triennially. In addition, a special encouragement prize of 7,500 guilders is given to a young person in the field. Established in 1972 in memory of H.N. Werkman (1882-1945), graphic artist and printer.

9653
Wibautprijs
For recognition of a project in Amsterdam in the field of architecture, in which the participation of the future users is clearly visible. A monetary prize of 15,000 Dutch guilders is awarded triennially. In addition, a special encouragement prize of 7,500 guilders is given to a young person in the field. Established in 1977 in memory of F.M. Wibaut (1859-1939), a social democrat. Awarded alternately with the Stamprijs and the Merkelbachprijs.

9654
Stichting Edmond Hustinx
Hondertmarkt 446
NL-6211 MB Maastricht, Netherlands   Phone: 43 21 44 73

9655
Edmond Hustinxprijs
To recognize Dutch and Belgian authors of plays and television dramas. A jury makes the selection. Two prizes are awarded biennially, one to someone Dutch and one to someone Flemish. This award is given jointly with the Algemeen Nederlands Verbond and Stichting Dramaastricht.

9656
Stichting Frans Erensprijs
Europalaan 49
NL-6226 CN Maastricht, Netherlands   Phone: 43 63 53 40

9657
Frans Erensprijs
To recognize a Dutch author for memoirs, essays, or creative literary works in prose or poetry. A monetary prize of 10,000 Dutch guilders is awarded every three years. Established in 1986 and named for Frans Erens, a Dutch author (1857-1935).

9658
Stichting Internationaal Orgelconcours
Stadhuis
Postbus 3333   Phone: 23 160574
NL-2001 DH Haarlem, Netherlands   Fax: 23 160576

9659
Stichting Internationaal Orgelconcours
To recognize outstanding organists. The deadline for applications is December 15. A monetary prize of 7,500 Dutch guilders is awarded to the winner and each finalist receives 1,500 Dutch guilders. Awarded biennially. Established in 1951. Sponsored by Ahrend Groep N.V., Amsterdam.

9660
Stichting Koningin Wilhelmina Fonds
Dutch Cancer Society
Sophialaan 8   Phone: 20 5700500
NL-1075 BR Amsterdam, Netherlands   Fax: 20 6750302

9661
Prof. Dr. P. Muntendamprijs
For recognition of contributions to the fight against cancer in the Netherlands, in the fields of cancer research, treatment, nursing, professional and non-professional care of cancer patients, journalism, public information, patient education, or in organizational aspects. There are no restrictions as to age. Nominations may be made by anyone or any group before March 1. A scroll and bronze plaque are awarded annually at the convention of members of the Society. The winner may allocate $30,000 to goal within the field of cancer control after board approval. Established in 1975 in memory of Professor Dr. P. Muntendam, former President of the Board of the Society.

9662
Stichting Liszt Concours
Muziekcentrum Vredenburg
PO Box 550
NL-3500 AN Utrecht, Netherlands
Phone: 30 334 344
Fax: 30 316 522

9663
International Franz Liszt Piano Competition
(Internationaal Franz Liszt Pianoconcours)
For recognition of an extraordinary interpretation of the piano music by Franz Liszt, and as a contribution for further study. Candidates should be no younger than 16 years of age and no older than 30 years of age. The following prizes are awarded: (1) First prize - 25,000 guilders; (2) Second prize - 15,000 guilders; (3) Third prize - 10,000 guilders; and (4) Fourth to Sixth prizes - 7,500 guilders. Awarded triennially. Established in 1986.

9664
Stichting P.C. Hooftprijs voor Letterkunde
Nederlands Letterkundig Museum et
    Documentatie Centrum
Prinses Irenepad 10
Postbus 90515
NL-2509 LM The Hague, Netherlands
Phone: 070 347 11 14

9665
Pieter Cornelisz Hooft Prize
For recognition of important and original literary works by individuals of the Dutch nationality whose literary work was written principally in Dutch. Awards are presented in the following categories on a rotating basis: poetry, fiction, and nonfiction. A monetary prize of 75,000 guilders is awarded annually. Established in 1947. Formerly: State Prize for Literature.

9666
Theo Thijssenprijs
For recognition of the best books for children and young people. A monetary prize of 75,000 guilders is awarded triennially. Established in 1964.

9667
Stichting Wonen
Address unknown.

9668
Biennial of Young Dutch Architects
(Biennale Jonge Nederlandse Architecten)
To encourage professional development in the field of architecture. Individual architects are selected to be honored by an exhibition biennially. Established in 1983.

9669
Stichting World Wide Video Centre
Spui 189
NL-2511 BN The Hague, Netherlands
Phone: 31 70 3644805
Fax: 31 70 3614448

Formerly: Stichting Kijkhuis/World Wide Video Festival.

9670
World Wide Video Festival
For recognition of achievement in the field of video and to encourage professional development. Independent video productions not shown in Holland publicly and not older than a year are eligible. Monetary prizes and certificates are awarded annually. Special awards include: Canon Europa Award; Sony Industrial Award; Prize of the City of The Hague; and Art Centre Delft Prize. Established in 1987. Sponsored by the City of The Hague, Sony Industrial, Canon Europa, and Art Centre Delft.

9671
Stichting Woutertje Pieterse Prijs
Sparreniaan 37
NL-3742 WD Baarn, Netherlands
Phone: 2154 20820

9672
Libris Woutertje Pieterse Prijs
To recognize an individual for contributions to children's literature. A monetary prize of 10,000 Dutch guilders is awarded. Established in 1988.

9673
Tilburg University
Faculty of Letters
PB 90153
NL-5000 LE Tilburg, Netherlands
Phone: 13 662773

9674
E. Du Perron Award
(E. Du Perron-Prijs)
For recognition of achievements in the cultural field concerned with improving the mutual understanding between ethnic groups. Selection is by nomination. A monetary prize of 1,500 Dutch guilders is awarded annually. Established in 1986 in honor of E. Du Perron. Sponsored by the City Council of Tilburg.

9675
Marten Toonder Stichting
Rubensstraat 58
NL-1077 MV Amsterdam, Netherlands
Phone: 20 6794631

9676
Geertjan Lubberhuizen prijs
To encourage the writing of literary prose in Dutch. Dutch authors who haven't published any work yet or those who published their first work in the last year can submit manuscripts/books of at least 25,000 words. A monetary prize is awarded annually. Established in 1983 in honor of Geertjan Lubberhuizen, a publisher. Additional information is available from Martin Mooij, Operalaan 39, 2907 Capelle a/d IJssel, Netherlands. Formerly: (1985) Eenhoornprijs.

9677
Universal Esperanto Association
(Universala Esperanto-Asocio)
Nieuwe Binnenweg 176
NL-3015 BJ Rotterdam, Netherlands
Phone: 10 4361044
Fax: 10 4361751

9678
Deguchi Prize
(Premio Deguci)
To recognize individuals or organizations who have made a particularly outstanding contribution to the use of Esperanto for promoting international understanding and cooperation. A monetary prize of 4,000 Dutch guilders is awarded at the annual World Esperanto Congress in July or August. Established in 1987 at the initiative of the Japanese religious organization Omoto, for whose founder it is named.

9679
Zamenhof Award for International Understanding
(Premio Zamenhof por Internacia Komprenigo)
To support and give recognition to those members of the world community who have distinguished themselves by their efforts to create international understanding. Individuals or organizations of any country whose contributions to international understanding have been outstanding or exemplary and serve as an inspiration to others are considered. A monetary prize of $1,000 is awarded annually at a ceremony in December. Established in 1985 in memory of Dr. Ludwig L. Zamenhof (1859-1917), initiator of the international language, Esperanto. Additional information is available from Universal Esperanto Association, c/o Mrs. Rochelle F. Grossman, 777 United Nations Plaza, Suite 1, New York, NY 10017; telephone: (212) 687-7041.

9680
University of Limburg
(Rijksuniversiteit Limburg)
c/o College van Dekanen
PO Box 616
NL-6200 MD Maastricht, Netherlands
Phone: 43 882222
Phone: 43 887777
Fax: 43 252195

9681
Peter Debye Prize
For recognition of the scientist(s) who has/have made a fundamental contribution to medical research, forming a link between medicine and the basic disciplines. The particular subject is fixed once every two or three years. Individuals or a group of as many as three persons may be nominated by June 7 preceding the year of presentation. The next presentation will be in 1994, regarding research in the field of the molecular biology of cardiovascular diseases. An award of 20,000 Dutch guilders and a charter are presented biennially or triennially, usually at the Dies Natalis of the University. Established in 1977 by the Edmond Hustinx Foundation, Maastricht, in honor of the physicist, Peter J. W. Debye (1884-1966), a native of Maastricht, who was awarded the Nobel Prize for chemistry in 1936. Additional information is available from Dr. E. H. S. Drenthe, secretary of the jury for the Peter Debye Prize, Office of the Rector, telephone: 43 88 3110; fax: 43 252195.

9682
Edmond Hustinx Prize for Science
For recognition of the scientist who has made a fundamental contribution to the community. Once a year, the board of the Edmond Hustinx Foundation awards this prize. Additional information is available from the Secretariat of the Edmond Hustinx Foundation, P.O. Box 333, NL-6200 AH Maastricht, the Netherlands.

9683
Catharina Pijlsprijs
(Catharine Pijls Prize)
To recognize scientists who have made fundamental contributions to the health sciences, and to encourage professional development of the health sciences. A monetary award of 20,000 Dutch guilders is presented at the convention. Established in 1984 by the Catharina Pijls Foundation, Maastricht. Additional information is available from the Faculty of Health Sciences, phone: 43 881552.

9684
Therese van Duyl-Schwartze Foundation
(Therese van Duyl-Schwartze Stichting)
Herengracht 317
NL-1016 AV Amsterdam, Netherlands
Phone: 20 6232456
Fax: 20 6250442

9685
Therese van Duyl-Schwartze Portrait Award
(Therese van Duyl-Schwartze Portretprijs)
To recognize and encourage portrait painting. A bronze medal designed by Erik Claus is awarded. Established in 1919 by the foundation in memory of Therese van Duyl-Schwartze (1851-1918), a woman portrait painter of considerable fame.

9686
Vereniging van Letterkundigen
Huddestraat 7
NL-1018 HB Amsterdam, Netherlands
Phone: 20 6240803

9687
Charlotte Kohlerprijs
To recognize the author of a Dutch novel, poetry, or drama. A monetary prize of 25,000 Dutch guilders is awarded every five years. Sponsored by Stichting Charlotte Kohler.

9688
H. G. van der Viesprijs
To encourage professional development in the field of drama. A monetary prize is awarded triennially through a bequest of H. G. van der Vies. Established in 1982.

9689
Vereniging van Schouwburg - en Concertgebouwdirecties in Nederland
Paulus Potterstraat 12
NL-1071 CZ Amsterdam, Netherlands
Phone: 20 64 72 11

9690
Prosceniumprijs
To recognize a person or group for distinguished contribution to the areas of costume, drama, or music of a Dutch stage production. A bronze figurine by the sculptor, Jan Spiering, is given together with the other Dutch theatre prizes. Every year, three juries are set up: (1) for stage; (2) for dance; and (3) for the Hans Snoekprijs. In addition, the organization also gives a gold and silver Krommert Award for theatre technique.

9691
World-Association for the History of Veterinary Medicine
c/o Library of the Faculty of Veterinary
  Medicine
Yalelaan 1
PO Box 80159
NL-3508 TD Utrecht, Netherlands
Phone: 30 534603
Fax: 30 531407

9692
Cheiron Medal
To recognize individuals for contributions of special merit involving the advancement of the history of veterinary medicine. A silver medal and a certificate are awarded at meetings of the World Association; as a rule, not more than two medals are awarded annually. Established in 1989 to commemorate the 20th anniversary of the Association.

Netherlands

9693

World Music Contest Foundation, Kerkrade
(Stichting Wereld Muziek Concours Kerkrade)
PO Box 133
NL-6460 AC Kerkrade, Netherlands
Phone: 45 455000
Fax: 45 353111

9694

International Conductors' Competition
For recognition of outstanding conducting. Participation is open to conductors of woodwind and brassbands, Continental-style brassbands and other brassbands, who are not older than 30 years of age. Each candidate must be able to communicate in one of the following languages: Dutch, English, French, or German. The following prizes are awarded: First Prize - a Gold Baton; Second Prize - a Silver Baton; and Third Prize - a Bronze Baton. Awarded every four years.

9695

Kerkrade World Music Contest
(Wereld Muziek Concours Kerkrade)
For recognition of outstanding amateur bands and orchestras. Participants may enter one or more of the following competitions: (1) concert competitions - participation in the concert competition is open to the following amateur orchestral categories: symphonic windbands, including harmony-orchestras of the French and Dutch variety as well as American style symphonic windbands; brassbands of the continental type, also known as fanfare orchestras; and brassbands of the English type; (2) marching competitions - participation in the marching competitions is open to all bands of the above mentioned categories and drumbands of various compositions, such as drum and bugle bands, pipebands, etc.; and (3) show competitions - participation in the show competitions is open to bands and orchestras with or without majorettes and/or showgirls. A first prize with distinction, first prize, second prize, and third prize are awarded every four years in each competition.

9696

World Press Photo Foundation
Van Baerlestraat 144
NL-1071 BE Amsterdam, Netherlands
Phone: 20 6 76 60 96
Fax: 20 6 76 44 71

9697

World Press Photo Contest
For recognition of the best press photographs of the preceding year. Single pictures and picture stories (or sequences), black-and-white or color, prints or 35mm slides may be entered in the following categories: General News - planned and/or organized events; Spot News - unscheduled events for which no advance planning was possible; People in the News - pictures or stories of people playing a part in the news; Sports - action or feature pictures or stories; The Arts - any performance, development, or highlight in fashion, architecture, visual and performing arts, etc.; Science and Technology - any achievement, development, or highlight in science or technology; Nature and the Environment - natural or environmental subjects, e.g., flora and fauna, landscapes, ecology, etc.; Daily Life - pictures or stories illustrating the richness and diversity of everyday life. A series is limited to 12 pictures. The World Press Photo of the Year award goes to the photographer who has best succeeded in portraying the essence of an event or a situation. The photographer receives the Premier Award - a cash prize of 15,000 Dutch guilders, a Diploma of Excellence, and an invitation to Amsterdam, including a return flight and hotel accommodation, to attend the awards ceremony at the end of April. First prize winners in each category of best single picture and best picture story receive a Golden Eye Trophy, a cash prize of 2,500 Dutch guilders, a Grand Diploma, and an invitation to Amsterdam (with the same details as above). Second and third prize winners receive a Golden Eye Medal and a Diploma. An additional prize is the World Press Photo Children's Award, given for the best press photo of the year as selected by an international children's jury. The Award includes the Volkskrant Trophy, a cash prize of 2,500 Dutch guilders, and an invitation to Amsterdam (with the same details as above).

New Caledonia

9698

THESE-PAC Association
(Association pour la Diffusions des Theses sur le Pacifique Francophon e)
BP 920
Noumea, New Caledonia
Phone: 2 51 5 98
Fax: 28 3113

9699

THESE-PAC Awards
To recognize outstanding university work on the South Pacific area and New Caledonia. Two first prizes of 100,000 CFP francs ($1,000 US) are awarded annually: Prix C.P.S. - for the best university work on Australia, New Zealand, Hawaii, and the area served by the South Pacific Commission (American Samoa, Cook Islands, Federated States of Micronesia, Fiji, French Polynesia, Guam, Kuribati, Northern Mariana Islands, Marshall Islands, Nauru, Niue, Palau, Papua New Guinea, Pitcairn Island, Solomon Islands, Tokelau, Tonga, Tuvalu, Vanuatu, Wallis and Futuna, and Western Samoa), and Prix Nouvelle-Caledonia - for the best university work about New Caledonia. Second and third place winners in each of the two categories receive 10,000 CFP francs. Additional awards include: a special prize on the French-speaking Pacific for one of the competing university works that did not win one of the first two prizes; and health and/or social prizes of a total amount of 50,000 CFP francs for the best work or thesis either in general medicine or specialized medicine, such as pharmacy, and veterinarian medicine; and the best third-year thesis for a degree or diploma in a social, medical, or related field. Established in 1987.

New Zealand

9700

American Express South Pacific Credit Card
345 Queen St.
PO Box 4005
Auckland 6, New Zealand
Phone: 9 793 441
Fax: 9 370 312

9701

American Express Short Story Award
For recognition of unpublished short stories of up to 6,000 words. First and second monetary prizes of $5,000 and $2,000 were awarded annually. (Discontinued in 1989)

9702

Australasian Seabird Group
PO Box 12397
Wellington North, New Zealand

9703

Australasian Seabird Group Awards
For recognition of accomplishments in the field of seabirds of the South Pacific. Awards are presented.

9704

Book Publishers Association of New Zealand
Level 8, Norwich House
Chr Queen & Durham St.
PO Box 386
Auckland 1, New Zealand
Phone: 9 309 2561
Fax: 9 309 7798

Formed by merger of: (1977) New Zealand Book Publishers Association; Book Publishers Representatives Association.

9705
Montana Book Awards
For recognition of the best book written by a New Zealander or New Zealand resident and published during the preceding year. Publishers must submit books by April. The following awards are presented: a monetary award of $20,000 and a scroll - first prize; $10,000 and a scroll - second prize; and $5,000 and a scroll - third prize. In addition to prizes for the authors, the winning publishers receive scrolls. Awarded annually in June. Established in 1968 by Sir James Wattie in association with the Book Publishers Association of New Zealand. Sponsored by Montana Wines. Formerly: Goodman Fielder Wattie Book Award.

9706
Booksellers of New Zealand
PO Box 11-377
Wellington, New Zealand
Phone: 4 728 678
Fax: 4 728 628

Formerly: (1991) Booksellers Association of New Zealand.

9707
AIM Children's Book Awards
To recognize the best children's books published annually, and to stimulate children's authors and publishers to strive for excellence. Eligible books must have been published during the preceding year and must be a New Zealand edition by a New Zealand author, or New Zealand resident. Reprints are not eligible. Books must contain 16 or more pages of text and illustration. Monetary prizes are awarded for the Best Story Book and Best Picture Book annually in April. Established in 1990 jointly by the Booksellers Association of New Zealand, the Book Publishers Association of New Zealand, and the Queen Elizabeth II Arts Council of New Zealand. Sponsored by Unilever New Zealand Ltd.

9708
Canterbury Historical Association
Dept. of History
Univ. of Canterbury
Private Bag
Christchurch 1, New Zealand
Phone: 3 642283
Fax: 3 642003

9709
J. M. Sherrard Awards
To encourage scholarly research and publication in the field of New Zealand regional history. Amateur and professional historians are eligible. Regional history titles included in the National Bibliography for the preceding two years are considered. A monetary award of approximately $1,000 (New Zealand) is awarded biennially as one major award, and may be divided equally among as many as four winners. Established in 1972 in honor of J. M. Sherrard.

9710
Christchurch International Amateur Film Festival
Christchurch Movie and Video Society, Inc.
PO Box 2006
Christchurch, New Zealand
Phone: 3 388 776

9711
Christchurch International Amateur Film Festival Awards
For recognition of the best amateur films not exceeding 30 minutes, in the following categories: (1) fiction; (2) documentary; and (3) travel or genre (including animation and experimental films). Films may be submitted by September 30. Sponsored trophies are awarded at the discretion of the judges for editing, photography, animation, sound, nature, and scenario. The Hei Tiki Trophy is presented to the overall festival winner. Awarded annually. Established in 1967.

9712
Dairy Industry Association of New Zealand
1/136 Calliope Rd.
Devonport, New Zealand
Phone: 9 4456267

Formerly: Dairy Technology Society (New Zealand).

9713
Chemical Cleaning/Trigon Packaging Achievement Award
To recognize innovative product development.

9714
Dairy Industry Quality Performance Awards
To recognize four dairy production plants each year in the areas of cream products, cheese, milk powders, and protein products. Sponsored by PRINTPAC-UEB, CHRISTIAN HANSEN, and APV-BAKER.

9715
Distinguished Service Award
To recognize distinguished service and outstanding achievement in the dairy industry. Anyone associated with the New Zealand dairy industry is eligible. A trophy and a certificate are awarded annually. Established in 1967.

9716
Gold Medal Award
To recognize the highest total marks in the Diploma in Dairy Technology at Massey University, Palmerston North.

9717
Outstanding Achievement Award
To recognize an outstanding achievement within the dairy industry. In addition, a Study Award, Young Achievers Award, and Management Development Award are presented.

9718
Riddet Award
To encourage younger persons to publish articles relating to the dairy industry. A monetary prize and a certificate were awarded annually. Established in 1971, to honor Dr. W. Riddet. (Discontinued in 1991)

9719
Designers Institute of New Zealand
PO Box 5521
Wellesley St.
Auckland, New Zealand
Phone: 9 776012
Fax: 9 3664713

Formerly: New Zealand Society of Industrial Design.

9720
New Zealand Society of Designers Awards
To recognize professional designers, students, and oranizations in New Zealand and to strengthen the design profession by promoting high standards in the design field. Formerly: New Zealand Society of Designers Awards.

9721
Fletcher Challenge International Exhibition and Competition
PO Box 33-1425
Takapuna, New Zealand
Phone: 9 6308581
Fax: 9 6308581

9722
Fletcher Challenge International Ceramics Award
To encourage excellence in all forms of ceramic art. Slides of up to three different views of one work only may be submitted by December 1. Slides submitted must be of the actual work or indicative of the work that is intended to be sent. Each entry is judged on excellence. A monetary prize

of $10,000 NZ is awarded annually as the Premier Award and up to five merit awards of $2,000 NZ each are also awarded. In addition, the winner of the Premier Award may receive assistance to travel to Auckland, New Zealand to receive the award in person at the official opening of the Exhibition. Established in 1977 by Fletcher Brownbuilt.

9723
Historical Branch Advisory Committee
Historical Branch
Department of Internal Affairs
PO Box 805
Wellington, New Zealand
Phone: 4 4957200
Fax: 4 4991943

9724
Awards in History
To encourage and support research into, and the writing of, the history of New Zealand. Applications from researchers and writers of projects relating to New Zealand history must be submitted by October 15 each year. Assistance is not normally available for projects that are eligible for university research funds, nor for university theses. Grants are awarded annually in December. Established in 1988 by the New Zealand Department of Internal Affairs.

9725
Awards in Oral History
To provide financial help for projects using oral resources relating to the history of New Zealand/Aoetearoa and New Zealand's close connections with the Pacific. Awards are made to individuals, groups, communities, and institutions. Residents of New Zealand must apply by April 30. Grants are awarded annually. Established in 1990 by the Australian people to commemorate New Zealand's sesquicentennial. Sponsored by Australian Sesquicentennial Gift Trust for Oral History.

9726
Institution of Professional Engineers New Zealand
PO Box 12241
101 Molesworth St.
Wellington, New Zealand
Phone: 4 4739444
Fax: 4 4732324

9727
Angus Award
To recognize the author of the best paper submitted during the three years preceding the date of the award on a subject possessing a substantial mechanical interest. Members are eligible. A monetary prize and a certificate are awarded annually. Established in 1959 and endowed by the late P.R. Angus, a former Chief Mechanical Engineer of the New Zealand Railways, and a Past-President of the Institution.

9728
W. H. M. Blackwell Memorial Lecture
Awarded annually. Established in 1991 as a memorial to W.H.M. Blackwell for his pioneering work in the field of continuing education.

9729
John Cranko Memorial Award
To recognize members of the Institution and/or the New Zealand Institute of Refrigeration Heating and Air Conditioning Engineers. Awarded when merited. Established in 1979 as a memorial by friends, clients, and family of John Eardley Cranko after his death in August, 1978. Co-sponsored by the New Zealand Institute of Refrigeration Heating and Air Conditioning Engineers.

9730
Dobson Lecture
A public lecture on a subject of current public interest related to engineering. Established in 1974.

9731
Environmental Award
To recognize predominantly engineering work that best exemplifies care for and consideration of environmental values. Account is taken of the indentification of environmental values in the design, the manner in which the resulting problems were resolved, and the overall contribution of the end result to environmental values and public enjoyment. Projects to qualify for the award do not have to be of national importance but must be of significance in their immediate locality. An individual or public or private body is eligible and, in the case of an individual, the person need not necessarily be an engineer or a member of the Institution. A plaque is presented to the individual or organization responsible for the work. In addition, a certificate is presented to the person or persons predominantly responsible for the design and execution of the project. Awarded biennially. Established in 1971.

9732
Freyssinet Award
To recognize a member of the Institution for the best paper published during the three years preceding the year for which the award is made on a subject dealing with some aspects of engineering, structural design, or erection. A monetary prize and a certificate are awarded annually. Established in 1965 in memory of Eugene Freyssinet, a French engineer. Sponsored by the New Zealand Concrete Society and the Cement and Concrete Association of New Zealand.

9733
Fulton-Downer Award
To recognize the best papers on technical subjects presented at the annual IPENZ Conference. Two awards are given: the Fulton-Downer Gold Medal and a monetary prize are awarded to the member winner and the Fulton-Downer Silver Medal and a monetary prize are awarded to the student or graduate member. Awarded annually. Established in 1929 by a bequest from the late J.E. Fulton to which was added, in 1973, a donation from A.F. Downer.

9734
Furkert Award
For recognition of the best paper by a member submitted within the three years preceding the date of the award on a subject dealing with the action of water on the faces of nature, particularly such faces of nature as are connected with the works of man. A monetary prize and a certificate are awarded annually. Established in 1951 by the late F.W. Furkert, a former Engineer-in-Chief of the Ministry of Works and Past-President of the Institution.

9735
Hopkins Lecture
To encourage discussion of engineering within the profession and to encourage public understanding of engineering issues. The lecture is given by an eminent speaker with a high reputation in his field and with a knowledge of engineering, although not necessarily an engineer. The lecture is held each year in Christchurch and covers broad and social engineering issues rather than purely technical. Established in 1978 by the Institution and the University of Cambridge in honor of Professor H.J. Hopkins.

9736
IPENZ Craven Post-Graduate Research Scholarship
To encourage research in engineering, particularly that which may have application to the future development of New Zealand. Candidates who are taking the final examination for the Degree of Bachelor of Engineering at the University of Auckland or the University of Canterbury, and also graduates in engineering of any university within the British Commonwealth are eligible. The scholarship of $1,000 is tenable for one year and shall be held by a candidate who during the tenure of his scholarship is pursuing postgraduate studies for a Masters degree in engineering at either the University of Auckland or the University of Canterbury. Awarded annually. Established in 1980.

9737
IPENZ Structural Award
To recognize the best paper published by the Institution during the three-year period ending on July 31 preceding the conference at which the award is made on some aspect of structural engineering design or construction in which materials other than prestressed or reinforced concrete fulfill a major role. Awarded annually. Established in 1988.

9738
MacLean Citation
To recognize persons who have rendered exceptional and distinguished service to the profession. A citation is awarded when merited. Established in 1954 in memory of Francis William MacLean, a former President of the Institution, who displayed exceptional devotion to the profession of engineering and to his fellow engineers.

9739
W. L. Newnham Memorial Lecture
An annual lecture series, given on the first day of the Institution's annual conference. Established in 1970.

9740
Evan Parry Award
For recognition of the best paper by a member on an electrical engineering subject submitted to the Institution during the three years preceding the date of the award. A monetary award and a certificate are awarded annually. Established in 1965 by the late R.S. Maunder, a Past-President of the Institution, in memory of Evan Parry, a former Chief Electrical Engineer of the Public Works Department. Sponsored by Electricorp Production.

9741
President's Award
To recognize a member or group of members who has done something outstanding particularly in the role of the engineers public service. The award is made from time to time at the sole discretion of the President. Established in 1990.

9742
Professional Commitment Award
To recognize a corporate member of the Institution for his continuing contribution to the profession of engineering, to the activities of the Institution, and to society. The recipient should be over the age of 40 years. The following attributes are sought in nominees for this award: upholding the image of the profession, publicizing engineering achievement and promoting the interests of the profession and industry, emphasis of the Institution's code of ethics and the profession's expertise and experience, encouragement to young people to enter the profession and young engineers to take an active role in Institution affairs, participation in community affairs, assistance with career counseling and recruitment to the Institution, and dissemination of technical and welfare information within the profession. A certificate is presented annually at the Institution's annual conference. Established in 1981 by R.J. McCarten.

9743
Rabone Award
To recognize members submitting papers of exceptional merit which do not come within the conditions of other awards or which otherwise justify recognition. The paper must be published by the Institution during the three year period ending July 31 preceding the conference at which the award is given. A monetary award and a certificate are presented annually. Established in 1932. In 1969, the award was endowed to recognize papers of special merit by members under 40 years of age in categories other than those covered by the awards existing at the time.

9744
Skellerup Award
To recognize the member presenting the best paper during the three years preceding the year of the award on a subject dealing with the development of New Zealand's natural resources or the development of New Zealand's chemical process industry. The paper must be published by the Institution during the five year period ending July 31 preceding the conference at which the award is given. A monetary prize and a certificate are awarded annually. Established in 1977 in memory of George Waldemar Skellerup, who initiated development of Lake Grassmore Solar Salt Works. Sponsored by Dominion Salt Limited.

9745
Steel and Tube Travelling Scholarship
To assist engineering graduates desiring to improve their skills in the areas of management, finance, or administration. It is likely that these skills would be acquired by formal courses at an approved institution in New Zealand or overseas. Both graduate and corporate members of the Institution who have had at least two years post-graduate experience in the engineering or manufacturing industries in New Zealand are eligible for the scholarship, though preference is given to corporate members preparing for wider responsibilities. A scholarship is awarded annually. Established in 1982.

9746
Turner Lecture
To promote and extend the knowledge of contract, particularly relating to building and engineering. Established in 1985 by C.W.O. Turner.

9747
New Zealand
Department of Internal Affairs
ANZAC Fellowship Selection Committee
PO Box 805
Wellington, New Zealand
Phone: 4 4957200
Fax: 4 4991865

9748
ANZAC Fellowships
To enable New Zealanders in all walks of life, who have already made a mark in their profession, trade, or calling, to study or train in Australia to the benefit of themselves, their families, New Zealand, and the furtherance of good relations between Australia and New Zealand. Preference is given to applicants whose programs are in fields where equivalent training or experience cannot be obtained in New Zealand, or where closer liaison between Australia and New Zealand is desirable. The scheme is not intended to give fellowships solely for academic study nor to members of the academic staff of institutions of higher education for the purpose of furthering their academic studies. Permanent residents New Zealand are eligible. The New Zealand selection committee makes nominations to the Australian selection committee, which makes the final selection of four to six candidates to hold the fellowships for periods of 1-12 months in Australia. Monetary grants, travel expenses, and allowances for dependents are awarded annually. Established in 1967 to commemorate the friendship between Australia and New Zealand.

9749
New Zealand Academy of Fine Arts
Dominion Museum Bldg.
Buckle St.
PO Box 467
Wellington, New Zealand
Phone: 4 385 9267
Phone: 4 384 4911
Fax: 4 385 7175

9750
Academy Awards
To recognize New Zealand artists whose works are considered to be of merit, and worthy of recognition, and to enable exceptionally promising exhibitors to work towards further development within their chosen medium. The following awards are given: Governor General Art Award - to give recognition to New Zealand artists who consistently produce work of the highest standard, and who through their work have contributed towards the development of the visual arts in New Zealand. Awarded annually. Established in 1983. National Bank Art Award - two $2,000 awards for art in abstract form. In addition, two special awards for exhibitors up to and including 18 years of age are presented. Established in 1985. The Academy Awards program was established in 1979.

9751
New Zealand Association of Scientists
PO Box 1874
Wellington, New Zealand
Phone: 4 3855999
Fax: 4 3895095

9752
Sir Ernest Marsden Medal for Outstanding Service to Science
For recognition of a meritorious contribution to the cause and/or the development of science. Any person who has made an outstanding contribution to science is eligible. An engraved medal is awarded annually. Established in 1973.

9753
New Zealand Association of Scientists Certificate for Science Journalism
To encourage public appreciation of scientific objectives, methods and achievements through recognition of outstanding science journalism in broadcasting, newspapers, and magazines. Writing produced in New Zealand for the non-scientific audience, published during the preceding year, may be submitted by May 10. A certificate is awarded annually at the Association's annual general meeting. Established in 1979.

9754
New Zealand Association of Scientists Prize for Science Communication
To encourage public appreciation of scientific objectives, methods and achievements through recognition of outstanding science communication by scientists in newspapers, magazines, and broadcasting. Items produced in New Zealand for a general audience by a scientist (understood to include technologists) are eligible. Persons employed in a journalistic capacity are ineligible. A monetary award of $1,000 (New Zealand), and two merit awards of $100 (New Zealand) each are presented annually at the annual general meeting of the Association. Established in 1990.

9755
Research Medal
To provide recognition for outstanding research work in the fields of natural, physical, or social sciences. Individuals less than 40 years of age are eligible. An engraved medal is awarded annually. Established in 1951.

9756
New Zealand Council for Educational Research
Education House
PO Box 3237
178-182 Willis St.
Wellington, New Zealand
Phone: 4 3847939
Fax: 4 3847933

9757
J. R. McKenzie Senior Fellowship in Educational Research
To provide an opportunity for a teacher or scholar to complete a survey or prepare a report for publication, usually in an area of educational research. Applications are accepted from New Zealand residents who are university graduates with at least a master's degree. A salary while engaged in the research and travel and secretarial assistance are awarded biennially. Established in 1962 by the J.R. McKenzie Trust Board in memory of Sir John McKenzie.

9758
New Zealand Dental Association
PO Box 28084
Remeura
Auckland 5, New Zealand
Phone: 9 5205256
Fax: 9 5205256

9759
New Zealand Dental Association Awards
To recognize registered dental practitioners in New Zealand. Awards are given annually.

9760
New Zealand Library Association
20 Brandon St.
PO Box 12-212
Wellington, New Zealand
Phone: 4 473 5834
Fax: 4 499 1480

9761
Russell Clark Award
For recognition of the most distinguished illustrations in a children's book with or without text. The illustrator must be a citizen of New Zealand, and the book must have been published during the preceding year. A monetary award and a bronze medal are presented annually. Established in 1978 in memory of Russell Clark (1905-1966), a New Zealand illustrator, artist and sculptor.

9762
Esther Glen Award
To recognize the author of the most distinguished contribution to literature for children. Authors of books published during the preceding year who are citizens or residents of New Zealand are eligible. A monetary award and a bronze medal are awarded annually. Established in 1945 in memory of Esther Glen (1881-1940), a New Zealand journalist and editor active in promoting children's literature.

9763
New Zealand Library Association Non-Fiction for Young People Award
To recognize a distinguished contribution to nonfiction for young people. Citizens or residents of New Zealand are eligible. A monetary award and a medal are presented annually. Established in 1987.

9764
New Zealand Maori Arts and Crafts Institute
PO Box 334
Hemo Gorge Rd.
Rotorua, New Zealand
Phone: 73 489047
Fax: 73 489045

Formerly: Rotorua Maori Arts and Crafts Institute.

9765
Sir Henry Kelliher Student of Honour
To encourage professional development in the prestige art of Maori carving and other arts of the Maori people. Students who complete the three year training period at the Institute are eligible. A certificate by the Institute, and a monetary award by a donor are awarded. The graduate of honor is requested to carve a plaque for display in the chambers of Hotel Rotorua, which has become a hall of honor. Awarded annually in December at the graduation ceremony. Established in 1969 by Sir Henry Kelliher of Dominion Breweries. Sponsored by Hotel Rotorua, New Zealand.

9766
New Zealand National Society for Earthquake Engineering
PO Box 312
Walkanae, New Zealand
Phone: 4 293 3059
Fax: 4 293 3059

9767
Otto Glogau Award
To recognize the author(s) who submits the best paper. Authors are considered for the following: any paper published in the bulletin whether by members or non-members within the previous three years and any paper published elsewhere, provided at least one author is a member and the paper is nominated in writing by a member during the current

year. A monetary award of $300 for the purchase of books and a certificate are awarded annually at the convention. Established in 1978, and renamed in 1981 to honor Otto Glogau, former president of the Society. Formerly: (1981) NZNSEE Award.

9768
New Zealand Theatre Federation
PO Box 3037
Christchurch 1, New Zealand
Phone: 3 3772303
Fax: 3 3772304

9769
Annual One-Act Play Festival Award
To recognize an outstanding one-act play. Amateur societies may enter. The festival is organized on a national basis on three levels: district, Regional, and national. A Book of Honor is awarded annually.

9770
Shell Playwrights Award
To recognize an original play written by a New Zealand playwright participating in the one-act play competition. A monetary prize of $1,000 NZ is awarded annually. Established in 1986 in honor of Olga E. Harding, who contributed to amateur theatre in New Zealand.

9771
New Zealand Tourist Industry Federation and New Zealand Tourism Department
Education House (West Tower), 9th Fl.
178-182 Willis St.
PO Box 1697
Wellington, New Zealand
Phone: 4 385 8019
Fax: 4 385 8047

9772
American Express New Zealand Tourism Awards
To encourage and recognize excellence in tourism and tourist products in New Zealand; to improve and enhance the quality of the New Zealand experience offered; and to encourage significant initiatives taken by individuals and/or organizations to develop tourism and tourist products in New Zealand. Open to any individual, company or organization. Entries must be completed, operating and open to the public. Entries may be submitted by October 4. Awards are presented in the following categories: (1) Tourist Attractions; (2) Tourist Activities; (3) Accommodation: International, Boutique, Moderate, Specialist, and Recreational; (4) Tourist Retailer; (5) Souvenir; (6) Tourist Transportation; (7) Heritage Tourism; (8) Culture Tourism; (9) Regional/Local Tourism Organization; (10) Special Events; (11) Festivals; (12) Tourism Development Project; (13) Tourism Media; (14) Education or Training; and (15) Sir Jack Newman Award. Established in 1991. Sponsored by American Express. Additional information is available from Susan Henagham, New Zealand Tourism Department, PO Box 95, Wellington, Phone: (04) 728 860, fax: (04) 781 736.

9773
New Zealand Women Writers' Society
GPO Box 11-352
Wellington, New Zealand
Phone: 4 888 140

9774
Bank of New Zealand Katharine Mansfield Award
For recognition of an unpublished short story of not more than 5,000 words. Open to all New Zealanders by birth, naturalization, or by residence in New Zealand for five years continuously immediately prior to the closing date of the competition. Monetary awards of $4,000 for first prize and $1,500 for second prize are presented biennially. Established in 1959 in memory of Katherine Mansfield, a New Zealand writer. Sponsored by the Bank of New Zealand. Formerly: Katherine Mansfield and Bank of New Zealand Short Story Award.

9775
Bank of New Zealand Novice Writers' Awards
For recognition of an unpublished short story. Writers over 13 years of age who have not previously had work published may submit short stories of 3,000 words. Open to all New Zealanders by birth, naturalization, or by residence in New Zealand for five years continuously immediately prior to the closing date of the competition. A monetary prize of $1,000 is awarded biennially. Established in 1959. Sponsored by the Bank of New Zealand.

9776
Bank of New Zealand Young Writers' Award
For recognition of an unpublished short story. Secondary school pupils between 13 and 19 years of age may submit a short story of 2,000 words. The winner must still be enrolled in school at the time of the presentation. Open to all New Zealanders by birth, naturalization, or by residence in New Zealand for five years continuously immediately prior to the closing date of the competition. A monetary prize of $1,000 for the winner and $500 for his school are awarded biennially. Established in 1959. Sponsored by the Bank of New Zealand.

9777
PEN New Zealand, Inc.
PO Box 67 013
Mt. Eden
Auckland, New Zealand
Phone: 9 630 8077
Fax: 9 630 8077

9778
PEN Best First Book of Fiction Award
For recognition of the best first book of fiction published by a New Zealander during the calendar year prior to the award. A monetary prize of $1,000 NZ is awarded annually. Established in 1944 in memory of Hubert Church. Formerly: Hubert Church Prose Memorial Prize.

9779
PEN Best First Book of Non-fiction Award
For recognition of the best first book of non-fiction published by a New Zealander during the calendar year prior to the award. A monetary prize of $1,000 NZ is awarded annually. Established in 1992 in recognition of E. H. McCormick.

9780
PEN Best First Book of Poetry Award
For recognition of the best first book of poetry published by a New Zealander during the calendar year prior to the award. A monetary prize of $1,000 NZ is awarded annually. Established in 1940 in memory of Jessie Mackay. Formerly: Jessie Mackay Memorial Prize.

9781
PEN Young Writers' Incentive Awards
For recognition of a work of prose or poetry by New Zealand writers between 8 and 19 years of age. The award was given in the categories of prose and poetry. Monetary awards were presented annually. Established in 1973. (Discontinued)

9782
Lilian Ida Smith Award
To assist people 35 years of age or older to embark on or further a literary career. Recipients must be either embarking on their careers or not have yet had sufficient opportunity to fulfill their potential. An award of $3,000 NZ is made biennially to assist a writer in the completion of a specific writing project. Projects may be nonfiction, fiction, poetry, or drama for children or adults. Recipients must be PEN NZ members. Application deadline is January 30. Established in 1986 from a bequest made by Lillian Ida Smith, a music teacher who had an interest in the arts.

9783
Playmarket
PO Box 9767
Wellington, New Zealand
Phone: 4 828461
Fax: 4 828461

9784
The Sunday Times Bruce Mason Playwrights' Award
To recognize a playwright of promise at the beginning of his or her career. New Zealand citizens are eligible. A monetary award of $4,000 NZ is awarded annually. Established in 1983 by Playmarket to honor Bruce Mason, one of New Zealand's finest playwrights and theater critics. Sponsored by *The Sunday Times*. Formerly: *The Dominion Sunday Times Bruce Mason Playwrights Award*.

9785
Polynesian Society Incorporated
c/o Maori Studies Dept.
Univ. of Auckland
Private Bag 92019
Auckland 1, New Zealand
Phone: 9 737999
Fax: 9 3023245

9786
Elsdon Best Memorial Medal
For recognition of excellence of published ethnography or related work dealing with New Zealand Maori peoples. Published authors are eligible. A medal is awarded annually when merited. Established in 1970 in honor of Elsdon Best, a New Zealand ethnographer.

9787
Nayacakalou Medal
For recognition of recent significant scholarly publications on the Pacific Islands relevant to the aims and purposes of Polynesian society and the interests and concerns of the late Dr. Rusiate Nayacakalou, Fijian scholar and statesman, in whose honor the award is given. Established in 1992.

9788
Postal History Society of New Zealand
PO Box 99-673 Newmarket
Auckland, New Zealand
Phone: 9 4164850

9789
Annual Club Competition
To recognize the winners of the annual club competition in the field of postal history, especially of New Zealand and the South Pacific. The following awards are presented: Literature Award, Marcophily Prize, Marcel Stanley Novice Award, and open class.

9790
Queen Elizabeth II Arts Council of New Zealand
Old Public Trust Bldg.
131-135 Lambton Quay
Box 3806
Wellington, New Zealand
Phone: 4 730 880
Fax: 4 712 865

9791
Air New Zealand Award
To enable New Zealand artists to further their careers by overseas study and experience. Up to four awards may be given annually and are open to both established artists for refresher courses following a distinguished contribution to the arts in New Zealand, and artists with known potential who would gain significantly from their experience, and who would have a demonstrable impact on their disciplines upon their return to New Zealand. Individuals cannot apply in their own right. Candidates must be nominated by some other person or group. The awards provide travel on approved Air New Zealand international routes plus a cash grant towards expenses. These awards established in 1978, are administered on behalf of Air New Zealand by the Queen Elizabeth II Arts Council of New Zealand.

9792
Allan Highet Award
To provide recognition and support for emerging artists with ability and potential. The award provides assistance to enable artists to undertake a major project which would otherwise not be possible given the range and level of alternative support available in New Zealand. The award is not subject to application. The award is intended primarily to assist individual artists. However, individuals who work in a creative partnership with other artists will not be excluded from consideration. The award of $25,000 is tenable either within New Zealand or abroad. Awarded annually when merited. Established in 1984 in honor of Allan Highet, a Foundation member of the Council and first government Minister for the Arts in New Zealand from 1974-84.

9793
Jack McGill Music Scholarship
To assist individuals of outstanding musical ability to undertake musical studies, to make investigations into music or any particular field thereof or to gain further musical experience in any part of the world. The Scholarships are offered annually by the Arts Council in association with the Public Trust Office which administers the estate of the late Jack McGill, a former Wellington oil company executive, and his sister, Maud Field. The number of Scholarships and the value of each vary from year to year depending on the income from the estate and the calibre of the applications.

9794
Carl Ludwig Pinschof Scholarship
To provide young New Zealand performing musicians aged 19-35 with a scholarship to undertake study at an Austrian conservatorium of music for a 12 month period. The scholarship takes the form of a monthly living allowance provided through the Austrian Government and travel assistance to a successful New Zealand candidate from the Arts Council.

9795
Queen Elizabeth II Arts Council of New Zealand
Literature Programme
PO Box 3806
Wellington, New Zealand
Phone: 4 730880
Fax: 4 712865

9796
Adam Prize
To recognize the book of prose (fiction or nonfiction) that the selection panel felt had made the greatest contribution to New Zealand literature. Awarded biennially. Sponsored by the Adam Trust. (Discontinued)

9797
AIM Children's Book Awards
To promote excellence in children's literature and provide prizes for the best children's novel and best children's picture book of the year. The deadline is in mid-November. Sponsored by Lever Rexona Ltd., administered by Booksellers New Zealand, and managed by a partnership of Booksellers of New Zealand, the Book Publishers' Association, and the Literature Programme of the Queen Elizabeth II Arts Council. Additional information is available from Booksellers New Zealand, PO Box 11-377, Wellington.

9798
Arts Council Writing Grants
To provide grants for writers in four separate categories. Creative Writing Grants are available for leading, established, and new writers, writers of fiction, poetry, or drama for adults. Children's Writers' Grants are available for adult writers for children of any age (closing date is September 15). Nonfiction Grants are available for nonfiction projects that pertain to literature. Priority is given to subjects such as literary biography and criticism (closing date is January 31). Te Hunga Taunaki Kaituhi Maori is also available to promote and encourage original work in Te Reo

Maori. Monetary awards are presented annually. Established in 1973. Formerly: Literary Fund Writing Grants.

9799
Award for Achievement
For recognition of a contribution to literature. A monetary prize was awarded annually. Established in 1956. (Discontinued)

9800
Katherine Mansfield Memorial Fellowship
To enable a writer to spend up to four months at the Villa Isola Bella at Menton, France, where Katherine Mansfield once lived. Guidelines and application forms should be obtained before applying. The closing date is July 31. Sponsored by ECNZ and managed by the Katherine Mansfield Fellowship Board of Trustees.

9801
New Zealand Book Awards
For recognition of the best books published in fiction, poetry, nonfiction, and book production. New Zealand authors are eligible. Monetary prizes for each category are presented annually. Sponsored by Queen Elizabeth II Arts Council.

9802
Reed Publishing (NZ) Ltd.
39 Rawene Rd., Birkenhead
Auckland 10, New Zealand
Phone: 9 480 6039
Fax: 9 419 1212

Formerly: (1991) Reed Methuen Publishers.

9803
Reed Fiction Award
To promote the publication of New Zealand fiction and to encourage new fiction writers. Authors must be New Zealanders or Pacific Islanders and unpublished in volume form. Manuscripts must be at least 40,000 words. A monetary award of NZ$5,000 is presented annually. Established in 1989. Formerly: (1991) Heinemann/Reed Fiction Award.

9804
A. W. Reed Memorial Book Award
For recognition of the company's best completed manuscript in nonfiction. A monetary award of NZ$5,000 was awarded annually. Established in 1980 in memory of the co-founder of the company, A.W. Reed. Sponsored by the Reed Trust. (Discontinued in 1987)

9805
A. W. Reed Memorial Children's Book Award
For recognition of the company's best completed manuscript in children's fiction. New Zealand citizens or residents are eligible. A monetary award of NZ$2,500 is awarded annually. Established in 1984 in memory of the co-founder of the company, A.W. Reed. (Discontinued in 1987)

9806
Royal New Zealand Aero Club
PO Box 402
Timaru, New Zealand
Phone: 3 688 2069
Fax: 3 688 2069

9807
Aero Engine Services Trophy
For recognition of achievement in aerobatics by nonprofessional pilots. Entrants in the competition are eligible. A trophy is awarded annually. Established in 1969.

9808
Airways Corporation Trophy
For recognition of achievement in general flying. Entrants in the competition are eligible. A cup is awarded annually. Established in 1991 by Airways Corporation of New Zealand Ltd.

9809
Airwork Cup
For recognition of achievement in aircraft preflight inspection. Affiliated club members not competing for the C.A.D. Trophy are eligible. A cup is awarded annually.

9810
D. M. Allan Memorial Cup
For recognition of achievement in aerobatics for New Zealand professional club pilots. Entrants in the competition are eligible. A cup is awarded annually. Established in 1949 in honor of D.M. Allan.

9811
Jean Batten Memorial Trophy
For recognition of achievement in takeoff, circuit, preflight inspection, and landing. Female pilots of affiliated clubs who hold student pilot licenses are eligible. A monetary grant and trophy are awarded annually. Established in 1989 in honor of Jean Batten.

9812
Bledisloe Aviation Trophy
For recognition of achievement in airmanship, landings, and navigation for pilots who have gone solo in the preceding year. A trophy is awarded annually. Established in 1975.

9813
Sir Francis Boys Cup
For recognition of achievement in takeoff, circuit, and landing for club-trained pilots. Entrants in the competition are eligible. A cup is awarded annually. Established in 1975.

9814
C. A. D. Trophy
For recognition of achievement in aircraft preflight inspections. All RNZAC National Championship competing pilots are eligible. A trophy is awarded annually.

9815
Cory - Wright Cup
For recognition of achievement in navigation for club-trained pilots. Entrants in the competition are eligible. A cup is awarded annually. Established in 1975.

9816
Oscar Garden Trophy
For recognition of achievement in full panel instrument flying. Entrants in the competition are eligible. A trophy is awarded annually. Established in 1975. Formerly: Air Service Training Blind Flying Trophy.

9817
Gloucester Navigation Trophy
For recognition of achievement in direct route navigation for holders of a commercial pilot's license. Entrants in the competition are eligible. A trophy is awarded annually. Established in 1975.

9818
Jubilee Trophy
For recognition of achievement in aerobatic flying. Any licensed pilots of affiliated clubs are eligible. A trophy is awarded annually.

9819
W. A. Morrison Trophy
For recognition of achievement in three aircraft flying in formation. Private or commercial pilot license holders in affiliated clubs are eligible. A trophy is awarded annually.

9820
New Zealand Herald Challenge Trophy
For recognition of achievement in navigation, pilotage, and landing for nonprofessional pilots. Entrants in the competition are eligible. A trophy is awarded annually. Established in 1975.

9821
"New Zealand Wings" Trophy
For recognition of achievement in landing, formation flying, and aerobatics. Entrants in the competition are selected by the aero club bodies of New Zealand and Australia. The competition is conducted in New Zealand and Australia on a "year about" basis. A trophy is awarded annually. Established in 1993.

9822
Newman Cup
For recognition of achievement in takeoff, circuit, and landing for women pilots. Entrants in the competition are eligible. A cup is awarded annually. Established in 1975.

9823
North Shore Trophy
For recognition of achievement for the most points amassed by a club at the RNZAC Annual National Championships. Clubs with pilots competing at the National Championships are eligible. A trophy is awarded annually.

9824
Rotorua Trophy
For recognition of achievement in a mock bombing competition. Student or private pilot license holders who are Club members are eligible. A trophy is awarded annually.

9825
G. M. Spence Trophy
For recognition of achievement in forced landings. Entrants in the competition are eligible. A trophy is awarded annually. Established in 1931 by G.M. Spence.

9826
Waitemata Aero Club Cup
For recognition of achievement in CIVA Sportsman aerobatics. Entrants in the competition are eligible. A trophy is awarded annually. Established in 1993.

9827
Wanganui Trophy
For recognition of achievement in a low-flying competition. The competition is open to pilots of affiliated clubs who hold a commercial pilot's license and who are not in full-time employment as pilots. A trophy is awarded annually. Established in 1989.

9828
Ivon Warmington Trophy
For recognition of achievement in liferaft dropping from a plane. Club pilots who hold private pilot licenses are eligible. A trophy is awarded annually.

9829
Wigram Cup
For recognition of achievement in landing, instrument flying, and noninstrument circuit flying for nonprofessional pilots. Entrants in the competition are eligible. A cup is awarded annually. Established in 1975.

9830
Wigram Cup (Sub-Competition) - Instrument Flying
For recognition of achievement in flying using a limited panel of flight instruments. Entrants in the competition are eligible. A cup is awarded annually. Established in 1991.

9831
Wigram Cup (Sub-Competition) - Junior Landing
For recognition of achievement in landing. Entrants in the competition are eligible. A cup is awarded annually. Established in 1956.

9832
Wigram Cup (Sub-Competition) - Non-instrument Circuits
For recognition of achievement in flying two circuits without the assistance of flight instruments. Entrants in the competition are eligible. A cup is awarded annually. Established in 1991.

9833
Wigram Cup (Sub-Competition) - Senior Landing
For recognition of achievement in landing. Entrants in the competition are eligible. A cup is awarded annually. Established in 1956.

9834
Royal Society of New Zealand
PO Box 598
Wellington, New Zealand
Phone: 4 4727421
Fax: 4 4731841

9835
Leonard Cockayne Memorial Lecture
For encouragement of botanical research in New Zealand. An invitation to deliver a lecture is awarded triennially. Established in 1964 to commemorate the life and work of the late Leonard Cockayne.

9836
E. R. Cooper Memorial Medal and Prize
For the encouragement of scientific research in the fields of physics or engineering. The award consists of a medal and prize - a book or books, suitably inscribed - and is made every two years to the persons who, in the opinion of the Selection Committee, published the best single account of original research in physics or engineering. Preference is given to contributions to the development of New Zealand natural resources. Established in 1958 by the Dominion Physical Laboratory in memory of E. R. Cooper.

9837
Hamilton Memorial Prize
For the encouragement of beginners in scientific research in New Zealand or in the islands of the South Pacific. Works published within seven years preceding the last day of January prior to the annual meeting where the award is made are eligible. Such publications must include the first investigation published by the candidate. Candidates for the prize must send an intimation of candidature to the Executive Officer before June 30, with two copies of each published work. In addition, any fellow or member may nominate one or more candidates for the prize.

9838
Hector Memorial Medal and Prize
To recognize advancement and achievement, on a rotating basis, in the following scientific areas: plant sciences, chemical sciences, human sciences, solid earth sciences, mathematical sciences, physical sciences, engineering sciences, and animal sciences. Investigators working within New Zealand are considered for the award. A monetary prize of $500 and a bronze medal are awarded annually. Established in 1910 by the Hector Memorial Fund of the New Zealand Institute in memory of Sir James Hector, K.C.M.G., M.D., F.R.S., the second President of the New Zealand Institute.

9839
Hutton Memorial Medal and Prize
To recognize and encourage research in zoology, botany, or geology in New Zealand. Researchers who have received the greater part of their education in New Zealand or who have resided in New Zealand for not less than ten years are eligible for the award. A bronze medal and grants are awarded triennially. Established in 1909 by the New Zealand Institute

in memory of Professor Sir Frederick Wollaston Hutton, F.R.S., its first President.

9840
New Zealand Science and Technology Post-Doctoral Fellowship
To provide early career support for New Zealand Scientists, engineers, and social scientists of outstanding talent. New Zealand citizens and permanent residents, preferably under 36 years of age, who have their Ph.D. or equivalent degree are eligible. Fellows are selected based on their academic record and the scientific excellence of the proposed research. The deadline for applications is January 20. Seventeen stipends of approximately $40,500 each, plus research and hosting expenses are awarded annually.

9841
T. K. Sidey Medal and Prize
For the promotion and encouragement of scientific research in the study of light visible and invisible, and other solar radiations in relation to human welfare, or, at the discretion of the Society, of research on radiations of any kind. A medal and monetary prize, not be less than $200, are awarded at irregular intervals as the state of the fund permits. Established in 1933 by the transfer to the New Zealand Institute of £500 collected to commemorate the passing of the Summer-Time Act (1927) through the instrumentality of Sir Thomas A. Sidey.

9842
Thomson Medal
For recognition of outstanding contributions to the organization, administration, or application of science. Established in 1985 to commemorate the contributions made to science by George Malcolm Thomson (1848-1933) and his son, James Allan Thomson (1881-1928). Both are former Presidents of the Royal Society of New Zealand. Establishment of the medal was made possible by the generosity of A. P. Thomson, son of J. A. Thomson.

9843
Sargeson Trust
The Secretary
50 Lake Rd.
Devonport
Auckland, New Zealand

9844
Sargeson Writer's Fellowship
To recognize and encourage a fiction writer of proven ability. New Zealand citizens are eligible. Accommodation in a furnished flat in central Auckland for nine months, plus an annual stipend of $10,000 (New Zealand). Established in 1987 by the Sargeson Trust to honor the New Zealand fiction writer, Frank Sargeson. Additional information is available from Christine Cole Catley, PO Box 199, Picton, NZ.

9845
Trustees Executors and Agency Company of New Zealand
PO Box 760
24 Water St.
Dunedin 9001, New Zealand
Phone: 24 779 466
Fax: 24 779 466

9846
Buckland Literary Award
To recognize the author of a novel, poem, article, essay, biography or play which is of the highest literary merit. The award is designed to encourage the advancement and betterment of New Zealand literature. Works by New Zealand authors written during the preceding year may be nominated. A monetary award of the income from the trust of $5,000 (New Zealand) is awarded annually when merited. Established in 1966 by the late Freda Mary Buckland.

9847
University of Canterbury
Private Bag 4800
Christchurch 1, New Zealand
Phone: 3 667001
Fax: 3 642999

9848
Margaret Condliffe Memorial Prize
To recognize and encourage creative achievement that shows promise of marked distinction in letters, the fine arts, or the service of humanity. Residents of New Zealand are eligible. No application is required. Awarded by the University Council on the recommendation of the Academic Board. Established in 1945 by Professor J.B. Condliffe of the University of Canterbury and Mrs. Condliffe in memory of Margaret Condliffe, his mother.

9849
University of Otago
PO Box 56
Dunedin, New Zealand
Phone: 3 4791100
Fax: 3 4741607

9850
Mechaelis Memorial Prize
This, the premier award in New Zealand for physics, is given for recognition of the most valuable original contribution towards the advancement of physics, or astronomy and astrophysics. Awards are given in alternate years for physics or astronomy. Residents of New Zealand for at least five years preceding the date of selection may apply by June 1. A monetary award and a gold medal are awarded biennially. Established in 1949 by Mrs. Jessie Mechaelis in honor of William R. Mechaelis.

9851
Philip Neill Memorial Prize in Music
For recognition of excellence in original composition. The test is the composition of a work in a form of structure prescribed by the examiners, such prescription to vary from year to year. The competition is open to all past and present students of a university in New Zealand, but a winner of the prize in any year is not eligible to compete again until five complete years have elapsed since the year the candidate was awarded the prize. A monetary prize is awarded annually. Established in 1943 in memory of Philip Foster Neill, a medical student of the University of Otago, by his sister.

9852
Percy Smith Medal in Anthropology
For recognition of published research work in anthropology. Where two researches are judged of equal merit, preference is given to the one based on material from the Pacific. Past or present students or staff members of the University of Otago, or past or present staff members of the Otago Museum are eligible. A medal is awarded not more than once every four years. Established in 1920 by Mr. S. Percy Smith.

9853
World Council of Young Men's Service Clubs
(Conseil Mondial des Clubs d'Entraide de Jeunes Gens)
8 Whitney St.
Box 240
Blenheim 7301, New Zealand
Phone: 57 87159
Fax: 57 88968

9854
World Council of Young Men's Service Clubs Awards
To recognize individuals who and facilitate international goodwill. Competitions are held and awards are given annually.

Nigeria

9855
Association of Nigerian Authors
Address unknown.

9856
ANA Literary Prize
To encourage Nigerian writing in all Nigerian languages including English, Yoruba, Hausa, Igbo, and others. Plays, novels, collections of short stories, or collections of essays may be considered. Nigerian authors may submit work by June 30. A monetary prize of 1,000 nairas is awarded annually. Established in 1983.

9857
Centre for Management Development
Management Village, Shangisha
P.M.B. 21578 Ikeja
Lagos, Nigeria   Phone: 1 961130

9858
Best Management Essay Award
To encourage management students, promote their professional development and excite in them the spirit of research and scholarship. Students in management and allied fields in any of the country's universities may submit essays. A monetary prize is awarded annually. Established in 1985.

9859
Best MBA Student Award
To recognize the best MBA student and the runner-up in the business schools in Nigerian universities. MBA students in any of the Nigerian universities are eligible. A monetary prize is awarded annually. Established in 1985.

9860
Concord Press Board of Trustees
Enuwa Sq.
PO Box 845
Ile-Ife, Nigeria   Phone: 36 230190

9861
Concord Press Award for Academic Publishing
To encourage publication of works by Nigerian authors and scholars that are suitable as textbooks at the University level. Subjects may include science, medicine, pharmacy, accounting, engineering, and environmental design. Nigerian authors and Nigerian publishers may submit works published during the preceding year. A monetary prize of N25,000 and a plaque are awarded annually. Established in 1984. Sponsored by Chief M.K.O. Abiola.

9862
Delta Publications (Nigeria) Limited
172 Ogui Road
PO Box 1172
Enugu, Enugu, Nigeria   Phone: 42 253215

Formerly: Delta Publications (Nigeria).

9863
Delta Fiction Award
For recognition of an outstanding work of fiction. Applicants must be Nigerian and must submit typed manuscripts by November 30. A monetary prize is awarded annually. Established in 1983. In 1987, the Delta Students Award was established to recognize Nigerian students from 13 years of age and older.

9864
Nigerian Academy of Science
P.M.B. 1004
Univ. of Lagos
Lagos, Lagos, Nigeria

9865
MAN National Science Prize
To recognize and encourage scientists and technologists in Nigeria. Contributions that have a strong impact on the Nigerian economy and represent a significant breakthrough, such as invention of a new technology or a process of innovative adaptation are considered. A monetary award of N5,000 and a certificate are presented annually. Established in 1987. Sponsored by the Manufacturers Association of Nigeria.

9866
Pharmaceutical Society of Nigeria
52A Ikorodu Road, Fadey
Yaba
Lagos, Lagos, Nigeria   Phone: 1 864267

9867
Fellowship Award
For recognition of contributions to the pharmaceutical profession and service to the Society. Members of the Society with ten years post qualification experience who are citizens may be nominated. A medal is awarded every five years at the fellowship award ceremony. Established in 1970.

9868
West African College of Surgeons
(College Ouest Africaine des Chirurgiens)
W. African Health Committee Bldg.
6 Taylor Drive, Edmond Cresent
Private Mail Bag 1067
Yaba, Lagos, Nigeria   Phone: 1 800140

9869
Best Paper Award
For recognition of the best paper presented at scientific meeting. Grants and scholarships are also awarded.

Norway

9870
Association for Promotion of Skiing
(Foreningen til Ski-Idrettens Fremme)
Kongevein 5
N-0390 Oslo 3, Norway   Phone: 2 14 16 90

9871
Holmenkoll Medal
(Holmenkollmedaljen)
To recognize outstanding skiers and to promote the sport of skiing. Individuals who have been active in skiing in Holmenkollen for at least one year are eligible. A medal is awarded annually when merited. Established in 1895.

9872
Holmenkollen Ski Festival
To recognize outstanding skiers at the annual Ski Festival. The following events are held: Combined, Jump, Men's 50 Km, Men's 18 Km, Men's 15 Km, Women's 30, Women's 20 Km, Women's 10 Km, Women's 5 Km, Women's Relay and Men's Relay. The Trophy of Holmenkollen (Holmenkollpokal) is awarded annually. Established in 1892.

9873
Bergen International Festival
(Festspillene I Bergen)
PO Box 183
Lars Hillesgt. 3A
N-5001 Bergen, Norway
Phone: 5 21 61 00
Fax: 5 31 55 31

9874
Robert Levins Festspillfond
To encourage and promote a higher level of quality among younger, Norwegian pianists. Norwegian citizens are eligible. A monetary prize of 15,000 Norwegian kroner is awarded annually during the Festival in May/June. Established in 1985 in honor of Robert Levin.

9875
Operasangerinnen Fanny Elstas Fond
To encourage, promote and improve Norwegian vocal music, both composition and singing. Stipends, scholarships, and invitations to master classes are awarded annually during the Festival in May/June. Established in 1979 in honor of Fanny Elsta.

9876
Sigbjorn Bernhoft Osas Festspillfond
For recognition of outstanding achievements within the field of Norwegian folk-music. A monetary prize is awarded annually during the Festival in May/June. Established in 1986 in honor of Sigbjorn Bernhoft Osa.

9877
Birkebeiner-Rennet
Postboks 94
N-2451 Rena, Norway
Phone: 64 40825

9878
Birkebeinerrennet Ski Race
To recognize the best skiiers in a 35-mile cross country race. Cups, trophies, and plaques are awarded annually. Established in 1932.

9879
N. W. Damm & Son A.S
Kristian August gt. 3
PO Box 1755 Vika
N-0122 Oslo, Norway
Phone: 2 941500
Fax: 2 360874

9880
Damm prize
(Damm-prisen)
To recognize outstanding authors of children's books and to offer first class books for children and young adults. Anyone may contribute works by February 7 of every second year. Established in 1952 by N.W. Damm & Son, in memory of the founder of the publishing company, which was founded in 1843.

9881
European Movement in Norway
(Europabevegelsen i Norge)
Welhavensgt 1b
N-0166 Oslo 1, Norway
Phone: 2 467880
Fax: 2 206436

9882
Culture Prize
(Kulturprisen)
To recognize a young artist who has the potential to be internationally known. A monetary prize for travel abroad is awarded annually when merited. Established in 1980. (Temporarily discontinued)

9883
Golden Pen
(Gullpennen)
For recognition of service to the European Movement by members. A Golden Pen is awarded annually when merited. Established in 1970. (Temporarily discontinued)

9884
Press Prize
To recognize a journalist who has written objectively about Europe during the preceding year. A painting by a well known Norwegian artist is awarded annually when merited. Established in 1975.

9885
Federation of Norwegian Industries
(Norges Industriforbund)
Postboks 2435 - Solli
N-0202 Oslo 2, Norway
Phone: 2 43 70 00

Defunct organization.

9886
Federation of Norwegian Industries Prize
To recognize a journalist working for a newspaper, radio, or television station who has prepared the best program of the year on an industrial theme. A monetary prize of 10,000 Norwegian kroner was awarded annually. (Discontinued)

9887
Industriforbundets Miljovernpris
(Federation of Norwegian Industries Environment Prize)
For recognition of the industrial company that contributed most to environmental protection. A diploma and a graphic print, designed especially for this prize, were awarded annually. Established in 1972. (Discontinued in 1989)

9888
International Animated Film Association
(Association Internationale du Film d'Animation)
N-6100 Volda, Norway
Phone: 47 70 77066
Fax: 47 70 77331

9889
ASIFA Special Award
(Prix Special ASIFA)
To recognize a film or person or entity for the best contribution to international understanding through the art of animation. Nomination may be made to the ASIFA Board. A trophy of a silver marabout created by Georgi Tshapkanov, a Bulgarian sculptor, is awarded at ASIFA patronized festivals. Established in 1985.

9890
International Bandy Federation
(Internationella Bandyforbundet)
Hauger Skolvei 1
N-1351 Rud, Norway
Phone: 2 518800
Fax: 2 132989

9891
Competitions and Tournaments
To promote the game of Bandy, a sport related to ice hockey, but played on a larger ice rink, with 11 players on a team, using a plastic ball and curved sticks and no play behind goals. The Federation sponsors the Senior World Championship and a Junior Boys Championship for boys between 17 and 19 years of age. Awarded biennially. Established in 1957.

9892
IBF Gold Medal
For recognition of contributions to the sport of bandy.

9893
International Organization of Good Templars
Keysersgate 1
N-0165 Oslo 1, Norway
Phone: 2 208021
Fax: 2 206101

9894
IOGT International August Forell Award
For recognition of achievement in, and/or a contribution to a relevant field of activity of the organization. Selection is by nomination. A plaque is awarded every four years. Established in 1986.

9895
International Political Science Association
Institute of Political Science
Univ. of Oslo
Postboks 1097
Blindern
N-0317 Oslo 3, Norway
Phone: 2 85 51 68
Fax: 2 85 44 11

9896
Stein Rokkan Fellowship
To enable graduate students to attend IPSA World Congresses and to encourage their development as political scientists. Students engaged in post-graduate studies or research in political science are eligible. Travel expenses and a certificate are presented triennially at World Congresses. Established in 1980 in honor of Stein Rokkan.

9897
International Society of Chemotherapy
(Societe Internationale de chimiotherapie)
Tom Bergan
Institute of Medical Microbiology,
 Rikshospitalet
N-0027 Oslo, Norway
Phone: 22 200108
Fax: 22 200108

9898
Hamao Umezawa Prize for Chemotherapy
For recognition of outstanding research and life's work in chemotherapy. Nominations are accepted one and a half years before the award is given. A monetary prize and a document are presented biennially. Established in 1979 in honor of Professor Dr. Hamao Umezawa.

9899
Anders Jahres Humanitaere Stiftelse
PO Box 2100
N-3201 Sandefjord, Norway
Phone: 33 463000
Fax: 33 464900

9900
Anders Jahre Prize for Contributions to Norwegian Culture
To recognize an individual for outstanding contributions to Norwegian culture. A monetary award of $60,000 US is awarded.

9901
National Association of Norwegian Architects
(Norske Arkitekters Landsforbund)
Josefinesgt. 34
N-0351 Oslo 3, Norway
Phone: 2 60 22 90
Fax: 2 69 59 48

9902
Concrete Element Prize
For recognition of creative architectural and/or technical use of concrete elements. A monetary prize is awarded. Established in 1986.

9903
Concrete Structure Plaque
For recognition of environmental, aesthetic and technical uses of concrete structures. An honorary prize is awarded annually.

9904
Glass Prize
For recognition of the use of building-glass in a distinguished architectural or technical way in Norway. A monetary prize is awarded biennially.

9905
Masonry Prize
For stimulating and developing the use of masonry in Norwegian buildings. A monetary prize and a plaque are awarded when merited.

9906
National Prize for Good Building
For recognition of a building or group of buildings which raise the level of common building in Norway. A monetary prize and a plaque are awarded annually.

9907
Stone Prize
To recognize architects for distinguished use of Norwegian natural stone as a building material. A monetary prize is awarded annually.

9908
Wood Prize
For recognition of the creative and imaginative use of wood as an element in modern architecture. A monetary prize is awarded annually.

9909
Nordkapp Culture Office - the North Cape Festival
(Nordkapp Kulturkontor - Nordkapp Festivalen)
Mailboks 114
N-9750 Honningsvag, Norway
Phone: 84 72477

9910
World Champion Trolling Fisherline Bucket
(VM i Linestampkasting)
For recognition of outstanding trolling. A medal and a plaque are awarded annually at the North Cape Festival.

9911
Norpress - Norsk Pressebyra
Grensen 18
PO Box 6864
N-0130 St. Olaus Mas 1, Norway
Phone: 22 411050
Fax: 22 424619

Formerly: Hoyres Pressebyra.

9912
Norpress Press Prize
To recognize outstanding achievement in journalism within the conservative press. A monetary award of 8,000 Norwegian kroner and a diploma are awarded annually at the general meeting of Norpress (Norwegian Press Agency). Established in 1972. Formerly: Hoyres Pressebyra Press Prize.

9913
Norsemen's Federation
(Nordmanns-Forbundet)
Radhusgt. 23 b
N-0158 Oslo 1, Norway
Phone: 2 24 27 514
Fax: 2 24 25 163

9914
Norsemen's Federation Translation Grant
(Nordmanns-Forbundet oversetterstotte)
To increase the knowledge of Norwegian literature abroad. Publishing houses that introduce Norwegian fiction or poetry in translation are eligible. A grant of 15,000 Norwegian kroner is awarded annually to one or more houses. Application deadline is December 15. Established in 1978. Applications should be sent to NORLA, PO Box 239 Sentrum, N-0103 Oslo, Norway.

9915
Norway
Ministry of Cultural and Scientific Affairs
Norwegian Directorate for Public & School
   Libraries
Munkedamsveien 62
PO Box 8145 DEP
N-0033 Oslo 1, Norway
Phone: 2 83 25 85
Fax: 2 83 15 52

9916
Literature Awards for Children and Young People
(Premie for barne-og ungdomslitteratur)
To promote and encourage the creation and publication of quality literature for children and young people. Original books in Norwegian, translations into Norwegian, and Norwegian comics issued during the preceding year are eligible. Illustrators are also eligible. Awards cannot be given to the same author two years in succession. Monetary prizes are awarded in the following categories: (1) Best Children's Book - established in 1948; (2) Best Illustration - established in 1957; (3) Best Picture Book - established in 1961; (4) Best Translation - established in 1972; (5) Best Comic Animation - established in 1973; (6) Outstanding Young Author - established in 1977; and (7) Best Nonfiction. The awards for Outstanding Young Author and Best Nonfiction are awarded only in special cases. Monetary awards are presented annually. Established in 1948.

9917
Norway
Ministry of Foreign Affairs
7. juni plassen 1
POB 8114 Dep.
N-0032 Oslo 1, Norway
Phone: 22 343600
Fax: 22 349580

9918
King's Cross for Distinguished Service
To recognize individuals who have distinguished themselves in war activities. Formerly: King's Medal for Distinguished Service.

9919
Medal for a Noble Deed
To recognize an individual for having shown great courage in saving someone else's life at the risk of his own. Gold or silver medals are awarded when merited. (Discontinued)

9920
Medal for Civic Virtue
To recognize an individual for diligence and ability in the mediation board system (pre-court cases, local government) and for contributions as a citizen to the country. The award has been expanded to include zealous discharge of office and any meritorious activity that merits public recognition. Gold and silver medals are awarded annually.

9921
Royal Norwegian Order of Merit
To recognize individuals for service. Consuls who have served a minimum of eight years and foreign nationals are eligible. The Order has five classes: Grand Cross, Commander with Stars, Commander, Officer and Knight. The insignia of Officer of the Royal Norwegian Order of Merit ("Ridder I" in Norwegian) consists of a gold cross. The insignia of Knight ("Ridder" in Norwegian) are silver. Established in 1985.

9922
Royal Norwegian Order of St. Olav
To recognize individuals for outstanding service to their native country and humanity. A decoration and a diploma are awarded when merited in the following ranks: Grand Cross; Commander - 1st and 2nd class; and Knight - 1st and 2nd class. Established in 1847 by King Oscar I.

9923
St. Olav Medal
To recognize individuals who have promoted knowledge of Norway abroad or have strengthened the ties between Norwegian emigrants and their home country. A silver medal is awarded annually. Established in 1939 by H.M. King Haakon VII.

9924
Norwegian Academy for Language and Literature
(Norske Akademi for Sprog og Litteratur)
Inkognitogt 24
N-0256 Oslo 2, Norway

9925
Norske Akademis Pris Til Minne om Thorleif Dahl
For recognition of achievement in the following fields of literature: fiction, poetry, essays and translation. Individuals may be nominated. A monetary prize and a sculpture are awarded annually in November. Established in 1982 by the Norwegian Academy and Thorleif Dahl's Cultural Library in honor of Thorleif Dahl.

9926
Norwegian Academy of Science and Letters
(Norske Videnskaps-Akademi)
Drammensveien 78
N-0271 Oslo 2, Norway
Phone: 2 44 42 96
Fax: 256 26 56

9927
Fridtjof Nansen Award
For recognition of outstanding contributions to the sciences or humanities. Norwegian scientists and research workers are eligible. A monetary prize of 30,000 Norwegian kroner and a certificate are awarded annually. Established in 1896 in memory of Fridtjof Nansen, a scientist, explorer, and diplomat. Sponsored by the Fridtjof Nansen Fund and affiliated funds for the advancement of science and letters.

9928
Norwegian Authors' Union
(Norske Forfatterforening)
Radhusgata 7
Oslo 1, Norway

9929
Rolf Stenersen Prize
To provide recognition for the best drama by a young playwright. A monetary prize is awarded biennially.

9930
Tarjei Vesaas Debutant Prize
To recognize a young writer under 30 years of age for his best first book of prose or poetry. A monetary prize of 14,000 Norwegian kroner is awarded annually.

9931
Norwegian Chemical Society
(Norsk Kjemisk Selskap)
Postboks 1107 Blindern
N-0317 Oslo, Norway
Phone: 22 855531
Fax: 22 855441

9932
Guldberg and Waage's Law of Mass Action Memorial Medal
(Medalje til minne om Guldberg og Waages Massevirkningslov)
To recognize Norwegian chemists for a scientific or technical-chemical work that is carried out in Norway. The study may have been done in cooperation with other research workers, but it must be obvious that the work of the honored chemist has been considerable and deserves the award. Only Norwegian chemists are eligible. A silver medal mounted on a wooden plate is awarded irregularly. Established in 1964.

9933
Norwegian Cultural Council
(Norsk Kulturrad)
Grev Wedels plass 7
N-0151 Oslo 1, Norway
Phone: 22 423919
Fax: 22 334042

9934
Culture Prize
For recognition of outstanding contributions to Norwegian culture. Individuals are eligible. A monetary prize of 100,000 Norwegian kroner is awarded annually. Established in 1968.

9935
Prize for Journalism on Arts and Culture
(Norsk kulturrads pris for kulturjournalistikk)
To recognize outstanding journalistic contributions in the field of arts and culture. A prize of 25,000 Norwegian kroner is awarded annually. Established in 1992.

9936
Translation Prize
(Norsk kulturrads oversettespris)
For recognition of a long production of qualified translations or, infrequently, for one excellent book translated from a foreign language in the preceding year. A monetary prize of 50,000 Norwegian kroner is awarded annually. Established in 1968.

9937
Norwegian Film Festival
(Norske Filmfestivalen)
PO Box 145
N-5501 Haugesund, Norway
Phone: 52 734430
Fax: 52 734420

9938
Amanda Award for Television and Cinematographic Merit
(Amanda Film - OG Fjernsynspris)
For recognition of outstanding achievement in the preceding season's (July-July) national film and television production. Norwegian film and television productions may be submitted to the appointed "Amanda" jury/juries. Awards are given in the following categories: Best Norwegian Feature, Best Dramatic Television Production, Best Documentary/TV Report, Best Artistic Short Film/Program, Best Entertainment Production for Television, Best Children's/Youth Film/TV Program, Best Actor, Best Actress, Best Professional Achievement, Best Foreign Feature, Gullklapperen (Honorary Award to Filmmakers), and Amanda-Komiteens Aerespris (Special Honorary Award). A bronze statuette awarded annually. Established in 1985.

9939
Norwegian Master-Painter Organization
(Norsk Malermestrenes Landsforbund)
PO Box 5479 Majorstua
N-0305 Oslo, Norway
Phone: 22 961160
Fax: 22 961161

9940
Norwegian Master-Painter Organization Awards
To recognize and further the interests of painters in Norway. Awards are given annually at competitions.

9941
Norwegian Press Association
(Norsk Presseforbund)
Storgt. 14
N-0184 Oslo 1, Norway
Phone: 2 2170117
Fax: 2 2176332

9942
Tor Gjesdals Prize
(Tor Gjesdals pris)
To reward personal activity in mass media or other channels of communication aimed at the promotion of international solidarity, thereby supporting such activity in the UN or UNESCO. Members of press organizations in Norway or other cultural workers are eligible. A monetary prize and a plaque are awarded annually. Established in 1979 by Anne Margret Gjesdal in memory Tor Gjesdal, former Director of Information in UNESCO.

9943
Grand Journalism Prize
(Den Store Journalistprisen)
For recognition of outstanding efforts in journalism by Norwegian citizens. A monetary prize and a plaque are awarded annually when merited. Sponsored by the Norwegian Union of Journalists, the Editors Association, the Norwegian Newspaper Publishers Association, and the Norwegian Broadcasting Corporation. Established in 1991.

9944
Narvesen-prisen
(Narvesen Prize)
For recognition of outstanding efforts in journalism by Norwegian citizens. A monetary prize and a plaque were awarded annually when merited. Sponsored by Narvesen Ltd. Established in 1954. (Discontinued)

9945
Norwegian Section of the International Board on Books for Young People
Norsk barnebokforum
Pilestredet 63, B,I
N-0350 Oslo 3, Norway
Phone: 2 46 70 31

9946
Kari Medal
To promote the art of illustration and picture-books for children. (Discontinued in 1961 when the Royal Ministry of Education and Ecclesiastical Affairs Prize was extended to the field of illustrations)

9947
Norwegian Short Film Festival
(Stiftelsen Kortfilmfestivalen)
Storengvn. 8 B
N-1342 Jar, Norway
Phone: 2 12 20 13
Fax: 2 12 48 65

9948
Short Film Festival Prize
(Stiftelsen Kortfilmfestivalen)
To recognize the best short film of the Festival. The film director must be a Norwegian citizen. A monetary award of 20,000 Norwegian kroner and a trophy of a director's chair in gold are awarded. Established in 1983.

9949
Trondheim City Council Prize
(Trondheim Kommunes Pris)
To recognize the best short film for distribution to cinemas/movie theatres. A monetary award of 5,000 Norwegian kroner was presented. Awarded annually. Established in 1985 by the Trondheim City Council. The Festival was held annually. (Discontinued in 1987)

9950
Terje Vigen Prize
(Terje Vigen-Prisen)
This is a special jury prize of the Festival. There are no conditions; the jury may award the prize to whomever it finds suitable. A statuette in bronze of Terje Vigen, a person from one of Henrik Ibsen's poems, is awarded annually. Established in 1988 by the Grimstad City Council.

9951
Norwegian Society of Chartered Engineers
(Norske Sivilingeniorers Forening)
PO Box 2312 Solli
N-0201 Oslo 2, Norway
Phone: 2 838330
Fax: 2 830746

9952
Gold Medal for Development of the Technological Environment
(Gullmedalje for Utvikling av det Teknologiske Miljo)
To recognize and encourage Norwegian leaders or businesses/civil departments for important achievements in Norwegian technology. A gold medal is awarded when merited. Established in 1975.

9953
Generaldirektor Aage W. Owe's Prisbelonningsfond
To recognize an individual for outstanding achievements in Norwegian industry through research and development, eminent leadership, and administration. A monetary award is presented when merited. Established in 1964.

9954
Prisbelonning - Eydes Pris
To recognize civil engineers for outstanding achievements in the field of building and construction work in Norway. A monetary award is presented when merited. Established in 1916.

9955
Technology Prize
(Norske Sivilingeniorers Forenings Teknologipris)
To recognize an individual for a contribution to technology. A monetary award is presented. Established in 1976. Formerly: Miljovernpris.

9956
Norwegian Translators' Association
(Norsk Oversetterforening)
Postboks 579 Sentrum
N-0105 Oslo 1, Norway
Phone: 22 33 45 56
Fax: 22 42 03 56

9957
Bastian Prize
(Bastian-prisen)
To recognize outstanding translations published during the preceding year. Awards are presented in two categories, adult books, and books for children and young adults. Members may submit entries by September 15. A monetary award and a trophy designed by Ornulf Bast are presented annually in January. Established in 1951. Since 1984, a prize for translations of books for children and young adults has been awarded.

9958
Oslo Kommune
Kultur-og Utdanningskomiteen
Radhuset
N-0037 Oslo 1, Norway
Phone: 2 2861600
Fax: 2 2861846

9959
Culture Prize
(Oslo Bys Kulturpris)
For recognition of outstanding achievement in art, science, or other cultural work. A monetary prize of 50,000 Norwegian kroner and a medal are awarded annually in December. Established in 1966.

9960
Oslo University
(Universitetet I Oslo)
Rector's Office
Box 1072, Blindern
N-0316 Oslo 3, Norway
Phone: 22 855050
Fax: 22 854442

9961
Anders Jahre Prize in Medicine
To recognize individuals for distinguished work or significant findings in medicine relevant to Scandinavia. Applications are not accepted for this prize. The following prizes are awarded: first prize - 600,000 Norwegian kroner, a gold medal and a diploma; second prize - 300,000 Norwegian kroner, a gold medal and a diploma. (If two individuals are awarded first prize, each will receive 300,000 Norwegian kroner. If two individuals are awarded second prize, each will receive 150,000 Norwegian kroner.) One of the prizes is awarded to an individual under 40 years of age. Awarded annually.

9962
The Queen Sonja International Music Competition
PO Box 5190 Majorstua
N-0302 Oslo, Norway
Phone: 2 2464055
Fax: 2 2463630

Formerly: Crown Princess Sonja International Music Competition.

9963
Crown Princess Sonja International Music Competition
To enhance Norwegian music internationally. The competition in 1995 is open to singers from all parts of the world who are born after January 1, 1963. The deadline for applications is March 15, 1995. The following prizes (totaling approximately $40,000 US) are awarded: first prize - 125,000 kroner; second prize - 75,000 kroner; third prize - 50,000 kroner; fourth prize - 25,000 kroner; and concert engagements. Established in 1988. The competition is held every three years in August.

9964
Research Council of Norway
(Norges Forskningsraad)
Stensberggata 26
PO Box 2700
St. Hanshauger
N-0131 Oslo, Norway
Phone: 2 2037000
Fax: 2 2037001

9965
Honorary Award
(Aerespris)
For recognition of outstanding contribution to the creation of new industrial production in Norway, based on innovations in science and technology. Candidates may be nominated by December 31. A monetary prize of

25,000 Norwegian kroner and a trophy are awarded annually at the Council's Convention. Established in 1966. (Discontinued)

9966
Inventiveness Prize
(Idepris)
For recognition of inventiveness in the fields of science and technology. Established in 1991. (Discontinued)

9967
Royal Norwegian Society of Sciences and Letters
(Kongelige Norske Videnskabers Selskab)
Erling Skakkes gt. 47 B Phone: 7 3592157
N-7013 Trondheim, Norway Fax: 7 3595895

9968
J. E. Gunnerus Medal
(Gunnerusmedaljen)
To recognize individuals for scientific and personal achievements in human society. Members of the Society may make nominations. A medal is awarded annually when merited. Established in 1935 in memory of Bishop Johan Ernst Gunnerus (1718-1773).

9969
Society of Norwegian Composers
(Norsk Komponistforening)
Postboks 9171 Vaterland
Toyenbekken 21 Phone: 22 170190
N-0134 Oslo 1, Norway Fax: 22 170500

9970
Composition of the Year
(Arets Verk)
To encourage professional development and to make contemporary music known to the public. Members are eligible. Monetary awards are presented annually at the general assembly. Established in 1965.

9971
Musician of the Year
To encourage musicians (soloists/ensembles/choirs) to perform contemporary music. The award is presented annually in December.

9972
Ullensaker Cykleklub
Postboks 138
N-2051 Jessheim, Norway Phone: 6 97 25 26

9973
Postgiro Norway
For recognition of achievement in an international bicycle race for women. A monetary prize and trophy are awarded annually. Established in 1983 by Ullensaker Cykleklub and Postgiro. Sponsored by Postgiro. Formerly: (1986) Postgiro Grand Prix.

Pakistan

9974
Hamdard Foundation Pakistan
Hamdard Centre
Nzimabad Phone: 21 6616004
Karachi 74600, Pakistan Fax: 21 6641766

Formerly: (1981) Hamdard National Foundation.

9975
Hamdard Foundation Pakistan Awards
To recognize individuals who encourage international understanding and work to improve education, health, medical care, and emergency relief. The Foundation gives grants, fellowships, and scholarships.

9976
Institution of Engineers, Pakistan
Engineering Centre
Gulberg-III, Lahore, Pakistan Phone: 42 872927

9977
Gold Medal
To encourage, regulate and elevate technical and general engineering knowledge. The award is given in two categories: (1) for meritorious service rendered to the Institution and the engineering profession; and (2) for technical papers or books in different disciplines of engineering. A gold medal is awarded for meritorious service. An Honorary Fellowship Diploma is awarded for technical papers or books. Awarded irregularly at the convention. Established in 1980.

9978
Iqbal Academy Pakistan
PO Box 1308, G.P.O.
Lahore, Pakistan Phone: 42 57214

9979
Iqbal Award
For promotion and recognition of original research work of high calibre to the field of Iqbal studies. A monetary prize and a medal are awarded triennially. Established in 1977 by the President of Pakistan in honor of Dr. Sir Allama Mohammad Iqbal. Sponsored by the Pakistan - Ministry of Education.

9980
National Book Council of Pakistan
Saeed Plaza Blue Area
Islamabad, Pakistan Phone: 51 816420

9981
Best Published Book Award (Publisher and Author)
To recognize a quality publication and an outstanding contribution in writing. Authors and publishers are eligible for books published and printed in Pakistan by citizens of Pakistan. A monetary prize is awarded annually. Established in 1988 by the National Book Council of Pakistan in the Ministry of Education.

9982
Incentive for Publications of Articles in International Journals
For recognition of achievement in the sciences. Citizens of Pakistan are eligible. A monetary prize is awarded annually. Established in 1986 by the National Book Council of Pakistan in the Ministry of Education.

9983
Scientist of the Year and Best Author
To promote serious writing in the sciences and other fields. Citizens of Pakistan are eligible. Cash awards, medals, certificates of commendation, and purchase of the first edition to support the book are awarded annually. Established in 1984. Sponsored by the Pakistan - Ministry of Education.

9984

National Institute of Folk and Traditional Heritage
Lok Virsa - LV
60 St. 63, F-7/3
PO Box 1184
Islamabad, Pakistan   Phone: 51 812578

9985

National Institute of Folk and Traditional Heritage Awards
To recognize individuals who nurture the roots of Pakistani culture and conduct research on traditional folklore. The Institute sponsors competitions and bestows awards.

9986

Nigar Weekly
Victoria Mansion
Abdullah Haroon Road
PO Box No. 3948
Karachi 4, Pakistan   Phone: 21 510020

9987

Nigar Public Film Awards
To encourage professional development in film, radio, television and stage. Individuals are selected by readers and judges. A trophy is awarded annually. Established in 1957 by Elias Rashidi. Formerly: *Nigar Weekly* Public Film Awards.

9988

Nigar Weekly **Song Award**
To recognize the singer of the best film song. Awarded annually.

9989

Pakistan
Ministry of Education
Block D
Pakistan Secretariat
Islamabad, Pakistan   Phone: 51 825001

9990

National Award for Painting and Graphics
To recognize the best painter and graphic artist of the year, and to encourage art and artists. Awarded annually.

9991

National Theatre Awards
For recognition of contributions to the theatre. Awards are given in the following categories: (1) play; (2) playwright; and (3) director of a stage play. Awarded annually.

9992

Pakistan Academy of Sciences
Constitution Ave., Sector G-5   Phone: 51 827789
Islamabad 44000, Pakistan   Phone: 51 824843

9993

Gold Medal
To recognize achievements in scientific and technological research in various disciplines of science, and in engineering and technology for those who have developed patents and processes of far-reaching national importance. Medals are given in the following categories: (1) Physical/Biological Science; (2) Physical/Biological Science (for scientists under 40 years of age); (3) Engineering and Technology; (4) Water Management; (5) Agricultural Science; (6) Energy; and (7) Earth Sciences. Pakistani scientists must be nominated by a Fellow of the Academy or rector/head of a university or scientific organization, within the time period specified. A gold medal is awarded annually at an investiture ceremony. Established in 1967 in the sciences, with the additional categories added in 1975 and 1990.

9994

Pakistan Government
Cabinet Division
Islamabad, Pakistan

9995

Pakistan Civil Awards
There are five Orders: (1) Order of Pakistan - only foreign nationals are eligible; (2) Order of Shujaat; (3) Order of Imtiaz; (4) Order of Quaid-i-Azam - only foreign nationals are eligible; and (5) Order of Khidmat - only foreign nationals are eligible. Foreign nationals can be given civil awards in any Order for eminence and outstanding services to Pakistan in a significant field of activity. Civil awards are conferred on citizens of Pakistan in recognition of: (1) Gallantry - awards in the Order of Shujaat; and (2) Academic distinction in the fields of medicine, science, engineering, technology, philosophy, history, literature or the arts - awards in the Order of Imtiaz. In addition, the President's Award for Pride of Performance can be conferred for outstanding achievements in the fields of art (including the performing arts), literature, science, sports and nursing. Established in 1958.

9996

Pakistan Military Awards
For recognition of gallantry performed while serving in the Armed Forces. Awarded when merited. Nishan-i-Haider is the highest award given for gallantry, followed by Nishan-i-Shujaat and Nishan-i-Imtiaz.

9997

Quaid-i-Azam Police Medal for Gallantry
For recognition of outstanding gallantry performed while serving on the Police Force. Awarded when merited. The President's Police Medal for Gallantry is also awarded.

9998

Pakistan Television Corporation
Federal TV Complex
Constitution Ave.
PO Box 1221   Phone: 51 828655
Islamabad, Pakistan   Fax: 51 823406

9999

Best Television Commercial/Advertising Film of the Year
To improve the standard of television advertising in Pakistan and to encourage the talent and technical skill available in the country. Only advertising agencies are eligible. Monetary prizes, plaques, and certificates are awarded annually.

10000

Documentary of the Year
To recognize the best producer, cameraman, and film editor of the best television documentary of the year; to encourage talent in Pakistan television; and to achieve international standards in all spheres of documentary film production. Trophies and certificates are awarded annually.

10001

Drama Festival (Jashan-E-Tamseel) Awards
To provide incentives to producers of dramas and to their production teams, and to meet international standards in the various spheres of television drama production. Awards are presented to the best play, best producer, best script, best actor, and best actress. Trophies and certificates are usually awarded annually.

Pakistan

10002

PTV Annual Award
To recognize achievement in the field of television production, and to encourage professionals in that field. Directors, producers, cameramen, engineers, designers and other professionals including writers, actors, composers, singers, and instrumentalists are eligible. Nominations, based on outstanding performances and productions in the preceding years, are accepted. Monetary awards, trophies, and certificates are awarded annually. Established in 1980.

10003

Pakistan Writers' Guild
11 Abbok Rd.
Anarkali, Lahore, Pakistan

10004

Awards for Regional Literature
For recognition of the best literary works, including the novel, short story, drama, poetry, biography, travel, literary criticism or research work in each of the four regional languages of Punjabi, Pushto, Sindhi and Gujrati. A monetary prize is awarded for work in each language annually.

10005

Dawood Prize for Literature
For reocgnition of the best literary works. Awards are given in the following categories: (1) books on literary research, literary history, literary cricitism; (2) research works on the ideological, historical or cultural aspects of the Pakistan movement in the pre-or post-independence period; and (3) translations. Monetary prizes are awarded in each category. Sponsored by the Dawood Foundation. Awarded annually.

10006

Habib Bank Prize for Literature
For recognition of the best translation or adaptation of the year (into English or a Pakistani language) of a modern or classical work in any Pakistani language. A monetary prize of 25,000 rupees is awarded annually. Established in 1968.

10007

National Bank of Pakistan Prize for Literature
For recognition of the best books on economics, scientific, technical and other professional subjects. Monetary prizes are awarded in each category annually. Sponsored by the National Bank of Pakistan.

10008

Prizes for Manuscripts for Juveniles
For recognition of creative writing in the field of children's literature in the Urdu language comprising history, geography, science, stories, poems. Six monetary prizes are awarded annually.

10009

Quaid-i-Azam Academy
297 M.A. Jinnah Rd.
Karachi 5, Pakistan
Phone: 718184
Phone: 719175

10010

Presidential Award on Best Book on Quaid-i-Azam and Pakistan
To encourage research and writing. All persons irrespective of their nationality, race, creed or sex are eligible. A monetary prize and a medal are awarded triennially. Established in 1981 by the President of Pakistan in honor of Quaid-i-Azam Mohammad Ali Jinnah, the founder of the State of Pakistan. Sponsored by the Pakistan Ministry of Education.

Paraguay

10011

Latin American Association of Freight and Transport Agents (Asociacion Latinoamericana de Agentes de Carga Aerea y Transporte)
Pte. Franco 663
Casilla de Correo 1126
Asuncion, Paraguay
Phone: 21 205269
Fax: 21 201786

10012

Competitions
To promote activities of Latin American and Caribbean air cargo agents' associations. Competitions are held.

Peru

10013

Colegio de Arquitectos del Peru
Av. San Felipe 999
Lima 11, Peru
Phone: 14 713778

10014

Hexagono de Oro
For recognition of the best executed project of architecture at the Biennial of Architecture. Society members are eligible. A bronze trophy in the shape of an hexagon as the symbol of the Colegio de Arquitectos del Peru is awarded when merited at the Biennial of Architecture. Established in 1970.

10015

Geographic Society of Lima (Sociedad Geografica de Lima)
Casilla 1176
Jiron Puno No. 456
Lima 100, Peru
Phone: 14 273723

10016

Medallas de Geografia Fisica, Humana, Economica
For recognition of meritorious work in the fields of physical geography, sociology, and economics. Medals are awarded annually when merited.

10017

Regional Centre for Seismology for South America (Centro Regional de Sismologia para America del Sur)
Apartado 14-0363
Lima, Peru
Phone: 14 321824
Fax: 14 336750

10018

Ceresis Award (Premio Ceresis)
For recognition of exceptional contributions to the advancement of seismology and related fields, relevant to South America. Selection is by nomination and unanimous approval of the member states. A plaque and a diploma are awarded biennially. Established in 1979.

Philippines

10019

Asian NGO Coalition for Agrarian Reform and Rural Development
ANGOC Regional Secretariat
Matrincc Bldg., Ste. 47
2178 Pasong Tamo Makati
Manila 1200, Philippines
Phone: 2 8163033
Fax: 2 9215122

10020

ANGOC Award for Rural Development
For recognition of village-level primary organizations that have made an outstanding contribution to rural development in their own community. In so doing, the successful experience of the primary organization is shared with other NGOs in the region. Development-oriented associations engaged in rural development at the village level are considered. A plaque is awarded and one issue of the ANGOC Monograph Series is devoted to the program or project. The monograph is disseminated globally. Awarded annually at a special occasion arranged by the Coalition. Established in 1985.

10021

Asian-Pacific Weed Science Society
Bio-Science Bldg. C-214
U.P. at Los Banos College
Laguna 4031, Philippines
Phone: 3397

10022

Best Paper Award
For recognition of outstanding contributions to research in weed science. Papers presented during the biennial conference are considered. A monetary prize and a plaque are awarded biennially during the conference. Established in 1983.

10023

Association of Development Financing Institutions in Asia and the Pacific
2F Skyland Plaza
Sen. Gil Puyat Ave.
Makati, Metro Manila, Philippines
Phone: 2 8161672
Fax: 2 8176498

10024

Honorary Member
For recognition of achievement or contribution to the advancement of the development banking profession in the Asia-Pacific region. Individuals may be nominated if they have gained recognition in the field on development banking because of any of the following services: they have created, developed, and actualized an innovative concept, system, or technology that has been responsible for the improvement of development financing in the region; they have been the leading figure in the founding, development, and the operation of a pioneering institution that provides either development, financing or support, and assistance to other development financing institutions; or they have been recognized by peers and the leaders of their country for outstanding contributions to the field of development financing. A life-time membership in the Association is awarded when merited. Established in 1983.

10025

Association of Special Libraries in the Philippines
PO Box 4118
Manila, Philippines
Phone: 2 590177

10026

ASLP Professional Award
To recognize professional librarians who have made significant contributions to special librarianship. Awarded biannually.

10027

ASLP Service Award
To recognize professional librarians, library or information science graduates, and individuals who have made significant contributions to special librarianship. Awarded biannually.

10028

ASLP Special Citizen Awards
To recognize professional librarians, library or information science graduates, and individuals who have made significant contributions to special librarianship.

10029

Cultural Center of the Philippines
CCP Complex, Roxas Boulevard
PO Box 310
Metro Manila 1004, Philippines
Phone: 2 832 1125

10030

ASEAN Award for Literature
To recognize individual literary artists/groups who have produced a signficiant body of works in either poetry, fiction, drama, essay, children's literature or other works of non-fiction with literary merit that use cultural traditions relating to the other cultures of ASEAN. Other criteria in the selection of Filipino winners include the following: the literary artist/group should be a living citizen(s) of the Philippines; the artist should have been recognized by peers and by the country as a whole, through previous prestigious literary awards, fellowships, or other forms of recognition; the literary artist/group should have contributed significantly to the development of the Filipino nation through works that portray and crystallize personal insights on Filipino culture; and the artist's/group's medium should be any of the major Philippine languages. Institutions or professional groups/organizations are invited to submit a maximum of three nominations by March 16. A monetary award of $1,500 and a trophy are awarded triennially. Established in 1987.

10031

ASEAN Award for the Performing Arts
To recognize individual performing artists or groups in the field of dance, musical arts or theater who have created and produced an outstanding body of work in a style signficiant to the culture and tradition of the country that relates to the other ASEAN cultural tradition. Other criteria in the selection of Filipino winners include the performing artist/group should be a living citizen(s) of the Philippines, and the awardee should be nationally recognized as an outstanding artist/performing group of the country. Nominated performing troupes or companies, in addition, should have produced and presented through the years an outstanding repertoire that uses traditions that relate to other ASEAN cultural traditions and innovations in response to contemporary needs and tempers. Institutions or professional groups/organizations are invited to submit a maximum of three nominations by March 16. A monetary award of $1,500 and a trophy are awarded triennially. Established in 1987.

10032

ASEAN Award for Visual Arts
For recognition of outstanding work in the field of visual arts. Individual artists/groups from any of the following fields: painting (including calligraphy, graphics and photography), sculpture, handicraft (traditional or modern), or architecture are eligible. The artist/group should have contributed to the development of his nation and culture through works that do not merely preserve its cultural heritage but more so transform the same into a living, growing tradition reflective of and responsive to the contemporary needs of people, nation and culture. Other criteria in the selection of Filipino winners include the following: the artist/group should be citizen(s) of the Philippines and should have created an outstanding collection of works in a style significant to Filipino culture and related to the other ASEAN cultures; and the artist/group should have been recognized by peers and by the country as a whole through critical acclaim or through awards in prestigious competitions or from cultural organizations or institutions, national and/or international. Institutions and professional groups/organizations are invited to submit a maximum

10033
CCP Awards for Television
To encourage the TV stations to prioritize airing of quality Filipino production and artists by recognizing their works that truly reflect Filipino values, way of life, arts and culture. Filipino-produced TV programs that have been continuously aired for at least two months in any channel (for TV specials) are eligible. An originally sculptured trophy by a famous Filipino artist for ten outstanding TV programs and TV special; and plaques for significant individual awardees are awarded annually, usually in the first quarter of the succeeding year. Established in 1987. Additional information is available from Ma. Lourdes I. Jacob, Associate Artistic Director, Visual, Literary and Media Arts Dept. - Cultural Center of the Philippines.

10034
CCP Literary Awards
(Gawad CCP Sa Panitikan)
For recognition of achievement in literature and writing, and to encourage professional development. Awards are given for works in Filipino in the following categories: Poetry Short Story, Critical Essay on the Performing Arts; and Three-act Play. The contest is open to all Filipino citizens, except employees of CCP and their family members. Entries in the play category must not have been produced previously; entries in poetry, short story and essay categories may be published or unpublished works. Entries must be received by January 31. Filipino citizens are eligible. A monetary prize and a certificate are awarded annually for playwriting, and every five years for the other four categories. Established in 1969 by the Cultural Center of the Philippines Coordinating Center for Literature.

10035
International Federation of Asian and Western Pacific Contractors' Associations
3/F Padilla Bldg.
Ortigas Commercial Complex
Emerald Ave.
Pasig, Metro Manila, Philippines
Phone: 2 632782
Fax: 2 6312789

10036
Builders' Awards
To promote the development of operational and technical advancement in the field of construction, and to encourage the involvement of the construction industry in national welfare. Association members are eligible. A gold or silver medal is awarded at the Association's convention. Established in 1964.

10037
IFAWPCA-CHOI Fieldman Award
To encourage the development of construction field management systems, procedures, construction methods, and techniques; and to promote the cause of man-made power training. Candidates may be nominated. A monetary award or a citation is presented at the convention. Established in 1982 by Mr. Choi Chong-Whan, Past President of IFAWPCA, and President of Samwhan Corporation of Korea.

10038
IFAWPCA-PCA Foundation Research Award
To encourage the development of applied research in construction materials, methods, and systems, and to promote construction technology in the IFAWPCA region. A monetary award is presented at the convention. Established in 1971 by Mr. Domingo V. Poblete.

10039
International PEN - Philippines
PO Box 3959
Manila, Philippines
Phone: 2 591241
Fax: 2 586581

10040
International PEN - Philippines Awards
To recognize individuals who promote mutual understanding among countries and to provide for freedom of thought and expression within and between nations. Awards are given annually.

10041
Ramon Magsaysay Award Foundation
Ramon Magsaysay Center
1680 Roxas Blvd.
Manila 1004, Philippines
Phone: 2 591959
Fax: 2 5218105

10042
Ramon Magsaysay Awards
For recognition of service to the people of Asia in the following fields: Government Service - outstanding service in the public interest in any branch of government, including executive, judicial, legislative, or military; Public Service - outstanding service for the public good by a private citizen; Community Leadership - leadership of a community, whether local, national or international, especially toward action that would help the man on the land to have fuller opportunities and a better life; Journalism, Literature, and Creative Communication Arts - effective writing and publishing as a power for public good. Other forms of communication, such as radio, TV, theater, and cinema are included; and International Understanding - advancement of amity and understanding between peoples of different countries. Persons in Asia, regardless of race, creed, sex, or nationality are eligible. Institutions, associations, or organizations are eligible for the award also. The Board of Trustees is responsible for the final selection of awardees. The Board of Trustees invites nominators from each country covered by the program to nominate in a given category by January 15. A maximum of five monetary awards of $50,000 each is awarded annually when merited. In addition, a gold medal and a certificate are issued to each recipient with inscriptions indicating the basis of selection. Presented at a ceremony in Manila on August 31st, the anniversary of the birth of Ramon Magsaysay, the late President of the Philippines, who exemplified the highest type of democratic leadership.

10043
Multi-Color Exhibitors Association
PO Box 2748
Manila, Philippines

10044
Manila International Exhibition of Photography
For recognition in the field of photography. Awards are given in the following categories: (1) Color Slides; (2) Color Prints; and (3) Monochrome Prints. In the color slide category, the following prizes are presented: (1) FIAP Gold Medal for Best Set of Four Entries; (2) PSA-CSD Gold Medal for Best Slide of the Show; (3) PSA-CSD Gold Medal (Contemporary) for Best Contemporary Slide of the Show; (4) Alfred Jendroszek Award for Best Contemporary Slide of Asia; (5) Dr. G.C. Tansiongkun Award for Best Human Figure Study; (6) Lim Kwong Ling Award for Best Human Interest; (7) AGFA-Photokina Mktg. Corp. Award for Best Local Entry; (8) MCE Awards for Outstanding Entries; (9) FIAP Honorable Mentions; and (10) MCE Special Award for Best Entry of MCE Member. In the color print category, the following prizes are awarded: (1) FIAP Gold Medal for Best Set of Four Entries; (2) PSA-PPD Gold Medal for Best of Show; (3) MCE-Award for Best Human Interest; (4) Wellington Lee Award for Best Creative Entry; (5) James Turnbull Award for Best Portrait; (6) AGFA-Photokina Mktg. Corp. Award for Best Local Entry; (7) MCE Awards for Outstanding Entries; (8) FIAP Honorable Mentions; and (9) MCE Special Award for Best Entry of MCE Members. In the monochrome print category, the following prizes are awarded: (1) FIAP Gold Medal for Best Set of Four Entries; (2) T. Angsin Award for Best of Show; (3) James Turnbull Award for Best Portrait; (4) Kok Noun Ho Award for Best Landscape; (5) AGFA-Photokina Marketing. Award for Best Local Entry; (6) MCE Awards for Outstanding Entries; (7) FIAP Honorable Mentions; and (8) MCE Special Award for Best Entry of MCE Member. Awarded annually. Established in 1982 as a color slide competition. The color print and monochrome print categories were added in 1984 and 1986, respectively.

10045
National Commission on Culture and the Arts
House No. 8 Casa Blanca Plaza
San Luis Complex, General Luna St.
Intramuros
Manila, Philippines
Phone: 632 405761
Fax: 632 405765

10046
CCP Awards for Alternative Film and Video
(Gawad CCP Para sa Alternatibong Pelikula at Video)
To recognize outstanding works in film and video. The award is given in four categories: feature; experimental; animation; and documentary for both film and video. Works should not have been made for commercial screening. Each winner receives certificates and cash prizes. Given by the Coordinating Center for Film of the Cultural Center of the Philippines.

10047
CCP Awards for Radio
(Gawad CCP Para sa Radyo)
To encourage radio stations and independent producers to prioritize airing of quality Filipino productions that truly reflect Filipino way of life, values, and culture. The award is given in three categories: Best Radio Drama Program; Best Radio Documentary Program; and Best Radio Special. An award is also given to the Best Musical Program aside from the Significant Contribution Awards. Award offered biennially. Additional information is available from Ma. Lourdes I. Jacob, Associate Artistic Director, Visual, Literary, and Media Arts Department, Cultural Center of the Philippines.

10048
CCP Awards for the Arts
(Gawad CCP Para sa Sining)
To recognize Filipino artists or group of artists who have made outstanding contributions to their particular art form. The award is given in three categories. Category A: Artists or group of artists who have/had consistently produced outstanding works in their particular art form or have/had evolved a distinct style or technique that enriches the development of their particular art form; and artists or group of artists who are nationally recognized as outstanding in their field by virtue of winning in prestigious national or international art or literary competitions or being acknowledged as such by critic circles or by their peers. Category B: Artists or group of artists who have made outstanding contributions to the culture of the region of their birth or residence through: Outstanding works that cull and draw inspiration from the cultural heritage, tradition and experiences of the people of their region or locality; outstanding works that manifest or develop a particular style or form significant to their particular region or locality; trailblazing works contemporaneous or innovative in style or form but somehow incorporating elements of their region's heritage and tradition; pioneering or innovative works that have influenced the other artists of their region to explore and develop a particular style or form significant to their locality or have/had inspired revitalization or art-making in their region; outstanding works that draw national attention or popularize particular aesthetic forms indigenous or endemic to the region; outstanding work/works that has/have earned for the regional artists national or international prestige and honor in reputable or recognized national or internatioal art and literary competition, thereby bringing honor not only to themselves but to the other artists and the people of their region as well. Category C: Outstanding cultural workers who, through their works either in research, curatorship or administration have helped to develop or enrich particular art forms or Philippine culture in general. Each awardee receives a medal of recognition, honor, and distinction designed by National Artist Napoleon Abueva, a citation scroll, and a gift check of 10,000.00 pesos.

10049
National Artist Award/International Artist Award
For recognition of a contribution to the advancement of the arts and of the culture of the Philippines. Awards are given in the categories of national artist and international artist. A monetary award, a medal, medical and hospitalization benefits, and a place of honor in state and national ceremonies are awarded annually. Established in 1972.

10050
Nutrition Foundation of the Philippines
107 Eulogio Rodriguez, Sr. Blvd.
Quezon City 1102, Philippines
Phone: 711 3980
Fax: 711 3980

10051
Dr. Juan Salcedo, Jr. Memorial Lecturer
For recognition of contributions to nutrition and allied fields. Individuals who are eminent in nutrition and allied fields are eligible for selection by the Board of Trustees. A monetary prize and a plaque are awarded annually. Established in 1985 in honor of Dr. Juan S. Salcedo, Jr., national scientist and founder of the Foundation.

10052
Carlos Palanca Foundation and La Tondena, Inc.
Carlos Palanca Memorial Awards for
Literature
Ground Floor, CPJ Bldg.
105 Carlos Palanca, Jr. St., Legaspi
Village
Makati, Metro Manila, Philippines
Phone: 2 8183681
Fax: 2 8174045

10053
Don Carlos Palanca Memorial Awards for Literature
For recognition of outstanding novels, short stories, poetry, essays, one-act plays, three-act plays, short stories for children, teleplays, and screenplays written in the English and Pilipino languages. Filipino citizens and Philippine publishers may submit entries by May 31. Monetary prizes and certificates are awarded for first, second and third prize annually on September 1. Established in 1951 to honor Don Carlos Palanca (1869-1950), businessman, philanthropist and a staunch advocate of education for Chinese youth.

10054
Philippine Numismatic and Antiquarian Society
Address unknown.

10055
Bantug Award
This, the highest award in Philippine numismatics, is given for recognition of outstanding achievements contributing to the development and enhancement of Philippine numismatics. A trophy is awarded.

10056
Philippines
Department of Science and Technology
Science Education Institute
Bicutan, Taguig
PO Box 1412
Metro Manila, Philippines
Phone: 2 8221333
Fax: 2 8221924

10057
Gawad AGKATEK (Agham, Kapaligiran at Teknolohiya)
To strengthen the role of science clubs in the promotion of public understanding of science, technology, and environment (STE) in the community and to encourage science club members to initiate/undertake community-based projects on STE. Cash prizes and trophies are awarded annually.

10058
The Outstanding Youth Science Researchers
To recognize Philippine youth under the age of 21 who demonstrate scientific talent with constructive and innovative creativity and to encourage pursuit of research and development. Competitors are screened from a series of Science Fairs held at the municipal, provincial, city, regional and national levels. Only the First Place winners qualify for the next higher level of competition. The following National prizes are

awarded in the elementary, secondary and college categories: monetary prizes to the top three winners; medals to all the national finalists; trophies to the top three winners; plaques of participation to schools of the top three winners; plaques of recognition to the advisers of the top three winners. In addition, the APPROTECH ASIA Special Award is given by APPROTECH ASIA in support of projects which are shown to promote or improve environmental preservation, protection and management. Awarded annually. Established in 1969 by the Science Foundation of the Philippines. Co-sponsored by the Philippines - Department of Education, Culture and Sports, and the Science Education Institute and Filipinas Shell Foundation. Formerly: (1983) The Outstanding Young Scientists (TOYS).

10059

Philippine Mathematical Olympiad
To recognize secondary students with mathematical talents. Certificates of achievement, monetary prizes, trophies, medals, and plaques are awarded bi-annually. Established in 1984. Jointly sponsored by the Department of Science and Technology through the Science Education Institute, the Department of Education, Culture, and Sports, and the Mathematical Society of the Philippines.

10060

Philippine Physics Olympiad
To recognize Philippine secondary school students with talent in physics and to stimulate the improvement of physics education. Certificates of merit, monetary prizes, trophies, medals, and plaques are awarded bi-annually. Established in 1992. Sponsored jointly by the Department of Science and Technology through the Science Education Institute, the Department of Education, Culture, and Sports, and the Samahang Pisika ng Pilipinas.

10061

Dr. Juan S. Salcedo Jr. Science Education Award
For recognition of outstanding contributions made by science or mathematics teachers or supervisors in advancing science/mathematics instruction in the areas of research, development of instructional materials, and teaching/learning aids, use of innovative teaching strategies, and meaningful involvement in professional activities that contributed to the promotion of science and technology consciousness. Filipino citizens who teach full-time science or math in the elementary or secondary level in any public or government-recognized private school in the country, may be nominated by the school administrator. At the college level, nomination is limited to institutions offering science/math teacher education degree programs. Monetary prizes, a Presidential Trophy and certificates of recognition for the nominating school are awarded annually. Established in 1985 in honor of Dr. Juan S. Salcedo Jr., a national scientist. Sponsored by Philippines - Department of Science and Technology and the Boto-Balani Foundations, Inc., in cooperation with the Philippines - Department of Education, Culture, and Sports. Formerly: (1990) Search for Outstanding Contributions to Science Education.

10062

South East Asia Iron and Steel Institute
Ortigas Bldg., Rm. 507
Ortigas Ave.
Pasig, Metro Manila, Philippines
Phone: 2 6315782
Fax: 2 6315781

10063

Friends of SEAISI Award
To recognize contributions to the development of the iron and steel industry in the region and of the Institute. Former chairmen who served full term, contributed to the advancement of SEAISI and played a promotional role are eligible. A medal and benefits as members at conferences are awarded. Established in 1980.

10064

Mt. Newman Iron Ore Award
For recognition of a technical paper on the subject of iron and steel presented during the SEAISI conference. The paper must be written by a non-expatriate from a SEAISI member country to be considered. A monetary prize and a plaque are awarded annually. Established in 1979. Sponsored by the Mt. Newman Iron Ore Project.

Poland

10065

Frederic Chopin Society
(Towarzystwo im. Fryderyka Chopina w Warszawie)
ul. Okolnik 1
PL-00-368 Warsaw, Poland
Phone: 22 275471
Fax: 22 279599

10066

Grand Prix du Disque Frederic Chopin
To recognize an outstanding recording of a work by Chopin. Medals and diplomas are awarded biennially. Established in 1985.

10067

International Frederic Chopin Piano Competition
To recognize the best artistic interpretation of the music of Chopin and to encourage professional development. Pianists of all nationalities between 18 and 30 years of age may apply by April 1, 1995 for the next competition. The following prizes are awarded: first prize - 150 million zlotys and a gold medal; second prize - 100 million zlotys and a silver medal; third prize - 75 million zlotys and a bronze medal; fourth prize - 50 million zlotys; fifth prize - 40 million zlotys; sixth prize - 30 million zlotys; Award for Best Performance of a Polonaise - 20 million zlotys; Polish Radio Award for the Best Performance of Mazurkas - 20 million zlotys; and National Philharmonic Award for the Best Performance of a Concerto - 20 million zlotys. Awards of 25 million zlotys are presented to the four best competitors in the third stage not admitted to the final. Competitors in the second stage not admitted to the third stage are awarded diplomas. Additional awards sponsored by private individuals from Poland and other countries and by institutions are presented. Awarded every five years at the National Philharmonic Hall. Established in 1927 by Professor Jerzy Zurawlew in memory of Frederic Chopin. Co-sponsored by Poland - Ministry of Culture and Arts.

10068

Cracow International Festival of Short Films
ul. Mazowiecka 6/8
PO Box 127
PL-00-950 Warsaw, Poland
Phone: 22 26 40 51

10069

Cracow International Festival of Short Films
For recognition of short films of all kinds, especially those which, in their human, social and artistic aspects, reveal the changes, trends and achievements of the 20th century. The following prizes are awarded: (1) Grand Prix - a Golden Dragon statuette and 40,000 zlotys for the best film; (2) two Special Prizes - Golden Dragon statuettes and 30,000 zlotys each; (3) four Main Prizes - Silver dragon statuettes and monetary prizes of 25,000 zlotys each; (4) three Bronze Dragon statuettes and 15,000 zlotys; (5) a silver medal of the International Committee for the Diffusion of Arts and Literature through the Cinema (CIDALC) - for the best short film; and (6) International Federation of Cinematographic Press (FIPRESCI Diploma) - for the best short. Awarded annually in June. Established in 1961. Sponsored by the Ministry of Culture and Art and the City Council of Cracow.

10070

International Association of Teachers of German
(Internationale Deutschlehrerverband)
Adam-Mickiewicz-Universitet Poznan
Uniwersytet im. Adama Mickiewicza
H. Wieniawskiego 1
PL-61-712 Poznan, Poland
Phone: 61 23 25 8°
Fax: 61 5°

10071

Ehrenmitgliedschaft im IDV
For recognition of achievement in developing the association. A diploma is awarded at the convention every three years. Established in 1974.

10072

**International Henryk Wieniawski Competitions
(Miedzynarodowe Konkursy Im. Henryka Wieniawskiego)**
ul. Swietoslawska 7
PL-61-840 Poznan, Poland
Phone: 61 52 26 42
Fax: 61 52 26 42

10073

International Henryk Wieniawski Composers Competition
To recognize a composer for the best violin compositions. Composers of all nationalities and ages are eligible. Awards are presented in two categories: (1) compositions for violin and orchestra; and (2) compositions for violin solo or with an accompanying instrument, or violin and any electro-acoustic instrument. Monetary prizes are awarded every five years. Established in 1956.

10074

International Henryk Wieniawski Violin Competition
To recognize a violinist for the best violin performance. Violinists of all nationalities who are under 30 years of age are eligible. Monetary awards for the six main prizes and medals are presented every five years. Established in 1935.

10075

International Henryk Wieniawski Violinmakers Competition
To encourage creative contributions to the tradition of violin making. Violin makers of all ages and nationalities are eligible. Monetary awards totaling 3,500,000 zlotys are presented every five years. Additional awards are presented, including medals presented by violin makers' unions. The violin maker possessing the most outstanding artistic individuality is awarded a Golden Groblicz by the National Museum of Poznan. Established in 1957 by the Henryk Wieniawski Music Society in Poznan.

10076

**International Print Triennial
(Miedzynarodowe Triennale Grafiki)**
Vl. Dunajewskiego 2/6
PL-31-133 Krakow, Poland
Phone: 12 221903
Fax: 12 217123

Formerly: (1988) International Print Biennale.

10077

**International Print Triennial
(Miedzynarodowe Triennale Grafiki)**
For recognition of outstanding prints. Monetary awards and medals are presented for the Grand Prix and First, Second and Third Prize. Awarded triennially. Established in 1966. Sponsored by the Ministry of Culture and Art. Formerly: International Print Biennale.

10078

**Lublin Scientific Society
(Lubelskie Towarzystwo Naukowe)**
Pl. Litewski 2
PL-20-080 Lublin, Poland
Phone: 81 21300

10079

Honorary Member
For recognition in the field of science. Honorary membership is awarded when merited.

10080

**Modern Language Association of Poland
(Polskie Towarzystwo Neofilologiczne)**
ul. Mielzynskiego 27/29
PL-61-725 Poznan, Poland
Phone: 61 532 682

10081

**Honorary Member
(Czlonkostwo Honorowe)**
To promote foreign language teaching in Poland and for contributions to PTN activities. Selection is by nomination. A medal is awarded at the convention. Established in 1986.

10082

**Prof. Ludwik Zabrocki Medal
(Medal im. prof. Ludwika Zabrockiego)**
To promote foreign language teaching in Poland and for contributions to PTN activities. Selection is by nomination. A medal is awarded at the convention. Established in 1986 in honor of Prof. Ludwik Zabrocki.

10083

**Pax Association
(Stowarzyszenie Pax)**
c/o Pax Publishing Institute
ul. Chocimska 8/10
PL-00 791 Warsaw, Poland

10084

Pietrzak Award
For recognition of outstanding achievements in the fields of literature, journalism, criticism, film, fine arts, theatre, architecture and science. Polish and foreign artists, writers and scientists whose work contributes to peace in the world are eligible. Monetary prizes are awarded annually. Established in 1948 by Pax Association and the Pax Publishing Institute (Instytut Wydawniczy Paz).

10085

**Photographic Society of Poznan
(Poznanskie Towarzystwo Fotograficzne)**
Organizing Committee
ul. Paderewskiego 7
PL-61-770 Poznan, Poland

10086

International Art Photography Exhibition "Foto Expo"
For recognition of the best achievements of photographic art. Both professional and amateur photographers may submit photographs in three sections: (1) black and white photographs - not more than four pictures, dimensions from 24x30 up to 40x50cm; (2) color photographs - not more than four pictures, dimensions 24x30cm or larger; and (3) series - not more than six photographs but regarded as one unit. The following awards are presented: (1) Grand Prix; (2) Gold Medal; (3) Silver Medal; (4) Bronze Medal; and (5) FIAP Medals. The Winner of the Grand Prix and the Medallists are invited to Poznan, and the organizers cover all costs of staying, excluding traveling costs. Awarded biennially. Established in 1967. Co-sponsored by The Department of Culture and Art and the City Council of the Town of Poznan.

10087

**Poland
Ministry of Culture and Art
(Poland
Ministerstwo Kultury i Sztuki)**
ul. Krakowskie Przedmiescie 15/17
PL-00-071 Warsaw, Poland
Phone: 4822 200231
Fax: 4822 261922

10088
Badge for the Protection of Monuments
To recognize individuals for outstanding contributions in the conservation of monuments. Honorable distinction and silver and golden badges are awarded when merited. Established by the Minister of Culture in 1963.

10089
Cultural Merit Award
(Zasluzony Dzialacz Kultury)
For recognition of meritorious work in the field of culture. Polish citizens are eligible. A badge is awarded when merited. Established in 1993 by the Council of Ministers.

10090
Medal for Outstanding Sports Achievements
(Medal Za Wybitne Osiagniecia Sportowe)
To recognize individuals for outstanding sport's achievements. Established in 1984. Sponsored by the Director of the Physical Culture and Tourism Agency.

10091
Merit of Polish Culture Badge
For recognition of the popularization of Polish culture and art abroad and contributions to the development of cultural relations with Poland. Foreigners living abroad, employees of foreign diplomatic missions and foreign cultural and scientific institutions in Poland, cultural activists, and unions of foreigners of Polish origin are eligible. A badge is awarded when merited. Established in 1969 by the Council of Ministers. Since the name and the emblem of the Polish State changed, the new project of the badge has been submitted to the Council of Ministers.

10092
Poland
Ministry of National Defense Publishing House
(Poland
Wydawnictwo Ministerstwa Obrony Narodowej)
ul. Grzybowska 77
PL-00-950 Warsaw, Poland   Phone: 22 20 12 61

10093
Medal for Armed Forces in the Service of the Fatherland
(Sily Zbrojne w Sluzbie Ojczyzny)
To recognize 25, 15, and 5 years of exemplary service in the Polish Army.

10094
Medal for Participation in the Battle for Berlin
(Medal Za Udzial w Walkach o Berlin)
To recognize participants in the Battle for Berlin. Established in 1966.

10095
Minister of National Defense Prize
(Nagroda Ministra Obrony Narodowej)
For recognition of the best books on the subjects of military history, strategy, art of operation, tactics, and military techniques. Books may be documentary papers, memoirs, or belles-lettres. A monetary prize and a diploma are awarded. Established in 1958.

10096
Poland
Office of the President
(Poland
Kancelaria Prezydenta)
ul. Wiejska 10   Phone: 22 6284785
PL-00-902 Warsaw, Poland   Fax: 22 216180

10097
Anniversary of People's Poland Awards
(Medal Polski Ludowej)
To recognize individuals who contributed to the strengthening of the national economy and culture. Awarded on the 10th, 30th, and 40th anniversaries of the people's Poland. Established in 1943. (Discontinued in 1992)

10098
Cross for Military Action of the Polish Armed Forces in the West
(Krzyz Czynu Bojowego Polskich Sil Zbrojnych na Zachodzie)
To recognize participants of military actions waged by the Polish Armed Forces in the West in the years 1939-1945. Established in 1989.

10099
Cross for Participation in the War of 1918-1921
(Krzyz Za Udzial w Wojnie 1918-1921)
To recognize individuals whose service in the years 1918-1921 helped to establish the independence of Poland. Established in 1990.

10100
Cross of Auschwitz
(Krzyz Oswiecimski)
To recognize individuals who had been imprisoned in Nazi concentration camps. Established in 1985.

10101
Cross of Merit
(Krzyz Zaslugi)
For recognition of accomplishments in professional work and social activity. Gold, silver, and bronze crosses are awarded when merited. Established in 1923.

10102
Cross of Merit for Bravery
(Krzyz Zaslugi za Dzielnosc)
For recognition of accomplishments by soldier and paramilitary organization members and outstanding bravery during difficult conditions. A cross is awarded when merited. Established in 1928.

10103
Cross of Merit with Swords
(Krzyz Zaslugi z Mieczami)
For recognition of heroism and bravery during the war but not on the field of battle. Gold, silver, and bronze crosses are awarded when merited. Established in 1942.

10104
Cross of the Battle of Lenino
(Krzyz Bitwy pod Lenino)
To recognize participants in the Battle of Lenino. Established in 1988.

10105
Cross of the Warsaw Uprising
(Warszawski Krzyz Powstanczy)
To recognize participants in the Warsaw Uprising of 1944. Established in 1981.

10106
Cross of Valour
(Krzyz Walecznych)
To recognize individuals for courage on the battle field. Established in 1920.

10107
Home Army Cross
(Krzyz Armii Krajowej)
To recognize soldiers of the Home Army. Established in 1966.

10108

Medal for Long Marital Life
(Medal Za Dlugoletnie Pozycie Malzenskie)
To recognize couples who have been happily married for 50 years. A medal is awarded when merited. Established in 1960.

10109

Medal for Merit in Action
(Medal Zasluzonym na Polu Chwaly)
To recognize individual courage on the field of battle. Gold, silver, and bronze medals are awarded. Established in 1943 by the Command of the Tadeusz Kosciuszko 1st Infantry Division. (Discontinued in 1992)

10110

Medal for Participation in the War of 1939
(Medal Za Udzial w Wojnie Obronnej 1939)
To recognize individuals who participated in the defensive war against the Nazis from September 1, 1939 to October 6, 1939. Established in 1981.

10111

Medal for Self-Sacrifice and Courage
(Medal Za Ofiarnosc i Odwage)
To recognize individuals who have risked their lives saving others from drowning, helped victims of natural disasters and fires, or have saved the property of others from destruction. A medal is awarded when merited. Established in 1960.

10112

Medal for the Services to the Country's Defense
(Za Zaslugi dla Obronnosci Kraju)
To recognize individuals who have contributed to the strengthening and development of Poland's defensive capability.

10113

Medal for Your Freedom and Ours
(Medal Za Wasza Wolnosc i Nasza)
To recognize those who fought in the army of the Spanish Republic in the years 1936-39 and those who showed outstanding assistance to them. Established in 1956. (Discontinued in 1992)

10114

Medal of Commission of National Education
(Medal Komisji Edukacji Narodowej)
To recognize contributions to education, especially in the following fields: pedagogical sciences, art and books for children and youth, and didactic activity. Established in 1991.

10115

Military Decorations
To recognize participants in the victorious offensive of the Polish and Soviet armies, and of the various battles and campaigns of the Second World War. The following medals were presented: Medal for Warsaw (Medal za Warszawe) 1939-1945 and Medal for the Odra, Nysa and Baltic Sea (Medal za Odre, Nyse, Batlyk), established in 1945.

10116

National Armed Act Cross
(Krzyz Narodowego Czynu Zbrojnego)
To recognize soldiers of the National Armed Forces. Established in 1944.

10117

Order of Merit of the Republic of Poland
(Order Zaslugi Rzeczypospolitej Polskiej)
For recognition of outstanding political, social, economic, or cultural activities that have contributed to the development of international cooperation and friendship between Poland and other nations. Foreign citizens or Poles living abroad are eligible. A medal is awarded when merited. Established in 1974.

10118

Order of the Cross of Grunwald
(Order Krzyza Grunwaldu)
For recognition of military service during the war and for a contribution to the creation and development of the Armed Forces of the Polish People's Republic. A medal in the form of a cross was awarded in three classes when merited. Established in 1944. (Discontinued in 1992)

10119

Order of the Rebirth of Poland
(Order Odrodzenia Polski)
For recognition of important contributions in the following fields: education, science, culture and arts, national economy, governmental service, and social activity. A medal is awarded in five classes when merited. Established in 1921.

10120

Partisans' Cross
(Krzyz Partyzancki)
To recognize participation in the guerrilla warfare waged against the Nazis.

10121

Peasantry Batallion Cross
(Krzyz Batalonow Chlopskich)
To recognize soldiers of peasantry military organizations. Established in 1989.

10122

Silesian Insurrectionary Cross
(Slaski Krzyz Powstanczy)
To recognize individuals for participation in the Silesian risings of 1919-21 or in the underground movement in Silesia in the years 1939-45. Established in 1946.

10123

War Order Virtuti Militari
(Order Wojenny Virtuti Militari)
For recognition of outstanding heroism and bravery during the war and for distinguished military merit. A cross is awarded in five classes when merited. Established in 1792 by King Stanislav August Poniatowski. First awarded in 1792 to Prince Josef Poniatowski and Tadeusz Kosciuszko.

10124

Wielkopolska Insurrectionary Cross
(Wielkopolski Krzyz Powstanczy)
To recognize participants in the Wielkopolska rising in the years 1918-19. Established in 1957.

10125

Poland
Office of the Prime Minister
(Poland
Urzad RADY Ministrow)
Al. Ujazdowskie 1/3
PL-00-583 Warsaw, Poland

10126

Polish Prime Minister Award for Literature for Children and Youth
To recognize an outstanding author of books for children and young people for his entire work. A monetary prize is awarded biennially. (Discontinued)

10127

Polish Academy of Sciences
(Polska Akademia Nauk)
Palac Kultury i Nauki
PL-00-901 Warsaw, Poland   Phone: 22 203380

10128
Scientific Secretary of the Polish Academy of Sciences Award
(Nagroda Sekretarza Naukowego Polskiej Akademii Nauk)
For recognition of achievement in the field of history. Selection is by nomination or application. A monetary prize is awarded annually. Established in 1982. Additional information is available from Instytut Historii, Rynek Starego Miasta, 29/31, 00 272 Warsaw, Poland.

10129
Polish Artistic Agency PAGART
International Song Festival Sopot
Impresariat Miedzynarodowego Festiwalu
 Piosenki
Pl. Zwyciestwa 9
PL-00-078 Warsaw, Poland   Phone: 22 26 09 95

10130
Sopot International Song Festival
To promote song as well as cultural exchange and friendship among nations. Singers and vocal-instrumental groups can take part in the festival when introduced by record companies, radio and TV organizations, and artist agencies. The participants are obliged to participate in two contests: (1) the contest of the Grand Prix of the Festival - SOPOT. Each performer or group is to sing two songs that are considered the hits of the season by the sponsoring institution. The well known melodies (light music standards) are excluded from the competition. The international jury awards prizes estimating artistic value of the song as well as its attraction and interpretation; and (2) the contest of the Amber Nightingale. Each performer or group is to sing one song by a Polish composer in any language (excluding Polish). The organizers will send the list of Polish songs to choose from. A Gala Concert with the participation of all the winners takes place in August. All festival concerts are broadcast by radio and TV and transmitted to the countries belonging to Intervision and Eurovision. Entries of the performers must be received by the announced deadline. The following prizes are awarded: (1) Grand Prix of SOPOT - the Amber Record and 200,000 zlotys; Second Prize - 100,000 zlotys; and (2) Amber Nightingale and 200,000 zlotys; Second Prize - 100,000 zlotys; and Third Prize - 50,000 zlotys. The winners of both contests receive the following monetary prizes: singers - soloists, 10,000 zlotys; group members, 7000 zlotys each; and the representatives of sponsoring institutions - 5000 zlotys. A Crystal Tuning Fork is granted for the best arrangement of a Polish song; a Special Prize is presented by the journalists covering the festival, and independent awards may be granted if approved by the Organizing Committee. Awarded annually. Established in 1963.

10131
Polish Association of Pediatric Surgeons
(Polskie Towarzystwo Chirurgow Dzieciecych)
ul. Inspektowa 21   Phone: 22 482925
PL-02-944 Warsaw, Poland   Fax: 22 152812

10132
Czlonek Honorowy
(Honorary Member)
For recognition of work for sick children. A plaque is awarded triennially at the convention of the Association. Established in 1967.

10133
Polish Chemical Society
(Polskie Towarzystwo Chemiczne)
ul. Freta 16
PL-00-227 Warsaw, Poland   Phone: 22 311304
                                     Fax: 2 6358556

10134
Jan Harabaszewski Medal
For recognition of outstanding contributions to the field of chemistry education. Nominees for the awards are named by the Presidium of General Council of the Society or by Division of Educational Chemistry. A medal is awarded annually. Established in 1989 in honor of Jan Harabaszewski, a Polish scientist.

10135
Honorary Membership
To recognize distinguished chemists, regardless of their nationality and affiliation, for outstanding scientific achievements and contributions to the development of the Society and chemistry in Poland. Nominees for the awards are named by the Presidium of General Council of the Society or by its regional councils and are determined by the General Assembly.

10136
Stanislaw Kostanecki Medal
For recognition of contributions to the fields of physical and inorganic chemistry. Nominees for the awards are named by the Presidium of General Council of the Society or by its regional councils.

10137
Polish Chemical Society Medal
In recognition of outstanding foreign chemists who have made significant contributions to science and/or technology and have strong ties with Polish chemical institutions, particularly academic. Awarded by the General Assembly of the Society.

10138
Jedrzej Sniadecki Medal
For recognition of superior scientific achievements. Nominees for the awards are named by the Presidium of General Council of the Society or by its regional councils.

10139
Jan Zawidzki Medal
For recognition of outstanding contributions to the fields of physical and inorganic chemistry. Nominees for the awards are named by the Presidium of General Council of the Society or by its regional councils.

10140
Polish Composers Union
(Zwiazek Kompozytorow Polskich)
                                     Phone: 22 31 17 41
Rynek Starego Miasta 27   Phone: 22 31 16 34
PL-00-272 Warsaw, Poland   Fax: 22 31 06 07

10141
Tadeusz Baird Memorial Competition for Young Composers
(Konkurs Mlodych Kompozytorow im. Tadeusza Bairda)
For recognition of outstanding young composers. In 1994, the composition was a piece for symphonic orcestra. Polish citizens who are 35 years of age or younger are eligible. Monetary prizes are awarded annually in November. Established in 1958 by the Board of the Polish Composers Union and renamed in 1990 in honor of Tadeusz Baird.

10142
Polish Composers Union Prize
(Nagroda Muzyczna Zwiazku Kompozytorow Polskich)
For recognition of outstanding achievements in creating and performing music, in musicology, and in organizing activities. Polish citizens are eligible. A monetary award and a diploma are presented annually in January. Established in 1949 by the Polish Composers Union to commemorate the liberation of Warsaw on January 17, 1945.

10143
Polish Film Festival
Piwna 22
PO Box Nr. 192   Phone: 58 315244
PL-80-831 Gdansk, Poland   Fax: 54 313744

10144
Gdansk Golden Lions
(Zlote Lwy Gdanskie)
To recognize the best polish film at the festival. Approximately twenty monetary awards and trophies given annually at the November festival. Established in 1974. Sponsored by Komitet Kinematografii - Warszawa, Urzad Wojewodzki - Gdansk, and Urzad Miasta - Gdynia.

10145
Polish Geographical Society
(Polskie Towarzystwo Geograficzne)
ul. Krakowskie Przedmiescie 30
PL-00-325 Warsaw, Poland
Phone: 22 261794
Fax: 22 267267

10146
Gold Award
(Zlota Odznaka)
For recognition of contribution to the Society. Society members or other persons or institutions are eligible. Badges are awarded annually. Established in 1968.

10147
Honorary Member
(Czlonkostwo Honorowe)
For recognition of outstanding achievements in the field of geography and geography education as well as contributions to the Society. Citizens of Poland and foreigners are eligible. A diploma is awarded annually. Established in 1918.

10148
Medal of the Polish Geographical Society
(Medal Polskiego Towarzystwa Geograficznego)
For recognition of contributions to developing and promoting geography and the Polish Geographical Society. Citizens of Poland and foreigners are eligible. A medal is awarded annually. Established in 1962.

10149
Polish Geological Society
(Polskie Towarzystwo Geologiczne)
Oleandry 2a
PL-30-063 Krakow, Poland
Phone: 12 332041

10150
Nagroda im. Henryka Swidzinskiego
(Henryk Swidzinski Award)
To stimulate geological research on the Carpathians and Holy Cross (Swiety Krzyz) Mountains. Scientists, excluding professors, who are under 40 years of age are eligible. A monetary award, a diploma, and honorable mention in *Annales Societatis Geologorum Poloniae* are awarded annually. Established in 1970 by Lucyna Swidzinski, widow of Professor Swidzinski, president of the Polish Geological Society.

10151
Nagroda im. Ludwika Zejsznera
(Ludwik Zejszner Prize)
This, the highest prize of the society, is presented in recognition of the best paper printed in *Annales Societatis Geologorum Poloniae*. A scientist who has not yet received the title of professor is eligible. A monetary award, a diploma, and honorable mention in the annals are awarded annually. Established in 1964 in memory of Ludwik Zejszner, an outstanding Polish geologist of the nineteenth century. Sponsored by the Polish Academy of Sciences.

10152
Polish Librarians Association
(Stowarzyszenie Bibliotekarzy Polskich)
ul. Konopczynskiego 5/7
PL-00-953 Warsaw, Poland
Phone: 22 275296

10153
Literary Prize of PLA
(Nagroda Literacka SBP)
For recognition of work that has had an impact on publishing activity. Outstanding works of fiction and nonfiction are considered. Opinions of the local branches of PLA are sought in the selection process. A plaque, diploma and registration of the honored book are awarded annually. Established in 1983.

10154
Adam Lysakowski Scientific Prize
(Nagroda Naukowa im. Adama Lysakowskiego)
To encourage library and information science in Poland. Research in practical current problems may be nominated for the awards. A plaque and a diploma are awarded annually. Established in 1983 in memory of Adam Lysakowski, an outstanding Polish librarian (1895-1952).

10155
Polish Mathematical Society
(Polskie Towarzystwo Mathematyczne)
ul. Sniadeckich 8
PL-00-950 Warsaw, Poland
Phone: 22 29 95 92

10156
Banach Award
(Nagrody im. S. Banacha)
For recognition of achievement in mathematics. Polish citizens may apply by November 30. A monetary prize is awarded annually. Established in 1946.

10157
Mazurkiewicz Award
(Nagrody im. S. Mazurkiewicza)
For recognition of achievement in mathematics. Polish citizens may apply by November 30. A monetary prize is awarded annually. Established in 1946.

10158
Sierpinski Award
(Nagrody im. W. Sierpinskiego)
For recognition of achievement in mathematics. Polish citizens may apply by November 30. A monetary prize is awarded annually. Established in 1971.

10159
Zaremba Award
(Nagrody im. S. Zaremby)
For recognition in mathematics. Polish citizens may apply by November 30. A monetary prize is awarded annually. Established in 1946.

10160
Polish Medical Society of Radiology
(Polskie Lekarskie Towarzystwo Radiologiczne)
ul. Banacha 1a
PL-02-097 Warsaw, Poland
Phone: 22 223005
Fax: 22 223005

10161
Honorary Member
For recognition of contributions to radiology. Members are selected for honorary membership when merited.

10162
Scientific Award in the Field of Radiology
(Nagroda naukowa w dziedzinie radiologii)
For recognition of research or a series of researches in the field of roentgenology, nuclear medicine, and other radiological imaging. Individual or collective scientific papers published between the congresses of the society are eligible for consideration. A monetary prize and publication in the society magazine, the *Polish Review of Radiology*, are awarded triennially (biennially before 1977) at the convention. Established in 1965.

10163
Polish Musicians Association
(Stowarzyszenie Polskich Artystow Muzykow)
ul. Krucza 24/26
PL-00-526 Warsaw, Poland   Phone: 22 6212802

10164
International Warsaw Autumn Festival of Contemporary Music
To recognize individuals at the annual music festival. The following awards are presented: Orpheus Award (Orfeusz) - for the best performance of a contemporary Polish musical composition by soloists, choirs, orchestras, or conductors, a bronze statuette of Orpheus is awarded; the Gold Award (Zlota Odznaka Spam) - for the most meritorious member of the Polish Musicians Association a medal is awarded; and the Annual Award (Doroczna Nagroda Spam) - for promotion of music culture in Poland. A monetary award is presented. Established in 1960.

10165
Polish Nurses Association
(Polskie Towarzystwo Pielegniarskie)
ul Koszykowa 8
PL-00-564 Warsaw, Poland   Phone: 22 21 50 66

10166
Honour Distinctions
To recognize members for contributions to the Association; and to recognize individuals and institutions outside the Polish Nurses Association for contributions to the nursing profession. From 1974 through 1988, 1,112 distinctions have been awarded. In addition, members may be awarded regional distinctions, state distinctions (Chivalry Cross of the Order of Polish State Renascence), and distinctions granted by the Ministry of Health for exemplary work in health promotion and service. Established in 1974.

10167
Polish PEN Club
(Polshi PEN Club)
Krakowskie Przedmiescie 87/89   Phone: 22 265784
PL-00-078 Warsaw, Poland   Fax: 22 260589

10168
Polish PEN Centre Prizes
For recognition of outstanding contributions to Polish literature. The following prizes are awarded: prize for translators of Polish literature into foreign languages, established in 1948; prize for translators of foreign literature into Polish, established in 1949; Jan Parandowski Prize, established in 1988; literary prize for editors, established in 1978; Ksawery Pruszynski Prize, established in 1988; Jan Strzelecki Prize, established in 1990; Commander Kazimierz Szczesny Prize, established in 1989; and special prize, established in 1989.

10169
Polish Phonetic Association
(Polskie Towarzystwo Fonetyczne)
ul. Noskowskiego 10   Phone: 61 483374
PL-61-704 Poznan, Poland   Fax: 61 520671

10170
Polish Phonetic Association Award
(Nagroda Polskiego Towarzystwa Fonetycznego)
For recognition of outstanding dissertations in the field of phonetics. Members of the Society are eligible. A monetary award and a diploma are awarded biennially. Established in 1984. The next award is scheduled for 1994.

10171
Polish Physical Society
(Polskie Towarzystwo Fizyczne)
ul. Hoza 69   Phone: 2 6212668
PL-00-681 Warsaw, Poland   Fax: 2 6212668

10172
Marian Smoluchowski Medal
(Medal Mariana Smoluchowskiego)
For recognition of a splendid contribution to science and to international scientific cooperation in physics. Scientists may be nominated. A medal and a special diploma in Polish and Latin are awarded annually when merited. Established in 1967 in memory of Marian Smoluchowski, a Polish physicist famous for his achievements in the kinetic theory of matter.

10173
Polish Psychological Association
(Polskie Towarzystwo Psychologiczne)
ul. Stawki 5/7   Phone: 22 311368
PL-00-183 Warsaw, Poland   Fax: 22 311368

10174
Professor Stefan Blachowski Award
(Nagroda im. Profesora Stefana Blachowskiego)
To encourage the professional development of young psychologists. Members of the Association who are no more than 35 years of age are eligible. A monetary prize is awarded annually. Established in 1963 in honor of Professor Stefan Blachowski who renewed the activity of the Association after World War II.

10175
Prof. Bohdan Zawadzki Award
(Nagroda im. Bohdana Zawadzkiego)
To encourage development of applied psychology all over the country and to encourage psychologists to establish new ways of psychological assistance. Members of the Association are eligible. A monetary prize is awarded annually. Established in 1988.

10176
Polish Rheumatological Society
(Polskie Towarzystwo Reumatologiczne)
ul. Spartanska 1
PL-02-637 Warsaw, Poland   Phone: 22 44 42 41

10177
Polish Rheumatological Society Award
(Nagroda Polskiego Towarzystwa Reumatologicznego)
For recognition of contributions to rheumatology. Scientific papers or contributions to improved patient care are considered. A monetary award is presented every four years at the convention. Established in 1983.

10178
Polish Section of the International Board on Books for Young People
(Polska Sekcja IBBY)
Hipoteczna 2
PL-00-950 Warsaw, Poland   Phone: 22 27 58 82

10179
Janusz Korczak Literary Award
(Nagroda literacka im. Janusza Korczaka)
For recognition of achievement in the human and moral field in literature for or about young people. Selection is by international nomination. A monetary prize and a medal are awarded biennially. Established in honor of Dr. Janusz Korczak.

10180
Polish Society for Commodity Science
(Polskie Towarzystwo Towaroznawcze)
ul. Sienkiewicza 4   Phone: 12 33 08 21
PL-30-033 Krakow, Poland   Fax: 12 33 57 33

10181
Honorary Member
For recognition of a special activity and achievements in the development of commodity science, particularly in raising the quality of goods. A diploma is awarded every five years. Established in 1970.

10182
Polish Society for Contemporary Music
ul. Mazowiecka 11   Phone: 22 27 69 81
PL-00-052 Warsaw, Poland   Fax: 22 27 78 04

10183
International Composers Competition Kazimierz Serocki
To recognize a work for chamber orchestra with or without a soloist. Open to composers of all nationalities and with no age limits. Works for a chamber orchestra of 15 to 30 performers, lasting from 10 to 25 minutes, may be submitted by November 30, 1995 for the 1996 competition. Works submitted should not have been either published or performed before the end of the competition. A monetary award of Moeck Verlag is 3000 DM. Amount of the rest of awards will be published. Established in 1984.

10184
Polish Society of Endocrinology
(Polskie Towarzystwo Endokrynologizne)
ul. Starynkiewicza 3
PL-02-015 Warsaw, Poland   Phone: 22 28 11 59

10185
Honorary Member
(Czlonkostwo Honorowe)
To recognize achievements in the field of experimental and clinical endocrinology and contributions to the development of endocrinology in Poland. Nominations by the Society members are considered by the Executive Committee and accepted by the members of the General Assembly. A special diploma is awarded triennially on the occasion of the Society's scientific meeting. Established in 1962.

10186
Polish Society of Epidemiologists and Infectionists
(Polskie Towarzystwo Epidemiologow i Lekarzy Chorob Zakaznych)
c/o National Institute of Hygiene
ul. Chocimska 24   Phone: 22 49 77 02
PL-00-791 Warsaw, Poland   Fax: 22 49 74 84

10187
Professor Jozef Kostrzewski Award
(Nagroda im. Jozefa Kostrzewskiego)
For recognition of achievement in epidemiology and infectious diseases. Members of the Society are eligible. Monetary prizes are awarded triennially. Established in 1954 in honor of Professor Jozef Kostrzewski.

10188
Professor Feliks Przesmycki Award
(Nagroda im. Professor Feliksa Przesmyckiego)
For recognition of achievement in virology and clinical virology of neuroinfections. Members of the Society are eligible. Monetary prizes are awarded triennially. Established in 1975 by the family foundation of Professor Feliks Przesmycki in honor of Professor Feliks Przesmycki.

10189
Polish Society of Hygiene
(Polskie Towarzystwo Higieniczne)
ul. Karowa 31   Phone: 22 266320
PL-00-324 Warsaw, Poland   Fax: 22 266320

Formerly: (1934) Warszawskie Towarzystwo Higieniczne.

10190
Honorary Member
For recognition of contributions to the field of hygiene and public health. Members of the Society may be nominated for honorary membership annually. Established in 1978.

10191
Medal: 80 Years of the Polish Society of Hygiene
(Medal: 80 lat PTH)
For recognition of contributions to the field of hygiene and public health. Members of the Society may be nominated. A medal is awarded annually. Established in 1978 to commemorate the 80th anniversary of the Society.

10192
Medal Jubilee: One Hundred Years of the PSH
(Medal Jubileuszowy: 100 lat PTH)
For recognition of contributions to the field of hygiene and public health. Members of the Society may be nominated. A medal is awarded annually. Established in 1994 to commemorate the 100th anniversary of the Society.

10193
Medal Jubileuszowy: 90 Lat PTH
For recognition of contributions to the field of hygiene and public health. Members of the Society may be nominated. A medal is awarded annually. Established in 1988 to commemorate the 90th anniversary of the Society.

10194
One Hundred Years of the Periodical *Health* Medal
(100-lecie czasopisma *Zdrowie*)
For recognition of contributions to the field of hygiene and public health. Members of the Society may be nominated. Established in 1985.

10195
Plaques
For recognition of contributions to the field of hygiene and public health. Members of the Society may be nominated. Gold and silver plaques are awarded annually. Established in 1978.

10196
Polish Society of Veterinary Science
(Polskie towarzystwo Nauk Weterynaryjnych)
ulica Grochowska 272
PL-03-849 Warsaw, Poland   Phone: 22 103397

10197
Polish Society of Veterinary Science Awards
To recognize veterinarians in Poland who work towards excellence in veterinary medicine. Awards are presented.

10198
Polish Sociological Association
(Polskie Towarzystwo Socjologiczne)
Nowy Swiat 72, p. 216
PL-00-330 Warsaw, Poland   Phone: 22 26 77 37

10199
Honorary Member
(Czlonek Honorowy)
For recognition of outstanding sociologists. A Foreign Honorary Member award may also be awarded to foreign sociologists. A diploma is awarded irregularly. Established in 1977.

10200
Stanislaw Ossowski Award
(Nagroda im. Stanislawa Ossowskiego)
For recognition of the best book(s) in the field of sociology by Polish authors published in the five years preceding the year for which the award is given. Younger sociologists are given preference. A monetary prize and a diploma are awarded annually at the Convention of the Association. Established in 1973 in honor of Stanislaw Ossowski.

10201
Polish Theological Association in Cracow
(Polskie Towarzystwo Teologiczne w Krakowie)
ul. Augustianska 7
PL-31-064 Krakow, Poland   Phone: 12 66 25 07

10202
Honorary Life Member
(Czlonek honorowy dozywotni)
For recognition of a contribution in the field of theology. Members of the Society are eligible. A medal and a plaque are awarded at the convention. Established in 1978.

10203
Secretariat of the Committee of State Prizes
(Komitet Nagrod Panstwowych)
Palac Kultury i Nauki
PL-00-901 Warsaw, Poland   Phone: 22 20 26 29

10204
State Prize
(Nagroda Panstwowa)
To promote and stimulate the development of exact natural and social sciences, medicine, technology, agriculture, literature and arts in Poland. Nominations may be sent to the Committee of State Prizes by December 15 by persons entitled in the establishing act. Monetary prizes, gold or silver medals, and certificates are awarded biennially. Established in 1948 by the Ministers Committee for Culture Affairs - Council of Ministers.

10205
Society of Authors (ZAiKS)
(Stowarzyszenie Autorow (ZAiKS))
ul. Hipoteczna 2   Phone: 22 276061
PL-00-092 Warsaw, Poland   Fax: 22 6351347

10206
Award for the Promotion of Polish Entertainment Creativity
(Nagroda za popularyzacje polskiej tworczosci rozrywkowej)
To encourage and to recognize the popularization of Polish creativity in the entertainment field in Poland and abroad. The award is presented to Polish citizens and foreigners. A monetary award and diploma are awarded annually. Established in 1990.

10207
Karol Malcuzynski Award
(Nagroda imienia Karola Malcuzynskiego)
For recognition of creativity by residents of Warsaw in the fields of literature, publicity, film, television, and photography. A monetary award and a diploma are awarded biennially on the anniversary of the death of Mr. Malcuzynski. Established in 1988 in memory of Karol Malcuzynski, former president of the Council of ZAiKS and famous publicist and resident of Warsaw.

10208
ZAiKS Awards for Translators
To recognize translators for a particular literary work or for their entire body of work. Awards are presented in two categories: polish translators into foreign languages and foreign translators into Polish (ZAiKS Literary Award for Translation's Output). Monetary prizes of 120,000 zlotys are awarded annually. Established in 1966 for foreign translators and in 1972 for Polish translators.

10209
Society of Friends of the Polish Language
(Towarzystwo Milosnikow Jezyka Polskiego)
ul. Straszewskiego 27, II p.
PL-31-113 Krakow, Poland   Phone: 12 22 26 99

10210
Honorary Member
(Czlonkostwo Honorowe)
To recognize an individual for contributions toward popularizing learning about the Polish language. Awarded when merited.

10211
State Silesian Philharmonic Orchestra
(Panstwowa Filharmonia Slaska)
ul. A. Zawadzkiego 2
PL-40-084 Katowice, Poland   Phone: 32 58 98 85

10212
International Grzegorz Fitelberg Competition for Conductors in Katowice
(Miedzynarodowy Konkurs Dyrygentow im. Grzegorza Fitelberga)
To encourage professional development of conductors under 35 years of age. Monetary prizes and medals are awarded every four years. Established in 1979 by Prof. Karol Stryja in honor of Grzegorz Fitelberg, a famous Polish conductor. Sponsored by the Warsaw Ministry of Culture and the Arts.

10213
Warsaw Philharmonic
(Filharmonia Narodowa w Warszawie)
ul. Jasna 5   Phone: 22 268311
PL-00-950 Warsaw, Poland   Phone: 22 265617

10214
Witold Lutoslawski International Composers Competition
(Miedzynarodowy Konkurs Kompozytorski im-Witolda Lutoslawskiego)
To stimulate and promote music composition for symphony orchestra. Compositions may be submitted in the following categories: symphony

orchestra; choir and symphony orchestra; solo voice or voices and symphony orchestra; solo instrument or instruments and symphony orchestra; and choir, solo voice or voices and symphony orchestra. Composers of all ages and nationalities may submit scores by December 31. Pieces not performed in public and not rewarded at any other competition are eligible. The following monetary prizes are awarded biennially in odd-numbered years: 25,000,000 Zlotys - First prize; 20,000,000 Zlotys - Second prize; and 15,000,000 Zlotys - Third prize. Established in 1988. For more information contact the Secretary of the International Witold Lutoslawski Composer's Competition.

10215
Wloclawek Scientific Society
(Wloclawskie Towarzystwo Naukowe)
Pl. Wolnosci 1
PL-87-800 Wloclawek, Poland   Phone: 228 08

10216
Honorary Diploma
(Dyplom Honorowy)
For recognition of achievement in a field of science. Members of the Society are eligible. A diploma is awarded every four years at the convention. Established in 1984.

10217
Wroclaw International Triennial of Drawing
ul. Swidnicka 2/4   Phone: 71 31395
PL-50-067 Wroclaw, Poland   Fax: 71 447324

10218
Wroclaw International Trienniale of Drawing
(Miedzynarodowe Triennale Rysunku - Wroclaw)
To provide recognition for the best drawings submitted to the competition. Works should have been created during the preceding three years. The following monetary prizes are awarded: Grand Prix - 10 million zlotys; five equivalent prizes of 5 million zlotys each; and medals. Cosponsored by the Ministry of Culture and Art, Wroctaw Voivode, and Wroctaw Municipality.

10219
Wroclaw Scientific Society
(Wroclawskie Towarzystwo Naukowe)
ul. Rosenbergow 13
PL-51-616 Wroclaw, Poland   Phone: 22 48 40 61

10220
Honorary Member
For recognition of a special a contribution to science. Nomination by the general meeting of the Society is required. A diploma is awarded at the convention. Established in 1965.

Portugal

10221
Association of Latin Languages Allergologists and Immunologists
(Groupement des Allergologistes et Immunologistes de Langues Latines)
CAIC
Rua Sampaio e Pina 16-4th Fl.   Phone: 1 658202
P-1000 Lisbon, Portugal   Fax: 1 658202

10222
Association of Latin Languages Allergologists and Immunologists Award
To recognize medical doctors and holders of doctoral and master's degrees for exchanging and disseminating information on allergic and immunologic diseases. Awards are given at an annual conference in October.

10223
Camara Municipal de Coimbra
c/o Departamento de Cultura
Praca 8 de Maio   Phone: 39 22177
P-3000 Coimbra, Portugal   Phone: 39 22178

10224
Premio Literario Miguel Torga - Cidade de Coimbra
To encourage literary activity and young authors. To be considered, the literary work must be a work of fiction written in the Portuguese language and must also be original. A monetary prize of 400,000 escudos is awarded biennially in even-numbered years. Established in 1984 in honor of Miguel Torga, a writer and poet.

10225
CINANIMA - International Animated Film Festival
(CINANIMA - Festival Internacional de Cinema de Animacao)
Apartado 43   Phone: 2 724611
4501 Espinho Codex, Portugal   Fax: 2 726015

10226
CINANIMA
To encourage the development of and to recognize outstanding animated films. Films produced for cinema or televison in 35mm (optical sound), 16mm (optical or magnetic sound), and video (formats U-matic 3/4LB PAL, SECAM, NTSC, U-matic LB/SP, VHS multisystem, and Super VHS) made during the preceding two years are eligible. A trophy is presented in each of the following categories: best film under 5 minutes; best film between 5 and 10 minutes; best film between 10 and 40 minutes; best feature film; best advertising film; best didactic and informative film; best first film; best experimental film; and best film for children and youth. The following prizes are awarded annually: Grand Prix of the Festival - PTE 500,000; Institute of Youth Prize - PTE 250,000; City of Espinho - PTE 250,000; and Young Portuguese Director, sponsored by the Institute of Youth - PTE 200,000. Established in 1977 by NASCENTE - Cooperative Society with Cultural Purposes.

10227
Vianna da Motta International Piano and Violin Competition
(Concurso Internacional Vianna da Motta Piano e Violino)
Rua Actonio Maria Cardoso 60, piso 2 Phone: 1 372620
P-1200 Lisbon, Portugal   Fax: 1 372013

10228
Vianna da Motta International Competition
(Concurso Internacional Vianna da Motta)
To recognize the best performers of the competition between 16 and 30 years of age. Awards are presented alternately to pianists and violinists. The following monetary prizes are awarded: (1) Grand Prix - $8,000 US; (2) Second prize - $5,000 US; and (3) Third prize - $2,500 US. Awarded every four years. Established in 1957 in memory of Vianna da Motta (1868-1948). Sponsored by Lisbon City Hall and City of Lisbon Foundation.

10229
International Cinema Festival of Algarve
(Festival Internacional de Cinema do Algarve)
PO Box 8091   Phone: 1 8513615
P-1801 Lisbon, Portugal   Fax: 1 8521150

10230
International Cinema Festival of Algarve
(Festival Internacional de Cinema do Algarve)
To recognize outstanding films. Portuguese or foreign filmmakers may submit Super 8, 16mm and 35mm films in color and black and white. Films

are admitted in two sections: (1) Non-professional; and (2) Independent. Awards are presented in the following categories: (1) Festival Grand Prize; (2) Best Fiction Film; (3) Best Documentary Film; (4) Best Cartoon; (5) Best Experimental Film; (6) Antonio Bernardo Trophy - to the first work of a Portuguese moviemaker; (7) Best Film on the Algarve - for the best film on a regional subject about Algarve; and (8) Special Jury Awards. A trophy and 75,000 Portuguese escudos are awarded to the winners of the two sections in each category. The Festival Grand Prize and Antonio Bernardo Trophy winner are awarded trophies. Awarded annually.

10231

International Festival of Cinema for Children and Youth - Tomar
(Festival Internacional de Cinema para a Infancia e Juventude - Tomar)
Camara Municipal de Tomar
Codigo Postal 2300
P-2300 Tomar, Portugal   Phone: 3 32 47

10232

International Festival of Cinema for Children and Youth
(Festival Internacional de Cinema para a Infancia e Juventude - Tomar)
To present films for children and young people and to develop this kind of cinema in its quality and quantity. The Festival has the following sections: Section A - Films for Children; Section B - Films for Young People; and Section C - Informative films (not competitive). The films presented in sections A and B must havde been shot during the preceding two years. Films which have been shown in public cinemas in Portugal are admitted in these sections. In section C, all kinds of films for children, young people or educators can be accepted, as far as the Festival rules are concerned. Feature films, medium films and short films can be presented in each one of these sections. The deadline for entries is November 15. The International Jury of the IFCCY awards the following prizes: Section A (Children) - Janela de Prata, first prize; and Tabuleiro, second prize, to one film, or two films equally; Section B (Young People) - Janela de Prata, first prize; and Tabuleiro, second prize to one film, or two films equally; Prize Roda Do Nabao - to one film from a young director, aged less than twenty-six years, enrolled in one of the sections Children or Young People; and The Jury Prize, called Caravela, to a person, organization or representative of a country-participating or otherwise connected with the Festival, whose activities on the favor of the Cinema for Children and the Young are remarkable and relevant. The Children's Jury awards the Pequena Janela de Prata to a film of Section B. Awarded annually. Established in 1979. (Inactive in 1990)

10233

International Film Festival of Figueira da Foz
(Festival Internacional de Cinema da Figueira da Foz)
Apartado 50407   Phone: 1 346 95 56
P-1709 Lisbon Codex, Portugal   Fax: 1 342 08 90

10234

International Film Festival of Figueira da Foz
To recognize films of outstanding expressive and aesthetic value. Awards are presented in the categories of fiction films, documentary films (preferably about social themes), short films (12 minutes maximum duration), and films for children. The Festival is open to films in 35mm and 16mm completed during the previous year. The following awards are presented when merited: Grand-Prix of the International Film Festival of Figueira da Foz - for one or two feature films and one or two documentary films; Prize of the International Film Festival of Figueira da Foz - for one or two short films; Silver Plates - three awards for fiction and documentary films; Prize of the City of Figueira da Foz - for a first work; Glauber Rocha Prize - for a film coming from the continents of Latin America, Africa, or Asia; Prize of the Regional Tourism Office - for innovative film; Environment Prize - for the best film about the environment; Women Prize - for a film about the condition of women; Youth Prize - for a film about the world of young people; Jury Prize - awarded to a personality, a department, or a representative from a participating country or in any way connected with the Festival; Prize of the International Film Festival of Figueira da Foz - for films for children; and Dr. Joao dos Santos Prize - for a film about education for liberty. Awarded annually. Established in 1972. Sponsored by the Centro de Estudos e Animacao Cultural, the Ministry of Foreign Affairs, the National Department of Culture, the National Department of Tourism, the Portuguese Film Institute, the District Government of Coimbra, the Figueira da Foz Municipality, and the Calouste Gulbenkian Foundation.

10235

International Film Festival of Santarem
(Festival Internacional de Cinema de Santarem)
Rua Conselheiro Figueiredo Leal 1   Phone: 43 22130
2000 Santarem, Portugal   Fax: 43 27643

10236

International Film Festival of Santarem
(Festival Internacional de Cinema de Santarem)
For recognition of achievement in film and video production. The Festival is divided into four sections, as follows: (1) Feature Films - the copy must be in 35mm; it must have optical sound and it has to be subtitled in Portuguese, Spanish, or French except those which in the original version are spoken in Portuguese or Spanish; the copy must not have been commercially presented in Portugal; (2) Festival of Agricultural and Enviromental Short Films - the aim is to facilitate a panoramic view on agricultural and environment pictures; to contribute to a better knowledge and a better study of agricultural and environment problems; to collaborate on the divulging of agricultural productions techniques; to stimulate the film production either on agriculture or rural themes or on environment themes; and to promote its quality through a comparison at an international level. In this section, there are two contest sectors: agricultural films and environment films. The copy of the film may be in 35mm with optical sound, or magnetic sound included, subtitled in Portuguese, Spanish, French, or English except those which, in the original version, are spoken in Portuguese or Spanish. The films must not be more than 45 minutes; (3) Documentary - on the theme "Man and the Earth"; and (4) Video Festival - that two sections: Video Free Show open to any participant and any thematic; and Video Festival on Environment and Agriculture. The video cassettes may be U-Matic, V.H.S. or Betamax and recorded in Pal-M system. Each video cassette must contain only one production. Entry forms must be submitted by February 26. Two International Juries will present the following awards: for short films in each section: Cacho de Ouro (Golden Bunch), Cacho de Prata (Silver Bunch), and Cacho de Bronze (Bronze Bunch); and for feature films: Cacho de Ouro (Golden Bunch), Cacho de Prata (Silver Bunch), Cacho de Bronze (Bronze Bunch), and Prize "Cidade de Santarem" - attributed to human values; Prize "Fernando Duarte" - for the best director, Prize "Manuel Alves Castela" - for the best script, Prize for the best actor, Prize for the best actress, Prize of the critic - to be attributed by the critics, and other special prizes at the Jury's disposal. In the documentary and Video Sections, the Golden Bunch, Silver Bunch, and Bronze Bunch are awarded. The International Festival and the Agricultural and Environment Film Festival were established in 1971 by Fernando Duarte. The Video Free Show was established in 1984. Sponsored by Camara Municipal de Santarem. (Inactive in 1990)

10237

International Film Festival of the Estoril Coast
(Festival Internacional de Cinema da Costa do Estoril)
Quinta da Bicuda, 46
P-2750 Cascais, Portugal

10238

International Film Festival of the Estoril Coast
(Festival Internacional de Cinema da Costa do Estoril)
For recognition of outstanding films. Gold and silver seagull trophies are awarded for first and second prize, respectively. In addition, several special prizes are awarded annually. Established in 1989. (Discontinued)

10239
International Society for Rock Mechanics
(Societe Internationale de Mecanique des Roches)
c/o Laboratorio Nacional de Engenharia
   Civil
101 Av. do Brasil   Phone: 1 8482131
P-1799 Lisbon Codex, Portugal   Fax: 1 8478187

10240
Muller Award
To recognize an individual for a contribution in the field of rock mechanics. Nominations or applications must be submitted 18 months in advance of the ISRM Congress. A medal and travel expenses are awarded every four years at the ISRM Congress. Established in 1991 to honor Prof. Leopold Muller.

10241
Manuel Rocha Medal
For recognition of an outstanding doctoral thesis in the field of rock mechanics that is accepted during the two years preceding the conferment. A monetary prize, a bronze medal, and travel expenses to receive the award are presented annually. Established in 1982 in honor of Manuel Rocha, past president of the Society and Portuguese scientist.

10242
Latin Languages Allergists and Immunologists Group
(Groupement des Allergologistes et Immunologistes de Langues Latines)
Rua Sampaio e Pina, 16, 4   Phone: 1 3874201
P-1000 Lisbon, Portugal   Fax: 1 658202

10243
Dagra Prize
(Premio Dagra)
To recognize an individual for achievement in asthma and respiratory allergy treatment. A monetary award of 200,000 Spanish pesetas is presented biennially. Established in 1982.

10244
Lisbon Academy of Sciences
(Academia das Ciencias de Lisboa)
Rua da Academia das Ciencias 19   Phone: 1 3463866
P-1200 Lisbon, Portugal   Fax: 1 3420395

10245
Carlos Teixeira Prize
(Premio Carlos Teixeira)
For recognition of outstanding works in the field of Portuguese geology by Portuguese or international scientists. Monetary prizes totaling 100,000 escudos are awarded every three years. Established in 1986.

10246
Laranjo Coelho Prize
(Premio Laranjo Coelho)
To recognize a Portuguese author for an outstanding historical study, published or unpublished. A monetary prize of 30,000 escudos is awarded biennially. Established in 1972.

10247
General Casimiro Dantas Prize
(Premio General Casimiro Dantas)
To recognize authors of outstanding literary works, and to stimulate cultural growth and creative literature in Portugal. A monetary prize of 8,000 escudos is awarded biennially. Established in 1963.

10248
Antonio Alves de Carvalho Fernandes Prize
(Premio Antonio Alves de Carvalho Fernandes)
To recognize Portuguese scientists for an original work on electronics and telecommunications. A monetary prize of 100,000 escudos is awarded biennially. Established in 1984 by Academia das Ciencias de Lisboa and Standard Electrica Portuguesa.

10249
Alvarenga do Piaui (Brasil) Prize
(Premio Alvarenga do Piaui)
To stimulate progress in the medical sciences in Portugal by recognizing the Portuguese authors of original, unpublished works in one of the medical fields, including Portuguese medical history. The submitted works may not have won previous prizes. A monetary prize of 2,500 escudos is awarded annually. Established in 1898.

10250
Abilio Lopes do Rego Prize
(Premio Abilio Lopes do Rego)
To recognize the author of an original work on any theme related to the history of Portuguese colonization, published in Portuguese during the year of the prize, or presented as a manuscript to the jury. The following prizes are awarded: first prize - 50,000 escudos, and second prize - 30,000 escudos. Awarded annually. Established in 1950.

10251
Calouste Gulbenkian Translation Prize
(Premio de Traducao Calouste Gulbenkian)
To recognize the best translator of a work of fiction, a play, or a work of poetry from a foreign language into Portuguese. Aesthetic and vernacular qualities of the translation are considered by the jury. Portuguese translators whose works are published during the year of the award are eligible. Two prizes of 20,000 escudos each, one for prose and one for poetry, are awarded annually. Established in 1975 by the Calouste Gulbenkian Foundation.

10252
International Vasco Vilalva Prize
(Premio Internacional Vasco Vilvalva)
For recognition of outstanding unpublished, unrewarded works by Portuguese or international scientists in the field of Portuguese agriculture. A monetary prize in escudos comparable to $10,000 US is awarded triennially. Established in 1986.

10253
Antonio Larragoiti Prize
(Premio Larragoiti)
To recognize the author of the best original work on a Portuguese-Brazilian theme in the field of literature, philology, history, law, politics, and the social sciences published during the year of the prize or during the preceding year. Portuguese and Brazilian authors, alternately, are eligible for the prize. A monetary prize of 12,000 escudos is awarded biennially, alternately by Academia das Ciencias de Lisboa and Academia Brasileira de Letras. Established in 1945 by Antonio Larragoiti. Cosponsored by the Brazilian Academy of Letters.

10254
Aboim Sande Lemos Prize
(Premio Aboim Sande Lemos)
To recognize the author of the best published or unpublished work on balanced and rational nutrition, especially in relation to the nutritional problems of the Third World, or to honor work connected with professional hygiene. Portuguese scientists are eligible for works written during the preceding two years. A monetary prize of 20,000 escudos is awarded biennially. Established in 1976.

10255
Artur Malheiros Prize
(Premio Artur Malheiros)
To recognize Portuguese authors of unpublished works in the sciences, particularly in physics, chemistry, pure and applied mathematics, scientific engineering, biology, medicine, jurisprudence, or economics. A monetary prize of 6,000 escudos is awarded annually. Established in 1937.

10256
Ricardo Malheiros Prize
(Premio Ricardo Malheiros)
To recognize the author of the best original work of fiction in the categories of the novel, novella, or short story, written in Portuguese and published during the year of the prize. A monetary award of 5,000 escudos is awarded annually. Established in 1933.

10257
Manuel Alves Monteiro Prize
(Premio Manuel Alves Monteiro)
To recognize Portuguese authors of outstanding works in hygiene, social medicine, or public health. A monetary prize of 20,000 escudos is awarded. Established in 1966.

10258
Ramos Paz Prize
(Premio Ramos Paz)
To recognize the Portuguese author of the best original unpublished work on some aspect of Brazilian literature or on Portuguese-Brazilian literary relationships. A monetary prize of 3,000 escudos is awarded. Established in 1943.

10259
Aquilino Ribeiro Literary Prize
(Premio Aquilino Ribeiro)
To recognize the author of the best literary work of prose (a novel or a collection of stories or short stories) from any Portuguese speaking country. The work should have been published during the preceding two years, or it may be an original, unpublished manuscript. A monetary prize of 100,000 escudos is awarded biennially. Established in 1979 by the Academy of Science of Lisbon and the Calouste Gulbenkian Foundation.

10260
Madeira, Regional Secretary of Tourism, Culture and Emigration
(Madeira, Secretaria Regional do Turismo, Cultura e Emigracao)
Avenido Arriaga 18
P-9000 Funchal, Madeira, Portugal
Phone: 91 2 90 57
Fax: 91 32 151

10261
Estrelicia Dourada
For recognition of a contribution to tourism activities and to encourage professional development in the field of tourism. Nomination is by the Tourism Authority. A trophy is awarded when merited. Established in 1982 by the Tourism Authority of the Regional Government of Madeira.

10262
Medalha de Merito Turistico
To recognize individuals or associations for their outstanding contributions and dedication to the tourism of Madeira. Individuals or associations may be nominated by the Tourism Authority. A medal is awarded when merited. Established in 1982 by the Tourism Authority of the Regional Government of Madeira.

10263
Municipality of Lisbon
(Camara Municipal de Lisboa)
Dept. of Cultural Patrimony
Pacos do Concelho - Praca do Municipio
P-1100 Lisbon, Portugal
Phone: 1 346 29 51
Fax: 1 346 75 48

10264
Premio Municipais Joshua Benoliel de Fotografia
To recognize a photographer for the best color, and black and white photography. Portuguese citizens are eligible. A monetary award of 250,000 escudos is awarded annually in each category, at a special ceremony at City Hall. Established in 1989 in memory of Joshua Benoliel, journalist and photographer (1873-1939), whose work marks the beginning of photographic history in Portugal.

10265
Premio Municipal Alfredo Marceneiro de Fado
To recognize the best Portuguese folk song. Unedited folk songs with a duration of 3-6 minutes may be submitted. A monetary award of 500,000 escudos is presented annually at a special ceremony at City Hall. Established in 1989 in memory of Alfredo Duarte Marceneiro (1891-1982), a distinguished Portuguese folk singer.

10266
Premio Municipal Augusto Vieira da Silva de Investigacao
To recognize the best research work on the subject of Lisbon. Unedited works may be submitted. Portuguese citizens are eligible. A monetary award of 250,000 escudos is presented annually, at a special ceremony at City Hall. Established in 1989 in memory of Augusto Vieira da Silva (1869-1951), a distinguished scholar on the history of Lisbon.

10267
Premio Municipal Carlos Botelho de Pintura
To recognize the best painting on the subject of Lisbon. Portuguese painters may submit applications. A monetary award of 500,000 escudos is presented annually, at a special ceremony at City Hall. Established in 1989 in memory of Carlos Botelho (1899-1982), a well-known Portuguese painter known as the "painter of Lisbon."

10268
Premio Municipal Fernando Amado de Encenacao Teatral
To recognize the best staging exhibited in Lisbon during the preceding year. A monetary award of 250,000 escudos is presented annually, at a special ceremony at City Hall. Established in 1989 in memory of Fernando Alberto da Silva Amado (1899-1968), critic, dramatist, politician, author of *O Livro e o Pensador*, *O Segredo de Polichinelo*, and teacher of theatre in school arts.

10269
Premio Municipal Francisco da Conceicao Silva de Espacos Interiores abertos ao publico
To recognize the best project of construction, adaptation or recovery of an interior space. Hotels, theaters, cinemas, banks, and other buildings open to the public are eligible. A monetary award of 600,000 escudos is presented annually at a special ceremony at City Hall. Established in 1989 by Francisco da Conceicao Silva, an important figure of modern Portuguese architecture.

10270
Premio Municipal Joao Baptista Rosa de Video
To recognize the best video on the subject of Lisbon. Unedited videos with a duration of 20-30 minutes may be submitted. A monetary award of 500,000 escudos is presented annually, at a special ceremony at City Hall. Established in memory of Joao Baptista Rosa (1925-1982), journalist, producer, television and cinema reporter and the author of *A Pintura de Vieira da Silva* and *Azulejos Portugueses*. His work marks a significative moment in Portuguese cinema.

10271

Premio Municipal Jorge Colaco de Azulejaria
For recognition of the best work in decorative glazed-tiles used on the facade of a building constructed in Lisbon during the preceding year. A monetary prize of 600,000 escudos is divided among the author of the work, the author of the project of the building and the makers of the glazed tiles. Awarded annually. Established in 1985. Renamed in 1989 to honor Jorge Colaco (1868-1942), a distinguished caricaturist and tile-maker, whose tiles decorate Windsor Palace, the medical school at Lisbon, and Sao Bento Station at Porto.

10272

Premio Municipal Jose Simoes de Almeida de Escultura
To recognize the best piece of sculpture. Portuguese sculptors are eligible. A monetary award of 1,000,000 escudos is presented annually, at a special ceremony at City Hall. Established in 1989 in memory of Jose Simoes de Almeida (1844- 1926), a sculptor famous for *Duque de Terceira*, and *O Genio da Vitoria* (Restauradores), among others.

10273

Premio Municipal Julio Cesar Machado de Jornalismo
For recognition of the best report on Lisbon published in newspapers or magazines during the preceding year. Portuguese journalists are eligible. A monetary prize of 250,000 escudos is awarded annually. Established in 1951 in memory of Julio Cesar Machado (1835-1890), a well-known Lisbon journalist. Re-established in 1982.

10274

Premio Municipal Julio de Castilho de Olisipografia
For recognition of the best research work on the history or archaeology of Lisbon published during the preceding year. Portuguese scholars are eligible. A monetary prize of 250,000 escudos is awarded annually. Established in 1939 in memory of the Viscount of Castilho, Julio de Castilho, a distinguished scholar and writer, particularly on the history of Lisbon. Re-established in 1982.

10275

Premio Municipal Maria Leonor Magro de Radio
To recognize the best radio broadcast on the subject of Lisbon. A monetary award of 250,000 escudos is presented annually, at a special ceremony at City Hall. Established in 1989 in memory of Maria Leonor Magro (1920-1988), journalist, producer, and one of the most popular figures of Portuguese broadcasting.

10276

Premio Municipal Rafael Bordalo Pinheiro de Banda Desenhada, Cartoon e Caricaturista
To recognize the best work of animated cartoon and caricature. Portuguese citizens are eligible. A monetary award of 250,000 escudos is presented annually, at a special ceremony at City Hall. Established in 1989 in memory of Rafael Bordalo Pinheiro, the most popular Portuguese caricaturist (1846- 1905).

10277

Premio Municipal Roberto de Araujo Pereira de Design
To recognize the best design project which tends to improve the Lisbon urban context. A monetary award of 500,000 escudos is awarded annually, at a special ceremony at City Hall. Established in 1989 to honor Roberto de Araujo Pereira, painter, scenographist, and a pioneer of Portuguese design.

10278

Premio Municipal Trabalho e Estudo
For recognition of the best essay written about Lisbon, by a member of the City's staff who is pursuing his studies at the University level. A monetary prize of 50,000 escudos is awarded annually. Established in 1987 by Camara Municipal de Lisboa to commemorate student's National Day, March 24.

10279

Premio Valmor e Municipal de Arquitectura
To recognize the owner of and the architect responsible for a building which unites esthetic and architectonic values, constructed or restored in Lisbon during the preceding year. Portuguese architects are eligible. A monetary prize of 800,000 escudos is awarded annually. Established in 1903 to honor the Viscount Valmor (1837-1897), public benefactor.

10280

Premios Municipais Eca de Queiroz de Literatura
For recognition of the best work in poetry, the best novel, the best literary or biographical essay and the best theatrical play published (first edition) during the preceding year. Portuguese writers are eligible. Monetary prizes of 250,000 escudos each are awarded annually. Established in 1982. Renamed in 1989 to honor Eca de Queiroz (1845-1900), one of the most important Portuguese writers.

10281

Premios Municipais Joly Braga Santos de Musica
To recognize the best symphony and chamber music composition. Unedited works may be submitted. A monetary prize of 750,000 escudos is presented annually, at a special ceremony at City Hall. Established to honor Joly Braga Santos, a distinguished composer, teacher and orchestrator.

10282

Premios Municipais Palmira Bastos e Antonio Silva de Interpretacao Teatral
To recognize the best theatrical interpretation made by an actor and an actress in Lisbon during the preceding year. Portuguese performers are eligible. A monetary award of 250,000 escudos is awarded to both an actor and an actress. Awarded annually at a special ceremony at City Hall. Established in 1989 in memory of Palmira Bastos (1875-1967) and Antonio Silva (1886-1971), two important figures in Portuguese theater and cinema.

10283

National Academy of Fine Arts
(Academia Nacional de Belas-Artes)
Largo da Academia Nacional de Belas-
 Artes
P-1200 Lisbon, Portugal

10284

Jose de Figueiredo Prize
To recognize the author of the best work on the subject of fine arts which combines historical research with analytical and critical insight. The work may be written by Portuguese or foreign art critics, providing they deal with Portuguese art. A monetary prize of 3,975 escudos is awarded annually. Established in 1940 in memory of Dr. Jose de Figueiredo, an art critic.

10285

Premio Anual de Aquisicao
To recognize Portuguese artists in the field of architecture, sculpture, and painting for outstanding works relevant to the national culture. A monetary prize of 100,000 escudos is awarded. Established in 1983.

10286

Premio Anual de Investigacao
To recognize graduates of the Escolas Superiores de Belas-Artes of Lisbon or Porto. Graduates who for at least five and no longer than ten years after certification have maintained creative activity in the fields of architecture, sculpture, or painting may enter the public contest. A monetary prize of 100,000 escudos is awarded. Established in 1983.

10287

Doctor Gustavo Cordeiro Ramos Prize
For recognition of the best painting or sculpture which either appeared in a public exhibition within the established period, which has been integrated in the public or private building for which it was executed, or which constitutes a part of a monument. Portuguese artists, preferably the graduates of schools of fine arts in Lisbon and Porto, are eligible. A monetary prize of 19,000 escudos is paid to the artist during the year. Awarded annually. Established in 1977.

10288

National Institute for the Environment
(Instituto Nacional do Ambiente)
Rua Carlos Testal 1
P-1000 Lisbon, Portugal
Phone: 1 562001
Fax: 1 561102

10289

Environment in Children's Literature Award
(Ambiente na Literatura Infantil)
To recognize original works of prose or poetry which best illustrate the importance of the relationship between Man and Nature, with special emphasis on the relevant role played by Man. Work carried out in Portugal, or work that addresses concrete global problems that may influence Portugal, is eligible. Papers must be written in Portuguese, regardless of the nationality of the author. Awards are presented in two categories: (1) unpublished works; and (2) works published for the first time during the year considered for the prize. Two monetary prizes of 250,000 escudos each are awarded on June 5, World Environment Day. First awarded in 1977 for works published in 1976.

10290

Oporto Internacional Film Festival - Fantasporto
(Festival Internacional de Cinema do Porto-Fantasporto)
Rua da Constituicao, 311
P-4200 Porto, Portugal
Phone: 2 5508990
Fax: 2 5508210

10291

Oporto International Film Festival - Fantasporto
(Festival Internacional de Cinema do Porto - Fantasporto)
To promote imaginary films on an international level that seek new forms and methods of filmmaking, and in which the creative powers of the imagination have a treatment of quality. The Festival has four sections: Retrospective Section, Informative Section, Competitive Section, and Portuguese Cinema. Trophies are awarded annually in the following categories: Fantasporto Best Film Award, Best Director, Best Actor, Best Actress, Best Screenplay, Best Special Effects, Best Short Film, Special Award - to a film whose artistic and technical aspects present a high level of originality, New Directors Award, Critics Award, and Audience Award. Diplomas are given to all films participating in the competitive section. The Festival is held annually in February. Established in 1980 by the magazine, *Cinema Novo*.

10292

PEN Clube Portugues
York House
Rua das Janelas Verdes 32
P-1200 Lisbon, Portugal
Phone: 1 3505175
Fax: 1 576578

10293

PEN Prizes (Poetry, Essay, Novel)
(Premios PEN)
For recognition of achievements in the writing of poetry, essays, and novels. Monetary prizes are awarded in each category annually. Established in 1980.

10294

Portugal
Ministry of Education and Culture
(Portugal
Ministerio da Educacao y Cultura)
Avenida 5 de Outubro 107
P-1000 Lisbon, Portugal
Phone: 1 677 001

10295

Visconde de Sousa Prego Freedom Prize
(Premio Liverdade-Visconde de Sousa Prego)
To recognize primary school teachers who distinguished themselves by their fine teaching and scholarly skills. Portuguese teachers of elementary schools on the continent (not in Portuguese overseas territories) are eligible. Four monetary prizes of 7,500 escudos each are awarded annually. Established in 1978 by Visconde de Sousa Prego.

10296

Portugal
State Secretariat of Culture
Palacio Nacional da Ajuda
1300 Lisbon, Portugal
Phone: 1 3649867
Fax: 1 3621832

10297

Camoes Prize
(Premio Luis de Camoes)
For recognition of the best work written on Portuguese life and culture by a Portuguese writer, published in or outside of Portugal. Works written by authors from countries whose official language is Portuguese are also eligible. A monetary prize of 1,000,000 Portuguese escudos is awarded annually. Established in 1983 by the Ministry of Culture.

10298

Critics Prize
(Premio da critica)
To recognize a literary personality for the totality of his/her work and to recognize a work of fiction, poetry, or a play. A monetary prize is awarded annually. Established in 1979 by the Portuguese Center of the International Association of Literary Critics and the State Secretary of Culture.

10299

Portuguese Academy of History
(Academia Portuguese da Historia)
Palacio da Rosa
Largo da Rosa 5
P-1100 Lisbon, Portugal

10300

Augusto Botelho da Costa Veiga Prize
For recognition of the best published work on the history of Portugal. Portuguese historians and members of the Academy are eligible. A monetary prize of 36,240 escudos is awarded triennially. Established in 1967 by Tenente-coronel Augusto Botelho da Costa Veiga.

10301

Ferreira Chavez Prize
To recognize a student of painting of the Higher School of Fine Arts in Lisbon who has distinguished himself during the academic year. Awarded annually.

10302

Luciano Freire Prize
To recognize an author of an art work whose concept and technique has been judged the most exceptional, and whose work was exhibited in Portugal. Honorary recognition is awarded annually. Established in 1934 in memory of Professor Luciano Freire.

10303
Calouste Gulbenkian Prizes for History
For recognition of the best published works on the history of the Portuguese presence in the world and on the history of Portugal from the 16th to the 20th century. A monetary prize of 20,000 escudos is awarded to the winner of each competition. Established in 1975 by the Calouste Gulbenkian Foundation.

10304
Lupi Prize
To recognize students of painting of the Higher School of Fine Arts in Lisbon for the best painting (executed during eight sessions of three hours each) representing a male or female nude model. Awarded annually.

10305
Julio Mardel Prize
For recognition of the best work of painting or sculpture. Young Portuguese artists are eligible. A monetary prize of 16,000 escudos is awarded biennially. Established in 1957 by the painter, Fernando Mardel.

10306
Soares Dos Reis Prize
To recognize students of the Higher School of Fine Arts in Porto for outstanding composition and preparatory drawing for their paintings, sculptures and architectural projects. Awarded annually.

10307
Portuguese Association of Writers
Rua de S. Domingos a Lapa 17
P-1200 Lisbon, Portugal   Phone: 1 320467

10308
City of Lisbon Literary Prize
(Premio Cidade de Lisboa)
For recognition of the best work of fiction written by a Portuguese author during the year preceding the prize. A monetary prize of 75,000 escudos is awarded annually. Established in 1977. Co-sponsored by the Municipality of Lisbon.

10309
Grande Premio de Romance e Novela da Associacao Portuguesa de Escritores
For recognition of an outstanding work of fiction published during the preceding year. Works of fiction may be submitted to the jury. A monetary prize of 750,000 escudos and a trophy are awarded annually. Established in 1982.

10310
Revelation Prize for Children's Literature
To recognize the Portuguese author of the best unpublished work of children's literature. A monetary prize of 100,000 escudos is awarded annually. Established in 1978. Co-sponsored by the Portuguese Ministry of Culture.

10311
Revelation Prize for Essay
(Premio de Revelacao de Ensaio)
To recognize the Portuguese author of the best unpublished essay. A monetary prize of 100,000 escudos is awarded annually. Established in 1978. Co-sponsored by the Portuguese Ministry of Culture.

10312
Revelation Prize for Fiction
(Premio de Revelacao de Ficcao)
To recognize the Portuguese author of the best unpublished work of fiction. A monetary prize of 100,000 escudos is awarded annually. Established in 1978. Co-sponsored by the Portuguese Ministry of Culture.

10313
Revelation Prize for Poetry
(Premio de Revelacao de Poesia)
To recognize the Portuguese author of the best unpublished work of poetry in Portugal. A monetary prize of 100,000 escudos is awarded annually. Established in 1978. Co-sponsored by the Portuguese Ministry of Culture.

10314
Portuguese League Against Cancer
Rua Prof. Lima Bastos
P-1000 Lisbon, Portugal

10315
Fernando Fonseca Prize
To provide recognition for the best original work on clinical or experimental approaches to fighting cancer. Physicians and scientists educated in Portuguese universities and medical schools who participated in the competition organized by the Portuguese League are eligible. A monetary prize of 50,000 Portuguese escudos is awarded biennially. Established in 1979.

10316
Sociedade de Geografia de Lisboa
Rua das Portas Santo Antao 100
P-1100 Lisbon, Portugal   Phone: 1 325401

10317
Admiral Gago Coutinho Prize
(Premio Internacional Almirante Gago Coutinho)
For recognition of geographical field work. The deadline for consideration is December 31 each year. A monetary award is presented annually. Established in 1964 in honor of Admiral Carlos Viegas Gago Coutinho, geographer and aviator.

10318
Sociedade Portuguese de Autores
Avenida Duque de Loule 31   Phone: 578320
P-1000 Lisbon, Portugal   Fax: 530257

10319
Camilo Castelo Branco Prize
For recognition of the best work of fiction by a Portuguese author. A monetary prize of 50,000 Portuguese escudos is awarded annually. Established in 1959.

10320
Universidade de Lisboa
c/o Faculty of Law
Alameda da Universidade
P-1699 Lisbon, Portugal   Phone: 767624

10321
Insurance Law Prize
(Premio Direito dos Seguros)
To provide recognition for the best works in the field of insurance law. Students, of any nationality, of the Department of Law in Lisbon and in Canada are eligible. A monetary prize of 15,000 Portuguese escudos is awarded annually. Established in 1973 by the International Association for Insurance Law - Portuguesa Section.

Romania

10322
Academy of Medical Sciences
(Academia de Stiinte Medicale)
Blvd. 1 Mai 11
79173 Bucharest, Romania

10323
Medical Sciences Award
For recognition of outstanding research in medicine. A monetary prize and honorary recognition are awarded annually.

10324
Festival of Contemporary Theatre
(Festivalul de Teatru Contemporan)
c/o Teatru Dramatic Brasov-Piata
Teatrului 1   Phone: 68 151486
2200 Brasov, Romania   Fax: 68 151486

10325
Festival of Contemporary Theatre
(Festivalul de Teatru Contemporan)
To recognize contributions and achievement in drama. Awards are presented in the following categories: best show, actor, actress, originality, direction, and other special awards. Monetary awards, bronze statues, and diplomas are presented annually. Established in 1978. Sponsored by UNITER (The National Theatre Organizaion) and the Ministry of Culture.

10326
Radiodifuziunea Romana
Str. Gral Berthelot 60-62   Phone: 6 503055
Bucharest, Romania   Fax: 3 123640

10327
Romanian Radio and Television Award
To provide recognition for the most outstanding radio and television programs, and for dramatic works and musical compositions prepared for radio or television. A monetary award and honorary recognition are granted annually.

10328
Romanian Academy
(Academia Romana)
Calea Victoriei 125   Phone: 0 502248
71102 Bucharest, Romania   Fax: 1 3120209

10329
Ion Andreescu Prize
For recognition of an exceptional work in plastic art works. Romanian artists are eligible. A monetary award of 10,000 lei and a diploma are awarded annually. Established in 1948.

10330
Grigore Antipa Prize
To recognize works in environmental research. A monetary prize of 10,000 lei is awarded annually.

10331
Petre S. Aurelian Prize
For recognition of outstanding work in economics. Young Romanian economists are eligible. A monetary award of 10,000 lei and a diploma are awarded annually. Established in 1948.

10332
Victor Babes Prize
For recognition of an outstanding achievement in the medical sciences. Young Romanian physicians and researchers are eligible. A monetary prize of 10,000 lei and a diploma are awarded annually. Established in 1948.

10333
Nicolae Balcescu Prize
For recognition of outstanding works in historical sciences. Young Romanian historians are eligible. A monetary prize of 10,000 lei and a diploma are awarded annually. Established in 1948.

10334
Gheorghe Baritiu Prize
To recognize scientific works in history. A monetary prize of 10,000 lei is awarded annually.

10335
Simion Barnutiu Prize
To recognize a young Romanian writer for outstanding works in juridical sciences. A monetary award of 10,000 lei and a diploma are awarded annually. Established in 1948.

10336
Constantin Budeanu Prize
For recognition of technical and technological works. A monetary prize of 10,000 lei is awarded annually.

10337
Ion Luca Caragiale Prize
For recognition of the best Romanian drama. Young Romanian playwrights are eligible. A monetary prize of 10,000 lei is awarded annually. Established in 1948.

10338
George Cartianu Prize
To recognize outstanding works in communication technology. A monetary prize of 10,000 lei is awarded annually.

10339
Timotei Cipariu Prize
For recognition of works in philology. Young Romanian literary critics or scholars are eligible. A monetary prize of 10,000 lei is awarded annually. Established in 1948.

10340
Henri Coanda Prize
For recognition of remarkable contributions to the development of the technical sciences. A monetary prize of 10,000 lei is awarded annually.

10341
Grigore Cobalcescu Prize
For recognition of work in geology. Young Romanian research workers are eligible. A monetary prize of 10,000 lei and a diploma are awarded annually. Established in 1948.

10342
Vasile Conta Prize
To recognize works in philosophy or psychology. A monetary prize of 10,000 lei is awarded annually.

10343
Ion Creanga Prize
For recognition of the most outstanding work of prose. Young Romanian writers are eligible. A monetary prize of 10,000 lei is awarded annually. Established in 1948.

10344
Daniel Danielopolu Prize
To recognize works in the medical sciences, particularly physiology. A monetary prize of 10,000 lei is awarded annually.

10345
Marin Dracea Prize
For recognition of works in forestry science. A monetary prize of 10,000 lei is awarded annually.

10346
Mihail Eminescu Prize
For recognition of the best published collection of poems. Young Romanian poets are eligible. A monetary prize of 10,000 lei is awarded annually. Established in 1948.

10347
George Enescu Prize
For recognition of superior musical compositions. Young Romanian musicians are eligible. A monetary prize of 10,000 lei and a diploma are awarded annually. Established in 1956.

10348
Mircea Florian Prize
To recognize outstanding philosophical works. A monetary prize of 10,000 lei is awarded annually.

10349
Stefan Gheorghiu Prize
For recognition of published works on modern history. A monetary prize of 10,000 lei and a diploma were awarded annually. Established in 1948. (Discontinued)

10350
Dimitrie Gusti Prize
To recognize scientific works in sociology. A monetary prize of 10,000 lei is awarded annually.

10351
Spiru Haret Prize
For recognition of a contribution to mathematical sciences. A monetary prize of 10,000 lei is awarded annually.

10352
Bogdan Petriceicu Hasdeu Prize
For recognition of work in philology. Young Romanians are eligible. A monetary prize of 10,000 lei is awarded annually. Established in 1948.

10353
Iuliu Hatieganu Prize
For recognition of scientific works in clinical medicine. A monetary prize of 10,000 lei is awarded annually.

10354
Stefan Hepites Prize
To recognize outstanding work in geophysics. A monetary prize of 10,000 lei is awarded annually.

10355
Horia Hulubei Prize
To recognize works in physical sciences. A monetary prize of 10,000 lei is awarded annually.

10356
Eudoxiu Hurmuzachi Prize
For recognition of historical works. A monetary prize of 10,000 lei is awarded annually.

10357
Dragomir Hurmuzescu Prize
For recognition of outstanding contributions to the physical sciences. Young Romanian scientists. A monetary prize of 10,000 lei and a diploma are awarded annually. Established in 1948.

10358
Ion Ionescu de la Brad Prize
To recognize outstanding work in agricultural science, and to reward contributions to the scientific, technical, and cultural development of the country. Young Romanian scholars are eligible. A monetary prize of 10,000 lei and a diploma are awarded annually. Established in 1948.

10359
Gheorge Ionescu-Sisesti Prize
To recognize agricultural works. A monetary prize of 10,000 lei is awarded annually.

10360
Nicolae Iorga Prize
For recognition of contributions in the field of historical sciences. Romanian research workers, writers, or critics are eligible. A monetary prize of 10,000 lei and a diploma are awarded annually. Established in 1948.

10361
Mihail Kogalniceau Prize
To recognize scientific works in history. A monetary prize of 10,000 lei is awarded annually.

10362
Gheorghe Lazar Prize
For recognition of outstanding works in mathematics and astronautics. Young Romanian mathematicians and scientists are eligible. A monetary prize of 10,000 lei and a diploma are awarded annually. Established in 1948.

10363
Virgil Madgearu Prize
To recognize outstanding works in economics. A monetary prize of 10,000 lei is awarded annually.

10364
Simion Florea Marian Prize
To recognize works in ethnography and folklore. A monetary prize of 10,000 lei is awarded annually.

10365
Gheorghe Marinescu Prize
For recognition of a contribution to medicine. A monetary prize of 10,000 lei are awarded annually. Established in 1948.

10366
Simion Mehedinti Prize
For recognition of work in geography. A monetary prize of 10,000 lei is awarded annually.

10367
Constantin Miculescu Prize
For recognition of original research in physics. Romanian scientists are eligible. A monetary prize of 10,000 lei and a diploma are awarded annually. Established in 1948.

10368
Constantin Radulescu Motru prize
Fo recognition of works in philosophy or psychology. A monetary prize of 10,000 lei is awarded annually.

10369
Ludovic Mrazec Prize
For recognition of work in geology. A monetary prize of 10,000 lei is awarded annually.

10370
Gheorghe Murgoci Prize
For recognition of works in the geological or geographical sciences. Young Romanian scientists are eligible. A monetary prize of 10,000 lei and a diploma are awarded annually. Established in 1948.

10371
C. D. Nenitescu Prize
To recognize works in the chemical sciences. A monetary prize of 10,000 lei is awarded annually.

10372
Stefan S. Nicolau Prize
For recognition of works in the medical field, particularly infectious pathology. A monetary prize of 10,000 lei is awarded annually.

10373
Dimitrie Onciul Prize
To recognize scientific works in history. A monetary prize of 10,000 lei is awarded annually.

10374
George Oprescu Prize
For recognition in the field of art history and art criticism. A monetary prize of 10,000 lei is awarded annually.

10375
Constantin I. Parhon
To recognize works in medical sciences, particularly endocrinology. A monetary prize of 10,000 lei is awarded annually.

10376
Vasile Parvan Prize
For recognition of distinguished contributions to history or archaeology. A monetary prize of 10,000 lei is awarded annually. Established in 1948.

10377
Ion Petrovici Prize
For recognition of works in philosophy or psychology. A monetary prize of 10,000 lei is awarded annually.

10378
Ciprian Porumbescu Prize
For recognition of work in musicology. Young Romanian musicologists are eligible. A monetary prize of 10,000 lei and a diploma are awarded annually. Established in 1956.

10379
Stefan Procopiu Prize
To recognize works in physical sciences. A monetary prize of 10,000 lei is awarded annually.

10380
Emil Racovita Prize
For recognition of work in biology. Young Romanian research workers are eligible. A monetary prize of 10,000 lei and a diploma are awarded annually. Established in 1948.

10381
Anghel Saligny Prize
For recognition of original research or applied works in the field of technology. A monetary prize of 10,000 lei and a diploma are awarded annually. Established in 1989.

10382
Traian Savulescu Prize
For recognition of original research or applied works in the field of agriculture. Young Romanian research workers are eligible. A monetary prize of 10,000 lei and a diploma are awarded annually. Established in 1948.

10383
Gheorghe Spacu Prize
For recognition of outstanding achievement in chemistry. Young scientists in Romania are eligible. A monetary prize of 10,000 lei and a diploma are awarded annually. Established in 1948.

10384
Simon Stoilov Prize
For recognition of a contribution to mathematical sciences. Young Romanian mathematicians are eligible. A monetary prize of 10,000 lei and a diploma are awarded annually. Established in 1948.

10385
Tudor Tanasescu Prize
For recognition of outstanding works in information sciences. A monetary prize of 10,000 lei is awarded annually.

10386
Nicolae Teclu Prize
For recognition of a contribution to chemistry. A monetary prize of 10,000 lei and a diploma are awarded annually. Established in 1948.

10387
Emanoil Teodorescu Prize
For recognition of work in the biological sciences. A monetary prize of 10,000 lei and a diploma are awarded annually. Established in 1948.

10388
Gheorghe Titeica Prize
For recognition of work in mathematics. A monetary prize of 10,000 lei and a diploma are awarded annually. Established in 1948.

10389
Nicholae Titulescu Prize
For recognition of works in economic, juridical, and political science. A monetary prize of 10,000 lei is awarded annually.

10390
Aurel Vlaicu Prize
For recognition of an outstanding contribution to technology. A monetary prize of 10,000 lei and a diploma are awarded annually. Established in 1948.

10391
Traian Vuia Prize
For recognition of work in technology. A monetary prize of 10,000 lei and a diploma are awarded annually. Established in 1948.

10392
Alexandru Xenopol Prize
To recognize scientific works in history. A monetary prize of 10,000 lei is awarded annually.

10393
Romanian Fine Arts Union
(Uniunea Artistilor Plastici din Romania)
Str. Nicolae Iorga 21, Sector 1   Phone: 0 50 73 15
71118 Bucharest, Romania   Phone: 0 50 71 80

10394
ARTA Magazine Awards
To recognize an outstanding painter or graphic artist. Awarded annually. Established in 1986. Sponsored by ARTA Magazine.

10395
Fine Arts Union Prize
To recognize an individual for outstanding accomplishments in art over a long period of time. Painters, sculptors, graphic artists, decorative artists and art critics are eligible. Awarded annually. Established in 1986. In addition, a Special Prize may be awarded.

10396
Prize for Art Critique
To recognize outstanding achievements in art critique. Union members are eligible. A monetary award is presented annually. Established in 1968.

10397
Prize for Decorative Arts
To recognize outstanding achievements in decorative arts. Union members are eligible. monetary award is presented annually. Established in 1968.

10398
Prize for Design
To recognize outstanding achievements in design. Union members are eligible. A monetary award is presented annually. Established in 1968.

10399
Prize for Graphic Arts
To recognize outstanding achievements in graphic arts. Union members are eligible. A monetary award is presented annually. Established in 1968.

10400
Prize for Monumental Art
To recognize outstanding achievements in monumental art. Union members are eligible. A monetary award is presented annually. Established in 1968.

10401
Prize for Painting
To recognize outstanding achievements in painting. Union members are eligible. A monetary award is presented annually. Established in 1968.

10402
Prize for Scenography
To recognize outstanding achievements in scenography. Union members are eligible. A monetary award is presented annually. Established in 1968.

10403
Prize for Sculpture
To recognize outstanding achievements in sculpture. Union members are eligible. A monetary award is presented annually. Established in 1968.

10404
Young Artists Prize
To recognize an outstanding young artist. Awarded annually. Established in 1986.

10405
Romanian Union of Composers and Musicologists
(Uniunea Compozitorilor si Musicologilor din Romania)
Caleo Victoriei 141
71102 Bucharest 1, Romania
Phone: 650 28 38
Fax: 650 28 25

10406
Romanian Union of Composers Prizes
For recognition of the most outstanding works in composition and musicology. Several monetary awards, subscriptions to Actualitatea Muzicala, and sponsoring for various music festivals in Romania (depending upon the kind of musical work) are awarded annually. Established in 1968.

10407
Union of Architects of Romania
(Uniunea Arhitectilor din Romania)
18-20 Academiei St.
79182 Bucharest, Romania
Phone: 0 15 84 72
Phone: 0 14 07 43
Fax: 0 15 84 72

Formerly: (1991) Union of Architects of the SRR.

10408
Union of Architects of Romania Prize
For recognition of the outstanding design and execution of buildings and ensembles of buildings as well as planning works. Functionality, originality, and style are considered. Union members are eligible. A monetary prize and an honorary recognition are awarded annually. Established in 1953. Formerly: Union of Architects of the SRR Prize.

10409
Writer's Union of the SRR
(Uniunea Scriitorilor din Romania)
Calea Victoriei 133
71102 Bucharest, Romania
Phone: 0 50 72 45
Fax: 0 50 55 94

10410
Brasov Writers Association Award
For recognition of outstanding contributions to Romanian literature. Monetary awards and honorary recognition are granted annually.

10411
Bucharest Writers Association Award
For recognition of outstanding literary works in the following categories: poetry, prose, criticism and history of literature, literature for children and youth, translation from the world literature, and drama. Monetary prizes and honorary recognition are awarded annually.

10412
Cluj Writers Association Award
For recognition of outstanding literary activity and achievements. A monetary award and honorary recognition are awarded annually.

10413
Jassy Writers Association Award
For recognition of outstanding literary activity and achievements. A monetary award and honorary recognition are granted annually.

10414
Romanian Writers' Union Prizes
To recognize outstanding literary works in the following categories: poetry, prose, drama, literary criticism, history of literature, journalism, literature for children and youth, translations from world literature, and a new literary work written by a young writer. Monetary prizes and honorary recognition are awarded annually. Established in 1964.

10415 Timisoara Writers Association Award
For recognition of outstanding contributions to Romanian literature. A monetary award and honorary recognition are awarded annually.

10416 Tirgu Mures Writers Association Award
For recognition of outstanding contributions to Romanian literature. Monetary prizes and honorary recognition are awarded annually.

Russia

10417
Academy of Sciences, Moscow
Leninskii prosp. 14   Phone: 234 35 06
117901 Moscow, Russia   Phone: 234 21 53

10418 International Geological L. A. Spendiarov Prize of the USSR Academy of Sciences
For recognition of advanced scientific research, and to strengthen international cooperation in the field of geosciences. Citizens of the country which is the organizer of the International Geological Congress at which the prize is awarded are eligible. A monetary prize and a diploma are awarded every four years. Established in 1897 by A. Spendiarov, in memory of his son, Leonid A. Spendiarov, who perished during a geological excursion at the 7th IGC in St. Petersburg. Additional information is available from Dr. Ruslan I. Volkov, Exec. Sec. of the National Committee of Geologists, Pyzhevsky 7, 109017 Moscow Zh-17, Russia.

10419 Lomonosov Gold Medal
For recognition of outstanding works in the natural, physical, and social sciences. Two gold medals with the profile of the Russian scientist, M.V. Lomonosov, are awarded annually: one to a Soviet scientist; and one to a foreign scholar. Established in 1956 by the Council of Ministers of the USSR. First awarded in 1959.

10420
Academy of Sciences, Moscow
Section of Social Science
Dept. of Literature and Languages
Volkhonka 18/2
121019 Moscow, Russia   Phone: 202 66 25

10421 Belinsky Prize
For recognition of the best works of literary criticism, and the theory and history of literature. A monetary prize is awarded annually.

10422 N. A. Dobrolyubov Prize
To recognize Soviet scientists for outstanding work in literary criticsm. A monetary prize of 2,000 rubles is awarded triennially. Established in 1969 by the Council of Ministers.

10423 Alexander Sergeovich Pushkin Prize
To recognize Soviet scientists for outstanding work in the Russian language. A monetary prize of 2,000 rubles is awarded triennially. Established in 1969 by the Council of Ministers.

10424
All-Union Leninist Young Communist League
c/o Committee of Youth Organizations of
  the USSR
ul. Bogdana Chmelnitskovo 7/8
101846 Moscow, Russia   Phone: 206 85 42

Defunct organization.

10425 Agriculture Award
To recognize young people who work well in agriculture, and the citizens of big cities who help them.

10426 Certificate of Honor
To recognize individuals in all areas of endeavor for doing their job well.

10427 Chronicle of Komsomol Honor
To recognize collectives that work well in all kinds of areas such as agriculture, industry, and sports. The name of the collective is inscribed in the honor book of Komsomol.

10428 Efficiency of Labor Award
To recognize individuals who have raised the quality and effectiveness of labor.

10429 Environmental Protection Award
To recognize young people, adults, and foreigners for active participation in guarding the natural environment.

10430 Friendship Medal
To recognize individuals and organizations for outstanding contributions to improve the friendship of young people in all countries.

10431 Gaydar Award
To recognize adults for work with young peopol in schools, children's homes (orphanages), and in special schools. The award is named for Gaydar, a patriotic writer for young people, who was killed in World War II.

10432 High Quality of Work Award
To recognize young people for contributions to science, culture, sports, and military service. The Honoree's name is inscribed in an honor book.

10433 Komsomol Medal
This, the highest medal of Komsomol is given to a Komsomol member, or young party member, for outstanding accomplishments in all areas of the economy, military, or sports. Young people, or the adults who worked with them and also foreign citizens who did something to improve the friendship between many people, are eligible. A medal is awarded on October 29, the anniversary of the establishment of the Komsomol.

10434 Komsomol Propagandist Award
To recognize individuals for all kinds of propaganda.

10435 Komsomol Special Award for Science and Technology
To recognize outstanding young science workers, college teachers, engineers and agricultural workers. Monetary awards are presented.

10436
Komsomol Work Award
To recognize individuals who work well in Komsomol jobs.

10437
Labor Courage Award
To recognize young people and adults for work in the military, agriculture, art, literature, journalism, and sports.

10438
Literature, Art, Journalism, and Architecture Awards
To recognize young people and adults who help young people in the fields of: literature, art, journalism, and architecture.

10439
Master - Gold Hands Award
To recognize young professional craftsmen for creative work for the national economy, military and railroads.

10440
Military Awards
Three types of military awards are presented to recognize: (1) military young people for courage and skills in all military specialties; (2) generals and admirals who work with young people; and (3) foreign military personnel, e.g., Warsaw Block.

10441
My Country - USSR Award
To recognize patriotic young people who learn about their country and native area, its history, party history, and the revolutionary history.

10442
My Country - USSR Award
To recognize youth and adult organizers of youth tourism, such as coaches and instructors.

10443
Pedagogy Award
To recognize teachers of young people in all types of schools such as, colleges, recreation centers and professional institutes.

10444
Railroad Construction Award
To recognize young workers for construction of the BAM Railroad, which was built under difficult conditions in the north.

10445
Scout Leader Award
To recognize supervisors of scout groups.

10446
Sports Award
To recognize outstanding Soviet sportsmen and coaches. A medal is awarded.

10447
Training Award
To recognize instructors of young people.

10448
Young People and Adult Supervisors Award
To recognize active work by student groups during the summer when the groups assist in all areas of agriculture, building, and railroad construction.

10449
Young Teacher's Award
To recognize teachers under the age of 28 for work in all kinds of schools, colleges, and professional schools.

10450
International Association of Teachers of Russian Language and Literature
ul. Volgina, 6
117485 Moscow, Russia
Phone: 330 89 92
Fax: 330 85 65

10451
A. S. Pushkin's Medal
For recognition of contributions to teaching the Russian language and scientific research concerning the Russian language. A medal is awarded annually. Established in 1977 by IATR and the Ministry of Higher Education of USSR in memory of A.S. Pushkin, a famous Russian poet of the 19th century.

10452
International Dmitri Shostakovich Competition of String Quartets
Organizing Committee
15 Neglinnaya St.
Moscow, Russia
Phone: 925 96 49
Fax: 288 95 88

10453
International Dmitri Shostakovich Competition of String Quartets
For recognition of outstanding string quartets. The competition is open to quartets the aggregate age of whose performers does not exceed 150 years, while each player in the quartet should not be over 45 years old at the time of the Competition. The deadline for application is June 31. The following prizes are awarded: (1) First Prize - 4,000 rubles and a gold medal; (2) Second Prize - 3,200 rubles and a silver medal; (3) Third Prize - 2,000 rubles and a bronze medal; (4) Two certificates and 1,000 rubles each; and (5) 800 rubles to the best performer of the work by a Soviet composer.

10454
International Tchaikovsky Competition
ul. Neglinnaya 15
103051 Moscow, Russia
Phone: 925 96 49
Fax: 288 95 88

10455
International Tchaikovsky Competition
To recognize the best pianists, violinists, cellists, and vocalists of the Competition. Prizes are also awarded for meritorious performances of Tchaikovsky's music. Instrumentalists who are between 18 and 32 years of age and singers between 18 and 34 years of age are eligible. The Organizing Committee of the International Tchaikovsky Competition offers eight prizes and four certificates to pianists; eight prizes and four certificates to violinists; eight prizes and four certificates to cellists; six prizes and two certificates to female singers, and six prizes and two certificates to male singers. The following monetary awards are presented: (1) First Prize - 5,000 rubles and a Gold Medal; (2) Second Prize - 4,000 rubles and a Silver Medal; (3) Third Prize - 3,000 rubles and a Bronze Medal; (4) Fourth Prize - 2,400 rubles and an honorary badge; (5) Fifth Prize - 2,000 rubles and an honorary badge; (6) Sixth Prize - 1,600 rubles and an honorary badge; (7) Seventh Prize - 1,200 rubles and an honorary badge; and (8) Eighth Prize - 800 rubles and an honorary badge. The recipients of certificates receive a prize of 250 rubles each. A prize of 250 rubles is also awarded in each group to the best performer of obligatory work by a Soviet composer. In the solo voice group, a prize is also awarded for the best performance of compositions by M. Mussorgsky. The first three laureates are engaged in concert tours in the USSR. The Competition is held every four years. Established in 1958.

10456
Moscow International Ballet Competition
ul. Neglinnaya 15
103051 Moscow, Russia

10457
Moscow International Ballet Competition
For recognition of outstanding contributions to choreography which express a realistic approach to the art of ballet. Dancers (soloist and duets) between 17 and 27 years of age, and choreographers are eligible. Gold, silver, and bronze medals, and monetary prizes are awarded. Awards for choreography and for accompanianists are presented every four years. Established in 1969. Moscow is one of four locations for the International Ballet Competition, the others being Varna, Bulgaria; Jackson, Mississippi, U.S.A.; and Helsinki, Finland. The competition was held in Moscow in 1989.

10458
Presidium of the Supreme Soviet of the USSR
Kremlin
Moscow, Russia   Phone: 925 9051

Defunct organization.

10459
Gold Star Medal
For recognition of outstanding public service to the country through the performance of an heroic deed. The title "Hero of the Soviet Union," the Order of Lenin and a Gold Star Medal are awarded when merited. Established in 1934. In addition, since 1936, over 47 medals have been established by the State to recognize citizens for special service, particularly military service in various battles.

10460
Hammer and Sickle Gold Medal
For recognition of outstanding service to the Soviet state and contributions to its economic and cultural development. Awards are given in the following categories: (1) achievements in science; (2) improvement of production in industry; (3) important contribution in the development of Soviet literature and to authors active in the public life of the country; (4) scholarly works in the field of international relations; (5) development of Soviet cinematography; (6) music; and (7) architecture. Soviet Union citizens and sometimes foreigners are eligible. The title "Hero of Socialist Labor," the Order of Lenin and a medal of gold with a likeness of Lenin in platinum and gold, embossed with a hammer and sickle (symbol of cooperation of workers and peasants) are awarded. Established in 1938.

10461
Honorary Titles of the USSR
For recognition of the achievements of outstanding citizens and groups. The Presidium of the Supreme Soviet established and awards the following titles: Hero of the Soviet Union, Hero of Socialist Labor, Hero City, Hero Fortress, Pilot-Cosmonaut of the USSR, Mother- Heroine, People's Artist of the USSR, People's Architect of the USSR, Honored Military Pilot of the USSR, Honored Military Navigator of the USSR, Honored Test Pilot of the USSR, Honored Test Navigator of the USSR, Honored Pilot of the USSR, and Honored Navigator of the USSR. In addition, the Presidium of the Supreme Soviet of the Republics have established and awarded honorary titles.

10462
Order of Friendship of Peoples
To recognize citizens, organizations, societies, businesses, departments, and foreign citizens for outstanding work toward the strengthening of friendship and brotherly cooperation between socialist nations and peoples, for promoting the cultural development of the Soviet Union, or for promoting the fraternal friendship and cooperation between the socialist countries. A medal is awarded. Established in 1972.

10463
Order of Lenin
This, the highest decoration in the USSR, is given for: (1) outstanding service to the development of public health care and medical care; (2) contribution to science and technology and training of research personnel; (3) distinguished public service to the Soviet state and to the Communist party; (4) contribution to the cause of strengthening the Soviet defense capabilities; (5) achievements in the development of Soviet agriculture; (6) education; (7) construction; (8) social sciences and philosophy; (9) outstanding efforts in the fine arts; (10) music; (11) film; (12) theatre; (13) literature; and (14) architecture. Individuals, collectives, enterprises and social organizations are eligible. A medal of gold with a likeness of Lenin in platinum is awarded when merited. Recipients receive rights to income tax exemption, pension rights, transportation privileges and monthly payments. Established in 1930. Since 1924, approximately 20 orders of the USSR have been established.

10464
Order of the Glory of Labor
To recognize workers displaying selfless, highly productive, long-term labor at the same factory, construction site or farm. A medal is awarded. The following privileges accompany the medal: (1) an additional 15 percent on the winner's pension; (2) first priority for living space; (3) one free round-trip voyage per year in first class by rail, boat or airplane (within the Soviet Union); (4) free use of all public transport; (5) free stay, once a year, in a sanitorium or rest home; and (6) the right to receive public services or buy tickets at cultural events without waiting in line. Established in 1974.

10465
Order of the October Revolution
For recognition of revolutionary activity and outstanding contributions in building and strengthening Soviet power and the socialistic system, and constructing communism. Citizens, enterprises, offices, organizations and military units as well as republics, regions and cities and foreigners are eligible for the Order. A medal made of silver is awarded. Established in 1967 to commemorate the 50th anniversary of the October Revolution.

10466
Order of the Red Banner
To recognize individuals and military units for unusual courage and heroism in war actions against the enemies of the Soviet Union and for successes in military and political training. A silver medal is awarded when merited. Established in 1924.

10467
Order of the Red Banner of Labor
For recognition of an outstanding contribution to the cultural and economic development of the Soviet Union as well as for scientific and literary achievements. A medal is awarded. Established in 1928.

10468
Presidium of the Supreme Soviet of the USSR
Committee on Lenin and USSR State Prizes in the Fields of Science and Technology
S-ya Tvyerskaya-Yamskaya D.46
125047 Moscow, Russia   Phone: 972 35 23

Defunct organization.

10469
Lenin Prize
For recognition of outstanding achievement in the humanities. Government and non-government associations may nominate Soviet and foreign citizens. A monetary award of 20,000 rubles to a group of four or fewer individuals, a breastplate and a diploma are awarded biannually in even-numbered years on the occasion of Lenin's birthday.

10470

State Prize in Science and Technology
To recognize outstanding achievement in the natural sciences. Government and non-government associations may nominate Soviet and foreign citizens. A monetary prize of 10,000 rubles to a group of eight or fewer individuals, a breastplate and a diploma are awarded annually on the date of the October Revolution.

10471

Presidium of the Supreme Soviet of the USSR International Lenin Peace Prize Committee
Kremlin
Moscow, Russia

Defunct organization.

10472

International Lenin Peace Prize
For recognition of outstanding services performed in the struggle for preserving and strengthening peace. A monetary prize of 25,000 rubles, a gold medal, and a diploma are presented. Up to five prizes are awarded annually by the International Committee. Established in 1950.

10473

Sovinterfest
International Film Festivals and Exhibitions
  Goskino
10 Khokhlovsky Pereulok   Phone: 297 76 45
109028 Moscow, Russia   Phone: 227 89 24

10474

Moscow International Film Festival
To provide recognition for the best full-length feature films. The following prizes are awarded: (1) Grand Prize - for the best feature film; (2) Special Prize of the Jury; (3) Best actor; and (4) Best actress. In addition, a Grand Prix and a Special Prize are awarded by the International Jury of Film Clubs. Awarded biennially. Established in 1959.

10475

Union of Soviet Architects
ul. Shchuseva 3
103889 Moscow, Russia   Phone: 290 25 79

10476

Union of Soviet Architects Prizes
For recognition of the best architectural and artistic accomplishment in the construction of industrial and civil units presented during the exhibition of creative achievements in Soviet architecture. Monetary prizes of up to 1,000 rubles and diplomas are awarded biennially.

10477

Union of Soviet Journalists
bul'var Zubovskiy 4   Phone: 201 77 70
95 2017770 Moscow, Russia   Fax: 200 42 37

10478

Best Journalist Work of the Year
For recognition of the best work by a journalist during the preceding year. Fifteen prizes, each 1,000 rubles including one prize for young journalists under 30, one prize for journalists of regional, city and union newspapers, and one each for the best sketch, the best reporting, and fuilleton (cultural section of a newspaper). Recipients may not have received a union prize within the last five years. Groups of more than three are not eligible.

10479

Soviet Journalists Media Prize
To recognize Soviet Journalists for contributions in the following areas: history, theory and practice in the area of the Soviet press, television, and radio. A monetary prize of 1,000 rubles is awarded every five years.

10480

Ulianova Prize
For recognition of the best contribution in the area of mass propaganda. Prizes are divided into the following categories: (1) Central Publications - 700 rubles; (2) Republic Publications - 2 x 600 rubles; (3) Oblast, city, and evening newspapers - 3 x 500 rubles; (4) Regional and Union - 3 x 400 rubles; (5) Syndicated Newspapers - 3 x 200 rubles. Works of outstanding professionals reflecting the struggle of the Soviet people as promulgated by the recent plenums and party congresses and the transformations taking place in society are eligible.

10481

Union Prize for Publicistic (Publishers)
Open to Journalists in the following categories: Editorial Collectives of the Central Republic, Kray, city, and county Rayon syndicated newspapers, journals and television and radio committees as well as information agencies. Competition winners receive: Central Press Publications - 1,000; Pubs. of Union Republics 2 x 800 rubles; Pubs. of Autonomous Republics, Krays and Obelasts, 4 x 600 rubles; Akrugs, union, city, and regional newspapers 5 x 400 rubles; syndicated newspapers, or factory newsbroadcasts 3 x 200 rubles.

10482

Vorovsky Prizes
To recognize Soviet and foreign journalists who have made significant contributions in international journals. Three prizes of 1,000 rubles are awarded annually.

10483

USSR Council of Ministers
Kremlin
Moscow, Russia   Phone: 925 9051

Defunct organization.

10484

Best Project of the Year Prize
For recognition of construction of large industrial and civil units of excellent quality by collectives of architects and builders. A monetary prize, amounting to as much as 20,000 rubles and a diploma are awarded annually.

10485

USSR Council of Ministers and the Central Committee of the Communist Party of the Soviet Union
Staraya pl. 4
103132 Moscow, Russia   Phone: 206 2511

Defunct organization.

10486

USSR State Prize for Architecture
For recognition of the best work in the field of architecture of importance throughout the Soviet Union. A monetary prize of 2,500 rubles, the honorary title "State Prize of the USSR Laureate," and investiture with the breast-plate are awarded annually.

Saudi Arabia

10487
Islamic Development Bank
Islamic Research and Training Institute
PO Box 9201
Jeddah 21413, Saudi Arabia
Phone: 2 6361400
Fax: 2 6378927

10488
Islamic Development Bank Prizes in Islamic Economics and Islamic Banking
To recognize, reward, and encourage creative efforts of outstanding merit in the fields of Islamic economics and Islamic banking. Such efforts may take the form of research, teaching, training, mobilization of intellectual and scientific capabilities that would contribute to the promotion of Islamic values in economics and banking, or any other related activity. Individuals, universities, academic, financial, and Islamic institutions throughout the world may nominate whoever they deem eligible. One prize is awarded annually, alternating between Islamic economics and Islamic banking. A monetary award of 30,000 Islamic dinars (equivalent to US $42,250 approximately) and a citation are awarded for each. Established in 1986.

10489
Islamic Foundation for Science, Technology and Development
(Fondation Islamique pour la Science, la Technologie et le Developpement)
PO Box 9833
Jeddah 21423, Saudi Arabia
Phone: 2 6322292
Fax: 2 6322274

10490
Islamic Foundation Awards
To provide advisory services in science and technology, promote coordination of scientific and technological research and its applications to the Muslim world, and work to ensure the integration of science and technology in the socio-economic plans of Muslim states. Scholarships are presented.

10491
Islamic States Broadcasting Services Organization
(Organisation des Radiodiffusions des Etats Islamiques)
PO Box 6351
Jeddah 21442, Saudi Arabia
Phone: 2 6722269
Fax: 2 672600

10492
Islamic Countries Festival for Radio Production
To promote Islamic ideals through broadcasting services, to produce Islamic radio programs, and to coordinate program exchanges among member states. The Organization sponsors competitions for the production of Islamic programs of high standards. Programs produced by member states' official broadcasting services are eligible. A Certificate of Honour is awarded biennially. Established in 1983. (Inactive since 1986)

10493
King Abdul Aziz Research Centre
PO Box 2945
Riyadh 11461, Saudi Arabia
Phone: 1 4412318
Fax: 1 4412316

10494
King Abdul Aziz Prize
To provide recognition for the best book on the history of the Kingdom of Saudi Arabia and the history of the Saudi dynasty in particular. Two monetary prizes of 40,000 Saudi riyals each and a third prize of 25,000 Saudi riyals are awarded annually. Established in 1972. (Inactive since 1982) Formerly: King Faisal Prize.

10495
King Faisal International Prize General Secretariat
(Al Amanah Al Ammah Li Jaezat Al Malik Faisal Al Alamiyyah)
PO Box 22476
Riyadh 11495, Saudi Arabia
Phone: 1 4652255
Fax: 1 4658685

10496
King Faisal International Prize for Arabic Literature
(Jaezat Al Malik Faisal Al Alamiyyah Lil Adab Al Arabi)
To provide recognition for achievement in the field of Arabic literature, and to encourage studies and creativity in this field. Individuals may be nominated by universities, academies, educational institutions and research centers throughout the world. A monetary award of 350,000 Saudi riyals, a certificate, and a gold medal are awarded annually in a special official ceremony. Established in 1977, and first awarded in 1980 in memory of King Faisal Ibn Abdul Azia al-Saud, former King of Saudi Arabia.

10497
King Faisal International Prize for Islamic Studies
(Jaezat Al Malik Faisal Al Alamiyyah Lil Derasat Al Islamiyyah)
To recognize individuals for scientific activities in the field of Islamic Studies. Scholars may be nominated by universities, academies, educational institutions and research centers throughout the world. A monetary award of 350,000 Saudi riyals, a certificate, and a gold medal are awarded annually in a special official ceremony. Established in 1977, and first awarded in 1979 in memory of the late King Faisal Ibn Abdul Azia al-Saud, former King of Saudi Arabia.

10498
King Faisal International Prize for the Service of Islam
(Jaezat Al Malik Faisal Al Alamiyyah Li Khidmt Al Islam)
To recognize individuals who have performed exceptional services for the benefit of Islam and Muslims. Individuals may be nominated by Islamic organizations, societies, and unions from all parts of the world. A monetary award of 350,000 Saudi riyals, a certificate, and a gold medal are awarded annually in a special official ceremony. Established in 1977, and first awarded in 1979 in memory of King Faisal Ibn Abdul Azia al-Saud, former King of Saudi Arabia.

10499
King Faisal International Prize in Medicine
(Jaezat Al Malik Faisal Al Alamiyyah Lil Tib)
To recognize individuals for a published work in the field of medicine leading to the benefit of mankind and the enrichment of human thought. Individuals may be nominated by universities, academies, educational institutions and research centers throughout the world. The deadline for submissions is September 1. A monetary award of 350,000 Saudi Riyals, a certificate, and a gold medal are awarded annually in a special official ceremony. Established in 1980, and first awarded in 1982 in memory of King Faisal Ibn Abdul Azia al-Saud, former King of Saudi Arabia.

10500
King Faisal International Prize in Science
(Jaezat Al Malik Faisal Al Alamiyyah Lil Ulum)
To recognize individuals for a published work in the field of science leading to the benefit of mankind and the enrichment of human thought. Individuals may be nominated by universities, academies, educational institutions and research centers throughout the world. The deadline for submissions is September 1. A monetary award of 350,000 Saudi riyals, a certificate, and a gold medal are awarded annually in a special official ceremony. Established in 1980, and first awarded in 1983 in memory of King Faisal Ibn Abdul Azia al-Saud, former King of Saudi Arabia.

10501
Organization of Islamic Capitals and Cities (OICC)
PO Box 13621
Jeddah 21414, Saudi Arabia
Phone: 2 6655896
Fax: 2 6657516

Formerly: (1984) Islamic Capitals Organization.

10502

Book Awards
To recognize the best books on urban and city planning, architecture, municipal services, utilities, heritage preservation, environmental protection, and municipal administration. Prizes are awarded every 3 years.

10503

Union of Arab Football Associations
Olympic Complex
Deriyyah Rd.
PO Box 62997
Riyadh 11595111, Saudi Arabia
Phone: 1 4820920
Fax: 1 4823196

10504

Arab Sports Pressman Award
To recognize an Arab sports pressman for contributions to Arab football for at least 15 years. Candidates may be submitted by the Arab Football Federations. Established in 1987.

Scotland

10505

Association for the Protection of Rural Scotland
Gladstone's Land, 3rd Fl.
483 Lawnmarket
Edinburgh EH1 2NT, Scotland
Phone: 31 2257012
Fax: 31 2256592

10506

APRS Annual Award
To encourage good planning and to recognize structures that make a contribution to the appearance and amenity of the countryside in Scotland. New or reconstructed buildings, works, or other structures in the Scottish countryside, completed within four years of entry, are eligible. Entries must be submitted by July 31. A plaque to be affixed to the building externally or internally; a diploma to the promoter, contractor, and architect; and a certificate of commendation to the runner-up are awarded annually in November. The award alternates each year between a new work and a work of reconstruction. Established in 1975 in connection with Scotland's participation in the European Architectural Heritage Year.

10507

Eyebright Award
To encourage environmental improvements of areas of dereliction in rural settings in Scotland. A specially designed trophy and scroll were awarded to the winning entry and scrolls to runners-up. Awarded triennially. Established in 1987 to commemorate the European Year of the Environment. (Discontinued)

10508

Association in Scotland to Research Into Astronautics
16 Oakfield Ave.
Glasgow G12 8JE, Scotland
Phone: 41 339 2558

10509

Astra Trophy
To recognize members who have significantly contributed to ASTRA activities during the year. Awarded annually at the Association's anniversary dinner.

10510

Victor Hirt Prize
To recognize the best individual flight at the Scottish Rocket Weekend Aquajet Contest. Awarded annually.

10511

Honorary Member
To recognize major achievements in astronautics and significant contributions to Association activities. Life membership is awarded by vote of the Council or general meeting. Established in 1963.

10512

Oscar Schwiglhofer Trophy
To recognize the winning team in the Scottish Rocket Weekend Aquajet Contest. Awarded annually.

10513

Book Trust (Scotland)
Scottish Book Center
137 Dundee St.
Edinburgh EH11 1BG, Scotland
Phone: 31 2293663
Fax: 31 2281293

Formerly: National Book League (Scotland).

10514

Kathleen Fidler Award
To encourage writers for children ages eight to twelve years old. Novels that are 20,000 words or more, unpublished, and the first work attempted for this age group by the author may be submitted by October 31 each year. A monetary prize of £1,000, a rosewood and silver trophy, and publication by Blackie are awarded annually in October. Established in 1983 by Blackie and Son Limited, the Federation of Children's Book Groups and the Book Trust Scotland in honor of Kathleen Fidler, a Scottish children's author. Sponsored by Blackie and Son Limited.

10515

British Association of Paediatric Surgeons
Royal College of Surgeons of Edinburgh
Nicolson St.
Edinburgh EH8 9DW, Scotland
Phone: 31 6683975

10516

British Association of Paediatric Surgeons Awards
To recognize individuals who work to improve the techniques of study, practice, and research in pediatric surgery. The BAPS Annual Prize, John Grant Memorial Prize, and the Denis Browne Gold Medal are awarded annually.

10517

British Broadcasting Corporation
BBC Educational Radio
Broadcasting House
5 Queen St.
Edinburgh EH2 1JF, Scotland
Phone: 31 2431274

10518

A Kelpie for the Nineties
To recognize an author for a new work of fiction for children. Previously published work cannot be entered. The winning novel is published by Canongate Publishing Ltd. and dramatized on BBC Radio Scotland. Awarded biennially. Established in 1985. Co-sponsored by the Scottish Libraries Association. Formerly: (1989) A Quest for a Kelpie.

10519

British Society of Animal Production
PO Box 3
Penicuik, Lothian EH26 ORZ, Scotland
Phone: 31 4454508
Fax: 31 4455636

10520
Sir John Hammond Memorial Prize
To recognize an individual who works or has worked in the United Kingdom or Ireland in research, teaching, advising, farming, or affiliated professions, and has made a significant contribution to the development of animal production based on the application of knowledge of animal physiology. Individuals under 45 years of age may be nominated. A monetary award and a certificate are presented annually at the winter meeting of the Society. Established in 1968 to honor Sir John Hammond.

10521
Celtic Film and Television Association
c/o The Library, Farraline Park
Inverness IV1 1LS, Scotland
Phone: 463 226189
Fax: 463 237001

Formerly: (1988) Association for Film and Television in the Celtic Countries.

10522
International Festival of Film and Television in the Celtic Countries
For recognition of achievement by outstanding filmmakers and to encourage younger filmmakers. Individuals who reside or work in Celtic countries may apply. Awards are given in the following categories: (1) Documentary and Features; (2) Starting Out; (3) News and Current Affairs; (4) Drama; (5) Made for Young People; (6) Entertainment; and (7) Spirit of the Festival - to the overall winner. Trophies are awarded annually. Established in 1985.

10523
College of Piping
16-24 Otago St.
Glasgow G12 8JH, Scotland
Phone: 41 3343587
Fax: 41 3373024

10524
Balvenie Medal
For recognition of services to piping. A silver medal, struck in Edinburgh, which carries a likeness of William Grant, the founder of The Glenfiddich Distillery, on the face is awarded annually. Established in 1985.

10525
Glenfiddich Trophy
For recognition of outstanding piping. There are two panels of three judges for each of the two sections of the championships: piobaireachd, with each piper submitting six tunes in advance from which the judges will select one; and march, strathspey, and reel with the judges selecting three tunes from those submitted. The following prizes are awarded: first overall prize - one year's retention of the Glenfiddich Trophy, £600, and an inscribed sgian dhu; second prize - £300; and third prize - £150. Additional prizes are also awarded annually. Established in 1974.

10526
Collegium Internationale Neuro-Psychopharmacologicum
c/o Gill Houston
Office of the President
51 Sunnybank Dr.
Clarkston
Glasgow G76 7SS, Scotland
Phone: 41 6202026
Fax: 41 6380931

10527
Max Hamilton Memorial Prize
To recognize a young scientist under 40 years of age for outstanding contributions to psychopharmacology. Contributions may be in clinical evaluation or services, preclinical or clinical research, or any combination of these; based on a single discovery or a cumulative body of work; or empirical advances or a theoretical construct. A monetary prize of $10,000 and an engraved plaque are awarded. Established in honor of Max Hamilton for his assessment of depressive illness through psychometrics. Sponsored by Bristol-Myers Squibb.

10528
Rafaelsen Fellowship Award
To support the attendance of young scientists at the 15th CINP Congress in San Juan, Puerto Rico. Researchers or clinicians under 36 years of age who are committed to the field of neuropsychopharmacology are eligible. Nominations must be made by CINP members. A stipend and a plaque are awarded. Established in 1986 by Ole Rafaelson and William Bunney and named for Dr. Rafaelson posthumously in 1987.

10529
Design Council - Scotland
Ca' d'Oro Bldg.
45 Gordon St.
Glasgow G1 3LZ, Scotland
Phone: 41 221 6121
Fax: 41 221 8799

10530
Scottish Annual Report Prize
For recognition of an annual report of outstanding design and presentation produced by a Scottish based or registered company or organization. Either the designer or the client may enter the report. A trophy is presented at an annual awards ceremony. Established in 1985 by Scottish Business Insider and the Design Council - Scotland. Sponsored by Price Waterhouse.

10531
Scottish Designer of the Year Award
For recognition of outstanding standards of creative skill in design work in the following areas: Product/Engineering, Industrial/Furniture, Graphic/Exhibition, and Textile/Fashion Design. Candidates must be residents of Scotland. A monetary award and a trophy are presented biennially at an award ceremony. Established in 1978. Sponsored by the Clydesdale Bank PLC, Buchanan Street, Glasgow.

10532
Edinburgh Architectural Association
15 Rutland Sq.
Edinburgh EH1 2BE, Scotland
Phone: 31 225 7545
Fax: 31 228 2188

10533
EAA Award for Architecture
To encourage professional development and to recognize outstanding design by a chartered architect within the Chapter. The design must have been built within the Chapter during the preceding year from November 1 to October 31. A medal is awarded annually. Established in 1984.

10534
Edinburgh Festival Fringe
180 High St.
Edinburgh EH1 1QS, Scotland
Phone: 31 2265257
Fax: 31 2204205

10535
Guardian Student Drama Award
To encourage the best in student theater on the Fringe. Winners receive £1,000 and give a special one-off performance of the winning show in the final week of the Fringe. Additional information can be obtained from The Guardian Press Office, 119 Farringdon Rd., London EC1R 3ER.

10536
Independent Theatre Award
To encourage fringe companies to stage new productions at the annual Edinburgh Festival Fringe. The production must run for a minimum of 10 days over the three weeks of the Festival. A monetary prize of £1,000 plus a three week run at the Hampstead Theatre in London are awarded annually in August. Established in 1988 by *The Independent*. Sponsored by *The Independent* and the Hampstead Theatre. Additional information is available from *The Independent*, 40 City Road, London EC1Y 2DB, England.

10537

Perrier Award
For recognition of the most outstanding revue/cabaret in the Edinburgh Festival Fringe. Judging is by a panel of experts and three members of the public. The winner leads the Perrier Pick of the Fringe Season at a leading London theater and receives a monetary award of £3,000. Established in 1981.

10538

Scotsman Fringe First Awards
To encourage presentation of new works of drama. Eligible plays must have been performed not more than six times in the United Kingdom and must be entered in the Fringe Program. Awarded annually. Established in 1974.

10539

***Scottish Daily Express* New Names Awards**
To provide recognition for three fringe companies each year who promote new work in theater and music at the annual Edinburgh Festival Fringe. Performing companies staging new work are considered. Monetary prizes of £1,500 for first prize, £750 for second prize, £250 for third prize are awarded annually in August. Established in 1987 by the *Scottish Daily Express*. Sponsored by the *Scottish Daily Express* newspaper. Additional information is available from the *Scottish Daily Express*, Park House, Park Circus Place, Glasgow G3 6AF, Scotland.

10540

Edinburgh International Film Festival
Eiff Filmhouse
88 Lothian Rd.
Edinburgh EH3 9BZ, Scotland
Phone: 31 2284051
Fax: 31 2295501

10541

Edinburgh International Film Festival
For recognition of outstanding films screened at the Festival. The following prizes are awarded: Charles Chaplin Award - for the best film by a new director; Michael Powell Award - for an outstanding British film; Post Office McLaren Award - for outstanding British animation; and Young Filmmaker of the Year Award - for the best student filmmaker.

10542

European Committee for Young Farmers and 4H Clubs
11 Queensferry Rd.
Edinburgh EH4 3HB, Scotland
Phone: 31 3321874
Fax: 31 3321874

10543

European Committee for Young Farmers and 4H Clubs Awards
To further the work of 4H Clubs and related rural and farming organizations by recognizing young people living in rural areas.

10544

The Fell Pony Society
Riccarton Mill
Newcastleton TD9 0SN, Scotland
Phone: 3873 76251
Fax: 3873 76251

10545

Fell Pony Society Ridden Championship
For recognition of the best Fell Pony shown under saddle. An animal must be fully pedigreed and four years old or over to be eligible. A monetary prize and a trophy are awarded annually. Established in 1973.

10546

The Glasgow Herald
195 Albion St.
Glasgow, Scotland
Phone: 41 552 6255

10547

***The Glasgow Herald* Science Fiction Short Story Competition**
To encourage new writers of science fiction and fantasy, and to recognize the best original short science fiction story (2000 words) in the annual newspaper competition for new writers. A word processor was awarded annually, usually at the science fiction convention. Established in 1986 by the Albacon III Convention. (Discontinued)

10548

Guild of Taxidermists
Glasgow Art Gallery & Museum
Kelvingrove
Glasgow G3 8AG, Scotland
Phone: 41 3573929
Fax: 41 3574537

10549

Professional Member
To recognize an individual for outstanding work in the field of taxidermy. Members of the Guild must submit six examples of their work for judging. Scrolls are presented at the Conference of the Guild. Established in 1983.

10550

Hawthornden Literary Institute
c/o Hawthornden Castle International
 Retreat for Writers
Lasswade
Midlothian EH18 1EG, Scotland
Phone: 31 4402180

10551

Hawthornden Prize
This, the oldest of the British literary prizes, is given for recognition of the best work of imaginative literature published during the previous year. British authors are eligible. It is especially designed to encourage young authors and the word "imaginative" is given a broad interpretation. Biographies are not necessarily excluded. Books do not have to be submitted for the prize. A monetary prize of £2,000 is awarded, usually annually. Established in 1919 by Alice Warrender. Additional information is available from the Hawthornden Prize, 43 Hays Mews, Berkeley Square, London W1X 7RU, England. The Institute also offers its facilities as a retreat to a number of selected Fellows in the spring or autumn.

10552

Institute of Chartered Accountants of Scotland
27 Queen St.
Edinburgh EH2 1LA, Scotland
Phone: 31 2255673
Fax: 31 2253813

10553

The David J Bogie Prize
To recognize the candidate whose performance in the papers in Auditing is the most meritorious. An award of £100 is presented.

10554

The J. C. Burleigh Prize
To award the candidate whose performance in the papers in Information Technology is the most meritorious. £75 is awarded.

10555

The Canadian Prize
To reward the winner of the Institute's Gold Medal. A monetary award of £100 is presented. Established 1967.

10556

The Walid Chorbachi Prizes
To recognize the candidates who placed first, second, and third at the Test of Professional Competence. Awards of £250, £150, £100 are presented.

10557

The James M. Cowie Prize
To award the candidate in Part I who is judged to be second in merit for the Winter Diet. £100 is presented.

10558

Gold Medal
To encourage the professional development of the Institute's students. The award is given to the candidate whose performance, over all parts of the Institute's professional examinations, is judged to be most meritorious. A gold medal is awarded annually. Established in 1961 by Mr. Albert J. Watson, CA. of Hillsborough, U.S.A.

10559

The Guthrie Prize
To award the candidate in Part II who is fourth in order of merit in the Spring Diet.

10560

Lady Members Group
To recognize the TOPP's candidate at Part II whose performance is judged to be first in order of merit. £75 is awarded.

10561

The John Mann Prize
To recognize the candidate whose performance in the papers in Taxation is the most meritorious. An award of £100 is presented.

10562

The Robert McArthur Prize
To award the candidate at Part I who is judged to be third in order of merit in the Spring Diet. £100 is presented.

10563

The Sir William McLintock Prize
To recognize the person who is second in order of merit in the Test of Professional Competence Part I. £100 is awarded.

10564

The Forbes Murphy Prize
To recognize the candidate in Part II whose performance in the paper in Professional Organization and Ethics is the most meritorious. A monetary award of £50 is presented.

10565

The Forbes Murphy Prize
To recognize the candidate whose performance in the Test of Professional Competence Part I is fourth in order of merit. £50 is awarded.

10566

Patrick O'Brien
To recognize the candidate at Part II whose performance is judged to be fifth in order of merit in the Spring Diet. £50 is awarded.

10567

The John Munn Ross Prize
To recognize the candidate whose performance was third in order of merit in the Test of Professional Competence Part I. £100 is awarded.

10568

Helen Sommerville Prize
To recognize the candidate in Part II of the Winter Diet who is fifth in order of merit. £50 is awarded.

10569

The Albert J Watson Prize
To recognize meritorious performance in the Test of Professional Competence Part I. A prize of £200 is awarded.

10570

The C. J. Weir Prize
To award the fourth place winner in the Winter Diet. £50 is presented.

10571

The Ronald Williamson Prize
To provide recognition to the candidate whose performance in the papers in Financial Reporting warrants merit. £100 is awarded.

10572

International Association of Music Libraries
United Kingdom Branch
c/o Richard Turbet
Aberdeen Univ. Library
Queen Mother Library, Meston Walk
Aberdeen AB9 2UE, Scotland
Phone: 224 272592
Fax: 224 487048

10573

C. B. Oldman Prize
For recognition of the best work of music bibliography, librarianship, or reference. Individuals domiciled in the United Kingdom are eligible. A monetary prize of £150 is awarded annually at the IAML (UK) annual study weekend. Established in 1988 in memory of C. B. Oldman.

10574

International Association of Technological University Libraries
Heriot-Watt Univ. Library
Riccarton
Edinburgh EH14 4AS, Scotland
Phone: 31 4495111
Fax: 31 4513164

10575

IATUL Essay Prize
To stimulate young librarians to contribute a paper at an IATUL conference or seminar on some aspect of library development of interest to people who work in technological university libraries. A monetary prize of $500 is awarded annually. Established in 1986.

10576

Travelling Fellowship and Research Grants
To enable staff from member libraries of IATUL to undertake research into management problems of university libraries. Staff from member libraries are eligible. A grant is awarded annually. Established in 1986. (Discontinued)

10577

International PEN - Scotland
33 Drumsheugh Gardens
Edinburgh EH3 7RN, Scotland
Phone: 31 225 1038

10578

Frederick Niven Award
For recognition of an outstanding work of fiction by a Scottish writer published during the preceding three years. A monetary award of £100 was awarded triennially. Established in 1956 with a fund left to Scottish PEN by Mrs. Pauline Niven, widow of the author. (Discontinued in 1984)

10579

International Society on Electrocardiology
Univ. Dept. of Medical Cardiology
Royal Infirmary
10 Alexandra Parade
Glasgow G31 2ER, Scotland
Phone: 41 552 3535
Fax: 41 552 6114

10580

Siemens Elema Young Investigators Award
To encourage young research workers in the field of electrocardiology. Individuals who are under 40 years of age are eligible. The following monetary prizes are awarded annually at the congress: first prize - $500 US; second prize - $300 US; and third prize - $200 US. Established in 1986.

10581

Michael Kelly Associates
Scottish Legal Bldg.
95 Bothwell St.
Glasgow G2 7HY, Scotland
Phone: 41 2042580
Fax: 41 2040245

10582

McVitie's Prize for the Scottish Writer of the Year
To reward excellence in Scottish writing. Any substantial work of an imaginative nature may be entered; for example, novel, poetry, biography, radio and TV scripts, or children's fiction. Works must have been published between September 1 of the previous year and August 31 of the current year. Writers born in Scotland, or who have Scottish parents, or who are or have been residents in Scotland, or who take Scotland as an inspiration are eligible. The deadline for entry is August 31. A monetary prize of £10,000 and a trophy are awarded annually in November. Additional awards of £500 each are presented to four writers. Established in 1987 by United Biscuits (Holdings) PLC. Sponsored by United Biscuits (Holdings) PLC.

10583

Keltic Society and the College of Druidism
PO Box 307
Edinburgh EH9 1XA, Scotland
Phone: 31 6675788

10584

Keltic Society Awards
To promote interest in all branches of Keltic culture and to show its relevance in modern society, and for recognition of new expressions of Keltic art, music, and poetry.

10585

Kevock Choir Midlothian Scotland
185 Causewayside IFI
Edinburgh EH9 1PH, Scotland
Phone: 31 668 2728

10586

Kevock Choir and Bank of Scotland Scottish Folk Song Arrangement Competition
To encourage present day composers to write new arrangements for traditional Scottish folk songs. Entries are accepted. A monetary prize of £200 is awarded for the Judges' Choice Award. An Audience Choice Award is also presented. The Competition was held in 1988, and is to be held again in 1993. Established in 1987.

10587

Ladies' Golf Union
The Scores
St. Andrews, Fife KY16 9AT, Scotland
Phone: 334 75811
Fax: 334 72818

10588

Ladies' British Open Amateur Championship
To recognize the winner of the annual amateur golf championship. A Challenge Cup is awarded. Established in 1893.

10589

Women's British Open Championship
To recognize the winners of the annual golf championship. Two trophies are awarded: (1) Hickson Trophy (The Championship Trophy) - presented by Miss Gillian Hickson to the player returning the lowest score for the 72 holes, and held for one year. The winner is the Women's British Open Champion. If a professional golfer, she receives a check for the first prize, and if an amateur, a voucher; (2) Smyth Salver - presented by Miss Moira Smyth to the amateur competitor returning the lowest score for the 72 holes, and held for one year. The winner also receives a voucher. The Trophies may not leave Great Britain or Ireland. In 1991, the prize fund totaled £150,000. Established in 1976.

10590

National Association of Youth Orchestras
Ainslie House
11 St. Colme St.
Edinburgh EH3 6AG, Scotland
Phone: 31 2254606
Fax: 31 2253568

10591

British Reserve Insurance Conducting Prize
To encourage professional development of young British conductors. UK citizens between 18 and 26 years of age inclusive are eligible. A monetary prize of £400 is awarded biennially. Established in 1988. Sponsored by British Reserve Insurance.

10592

British Reserve Insurance Youth Orchestra Award
To encourage youth orchestra development. Members of the Association are eligible. A monetary prize of £250 each is awarded annually to approximately 10 youth orchestras. Established in 1990. Sponsored by British Reserve Insurance.

10593

Novello Youth Orchestra Award
To stimulate interest in contemporary repertoire and to support youth orchestras in performance. A monetary prize of £1,000 was awarded annually. Established in 1989. Sponsored by Novello & Company Ltd, Music Publishers. (Discontinued)

10594

Dr. William Baird Ross Trust
10 Strathalmond Park
Edinburgh EH4 8AL, Scotland

10595

Dr. William Baird Ross Trust Competition
To encourage the study of church music. Offers a prize every third year for a composition in church music. Amateur or professional musicians who are living and working in Scotland are eligible. Established in 1965 in memory of Dr. William Baird Ross by his daughters.

10596

Royal and Ancient Golf Club of St. Andrews
St. Andrews, Fife KY16 9JD, Scotland
Phone: 334 72112
Fax: 334 77580

10597

British Open Golf Champion
To recognize the winner of the annual golf tournament. Amateur and professional golfers are eligible. Entries must be submitted by June 1. The competition is held in three stages: Regional Qualifying Competitions, Final Qualifying Competitions, and Open Championship. A maximum of 156 competitors participate in the Open Championship. The winner is designated Champion Golfer of the Year and receives the Championship Trophy to retain for one year and the Championship Gold Medal. The first amateur in the Championship, unless he or she is the

winner, receives a Silver Medal, provided that 72 holes have been completed. Other amateurs who complete 72 holes receive a Bronze Medal. Prize money is awarded only to professional golfers. In 1994, monetary awards totaling £1,000,000 will be presented. The Champion Golfer of the Year receives £100,000 for first place. In addition, the Professional Golfers Association awards various trophies at the competition. Established in 1860 by the Prestwick Golf Club, Ayrshire, Scotland.

10598
Royal College of Physicians and Surgeons of Glasgow
234-242 St. Vincent St. Phone: 41 221 6072
Glasgow G2 5RJ, Scotland Fax: 41 221 1804

10599
Ethicon Fellowship
To encourage young fellows and members of the College to further their education by visits to centers abroad or in the United Kingdom. Applications are accepted from fellows and members in Dental Surgery of the Royal College of Physicians and Surgeons of Glasgow. An award of up to £2,000 is granted to defray expenses of travel and subsistence. Applicants are required to submit a report to the Council of the College within two months of return. Application deadline is January 14.

10600
Alexander Fletcher Memorial Prize Lecture
To recognize a medical graduate of Glasgow, St. Andrew's, or Dundee Universities of not more than 10 years standing for a lecture on a subject related to original research done by the lecturer. A monetary prize of £100 is awarded. Established in 1966.

10601
Travelling Fellowships
To encourage the professional development of Fellows, Members or Fellows in Dental Surgery of the College. Fellowship awards of up to £1,500 each for travel and expenses are awarded annually. Established in 1988.

10602
Watson Prize Lecture
To recognize Fellows or Members of the College who are medical graduates of not more than 10 years standing for original work. The award consists of £1,000 and the opportunity to present a lecture. Established in 1893.

10603
T. C. White Prize Lecture
To recognize a dental graduate of not more than 10 years standing. An invitation to deliver a lecture on a subject related to the original work done by the prize winner is awarded. Established in 1984.

10604
T. C. White Travelling Fellowship
To encourage Fellows and Diplomates in Dental Surgery of the College to further their education and experience by visits to centers abroad or in the United Kingdom. Travel expenses up to £1,500 are awarded annually. Established in 1986 in honor of Prof. T.C. White. A T.C. White Visiting Scholarship is also awarded for travel in the United Kingdom.

10605
Royal College of Surgeons of Edinburgh
Nicolson St.
Edinburgh EH8 9DW, Scotland Phone: 31 556 6206

10606
Honorary Fellow
To recognize distinguished persons who have made notable contributions to the science and practice of surgery or to recognize distinguished persons outside the profession of surgery, who have made notable contributions to the College. Individuals are nominated. A diploma of Honorary Fellowship is presented when merited. Established in 1671.

10607
Lister Professorship
To select a lecturer for the Clinical and Scientific Meeting. An honorarium, a travel allowance, and an invitation to deliver a lecture at the Clinical and Scientific Meeting are awarded annually. Established in 1982 in honor of Baron Joseph Lister of Lyme Regis, Fellow and Honorary Fellow of the College, and a leading figure in the history of surgery, especially noted for the antiseptic method.

10608
Syme Professorship
To recognize the Fellow who presents the best paper at a special session during the annual Clinical and Scientific Meeting. Selection is limited to Fellows of the College for research in the practice and science of surgery. The work should not have been published elsewhere prior to the date of completion. There is no age limit. The Award, which includes a medal and travel allowance, is presented at the Meeting. Established in 1986 in honor of Professor James Syme (1799-1870), President of the College, 1849-50, and Professor of Clinical Surgery, University of Edinburgh.

10609
Royal Incorporation of Architects in Scotland
15 Rutland Sq. Phone: 31 2297545
Edinburgh EH1 2BF, Scotland Phone: 31 2292188

10610
Sir Rowand Anderson Silver Medal
To recognize the best student member of Scotland. Portfolios must be submitted to the Secretary of the RIAS by October 31. Candidates, who must be within a year of passing Part II, would normally be sponsored by a school of architecture. A monetary award of £300, a silver medal, and a certificate are awarded annually. Established in 1966.

10611
Sir John Burnet Memorial Award
To test students' skill in architectural design and ability to communicate their proposals in response to a client's brief through drawings, prepared within a predetermined time limit. Competitors must be student members of the RIAS who have passed the Part I examination or equivalent and who have not passed the RIBA Part III examination or equivalent. Arrangements are made by each school to hold the *en loge*, normally in February. A monetary prize of £150 and a certificate are awarded annually.

10612
Sir Robert Lorimer Memorial Award
For recognition of the best set of freelance sketches. Applications must be submitted to the Secretary, RIAS, by January 31 of each year. Competitors must be members or student members who are under the age of 29 years. The sketches should be analytical and illustrate in graphic form any architectural subject either existing or projected, and can be in any medium. A book voucher of £125 and a certificate are awarded annually. Established in 1933.

10613
Regeneration of Scotland Design Award
To recognize the increasing importance of good design to the Scottish economy. A trophy, scroll, and a plaque are awarded annually. Established in 1985. This award is a joint initiative of the Scottish Enterprise and the Royal Incorporation of Architects in Scotland. Additional information is available from Kate Comfort, Director of Public Affairs.

10614
RIAS Award for Measured Drawing
To encourage and recognize measured drawing as essential to an architect's training. The committee judges competitors on the following points: the choice of architectural fabric, for the measured study, such

buildings as under threat (buildings need not be old); the clarity of understanding and accuracy revealed by the drawing; and the elegance with which the analysis is presented. Student members, and member of the RIAS under the age of 29 may submit entries by January 31. Monetary awards of £150 to £400 and certificates are presented annually. Formerly: RIAS/Acanthus Award for Measured Drawing.

10615

RIAS/John Maclaren Travelling Fellowship
To provide for the study of contemporary architectural design and construction outside the United Kingdom. The money may be used to assist with study at a School of Architecture or Engineering, to take up a paid position in practice in the country chosen for study, or as a reward for work that has included study overseas. Applicants must be on the Register of Registered Architects, and Corporate Members of the Royal Incorporation. Either a completed study in the form of appropriate written and illustrated material or a written statement outlining the proposed nature and purpose of the study must be submitted by January 31. A monetary award of £600 and a certificate are awarded biennially. At the outset, the winner of the fellowship is paid a sum of £500. The issue of the certificate and the balance is made upon receipt of the report and material and delivery of the dissertation as appropriate. Established in 1952.

10616

RIAS/Whitehouse Studio Award for Architectural Photography
To recognize that architectural photography is a distinct art, and to encourage its appreciation and development. Student members and members of the RIAS under the age of 29 may submit entries by January 31. Competitors may submit a set of not more than six related photographs in color, or black and white. A monetary award of £250 and a certificate are presented annually. Formerly: RIAS/Dunedin Award for Architectural Photography; RIAS/Alastair Hunter Award for Architectural Photography.

10617

Thomas Ross Award
To provide for the production of a thesis or report resulting from research or study of: ancient Scottish buildings or monuments, or matters pertaining particularly to Scotland and to Scottish architecture and/or environment. Candidates must be members of the RIAS, be otherwise of graduate status, or submit other evidence of their qualifications as may satisfy the requirements of RIAS. An outline of the proposed subject of study must be submitted by January 31. A monetary prize of £600, with the possibility of additional help towards publication, and a certificate are awarded biennially. At the outset of the study, the nominee for the award is paid the sum of £300 which must be repaid if an acceptable study is not submitted within a two-year period. The final bound report must be presented for consideration by the first day in March two years following. If acceptable, the balance of £300 is paid. Established in 1966.

10618

Royal Scottish Academy of Painting, Sculpture and Architecture
The Mound
Edinburgh EH2 2EL, Scotland   Phone: 31 225 6671

10619

Annual Exhibition of the Royal Scottish Academy
To recognize outstanding art at the Annual Exhibition. Exhibits may be submitted in oil, water-colour, acrylic, pastel, drawings, prints, sculpture and architecture. The following major awards are presented: RSA Medal for Architecture - for recognition of outstanding work, preferably a drawing, and to encourage younger architects. A gold medal is awarded annually and presented privately by the President of the Academy. Established in 1968 by an anonymous donor; RSA Guthrie Award - for the best work by a young artist (under 33 years of age who has passed the usual years of training in painting, sculpture or architecture). A monetary award of £500 and a medal are presented annually. Established in 1918 as a tribute to Sir James Guthrie, President of the RSA from 1902 to 1919; and RSA Benno Schotz Prize - for promising work by a young sculptor domiciled in Scotland. Open to artists who are under 33 years of age. A monetary award of £250 is presented annually. Established in 1965 by a donation from the sculptor, Benno Schotz. Additional awards are presented. The Exhibition was established in 1826.

10620

Royal Scottish Automobile Club
11 Blythswood Sq.   Phone: 41 2213850
Glasgow G2 4AG, Scotland   Fax: 41 2213805

10621

Jim Clark Trophy
To recognize the Scottish driver contributing most to motor sport during the year. A competitor in international motor sport of Scottish nationality may be nominated. A trophy and souvenir plaque are awarded annually when merited. Established in 1965 in memory of Jim Clark, O.B.E., world champion driver in 1963 and 1965, and winner of 25 Grands Prix and the Indianapolis 500 in 1965.

10622

Royal Scottish Forestry Society
65 Queen St.   Phone: 31 225 8142
Edinburgh EH2 4NA, Scotland   Fax: 31 225 8142

10623

Ballogie Cup
For recognition of achievement by a student at the supervisory level at the Scottish School of Forestry Inverness Technical College, Scotland. A trophy and book prize are awarded annually. Established in 1983.

10624

Hunter Blair Trophy
To encourage good woodland management in Scotland. Applications are accepted. A trophy is awarded annually. Established in 1964 in honor of Sir James Hunter Blair of Blairquhan. Sponsored by Royal Highland and Agricultural Society of Scotland.

10625

Sir George Campbell Memorial Trophy
To recognize a member for contributing a short article to the Society's Journal, *Scottish Forestry*. A trophy is awarded annually. Established in 1969 in honor of Sir George Campbell of Crarae, Argyllshire, Scotland.

10626

Duke of Buccleuch Memorial Trophy
For recognition of achievement by a student at the craft level at the Scottish School of Forestry, Inverness Technical College, Scotland. A trophy and book prize are awarded annually. Established in 1977 in memory of Walter John, Duke of Buccleuch and Queensberry K.T. G.C.V.O. who died in 1973.

10627

Royal Scottish Geographical Society
Graham Hills Bldg.
40 George St.   Phone: 41 5523330
Glasgow G1 1QE, Scotland   Fax: 41 5523331

10628

Associateship of the Society
To provide further training in geography. Individuals who have academic training as geographers, plus at least three years of relevant employment experience are eligible. Recipients are selected based on recommendations of the validating committee of the Society.

10629

Centenary Medal
For recognition of work in either of the fields covered by the Society, but where the standard of merit does not attain that of a gold medal.

Individuals of any nationality are eligible. A silver gilt medal is awarded irregularly. Established in 1931. Formerly: Research Medal.

10630
Honorary Fellow
To recognize an individual for contributions to geography and/or public life in Scotland that has an impact on the geography of Scotland and furthers the work of the Society. Applications and nominations are not accepted. A certificate of Fellowship is awarded. Re-established in 1984.

10631
Livingstone Gold Medal
For recognition of outstanding public service in which geography has played an important part, either by exploration, by administration, or in other areas where its principles have been applied to the benefit of the human race. Individuals of any nationality are eligible. No nominations or applications are accepted. A gold medal is awarded irregularly. Established in 1901 by Mrs. A. Livingstone Bruce to honor David Livingstone.

10632
Mungo Park Medal
For recognition of work in either of the fields covered by the Gold Medal or the Livingstone Gold Medal awards, but where the standard of merit does not attain that of a gold medal. Individuals of any nationality are eligible. A silver medal is awarded irregularly. Established in 1930.

10633
Newbigin Prize
To recognize the author of the most meritorious learned article published in each volume of Scottish Geographical magazine as judged by the Publication Committee of the Society. A monetary award of £100 is presented. Established in 1950 in memory of Marion Newbigin, Editor of the *Scottish Geographical* magazine.

10634
President's Award
To recognize the research contribution of researchers in mid-career.

10635
Scottish Geographical Medal
To recognize work of conspicuous merit within the science of geography. Research, whether in the field or otherwise, or any other contribution or cumulative service to the advancement of science is considered. Individuals of any nationality are eligible. A gold medal is awarded irregularly. Established in 1890. Formerly: Gold Medal.

10636
Royal Society of Edinburgh
22/24 George St.
Edinburgh EH2 2PQ, Scotland
Phone: 31 2256057
Fax: 31 2206889

10637
David Anderson-Berry Medal
For recognition of recent work on the effects of X-rays and other forms of radiation on living tissues. Published work will be taken into consideration if submitted to the Society with the application. A medal is awarded.

10638
BP Prize Lectureship in the Humanities
To recognize an individual under 40 years of age in a Scottish educational institution. Awards are given in alternate years in the following categories: languages, literature, and the arts; archaeological and historical studies; social studies; and philosophy, theology, and law. A monetary prize of £500 plus a lecture to be held at the society is awards biennially. Established in 1990 and sponsored by British Petroleum (BP).

10639
W. S. Bruce Medal
For recognition of some notable contribution to the natural sciences, such as zoology, botany, geology, meteorology, oceanography, and geography. The contributions must be in the nature of new knowledge and be the outcome of a personal visit to polar regions on the part of the recipient. The recipient should preferably be at the outset of his or her career as an investigator. Open to workers of all nationalities, with a preference for those of Scottish birth or origin. The Committee of Awards is appointed jointly by the Royal Society of Edinburgh, the Royal Physical Society, and the Royal Scottish Geographical Society. A medal is awarded every five years. Established in 1923 to commemorate the work of Dr. W. S. Bruce as an explorer and scientific investigator in polar regions.

10640
Alexander Ninian Bruce Prize
For recognition of meritorious research in medical or veterinary physiology. Individuals under 40 years of age and working in a Scottish institution are eligible. A monetary prize of £250 is awarded quadriennially. Established in 1991.

10641
Caledonian Research Foundation Prize Lecturehip
To recognize an individual who has an international reputation in the fields of biological, biochemical, physical, and clinical sciences related to medicine. A monetary prize of £1,000 plus a lecture to be given by the winner at various locations throughout Scotland is awarded annually. Established in 1990 and sponsored by Caledonian Research Foundation.

10642
Henry Dryerre Prize Lecture
To recognize a distinguished scholar in the field of medical research. A monetary prize of £500 plus a lecture to be held at the Society is awarded quadriennially. Established in 1991 in honor of Professor Henry Dryerre.

10643
Henry Duncan Prize Lectureship
For recognition of a work of a scholar of any nationality for work of international reputation in Scottish studies. A monetary prize of £500 plus a lecture to be held at the Society is awarded triennially. Established in 1990 by Trustees Savings Bank (TSB) Scotland in memory of the Reverend Henry Duncan who founded the first TSB.

10644
Gunning Victoria Jubilee Prize Lectureship
In recognition of original work in physics, chemistry, or pure or applied mathematics. A monetary prize for a lecture is awarded quadriennially to scientists resident in or connected with Scotland. Established in 1887 by Dr. R. H. Gunning.

10645
Keith Medal
For recognition of a communication on a scientific subject presented to the Royal Society of Edinburgh. Preference is given to a paper containing a discovery. The medal is awarded alternately in quadrennial periods, provided papers worthy of recommendation have been communicated to the society for publications in: Proceedings A (Mathematics) or Proceedings B (Biological Sciences) or Transactions (Earth Sciences).

10646
MakDougall-Brisbane Prize
For promotion of research in science. The Society is not compelled to award the prize unless there is an individual engaged in scientific pursuit, a paper written on a scientific subject, or a discovery in science made during the biennial period of sufficient merit or importance in the opinion of the Society to be entitled to the prize. Preference is given to a person under 40 years of age working in Scotland. Awarded in successive biennial periods in the following subjects: physical sciences, engineering sciences, and biological sciences.

10647

Neill Medal

For recognition of a work or publication by some Scottish naturalist, on some branch of natural history completed or published within five years of the time of award. A medal is awarded triennially. Established by a bequest from the late Dr. Patrick Neill.

10648

Bruce-Preller Prize Lectureship

To recognize an outstanding scientist. The subject is to be, in sequence, earth science, engineering, medical, or biological sciences. An honorarium is awarded biennially. Established in 1929 by the bequest of the late Dr. Charles Du Riche Preller.

10649

James Scott Prize Lectureship

To provide for a lecture on the fundamental concepts of natural philosophy. Awarded quadriennially. Established in 1918 by the Trustees of the James Scott Bequest.

10650

Saltire Society
9 Fountain Close
22 High St.
Edinburgh EH1 1TF, Scotland
Phone: 31 5561836
Fax: 31 5571675

10651

Art and Craft in Architecture Award

For recognition of works of art that are designed and incorporated as intrinsic parts of buildings. The competition is open to all craft workers and artists. Work must be located in Scotland and be an intrinsic part of a building or group of buildings. Awarded biennially. Established in 1971.

10652

Civil Engineering Award

To encourage the highest standards in the design and construction of civil engineering projects in Scotland. Commendations are also made for conservation projects. Awarded annually. Established in 1981. Sponsored jointly by the Scottish Association of the Institution of Civil Engineers.

10653

Patrick Geddes Planning Award

To encourage modern environmental planning and to keep the cultural traditions alive. Made in conjunction with the Royal Town Planning Institute and the Sir Patrick Geddes Memorial Trust to promote public interest and to encourage professional excellence in the art of town and country planning. Financed by the Glasgow Development Agency, and the Lothian and Edinburgh Enterprise Limited. Established in 1984, in memory of Patrick Geddes.

10654

Housing Design Award

For recognition of housing design in Scotland. Entries may be submitted by owners, builders, public or semi-public bodies and individuals who have commissioned works in Scotland, or by the architects employed by them. Awarded annually. Established in 1937.

10655

Agnes Mure MacKenzie Award

For recognition of a published work of Scottish historical research, including intellectual history and the history of science. A monetary prize is awarded triennially. Established in 1965 in memory of Agnes Mure MacKenzie.

10656

National Scots Song Competition

To recognize choirs singing songs in Scots who are the winners of first and second places at their local music competition festival. Certificates were awarded annually. Established in 1980. In 1987, the Competition was extended to include Junior choirs and unconducted vocal ensembles, not eligible to enter the above category. (Temporarily discontinued)

10657

Saltire Society and The Royal Bank of Scotland - Scottish Science Award

To recognize distinguished scientists of Scottish descent or living in Scotland. Nominations for the Awards are recommended to the Society's Science Committee by the Royal Society of Edinburgh. Disciplines cover medicine and veterinary medicine, physical sciences, biological and earth sciences. Established in 1989.

10658

Scottish Book of the Year Award

For recognition of the Scottish Book of the Year and the Scottish First Book of the Year. The competition is open to any author of Scottish descent or living in Scotland, or for a book by anyone which deals with the work or life of a Scot or with a Scottish problem, event or situation. In 1988, the Award was extended to include the first published work by a new author. Entries are submitted to the Society by literary editors of leading newspapers, magazines and periodicals. Nominations are presented for consideration by the end of September. A monetary prize of £5,000 is awarded for the Book of the Year, and £1,500 for the First Book of the Year. Awarded annually. Established in 1982. Sponsored by *The Scotsman* and Scottish Television. Formerly: Saltire Society Scottish Literary Awards.

10659

Scottish Arts Council
Literature Dept.
12 Manor Pl.
Edinburgh EH3 7DD, Scotland
Phone: 31 2266051

10660

Book Awards

To recognize authors of newly published books. Authors should be Scottish, residents in Scotland, or have written books of Scottish interest. Applications, from publishers, are considered by a special panel. Usually six monetary awards of £1,000 each are awarded biannually. In addition, grants and bursaries are awarded to assist writers of professional status.

10661

Neil Gunn International Fellowship

For recognition of achievement in literature. Writers who are not British and are not living in the United Kingdom are eligible for consideration by invitation only. A monetary prize is awarded biennially. Established in 1973 in honor of Neil M. Gunn.

10662

Scottish Bowling Association
50 Wellington St.
Glasgow G2 6EF, Scotland
Phone: 41 2218999
Fax: 41 2218999

10663

National Championships

For recognition of championship winners in bowling. Awards are given in the following competitions: Fours Championship, Triples Championship, Pairs Championship, Singles Championship, Seniors' Fours Championship, and Junior Singles Championship. Members of the Association are eligible. Monetary prizes, medals, and trophies are awarded annually. Established in 1892. Sponsored in 1994 by Scottish Power PLC.

10664

Scottish Canoe Association
Caledonia House
South Gyle
Edinburgh EH12 9DQ, Scotland
Phone: 31 3177314
Fax: 31 3177319

10665

Canoeist of the Year
For recognition of the outstanding, all-around male canoeist competitor in Scotland. The awardee must be a member of the Association. A trophy is presented annually. Established in 1960 by Fred Westington.

10666

Lady Canoeist of the Year
For recognition of the outstanding, all-around female canoeist competitor in Scotland. The awardee must be a member of the Association. A trophy is presented annually. Established in 1986 by Mr. and Mrs. K. Brown.

10667

Scottish Football Association
6 Park Gardens
Glasgow G3 7YF, Scotland
Phone: 41 3326372
Fax: 41 3327559

10668

Honorary Long Service Award
For recognition of exceptionally long service to the game of football (soccer) in Scotland. Established in 1980.

10669

Service Award for the Promotion and Teaching of Football
For contributions to Scottish football (soccer). Awarded annually. Established in 1985.

10670

Scottish Industrial and Trade Exhibitions
c/o John Todd
10 Blenheim Pl.
Edinburgh EH7 5JH, Scotland
Phone: 31 556 5152
Fax: 31 556 8896

10671

Scottish Marketing Awards
To recognize the best in Scottish marketing. The following awards are presented: Best Small Company - annual turnover under £2 million; Best Medium Company - annual turnover from £2-25 million; Best Large Company - awards are presented to a business in the manufacturing sector and the service sector with annual turnover above £25 million; and three Public Sector Awards for organizations responsible for budgets over £25 million. The Awards are open to all organizations operating in Scotland, whether their major market is in the UK or overseas. A handcrafted engraved trophy, stand space at an exhibition organized by SITE, and the opportunity to attend a Chartered Institute of Marketing training seminar are awarded at the Awards Presentation Dinner. The deadline is February 1.

10672

Scottish International Piano Competition
Royal Scottish Academy of Music & Drama
100 Renfrew St.
Glasgow G2 3DB, Scotland
Phone: 41 3324101
Fax: 41 3328901

10673

Scottish International Piano Competition
For recognition of achievement in the piano competition. Applications are accepted from individuals up to 32 years of age of any nationality. A monetary prize of £10,000 plus engagements in Britain are awarded triennially. Established in 1986 in memory of Frederic Lamond (1868-1948). Sponsored by BT and associated sponsors.

10674

Scottish Opera
39 Elmbank Crescent
Glasgow G2 4PT, Scotland
Phone: 41 2484567

10675

John Noble Bursary
To recognize and develop potential in the field of opera. Individuals from 18 to 26 years of age with Scottish connections through birth, residence, or training may apply with two written references from professionals. A monetary award of £1,500 is presented annually. Established in 1973 in honor of John Noble, a supporter of Scottish Opera.

10676

Scottish Photographic Federation
Jensara, Torthorwald
Dumfries DG1 3QA, Scotland
Phone: 387 75434

10677

Scottish Salon of Photography
For recognition of outstanding photography. Awards are given in the following categories: FIAP Gold Medals for Best Colour Print, Best Monochrome Print, and Best Slide; PSA Gold Medals for Best Nature Print, Best Nature Slide, Best Landscape Print, and Best Landscape Slide; SPF Gold Medals for Best Portrait Print, Best Portrait Slide, Best Contemporary Print, and Best Contemporary Slide; Judges Choice - FIAP Blue Ribbon; SPF Gold Medals & Honourable Mention for Best Colour Print by a Scottish resident, Best Monochrome Print by a Scottish resident, and Best Slide by a Scottish resident; SPF Gold Medal for Best Club Entry; Dumfries Octocentenary Trophy for Best Scottish Club Entry; and Honourable Mentions for Monochrome Prints, Colour Prints, and Slides. Awarded annually. Established in 1917.

10678

Scottish Tartans Society
The Administrator
Scottish Tartans Museum
Drummond St.
Comrie
Perthshire PH6 2DW, Scotland
Phone: 764 70779
Fax: 764 70779

10679

Fellowship of the Scottish Tartans Society
For recognition of outstanding scholarly work in the field of Tartans and Highland Dress. Original research which makes a significant contribution is considered. The title of Fellow of the Scottish Tartans Society is awarded when merited.

10680

Society of Antiquaries of Scotland
Royal Museum of Scotland
Queen St.
Edinburgh EH2 1JD, Scotland
Phone: 31 225 7534

10681

Honorary Fellow
To recognize contributions to the field of archaeology/history. Members are eligible. Honorary Fellows are elected annually in November.

10682

UK Committee for the Thouron Awards
Univ. of Glasgow
Glasgow G12 8QQ, Scotland
Phone: 41 339 8855

10683
Thouron Fellowship
To provide for U.S.-U.K. student exchange and to promote good relations between people in the two countries. Graduates of United Kingdom universities or of the University of Pennsylvania are eligible. A monetary award for fees and maintenance including travel are presented annually. Established in 1960 by Sir John Thouron.

10684
University of Edinburgh
Dept. of English Literature
David Hume Tower, George Sq.
Edinburgh EH8 9JX, Scotland
Phone: 31 667 1000
Fax: 31 662 0772

10685
James Tait Black Memorial Prizes
For recognition of the best biography or work of that nature, and the best work of fiction, published during the calendar year. Publishers are invited to submit a copy of any work of fiction or biography for consideration by November 30. Consideration will not be limited to those books of which copies are submitted; but submission considerably improves the chance of success. Works of fiction and biographies written in English, originating with a British publisher, and first published in Britain in the year of the award are eligible, but technical publication elsewhere, simultaneously or even a little earlier, does not disqualify. The nationality of the writer, however, is irrelevant. Both prizes may go to the same author; but neither to the same author a second time. The closing date for submissions is November 30. Two monetary prizes of £1,500 each are awarded annually. Established in 1918 in memory of James Tait Black, a partner in the publishing house of A.C. Black, Ltd, and supplemented since 1979 by the Scottish Arts Council.

Senegal

10686
African Cultural Institute
(Institut Culturel Africain et Mauricien)
13, avenue Bourguiba
PO Box 1
Dakar, Senegal
Phone: 24 78 82

10687
Grand Prix ICA - Prix de la Meilleure Chanson en Langue Traditionnelle
To recognize the best song in a traditional language entered in the Concours Decouvertes (discovery competition) organized by Radio French Internationale. The organization of the Concours de Musique Africaine is a project that is carried out in collaboration with URTNA. Members are eligible. The following monetary prizes are awarded: 1st prize - 250,000 CFA francs; 2nd prize - 150,000 CFA francs; and 3rd prize - 100,000 CFA francs. Awarded annually. Established in 1980 by Radio France Internationale.

10688
Grand Prix ICA - Prix de la Recherche Scientifique
For recognition of works that have contributed to the advancement of research in the fields of social science and humanities in the development of Africa. Essays, memoirs or dissertations that have been published are eligible. The following monetary awards are presented: 1st prize - 250,000 CFA francs; 2nd prize - 150,000 CFA francs; and 3rd prize - 100,000 CFA francs. Awarded annually at the Convention. Established in 1982.

10689
Grand Prix ICA - Prix de Sculpture
To recognize artists for works of sculpture, ceramic or painting on themes of African culture and Africa. Members are eligible. The following monetary awards are given: 1st prize - 250,000 CFA francs; 2nd prize - 150,000 CFA francs; and 3rd prize - 100,000 CFA francs. Awarded annually. Established in 1974.

10690
Grand Prix ICA - Prix du Meilleur Film Documentaire
To recognize the best documentary film in the Festival Panafricain de Ougadougou (Haute Volta) FESPACO. A monetary award of 500,000 CFA francs is awarded biennially. Established in 1981 by ICA. Sponsored by Festival Pan Africain du Cinema (FESPACO).

10691
Prix Alioune Diop pour les Lettres Africaine
For recognition of writers of literary works on African culture. Works already published, novels or poetry in French or English, are eligible. The following monetary awards are presented: 1st prize - 250,000 CFA francs; 2nd prize - 150,000 CFA francs; and 3rd prize - 100,000 CFA francs. Awarded annually at the Convention. Established in 1982 to honor Alioune Diop, former Director of Presence Africaine. Formerly: (1981) Grand Prix ICA.

10692
African Regional Centre for Technology
(Centre Regional Africain de Technologie)
Boite Postale 2435
Dakar, Senegal
Phone: 237712
Fax: 237713

10693
African Regional Centre for Technology Awards
To recognize efforts by member countries of the Economic Commission for Africa and the Organization of African Unity to strengthen African technological capabilities, and to use technology to stimulate socioeconomic growth. Awards are presented.

Serbia

10694
Belgrade City Council
Secretariat for Education and Culture
Trg Marksa i Engelsa br. 6
YU-11000 Belgrade, Serbia

10695
ATELJE 212 on the Bitef Award
To recognize a performance which expresses the best new trends in the contemporary theatre. A sculpture by Nebojsa Mitric is awarded annually.

10696
October Prizes of the City of Belgrade
For recognition of achievements in science and the arts. Two prizes are given for outstanding contributions to sociology; two for mathematics, technology and physics; two for biology and medical sciences; one for literature and translation; one for fine and applied arts; one for music; one for architecture and town planning; one for film; and one for theatre. Individuals and groups are eligible, but either the author must be from Belgrade, or his work must in some way be connected with the City. Monetary prizes of 10,000 dinars are awarded to individuals and 15,000 dinars to groups. Awarded annually.

10697
October Show Awards
For recognition of outstanding contributions to the contemporary fine and applied arts in the Republic of Serbia. The Organizing Committee of 12 to 21 members, who are artists, critics, public, and cultural workers, is in charge of the show. Works must have been completed within the preceding two years. Six monetary awards are given annually to commemorate the anniversary of the liberation of Belgrade.

10698

**Belgrade International Festival of Scientific Films
(Medunarodni Festival Naucnog Filma Beograd)**
Drustovo "Nikola Tesla"
Kneza Milosa 10
YU-11000 Belgrade, Serbia
Phone: 11 330 641

10699

**Belgrade International Festival of Scientific Films
(Medunarodni Festival Naucnog Filma Beograd)**
For recognition of outstanding scientific and technical films. The Nikola Tesla Award, the grand prize, consisting of a gold statuette of Nikola Tesla, is awarded for the best film of the Festival. Gold, silver and bronze medals are awarded for scientific documentary films, television science films, scientific research films and scientific popular films. Special prizes and certificates are presented to films outstanding by their topical, scientific and artistic values. This prize is awarded by the Council of the Trade Union Confederation of Yugoslavia, Narodna Tehnika of Yugoslavia, Newspaper Publishing House "Politika," Yugoslav Council for Environment Protection and Advancement, Television Beograd, and the Association of Engineers and Technicians of Yugoslavia. Awarded biennially. Established in 1960.

10700

Belgrade International Film Festival
Sava Center
Milentija Popovica 9
YU-11070 Belgrade, Serbia
Phone: 11 222 49 61
Fax: 11 222 11 56

10701

Yugoslav Documentary and Short Films Festival Awards
For recognition of the best documentary, short and animated (cartoon) films produced during the year. Individuals and film production companies, directors, script writers, and directors of photography are eligible. Gold and silver medals and diplomas are awarded annually. The following prizes are also given: (1) special awards of the International Committee for the dissemination of Arts and Culture Through Film (CIDALC); (2) the Kekec Award of the Council for Education and Care of Children of Yugoslavia for the best film for children and youth; (3) the award of the Central Committee of the Union of Youth of Yugoslavia; (4) the award of the Ljubljana review *Ekran*; and (5) the award of the Yugoslav Association of Organizations for Physical Culture.

10702

Borba
Trg Marksa i Engelsa 7
Belgrade, Serbia
Phone: 11 334531
Fax: 11 344913

10703

***Borba* Award**
For recognition of achievements in the field of architecture. The award consists of one federal and six republic awards. The republic awards are given for excellence in the individual republic, and the federal award is given to one of the architects who has received the republic prize. The federal award consists of a sum of money and a scroll.

10704

Dramatic Festival
(Sterijino pozorje)
Katarina Ciric-Petrovic, Dept. of
  International Relations
Zmaj Jovina 22/I
YU-21000 Novi Sad, Serbia
Phone: 21 51 077
Phone: 21 51 273
Fax: 21 615 976

Formerly: Yugoslav Theatre Festival.

10705

**Sterijina Nagrada
(Sterija Award)**
To foster the growth and creative reputation of Yugoslav dramatic literature and theatre. Awards are given for the following: (1) the best production as a whole; (2) the best modern Yugoslav dramatic text; (3) the best direction; (4) the best stage adaptation/dramatization; (5) five equal awards for the best acting; (6) the best stage design; (7) the best costume design; (8) special award for the best comedy; (9) the best drama review in the previous year; (10) the award of the Round Table of Critics; and (11) special award for stage music. Each professional theater in Yugoslavia and theatres from abroad performing a Yugoslav dramatic text are entitled to nominate any work by a contemporary or classical playwright provided that the stage version of the work is a modern vision and interpretation and that it has been performed by the company during the preceding two calendar years. The nominated plays are first viewed by special committees of theater professionals who choose the most significant ones. The Selector of the Festival views all performances that the critics have recommended and then he composes the final repertoire of the festival. Monetary awards, diplomas, and art object-statuettes are awarded annually at the Festival in the spring. Established in 1956 by Sterijino pozorje in honor of Jovan Sterija Popovic, one of the greatest Serbian comedy writers of the late 19th century. In addition, the following awards are presented: (1) *Scena* theater journal award for books in the field of theater studies; and (2) an award for special merit for the advancement of Yugoslav theater art and culture.

10706

**Federation of Veterans' Associations of the People's Liberation War of Yugoslavia
(Savez Udruzenja Boraca Narodnooslobodilackog Rata Jugoslavije)**
Lenjinov bulevar 6/III
YU-11070 Belgrade, Serbia
Phone: 11 629149
Phone: 11 626623

10707

**Nagrada Saveta Fonda SO SUBNOR Cetvrti jul
(Fourth of July Prize)**
To encourage artistic and scientific creative work drawing from the people's liberation struggle and the socialist revolution in the fields of literature, political writings, historical and other social sciences, painting, music, theatre, film, radio and television. The quality of work determines its eligibility. Monetary prizes totaling 100,000 dinars are awarded annually. Established in 1968 by the Federal Committee of SUBNOR to commemorate the Uprising of the Nations and Nationalities of Yugoslavia.

10708

Plaques of SUBNOR
To recognize Yugoslav and foreign nationals and organizations for their special contribution to the work and development of the SUBNOR and the attainment of its aims. Plaques of SUBNOR are awarded annually. Established in 1973.

10709

International Centre for Heat and Mass Transfer
Postanski Fah 552
YU-11000 Belgrade, Serbia
Phone: 11 458 222

10710

ICHMT Fellows Awards
For recognition of a contribution to a field of heat and mass transfer science and for enhancement of the progress in scientific and technological cooperation connected to the ICHMT activities. Nominations are accepted. A certificate is awarded biennially. Established in 1975.

10711

Luikov Medal
For recognition of an outstanding contribution to the heat and mass transfer science and art. Nominations are accepted by January. A medal is awarded biennially. Established in 1975 in honor of A.V. Luikov.

10712
International Institute for the Science of Sintering
Postanski Fah 745 Phone: 11 637239
YU-11001 Belgrade, Serbia Fax: 11 182825

10713
Frenkel Prize
For recognition of a contribution to the science of sintering, to the affirmation of the science of sintering, and to the organized international cooperation of scientists in the field. Institute members must nominate individuals by April of the year of the award. Honorary membership in IISS and participation in the World Round Table Conference of Sintering without participation fees are awarded every four years at WRTCS. Established in 1976 in memory of Ya. I. Frenkel, a world known physicist and one of the founders of the science of sintering.

10714
G. C. Kuczynski Diploma
To recognize the author of a paper published in an eminent scientific journal that contributes to the development of the sintering theory. Institute members must nominate individuals by April of the year of the award. An honorary diploma is awarded every four years at WRTCS. Established in 1976 in memory of Professor G. C. Kuczynski, one of the founders of the science of sintering.

10715
Samsonov Prize
For recognition of the best paper published in the journal *Science of Sintering*. Institute members must nominate individuals by April of the year of the award. An honorary diploma is awarded every four years at WRTCS. Established in 1976 in memory of G. V. Samsonov, internationally known materials scientist.

10716
Jeunesses Musicales of Serbia
(Muzicka Omaladina Srbije)
Terazije 26/II Phone: 11 686380
YU-11000 Belgrade, Serbia Phone: 11 688860

10717
International Jeunesses Musicales Competition - Belgrade
(Concours International des Jeunesses Musicales - Belgrade)
For recognition of outstanding performance in the field of music. The categories change annually. Awards are given in the following categories: (1) Flute and woodwind quartet, 1992; (2) Solo voice, 1993; and (3) Piano and piano trio, 1994; (4) Violoncello and composition, 1995; (5) Violin and string orchestra, 1996; and (6) Oboe and woodwind quartet, 1997. Performers and composers under 30 years of age are eligible. For chamber ensembles, no player should be older than 35. Applications may be submitted by December 31. The following prizes are awarded: (1) First prize - 13,000 dinars and promotion through concerts and tours; (2) Second prize - 10,000 dinars; and (3) Third prize - 7,000 dinars. Awarded annually. Established in 1969. Sponsored by the Cultural Community of Belgrade, the Cultural Community of the Republic of Serbia, Yugoslavia Radio Television, and the Union of Organizational Yugoslav composers. Additional information is available from Mrs. Biljana Zdrakovic, Exec. Sec.

10718
Nedeljne Informativne Novine
Cetinjska 1 PO Box 208 Phone: 11 324410
YU-11000 Belgrade, Serbia Fax: 11 633368

10719
Dimitrije Tucovic Nonfiction Award
To promote Yugoslav nonfiction literature. Nonfiction books published for the first time in the year of the award are eligible. A monetary prize and a certificate are awarded annually in honor of Dimitrije Tucovic, a socialist militant and thinker in Serbia at the beginning of the century. Established in 1976.

10720
Novel of the Year Award
To stimulate modern Yugoslav literature. Yugoslav novels published for the first time in the year of the award are eligible. A monetary prize of 20,000 dinars and a certificate are awarded annually in October. Established in 1954.

10721
Prosvjta Publishing House
Cika Ljubina 1/I Phone: 11 629 843
YU-11000 Belgrade, Serbia

10722
Prosvjeta Prize
To provide recognition for the best contemporary Yugoslav novel. A monetary prize and publication of the novel are awarded annually.

10723
Serbian Academy of Sciences and Arts
(Srpska Akademij Naukai Umetnosti)
PO Box 366
Knez-Mihailova ulica 35 Phone: 11 187144
YU-11000 Belgrade, Serbia

10724
Serbian Academy of Sciences and Arts Awards
To recognize outstanding members for their contributions to the Academy's activities and role in the society. A plaque is awarded. To date, about 10 members of the Academy have been accorded such plaques.

10725
Serbian PEN Centre
Francuska 7
YU-11000 Belgrade, Serbia

10726
Yugoslav PEN Club Award
To recognize a translation of a book from and into languages spoken or used in Yugoslavia, and to promote and develop close and friendly relationships among literatures and writers of different countries. A monetary prize is awarded.

Singapore

10727
Asia Pacific Academy of Ophthalmology
No. 6A, Napier Rd.
Gleneagles Hospital
Annexe Block, 2nd Storey, No. 02-38 Phone: 4666 666
Singapore 0922, Singapore Fax: 7333360

10728
Holmes Lecture
To select a speaker from the Asia Pacific region to lecture on the subject of preventative ophthalmology. Established in 1983.

10729
Ocampo Lecture
To select a speaker from the Asia Pacific region to lecture on the subject of clinical or basic research in ophthalmology. Established in 1983.

10730
Jose Rizal Medal
To recognize excellence in ophthalmology in the countries of Asia and the Pacific. A silver medal is awarded every two to four years. Under exceptional circumstances, a Gold Jose Rizal Medal can be presented to an opthalmologist who practices ophthalmology outside member countries of the Academy and who has made exceptionally valuable contributions to ophthalmology in the region. Established in 1968 in memory of Dr. Jose Rizal.

10731
Asian Association of Occupational Health
Dept. of Social Medicine and Public Health
National Univ. of Singapore
Outram Hill
Singapore 0316, Singapore   Phone: 2226444

10732
Awards
To recognize young scientists, researchers, and Association members in the field of occupational health. Awards are presented.

10733
National Book Development Council of Singapore
Bukit Merah Branch Library
Bukit Mera Central   Phone: 2732730
Singapore 0315, Singapore   Fax: 2706139

10734
Book Awards
To develop local literary talent in the field of creative and noncreative writing in any of the four official languages (Malay, English, Chinese, and Tamil), and to stimulate public interest in and support for local literary achievements. Works published during the two years preceding the award year are eligible. The awards are given in five categories: fiction, poetry, nonfiction, children's and young people's books, and drama. Only first editions of original books by Singapore citizens or permanent residents published locally or abroad are eligible. An author who has received a National Book Development Council of Singapore Book Award is eligible for the same award again, upon the unanimous vote of the panel of judges. Translations, edited works, treatises, or research works written for a university degree or examination are not eligible. Works by any serving members of the National Book Development Council of Singapore are not eligible. As many as 20 monetary prizes of 2,000 Singapore dollars and a souvenir are awarded biennially at the opening ceremony of the annual Singapore Festival of Books and Book Fair. Established in 1976. Since 1982, the nonfiction has been sponsored by the Singapore Press Holdings.

10735
Singapore
Office of the Prime Minister
8 Shenton Way, 14-01
Treasury Bldg.   Phone: 3217415
Singapore 0106, Singapore   Fax: 3217412

10736
Certificate of Honor
(Sijil Kemuliaan)
For recognition of outstanding service. Individuals who are citizens of Singapore and, in special circumstances, persons who are not citizens of Singapore are eligible. No more than six Certificates of Honour are awarded in any one year. Established in 1962.

10737
Commendation Medal (Military)
(Pingat Kepujian (Tentera))
To recognize any member of the Singapore Armed Forces who has clearly placed himself above his peers through commendable achievements in military command or staff work, or performed service over and above the call of duty. A medal is awarded. Established in 1981.

10738
Conspicuous Gallantry Medal
(Pingat Gagah Perkasa)
For recognition of an act of conspicuous gallantry and courage in circumstances of extreme personal danger. Individuals who perfomed an act of bravery within the State of Singapore are eligible. Established in 1962.

10739
Distinguished Service Order
(Darjah Utama Bakti Chemerlang)
To recognize any person who has performed within Singapore, or in special circumstances outside Singapore, an act or a series of acts constituting distinguished conduct. An enamelled bronze medal is awarded. Established in 1968.

10740
Efficiency Medal
(Pingat Berkebolehan)
For recognition of exceptional efficiency or devotion to duty or for work of special significance. Individuals in the following categories are eligible: (1) public officers; (2) officers employed by statutory authorities; and (3) any person in the service of any organization, association or body rendering services in the field of education. A bronze medal is awarded. Established in 1969.

10741
Medal for Valour
(Pingat Keberanian)
To recognize any person who has performed an act of courage and gallantry in circumstances of personal danger. A medal is awarded. Established in 1987.

10742
Medal of Honor
(Pingat Kehormatan)
For recognition of acts or a series of acts constituting distinguished conduct in active service in the field. In special circumstances, the Medal may be awarded to any person engaged in operational duties whose acts or series of acts constitute distinguished conduct. Members of the Singapore Armed Forces and the Singapore Police Force are eligible. A silver medal is awarded. Established in 1970.

10743
Meritorious Service Medal
(Pingat Jasa Gemilang)
To recognize a person who has perfomed within Singapore, or in special circumstances outside Singapore, service of conspicuous merit, characterized by resourceful devotion to duty, including long service marked by exceptional ability, merit and exemplary conduct. A silver medal is awarded. Established in 1962.

10744
Order of Nila Utama
(Darjah Utama Nila Utama)
For recognition of foreign dignitaries. Individuals are recommended by the Prime Minister. There are three grades of the Order of Nila Utama: (1) the First Class; (2) the Second Class; and (3) the Third Class. Awarded by the President. Established in 1975.

10745
Order of Temasek
(Darjah Utama Temasek)
For recognition of outstanding service to the country. The maximum number of persons admitted to the First Class of the Order of Temasek is limited to twelve. Ordinarily, only citizens of Singapore are admitted to the Order, but in special circumstances persons who are not citizens of Singapore may be admitted in an honorary capacity, provided that the maximum number of persons admitted to the First Class of the Order, not in an honorary capacity, does not exceed twelve. There shall be no limit to the number of persons admitted to the Second Class and Third Class of the Order of Temasek. A medal in the form of a silver gilt and enamelled five-pointed star with a wreath around it is conferred by the President on the advice of the Prime Minister. Established in 1975.

10746
Police Medal for Valour
(Pingat Polis Keberanian)
To recognize any police officer who has performed an act or series of acts displaying personal courage or constituting distinguished and gallant conduct in circumstances dangerous to himself or his fellow-beings. The Medal may be awarded posthumously. Established in 1988.

10747
Public Administration Medal
(Pingat Pentadbiran Awam)
For recognition of outstanding efficiency, competence and industry. Individuals in the following categories are eligible: (1) any public officer; (2) any officer employed by a statutory authority; or (3) any person in the service of any organization, association, or body rendering services in the field of education. Gold, silver, and bronze medals are awarded. Established in 1963.

10748
Public Service Medal
(Pingat Bakti Masharakat)
For recognition of commendable public services in Singapore or to any person for achievement in the field of the arts and letters, sports, the sciences, business, the professions, and the labor movements. A medal is awarded. Established in 1973.

10749
Public Service Star
(Bintang Bakti Masharakat)
For recognition of valuable public service to the people of Singapore or for recognition of a contribution in the field of arts and letters, sports, or the sciences. A silver star is awarded. When the star is awarded to a person to whom it has been previously awarded, a bar is attached to the ribbon from which the star is suspended. Established in 1963.

10750
Star of Temasek
(Bintang Temasek)
For recognition of acts of exceptional courage and skill or conspicuous devotion to duty in circumstances of extreme danger. Members of the Singapore Armed Forces and the Singapore Police Force are eligible. A silver star is awarded. Established in 1970.

10751
Singapore Chefs Association
24 Nassim Hill
Singapore 1025, Singapore

10752
Singapore Food and Hotel Asia Competition
To recognize outstanding culinary ability. The competition is built around research and development and establishing food trends for the future. Medals are awarded. Winners participate in the Culinary Olympics held every four years in Frankfurt, Germany, with the winners of the other international regional competitions: Culinary World Cup (Luxembourg); Salon Culinaire Mondial (Basel, Switzerland); Culinary Arts Salon (USA); Hotelympia (London); Chef Ireland (Ireland); and Culinary Masters (Canada). Established in 1900.

Slovakia

10753
Association of Slovak Writers
(Spolak slovenskych spisovatelov)
Stefanikova 14
815 08 Bratislava, Slovakia   Phone: 7 436 15

10754
Bratislava Literary Prize
For recognition of the best literary work relating to the town of Bratislava written during the preceding five years. A monetary prize is awarded annually.

10755
Cena Vilenica
For recognition of a literary work of central Europe. Open to poets and authors of central European countries. Awarded annually in September. Established in 1986.

10756
Cena Zvazu slovenskych spisovatelov
For recognition of outstanding works of original Slovak poetry, prose, literary science, drama, essays, and literature for children. Members of the Society are eligible. A monetary prize of 10,000 Czechoslovak crowns is awarded annually. Established in 1969.

10757
Jan Holly Prize
To recognize an outstanding translation of foreign literature into the Slovak language. A monetary award is presented annually. Established in 1967 to honor Jan Holly (1785-1949), a Slovak poet and translator.

10758
Pavol Orszagh Hviezdoslav Prize
(Cena Pavla Orszagha Hviezdoslava)
To recognize the outstanding translation of Slovak literature into foreign languages. The publication of several translations of Slovak literature abroad are required for consideration. A monetary award and a fortnight stay in Slovakia are awarded annually. Established in 1970 to honor Pavol Orszagh Hviedzdoslav, an outstanding Slovak poet (1848-1921).

10759
Bibiana, International House of Art for Children
(Bibiana, Medzinarodny dom umenia pre deti)
Panska 41
814 99 Bratislava, Slovakia   Phone: 7 331314
    Fax: 7 334986

10760
Most Beautiful and the Best Children's Book of spring, summer, autumn, winter in Slovakia
(Najkrajsia a najlepsia detska kniha jari, leta, jesene a zimy na Slovensku)
To recognize Slovak publishing companies for the most artistically valuable books produced for children and youth each spring, summer, autumn, and winter. A plaque is awarded quarterly. Established in 1990.

10761
Ludmila Podjavorinska Plaque
No further information was available for this edition.

10762
Triple Rose Prize
No further information was provided for this edition.

10763
L'udovit Fulla Prize
No further information was provided for this edition.

10764
Friends of Children's Books
(Priateia detskaj knihy)
Bibiana, International House of Art for
  Children
Penska 41
814 99 Bratislava, Slovakia
Phone: 7 33 13 14
Fax: 7 33 49 86

10765
L'udovit Fulla Prize
(Cena L'dovita Fullu)
For recognition of outstanding achievements in the field of illustrations of children's books. Czechoslovak citizens are eligible. The deadline is March 31. A monetary prize, medal, and diploma are awarded annually in May. Established in 1965 and renamed in 1977 in honor of L'udovit Fulla (1902-1976), an outstanding Slovak illustrator and painter. Sponsored by the Slovak Fund of Creative Arts.

10766
Ludmila Podjavorinska Plaque
(Plaketa Ludmily Podjavorinskej)
To recognize individuals or institutions for the popularization of Slovak children's books abroad. A plaque, and a diploma are awarded biennially by the Ministry of Culture of Slovak Republic. Established in 1972 by Circle of Children's Book Friends in Slovakia and Mlade Leta Publishing House in memory of Ludmila Podjavorinska (1872-1951), Slovak witer, national artist, and founder of Slovak literature for children and youth. Sponsored by Mlade Leta Publishing House.

10767
Triple Rose Prize
(Cena Trojruza)
To recognize writers or illustrators for their life-long work in the field of art and literature for children. Czechoslovak citizens may be nominated by March 31. A monetary award, a medal and a diploma are presented annually. Established in 1965 to honor Frano Kral (1903- 1955), a national artist and an important Slovak writer for children and youth. Co-sponsored by Slovak Literary Fund and Friends of Children's Books. Formerly: Cena Frana Kral'a.

10768
National Committee of the Capital of Slovakia Bratislava
(Narodny vybor hlavneho mesta SSR Bratislavy)
Primacialne namestie c.1
811 01 Bratislava, Slovakia
Phone: 7 356 111

Defunct organization.

10769
Prize of National Committee of the Capital of Slovakia Bratislava
(Cena Narodneho vyboru hlavneho mesta Bratislavy)
For recognition of achievements in scientific, technical, artistic, and other socially beneficial activities important for the economic, cultural and social development of the capital. Up to five monetary prizes with diplomas were awarded annually. Established in 1977 in honor of the liberation of the city by the Soviet Army on April 4, 1945. (Discontinued in 1991)

10770
Slovak Music Fund
(Slovensky hudobny fond)
Medena 29
811 02 Bratislava, Slovakia
Phone: 7 331380
Fax: 7 333569

10771
Jan Levoslav Bella Prize
(Cena Jana Levoslava Bellu)
For recognition of achievement in music composition. Composers of Slovakia are eligible. Monetary prizes and publicity are awarded annually on October 1, International Music Day. Established in 1963, in honor of one of the first Slovak composers, Jan Levoslav Bella.

10772
Frico Kafenda Prize
(Cena Frica Kafendu)
For recognition of achievement in the field of concert music. Performers of Slovakia are eligible. A monetary prize and publicity are awarded annually on October 1, International Music Day. Established in 1964 in honor of one of the first Slovak composers, Frico Kafenda.

10773
Jozef Kresanek Prize
To honor accomplishments in musicology. A monetary prize and certificate are awarded annually on October 1, the International Day of Music. Established in 1991 in honor of Slovak musicologist and composer Jozef Kresanek.

10774
Ladislav Martonik Prize
To recognize outstanding accomplishments at home and abroad in jazz music. A monetary award and a certificate are presented annually on the International Day of Music, October 1. Established in 1991 in honor of Slovak jazz musician Ladislav Martonik.

10775
Karol Padivy Prize
To acknowlege outstanding accomplishments in brass-band music, at home and abroad. A monetary prize and certificate are awarded annually on October 1, the International Day of Music. Established in 1991 in honor of brass-band music composer and conductor Karol Padivy.

10776
Pavol Tonkovic Prize
To recognize creative activity at home and abroad in the field of folk music. A monetary award and certificate are presented annually on the 1st of October, the International Day of Music. Established in 1991 in honor of Pavol Tonkovic, conductor, composer, and folk music expert.

10777
Slovak Radio, Bratislava
(Slovensky Rozhlas, Bratislava)
c/o Executive Committee of Prix Bratislava
Mytna 1
812 90 Bratislava, Slovakia
Phone: 7 494462
Fax: 7 498923

10778
Bratislava Radio Prize for Folklore Music
(Prix de Musique Folklorique de Radio Bratislava)
For recognition of the best tape recording of musical folklore in the categories of stylized folklore and authentic folklore. European radio stations are invited to participate. The following prizes are awarded in each category: First prize - 15,000 Czechoslovak crowns, a gold medal, and a certificate; Second prize - 12,000 Czechoslovak crowns, a silver medal, and a certificate; Third prize - 8,000 Czechoslovak crowns, a bronze medal, and a certificate; works of art for performers and composers in the stylized folklore category; and special prizes for other

10779
Slovak Television, Bratislava
(Slovenska televizia, Bratislava)
Asmolovova 28
CS-845 45 Bratislava, Slovakia
Phone: 7 721940
Fax: 7 729440

10780
Prix Danube Festival, Bratislava
To encourage quality television production for children and youth. The Festival takes place under the motto: "In furtherance of a progressive relationship of children and youth to life". The competition is divided into four categories: documentary and informative programs for children and youth, magazine programs, dramatic programs for children and youth, and animated programs for children and youth. Each participating television organization may enter the competition in all four categories with independent entries, or individual parts of a serial, the total duration of which must not exceed 90 minutes. It is possible to submit several entries in one category. Only original television programs produced during the preceding two years and telecast in the respective country are eligible for entry by June 30. No programs may be entered for the competition that have been awarded a prize at other international festivals. The following awards are presented: Danube Prize - the main prize awarded in each category by the two international juries; Honorable Mention - awarded in each category for outstanding individual achievements of the creators of the program or for the program itself; Critics Prize - by the International Jury of Journalists; CIFEJ Prize - Centre International des Films pour Enfants et Jeunesse; and Prize of Slovak TV Artists Union. Awarded biennially. Established in 1971.

10781
Slovakia
Ministry of Culture, Slovak
Sprava Kulturnych zariadeni MK SSR
Dobsinskeho nam. 1
813 49 Bratislava, Slovakia
Phone: 7 333 550

10782
International Biennial of Illustrations Bratislava
For recognition of the best illustrations in children's books. Illustrations which have won national or international awards, and those which have not yet received any prizes are eligible. The following prizes are awarded: (1) Grand Prix - a trophy and 35,000 Czechoslovak crowns; (2) five Golden Apples and 15,000 Czechoslovak crowns each; (3) ten plaques and 5,000 Czechoslovak crowns each; and (4) four honorary diplomas. Awarded biennially.

10783
Slovkoncert, Slovak Artist Management
Michalska 10
815 36 Bratislava, Slovakia
Phone: 7 334561
Phone: 7 334538
Fax: 7 332652

Formerly: Slovkoncert, Czechoslovakia Artists Agency.

10784
International Rostrum of Young Performers/UNESCO
(Medzinarodna tribuna mladych interpretov/UNESCO)
To promote outstanding young artists by helping them gain access to the concert or operatic stage at the beginning of their artistic careers. The IRP is divided into Concert Rostrum for instrumentalists and concert singers. Candidates under the age of 30 who are nominated by a radio corporation must submit sound recordings. On the basis of the audition of the sound recording, 12 young soloists and chamber ensembles are selected. A diploma, a plaque, and the distribution of recording and publicity material through the International Music Council and UNESCO, Paris, are presented biennially. Winners of the prizes are given the title, Laureate. Established in 1969 by the International Music Council. Sponsored by UNESCO. Additional information is available from International Music Council Paris, Guy Hout, Executive Secretary, 1 rue Miollis, 75 732 Paris, France, or Dr. Ladislav Mokry, Vice President International Music Council coordinator IRP/TIJI/, Palackeho 2, 816 01 Bratislava, Slovak Republic.

10785
Young Years Publishing House
(Mlade leta, slovenske vydavatel'stvo knih pre mladez)
Nam. SNP 12
CS-815 19 Bratislava, Slovakia
Phone: 364475
Fax: 364563

10786
Mlade leta Prize
(Cena Vydavatel'stva Mlade leta)
For recognition of the best book of juvenile literature. Prose, poems, literature of popular science, illustrations, and translations, as well as outstanding editorial works by Slovak authors are eligible. A monetary prize and a diploma are awarded annually in May. Established in 1953; the illustration category was added in 1961. Formerly: (1965) Frano Kral Prize.

Slovenia

10787
European Society for Noninvasive Cardiovascular Dynamics
Institute of Physiology, Faculty of Medicine
Zaloska 4
61105 Ljubljana, Slovenia
Phone: 61 317152
Fax: 61 311540

Formerly: (1978) European Society for Ballistocardiography and Cardiovascular Dynamics.

10788
Burger Memorial Award
To recognize scientists who have contributed to important and generally accepted progress in the field of noninvasive cardiography. Selection is by nomination. A medal is awarded every five years at a meeting of the Society. Established in 1975 in honor of Professor H. C. Burger, the founder of medical physics in the Netherlands.

10789
Young Scientist Award in Noninvasive Cardiovascular Dynamics
To recognize young scientists who have contributed to noninvasive cardiovascular dynamics. Individuals under 30 years of age may be nominated. A certificate is awarded every five years at a meeting of the Society. Established in 1991.

10790
Interfilm Festival
Presernova 30
61104 Ljubljana, Slovenia
Phone: 61 317340
Fax: 61 317645

10791
International Festival of Ecological Film Events
To recognize films in the categories of documentary, educational and scientific on the subject of ecology. The Gold, Silver, and Bronze Biharnick are awarded for Best Screenplay, Direction and Photography. Medals are awarded biennially. Established in 1983.

10792
International Festival of Sports and Tourist Films
For recognition of outstanding films. Documentaries, animated cartoons, and educational films may be entered. Awards are presented in the following categories: (1) Grand Prix - Golden Triglav, Silver Triglav, and Bronze Triglave are awarded to the best three films: (2) the film which shows the connection between alpinism, sport and tourism most suc-

10793 Slovenia — Awards, Honors & Prizes, 1995-96

cessfully - UNESCO-CIDALC Prize donated by the Committees for Sport and Tourism of UNESCO; (3) Best Camera Work; (4) Best Screenplay; (5) Best Educational Film; and (6) the country presenting the best selection of films - Grand Medal of the City of Kranj. The festival is organized biennially. Established in 1966. The Festival is co-sponsored by the Cultural Community of Slovenia and private organizations.

10793
International Centre of Graphic Arts
(Mednarodni Graficni Likovni Center)
Pod turnom 3, Grad Tivoli
61000 Ljubljana, Slovenia
Phone: 61 225 632
Fax: 61 215 304

10794
Grand Prix of Honour for a Yugoslav Artist
For recognition of contributions to the field of graphic arts. Citizens of Yugoslavia are eligible. A medal is awarded. Established in 1991. Formerly: Velika Castna Nagrada za Jugoslovanskega Umetnika.

10795
International Biennial of Graphic Art
(Biennale Internationale de Gravure)
For recognition of achievement in the field of graphic art. Both black-and-white and color reproductive printmaking techniques (monotype excluded) are taken into consideration, regardless of style and technical execution. Each entrant should forward three prints. Apart from works by invited exhibitors, works forwarded by artists upon their own initiative are accepted. These, however, are submitted to the selection of a jury. The deadline is December 20. Monetary prizes are awarded for the Grand Prix and the second and third prizes. The Grand Prix d'Honneur (Grand Prize of Honor) is given to artists who prove their constant high level during the years of participating in the biennial. Awarded biennially. Established in 1955.

10796
Library Association of Slovenia
(Zveza bibliotekarskih drustev Slovenije)
Turjaska 1
61001 Ljubljana, Slovenia
Phone: 61 332853

10797
Copova Diploma
For recognition of an outstanding contribution in the field of libraries. Members of the Association are eligible. A plaque and a diploma are awarded annually. Established in 1967 in honor of Matija Cop (1797-1835), Slovenian librarian.

10798
Preseren Fund
Cultural Community of Slovenia
(Presernov Sklad)
Republike Slovenije
Republiski Sekretariat Za Kulturo
Cankarjeva 5
61000 Ljubljana, Slovenia
Phone: 61 210914
Fax: 61 210814

10799
Preseren Award
(Presernova Nagrada)
This, the highest acknowledgment of the Republic of Slovenia, is given for recognition of achievements in the arts that includes letters, drama, music, dance, plastic and graphic arts, film, radio and television, architecture, and design. The works should be notable contributions to Slovene culture and should reflect outstanding lifetime work. The works considered also should have been published, exhibited, or performed two years before the award is given. Monetary awards and plaques are given annually at the central celebration of the cultural holiday (February 8th). Established in 1946 on the occasion of the anniversary of the death of France Preseren (1800-1849), the Slovene poet.

10800
Slovenia Writers Association
(Drustvo Slovenskih Pisateljev)
Tomsiceva 12
61001 Ljubljana, Slovenia
Phone: 61 21318
Phone: 61 214144

10801
International Literary Award Vilenica
To recognize exceptional artistic achievements in poetry, fiction, drama and essay originating in the Middle European cultural environment. Authors from the Middle European cultural environment are eligible. A monetary award is presented annually in September. Established in 1986.

10802
Slovensko Farmacevtsko Drustvo
(Pharmaceutical Society of Slovenia)
Ptuska 21
61000 Ljubljana, Slovenia
Phone: 61 344 085

10803
Minarikovo Odlicje
(Award of Minarik)
For recognition of achievement in the field of pharmacy. A plaque and trophy are awarded annually. Established in 1975 in honor of Franc Minarik, a world famous person in the history of pharmacy.

10804
Speculative Arts Association
(Sekcija Za Spekulativno Umetnost)
Kersnikova 4
6000 Ljubljana, Slovenia
Phone: 61 329850

10805
***Pasja Dlaka*, Slovenian/Universal Science Fiction Award**
(*Pasja Dlaka*, Slovenska/Svetovna Znanstvenofantasticna Nagrada)
To further Slovenian science fiction in the world, and the creative use of Slovenia, Slovenian language and Slovenians in science fiction written in non-Slovenian languages. Nomination is by members of the Association. No age or citizenship requirements are necessary. Established in 1983 in honor of the science fiction novel, *Pasja Dlaka*, by Damir Feigel, father of Slovenian science fiction.

10806
Zalozba Mladinska Knjiga
(Mladinska Knjiga)
Slovenska 29
61000 Ljubljana, Slovenia
Phone: 61 221233
Fax: 61 215320

Formerly: Youth Book Publishing House.

10807
Fran Levstik Prize
For recognition of the best Slovene children's or young adults' book. Entries are judged in the following areas: text - for fiction, a collection of poems and songs, illustrations, and text - for non-fiction. A monetary award, a diploma, and a memorial plaque are awarded biennially.

South Africa, Republic of

10808

AA Life
Arts Fund
PO Box 11159
Johannesburg 2000, Republic of South
 Africa

Phone: 11 492 1420
Fax: 11 836 9117

Formerly: (1987) AA Mutual Life.

10809

AA Life Vita Art Now

For recognition of outstanding achievement in the fine arts. Four quarterly awards and annual overall awards are presented. The year culminates in an exhibition of contemporary South African Art - the AA Life Vita Art Now Exhibition, which includes paintings, ceramics, sculpture, performance art, photography, mixed-media, etc. Established in 1987.

10810

AA Life Vita Ballet and Opera Awards

For recognition of outstanding achievement in ballet and opera in the Transvaal region. Awards are presented in the following categories: (1) Opera: (a) Most Outstanding Performance by a Male Singer; (b) Most Outstanding Performance by a Female Singer; and (2) Ballet; (a) Most Outstanding Performance by a Male Dancer; (b) Most Outstanding Performance by a Female Dancer; (c) Most Outstanding Performance by a Male Dancer in a Supporting Role; (d) Most Outstanding Performance by a Female Dancer in a Supporting Role; and (e) Most Outstanding Performance by a Dancer in a Character Role.

10811

AA Life Vita Contemporary Choreography and Dance Awards

For recognition of outstanding choreography and dance performance. All choreographers and dancers in original contemporary works, initiated and performed during the preceding year, are eligible. This includes work presented during individual choreographers' seasons, contemporary dance companies' seasons and the inaugural Dance Umbrella. The following awards are presented: (1) Most Promising Male Dancer; (2) Most Promising Female Dancer; (3) Best Female Dancer; (4) Best Male Dancer; and (5) Best Contemporary Choreography. Awarded annually. Established in 1985.

10812

AA Life Vita National Theatre Awards

For recognition of outstanding work in the theater. Winners from each province, in the relevant categories, are considered for the National Theatre Awards. The following awards are made annually: (1) Play of the Year - 10,000 rand; (2) Actor of the Year - 5,000 rand; (3) Actress of the Year - 5,000 rand; (4) Supporting Actor of the Year - 3,000 rand; (5) Supporting Actress of the Year - 3,000 rand; (6) Director of the Year - 5,000 rand; (7) South African Playwrights of the Year - 6,000 rand; and (8) New South African Play of the Year - 5,000 rand; and (9) Musical of the Year.

10813

AA Life Vita Regional Theatre Awards

For recognition of outstanding work in the theatre. Awards are presented for the Cape, Natal, and Orange Free State in the following categories: (1) Best Production of a Play or Musical; (2) Best Performance by an Actor; (3) Best Performance by an Actress; (4) Best Performance by an Actor in a Supporting Role; (5) Best Performance by an Actress in a Supporting Role; (6) Best Script; (7) Excellence in Direction; (8) Best Original Design: Costumes; (9) Best Original Design: Lighting; (10) Best Original Design: Set; and (11) Special Awards.

10814

M-Net Vita Film Award

To promote the South African film industry by rewarding excellence in the various facets of filmmaking. Films completed during the preceding year should be submitted by April 30. No made-for-television films and television programs qualify for entry. Films may be entered for consideration in the categories rewarding individual merit, provided that the individual concerned is an SA citizen or permanent resident. Awards are given in the following categories: (1) Best South African Film - first prize 100,000 rand; second prize - 50,000 rand; and third prize - 30,000 rand. To be entered for this award, at least four of the six major credits (producer, director, scriptwriter, cinematographer, editor, lead actor/actress) must be South African citizens, or permanent residents; (2) Best Director; (3) Best Actor; (4) Best Actress; (5) Best Scriptwriter; (6) Best Editing; (7) Best Sound; (8) Best Cinematography; (9) Best Art Direction; (10) Best Music Score; and (11) Best Performance in a Supporting Role - four awards. Awarded annually. Established in 1988 by AA Life. Since 1991, the sponsorship is by M-Net in consultation with AA Life Vita Awards. Formerly: (1991) AA Life/M-NET Vita Film Awards.

10815

Associated Scientific and Technical Societies of South Africa
PO Box 93480
Yeoville 2143, Republic of South Africa

Phone: 11 4871512
Fax: 11 6481876

10816

Scientific/Engineering Award

To recognize outstanding national contributions toward the advancement of scientific and technological knowledge. Awards are presented annually.

10817

Association of South African Quantity Surveyors (Vereniging van Suid-Afrikaanse Bourekenaars)
PO Box 3527
Halfway House 1685, Republic of South
 Africa

Phone: 315 4140
Fax: 315 3785

10818

Gold Medal of Honour

This, the Association's highest honor, is given for outstanding service to the building industry in general and to quantity surveying in particular. Members are eligible. A gold medal and a citation are awarded when merited. Established in 1977.

10819

Association of Surgeons of South Africa
Box 52027
Saxonwold
Johannesburg 2132, Republic of South
 Africa

Phone: 11 837 1011

10820

Bronze Medal

To provide recognition for the best publication in the Asociation's *South African Journal of Surgery*. Registrars-in-training are eligible. Awarded annually.

10821

Astronomical Society of Southern Africa
Assoc. Scientific & Technical Societies of
 South Africa
18A Gill St.
Observatory 2198, Republic of South Africa

Phone: 11 487 1512

10822

Gill Medal

For recognition of services to astronomy. Preference is given to work done in Southern Africa. Society members and non-members are eligible. Awarded annually when merited.

10823

McIntyre Award
For recognition of significant contributions to the history of astronomy in the form of: (1) a work to be published or which has been published in book form; or (2) a journal of recognized standing within the previous five years. Living persons of any nationality are eligible. A monetary prize of not less than 200 rand, derived from the interest on the bequest made to the Society by the late Donald G. McIntyre, is awarded irregularly.

10824

Recognition of Long Service to the Society
For recognition of individuals who have rendered invaluable service to the Society for at least 20 years. A book, suitably inscribed and valued up to 50 rand, is awarded annually.

10825

Cancer Association of South Africa
PO Box 2000
Johannesburg 2000, Republic of South Africa
Phone: 11 403 2825
Fax: 11 403 1946

10826

Lady Cade Memorial Fellowship
To encourage professional development in cancer research for senior scientists resident in South Africa. Open to medical graduates of senior status who are resident in South Africa, or South African nationals who are domiciled in the British Commonwealth, or in some cases, elsewhere. Preference is given to those holding senior posts at approved universities or other institutions to which the Fellows will be expected to return within six months of the termination of the Fellowship and work there, for a period of not less than two years. A monetary award and travel expenses to the United Kingdom for a minimum period of one year are presented biennially. Established in 1952 by the Medical Faculty of the University of the Witwatersrand, Johannesburg, South Africa, in memory of Lady Cade, who died while visiting South Africa with her cancer surgeon husband, Sir Stanford Cade. Sponsored by the Cancer Association of South Africa and the Cancer Research Campaign in London.

10827

Cape Tercentenary Foundation
PO Box 1506
Cape Town 8000, Republic of South Africa
Phone: 21 794 5829

10828

Award of Merit
To provide recognition for outstanding services to the cultural, artistic, historic, dramatic and conservation fields. Persons who have rendered outstanding services in one of the activities in which the Foundation is interested are eligible. Monetary awards and certificates are presented annually, usually in February. Established in 1953.

10829

Central News Agency Ltd.
c/o The Organizer
PO Box 7724
Johannesburg 2000, Republic of South Africa
Phone: 11 726 4521
Fax: 11 725 7119

10830

CNA Literary Award
To provide recognition for the best original works in English and Afrikaans written by South African authors. Accepted books must fall into the following categories: novels and short stories, poetry, biography, drama, history and travel. Monetary prizes of 500 rand are awarded annually to each of three shortlisted authors in English and Afrikaans, and 7,500 rand to the winner as well as a commemorative bronze plaque. Established in 1961.

10831

Chamber of Mines of South Africa
5 Holland St.
Johannesburg 2001, Republic of South Africa
Phone: 11 8388211
Fax: 11 8341884

10832

Awards for Bravery
To recognize an individual for bravery, outstanding first aid, or meritorious conduct in the industry. Prizes are awarded in the following categories: Bravery of the Highest Degree - for a deliberate and premeditated assumption of risk that, to the knowledge of the person concerned, might prove fatal. A monetary prize, a bronze medal, a gold watch, an honor tie, a certificate, and a framed photograph of the presentation; Outstanding Bravery - a monetary prize, a gold watch, an honor tie, a certificate and a framed photograph; Bravery - a monetary prize, a stainless steel watch, an honor tie, a certificate, and a framed photograph; Lesser Acts of Bravery - a monetary prize, an honor tie, a briefcase, and a letter of commendation.

10833

Chiropractic Association of South Africa
(Chiropraktiese Vereniging van Suid-Afrika)
121 Clarence Rd.
Morningside
Durban 4001, Republic of South Africa
Phone: 31 3091480
Fax: 31 3091480

10834

Chiropractor of the Year
To recognize a member who has shown meritorious service to his profession. Awarded irregularly.

10835

Concrete Society of Southern Africa
(Betonvereniging van Suidelike Afrika)
Portland Park
PO Box 168
Halfway House 1685, Republic of South Africa
Phone: 11 315 0300
Phone: 11 315 0314
Fax: 11 315 0054

10836

Concrete Man of the Year
For recognition of the person doing the most to promote the use of concrete and the standards of excellence in its use. Established in 1982 by the Transvaal Branch.

10837

Fulton Awards
(Fulton Toekenning)
This premier civil engineering award in Southern Africa, is presented for recognition of excellence in the use of concrete in three categories: civil engineering structures, building structures, and concrete sculptures. A project that is made substantially of concrete and has been completed in the year of the award is eligible. Plaques are awarded annually. Established in 1979 in honor of Dr. Sandrock Fulton.

10838

Dental Association of South Africa
(Tandheelkundige Vereniging van Suid-Afrika)
Private Bag 1
Houghton 2041, Republic of South Africa
Phone: 642 4687
Fax: 642 5718

10839

J.C. Middleton Shaw Fellowshipq
To recognize an individual for achievement in post-graduate dental education. Applicants must be, except under special circumstances, members. Applications must be submitted by July 31. The award pro-

vides for education in the Republic of South Africa or abroad. A monetary award of 6,000 rand ($5,000 U.S. if project is overseas) is presented.

10840
Elida Pond's Fellowship and Other Awards in Dentistry
To encourage the development of dental research and ensure its continuation in the Republic of South Africa. The Fellowship is intended for research in any field related to dentistry. Applicants must be South African Nationals or hold permanent residence status. Applications must be supported by a university or other such institution. Applications must be submitted by July 31. Awards are usually made for one year only, but may be extended for a further period of one year. A maximum of 10,000 rand is available for the Fellowship and any other awards which may be granted.

10841
Julius Staz Scholarship for Dental Research
To provide an opportunity for a qualified person to study a research technique of relevance to dentistry. Applications are considered from individuals who have a proven record of research or who are sponsored by an individual with such a record. The applicant or his/her sponsor must be a member who has been in good standing for two or more consecutive years. Applications must be submitted by July 31. A monetary award of 3,000 rand ($2,500 U.S. if project is abroad) is presented.

10842
Dohne Merino Breeder's Society of South Africa
PO Box 61
Stutterheim 49309, Republic of South Africa
Phone: 436 31330
Fax: 436 31931

10843
IVOMEC Award for Effective Sheep Breeding
To recognize the most successful Dohne Merino ram breeder of South Africa. Members of the Society are eligible. A floating trophy and monetary prize are awarded biennially. Established in 1977. Sponsored by Logos Agvet.

10844
Durban Camera Club
PO Box 1594
Durban 4000, Republic of South Africa

10845
Durban International Exhibition of Photography
For recognition of outstanding photography. Awards are presented in the following categories: (1) Colour Slides; (2) Nature Slides; (3) Monochrome Prints; (4) Colour Prints; and (5) Nature Prints. Photographers may submit up to four pictures in any or all sections. Gold, silver and bronze medals are awarded in each category biennially. Established in 1976.

10846
Durban International Film Festival
University of Natal
King George V Ave.
Durban 4001, Republic of South Africa
Fax: 31 2617107

10847
Durban International Film Festival Awards
To honor outstanding achievement in film. Awards are presented for best film, best director, best actor, best supporting actor, and best documentary. A certificate is awarded in each category annually during the festival. Established in 1978.

10848
Eighteen-twenty Foundation
1820 Settlers National Monument, Gunfire Hill
PO Box 304
Grahamstown 6140, Republic of South Africa
Phone: 461 27115

10849
Standard Bank Young Artists' Awards
For recognition of outstanding contributions to South African fine and performing arts. Individuals under 40 years of age are eligible. Awards are given in the following categories: (1) music; (2) fine arts; and (3) drama. Individuals must be nominated by the Arts Festival Committee. A monetary award, a sponsored exhibition or production at the National Festival of the Arts, and a national tour are awarded annually. Established in 1981. Sponsored by the Standard Bank Investment Corporation.

10850
English Academy of Southern Africa
PO Box 124
Univ. of Witwatersrand
Johannesburg 2050, Republic of South Africa
Phone: 11 7163683

10851
English Academy Medal
To recognize an individual who has conspicuously served the cause of English over a number of years, or performed signal service in the cause of English. A medal is awarded annually. Established in 1989.

10852
Thomas Pringle Award
For recognition of work written in English and published in newspapers and periodicals in Southern Africa. Material published in the following categories is considered: reviews of books, plays, films, and television in newspapers or periodicals; literary articles or substantial book reviews; articles on language, the teaching of English, and educational topics in academic, teachers', and other journals, and in newspapers; short stories and one act plays in periodicals; and poetry in periodicals (a single poem could be sufficient for an award). The first category is considered annually for an award. The other four categories are considered in alternate years over a two-year period. Monetary prizes of 500 rand each and an illuminated certificate are awarded. A maximum of three awards is made annually. Sponsored by The Achievement Management Group of Companies.

10853
Olive Schreiner Prize
To recognize the first major work in English by a new South African writer. Awards are given in one of three categories: poetry, drama, and prose (rotating in the order given). South Africans and citizens of the territories administered (or formerly administered) by South Africa are eligible for work published in South Africa. A monetary prize of 1,000 rand and an illuminated certificate are awarded annually. Established in 1961 by the South African Academy for Sciences and Arts and transferred in 1972 to the English Academy of Southern Africa. Sponsored by The Achievement Management Group of Companies.

10854
English Association
B204 Devonshire Hill
Grotto Rd.
Rondebosch
Cape Town 7700, Republic of South Africa
Phone: 21 68 54242

10855
English Association Literary Competition
To promote and encourage creative writing in the English language. The nature of the competition varies from year to year and may be for poetry, a short story, a one-act play, an essay, novel, profile of a writer, radio plays or full-length plays. South African writers may submit original, unpublished works only. Monetary prizes totaling 2,000 rand are awarded. Established in 1963.

10856
Federation of Afrikaans Cultural Societies
(Federasie van Afrikaanse Kultuurvereniginge)
PO Box 91050
Aucklandpark 2006, Republic of South Africa   Phone: 11 7262073

10857
Federation of Afrikaans Cultural Societies Awards
To recognize and encourage research of Afrikaans culture. The Federation sponsors competitions and bestows awards and scholarships.

10858
Fertilizer Society of South Africa
(Misstofvereniging van Suid-Afrika)
PO Box 7438
Hennopsmeer 0046, Republic of South Africa   Phone: 12 6633110
                                                    Fax: 12 6633921

10859
Jan De Waal Memorial Award
(Jan De Waal Gedenktoekenning)
For recognition of the best agricultural research paper presented or published by a researcher under the age of 40 years during the year. The deadline for nominations is August. A medal is awarded annually at the general meeting of the Society. Established in 1974 in memory of Jan De Waal, former chairman of the Society.

10860
FSSA Gold Medal
(MVSA Goue Medalje)
For recognition of contributions to agriculture in South Africa over a long period of time. The deadline for nomination is August. A medal is awarded annually at the general meeting of the Society. Established in 1968.

10861
FSSA Silver Medal (Extension)
(MUSA Silwer Medalje (Voorligting))
For recognition of contributions to agricultural extension in South Africa. The deadline for nomination is August. A medal is awarded annually at the general meeting of the Society. Established in 1968.

10862
FSSA Silver Medal (Research)
(MVSA Silwer Medalje (Navorsing))
For recognition of contributions to agricultural research in specific fields. The deadline for nominations is August. A medal is awarded annually at the general meeting of the Society. Established in 1968.

10863
FSSA Silver Medal (Research and Extension)
(MUSA Silwer Medalje (Navorsing en Voorligting))
For recognition of contributions to agricultural research and extension in South Africa. The deadline for nominations is August. A medal is awarded annually at the general meeting of the Society. Established in 1972.

10864
Free Market Foundation of Southern Africa
PO Box 785121
Sandton
Johannesburg 2146, Republic of South Africa   Phone: 11 8840270
                                                     Fax: 11 8845672

10865
Free Market Award
To honor individuals who have made an outstanding contribution to the cause of economic freedom in South Africa. Selection is by nomination. A certificate and Kruger Rand are awarded annually. Established in 1980.

10866
Geological Society of South Africa
(Geologiese Vereniging van Suid-Afrika)
PO Box 44283   Phone: 11 8882288
Linden 2104, Republic of South Africa   Fax: 11 8881632

10867
Corstorphine Medal
To provide recognition for the best student thesis embodying the results of original research on geological subjects. Students of any university in Southern Africa are eligible. A bronze medal is awarded annually when merited. Established in 1925 to honor Geo. S. Corstorphine, Honorary Editor of the *Transactions of the Geological Society of South Africa* (1903-1905 and 1910-1915).

10868
Draper Memorial Medal
For recognition of a past record of research with particular reference to the advancement of South African geology. Members of the Society for at least five years are eligible. A bronze medal showing a bust of Dr. David Draper, the first Honorary Secretary of the Society, is awarded annually. Established in 1932.

10869
Alex L. Du Toit Memorial Lecturer
To recognize an individual who has distinguished him or herself in the fields in which Alex Du Toit was active, i.e. continental drift, geology of South Africa and particularly its relation to hydrology, and archaeology. If circumstances permit, and at the discretion of the Council, the lecturer alternates from South Africa and overseas. Awarded biennially. Established in 1949 to honor the life and work of Dr. Alexander Logi Du Toit, distinguished South African geologist.

10870
Honorary Member
To recognize outstanding contributions to the field of geology. Awarded when merited.

10871
Honours Award
To recognize a member or group of members of the Society who has made a particularly meritorious contribution to the Geological Society of South Africa or the Geological Fraternity of South Africa. A shield on which the recipient's name is inscribed is awarded when merited. Established in 1978.

10872
Jubilee Medal
For recognition of a paper of particular merit published by the Society in any year. Members of the Society are eligible. A gold medal weighing one ounce is awarded annually. Established in 1945 on the 50th anniversary of the founding of the Society.

10873

Grassland Society of Southern Africa
(Weidingsvereniging van Suidelike Afrika)
University of Natal
PO Box 375
Pietermaritzberg 3200, Republic of South Africa
Phone: 31 2605268
Fax: 31 2605067

10874

Grassland Society of Southern Africa Awards
To recognize individuals interested in grassland (or rangeland) science. Young scientists who have made outstanding contributions in the field are eligible.

10875

Institute of Marketing Management
(Instituut van Bemarkingsbestuur)
PO Box 91820
Auckland Park 2006, Republic of South Africa
Phone: 11 482 1419
Fax: 11 482 3190

10876

Raymond Ackerman Marketing Director of the Year
To recognize men and women of South Africa for personal achievements in marketing. A monetary prize of 1,000 rands, a trophy, and a certificate were awarded, and the two semi-finalists received certificates. Awarded annually. Established in 1981. (Discontinued in 1987)

10877

Emergent Entrepreneur Award
To motivate and recognize the successful small business entrepreneurs in South Africa. The award reflects recognition of the socio political context in which the small business venture purports to provide an economic service. The business must meet the following composite criteria: (1) established for at least two years; (2) comprised of up to a maximum of twenty employees; (3) prove profitability of the venture at least by the end of the second financial year; (4) particular recognition to the entrepreneur who has spotted a unique gap in the market place; (5) provide employment; and (6) evidence that the human resources deployed in the enterprise are developed. Three nominees are selected to attend the Institute's Awards Banquet held annually in September. The winner receives a monetary award of 10,000 rand as an injection of capital to the winner's business and a certificate. Established in 1987. Sponsored by Shell South Africa in conjunction with the Institute.

10878

Marketing Man/Woman of the Year Award
For recognition of outstanding success in marketing that resulted in a noteworthy and profitable success in the production, distribution or sales turnover of one or more products or services provided by a business, corporate body, industry, or administrative department. Chief executives of companies who display inventiveness, initiative, planning and motivation are eligible. Nominations are open to members of all racial groups. Three finalists are guests of the Institute of the National Marketing Awards Banquet in September. A certificate is awarded annually. Established in 1962.

10879

Institute of South African Architects
PO Box 2093
Houghton 2041, Republic of South Africa
Phone: 11 4861683
Fax: 11 4861683

10880

Architectural Critics and Writers Award
For recognition of a distinguished contribution to architectural criticism and/or writing. Established in 1977.

10881

Gold Medal
For recognition of an outstanding contribution to architecture through practice and design. Members of the Institute are eligible. A silver gilt medal is awarded when merited. Established in 1958.

10882

Medal of Distinction
For recognition of services to the profession of architecture. Members of the Institute are eligible. A medal is awarded when merited. Established in 1981.

10883

Patron of Architecture Award
For recognition of achievement in architecture and allied fields. An individual, government, department, or other organization is eligible. Awarded when merited. Established in 1981.

10884

Institute of Traffic Officers of Southern Africa
(Instituut van Verkeersbeamptes van Suider-Africa)
Gluckman St.
Private Bag X1258
Potchefstroom 2520, Republic of South Africa
Phone: 148 995301
Fax: 148 26388

10885

Institute of Traffic Officers of Southern Africa Awards
To recognize professional law enforcement officers in South Africa.

10886

Medical Association of South Africa
(Mediese Vereniging van Suid-Afrika)
PO Box 20272
Alkantrant 0005
Pretoria, Republic of South Africa
Phone: 12 47 6101

10887

Andries Blignault Medal
For recognition of the best contribution of the year by multi-authors published in the *South African Medical Journal*. A medal is awarded annually.

10888

Louis Leipoldt Memorial Medal
For recognition of the best manuscript submitted to the *South African Medical Journal* by a general practitioner. A medal is awarded annually.

10889

Hamilton Maynard Memorial Medal
For recognition of the best manuscript by a single author published in the *South African Medical Journal*. A medal is awarded annually.

10890

Medical Association of South Africa Awards for Excellence in Medical Reporting (Press, Radio, Television)
For recognition of outstanding medical reporting on television, in the press or on radio. Journalists from all the media are eligible. A plaque and cash prizes in each category are awarded annually.

10891

Medical Association of South Africa Branch Award for Meritorious Service
To recognize members who voluntarily serve their Association in their own branches or divisions, and whose service is perhaps known only to their own local colleagues. Members of the Association for at least fifteen

years are eligible. Lapel badges and certificates are awarded when merited. Established in 1972.

10892
Medical Association of South Africa Bronze Medal Award
To recognize members of the Associaton for signal service to the Association. Not more than four bronze medals and certificates are awarded annually. Established in 1948.

10893
Medical Association of South Africa Gold Medal Award
To recognize members of the Association who have rendered services of outstanding value to the medical profession. A gold medal and a certificate are awarded annually. Established in 1930.

10894
Medical Association of South Africa Group Award for Meritorious Service
For recognition of outstanding service to a specific group of the Association. Members of at least 15 years standing are eligible. A lapel badge and a certificate are awarded annually when merited. Established in 1980.

10895
Medical Association of South Africa Pro Meritis Award
To recognize members of the Medical Association of South Africa or any other persons who by means other than original research have made valuable contributions to medical science and the art of healing in South Africa. No more than two plaques and certificates are awarded annually. Established in 1976.

10896
Medical Association of South Africa Silver Medal Award
To recognize members of the Association or other residents in South Africa who, through original research, have made valuable contributions to the advancement of medical science and the art of healing. No more than two silver medals and certificates are awarded annually. Established in 1956.

10897
Medical Students' Prize
For recognition of the best article published in the *South African Journal* by a medical student. A cash prize is awarded annually.

10898
National Association for Clean Air
PO Box 2036
Parklands 2121, Republic of South Africa
Phone: 11 6462210
Fax: 11 6462210

10899
NACA Clean Air Award
To recognize the contributions of any individual or organization to the cause of clean air in South Africa. Members of the Association may make nominations. A framed certificate is awarded annually. Established in 1986.

10900
National Wool Growers' Association
PO Box 2242
Port Elizabeth 6056, Republic of South Africa
Phone: 41 541536
Fax: 41 545698

10901
Golden Ram Award (Goueram-Toekenning)
To recognize members of the Association who have delivered exceptional service to the wool industry. The Central Executive may nominate presidents of the Association, chairmen of the South African Wool Board, or persons who have delivered exceptional service to the industry. A medal and certificate are awarded when merited at the Congress. Established about 1964.

10902
Nematological Society of Southern Africa
Outspan Citrus Centre
PO Box 28
Nelspruit 1200, Republic of South Africa
Phone: 1311 53731
Fax: 1311 552281

10903
George C. Martin Memorial Scholarship
To encourage studies and professional development in the field of nematology. Applications are accepted before February of each year. A monetary prize is awarded annually. Established in 1982 in honor of George C. Martin. Sponsored by various chemical companies.

10904
W. J. van der Linde Memorial Award
For recognition of the best paper in the field of nematology read at the NSSA Symposium. Papers displaying original research and good presentation are eligible. A medal is awarded biennially. Established in 1983 in honor of W. J. van der Linde.

10905
Perskor Publishers
PO Box 845
Johannesburg 2000, Republic of South Africa
Phone: 11 776 9111

10906
Perskor Prize for Leisure Reading
For recognition of the best book published by Perskor during the preceding three years. A monetary prize of 5,000 rand is awarded. Established in 1985.

10907
Perskor Prize for Literature
For recognition of the best literary work published by Perskor during the preceding three years. A monetary prize of 5,000 rand is awarded biannually.

10908
Perskor Prize for Youth Literature
For recognition of the best youth book published by Perskor during the preceding three years. A monetary prize of 5,000 rand is awarded biannually. Established in 1979.

10909
Pretoria International Exhibition of Photography
PO Box 20048
Alkantrant 0005, Republic of South Africa
Phone: 12 57 4315

10910
Pretoria International Exhibition of Photography
To recognize outstanding photography. Open to photographers from any country. Entries may be submitted in the following categories: (1) Contemporary Sections - Prints and Color Slides; (2) Color Transparencies; (3) Monochrome and Color Prints; (4) Color Slides; and (5) Nature Slides and Prints. Medals are awarded by the Photographic Society of Southern Africa and the Photographic Society of America. Additional medals and plaques are awarded. The exhibition is held biennially. Established in 1971 by Interfoto.

10911
Public Relations Institute of Southern Africa
(Openbare Skakelinstituut van Suidelike Afrika)
PO Box 31749
Braamfontein 2017, Republic of South Africa
Phone: 11 7267356
Fax: 11 7267082

Formerly: (1988) Public Relations Institute of South Africa.

10912
Public Relations Institute of Southern Africa Awards
To recognize students and professionals in the public relations field.

10913
Republic of South Africa
Department of Foreign Affairs
c/o Protocol Section
Private Bag X152
Pretoria 0001, Republic of South Africa
Phone: 12 3233717
Fax: 12 3231011

10914
Order of Good Hope
To recognize civilian and military citizens of foreign countries who have distinguished themselves by their services in the promotion of the international relations of South Africa. Individuals who have earned the respect and gratitude of the Republic of South Africa may be recommended by the Executive Council of the Republic of South Africa. The Order is available for award in five classes appertaining, in the case of foreign functionaries and persons of rank and station, to the following categories: (1) Special Class - Grand Collar, for Heads of State only; (2) First Class - Grand Cross, for Prime Ministers, Ministers, Ministers of State, Supreme Court Judges, Presidents of Legislative Bodies, Secretaries of State, Ambassadors, and Commanders in Chief and other functionaires of comparable rank; (3) Second Class - Grand Officer, for Members of Legislative Bodies, Envoys Extraordinary, Ministers Plenipotentiary, officers other than Commanders in Chief, and other functionaries of comparable rank; (4) Third Class - Commander, for Charge d'Affaires, Counsellors of diplomatic missions, Consuls General, Colonels and Lieutenant Colonels; and (5) Fourth Class - Officers, for secretaries of diplomatic missions, Consuls, and lower ranking officers of armed forces. Medals are awarded when merited by the State President. Established in 1973.

10915
Republic of South Africa
Department of National Education
c/o Frans du Toitgebou Bldgs.
Schoeman St., Private Bag X122
Pretoria 0001, Republic of South Africa
Phone: 12 314 6337

10916
South African Sports Merit Award
For recognition of competitive sports achievements within the boundaries of the Republic of South Africa. The award recognizes coaches who brought about outstanding sports achievements by South African sportsmen/sportswomen at the international and/or national level, and sports administrators/officials who contributed to the promotion and furtherance of the sport concerned. A silver medal is awarded when merited.

10917
State President's Sport Award
To recognize an individual or team for achievements in sport of the highest international order. This includes an improvement of an existing world record or the winning of a world championship in an established prestige sport or other achievements equal to these. South African citizens are eligible. A gold medal is awarded when merited.

10918
Republic of South Africa
South African Defense Force
Private Bag X159
Pretoria 0001, Republic of South Africa
Phone: 12 4284105

10919
Ad Adstra Decoration
To recognize members of the SA Defence Force who have distinguished themselves on board aircraft by their excellent flying skill, outstanding ingenuity, or skill during emergencies or unusual situations. A gold star with an eagle displayed in the center and worn from a white and grey striped ribbon is bestowed.

10920
Air Force Cross
To recognize members of the SA Air Force who have distinguished themselves among the air defence by their exceptional courage, leadership, skill, ingenuity, or tenacity in the handling of personnel, weaponry, or other equipment in dangerous situations. A silver cross with a blue gem center displaying an eagle and worn from a white, blue, and yellow striped ribbon is bestowed. A bar is issued for successive awards.

10921
Army Cross
To recognize members of the SA Army who have distinguished themselves in dangerous situations by their exceptional courage, leadership, skill, ingenuity, or tenacity in the handling of personnel, weaponry, or other equipment. A silver cross with a red gem center displaying a horse and worn from a white and red striped ribbon are bestowed. A bar is presented for successive awards.

10922
Castle of Good Hope Decoration
For recognition of single acts of valor or most conspicuous bravery or some daring or pre-eminent act of self-sacrifice or extreme devotion to duty in the presence of an enemy. All ranks of the SA Defense Force are eligible. A bar may be awarded should the recipient again perform such an act that would have made him eligible to receive the decoration. The post-nominal letters of CGH and a gold pentagon worn from a ribbon of green silk are awarded. Established in 1952.

10923
John Chard Decoration
To recognize individuals from all ranks of the Citizen Force for long (20 years) and efficient service. An oval silver medal worn from a red, white, and blue ribbon is awarded. Established in 1952 and named in honor of Lieutenant John Rouse Marriot Chard, who in 1879 commanded the defense of Rorke's Drift.

10924
John Chard Medal
To recognize individuals from all ranks of the Citizen Force who have distinguished themselves for rendering 10 years of long and efficient service. A bronze oval medal worn from a red, white, and blue ribbon is awarded. Established in 1952.

10925
De Wet Decoration
To recognize officers of the Commandos for distinguishing themselvers for twenty years of long and efficient service. A round silver medal worn from a green, blue, and yellow ribbon is awarded. Established in 1965.

10926
De Wet Medal
For recognition of commandos who have distinguished themselves through 10 years of long and efficient service. A round medal displaying a soldier leading the charge worn from a green, white, blue, and yellow ribbon is awarded.

10927
General Service Medal
To recognize members of the SA Defence Force who have rendered service as part of military operations within the borders of the Republic of South Africa for the prevention or suppression of terrorism or internal disorder or who have served for the preservation of life, health or property, or maintenance of essential services, including the maintance of law and order or the prevention of crime in co-operation with the South Africa Police. A silver medal displaying a star and wreath, worn from a red, white, and blue ribbon is bestowed. Established January 1983.

10928
Honoris Crux
To recognize individuals from all ranks of the SA Defense Force for deeds of bravery, while endangering themselves against an armed enemy. A bar may be awarded for a further similar deed of bravery. The post-nominal letters of HC and a Maltese cross and wreath with a red, white, and blue enamel center worn from an orange and white ribbon are awarded. Established in 1952.

10929
Honoris Crux Diamond
To recognize individuals from all ranks for death-defying heroic deeds of bravery while in extreme danger. The post-nominal letters of HCD and a green and gold Maltese cross worn from an orange vertical ribbon are awarded. A bar is issued for successive awards. Established in 1975. (Discontinued)

10930
Honoris Crux Gold
To recognize individuals from all ranks for outstanding deeds of bravery while in extreme danger. The post-nominal letters of HCG and a green Maltese cross, against a silver wreath, with a red, white, and blue enamel center worn from an orange ribbon with white stripe are awarded. A bar is issued for successive awards. Established in 1975. (Discontinued)

10931
Honoris Crux Silver
To recognize individuals from all ranks of the SA Defense Force for exceptional deeds of bravery, while greatly endangering their lives during military operations against an armed enemy. The post-nominal letters of HCS and a green Maltese cross, against a silver wreath, with a red, white, and blue enamel center worn from an orange ribbon with two white stripes is awarded. A bar is issued for successive awards. Established in 1975.

10932
Honourably Mentioned in Despatches
To recognize individuals from all ranks of the SA Defense Force, who in time of war or emergency distinguish themselves by brave or gallant conduct, meritorious service or devotion to duty in the field, whether in combat against an enemy or otherwise and for which no medal is warranted. Established in 1967.

10933
Medal for Distinguished Conduct and Loyal Service
To recognize members of the SA Defence Force who have distinguished themselves in conduct and loyal service of forty years. A round medal worn from a red, white, and blue ribbon is bestowed.

10934
Medical Services Cross
To recognize members of the SA Medical Services who have distinguished themselves in dangerous situations by their exceptional courage, leadership, skill, ingenuity, or tenacity in the handling of personnel, weaponry, or other equipment. A silver cross with a red gem center diplaying a staff and snake, worn from a white and red striped ribbon is bestowed. A bar is presented for successive awards.

10935
Military Merit Medal
To recognize members of the SA Defence Force who have distinguished themselves by the rendering of services of a high order. A medal worn from a blue and red striped ribbon is bestowed. A bar is presented for successive awards. Formerly: C SADF Commendation Medal; Chief of the South African Defense Force Commendation Medal.

10936
National Cadet Bisley Grand Champion Medal
To recognize a person who, as a member of the Cadet Corps of the SA Defence Force, has distinguished himself as the champion shot at the National Cadet Bisley. Awarded annually.

10937
Navy Cross
To recognize members of the SA Navy who have distinguished themselves in dangerous situations by their exceptional courage, leadership, skill, ingenuity, or tenacity in the handling of personnel, weaponry, or other equipment. A silver cross with a blue gem center displaying a gargoyle and worn from a white and blue striped ribbon is bestowed. A bar is presented for successive awards.

10938
Pro Merito Decoration
To recognize other ranks of the SA Defense Force who have distinguished themselves for outstanding service of the highest order and utmost devotion to duty. A white enameled Maltese cross edged in gold is awarded. A bar is issued for successive awards. Established in 1975.

10939
Pro Merito Medal
For recognition of other members of the SA Defence Force who have distinguished themselves through exceptional, meritorious service and diligence. A rounded medal with five points and an enamel center, worn from a blue and white ribbon is awarded. A bar is presented for successive awards.

10940
Pro Patria Medal
To recognize individuals from all ranks of the SA Defense Force for services rendered in connection with the prevention or combating of terrorism, or services in the defense of the Republic of South Africa. A bronze octagonal medal worn from an orange, white, and blue striped ribbon are awarded. Established in 1974.

10941
Pro Virtute Decoration
To recognize officers for distinguished conduct and exceptional combat leadership in action. A silver cross-like medal with a red enamel center, worn from a red and white ribbon is awarded. A bar is issued for successive awards.

10942
Pro Virtute Medal
For recognition of other members of the SA Defence Force who have distinguished themselves through conduct and conspicuous leadership in action. A silver medal worn from a red and white ribbon is bestowed.

10943
South African Defence Force Champion Shot Medal
For recognition of four SA Defense Force members who have distinguished themselves as champion shots in service shooting, full-bore shooting, small-bore shooting, and pistol shooting. A round medal worn from an aqua, red, and navy ribbon is awarded annually. Established in 1972.

10944
South African Defence Force Good Service Medal
To recognize permanent SADF members who have distinguished themselves through years of service. A gold medal is bestowed for 30 years of service, a silver for 20 years of service, and a bronze for 10 years of service. Formerly: (1975) Permanent Force Good Service Medal.

10945
Southern Africa Medal
To recognize members of the SA Defence Force who rendered service in connection with the suppression of terrorism and who have participated in an operation across the border. A silver hexagonal medal worn from a red, yellow, blue, and white stiped ribbon is bestowed.

10946
Southern Cross Decoration
To recognize officers for outstanding service of the highest order and utmost devotion to duty. The post-nominal title of SD and a gold Maltese cross with a blue enamel center adorned with five stars is awarded. A bar is issued for successive awards. Established in 1975.

10947
Southern Cross Medal
For recognition of SA Defence Force officers who have distinguished themselves through exceptional, meritorious service and diligence. A silver medal with a blue enamel center displaying five stars and worn from a blue and white ribbon is awarded. A bar is presented for successive awards.

10948
Danie Theron Medal
To recognize individuals from all ranks of the Commandos for exceptionally diligent and outstanding service (of no less than ten years). A round silver medal worn from a green and yellow striped ribbon is awarded. Established in 1970 and named for Captain Danie Theron, Master Scout of the Anglo-Boer War. (Discontinued)

10949
Republic of South Africa
South African Railways Police
c/o Office of the Commissioner
PO Box 711
Johannesburg 2000, Republic of South
   Africa   Phone: 11 32830

10950
Decoration for Distinguished Service in the South African Railways Police Force
For recognition of distinguished service rendered or gallantry displayed by a member of the South African Railways Police Force who by protecting or saving of life or property, displayed particular gallantry or exceptional ingenuity, proficiency or perseverance; or who distinguished himself by displaying outstanding resourcefulness or outstanding leadership or particular conscientiousness and personal example in any section or branch of the Force. A gilded silver five-pointed star is awarded when merited.

10951
Medal for Bravery
In recognition of cases of exceptional merit such as bravery involving the risk of life, although not necessarily involving the saving of life. Any South African Railway servant, except members of the South African Railways Police Force, who displays outstanding bravery is eligible. A bronze medal is awarded when merited.

10952
South African Police Cross for Valour
This, the highest decoration or medal, is given for recognition of acts of valor by a member of the South African Railways Police Force who displayed conspicuous and exceptional gallantry or who has performed a fearless or pre-eminent act whereby he has lost or actually imperilled his own life in the performance of any of his duties or in protecting or saving or endeavoring to protect or save life or property. A gold and white enameled double pointed Maltese cross is awarded when merited. Established in 1980.

10953
South African Railways Police Medal for Combating Terrorism
To recognize a member of the South African Railways Police Force who has been involved in combat with terrorists, or who has, in the course of duty in connection with the prevention and combating of terrorism, sustained injuries arising from terrorist activities, or who in execution of such duties, displayed exceptional vigilance, zeal, ingenuity, skill or leadership; or to recognize a member who in support of the Force has performed counterinsurgency duty for at least 60 days. A circular bronze medal is awarded when merited, and may be awarded posthumously. Established in 1974.

10954
South African Railways Police Star for Distinguished Leadership
To recognize an officer of the general staff of the South African Railways Police Force who has distinguished himself through leadership, meritorious service contributing to the security of the State, or service to members of a dynasty or to Heads of State or Governments. An eight pointed star of silver with an eight pointed star of gold thereon and a small silver star in the middle set with diamonds is awarded when merited, and may be awarded posthumously. Established in 1979.

10955
South African Railways Police Star for Distinguished Service
To recognize an officer of the general staff in the South African Railways Police Force who has distinguished himself through meritorious service promoting the efficiency of the Force or who has contributed actively to the security of the Republic of South Africa. In addition, it may be awarded to a high ranking South African citizen who has rendered meritorious service to the Republic of South Africa. An eight pointed star of silver with a smaller eight pointed star of gold in the middle is awarded when merited, and may be awarded posthumously. Established in 1979.

10956
Star for Merit in the South African Railways Police Force
In recognition of outstanding devotion to duty by a member who rendered services of a particularly meritorious or exemplary nature or distinguished himself by personal heroism; or for service during a period of not less than thirty years, which need not be continuous, in which the individual displayed an irreproachable character and exemplary conduct. A silver medal shaped like a five-pointed star is awarded when merited. Established in 1963.

10957
Republic of South Africa
State President's Office
Chancery of Orders
Private Bag X1000
Pretoria 0084, Republic of South Africa   Phone: 12 3252000

10958
Order for Meritorious Service
For recognition of outstanding merit and exceptionally distinguished services to the Republic. The Order is available for award in two classes to South African citizens in the following categories: Class I, Gold - to South African citizens who have distinguished themselves by exceptional merit by rendering exceptionally meritorious service in the general public interest; and Class II, Silver - to South African citizens who have distinguished themselves by outstanding merit by rendering meritorious service in the general public interest. A cross enamelled in white, charged with a cross nowy couped, surmounted by a circular medallion of the shield of the Coat of Arms of the Republic of South Africa, enamelled proper is awarded. The Order is worn on a pendant from a blue, white, and orange ribbon. The recipient may append the post-nominal title of OMSG or OMSS to his or her name. Awarded when merited by the State

President. Established in 1986. Formerly: (1986) Decoration for Meritorious Service.

10959
Order of Good Hope
To recognize citizens of foreign countries who have distinguished themselves by their services in the mutual promotion of South African international relations or have promoted the interests of the Republic. The Order is available for an award in five classes: Class I, Grand Cross (Gold) - to heads of state, and in special cases heads of government and other persons who have promoted the interests of the Republic through excellent meritorious service; Class II, Grand Officer (Silver) - to heads of government and other ministers of state, supreme court judges, presidents of legislative bodies, secretaries of state, ambassadors extraordinary and plenipotentiary, commanders in chief of the armed forces, and other functionaries and persons of comparable rank and station according to the rules and practices of each country who have promoted the interests of the Republic through outstanding meritorious service; Class III, Commander - to members of legislative bodies, envoys extraordinary and ministers plenipotentiary, general officers of the armed forces other than commanders in chief, and other functionaries and persons of comparable rank and station according to the rules and practices of each country who have promoted the interests of the Republic through exceptionally meritorious service; Class IV, Officer - to charges d'affaires, counsellors of diplomatic missions, Consuls General, Colonels and Lieutenant-Colonels or persons of equivalent rank, and other functionaries and persons of comparable rank and station according to the rules and practices of each country who have promoted the interest of the Republic through meritorious service; Class V, Member - to secretaries of diplomatic missions, consuls, lower ranking officers of the armed forces, and other functionaries and persons of comparable rank and station according to the rules and practices in each country who have promoted the interest of the Republic through exceptional service. Awarded when merited by the State President. Established in 1988.

10960
Order of the Southern Cross
The Order is available for award in two classes to South African citizens in the following categories: Class I, Gold - to those whose unique achievement of the highest standard has served the interest of the Republic of South Africa; and Class II, Silver - to those whose outstanding achievement of a high standard has served the interest of the Republic of South Africa. A five armed ball-tipped Maltese Cross, enamelled in white, charged in the centre with a diamond surmounting a faceted five pointed star inverted, enamelled in blue is awarded. The Order is worn on a pendant from a ribbon of orange, white, and blue. The recipient may append the post-nominal title of OSG or OSS to his or her name. Awarded when merited by the State President. Established in 1986.

10961
Order of the Star of South Africa (Military)
To recognize officers of the South African Defence Force in the following categories: Class I, Gold - to major generals and higher officers or officers of comparable ranks who distinguish themselves by meritorious military service that promotes the efficiency and preparedness of the South African Defence force and contributes lastingly to the security of the Republic of South Africa; and Class II, Silver - to brigadiers and higher officers or officers of comparable ranks who distinguish themselves by exceptionally meritorious service of major military importance. A circular protea wreath, with a blue Maltese Cross surmounted by an eight pointed star with alternate long and short rays and with a diamond in the center is awarded. The Gold Order is attached to a gold pendant from a blue ribbon and the Silver Order is attached to a pendant from a blue and white ribbon. The recipient may append the post-nominal title of SSA or SSAS to his or her name. Awarded when merited by the State President. Established in 1983.

10962
Order of the Star of South Africa (Non-Military)
For recognition of service of military importance to South Africa. Officers of the various service departments excluding the South African Defence Force or persons of comparable rank in other departments and institutions, as well as South African citizens are eligible. The following awards are presented: Class I, Grand Cross (Gold) - to major generals and higher officers or persons of equivalent ranks and other South African citizens who distinguish themselves by excellent meritorious service that contributes significantly to the security and/or general national interest of the Republic of South Africa; Class II, Grand Officer (Silver) - to brigadiers and higher officers or persons of equivalent ranks and other South African citizens who distinguish themselves by outstanding meritorious service that contributes significantly to the security and/or general national interest of the Republic of South Africa; Class III, Commander - to South African citizens who distinguish themselves by exceptionally meritorious service that contributes meaningfully to the security and/or general national interest of the Republic of South Africa; Class IV, Officer - to South African citizens who distinguish themselves by rendering meritorious service that contributes to the security and/or general national interest of the Republic of South Africa; and Class V, Member - to South African citizens who distinguish themselves by rendering exceptional service that contributes to the security and/or general national interest of the Republic of South Africa. A circular protea wreath in gold, with a blue Maltese Cross bordered in gold, surmounted by an eight pointed star with alternate long and short rays and with a diamond in the center is awarded. The Order is attached to a gold pendant from a gold and blue ribbon. The recipient may append the post-nominal title of SSA or SSAS in the first two classes. Awarded when merited by the State President. Established in 1988.

10963
Woltemade Cross for Bravery
This is the highest of the National Orders. It is given for recognition of gallantry displayed in circumstances of extreme danger to save or to protect or endeavor to save or protect the lives of South African citizens or property belonging to the Republic. South African citizens who have distinguished themselves by conspicuous bravery within or outside the Republic of South Africa, and other persons who have distinguished themselves in this manner in the Republic or in territories belonging to or administered by the Republic are eligible. A silver or gold decoration bears in relief, on the obverse, a representation of the act of heroism performed by Wolraad Woltemade in the year 1773 when, on horseback, he rescued shipwrecked persons in Table Bay. The reverse side of the decoration consists of the embellished Coat of Arms of the Republic of South Africa. Awarded when merited by the State President. Formerly: (1991) Woltemade Decoration for Bravery.

10964
Royal Society of South Africa
P.D. Hahn Bldg.
PO Box 594
Capetown 8000, Republic of South Africa

Phone: 21 6502543
Fax: 21 6503726

10965
John F. W. Herschel Medal
To recognize persons or teams who have made outstanding contributions in a wide range of fields, especially those of a multidisciplinary scientific nature that have been completed in South Africa or that are relevant to South Africa. A medal is awarded annually when merited. Established in 1984 in honor of John F. W. Herschel, a scientist and a renowned polymath.

10966
Meiring Naude Medal
To recognize persons or teams who have made outstanding contributions to science, especially those of a multidisciplinary scientific nature that have been completed in South Africa or that are relevant to South Africa. Scientists under 35 years of age who are residents or who are visiting South Africa are eligible. A medal is awarded annually when merited. Established in 1984 in honor of Stefan Meiring Naude, a renowned South African scientist, discoverer of the N15 isotope, and past president of the Society.

10967

**SA Holstein Friesland Society
(Friestelersvereniging van Suid-Afrika)**
PO Box 544
52 Aliwal St.
Bloemfontein 9300, Republic of South
  Africa   Phone: 51 479123
                                           Fax: 51 304224

10968

Gold Medal
To encourage and improve the breeding of Friesland cattle in South Africa, and maintain unimpaired the purity of the breed. Friesland cattle at the various agricultural schools and colleges throughout the Republic of South Africa are considered. Friesland shields are awarded annually.

10969

Society of Medical Laboratory Technologists of South Africa
PO Box 6014
Roggebaai   Phone: 21 4194857
Cape Town 8012, Republic of South Africa   Fax: 21 212566

10970

Irene Aitken Memorial Award
To recognize a member of the SMLTSA for papers, posters, or publications in a recognized journal on haematological subjects. The recipient must be qualified for a period of at least 5 years. Preference is given to original work. Business class return airfare from JHB to London to attend a congress or for further study, and a certificate are awarded annually. The award is presented at the National Congress of the SMLTSA. If no congress is held that year, the presentation is made at an appropriate regional or branch function.

10971

Ames Histology Award
To recognize achievement in the field of histology. A monetary award of 600 rand is awarded annually at the National Congress. If no congress is held that year, then presentation is made at an appropriate regional or branch meeting.

10972

Bactlab Systems Gold Award
To recognize the person who made significant contributions to the academic improvement of posters presented in either of the following categories: microbiology, serology, or flow-cytometry. Preference will be given to original work. The recipient should be a member in good standing of the SMLTSA and must have been qualified for a period of at least 3 years. The recipient is not restricted to the number of awards. A check for 500 rand, a floating trophy, and a miniature are awarded biannually at the SMLTSA National Congress.

10973

Bactlab Systems Premier Award
To recognize the person who has contributed most to improving the standard of academic papers in the category of microbiology. Preference will be given to authors or co-authors who have completed their papers with minimal outside help. The recipient should be a member of the SMLTSA in good standing and should have been qualified for a period of at least 5 years. The prize, which is awarded annually, includes a return airfare to the U.S. to present a paper or poster at either the American Society for Microbiology Congress or the American Society of Medical Technologists Annual Congress. The prize also included a floating trophy, miniature, and certificate.

10974

Behring Diagnostics Award
To recognize the best immunology student. 500 rand is awarded to the student and 250 rand is awarded to the branch at which the student is a member. Awards are presented annually at the National Congress. If a Congress is not held that year, the prize will be presented at an appropriate regional or branch meeting.

10975

Boehringer Mannheim S.A. Award
To recognize a member of the Society who has contributed most significantly toward the aims of medical technology. 1,000 rand is awarded biannually. Formerly: Boehringer Mannheim Prize.

10976

Johnson and Johnson Award
To recognize achievements in higher education (H.D. Med Tech, M. Tech or Laureates) and/or service to the profession in one of the following categories: blood transfusion, serology, virology, and haematology. A monetary prize of 500 rand and a copper plaque are presented annually at the National Congress. If no congress is held that year, presentation is made at an appropriate regional or branch meeting.

10977

Joseph Prize
To recognize the author or authors of the highest standard paper published in *Medical Technology: SA Journal*. A monetary prize of 800 rand is presented at SMLTSA National Congress.

10978

Merck Award
To recognize the most successful candidate in the categories of cytopathology or microbiology. A monetary prize of 1,000 rand is awarded biannually at the National Congress of the SMLTSA.

10979

Orthodiagnostic Prizes
To recognize the best medical technologists in chemical pathology and haematology and blood transfusion. A monetary prize is awarded annually. Also, twice per year, a monetary prize is awarded to the most deserving technologist in each branch of the Society.

10980

Premier Technology Shandon Award
To recognize achievement in the field of cytology, service to the profession, original research, and publication of outstanding papers. A monetary prize of 1,000 rand is awarded biannually at the SMLTSA National Congress.

10981

Public Relations Award
To recognize the Technologist of the Year. 1,000 rand is awarded annually at the National Congress. If no congress is held that the year, the presentation will be made at an appropriate regional or branch function.

10982

Technicon 50th Anniversary Award (Bayer Diagnostics Award)
To recognize the author or co-author of a paper published in any recognized journal or presentation at Congress in the fields of haematology, immunology clinical chemistry, or laboratory computers. Candidates must show why the award should be made to them, how the award will be used, and what benefit will be gained from it. 5,000 rand is awarded biannually toward study or as a travel grant to further professional career. Presented at the National Congress of the SMLTSA. Sponsored by Bayer Miles.

10983

Wellcome Diagnostics Student Award
To recognize the academic achievement of students at the relevant Technikon. Recipient must be a pre-diplomat and must have been a member of the Society for a period of not less than one year. A trophy, which remains the property of the relevant Branch, a miniature, and 100 rand is awarded annually.

10984

**South African Academy of Science and Arts
(Suid-Afrikaanse Akademie vir Wetenskap en Kuns)**
Kuns, Engelenburghurs, Hamiltonstraat
PO Box 538
Pretoria 0001, Republic of South Africa
Phone: 12 285082
Fax: 12 285091

10985

Annual Award of the S.A. Transport Services/Transnet
To provide recognition for publications of a high standard in the field of railway administration. A medal is awarded annually.

10986

Alba Bouwer Prize
For recognition of Afrikaans literature for children in the category 7-12 years of age. A prize is awarded triennially.

10987

D. F. du Toit Malherbe Prize for Genealogical Research
To provide recognition for publications of a high standard in Afrikaans in the field of genealogy. Awarded triennially.

10988

Frans du Toit Medal
To recognize an individual for creative contributions to South African business, sustained contribution over a long period to the areas in which Frans du Toit was engaged, and leadership and the impetus for further development of those areas that he inspired. A gold medal is awarded annually.

10989

Gold Medal for Achievement in Science and Technology
To provide recognition for creative work in the fields of science and technology. A gold medal donated by the South African Chamber of Mines is awarded annually.

10990

Havenga Prize for Science and Technology
For recognition of outstanding work in science and technology. The candidate must have published work of a high standard in Afrikaans. The prize is awarded in eight fields that are rotated every three years. A gold medal is awarded annually.

10991

Hertzog Prize
For recognition of the best literary work written in Afrikaans during the three years preceding the award. The prize rotates in the following categories: poetry, drama, and prose. A monetary prize of 2,000 rand is awarded annually.

10992

Tienie Holloway Medal
To recognize writers who have written the best work for children under eight years of age. A medal is awarded every three years.

10993

Junior Captain Scott Commemorative Medal
To recognize the best thesis for the Master of Science degree in zoology and botany. Awarded in rotation beginning in 1994 with zoology.

10994

C. J. Langenhoven Prize
For recognition of an outstanding work on Afrikaans linguistics. Awarded every three years.

10995

Literary Prize
To encourage amateur talent. The prizes are awarded alternately in the following categories: poetry, drama, and prose. Monetary prizes of 500 rand are awarded annually. Also known as the Poort-Prize.

10996

Literary Prize for Translation
To recognize a translation from any language into Afrikaans of a work of prose, poetry, or drama. A monetary prize is awarded annually. Established in 1948.

10997

D. F. Malan Medal
For recognition of outstanding contributions in the advancement of the Afrikaans language and culture. A gold medal is awarded every three years in memory of Dr. D.F. Malan for his outstanding services in the advancement of the Afrikaans language and culture.

10998

Eugene Marais Prize
For recognition of an early or first work in belles lettres written in the Afrikaans language. A monetary prize is awarded annually.

10999

Medal of Honor
For recognition of achievement in the following fields: theatre and recital, music and ballet, art and sculpture, architecture, film, promotion of social work, and other disciplines. Awarded when merited.

11000

Medal of Honor for Promotion of a Scientific Field
For promotion of a specific field of study of education, from the secondary to the tertiary level.

11001

Medal of Honor of the Physical Sciences and Technique
For recognition of achievement in any field of study in the physical sciences and technique not already covered by the named prizes.

11002

Gustav Preller Prize
To provide recognition for works of literary science and criticism in Afrikaans. A monetary prize is awarded every three years.

11003

**SAUK Prys vir Televisie en Radio
(SABC Prize for Television and Radio)**
For recognition of a radio or TV play in Afrikaans or English. Individuals may be nominated. A monetary award donated by the SABC is presented annually. Established in 1961.

11004

Scheepers Prize
To provide recognition for the advancement of Afrikaans literature for young people. Works must be of literary and educational value to the young reader and aimed at the older child. A monetary prize is awarded every three years, since 1974. Established in 1956.

11005

Senior Captain Scott Commemoration Medal
To recognize any biologist in Southern Africa for outstanding achievement. Awarded annually.

11006

Stals Prize for the Humanities
To provide recognition for publications of a high standard in the humanities that are written in Afrikaans. The prize is awarded in twelve fields that rotate every three years. Awarded annually.

11007
M. T. Steyn Prize for Achievement in Science and Technology
For recognition of leadership at the highest level in the fields of natural sciences and technology. The prize may be awarded only once to a candidate, as it is regarded as a seal of excellence on his or her career. A gold medal is awarded annually. Established in 1964.

11008
Albert Strating Prize
To recognize achievement in preventive medicine. A medal is awarded every three years. Established in 1993 in honor of Dr. Albert Strating.

11009
Totius Prize for Theology and the Original Languages of the Bible
For recognition of publications in Afrikaans in the field of Christian theology and the original languages of the Bible. Awarded biennially.

11010
Toon Van Den Heever Prize for Jurisprudence
To provide recognition for an original work on jurisprudence in the Afrikaans language. Awarded every three years.

11011
Rev. Pieter van Drimmelen Medal
To recognize the work of an individual in the following fields: translation of the Bible, theological textbooks in Afrikaans for the use of university students, published books of sermons, religious instruction (teaching), and writing, translating, composing, or other improvements to the Afrikaans Psalms en Gesange (Hymns). Awarded annually.

11012
N. P. van Wyk Louw Prize
To recognize an individual for a creative contribution to the development, organization, and sustained extension of a branch/branches of the human sciences. The contribution must be fundamental and important to the promotion of the human sciences and to their successful application in the national interest. A medal is awarded annually. Established in 1991 in honor of N. P. van Wyk Louw, Africaans poet, dramatist, essayist, and man of letters (1906-1970).

11013
Markus Viljoen Medal for Journalism
To provide recognition for work of long duration and high standard in Afrikaans journalism. A gold medal is awarded every three years.

11014
South African Association for Learning and Educational Disabilities
Div. of Specialised Education
Univ. of the Witwatersrand
PO Box WITS
Johannesburg, Republic of South Africa   Phone: 11 716 5295

11015
Irma Roth/Saaled Bursary
To encourage students to work with disadvantaged/learning-disabled children. An experienced teacher who wishes to pursue a diploma in specialised/remedial education may apply. A monetary prize of 1,000 rand is awarded annually. Established in 1986 in honor of Irma Roth. Formerly: Saaled Bursary.

11016
South African Association for the Advancement of Science
Medals and Merit Committee
PO Box 31226
Totiusdal
Pretoria 0134, Republic of South Africa   Phone: 12 735978

11017
British Association Medal
To recognize an outstanding researcher under the age of 40, working in any branch of science. Awarded annually.

11018
Certificate of Merit
To recognize persons who have contributed materially one way or another to the advancement of science in South Africa. Awarded when merited.

11019
Durban Medal
To recognize a paper of particular merit presented to the Humanistic and Social Sciences Sections of the Association. A medal and publication of the paper in *South African Journal of Science* were awarded annually. (Discontinued)

11020
South Africa Medal
To recognize a senior scientist for contributions to the advancement of science in South Africa. Awarded annually.

11021
South African Association of Botanists
Address unknown.

11022
SAAB Junior Medal for Botany
For recognition of the best thesis on a botanical subject at a Southern African university. Only South African botany students are eligible. A bronze medal is awarded annually. Established in 1979.

11023
SAAB Senior Medal for Botany
For recognition of outstanding research and/or other contributions to the advancement of botany in South Africa. South African botanists are eligible. A silver medal is awarded annually. Established in 1980.

11024
South African Medal for Botany
For recognition of outstanding contributions to South African botany. South African botanists are eligible. A gold medal is awarded annually. Established in 1973.

11025
South African Association of Consulting Engineers
(Suid-Afrikaanse Vereniging van Raadgewende Ingenieurs)
367 Surrey Ave.
PO Box 1644
Ferndale   Phone: 11 7875944
Randberg 2125, Republic of South Africa   Fax: 11 7895264

11026
SAACE/SA Construction World Awards for Excellence in Engineering
To recognize outstanding engineering design in the following categories: (1) Civil/structural engineering; (2) Electrical/electronic/mechanical engineering; (3) Multi-disciplinary engineering; and (4) any other branch of engineering. The Award is a stainless steel sculpture by Eduardo Villa. The winners in the various categories are presented with inscribed photographs while the Award itself remains in the Boardroom at the offices of the Association's Secretariat. Estblished in 1972.

11027
South African Association of Occupational Therapists
(Suid Afrikaanse Vereniging van Arbeidsterapeute)
PO Box 17289
Hillbrow
Johannesburg 2036, Republic of South
   Africa
Phone: 31 8202310
Fax: 31 8202872

11028
South African Association of Occupational Therapists Awards
To recognize occupational therapists and assistants. Awards are presented.

11029
South African Association of University Women
PO Box 6638
Johannesburg 2000, Republic of South
   Africa
Phone: 11 884 2748
Fax: 11 444 9206

11030
Hansi Pollak Fellowship
To provide for post graduate study in the field of social sciences devoted to the practical purpose of ameliorating social conditions in South Africa. Degreed women who are members of the Association are eligible. A fellowship of 3,500 rand each year for two years is awarded biennially. Established in 1985 by a bequest of Dr. Hansi Pollak. (Discontinued)

11031
South African Biological Society
(Suid-Afrikaanse Biologiese Vereniging)
PO Box 820
Pretoria 0001, Republic of South Africa

11032
Junior Captain Scott Memorial Medal
To provide recognition for the best thesis presented at a South African university for the Master's degree in zoology or botany. Awarded annually, in alternate years for botany and zoology.

11033
Senior Captain Scott Memorial Medal
To recognize the best candidate in biology during the South African Science Week. Awarded annually.

11034
Fitz Simons Medal
To recognize the best candidate in biology during the South African Science Week. Awarded annually.

11035
Theiler Memorial Medal
To recognize the best students who pass with distinction in the B.V.Sc. final examination in South Africa. Awarded annually upon recommendation of the dean of the faculty of Veterinary Science.

11036
South African Broadcasting Corporation
Radio Park
Private Bag X1
Auckland Park 2006, Republic of South
   Africa
Phone: 11 7149111
Fax: 11 71443106

11037
Artes Awards
To recognize outstanding work, to promote the quality of radio and television programs, and to stimulate discussion between those creatively engaged in broadcasting. Awards are presented in 25 categories for radio and 21 for television. A trophy and a monetary prize of 2,000 rand are awarded in each category annually.

11038
Prize for Colored Musicians
To encourage colored musicians in South Africa. A monetary prize of 500 rand was awarded for each language annually. (Discontinued)

11039
Prize for Composers and Performers of Afrikaans Folk Musik
To recognize the performers and composers of the best Afrikaans folk music. A monetary prize of 5,000 rand was awarded.

11040
Prize for Performers of Classical Music
To encourage musicians performing serious music. A monetary prize of 18,000 rand is awarded annually.

11041
Radio Bantu Prize for Works Written for the Radio
To provide recognition for plays, serials, legends, songs, or documentary programs written especially for the radio. A monetary prize of 1,400 rand is awarded annually.

11042
South African Broadcasting Corporation Prize
To provide recognition for the best radio and the best television drama and documentary programs broadcast. Monetary prizes of 2,000 rand each are awarded annually by the South African Academy of Science and Arts. Established in 1961 for radio; and in 1977 for television.

11043
Springbok Radio Sarie Awards
To encourage local musical talent in the field of light music. Awards are presented in the following classes: (1) top female vocalist; (2) top male vocalist; (3) top instrumental group; (4) top beat group; (5) top band; (6) top vocal group; (7) best song of the year; (8) best English long playing record of the year; (9) best Afrikaans long playing record of the year; and (10) best long playing record of the year. Silver and gold Springbok trophies are awarded annually.

11044
South African Chemical Institute
(Suid-Afrikaanse Chemiese Instituut)
Admin. Sec.
PO Box 93480
Yeoville
Johannesburg 2143, Republic of South
   Africa
Phone: 11 4871543

11045
AECI Medal
To recognize the senior author of a research paper in a prescribed field for a particular year that has been published in the *South African Journal of Chemistry* and is considered to have made the most significant contribution to scientific knowledge in that field of chemistry. Each year, the award is considered for papers in one of the following four fields of chemistry: analytical, organic, physical, and inorganic, in the defined sequence. A gold medal is awarded annually when merited. Established in 1961. Sponsored by AECI Limited.

11046
Chemical Education Medal
To recognize a person who has made an outstanding contribution to chemical education, as judged by works published within the previous five years. Published works may be in any form and may be related to any level or education context. The deadline for applications and nominations is March 31. A medal struck in silver bearing the Institute's crest and name on the obverse is awarded.

11047
Gold Medal
To recognize an individual whose scientific contributions in the field of chemistry or chemical technology are adjudged to be of outstanding merit. A member of the South African Chemical Institute may nominate individuals. A gold medal is awarded annually when merited. Established in 1967.

11048
Industrial Chemistry Medal
To recognize an individual who has conducted novel research or enhanced existing chemical research in a particular field in an industrial laboratory that is judged to be of outstanding merit, taking into account the benefits to the individual's company and the chemical community at large. The deadline for nominations and applications is March 31. A medal struck in silver bearing the Institute's crest and name on the obverse is awarded.

11049
Mischa Mrost Prize
To recognize the senior author of the best paper published during the previous year in *ChemSA*. Any paper of general interest to chemistry, the chemical profession, or the chemical industry is eligible, and is judged in terms of quality, topicality, and relevance. A monetary prize of 250 rands is awarded annually when merited. Established in 1977 in honor of Mischa Mrost, former President of the South African Chemical Institute.

11050
Raikes Medal
To recognize an individual whose original chemical research shows outstanding promise, as adjudged by publication in reputable journals. The research must have been performed in South Africa. Individuals under the age of 35 on March 31 during the year of the award may be nominated by a member of the South African Chemical Institute, or may apply. A gold medal is awarded annually when merited. Established in 1960 in honor of Humphrey Raikes, a former professor of Chemistry at the University of the Witwatersrand.

11051
Hendrik Van Eck Medal
To recognize a member of the Institute who has made exceptional contributions in the business or industrial sectors and/or to the community as a whole in South Africa. Members of the South African Chemical Institute may be nominated by a member of the SACI. A gold medal is awarded annually when merited. Established in 1983 in honor of Hendrik van Eck, a major South African industrialist.

11052
South African Geographical Society
PO Box 128
Wits 2050, Republic of South Africa   Phone: 11 3391951

11053
Bronze Medal
To recognize an individual for an outstanding M.A./M.Sc. thesis in the field of geography. Awarded annually. Established in 1981.

11054
Fellow
For recognition of sustained and outstanding intellectual contributions and productivity in any field of geography as demonstrated in a substantial number of scholarly publications. Nominations are accepted by the Fellowships Committee at least two months before the annual general meeting (customarily held in August of any year). A citation and an illuminated certificate are awarded when merited. Established in 1975.

11055
Gold Medal
For recognition of outstanding contributions and service in the development of geography in South Africa. Nominations are accepted by the Fellowships Committee at least two months before an annual general meeting (customarily held in August of any year). A gold medal and a citation are awarded when merited. Established in 1967 to mark the 50th Anniversary of the founding of the society.

11056
South African Institute for Librarianship and Information Science (Suid-Afrikaanse Instituut vir Biblioteek-en Inligtingwese)
Hon. Sec.
PO Box 36575
Menlo Park   Phone: 12 464967
Pretoria 0102, Republic of South Africa   Fax: 12 464967

11057
Percy Fitzpatrick Award
For recognition of a children's book written in English. Books published in South Africa are eligible. A medal is awarded biennially when merited. Established in 1975.

11058
**Katrine Harries Award
(Katrine Harriestoekenning)**
For recognition of illustrations in children's books. Books published in South Africa are eligible. A medal is awarded annually. Established in 1974.

11059
**C. P. Hougenhout Award
(C.P. Hoogenhouttoekenning)**
For recognition of a children's book written in Afrikaans. Books published in South Africa are eligible. A medal is awarded annually. Established in 1960 in honor of C.P. Hoogenhout, the author of the first Afrikaans children's book.

11060
Carl Lohann Prize
To recognize an individual for a contribution to the promotion of children's books. A monetary award and a certificate are presented annually. Established in 1991 by Dean Retief of HAUM Publishers to honor Prof. C.A. Lohann. Sponsored by HAUM Publishers.

11061
**SABINET Prize
(SABINET-Prys)**
To encourage the publicqtion of articles of high quality. A monetary award and a certificate are awarded annually. Established in 1988 by SABINET. Sponsored by the SA Bibliographic and Information Network (SABINET).

11062
**SAILIS Bibliographic Award
(SAILIS Bibliografiese Toekenning)**
For recognition of achievement in the field of bibliography. Selection is by nomination. A certificate is awarded biennially. Established in 1985.

11063
SAILIS Research Award
For recognition of outstanding research in the field of librarianship and/or information science. A certificate is awarded when merited. Established in 1981.

11064
SAILIS Research Certificate
For recognition of a scientific contribution to the advancement of library and information science. Established in 1981.

11065

South African Institute of Civil Engineers
(Suid-Afrikaanse Instituut var Siviele Ingenieurs)
PO Box 31257
Braamfontein 2017, Republic of South Africa
Phone: 11 6481184
Fax: 11 6487427

Formerly: South African Institute of Civil Engineering Technicians and Technologists.

11066

South African Institute of Civil Engineering Technicians and Technologists Awards
To recognize individuals for outstanding contributions to the field of civil engineering. Awards are presented annually.

11067

South African Institute of Electrical Engineers
PO Box 93541
Yeoville 2143, Republic of South Africa

11068

South African Institute of Electrical Engineers Awards
For recognition of worthy papers, contributions and other items of interest published in the Institute's *Transactions*. Monetary awards or certificates and medals are awarded annually.

11069

South African Institute of Physics
(Suid-Afrikaanse Instituut vir Fisika)
Univ. of Zululand
Private Bag
Kwa Dlangezwa 3886, Republic of South Africa
Phone: 351 93911
Fax: 351 93571

11070

Nuclear Physics Postgraduate Student Awards
For postgraduate study towards a higher degree in the fields of nuclear, particle, and radiation physics. A monetary award is presented annually. Established in 1985.

11071

SAIP - De Beers Gold Medal Award
For recognition of outstanding achievement in any branch of physics. Residents of South Africa are eligible. A gold medal with the SAIP emblem and inscription is awarded biennially. Established in 1978. Sponsored by De Beers Industrial Diamond Division.

11072

SAIP Science Olympiad Medal
To recognize the winner of the physics section of the annual schools science Olympiad organized by the Foundation for Science, Education and Technology. A monetary award and a bronze medal with the SAIP emblem and inscription are presented annually. Sponsored by SAIP.

11073

SAIP - Silver Jubilee Medal Award
For recognition of outstanding achievement in any branch of physics. Scientists under 35 years of age who are residents of South Africa are eligible. A silver medal with the SAIP emblem and inscription is awarded biennially. Established in 1980.

11074

SAMES Postgraduate Student Award
To recognize the most outstanding work in the field of semiconductor/integrated circuit technology and/or physics. Publications originating from a recent thesis to a South African university may be submitted. A monetary award is presented annually. Established in 1983.

11075

SMM Postgraduate Student Award
To recognize the most outstanding work in the field of solid state physics and/or materials science by a postgraduate student. Publications originating from a recent thesis presented to a South African university may be submitted. A monetary award is presented annually. Established in 1982. Sponsored by SMM Instruments (Pty) Ltd.

11076

SMM Prize
To recognize the best publication in the *South African Journal of Physics*. A monetary award is presented annually. Established in 1980. Sponsored by SMM Instruments (Pty) Ltd.

11077

Solid State Physics and Materials Science Essay Prize
To recognize the most outstanding essay written by a student at the undergraduate or honors level. A monetary award is presented annually. Established in 1983. Sponsored by De Beers Industrial Diamond Division (Pty) Ltd., and Industrial Development Corporation of SA Ltd.

11078

South African National Committee on Illumination
(Suid-Afrikaanse Nasionale Komitee vir Verlingting)
PO Box 36320
Menlo Park
Pretoria 0102, Republic of South Africa

11079

Anode Trophy
For recognition of the best paper on lighting research and practice delivered at the annual congress of the Committee. A trophy is awarded annually at the Congress. Established in 1977 by Anode Electrical Contractors.

11080

Communications Group Trophy
For recognition of the most outstanding contribution to the art and science of lighting. Projects originated in South Africa during the preceding year are eligible. A monetary prize is awarded annually. Established in 1984 by the Communications Group.

11081

South African National Council for the Blind
PO Box 11149
Brooklyn 0011, Republic of South Africa
Phone: 12 3461171
Fax: 12 3461177

11082

R. W. Bowen Medal
For recognition of lifelong meritorious service to the visually disabled people of South Africa. South Africans of any group and age may be nominated. A medal and citation are awarded biennially. Established in 1962 in memory of R. W. Bowen, a blinded veteran of the 1914-1918 War, and first chairman of the South African National Council for the Blind.

11083

South African Optical Society
c/o CSIR
PO Box 395
Pretoria 0001, Republic of South Africa
Phone: 12 841 4352

11084

Prize for Optics
For recognition of an outstanding performance in the field of optics. Contributions may be: (1) an improvement in the production ability (quantitative or qualitative) of a South African industry; (2) greater independence of South African industry in strategic technology; and (3) an

invention or publication of outstanding quality. The deadline is July 31. A monetary prize of 500 rand and a certificate are awarded annually.

11085

South African Society of Dairy Technology
PO Box 1284
Pretoria 0001, Republic of South Africa   Phone: 12 286 400

11086

Dairy Technology Awards
For recognition of meritorious research work pertaining to dairy technology, or for outstanding services rendered to the dairy industry. Awarded annually to no more than two persons.

11087

South African Society of Music Teachers
(Suid-Afrikaanse Vereniging van Musiekonderwysers)
PO Box 5318   Phone: 41 361555
Walmer 6065, Republic of South Africa   Fax: 41 560448

11088

Ellie Marx Memorial Scholarship
To recognize an exceptionally talented young South African student, who shows promise of becoming an outstanding solo performer, and to provide for study of the performance of stringed musical instruments (particularly the violin). Individuals who have studied a stringed instrument in South Africa for three years and who are under 25 years of age are eligible. A monetary prize of 5,000 rand is awarded annually. Established in 1960 by Ellie Marx.

11089

South African Sugar Technologists' Association
c/o SASA Experiment Sta.
Private Bag X02
Mount Edgecombe 4300, Republic of South   Phone: 31 593205
   Africa   Fax: 31 595406

11090

Gold Medal
For recognition of outstanding contributions to technology in the South African sugar industry. Members of the Association are eligible. A gold medal is awarded irregularly at the annual general meeting. Established in 1968.

11091

South African Veterinary Association
Address unknown.

11092

Boswell Award
To recognize individuals for selfless service to the Association.

11093

SAVA Gold Medal
This, the Association's highest award, is given to provide recognition for contributions to veterinary science in South Africa.

11094

Southern Africa Road Federation
PO Box 8189
Johannesburg 2000, Republic of South
   Africa   Phone: 11 29 9181

11095

SARF Bursary
For recognition of advanced study in road engineering subjects, traffic police administration or transport management or economics. South African citizens interested in full-time study may apply. A grant is awarded annually. Established in 1950.

11096

Southern African Association of Industrial Editors
(Suider-Afrikaanse Vereniging vir Bedryfsredakteurs)
PO Box 6193
Birchleigh 1620, Republic of South Africa   Phone: 11 3913316

11097

Communicator of the Year Award
To recognize industrial editors, educational institutions, and editorial students in South Africa. The Communicator of the Year Award is given annually. In addition, the National House Journal Competition is held annually.

11098

Southern African Institute of Forestry
(Suider-Afrikaanse Instituut van Boswese)
PO Box 1022   Phone: 12 473479
Pretoria 0001, Republic of South Africa   Fax: 12 3286041

11099

Suider-Afrikaanse Instituut van Boswese Toekenning
(Southern African Institute of Forestry Award)
To recognize a forestry scientist or leader for an outstanding contribution to forestry or the application of forestry in Southern Africa. Nominations must be made by the Council of the Institute, or one of its branches. An illuminated scroll is awarded annually if merited. Established in 1975.

11100

Southern African Ornithological Society
PO Box 84394   Phone: 11 8884147
Greenside 2034, Republic of South Africa   Fax: 11 7827013

11101

Gill Memorial Medal
For recognition of an outstanding contribution to ornithology in South Africa (the area south of the Zambezi and Cunene Rivers). A bronze medal was awarded usually every three years. Established in 1960 in honor of E.L. Gill. (Discontinued)

11102

Southern African Society for Plant Pathology
INFRUITEC
Private Bag X5013
Stellenbosch 7600, Republic of South   Phone: 51 4012466
   Africa   Fax: 51 4012117

Formerly: South African Society for Plant Pathology and Microbiology; South African Society for Plant Pathology.

11103

Fellow
For recognition of service to the Society and to teaching and/or research in plant pathology. Individuals who have ten years of uninterrupted membership may be nominated by the members and elected by the Council. A certificate is awarded when merited. Established in 1984.

11104

Honorary Member
For recognition of an outstanding contribution to plant pathology or the Society. Election is by ballot at the annual general meeting. A certificate is awarded. Established in 1963.

11105

Christiaan Hendrik Persoon Medal
For recognition of an outstanding achievement in the field of plant pathology. Nominations are accepted. A medal is awarded triennially. Established in 1979.

11106

Stellenbosch Farmers' Winery
PO Box 46
Stellenbosch 7600, Republic of South Africa
Phone: 21 8087911
Fax: 21 8871355

11107

Nederburg Opera and Ballet Award
For recognition of outstanding achievement in the fields of ballet and opera in South Africa. Selection is by nomination. Artists living and working in South Africa are taken into consideration. (This includes South Africans living overseas but who have taken part in a production in South Africa in the specific year. It also includes overseas artists who have worked in South Africa for at least three years.) Artists who have taken part in professional productions (opera, ballet, operetta, musical) in any theater in the country may be considered for the prize. A monetary prize and a trophy are awarded for the artist who, in the previous calendar year, has made the greatest contribution to opera and ballet in the province concerned. A special prize, with no specific conditions attached, is awarded for any distinctive opera or ballet contribution. In addition, a prize is awarded to the most promising young artist in every province. The adjudication should be aimed at artists who have made a "visible" artistic contribution to opera or ballet. Awarded annually. Established in 1971.

11108

Sunday Times Business Times
Editor
PO Box 1090
Johannesburg 2000, Republic of South Africa
Phone: 11 4972711
Fax: 11 4972327

11109

Royal Companies Award
To recognize companies that have performed outstandingly for shareholders. Companies must rank in the top 20 companies for three consecutive years to be considered. A certificate is awarded annually. Established in 1968.

11110

Top 100 Companies Award
To recognize Johannesburg Stock Exchange-listed companies that have achieved high returns for shareholders over a five-year period. Companies are ranked in the top 100 companies by average annual compound rate of return to shareholders. A certificate is awarded annually. Established in 1968.

11111

Top Five Businessmen Award
To recognize outstanding achievement by company executives. Individuals with a long term record of achievement in business and public affairs are considered. A certificate is awarded annually. Established in 1968.

11112

Tafelberg Publishers Ltd.
28 Wale St.
PO Box 879
Capetown 8000, Republic of South Africa
Phone: 21 241320
Fax: 21 242510

11113

W. A. Hofmeyr Prize
(W. A. Hofmeyr-prys)
For recognition of the best literary work in Afrikaans or English published in the preceding year by one of the publishers in the Nasionale Pers group which consists of Tafelberg, Human and Rousseau, Nasou, Van Schaik, and Via Afrika. A monetary prize of 5,000 rand and a gold medal are awarded annually. Established in 1954 in memory of W. A. Hofmeyr, a past Chairman of the Nasionale Pers group.

11114

M. E. R. Prize
(M. E. R.-prys)
For recognition of the most deserving children's book published in Afrikaans or English during the preceding year by the publishing houses of the Nasionale Boekhandel Publishing Group. A monetary prize of 5,000 rand and a gold medal are awarded annually. Established in 1984 in memory of Maria Elizabeth Rothman, a pioneer in the field of Afrikaans children's literature.

11115

Recht Malan Prize
(Recht Malan-prys)
For recognition of the most deserving book of non-fiction in Afrikaans or English published in the preceding year by the publishing houses of the Nasionale Boekhandel Publishing Group. A monetary prize of 5,000 rand and a gold medal are awarded annually. Established in 1978 in memory of Recht Malan, a past Chairman of the Nasionale Pers group.

11116

Technikon Witwatersrand
PO Box 17011
Doornfontein 2028, Republic of South Africa
Fax: 11 4020475

11117

Rector's Medal
For recognition of extraordinary achievement in the fields of science or commerce. Individuals who have demonstrated overall dedication and research over a minimum of 10 years are eligible. A gold medal is awarded annually. Established in 1986 by Dr. D. H. Wiid, past Rector. Additional information is available from the Director, Corporate Comunications, Technikon Witwatersrand.

11118

Simon Van der Stel Foundation
(Stigting Simon Van der Stel)
PO Box 1743
Pretoria 0001, Republic of South Africa
Phone: 21 268651

11119

Simon Van der Stel Foundation Medal
(Stigting Simon Van der Stel Medalje)
For recognition of an individual or institution which has rendered outstanding service to conservation and renovation of buildings and towns in South Africa. The National Council may make nominations. A gilded medal is awarded annually. Established in 1961.

| 11120 |

Water Institute of Southern Africa
(Water Instituut van Suidelike Africa)
PO Box 1948
Parklands
Johannesburg 2121, Republic of South Africa
Phone: 11 7284303
Fax: 11 4831253

| 11121 |

C. G. Cillie Award
To recognize the best contribution to anaerobic research in Southern Africa by a university student. A floating trophy, a book prize valued at 250 Rand, and a certificate are awarded annually. Established in 1989 to honor the research contributions on water treatment by Dr. C. G. Cillie.

| 11122 |

Umgeni Award
To encourage excellence in the fields of water science and engineering by recognizing a paper that makes a noteworthy contribution to water science or engineering. Members are eligible for papers published through WISA. A monetary award of 1,000 rand is awarded annually. Established in 1988 to mark the inauguration of the Water Institute of Southern Africa. Sponsored by Umgeni Water.

| 11123 |

Wilson Award
(Wilson - Toekenning)
To recognize the combined competence and initiative of the owner and works manager of a Waste Water Treatment Works, having a total design capacity of up to 25,000 kl/day average DWF. The criteria that are considered include treatment and operating efficiency, maintenance and servicing, laboratory control, housekeeping, safety, and administration. A certificate is awarded biennially at the Conference. Established in 1976 to honor Dr. Harold Wilson (1887-1974), a founding member and first Chairman of the South African Branch of the Institute of Water Pollution Control in 1937.

| 11124 |

Weekly Mail & Guardian Film Festival
139 Smit Str.
Braamfontein
Johannesburg 2001, Republic of South Africa
Phone: 11 4037111
Fax: 11 4031025

| 11125 |

Weekly Mail and Guardian Short Film Competition
To encourage aspirant filmmakers with limited resources to make films. Open to filmmakers from South Africa, Mozambique, Angola, Namibia, Zimbabwe, Tanzania, and Botswana. Awards are presented to the directors of films in the following categories: best overall film, best fiction under 30 minutes, and best docmentary under 30 minutes. Three monetary awards and certificates are presented annually. A trip to the International Film Festival is awarded to the winner of the best overall film. Established in 1988. Cosponsored by AGFA, Panorama Sound, Mail and Guardian Newspaper, and Logical Designs. Formerly: Fano/Weekly Mail Short Film Competition.

| 11126 |

Wildlife Society of Southern Africa
(Natuurlewevereniging van Suidelike Afrika)
PO Box 44189
Linden 2104, Republic of South Africa
Phone: 11 7824716
Fax: 11 7827216

| 11127 |

Conservationist of the Year
To recognize the outstanding conservationist as selected by the Natal Branch of the Wildlife Society of Southern Africa.

| 11128 |

Gold Medal
To recognize individuals who have made an outstanding contribution to the cause of conservation. Individuals may be nominated. A gold-plated sable head mounted on tamboti wood is awarded when merited. The award was designed and donated by Otto Poulsen, a Durban jeweler and wildlife enthusiast. In addition, a scroll is awarded to corporate bodies that may be nominated. Established in 1976.

| 11129 |

Charles Thomas Astley Maberley Memorial Scholarships
To enable students to undertake postgraduate research in any aspect of South Africa's indigenous fauna. Postgraduate students who are citizens of any Southern African State and registered at a university in the Transvaal are eligible. A monetary award is presented annually in two installments. Established in 1972 by the Transvaal Branch of the WLS to honor Charles Maberley for his contribution to conservation in Southern Africa.

| 11130 |

Zoological Society of Southern Africa
(Dierkundige Vereniging Van Suidelike Afrika)
c/o Dept. of Zoology
Univ. of Stellenbosch
Stellenbosch 7600, Republic of South Africa
Phone: 021 8083222
Phone: 021 8083236
Fax: 021 8084336

| 11131 |

Certificate of Merit
Awarded each year to the best third-year and honors students in zoology at each of the universities in southern Africa. Each students also receives free membership for one year. Awards are based on the recommendation of department heads.

| 11132 |

Gold Medal
To recognize a zoologist of exceptional merit in the field of zoology in southern Africa. A medal is awarded annually if merited. Established in 1970.

| 11133 |

Stevenson - Hamilton Award
To recognize an amateur zoologist for exceptional contributions to zoology in southern Africa. Individuals may be nominated by members of the Society before May of each year. A medal is awarded annually if merited. Established in 1988.

Spain

| 11134 |

AEDOS S.A.
Consejo de Ciento 391
E-08009 Barcelona 9, Spain
Phone: 3 301 28 45
Phone: 3 301 86 15
Fax: 3 317 01 41

| 11135 |

AEDOS Agricultural Award
(Premio Agricola AEDOS)
To stimulate the writing of original works dealing with agricultural and cattle raising subjects. A monetary prize was awarded. Awarded annually. Established in 1960. (Discontinued in 1982)

| 11136 |

Catalan Biography Award
(Premio de Biografia Catalana AEDOS)
To stimulate the writing of biographies of Catalan celebrities, especially those who distinguished themselves in the fields of politics, literature,

Spain — Awards, Honors & Prizes, 1995-96

arts, and science. A monetary award of 100,000 pesetas was awarded irregularly. Established in 1952. (Discontinued in 1975)

11137

Alcances/Muestra Cinematografica del Atlantico
Gran Via, 43, 9F
E-28013 Madrid, Spain
Phone: 1 247 98 62
Phone: 1 247 95 19
Fax: 1 542 001

11138

Alcanes/Muestra Cinematografica de Atlantico
For recognition of outstanding cinematography of the Atlantic.

11139

Asamblea de Directores-Realizadores Cinematograficos y Audio-visuales Espanoles (ADIRCAE)
San Lorenzo 11
E-28004 Madrid, Spain
Phone: 1 3196844
Fax: 1 3196844

11140

ADIRCAE Prizes
(Premios ADIRCAE)
For recognition of outstanding contributions to film and television. Awards are given for performance and directing. Members are eligible. Trophies are awarded annually. Established in 1985. Sponsored by Sociedad General de Autores Espanoles.

11141

Asociacion Amigos de Arco
Avda. Portugal, s/n
E-28011 Madrid, Spain
Phone: 1 470 10 14
Fax: 1 464 33 26

11142

Becas de Creacion Artistica
To recognize outstanding works of art. Awards are presented in two categories: painting and sculpture. Spanish citizens between the ages of 24 and 40 are eligible. The deadline is June 5. A monetary award of 100,000 pesetas is presented annually. Established in 1988 by Mario Conde.

11143

Asociacion Hispanoamericana de Centros de Investigacion y Empresas de Telecomunicaciones
Vitrubio, No. 7
E-28006 Madrid, Spain
Phone: 1 4419500

11144

Premio de Investigacion Ahciet
To recognize and encourage research in the field of telecommunications. Members of the Association are eligible. A monetary prize and diploma are awarded annually. Established in 1984.

11145

Premio Revista Ahciet
For recognition of the best article in *Ahciet Magazine*. Members of the Association are eligible. A monetary prize and diploma are awarded annually. Established in 1983.

11146

Ateneo de Valladolid
General Ruiz 1
E-47004 Valladolid, Spain

11147

Premio Ateneo de Valladolid de Novela Corta
For recognition of literary creativity in the short novel form. Authors may present more than one work. Works must be in Spanish and from 75 to 100 pages in length. The deadline is December 31. A monetary prize of 100,000,000 Spanish pesetas and publication of the book are awarded annually by the City Council of Valladolid, Spain. Established in 1950.

11148

Ateneo Feminista Festival Internacional de Cine Realizado por Mujeres
C/. Barquillo 44-2 Izda.
E-28004 Madrid, Spain
Phone: 1 3086935
Fax: 1 3196902

11149

International Festival of Films Directed by Women
(Festival Internacional de Cine Realizado por Mujeres)
For recognition of films directed by women. Awards are given in the following categories: (1) Feature; (2) Short; (3) Documentary; and (4) Video. The public votes for the best film in each category. The Premio del Publico and a monetary prize of $1,000 is awarded in each category annually. Established in 1991.

11150

Ateneo Santander
Plaza Porticada
Santander, Spain

11151

Santander Athenaeum Novel Award
For recognition of an outstanding novel. A monetary prize of 1,000,000 pesetas is awarded. Established in 1974.

11152

Ayuntamiento de Benicasim
Presidente de la Comision Organizadora
Medico Segarra 4
E-12560 Benicasim (Castellon), Spain
Phone: 964 300962

11153

Francisco Tarrega International Guitar Competition
(Certamen Internacional de Guitarra Francisco Tarrega)
To promote the interpretation of works for guitar, especially those of Francisco Tarrega by concert guitar players. Guitarists who are 32 years of age or under may enter by August 1. The following prizes are awarded: (1) First Prize - 1,000,000 pesetas, concerts and a CD recording; (2) Second Prize - 600,000 pesetas; (3) Special Prize for the interpretation of Francisco Tarrega - 300,000 pesetas; (4) Special Prize for a Spanish interpreter born or resident in Comunidad Valenciana, who has passed the preliminary phase - 100,000 pesetas; (5) Prize of the Public - 200,000 pesetas. Awarded annually. Established in 1966 in honor of the guitarist, Francisco Tarrega.

11154

Barcelona Film Festival, Films and Directors
(Festival de Cinema de Barcelona, Films i Directors)
Lluria 67
E-08007 Barcelona, Spain
Phone: 3 215 24 24
Fax: 3 215 29 66

Formerly: Setmana Internacional de Cinema de Barcelona.

11155

Barcelona Film Festival
For recognition in the competitive section of the festival. European productions are eligible. The entry deadline is in March. DRAC d'Argent awards are presented in the following categories: (1) best actor; (2) best

actress; (3) best short; (4) best technical or artistic contribution to a film; and (5) Jury's Special Prize. Trophies are awarded. The Europa Award (Premi Europe) is awarded to the best picture. A monetary award of 200,000 ECUS to be invested in a movie by the winning film's director, and a trophy are presented. Awarded annually. Established in 1959. Re-established in 1987. Sponsored by the Catalan Board of Cinema, local and national authorities, and private corporations. Formerly: (1987) Dama del Paraigues (Lady with the Umbrella); Barcelona International Week of Cinema in Color Awards.

11156

Barcelona Theatre Institute
(Institut del Teatre de la Diputacio de Barcelona)
Sant Pere mes Baix 7
E-08003 Barcelona, Spain
Phone: 3 268 20 78
Fax: 3 268 10 70

11157

Premi Adria Gual
For recognition of the best performing project. The winning project is included in the program planning of the Centre Dramatic de la Generalitat during the next season. Foreign entries are not eligible. A monetary prize of 5,000,000 pesetas maximum is awarded annually. Established in 1977 by Generalitat de Catalunya and Diputacio de Barcelona in memory of Adria Gual (1872-1943), a playwright, director, scene designer, theatre theoretician, and founder of Teatre Intim in 1898.

11158

Premi Ignasi Iglesias
For recognition of the best new Catalan play of the year. A monetary prize of 1,000,000 pesetas is awarded annually. Established in 1932 to 1938 and re-established in 1977 in memory of Ignasi Iglesias (1871-1928), a Catalan playwright who was influenced by Ibsen and wrote many plays for the social theatre.

11159

Premi Josep M. Carbonell
For recognition of the best puppetry performance project. A monetary prize of 1,500,000 pesetas is awarded biennially. The winning project is included in the program planning of the International Puppet Theatre Festival of Barcelona. Established in 1993 by Generalitat de Catalunya and Diputacio de Barcelona in memory of Josep M. Carbonell (1945-1992). Carbonell was puppeteer and director of the International Puppet Theatre Festival of Barcelona since 1982.

11160

Premi Josep Maria de Sagarra
For the recognition of the best play translated into Catalan. A monetary prize of 1,000,000 pesetas is awarded biennially. Established in 1980 by Generalitat de Catalunya and Diputacio de Barcelona in memory of Josep Maria de Sagarra (1894-1961), a Catalan poet, novelist, playwright and translator of Shakespearean plays.

11161

Premi Nacional d'Arts Esceniques
For recognition of the most outstanding contribution to the theatre during the year. A trophy, a sculpture by Subirachs, is awarded annually. Established in 1983 by Generalitat de Catalunya and Diputacio de Barcelona. Formerly: (1989) Premi Nacional d'Activitats Teatrals.

11162

Premi Nacional d'Interpretacio Teatral i de Dansa
To recognize the best actor, best dance contribution, best theater director, or best scenic designer of the year. A trophy, a sculpture by Subirachs, is awarded annually each December. Established in 1983 by Generalitat de Catalunya and Diputacio de Barcelona as four awards: Premi Nacional de Dansa, Premi Nacional de Direccio, Premi Nacional d'Escenografia, and Premi Nacional d'Interpretacio. These four were combined in 1989.

11163

Premi Ricard Moragas
For recognition of the best dance choreography, original and unique. Monetary prizes of 1,000,000 pesetas for the winner and 500,000 pesetas for the second prize are awarded annually. Established in 1987 by the Generalitat de Catalunya and Diputacio de Barcelona by combining three prizes: Premi Roseta Mauri, Premi Tortola Valencia, and Premi Vicente Escudero. Established in memory of Ricard Moragas (1829-1899), a Catalan choreographer, dancer and scene designer.

11164

Premi Xavier Fabregas
For recognition of the best essay or research in the field of the performing arts in any of its aspects, historical, sociological, aesthetic, theoretical, or documentary. The research must be endorsed by a University or higher institution. A monetary prize of 1,000,000 pesetas is awarded biennially. Established in 1986 by Generalitat de Catalunya and Diputacio de Barcelona in memory of Xavier Fabregas, i Surroca (1931-1985), critic, researcher and historian on performing arts, especially in the Catalan theatre.

11165

Bienal de Cine y Video Cientifico
(Festival de Cine Cientifico)
c/o Servicio Cultural de la Caja de
  Ahorros de
la Immaculata
Avda. Independencia 10
E-50004 Zaragoza, Spain

11166

Bienal de Cine y Video Cientifico
For recognition of outstanding films and videos on science. Educational, documentary, or biographical subjects are considered. Trophies are awarded biennially. Sponsored by Servicio Cultural de la Caja de Ahorros de la Immaculata. Formerly: (1991) Festival de Cine Cientifico.

11167

Maria Canals International Music Competition, Barcelona
(Concurs Internacional Maria Canals de Barcelona)
Gran Via de les Corts Catalanes 654, pral.
E-08010 Barcelona, Spain
Phone: 3 318 7731

11168

Maria Canals International Music Competition for Musical Performance, Barcelona
(Concours Internacional Maria Canals de Barcelona)
To recognize the best performers in the Competition. The ages are 18 to 32 years old for instrumentalists, and 18 to 35 years old for singers. The prize categories rotate annually. The deadline is January 19. The following monetary prizes are awarded: (1) First prize - 500,000 Spanish pesetas; (2) Second prize - 250,000 Spanish pesetas; and (3) Third prize - 100,000 Spanish pesetas. Medals and diplomas are also awarded. The competition is held annually. Established in 1954.

11169

Catalonia
Department of Agriculture, Stock Farm and Fishing
(Generalitat de Catalunya
Department d'Agricultura, Ramaderia i Pesca)
Passeig de Gracia 105
E-08008 Barcelona, Spain
Phone: 3 2378625
Fax: 3 2373361

11170

Catalonian Agriculture, Stock Farm, Forestry, Conservation of Nature and Fishing Awards
(Guardons de l'Agricultura, Ramaderia, Forest, Conservacio de la Natura i Pesca Catalana)
For recognition of the effort and the dedication of persons and of public and private institutions to improve the agricultural and fishing sectors of Catalonia. Candidates are nominated by the Minister of Agriculture, Stock Farm and Fishing of the Generalitat of Catalonia. A medal is awarded to persons, and a plaque is awarded to institutions annually. Established in 1988.

11171

Catalonia
Department of Youth
(Generalitat de Catalunya
Direccio General de Joventut)
Secretaria General de Joventut
Calabria, 147
E-08015 Barcelona, Spain
Phone: 3 4838383
Fax: 3 4838300

11172

Premi Artur Martorell
To promote studies related to young peoples' leisure time. A monetary prize is awarded biennially. Established in 1984.

11173

Youth Studies Prize
(Premi Joventut)
To promote studies related to youth. A monetary prize is awarded biennially. Established in 1984.

11174

Catalonia
Office of the President
(Generalitat de Catalunya
Department de la Presidencia)
Placa de Sant Jaume, s/n
E-08002 Barcelona, Spain
Phone: 3 302 47 00

11175

Catalonia International Award
(Premi Internacional Catalunya)
For recognition of a contribution of creative works and the development of human cultural values. Individuals must be nominated by institutions or members of the advisory council. A monetary prize of $100,000 US is awarded annually. Established in 1989. Additional information is available from Institut Catala, d'Estudis Mediterranis, C. Bailen, 9 2n., E-08010 Barcelona, Spain.

11176

Catalonian Certificate of Merit for Promotion of the Catalan Culture
(Diploma de Reconeixements de Merits en favor del Patronomi Cultural de la Generalitat de Catalunya)
To recognize persons or institutions who have dedicated themselves to the protection and the conservation of the Catalonian culture. A certificate is awarded annually. Established in 1982.

11177

Catalonian Government Prize for Tourism
(Premio en Favor del Foment del Turisme)
To recognize individuals and establishments dedicated to the promotion of Catalonian tourism. A medal of honor and a plaque are awarded annually. Established in 1981.

11178

Catalonian Government Prizes for Economic Energy Consumption and Diversification
For recognition of outstanding works which promote energy conservation and diversification of energy use to incorporate methods other than dependence on petroleum. Monetary prizes ranging from 200,000 to 500,000 pesetas are awarded. Established in 1985.

11179

Catalonian Prize for Technical Application and Industrial Products
(Premi a l'Aplicado de la Tecnologia al Proceso o al Producto Industrial de la Generalitat de Catalunya)
To stimulate interest and recognize the merits of Catalonian producers and industries who maintain intellectual creativity in industry. Monetary prizes ranging from 1,000,000 to 3,000,000 pesetas are awarded annually. Established in 1983.

11180

Catalonian Prizes for Catalan Literature
(Premios de Literatura Catalana de la Generalitat de Catalunya)
For recognition and promotion of the outstanding literary works published in the Catalan language during the previous year. Prizes are awarded in the following categories: novel, poetry, narrative, short story, travel, memoirs, essay, investigation of the Catalan language or literature, children's literature, translation to Catalan from another language, and translation from Catalan to another language. Honorable mentions are awarded for books or collections of books of outstanding literary quality or graphics and drawing design, and for the best publication with an artistic theme. Eight monetary prizes of 300,000 pesetas each are awarded annually. Established in 1981.

11181

Catalonian Prizes for Cinematography
(Premios de Cinematografia de la Generalitat de Catalunya)
To encourage Catalonian film production, and for recognition of outstanding works in Catalonian films of the previous year in the following categories: full and short feature films, producers who promote the advancement of film in Catalonia, movie theaters which promote premieres of Catalan films, the best director, the best technical skills, best actor and actress, personal or collective contributions to Catalan cultural films, and filmclubs which best promote the advancement of cinematographic expression in Catalonia. The above-mentioned parties must be registered with the department of film production in Catalonia. The prizes must be awarded. Monetary prizes ranging from 250,000 to 5,000,000 pesetas are awarded annually. Established in 1983.

11182

Catalonian Prizes for Music
(Premio de Musica de la Generalitat de Catalunya)
To recognize and promote outstanding musical creation by Catalan composers, such as music for choirs, soloists, or quartets with the original text in Catalan. Works must be 10-15 minutes long and unpublicized. A monetary prize of a varying sum from 500,000 pesetas is awarded annually. Established in 1982.

11183

Catalonian Prizes for Videography
(Premios de Videografia de la Generalitat de Catalunya)
To encourage videographic production and recognize outstanding video producers. Videos in Catalan and produced by Catalonian residents in the previous year are eligible. The categories, which may vary annually, are: the test video overall; best producer-director; best technical skills; and best post-production promotion. Monetary prizes ranging from 500,000 to 1,000,000 pesetas are awarded. Established in 1988.

11184

Council of Catalonia Prize for Export
(Premi de la Generalitat de Catalunya al Foment de l'Exportacio)
To recognize residents and establishments who promote the export of Catalan goods. A black marble plaque is awarded annually. Established in 1982.

11185

Creu de Sant Jordi
To recognize individuals and institutions who have contributed services to Catalonia to defend their identity and to restore their personality or, more generally, individuals that have made an important work in civic and cultural fields. A medal is awarded annually. Established in 1981.

11186

Jordi Lluch Prize
(Premi Jordi Lluch i de Andres)
For recognition of outstanding unpublished studies or works directly related to the finance and the economy of independent communities. An indivisible monetary prize of 500,000 pesetas is awarded annually. Established in 1985. Further information is available from the Department of Economy and Finances of Catalonia, Barcelona.

11187

Medalla de la Generalitat de Catalunya
For recognition of individuals and institutions that stand out in a special way in the field of Arts and Sciences, improving the spiritual, artistic and cultural patrimony of Catalonia. Gold, silver and bronze medals are awarded at the convention. Established in 1978.

11188

Narcis Monturiol Medal and Plaque for Science and Technology
(Medalla i Placa Narcis Monturiol al merit cientific i technologic)
To recognize scientific or juridical organizations or individuals who have distinguished themselves with outstanding works of scientific and technological merit in the province of Catalonia. A medal honoring the scientists and a plaque honoring the jurists are awarded annually. Established in 1982.

11189

President Macia Plaque and Medal
(Placa i Medalla President Macia)
To recognize meritorious work strengthening or advancing economic activity in the area by individuals or institutions. A bronze medal is awarded annually. Established in 1982.

11190

Sport Medal of Catalonia
(Medalla de l'Esport de la Generalitat de Catalunya)
To recognize persons who have dedicated themselves to the promotion of sports in Catalonia. A medal is awarded annually. Established in 1980.

11191

Catalonia Institute of Technology of Construction
(Institut de Tecnologia de la Construccio de Catalunya (ITEC))
Bon Pastor 5, 4t
E-08021 Barcelona, Spain   Phone: 3 209 60 99

11192

Construmat Award
(Premis Construmat)
For recognition of Spanish achievement in civil engineering, residential construction and renovation, journalistic coverage of construction, industrial products, and construction processes. Civil engineering projects constructed during the recent year are eligible. The civil engineering prize is given in the categories of maritime, hydraulic, subterranean traffic engineering and structures. A trophy is awarded biennially. Established in 1985.

11193

Catalonian Council of Books for Young People
(Consell Catala del Llibre per a Infants)
Portal de Santa Madrona, 6-8
E-08001 Barcelona, Spain   Phone: 3 4125640
                                        Fax: 3 4121958

11194

Catalonia Illustration Prize
(Premi Catalonia d'illustracio)
To encourage professional development, and for recognition of the best illustrations for children's books published anywhere in the world in any language. Illustrations submitted for the award must have been published for the first time during the preceding two years. Comics and collector's books are expressly excluded. A monetary prize of 1,000,000 pesetas and a trophy are awarded. The publisher of the prize-winning book is given an honorary mention. Three plaques to the runners-up and five certificates to other illustrations considered to be of special merit are given to publishers of the prize-winning works. Established in 1984.

11195

Center of Tourist Initiatives
(Centro de Iniciativas Turisticas)
Calle San Juan, 2F   Phone: 43 650414
E-20400 Tolosa, Spain   Fax: 43 654655

11196

Competition of Composition for Choirs
(Concurso de Composicion Vasca Para Masas Corales)
To recognize original and unpublished compositions for choirs of four or more mixed voices, "a capella." Compositions may be submitted in two theme categories: (1) Folk Basque Song - theme can be popular Basque or from another composer of Basque inspiration or from own creation; and (2) Polyphony - theme can be from one's own inspiration, of sacred or profane nature. A monetary award of 100,000 pesetas is presented annually in each category. Established in 1972. Sponsored by the Basque Government, the Deputation of Guipuzcoa, and Town Hall.

11197

International Choral Competition of Tolosa
(Certamen Internacional de Masas Corales de Tolosa)
To encourage the choir movement and to recognize outstanding choral groups in the following categories: (1) Folklore - Male or Female Voices; (2) Folklore - Mixed Voices; (3) Polyphony - Male or Female Voices; (4) Polyphony - Mixed Voices; (5) Gregorian; and (6) Children's Choirs. All choirs may submit applications. Open to amateur choirs. All singers must sing without musical accompaniment. Monetary prizes and medals are awarded annually. Established in 1969. Sponsored by the Basque Government, the Deputation of Guipuzcoa, and Town Hall.

11198

Centro de Medios Audiovisuales
Avda. Carlos Haya, 25   Phone: 52 30 68 94
E-29010 Malaga, Spain   Fax: 52 21 14 11

11199

International Week of Scientific Films
(Semana Internacional de Cine Cientifico)
For recognition of outstanding films or videos on scientific subjects. Each country is authorized to present films or videos with up to a maximum screening time of 2 hours, in any case not to exceed 4 items (i.e. 2 hours films/videos, or 4 films/videos). The selection of films/videos entered by member countries of the International Scientific Film Association is made by the national branch. The deadline is September 1. The following prizes are awarded by the International Jury: (1) First Prize to the best humanistic film/video consists of a diploma and the Trophy "Juan de la Rosa"; (2) First Prize to the best films/video of research, popular science, or television program consists of a diploma and trophy; and (3) Honorable Mentions for the best cinematography technique, best artistic innovation, best scientific entry, best naturalist entry and best technological entry. The National Jury awards: (1) First Prize to the best film/video of higher education, secondary education, primary education; and (2) Honorable Mentions to the best script, best photography, best editing, and best special effect. The A.S.E.C.I.C. Jury (National branch of the ISFA-AICS) awards a diploma and the Trophy "Guillermo F. Zuniga." Sponsored by Obra Cultural of the Montes de Piedad and Caja de Ahorros de Ronda, Cadiz, Almeria, Malaga y Antequera.

11200

Centro Regional Para la Ensenanza de la Informatica
Apartado de Correos 232
E-28080 Madrid, Spain
Phone: 1 410 02 81
Fax: 1 419 67 56

11201

Premio CREI de Informatica
To promote the teaching of information systems and their educational and professional application in the Latin American countries. To recognize the best text, method outline, or study for information systems. A golden award and $5,000 for first prize, and three successive prizes of $1,000 each were awarded annually. Established in 1982. (Discontinued in 1988)

11202

Certamen Internacional de Cine Amateur Ciutat d'Igualada
Apartado de Correos 378
E-08700 Barcelona, Spain
Phone: 93 804 6907
Fax: 93 804 4362

11203

Certamen Internacional de Cine Amateur Ciutat d'Igualada
To recognize outstanding amateur films. Non-professional film directors from all over the world may submit entries by July 20. Films are divided into two groups: Super 8mm and 16mm. Films are classified by content: (1) argument; (2) fantasy and animation; and (3) documentary-record. A monetary prize of 200,000 pesetas and a gold medal are awarded for the Ciutat d'Igualada Grand Prize. In the 16mm category, the following prizes are awarded in each content area: (1) First prize - 30,000 pesetas and a silver medal; and (2) Second prize - a bronze medal. In the Super 8mm category, the following prizes are awarded in each content area: (1) First prize - 25,000 pesetas and a silver medal; and (2) Second prize - a bronze medal. Additional special awards may be presented: (1) Generalitat de Catalunya Trophy - to the film in the Catalan language which best highlights the ethnographical and/or patrimonial values of Catalunya; (2) Josep Castelltort I Ferrer Trophy - to the best cutting work; (3) other special prizes for work of technical or artistic merit; and (4) Televisio de Catalunya (TV3) Award - to one of the 16mm films which in addition to quality is of interest and lends itself to broadcasting by TV3. Established in 1979.

11204

Cineistes Independent de Badalona
PO Box 286
E-08911 Badalona, Spain
Phone: 464 0191
Fax: 464 0450

11205

Badalona Short Film and Video Festival
(Certamen Internacional de Curtmetratges i Video)
For recognition of outstanding short films and videos. Awards are given in the following categories: Independents and film clubs; Schools of cinematography; and Videos. A trophy of "Venus de Badalona" is awarded annually for the Premi Extraordinari Ciutat de Badalona to the best film or video of the festival. In addition, the following prizes are awarded: Premi Generalitat de Catalunya - to the best film or video of Catalunya; Premi Excm. Ajuntament de Badalona - to the best director of a Badalonian film or video; and Premi especial ASIFA (Asociacio Internacional Cinema d'Animacio) - to the best animated film. Established in 1969. Co-sponsored by Cineistes Independents de Badalona, Ajuntament de Badalona, TV3, TV Catalunya, Generalitat de Catalunya, and ASIFA.

11206

College of Technical Architects and Buildings Foremen of Barcelona
(Colilegi d'Aparelladors i Arquitectes Tecnics de Barcelona)
Bon Pastor 5
E-08021 Barcelona, Spain
Phone: 3 2098299
Fax: 3 4143434

11207

Elies Rogent Video Competition on Rehabilitation and Restoration
(Certamen de video Elies Rogent de Rehabilitacio i Restauracio)
To recognize outstanding video productions that show contributions to the field of rehabilitation of buildings and cultural heritage. Categories include the Section in Competition, open to specific productions of noncommercial content lasting from 10 minutes to an hour, and the Section for Display, for productions made by insitutions, companies to advertise their products, those commercialized as a means of presentation, and those that, due to specific reasons, the producers do not wish to present in the competition. Monetary awards are presented biennially the first week of April. Established in 1990 to honor Elies Rogent, an architect.

11208

Comision "Justicia y Paz" de Espana
Francisco Silvela 77 bis, 1 dcha.
E-28028 Madrid, Spain
Phone: 1 5611214
Fax: 1 5611214

11209

Justice and Peace Prize for Human Values
(Premio Justicia y Paz a los Valores Humanos)
To recognize persons or organizations who distinguish themselves in the defense and promotion of human values in any part of the world. A monetary prize and a medal are awarded annually. Established in 1987.

11210

Confederacion Espanola de Cajas de Ahorros
Departamento de Comunicacion y
  Relacioues Externas
Alcala 27
E-28014 Madrid, Spain
Phone: 1 5965628
Fax: 1 5965737

11211

Premio de Cuentos Hucha de Oro
To recognize outstanding unpublished short stories written in Castillian Spanish. Multiple entries are accepted on any theme. The following prizes are awarded: a monetary prize of 1,000,000 Spanish pesetas and a Golden Money Box - First prize; 500,000 Spanish pesetas and a replica of the Golden Money Box - Second prize; and 20 awards of 25,000 pesetas each and a Silver Money Box. Awarded annually. Established in 1966.

11212

Conservatorio Profesional de Musica i Danza Les Illes Baleares
Placa de l'Hospital 4
E-07012 Palma de Mallorca, Spain
Phone: 71 1157
Fax: 71 726612

11213

Concurso Internacional de Piano Frederic Chopin
To recognize pianists at the competition. Individuals must be under 30 years of age and may be from any country. The deadline for applications is November 7. A medal and the following monetary prizes are awarded: first prize - 1,000,000 pesetas and recitals; second prize - 500,000 pesetas; and third prize - 250,000 pesetas. Awarded triennially. Established in 1981.

11214

Destino Publishing House
(Ediciones Destino, S.A.)
Consejo de Ciento 425, 5a planta
E-08009 Barcelona, Spain
Phone: 3 265 23 05
Fax: 3 265 75 37

11215
Apel Les Mestres Prize
(Premi Apel Les Mestres)
For recognition of the best illustrated and written book in any language for children or youth. A writer-illustrator, or a writer and an illustrator may be honored. A monetary award of 750,000 Spanish pesetas and publication of the book are awarded annually. Established in 1981 in memory of Apel Les Mestres, a Catalan illustrator and writer (1854-1936).

11216
Nadal Prize
(Premio Nadal)
For recognition of the best unpublished novel written in Spanish. A monetary prize of 3,000,000 Spanish pesetas and publication of the novel are awarded annually. Established in 1944 in memory of Eugenio Nadal, a Catalan intellectual, and editorial secretary of the weekly *Revista Destino*, who died in 1944.

11217
Josep Pla Prize
(Premi Josep Pla)
For recognition of the best unpublished book in the Catalan language. A monetary award of 1,000,000 Spanish pesetas and publication of the book are awarded annually. Established in 1968 in honor of Josep Pla, a Catalan intellectual and writer.

11218
Diputacion Provincial de Valencia
Plaza de Manises 4
E-46003 Valencia, Spain
Phone: 96 3913790
Fax: 96 3910989

11219
Jose Iturbi International Piano Competition
(Concurso Internacional de Piano Jose Iturbi)
For recognition of an outstanding piano performance. Pianists of any nationality who are under 31 years of age on the date of the final event may take part in the contest. The following prizes are awarded: Grand Prize - 1,500,000 pesetas from the Ministry of Culture; Second Prize - 1,000,000 pesetas from the Valencia County Council, recitals throughout Spain, a concert with the Municipal Orchestra of Valencia, and a recital for the Philharmonic Society of Valencia; Third Prize - 750,000 pesetas from Bancaja and recitals sponsored by the Culture Conselleria in the Valencian community; Fourth Prize - 500,000 pesetas from the Town Hall of Valencia and recitals sponsored by the Valencia County Council; Fifth Prize - 300,000 pesetas from the Philharmonic Society of Valencia; Sixth Prize - 250,000 pesetas form Bancaja; and Special Prize - 250,000 for the best interpretation of Spanish music from the Valencia County Council. The deadline for applications is June 30. Established in honor of Jose Iturbi, a famous Valencian musician. Sponsored by the Valencia County Council.

11220
Editorial Planeta
Corcega 273-279
E-08008 Barcelona, Spain
Phone: 3 4154100
Fax: 3 2177140

11221
Mirror of Spain Prize
(Premio Espejo de Espana)
To recognize authors of any nationality for unpublished biographies, memoirs, reports, studies, essays, inquiries, or other endeavors that reveal the Iberian culture from any point of view - historical, political, sociological, or economic. Preference is given to work covering aspects of the past that influenced the present and help shape the future. Works must be written in Castillian Spanish, be at least 250 pages long, and be unpublished, except for works by authors deceased before the announcement of the contest. A monetary prize of 4,000,000 Spanish pesetas and publication of 25,000 copies is awarded. The prize must be awarded each year and cannot be divided. Established in 1975.

11222
Planeta Prize
(Premio Planeta de Novela)
For recognition of the best unpublished novel. Writers of Spanish speaking countries who write in Castillian Spanish are eligible. A monetary award of 50,000,000 Spanish pesetas for first prize and a minimum of 12,000 copies and a maximum of 2,000,000 copies for the first edition is awarded. The winner receives royalties on all copies over 222,000 sold. A second prize of 6,000,000 Spanish pesetas and royalties on all copies over 55,000 sold are also awarded. The prize must be awarded each year and cannot be divided. Established in 1952 by Jose Manuel Lara Hernandez, director of Editorial Planeta.

11223
Premio de Novela Ateneo de Sevilla
For recognition of unpublished novels of at least 200 pages written in Castillian Spanish by authors of any nationality. A monetary prize of 10,000,000 Spanish pesetas, publication of 50,000 copies, and 10 percent of the royalties are awarded annually. The prize must be awarded each year and cannot be divided. Established in 1969.

11224
Premio Literario Ramon Llull
To recognize an author of any nationality for an outstanding novel of at least 200 pages, written in Catalonian Spanish, and to promote the production of novels in Catalonian Spanish. A monetary prize of 3,000,000 Spanish pesetas is awarded. The prize must be awarded each year and cannot be divided. Established in 1968, and re-established in 1980.

11225
Euroarabe-Audiovisuals Communications Center
(Centro Euroarabe para las Comunicaciones Audiovisuales)
Paseo de la Castellana 164, 17A
E-28046 Madrid, Spain
Phone: 1 3594353
Fax: 1 3595259

11226
Euroarabe and Television Festival
(Festival de Cine y TV Euroarabe)
For recognition and promotion of the best Spanish-Arab films. Awards are presented biennially. Established in 1980.

11227
Festival de Cine de Alcala de Henares
Cine-Club Nebrija
Plaza Atilano Casado 2
Alcala Henares (Madrid), Spain
Phone: 8 81 02 97

11228
Festival de Cine de Alcala de Henares
For recognition of outstanding short films.

11229
Festival Internacional de Cine Arte
Centro Cultural de la Fundacio Caixa de Pensiones
Passeig de Sant joan 108
E-08037 Barcelona, Spain
Phone: 3 258 89 06
Fax: 3 258 75 82

11230
Festival Internacional de Cine Arte
For recognition of films and videos related to the plastic arts. Honorary prizes were given biennially in November. (Discontinued)

11231

Festival Internacional de Cine Ecologico y de la Naturaleza
Gran Via 43, 9 piso F
E-28013 Madrid, Spain
Phone: 1 542 42 53
Phone: 1 542 10 05
Fax: 1 542 07 01

11232

Festival Internacional de Cine Ecologico y de la Naturaleza
For recognition of outstanding ecology and nature films. Sponsored by Gobierno Autonomo de Canarias, Ayuntamiento del Puerto de la Cruz, ICONA, and Instituto de la Juventud del Ministerio de Cultura.

11233

Festival Turolense de Cine Superocho y Video
El Pozo 3
E-44001 Teruel, Spain
Phone: 78 600012
Fax: 78 600012

11234

International Video Contest
(Certamen Internacional de Video)
For recognition of outstanding videos of less than 30 minutes. Awards are given in the following categories: Animation, Fiction, Documentary, and Experimental. A monetary prize of 300,000 pesetas and a Torico Trophy are awarded for the Best Video, and monetary prizes of 100,000 pesetas each are awarded for the second place video, the best documentary film, and the best animation film.

11235

Film Festival of Huesca
(Certamen Internacional de Films Cortos, Ciudad de Huesca)
Aptdo. de Correos 174
Duquesa Villahermosa, 1
E-22002 Huesca, Spain
Phone: 74 227058
Fax: 74 246600

11236

International Contest of Short Films, City of Huesca
(Certamen International de Films Cortos, Ciudad de Huesca)
To promote the diffusion of short films in Spain. Any Spanish foreign short film accepted by the Selection Committee can take part in the Contest. Although there are no restrictions in the choice of theme, those that deal exclusively with tourism or publicity cannot be presented. The following prizes are awarded annually: Prix Ciudad de Huesca, Golden Danzante - 500,000 pesetas to the most outstanding film; Silver Danzante to the best film with plot; Silver Danzante to the best animated film; Silver Danzante, to the best documentary film; Bronze Danzante; Premio Cacho Pallerocici - 500,000 pesetas to the best Iberoamerican short film; and (7) Premio Jinete Iberico.

11237

Fundacio Enciclopedia Catalana
Address unknown.

11238

Carles Riba Poetry Prize
(Premi de Poesia Carles Riba)
For recognition of the best unpublished poetry in Catalonian Spanish. The entries may not have won other literary prizes. A monetary prize of 500,000 Spanish pesetas is awarded annually. Established in 1959. Co-sponsored by Edicions Proa S.A., Disputacio 250, 1 piso, E-08007 Barcelona, Spain.

11239

Sant Jordi
For recognition of the best Catalan novel of the year. Novels written in the Catalan language may be submitted to Fundacio Enciclopedia Catalana. A monetary prize of $12,890 is awarded annually. Established in 1960 by Omnium Cultural.

11240

Fundacion Jacinto e Inocencio Guerrero
Gran Via 78
E-28013 Madrid, Spain
Phone: 1 247 66 18

11241

International Guitar Contest
(Premio Internacional de Guitarra S.A.R. La Infanta Dona Christina)
Guitar players of any nationality or age are eligible. A monetary prize of 1,000,000 pesetas is awarded annually. A second prize of 500,000 pesetas can be awarded also. Established in 1985.

11242

Premio Internacional de Canto Fundacion Guerrero
For recognition of outstanding singing performances. The competition is open to singers of any type of voice or nationality who are under 30 years of age. The deadline for entry is November 11. A monetary prize of 1,000,000 pesetas is awarded for First Prize, and a premium of 250,000 pesetas is awarded to the best interpreter of works of Jacinto and Inocencio Guerrero. Awarded biennially. Established in 1984 in memory of Maestros Jacinto and Inocencio Guerrero.

11243

Premio Internacional de Piano Fundacion Guerrero
For recognition of outstanding piano performances. Players of any nationality or age may apply by October 1. A monetary prize of 1,000,000 pesetas is awarded for First Prize, and 500,000 pesetas is awarded for Second Prize at the Jury's discretion. Awarded biennially. Established in 1987.

11244

Fundacion Pedro Barrie de la Maza, Conde de Fenosa
Canton Pequeno 1
E-15003 La Coruna, Spain
Phone: 22 54 073

11245

Premios Vitalicios
For recognition of outstanding cultural contributions through creative literature and/or scientific investigation. A monetary prize of 1,000,000 Spanish pesetas is awarded annually. Established in 1976.

11246

Queen Sofia Award for Research into Mental Retardation
(Premio Reina Sofia de Investigacion sobre prevencion de la sub-normalidad)
For recognition of productive investigations into the causes and prevention of metabolic sub-normality. A monetary prize of 5,000,000 Spanish pesetas is awarded biennially. Established in 1982 in honor of Pedro Barrie de la Maza.

11247

Fundacion Principado de Asturias
Suarez de la Riva 11
E-33071 Oviedo, Spain

11248

Prince of Asturias Prizes
(Premios Principe de Asturias)
For recognition of outstanding accomplishments in the fields of Spanish and Latin American culture and science. The following awards are given in the following categories: (1) Prince of Asturias Arts Prize; (2) International Co-operation Prize; (3) Prince of Asturias Prize for Scientific and Technical Research; (4) Social Science Prize; (5) Prince of Asturias Sports Prize; (6) Prince of Asturias Prize for Literature; (7) Prince of Asturias Media and Humanities Prize; and (8) Prince of Asturias Prize for Concord. A monetary prize of 2,000,000 pesetas and a statue designed by Joan Miro are awarded annually to each winner. Established in 1980.

11249

General Society of Spanish Authors
(Sociedad General de Autores de Espana)
Fernando VI 4, Apdo. 484
E-28004 Madrid, Spain   Phone: 1 419 21 00

11250

Galardones SGAE
To recognize individuals or organizations that have significantly protected the royalties of authors. A trophy is awarded annually. Established in 1981.

11251

Gijon International Film Festival for Young People
(Festival Internacional de Cine para la Juventud de Gijon)
Paseo de Begona, 24 Entresuelo   Phone: 98 5343739
E-33205 Gijon-Asturias, Spain   Fax: 98 5354152

Formerly: (1986) Certamen Internacional de Cine para la Infancia y la Juventud de Gijon.

11252

Gijon International Film Festival for Young People
(Festival Internacional de Cine para la Juventud de Gijon)
For recognition of the best full-length and short films for young people. Films may be entered by countries, organizations, and individuals that are specially adapted to young people. Long or short films in 35mm and 16mm made during the preceding year may be submitted by June 20. Exhibitors must submit their films in Spanish, French, or English, or subtitled in any one of these three languages. The different National Centres are invited to select one or several films of each country to participate. The Principado de Asturias Prize is awarded to the Best Feature and Best Short Film. In addition, the following prizes are awarded: Best Director, Best Actor, Best Actress, Daniel Toradash Prize to the Best Script, Gil Parrondo Prize to the Best Art Director, Special Prize of the Jury awarded by an International Jury; and Prize of the Young Jury awarded to the best short film and best feature selected by a jury of 150 young people between 15 and 21 years of age. Awarded annually. Established in 1962.

11253

Government of Navarra
Departamento de Educacion y Cultura
Ansoleaga 10   Phone: 48 107806
E-31001 Pamplona, Spain   Fax: 48 223906

11254

Julian Gayarre International Singing Competition
(Concurso Internacional de Canto Julian Gayarre)
To encourage professional development of young opera singers. The deadline for enrollment is July 31. Monetary awards are presented biennially. Established in 1986 by the Government of Navarre with singer Jose Carreras to honor Julian Gayarre, a Navarrese tenor.

11255

Pablo Sarasate International Violin Competition
(Concurso Internacional de Violin Pablo Sarasate)
To recognize and encourage the professional development of young violinists. Open to violinists of any nationality who are 30 years of age or younger. The deadline for enrollment is in July. Monetary prizes of over 5 million pesetas and later performances for the winners are awarded biennially. Established in 1991 to honor Pablo Sarasate, a Pamplonese violinist and composer, 1844-1908.

11256

Gran Canaria International Short Film Festival
(Festival Internacional Cortometrajes de las Palmas Gran Canaria)
Centro Insular de Cultura   Phone: 28 37 10 11
Perez Galdoz 53   Phone: 28 37 10 23
E-35002 Las Palmas Gran Canaria, Spain   Fax: 28 36 29 19

11257

Gran Canaria International Short Film Festival
(Festival Internacional Cortometrajes de las Palmas Gran Canaria)
For recognition of short films in the categories of fiction and animation. Camara Awards and monetary prizes are awarded for best of category and best of genre. Sponsored by Cabildo Insular de Gran Canaria.

11258

Ibero-American Institute of Aeronautic and Space Law
(Instituto Iberoamericano de Derecho Aeronautico y del Espacio)
c/o E.T.S.I.A.
Plaza del Cardenal Cisneros 3
E-28040 Madrid, Spain   Phone: 3366374

11259

Miembro de Honor
For recognition of contributions to the studies of aeronautical and spatial law. A medal and a diploma are awarded when merited. Established in 1962. A Medalla al Merito is also awarded.

11260

Iberoamerican Film Festival
(Festival Internacional de Cine Iberoamericano)
Hotel Tartesos
Avda. Martin Alonso Pinzon 13
E-21003 Huelva, Spain   Phone: 955 24 56 11

11261

Iberoamerican Film Festival
(Festival Internacional de Cine Iberoamericano)
For recognition of outstanding films from Latin America and the Spanish penisula.

11262

IMAGFIC International Film Festival of Madrid
(IMAGFIC Festival Internacional de Cine de Madrid)
    Phone: 1 541 55 45
Gran Via 62, 8 Izda.   Phone: 1 241 55 45
E-28013 Madrid, Spain   Fax: 1 542 54 95

Formerly: Festival Internacional de Cine Imaginario y de Ciencia Ficcion de la Villa de Madrid.

11263

IMAGFIC International Film Festival of Madrid
(IMAGFIC Festival Internacional de Cine de Madrid)
To promote cinema of the imagination, expressed in the following genres: science fiction, horror, thriller and mystery films. The Official Section is open to 35 and 70 mm films in their original languages and preferably with Spanish subtitles. Short films of less than 15 minutes may also be submitted. Films must not have been shown publicly and must not have participated at other Spanish festivals or have won prizes at other international festivals recognized by the I.F.F.P.A. IMAGFIC trophies are awarded in the following categories: (1) Best Feature Length Film; (2) Best Direction; (3) Best Screenplay; (4) Best Acting; (5) Best Photography; (6) Special Prize for Technical Achievement; and (7) Best Short film. In addition, the following special awards are presented: (1) Great Audience Award; and (2) Critic Award (FIPRESCI) - established in 1981. In addition to the Official Section, three Parallel Sections are held: (1) Animation Film Section - features, medium-length films and short films, using any animation techniques; (2) New Barbarians Section - independent feature

and short films (less than 15 minutes), made with experimental or avantgarde criteria; and (3) Imagfic Midnight - this selection pursues the recovery of feature films that haven't been shown in commercial exhibition or haven't been correctly shown. Trophies are awarded in the Animated and New Barbarian Sections. In addition, the Jorge Lluesma Award, established in 1985 to honor the founder of IMAGFIC, is awarded to a film (other than a fantastic or science fiction film), found to have outstanding qualities. The festival is held annually. Established in 1980.

11264

International Association for Shell and Spatial Structures
Alfonso XII 3
E-28014 Madrid, Spain
Phone: 1 3357400
Fax: 1 3357422

Formerly: (1960) International Committee for Shell Structures.

11265

Eduardo Torroja Medal
To recognize outstanding contributions in the design or construction of shell or spatial structures, or for distinguished services to the Association. Members of IASS for at least five years are eligible. Nominations must be supported by at least three Executive Council members and be submitted at least one year before the award is given. A medal is awarded triennially. Established in 1974 in memory of Eduardo Torroja (1899-1961), founder of the Association. Sponsored by Spain - Ministry of Public Works. (Inactive in 1991)

11266

International Documentary and Short Film Festival of Bilbao
(Festival Internacional de Cine de Bilbao Documental y Cortometraje)
Colon de Larreategui, 37-46 drcha.
Apro. de correos 579
E-48009 Bilbao, Spain
Phone: 4 247860
Fax: 4 245624

11267

International Documentary and Short Film Festival of Bilbao
(Festival Internacional de Cine de Bilbao Documental y Cortometraje)
For recognition of the best documentary and short fiction or animated films. Foreign films produced within the preceding two years and films from Spain produced within the preceding year must be entered by producers by September 15. The maximum duration of the films is thirty minutes. Films awarded prizes by international juries at European Festivals recognized by the International Film Producers Associations Federations (FIAPF) will not be selected for the competition. Films must be entered in 16 to 35mm format. The following awards are presented: Gran Premio del Festival de Bilbao - 400,000 pesetas; Gran Premio de Cine Espanol - 350,000 pesetas; Gran Premio de Cine Vasco - 350,000 pesetas; Premios Mikeldi de Oro for the categories of documentary, fiction, and animation - 250,000 pesetas each; and Premios Mikeldi Plata for the categories of documentary, fiction, and animation - 150,000 pesetas each. Established in 1958.

11268

International Medical Film and Health Education Week
(Semana Internacional de Cine Medico y de Educacion Sanitaria)
Congresos GESTAC
Gran Capitan 12
E-18002 Granada, Spain
Phone: 58 295108

11269

International Medical and Health Education Film Week
(Semana Internacional de Cine Medico y de Educacion Sanitaria)
To recognize doctors of medicine of any nationality for outstanding films and videos on medicine, surgery, research, higher education or public health, and ecology. Prizes are awarded.

11270

International Nut Council
(Consejo Internacional de Los Frutos Secos)
Calle Boule 4
E-43201 Reus, (Tarragona), Spain
Phone: 77 33 14 16
Fax: 77 31 50 28

11271

Golden Nut Award
For recognition of efforts to promote world consumption of edible nuts. Selection is by nomination. A trophy with a gold almond in the center is awarded annually during the convention/congress. Established in 1984.

11272

International Pilar Bayona Piano Competition
(Concurso Internacional de Piano Pilar Bayona)
Calle Coso 57, 2 piso
E-50001 Zaragoza, Spain
Phone: 76 29 68 38
Fax: 76 29 20 87

11273

International Pilar Bayona Piano Competition
(Concurso Internacional de Piano Pilar Bayona)
For recognition of outstanding piano performances. Individuals from 16 to 32 years of age are eligible to enter by September 15. The following monetary prizes are awarded: (1) First Prize - 1,500,000 pesetas; (2) Second Prize - 800,000 pesetas; (3) Third Prize - 500,000 pesetas; and (4) Prix special Eduardo Fauquie - 100,000 pesetas. Awarded biennially.

11274

International Singing Competition of Bilbao
(Bilboko Nazioarteko Kantu Lehiaketa)
Aparta de Correos 1532
Ibanez de Bilbao, 2 Izda
E-48001 Bilbao, Spain
Phone: 4 4246533
Fax: 4 4246454

11275

International Voice Competition of Bilbao
(Concurso Internacional de Canto de Bilbao)
To recognize outstanding singers for musicality, quality of voice, and interpretation, particularly in opera. Contestants must be between 18 and 33 years of age. Entries may be submitted by October 1. The following awards are presented. Male Voices: First Prize - 800,000 pesetas; Second Prize - 500,000 pesetas; and Third Prize - 300,000 pesetas. Female Voices: First Prize - 800,000 pesetas; Second Prize - 500,000 pesetas; and Third Prize - 300,000 pesetas. Every finalist who has failed to receive any of the prizes mentioned will receive 75,000 pesetas. In addition, the winners of the two First Prizes receive a contract to give two opera recitals in the following season. Special Prizes are also awarded, and include a scholarship of 1,200,000 pesetas sponsored by the City Hall of Bilbao for completion of studies with a conductor of international prestige; 300,000 pesetas for the finest interpretation of a lieder, song, or oratorio aria; and 500,000 pesetas offered by the Diputacion Foral de Bizkaia for the best interpretation of a work in Basque. The Competitions is held biennially. Established in 1986. Sponsored by Diputacion Foral de Vizcaya.

11276

International Sociological Association
(Asociacion Internacional de Sociologia)
Faculty Political Sciences and Sociology
  University
Complutense
28223 Madrid, Spain
Phone: 1 3527650
Fax: 1 3524945

11277

Worldwide Competition for Young Sociologists
To recognize young scholars engaged in social research. Individuals under 35 years of age who hold a Master's degree (or an equivalent graduate diploma) in sociology or in a related discipline may submit essays focusing on socially relevant issues. Essays may be written in one

of the following languages: English, French, Spanish (the three languages of the ISA) as well as Arabic, Chinese, German, Italian, Japanese, Portuguese, and Russian. A Merit Award certificate, a four-year membership in the ISA, and an invitation to attend the World Congress, of Sociology are awarded every four years. Established in 1987. Additional information may be obtained from ISA in Madrid.

11278

International Week of Sea and Marine Cinema - Cartagena (Semana Internacional de Cine Naval y del Mar)
Ramon y Cajal 94
E-30204 Cartagena, Spain   Phone: 68 51 20 99

11279

International Week of Sea and Marine Cinema - Cartagena (Semana Internacional de Cine Naval y del Mar - Cartagena)
For recognition of films in which the sea or continental waters are the stage or background for any real or imaginary personal life occurrence. Films may be submitted by January 1. The following prizes are awarded for long films: (1) Premio Carabela Ciudad de Cartagena - for the best film of any size or format; (2) Premio Hannon el Navegante - for the best director; (3) Premio Sirena - for the best actress; (4) Premio Isidoro Maiquez - for the best actor; (5) Premio Faro Cabo de Palos - for the best photography. The following prizes are awarded for short films: (1) Premio Isaac Peral - for the best argumentative short; (2) Premio Mar Menor - for the best documentary short; and (3) Premio Caracola de Mar - for the best animation and experimental short. All awards are determined by an international jury. Awarded annually in November. Established in 1971.

11280

Jaen International Piano Competition, Jaen Prize (Concurso Internacional de Piano Premio Jaen)
Instituto de Estudios Giennenses
Palacio Provincial
E-23002 Jaen, Spain

11281

Jaen Prize (Premio Jaen)
For recognition of the best piano performance by pianists of both sexes and of any nationality. Applications may be submitted by March 14. The following awards are presented: (1) First Prize - 2,000,000 Spanish pesetas, a gold medal, and concerts; (2) Second Prize - 1,000,000 Spanish pesetas; (3) Third Prize - 400,000 Spanish pesetas; (4) Rosa Sabater Prize - for the best interpretation of Spanish music, 500,000 Spanish pesetas. Awarded annually. Established in 1956.

11282

Jornadas Internacionales de Cine Medico de San Sebastian
Address unknown.

11283

Torreon de Igueldo
For recognition of the best medical film or video in various specialties. The film must successfully divulge medical information. A trophy is awarded annually. Established in 1966 by Asociacion Cine Medico de San Sebastian. Co-sponsored by Gobierno Vasco and Sebastian-Colegio Medico de Guipuzcoa. Additional information is available from Jose Luis Munoa Roig, Hernani no. 2, San Sebastian, Spain.

11284

Juventudes Musicales de Espana
Girona 10, Numero 3   Phone: 3 2652371
E-08010 Barcelona, Spain   Fax: 3 2659080

11285

Concurso Permanente De Jovenes Interpretes
To recognize and encourage the artistic development of young Spanish musicians. Musicians in the following areas are eligible: accordion, harp, voice, chamber ensembles, choral ensembles, flute, guitar, organ, percussion, trombone, French horn, trumpet, violin, piano, and cello. Spanish citizens under 25 years of age may apply. The following awards are presented annually: First Prize - 150,000 pesetas, a diploma, a concert in the National Auditori in Madrid, and a tour with ten concerts in Spain; and Second Prize - 75,000 pesetas and a diploma. Established in 1978. Sponsored by the Spanish Ministry of Culture.

11286

Madrid
Departamento de Auditorios y Centros Culturales (Ayuntamiento de Madrid)
Conde Duque, 9-11   Phone: 1 5885301
E-28015 Madrid, Spain   Fax: 1 5885749

11287

Premio Antonio de Lara "Tono" de Humor Grafico
For recognition of works published during the preceding year on the city of Madrid that best display graphic humor. Publications must be in Castilian. A monetary prize of 500,000 pesetas is awarded annually.

11288

Premio Antonio Maura
For recognition of the best investigative essays on the problems related to life in Madrid, its urbanization, government, education, sanitation, or transport systems, and solutions to these problems. Essays must be ritten in Castilian. A monetary prize of 2,000,000 pesetas is awarded annually. The prize may be divided. Established in 1966.

11289

Premio Daniel Zuloaga
To recognize the best ceramicists of Madrid and to stimulate innovative creations in ceramics. Ceramicists resident in Madrid may submit only one work not larger than 150 cm in any direction and must not have won a previous prize. A monetary prize of 500,000 pesetas is awarded annually. Established in 1986 on the 75th anniversary of the Madrid School of Ceramics.

11290

Premio Francisco de Goya
For recognition of the best painting by an artist who is a resident of Madrid. Only one painting may be submitted by each artist. The painting's sides must be less than two meters long. A monetary prize of 1,500,000 pesetas is awarded annually. Established in 1977.

11291

Premio Francisco de Quevado
To recognize Spanish or Spanish-American poets for outstanding poetry written in Castillian. Poems that have not been published in a book, nor have won prizes in any other contest are considered. The length is restricted to between 600 and 1,000 verses. A monetary prize of 1,000,000 pesetas is awarded annually. Established in 1973.

11292

Premio Guillermo Marconi
To recognize the radio program broadcast in Castilian that best depicts the city of Madrid and its personality. A monetary prize of 500,000 pesetas is awarded. Established in 1986. Formerly: Premio de Radio Villa de Madrid.

11293

Premio Kaulak
For recognition of the best photography of Madrid based on urban, artistic, cultural, sociological, or human aspects. Photographers must be residents of Madrid. A minimum of three to a maximum of five color

photographs may be submitted. A monetary prize of 500,000 pesetas is awarded annually. Established in 1971.

11294

Premio Lope de Vega

For recognition of the best unpublished, unperformed play submitted by Spanish or Latin American authors. Plays must be written in Castillian. Translations and adaptations are not eligible. A monetary prize of 2,000,000 pesetas and production of the play at the Teatro Espanol in Madrid is awarded annually. Established in memory of Lope Felix de Vega Carpio (1562-1635), a dramatist.

11295

Premio Luis Bunuel

To recognize the best Spanish cinematographer. Short films that have been completed during the preceding year and are a maximum of 30 minutes in length are eligible for consideration. A monetary prize of 1,00,000 pesetas is awarded annually. Established in 1983.

11296

Premio Maestro Villa

For recognition of the best original musical score. Musical scores of the symphonic genre such as symphonies, suites, symphonic poems, but excluding those in which vocal parts appear, are considered. Composers must residents of Madrid. A monetary prize of 1,500,000 pesetas is awarded annually. Established in memory of Maestro Ricardo Villa, founder of the Municipal Symphonic Band of Madrid.

11297

Premio Mariano Benlliure

For recognition of the best sculpture in a city exhibition. The sculptor must be a resident of Madrid. Only one work may be submitted by an artist. A monetary prize of 1,500,000 pesetas is awarded annually. Established in 1980. Formerly: Premio de Escultura Villa de Madrid.

11298

Premio Mesonero Romanos

To recognize an author of the best periodical articles featuring the city of Madrid that have been published during the preceding year. A monetary prize of 500,000 pesetas is awarded annually. Established in 1971.

11299

Premio Ortega y Gasset

To recognize authors of outstanding essays concerning Madrid written from an economic, sociological, cultural, or artistic point of view. Essays must be written in Castilian. A monetary award of 2,000,000 pesetas is awarded annually. Established in 1972.

11300

Premios Maria Guerrero y Ricardo Calvo

To recognize actresses and actors for outstanding dramatic interpretation. The performance must have been presented in Madrid during the preceding year. Monetary prizes of 500,000 pesetas each are awarded annually. Established in 1977.

11301

Prenio Ramon Gomez de la Serna

To recognize the best narrative written in Castilian that has not been previously entered in another competition. Works must be between 150 and 250 pages in length. A monetary prize of 2,000,000 pesetas is awarded annually.

11302

Malaga International Week of Author Films
(Semana Internacional de Cine de Autor)
Concepcion Arenal 63
Apartado Correos 155
E-27080 Lugo, Spain   Phone: 982 212919

11303

Malaga International Week of Author Films
(Semana Internacional de Cine de Autor de Malaga)
For recognition of the best films. Awarded annually. Established in 1969. Sponsored by Grupo Fotocinematografico Fonmina.

11304

Mostra de Valencia, Cinema del Mediterrani
Plaza del Arzobispo 2, acc. B   Phone: 6 3921506
E-46003 Valencia, Spain   Fax: 6 3915156

11305

Valencia Film Festival, Golden Palm Award
(Mostra de Valencia, Palmero de Oro)
For recognition of the best Mediterranean film presented in the competition, and to encourage Mediterranean cinematography. The Festival is composed of the following sections: Official Section, Informative Section, Special Section, Retrospective, Homage, Director's Retrospective, Spanish Cinema, Actor/Actress Tribute, and Festival for Children. Feature films made in the Mediterranean area during the preceding year may enter the competition. Monetary prizes totaling 3,300,000 pesetas, trophies, and plaques are awarded annually in October. The following prizes are awarded: Golden Palm - 2,000,000 pesetas, Silver Palm - 800,000 pesetas, Bronze Palm - 500,000 pesetas, The International Jury Awards of the Mostra de Valencia, Pierre Kast Award to the Best Screenplay, Best Actor's Award, Best Actress' Award, and Special Mention to the Best Sound Track. Established in 1980 by Fundacion Municipal de Cine and the Town Council of Valencia. The next film festival is scheduled for October 13th-20th, 1994.

11306

Museo Angel Orensanz y Artes de Serrablo
Ayuntamiento de Sabinanigo
E-Huesca, Spain

11307

Museo Angel Orensanz and Artes del Serrablo International Sculpture Award
For recognition of an outstanding sculpture. Artists from all countries may send up to two pieces in any material and style of no less than 1 foot and 67 inches. The deadline is May 20. A monetary award of $1,250 plus an exhibition at the Galerie du Marais, Paris, France, are awarded. Established in 1983. Additional information is available from A. Orensanz, 193 Tenth Avenue, New York, NY 10011, U.S.A., (212) 255-7749.

11308

Omnium Cultural
carrer dels Montcada 20 pral.
palau Dalmases
E-08003 Barcelona, Spain   Phone: 3 319 80 50

11309

Premi Sant Jordi
For recognition of the outstanding novel of the year. Unpublished novels, written in Catalan, which have won no other prizes are eligible. A monetary prize of 5,000,000 pesetas and publication of the novel are awarded annually. Established in 1960 in honor of the patron saint of Catalonia.

11310

Prize of Honor for Catalan Letters
(Premi d'Honor de les Lletres Catalanes)
For recognition of outstanding literary or scientific works which promote or advance Catalonian culture. It is the region's highest honor. A monetary prize of 1,000,000 pesetas and a plaque are awarded annually. Established in 1969.

11311
Organization of Ibero-American States for Education, Science and Culture
(Organizacion de Estados Iberoamericanos Para la Educacion, la Ciencia y la Cultura)
Ciudad Universitaria
E-28040 Madrid, Spain
Phone: 1 5496954
Fax: 1 5493678

11312
OEI Gold Medal
(OEI Medalla de Oro)
To recognize individuals who have made an outstanding contribution either to the Bureau itself or to the field of education within the Ibero-American region. Individuals may be nominated by the Executive Council. A gold medal is awarded annually. Established in 1960.

11313
Peace and Cooperation
(Paz y Cooperacion)
Melendez Valdes 68, 4 Piso Izda
28015 Madrid, Spain
Phone: 1 5435282
Fax: 1 5435282

11314
Peace and Cooperation School Award
(Premio Escolar Paz y Cooperacion)
For recognition of students and teachers in the field of peace education. Individuals in primary or secondary education are eligible. A monetary prize and several diplomas are awarded annually. Established in 1986 in honor of United Nations events. Sponsored in different years by UNICEF, Red Cross, UNHCR, ILO, and UNESCO.

11315
Prensa Espanola
Josefa Valcarcel 21
E-28027 Madrid, Spain
Phone: 1 320 08 18
Fax: 1 320 36 80

11316
Premio Blanco y Negro de Pintura
To recognize outstanding painting. Works by Spanish artists under 35 years of age, on any theme and using any technique, may be submitted. A monetary award of 1,000,000 pesetas is presented biennially. Established in 1970 to commemorate the profound artistic involvement of *Blanco y Negro*, a magazine to which the most outstanding Spanish painters and illustrators have contributed since 1891.

11317
Premio Luca de Tena
To recognize the best unsigned literary article published in any Spanish newspaper during the previous year. The author or any other individual or organization may submit a nomination. A monetary award of 1,000,000 pesetas is presented annually. Established in 1929 to honor Torcuato Luca de Tena, founder of *Prensa Espanola*.

11318
Premio Mariano de Cavia
To recognize the best signed literary article published by any Spanish newspaper during the previous year. The author or any other individual/organization may submit a nomination. A monetary award of 1,000,000 pesetas is presented annually. Established in 1920 to honor Mariano de Cavia, a famous writer and journalist, and a regular contributor of ABC.

11319
Premio Mingote
To recognize the best journalistic photograph or cartoon printed by any Spanish newspaper during the previous year. The photographer/artist or another individual or organization may submit a nomination. A monetary award of 1,000,000 pesetas is presented annually. Established in 1966 to honor Antonio Mingote, the famous ABC cartoonist.

11320
PRISA
Calle de Miguel Yuste 40
E-28037 Madrid, Spain

11321
Ortega y Gasset Award for Journalism
For recognition of outstanding articles that have appeared in a Spanish-language newspaper or magazine in any country during the previous year. Particular attention is given to investigative reporting, journalistic innovation, and the development of new professional techniques. A prize is also given for television. A monetary prize of 1 million pesetas and a sculpture by Pablo Serrano are awarded annually. Established in 1983 in honor of Jose Ortega y Gasset, a great thinker, author, and journalist, by PRISA, publisher of the Madrid daily, *El Pais*.

11322
Radio Exterior de Espana
Apartado 156.202
E-28080 Madrid, Spain
Phone: 1 711 2742
Fax: 1 711 2906

11323
Euromusica Competition
To discover Spanish musical talent living in Europe and to promote these musicians in broadcasts.

11324
Radio Exterior de Espana Prize
For recognition of an outstanding actor in a film entered in the Latin American Film Festival. An original bronze sculpture is awarded.

11325
Margarita Xirgu Radio Drama Prize
For recognition of a radio script, on any subject, lasting no longer than 30 minutes and no less than 25. A monetary prize of 500,000 pesetas is awarded annually when merited. Sponsored by the Institute for Latin American Cooperation.

11326
Rialp Publishing House
(Ediciones Rialp, S.A.)
Akcaka, 250
E-28027 Madrid, Spain
Phone: 1 3260504
Fax: 1 3261321

11327
Premio Adonais de Poesia
For recognition of the best poetry by young Spanish speaking poets. Young Spanish and Latin American poets under 35 years of age may submit poems by September 30. The following awards are presented: first prize - 25,000 pesetas and a statuette and two honorable mentions - 10,000 pesetas each. Prize winning works are published in the *Adonais Collection*, a series that brings new poets to public attention. Awarded annually in December. Established in 1943. Additional information is available from Coleccions Adonais: 500 titulos.

11328
Fernando Rielo Foundation
Jorge Juan 102, Numero 2B
E-28009 Madrid, Spain
Phone: 1 5754091
Fax: 1 4352351

11329
Fernando Rielo World Prize for Mystical Poetry
For recognition of outstanding mystical poetry (poetry expressing humanity's spiritual values in their profound religious significance). Any previously unpublished poem or group of poems with a total length of 600 to 1300 lines and written or translated into Spanish is eligible. The deadline is October 15. A monetary award of 600,000 pesetas and

publication of the entry are awarded when merited. Established to honor Fernando Rielo, a Spanish philosopher and poet.

11330
Royal Academy of Pharmacy
(Real Academia de Farmacia)
c/ Farmacia 11
E-28004 Madrid, Spain   Phone: 1 531 03 07

11331
Premio Alberto Comenge
For recognition of an outstanding work in the field of pharmacology. Pharmacologists from Spain, Portugal, the Americas and the Phillipines are eligible. Works must be in Spanish or Portuguese, unpublished, and may not have won previous prizes. The deadline for submission is October 31. A monetary prize of 50,000 pesetas is awarded.

11332
Premio Alter
For recognition of a work in the field of drug research. Pharmacologists from Spain, Portugal, the Americas and the Phillipines are eligible. Works must be in Spanish or Portuguese, unpublished, and may not have won previous prizes. The deadline for submission is October 31. A monetary prize of 100,000 pesetas is awarded.

11333
Premio Antibioticos
For recognition of an outstanding work in the field of pharmacology. Pharmacologists from Spain, Portugal, the Americas and the Phillipines are eligible. Works must be in Spanish or Portuguese, unpublished, and may not have won previous prizes. The deadline for submission is October 31. A monetary prize of 100,000 pesetas is awarded for First prize, and two prizes of 25,000 pesetas each are also awarded.

11334
Premio de la Compania Espanola de Penicilina y Antibioticos
For recognition of an outstanding work in the field of pharmacology. Pharmacologists from Spain, Portugal, the Americas and the Phillipines are eligible. Works must be in Spanish or Portuguese, unpublished, and may not have won previous prizes. The deadline for submission is October 31. A monetary prize of 25,000 pesetas is awarded.

11335
Premio de la Real Academia de Farmacia
For recognition of outstanding works in the field of pharmacology. Pharmacologists from Spain, Portugal, the Americas and the Phillipines are eligible. Works must be in Spanish or Portuguese, unpublished, and may not have won previous prizes. The deadline for submission is October 31. A monetary prize of 150,000 pesetas is awarded for first prize, and two prizes of 50,000 pesetas each are also awarded.

11336
Premio del Colegio Oficial de Farmaceuticos
For recognition of the best work in pharmacology at the College by a Madrid resident. Pharmacologists from Spain, Portugal, the Americas and the Phillipines are eligible. Works must be in Spanish or Portuguese, unpublished, and may not have won previous prizes. The deadline for submission is October 31. A monetary prize of 100,000 pesetas is awarded.

11337
Premio del Consejo General de Colegios Oficiales de Farmaceuticos de Espana
For recognition of outstanding pharmaceutical research. Pharmacologists from Spain, Portugal, the Americas and the Phillipines are eligible. Works must be in Spanish or Portuguese, unpublished, and may not have won previous prizes. The deadline for submission is October 31. A monetary prize of 100,000 pesetas is awarded for First prize, and two prizes of 50,000 each are also awarded.

11338
Premio Fabrica Espanola de Productos Quimicos y Farmaceuticos
For recognition of an outstanding work in drug research. Pharmacologists from Spain, Portugal, the Americas and the Phillipines are eligible. Works must be in Spanish or Portuguese, unpublished, and may not have won previous prizes. The deadline for submission is October 31. A monetary prize of 150,000 pesetas is awarded for First prize, and two prizes of 25,000 pesetas each are also awarded.

11339
Premio Fundacion Rafael Folch
To recognize the author of an outstanding work on the history of pharmacology or affiliated sciences. Pharmacologists from Spain, Portugal, the Americas and the Phillipines are eligible. Works must be in Spanish or Portuguese, unpublished, and may not have won previous prizes. The deadline for submission is October 31. A medal is awarded.

11340
Premio Guillermo Tena
For recognition of research in toxicology. Pharmacologists from Spain, Portugal, the Americas and the Phillipines are eligible. Works must be in Spanish or Portuguese, unpublished, and may not have won previous prizes. The deadline for submission is October 31. A monetary prize of 100,000 pesetas is awarded.

11341
Premio Juan Abello
For recognition of an outstanding work in the field of pharmacology. Pharmacologists from Spain, Portugal, the Americas and the Phillipines are eligible. Works must be in Spanish or Portuguese, unpublished, and may not have won previous prizes. The deadline for submission is October 31. A monetary prize of 25,000 pesetas is awarded.

11342
Premio Juan de la Serna
For recognition of the promotion of studies about environmental pollution. Pharmacologists from Spain, Portugal, the Americas and the Phillipines are eligible. Works must be in Spanish or Portuguese, unpublished, and may not have won previous prizes. The deadline for submission is October 31. A monetary prize of 50,000 pesetas is awarded.

11343
Premios de la Cooperativa Farmaceutica Espanola
For recognition of outstanding work in the following two categories: (1) pharmaceutical and technical instruments; and (2) pharmaceutical history. Pharmacologists from Spain, Portugal, the Americas and the Phillipines are eligible. Works must be in Spanish or Portuguese, unpublished, and may not have won previous prizes. The deadline for submission is October 31. A monetary prize of 200,000 pesetas is awarded for First prize in the first category, and 150,000 pesetas for the second category. In addition, a prize of 50,000 pesetas is awarded in both categories.

11344
Royal Spanish Academy
(Real Academia Espanola)
Felilpe IV No. 4   Phone: 1 4203613
Madrid, Spain   Fax: 1 4200079

11345
Fundacion del Premio Fastenrath
To recognize Spanish authors for works of excellence written in the Spanish language. Works published or performed during the preceding five-year period are eligible. Awards are given in alternate years in the following categories: poetry, essays or criticism, novel or story, history or biography, and drama. A monetary prize of 500,000 Spanish pesetas is awarded annually. Established in 1909 by King Alfonso XIII.

11346
Premio Alvarez Quintero
For recognition of the best novel, story collection, or theatrical work. Awards are given alternately for novel or story collection and theatrical works. A monetary prize of 100,000 Spanish pesetas is awarded biennially. Established in 1949.

11347
Premio Menendez Pidal
(Menendez Pidal Prize)
For recognition of an outstanding published or unpublished work in the fields of Spanish linguistics or Spanish literature. Works by Spanish or foreign authors in the vocabulary of a Spanish region that has not been studied sufficiently are eligible. A monetary prize of 300,000 Spanish pesetas is awarded biennially. Established in 1958.

11348
Premios de la Fundacion Conde de Cartagena
(Count of Cartagena Prizes)
For recognition of unpublished works written in Castilian Spanish by Spanish citizens and Hispanic Americans on a theme to be decided for each competition. The current theme is a compilation of Spanish vocabulary in two categories: words in present use but not in the academic dictionary and words pertaining to the economics and trade from the sixteenth century to the eighteenth century. Monetary prizes of 500,000 Spanish pesetas are awarded annually. Established in 1929.

11349
Rivadeneira Prizes
For recognition of the best work on any theme in the fields of Spanish literature and linguistics. Two monetary prizes, one of 300,000 Spanish pesetas, another of 200,000 Spanish pesetas, are awarded annually. Established in 1940.

11350
San Sebastian International Film Festival
(Festival Internacional de Cine de San Sebastian)
Apart. Correos 397 Phone: 43 481212
E-20080 San Sebastian, Spain Fax: 43 481218

11351
Festival Internacional de Cine de San Sebastian
For recognition of the best films of the festival. The following prizes are among those presented: Gold Shell (Concha de Oro) - to the best film; Silver Shell (Concha de Plata) - to the best director; Special Jury Prize; San Sebastian Prize - to the best actress; and San Sebastian Prize - to the best actor. Awarded annually in September. Established in 1953.

11352
San Sebastian Underwater Film Cycle
(Ciclo Internacional de Cine Submarino)
Apartado de Correos 979 Phone: 43 428858
E-20080 San Sebastian, Spain Fax: 43 450794

11353
San Sebastian Underwater Film Cycle
(Ciclo Internacional de Cine Submarino)
For recognition of films that have underwater scenes or deal with this subject. Films of 16mm must be submitted by March 10. Trophies and medals are awarded annually. Established in 1975. Sponsored by Entidades Oficiales del Gobierno Vasco.

11354
Santander International Piano Competition
(Concurso Internacional de Piano de Santander)
Hernan Cortes 3 Phone: 42 311266
E-39003 Santander, Spain Fax: 42 314816

11355
Santander International Piano Competition
(Concurso Internacional de Piano de Santander)
To give international support to young pianists of great talent. Pianists of all nationalities between 16 and 30 years of age may apply. The following prizes are awarded: Santander Grand Prize and Gold Medal - 2,000,000 pesetas, world-wide concert engagements, and a recording. It may, exceptionally, be awarded to one or two pianists and requires a majority of at least 75 percent of the Jury's votes; Santander Prize of Honour - 1,300,000 pesetas and recitals to one or two pianists by the Jury's majority vote; Finalist Prize - 750,000 pesetas and recitals to those participants who reach the Final Stage; and Special and Scholarship Prizes. Awarded triennially. Closing date is January 15. Established in 1974 and held under the auspices of Spain - Ministry of Culture and the Santander International Festival. For further information, contact Isaac Albeniz at the above address or Mrs. Brookes McIntyre, 1000 Brickell Ave., Miami, FL 33131, (305) 530-2910, Fax (305) 530-2905.

11356
Semana Internacional de Cine de Autor
Apartado De Correos 24
E-29080 Malaga, Spain

11357
Hercules Award
For recognition of the best film in the film festival Semana Internacional de Cine de Autor, and for the best film in the Spanish language. Only films presented in the Competition are considered. A trophy is awarded annually. Established in 1986. Additional information is available from Junta de Andalucia, Larios, 9, Malaga, Spain.

11358
Sitges International Fantasy Film Festival
(Festival Internacional de Cinema Fantastic de Sitges)
Calle Disputacion 279 Bajos Phone: 3 317 35 85
E-08007 Barcelona, Spain Fax: 3 301 22 47

11359
Sitges International Fantasy Film Festival Awards
(Premi Festival Internacional de Cinema Fantastic de Sitges)
To provide recognition for the best long or short 35mm films of the fantastic and horror genre produced by any organization, company, individual, etc. Awards are presented to the best actress, actor, script, photography, special effects, and director of the best long film and the best short film. Trophies are awarded annually. Established in 1968.

11360
Spain
Ministry of Foreign Affairs
c/o Instituto de Cooperacion
 Iberoamericana
Plaza de la Provincia 1 Phone: 91 5838100
12 Madrid, Spain Fax: 91 5838310

11361
King of Spain Journalism Prizes
(Premios Rey de Espana de Periodismo)
For recognition of outstanding achievement by Spanish or Portuguese-speaking professionals in the fields of radio, press, television, and photography. A monetary prize of 800,000 Spanish pesetas and a statuette are awarded annually. Established in 1983 in cooperation with the EFE News Agency.

11362
Premio Bartolome de las Casas
To recognize Latin-American individuals or institutions for outstanding work in defense of the indigenous villages and their rights and values. Established by the Instituto de Cooperacion Iberoamericana and la

Secretaria de Estado para la Cooperacion Internacional y para Iberoamerica. For additional information call: 91 5760005.

11363

Premio Maria Guerrero a la Labor Teatral
For recognition of the most outstanding Argentinian theatrical work of the year. Established by the joint efforts of Asociacion Amigos del Teatro Nacional Cervantes de Buenos Aires, the Instituto de Cooperacion Iberoamericana, and the Ministry of Culture of Spain.

11364

Premio Teatral Tirso de Molina
To recognize playwrights, regardless of nationality, for outstanding works in the Castillian language. Playwrights who have not been honored or published in the past are eligible.

11365

Spain
Ministry of Industry, Trade and Tourism
(Spain
Ministerio de Industria, Comercio y Turismo)
Secretaria General de Turismo
Paseo de la Castellana 160
E-28046 Madrid, Spain   Phone: 1 4588010

11366

Orden al Merito Turistico
For recognition of special services to Spanish tourism by persons and institutions. Gold, silver and bronze medals to individuals and plaques to institutions are awarded annually. Established in 1962.

11367

Spain Ministry of Culture
(Spain Ministerio de Cultura)
Direccion General del Libro y Bibliotecas
Plaza del Rey 1   Phone: 1 5325089
E-28004 Madrid, Spain   Fax: 1 5321222

11368

Miguel Cervantes Prize for Literature
(Premio Miguel de Cervantes)
This, the most esteemed of the literary prizes of Spain, is given to recognize an author whose total life's published work in the Castilian language has contributed to the enrichment of the Spanish and Hispanic American culture. The prize must be given and cannot be divided. A monetary prize of 15,000,000 Spanish pesetas is awarded annually. Established in 1976.

11369

National Plastic Arts Prize
(Premio Nacional de Artes Plasticas)
For recognition of contributions in the field of sculpture. A monetary prize of 5,000,000 pesetas is awarded. Additional information is available from D.G. de Bellas Artes y Archivos at the Ministry of Culture.

11370

National Prize for Illustration of Literature for Children and Young People
(Premio Nacional de Illustracion de Libros Infantiles y Juveniles)
For recognition of the best illustration of children's literature published during the preceding year. Spanish illustrators are eligible. The prizes cannot be divided. A monetary prize of 500,000 Spanish pesetas is awarded annually in each of the categories of literature for children and literature for young people. Established in 1978. Additional information is available from Centro del Libro y la Lectura, Santiago Rusinol 8, E-28040 Madrid, Spain, phone: 253 92 66.

11371

Premio Nacional de Cinematografia
For recognition of outstanding work in the field of films. A monetary prize of 2,500,000 pesetas is awarded. Additional information is available from Instituto de la Cinematografia y de las Artes Audiovisuales at the Ministry of Culture.

11372

Premio Nacional de Danza
For recognition in the field of dance. A monetary prize of 2,500,000 pesetas is awarded.

11373

Premio Nacional de Historia de Espana
To encourage research in and publication about the history of Spain. Awarded for the best book by Spanish or foreign authors published in Spain in the previous year. The deadline is March 31. An indivisible monetary prize of 2,500,000 Spanish pesetas is awarded annually.

11374

Premio Nacional de las Letras Espanolas
To recognize an outstanding living Spanish author whose works in a Spanish language are considered an integral part of Spanish literature as a whole. An indivisible monetary prize of 5,000,000 Spanish pesetas is awarded annually. Established in 1984.

11375

Premio Nacional de Literatura
To recognize outstanding works in Spanish literature in the fields of poetry, narration, and essay. Spanish authors of books published during the preceding year are eligible. Monetary prizes of 2,500,000 Spanish pesetas for each category are awarded annually. Established in 1984.

11376

Premio Nacional de Teatro
For recognition in the field of theatre. A monetary prize of 2,500,000 pesetas is awarded.

11377

Premio Nacional de Traduccion
To recognize outstanding Spanish translators for the best work edited in the previous year. The prize may be divided equally or not awarded at the discretion of the jury. A monetary prize of 2,500,000 Spanish pesetas is awarded annually. Established in 1956 by the Ministry of National Education.

11378

Premio Nacionales de Musica
For recognition in the field of music. Two monetary prizes of 2,000,000 pesetas each are awarded.

11379

Premios Nacionales de Literatura Infantil y Juvenil
To recognize outstanding works of the previous year in the field of children's literature and its translation. Authors or translators of Spanish origin are eligible. The prize for creation is indivisible, although the prize for translation may be divided at the jury's discretion. Monetary prizes of 1,500,000 Spanish pesetas for creation and 1,000,000 Spanish pesetas for translation are awarded in alternate years for each category. Established in 1978. Additional information is available from Centro del Libro y la Lectura, Santiago Rusinol, 8, E-Madrid, Spain.

11380

Spanish Association of Painters and Sculptors
(Asociacion Espanola de Pintores y Escultores)
Infantas 30   Phone: 1 5224961
E-28004 Madrid, Spain   Fax: 1 5224961

11381
Spanish Association of Painters and Sculptors Prizes
To recognize members for excellence in oil painting, sculpture, watercolor painting, drawing, and engraving. Medals, some with a trophy and a few with monetary prizes, are awarded annually at the Salon de Otono which was established in 1920. The Medalla de Honor also carries official civil honors.

11382
Spanish Organization for Children's and Juvenile Literature
(Organizacion Espanola para el Libro Infantil y Juvenil)
Santiago Rusinol 8
E-28040 Madrid, Spain
Phone: 1 533 08 02
Fax: 1 253 99 90

11383
Illustration Award
(Concurso de Ilustraciones)
To encourage good quality illustrations and to promote Children's Book Week. Original unpublished works may be submitted by February 28. A monetary prize of 300,000 Spanish pesetas is awarded annually. Established in 1985. Sponsored by Centro del Libro y de la Lectura (Ministerio de Cultura).

11384
Lazarillo Prize
(Premio Lazarillo)
To promote and to recognize literature and quality illustration for children and teenagers. Awards are given in the following categories: best book; and best illustration of a book. Unpublished works, written in Spanish, for young children and teenagers are eligible. The deadline for nominations is July 15. A monetary prize of 1,000,000 Spanish pesetas for each category and certificates are awarded annually. Established in 1958 (and administered until 1986) by the Instituto Nacional del Libro Espanol, Ministerio de Cultura of Spain. Sponsored by Centro del Libro y de la Lectura (Ministerio de Cultura).

11385
Torello Film Festival
PO Box 19
Anselm Clave 5, 3er
E-08570 Torello (Barcelona), Spain
Phone: 3 8592899
Fax: 3 8593000

Formerly: Torello Excursionist Center.

11386
International Festival of Mountain Films, Vila de Torello
(Concurs International de Cinema de la Montagne Vila de Torello)
An international film contest of mountain cinema. Films related to mountains and ecology, such as alpinism, climbing, excursions, expeditions, mountain sports, skiing, speleology, and protection of nature, flora, and fauna are considered. Films presented to the competition must go through the selection committee. Foreign films that are not presented dubbed or subtitled in Castilian are to be accompanied by a large synopsis in Castilian, French, or English. Films in 35mm, 16mm, or video must be submitted by October 5. Films made before 1988 or already presented in other competition editions are not accepted. The following prizes are awarded: Grand Prix Vila de Torello - Gold Edelweiss and 400,000 pesetas to the best film; Silver Edelweiss and 150,000 pesetas to the best mountaineering film; Silver Edelweiss and 150,000 pesetas to the best mountain environment film; Silver Edelweiss and 150,000 pesetas to the best film of mountain sports; Silver Edelweiss and 150,000 pesetas for the jury prize; Medal Federacion Espanola de Montanismo and 75,000 pesetas for the best film by a Spanish director; and Silver Edelweiss and 50,000 pesetas each for best photography, script, and editing. Awarded annually. Established in 1983 by Torello Excursionist Centre. Sponsored by the City Council.

11387
Tusquets Editores S.A.
Iradier 24 bajos
E-08017 Barcelona, Spain
Phone: 3 417 41 70
Fax: 3 417 67 03

11388
Premio Comillas de Biografia, Autobiografia y Memorias
To promote unpublished biographies, memoirs, and autobiographies written in the Castillian Spanish language. A monetary award of 2,000,000 Spanish pesetas and a trophy are presented annually when merited. Established in 1988.

11389
Premio Tusquets Editores de Novela
To promote the unpublished work of unknown young authors. Works must be first, or at most, second novels written in Castilian Spanish language. A monetary award of 1,000,000 pesetas and an art object are awarded bienially when merited. Established in 1993.

11390
Vertical Smile
(Premio La Sonrisa Vertical)
To promote the knowledge of great erotic authors and revitalize this marginal genre of Castilian literature. Works must be written in Spanish to be considered. A monetary award of 1,000,000 pesetas and an art object are awarded annually in January. Established in 1978 in honor of Lopez Barbadillo, the first to publish a collection of erotic narratives.

11391
Valladolid International Film Festival
(Semana Internacional de Cine de Valladolid)
PO Box 646
E-47080 Valladolid, Spain
Phone: 83 305700
Fax: 83 309835

11392
Valladolid International Film Festival
For recognition of the best films of the festival. An international jury decides the winners of the following awards from those feature-lengths and shorts selected for participation in competition in the official section: Golden Spike and Silver Spike to the two best feature-lengths. The Spanish distributor of the winner of the Golden Spike receives $30,000 US; Prize to the Best New Director, competing with a first or second feature-length receives $10,000 US; Best Actress; Best Actor; Best Director of Photography Award; Golden Spike and Silver Spike to the two best short films. The filmmaker of the top prizewinner receives $5,000 US; Jury Prize to short and feature-length films. No more than one "ex aequo" is permitted within each category. Cash prizes, in this case, will be split equally; and another jury, independent from the one in the official section awards a prize of $10,000 US to the Best Documentary in the Time of History section. This jury may also award two special mentions. The prize must be conferred. Established in 1956 by Antolin de Santiago y Juarez.

11393
Francisco Vinas International Singing Competition
(Concurs Internacional de Cant Francesc Vinas)
Bruc 125
E-08037 Barcelona, Spain
Phone: 3 2154227

11394
Francisco Vinas International Singing Competition
(Concurs Internacional de Cant Francesc Vinas)
To encourage talented young singers all over the world. Female singers between 18 and 32 years of age, and male singers between 20 and 35 years of age are eligible. Applications must be submitted by October 17. A monetary prize of 1,100,000 pesetas and a gold plated silver medal are awarded to the grand prize winners in the male and female categories (Gran Premio Generalitat de Catalunya). Other official, special, and extraordinary prizes for a total amount of over 8,000,000 Spanish pesetas are awarded. The competition is held annually. Established in 1963 by Dr.

11395

World Veterinary Association
(Association Mondiale Veterinaire)
Calle Pricipe de Vergara 276
E-28016 Madrid, Spain   Phone: 1 2471838

11396

Gamgee Medal
For recognition of outstanding services to veterinary science and the profession. Veterinary doctors in World Veterinary Association member-countries are eligible. A gold medal is awarded at irregular intervals and on the occasion of a World Veterinary Congress. Established in 1963 and awarded in 1963, 1975, and 1983. Named for Dr. John Gamgee, Edinburgh veterinarian, who organized the first international Veterinary Congress in 1863 in Hamburg.

11397

Zaragoza Fair
Catalogue and Statistics
PO Box 108
Carretera Nacional II, Km. 311   Phone: 76 701100
E-50012 Zaragoza, Spain   Fax: 76 330649

Formerly: (1991) Zaragoza Institution for Fairs and Exhibitions.

11398

International Contest of Agrarian Cinema and Video
(Certamen International de Cine y Video Agrario)
To give a panoramic vision of the international production on agrarian matters, to collaborate in the agrarian extension in general, and to contribute to a better knowledge of the country and its problems. Awards are given in two sections (for film and for video) in the following categories: Mechanization - those productions whose main theme is related to the use of machinery in any sector of agriculture, cattle rearing, or forestry production; Country in General - those productions that cannot be included in the previous section and whose theme is related to the agrarian production or the different aspects of life in the country in its fullest sense, such as preservation of nature, rural domestic economy, food, cooperativism, and development of the rural community; and Special Group - productions whose theme corresponds to either of the above section but in which the commercial or publicity character stands out. A gold trophy is presented to the best overall winner, and silver and bronze trophies are presented in each section of the three categories. The biennial film competion was established in 1975. In 1986, the video competition was established and held biennially in alternate years. In 1991, the Competitions were combined and held annually. (Discontinued)

Sri Lanka

11399

Foundation of Socio-Cultural Services
Dambulla Rd. 55/4
Kurunegala, Sri Lanka

Formerly: (1980) Karanegala Maha Sahithya Sangamaya.

11400

Foundation of Socio-Cultural Services Competitions
To recognize individuals concerned with cultural advancement and socio-economic development in Sri Lanka. The Foundation Sponsors competitions.

11401

Institution of Engineers, Sri Lanka
                                          Phone: 1 685490
120/15 Wijerama Mawatha   Phone: 1 698426
Colombo 7, Sri Lanka   Fax: 1 699202

11402

Ceylon Development Engineering Award
To recognize the author(s) of the best article in the quarterly journal, Engineer published each year. Expertise in the relevant field is necessary for consideration. A monetary prize of 3,000 Sri Lanka rupees is awarded annually at the convention. Established in 1980. Sponsored by the Ceylon Development Engineering Company, Ltd.

11403

IESL Award
For recognition of achievement in the Institution Part I Examination. Individuals who pass all subjects and reach an aggregate of 65 percent are eligible. Awarded annually at the convention. Established in 1986.

11404

Junior Inventor of the Year
To encourage originality and inventiveness of technical minded and talented students. Sri Lankan students between 12 and 20 years of age must be nominated by April 30. Monetary prizes, medals, and certificates are awarded annually. Established in 1988. Co-sponsored by Lanka Electricity Company (Private) Ltd.

11405

T. P. de S. Munasinghe Memorial Award
To recognize the best student in civil engineering at the Institution Part II Examination. Students must obtain a minimum average of 65 percent marks and should have passed the Part I Examination or be exempted from it. A monetary prize of 1,000 Sri Lanka rupees is awarded annually at the convention. Established in 1984 in honor of T.P. de S. Munasinghe, a Fellow and past president of the Institution. Sponsored by Mrs. T.P. de S. Munasinghe and family.

11406

Professor E. O. E. Pereira Award
To recognize the author(s) of the best paper in the field of engineering at the annual convention of the Institution. Members of the Institution may submit papers by June 30 every year. Books or publications valued at 1,000 Sri Lanka rupees are awarded annually at the convention. Established in 1973 in honor of Professor E.O.E. Pereira, first Dean, Faculty of Engineering and first Engineer Vice Chancellor of the Peradeniya Campus of the University of Ceylon (now University of Peradeniya, Sri Lanka). Sponsored by the Faculty of Engineering, University of Peradeniya, Sri Lanka.

11407

Aylet Lilly Perera Memorial
For recognition of achievement in the Institution Part II Examination in Mechanical Engineering. Individuals who pass all subjects and reach an aggregate of 65 percent are eligible. Books are awarded annually at the convention. Established in 1987 in honor of Mrs. Aylet Lilly Perera, mother of L.R.L. Perera, past president of the Institution.

11408

State Development and Construction Corporation Award
To recognize the author(s) of the best article in the field of engineering in the quarterly journal, Engineer. Associate Members of the Institution are eligible. A monetary prize of 1,000 Sri Lanka rupees is awarded annually at the convention. Established in 1980. Sponsored by the State Department and Construction Corporation, Sri Lanka.

11409

D. J. Wimalasurendra Memorial Award
To recognize the best student in electrical engineering at the Institution's Part II Examination. Students must obtain a minimum average of 65 percent marks and should have passed the Part I Examination or be

exempted from it. A monetary prize of 1,000 Sri Lanka rupees is awarded annually at the convention. Established in 1984 in honor of D.J. Wimalasurendra, a member of the Institution and an electrical engineer who is considered the father of hydro-electricity in Sri Lanka. Sponsored by the Central Engineering Consultancy Bureau of Sri Lanka and the Ceylon Electricity Board.

11410
Young Engineer of the Year
To identify the original and innovative work and ideas of young people, and to assist their original thinking and development by highlighting their activities and providing them with encouragement and motivation. Sri Lankan citizens between 20 and 35 years of age must be nominated by June 30. Monetary prizes, a trophy, and certificates are awarded annually. Established in 1989.

11411
Lanka Mahila Samiti
UDA Bldg., 7th Fl.
2 Galle Rd.
Colombo 4, Sri Lanka   Phone: 1 502537

11412
Lanka Mahila Samiti Awards
To recognize individuals who work to improve the quality of life in rural communities at the familial, employment, and social levels. Awards are presented.

11413
Royal Asiatic Society of Sri Lanka
Mahaweli Centre & R. A. S Building
86 Ananda Coomaraswamy Mawatha
Colombo 7, Sri Lanka   Phone: 1 699249

11414
Royal Asiatic Society Medal
To recognize outstanding contributions pertaining to the objectives of the Society: inquiries into the history, religions, languages, literature, arts, sciences and the social conditions of the present, and former inhabitants of Sri Lanka and connected cultures. Members of the Society are eligible. A medal is awarded triennially at the annual convention. Established in 1946.

11415
Abdul Majeed Mohamed Sahabdeen Trust Foundation
The Secretary
86, Galle Rd.   Phone: 1 327368
Colombo 3, Sri Lanka   Fax: 1 440523

11416
Mohamed Sahabdeen Award for International Understanding
To recognize any person or association of persons who has, during the preceding three years, made an outstanding contribution to the furtherance of intercultural, interdisciplinary, or international understanding. Any person or association of persons from Sri Lanka or other South Asian countries is eligible to apply or be nominated. Nominations may be made by an individual or an organization by August 30. A grant, a citation, and a certificate are awarded. Established by Act of Parliament No. 3 of 1991 - Sri Lanka.

11417
Mohamed Sahabdeen Award for Literature
To recognize any person or association of persons who has, during the preceding three years, made an outstanding contribution to creative literature, history, philosophy, law, religion, or mass media. Any person or association of persons from Sri Lanka or other South Asian countries is eligible to apply or be nominated. Nominations may be made by an individual or an organization by August 30. Established by Act of Parliament No. 3 of 1991 - Sri Lanka.

11418
Mohamed Sahabdeen Award for Science
To recognize any person or association of persons who has, during the preceding three years, made an outstanding contribution to the advancement of science, including socioeconomic, medical, and engineering sciences. Any person or association of persons from Sri Lanka or any other SAARC countries (India, Pakistan, Bangladesh, Nepal, Maldive Islands, and Bhutan) is eligible to apply or be nominated. Nominations may be made by an individual or an organization by August 30. Established by Act of Parliament No. 3 of 1991 - Sri Lanka.

11419
Sri Kapila Humanitarian Society
257 Circular Rd.
Magalle
Galle, Sri Lanka

11420
Sri Kapila Humanitarian Society Competitions
To recognize individuals for their awareness and perpetuation of the economic, medical, ethical, and religious advantages of a vegetarian diet and efforts to prevent any form of cruelty towards animals. The Society organizes competitions.

11421
Sri Lanka
Ministry of Cultural Affairs
34 Malay St.
Colombo 2, Sri Lanka   Phone: 1 545777

11422
Kala Bhushana Honours
To honor traditional artistes who have been engaged in the local traditional arts for a considerable length of time. About 25-50 artists are honored. A silver medal and $10,000 rupees are awarded annually.

11423
Literary Awards and Prizes for Sinhalese Literature
For recognition of the best books published during the previous year in the Sinhala language. Awards are given in the following categories: novels, short stories, poetry, translations, children's literature, scientific literature, drama, music, miscellaneous literary areas, and original works in the Pali, Sanscrit and Arabic languages. Monetary prizes of 1,000 Sri Lanka rupees and a citation are awarded in each category annually.

11424
Literary Prizes for Tamil Literature
For recognition of the best books published in Sri Lanka during the previous year in the Tamil language in the following categories: novels, short stories, poetry and miscellaneous literary areas. Monetary prizes of 1,000 Sri Lanka rupees and a citation are awarded in each category annually.

11425
Don Pedrick Memorial Literary Award
To provide recognition for the best original literary work in the Sinhala language. A monetary prize of 1,000 Sri Lanka rupees is awarded annually. (Inactive)

11426
Sinhala Drama Awards
For recognition in the field of drama. Awards are given in the following categories: Best Actor, Best Actress, Best Make-up, Best Costume Design, Best Music Direction, Best Play, Best Stage Direction, Best Stage Lighting, Best Stage Decor, Best Choreography, Best Supporting Ac-

tress, Best Supporting Actor, and Best Play Script (translation). Only plays written and produced in the Sinhala language are considered. Monetary prizes of 1,000 rupees each are awarded annually.

11427
Tamil Drama Award
For recognition in the field of drama. Awards are given in the following categories: Best Actor; Best Actress; Best Music for a Play; Best Stage Decoration; Best Play; and Best Production of a Modern or Tamil Play. Only plays written or produced in the Tamil language are considered. Monetary prizes of 1,000 rupees each are awarded annually.

11428
Sri Lanka
Office of the President
Republic Sq.
Colombo 1, Sri Lanka Phone: 1 24801

11429
Deshabandu
For recognition of outstanding contributions to the country. Awards are given in three classes: Class I; Class II; and Class III.

11430
Deshamanya
For recognition of outstanding contributions to the country.

11431
Kalakirthi
For recognition of outstanding contributions to the country.

11432
Kalashoori
For recognition of outstanding contributions to the country. Awards are given in three classes: Class I; Class II; and Class III.

11433
Lanka Sikkhamani
For recognition of outstanding contributions to the country.

11434
Sri Lanka Abhimanya
For recognition of outstanding contributions to the country.

11435
Sri Lankatillaka
For recognition of outstanding contributions to the country.

11436
Vidyajothi
For recognition of outstanding contributions to the country.

11437
Vidyanidhi
For recognition of outstanding contributions to the country.

11438
United Nations Association of Sri Lanka
39/1 Cyril Jansz Mawatha Phone: 94 3432123
Panadura, Sri Lanka Fax: 94 331617

11439
UNA Awards
For recognition of outstanding service to the Association and to world peace. The following awards are presented: Honorary Membership, Special Meritorious Service Award, Meritorious Service Award, Volunteer of the Year, Most Distinguished Service Award, Distinguished Service Award, and the National Peace Prize of Sri Lanka. Medals and certificates are presented for each award. In addition, the winner of the Peace Prize receives a monetary award and the Volunteer of the Year receives a certificate and a gift. Awards are presented at the annual general meeting of the Association. Established in 1990.

11440
UNA Study Circles Challenge Trophys
To recognize the four best UNA Study Circles in participating high schools. Four trophys are awarded. Certificates are also presented for the following inter Study Circle competitions: Essays on the United Nations; General Knowledge Prize on the UN; Best Speakers in an Oratorical Contest; Best Essay on Population and Sustainable Development; Best Suggestions for the Improvement of the Program; General Knowledge Quiz on International Flags, National Emblems, Coat-of-Arms, and National Anthems of UN Member States. Teachers in charge of the study groups and six runners-up also receive certificates.

Sweden

11441
Carina Ari Foundation
(Carina Ari Stiftelsen)
c/o Carina Ari Library of Dance
Sehlstedtsgatan 4 Phone: 8 6626570
S-11528 Stockholm, Sweden Fax: 8 6674963

11442
Carina Ari Medal of Merit
(Carina Ari Medaljen)
For recognition of outstanding contributions to the art of dance in Sweden. A gold medal is awarded annually. Established in 1961 in memory of Carina Ari, a Swedish ballerina and choreographer of international career, especially in Paris in the 1920s and 1930s.

11443
Association of Swedish Amateur Orchestras
(Riksforbundet Sveriges Amatororkestrar)
Postfack 3128
S-580 03 Linkoping, Sweden Phone: 13 149590

11444
Association of Swedish Amateur Orchestras Awards
To recognize Swedish amateur orchestras. Awards are given triennially.

11445
Blekinge County Council
(Blekinge Lans Landsting)
Kansliet Phone: 455 88000
S-371 81 Karlskrona, Sweden Fax: 455 80250

11446
Blekinge County Council Culture Prize
(Blekinge lans landstings kulturpris)
To recognize a person or organisation for a valuable contribution to science, technology, literature, art, music, dance, drama, journalism, free education, environmental control or to recognize an important humanitarian achievement. Individuals who were born or are living in the county are eligible. A monetary prize of 30,000 Swedish kronor is awarded annually. Established in 1964.

11447
Blekinge County Council Environment Prize
(Blekinge Lans landstings Miljo vardspris)
To stimulate environmental protection in Blekinge county. A monetary prize of 10,000 Swedish kroner is awarded annually. Established in 1986.

11448

Charta 77 Foundation
Norrtullsgatan 65
S-113 45 Stockholm, Sweden

Phone: 8 334822
Fax: 8 324096

11449

Dr. Frantisek Kriegel Prize
(Cena Frantisek Kriegel)
For recognition of contributions to the human and civil rights movement and civil courage in the Czech Republic and the Slovak Republic. Individuals who promote human rights and civic freedom are considered. A monetary prize is awarded annually. Established in 1987 in memory of Frantisek Kriegel (1908-1978), a promoter of Prague spring and the only leader who refused to sign the acceptance of Soviet rule in August 1968.

11450

Jaroslav Seifert Prize
(Cena Jaroslava Seiferta)
For recognition of the best work in Czech and Slovak literature. A monetary award of 250,000 Czech crowns and a diploma made by one of the well known Czechoslovak artists are awarded. Established in 1986 in memory of Jaroslav Seifert, Nobel Prize Winner (1984) and Czech poet.

11451

Confederation of Nordic Bank Employees' Unions
(Nordiska Bankmannaunionen)
Birger Jarlsgatan 31
Box 7375
S-103 91 Stockholm, Sweden

Phone: 8 614 03 00
Fax: 8 611 38 98

11452

NBU Scholarship
To provide members with the opportunity to follow the professional and trade union development in and outside the Nordic countries. Applications are accepted. A scholarship is awarded for a study visit annually at the spring meeting of the Executive Committee. Established in 1979.

11453

European Human Rights
Marknadsvagen 289
S-183 34 Taby, Sweden

Phone: 8 7681398

11454

Award for Human Rights in Europe
For recognition of unselfish work in the defense of human rights in Europe. A plaque is awarded annually. Established in 1983 by Ditlieb Felderer.

11455

European Society for Neurochemistry
Dept. of History
Institute of Neurobiology
Univ. of Goteborg
Postfach 33031
S-40023 Goteborg, Sweden

Phone: 31 853378
Fax: 31 829690

11456

Porcellati Award
To permit a young neurochemist to travel to the biennial meetings of the Society, probably to deliver a paper/poster. Members who are 40 years of age or younger are eligible. A monetary award for travel is awarded biennially. Established in 1987 by ISN in association with Fidia S.p.a. in memory of Professor Guiseppe Porcellati, a former chairman of the Society.

11457

Filmtidskriften Chaplin
PO Box 27126
S-102 52 Stockholm, Sweden

Phone: 8 6651100
Fax: 8 6638009

11458

Chaplin Prize
For recognition of distinguished accomplishments in Swedish films. Directors, actors, actresses, cameramen, among others, are eligible. A sculpture is awarded annually by the Swedish film magazine, *Film Tidskriften Chaplin*. Established in 1959 by Bengt Forslund, the magazine's first editor.

11459

Geological Society of Sweden
(Geologiska Foreningen)
c/o SGU, Box 670
S-751 28 Uppsala, Sweden

Formerly: Geologiska Foreningen i Stockholm.

11460

Geologiska Foreningens Medaljfondsstipendium
To recognize the best contribution to the Society's journal during a two-year period. Authors who have not yet defended their Ph.D. thesis at the time of publication are eligible. A monetary award and a diploma are presented biennially at the annual meeting of the Society. Established in 1970.

11461

International Association of Logopedics and Phoniatrics
c/o dr. Ewa Soderpalm
Nilssonsberg 21
S-411 Goteborg, Sweden

Fax: 31 823415

11462

Manuel Garcia Prize
To recognize distinguished contributions to scientific studies that attempt to diminish the disorder in human vocal communications. Papers published in *Folia Phoniatrica* are considered. A monetary prize of 1,000 Swiss francs is awarded triennially at the International Congress. Established in 1968 by the Association and Sandoz AG in honor of Manuel Garcia, a singer and founder of laryngoscopy.

11463

International Association of Medical Laboratory Technologists
(Association Internationale des Techniciens de Laboratoire Medical)
Executive Office
Ostermalmsgatan 19
S-114 26 Stockholm, Sweden

Phone: 8 103031
Fax: 8 109061

11464

Baxter Diagnostics Award
To recognize an individual for outstanding services to medical laboratory technology. The following are conditions of entry: membership of at least five years in one of the national associations; full-time occupation in a medical laboratory; proper professional qualifications; and activity in own professional organization. Entries must be submitted by November 1. A monetary award of 4,000 Swiss francs is presented. Established in 1966. Sponsored by Baxter-Dade Inc. Formerly: Merz and Dade Award; Baxter-Dade Award.

11465

Biomerieux Award
To encourage work in research and experimentation in all areas of clinical diagnosis: microbiology, clinical chemistry, coagulation, immu-

nology, or radioimmunology. Members of a constituent member society of IAMLT are eligible. A monetary award of 8,000 French francs is awarded. The deadline for applications is November 1.

Boehringer Mannheim GmbH Award
To recognize outstanding work in the field of clinical chemistry and immunodiagnostics. Active membership in a constituent society of IAMLT is required. Entries must be submitted by November 1 to the Executive Office. A monetary award of 5,000 German marks is presented at the IAMLT Congress. Established in 1990.

Nordic Award
To enable an official representative from a constituent society of IAMLT with economical difficulties to attend the General Assembly of Delegates. Applicant must be officially appointed by his or her society to be the chief delegate at the Assembly. The deadline for applications is in November. A monetary prize of 15,000 Swedish crowns is awarded.

Ortho Diagnosis Systems Educational Award
To further the education of qualified medical technologists who are active members of IAMLT and fluent in English. Applications must be submitted by November 1. Two monetary prizes of $1,000 US each are awarded biennially.

International Association of Museums of Arms and Military History
Armemuseum
PO Box 14095
S-10441 Stockholm, Sweden
Phone: 8 6603853
Fax: 8 6626831

Honorary Member
To recognize individuals for contributions to the Association.

International Braille Chess Association
(Association Internationale des Echecs en Braille)
Box 64
S930 90 Arjeplog, Sweden
Phone: 9 6110017
Fax: 9 6111002

Chess Olympiad for the Blind
To promote individual and team tournaments in chess for the blind. Awards are given to tournament winners.

International Braille Chess Association Awards
For recognition of services rendered to the Association and its work with Braille chess.

International Commission for the Eriksson Prize Fund
Dept. of Plant & Forest Protection
Swedish Univ. of Agricultural Sciences
Box 7044
S-750 07 Uppsala, Sweden
Phone: 18 132258
Fax: 18 672890

Jakob Eriksson Prize Medal
For recognition of research in mycology, plant pathology, or virus diseases. Young researchers may be nominated. A medal is awarded every five to six years at the International Congress of Plant Pathology. Established in 1950 by The Botanical Section of the International Union of Biological Sciences in honor of Dr. Jakob Eriksson. Additional informa-

tion is available from The Royal Swedish Academy of Sciences, P.O. Box 50005, S-10 405 Stockholm, Sweden; telephone: 8 150430.

International Orienteering Federation
(Internationale Orientierungslauf Foderation)
Box 76
S-191 21 Sollentuna, Sweden
Phone: 8 353455
Fax: 8 357168

IOF Pins of Honour
To recognize officials and members of the IOF for contributions to the development and popularization of the orienteering sport, as well as to individuals working for many years, promoting various IOF activities. Silver and bronze pins are awarded. Additional information is available from Berit Pehrson.

International Powerlifting Federation
Postfack 6007
S-126 06 Hagersten, Sweden

International Powerlifting Federation Awards
To promote the sport of powerlifting internationally at World Championships for men, women, juniors, and masters. (Powerlifting consists of three lifts performed with a standard barbell: squat, bench press, and deadlift. Three attempts are made of each lift, and the highest scores in each category are added together for best total.) A Champion of Champions award is given to the athlete with the top performance of the meet. IPF medals are presented to first, second, and third place winners at World Championships. IPF participation certificates are presented to all athletes, coaches, and managers at the Championships.

IPF Hall of Fame
To honor exceptional and outstanding achievement and contributions in and to powerlifting internationally. An election of the Congress determines those elected annually with a maximum of one official and two athletes elected each year. A certificate of achievement is awarded. A maximum of 2 men and 1 woman may be admitted to the Hall of Fame each year. Established in 1977.

International Research Group on Wood Preservation
Box 5607
S-114 86 Stockholm, Sweden
Phone: 8 101453
Fax: 8 108081

Ron Cockcroft Award
To promote international wood preservation research through the Research Group by assisting selected individuals to attend IRG congresses. The award is intended to be particularly available to postgraduate students and active scientists and also non-members who otherwise cannot attend an IRG meeting. Applications must be submitted by December 31. Travel assistance is awarded annually prior to each congress. Established in 1988 in memory of Ron Cockcroft, secretary-general of the IRG.

International Union of Pure and Applied Physics
(Union Internationale de Physique Pure et Appliquee)
Gothenburg Univ.
Vasaparken
S-412 24 Goteborg, Sweden
Phone: 31 18 27 54

11484
Boltzmann Medal
To recognize outstanding achievements in thermodynamics or statistical mechanics. A gold medal is awarded triennially by the International Commission on Thermodynamics and Statistical Mechanics. Additional information is available from Prof. J.M.J. van Leeuwen, Chairman of IUPAP Com. on Thermodynamics and Statistical Mechanics (C3), Instituut-Lorentz, Nieuwsteeg 18, NL-2311 SB Leiden, Netherlands.

11485
ICO Prize
To recognize outstanding achievements in optics. Awarded annually. Established in 1982. Sponsored by the International Commission for Optics. Additional information is available from Prof. J.C. Dainty, Secretary-General of ICO, Imperial College of London, Blackett Laboratory, London SW7 2BZ, England, fax: 1 5847596.

11486
ICPE Medal for Physics Teaching
To improve the teaching of physics at all levels of education and on an international basis, and to recognize an outstanding contribution to physics education. The contribution should be major in scope and impact and should have been extended over a considerable period of time. A medal designed by the Hungarian artist Miklos Borsos is awarded biennially. Established in 1980 by the International Commission on Physics Education. Additional information is available from Prof. E.L. Jossem, Chairman of IUPAP Com. on Physics Education (C14), Department of Physics, The Ohio State University, 174 West 18th Avenue, Columbus, Ohio 43210-1106, U.S.A., fax: (614) 292-8261.

11487
London Award
For recognition of outstanding work in the field of low temperature physics. Awarded by the International Commission on Very Low Temperature Physics. Established in 1958. Additional information is available from Prof. W.F. Vinen, Chairman of IUPAP Com. on Low Temperature Physics (C5), Dept. of Physics, University of Birmingham, P.O. Box 363, Birmingham B15 2TT, United Kingdom, fax: 021 414 6709.

11488
SunAmco Medal
To recognize achievements and contributions to metrology, the measurement of atomic masses and fundamental principal constants and the units and nomenclature of physics. A medal is awarded as appropriate. Established in 1990 by IUPAP Commission C2: Sun Amco. Additional information is available from Professor A. H. Wapstra, Secretary, IUPAP Commission C2: SunAmco, National Institute for Physics and High Energy Physics, Section K, P.O. Box 41882, 1009 DB Amsterdam, Netherlands.

11489
Kaleidoscope, Immigrant Filmmakers Association
(Kaleidoscope, Ivandrar Filmarnas forening)
PO Box 2260
S-103 16 Stockholm, Sweden   Phone: 8 19 31 89

11490
Kaleidoscope Immigrantfilmfestival
To recognize short films by and about immigrants and to help them reach a wider audience. Films suitable for inclusion in the festival may be in two categories: those taking up questions concerning immigration, immigration problems and knowledge concerning immigrants; and films on other free topics. The following prizes are awarded: (1) Grand Prix; (2) Diploma of Honour; (3) Best Documentary; (4) Special Prize of the Jury; (5) Honourable Mention; and (6) The Kaleidoscope Prize. A trophy and diplomas are awarded biennially. Established in 1982. Sponsored by the Swedish Film Institute and other cultural administrations and organizations.

11491
National Association of Swedish Architects
(Svenska Arkitekters Riksforbund)
Norrlandsgatan 18, 2 tr   Phone: 8 6792760
S-111 43 Stockholm, Sweden   Fax: 8 6114930

11492
Kasper Salin Prize
(Kasper Salinpriset)
For recognition of the best Swedish architecture. Any building completed during the preceding year is eligible for consideration. A plaque is awarded annually. Established in 1961 by the Kasper Salin Foundation in memory of Kasper Salin, a city planning architect of Stockholm, Sweden (1898-1919).

11493
Nobel Foundation
(Nobelstiftelsen)
PO Box 5232
Sturegatan 14   Phone: 8 663 09 20
S-102 45 Stockholm, Sweden   Fax: 8 660 38 47

11494
Bank of Sweden Prize in Memory of Alfred Nobel
For recognition of contributions in the field of economic sciences. A monetary prize of 6,700,000 Swedish kronor in 1993, a gold medal and a diploma are awarded annually by the Royal Swedish Academy of Sciences. Instituted in 1968 by the Central Bank of Sweden at their tercentary, which placed an annual amount of money at the disposal of the Nobel Foundation as the basis for a prize to be awarded in economic sciences.

11495
Nobel Peace Prize
To recognize an individual who is a champion of peace, and who has done the most for the promotion of the fraternity of nations, for the abolition or reduction of standing armies, and for the holding and promotion of peace congresses. A monetary prize of 6,700,000 Swedish kronor in 1993, a gold medal, and a diploma are awarded annually by the Norwegian Nobel Committee, 19 Drammensveien, N-0255 Oslo 2, Norway. First awarded in 1901.

11496
Nobel Prize for Chemistry
To recognize the individual who has made the most important discovery or improvement in the field of chemistry. A monetary prize of 6,700,000 Swedish kronor in 1993, a gold medal, and a diploma are awarded annually. First awarded in 1901. Presented by the Royal Swedish Academy of Sciences, PO Box 50005, S-1043 05 Stockholm.

11497
Nobel Prize for Literature
To recognize a person who has produced the most distinguished work of an idealistic nature in the field of literature. Authors, regardless of nationality, are considered for their complete work. A monetary prize of 6,700,000 Swedish kronor in 1993, a gold medal, and a diploma are awarded annually. First awarded in 1901. Presented by the Swedish Academy, Box 2118, S-103 13 Stockholm.

11498
Nobel Prize for Physics
To recognize an individual who has made the most important discovery or improvement in the domain of physics. A monetary prize of 6,700,000 Swedish kronor in 1993, a gold medal, and a diploma are awarded annually. First awarded in 1901. Presented by the Royal Swedish Academy of Sciences, Box 50005, S-104 05 Stockholm.

11499
Nobel Prize for Physiology or Medicine
To recognize an individual who has made the most important discovery in the field of physiology and medicine. A monetary prize of 6,000,000 Swedish kronor in 1991, a gold medal and a diploma are awarded annually. Established in 1895 and first awarded in 1901. The prize is presented by the Nobel Assembly at the Karolinska Institute, Box 60250, S-104 01 Stockholm.

11500
NOMUS - Nordic Music Committee
(NOMUS - Nordisk Musikkomite)
Schonfeldts grand 1 Phone: 8 7914680
S-111 27 Stockholm, Sweden Fax: 8 213468

11501
Nordic Council Music Prize
(Nordisk Rads Musikpris)
To recognize a living Nordic composer for a recent musical work and in alternate years a living Nordic performer. The selection is made by NOMUS - Nordic Music Committee, which is an expert committee consisting of two members from each Nordic country. Candidates for the prize are nominated by the delegates of the respective countries. A monetary prize of 200,000 Danish kroner is awarded annually. Established in 1965. Sponsored by the Nordic Council.

11502
Nordic Council (Sweden)
(Nordiska Radet - Sweden)
PO Box 2082 Phone: 8 7865040
S-103 12 Stockholm, Sweden Fax: 8 105429

11503
Nordic Council Literature Prize
(Nordiska Radets Litteraturpris)
To increase the interest in the literature of the Nordic countries. Works by living authors from Nordic countries (Denmark, Finland, Greenland, Iceland, Norway, and Sweden), which have been produced during the preceding two years are eligible. The literary work may be in one of the languages of the Nordic region, including Faeroese, Greenlandic, and Sami. A monetary prize of 200,000 Danish kroner is presented annually at the time of the Nordic Council's session. Established in 1962 by the Nordic governments.

11504
Nordic Council Music Prize
To increase the interest in the music of the Nordic countries. Awarded biennially.

11505
Olof Palme Memorial Fund for International Understanding and Common Security
Sveavagen 68 Phone: 8 7002600
S-105 60 Stockholm, Sweden Fax: 8 204257

11506
Olof Palme Memorial Fund Scholarships
To encourage the study of peace and disarmament and for work against racism and hostility to foreigners. Scholarships are awarded annually. Established in 1986.

11507
Olof Palme Prize
For recognition of an outstanding achievement in the areas of peace, disarmament, international understanding and common security. The Board of the Fund makes the selection. A monetary prize and diploma are awarded annually. Established in 1987 in honor of Olof Palme, former Prime Minister of Sweden.

11508
Right Livelihood Awards Foundation
Administrative Office
PO Box 15072 Phone: 8 7020340
S-10465 Stockholm, Sweden Fax: 8 7020338

11509
Right Livelihood Award
To honor and support those working on exemplary and practical solutions to the real problems in the world today, thereby forming an essential contribution to making life more whole and healing our planet. The awards have become known as the Alternative Nobel Prize. Selection is by a jury that accepts nominations (no self-nomination). Three monetary prizes totaling $200,000 and one honorary award are presented annually on December 9 in Stockholm, Sweden. The cash prizes are for a specific project, not for personal use. Established in 1980 by Jakob von Uexkull, a Swedish-German writer and philatelic expert, who is Chairman of the Foundation and a former member of the European Parliament. Additional information is available from the Right Livelihood Award Stiftelsen, Kerstin Bennett, Admin. Dir.

11510
Royal Academy of Fine Arts
(Kungl. Akademien for de Fria Konsterna)
Box 16317 Phone: 8 232945
S-103 26 Stockholm, Sweden Fax: 8 7905924

11511
Sergel Prize
(Sergelpriset)
To recognize the most prominent Swedish sculptor. A monetary prize of 5,000 Swedish kronor and a gold medal are awarded every five years. Established in 1943 in memory of Johan Tobias Sergel, sculptor (1740-1814).

11512
Royal Physiographical Society of Lund
(Kungliga Fysiografiska Sallskapet i Lund)
Stortorget 6 Phone: 46 132528
S-222 23 Lund, Sweden Fax: 46 131944

11513
Engestromska medaljen for tillampad naturvetenskap
For recognition in the field of applied science. A medal is awarded triennially. Established in 1917.

11514
Fabian Gyllenbergs pris
For recognition of the best thesis in the field of chemistry in the last three years at the University of Lund. Awarded triennially. Established in 1972.

11515
Assar Haddings pris
For recognition in the field of geology. Awarded triennially. Established in 1959.

11516
Bengt Jonssons pris
For recognition of meritorious work in the field of botany by young scientists at the University of Lund. Awarded every five years. Established in 1940.

11517

Linnemedaljen for botanik
For recognition in the field of botany. A medal is awarded triennially. Established in 1939.

11518

Linneprisen
For recognition in the fields of botany and zoology. Awarded triennially. Established in 1935.

11519

Minnesmedaljen i guld
For recognition of outstanding merit in the fields of science and medicine. Established in 1915.

11520

Thunbergmedaljen
For recognition in the field of physiology. Scandinavian scientists are eligible. A medal is awarded biennially. Established in 1954.

11521

Wilhelm Westrups beloning
For recognition in the field of applied science, especially benefitting the economy of the Swedish province of Skane (Scania). Awarded every five years. Established in 1923.

11522

Royal Swedish Academy of Engineering Sciences
(Ingenjorsvetenskapsakademien)
Box 5073
S-102 42 Stockholm, Sweden
Phone: 8 7912900
Fax: 8 6115623

11523

Brinell Medal
For research and publication in mining, metallurgy, and processing of iron and steel. A gold medal is awarded every second or third year upon the academy's anniversary. Established as an international prize in 1954.

11524

De Lavalforelasning
To recognize a person who worked on the turbine technique or the technique of separation. A gold medal was awarded biennially. The recipient was invited to deliver a lecture. Established in 1968. (Discontinued in 1984)

11525

Axel F. Enstrommedalj
To recognize persons who, without necessarily being scientists, were responsible for successfully promoting technical research and development in private and governmental service. A gold medal with a portrait of Axel Enstrom, first leader of the academy, was awarded when merited. Established in 1958. (Discontinued in 1989)

11526

Gold Plaque
For recognition of meritorious work in the service of scientific or technological research. A gold plaque is awarded annually. Established in 1951.

11527

Great Gold Medal
This, the highest award of the academy, is given to recognize outstanding scientific and technological achievements within the academy's sphere of activity. The Great Gold Medal is awarded to a member of the academy when merited. Another medal, the Gold Medal, is given for meritorious contributions in the academy's sphere of activity. Awarded annually. Established in 1921.

11528

Axel Ax:son Johnson Lecture
To recognize a prominent scientist. The recipient is invited to give a lecture in the field of energy or fuel. A silver plaquette is awarded triennially. Established in 1955.

11529

Royal Swedish Academy of Music
Blasieholmstorg 8
S-111 Stockholm, Sweden

11530

Polar Music Prize
To recognize contributions to music. A monetary prize is awarded biennially. Established in 1992 by Stig Anderson, the man behind the pop group, ABBA.

11531

Royal Swedish Academy of Sciences
(Kungl. Vetenskapsakademien)
PO Box 50005
S-104 05 Stockholm, Sweden
Phone: 8 150430
Fax: 8 155670

11532

Adelskoldska Medaljen
For outstanding invention or work in the technical sciences. Awarded once in a ten-year period.

11533

Aldre Linnemadeljen i guld
For recognition of outstanding service to the Academy or its related institutions. A silver medal is also awarded to persons in Sweden or foreign countries.

11534

Arnbergska Priset
For recognition of outstanding work on the technical, economic, or statistical sciences. Awarded in varying years as set by the Academy.

11535

Berzeliusmedaljen i guld
For recognition in the field of science.

11536

Carl XVI Gustavs Medalj
To recognize Swedish or foreign citizens for outstanding contributions regarding the environment or written work on that topic.

11537

Crafoord Prize
For recognition of excellence in mathematics, astronomy, biosciences (particularly ecology), geosciences, and polyarthritis. A monetary prize of $125,000 and a gold medal are awarded annually. Established in 1980 by Anna-Greta and Holger Crafoord, chairman of the medical supply firm Gambro AB, to help the areas of science not covered by the Nobel prizes.

11538

Edlundska Priset
For outstanding research in mathematics, astronomy, physics, or chemistry. Swedish citizens are eligible.

11539

Jakob Eriksson Prize
For recognition of research in mycology, plant pathology, or virus diseases. Young researchers may be nominated. A medal is awarded every five to six years at the International Botanical Congress. Estab-

lished in 1950 by the Botanical Section of the International Union of Biological Sciences in honor of Dr. Jakob Eriksson. Additional information is available from Prof. Vilhelm Umaerus, Chairman of the International Commission for the Eriksson Prize Fund, P.O. Box 7044, S-750 07 Uppsala, Sweden.

11540
Hilda och Alfred Erikssons Pris
For recognition of outstanding research into the aid of suffering in man or animals. Swedish citizens are eligible. Awarded annually.

11541
Flormanska Beloningen
For recognition of an outstanding printed thesis in anatomy or physiology. Swedish citizens are eligible. Awarded when decreed by the Academy.

11542
Gregori Aminoffs Pris
For recognition of an outstanding thesis on a theme in crystallography.

11543
Letterstedtska Forfattarpriset
For recognition of outstanding original work in the fields of literature, science, or the arts, or an invention of practical value to humanity. Swedish citizens are eligible. Awarded annually.

11544
Letterstedtska Medaljen i guld
For recognition in the field of science.

11545
Letterstedtska Priset for Oversattningar
For recognition of the translation to Swedish of an excellent foreign work in the field of literature, industry, science, or young people's education. Awarded annually.

11546
Lindbomska Beloningen
For recognition of particularly meaningful work in physics or chemistry.

11547
Lovenmedaljen
For recognition of outstanding work in the zoological sciences. Swedish citizens are eligible.

11548
Naturskyddsmedaljen
For recognition of outstanding work in conservation.

11549
Nobel Prizes
The Nobel Prizes in physics and chemistry have been awarded by the Academy since their inception in 1901. Since 1968 the Prize in Economic Sciences in Memory of Alfred Nobel has also been awarded by the Academy. The prize-giving ceremony takes place on December 10, the anniversary of Nobel's death. (The prizes are described under the Nobel Foundation in Sweden.)

11550
Soderbergs Pris
To recognize a Swedish citizen or resident of Sweden for outstanding work in economic science or law.

11551
Soderstromska Medaljen i guld (Soderstrom Gold Medal)
To recognize outstanding contributions within the national economic field. Members of the Academy nominate candidates and decide the winners. A gold medal is awarded annually. Established in 1904 by a donation from Carl Christian Soderstrom.

11552
Sparreska Priset
For recognition of outstanding scientific accomplishment or research. Recipients must be under 25 years of age. Awarded once within a five-year period.

11553
Stockholm Water Prize
To stimulate and reward distinguished achievements in the field of water management. Laureates may include individuals, companies, or organizations. Achievements rewarded may be political, technological, practical, or pedagogical. The winner of the prize is chosen each year by a nominating committee. A monetary prize of $150,000 is awarded annually. Co-sponsored by the International Association on Water Pollution Research and Control (IAWPRC), the International Water Supply Association (IWSA) and the Worldwide Fund for nature (WWF).

11554
Stora Linnemedaljen i guld
For recognition of outstanding research by a Swedish scientist in the fields of botany or zoology. Awarded triennially.

11555
Stromer-Ferrnerska Beloningen
To recognize a Swedish scientist for outstanding scientific work in the field of mathematics. Awarded as decreed by the Academy.

11556
Sture Centerwalls Pris
To recognize conservationists who best promote the protection of animal life in Sweden.

11557
Svante Arrhenius Medaljen
To recognize native or foreign scientists in physics or chemistry for outstanding research. Awarded every fifth year.

11558
Verner von Heidenstams Guldmedalj
For recognition of meaningful work and dedication to the relief of animal suffering, particularly during severe winters. Awarded annually.

11559
Wahlbergska Minnesmedaljen i guld
For recognition of accomplishment in the natural sciences. Open to Swedish or foreign citizens. Awarded every fifth year.

11560
Wallmarkska Priset
For recognition of an invention or accomplishment that promotes progress in the areas of mathematics, astronomy, applied mechanics, physics, chemistry, minerology, or technology. Awarded annually.

11561
The Scandinavian Journal of Economics
Dept. of Economics
Univ. of Stockholm
S-106 91 Stockholm, Sweden
Phone: 8 163042
Fax: 8 159061

11562
David Davidson Prize in Economics
To provide recognition for the most outstanding contribution published in *The Scandinavian Journal of Economics* during the preceding two year period. Regularly submitted articles by Nordic authors who are citizens of Denmark, Finland, Iceland, Norway, and/or Sweden are eligible. A mone-

tary prize is awarded biennially. Established in 1971 in memory of David Davidson, a Swedish economist and founder of *Ehonomisk Tidskrift* (now *The Scandinavian Journal of Economics*) in 1899.

11563

**Scandinavian Research Council for Criminology
(Nordiska Samarbetsradet for Kriminologi)**
University of Oslo
Faculty of Law, Dept. of Criminology
N-0162 Oslo, Sweden
Phone: 22 859300
Fax: 22 859346

11564

Scandinavian Research Council for Criminology Awards
To recognize contributions in the field of criminology. The Council bestows research grants and awards annually.

11565

**Scandinavian Society for Plant Physiology
(Societas Physiologiae Plantarum Scandinavica)**
Dept. of Botany
Univ. of Stockholm
S-106 91 Stockholm, Sweden
Phone: 8 163765
Fax: 8 165525

11566

**Framstaende Popularvetenskapug Publicering I Vaxtfyscologi
(Distinguished Popular Scientific Publishing of Plant Physiology)**
To recognize individuals who promote the knowledge of plant physiology to the general public. Scandinavians are eligible. Awarded triennially when merited. Established in 1976.

11567

Sjostrands Forlag
Hasselby Strandvag 22
S-162 39 Vallingby, Sweden
Phone: 8 38 38 56
Fax: 8 98 46 45

11568

**Golden Cat Award
(Arets Katt)**
For recognition of outstanding achievements in the field of children's and young adult literature. A jury consisting of three persons makes the selection. Applications are not accepted. A round trip to Stockholm with a three to four days stay and a statuette are awarded annually. Established in 1984 by Sjostrands Forlag AB and Ulla-Britt Sjostrand.

11569

Svenska Dagbladet
Ralambsvagen 7
S-105 17 Stockholm, Sweden
Phone: 8 135000
Fax: 8 523497

11570

Design Management Prize
To encourage Swedish companies to work with design management as means of competition and strategy and to recognize a company which is treating all the aspects of design in a skillful and creative way. A crystal sculpture is awarded biennially. Established in 1988 by *Svenska Dagbladet* and Svensk Form.

11571

Gold Medal
For recognition of the year's foremost athletic accomplishment. A gold medal is awarded annually by the daily paper, *Svenska Dagbladet*. Established in 1925.

11572

Literary Award
To encourage an outstanding individual contribution to Swedish literature during the preceding year. A monetary prize of 25,000 Swedish kronor is awarded annually. Established in 1944.

11573

Opera Prize
To encourage Swedish opera and ballet, and to recognize outstanding contributions in these fields during the preceding theatre season. A monetary prize of 10,000 Swedish kronor is awarded annually. Established in 1977.

11574

Poppe Prize
To encourage high quality contributions within revue, cabaret, and show business. Comedians are eligible. A sculpture representing Nils Poppe, made by the artist Thomas Qvarsebo, is awarded annually in June. Established in 1984 for the legendary Swedish comedian, Nils Poppe, who was the first to receive the award.

11575

Stockholm Prize
To support the development of the inner city environment and also other attractive parts of the country, and to recognize the persons who have contributed with the most qualified proposals. A monetary prize of 50,000 Swedish kronor is awarded annually.

11576

Thalia Prize
To encourage Swedish theatre design, and to recognize contributions during the preceding theatre season. A monetary prize of 10,000 Swedish kronor is awarded annually. Established in 1951.

11577

**Sweden
Chancery of the Royal Orders
(Sweden
Utrikesdepartementet)**
Royal Palace
S-111 30 Stockholm, Sweden

11578

Gold Medal of the Royal Order of the Polar Star
For recognition of personal services rendered to Sweden or Swedish interests. The medal can be awarded only to foreign citizens. Established in 1986.

11579

Royal Order of the Polar Star
For recognition of personal services rendered to Sweden or Swedish interests. The Order is divided into the following classes: Commander Grand Cross, Commander First Class, Commander, Officer or Member of the First Class, Officer, or Member. Foreign citizens are eligible. Awarded when merited. Established in 1748 to reward contributions, civic merits, and services rendered by civil servants or men of letters and science, to the Swedish nation. From 1975 on, this award has been conferred only upon foreign citizens.

11580

Royal Order of the Seraphim
For recognition of personal services to Sweden or for the promotion of Swedish interests. The Order has one class only with the dignity of Knight or Member. Foreign heads of state or persons of equal status are eligible. Awarded when merited. Established in 1748 to recognize distinguished service to the King or to Sweden. From 1975 on, this award has been conferred only upon a foreign head of state or a person of equal status.

11581
Swedish Academy
(Svenska Akademien)
PO Box 2118
S-103 13 Stockholm, Sweden
Phone: 8 106524
Fax: 8 244225

11582
Carl Akermarks stipendium
For recognition of outstanding achievements in Swedish theatre. Five monetary prizes of 20,000 Swedish kronor are awarded annually. Established in 1984 by Carl Akermark.

11583
Ida Backmans stipendium
For recognition of a work of Swedish literature or journalism that represents an idealistic view of the world. A monetary prize of 50,000 Swedish kronor is awarded biennially. Established in 1953 by Ida Backman in memory of the Swedish writers, Gustaf Froding (1860-1911) and Selma Lagerlof (1858-1940).

11584
Bellmanpriset
To recognize a truly outstanding Swedish poet. A monetary prize of 100,000 Swedish kronor is awarded annually. Established in 1920 by the Swedish painter, Anders Zorn.

11585
Beskowska resestipendiet
For recognition of a literary work by a Swedish writer. A monetary prize of 30,000 Swedish kronor for travel expenses is awarded biennially. Established in 1873 by Bernhard von Beskow.

11586
Blomska stipendiet
For recognition of scientific work on the Swedish language. A monetary prize of 25,000 Swedish kronor is awarded annually. Established in 1945 by Edward and Eva Blom.

11587
Gerard Bonniers Pris
To recognize writers working within a field of interest of the Academy. A monetary prize of 100,000 Swedish kronor is awarded annually. Established in 1988 by Gerard Bonnier.

11588
Doblougska priset
For recognition of outstanding literary works by Norwegian and Swedish writers. Two monetary prizes of 60,000 Swedish kronor each are awarded annually for each category. Established in 1951.

11589
Signe Ekblad-Eldhs pris
To recognize an eminent Swedish writer. A monetary prize of 80,000 Swedish kronor is awarded annually. Established in 1960.

11590
Lydia och Herman Erikssons stipendium
For recognition of poetry or prose by a Swedish author. A monetary prize of 60,000 Swedish kronor is awarded biennially. Established in 1976.

11591
Karin Gierows pris for hangiven bildningsverksamhet
To recognize dedicated individuals who promote the spread of information on Swedish culture. Writers, journalists, and teachers are eligible. Two monetary prizes of 25,000 Swedish kronor each are awarded annually. Established in 1976 by Karl Ragnar Gierow.

11592
Karin Gierows pris for kunskapsformedlande framstallningskonst
To recognize Swedish journalists who promote knowledge by means of writing. Three monetary prizes of 25,000 Swedish kronor each are awarded annually. Established in 1976 by Karl Ragnar Gierow.

11593
Gun och Olof Engqvists stipendium
For recognition of a work of Swedish literature, or to recognize a journalist who writes about Swedish culture. A monetary prize of 100,000 Swedish kronor is awarded annually. Established in 1975 by Gun and Olof Engqvist.

11594
Axel Hirschs pris
For recognition of biographical or historical work by Swedish writers or scientists. Monetary prizes totaling 140,000 Swedish kronor are awarded annually. Established in 1967.

11595
Kallebergerstipendiet
For recognition of a work of prose or poetry. A monetary prize of 30,000 Swedish kronor is awarded annually. Established in 1977 by Gosta Ronnstrom and Tekla Hansson.

11596
Kellgrenpriset
For recognition of important achievements in any of the fields of the Academy. A monetary prize of 75,000 Swedish kronor is awarded annually. Established in 1980 by Karl Ragnar Gierow.

11597
Ilona Kohrtz' stipendium
For recognition of a work of prose or poetry in Swedish. A monetary prize of 20,000 Swedish kronor is awarded annually. Established in 1962.

11598
Kungliga priset
For recognition of a contribution to Swedish culture or for a literary or artistic work. A monetary prize of 40,000 Swedish kronor is awarded annually. Established in 1835 by King Karl XIV Johan of Sweden.

11599
Margit Pahlsons pris
For recognition of works on linguistics or Swedish language cultivation. A monetary prize of 100,000 Swedish kronor is awarded annually. Established in 1981 by Ms. Margit Pahlson.

11600
Birger Scholdstroms pris
For recognition of a work on the history of literature, or for a biography written by a Swedish author. A monetary prize of 30,000 Swedish kronor is awarded every four years. Established in 1960.

11601
Schuckska priset
For recognition of a work on the history of Swedish literature. A monetary prize of 60,000 Swedish kronor is awarded annually. Established in 1946.

11602
Stiftelsen Natur och Kulturs oversattarpris
For recognition of good translations of foreign literature into Swedish or of Swedish literature into foreign languages. Two monetary prizes of 30,000 Swedish kronor are awarded annually. Established in 1985 by the Natur och Kultur Foundation.

11603
Stipendium ur Lena Vendelfelts minnesfond
For recognition of a literary work, particularly poetry. A monetary prize of 30,000 Swedish kronor is awarded annually. Established in 1981 by Mr. and Mrs. Erik Vendelfelt.

11604
Stora priset
For recognition of an outstanding contribution to Swedish culture. A gold medal is awarded when merited. During the 20th century, 20 persons received the medal. Established in 1786 by King Gustavus III of Sweden.

11605
Svenska Akademiens Finlandspris
For recognition of important achievements in promotion of Swedish culture in Finland. Finnish citizens are eligible. A monetary prize of 50,000 Swedish kronor is awarded annually. Established in 1966.

11606
Svenska Akademiens nordiska pris
For recognition of important achievements in any of the fields of interest of the Academy. Citizens of any of the Scandinavian countries are eligible. A monetary prize of 250,000 Swedish kronor is awarded annually. Established in 1986 by the Academy in connection with its 200th anniversary.

11607
Svenska Akademiens oversattarpris
For recognition of the best translations of foreign literature into the Swedish language. Translations in other humanistic disciplines are also eligible. A monetary prize of 30,000 Swedish kronor is awarded annually. Established in 1953.

11608
Svenska Akademiens sprakvardspris
For recognition of outstanding works on linguistics or language cultivation by a Swedish author. A monetary prize of 25,000 Swedish kronor is awarded annually. Established in 1953.

11609
Svenska Akademiens svensklararpris
To recognize teachers for stimulating young people's interest in the Swedish language and literature. Two monetary prizes of 25,000 Swedish kronor each are awarded annually. Established in 1987 by the Crafoord Foundation.

11610
Svenska Akademiens teaterpris
To recognize actors, actresses, producers, and playwrights who have made outstanding achievements in the Swedish theater. A monetary prize of 40,000 Swedish kronor is awarded annually. Established in 1963.

11611
Svenska Akademiens tolkningspris
For recognition of translations of Swedish literature into foreign languages. A monetary prize of 30,000 Swedish kronor is awarded annually. Established in 1965.

11612
Zibetska priset
For recognition of a work on the history or culture of the period of King Gustavus III, or for a literary work with special regard to this period. A monetary prize of 30,000 Swedish kronor is awarded approximately every second year. Established in 1809 in memory of King Gustavus III.

11613
Zornska priset
For recognition of an outstanding literary work. A monetary prize of 20,000 Swedish kronor was awarded annually. Established in 1969. (Discontinued)

11614
Swedish Academy of Pharmaceutical Sciences
(Apotekarsocieteten)
PO Box 1136
S-111 81 Stockholm, Sweden
Phone: 8 245080
Fax: 8 205511

11615
Scheele-priset
(Scheele Award)
For recognition of outstanding scientific contributions in the field of pharmaceutical sciences. Nominations must be submitted by March 1. A monetary prize of 100,000 Swedish kroner and a medal are awarded and the winner presents the Scheele Memorial Lecture. Awarded annually in October in connection with the annual congress. Established in 1961 in memory of C. W. Scheele (1742-1786).

11616
Swedish Association for Water Hygiene
(Foreningen for Vattenhygien)
Valsarevagen 8
S-155 00 Nykvarn, Sweden
Phone: 75 54 09 41

11617
FVH-priset
(FVH Award)
For recognition of a person (or group of persons) in the Nordic countries who by idea, construction, practical application, research, or thesis served the development of water management. Nordic citizenship is necessary for consideration. A plaque is awarded annually. Established in 1986.

11618
Swedish Authors' Fund
(Sveriges Forfattarfond)
Schonfeldts grand 1-3
S-111 27 Stockholm, Sweden
Phone: 8 7914780
Fax: 8 206178

11619
Swedish Authors' Fund Awards
To recognize authors, translators, and illustrators who have made special contributions within their own fields. Awards of 20,000 Swedish kronor each are awarded annually. The main purpose of the fund is to administer the Swedish system of library loan compensation to authors, translators, and book illustrators.

11620
Swedish Economic Association
(Nationalekonomiska Foreningen)
Stockholm School of Economics
c/o Anders Paalzow
PO Box 6501
S-113 83 Stockholm, Sweden
Phone: 8 162225
Fax: 8 313207

11621
Gunnar Myrdal Prize
(Gunnar Myrdals och sparbankernas pris for basta artikel)
For recognition of the best article in *Ekonomisk Debatt*. A monetary prize is awarded annually. Established in 1984 by Svenska Sparbanksforeningen in honor of Gunnar Myrdal, the Swedish economist and social scientist.

11622

Swedish Federation of Film and Video Amateurs
(Sveriges Film- och Videoamatorer)
Abiskovagen 18
S-162 25 Vallingby, Sweden
Phone: 8 7391543
Fax: 8 330218

11623

UNICA Medal
(UNICA-medaljen)
To recognize an individual or an organization that has contributed to the spread of amateur film/video making. Nominations are accepted. A medal is awarded annually. Established in 1986.

11624

Swedish Film Institute
(Svenska Filminstitutet)
Filmhuset
Borgvagen 1-5
PO Box 27126
S-102 52 Stockholm, Sweden
Phone: 8 6651140
Fax: 8 6611820

11625

Ingmar Bergman Plaquette
For recognition of an outstanding artistic and/or technical contribution to the cinematographic art. Swedish or foreign filmmakers are eligible. A plaquette and travel allowance are awarded annually. Established in 1978.

11626

Golden Bug Statuette
(Guldbaggar)
For recognition of meritorious contributions to Swedish film. Awards are given in the following categories: Best Picture, Best Director, Best Actor, and Best Actress, Best Manuscript, Best Cameraman, and Best Foreign Film. Three additional awards may be given for important contributions to the Swedish cinema. Seven to ten Golden Bug Statuettes are awarded annually. Established in 1963.

11627

Robin Hood Plaquette
To provide recognition for historical research in the field of the cinema. A plaquette is awarded annually when there is a suitable candidate. Established in 1974.

11628

Swedish Insurance Society
(Svenska Forsakringsforeningen)
Slojdgafan 9
S-115 87 Stockholm, Sweden
Phone: 8 242860
Fax: 8 241320

11629

Arets pris i svensk forsakring
For recognition of achievement in the sound development of the Swedish insurance industry. A monetary prize and a diploma are awarded annually. Established in 1970.

11630

Swedish Library Association
(Sveriges Allmanna Biblioteksforening)
PO Box 3127
S-103 62 Stockholm, Sweden
Phone: 8 7230082
Fax: 8 7230038

11631

Aniara Prize
(Aniara Priset)
For recognition of the best book written in Swedish by a Swedish author. A trophy is awarded annually. Established in 1974 in honor of Swedish author, Harry Martinsson, and his book *Aniara*.

11632

Elsa Beskow Plaque
(Elsa Beskow Plaketten)
To recognize the illustrator of the best children's book published during the preceding year. A plaque of glass is awarded annually. Established in 1958 in honor of Elsa Beskow, well known children's book designer.

11633

Nils Holgersson Plaque
(Nils Holgersson Plaketten)
To recognize the author of the best book for youth published during the preceding year. A plaque of glass is awarded annually. Established in 1950 in honor of Swedish author, Selma Lagerlof.

11634

Swedish Mathematical Society
(Svenska Matematikersamfundet)
Dept. of Mathematics
Royal Institute of Technology
S-10044 Stockholm, Sweden
Phone: 8 7906148
Fax: 8 7231788

11635

Swedish Mathematical Society Fellowship
(Wallenbergstipendiet)
To recognize younger mathematicians. Selection is by nomination; no applications are accepted. A monetary award is presented annually. Established in 1983. Sponsored by Wallenbergs Stiftelse.

11636

Swedish Section of the International Board on Books for Young People
(Barn-och ungdomsboksradet)
Odengat 61
S-113 22 Stockholm, Sweden

11637

Gulliver Award
For recognition in the field of children's literature. Selection is made by nomination. A monetary prize and a diploma are awarded annually. Established in 1969 to commemorate *Gulliver's Travels*. Sponsored by different publishing houses. Additional information is available from Birgitta Fransson, Vikbyvagen 9, S-181 43 Lidingo, Sweden, telephone: 8 7659280.

11638

Swedish Society Against Painful Experiments on Animals
(Nordiska Samfundet Mot Plagsamma Dourfarsak)
Edelcrantzvagen 2
S-129 38 Hagersten, Sweden
Phone: 8 880790
Fax: 8 6465470

11639

Anti-Prize
(Anti-Priset)
For recognition of the worst possible achievement in animal experiments during the year. Animal experimenters, individual or company, are considered. A disarmed rat trap and a plaque citing the reason for choice of recipient are awarded annually at the general assembly. Established in 1984.

11640
Positive Prize
(Positiva Priset)
For recognition of long-standing in the struggle for animal rights. Individuals who perform deeds in the interests of animals are eligible. Diverse objects and a plaque are awarded annually at the general assembly. Established in 1987.

11641
Swedish Society for Promotion of Literature
(Stiftelsen Litteraturframjandet)
Alsonogatan 11 Phone: 8 7437340
S-116 85 Stockholm, Sweden Fax: 8 7430315

Defunct organization.

11642
Children's Book Prize
To provide recognition for writers and illustrators of books for children. A monetary prize of 20,000 Swedish kronor was divided among various prize recipients. Awarded annually. (Discontinued in 1992)

11643
Carl-Emil Englund Prize
To provide recognition for the best collection of Swedish poems of the year. A monetary prize of 25,000 Swedish kronor was awarded annually. (Discontinued in 1992)

11644
Grand Prize for a Novel
To provide recognition for the best Swedish novel of the year. A monetary prize of 25,000 Swedish kronor was awarded annually. (Discontinued in 1992)

11645
Grand Prize for Literature
For recognition of outstanding literary work written in Swedish. A monetary prize of 50,000 Swedish kronor was awarded annually. (Discontinued in 1992)

11646
Testimonial Prize
To provide recognition for an individual of outstanding culture, especially in the field of literature. A golden miniature sculpture was awarded annually. (Discontinued in 1992)

11647
Swedish Society of Aeronautics and Astronautics
(Flygtekniska Foreningen)
Rymdbolaget
PO Box 4207 Phone: 8 6276298
S-171 54 Solna, Sweden Fax: 8 987069

11648
Jetfoundation
(Jetfonden)
For recognition of advances in the economics and safety of jet flying in its widest meaning. Individuals working in Sweden are eligible. A monetary prize is awarded annually. Established in 1984 by Tord Angstrom, other individuals, and other companies.

11649
Thulinmedaljen
For recognition of outstanding achievement in the field of aeronautics. The following awards are presented: a gold medal for achievement of the highest merit; a silver medal for an independent work, thesis, or design to aeronautical development; and a bronze medal for the furtherance of the goals of the Society. Awarded annually. The bronze medal may be given more often. Established in 1944 by Tord Angstrom.

11650
Swedish Society of Crafts and Design
(Foreningen Svensk Form)
Renstiernas Gata 12 Phone: 8 6443303
S-116 28 Stockholm, Sweden Fax: 8 6442285

11651
Excellent Swedish Design Prize
(Utmarkt Svensk Form)
For recognition of outstanding Swedish design products during the preceding year. Products should be well designed and of high quality with regard to function, materials, and manufacture. The jury also takes resources and environmental factors into account. The products should be produced in quantity and available on the market. Products may be entered by application or nomination. Swedish manufacturers and designers are eligible. Plaques are awarded annually. Established in 1983. Formerly: Excellence in Swedish Design Prize.

11652
Scandinavian Design Prize
To stimulate interest in good product design, graphic design, and architecture in Scandinavian industry. The objective is to make good design a part of the strategy for future development in Scandinavian companies. The prize is awarded through national nominations from the five Scandinavian countries. Prizes are awarded in the categories of design-based business management and product design. The prize for design-based business management is awarded to a Scandinavian company that has made a mark in the three design fields of product design, graphic communication, and architecture. Established in 1992. Formerly: Design Management Prize.

11653
Uppsala Film Festival
PO Box 1746 Phone: 18 120025
S-751 47 Uppsala, Sweden Fax: 18 121350

11654
Uppsala Filmkaja
To recognize outstanding films and to encourage professional development. The dealine is August 1. Awards are presented in the following categories: Fiction Films A (maximum 20 minutes), Fiction Films B (20-60 minutes), Animation Films (maximum 60 minutes), Documentary Films (maximum 60 minutes), Experimental Films (maximum 60 minutes), and Children and Young People's Films (maximum 60 minutes). The Uppsala Filmkaja statuette, sculpted by Folke Soogren is awarded annually. Established in 1983.

Switzerland

11655
Aga Khan Trust for Culture
32, chemin des Crets-de-Pregny
Grand Saconnex Phone: 22 7989070
CH-1218 Geneva, Switzerland Fax: 22 7989391

Formerly: Aga Khan Awards Foundation.

11656
Aga Khan Award for Architecture
For recognition of architectural excellence; to nurture a heightened awareness of Islamic culture within the architectural profession, related disciplines, and society; and to encourage buildings for tomorrow's needs. In its selection process, the award committee considers the context in which architecture is practiced, and the social, economic,

technical, and environmental factors to which the project responds. Particular consideration is given to those projects that use available resources and initiatives appropriately and creatively, that meet both the functional and cultural needs of their users, and that have the potential to stimulate related development elsewhere. Projects that have been completed within the past 25 years and that have been in use for at least two years may be nominated. The projects must be located in the Islamic world or intended for use primarily by Muslims. Monetary prizes totaling $500,000 US, trophies, and certificates are awarded to those contributors including architects, construction professionals, craftsmen, and clients who are considered most responsible for the success of a project. Awarded triennially. Established in 1977 by His Highness the Aga Khan, chairman of the Awards Steering Committee.

11657

**Association des Musiciens Suisses
(Schweizerischer Tonkunstlerverein)**
Secretariat
11 bis, avenue du Grammont
CH-1000 Lausanne 13, Switzerland

Phone: 21 6166371
Fax: 21 6176382

11658

**Prix de Compositeur de l'AMS
(Komponistenpreis des STV)**
For recognition of the total work of a Swiss composer. Members of the Association are eligible. A monetary prize of 20,000 Swiss francs is awarded annually when merited. Established in 1944.

11659

**Prix de Soliste de l'AMS
(Solistenpreis des STV)**
To recognize a young Swiss soloist for the quality of the musical presentation. Awards are given each year for different instruments or for singing. Instrumentalists must be less than 30 years of age, and singers less than 32 years of age, and at the beginning of their careers. A monetary prize of 8,000 Swiss francs is awarded annually. Established in 1942.

11660

Association du Festival International du Film de Comedie de Vevey
LA GRENETTE Graude Place 29
CH-1800 Vevey, Switzerland

Phone: 21 922 20 27
Fax: 21 922 20 24

11661

Festival International du Film de Comedie de Vevey
For recognition of outstanding comedy films. Films selected for the competitive section of the Festival are eligible. The following prizes are awarded: Grand Prix de Vevey - for the best film; Prix d'interpretation - two prizes for interpretation by a man and a woman; Prix du Public; Prize for the Best Swiss film; and Prize for the Best Short Film. Canne d'Or trophies are awarded annually. Established in 1981 in memory of Charlie Chaplin, who spent 25 years in Corsier sur Vevey.

11662

Association du Festival Tibor Varga Sion - Valais
Case Postale 954
CH-1951 Sion VS, Switzerland

Phone: 27 234317
Fax: 27 234662

11663

**International Record Critics Award
(Prix International des Critiques de Disques)**
To recognize the best recording of the year. The Prix International du Disque Serge et Olga Koussevitzky was also awarded to recognize the first recording of an orchestral work by a living composer. Awarded annually at the Festival Tibor Varga. Established in 1968 by a group of international critics. Sponsored by the Ville de Sion. (Discontinued)

11664

**Tibor Varga International Competition for Violin
(Concours International de Violon Tibor Varga)**
For recognition of achievement in violin performance. Violinists between 15 and 32 years of age are eligible. The deadline for applications is May 1. The following monetary prizes are awarded: first prize - 10,000 Swiss francs by Etat du Valais; second prize - 7,500 Swiss francs by Municipalite de Sion; third prize - 5,000 Swiss francs by Bourgeoisie de Sion; fourth prize - 2,000 Swiss francs by Loterie Romande; and special prizes ranging from 1,000 to 2,000 Swiss francs. Established in 1966 by Maestro Tibor Varga.

11665

**Association for the Furtherance of Professional Women Musicians
(Verein zur Forderung von Berufsmusikerinnen)**
Postfach 118
CH-8057 Zurich, Switzerland

11666

International Women-Composer's Competition
For recognition of an outstanding composition for string chamber orchestra (12-14 players) by a woman of any nationality. Works should be 10-15 minutes in length, must be unpublished and must not have been publicly performed. The deadline for entries is September 1. A monetary prize of 2,000 Swiss francs is awarded.

11667

**Marcel Benoist Foundation
(Marcel Benoist Stiftung)**
Federal Office for Education and Science
PO Box 5675
CH-3001 Berne, Switzerland

Phone: 31 3229680
Fax: 31 3227854

11668

Marcel Benoist Prize
To recognize outstanding scientific research in Switzerland. Scholars living in Switzerland are eligible. A monetary prize is awarded annually. Established in 1920.

11669

Martin-Bodmer-Stiftung fur einen Gottfried Keller-Preis
c/o Dr. Daniel Bodmer
Ramistrasse 18
CH-8001 Zurich, Switzerland

Phone: 1 2515348

11670

Gottfried Keller Prize
To recognize writers for works on Switzerland. Selection is by nomination. A monetary award of 15,000 Swiss francs is presented biennially. Established in 1921 by Martin Bodmer.

11671

Centre de Ballet Contemporain
9, rue Juste-Olivier
CH-1260 Nyon, Switzerland

Phone: 22 61 09 39

11672

Concours International de Choregraphie du CBC, Nyon
For recognition of outstanding works of choreography in several categories. International recognition and the opportunity for performances are awarded annually. Established in 1977.

11673

CIBA-GEIGY ILAR Rheumatology Prize
c/o CIBA-GEIGY Limited
PO Box
CH-4002 Basel, Switzerland
Phone: 61 696 7859
Fax: 61 696 6029

11674

CIBA-GEIGY ILAR Rheumatology Prize
To encourage research in rheumatology within the widest meaning of the term. For recognition of an outstanding achievement in the field of rheumatology and to support the continuation of research underlying this achievement. Individuals who contribute to progress in the field of rheumatology are eligible. A monetary prize is awarded every four years.

11675

Concours Geza Anda
Bleicherweg 18
CH-8002 Zurich, Switzerland
Phone: 1 2051423
Fax: 1 2051429

11676

**Geza Anda International Piano Competition
(Concours Geza Anda)**
To sponsor young pianists in the musical spirit of Geza Anda. Pianists who are under 32 years of age are eligible. Besides concert engagements in international music centers for the three prize winners, the following monetary prizes are awarded: 30,000 Swiss francs - first prize; 20,000 Swiss francs - second prize; and 10,000 Swiss francs - third prize. The following special prizes are also awarded: the Geza Anda Audience Prize, sponsored by BALLY; and the Mozart-Prize awarded by the Zurich Opera. Awarded triennially. Established in 1978 by the Geza Anda Foundation in memory of Geza Anda, a pianist. The competition was founded by Mrs. Hortense Anda-Buhrle. The next competition will be held in June, 1994.

11677

Concours International de Composition Musicale Opera et Ballet Geneve
Radio Television Suisse Romande
Maison de la Radio
Case Postale 233
66 Boulevard Carl-Vogt
CH-1211 Geneva 8, Switzerland
Phone: 22 29 23 33
Fax: 22 781 52 18

11678

Concours International de Composition Musicale Opera et Ballet Geneve
To encourage the composition of musical and theatrical works. The Competition is designed to stimulate the creation of orchestral works of special interest in the musical and/or choreographic field with scores for ballet or alternately for opera. Composers of all ages and nationalities may submit anonymously a work which is original, unpublished, and has not been performed by September 30. A monetary prize of 20,000 Swiss francs and the possibility of production are awarded for first place, Premier Prix de Composition. Monetary prizes totaling 10,000 Swiss francs are awarded for second and third place at the discretion of the International Jury. The Competition is organized biennially by the City of Geneva and the Radio-Television Suisse Romande. (Temporarily suspended in 1993)

11679

Concours International de Musique de Chambre pour Ensembles d'Instruments a Vent
Case postale 370
CH-1920 Martigny, Switzerland
Phone: 26 2 55 14

11680

Concours International de Musique de Chambre pour Ensembles d'Instruments a Vent
For recognition of outstanding wind instrument ensembles. Ensembles of three to eight performers are eligible. Prizes totaling 20,000 Swiss francs with a first prize of 10,000 Swiss francs are awarded annually. Established in 1978.

11681

Concours National Feminin de Musique du Lyceum de Suisse
8, rue Leon-Berthoud
CH-2000 Neuchatel, Switzerland
Phone: 38 25 87 07

11682

Concours National Feminin de Musique du Lyceum de Suisse
For recognition of the best execution of contemporary music by women performers on different instruments in alternating years. Women of Swiss nationality or foreigners living in Switzerland and practicing their music in Switzerland are eligible. The following prizes are awarded: (1) First Prize - 5,000 Swiss francs; (2) Second Prize - 3,000 Swiss francs; and (3) Special Prize - 500 Swiss francs. Awarded triennially. Established in 1936.

11683

Credit Suisse
2, Place Bel-Air
PO Box 2153
CH-1211 Geneva 22, Switzerland
Phone: 22 391 21 11
Fax: 22 391 25 91

11684

**Credit Suisse Design Prize for Technical and Industrial Innovation in Geneva
(Prix Credit Suisse de la Creation technique, et industrielle a Geneve)**
To encourage applied research in Geneva by awarding the best creations in the technical and industrial fields. The creators must reside in the Canton of Geneva. A monetary prize is awarded annually. Established in 1981 on the occasion of the 75th anniversary of Credit Suisse Geneva.

11685

**E.A.F.O.R.D.
International Secretariat**
5, Rte. des Morillions, Burea No. 475
Case Postale 2100
1211 Geneva 2, Switzerland
Phone: 22 7886233
Fax: 22 7886245

Formerly: International Organisation for the Elimination of All Forms of Racial Discrimination..

11686

International Award for the Furtherance of Human Understanding
For recognition of the furtherance of human understanding in the field of literature. Applications must be submitted. A monetary award and certificate are presented periodically. Established in 1978.

11687

Editions vwa
C. P. 172
8, rue de l'Hotel-de-Ville
CH-2301 CH-2301 La Chaux-de-Fonds,
Switzerland
Phone: 39 282418
Fax: 39 282750

11688

Prix litteraire de la Ville de La Chaux-de-Fonds et de la revue vwa
To recognize outstanding literary work: novels, short stories, poems, or plays. Awards are given to authors from Switzerland and alternately:

France, Belgium, Algeria, French-speaking Canada and Senegal. For 1994, the prize is for a Swiss citizen and a citizen from Senegal living in Switzerland or Senegal. A monetary prize of 10,000 Swiss francs, a watch, and publication in the magazine *vwa* are awarded biennially. In addition, the six or eight best works are published in a special issue of the *Revue Litteraire vwq*. Established in 1986 by *vwa* magazine and the City of La Chaux-de-Fonds. Sponsored by Montres Ebel, La Chaux-de-Fonds (Ebel Watch).

11689
European Association for Signal Processing
(Association Europeenne de Traitement de Signaux)
Case Postale 134
CH-1000 Lausanne 13, Switzerland   Phone: 21 6932626

11690
European Association for Signal Processing Awards
To recognize engineers, scientists, and industrial firms for contributions to signal processing. Awards are presented biennially.

11691
European Broadcasting Union
(Union Europeene de Radio-Television)
Ancienne Route 17A
Case postale 67
CH-1218 Grand Saconnex/Geneva,   Phone: 22 7172111
  Switzerland   Fax: 22 7172481

11692
Eurovision Song Contest
To encourage the creation of original songs. Awarded annually. Established in 1955. Additional information is available from Christian Clausen, phone: 22 7172881; fax: 22 7172810.

11693
Geneva-Europe Prizes for Television Writing
To assist in discovering new talents and to stimulate the growth of audiovisual culture in Europe. The following awards are presented: the Assistance Prizes for Television Writing (bursaries) and the Grand Prize for Television Writing. The Grand Prize is awarded, at least one year after the Assistance Prizes are awarded, to the best full script based on the synopses of writers who won Assistance Prizes. Entrants may not be more than 35 years of age during the year of the Assistance Prizes competition. The following awards will be presented at a public ceremony each year: Assistance Prizes - a training period and a monetary award; and the Grand Prize for Television Writing - a monetary award and production of his/her script within the limits of available funds.

11694
European Coordinating Committee for Artificial Intelligence
ISSCO
54, route des Acacias
CH-1227 Geneva, Switzerland   Phone: 22 209333

11695
European Coordinating Committee for Artificial Intelligence Awards
To recognize and encourage scientific and technological advances in the field of artificial intelligence. Awards are bestowed biennially at the European Conference on Artificial Intelligence.

11696
European Environmental Mutagen Society
c/o F. Hoffmann LaRoche, Ltd.
CH-4002 Basel, Switzerland   Phone: 67 6884797

11697
EEMS Award
For recognition of an excellent scientific contribution in the field of environmental mutagenesis. The Council of the Society makes the selection. A monetary prize of 2,500 Swiss francs is awarded and travel expenses are awarded annually. Established in 1986.

11698
EEMS Award to Young Scientists
For recognition of creative research in the field of environmental mutagenesis by scientists who are 35 years of age or younger. The Council of the Society makes the selection. A monetary prize of 500 Swiss francs and travel expenses are awarded annually. Established in 1980.

11699
European Free Trade Association
(Association Europeenne de Libre-Echange)
Press and Information Service
9-11, rue de Varembe   Phone: 22 7491111
CH-1211 Geneva 20, Switzerland   Fax: 22 7339291

11700
EFTA Awards
To encourage young scholars to submit papers on topics within the confines of the following theme: relations between the EFTA Countries and the Emerging Market Economies in Central and Eastern Europe. This theme may be treated from different angles: economic, legal, trade policy, and political or general issues. Candidates should hold at least one university level degree and be under 30 years of age. The paper should not exceed 50 pages and must be submitted in English by August 15. The winners receive awards of between 5,000 and 10,000 Swiss francs. EFTA reserves the right to publish the winning entries.

11701
European Nuclear Society
(Europaische Kernenergie-Gesellschaft)
Postfach 5032   Phone: 31 216111
CH-3001 Bern, Switzerland   Fax: 31 229203

11702
European Nuclear Society Awards
To recognize scientific and engineering progress in the peaceful use of nuclear energy.

11703
European Physical Society
PO Box 69   Phone: 22 7931130
CH-1213 Petit-Lancy 2, Switzerland   Fax: 22 7931317

11704
Hewlett-Packard Europhysics Prize
For recognition of outstanding achievement in solid state physics. Europeans must be nominated by August 31. Nominations are submitted to the EPS Secretariat for the Selection Committee. A monetary prize of 48,000 Swiss francs and a certificate are awarded annually at the Conference. Established in 1975.

11705
High Energy and Particle Physics Prize
For recognition of important contributions to theoretical or experimental particle physics. Nominations are invited. A monetary prize is awarded biennially at the EPS HEPP Conference. Established in 1989 by the EPS High Energy and Particle Physics (HEPP) Division. Sponsored by Cray Research France, Digital Equipment Corporation Europe (Switzerland), Interatom (Federal Republic of Germany), Le Croy Corporation (USA), Philips (The Netherlands), Siemens AG (Federal Republic of Germany), and Thomson Tubes Electroniques (France).

11706

European Thyroid Association
(Association Europeenne Thyroide)
Unite de Thyroide, Lab 4-767
Hopital Cantonal Universitaire
CH-1211 Geneva 4, Switzerland
Phone: 22 227648
Fax: 22 476486

11707

European Thyroid Association Awards
To recognize physicians and research scientists who are involved in work on the thyroid gland and its diseases. Awards are presented.

11708

EUROTOX
Sandoz, Ltd.
Toxicology, Building 881
CH-4002 Basel, Switzerland
Phone: 61 62 56 47
Fax: 61 61 00 02

Formerly: (1989) European Society of Toxicology.

11709

EUROTOX Young Scientist's Poster Award
To recognize the author of the best poster in the Competition. Posters are evaluated for both scientific content and technical aspects of the presentations. Individuals under 35 years of age are eligible for consideration. A monetary prize of 1,000 Dutch guilders and a certificate are awarded annually. Established in 1974. Formerly: (1990) Young Scientist Award.

11710

Special EST Prize
For recognition of an outstanding paper describing a new toxicity test that used less animals than conventional testing. A monetary prize of 5,000 Swiss francs was awarded when merited. Established in 1984. (Discontinued in 1989)

11711

Federation Internationale de Football Association
FIFA House
Hitzigweg 11
PO Box 85
CH-8030 Zurich, Switzerland
Phone: 1 3849595
Fax: 1 3849696

11712

FIFA Futsal (Indoor Football) World Championship
To recognize the futsal (indoor football/soccer) champions. Awarded every four years. Established in 1989 in Holland. Formerly: FIFA Five-a-Side (Indoor Football) World Championship.

11713

FIFA U-17 World Championship
To recognize the football (soccer) champions in the tournament. Awarded biennially. Established in 1985 in China. Formerly: FIFA U-17 World Tournament.

11714

FIFA Women's World Football Championship
To recognize the women's football (soccer) champions. Established in Peoples' Republic of China in 1991.

11715

FIFA World Cup Trophy
For recognition of the world football (soccer) champions. A gold trophy is engraved with winning team's name and a replica in gold plate is awarded at the tournament held every four years. Established in 1930. Formerly: Jules Rimet Cup.

11716

Olympic Football Tournaments (Men and Women)
To recognize the football (soccer) champions in the Olympic Games. Awarded every four years. The Olympics were established in 1896. Football was first included in the program in 1904. Women's football tournament will be included in Atlanta 1996 Olympics.

11717

U-20 World Youth Championship for the FIFA/Coca-Cola Cup
To recognize the world youth football (soccer) champions. Awarded biennially. Established in 1977 in Tunisia.

11718

Edwin Fischer Stiftung Luzern
Reussteg 3
CH-6003 Luzern, Switzerland
Phone: 41 23 38 10

11719

Edwin Fischer Memorial Prize
(Edwin Fischer - Gedenkpreis)
To recognize outstanding students of the conservatory. To be eligible, students must have earned their concert diploma with honors. A monetary prize of 3,000 Swiss francs is awarded annually. Established in 1968 in honor of Edwin Fischer, a pianist.

11720

Fondation Armleder
Hotel Richemond
CH-1206 Geneva, Switzerland
Phone. 22 7311400
Fax: 22 7312414

11721

Prix Liberte Litteraire
A monetary prize of 35,000 Swiss francs is awarded annually. Established in 1989 in memory of Colette, a French writer. The award name changed after Salmau Rushdie's 1993 recognition by the Prix Colette. Formerly: Prix Colette.

11722

Fondation C. F. Ramuz
Case Postale 181
CH-1009 Pully, Switzerland

11723

Grand Prix C. F. Ramuz
To recognize a writer for his entire work. Swiss authors writing in the French language are eligible. A monetary prize of 15,000 Swiss francs is awarded every five years. Established in 1955.

11724

Fondation en faveur de l'Art Choregraphique
Palais de Beaulieu
Au. Bergieres 6
CH-1004 Lausanne, Switzerland
Phone: 21 6432405
Fax: 21 6432409

11725

Prix de Lausanne
To help promising young dancers between 15 and 18 years of age to embark on a professional career. Up to six scholarships for a year's study in the best schools of dance in the world and a medal are awarded. Winners choose the schools they wish to attend from a list furnished by the competition. In addition, monetary prizes and professional prizes are awarded as well as a gold medal, on occasion, to someone exceptional. Established in 1973 by Philippe Braunschweig.

Switzerland — Awards, Honors & Prizes, 1995-96

11726
Fondation Louis Jeantet de Medecine
Case postale 277
CH-1211 Geneva 17, Switzerland
Phone: 22 3105669
Fax: 22 3105669

11727
Louis Jeantet Prize for Medicine
(Prix Louis Jeantet de Medecine)
To enable researchers to continue biomedical research projects, either fundamental or clinical, of a very high level. Individuals or groups must be proposed by scientists, doctors, or institutions who are familiar with the work of the candidates. To be eligible, researchers must be working in a European country that is a member of the Council of Europe. The deadline for entry is February 15. Monetary awards totaling 2 million Swiss francs are awarded annually. Established in 1986.

11728
Fondation Schiller Suisse
(Schweizerische Schillerstiftung)
Im Ring 2
CH-8126 Zumikon, Switzerland
Phone: 1 9182580

11729
Grosser Schillerpreis
For recognition of outstanding literary achievement. Swiss citizens are eligible. A monetary prize is awarded at irregular intervals. Established in 1905.

11730
Preis der Schweizerischen Schillerstiftung
For recognition of outstanding literary achievement. Swiss citizens or foreign authors who are residents of Switzerland are eligible. A monetary prize of 5,000 to 10,000 Swiss francs is awarded annually. Established in 1905 in memory of Friedrich Schiller, a German poet.

11731
Foundation Dr. A. Hedri-Stiftung, Zurich
Industriestrasse 5
2555 Brugg, Switzerland
Phone: 32 53 20 53

11732
Dr. A. Hedri-Preis
For recognition in the field of exopsychology, the science of extraterrestrial consciousness, and epipsychology, the science of post-mortal consciousness. Two monetary prizes and diplomas are awarded annually. Established in 1990.

11733
Anne Frank-Fonds
Hohe Winde-Str. 104
CH-4059 Basel, Switzerland
Phone: 61 357391
Fax: 61 357970

11734
Anne Frank Literary Award
(Anne Frank-Literaturpreis)
For recognition of a literary work comparable in significance with the *Diary of Anne Frank* by a less known author. A monetary prize was awarded one time in 1985. The prize will be awarded again in 1994. Established in 1984 in memory of Anne Frank and her diary.

11735
Fribourg Festival of Sacred Music
(Festival de Musique Sacree de Fribourg)
PO Box 292
CH-1701 Fribourg, Switzerland
Phone: 37 224800
Fax: 37 228331

11736
International Competition in Composition of Sacred Music
(Concours International de Composition de Musique Sacree)
To encourage the creation of original works taking their inspiration from sacred texts of the Christian tradition. The competition is open to composers of all ages and nationalities. A new theme is chosen biennially. The next competition is in 1995. First prize, a monetary prize of 10,000 Swiss francs, is awarded biennially for the Prize of the City of Fribourg; second and third prize are also awarded. Established in 1985. Sponsored by Jeunesses Musicales de Suisse and Radio Suisse Romande "Espace 2."

11737
Golden Ring Organizing Committee
(Comite d'Organisation de l'Anneau d'Or)
2, avenue de Rhodanie
PO Box 248
CH-1000 Lausanne 6, Switzerland
Phone: 21 617 73 21
Fax: 21 26 86 47

11738
Golden Ring - International Contest of Televised Sports, Lausanne
(Anneau d'Or - Concours International d'Emissions Sportives en Television)
To promote sports programs and improve general knowledge of sports. The following categories of programs are eligible to compete: (1) Category I - news coverage: coverage of sports news destined for a TV News program or for a program giving sports results; This report should last a maximum of 10 minutes and be the best possible reflection of a sports event. Cuts and editing are admissible; (2) Category II - magazine programs: in the form of reports, investigations or files, lasting a maximum of 60 minutes; and (3) Category III - the best sports action sequences: the International Olympic Committee awards an Olympic golden ring, an Olympic silver ring and an Olympic bronze ring for the best real-life sports action sequences. These sequences, filmed on the occasion of a sports event, should be of an unusual nature and should not exceed a maximum of 30 seconds. No editing is allowed. All programs presented must be free of commercials and should not have won any international award. They should have been broadcast for the first time during the eighteen months prior to the award. Participation is open to all organizations operating a national or private television network. Each organization is allowed to enter one program in Category I and Category II and can present up to threesequences in Category III. The International Jury awards a golden ring and a silver ring in Category I and II. A special jury, nominated by the IOC, awards the prizes in Category III. Awarded biennially at the closing ceremony of the Competition. Established in 1976. Organized by the city of Lausanne, and co-sponsored by the European Broadcasting Union, the International Olympic Committee, and the Swiss Broadcasting Corporation.

11739
Green Meadow Foundation
(Stiftung im Gruene)
Pressestelle
CH-8803 Ruschlikon, Switzerland
Phone: 1 7246111
Fax: 1 7246262

11740
Gottlieb Duttweiler Prize
For recognition of individuals who have made a commendable contribution, either academic or in practice, toward the realization of a cultural, social, or economic environment that permits self-expression and participation by all in its continual shaping. A monetary prize is awarded every two to three years. Established in 1958 on the occasion of the 70th anniversary of Gottlieb Duttweiler, the founder of Migros.

11741
Paul Guggenheim Foundation
(Fondation Paul Guggenheim)
c/o Inst. Universitaire de Hautes Etudes
  Intl.
132, rue de Lausanne
CH-1211 Geneva 21, Switzerland
Phone: 22 7311730
Fax: 33 7384306

11742
Paul Guggenheim Prize
(Prix Paul Guggenheim)
To encourage young academics by awarding a prize for a major monograph in the field of public international law. Applications are accepted. A monetary prize of 12,000 Swiss francs is awarded biennially. Established in 1979 in honor of Paul Guggenheim, an outstanding Swiss international lawyer.

11743
Clara Haskil Association
40, rue du Simplon
Case postale 234
CH-1800 Vevey, Switzerland
Phone: 21 9226704
Fax: 21 9226734

11744
Clara Haskil Competition
(Concours Clara Haskil)
To recognize and help a young pianist whose approach to piano interpretation is "of the same spirit that constantly inspired Clara Haskil and that she illustrated so perfectly." Male and female pianists from any country who are 30 years of age or younger are eligible to apply by July 1. A monetary prize of 15,000 Swiss francs, a broadcasted public concert (together with the second and third finalists), a concert engagement during the Festival, and concerts at other music centers in Europe are awarded biennially in September. Established in 1963 by the Clara Haskil Association and the Lucerne Festival in memory of Clara Haskil, a Romanian pianist famous for her interpretive skills. From 1973 through 1984 the Competition was organized by the Montreux-Vevey Music Festival. Since 1985, the Competition has been organized independently.

11745
Hildegard Doerenkamp and Gerhard Zbinden Foundation for Realistic Animal Protection in Bio-Medical Research
(Hildegard Doerenkamp/Gerhard Zbinden Stiftung fur realistischen Tierschutz)
c/o Dr. Beat Gahwiler
Brain Research Institute, University of
  Zurich
August Forel Str. 1
CH-8029 Zurich, Switzerland
Phone: 1 3856350
Fax: 1 3856504

11746
Scientific Award
To recognize individuals for scientific contributions to the reduction of dependence on laboratory animals in biomedical research, and improvement of experimental techniques aimed at alleviating experimental pain and stress in laboratory animals used in scientific studies. A monetary award of 50,000 German marks was awarded annually. Established in 1985. (Discontinued)

11747
Inner Swiss Cultural Foundation
(Innerschweizerische Kulturstiftung)
Erziehungsdepartement des Kantons
  Luzern
Postfach
CH-6002 Lucerne, Switzerland
Phone: 41 245111
Fax: 41 245178

11748
Inner Swiss Culture Award
(Innerschweizerischer Kulturpreis)
For recognition of important scientific or cultural achievements which concern Inner Switzerland or which are brought forth by the Inner Swiss. Individuals regardless of nationality are eligible. A monetary award of 75,000 Swiss francs and a certificate are awarded biennially, alternating with the Inner Swiss Literature Award. Established in 1951.

11749
Inner Swiss Literature Award
(Innerschweizerischer Literaturpreis)
For recognition of outstanding literary work. Authors living in the central part of Switzerland (Innerschweiz cantons: Lucerne, Uri, Schwyz, Obwalden, Nidwalden, and Zug) or who originate from those areas are eligible. A monetary prize of 15,000 Swiss francs and a certificate are awarded annually. Established in 1951.

11750
Institute of International Law
(Institut de Droit International)
10, chemin des Limites
CH-1293 Bellevue, Switzerland
Phone: 22 7311730
Fax: 22 7384306

11751
James Brown Scott Prizes
For recognition of contributions to international law in theory and practice. Thirteen prizes are designed to reward the authors of the best dissertations devoted to a specific topic of public international law. These prizes bear the following names: Prix Andres Bello, Prix Carlos Calvo, Prix Grotius, Prix Francis Lieber, Prix Frederic de Martens, Prix Mancini, Prix Samuel Pufendorf, Prix Louis Renault, Prix G. Rolin-Jaequemyns, Prix Emer de Vattel, Prix Vitoria, Prix John Westlake, and Prix Henri Wheaton. The prizes are offered for competition in rotation so that one prize may, where appropriate, be awarded every four years. The prize awarded in 1950 bore the name of Grotius. Thereafter, the order of rotation was in the alphabetical order of the names. The competition is open to any person, except members and former members, associates and former associates of the institute. Dissertations must be submitted by December 31 of the preceding year. The amount of each prize is determined by the Bureau of the Institute on the basis of the income of the Special James Brown Scott Prize Fund. The prizes were established in 1931 by James Brown Scott in memory of his mother and his sister, Jeannette Scott.

11752
International Amateur Swimming Federation
(Federation Internationale de Natation Amateur)
Ave. de Beaumont 9
1012 Lausanne, Switzerland
Phone: 21 3126602
Fax: 21 3126610

11753
FINA Prize
This, the highest award of the swimming world, is given for recognition of national or international achievement in, or contribution to, the aquatic disciplines of swimming, diving, synchronized swimming, and water polo. The FINA Prize is awarded annually. In addition, FINA Gold Pins, FINA Silver Pins, FINA Diplomas (Certificate of Merit), and FINA Honor Plaques are awarded when deemed appropriate by the FINA Bureau. Established in 1973. Formerly: (1985) FINA Prize Eminence.

11754
International Association for Bridge and Structural Engineering
(Association Internationale des Ponts et Charpentes)
ETH-Honggerberg
CH-8093 Zurich, Switzerland
Phone: 1 6332647
Fax: 1 3712131

11755
IABSE Prize
To honor an individual early in his or her career for an outstanding achievement in the field of structural engineering. Members forty years of age or younger are eligible. A medal and a certificate are awarded annually at the conference. Established in 1983.

11756
International Award of Merit in Structural Engineering
For recognition of outstanding contributions in the field of construction engineering, with special reference to their usefulness to society. Contributions may include the following aspects: planning, design, and construction; materials and equipment; and education, research, government, and management. Structural engineers who are members or nonmembers of the Association are eligible. A medal and a certificate are awarded annually at the meeting of the Permanent Committee. Established in 1975.

11757
Outstanding Paper Award
To recognize an outstanding article published in *Structural Engineering International*. Established in 1993.

11758
International Association for the Defense of Religious Liberty
(Association Internationale pour la defense de la Liberte Religieuse)
Schosshaldenstrasse 17
CH-3006 Bern, Switzerland
Phone: 31 446262
Fax: 31 446266

11759
Essay Prize
To recognize an outstanding essay on defending religious freedom and fighting against intolerance and fanaticism. Awarded at the quinquennial world congress.

11760
International Association for the Study of Insurance Economics (Geneva Association)
(Association Internationale pour l'Etude de l'Economie de l'Assurance (Association de Geneve))
18, chemin Rieu
CH-1208 Geneva, Switzerland
Phone: 22 3470938
Fax: 22 3472078

11761
Ernst Meyer Prize
(Prix Ernst Meyer)
To recognize university research work that makes a significant and original contribution to the study of risk and insurance economics. Students or researchers may apply for the award mainly by the presentation of a Ph.D. thesis. A monetary prize of 5,000 Swiss francs is awarded annually. Established in 1974 by the Geneva Association. The award honors Ernst Meyer, former Managing Director of the Allianz and founding father of the Geneva Association. The Association also awards research grants and subsidies for thesis publication.

11762
International Association of Professional Numismatists
(Association Internationale des Numismates Professionels)
Lowenstrasse 65
CH-8001 Zurich, Switzerland
Phone: 1 22 118 85
Fax: 1 21 129 76

11763
Medal of Honor
For recognition of distinguished service by a member of the numismatic trade profession. A medal is awarded.

11764
International Balint Society
(Federation Internationale Balint)
Monte Verita
CH-6612 Ascona, Switzerland

11765
Award for Medical Students
To recognize the medical students presenting the best papers based upon the writer's own experience of the doctor-patient relationship during medical training. Papers must be based on the personal experience of a student-patient relationship and how the student experiences the relationship, individually or in a team. This process is seen to reflect the multiple relations between the student, the personnel, the working routines, and different institutions. How the student perceives, and consequently acts upon, the demands he or she is exposed to, and future possibilities of using training facilities that take into account individual states of awareness presently neglected in medical decision must also be discussed. The deadline for submissions is January 31. A monetary prize of 10,000 Swiss francs is awarded annually.

11766
International Board on Books for Young People
(Internationales Kuratorium fur das Jugendbuch)
IBBY Secretariat
Nonnenweg 12
Postfach
CH-4003 Basel, Switzerland
Phone: 61 2722917
Fax: 61 2722757

11767
Hans Christian Andersen Awards
These, the highest international distinctions in children's literature, are given to recognize an author and an illustrator, living at the time of the nomination, who by the outstanding value of their work are judged to have made a lasting contribution to literature for children and young people. The complete works of the author and the illustrator are taken into consideration. Each National Section of IBBY is invited to propose a candidate for each medal. A person who has been awarded the Hans Christian Andersen Medal should not be proposed for the medal again. A medal and diploma are awarded biennially to an author and an illustrator. Established in 1956 for authors, and in 1966 for illustrators. Formerly: International Hans Christian Andersen Awards.

11768
IBBY - Asahi Reading Promotion Award
To recognize a group or an institution that has made a lasting contribution to the for development of book programs for children and young people. A monetary prize of 1,000,000 Japanese yen and a diploma are awarded. Established in 1986. Sponsored by the Japanese newspaper company, Asahi Shimbun Publishing Company. Formerly: Rising Sun Prize.

11769
IBBY Honour List
To recognize recent children's books for excellence in writing, illustration, and translation and to encourage international understanding through children's literature. Each National Section is invited to name books considered to be characteristic of its country and suitable to be recommended by IBBY for publication in other languages. One book is to be named for writing and one for illustration. For a country with a substantial and continuing production of children's books in more than one language, up to three books may be submitted for writing. The books selected for the Honour List must have been first published no earlier than three years before their nomination. Each National Section is also invited to submit the name of a translator whose work is of outstanding quality and to specify one book, first published no earlier than three years before its nomination. Diplomas are awarded biennially. Established in 1956 for authors, 1974 for illustrators, and 1978 for translators. Formerly: Hans Christian Andersen Honour Diploma.

11770
International Committee of the Red Cross
(Comite International de la Croix-Rouge)
19, Avenue de la Paix Phone: 22 7346001
CH-1202 Geneva, Switzerland Fax: 22 7332057

11771
Florence Nightingale Medal
(Medaille Florence Nightingale)
To recognize qualified male or female nurses and voluntary nursing aids who are active members or regular helpers of a National Red Cross or Red Crescent Society, or an affiliated medical or nursing institution, for having distinguished themselves in time of peace or war, by their exceptional courage and devotion to wounded, sick, or disabled persons or to civilian victims of a conflict or disaster. The medal may be awarded posthumously if the prospective recipient has fallen on active service. The award is presented by the International Committee of the Red Cross (ICRC) on proposals made to it by National Red Cross and Red Crescent Societies. The deadline is March 1. A medal and a diploma are awarded biennially. The medal is silver-gilt with a portrait of Florence Nightingale and the words "Ad memoriam Florence Nightingale 1820-1910" inscribed on the obverse, and "Pro vera misericordia et cara humanitate perennis decor universalis" on the reverse. The name of the holder and the date of the award are engraved in the center. The medal is attached by a red and white ribbon to a laurel crown surrounding a red cross. No more than 50 medals are issued at any one distribution. Established in 1912 by contributions from National Societies of the Red Cross in memory of the distinguished services of Florence Nightingale for the improvement of the care of the wounded and sick.

11772
Paul Reuter Prize
To recognize a work aimed at improving knowledge or understanding of international humanitarian law. The work must either be unpublished or have been published during the preceding two years of the award year. The deadline for applications is November 15 of the year preceding the award of the prize. A certificate and 2,000 Swiss francs are awarded biennially. The name of the prizewinner will be announced by the President of the ICRC on February 12 of the year the prize is awarded. Established by Paul Reuter, Honorary Professor of the University of Paris, member of the Institute of International Law, and President of the U.N. Commission for International law.

11773
International Competition for Musical Performers - Geneva
(Concours International d'Execution Musicale - Geneve)
104, rue de Carouge Phone: 22 3286208
CH-1205 Geneva, Switzerland Fax: 22 3204366

11774
International Competition for Musical Performers - Geneva
(Concours International d'Execution Musicale - Geneve)
For recognition of the best musical performances of the Competition. Individuals 30 years of age or younger must submit registration forms by May 31. Awards are given in alternate years in the following categories: 1994 - Orchestral Direction Competition in "Hommage a Ernest Ansermet"; 1995 - violoncello, saxophone, double-bass, and guitare; and 1996 - piano, viola, trumpet, and harp. The following prizes are awarded: first prize - 15,000 Swiss francs; second prize - 10,000 Swiss francs; and third prize - 8,000 Swiss francs. First, second, and third prizes consisting of 50,000 Swiss francs, 30,000 Swiss francs, and 20,000 Swiss francs, respectively, are awarded for the Orechestral Direction Competition. Also awarded are: Prix Suisse - 10,000 Swiss francs, Bunkamura Orchard Hall Award - 30,000 Swiss francs, Scholarship of Rentes Genevoise - 10,000 Swiss francs, Prix de l'Association des Musiciens de Geneve - 2,000 Swiss francs, and Prix Paul Streit - 3,000 Swiss francs. A Rolex watch is also presented to each first place winner. Competitions are held annually. Established in 1939 by Dr. F. Liebstoeckl and H. Gagnebin.

11775
International Council of French-Speaking Radio and Television
(Conseil International des Radios - Televisions d'Expression Francaise)
23, rue Gourgas Phone: 22 28 12 11
CH-1205 Geneva, Switzerland Fax: 22 20 51 77

11776
Prix CIRTEF de Corealisation
For recognition of the best radio and television co-production between its members, and to encourage professional development. Organizations participating in the co-production must all be members of CIRTEF. Productions must have been produced in the preceding two years. A trophy is awarded biennially at the General Conference. Established in 1981.

11777
International Council of Nurses
(Conseil International des Infirmieres)
3, pl. Jean-Marteau Phone: 22 7312960
CH-1201 Geneva, Switzerland Fax: 22 7381036

11778
Christiane Reimann Prize
To recognize one or more nurses, who, during the years immediately preceding the award, have made a significant contribution either within the nursing profession through research or practical nursing for the benefit of humanity or for the nursing profession. In special cases, the prize may be given to two or three recipients who have collaborated or worked on the same task. Nominations may be submitted by individuals or groups of individuals, with the exception of ICN Board, Standing Committee, and staff members. The nominee must meet the following criteria: have current membership in a national nurses' association in membership with ICN and have made a significant contribution within the nursing profession for the benefit of humanity or for the nursing profession. A monetary prize is presented every four years at the ICN congress. Established in 1984 by Christiane Reimann, the first full time executive secretary of the ICN.

11779
International Equestrian Federation
(Federation Equestre Internationale - FEI)
Bolligenstrasse 54 Phone: 31 42 93 42
CH-3000 Berne 32, Switzerland Fax: 31 42 89 27

11780
Federation Equestre Internationale Awards
For recognition of outstanding achievements in equestrian sports. Competitions are held.

11781
International Exhibition Logistics Associates
Case Postale 1629 Phone: 22 8277010
CH-1211 Geneva 26, Switzerland Fax: 22 3438874

11782
International Exhibition Logistics Associates Awards
To recognize outstanding contributions in the field of exhibition organization.

11783
International Federation for Information Processing
16, place Longemalle Phone: 22 3102649
CH-1204 Geneva, Switzerland Fax: 22 7812322

11784
Outstanding Service Award
In recognition of services rendered to IFIP by Technical Committee and Working Group members not normally eligible for the Silver Core Award. Certificates are given.

11785
Silver Core Award
For recognition of outstanding contributions to computer science. Scientists of any nationality are eligible.

11786
International Federation of Aero-Philatelic Societies
(Federation Internationale des Societes Aerophilateliques)
PO Box 1359
CH-8058 Zurich Airport, Switzerland

11787
FISA Medal
(Medaille de la FISA)
For recognition of merits in the field of aerophilately. Individuals may be nominated by the Directorium of FISA. A medal is awarded annually at the congress. Established in 1961.

11788
International Federation of University Women
37, Quai Wilson   Phone: 22 7312380
CH-1201 Geneva, Switzerland   Fax: 22 7380440

11789
IFUW Awards Competition
To encourage advanced scholarship by enabling university women to undertake original research in some country other than that in which they have received their education or habitually reside. Members must apply by November 1. Applicants must be members of the Federation and be well started on the research program. A fellowship is not awarded for the first year of a Ph.D. program. The following fellowships and grants are awarded biennially: IFUW Ida Smedley MacLean International Fellowship - 8,000 to 10,000 Swiss francs; CFUW A. Vibert Douglas International Fellowship - $6,000 Canadian; AFUW - Queensland International Fellowship - $12,000 Australian; British Federation Crosby Hall Fellowship - £2,500; NZFUW/Wellington Suffrage Fellowship - $10,000 New Zealand; and a number of Winifred Cullis and Dorothy Leet Grants - stipend is determined according to need, normally between 3,000 and 6,000 Swiss francs. The Winifred Cullis Grants assist women graduates to obtain specialized training essential to their research; train in new techniques in the humanities, social sciences, and natural sciences; and carry out independent research, including completion of a piece of research well advanced. The Dorothy Leet Grants assist women graduates of countries with a comparatively low per capita income. Grants are also given to other women graduates who wish to work as experts in these countries or whose research is of value to such countries. For further information for U.S. residents, contact AAUW/IFUW Liaison American Association of University Women, 1111 16th St., NW, Washington, D.C. 20036; for all others, contact IFUW headquarters.

11790
International Festival of Alpine Films Les Diablerets, Switzerland
(Festival International du Film Alpin Les Diablerets, Suisse)
PO BOX 125   Phone: 25 53 1358
CH-1865 Les Diablerets, Switzerland   Fax: 25 53 2348

11791
International Festival of Alpine Films Les Diablerets, Switzerland
(Festival International du Film Alpin Les Diablerets, Suisse)
To encourage and develop the production of films which will stimulate, both in Switzerland and abroad, an interest in the Alps and in the people who live and work in the mountains. An "Alpine Film" is to be understood as any film or video tape whose action could be situated only in the mountains and a "Mountain Environment Film" as any production focusing attention on, or portraying, a place or region which deserves to be preserved or which is already protected. The entries are divided into six categories: (1) Climbing - mountaineering technique or ski-alpinism; (2) Climbing and free climbing; (3) Expedition; (4) Documentary; (5) Scenario; and (6) Protection and preservation of the mountain environment. The Festival is open to all filmmakers, professional, free-lance, or amateurs. Films must be submitted in 16mm or 35mm formats, with optical magnetic or double band (sepmag) sound. Videotapes should be system U-matic or VHS. The following prizes are awarded: (1) Grand Prix des Diablerets - for the film receiving the unanimous votes of the Jury. The winning of this prize automatically excludes the film from consideration for further awards (except the Public's Prize); (2) Diables d'Or - one Diable (Devil) for each of the six categories; (3) Grain d'Or - to a film that offers something new for adventure films; (4) Special Prizes - donated by various organizations outside the Festival, who stipulate the rules for the award; and (5) Public's Prize - awarded by the Festival Organizing Committee according to votes received from the public after each viewing. Established in 1975.

11792
International Festival of Films on Architecture and Town-planning of Lausanne
(Festival International du Film d'Architecture et d'Urbanisme de Lausanne)
Case Postale 2756   Phone: 21 8019606
CH-1002 Lausanne, Switzerland   Fax: 21 8034053

11793
International Festival of Films on Architecture and Town-planning of Lausanne
(Festival International du Film d'Architecture et d'Urbanisme de Lausanne)
To offer film producers throughout the world a forum where various kinds of films dealing with the theme of architecture and town-planning may be screened and compared in an atmosphere of mutual understanding. In promoting films of high quality in this particular field, the festival aims to encourage discussion and to stimulate a closer relationship between the public and experts on architecture and town-planning. Films having the central theme of architecture and town-planning produced in 35mm, 16mm, or in video, with optical or magnetic sound incorporated may participate. All films up to a maximum of 60 minutes screening time produced during the previous five-year period are eligible. The following prizes are awarded biennially: Grand Prix du FIFAL, Prix du Canton de Vaud, Prix de la Ville de Lausanne, Prix Special du Jury, Prix de L'EPFL, Prix de L'Associati on Suisse Pour le Film Scientifique, Prix du Public, and prizes for the Best Documentary Film, Best Fiction Film, and Best Experimental Film. Established in 1987. Organized by the Swiss Association for the Scientific Films (ASFS), under the patronage of the General Secretary of the Council of Europe, the Swiss Federal Government, the State of Vaud, the City of Lausanne, and the Swiss Federal Institute of Technology, Lausanne.

11794
International Festival of Films on Art
C.P. 2783
CH-1002 Lausanne, Switzerland   Fax: 21 8034053

11795
Grand Prix FIFART
To recognize the best film on art. First place winners receive a diploma and a monetary prize of 3,000 francs; gold watches are awarded for second and third place. The festival is held every two years in October. Established in 1992. For more information, contact Mariela Agostinho.

11796

International Festival of Films on Energy Lausanne
(Festival International du Film sur l'Energie Lausanne)
PO Box 88 (Chauderon) Phone: 21 312 90 69
CH-1000 Lausanne 9, Switzerland Fax: 21 320 10 19

11797

International Festival of Films on Energy Lausanne
(Festival International du Film sur l'Energie Lausanne)
To offer to film producers throughout the world a forum where all films having an energy theme may be screened and compared in an atmosphere of mutual understanding. In promoting films of high quality in this particular filed, the Festival aims to encourage discussion and to stimulate a closer relationship between the public and energy experts. Films produced in the period covering the four previous editions of the festival, of which the central theme is primary energies (coal, petrol, natural gas, geothermal energy, wind energy, sea energy, vegetal and organic fuel, etc.), production of electricity, and environment may be submitted. Films produced in 35mm, 16mm, or in video, with optical or magnetic sound incorporated and up to a maximum of 60 minutes screening time may participate. The following prizes are awarded: Grand Prix of the International Film Festival on Energy, Lausanne; Award of the State of Vaud; Award of the City of Lausanne; Award UNIPEDE; Award for the best documentary film; Award for the best fiction film; Award for the best animated cartoon film; and Award of the Press. Established in 1986. Since 1991, organized by the FIFEL Foundation and placed under the high patronage of the International Energy Agency, the Organisation for Economic Co-operation and Development, the Swiss Confederation, the State of Vaud, the Town of Lausanne, the Federal Institute of Technology of Lausanne (EPFL), the Western Switzerland Energy Board (EOS), and Mrs. Catherine Lalumiere, General Secretary of the Council of Europe.

11798

International Handball Federation
Lange Gasse 10 Phone: 61 331 50 15
CH-4052 Basel, Switzerland Fax: 61 23 13 44

11799

Hans-Baumann-Trophy
To recognize the member association of the IHF that has most successfully contributed to the development and propagation of handball in their country or in the whole world. A trophy is awarded biennially at the ordinary IHF Congress. Established in memory of Hans Baumann, former president of the International Handball Federation.

11800

European Cup Competitions
To recognize the winners of the European Cup Competitions in handball. The Federation organizes European Cup Competitions for men and women: for National Champions, for Cup winners, and for the IHF Cup. Winners of the individual European Cup Competitions qualify automatically for the following year's competition. Also entitled to participate in the EC are the current National Champions and Cup winners (men and women) of each European national association and any additional associations decided upon by the IHF Congress. The choice of teams to be entered for the IHF Cup (men and women) is left to the national associations. Entries for teams to take part in European Cup Competitions must be in the hands of the IHF General Secretariat in Basel by August 15, each year. The following Challenge Trophies are awarded: (1) Men's National Champions; (2) Ladies' National Champions; (3) Men's Cup winners; (4) Ladies' Cup winners; (5) IHF-Cup, Men; and (6) IHF-Cup, Ladies. Awarded annually. Established in 1957 for men and in 1961 for women.

11801

World Championships
To recognize the winners of handball in world championships. Any member of the IHF which has met its obligations to the IHF is entitled to participate in a World Championship. Temporary members may be given special permission by the Council. Entries for World Championships are to be sent to the General Secretariat of the IHF within the period fixed. The Congress or the Council decides on the number of teams participating and any qualifying matches before every World Championship. All A-and B-WC and ladies' and men's juniors WC should have 16 teams competing if possible. The minimum number of teams for a World Championship is eight. Prizes are awarded to teams as follows: (1) the first three teams receive for up to 16 players and a number of officials (to make a total of 20 altogether) medals and diplomas: first place and World Champion - gold; second place - silver; and third place - bronze; and (2) all other teams and officially appointed IHF officials receive commemorative medals. Established in 1938.

11802

International Ice Hockey Federation
Todistrasse 23 Phone: 1 2811430
Ch-8002 Zurich, Switzerland Fax: 1 2811433

11803

International Ice Hockey Federation Competition
To encourage the playing of ice hockey by organizing regular international competitions and championships. European Championships have been held since 1910, and World Championships since 1920.

11804

International Institute for Promotion and Prestige
(Institut International de Promotion et de Prestige)
Fondation du Centre International de
 Geneve
1, rue de Varembe Phone: 22 7338614
CH-1202 Geneva, Switzerland Fax: 40 539465

11805

International Institute for Promotion and Prestige Awards
To honor and encourage individuals, groups, firms, and institutions that contribute to international exchange and work to improve living conditions for all mankind in industrial, scientific, and technological areas. Awards are presented in the following categories: economics, ecology, industrial, humanitarian, cultural, and scientific. In the industrial category, two levels of awards are presented: Trophee International and Prix de Promotion Internationale. The Encourgement Award is presented to middle-size companies in all areas. Awarded annually. Established in 1967.

11806

International Labour Organization
4 rue des Morillons Phone: 22 996111
CH-1211 Geneva 22, Switzerland Fax: 22 7988685

11807

Workers' Education Fellowships
To promote trade union education. Individuals who hold trade union leadership functions are eligible. Travel and expenses are awarded.

11808

International Motorcycle Federation
(Federation Internationale Motocycliste)
19, chemin William-Barbey Phone: 22 7581960
CH-1292 Chambesy-Geneva, Switzerland Fax: 22 7582180

11809

FIM Fair Play Trophy
(Trophee du Fairplay FIM)
For recognition of fair play in the world of motorcycling. Awarded when merited. Established in 1983.

11810

Gold Medal of the FIM
For recognition of outstanding accomplishments in the sport of motorcycling. Awarded when merited. Established in 1963.

11811

Prix au Merite Motocycliste
For recognition of contributions to the sport of motorcycling. Gold, silver, and bronze medals are awarded when merited. Established in 1983.

11812

World Motorcycle Championships
To encourage and draw up regulations for the sport of motorcycling in all of its disciplines by controlling worldwide through its members the application of rules, standards, and, in particular, its codes. The FIM is the sole international authority empowered to control international motorcycling activities organized under its jurisdiction throughout the world. The official titles of World Championships, Intercontinental Championships, Continental Championships, and FIM Prize Events, in all disciplines of the motorcycle sport belong to the FIM. Some of the motorcycling events held each year determine: Road Racing World Champions, World Champions Motocross and Supercross, FIM Rally, Trial World Champions, Enduro World Champions, and World Track Racing Champions.

11813

International Olympic Committee
(Comite International Olympique)
Chateau de Vidy
CH-1007 Lausanne, Switzerland
Phone: 21 25 32 71
Fax: 21 24 15 52

11814

Olympic Cup
(Coupe Olympique)
For recognition of an institution or association with a general reputation for merit and integrity that has been active and efficient in the service of sport and has contributed substantially to the development of the Olympic Movement. The Cup remains at the Chateau de Vidy, and a reproduction is awarded annually. Established by the Baron de Coubertin in 1906.

11815

Olympic Medals and Diplomas
(Medailles et Diplomes Olympique)
To recognize winners of individual and team events at the summer and winter Olympics. The following awards are given: first prize - a silver-gilt medal and a diploma; second prize - a silver medal and a diploma; and third prize - a bronze medal and a diploma. The medals must bear the name of the sport concerned and be fastened to a detachable chain or ribbon to be hung around the neck of the athlete. Diplomas, not medals, are also awarded for the fourth, fifth, sixth, seventh and eighth places, if any. All participants in a tie for first, second and third places are entitled to receive a medal and a diploma. The names of all winners are inscribed upon the walls of the main stadium where the Olympic Games have taken place. Awarded every four years. Established in 1896.

11816

Olympic Order
(Ordre Olympique)
To recognize an individual who has illustrated the Olympic ideal through his action, has achieved remarkable merit in the sporting world, or has rendered outstanding services to the Olympic cause, either through his own personal achievement or his contribution to the development of sport. Nominations are proposed by the Olympic Order's Council and decided upon by the Executive Board. Active members of the IOC may not be admitted as such into the Olympic Order. From 1974 through 1984, the award was presented in three Orders: gold, silver and bronze. Since 1984, there has been no distinction between the silver and bronze Order. The insignia of the Olympic Order and the diploma are conferred upon the recipient by the President, by a member of the IOC nominated by him, or, failing that, by someone approved by the President. Awarded annually. Established in 1974.

11817

International Photobiology Association
Swiss Institute for Experimental Cancer
 Research
CH-1066 Epalinges, Switzerland
Fax: 21 32 69 33

11818

Finsen Prize
To recognize scientists who have made an outstanding contribution to photobiology. Photobiologists may be nominated by the Finsen Committee. A gold medal, an opportunity to deliver the Finsen lecture during the Photobiology Congress, and a grant are awarded every four years. Established in 1937 by the Comite International de la Lumiere (C.I.L.) in memory of Niels Finsen, Nobel Prize winner for Medicine and Physiology in 1903.

11819

International Potash Institute
(Institut International de la Potasse)
Postfach 121
Worblaufen
CH-3048 Berne, Switzerland
Phone: 31 58 53 73
Fax: 31 58 41 29

11820

Competition for Young Researchers
To recognize young research workers who promote research in areas such as crop fertilization, plant nutrition, and soil science, particularly in connection with the role of potassium as one of the major plant nutrients. Research may be written in English, French, German, or Spanish. Individuals under 40 years of age are eligible. A jury of the Scientific Board of the Institute makes the selection. A monetary prize of 5,000 Swiss francs is awarded. Awarded every three to four years. Established in 1963.

11821

International Public Relations Association
Case Postale 2100
CH-1211 Geneva 2, Switzerland
Phone: 22 7910550
Fax: 22 7880336

11822

IPRA Golden World Awards for Excellence
To recognize excellent public relations programs carried out at least partially during the preceding two-year period. Business corporations, associations, institutions, and governments anywhere in the world may submit entries. Public relations firms and consultancies can enter in behalf of clients and share honors with them. The public relations program can be of any kind and be local, regional, national, or international in scope. Entries must be submitted by November 30. Awards are presented in the following categories: overall institutional, international, public service, public affairs, issue management, emergency, community relations, employee relations, investor relations, marketing - new product, marketing - established product, marketing - new service, marketing - established service, special event/observance - under eight days, special event/observance - eight days or more, environmental, and other - aimed at dealers, members, educators, youth, or other special public. Sponsored by NEC Corp.

11823

IPRA President's Award
To recognize contributions to a better world understanding. A trophy is awarded annually. Established in 1977.

11824

International Road Transport Union
(Union Internationale des Transports Routiers)
Postbox 44
CH-1211 Geneva 20, Switzerland
Phone: 22 7341330
Fax: 22 7330660

11825
Grand Prix d'Honneur
To recognize an act of outstanding bravery by a professional road transport driver of a bus, coach, or truck accomplished in the course of professional duties. Candidates may be nominated by IRU member associations (in the United States, the American Trucking Associations). A monetary prize, a diploma, and a gold button badge are awarded biennially at the IRU Congress. Established in 1968.

11826
International Savings Banks Institute
(Institut International des Caisses d'Epargne)
1-3, rue Albert-Gos
Case Postale 355
CH-1211 Geneva, Switzerland
Phone: 22 477466
Fax: 22 467356

11827
Awards for Contributions in Banking
To recognize and promote the interests of savings banks and their clients.

11828
International Skating Union
Promenade 73, Postfach
CH-7270 Davos Platz, Switzerland
Phone: 81 437577
Fax: 81 436677

11829
Jacques Favart Trophy
For recognition of outstanding accomplishments in the field of skating. Members are invited to propose nominees. The nominees are considered by the appropriate Technical Committee and recommendations are made to the ISU Council, which makes the final decision. A trophy is awarded. Established in 1981 to honor Jacques Favart, the former ISU President (1967 to 1980).

11830
Georg Hasler Medal
For recognition of contributions to the sport of skating. Up to four awards are made annually: two to skaters, either Speed or Figure Skating; and two to administrators. Members are invited to propose nominees. Nominations must be received by the ISU secretariat not later than April 30 in each year. A medal is awarded. Established in 1985 in memory of Mr. Georg Hasler, for his outstanding service and personal dedication to the ISU as Honorary Secretary from 1947 to 1975.

11831
ISU Speed and Figure Skating Championships
To recognize the winners of the speed skating and figure skating championships. The following Speed Skating Championships are held: (1) World Speed Skating Championship for Men; (2) World Speed Skating Championship for Ladies; (3) European Speed Skating Championships for Ladies and Men; (4) World Sprint Speed Skating Championships for Ladies and Men; (5) World Junior Speed Skating Championships for Ladies and Men; (6) World Short Track Speed Skating Championships for Ladies and Men; and (7) World Short Track Speed Skating Team Championships. The following Figure Skating Championships are held for Men, Women, Pairs and Dance: (1) World Figure Skating Championships; (2) European Figure Skating Championships; and (3) World Junior Figure Skating Championships. Awarded annually. Established in 1906.

11832
International Ski Federation
(Federation Internationale de Ski)
Blochstrasse 2
CH-3653 Oberhofen, Switzerland
Phone: 33 446161
Fax: 33 435353

11833
Alpine World Cup Champions
To recognize the men's and women's overall champion in the ski racing competition. In addition, the following awards are presented: Alpine World Cup Medals - to recognize men and women in four categories: slalom, giant slalom, downhill, and super 6; The Nations Cup - to recognize the country whose skiers accumulate the most points in the competition; World Cup Jumping Leaders - established in 1981; Nordic World Cup Leaders - established in 1974; Nordic Combined World Cup Leaders - established in 1984; and Skier of the Year - established in 1975. Awarded annually. Established in 1967.

11834
International Ski Writers Association
Rheintalweg 106
CH-4125 Riehen, Switzerland
Phone: 61 6410088
Fax: 61 6410087

11835
Golden Skier Award
To recognize full-time writers, reporters, and commentators working in all branches of the media, who specialize in writing about ski racing. The Golden Skier Award is given annually to the best personality in the field of ski racing.

11836
International Social Security Association
(Association Internationale de la Securite Sociale)
4, route des Morillons
Case postale 1
CH-1211 Geneva 22, Switzerland
Phone: 22 7996617
Fax: 22 7986385

Formerly: (1947) Conference Internationale de la Mutualite et des Assurances Sociales.

11837
International Social Security Association Medal
(Medaille de l'AISS)
For recognition of exceptional service and devotion to ISSA during the active life of the recipient. A medal and diploma are awarded after the retirement of the recipient. Established in 1967 in honor of the 40th anniversary of ISSA.

11838
Leo Wildmann Prize
(Prix Leo Wildmann)
To recognize meritorious investigative work in the field of social security. A monetary award of 4,000 Swiss francs is awarded triennially to each of two winners, one from a developing country and another from an industrialized country. Established in 1986 in honor of Leo Wildmann, former Secretary General of the Association. (Discontinued)

11839
International Society of Electrochemistry
(Societe Internationale d'Electrochimie)
Postfach 475
CH-8501 Frauenfeld, Switzerland

11840
International Society of Electrochemistry Awards
To recognize contributions in the field of electrochemistry. The Society bestows the Pergamon Electrochimie Gold Medal biennially, the Tajima Prize annually, and the Prix Jacques Tacussel biennially.

11841

International Society of Radiology
Dept. of Medical Radiology
Unive. Hospital
CH-8091 Zurich, Switzerland
Phone: 1 255 29 00
Fax: 2 255 44 43

11842

Antoine Beclere Prize
For recognition of outstanding contributions in the scientific fields of interest to medical radiology. National Radiological Societies that are members of the ISR may make nominations. A monetary prize of $5,000 US and a medal are awarded every four years at the International Congress. Established in 1979 by Antoinette Beclere in memory of Antoine Beclere, the eminent French pioneer and scientist of international radiology. Sponsored by the Antoine Beclere Foundation.

11843

International Society of Surgery (ISS/SIC)
(Societe Internationale de Chirurgie)
RUMA-Haus
Netzibodenstrasse 34
CH-4133 Pratteln, Switzerland
Phone: 61 8114770
Fax: 61 8114775

11844

Robert Danis Prize
To recognize the surgeon/author of the most important and personal work in connection with surgical treatment of fractures (orthopaedic treatment excluded). Surgeon nationals of one of the countries represented at the ISS/SIC are eligible. Work can be in connection with either technics, clinics, or experimentation. A monetary prize for the purchase of instruments, or to finance an educational tour is awarded annually. Established in 1947.

11845

Rene Leriche Prize
For recognition of the most valuable work on the surgery of arteries, veins, or the heart which has appeared in the previous few years. Awarded annually. Established in 1947.

11846

Prize of the Societe Internationale de Chirurgie
To recognize the surgeon who has a published work that has made the most notable and useful contribution to surgical science. The prize winner need not necessarily be a member of the Society. Nominations are considered and voted upon at the meeting of the Executive Committee that is always held before the General Assembly of the Congress. A medal is awarded biennially at the General Assembly. Established in 1953.

11847

International Telecommunications Union
(Union Internationale des Telecommunications)
Telecom 91 Secretariat
Place des Nations
CH-1211 Geneva 20, Switzerland
Phone: 22 7305243
Fax: 22 7306444

11848

Golden Antenna - International Film/Video Festival on Telecommunications and Electronics
(Antenne d'or Festival international du film et de la bande video sur les telecommunictions et l'electronique)
To encourage world-wide production of high-quality films and videotape recordings covering all fields of telecommunications and electronics and their applications. Outstanding films and videotape are recognized in the following categories: (1) Productions on telecommunications and electronics in general made for public information; (2) Productions on specific telecommunication services made for public information; (3) Publicity, advertising or promotional productions on telecommunications or electronics; (4) Productions concerned with technical research and/or with specific telecommunications or electronics techniques; and (5) Vocational training productions in the field of telecommunications and electronics and those produced under the Union's technical cooperation program for the development of telecommunications in Member countries. The following are eligible to submit entries: (1) governments of the member countries of ITU (maximum of 5 films, cassettes, or slide programs); (2) commercial enterprises participating in TELECOM (maximum of 3 entries); (3) scientific or industrial organizations participating in the work of ITU; and (4) the United Nations family of organizations. Commercial films must be less than five years old. The deadline is April 30. The following awards are presented: (1) Golden Antenna - to the best of the Festival; (2) Silver Antennae - to the best production in each of the five categories of the Festival; (3) the Bronze Antennae - second prize in the five categories; and (4) Special Mentions or Honorable Mentions - to outstanding productions for their artistic, technical or other qualities. The Golden Antenna is a gold-plated radio antenna (model of two-dish antennae mounted on a tower). The silver-plated Silver Antennae and the Bronze Antennae are model earth stations for communication with satellites, with dish antennae. Awarded at the film festival which is held every four years in conjunction with TELECOM, the World Telecommunication Exhibition. Established in 1971. (Discontinued)

11849

ITU Centenary Prize
To recognize individuals in the telecommunications field. Citizens of the member states of the ITU are eligible. A monetary award of 15,000 Swiss francs and a gold medal are awarded every four years at the World Telecommunications Exhibition. Established in 1979 to commemorate the first centenary of the ITU and international cooperation in telecommunications.

11850

International Television Symposium and Technical Exhibition - Montreux
(Symposium International et Exposition technique de Television - Montreux)
5, rue du Theatre
PO Box 1451
CH-1820 Montreux, Switzerland
Phone: 21 9633220
Fax: 21 9638851

11851

Montreux Achievement Gold Medal
For recognition of an achievement in the development or application of new systems, technologies, or equipment that has significantly contributed to the improvement of television engineering. A gold medal is awarded biennially at the Montreux International Television Symposium. Established in 1977.

11852

Montreux International Electronic Cinema Festival
For recognition of high definition television productions screened during the Festival in the following categories: dramas; documentaries; sports and events; music, variety, and light entertainment; and commercial advertising and promotional announcements. An International Nomination Committee pre-screens all productions entered in the Festival and nominates the final selection of productions to be accepted for screening by the International Jury. An Astrolabium is awarded to the best production in each category and to the production, out of all accepted productions, that has made the most effective and innovative use of high definition television production technology. Festival citations, if appropriate, are awarded to individuals considered to be worthy of recognition for their outstanding contribution to an HDTV production. Established in 1987.

11853

International Triennial Exhibition of Photography
(Triennale internationale de la photographie)
Musee d'Art et d'Histoire
12, rue de Morat
CH-1700 Fribourg, Switzerland
Phone: 37 228571
Fax: 37 231672

11854
International Triennial Exhibition of Photography Prizes
To recognize the best photographers of all continents. Recognized and unknown artists and professional and amateur photographers are eligible. The following prizes are presented: Grand Prize of 10,000 Swiss francs - the Golden Diaphragm; First Prize of 5,000 Swiss francs - the Silver Diaphragm; Second Prize of 3,000 Swiss francs - the Bronze Diaphragm; Kodak Prize for the most talented young professional photographer - 5,000 Swiss francs; Polaroid Prize for the author of the best instantly-developed photograph - 5,000 Swiss francs; and Ilford Prize for the best non-professional photographer - 5,000 Swiss francs. The Jury may award three special mentions of 1,000 Swiss francs each. The photographs selected for the Exhibition are exhibited in the Museum of Art and History in Fribourg. Awarded triennially in autumn. Held under the patronage of the Swiss Confederation, the Canton and City of Fribourg. Established in 1975. Sponsored by Kodak, Polaroid and Ilford. (Temporarily Discontinued)

11855
International Union Against Cancer
(Union Internationale Contre le Cancer)
3, rue du Conseil-General Phone: 22 3201811
CH-1205 Geneva, Switzerland Fax: 22 3201810

11856
American Cancer Society International Cancer Research Fellowships
To enable senior investigators from any country, who have been actively engaged in cancer research for at least five years, to work in collaboration with outstanding scientists. The fellowships are not for postdoctoral or special training but for original work in the basic, clinical or behavioral areas of cancer research. The applications deadline is October 1. Between 12 to 15 Fellows are selected annually from about 50 candidates. The average award value for a 12 month fellowship is $30,000 US. Sponsored by the American Cancer Society. Formerly: American Cancer Society Eleanor Roosevelt International Cancer Fellowships.

11857
Mucio Athayde International Cancer Prize
For recognition of the most outstanding contribution to the fight against cancer. A monetary prize of $100,000 and a gold medal were awarded at a ceremony during the International Cancer Congress. Established in 1981 by Mucio Athayde, a Brazilian multi-millionaire property developer. (Discontinued in 1982)

11858
Cancer Research Campaign International Fellowships
To enable investigators to work abroad in clinical or basic research in cancer. The fellowships were also open to investigators in the behavioral and social sciences related to cancer. Sponsored by the Cancer Research Campaign (UK). (Discontinued)

11859
International Cancer Research Technology Transfer Project
To enable scientifically or medically qualified investigators and specialists from any country who are actively engaged in cancer research or clinical management in the field to spend time in an appropriate foreign institution to exchange information on new or improved techniques, to compile data in the basic, clinical or behavioral areas of cancer research, or to acquire knowledge and skills of appropriate, up-to-date clinical management techniques. Applications may be submitted at any time of the year. Awards are for one to three months. Contributions are awarded towards living costs. Over 150 awards are made each year. The maximum award is US $1,600, plus airfare. Funded jointly by the Office of International Affairs at the National Cancer Institute of the United States of America, and by certain Member Organizations of the UICC.

11860
International Oncology Nursing Fellowships
To provide an opportunity for qualified nurses to augment their professional knowledge and experience through a short-term observership at a renowned comprehensive cancer centre in North America or the United Kingdom. English-speaking registered nurses, who are actively engaged in the management of cancer patients in their home institutes and who come from regions of the world where specialist cancer nursing training is not yet widely available, are eligible to apply, as are established oncology nurses who wish to disseminate their skills in these regions. Applications, complete with all supporting documentation, must be received by the UICC Geneva Office by November 15. About five fellowships with an average value of $2,800 US are awarded annually. Sponsored by the Oncology Nursing Society (U.S.A.).

11861
Hussain Makki Al Juma International Cancer Prize
To provide recognition for outstanding scientific achievement in cancer research in the basic science or clinical field as identified by scientific publications. A monetary prize of $120,000 was awarded in 1984. Co-sponsored by the Kuwait Foundation for the Advancement of Sciences. (Discontinued)

11862
UICC Award
A special award to recognize individuals for exceptional contributions to cancer prevention.

11863
Yamagiwa-Yoshida Memorial International Cancer Study Grants
To enable cancer investigators from any country who are actively engaged in cancer research to undertake joint research/study abroad or to establish bilateral research projects, including advanced training in experimental methods and special techniques. The applications deadline is January 1 or July 1. About 15 grants with an average value for 3 months of $8,000 US are made annually. Selections take place twice a year, in spring and autumn. Sponsored by the Japan National Committee for UICC and the Olympus Optical Company in Tokyo.

11864
International Video Week of Geneva
(Semaine Internationale de Video de Geneve)
St. Gervais Geneve
5, rue du Temple Phone: 22 732 20 60
CH-1201 Geneva, Switzerland Fax: 22 738 42 15

11865
International Video Week of Geneva
(Semaine Internationale de Video de Geneve)
To give artists from all countries an opportunity to present their videos and to get to know the works of others. The videos presented must be original and display a personal approach with regard to both form and subject-matter. The competition is open to video artists and directors from all over the world, without distinction of genre, language or duration. Participants may submit only one entry each. Entries must have been made during the preceding two years. The following prizes are awarded: (1) Grand Prix de la Ville de Geneve - 10,000 Swiss francs; (2) Prix "Jeune Createur" - 4,000 Swiss francs given by the Departement de l'Instruction Publique de Geneve; (3) Prix St-Gervais MJC - 1,500 Swiss francs; and (4) Prix Gestronic S.A. - 1,500 Swiss francs. Awarded biennially. Established in 1985.

11866
INTERPHIL
CIC Case 20 Phone: 22 733 67 17
CH-1211 Geneva 20, Switzerland Fax: 22 734 70 82

11867
Sforza Award in Philanthropy
To recognize an individual, pre-eminent in modern philanthropy, of international standing who has furthered the cause of philanthropic activity in more than one country. Members may make nominations. A medal is awarded occasionally at the World Conference. Established in 1983 in memory of Count S.G. Sforza (1916-77).

11868

Italian and Romansh PEN Centre of PEN International
(PEN Club della Svizzera Italiana e Retoromancia)
Case Postale 2126
CH-6901 Lugano 1, Switzerland

11869

Ascona Prize for a Narrative Work in Literature
For recognition of narrative works (novels or short stories) written in Italian. A monetary prize of 8,000 Swiss francs was awarded to each of the two winners. Established in 1983. (Discontinued)

11870

Heinz Karger Memorial Foundation
(Heinz Karger-Gedaechtnis-Stiftung)
c/o S. Karger AG
Allschwilerstrasse 10
CH-4009 Basel, Switzerland
Phone: 61 306 11 11
Fax: 61 306 12 34

11871

Heinz Karger Memorial Foundation Annual Award
To recognize an individual scientist for his or her contribution to original research work on a designated scientific subject in the field of medical or natural sciences. A monetary prize of 20,000 Swiss francs is awarded when merited. Established in 1960 by Dr. Thomas Karger in memory of his father, Heinz Karger of Basel.

11872

Ludwig Keimer Foundation for Comparative Research in Archaeology and Ethnology
Picassoplatz, 8
CH-4052 Basel, Switzerland
Phone: 61 23 27 09
Phone: 61 23 27 10

11873

Ludwig Keimer Foundation Prizes
To honor individuals and institutions for high achievements in social, economic and cultural fields. Monetary prizes are awarded annually. Established in 1971.

11874

Locarno Internationale Film Festival
(Festival Internazionale del Film Locarno)
Via Della Posta 6
CH-6600 Locarno, Switzerland
Phone: 93 31 02 32
Fax: 93 31 74 65

11875

Locarno International Film Festival
(Festival Internazionale de Film Locarno)
For recognition of outstanding films by new directors and growing national film industries. All films should be submitted in the original language and with French subtitles. The competition is open to films that respect the purpose of the Festival and are over 60 minutes in length. Films must have been completed no more than twelve months earlier and must not have been shown publicly in Europe before their official presentation at the Festival. Films that have won prizes at other non-European international festivals recognized by the F.I.A.P.F. are not eligible. Preference is normally given to world or international premieres. Educational, scientific, and advertising films are not eligible for the competition. Films may be submitted by producers, television networks as co-producers, or official national or professional organizations from each country. Countries making official entries and national and professional organizations may submit a choice of several films. The following prizes are awarded: the Grand Prize of the Festival - the Golden Leopard and the Grand Prize of the City of Locarno (30,000 Swiss francs) to the best film in competition; the Special Prize of the Festival - the Silver Leopard and the Second Prize of the City of Locarno (15,000 Swiss francs) to the second best film; the Grand Prize of the Award Committee - the Bronze Leopard and the Third Prize of the City of Locarno (5,000 Swiss francs) to a director, actor, or actress considered to be of exceptional merit; the Bronze Leopard and the Fourth Prize of the City of Locarno; the Swissair/Crossair Special Prize (10,000 Swiss francs) for the film that best translates the spirit of communication among peoples and cultures; and three honorable mentions. The Leopard sculpture is designed by the Swiss artist, Remo Rossi, and is paid for by the town of Locarno. Awarded annually in August. Established in 1946 by the town of Locarno, the canton of Tessin, and the Swiss Government.

11876

Masterplayers International Music Academy
Via Losanna 12
CH-6900 Lugano, Switzerland
Phone: 91 233063
Fax: 91 233063

11877

Masterplayers International Music and Conductors Competition
To provide international support for artists of great talent in the fields of instrumentalists, conductors, singers, choirs, and chamber music. Applications are accepted from any country. The Masterplayers Prize, monetary prizes, trophies, diplomas, and engagements are awarded annually in August/September. Established in 1977.

11878

Montreux International Choral Festival
(Rencontres chorales internationales de Montreux)
Avenue Bel-Air 112
CH-1814 Tour-de-Peilz, Switzerland
Fax: 21 9638851

11879

Montreux International Choral Festival
(Rencontres chorales internationales de Montreux)
To enable choral groups from all over the world to meet in friendly competition. Each choir is free to take part in the contest and have its performance judged by the votes of the jury and the public or to perform outside the contest. There is no restriction on the choice of choral works. The maximum time allowed is 20 minutes of actual music. The following prizes are awarded: The Jury's Prize - 8,000 Swiss francs; The Public's Prize - 2,000 Swiss francs; The OTM Prize (Montreux Tourist Office) - 2,000 Swiss francs is awarded each year to one of the following: mixed voice choir, male voice choir, or ladies and children's choirs; and The Editions Barenreiter, Basle & Kassel Prize - 2,000 Swiss francs. Awarded annually. Established in 1964 by Paul-Andre Gaillard. Sponsored by the City of Montreux. Additional information is available from the Office of Tourism, CP 97, CH-1820 Montreux, Switzerland, phone: 21 963 12 12.

11880

Mother and Child International
Ch. Grande-Gorge 16
CH-1255 Veyrier, Switzerland
Phone: 22 7840658
Fax: 22 7840658

Formerly: International Association for Maternal and Neonatal Health - IAMANEH.

11881

Mother and Child International Award
For recognition of the most outstanding contribution in the field of maternal and child health or in the field of reproductive health and family planning. A monetary prize and a plaque are awarded triennially at the IAMANEH Congress. Established in 1984 by IAMANEH. Formerly: (1990) IAMANEH Award.

11882

Nestle Foundation
(Fondation Nestle)
PO Box 581
CH-1001 Lausanne, Switzerland
Phone: 21 3203351
Fax: 21 3203392

11883
FENS European Nutrition Award
For recognition of achievement in the area of nutrition research. Individuals who reside in Europe may be nominated by European nutrition societies. FENS officers and Council members of the Nestle Foundation are excluded. A monetary prize and a medal are awarded at each European Nutrition Conference. Established in 1982.

11884
New Swiss Chemical Society
(Neue Schweizerische Chemische Gesellschaft)
K-25.5.02   Phone: 61 696 66 26
CH-4002 Basel, Switzerland   Fax: 61 696 69 85

Formerly: Swiss Chemical Society; Swiss Association of Chemists.

11885
Dr. Max-Luthi Auszeichnung
(Prix Dr. Max-Luthi)
To recognize the author of a work of exceptional quality in the Department of Chemistry in a technical Swiss school. Applications must be filed by December.

11886
Paracelsus-Preis
For recognition of outstanding research in the field of chemistry. A monetary prize, a medal and a diploma are awarded biennially. Established in 1938 in honor of Paracelsus.

11887
Sandmeyer-Preis
(Prix Sandmeyer)
To recognize a researcher or a group of researchers for outstanding work in the chemical industry field or studies. The work must take place in Switzerland, or in a foreign country by a group of researchers with participation of Swiss citizens. Application deadline is October.

11888
Werner-Preis
To recognize a young member of the Society who, during the current year, has obtained very good research results in the field of chemistry. A monetary prize, a medal, and a diploma are awarded annually. Established in 1915 in honor of Professor Werner. In 1966, a one-time Golden Werner-Medaille was awarded.

11889
New Swiss Chemical Society Symposia
(Neue Schweizerischer Chemische Gesellschaft)
Inst. of Organic Chemistry
Freiestrasse 3
Univ. of Bern   Phone: 41 6314311
CH-3012 Bern, Switzerland   Fax: 41 6318057

Formerly: (1991) Swiss Association of Chemists.

11890
New Swiss Chemical Society Prizes
To recognize contributions by active or retired academic and industrial chemists, chemistry students, and chemical firms. The New Swiss Chemical Society the following awards: Paracelsus Preis, Werner Preis, Sandmeyer Preis, and the Dr. Max Luthi Preis. For additional information, contact the Society. Formerly: Swiss Association of Chemists Prizes.

11891
Nyon International Documentary Film Festival
PO Box 98   Phone: 22 3616060
CH-1260 Nyon, Switzerland   Fax: 22 3617071

11892
Nyon International Documentary Film Festival
For recognition of documentary films dealing with the social and psychological aspects of human life. The emphasis is on those films most likely to command specialized, rather than traditional, distribution with the object of promoting better international comparisons. Priority is also given to those films that deal with contemporary issues. Documentary films of any length may be entered. Films must have been produced during the 12 months preceding the Festival. The following awards are presented annually: Gold Sesterce for the best film; a maximum of three Silver Sesterces for different groups of documentaries (ethnological, newsreels, etc.); and certificates of merit. Established in 1968, and recognized by the International Federation of Film Producers Associations. Sponsored by the Swiss Federal Office for Cultural Affairs.

11893
Office of the Mayor of Zurich
(Prasidialabteilung der Stadt Zurich)
Postfach   Phone: 1 2163125
CH-8022 Zurich, Switzerland   Fax: 1 2121404

11894
Kunstpreis der Stadt Zurich
For recognition of achievement in art, music, or literature. Citizens of Zurich are eligible. Applications are not accepted. A monetary award of 40,000 Swiss francs is awarded annually. Established in 1932.

11895
Queen Marie Jose International Musical Composition Prize
(Prix de Composition Musicale Reine Marie-Jose)
Secretariat of the International Musical
  Prize Contest
Box 19
CH-1252 Meinier/Geneva, Switzerland

11896
Queen Marie Jose International Musical Composition Prize
(Prix de Composition Musicale Reine Marie Jose)
For recognition of a musical composition. The contest is open to composers of all nationalities without age limit. The winners of the former International Musical Composition Prize Contest, Queen Marie Jose, are not eligible. Composition length must be between 12 minutes and 25 minutes. Scores and tapes must be submitted by May 31. A monetary award of 10,000 Swiss francs is presented when merited. Should the jury decide not to award this prize, it can either award a prize of 7,000 Swiss francs called the Merlinge Prize, or forego awarding a prize. The award-winning composition is performed as part of the Merlinge concerts in cooperation with the Radio - Television Suisse Romande. The competition is held biennially. Established in 1960 by Queen Marie Jose.

11897
Rolex Awards for Enterprise
PO Box 1311   Phone: 22 3082200
CH-1211 Geneva 26, Switzerland   Fax: 22 3002255

11898
Rolex Awards for Enterprise
To encourage outstanding personal enterprise and to provide financial support for the implementation of projects. These should break new ground in one of the following major sectors of human endeavor: Applied Sciences and Invention - projects must be aimed at innovative progress in experimental or applied research; Exploration and Discovery - projects must be aimed at inspiring our imagination or expanding our knowledge of the world we live in; and Environment - projects must be aimed at protecting, preserving, or improving the world around us. Individuals must submit an official application form by the end of March of the year preceding the award year. The only language accepted is English. Only one application may be submitted by any one person or by any one group. Five monetary awards, each consisting of approximately

50,000 Swiss francs and a specially engraved gold Rolex chronometer are awarded triennially in April or May. A steel and gold chronometer is awarded to honorable mentions. Established in 1976 by Montres Rolex S.A., Geneva, on the occasion of the 50th anniversary of the invention of the Rolex Oyster case, the world's first waterproof watch case.

11899

Max Schmidheiny Foundation
(Max Schmidheiny Stiftung)
St. Gallen Graduate School
PO Box 752
Dufourstrasse, 83
CH-9001 St. Gallen, Switzerland   Phone: 71 23 28 14

11900

Freedom Prize
(Freiheitspreis)
To promote and encourage especially praiseworthy efforts to preserve and develop the free market economy and society and, in particular, endeavors to safeguard personal liberty and individual responsibility, and to guarantee social security. To ensure that support is given with complete objectivity, an independent international group of experts is appointed to examine and evaluate all achievements submitted for awards. Scientists, politicians, journalists and/or entrepreneurs, as well as any individual with a special commitment to the cause of liberty, are eligible. A monetary prize and certificate are awarded annually in May. Established in 1977 by Dr. h.c. Max Schmidheiny. Formerly: Max Schmidheiny Prize for Free Enterprise and Political Liberty.

11901

Schweizerische Gesellschaft fur Innere Medizin
Medizinische Klinik   Phone: 63 293102
CH-4900 Langenthal, Switzerland   Fax: 63 293112

11902

Swiss Society for Internal Medicine Prize
(Preis der Schweizerischen Gesellschaft fur Innere Medizin)
To stimulate scientific work by young Swiss or Swiss domiciled researchers. Original articles either already published in a scientific medical journal or accepted by such a journal, are considered. Also, articles based on work performed in Switzerland by a non-resident are considered. A monetary prize is awarded annually.

11903

SGD Swiss Graphic Designers
Limmatstrasse 63
CH-8005 Zurich, Switzerland   Phone: 1 2724555

Formerly: Arbeitsgemeinschaft Schweizer Grafiker.

11904

SGD Swiss Graphic Designers
To recognize contributions by certified graphic designers through association sponsored competitions. Formerly: Arbeitsgemeinschaft Schweizer Grafiker Competitions.

11905

Societe de Geographie de Geneve
2, rue de l'Athenee
CH-1205 Geneva, Switzerland

11906

Medaille d'Or
To recognize an explorer who has made a great discovery or to recognize a scholar who is the author of an outstanding work. A gold medal is awarded very infrequently. Established in 1910 by Arthur de Claparede of Geneva. (The award was given seven times between 1912 and 1958.)

11907

Society of Laboratory Animal Science
(Gesellschaft fur Versuchstierkunde - GV SOLAS)
BRL Ltd
Wolferstrasse 4   Phone: 61 901 42 42
CH-4414 Fullinsdorf, Switzerland   Fax: 61 901 25 65

11908

GV-SOLAS Competition
(GV-SOLAS Preisausschreiben)
To recognize outstanding dissertations as well as guiding publications in the field of laboratory science. Applicants for the award on outstanding dissertations on laboratory animal science are requested to submit a copy of their dissertation, their curriculum vitae, a copy of their degree certificate (not older than 3 years), and the report on the thesis, via their dissertation supervisor. Applicants for the award on pathbreaking work in laboratory science, who have not yet reached the age of 45 by closing date, are requested to submit a copy of their most important publication, their curriculum vitae as well as a presentation of their scientific career. Closing date is December 31. A monetary prize of 15,000 German marks is awarded triennially. Established in 1991. Sponsored by GV-SOLAS.

11909

Honorary Member
(Ehrenmitglied)
For recognition of achievement in laboratory animal science. Individuals may be nominated. A certificate is awarded when merited. Established in 1978.

11910

Society of Swiss Cuisiniers
PO Box 4870
CH-6002 Lucerne, Switzerland

11911

Basel Salon Culinaire Mondial
To recognize outstanding culinary ability. The competition is built around research and development and establishing food trends for the future. Medals are awarded. Winners participate in the Culinary Olympics held every four years in Frankfurt, Germany, with the winners of the other international regional competitions: Culinary World Cup (Luxembourg); Food & Hotel Asia Competition (Singapore); Culinary Arts Salon (USA); Hotelympia (London); Chef Ireland (Ireland); and Culinary Masters (Canada). Established in 1900.

11912

Solothurner Filmtage
Postfach 1030   Phone: 65 233161
CH-4052 Solothurn, Switzerland   Fax: 65 236410

11913

Stanley Thomas Johnson Award
(Stanley Thomas Johnson Forderpreis/Prix Cinegramm)
To encourage professional development. Swiss films made by film students are eligible. A maximum monetary prize of 20,000 Swiss francs is awarded for a film with a total of 60,000 Swiss francs awarded annually. Established in 1987. Sponsored by Stanley Thomas Johnson Foundation, Berne, Switzerland.

11914

Standing Commission of the Red Cross and Red Crescent
(Commission Permanente de la Croix-Rouge et du Croissant-Rouge)
International Fondation des Societes de La
  Croix-Rouge
et du Croissant-Rouge
17, chemin des Crets, BP 372
Petit-Saconnex
CH-1211 Geneva 19, Switzerland

Phone: 22 734 04 222
Fax: 22 733 0395

Formerly: (1986) Commission Permanente de la Croix-Rouge Internationale.

11915

Medaille Henry Dunant
For recognition of outstanding services and acts of great devotion, mainly of international significance, to the cause of the Red Cross. Criteria for the award of the Medal include risks run and arduous conditions endangering life, health, and personal freedom. It may also be awarded for a long period of devoted service to the International Red Cross and Red Crescent Movement. Members of the Movement (or recently deceased members for a posthumous award) may be proposed by National Red Cross or Red Crescent Societies, the ICRC, the International Federation of Red Cross and Red Crescent Societies, or a member of the Standing Commission. Not more than five medals, which are red crosses bearing the profile of Henry Dunant in relief attached to a green ribbon, are normally awarded biennially. The Standing Commission may also, provided all its members expressly agree, award the Medal at once without regard to the two-year interval and without meeting in plenum. Established in 1965 by the International Conference of the Red Cross on the initiative of the Australian Red Cross in memory of Henry Dunant, founder of the Red Cross. Sponsored by the Australian Red Cross.

11916

Swiss Academy of Medical Sciences
(Schweizerische Akademie der Medizinischen Wissenschaften)
Petersplatz 13
CH-4051 Basel, Switzerland

Phone: 61 2614977
Fax: 61 2614934

11917

Robert Bing Prize
To encourage scientists who have done outstanding work that has helped in the recognition, treatment and cure of neurological diseases. Nominations or personal applications are accepted. A monetary prize and a certificate are awarded biennially. Established in 1956 by Professor Robert Bing.

11918

Jakob Klaesi Awards
(Jakob Klaesi-Preis)
To recognize younger medical scientists for substantial scientific contributions to clinical research in the fields of mental depression or schizophrenia. Two to three monetary prizes of 30,000 Swiss francs will be awarded. Established in memory of Jakob Klaesi, late director of the Clinic of Psychiatry of the University of Bern.

11919

Theodore Ott Prize
(Prix Theodore Ott)
To encourage outstanding younger scientists and medical researchers who have performed scientific work with major impact on recognition and understanding of the etiology or therapy of neurological disorders. Nominations or personal applications are accepted. A monetary prize will be awarded approximately every five years. Established in 1992.

11920

Swiss Association for Theatre Studies
(Schweizerische Gesellschaft fur Theaterkultur)
Theaterkultur Verlag
Postfach 180
CH-6130 Willisau, Switzerland

Phone: 45 81 39 22

11921

Hans Reinhart Ring
To recognize an artist for an outstanding theatrical performance. Swiss stage artists or foreign artists performing in Switzerland are eligible. A gold ring is awarded annually. Established in 1957 in memory of the society's founder, Winterthur poet, Hans Reinhart.

11922

Swiss Biochemical Society
(Schweizerische Gesellschaft fur Biochemie)
Institut fur Biochemie und
  Molekularbiologie
Universitat Bern
Freiestrasse 3
CH-3012 Buhlstrasse 28, Switzerland

Phone: 31 6314111
Fax: 31 6313737

11923

Friedrich Miescher Prize
For recognition of outstanding achievement in biochemistry. Biochemists under 40 years of age who are of Swiss nationality or are working in Switzerland are eligible. A monetary prize of 10,000 Swiss francs and a medal are awarded annually. Established in 1969 in memory of the Swiss physiologist, Friedrich Miescher, who discovered the nucleic acids in 1869. Sponsored by the Friedrich Miescher Institute of CIBA-GEIGY, Basel, Switzerland.

11924

Swiss Broadcasting Corporation and the City of Montreux
(Societe Suisse de Radiodiffusion et Television et la Ville de Montreux)
Rose d'Or de Montreux
c/o SBC Headquarters
Giacomettistrasse 1-3
CH-3000 Berne 15, Switzerland

Phone: 31 43 91 11
Fax: 31 43 94 74

11925

Golden Rose of Montreux Award
To promote a better knowledge of light entertainment programs on an international level, to assist program exchanges, and to encourage the creation of original works of high quality. Light entertainment programs are judged in the following categories: Music - songs, light music, jazz, pop, rock, and variety shows; Comedy - humor and situation comedy; and Miscellaneous - any entry not included in Music or Comedy such as game shows, circus, and light entertainment documentaries. Eligible recipients fall into two categories: Broadcasters - organizations which operate a television service of national importance may enter one program in each category. In the case of countries where there are several television organizations linked by a national association, this association, representing all the organizations, shall be entitled to enter one program in each category; and Independent Producers - independent producers may enter one program in the category of their choice. Competitors should select the most suitable category. The presented programs can be intended for any kind of transmission and must have been produced or televised for the first time in the 14 months. Entries composed of several parts of the same program are not eligible. The length of the program must be at least 20 minutes but not more than 60 minutes. Edited versions of longer programs are permitted. Entries are submitted to an international pre-selection committee which will then determine the programs to be presented in the official selection. Deadline for inscriptions is February 21 and deadline for material is March 4. Programs admitted to the competition are submitted to three international juries, one for each category. Each jury can award two prizes in its category: First Prize - The Silver Rose; Second Prize - The Bronze Rose. In the Comedy category,

the First Prize is the special prize of the City of Montreaux. At the end of this competition, the three First Prize winners then compete for the Golden Rose of Montreaux Award which goes to the best entertainment program of all categories. This award also carries a monetary prize of 10,000 Swiss francs. In addition, the program which best reflects human values can be awarded the Prix UNDA. This prize can be awarded along with the Rose.

Press Prize for Broadcasters
(Prix de la Presse des radiodiffuseurs)
For recognition of the program selected as outstanding by the journalists accredited to the Golden Rose of Montreux contest. Awards are given in two categories, Official Television Organization and Independent Producer. The Press is composed of trade press and newspaper journalists and TV critics who must sign a statement agreeing to watch all programs accepted for the contest, and must attend the first meeting of the Press jury. Not more than one-third of the total members of the Press jury may come from any one country. Journalists who have assisted in any capacity in the production of a program shown at the contest may not be members of the Press jury. The Press prize presentation takes place at the same time as the presentation of the awards made by the International jury. Established in 1961.

Swiss Federal Institute of Technology Zurich
(Eidgenossische Technische Hochschule Zurich)
ETH-Zentrum   Phone: 1 2562057
CH-8092 Zurich, Switzerland   Fax: 1 2625814

ASEA-Brown Boveri-Forschungspreis
For recognition of outstanding student scientific works. In particular, diploma theses or doctoral dissertations in mechanical engineering and informatics are considered. Candidates must be under 34 years of age. Monetary prizes ranging from 2,000 to 10,000 Swiss francs are awarded biennially to one or more candidates on ETH-Day (Dies Academicus). Established in 1984 by BBC AG, Brown, Boverie and Cie, CH-Baden, Switzerland. Formerly: Brown Boveri-Forschungspreis fur Energietechnik.

Heinrich Hatt-Bucher Prize
For recognition of outstanding student scientific work in the final diploma in the field of architecture and civil engineering. Two monetary prizes of 3,000 Swiss francs and 2,000 Swiss francs, respectively, are awarded annually at ETH-Day (Dies-Academicus). Established in 1986 by Heinrich Ernst Hatt-Bucher.

Georg A. Fischer-Preis
For recognition of outstanding student scientific works. In particular, diploma theses or doctoral dissertations in mechanical engineering are considered. Monetary prizes of 2,500 to 5,000 Swiss francs are awarded to one or more candidates annually on ETH-Day (Dies Academicus) and Promotion-Day. Established in 1970 by Mrs. Katja Fischer in honor of Mr. Georg A. Fischer, a mechanical engineer at ETH.

Hilti-Preis fur Innovative Forschung
For recognition of a scientifically outstanding diploma or Ph.D. thesis in applied research. A prize of 5,000 Swiss francs is awarded annually on the ETH-Day (Dies Academicus) or at a Promotion Ceremony. Established in 1989 by Hilti AG, Schaan, FL.

Otto Jaag-Gewasserschutz-Preis
For recognition of outstanding student scientific works, particularly for diploma theses or doctoral dissertations. A monetary prize of 1,000 Swiss francs is awarded annually on ETH-Day (Dies Academicus). Established in 1980 in honor of Professor Dr. Otto Jaag.

Fritz Kutter-Preis
For recognition of an outstanding diploma or Ph.D. thesis in computer science, with a significant contribution in information processing or a valuable implementation of know-how, at a Swiss University or Swiss Federal Institute of Technology. The monetary prize is awarded at some academic event. Established in 1975.

Latsis-Preis
For recognition of outstanding scientific work. Candidates who are 40 years of age and younger are eligible. The candidates are evaluated by the Research Committee of the ETH Zurich. A monetary prize of 25,000 Swiss francs is awarded annually. Established in 1984 by Fondation Latsis Internationale in honor of Dr. John Latsis. Sponsored by Forschungskommission ETH Zurich.

Preis der Stiftung Kunststoff-Technik
For recognition of outstanding student scientific dissertations in the field of materials science. Students of the Swiss Federal Institute of Technology Zurich are eligible. A monetary award of 1,000 Swiss francs is awarded annually on ETH-Day. Established in 1985 by the Verband Kunststoffverarbeitender Industriebetriebe der Schweiz VKI. Additional information is available from VKI, Turnerstrasse 10, CH-8006 Zurich, Switzerland.

Ruzicka-Prize
(Ruzicka-Preis)
For recognition of an outstanding work in the field of chemistry. Work that has already been published and completed in Switzerland or by a Swiss national abroad under 40 years of age is eligible. A monetary prize, medal, document, and colloquium are awarded annually in September. Established in 1957 by Schweizerische Chemische Industrie in memory of Dr. Leopold Ruzicka, winner of the Nobel Prize for Chemistry, 1945.

Hans Vontobel-Fonds
For recognition of the best student scientific thesis or dissertation in the fields of agriculture or animal husbandry. A monetary prize of up to 5,000 Swiss francs is awarded at least every three years if not annually.

Swiss Foundation for Parapsychology
(Schweizerische Stiftung fur Parapsychologie, Brugg/Biel)
Industriestrasse 5
CH-2555 Brugg/Biel, Switzerland   Phone: 32 53 20 53

Swiss Prize for Parapsychology
(Schweizer-Preis fur Parapsychologie)
For recognition of research in the field of parapsychology. A monetary prize of 8,000 Swiss francs and a certificate are awarded to each winner annually in February. Established in 1968.

Swiss Music - Edition
(Schweizer Musikedition)
Postfach   Phone: 41 23 60 70
CH-6000 Lucerne 7, Switzerland   Fax: 41 22 43 34

Swiss Music - Edition
(Schweizer Musikedition)
For recognition of compositions of contemporary music. Swiss citizens or other citizens living in Switzerland are eligible. A monetary award to print the work and promotion for selected works are awarded annually.

11942
Swiss Neurological Society
(Schweizerische Neurologische Gesellschaft)
Kant. Spital Aarau
CH-5001 Aarau, Switzerland

11943
Mogens and Wilhelm Ellermann Foundation Prize
(Preis der Mogens und Wilhelm Ellermann-Stiftung)
For recognition of an outstanding publication on neurological sciences. Residents or citizens of Switzerland who are under 35 years of age are eligible. A monetary prize of 14,000 Swiss francs is awarded biennially as well as 2,000 Swiss francs for a lecture on the subject of the prize winning essay. Established in 1984 in honor of Mogens and Wilhelm Ellermann. Sponsored by the Mogens and Wilhelm Ellermann Foundation.

11944
Swiss Organ Competition
(Concours Suisse de l'orgue)
Place du Prieur   Phone: 24 531718
CH-1323 Romainmotier, Switzerland   Fax: 24 531150

11945
Swiss Organ Competition
(Concours Suisse de l'orgue)
To encourage professional development. The competition is open to everyone without discrimination of age or nationality. A monetary award is presented annually when merited at the Swiss Organ Festival. Established in 1983 by Bernard Heiniger.

11946
Swiss Teachers' Association
(Lehrerinnen und Lehrer Schweiz)
Ringstrasse 54
Postfach 189   Phone: 1 3118303
CH-8057 Zurich, Switzerland   Fax: 1 3118315

Formerly: (1989) Schweizerischer Lehrerverein.

11947
Swiss Children's Book Prize
(Schweizerischer Jugendbuchpreis)
To promote good literature for young people. Swiss authors, illustrators and publishing firms only are eligible. Members of the commission may propose the nominees. The commission nominates the winner by secret ballot. A monetary prize of 5,000 Swiss francs is awarded annually when merited. Established in 1943.

11948
Tirreno Gruppo Editoriale
Via Valeggia 12
6926 Montagnola-Lugano, Switzerland

11949
Ernest Bloch International Competition for Musical Composition
To recognize individuals for music composition. The competition is limited for a composition for string orchestra, for a duration of 8 - 15 minutes. Entries should not be published or performed previously. Competition is open to citizens of any country, regardless of age. The jury will select three finalists whose competitions will be performed at the Settimane Musicaldi di Lugano, at the end of which a first prize of 7,000 CHF, second prize of 3,000 CHF, third prize of 1,000 CHF, and publication and CD recording by Tirreno Gruppo Editoriale (TGE) will be awarded. In addition to the three winners, 21 semifinalists compositions may be published, be given a first performance by the affiliated orchestras, and possibly be recorded on a CD by TGE. Scores submitted should have a nome-de-plume and the year of its writing in a sealed envelope, with the nome-de-plume on it. On separate paper give personal details of the composer including name, address, telephone, fax, birthplace, birthdate, nationality, and nome-de-plume. Include a check in the amount of $50 U.S. currency for each work submitted. Deadline is May 30. Formerly: Georges Enesco International Composition Competition.

11950
Union Bank of Switzerland
(Schweizerische Bankgesellschaft)
Bahnhofstr. 45   Phone: 1 2341111
CH-8021 Zurich, Switzerland   Fax: 1 23651111

11951
Swiss Grand Prize Photo Competition - Youth in Switzerland
(Grand Prix Suisse de la Photographie - Jeunesse en Suisse)
To recognize excellence in the photography of young people. The following monetary prizes were awarded biennially: 12,000 Swiss francs - First Prize; 11,000 Swiss francs - Second Prize; 10,000 Swiss francs - Third Prize; and 20,000 Swiss francs - Forderungs-preise or Encouragement prizes. Established in 1973. (Discontinued)

11952
United Nations
Centre for Human Rights
(Center pour les Droits de l'Homme)
Palais de Nations   Phone: 22 7346011
CH-1211 Geneva 10, Switzerland   Fax: 22 7339879

11953
Human Rights Prize
(Prix pour les Droits de l'Homme)
To recognize individuals and organizations who have made outstanding contributions to the promotion of the protection of human rights and fundamental freedoms. Nominations obtained from member states of the United Nations, specialized agencies, international non-governmental organizations, in consultative status with the Economic and Social Council, are presented to the selection committee composed of the President of the United Nations General Assembly, the President of the Economic and Social Council, the Chairman of the Commission on Human Rights, the Chairman of the Sub-Commission on Prevention of Discrimination and Protection of Minorities, and the Chairman of the Commission on the Status of Women. A citation on a plaque is awarded at intervals of not less than every five years.

11954
United Nations
High Commission for Refugees
Nansen Committee
UNHCR Headquarters
Case Postale 2500   Phone: 22 7398111
CH-1211 Geneva 2, Switzerland   Fax: 22 7319546

11955
Nansen Medal
To recognize individuals who have rendered outstanding service to the cause of refugees. No age restrictions apply. Individuals, nations, and voluntary agencies are eligible. The Nansen Medal and a monetary prize of $50,000 US to pursue refugee assistance projects drawn up in consultation with UNHCR are awarded. Awarded annually, usually in the last quarter. Established in 1954 by Dr. G.J. Van Heuven Goedhart, the first United Nations High Commissioner for Refugees, in memory of Dr. Fridtjof Nansen, Norwegian explorer and former High Commissioner for Refugees of the League of Nations.

11956

Universal Postal Union
(Union Postale Universelle)
Bureau International
Weltpoststrasse 4
CH-3000 Berne 15, Switzerland
Phone: 31 3503111
Fax: 31 3503110

11957

International Letter-Writing Competition for Young People
To develop young people's facility in composition and the subtlety of their thought and to contribute to the strengthening of international friendship which is one of the essential missions of the Universal Postal Union. Individuals who are 15 years of age and under may participate in the Competition organized at the national level by Postal Administrations belonging to the UPU. Letters may be submitted until May 30 each year. Gold-plated, silver and bronze medals, diplomas, and postage stamp albums are awarded annually. A jury of UNESCO, which chooses the winning letters, also awards three bronze medals. Ceremonies are organized by the winning Postal Administrations and prizes are presented to the winners on October 9, the anniversary of the founding of the UPU. Established in 1972.

11958

Universite de Geneve
Bureau Universitaire d'Information Sociale
4, rue de Candolle
CH-1211 Geneve 4, Switzerland
Phone: 22 7057779

11959

Prix Latsis
For recognition of an exceptional scientific thesis on completed research work that presents a marked advance in economics, social science, political science, comparative civilizations, linguistics, and information. Applications must be submitted by January 15. The faculty of the economic and social sciences departments of the University selects candidates who are less than 40 years old. A monetary prize of 25,000 Swiss francs is awarded annually in June. Established in 1982 by the Fondation Latsis. Co-sponsored by the Faculty of Economic and Social Sciences. Additional information is available from Secretariat de la Fondation, c/o Madame Lenz, Verena, 3-5 Chemin des Tuileries, 1-293 Bellevue, Oeweke, Switzerland.

11960

Prix Mondial Nessim Habif
For recognition in the field of international studies. A monetary prize of 10,000 Swiss francs is awarded every year by another facility or institute. Established in 1958. Sponsored by Monsieur Nessim Habif. Additional information is available from Bureau d'Information sociale de l'Universite, 4, rue de Candolle, CH-1211 Geneve 4, Switzerland.

11961

University of Basel
(Universitat Basel)
Petersplatz 1
CH-4003 Basel, Switzerland
Phone: 61 267 30 28

11962

Amerbach-Preis
For recognition of the best essay written by a young scholar. Students or alumni of the various departments of the University are eligible. A monetary award of 5,000 Swiss francs and a medal are awarded annually on the occasion of the Dies Academicus. Established in 1962.

11963

Cooperative Prize
(Genossenschaftspreis)
For recognition of an outstanding dissertation or essay. Faculty members of the Departments of Law, Social Sciences, Philosophy, and History are eligible. A monetary prize of 10,000 Swiss francs is awarded annually on the occasion of the Dies Academicus to each of two winners. Established in 1960 by the Organization of Swiss Consumers. Additional information is available from the Swiss Cooperative Society and similar societies, Coop Schweiz, Thiersteinerallee 12, CH-4002 Basel, Switzerland, phone (61) 20 61 11.

11964

University of Berne
Hochschulstrasse 4
CH-3012 Berne, Switzerland
Phone: 31 65 81 11
Fax: 31 65 39 39

11965

University of Berne Prizes
To recognize students and faculty members for outstanding essays, articles, dissertations, and other scholarly research in the following fields: biology, chemistry, physics, medicine, veterinary medicine, and other branches of science and technology, insurance, translation, education, economics, philosophy, ethics, psychology, industry and trade, theology, sociology, and politics. Every three years, the Theodor Kocher Fund of the Research Institute for Biology awards a prize of 3,000 Swiss francs for meritorious scholarly work or to further scientific investigation. The Travers-Borgstroem Foundation awards a prize of a maximum of 5,000 Swiss francs for an essay on the financing of water preservation in Switzerland.

11966

Charles Veillon Foundation
(Fondation Charles Veillon)
Route de Crissier
CH-1030 Bussigny-pres-Lausanne,
  Switzerland
Phone: 21 701 41 47

11967

Charles Veillon European Essay Prize
For recogniton of any work offering productive criticism of contemporary societies, of their ways of life, and of their ideologies. European authors are eligible. A monetary prize of 20,000 Swiss francs is awarded annually. The jury may recommend to the Foundation that a monograph on the winning author be distributed to universities, institutes, libraries and bookstores. Established in 1974 in memory of Charles Veillon. Formerly: Prix Europeen de l'Essai Charles Veillon.

11968

World Conservation Union
(Alliance mondiale pour la nature)
Centre Mondial de la Conservation
Avenue du Mont Blanc
CH-1196 Gland, Switzerland
Phone: 22 64 91 14
Fax: 22 64 29 26

11969

Honorary Member
To recognize individuals for outstanding service in furthering the conservation objectives of protected areas of society.

11970

Fred M. Packard International Parks Merit Award/Commission on Parks and Protected Areas
To recognize park wardens, rangers, and managers from anywhere in the world for contributions in the following areas: valor; advocacy for parks and their values; innovative management; communicating park ideals and objectives to the public; conscientious application to park work in the face of difficult and dangerous circumstances; teaching and training park personnel; research; and administrative service. Awards are given in the following categories: (1) Valor - to recognize personnel who have acted with physical or moral courage beyond the call of duty; (2) Service - to recognize personnel for long and distinguished service; (3) Special Achievement - to recognize personnel for outstanding performance, although their jobs did not call for acts of personal bravery or daring. Nominations are accepted. A certificate and medal are pre-

sented. In some cases, a monetary award is also presented. Established in 1979 and now given in honor of Fred M. Packard, who initiated the award. Formerly: (1982) Valor Award.

11971

John C. Phillips Memorial Medal
For recognition of distinguished service in international conservation. A sterling silver medal is awarded triennially at ordinary sessions of the IUCN General Assembly. Established in 1963 by Friends of John C. Phillips and the American Committee for International Wild Life Protection in memory of John C. Phillips, distinguished United States naturalist, explorer, author and conservationist.

11972

World Health Organization
(Organisation Mondiale de la Sante)
Avenue Appia Phone: 22 791 21 11
CH-1211 Geneva 27, Switzerland Fax: 22 791 07 46

11973

Leon Bernard Foundation Prize
For recognition of outstanding service in the field of social medicine. No condition is made as to age, sex, profession or nationality. Only nominations put forward by national health administrations of WHO Member States and by former recipients of the awards are acceptable. A monetary prize of 1,000 Swiss francs and a bronze medal are awarded irregularly.

11974

Darling Foundation Prize
For recognition of outstanding work in the control of malaria. Only nominations put forward by national health administrations of WHO Member States and by former recipients of the awards are acceptable. A monetary award of 1,000 Swiss francs and a bronze medal are awarded irregularly. Established in memory of Dr. Samuel Taylor Darling, a noted malaria researcher.

11975

Sasakawa Health Prize
To recognize an individual for outstanding innovative work in health development. Established upon the initiative of Mr. Ryoichi Sasakawa of Japan, a great supporter of WHO, President of the Sasakawa Memorial Health Foundation and WHO Goodwill Ambassador.

11976

Dr. A. T. Shousha Foundation Prize
For recognition of the most significant contribution to any health problem in the geographical area in which Dr. Shousha served the WHO. Only nominations put forward by national health administrations of WHO Member States and by former recipients of the awards are acceptable. A monetary prize of 1,000 Swiss francs and a bronze medal are awarded irregularly, but not more often than once a year. Established in 1966.

11977

World Meteorological Organization
(Organisation Meteorologique Mondiale)
41 Avenue Giuseppe-Motta
Case Postale 2300 Phone: 22 7308111
CH-1211 Geneva 2, Switzerland Fax: 22 7342326

11978

International Meteorological Organization Prize
For recognition of outstanding work in the field of meteorology or in any related field. A monetary prize of $1,200, a gold medal, and a parchment scroll with a citation are given annually. Established in 1956 to commemorate the International Meteorological Organization which was established in 1873, and succeeded by the WMO in 1951.

11979

Prof. Dr. Vilho Vaisala Award
To encourage and stimulate interest in important research programs in the field of instruments and methods of observation in support of WMO programs. Scientists may submit papers through the permanent representatives of members of WMO by November 30. A monetary prize of $1,000 US and a diploma are awarded annually. Established in 1986 in honor of Dr. Vilho Vaisala, founder of the Vaisala Oy.

11980

WMO Research Award for Young Scientists
To encourage young scientists, preferably in developing countries, who are working in the field of meteorology. Individuals who are under 35 years of age may be nominated by permanent representatives of WMO. A monetary award of $1,000 and a citation are awarded annually. Established in 1970.

11981

World Organization of the Scout Movement
Honors and Awards Committee
Case Postale 241 Phone: 22 3204233
CH-1211 Geneva 4, Switzerland Fax: 22 7812053

11982

Bronze Wolf
(Loup de Bronze)
To recognize an individual for outstanding services of the most exceptional character to the world scout movement. A bronze medal in the form of an animal is awarded triennially at the World Scout Conferences. Established in 1935 by Robert Baden-Powell, founder of the Scout movement.

11983

Worlddidac Foundation
Bollwerk 21
PO Box 8866 Phone: 41 313117682
CH-3001 Berne, Switzerland Fax: 41 31312171

11984

Worlddidac Award
To promote the quality improvement and the creativity of the international educational materials industry. The products entered are divided into the following entry groups: preschools, elementary schools, secondary/senior schools, vocational and adult education, and special education. Within these entry groups there is a further classification into the following product groups: teaching and learning aids for general education, including books, educational games, demonstration material (charts, globes, etc.); scientific and technological apparatus and equipment for student or classroom use, including models; AV and computer software; AV and computer hardware; and educational furniture. Products newly released in the past two years are eligible. Gold, silver, or bronze award certificates are presented biennially at the International Education and Training Exhibition Worlddidac in Basle. Established in 1984.

11985

WWF World Wide Fund for Nature
 Phone: 22 3649111
CH-1196 Gland, Switzerland Fax: 22 3645358

Formerly: World Wildlife Fund.

11986

Gold Medal
This, WWF's highest award, is given for highly meritorious and strictly personal services to the conservation of wildlife and natural resources. The WWF awards cannot be applied for. Nominations are made, screened, and judged through an internal consultative process. A gold medal is awarded. Established in 1970.

11987

International Conservation Roll of Honour
A posthumous honor for people having rendered outstanding services to the cause of conservation, not only to WWF. The WWF awards cannot be applied for. Nominations are made, screened, and judged through an internal consultative process. Established in 1973.

11988

Members of Honour
Appointed from amongst persons of great distinction in conservation or fields related to conservation, and from retiring Board Members in recognition of outstanding services to WWF. The WWF awards cannot be applied for. Nominations are made, screened, and judged through an internal consultative process. Established in 1969.

11989

Y's Men International
Service Club to the YMCA
37, quai Wilson
CH-1201 Geneva, Switzerland
Phone: 22 7323100
Fax: 22 7384015

11990

Harry M. Ballantyne Award
This, the highest honor of the Y's Men International, is given to recognize especially deserving friends of Y's Men International who over a long period of time have rendered service of special value and helpfulness to the Y's Men's movement. A medal, a trophy, and a framed diploma are awarded annually. Established in 1957.

Taiwan

11991

Center for Chinese Studies
20 Chungshan South Road
Taipei 100 40, Taiwan
Phone: 2 3147321
Fax: 2 3712126

Formerly: (1987) Resource and Information Center for Chinese Studies.

11992

Award Program to Assist Foreign Scholars in Carrying Out Sinological Research in the R.O.C.
To enhance scholarly communication in the field of Chinese studies and encourage foreign scholars of Chinese studies to carry out research work in the Republic of China. Ph.D. candidates, assistant professors, associate professors, professors, and researchers at institutes who plan to do research in the R.O.C. are eligible to apply. The deadline is October 31 for research projects proposed to begin on or after July of the following year. Research grants for 3 to 12 months are awarded annually. The amount of each grant is determined by the candidate's rank at the time of application. Established in 1988 by the R.O.C. Ministry of Education. Formerly: Program to Assist Foreign Sinologists Carry Out Research in the R.O.C..

11993

Chia Hsin Foundation
96, Chung Shan Road N., Sec. 2
Taipei 10449, Taiwan
Phone: 2 523 1461
Fax: 2 523 1204

11994

Chia Hsin Prize
For recognition of outstanding new literary and scholarly works published during the preceding year. A monetary prize of $500,000 (new Taiwan dollars) is awarded annually. Established in 1963. Sponsored by Chia Hsin Cement Corporation.

11995

Chinese Acupuncture Science Research Foundation
8-7, Hang-Chow Building
23, Hang-Chow South Road, Section 1
Taipei 100, Taiwan
Phone: 2 351 5248

11996

Award for Outstanding Achievement in Acupuncture Research
To assist the scientific study of acupuncture and to recognize outstanding results in acupuncture research. Completed acupuncture research projects are eligible. A monetary prize is awarded annually in July. Established in 1978 by Dr. George Yeh.

11997

Chungshan Cultural Foundation
225 Sec. 3, Pei Yi Road, Hsintien
Taipei, Taiwan

11998

Chungshan Cultural Foundation Prizes
To provide recognition for outstanding academic and literary publications and inventions. A monetary prize of 50,000 new Taiwan dollars, a plaque and a citation are awarded annually.

11999

Importers and Exporters Association of Taipei
350 Sungkiang Rd.
Taipei 10477, Taiwan
Phone: 2 5813521
Fax: 2 5423704

12000

Importers and Exporters Association of Taipei Competitions
To recognize exporters, importers, and manufacturers in Taiwan. Competitions are sponsored and awards are bestowed. Scholarships are awarded to students in international trade.

12001

National Fund for Literature and Art
Board of Trustees
17 Chinhua St., 9th Fl.
Taipei 10726, Taiwan
Phone: 2 396 3874
Phone: 2 396 6626
Fax: 2 397 9144

12002

National Award for Literature and Arts
To reward and encourage outstanding creative work in 12 categories: literary and artistic theory, poetry, essays, fiction, journalism, biography, children's literature, fine arts, music, dance, theater, and performing arts. Chinese citizens and foreigners living in Taiwan for more than three years may be nominated by August 15. A monetary award of $400,000 NT and a plaque are awarded annually to each recipient. Established in 1974. In addition, Special Achievement Awards are granted to those who have made special contributions to literature and the arts or to national cultural development or to those who have made major contributions through long-term participation in Literature and the arts. Awards are also available to assist creative writers in the of their first book and to assist them in visiting the front line, rural areas, Taiwan aborigine communities, and other important areas of national reconstruction for the production of fine works of literature. Further awards are given to encourage your people with creative potential to create literary and artistic works, including grants to colleges and universities to set up literary prizes, to the Central Daily News to sponsor the national student literature prize, and others. Additional information is available from the Council for Cultural Planning and Development, Executive Yuan of R.O.C.

12003

Translation Awards
To reward and assist outstanding translators from the R.O.C. and accomplished translators from other countries. Awards are given for translation

of a work of Chinese literature into a foreign language (essays, fiction, poetry, drama, literary criticism); translation of a work of foreign literature into Chinese (essays, fiction, poetry, drama, literary criticism); and translation of a work of general nature (with academic value). In addition, Translator Achievement Awards are awarded to translators who have made special contributions throughout a distinguished career.

12004

Pacific Cultural Foundation
Palace Office Bldg., Ste. 807
346 Nanking E. Rd., Section 3
Taipei, Taiwan

Phone: 2 7527424
Fax: 2 7527429

12005

Pacific Cultural Foundation Awards
To recognize individuals who work towards mutual understanding among countries and regions throughout the world, and to provide grants for foreign scholars to study Chinese culture, history, and contemporary problems.

12006

Taipei City Symphony Orchestra
7F, 25, Pa-Teh Rd., Sec. 3
Taipei, Taiwan

Phone: 2 752 3731

12007

Taipei International Music Competition
To offer young, talented musicians from around the world the opportunity to display their virtuosity and launch a career in classical music. The competition is held in alternate years in voice and cello. Musicians between 17 and 30 years of age are eligible for the cello competition. Female singers, between 20 and 30 years of age, and male singers between 20 and 32 are eligible for the vocal competition. The deadline for entry is March 1. The following monetary prizes are awarded: (1) First Prize - $10,000; (2) Second Prize - $7,500; (3) Third Prize - $5,000; and (4) Fourth Prize - $3,000. Awarded annually. Established in 1988. Sponsored by Taipei City Government.

12008

Taipei Golden Horse Film Festival
No. 45, Chilin Rd., No. 7F
Taipei, Taiwan

Phone: 2 5675861
Fax: 2 5318966

Formerly: Taipei International Film Exhibition.

12009

Golden Horse Awards
To encourage film production in Taiwan and Hong Kong. The Festival is comprised of three major events each year: Golden Horse Awards - a prestigious competition designed to promote the production of Chinese-language cinema; International Film Exhibition - a non-competitive annual showcase of a wide range of the most outstanding films from around the world to enhance the public's appreciation of cinematic art and to foster understanding among diverse cultures; and Chinese Film Exhibition - a showcase of Chinese films retrospectively on different topics, recent products and overseas Chinese film production. Awards are given in the following categories: Best Feature Film; Best Actor; Best Actress; Best Supporting Actor; Best Supporting Actress; Best Feature Film Director; Best Feature Film Photography; Best Screenplay; Best Adapted Script; Best Feature Film Art Design and Achievement in Costume Design; Best Feature Film Original Score, Musical Adaptation and Song; and Best Feature Film Editor and Recording. Awarded annually. Established in 1980. Sponsored by the Government Information Office and the Republic of China Motion Picture Development Foundation.

12010

Taiwan
Ministry of Education
Bureau of Cultural Affairs
5 Chungshan South Road
Taipei 10040, Taiwan

Phone: 2 351 3111

12011

Literature and Art Awards
For recognition of contributions to literature and the arts. Awards are given in the following categories: literature; drama; music; art; calligraphy; dance; and photography. A monetary award of 100,000 new Taiwan dollars and a gold medal are awarded in each field annually.

Tanzania, United Republic of

12012

National Kiswahili Council
(Baraza la Kiswahili la Taifa)
PO Box 4766
Dar es Salaam, United Republic of
  Tanzania

Phone: 24139

12013

Outstanding Kiswahili Scholars
(Mabingwa wa Kiswahili)
For recognition of contributions towards Kiswahili development, particularly in the field of literature. Selection is by nomination. A monetary prize and certificate are awarded every five years. Established in 1988 to commemorate five years of Kiswahili development.

Thailand

12014

Isara Amantakul Foundation
c/o Press Association of Thailand
299 Ratchasima Rd.
Dusit
Bangkok 3, Thailand

Phone: 2 241 0766

12015

Isara Amantakul Prize
To recognize Thai reporters and photographers for outstanding contributions in the field of journalism. Monetary awards of 5,000 baht each for the best reporter and best photographer are awarded annually.

12016

Asian Institute of Technology
Media and Information Services
Km. 41, Phaholyothin Road, Pathumthani
PO Box 2754
Bangkok 10501, Thailand

Phone: 2 516 0110 44
Phone: 2 516 2126

12017

Gold Medal Award for Outstanding Leadership in Rural Development
For recognition of leadership and accomplishments in rural development. A monetary prize and a gold medal were awarded when merited. Established in 1987 on the occasion of the birthday of His Majesty, the King of Thailand, King Bhumibol Adulyadej. This was presented once in 1987.

Thailand

12018
Association of Southeast Asian Institutions of Higher Learning
Ratasastra Bldg. 2
Chulalongkorn Univ. Phone: 2 516966
Bangkok 10330, Thailand Fax: 2 225007

12019
Association of Southeast Asian Institutions of Higher Learning Awards
To recognize individuals for teaching, research, and public service. The Association sponsors competitions and gives fellowships.

12020
Bangkok Bank Limited
333 Silom Rd. Phone: 2 234 3333
Bangkok 10500, Thailand Fax: 2 236 5913

12021
Bangkok Bank Documentary Film Competition Prizes
To promote excellence in documentary films and their role in the social and economic development of Thailand. Local 16mm documentary film producers or other sponsoring agencies are eligible. Two monetary prizes of 75,000 baht each are awarded annually. Established in 1977.

12022
Bangkok Bank Prize for Thai Literature Competition
To promote Thai literature and to maintain the Thai tradition. Prose or poetic work in the Thai language, in narrative style, concerning history, art, culture, religion, social affairs, philosophy or new creative ideas may be submitted. Monetary awards of 50,000 baht each for prose and poetry are awarded annually.

12023
Bua-Luang Art Competition Prize
To encourage Thai artists to display their talent in traditional styles of Thai painting. A monetary award and a Bua-Luang medal are awarded annually.

12024
Foundation for the Promotion of Science and Technology under the Patronage of H.M. the King
Faculty of Science
Chulalongkorn Univ.
Phyathai Rd. Phone: 2 252 7987
Bangkok 10330, Thailand Fax: 2 215 4804

12025
Outstanding Scientist Award
To recognize an individual or a group of individuals for an outstanding contribution to the development of basic science in Thailand. A monetary prize of 200,000 Baht, a plaque and a certificate are awarded annually on National Science Day. Established in 1982 by the Science Society of Thailand. Sponsored by the Siam Cement Company.

12026
International Association of University Presidents
Thai Bldg., 7th Fl.
1400 Rama IV Rd.
Klong Toey
Bangkok 10110, Thailand

12027
International Association of University Presidents Awards
To recognize members of the Association for promoting peace, welfare, and security for mankind through education, and to improve the quality of higher education through mutual cooperation among member institutions of higher learning.

12028
Royal Institute
The Grand Palace
Na Phra Lan Road Phone: 2 214822
Bangkok 10200, Thailand Phone: 2 220189

12029
Writing Competition on the Teaching of Buddhism for Children
For recognition of written work on the teaching of Buddhism to children. Works must be submitted by the end of October each year. A monetary prize is awarded annually. Established in 1928 by His Majesty the King Prajadhipok Rama VII. Sponsored by His Majesty the King of Thailand.

12030
Southeast Asian Ministers of Education Organization
Darakarn Bldg.
920 Sukhumvit Rd. Phone: 2 391 0144
Bangkok 10110, Thailand Fax: 2 381 2587

12031
SEAMEO Testimonial for the Southeast Asian Ministers of Education Council (SEAMEC) President
To recognize the president of the Council for encouraging professional development of the Southeast Asian region through regional cooperation via education, science, and culture. Membership in the Council is necessary to be elected as President by the Council members. A plaque is awarded annually at the Conference. Established in 1984 in honor of SEAMEO, which is dedicated to the cause of regional cooperation in education, science, and culture and for peace and prosperity in Southeast Asia.

Trinidad and Tobago

12032
Trinidad and Tobago Government
Prime Minister's Office
Central Bank Tower
Eric Williams Plaza
Independence Sq.
Port of Spain, Trinidad and Tobago Phone: 809623-3653

12033
Chaconia Medal of the Order of the Trinity
For recognition of long and meritorious service to Trinidad and Tobago in the field of social work; and community service which promotes community spirit and national welfare. Non-citizens may be conferred with honorary awards. No more than ten gold, silver and bronze medals are awarded annually.

12034
Hummingbird Medal of the Order of the Trinity
For recognition of loyal and devoted service in various fields of endeavor which benefits or adds to the prestige of the community or country; and for outstanding human action. Non-citizens may be conferred with honorary awards. No more than fifteen gold, silver and bronze medals are awarded annually.

12035
Public Service Medal of Merit of the Order of the Trinity
For recognition of outstanding and meritorious public service by citizens who are members of the public sector, such as the Defense and Protective Services, members of Statutory Boards and Committees, and other quasi public services. Only citizens of Trinidad and Tobago are eligible. Gold, silver and bronze medals are awarded annually.

12036
Trinity Cross of the Order of the Trinity
This, the most prestigious award of the Order, is given for recognition of distinguished and outstanding service to Trinidad and Tobago by citizens; and for gallantry in the face of the enemy, or for gallant conduct beyond the call of duty. Non-citizens who have rendered distinguished service are also eligible. A gold cross is awarded annually. The medal is limited to five recipients a year.

12037
West Indian Tobacco Company
Eastern Main Rd.
PO Box 177
Port-of-Spain, Trinidad and Tobago   Phone: 809662-2271

12038
Sports Hall of Fame
To recognize outstanding sporting personalities and, at the same time, ensure a permanent record of their achievements. The Sports Hall of Fame is open to Sportsmen, Sportswomen, and Administrators who have made an outstanding contribution to sports. The nominee must be a national of Trinidad and Tobago, resident or represented Trinidad and Tobago, and must have retired from active open international sport before being considered for selection. Established in 1984.

12039
Jeffrey Stollmeyer Memorial Award
To recognize an individual for outstanding service to any particular sport as an administrator for the past year. The nomination is open only to nationals of Trinidad & Tobago or persons with such residential status. A plaque is awarded annually.

12040
West Indian Tobacco Sports Foundation Award
To recognize the top sportsman and sportswoman of the year. Individuals are nominated by the associations representing their particular sport and the winners are chosen, by majority vote, by a panel of sports officials and sports writers and broadcasters. Trophies are awarded annually. The award was first given in 1962, the year of the nation's independence. It was won exclusively by men until 1971, when awards were given to the top sportsman and sportswoman of the year.

Tunisia

12041
Festival International du Film Amateur
(Journees Cinematographique de Carthage)
PO Box 116
1015 Tunis, Tunisia   Phone: 1 280 298

12042
Festival International du Film Amateur
For recognition of outstanding films, and to encourage Arab and African film production. Arab or African citizens may submit films. Awards are given for: (1) Best Film; (2) Best Actor; (3) Best Actress; (4) Best Short Film; (5) Prize for a First Time Director; (6) Special Jury Prize; and (7) Best Photography. A monetary prize and a medal are awarded biennially. Established in 1966 by the Minister of Culture, La Kasbah, Tunis, Tunisia, in honor of the goddess of Carthage. Sponsored by the Ministry of Cultural Affairs, and the Tunisian Federation of Amateur Filmmakers.

Turkey

12043
Ataturk Supreme Council for Culture, Language and History
(Ataturk Kultur, Dil ve Tarih Yuksek Kurumu)
217 Ataturk Bulvari
Kavaklidere   Phone: 41 128 61 00
TR-06680 Ankara, Turkey   Phone: 41 126 71 25

12044
Ataturk International Peace Prize
(Ataturk Uluslararasi Baris Odulu)
To recognize an individual who has served world peace and the development of friendship, understanding, and goodwill in international relations, through his political, scientific, scholarly, artistic and other works. Contributions should be in conformity with Ataturk's "Peace at Home, Peace in the World" principle. Applications may be submitted by December 31. A monetary award, a gold prize badge, and an engraved silver plaque are awarded annually on May 19 on the occasion of the Commemoration of Ataturk on Youth and Sports Day. The Prize winner is invited to attend the ceremony and deliver a lecture on "Ataturk and World Peace" or on the works, services, and activities which have earned him the Prize. Established in 1986.

12045
Chamber of Geological Engineers of Turkey
(Tmmob Jeoloji Muhendisleri Oiasi)
PK 464 Kizilay   Phone: 4 134 36 01
TR-06424 Ankara, Turkey   Fax: 4 134 23 88

Formerly: (1989) Geological Society of Turkey.

12046
Hamit Nafiz Pamir Hizmet Odulu
For recognition of contributions to professional and educational developments in the earth sciences. A plaque was awarded annually at the convention. Established in 1981 in honor of Professor Dr. Hamit Nafiz Pamir, the founder of the Geological Society of Turkey (which was disbanded in 1989, and its award cancelled).

12047
Service Award of Chamber of Geological Engineers
(Jeoloji Muhendisleri Odasi Emek Odulu)
To recognize individuals for 25, 30, 40 and 50 years service in the field of geology. Established in 1983.

12048
***Cumhuriyet* Newspaper**
(Cumhuriyet Matbaacilik ve Gazetecilik T.A.S.)
Yenigun A.s,, Turkocagi Cad. 39/41
Cagaloglu
TR-34334 Istanbul, Turkey   Phone: 1 512 05 05

12049
Yunus Nadi Yarismasi
(Yunus Nadi Prize)
To encourage the literary and intellectual development of the new generation of Turkish people. All professional or non-professional persons interested can apply for the award. A monetary award of 10,000,000 Turkish liras is given to the winner in each of the eight categories: short stories, novel, poetry, poster, photography, cartoon, long footage film scenario, and study on social sciences. Awarded annually on June 29. Established in 1946-47 in memory of Yunus Nadi, founder of *Cumhuriyet* Newspaper. Formerly: (1990) Yunus Nadi Gift.

12050

**Darussafaka Association
(Darussafaka Cemiyeti)**
Halaskargazi Cad. 291
TR-Sisli, Istanbul, Turkey

Phone: 2 484810
Fax: 2 338023

12051

**Sait Faik Prize
(Sait Faik Odulu)**
To recognize the best short story writer. A monetary prize of 5,000,000 Turkish liras and a plaquette are awarded annually. Established in 1965.

12052

**Hurriyet Foundation
(Hurriyet Vakfi)**
Babiali Cad. 15-17
Cagaloglu
TR-34360 Istanbul, Turkey

Phone: 1 5120000
Fax: 1 5120026

Formerly: (1982) Erol Simavi Hurriyet Vakfi.

12053

**International Simavi Cartoon Competition
(Uluslarasi Simavi Karikatur Yarismasi)**
To encourage and recognize an outstanding international cartoonist. Competitors may submit entries by June 1 of each year. The following awards are presented: (1) first prize - a monetary award of US $5,000, a golden plaque and Ministry of Culture and Tourism Prize; (2) second prize - a monetary award of US $3,000, a silver Plaque and *Hurriyet Newspaper* Golden Plaque; (3) third prize - a monetary award of US $2,000, Hurriyet Foundation Bronze Plaque and *Carsaf* Magazine Silver Plaque; and (4) 10 honorable mentions. Awarded annually on June 27, the anniversary of the Foundation. Established in 1983.

12054

International Commission for the Preservation of Islamic Cultural Heritage (ICPICH)
Research Centre for Islamic History, Art
and Culture
Barbaros Bulvari
Yildiz Sarayi, Seyir Kosku
PO Box 24, Besiktas
TR-80692 Istanbul, Turkey

Phone: 212 2605988
Fax: 212 2584365

12055

Award for Distinction in Islamic Science
To recognize individuals who have made contributions in the field of Islamic science history, art, and literature. (Currently inactive)

12056

International Calligraphy Competition
To revive and encourage the development of the classical Islamic calligraphy within the framework of its original principles and traditional spirit. The Competition covers the following styles: Jaly Thuluth, Thuluth, Naskh, Jaly Ta'lik, Ta'lik, Jaly Diwani, Diwani, Qufi, Muhaggag, Reyhani, Rikaa, Riq'a, Maghrebi, and Hurde Ta'lik. Entries submitted in any one of these styles should be written in the classical way and according to the classical rules of calligraphy. The work must be written with a reed pen using classical ink. A monetary prize and a certificate are awarded triennially. Established in 1986, and in 1989 held in honor of Yaqut Al-Mustasimi, an Abbasid calligrapher of Turkish origin who lived in the 13th century A.D. The first competition was held in honor of Hamid El-Amidi, the last famous calligrapher of Turkey. The third competition honored Ibn Al-Bawab on the millenium of his death.

12057

International Photographic Competition to Commemorate Islamic Heritage
To promote the unique qualities of Islamic cultural heritage through a contemporary visual medium-like photography. Awards are given for color prints, black and white prints, and transparencies. A monetary prize and a certificate are awarded for Grand Prize, first place, second place, and third place in each category. Established in 1989. Co-sponsored by the Secretariat of the International Commission for the Preservation of Islamic Cultural Heritage and the Research Centre for Islamic History, Art and Culture.

12058

King Fahd Awards for Design and Research in Islamic Architecture
For recognition of contributions to the conservation, restoration, and reconstruction of monuments representing Islamic Cultural Heritage, and to recognize the emerging design talent and scholarship aimed at the issues of Islamic architecture. Open to architectural students and recent graduates from all over the world who have completed their education within three years prior to the submission. The following prizes are awarded: King Fahd Award for the Design of Islamic Architecture - $10,000; Major Awards - four at $4,000 each; Minor awards - six at $2,000 each; Design tutor for the King Fahd Award - $2,000; and Design tutors of each winning design are awarded an Honorarium of $1,000. Established in 1985 by His Majesty King Fahd Bin Abdul Aziz, King of the Kingdom of Saudi Arabia. (Inactive since 1986)

12059

**Istanbul Foundation for Culture and Arts
(Istanbul Kultur ve Sanat Vakfi)**
Yildiz Kultur ve Sanat Merkezi
Babaros Bulvari
Besiktas
TR-80700 Istanbul, Turkey

Phone: 1 160 90 72
Phone: 1 160 45 33
Fax: 1 161 88 23

12060

**Istanbul International Film Festival
(Uluslararasi Istanbul Sinema Gunleri)**
For recognition of contributions to the field of cinema; to encourage cooperation between the arts and the cinema; and to promote the distribution of films of outstanding quality in Turkey. The program consists of the following sections: (1) an international competiton for the Golden Tulip Award open to feature films on such subjects as literary adaptations, filmed versions of the performing arts, biographies of artists and writers, and films on creativity in the arts; (2) films on a specific theme such as music and the movies; (3) tributes to directors; and (4) Turkish cinema. Feature films in 35mm with a minimum length of 1,600 m. produced during the preceding two years are eligible for presentation in the competition. Films of the competition are selected by the Program Committee. Producers, directors, distributors, national film institutes and foreign embassies may submit titles. Films in the competition are judged by an international jury composed of directors, producers, actors, film critics, and cinema-historians. The Golden Tulip Award (Altin Lale Odulu, the Grand Prix of the festival) is awarded annually. Established in 1985.

12061

Milliyet
Nuriosmaniye Caddesi 65
Istanbul, Turkey

Phone: 1 511 4410

12062

Karacan Prize
For recognition of articles which draw the attention of readers to important current problems of Turkey. Monetary prizes and publishing rights are awarded annually in memory of the founder of the newspaper, A.N. Karacan.

12063

Sportsman of the Year Award
To recognize the best sportsman of the year and to encourage sports. A cup is awarded to the best sportsman annually.

12064

Scientific and Technical Research Council of Turkey (Tubitak)
(Turikiye Bilimsel ve Teknik Arastirna Kurumu)
Ataturk Bulvari 221
Kavaklidere
TR-06100 Ankara, Turkey
Phone: 1685300
Fax: 41277489

12065

Bilim Odulu
(Science Award)
For recognition of contributions to scientific research at the international level, or to the development of the country. Living Turkish scientists are eligible. A monetary prize of 6,000,000 Turkish liras, a golden plaque and a certificate are awarded annually. Established in 1965.

12066

Hizmet Odulu
(Service Award)
For recognition of contributions to science and technology at the national level through scientific research or through training of young scientists, and for helping the development of a scientific field. Turkish scientists, living or dead, are eligible. A monetary prize of 4,000,000 Turkish liras, a silver plaque and a certificate are awarded annually. Established in 1968.

12067

Tesvik Odulu
(Encouragement Award)
To recognize and encourage outstanding scientific research, particularly research work carried out within the last five years which is highly scientific or has contributed to the development of the country. Living Turkish scientists under 40 years of age are eligible. A monetary prize of 2,000,000 Turkish liras, a silver plaque, and a certificate are awarded annually. Established in 1968.

12068

TUBITAK Husamettin Tugac Award
(TUBITAK Husamettin Tugac Odulu)
For recognition of contributions to technology by researchers. Turkish scientists are eligible. A monetary prize, a plaque and a certificate are awarded annually. Established in 1981 in memory of Husamettin Tugac. Sponsored by Husamettin Tugac Foundation.

12069

Tercuman
Tercuman Tesisleri
Davutpasa Cad. 115
Topkapi
TR-Istanbul, Turkey
Phone: 1 5821212

12070

Best Critic Prize
To encourage an interest in literary criticism among readers and to promote the publication of the newspaper granting the award. Monetary prizes of 2,500, 1,500, and 1,000 Turkish liras are awarded on the 15th and 30th of every month.

12071

Turkish Historical Society
(Turk Tarih Kurumu)
Kizilay Sok. 1
TR-Ankara 1, Turkey
Phone: 41 3102368

12072

Orhan Kemal Award
To encourage the publication of novels which reflect the views of Orhan Kemal. A shield is awarded annually. Sponsored by the family and friends of the late Orhan Kemal.

12073

Fikret Madarali Prize
For recognition of the best novel, preferably having as a theme contemporary national problems. Three monetary prizes of 10,000, 5,000 and 3,000 Turkish liras are awarded annually. Sponsored by the family and friends of the late Madarali, a renowned Turkish literature teacher.

12074

Turkish Language Institute
(Turk dil Karumu)
Ataturk Bulvari 217
Kavaklidere
TR-06680 Ankara, Turkey
Phone: 41 1268124
Fax: 41 285288

12075

Literature Prize
To recognize outstanding contributions to Turkish Literature in poetry, research, the short story, the novel, criticism, essay, translation, memoirs, children's literature, and drama. A monetary award of 10 million Turkish liras, a certificate and a plaque are awarded every four years. Established in 1955. Reorganized in 1990. Formerly: (1983) Award for Literature.

12076

Press Language Prize
To recognize the best and most accurate use in the press of the Turkish language as regards the news, articles and sports news. A monetary award of 10 million Turkish liras, a certificate, and a plaque are awarded every four years. Established in 1955. Reorganized in 1990. Formerly: (1983) Newspaper Language Prize.

12077

Prize for Social Sciences and Humanities
For recognition of outstanding contributions to the social sciences and humanities. A monetary prize of 10,000 Turkish liras and a medal were awarded annually. Established in 1955 in memory of Kemal Ataturk, founder of the Turkish Republic and of the Society. (Discontinued in 1983)

12078

Radio and Television Language Prize
To recognize the best and most accurate use on radio and television of the Turkish language. A monetary award of 10 million Turkish liras, a certificate and a plaque are awarded every four years. Established in 1955. Reorganized in 1990.

12079

Scholarly Studies Prize
To recognize outstanding scholarly studies in the Turkish language and literature. A monetary award of 10 million Turkish liras, a certificate, and a plaque are awarded every four years. Established in 1990.

12080

Turkish Language Prize
To recognize outstanding scholarly contributions to the Turkish language in the fields of lexicography, grammar, source books, turcology, dialectology, and terminology. A monetary award of 10 million Turkish liras, a certificate and a plaque are awarded every four years. Established in 1990.

12081
Turkish Society of Plastic Surgeons
(Turk Plastik Cerrahi Dernegi)
Billur Sokak 35/3, Kavaklidere
TR-06700 Ankara, Turkey   Phone: 4 127 22 23

12082
Best Chief Resident Paper
(En iYi Bas Asistan Tebligi)
To encourage professional development in the field of plastic surgery. Candidates for membership may submit papers two months before each National Congress. A certificate and subscription to journals are awarded annually. Established in 1990.

12083
Turkiye Radyo Televizyon Kurumu
Nevzat Tandogan Caddesi 2
Kavaklidere   Phone: 4 128 2230
Ankara, Turkey   Fax: 4 142 767

12084
Turkish Radio and Television Culture, Art and Science Prizes
To recognize the best literary and scientific works for radio and television. Monetary prizes of 500,000 Turkish liras are awarded.

Uganda

12085
Uganda Association for the Mentally Handicapped
(Ekibiina Ekiyamba Abantu Abayiga Empola)
PO Box 9177   Phone: 41 235364
Kampala, Uganda   Fax: 41 245580

12086
Travel Prize
(Kutambula)
For recognition of achievement and contribution in the field of serving persons with mental disabilities. Individuals must be nominated. A monetary prize for travel expenses is awarded annually. Established in honor of Bertha Kawooya, founder of the Association.

Uruguay

12087
Academia Nacional de Medicina del Uruguay
18 de Julio 2175
Montevideo, Uruguay   Phone: 2 40 14 44

12088
Gran Premio Nacional de Medicina
To stimulate scientific works among the medical profession of Uruguay. Established in 1977 by the Ministerio de Educacion y Cultura.

12089
Concurso Internacional de Piano Ciudad de Montevideo
Santiago Vazquez 1178
Montevideo, Uruguay   Phone: 2 78 18 55

12090
Concurso Internacional de Piano Ciudad de Montevideo
For recognition of outstanding piano performances. Pianists under 33 years of age of all nationalities may apply. Monetary prizes totaling $4,000 and medals are awarded triennially. Established in 1964 by Eliane Richepin.

12091
Mutual Assistance of Latin American State Owned Companies
(Asistencia Reciproca Petrolera Estatal Latin)
Javier de Viana 2345
Montevideo, Uruguay   Phone: 2 40 74 54

12092
Premio Petrocanada
For recognition of the best paper presented in technical meetings. Society members may be nominated. Three or four monetary prizes, medals, and certificates are awarded annually at the Annual Assembly. Established in 1984 by Petrocanada.

12093
Panamerican Federation of Architects' Associations
(Federacion Panamericana de Asociaciones de Arquitectos)
25 de Mayo 444, Piso 5
Montevideo, Uruguay   Phone: 2 91 07 20

12094
Federacion Panamericans de Asociaciones de Arquitectos Premios
To recognize the winners of competitions in the field of architecture.

Vatican City

12095
International Federation of Catholic Medical Associations
(Federation Internationale des Associations Medicales Catholiques)
Palazzo San Calisto   Phone: 6 63887372
CV-00120 Vatican City, Vatican City   Fax: 6 3789829

12096
Pope John XXI Prize
To encourage original work in Catholic medical ethics. Medical practitioners of any nationality are eligible. A monetary prize and a medal are awarded every four years. Established in 1950 by the Portuguese Catholic doctors organization in memory of Pope John XXI, a Portuguese physician who wrote medical treatises and books. His Pontificate was short.

12097
Pontifical Academy of Sciences
(Pontificia Academia Scientiarum)
    Phone: 6 69883451
Casina Pio IV   Fax: 6 69885218

12098
Pius XI Gold Medal
(Medaglia d'Oro Pio XI)
For recognition of outstanding research in the field of mathematical and natural sciences. Important scientific research by scientists under 45 years of age is considered by the Academic Council. A gold medal is awarded biennially at the Plenary Session. Established in 1961 by Pope John XXIII in memory of Pope Pius XI.

12099
The Vatican
Papal Secretariat of State
I-00120 Vatican City, Vatican City

12100
Benemerenti Medals
To recognize a well deserving person for exceptional accomplishment and service. Men and women are eligible. Medals of gold, silver or bronze, bearing the likeness of the reigning Pope on one side and a laurel crown and the letter B on the other, are conferred by the Pope.

12101
Order of Pius IX
For recognition of outstanding service to the Church and society. Four classes of knighthood may be awarded: (1) the Class of the Grand Collar; (2) Knights of the Grand Cross; (3) Knights of the Second Class; and (4) Commander and Knights of the Third Class. Christian or non-Christian heads of state are eligible. Membership is determined by the Pope. Pontifical Orders of Knighthood are awarded. Founded in 1847, and restricted to heads of state in 1966 by Paul VI.

12102
Order of St. Gregory the Great
To recognize people who are distinguished for personal character and reputation, and for notable accomplishment. This secular honor of merit has civic and military divisions. Membership is determined by the Pope. Pontifical Orders of Knighthood are awarded. Established in 1831.

12103
Order of St. Sylvester
For recognition of outstanding service to the Church. A secular honor of merit, formerly a part of the Order of the Golden Spur, is now awarded separately with three possible degrees: (1) Knights of the Grand Cross; (2) Knight Commanders, with or without emblem; and (3) Knights. Membership is determined by the Pope. Pontifical Orders of Knighthood are awarded. Established in 1841 by Gregory XVI and redefined in 1905 by Pius X.

12104
Order of the Golden Spur (Golden Militia)
To recognize Christian heads of state. This secular honor of merit is one of the oldest knighthoods. The award was restricted in 1966 by Paul VI to Christian heads of state. Membership is determined by the Pope. Pontifical Orders of Knighthood are awarded. Established in 1841 by Gregory XVI as the Order of St. Sylvester. In 1905, Pius X restored the Order of the Golden Spur, separating it from the Order of Sylvester.

12105
Pope John XIII Peace Prize
For recognition of outstanding contributions to world peace. Men and women are eligible. A monetary prize of $25,000 and a citation are awarded triennially by the Pope.

12106
Pro Ecclesia et Pontifice Medal
For recognition of outstanding service to the Church and the papacy. Men and women are eligible. A gold medal with the likeness of Leo XIII is awarded. Established in 1888.

12107
Supreme Order of Christ (Militia of Our Lord Jesus Christ)
For recognition of a Christian head of state. A secular honor of merit, originally meant to continue the suppressed Order of Templars in Portugal during the 14th and 15th centuries, this Order is now restricted to Christian heads of state. Membership in this highest and most exclusive Pontifical Order of Knighthood is determined by the Pope. Founded in 1319, and restricted to heads of state in 1966 by Paul VI.

Venezuela

12108
Festival del Cine Nacional
Departamento de Cine, Universidad de
 Los Andes
Chorros de Milla, Altos Comedor
 Universitario
Merida Edo, Merida, Venezuela   Phone: 74 441514

12109
Festival del Cine Nacional
To encourage professional development and to recognize the outstanding films of the festival. Super 8, 16mm, or 35mm films produced during the preceding year may be entered by Venezuelan citizens or foreigners who have resided in Venezuela for three years. The following prizes are awarded: (1) Gran Premio Libertador Simon Bolivar - monetary prizes of 30,000, 40,000, and 60,000 bolivares for the best documentary or fictional films of short, medium or full length; (2) Special Jury Prize for fictional films; (3) Special Jury Prize for documentary films; (4) Special Prize for the best film for children or young people - 10,000 bolivares; (5) monetary prizes of 5,000 bolivares each in the categories of camera, direction, photography, scenery, music and sound; (6) Prize of the People; and (7) Best Actor and Actress, Best Supporting Actor and Actress, Photography, Feature, Documentary, and Cinematography - works of art are awarded. Awarded biennially. Established in 1980 by Concejo Municipal de Libertador del Edo. Merida, Gobernacion del Edo. Merida, Asamblea Legislativa del Edo. Merida, Fondo de Formento Cinematografico, and Universidad de Los Andes, in memory of Simon Bolivar.

12110
Gobernacion Del Estado Tachira - Venezuela
Address unknown.

12111
Orden Francisco Javier Garcia de Hevia
To recognize and promote persons and institutions whose initiatives have contributed to the progress of the Tachira region. Either Venezuelans or distinguished foreign persons are eligible. Gold, silver, and bronze medals are awarded at irregular intervals by the regional government and presiding governor, Luisa T. Pacheco de Chacon. Established in 1982 by Dr. Ildefonso Moreno Mayo, Governor of Tachira, in memory of Dr. Francisco Javier Garcia de Hevia, distinguished Venezuelan lawyer and educational leader.

12112
Orden Manuel Felipe Rugeles
To honor and promote individuals who have distinguished themselves in the cultural, artistic, or educational development of Tachira. Venezuelan or foreign individuals are eligible. A gold medal with the likeness of Dr. Rugeles is awarded at irregular intervals. Established in 1981 by Dr. Mayo, governor of Tachira, in honor of the author-poet of Tachira, Dr. Manuel Felipe Rugeles.

12113
International Festival of the New Super 8 Cinema and Video (Festival Internacional del Nuevo Cine Super 8 y Video)
Apartado: 61.482 - Chacao 1060
Caracas, Venezuela   Phone: 2 77 13 67

12114
Festival Internacional del Nuevo Cine Super 8 y Video (International Festival of the New Super 8 Cinema and Video)
To recognize filmmakers and video makers from all over the world, working with Super-8 or video, and to show the different forms of expression in films and videos as art. The films are evaluated according to their form, language, contents and technical aspects. The films can be either black and white or color; silent or with magnetic sound. Awards are

given to the three best films. Honorable mentions are also awarded. Awarded annually in November.

12115

National Council for Culture
(Consejo Nacional de la Cultura)
Torre Norte, Piso 16
Centro Simon Bolivar
Apdo 50995
Caracas, Venezuela

12116

Carmen Teresa du Hurtado Machado Latin American Competition for Voice
To promote and reward talented male and female singers for opera, oratorio and concert. Singers of both sexes, born or naturalized in any Latin American country, between 18 and 32 years of age for women and 30 and 35 years of age for men are eligible. The following prizes are awarded to each a man and a woman: (1) first prize - 12,000 bolivares; (2) second prize - 8,000 bolivares; and (3) third prize - 5,000 bolivares. Gold, silver and bronze medals and the corresponding diplomas for first, second and third place are also given. Awarded biennially. Established in memory of Sra. Carmen Teresa de Hurtado Machado (b. 1892) who pioneered academic voice training in Venezuela with Maestro Vincente Emilio Sojo. The Competition was first held in March, 1980.

12117

Inocente Carreno Competition for Composers
For promotion and recognition of symphonic compositions (symphonies, symphonic poems, symphonic suites, oratorios, religious and other cantatas, concertos for one or more instruments and orchestra, etc.). Composers from the following countries are members of the "Andres Bello" Covenant: Chile, Peru, Ecuador, Colombia, Venezuela and Panama. A jury formed by one representative of each of the signatory countries and the Secretary General deliberate on the respective merits of the compositions submitted. A monetary prize of US $10,000, a gold medal, and a diploma are awarded at a public ceremony. The Secretariat offers the publication of the winning composition and its promotion by means of plate or magnetic tape recording. Awarded biennially. Established at the second meeting of the "Andres Bello" Covenant's Cultural Committee to honor Venezuela's composer Inocente Carreno. The Competition was first held in 1981. Sponsored by the Venezuelan National Council for Culture and coordinated by the Instituto Latinoamericano de Investigaciones y Estudios Musicales "Vicente Emilio Sojo."

12118

Teresa Carreno Latin American Competition for Piano
To promote and reward talented young pianists from Latin America. Pianists born or naturalized in any Latin American country, between the ages of 18 and 30 are eligible. The following prizes are awarded: (1) first prize - 12,000 bolivares, a gold medal and a diploma; (2) second prize - 8,000 bolivares, a silver medal and a diploma; and (3) third prize - 5,000 bolivares, a bronze medal and a diploma. Awarded biennially. Sponsored by CONAC. Established in 1974 in memory of Teresa Carreno, a pianist from Venezuela (1853-1917).

12119

Alirio Diaz International Competition for Guitar
For recognition of the best performance by a classical guitar player. Guitar players between the ages of 18 and 35 of any nationality are eligible. The following prizes are awarded: (1) first prize - 20,000 bolivares, a gold medal and a diploma; (2) second prize - 10,000 bolivares, a silver medal and a diploma; and (3) third prize - 5,000 bolivares, a bronze medal and a diploma. Awarded every two years. Sponsored by CONAC.

12120

Romulo Gallegos Novel Prize
To recognize and to stimulate the creative activity of Spanish-language authors. Writers from Latin America, Spain or the Philippines, regardless of their country of residence, may submit a first edition of a Spanish novel. The prize may not be divided among authors or be awarded more than once to an author. A monetary prize of 100,000 bolivares is awarded once every five years. Established in honor of Romulo Gallegos.

12121

Journalism Competition Prizes
To stimulate the work of promotion, diffusion, disclosure and interpretation of art and literature in Venezuela. The competition is open to Venezuelans and foreigners resident in Venezuela. The following prizes are awarded: (1) first prize, Andres Bello Award - to the writer of art or literature who has most distinguished himself on behalf of Venezuelan culture through the medium of the press; (2) second prize, Mariano Picon Salas Award - to the magazine which has most distinguished itself for work in the promotion and disclosure of the different artistic manifestations; (3) third prize, Gabriel Espinoza Award - to an art or literature critic who has most distinguished himself through either print or audiovisual media; (4) fourth prize, Ramon Diaz Sanchez Award - to the television program which has most contributed to the development of Venezuelan culture and to the improvement of television's quality; and (5) fifth prize - Rafael Guinand Award - to the radio program which has most contributed to the development of Venezuelan culture and to the improvement of radio broadcasting. Awarded annually.

12122

National Prize for Literature
To recognize a Venezuelan author for an outstanding book published during the preceding three years. Awards are given in alternate years in the following categories: (1) poetry; (2) prose; and (3) essay and scientific literature. A monetary prize of 20,000 bolivares, a gold medal and a diploma are awarded annually.

12123

National Prize for Music Maestro Sojo
To reward native born and naturalized Venezuelan musicians. The following prizes are awarded: (1) First prize, Jose Angel Lamas - to the best symphonic work, symphonic suite, oratorio or cantata, religious or profane, concerts for one or more instruments, solo or orchestral - 12,000 bolivares, a gold medal and a diploma of honor; (2) second prize, Juan Bautista Plaza - to short works of a symphonic suite, etc. - 6,000 bolivares, a medal and a diploma; (3) third prize, Caro de Boesi - to the best work for small instrumental groups (chamber groups, trios, quartets, duos, vocalists with instrumentalists) - 4,000 bolivares, a medal and a diploma; and (4) fouth prize, Jose Angel Montero - to the best work of pure vocal nature, a capella, or soloist with piano accompaniment - 3,000 bolivares, a gold medal and a diploma. Awarded annually.

12124

National Prize for Theatre Juana Sujo
To stimulate and increase theatre production among native born or naturalized Venezuelan authors. A monetary prize of 5,000 bolivares, a gold medal and a diploma are awarded annually on March 27 (International Theatre Day).

12125

National Council for Scientific and Technological Research
(Consejo Nacional de Investigaciones Cientificas y Tecnologicas - CONICIT)
Apartado 70617
Los Ruices
Caracas, Venezuela   Fax: 2398677

12126

Annual Prize for Scientific Works
(Premios Anuales a los Mejores Trabajos Cientificos)
For recognition of outstanding work in scientific research in biology, medicine, physics, chemistry, mathematics, engineering, and social sciences. An indivisible monetary prize of 30,000 bolivares and a certificate are awarded annually.

12127
Best Scientific or Technological Journal Prize
(Premio a la Mejor Revista Cientifica o Tecnologica)
To recognize the best Colombian scientific journal complying with norms set by UNESCO published in the previous year. Established in 1987.

12128
National Prize for Technical Development/Colombia
(Premio Nacional a Desarollo Tecnologico)
For outstanding technical research. A fellowship of 50,000 bolivares for further investigation is awarded annually. Established in 1979.

12129
National Science Prize
(Premio Nacional de Ciencia)
For recognition of outstanding scientific research. Awarded annually. Established in 1978 by the Council.

12130
Luis Zambrano National Prize for Inventive Technology
(Premio Luis Zambrano a la Inventiva Tecnologica Nacional)
Tor recognize scientists who promote the development of technology through invention rather than research. A monetary prize of 20,000 bolivares is awarded annually. Established in 1984.

12131
Pan American Federation of Engineering Societies
(Union Pan-American de Asociaciones de Igenieros)
Apartado de Correos 17451
Caracas 1010, Venezuela
Phone: 2 5075423
Fax: 2 5749843

12132
Competitions
For recognition in the field of engineering. Competitions are held.

12133
Panamerican Federation of Associations of Medical Schools
(Federacion Panamericana de Asociaciones de Facultades (Escuelas) de Medicina)
Apartado 60411
Caracas 1060-A, Venezuela
Phone: 2 93 08 75
Phone: 2 93 62 71
Fax: 2 93 63 46

12134
Francisco Hernandez Award
(Orden Francisco Hernandez)
For recognition of contributions in the medical education field. Individuals dedicated to teaching and allied health disciplines with the highest levels of quality and professional ethics in the American continent are eligible. A plaque is awarded biennially at the Panamerican Conference of Medical Education. Established in 1984 in honor of Dr. Francisco Hernandez.

12135
Venezuela
Office of the President
(Republica de Venezuela
Despacho del Presidente)
Palacio de Miraflores
Avenida Urdaneta
Caracas 1010, Venezuela
Phone: 2 81 08 11

12136
Order for Merit in Work
To reward employees and workers who have distinguished themselves for efficiency, preparation, and perseverance in work and for exemplary civic and family conduct. Employees and workers of the government and others of merit are eligible. The following awards are presented: (1) first class order to workers with 30 years of service; (2) second class order to workers with between 20 and 30 years; and (3) third class order to workers with 20 years of service.

12137
Order of Andres Bello
To reward individuals who have distinguished themselves in teaching, science, literature, art or generally in the development of culture. The order includes four classes: (1) Collar; (2) Band of Honor; (3) Tie; and (4) Medal. Awarded annually by the President of the Republic or the Minister of Education.

12138
Order of Francisco de Miranda
To reward service to science, to the progress of the nation and for outstanding merit. Orders of first, second and third class are awarded. The President of the Republic receives by right the first class order and awards the second and third class to others.

12139
Order of the 27th of June
To reward distinguished service during years of teaching. The following awards are presented: (1) a gold medal for 30 consecutive years or a total of 35 years; (2) a silver medal for 20 consecutive years or a total of 25 years; and (3) a bronze medal for 10 consecutive years or a total of 15 years.

12140
Order of the Liberator
To reward distinguished servants of the nation for outstanding merit and service to humanity. The order includes several classes: (1) Collar - awarded to chiefs of state and hereditary rulers; (2) First class - awarded to vice presidents of the Republic, presidents of the houses of legislature, president of the federal court, executive ministers, ministers of other nations, ambassadors, governor of the federal district and the general secretary of the president of the Republic; (2) Second class - awarded to members of the federal court, vice presidents of the houses of legislature, attorney general, inspector general of the Army, presidents of states, diplomatic ministers and chiefs of mission accredited in other nations and the Archbishop of Caracas; (4) Third class - awarded to senators and deputies, general officials, secretaries of state governments, national health directors, director and consultants of ministries, presidents of state legislatures, prelates of dioceses, secretaries of the houses of state legislature, secretaries of delegations, charge d'affaires, mayors and governors, presidents or directors of academies and associations either scientific or literary; (5) Fourth class - awarded to consuls and vice consuls, employees who exercise jurisdiction in the states, members of the legislative bodies, secondary school educators, colonels or equivalent in the Navy; and (6) Fifth class - awarded to employees or functionaries who do not exercise jurisdiction in any branch of the administration, all other officials of the Army, journalists, artists, industrialists, and any other persons who might distinguish themselves in the sciences, literature or art.

12141
Venezuelan Architectural Association
(Colegio de Arquitectos de Venezuela)
Avda Colegio de Arquitectos
Urb. La Urbina, Sector Norte
Prolongacion Antiqua Carretera Pet.-
  Guacenos
Caracas 1070, Venezuela
Phone: 2 41 80 07

12142
National Prize for Architecture
To recognize an architect for the most distinguished architectural work completed during the two-year period. Candidates must reside in Venezuela and be members of the Colegio. A monetary prize of 10,000 bolivares, a gold medal and a diploma are awarded biennially. Established in 1963.

Venezuela

12143
Venezuelan Geological Society
(Sociedad Venezolana de Geologos)
Apartado 2006
Caracas 1010-A, Venezuela
Phone: 2 672 0734
Fax: 2 606 4963

12144
Servicios Distinguidos
For recognition of distinguished contributions in the development and realization of the activities of the Venezuelan Society of Geologists. Individuals must be approved by the Board and the Convention. A plaque is awarded irregularly. Established in 1968. Formerly: (1985) Miembro Honorario.

12145
Venezuelan Section of the International Board on Books for Young People
Banco del Libro
Final Avenida Luis Roche - Altamira Sur/
 Apartado 5893
Caracas 1010-A, Venezuela
Phone: 2 333621
Fax: 2 334272

12146
Best Books for Children Awards
(Diez Mejores Libros para Ninos)
To recognize the ten best books for children published in Spanish. Five books originally published in Spanish and five books translated from other languages into Spanish are selected by librarians, reading specialists, and children. Honorable Mention awards are presented annually. Established in 1980 by Banco del Libro to celebrate the Day of the Book.

12147
Venezuelan Society of Civil Engineers
(Sociedad Venezolana de Ingenieros Civiles)
c/o Colegio de Ingenieros de Venezuela
Apdo 2006
Caracas, Venezuela

12148
Venezuelan Society of Civil Engineers Award
To recognize Venezuelan highway engineers, and to stimulate study and research in highway engineering, particularly in Venezuela. A plaque is awarded annually. Established in 1975.

Wales

12149
Arts Council Council of Wales
(Cyngor Celfyddydau Cymru)
Holst House
Museum Pl.
Cardiff CF1 3NX, Wales
Phone: 222 394711
Fax: 222 221447

Formerly: Welsh Arts Council.

12150
Arts Council of Wales Book of the Year Awards
To recognize works of exceptional merit by Welsh authors (by birth or residence) that have been published during the previous calendar year. Works may be written in Welsh or English. Awards are presented in the categories of poetry, fiction, and creative non-fiction, including literary criticism, biography, and autobiography. In the case of non-fiction, the subject matter must be concerned with Wales. Two prizes of £3,000 are awarded to the first place winners and £1,000 to four other short-listed authors in the above categories. In addition, Bursaries are awarded to writers who have resided in Wales for at least two years to undertake specific literary work on a full-time basis for up to six months. Formerly: Welsh Arts Council Prizes.

12151
Welsh Arts Council Drama Prize
To recognize an outstanding playwright at the Welsh National Eisteddfod. A monetary prize and performance of the winning play at the North Wales Theatre Gynedd Company are awarded. (Discontinued)

12152
British Association for Applied Linguistics
Cals. Univ. College Swansea
Swansea, W. Glam SA2 8PP, Wales
Phone: 792 295391
Fax: 792 295641

12153
BAAL Book Prize
For recognition of an outstanding book in applied linguistics. Books published during the preceding calendar year are eligible. The deadline for nomination is April 30. Established in 1984.

12154
British Broadcasting Corporation and Welsh National Opera
Broadcasting House
Cardiff CF5 2YQ, Wales
Phone: 222 572888
Fax: 222 552973

12155
Cardiff Singer of the World Competition
To recognize outstanding singers at the beginning of their professional careers. Individuals who are at least 18 years of age may be nominated by the national broadcasting organization or other national organization. (One individual may be nominated from each country.) A monetary award of £10,000, a trophy, a London recital sponsored by British Petroleum, and a BBC engagement are awarded biennially. Established in 1983. Supported by British Petroleum. Additional information is available from the Richard Tucker Music Foundation, c/o Exec. Dir., 1790 Broadway, Ste. 715, New York NY 10019-1412.

12156
British Hang Gliding Association
2 Lion Terr. Gilwern
Abergavenny, Gwent NP7 OBU, Wales
Phone: 873 831667
Fax: 873 831068

12157
British Hang Gliding Association Trophy
For recognition of outstanding contributions to hang gliding. A trophy is awarded when merited. Established in 1985.

12158
National Cross Country Trophy
To recognize the hang glider pilot who has flown the most miles/kilometers during the year in British skies. A trophy is awarded annually. Established in 1982.

12159
President's Trophy
To recognize the pilot who has flown the single longest flight of the year provided that it is longer than the previous longest flight. The recipient is also the holder of the British Distance Record. On years when the distance record is not broken, the award is presented to someone for services to hang gliding. A trophy is awarded annually. Established in 1976.

12160
Alvin Russell Trophy
To recognize the British Hang Gliding Champion. A trophy is awarded annually. Established in 1977 in memory of Alvin Russell, multi-talented

hang glider pilot and the Association's first training officer who died on December 24, 1976.

12161
British Numismatic Society
c/o Royal Mint
Llantrisant
Pontyclun, M. Glam CF7 8YT, Wales
Phone: 443 222111
Fax: 443 228799

12162
Sanford Saltus Medal
To recognize the member of the Society whose paper or papers appearing in the Society's publications are in the best interest of numismatic science. Members of the Society vote for the best paper. A gold medal is awarded triennially. Established in 1910 by John Sanford Saltus.

12163
Campaign for the Protection of Rural Wales
(Ymgyrch Diogelu Cymru Wledig)
Ty Gwyn
31 High St.
Welshpool, Powys SY21 7JP, Wales
Phone: 938 552525
Phone: 938 556212
Fax: 938 552741

Formerly: Council for the Protection of Rural Wales.

12164
Rural Wales Award
To recognize work by individuals and organizations that is consciously intended to enhance the appearance or amenities of the Welsh countryside. Local branches of the organization make the awards. Framed certificates and a brass plaque are awarded annually. Established in 1984.

12165
Commonwealth Weightlifting Federation
(Federation Halterophile du Commonwealth)
Pennant, Blaenau
Ammanford, Dyfed, Wales
Phone: 269 850390

12166
Commonwealth Weightlifting Federation
To promote weightlifting in the British Commonwealth and to recognize the winners of championship contests. Certificates are awarded annually. No further information on awards is available for this edition.

12167
Ryan Davies Memorial Fund
Dinefwr House
Llandeilo, Dyfed SA19 6RT, Wales
Phone: 558 823864
Fax: 558 823867

12168
Ryan Davies Awards
To assist young Welsh talent in music and drama. Individuals under 30 years of age of Welsh birth are eligible. Monetary prizes are awarded annually in August. Established in 1980 in memory of Ryan Davies, the Welsh entertainer.

12169
Drama Association of Wales
Chapter Arts Centre
Market Rd.
Canton
Cardiff, S. Glam CF5 1QE, Wales
Phone: 222 43794
Fax: 222 225901

12170
D. T. Davies Memorial Award for Playwriting
For recognition of outstanding achievement in the writing of a one-act play. Candidates are selected by ajudicators of One-Act Playwriting Competitions. A plaque is awarded annually. Established in 1962 in memory of the playwright, D.T. Davies.

12171
Maynard Cup
For recognition of outstanding achievements in drama production in the Wales One-Act Play Festival. Candidates are selected by adjudicators at local One-Act Play Festivals. A cup is awarded annually in May. Established in 1935.

12172
European Surfing Federation
77 Fairway
Port Talbot SA12 7HW, Wales
Phone: 639 886246
Fax: 656 647851

12173
European Surfing Championships - Open Champion
To recognize the winners of the annual European surfing championships. A trophy is awarded biennially. Established in 1965.

12174
Historical Metallurgy Society
22 Easterfield Dr.
Southgate
Swansea SA3 2DB, Wales
Phone: 656 880766

12175
Historical Metallurgy Society Grants
To encourage the preservation and study of all aspects of metallurgical history, including the extraction of ores and minerals, the melting and working of metals, and the preservation of archaeological and historical sites and objects. Grants for research and excavations are awarded.

12176
Llangollen International Musical Eisteddfod
c/o Eisteddfod Office
Llangollen, Clwyd LL20 8NG, Wales
Phone: 978 860236
Fax: 978 861300

12177
Llangollen International Musical Eisteddfod
For recognition of the best performances in the following categories: folk songs solo/group, folk dance groups, children's choirs, vocal soloists, instrumental solo/group, International Young Instrumentalist of the Year, chamber choirs, youth choirs, mixed choirs, female choir, male choir, folk dance group, International Young Singer of the Year, Princeps Cantorum, and Gwynne William Prize. The festival provides "an opportunity for peoples of the world to gather together to make music in a spirit of harmony and friendship...that we might learn to live in peaceful coexistence with one another." All competitors, except the choir conductors and accompanists, must be amateurs. International Eisteddfod Trophies and monetary prizes ranging from £10 to £3,000 are awarded annually. A "Choir of the World at Llangollen" is also named. Established in 1947.

12178
Newport International Competition for Young Pianists Committee
Leisure and Amenities
Newport Borough Council, Civic Centre
Newport, Gwent NP9 4UR, Wales
Phone: 633 232801
Fax: 633 244721

Formerly: Newport Pianoforte Competition.

12179
Newport International Competition for Young Pianists
To provide a platform for young pianists at the start of their professional careers. Individuals must be under 25 years of age at the time of competition to be eligible. The following monetary prizes are awarded: first prize - £2,000 and a series of concerts at Wales; second prize - £1,250; third prize - £750; and three other competitors in the second round - £300 each. Each of the six final competitors also receives a Certificate of Merit. The competition is held triennially. Established in 1979.

12180
North Wales Arts Association
(Cymdeithas Gelfyddydau Gogledd Cymru)
10 Wellfield House
Bangor, Gwynedd LL57 1ER, Wales
Phone: 248 353248
Fax: 248 351077

12181
Alun Llywelyn-Williams Memorial Award
(Gwobr Goffa Alun Llywelyn-Williams)
To enable an artist from any artistic field to complete a specific piece of work. One artistic field is selected each year. Open to artists living in Wales or who were born and brought up in Wales. A monetary award of £500 to £1,000 is presented annually. Established in 1989 by HTV Cymru/Wales to honor Prof. Alun Llywelyn-Williams (1913-1988), poet and literary critic. Sponsored by HTV Cymru/Wales.

12182
Prince of Wales' Committee
(Pwyllgor Tywysog Cymru)
Empire House, 4th Fl.
Mount Stuart Sq.
Cardiff CF1 6DN, Wales
Phone: 222 471121
Fax: 222 482086

12183
Prince of Wales' Awards
(Gwobrau Tywysog Cymru)
To recognize projects that have improved the environment in Wales or human understanding of the environment. Open to everyone, young or old, town dwellers, schools, multinational companies, or community groups. Projects must be in Wales and completed within 18 months of the June 15 deadline. Award certificates are signed and presented by HRH The Prince of Wales at a special annual ceremony. Established in 1970. Sponsored by Welsh Water since 1981.

12184
Royal National Eisteddfod of Wales
(Eisteddfod Genedlaethol Frenhinol Cymr)
Eisteddfod Office
40 Parc Ty Glas, Llanishen
Cardiff, S. Glam CF1 3BN, Wales
Phone: 222 763 777

12185
Membership of the Gorsedd of Bards of Great Britain
(Aelod o Orsedd Beirdd Ynys Prydain)
In recognition of service to Wales, its language and culture, and also to honor Welshmen prominent in other fields of endeavor. Familiarity with the Welsh language, the oldest living language in Europe, is required. Membership entitles the holders to take part in the colorful ceremonial at the Royal National Eisteddford. Bestowed annually during the first week of August. Established in 1772 by Iolo Morgannwg. Sponsored by the Gorsedd Board. Additional information is available from the Recorder, Mr. James Nicholas, B.Sc., Plas Maes-y-Groes, Talybont, Bangor, Gwynedd.

12186
W. Towyn Roberts Scholarship
(Ysgoloriaeth W. Towyn Roberts)
To promote solo singing in Wales and to enable the most promising competitor in a special competition to follow a course of vocal instruction in a recognized school or college of music. The scholarship is open to those born in Wales or of Welsh parents, any person who has resided or worked in Wales for the three years prior to the date of the Eisteddfod, or any person able to speak or write the Welsh language. Competitors are expected to prepare a contrasting program of songs from different periods to be sung in Welsh. The program must include one song by a contemporary Welsh composer. A scholarship of £3,000 is awarded annually during the first week of August. Established in 1982 by W. Towyn Roberts in memory of Violet Jones, Nantclwyd, the founder's wife.

12187
Royal Welsh Agricultural Society
(Cymdeithas Amaethyddol Frenhinol Cymru)
Llanelwedd
Builth Wells, Powys LD2 3SY, Wales
Phone: 982 553683
Fax: 982 553563

Formerly: Welsh National Agricultural Society.

12188
Sir Bryner Jones Perpetual Memorial Award
(Gwobr Goffa Sir Bryner Jones)
For recognition of exceptional achievement in agricultural practice within the principality. Individuals may be nominated. A trophy is awarded annually. Established in 1957 by Miss Bertha Bryner Jones in memory of Sir Bryner Jones, CBE, MSc.

12189
Society of Architects in Wales
75a Llandennis Rd.
Cardiff CF2 6EE, Wales
Phone: 222 762215
Fax: 222 747354

12190
Welsh Housing Design Awards
(Gwobrau Cynllunwaith Tai yng Nghymru)
To focus attention on and to promote higher standards of design, specification and construction in housing projects, both in the public and private sectors. In judging the quality of entries, attention is paid not only to external appearance, layout, landscaping and grouping of buildings, but also to design, building quality, workmanship, choice of building materials, maintenance and user satisfaction. The planning of residential roads and footpaths, the siting and integration of garages, and the provision of parking spaces, landscaping and play spaces are also taken into account. Houses must have been completed within a specified time. Awards are given in the following categories: (1) Private Sector: New Housing; (2) Public and Private Sector: Improvement or conversion; and (3) Public and Private Sector: New Housing. Medals are awarded to Housing Schemes judged to have reached high standards of excellence; such schemes are awarded a building plaque and diploma. Schemes just failing to qualify for a Medal Award may be Highly Commended and recognized by the award of a diploma. Awarded biennially. Established in 1961 by the Royal Institute of British Architects, Welsh Region and National Housebuilding Council.

12191
Thomson Foundation
68 Park Pl.
Cardiff CF1 3AS, Wales
Phone: 222 874873
Fax: 222 225194

12192
Thomson Foundation Fellowships
To enable print and television/radio journalists in full-time employment in developing countries to attend 12-week advanced courses in journalism in Cardiff. Applicants must have a good understanding of English. Awards vary in number each year according to resources available. The

award covers tuition fees, accommodation, subsistence allowance, travel within Britain, and some meals, but not air travel. Established in 1962 by Lord Thomson of Fleet. Enquiries can be made at British High Commissions and Embassies as well as British Council offices.

12193

Welsh Academy
Mount Stuart House, 3rd Fl.
Mount Stuart Sq.
Cardiff CF1 6DQ, Wales   Phone: 222 492025

12194

City of Cardiff International Poetry Competition
For recognition in the field of poetry at the Cardiff Literature Festival. Entrants must be new writers who have not published a full collection of poetry. Monetary prizes of £1,000, £500, £300, £200 are awarded annually. Established in 1986. Sponsored by the Cardiff City Council.

12195

Welsh Books Council
(Cyngor Llyfrau Cymraeg)
Castell Brychan, Heol-y-Bryn
Aberystwyth, Cymru, Dyfed SY23 2JB,   Phone: 970 624151
  Wales   Fax: 970 625385

Formerly: (1990) Welsh National Centre for Children's Literature.

12196

Gwobrau Tir na n-og
(Tir Na N-Og Awards)
To raise the standard of children's and young people's books and to encourage the buying and reading of good books. Awards are given in the following categories: fiction - original Welsh language novels, stories and picture-books are considered; other books published during the year - every other Welsh language book published during the relevant year is considered with the exception of those translations produced overseas in the form of international editions, and also packs and pamphlets; and the best English language book of the year with an authentic Welsh background - fiction and factual books originated in English are eligible. Translations from Welsh or any other language are not eligible. Books published during the preceding year may be chosen by a selection panel. Monetary prizes totaling £1,000 are shared equally among the three categories. Awarded annually. Established in 1976 by the Welsh Arts Council, the Welsh Joint Education Committee, and the Welsh Youth Libraries Group.

12197

Mary Vaughan Jones Award
For recognition of outstanding services to the field of children's literature in Wales over a period of time. The winner is chosen by a panel. A silver trophy is awarded triennially in November. Established in 1985 in memory of Mary Vaughan Jones, one of the main benefactors of children's literature in Wales for a period of over 30 years.

12198

YR Academi Gymreig
Mount Stuart House
Mount Stuart Sq., the Docks   Phone: 222 492064
Cardiff CF1 6DQ, Wales   Fax: 222 49930

12199

Griffith John Williams Memorial Prize
(Gwobr Goffa Griffith John Williams)
For recognition of the best published work in the Welsh language. Works published during the previous year by individuals who are not members of the Academi are considered. Children's literature is also excluded. A monetary prize is awarded annually. Established in 1966 in honor of Professor Griffith John Williams.

Zambia

12202

Wildlife Conservation Society of Zambia
PO Box 30255
Lusaka, Zambia   Phone: 1 254226

12203

University Biological Prize Award
To encourage biology students in their work. A monetary prize was awarded annually. Established in 1974. (Discontinued in 1991)

Zimbabwe

12204

Arthur Bensusan Memorial Fund
PO Box 405   Phone: 4 46501 Harare
Harare, Zimbabwe   Fax: 4 46504 Harare

12205

Arthur Bensusan Memorial Fund Prize
To advance the science and practice of mining and the minerals industries. Graduates in the minerals industry are eligible. A monetary prize is awarded annually. Established in 1980 by Mrs. C. Bensusan in memory of Arthur Bensusan. Sponsored by the Institution of Mining and Metallurgy.

12206

National Arts Council of Zimbabwe
144 Sinoia St.
PO Box UA463
Harare, Zimbabwe   Phone: 0707898

12207

National Arts Council of Zimbabwe Competitions
To recognize and promote the arts in Zimbabwe.

12208

Wildlife Society of Zimbabwe
PO Box 3497
Harare, Zimbabwe   Phone: 700451

12209

Wildlife Society of Zimbabwe Competitions
To recognize groups and individuals united to preserve wildlife in Zimbabwe, and to encourage all Zimbabweans to take an active interest in conservation through increased public awareness and use of available conservation educational facilities. The Society sponsors annual wildlife photography competitions and an annual environmental quiz for school-age children.

12210

Young Women's Christian Association Council of Zimbabwe
PO Box AY 154
Amby
Harare, Zimbabwe   Phone: 0 44124

12211

Young Women's Christian Association Council of Zimbabwe Competitions
To recognize individuals for contributions to peace and justice. The Council organizes competitions and meets annually at a conference.

12212

Zimbabwe Institution of Engineers
PO Box 660
Harare, Zimbabwe   Phone: 0 707388

12213

Engineering Achievement Award
To provide public recognition of noteworthy engineering achievements in Zimbabwe with the two-fold aim of challenging and encouraging engineers to strive for professional excellence, and drawing public attention to the contribution the engineering profession makes to the quality of life. Nominees do not have to be members of this Institution but the submission must be by a member of the Zimbabwe Institution of Engineers. Nominations for achievements in every branch of engineering and in such fields as research, invention, construction or design, amongst others may be submitted by March 31. A certificate and an inscribed plaque are awarded.

12214

P. H. Haviland Award
To recognize an individual who has made an outstanding contribution in the field of water engineering, irrigation, or the prevention of water pollution and allied fields. Such contribution may be either in engineering or in administration and may arise from outstanding work in a person's field of employment. Nominations are accepted for the award before March 31. The Award consists of a plaque, framed in wood, and a check in the value of $100.

12215

K. G. Stevens Award
To encourage the presentation of papers of outstanding merit. Corporate members of the Institution may make nominations by April 30. A monetary prize of $200 and a bookplate are awarded annually. Established in 1981 in honor of K.G. Stevens. Sponsored by K.G. Stevens Trust.

12216

Wingquist Award
For recognition of a service to engineering, noteworthy achievements, or unpaid social or public service. Members of any grade of the Institution are eligible for nomination by March 31. A monetary prize of $300 is awarded annually. Established in 1982 in honor of Wingquist. Sponsored by SKF Limited.

12217

Zimbabwe Literature Bureau
PO Box 749 Causeway
Harare, Zimbabwe   Phone: 0 726929

12218

Literary Competition
To encourage professional writing and to recognize the best novel, play, translation, or short story of the competition. Zimbabwean Shona and Ndebele writers are eligible. Two monetary awards are presented annually. Established in 1956.

12219

Zimbabwe National Traditional Dance Association
National Arts Council of Zimbabwe
PO Box CY 520
Causeway   Phone: 0 707898
Harare, Zimbabwe   Phone: 0 793343

Formerly: (1988) Harare African Traditional Dance Association.

12220

Neshamwari Traditional Music and Dance Festival
To recognize achievement and to encourage professional development in traditional music and dance. Elimination contests are held throughout all eight provinces in August. Monetary prizes and trophies are awarded annually. Established in 1966 by the Department of Community Services, City of Harare. Sponsored by Chibuku Breweries.

12221

Zimbabwe Scientific Association
PO Box 8351
Causeway
Harare, Zimbabwe   Phone: 4 42832

12222

Fellow
To recognize individuals who have actively contributed to the advancement of science in Zimbabwe. Persons of high standing who may or may not be members of the Association are eligible for nomination. A certificate and lifetime membership are awarded annually when merited. Established in 1968.

12223

Gold Medal
For recognition of a paper, series of papers, published report, thesis, invention, design or similar achievement which has made an outstanding contribution to the advancement of science in Zimbabwe. Members and non-members of the Association are eligible for nomination. A gold medal and a certificate are awarded annually when merited. Established in 1975.

12224

Zimbabwe Teachers Association
Longman Bldg.
Harare Dr./Tourie Rd.
Box 1440
Harare 263, Zimbabwe   Phone: 0 466392

12225

Zimbabwe Teachers Association Awards
To recognize individuals who promote the economic, social, and professional welfare of members of the Association and advocate the educational interests of the people of Zimbabwe. The Association sponsors competitions and bestows awards.

Subject Index of Awards

The Subject Index of Awards classifies all awards described in this volume by their principal areas of interest. The index contains some 400 subject headings, and each award is indexed under all relevant headings. The index also contains *see* and *see also* references. Awards are arranged alphabetically under each subject heading. Identically named awards are followed by an indented alphabetical list of the organizations administering an award by that name. The numbers following award and organization names are book entry numbers, not page numbers.

Academic achievement (See also Professional and personal achievement)
ANZAC Fellowships 9748
British Mexican Society Postgraduate Prize 2457
Civil Engineering Prizes for Students 3232
Concord Press Award for Academic Publishing 9861
Distincion Universidad Nacional para Jovenes Academicos 9181
Exchange Fellowships 7842
Fondation Laplace 5612
Fulbright Awards - American Program 185
Fulbright Awards - Australian Program 186
Gran Cruz de la Universidad del Valle 1754
IEE Benefactors Prize 3283
IEE Prize 3285
Herbert-Kind-Preis der ETG 6696
Outstanding Kiswahili Scholars 12013
President's Prize 2596
Prix de l'Ecole Centrale 5688
Prix L. E. Rivot 5698
RAF Apprentice Engineering Technician Prize 3300
University of Berne Prizes 11965

Accounting
Awards for Published Accounts 3080
The David J Bogie Prize 10553
The J. C. Burleigh Prize 10554
The Canadian Prize 10555
Charity Accounts Award 3081
The Walid Chorbachi Prizes 10556
Concurso Anual de Tesis Profesionales 8937
The James M. Cowie Prize 10557
Founding Societies' Centenary Award 3082
Gold Medal 10558
The Guthrie Prize 10559
Institute of Financial Accountants Awards 3100
Jorg Kandutsch Preis 846
Lady Members Group 10560
The John Mann Prize 10561
The Robert McArthur Prize 10562
The Sir William McLintock Prize 10563
The Forbes Murphy Prize
    Institute of Chartered Accountants of Scotland 10565
    Institute of Chartered Accountants of Scotland 10564
Patrick O'Brien 10566
Premio Carlos Perez del Toro 8954
Premio el Professor Distinguido 9035
Premio Nacional de la Contaduria Publica 9036
The John Munn Ross Prize 10567
Helen Sommerville Prize 10568

Elmer B. Staats International Journal Award 847
The Albert J Watson Prize 10569
The C. J. Weir Prize 10570
The Ronald Williamson Prize 10571

Acoustics
Simon Alport Memorial Prize 3052
Bekesy Prize 7445
Medailles d'Argent de la SFA 6350
Jozsef Petzval Medal 7446
Prix Chavasse de la SFA 6351
Prix Jeune Chercheur 6352
Prix Philips - France 6353
Prix Thomson Sintra 6354
Pro Silentio 7447
Rayleigh Medal 3053
Stephens Lecture 3054
Tyndall Medal 3055
A. B. Wood Medal and Prize 3056

Actuary See Insurance

Addiction See Drug addiction; Alcoholism treatment

Administration See Management

Adoption See Family relations

Adult and continuing education
Nehru Literacy Award 7566
Franz Stangler Memorial Prize for Adult Education 861
Tagore Literacy Award 7567

Advertising (See also Marketing; Public relations; Publicity)
Advertising Grand Prize 5319
AFN - AGFA Awards 2127
Asian Advertising Award 4479
Best Television Commercial/Advertising Film of the Year 9999
Certamen Nacional la Letra Impresa 9251
Antonina Colonna Prize 8448
Color Television Advertising Award 4534
Dentsu Advertising Awards 8524
Euro Best Awards 3362
Fox of Poster for Books for the Young 6203
Golden Nut Award 11271
International Advertising Award 3753
International Advertising Festival, Cannes 3363
International Advertising Festival of Ireland 7785
International Advertising Press & Poster Festival 3364
IPA Advertising Effectiveness Awards 3200

Lauriers de la FM 6116
Mc Connell Award 7751
National Business Calendar Awards 2483
Newspaper Advertising Prize 8626
Nikkei Advertising Awards 8707
Osterreichischer Staatspreis fur den Werbefilm
    Austria - Ministry of Economic Affairs 745
    Austrian Society of Film Sciences, Communications and Media Research 784
Premio Comunicacao 1408
Premio Nacional Teponaxtli de Malinalco 8932
Primo Scolastico di Raccordo 8014
Staatspreis fur Radiowerbung 749
State Emblems for Economic Advertising (Domestic/Foreign) and Advertising for Social Matters 754
Sunday People Tattersall Trophy 3659

Aeronautical engineering
L.P. Coombes Medal 434
Hartnett Award 658
Institution of Engineers, Australia Award - University of Canberra 455
Henry Mignet Diploma 5160
National Aeronautical Prize 7476
Frank Radcliffe Travelling Fellowship 3902
George Taylor (of Australia) Prize 3912

Aeronautics and aviation (See also Aeronautical engineering; Aviation safety; Flying; Helicopters)
AAHS Trophy (American Aviation Historical Society) 2041
Air League Challenge Trophy 2044
Air League Founders' Medal 2045
Airwork Cup 9809
R. P. Alston Medal 3881
AOPA Awards for Achievement & Endeavor in Light Aviation 2049
Awards 5987
Leon Biancotto Diploma 5138
Louis Bleriot Medal 5139
Samuel M. Bosch Prize 70
British Gold Medal 3884
British Silver Medal 3885
John Britten Prize 3886
Sir Vernon Brown Prize 3887
Busk Prize 3888
C. A. D. Trophy 9814
Civil Aeronautics Cross of Merit 1598
Colibri Diploma 5140
Contact Vamp Trophee 9400
Cory - Wright Cup 9815
De La Vaulx Medal 5142
Diploma for Outstanding Airmanship 5143
Engineering Prize - Dov Hoz Prize 7951

Aerospace — Awards, Honors & Prizes, 1995-96

Aeronautics (continued)
Excellence in Aerospace Education   7474
FAI Bronze Medal   5146
FAI Gold Air Medal   5147
FISA Medal   11787
Flight Simulation Silver Medal   3891
Fondation Alexandre Darracq   5480
Dr. V. M. Ghatage Award   7475
Gloucester Navigation Trophy   9817
Grand Prix   4902
Hafner VTOL Prize   3892
Hodgson Prize   3893
Honorary Group Diploma   5153
IFA Len Gore Scholarship   3413
IFALPA Scroll of Merit   3409
International Scientific and Technical Gliding Organisation Awards   6981
Jetfoundation   11648
Herbert Le Sueur Award   3894
Charles Lindberg Diploma   5157
Meteorology Prize   4104
Miembro de Honor   11259
National Aeronautical Prize   7476
New Zealand Herald Challenge Trophy   9820
North Shore Trophy   9823
Alphonse Penaud Diploma   5164
Phoenix Diploma   5165
Pilcher-Usborne   3899
Polaris Award   3410
Presidential Sword   3900
Prix d'Aeronautique   4903
Prix des Jeunes   4905
R38 Memorial Prize   3901
N. E. Rowe Medals   3903
Dr. Biren Roy Trust Award   7478
Royal Aeronautical Society Bronze Medal   3904
Clarence N. Sayen Award   3411
Silver Turnbuckle   3909
Simms Prize   3910
Akroyd Stuart Prize   3911
Thulinmedaljen   11649
Paul Tissandier Diploma   5166
B. W. O. Townshend Award   3913
Wilbur and Orville Wright Memorial Lecture   3915
Writer's Trophy   2042
Young FAI Artists Contest   5169

Aerospace (*See also* Aerospace medicine)
Peter Allard Silver Medal   3880
Antonov Aeromodelling Diploma   5137
British Bronze Medal   3883
Certificate of Honor   6031
J. R. Cooper Prize   3889
COSPAR Award   5062
COSPAR Distinguished Service Medal   5063
Design Council British Aerospace Engineering Design Prizes   2739
Allan D. Emil Memorial Award   5972
FAI Aeromodelling Gold Medal   5144
FAI Airsport Medal   5145
Sir Roy Fedden Award   3890
Fondation Edmond Brun   5549
Fono Award   7319
Yuri A. Gagarin Gold Medal   5150
Dr. V. M. Ghatage Award   7475
Gold Medal   7215
Gold Space Medal   5151
Grand Prix   4902
Daniel and Florence Guggenheim International Astronautics Award   5944
Honorary Fellow   2422
Honorary Group Diploma   5153
Honorary Member   10511

International Academy of Astronautics Book Awards   5945
International Academy of Astronautics Section Awards   5946
International Cooperation Medal   5064
V. M. Komarov Diploma   5154
Korolev Diploma   5155
Gheorghe Lazar Prize   10362
Lifetime Achievement Award   6032
Massey Award   5065
Miembro de Honor   11259
Nagy Award   7320
Nile Gold Medal   5162
Nordberg Medal   5066
Odyssey Diploma   5163
Pardoe Space Award   3898
Preise fur herausragende wissenschaftliche Leistungen   6772
Prix d'Astronautique   4904
Dr. Biren Roy Space Science and Design Award   7477
Dr. Biren Roy Trust Award   7478
Royal Aeronautical Society Companion   3905
Royal Aeronautical Society Gold Medal   3906
Royal Aeronautical Society Honorary Fellow   3907
Royal Aeronautical Society Silver Medal   3908
Vikram Sarabhai Medal   5067
Silver Plaque   2423
Space Achievement Medal   2424
Andrei Tupolev Diploma   5167
Andrei Tupolev Medal   5168
Von Karman Award   5947
Wakefield Gold Medal   3914
Young FAI Artists Contest   5169
Zeldovich Medals   5068

Aerospace medicine
Buchanan Barbour Award   3882

African art (*See also* African studies)
Award of Merit   10828
Biennial of Bantu Contemporary Art   6507
Grand Prix ICA - Prix de Sculpture   10689
National Arts Council of Zimbabwe Competitions   12207

African studies (*See also* African art)
African Centre for Applied Research and Training in Social Development Awards   8851
Award of Merit   10828
Prix Albert Bernard   6134
Prix Robert Cornevin   6137
Prix Robert Delavignette   6138
Federation of Afrikaans Cultural Societies Awards   10857
Fondazione Giorgio Maria Sangiorgi   8055
Grand Prix ICA - Prix de la Meilleure Chanson en Langue Traditionnelle   10687
Grand Prix ICA - Prix de la Recherche Scientifique   10688
Grand Prix ICA - Prix du Meilleur Film Documentaire   10690
Grand Prix Litteraire de Madagascar   4921
D. F. Malan Medal   10997
Kwame Nkrumah Prize in African Studies   7177
Noma Award for Publishing in Africa   2039
Prix Alioune Diop pour les Lettres Africaine   10691
Amaury Talbot Prize for African Anthropology   3930

Agricultural economics
Octaaf Callebaut Prize   1252
Fondation Foulon   5558
Fondation Nicolas Zvorikine   5640
Fondation Rene Dujarric de la Riviere   5659
Honorary Member   7852
Premio Jose Maria Bustillo   13
Prix de la Fondation Xavier - Bernard   4770

Agricultural education
Membre d'honneur   4951

Agricultural engineering
Agricultural Engineering Award   421
Armand Blanc Prize   1177
Sir Roland Burke Trophy   3919
Machinery Award Scheme   3922
Perkins Power Award   3777
Technology Award   3924
D. H. Trollope Medal   491

Agriculture (*See also* Agricultural economics; Agricultural education; Agricultural engineering; Agronomy; Animal husbandry; Dairy industry; Forestry; Poultry science; Rural economics)
Agriculture Award   10425
Agrofilm International Short Film Festival   1873
Akzo prijs   9389
Alejandro Angel Escobar Science Prize   1584
Asahi Nogyo Sho   8490
Awards
   Association for Cooperation in Banana Research in the Caribbean and Tropical America   7236
   European Confederation of Agriculture   1127
R. B. Bennett Commonwealth Prize   4319
Best Paper Award
   Asian-Pacific Weed Science Society   10022
   European Weed Research Society   6735
Blount Memorial Scholarship   2085
British Grassland Society Award   2389
Caldas Science Prize   1688
Catalonian Agriculture, Stock Farm, Forestry, Conservation of Nature and Fishing Awards   11170
Chronicle of Komsomol Honor   10427
Concorso Esercitazioni agrarie   8007
Dalgety Farmers Limited Awards for Excellence in Rural Journalism   353
Frederico de Menezes Veiga Prize   1447
Jan De Waal Memorial Award   10859
Diplomes de Medailles   4769
Dissertation Honors   6998
European Committee for Young Farmers and 4H Clubs Awards   10543
FAI Silver Jubilee Award   7499
FAO Technical Assistance Fellowship   8268
Farm Buildings Award Scheme   2705
Farrer Memorial Medal   367
Federacion Nacional de Cultivadores de Cereales Competitions   1697
Fellows and Associates of Royal Agricultural Societies   2691
Fondation Bigot de Morogues   5503
Fondation Demolombe   5538
Fondation Paul Marguerite de la Charlonie   5647
Fondazione Valeria Vincenzo Landi   8065
FSSA Gold Medal   10860
FSSA Silver Medal (Extension)   10861
FSSA Silver Medal (Research)   10862

FSSA Silver Medal (Research and Extension) 10863
Fujihara Award 8527
Gold Medal 9993
Gold Medal for Distinguished Services to Agriculture 3920
Honorary Fellow 3921
Honorary Life Members 1119
Honorary Member 6633
Inter-American Agricultural Award for Young Professionals 1774
Inter-American Agricultural Medal 1776
Inter-American Award for the Participation of Women in Rural Development 1777
International DLG Prize 6774
International Vasco Vilalva Prize 10252
Ion Ionescu de la Brad Prize 10358
Gheorge Ionescu-Sisesti Prize 10359
Israel Prize 7906
Sir Bryner Jones Perpetual Memorial Award 12188
Armando Kaminitz Research Awards 7981
Kaplan Prize 7892
The Kharazmi Prize 7737
Knight of African Agriculture 2019
Prof. L. S. S. Kumar Memorial Award 7655
Labor Courage Award 10437
Loraine Award for Nature Conservation 4472
Massey Ferguson National Agricultural Award 3635
Andre Mayer Research Fellowship 8269
Manuel Mejia Medal of Merit in the Coffee Industry 1734
National Distinction of the Environment 1600
Netherthorpe Award 2959
Order of Lenin 10463
Order of Merit in Agriculture 1602
Ordre du Merite Agricole
  Cote d'Ivoire - Presidency of the Republic 1793
  France - Ministry of Agriculture and Forestry 5240
Osiris Award 8270
Perkins Power Award 3777
Poggendorff Memorial Lecture 629
Dr. Rajendra Prasad Award 7575
Premi Anita Vecchi 8020
Premio Academia Nacional de Agronomia y Veterinaria 6
Premio Bolsa de Cereales de Buenos Aires 8
Premio Carlotta Strampelli 8008
Premio del Seminario de Economia Agricola del Tercer Mundo 9190
Premio Fundacion Rene Baron 12
Premio Massey Ferguson 14
Prix Blaise des Vosges 5719
Prix Corbay 5727
Prix de la Fondation Xavier - Bernard 4770
Prix Jean Dufrenoy 4771
Research Medal for Research Work of Benefit to Agriculture 3923
Royal Bath and West Scholarship Awards (World and European) 3947
Royal Society of Victoria Medal 638
Moinho Santista Prizes for Young People 1496
Moinho Santista Prizes 1497
Edouard Saouma Award 8271
Traian Savulescu Prize 10382
B. R. Sen Award 8272
Silver Jubilee Commemoration Medal 7672
Sinden Award 3664
Soil Association Awards for Organic Food Products 4473
State Prize 10204
Sulphur Institute Award 7500
Technology Award 3924
Johann Heinrich von Thunen Gold Medal 7127
TWNSO Award in Agriculture 8457
Justus Von Liebig Prize 7131
Hans Vontobel-Fonds 11937
C. A. Weber Medaille 6634
Wolf Foundation Prizes 7987
World Food Day Award 7569
World Ploughing Championship Awards 4626
Young Scientist or Grower of the Year Award 3665

Agronomy
Competition for Young Researchers 11820
Diplomes de Medailles 4769
Fondation de Madame Albert Demolon 5533
Japanese Society of Soil Science and Plant Nutrition Award 8666
Jubilee Prize 2542
Premio Vilfred Baron 15
Prix du Troisieme Cycle 4952
Progress Award of Japanese Society of Soil Science and Plant Nutrition 8667
Dr. Arthur Ruppin Prize 7885

Air pollution See Environmental conservation

Alcoholism treatment
IOGT International August Forell Award 9894
Man for Mankind Awards 938
Mrs. James Nelson Award 716
Prix Lutte Contre L'Alcoolisme 4858
Ulster Award 717

Animated films
Annecy International Animated Film Festival 5957
ASIFA Special Award 9889
Asolo International Animation Festival 8100
Australian Film Institute Awards 221
Badalona Short Film and Video Festival 11205
Belgrade International Festival of Scientific Films 10699
Bombay International Film Festival 7529
British Academy of Film and Television Arts Awards - Film 2233
Certamen Internacional de Cine Amateur Ciutat d'Igualada 11203
Cesar Awards 4793
CINANIMA 10226
Edinburgh International Film Festival 10541
Gran Canaria International Short Film Festival 11257
Holland Animation Film Festival Awards 9454
Huy - World Festival of Movies of Short Films Awards 1160
International Animation Festival in Japan, Hiroshima 8531
International Documentary and Short Film Festival of Bilbao 11267
International Festival of Ecological Film Events 10791
International Festival of Films on Energy Lausanne 11797
International Film and Student Directors Festival 6020
International Leipzig Documentary and Animation Film Festival 7035
International Odense Film Festival 1963
International Video Contest 11234
International Visual Communications Association Awards 3502
Mari Kuttna Award 2348
Medal for Postal Merit 1604
Monte Carlo International Forum for New Images Imagina 9321
Stuttgart International Festival of Animated Film 7142
Svjetski Festival Animiranih Filmova, Zagreb 1816
Tampere International Short Film Festival 4758
Wattrelos Short Film and Video Festival 6477

Anatomy
Broca Prize 4897
Flormanska Beloningen 11541
Fondation Godard 5569
Avelino Gutierrez Prize 80
John Hunter Medal and Triennial Prize 3976
Hunterian Oration 3977
Sobotta Preis 6521

Anesthesiology
Drummond-Jackson Prize 4372
Henry Hill Hickman Medal 4253
ICI Research Scholarship 6701
Karl Koller Gold Medal 1142
RSM May and Baker Pharmaceuticals Prizes 4265

Animal care and training (See also Animal husbandry; Animal rights; Horsemanship; Poultry science; Veterinary medicine)
Marchig Animal Welfare Award 4633
Prix Botiaux-Dulac 5339
Prix de Biologie Alfred Kastler 5271
PRO Dogs National Charity Open Creative Writing & Photographic Competition 3802
Dorothy Sidley Memorial Award 3031
Small Project Grants 4571
Supreme Champion 3464
Young Handler Award 3465
Zoo Animal Welfare Award 4572

Animal husbandry
A. D. and P. A. Allen Memorial Fellowship 2084
Alejandro Angel Escobar Science Prize 1584
Bledisloe Gold Medal for Landowners 3917
Blount Memorial Scholarship 2085
Frederico de Menezes Veiga Prize 1447
Distinguished Service Award 8229
EAAP Annual Meeting Awards 8230
Fellows and Associates of Royal Agricultural Societies 2691
Gold Medal 10968
Golden Ram Award 10901
Sir John Hammond Memorial Prize 10520
George Hedley Award 3708
Herds Competition 2393
Herdsman of the Year 2391
IVOMEC Award for Effective Sheep Breeding 10843
Prof. L. S. S. Kumar Memorial Award 7655
A. M. Leroy Fellowship 8231
Andre Mayer Research Fellowship 8269
Premio Dr. Francisco C. Rosenbusch 9
Premio Fundacion Rene Baron 12
Premio Internazionale per la Zootecnia Uovo d'Oro 8151
Dorothy Sidley Memorial Award 3031
Hans Vontobel-Fonds 11937

Animal rights
Anti-Prize 11639
Gwen Barter Award 3543
GV-SOLAS Competition 11908
Houghton Award 3544
Order of Nature Award 8871
Positive Prize 11640
Dorothy Sidley Memorial Award 3031
Lord Soper Award 3545
Sri Kapila Humanitarian Society Competitions 11420
Peter Wilson Award 3546

Anthropology
Bertillon Prize 4896
Broca Prize 4897
Curl Bequest Prize 3926
J. B. Donne Essay Prize on the Anthropology of Art 3927
Festival dei Popoli 8239
Fondation Andre C. Bonnet 5488
Arthur Maurice Hocart Prize 3928
Huxley Memorial Medal and Lecture 3929
International Prize 5301
Simion Florea Marian Prize 10364
Prix de Monsieur et Madame Louis Marin 6141
Mueller Medal 190
National Prize for Anthropology 1623
Premio Juan Comas 9057
Premio Miguel Othon de Mendizabal 9060
Premio Nicolas Leon 9061
Royal Society of Victoria Medal 638
Percy Smith Medal in Anthropology 9852
Amaury Talbot Prize for African Anthropology 3930
Vallois Prize 4898
Wellcome Medal for Anthropological Research as applied to Medical Problems 3931

Antiquity
Concours des Antiquites de la France 5431
Prix Bordin 5439
Prix de La Fons-Melicocq 5447
Prix du Budget 5452
Prix Gustave Mendel 5461
Prix Roman et Tania Ghirshman 5471
Prix Saintour 5472
Viking Society for Northern Research Awards 4599

Apparel See Fashion

Arabic culture
Baghdad Prize for Arab Culture 6410
Certificate of Honor 7550
Euroarabe and Television Festival 11226
Fondation Edmond Fagnan 973
King Abdul Aziz Prize 10494
Medal of Distinction 7749

Archaeology
Eduard-Anthes-Preis fur Archaologische Forschungen 7150
Archaeological Book Award 2245
Archaeological Fieldwork Grants 8176
R. M. Baguley Award 3799
Balsdon Fellowship 8177
BP Award 2246
BP Prize Lectureship in the Humanities 10638
Brussels International Art and Archaeology Film Festival 1162
Channel 4 Film Awards 2693
Dr. M. Aylwin Cotton Foundation Fellowship Awards 2688
Dr. M. Aylwin Cotton Foundation Publication Grants 2689
Alex L. Du Toit Memorial Lecturer 10869
Egypt Exploration Society Centenary Studentship 2762
Eric Fletcher Award 4362
Frend Medal 4383
Gold Medal 4384
Grand Prix National de l'Archeologie 5284
Heritage in Britain Award 2247
Honorary Fellow 10681
Hugh Last Award 8178
International Prize 5301
Ironbridge Award 2248
Mansel-Pleydell and Cecil Trusts 2749
Medaille d'Archeologie 4773
Medaille Georges Perrot 5432
Medieval Archaeology Research Fund 4363
Mythic Society Scholar 7713
Nationwide Silver Trowel Award 2249
Vasile Parvan Prize 10376
Pitt-Rivers Award 2250
Premio Alfonso Caso 9053
Premio Municipal Julio de Castilho de Olisipografia 10274
Prix Adolphe Noel-des-Vergers 5433
Prix Ambatielos 5437
Prix de la Fondation Emile Senart 5445
Prix de la Fondation Louis de Clercq 5446
Prix du Duc de Loubat 5453
Prix Emile Le Senne 5456
Prix Gustave Mendel 5461
Prix Gustave Schlumberger 5462
Prix Hercule Catenacci
  Institut de France 5343
  Institut de France - Academie Francaise 5867
Prix Joseph-Edmond Marchal 962
Prix L.-Pierre Descamps 1051
Prix Lavalleye-Coppens 964
Prix Raoul Duseigneur 5470
Prix Simone Bergmans 949
Regional Production Prizes 23
Research Grants 8179
Royal Society of Victoria Medal 638
Percia Schimmel Award for Distinguished Contribution to Archaelogy in Israel 7931
Bob Smith Award 3800
Sponsorship Award 2251
Sudrey's Fund 4364
Reginald Taylor Essay Prize 2243
Michael Ventris Memorial Award 2093
Virgin Group Award 2252
Bernard Webb Studentship 2094
Erik Westerby Prize 2013
J. J. A. Worsaae Medal 1978

Archery
Individual Championships 4568
Team Championships (non-divisional) 4569

Architectural criticism
Architectural Critics and Writers Award 10880
Pierre Bayle Prijs 9580
Jean Tschumi Prize 6062

Architecture (See also Architectural criticism; Construction; Historic preservation; Housing; Landscape architecture; Monument restoration; Park planning; Planning)
Aanmoedigingsprijzen 9635
Aga Khan Award for Architecture 11656
Sir Rowand Anderson Silver Medal 10610
Annual Environmental Awards 3755
Annual Exhibition of the Royal Scottish Academy 10619
Annual Prize of the Society of Czech Architects 1882
APRS Annual Award 10506
Architectural Awards 8840
Architecture Award 2886
Art and Craft in Architecture Award 10651
Arte in Piazza International Competition 8098
ASEAN Award for Visual Arts 10032
Berlin Art Prizes 6509
Best Project of the Year Prize 10484
BIAT Student Award 2397
Biennial of Young Dutch Architects 9668
BNA - Kubus 9590
Paul Bonatz Preis 7135
Book Awards 10502
Borba Award 10703
Brick Design Awards 2215
Heinrich Hatt-Bucher Prize 11929
Sir John Burnet Memorial Award 10611
City of Munich Prizes 7019
City of Vienna Prizes for Art, Science, and Humanities 789
Civic Trust Awards 2636
Community Enterprise Scheme 4073
Concrete Element Prize 9902
Construmat Award 11192
Dr. M. Aylwin Cotton Foundation Fellowship Awards 2688
Dr. M. Aylwin Cotton Foundation Publication Grants 2689
Distinguished Professional Contribution Award 8805
EAA Award for Architecture 10533
Eckersberg Medal 1897
Education School Design Award 2757
Europa Nostra Awards 9402
European Prize for the Preservation of Historic Monuments 7110
James Alfred Ewing Medal 3236
Farm Buildings Award Scheme 2705
Federacion Panamericans de Asociaciones de Arquitectos Premios 12094
Harold Fern Award 2067
Festival International du Film d'Architecture d'Urbanisme et d'Environement Urbain de Bordeaux 6018
Sir Banister Fletcher Prize Trust 2150
Fondation Dulac 5351
Forderpreis des Landes Nordrhein-Westfalen fur junge Kunstlerinnen und Kunstler 7026
Forderpreis fur bildende Kunst der Landeshauptstadt Dusseldorf 6682
Glass Prize 9904
Gold Medal 10881
Gold Medal Conanti Award 1898
Gold Medal for Outstanding Architectural Achievement 6059
Grand Prix d'Architecture de l'Academie des Beaux-Arts 5352
Grand Prix de l'Architecture de la Ville de Paris 6091
Grand Prix National de l'Architecture 5285
Hammer and Sickle Gold Medal 10460
C. F. Hansen Medal 1899
Hexagono de Oro 10014
Housing Design Award 10654
Housing Design Awards 4068
IFHP International Student Competition 9487
IFI Award 9489
International Festival of Films on Architecture and Town-planning of Lausanne 11793

Subject Index of Awards
Volume 2: International and Foreign

Art

International Prize for Architecture of the National Housing Institute   1227
Nami Jafet Prize   1488
Kaleidoscope of Honor   1946
King Fahd Awards for Design and Research in Islamic Architecture   12058
Charlotte Kohler Prijs   9571
Peter Joseph Lenne Prize   6562
Literature, Art, Journalism, and Architecture Awards   10438
London Awards   3038
Sir Robert Lorimer Memorial Award   10612
Robert Matthew Award   2644
Sir Robert Matthew Prize   6060
Medaille d'Archeologie   4773
Medaille d'Architecture Fondation le Soufache   4774
Medaille d'Architecture Prix Dejean ou Prix Delarue   4775
Medaille de la Jurisprudence   4776
Medaille de la Recherche et de la Technique   4777
Medaille de la Restauration   4778
Medaille de l'Academie d'Architecture   4779
Medaille de l'Analyse Architecturale   4780
Medaille de l'Architecture d'Accompagnement   4781
Medaille de l'Urbanisme   4783
Medaille des Arts Plastiques   4784
Medaille des Publications   4785
Medaille d'Honneur de l'Academie d'Architecture   4786
Medaille d'Or de l'Academie d'Architecture   4787
Medal of Distinction   10882
Medal of Honor
   Federation of Danish Architects   1947
   South African Academy of Science and Arts   10999
Medals of Honour   9404
Johann-Heinrich-Merck Ehrung   6602
Merit Plaque Award   7260
Merkelbachprijs   9642
NAS Design Prize   3676
National Architecture Awards   609
National Prize for Architecture   12142
National Prize for Good Building   9906
National Prize for Industrial and Commercial Building   743
October Prizes of the City of Belgrade   10696
George Oprescu Prize   10374
Order of Culture   8586
Order of Lenin   10463
Parsonage Design Award   2619
Patron of Architecture Award   10883
Pelles Prize   7865
Auguste Perret Prize   6061
Pietrzak Award   10084
Anthony Pott Memorial Award   2092
Praemium Imperiale   8599
Premio Anual de Aquisicao   10285
Premio Anual de Investigacao   10286
Premio de Composicion Arquitectonica Alberto J. Pani   9189
Premio La Ceramica n la Arquitectura   9302
Premio Municipal Francisco da Conceicao Silva de Espacos Interiores abertos ao publico   10269
Premio Valmor e Municipal de Arquitectura   10279
Preseren Award   10799
Prix Achille Leclere   5354
Prix Antoine-Nicolas Bailly   5359
Prix Baron Horta   952
Prix Bordin   5364
Prix Catenacci   5367

Prix Chaudesaigues   5370
Prix Claude Berthault   5371
Prix COGEDIM   5040
Prix de Rome   9578
Prix Duc   5384
Prix Ernest Acker   958
Prix Estrade-Delcros   5387
Prix et Fondations Concernant l'Academie de France a Rome   5388
Prix Fondation Bernard Hamburger   4788
Prix Fondation Richard Lounsbery   4789
Prix Francoise Abella   5391
Prix Georges Wildenstein   5395
Prix Hector Lefuel   5399
Prix Henri Dauberville   5400
Prix Houllevigue   5403
Prix Nature et Patrimoine   5080
Prix Paul Bonduelle   967
Prix Paul de Pessemier   1053
Prix Pierre Carsoel   968
Prix Rouyer   5424
Prix Ruhlman   5425
Prize Mission Special Japan   8733
Prize of Architecture   1948
Quality Brickwork Award   2216
RAIA Gold Medal   610
Zeev Rechter Award   7866
Redland Pitched Roof Awards   3841
Regeneration of Scotland Design Award   10613
RIAS Award for Measured Drawing   10614
RIAS/John Maclaren Travelling Fellowship   10615
RIAS/Whitehouse Studio Award for Architectural Photography   10616
RIBA Architecture Awards   4069
David Roell Prijs   9575
Elies Rogent Video Competition on Rehabilitation and Restoration   11207
Thomas Ross Award   10617
Rotterdam-Maaskant Award   9583
Rotterdam Maaskant Award for Young Architects   9584
Royal Academy Summer Exhibition   3864
Royal Gold Medal for Architecture   4071
Kasper Salin Prize   11492
Scandinavian Design Prize   11652
Scholarship Prizes   6512
Fritz Schumacher Prizes   7122
Sendai International Design Competition   8760
Sikkensprijs   9621
Soares Dos Reis Prize   10306
State Prize in Science and Technology   10470
Stone Prize   9907
Toros Toramanian Prize   114
Eduardo Torroja Medal   11265
Alfred H. Turner Award   2074
UNESCO Prize for Architecture   6423
Union of Architects of Romania Prize   10408
Union of Soviet Architects Prizes   10476
Upper Austria Prize for Architecture   906
USSR State Prize for Architecture   10486
A. J. Van Eck Prize   9591
Michael Ventris Memorial Award   2093
Bernard Webb Studentship   2094
Welsh Housing Design Awards   12190
Wibautprijs   9653
Wolf Foundation Prizes   7987
Charles Wollaston Award   3865
Wood Prize
   Danish Timber Information Council   1922
   National Association of Norwegian Architects   9908
Miklos Ybl Prize for Architecture   7392

Archival science See Library and information services

Art (See also African art; Art education; Art history; Design; Exhibiting; Photography; specific disciplines, e.g. Ceramics)
AA Life Vita Art Now   10809
AA Life Vita Contemporary Choreography and Dance Awards   10811
ACTA Australian Maritime Art Award   116
Adam and Company/Spectator Art Award   4483
Air New Zealand Award   9791
Altmeier-Medaille Europamunze der EVBK   6723
Amsterdam Prize   9451
Amsterdam Prize for Art   9593
Ion Andreescu Prize   10329
Annual Exhibition of the Royal Scottish Academy   10619
Antwoorden Prijsvragen, Klasse der Schone Kunsten   1250
Gerardo Arellano Cultural Merit Medal   1651
Art and Education Prize   9333
Art Scholarship   3946
Artist of the Year, Helsinki Festival   4720
Artists Association of Finland Award   4665
Arts Council of Northern Ireland Bursaries and Awards   7854
Arts Prize - Meir Dizengoff Prize   7947
ASEAN Award for Visual Arts   10032
Athena Arts Prize   2141
Australian Artists Creative Fellowships   160
Australian Arts Award   414
Austrian State Encouragement Prizes   758
Austrian State Grand Prize   759
Austrian State Recognition Prizes   765
Award for Distinction in Islamic Science   12055
Award for Distinguished Services to Art   8784
Awards
   Fondazione Anna Pane   8241
   International Society for Education Through Art   3467
Awards for the Best Produced Books in Hong Kong   7277
Bangkok Bank Prize for Thai Literature Competition   12022
Bass Arts Award   7855
Pierre Bayle Prijs   9580
Berlin Art Prizes   6509
Bharat Ratna   7549
Bienal de Iberoamericana de Arte   9029
Bienal de Pintores Rufino Tomayo   9206
Bienal Iberoamericana de Arte   9207
Bienal Nacional Diego Rivera for Drawings and Prints   9208
Biennale Internationale de Limoges   5299
Black Panel World Foundation Awards   6571
Blake Prize for Religious Art   285
Blekinge County Council Culture Prize   11446
Ros Bower Memorial Award
   Australia Council - Community Cultural Development Board   151
   Australia Council for the Arts - Visual Arts/Craft Board   163
Brussels International Art and Archaeology Film Festival   1162
Johan en Titia Buning-Brongers prys   9344
Bursaries, Scholarships, and Travel Awards   7755
Cacique's Crown of Honor   7243
George Campbell Memorial Travel Award   7756

Art

Awards, Honors & Prizes, 1995-96

Art (continued)

George Campbell Memorial Travel Grant 7856
Gustavo Capanema Prize 1430
CCP Awards for the Arts 10048
Centre of Art and Communication Awards 42
Ferreira Chavez Prize 10301
Citation of Merit 577
City of Munich Prizes 7019
City of Vienna Prizes for Art, Science, and Humanities 789
City of Vienna Promotional Prizes 791
Concurso Nacional para Estudiantes de Artes Plasticas en Aguascalientes 9211
Concurso Universitario de Artes Plasticas 9178
Condecoracion al Merito Social 9013
Lovis-Corinth-Preis 6523
Dr. M. Aylwin Cotton Foundation Fellowship Awards 2688
Dr. M. Aylwin Cotton Foundation Publication Grants 2689
Culture Prize
   European Movement in Norway 9882
   Oslo Kommune 9959
Leonardo Da Vinci World Award of Arts 9306
Jose de Figueiredo Prize 10284
George de Menasce Memorial Trust 3749
Hendrik de Vries Award 9362
Hendrik de Vries Stipend 9363
Distinguished Professional Contribution Award 8805
DMAS Annual Art Awards 355
J. B. Donne Essay Prize on the Anthropology of Art 3927
Dublin Corporation Arts Scholarship 7758
Aquileo J. Echeverria Prize 1761
Eckersberg Medal 1897
Encuentro Nacional de Arte Joven 9212
Federation of British Artists Prizes and Awards 2870
Fellow 642
Fellowships and Scholarships 146
Fellowships in Arts and Crafts 2657
Festival dei Popoli 8239
Fine Arts Association of Finland Awards 4676
Fine Arts Prize 8829
Fine Arts Union Prize 10395
Sir Banister Fletcher Prize Trust 2150
Fondation Charles Fremont 5516
Fondation Kastner-Boursault 5605
Fondation Thorlet 5710
Fondation Tremont 5673
Forderpreis fur bildende Kunst der Landeshauptstadt Dusseldorf 6682
Fox of Poster for Books for the Young 6203
Luciano Freire Prize 10302
Galardon Estado de Mexico 9008
Dr. Haim Gamzu Prize 7965
Joaquin Garcia Monge Prize 1762
Goethepreis 6612
Gold Medal 930
Golden Aesop Prize 1521
Golden Award of the Micro Hall Art Center 7048
Grand Prix National des Metiers d'Art 5289
Grenfell Henry Lawson Festival of Arts Awards 415
Will Grohmann Prize 6511
Grote Prys Alfons Blomme 1231
Calouste Gulbenkian Foundation Grants 2981
Alice Berger Hammerschlag Trust Award 7857

Higgs and Hill Bursary 4178
Honorary Fellow 7922
Honorary Rings of the City of Salzburg 865
N. L. Hoyen Medal 1900
Ikarus Medaille 7050
Inaugural Red Ochre Award 165
Inter Nations Culture Prize 6927
International Biennial Exhibition of Humour in Art 8282
International Ceramic Art Competition 8309
International Print Biennal - Varna 1532
International Print Triennial 10077
Internationale Eugene Baieprijs 1243
Israel Discount Bank Prize 7924
Israel Prize 7906
Israeli Discount Bank Prize 7966
Nami Jafet Prize 1488
Japan Art Academy Prize 8597
Japan Art Award 8742
Kala Bhushana Honours 11422
Keltic Society Awards 10584
Charlotte Kohler Prijs 9571
Beatrice S. Kolliner Award for a Young Israeli Artist 7927
Kraszna-Krausz Award 3527
Kungliga priset 11598
Kunst-und Kulturpreis des Groupement 6724
Kunstpreis der Stadt Darmstadt 6600
Kunstpreis der Stadt Zurich 11894
Kunstpreis des Landes Bremen 6581
Kyoto Prizes 8539
Labor Courage Award 10437
Laing Collection Art Competition 3531
Laureate of the Triennial of the Realistic Painting 1533
Leeds Philosophical and Literary Society Medal 3548
Letterstedtska Forfattarpriset 11543
Judith Leysterprijs 9448
Literature and Art Awards 12011
Literature, Art, Journalism, and Architecture Awards 10438
Alun Llywelyn-Williams Memorial Award 12181
Kaiser-Lothar-Preis 6725
Lower Austria Prize for the Advancement of Fine Arts and Literature 859
Lower Austria Recognition Prize in Arts and Sciences 860
Macaulay Fellowship 7760
Manu Daula Frigate Bird Award 578
Medal of Honor 10999
Medalla Eduardo Neri 9124
Meijimura Prize 8698
Member 4468
Johann-Heinrich-Merck Ehrung 6602
Merit of Polish Culture Badge 10091
Mobil Business in the Arts Awards 529
Hans-Molfenter-Preis der Landeshauptstadt Stuttgart/Galerie 7137
Piet Mondriaan Lecture 9620
Monte Carlo International Prize of Contemporary Art 9310
Moon Fish Award 7052
Douglas J. Moran Portraiture Prize 693
Musgrave Medal 8482
Nagrada Saveta Fonda SO SUBNOR Cetvrti jul 10707
National Annual Exhibition of Fine Arts 1436
National Art Collections Awards 3671
National Artist Award/International Artist Award 10049
National Arts Council of Zimbabwe Competitions 12207

National Award for Literature and Arts 12002
National Award for Painting and Graphics 9990
National Cultural Awards 1413
National Prize for Arts 1660
National Prize for Fine Arts 9146
National Prize in Science and Art 9152
National Salon of Fine Arts Prizes 1441
National Science, Literature and Art Prize 7183
Northern Telecom Arts Europe 4488
October Prizes of the City of Belgrade 10696
October Show Awards 10697
Jacques and Eugenie O'Hana Prize 7968
Old Masters Award 3428
Oppenheim John Downes Memorial Trust 3738
George Oprescu Prize 10374
Orden Manuel Felipe Rugeles 12112
Order Ingenio et Arti 1939
Order of Andres Bello 12137
Order of Cultural Merit 8579
Order of Merit 2378
Order of the Crown 1074
Order of the Netherlands Lion 9358
Order of the Rebirth of Poland 10119
Karl Ernst Osthaus Prize 7068
Outstanding Artist of Hungary 7411
Pakistan Civil Awards 9995
Jan Palach Prize 5993
Panorama of Actual Brasilian Art 1492
George F. Papentuss Poster Award 3454
Paracelsusring der Stadt Villach 888
Peace Prize of the German Book Trade 6776
Pietrzak Award 10084
Preis der Landeshauptstadt Innsbruck fur Kunstlerisches Schaffen 891
Preis der Stadt Mannheim fur junge Kunstler 7099
Premi 8030
Premi Antonio Feltrinelli 8069
Premio Cavolini - De Mellis 8087
Premio Iglesias 8118
Premio MEC de Arte 1442
Premio Mixcoatl 9255
Premio Nacional de Arte 1545
Premio Napolitain Illustri 8257
Premio Sinaloa de Ciencias y Artes 9015
Premio Tenore 8088
Premio Tetradramma d'oro 8034
Preseren Award 10799
Prince of Asturias Prizes 11248
Prix Alfred Verdaguer
   Institut de France 5336
   Institut de France - Academie des Beaux Arts 5355
   Institut de France - Academie des Sciences 5683
Prix Antoine Girard 5815
Prix Claude Berthault 5726
Prix Corbay 5727
Prix de l'Academie des Sciences, Arts et Belles Lettres de Dijon 4795
Prix de l'Illustration des Arts 5049
Prix de Rome 9578
Prix de Stassart 983
Prix d'Histoire de la Vallee aux Loups 6102
Prix Diderot Universalis 5112
Prix Emile Le Senne 5456
Prix Eugene Carriere 5850
Prix Fraternite Gaby Archenbaud 6124
Prix Gustave-Francois Redon 5397
Prix Henri Hertz 5204
Prix Houllevigue 5403

Prix J. J. Berger 5404
Prix Jean Reynaud 5406
Prix Jules et Louis Jeanbernat et Barthelemy de Ferrari Doria 5346
Prix Jules et Louis Jeanbernat et Barthelemy de Ferrari Doria
 Institut de France - Academie des Sciences Morales et Politiques 5768
 Institut de France - Academie Francaise 5874
Prix Jules Raeymaekers 963
Prix Lavalleye-Coppens 964
Prix Osiris 5347
Prix Osiris 5703
Prix Paul Marmottan 5419
Prix Raoul Duseigneur 5470
Prix Science pour l'Art - Moet-Hennessy - Louis Vuitton 6122
Prix Simone Bergmans 949
Prix Valentine Abraham Verlain 5926
Prize for Art Critique 10396
Prize for Decorative Arts 10397
Prize for Monumental Art 10400
Prize for Revolutionary Song 8882
Promotional Prizes 7022
Prudential Awards for the Arts 3826
Public Service Medal 10748
Public Service Star 10749
Mendel Pundik Fund 7970
Tom Roberts Award 650
David Roell Prijs 9575
Annie Romein Prys 9426
Royal Academy Summer Exhibition 3864
Salon Anual de Artes Plasticas Premios Pedro Domingo Murillo 1389
Salon Nacional de Artes Plasticas - Espacios Alternativos 9242
Salzburg Prize for the Promotion of the Arts, Science and Literature 869
Sandberg Prize for Israeli Art 7930
Sandbergprijs 9647
Sandoz Preis 878
Moinho Santista Prizes for Young People 1496
Moinho Santista Prizes 1497
Scholarship Prizes 6512
Scholarships of the City of Munich 7023
Shincho Art and Science Award 8744
Sikkensprijs 9621
Singer-Polignac Grants 5226
Jill Smythies Award 3589
Society for Italic Handwriting Award 4358
Soviet Land Nehru Award 7722
Spurs of Criticism 4760
Standard Bank Namibia Biennale 9326
Standard Bank Young Artists' Awards 10849
State Prize 10204
State Prize in Science and Technology 10470
Storywriting and Art Project 144
Sir Arthur Streeton Award 651
Suntory Prize for Social Sciences and Humanities 8764
Thorvaldsen Medal 1902
Tiroler Landespreis fur Kunst 732
Marten Toonder Award 7762
Trade Union's Art and Cultural Prize 7442
Turner Prize 3764
Union of Writers and Artists of Albania Competitions 2
Visual Arts/Craft Board Emeritus Award 167
Visual Arts/Craft Board Emeritus Medal 168
Visual Arts/Craft Board's Emeritus Fellowships and Medals 169
Konrad-von-Soest-Preis 7029

Warringah Art Prize 706
Rudolf-Wilke-Preis 6576
Wolf Foundation Prizes 7987
Charles Wollaston Award 3865
Wurdigungspreis 862
Yorkshire Post Art and Music Award 4645
Young Artists Prize 10404

Art education
NSEAD/Berol Curriculum Development Award for Art and Design Teachers 3712
Jozef Van Ginderachter Prize 1278

Art history
ASDA Prize 4909
CINOA Award 3391
Jose de Figueiredo Prize 10284
Hans Janssen Prize 6909
Medaille de l'Histoire de l'Art 4782
Medaille Georges Perrot 5432
Michaly Munkacsy Prize for Visual and Applied Arts 7406
Premio de Critica de Arte Luis Cardoza y Aragon 9216
Prix Charles and Marguerite Diehl 5441
Prix du Baron de Joest 5383
Prix Elie Faure 4985
Prix Houllevigue 5403
Prix Jules et Louis Jeanbernat et Barthelemy de Ferrari Doria 5407
Prix Louis Fould 5469
Prix Minda de Gunzburg 4910
Prix Paul Cailleux 5058
Prix Richtenberger 5422
Prix Roman et Tania Ghirshman 5471
Prix Thorlet 5428
State Prize in Science and Technology 10470

Arts and humanities (*See also* Antiquity; Archaeology; Ethics; Humanities research; Museums; Philosophy; Philosophy of science; Religion)
ABSA Business Awards 2030
Konrad Adenauer Research Award 7154
Albert Medal 4318
The Arthur Andersen Award for the Business in the Arts Advisor of the Year 2031
Antwoorden Prijsvragen, Klasse der Letteren 1249
Austrian Medal of Honor in the Arts and Sciences 756
Award of Merit 10828
Eugenio Balzan Prize 8280
R. B. Bennett Commonwealth Prize 4319
BP Arts Award 2032
BP Prize Lectureship in the Humanities 10638
British Academy Fellowship 7840
British Academy Research Awards 2222
Brussels International Festival of Scientific and Technical Films 1098
Hedwig-Burgheim Medaille 7040
Miguel Antonio Caro and Rufino Jose Cuervo National Order 1711
City of Vienna Prizes for Art, Science, and Humanities 789
Margaret Condliffe Memorial Prize 9848
Crawford Medal 183
Cymmrodorion Medal 3023
The Daily Telegraph Award 2033
De la Court Prize 9599
Elf Arts Award 2034
Fondation Alhumbert 5484
Fondation Montyon des Arts Insalubres 5638
Benjamin Franklin Medal 4322

Humboldt Research Awards to Foreign Scholars 7155
IFUW Awards Competition 11789
Imperial Prize 8594
Israel Prize 7906
Japan Academy Prize 8595
Kossuth Prize 7410
Kuwait Prize 8844
Lenin Prize 10469
Libraries Prize 8153
Medalla de la Generalitat de Catalunya 11187
Montaigne Prize 7117
Fridtjof Nansen Award 9927
National Prizes for Culture 1391
Order of Merit in the Sciences and Arts 6743
Jan Palach Prize 5993
Premi Antonio Feltrinelli 8069
Premio di Laurea Luigi Casati in Discipline Uranistiche 8075
Premio Maria Teresa Messori Roncaglia and Eugenio Mari 8077
Prince of Asturias Prizes 11248
Prix Mondial Cino del Duca 5224
Prize for Journalism on Arts and Culture 9935
Prize for Research and Studies of the Repercussions of the Iraqi Invasion of Kuwait 8845
Schiller-Gedachtnispreis des Land Baden-Wurttemberg 7055
Scholastic Award 8808
Serbian Academy of Sciences and Arts Awards 10724
Shakespeare Prize 7124
Stals Prize for the Humanities 11006
The Times Critics' Award 2035
Tiroler Landespreis fur Wissenschaft 733
Upper Austria Culture Prize for Fine Arts 902
Upper Austria Culture Prize for Science 905
Franz Vogt-Preise 7005
Joost van den Vondel Prizes 7133

Asian studies (*See also* Japanese culture)
APO National Award 8504
APO Regional Award 8505
Association of Southeast Asian Institutions of Higher Learning Awards 12019
Award Program to Assist Foreign Scholars in Carrying Out Sinological Research in the R.O.C. 11992
BCLA Translation Competition (EC Languages) 2318
BCLA Translation Competition (Non-EC Languages) 2319
Burton Memorial Medal 3933
Certificate of Honor 7550
George de Menasce Memorial Trust 3749
Gold Medal 3934
Honorary Fellow 3935
Indian Books Centre Oriental Studies Award 7571
Iqbal Award 9979
Japan Foundation Grant Programs 8613
Pacific Cultural Foundation Awards 12005
Prix Bordin 5439
Prix Delalande-Guerineau 5449
Prix du Budget 5452
Prix Herbert Allen Giles 5463
Prix Litteraire de l'Asie 4927
Prix Saintour 5472
Prix Stanislas Julien 5473

Astronautics *See* Aerospace

Astronomy

Astrological Association Awards 2137
Sir David Bates Medal 6715
Lydia Brown Award for Meritorious Service 2285
Crafoord Prize 11537
Discovery of New Celestial Bodies Award 8507
Eddington Medal 3938
Edlundska Priset 11538
Arthur Farrant Award 137
Fondation Ancel 5487
Fondation Andre Lallemand 5489
Fondation Antoine d'Abbadie 5493
Fondation Antoinette Janssen 5494
Fondation Arago 5495
Fondation Damoiseau 5528
Fondation Ernest Dechelle 5553
Fondation Frederic Forthuny 5561
Fondation G. de Pontecoulant 5562
Fondation Henry Wilde 5583
Fondation Janssen 5591
Fondation La Caille 5608
Fondations Lalande - Benjamin Valz 5681
Gill Medal 10822
Gold Medal
  Royal Astronomical Society 3939
  Scientific Group for Space Research 7215
Walter Goodacre Medal and Gift 2286
Herschel Medal 3940
INSA - Vainu Bappu Memorial Award 7653
Hannah Jackson (nee Gwilt) Gift and Medal 3941
McIntyre Award 10823
Mechaelis Memorial Prize 9850
Medaille des Anciens Presidents 6217
Medaille des Soixante Ans et Fondation Manley-Bendall 6218
Merlin Medal and Gift 2287
Plaquette du Centenaire de Camille Flammarion 6219
Prix Agathon De Potter 1007
Prix des Dames 6220
Prix Dorothea Klumpke - Isaac Roberts 6221
Prix du Commisariat a l'Energie Atomique 5693
Prix Edmond Girard 6222
Prix Edouard Mailly 1018
Prix G. Bidault de l'Isle 6223
Prix Gabrielle et Camille Flammarion 6224
Prix Henri Rey 6225
Prix Janssen 6226
Prix Julien Saget 6227
Prix Marcel Moye 6228
Prix Marius Jacquemetton 6229
Prix Paul and Marie Stroobant 1033
Prix Pol and Christiane Swings 1035
Prix Viennet-Damien 6230
Recognition of Long Service to the Society 10824
Research Award 8508
Research Award for Amateurs 8509
Research Award for Junior Astronomers 8510
Royal Society of Victoria Medal 638
Steavenson Memorial Award 2288
H. L. Vanderlinden Prize 1262
Wallmarkska Priset 11560
Frederick White Prize 181

Athletics See **Physical education; Sports; Track and field**

Atmospheric science See **Meteorology**

Atomic energy (See also Nuclear engineering)

Octacilio Cunha Award 2027
European Nuclear Society Awards 11702
Carneiro Fellipe Medal 2028
FORATOM Award 2125
Plowden Prize 2462

Audiology See **Speech and hearing**

Audiovisuals

Ermanno Acanfora International Prize 8435
City of Sorrento Prize 8436
Dance Screen Award 842
Festival National de l'Audiovisuel d'Entreprise 5007
International Advertising Festival, Cannes 3363
International Diaporama Festival 1224
International Festival of Economics and Training Films 1191
Journalism Competition Prizes 12121
Aldo Merola International Prize 8437
Opera Screen Award 844
Phenix - U.D.A. 6429
Prix Albert Londres 4940
Salon Nacional de Artes Plasticas - Espacios Alternativos 9242
Worlddidac Award 11984

Auto racing

Armstrong Siddeley Car Rally Prizes 2098
Awards at the AGM and the Concours 3533
Challenge Shield 3661
Jim Clark Trophy 10621
Driver of the Year Award 2971
East Anglian Trophy 3662
Golden Sands Rally 1535
Lancia Motor Club Trophies 3534
Le Mans 24-hour Grand Prix d'Endurance 4979

Automobiles

Automobilclub Von Deutschland Awards 6549
British Petroleum Build A Car Competition 4301
Driver of the Year 2145
Excelsior Endurance Award 2165
Foundation Award to the Technician of the Year in the Rolls-Royce Dealer Network Chosen by a Craft Competition 4303
Foundation Prestige Lectures 4304
Horace Grimley Award 3519
Ruth and Jim Hulbert Memorial Trophy 2060
Sir William Lyons Award 2972
Ministry of Defence Medal 4305
MOC Cup 3647
Pemberton Trophy 2973
Rolls-Royce Enthusiasts Awards 3855
IIE Sir Henry Royce Award for Achievement 4308
Sir Henry Royce Memorial Lecture 4313
Sir Henry Royce Pupil Prize 4315
Sir Henry Royce Trophy for the Pursuit of Excellence 4316
Segrave Trophy 3944
Ken Warren Memorial Trophy 2143

Automotive engineering

J. E. Batchelor Award 655
FISITA Travelling Fellowship 656
Fondation Alexandre Darracq 5480
Gas Turbine Award 657
Hartnett Award 658
Land-Rover Register Shield 3536
Oliver Lucas Automotive Electronic Engineering Award 3293
O'Shannessy Award 659
Rodda Award 660

Automotive safety

Challenge for Road Safety 5974
FIA F3000 International Champion 5975
FIA Formula 1 World Champion 5976
FIA World Rally Champion 5977

Aviation See **Aeronautics and aviation**

Aviation safety

Aircraft Safety Prize 4103
R. P. Alston Medal 3881
Jetfoundation 11648
Handley Page Award 3897

Aviculture See **Ornithology**

Bacteriology See **Microbiology**

Badminton

Distinguished Service Award 3377
Divisional Team Championships 4567
English Badminton Award 2153
Honorary Life Vice-Presidents 3378
Individual Championships 4568
Meritorious Service Award 3379
Herbert Scheele Medal 2154
Herbert Scheele Trophy 3380

Ballet

AA Life Vita Ballet and Opera Awards 10810
H. C. Andersen Ballet Award 2003
The Phyllis Bedells Bursary 3867
The Grace Busustow Award 3868
City of Sydney Ballet Scholarship 320
Concours International de Composition Musicale Opera et Ballet Geneve 11678
Adeline Genee Award 3869
Helsinki International Ballet Competition 4734
Moscow International Ballet Competition 10457
Nederburg Opera and Ballet Award 11107
The President's Award 3870
Queen Elizabeth II Coronation Award 3871
Alexandra Radius Prize 9436
Varna International Ballet Competition 1539

Banking

Awards for Contributions in Banking 11827
Honorary Member 10024
Islamic Development Bank Prizes in Islamic Economics and Islamic Banking 10488
NBU Scholarship 11452

Baseball

CEBA Honour List 1116
European Baseball Championships 1117

Basketball

Coach of the Year 2775
Competitions 559
Divisional Team Championships 4567
Fair Play Award 2776
National Championship Cup Finals 2777
National League Player of the Year 2778
National Trophy (Men and Women) 2779
Player of the Year (Men and Women) 2780

Bibliography

Redmond Barry Award 239
Besterman Medal 3564

Howard Drake Memorial Award   3064
Medal for Services to Bibliography   2167
C. B. Oldman Prize   10573
Prix Brunet   5440
SAILIS Bibliographic Award   11062
Walter Stone Memorial Award   369
Triennial Prize of Bibliography   6970

Bicycling
Gold Badge of Honour   2327
El Heraldo Sport Prizes   9022
Individual Championships   4568
International Popular Sports Achievement Award   6948
Newcomers Award   3804
Postgiro Norway   9973
Professional of the Year   3805
Team Champions   3806
Team Championships (non-divisional)   4569
Tour de France   6348
Wilkinson Sword Award of Merit   2325

Biochemistry
ACB Foundation Award   2114
Ames Medal and Award   2115
Boehringer Mannheim Award   2116
Caledonian Research Foundation Prize Lecturehip   10641
Jagdish Chandra Bose Medal   7642
CIBA Medal and Prize   2170
Colworth Medal   2171
Corning Award   2117
ESCPB Young Scientists Awards   1138
Fondation Andre Policard-Lacassagne   5490
Fondation Charles Dhere   5514
Fondation Charles-Leopold Mayer   5518
Fondation du Docteur et de Madame Henri Labbe   5543
Fondation Jean-Marie Le Goff   5598
Fondation Laura Mounier de Saridakis   5613
Fondation Leon Velluz   5619
Fondation Max-Fernand Jayle   5630
Forderungspreis der Osterreichische Geselschaft fur Klinische Chemie   876
Luigi Galvani Prize   6569
Bires Chandra Guha Memorial Lecture   7648
Dr. H. P. Heineken Prize
  Heineken Foundation   9452
  Royal Netherlands Academy of Arts and Sciences   9600
Hestrin Prize   7915
Honorary Member   2172
Sir Frederick Gowland Hopkins Memorial Lecture   2173
Japanese Biochemical Society's Shorei-Sho Awards   8650
Jubilee Lecture and Harden Medal   2174
Keilin Memorial Lecture   2175
Kone Award   2118
Krebs Memorial Scholarship   2176
Richard-Kuhn-Medaille   6786
Rudi Lemberg Travelling Fellowship   175
Friedrich Miescher Prize   11923
Morton Lecture   2177
National Committee for Biochemistry Award   7843
Premio Europeo Prof. D. Ganassini   8259
Prix Andre Lichtwitz   5942
Prix Dina Surdin   6234
Prix du Groupe d'Etudes et de Recherches sur les Lipides et les Lipoproteines   6235
Prix Leon et Henri Fredericq   1030
Prix Maurice Nicloux   6236
Prix Nine Choucroun   5332
Prix Roussel   6205
Royal Society of Victoria Medal   638
SSIEM Award   4378
Travel Fund   2178
Prijs J. B. Van Helmont   1319
A. I. Virtanen - Award   4671
Otto-Wallach-Plakette   6793
Otto-Warburg-Medaille   6892
Wellcome Trust Award for Research in Biochemistry Related to Medicine   2179
Heinrich-Wieland Preis   7017

Biography
J. R. Ackerley Prize   2782
The Age Book of the Year Awards   118
Arts Council of Great Britain Schemes   2100
Arts Council of Wales Book of the Year Awards   12150
Awards for Regional Literature   10004
Benson Medal   4231
James Tait Black Memorial Prizes   10685
Buckland Literary Award   9846
Buenos Aires Literary Prizes   36
Giosue Carducci Prize   8174
Category A Fellowships   155
Category B Fellowships   156
CCP Literary Awards   10034
CNA Literary Award   10830
Duff Cooper Prize   2686
FAW Christina Stead Award   385
FAW Herb Thomas Literary Award   390
Dr. Wijnaendts Francken-prijs   9626
Fundacion del Premio Fastenrath   11345
GPA Book Award   7777
Thomas Hardy Society Book Prize   2983
Axel Hirschs pris   11594
Busken Huetprijs   9639
Kerala Sahitya Akademi Awards   7703
Literary Prizes   7192
Somerset Maugham Awards   4390
McVitie's Prize for the Scottish Writer of the Year   10582
Mirror of Spain Prize   11221
National Award for Literature and Arts   12002
National Prize for Linguistics and Literature   9148
Nelson Hurst & Marsh Biography Award   2151
Premio Comillas de Biografia, Autobiografia y Memorias   11388
Premio de Biografia   9215
Premio Editiorial Costa Rica   1770
Premio Republica Argentina   19
Premios Literarios Nacionais   1474
Premios Municipais Eca de Queiroz de Literatura   10280
Prix Carton de Wiart   1294
Prix Cazes-Brasserie Lipp   6164
Prix Claire Virenque   5829
Prix de la Biographie   5833
Prix de l'Histoire Vecue   6503
Prix de Litterature des Alpes et du Jura   4923
Prix Europeen de l'ADELF   4924
Prix Jacqueline Mompezat   6335
Birger Scholdstroms pris   11600
Walter Stone Memorial Award   369
Strega Prize   8439
Whitbread Literary Awards   2211
Yomiuri Literature Prize   8795

Biology (See also Anatomy; Biochemistry; Biophysics; Biomedical engineering; Biotechnology; Botany; Genetics; Marine biology; Microbiology; Mycology; Nature; Ornithology; Physiology; Zoology)
Akzo prijs   9389
Bancroft - Mackerras Medal of the Australian Society for Parasitology   264
Bhatnagar Award   7532
Bicentenary Medal   3584
Biodeterioration Society Awards   2181
Biological Council Awards   2183
Anil Kumar Bose Memorial Award   7641
Osvaldo L. Bottaro Prize   71
Caledonian Research Foundation Prize Lecturehip   10641
Eliseo Canton Prize   74
Jagdish Chandra Bose Medal   7642
Bashambar Nath Chopra Lecture   7644
Colombian Academy of Science Third World Prize   1579
Conway Lecture   7830
Crafoord Prize   11537
Oswaldo Cruz Prize   1411
Darwin Medal   4146
EEMS Award   11697
EEMS Award to Young Scientists   11698
Pedro I. Elizalde Prize   77
EMBO Medal   6727
EUROSON Young Persons Award   2829
Finsen Prize   11818
Premio Lola e Igo Flisser   9182
Fondation Aime Berthe   5477
Fondation Alhumbert
Fondation Charles-Leopold Mayer   5518
Fondation Da Gama Machado   5527
Fondation du Baron de Joest   5541
Fondation Georges Deflandre et Marthe Deflandre-Rigaud   5567
Fondation Grammaticakis-Neuman   5570
Fondation Langevin   5610
Fondation Laura Mounier de Saridakis   5613
Fondation Louis Armand   5621
Fondation Mergier-Bourdeix   5633
Fondation Parkin   5642
Fondation Paul Gallet   5646
Fondation Roy-Vaucouloux   5663
Fondation Tregouboff   5672
Fondazione Guido Lenghi e Flaviano Magrassi   8060
Fujihara Award   8527
Gabor Medal   4150
Gold Medal   9993
Golden Jubilee Commemoration Medal for Biology   7646
Gottingen Academy of Sciences Prize for Biology   6904
Gottschalk Medal   174
William Bate Hardy Prize   2566
Hector Memorial Medal and Prize   9838
Steven Hoogendijk Prijs   9420
International Prize for Biology   8636
Tadas Ivanausko premija   8855
Louis Jeantet Prize for Medicine   11727
Keilin Memorial Lecture   2175
Keith Medal   10645
Kshanika Oration Award to a Woman Scientist for Research in the Field of Biomedical Sciences   7593
Rudi Lemberg Travelling Fellowship   175
Morris L. Levinson Prizes   7982
Linacre Lecture and Award   4330
MacLeod prijs   1258
MakDougall-Brisbane Prize   10646
Artur Malheiros Prize   10255
Mendel Medal   6625
Naito Foundation Research Prize   8705
October Prizes of the City of Belgrade   10696
Pfizer Academic Awards   3779
Bruce-Preller Prize Lectureship   10648
Premio de Ciencias Morfologicas Dr. Enrique Acosta Vidrio   9188

Biomedical   **Awards, Honors & Prizes, 1995-96**

Biology (continued)
Premio Dr. Eduardo Liceaga   9114
Premio Europeo Prof. D. Ganassini   8259
Premio Federico Nitti   8382
Premio Nacional de Desarrollo Quimico Cosmetico   9272
Prix Albert Brachet   1008
Prix de Biologie Alfred Kastler   5271
Prix de la Fondation du 150e anniversaire de la Societe royale des Sciences de Liege   1368
Prix des Sciences Biologiques et Medicales   5050
Prix des Sciences de la Mer   5692
Prix du Commisariat a l'Energie Atomique   5693
Prix du Ministere de la Jeunesse et des Sports   4834
Prix Dubois - Debauque   1016
Prix Fonde par l'Etat   5695
Prix Lamarck   1028
Prix Leo Errera   1029
Prix Michel Noury   4865
Prix P. J. et Edouard Van Beneden   1032
Prix Richard Lounsbery   5705
Emil Racovita Prize   10380
Prof. G. N. Ramachandran 60th Birthday Commemoration Medal Award   7664
Roentgen-Preis   7001
Carl Asmund Rudolphi Medal   6636
Saltire Society and The Royal Bank of Scotland - Scottish Science Award   10657
Sandoz Preis   878
Moinho Santista Prizes for Young People   1496
Moinho Santista Prizes   1497
Scholastic Award   8808
H. Schoutedenprijs   1259
Scientific Research Prizes   8919
Senior Captain Scott Memorial Medal   11033
Senior Captain Scott Commemoration Medal   11005
Fitz Simons Medal   11034
John Frederick Adrian Sprent Prize   265
Egon Stahl Award   7082
Jan Swammerdam Medal   9559
David Syme Research Prize   697
Emanoil Teodorescu Prize   10387
Trail - Crisp Award   3590
TWAS Award in Biology   8451
University of Berne Prizes   11965
Paul van Oyeprijs   1261
Franz Vogt-Preise   7005
Frederick White Prize   181

Biomedical engineering
Butterworth Hrinemann Prize   2185
C. J. Martin Fellowships   542
Dr. V. K. Zworykin Premium   3312

Biophysics
Jagdish Chandra Bose Medal   7642
Fondation Andre Policard-Lacassagne   5490
Fondation Charles-Leopold Mayer   5518
Dr. H. P. Heineken Prize
  Heineken Foundation   9452
  Royal Netherlands Academy of Arts and Sciences   9600
Prix Leon et Henri Fredericq   1030
Prof. G. N. Ramachandran 60th Birthday Commemoration Medal Award   7664
Prijs J. B. Van Helmont   1319

Biotechnology
DECHEMA Honorary Membership   6615
DECHEMA Medal   6616
DECHEMA Preis der Max Buchner Forschungsstiftung   6617
ESB Clinical Biomechanics Award   6729
ESB Poster Award   6730
ESB Research Award in Biomechanics   6731
Premio Miguel Otero   9131
Prix Moet-Hennessy Louis-Vuitton   5933
Prix Protex   6386
WFCC Skerman Award for Taxonomy   712

Blindness
Apple Tree Award   3691
Australian Audio Book-of-the-Year   548
R. W. Bowen Medal   11082
Braille and Talking Book Library Award   290
Chess Olympiad for the Blind   11472
John William Clark Award   2432
Baudilio Courtis Prize   76
IAPB Awards   3366
International Braille Chess Association Awards   11473
Prix Pierre Villey   5911
Young Deaf Achiever   2732

Boating (See also Rowing)
Award for Valour   2299
Award of Honour   2300
Award of Merit   2301
Book of the Sea Award   3521
Canoeist of the Year   10665
European Finn Seniors Championship   9507
European Junior Finn Championship   9508
Federation Internationale de Canoe   8284
Flying Fifteen World Championship   2898
Individual Championships   4568
International Fireball Worlds Trophy   2894
International Sailing Film Festival in La Rochelle   6044
Lady Canoeist of the Year   10666
Presidential Commendation   2302
Rassegna Internazionale dei Documentari Cine-TV Marinari   8295
RYA Award   4299
Team Championships (non-divisional)   4569
Mark Thornton Gold Challenge Award   3430
World Championship   9509
Yachtsman of the Year Award   4640
Young Sailor of the Year Award   4641

Book and newspaper design
Book Design Awards   193
British Book Design and Production Awards   2482
Walter Tiemann Award   7033

Book illustration See Illustration

Books See Publishing

Botany
Otto-Appel-Denkmunze   6667
Arboricultural Association Award   2089
Bacteria Section Awards   6052
H. H. Bloomer Award   3585
British Lichen Society Awards   2426
W. S. Bruce Medal   10639
Cactus d'Or   3452
Prof. Hira Lal Chakravarty Awards   7683
Clarke Medal   623
Leonard Cockayne Memorial Lecture   9835
Anton-de-Bary-Medaille   6668
Engler Gold Medal   6932
Jakob Eriksson Prize   11539
Jakob Eriksson Prize Medal   11475
Fellow   11103
FESPP Award   9424
Flintoff Medal and Prize   4196
Fondation Auguste Chevalier   5498
Fondation Barbier   5500
Fondation de Coincy   5531
Fondation de la Fons-Melicocq   5532
Fondation Desmazieres   5540
Fondation Foulon   5558
Fondation Jean de Rufz de La Vison   5595
Fondation Jean Thore   5600
Fondation Montagne   5635
Fondation Paul Bertrand   5643
Framstaende Popularvetenskapug Publicering I Vaxtfyscologi   11566
Hector Memorial Medal and Prize   9838
Dr. H. P. Heineken Prize
  Heineken Foundation   9452
  Royal Netherlands Academy of Arts and Sciences   9600
Honorary Member
  Society of Applied Botany   7088
  Southern African Society for Plant Pathology   11104
Hutton Memorial Medal and Prize   9839
Bengt Jonssons pris   11516
Junior Captain Scott Commemorative Medal   10993
Julius-Kuhn-Preis   6669
Prof. L. S. S. Kumar Memorial Award   7655
Life Membership   8551
Linnean Medal   3587
Linnemedaljen for botanik   11517
Linneprisen   11518
Prof. Panchanan Maheshwari Memorial Lecture Award   7657
Irene Manton Prize   3588
Medaille d'Or   5114
Mueller Medal   190
Hugo Muller Lectureship   4211
OPTIMA Gold Medal   7065
OPTIMA Silver Medal   7066
George F. Papentuss Poster Award   3454
Christiaan Hendrik Persoon Medal   11105
Phytopathological Society of Japan Prize   8724
Phytopathological Society of Japan Scientific Research Promotion Award   8725
Premio Efraim Hernandez Xolocotzi   8956
Prix Agathon De Potter   1007
Prix de Coincy   4993
Prix de l'adjudant Hubert Lefebvre   1015
Prix du Conseil de la Societe   4994
Prix Edmond de Selys Longchamps   1017
Prix Emile Laurent   1019
Prix Gandoger   4995
Prix Joseph Schepkens   1027
Royal Society of Victoria Medal   638
SAAB Junior Medal for Botany   11022
SAAB Senior Medal for Botany   11023
Prof. T. S. Sadasivan Lecture Award   7668
Schleiden Medal   6626
Junior Captain Scott Memorial Medal   11032
Jill Smythies Award   3589
South African Medal for Botany   11024
Egon Stahl Award   7082
Stora Linnemedaljen i guld   11554
Sulphur Institute Award   7500
Sunder Lal Hora Medal   7674
Superior Scientist Award   5326
Whitley Awards   646

Bowling
Individual Championships   4568
International Federation of Bowlers Awards   4725
National Championships   10663
Team Championships (non-divisional)   4569

Boxing
El Heraldo Sport Prizes 9022
World Boxing Council Awards 9304

Bravery *See* **Heroism**

Bridge
European Bridge Champion 7875

Broadcast journalism
Benson and Hedges Media Awards 7781
BP Arts Media Awards 210
CRPLF Awards 5070
Ludwig-Erhard-Preis fur Wirtschaftspublizistik 6699
Guillermo Gonzalez Camarena 9087
Journalism Prize 1062
Alfonso Sordo Noriega Prize 9090
Prix de la Memoire 5206
Prix Ringier 6194
Reuter Foundation Fellowship 3850
Royal Television Society Television Journalism Awards 4288
Television Journalism Prize 40

Broadcasting (*See also* Broadcast journalism; Cable television; Media; Radio; Sports broadcasting; Television; Video)
ABU Engineering Award 8888
Akashvani Annual Awards for Technical Excellence 7481
Danmarks Radio TV Award 1991
FES Award 8890
Golden Harp Television Festival 7824
Bharatendu Harishchandra Award 7530
IBC John Tucker Award 3384
IERE Benefactors Premium 3290
International Radio and Television Festivals and Competitions 1867
Kikuchi Prize 8752
Kryger Prize 1992
NHK Broadcast Cultural Award 8601
Nihon Shinbun Kyokai Awards 8628
Order of Cultural Merit 8579
P1-Prize 1993
Radio Denmark Language Award 1994
Regional Radio and Television Awards 1108
South African Broadcasting Corporation Prize 11042
Special Awards 2659

Brotherhood
Eugenio Balzan Prize 8280
Cruz de Boyaca 1618
Friendship Medal 10430
International Youth Award 7687
Jawaharlal Nehru Award for International Understanding 7573
Order of Friendship of Peoples 10462
Premio Mixcoatl 9255

Business (*See also* Accounting; Advertising; Business history; Business journalism; Consumer affairs; Economics; Management; Manufacturing; Marketing)
Albert Medal 4318
Best MBA Student Award 9859
Business Enterprise Awards 4163
Businessperson of the Year 925
Frans du Toit Medal 10988
Emergent Entrepreneur Award 10877
European Businesswoman of the Year 2281
European Grand Prix of Corporate Image 5006
European Markstrat Competition 6402
Exporters Medal 1609
Festival National de l'Audiovisuel d'Entreprise 5007
Fondation Kastner-Boursault 5605
Benjamin Franklin Medal 4322
Gallaher Business Challenge 7859
Graduateship of the City and Guilds of London Institute 2624
Guildhall Helping Hand Awards 2878
International Festival of Economics and Training Films 1191
International Industrial Film and Video Awards 2703
Joyce Award 2282
Licentiateship of the City and Guilds of London Institute 2625
Livewire Start-up Awards 3596
Medals for Excellence 2626
Membership of the City and Guilds of London Institute 2627
Mercury Business Book Award 3642
Mobil Business in the Arts Awards 529
National Prize for Quality 9261
Order of Merit in Commerce 1613
Sir Peter Parker Awards for Spoken Business Japanese 4335
Prix Corbay 5727
Prix Herman Schoolmeesters 991
Prize Mission Special Japan 8733
Prize Objective Japan 8734
Public Service Medal 10748
Rector's Medal 11117
Rising Star Award 2283
Rookie Businessperson of the Year 926
Royal Companies Award 11109
Top 100 Companies Award 11110
Top Five Businessmen Award 11111
Woman of the Year in Finland 4752
Worldaware Business Awards 4635
Young Businessman of the Year Award 2957

Business administration *See* Management

Business history
Wadsworth Prize for Business History 2564

Business journalism
Accountancy Journalist of the Year 2579
BAIE Editing for Industry Awards 2266
Construmat Award 11192
David Davidson Prize in Economics 11562
Ludwig-Erhard-Preis fur Wirtschaftspublizistik 6699
Grand Prix du Journal d'Entreprise 6434
Guildhall Helping Hand Awards 2878
Journalism Prize 1062
Sir William Lyons Award 2972
PPA Magazines Awards for Editorial and Publishing Excellence 3774
Worldaware Business Awards 4635
Young Business Writer 2890

Cable television (*See also* Television)
NHK Japan Prize Contest 8602

Calligraphy *See* **Graphic arts**

Camping *See* **Recreation**

Canadian literature
Canada-Australia Literary Award 154
Prix France-Acadie 4894

Cancer (*See also* Radiology)
American Cancer Society International Cancer Research Fellowships 11856
Awards 1140
Karl Heinrich Bauer Prize for Surgical Tumor Research 6874
Doctor Raoul Biltris Prize 1309
Bourse Gonzague Mulliez 4802
Bourse Veronique Dejouany 4803
Lady Cade Memorial Fellowship 10826
Cancer Campaign Medals of Merit 4673
Cecilia Cioffrese Prizes for Health Care 8225
Dr. Roland De Ruyck Prize 1311
EACR Italian Fellowship Program 2819
EACR Travel Fellowships 2820
Paul Ehrlich - und Ludwig Darmstaedter Preis 6691
Fondation Dandrimont-Benicourt 5529
Fondation du Docteur et de Madame Peyre 5544
Fondation Eugene et Amelie Dupuis 5554
Fondation Gustave Roussy 5572
Fondation Henriette Regnier 5579
Fondation Leon-Alexandre Etancelin 5616
Fondation Louise Darracq 5623
Fondation Marie Leon-Houry 5626
Fondation Odette Lemenon 5641
Fondation Roberge 5660
Fondation Roy-Vaucouloux 5663
Fondazione Wilhelm Conrad Rontgen 8066
Fernando Fonseca Prize 10315
Garrod Medal 2515
Edgar Gentilli Prize 3955
T. P. Gunton Award 2437
Alexander Haddow Lecture 4250
Honorary Member 5963
International Association for the Study of Lung Cancer Awards 1956
International Cancer Research Technology Transfer Project 11859
International Oncology Nursing Fellowships 11860
Leah Lederman Memorial Lectures 4259
Albert McMaster Award 2447
Prof. Dr. P. Muntendamprijs 9661
Raul Nicolini Prize 90
Nycomed Prize 9528
Pezcoller Recognition for Dedication to Oncology 8398
Prix Alexander Straetmans 1324
Prix Amelie Marcel 4808
Prix Antoine et Claude Beclere 4810
Prix Berthe Pean 4813
Prix Cancer 4814
Prix Cordier 4818
Prix Cornelis - Lebegue 1328
Prix Delahautemaison 5264
Prix Drieu-Cholet 4831
Prix Fauconnier 4839
Prix Gallet et Breton 4840
Prix Griffuel 4942
Prix Gustave Roussy 4841
Prix Henry et Mary Jane Mitjaville 4845
Prix Henry Fauconnier 1335
Prix Paul Mathieu 4869
Prix Rosen de Cancerologie 5265
Prix Specia 4874
Prix Yvonne Foulley 4878
Research Training Fellowship 6485
Bernandino Rivadavia Prize 98
Saint Luke's Lecture 7832
Sandoz Oration Award for Research in Cancer 7605
Erkki Saxen Medal 4674
Schweisguth Prize 9529
Rabbi Shai Shacknai Memorial Prize and Lectureship 7888
Raja Ravi Sher Singh of Kalsia Memorial Cancer Research Award 7609
Helen Tomkinson Award 2452

Cancer (continued)
Alexandre and Gaston Tytgat Prize 1360
Eufemio Uballes Prize 101
UICC Award 11862
Hamao Umezawa Prize for Chemotherapy 9898
Visiting Scientist Award 6486
Walker Prize 3981
Premio Aida Weiss 9200
Michael Williams Lecture 4273
Yamagiwa-Yoshida Memorial International Cancer Study Grants 11863

Canoeing See **Boating**

Cardiology
Richard J. Bing Award 3469
Rafael A. Bullrich Prize 73
Burger Memorial Award 10788
Professor Ignacio Chavez Young Investigator Award 9073
Rosalia Feldblit de Garfunkel Prize 78
R. T. Hall Prize 305
Peter Harris Award 3470
Geoffrey Holt Award 2443
Amrut Mody-Unichem Prize for Research in Cardiology, Neurology and Gastroenterology 7596
Claude-Adolphe Nativelle Prize for Medicine 6128
Premio Maestro Arturo Rosenblueth 9276
Premio Maestro Ignacio Chavez 9277
Premio Maestro Manuel Vaquero 9278
Premio Maestro Salvador Aceves 9279
Premio Sor Maria del Roble 9280
Prix Jean Escalle 4847
Prix Lian 4857
Dos Santos Prize 5128
Edith Walsh Award 2454
Young Scientist Award in Noninvasive Cardiovascular Dynamics 10789

Career achievement See **Academic achievement; Professional and personal achievement**

Cars See **Automobiles**

Cartography (See also Geography)
Awards 3440
John Bartholomew Award 2304
British Cartographic Society Design Award 2305
Fondation de Madame Edmond Hamel 5534
Keuffel and Esser Awards 2306
Laser Scan Award in Digital Cartography 2307
Deak Lazar Memorial Medal 7310
Diaconus Lazarus Commemorative Medal 7395
National Geographic Society Award 2308
Pyser-SGI Award 2309

Cartoons (See also Animated films; Drawing; Humor)
AMP W.G. Walkley Awards for Journalism 523
Constantino Escalante Prize 9085
Golden Aesop Prize 1521
International Simavi Cartoon Competition 12053
Kodanasha Prize for Cartoon Book 8688
Yunus Nadi Yarismasi 12049
National Prize for Journalism and Information 9140
Newspaper Cartoon Competition 9167
Premio Mingote 11319
Premio Municipal Rafael Bordalo Pinheiro de Banda Desenhada, Cartoon e Caricaturista 10276
Prix Henri Lehmann 5401
Yomiuri International Cartoon Contest 8794

Catholic literature
Prix Constant Dauguet 5830
Prix Gallet 5747
Prix Juteau-Duvigneaux 5877

Cats See **Animal care and training**

Ceramic engineering
Goldene Gehlhoff-Ring 6638
Industriepreis fur technisch-wissenschaftliche Arbeiten 6639
Premio La Ceramica n la Arquitectura 9302
Otto Schott Denkmunze 6640

Ceramics (See also Glass)
Academy Awards 9750
Biennale Internationale de Limoges 5299
Fletcher Challenge International Ceramics Award 9722
Grand Prix ICA - Prix de Sculpture 10689
International Ceramic Art Competition 8309
Medaille des Arts Plastiques 4784
Premio Daniel Zuloaga 11289
Royal Dublin Society Crafts Competition 7835
Salon Nacional de Artes Plasticas - Ceramica 9239

Charity activities See **Philanthropy; Volunteerism**

Chemical engineering
Brennan Medal 3214
John A. Brodie Medal 427
Chemeca Medal 431
Chemeca Student Design Prize 432
Council Medal 3215
CRA Award 436
George E. Davis Medal 3216
DECHEMA Honorary Membership 6615
DECHEMA Medal 6616
DECHEMA Preis der Max Buchner Forschungsstiftung 6617
Donald Medal 3217
Esso Award 439
Ned Franklin Medal 3218
Gold Medal 2882
Graduate Prizes 4332
Arnold Greene Medal 3219
Hanson Medal 3220
John William Hinchley Medal 3221
Hutchison Medal 3222
ICI Award 441
Junior Moulton Medal 3223
Leverhulme Medal 4152
Macnab Medal 3224
Mencion IMIQ 9105
Premio IMIQ 9106
Premio IMIQ-CONACYT 9107
Premio IMIQ, ING. Estanislao Ramirez 9108
Premio IMIQ, Victor Marquez Dominguez 9109
Premio para el Estimulo de Docencia e Investigacion en Ingenieria Quimica 9110
Queensland Division Chemical Branch Award 482
Senior Moulton Medal 3225
Shedden Pacific Medal and Prize 487
Skellerup Award 9744
H. K. Suttle Award 2883
Karoly Than Medal 7323
Travel and Study Abroad 2884

Chemical industry
Baekeland Lecture 4401
Canada Lecture and Medal 4403
Cavallaro Medal
 European Federation of Corrosion 6710
 Universita di Ferrara - Centro di Studi sulla Corrosione 8464
CEFIC Environment Award 1129
Centenary Medal and Lecture 4405
Chemical Industry Medal 4406
Chemical Society of Japan Award for Technological Development 8515
European Federation of Corrosion Medal 6711
Ferroguard Award in Electrochemical Technology 7495
Hellmuth Fischer-Medaille 6618
Industrial Chemistry Medal 11048
Lampitt Medal 4412
Mascot National Award 7496
Messel Medal and Lecture 4418
Alwin Mittasch-Medaille 6619
Perkin Medal 4420
Ignac Pfeifer Medal 7322
President's Medal 4421
Arthur B. Purvis Lecture 4422
Andres Manuel del Rio National Prize in Chemistry 8948
Richard Seligman Lecture 4425
Society's Medal and Lecture 4426
Charles Tennant Memorial Lecture 4427
Hendrik Van Eck Medal 11051

Chemistry (See also Biochemistry; Chemical engineering; Chemical industry; Color technology; Fiber science; Geochemistry; Industrial chemistry)
ACHEMA Plaque in Titanium 6614
AECI Medal 11045
Akzo prijs 9389
Adrien Albert Lectureship 4183
Analar Lectureship 4184
Alejandro Angel Escobar Science Prize 1584
Applied Research Medal 597
Armstrong Lecture 4400
Dr. Max-Luthi Auszeichnung 11885
Bader Award 4185
Barrer Award 4186
Beilby Medal and Prize 4187
Gmelin-Beilstein-Denkmunze 6778
Ronald Belcher Memorial Lectureship 4188
Ernst David Bergmann Prize 7978
Ellen and Niels Bjerrum Award for Chemists 1980
Bourke Lectureship 4189
Robert Boyle Medal in Analytical Chemistry 4190
S. F. Boys - A Rahman Lectureship 4191
Bunsen-Denkmunze 6628
Canada International Lecture 4402
Carbohydrate Chemistry Award 4192
Castner Lecture and Medal 4404
Centenary Lectureship 4193
Chemical Education Medal 11046
Chemical Society of Japan Award 8512
Chemical Society of Japan Award for Chemical Education 8513
Chemical Society of Japan Award for Distinguished Technical Achievements 8514
Chemical Society of Japan Award for Young Chemists 8516
Chemical Society of Japan Award of Merits for Chemical Education 8517

Subject Index of Awards
Volume 2: International and Foreign
Chemistry

Chemical Technology Award 8941
Chinese Chemical Society Awards 1572
Colombian Academy of Science Third World Prize 1579
Corday-Morgan Medal and Prize 4194
Cornforth Medal 598
Davy Medal 4147
DECHEMA Honorary Membership 6615
DECHEMA Medal 6616
Distinguished Clinical Chemist Award 7896
Distinguished International Services Award 7897
Divisional Award of the Chemical Society of Japan 8518
Carl-Duisberg-Gedachtnispreis 6779
Carl-Duisberg-Plakette 6780
Edlundska Priset 11538
Ellinger-Gardonyi Award 3730
Ewald Prize 3498
Faraday Medal and Lectureship 4195
Emil-Fischer-Medaille 6781
Hellmuth Fischer-Medaille 6618
Flintoff Medal and Prize 4196
Fondation Aime Berthe 5477
Fondation Alexandre Darracq 5480
Fondation Alhumbert 5484
Fondation Andre Policard-Lacassagne 5490
Fondation Aniuta Winter-Klein 5492
Fondation Berthelot 5502
Fondation Cahours, Houzeau 5508
Fondation Charles-Adam Girard 5513
Fondation Clavel 5522
Fondation du Baron de Joest 5541
Fondation Emile Jungfleisch 5552
Fondation Gabrielle Sand 5563
Fondation Grammatickakis-Neuman 5570
Fondation Henry Wilde 5583
Fondation Jean-Baptiste Dumas 5592
Fondation Jean Reynaud 5599
Fondation Jecker 5601
Fondation Jerome Ponti 5602
Fondation L. La Caze 5607
Fondazione Langevin 5610
Fondation Lavoisier 5614
Fondation Le Conte 5615
Fondation Leon Velluz 5619
Fondation Louis Armand 5621
Fondation Marie Guido Triossi 5625
Fondation Mergier-Bourdeix 5633
Fondation Paul Gallet 5646
Fondation Paul Marguerite de la Charlonie 5647
Fondation Paul Pascal 5648
Fondation Philippe A. Guye 5651
Fondation Pierre Desnuelle 5652
Fondation Rochat-Juliard 5661
Fondation Schutzenberger 5666
Fondation Vaillant 5674
Fondations Estrade Delcros, Houllevigue, Saintour, Jules Mahyer 5679
Fondazione Guido Donegani 8059
Forderungspreis der Osterreichische Gesellschaft fur Klinische Chemie 876
Theodor Forster Memorial Lecture 6629
Francqui Prize 1156
Sir Edward Frankland Fellowship 4197
Sir Edward Frankland Prize Lectureship 4198
Fresenius-Preis 6782
Fujihara Award 8527
GAMS Prize 5324
Gold Medal 11047
Golden Jubilee Commemoration Medal for Chemistry 7647
Gottingen Academy of Sciences Prize for Chemistry 6905
Graduate Prizes 4332

Gregori Aminoffs Pris 11542
Guldberg and Waage's Law of Mass Action Memorial Medal 9932
Gunning Victoria Jubilee Prize Lectureship 10644
Fabian Gyllenbergs pris 11514
Otto-Hahn-Preis fur Chemie und Physik
  Deutsche Physikalische Gesellschaft 6658
  German Chemical Society 6783
Carl Hanson Medal 4408
Jan Harabaszewski Medal 10134
Harrison Memorial Prize 4199
Haworth Memorial Lectureship and Medal 4200
Hector Memorial Medal and Prize 9838
Helmholtz Prizes 6914
Prijs Jan-Frans Heymans 1313
Hickinbottom Fellowship 4201
Hilditch Lecture 4409
Gilles Holst Medal 9601
Honorary Member 6630
Honorary Membership 10135
Robert Horne Lecture 4410
Hurter Lecture 4411
ICTA Young Scientist Award 3389
IFEAT Distinguished Service Medal 3415
IFSCC Award and IFSCC Honorary Mention 3421
IFSCC Poster Prize 3422
Industrial Chemistry Medal 11048
Industrial Lectureship 4202
Ingold Lectureship 4203
International Organization for Chemical Sciences in Development Awards 9077
International Society of Electrochemistry Awards 11840
Japan Society for Analytical Chemistry Award 8634
John Jeyes Lectureship 4204
Jordan Award 3731
Kaufmann Memorial Lecture 6838
H. P. Kaufmann-Preis 6839
Earl King Prize 3170
Wilhelm-Klemm-Preis 6784
KNCV Gold Medal 9609
Joseph-Konig-Gedenkmunze 6785
Stanislaw Kostanecki Medal 10136
Le Sueur Lecture 4413
Leighton Memorial Medal 599
Leverhulme Lecture 4414
Leverhulme Medal 4152
Ivan Levinstein Memorial Lecture 4415
Julius Lewkowitsch Memorial Lecture 4416
Liebig-Denkmunze 6787
Lindbomska Beloningen 11546
Listar Memorial Lecture 4417
Liversidge Lectureship 4205
Liversidge Memorial Lectureship 627
Longstaff Medal 4206
Josepf Loschimidt Prize 4207
Artur Malheiros Prize 10255
Marlow Medal and Prize 4208
Medaglia Amedeo Avogadro 8378
Medaglia Emanuele Paterno 8337
Medaglia Stanislao Cannizzaro 8340
Meldola Medal and Prize 4209
Ludwig Mond Lectureship 4210
Mischa Mrost Prize 11049
Hugo Muller Lectureship 4211
National Prize for Chemistry 1737
C. D. Nenitescu Prize 10371
Nernst - Haber - Bodenstein-Preis 6631
Nobel Prize for Chemistry 11496
Nobel Prizes 11549
W. Normann-Medaille 6840
Nyholm Lectureship 4212

Oils and Fats Group International Lecture 4419
H. C. Orsted Medal 2007
Paracelsus-Preis 11886
Partington Prize 4374
Pedler Lectureship and Medal 4213
Jozsef Petzval Medal 7446
Pfizer Academic Awards 3779
C. S. Piper Prize 600
Polish Chemical Society Medal 10137
Porter Medal 3500
Preis der Gesellschaft Deutscher Chemiker fur Journalisten und Schriftsteller 6788
Premio Federico Nitti 8382
Premio Nacional de Desarrollo Quimico Cosmetico 9272
Prix Agathon De Potter 1007
Prix Barrabe 5304
Prix Chimie 4816
Prix de Boelpaepe 1013
Prix de la Fondation de la Maison de la Chimie 5201
Prix de la Fondation du 150e anniversaire de la Societe royale des Sciences de Liege 1368
Prix de l'Institut Francais du Petrole 5690
Prix des Sciences de la Mer 5692
Prix du Commisariat a l'Energie Atomique 5693
Prix du Gaz de France 5694
Prix Fonde par l'Etat 5695
Prix Frederic Swarts 1022
Prix Georges Millot 5309
Prix Jean-Servais Stas 1026
Prix Le Bel 6357
Prix Louis Melsens 1031
Prix Paul Janssen 1365
Prix Pierre Sue 6358
Prix Protex 6386
Prix Raymond Berr Atochem 6359
Prix Triennal de la Societe Royale de Chimie 1366
Raikes Medal 11050
Ramachar Award in Electrochemical Science 7497
Ramsay Memorial Fellowship for Chemical Research 3837
Theophilus Redwood Lectureship 4214
Rennie Memorial Medal 601
Rhone - Poulenc Lectureship 4215
Rideal Memorial Lecture 4423
Robert Robinson Lectureship 4216
R. A. Robinson Memorial Lectureship 4217
Bakhuis Roozeboom Medal 9604
Royal Society of Victoria Medal 638
RSC Interdisciplinary Awards 4218
RSC Sponsored Awards 4219
Ruzicka-Prize 11936
SAC Gold Medal 4220
SAC Silver Medal 4221
Sandmeyer-Preis 11887
Sandoz Preis 878
Moinho Santista Prizes for Young People 1496
Moinho Santista Prizes 1497
Gerhard M. J. Schmidt Memorial Prize 7984
SCI International Medal 4424
Scientific Research Prizes 8919
Seligman Crystal 3426
Professor T. R. Seshadri Seventieth Birthday Commemoration Medal 7669
Simonsen Lectureship 4222
H. G. Smith Medal 602
Jedrzej Sniadecki Medal 10138
Somach - Sachs Memorial Award 7985
Gheorghe Spacu Prize 10383
Spiers Memorial Lectureship 4223

729

Chemistry (continued)
Hermann-Staudinger-Preis 6789
Alfred-Stock-Gedachtnispreis 6790
Svante Arrhenius Medaljen 11557
David Syme Research Prize 697
Nicolae Teclu Prize 10386
Dr. Edmund-Thiele-Denkmunze 6545
Tilden Lectureship 4224
TWAS Award in Chemistry 8452
University of Berne Prizes 11965
Van Marum Medal 9610
A. I. Virtanen - Award 4671
Franz Vogt-Preise 7005
Adolf-von-Baeyer-Denkmunze 6791
August-Wilhelm-von-Hofmann-Denkmunze 6792
Otto-Wallach-Plakette 6793
Wallmarkska Priset 11560
Vince Wartha Medal 7324
Werner-Preis 11888
Roy L. Whistler Award 3386
Heinrich-Wieland Preis 7017
Wolf Foundation Prizes 7987
Young Scientist Award 1968
Jan Zawidzki Medal 10139
Karl-Ziegler-Preis 6794

Chess
Alexander Shield 2786
BCF Player of the Year 2311
Chess Awards 7521
Chess Olympiad for the Blind 11472
Chess World Champions 7224
Club of the Year 2312
FIDE Master 7225
Gelsthorpe Cup 2787
Gold Diploma of Honor 7226
Grandmaster 7227
International Arbiter 7228
International Braille Chess Association Awards 11473
International Master 7229
President's Award for Services to Chess 2313
Woman FIDE Master 7230
Woman Grandmaster 7231
Woman International Master 7232

Child welfare (See also Youth work)
Jamnalal Bajaj Foundation Awards 7693
Man for Mankind Awards 938

Children and youth
Cork Youth International Video and Film Festival 7812
Creative Writing Junior Competition 2219
Fox of Poster for Books for the Young 6203
Frankfurter Guckkastenmennchen 6592
International Festival of Cinema for Children and Youth 10232
Prix Danube Festival, Bratislava 10780
Prix Jeunesse International Munchen 7076

Children's literature
AIM Children's Book Awards
  Booksellers of New Zealand 9707
  Queen Elizabeth II Arts Council of New Zealand - Literature Programme 9797
Hans Christian Andersen Awards 11767
Andersen Prize 8422
ASEAN Award for Literature 10030
Austrian National Book Award for Children's Literature 757
Austrian State Prize for Poetry for Children 764
Award of the Circle of the Greek Children's Book 7188

Awards for the Best Produced Books in Hong Kong 7277
Bancarellino Prize 8163
Bangla Academy Literary Award 934
Bastian Prize 9957
Elsa Beskow Plaque 11632
Best Books for Children Awards 12146
Book Awards 10734
Book of the Year Award: Older Readers 310
Book of the Year Award: Younger Readers 311
Book Prizes of the Circle of the Greek Children's Book 7189
Alba Bouwer Prize 10986
Brothers Grimm Prize 6561
Bucharest Writers Association Award 10411
Buxtehuder Bulle 7094
Carnegie Medal 3566
Castello-Sanguinetto Prize 8197
Catalonia Illustration Prize 11194
Cena Zvazu slovenskych spisovatelov 10756
Children's Book Award 2874
Children's Book Council Award 7735
Children's Novel Writing Competition 8902
Children's Story Prize 9047
City of Vienna Prizes for Books for Children and Young People 790
Russell Clark Award 9761
Competition for Children's Theater or Stories 9012
Concurso Carmen Lyra 1768
Critici in Erba Prize 8171
Croatian Socialist Republic Prizes 1808
Lady Cutler Award 315
Damm prize 9880
Danish Prize for Children's Literature 1936
Danmarks Skolebibliotekarforenings Bornebogspris 1920
Penelope Delta 7190
Dromkeen Librarian's Award 411
Dromkeen Medal 412
EARTHWORM Children's Book Award 2913
Environment in Children's Literature Award 10289
Excursions and Journeys in Greece Award 7219
Eleanor Farjeon Award 2617
FAW Mary Grant Bruce Award for Children's Literature 397
Festival Awards for Literature 673
Kathleen Fidler Award 10514
FIT Astrid Lindgren Translation Prize 823
Percy Fitzpatrick Award 11057
Fox of Poster for Books for the Young 6203
German Youth Literature Prize 6833
Friedrich-Gerstaecker-Preis 6573
Glazen Globe 9586
Esther Glen Award 9762
Gold Paintbrush 9365
Gold Pencil 9366
Gold Ribbon 1840
Golden Cat Award 11568
Grand Prix des Treize 5030
Grands Prix Litteraire de la Ville de Paris 6095
Graphics Prize Fiera di Bologna for Children and Young Adults 8172
Kate Greenaway Medal 3568
The Guardian Children's Fiction Award 2954
Gulliver Award 11637
Gwobrau Tir na n-og 12196
Katrine Harries Award 11058
Historic Novel Award 7220
Nils Holgersson Plaque 11633

Tienie Holloway Medal 10992
Hong Kong Biennial Awards for Chinese Literature 7278
C. P. Hougenhout Award 11059
IBBY-Asahi Reading Promotion Award 8494
IBBY - Asahi Reading Promotion Award 11768
IBBY Honour List 11769
Illustration Award 11383
International Biennial of Illustrations Bratislava 10782
Mary Vaughan Jones Award 12197
A Kelpie for the Nineties 10518
Sir Peter Kent Conservation Book Prize 2200
Rudolf Koivu Prize 4687
Janusz Korczak Literary Award 10179
Lazarillo Prize 11384
Fran Levstik Prize 10807
Libris Woutertje Pieterse Prijs 9672
Literary Awards and Prizes for Sinhalese Literature 11423
Literary Competition 357
Literature Awards for Children and Young People 9916
Monteiro Lobato Prize 1424
Carl Lohann Prize 11060
Lydecken - palkinto 4667
M. E. R. Prize 11114
Macmillan Prize for a Children's Picture Book 3757
Kurt Maschler Award 2202
McVitie's Prize for the Scottish Writer of the Year 10582
Apel Les Mestres Prize 11215
Mlade leta Prize 10786
Mobil Children's Culture Award 8702
Most Beautiful and the Best Children's Book of spring, summer, autumn, winter in Slovakia 10760
Mother Goose Award 2209
Myrto's Book Award 7221
National Award for Literature and Arts 12002
National Book Institute Juvenile Literature Award 1472
National Prize for Illustration of Literature for Children and Young People 11370
National Short Story Competition 1757
New South Wales State Literary Awards 147
New Zealand Library Association Non-Fiction for Young People Award 9763
Noma Award for Publishing in Africa 2039
Noma Concours for Picture Book Illustrations 8500
Noma Illustration Prizes 8689
Noma Prize for Juvenile Novel 8690
Laura Orvieto Prize 8251
Paaskynen palkinto 4668
Don Carlos Palanca Memorial Awards for Literature 10053
Perskor Prize for Youth Literature 10908
Picture Book of the Year Award 312
Ludmila Podjavorinska Plaque Bibiana, International House of Art for Children 10761
Friends of Children's Books 10766
Eve Pownall Award: Information Books 313
Premio Antoniorrobles 9120
Premio FUNDALECTURA de Literatura Infantil y Juvenil Colombiana 1703
Premio Nacional de Cuento para Ninos Juan de la Cabada 9232
Premios Nacionales de Literatura Infantil y Juvenil 11379
Prijs van de Nederlandse Kinderjury 9367

Prix Bernard Versele 1219
Prix de Traduction de Litterature Enfantine 4991
Prix Helene Porges 5864
Prix SGDL du Livre Jeunesse 6296
Prizes for Manuscripts for Juveniles 10008
Recognition Prize for Children's and Youth's Literature 769
Revelation Prize for Children's Literature 10310
Romanian Writers' Union Prizes 10414
Bala Sahitya Award 7696
Sankei Jidoh Bunka Shuppan Shoh 8729
Scheepers Prize 11004
Shogakukan Bungaku-Sho 8747
Shogakukan Kaiga-Sho 8748
Short Stories for Small Children Award 7222
Signal Poetry Award 4537
Smarties Book Prize 2206
Jenny Smelik/IBBY Prize 9387
Sonderpreis 6834
Sree Padmanabha Swari Prize 7708
Staatsprijs voor Jeugdliteratuur 1081
Anni Swan Prize 4704
Swiss Children's Book Prize 11947
TES Information Book Awards 4548
TES Schoolbook Award 4549
Theo Thijssenprijs 9666
Topelius Prize 4689
Triple Rose Prize
  Bibiana, International House of Art for Children 10762
  Friends of Children's Books 10767
L'udovit Fulla Prize 10763
Urban Council Awards for Creative Writing in Chinese 7279
Nienke van Hichtum Prize 9351
Venz Kinder Boeken Prijs 9369
Pier Paolo Vergerio European Prize for Children's Literature 8466
Verlagspreis zur Forderung popularwissenschaftlicher Literatur fur das jungere Lesealter 7152
West Australian Young Readers' Book Award 249
Western Australian Premier's Book Awards 515
Whitbread Literary Awards 2211
White Ravens 6995
Young Australians Best Book Award 719

Chiropractic
Chiropractor of the Year 10834

Choral music
AGEC-Preis 9477
Akashvani Annual Awards 7480
Bela Bartok International Choir Contest 7296
Dietrich Buxtehude Prize 7037
Catalonian Prizes for Music 11182
Citibank Choral Awards 319
Competition of Composition for Choirs 11196
Composition Competition, Tours 5192
Cork International Choral Festival 7766
Crawley Plaque 2261
International Choir Festival 9478
International Choral Competition of Tolosa 11197
International Choral Competition, Tours 5193
International Competition for Choirs 797
International Composition Contest Guido d'Arezzo 8215

International Franz Schubert Male Choir Contest - Vienna 882
International Polyphonic Contest Guido d'Arezzo 8216
International Trophy Competition 7767
Iuventus Mundi Cantat Competition 1893
Llangollen International Musical Eisteddfod 12177
Masterplayers International Music and Conductors Competition 11877
Montreux International Choral Festival 11879
National Scots Song Competition 10656
Sacred Choral Chant National Competition 8468
Singing Youth International, Zoltan Kodaly Choral Competition 7423
Harold Smart Anthem Competition 4139
Tyneside Trophy 2262
Zelter Medal 6746

Choreography
AA Life Vita Contemporary Choreography and Dance Awards 10811
Aanmoedigingsprijzen 9635
Concorso Coreografico Internazionale di Modern Jazz Dance 8110
Concours International de Choregraphie du CBC, Nyon 11672
Dance Screen Award 842
Digital Dance Awards 2746
Ferenc Erkel Prize for Musical Composition 7400
Sonia Gaskellprijs 9637
Helsinki International Ballet Competition 4734
Leonida Massine Prize for the Art of the Dance 8156
Moscow International Ballet Competition 10457
Laurence Olivier Awards 4466
Premi Ricard Moragas 11163
Premio Nacional de Danza Clasica Contemporanea 9297
Premio Nacional de Danza Etnocoreografica 9298
Time Out Theatre, Dance and Comedy Awards 4545

Christianity (See also Catholic literature)
Collins Religious Book Award 2640
Deo Gloria Award 2198
Frend Medal 4383
Grand Prix des Treize 5030
Interfilm Award 9456
International Christian Television Week 7165
Mrs. James Nelson Award 716
Order of Pius IX 12101
Order of St. Sylvester 12103
Order of the Golden Spur (Golden Militia) 12104
Prix Cardinal Grente 5827
Prix Chretiente d'Orient 5011
Prix Claire Virenque 5829
Prix Vega et Lods de Wegmann 5928
Pro Ecclesia et Pontifice Medal 12106
Pro Ecelesia et Pontifice 8476
Dr. William Baird Ross Trust Competition 10595
Winifred Mary Stanford Prize 3019
Supreme Order of Christ (Militia of Our Lord Jesus Christ) 12107
Totius Prize for Theology and the Original Languages of the Bible 11009
Ulster Award 717
Unda Dove 1376

Rev. Pieter van Drimmelen Medal 11011
Young Women's Christian Association Council of Zimbabwe Competitions 12211

Church history
Hanns Lilje Prize 6910
Prix Georges Goyau 5859

Cinema See Films

Citizenship and patriotism
Cross of Merit for Moral and Civic Education 1432
Eichendorff Plakette 6742
King's Cross for Distinguished Service 9918
Medal for Civic Virtue 9920
Medal of Service 7251
Medalla Lazaro Cardenas del Rio 9300
My Country - USSR Award 10441
Orden Nacional al Merito 1619
Order of Excellence of Guyana 7254
Order of Orange-Nassau 9356
Order of Rio Branco 1417
Order of Roraima of Guyana 7255
Order of the Netherlands Lion 9358
Order of the October Revolution 10465
Premio Miguel Hidalgo 9141
Prix Audiffred 5715
Prix General Muteau 5749
Royal Norwegian Order of St. Olav 9922
St. Olav Medal 9923
Verdienstorden der Bundesrepublik Deutschland 6739

City management
Britain in Bloom Awards 4541

City planning (See also Park planning; Planning)
Sir Patrick Abercrombie Prize 6058
Annual Award for Planning Achievement 4290
Book Awards 10502
Civic Trust Awards 2636
Festival International du Film d'Architecture d'Urbanisme et d'Environement Urbain de Bordeaux 6018
Ford European Conservation Awards 2677
Forderpreis des Landes Nordrhein-Westfalen fur junge Kunstlerinnen und Kunstler 7026
Patrick Geddes Planning Award 10653
Gold Medal 4291
Ebenezer Howard Memorial Medal 4553
IFHP International Film/Video Competition 9486
IFHP International Student Competition 9487
International Festival of Films on Architecture and Town-planning of Lausanne 11793
Medaille des Arts Plastiques 4784
October Prizes of the City of Belgrade 10696
George Pepler International Award 4292
Premio Antonio Maura 11288
Prix de Rome 9578
Prix Nature et Patrimoine 5080
Rotterdam-Maaskant Award 9583
Sendai International Design Competition 8760
Stockholm Prize 11575
Simon Van der Stel Foundation Medal 11119
Edwin Williams Memorial Award 2862
Miklos Ybl Prize for Architecture 7392

Civil engineering (See also Construction)
Russell Allin Prize 3227
Alpar Medal 7449
Baker Medal 3228
Brunel Medal 3229
Heinrich Hatt-Bucher Prize 11929
Build a Building Competition 3230
Robert Alfred Carr Premium 3231
R. W. Chapman Medal 430
Civil Engineering Award 10652
Civil Engineering Prizes for Students 3232
Concrete Society Award 2673
Construmat Award 11192
Coopers Hill War Memorial Prize 3233
Crampton Prize 3234
Bill Curtin Medal 3235
ETE Merit Medal 7450
James Alfred Ewing Medal 3236
Fondation Camere 5509
James Forrest Medal 3237
Freyssinet Award 9732
Fulton Awards 10837
Furkert Award 9734
Geotechnical Research Medal 3238
Gold Medal 3359
Halcrow Premium 3239
T. K. Hsieh Award 3242
Renee Redfern Hunt Memorial Prize 3243
IABSE Prize 11755
Institution Gold Medal 3244
International Award of Merit in Structural Engineering 11756
Kelvin Medal 3248
Lindapter Award 3249
Manby Premium 3250
MERIT Competition 3251
Miller Prizes 3252
T. P. de S. Munasinghe Memorial Award 11405
National Engineering Excellence Awards 476
Outstanding Paper Award 11757
Overseas Premium 3253
Frederick Palmer Prize 3254
Parkman Medal 3255
Prisbelonning - Eydes Pris 9954
Prix Barbier 5303
Prix L. E. Rivot 5698
Reed and Mallik Medal 3256
SAACE/SA Construction World Awards for Excellence in Engineering 11026
Safety in Construction Medal 3257
SARF Bursary 11095
South African Institute of Civil Engineering Technicians and Technologists Awards 11066
Special Awards 3360
George Stephenson Medal 3258
Telford Medal 3259
Telford Premium 3260
Trevithick Premium 3261
Venezuelan Society of Civil Engineers Award 12148
W. H. Warren Medal 494
Garth Watson Medal 3262
Webb Prize 3264

Civil rights and liberties (See also Brotherhood; Child welfare; Citizenship and patriotism; Freedom; Heroism; Human relations; Human rights; Humanitarianism; Intellectual freedom; Women's rights)
Association for Civil Rights in Israel Awards 7863
Estrella de la Policia 1673
Fraenkel Prize in Contemporary History 3086

Frihedspris 1989
Libertarian Alliance Awards 3559

Coaching
Coach of the Year 2775

Coin collecting See Numismatics

Collectibles See Hobbies and clubs

Collegiate journalism
Concurso de Resena Teatral 9172

Color technology
George Douglas Lecture 4432
Ellinger-Gardonyi Award 3730
Honorary Fellow 4433
Honorary Member 4434
Jordan Award 3731
Judd AIC Award 9480
Medals of the Society of Dyers and Colourists 4435
Perkin Medal 4436
Sikkensprijs 9621
Turner - Scholefield Award 4437

Comedy See Entertainment; Humor

Commerce See Business; Finance

Communications (See also Audiovisuals; Broadcasting; Communications technology; Cybernetics; Human relations; Linguistics; Public relations; Public speaking)
Alejandro Angel Escobar Science Prize 1584
ATERB Medal Outstanding Young Investigator Telecommunications and Electronics 272
Columbus Prize 8325
Communicator of the Year 2267
Fondation Valentine Allorge 5675
Forderpreis der ITG 6530
Tor Gjesdals Prize 9942
Bharatendu Harishchandra Award 7530
International Advertising Festival, Cannes 3363
International Visual Communications Association Awards 3502
IPDC - UNESCO Prize for Rural Communication 6416
ITU Centenary Prize 11849
Harold Dwight Lasswell Award 922
Ian Murray Leslie Awards 2582
Ramon Magsaysay Awards 10042
Medalla Merito de las Comunicaciones Manuel Murillo Toro 1605
Medienpreis fur Sprachkultur 6894
Erich Pietsch Preis 6836
Plain English Award 3786
Pollak-Virag Award 7452
Premio de Investigacion Ahciet 11144
Premio Nacional de Trabajos Recepcionales escritos en Comunicacion 8971
Premio Revista Ahciet 11145
Prince of Asturias Prizes 11248
Prix France Telecom 5696
Puskas Tivadar Award 7453
Philipp Reis Medal 6748
Alexander Rhomberg Preis 6895
Prix Stendhal 6008
Guillermo Lee Stiles Medal 1606

Communications technology
Appleton Prize 1210
Nandor Barany Medal 7444
George Cartianu Prize 10338

Antonio Alves de Carvalho Fernandes Prize 10248
John Howard Dellinger Gold Medal 1211
Electronics and Communication Engineering Journal Premium 3274
Fondation Pierre Lafitte 5653
IERE Benefactors Premium 3290
Issac Koga Gold Medal 1212
Karl Kupfmuller Prize 6531
Montreux Achievement Gold Medal 11851
Jozsef Petzval Medal 7446
Premio Condumex 9187
Royal Television Society Technology Awards in Memory of Geoffrey Parr 4287
Balthasar van der Pol Gold Medal 1213

Community affairs (See also Citizenship and patriotism; Community service; Heroism; Humanitarianism; Organizational service; Public affairs)
Fellowship Scheme to Promote Commonwealth Understanding 2655
Wahidin Sudiro Husodo Award 7727
Sutomo Tjokronegoro Award 7730

Community service (See also Public service; Social service; Volunteerism)
Ros Bower Memorial Award 163
Businessperson of the Year 925
Chaconia Medal of the Order of the Trinity 12033
Civic Medal of Cartagena 1608
Commonwealth Youth Service Awards 2671
Community Enterprise Scheme 4073
Galardon Estado de Mexico 9008
Gem of Mexico City 8960
Hummingbird Medal of the Order of the Trinity 12034
Irish Life Pensioner of the Year Awards 7807
Israel Prize 7906
Ramon Magsaysay Awards 10042
Medals of Honor 8585
Mercury Communications Award for the Prince's Trust 4487
Mexico City Medal of Civic Merit 8961
National Community Service Prize 9135
Orden Francisco Javier Garcia de Hevia 12111
Orden Rafael Nunez 1705
Order of Orange-Nassau 9356
Order of the Netherlands Lion 9358
Prize of the Capital of Slovakia Bratislava 1830
Prize of the Mayor of the City of Bratislava 1831
Pedro Romero Medal 1615
Rookie Businessperson of the Year 926
Carmen and Aguiles Serdan Prize 9001
Shield of the Minister of Labour and Social Affairs 7911
Special Awards 2659
Ignacio Zaragosa Jewel 9002

Company publications
Annual Promotional Activity Award 8858

Composing See Music composition

Computer programming
Dantzig Prize 9548
Molster Fonds Prijs 9385
Orchard-Hays Prize 9550
Prix Ars Electronica 772

Computer science (See also Communications; Computer programming; Computers; Information management; Library and information services)
Simon Alport Memorial Prize 3052
BCS Awards 2321
European Coordinating Committee for Artificial Intelligence Awards 11695
Premio AEI - Milano Section 8349
Premio Condumex 9187
Prix Michel Monpetit 5701
Prix Scientifique IBM France 5330
Sociedad Cubana de Matematica y Computacion "Pablo Miguel" Awards 1823
Tudor Tanasescu Prize 10385
Alan Taylor Award 2322

Computers
Construction Industry Computing Association Awards 2682
Engineering Journals Premia 3277
Fritz Kutter-Preis 11933
Monte Carlo International Forum for New Images Imagina 9321
Outstanding Service Award 11784
Silver Core Award 11785
Wilkes Award 2323

Concrete
Concrete Element Prize 9902
Concrete Society Award 2673
Concrete Structure Plaque 9903
Fulton Awards 10837
Glass Prize 9904
Masonry Prize 9905
National Prize for Good Building 9906
Stone Prize 9907

Conducting
Annual Prize of the Czech Musical Fund 1854
Besancon International Competition for Young Conductors 5181
British Reserve Insurance Conducting Prize 10591
Guido Cantelli International Competition for Young Conductors 8158
Concorso Internazionale di Direzione d'Orchestra Vittorio Gui 8441
International Competition for Musical Performers - Geneva 11774
International Conductors' Competition 9694
International Conductors Competition of the Hungarian Television 7415
International Grzegorz Fitelberg Competition for Conductors in Katowice 10212
Nicolai Malko International Competition for Young Conductors 1982
Nordic Competition for Young Orchestra Conductors 1907
Antonio Pedrotti International Competition for Orchestra Conductors 8112
Prague Spring International Music Competition 1880
RPS Music Awards 4128
Leonie Sonning Music Award 2009
Hans Swarowsky International Conducting Competition 895
Tokyo International Music Competition 8770
Arturo Toscanini International Competition for Conductors 8393
Toti Dal Monte International Singing Competition 8222

Conservation (See also Ecology; Energy; Energy conservation; Environmental conservation; Environmental health; Forestry; Nature; Planning; Sanitary engineering; Water conservation; Water resources; Wildlife conservation)
Asahi Forestry Culture Prize 8489
BIR Gold Medal 1093
Christopher Cadbury Medal 4161
Council of Europe Museum Prize 5088
Eichendorff Plakette 6742
Environmental Protection Award 10429
Europa Nostra Awards 9402
European Nature Conservation Diploma 5094
Ford European Conservation Awards 2677
Honorary Member 11969
National Distinction of the Environment 1600
Fred M. Packard International Parks Merit Award/Commission on Parks and Protected Areas 11970
John C. Phillips Memorial Medal 11971
Premio de Ecologia 9263
Prix Nature et Patrimoine 5080
Simon Van der Stel Foundation Medal 11119

Construction (See also Architecture; Civil engineering; Concrete)
Alpar Medal 7449
Architectural Technician of the Year Award 2395
Arte in Piazza International Competition 8098
Best Project of the Year Prize 10484
BIAT/Pugh Award 2396
BIAT Student Award 2397
Build a Building Competition 3230
Builders' Awards 10036
Building Manager of the Year Awards 2581
Carpenters Award 3623
Concrete Man of the Year 10836
Construmat Award 11192
Contractors' Award 3762
Crampton Prize 3234
ETE Merit Medal 7450
Farm Buildings Award Scheme 2705
Fondation Camere 5509
Gold Medal of Honour 10818
Housing Design Awards 4068
IFAWPCA-CHOI Fieldman Award 10037
IFAWPCA-PCA Foundation Research Award 10038
Institution Gold Medal 3244
Ian Murray Leslie Awards 2582
Magnel Prize 1362
Master - Gold Hands Award 10439
National Contractors Travelling Scholarship 2560
National Engineering Excellence Awards 476
Order of Lenin 10463
Pin of Honour 6950
Plaisterers Trophy Competition 3686
Prisbelonning - Eydes Pris 9954
Safety in Construction Medal 3257
Peter Stone Award 2110
Eduardo Torroja Medal 11265
Verdeyen Prize for Soil Mechanics 1363

Consulting
ACEA Engineering Awards 135
National Prize for Consulting 742

Consumer affairs
International Advertising Festival, Cannes 3363

Cookbook writing
Glenfiddich Awards 2949
Prix Litteraires 4791
Andre Simon Fund Book Awards 4342

Cooking See Food

Copyright
CISAC Prize 5995
Copyright Prize 9381
Galardones SGAE 11250

Corrosion engineering
Sir Robert Hadfield Medal and Prize 3136

Cosmetology
Premio Nacional de Desarrollo Quimico Cosmetico 9272

Costume design
Cesar Awards 4793
Les Molieres 4970
Laurence Olivier Awards 4466
Premio Elio Costanzi 8001
Premio Francesco Compagna 8002
Premio Francesco Pistolese 8003
Premio Irene Brin 8004
Premio Mondo e Cultura 8005
Sinhala Drama Awards 11426

Crafts
Bremer Forderpreis fur Kunsthandwerk 6580
Cattell Cup 4452
Fellowships in Arts and Crafts 2657
Friendship Cup 4453
Haythorntwaite Cup 4454
Howe Cup 4455
Jowett Medal 4456
Kala Praveena Award 7544
Sir Henry Kelliher Student of Honour 9765
Marlowe Award 4429
Michaly Munkacsy Prize for Visual and Applied Arts 7406
NSEAD/Berol Curriculum Development Award for Art and Design Teachers 3712
Premio Mixcoatl 9255
President's Cup 4457
N. C. Roms Guldmedalje 1932
Standard Bank Namibia Biennale 9326
Storywriting and Art Project
  Australia - Department of Veterans' Affairs, Public Relations Dept. 144
  Heidelberg Repatriation Hospital - Department of Veterans' Affairs 417
TSB Award 4430
Tweddle Medal 4458
UNESCO Crafts Prize 6420
Visual Arts/Craft Board's Emeritus Fellowships and Medals 169
Warringah Art Prize 706

Craftsmanship
Contractors' Award 3762
Craftsman's Award 4683
Gold Medal for Craft Excellence 2623
Grand Prix des Metiers d'Art 6473
Queen Fabiola Prize 1168
Royal Dublin Society Crafts Competition 7835
State Prize for Arts and Crafts 776

Creative

Creative writing
The Age Book of the Year Awards 118
Apple Tree Award 3691
The Bridport Prize 2218
Bursaries, Scholarships, and Travel Awards 7755
Laurens Janszoon Coster Prize 9443
Creative Writing Junior Competition 2219
Czechoslovak National Artist 1856
Denman Cup 3688
Deux Magots Prize 5002
Jose F. Elizondo Prize 9084
Geneva-Europe Prizes for Television Writing 11693
Goncourt Prize 4798
Hadiah Cerpen Maybank - DBP 8903
Frans Kellendonk-prijs 9628
Lichfield Prize 3576
Magon National Prize of Culture 1763
Shiva Naipaul Memorial Prize 4484
National Competition in Teaching of Journalism Prize 1437
Nestroy-Ring der Stadt Wien 794
Premio Tusquets Editores de Novela 11389
Prijs voor Meesterschap 9630
Prize for Research in Education of the National Institute of the Book 1443
Prizes for Manuscripts for Juveniles 10008
Stipendien an Autoren/Autorinnen 6583
Svjetlost Prizes 1404
Jose Maria Vergara y Vergara Prize 1665
Yugoslav PEN Club Award 10726

Crime writing See **Mystery writing**

Criminology (See also **Law enforcement; Prisons**)
Lewis Minshall Award 2892
Scandinavian Research Council for Criminology Awards 11564

Culinary arts See **Food**

Culture (See also **African studies; Asian studies; Ethnic affairs; Folklore; Gypsies; Islamic culture; Mythology;** specific cultural groups, e.g. **Arabic culture**)
Australian Heritage Award 204
Bangkok Bank Prize for Thai Literature Competition 12022
Book Awards 10502
Bulgarian Academy of Science Honorary Badge - Marin Drinov Medal 1512
Miguel Antonio Caro and Rufino Jose Cuervo National Order 1711
Catalonia International Award 11175
CCP Awards for Radio 10047
Certificate of Honor 10426
Condor of the Andes 1393
Culture Prize
 Norwegian Cultural Council 9934
 Oslo Kommune 9959
Czechoslovak National Artist 1856
E. Du Perron Award 9674
Educational Merit Diploma 1656
Finnish Cultural Foundation's Prize 4693
Galardon Estado de Mexico 9008
Joaquin Garcia Monge Prize 1762
Golden Harp Television Festival 7824
Friedrich-Gundolf-Preis fur die Vermittlung deutscher Kultur im Ausland 6767
R. Lysholt Hansens Bibliotekspris 1915
High Quality of Work Award 10432
Inner Swiss Culture Award 11748
International Institute for Promotion and Prestige Awards 11805
Internationale Eugene Baieprijs 1243

Ion Ionescu de la Brad Prize 10358
Nami Jafet Prize 1488
Ludwig Keimer Foundation Prizes 11873
Kossuth Prize 7410
Kultureller Ehrenpreis 7020
Kulturpreis der Stadt Dortmund - Nelly-Sachs-Preis 7096
Kulturpreis der Stadt Villach 887
Medals of Honor 8585
Ministry of National Education Medal 1659
National Artist Award/International Artist Award 10049
National Order of the Southern Cross 1415
National Prize for Sciences 1663
November 17th Medal 1869
Oesterreichischer Auslandskulturpreis 767
Onassis Prize for Culture, Arts and Humanities 7208
Orden Manuel Felipe Rugeles 12112
Orden Rafael Nunez 1705
Order of Andres Bello 12137
Order of the Red Banner of Labor 10467
Outstanding Artist of Hungary 7411
Prague Literary Prize 1888
Preis der Justus-Liebig-Universitat Giessen 7000
Premi 8032
Premio Tetradramma d'oro 8034
Prix Chretiente d'Orient 5011
Prix de Jouy 5832
Prix Jean Mace 6083
Prix Medecine et Culture 5938
Prize for Journalism on Arts and Culture 9935
Karl Renner Preis 795
Silvio Romero Folklore Prize 1444
Pedro Romero Medal 1615
Royal Asiatic Society Medal 11414
Friedrich Ruckert Preis 7105
Salzburg Prize for the Promotion of the Arts, Science and Literature 869
Schiller Preis der Stadt Mannheim 7100
Scholarships of the City of Munich 7023
Geschwister-Scholl-Preis 7024
SEAMEO Testimonial for the Southeast Asian Ministers of Education Council (SEAMEC) President 12031
Silver Carnation 9576
Jose Vasconcelos World Award of Education 9308

Cybernetics
Norbert Wiener Memorial Gold Medal 6488

Cycling See **Bicycling**

Dairy industry
Chemical Cleaning/Trigon Packaging Achievement Award 9713
Dairy Industry Quality Performance Awards 9714
Dairy Technology Awards 11086
Distinguished Service Award 9715
Gold Medal Award 9716
Dr. Kurien Award 7617
Outstanding Achievement Award 9717
Patrons and Fellows 7618

Dance (See also **Ballet; Choreography**)
AA Life Vita Contemporary Choreography and Dance Awards 10811
Carina Ari Medal of Merit 11442
Stephen Arlen Memorial Fund Award 2096
Arts Council of Northern Ireland Bursaries and Awards 7854
Arts Festival Award 8576

ASEAN Award for the Performing Arts 10031
Award for Distinguished Cultural Service 8577
Pierre Bayle Prijs 9580
BDF Awards 2158
Blekinge County Council Culture Prize 11446
Bursaries, Scholarships, and Travel Awards 7755
City of Munich Prizes 7019
Concours International de Composition Musicale Opera et Ballet Geneve 11678
Concours International de Danse de Paris 5179
Dance Screen Award 842
Decorations and Medals 8578
Digital Dance Awards 2746
Dublin Corporation Arts Scholarship 7758
Folk Music Festival - Plaketti 4741
Forderpreis fur Musik der Landeshauptstadt Dusseldorf 6684
Gold Badge 2789
Golden Echo Prize 8371
Grand Prix International d'Arts et Lettres Notre-Dame et la Mer 4958
Grand Prix National de la Danse 5276
Grand Prix SACD 6395
International Video Dance Grand Prix 6465
Internationaler Fotosalon 6756
Bharta Kala Prapoorna in Dance 7541
Kala Praveena Award 7544
Franz Liszt Prize 7403
Literature and Art Awards 12011
Llangollen International Musical Eisteddfod 12177
The London Evening Standard Ballet and Opera Awards 3600
Leonida Massine Prize for the Art of the Dance 8156
Medal of Honor 10999
Mestaripelimanni, Mestarikansanlaulaja 4742
Miss Dance of Great Britain 3398
National Award for Literature and Arts 12002
National Classical Music Contest 8834
Neshamwari Traditional Music and Dance Festival 12220
Laurence Olivier Awards 4466
Opera Prize 11573
Order of Cultural Merit 8579
Order of the Golden Rose 7826
Premio Nacional de Danza 11372
Premio Nacional de Danza INBA-Sinaloa Jose Limon 9233
Preseren Award 10799
Prix de Lausanne 11725
Prix Talents Nouveau 6399
Promotional Prizes 7022
Prudential Awards for the Arts 3826
Regional Cultural Commendation 8580
Riccione TTVV - Teatro Televisione Video 8405
Scholarships of the City of Munich 7023
Split Summer Festival 1803
Time Out Theatre, Dance and Comedy Awards 4545
Traditional Irish Singing and Dancing Society Awards 7850
G. B. Viotti International Music and Dance Competition 8425
World Championships in Ballroom and Latin Dancing 4624

Data base management See **Information management**

Subject Index of Awards
Volume 2: International and Foreign — Documentary

Data processing See **Computer science**

Deafness (See also **Speech and hearing**)
Apple Tree Award 3691
CISS Medallions of Honor 1960
Medal of Honour 2329
NDCS Scholarship 3682
Prix Federation Mondiale des Sourds 4765
Rubens-Alcais Challenge 1961
Edith Whetnall Lectureship 4272
World Film Festival of ORL Scientific Films and Videotapes 1187
World Organization of Jewish Deaf Competitions 7993
Young Deaf Achiever 2732

Democracy See **Freedom**

Demography
Bertillon Prize 4896
Clarence James Gamble Award 920
ICOMP Population Programmes Management Award 8906
Prix Paul Leroy-Beaulieu 5785

Dental research
Colyer Prize 4237
Doubleday Lectureship 4241
International Miller Prize 3400
Johnson & Johnson Preventive Dentistry Awards 3402
Medical Postgraduate Research Scholarships and Dental Postgraduate Research Scholarships 543
ORCA Rolex Prize 2835
Elida Pond's Fellowship and Other Awards in Dentistry 10840
Research Project Grants 546
Julius Staz Scholarship for Dental Research 10841

Dentistry (See also **Dental research**; **History of dentistry**; **Orthodontistry**)
Cartwright Prize 3974
F. G. Christensen Memorial Prize 589
Colyer Gold Medal 3975
Drummond-Jackson Prize 4372
Ethicon Fellowship 10599
Honorary Gold Pin 6796
Honorary Member 6797
Honorary Plaque 6798
International Miller Prize 3400
Jessen Fellowship in Children's Dentistry 3401
Johnson & Johnson Preventive Dentistry Awards 3402
Fritz Linnert Honorary Award 6799
Bengt Magnusson Memorial Prize 3370
Merit Award 6800
J.C. Middleton Shaw Fellowshipq 10839
Dr. Erich Muller Prize 6801
New Zealand Dental Association Awards 9759
Odontological Commemorative Lecture 4262
Winifred E. Preedy Post-Graduate Bursary 219
Premio Prof. Dr. Alejandro Cabanne 44
Prix a un Etudiant de l'Ecole Dentaire 4805
Prix Helene Rubillard 4842
Prix Medecin General Inspecteur Raymond Debenedetti 4862
Socio Colabrador 45
Kenneth J. G. Sutherland Prize 590
Travelling Fellowships 10601
T. C. White Prize Lecture 10603
T. C. White Travelling Fellowship 10604

Dermatology
Argentinian Association of Dermatology Awards 33
British Association of Dermatologists Awards 2264
Castellani - Reiss Medal and Award 1721
Chilean Society Awards for Scientific Works 1555
Dowling Lectureships 4242
Dr. Antonio Gonzalez Ochoa Award 9099
Xavier Vilanova Prize 1462
Hugh Wallace Essay Prize 4268
Hugh Wallace's Registrars' Prize 4269

Design (See also **Art**; **Architecture**; **Book and newspaper design**; **Costume design**; **Fiber science**; **Fashion**; **Graphic arts**; **Industrial design**; **Interior design**; **Jewelry design**; **Lighting design**; **Set design**; **Textile design**)
Aanmoedigingsprijzen 9635
Awards 3467
Bicentenary Medal 4320
Brick Design Awards 2215
British Academy of Film and Television Arts Awards - Film 2233
British Academy of Film and Television Arts Awards - Television 2234
British Design Awards 2738
CERT/Irish Life Souvenir of Ireland Challenge 7802
City of Munich Prizes 7019
Community, Environment, Art, and Design (CEAD) Award 164
Crate and Barrel Israeli Product Design Award for the Home and its Surroundings 7920
Credit Suisse Design Prize for Technical and Industrial Innovation in Geneva 11684
CSD Medal 2607
Design Management Prize 11570
European Community Design Prize 6803
Excellent Swedish Design Prize 11651
German Design Prize 6804
German Prize for Design Promoters 6805
Dr. V. M. Ghatage Award 7475
Good Design Selection 8817
Grand Prix Amon Ra 5195
Frans Halsprijs voor Tentoonstellingsvormgeving 9447
Honorary Fellow 2608
International Design Award, Osaka 8605
International Design Competition, Osaka 8606
Jesselson Prize for Contemporary Judaica Design 7925
Charlotte Kohler Prijs 9571
Korea Good-Packaging Exhibition 8818
Label of the Year Competition 3529
Lighting Design Awards 3581
Minerva Awards 2609
Most Beautiful Books of Austria 741
NAS Design Prize 3676
New Designers 3027
New Zealand Society of Designers Awards 9720
NFWI Design Award 3689
NSEAD/Berol Curriculum Development Award for Art and Design Teachers 3712
PANPA Newspaper Awards 575
Premio Municipal Jorge Colaco de Azulejaria 10271
Premio Municipal Roberto de Araujo Pereira de Design 10277
Preseren Award 10799
Prince Philip Prize for the Designer of the Year 2742
Prize for Design 10398
Prize for Scenography 10402
Prize Mission Special Japan 8733
Dr. Biren Roy Trust Award 7478
Royal Designers for Industry 4323
Sandberg Grant for Research and/or Development 7929
Scandinavian Design Prize 11652
Scottish Annual Report Prize 10530
Sikkensprijs 9621
Staatspreis fur gestaltendes Handwerk 748
State Emblem for Outstanding Design 753
State Prize for Arts and Crafts 776
Tanner Award 2597
Eduardo Torroja Medal 11265
Emmy Van Leersumprijs 9650

Dietetics See **Nutrition**

Diplomacy See **International relations**

Diving safety See **Water safety**

Divorce See **Family relations**

Documentary films
Agrofilm International Short Film Festival 1873
Amanda Award for Television and Cinematographic Merit 9938
Amiens International Film Festival 4890
Australian Film Institute Awards 221
Bangkok Bank Documentary Film Competition Prizes 12021
Belgrade International Festival of Scientific Films 10699
Bienal de Cine y Video Cientifico 11166
Bombay International Film Festival 7529
British Academy of Film and Television Arts Awards - Television 2234
Certamen Internacional de Cine Amateur Ciutat d'Igualada 11203
Cesar Awards 4793
Dance Screen Award 842
Documentary Film Festival - Amsterdam 9376
Documentary of the Year 10000
European Film Awards (Felix Awards) 6713
Festival dei Popoli 8239
Film Competition 9265
Grand Prix ICA - Prix du Meilleur Film Documentaire 10690
Grand Prix of the Dutch Film Golden Calf 9383
Gulf of Salerno Grand Trophy 8417
Huy - World Festival of Movies of Short Films Awards 1160
Indonesian Film Festival 7733
International Documentary and Short Film Festival of Bilbao 11267
International Festival of Ecological Film Events 10791
International Festival of Films Directed by Women 11149
International Festival of Films on Architecture and Town-planning of Lausanne 11793
International Festival of Films on Energy Lausanne 11797
International Film and Student Directors Festival 6020
International Film Festival of Visual Anthropology and Social Documentation 5032
International Filmfestival Mannheim/Heidelberg 6954
International Leipzig Documentary and Animation Film Festival 7035

Drama — Awards, Honors & Prizes, 1995-96

Documentary (continued)
International Short Film Festival, Oberhausen 6984
International Video Contest 11234
International Visual Communications Association Awards 3502
International Women's Film Festival, Creteil 6072
Les Ecrans De L'Aventure International Festival of Adventure Documentaries 5328
Magnolia Prize 1576
Medal for Postal Merit 1604
Montreux International Electronic Cinema Festival 11852
Nyon International Documentary Film Festival 11892
Prix Danube Festival, Bratislava 10780
Rassegna Internazionale dei Documentari Cine-TV Marinari 8295
Sondrio Town Council International Festival of Documentary Films on Parks 8433
Tampere International Short Film Festival 4758
Techfilm International Film Festival 1874
Thessaloniki Film Festival 7217
Trento International Film Festival of Mountain and Exploration 8460
Uppsala Filmkaja 11654

Dogs See **Animal care and training**

Drama (See also **Drama criticism; Theater**)
Theodor W. Adorno Award 6611
All India Competition for Radio Playwrights 7482
ANA Literary Prize 9856
Angel Literary Award 2080
Annual One-Act Play Festival Award 9769
Stephen Arlen Memorial Fund Award 2096
Arts Achievement Award 8575
Arts Council of Northern Ireland Bursaries and Awards 7854
Arts Council Writing Grants 9798
ASEAN Award for Literature 10030
Awards for Regional Literature 10004
Awgie Awards 283
Arthur Azevedo Prize 1421
Bangla Academy Literary Award 934
Verity Bargate Award 4470
Blekinge County Council Culture Prize 11446
Boardman Tasker Memorial Award for Mountain Literature 2192
Book Awards 10734
Brothers Grimm Prize 6561
Bucharest Writers Association Award 10411
Buckland Literary Award 9846
Buenos Aires Drama Prize 35
Ion Luca Caragiale Prize 10337
Carlos Casavalle Prize 26
Category A Fellowships 155
Category B Fellowships 156
CCP Literary Awards 10034
Cena Zvazu slovenskych spisovatelov 10756
CNA Literary Award 10830
Commonwealth Writers Prize 2654
Competition for Children's Theater or Stories 9012
Concurso Anual de Literatura Premios Franz Tamayo 1388
Critics Prize 10298
Croatian Socialist Republic Prizes 1808
Ryan Davies Awards 12168
D. T. Davies Memorial Award for Playwriting 12170
Luisa Claudio de Sousa Prize 1451

Nestor de Tiere Prize 1269
George Devine Award 2794
Drama Festival (Jashan-E-Tamseel) Awards 10001
Johannes Ewald Prize 1927
FAW Adele Shelton-Smith Award for Play, Radio or Other Scripts for Young Writers 378
Festival of Contemporary Theatre 10325
Miles Franklin Literary Award 127
Fundacion del Premio Fastenrath 11345
Gold Medal 2979
Golden Chest International Television Festival 1518
Gran Premio de Honor Argentores 30
Grand Prix Amon Ra 5195
Grand Prix de la Mer 4918
Grand Prix Litteraire de Madagascar 4921
Grand Prix SACD 6395
Grands Prix Litteraire de la Ville de Paris 6095
Eric Gregory Awards 4389
Guardian Student Drama Award 10535
Calouste Gulbenkian Translation Prize 10251
Hebrew Radio Play Prize 7917
Hertzog Prize 10991
Edmond Hustinxprijs 9655
Independent Theatre Award 10536
Nataka Kala Prapoorna in Drama 7542
Kala Praveena Award 7544
Kalokerinos Foundation Prize 7212
Kerala Sahitya Akademi Awards 7703
Kikuchi Prize 8752
LEA Award 4696
Jessie Litchfield Award 557
Literary Awards and Prizes for Sinhalese Literature 11423
Literary Competition 12218
Literary Prize 10995
Literary Prize for Translation 10996
Literature and Art Awards 12011
The London Evening Standard Drama Awards 3601
Malaysian Literary Prize 8904
Malpertuis Prize 1288
Mambembe Trophy 1434
Arthur Markham Memorial Prize 4585
Maynard Cup 12171
McVitie's Prize for the Scottish Writer of the Year 10582
Mobil Playwriting Competition for the Royal Exchange Theatre, Manchester 4004
Natakavedi (Bombay) Award 7707
National Drama Contest 1439
National Operatic and Dramatic Association Awards 3695
National Prize for Linguistics and Literature 9148
National Theatre Awards 9991
New South Wales State Literary Awards 147
Noma Award for Publishing in Africa 2039
Order of Culture 8586
Don Carlos Palanca Memorial Awards for Literature 10053
Premi Adria Gual 11157
Premi Ignasi Iglesias 11158
Premi Josep Maria de Sagarra 11160
Premier's Literary Awards 149
Premio Alvarez Quintero 11346
Premio Argentores 31
Premio Editiorial Costa Rica 1770
Premio Hispanoamericano Xavier Villaurrutia 9267
Premio Litterario Viareggio 8407
Premio Lope de Vega 11294

Premio Municipal de Literatura 1568
Premio Nacional de Literatura 1548
Premio Nacional de Teatro 11376
Premio Riccione - ATER: per un teatro d'autore 8404
Premio Teatral Tirso de Molina 11364
Premios Municipais Eca de Queiroz de Literatura 10280
Preseren Award 10799
Thomas Pringle Award 10852
Prix Andre Praga 1292
Prix Brieux 5823
Prix Capuran 5826
Prix de Litterature des Alpes et du Jura 4923
Prix du Theatre 5844
Prix Emile Augier 5847
Prix Emile Hinzelin 5849
Prix Europeen de l'ADELF 4924
Prix France-Acadie 4894
Prix Gerard Philipe de la Ville de Paris 6096
Prix Paul Hervieu 5905
Prix Talents Nouveau 6399
Prix Toirac 5924
Prize for Literature of the Council of the French Community of Belgium 1110
Prizes for Theatrical Works 7193
Prosceniumprijs 9690
Radio Times Drama & Comedy Awards 2160
Wanda Reumer Prijs 9328
Riccione TTVV - Teatro Televisione Video 8405
Romanian Radio and Television Award 10327
Romanian Writers' Union Prizes 10414
Schiller-Gedachtnispreis des Land Baden-Wurttemberg 7055
Olive Schreiner Prize 10853
Scotsman Fringe First Awards 10538
Shell Playwrights Award 9770
Split Summer Festival 1803
Staatsprijs voor Toneelletterkunde 1085
Standard Bank Young Artists' Awards 10849
Rolf Stenersen Prize 9929
Sterijina Nagrada 10705
Stroud and District Festival 4497
The Sunday Times Bruce Mason Playwrights' Award 9784
Svenska Akademiens teaterpris 11610
Tamil Drama Award 11427
Thames Television Playwright Scheme 4535
Theatre Award 9398
Theatre Prize 7963
Time Out Theatre, Dance and Comedy Awards 4545
H. G. van der Viesprijs 9688
Georges Vaxelaire Prize 1307
Visser-Nederlandia dramaprijzen 9330
John Whiting Award 2101
Margarita Xirgu Radio Drama Prize 11325
Yomiuri Literature Prize 8795
Zilveren CJP 9422

Drama criticism
Arthur Azevedo Prize 1421
Pierre Bayle Prijs 9580
Prijs van de Kritiek 9360
Thomas Pringle Award 10852
Prix J. J. Weiss 5869

Drawing (See also **Cartoons; Graphic arts; Illustration**)
Academy Awards 9750

Bienal Nacional Diego Rivera for Drawings and Prints 9208
Cleveland International Drawing Biennale Prize 2638
Concurso Nacional para Estudiantes de Artes Plasticas en Aguascalientes 9211
Festival International du Dessin Humoristique 6132
Katanning Art Prize 511
National Akademi Award 7534
Premio Municipal Rafael Bordalo Pinheiro de Banda Desenhada, Cartoon e Caricaturista 10276
Prix de Dessin Pierre David - Weill 5375
Prix de Rome 9578
Prix Le Guay-Lebrun 5410
Salon Anual de Artes Plasticas Premios Pedro Domingo Murillo 1389
Salon Nacional de Artes Plasticas - Dibujo 9240
Spanish Association of Painters and Sculptors Prizes 11381
Storywriting and Art Project 417
Warringah Art Prize 706
Wroclaw International Triennale of Drawing 10218

Drug addiction
IOGT International August Forell Award 9894
Man for Mankind Awards 938
Prix Lutte Contre le Tabagisme 4859

Dutch literature
AKO Literatuur Prijs 9633
Lode Baekelmans Prize 1264
Dr. Karel Barbier Prize 1265
August Beernaert Prize 1266
Anna Bijnsprijs 9340
Henriette de Beaufort-prijs 9625
Frans Erensprijs 9657
Gouden Strop 9441
Franz Grillparzer Prize 7113
Henriette Roland Holst-prijs 9627
Charlotte Kohlerprijs 9687
Kruyskamp-prijs 9629
Geertjan Lubberhuizen prijs 9676
Arthur Merghelynck Prize 1274
Multatuliprijs 9644
Order of the Netherlands Lion 9358
Prijs der Nederlandse Letteren 9552
Prijs van de Nederlandse Kinderjury 9367
Prijs voor Meesterschap 9630
Prix des Ambassadeurs 9434
Strasbourg Prizes and Gold Medal 7126
Lucy B. and C. W. Van der Hoogt-prijs 9631
Jozef Van Ginderachter Prize 1278
Venz Kinder Boeken Prijs 9369
Visser-Neerlandiaprijs 9331

Earth science See **Geology and paleontology; Seismology**

East European culture
Booker Russian Novel Prize 2196
Lovis-Corinth-Preis 6523
Georg-Dehio-Preis 6524
Andreas-Gryphius-Preis 6525
Mesrop Mashtots Award 112
Stephan Shaumian Prize 113
Johann-Wenzel-Stamitz-Preis 6526
Toros Toramanian Prize 114

Ecology (See also Nature)
Agrofilm International Short Film Festival 1873
Amsterdam Prize 9451

Grigore Antipa Prize 10330
BES Fellowships and Grants 2333
Bienal Internacional del Cartel en Mexico 9285
Crafoord Prize 11537
Ecology Institute Prize 6688
Environment Medal 4407
Festival Internacional de Cine Ecologico y de la Naturaleza 11232
Fondation Georges Deflandre et Marthe Deflandre-Rigaud 5567
Fondation Georges Millot 5568
Fondation Jean Lebrun 1003
International Festival of Mountain Films, Vila de Torello 11386
International Institute for Promotion and Prestige Awards 11805
IRPE Prize (International Recognition of Professional Excellence) 6689
Mauriac International Medical Film Festival 6112
Medal for Distinguished Service to Tropical Ecology 7691
Medalla Alfonso L. Herrera al Merito en Ecologia y Conservacion 9040
OKOMEDIA International Ecological Film Festival 7063
Premio Omeyocan 9196
President's Medal 2334
Prix des Sciences de la Mer 5692
Sendai International Design Competition 8760
Trento International Film Festival of Mountain and Exploration 8460

Economic development
African Regional Centre for Technology Awards 10693
APO National Award 8504
APO Regional Award 8505
Artiste Europeen Prize 1125
Asian Advertising Award 4479
Carl Bertelsmann Prize 6566
Prix Pierre Chauleur 6136
CIB Developing Countries Fellowships 9482
Prix Robert Delavignette 6138
Foundation of Socio-Cultural Services Competitions 11400
Indira Gandhi Prize for Peace, Disarmament and Development 7502
General Award 8806
Nessim Habif Prize 6412
Hamdard Foundation Pakistan Awards 9975
Honorary Member 10024
Institute for University Cooperation Awards 8276
King Baudouin International Development Prize 1217
Komsomol Medal 10433
Legion of Honour Award 7724
Order of Merit in Commerce 1613
Order of National Hero 8484
Premio Nacional de Integracion Latinoamericana 8934
Premio Nacional Serfin, sobre Medio Ambiente 8935
Premio Visconde de Cairu 1464
President Macia Plaque and Medal 11189
Lanka Mahila Samiti Awards 11412
SEAMEO Testimonial for the Southeast Asian Ministers of Education Council (SEAMEC) President 12031
Solidarios Award to Latinoamerican and Caribbean Development 2015
Special Recognition Award 7725
A. Spinoy Award 1372
Third World Prize 4539

TWAS Award in Basic Medical Sciences 8450
TWAS Award in Biology 8451
TWAS Award in Chemistry 8452
TWAS Award in Mathematics 8453
TWAS Award in Physics 8454
TWAS History of Science Prize 8455
TWNSO Award in Agriculture 8457
TWNSO Award in Technology 8458
UNESCO Science Prize 6427
Freiherr Von Stein Prize 7132
Worldaware Business Awards 4635

Economic history
S. J. Butlin Prize 359

Economics (See also Agricultural economics; Economic development; Finance; International trade; Rural economics; Social science research)
Senator Giovanni Agnelli International Prize 8247
Amex Bank Review Awards 2078
P. W. S. Andrews Memorial Essay Prize 3517
Arnbergska Priset 11534
Petre S. Aurelian Prize 10331
BANAMEX Economics Prize 9202
Bank of Sweden Prize in Memory of Alfred Nobel 11494
Prix Georges Bruel 6135
Concurso Anual de Tesis Profesionales 8937
J. G. Crawford Award 256
Daeyang Prize in Economics 8815
David Davidson Prize in Economics 11562
Isaac Deutscher Memorial Prize 2744
Dissertation Prize in Economics 4736
Economics Prize 1226
EFTA Awards 11700
Eminent Activist Medal 7379
Ludwig-Erhard-Preis fur Wirtschaftspublizistik 6699
Fondation Ernest Mahaim 975
Fondazione Francesco Sarerio Nitti Prize 8054
Free Market Award 10865
Freedom Prize 11900
Rodrigo Gomez Prize 8944
Grand Prix de l'Academie des Sciences Morales et Politiques 5711
Bernhard-Harms-Preis 7007
David Horowitz Memorial Prize 7868
Institute for Latin American Integration Award 51
International Festival of Economics and Training Films 1191
International Industrial Film and Video Awards 2703
International Institute for Promotion and Prestige Awards 11805
Islamic Development Bank Prizes in Islamic Economics and Islamic Banking 10488
Yrjo Jahnsson Award in Economics 4737
Ludwig Keimer Foundation Prizes 11873
John W. Kendrick Prize 3853
Kuwait Prize 8844
Leverhulme Memorial Lecture 3554
Jordi Lluch Prize 11186
Virgil Madgearu Prize 10363
Artur Malheiros Prize 10255
Medal of Service 7251
Medallas de Geografia Fisica, Humana, Economica 10016
Johann-Heinrich-Merck Ehrung 6602
Ernst Meyer Prize 11761
Gunnar Myrdal Prize 11621

Editing   **Awards, Honors & Prizes, 1995-96**

Economics (continued)
Naples Prize for the Study of Southern and Northern Countries in the World 8254
National Bank of Pakistan Prize for Literature 10007
National Banking Commission Prize 8958
National Economics Prize 9095
National Institute of Insurance International Prizes 8067
Nobel Prizes 11549
Orden Rafael Nunez 1705
Order of Merit of the Republic of Poland 10117
Order of the Rebirth of Poland 10119
Order of the Red Banner of Labor 10467
Premio Anual de Investigacion Economica Jesus Silva Herzog 9184
Premio Banco de la Republica 1590
Premio Internacional Daniel Cosio Villegas 9287
Premio Internazionale di Meridionalistica Guido Dorso 8149
Premio Luis Elizondo - Premio Cientifico y Technologico 8989
Prix Charles Dupin 5722
Prix Charles Lyon-Caen 5725
Prix Demolombe 5731
Prix des Sciences Economiques et Sociales 5051
Prix du Budget 5734
Prix Emile Girardeau 5739
Prix Estrade-Delcros 5742
Prix Fabien 5854
Prix Grammaticakis-Neuman 5752
Prix Jean Reynaud 5762
Prix Joseph Dutens 5764
Prix Latsis 11959
Prix Le Dissez de Penanrun 5771
Prix Leon Faucher 5773
Prix Limantour 5774
Prix Rossi 5789
Prix Saintour 5790
Prix Ugo Papi - Gaston Leduc 5793
Prix Wolowski 5796
Prix Zerilli Marimo 5797
Karl Renner Preis 795
Royal Economic Society Prize 4000
Royal Society of Victoria Medal 638
Dr. Arthur Ruppin Prize 7885
Moinho Santista Prizes for Young People 1496
Schumpeter Prize 6962
Schunk-Preis fur Wirtschaftswissenschaften 7002
Science Prize - Peretz Naftali Prize 7962
Stephan Shaumian Prize 113
Soderbergs Pris 11550
Soderstromska Medaljen i guld 11551
State Prize 7412
Suntory Prize for Social Sciences and Humanities 8764
Nicholae Titulescu Prize 10389
University of Berne Prizes 11965

Editing
BAIE Editing for Industry Awards 2266
British Society of Magazine Editors Awards 3772
Communicator of the Year Award 11097
Gold Ribbon 1840
International Visual Communications Association Awards 3502
Mlade leta Prize 10786
Nihon Shinbun Kyokai Awards 8628
Lorenz Oken Medaille 6890
Juan Pablos Editorial Merit Prize 9154
Polish PEN Centre Prizes 10168

Prix de la Promotion Poetique 6329
TES Schoolbook Award 4549
Troubadour de la SABAM 1071

Editorial writing
AFN - AGFA Awards 2127
Jose Joaquin Fernandez de Lizaldi Prize 9086
National Prize for Journalism and Information 9140

Education (*See also* **Academic achievement; Educational research; Intellectual freedom; Learning disabled; Literacy; Scholarly works; Teaching; Training and development**)
Ermanno Acanfora International Prize 8435
Lady Allen of Hurtwood Trust Award 2055
Ignacio Manuel Altamarino Medal 9145
Janos Csere Apaczai Prize 7397
Art and Education Prize 9333
Awards
   Near East/South Asia Council of Overseas Schools 7204
   Women's International Zionist Organization 7989
Blekinge County Council Culture Prize 11446
Simon Bolivar Medal 1653
Augustin Nieto Caballero Medal 1654
Cenafor Prize for a Monograph 1431
Chemical Education Medal 11046
City of Sorrento Prize 8436
City of Vienna Prizes for Art, Science, and Humanities 789
Cross of Merit for Moral and Civic Education 1432
ECIS Awards 2827
Education Medal 8799
Education School Design Award 2757
Educational Merit Diploma 1656
Electronics Education Premium 3275
Fellow 333
Ivan Filipovic Awards 1809
Gold Book 1395
Calouste Gulbenkian Foundation Grants 2981
Soren Gyldendal Prisen 1954
Nessim Habif Prize 6412
Hodgson Prize 3893
Honorary Member 10147
INFOSTA Award 8541
International Association of University Presidents Awards 12027
International Visual Communications Association Awards 3502
Israel Prize 7906
Japan Foundation Grant Programs 8613
Antonio Machado Prize for Essay 1723
Mackie Medal 189
Medal of Commission of National Education 10114
Medals of Honor 8585
Aldo Merola International Prize 8437
Samuel Mikoviny Medal 7357
Mythic Society Scholar 7713
National Order of Education 1414
National Order of the Southern Cross 1415
NHK Japan Prize Contest 8602
Nile Gold Medal 5162
November 17th Medal 1869
OEI Gold Medal 11312
Orden Manuel Felipe Rugeles 12112
Order of Lenin 10463
Order of the Academic Palms 5295
Order of the Rebirth of Poland 10119
Ordre de l'Education Nationale 1792

Abraham Geza Pattantyus Award 7456
Personal Recognition Awards in Education 8367
Phenix - U.D.A. 6429
Premio a la Mejor Labor de Promocion de Lectura 1701
Premio Innovazione Elettronica 8326
Premio Internazionale di Meridionalistica Guido Dorso 8149
Premio Luis Elizondo - Premio Cientifico y Technologico 8989
Premio Nacional de Educaccion 923
Premio Romulo Garza para Publicaciones 9027
Prix Adrien Duvand 5713
Prix Ernest Thorel 5741
Prix Eugene Lameere 987
Prix Jean Mace 6083
Prix Louis Liard 5775
Prix Tobie Jonckheere 998
Pro Ecelesia et Pontifice 8476
Andres Manuel del Rio National Prize in Chemistry 8948
SEAMEO Testimonial for the Southeast Asian Ministers of Education Council (SEAMEC) President 12031
Sociedad Cubana de Matematica y Computacion "Pablo Miguel" Awards 1823
Special Awards 2659
State Prize 7412
TES Schoolbook Award 4549
J. P. Thomson Medal 617
Trade Union's Art and Cultural Prize 7442
University of Berne Prizes 11965
Jose Vasconcelos World Award of Education 9308
Worlddidac Award 11984
Yomiuri Education Prize 8792

Education, adult and continuing *See* **Adult and continuing education**

Education, agricultural *See* **Agricultural education**

Education, art *See* **Art education**

Education, elementary *See* **Elementary education**

Education, engineering *See* **Engineering education**

Education, geographic *See* **Geographic education**

Education, health *See* **Health education**

Education, higher *See* **Higher education**

Education, medical *See* **Medical education**

Education, music *See* **Music education**

Education, physical *See* **Physical education**

Education, science *See* **Science education**

Education, secondary *See* **Secondary education**

Education, special *See* **Special education**

Education, vocational *See* **Vocational education**

Educational films
Atom Awards 270
Educational Television Awards Scheme 2760
Goldschmidt-Clermont Prize 3434
Andre Leroy Prize 3436
NHK Japan Prize Contest 8602
Roshd International Educational Film Festival 7741

Educational research
Fondation Victor Thebault 5677
IEA - Bruce H. Choppin Memorial Award 9465
J. R. McKenzie Senior Fellowship in Educational Research 9757
Medellin University Prize 1752
UNESCO Prize for the Teaching of Human Rights 6426

Electrical engineering (See also Electronics)
Charles Babbage Premium 3268
Blathy Award 7326
Blumlein-Brown-Willans Premium Award 3269
Bridgeport Prize 3270
Centres Premium 3271
College of Electrical Engineers Student Prizes 433
Coopers Hill War Memorial Prize and Medal 3272
Csaki Award 7327
Deri Award 7328
Divisional Premium 3273
Electronics Letters Premium Awards 3276
Electrotechnical Award 7329
Engineering Journals Premia 3277
Epitoipar Kivalo Munkaert 7330
James Alfred Ewing Medal 3236
Faraday House Commemorative Prize 3278
Faraday Medal 3279
Fondations Gaston Plante, Francois Hebert-Paul Jousselin 5680
Harry Henniker Premium 3281
Honorary Ring 6528
IEE Achievement Medal 3282
IEE Benefactors Prize 3283
IEE Measurement Prize 3284
IEE Prize 3285
IEE Prize for Helping Disabled People 3286
IEE Prize for Innovation 3287
IEE Rayleigh Book Award 3288
IEE Scotland North Premium 3289
Institution Premium 3291
International Premium Awards 3292
Ipar Kivalo Munkaert 7331
Kalman Kando Award 7332
Herbert-Kind-Preis der ETG 6696
Kisz KB Aranykoszorus Kisz Jelveny 7333
Jozsef Liska Award 7334
Literaturpreis der ETG 6697
John Madsen Medal 472
Magyar Elektrotechnikai Egyesulet Mtezs 7335
Manufacturing Prize 3294
MEE Award 7336
Eric Megaw Memorial Prize 3295
George Montefiore Foundation Prize 1046
Enrique Morales Prize 1746
Henry Nimmo Premium 3297
Nivo Award 7337
Overseas Student Medallion 3299
Evan Parry Award 9740
Premio ABB 8346
Premio AEI Galileo Ferraris 8347
Premio AEI - Milano Section 8349
Premio Bottani 8351
Premio Maria Faletti-Nosari 8354
RAF Apprentice Engineering Technician Prize 3300
A. H. Reeves Premium 3301
IIE Sir Henry Royce Award for Achievement 4308
Sir Henry Royce Award 3303
SAACE/SA Construction World Awards for Excellence in Engineering 11026
M. A. Sargent Medal 486
J. D. Scaife Award 3304
Simms Prize 3910
South African Institute of Electrical Engineers Awards 11068
Sandor Straub Award 7338
Student Medallion Award 3305
Szocialista Kulturaert 7339
J. Langham Thompson Premium 3306
Janos Urbanek Award 7340
Laslo Verebely Award 7341
D. J. Wimalasurendra Memorial Award 11409
Young Engineer of the Year 3309
Younger Members' Premiums Awards 3311
Zipernowsky Prize 7342

Electrical industry
Anode Trophy 11079
Certamen Anual Nacional de Tesis de Ingenieria 9033
Communications Group Trophy 11080
Fondation Kastner-Boursault 5605
Lighting Design Awards 3581
Product of the Year 4507
Student Lighting Design Awards 3578

Electronics
ATERB Medal Outstanding Young Investigator Telecommunications and Electronics 272
Antonio Alves de Carvalho Fernandes Prize 10248
Electronics and Communication Engineering Journal Premium 3274
Electronics Education Premium 3275
Electronics Letters Premium Awards 3276
European Association for Signal Processing Awards 11690
Fondation Clement Felix 5523
Fondation du General Ferrie 5546
Armando Kaminitz Research Awards 7981
Literary Prize - Education and Instruction Prize 7954
Premio AEI Galileo Ferraris 8347
Premio AEI Guglielmo Marconi 8348
Premio AEI - Milano Section 8349
Premio Bonazzi 8350
Premio F. Cameli 8352
Premio F. Malusardi 8353
Premio Maria Faletti-Nosari 8354
J. Langham Thompson Premium 3306
J. J. Thomson Medal 3307
Dr. V. K. Zworykin Premium 3312

Elementary education
Visconde de Sousa Prego Freedom Prize 10295
Kenko Yuryo Gakko Hyosho 8495
Prix Halphen 5754
Prix Joseph De Keyn 992
TES Schoolbook Award 4549

Emergency medicine
Fondation Henri Mondor 5577
National Medal 208

Endocrinology
Fondation Janine Courrier 5590
Schoeller-Junkmann-Preis 6844
Marius-Tausk-Preis 6845
Von Basedow Prize for Research into the Thyroid Gland 6846
Von-Recklinghausen-Preis 6847

Energy
Achievement Through Action Award 508
Walter Ahlstrom Prize 4682
Australian Institute of Energy Medal 225
Farrington Daniels Award 509
Energy Prize 6383
Esso Energy Award and Medal 4148
Fondation Coron-Thevenet 5524
Fondation Ivan Peyches 5586
Gold Medal 9993
Heinrich Hertz Preis 7148
Institute of Energy Award 3088
International Festival of Films on Energy Lausanne 11797
Iwatani Naoji Memorial Prize 8573
James Prescott Joule Medal 3247
Armando Kaminitz Research Awards 7981
Maisons solaires, maisons d'aujourd'hui 5046
Prix du Gaz de France 5694
Willans Premium 3308

Energy, atomic See **Atomic energy**

Energy conservation
Catalonian Government Prizes for Economic Energy Consumption and Diversification 11178
Laszlo Dobo Prize 7378
Eminent Activist Medal 7379
Prix Nature et Patrimoine 5080
Janos Andras Segner Prize 7380
Geza Szikla Prize 7381

Engineering (See also Communications technology; Cybernetics; Electronics; Energy; Engineering education; Materials science; Mining and metallurgy; Photogrammetry; Robotics; Standards; Surveying; Testing; Water resources)
ABU Engineering Award 8888
ACEA Engineering Awards 135
Amsterdam Prize for the Environment 9596
Annual Award 2528
Applications Paper Prize 816
Armstrong Lecture 4400
The Associateship of the City and Guilds of London Institute 2621
Automatica Prize Paper Awards 817
Award for Achievement in Engineering Enterprise 424
Awards for Work Displaying Engineering Excellence 425
Donat Banki Award 7455
Barker Silver Medal 2590
Beilby Medal and Prize 4187
W. H. Bennett Travelling Fellowship 3316
Bhatnagar Award 7532
Birmingham Medal 3317
W. H. M. Blackwell Memorial Lecture 9728
Scott Blair Scholarship 2529
O. F. Blakey Memorial Prize 426
Paul Bonatz Preis 7135
Frederick Brough Memorial Prize 428
Brussels International Festival of Films on the Engineering Profession 1097
Caldas Science Prize 1688
Carter Bronze Medal 2591
Castrol Award 3090

Engineering — Awards, Honors & Prizes, 1995-96

Engineering (continued)

Celette Prize 3318
Certamen Anual Nacional de Tesis de Ingenieria 9033
Certificates of Merit 3091
Ceylon Development Engineering Award 11402
Churchill Medal 4441
Clark Travelling Fellowship 3319
Lorenzo Codazzi Prize 1745
Collacott Prize 3266
Competitions 12132
Control Engineering Textbook Prize 818
Convention Medal and Convention Certificate 936
E. R. Cooper Memorial Medal and Prize 9836
Jennifer Cox Memorial Prize 435
John Cranko Memorial Award 9729
E. H. Davis Memorial Lecture 437
Charles Deakin Award 7175
Dempster Travelling Fellowship 3320
Design Council British Aerospace Engineering Design Prizes 2739
Dieterichs/Maclay Memorial Prize 3321
Distinguished Professional Contribution Award 8805
Dobson Lecture 9730
Dufton Silver Medal Award 2592
Engineering 2000 Awards 438
Engineering Achievement Award 12213
Engineering Council Young Engineer for Britain Competition 4302
Engineering Prize - Israel Rokach Prize 7952
The Environment Award for Engineers 2769
Environmental Award 9731
Esso Energy Award and Medal 4148
Fondation Charles Fremont 5516
Fondation Tremont 5673
Foundation Prestige Lectures 4304
Fujihara Award 8527
Fulton-Downer Award 9733
Gairn E.E.C. Medal 4442
T. V. Garrud Fellowship 3323
Leon Gaster Bronze Medal 2593
Otto Glogau Award 9767
Gold Medal
 British Society of Rheology 2530
 Institution of Engineers, Pakistan 9977
 Pakistan Academy of Sciences 9993
Gold Medal for Development of the Technological Environment 9952
Frank Haskell Silver Medal 3092
P. H. Haviland Award 12214
Hector Memorial Medal and Prize 9838
Helmholtz Prizes 6914
Ian Henderson Memorial Prize 440
Honda Prize 8535
Hopkins Lecture 9735
Hosei International Fund Foreign Scholars Fellowship 8537
Humboldt Research Awards to Foreign Scholars 7155
Charles Hunt Memorial Medal 3324
IAHR-APD Award 9459
IESL Award 11403
IET Woman's Engineer Award 3093
Institution Bronze Medal 3325
Institution Gold Medal 3326
Institution Medal and Premium (Local Associations) Competition 3245
Institution Medal and Premium (Universities) Competition 3246
Institution of Engineers, Australia Award - Ballarat University College 443

Institution of Engineers, Australia Award - Curtin University of Technology 444
Institution of Engineers, Australia Award - James Cook University of North Queensland 445
Institution of Engineers, Australia Award - LaTrobe University College of Northern Victoria 446
Institution of Engineers, Australia Award - Monash University 447
Institution of Engineers, Australia Award - Monash University - Caulfield Campus 448
Institution of Engineers, Australia Award - Monash University Gippsland 449
Institution of Engineers, Australia Award - Queensland University of Technology 450
Institution of Engineers, Australia Award - Royal Melbourne Institute of Technology 451
Institution of Engineers, Australia Award - Swinburne Institute of Technology 452
Institution of Engineers, Australia Award - University College of Southern Queensland 453
Institution of Engineers, Australia Award - University of Adelaide 454
Institution of Engineers, Australia Award - University of College of Central Queensland 456
Institution of Engineers, Australia Award - University of Melbourne 457
Institution of Engineers, Australia Award - University of New South Wales 458
Institution of Engineers, Australia Award - University of Newcastle 460
Institution of Engineers, Australia Award - University of Queensland 461
Institution of Engineers, Australia Award - University of South Australia 462
Institution of Engineers, Australia Award - University of Sydney 463
Institution of Engineers, Australia Award - University of Tasmania 464
Institution of Engineers, Australia Award - University of Technology, Sydney 465
Institution of Engineers, Australia Award - University of Western Australia 466
Institution of Engineers, Australia Award - University of Wollongong 467
Institution of Engineers, Australia Award - Victoria University of Technology - Footscray Campus 468
Institution of Engineers Medal 469
Institution Silver Medal 3327
International Association of Engineering Geology Awards 5965
IPENZ Craven Post-Graduate Research Scholarship 9736
IPENZ Structural Award 9737
Arthur Thomas Ippen Award 9461
Jackson Silver Medal 3094
James Prescott Joule Medal 3247
Junior Inventor of the Year 11404
The Kharazmi Prize 7737
Maurice Lefranc Scholarships 1148
Local Government Engineering Medal 471
MacLean Citation 9738
MacRobert Award 3875
P. C. Mahalanobis Medal 7656
MakDougall-Brisbane Prize 10646
Artur Malheiros Prize 10255
Mendelssohn Award 6942
Mensforth International Gold Medal 3296
John Monash Medal 474
John E. Morgan Silver Cup 3095
Mullard Award and Medal 4153
Napier - Shaw Bronze Medal 2595

Kevin Nash Gold Medal 3473
National Engineering Excellence Awards 476
National Engineering Prize 1747
National Excellence Awards for Engineering Journalism 477
National Professional Young Engineer of the Year 478
NatWest Bank Engineering Marketing Award 2773
W. L. Newnham Memorial Lecture 9739
Orden al Merito Julio Garavito 1669
Pakistan Civil Awards 9995
R. W. Parsons Memorial Prize 479
Pelles Prize 7865
Professor E. O. E. Pereira Award 11406
Pergamon Scott Blair Biorheology Scholarship 2531
Manuel Ponce de Leon Prize 1748
Bruce-Preller Prize Lectureship 10648
Premio Luis Elizondo - Premio Cientifico y Technologico 8989
Premio Romulo Garza para Investigacion 9026
President's Award 9741
President's Medal 4443
President's Prize
 Chartered Institution of Building Services Engineers 2596
 Institution of Engineers, Australia 480
Prix Blaise Pascal du GAMNI-SMAI 5685
Prix Charles Lemaire 1012
Prix du Gaz de France 5694
Professional Commitment Award 9742
Professional Engineer of the Year 481
Giorgio Quazza Medal 819
Queen's Silver Jubilee Competition 4306
Rabone Award 9743
Railway Engineering Award 483
James Ransom Memorial Medals 3329
Rolls Royce Jubilee Award 3302
Royal Society of Victoria Medal 638
Sir Henry Royce Pupil Prize 4315
Sir Henry Royce Trophy for the Pursuit of Excellence 4316
Peter Nicol Russell Memorial Medal 485
SAACE/SA Construction World Awards for Excellence in Engineering 11026
Diodoro Sanchez Prize 1749
Scientific/Engineering Award 10816
Shanti Swarup Bhatnagar Medal 7670
Simms Medal 4444
Society's Prizes 4445
State Development and Construction Corporation Award 11408
Steel and Tube Travelling Scholarship 9745
K. G. Stevens Award 12215
Sugg Heritage Award 3330
Tanner Award 2597
Tasmania Division Award of Merit 489
Nikola Tesla Awards 1813
Tipping Bronze Apprentice Medal 3096
Transport Engineering Medal 490
Turner Lecture 9746
UNESCO Science Prize 6427
University of Tasmania - Launceston Award 492
Walsh - Weston Bronze Award 2598
Western Australian School of Mines Award 495
Gustave Willems Prize 1239
Wingquist Award 12216
Corbet and Henry Woodall, and William Cartwright Holmes Postgraduate Award 3331
Young Author Prize 820
Young Engineer of the Year 11410

Young Engineers for Britain 2771
Young Engineers Speaking Competition 496
Young Enterprise Award 3310
S. H. Zaheer Medal 7679

Engineering, aeronautical See **Aeronautical engineering**

Engineering, agricultural See **Agricultural engineering**

Engineering, automotive See **Automotive engineering**

Engineering, biomedical See **Biomedical engineering**

Engineering, ceramic See **Ceramic engineering**

Engineering, chemical See **Chemical engineering**

Engineering, civil See **Civil engineering**

Engineering, corrosion See **Corrosion engineering**

Engineering education
Engineering Journals Premia 3277
IAESTE Award Certificate 5959
ICI Award 441
IGIP Award 849
Institution of Engineers, Australia Award - Australian Maritime College 442

Engineering, electrical See **Electrical engineering**

Engineering, human See **Human engineering**

Engineering, industrial See **Industrial engineering**

Engineering, lubrication See **Lubrication engineering**

Engineering, marine See **Naval engineering**

Engineering, mechanical See **Mechanical engineering**

Engineering, military See **Military engineering**

Engineering, naval See **Naval engineering**

Engineering, nuclear See **Nuclear engineering**

Engineering, petroleum See **Petroleum engineering**

Engineering, sanitary See **Sanitary engineering**

English history
Alan Ball Local History Awards 3563
David Berry Prize 4020
Browne Medal for Original Research 4597
Cromwell Association Award 2720
Kernow Goth Trophy 2876
Walter Frewen Lord Prize 3998
Templer Medal 4350
Whitfield Prize 4021

English literature
Benson Medal 4231
Constable Trophy 2680
Rose Mary Crawshay Prize for English Literature 2225
Hawthornden Prize 10551
Enid McLeod Literary Prize 2908
Royal Society of Literature Award 4233
W. H. Smith Literary Award 4345

Engraving
Grand Prix des Arts de la Ville de Paris 6092
Prix Ary Scheffer 5360
Prix Auguste Durand et Edouard Ordonneau 5361
Prix Bordin 5364
Prix Breaute 5365
Prix Colmont 5373
Prix de Gravure Lacouriere 5198
Prix de la Fondation Florence Gould 5376
Prix de la Societe Francaise de Gravure 5377
Prix Estrade-Delcros 5387
Prix et Fondations Concernant l'Academie de France a Rome 5388
Prix Frederic et Jean de Vernon 5392
Prix Georges Wildenstein 5395
Prix Houllevigue 5403
Prix Paul-Louis Weiller 5418
Prix Pinet 5420
Prix Regner de gravure 4912
Salon Anual de Artes Plasticas Premios Pedro Domingo Murillo 1389
Spanish Association of Painters and Sculptors Prizes 11381

Entertainment (See also **Animated films; Humor**)
Award for the Promotion of Polish Entertainment Creativity 10206
Golden Rose of Montreux Award 11925
Grand Prix National du Cirque 5292
Order of Cultural Merit 8579
Pall Mall Export Swing Award 9566
Poppe Prize 11574

Entomology See **Zoology**

Entrepreneurship See **Business**

Environmental conservation
Ermanno Acanfora International Prize 8435
Walter Ahlstrom Prize 4682
Asahi Forestry Culture Prize 8489
Christopher E. Barthel, Jr. Award 3495
Blekinge County Council Culture Prize 11446
Blekinge County Council Environment Prize 11447
Blue Planet Prize 8486
Book Awards 10502
Britain in Bloom Awards 4541
Business and Industry Commitment to the Environment Awards 2562
Carl XVI Gustavs Medalj 11536
CEFIC Environment Award 1129
City of Sorrento Prize 8436
Concurso de Ecologia Cacique Chuira 1594
EARTHWORM Children's Book Award 2913
Ekofilm Awards 1862
Environment in Children's Literature Award 10289
Environmental Award 9731
Environmental Management Awards 4321
European Environmental Film Festival 5116

Fauna and Flora Preservation Society Grants 2866
Festival International du Film d'Architecture d'Urbanisme et d'Environement Urbain de Bordeaux 6018
Ford European Conservation Awards 2677
Ned Franklin Medal 3218
Grassland Society of Southern Africa Awards 10874
Elizabeth Haub Prize 6940
Honda Prize 8535
Honorary Life Member 1146
Institution of Environmental Sciences Awards 3314
International Festival of Alpine Films Les Diablerets, Switzerland 11791
International Film Festival - Nature, Man and His Environment 8301
Tadas Ivanausko premija 8855
Sir Peter Kent Conservation Book Prize 2200
Hans Klose Prize 7116
Medalla Alfonso L. Herrera al Merito en Ecologia y Conservacion 9040
Aldo Merola International Prize 8437
NACA Clean Air Award 10899
Naturskyddsmedaljen 11548
Sultan Oaboos Prize for Environmental Preservation 6418
Onassis Prize for the Environment 7210
Premio de Ecologia 9263
Premio Luis Elizondo - Premio Cientifico y Technologico 8989
Prince of Wales' Awards 12183
Prix de Centre International Humanae Vitae 5015
Prix de l'Institut Francais du Petrole 5690
Prix Nature et Patrimoine 5080
Queen's Awards for Environmental Achievement 3830
RICS Awards 4085
Rolex Awards for Enterprise 11898
Fritz Schumacher Prizes 7122
Sture Centerwalls Pris 11556
The Times/PM Environment Award 4551
Umweltpreis der Landeshauptstadt Stuttgart 7140
UNEP Sasakawa Environment Prize 8812
United Nations Environment Program Awards - Global 500 Roll of Honour 8813
Alexander Von Humboldt Medal 7130
World Clean Air Congress Award 3496
World Press Photo Contest 9697
Young Scientist Award 2822

Environmental health
Competitions 1206
Gawad AGKATEK (Agham, Kapaligiran at Teknolohiya) 10057
Latin American Federation of Thermalism and Climatism Awards 57
NACA Clean Air Award 10899

Equestrian See **Horsemanship**

Essays
Ablett Prize 3125
Actonian Prize 4087
Alexander Prize 4019
Russell Allin Prize 3227
Amerbach-Preis 11962
ANA Literary Prize 9856
ASEAN Award for Literature 10030
Austrian State Prize for Cultural Publications 760
Charles Babbage Premium 3268
Baker Medal 3228

Ethics   **Awards, Honors & Prizes, 1995-96**

Essays (continued)
Bangla Academy Literary Award   934
Barker Silver Medal   2590
Guy Bengough Medal and Prize   3126
David Berry Prize   4020
Bessemer Gold Medal   3127
Blumlein-Brown-Willans Premium Award   3269
Brunel Medal   3229
Buckland Literary Award   9846
Buenos Aires Literary Prizes   36
Robert Alfred Carr Premium   3231
Carter Bronze Medal   2591
Carlos Casavalle Prize   26
Category A Fellowships   155
Category B Fellowships   156
Cena Zvazu slovenskych spisovatelov   10756
Centres Premium   3271
Commonwealth Essay Competition   3997
Cooperative Prize   11963
Coopers Hill War Memorial Prize   3233
Coopers Hill War Memorial Prize and Medal   3272
Arthur H. Cornette Prize   1268
Crampton Prize   3234
Curl Bequest Prize   3926
Bill Curtin Medal   3235
Divisional Premium   3273
J. B. Donne Essay Prize on the Anthropology of Art   3927
Dufton Silver Medal Award   2592
Aquileo J. Echeverria Prize   1761
Joris Eeckhout Prize   1270
Electronics and Communication Engineering Journal Premium   3274
Electronics Education Premium   3275
Electronics Letters Premium Awards   3276
Engineering Journals Premia   3277
First Book Prize   21
Fondation Mege   5631
James Forrest Medal   3237
Dr. Wijnaendts Francken-prijs   9626
Fundacion del Premio Fastenrath   11345
Trench Gascoigne Prize Essay Competition   4295
Leon Gaster Bronze Medal   2593
GPA Book Award   7777
Grand Prix de la Mer   4918
Grand Prix Litteraire de l'Oceanie   4920
Grand Prix Litteraire de Madagascar   4921
Grand Prix Thyde Monnier   6266
Grands Prix Litteraire de la Ville de Paris   6095
J. Greshoff Prize   9349
Andreas-Gryphius-Preis   6525
Halcrow Premium   3239
Charles Hatchett Award   3137
Wilhelm-Heinse-Medaille   6514
Harry Henniker Premium   3281
Hermann Hesse Prize   7086
David Hislop Award   3240
Arthur Maurice Hocart Prize   3928
Howard Medal   3241
T. K. Hsieh Award   3242
Busken Huetprijs   9639
Renee Redfern Hunt Memorial Prize   3243
IAPH Essay Contest   8545
IEE Scotland North Premium   3289
IERE Benefactors Premium   3290
Institution Medal and Premium (Local Associations) Competition   3245
Institution Medal and Premium (Universities) Competition   3246
Institution Premium   3291
International Premium Awards   3292

Isle of Elba - Raffaello Brignetti Literary Award   8323
James Prescott Joule Medal   3247
John F. Kennedy Student Paper Competition   9462
Kerala Sahitya Akademi Awards   7703
C. B. Kumar Award   7704
Lindapter Award   3249
Jessie Litchfield Award   557
Literary Prizes   7192
Littre Prize   6501
Walter Frewen Lord Prize   3998
Oliver Lucas Automotive Electronic Engineering Award   3293
Malaysian Literary Prize   8904
Malpertuis Prize   1288
Manby Premium   3250
Arthur Markham Memorial Prize   4585
Maxwell Prizes   3475
Eric Megaw Memorial Prize   3295
Johann-Heinrich-Merck Preis   6768
Miller Prizes   3252
Mirror of Spain Prize   11221
Napier - Shaw Bronze Medal   2595
National Award for Literature and Arts   12002
National Prize for Linguistics and Literature   9148
National Prize for Literature   12122
Nautical Institute Competitions   3716
Henry Nimmo Premium   3297
Noma Award for Publishing in Africa   2039
Norske Akademis Pris Til Minne om Thorleif Dahl   9925
Overseas Premium   3253
Don Carlos Palanca Memorial Awards for Literature   10053
Frederick Palmer Prize   3254
Parkman Medal   3255
PEN Prizes (Poetry, Essay, Novel)   10293
Pfeil Medal and Prize   3144
Premio Antonio Maura   11288
Premio Editiorial Costa Rica   1770
Premio Hispanoamericano Xavier Villaurrutia   9267
Premio Internacional de Ensayo Literario Malcolm Lowry   9226
Premio Litterario Viareggio   8407
Premio Municipal de Literatura   1568
Premio Municipal Trabalho e Estudo   10278
Premio Nacional de Ensayo Literario Jose Revueltas   9234
Premio Nacional de Literatura
    Chile - Ministerio de Educacion   1548
    Spain Ministry of Culture   11375
Premio Ortega y Gasset   11299
Premios Literarios Nacionais   1474
Premios Municipais Eca de Queiroz de Literatura   10280
Prix biennal Marcel Thiebaut   6273
Prix Cazes-Brasserie Lipp   6164
Prix Constant de Horion   1041
Prix de l'Essai   5836
Prix de Litterature des Alpes et du Jura   4923
Prix Franz de Wever   1297
Prix Leopold Rosy   1303
Prix Litteraire des Mascareignes, des Seychelles et des Comores   4929
Prix Medicis de l'Essai   6175
Prix Medicis Etranger   6176
Prix Roger Nimier   6121
Prix SGDL de l'Essai   6293
Prize for Literature of the Council of the French Community of Belgium   1110
Reed and Mallik Medal   3256
A. H. Reeves Premium   3301

Revelation Prize for Essay   10311
Ricardo Rojas Prize   38
Safety in Construction Medal   3257
Ary Sleeks Prize   1276
Staatsprijs voor Kritiek en Essay   1082
Gyorgy Striker Junior Paper Award   7429
Student Medallion Award   3305
Telford Medal   3259
Telford Premium   3260
J. Langham Thompson Premium   3306
Trevithick Premium   3261
Charles Veillon European Essay Prize   11967
Jose Verissimo Prize   1445
Walsh - Weston Bronze Award   2598
James Watt Medal   3263
Webb Prize   3264
Willans Premium   3308
Wolskel Industrial Chemistry Essay Award   603
Yomiuri Literature Prize   8795
Young Lighters of the Year   2599
Younger Members' Premiums Awards   3311
Dr. V. K. Zworykin Premium   3312

Ethics
Senator Giovanni Agnelli International Prize   8247
Fondazione Premio Dotte Giuseppe Borgia   8063
Italian Minister for Culture and the Environment Prizes   8365
Anatoly Koryagin Award   9472
Littre Prize   6501
Prix de Centre International Humanae Vitae   5015
University of Berne Prizes   11965

Ethnic affairs (See also Culture)
Elsdon Best Memorial Medal   9786
Prix Georges Bruel   6135
Prix Robert Delavignette   6138
Ethnic Affairs Commission of New South Wales Award   686
Haifa Prize   7878
International Film Festival of Visual Anthropology and Social Documentation   5032
Prix de Monsieur et Madame Louis Marin   6141
Phenix - U.D.A.   6429
Premio Fray Bernardino de Sahagun   9056
Prix Henri Lavachery   990
Regional Production Prizes   23
Dr. Arthur Ruppin Prize   7885
Shibusawa Memorial Prize   8738

European culture (See also East European culture)
Hamburg Max Brauer Prize   7108
Henry Duncan Prize Lectureship   10643
Erasmus Prize   9396
European Music and Poetry Competitions   1121
European Prizes for Folk Art   7111
Dr. Wijnaendts Francken-prijs   9626
Goethe Medaille   6901
Anders Jahre Prize for Contributions to Norwegian Culture   9900
John Lotz Commemorative Medal   7420
Somerset Maugham Awards   4390
Maxwell Prizes   3475
Membership of the Gorsedd of Bards of Great Britain   12185
Press Prize   9884
Prix International de la Societe Europeenne de Culture   8233
Fritz Reuter Prize   7121

Sonning Prize 2011
Henrik Steffens Prize 7125
Endre Szirmai Prize 7421
Gottfried Von Herder Prizes 7129
Joost van den Vondel Prizes 7133

European history
Amsterdam Prize for History 9594
Norman Hepburn Baynes Prize 4578
Edmund Curtis Memorial Prize 7841
Georg-Dehio-Preis 6524
Fraenkel Prize in Contemporary History 3086
Dr. Wijnaendts Francken-prijs 9626
History Prize 1061
Hans Janssen Prize 6909
Eoin O'Mahony Bursary 7844
Premio Municipal Augusto Vieira da Silva de Investigacao 10266
Prijs voor wetenschappelijk Werk van de Stad Lier 1382
Prix Anton Bergmann 978
Trevor Reese Memorial Prize 4581
Endre Szirmai Prize 7421
Herbert Weichmann-Preis 7013

European integration
Joseph Bech Prize 7107
Emile Bernheim European Prizes 1378
Coudenhove-Kalergi Award 7070
EFTA Awards 11700
Europe Prize 5089
Europe Prize - Flag of Honor 5090
Europe Prize - Plaque of Honor 5091
European Merit Award 8862
European Prize for Statesmanship 7109
Golden Pen 9883
International Charlemagne Prize of Aachen 7092
Louis Michel Prize 5013
Prix Adolf Bentinck 6160
Robert Schumann Prize 7123
Prix Stendhal 6008
Gottfried Von Herder Prizes 7129

European literature (See also **Dutch literature; English literature; French literature; Irish literature; Italian literature; Spanish literature**)
Aniara Prize 11631
Austrian State Grand Prize 759
Austrian State Prize for European Literature 762
Booker Russian Novel Prize 2196
City of Munich Prizes 7019
Europalia Literary Prize of the European Community 1154
Isle of Elba - Raffaello Brignetti Literary Award 8323
John Lotz Commemorative Medal 7420
Nordic Council Literature Prize 11503
Norsemen's Federation Translation Grant 9914
Promotional Prizes 7022
Rauriser Literaturpreis 723
Sant Jordi 11239
Schlegel - Tieck Prize 4398
Shakespeare Prize 7124
Otto Stoessl-Preis 893
Adelbert-von-Chamisso-Preis 6553

Exhibiting
Annual Promotional Activity Award 8858
ASDA Prize 4909
International Exhibition Logistics Associates Awards 11782
Union of International Fairs Awards 6457

Exploration (See also **Geography**)
Antarctic Medal 206
Butsuri-Tansa Gakkai-sho 8756
Livingstone Gold Medal 10631
Medaille d'Or 11906
Mungo Park Medal 10632
Polar Medal 2380
Rink Medal 1952
Rolex Awards for Enterprise 11898
Trento International Film Festival of Mountain and Exploration 8460

Export See **International trade**

Family planning
Mother and Child International Award 11881
R. Wasito Award 7731

Family relations (See also **Child welfare**)
Medal for Long Marital Life 10108
Prix Malouet 5780

Fashion (See also **Cosmetology; Design; Hairstyling**)
Forderpreis des Landes Nordrhein-Westfalen fur junge Kunstlerinnen und Kunstler 7026
Lloyds Bank British Fashion Awards 2338
Premio Elio Costanzi 8001
Premio Francesco Compagna 8002
Premio Francesco Pistolese 8003
Premio Irene Brin 8004
Premio Mondo e Cultura 8005
Prize Mission Special Japan 8733
Woman's Journal British Fashion Award 4610

Feminism See **Women**

Fencing
Divisional Team Championships 4567
Individual Championships 4568
International Fencing Federation Awards 6012
National Order of the Southern Cross 1415

Fiber science (See also **Textile design; Textile industry**)
George Douglas Lecture 4432
Preis der Stiftung Kunststoff-Technik 11935
S. G. Smith Memorial Medal 4523
Textile Institute Jubilee Award 4526
Textile Technology Award 8942
Worshipful Company of Feltmakers Research Medal 4439

Fiction (See also **Science fiction; Short stories**)
The Age Book of the Year Awards 118
ANA Literary Prize 9856
Angel Literary Award 2080
Graca Aranha Prize 1450
Afonso Arinos Prize 1420
Arts Council of Great Britain Schemes 2100
Arts Council of Wales Book of the Year Awards 12150
Arts Council Writing Grants 9798
ASEAN Award for Literature 10030
Australian/Vogel Literary Award 120
Authors' Club First Novel Award 2149
Award for Original Hebrew Novel 7872
Awards for Regional Literature 10004
Bagutta Prize 8160
Bangla Academy Literary Award 934
Benson Medal 4231
Bicentennial Fiction Award 196
James Tait Black Memorial Prizes 10685

Boardman Tasker Memorial Award for Mountain Literature 2192
Book Awards 10734
Booker Prize 2195
F. Bordewijk Prize 9346
Bourses de la Vocation 5212
British Fantasy Awards 2336
Buckland Literary Award 9846
Buenos Aires Literary Prizes 36
Carlos Casavalle Prize 26
Camilo Castelo Branco Prize 10319
Category A Fellowships 155
Category B Fellowships 156
CCP Literary Awards 10034
City of Lisbon Literary Prize 10308
CNA Literary Award 10830
Commonwealth Writers Prize 2654
Concurso Anual de Literatura Premios Franz Tamayo 1388
Concurso Literario Premio Emece 47
Concurso Nacional de Novela Erich Guttentag 1398
Constable Trophy 2197
Critics Prize 10298
Croatian Socialist Republic Prizes 1808
Luisa Claudio de Sousa Prize 1451
Delta Fiction Award 9863
Aquileo J. Echeverria Prize 1761
Elle Literary Prize 5110
Euro Best Awards 3362
Geoffrey Faber Memorial Prize 2860
Fawcett Book Prize 2868
Festival Awards for Literature 673
Finlandia Prize 4686
Fundacion del Premio Fastenrath 11345
Romulo Gallegos Novel Prize 12120
Goncourt Prize 4798
GPA Book Award 7777
Grand Prix de la Litterature 6260
Grand Prix du Roman 5806
Grand Prix Thyde Monnier 6266
Grande Premio de Romance e Novela da Associacao Portuguesa de Escritores 10309
Grands Prix Litteraire de la Ville de Paris 6095
Andreas-Gryphius-Preis 6525
The Guardian Fiction Prize 2955
Calouste Gulbenkian Translation Prize 10251
Gunzo Fiction Prize 8685
Soren Gyldendal Prisen 1954
Hermann Hesse Prize 7086
David Higham Prize for Fiction 2199
Winifred Holtby Memorial Prize 4232
Hong Kong Biennial Awards for Chinese Literature 7278
Pieter Cornelisz Hooft Prize 9665
The Independent Foreign Fiction Award 3044
Orhan Kemal Award 12072
Kerala Sahitya Akademi Awards 7703
Korean National Literary Award 8823
Fran Levstik Prize 10807
Literary Awards and Prizes for Sinhalese Literature 11423
Literary Competition 12218
Literary Prizes 7192
Literary Prizes for Tamil Literature 11424
Literaturpreis der Bundesarztekammer 6816
Julia Lopes of Ameida Prize 1425
Fikret Madarali Prize 12073
Ricardo Malheiros Prize 10256
Antonio Maria Special Award 1471
Arthur Markham Memorial Prize 4585
Somerset Maugham Awards 4390

Fiction (continued)
McVitie's Prize for the Scottish Writer of the Year 10582
Netta Muskett Award 3857
Nadal Prize 11216
Naoki Prize 8753
National Award for Literature and Arts 12002
National Prize for Linguistics and Literature 9148
New South Wales State Literary Awards 147
New Zealand Book Awards 9801
Noma Award for Publishing in Africa 2039
Noma Prize for Literature 8691
Norske Akademis Pris Til Minne om Thorleif Dahl 9925
Novel of the Year Award 10720
Don Carlos Palanca Memorial Awards for Literature 10053
Parnassos Foundation Prize 7213
PEN Best First Book of Fiction Award 9778
PEN Prizes (Poetry, Essay, Novel) 10293
Josep Pla Prize 11217
Planeta Prize 11222
Premier's Literary Awards 149
Premio Alvarez Quintero 11346
Premio Ateneo de Valladolid de Novela Corta 11147
Premio de Novela Ateneo de Sevilla 11223
Premio de Novela Jose Ruben Romero 9218
Premio Editiorial Costa Rica 1770
Premio Iberoamericano de Primeras Novelas 1564
Premio Juan Rulfo Para Primera Novela 9228
Premio Literario Ramon Llull 11224
Premio Litterario Viareggio 8407
Premio Nacional de Literatura
 Chile - Ministerio de Educacion 1548
 Spain Ministry of Culture 11375
Premio Poesia y Narrativa 1772
Premios Literarios Nacionais 1474
Premios Municipais Eca de Queiroz de Literatura 10280
Prix Alex Pasquier 1040
Prix ALPHA de la Nouvelle 4900
Prix Cazes-Brasserie Lipp 6164
Prix Claire Virenque 5829
Prix de la Meilleure Nouvelle Francophone 4883
Prix de la Nouvelle de la France 5253
Prix des Maisons de la Presse Prize 6106
Prix *Femina* 6168
Prix George Garnir 1299
Prix Gilles Nelod 1042
Prix Interallie 5022
Prix Lucien Tisserand 5887
Prix Medicis 6174
Prix Medicis Etranger 6176
Prix Renaudot 6178
Prix Roberge 5916
Prix Roger Nimier 6121
Prix Sander Pierron 1306
Prix Sola-Cabiati 6097
Prix Sully-Olivier-de-Serres 5241
Prix Valery Larbaud 4987
Prix Victor Rossel 1247
Prize for Literature of the Council of the French Community of Belgium 1110
Prize for Novel 7793
Prizes for Literature 8884
Prosvjeta Prize 10722
Wilhelm-Raabe-Preis 6574
Reed Fiction Award 9803
Revelation Prize for Fiction 10312
Ritz Paris Hemingway Award 6199
Ricardo Rojas Prize 38
Romantic Novel of the Year 3858
Sargeson Writer's Fellowship 9844
Ary Sleeks Prize 1276
Lilian Ida Smith Award 9782
Southern Arts Literature Prize 4481
Staatsprijs voor Romans en Verhalend Proza 1084
Storywriting and Art Project 417
Strega Prize 8439
Sunday Express Book of the Year Award 4501
Betty Trask Award 4393
Urban Council Awards for Creative Writing in Chinese 7279
Western Australian Premier's Book Awards 515
Whitbread Literary Awards 2211
Yomiuri Literature Prize 8795
Yoshikawa Eiji Literary Prize 8693

Field hockey *See* **Hockey**

Film competitions *See* **Film festivals**

Film criticism
Pierre Bayle Prijs 9580

Film festivals
Agrofilm International Short Film Festival 1873
Airone 8319
Alcanes/Muestra Cinematografica de Atlantico 11138
Ales Film Festival 4886
Amiens International Film Festival 4890
Asolo International Animation Festival 8100
Australian International Widescreen Festival 281
Avoriaz Film Awards 4983
Award of Austrian Film Days 874
Badalona Short Film and Video Festival 11205
Barcelona Film Festival 11155
Berlin International Film Festival 6564
Bienal de Cine y Video Cientifico 11166
Bombay International Film Festival 7529
British Short Film Festival 2498
Brussels International Art and Archaeology Film Festival 1162
Brussels International Festival of Fantasy Thriller and Science-Fiction Films 1241
Brussels International Festival of Films on the Engineering Profession 1097
Brussels International Festival of Scientific and Technical Films 1098
Cannes International Film Festival 5004
Certamen Internacional de Cine Amateur Ciutat d'Igualada 11203
Chamrousse International Festival of Comedy Films 5028
Christchurch International Amateur Film Festival Awards 9711
CINANIMA 10226
City of Sacile Prize 8094
Clermont-Ferrand International Short Film Festival 6196
Clermont-Ferrand National Short Film Festival 6197
Competition for Films and Videos on Japan 8774
Concours Technique International du Film de l'UNIATEC 6436
Cork International Film Festival 7769
Cork Youth International Video and Film Festival 7812
Cracow International Festival of Short Films 10069
Dendy Awards for Australian Short Films 685
Documentary Film Festival - Amsterdam 9376
Durban International Film Festival Awards 10847
Edinburgh International Film Festival 10541
Ekofilm Awards 1862
Ethnic Affairs Commission of New South Wales Award 686
Euroarabe and Television Festival 11226
European Environmental Film Festival 5116
European Grand Prize of Corporate Image 5006
Fantasy Film Awards 1091
Festival de Biarritz du Film Iberique et Latino-Americain 4968
Festival de Cine de Alcala de Henares 11228
Festival del Cine Nacional 12109
Festival du Court-Metrage en Plein Air 5173
Festival du Film Court de Villeurbanne 5175
Festival du Film de Fin d'Etudes Cinematographiques 6024
Festival Internacional de Cine de San Sebastian 11351
Festival Internacional de Cine Ecologico y de la Naturaleza 11232
Festival Internacional del Nuevo Cine Super 8 y Video 12114
Festival International de Films de Femmes 1384
Festival International de Paris du Film Fantastique et de Science-Fiction 6149
Festival International du Film d'Architecture d'Urbanisme et d'Environement Urbain de Bordeaux 6018
Festival International du Film de Comedie de Vevey 11661
Festival International du Film de Vol Libre 5184
Festival International du Film d'Histoire 5186
Festival International du Film et des Medias de Tourisme 6056
Festival of Nations 803
Filmotheque of the Youth 6983
Frankfurter Guckkastenmennchen 6592
Gdansk Golden Lions 10144
Gijon International Film Festival for Young People 11252
Golden Butterfly 7739
Golden Horse Awards 12009
Golden Knight International Amateur Film and Video Festival 8912
Golden R 8415
Golden Toucan 1482
Gottwaldov Festival of Children's Films 1890
Gran Canaria International Short Film Festival 11257
Grand Prix FIFART 11795
Grand Prix of the European Festival 5126
Grand Prize 8095
Grand Prize of the National Festival of Hungarian Non-professional Film and Videomakers 7315
Gulf of Salerno Grand Trophy 8417
Hercules Award 11357
Hiroshima International Amateur Film and Video Festival 8533
Holland Animation Film Festival Awards 9454

Subject Index of Awards
Volume 2: International and Foreign — Films

Hong Kong Independent Short Film Competition/Urban Council Short Film Awards 7265
Huy - World Festival of Movies of Short Films Awards 1160
IAC International Film and Video Competition 3067
Iberoamerican Film Festival 11261
IMAGFIC International Film Festival of Madrid 11263
Impact of Music on Film Competition 1193
Indonesian Film Festival 7733
Interfilm Award 9456
International Advertising Festival, Cannes 3363
International Amateur Film Festival, Golden Diana 897
International Animation Festival in Japan, Hiroshima 8531
International Children's Film and Video Festival 675
International Children's Film Festival of India 7715
International Cinema Festival of Algarve 10230
International Documentary and Short Film Festival of Bilbao 11267
International Festival of Alpine Films Les Diablerets, Switzerland 11791
International Festival of Cinema for Children and Youth 10232
International Festival of Ecological Film Events 10791
International Festival of Economics and Training Films 1191
International Festival of Film and Television in the Celtic Countries 10522
International Festival of Films Directed by Women 11149
International Festival of Films on Architecture and Town-planning of Lausanne 11793
International Festival of Films on Energy Lausanne 11797
International Festival of Maritime and Exploration Films 6014
International Festival of Mountain Films, Vila de Torello 11386
International Festival of Red Cross and Health Films 1528
International Festival of Sport Films 5248
International Festival of Sports and Tourist Films 10792
International Festival of Tourist Films - Tourfilm 1852
International Festival on General Health, the Red Cross and Environmental Protection Amateur Films 7440
International Film and Student Directors Festival 6020
International Film Festival Bludenz 721
International Film Festival - Nature, Man and His Environment 8301
International Film Festival of Figueira da Foz 10234
International Film Festival of India 7689
International Film Festival of Santarem 10236
International Film Festival of Visual Anthropology and Social Documentation 5032
International Filmfestival Mannheim/Heidelberg 6954
International Industrial Film and Video Awards 2703
International Leipzig Documentary and Animation Film Festival 7035

International Medical and Health Education Film Week 11269
International Multimedia Science Film Festival 8375
International Odense Film Festival 1963
International Prize Paladino D'Oro 8313
International Sailing Film Festival in La Rochelle 6044
International Short Film Festival, Oberhausen 6984
International Sports Film Festival 8317
International Sports Film Festival in Budapest 7431
International Student Film Festival 7903
International Week of Scientific Films 11199
International Week of Sea and Marine Cinema - Cartagena 11279
International Women's Film Festival, Creteil 6072
Istanbul International Film Festival 12060
Japan International Film - Video Festival of Adventure and Sports in Hakuba 8622
Stanley Thomas Johnson Award 11913
Jury Award 8096
Kaleidoscope Immigrantfilmfestival 11490
Karibu 1102
Les Ecrans De L'Aventure International Festival of Adventure Documentaries 5328
Lille Sport Film Festival 5038
Locarno International Film Festival 11875
Malaga International Week of Author Films 11303
Mauriac International Medical Film Festival 6112
Melbourne International Film Festival Shorts Awards 525
Moomba International Amateur Film Festival 527
Moscow International Film Festival 10474
Mostra Internazionale del Film d'Autore Gran Premio 8297
Munich International Filmschool Festival 7059
Mystery Prize 8388
New South Wales Film and Television Office Rouben Mamoulian Award 687
Nyon International Documentary Film Festival 11892
OKOMEDIA International Ecological Film Festival 7063
Oporto International Film Festival - Fantasporto 10291
Panafrican Film and Television Festival of Ouagadougou 1541
Joseph Plateau Prize 1194
Premio CORAL 1828
Prize of the Audience 6956
Prize of the Best National Collection 7316
Radio Exterior de Espana Prize 11324
Rassegna Internazionale dei Documentari Cine-TV Marinari 8295
Stefano Reggiani Prize 8291
Roshd International Film Festival Awards 7743
St. Kilda Film Festival 648
San Sebastian Underwater Film Cycle 11353
Sao Paulo International Film Festival 1499
Short Film Festival Prize 9948
Sofia International Film Festival on Organization and Automation of Production and Management Awards 1530
Star Boy Award 4754
Stuttgart International Festival of Animated Film 7142
Svjetski Festival Animiranih Filmova, Zagreb 1816

Tampere International Short Film Festival 4758
Techfilm International Film Festival 1874
Thessaloniki Film Festival 7217
Tokyo International Film Festival 8768
Torreon de Igueldo 11283
Trento International Film Festival of Mountain and Exploration 8460
Turin International Festival of Young Cinema 8462
UNICA Prize for the Best National Collection 7317
Uppsala Filmkaja 11654
Valencia Film Festival, Golden Palm Award 11305
Valladolid International Film Festival 11392
Karlovy Vary International Film Festival 1891
Venice International Film Festival 8470
Terje Vigen Prize 9950
W. A. Film and Video Festival 404
Wattrelos Short Film and Video Festival 6477
Weekly Mail and Guardian Short Film Competition 11125
World Festival of Mountain Pictures 6481
World Festival of Underwater Pictures 6483
World Film Festival of ORL Scientific Films and Videotapes 1187
Youth Award 5249
Yugoslav Documentary and Short Films Festival Awards 10701

Films (See also **Animated films; Audiovisuals; Cable television; Documentary films; Educational films; Entertainment; Film criticism; Film festivals; Television; Video**)
Aanmoedigingsprijzen 9635
ADIRCAE Prizes 11140
Theodor W. Adorno Award 6611
Age d'Or Prijs 1352
Amanda Award for Television and Cinematographic Merit 9938
Arts Festival Award 8576
Australian Film Institute Awards 221
Austrian State Encouragement Prizes 758
Austrian State Grand Prize 759
Austrian State Recognition Prizes 765
Awgie Awards 283
BAFTA Scholarship 2232
Bela Balanzs Prize for Cinematography 7399
Bangkok Bank Documentary Film Competition Prizes 12021
Belgian Film Archive Prizes for the Distribution of Quality Films 1353
Belgrade International Festival of Scientific Films 10699
Ingmar Bergman Plaquette 11625
Berlin Art Prizes 6509
Best Film Script in the Dutch Language 1077
BFI Fellowships 2344
BFI Film Award 2345
BFI Special Awards 2346
Biennale Internationale du Cinema Humain Marcel Mignon 1095
BMA Film and Video Competition 2429
BMA Medicine in the Media Award 2430
British Academy of Film and Television Arts Awards - Film 2233
British Fantasy Awards 2336
Bursaries, Scholarships, and Travel Awards 7755
Catalonian Prizes for Cinematography 11181

Finance   Awards, Honors & Prizes, 1995-96

Films (continued)
CCP Awards for Alternative Film and Video   10046
Cesar Awards   4793
Channel 4 Film Awards   2693
Chaplin Prize   11458
Charlie Chaplin Prize   1520
Dance Screen Award   842
David Film Awards   8218
Georges de Beauregard Prize   4962
Deutscher Filmpreis   6741
Ecumenical Prize   1172
European Film Awards (Felix Awards)   6713
FAW Adele Shelton-Smith Award for Play, Radio or Other Scripts for Young Writers   378
Festival International du Film Amateur   12042
Festival National de l'Audiovisuel d'Entreprise   5007
Film Competition   9265
Film Society of the Year Award   2340
Filmpreis der Bundesarztekammer   6814
FIPRESCI Prize   6944
Forderpreis des Landes Nordrhein-Westfalen fur junge Kunstlerinnen und Kunstler   7026
Golden Bug Statuette   11626
Golden Deer   7314
Gran Premio de Honor Argentores   30
Grand Prix de l'Oeuvre Musicale Audiovisuelle   6254
Grand Prix ICA - Prix du Meilleur Film Documentaire   10690
Grand Prix National du Cinema   5291
Grand Prix of the Dutch Film Golden Calf   9383
Grand Prix SACD   6395
Grierson Award   2347
Hammer and Sickle Gold Medal   10460
El Heraldo Prizes   9021
Hong Kong Film Awards   7264
IFHP International Film/Video Competition   9486
International Advertising Festival of Ireland   7785
International Contest of Short Films, City of Huesca   11236
International Visual Communications Association Awards   3502
Nami Jafet Prize   1488
L. J. Jordaanprijs   9640
Cherry Kearton Medal and Award   4012
Byron Kennedy Memorial Prize   222
Kikuchi Prize   8752
Leonide Moguy CIDALC Prize   5991
Literavision Preis   7021
Raymond Longford Award   223
M-Net Vita Film Award   10814
Ramon Magsaysay Awards   10042
Karol Malcuzynski Award   10207
Medaille des Publications   4785
Medal of Honor   10999
Milli Award   199
Jean Mitry Award   8400
Yunus Nadi Yarismasi   12049
Nagrada Saveta Fonda SO SUBNOR Cetvrti jul   10707
National Cultural Awards   1413
National Prize for Journalism and Information   9140
National Prize for Linguistics and Literature   9148
Vladimir Nazor Awards   1812
Nigar Public Film Awards   9987
OCIC-Prize   1173
October Prizes of the City of Belgrade   10696
Orbit Award of the ANZAAS International Scientific Film Exhibition and Competition   191
Order of Cultural Merit   8579
Order of Lenin   10463
Osterreichischer Staatspreis fur den Werbefilm
   Austria - Ministry of Economic Affairs   745
   Austrian Society of Film Sciences, Communications and Media Research   784
Pietrzak Award   10084
Roquette Pinto Prize   1418
Michael Powell Book Award   2349
Praemium Imperiale   8599
Preis fur Film und Fernsehforschung   785
Premio Anna Magnani   8122
Premio Argentores   31
Premio Ariel de Cinematografia   9097
Premio Cinema d'Essai - Targa AIACE   8124
Premio Internazionale Enno Flaiano   8114
Premio Luis Bunuel   11295
Premio Nacional de Cinematografia   11371
Premio Nacional de Television Simon Bolivar   1596
Premios Diosa de Plata   9257
Preseren Award   10799
President's Gold Medal   7559
Prix Andre Jullien du Breuil   5813
Prix de la Promotion Cinematographique   6328
Prix Diderot Universalis   5112
Prix du Cinema - Prix Jean Leduc   5843
Prix Georges Sadoul   6170
Prix Georges Wildenstein   5395
Prix Jean Vigo   5190
Prix Talents Nouveau   6399
Prize for a Flemish Short Film   1079
Prize for Theatre or Cinema   8832
Promotional Prizes   7022
Robin Hood Plaquette   11627
Rosa Camuna   8166
Sammy Awards   653
Scholarship Prizes   6512
Sitges International Fantasy Film Festival Awards   11359
Spurs of Criticism   4760
State Prize in Science and Technology   10470
Salvador Toscano Medal   8952
Trade Union's Art and Cultural Prize   7442
UNICA Awards   9537
UNICA Medal   11623
Upper Austria Culture Prize for Film   901
The Vercorin Manuscript Writing Award   8472
Clifford Wheeler Award   2880

Finance (See also **Accounting; Banking; Business; Economics; Insurance; Public finance**)
Banker of the Year   2812
Borrower of the Year   2813
Central Banker of the Year   2814
EIB Prize   8860
Finance Minister of the Year   2815
Fondazione Francesco Sarerio Nitti Prize   8054
Global Equity Awards   2816
Rodrigo Gomez Prize   8944
Bernhard-Harms-Preis   7007
IMEF National Prize for Financial Research   9038
National Banking Commission Prize   8958
National Institute of Insurance International Prizes   8067
Premio Nacional del Mercado de Valores   9042
Royal Companies Award   11109
Top 100 Companies Award   11110
Worst Finance Minister of the Year   2817

Financial journalism *See* **Business journalism**

Financial law *See* **Law**

Fine arts *See* **Art; Arts and humanities; Music**

Fire fighting
Australian Fire Service Medal   335
Disciplined Services Medal for Long Service and Good Conduct   7245
Disciplined Services Medal for Meritorious Service   7246
Disciplined Services Star for Distinguished Service   7247
Gallantry Medal   2351
Meritorious Service Decoration   2352
National Medal   208
Queen's Fire Service Medal for Gallantry   2381

Fire prevention
Fire Safety Award   2109

Firearms
Queen's Prize NRA Gold Medal   3706

Fishing
Catalonian Agriculture, Stock Farm, Forestry, Conservation of Nature and Fishing Awards   11170
FAO Technical Assistance Fellowship   8268
Osiris Award   8270
World Champion Trolling Fisherline Bucket   9910

Fishing industry
Chandrakala Hora Medal   7649
Peter Jones Memorial Award   2896

Fitness *See* **Health and fitness**

Flying
Aero Engine Services Trophy   9807
Airtour Sword   2999
Airways Corporation Trophy   9808
D. M. Allan Memorial Cup   9810
AOPA Awards for Achievement & Endeavor in Light Aviation   2049
Auto-Alloys Precision Trophy   3000
Babcock and Wilcox Trophy   3001
Jean Batten Memorial Trophy   9811
Bledisloe Aviation Trophy   9812
Sir Francis Boys Cup   9813
British Hang Gliding Association Trophy   12157
British Helicopter Advisory Board (BHAB) Trophy   3002
Leonardo Da Vinci Diploma   5141
Everard Trophy   3003
FAI Gold Parachuting Medal   5148
FAI Gold Rotorcraft Medal   5149
Famous Grouse Trophy   3004
Festival International du Film de Vol Libre   5184
Oscar Garden Trophy   9816
Grand Prix de Vitesse en Planeur a Luchon   5171
Hang Gliding Diploma   5152
Helicopter Club of Great Britain Championship Trophy   3005
Imperial Tobacco Trophy   3006

Jubilee Trophy 9818
Lilienthal Medal 5156
Livingston and Doughty Trophy 3007
Pepe Lopes Medal 5158
Pelagia Majewska Medal 5159
Montgolfier Diploma 5161
W. A. Morrison Trophy 9819
National Cross Country Trophy 12158
"New Zealand Wings" Trophy 9821
Newman Cup 9822
Precision Timing Trophy 3008
President's Trophy 12159
Rotorua Trophy 9824
Alvin Russell Trophy 12160
G. M. Spence Trophy 9825
Paul Tissandier Diploma 5166
Waitemata Aero Club Cup 9826
Wanganui Trophy 9827
Ivon Warmington Trophy 9828
Wigram Cup 9829
Wigram Cup (Sub-Competition) - Instrument Flying 9830
Wigram Cup (Sub-Competition) - Junior Landing 9831
Wigram Cup (Sub-Competition) - Non-instrument Circuits 9832
Wigram Cup (Sub-Competition) - Senior Landing 9833

Folklore
Bratislava Radio Prize for Folklore Music 10778
Katharine Briggs Folklore Award 2902
City of Vienna Promotional Prizes 791
Coote-Lake Medal for Folklore Research 2903
Ehrennadel fur Verdienste um die Osterreichische Volkskunde Huterstern 908
Folk Music Festival - Plaketti 4741
Michael Haberlandt Medal 909
El Heraldo Music Prizes 9020
Magical Folklore of Choco Prize 1658
Simion Florea Marian Prize 10364
Mestaripelimanni, Mestarikansanlaulaja 4742
National Institute of Folk and Traditional Heritage Awards 9985
Noordstarfonds - Dr. Jan Grauls Prize 1275
Order of the Golden Rose 7826
Premio MEC de Arte 1442
Premio Vicente T. Mendoza 9063
Regional Production Prizes 23
Silvio Romero Folklore Prize 1444
Franz Stangler Memorial Prize for Adult Education 861
Trento International Film Festival of Mountain and Exploration 8460
Jozef Van Ginderachter Prize 1278

Food (See also Cookbook writing; Dairy industry; Food processing; Nutrition; Restaurants; Wine)
Agrofilm International Short Film Festival 1873
Basel Salon Culinaire Mondial 11911
A. H. Boerma Award 8267
Chef Ireland 7817
Concours du Meilleure Jeune Commis Rotisseur 5024
Culinary Military Cup 8873
Culinary Olympics 7090
Culinary World Cup 8874
FAO Technical Assistance Fellowship 8268
Glenfiddich Awards 2949
Bires Chandra Guha Memorial Lecture 7648
Honorary Fellow 3102
Hotelympia Competition 2611
Joseph-Konig-Gedenkmunze 6785
Dr. V. N. Patwardhan Prize in Nutritional Sciences 7598
Premio del Seminario de Economia Agricola del Tercer Mundo 9190
Edouard Saouma Award 8271
B. R. Sen Award 8272
Andre Simon Medal 3506
Singapore Food and Hotel Asia Competition 10752

Food processing
Agrofilm International Short Film Festival 1873
Clyde H. Bailey Medal 807
Certificate of Appreciation 7745
Louis de Saint Rat Award 7373
Tamas Kosutany Memorial Medal 7374
Harald Perten Award 808
Premio Luis Elizondo - Premio Cientifico y Technologico 8989
Prix Litteraires 5026
Royal Bath and West Scholarship Awards (World and European) 3947
Friedrich Schweitzer Medal 809
Richard Seligman Lecture 4425
Elek Sigmond Memorial Medal 7375
Gabor Torok Memorial Medal 7376

Food service (See also Restaurants)
Acorn Awards 2571
Catey Awards 2572

Food technology See Food processing

Football (See also Soccer)
Divisional Team Championships 4567
Honorary Long Service Award 10668
Service Award for the Promotion and Teaching of Football 10669
Team Championships (non-divisional) 4569

Foreign policy
Christopher Ewart-Biggs Memorial Prize 2851
National Essay Contest on Colombian Foreign Policy 1592
Order of Nila Utama 10744
Prix Lucien de Reinach 5777

Forestry (See also Paper industry; Wood and wood products)
Ballogie Cup 10623
Albert Bedo Award 7344
Hunter Blair Trophy 10624
Sir George Campbell Memorial Trophy 10625
Catalonian Agriculture, Stock Farm, Forestry, Conservation of Nature and Fishing Awards 11170
Marin Dracea Prize 10345
Duke of Buccleuch Memorial Trophy 10626
FAO Technical Assistance Fellowship 8268
Tom Gill Memorial Award 2650
Karoly Kaan Award 7346
Osiris Award 8270
Wilhelm Leopold Pfeil Prize 7119
Premio Fundacion Celulosa Argentina 10
Queen's Award for Forestry 2651
Royal Bath and West Scholarship Awards (World and European) 3947
Royal Society of Victoria Medal 638
Schlich Memorial Trust Award 2652
Scientific Achievement Award 851
Suider-Afrikaanse Instituut van Boswese Toekenning 11099

Freedom
Annual Literary Festival 782
Chartered Institute of Journalists Gold Medal 2584
Commonwealth Press Union Scholarships 2669
Czechoslovak Association of Liberty and Anti-Fascist Fighters Awards 1846
Essay Prize 11759
European Parliament Sakharov Prize for Freedom of Thought 2841
Free Market Award 10865
Freedom Prize 11900
Front de l'Independence Awards 1158
Human Rights Prize 11953
International PEN - Philippines Awards 10040
International Simon Bolivar Prize 6415
Jerusalem Prize for the Freedom of the Individual in Society 7934
Journalism Prize 6003
Justice and Peace Prize for Human Values 11209
Airey Neave Research Award 3718
Plume d'Or de la Liberte 6007
Prix de la Liberte 6155
Prix de la Presse Libre - Les Libertes d'Or 5217
Prix Henri Texier 5755
Prize for Freedom 3557
Albert Schweitzer Award 3368
Young Women's Christian Association Council of Zimbabwe Competitions 12211

French-Canadian culture
Grand Prix de la Francophonie 5800

French culture
Fondation General Muteau 5799
Grand Prix National de l'Entreprise Culturelle 5286
Grand Prix National du Patrimoine 5293
International Council of the French Language Competitions 5999
Nouveau Prix Populiste 6130
Phenix - U.D.A. 6429
Prix 2000 SG 6384
Prix Diderot Universalis 5112
Prix du Chanoine Delpeuch 5735
Prix du PEN Club 6156
Prix Jean Mermoz 5267
Prix Lange 5881
Prix Leopold Sedar Senghor 5268
Prix Litteraire International Charles-Helou 4884
Prize for Literature of the Council of the French Community of Belgium 1110
UCTF Awards 5269

French history
Grand Prix d'Histoire Nationale Maurice Payard 4881
Grands Prix de la Fondation Napoleon 5214
Prix de La Fons-Melicocq 5447
Prix de Litterature des Alpes et du Jura 4923
Prix d'Histoire de la Vallee aux Loups 6102
Prix du Baron de Courcel
    Institut de France - Academie des Inscriptions et Belle-Lettres 5450
    Institut de France - Academie des Sciences Morales et Politiques 5733
Prix du Baron de Courcel 5842
Prix Emile Le Senne 5456

French   **Awards, Honors & Prizes, 1995-96**

French (continued)
Prix Eugene Colas   5851
Prix Eugene Piccard   5852
Prix Europeen de l'ADELF   4924
Prix Feydau de Brou   5855
Prix Gabriel Monod   5746
Prix Gobert
    Institut de France - Academie des Inscriptions et Belle-Lettres   5460
    Institut de France - Academie Francaise   5860
Prix Henri Hertz   5204
Prix Marcelin Guerin   5890
Prix Rene Petiet   5915
Prix Richelieu   6126
Prix Toutain-Blanchet   5474

French literature
Concours Max-Pol Fouchet   4974
Concours Promethee   4975
Fondation du General Muteau   5547
French Booksellers Prize   5257
Grand Prix de la Francophonie   5800
Grand Prix de la Mer   4918
Grand Prix de Litterature Francaise hors de France   1287
Grand Prix de Litterature Paul Morand   5802
Grand Prix Litteraire de l'Afrique Noire   4919
Grand Prix Litteraire de l'Oceanie   4920
Grand Prix Litteraire de Madagascar   4921
Grand Prix National de la Poesie   5281
Grand Prix National des Lettres   5288
Hassan II des Quatre Jurys   5232
International Prize for the First Novel   6042
Littre Prize   6501
Scott Moncrieff Prize   4397
Prix Alfred Verdaguer   5336
Prix Alice Louis Barthou   5810
Prix Andre Jullien du Breuil   5813
Prix Andre Lequeux   5714
Prix Antoine Girard   5815
Prix Biguet   5819
Prix Boudenoot   5822
Prix Chateaubriand   5048
Prix de la Meilleure Nouvelle Francophone   4883
Prix de la Resistance   5044
Prix de l'Academie des Sciences, Arts et Belles Lettres de Dijon   4795
Prix de l'Afrique Mediterraneenne/Maghreb   4922
Prix de Litterature des Alpes et du Jura   4923
Prix d'Histoire de la Vallee aux Loups   6102
Prix du Baron de Courcel   5450
Prix du Jeune Ecrivain "BNP" avec Le Monde   6438
Prix du Jeune Ecrivain Francophone   6439
Prix Dumas-Millier   5845
Prix Ernest Discailles   986
Prix Estrade-Delcros   5457
Prix Europeen de l'ADELF   4924
Prix Felix Feneon   5203
Prix Fernand Mery-Prix Animalier   6504
Prix France - Belgique   4925
Prix Guizot   5861
Prix Halphen   5863
Prix Henri Hertz   5204
Prix Heredia   5868
Prix Jean Jacques Berger   5465
Prix Jean-Jacques Berger   5871
Prix Jean Reynaud   5466
Prix Jules et Louis Jeanbernat et Barthelemy de Ferrari Doria
    Institut de France - Academie des Inscriptions et Belle-Lettres   5467

Institut de France - Academie Francaise   5874
Prix Liberte Litteraire   11721
Prix litteraire de la Ville de La Chaux-de-Fonds et de la revue vwa   11688
Prix Litteraire de l'Asie   4927
Prix Litteraire des Caraibes   4928
Prix Litteraire des Mascareignes, des Seychelles et des Comores   4929
Prix Litteraire France - Quebec/Jean Hamelin   4930
Prix Litteraire Prince Pierre-de-Monaco   9312
Prix Louis Barthou   5884
Prix Marcelin Guerin   5890
Prix Marcelle Millier   5891
Prix Marie Havez-Planque   5894
Prix Maujean   5895
Prix Max Barthou   5897
Prix Mediterranee   6187
Prix Montyon   5899
Prix Mottart   5900
Prix Narcisse Michaut   5901
Prix Pierre Benoit   5909
Prix Pierre de Regnier   5910
Prix Roland de Jouvenal   5917
Prix SGDL des Arts   6294
Prix SGDL du Roman   6297
Marcel Proust Prize   6182
Strasbourg Prizes and Gold Medal   7126

Friendship See Brotherhood

Furniture (See also Interior design; Industrial design)
The Daily Mail Awards of Excellence   2727
New Designers   3027

Gardening See Horticulture

Gastronomy See Food; Restaurants

Genealogy
Prix Paul Adam-Even   943
Julian Bickersteth Memorial Medal   3104
D. F. du Toit Malherbe Prize for Genealogical Research   10987
Alexander Henderson Award   227
Eoin O'Mahony Bursary   7844
Prix Amerlinck   944
Prix Arvid Berghman   945
Prix Riquer   946

Genetics
Darwin - Wallace Medals   3586
Gabor Medal   4150
Japan Society of Human Genetics Award   8641
Kihara Award   8529
Prix Joseph Schepkens   1027

Geochemistry
Verdeyen Prize for Soil Mechanics   1363

Geographic education
Commission Geographical Education Awards   6960

Geography (See also Cartography; Exploration; Geographic education)
Academico Honorario   7238
Associateship of the Society   10628
Back Award   4006
Vitus Bering Medal   1997
Hans Bobek Preis   779
Bronze Medal   11053
W. S. Bruce Medal   10639

Prix Georges Bruel   6135
Busk Medal   4007
Centenary Medal   10629
Agustin Codazzi Medal   1718
Congress Prizes   3393
Admiral Gago Coutinho Prize   10317
Andre H. Dumont Medal   1057
Egede Medal   1998
Fellow
    Royal Geographical Society of Queensland   616
    South African Geographical Society   11054
Fennia Gold Medal   4712
Fennia Silver Medal   4713
Fondation Aime Laussedat   5478
Fondation Binoux   5504
Fondation Gay   5565
Fondation Jacques Bourcart   5587
Fondation Jean Lebrun   1003
Founder's Medal   4008
Galathea Medal   1999
Geographical Award   4009
Gill Memorial   4010
Gold Award   10146
Gold Medal
    Chilean Society of History and Geography   1557
    South African Geographical Society   11055
Grand Prix Litteraire de Madagascar   4921
Edward Heath Award   4011
Honorary Fellow   10630
Honorary Member
    Chilean Society of History and Geography   1558
    Polish Geographical Society   10147
    Royal Danish Geographical Society   2000
Ragnar Hult Medal   4714
Laureat d'Honneur of the International Geographical Union   6958
Deak Lazar Memorial Medal   7310
Livingstone Gold Medal   10631
Medaille d'Or   11906
Medal of the Polish Geographical Society   10148
Medal of the Tokyo Geographical Society   8766
Medallas de Geografia Fisica, Humana, Economica   10016
Simion Mehedinti Prize   10366
Mungo Park Medal   10632
Murchison Award   4013
Gheorghe Murgoci Prize   10370
Mrs. Patrick Ness Award   4014
Newbigin Prize   10633
Niels Nielsen Award   2001
Patron's Medal   4015
Pocasni Clan   1400
Cuthbert Peek Award   4016
President's Award   10634
Prix du Duc de Loubat   5453
Prix Saintour   5790
Royal Society of Victoria Medal   638
Scottish Geographical Medal   10635
J. P. Thomson Medal   617
Victoria Medal   4017
Franz von Hauer Medaille   780
D. N. Wadia Medal   7678
Belisario Ruiz Wilches Award   1719

Geology and paleontology (See also Geochemistry; Geophysics; Photogrammetry; Seismology)
Aberconway Medal   2919
Major John Sacheverell A'Deane Coke Medal   2920

Akzo prijs   9389
Awards and Grants   1958
Bhatnagar Award   7532
Bigsby Medal   2921
Bourse Prince Rainier III de Monaco   5935
W. S. Bruce Medal   10639
Carlos Teixeira Prize   10245
Ceresis Award   10018
Clarke Medal   623
Clarke Memorial Lectureship   624
Grigore Cobalcescu Prize   10341
Corstorphine Medal   10867
Crafoord Prize   11537
Sir Charles Darwin International Medal for Science and Environment   7717
Draper Memorial Medal   10868
Alex L. Du Toit Memorial Lecturer   10869
Andre H. Dumont Medal   1057
Ehrenmitglied   6533
Carl Engler Medal   6861
Professor Gunnar Erdtman International Award for Palynology   7718
Eskola Medal   4716
Major Edward D'Ewes Fitzgerald Coke Medal   2922
Fondation Andre C. Bonnet   5488
Fondation Charles Jacob   5517
Fondation Cuvier   5526
Fondation Delesse   5537
Fondation Demolombe   5538
Fondation Fontannes   5557
Fondation Georges Deflandre et Marthe Deflandre-Rigaud   5567
Fondation Georges Millot   5568
Fondation Henry Wilde   5583
Fondation James Hall   5589
Fondation Jean Cuvillier   5593
Fondation Joseph Labbe   5603
Fondation Leon Lutaud   5618
Fondation Louis Armand   5621
Fondation Lucien Cayeux   5624
Fondation Paul Bertrand   5643
Fondation Paul Fallot-Jeremine   5645
Fondation Victor Raulin   5676
Foreign Honorary Fellow   5132
Sue Tyler Friedman Medal   2923
Geologiska Foreningens Medaljfondsstipendium   11460
Otto Glogau Award   9767
Gold Medal   9993
Assar Haddings pris   11515
Hector Memorial Medal and Prize   9838
G. Vernon Hobson Bequest   3339
Arthur-Holmes Medal   5133
Honorary Member
  Geological Society of South Africa   10870
  International Union for Quaternary Research   3489
Honours Award   10871
Hutton Memorial Medal and Prize   9839
ICTA DuPont Award   3388
International Association of Engineering Geology Awards   5965
International Geological L. A. Spendiarov Prize of the USSR Academy of Sciences   10418
International Prize   5301
Jubilee Medal   10872
Keith Medal   10645
Korrespondierendes Mitglied   6534
Lyell Medal   2924
Mansel-Pleydell and Cecil Trusts   2749
Mawson Lecture   177
Ludovic Mrazec Prize   10369
Mueller Medal   190
Murchison Medal   2925
Gheorghe Murgoci Prize   10370

Nagroda im. Henryka Swidzinskiego   10150
Nagroda im. Ludwika Zejsznera   10151
Kevin Nash Gold Medal   3473
Edgar Pam Fellowship   3342
Bruce-Preller Prize Lectureship   10648
Premio Florentino Ameghino   28
Premio Giorgio Dal Piaz   8427
Premio Ricardo Monge Lopez   9289
Premio Union Geofisca Mexicana   9290
President's Awards   2926
Prestwich Medal   2927
Prix Barbier   5303
Prix Baron Van Ertborn   1010
Prix Barrabe   5304
Prix de Lamothe   5305
Prix Fondation Pierre Pruvost   5306
Prix Fontannes   5307
Prix Gaudry   5308
Prix Georges Millot   5309
Prix Gosselet   5310
Prix Henri Buttgenbach   1024
Prix Jacques Bourcart   5311
Prix Leon Bertrand   5312
Prix Paul Fourmarier   1034
Prix Prestwich   5313
Prix Raymond et Madeleine Furon   5314
Prix Viquesnel   5315
Prix Wegmann   5316
Royal Society of Victoria Medal   638
Saltire Society and The Royal Bank of Scotland - Scottish Science Award   10657
Service Award of Chamber of Geological Engineers   12047
Servicios Distinguidos   12144
William Smith Medal   2928
Steno Medal   1950
Prix van Straelen   5317
David Syme Research Prize   697
Thorarinsson Medal   500
Trento International Film Festival of Mountain and Exploration   8460
Van Waterschoot van der Gracht Plaque   9588
Karl Alfred von Zittel Medaille   6535
D. N. Wadia Medal   7678
L. R. Wager Prize   501
Alfred-Wegener Medal   5135
Frederick White Prize   181
Wollaston Medal   2929
R. H. Worth Prize   2930

Geophysics (*See also* **Physics; Geology and paleontology**)
Sir David Bates Medal   6715
Best First Presentation   7285
Best Papers of the Year   7286
Guy Bomford Prize   5967
Butsuri-Tansa Gakkai-sho   8756
Chapman Medal   3937
Charles Chree Medal and Prize   3187
East European Support Award   6716
EGS Badge Award   6717
Laszlo Egyed Memorial Award   7287
Carl Engler Medal   6861
Lorand Eotvos Memorial Medal   7288
European Geophysical Society Honorary Membership   6718
Fondation Antoine d'Abbadie   5493
Gold Medal   3939
Hagedoorn Award   9406
Stefan Hepites Prize   10354
Honorary Membership   7289
Milutin Milankovitch Medal   6719
Price Medal   3942
Prix Barrabe   5304
Prix Fondation Pierre Pruvost   5306
Prix Georges Millot   5309

Prix Gosselet   5310
Prix Jacques Bourcart   5311
Prix Leon Bertrand   5312
J. Renner Memorial Award   7290
Royal Society of Victoria Medal   638
Conrad Schlumberger Award   9407
Van Weelden Award   9408
D. N. Wadia Medal   7678
Young Scientists Publication Awards   6720
Young Scientists Travel Awards   6721

Geriatrics (*See also* **Gerontology**)
A. C. Comfort Memorial Award   4238
Philip Davis Prize in Old Age Psychiatry   3960
Prof. Surindar Mohan Marwah Award   7594
Theodor Naegeli Prize   6880
Sandoz Prize for Gerontological Research   7418
Fund Professor Doctor G. Verdonk   1320

Gerontology (*See also* **Geriatrics**)
Lord Cohen of Birkenhead Medal   2517
Theodor Naegeli Prize   6880
Sandoz Prize for Gerontological Research   7418

Glass (*See also* **Ceramics**)
Bibby Cup   2533
British Glass Manufacturers Confederation Awards   2354
Norman Collins Memorial Award   2534
David Flack Memorial Trophy   2535
Literary Prizes   2536
Medaille des Arts Plastiques   4784
Lucy Oldfield Cup (Premier Award)   2537
Royal Dublin Society Crafts Competition   7835
Thames Valley Award   2538
TSL Trophy   2539
A. D. Wood Cup   2540

Golf
Peter Alliss and Roy Beckett Crystal Rose Bowl   3673
ASEAN Award for Visual Arts   10032
British Open Golf Champion   10597
Championship Silver Challenge Trophy   3674
Divisional Team Championships   4567
Golfer of the Year   2129
Individual Championships   4568
Japan Golf Championships   8617
Ladies' British Open Amateur Championship   10588
Lord Derby's Knowsley Safari Park Tournament   3808
National Pro-Am Championship   3809
Jack Nicklaus Best Junior Golfer   8618
PGA Club Professional Championship   3810
PGA Cup   3811
PGA Fourball Championship   3812
PGA Junior Championship   3813
PGA National Assistants' Championship   3814
PGA Pro-Am Matchplay Championship   3815
PGA Pro-Captain Challenge   3816
PGA Regional Team Championship   3817
PGA Seniors' Championship   3818
Ryder Cup   3819
Ryle Memorial Medal   3820
Braid Taylor Memorial Medal   3821
Teachers Scramble   4489
Tooting Bec Cup   3822
Harry Vardon Trophy   3823
Whitcombe-Cox Trophy   3824
Women's British Open Championship   10589

Government

Government service (*See also* **Public service**)
Cacique's Crown of Honor 7243
European Prize for Statesmanship 7109
King's Cross for Distinguished Service 9918
Ramon Magsaysay Awards 10042
Marianne d'Or 6099
Medal for Civic Virtue 9920
Medal of Service 7251
Order of Merit of the Republic of Poland 10117
Order of the Rebirth of Poland 10119
Padma Bhushan 7554
Padma Shri 7555
Padma Vibhushan 7556
Prix Territoria 6100

Graphic arts
Gerardo Arellano Cultural Merit Medal 1651
ARTA Magazine Awards 10394
ASEAN Award for Visual Arts 10032
Association of Finnish Graphic Design Awards 4718
Bienal Internacional del Cartel en Mexico 9285
Thorvald Bindesboll Medal 1896
British Press Awards 4561
Concurso Nacional de Artes Plasticas - Grafica (Mini Estampa) 9210
Concurso Nacional para Estudiantes de Artes Plasticas en Aguascalientes 9211
Excellence Awards 3395
Forderpreis des Landes Nordrhein-Westfalen fur junge Kunstlerinnen und Kunstler 7026
Grand Prix National des Arts Graphique 5287
Grand Prix of Honour for a Yugoslav Artist 10794
International Biennial of Graphic Art 10795
International Calligraphy Competition 12056
International Design Competition, Osaka 8606
International Visual Communications Association Awards 3502
Internationaler Plakatpreis fur Figurentheater 6675
Eugene Kolb Prize 7967
Monte Carlo International Forum for New Images Imagina 9321
National Akademi Award 7534
National Award for Painting and Graphics 9990
Nederlandse Grafiekprijs 9623
Osterreichischer Graphikwettbewerb 729
Preseren Award 10799
President's Trophy 3396
Prix Ars Electronica 772
Prix de Rome 9578
Prize for Graphic Arts 10399
Royal Dublin Society Crafts Competition 7835
Salon Nacional de Artes Plasticas - Graphic Art 9244
Salon Nacional de Artes Plasticas - Graphica (Interpretacion del Quijote de la Mancha) 9245
Santa Rosa Award 1475
Scandinavian Design Prize 11652
Scottish Designer of the Year Award 10531
SGD Swiss Graphic Designers 11904
Storywriting and Art Project 417
Triennale-India Award of Lalit Kala Akademi 7535
Konrad-von-Soest-Preis 7029

Awards, Honors & Prizes, 1995-96

Greek culture
Academy of Athens Medal 7181
Excursions and Journeys in Greece Award 7219
Gold Medal of the Academy of Greece 7202
Greek National Tourist Organization Awards 7198
Historic Novel Award 7220
National Science, Literature and Art Prize 7183
Prix Alfred Croiset 5434
Prix Ambatielos 5437
Prix de Chenier 5443
Prix Gustave Mendel 5461

Gymnastics
El Heraldo Sport Prizes 9022

Gypsies
Prix Romanes International 6114

Hairstyling
Guild-CAT National Open Presentation Trophy 2963
Guild College Fantasy Championship 2964
Guild under "18" Styling Award 2965
Men's National Young Hairstyling Championship 2966
National Young Hairstyling Championship 2967

Handball
Hans-Baumann-Trophy 11799
European Cup Competitions 11800
World Championships 11801

Handicapped (*See also* **Blindness; Deafness; Mentally disabled; Rehabilitation and therapy; Speech and hearing**)
3M Talking Book of the Year 612
Apple Tree Award 3691
Decorations 6946
Disability Award 8801
DPI-ACOPIM Journalism Award 1684
Harding Award 2037
IEE Prize for Helping Disabled People 3286
Jose M. Jorge Prize 84
Korea Polio Association Awards 8820
Oita International Wheelchair Marathon 8711
James D. Wolfensohn Award 3419
Young Deaf Achiever 2732

Health and fitness
Dower Prize 3048
Armando Kaminitz Research Awards 7981
Prof. Henry Neufeld Memorial Research Grant 7976
Catharina Pijlsprijs 9683
Premio Gea Gonzalez - PUIC 9024
Prix 2000 SG 6384
Prix Sante Publique 5940

Health care (*See also* **Health and fitness; Health education; Health care administration; Hospital administration; Medicine; Preventive medicine**)
Jorge Bejarano Civic Medal for Health and Welfare Merits 1667
Lord Cohen Award 4226
Egyptian Red Crescent Society Competitions 2021
Prix Eugene Etienne 6139
Gold Medal 4227
Grand Prior's Trophies 3742
Wahidin Sudiro Husodo Award 7727

International Festival of Red Cross and Health Films 1528
Aboim Sande Lemos Prize 10254
Life-Saving Medal of the Order 3743
Premio Domenico Marotta 8381
Prix Melsens 1337
Rogers Prize 4638
Sasakawa Health Prize 11975
Service Medal of the Order 3745
Special Awards 2659
John Edward Worth Prize 4229

Health care administration
Baxter Award for Healthcare Management in Europe 7775

Health education
CIERSES Awards 6022
T. P. Gunton Award 2437
International Festival of Red Cross and Health Films 1528
Kenko Yuryo Gakko Hyosho 8495
Mauriac International Medical Film Festival 6112
Prix Sante et Entreprise 5036

Hearing *See* **Speech and hearing**

Helicopters
Airtour Sword 2999
Auto-Alloys Precision Trophy 3000
Babcock and Wilcox Trophy 3001
British Helicopter Advisory Board (BHAB) Trophy 3002
Everard Trophy 3003
Famous Grouse Trophy 3004
Helicopter Club of Great Britain Championship Trophy 3005
Imperial Tobacco Trophy 3006
Livingston and Doughty Trophy 3007
Alan Marsh Award 3895
Alan Marsh Medal 3896
Precision Timing Trophy 3008

Heroism
Albert Medal 2358
Ashok Chakra 7547
Australian Bravery Decorations 207
Award for Valour 2299
Awards for Bravery 10832
Binney Memorial Award 2945
Cacique's Crown of Valor 7244
Castle of Good Hope Decoration 10922
Certificate of Commendation 4100
Condecoracion al Merito Social 9013
Conspicuous Gallantry Medal 10738
Cross of Merit for Bravery 10102
Cross of Merit with Swords 10103
Cross of Valour 10106
Cruz de Boyaca 1618
Decoration for Distinguished Service in the South African Railways Police Force 10950
Diploma for Outstanding Airmanship 5143
Distinguished Service Medal 7789
Distinguished Service Order 2366
Edward Medal 2367
Fondation du General Muteau 5547
Gallantry Decorations 342
George Cross 2368
George Medal 2369
Golden Arrow of Courage 7250
Grand Prix d'Honneur 11825
Honoris Crux 10928
Honoris Crux Diamond 10929
Honoris Crux Gold 10930
Honoris Crux Silver 10931
Jeevan Raksha Padak 7551

King's Cross for Distinguished Service 9918
Kirti Chakra 7552
Life-Saving Honorary Medal 7402
Life-Saving Medal of the Order 3743
Maha Vir Chakra 7553
Medaille Henry Dunant 11915
Medal for a Noble Deed 9919
Medal for Brave Performance in Mining 740
Medal for Bravery
 Colombia - Ministry of Justice 1629
 Republic of South Africa - South African Railways Police 10951
Medal for Courage 8915
Medal for Self-Sacrifice and Courage 10111
Medal for Valour 10741
Medalla al Valor 1674
Medals for Acts of Distinction 8369
Medals of Honor 8585
Military Medal for Gallantry 7790
Military Order of William 9355
Mountbatten Medal 4101
National Order of the Liberation 5238
Florence Nightingale Medal 11771
Order of the Red Banner 10466
Outstanding Young Citizen Award 7882
Fred M. Packard International Parks Merit Award/Commission on Parks and Protected Areas 11970
Pakistan Military Awards 9996
Param Vir Chakra 7557
Polaris Award 3410
Police Medal for Valour 10746
Premio Luis Elizondo - Premio Humanitario 8990
Premio Miguel Hidalgo 9141
President's Commendation for Brave Conduct 7256
Prix Courage Quotidien 5098
Prix d'Honneur Courage Quotidien 5099
Prix Dulac 5736
Prix Eugene Salvan 5743
Provincial Police Award 2112
Quaid-i-Azam Police Medal for Gallantry 9997
Queen's Gallantry Medal 2382
Righteous Among the Nations 7995
Royal Humane Society Awards 4066
Sarvotten Jeevan Raksha Padak 7560
Sea Gallantry Medal 2386
Shaurya Chakra 7561
South African Police Cross for Valour 10952
South African Railways Police Medal for Combating Terrorism 10953
Star for Merit in the South African Railways Police Force 10956
Star of Temasek 10750
Trinity Cross of the Order of the Trinity 12036
Uttam Jeevan Raksha Padak 7562
Victoria Cross 2387
Victoria Cross for Australia 348
Vir Chakra 7563
War Order Virtuti Militari 10123
Woltemade Cross for Bravery 10963

Higher education
AFUW-SA Inc. Trust Fund Bursary 216
Association of Southeast Asian Institutions of Higher Learning Awards 12019
Australian College of Education Medal 201
Thenie Baddams Bursary 217
Concord Press Award for Academic Publishing 9861
Concurso la Mejor Tesis sobre la Mujer in la UNAM 9173
Condecoracion del Merito Universitario 1751

Distincion Felix Restrepo 1740
Ethicon Fellowship 10599
Fellowship of the Australian College of Education 202
Jean Gilmore Bursary 218
Harkness Fellowships 2985
IAHR Lecturer Award 9460
Medellin University Prize 1752
Orden Universidad Javeriana 1741
Premio Municipal Trabalho e Estudo 10278
Society for Research into Higher Education Awards 4368
Georgina Sweet Fellowship 212
Thouron Fellowship 10683
Watson Prize Lecture 10602

Highway safety
Automobilclub Von Deutschland Awards 6549
Awards 8547
SARF Bursary 11095

Hiking *See* **Recreation**

Hispanic culture
Hispanic Culture Gold Medal 53
Medalla Instituto Colombiano de Cultura 1713
Guillermo Valencia Prize for Hispanic Culture 1621

Historic preservation (*See also* **Monument restoration**)
AIA Award for Fieldwork 2105
AIA Conference Award 2106
Annual Prize for Best Restoration Program 5106
APRS Annual Award 10506
Australian Heritage Award 204
Award of Merit 10828
Badge for the Protection of Monuments 10088
Concours de Sauvegarde Vieilles Maisons Francaises 6467
Dorothea Award for Conservation 2107
Europa Nostra Awards 9402
European Prize for the Preservation of Historic Monuments 7110
FCI Competition Essay 2864
Gazzola Prize 6001
Heritage in Britain Award 2247
ICCROM Award 8286
International Association for the Protection of Monuments and Restoration of Buildings Awards 6934
Ironbridge Award 2248
King of Prussia's Gold Medal 3015
Maritime Heritage Award Medal 4628
Medaille de la Restauration 4778
Medals of Honour 9404
Onassis Prize for Culture, Arts and Humanities 7208
Premio Francisco de la Maza 9054
Premio Internazionale Paolo Gatto 8076
Premio Manuel Toussaint 9058
Premio Paul Coremans 9062
Premio Umberto Zanotti Bianco 8361
Prix Henri Texier II 5756
Prix Master Foods des Demeures Historiques 1052
Prix Paul de Pessemier 1053
Elies Rogent Video Competition on Rehabilitation and Restoration 11207
Rural Wales Award 12164
Simon Van der Stel Foundation Medal 11119
Jozef Van Ginderachter Prize 1278

History (*See also* **Antiquity; Biography; Culture; Genealogy; Historic preservation; History of dentistry; History of medicine; History of pharmacy; History of science; History of technology; Medieval studies; Monument restoration; Social science research**)
Academico Honorario 7238
The Age Book of the Year Awards 118
Alexander Prize 4019
Amsterdam Prize 9451
Anderson Prize Essay 4366
Australian Society of Archivists Award 267
Australian/Vogel Literary Award 120
Award for Historical Works Pertaining to Justus-Liebig University 6997
Awards 3795
Awards in History 9724
Awards in Oral History 9725
Arthur Azevedo Prize 1421
Nicolae Balcescu Prize 10333
Bangkok Bank Prize for Thai Literature Competition 12022
Gheorghe Baritiu Prize 10334
Augusto Botelho da Costa Veiga Prize 10300
BP Prize Lectureship in the Humanities 10638
Prix Georges Bruel 6135
Bucharest Writers Association Award 10411
Category A Fellowships 155
Category B Fellowships 156
CNA Literary Award 10830
Laranjo Coelho Prize 10246
Duff Cooper Prize 2686
J. Coppens Prize 1253
Correspondent Membership 4698
Dr. M. Aylwin Cotton Foundation Fellowship Awards 2688
Dr. M. Aylwin Cotton Foundation Publication Grants 2689
C. H. Currey Memorial Fellowship 683
Cutty Sark Medal 3633
Dawood Prize for Literature 10005
C. De Clercq Prize 1254
Abilio Lopes do Rego Prize 10250
Aquileo J. Echeverria Prize 1761
Prof. Leon Elaut Prize 1271
Fellowship of the Scottish Tartans Society 10679
Fellowships and Scholarships 146
Festival dei Popoli 8239
Fondation Henri Pirenne 976
Fondation Thorlet 5710
Fondazione Premio Dotte Giuseppe Borgia 8063
Fraenkel Prize in Contemporary History 3086
Fundacion del Premio Fastenrath 11345
Gottingen Academy of Sciences Prize 6903
Gottingen Academy of Sciences Prize for German History 6906
GPA Book Award 7777
Grand Prix de l'Academie des Sciences Morales et Politiques 5711
Grand Prix de l'Histoire - Moet-Hennessy 6120
Grand Prix Litteraire de Madagascar 4921
Grand Prix National d'Histoire 5290
Grands Prix Litteraire de la Ville de Paris 6095
Calouste Gulbenkian Prizes for History 10303
Axel Hirschs pris 11594
Historical Literature Award 8740
Hodgson Prize 3893
Honorary Fellow 10681

History — Awards, Honors & Prizes, 1995-96

History (continued)
- Honorary Member 268
- Eudoxiu Hurmuzachi Prize 10356
- Inter Nations Culture Prize 6927
- Nicolae Iorga Prize 10360
- Italian Minister for Culture and the Environment Prizes 8365
- Genyoshi Kadokawa Prize 8679
- Kellgrenpriset 11596
- King Abdul Aziz Prize 10494
- Mihail Kogalniceau Prize 10361
- Antonio Larragoiti Prize
  - Brazilian Academy of Letters 1423
  - Lisbon Academy of Sciences 10253
- Jessie Litchfield Award 557
- Agnes Mure MacKenzie Award 10655
- Mansel-Pleydell and Cecil Trusts 2749
- Somerset Maugham Awards 4390
- Norton Medlicott Medal 3017
- Mythic Society Scholar 7713
- Nagrada Saveta Fonda SO SUBNOR Cetvrti jul 10707
- National Prize for History 1661
- National Prize for History, Social Sciences and Philosophy 9147
- National Prize in Science and Art 9152
- National Prize of the President of the Republic 8068
- National Science, Literature and Art Prize 7183
- Dimitrie Onciul Prize 10373
- Pakistan Civil Awards 9995
- Vasile Parvan Prize 10376
- Thomas Eric Peet Travelling Prize 4576
- Samuel Pepys Medal 2764
- Premio Academia Nacional de la Historia 17
- Premio Editorial Costa Rica 1770
- Premio Enrique Pena 18
- Premio Francisco de la Maza 9054
- Premio Francisco Javier Clavijero 9055
- Premio Manuel Toussaint 9058
- Premio Marcos y Celia Mauss 9194
- Premio Mario di Nola 8078
- Premio Municipal Julio de Castilho de Olisipografia 10274
- Premio Nacional de Historia 1547
- Premio Nacional de Historia de Espana 11373
- Premio Rafael Heliodoro Valle 9249
- Premios Literarios Nacionais 1474
- Prijs voor Meesterschap 9630
- Prix Adolf Bentinck 6160
- Prix Alberic Rocheron 5807
- Prix Ambatielos 5437
- Prix Auguste Gerard 5716
- Prix Aujourd'hui 6162
- Prix Cazes-Brasserie Lipp 6164
- Prix Charles and Marguerite Diehl 5441
- Prix Charles Clermont-Ganneau 5442
- Prix Charles Duvivier 980
- Prix Charles Lyon-Caen 5725
- Prix Constant de Horion 1041
- Prix de la Resistance 5044
- Prix de M. et Mme. Louis Marin 5837
- Prix de Saint-Genois 982
- Prix de Stassart 983
- Prix de Stassart pour Histoire Nationale 984
- Prix Demolombe 5731
- Prix Diane Potier-Boes 5839
- Prix Drouyn de Lhuys 5732
- Prix du Budget 5734
- Prix du Duc de Loubat 5453
- Prix du Livre Historique d'Investigation - Les Libertes d'Or 5219
- Prix Dupin Aine 5737
- Prix Ernest Discailles 986
- Prix Estrade-Delcros 5742
- Prix Eugene Lameere 987
- Prix Eugene Piccard 5852
- Prix France-Acadie 4894
- Prix Gabriel-Auguste Prost 5458
- Prix Gabriel Monod 5746
- Prix Gaston Maspero 5459
- Prix Georges Mauguin 5750
- Prix Gustave Chaix d'Est Ange 5753
- Prix Gustave Schlumberger 5462
- Prix Hercule Catenacci
  - Institut de France 5343
  - Institut de France - Academie des Sciences Morales et Politiques 5757
  - Institut de France - Academie Francaise 5867
- Prix Jacques Flach 5758
- Prix Jean Reynaud 5762
- Prix Joseph du Teil 5763
- Prix Jules Duculot 994
- Prix Koenigswarter 5770
- Prix Lavalleye-Coppens 964
- Prix Le Dissez de Penanrun 5771
- Prix Leon Leclere 995
- Prix Limantour 5774
- Prix Litteraire de l'Asie 4927
- Prix Litteraire des Mascareignes, des Seychelles et des Comores 4929
- Prix Marcel Flach 5781
- Prix Marie-Eugene Simon Henri Martin 5893
- Prix Maurice Travers 5783
- Prix Monseigneur Marcel 5898
- Prix Paul-Michel Perret 5786
- Prix Roman et Tania Ghirshman 5471
- Prix Saintour 5790
- Prix SGDL du Livre d'Histoire 6295
- Prix Sola-Cabiati 6097
- Prix Suzanne Tassier 997
- Prix Therouanne 5922
- Prix Thiers 5923
- Prix Toutain 5925
- Prix Victor Cousin 5794
- Prix XVII Siecle 6346
- Prix Yvan Loiseau 5931
- Regional Production Prizes 23
- Romanian Writers' Union Prizes 10414
- Routledge Ancient History Prize 3861
- Royal Australian Historical Society Competitions 607
- Royal Society of Literature Award 4233
- Mohamed Sahabdeen Award for Literature 11417
- Birger Scholdstroms pris 11600
- Schuckska priset 11601
- Scientific Secretary of the Polish Academy of Sciences Award 10128
- Stephan Shaumian Prize 113
- J. M. Sherrard Awards 9709
- Society of the Friends of History Award 4756
- Lee Steere History Essay Competition 644
- Suntory Prize for Social Sciences and Humanities 8764
- Svenska Akademiens nordiska pris 11606
- Dirk Jacob Veegens-Prijs 9394
- G. Vitelli Prize 8332
- Wolfson Foundation Literary Awards for History 4608
- Alexandru Xenopol Prize 10392
- Zibetska priset 11612

History, art See Art history

History, business See Business history

History, church See Church history

History, English See English history

History, European See European history

History, French See French history

History, Italian See Italian history

History, Jewish See Jewish history

History, Latin American See Latin American history

History, library See Library history

History, military See Military history

History of art See Art history

History of dentistry
- C. E. Wallis Lecture 4270

History of medicine
- Alvarenga do Piaui (Brasil) Prize 10249
- Fondation Mege 5631
- Prix du Docteur Frans Johnckheere sur l'Historie de la Medecine 1330
- Prix Jean-Francois Coste 4849

History of pharmacy
- Schelenz Plaque 6986
- Ludwig Winkler Plaque 6987

History of science
- Dr. Enrique Beltran Prize of the History of Science and Technology 9122
- Fondation Binoux 5504
- J. Gillis Prize 1256
- Alexander Koyre Medal 5949
- Kuwait Prize 8844
- Partington Prize 4374
- Prix Franz Cumont 988
- Prize for Young Historians of Science 5950
- Singer Prize 2523
- TWAS History of Science Prize 8455

History of technology
- Dr. Enrique Beltran Prize of the History of Science and Technology 9122

Hobbies and clubs (See also Animal care and training; Automobiles; Crafts; Genealogy; Horticulture; Numismatics; Philately; Photography; Recreation)
- Crossword Champion 2641
- Crossword Club Competitions 2722
- IOF Pins of Honour 11477
- National Bottle Show Champion 3733
- National Model Car Racing Champion 2505

Hockey
- Asian Winter Games, Sapporo 8713
- Championnats d'Europe de Rink-Hockey 5118
- Divisional Team Championships 4567
- International Ice Hockey Federation Competition 11803
- Team Championships (non-divisional) 4569

Horse racing
- National Hunt Champion Award 3834
- Racehorse of the Year Award 3835

Horsemanship
- Annual Awards 2493

Breed Horse Show Awards 2544
British Appaloosa Society National Champions 2240
British Show Pony Society Rosettes 2500
Cubitt Award 3797
Dublin Horse Show 7834
Federation Equestre Internationale Awards 11780
Fell Pony Society Ridden Championship 10545
National Champion Challenge Cup 2241
NPS Medal of Honour 3701
NPS Stud Assistant's Certificate 3702
Perpetual Trophy Awards 2494
Show Hunter Ponies Awards 2501
Show Ponies Awards 2502
Supreme Champion Awards 2545
Working Hunter Ponies Awards 2503

Horticulture
Affiliated Societies' Cup 4023
Associates of Honour 4024
Lady Astor Presidents Cup 2470
Award of Merit Scheme 4339
Peter Barr Memorial Cup 4025
Bowles Cup 4026
British National Carnation Society Award 2726
Certificate of Honour 2057
Stephenson R. Clarke Cup 4027
Reginald Cory Memorial Cup 4028
Crosfield Cup 4029
Lionel de Rothschild Cup 4030
Delphinium Society Awards 2736
Devonshire Trophy 4031
Dublin Horse Show 7834
E. H. Trophy 4032
Engleheart Cup 4033
Farrer Trophy 4034
Fleuroselect Gold Medal 9428
Foremarke Cup 4035
Franco-British Landscape Gardening Award 2907
Gladiolia Society Award 2728
Gordon-Lennox Cup 4036
Grand Prix SOPEXA du Sommelier 5228
Grand Prize of AIPM/Grand Prize of Excellence 9467
Holford Medal 4037
Honorary Fellow 4038
International Floral Decoration Competition 1067
Jones-Bateman Cup 4039
Lawrence Medal 4040
Leonardslee Bowl 4041
Loder Cup 4042
Loder Rhododendron Cup 4043
Long-Service Medal 4044
Lyttel Lily Cup 4045
Lyttel Trophy 2058
McLaren Cup 4046
George Monro Memorial Cup 4047
George Moore Medal 4048
Premi internazionali vitivinicoli 8092
President's International Trophy 4109
RHS Vegetable Cup 4049
Richardson Trophy 4050
Riddell Trophy for Vegetables 4051
Mrs. F. E. Rivis Prize 4052
Rose Gold Medal 109
Rose Pin 110
Rosette Awards 4340
Rosse Cup 4053
Rothschild Challenge Cup 4054
Royal Bath and West Scholarship Awards (World and European) 3947
Sewell Medal 4055
Simmonds Medal 4056
Roza Stevenson Cup 4057
Veitch Memorial Medal 4058
Victoria Medal of Honour in Horticulture - V.M.H. 4059
A. J. Waley Medal 4060
Westonbirt Orchid Medal 4061
Wigan Cup 4062
Williams Memorial Medal 4063
Guy Wilson Memorial Vase 4064
Eric Young Trophy 3740

Hospital administration
Essay Competition 7620
Coronel Medico Jorge Esguerra Lopez Award 1708

Hotels See Travel

Housing
Economics Prize 1226
Housing Design Awards 4068
IFHP International Film/Video Competition 9486
IFHP International Student Competition 9487
Law Prize 1228
Sociology Prize 1229

Human engineering
Ulf Aberg Post Graduate Award 2798
Applications Award 2799
Sir Frederic Bartlett Medal 2800
Otto Edholm Award 2801
Ergonomics Society Special Award 2802
Ergonomics Society's Meritorious Service Award 2803
Honorary Fellow 2804
Hywel Murrell Award 2805
President's Medal 2806
Society Lecturer 2808

Human relations
Simon Bolivar Medal 1653
Hedwig-Burgheim Medaille 7040
Dobinson Award 2695
E. Du Perron Award 9674
Gottlieb Duttweiler Prize 11740
Friendship Medal 10430
Haifa Prize 7878
Heinrich Heine Prize 6686
International Award for the Furtherance of Human Understanding 11686
International Simon Bolivar Prize 6415
Kulturpreis der Stadt Dortmund - Nelly-Sachs-Preis 7096
Olof Palme Memorial Fund Scholarships 11506
Olof Palme Prize 11507
Prix Paul Vigne d'Octon 5787
Rose of Tralee 7827
Mohamed Sahabdeen Award for International Understanding 11416
Vaughn - Ueda Prize 8629

Human resource management See Personnel management

Human rights (See also Civil rights and liberties)
Award for Human Rights in Europe 11454
Awards 1355
Commission for the Defense of Human Rights in Central America Awards 1759
Competitions 8104
Concurso Anual de Tesis Profesionales 8937
European Human Rights Prize 5093
European Parliament Sakharov Prize for Freedom of Thought 2841
Frihedspris 1989
Heinrich Heine Prize 6686
Human Rights Medal 6026
Human Rights Prize 11953
Inter-American Institute of Human Rights Awards 1779
Dr. Frantisek Kriegel Prize 11449
Ross McWhirter Foundation Awards 4613
Airey Neave Research Award 3718
Onassis Competition for the Letters, the Sciences and the Arts 7207
Premio Derechos Humanos 9191
Premio Facultad de Derecho a la Mejor Tesis 9192
Premio Felipe Tena Ramirez 9193
Prince of Asturias Prizes 11248
Prix des droits de l'homme 5251
Right Livelihood Award 11509
Soroptimist International of the South West Pacific Awards 668
UNESCO Human Rights Prize 6034
UNESCO Prize for the Teaching of Human Rights 6426

Humanitarianism
Antarjatik Beshamarik Sheba Sangstha Competitions 932
Asahi Shakai Fukushi Sho 8491
Blekinge County Council Culture Prize 11446
Miguel Antonio Caro and Rufino Jose Cuervo National Order 1711
Fondation Bordin 5506
Fondation Gabrielle Sand 5563
Galardon Estado de Mexico 9008
Hanseatic Goethe Prize 7112
Gold Medal 7206
International Dag Hammarskjold Award 1237
International Institute for Promotion and Prestige Awards 11805
International Institute of Humanitarian Law Prize 8307
Medals for Acts of Distinction 8369
Montaigne Prize 7117
Nansen Medal 11955
National Prize for Civic Merit 9139
Order of St. John 3744
Phenix - U.D.A. 6429
Premio Corazon de Oro 9270
Premio Luis Elizondo - Premio Humanitario 8990
Premio Miguel Hidalgo 9141
Prix d'Aschen-Presles 5340
Prix Felix de Beaujour 5745
Prix Jean Finot 5760
Prix Marie Laurent 5782
Paul Reuter Prize 11772
Fernando Rielo World Prize for Mystical Poetry 11329
Royal Norwegian Order of St. Olav 9922
Friedrich Ruckert Preis 7105
Solidarity Prize 8963
Sovereign Western Order 1370
Henrik Steffens Prize 7125

Humanities See Arts and humanities

Humanities research
Eichendorff Medal 6693
Grand Prix ICA - Prix de la Recherche Scientifique 10688
Hosei International Fund Foreign Scholars Fellowship 8537

Humanities (continued)
Reuchlinpreis der Stadt Pforzheim 7102
Oskar Seidlin Preis 6694

Humor (See also Cartoons; Entertainment)
Booby Prize 4944
Chamrousse International Festival of Comedy Films 5028
Charlie Chaplin Prize 1520
CWA Last Laugh Award 2714
Jose F. Elizondo Prize 9084
Festival International du Dessin Humoristique 6132
Festival International du Film de Comedie de Vevey 11661
Golden Aesop Prize 1521
Grand Prix de l'Humour 6253
Hitar Petar/Artful Peter/Grand Prize for Humor and Satire in Literature 1522
International Short Film Festival, Oberhausen 6984
Les Molieres 4970
Noble Prize 4945
Photo-Jokes Competition 1523
Premio Antonio de Lara "Tono" de Humor Grafico 11287
Radio Times Drama & Comedy Awards 2160
Theatre Production Prize 24
Time Out Theatre, Dance and Comedy Awards 4545

Hunting
International Council for Game and Wildlife Conservation Awards 5997

Hydrography (See also Oceanography)
Odon Bogdanfy Medal 7348
Commodore A. H. Cooper Medal 9319
Hugo Lampl Prize 7350
President's Prize 3035
Ferenc Schafarzik Medal 7351
Society Awards for Journal Articles 3036

Hypnosis
International Society for Medical and Psychological Hypnosis Awards 8311

Ice hockey See Hockey

Ice skating
Asian Winter Games, Sapporo 8713
Jacques Favart Trophy 11829
Georg Hasler Medal 11830
ISU Speed and Figure Skating Championships 11831

Illustration
AIM Children's Book Awards
  Booksellers of New Zealand 9707
  Queen Elizabeth II Arts Council of New Zealand - Literature Programme 9797
Hans Christian Andersen Awards 11767
Association of Finnish Graphic Design Awards 4718
Austrian National Book Award for Children's Literature 757
Award of the Circle of the Greek Children's Book 7188
Elsa Beskow Plaque 11632
Bird Illustrator of the Year 2292
Book Prizes of the Circle of the Greek Children's Book 7189
Catalonia Illustration Prize 11194
Children's Book Award 2874
Children's Book Council Award 7735
City of Vienna Prizes for Books for Children and Young People 790
Russell Clark Award 9761
Laurens Janszoon Coster Prize 9443
Bertram Cox Bequest 4131
Critici in Erba Prize 8171
L'udovit Fulla Prize 10765
Glenfiddich Awards 2949
Gold Paintbrush 9365
Gold Ribbon 1840
Golden Cat Award 11568
Graphics Prize Fiera di Bologna for Children and Young Adults 8172
Kate Greenaway Medal 3568
Katrine Harries Award 11058
IBBY Honour List 11769
Illustration Award 11383
Illustratorprisen 1938
International Biennial of Illustrations Bratislava 10782
International Print Biennial - Varna 1532
Kodansha Prize 8687
Rudolf Koivu Prize 4687
Lazarillo Prize 11384
Fran Levstik Prize 10807
Literature Awards for Children and Young People 9916
Macmillan Prize for a Children's Picture Book 3757
Kurt Maschler Award 2202
Apel Les Mestres Prize 11215
Mlade leta Prize 10786
Mother Goose Award 2209
National Business Calendar Awards 2483
National Prize for Illustration of Literature for Children and Young People 11370
Noma Concours for Picture Book Illustrations 8500
Noma Illustration Prizes 8689
Professor Pi-Prijs 9646
Picture Book of the Year Award 312
Premio Antoniorrobles 9120
Prix Catenacci 5367
Prix GLM 4954
Prix Hercule Catenacci
  Institut de France 5343
  Institut de France - Academie des Sciences Morales et Politiques 5757
Publieksprijs voor het Nederlandse Boek 9368
Sankei Jidoh Bunka Shuppan Shoh 8729
Shogakukan Kaiga-Sho 8748
Jenny Smelik/IBBY Prize 9387
W. H. Smith Illustration Award 4595
W. H. Smith Illustration Awards 4344
Storywriting and Art Project 417
Suomalainen kuvakirja palkinto 4669
Swedish Authors' Fund Awards 11619
Swiss Children's Book Prize 11947
TES Information Book Awards 4548
TES Schoolbook Award 4549
Triple Rose Prize 10767
Pier Paolo Vergerio European Prize for Children's Literature 8466
Verlagspreis zur Forderung popularwissenschaftlicher Literatur fur das jungere Lesealter 7152
White Ravens 6995
Young Australians Best Book Award 719

Individual rights See Civil rights and liberties

Industrial arts
Prix Joseph De Keyn 992

Industrial chemistry
Grand Prix Chimie Industrielle 6356
Industrial Lectureship 4202
Prix Frederic Swarts 1022
RSC Sponsored Awards 4219
Wolskel Industrial Chemistry Essay Award 603

Industrial design
Architecture Award 2886
Bimcam Ardley Prize 3157
Awards for Innovation 7771
Thorvald Bindesboll Medal 1896
British Design Awards 2738
Design Council British Aerospace Engineering Design Prizes 2739
Garden Machinery Annual Awards 2238
Grand Prix Amon Ra 5195
Grand Prix National de la Creation Industrielle 5275
ICSID/Compiegne Industrial Design Award 6461
International Design Competition, Osaka 8606
Kho Liang le-prijs 9641
Mexinox Prize 9158
National Design Competition for the Use of Aluminum 9018
New Designers 3027
Oscar la Villette du Jeu et Jouet a Caractere Scientifique et Technique 5009
Premi e Concorsi il Compasso d'oro 8147
Premio Beca Nacional de Diseno Industrial Clara Porset 9186
Prince Philip Prize for the Designer of the Year 2742
Redland Pitched Roof Awards 3841
Royal Designers for Industry 4323
Scottish Designer of the Year Award 10531
State Prize for Design 777
Student Lighting Design Awards 3578
Zinc Castings 86 4654

Industrial engineering
Brussels International Festival of Films on the Engineering Profession 1097
Fondation Henry Giffard 5581
Members Prize 3357
Generaldirektor Aage W. Owe's Prisbelonningsfond 9953
Premio Condumex 9187

Industries and trades (See also Business; Craftsmanship; specific industries and trades, e.g. Dairy industry)
Alejandro Angel Escobar Science Prize 1584
Australasian Corrosion Association Awards 139
Bablik Medal 2831
R. B. Bennett Commonwealth Prize 4319
Carl Bertelsmann Prize 6566
Best Apprentice Competition 5060
BIMCO/Lloyd's List Maritime Book Prize 3598
Carothers Medal 4514
Catalonian Prize for Technical Application and Industrial Products 11179
Certificates of Merit 3091
Chronicle of Komsomol Honor 10427
Communicator of the Year Award 11097
Credit Suisse Design Prize for Technical and Industrial Innovation in Geneva 11684
EGGA Pin 2832
European Disposables and Nonwovens Association Awards 1133
Fondation Ayme Poirson 5499

Fondation Petit d'Ormoy 5649
Franck Award 6054
Benjamin Franklin Medal 4322
Golden Ram Award 10901
Graduateship of the City and Guilds of London Institute 2624
Haifa Prize 7878
Hammer and Sickle Gold Medal 10460
Honorary Member
　European General Galvanizers Association 2833
　International Primary Aluminum Institute 3458
Institute of Quarrying Awards 3206
Institute of the Furniture Warehousing and Removing Industry Awards 3212
International Dag Hammarskjold Award 1237
International Industrial Film and Video Awards 2703
International Institute for Promotion and Prestige Awards 11805
International Institute of Refrigeration Prize 6028
International Union for Surface Finishing Awards 3491
Kaplan Prize 7892
Licentiateship of the City and Guilds of London Institute 2625
MAGB Malting Diploma 3625
Medals for Excellence 2626
Membership of the City and Guilds of London Institute 2627
Messel Medal and Lecture 4418
National Prize of Quality 1611
Order of Merit in Industry 1614
Premio Mixcoatl 9255
Presidents Paper Trophy Award 3508
President's Trophy - Papers Award 3487
Prix Corbay 5727
Prix de la Fondation Jean-Bernard Verlot 4949
Prix Osiris 5347
Prix Science pour l'Art - Moet-Hennessy - Louis Vuitton 6122
Professional Member 10549
Queen's Awards for Environmental Achievement 3830
Erik Rotheim Medal 1150
Royal Companies Award 11109
Silver Medal 2315
Top 100 Companies Award 11110
Trophees de l'Initiative 5104
University of Berne Prizes 11965
Vishwakarma Medal 7677
Ian William Wark Medal and Lecture 180

Information management
Annual Award for Outstanding Achievement in the Field of Information Science 3106
INFOSTA Award 8541
Fritz Kutter-Preis 11933
Rolf Nevanlinna Prize 4732
Erich Pietsch Preis 6836

Innovation *See* Inventions

Instructional films *See* Audiovisuals; Educational films

Insurance
African Insurance Organization Awards 1543
Arets pris i svensk forsakring 11629
Ellis Carson Award 2601
Finlaison Medal 3058
Gold Medal 3059

Paul Golmick Scholarship 2602
Walter T. Greig Scholarship 2603
Insurance Law Prize 10321
Messenger and Brown Prize 3060
Ernst Meyer Prize 11761
National Institute of Insurance International Prizes 8067
Morgan Owen Medal 2604
Prix Jules Lefort 5769
Rutter Gold Medal and Prize 2605
University of Berne Prizes 11965

Intellectual freedom
Libertarian Alliance Awards 3559

Intellectual property *See* Copyright; Inventions

Intelligence *See* National security

Interior design
BDIA-Preis 6809
The *Daily Mail* Awards of Excellence 2727
Forderpreis des Landes Nordrhein-Westfalen fur junge Kunstlerinnen und Kunstler 7026
Forderpreis fur hervorragende Diplomarbeiten auf dem Gebiet der Innenarchitektur 6810
IFI Award 9489
International Design Competition, Osaka 8606
International Union of Master Painters Competitions 6993
New Designers 3027
Scottish Designer of the Year Award 10531
Mark Stamprijs 9648

International law
Mitchell B. Carroll Prize 9511
Fondation Ernest Mahaim 975
Fondazione Professor Giuseppe Ciardi 1204
Francoisprijs 9554
Hague Academy of International Law Scholarships 9445
International Institute of Humanitarian Law Prize 8307
Immanuel Kant Prize 7114
Georg Schwarzenberger Prize in International Law 3065
James Brown Scott Prizes 11751

International relations (*See also* European integration; World peace)
ANZAC Fellowships 9748
Atlantic Award 1233
Awards
　Global Futures Network 7506
　World League for Freedom and Democracy 8836
Concurso Anual de Tesis Profesionales 8937
J. G. Crawford Award 256
Deguchi Prize 9678
Indira Gandhi Prize for Peace, Disarmament and Development 7502
Tor Gjesdals Prize 9942
Good Neighbor Award 9075
Calouste Gulbenkian Foundation Grants 2981
Hammer and Sickle Gold Medal 10460
Harkness Fellowships 2985
International Dag Hammarskjold Award 1237
International Librarian of the Year 3569
IPRA President's Award 11823

Jamnalal Bajaj International Award for Promoting Gandhian Values Outside India 7694
Japan Foundation Award 8612
Japan Foundation Prize for the Promotion of Community-Based Cultural Exchange 8614
Japan Foundation Special Prizes 8615
King Baudouin International Development Prize 1217
Prix Marechal Lyautey 6140
Antonio Machado Prize for Essay 1723
Ramon Magsaysay Awards 10042
Merit of Polish Culture Badge 10091
Jawaharlal Nehru Award for International Understanding 7573
Order of Good Hope
　Republic of South Africa - Department of Foreign Affairs 10914
　Republic of South Africa - State President's Office 10959
Order of Merit of the Republic of Poland 10117
Order of San Carlos 1620
Prix Adolf Bentinck 6160
Prix Jules Voncken 1181
Prix Mondial Nessim Habif 11960
Prizes for Excellence in the Study of International Affairs 229
St. Olav Medal 9923
SCI International Medal 4424
Thouron Fellowship 10683
Eric M. Warburg Prize of Atlantic Bridge 6547
David Watt Memorial Prize 4327
Herbert Weichmann-Preis 7013
Yomiuiri International Cooperation Prize 8781
Zamenhof Award for International Understanding 9679

International trade
Concurso Anual de Tesis Profesionales 8937
Council of Catalonia Prize for Export 11184
Export Awards for Small Businesses 3649
Exporters Medal 1609
Bernhard-Harms-Preis 7007
Importers and Exporters Association of Taipei Competitions 12000
Institute of Export Prizes 3098
Queen's Awards for Export Achievement 3831

International understanding (*See also* Brotherhood; Human relations; Humanitarianism)
ECIS Award For International Understanding 2826
Hamdard Foundation Pakistan Awards 9975
International Simon Bolivar Prize 6415
International Television Festival Golden Prague 1844
Arthur Thomas Ippen Award 9461
Rufus Jones Award 921
John F. Kennedy Student Paper Competition 9462
Laureat d'Honneur of the International Geographical Union 6958
Onassis Prize for International Understanding and for Social Achievement 7209
Pacific Cultural Foundation Awards 12005
Mohamed Sahabdeen Award for International Understanding 11416
Strasbourg Prizes and Gold Medal 7126
Philipp Franz von Seibold Award 7161
Yomiuiri International Cooperation Prize 8781

Inventions (See also Technology)
Bessemer Gold Medal 3127
Chungshan Cultural Foundation Prizes 11998
Concours Lepine 4938
Craftsman's Award 4683
Credit Suisse Design Prize for Technical and Industrial Innovation in Geneva 11684
Ya'acov Dori Prize 7877
Fondation du General Muteau 5547
Fondation Theurlot 5670
William Hopkins Prize 2567
IEE Prize for Innovation 3287
Junior Inventor of the Year 11404
Letterstedtska Forfattarpriset 11543
MacRobert Award 3875
Paterson Medal and Prize 3195
Richardson Gold Medal 3179
Rolex Awards for Enterprise 11898
SMART (Small Firms Merit Awards for Research & Technology) 4559
State Emblem for Innovation 752
Vishwakarma Medal 7677
World First Postal Automatization Award 1386
Luis Zambrano National Prize for Inventive Technology 12130

Investment See Finance

Irish culture
CERT/Irish Life Souvenir of Ireland Challenge 7802
Order of the Golden Rose 7826
Traditional Irish Singing and Dancing Society Awards 7850

Irish literature
Christopher Ewart-Biggs Memorial Prize 2851
Eric Gregory Medal 7792
Prize for Novel 7793
Rooney Prize for Irish Literature 7848

Iron and steel industry
Bessemer Gold Medal 3127
Friends of SEAISI Award 10063
Hattori Prize 8561
Honorary Member 8562
Howard Medal 3241
Iron and Steel Development Award 8563
Komura Prize 8564
Mt. Newman Iron Ore Award 10064
Nishiyama Medal 8565
Noro Prize 8566
Tawara Gold Medal 8567
G. Watanabe Medal 8568
Williams Prize 3155

Islamic culture
Aga Khan Award for Architecture 11656
Arab Book Fair Prize 8842
International Photographic Competition to Commemorate Islamic Heritage 12057
King Faisal International Prize for Arabic Literature 10496
King Faisal International Prize for Islamic Studies 10497
King Faisal International Prize for the Service of Islam 10498
Kuwait Prize 8844

Israeli culture
Association for Civil Rights in Israel Awards 7863
Honorary Fellow 7922
Jerusalem Municipality Awards 7936
Percia Schimmel Award for Distinguished Contribution to Archaeology in Israel 7931

Italian culture
Awards 8241
Golden Pen Prize 8343
Premi 8142
Premi culturali 8038
Premio Cavolini - De Mellis 8087
Premio Internazionale di Meridionalistica Guido Dorso 8149
Premio Luigi Prete 8040
Premio Maria Cianci 8304
Premio Napoli - Mezzogiorno 8256
Premio Tenore 8088
Premio Umberto Zanotti Bianco 8361
Nicoletta Quinto Prize 8305
Serena Medal for Italian Studies 2230

Italian history
Balsdon Fellowship 8177
Fondazione Contessa Caterina Pasolini Dall'Onda Borghese Prize 8050
Galileo Galilei International Prize of the Rotary Club of Italy 8303
Premio Maria Cianci 8304
Nicoletta Quinto Prize 8305
Villa I Tatti Fellowships 8474

Italian literature
Andersen Prize 8422
Awards 8241
Bagutta Prize 8160
Balsdon Fellowship 8177
Campiello Prize 8185
Certamen Capitolinum 8330
John Florio Prize 4396
Golden Pen Prize 8343
Grinzane Cavour Prize 8187
Italian PEN Prize 8363
Naples Prize for Literature 8253
Premi
  Accademia di Scienze, Lettere e Arti di Palermo 8030
  Accademia Internazionale della Tavola Rotonda 8036
Premi Concorsi Letterari 8012
Premi del Ministro per i Beni Culturali e Ambientali 8070
Premi Nazionali Paestum 8028
Premio Bancarella 8164
Premio Ceppo Proposte Nicola Lisi 8084
Premio Iglesias 8118
Premio Il Ceppo 8085
Premio Letterario del Frignano Riccio d'Oro 8016
Premio Letterario Racconti di Carnevale 8116
Premio Nazionale di Narrativa 8144
Premio Nazionale di Poesie 8145

Japanese culture (See also Asian studies)
Asahi Fellowship 8488
Asahi Sho 8492
Competition for Films and Videos on Japan 8774
Concoulrs Reportage Seer le Japon 4907
Daiwa Scholarships 2730
Historical Literature Award 8740
International Publications Cultural Award 8727
Japan Foundation Award 8612
Japan Foundation Grant Programs 8613
Japan Foundation Prize for the Promotion of Community-Based Cultural Exchange 8614
Japan Foundation Special Prizes 8615
Genyoshi Kadokawa Prize 8679
Yukio Mishima Award 8743
Mobil Children's Culture Award 8702
Mobil Music Award 8703
Sir Peter Parker Awards for Spoken Business Japanese 4335
Prize Mission Special Japan 8733
Prize Objective Japan 8734
Suntory Prize for Community Cultural Activities 8763
Suntory Prize for Social Sciences and Humanities 8764
Philipp Franz von Seibold Award 7161
Shugoro Yamamoto Award 8745
Yoshikawa Elji Prize 8694

Jewelry design
Prix Jacque Gautier 4914
Royal Dublin Society Crafts Competition 7835

Jewelry industry
Hermann Bank Senior Silver Medal 6763
National Prize for Jewelry 744
Tully Medal 2917

Jewish culture
Award for Book Review in the Daily Press 7870
Award for Original Hebrew Novel 7872
Award for Original Hebrew Poetry 7873
Awards 7989
BCLA Translation Competition (EC Languages) 2318
BCLA Translation Competition (Non-EC Languages) 2319
A. S. Diamond Memorial Prize 3515
Fondation Edmond Fagnan 973
Honorary Life Member 1146
International Center for Peace in the Middle East Awards 7894
Israel Prize 7906
Jesselson Prize for Contemporary Judaica Design 7925
Yehoshua Kaniel Prize 7879
Marc Lavry Prize 7880
Literary Prize - Bialik Prize for Literature 7953
Literary Prize - Mendele Prize 7955
David Pinski Prize 7884
Prix de l'Education Alfred Weichselbaum 5124
Leib Yaffe Prize 7973

Jewish history
Fraenkel Prize in Contemporary History 3086
Israel Archives Association Awards 7913
Walter-Meckauer-Plakette 7042
Righteous Among the Nations 7995
Dr. Arthur Ruppin Prize 7885
Zalman Shazar Award for Research in Jewish History 7940
World Federation of Jewish Fighters, Partisans, and Camp Inmates Award 7991
Leib Yaffe Prize 7973

Journalism (See also Literature; Cartoons; Editing; Editorial writing; Media; Publications; Radio; Television; Travel literature; specific types of journalism, e.g. Broadcast journalism)
AAHS Trophy (American Aviation Historical Society) 2041
AFN - AGFA Awards 2127
Jose Antonio Alzate Prize 9079
Isara Amantakul Prize 12015

Subject Index of Awards
Volume 2: International and Foreign

Latin

AMP W.G. Walkley Awards for Journalism 523
Angel Literary Award 2080
Aranytoll 7292
Ida Backmans stipendium 11583
Bagutta Prize 8160
Benson and Hedges Media Awards 7781
Best Journalist Work of the Year 10478
Blekinge County Council Culture Prize 11446
A. H. Boerma Award 8267
BP Arts Media Awards 210
British Press Awards 4561
British Society of Magazine Editors Awards 3772
Juan Ignacio Castorena y Urzua 9082
Certamen Nacional de Periodismo Rogelio Cantu Gomez 8978
Chartered Institute of Journalists Gold Medal 2584
City of Munich Prizes 7019
City of Vienna Prizes for Art, Science, and Humanities 789
Commonwealth Press Union Scholarships 2669
Concoulrs Reportage Seer le Japon 4907
Concourt Fellowship 4797
Concurso Anual de Tesis Profesionales 8937
Concurso Nacional Carta a mi Hijo 9252
Dalgety Farmers Limited Awards for Excellence in Rural Journalism 353
Arthur Desguin International Prize 1104
Bernal Diaz del Castillo Prize 9083
Gilberto Figueroa Nogueron Prize 8998
Julius Fucik Honorary Medal 1864
Joaquin Garcia Monge Prize 1762
C. Oswald George Prize 3210
Karin Gierows pris for hangiven bildningsverksamhet 11591
Karin Gierows pris for kunskapsformedlande framstallningskonst 11592
Tor Gjesdals Prize 9942
Grand Journalism Prize 9943
Jose Guadelupe Posada Prize 9088
Gun och Olof Engqvists stipendium 11593
Bharatendu Harishchandra Award 7530
Innovation Writer of the Year 3773
International Dag Hammarskjold Award 1237
International Journalism Prize 1865
International Publications Cultural Award 8727
Journalism Competition Prizes 12121
Journalism Prize
  Belgian Municipal Credit Institution 1062
  International Federation for the Rights of Man 6003
Journalist Prize of the DGE 6857
Karacan Prize 12062
Kellgrenpriset 11596
Kikuchi Prize 8752
King of Spain Journalism Prizes 11361
Labor Courage Award 10437
Literary Prize - Nachum Sokolov Prize 7956
Literature, Art, Journalism, and Architecture Awards 10438
Ramon Magsaysay Awards 10042
Medaille des Publications 4785
Medienpreis fur Sprachkultur 6894
Mlada Fronta Award 1887
Mobral Journalism Prize 1412
Magdalena Mondragon Medal 8922
National Award for Literature and Arts 12002
National Prize for Journalism and Information 9140

National Prize for Journalism for Young People 8946
Netherthorpe Award 2959
Newspaper Cartoon Competition 9167
Newspaper Culture Award 8627
Carlos Noria de Bustamente Prize 9089
Norpress Press Prize 9912
Ortega y Gasset Award for Journalism 11321
Catherine Pakenham Memorial Award 3602
Pascall Prize 580
Pietrzak Award 10084
Plume d'Or de la Liberte 6007
PPA Magazines Awards for Editorial and Publishing Excellence 3774
Premio de Periodismo Cultural 9221
Premio de Periodismo Rosario Castellanos 8928
Premio Esso de Jornalismo 1456
Premio Litterario Viareggio 8407
Premio Luca de Tena 11317
Premio Manuel Buendia 9294
Premio Mariano de Cavia 11318
Premio Mesonero Romanos 11298
Premio Mixcoatl 9255
Premio Municipal Julio Cesar Machado de Jornalismo 10273
Premio Nacional de Periodismo 1549
Premio Nacional de Periodismo Pio Viquez 1765
Premio Napoli di Giornalismo 8255
Premio Periodismo Cultural 9238
Premio Sinaloa de Periodismo 9016
Press Language Prize 12076
Press Prize 9884
Press Prize for Broadcasters 11926
Thomas Pringle Award 10852
Prix Albert Londres 4940
Prix Andre Jullien du Breuil 5813
Prix de la Fondation Mumm pour la Presse Ecrite 5101
Prix de la Meilleure une Journalistique - Les Libertes d'Or 5216
Prix de la Memoire 5206
Prix de la Press Poetique 6327
Prix de la Presse Libre - Les Libertes d'Or 5217
Prix du Journalisme d'Investigation - Les Libertes d'Or 5218
Prix du Livre Historique d'Investigation - Les Libertes d'Or 5219
Prix du Livre Media ou du Livre d'Investigation - Les Libertes d'Or 5220
Prix Mumm Kleber-Haedens 5102
Prize for Journalism on Arts and Culture 9935
Ignacio Ramirez Prize 9091
Reuter Foundation Fellowship 3850
Margaret Rhondda Award 4391
RICS Awards 4085
Romanian Writers' Union Prizes 10414
Royal Television Society Television Journalism Awards 4288
Ferenc Rozsa Prize 7407
Alejandro Silva de la Fuente Award 1553
Soviet Journalists Media Prize 10479
Soviet Land Nehru Award 7722
Prix Stendhal 6008
Student Media Awards 2956
Svenska Akademiens nordiska pris 11606
Thomson Foundation Fellowships 12192
Trade Union's Art and Cultural Prize 7442
Transport Journalist of the Year 2587
Ulianova Prize 10480
Union Prize for Publicistic (Publishers) 10481
Vaughn - Ueda Prize 8629

Markus Viljoen Medal for Journalism 11013
Vorovsky Prizes 10482
What the Papers Say Award 2947
Writer's Trophy 2042
Francisco Zarco Prize 9093

Judaism
Literary Prize - Rav Kook Prize 7957

Judo See **Martial arts**

Justice See **Civil rights and liberties**

Juvenile literature See **Children's literature**

Karate See **Martial arts**

Kayak See **Boating**

Labor (See also **Occupational health; Occupational safety**)
Efficiency of Labor Award 10428
Wenzel-Jaksch-Gedachtnis-Preis 7080
Medaille d'Honneur du Travail 1790
National Labor Prize 9137
NBU Scholarship 11452
Order of Labor 1632
Order of the Glory of Labor 10464
Prix Blaise des Vosges 5719
Public Service Medal 10748
Workers' Education Fellowships 11807

Laboratory technology
Gold Plaque 11526
Honorary Fellow 3169
R. J. Lavington Prize 3171
Life Membership of IMLS 3172
Membership in Retirement 3173
Sims Woodhead Medal 3175

Lacrosse
Divisional Team Championships 4567
Team Championships (non-divisional) 4569

Landscape architecture (See also **Horticulture**)
Annual Environmental Awards 3755
BALI National Landscape Awards 2269
Paul Bonatz Preis 7135
Britain in Bloom Awards 4541
Civic Trust Awards 2636
Engineering Prize - Avraham Cravenne Prize 7950
Forderpreis des Landes Nordrhein-Westfalen fur junge Kunstlerinnen und Kunstler 7026
IFLA Competitions 6005
Peter Joseph Lenne Prize 6562
Prix de Rome 9578
Rural Wales Award 12164
UNESCO Prize for Landscape Architecture 6424
Alexander Von Humboldt Medal 7130
Friedrich Ludwig von Sckell Ehrenring 6554

Language See **Linguistics; Translations**

Latin American history
Gold Medal 1557
Honorary Member 1558
Jabuti Prize 1470
Carlos Pereyra Prize 8994
Premio BANAMEX Atanasio G. Saravia de Historia Regional Mexicana 9204

Law

Law (*See also* Civil rights and liberties; Consumer affairs; Copyright; Criminology; Firearms; International law; Inventions; Law enforcement; Legal literature; Legislative improvement; Prisons)
Simion Barnutiu Prize   10335
BP Prize Lectureship in the Humanities   10638
John Brooke Scholarship   7783
Otto Brusiin Award   4706
Certificate of Honor   6031
Commonwealth Magistrates' Hall of Fame   2666
Jose Ignacio De Marquez, Santiago Perez, and Antonio Ricaurte Prizes   1625
Defenders of Justice   1626
Dissertation Honors   6998
Howard Drake Memorial Award   3064
Forensic Science Society Awards   2905
Grand Prix de l'Academie des Sciences Morales et Politiques   5711
Paul Guggenheim Prize   11742
Hodgson Prize   3893
Honorary Member   5969
Humboldt Research Awards to Foreign Scholars   7155
Insurance Law Prize   10321
International Legal Aid Award   3382
Israel Prize   7906
Antonio Larragoiti Prize
  Brazilian Academy of Letters   1423
  Lisbon Academy of Sciences   10253
Law Books in Hindu Prize   7516
Law Prize   1228
Artur Malheiros Prize   10255
Medaille de la Jurisprudence   4776
Miembro de Honor   11259
C. H. Milburn Award   2449
National Institute of Insurance International Prizes   8067
Preis der Justus-Liebig-Universitat Giessen   7000
Premio Juridico Mtro. Jorge Sanchez Cordero   8987
Prix Charles Duvivier   980
Prix Corbay   5727
Prix Demolombe   5731
Prix du Budget   5734
Prix Dupin Aine   5737
Prix Estrade-Delcros   5742
Prix Jean Reynaud   5762
Prix Jules Voncken   1181
Prix Le Dissez de Penanrun   5771
Prix Maurice Travers   5783
Prix Rene Cassin   5788
Prix Saintour   5790
Prix Suzanne Tassier   997
Prix Wolowski   5796
Prize Mission Special Japan   8733
Mohamed Sahabdeen Award for Literature   11417
Peter Scott Memorial Scholarship   3969
Soderbergs Pris   11550
George Stavros Gold Medal   7195
George Stavros Silver Medal   7196
Swiney Prize for a Work on Jurisprudence   4325
Nicholae Titulescu Prize   10389
Toon Van Den Heever Prize for Jurisprudence   11010

Law enforcement
Australian Police Medal   336
Diploma of Honour and Medal   3456
Disciplined Services Medal for Long Service and Good Conduct   7245
Disciplined Services Medal for Meritorious Service   7246
Disciplined Services Star for Distinguished Service   7247
Distintivo al Merito Canino   1671
Distintivo al Merito Docente Gabriel Gonzales   1672
Estrella de la Policia   1673
Institute of Professional Investigators Awards   3202
Institute of Traffic Officers of Southern Africa Awards   10885
Medaille d'Honneur de la Police   1788
Medalla al Valor   1674
Medallos de los Servicios   1675
National Medal   208
Police Overseas Service Medal   345
Quaid-i-Azam Police Medal for Gallantry   9997
Queen's Police Medal for Gallantry   2383
Roll of Honor   3460
General Santander Medal   1676
Servicios Distinguidos   1677
South African Police Cross for Valour   10952
South African Railways Police Medal for Combating Terrorism   10953
South African Railways Police Star for Distinguished Leadership   10954
South African Railways Police Star for Distinguished Service   10955
Star for Merit in the South African Railways Police Force   10956

Leadership (*See also* Academic achievement; Professional and personal achievement)
Decoration for Distinguished Service in the South African Railways Police Force   10950
Distinguished Service Decorations   341
Gold Medal for Development of the Technological Environment   9952
National Leadership Award   7796
Order of National Hero   8484
Generaldirektor Aage W. Owe's Prisbelonningsfond   9953
Pro Virtue Decoration   10941
South African Railways Police Medal for Combating Terrorism   10953
South African Railways Police Star for Distinguished Leadership   10954

Learning disabled
Irma Roth/Saaled Bursary   11015

Legal literature
Dissertation Prize   5255
Prix Berriat Saint-Prix   5717
Prix Charles Lyon-Caen   5725
Prix Dupin Aine   5737
Prix Gallet   5747
Prix Jean-Baptiste Chevallier   5759
Prix Joseph Hamel   5765
Prix Koenigswarter   5770
Prix Limantour   5774
Prix Maurice Travers   5783
Prix Odilon Barrot   5784
Prix Rene Cassin   5788
Prix Wolowski   5796

Legislative improvement
Guildhall Helping Hand Awards   2878
Prix Lucien Dupont   5778

Library and information services (*See also* Bibliography; Information management; Library history; Literacy; Reference)
H. C. L. Anderson Award   237
Ellinor Archer Award   238
ASLP Professional Award   10026
ASLP Service Award   10027
ASLP Special Citizen Awards   10028
Redmond Barry Award   239
Besterman Medal   3564
Bibliotheconomy and Documentation National Award   1469
Dr. Josef Bick Ehrenmedaille   738
J. D. Stewart Bursary Award   3565
Carey Award   4447
Carnegie Medal   3566
Daphne Clark Award   3561
Copova Diploma   10797
Howard Drake Memorial Award   3064
T. C. Farries Public Relations and Publicity Awards   3567
Fellow   240
Finnish Library Association Awards   4700
Maria Gemenis Award   241
R. Lysholt Hansens Bibliotekspris   1915
Honorary Fellow
  International Federation of Library Associations and Institutions   9491
  Library Association of Ireland   7814
Honorary Member   4663
Honorary President   9492
IATUL Essay Prize   10575
IFLA Medal   9493
International Book Award   899
International Librarian of the Year   3569
Holt Jackson Community Initiative Award   3570
Professor Kaula Gold Medal   7698
Kaula - Ranganathan Gold Medal   7699
Kukuljeviceva povelja   1799
Letter of Recognition   242
Library Contest Awards   8154
Library Manager of the Year   243
Library Technician of the Year   244
Literary Prize of PLA   10153
Adam Lysakowski Scientific Prize   10154
McColvin Medal   3571
Alfred McMicken Award   251
Meckler Award for Innovation Through Information Technology   3572
Medal for Serving the Association of Hungarian Librarians   7294
Metcalfe Medallion   245
Mita Society for Library and Information Science Prize   8700
Ulverscroft Munford Research Fellowship   3573
C. B. Oldman Prize   10573
Edvard Pedersens Biblioteksfonds Forfatterpris   1916
Ruben Perez Ortiz Prize   1686
Prix de la Promotion Poetique   6329
Ranganathan Award for Classification Research   7493
SABINET Prize   11061
SAILIS Bibliographic Award   11062
SAILIS Research Award   11063
SAILIS Research Certificate   11064
Franz Stangler Memorial Prize for Adult Education   861
Study Grant Awards   246
Ervin Szabo Medal   7408
Robert Vosper IFLA Fellows Program   9496
WA Special Librarian Award   247
Wheatley Medal
  Library Association   3574
  Society of Indexers   4448
Harold White Fellowship   549

Library history
National Library of Colombia Prize   1714

Literature

Library services *See* **Library and information services**

Lighting design
Design & Light Competition 8274
Leon Gaster Bronze Medal 2593
Lighting Award 2594
Laurence Olivier Awards 4466
Student Lighting Design Awards 3578
Walsh - Weston Bronze Award 2598
Young Lighters of the Year 2599

Limnology *See* **Hydrography**

Linguistics
BAAL Book Prize 12153
Blomska stipendiet 11586
Certamen Capitolinum 8330
Certificate of Merit 4563
Timotei Cipariu Prize 10339
CISLB Awards 1179
Dr. M. Aylwin Cotton Foundation Fellowship Awards 2688
Dr. M. Aylwin Cotton Foundation Publication Grants 2689
Albert Counson Prize 1284
Deguchi Prize 9678
Konrad Duden Preis der Stadt Mannheim 7098
Ehrenmitgliedschaft im IDV 10071
English Academy Medal 10851
Esperantista Go-Ligo Internacia Competitions 8549
Esperanto Diploma 7425
Gottingen Academy of Sciences Prize 6903
Grand Prix Amon Ra 5195
Grand Prix du Rayonnement de la Langue Francaise 5805
Bogdan Petriceicu Hasdeu Prize 10352
Honorary Member 10081
Italian Minister for Culture and the Environment Prizes 8365
Kellgrenpriset 11596
C. J. Langenhoven Prize 10994
Antonio Larragoiti Prize
    Brazilian Academy of Letters 1423
    Lisbon Academy of Sciences 10253
John Lotz Commemorative Medal 7420
D. F. Malan Medal 10997
National Competition in Teaching of Journalism Prize 1437
National Prize for Linguistics and Literature 9148
National Prize in Science and Art 9152
National Prize of the President of the Republic 8068
Noordstarfonds - Dr. Jan Grauls Prize 1275
Margit Pahlsons pris 11599
Polish Phonetic Association Award 10170
Preis der Justus-Liebig-Universitat Giessen 7000
Premio Menendez Pidal 11347
Press Language Prize 12076
Prijs voor Meesterschap 9630
Thomas Pringle Award 10852
Prix Alfred Croiset 5434
Prix Alfred Dutens 5435
Prix Antoine Meillet 5438
Prix de la Fondation Emile Benveniste 5444
Prix Honore Chavee 5464
Prix Joseph Gantrelle 993
Prix Latsis 11959
Prix Pol Comiant 5912
Prix Roman et Tania Ghirshman 5471
Prix Saintour 5919
Prix Suzanne Tassier 997
Prix Volney 5349

Prix Volney 5475
Pushkin Institute Scholarship, Moscow 4352
Alexander Sergeovich Pushkin Prize 10423
A. S. Pushkin's Medal 10451
Radio and Television Language Prize 12078
Felix Restrepo Prize for Philology 1679
Rivadeneira Prizes 11349
Schiller-Gedachtnispreis des Land Baden-Wurttemberg 7055
George Stavros Gold Medal 7195
George Stavros Silver Medal 7196
Svenska Akademiens nordiska pris 11606
Svenska Akademiens sprakvardspris 11608
Theatre Award 9398
Turkish Language Prize 12080
UMEA-Shinoda-Premio 8778
Jozef Van Ginderachter Prize 1278
Verbatim Award 1944
Jozef Vercoullie Prize 1279
Leonard Willems Prize 1280
Prof. Ludwik Zabrocki Medal 10082
Zamenhof Award for International Understanding 9679

Literacy
ACCU Prizes for Fully-Illustrated Literacy Follow-up Materials 8498
Escorts Book Award 7491
International Book Award 899
Mobral Journalism Prize 1412
Nehru Literacy Award 7566
November 17th Medal 1869
Tagore Literacy Award 7567
UNESCO Literacy Prizes 6422

Literary criticism
All Japan Description Contest from A Pocket Book Reading 8675
Arts Council of Wales Book of the Year Awards 12150
Austrian State Prize for Cultural Publications 760
Award for Book Review in the Daily Press 7870
Awards for Regional Literature 10004
Pierre Bayle Prijs 9580
Belinsky Prize 10421
Best Critic Prize 12070
Bucharest Writers Association Award 10411
Buenos Aires Literary Prizes 36
Category A Fellowships 155
Category B Fellowships 156
CCP Literary Awards 10034
Rose Mary Crawshay Prize for English Literature 2225
Dawood Prize for Literature 10005
Alonso de Ercilla Award 1552
Luisa Claudio de Sousa Prize 1451
N. A. Dobrolyubov Prize 10422
Dr. Wijnaendts Francken-prijs 9626
GPA Book Award 7777
Grand Prix de la Critique Litteraire 4956
Grands Prix Litteraire de la Ville de Paris 6095
Journalism Competition Prizes 12121
Kamei Katsuichiro Prize 8686
Korean National Literary Award 8823
Kuttippuzha Award 7705
Literary Prizes 7192
Somerset Maugham Awards 4390
Walter McRae Russell Award 132
Johann-Heinrich-Merck Preis 6768
National Award for Literature and Arts 12002
Pietrzak Award 10084

Pramie fur die Beantwortung einer Literarischen oder Philologischen Frage 6769
Gustav Preller Prize 11002
Premio Nacional de Critica Literaria Mirta Aguirre 1820
Premio Nacional de Literatura 1548
Thomas Pringle Award 10852
Prix Alberic Rocheron 5807
Prix Alfred Croiset 5434
Prix biennal Marcel Thiebaut 6273
Prix Constant de Horion 1041
Prix de la Critique 5834
Prix de la Critique Poetique 6326
Prix Emile Faguet 5848
Prix J. J. Weiss 5869
Ricardo Rojas Prize 38
Romanian Writers' Union Prizes 10414
Royal Society of Literature Award 4233
Staatsprijs voor Kritiek en Essay 1082
Suntory Prize for Social Sciences and Humanities 8764
Yomiuri Literature Prize 8795

Literature (*See also* **Creative writing; Drama criticism; Editing; Essays; Editorial writing; Humor; Illustration; Linguistics; Literacy; Literary criticism; Mystery writing; Scholarly works; Translations; specific literary genres, e.g. Biography**)
3M Talking Book of the Year 612
Academy of Athens Prize 7182
ACUM Medal for Performing and Distribution of Israeli Works, Music and Literature 7942
ACUM Prizes for Literature and Music 7943
Akutagawa Prize 8750
Alice Award 662
Annual Literary Award 8849
Annual Literary Festival 782
Anugerah Sastera Negara 8901
Arab Book Fair Prize 8842
Gerardo Arellano Cultural Merit Medal 1651
Arts Achievement Award 8575
Arts Council of Northern Ireland Bursaries and Awards 7854
Arts Council of Wales Book of the Year Awards 12150
Jozsef Attila Prize 7398
Australia-New Zealand Literary Exchange 153
Australian Literature Society Gold Medal 130
Austrian State Encouragement Prizes 758
Austrian State Grand Prize 759
Austrian State Recognition Prizes 765
Award for Aboriginal and Torres Strait Islander Writers 554
Award for Distinction in Islamic Science 12055
Awards for the Best Produced Books in Hong Kong 7277
Ida Backmans stipendium 11583
Eugenio Balzan Prize 8280
Bangkok Bank Prize for Thai Literature Competition 12022
Bangla Academy Literary Award 934
Banjo Awards 534
Beernhaert Prize 1282
Berlin Art Prizes 6509
Beskowska resestipendiet 11585
Best Published Book Award (Publisher and Author) 9981
Bharat Ratna 7549
Blekinge County Council Culture Prize 11446

Literature

Awards, Honors & Prizes, 1995-96

Literature (continued)
K. Blundell Trust 4386
BMEC Donald Maxwell Award 3115
Bodensee-Literaturpreis der Stadt Uberlingen 7146
Gerard Bonniers Pris 11587
Book Awards 10660
Book of the Year 7371
Ernest Bouvier-Parviliez Prize 1283
BP Prize Lectureship in the Humanities 10638
Braille and Talking Book Library Award 290
Brasov Writers Association Award 10410
Bratislava Literary Prize 10754
Bremen Literary Prize 6578
Brenner Prize 7890
Brno Literary Prize 1886
John Buchanan Prize in Esperanto 4574
Bucharest Writers Association Award 10411
Georg-Buchner-Preis 6765
Bungakukai Shinjin Sho 8751
H. M. Butterley - F. Earle Hooper Award 363
Canada-Australia Literary Award 154
Canberra Book of the Year Award 331
Carlos Casavalle Prize 26
Grinzane Cavour Prize 8187
Cena Vilenica 10755
Cena Zvazu slovenskych spisovatelov 10756
I. C. Chacko Award 7701
Chia Hsin Prize 11994
Chilean Academy of Language Prize 1551
Chungshan Cultural Foundation Prizes 11998
City of Vienna Prizes for Art, Science, and Humanities 789
City of Vienna Promotional Prizes 791
Cluj Writers Association Award 10412
Concurso Nacional de Novela Erich Guttentag 1398
Margaret Condliffe Memorial Prize 9848
Ion Creanga Prize 10343
Cymmrodorion Medal 3023
Fondazione Contessa Caterina Pasolini Dall'Onda Borghese Prize 8050
Danish Academy Prize for Literature 1909
General Casimiro Dantas Prize 10247
Dawood Prize for Literature 10005
Luisa Claudio de Sousa Prize 1451
Hendrik de Vries Award 9362
Hendrik de Vries Stipend 9363
Felix Denayer Prize 1285
Denny Gold Medal 3116
Deo Gloria Award 2198
Henri Deschamps Literary Prize 7258
Alfred Doblin Prize 6510
Doblougska priset 11588
Ya'acov Dori Prize 7877
Dublin Corporation Arts Scholarship 7758
Aquileo J. Echeverria Prize 1761
Eichendorff Medal 6693
Signe Ekblad-Eldhs pris 11589
Camille Engelman Prize 1286
English Association Literary Competition 10855
Lydia och Herman Erikssons stipendium 11590
Eugenio Espejo National Prize for Culture 2017
Johannes Ewald Prize 1927
FAW Adele Shelton-Smith Award for Play, Radio or Other Scripts for Young Writers 378
FAW Australian Unity Award 381
FAW Di Cranston Awards 387
FAW Patricia Weickhardt Award 398

Fellowships and Scholarships 146
Female Writers Literary Award 8520
Festival da Torneira Poetica 1406
First Book Prize 21
Forderpreis des Landes Nordrhein-Westfalen fur junge Kunstlerinnen und Kunstler 7026
Forderpreis fur Literatur der Landeshauptstadt Dusseldorf 6683
Anne Frank Literary Award 11734
Miles Franklin Literary Award 127
Joaquin Garcia Monge Prize 1762
Geeta Award 7510
Karin Gierows pris for hangiven bildningsverksamhet 11591
Goethepreis 6612
Grand Prix Amon Ra 5195
Grand Prix C. F. Ramuz 11723
Grand Prix de Litterature 5801
Grand Prix International d'Arts et Lettres Notre-Dame et la Mer 4958
Grand Prix Paul Feval de Litterature Populaire de la Societe des Gens de Lettres 6264
Grand Prix Poncetton de la Societe des Gens de Lettres 6265
G. H.'s - Gravesande Prize 9348
Eric Gregory Awards 4389
Grenfell Henry Lawson Festival of Arts Awards 415
Grosse Literaturstipendien des Landes Tirol 728
Grosser Literaturpreis der Bayerische Akademie der Schonen Kunste 6552
Grosser Schillerpreis 11729
Gun och Olof Engqvists stipendium 11593
Neil Gunn International Fellowship 10661
Hali Award 7511
Hammer and Sickle Gold Medal 10460
Thomas Hardy Society Book Prize 2983
Haryana Sahitya Award 7512
Johann-Peter-Hebel-Preis 7054
Hertzog Prize 10991
Historical Literature Award 8740
Hitar Petar/Artful Peter/Grand Prize for Humor and Satire in Literature 1522
W. A. Hofmeyr Prize 11113
Holberg Medal 1928
Hong Kong Biennial Awards for Chinese Literature 7278
Ricarda-Huch-Preis 6599
Huh Kyun Literary Award 8825
Constantijn Huygens Prize 9350
Inner Swiss Literature Award 11749
Institute Silver Medal 3119
Inter Nations Culture Prize 6927
International Award for the Furtherance of Human Understanding 11686
International Dag Hammarskjold Award 1237
International Literary Award Vilenica 10801
International PEN - Philippines Awards 10040
International Publications Cultural Award 8727
Internationale Eugene Baieprijs 1243
The Irish Times Literature Prizes 7810
Israel Prize 7906
Jabuti Prize 1470
Percy Jackson Award 3120
Jassy Writers Association Award 10413
Jerusalem Prize for the Freedom of the Individual in Society 7934
Jnanpith Award 7486
Genyoshi Kadokawa Prize 8679
Takeshi Kaiko Award 8762
Kallebergerstipendiet 11595
Gottfried Keller Prize 11670

Kellgrenpriset 11596
Kikuchi Prize 8752
King Faisal International Prize for Arabic Literature 10496
Ilona Kohrtz' stipendium 11597
Kordelin Prize 4744
Kossuth Prize 7410
Kungliga priset 11598
Kunstpreis der Stadt Zurich 11894
Labor Courage Award 10437
Antonio Larragoiti Prize
    Brazilian Academy of Letters 1423
    Lisbon Academy of Sciences 10253
Letterstedtska Forfattarpriset 11543
Fran Levstik Prize 10807
LiBerature Prize 6923
Libraries Prize 8153
Lichfield Prize 3576
Hilarie Lindsay Award 665
Jessie Litchfield Award 557
Literary Award 11572
Literary Awards 7404
Literary Prize
    National Academy of Arts 8830
    South African Academy of Science and Arts 10995
Literary Prize for Translation 10996
Literary Prize of PLA 10153
Literature and Art Awards 12011
Literature, Art, Journalism, and Architecture Awards 10438
Literature Board's Emeritus Fellowship Awards 166
Literature Prize 12075
Literaturpreis des Kranichs mit dem Stein 6672
Alun Llywelyn-Williams Memorial Award 12181
Lower Austria Prize for the Advancement of Fine Arts and Literature 859
Lower Austria Recognition Prize in Arts and Sciences 860
Macaulay Fellowship 7760
Machado de Assis Prize 1426
Ramon Magsaysay Awards 10042
The Mail on Sunday - John Llewellyn Rhys Prize 2201
Karol Malcuzynski Award 10207
Thomas Mann Prize 7038
Katherine Mansfield Memorial Fellowship 9800
Eugene Marais Prize 10998
Somerset Maugham Awards 4390
Walter-Meckauer-Plakette 7042
Messel Medal and Lecture 4418
Mlada Fronta Award 1887
Montaigne Prize 7117
Montana Book Awards 9705
Moortidevi Sahitya Puraskar 7487
Musgrave Medal 8482
Mythic Society Scholar 7713
Yunus Nadi Yarismasi 12049
Nagrada Saveta Fonda SO SUBNOR Cetvrti jul 10707
K. R. Namboodiri Award 7706
National Cultural Awards 1413
National Order of the Southern Cross 1415
National Prize Competition for Literature for Neo-Literates 7527
National Prize for Literature
    Argentina - Ministry of Education and Justice 22
    Colombia - Ministry of National Education 1662
    National Council for Culture 12122
National Prizes for Culture 1391

Subject Index of Awards
Volume 2: International and Foreign

Literature

National Science, Literature and Art Prize 7183
Vladimir Nazor Awards 1812
New South Wales State Literary Awards 147
Martin Andersen Nex Prize 1929
Nobel Prize for Literature 11497
Northern Arts Literary Fellowship 3725
Northern Arts Writers' Awards 3726
October Prizes of the City of Belgrade 10696
Adam Oehlenschlager Prize 1930
Order of Andres Bello 12137
Order of Cultural Merit 8579
Order of Culture 8586
Order of Lenin 10463
Order of Merit 2378
Order of the Crown 1074
Order of the Red Banner of Labor 10467
Osaragi Jiro Prize 8496
Outstanding Kiswahili Scholars 12013
Oya Soichi Non-Fiction Prize 8754
Pakistan Civil Awards 9995
Jan Palach Prize 5993
Ramos Paz Prize 10258
Peace Prize of the German Book Trade 6776
Edvard Pedersens Biblioteksfonds Forfatterpris 1916
Don Pedrick Memorial Literary Award 11425
PEN Literary Award 8827
Perskor Prize for Leisure Reading 10906
Perskor Prize for Literature 10907
A. A. Phillips Award 133
Pietrzak Award 10084
David Pinski Prize 7884
Polish PEN Centre Prizes 10168
Prague Literary Prize 1888
Preis der Schweizerischen Schillerstiftung 11730
Gustav Preller Prize 11002
Premi Antonio Feltrinelli 8069
Premio de la Critica a los Mejores Libros Publicados 1819
Premio Hispanoamericano Xavier Villaurrutia 9267
Premio Internacional Alfonso Reyes 9268
Premio Internazionale Enno Flaiano 8114
Premio Latinoamericano de Narrativa, Colima 9230
Premio Literario Miguel Torga - Cidade de Coimbra 10224
Premio Mario di Nola 8078
Premio Mixcoatl 9255
Premio Municipal de Literatura 1568
Premio Nacional de Literatura
   Angolan Writers Union 4
   Cuban Book Institute 1821
Premio Nacional de Literatura Paula Allende 9295
Premio Pablo Neruda 1566
Premio Rafael Heliodoro Valle 9249
Premio Revista Punto de Partida 9198
Premio Tusquets Editores de Novela 11389
Premios Vitalicios 11245
Preseren Award 10799
Presidential Award on Best Book on Quaid-i-Azam and Pakistan 10010
Prime Minister's Prize 7907
Prince of Asturias Prizes 11248
Prix Alfred Nee 5808
Prix Alfred Verdaguer
   Institut de France - Academie des Sciences 5683
   Institut de France - Academie Francaise 5809

Prix Alioune Diop pour les Lettres Africaine 10691
Prix Alix Charlier-Anciaux 1291
Prix Anais Segalas 5811
Prix Andre Barre 5812
Prix Andre Lequeux 5337
Prix Auguste Michot 1293
Prix Auguste Teirlinck 979
Prix Balzac 6248
Prix Bordin 5820
Prix Botta 5821
Prix Broquette-Gonin 5824
Prix Calmann-Levy 5825
Prix Carton de Wiart 1294
Prix Charles Blanc 5828
Prix de Joest 5831
Prix de la Liberte 6155
Prix de M. et Mme. Louis Marin 5837
Prix de Saint-Genois 982
Prix de Stassart 983
Prix Diderot Universalis 5112
Prix Docteur Binet-Sangle 5840
Prix du Palais Litteraire 6166
Prix Durchon-Louvet 5846
Prix Emmanuel Vossaert 1295
Prix Eugene Schmits 1296
Prix Eve Delacroix 5853
Prix Fontannes 5307
Prix France - Liban 4926
Prix Fraternite Gaby Archenbaud 6124
Prix Furtado (de Bayonne) 5857
Prix Gaston et Mariette Heux 1298
Prix Georges Dupau 5858
Prix Gustave Le Metais Lariviere Fils (Prix d'Academie) 5862
Prix Hercule Catenacci
   Institut de France 5343
   Institut de France - Academie Francaise 5867
Prix Hubert Krains 1043
Prix J. J. Weiss 5869
Prix Jean Reynaud 5872
Prix Jules et Louis Jeanbernat et Barthelemy de Ferrari Doria 5346
Prix Jules et Louis Jeanbernat et Barthelemy de Ferrari Doria 5768
Prix Jules Favre 5875
Prix Kastner-Boursault 5878
Prix Lafontaine 5879
Prix Lambert 5880
Prix Louis P. Miller 5886
Prix Maille-Latour-Landry 5888
Prix Maurice-Edgar Coindreau 6290
Prix Maurice Trubert 5896
Prix Osiris 5347
Prix Osiris 5703
Prix Paul Flat 5904
Prix Paul Teissonniere 5907
Prix Sobrier-Arnould 5921
Prix Thyde Monnier 6298
Prix Toutain 5925
Prix Valentine Abraham Verlain 5926
Prix Valentine de Wolmar 5927
Prix Vega et Lods de Wegmann 5928
Prix Vitet 5929
Prix Xavier Marmier 5930
Prize for Better Work 8886
Prize for Literature of the Council of the French Community of Belgium 1110
Prize for the Best Foreign Book 6180
Public Service Medal 10748
Public Service Star 10749
Publieksprijs voor het Nederlandse Boek 9368
Alexander Puschkin Prize 7120
Regional Production Prizes 23
Aquilino Ribeiro Literary Prize 10259

Collin Roderick Lectures 406
Romanian Writers' Union Prizes 10414
Annie Romein Prys 9426
Routledge Ancient History Prize 3861
Juan Rulfo Latin American and Caribbean Prize for Literature 9259
Mohamed Sahabdeen Award for Literature 11417
Sahitya Akademi Awards 7537
Sahitya Akademi Fellowship 7538
Salzburg Prize for the Promotion of the Arts, Science and Literature 869
Sandoz Preis 878
Santander Athenaeum Novel Award 11151
Moinho Santista Prizes for Young People 1496
Moinho Santista Prizes 1497
Schiller-Gedachtnispreis des Land Baden-Wurttemberg 7055
Harold Jan Schoemaker Award 9463
Scholarship Prizes 6512
Scholarships of the City of Munich 7023
Birger Scholdstroms pris 11600
Geschwister-Scholl-Preis 7024
Olive Schreiner Prize 10853
Schuckska priset 11601
Robert Schumann Prize 7123
Scottish Book of the Year Award 10658
Oskar Seidlin Preis 6694
Jaroslav Seifert Prize 11450
Stephan Shaumian Prize 113
Singer-Polignac Grants 5226
Bhai Santokh Singh Award 7513
W. H. Smith Young Writers' Competition 4346
Society of Writers of Macedonia Awards 8876
Soviet Land Nehru Award 7722
Spurs of Criticism 4760
Staatsprijs ter Bekroning Van een Schrijverscarriere 1080
State Grand Prize for Literature 1087
State Prize 10204
State Prize in Science and Technology 10470
Stipendium ur Lena Vendelfelts minnesfond 11603
Herbert Akroyd Stuart Award 3121
Stuttgart Literary Prize 7139
Sur Award 7514
Svenska Akademiens nordiska pris 11606
Svenska Akademiens svensklararpris 11609
Svjetlost Prizes 1404
Swedish Authors' Fund Awards 11619
Junichiro Tanizaki Award 8521
Sidney Gilchrist Thomas Medal and Prize 3152
Timisoara Writers Association Award 10415
Tirgu Mures Writers Association Award 10416
Tiroler Landespreis fur Kunst 732
Marten Toonder Award 7762
Townsville Foundation for Australian Literary Studies Award 407
Trade Union's Art and Cultural Prize 7442
Travelling Scholarships 4394
Thaddaus-Troll-Preis 6754
Troubadour de la SABAM 1071
Turkish Radio and Television Culture, Art and Science Prizes 12084
Union of Writers and Artists of Albania Competitions 2
Upper Austria Culture Prize for Literature 903
Urban Council Awards for Creative Writing in Chinese 7279
Jose Maria Vergara y Vergara Prize 1665

761

Literature (continued)
Vertical Smile 11390
Tarjei Vesaas Debutant Prize 9930
Viking Society for Northern Research Awards 4599
Joost van den Vondel Prizes 7133
Walmap Prize 1494
Patrick White Literary Award 708
Christoph-Martin-Wieland-Preis 6761
Anton Wildgans Prize of Austrian Industry 736
Griffith John Williams Memorial Prize 12199
Karl Wolfskehl Preis fur Exilliteratur 6555
Abraham Woursell Prize 799
Wurdigungspreis 862
Leib Yaffe Prize 7973
Yorkshire Post Art and Music Award 4645
Yorkshire Post Best First Work Award 4646
Yorkshire Post Book of the Year Award 4647
Yugoslav PEN Club Award 10726
Zibetska priset 11612

Literature, Canadian *See* Canadian literature

Literature, Catholic *See* Catholic literature

Literature, Children's *See* Children's literature

Literature, Dutch *See* Dutch literature

Literature, English *See* English literature

Literature, European *See* European literature

Literature, French *See* French literature

Literature, Irish *See* Irish literature

Literature, Italian *See* Italian literature

Literature, legal *See* Legal literature

Literature, Mexican *See* Mexican literature

Literature, religion *See* Religion literature

Literature, Spanish *See* Spanish literature

Literature, travel *See* Travel literature

Lubrication engineering
JSLE Best Paper Award 8669

Magazines *See* Journalism; Publications

Management (*See also* Health care administration; Hospital administration; Human relations; Information management; Leadership; Operations research; Planning; Public administration)
Alejandro Angel Escobar Science Prize 1584
APO National Award 8504
APO Regional Award 8505
Baxter Award for Healthcare Management in Europe 7775
Belgian Institute of Administrative Sciences Prize 1059
Best Management Essay Award 9858
Best MBA Student Award 9859
Book Awards 10502
Bridgeport Prize 3270
Building Manager of the Year Awards 2581
Chemical Industry Medal 4406
CIOS Gold Medal 8908
Design Management Prize 11570
Emergent Entrepreneur Award 10877
Environmental Management Awards 4321
European Businesswoman of the Year 2281
Fellow 333
Fellowship of the City and Guilds of London Institute 2622
Fellowships and Training Programmes 2656
Garner-Themoin Medal 9504
Gold Medal 3110
Hall of Fame 7710
Elizabeth Haub Prize 6940
Hegarty Prize 574
Hodgson Prize 3893
IFAWPCA-CHOI Fieldman Award 10037
Institute of Administrative Management Competitions 3062
International Association of University Presidents Awards 12027
Library Manager of the Year 243
Management Expert 7711
Maple Leaf Award 9505
Mensforth International Gold Medal 3296
MERIT Competition 3251
Minit/EMJ Trophy 3657
Parkman Medal 3255
Premio Internazionale di Meridionalistica Guido Dorso 8149
Premio Luis Elizondo - Premio Cientifico y Technologico 8989
Premio Mixcoatl 9255
Prince Philip Medal 2628
Rising Star Award 2283
Sofia International Film Festival on Organization and Automation of Production and Management Awards 1530
Jeffrey Stollmeyer Memorial Award 12039
John Storey Medal 231
Verulam Medal 3111

Manufacturing (*See also* Industries and trades)
Albert Medal 4318
Fellowships and Training Programmes 2656
Garden Machinery Annual Awards 2238
Dr. V. M. Ghatage Award 7475
Tony Goldsmith Cup 3280
Importers and Exporters Association of Taipei Competitions 12000
Institute of Manufacturing Awards 3113
Mensforth International Gold Medal 3296
Nuffield Silver Medal 3298
Rolls Royce Jubilee Award 3302
Dr. Biren Roy Trust Award 7478

Marine biology
International Seaweed Association Awards 1484
Ray Lankester Investigatorship 3631

Marine engineering *See* Naval engineering

Marketing (*See also* Advertising; Public relations; Merchandising)
Best of Europe - International Direct Marketing Awards 1131
DMA/Royal Mail Direct Marketing Awards 2331
ESOMAR Awards 9418
Honorary Member 10181
IEC Promotion and Marketing Award 3405
Institute of Marketing Awards 3123
International Festival of Economics and Training Films 1191
International Markstrat Competition 6403
Marketing Man/Woman of the Year Award 10878
NatWest Bank Engineering Marketing Award 2773
PPA Subscription Awards 3775
Scottish Marketing Awards 10671
Lawrie Waddams Award 2824

Martial arts
Budo Koro Sho 3442
Competitions 8838
World Union of Karatedo Organizations Championships 6497

Materials science (*See also* Ceramic engineering; Mining and metallurgy)
Ablett Prize 3125
Peter Allard Silver Medal 3880
Armourers & Brasiers' Award 4142
Beilby Medal and Prize 4187
Guy Bengough Medal and Prize 3126
G. D. Birla Memorial Gold Medal 7625
Bulk Materials Handling Award 429
Andrew Carnegie Research Fund 3128
Tom Colclough Medal and Prize 3129
Cook Prize 3130
Elegant Work Prize 3132
A. A. Griffith Medal and Prize 3134
Charles Hatchett Award 3137
Leslie Holliday Prize 3138
INSA Prize for Material Sciences 7651
Institute of Ceramics Awards 3078
Italian Association for Metallurgy Awards 8334
T.B. Marsden Professional Award 3141
National Lecture Competition 3143
Prix Charles Lemaire 1012
Prix du Gaz de France 5694
Prix Professeur Louis Baes 1036
Prix Scientifique IBM France 5330
RILEM Award 6068
A.W. Roberts Award 484
Rosenhain Medal and Prize 3148
Royal Charter Prize 3149
SMM Postgraduate Student Award 11075
Solid State Physics and Materials Science Essay Prize 11077
Technician of the Year Award 3151
Sidney Gilchrist Thomas Medal and Prize 3152
Urethane Medal 3153
Verulam Medal and Prize 3154

Mathematics (*See also* Statistics; Surveying)
Australian Mathematical Society Medal 253
Eugenio Balzan Prize 8280
Banach Award 10156
Berwick Prize 3608
Bhatnagar Award 7532
Guy Bomford Prize 5967
CASTME Awards 2646
T. M. Cherry Student Prize 122
Colombian Academy of Science Third World Prize 1579
Crafoord Prize 11537
Dantzig Prize 9548
De Morgan Medal 3609
Dirac Medal 8288
Edlundska Priset 11538
Fields Medal 4731
Fondation Aime Berthe 5477
Fondation Carriere de Mathematiques 5511
Fondation du Baron de Joest 5541
Fondation Elie Cartan 5550
Fondation Emil Picard 5551
Fondation Ernest Dechelle 5553

Subject Index of Awards
Volume 2: International and Foreign

Medical

Fondation Francoeur 5560
Fondation Gabrielle Sand 5563
Fondation Grammatickakis-Neuman 5570
Fondation Henri Poincare 5578
Fondation Jean du Hamel de Breuil 5596
Fondation Jean Reynaud 5599
Fondation Jerome Ponti 5602
Fondation Langevin 5610
Fondation Le Conte 5615
Fondation Louis Armand 5621
Fondation Marie Guido Triossi 5625
Fondation Mergier-Bourdeix 5633
Fondation Paul Gallet 5646
Fondation Poncelet 5656
Fondation Servant 5668
Fondation Tchihatchef 5669
Fondation Vaillant 5674
Fondation Victor Thebault 5677
Fondations Estrade Delcros, Houllevigue, Saintour, Jules Mahyer 5679
Fondazione Premio Dotte Giuseppe Borgia 8063
Forder Lectureship 3610
Francqui Prize 1156
Fujihara Award 8527
Fulkerson Prize 9549
Gunning Victoria Jubilee Prize Lectureship 10644
Hardy Lectureship 3611
Spiru Haret Prize 10351
Hector Memorial Medal and Prize 9838
William Hopkins Prize 2567
ICTP Prize 8289
Italian Minister for Culture and the Environment Prizes 8365
Junior Berwick Prize 3612
Junior Whitehead Prize 3613
Keith Medal 10645
Gheorghe Lazar Prize 10362
Morris L. Levinson Prizes 7982
Thomas Ranken Lyle Medal 176
Artur Malheiros Prize 10255
Mazurkiewicz Award 10157
Medals of the National Academy of Science 8379
National Institute of Insurance International Prizes 8067
National Prize for Physics, Mathematics and Natural Sciences 9149
National Prize in Science and Art 9152
National Prize of the President of the Republic 8068
Naylor Prize in Applied Mathematics 3614
Bernhard H. Neumann Prize 254
Rolf Nevanlinna Prize 4732
Nihon Sugakukai Iyanaga Sho 8696
October Prizes of the City of Belgrade 10696
Olimpiada de Matematicas Mexicana 9282
Orchard-Hays Prize 9550
Philippine Mathematical Olympiad 10059
Pius XI Gold Medal 12098
Polya Prize 3615
Premi Antonio Feltrinelli 8069
Premi del Ministro per i Beni Culturali e Ambientali 8070
Premio Bartolozzi 8358
Premio Caccioppoli 8359
Premio Sotero Prieto a la Mejor Tesis de Licenciatura en Matematicas 9283
Prix Adolphe Wetrems 1006
Prix Agathon De Potter 1007
Prix Ampere d'Electricite de France 5684
Prix Barrabe 5304
Prix Blaise Pascal du GAMNI-SMAI 5685
Prix Charles Lagrange 1011

Prix de la Fondation du 150e anniversaire de la Societe royale des Sciences de Liege 1368
Prix des Sciences Physiques et Mathematiques 5052
Prix Eugene Catalan 1020
Prix Fonde par l'Etat 5695
Prix Francois Deruyts 1021
Prix Jacques Deruyts 1025
Prix Scientifique IBM France 5330
Prix Theophile de Donder 1037
Royal Society of Victoria Medal 638
Dr. Juan S. Salcedo Jr. Science Education Award 10061
Moinho Santista Prizes for Young People 1496
Moinho Santista Prizes 1497
Scientific Research Prizes 8919
Senior Whitehead Prize 3616
Sierpinski Award 10158
Sociedad Cubana de Matematica y Computacion "Pablo Miguel" Awards 1823
Srinivasa Ramanujan Medal 7673
George Stavros Gold Medal 7195
George Stavros Silver Medal 7196
Simon Stoilov Prize 10384
Stromer-Ferrnerska Beloningen 11555
Swedish Mathematical Society Fellowship 11635
Sylvester Medal 4158
Gheorghe Titeica Prize 10388
TWAS Award in Mathematics 8453
Wallmarkska Priset 11560
Carl-Walther-Preis 6807
Wolf Foundation Prizes 7987
Zaremba Award 10159

Mechanical engineering
Alejandro Angel Escobar Science Prize 1584
Angus Award 9727
ASEA-Brown Boveri-Forschungspreis 11928
Australian Geomechanics Award - John Jaeger Memorial Award 423
James Alfred Ewing Medal 3236
Georg A. Fischer-Preis 11930
Fondation Alexandre Darracq 5480
Fondation Fourneyron 5559
Fondation Henri de Parville 5576
Fondation Henry Wilde 5583
Fondation Jean du Hamel de Breuil 5596
Fondation Louis Armand 5621
Fondation Petit d'Ormoy 5649
Institution of Mechanical Engineers Awards 3333
Thomas A. Jaeger Prize 8543
JSME Medal 8643
George Julius Medal 470
A. G. M. Michell Medal 473
Aylet Lilly Perera Memorial 11407
Premio Internazionale con Medaglia d'oro, Professor Modesto Panetti 8024
Prix Auguste Sacre 1009
Prix du Commisariat a l'Energie Atomique 5693
Prix Montyon de Mecanique 5702
Rover Midlander Open Design Award 4307
Sir Henry Royce Initiative Award 4309
Sir Henry Royce Memorial Lecture 4312
Sir Henry Royce Prestige Lecture on the Institution of Incorporated Engineers 4314
SAACE/SA Construction World Awards for Excellence in Engineering 11026
Wallmarkska Priset 11560
Warman International Students Design Award Competition 493
James Watt International Medal 3334

James Watt Medal 3263

Media (See also Cable television; Communications; Journalism; Radio; Television)
Tor Gjesdals Prize 9942
Premio Nacional Teponaxtli de Malinalco 8932
Mohamed Sahabdeen Award for Literature 11417
Science and Technology Media Fellowships 2255
Thomson Foundation Fellowships 12192
World Food Day Award 7569

Medical education
BMA Film and Video Competition 2429
BMA Medicine in the Media Award 2430
Fondation Jean Dagnan-Bouveret 5594
Francisco Hernandez Award 12134
International Medical and Health Education Film Week 11269
International Multimedia Science Film Festival 8375
Medical Electives Bursaries 2658
Premio Dr. Manuel J. Castillejos 9103
Torreon de Igueldo 11283
University Commemorative Medal 7462

Medical journalism (See also Science journalism)
Andries Blignault Medal 10887
BUPA Prizes for Medical Writing and Illustration 4387
Fondation Alfred Dutens 5483
Fondation Chaussier 5520
Fondation Dusgate 5548
Margaret Holroyd Prize 2519
Louis Leipoldt Memorial Medal 10888
Michael Mason Prize 2520
Hamilton Maynard Memorial Medal 10889
Medical Association of South Africa Awards for Excellence in Medical Reporting (Press, Radio, Television) 10890
Medical Students' Prize 10897
Minkowski Prize 6705
Dr. Erich Muller Prize 6801
Prof. Dr. P. Muntendamprijs 9661
Prix Alvarenga de Piauhy 1325
Prix Denis Thienpont 1329
Prix du Docteur Frans Johnckheere sur l'Historie de la Medecine 1330
Prix du Docteur Jules Deminne et sa femme nee Anne Fabry 1331
Prix du Docteur Louis de Give de Muache 1332
Prix Hamoir 1333
Prix Henriette Simont 1334
Prix Henry Fauconnier 1335
Prix Joseph Lepoix 1336
Prix Melsens 1337
Prix Pfizer 1338
Prix Quinquennal des Sciences Pharmaceutiques et Therapeutiques 1339
Prix Triennal Professeur Pierre Rijlant pour l'Electrophysiologie Cardiaque 1343
Sudjono Djuned Poesponegoro Award 7729

Medical research (See also Scientific research)
Professor B. K. Aikat Oration Award 7577
Basanti Devi Amir Chand Prize 7578
Shakuntala Amir Chand Prizes 7579
Dr. Nitya Anand Endowment Lecture 7636
John Arderne Medal and Prize 4235
Elsa E. Arini de Masnatta Prize 65
Astra Award 1970

Medical — Awards, Honors & Prizes, 1995-96

Medical (continued)

Australian Applied Health Sciences Fellowships 538
Australian Post-Doctoral Fellowships 539
Bacteriology Prize of the IMLS 3166
Bernhard Baron Travelling Scholarship in Obstetrics and Gynaecology 3949
BGRC Silver Jubilee Oration Award 7580
Richard J. Bing Award 3469
Robert Bing Prize 11917
Florence and William Blair-Bell Memorial Fellowship 3951
Juan Bonorino Cuenca Prize 68
Brackenbury Award 2431
Alexander Ninian Bruce Prize 10640
Donal Burke Memorial Lecture 7829
Lady Cade Memorial Fellowship 10826
Caldas Science Prize 1688
Mariano R. Castex Prize 75
Chalmers Memorial Medal 4276
Jean-Martin Charcot Award 3417
CIBA-GEIGY Award for Best Controlled Clinical Trial 6968
CIBA-GEIGY ILAR Rheumatology Prize 11674
Cecilia Cioffrese Prizes for Health Care 8225
Annie Clegg Award 2433
Lord Cohen of Birkenhead Medal 2517
Cothenius Medal 6622
Dalby Prize 4239
Chaturvedi Kalawati Jagmohan Das Memorial Award 7583
Dr. Dharamvir Datta Memorial Oration Award 7584
Arthur de Falloise Quinquennial Prize 1065
Peter Debye Prize 9681
Smt. Swaran Kanta Dingley Oration Award 7586
W. E. Dixon Lecture 4240
Vera Down Award 2434
Downs Travelling Scholarship 4243
Henry Dryerre Prize Lecture 10642
Jacqueline du Pre Award 3418
Eden Travelling Fellowship in Obstetrics and Gynaecology 3953
Edgar Research Fellowship 3954
Hilda och Alfred Erikssons Pris 11540
European Thyroid Association Awards 11707
Francis Hardy Faulding Memorial Fellowship 605
Enrique Finochietto Prize 79
Ernest Fletcher Memorial Lecture 4246
Fondation Aime Berthe 5477
Fondation Alexandre Joannides 5481
Fondation Argut 5496
Fondation Bariot-Faynot 5501
Fondation Breant 5507
Fondation Carre-Bessault 5510
Fondation du Docteur Jean Toy 5545
Fondation Eugene et Amelie Dupuis 5554
Fondation Gustave Roussy 5572
Fondation Henriette Regnier 5579
Fondation Jean-Marie Le Goff 5598
Fondation Le Conte 5615
Fondation Leon-Alexandre Etancelin 5616
Fondation Lonchampt 5620
Fondation Marie Leon-Houry 5626
Fondation Maujean 5629
Fondation Memain-Pelletier 5632
Fondation Odette Lemenon 5641
Fondation Parkin 5642
Fondation Roberge 5660
Fondation Roy-Vaucouloux 5663
Fondazione Giovanni Di Guglielmo 8057
Manuel Forero Prize 1728

French Society for Medical Hydrology and Climatology Prize 5297
Norman Gamble Research Prize 4247
Manuel Garcia Prize 11462
Edgar Gentilli Prize 3955
William Gibson Research Scholarship for Medical Women 4248
Gold Medal of the Royal Society of Medicine 4249
Maurice Goldblatt Cytology Award 6929
Grand Prix de la Fondation pour la Recherche Medicale 5262
Graves Lecture 7831
Green-Armytage and Spackman Travelling Scholarship 3956
R. T. Hall Prize 305
Katherine Bishop Harman Award 2438
Nathaniel Bishop Harman Award 2439
Peter Harris Award 3470
W. J. Harrison Prize (Laryngological Section) 4251
Sir Charles Hastings Award 2440
Charles Oliver Hawthorne Award 2441
Richard Hewitt Award 4252
Doris Hillier Award 2442
Geoffrey Holt Award 2443
Casey Holter Memorial Prize 4370
Honorary Member 10185
IBRO/UNESCO Fellowship Programme 5980
ICMR Prize for Biomedical Research Conducted in Underdeveloped Areas 7587
ICMR Prize for Biomedical Research for Scientists belonging to Under-privileged Communities 7588
Angela Iglesia de Llano Prize 82
Imamura Memorial Prize 8652
INSA - T. S. Tirumurti Memorial Lecture 7652
Insole Award 2444
The Islamic Organization for Medical Sciences Prizes 8843
Dr. M. O. T. Iyengar Memorial Award 7589
Dr. C. G. S. Iyer Oration Award 7590
T. V. James Fellowship 2445
Louis Jeantet Prize for Medicine 11727
Jewish Colonization in the Argentine Republic Prize 83
Lala Ram Chand Kandhari Award 7592
Heinz Karger Memorial Foundation Annual Award 11871
Jakob Klaesi Awards 11918
Richard Kovacs Prize 4258
August Krogh Lecture and Award 1986
Life Membership of IMLS 3172
Eli Lilly/EASD Research Fellowship in Diabetes & Metabolism 6704
Dora Lush Biomedical Postgraduate Scholarships 541
George Macdonald Medal 4279
Donald Mackay Medal 4280
Maddison Prize 4461
C. J. Martin Fellowships 542
Quinquela Martin Foundation Prize 49
Prof. Surindar Mohan Marwah Award 7594
Medical Association of South Africa Pro Meritis Award 10895
Medical Association of South Africa Silver Medal Award 10896
Medical Postgraduate Research Scholarships and Dental Postgraduate Research Scholarships 543
Medical Research Grants 4739
Medical Sciences Award 10323
Merck, Sharp and Dohme International Award 1971
Michael Award 6925

Mogens and Wilhelm Ellermann Foundation Prize 11943
Mollegaard BB RAT Travel Fellowship 6706
Juan Jose Montes de Oca Prize 86
National Back Pain Association Medal 3678
National Vaccine and Serum Institute Award 1574
Claude-Adolphe Nativelle Prize for Medicine 6128
Nichols Fellowship 4260
Angelica Ocampo Prize 92
O'Connor Award 3424
Theodore Ott Prize 11919
Pfizer Award Fellowship 1972
Catharina Pijlsprijs 9683
Polish Rheumatological Society Award 10177
Dr. D. N. Praad Memorial Oration Award 7599
Preis der Justus-Liebig-Universitat Giessen 7000
Bruce-Preller Prize Lectureship 10648
Premio Anual de Investigacion en Epilpsia 9065
Premio Anual de Investigacion Medica Dr. Jorge Rosenkranz 9071
Premio Dr. Eduardo Liceaga 9114
Premio Gea Gonzalez - PUIC 9024
Premios a la Investigacion Medica 9044
Prix Albert-Pierre-Jean Dustin 1323
Prix Anonyme 1326
Prix de Biologie Alfred Kastler 5271
Prix de la Fondation Athena 5687
Prix de la Fondation pour la Recherche Medicale 5263
Prix de la Societe des Eaux Minerales d'Evian-des-Bains 4820
Prix Delahautemaison 5264
Prix des Sciences Biologiques et Medicales 5050
Prix Fonde par l'Etat 5695
Prix O.R.L. 4868
Prix Quinquennal Docteur Albert Dubois pour la Pathologie tropicale 1340
Prix Quinquennaux des Sciences Medicales du Gouvernement 1341
Prix Recherche et Medecine 5939
Prix Rosen de Cancerologie 5265
Prix SmithKline Beecham 1342
Prix Triennal Professeur Pierre Rijlant pour l'Electrophysiologie Cardiaque 1343
Public Education Prize 1730
Queen Sofia Award for Research into Mental Retardation 11246
R. R. Race Prize 3174
Alejandro A. Raimondi Prize 97
Dr. T. Ramachandra Rao Award 7601
Ralph Reader Prize 306
Albert Renold Fellowship 6708
Research Program Grants 545
Research Project Grants 546
H. C. Roscoe Fellowship 2451
Sandoz Prize for Gerontological Research 7418
Dos Santos Prize 5128
Smt. Kamal Satbir Award 7606
Schering Plough International Award Fellowship 1973
Georg-Schmorl-Preis 7084
Ludwig Schunk Prize for Medicine 7003
Shri Dhanwantari Prize 7671
Siemens Elema Young Investigators Award 10580
SmithKline Beecham Pharmaceuticals Young Investigator 1974
Maj. Gen. Saheb Singh Sokhey Award 7610
Smt. Pushpa Sriramachari Award 7611

Medicine

SSIEM Award 4378
Albert Szent-Gyorgyi Commemorative Medal 7461
E. Townsend Award 2453
Joseph Toynbee Memorial Lectureship 4267
Usui Foundation for Hematological Research 8656
Prijs Albert Van Dyck 1317
Dr. Karel Verleysen Prize 1321
Franz Volhard Award 1975
Dr. Prem Nath Wahi Award for Cytology and Preventive Oncology 7614
Edith Walsh Award 2454
Wellcome Trust Award for Research in Biochemistry Related to Medicine 2179
Elizabeth Wherry Award 2455
Young Investigator Award
 Japanese Society of Hematology 8657
 World Organization of Gastroenterology 7169
Young Investigator Awards of the Dr. C. and F. Demuth Medical Foundation 1976
Young Scientist Award 1968
Young Scientists for Rainforests 2678

Medical technology (See also **Biomedical engineering; Biotechnology**)
Irene Aitken Memorial Award 10970
Ames Histology Award 10971
Bactlab Systems Gold Award 10972
Bactlab Systems Premier Award 10973
Baxter Diagnostics Award 11464
Behring Diagnostics Award 10974
Biomerieux Award 11465
Boehringer Mannheim GmbH Award 11466
Boehringer Mannheim S.A. Award 10975
International Cytotechnology Award of the IAC 6930
Johnson and Johnson Award 10976
Joseph Prize 10977
Merck Award 10978
Nordic Award 11467
Ortho Diagnosis Systems Educational Award 11468
Orthodiagnostic Prizes 10979
Premier Technology Shandon Award 10980
Public Relations Award 10981
Technicon 50th Anniversary Award (Bayer Diagnostics Award) 10982
Wellcome Diagnostics Student Award 10983
Dr. V. K. Zworykin Premium 3312

Medicine (See also **Biomedical engineering; Biotechnology; Health care; History of medicine; History of pharmacy; Occupational health; Rehabilitation and therapy; Toxicology; specific fields of medicine, e.g. Anesthesiology**)
Akzo prijs 9389
Elena Allemand de Gunche Prize 62
Geronimo H. Alvarez Prize 63
Amsterdam Prize 9451
Amsterdam Prize for Medicine 9595
Alejandro Angel Escobar Science Prize 1584
Annual Stimulus Subprize 64
Padre Fermin G. Arnau S.J. - Obra De San Lazaro Prize 66
Association of Latin Languages Allergologists and Immunologists Award 10222
Award for Medical Students 11765
Awards 9416
Victor Babes Prize 10332
Balint Society Prize Essay 2156
Eugenio Balzan Prize 8280

Lister Boyd Beaver Award 2990
Jorge Bejarano Civic Medal for Health and Welfare Merits 1667
Leon Bernard Foundation Prize 11973
Claude Bernard Lecturer 6703
Best Research Lectures on Sarcoidosis 4620
Bhatnagar Award 7532
Malcolm Black Travel Fellowship 3950
Blair-Bell Medal 4236
William Blair-Bell Memorial Lectureship in Obstetrics and Gynaecology 3952
H. L. Bockus Medal 7167
Carlos Bonorino Udaondo Prize 69
Samuel M. Bosch Prize 70
Osvaldo L. Bottaro Prize 71
Brohee Medal 7168
Buckston Browne Prize Medal 2991
Buchanan Medal 4144
Caledonian Research Foundation Prize Lecturehip 10641
Carus Medal 6621
Carus Preis 7104
Castellani - Reiss Medal and Award 1721
Chilean Society Awards for Scientific Works 1555
Sir Rickard Christophers Medal 4277
City of Vienna Prizes for Art, Science, and Humanities 789
Concurso Nacional de Obras Medicas 1725
Oswaldo Cruz Prize 1411
Dagra Prize 10243
Daniel Danielopolu Prize 10344
Darling Foundation Prize 11974
Chaturvedi Ghanshyam Das Jaigopal Memorial Award 7582
Reynier De Graaff Medal 9556
Dissertation Honors 6998
Distinguished Clinical Chemist Award 7896
Distinguished International Services Award 7897
Alvarenga do Piaui (Brasil) Prize 10249
Educational Foundation Grant 1183
Alan Edwards Prize 4244
Paul Ehrlich - und Ludwig Darmstaedter Preis 6691
Ellison-Cliffe Medal and Lecture 4245
Carlos Esguerra Prize 1727
ESM Career Development Award 2845
European Rhinologic Society Prizes 9414
EUROSON Young Persons Award 2829
Charlotte Eyck Award 2435
Neil Hamilton Fairley Fellowships 540
Fellow 7281
Filmpreis der Bundesarztekammer 6814
Alexander Fletcher Memorial Prize Lecture 10600
Fondation Alfred Dutens 5483
Fondation Barbier 5500
Fondation Bordin 5506
Fondation Chaussier 5520
Fondation du Baron de Joest 5541
Fondation du Baron Larrey 5542
Fondation du Docteur et de Madame Peyre 5544
Fondation Dusgate 5548
Fondation Gaston Rousseau 5564
Fondation Lannelongue 5611
Fondation Laura Mounier de Saridakis 5613
Fondation Louis-Daniel Beauperthuy 5622
Fondation Memain-Pelletier 5335
Fondation Mergier-Bourdeix 5633
Fondation Montyon de Medicine et Chirugie 5636
Fondation Paul Gallet 5646
Fondation Petit d'Ormoy 5649
Fondation Rochat-Juliard 5661

Fondation Serres 5667
Fondations Bellion - Charles Bouchard 5678
Fondazione Eugenio Morelli 8053
Fothergillian Medal 3637
Roberto Franco Prize 1729
Francqui Prize 1156
French Society for Medical Hydrology and Climatology Prize 5297
Fujihara Award 8527
Fund Dr. en Mevr. Schamelhout-Koettlitz 1312
Gold Medal for Distinguished Merit 2436
Gottschalk Medal 174
Gran Premio Nacional de Medicina 12088
Pablo Elias Gutierrez Award 1707
Iuliu Hatieganu Prize 10353
Hippocrates Medal 6916
Honorable Mention 6815
Honorary Fellow 4278
Honorary Life Direct Member 7282
Honorary Member 7044
Steven Hoogendijk Prijs 9420
Butterworth Hrinemann Prize 2185
Humboldt Research Awards to Foreign Scholars 7155
Hunterian Medal 3033
Samuel Hyde Memorial Lecture 4254
IAMP Awards 498
IFOS Golden Award 1185
IFOS Thanking Award 1186
International Association for the Study of Lung Cancer Awards 1956
ISHAM Lucille K. Georg Award 1202
The Islamic Organization for Medical Sciences Prizes 8843
Israel Prize 7906
Anders Jahre Prize in Medicine 9961
JALMA Trust Fund Oration Award In The Field Of Leprosy 7591
Miklos Jancso Commemorative Medal 7459
Jephcott Lectures 4257
Jean Julliard Prize 3477
The Kharazmi Prize 7737
King Faisal International Prize in Medicine 10499
Mary Kingsley Medal 3594
M. Kodiat Award 7728
Professor Jozef Kostrzewski Award 10187
Kshanika Oration Award to a Woman Scientist for Research in the Field of Biomedical Sciences 7593
LEPRA Essay Competition 3552
Lettsomian Medal 3638
Littre Prize 6501
Artur Malheiros Prize 10255
Harold Malkin Prize 3957
Malpighi Prize 2846
Manson Medal 4281
Gheorghe Marinescu Prize 10365
Mauriac International Medical Film Festival 6112
Medical Academy of Sao Paulo Prize 1490
Medical Association of South Africa Bronze Medal Award 10892
Medical Association of South Africa Gold Medal Award 10893
Medical Association of South Africa Group Award for Meritorious Service 10894
Medical Services Cross 10934
Member of Honour 7045
Dr. Kamala Menon Medical Research Award 7595
C. H. Milburn Award 2449
Minnesmedaljen i guld 11519

Medicine (continued)

Amrut Mody-Unichem Prize for Research in Cardiology, Neurology and Gastroenterology 7596
Amrut Mody-Unichem Prize for Research in Maternal and Child Health and Chest Diseases 7597
MOTESZ Prize 7308
National Academy of Medicine Prize 87
Edgardo Nicholson Prize 89
Stefan S. Nicolau Prize 10372
Raul Nicolini Prize 90
Nobel Prize for Physiology or Medicine 11499
Novo Nordisk Prize 1987
Nuffield Lecture 4261
October Prizes of the City of Belgrade 10696
Lorenz Oken Medaille 6890
Order of Lenin 10463
Outstanding Instructor 7460
Pakistan Civil Awards 9995
John Panchaud Medallions 2724
Paracelsus Medaille 6817
Constantin I. Parhon 10375
Dr. V. N. Patwardhan Prize in Nutritional Sciences 7598
Castelli Pedroli Prize 6707
Alberto Peralta Ramos Prize 93
Pezcoller Prize 8397
Pietro Caliceti International Prize 8249
Jorge E. Pons Goldaracena Prize 95
Pope John XXI Prize 12096
Porcellati Award 11456
Premi 8026
Premi Antonio Feltrinelli 8069
Premio Consagracion Rodolfo A. Vaccarezza 59
Premio Domenico Marotta 8381
Premio Europeo Prof. D. Ganassini 8259
Premio Federico Nitti 8382
Premio Luis Elizondo - Premio Cientifico y Technologico 8989
Premio Nipiol-Buitoni 8431
Premio Profesor Dr. Ricardo Hansen 60
Prix a l'Etudiant Medaille d'Or de l'Internat 4804
Prix Aimee et Raymond Mande 4807
Prix Alvarenga de Piauhy 1325
Prix Andre Batel-Rouvier 4809
Prix Artois - Baillet Latour de la Sante 1327
Prix Auguste Secretan 4811
Prix Celine 6232
Prix Charles Achard 4815
Prix CIBA-GEIGY 4817
Prix Clement Marot de Poesie 6502
Prix de Bruxelles 1089
Prix de la Ville de Paris 4821
Prix de l'Academie Nationale de Medecine 4822
Prix de l'Histoire Vecue 6503
Prix Denis Thienpont 1329
Prix Dermatologie Immunologie 4824
Prix Dermatologie Syphiligraphie 4825
Prix Deschiens 4827
Prix Devouement 4828
Prix Docteur Darolles 4830
Prix Drieu-Cholet 4831
Prix du Commisariat a l'Energie Atomique 5693
Prix du Docteur Jules Deminne et sa femme nee Anne Fabry 1331
Prix du Docteur Louis de Give de Muache 1332
Prix d'Urologie 4835
Prix Electrotherapie 4836
Prix Europe et Medecine 5937
Prix Henriette Simont 1334
Prix Jansen 4846
Prix Joseph-Antoine Maury 4853
Prix Joseph Lepoix 1336
Prix Jules Perreau 4854
Prix Jules Voncken 1181
Prix Leon Baratz 4855
Prix Leon Launoy 4856
Prix Maurice-Louis Girard 4861
Prix Medecin General Inspecteur Raymond Debenedetti 4862
Prix Medecine 4863
Prix Medecine et Culture 5938
Prix Michel Noury 4865
Prix Neurologie 4866
Prix Obstetrique 4867
Prix Osiris 5703
Prix Prince Albert Ier de Monaco 4872
Prix Prosper Veil 4873
Prix Quinquennal des Sciences Pharmaceutiques et Therapeutiques 1339
Prix Raoul Follereau 5913
Prix Richard Lounsbery 5705
Prix Roussel 6205
Prix SmithKline Beecham 1342
Prix Tuberculose 4876
Prix Victor et Clara Soriano 4877
Professor Feliks Przesmycki Award 10188
Marcial V. Quiroga Prize 96
Dr. P. N. Raju Oration Award 7600
Tilak Venkoba Rao Award 7602
Raven Lecturer 1967
Franz Redeker Preis 6680
Lloyds Roberts Lecture 4264
Rogers Prize 4579
Royal College of Surgeons of England Honorary Medal 3980
Carl Asmund Rudolphi Medal 6636
Saltire Society and The Royal Bank of Scotland - Scottish Science Award 10657
Sandoz Preis 878
Moinho Santista Prizes for Young People 1496
Moinho Santista Prizes 1497
Federico Guillermo Schlottmann Prize 99
Ludwig Schunk Prize for Medicine 7003
Paul Schurmann-Medaille 6853
Paul Schurmann-Preis 6854
Science Prize - Dr. Moshe Einhorn Prize 7960
Science Prize - Henrietta Szold Prize 7961
M. N. Sen Oration Award for Practice of Medicine 7607
John Sheppard Memorial Lecture 7753
Short Story Award 6505
Dr. A. T. Shousha Foundation Prize 11976
Sidmar Prize 1315
S.I.N.U.S. Association Prize 6213
Dr. J. B. Srivastav Award in the Field of Virology 7612
State Prize
  Hungary - Office of the Prime Minister 7412
  Secretariat of the Committee of State Prizes 10204
Subvention de l'Academie Nationale de Medecine 4879
Swiney Prize for a Work on Jurisprudence 4325
Swiss Society for Internal Medicine Prize 11902
THESE-PAC Awards 9699
Denis Thienpont Prize 1316
Sutomo Tjokronegoro Award 7730
Enrique Tornu Prize 100
Travel Awards 2847
Travelling Fellowships 10601
TWAS Award in Basic Medical Sciences 8450
UMEA-Shinoda-Premio 8778
University of Berne Prizes 11965
Leopoldo Uriarte Y Pineiro Prize 102
Roberto A. Vacarezza Prize 103
Premio Miguel Aleman Valdes 8992
Prijs Franz Van Goidsenhoven 1318
Franz Vogt-Preise 7005
Ernst von Bergmann Plakette 6818
Albert Wander Lecture 4271
R. Wasito Award 7731
Wellcome Foundation Prize and Lecture 4159
Wellcome Medal for Anthropological Research as applied to Medical Problems 3931
Winsbury-White Lecture 4274
Wissenschaftlicher Wettbewerb der ZFA 6917
Wolf Foundation Prizes 7987
WONCA Foundation Award 7283
World Film Festival of ORL Scientific Films and Videotapes 1187

Medicine, aerospace See **Aerospace medicine**

Medicine, emergency See **Emergency medicine**

Medicine, preventive See **Preventive medicine**

Medicine, sports See **Sports medicine**

Medicine, veterinary See **Veterinary medicine**

Medieval studies
Prix Bordin 5439
Prix du Budget 5452
Prix Saintour 5472

Mental health (See also Psychiatry)
Jakob Klaesi Awards 11918
MIND Book of the Year - Allen Lane Award 3651
Doris Odlum Award 2450
Theodore Ott Prize 11919
Dr. Vidya Sagar Award 7604
John William Starkey Award 4228
Stengel Research Award 811
Stengel Service Award 812

Mentally disabled
Awards 5961
Natalie Cobbing Travelling Fellowship (Psychiatry of Mental Handicap) 3959
Philip Davis Prize in Old Age Psychiatry 3960
DPI-ACOPIM Journalism Award 1684
Making the Difference 536
Brian Oliver Prize in the Psychiatry of Learning Disabilities 3965
Prix Bernard Ladougne 4812
Prix Jocelyn Chedoudi 4852
Prix Maladies Mentales 4860
Travel Prize 12086

Merchandising
Independent Retailer Organisation Awards 3046

Metallurgy See **Mining and metallurgy**

Meteorology
Alejandro Angel Escobar Science Prize 1584
Barringer Medal 3644
W. S. Bruce Medal 10639
Prix Georges Bruel 6135
Deutsche Meteorologische Gesellschaft Ehrenmitgliedschaft 6643
Deutsche Meteorologische Gesellschaft e.V. Forderpreis 6644
Fondation Leon Grelaud 5617
Fondation Parkin 5642
Fondation Victor Raulin 5676
Helmholtz Prizes 6914
International Meteorological Organization Prize 11978
Leonard Medal 3645
Meteorology Prize 4104
K. R. Ramanathan Medal 7666
Royal Society of Victoria Medal 638
Symons Memorial Medal 4105
Prof. Dr. Vilho Vaisala Award 11979
Alfred Wegener-Medaille 6645
WMO Research Award for Young Scientists 11980

Mexican literature
Ignacio Manuel Altamirano Prize for Novel 9046
Certamen Nacional de Literatura *El Porvenir* 8977
Competition for Children's Theater or Stories 9012
Concurso Nacional de Escritores de Teatro 9274
Concurso Univeritario de Cuento 9177
Condecoracion al Merito Social 9013
Jorge Cuesta National Poetry Prize 9006
Magda Donato Prize 8930
Editorial Planeta - Joaquin Mortiz International Prize for Novel 8980
Juegos Florales Prize of San Juan del Rio, Queretaro 9162
Angel Maria Garibay Kintana Prize for Literary Essay 9048
Efrain Huerta National Prize for Short Story and Poetry 9164
Instituto de Bellas Artes Concurso de Becas Literarias 9213
Miguel N. Lira Poetry Prize 9004
Josue Mirlo Poetry Prize 9049
National Prize for Linguistics and Literature 9148
National Prize in Science and Art 9152
Gilbert Owen National Prize for Literature 9014
Premio Antoniorrobles 9120
Premio de Narrativa Jorge Ibarguengoitia 9217
Premio de Novela Jose Ruben Romero 9218
Premio de Testimonio 9224
Premio Josefina Vicens para Novela Breve 9227
Premio Juan Rulfo Para Primera Novela 9228
Premio Nacional de Literatura Jose Fuentes Mares 9292
Premio Nacional de Novela 9235
Agustin Yanez First Novel Prize 8981

Microbiology
Arima Award 6064
Alois Bachmann Prize 67
Bactlab Systems Premier Award 10973
M. W. Beijerinck Virology Medal 9598
Malcolm Breach Award 3167
Colworth Prize Lecture 4354
Paul Ehrlich - und Ludwig Darmstaedter Preis 6691
Carlos J. Finlay Prize 6411
Fleming Award 4355
Fondation Andre-Romain Prevot 5491
Fondation Costantino Gorini 5525
Fondation Salman A. Waksman 5664
Garrod Medal 2515
Emil Christian Hansen Foundation for Microbiological Research Award 1904
Dr. H. P. Heineken Prize
  Heineken Foundation 9452
  Royal Netherlands Academy of Arts and Sciences 9600
Merck Award 10978
Stuart Mudd Award 6065
W. H. Pierce Memorial Prize 4348
Dr. Y. S. Narayana Rao Oration Award in Microbiology 7603
Marjory Stephenson Prize Lecture 4356
Leopoldo Uriarte Y Pineiro Prize 102
Van Leeuwenhoek Medal 9605
Van Niel Prize 6066
A. I. Virtanen - Award 4671

Microfilms *See* **Information management**

Military engineering
Institution of Engineers, Australia Award - University of New South Whales - Australian Defence Force Academy 459

Military history
Browne Medal for Original Research 4597
European Cup of Wargame 5321
Honorary Member 11470
Minister of National Defense Prize 10095
Templer Medal 4350
Tournoi de Paris de Jeux d'Histoire Antico - medieval 5322

Military service
Ad Adstra Decoration 10919
Air Force Cross
  British Government 2356
  Republic of South Africa - South African Defense Force 10920
Air Force Medal 2357
Army Cross 10921
Ashok Chakra 7547
Ati Vishisht Seva Medal 7548
Australian Service Medals 337
Castle of Good Hope Decoration 10922
Certificate of Honor 10426
John Chard Decoration 10923
John Chard Medal 10924
Chesney Memorial Gold Medal 4294
Commendation Medal (Military) 10737
Condecoracion Servicios Distinguidos en Guerra Exterior 1634
Conspicuous Gallantry Medal 2360
Conspicuous Service Decorations 339
Croix de Guerre 5243
Cross for Military Action of the Polish Armed Forces in the West 10098
Cross for Participation in the War of 1918-1921 10099
Cross of Merit for Bravery 10102
Cross of the Battle of Lenino 10104
Cross of the Warsaw Uprising 10105
Cross of Valour 10106
De Wet Decoration 10925
De Wet Medal 10926
Defence Force Service Awards 340
Distinguished Conduct Medal 2361
Distinguished Flying Cross 2362
Distinguished Flying Medal 2363
Distinguished Service Cross 2364
Distinguished Service Decorations 341
Distinguished Service Medal 2365
Efficiency Medal 7248
Ehrenzeichen der Bundeswehr 6737
Fondation du Baron Larrey 5542
Trench Gascoigne Prize Essay Competition 4295
General Service Medal 10927
High Quality of Work Award 10432
Home Army Cross 10107
Honoris Crux 10928
Honoris Crux Diamond 10929
Honoris Crux Gold 10930
Honoris Crux Silver 10931
Honourably Mentioned in Despatches 10932
Kirti Chakra 7552
Labor Courage Award 10437
Maha Vir Chakra 7553
Medaille Militaire 5244
Medal for Armed Forces in the Service of the Fatherland 10093
Medal for Distinguished Conduct and Loyal Service 10933
Medal for Participation in the Battle for Berlin 10094
Medal for Participation in the War of 1939 10110
Medal for the Services to the Country's Defense 10112
Medalla al Merito Logisgtico y Administrativo Contralmirante Rafael Tono 1635
Medalla Militar Francisco Jose de Caldas 1636
Medalla Militar Soldado Juan Bautista Solarte Obando 1637
Medalla Servicios Distinguidos a la Aviacion Naval 1638
Medalla Servicios Distinguidos en Orden Publico 1639
Medalla Servicios Distinguidos Infanteria de Marinia 1640
Medalla Servicios Distinguidos la Fuerza de Superficie 1641
Medalla Tiempo de Servicio 1642
Medical Services Cross 10934
Military Awards 10440
Military Cross 2371
Military Decorations 10115
Military Medal 2372
Military Merit Medal 10935
Military Service Medal 7252
Military Service Star 7253
Most Excellent Order of the British Empire 2375
National Armed Act Cross 10116
National Cadet Bisley Grand Champion Medal 10936
National Medal 208
National Order of the Liberation 5238
Navy Cross 10937
Orden del Merito Aeronautico Antonio Ricaurte 1643
Orden del Merito Jose Maria Cordoba 1644
Orden del Merito Militar Antonio Narino 1645
Orden del Merito Naval Almirante Padilla 1646
Orden del Merito Sanitario Jose Fernandez Madrid 1647
Orden Departmental de Bolivar 1612
Orden Militar San Mateo 1648
Order of Australia 344
Order of Merit 2378
Order of the Cross of Liberty 4678
Order of the Lion of Finland 4679

Mineralogy   **Awards, Honors & Prizes, 1995-96**

Military (continued)
Order of the Red Banner 10466
Order of the Star of South Africa (Non-Military) 10962
Pakistan Military Awards 9996
Param Vir Chakra 7557
Param Vishisht Seva Medal 7558
Partisans' Cross 10120
Peasantry Batallion Cross 10121
Plaques of SUBNOR 10708
H.R.H. Prince Peter Award 1164
Prix Edmond Freville 5738
Prix Lazare Carnot 5699
Prix Medecin General Inspecteur Raymond Debenedetti 4862
Pro Merito Decoration 10938
Pro Merito Medal 10939
Pro Patria Medal 10940
Pro Virtute Decoration 10941
Pro Virtute Medal 10942
C. P. Robertson Memorial Trophy 2047
Paul Schurmann-Medaille 6853
Paul Schurmann-Preis 6854
Servicios Distinguidos a la Fuerza Submarina 1649
Shaurya Chakra 7561
Silesian Insurrectionary Cross 10122
South African Defence Force Champion Shot Medal 10943
South African Defence Force Good Service Medal 10944
Southern Africa Medal 10945
Southern Cross Decoration 10946
Southern Cross Medal 10947
Danie Theron Medal 10948
Unit Citations 347
Vietnam Medal 349
Vir Chakra 7563
Vishisht Seva Medal 7564
War Order Virtuti Militari 10123
Wielkopolska Insurrectionary Cross 10124

Mineralogy
Georg-Agricola-Medaille 6647
Hermann Bank Senior Silver Medal 6763
Andre H. Dumont Medal 1057
Eskola Medal 4716
Fondation Carriere de Mineralogie 5512
Fondation Delesse 5537
Fondation Henry Wilde 5583
Fondation Joseph Labbe 5603
Fondation Victor Raulin 5676
Viktor-Moritz-Goldschmidt Preis 6648
Muller Award 10240
Hugo Muller Lectureship 4211
Prix Agathon De Potter 1007
Prix Henri Buttgenbach 1024
Manuel Rocha Medal 10241
Wallmarkska Priset 11560
Abraham-Gottlob-Werner Medaille 6649

Mining and metallurgy (See also **Materials science**)
Georg Agricola Denkmunze 6849
Australian Geomechanics Award - John Jaeger Memorial Award 423
Bablik Medal 2831
Arthur Bensusan Memorial Fund Prize 12205
Vidy Bharati Prize 7622
Bhoruka Gold Medal 7623
Binani Gold Medal 7624
G. D. Birla Memorial Gold Medal 7625
Bralco Gold Medal 7626
Brinell Medal 11523
British Foundry Medal and Prize 3069
Arthur Claudet Student's Prize 3336

Consolidated Gold Fields Gold Medal 3337
Aldo Dacco Award 8126
Felice de Carli Award 8127
Marton Debreczeni Medal 7353
Christoph Traugott Delius Medal 7354
Dowding Medal and Prize 3131
EGGA Pin 2832
Stanley Elmore Fellowships 3338
Fondation Camere 5509
Fondation Georges Millot 5568
Foundry Industry Award 3070
E. J. Fox Gold Medal 3071
Frenkel Prize 10713
Sir Padamji Ginwala Gold Medal 7627
Federico Giolitti Steel Medal 8128
Dr. Paul Grunfeld Memorial Award and Medal 3135
Paul Grunfeld Prize 6850
Sir Robert Hadfield Medal and Prize 3136
Historical Metallurgy Society Grants 12175
G. Vernon Hobson Bequest 3339
Honorary Member
  European General Galvanizers Association 2833
  Indian Institute of Metals 7628
  Institute of British Foundrymen 3072
Hume-Rothery Prize 3139
IIM Platinum Medal 7629
IIM Rolling Trophy 7630
IMM Gold Medal 3340
IMM Honorary Fellow 3341
International Committee for Studies of Bauxites and Aluminum-Oxides-Hydroxides Medal 7355
Italian Association for Metallurgy Awards 8334
Antal Kerpely Medal 7356
Voya Kondic Medal 3073
Kroll Medal and Prize 3140
G. C. Kuczynski Diploma 10714
Lessing Memorial Medal 3653
Luigi Losana Gold Medal 8129
Eugenio Lubatti Award 8130
Carl Lueg Commemoration Medal 6812
MECON Award 7631
Medaglia d'Oro Aim ai Soci Fondtori 8131
Medal for Brave Performance in Mining 740
Meritorious Services Medal 3074
Metaserv Awards 3142
Samuel Mikoviny Medal 7357
Edgar Pam Fellowship 3342
Papers and Publications Committee Prizes 3654
Antal Pech Medal 7358
Pfeil Medal and Prize 3144
Platinum Medal 3145
Prain Medal and Prize 3147
Premio Condumex 9187
Prix Barbier 5303
Prix Pechiney 5704
Reden Plakette 6851
Rosenhain Medal and Prize 3148
Sail Gold Medal 7632
Samsonov Prize 10715
Silver Medal 419
Bosworth Smith Trust Fund 3343
Vilmos Soltz Medal 7359
Steel Eighties Award 7633
Stokowiec Medal and Prize 3150
Oliver Stubbs Gold Medal 3075
Zsigmond Szentkiralyi Medal 7360
Tata Gold Medal 7634
Technician of the Year Award 3151
Travel Award 3655
Van Waterschoot van der Gracht Plaque 9588
Aladar Wahlner Medal 7361

Western Australian School of Mines Award 495
World Phosphate Institute Awards 9324
Worshipful Company of Ironmongers Jubilee Award 3076
Zinc Castings 86 4654
Samu Z. Zorkoczy Medal 7362
Vilmos Zsigmondy Medal 7363

Minority groups See **Ethnic affairs**

Monument restoration
Badge for the Protection of Monuments 10088
Gazzola Prize 6001
Prins Bernhard Fonds Monumenten Prijs 9573
Fritz Schumacher Prizes 7122

Motion pictures See **Films**

Motorcycle racing
FIM Fair Play Trophy 11809
Gold Medal of the FIM 11810
Prix au Merite Motocycliste 11811
Vincent Owners Club Awards 4601
World Motorcycle Championships 11812

Museums
Council of Europe Museum Prize 5088
Fellow 531
Finnish Museums Association 50th Anniversary Medal 4702
Grand Prix National de la Museographie 5277
Jabach Medal 6596
Ferenc Mora Memorial Medal 7405
Museum of the Year Awards 532
Premio Miguel Covarrubias 9059
Prins Bernhard Fonds Museum Prijs 9574

Music (See also **Conducting; Music competitions; Music composition; Music education; Musical instruments; Musicology; Opera; Performing arts; Recording industry**; specific types of music, e.g. **Choral music**)
Aanmoedigingsprijzen 9635
ACUM Medal for Performing and Distribution of Israeli Works, Music and Literature 7942
ACUM Prizes for Literature and Music 7943
Theodor W. Adorno Award 6611
Alpenlandischer Volksmusikwettbewerb 726
Annual Prize of the Czech Musical Fund 1854
Antwoorden Prijsvragen, Klasse der Schone Kunsten 1250
Gerardo Arellano Cultural Merit Medal 1651
Stephen Arlen Memorial Fund Award 2096
Arts Achievement Award 8575
Arts Council of Northern Ireland Bursaries and Awards 7854
ASEAN Award for the Performing Arts 10031
Association of Swedish Amateur Orchestras Awards 11444
Australian Gumleaf Playing Championship 521
Australian Musical Foundation in London Award 2147
Austrian State Encouragement Prizes 758
Austrian State Grand Prize 759
Austrian State Recognition Prizes 765
Awards 1196
Bach Festival 8985

Music

Balvenie Medal 10524
Gregorio Becerra Duque Trophy 1587
Emil Berlanda Preis 727
Berlin Art Prizes 6509
Blekinge County Council Culture Prize 11446
Bratislava Radio Prize for Folklore Music 10778
BRIT Awards 2478
British Reserve Insurance Youth Orchestra Award 10592
Buenos Aires Music Prize 37
Bursaries, Scholarships, and Travel Awards 7755
Dietrich Buxtehude Prize 7037
Cesar Awards 4793
Chopin Piano Competition, Czechoslovakia 1833
City of Munich Prizes 7019
City of Vienna Prizes for Art, Science, and Humanities 789
City of Vienna Promotional Prizes 791
Companion 4111
Concurso de Jovenes Solistas 9171
Concurso Nacional de Cuartetos de Cuerdas 9174
Contest for Piano Accompanists 1453
CRPLF Awards 5070
Ryan Davies Awards 12168
Distinguished Musician Award 3041
Dublin Corporation Arts Scholarship 7758
Dusek Competition of Musical Youth 1876
Aquileo J. Echeverria Prize 1761
Euromusica Competition 11323
European Music and Poetry Competitions 1121
European Prizes for Folk Art 7111
Fellow 4112
Fellowships and Scholarships 146
Festival dei Popoli 8239
Edwin Fischer Memorial Prize 11719
Folk Music Festival - Plaketti 4741
Forderpreis des Landes Nordrhein-Westfalen fur junge Kunstlerinnen und Kunstler 7026
Forderpreis fur Musik der Landeshauptstadt Dusseldorf 6684
Glenfiddich Trophy 10525
Gold Badge 2789
Gold Medal
    Guildhall School of Music and Drama 2979
    Royal Philharmonic Society 4126
Golden Harp 9372
Goldene Mozart-Medaille 826
Goldene Mozart-Nadel 827
Grand Prix de la Musique Symphonique 6251
Grand Prix de l'Edition Musicale 6252
Grand Prix d'Interpretation de la Musique Francaise d'Aujourd'hui 6256
Grand Prix du Disque Frederic Chopin 10066
Grand Prix National de la Musique 5278
Grand Prix SACD 6395
Grant or Prize 4710
Hammer and Sickle Gold Medal 10460
El Heraldo Music Prizes 9020
Hit of the season 1402
Honorary Member
    Incorporated Society of Musicians 3042
    International Society for Contemporary Music 9526
    Royal Academy of Music 3877
    Royal Northern College of Music 4113
    Franz Schmidt Society 880
Honorary Member and Honorary Associate 3788

Impact of Music on Film Competition 1193
Innsbruck Radio Prize for Early Music 843
International Grand Prix for Liszt Records 7438
International Guitar Contest 11241
International Tchaikovsky Competition 10455
International Warsaw Autumn Festival of Contemporary Music 10164
Internationaler Fotosalon 6756
Interpreters Competition of Slovak Republic 1871
Julius Isserlis Scholarship 4127
Nami Jafet Prize 1488
Jazzpar Prize 1913
Frico Kafenda Prize 10772
Gana Kala Prapoorna in Music 7543
Kala Praveena Award 7544
Keltic Society Awards 10584
Kunstpreis der Stadt Zurich 11894
Kyoto Prizes 8539
Sascha Lasserson Memorial Trust Prize 3538
Lilli-Lehmann-Medaille 828
R. Lenaerts Prize 1257
Franz Liszt Prize 7403
Literarischer Marz 6601
Literature and Art Awards 12011
LITERATURIUMS Kabarett Award 7051
Lower Austria Prize for the Advancement of Fine Arts and Literature 859
Lower Austria Recognition Prize in Arts and Sciences 860
Ladislav Martonik Prize 10774
Ellie Marx Memorial Scholarship 11088
Leonida Massine Prize for the Art of the Dance 8156
Jack McGill Music Scholarship 9793
Medaille d'Or de la Communication Musicale 6258
Medal of Honor 10999
Medal of the Mozart City of Salzburg 867
Mobil Music Award 8703
Mozart Medal
    Instituto Cultural Domecq, A.C. 9030
    Vienna Mozart Society 913
Music Critics Prizes 6406
Music Prize 8831
Musician of the Year 9971
Musicians Benevolent Fund Awards 3669
Nagrada Saveta Fonda SO SUBNOR Cetvrti jul 10707
National Award for Literature and Arts 12002
National Cultural Awards 1413
National Music Award 1440
Vladimir Nazor Awards 1812
Nordic Biennial for Young Soloists 1906
Nordic Council Music Prize 11504
October Prizes of the City of Belgrade 10696
Order of Cultural Merit 8579
Order of Culture 8586
Order of Lenin 10463
Karol Padivy Prize 10775
Dorothy Parkinson Award for Young British Musicians 2987
Bernhard-Paumgartner-Medaille 829
Perspektiefprys 9335
Carl Ludwig Pinschof Scholarship 9794
Pisuisse Prize 9616
Joseph Plateau Prize 1194
Polar Music Prize 11530
Praemium Imperiale 8599
Preis der Landeshauptstadt Innsbruck fur Kunstlerisches Schaffen 891
Premio Iglesias 8118

Premio MEC de Arte 1442
Premio Nacional de Arte 1545
Premio Nacionales de Musica 11378
Premio Tenco 8193
Premio Trienal Instituto Torcuato di Tella Mozarteum Argentina 55
Preseren Award 10799
Prix Bordin 5364
Prix Estrade-Delcros 5387
Prix Georges Wildenstein 5395
Prix Henri Dauberville 5400
Prix Hercule Catenacci
    Institut de France 5343
    Institut de France - Academie Francaise 5867
Prix Musical de Radio Brno 1848
Prix Talents Nouveau 6399
Prize for Composers and Performers of Afrikaans Folk Musik 11039
Prize for Mozart Interpretation 914
Prize for Performers of Classical Music 11040
Pro Musica Medal 6744
Promotional Prizes 7022
Prosceniumprijs 9690
PRS Enterprise Awards 3770
Prudential Awards for the Arts 3826
Queen's Commendation for Excellence 3878
Record of the Year Prize 4691
Royal Orchestral Society Medal 4115
RPS Music Awards 4128
Salzburg Prize for the Promotion of the Arts, Science and Literature 869
Sandoz Preis 878
Annie M. G. Schmidt Prize 9373
Scholarship Prizes 6512
Scholarships of the City of Munich 7023
Scottish Daily Express New Names Awards 10539
Francois Shapira Prize 7971
Shell - LSO Music Scholarship 3618
Singer-Polignac Grants 5226
Leonie Sonning Music Award 2009
Sounds Australian Awards 671
Ludwig-Spohr-Preis 6575
Springbok Radio Sarie Awards 11043
Spurs of Criticism 4760
Jakob Stainer Preis 730
Johann-Wenzel-Stamitz-Preis 6526
Standard Bank Young Artists' Awards 10849
Jani Strasser Award 2942
Tiroler Landespreis fur Kunst 732
Pavol Tonkovic Prize 10776
Donald Tovey Memorial Prize 4583
Trade Union's Art and Cultural Prize 7442
Traditional Irish Singing and Dancing Society Awards 7850
TRIC Annual Celebrity Awards 4508
Troubadour de la SABAM 1071
Upper Austria Culture Prize for Music 904
Ernst Von Siemens Music Prize 7163
Joost van den Vondel Prizes 7133
Wettbewerb "Jugend musiziert" 734
Sir Thomas White's Music Scholarship 2707
Clive Wilson Award for Young Musicians 2988
Wolf Foundation Prizes 7987
Hugo Wolf-Medaille 834
World Festival of Underwater Pictures 6483
Wurdigungspreis 862
Yorkshire Post Art and Music Award 4645
Zauberfloten-Medaille 830

Music Awards, Honors & Prizes, 1995-96

Music competitions (*See also* Opera; Piano competitions; Violin competitions; Vocal music)
AT&T Istel Young Musicians Awards 3839
BBC Television Young Musician of the Year 2297
British Music Society Awards 2459
Bromsgrove Festival Young Musicians' Platform 2558
Valentino Bucchi Prize of Rome Capital City 8263
Budapest International Music Competition 7414
Maria Callas Grand Prix, Opera, Oratorio-Lied 7186
Maria Canals International Music Competition for Musical Performance, Barcelona 11168
Teresa Carreno Latin American Competition for Piano 12118
Chartres International Organ Competition 4936
CIA Merit Awards 814
City of Alessandria International Competition in Classical Guitar 8201
Concertino Prague International Radio Competition for Young Musicians 1838
Concorso Internationale di Musica da Camera "Palma d'Oro" di Citta di Finale Lingure 8120
Concorso Internazionale di violoncello Gaspar Cassado 8442
Concorso Internazionale Mauro Giuliani Duo di Chitarre 8183
Concours D'Orgue Europeen de Beauvais 5108
Concours International de Clavecin de Paris 5177
Concours International de Harpe Louise Charpentier 5210
Concours International de Musique de Chambre de Paris 6432
Concours International de Musique de Chambre pour Ensembles d'Instruments a Vent 11680
Concours International d'Ensembles de Musique de Chambre de Colmar 5042
Concours International du Festival de Musique de Toulon 5076
Concours International Printemps de la Guitare 1106
Concours National Feminin de Musique du Lyceum de Suisse 11682
Concurso de Jovenes Solistas 9171
Concurso Internacional de Piano Ciudad de Montevideo 12090
Concurso Permanente De Jovenes Interpretes 11285
Conquest of the Classical Guitar International Competition 8018
CRPLF Awards 5070
Alirio Diaz International Competition for Guitar 12119
Early Music Festival - Bruges 1152
The Essex Chronicle Awards for the Essex Schools Musician of the Year 3735
European Chopin Piano Competition 6594
European Piano Competition 4916
Evian International String Quartet Competition 6192
Finale Ligure International Chamber Music Competition 8106
Cesar Franck Organ Competition 9432
Grand Prix de la Melodie Francaise 6408
Grand Prix de la Ville de Paris 5034
Harveys Leeds International Pianoforte Competition 2994
Heran Violoncello Competition 1835
Paul Hofhaimer Prize of the Tyrolian Capital City Innsbruck 890
Vaclav Huml International Violin Competition 1801
International Competition for Chamber Music Ensembles 8102
International Competition for Musical Performers - Geneva 11774
International Competition for Violin and Viola Makers 1516
International Competition of Franz Schubert and Twentieth Century Music 805
International Dmitri Shostakovich Competition of String Quartets 10453
International Double Bass Competition Giovanni Bottesini 8168
International Electroacoustic Music Competition Bourges 4999
International Gaudeamus Interpreters Competition 9438
International Harp Contest in Israel 7899
International J. S. Bach Competition 6936
International Jeunesses Musicales Competition - Belgrade 10717
International Karl Richter Organ Competition 6899
International Kuhlau Competition for Flautists 6966
International Musical Contest Dr. Luis Sigall Competition 1570
International Organ Competition, Odense 1965
International Paulo Cello Competition 4750
International Robert Schumann Choir Competition 6978
International Rostrum of Young Performers/UNESCO 10784
International String Quartet Competition 8444
International Tchaikovsky Competition 10455
International Villa-Lobos Guitar Competition 1501
International Warsaw Autumn Festival of Contemporary Music 10164
Internationaler Musikwettbewerb der ARD 6974
Interpretation Competition 3448
Irino Prize 8559
Philip Jones International Brass Chamber Music Competition, Barcs 7416
Jugend musiziert Preis 853
Jury's Special Award 3449
Kerkrade World Music Contest 9695
Kobe International Flute Competition 8683
Kranichsteiner Musikpreis 6976
Lahti International Organ Competition 4746
Robert Levins Festspillfond 9874
John Lill Awards for Essex Young Musician of the Year 3736
Linz International Anton Bruckner Organ Competition 857
Liszt Society Prize 3592
Llangollen International Musical Eisteddfod 12177
London International String Quartet Competition 3606
Masterplayers International Music and Conductors Competition 11877
Mathy & Opera Awards 262
National Classical Music Contest 8834
Neshamwari Traditional Music and Dance Festival 12220
NFMS/ESSO Young Concert Artists 3684
Sigbjorn Bernhoft Osas Festspillpfond 9876
Prague Spring International Music Competition 1880
Prix de Soliste de l'AMS 11659
Prize for Performance of Israeli Works 7909
Puy of Electroacoustic Music Competition 5000
Queen Elisabeth International Music Competition of Belgium Prizes 1245
Rostropovitch International Cello Competition 6201
Royal Over-Seas League Music Competition 4117
Santander International Piano Competition 11355
Scheveningen International Music Competition 9614
Stichting Internationaal Orgelconcours 9659
Stroud and District Festival 4497
Swiss Organ Competition 11945
Taipei International Music Competition 12007
Francisco Tarrega International Guitar Competition 11153
Lionel Tertis International Viola Competition and Workshop 3627
Tokyo International Competition for Chamber Music 8624
Tokyo International Music Competition 8770
Tokyo Music Festival 8772
Tournemire Prize 3450
Triennial International Carillon Competition - Queen Fabiola 1348
Tunbridge Wells International Young Concert Artist Competition 4557
Maurice Vieux International Alto Competition 6469
Young Artists' Competition of Kol Israel 7918
Young Concert Artists Trust Award 4649
Young Performers Award 197

Music composition
AGEC-Preis 9477
Ancona International Music Composition Competition for Wind Instruments 8191
Arts Prize - Yoel Engel Prize 7949
Austrian State Prize for European Composers 761
Tadeusz Baird Memorial Competition for Young Composers 10141
Don Banks Composer Fellowship 158
Don Banks Fellowship 162
BBC Television Young Musician of the Year 2297
Jan Levoslav Bella Prize 10771
Ernest Bloch International Competition for Musical Composition 11949
Leslie Boosey Award 3768
Karel Boury Prize 1267
British Academy of Film and Television Arts Awards - Film 2233
British Academy of Film and Television Arts Awards - Television 2234
Benjamin Britten Composers' Competition 2556
Valentino Bucchi Prize of Rome Capital City 8263
Budapest International Composers' Competition 7365
Inocente Carreno Competition for Composers 12117
Catalonian Prizes for Music 11182
Colombian Composers Competition Prizes 1655
Competition for Composers 7015
Competition of Composition for Choirs 11196

770

Composition Competition, Tours 5192
Composition Competitions 4376
Composition of the Year 9970
Composition Prize 4125
Composition Prize for Young European Composers 9337
Concorso Internazionale di Composizione Organistica Oliver Messiaen 8203
Concorso Internazionale Luigi Russolo 8261
Concours International de Composition Musicale, Avray 4977
Concours International de Composition Musicale Opera et Ballet Geneve 11678
Defresne Prize 9607
Vivian Ellis Prize 3769
George Enescu Prize 10347
Ferenc Erkel Prize for Musical Composition 7400
Eurovision Song Contest 11692
Forderpreis des Landes Nordrhein-Westfalen fur junge Kunstlerinnen und Kunstler 7026
Grand Prix de la Chanson Francaise 6250
Grand Prix de l'Oeuvre Musicale Audiovisuelle 6254
Grand Prix du Jazz 6257
Grand Prix Musical de la Ville de Paris 6093
Grant or Prize 4710
El Heraldo Music Prizes 9020
Prix International Arthur Honegger de Composition Musicale 5197
International Carl Maria von Weber Competition, Dresden 6921
International Competition for Original Composition for Band 8409
International Competition for Symphonic Composition, Trieste 8402
International Competition in Composition of Sacred Music 11736
International Competition of Music Composition 5182
International Composers Competition Kazimierz Serocki 10183
International Composition Contest Guido d'Arezzo 8215
International Contest for Carillon Composition 1347
International Electroacoustic Music Competition Bourges 4999
International Gaudeamus Musicweek for Young Composers Award 9439
International Henryk Wieniawski Composers Competition 10073
International Piano Composition Contest 6040
International Songwriters' Association Awards 7787
International Women-Composer's Competition 11666
Irino Prize 8559
Kevock Choir and Bank of Scotland Scottish Folk Song Arrangement Competition 10586
Korean Composition Award 8822
Kranichsteiner Musikpreis 6976
Ernst Krenek-Preis der Stadt Wien 793
Marc Lavry Prize 7880
Paul Lowin Orchestral Prize 517
Paul Lowin Song Cycle Prize 518
Witold Lutoslawski International Composers Competition 10214
Macaulay Fellowship 7760
Masterplayers International Music and Conductors Competition 11877
Mozart Medal 9030
Music Prize 8831
Musician of the Year 9971

National Prize for Music Maestro Sojo 12123
Philip Neill Memorial Prize in Music 9851
Nordic Council Music Prize 11501
Olympia International Composition Prize 7200
Operasangerinnen Fanny Elstas Fond 9875
Goffredo Petrassi International Competition for Composers 8392
Polish Composers Union Prize 10142
Premio Maestro Villa 11296
Premio Municipal Alfredo Marceneiro de Fado 10265
Premio Nazionale Composizione 8245
Premios Municipais Joly Braga Santos de Musica 10281
Prime Minister's Prize for Composition 7908
Prix Andre Caplet 5358
Prix Ars Electronica 772
Prix Arthur De Greef 951
Prix Ch. M. Tornov-Loeffler 5368
Prix Chartier 5369
Prix de Compositeur de l'AMS 11658
Prix de Composition Musicale 9311
Prix de la Fondation Florence Gould 5376
Prix de Soussay 5379
Prix Florent Schmitt 5390
Prix Georges Bizet
  Institut de France 5342
  Institut de France - Academie des Beaux Arts 5394
Prix Hector Lefuel 5399
Prix Henriette Renie 5402
Prix Houllevigue 5403
Prix Irene Fuerison 960
Prix Jacques Durand 5405
Prix Monbinne 5415
Prix Nicolo 5416
Prix Paul-Louis Weiller 5418
Prix Quadriennal de Composition Musicale Camille Huysmans 1055
Prix Rene Dumesnil 5421
Prix Rossini 5423
Prix Samuel - Rousseau 5426
Prize for Composers and Performers of Afrikaans Folk Musik 11039
Prize for Revolutionary Song 8882
Puy of Electroacoustic Music Competition 5000
Queen Elisabeth International Music Competition of Belgium Prizes 1245
Queen Marie Jose International Musical Composition Prize 11896
Romanian Radio and Television Award 10327
Romanian Union of Composers Prizes 10406
Dr. William Baird Ross Trust Competition 10595
Royal Over-Seas League Music Competition 4117
RPS Music Awards 4128
Sinhala Drama Awards 11426
Harold Smart Anthem Competition 4139
Leonie Sonning Music Award 2009
Sopot International Song Festival 10130
Sounds Australian Awards 671
Ludwig-Spohr-Preis 6575
Stroud and District Festival 4497
Stuttgart City Prize for Young Composers 7138
Swiss Music - Edition 11941
Tamil Drama Award 11427
Camillo Togni International Composers Competition 8133
Marten Toonder Award 7762

Troubadour de la SABAM 1071
Matthijs Vermeulenprijs 9651
Vienna International Composition Contest 774
Sir Thomas White's Music Scholarship 2707
Wihuri Sibelius Prize 4763
Yorkshire & Humberside Arts Young Composers Awards 3029

Music education
Leo Kestenberg Medal 6870
Sir George Thalben-Ball Memorial Scholarships 4532
UNESCO - International Music Council Music Prize 6421
Young Pianists Yearly Award 2843

Musical instruments
Early Music Festival - Bruges 1152
International Guitar Makers Competition 6185
International Henryk Wieniawski Violinmakers Competition 10075
International Society of Violin and Bow Makers Competitions 9531
International Triennial of Stringed Instruments 8321
Oskar Nedbal Award 1850
Prize for Fabrication of Traditional Musical Instrument 8881
Royal Dublin Society Crafts Competition 7835

Musicology
Derek Allen Prize 2221
Arts Prize - Yoel Engel Prize 7949
Dent Medal 4107
Ferenc Erkel Prize for Musical Composition 7400
Grant or Prize 4710
Jozef Kresanek Prize 10773
National Music Award 1440
Parma Rotary Club International Prize "Giuseppe Verdi" 8386
Frank Peleg Prize 7883
Polish Composers Union Prize 10142
Ciprian Porumbescu Prize 10378
Prix Kastner-Boursault 5409
Prix Rene Dumesnil 5421
Prize for Musicology 915
Romanian Union of Composers Prizes 10406
UNESCO - International Music Council Music Prize 6421
Floris van der Mueren Prize 1260

Mycology
Clusius Carolus Award 7345
ISHAM Lucille K. Georg Award 1202
Prix Denis Thienpont 1329
Schoenlein-Plakette 6872

Mystery writing
CWA/Cartier Diamond Dagger Award 2710
CWA Gold Dagger Award 2711
CWA John Creasey Memorial Award 2713
CWA Last Laugh Award 2714
CWA Rumpole Award 2715
Hammett Award 1825
Suntory Awards for Mystery Fiction 8525
Alexei Tolstoi Award 1826

Mythology
Prix Le Fevre-Deumier (de Pons) 5468
Prix Lefevre-Deumier de Pons 5772

National

National security
Fondation Alexandre Darracq 5480
Fondation du General Muteau 5547
Fondation Lamb 5609
Institute of Civil Defence and Disaster Studies Competitions 3084
Medal for the Services to the Country's Defense 10112
Order of Lenin 10463
Prix Amiral Castex 5230
Prix Marechal Foch 5892
Prix Science et Defense 5246

Natural history See Science

Natural science See Science

Nature
INF-Press Prize 1198
Natural World Book of the Year Award 3714
Verlagspreis zur Forderung popularwissenschaftlicher Literatur fur das jungere Lesealter 7152

Nature photography
Birkenhead International Colour Salon 2190

Naval architecture See Naval engineering

Naval engineering
Samuel Baxter Prize 4089
BMEC Donald Maxwell Award 3115
Calder Bequest 4090
Denny Gold Medal 3116
Fondation Plumey 5655
William Froude Medal 4091
Froude Research Scholarship in Naval Architecture 4092
Stanley Gray Award 3117
Stanley Gray Fellowships 3118
David Hislop Award 3240
Institute Silver Medal 3119
Percy Jackson Award 3120
RINA Gold, Silver and Bronze Medals 4093
RINA Small Craft Group Medal 4094
Kevin Stark Memorial Award 488
Herbert Akroyd Stuart Award 3121
Trusler Prize 4095
Wakeham Prize 4096
Watts Prize 4097
Sir William White Post-Graduate Scholarship in Naval Architecture 4098

Navigation
Lode Baekelmans Prize 1264
Bronze Medal 4075
Fellow 4076
Fondation Binoux 5504
Fondation de Madame Edmond Hamel 5534
Fondation Jean du Hamel de Breuil 5596
Gold Medal 4077
Honorary Member 4078
Nautical Institute Competitions 3716
Order for Industrial Merit 1732
Premio F. Cameli 8352
Silver Medal 4079
Gustave Willems Prize 1239

Neurology
Hughlings Jackson Lecture and Medal 4255
Amrut Mody-Unichem Prize for Research in Cardiology, Neurology and Gastroenterology 7596
Raven Lecturer 1967
Sherrington Memorial Lecture 4266
Young Scientist Award 1968

Awards, Honors & Prizes, 1995-96

Newspapers See Journalism

Non-destructive testing See Testing

Nonfiction
Angel Literary Award 2080
Arts Council of Wales Book of the Year Awards 12150
ASEAN Award for Literature 10030
BIMCO/Lloyd's List Maritime Book Prize 3598
Boardman Tasker Memorial Award for Mountain Literature 2192
Book Awards 10734
Book of the Sea Award 3521
Buckland Literary Award 9846
CWA Gold Dagger Award for Non-Fiction 2712
Dimitrije Tucovic Nonfiction Award 10719
Escorts Book Award 7491
Fawcett Book Prize 2868
Festival Awards for Literature 673
Calvin and Rose G. Hoffman Prize for Distinguished Publication on Christopher Marlowe 3525
Pieter Cornelisz Hooft Prize 9665
Japanese Non-Fiction Prize 8678
Kodansha Prize 8687
Fran Levstik Prize 10807
Recht Malan Prize 11115
Mercury Business Book Award 3642
Natural World Book of the Year Award 3714
NCR Book Award 2139
New South Wales State Literary Awards 147
New Zealand Book Awards 9801
Oya Soichi Non-Fiction Prize 8754
PEN Best First Book of Non-fiction Award 9779
Eve Pownall Award: Information Books 313
Premier's Literary Awards 149
Premio a las Mejores Obras Cientificas o Tecnicas Publicadas en el Ano 1818
Prix Aujourd'hui 6162
Prix des Maisons de la Presse Prize 6106
Prix Louis Castex 5885
Prix Valery Larbaud 4987
Science Book Prizes 4157
Lilian Ida Smith Award 9782
Southern Arts Literature Prize 4481
Storywriting and Art Project 417
Strega Prize 8439
Tieto-Finlandia Prize 4688
Time-Life Silver Pen Award for Non-Fiction 2784
Western Australian Premier's Book Awards 515
Whitfield Prize 4021
Yomiuri Human Document Prize 8793

Nuclear disarmament See World peace

Nuclear engineering (See also Atomic energy)
Gold Plate of ANDIN 8384
Graduate Award 3345
Hinton Medal 3346
HMS Sultan Prize 3347
Honorary Fellowship 3348
Nuclear Physics Postgraduate Student Awards 11070
Pinkerton Award 3349
Royal Naval College, Greenwich Prize 3350
Rutherford Medal and Prize 3196
Gilbert Tomes Award 3351
University of Cambridge Arthur Shercliff Prize 3352

University of Manchester Prize 3353
Bruce Youngman Award 3354

Numismatics
Annual Club Competition 9789
Prix Babut 6361
Bantug Award 10055
Bronze Medal 258
Gold Medal 259
Jeton de Vermeil 6362
Medal of Honor 11763
Prix Allier de Hauteroche 5436
Prix Duchalais 5454
Prix Edmond Drouin 5455
Prix Quinquennal de Numismatique 1100
Prix Roman et Tania Ghirshman 5471
Prix Victor Tourneur
  Academie Royale de Belgique - Classe des Beaux-Arts 970
  Academie Royale de Belgique - Classe des Lettres et des Sciences Morales et Politiques 999
Quadrennial Prize of the Royal Belgian Numismatic Society 1345
Sanford Saltus Medal 12162
Silver Medal 260

Nursing
Auxiliar de Enfermera Lucia Salcido 9126
Honour Distinctions 10166
International Oncology Nursing Fellowships 11860
Florence Nightingale Medal 11771
Nursing Service Cross 343
Pakistan Civil Awards 9995
Premio al Merito Nacional Enfermera Isabel Cendala Gomez 9128
Christiane Reimann Prize 11778
Royal Red Cross 2384
Special Awards 2659

Nutrition
FENS European Nutrition Award 11883
Fondation du Docteur et de Madame Henri Labbe 5543
German Nutrition Foundation Travel Scholarship 6856
Journalist Prize of the DGE 6857
Armando Kaminitz Research Awards 7981
Hans Adolf Krebs-Preis 6858
Aboim Sande Lemos Prize 10254
Premio Nacional de Ciencia y Tecnologia de Alimentos 8965
Prix du Centre de Recherches Cliniques et Biologiques sur la Nutritiotion de l'Homme 4832
Prix Pierre et Celine Lhermite 4871
Max Rubner-Preis 6859
Dr. Juan Salcedo, Jr. Memorial Lecturer 10051
Fund Professor Doctor G. Verdonk 1320
A. I. Virtanen - Award 4671

Occupational health
Distinguished Service Awards 4165
Eagle Star Training Award 4166
Sir George Earle Trophy 4167
Fondation Montyon des Arts Insalubres 5638
Ned Franklin Medal 3218
Gold, Silver, Bronze and Merit Awards 4168
International Industrial Film and Video Awards 2703
Kimberly-Clark Special Award 4170
Sector Awards 4172

Subject Index of Awards
Volume 2: International and Foreign

Painting

Occupational safety
Distinguished Service Awards 4165
Eagle Star Training Award 4166
Sir George Earle Trophy 4167
Fondation Maujean 5629
Ned Franklin Medal 3218
Gold, Silver, Bronze and Merit Awards 4168
International Industrial Film and Video Awards 2703
Kimberly-Clark Special Award 4170
Safety Awards 2484
Sector Awards 4172

Occupational therapy See **Rehabilitation and therapy**

Oceanography (See also **Hydrography**)
Cath Allen Prize 2576
W. S. Bruce Medal 10639
Albert Defant-Medaille 6642
Fondation Georges Millot 5568
Fondation Jacques Bourcart 5587
Norman Heaps Prize 2577
International Festival of Maritime and Exploration Films 6014
National Marine Science Prize 1690
Prix de la Belgica 1014
Prix des Sciences de la Mer 5692
Royal Society of Victoria Medal 638

Oil painting See **Painting**

Oncology See **Cancer**

Opera (See also **Vocal music**)
AA Life Vita Ballet and Opera Awards 10810
AA Life Vita Contemporary Choreography and Dance Awards 10811
American Institute of Musical Studies Award 565
Austrian Operatic Award 566
Bayreuth Scholarship 567
Dame Mabel Brookes Memorial Fellowship 568
Bursaries, Scholarships, and Travel Awards 7755
Maria Callas Grand Prix, Opera, Oratorio-Lied 7186
John Christie Award 2938
Concorso Internazionale Musicale Francesco Paolo Neglia 8205
Concours International de Chant de Paris 6431
Concours International de Chant Lyrique de Verviers 1215
Concours International de Composition Musicale Opera et Ballet Geneve 11678
Concurso Internazionale per Cantanti Lirici Citta di Ercolano 8480
Carl Ebert Award 2939
Esso - Glyndebourne Touring Opera Singers' Award 2940
Lady Galleghan Encouragement Award 569
Julian Gayarre International Singing Competition 11254
German Operatic Award 570
Glyndebourne Peter Stuyvesant Award 2941
International Belvedere Competition for Opera Singers 911
International Competition for Verdian Voices 8293
International Competition for Young Opera Singers - Sofia 1525
International Competition, Opera and Bel Canto 1069

International Gaudeamus Musicweek for Young Composers Award 9439
International Rostrum of Young Performers/UNESCO 10784
International Vocal Competition 's-Hertogenbosch 9539
International Voice Competition of Bilbao 11275
The London Evening Standard Ballet and Opera Awards 3600
Mathy & Opera Awards 262
Metropolitan Opera Auditions - Australian Regional Finals 571
National Contest for Opera Singers 1438
National Music Award 1440
National Operatic and Dramatic Association Awards 3695
Nederburg Opera and Ballet Award 11107
New Voices - European Singing Contest 6567
John Noble Bursary 10675
Laurence Olivier Awards 4466
Opera Prize 11573
Opera Screen Award 844
Premio Biella 8010
Prix de Soussay 5838
Prix Monbinne 5415
Prix Samuel - Rousseau 5426
Prudential Awards for the Arts 3826
RPS Music Awards 4128
Shell, Royal Opera House, Covent Garden Scholarship 572
Split Summer Festival 1803
Televised Opera Prize of the City of Salzburg 870
Toti Dal Monte International Singing Competition 8222
Treviso Lyric Prize 8223
Erich Vietheer Memorial Award 2943

Operations research
Distinguished Principal Founding Member 836
EURO Golden Medal 6010
Hodgson Prize 3893
Honorary Scholar 837
Peccei Scholar 838

Ophthalmology
Charamis Medal 1135
Sir Stewart Duke Elder International Medal 9500
Jules Francois Medal 9501
Gold Medal 2023
Gonin Medal 9502
Helmholtz Medal 1136
Holmes Lecture 10728
International Council of Ophthalmology Awards 9484
IOOL Medal 3446
Middlemore Award 2448
Adolfo Noceti and Atilio Tiscornia Prize 91
Ocampo Lecture 10729
Ophthalmology Fund Prizes and Lectures 4263
Prix du Docteur Robert Netter 4833
Prix Prosper Veil 4873
Ridley Medal 3438
Jose Rizal Medal 10730
Trachoma Gold Medal 6036

Optics
Nandor Barany Medal 7444
ICO Galileo Galilei Medal 5984
ICO Prize
 International Commission for Optics 5985

International Union of Pure and Applied Physics 11485
Jozsef Petzval Medal 7446
Prize for Optics 11084
Thomas Young Medal and Prize 3198

Optometry
International Optometrist of the Year 3444
IOOL Emeritus 3445
IOOL Medal 3446

Orchestral conducting See **Conducting**

Organizational service
Award of Merit 2472
Harry M. Ballantyne Award 11990
Eminent Activist Medal 7379
International Social Security Association Medal 11837
Medaille Henry Dunant 11915
Medical Association of South Africa Branch Award for Meritorious Service 10891
Ministry of National Education Medal 1659

Oriental culture See **Asian studies; Japanese culture**

Ornithology
Australasian Seabird Group Awards 9703
Australian Bird Call Championship 520
Best Annual Bird Report 2290
Best Bird Book of the Year 2291
Bird Illustrator of the Year 2292
Bird Photograph of the Year 2293
Birdlife International/FFPS Conservation Expedition Competition 2188
Foederpreis Vogelschutz 6651
Godman-Salvin Medal 2464
Jubilee Medal 2551
David Lack Studentship 2465
Ornithologen-Preis 6652
RSPB Medal 4175
Erwin-Stresemann-Preis 6653
Werner Sunkel Stiftung 6654
Bernard Tucker Medal 2552
Union Medal 2466
Wildlife Action Award 4652

Orthodontistry
Chapman Prize Essay 2525
Ernest Sheldon Friel Memorial Lecture 2837
W. J. B. Houston Research Awards 2838
Northcroft Memorial Lecture 2526
Georges Villain Prize 3403

Packaging
Deutscher Verpackungs-Wettbewerb 7078
Euro Best Awards 3362
Eurostar Awards for Packaging 9412
Good Design Selection 8817
International Design Competition, Osaka 8606
Korea Good-Packaging Exhibition 8818
Scanstar Packaging Competiton 2005
State Emblem for Adequate Packaging 750
Worldstars for Packaging 6490

Painting (See also **Watercolor painting**)
Academy Awards 9750
Archibald Prize 124
ARTA Magazine Awards 10394
ASEAN Award for Visual Arts 10032
Becas de Creacion Artistica 11142
Bienal de Pintores Rufino Tomayo 9206
Biennial of Bantu Contemporary Art 6507
BP Portrait Award 3704

Painting (continued)
Bremer Forderpreis fur Bildende Kunst 6579
Bua-Luang Art Competition Prize 12023
City of Vienna Prizes for Art, Science, and Humanities 789
Concurso Nacional para Estudiantes de Artes Plasticas en Aguascalientes 9211
De Laszlo Medal 4177
Federation of British Artists Prizes and Awards 2870
Fine Arts Prize 8829
Forderpreis des Landes Nordrhein-Westfalen fur junge Kunstlerinnen und Kunstler 7026
Portia Geach Memorial Award 128
Gold Medal Conanti Award 1898
Grand Prix des Arts de la Ville de Paris 6092
Grand Prix ICA - Prix de Sculpture 10689
Grand Prix International d'Arts et Lettres Notre-Dame et la Mer 4958
Grand Prix National de la Peinture 5279
Grote Prys Alfons Blomme 1231
Hunting/*Observer* Art Prizes 3760
Douglas Hyde Gold Medal 7759
International Print Biennal - Varna 1532
Katanning Art Prize 511
Stephan Lochner Medal 6597
Lupi Prize 10304
Julio Mardel Prize 10305
Medaille des Arts Plastiques 4784
Michaly Munkacsy Prize for Visual and Applied Arts 7406
National Akademi Award 7534
National Award for Painting and Graphics 9990
Vladimir Nazor Awards 1812
Norwegian Master-Painter Organization Awards 9940
Order of Culture 8586
Panorama of Actual Brasilian Art 1492
Praemium Imperiale 8599
Preis der Neuen Darmstadter Sezession fur Junge Kunstler 6603
Premio Anual de Aquisicao 10285
Premio Anual de Investigacao 10286
Premio Blanco y Negro de Pintura 11316
Premio Francisco de Goya 11290
Premio Municipal Carlos Botelho de Pintura 10267
Premio Regional de Pintura 9165
Prix Achille Fould-Stirbey 5353
Prix Alphonse Cellier 5356
Prix Alphonse de Neuville et Sanford Saltus 5357
Prix Balleroy
  Institut de France 5338
  Institut de France - Academie des Beaux Arts 5362
Prix Bastien-Lepage 5363
Prix Bordin 5364
Prix Breaute 5365
Prix Brizard 5366
Prix Charles Caty 953
Prix Claude Berthault 5371
Prix Colmont 5373
Prix Constant Montald 954
Prix Dagnan-Bouveret 5374
Prix de Peinture Andre et Berthe Nouflard 5199
Prix de Portrait Paul-Louis Weiller 5378
Prix de Rome 9578
Prix Dulac 5385
Prix Dumas-Millier 5386
Prix E. du Cayla-Martin 955
Prix Elie Faure 4985
Prix Emile Sacre 957

Prix Estrade-Delcros 5387
Prix et Fondations Concernant l'Academie de France a Rome 5388
Prix Eugene Piot 5389
Prix Felix Feneon 5203
Prix Gabriel Ferrier 5393
Prix Georges Wildenstein 5395
Prix Gustave Camus 959
Prix Gustave Courtois 5396
Prix Haumont 5398
Prix Hector Lefuel 5399
Prix Henri Lehmann 5401
Prix Houllevigue 5403
Prix Jeanne Burdy 5345
Prix Jos Albert 961
Prix Karl Beule 5408
Prix Le Guay-Lebrun 5410
Prix Leclerc - Maria Bouland 5411
Prix Louise Dehem 965
Prix Maurice R... D... 5412
Prix Maxime David 5413
Prix Meurand 5414
Prix Paul Artot 966
Prix Paul Chabas 5417
Prix Paul-Louis Weiller 5418
Prix Rene Janssens 969
Prix Troyon et Edouard Lemaitre 5429
Prize for Painting 10401
Doctor Gustavo Cordeiro Ramos Prize 10287
Royal Academy Summer Exhibition 3864
Royal Hibernian Academy of Arts Awards 7837
Royal Subsidy for Modern Painting 9612
Salon Anual de Artes Plasticas Premios Pedro Domingo Murillo 1389
Salon Nacional de Artes Plasticas - Pintura 9246
Soares Dos Reis Prize 10306
Spanish Association of Painters and Sculptors Prizes 11381
Standard Bank Namibia Biennale 9326
Storywriting and Art Project
  Australia - Department of Veterans' Affairs, Public Relations Dept. 144
  Heidelberg Repatriation Hospital - Department of Veterans' Affairs 417
Sulman Prize 125
Triennale-India Award of Lalit Kala Akademi 7535
Willink Van Collen Prize 9545
Therese van Duyl-Schwartze Portrait Award 9685
Paul Tetar Van Elven Fund Prize 9546
Wolf Foundation Prizes 7987
Charles Wollaston Award 3865

Paleontology See **Geology and paleontology**

Paper industry (*See also* **Forestry; Wood and Wood products**)
Walter-Brecht-Denkmunze 6537
Hans-Clemm-Denkmunze 6538
Ehrenring der ehemaligen Forschungsstelle Papiergeschichte 6539
Goldene Vereinsnadel 6540
Honorary Member 6541
Valentin-Hottenroth-Denkmunze 6542
Eugen-Lendholt-Denkmunze 6543
Alexander-Mitscherlich-Denkmunze 6544
Paper Industry Gold Medal 2468
Technical Association of the Australian and New Zealand Pulp and Paper Industry Awards 689
Dr. Edmund-Thiele-Denkmunze 6545

Parachuting See **Flying**

Parenting See **Family relations**

Park planning (*See also* **City planning**)
Peter Joseph Lenne Prize 6562

Parks See **Recreation**

Patents See **Inventions**

Pathology
Otto-Appel-Denkmunze 6667
Domingo J. Brachetto Brian Prize 72
Cellular Pathology Prize 3168
Dautrebande Physiopathology Foundation Prize 1112
Arthur de Falloise Quinquennial Prize 1065
Distinguished Fellow 614
Pedro I. Elizalde Prize 77
Fondation Alphonse Laveran 5485
Fondation Godard 5569
Gold Headed Cane 8788
Medaille d'Or Laveran 6241
Prix Albert-Pierre-Jean Dustin 1323
Prix Noury-Lemarie 6242
Prix Pfizer 1338
Prix Quinquennal Docteur Albert Dubois pour la Pathologie tropicale 1340
Gordon Signy Foreign Fellowship 8789
Smt. Pushpa Sriramachari Award 7611
Prijs J. B. Van Helmont 1319

Patriotism See **Citizenship and patriotism**

Peace See **World peace**

Pediatrics
British Association of Paediatric Surgeons Awards 10516
Adalbert Czerny Preis 6820
Czlonek Honorowy 10132
Dr. H. B. Dingley Memorial Award 7585
Marcellino Herrera Vegas Prize 81
Otto Heubner Preis 6821
IPA Medal 6038
Jacques Lefebvre Memorial Award 5130
Dr. Kamala Menon Medical Research Award 7595
Mother and Child International Award 11881
Juan Carlos Navarro Prize 88
Nycomed Prize 9528
Prix Etienne Chabrol 4838
Schweisguth Prize 9529
Calixto Torres Umana Award 1692
Edith Whetnall Lectureship 4272

Performing arts (*See also* **Ballet; Choreography; Costume design; Dance; Drama; Entertainment; Music; Puppetry; Theater**)
Arts Achievement Award 8575
Arts Council of Northern Ireland Bursaries and Awards 7854
Arts Prize - Moshe Halevi Prize 7948
Awards 1196
The Bathurst: Narrator of the Year 288
Berlin Art Prizes 6509
British Academy of Film and Television Arts Awards - Film 2233
British Academy of Film and Television Arts Awards - Television 2234
Hamilton Deane Award 2753
European Prizes for Folk Art 7111
European Showmen's Union Awards 8864
Export Prize 9371

Philosophy

Fellowships and Scholarships 146
El Heraldo Prizes 9021
International Dag Hammarskjold Award 1237
Mari Jaszai Prize 7401
National Award for Literature and Arts 12002
Nordic Council Music Prize 11501
Pakistan Civil Awards 9995
Perspektiefprys 9335
Polish Composers Union Prize 10142
Premi Xavier Fabregas 11164
Premio Nacional de Arte 1545
Premios Municipais Palmira Bastos e Antonio Silva de Interpretacao Teatral 10282
Alfonso Reyes Prize 9156
Salzburg Prize for the Promotion of the Arts, Science and Literature 869
Sargeet Natak Akademi Fellowships 7545
Annie M. G. Schmidt Prize 9373
Scholarship Prizes 6512
Silver Harp 9374
Sinhala Drama Awards 11426
Time Out Theatre, Dance and Comedy Awards 4545

Perfumes *See* **Cosmetology**

Personal achievement *See* **Professional and personal achievement**

Personnel management (*See also* **Training and development**)
Awards for Exemplary Contributions to the Human Resource Management Field 714
Manpower Society Essay Competition 3629

Pest control *See* **Public health**

Petroleum engineering
Cadman Memorial Medal 3181
Redwood Medal 3182

Petroleum industry
Carl Engler Medal 6861
H. E. Jones London Medal 3328
Sugg Heritage Award 3330
Carl Zerbe Prize 6862

Pets *See* **Animal care and training**

Pharmacology
Akzo prijs 9389
Dr. Nitya Anand Endowment Lecture 7636
Award for Drug Discovery 4360
Awards in Recognition of Excellence 9516
Andre Bedat Award 9517
Development Grants 9518
Distinguished Service Certificate 582
Distinguished Service Medal 583
Franz-Dittrich-Ehrenring 801
W. E. Dixon Lecture 4240
Julije Domac Medal 1805
Ehrennadel der Deutschen Apotheker 6585
Fellow 7179
Fellowship Award 9867
FIP Fellowships 9519
FIP International Travel Scholarships 9520
Fluckiger Medaille 6586
Fondation Barbier 5500
Galen Medal 4637
Max Hamilton Memorial Prize 10527
Prijs Jan-Frans Heymans 1313
Honorary Life Member
　International Pharmaceutical Students' Federation 7901
　Pharmacy Guild of Australia 584

Honorary Member 585
Host-Madsen Medal 9521
Lesmuller-Medaille 6587
Carl Mannich Medal 6823
Medaglia d'Oro Icilio Guareschi 8237
Hans Meyer Medaille 6588
Minarikovo Odlicje 10803
Pfizer Academic Awards 3779
Dr. D. N. Praad Memorial Oration Award 7599
Preis fur Pharma-Technik 7072
Premio Alberto Comenge 11331
Premio Alter 11332
Premio Antibioticos 11333
Premio de la Compania Espanola de Penicilina y Antibioticos 11334
Premio de la Real Academia de Farmacia 11335
Premio del Colegio Oficial de Farmaceuticos 11336
Premio del Consejo General de Colegios Oficiales de Farmaceuticos de Espana 11337
Premio Fabrica Espanola de Productos Quimicos y Farmaceuticos 11338
Premio Fundacion Rafael Folch 11339
Premio Guillermo Tena 11340
Premio Juan Abello 11341
Premio Juan de la Serna 11342
Premio Martin de la Cruz 9130
Premios CANIFARMA 8939
Premios de la Cooperativa Farmaceutica Espanola 11343
Prix de Biologie Alfred Kastler 5271
Prix d'Encouragement a la recherche en Chimie Therapeutique 6238
Prix G. Zambon 1200
Prix Leon et Henri Fredericq 1030
Prix Medecin General Inspecteur Raymond Debenedetti 4862
Prix Mentzer des Rencontres de Chemie Therapeutique 6239
Prix Pharmacie 4870
Prix Quinquennal des Sciences Pharmaceutiques et Therapeutiques 1339
Prix SmithKline Beecham 1342
PSJ Award 8715
PSJ Award for Distinguished Service 8716
PSJ Award for Divisional Scientific Contributions 8717
PSJ Award for Drug Research and Development 8718
PSJ Award for Educational Services 8719
PSJ Award for Young Scientists 8720
Publisher's Prizes 9522
Rafaelsen Fellowship Award 10528
Redi Award 6989
Dr. Rio de La Loza Prize 9118
Scheele Plakette 6589
Scheele-priset 11615
Ferdinand Schlemmer Medal 6824
Paul Schurmann-Medaille 6853
Paul Schurmann-Preis 6854
Serturner Medal 6825
Societas Pharmaceutica Hungarica, and Kazay Endre Award 7369
Egon Stahl Award 7082
Hermann Thoms Medal 6826

Philanthropy
Alejandro Angel Escobar Charity Prizes 1583
Award for Distinction in Islamic Science 12055
Charity Accounts Award 3081
Premio Luis Elizondo - Premio Humanitario 8990

Sforza Award in Philanthropy 11867
Young Scientists for Rainforests 2678

Philately
Award of Merit 2472
Congress Medal 2473
Crawford Medal 4119
Distinguished Philatelist 2474
FISA Medal 11787
Honorary Member 2475
Melville Junior Stamp Competition 2476
Royal Philatelic Society, London Medal 4121
Stampex Exhibition Awards 3781
Tapling Medal 4122
Tilleard Medal 4123
Wilde Cup and Webb Cup 3021
World First Postal Automatization Award 1386

Philology *See* **Linguistics**

Philosophy
Theodor W. Adorno Award 6611
Austrian State Prize for Cultural Publications 760
Eugenio Balzan Prize 8280
Benelux Libertarian Award 1222
Prix Robert Blanche 5707
BP Prize Lectureship in the Humanities 10638
Collins Religious Book Award 2640
Vasile Conta Prize 10342
Isaac Deutscher Memorial Prize 2744
Dissertation Honors 6998
Mircea Florian Prize 10348
Gottingen Academy of Sciences Prize 6903
Grand Prix de l'Academie des Sciences Morales et Politiques 5711
Grand Prix de Philosophie 5803
Kyoto Prizes 8539
Somerset Maugham Awards 4390
Constantin Radulescu Motru prize 10368
National Prize for History, Social Sciences and Philosophy 9147
National Prize in Science and Art 9152
Neometaphysical Merit Award 4450
Order of Lenin 10463
Pakistan Civil Awards 9995
Ion Petrovici Prize 10377
Premi del Ministro per i Beni Culturali e Ambientali 8070
Premio Mario di Nola 8078
Premio Norman Sverdlin 9195
Prix Charles Lambert 5723
Prix Charles Leveque 5724
Prix Charles Lyon-Caen 5725
Prix Crouzet 5728
Prix Demolombe 5731
Prix du Budget 5734
Prix du l'Union Rationaliste 6459
Prix Estrade-Delcros 5742
Prix Fraternite Gaby Archenbaud 6124
Prix Gegner 5748
Prix Grammatikakis-Neuman 5752
Prix Jean Jacques Berger 5761
Prix Jean Reynaud 5762
Prix Joseph Saillet 5766
Prix Jules Duculot 994
Prix Le Dissez de Penanrun 5771
Prix Le Fevre-Deumier (de Pons) 5468
Prix Lefevre-Deumier de Pons 5772
Prix Louis Liard 5775
Prix Polydore de Paepe 996
Prix Saintour 5790
Prix Stassart 5791
Prix Victor Cousin 5794

Philosophy (continued)
Prix Victor Delbos 5795
Royal Society of Literature Award 4233
Friedrich Ruckert Preis 7105
Mohamed Sahabdeen Award for Literature 11417
Moinho Santista Prizes for Young People 1496
Moinho Santista Prizes 1497
Sarton Chair 1357
Sarton Medal 1358
Stephan Shaumian Prize 113
George Stavros Gold Medal 7195
George Stavros Silver Medal 7196
University of Berne Prizes 11965

Philosophy of science
Fondation Binoux 5504
Fondation Charles Eugene Guye 5515
Fondation Grammaticakis-Neuman 5570
J. Gillis Prize 1256
James Scott Prize Lectureship 10649

Photogrammetry
Brock Gold Medal Award 8553
Leonard Curtis European Award 3843
Sam G. Gamble Award 8554
Deak Lazar Memorial Medal 7310
Poster Paper Prize 3844
President's Award 3845
President's Medal 3783
President's Prize 3784
Remote Sensing Society Medal 3846
Remote Sensing Society Student Awards 3847
Schermerhorn Award 8555
Schwidefsky Medal 8556
Taylor and Francis Best Letter Award 3848
Otto von Gruber Award 8557

Photographic prints
PSI Gold Medals 7819
PSI Medals 7820

Photography (See also Nature photography; Photogrammetry; Photographic prints; Photojournalism; Slide photography)
Aanmoedigingsprijzen 9635
Academy Awards 9750
Isara Amantakul Prize 12015
Asia and the Pacific Photography Contest 8499
Associate of the Photographic Salon Exhibitors Association 7267
Association Award 7268
Association Awards 2131
Association Internationale de la Presse Sportive Awards 8315
Association of Photographers/Kodak Student Competition 2132
Association Seal 7269
Austrian State Encouragement Prizes 758
Maria Austriaprijs 9636
Awards of E.A. International Salon of Photography 7270
BAIE Editing for Industry Awards 2266
Bandeirante Trophy 1458
Bienal de Fotografia 8967
Bienal Internacional del Cartel en Mexico 9285
Biennale Internationale du Cinema Humain Marcel Mignon 1095
Bird Photograph of the Year 2293
British Academy of Film and Television Arts Awards - Film 2233
British Academy of Film and Television Arts Awards - Television 2234
Augustin Casasola Prize 9081
Centenary Medal 4130
Concurso Nacional de Fotografia Cientifica 9175
Concurso Universitario de Fotografia 9179
Bertram Cox Bequest 4131
Daguerre-Preis 6605
Durban International Exhibition of Photography 10845
Essex International Salon of Photography 2810
Fellow of the Photographic Salon Exhibitors Association 7271
Fenton Medal 4132
Marc Ferrez Photography Award 1433
FIAP Awards 8866
FIAP Medals 8867
FIAP Service Awards 8868
FIAP World Cups 8869
Forderpreis fur bildende Kunst der Landeshauptstadt Dusseldorf 6682
La Galerie d'Essai 6189
Grand Prix Amon Ra 5195
Grand Prix de la Photographie de la Ville de Paris 6089
Grand Prix International d'Arts et Lettres Notre-Dame et la Mer 4958
Grand Prix National de la Photographie 5280
Greek National Tourist Organization Awards 7198
Honorary Fellow 7272
Honorary Fellowship 4133
Honorary Member 7273
Honorary Membership 4134
Hood Medal 4135
International Art Photography Exhibition "Foto Expo" 10086
International Photographic Competition to Commemorate Islamic Heritage 12057
International Sailing Film Festival in La Rochelle 6044
International Student Salon of Photography 7275
International Triennial Exhibition of Photography Prizes 11854
International Visual Communications Association Awards 3502
Internationaler Fotosalon 6756
Interphot - Adelaide International Exhibition of Photography 677
Enrique Kavlin Photography Grant 7926
Cherry Kearton Medal and Award 4012
Kodansha Prize 8687
Kraszna-Krausz Award 3527
Gerard Levy Prize for a Young Photographer 7928
Literature and Art Awards 12011
Magnolia Prize 1576
Karol Malcuzynski Award 10207
Manila International Exhibition of Photography 10044
Yunus Nadi Yarismasi 12049
National Business Calendar Awards 2483
National Photography Competition 1756
National Prize for Journalism and Information 9140
Photo-Jokes Competition 1523
Photographic Society of Japan Awards 8722
Rita Poretsky Prize in Photography 7969
Premio dos Culturas en Origen 8969
Premio Esso de Jornalismo 1456
Premio Kaulak 11293
Premio Mingote 11319
Premio Municipais Joshua Benoliel de Fotografia 10264
Premios Asociacion de Reporteros Graficos 8924
Pretoria International Exhibition of Photography 10910
Prix de Boelpaepe 1013
Prix de Rome 9578
Prix du Livre de Photographies 6190
PRO Dogs National Charity Open Creative Writing & Photographic Competition 3802
Progress Medal 4136
PSI Gold Medals 7819
PSI Medals 7820
RIAS/Whitehouse Studio Award for Architectural Photography 10616
Rodman Medal 4137
Rosario International Photographic Salon 105
Salon International de la Recherche Photographique 6215
Salon International diapositives d'Auvergne 4888
Salon Nacional de Artes Plasticas - Fotografia 9243
Scottish Salon of Photography 10677
Standard Bank Namibia Biennale 9326
Sun Life/*Amateur Photographer* Monochrome Awards 4499
Time Out Travel Writer and Photographer of the Year 4546
Trade Union's Art and Cultural Prize 7442
Transport Photographer of the Year 2588
Wildlife Photographer of the Year Competition 2162
World Festival of Mountain Pictures 6481
World Festival of Underwater Pictures 6483
Young Wildlife Photographer of the Year Competition 2163

Photojournalism
AFN - AGFA Awards 2127
AMP W.G. Walkley Awards for Journalism 523
BCPA International Salon of Colour Slides 7489
British Press Awards 4561
Essex International Salon of Photography 2810
Alan Harper Bursary 2888
Ing. Salvador Toscano Prize 9092
Willie Vicoy Reuter Fellowship 3851
World Press Photo Contest 9697

Physical education
Philip Noel Baker Research Award 4722
Honorary Member 7822
International Jose Maria Cagigal Award in Physical Education 1166
Official UNESCO Award for Distinguished Services to Physical Education and Sport 6419
Sport Science Award of the IOC President 4723

Physical fitness See Health and fitness

Physical medicine See Rehabilitation and therapy

Physical science
Bhatnagar Award 7532
Anil Kumar Bose Memorial Award 7641
Caledonian Research Foundation Prize Lecturehip 10641
Fondation Aime Berthe 5477
Fondation Tchihatchef 5669

Fondazione Premio Dotte Giuseppe
 Borgia 8063
William Hopkins Prize 2567
Dragomir Hurmuzescu Prize 10357
Lomonosov Gold Medal 10419
MakDougall-Brisbane Prize 10646
Medals of the National Academy of Science 8379
National Prize in Science and Art 9152
Bruce-Preller Prize Lectureship 10648
Research Medal 9755
Saltire Society and The Royal Bank of Scotland - Scottish Science Award 10657
Scholastic Award 8808
Frederick White Prize 181

Physical therapy See **Rehabilitation and therapy**

Physics
Akzo prijs 9389
Alejandro Angel Escobar Science Prize 1584
Appleton Prize
  International Union of Radio Science 1210
  Royal Society 4141
Prof. R. K. Asundi Memorial Lecture 7638
Homi J. Bhabha Medal 7639
R. D. Birla Award 7681
Walter Boas Medal 233
Boltzmann Medal 11484
Max Born Medal and Prize 3184
Max-Born-Preis 6656
Satyendranath Bose Medal 7640
Charles Vernon Boys Medal and Prize 3185
Bragg Gold Medal for Excellence in Physics 234
Bragg Medal and Prize 3186
A. N. Chatterjee Memorial Medal 7469
Colombian Academy of Science Third World Prize 1579
E. R. Cooper Memorial Medal and Prize 9836
Dirac Medal
  International Centre for Theoretical Physics 8288
  University of New South Wales 699
Paul Dirac Medal and Prize 3188
Duddell Medal and Prize 3189
Edlundska Priset 11538
Fondation Anatole et Suzanne Abragam 5486
Fondation Arthur du Fay 5497
Fondation Boileau 5505
Fondation Danton 5530
Fondation Deslandres 5539
Fondation du Baron de Joest 5541
Fondation Edmond Brun 5549
Fondation Ernest Dechelle 5553
Fondation Fernand Holweck 5556
Fondation Gabrielle Sand 5563
Fondation Gustave Ribaud 5571
Fondation Henri de Parville 5576
Fondation Henry Bazin 5580
Fondation Henry Wilde 5583
Fondation Hughes 5585
Fondation Jean Reynaud 5599
Fondation Jerome Ponti 5602
Fondation Kodak-Pathe-Landucci 5606
Fondation L. La Caze 5607
Fondation Langevin 5610
Fondation Laura Mounier de Saridakis 5613
Fondation Le Conte 5615
Fondation Louis Armand 5621
Fondation Marie Guido Triossi 5625
Fondation Mergier-Bourdeix 5633

Fondation Paul Gallet 5646
Fondation Paul Marguerite de la Charlonie 5647
Fondation Pierson-Perrin 5654
Fondation Rochat-Juliard 5661
Fondation Servant 5668
Fondation Vaillant 5674
Fondation Victor Raulin 5676
Fondations Estrade Delcros, Houllevigue, Saintour, Jules Mahyer 5679
Francqui Prize 1156
Fujihara Award 8527
K. L. Garg Memorial Award 7470
Stern-Gerlach-Medaille 6657
Glazebrook Medal and Prize 3190
Gottingen Academy of Sciences Prize for Physics 6907
Grand Prix de Physique Jean Ricard 6364
Gregori Aminoffs Pris 11542
Gunning Victoria Jubilee Prize Lectureship 10644
Guthrie Medal and Prize 3191
Otto-Hahn-Preis fur Chemie und Physik
  Deutsche Physikalische Gesellschaft 6658
  German Chemical Society 6783
Helmholtz Prizes 6914
Gustav-Hertz-Preis (Physik-Preis) 6659
Hewlett-Packard Europhysics Prize 11704
High Energy and Particle Physics Prize 11705
Gilles Holst Medal 9601
Holweck Medal and Prize 3192
Butterworth Hrinemann Prize 2185
Hughes Medal 4151
Horia Hulubei Prize 10355
ICHMT Fellows Awards 10710
ICPE Medal for Physics Teaching 11486
ICTP Prize 8289
Indradipta Memorial Medal 7471
Italian Minister for Culture and the Environment Prizes 8365
Gentner-Kastler-Prize 6660
Kini Family Award 7472
Morris L. Levinson Prizes 7982
Lindbomska Beloningen 11546
London Award 11487
Lorentz Medal 9602
Luikov Medal 10711
Thomas Ranken Lyle Medal 176
Artur Malheiros Prize 10255
Marlow Medal and Prize 4208
Harrie Massie Medal and Prize 3193
Harrie Massie Medal 235
Matteucci Medal 8377
Maxwell Medal and Prize 3194
Mechaelis Memorial Prize 9850
Medaille fur Naturwissenschaftliche Publizistik 6661
Medaille Rammal 6365
Constantin Miculescu Prize 10367
National Prize for Physics, Mathematics and Natural Sciences 9149
National Prize of the President of the Republic 8068
Nobel Prize for Physics 11498
Nobel Prizes 11549
Nuclear Physics Postgraduate Student Awards 11070
October Prizes of the City of Belgrade 10696
H. C. Orsted Medal 2007
Paterson Medal and Prize 3195
Pawsey Medal 178
Philippine Physics Olympiad 10060
Max-Planck-Medaille 6662
Robert-Wichard-Pohl-Preis 6663

Premio Triennale per la Fisica Francesco Somaini 8243
Prix Agathon De Potter 1007
Prix Aime Cotton 6366
Prix Ampere d'Electricite de France 5684
Prix Barrabe 5304
Prix Daniel Guinier 6367
Prix de la Fondation du 150e anniversaire de la Societe royale des Sciences de Liege 1368
Prix des Sciences Physiques et Mathematiques 5052
Prix du Commisariat a l'Energie Atomique 5693
Prix du Gaz de France 5694
Prix Esclangon 6368
Prix Felix Robin 6369
Prix Fonde par l'Etat 5695
Prix Foucault 6370
Prix Gentner-Kastler 6371
Prix Georges Millot 5309
Prix Georges Vanderlinden 1023
Prix Holweck 6372
Prix IBM 6373
Prix Jean Perrin 6374
Prix Jean Ricard 6375
Prix Jeune Chercheur IBM 6376
Prix Joliot-Curie 6377
Prix Langevin 6378
Prix Louis Ancel 6379
Prix Louis Melsens 1031
Prix Mesucora 5700
Prix Plasma 6380
Prix Pol and Christiane Swings 1035
Prix Scientifique IBM France 5330
Prix Theophile de Donder 1037
Prix Yves Rocard 6381
Stefan Procopiu Prize 10379
Prof. G. N. Ramachandran 60th Birthday Commemoration Medal Award 7664
Prof. K. Rangadhama Rao Memorial Lecture 7667
Roentgen-Preis 7001
Rontgen Prize 2416
Royal Society of Victoria Medal 638
Rumford Medal 4156
Rutherford Medal and Prize 3196
SAIP - De Beers Gold Medal Award 11071
SAIP Science Olympiad Medal 11072
SAIP - Silver Jubilee Medal Award 11073
SAMES Postgraduate Student Award 11074
Moinho Santista Prizes for Young People 1496
Moinho Santista Prizes 1497
Karl-Scheel-Preis 6664
Walter-Schottky-Preis fur Festkorperforschung 6665
Scientific Research Prizes 8919
Simon Memorial Prize 3197
SMM Postgraduate Student Award 11075
SMM Prize 11076
Marian Smoluchowski Medal 10172
Snellius Medal 9558
Solid State Physics and Materials Science Essay Prize 11077
SunAmco Medal 11488
Svante Arrhenius Medaljen 11557
David Syme Research Prize 697
TWAS Award in Physics 8454
University of Berne Prizes 11965
Gleb Wataghin Award 1460
Welch Foundation Scholarship 3493
Wolf Foundation Prizes 7987

Physiology
Broca Prize 4897
Alexander Ninian Bruce Prize 10640

Physiology (continued)
Dautrebande Physiopathology Foundation Prize 1112
Arthur de Falloise Quinquennial Prize 1065
O. Dupont Prize 1255
ESCPB Young Scientists Awards 1138
Flormanska Beloningen 11541
Fondation Claude Lallemand 5521
Fondation du Docteur et de Madame Peyre 5544
Fondation Fanny Emden 5555
Fondation Godard 5569
Fondation Jean de Meyer 1002
Fondation L. La Caze 5607
Fondation Martin-Damourette 5628
Fondation Max-Fernand Jayle 5630
Fondation Montyon de Physiologie 5637
Fondation Octave Dupont 1005
Fondation Philipeaux 5650
Fondation Pourat 5658
Fondation Serres 5667
Luigi Galvani Prize 6569
John Hunter Medal and Triennial Prize 3976
Hunterian Oration 3977
Nobel Prize for Physiology or Medicine 11499
Premio Internazionale Amedeo e Frances Herlitzka per la Fisiologia 8023
Prix Leon et Henri Fredericq 1030
Prix Theophile Gluge 1038
Royal Society of Victoria Medal 638
Sherrington Memorial Lecture 4266
Thunbergmedaljen 11520
Heinrich-Wieland Preis 7017

Piano competitions
Geza Anda International Piano Competition 11676
BBC Television Young Musician of the Year 2297
Valentino Bucchi Prize of Rome Capital City 8263
Budapest International Music Competition 7414
F. Busoni Prize 8181
Maria Callas Grand Prix for Pianists 7185
Alessandro Casagrande International Piano Competition 8207
Alfredo Casella International Piano Competition 8048
Dino Ciani International Competition for Young Pianists 8189
City of Sydney Piano Scholarship 321
Cologne International Pianoforte Competition 6607
Concertino Prague International Radio Competition for Young Musicians 1838
Concorso Internationale di Musica da Camera "Palma d'Oro" di Citta di Finale Lingure 8120
Concorso Internazionale Musicale Francesco Paolo Neglia 8205
Concorso Internazionale Vincenzo Bellini per Pianisti e Cantanti Lirici 8108
Concorso nazionale pianistico Premio Rendano 8138
Concours Internationale de Piano, Epinal 5074
Concours International d'Ensembles de Musique de Chambre de Colmar 5042
Concurso Internacional de Piano Frederic Chopin 11213
Crown Princess Sonja International Music Competition 9963
Vianna da Motta International Competition 10228
Dudley International Piano Competition 2755
Early Music Festival - Bruges 1152
Ettlingen International Competition for Young Pianists 7061
Finale Ligure International Chamber Music Competition 8106
Rina Sala Gallo International Piano Competition 8140
GPA Dublin International Piano Competition 7779
Grand Prix de la Ville de Paris 5034
Harveys Leeds International Pianoforte Competition 2994
Clara Haskil Competition 11744
International Beethoven Piano Competition 918
International Competition for Musical Performers - Geneva 11774
International Competition of Franz Schubert and Twentieth Century Music 805
International Franz Liszt Piano Competition 9663
International Frederic Chopin Piano Competition 10067
International J. S. Bach Competition 6936
International Kuhlau Competition for Flautists 6966
International Mozart Competition 872
International Music Competition of Japan 8608
International Piano Competition Liszt - Mario Zanfi Prize 8169
International Pilar Bayona Piano Competition 11273
International Robert Schumann Competition 6979
International Villa-Lobos Piano Contest 1502
Internationaler Musikwettbewerb der ARD 6974
Jose Iturbi International Piano Competition 11219
Jaen Prize 11281
Marguerite Long and Jacques Thibaud International Competition 6085
National Power World Piano Competition London 3604
Newport International Competition for Young Pianists 12179
NFMS/ESSO Young Concert Artists 3684
Vlado Perlemuter Piano Scholarship 2909
Ettore Pozzoli International Piano Competition 8199
Premio Internacional de Piano Fundacion Guerrero 11243
Premio Internazionale Accademia Musicale Chigiana Siena 8046
Prix Arthur De Greef 951
Queen Elisabeth International Music Competition of Belgium Prizes 1245
Royal Over-Seas League Music Competition 4117
Arthur Rubinstein International Piano Master Competition 7938
Scottish International Piano Competition 10673
Senigallia International Meeting of Young Pianists 8419
Senigallia International Piano Competition 8420
Smetana Piano Competition 1894
Sydney International Piano Competition of Australia 326
Tunbridge Wells International Young Concert Artist Competition 4557
G. B. Viotti International Music and Dance Competition 8425
Pancho Vladiguerov International Competition for Pianists 1526
World Music Masters 5234
Young Concert Artists Trust Award 4649

Ping pong *See* Table tennis

Planning (*See also* City planning; Park planning)
Patrick Geddes Planning Award 10653
The Long Range Planning Award 4495

Plays *See* Drama; Theater

Playwriting *See* Drama

Poetry
Emil Aarestrup Prize 1924
The Age Book of the Year Awards 118
Aldeburgh Poetry Festival Prize 2051
Angel Literary Award 2080
Annual Competition Awards 3479
Kitty Archer-Burton Poetry Competition 663
Rosemary Arthur Award 3697
Arts Council of Great Britain Schemes 2100
Arts Council of Wales Book of the Year Awards 12150
Arts Council Writing Grants 9798
Arvon Foundation International Poetry Competition 2103
ASEAN Award for Literature 10030
Jozsef Attila Prize 7398
Austrian State Prize for Poetry for Children 764
Joseph Autran Prize 6304
Award for Aboriginal and Torres Strait Islander Writers 554
Award for Original Hebrew Poetry 7873
Awards 1196
Awards for Regional Literature 10004
Bagutta Prize 8160
Bangkok Bank Prize for Thai Literature Competition 12022
Bangla Academy Literary Award 934
Alice Hunt Bartlett Prize 3790
Bellmanpriset 11584
Benson Medal 4231
Horst Bienek Preis fur Lyrik 6551
Olavo Bilac Prize 1422
Boardman Tasker Memorial Award for Mountain Literature 2192
Pascal Bonetti Grand Prize 6305
Book Awards 10734
Bourses de la Vocation 5212
The Bridport Prize 2218
Bronze Swagman Award 710
Bucharest Writers Association Award 10411
Georg-Buchner-Preis 6765
Buenos Aires Literary Prizes 36
Jan Campert Prize 9347
Giosue Carducci Prize 8174
Carlos Casavalle Prize 26
Category A Fellowships 155
Category B Fellowships 156
CCP Literary Awards 10034
Cena Zvazu slovenskych spisovatelov 10756
Certamen Nacional de Poesia, Alfonso Reyes 9160
Chateauneuf-du-Pape Grand Prize 6306
Choku Prize 8676
Cholmondeley Award for Poets 4388
City of Cardiff International Poetry Competition 12194
CNA Literary Award 10830

Poetry

Tom Collins Poetry Award 375
Concours Max-Pol Fouchet 4974
Concurso Anual de Literatura Premios Franz Tamayo 1388
Concurso Joven Creacion 1769
Creative Writing Junior Competition 2219
Creativity Centre Inc. Poetry Prize 351
Critics Prize 10298
Croatian Socialist Republic Prizes 1808
Jorge Cuesta National Poetry Prize 9006
Dakotsu Prize 8677
Albert Dauzat Prize 6307
Deldebat de Gonzalya Foundation Prize 6308
De Pimodan Foundation Prize 6309
Denis Devlin Memorial Award for Poetry 7757
Alfred Doblin Prize 6510
Aquileo J. Echeverria Prize 1761
Jose F. Elizondo Prize 9084
Mihail Eminescu Prize 10346
Environment in Children's Literature Award 10289
Lydia och Herman Erikssons stipendium 11590
Erlanger Foundation Prize 6310
European Music and Poetry Competitions 1121
European Poetry Translation Prize 3791
Johannes Ewald Prize 1927
Geoffrey Faber Memorial Prize 2860
Prudence Farmer Award 3720
FAW Anne Elder Poetry Award 380
FAW Christopher Brennan Award 386
FAW Fedora Anderson Young Writers Poetry Award 388
FAW Kate Tracy Memorial Young Writers Award 395
Festival Awards for Literature 673
First Book Prize 21
Ernest Fleury Prize 6311
Juegos Florales Prize of San Juan del Rio, Queretaro 9162
Forderpreis des Landes Nordrhein-Westfalen fur junge Kunstlerinnen und Kunstler 7026
Fouraignan Foundation Prize 6312
Fundacion del Premio Fastenrath 11345
Guido Gezelle Prize 1272
Maurice Gilliams Prize 1273
Mary Gilmore Award 131
Golden Poet-Tree Award 7049
Herman Gorterprijs 9638
GPA Book Award 7777
Grand Prix Amon Ra 5195
Grand Prix de la Maison de Poesie 6104
Grand Prix de la Mer 4918
Grand Prix de la Poesie 6261
Grand Prix de Poesie 5804
Grand Prix des Biennales Internationales de Poesie 1170
Grand Prix des Poetes 6255
Grand Prix International d'Arts et Lettres Notre-Dame et la Mer 4958
Grand Prix International de Poesie de la Ville de Grenoble 6302
Grand Prix Litteraire de l'Oceanie 4920
Grand Prix Litteraire de Madagascar 4921
Grand Prix National de la Poesie 5281
Grand Prix RTL/Poesie 1 6207
Grand Prix Thyde Monnier 6266
Grand Prize of French Poets 6313
Grands Prix Litteraire de la Ville de Paris 6095
Robert Graves Prize 7390
Eric Gregory Awards 4389
Grenfell Henry Lawson Festival of Arts Awards 415

Andreas-Gryphius-Preis 6525
Calouste Gulbenkian Translation Prize 10251
Edmond Haraucourt Prize 6314
Felicia Hemans Prize for Lyrical Poetry 4575
Hertzog Prize 10991
Hermann Hesse Prize 7086
Hong Kong Biennial Awards for Chinese Literature 7278
Pieter Cornelisz Hooft Prize 9665
Peter-Huchel-Preis fur Lyrik 7144
Efrain Huerta National Prize for Short Story and Poetry 9164
Clovis Hugues Prize 6315
International Vaptsarov Prize 1537
Isle of Elba - Raffaello Brignetti Literary Award 8323
Max Jacob Poetry Prize 6081
Jean-Christophe Prizes 6316
Kallebergerstipendiet 11595
Kanakasree Award 7702
Frans Kellendonk-prijs 9628
Kellgrenpriset 11596
Keltic Society Awards 10584
Kerala Sahitya Akademi Awards 7703
Ilona Kohrtz' stipendium 11597
Korean National Literary Award 8823
Georges Lafenestre Foundation Prize 6317
Eugene Le Mouel Foundation Prize 6318
Le Prix de Poesie Charles Vildrac 6267
Sebastien-Charles Leconte Foundation Prize 6319
Grace Leven Prize for Poetry 513
Fran Levstik Prize 10807
Liechtenstein-Preis zur Forderung junger Lyriker 8853
Miguel N. Lira Poetry Prize 9004
Jessie Litchfield Award 557
Literary Awards and Prizes for Sinhalese Literature 11423
Literary Competition 357
Literary Prize 10995
Literary Prize for Translation 10996
Literary Prizes 7192
Literary Prizes for Tamil Literature 11424
Literaturpreis der Bundesarztekammer 6816
Paul Lofler Foundation Prize 6320
Malaysian Literary Prize 8904
Malpertuis Prize 1288
Mandat des Poetes 6108
Arthur Markham Memorial Prize 4585
Somerset Maugham Awards 4390
McVitie's Prize for the Scottish Writer of the Year 10582
Charles Meeking Award for Poetry 666
Arthur Merghelynck Prize 1274
Mlada Fronta Award 1887
Mlade leta Prize 10786
Albert Mockel Grand Prize for Poetry 1289
Modern Poet Prize 8631
Mr. H's Prize 8632
Ian Murdie Memorial Awards 373
Yunus Nadi Yarismasi 12049
National Award for Literature and Arts 12002
National Poetry Competition 3792
National Poetry Foundation 3698
National Prize for Linguistics and Literature 9148
National Prize for Literature
   Argentina - Ministry of Education and Justice 22
   National Council for Culture 12122
New South Wales State Literary Awards 147

New Zealand Book Awards 9801
Noma Award for Publishing in Africa 2039
Norske Akademis Pris Til Minne om Thorleif Dahl 9925
Outpost's Poetry Competition 3012
Gilbert Owen National Prize for Literature 9014
Don Carlos Palanca Memorial Awards for Literature 10053
Parnassos Foundation Prize 7213
PEN Best First Book of Poetry Award 9780
PEN Prizes (Poetry, Essay, Novel) 10293
Phenixprijs 9581
Charles Pitou Foundation Prize 6321
Poetic Prose Prize 6322
Poetry International Award 9568
Poetry International/Poetry on the Road Festival 9569
Poets International Organization Awards 7720
Emil Polak Prize 1290
Preis der Landeshauptstadt Innsbruck fur Kunstlerisches Schaffen 891
Premier's Literary Awards 149
Premier's Poetry Award 293
Premio Adonais de Poesia 11327
Premio Biella 8010
Premio Ceppo Proposte Nicola Lisi 8084
Premio de Poesia Carlos Pellicer 9222
Premio de Poesia Joven de Mexico Elias Nandino 9223
Premio de Traduccion de Poesia 9225
Premio Editiorial Costa Rica 1770
Premio Francisco de Quevado 11291
Premio Hispanoamericano Xavier Villaurrutia 9267
Premio Il Ceppo 8085
Premio Litterario Viareggio 8407
Premio Municipal de Literatura 1568
Premio Nacional de Literatura
   Chile - Ministerio de Educacion 1548
   Spain Ministry of Culture 11375
Premio Nacional de Poesia 9236
Premio Nacional de Poesia Ciudad de la Paz 8996
Premio Nacional de Poesia Joven Francisco Gonzalez de Leon 9237
Premio Nazionale di Poesie 8145
Premio Poesia y Narrativa 1772
Premios Literarios Nacionais 1474
Premios Municipais Eca de Queiroz de Literatura 10280
Prijs de Vlaamse Gids 1374
Thomas Pringle Award 10852
Prix Anick Campion-Guillaumet et Bernard Guillaumet 6323
Prix Annuel de Poesie 5814
Prix Antonin Artaud 4932
Prix Antony Valabregue 5816
Prix Auguste Capdeville (De Beziers) 5817
Prix Auguste Michot 1293
Prix Balleroy 5338
Prix Balleroy 5818
Prix Capuran 5826
Prix Claire Virenque 5829
Prix Claude Sernet 4933
Prix Clement Marot de Poesie 6502
Prix de Fondation Duchesse de Rohan 6324
Prix de Fondation Labbe-Vauquelin 6325
Prix de la Critique Poetique 6326
Prix de La Grange 5448
Prix de la Press Poetique 6327
Prix de la Promotion Cinematographique 6328
Prix de la Promotion Poetique 6329
Prix de la Promotion Radiophonique de la Poesie 6330

Poetry (continued)
Prix de la Promotion Televisuelle de la Poesie 6331
Prix de l'Academie Mallarme 4800
Prix de Litterature des Alpes et du Jura 4923
Prix de Poesie Louis Montalte 6277
Prix de Poesie Roger Kowalski 6475
Prix de Poesie *SEPIA* 6211
Prix des Chants Perdus 6332
Prix Emile Hinzelin 5849
Prix Emmanuel Vossaert 1295
Prix Eugene Schmits 1296
Prix Europeen de l'ADELF 4924
Prix France-Acadie 4894
Prix Francois Coppee 5856
Prix Franz de Wever 1297
Prix Georges Lockem 1300
Prix GLM 4954
Prix Guillaume Apollinaire 6172
Prix Helene Seguin 6333
Prix Henri Jousselin 5865
Prix Henri Mondor 5866
Prix Hercule Catenacci
 Institut de France 5343
 Institut de France - Academie Francaise 5867
Prix Heredia 5868
Prix Hubert Krains 1043
Prix Ilarie Voronca 4934
Prix International des Amities Francaises 6334
Prix Jacques Raphael-Leygues 6336
Prix Jean Bouscatel 5870
Prix Jean Kobs 1302
Prix Le Fevre-Deumier (de Pons) 5883
Prix Litteraire des Mascareignes, des Seychelles et des Comores 4929
Prix Maise Ploquin-Caunan et Docteur Jacques Perdrizet 5889
Prix Marc Chesneau 6337
Prix Marcel Mompezat 6338
Prix Marceline Desbordes-Valmore 6339
Prix Marie Havez-Planque 5894
Prix Marthe Ripert-Sarrut 6340
Prix Mounet-Sully 6341
Prix Nicole Houssa 1304
Prix Pascal Fortuny 5903
Prix Paul Labbe-Vauquelin 5906
Prix Paul Verlaine 5908
Prix Rene Bardet 5914
Prix Rene Lyr 1044
Prix Roberge 5916
Prix Rossini 5423
Prix Sabine Sicaud 6342
Prix Saint-Cricq-Theis 5918
Prix Sivet 5920
Prix Valentine de Wolmar 5927
Prix Victor Bernard 6343
Prize for Literature of the Council of the French Community of Belgium 1110
Prize for Poetry in Irish 7761
PRO Dogs National Charity Open Creative Writing & Photographic Competition 3802
Publieksprijs voor het Nederlandse Boek 9368
Queen's Gold Medal for Poetry 4555
Red Earth Poetry Award 555
Revelation Prize for Poetry 10313
Carles Riba Poetry Prize 11238
Fernando Rielo World Prize for Mystical Poetry 11329
Romanian Writers' Union Prizes 10414
Rose of French Poets Prize 6344
Royal Society of Literature Award 4233
Olive Schreiner Prize 10853
Howard Sergeant Memorial Award 3013
Signal Poetry Award 4537
Lilian Ida Smith Award 9782
Southern Arts Literature Prize 4481
Staatsprijs voor Poezie 1083
Stipendium ur Lena Vendelfelts minnesfond 11603
Storywriting and Art Project
 Australia - Department of Veterans' Affairs, Public Relations Dept. 144
 Heidelberg Repatriation Hospital - Department of Veterans' Affairs 417
Stroud and District Festival 4497
Svenska Akademiens nordiska pris 11606
Dylan Thomas Award 3793
Anne Tibble Poetry Competition 3723
Georg Trakl Prize for Poetry 724
Dorothy Tutin Award 3699
Urban Council Awards for Creative Writing in Chinese 7279
Karel van de Woestijne Prize 1277
Lucy B. and C. W. Van der Hoogt-prijs 9631
VER Poets Open Competition 4593
Tarjei Vesaas Debutant Prize 9930
Annette-von-Droste-Hulshoff-Preis 7028
Western Australian Premier's Book Awards 515
Whitbread Literary Awards 2211
Wesley Michel Wright Prize for Poetry 695
Yeats Club Open Poetry Competition 4643
Yomiuri Literature Prize 8795

Police *See* Law enforcement

Polish culture
Award for the Promotion of Polish Entertainment Creativity 10206
Cross of Auschwitz 10100
Cultural Merit Award 10089
International Warsaw Autumn Festival of Contemporary Music 10164
Merit of Polish Culture Badge 10091
Order of Merit of the Republic of Poland 10117
Order of the Rebirth of Poland 10119

Political science (*See also* European integration; Foreign policy; Human relations; International relations; Legislative improvement; National security; Social science research; World peace)
Crisp Medal 141
Dissertation Honors 6998
Antonio Larragoiti Prize
 Brazilian Academy of Letters 1423
 Lisbon Academy of Sciences 10253
W. J. M. MacKenzie Book Prize 7861
Medalla Eduardo Neri 9124
Nagrada Saveta Fonda SO SUBNOR Cetvrti jul 10707
Naples Prize for the Study of Southern and Northern Countries in the World 8254
National Essay Contest on Colombian Foreign Policy 1592
Premio Internazionale di Meridionalistica Guido Dorso 8149
Prix Aujourd'hui 6162
Prix Charles Dupin 5722
Prix Charles Lyon-Caen 5725
Prix Emile de Laveleye 985
Prix Ernest Lemonon 5740
Prix Grammaticakis-Neuman 5752
Prix J. J. Weiss 5869
Prix Jean Jacques Berger 5761
Prix Joseph Dutens 5764
Prix Latsis 11959
Prix Leon Faucher 5773
Prix Limantour 5774
Prix Rossi 5789
Prix Saintour 5790
Stein Rokkan Fellowship 9896
Dr. Arthur Ruppin Prize 7885
Robert Schumann Prize 7123
George Stavros Gold Medal 7195
George Stavros Silver Medal 7196
Suntory Prize for Social Sciences and Humanities 8764
Nicholae Titulescu Prize 10389
University of Berne Prizes 11965
T. E. Utley Memorial Award 4591
David Watt Memorial Prize 4327
Women and Politics Prize 142

Pollution control *See* Environmental conservation; Water conservation

Population *See* Demography; Family planning

Portuguese culture
Camoes Prize 10297

Poultry science
Blount Memorial Scholarship 2085
Macdougall Medal 7173
Tom Newman International Memorial Award 2480
Dr. Bart Rispens Research Award 7171
Santa Rosa Award 1475

Poverty *See* Humanitarianism

Preventive medicine
Gold Medal of the Royal Society of Medicine 4249
Insole Award 2444
Jenner Medal 4256
Albert Strating Prize 11008

Printed materials *See* Publications

Printing industry
Awards for the Best Produced Books in Hong Kong 7277
Gutenberg Award 6912
National Business Calendar Awards 2483
Charles Nypels Prijs 9564
Printing Culture Prize 8610
Safety Awards 2484

Prints *See* Graphic arts; Photographic prints

Prisons
Disciplined Services Medal for Long Service and Good Conduct 7245
Disciplined Services Medal for Meritorious Service 7246
Disciplined Services Star for Distinguished Service 7247
Distinction for Distinguished Services 1627
Distinction for Time of Service 1628
Medal for Bravery 1629
Penitentiary Order of Merit 1630

Professional and personal achievement (*See also* Academic achievement; Leadership)
Astra Trophy 10509
Andres Bello Medal 1652
Bourses de la Vocation 5212
Businessperson of the Year 925
City of Munich Prizes 7019
Conspicuous Service Decorations 339
Cross of Merit 10101

Faraday Medal 3279
For Budapest Award 7300
Gieh ir-Repubblika Honor Society 8914
J. E. Gunnerus Medal 9968
Honorary Member 10210
IEE Achievement Medal 3282
International Federation of Shorthand and Typewriting Competitions 6952
Anders Jahre Prize for Contributions to Norwegian Culture 9900
Kultureller Ehrenpreis 7020
Mensa International Competitions 3640
Mercury Communications Award for the Prince's Trust 4487
National Labor Prize 9137
Onassis Prize for International Understanding and for Social Achievement 7209
Ordre de Merit de Madagascar 8878
Francis Ormond Medal 620
Pro Urbe Budapest Award 7304
Rafael Ramirez Medal 9155
Rolls Royce Jubilee Award 3302
Rookie Businessperson of the Year 926
Sir Henry Royce Award 3303

Psychiatry (See also Mental health)
Natalie Cobbing Travelling Fellowship (Psychiatry of Mental Handicap) 3959
Philip Davis Prize in Old Age Psychiatry 3960
Gaskell Medal and Prize 3961
Max Hamilton Memorial Prize 10527
Anatoly Koryagin Award 9472
Laughlin Prize 3962
Lilly Travelling Fellowships 3963
Lucio V. Lopez Prize 85
Morris Markowe Public Education Prize 3964
Anna Monika Foundation Prize 7057
Brian Oliver Prize in the Psychiatry of Learning Disabilities 3965
President's Essay Prize 3967
Rafaelsen Fellowship Award 10528
Ramaermedaille 9562
Research Prize and Bronze Medal 3968
Werner Schwidder Award 4727
Peter Scott Memorial Scholarship 3969
Woodford-Williams Prize 3970

Psychology
Bartlett Lecture 2856
Professor Stefan Blachowski Award 10174
Book Award 2486
Bourse Marcelle Blum 5708
British Psychological Society Prize for "A" Level Psychology 2487
Vasile Conta Prize 10342
Kenneth Craik Award 4329
Prix Dagnan-Bouveret 5709
Experimental Psychology Society Prize 2857
Mircea Florian Prize 10348
Fondation Fanny Emden 5555
Dr. A. Hedri-Preis 11732
Honorary Fellow 2488
Honorary Life Member 2489
IAMP Awards 498
International Prize 5301
Constantin Radulescu Motru prize 10368
Ion Petrovici Prize 10377
Presidents' Award 2490
Prix de Psychologie 981
Quinquennial Award in the Psychology of Religion 1175
Royal Society of Victoria Medal 638
Spearman Medal 2491
Swiss Prize for Parapsychology 11939

University of Berne Prizes 11965
Prof. Bohdan Zawadzki Award 10175

Public administration (See also City management; Government service; Historic preservation; Planning; Public finance; Public works)
Concurso Anual de Tesis Profesionales 8937
Alexis de Tocqueville Prize 9410
Haldane Essay Competition Medal 4081
"Honorary Citizen" Title 7301
Orden Departmental de Bolivar 1612
Premio del Instituto Nacional de Administracion Publica 9051
Prix Charles Duvivier 980
Prix Edmond Freville 5738
Prix Odilon Barrot 5784

Public affairs (See also Community affairs; Consumer affairs; Housing; Leadership; Legislative improvement; Military service)
Astor Award 2668
Messel Medal and Lecture 4418

Public finance
Jordi Lluch Prize 11186

Public health
Jorge Bejarano Civic Medal for Health and Welfare Merits 1667
Brackenbury Award 2431
Buchanan Medal 4144
Condecoracion Dr. Eduardo Liceaga 9127
Prix Eugene Etienne 6139
Fondation Maujean 5629
Honorable Mention 6815
Honorary Member 10190
John Kershaw Award 4460
Donald Mackay Medal 4280
Maddison Prize 4461
Medal: 80 Years of the Polish Society of Hygiene 10191
Medal Jubilee: One Hundred Years of the PSH 10192
Medal Jubileuszowy: 90 Lat PTH 10193
Manuel Alves Monteiro Prize 10257
Morishita Prize 8502
Prof. Dr. P. Muntendamprijs 9661
Neech Prize 4462
Arthur Newth Memorial Prize 4463
One Hundred Years of the Periodical *Health* Medal 10194
Order of Lenin 10463
Ordre de la Sante Publique 1791
Plaques 10195
Pras Harvey 7945
Premio Dr. Francisco C. Rosenbusch 9
Premio Fundacion Manzullo 11
Premio Gerardo Varela 9129
Premios a la Investigacion Medica 9044
Public Health Award 4464
Public Health Travelling Fellowships 544
Dr. P. N. Raju Oration Award 7600
Royal Institute of Public Health and Hygiene Awards 4083
Moinho Santista Prizes for Young People 1496
Moinho Santista Prizes 1497
Science Prize - Henrietta Szold Prize 7961
Dr. M. K. Seshadri Prize in the Field of Practice of Community Medicine 7608
Prof. B. C. Srivastava Foundation Award 7613
Premio Miguel Aleman Valdes 8992

Public relations (See also Advertising; Publicity)
ABSA Business Awards 2030
Awards for Outstanding Consultancy Practice 3828
T. C. Farries Public Relations and Publicity Awards 3567
Fashion Awards 8235
Karin Gierows pris for hangiven bildningsverksamhet 11591
International Visual Communications Association Awards 3502
IPRA Golden World Awards for Excellence 11822
Michel Linon Prize 5122
President's Award 7815
Prix Herman Schoolmeesters 991
Public Relations Institute of Southern Africa Awards 10912
Public Relations State Emblem 746
C. P. Robertson Memorial Trophy 2047
Sword of Excellence Awards 3204

Public sanitation See Sanitary engineering

Public service (See also Community service; Government service)
Academy of Athens Medal 7181
Australian Bravery Decorations 207
Benemerenti Medals 12100
Bharat Ratna 7549
British Empire Medal 2359
Cacique's Crown of Honor 7243
Cavaliere of the Order Star of Italian Solidarity 8373
Certificate of Honor 10736
Collar of the Supreme Order of the Chrysanthemum 8582
Condecoracion al Merito Social 9013
Creu de Sant Jordi 11185
Croix de Guerre 5243
Deshabandu 11429
Deshamanya 11430
Distinguished Service Order 10739
Belisario Dominguez Medal of Honor 9143
Efficiency Medal 10740
Eminent Activist Medal 7379
First Class Order of the Rising Sun Paulownia Flowers 8583
Fondation Delalande-Guerineau 5536
Fondation Gabrielle Sand 5563
Fondation Jaffe 5588
Fondation Jean-Jacques Berger 5597
Fondation Marie Guido Triossi 5625
Fondation Paul Gallet 5646
Gold Medal of the Royal Order of the Polar Star 11578
Gold Star Medal 10459
Golden Arrow of Achievement 7249
Graduateship of the City and Guilds of London Institute 2624
Grand Collier 1787
Grand Cordon of the Supreme Order of the Chrysanthemum 8584
Honorary Citizen of the City of Salzburg 864
"Honorary Citizen" Title 7301
Honorary Titles of the USSR 10461
Wahidin Sudiro Husodo Award 7727
Imperial Service Order 2370
Israel Prize 7906
Kalakirthi 11431
Kalashoori 11432
King's Cross for Distinguished Service 9918
Komsomol Work Award 10436
Madarski Konnik Order 1506
Lanka Sikkhamani 11433

Public — Awards, Honors & Prizes, 1995-96

Public (continued)
Letter of Citizenship of the City of Salzburg   866
Licentiateship of the City and Guilds of London Institute   2625
Ramon Magsaysay Awards   10042
Medaille d'Honneur des Douanes   1789
Medal for Postal Merit   1604
Medal for Service to the Republic   8916
Medal of Honor   10742
Medal of Service   7251
Medal of the French Resistance   5245
Medals for Excellence   2626
Membership of the City and Guilds of London Institute   2627
Meritorious Service Medal   10743
Mexican Order of the Aztec Eagle   9133
Most Ancient and Most Noble Order of the Thistle   2373
Most Distinguished Order of St. Michael and St. George   2374
Most Excellent Order of the British Empire   2375
Most Honourable Order of the Bath   2376
Most Noble Order of the Garter   2377
National Order of Merit   5236
National Order of the Legion of Honor   5237
National Prize for Civic Merit   9139
Onassis Prize for the Environment   7210
Orden al Merito Julio Garavito   1669
Order for Merit in Work   12136
Order for Meritorious Service   10958
Order of Australia   344
Order of Francisco de Miranda   12138
Order of Lenin   10463
Order of Leopold   1073
Order of Nila Utama   10744
Order of Pius IX   12101
Order of Roraima of Guyana   7255
Order of St. Gregory the Great   12102
Order of Temasek   10745
Order of the Companions of Honour   2379
Order of the Cross of Liberty   4678
Order of the Dannebrog   1941
Order of the Elephant   1942
Order of the Falcon   7464
Order of the Liberator   12140
Order of the Lion of Finland   4679
Order of the Rose   1507
Order of the Southern Cross   10960
Order of the Star of South Africa (Military)   10961
Order of the Star of South Africa (Non-Military)   10962
Order of the White Rose of Finland   4680
Orders of the Precious Crown   8587
Orders of the Rising Sun   8588
Orders of the Sacred Treasure   8589
Ordre de Leopold II   1075
Ordre du Merite des P. et T.   1794
Ordre du Merite Ivoirien   1795
Ordre Nacional de Madagascar   8879
Ordre National   1797
Padma Bhushan   7554
Padma Shri   7555
Padma Vibhushan   7556
Premio Derechos Humanos   9191
Premio Mixcoatl   9255
President's Award   9741
Prix Bordin   5720
Prix de Joest   5730
Prix du Baron de Joest   5451
Prix Rene Cassin   5788
Prize of the Capital of Slovakia Bratislava   1830
Prize of the Mayor of the City of Bratislava   1831

Public Administration Medal   10747
Public Service Medal
  Council for the Order of Australia   346
  Singapore - Office of the Prime Minister   10748
Public Service Medal of Merit of the Order of the Trinity   12035
Public Service Star   10749
Right Livelihood Award   11509
Royal Norwegian Order of Merit   9921
Royal Norwegian Order of St. Olav   9922
Royal Order of the Polar Star   11579
Royal Order of the Seraphim   11580
Royal Victorian Order   2385
Salzburg Heraldic Medal   868
Spectator/Highland Park Parliamentarian of the Year Awards   4485
Sri Lanka Abhimanya   11434
Sri Lankatillaka   11435
Stara Planina Order   1508
Thirteen Centuries of Bulgaria Order   1509
Trinity Cross of the Order of the Trinity   12036
Hendrik Van Eck Medal   11051
Vidyajothi   11436
Vidyanidhi   11437
Heinrich von Stephan Medal   6749

Public speaking
Faraday House Commemorative Prize   3278
Alexander Fletcher Memorial Prize Lecture   10600
Guild of Professional Toastmasters Best After Dinner Speaker of the Year   2975
IAHR Lecturer Award   9460
Eric Megaw Memorial Prize   3295
National Lecture Competition   3143
Prix Marcelin Guerin   5890
Rosenkjaer Prize   1995
Watson Prize Lecture   10602
T. C. White Prize Lecture   10603
Younger Members' Premiums Awards   3311

Public works
National Engineering Excellence Awards   476

Publications (See also Company publications; Travel literature)
3M Talking Book of the Year   612
Arab Book Fair Prize   8842
Book Award   2486
British Society of Magazine Editors Awards   3772
Concord Press Award for Academic Publishing   9861
Dalgety Farmers Limited Awards for Excellence in Rural Journalism   353
IEE Rayleigh Book Award   3288
National Prize of the President of the Republic   8068
PPA Magazines Awards for Editorial and Publishing Excellence   3774
PPA Subscription Awards   3775
Premio Antonio de Lara "Tono" de Humor Grafico   11287
Premio Romulo Garza para Publicaciones   9027
Prix Danube Festival, Bratislava   10780

Publicity (See also Advertising; Public relations)
T. C. Farries Public Relations and Publicity Awards   3567
Komsomol Propagandist Award   10434
Primo Scolastico di Raccordo   8014
Lord Soper Award   3545

Publishing (See also Bibliography; Book and newspaper design; Editing; Illustration; Printing industry; Publications; Reference; Typography)
Arab Book Fair Prize   8842
Awards for the Best Produced Books in Hong Kong   7277
Banjo Awards   534
Best Published Book Award (Publisher and Author)   9981
Book Design Awards   193
British Book Design and Production Awards   2482
Laurens Janszoon Coster Prize   9443
Critici in Erba Prize   8171
Editorial Fellowship Program   7933
Galley Club Award for Excellence   409
Golden Book Prize   8342
Graphics Prize Fiera di Bologna for Children and Young Adults   8172
Hegarty Prize   574
Innovation Writer of the Year   3773
Inter Nations Culture Prize   6927
International Book Award   899
Kodansha Prize   8687
Kraszna-Krausz Award   3527
Ralph Lewis Award   4587
Montana Book Awards   9705
Most Beautiful and the Best Children's Book of spring, summer, autumn, winter in Slovakia   10760
Most Beautiful Books of Austria   741
New Zealand Book Awards   9801
Nihon Shinbun Kyokai Awards   8628
PANPA Newspaper Awards   575
PPA Magazines Awards for Editorial and Publishing Excellence   3774
Premio Internazionale di Meridionalistica Guido Dorso   8149
Prix Bordin   5364
Prix du Livre de Photographies   6190
Sunday Times Small Publishers Award   4504
Swiss Children's Book Prize   11947
Walter Tiemann Award   7033
Trophee International de la Reliure D'Art   4892

Puppetry
Bochumer Textpreis fur Figurentheater   6674
Brothers Grimm Prize   6561
Jan Nelissenprijs   9645
Premi Josep M. Carbonell   11159
Fritz Wortelmann Preis of the City of Bochum for Amateur Puppetry   6676

Quality control See Standards

Race relations See Ethnic affairs

Radio (See also Broadcasting; Cable television; Media; Television)
ABU Prize Competitions for Radio and Television Programmes   8889
Akashvani Annual Awards   7480
Akashvani Annual Awards for Technical Excellence   7481
All India Competition for Radio Playwrights   7482
AMP W.G. Walkley Awards for Journalism   523
Artes Awards   11037
Arts Festival Award   8576
Awgie Awards   283
Berlin Art Prizes   6509

Bratislava Radio Prize for Folklore Music 10778
CCP Awards for Radio 10047
Laurens Janszoon Coster Prize 9443
CRPLF Awards 5070
Danmarks Radio TV Award 1991
Dentsu Advertising Awards 8524
Esperanto Diploma 7425
FAW Adele Shelton-Smith Award for Play, Radio or Other Scripts for Young Writers 378
Glenfiddich Awards 2949
Golden Aztec Calendar Prize 8926
Gran Premio de Honor Argentores 30
Grand Prix SACD 6395
Bharatendu Harishchandra Award 7530
Hebrew Radio Play Prize 7917
Innsbruck Radio Prize for Early Music 843
International Advertising Festival of Ireland 7785
International Radio and Television Festivals and Competitions 1867
Islamic Countries Festival for Radio Production 10492
Journalism Competition Prizes 12121
Journalist Prize of the DGE 6857
Kryger Prize 1992
Lauriers de la FM 6116
Ramon Magsaysay Awards 10042
Medienpreis fur Sprachkultur 6894
Nagrada Saveta Fonda SO SUBNOR Cetvrti jul 10707
NHK Japan Prize Contest 8602
Nigar Public Film Awards 9987
Alfonso Sordo Noriega Prize 9090
P1-Prize 1993
Premio Argentores 31
Premio Guillermo Marconi 11292
Premio Municipal Maria Leonor Magro de Radio 10275
Preseren Award 10799
Prix CIRTEF de Corealisation 11776
Prix de la Promotion Radiophonique de la Poesie 6330
Prix Futura Berlin 7074
Prix Italia 8413
Prix Musical de Radio Brno 1848
Prix Talents Nouveau 6399
Radio and Television Language Prize 12078
Radio Bantu Prize for Works Written for the Radio 11041
Radio Denmark Language Award 1994
Radio Times Drama & Comedy Awards 2160
Regional Radio and Television Awards 1108
Romanian Radio and Television Award 10327
SAUK Prys vir Televisie en Radio 11003
Scholarship Prizes 6512
Sony Radio Awards 4477
South African Broadcasting Corporation Prize 11042
Staatspreis fur Radiowerbung 749
Trade Union's Art and Cultural Prize 7442
TRIC Annual Celebrity Awards 4508
Turkish Radio and Television Culture, Art and Science Prizes 12084
Unda Dove 1376
WACRAL Award Certificate 4618
Margarita Xirgu Radio Drama Prize 11325

Radiology
3M Mayneord Memorial Lecture 2404
Heinrich-E.-Albers-Schonberg Medaille 6828
David Anderson-Berry Medal 10637
Thomas Baker Memorial Fellowship for Radiologists 592
Barclay Medal 2405
Barclay Prize 2406
Antoine Beclere Prize 11842
BIR Travel Bursaries 2407
Clinical MRI Prize 2408
Mackenzie Davidson Lecture 2409
Paul De Backer Prize 1310
Flude Memorial Prize 2410
Hermann-Holthusen-Ring 6829
Honorary Member 10161
Junior Member and Travel Awards 593
Jacques Lefebvre Memorial Award 5130
Leonard Levy Memorial Prize 2411
Nic McNally Memorial Prize 2412
Medaille Boris Rajewsky 1123
Stanley Melville Award 2413
Nycomed Scandinavian Scholarships 2414
Prix Antoine et Claude Beclere 4810
Prix de l'APERR 4966
Prix Jean-Francois Ginestie 4850
RAD Magazine Best Poster Prize 2415
Hermann-Rieder-Medaille 6830
Roentgen-Preis 7001
Rontgen Plakette 6678
Wilhelm Conrad Rontgen-Preis 6831
Rontgen Prize 2416
Royal College of Radiologists Award 3972
Scientific Award in the Field of Radiology 10162
Sievert Award 9524
Silvanus Thompson Memorial Lecture 2417
Tubiana Award 2418
Hamao Umezawa Prize for Chemotherapy 9898

Radiotherapy See **Cancer**

Railway transportation
Railway Engineering Award 483
Webb Prize 3264

Recording industry
Arts Festival Award 8576
Bratislava Radio Prize for Folklore Music 10778
BRIT Awards 2478
Class Prizes in British Amateur Tape Recording Contest 2872
Export Prize 9371
Grand Prix du Disque Frederic Chopin 10066
El Heraldo Music Prizes 9020
International Grand Prix for Liszt Records 7438
International Songwriters' Association Awards 7787
National Record Award 1416
Record of the Year Prize 4691
Sopot International Song Festival 10130
Springbok Radio Sarie Awards 11043
Jean Thevenot Medal 9533
Wiener Flotenuhr 916

Recreation (See also **Hobbies and clubs**)
Eichendorff Plakette 6742
Premi Artur Martorell 11172
Sondrio Town Council International Festival of Documentary Films on Parks 8433
Youth Studies Prize 11173

Reference
McColvin Medal 3571
Wheatley Medal 3574

Refugees See **Humanitarianism**

Rehabilitation and therapy
Awards 10732
Boehm Medal 6864
Corresponding Members 6865
Decorations 6946
Mildred Elson Award for International Achievement in Physical Therapy 4622
Honorary Member 6866
Samuel Hyde Memorial Lecture 4254
Jose M. Jorge Prize 84
Richard Kovacs Prize 4258
South African Association of Occupational Therapists Awards 11028
WVF Rehabilitation Prize 6499

Religion (See also **Catholic literature; Christianity; Church history; Judaism; Religion literature; Theology**)
Actonian Prize 4087
Bangkok Bank Prize for Thai Literature Competition 12022
Blake Prize for Religious Art 285
Collins Religious Book Award 2640
C. De Clercq Prize 1254
Ecumenical Prize 1172
IABO Awards 8278
ICCJ - Sternberg Award 6938
Indian Books Centre Oriental Studies Award 7571
OCIC-Prize 1173
Prix Crouzet 5728
Prix des Cathedrales 5380
Prix Emile de Laveleye 985
Prix Franz Cumont 988
Prix Goblet d'Alviella 989
Prix Le Fevre-Deumier (de Pons) 5468
Prix Lefevre-Deumier de Pons 5772
Prix Roman et Tania Ghirshman 5471
Prix Victor Delbos 5795
Quinquennial Award in the Psychology of Religion 1175
Regional Ecumenism Award 941
Mohamed Sahabdeen Award for Literature 11417
Albert Schweitzer Award 3368
Templeton Prize for Progress in Religion 928
Writing Competition on the Teaching of Buddhism for Children 12029

Religion literature
Prix de Pays Protestants 6153
Prix Henri Davignon 1301
Winifred Mary Stanford Prize 3019

Research (See also **Dental research; Educational research; Humanities research; Medical research; Scientific research; Social science research**)
Arata Award 3432
Bialik Prize for Research 7905
Bicentennial Fellowship 7839
J. D. Stewart Bursary Award 3565
Concours Seymour Cray France 5078
Diploma al Merito Universitario 9180
Dufton Silver Medal Award 2592
Elegant Work Prize 3132
Entwicklungslanderpreises der Justus-Liebig-Universitat Giessen 6999
James Alfred Ewing Medal 3236
FENS European Nutrition Award 11883
Fondation Montyon des Statistiques 5639
Leon Gaster Bronze Medal 2593
Geotechnical Research Medal 3238
Stanley Gray Fellowships 3118
Ulverscroft Munford Research Fellowship 3573

Research (continued)
Napier - Shaw Bronze Medal 2595
National Engineering Excellence Awards 476
National Prize for Technology and Design 9151
National Prize of the President of the Republic 8068
Okuma Academic Commemorative Prize 8785
Okuma Academic Encouragement Prize 8786
Premio Napolitain Illustri 8257
Premio Universidad Nacional 9199
Prix Prestwich 5313
Research Grant 2915

Restaurants
Glenfiddich Awards 2949
Time Out Eating and Drinking Awards 4544

Retailing See Merchandising

Rhetoric See Public speaking

Riflery See Firearms; Hunting; Shooting

Robotics
Premio Condumex 9187

Rowing
Team Championships (non-divisional) 4569

Rugby
FIRA Championship Awards 5952
Medailles de la FIRA 5953
Medailles du Merite 5954
Rugby World Juniors Championship Awards 5955

Rural economics
ANGOC Award for Rural Development 10020
FAO Technical Assistance Fellowship 8268
Inter-American Agricultural Award for Young Professionals 1774
Inter-American Agricultural Medal 1776
Inter-American Award for the Participation of Women in Rural Development 1777
IPDC - UNESCO Prize for Rural Communication 6416
Osiris Award 8270
Premio Bartolome de las Casas 11362
Premio Mariano Ospina Perez 1699
Prof. B. D. Tilak Lecture Award 7676

Safety (See also Environmental health; Fire fighting; Fire prevention; Sanitary engineering; specific types of safety, e.g. Automotive safety)
International Festival of Economics and Training Films 1191
International Visual Communications Association Awards 3502
Magnel Prize 1362
Safety in Construction Medal 3257
Verdeyen Prize for Soil Mechanics 1363

Salesmanship See Marketing; Merchandising

Sanitary engineering (See also Public works)
Fondation Alfred Durand-Claye 5482

Scholarly works
AFUW - QLD Freda Bage Fellowship 214
The Age Book of the Year Awards 118
Chia Hsin Prize 11994
Chungshan Cultural Foundation Prizes 11998
Concord Press Award for Academic Publishing 9861
Cornforth Medal 598
Belisario Dominguez Medal of Honor 9143
Charles Douglas-Home Memorial Award 2751
Fondation James Hall 5589
Eric Gregory Medal 7792
Kenyon Medal for Classical Studies 2229
Meijimura Prize 8698
Pierre Mendes France Prize 6118
Nayacakalou Medal 9787
A. A. Phillips Award 133
C. S. Piper Prize 600
Premio di Laurea Luigi Casati in Discipline Scientifiche 8074
Premio Municipal Augusto Vieira da Silva de Investigacao 10266
Premio Romulo Garza para Publicaciones 9027
Prix d'Aumale 5341
Prix d'Aumale 5729
Prix Pierre Villey 5911
Scholarly Studies Prize 12079
Scientist of the Year and Best Author 9983
THESE-PAC Awards 9699
Jose Verissimo Prize 1445
Young Enterprise Award 3310

Science (See also History of science; Science education; Scientific research; Technology; specific fields of science, e.g. Astronomy)
Academy of Athens Prize 7182
Actonian Prize 4087
Aldre Linnemadeljen i guld 11533
Amsterdam Prize for the Environment 9596
Annual Award 2528
Antwoorden Prijsvragen, Klasse der Wetenschappen 1251
ANZAAS Medal 188
Istvan Apathy Commemorative Medal 7458
Aryabhata Medal 7637
Australian Natural History Medallion 402
Austrian Medal of Honor in the Arts and Sciences 756
Eugenio Balzan Prize 8280
Donat Banki Award 7455
Bavarian Academy of Science Competition Prize 6557
Bavarian Academy of Science Prize 6558
Belgrade International Festival of Scientific Films 10699
Benemerenti Medals 6559
Prof. E. D. Bergmann Memorial Award 7975
Berzeliusmedaljen i guld 11535
Bharat Ratna 7549
Scott Blair Scholarship 2529
Blekinge County Council Culture Prize 11446
Rudjer Boskovic Awards 1807
Brazilian Association for the Advancement of Science Awards 1428
British Association Film and Television Awards 2254
British Association Medal 11017
Brussels International Festival of Scientific and Technical Films 1098
Bulgarian Academy of Science Honorary Badge - Marin Drinov Medal 1512
Burnet Lecture 171
Cacique's Crown of Honor 7243
Caldas Science Prize 1688
Miguel Antonio Caro and Rufino Jose Cuervo National Order 1711
Carus Medal 6621
Carus Preis 7104
Certificate of Honor 10426
Certificate of Merit 11018
Dr. G. P. Chatterjee Memorial Lecture 7643
City of Vienna Promotional Prizes 791
Sir Charles Clore Prize for Distinguished Service of Science to the Society 7979
Lorenzo Codazzi Prize 1745
Fernand Colin-Prijs 1379
Collins Religious Book Award 2640
Commendation by the Minister of State for Science and Technology 8591
Condecoracion al Merito Social 9013
James Cook Medal 625
Culture Prize 9959
Cymmrodorion Medal 3023
John Howard Dellinger Gold Medal 1211
Dissertation Honors 6998
N. A. Dobrolyubov Prize 10422
Educational Merit Diploma 1656
Albert Einstein World Award of Science 9307
Engestromska medaljen for tillampad naturvetenskap 11513
Esso Energy Award and Medal 4148
Michael Faraday Award 4149
Fellow 12222
Fellowship of the City and Guilds of London Institute 2622
Matthew Flinders Lecture 172
Fondation Albert I de Monaco 5479
Fondation Alexandre Darracq 5480
Fondation Alhumbert 5484
Fondation Ayme Poirson 5499
Fondation Bordin 5506
Fondation Charles Fremont 5516
Fondation de Madame Victor Noury 5535
Fondation Delalande-Guerineau 5536
Fondation Ernest Dechelle 5553
Fondation Gabrielle Sand 5563
Fondation Gustave Roux 5573
Fondation Helene Helbronner-Fould 5574
Fondation Henri Becquerel 5575
Fondation Jaffe 5334
Fondation Jaffe 5588
Fondation Jean Reynaud 5599
Fondation Jerome Ponti 5602
Fondation Jules et Louis Jeanbernat et Barthelemy de Ferrari Doria 5604
Fondation Lannelongue 5611
Fondation Laplace 5612
Fondation Le Conte 5615
Fondation Marie Guido Triossi 5625
Fondation Paul Doistau - Emile Blutet 5644
Fondation Paul Gallet 5646
Fondation Petit d'Ormoy 5649
Fondation Thorlet 5671
Fondation Tremont 5673
Fondations Estrade Delcros, Houllevigue, Saintour, Jules Mahyer 5679
Fondazione Premio Dotte Giuseppe Borgia 8063
Forderpreis fur Wissenschaften 6685
Francqui Prize 1156
Geoffrey Frew Fellowship 173
Fujihara Award 8527
Galardon Estado de Mexico 9008
Joaquin Garcia Monge Prize 1762
Gawad AGKATEK (Agham, Kapaligiran at Teknolohiya) 10057
Genootschapsmedaille 9557
Goethepreis 6612
Gold Medal
British Society of Rheology 2530

Subject Index of Awards
Volume 2: International and Foreign
Science

Pakistan Academy of Sciences 9993
Zimbabwe Scientific Association 12223
Gold Medal for Achievement in Science and Technology 10989
Grand Prix Scientifique de la Ville de Paris 6094
J. E. Gunnerus Medal 9968
Soren Gyldendal Prisen 1954
Hamilton Memorial Prize 9837
Hammer and Sickle Gold Medal 10460
Havenga Prize for Science and Technology 10990
Hegel-Preis der Landeshauptstadt Stuttgart 7136
Dannie Heineman Prize 6908
John F. W. Herschel Medal 10965
High Quality of Work Award 10432
Dr. Hirata Award 8662
Honorable Mention 6815
Honorary Diploma 10216
Honorary Fellow 8807
Honorary Member
 Lublin Scientific Society 10079
 Wroclaw Scientific Society 10220
Honorary Rings of the City of Salzburg 865
Steven Hoogendijk Prijs 9420
Humboldt Research Awards to Foreign Scholars 7155
Hungarian Academy of Sciences Gold Medal 7312
Javed Husain Prize for Young Scientists 6414
Edmond Hustinx Prize for Science 9682
IFUW Awards Competition 11789
Imperial Prize 8594
Incentive for Publications of Articles in International Journals 9982
INSA Medal for Young Scientists 7650
Inter Nations Culture Prize 6927
International Dag Hammarskjold Award 1237
International Institute for Promotion and Prestige Awards 11805
Ion Ionescu de la Brad Prize 10358
ISCA Young Scientists' Awards 7684
Islamic Foundation Awards 10490
Israel Prize 7906
Italian Minister for Culture and the Environment Prizes 8365
Otto Jaag-Gewasserschutz-Preis 11932
Nami Jafet Prize 1488
Jamnalal Bajaj Foundation Awards 7693
Japan Academy Prize 8595
Japan Prize 8736
Axel Ax:son Johnson Lecture 11528
R. M. Johnston Memorial Medal 634
Kalinga Prize 6417
Alexander Petrowitsch Karpinskij Prizes 7115
Cherry Kearton Medal and Award 4012
The Kharazmi Prize 7737
King Faisal International Prize in Science 10500
Issac Koga Gold Medal 1212
Komsomol Special Award for Science and Technology 10435
Kossuth Prize 7410
K. S. Krishnan Memorial Lecture 7654
Kultureller Ehrenpreis 7020
Kulturpreis der Stadt Villach 887
Kuwait Prize 8844
Kyoto Prizes 8539
Latsis-Preis 11934
Leeds Philosophical and Literary Society Medal 3548
Letterstedtska Forfattarpriset 11543
Letterstedtska Medaljen i guld 11544

Leverhulme Tercentenary Medal 3555
Life Achievement Award 1811
Literary Awards and Prizes for Sinhalese Literature 11423
Lomonosov Gold Medal 10419
Clive Lord Memorial Medal 635
Lower Austria Prize for the Advancement of Fine Arts and Literature 859
Magon National Prize of Culture 1763
MAN National Science Prize 9865
Mansel-Pleydell and Cecil Trusts 2749
Sir Ernest Marsden Medal for Outstanding Service to Science 9752
Nic McNally Memorial Prize 2412
Medal of Honor for Promotion of a Scientific Field 11000
Medal of Honor of the Physical Sciences and Technique 11001
Medal of Merit 6624
Medalla de la Generalitat de Catalunya 11187
Medals of the National Academy of Science 8379
Meghnad Saha Medal 7658
Johann-Heinrich-Merck Ehrung 6602
Messel Medal and Lecture 4418
Minnesmedaljen i guld 11519
Sisir Kumar Mitra Memorial Lecture 7659
Mlada Fronta Award 1887
Mlade leta Prize 10786
Narcis Monturiol Medal and Plaque for Science and Technology 11188
Mullard Award and Medal 4153
Musgrave Medal 8482
Fridtjof Nansen Award 9927
National Bank of Pakistan Prize for Literature 10007
National Cultural Awards 1413
National Marine Science Prize 1690
National Order of the Southern Cross 1415
National Prize for Physics, Mathematics and Natural Sciences 9149
National Prize for Sciences 1663
National Prize for Technical Development/ Colombia 12128
National Prize in Science and Art 9152
National Prize of the President of the Republic 8068
National Prizes for Culture 1391
National Science, Literature and Art Prize 7183
Natural World Book of the Year Award 3714
Meiring Naude Medal 10966
Jawaharlal Nehru Birth Centenary Lectures 7660
Jawaharlal Nehru Birth Centenary Medal 7661
Jawaharlal Nehru Birth Centenary Visiting Fellowship 7662
Neill Medal 10647
Niwa Prize 8620
Professor E. J. Nystroms Prize 4708
October Prizes of the City of Belgrade 10696
Lorenz Oken Medaille 6890
Orbit Award of the ANZAAS International Scientific Film Exhibition and Competition 191
Order Ingenio et Arti 1939
Order of Andres Bello 12137
Order of Culture 8586
Order of Francisco de Miranda 12138
Order of Lenin 10463
Order of Merit 2378
Order of Merit in the Sciences and Arts 6743
Order of the Crown 1074

Order of the Netherlands Lion 9358
Order of the Rebirth of Poland 10119
Order of the Red Banner of Labor 10467
H. C. Orsted Medal 2007
Oscar la Villette du Jeu et Jouet a Caractere Scientifique et Technique 5009
Outstanding Scientist Award 12025
The Outstanding Youth Science Researchers 10058
Pakistan Civil Awards 9995
Jan Palach Prize 5993
Paracelsusring der Stadt Villach 888
Abraham Geza Pattantyus Award 7456
Swraj Paul Award for the Promotion of Science & Technology Policy 3462
Peace Prize of the German Book Trade 6776
Peccei Scholar 838
Pergamon Scott Blair Biorheology Scholarship 2531
Pietrzak Award 10084
Pras Harvey 7945
Preis der Stiftung Kunststoff-Technik 11935
Premi
 Accademia di Scienze, Lettere e Arti di Palermo 8030
 Accademia di Studi Storici Aldo Moro 8032
Premi Antonio Feltrinelli 8069
Premi del Ministro per i Beni Culturali e Ambientali 8070
Premio a las Mejores Obras Cientificas o Tecnicas Publicadas en el Ano 1818
Premio Anton Mario Lorgna 8380
Premio Atomo D'oro 8090
Premio Cavolini - De Mellis 8087
Premio di Laurea Luigi Casati in Discipline Scientifiche 8074
Premio Efraim Hernandez Xolocotzi 8956
Premio Federico Nitti 8382
Premio Internazionale di Meridionalistica Guido Dorso 8149
Premio Internazionale per un Articolo o Studio Scientifico o Tecnico 8265
Premio Luigi Prete 8040
Premio Luis Elizondo - Premio Cientifico y Technologico 8989
Premio Maria Teresa Messori Roncaglia and Eugenio Mari 8077
Premio Nacional de Ciencias 1546
Premio Nacional de Ciencias y Tecnologia Clodomiro Picado Twight 1764
Premio Nacional de Medicina, Dr. Luis Edmundo Vasquez 2025
Premio Napolitain Illustri 8257
Premio scientifico-technico 8136
Premio Sinaloa de Ciencias y Artes 9015
Premio Tenore 8088
Premio Tetradramma d'oro 8034
Premios Vitalicios 11245
Prince Philip Medal 2628
Prix Adolphe Wetrems 1006
Prix Adrien Constantin de Magny 5682
Prix Alfred Verdaguer
 Institut de France 5336
 Institut de France - Academie des Sciences 5683
Prix Andre Lequeux
 Institut de France 5337
 Institut de France - Academie des Sciences Morales et Politiques 5714
Prix Antoine Girard 5815
Prix Claude Berthault 5726
Prix Corbay 5727
Prix d'Aumale 5686
Prix de l'Academie des Sciences, Arts et Belles Lettres de Dijon 4795

Science

Science (continued)
Prix de Madame Claude Berthault 5691
Prix de Stassart 983
Prix Franco-Britannique de l'Academie des Sciences 5697
Prix Fraternite Gaby Archenbaud 6124
Prix Gegner 5748
Prix Jules et Louis Jeanbernat et Barthelemy de Ferrari Doria 5346
Prix Jules et Louis Jeanbernat et Barthelemy de Ferrari Doria
   Institut de France - Academie des Sciences Morales et Politiques 5768
   Institut de France - Academie Francaise 5874
Prix Mondial Cino del Duca 5224
Prix Osiris 5347
Prix Osiris 5703
Prix Science et Defense 5246
Prix Science pour l'Art - Moet-Hennessy - Louis Vuitton 6122
Prize for Better Work 8886
Prize for Junior Scientists 6517
Prize of Honor for Catalan Letters 11310
Prizes to Young Graduates 6029
Public Service Medal 10748
Alexander Sergeovich Pushkin Prize 10423
Chandrasekhara Venkata Raman Medal 7665
Rector's Medal 11117
Regional Production Prizes 23
Research Medal 9755
Kurt P. Richter Prize 1208
Rolex Awards for Enterprise 11898
Royal Society of Western Australia Medal 640
Friedrich Ruckert Preis 7105
Mohamed Sahabdeen Award for Science 11418
Salzburg Prize for the Promotion of the Arts, Science and Literature 869
Moinho Santista Prizes for Young People 1496
Moinho Santista Prizes 1497
Sarton Chair 1357
Sarton Medal 1358
Walter Schall-Preis 6897
Science and Technology Media Fellowships 2255
Science Award 8663
Science Prize 8080
Science Prize - Dr. Chaim Weizman Prize 7959
Scientific/Engineering Award 10816
Scientific Merit Award 1681
Scientist of the Year and Best Author 9983
SEAMEO Testimonial for the Southeast Asian Ministers of Education Council (SEAMEC) President 12031
Selby Fellowship 179
Serbian Academy of Sciences and Arts Awards 10724
Service Award 8664
Shincho Art and Science Award 8744
Singer-Polignac Grants 5226
Society Medal 630
Sofia International Film Festival on Organization and Automation of Production and Management Awards 1530
South Africa Medal 11020
Sparreska Priset 11552
State Prize
   Hungary - Office of the Prime Minister 7412
   Secretariat of the Committee of State Prizes 10204
George Stavros Gold Medal 7195
George Stavros Silver Medal 7196
M. T. Steyn Prize for Achievement in Science and Technology 11007
Techfilm International Film Festival 1874
Third World Academy of Science Prize 8910
Thomson Medal 9842
Prof. B. D. Tilak Lecture Award 7676
Tiroler Landespreis fur Wissenschaft 733
Trophees de l'Initiative 5104
Fran Tucan Award 1814
Turkish Radio and Television Culture, Art and Science Prizes 12084
UNESCO Science Prize 6427
University of Berne Prizes 11965
Upper Austria Culture Prize for Science 905
Balthasar van der Pol Gold Medal 1213
Sir Joseph Verco Medal 632
Verlagspreis zur Forderung popularwissenschaftlicher Literatur fur das jungere Lesealter 7152
Franz Vogt-Preise 7005
Pran Vohra Award 7685
Wahlbergska Minnesmedaljen i guld 11559
Ian William Wark Medal and Lecture 180
Weizmann Prizes of the Academy of Scientific Research 8920
Wilhelm Westrups beloning 11521
Woman of the Year in Finland 4752
Asa Wright Honorary Award 7467
Wurdigungspreis 862

Science education
Bienal de Cine y Video Cientifico 11166
Bragg Medal and Prize 3186
British Association Film and Television Awards 2254
CASTME Awards 2646
Chemical Society of Japan Award for Chemical Education 8513
Chemical Society of Japan Award of Merits for Chemical Education 8517
Excellence in Aerospace Education 7474
Jan Harabaszewski Medal 10134
Hizmet Odulu 12066
ICPE Medal for Physics Teaching 11486
International Multimedia Science Film Festival 8375
International Week of Scientific Films 11199
Medal of Honor for Promotion of a Scientific Field 11000
PSJ Award for Educational Services 8719
Dr. Juan S. Salcedo Jr. Science Education Award 10061
Science Book Prizes 4157
Sony Science Education Promotion Fund 8758
Worlddidac Award 11984

Science fiction
Avoriaz Film Awards 4983
Belgrade International Festival of Scientific Films 10699
British Fantasy Awards 2336
British Science Fiction Association Awards 2496
Brussels International Festival of Fantasy Thriller and Science- Fiction Films 1241
Arthur C. Clarke Award 4337
Concurso de Cuento de Ciencia Ficcion 9170
Festival International de Paris du Film Fantastique et de Science-Fiction 6149
Harry Harrison Award 6492
IMAGFIC International Film Festival of Madrid 11263
Pasja Dlaka, Slovenian/Universal Science Fiction Award 10805

Prix Cosmos 2000 6079
Prix Julia Verlanger 6463
Special President's Award 6494
World SF President's Award 6495

Science journalism (*See also* **Medical journalism**)
Best Paper Award 7616
Best Scientific or Technological Journal Prize 12127
Fondation Da Gama Machado 5527
Fondation Damoiseau 5528
Fondation Desmazieres 5540
Forderpreis der ITG 6530
Sigmund-Freud-Preis 6766
Indira Gandhi Prize for Popularization of Science 7645
Glaxo Science Writers Awards 2936
Jabuti Prize 1470
Literaturpreis der ETG 6697
Lower Austria Recognition Prize in Arts and Sciences 860
Medaille fur Naturwissenschaftliche Publizistik 6661
National Excellence Awards for Engineering Journalism 477
New Zealand Association of Scientists Certificate for Science Journalism 9753
New Zealand Association of Scientists Prize for Science Communication 9754
Newbigin Prize 10633
Antal Pech Medal 7358
Perkins Power Award 3777
Preis der Gesellschaft Deutscher Chemiker fur Journalisten und Schriftsteller 6788
Premio Romulo Garza para Publicaciones 9027
President's Medal 4443
Prix de l'Information Scientifique 5689
Simms Medal 4444
Society's Prizes 4445
Spearman Medal 2491
Warner Memorial Medal 4527

Scientific research
Adelskoldska Medaljen 11532
AIPEA Medals 1048
Akzo prijs 9389
Ames Prize for Investigation in the field of Basic Health Sciences 1581
Annual Prize for Scientific Works 12126
Grigore Antipa Prize 10330
Arabization Prizes 7747
Arnbergska Priset 11534
Australian Applied Health Sciences Fellowships 538
Award for Outstanding Achievement in Acupuncture Research 11996
Marcel Benoist Prize 11668
Bilim Odulu 12065
Charles Vernon Boys Medal and Prize 3185
Bradley Award 1049
Walter Burfitt Medal and Prize 622
Castner Lecture and Medal 4404
Charles Chree Medal and Prize 3187
Agustin Codazzi Medal 1718
Colombian Academy of Science Prize 1578
Colombian Academy of Science Third World Prize 1579
Copley Medal 4145
CORESTA Prize 5082
Cothenius Medal 6622
Darwin Plaque 6623
Edgeworth David Medal 626
Peter Debye Prize 9681
Defenders of Justice 1626
EACR Italian Fellowship Program 2819

Subject Index of Awards
Volume 2: International and Foreign

EACR Travel Fellowships 2820
Hilda och Alfred Erikssons Pris 11540
Neil Hamilton Fairley Fellowships 540
Carlos J. Finlay Prize 6411
Fondation Alexandre Joannides 5481
Fondation Anatole et Suzanne Abragam 5486
Fondation Andre Policard-Lacassagne 5490
Fondation Andre-Romain Prevot 5491
Fondation Cahours, Houzeau 5508
Fondation Camille Liegeois
  Academie Royale de Belgique - Classe des Lettres et des Sciences Morales et Politiques 972
  Academie Royale de Belgique - Classe des Sciences 1001
Fondation Charles-Adam Girard 5513
Fondation Charles-Louis de Saulses de Freycinet 5519
Fondation Clement Felix 5523
Fondation Dandrimont-Benicourt 5529
Fondation Danton 5530
Fondation Fernand Holweck 5556
Fondation G. de Pontecoulant 5562
Fondation Gaston Rousseau 5564
Fondation Gegner 5566
Fondation Henry Le Chatelier 5582
Fondation Hirn 5584
Fondation Janine Courrier 5590
Fondation Jecker 5601
Fondation Joseph Labbe 5603
Fondation Kodak-Pathe-Landucci 5606
Fondation La Caille 5608
Fondation Lucien Cayeux 5624
Fondation Marquet 5627
Fondation Millet-Ronssin 5634
Fondation Paul Fallot-Jeremine 5645
Fondation Paul Pascal 5648
Fondation Pierre Lafitte 5653
Fondation Rogissart-Sarazin-Vandevyere 5662
Fondation Salman A. Waksman 5664
Fondation Schutzenberger 5666
Fondation Vaillant 5674
Granjon Prize 3435
Grants for Field Research 7234
Great Gold Medal 11527
GV-SOLAS Competition 11908
Otto-Hahn-Preis fur Chemie und Physik 6658
Hilti-Preis fur Innovative Forschung 11931
Hizmet Odulu 12066
Honorary Member 9458
Hosei International Fund Foreign Scholars Fellowship 8537
W. J. B. Houston Research Awards 2838
Humboldt Research Fellowships 7156
Javed Husain Prize for Young Scientists 6414
International Hydrology Prize 9469
International Industrial Film and Video Awards 2703
Arthur Thomas Ippen Award 9461
Islamic Foundation Awards 10490
Japan Society for the Promotion of Science Research Fellowships Science and Technology 7157
Heinz Karger Memorial Foundation Annual Award 11871
John F. Kennedy Student Paper Competition 9462
Kuwait Prize 8844
Pieter Langerhuizen Prize 9391
Le Cristal du CNRS 5017
Lower Austria Recognition Prize in Arts and Sciences 860

Jeannette and Samuel L. Lubell Memorial Award 7983
Feodor Lynen Research Fellowships 7158
Art Manzelli Prize 5083
C. J. Martin Fellowships 542
Michael Mason Prize 2520
Medaille d'Argent du CNRS 5018
Medaille de Bronze du CNRS 5019
Medaille d'Or du CNRS 5020
Medal of Merit 4684
Samuel Mikoviny Medal 7357
National Prize for Physics, Mathematics and Natural Sciences 9149
National Research Council Stimulation Prize 7466
National Science Prize 12129
New Zealand Science and Technology Post-Doctoral Fellowship 9840
Non-Clinical Bursary 2521
OAPEC Award for Scientific Research 8847
Archibald D. Olle Prize 628
Outstanding Young Scientist Award 5134
Aurelio Peccei Prize 8227
Pius XI Gold Medal 12098
Max Planck Research Awards 7159
Preis der Justus-Liebig-Universitat Giessen 7000
Premio Innovazione Elettronica 8326
Premio Romulo Garza para Investigacion 9026
Premio TWAS (Third World Academy of Sciences) 8918
Premios CANIFARMA 8939
Presidents' Award 2490
Prix Ampere d'Electricite de France 5684
Prix Blaise Pascal du GAMNI-SMAI 5685
Prix de Biologie Alfred Kastler 5271
Prix de l'Institut Francais du Petrole 5690
Prix des Jeunes 4905
Prix des Sciences Biologiques et Medicales 5050
Prix des Sciences Physiques et Mathematiques 5052
Prix du Salon du Laboratoire 6209
Prix Franco-Britannique de l'Academie des Sciences 5697
Prix Nicolas Missarel 5902
Prix Pechiney 5704
Prix Quinquennaux des Sciences Medicales du Gouvernement 1341
Prix Scientifique Philip Morris 4964
Prize 5120
Prize for Research and Studies of the Repercussions of the Iraqi Invasion of Kuwait 8845
Andres Manuel del Rio National Prize in Chemistry 8948
Royal Dutch Shell Prize 9392
Royal Medals 4154
Royal Society Fellowship/Study Visit 7845
Royal Society Grants 4155
Royal Society of Tasmania Medal 636
Senior Visiting Fellowship 7846
T. K. Sidey Medal and Prize 9841
Sparreska Priset 11552
George Stavros Gold Medal 7195
George Stavros Silver Medal 7196
Stora Linnemedaljen i guld 11554
Swiss Prize for Parapsychology 11939
Tesvik Odulu 12067
Textile Institute Jubilee Award 4526
Thorarinsson Medal 500
Tison Award 9470
TWNSO Award in Agriculture 8457
TWNSO Award in Technology 8458
Alexander von Humboldt Award for Scientific Cooperation 7160

Philipp Franz von Seibold Award 7161
L. R. Wager Prize 501
Wahlbergska Minnesmedaljen i guld 11559
Wihuri International Prize 4762

Sculpture

Aanmoedigingsprijzen 9635
Academy Awards 9750
Annual Exhibition of the Royal Scottish Academy 10619
Arts Prize - Meir Dizengoff Prize 7947
ASEAN Award for Visual Arts 10032
Becas de Creacion Artistica 11142
Otto Beit Award 4180
Biennial of Bantu Contemporary Art 6507
Buhrmann-Ubbens Papierprijs 9342
City of Vienna Prizes for Art, Science, and Humanities 789
Concurso Nacional para Estudiantes de Artes Plasticas en Aguascalientes 9211
De Laszlo Medal 4177
Fine Arts Prize 8829
Forderpreis des Landes Nordrhein-Westfalen fur junge Kunstlerinnen und Kunstler 7026
Forderpreis fur bildende Kunst der Landeshauptstadt Dusseldorf 6682
Gold Medal Conanti Award 1898
Jack Goldhill Award for Sculpture 3863
Grand Prix des Arts de la Ville de Paris 6092
Grand Prix ICA - Prix de Sculpture 10689
Grand Prix International d'Arts et Lettres Notre-Dame et la Mer 4958
Grand Prix National de la Sculpture 5282
International Sculpture Competition in Madera 9009
Wilhelm Lehmbruck Prize 7031
Judith Leysterprijs 9543
Stephan Lochner Medal 6597
Julio Mardel Prize 10305
Medaille des Arts Plastiques 4784
Medal of Honor 10999
Michaly Munkacsy Prize for Visual and Applied Arts 7406
Museo Angel Orensanz and Artes del Serrablo International Sculpture Award 11307
National Akademi Award 7534
National Plastic Arts Prize 11369
Order of Culture 8586
Panorama of Actual Brasilian Art 1492
Praemium Imperiale 8599
Preis der Neuen Darmstadter Sezession fur Junge Kunstler 6603
Premio Anual de Aquisicao 10285
Premio Anual de Investigacao 10286
Premio Mariano Benlliure 11297
Premio Municipal Jose Simoes de Almeida de Escultura 10272
Prix Bordin 5364
Prix Breaute 5365
Prix Claude Berthault 5371
Prix Colmont 5373
Prix de Portrait Paul-Louis Weiller 5378
Prix de Rome 9578
Prix des Cathedrales 5380
Prix Desprez 5381
Prix Doublemard 5382
Prix Dumas-Millier 5386
Prix Egide Rombaux 956
Prix Estrade-Delcros 5387
Prix et Fondations Concernant l'Academie de France a Rome 5388
Prix Eugene Piot 5389
Prix Felix Feneon 5203
Prix Frederic et Jean de Vernon 5392
Prix Georges Wildenstein 5395
Prix Hector Lefuel 5399

787

Sculpture (continued)
Prix Houllevigue 5403
Prix Injalbert 5344
Prix Le Guay-Lebrun 5410
Prix Paul Belmondo 5348
Prix Paul-Louis Weiller 5418
Prix Susse Freres 5427
Prize for Sculpture 10403
Doctor Gustavo Cordeiro Ramos Prize 10287
Rolandpreis fur Kunst im offentlichen Raum 6582
Royal Academy Summer Exhibition 3864
Royal Hibernian Academy of Arts Awards 7837
Salon Anual de Artes Plasticas Premios Pedro Domingo Murillo 1389
Salon Nacional de Artes Plasticas - Escultura 9241
Sandbergprijs 9647
Sergel Prize 11511
Silver Medal 4181
Soares Dos Reis Prize 10306
Spanish Association of Painters and Sculptors Prizes 11381
Standard Bank Namibia Biennale 9326
Prof. Hermann Struck Prize 7886
Thorvaldsen Medal 1902
Triennale-India Award of Lalit Kala Akademi 7535
Jacobus van Looyprijs 9449
Wolf Foundation Prizes 7987
Charles Wollaston Award 3865

Secondary education
Prix Joseph De Keyn 992
TES Schoolbook Award 4549

Seismology
Keith Medal 10645

Set design
Laurence Olivier Awards 4466

Shooting
Asian Winter Games, Sapporo 8713
Champion Shots Medal 338

Short stories
The Age Book of the Year Awards 118
ANA Literary Prize 9856
Angel Literary Award 2080
Annual Competition Awards 3479
Arafura Short Story Award 553
Asiaweek Short Story Competition 7262
Award for Aboriginal and Torres Strait Islander Writers 554
Awards for Regional Literature 10004
Bangla Academy Literary Award 934
Bank of New Zealand Katharine Mansfield Award 9774
Bank of New Zealand Novice Writers' Awards 9775
Bank of New Zealand Young Writers' Award 9776
Dr. Karel Barbier Prize 1265
H. E. Bates Short Story Competition 3722
The Bridport Prize 2218
British Fantasy Awards 2336
Canberra Times and Commonwealth Bank National Short Story of the Year 302
Carson Gold Memorial Short Story Competition Awards 371
City of Brisbane Short Story Award 292
City of Springvale Short Story Awards 317
CNA Literary Award 10830
Commonwealth Writers Prize 2654
Concours de Nouvelles 6087
Concourt Fellowship 4797
Concurso Anual de Literatura Premios Franz Tamayo 1388
Concurso Joven Creacion 1769
Concurso Latinoamericano de Cuento 9209
Concurso Literario Premio Emece 47
Catherine Cookson Cup 2996
Creative Writing Junior Competition 2219
Aquileo J. Echeverria Prize 1761
Sait Faik Prize 12051
FAW Kate Tracy Memorial Young Writers Award 395
Festival Awards for Literature 673
Fundacion del Premio Fastenrath 11345
David Gemell Cup 2997
Grand Prix de la Mer 4918
Grand Prix Litteraire de l'Oceanie 4920
Lyndall Hadow/Donald Stuart Short Story Award 376
Dame Alexandra Hasluck Short Story Competition 664
David Higham Prize for Fiction 2199
The Independent Foreign Fiction Award 3044
Kerala Sahitya Akademi Awards 7703
Jessie Litchfield Award 557
Literary Awards and Prizes for Sinhalese Literature 11423
Literary Competition
  Eaglehawk Dahlia and Arts Festival 357
  Zimbabwe Literature Bureau 12218
Literary Prizes 7192
Literary Prizes for Tamil Literature 11424
Julia Lopes of Ameida Prize 1425
Macmillan Silver Pen Award for Fiction 2783
Malaysian Literary Prize 8904
Ricardo Malheiros Prize 10256
Malpertuis Prize 1288
Arthur Markham Memorial Prize 4535
Ian Murdie Memorial Awards 373
Gilbert Owen National Prize for Literature 9014
Don Carlos Palanca Memorial Awards for Literature 10053
Premio Alvarez Quintero 11346
Premio de Cuentos Hucha de Oro 11211
Premio Editiorial Costa Rica 1770
Premio Latinoamericano de Cuento 9229
Premio Nacional de Cuento 9231
Premio Poesia y Narrativa 1772
Premios Literarios Nacionais 1474
Thomas Pringle Award 10852
Prix Carton de Wiart 1294
Prix Cazes-Brasserie Lipp 6164
Prix de la Nouvelle 5835
Prix de Litterature des Alpes et du Jura 4923
Prix Europeen de l'ADELF 4924
Prix Franz de Wever 1297
Prix George Garnir 1299
Prix Gilles Nelod 1042
Prix Litteraire des Mascareignes, des Seychelles et des Comores 4929
Prix Marie Havez-Planque 5894
Prix Robert Duterme 1305
Prix Sander Pierron 1306
Prix SGDL de la Nouvelle 6292
Prix Stendhal de la Nouvelle 6471
Prix Victor Rossel 1247
Prize for Literature of the Council of the French Community of Belgium 1110
PRO Dogs National Charity Open Creative Writing & Photographic Competition 3802
Aquilino Ribeiro Literary Prize 10259
Steele Rudd Award 294
Ian St. James Literary Award 2642
Short Story Award 6505
Ary Sleeks Prize 1276
Lilian Ida Smith Award 9782
Stand International Short Story Competition 4492
Storywriting and Art Project 144
Sydney PEN Short Story Award 506
Dylan Thomas Award 3793
Tom-Gallon Trust 4392
Whitbread Literary Awards 2211

Skiing
Alpine World Cup Champions 11833
Asian Winter Games, Sapporo 8713
Birkebeinerrennet Ski Race 9878
Golden Skier Award 11835
Holmenkoll Medal 9871
Holmenkollen Ski Festival 9872
International Popular Sports Achievement Award 6948
Sapporo International Ski Marathon 8731
Team Championships (non-divisional) 4569

Slide photography
Associate of the Photographic Salon Exhibitors Association 7267
Association Award 7268
Association Seal 7269
Australian International Widescreen Festival 281
BCPA International Salon of Colour Slides 7489
Durban International Exhibition of Photography 10845
Fellow of the Photographic Salon Exhibitors Association 7271
FIAP World Cups 8869
International Festival of the Image 6016
International Student Salon of Photography 7275
PSI Gold Medals 7819
PSI Medals 7820
Rosario International Photographic Salon 105
World Festival of Mountain Pictures 6481
World Festival of Underwater Pictures 6483

Soccer
Afro-Asia Club Championship 8892
Afro-Asia Nations Cup 8893
Arab Sports Pressman Award 10504
Asian Club Championship 8894
Asian Cup 8895
Asian Cup Winners Championship 8896
Asian Cup Women's Football Championship 8897
Asian Youth Football Championship (Under 16) 8898
Asian Youth Football Championship (Under 19) 8899
Awards 7773
FIFA Futsal (Indoor Football) World Championship 11712
FIFA U-17 World Championship 11713
FIFA Women's World Football Championship 11714
FIFA World Cup Trophy 11715
Honorary Long Service Award 10668
Olympic Football Tournaments (Men and Women) 11716
Service Award for the Promotion and Teaching of Football 10669
U-20 World Youth Championship for the FIFA/Coca-Cola Cup 11717

Social science (*See also* **Anthropology; Archaeology; Criminology; Demography; Economics; Genealogy; Geography; History; Political science; Psychology; Social science research; Sociology**)
  Konrad Adenauer Research Award   7154
  Administrative Visitors Fellowship Programme   1860
  Amsterdam Prize for the Environment   9596
  Caldas Science Prize   1688
  De la Court Prize   9599
  Dissertation Honors   6998
  Erasmus Prize   9396
  Fondation Emile Waxweiler   974
  Francqui Prize   1156
  Hosei International Fund Foreign Scholars Fellowship   8537
  Humboldt Research Awards to Foreign Scholars   7155
  IFUW Awards Competition   11789
  Imperial Prize   8594
  Israel Prize   7906
  Japan Academy Prize   8595
  Alexander Petrowitsch Karpinskij Prizes   7115
  Bartol Kasic Award   1810
  Ludwig Keimer Foundation Prizes   11873
  Kuwait Prize   8844
  Antonio Larragoiti Prize
    Brazilian Academy of Letters   1423
    Lisbon Academy of Sciences   10253
  Lomonosov Gold Medal   10419
  Medalla Eduardo Neri   9124
  Nagrada Saveta Fonda SO SUBNOR Cetvrti jul   10707
  National Cultural Awards   1413
  National Prize for History, Social Sciences and Philosophy   9147
  National Prize in Science and Art   9152
  National Science, Literature and Art Prize   7183
  Nyon International Documentary Film Festival   11892
  Order of Lenin   10463
  Order of Merit in the Sciences and Arts   6743
  Premio Luis Elizondo - Premio Cientifico y Technologico   8989
  Prince of Asturias Prizes   11248
  Prix Adelson Castiau   977
  Prix des Sciences Economiques et Sociales   5051
  Prix Emile de Laveleye   985
  Prix France-Acadie   4894
  Prix Latsis   11959
  Prix les Transports, l'Homme et la Ville   6151
  Prix Louis Marin   5776
  Prix Sante Publique   5940
  Prix Suzanne Tassier   997
  Research Medal   9755
  Dr. Arthur Ruppin Prize   7885
  Moinho Santista Prizes for Young People   1496
  Moinho Santista Prizes   1497
  Science Prize - Peretz Naftali Prize   7962
  Scientific Research Prizes   8919
  State Prize   10204
  George Stavros Gold Medal   7195
  George Stavros Silver Medal   7196
  Trade Union's Art and Cultural Prize   7442
  N. P. van Wyk Louw Prize   11012
  Sakuzo Yoshino Award   8522

Social science research
  Grand Prix ICA - Prix de la Recherche Scientifique   10688

  Grants for Field Research   7234
  Yunus Nadi Yarismasi   12049
  Prix Auguste Pavie   6142
  Preis der Justus-Liebig-Universitat Giessen   7000
  Prix Paul Rivet   6143
  Stein Rokkan Prize in Comparative Research   6050
  Royal Dutch Shell Prize   9392
  Johannes Cornelis Ruigrok-Prijs   9393
  Social Inventions Prizes   3050

Social service (*See also* **Community affairs; Public affairs; Child welfare; Family relations; Handicapped; Social work; Youth work**)
  Awards   7989
  Cross of Merit   10101
  Jamnalal Bajaj Foundation Awards   7693
  Kossuth Prize   7410
  National Youth Awards   7524
  Premio Anual de Servicio Social Gustavo Baz Prada   9185
  Prix Dodo   5841
  Prix Felix de Beaujour   5745
  Prix Georges Picot   5751
  Prix Jean Mace   6083
  Prix Jules Andeoud   5767
  Freiherr Von Stein Prize   7132
  Prix Emmanuel-Andre You   6144

Social work
  Chaconia Medal of the Order of the Trinity   12033
  Calouste Gulbenkian Foundation Grants   2981
  Jamnalal Bajaj Foundation Awards   7693
  Jamnalal Bajaj International Award for Promoting Gandhian Values Outside India   7694
  Medal of Honor   10999
  Premio Mixcoatl   9255
  Prix Fanny et Maurice Baumont   5744

Sociology
  Bangkok Bank Prize for Thai Literature Competition   12022
  Collins Religious Book Award   2640
  Festival dei Popoli   8239
  Dimitrie Gusti Prize   10350
  Honorary Member   10199
  International Film Festival of Visual Anthropology and Social Documentation   5032
  Prix Docteur Rene-Joseph Laufer   5712
  Leverhulme Memorial Lecture   3554
  Medallas de Geografia Fisica, Humana, Economica   10016
  October Prizes of the City of Belgrade   10696
  Stanislaw Ossowski Award   10200
  Prix Bigot de Morogues   5718
  Prix Carlier   5721
  Prix Emile Girardeau   5739
  Prix France-Acadie   4894
  Prix Maisondieu   5779
  Prix Rossi   5789
  Royal Society of Victoria Medal   638
  Sociology Prize   1229
  University of Berne Prizes   11965
  Viareggio Prize   8390
  Worldwide Competition for Young Sociologists   11277

Spanish culture
  Catalonian Certificate of Merit for Promotion of the Catalan Culture   11176

  Euroarabe and Television Festival   11226
  International Contest of Short Films, City of Huesca   11236
  Mirror of Spain Prize   11221
  Orden Rodrigo Correa Palacio   1588
  Premio Antonio de Lara ''Tono'' de Humor Grafico   11287
  Premio Municipal Julio de Castilho de Olisipografia   10274
  Premio Ortega y Gasset   11299
  Premio Rafael Heliodoro Valle   9249

Spanish literature
  Catalonian Prizes for Catalan Literature   11180
  Miguel Cervantes Prize for Literature   11368
  Concurso Nacional de Cuento Periodico *Prensa Nueva*   1743
  National Prize for Illustration of Literature for Children and Young People   11370
  Premi Sant Jordi   11309
  Premio de la Critica a los Mejores Libros Publicados   1819
  Premio Internacional de Ensayo Literario Malcolm Lowry   9226
  Premio Internacional de Novela, Nuevo Leon   8973
  Premio Literario Internacional *Novedades* y Diana
    Editorial Diana   8975
    Novedades   9253
  Premio Lope de Vega   11294
  Premio Menendez Pidal   11347
  Premio Nacional de Historia de Espana   11373
  Premio Nacional de las Letras Espanolas   11374
  Premio Nacional de Literatura   11375
  Premios de la Fundacion Conde de Cartagena   11348
  Premios Nacionales de Literatura Infantil y Juvenil   11379
  Prenio Ramon Gomez de la Serna   11301
  Prize of Honor for Catalan Letters   11310
  Fernando Rielo World Prize for Mystical Poetry   11329
  Rivadeneira Prizes   11349

Special education
  Making the Difference   536
  Irma Roth/Saaled Bursary   11015

Spectroscopy *See* **Optics**

Speech and hearing (*See also* **Deafness**)
  Manuel Garcia Prize   11462
  Prix Henri Baruk   4843

Speleology *See* **Geology and paleontology**

Sports (*See also* **Coaching; Physical education; Sports broadcasting; Sports journalism; Sports medicine; Sportsmanship; Water sports; specific sports, e.g. Auto racing**)
  ABC Sports Award of the Year   195
  Arjuna Awards   7518
  Asahi Sports Prize   8493
  Association Internationale de la Presse Sportive Awards   8315
  Award for Distinguished Service to Sport   8783
  Badge of Honour   9513
  Philip Noel Baker Research Award   4722
  Billiards and Snookers Awards   7519
  John Budgen Award   2122
  Cacique's Crown of Honor   7243

Sports

Sports (continued)
Cash Prizes to Universities 7520
Chronicle of Komsomol Honor 10427
CISS Medallions of Honor 1960
Commonwealth Games Federation 2661
Competitions and Tournaments 9891
Divisional Team Championships 4567
Dronacharya Award 7522
Engineering Prize - Dov Hoz Prize 7951
European Sportsman and Sportswoman of the Year 1144
Gold Medal 11571
Golden Ring - International Contest of Televised Sports, Lausanne 11738
High Quality of Work Award 10432
William Hill Sports Book of the Year 3010
Victor Hirt Prize 10510
Honorary Member 9514
Honour Roll 840
IAAF World Athletic Series 9314
IBF Gold Medal 9892
Individual Championships 4568
International Bocce Federation Competitions 1477
International Federation of Netball Associations Awards 503
International Federation of Netball Associations Service Awards 504
International Festival of Sport Films 5248
International Festival of Sports and Tourist Films 10792
International Judo Federation 6964
International Prize Paladino D'Oro 8313
International Sports Film Festival 8317
International Sports Film Festival in Budapest 7431
Japan International Film - Video Festival of Adventure and Sports in Hakuba 8622
Japan Sports Prize 8791
Komsomol Medal 10433
Labor Courage Award 10437
Lille Sport Film Festival 5038
Maulana Abul Kalam Azad Trophy 7523
Medal for Outstanding Sports Achievements 10090
Medal of Honour 6991
National Prize for Sports 9150
National Westminster Bank Trophy 4512
National Youth Awards 7524
Official UNESCO Award for Distinguished Services to Physical Education and Sport 6419
Oita International Wheelchair Marathon 8711
Olympic Cup 11814
Olympic Medals and Diplomas 11815
Olympic Order 11816
Ordre du Merite Sportif 1796
Outstanding Sportsman Award 7881
Pakistan Civil Awards 9995
Per Ludos Fraternitas 9317
Phenix - U.D.A. 6429
Premio al Deportista Universitario 9183
Premio Mixcoatl 9255
Premio Puma 9197
Prince of Asturias Prizes 11248
Public Service Medal 10748
Pedro Romero Medal 1615
Rubens-Alcais Challenge 1961
Oscar Schwiglhofer Trophy 10512
Arthur Sims Award 2123
South African Sports Merit Award 10916
Special Awards to Winners of International Sports Events 7525
Special Service Awards 3710
Sport Australia Hall of Fame 681
Sport Medal of Catalonia 11190

Awards, Honors & Prizes, 1995-96

Sport Science Award of the IOC President 4723
Sportplakete des Bundespraesidenten 6745
Sports Award 10446
Sports Hall of Fame 12038
State President's Sport Award 10917
Jeffrey Stollmeyer Memorial Award 12039
The Sunday Times Sportswomen of the Year Award 4505
Team Championships (non-divisional) 4569
Trento International Film Festival of Mountain and Exploration 8460
UK Cup 3680
West Indian Tobacco Sports Foundation Award 12040
World Games Competitions 9541

Sports broadcasting
Awards 7773

Sports journalism
Arab Sports Pressman Award 10504
Bancarella Sport Prize 8162
Benson and Hedges Media Awards 7781
Golden Skier Award 11835
Journalism Prize 1062
Peter Wilson Award 3546

Sports medicine
Bronze Medal 1479
Joachim Cabot and Louis Delezenne/Prize of the LMGMS 6077
Gold Medal 1480

Sportsmanship
Fair Play Award 2776
Pursuit Trophy 3481
Sportsman of the Year Award 12063
Trophee International du Fair Play Pierre de Coubertin 5989

Stamp collecting See **Philately**

Standards
Bimcam Ardley Prize 3157
Callendar Medal 3158
Deming Prize 8776
Distinguished Service Award 7428
Sir Harold Hartley Medal 3159
Honeywell International Medal 3160
Honeywell Prize 3161
Alec Hough-Grassby Memorial Award 3162
ICI Prize 3163
National Prize for Quality 9261
Staatspreis fur geprufte Qualitat 747
Sir George Thomson Gold Medal 3164

Statistics
Arnbergska Priset 11534
Association of Track and Field Statisticians Honorary Member 2134
Competition for Young Statisticians from Developing Countries 9535
Fondation Montyon des Statistiques 5639
Fondazione Francesco Sarerio Nitti Prize 8054
C. Oswald George Prize 3210
Honorary Member 787
Medaille Bourdin 6388
National Institute of Insurance International Prizes 8067
Jan Popper Memorial Prize 2135
Prix Charles Dupin 5722
Prix Coste 6389
Prix du Statisticien d'Expression Francaise 6390
Prix Edmond Michel 6391

Prix Emile Mercet 6392
Prix Michel Huber 6393

Steel industry See **Iron and steel industry**

Surfing
European Surfing Championships - Open Champion 12173

Surgery
Alejandro Angel Escobar Science Prize 1584
BAAPS Senior Registrar's Prize 2258
Bard Award 2271
Karl Heinrich Bauer Prize for Surgical Tumor Research 6874
BAUS Travelling Fellowship 2272
Best Chief Resident Paper 12082
Best Paper Award 9869
Samuel M. Bosch Prize 70
British Association of Paediatric Surgeons Awards 10516
British Journal of Urology Travelling Fellowship 2273
Bronze Medal 10820
William Cook Travelling Fellowship 2274
Juan N. Corpas Prize 1726
John Mitchell Crouch Fellowship 595
Czlonek Honorowy 10132
Robert Danis Prize 11844
Filmpreis 6875
Enrique Finochietto Prize 79
Fondation Barbier 5500
Fondation du Baron Larrey 5542
Fondation Dusgate 5548
Fondation Henri Mondor 5577
Fondation Montyon de Medicine et Chirugie 5636
Fondations Bellion - Charles Bouchard 5678
Fothergillian Medal 3637
Gold Medal of the Royal Society of Medicine 4249
Grassi Prize 8195
Avelino Gutierrez Prize 80
Hackett Memorial Prize 2259
Marcellino Herrera Vegas Prize 81
Honorary Fellow 10606
Hunterian Oration 3977
Jacksonian Prize 3978
Jubilaumspreis 6877
Werner Korte Medaille 6878
Fund Professor Doctor A. Lacquet 1314
Rene Leriche Prize 11845
Lewis Medical Travelling Scholarship 2275
Erich Lexer Preis 6879
Lister Memorial Medal 3979
Lister Professorship 10607
Theodor Naegeli Prize 6880
Lope Carvajal Peralta Award 1709
Pietro Caliceti International Prize 8249
Ignacio Pirovano Prize 94
Preis fur Poster - Ausstellungen 6881
Preis fur Wissenschaftliche Ausstellungen 6882
Premio Dr. Gonzalo Castaneda 9101
Premio Dr. Jose Aguilar Alvarez Prize 9102
Premio Dr. Manuel J. Castillejos 9103
Prix a l'Etudiant Medaille d'Or de l'Internat 4804
Prix a un Etudiant en Chirurgie 4806
Prix de la Mutualite Interprofessionnelle 4819
Prix de l'Union Nationale des Caisses Chirurgicales Mutualistes 4823
Prix des Fondations Oulmont, Zaval, Dreyfous 4826

Prix Docteur Albert Belgrand 4829
Prix Emile Delannoy-Robbe 4837
Prix Henri Mondor 4844
Prix Jean-Etienne Marcel 4848
Prix Jeanne et Maurice Chevassu 4851
Prix Osiris 5703
Prix Specialities Chirurgicales 4875
Prize of the Societe Internationale de Chirurgie 11846
Rogers Prize 4579
Seal of the German Surgical Society 6883
Shackman Travelling Fellowship 2276
Syme Professorship 10608
Tilanus Medal 9560
Joseph Toynbee Memorial Lectureship 4267
Travelling Fellowships 10601
Ernst Von Bergmann Gedenkmunze 6884
Von Langenbeck Preis 6885
Hans von Seemen Preis 6868

Surveying
Aubrey Barker Awards 2648
Gold Medal of Honour 10818
Guild Silver Medal 2969

Swedish culture
Karin Gierows pris for hangiven bildningsverksamhet 11591
Gun och Olof Engqvists stipendium 11593
Kellgrenpriset 11596
Kungliga priset 11598
Stora priset 11604
Svenska Akademiens Finlandspris 11605
Svenska Akademiens nordiska pris 11606

Swimming (See also Surfing; Water polo)
Henry Benjamin National Memorial Trophy 2064
G. Melville Clark National Memorial Trophy 2065
Dawdon Trophy 2066
Harold Fern Award 2067
Harold Fern National Trophy 2068
FINA Prize 11753
George Hearn Cup 2069
Alan Hime Memorial Trophies 2070
International Popular Sports Achievement Award 6948
Swimming Enterprises Trophy for Synchronised Swimmer of the Year 2071
Team Championships (non-divisional) 4569
Norma Thomas National Memorial Trophy 2073
Alfred H. Turner Award 2074
Belle White National Memorial Trophy 2075
T. M. Yeadon Memorial Trophy 2076

Systems management See Information management; Operations research

Table tennis
Divisional Team Championships 4567
European Competitions 2849
Individual Championships 4568

Tapestry See Textile design

Tattooing See Cosmetology

Teaching (See also Education)
Janos Csere Apaczai Prize 7397
Gabino Barreda 9000
Bragg Medal and Prize 3186
Visconde de Sousa Prego Freedom Prize 10295
Diploma al Merito Universitario 9180

Ehrenmitgliedschaft im IDV 10071
Excellence in Aerospace Education 7474
Ivan Filipovic Awards 1809
Karin Gierows pris for hangiven bildningsverksamhet 11591
Grant or Prize 4710
Honorary Member 10081
ICPE Medal for Physics Teaching 11486
Japan Foundation Grant Programs 8613
National Competition in Teaching of Journalism Prize 1437
NDCS Scholarship 3682
Order of Andres Bello 12137
Order of the 27th of June 12139
Outstanding Instructor 7460
Pedagogy Award 10443
Robert-Wichard-Pohl-Preis 6663
Premio Derechos Humanos 9191
Premio el Professor Distinguido 9035
Premio Universidad Nacional 9199
Thomas Pringle Award 10852
Prix de Chenier 5443
Prix de la Promotion Poetique 6329
Prix Malouet 5780
A. S. Pushkin's Medal 10451
Irma Roth/Saaled Bursary 11015
Dr. Juan S. Salcedo Jr. Science Education Award 10061
Sony Science Education Promotion Fund 8758
Svenska Akademiens svensklararpris 11609
Training Award 10447
Young Teacher's Award 10449
Prof. Ludwik Zabrocki Medal 10082
Zimbabwe Teachers Association Awards 12225

Technology (See also Biotechnology; Computer science; Engineering; History of technology; Industrial arts; Inventions; Robotics; Science; Standards; Testing)
Adelskoldska Medaljen 11532
African Regional Centre for Technology Awards 10693
Walter Ahlstrom Prize 4682
Akzo prijs 9389
Arnbergska Priset 11534
Awards for Innovation 7771
Belgrade International Festival of Scientific Films 10699
Carl Bertelsmann Prize 6566
Blekinge County Council Culture Prize 11446
British Association Film and Television Awards 2254
Brussels International Festival of Films on the Engineering Profession 1097
Brussels International Festival of Scientific and Technical Films 1098
Constantin Budeanu Prize 10336
Caldas Science Prize 1688
CASTME Awards 2646
Catalonian Prize for Technical Application and Industrial Products 11179
City of Vienna Prizes for Art, Science, and Humanities 789
Henri Coanda Prize 10340
Commendation by the Minister of State for Science and Technology 8591
CORESTA Prize 5082
Craftsman's Award 4683
Credit Suisse Design Prize for Technical and Industrial Innovation in Geneva 11684
Educational Merit Diploma 1656
Albert Einstein World Award of Science 9307
Environmental Management Awards 4321

Esso Energy Award and Medal 4148
Fellowship of the City and Guilds of London Institute 2622
Fellowships and Training Programmes 2656
Galardon Estado de Mexico 9008
Gawad AGKATEK (Agham, Kapaligiran at Teknolohiya) 10057
Gold Medal
  Pakistan Academy of Sciences 9993
  South African Sugar Technologists' Association 11090
Gold Medal for Achievement in Science and Technology 10989
Gold Medal for Craft Excellence 2623
Gold Medal for Development of the Technological Environment 9952
Grand Prix de la Technique de la Ville de Paris 6090
Great Gold Medal 11527
Havenga Prize for Science and Technology 10990
Heinrich Hertz Preis 7148
Hizmet Odulu 12066
Honda Prize 8535
Honorary Fellow 8807
IAESTE Award Certificate 5959
IBC John Tucker Award 3384
INSA Medal for Young Scientists 7650
International Design Competition, Osaka 8606
International Industrial Film and Video Awards 2703
Ion Ionescu de la Brad Prize 10358
Islamic Foundation Awards 10490
Nami Jafet Prize 1488
Jamnalal Bajaj Foundation Awards 7693
Japan Prize 8736
Kalinga Prize 6417
Komsomol Special Award for Science and Technology 10435
Kyoto Prizes 8539
MacRobert Award 3875
P. C. Mahalanobis Medal 7656
MAN National Science Prize 9865
J. N. McNicol Prize 619
Medal of Merit 4684
Medalla Juan de Dios Batiz 9069
Narcis Monturiol Medal and Plaque for Science and Technology 11188
Mullard Award and Medal 4153
National Bank of Pakistan Prize for Literature 10007
National Marine Science Prize 1690
National Prize for Technical Development/Colombia 12128
National Prize for Technology and Design 9151
National Prize in Science and Art 9152
National Prize of Quality 1611
National Research Council Stimulation Prize 7466
National Technology Competition 8950
Jawaharlal Nehru Birth Centenary Medal 7661
Niwa Prize 8620
October Prizes of the City of Belgrade 10696
Order of Lenin 10463
Francis Ormond Medal 620
Pakistan Civil Awards 9995
Swraj Paul Award for the Promotion of Science & Technology Policy 3462
Robert-Wichard-Pohl-Preis 6663
Pras Harvey 7945
Preis der Stiftung Kunststoff-Technik 11935
Premio a las Mejores Obras Cientificas o Tecnicas Publicadas en el Ano 1818

Television   **Awards, Honors & Prizes, 1995-96**

Technology (continued)
Premio di laurea 8135
Premio Internazionale per un Articolo o Studio Scientifico o Tecnico 8265
Premio Luis Elizondo - Premio Cientifico y Technologico 8989
Premio Nacional de Ciencias y Tecnologia Clodomiro Picado Twight 1764
Premio Petrocanada 12092
Premio Romulo Garza para Investigacion 9026
Premio scientifico-technico 8136
Prince Philip Medal 2628
Prix 2000 SG 6384
Prix de la Promotion Televisuelle de la Poesie 6331
Prize for Junior Scientists 6517
Queen's Awards for Environmental Achievement 3830
Queen's Awards for Technological Achievement 3832
Anghel Saligny Prize 10381
Scholastic Award 8808
Science and Technology Media Fellowships 2255
Scientific/Engineering Award 10816
Scientific Merit Award 1681
Scientific Research Prizes 8919
Self-Adhesive Labelling Awards 9498
Shanti Swarup Bhatnagar Medal 7670
SMART (Small Firms Merit Awards for Research & Technology) 4559
Sofia International Film Festival on Organization and Automation of Production and Management Awards 1530
State Prize
   Hungary - Office of the Prime Minister 7412
   Secretariat of the Committee of State Prizes 10204
M. T. Steyn Prize for Achievement in Science and Technology 11007
Techfilm International Film Festival 1874
Technological Innovation Award 1682
Technology Prize 9955
Nikola Tesla Awards 1813
Textile Technology Award 8942
Prof. B. D. Tilak Lecture Award 7676
Tiroler Erfinderpreis Josef Madersperger 731
Triennial Challenge Cup 1486
TUBITAK Husamettin Tugac Award 12068
TWNSO Award in Technology 8458
UNESCO Science Prize 6427
University of Berne Prizes 11965
Verlagspreis zur Forderung popularwissenschaftlicher Literatur fur das jungere Lesealter 7152
Aurel Vlaicu Prize 10390
Traian Vuia Prize 10391
Wallmarkska Priset 11560
Wurdigungspreis 862
S. H. Zaheer Medal 7679
Luis Zambrano National Prize for Inventive Technology 12130

Technology, color See **Color technology**

Technology, medical See **Medical technology**

Telecommunications See **Communications**

Television (See also **Broadcasting; Cable television; Media; Radio; Video**)
ABU Prize Competitions for Radio and Television Programmes 8889
ADIRCAE Prizes 11140
Amanda Award for Television and Cinematographic Merit 9938
AMP W.G. Walkley Awards for Journalism 523
Annual Awards 2977
Artes Awards 11037
Arts Festival Award 8576
Australian Film Institute Awards 221
Awgie Awards 283
Emilio Azcarraga Vidaurreta Prize 9080
BAFTA Scholarship 2232
Bela Balanzs Prize for Cinematography 7399
Berlin Art Prizes 6509
Best Television Commercial/Advertising Film of the Year 9999
BFI Fellowships 2344
BFI Film Award 2345
BFI Special Awards 2346
British Academy of Film and Television Arts Awards - Television 2234
CCP Awards for Television 10033
Charlie Chaplin Prize 1520
CINANIMA 10226
Color Television Advertising Award 4534
Laurens Janszoon Coster Prize 9443
Danmarks Radio TV Award 1991
Dentsu Advertising Awards 8524
Documentary of the Year 10000
Drama Festival (Jashan-E-Tamseel) Awards 10001
Educational Television Awards Scheme 2760
Euro Best Awards 3362
European Environmental Film Festival 5116
FAW Adele Shelton-Smith Award for Play, Radio or Other Scripts for Young Writers 378
Festival International du Film d'Histoire 5186
Geneva-Europe Prizes for Television Writing 11693
Glenfiddich Awards 2949
Golden Aztec Calendar Prize 8926
Golden Chest International Television Festival 1518
Golden Harp Television Festival 7824
Golden Ring - International Contest of Televised Sports, Lausanne 11738
Golden Toucan 1482
Guillermo Gonzalez Camarena 9087
Gran Premio de Honor Argentores 30
Grand Prix National de la Creation Audiovisuelle 5274
Bharatendu Harishchandra Award 7530
El Heraldo Prizes 9021
International Advertising Festival of Ireland 7785
International Christian Television Week 7165
International Competition of Video Works 6070
International Conductors Competition of the Hungarian Television 7415
International Festival of Film and Television in the Celtic Countries 10522
International Leipzig Documentary and Animation Film Festival 7035
International Radio and Television Festivals and Competitions 1867
International Television Festival Golden Prague 1844
International Video Dance Grand Prix 6465
International Visual Communications Association Awards 3502
Journalism Competition Prizes 12121
Journalist Prize of the DGE 6857
Byron Kennedy Memorial Prize 222
Literavision Preis 7021
Magnolia Prize 1576
Ramon Magsaysay Awards 10042
Karol Malcuzynski Award 10207
Mastermind Award 2295
Medienpreis fur Sprachkultur 6894
Montreux Achievement Gold Medal 11851
Montreux International Electronic Cinema Festival 11852
Mounte Carlo Television Festival 9322
Nagrada Saveta Fonda SO SUBNOR Cetvrti jul 10707
NHK Japan Prize Contest 8602
Nigar Public Film Awards 9987
Panafrican Film and Television Festival of Ouagadougou 1541
Penguin Awards 691
Joseph Plateau Prize 1194
Michael Powell Book Award 2349
Premio Anna Magnani 8122
Premio Argentores 31
Premio Internazionale Enno Flaiano 8114
Premio Nacional de Television Simon Bolivar 1596
Preseren Award 10799
Press Prize for Broadcasters 11926
Prix CIRTEF de Corealisation 11776
Prix Danube Festival, Bratislava 10780
Prix Futura Berlin 7074
Prix Italia 8413
Prix Jeunesse International Munchen 7076
PTV Annual Award 10002
Radio and Television Language Prize 12078
Radio Times Drama & Comedy Awards 2160
Rassegna Internazionale dei Documentari Cine-TV Marinari 8295
Regional Radio and Television Awards 1108
Romanian Radio and Television Award 10327
Royal Television Society Gold Medal 4283
Royal Television Society Programme Awards 4284
Royal Television Society Student Director Award 4286
Royal Television Society Television Journalism Awards 4288
Sammy Awards 653
SAUK Prys vir Televisie en Radio 11003
Scholarship Prizes 6512
South African Broadcasting Corporation Prize 11042
Teleconfronto 8446
Television Journalism Prize 40
Thomson Foundation Fellowships 12192
Trade Union's Art and Cultural Prize 7442
TRIC Annual Celebrity Awards 4508
Turkish Radio and Television Culture, Art and Science Prizes 12084
TV Week Logie Awards 679
Unda Dove 1376
Venice International Film Festival 8470

Tennis (See also **Table tennis**)
The Championships, Wimbledon 2053
Raymond Egan Memorial Trophy 7800
French Open 5259
Grand Slam of Tennis 3483
El Heraldo Sport Prizes 9022
ITF Award for Services to the Game 3484
Lawn Tennis Association National Awards 3540
LTA International Award 3541
Paris Open 5260

792

Tennis World Champions 3485

Testing
Berthold-Preis 6842
Angela Cevenini Prize 8356
John Grimwade Medal 2399
Hugh MacColl Award 2400
Nemet Award 2401
Roy Sharpe Prize 2402

Textile design
Royal Dublin Society Crafts Competition 7835
Salon Nacional de Artes Plasticas - Tapiz y Arte Textil 9247
Scottish Designer of the Year Award 10531
Textile Institute Design Medal 4524
Warringah Art Prize 706

Textile industry (See also **Fiber science**)
Companion Membership 4515
Holden Medal 4516
Honorary Fellow 4517
Honorary Life Member 4518
Institute Medal 4519
Kivalo Egyesuleti Munkaert Erem 7385
Lehr Ferenc Textilipari Ifjusagi Erem 7386
Lemkin Medal 4520
Section Awards 4521
Service Medal 4522
S. G. Smith Memorial Medal 4523
Textile Institute Development Award 4525
Textile Institute Jubilee Award 4526
A Textilipar Fejleszteseert Erem 7387
Warner Memorial Medal 4527
Weaver's Company Medal and Prize 4528

Theater
AA Life Vita National Theatre Awards 10812
AA Life Vita Regional Theatre Awards 10813
Aanmoedigingsprijzen 9635
Carl Akermarks stipendium 11582
Gerardo Arellano Cultural Merit Medal 1651
Arts Festival Award 8576
ASEAN Award for the Performing Arts 10031
ATELJE 212 on the Bitef Award 10695
Bellonci Scholarship 3407
Black Curtain Award 7047
City of Munich Prizes 7019
Cladan Award 325
CVB Amateur Theatre Award 9379
Clarence Derwent Award (British) 2236
George Devine Award 2794
Magda Donato Prize 8930
Drama Critics Prizes 6405
Drama Magazine Awards 2547

Aquileo J. Echeverria Prize 1761
European Theatre Prize 5095
Forderpreis des Landes Nordrhein-Westfalen fur junge Kunstlerinnen und Kunstler 7026
Grand Prix International d'Arts et Lettres Notre-Dame et la Mer 4958
Grand Prix National du Theatre 5294
Guardian Student Drama Award 10535
El Heraldo Prizes 9021
Allan Highet Award 9792
Independent Theatre Award 10536
Irish Life Festival Choice Awards 7805
Mari Jaszai Prize 7401
Josef Kainz-Medaille der Stadt Wien 792
Frans Kellendonk-prijs 9628
Kinokuniya Theatre Awards 8681
Charlotte Kohler Prijs 9571
LITERATURIUMS Kabarett Award 7051
The London Evening Standard Drama Awards 3601
Ramon Magsaysay Awards 10042
Mambembe Trophy 1434
Medal of Honor 10999
Mimografieprijs Amsterdam 9643
Les Molieres 4970
Nagrada Saveta Fonda SO SUBNOR Cetvrti jul 10707
National Award for Literature and Arts 12002
National Cultural Awards 1413
National Drama Contest 1439
National Prize for Theatre Juana Sujo 12124
National Theatre Awards 9991
Vladimir Nazor Awards 1812
John Newson Award 2911
Nigar Public Film Awards 9987
October Prizes of the City of Belgrade 10696
Laurence Olivier Awards 4466
OPUS Prizes 7240
Order of Cultural Merit 8579
Order of Lenin 10463
Order of the Golden Rose 7826
Perrier Award 10537
Perspektiefprys 9335
Pietrzak Award 10084
Pisuisse Prize 9616
William Poel Memorial Festival 4380
Praemium Imperiale 8599
Premi Nacional d'Arts Esceniques 11161
Premi Nacional d'Interpretacio Teatral i de Dansa 11162
Premio Anna Magnani 8122
Premio de Obra de Teatro 9219
Premio de Obra de Teatro para Ninos 9220
Premio Internazionale Enno Flaiano 8114
Premio Maria Guerrero a la Labor Teatral 11363
Premio Municipal Fernando Amado de Encenacao Teatral 10268
Premio Nacional de Teatro
  Costa Rica - Ministry of Culture, Youth and Sport 1766
  Spain Ministry of Culture 11376
Premio Norma Padilla 7241
Premios Maria Guerrero y Ricardo Calvo 11300
Prix Andre Jullien du Breuil 5813
Prix de Rome 9578
Prize for Theatre or Cinema 8832
Prizes for a Theatrical Play 8883
Prizes for Theatrical Works 7193
Prudential Awards for the Arts 3826
Hans Reinhart Ring 11921
Research Awards 4381
Riccione TTVV - Teatro Televisione Video 8405
Scholarships of the City of Munich 7023
Scottish Daily Express New Names Awards 10539
Sinhala Drama Awards 11426
Albin Skoda Ring 770
Spurs of Criticism 4760
State Prize in Science and Technology 10470
Sterijina Nagrada 10705
Svenska Akademiens teaterpris 11610
Tamil Drama Award 11427
Thalia Prize 11576
Theatre Prize 7963
Theatre Production Prize 24
Trade Union's Art and Cultural Prize 7442
Albert Van Dalsumprijs 9649

Joost van den Vondel Prizes 7133

Theology
BP Prize Lectureship in the Humanities 10638
Honorary Life Member 10202
George Stavros Gold Medal 7195
George Stavros Silver Medal 7196
University of Berne Prizes 11965
Rev. Pieter van Drimmelen Medal 11011

Therapy See **Rehabilitation and therapy**

Third world See **Economic development**

Tourism See **Travel**

Town planning See **City planning**

Toxicology
EUROTOX Young Scientist's Poster Award 11709
Redi Award 6989

Track and field
Association of Track and Field Statisticians Honorary Member 2134
IAAF World Championships 9315
Individual Championships 4568
C. N. Jackson Memorial Cup 2062
Jan Popper Memorial Prize 2135
Team Championships (non-divisional) 4569

Trade See **Business; Finance; International trade**

Trade unions See **Labor**

Trades See **Industries and trades**

Training and development
International Festival of Economics and Training Films 1191
International Visual Communications Association Awards 3502
National Training Award for Individual Achievement 2766
National Training Awards 2767
Ivor Spencer Top Butler of the Year Award 2961

Translations
Arab Book Fair Prize 8842
Austrian State Prize for Literary Translators 763
Award of the Circle of the Greek Children's Book 7188
Bangla Academy Literary Award 934
Bastian Prize 9957
BCLA Translation Competition (EC Languages) 2318
BCLA Translation Competition (Non-EC Languages) 2319
Helmut M. Braem-Preis 6760
John Buchanan Prize in Esperanto 4574
Bucharest Writers Association Award 10411
Pierre Francois Caille Memorial Medal 822
Catalonian Prizes for Catalan Literature 11180
Paul Celan-Preis 6671
Children's Book Council Award 7735
Croatian Socialist Republic Prizes 1808
Danish Academy Prize for Literature 1909
Dansk Oversaetterforbunds Aerespris
  Danish Writers' Association 1926
  Denmark - Ministry of Cultural Affairs 1937

Translations (continued)
Dawood Prize for Literature 10005
Alfred Doblin Prize 6510
European Poetry Translation Prize 3791
FIT Astrid Lindgren Translation Prize 823
FIT - UNESCO Translation Prize 824
John Florio Prize 4396
''Forintos''-Prize 7389
Grand Prix National de la Traduction 5283
Calouste Gulbenkian Translation Prize 10251
Habib Bank Prize for Literature 10006
Jan Holly Prize 10757
Hungarian PEN Club Medal 7367
Pavol Orszagh Hviezdoslav Prize 10758
IBBY Honour List 11769
Inter Nations Culture Prize 6927
Japan Foundation Grant Programs 8613
Japan Translation Culture Prize 8638
Japan Translation Prize for Publishers 8639
Karel Award 6493
Koopal Bursary for Literature 1078
Korea Translation Award 8826
Letterstedtska Priset for Oversattningar 11545
Literary Awards and Prizes for Sinhalese Literature 11423
Literary Competition 12218
Literary Prize for Translation 10996
Literary Prize - Tchernichowsky Prize 7958
Literature Awards for Children and Young People 9916
Malaysian Literary Prize 8904
Odorico Mendes Prize 1435
Mlada Fronta Award 1887
Mlade leta Prize 10786
Scott Moncrieff Prize 4397
National Translation Award 1473
Martinus Nijhoff Prijs voor Vertalingen 9572
Noma Prize for Translation 8692
Norsemen's Federation Translation Grant 9914
Norske Akademis Pris Til Minne om Thorleif Dahl 9925
Nossack Academy Writers Award 6515
October Prizes of the City of Belgrade 10696
Polish PEN Centre Prizes 10168
Premi Ignasi Iglesias 11158
Premi Josep Maria de Sagarra 11160
Premier's Literary Awards 149
Premio Alfonso X de Traduccion Literaria 9214
Premio de Traduccion de Poesia 9225
Premio Istituto Italo-Latino Americano 8328
Premio Nacional de Traduccion 11377
Prix Baudelaire 6272
Prix de Traduction de Litterature Enfantine 4991
Prix de Traduction Pierre-Francois Caille 6278
Prix Gerard de Nerval 6281
Prix GLM 4954
Prix Halperine-Kaminsky/Societe de Gens de Lettres de France 6282
Prix Jeanne Scialtel 5873
Prix Jules Janin 5876
Prix Langlois 5882
Prix Maurice Edgar Coindreau 6246
Prix Medicis Etranger 6176
Prix Tristan Tzara de Traduction (Franco-Hongrois) 6299
Prize for the Best Foreign Book 6180
Romanian Writers' Union Prizes 10414
Sahitya Akademi Prize for Translation 7539
Schlegel - Tieck Prize 4398
Aleida Schot Award 9618
Staatsprijs Voor Vertaling Van Nederlandse Letterkunde 1086
Stiftelsen Natur och Kulturs oversattarpris 11602
Stuttgart Literary Prize 7139
Svenska Akademiens oversattarpris 11607
Svenska Akademiens tolkningspris 11611
Swedish Authors' Fund Awards 11619
Translation Awards 12003
Translation Prize 9936
University of Berne Prizes 11965
Johann-Heinrich-Voss-Preis fur Ubersetzung 6770
Christoph-Martin-Wieland-Preis 6761
Yeats Club Open Poetry Competition 4643
Yomiuri Literature Prize 8795
ZAiKS Awards for Translators 10208

Transportation (See also Aeronautics and aviation; Automobiles; Automotive engineering; Automotive safety; Aviation safety; Helicopters; Highway safety; Navigation; Railway transportation)
Airline of the Year 2853
Annual Award of the S.A. Transport Services/Transnet 10985
Australian Transport Industry Award 308
Castrol Gold Medal 3177
Competitions 10012
Foundation Award to the Technician of the Year in the Rolls-Royce Dealer Network Chosen by a Craft Competition 4303
Foundation Prestige Lectures 4304
Grand Prix d'Honneur 11825
Mackenzie Junner Rose-Bowl Trophy 3208
Prix de la Belgique 6158
Railroad Construction Award 10444
Sir Henry Royce Memorial Award of the Worshipful Company of Carmen 4310
Sir Henry Royce Memorial Award 4311
Sir Henry Royce Trophy for the Pursuit of Excellence 4316
SARF Bursary 11095
Segrave Trophy 3944
Henry Spurrier Memorial Lecture 2586
Transport Journalist of the Year 2587
Transport Photographer of the Year 2588

Travel
Acorn Awards 2571
Airline of the Year 2853
Airone 8319
American Express New Zealand Tourism Awards 9772
Beca Eugenia Gomez Sierra 1586
Burton Memorial Medal 3933
Catalonian Government Prize for Tourism 11177
Catey Awards 2572
Concurso Anual de Tesis Profesionales 8937
Estrelicia Dourada 10261
Festival International du Film et des Medias de Tourisme 6056
Golden Apple 6479
Golden Bowl 1694
Greek National Tourist Organization Awards 7198
Hotel of the Year Awards 2854
Hotelier of the Year Award 2573
Huy - World Festival of Movies of Short Films Awards 1160
International Dag Hammarskjold Award 1237
International Festival of Sports and Tourist Films 10792
International Festival of Tourist Films - Tourfilm 1852
IYHF Certificate of Merit 3510
IYHF Roll of Honour 3511
Billy Kelly Award of Excellence 7798
Medal of Merit for Tourism 1695
Medal of Merit in Tourism 1610
Medalha de Merito Turistico 10262
National Aquarell Contest 9010
National Hotel Receptionist Award 2574
Orden al Merito Turistico 11366
Premio Mixcoatl 9255
Tourism Research Prize and Medal of Merit 1616
Trento International Film Festival of Mountain and Exploration 8460

Travel literature
Awards for Regional Literature 10004
CNA Literary Award 10830
Thomas Cook Travel and Guide Book Awards 2684
Greek National Tourist Organization Awards 7198
Literary Prizes 7192
Somerset Maugham Awards 4390
Prix J. J. Weiss 5869
Time Out Travel Writer and Photographer of the Year 4546
Yomiuri Literature Prize 8795

Typography
Gutenberg Award 6912
Prix GLM 4954
Triennial Prize of Bibliography 6970
H. N. Werkmanprijs 9652

Uniforms See **Fashion**

Unions See **Labor**

Urban development See **City planning**

Veterans See **Military service**

Veterinary medicine
Akzo prijs 9389
Amoroso Award 2507
AVA Prize for Undergraduates 274
AVA Student Award 275
Blaine Award 2508
Bledisloe Veterinary Award 3918
Boswell Award 11092
Bourgelat Award 2509
Alexander Ninian Bruce Prize 10640
Cheiron Medal 9692
Robert Daubney Research Fellowship in Virology and Helminthology 3983
Dunkin Award 2510
DUPHAR Award 3984
J. T. Edwards Memorial Medal 3985
Hilda och Alfred Erikssons Pris 11540
Fondation Rene Dujarric de la Riviere 5659
Gamgee Medal 11396
Gilruth Prize 276
G. Norman Hall Medal for Research into Animal Diseases 3986
R. W. Hall of Barry, Glamorgan, Prize 3987
Francis Hogg Prize 3988
Honorary Member 11909
ISHAM Lucille K. Georg Award 1202
Japanese Society of Veterinary Science Award 8671
Kendall Oration and Medal 277
Kesteven Medal 278
Martin Lerche Forschungspreis 6887
Livesey Medal 3989

Livesey Research Fellowship 2086
MacKellar Award 3990
Medaille d'Honneur du Comite Francais de l'AMV 5056
D. R. Melrose Memorial Trust 3991
Melton Award 2511
Meritorious Service Award 279
Prof. W. M. Mitchell Memorial Fund 3992
Polish Society of Veterinary Science Awards 10197
Prof. M. R. N. Prasad Memorial Lecture Award 7663
Preis der DVG zur Forderung von Nachwuchswissenschaftlern 6888
Premio Bayer en Ciencias Veterinarias 7
Premio Vilfred Baron 15
Premios CANIFARMA 8939
Prix Fernand Mery-Prix Animalier 6504
Prix Hamoir 1333
Prix Medecin General Inspecteur Raymond Debenedetti 4862
Prix Medecine Veterinaire 4864
Prix Michel Noury 4865
Prix SmithKline Beecham 1342
Dr. Bart Rispens Research Award 7171
Saltire Society and The Royal Bank of Scotland - Scottish Science Award 10657
Sandoz Preis 878
SAVA Gold Medal 11093
Ludwig Schunk Prize for Veterinary Medicine 7004
Share-Jones Lectureship in Veterinary Anatomy 3993
Dorothy Sidley Memorial Award 3031
Simon Award 2512
Sir Frederick Smith and Miss Aleen Cust Research Fellowships of the RCVS 3994
John Henry Steel Memorial Medal 3995
Harry Steele-Bodger Memorial Scholarship 2554
Theiler Memorial Medal 11035
University of Berne Prizes 11965
Wellcome Foundation Prize and Lecture 4159
Woodrow Award 2513
Wooldridge Farm Livestock Research Fellowship 2087
WSAVA International Prize for Scientific Achievement 4630
WSAVA International Prize for Service to the Profession 4631

Video
Aanmoedigingsprijzen 9635
Agrofilm International Short Film Festival 1873
AMP W.G. Walkley Awards for Journalism 523
Apple Tree Award 3691
ATOM Awards 270
Australian International Video Festival 361
Austrian State Encouragement Prizes 758
Badalona Short Film and Video Festival 11205
BAIE Editing for Industry Awards 2266
Bienal de Cine y Video Cientifico 11166
BMA Film and Video Competition 2429
BRIT Awards 2478
British Academy of Film and Television Arts Awards - Television 2234
British Amateur Video Awards 4603
Brussels International Art and Archeaology Film Festival 1162
Brussels International Festival of Films on the Engineering Profession 1097
Brussels International Festival of Scientific and Technical Films 1098

Catalonian Prizes for Videography 11183
CCP Awards for Alternative Film and Video 10046
Channel 4 Film Awards 2693
Class Prizes in British Amateur Tape Recording Contest 2872
Competition for Films and Videos on Japan 8774
Cork Youth International Video and Film Festival 7812
Dance Screen Award 842
Deutscher Jugend-Video-Preis 6591
Educational Television Awards Scheme 2760
Ekofilm Awards 1862
European Grand Prize of Corporate Image 5006
Festival Internacional del Nuevo Cine Super 8 y Video 12114
Festival International du Film et des Medias de Tourisme 6056
Festival National de l'Audiovisuel d'Entreprise 5007
Festival of Nations 803
Filmotheque of the Youth 6983
Golden Knight International Amateur Film and Video Festival 8912
Golden Toucan 1482
Goldschmidt-Clermont Prize 3434
Grand Prix of the European Festival 5126
Grand Prize of the National Festival of Hungarian Non-professional Film and Videomakers 7315
Hiroshima International Amateur Film and Video Festival 8533
IAC International Film and Video Competition 3067
IFHP International Film/Video Competition 9486
International Animation Festival in Japan, Hiroshima 8531
International Children's Film and Video Festival 675
International Competition of Video Works 6070
International Festival of Alpine Films Les Diablerets, Switzerland 11791
International Festival of Films Directed by Women 11149
International Festival of Films on Architecture and Town-planning of Lausanne 11793
International Festival of Films on Energy Lausanne 11797
International Festival of Mountain Films, Vila de Torello 11386
International Festival of Sport Films 5248
International Film Festival of Santarem 10236
International Industrial Film and Video Awards 2703
International Medical and Health Education Film Week 11269
International Multimedia Science Film Festival 8375
International Prize Paladino D'Oro 8313
International Sailing Film Festival in La Rochelle 6044
International Short Film Festival, Oberhausen 6984
International Sports Film Festival 8317
International Video Contest 11234
International Video Dance Grand Prix 6465
International Video Week of Geneva 11865
International Visual Communications Association Awards 3502
International Week of Scientific Films 11199

Japan International Film - Video Festival of Adventure and Sports in Hakuba 8622
L. J. Jordaanprijs 9640
Moomba International Amateur Film Festival 527
Opera Screen Award 844
Premio Municipal Joao Baptista Rosa de Video 10270
Elies Rogent Video Competition on Rehabilitation and Restoration 11207
Roshd International Educational Film Festival 7741
Jean Thevenot Medal 9533
Tokyo Video Festival 8780
Torreon de Igueldo 11283
Trento International Film Festival of Mountain and Exploration 8460
UNICA Medal 11623
W. A. Film and Video Festival 404
Wattrelos Short Film and Video Festival 6477
Clifford Wheeler Award 2880
World Festival of Mountain Pictures 6481
World Festival of Underwater Pictures 6483
World Film Festival of ORL Scientific Films and Videotapes 1187
World Wide Video Festival 9670

Visually impaired See **Blindness**

Violin competitions
Beethoven's Hradec Music Competition 1858
Valentino Bucchi Prize of Rome Capital City 8263
City of London Carl Flesch International Violin Competition 2630
Cologne International Violin Competition/Foundation/Shiflung Georg Kulenkampff 6609
Concertino Prague International Radio Competition for Young Musicians 1838
Concorso Internationale di Musica da Camera "Palma d'Oro" di Citta di Finale Lingure 8120
Concurso Nacional de Violin 9176
Alberto Curci International Violin Competition 8211
Vianna da Motta International Competition 10228
Finale Ligure International Chamber Music Competition 8106
Folkestone Menuhin International Violin Competition 2900
Hanover International Violin Competition 6758
Vaclav Huml International Violin Competition 1801
International Competition for Musical Performers - Geneva 11774
International Competition M. Abbado for Violinists 7999
International Henryk Wieniawski Composers Competition 10073
International Henryk Wieniawski Violin Competition 10074
International Henryk Wieniawski Violinmakers Competition 10075
International J. S. Bach Competition 6936
International Jean Sibelius Violin Competition 4729
International Jeunesses Musicales Competition - Belgrade 10717
International Ludwig Spohr Violin Competition 6972
International Mozart Competition 872

Vocal   **Awards, Honors & Prizes, 1995-96**

Violin (continued)
International Music Competition of Japan   8608
International Violin Competition Rodolfo Lipizer Prize   8209
International Violin Competition Zino Francescatti   4972
Internationaler Musikwettbewerb der ARD   6974
Internationaler Wettbewerb fur Streichquartett Karl Klinger Preis   7009
Kocian Violin Competition   1836
Fritz Kreisler International Competition Prizes   855
Marguerite Long and Jacques Thibaud International Competition   6085
National Violin Competition   9338
Carl Nielsen International Violin Competition   1984
Nicolo Paganini International Violin Competition   8395
Prague Spring International Music Competition   1880
Premio Internazionale Accademia Musicale Chigiana Siena   8046
Queen Elisabeth International Music Competition of Belgium Prizes   1245
Pablo Sarasate International Violin Competition   11255
Tunbridge Wells International Young Concert Artist Competition   4557
Tibor Varga International Competition for Violin   11664
G. B. Viotti International Music and Dance Competition   8425

Vocal music (See also **Choral music; Opera**)
Annual Prize of the Czech Musical Fund   1854
Australian Musical Foundation in London Award   2147
Gregorio Becerra Duque Trophy   1587
Budapest International Music Competition   7414
Maria Callas Grand Prix, Opera, Oratorio-Lied   7186
Maria Canals International Music Competition for Musical Performance, Barcelona   11168
Cardiff Singer of the World Competition   12155
Carmen Teresa du Hurtado Machado Latin American Competition for Voice   12116
City of London Walther Gruner International Lieder Competition   2632
Carlo Coccia International Singing Competition   8220
Concorso Internationale di Musica da Camera "Palma d'Oro" di Citta di Finale Lingure   8120
Concorso Internazionale Vincenzo Bellini per Pianisti e Cantanti Lirici   8108
Concours International de Chant de Paris   6431
Concours International de Chant Lyrique de Verviers   1215
Concours International de Chant Offenbach   5072
Concurso de anto Beca Francsco Araiza   9169
Dusek Competition of Musical Youth   1876
Early Music Festival - Bruges   1152
Eurovision Song Contest   11692
Gold Medal   2979
Grand Prix ICA - Prix de la Meilleure Chanson en Langue Traditionnelle   10687
Grand Prix National de la Chanson   5273
Grenfell Henry Lawson Festival of Arts Awards   415
Mirjam Helin International Singing Competition   4694
El Heraldo Music Prizes   9020
International Choral Competition of Tolosa   11197
International Competition of Franz Schubert and Twentieth Century Music   805
International Composition Contest Guido d'Arezzo   8215
International Franz Schubert Male Choir Contest - Vienna   882
International J. S. Bach Competition   6936
International Mozart Competition   872
International Musical Contest Dr. Luis Sigall Competition   1570
International Oratorio and Lied Competition   4981
International Robert Schumann Choir Competition   6978
International Singing Competition of Toulouse   6048
International Tchaikovsky Competition   10455
International Vocal Competition 's-Hertogenbosch   9539
International Voice Competition la Plaine-Atlantique   5188
International Voice Competition of Bilbao   11275
Internationaler Musikwettbewerb der ARD   6974
Jugend musiziert Preis   853
Lapeenranta National Singing Competition Awards   4748
Llangollen International Musical Eisteddfod   12177
Masterplayers International Music and Conductors Competition   11877
Mathy & Opera Awards   262
McDonald's Operatic Aria   323
Mestaripelimanni, Mestarikansanlaulaja   4742
Mozart Festival Competition for Young Artists   6919
National Classical Music Contest   8834
NFMS/ESSO Young Concert Artists   3684
Nigar Weekly Song Award   9988
Operasangerinnen Fanny Elstas Fond   9875
Premio Internacional de Canto Fundacion Guerrero   11242
Prix de Soliste de l'AMS   11659
Prize for Revolutionary Song   8882
Giacomo Puccini Prize   8411
Queen Elisabeth International Music Competition of Belgium Prizes   1245
Alec Redshaw Memorial Award   2951
W. Towyn Roberts Scholarship   12186
Royal Over-Seas League Music Competition   4117
RPS Music Awards   4128
Leonie Sonning Music Award   2009
Sopot International Song Festival   10130
Springbok Radio Sarie Awards   11043
Taipei International Music Competition   12007
Richard Tauber Prize   2082
Maggie Teyte Prize Competition   4530
Theatre Production Prize   24
Tokyo International Music Competition   8770
Tokyo Music Festival   8772
Tunbridge Wells International Young Concert Artist Competition   4557
Francisco Vinas International Singing Competition   11394

G. B. Viotti International Music and Dance Competition   8425
Sir Thomas White's Music Scholarship   2707
Young Artists' Competition of Kol Israel   7918
Young Concert Artists Trust Award   4649
Young Performers Award   197

Vocational education (See also **Industrial arts**)
Komsomol Medal   10433

Volleyball
Divisional Team Championships   4567

Volunteerism
Certificate of Outstanding Work in the Field of Voluntary Service   5085
National Community Service Prize   9135
Outstanding Young Citizen Award   7882
Shield of the Minister of Labour and Social Affairs   7911

Walking See **Track and field**

Water conservation
Agrofilm International Short Film Festival   1873
Dunbar Award   6733
P. H. Haviland Award   12214
Honorary Member   3372
IAWQ Pergamon Publications Medal   3373
Karl Imhoff - Pierre Koch Medal   3374
Samuel H. Jenkins Medal   3375
Stockholm Water Prize   11553

Water polo
Divisional Team Championships   4567
The Swimming Times Water Polo Award   2072

Water resources (See also **Sanitary engineering**)
G.N. Alexander Medal   422
C. G. Cillie Award   11121
FVH-priset   11617
Gold Medal   9993
P. H. Haviland Award   12214
IAHR-APD Award   9459
Arthur Thomas Ippen Award   9461
Jeno Kvassay Prize   7349
C. H. Munro Oration   475
Maarten Schalekamp Award   3504
Stockholm Water Prize   11553
Umgeni Award   11122
Wilson Award   11123

Water safety
Certificate of Commendation   4100
FIS Medal of Merit   6751
Inspecteur Honoraire de la Federation Internationale de Sauvetage Aquatique   6752

Water sports (See also **Boating; Fishing; Rowing; Surfing; Swimming; Water polo**)
Divisional Team Championships   4567
Team Championships (non-divisional)   4569

Watercolor painting (See also **Painting**)
Hunting/*Observer* Art Prizes   3760
Katanning Art Prize   511
Royal Hibernian Academy of Arts Awards   7837
Royal Watercolour Society Award   4297
Salon Anual de Artes Plasticas Premios Pedro Domingo Murillo   1389

Spanish Association of Painters and Sculptors Prizes 11381
Warringah Art Prize 706

Waterfowl management See **Wildlife conservation**

Weather See **Meteorology**

Weightlifting
Award of Merit 7433
Awards 561
Commonwealth Weightlifting Federation 12166
Individual Championships 4568
International Powerlifting Federation Awards 11479
IPF Hall of Fame 11480
IWF International Awards 7434
IWF National Awarwd 7435
President's Diploma of Honour 7436
Team Championships (non-divisional) 4569

Welding
Arata Award 3432
Edstrom Medal 3433
Goldschmidt-Clermont Prize 3434
Granjon Prize 3435
Japan Welding Society Award 8645
JWS Citation Award for Papers of the Year 8646
Kikundo Tanaka Memorial Award 8647
Andre Leroy Prize 3436
Sasaki Memorial Award 8648

Welfare See **Child welfare; Social service**

Wildlife conservation (See also **Environmental conservation**)
Birdlife International/FFPS Conservation Expedition Competition 2188
Conservationist of the Year 11127
Duke of Edinburgh Prize for the Japan Academy 8593
Fauna and Flora Preservation Society Grants 2866
Gold Medal
  Wildlife Society of Southern Africa 11128
  WWF World Wide Fund for Nature 11986
International Conservation Roll of Honour 11987
International Council for Game and Wildlife Conservation Awards 5997
Charles Thomas Astley Maberley Memorial Scholarships 11129
Members of Honour 11988
Order of the Golden Ark 9357
RSPB Medal 4175
Sture Centerwalls Pris 11556
Verner von Heidenstams Guldmedalj 11558
Wild Places 4651
Wildlife Action Award 4652
Wildlife Photographer of the Year Competition 2162
Wildlife Society of Zimbabwe Competitions 12209
Young Wildlife Photographer of the Year Competition 2163

Wine
English Wine of the Year Competition 2796
Grand Prix SOPEXA du Sommelier 5228
Premio A. Marescalchi 8042
Premio Internazionale di Viticoltura G. Dalmasso 8043
Premio P. G. Garoglio 8044
Andre Simon Medal 3506

Women
AFUW-SA Inc. Trust Fund Bursary 216
Alice Award 662
Asian Cup Women's Football Championship 8897
Thenie Baddams Bursary 217
Anna Bijnsprijs 9340
Bourse Marcelle Blum 5708
Concours National Feminin de Musique du Lyceum de Suisse 11682
Concurso la Mejor Tesis sobre la Mujer in la UNAM 9173
Rose Mary Crawshay Prize for English Literature 2225
Denman Cup 3688
Elle Literary Prize 5110
Engineering 2000 Awards 438
European Sportsman and Sportswoman of the Year 1144
Fawcett Book Prize 2868
Fellowships and Scholarships 146
Female Writers Literary Award 8520
Harold Fern National Trophy 2068
Festival International de Films de Femmes 1384
FIFA Women's World Football Championship 11714
William Gibson Research Scholarship for Medical Women 4248
Jean Gilmore Bursary 218
Dame Alexandra Hasluck Short Story Competition 664
Honor al Merito 1783
Honorary Member 7044
IET Woman's Engineer Award 3093
IFUW Awards Competition 11789
Inter-American Award for the Participation of Women in Rural Development 1777
International Festival of Films Directed by Women 11149
International Women-Composer's Competition 11666
International Women's Film Festival, Creteil 6072
Jamnalal Bajaj Foundation Awards 7693
Joyce Award 2282
Kshanika Oration Award to a Woman Scientist for Research in the Field of Biomedical Sciences 7593
Ladies' British Open Amateur Championship 10588
Judith Leysterprijs
  Frans Halsmuseum 9448
  Judith Leyster Stichting 9543
Hilarie Lindsay Award 665
Julia Lopes of Ameida Prize 1425
Pelagia Majewska Medal 5159
Medal of Distinction 7749
Charles Meeking Award for Poetry 666
Member of Honour 7045
Magdalena Mondragon Medal 8922
Newman Cup 9822
NFWI Design Award 3689
Orders of the Precious Crown 8587
Catherine Pakenham Memorial Award 3602
Jan Popper Memorial Prize 2135
Winifred E. Preedy Post-Graduate Bursary 219
Premio de Periodismo Rosario Castellanos 8928
Prix Anais Segalas 5811
Prix des Dames 6220
Prix *Femina* 6168
Prix Helene Seguin 6333
Prix Jules Favre 5875
Prix Marceline Desbordes-Valmore 6339
Prix Marcelle Millier 5891

Prix Suzanne Tassier 997
Prix Tanesse 5792
Margaret Rhondda Award 4391
Annie Romein Prys 9426
Rose of Tralee 7827
The Sunday Times Sportswomen of the Year Award 4505
Georgina Sweet Fellowship 212
Maggie Teyte Prize Competition 4530
Ulster Award 717
Woman of the Year in Finland 4752
Women and Politics Prize 142
Women's British Open Championship 10589

Women's rights
Soroptimist International of the South West Pacific Awards 668
Tagore Literacy Award 7567

Wood and wood products (See also **Forestry; Paper industry**)
Ron Cockcroft Award 11482
Wood Prize 9908

Work safety See **Occupational safety**

World peace
Anuvrat Award for International Peace 7484
Ataturk International Peace Prize 12044
Caribbean Prize for Peace Through the Pursuit of Justice 940
Indira Gandhi Prize for Peace, Disarmament and Development 7502
Felix Houphouet-Boigny Peace Prize 6413
International Association of University Presidents Awards 12027
International Center for Peace in the Middle East Awards 7894
International Dag Hammarskjold Award 1237
International Lenin Peace Prize 10472
IPRA President's Award 11823
Jamnalal Bajaj International Award for Promoting Gandhian Values Outside India 7694
Rufus Jones Award 921
Junior Research Fellowship 7508
Justice and Peace Prize for Human Values 11209
Immanuel Kant Prize 7114
Harold Dwight Lasswell Award 922
Niwano Peace Prize 8709
Nobel Peace Prize 11495
November 17th Medal 1869
Order of San Carlos 1620
Olof Palme Memorial Fund Scholarships 11506
Olof Palme Prize 11507
Peace and Cooperation School Award 11314
Peace Award 1235
Peace Prize of the German Book Trade 6776
Pope John XIII Peace Prize 12105
Premio Mixcoatl 9255
Prix Adolf Bentinck 6160
Prix Fraternite Gaby Archenbaud 6124
Prix Jean Mace 6083
Karl Renner Preis 795
Soroptimist International of the South West Pacific Awards 668
UNA Awards 11439
UNA Study Circles Challenge Trophys 11440
UNESCO Prize for Peace Education 6425
Wateler Peace Prize 9353

Youth

World (continued)
World Association for Celebrating Year 2000 Awards 4616
World Council of Young Men's Service Clubs Awards 9854
World Peace Council Awards 4767

Yachting See Boating

Youth achievement
Certificate of Honor 10426
Commonwealth Youth Service Awards 2671
European Committee for Young Farmers and 4H Clubs Awards 10543
Filmotheque of the Youth 6983
Harvey Essay Prize 2992
International Award 2932
International Letter-Writing Competition for Young People 11957
Livewire Start-up Awards 3596
My Country - USSR Award 10441
National Youth Awards 7524
National Youth Prize 9153
Outstanding Young Citizen Award 7882
The Outstanding Youth Science Researchers 10058
Queen's Award 2934
Young People and Adult Supervisors Award 10448

Youth work
Lady Allen of Hurtwood Trust Award 2055
Bronze Wolf 11982
Certificate of Honor 10426
Gaydar Award 10431
International Nathalie Masse Prize 5982
IYHF Certificate of Merit 3510
IYHF Roll of Honour 3511

My Country - USSR Award 10442
National Youth Awards 7524
Margaret O'Rourke Scholarship 2933
Premi Artur Martorell 11172
Prix Scientifique/Prix Innovante/Prix Media 5222
Scout Leader Award 10445
Training Award 10447
Young People and Adult Supervisors Award 10448
Youth of the Americas 1781
Youth Studies Prize 11173

Zoology (See also Ornithology)
Annual Award 3620
H. H. Bloomer Award 3585
W. S. Bruce Medal 10639
Certificate of Merit 11131
Clarke Medal 623
Fondation Cuvier 5526
Fondation Foulon 5558
Fondation Jean Thore 5600
Fondation Marc Poll 1004
Fondation Pouchard 5657
Fondation Savigny 5665
Frink Medal for British Zoologists 4656
Gold Medal 11132
Hector Memorial Medal and Prize 9838
Hutton Memorial Medal and Prize 9839
Thomas Henry Huxley Award 4657
International Centre of Insect Physiology and Ecology Awards 8803
International Federation of Beekeepers' Associations Awards 8299
Japanese Society of Sericultural Science Award 8659
Japanese Society of Zootechnical Science Award 8673

Junior Captain Scott Commemorative Medal 10993
Linnean Medal 3587
Linneprisen 11518
Lovenmedaljen 11547
George C. Martin Memorial Scholarship 10903
Mueller Medal 190
Nippon Oyo Dobutsu Konchu Gakkai Sho 8654
Louis Pasteur Prize 6046
Premio Maria Teresa e Allessandro Ghigi 8021
Prince Philip Prize 4658
Prix Adolphe Crevecoeur 1350
Prix Agathon De Potter 1007
Prix Lamarck 1028
Stamford Raffles Award 4659
Royal Society of Victoria Medal 638
Schleiden Medal 6626
Scientific Medal 4660
Junior Captain Scott Memorial Medal 11032
Sericultural Science Advancement Award 8660
Silver Medal 4661
P. Sivickio premija 8856
Stevenson - Hamilton Award 11133
Stora Linnemedaljen i guld 11554
Sunder Lal Hora Medal 7674
Dr. Har Swarup Memorial Lecture 7675
Roberto A. Vacarezza Prize 103
W. J. van der Linde Memorial Award 10904
Whitley Awards 646
Wigglesworth Medal 4002
Sir Charles Maurice Yonge Award 3621
Zoological Science Award 8797

Organization Index

The alphabetical Organization Index provides access to all sponsoring and administering organizations listed in both volumes, as well as to organization acronyms and alternate-language and former names. In the case of a sponsoring organization, the citation is to the specific award it sponsors. Each organization name is followed by the volume in which it appears. The numbers following the volume references are book entry numbers, not page numbers.

3M Company   Vol 1: 135, 2920, 20263
3M Healthcare   Vol 1: 10744
99 Company   Vol 1: 17977
187th Airborne Regimental Combat Team Association   Vol 1: 1
369th Veterans' Association   Vol 1: 6
AA Life   Vol 2: 10808
AA Mutual Life   Vol 2: 10808
AAFRC Trust for Philanthropy   Vol 1: 8
AAMR   Vol 2: 535
ABB Kent Taylor Ltd.   Vol 2: 4219
Abbado International Competition for Violinists; M.   Vol 2: 7998
Abbott Laboratories   Vol 1: 622, 4197
Abbott-Northwestern Hospital Sister Kenny Auxiliary   Vol 1: 17294
ABC - CLIO   Vol 1: 2827
ABC Color   Vol 1: 10511
Abrasive Engineering Society   Vol 1: 10
ABSA/Arthur Andersen Awards in Association with *The Times*   Vol 2: 2029
Abundantly Yours   Vol 1: 14
Academia Brasileira de Letras   Vol 2: 1419, 10253
Academia Chilena de la Lengua   Vol 2: 1550
Academia Colombiana de Ciencias Exactas, Fisicas y Naturales   Vol 2: 1577
Academia Colombiana de la Lengua   Vol 2: 1678
Academia das Ciencias de Lisboa   Vol 2: 10244
Academia de Geografia e Historia de Guatemala   Vol 2: 7237
Academia de la Investigacion Cientifica   Vol 2: 8917
Academia de Medicina de Sao Paulo   Vol 2: 1489
Academia de Stiinte Medicale   Vol 2: 10322
Academia Deletras Jose Dealencar   Vol 2: 1405
Academia Ludoviciana Gissensis   Vol 2: 6996
Academia Mexicana de Ciencias y Artes   Vol 2: 9096
Academia Mexicana de Cirugia   Vol 2: 9100
Academia Mexicana de Dermatologia   Vol 2: 9098
Academia Nacional de Agronomia y Veterinaria   Vol 2: 5
Academia Nacional de Belas-Artes   Vol 2: 10283
Academia Nacional de la Historia   Vol 2: 16
Academia Nacional de Medicina   Vol 2: 61, 1724
Academia Nacional de Medicina de Mexico   Vol 2: 9111
Academia Nacional de Medicina del Uruguay   Vol 2: 12087

Academia Portuguese da Historia   Vol 2: 10299
Academia Romana   Vol 2: 10328
Academie Bulgare des Sciences   Vol 2: 1511
Academie Canadienne du Cinema et de la Television   Vol 1: 24
Academie d'Agriculture de France   Vol 2: 4768
Academie d'Architecture   Vol 2: 4772
Academie de Gastronomie Brillat-Savarin   Vol 2: 4790
Academie des Arts et Techniques du Cinema   Vol 2: 4792
Academie des Sciences, Arts et Belles-Lettres de Dijon   Vol 2: 4794
Academie des Sciences Coloniales   Vol 2: 6133
Academie des sciences de l'Institut   Vol 1: 16954
Academie des Sciences d'Outre-Mer   Vol 2: 6133
Academie Diplomatique de la Paix, Pax Mundi   Vol 2: 1236
Academie Goncourt   Vol 2: 4796
Academie Internationale d'Heraldique   Vol 2: 942
Academie Internationale d'Histoire des Sciences   Vol 2: 5948
Academie Malgache   Vol 2: 8885
Academie Mallarme   Vol 2: 4799
Academie Nationale de Medecine   Vol 2: 4801
Academie Nationale de Reims   Vol 2: 4880
Academie Royale d'Archeologie de Belgique   Vol 2: 948
Academie Royale de Belgique - Classe des Beaux-Arts   Vol 2: 950
Academie Royale de Belgique - Classe des Lettres et des Sciences Morales et Politiques   Vol 2: 971
Academie Royale de Belgique - Classe des Sciences   Vol 2: 1000
Academie Royale de Langue et de Litterature Francaise   Vol 2: 1281
Academie Royale de Medecine de Belgique   Vol 2: 1322
Academy of American Franciscan History   Vol 1: 16
Academy of American Poets   Vol 1: 18
Academy of Applied Osteopathy   Vol 1: 650
Academy of Arts, Berlin   Vol 2: 6508
Academy of Athens   Vol 2: 7180
Academy of Canadian Cinema   Vol 1: 24
Academy of Canadian Cinema & Television   Vol 1: 24
Academy of Costume and Fashion   Vol 2: 8000
Academy of Country Music   Vol 1: 30

Academy of Country Music Entertainment   Vol 1: 6847
Academy of Criminal Justice Sciences   Vol 1: 32
Academy of Dentistry for the Handicapped   Vol 1: 39
Academy of Family Films and Family Television   Vol 1: 42
Academy of Fine Arts   Vol 2: 1895
Academy of International Business   Vol 1: 44
Academy of Management   Vol 1: 46
Academy of Medical Films   Vol 1: 54
Academy of Medical Sciences   Vol 2: 10322
Academy of Motion Picture Arts and Sciences   Vol 1: 56
Academy of Natural Sciences of Philadelphia   Vol 1: 67
Academy of Parish Clergy   Vol 1: 72
Academy of Religion and Psychical Research   Vol 1: 78
Academy of Science Fiction, Fantasy and Horror Films   Vol 1: 80
Academy of Sciences and Literature, Mainz - Section of Literature   Vol 2: 6513
Academy of Sciences and Technology in Berlin   Vol 2: 6516
Academy of Sciences, Armenia   Vol 2: 111
Academy of Sciences, Lithuania   Vol 2: 8854
Academy of Sciences, Moscow   Vol 2: 10417
Academy of Sciences, Moscow - Section of Social Science   Vol 2: 10420
Academy of Scientific Research   Vol 2: 8917
Academy of Security Educators and Trainers   Vol 1: 83
Academy of Television Arts and Sciences   Vol 1: 85
Academy of Tourism Organizations   Vol 1: 88
Academy of Wind and Percussion Arts   Vol 1: 13425
Acanthes; Association   Vol 2: 6200
Accademia Agraria   Vol 2: 8006
Accademia Biella Cultura   Vol 2: 8009
Accademia Culturale d'Europa   Vol 2: 8011
Accademia d'Arte Leonetto Cappiello per le Nuove Professioni e la Pubblicita   Vol 2: 8013
Accademia del Frignano Lo Scoltenna   Vol 2: 8015
Accademia della Chitarra Classica, Milan   Vol 2: 8017
Accademia delle Scienze Dell'Istituto di Bologna   Vol 2: 8019
Accademia delle Scienze di Torino   Vol 2: 8022
Accademia di Costume e di Moda   Vol 2: 8000
Accademia di Medicina di Torino   Vol 2: 8025

Accademia di Paestum - Eremo Italico   Vol 2: 8027
Accademia di Scienze, Lettere e Arti di Palermo   Vol 2: 8029
Accademia di Studi Storici Aldo Moro   Vol 2: 8031
Accademia il Tetradramma   Vol 2: 8033
Accademia Internazionale della Tavola Rotonda   Vol 2: 8035
Accademia Internazionale Medicea   Vol 2: 8037
Accademia Internazionale per l'Unita della Cultura   Vol 2: 8039
Accademia Italiana della Vite e del Vino   Vol 2: 8041
Accademia Musicale Chigiana   Vol 2: 8045
Accademia Musicale Napoletana   Vol 2: 8047
Accademia Nazionale dei Lincei   Vol 2: 8049
Accademia Nazionale Delle Scienze detta dei XL   Vol 2: 8376
Accademia Nazionale di Santa Cecilia   Vol 2: 8081
Accademia Pistoiese del Ceppo   Vol 2: 8083
Accademia Pontaniana   Vol 2: 8086
Accademia Romana di Scienze Mediche e Biologiche   Vol 2: 8089
Accademia Vitivinicola Daunia   Vol 2: 8091
Accounting Education Foundation of Alberta   Vol 1: 19810
Accreditation Board for Engineering and Technology   Vol 1: 90
Accurate Chemical and Scientific Corporation   Vol 1: 17548
Achievement Management Group of Companies   Vol 2: 10852, 10853
ACM SIGCOMM   Vol 1: 5477
Acoustical Society of America   Vol 1: 94
Acta Metallurgica   Vol 1: 105
ACTA Shipping   Vol 2: 115
Action for Children's Television   Vol 1: 110
Action for Nuclear Disarmament   Vol 1: 20406
Action Research   Vol 2: 2036
Action Research for the Crippled Child   Vol 2: 2036
Actors' Alley Repertory Theatre   Vol 1: 114
Actors' Equity Association   Vol 1: 116
Actors' Equity Foundation   Vol 1: 119
Actors' Fund of America   Vol 1: 123
Actors Theatre of Louisville   Vol 1: 125
ACTS Satellite Network   Vol 1: 127
Actuarial Education and Research Fund   Vol 1: 129
Addams Peace Association; Jane   Vol 1: 132
Adelaide Philosophical Society   Vol 2: 631
Adhesion Society   Vol 1: 134
adidas   Vol 1: 10538
ADIRCAE   Vol 2: 11139
Adirondack Council   Vol 1: 136
ADISQ (Association Quebecoise de L'Industrie du Disque, du Spectacle et de la Video)   Vol 1: 138
Administrative Management Society   Vol 1: 142
Adoptee-Birthparent Search   Vol 1: 145
Adrenal Metabolic Research Society of the Hypoglycemia Foundation   Vol 1: 147
Adult Education of the U.S.A.   Vol 1: 825
Advanced Centre of Cryogenic Research - Calcutta   Vol 2: 7468
Adventist World Headquarters   Vol 1: 16137
Advertising Age - Crain Communications   Vol 1: 149
Advertising and Design Club of Canada   Vol 1: 151
Advertising Association of the West   Vol 1: 743
Advertising Council   Vol 1: 153

Advertising Media Credit Executives Association   Vol 1: 155
Advertising Press Club of Ireland   Vol 2: 7750
Advertising Women of New York   Vol 1: 157
ADWEEK/East   Vol 1: 162
AECI Limited   Vol 2: 11045
AEDOS S.A.   Vol 2: 11134
Aero Club of America   Vol 1: 12721
Aero Club of Egypt   Vol 2: 5162
Aero Club of Poland   Vol 2: 5159
Aeronautical Research Laboratories   Vol 2: 434
Aeronautical Society of India   Vol 2: 7473
Aerospace Medical Association   Vol 1: 164, 167
Aestheticians International Association   Vol 1: 178
Affaire de Coeur   Vol 1: 181
Affiliate Artists   Vol 1: 183
AFL/CIO   Vol 1: 2950
Africa Travel Association   Vol 1: 186
African Book Publishing Record   Vol 2: 2038
African Centre for Applied Research and Training in Social Development   Vol 2: 8850
African Cultural Institute   Vol 2: 10686
African Farmers Association   Vol 2: 2018
African Governance Program   Vol 1: 11828
African Insurance Organization   Vol 2: 1542
African Regional Centre for Technology   Vol 2: 10692
African Studies Association   Vol 1: 190
Afro-American Patrolmen's League   Vol 1: 193
Afro-American Police League   Vol 1: 193
AFS Intercultural Programs   Vol 1: 195
AGA Education and Research Foundation   Vol 1: 5822
Aga Khan Awards Foundation   Vol 2: 11655
Aga Khan Trust for Culture   Vol 2: 11655
AGBU of America   Vol 1: 5269
AGCO   Vol 1: 4372
The Age   Vol 2: 117
Agence de Cooperation Culturelle et Technique   Vol 2: 4882
Agence de l'environnement et pour la maitrise de l'energie   Vol 2: 5046
AGFA   Vol 2: 281, 11125
Agfa Corporation   Vol 1: 17500
Agfa-Gevaert (HK) Ltd.   Vol 2: 7265
Agnelli; Fondazione Giovanni   Vol 2: 8246
Agri-Energy Roundtable   Vol 1: 197
Agrichemical Age   Vol 1: 13026
Agricultural Communicators in Education   Vol 1: 199
Agricultural Economics Society   Vol 2: 7851
Agricultural History Society   Vol 1: 205
Agricultural Institute of Canada   Vol 1: 209
Agricultural Pesticide Society   Vol 1: 7089
Agriservices Foundation   Vol 1: 13010
Aguda Ha'Biochimit Ha'Israelit   Vol 2: 7914
Aguda l'Haanakat Prasim Sifrutiim Al Shem Mordechai Bernstein   Vol 2: 7869
Ahlstrom Foundation; Walter   Vol 2: 4682
Ahrend Groep N.V.   Vol 2: 9659
Aim Quarterly Magazine   Vol 1: 214
Air and Waste Management Association   Vol 1: 216
Air-Britain (Historians) Ltd.   Vol 2: 2040
Air Canada   Vol 1: 6807, 8500
Air Force Association   Vol 1: 226
Air Force Association - Aerospace Education Foundation   Vol 1: 265
Air Force Historical Foundation   Vol 1: 267
Air League   Vol 2: 2043
Air Products and Chemicals, Inc.   Vol 1: 1519, 2598
Air Public Relations Association   Vol 2: 2046

Air Traffic Control Association   Vol 1: 270
Air Transport World   Vol 1: 280
Airco Distributor Gases   Vol 1: 5073
Aircraft Owners and Pilots Association   Vol 1: 282
Aircraft Technical Publishers   Vol 1: 12765, 16440
Airports Council International - North America   Vol 1: 286
Airtour International   Vol 2: 2999
Airways Corporation   Vol 2: 9808
Akademie der Kunste, Berlin   Vol 2: 6508
Akademie der Wissenschaften in Gottingen   Vol 2: 6902
Akademie der Wissenschaften und der Literatur zu Mainz - Klasse der Literatur   Vol 2: 6513
Akademie der Wissenschaften zu Berlin   Vol 2: 6516
Akademie voor Expressie door Woord en Gebaar   Vol 2: 9327
Akademie voor Kleinkunst   Vol 2: 9615
Akademiet for de skonne Kunster   Vol 2: 1895
Akademiet for de Tekniske Videnskaber   Vol 2: 1910
Akadimie Athinon   Vol 2: 7180
Akashvani   Vol 2: 7479
AKM   Vol 2: 774
Akzo Chemical America   Vol 1: 3316
Akzo Chemicals, Inc.   Vol 1: 1536
Akzo Company   Vol 2: 9389
Alabama Library Association   Vol 1: 290
Albany Institute of History and Art   Vol 1: 17090
Albany Trustee Company   Vol 2: 2687
Alberta Community Development   Vol 1: 292
Alberta Irrigation Projects Association   Vol 1: 299
Alberta Publishers Association   Vol 1: 6444
Alberta Theatre Projects   Vol 1: 301
Albright & Wilson Ltd.   Vol 2: 4219
Albright Institute of Archaeological Research; W.F.   Vol 1: 4009, 4010, 4014
Alcaldia Municipal   Vol 2: 1387
Alcan   Vol 1: 7491
ALCAN   Vol 1: 9173
Alcances/Muestra Cinematografica del Atlantico   Vol 2: 11137
Alco Control Company   Vol 1: 4570
Alcoa Company   Vol 1: 4671
Alcuin Society   Vol 1: 303
Aldeburgh Bookshop   Vol 2: 2051
Aldeburgh Poetry Trust   Vol 2: 2050
Aldrich Chemical Company, Inc.   Vol 1: 1522
Ales Film Festival   Vol 2: 4885
Alfa Laval Agri, Inc.   Vol 1: 1906
Algemeen Nederlands Verbond   Vol 2: 9329, 9655
Alger Association of Distinguished Americans; Horatio   Vol 1: 306
Alger Society; Horatio   Vol 1: 308
All-America Rose Selections   Vol 1: 314
All-America Selections   Vol 1: 318
All-American Collegiate Talent Search   Vol 1: 1763
All England Lawn Tennis and Croquet Club Wimbledon   Vol 2: 2052
All India Radio   Vol 2: 7479
All-Union Leninist Young Communist League   Vol 2: 10424
Allard Charitable Foundation; Pete   Vol 2: 3880
Allen & Hanburys, Division of Glaxo, Inc.   Vol 1: 1621
Allen & Unwin Pty Ltd   Vol 2: 119
Allen of Hurtwood Trust; Lady   Vol 2: 2054

Alliance for Children and Television   Vol 1: 320
Alliance for Community Media   Vol 1: 324
Alliance Francais   Vol 2: 4883
Alliance Internationale Jeanne d'Arc   Vol 2: 1354
Alliance mondiale pour la nature   Vol 2: 11968
Alliance of Canadian Cinema, Television and Radio Artists   Vol 1: 326
Alliance of Genetic Support Groups   Vol 1: 328
Allied Artists of America   Vol 1: 331
Allied Bendix   Vol 1: 17752
Allied Signal Corporation Foundation   Vol 1: 4070
AlliedSignal Foundation   Vol 1: 333
Allis Chalmers Corporation   Vol 1: 13031, 13032
Allport Memorial Fund of Harvard University; Gordon W.   Vol 1: 3813
Allstate Foundation   Vol 1: 13594
Allstate Life Insurance Company   Vol 1: 16394, 19428
ALPHA   Vol 2: 4900
Alpha Chi Sigma   Vol 1: 337
Alpha Chi Sigma Fraternity   Vol 1: 1541
Alpha Epsilon Rho - The National Broadcasting Society   Vol 1: 342
Alpha Kappa Alpha Sorority   Vol 1: 357
Alpha Kappa Delta International Sociology Honor Society   Vol 1: 359
Alpha Kappa Psi Foundation   Vol 1: 3961
Alpha Omega Alpha Honor Medical Society   Vol 1: 361, 5688
Alpha Omega Dental Fraternity   Vol 1: 365
Alpha Omega Fraternity   Vol 1: 365
Alpha Sigma Nu   Vol 1: 5838
Alpha Zeta Omega Pharmaceutical Fraternity   Vol 1: 368
Alpine Club of Canada   Vol 1: 373
Alpine Countries International Filmmaking and Writing Academy   Vol 2: 720
Alpine Garden Society   Vol 2: 2056
Alternative Energy Resources Organization   Vol 1: 377
Aluminum Association   Vol 1: 379
Aluminum Company of America   Vol 1: 381
Aluminum Company of Canada Limited   Vol 1: 6928, 7540
Alumni Association   Vol 1: 1658
Alumni Association of the City College of New York   Vol 1: 385
Alumni Federation of New York University   Vol 1: 390
Alva Foundation   Vol 1: 19881
Alvis Owner Club   Vol 2: 2059
Amado Foundation; Maurice   Vol 1: 11539
Amanah Al Ammah Li Jaezat Al Malik Faisal Al Alamiyyah; Al   Vol 2: 10495
Amantakul Foundation; Isara   Vol 2: 12014
AMARC   Vol 1: 6328
Amateur Astronomers Association of New York   Vol 1: 393
Amateur Athletic Association of England   Vol 2: 2061
Amateur Athletic Foundation of Los Angeles   Vol 1: 395
Amateur Athletic Union of the United States   Vol 1: 400
Amateur Boxing Federation; United States of America   Vol 1: 18990
Amateur Cinema League   Vol 1: 3143
Amateur Hockey Association of the United States   Vol 1: 19921
Amateur Softball Association of America   Vol 1: 461

Amateur Speedskating Union of the United States   Vol 1: 466
Amateur Swimming Association   Vol 2: 2063
Amateurs Photographes et Cineastes d'Auvergne   Vol 2: 4887
AMBAC Indemnity Corporation   Vol 1: 19065
Ambiente-Incontri   Vol 2: 8093
Ambulatory Pediatric Association   Vol 1: 468
Amelia Magazine   Vol 1: 473
America Forest and Paper Association   Vol 1: 475
America-Israel Cultural Foundation   Vol 1: 478
America the Beautiful Fund   Vol 1: 480
American Academy and Institute of Arts and Sciences   Vol 1: 493
American Academy for Cerebral Palsy   Vol 1: 482
American Academy for Cerebral Palsy and Developmental Medicine   Vol 1: 482
American Academy in Rome   Vol 1: 484, 14218
American Academy of Achievement   Vol 1: 486
American Academy of Allergy and Immunology   Vol 1: 488
American Academy of Arts and Letters   Vol 1: 493
American Academy of Arts and Sciences   Vol 1: 522
American Academy of Child and Adolescent Psychiatry   Vol 1: 529
American Academy of Child Psychiatry   Vol 1: 529
American Academy of Clinical Psychiatrists   Vol 1: 540
American Academy of Clinical Toxicology   Vol 1: 542
American Academy of Crown and Bridge Prosthodontics   Vol 1: 584
American Academy of Dental Electrosurgery   Vol 1: 545
American Academy of Dermatology   Vol 1: 547
American Academy of Dramatic Arts   Vol 1: 550
American Academy of Environmental Engineers   Vol 1: 553
American Academy of Environmental Medicine   Vol 1: 559
American Academy of Facial Plastic and Reconstructive Surgery   Vol 1: 563
American Academy of Family Physicians   Vol 1: 576
American Academy of Fixed Prosthodontics   Vol 1: 584
American Academy of Gnathologic Orthopedics   Vol 1: 586
American Academy of Implant Dentistry   Vol 1: 588
American Academy of Kinesiology and Physical Education   Vol 1: 591
American Academy of Medical Administrators   Vol 1: 593
American Academy of Neurological and Orthopaedic Surgeons   Vol 1: 603
American Academy of Neurological Surgery   Vol 1: 610
American Academy of Neurology   Vol 1: 612
American Academy of Nursing   Vol 1: 626
American Academy of Occupational Medicine   Vol 1: 1696
American Academy of Ophthalmology   Vol 1: 628
American Academy of Ophthalmology and Otolaryngology   Vol 1: 628
American Academy of Optometry   Vol 1: 635

American Academy of Oral Medicine   Vol 1: 644
American Academy of Orthopaedic Surgeons   Vol 1: 13089
American Academy of Osteopathic Surgeons   Vol 1: 1095
American Academy of Osteopathy   Vol 1: 650
American Academy of Otolaryngology - Head and Neck Surgery   Vol 1: 654
American Academy of Pediatrics   Vol 1: 660
American Academy of Periodontology   Vol 1: 687
American Academy of Physician Assistants   Vol 1: 699
American Academy of Psychiatrists in Alcoholism and Addictions   Vol 1: 705
American Academy of Psychiatry and the Law   Vol 1: 708
American Academy of Religion   Vol 1: 713
American Academy of Safety Education   Vol 1: 715
American Academy of Sanitarians   Vol 1: 718
American Academy of Somnology   Vol 1: 720
American Academy of the History of Dentistry   Vol 1: 722
American Academy on Mental Retardation   Vol 1: 725
American Accordion Musicological Society   Vol 1: 727
American Accordionists' Association   Vol 1: 729
American Action Fund for Blind Children and Adults   Vol 1: 13965
American Adoption Congress   Vol 1: 731
American Advertising Federation   Vol 1: 733
American Advertising Federation - Western Region Office   Vol 1: 742
American Agri-Women   Vol 1: 744
American Agricultural Economics Association   Vol 1: 748
American Agricultural Editors Association   Vol 1: 7684
American Airlines   Vol 1: 19575, 19576, 19577, 19578, 19579, 19580, 19581, 19582, 19588
American Alliance for Health, Physical Education, Recreation, and Dance   Vol 1: 757
American Alliance for Theatre & Education   Vol 1: 765
American Animal Hospital Association   Vol 1: 783, 9464
American Anthropological Association   Vol 1: 792
American Antiquarian Society   Vol 1: 798
American Arbitration Association   Vol 1: 800
American Architectal Foundation   Vol 1: 2526
American Armwrestling Association   Vol 1: 806
American Art Therapy Association   Vol 1: 809
American Artists Professional League   Vol 1: 811
American Assembly   Vol 1: 813
American Assembly for Men in Nursing   Vol 1: 815
American Assembly of Collegiate Schools of Business   Vol 1: 819
American Association for Adult and Continuing Education   Vol 1: 825
American Association for Aerosol Research   Vol 1: 829
American Association for Agricultural Education   Vol 1: 832
American Association for Automotive Medicine   Vol 1: 5606
American Association for Cancer Education   Vol 1: 836

American Association for Cancer Research Vol 1: 839
American Association for Clinical Chemistry, Inc. Vol 1: 845
American Association for Conservation Information Vol 1: 5478
American Association for Counseling and Development Vol 1: 1877, 12274
American Association for Crystal Growth Vol 1: 854
American Association for Geodetic Surveying Vol 1: 857
American Association for Hand Surgery Vol 1: 860
American Association for Laboratory Animal Science Vol 1: 862
American Association for Public Opinion Research Vol 1: 869
American Association for State and Local History Vol 1: 872
American Association for the Advancement of Science Vol 1: 877
American Association for the Advancement of Slavic Studies Vol 1: 890
American Association for the History of Medicine Vol 1: 894
American Association for the Study of Headache Vol 1: 898
American Association for Theatre in Secondary Education Vol 1: 765
American Association for Women Radiologists Vol 1: 904
American Association of Agricultural College Editors Vol 1: 199
American Association of Anatomists Vol 1: 908
American Association of Avian Pathologists Vol 1: 911
American Association of Bioanalysts Vol 1: 917
American Association of Blood Banks Vol 1: 919
American Association of Botanical Gardens and Arboreta Vol 1: 932
American Association of Bovine Practitioners Vol 1: 937
American Association of Cereal Chemists Vol 1: 944
American Association of Certified Orthoptists Vol 1: 952
American Association of Children's Residential Centers Vol 1: 956
American Association of College Baseball Coaches Vol 1: 1314
American Association of Colleges for Teacher Education Vol 1: 958
American Association of Collegiate Registrars and Admissions Officers Vol 1: 965
American Association of Community Theatre Vol 1: 970
American Association of Correctional Training Personnel Vol 1: 979
American Association of Cost Engineers Vol 1: 981
American Association of Dental Examiners Vol 1: 989
American Association of Electrodiagnostic Medicine Vol 1: 991
American Association of Electromyography and Electrodiagnosis Vol 1: 991
American Association of Endodontists Vol 1: 993
American Association of Engineering Societies Vol 1: 997
American Association of Fitness Directors in Business and Industry Vol 1: 5665

American Association of Genito-Urinary Surgeons Vol 1: 1002
American Association of Homes for the Aging Vol 1: 1005
American Association of Hospital Dental Chiefs Vol 1: 1015
American Association of Hospital Dentists Vol 1: 1015
American Association of Housing Educators Vol 1: 1019
American Association of Immunologists Vol 1: 1022
American Association of Individual Investors Vol 1: 9199, 9200
American Association of Industrial Physicians and Surgeons Vol 1: 1696
American Association of Law Libraries Vol 1: 1026
American Association of Managing General Agents Vol 1: 1032
American Association of Meat Processors Vol 1: 1034
American Association of Mental Health Professionals in Corrections Vol 1: 1037
American Association of Motor Vehicle Administrators Vol 1: 1039
American Association of Museums Vol 1: 1043
American Association of Neurological Surgeons - Joint Section on Spinal Disorders Vol 1: 8151
American Association of Neuropathologists Vol 1: 1047
American Association of Nurse Anesthetists Vol 1: 1051
American Association of Nurserymen Vol 1: 1062, 8946
American Association of Occupational Health Nurses Vol 1: 1073
American Association of Oral and Maxillofacial Surgeons Vol 1: 1083
American Association of Orthodontists Vol 1: 1089, 1353
American Association of Osteopathic Specialists Vol 1: 1095
American Association of Owners and Breeders of Peruvian Paso Horses Vol 1: 1099
American Association of Pathologists Vol 1: 4177
American Association of Pathologists and Bacteriologists Vol 1: 4177
American Association of Petroleum Geologists Vol 1: 1102
American Association of Petroleum Landmen Vol 1: 1115
American Association of Physical Anthropologists Vol 1: 1117
American Association of Physics Teachers Vol 1: 1124
American Association of Plastic Surgeons Vol 1: 1134
American Association of Political Consultants Vol 1: 1139
American Association of Psychiatric Services for Children Vol 1: 1141
American Association of Psychiatric Technicians Vol 1: 1147
American Association of Public Health Dentistry Vol 1: 1152
American Association of Public Health Physicians Vol 1: 1154
American Association of Retired Persons Vol 1: 1156
American Association of School Administrators Vol 1: 1170
American Association of School Personnel Administrators Vol 1: 1189

American Association of Sex Educators, Counselors and Therapists Vol 1: 1191
American Association of State Climatologists Vol 1: 1193
American Association of State Colleges and Universities Vol 1: 1196
American Association of State Highway and Transportation Officials Vol 1: 1200
American Association of Suicidology Vol 1: 1206
American Association of Surgeon Assistants Vol 1: 1209
American Association of Teacher Educators in Agriculture Vol 1: 832
American Association of Teachers of Arabic Vol 1: 1211
American Association of Teachers of German Vol 1: 1214
American Association of Teachers of Spanish and Portuguese Vol 1: 1217
American Association of Textile Chemists and Colorists Vol 1: 1219
American Association of Theatre for Youth Vol 1: 765
American Association of University Administrators Vol 1: 1223
American Association of University Administrators Foundation Vol 1: 1226
American Association of University Professors Vol 1: 1228
American Association of University Women Educational Foundation Vol 1: 1233
American Association of Veterinary Laboratory Diagnosticians Vol 1: 1238
American Association of Wardens and Superintendents Vol 1: 15397
American Association of Zoo Keepers Vol 1: 1240
American Association of Zoological Parks and Aquariums Vol 1: 1244
American Association on Mental Deficiency Vol 1: 1249
American Association on Mental Retardation Vol 1: 1249
American Astronautical Society Vol 1: 1251
American Astronomical Society Vol 1: 1235, 1263
American Athletic Association for the Deaf Vol 1: 1279
American Auto Racing Writers and Broadcasters Association Vol 1: 1282
American Automatic Control Council Vol 1: 1285
American Award Manufacturers Association Vol 1: 6203
American Badminton Association Vol 1: 19033
American Ballet Competition Vol 1: 1290
American Bandmasters Association Vol 1: 1292
American Baptist Churches in the U.S.A. - National Ministries Vol 1: 1294
American Baptist Historical Society Vol 1: 1294
American Baptist Homes and Hospitals Association Vol 1: 1303
American Bar Association Vol 1: 1305
American Baseball Coaches Association Vol 1: 1314
American Bashkir Curly Registry Vol 1: 1326
American Basketball Association Vol 1: 13442
American Beefalo Association Vol 1: 1332
American Beefalo World Registry Vol 1: 1332
American Begonia Society Vol 1: 1336
American Billiard Association Vol 1: 19044
American Biological Society Vol 1: 1340

American Birding Association   Vol 1: 1342
American Bison Association   Vol 1: 1345
American Blade Collectors Association and *The Blade Magazine*   Vol 1: 10799
American Blind Bowling Association   Vol 1: 1347
American Board for Occupational Health Nurses, Inc.   Vol 1: 1349
American Board of Orthodontics   Vol 1: 1352
American Board of Professional Psychology   Vol 1: 1355
American Board of Psychological Hypnosis   Vol 1: 1357, 17436
American Booksellers Association   Vol 1: 1359
American Bottled Water Association   Vol 1: 10810
American Bowling Congress   Vol 1: 1365, 13472
American Breeders Service   Vol 1: 1914, 4403
American Bridge Teacher's Association   Vol 1: 1370
American Buffalo Association   Vol 1: 1345
American Bugatti Club   Vol 1: 1373
American Bureau of Shipping   Vol 1: 1375
American Burn Association   Vol 1: 1377
American Business Press   Vol 1: 1386
American Camellia Society   Vol 1: 1389
American Camping Association   Vol 1: 1402
American Cancer Society   Vol 1: 840, 1409
American Carbon Committee   Vol 1: 1416
American Carbon Society   Vol 1: 1416
American Cartographic Association   Vol 1: 1422
American Catholic Historical Association   Vol 1: 1430
American Catholic Historical Society   Vol 1: 1434, 2297
American Catholic Philosophical Association   Vol 1: 1436
American Center for Children's Television   Vol 1: 1439
American Center for Design   Vol 1: 1442
American Ceramic Society   Vol 1: 1445
American Chamber of Commerce Executives   Vol 1: 1479
American Chemical Society   Vol 1: 3461
American Chemical Society - Divisional Activities   Vol 1: 1481
American Chemical Society - Research, Grants, and Awards   Vol 1: 1517
American Chess Foundation   Vol 1: 1574
American Children's Television Festival   Vol 1: 1439
American Chinese Medical Society   Vol 1: 7641
American Chiropractic Association   Vol 1: 1577
American Choral Foundation   Vol 1: 7655
American Cinema Editors   Vol 1: 1579
The American Civil Defense Association   Vol 1: 1581
American Civil Liberties Union   Vol 1: 1584
American Civil Liberties Union of the National Capital Area   Vol 1: 1586
American Cleft Palate Education Foundation   Vol 1: 7831
American Cockatiel Society   Vol 1: 1589
American Collectors Association   Vol 1: 1591
American College Health Association   Vol 1: 1595
American College of Allergy & Immunology   Vol 1: 1602
American College of Angiology   Vol 1: 1604
American College of Apothecaries   Vol 1: 1606

American College of Cardiology   Vol 1: 1609
American College of Chest Physicians   Vol 1: 1616
American College of Clinical Pharmacology   Vol 1: 1622
American College of Dentists   Vol 1: 1628
American College of Emergency Physicians   Vol 1: 1633
American College of General Practitioners in Osteopathic Medicine and Surgery   Vol 1: 1639
American College of Health Care Administrators   Vol 1: 1642
American College of Healthcare Executives   Vol 1: 1654
American College of Hospital Administrators   Vol 1: 1654
American College of Legal Medicine   Vol 1: 1666
American College of Medical Practice Executives   Vol 1: 1670
American College of Musicians   Vol 1: 1677
American College of Neuropsychiatrists   Vol 1: 1679
American College of Neuropsychopharmacology   Vol 1: 1685
American College of Nurse-Midwives   Vol 1: 1694
American College of Nursing Home Administrators   Vol 1: 1642
American College of Occupational and Environmental Medicine   Vol 1: 1696
American College of Occupational Medicine   Vol 1: 1696
American College of Oral and Maxillofacial Surgeons, Inc.   Vol 1: 1702
American College of Osteopathic Hospital Administrators; American Osteopathic Hospital Association and   Vol 1: 3355
American College of Osteopathic Surgeons   Vol 1: 1706
American College of Physicians   Vol 1: 1712
American College of Preventive Medicine   Vol 1: 1725
American College of Psychiatrists   Vol 1: 1729
American College of Psychoanalysts   Vol 1: 1733
American College of Radiology   Vol 1: 1736
American College of Sports Medicine   Vol 1: 1741
American College of Surgeons   Vol 1: 1747
American College of Utilization Review Physicians   Vol 1: 1750
American College Testing (ACT)   Vol 1: 12586, 12587
American College Theatre Festival   Vol 1: 1753
American Collegiate Talent Showcase   Vol 1: 1763
American Community Theatre Association   Vol 1: 970
American Comparative Literature Association   Vol 1: 1768
American Composers Alliance   Vol 1: 1771
American Concrete Institute   Vol 1: 1773
American Concrete Pipe Association   Vol 1: 1792
American Conference of Government Industrial Hygienists   Vol 1: 1797
American Congress of Rehabilitation Medicine   Vol 1: 1802
American Congress on Surveying and Mapping   Vol 1: 1810
American Conservatives for Freedom   Vol 1: 1822
American Consular Association   Vol 1: 2084

American Consulting Engineers Council   Vol 1: 1824
American Contract Bridge League   Vol 1: 1827
American Coon Hunters Association   Vol 1: 1829
American Correctional Association   Vol 1: 1831
American Corrective Therapy Association   Vol 1: 2765
American Cotswold Record Association   Vol 1: 1837
American Council for Better Broadcasts   Vol 1: 14883
American Council for Polish Culture   Vol 1: 1840
American Council for the Arts   Vol 1: 16268
American Council of Christian Churches   Vol 1: 1842
American Council of Learned Societies   Vol 1: 1845
American Council of Polish Cultural Clubs   Vol 1: 1840
American Council of the Blind   Vol 1: 1847
American Council on Alcoholism   Vol 1: 1853
American Council on Consumer Interests   Vol 1: 1859
American Council on Education   Vol 1: 1865
American Council on Industrial Arts Teacher Education   Vol 1: 8410
American Council on the Teaching of Foreign Languages   Vol 1: 1868
American Counseling Association   Vol 1: 1877
American Craft Council   Vol 1: 1888
American Crossword Puzzle Tournament   Vol 1: 1893
American Crystallographic Association   Vol 1: 1895
American Culinary Federation   Vol 1: 14623
American Custom Publishing   Vol 1: 12141
American Cyanamid Company   Vol 1: 4395
American Czech and Slovak Association   Vol 1: 1902
American Dairy Science Association   Vol 1: 1904
American Dance Festival   Vol 1: 1926
American Dance Guild   Vol 1: 1930
American Darts Organization   Vol 1: 1932
American Deafness and Rehabilitation Association   Vol 1: 1935
American Defense Preparedness Association   Vol 1: 1940
American Dental Association   Vol 1: 1942
American Dental Hygienists' Association   Vol 1: 1945
American Design Drafting Association   Vol 1: 1947
American Diabetes Association   Vol 1: 1949
American Die Casting Institute   Vol 1: 15411
American Dietetic Association Foundation   Vol 1: 1956
American Documentation Institute   Vol 1: 4156
American Donkey and Mule Society   Vol 1: 1960
American Economic Association   Vol 1: 1966
American Economic Development Council   Vol 1: 1971
American Educational Research Association   Vol 1: 1973
American Electronics Association   Vol 1: 1981
American Electroplaters' and Surface Finishers Society   Vol 1: 1983
American Electroplaters' Society   Vol 1: 1983

American Endurance Ride Conference   Vol 1: 1990
American Enterprise Institute for Public Policy Research   Vol 1: 1996
American Equilibration Society   Vol 1: 1998
American Ethical Union   Vol 1: 2002
American Evaluation Association   Vol 1: 2004
American Ex-Prisoners of War   Vol 1: 2010
American Express   Vol 2: 4466, 9402, 9772
American Express Bank Ltd.   Vol 2: 2077
American Express Canada   Vol 1: 18768
American Express Company   Vol 1: 7905, 11670
American Express South Pacific Credit Card   Vol 2: 9700
American Family Society   Vol 1: 2014
American Family Therapy Academy   Vol 1: 2016
American Family Therapy Association   Vol 1: 2016
American Fancy Rat and Mouse Association   Vol 1: 2018
American Farm Bureau Federation   Vol 1: 2020
American Farm Economics Association   Vol 1: 748
American Federation for Aging Research   Vol 1: 2022
American Federation of Information Processing Societies   Vol 1: 2024
American Federation of Labor and Congress of Industrial Organizations   Vol 1: 2028
American Federation of Mineralogical Societies   Vol 1: 2030
American Federation of Police   Vol 1: 3548
American Federation of School Administrators   Vol 1: 2032
American Federation of Teachers   Vol 1: 16698
American Federation of Teachers, AFL-CIO   Vol 1: 2034
American Fiction   Vol 1: 2036
American Fighter Aces Association   Vol 1: 2038
American Film and Video Association   Vol 1: 2044
American Film Institute   Vol 1: 2049
American Film Institute Alumni Association Writers Workshop   Vol 1: 20563
American Finance Association   Vol 1: 2054
American First Day Cover Society   Vol 1: 2056
American Fisheries Society   Vol 1: 2060
American Fishing Tackle Manufacturers Association   Vol 1: 4847
American Folklore Society   Vol 1: 2070
American Football Coaches Association   Vol 1: 2073
American Forage and Grassland Council   Vol 1: 2077
American Foreign Law Association   Vol 1: 2082
American Foreign Service Association   Vol 1: 2084
American Forensic Association   Vol 1: 2091
American Forest and Paper Association - American Wood Council   Vol 1: 2093
American Forestry Association   Vol 1: 2095
American Foundation for Polish-Jewish Studies   Vol 1: 2105
American Foundation for the Blind   Vol 1: 2107
American Foundation for Urologic Disease   Vol 1: 2110
American Friends of the Hebrew University   Vol 1: 2116

American Fund for Alternatives to Animal Research   Vol 1: 2125
American Furniture Manufacturers Association   Vol 1: 18526
American Gas Association   Vol 1: 14696
American Gastroenterological Association   Vol 1: 2127
American Gastroenterological Association Foundation   Vol 1: 2127
American Gear Manufacturers Association   Vol 1: 2140
American Gem Society   Vol 1: 2145
American Gem Trade Association   Vol 1: 2147
American Geographical Society   Vol 1: 2150
American Geophysical Union   Vol 1: 2159
American Geriatrics Society   Vol 1: 2173
American Grandprix Association   Vol 1: 2185
American Greyhound Track Operators Association   Vol 1: 2189
American Group Psychotherapy Association   Vol 1: 2191
American Guild of Authors and Composers   Vol 1: 18141
American Guild of Organists   Vol 1: 2193
American Guild of Patient Account Management   Vol 1: 2198
American Gynecological and Obstetrical Society   Vol 1: 2205
American Gynecological Society   Vol 1: 2205
American Handwriting Analysis Foundation   Vol 1: 2208
American Health Care Association   Vol 1: 2211
American Health Foundation   Vol 1: 2216
American Healthcare Radiology Administrators   Vol 1: 2219
American Heart Association   Vol 1: 2221
American Helicopter Society   Vol 1: 2245
American Helvetia Philatelic Society   Vol 1: 2260
American Hemerocallis Society   Vol 1: 2262
American Heritage Publishing Company   Vol 1: 2268, 17695
American Hiking Society   Vol 1: 2271
American Historic Inns, Inc.   Vol 1: 2277
American Historical Association   Vol 1: 2279, 6905, 11857, 14155
American Historical Association, Pacific Coast Branch   Vol 1: 2300
American Historical Print Collectors Society, Inc.   Vol 1: 2303
American Hockey Coaches Association   Vol 1: 2306
American Hockey League   Vol 1: 2315
American Home Economics Association Foundation   Vol 1: 2335
American Homebrewers Association   Vol 1: 2343
American Horse Shows Association   Vol 1: 2345
American Horticultural Society   Vol 1: 2351
American Hospital Association   Vol 1: 2367, 4138, 5387
American Hospital Radiology Administrators   Vol 1: 2219
American Hospital Supply Corporation   Vol 1: 7197
American Hosta Society   Vol 1: 2376
American Hotel & Motel Association   Vol 1: 2390
American Humane Association   Vol 1: 2396
American Humanics   Vol 1: 2406
American Humanist Association   Vol 1: 2408
American Indian Ethnohistoric Conference   Vol 1: 4128

American Indian Heritage Foundation   Vol 1: 2416
American Indian Horse Registry   Vol 1: 2419
American Indian Lore Association   Vol 1: 2424
American Indian Science and Engineering Society   Vol 1: 2427
American Industrial Arts Student Association   Vol 1: 18603
American Industrial Hygiene Association   Vol 1: 2429
American Institute for Decision Sciences   Vol 1: 8565
American Institute for Design and Drafting   Vol 1: 1947
American Institute for Public Service   Vol 1: 2439
American Institute of Aeronautics and Astronautics   Vol 1: 2442, 17762, 17766, 17775, 18915
American Institute of Architects   Vol 1: 2517, 2906, 5746, 8092, 18532
American Institute of Architects - New York Chapter   Vol 1: 2548
American Institute of Architects Foundation   Vol 1: 2550
American Institute of Architects - *Sunset Magazine*   Vol 1: 18531
American Institute of Biological Sciences   Vol 1: 2552
American Institute of Building Design   Vol 1: 2555
American Institute of Certified Planners   Vol 1: 3529, 3530
American Institute of Certified Public Accountants   Vol 1: 2557
American Institute of Chemical Engineers   Vol 1: 2562, 4458, 4468, 4683, 18914
American Institute of Chemists   Vol 1: 2609
American Institute of Cooperation   Vol 1: 13734
American Institute of Fishery Research Biologists   Vol 1: 2617
American Institute of Graphic Arts   Vol 1: 2619
American Institute of Industrial Engineers   Vol 1: 10353
American Institute of Iranian Studies   Vol 1: 2624
American Institute of Landscape Architects   Vol 1: 4637
American Institute of Mechanical Engineers   Vol 1: 4694
American Institute of Merchant Shipping   Vol 1: 1376, 2626
American Institute of Mining, Metallurgical and Petroleum Engineers   Vol 1: 2631, 4458
American Institute of Mining, Metallurgical, and Petroleum Engineers   Vol 1: 4468
American Institute of Mining, Metallurgical and Petroleum Engineers   Vol 1: 4681, 18914, 20227
American Institute of Mining, Metallurgical and Petroleum Engineers; Iron and Steel Society of the   Vol 1: 11456
American Institute of Mining, Metallurgical and Petroleum Engineers; Society of Petroleum Engineers of the   Vol 1: 17958
American Institute of Musical Studies   Vol 1: 13336, 15727
American Institute of Nutrition   Vol 1: 2646
American Institute of Physics   Vol 1: 1268, 2655, 3457
American Institute of Planners   Vol 1: 3527
American Institute of Plant Engineers   Vol 1: 2667

American Institute of Professional Geologists   Vol 1: 2670
American Institute of Real Estate Appraisers   Vol 1: 5189
American Institute of Steel Construction   Vol 1: 2677
American Institute of Stress   Vol 1: 2683
American Institute of the History of Pharmacy   Vol 1: 2685
American Institute of Ultrasound in Medicine   Vol 1: 2689
American Intellectual Property Law Association   Vol 1: 2694
American Interior Designers   Vol 1: 4620
American International Checkers Society   Vol 1: 2698
American Intraocular Implant Society   Vol 1: 4413
American Iris Society   Vol 1: 2700
American Irish Historical Society   Vol 1: 2705
American Iron and Steel Institute   Vol 1: 2707
American Israel Numismatics Association   Vol 1: 2711
American Italian Historical Association   Vol 1: 2714
American Jersey Cattle Club   Vol 1: 2716
American Jewish Committee   Vol 1: 2721
American Jewish Congress   Vol 1: 2727
American Jewish Historical Society   Vol 1: 2737
American Jewish Press Association   Vol 1: 2744
American Jewish Public Relations Society   Vol 1: 2748
American Journal of International Law   Vol 1: 4630
American Journal of Nursing   Vol 1: 2750
American Journalism Review   Vol 1: 2754
American Judicature Society   Vol 1: 2756
American Junior Bowling Congress   Vol 1: 20598
American Junior Shorthorn Association   Vol 1: 2760
American Kennel Club   Vol 1: 4986
American Kidney Fund   Vol 1: 2762
American Kinesiotherapy Association   Vol 1: 2765
American Kitefliers Association   Vol 1: 2777
American Korean Foundation   Vol 1: 11036
American Laryngological Association   Vol 1: 2779
American Lawn Bowls Association   Vol 1: 2785
American Lawyers Auxiliary   Vol 1: 2788
American League of Professional Baseball Clubs   Vol 1: 2797
American Leather Chemists Association   Vol 1: 2799
American Legion   Vol 1: 2803
American Legion Auxiliary   Vol 1: 2806
American Legislative Exchange Council   Vol 1: 2808
American Library Association   Vol 1: 2519, 2810, 7618
American Library Association - American Association of School Librarians   Vol 1: 2826
American Library Association - American Library Trustee Association   Vol 1: 2836
American Library Association - Armed Forces Libraries Round Table   Vol 1: 2841
American Library Association - Association for Library Collections and Technical Services   Vol 1: 2845
American Library Association - Association for Library Service to Children   Vol 1: 2852
American Library Association - Association of College and Research Libraries   Vol 1: 2865

American Library Association - Association of Specialized and Cooperative Library Agencies   Vol 1: 2879
American Library Association - Children's Services Division   Vol 1: 2852
American Library Association - Ethnic Materials Information Exchange Round Table   Vol 1: 2886
American Library Association - Exhibits Round Table   Vol 1: 2888
American Library Association - Federal Librarians Round Table   Vol 1: 2890
American Library Association - Government Documents Round Table   Vol 1: 2893
American Library Association - Intellectual Freedom Round Table   Vol 1: 2897
American Library Association - International Relations Committee   Vol 1: 2901
American Library Association - Junior Members Round Table Staff Liaison   Vol 1: 2919
American Library Association - Library Administration and Management Association   Vol 1: 2904
American Library Association - Library and Information Technology Association   Vol 1: 2907
American Library Association - Library History Round Table   Vol 1: 2912
American Library Association - Library Research Round Table   Vol 1: 2915
American Library Association - Map and Geography Round Table   Vol 1: 2917
American Library Association - New Members Round Table   Vol 1: 2919
American Library Association - Office for Library Personnel Resources   Vol 1: 2922
American Library Association - Office for Research and Statistics   Vol 1: 2925
American Library Association - Public Library Association   Vol 1: 2927
American Library Association - Publishing Committee   Vol 1: 2935
American Library Association - Reference and Adult Services Division   Vol 1: 2938
American Library Association - Resources and Technical Services Division   Vol 1: 2845
American Library Association - Social Responsibilities Round Table   Vol 1: 2952
American Library Association - Young Adult Library Services Association   Vol 1: 2956
American Library Association - Young Adult Services Division   Vol 1: 2956
American Library Association, Gay and Lesbian Task Force   Vol 1: 2953
American Library Association, Public Information Office   Vol 1: 2961
American Liszt Society   Vol 1: 2963
American Literary Translators Association   Vol 1: 2965
American Lithuanian Roman Catholic Women's Alliance   Vol 1: 11907
American Lung Association   Vol 1: 2969
American Lupus Society   Vol 1: 2973
American Machinist   Vol 1: 2976
American Machinist and Automated Manufacturing   Vol 1: 2976
American Management Association   Vol 1: 2978
American Management Systems   Vol 1: 2980
American Marketing Association   Vol 1: 2982
American Marketing Association - Academy for Health Services Marketing   Vol 1: 2993
American Marketing Association/New York   Vol 1: 2997
American Mathematical Association of Two Year Colleges   Vol 1: 2999

American Mathematical Society   Vol 1: 3001, 12683, 17510, 17520
American Meat Institute   Vol 1: 3012
American Medical Association   Vol 1: 672, 3016
American Medical Athletic Association   Vol 1: 3028
American Medical Joggers Association   Vol 1: 3028
American Medical Record Association   Vol 1: 3030
American Medical Technologists   Vol 1: 3035
American Medical Women's Association   Vol 1: 3048
American Medical Writers Association   Vol 1: 3055
American Mental Health Counselors Association   Vol 1: 3063
American Merchant Marine Library Association   Vol 1: 3067
American Meteorological Society   Vol 1: 3069
American MGB Association   Vol 1: 3099
American MGC Register   Vol 1: 3101
American Military Institute   Vol 1: 17553
American Milking Shorthorn Society   Vol 1: 3103
American Mining Congress   Vol 1: 3115
American Mizrachi Women   Vol 1: 5131
American Model Soldier Society and American Military Historical Society   Vol 1: 3118
American Morgan Horse Association   Vol 1: 3120
American Mosquito Control Association   Vol 1: 3128
American Mothers   Vol 1: 3137
American Mothers Committee   Vol 1: 3137
American Motion Picture Society   Vol 1: 3142
American Motorcyclist Association   Vol 1: 3145
American Movers Conference   Vol 1: 3148
American Museum of Natural History   Vol 1: 3151
American Music Awards   Vol 1: 3156
American Music Center   Vol 1: 3158
American Music Conference   Vol 1: 3160
American Music Scholarship Association   Vol 1: 3163
American Musical Instrument Society   Vol 1: 3165
American Musical Theater Festival   Vol 1: 3169
American Musicological Society   Vol 1: 3171
American National Standards Institute   Vol 1: 3177
American Nature Study Society   Vol 1: 3184
American Needlepoint Guild   Vol 1: 3186
American Network of Community Options and Resources   Vol 1: 3188
American Newspaper Publishers Association Foundation   Vol 1: 15352
American North Country Cheviot Sheep Association   Vol 1: 3195
American Nuclear Society   Vol 1: 19074, 20227
American Numismatic Association   Vol 1: 3197
American Numismatic Society   Vol 1: 3273
American Nurses' Association   Vol 1: 3279
American Nurses Foundation   Vol 1: 3290
American Occupational Medical Association   Vol 1: 1696
American Occupational Therapy Association   Vol 1: 3294
American Occupational Therapy Foundation   Vol 1: 3307
American Oil Chemists' Society   Vol 1: 3309

American Ophthalmological Society   Vol 1: 3317
American Optical Company   Vol 1: 15758
American Optical Corporation   Vol 1: 15747
American Optometric Association   Vol 1: 3319
American Optometric Foundation   Vol 1: 639
American Orchid Society   Vol 1: 3323
American Ornithologists' Union   Vol 1: 3344
American Orthopaedic Society for Sports Medicine   Vol 1: 3347
American Osteopathic Academy of Orthopedics   Vol 1: 3350
American Osteopathic College of Pathologists   Vol 1: 3353
American Osteopathic Healthcare Association and College of Osteopathic Healthcare Executives   Vol 1: 3355
American Osteopathic Hospital Association and American College of Osteopathic Hospital Administrators   Vol 1: 3355
American Otological Society   Vol 1: 3358
American Park and Recreation Society   Vol 1: 3361
American Parkinson Disease Association   Vol 1: 3364
American Patent Law Association   Vol 1: 2694
American Pediatric Society   Vol 1: 3366
American Petanque Association U.S.A.   Vol 1: 9156
American Petroleum Institute   Vol 1: 3368
American Pharmaceutical Association   Vol 1: 3370
American Pharmaceutical Association - Academy of Pharmacy Practice and Management   Vol 1: 3387
American Pharmaceutical Association - Academy of Students of Pharmacy   Vol 1: 3393
American Pharmaseal Corporation   Vol 1: 5577
American Philatelic Association   Vol 1: 3410
American Philatelic Congress   Vol 1: 3399
American Philatelic Society   Vol 1: 3410
American Philatelic Society Writers Unit Junior Division   Vol 1: 11631
American Philological Association   Vol 1: 3415
American Philosophical Association   Vol 1: 3418
American Philosophical Society   Vol 1: 3429
American Photographic Historical Society   Vol 1: 3439
American Physical Society   Vol 1: 3441
American Physical Therapy Association   Vol 1: 3474
American Physical Therapy Association - Private Practice Sector   Vol 1: 3494
American Physician's Art Association   Vol 1: 3496
American Physiological Society   Vol 1: 3498
American Phytopathological Society   Vol 1: 3516, 7094, 7685
American Pianists Association   Vol 1: 3525
American Pigeon Journal   Vol 1: 14469
American Planning Association   Vol 1: 3527
American Plant Life Society   Vol 1: 10816
American Plywood Association   Vol 1: 5742
American Podiatric Medical Association   Vol 1: 3544
American Podiatry Association   Vol 1: 3544
American Poetry Association   Vol 1: 3546
American Police Hall of Fame   Vol 1: 3548
American Political Science Association   Vol 1: 3566, 8173, 12698
American Political Science Association - Legislative Studies Section   Vol 1: 3587

American Political Science Association - Urban Politics and Urban Policy Section   Vol 1: 3589
American Pomological Society   Vol 1: 3594
American Poultry Historical Society - Watt Publishing Co.   Vol 1: 3598
American Power Boat Association   Vol 1: 3601
American Primrose Society   Vol 1: 3607
American Printed Fabrics Council   Vol 1: 3609
American Printing History Association   Vol 1: 3611
American Probation and Parole Association   Vol 1: 3614
American Protestant Health Association; College of Chaplains of the   Vol 1: 7914
American Psychiatric Association   Vol 1: 3620
American Psychological Association   Vol 1: 3657, 5658
American Psychological Association - Adult Development and Aging Division   Vol 1: 3677
American Psychological Association - American Psycholog-Law Society Division   Vol 1: 3680
American Psychological Association - Applied, Experimental and Engineering Psychology Division   Vol 1: 3683
American Psychological Association - Child, Youth, and Family Services Division   Vol 1: 3686
American Psychological Association - Clinical Psychology Division   Vol 1: 3689
American Psychological Association - Community Psychology Division   Vol 1: 3837
American Psychological Association - Consulting Psychology Division   Vol 1: 3700
American Psychological Association - Counseling Psychology Division   Vol 1: 3704
American Psychological Association - Developmental Psychology Division   Vol 1: 3710
American Psychological Association - Division of Independent Practice   Vol 1: 3712
American Psychological Association - Division of Psychopharmacology and Substance Abuse   Vol 1: 3715
American Psychological Association - Educational Psychology Division   Vol 1: 3719
American Psychological Association - Evaluation, Measurement, and Statistics Division   Vol 1: 3723
American Psychological Association - Excercise and Sport Psychology Division   Vol 1: 3725
American Psychological Association - Experimental Analysis of Behavior Division   Vol 1: 3727
American Psychological Association - Family Psychology Division   Vol 1: 3729
American Psychological Association - General Psychology Division   Vol 1: 3733
American Psychological Association - Health Psychology Division   Vol 1: 3735
American Psychological Association - History of Psychology Division   Vol 1: 3737
American Psychological Association - Media Psychology   Vol 1: 3739
American Psychological Association - Mental Retardation and Developmental Disabilities Division   Vol 1: 3743
American Psychological Association - Military Psychology Division   Vol 1: 3745
American Psychological Association - Peace Psychology Division   Vol 1: 3749

American Psychological Association - Physiological and Comparative Psychology Division   Vol 1: 3751
American Psychological Association - Population and Environmental Psychology Division   Vol 1: 3753
American Psychological Association - Psychological Hypnosis Division   Vol 1: 3755
American Psychological Association - Psychologists in Public Service Division   Vol 1: 3761
American Psychological Association - Psychologists Interested in Religious Issues Division   Vol 1: 3764
American Psychological Association - Psychology and the Arts Division   Vol 1: 3767
American Psychological Association - Psychology of Women Division   Vol 1: 3770
American Psychological Association - Psychotherapy Division   Vol 1: 3776
American Psychological Association - Rehabilitation Psychology Division   Vol 1: 3780
American Psychological Association - School Psychology Division   Vol 1: 3783
American Psychological Association - Society for Community Research and Action: Division of Community Psychology   Vol 1: 3786
American Psychological Association - Society for Consumer Psychology Division   Vol 1: 3792
American Psychological Association - Society for Industrial and Organizational Psychology   Vol 1: 3795
American Psychological Association - Society for Personality and Social Psychology Division   Vol 1: 3803
American Psychological Association - Society for Psychological Study of Lesbian and Gay Issues Division   Vol 1: 3806
American Psychological Association - Society for the Psychological Study of Social Issues   Vol 1: 3812
American Psychological Association - Society of Experimental Psychologists   Vol 1: 3816
American Psychological Association - State Psychological Association Affairs Division   Vol 1: 3819
American Psychological Association - Teaching of Psychology Division   Vol 1: 3823
American Psychological Association - Theoretical and Philosophical Psychology Division   Vol 1: 3825
American Psychological Association of Graduate Students   Vol 1: 3670
American Psychological Asssociation - Psychoanalysis Division   Vol 1: 3827
American Psychological Foundation   Vol 1: 3672, 3830
American Psychopathological Association   Vol 1: 3838
American Public Gas Association   Vol 1: 3841
American Public Health Association   Vol 1: 3844
American Public Power Association   Vol 1: 3851
American Public Welfare Association   Vol 1: 3865
American Public Works Association   Vol 1: 3871
American Radio Relay League   Vol 1: 3885
American Radio Theatre   Vol 1: 3896
American Radium Society   Vol 1: 3899
American Railway Development Association   Vol 1: 3903
American Recorder Society   Vol 1: 3905
American Red Cross   Vol 1: 3908

American Red Magen David for Israel   Vol 1: 3930
American Rehabilitation Association   Vol 1: 3932
American Revolution Round Table   Vol 1: 3948
American Rhinologic Society   Vol 1: 3951
American Rhododenron Society   Vol 1: 3955
American Riding Instructor Certification Program   Vol 1: 3958
American Risk and Insurance Association   Vol 1: 3960
American Road & Transportation Builders Association   Vol 1: 3965
American Road Builders Association   Vol 1: 3965
American Roentgen Ray Society   Vol 1: 1740
American Romanian Academy of Arts and Science   Vol 1: 3975
American Rose Society   Vol 1: 3977
American Rottweiler Club   Vol 1: 3979
American Rural Health Association   Vol 1: 14648
American Safety Video Publishers   Vol 1: 13099
American Saluki Association   Vol 1: 3983
American-Scandinavian Foundation   Vol 1: 3985
American School and Community Safety Association   Vol 1: 16981
American School and University   Vol 1: 3989
American School Food Service Association   Vol 1: 3993
American School Health Association   Vol 1: 4002
American Schools of Oriental Research   Vol 1: 4008
American Scientific Glassblowers Society   Vol 1: 4021
American Shetland Pony Club   Vol 1: 4025
American Sleep Disorders Association   Vol 1: 4027
American Social Science Association   Vol 1: 14239
American Society for Adolescent Psychiatry   Vol 1: 4029
American Society for Advancement of Anesthesia in Dentistry   Vol 1: 4034
American Society for Biochemistry and Molecular Biology   Vol 1: 4037
American Society for Bone and Mineral Research   Vol 1: 4044
American Society for Cell Biology   Vol 1: 4049
American Society for Clinical Nutrition   Vol 1: 4051
American Society for Clinical Pharmacology and Therapeutics   Vol 1: 4055
American Society for Cybernetics   Vol 1: 4060
American Society for Eighteenth-Century Studies   Vol 1: 799, 4064
American Society for Engineering Education   Vol 1: 4067
American Society for Enology and Viticulture   Vol 1: 4125
American Society for Ethnohistory   Vol 1: 4128
American Society for Experimental Pathology   Vol 1: 4177
American Society for Gastrointestinal Endoscopy   Vol 1: 4131
American Society for Health Care Marketing and Public Relations   Vol 1: 4137
American Society for Healthcare Education and Training   Vol 1: 4139

American Society for Horticultural Science   Vol 1: 4143
American Society for Hospital Marketing and Public Relations   Vol 1: 4137
American Society for Hospital Materials Management   Vol 1: 4154
American Society for Information Science   Vol 1: 4156
American Society for Investigative Pathology   Vol 1: 4177
American Society for Laser Medicine and Surgery   Vol 1: 4182
American Society for Legal History   Vol 1: 4184
American Society for Medical Technology   Vol 1: 4187
American Society for Metals   Vol 1: 5348, 12319
American Society for Microbiology   Vol 1: 4196, 19341
American Society for Nondestructive Testing   Vol 1: 4213
American Society for Parenteral and Enteral Nutrition   Vol 1: 4226
American Society for Personnel Administration   Vol 1: 17479
American Society for Pharmacology and Experimental Therapeutics   Vol 1: 4230
American Society for Photogrammetry and Remote Sensing   Vol 1: 4239
American Society for Psychoprophylaxis in Obstetrics   Vol 1: 5378
American Society for Public Administration   Vol 1: 4262, 9678, 12652, 13300
American Society for Public Administration - Section for Women in Public Administration   Vol 1: 4275
American Society for Quality Control   Vol 1: 4279, 19110
American Society for Surface Mining & Reclamation   Vol 1: 4289
American Society for Technion - Israel Institute of Technology   Vol 2: 7945
American Society for Testing and Materials   Vol 1: 6031
American Society for the Prevention of Cruelty to Animals   Vol 1: 4294
American Society for Theatre Research   Vol 1: 4296
American Society for Therapeutic Radiology and Oncology   Vol 1: 1740
American Society for Training and Development   Vol 1: 4299
American Society for Training and Development - Career Development Professional Practice Area   Vol 1: 4306
American Society for Training and Development - Council of Industry Groups   Vol 1: 4310
American Society for Training and Development - Council of Networks   Vol 1: 4312
American Society for Training and Development - Council of Regions and Chapters   Vol 1: 4314
American Society for Training and Development - Instructional Technology Professional Practice Area   Vol 1: 4316
American Society for Training and Development - International Professional Practice Area   Vol 1: 4319
American Society for Training and Development - Management Development Professional Practice Area   Vol 1: 4326
American Society for Training and Development - Mind/Brain Network   Vol 1: 4328

American Society for Training and Development - Multicultural Network   Vol 1: 4331
American Society for Training and Development - Organization Development Professional Practice Area   Vol 1: 4337
American Society for Training and Development - Quality of Work Life/Employee Involvement Network   Vol 1: 4339
American Society for Training and Development - Sales & Marketing Professional Practice Area   Vol 1: 4342
American Society for Training and Development - Technical and Skills Training Professional Practice Area   Vol 1: 4345
American Society for Training and Development - Women's Network   Vol 1: 4347
American Society of Abdominal Surgery   Vol 1: 4349
American Society of Agricultural Engineers   Vol 1: 4352, 8496
American Society of Agronomy   Vol 1: 4375, 7686, 18136
American Society of Animal Science   Vol 1: 4390
American Society of Artists   Vol 1: 4404
American Society of Association Executives   Vol 1: 4407
American Society of Biological Chemists   Vol 1: 4037
American Society of Business Press Editors   Vol 1: 4410
American Society of Cataract and Refractive Surgery   Vol 1: 4413
American Society of Certified Engineering Technicians   Vol 1: 4416
American Society of Church History   Vol 1: 4424
American Society of Civil Engineering   Vol 1: 4430
American Society of Civil Engineers   Vol 1: 4430, 18914, 20227
American Society of Clinical Pathologists   Vol 1: 4513
American Society of Composers, Authors and Publishers   Vol 1: 4522, 7654
American Society of Contemporary Artists   Vol 1: 4531
American Society of Contemporary Medicine and Surgery   Vol 1: 4534
American Society of Contemporary Medicine, Surgery and Ophthalmology   Vol 1: 4534
American Society of Contemporary Ophthalmology   Vol 1: 4534
American Society of Criminology   Vol 1: 4540
American Society of Cytology   Vol 1: 4545
American Society of Dentistry for Children   Vol 1: 4552
American Society of Electroencephalographic Technologists   Vol 1: 4554
American Society of Electroneurodiagnostic Technologists   Vol 1: 4554
American Society of Enologists   Vol 1: 4125
American Society of Farm Managers and Rural Appraisers   Vol 1: 4556
The American Society of Farm Managers and Rural Appraisers   Vol 1: 13029
American Society of Furniture Designers   Vol 1: 4561
American Society of Genealogists   Vol 1: 4565
American Society of Heating, Refrigerating and Air-Conditioning Engineers   Vol 1: 4567
American Society of Hematology   Vol 1: 4592
American Society of Hospital Pharmacists   Vol 1: 4598

American Society of Hospital Pharmacists Research and Education Foundation   Vol 1: 4602
American Society of Human Genetics   Vol 1: 4610
American Society of Ichthyologists and Herpetologists   Vol 1: 4612
American Society of Indexers   Vol 1: 4618
American Society of Interior Designers   Vol 1: 4620, 10569
American Society of International Law   Vol 1: 4628
American Society of Journalism School Administrators   Vol 1: 5952
American Society of Journalists and Authors   Vol 1: 4632
American Society of Landscape Architects   Vol 1: 4637
American Society of Law and Medicine   Vol 1: 4649
American Society of Limnology and Oceanography   Vol 1: 4651
American Society of Lubrication Engineers   Vol 1: 18078
American Society of Magazine Editors   Vol 1: 4654
American Society of Mammalogists   Vol 1: 4656
American Society of Mechanical Engineers   Vol 1: 2979, 4458, 4468, 4664, 17762, 17775, 18915, 20227
American Society of Mechanical Engineers - Gas Turbine Division   Vol 1: 4716
American Society of Mechanical Engineers - International Gas Turbine Institute   Vol 1: 4716
American Society of Music Arrangers   Vol 1: 4721
American Society of Naturalists   Vol 1: 4724
American Society of Naval Engineers   Vol 1: 4728
American Society of Neuroimaging   Vol 1: 4735
American Society of Newspaper Editors   Vol 1: 4738
American Society of Oral Surgeons   Vol 1: 1083
American Society of Parasitologists   Vol 1: 4741
American Society of Pharmacognosy   Vol 1: 3384, 4743
American Society of Photogrammetry   Vol 1: 4239
American Society of Physician Analysts   Vol 1: 4775
American Society of Planning Officials   Vol 1: 3527
American Society of Plant Physiologists   Vol 1: 4745
American Society of Plant Taxonomists   Vol 1: 4752, 6478
American Society of Plastic and Reconstructive Surgeons   Vol 1: 4756
American Society of Plastic and Reconstructive Surgeons - Plastic Surgery Educational Foundation   Vol 1: 4765
American Society of Podiatric Dermatology   Vol 1: 4771
American Society of Podiatric Medicine   Vol 1: 4773
American Society of Psychoanalytic Physicians   Vol 1: 4775
American Society of Psychopathology of Expression   Vol 1: 4777
American Society of Safety Engineers   Vol 1: 4779

American Society of Sanitary Engineering   Vol 1: 4789
American Society of Swedish Engineers   Vol 1: 4793
American Society of Traffic and Transportation   Vol 1: 4797
American Society of Transportation and Logistics   Vol 1: 4797
American Society of Travel Agents   Vol 1: 4805
American Society of Tropical Medicine and Hygiene   Vol 1: 4811
American Society of Ultrasound Technical Specialists   Vol 1: 17444
American Society of Zoologists   Vol 1: 4817
American Society on Aging   Vol 1: 4820
American Sociological Association   Vol 1: 4826
American Solar Energy Society   Vol 1: 4834
American Spectator   Vol 1: 4836
American Speech and Hearing Association   Vol 1: 4838
American Speech-Language-Hearing Association   Vol 1: 4838
American Spelean Historical Association   Vol 1: 14850
American Spice Trade Association   Vol 1: 4843
American Spinal Injury Association   Vol 1: 4845
American Sport Fishing Association   Vol 1: 4847
American Sportscasters Association   Vol 1: 4851
American Statistical Association   Vol 1: 4859
American Steamship and Tourist Agents Association   Vol 1: 4805
American Sterilizer Company   Vol 1: 10739
American String Teachers Association   Vol 1: 4866
American Studies Association   Vol 1: 4871
American Supplier Institute   Vol 1: 4878
American Swimming Coaches Association   Vol 1: 4880
American Symphony Orchestra   Vol 1: 4888
American Symphony Orchestra League   Vol 1: 4890
American Telemarketing Association   Vol 1: 4894
American Telephone and Telegraph Company   Vol 1: 12664
American Theatre Organ Society   Vol 1: 4896
American Theatre Wing   Vol 1: 4900, 11810
American Therapeutic Recreation Association   Vol 1: 4903
American Thyroid Association   Vol 1: 4905
American Tolkien Society   Vol 1: 4911
American Topical Association   Vol 1: 4913
American Translators Association   Vol 1: 4916
American Truck Historical Society   Vol 1: 4921
American Trucking Association   Vol 1: 4924
American Trucking Associations - National Accounting and Finance Council   Vol 1: 4932
American Trucking Associations - National Freight Claim and Security Council   Vol 1: 4935
American Tunaboat Association   Vol 1: 4937
American TV Commercials Festival   Vol 1: 15111
American Underground Association   Vol 1: 4939
American Underground-Space Association   Vol 1: 4939
American University - Department of Communications   Vol 1: 4944

American University - School of Communication   Vol 1: 4944
American University - School of Communication, ICI Education Foundation   Vol 1: 4946
American University - School of Public Affairs   Vol 1: 4948
American Urological Association   Vol 1: 4950
American Vacuum Society   Vol 1: 4958
American Vaulting Association   Vol 1: 4969
American Veterinary Epidemiology Society   Vol 1: 4971
American Veterinary Exhibitors Association   Vol 1: 4975
American Veterinary Medical Association   Vol 1: 4977, 9464
American Vocational Association   Vol 1: 4990
American Vocational Association/Motor Vehicle Manufacturers Association Industry Planning Council   Vol 1: 4993
American Water Resources Association   Vol 1: 4998
American Water Ski Association   Vol 1: 5009
American Water Works Association   Vol 1: 5011
American Watercolor Society   Vol 1: 5034
American Welding Society   Vol 1: 5069
American-Whig-Cliosophic Society   Vol 1: 5098
American Wine Society   Vol 1: 5100
American Women in Radio and Television   Vol 1: 5108
Americanism Educational League   Vol 1: 5112
Americans for a Sound AIDS/HIV Policy   Vol 1: 5114
Americans for Constitutional Action   Vol 1: 5116
Americans for Energy Independence   Vol 1: 5118
America's Cup Organizing Committee   Vol 1: 5120
America's Junior Miss Pagent   Vol 1: 5122
Americas Society   Vol 1: 5124
America's Young Woman of the Year   Vol 1: 5122
America's Youth on Parade   Vol 1: 5127
Ames Foundation for Investigation in the Field of Basic Health Science   Vol 2: 1580
AMF   Vol 1: 13002
Amgen   Vol 1: 15651
Amie de l'Orgue   Vol 2: 5107
Amiens International Film Festival   Vol 2: 4889
Amis de la Reliure d'Art   Vol 2: 4891
Amis d'Escoffier Society   Vol 1: 5129
AMIT Women   Vol 1: 5131
Amities Acadiennes   Vol 2: 4893
AMK Berlin, Ausstellungs - Messe - Kongress   Vol 2: 6518
AMK Berlin, Company for Exhibitions, Fairs and Congresses   Vol 2: 6518
Amoco Chemical Company   Vol 1: 18044
Amoco Foundation   Vol 1: 1539
Amoco Oil Company   Vol 1: 7341
Amsterdam Foundation for History   Vol 2: 9594
Amsterdam Foundation for Medicine   Vol 2: 9595
Amsterdam Foundation for the Environment   Vol 2: 9596
Amt der Niederosterreichischen Landesregierung, Kulturabteilung   Vol 2: 858
Amt der o.o. Landesregierung   Vol 2: 900
Amt der Salzburger Landesregierung - Kulturabteilung   Vol 2: 722

Amt der Tiroler Landesregierung, Kulturabteilung   Vol 2: 725
Amusement & Music Operators Association   Vol 1: 5138
AMVETS National Headquarters   Vol 1: 5142
Amy Foundation   Vol 1: 5146
ANAD - National Association of Anorexia Nervosa and Associated Disorders   Vol 1: 5148
Anaren Microwave, Inc.   Vol 1: 4118
Anatomical Society   Vol 2: 6520
Anatomische Gesellschaft   Vol 2: 6520
Ancient & Medieval History Book Club   Vol 2: 2245
Anda Audience Prize; Geza   Vol 2: 11676
Anda Foundation; Geza   Vol 2: 11676
Andersen Awards in Association with *The Times*; ABSA/Arthur   Vol 2: 2029
Anderson Cancer Center; M. D.   Vol 1: 19874
Anderson Production Company; J. Morris   Vol 1: 5152
Angel Escobar Foundation; Alejandro   Vol 2: 1582
Angel Hotel   Vol 2: 2079
Anglo-Austrian Music Society   Vol 2: 2081
Angolan Writers Union   Vol 2: 3
Anhinga Press   Vol 1: 5154
Animal Air Transportation Association   Vol 1: 5163
Animal Behavior Society   Vol 1: 5157
Animal Health Trust   Vol 2: 2083
Animal Protection Institute   Vol 1: 5161
Animal Protection Institute of America   Vol 1: 5161
Animal Transportation Association   Vol 1: 5163
Animal Welfare Institute   Vol 1: 5168
Animation Celebration   Vol 1: 5170
Ann Arbor Film Festival   Vol 1: 5173
Ann White Theatre   Vol 1: 20266
Annenberg Research Institute   Vol 1: 7438
Annual Reviews Inc.   Vol 1: 12678
Anrhydeddus Gymdeithas y Cymmrodorion   Vol 2: 3022
Antarjatik Beshamarik Sheba Sangstha   Vol 2: 931
Anthony Center for Women's Studies; Susan B.   Vol 1: 19866
Anthony J. Jannetti, Inc.   Vol 1: 13218, 15645
Anthropology Society of Paris   Vol 2: 4895
Anti-Defamation League of B'nai B'rith   Vol 1: 5175
Antioquia Society of Tourism   Vol 2: 1585
Antiquarian Field Club   Vol 2: 2748
Anuvrat Global Organization   Vol 2: 7483
Anuvrat Vishva Bharati (Anuvibha)   Vol 2: 7483
Anvil Press   Vol 1: 5183
ANZIAM-Australian and New Zealand Industrial and Applied Mathematics - Australian Mathematical Society   Vol 2: 121
AOAC International   Vol 1: 5185
APA Committee on Ethnic Minority Affairs   Vol 1: 3658
APA Committee on Gay and Lesbian Concerns   Vol 1: 3674
APA Committee on International Relations in Psychology   Vol 1: 3664
APA Committee on Women in Psychology   Vol 1: 3671
Apalachee Poetry Center   Vol 1: 5154
Apotekarsocieteten   Vol 2: 11614
Apothecaries Hall of Dublin   Vol 2: 7752
Appalachian Center   Vol 1: 6331
Appeal of Conscience Foundation   Vol 1: 5187
Applied Information Marketing   Vol 1: 8626

Appraisal Institute   Vol 1: 5189
Appraisal Institute Educational Trust   Vol 1: 5201
APPROTECH ASIA   Vol 2: 10058
APV-BAKER   Vol 2: 9714
Aquatic Hall of Fame and Museum of Canada   Vol 1: 5203
Arab Federation for Food Industries   Vol 2: 7744
Arab Towns Organization   Vol 2: 8839
Arango Design Foundation   Vol 1: 5205
Arbeitsgemeinschaft Europaischer Chorverbande   Vol 2: 9476
Arbeitsgemeinschaft fur Osterreichische Qualitatsarbeit   Vol 2: 747
Arbeitsgemeinschaft Schweizer Grafiker   Vol 2: 11903
Arbeitskreis fur Jugendliteratur   Vol 2: 6832
Arboricultural Association   Vol 2: 2088
The Arc   Vol 1: 5207
Arcane Order   Vol 1: 5221
Archaeological Institute of America   Vol 1: 5224
Architect's Journal   Vol 2: 2215
Architectural Association   Vol 2: 2091
Architectural League of New York   Vol 1: 5229
Architectural Record   Vol 1: 5232
Archival Association   Vol 2: 4662
Arcos Corporation   Vol 1: 5094
Arctic Institute of North America   Vol 1: 5235
Argentina - Ministry of Education and Justice   Vol 2: 20
Argentine Book Chamber   Vol 2: 25
Argentine Paleontological Association   Vol 2: 27
Argentine Society of Authors   Vol 2: 29
Argentinian Association of Dermatology   Vol 2: 32
Ari Foundation; Carina   Vol 2: 11441
Ari Stiftelsen; Carina   Vol 2: 11441
Aril Society International   Vol 1: 5237
Arisawa Memorial Fund; Hiroma   Vol 1: 5698
Aristech Chemical Corporation   Vol 1: 2593
Arizona Authors' Association   Vol 1: 5240
Arizona School for the Deaf & Blind   Vol 1: 8117
Arizona State Library Association   Vol 1: 5242
Arkansas Arts Center   Vol 1: 5253
Arkansas Elementary School Council - Arkansas Department of Education   Vol 1: 5256
Arkansas Historical Association   Vol 1: 5258
Arkansas Women's History Institute   Vol 1: 5261
Arkistoyhdistys r.y.   Vol 2: 4662
Arlen Memorial Fund; Stephen   Vol 2: 2095
ARMA International   Vol 1: 5934
Armed Forces Communications and Electronics Association   Vol 1: 5263
Armed Forces Military Association   Vol 1: 5267
Armemuseum   Vol 2: 11469
Armenian General Benevolent Union, Central Committee of America   Vol 1: 5269
Armstrong Memorial Research Foundation   Vol 1: 5271
Armstrong Siddeley Sapphire Owners Club   Vol 2: 2097
Arnold Air Society   Vol 1: 5273
Art and Education Foundation   Vol 2: 9332
Art Dealers Association of America   Vol 1: 5288
Art Direction Book Company   Vol 1: 5290
Art Directors Club, Inc.   Vol 1: 5292
Art Directors Club of Toronto   Vol 1: 151

Art Gallery of New South Wales   Vol 2: 123
Art Institute of Chicago   Vol 1: 5296
Art Libraries Society of North America   Vol 1: 5298
Art Society   Vol 2: 6522
Arte in Piazza   Vol 2: 8097
Arthritis Foundation   Vol 1: 5301
Arthroscopy Association of North America   Vol 1: 5306
Artisjus, Hungarian Organization for Defence of Copyright   Vol 2: 7371
Artists Association International   Vol 1: 5309
Artists Association of Finland   Vol 2: 4664
Artists' Fellowship   Vol 1: 5311
Artists International Presentations, Inc.   Vol 1: 5315
The Artist's Magazine   Vol 1: 5317
Arts & Crafts Exhibition Society   Vol 2: 4428
Arts & Science Center for Southeast Arkansas   Vol 1: 5319
Arts Council An Chomhairle Ealaion   Vol 2: 7754
Arts Council Council of Wales   Vol 2: 12149
Arts Council for Chautauqua County   Vol 1: 7529
Arts Council of Great Britain   Vol 2: 2099, 3826
Arts Council of Northern Ireland   Vol 2: 7853, 7856
Arts Council of Nothern Ireland   Vol 2: 7857
Arts Council of the Republic of Ireland   Vol 2: 7856, 7857
Arts Education Policy Review   Vol 1: 5321
Arts Encouragement Foundation   Vol 2: 9334
Arts Extension Service   Vol 1: 5324
Arts Foundation of Greater Toronto   Vol 1: 5326
Arts Guild of Old Forge   Vol 1: 5330
Arts Management   Vol 1: 5332
Arts Management Pty Limited   Vol 2: 126
Arts Midwest   Vol 1: 5336
Arvon Foundation   Vol 2: 2102
Asahi Breweries   Vol 2: 8770
Asahi Broadcasting Corporation   Vol 2: 8525
Asahi Glass Foundation   Vol 2: 8485
Asahi Shimbun Publishing Company   Vol 2: 8487, 8494, 11768
Asamblea de Directores-Realizadores Cinematograficos y Audiovisuales Espanoles (ADIRCAE)   Vol 2: 11139
Asbury Graphite Mills   Vol 1: 1417
ASC Committee on Corporation Associates   Vol 1: 1520
ASCAP Foundation   Vol 1: 4528
ASEE/ERM   Vol 1: 4119
Ashland Chemicals Inc.   Vol 1: 18044
Ashton-Drake Galleries   Vol 1: 5338
Asia Pacific Academy of Ophthalmology   Vol 2: 10727
Asia-Pacific Broadcasting Union   Vol 2: 8887
Asia/Pacific Cultural Centre for UNESCO   Vol 2: 8497
Asian American Journalists Association   Vol 1: 5340
Asian American Psychological Association   Vol 1: 5342
Asian Association of Occupational Health   Vol 2: 10731
Asian Cultural Centre for UNESCO   Vol 2: 8497
Asian Cultural Council   Vol 1: 5344
Asian Football Confederation   Vol 2: 8891
Asian Institute of Technology   Vol 2: 12016
Asian NGO Coalition for Agrarian Reform and Rural Development   Vol 2: 10019
Asian/Pacific American Librarians Association   Vol 1: 5346

Asian-Pacific Weed Science Society   Vol 2: 10021
Asian Parasite Control Organization   Vol 2: 8501
Asian Productivity Organization   Vol 2: 8503
Asiaweek Limited   Vol 2: 7261
ASIFA—Hollywood   Vol 1: 10603
Asistencia Reciproca Petrolera Estatal Latin   Vol 2: 12091
ASM International   Vol 1: 5348
Asociacion Amigos de Arco   Vol 2: 11141
Asociacion Amigos del Teatro Nacional Cervantes de Buenos Aires   Vol 2: 11363
Asociacion Argentina de Dermatologia   Vol 2: 32
Asociacion Colombiana de Bibliotecarios   Vol 2: 1685
Asociacion Colombiana de Personas Impedidas   Vol 2: 1683
Asociacion Colombiana de Universidades ASCUN   Vol 2: 1757
Asociacion Colombiana para el Avance de la Ciencia   Vol 2: 1680
Asociacion de Periodistas Universitarias   Vol 2: 8921
Asociacion de Reporteros Graficos de los Diarios de Mexico   Vol 2: 8923
Asociacion Espanola de Pintores y Escultores   Vol 2: 11380
Asociacion Farmaceutica Mexicana   Vol 2: 9117
Asociacion Hispanoamericana de Centros de Investigacion y Empresas de Telecomunicaciones   Vol 2: 11143
Asociacion Interamericana de Contabilidad   Vol 1: 10531
Asociacion Internacional de Escritores Policiacos   Vol 2: 1824
Asociacion Internacional de Sociologia   Vol 2: 11276
Asociacion Latinoamericana de Agentes de Carga Aerea y Transporte   Vol 2: 10011
Asociacion Mexicana de Periodistas de Radio y Television   Vol 2: 8925
Asociacion Mexicana para el Fomento del Libro Infantil y Juvenil   Vol 2: 9119
Asociacion Mundial de Mujeres Periodistas y Escritoras-Capitulo Mexico   Vol 2: 8927
Asociacion Nacional de Actores   Vol 2: 8929
Asociacion Nacional de la Publicidad   Vol 2: 8931
Asociacion Odontologica Argentina   Vol 2: 43
Asociacion Paleontologica Argentina   Vol 2: 27
Asociacion Quimica Colombiana   Vol 2: 1737
Asolo International Animation Festival   Vol 2: 8099
Aspects Artistiques, Litteraires et Photographiques de la region Hazebrouckoise   Vol 2: 4899
Aspen Filmfest   Vol 1: 5367
Aspen Institute   Vol 1: 5369
Asphalt Emulsion Manufacturers Association   Vol 1: 5372
Asphalt Recycling and Reclaiming Association   Vol 1: 5375
ASPO/Lamaze   Vol 1: 5378
Assembly of Hospital Schools of Nursing   Vol 1: 5387
Assembly of National Tourist Office Representatives   Vol 1: 89
Assessorato alla Cultura della Regione dell'Umbria   Vol 2: 8409
Associacao Brasileira de Propaganda   Vol 2: 1407
Associacao do Festrio, Festival Internacional de Cinema, Televisao e Video do Rio de Janeiro   Vol 2: 1481
Asociacion Internacional de la Seguridad Social   Vol 2: 11836
Associated Alumni of Brown University   Vol 1: 5389
Associated Builders and Contractors   Vol 1: 5392
Associated Church Press   Vol 1: 5394
Associated Colleges of the Midwest   Vol 1: 5398
Associated Collegiate Press   Vol 1: 7905
Associated Collegiate Press; National Scholastic Press Association/   Vol 1: 18506
Associated Exhibitors of the American Alliance for Health, Physical Education, Recreation and Dance   Vol 1: 5400
Associated General Contractors of America   Vol 1: 5402
Associated Landscape Contractors of America   Vol 1: 5404
Associated Master Barbers and Beauticians of America   Vol 1: 5407
Associated Medical Services   Vol 1: 16955
Associated Press - Managing Editors Association   Vol 1: 5409
Associated Press - Sports Department   Vol 1: 5414
Associated Press Broadcasters   Vol 1: 5416
Associated Scientific and Technical Societies of South Africa   Vol 2: 10815
Associated Writing Programs   Vol 1: 5418
Associates for the Advancement of Medical Instrumentation   Vol 1: 14776
Associates of Brand Library   Vol 1: 5420
Associates of National Agricultural Library   Vol 1: 5422
Associates of Saint Louis University Libraries   Vol 1: 5427
Association Acanthes   Vol 2: 6200
Association Aeronautique et Astronautique de France   Vol 2: 4901
Association canadienne d'economie familiale   Vol 1: 6910
Association canadienne des annonceurs   Vol 1: 5719
Association Canadienne des Editeurs de Quotidiens   Vol 1: 6850
Association Canadienne des Loisirs/Parcs   Vol 1: 7083
Association Canadienne des Producteurs Petroliers   Vol 1: 6796
Association Canadienne des Radiodiffuseurs   Vol 1: 6772
Association Canadienne des redacteurs scientifiques   Vol 1: 7125
Association Canadienne des Technologues en Radiation Medicale   Vol 1: 6782
Association Canadienne-Francaise pour l'Avancement des Sciences   Vol 1: 5429
Association Culture et Loisirs   Vol 2: 5042
Association de la Musique Country Canadienne   Vol 1: 6847
Association de l'industrie touristique du Canada   Vol 1: 18766
Association de Presse France - Japon   Vol 2: 4906
Association de Soutien et de Diffusion d'Art   Vol 2: 4908
Association des Amis d'Alfred-Georges Regner   Vol 2: 4911
Association des Amis de Jacques Gautier et Andree Gautier   Vol 2: 4913
Association des Anciens Eleves de Marcel Mercier   Vol 2: 4915
Association des Congres Belges de la Route   Vol 2: 6158
Association des Critiques de Theatre du Canada   Vol 1: 7252
Association des Ecrivains Belges de Langue Francaise   Vol 2: 1039
Association des Ecrivains de Langue francaise   Vol 2: 4917
Association des Ecrivains du Rouergue   Vol 2: 4931
Association des Grandes Orgues de Chartres   Vol 2: 4935
Association des hopitaux du Canada   Vol 1: 6920
Association des Ingenieurs-Conseils du Canada   Vol 1: 5756
Association des Ingenieurs Electriciens Sortis de l'Institut Montefiore   Vol 2: 1045
Association des Inventeurs et Fabricants Francais   Vol 2: 4937
Association des Musees Canadiens   Vol 1: 7039
Association des Musiciens Suisses   Vol 2: 11657
Association des traducteurs et traductrices litteraires du Canada   Vol 1: 11905
Association du Festival International du Film de Comedie de Vevey   Vol 2: 11660
Association du Festival Tibor Varga Sion - Valais   Vol 2: 11662
Association du Prix Albert Londres   Vol 2: 4939
Association Europeenne de Libre-Echange   Vol 2: 11699
Association Europeenne de Radiologie   Vol 2: 1122
Association Europeenne de Traitement de Signaux   Vol 2: 11689
Association Europeenne des Industries de la Galvanisation d'Articles divers   Vol 2: 2830
Association Europeenne pour la Promotion de la Poesie   Vol 2: 1120
Association Europeenne Thyroide   Vol 2: 11706
Association for Administration of Volunteer Services   Vol 1: 5651
Association for Advancement of Behavior Therapy   Vol 1: 5438
Association for Asian Studies   Vol 1: 5440
Association for Baha'i Studies   Vol 1: 5446
Association for Bridge Construction and Design   Vol 1: 5448
Association for Business Simulation and Experiential Learning   Vol 1: 5455
Association for Canadian Studies in the United States   Vol 1: 5458
Association for Children with Retarded Mental Development   Vol 1: 5461
Association for Civil Rights in Israel   Vol 2: 7862
Association for Commonwealth Literature and Language Studies   Vol 2: 2654
Association for Competition and Musical Review   Vol 2: 8101
Association for Computer Educators   Vol 1: 10610
Association for Computing Machinery   Vol 1: 5464, 10298
Association for Computing Machinery - Special Interest Group on Computer Graphics (ACM SIGGRAPH)   Vol 1: 5473
Association for Computing Machinery - Special Interest Group on Data Communication   Vol 1: 5476
Association for Conservation Information   Vol 1: 5478

Association for Consumer Research   Vol 1: 11611
Association for Convention Operations Management   Vol 1: 5480
Association for Cooperation in Banana Research in the Caribbean and Tropical America   Vol 2: 7235
Association for Documentary Editing   Vol 1: 5482
Association for Education and Rehabilitation of the Blind and Visually Impaired   Vol 1: 5487
Association for Education in Journalism   Vol 1: 5494
Association for Education in Journalism and Mass Communication   Vol 1: 5494
Association for Educational Communications and Technology   Vol 1: 5499
Association for Educational Communications and Technology and the ECT Foundation   Vol 1: 5505
Association for Electric Motors, Their Control, and Application   Vol 1: 5517
Association for Evolutionary Economics   Vol 1: 5520
Association for Film and Television in the Celtic Countries   Vol 2: 10521
Association for Fitness in Business   Vol 1: 5665
Association for Gerontology in Higher Education   Vol 1: 5523
Association for Gravestone Studies   Vol 1: 5525
Association for Healthcare Philanthropy   Vol 1: 5527
Association for Humanistic Education   Vol 1: 5529
Association for Indiana Media Educators   Vol 1: 5531
Association for Industrial Archaeology   Vol 2: 2104
Association for Information and Image Management   Vol 1: 5538
Association for Investment Management and Research   Vol 1: 5548
Association for Library and Information Science Education   Vol 1: 5557
Association for Library Collections and Technical Services   Vol 1: 2869
Association for Media and Technology in Education in Canada   Vol 1: 6857
Association for Media Psychology   Vol 1: 3739
Association for Mental Health Affiliation with Israel   Vol 1: 5565
The Association for Persons with Severe Handicaps (TASH)   Vol 1: 5567
Association for Practitioners in Infection Control   Vol 1: 5574
Association for Preservation Technology International   Vol 1: 5583
Association for Promotion of Skiing   Vol 2: 9870
Association for Puerto Rican-Hispanic Culture   Vol 1: 5586
Association for Recorded Sound Collection   Vol 1: 5588
Association for Research in Ophthalmology   Vol 1: 5590
Association for Research in Vision and Ophthalmology   Vol 1: 5590
Association for Retarded Citizens of the United States   Vol 1: 5207
Association for Social Anthropology in Oceania   Vol 1: 5595
Association for Social Economics   Vol 1: 5597

Association for Systems Management   Vol 1: 5601
Association for the Advancement of Automotive Medicine   Vol 1: 5606
Association for the Advancement of Health Education   Vol 1: 5610
Association for the Advancement of International Education   Vol 1: 5616
Association for the Advancement of Medical Instrumentation   Vol 1: 5619
Association for the Advancement of Medical Instrumentation Foundation   Vol 1: 5621
Association for the Development of Research on Cancer   Vol 2: 4941
Association for the Diffusion of Japanese Films Abroad   Vol 2: 8774
Association for the Education of Teachers in Science   Vol 1: 5629
Association for the Furtherance of Professional Women Musicians   Vol 2: 11665
Association for the History of Chiropractic   Vol 1: 5635
Association for the Promotion of Humor in International Affairs   Vol 2: 4943
Association for the Promotion of Humor in International Affairs (APHIA)   Vol 1: 5638
Association for the Protection of Rural Scotland   Vol 2: 10505
Association for the Study of Australian Literature   Vol 2: 129
Association for the Study of Connecticut History   Vol 1: 5641
Association for the Study of Higher Education   Vol 1: 5643
Association for the Study of the World Refugee Problem   Vol 2: 8103
Association for Theatre in Higher Education   Vol 1: 1759, 5645
Association for Volunteer Administration   Vol 1: 5651
Association for Women in Computing   Vol 1: 5655
Association for Women in Psychology   Vol 1: 5657
Association for Women in Science   Vol 1: 5660
Association for Women Veterinarians   Vol 1: 5662
Association for Worksite Health Promotion   Vol 1: 5665
Association Francaise d'Action Artistique   Vol 2: 5177
Association Francaise des Observateurs d'Etoiles Variables   Vol 2: 4946
Association Francaise du Froid   Vol 2: 4948
Association Francaise pour l'Etude du Sol   Vol 2: 4950
Association Guy Levis Mano   Vol 2: 4953
Association in Scotland to Research Into Astronautics   Vol 2: 10508
Association International du Tube   Vol 2: 3486
Association Internationale de Droit Penal   Vol 2: 5968
Association Internationale de Geodesie   Vol 2: 5966
Association Internationale de Geologie de l'Ingenieur   Vol 2: 5964
Association Internationale de la Couleur   Vol 2: 9479
Association Internationale de la Presse Sportive   Vol 2: 8314
Association Internationale de la Securite Sociale   Vol 2: 11836
Association Internationale de Pediatrie   Vol 2: 6037

Association Internationale de Police   Vol 2: 3455
Association Internationale de Sedimentologistes   Vol 2: 1957
Association Internationale des Cordeliers   Vol 2: 7786
Association Internationale des Critiques Litteraires   Vol 2: 4955
Association Internationale des Echecs en Braille   Vol 2: 11471
Association Internationale des Ecoles Superieures d'Education Physique   Vol 2: 1165
Association Internationale des Educateurs pour la paix   Vol 1: 10715
Association Internationale des Numismates Professionels   Vol 2: 11762
Association Internationale des Ponts et Charpentes   Vol 2: 11754
Association Internationale des Producteurs de l'Horticulture   Vol 2: 9466
Association Internationale des Receveurs de la Poste   Vol 1: 11299
Association Internationale des Techniciens de Laboratoire Medical   Vol 2: 11463
Association Internationale du Film d'Animation   Vol 2: 9888
Association Internationale les Amis d'Alto   Vol 2: 6469
Association Internationale Permanente des Congres de la Route   Vol 2: 6157
Association Internationale pour la defense de la Liberte Religieuse   Vol 2: 11758
Association Internationale pour l'Etude de l'Economie de l'Assurance (Association de Geneve)   Vol 2: 11760
Association Internationale pour L'Etude der Argiles   Vol 2: 1047
Association Internationale Pour l'Etude Scientifique de l'Arrieration Mentale   Vol 2: 5960
Association Internationale pour un Sport sans Violence   Vol 2: 9316
Association les Amis de Georges de Beauregard   Vol 2: 4961
Association Mondiale des Inventeurs   Vol 2: 1385
Association Mondiale des Radio-Amateurs et des Radioclubs Chretiens   Vol 2: 4617
Association Mondiale pour la Celebration de l'An 2000   Vol 2: 4615
Association Mondiale Veterinaire   Vol 2: 11395
Association Nazionale per la Tutela del Patrimonio Storico Artistico e Naturale della Nazione; Italia Nostra-   Vol 2: 8360
Association Notre-Dame et la Mer   Vol 2: 4957
Association of Accredited Cosmetology Schools   Vol 1: 5670
Association of Administrative Law Judges   Vol 1: 5672
Association of Air Medical Services   Vol 1: 5674, 5675
Association of American Colleges   Vol 1: 5676
Association of American Editorial Cartoonists   Vol 1: 5678
Association of American Geographers   Vol 1: 5681
Association of American Library Schools   Vol 1: 5557
Association of American Medical Colleges   Vol 1: 362, 5686
Association of American Physicians   Vol 1: 5690
Association of American Publishers   Vol 1: 5692

Association of American Publishers - Professional and Scholarly Publishing Division   Vol 1: 5694
Association of American University Presses   Vol 1: 5696
Association of Applied Insect Ecologists   Vol 1: 5699
Association of Area Business Publications   Vol 1: 5701
Association of Asian/Pacific American Artists   Vol 1: 5703
Association of Asphalt Paving Technologists   Vol 1: 5705
Association of Austrian Industrialists   Vol 2: 735
Association of Austrian Librarians   Vol 2: 737
Association of Belgian Historic Houses   Vol 2: 1050
Association of Black Nursing Faculty in Higher Education   Vol 1: 5709
Association of Boards of Certification   Vol 1: 5715
Association of Bone and Joint Surgeons   Vol 1: 5717
Association of Building Engineers   Vol 2: 2108
Association of Business Publishers   Vol 1: 1386
Association of Canadian Advertisers   Vol 1: 5719
Association of Canadian Orchestras   Vol 1: 15706
Association of Canadian Television and Radio Artists   Vol 1: 326
Association of Caribbean Historians   Vol 1: 5722
Association of Catholic Colleges and Universities   Vol 1: 5724
Association of Certified Accountants   Vol 2: 2578
Association of Chief Police Officers of England, Wales and Northern Ireland   Vol 2: 2111
Association of Clinical Biochemists   Vol 2: 2113
Association of Co-operative Educators   Vol 1: 5726
Association of College and University Housing Officers International   Vol 1: 5733
Association of College Unions - International   Vol 1: 5738
Association of Collegiate Schools of Architecture   Vol 1: 2518, 5741
Association of Comedy Artists   Vol 1: 5747
Association of Commonwealth Universities   Vol 2: 2658
Association of Community Travel Clubs   Vol 1: 5751
Association of Conservation Engineers   Vol 1: 5753
Association of Consulting Engineers Australia   Vol 2: 134
Association of Consulting Engineers of Canada   Vol 1: 5756
Association of Consulting Foresters of America, Inc.   Vol 1: 5760
Association of Cricket Umpires   Vol 2: 2121
Association of Departments of English   Vol 1: 5762
Association of Development Financing Institutions in Asia and the Pacific   Vol 2: 10023
Association of Earth Science Editors   Vol 1: 5764
Association of Energy Engineers   Vol 1: 5767
Association of Engineering Geologists   Vol 1: 5770

Association of Engineers and Architects in Israel   Vol 2: 7864
Association of Environmental Engineering Professors   Vol 1: 5777
Association of Episcopal Colleges   Vol 1: 5783
Association of European Aeronautical and Astronautical Students; Euroavia -   Vol 2: 9399
Association of European Atomic Forums   Vol 2: 2124
Association of European Operational Research Societies   Vol 2: 6010
Association of Fashion Advertising and Editorial Photographers   Vol 2: 2130
Association of Federal Investigators   Vol 1: 5786
Association of Field Ornithologists   Vol 1: 5796
Association of Film Commissioners International   Vol 1: 5798
Association of Finnish Writers for Children and Youth   Vol 2: 4666
Association of Food Journalists   Vol 1: 5801
Association of Fraternity Advisors, Inc.   Vol 1: 5803
Association of Free Community Papers   Vol 1: 5808
Association of Free Newspapers   Vol 2: 2126
Association of German Electrical Engineers   Vol 2: 6527
Association of German Electrical Engineers - Information Technology Society   Vol 2: 6529
Association of German Pharmacists   Vol 2: 6586
Association of Golf Writers   Vol 2: 2128
Association of Government Accountants   Vol 1: 5811
Association of Graduates   Vol 1: 5825
Association of Hungarian Geophysicists   Vol 2: 7284
Association of Hungarian Journalists   Vol 2: 7291
Association of Hungarian Librarians   Vol 2: 7293
Association of Hungarian Musicians   Vol 2: 7365
Association of Incentive Marketing   Vol 1: 5828
Association of Indians in America   Vol 1: 5831
Association of International Health Researchers   Vol 1: 5833
Association of Interpretive Naturalists   Vol 1: 13177
Association of Iron and Steel Engineers   Vol 1: 5835
Association of Jesuit Colleges and Universities   Vol 1: 5837
Association of Jewish Center Professionals   Vol 1: 5839
Association of Jewish Libraries   Vol 1: 5841
Association of Late-Deafened Adults   Vol 1: 5848
Association of Latin Languages Allergologists and Immunologists   Vol 2: 10221
Association of Lunar and Planetary Observers   Vol 1: 5852
Association of Marquette University Women   Vol 1: 5854
Association of Medical Illustrators   Vol 1: 5856
Association of Medical Rehabilitation Administrators   Vol 1: 5861
Association of Medical Rehabilitation Directors and Coordinators   Vol 1: 5861
Association of Mental Health Administrators   Vol 1: 5867

Association of Mental Health Clergy   Vol 1: 5869
Association of Military Colleges and Schools of the United States   Vol 1: 5871
Association of Military Surgeons of the United States   Vol 1: 5873
Association of Musical Culture   Vol 2: 8105
Association of National Olympic Committees   Vol 2: 4959
Association of Newspaper Classified Advertising Managers   Vol 1: 5901, 8833
Association of Nigerian Authors   Vol 2: 9855
Association of North American Radio Clubs   Vol 1: 5904
Association of Obedience Clubs and Judges   Vol 1: 5908
Association of Official Analytical Chemists   Vol 1: 5185
Association of Official Racing Chemists   Vol 1: 5910
Association of Official Seed Analysts   Vol 1: 5912
Association of Orthodox Jewish Teachers   Vol 1: 5914
Association of Palaeontology   Vol 2: 6532
Association of Performing Arts Presenters   Vol 1: 5916
Association of Photographers   Vol 2: 2130
Association of Physical Fitness Centers   Vol 1: 5919
Association of Private Enterprise Education   Vol 1: 5922
Association of Professional Engineers of Ontario   Vol 1: 16459
Association of Professional Genealogists   Vol 1: 5925
Association of Professors of Higher Education   Vol 1: 5643
Association of Psychologists of Nova Scotia   Vol 1: 5927
Association of Publicly Traded Companies   Vol 1: 5929
Association of Pulp and Paper Chemists and Engineers   Vol 2: 6536
Association of Railroad Advertising and Marketing   Vol 1: 5932
Association of Railroad Advertising Managers   Vol 1: 5932
Association of Records Managers and Administrators - ARMA International   Vol 1: 5934
Association of Retail Marketing Services   Vol 1: 5940
Association of Schools of Allied Health Professions   Vol 1: 5942
Association of Schools of Journalism and Mass Communication   Vol 1: 5952
Association of Scientists and Engineers of the Naval Sea Systems Command   Vol 1: 5954
Association of Sleep Disorders Centers   Vol 1: 4027
Association of Slovak Writers   Vol 2: 10753
Association of Social and Behavioral Scientists   Vol 1: 5961
Association of South African Quantity Surveyors   Vol 2: 10817
Association of Southeast Asian Institutions of Higher Learning   Vol 2: 12018
Association of Southern Baptist Campus Ministries   Vol 1: 5963
Association of Special Libraries in the Philippines   Vol 2: 10025
Association of Sports Museums and Halls of Fame   Vol 1: 10787
Association of State and Territorial Health Officials   Vol 1: 5965
Association of State and Territorial Local Liaison Officials   Vol 1: 13059

Organization Index
Volume 2: International and Foreign

Australian

Association of State Territorial and Health Officials   Vol 1: 13059
Association of Steel Distributors   Vol 1: 5968
Association of Surfing Professsionals   Vol 1: 5971
Association of Surgeons of South Africa   Vol 2: 10819
Association of Surgical Technologists   Vol 1: 5973
Association of Swedish Amateur Orchestras   Vol 2: 11443
Association of Teacher Educators   Vol 1: 5978
Association of the Friends of Georges de Beauregard   Vol 2: 4961
Association of the United States Army   Vol 1: 5982
Association of Third World Studies   Vol 1: 5984
Association of Track and Field Statisticians   Vol 2: 2133
Association of Travel Marketing Executives   Vol 1: 5988
Association of Ukrainian Sports Clubs in North America   Vol 1: 5991
Association of Universities and Colleges of Canada   Vol 1: 5994
Association of University Architects   Vol 1: 5996
Association of University Programs in Health Administration   Vol 1: 5999
Association of Visual Communicators   Vol 1: 6001
Association of Wall and Ceiling Industries - International   Vol 1: 6007
Association on Handicapped Student Service Programs in Postsecondary Education   Vol 1: 6018
Association on Higher Education and Disability   Vol 1: 6018
Association pour la Diffusions des Theses sur le Pacifique Francophon e   Vol 2: 9698
Association pour la Recherche sur le Cancer   Vol 2: 4941
Association pour l'avancement des sciences et des techniques de la documentation   Vol 1: 6020
Association pour le Developpement du Marche du Zinc   Vol 2: 4653
Association pour le Prix Scientifique Philip Morris   Vol 2: 4963
Association pour l'Etude et la Recherche en Radiologie   Vol 2: 4965
Association pour l'Organisation de Festivals a Biarritz   Vol 2: 4967
Association Professionnelle et Artistique du Theatre   Vol 2: 4969
Association Quebecoise des Critiques de Cinema   Vol 1: 6023
Association Raymond Berr Atochem   Vol 2: 6359
Association reconnue d'utilite publique   Vol 2: 4772
Association Royale des Demeures Historiques de Belgique   Vol 2: 1050
Association S.I.N.U.S.   Vol 2: 6212
Association Thalberg   Vol 2: 8048
Association Trends Weekly Newspaper   Vol 1: 6029
Association Zino Francescatti   Vol 2: 4971
Associazione Amici Della Musica Di Caltanissetta   Vol 2: 8107
Associazione Compagnia Jazz Ballet   Vol 2: 8109
Associazione Concorsi e Rassegne Musicali   Vol 2: 8101

Associazione Culturale Antonio Pedrotti   Vol 2: 8111
Associazione Culturale Ennio Flaiano e *Oggi E Domani*   Vol 2: 8113
Associazione Culturale Relazioni Inernazionali   Vol 2: 8115
Associazione Culturale Rodolfo Lipizer   Vol 2: 8208
Associazione di Cultura Lao Silesu   Vol 2: 8117
Associazione di Cultura Musica   Vol 2: 8105
Associazione di Cultural Musicale   Vol 2: 8119
Associazione Elettrotecnica ed Elettronica Italiana   Vol 2: 8344
Associazione Fra i Romani   Vol 2: 8121
Associazione Italiana Amici del Cinema d'Essai   Vol 2: 8123
Associazione Italiana di Metallurgia   Vol 2: 8125, 8333
Associazione Italiana par la Musica Contemporanea   Vol 2: 8132
Associazione Mineraria Subalpina   Vol 2: 8134
Associazione Musicale Alfonso Rendano   Vol 2: 8137
Associazione Musicale di Monza   Vol 2: 8139
Associazione Napoletana Amici di Malta   Vol 2: 8141
Associazione Nazionale di Ingegneria Nucleare   Vol 2: 8383
Associazione Nazionale Enrico Fermi   Vol 2: 8143
Associazione Nuovi Spazi Sonori   Vol 2: 8132
Associazione per Chianciano   Vol 2: 8446
Associazione per il Disegno Industriale   Vol 2: 8146
Associazione per Il Premio Internazionale di Meridionalistica Guido Dorso   Vol 2: 8148
Associazione Premio Grinzane Cavour   Vol 2: 8186
Associazione Premio Internazionale per la Zootecnia Uovo d'Oro   Vol 2: 8150
Associazione Turistica Pro Loco di Corciano   Vol 2: 8408
Associazone Italiana Biblioteche   Vol 2: 8152
ASTM   Vol 1: 6031
Astra USA, Inc.   Vol 1: 14041
Astrological Association   Vol 2: 2136
Astronomical League   Vol 1: 6088
Astronomical Society of Japan   Vol 2: 8506
Astronomical Society of Southern Africa   Vol 2: 10821
Astronomical Society of the Pacific   Vol 1: 6092
Astronomical Society of Western Australia   Vol 2: 136
AT & T Foundation   Vol 1: 8831
AT&T   Vol 2: 3839
AT&T Bell Laboratories   Vol 1: 3450, 3451, 10282, 10282, 15759
AT&T Foundation   Vol 1: 4068
AT&T Global Information Solutions Ltd.   Vol 2: 2138
Ataturk Kultur, Dil ve Tarih Yuksek Kurumu   Vol 2: 12043
Ataturk Supreme Council for Culture, Language and History   Vol 2: 12043
Atelier Imaginaire; L'   Vol 2: 4973
Atelier Musique de Ville d'Avray   Vol 2: 4976
Ateneo de Valladolid   Vol 2: 11146
Ateneo Feminista Festival Internacional de Cine Realizado por Mujeres   Vol 2: 11148
Ateneo Santander   Vol 2: 11150
Athena Poster and Print Company International   Vol 2: 2140

Athenaeum International Cultural Center   Vol 2: 7184
Athenaeum of Philadelphia   Vol 1: 6099
Athletes United for Peace   Vol 1: 6104
The Athletics Congress of the USA   Vol 1: 19930
Atlanta Apparel Mart   Vol 1: 19792
Atlanta Independent Film and Video Festival   Vol 1: 10091
Atlanta Tipoff Club   Vol 1: 6106, 12568
Atlantic Bridge   Vol 2: 6546
Atlantic Film Festival Association   Vol 1: 6112
Atlantic Monthly   Vol 1: 6114
Atlantic Offshore Fishermen's Association   Vol 1: 6116
Atlantic Richfield Company   Vol 1: 19953
Atlantic Salmon Federation   Vol 1: 6118
Atlantic Salmon Trust   Vol 1: 6119
Atlantik-Brucke   Vol 2: 6546
Atlantis Films   Vol 1: 6867
Atlas Economic Research Foundation   Vol 1: 6121
Atlas World Press Review   Vol 1: 20519
Atomic Industrial Forum   Vol 1: 19072
ATP Tour   Vol 1: 6123
Auburn University/*Southern Humanities Review*   Vol 1: 6125
Audience Development Committee (AUDELCO)   Vol 1: 6127
Audio Engineering Society   Vol 1: 6129
AudioVideo International   Vol 1: 6135
Audubon Artists, Inc.   Vol 1: 6139
Audubon Naturalist Society of the Central Atlantic States   Vol 1: 6141
Audubon Society of New Hampshire   Vol 1: 6143
Augusta National Golf Club   Vol 1: 6145
Augustan Society   Vol 1: 6147
Augustinians of the Assumption   Vol 1: 6149
Aujourd'hui Prize   Vol 2: 6161
Austen Society of North America; Jane   Vol 1: 6151
The Austin Chronicle   Vol 1: 6153
Austin Seven Clubs Association   Vol 2: 2142
Austin Ten Drivers Club Ltd.   Vol 2: 2144
Australasian Corrosion Association   Vol 2: 138
Australasian Institute of Metals   Vol 2: 418
Australasian Institute of Mining and Metallurgy   Vol 2: 423
Australasian Political Studies Association   Vol 2: 140
Australasian Seabird Group   Vol 2: 9702
Australia - Department of Veterans' Affairs, Public Relations Dept.   Vol 2: 143
Australia - New South Wales Ministry for the Arts   Vol 2: 145
Australia - Victorian Ministry for the Arts   Vol 2: 148
Australia Council   Vol 2: 670
Australia Council - Community Cultural Development Board   Vol 2: 150
Australia Council - Literature Board   Vol 2: 152
Australia Council - Performing Arts Board   Vol 2: 157
Australia Council for the Arts - Visual Arts/Craft Board   Vol 2: 159
Australian Academy of Science   Vol 2: 170
Australian Academy of the Humanities   Vol 2: 182
Australian-American Educational Foundation   Vol 2: 184
Australian and New Zealand Association for the Advancement of Science   Vol 2: 187
Australian Association for Corrosion Prevention   Vol 2: 138

Australian Book Publishers Association   Vol 2: 192
Australian Broadcasting Commission   Vol 2: 194
Australian Broadcasting Corporation   Vol 2: 194
Australian Cinematographers Society   Vol 2: 198
Australian College of Education   Vol 2: 200
Australian College of Veterinary Scientists   Vol 2: 278
Australian Council of National Trusts   Vol 2: 203
Australian Decorations Advisory Committee - Australian Bravery Decorations   Vol 2: 205
Australian Elizabethan Theatre Trust   Vol 2: 209
Australian Federation of University Women   Vol 2: 211
Australian Federation of University Women - Queensland Fellowship Fund   Vol 2: 213
Australian Federation of University Women - South Australia   Vol 2: 215
Australian Federation of University Women - South Australia Trust Fund   Vol 2: 215
Australian Film Commission   Vol 2: 675
Australian Film Institute   Vol 2: 220
Australian Geological Survey Organization   Vol 2: 499
Australian Historical Society   Vol 2: 606
Australian Institute of Energy   Vol 2: 224
Australian Institute of Genealogical Studies   Vol 2: 226
Australian Institute of International Affairs   Vol 2: 228
Australian Institute of Management   Vol 2: 230
Australian Institute of Physics   Vol 2: 232, 3193
Australian Institute of Physics (NSW Branch)   Vol 2: 699
Australian Library and Information Association   Vol 2: 236
Australian Library and Information Association - School Libraries Section (W.A. Group)   Vol 2: 248
Australian Library Promotion Council   Vol 2: 250
Australian Literature Society   Vol 2: 129
Australian Mathematical Society   Vol 2: 252
Australian Mathematical Society - Division of Applied Mathematics   Vol 2: 121
Australian Musical Foundation in London   Vol 2: 2146
Australian National University   Vol 2: 255
Australian Numismatic Society   Vol 2: 257
Australian Red Cross   Vol 2: 11915
Australian Sesquicentennial Gift Trust for Oral History   Vol 2: 9725
Australian Singing Competition   Vol 2: 261
Australian Society for Parasitology   Vol 2: 263
Australian Society of Archivists   Vol 2: 266
Australian Teachers of Media   Vol 2: 269
Australian Telecommunications and Electronics Research Board   Vol 2: 271
Australian Veterinary Association   Vol 2: 273
Australian Video Festival   Vol 2: 360
Australian Widescreen Association   Vol 2: 280
Australian Writers Guild   Vol 2: 282
Australian Writers Professional Service   Vol 2: 357
Austria - Bundesministerium fur Unterricht und Kunst   Vol 2: 755
Austria - Bundesministerium fur Wirtschaftliche Angelegenheiten   Vol 2: 739

Austria - Ministry of Economic Affairs   Vol 2: 739
Austria - Ministry of Education and Arts   Vol 2: 755
Austria - Ministry of Education, Arts and Sports   Vol 2: 884
Austrian Airlines   Vol 2: 918
Austrian Broadcasting Corporation - Upper Austrian Regional Studios   Vol 2: 771
Austrian Broadcasting Service   Vol 2: 843
Austrian Composers Association   Vol 2: 773
Austrian Design Institute   Vol 2: 775
Austrian Geographical Society   Vol 2: 778
Austrian Ministry of Economic Affairs   Vol 2: 776, 777
Austrian Ministry of Science and Research   Vol 2: 872
Austrian Pen Centre   Vol 2: 781
Austrian Radion-Studio Carinthia   Vol 2: 797
Austrian Society of Film Sciences, Communications and Media Research   Vol 2: 783
Austrian Statistical Society   Vol 2: 786
Austro Mechana   Vol 2: 774
Austro-Merck Vienna (Austria)   Vol 2: 876
Authors' Club   Vol 2: 2148
Auto-Alloys Ltd   Vol 2: 3000
Auto Club of Michigan   Vol 1: 12251
Automated Imaging Association   Vol 1: 6158
Automated Vision Association   Vol 1: 6158
Automatic Identification Manufacturers (AIM USA)   Vol 1: 6160
Automobilclub Von Deutschland   Vol 2: 6548
Automobile Club de l'Ouest   Vol 2: 4978
Automotive Advertisers Council   Vol 1: 11579
Automotive Hall of Fame   Vol 1: 6163
Automotive Organization Team   Vol 1: 6163
Automotive Service Industry Association - Young Executives Forum   Vol 1: 6168
Automotive Training Managers Council   Vol 1: 6170
Automotive Warehouse Distributors Association   Vol 1: 6172
Auvergne Lyric Center   Vol 2: 4980
Avenatech Inc.   Vol 1: 10741
AVI Publishing Company   Vol 1: 13013
Aviation Consulting   Vol 1: 2476
Aviation Distributors and Manufacturers Association   Vol 1: 6174
Aviation Hall of Fame   Vol 1: 13403
Aviation Hall of Fame and Museum of New Jersey   Vol 1: 6177
Aviation Safety Institute   Vol 1: 6181
Aviation/Space Writers Association   Vol 1: 6183
Aviation Technicians Education Council   Vol 1: 6195
Aviation Week & Space Technology   Vol 1: 6197, 9238
Avon Books   Vol 1: 6199
Avon Products   Vol 1: 6201
Avoriaz International Festival of Fantasy and Science-Fiction Films   Vol 2: 4982
Awards and Recognition Association   Vol 1: 6203
Ayrshire Breeders' Association   Vol 1: 6210
Ayuntamiento de Benicasim   Vol 2: 11152
Ayuntamiento de Guadalajara   Vol 2: 9259
Ayuntamiento de Madrid   Vol 2: 11286
Ayuntamiento de Monterrey   Vol 2: 9159
Ayuntamiento de San Juan del Rio   Vol 2: 9161
Ayuntamiento del Puerto de la Cruz   Vol 2: 11232
Azienda Autonoma di Soggiorno e Turismo   Vol 2: 8155
Azienda di Promozione Turistica di Montecatini Terme   Vol 2: 8319

Azienda di Promozione Turistica Novara   Vol 2: 8157
B. P. Chemicals Ltd.   Vol 2: 4219
Babcock and Wilcox Company   Vol 2: 3001
Babson College   Vol 1: 6212
Baby Talk Magazine   Vol 1: 11742
Bach Competition; International   Vol 2: 6935
Bach International Competition; Johann Sebastian   Vol 1: 6214
Bachauer International Piano Competition; Gina   Vol 1: 6216
Back Pain Association   Vol 2: 3677
Back Scholarship Foundation; Oskar   Vol 2: 9336
Badminton Association of England   Vol 2: 2152
Bagutta Restaurant   Vol 2: 8159
Bahamas Chamber of Commerce   Vol 2: 924
Bahrain Contemporary Art Association   Vol 2: 929
Bailey's Irish Cream   Vol 1: 13602
Bair Endowment; Clifford   Vol 1: 14406
Baird Corporation   Vol 1: 15749
Baker and Taylor   Vol 1: 2929, 2930
Baker and Taylor Books   Vol 1: 2829, 7000
Baker and Taylor Company   Vol 1: 2866, 2957, 9419
Baker, Inc.; J. T.   Vol 1: 1568
Balch Institute for Ethnic Studies   Vol 1: 6218
Bald Headed Men of America   Vol 1: 6220
Baldwin Piano and Organ Company   Vol 1: 12520
Balfour Beatty Ltd.   Vol 2: 3251
Balfour Foundation; L. G.   Vol 1: 13310
Balint Society   Vol 2: 2155
Ball State University - Department of Journalism   Vol 1: 6222
Ballet Makers Dance Foundation   Vol 1: 7295
Balloon Federation of America   Vol 1: 6232
Ballroom Dancers Federation   Vol 2: 2157
Baltic American Freedom League   Vol 1: 6245
Baltimore Film Forum   Vol 1: 6248
Baltimore Opera Company   Vol 1: 6250
The Baltimore Sun   Vol 1: 6252
Balzan Foundation; International   Vol 2: 8279
BANAMEX   Vol 2: 9201
Banca Promex   Vol 2: 9259
Banca Serfin   Vol 2: 8933
Bancarella Prize   Vol 2: 8161
Banco de Comercio   Vol 2: 9259
Banco de la Republica   Vol 2: 1589
Banco del Libro   Vol 2: 12146
Banco di Napoli   Vol 2: 8048
Banco Nacional de Comercio Exterior   Vol 2: 9259
Banco Nacional de Mexico   Vol 2: 9259
Banco Nacional de Mexico, S.N.C. (BANAMEX)   Vol 2: 9201
Banff Centre   Vol 1: 6254
Banff Centre - School of Management   Vol 1: 6798
Banff Centre for the Arts   Vol 1: 6254
Banff School of Fine Arts   Vol 1: 6254
Banff Television Festival   Vol 1: 6260
Bangkok Bank Limited   Vol 2: 12020
Bangla Academy   Vol 2: 933
Bank Marketing Association   Vol 1: 6262
Bank of Delaware   Vol 1: 6265
Bank of Ireland   Vol 2: 7796
Bank of Israel   Vol 2: 7867
Bank Street College   Vol 1: 7612
Bank Street College of Education   Vol 1: 6267
Banque Nationale de Paris   Vol 2: 6085
Banta Company, Inc.; George   Vol 1: 20345
Baraza la Kiswahili la Taifa   Vol 2: 12012

Barcelona Film Festival, Films and Directors   Vol 2: 11154
Barcelona Theatre Institute   Vol 2: 11156
Bard International; C. R.   Vol 2: 2271
Bard Urological Division   Vol 1: 5576
Barlow International Competition   Vol 1: 6269
Barn-och ungdomsboksradet   Vol 2: 11636
Barnes & Noble Bookstores   Vol 1: 6271
Barone Center on the Press, Politics and Public Policy; Joan Shorenstein   Vol 1: 9634
Baronial Order of Magna Charta   Vol 1: 6273
Bartholomew and Sons Ltd.; John   Vol 2: 2304
Bartlett; Elizabeth   Vol 1: 6275
Bartok Nemzetkozi Korusverseny Irodaja; Bela   Vol 2: 7295
Baruch Entertainment   Vol 1: 6277
Barwick - Howard Miller Clock Company   Vol 1: 12294
Baseball Writers Association of America   Vol 1: 6279, 13440, 13441
BASF Aktiengesellschaft   Vol 2: 6619
Bass'n Gal   Vol 1: 6285
Bataafsch Genootschap der Proefondervindelijke Wijsbegeerte   Vol 2: 9419
Bataan Relief Organization   Vol 1: 2010
Baudouin; Fondation Roi   Vol 2: 1216
Bausch & Lomb   Vol 1: 11223
Bavarian Academy of Fine Arts   Vol 2: 6550
Bavarian Academy of Science   Vol 2: 6556
Baxter-Dade Inc.   Vol 2: 11464
Baxter Diagnostics   Vol 1: 847
Baxter Foundation   Vol 1: 5687
Baxter Healthcare   Vol 2: 7775
Baxter Healthcare Corporation   Vol 1: 920, 4188
Baxter Healthcare Corporation, Dade Division   Vol 1: 926
Bay Area Book Reviewers Association   Vol 1: 6290
Bay Chamber Concerts   Vol 1: 6292
Bayer Miles   Vol 2: 10982
Bayerische Akademie der Schonen Kunste   Vol 2: 6550
Bayerische Akademie der Wissenschaften   Vol 2: 6556
Baylor University   Vol 1: 6294
Bayona Piano Competition; International Pilar   Vol 2: 11272
Baywood Publishing Company   Vol 1: 9590
BBC Magazines   Vol 2: 2159
BBC Wildlife Magazine   Vol 2: 2161
BDH Chemicals, Ltd   Vol 1: 7199
Beard Foundation; James   Vol 1: 6297
Bearn Mandat des Poetes; Fondation Pierre   Vol 2: 6107
Beauty and Barber Supply Institute   Vol 1: 6303
Beaux Arts Concerts   Vol 1: 6305
Bechtel Fund   Vol 1: 2856
Bechtel National, Inc.   Vol 1: 2566
Beclere Foundation; Antoine   Vol 2: 11842
Becton Dickinson and Company   Vol 1: 4202
Becton Dickinson Canada, Inc   Vol 1: 7200
Becton Dickinson VACUTAINER Systems   Vol 1: 846
Beebe Award; Frank Huntington   Vol 1: 6307
Beecham Clinical Laboratories   Vol 1: 849
Beecham Pharmaceuticals   Vol 2: 4219
Before Columbus Foundation   Vol 1: 6309
Behavioral Genetics Association   Vol 1: 6311
BEI Defense Systems Company   Vol 1: 12055
Belgian American Educational Foundation   Vol 1: 6315
Belgian Centre for Music Documentation   Vol 2: 1054

Belgian Geological Society   Vol 2: 1056
Belgian Government   Vol 2: 1160
Belgian Institute of Administrative Sciences   Vol 2: 1058
Belgian Municipal Credit Institution   Vol 2: 1060
Belgian National League Against Tuberculosis   Vol 2: 1064
Belgian National Office for the Promotion of Agricultural and Horticultural Products   Vol 2: 1066
Belgian Radio and Television   Vol 2: 1068
Belgische Radio en Televisie   Vol 2: 1068
Belgische Vereniging van Auteurs, Componisten en Uitgevers   Vol 2: 1070
Belgium - Ministere des Affaires Etrangeres   Vol 2: 1072
Belgium - Ministerie van de Vlaamse Gemeenschap   Vol 2: 1076
Belgium - Ministry of Foreign Affairs   Vol 2: 1072
Belgium - Ministry of the Flemish Community   Vol 2: 1076
Belgrade City Council   Vol 2: 10694
Belgrade International Festival of Scientific Films   Vol 2: 10698
Belgrade International Film Festival   Vol 2: 10700
Bell Association for the Deaf; Alexander Graham   Vol 1: 6317
Bell Canada   Vol 1: 16952
Bell Helicopter   Vol 1: 12068
Bell Laboratories; AT&T   Vol 1: 3450, 3451, 10268, 10282, 15759
Bellarmine College   Vol 1: 6322
Bello; Editorial Andres   Vol 1: 1563
Belted Galloway Society   Vol 1: 6324
Bendix; Allied   Vol 1: 17752
Beneath the Sea   Vol 1: 18871
Benelux Phlebology Society   Vol 2: 1088
Benevento; Strega Alberti   Vol 2: 8438
Benevolent and Loyal Order of Pessimists   Vol 1: 6326
Benn Brothers plc   Vol 2: 2468
Bennett Neuropsychiatric Research Foundation; A. E.   Vol 1: 17789
Benoist Foundation; Marcel   Vol 2: 11667
Benoist Stiftung; Marcel   Vol 2: 11667
Benson & Hedges Fireworks Competition   Vol 1: 6328
Benson & Hedges Inc. International   Vol 1: 6328
Bensusan Memorial Fund; Arthur   Vol 2: 12204
Bentinck; Prix Adolf   Vol 2: 6159
Berea College   Vol 1: 6330
Bergamo Film Meeting   Vol 2: 8165
Bergen International Festival   Vol 2: 9873
Berghman heraldiska Stiftelse; Arvid   Vol 2: 945
Berkeley Enthusiasts Club   Vol 2: 2164
Berlin City Hall   Vol 2: 6560
Berlin International Film Festival   Vol 2: 6563
Berlin Senate   Vol 2: 5096
Berlin; Senate of   Vol 2: 5096
Bernstein; Aguda l'Haanakat Prasim Sifrutiim Al Shem Mordechai   Vol 2: 7869
Bernstein Literary Prizes Association; Mordechai   Vol 2: 7869
Berntsen International   Vol 1: 1812
Berol Ltd.   Vol 2: 3712
Berr Atochem; Association Raymond   Vol 2: 6359
Bertelsmann Foundation   Vol 2: 6565
Bertelsmann Stiftung   Vol 2: 6565
Beta Beta Beta Biological Society   Vol 1: 6333

Beta Gamma Sigma   Vol 1: 6339
Beta Phi Mu International Library Science Honorary Society   Vol 1: 2813
Betonvereniging van Suidelike Afrika   Vol 2: 10835
Better Homes and Gardens   Vol 1: 16451
Better Roads and Transportation Council   Vol 1: 6342
Better World Society   Vol 1: 6345
Beverage Testing Institute   Vol 1: 6347
Beverly Hills Theatre Guild   Vol 1: 6349
Beyond War Foundation   Vol 1: 9346
Bharatiya Jnanpith   Vol 2: 7485
Bibby Scientific Products; J.   Vol 2: 2533
Bibiana, International House of Art for Children   Vol 2: 10759, 10764
Bibiana, Medzinarodny dom umenia pre deti   Vol 2: 10759
Bibliographic Institute of Mannheim   Vol 2: 7098
Bibliographical Society   Vol 2: 2166
Bibliographical Society of America   Vol 1: 6351
Biblioteca Nacional de Mexico   Vol 2: 9248
Biblioteca Provinciale G. D'Annunzio   Vol 2: 8212
Bibliotheque des Arts   Vol 2: 4984
Bibliotheque Municipale Valery Larbaud   Vol 2: 4986
Bibliotheque Nationale   Vol 2: 4988
Bibliotheque Nationale - Dep. Estampes Prix Lacouriere   Vol 2: 5198
Bibliotheque Publique d'Information   Vol 2: 5032
Bibliotheque Saint-John Perse Jeunesse   Vol 2: 4990
Bicycle Federation of America   Vol 1: 6353
Bicycle Institute of America   Vol 1: 6354
Bicycling Magazine   Vol 1: 6354
Bienal de Cine y Video Cientifico   Vol 2: 11165
Bienek Stiftung; Horst   Vol 2: 6551
Biennale di Venezia - Mostra Internazionale del Cinema   Vol 2: 8469
Biennale Internazionale dell'Umorismo Nell'Arte di Tolentino   Vol 2: 8281
Biennales Internationales de Poesie   Vol 2: 1169
Big Brothers/Big Sisters of America   Vol 1: 6355
Big Brothers of America   Vol 1: 6355
Big East Conference   Vol 1: 6359
Big Eight Conference   Vol 1: 6362
Big Muddy Film Festival   Vol 1: 6364
Big Sisters International   Vol 1: 6355
Bijns-Stichting; Anna   Vol 2: 9339
Bilboko Nazioarteko Kantu Lehiaketa   Vol 2: 11274
Bilingual Foundation of the Arts   Vol 1: 6366
Billboard   Vol 1: 6369
Billiard and Bowling Institute of America   Vol 1: 6372
Billiard Congress of America   Vol 1: 6374
Billiard Federation of the United States of America   Vol 1: 19044
BIMCO   Vol 2: 3598
Bingham Memorial Fund; Worth   Vol 1: 6376
Bio-Serv Company   Vol 1: 2647
Biochemical, Biophysical and Microbiological Society of Finland   Vol 2: 4670
Biochemical Society   Vol 2: 2168
Biodeterioration Society   Vol 2: 2180
Bioelectrochemical Society   Vol 2: 6568
Biological Council   Vol 2: 2182
Biological Engineering Society   Vol 2: 2184
Biomedical Engineering Society   Vol 1: 6378

Biomedical Marketing Association   Vol 1: 6383
Biometric Society   Vol 1: 8036
BirdLife International   Vol 2: 2187
Birkebeiner-Rennet   Vol 2: 9877
Birkenhead Photographic Association   Vol 2: 2189
Birmingham Opera Theater   Vol 1: 6385
Birmingham-Southern College   Vol 1: 6387
Black Bear Publications   Vol 1: 6389
Black Ice   Vol 1: 6391
Black Lung Association   Vol 1: 6393
Black Panel World Foundation   Vol 2: 6570
Black Theatre Network   Vol 1: 6395
Blackburn Prize; Susan Smith   Vol 1: 6397
Blackie and Son Limited   Vol 2: 10514
Blacks in Law Enforcement   Vol 1: 6399
Blackwell North America   Vol 1: 2847
Blake Society   Vol 2: 284
Blekinge County Council   Vol 2: 11445
Blekinge Lans Landsting   Vol 2: 11445
Blemont; Fondation Emile   Vol 2: 6103
Blessed Kateri Tekakwitha League   Vol 1: 6401
Blinded Veterans Association   Vol 1: 6403
Blues Alley Music Society   Vol 1: 6411
Blues Foundation   Vol 1: 6414
BNA   Vol 2: 9589
B'nai B'rith - Community Volunteer Services Commission   Vol 1: 6418
B'nai B'rith Foundation (Canada)   Vol 1: 6422
B'nai B'rith Foundation of the United States   Vol 1: 6425
B'nai B'rith Hillel Foundations   Vol 1: 6427
B'nai B'rith International - Commission on Continuing Jewish Education   Vol 1: 6430
B'nai B'rith International - King Center for Black-Jewish Relations; Don   Vol 1: 6433
B'nai B'rith Women   Vol 1: 6435
Boardman Tasker Memorial Trust   Vol 2: 2191
Boating Industry   Vol 1: 14337
Boating Writers International   Vol 1: 6437, 13275
BOC   Vol 1: 5073
Bodmer-Stiftung fur einen Gottfried Keller-Preis; Martin-   Vol 2: 11669
Boehringer Corporation Limited   Vol 2: 3170
Boehringer-Mannheim Canada   Vol 1: 7163
Boehringer-Mannheim Corporation   Vol 1: 853
Boeing Commercial Airplanes Group   Vol 1: 18788
Boeing Helicopter Company   Vol 1: 12066
Boise Peace Quilt Project   Vol 1: 6440
Boito Conservatory of Music Parma; A.   Vol 2: 8167
Bolivia - Ministry of Education and Culture   Vol 2: 1390
Bolivia - Office of the President   Vol 2: 1392
Bologna Children's Book Fair   Vol 2: 8170
Bologna University   Vol 2: 8173
Bombay Creative Photographers Association   Vol 2: 7488
Bonsai and Orchid Association   Vol 1: 6442
Book of the Month Club   Vol 1: 16020
Book Publishers' Association   Vol 2: 9797
Book Publishers Association of Alberta   Vol 1: 6444
Book Publishers Association of Israel   Vol 2: 7869
Book Publishers Association of New Zealand   Vol 2: 9704, 9707
Book Publishers Representatives Association   Vol 2: 9704
Book Trust   Vol 2: 4344
Book Trust (England)   Vol 2: 2193, 2616

Book Trust (Scotland)   Vol 2: 10513
Book Wholesalers   Vol 1: 2853
Bookbinders Guild of New York   Vol 1: 15226
Bookbuilders of Boston   Vol 1: 6446
Bookbuilders West   Vol 1: 6449
Booker PLC   Vol 2: 2195
Books Abroad   Vol 1: 20501
Books for Children   Vol 2: 2208
Books for Children Book Club   Vol 2: 2209, 2617
Books in Canada   Vol 1: 6452
Bookseller   Vol 2: 2734
Booksellers Association of Great Britain & Ireland   Vol 2: 2210
Booksellers Association of New Zealand   Vol 2: 9706
Booksellers New Zealand   Vol 2: 9797
Booksellers of New Zealand   Vol 2: 9706
Boosters Clubs of America   Vol 1: 6455
Boots Pharmaceuticals   Vol 2: 4219
Boots Pharmaceuticals, Inc.   Vol 1: 4907
Borba   Vol 2: 10702
Borden   Vol 1: 2337, 9334
Borden Foundation   Vol 1: 2431, 2648, 7143
The Boring Institute   Vol 1: 6457
Bosch Foundation Fellowship Program; Robert   Vol 1: 7421
Bosch Stiftung; Robert   Vol 2: 6553
Boston Athletic Association   Vol 1: 6459
Boston Ballet   Vol 1: 6461
Boston Film/Video Foundation   Vol 1: 5325
The Boston Globe   Vol 1: 6463
Boston University   Vol 1: 6466
Boston University - Pike Institute on Law and Disability   Vol 1: 6468
Boston University School of Music   Vol 1: 6470
Botanical Society of America   Vol 1: 6472, 8185
Botanical Society of France   Vol 2: 4992
Boto-Balani Foundations, Inc.   Vol 2: 10061
Boucheron Joaillier   Vol 2: 4996
Bound to Stay Bound Books, Inc   Vol 1: 2857
Bourges Experimental Music Group   Vol 2: 4998
Bowker; R. R.   Vol 1: 2831, 2848, 2945, 6493
Bowling Proprietors' Association of America   Vol 1: 6495
Bowling Writers Association of America   Vol 1: 6499
Box Office Management International   Vol 1: 6505
Boxoffice   Vol 1: 6510
Boy Scouts of America   Vol 1: 6513, 13974
Boy Scouts of America - National Jewish Committee on Scouting   Vol 1: 6523
Boynton Beach Recreation & Park Department   Vol 1: 6528
Boys & Girls Clubs of America   Vol 1: 6530
Boys Clubs of America   Vol 1: 6530
Bozena Slavinska   Vol 2: 8985
BP America, Inc.   Vol 1: 2569
BP Australia   Vol 2: 210
BP Exploration   Vol 2: 2246
BP Oil Ltd.   Vol 2: 3356
BP Peter Pears Award   Vol 2: 2212
BP Research   Vol 2: 4219
Brabender Instruments   Vol 1: 947
Braille and Talking Book Library   Vol 2: 286
Brain Research Foundation   Vol 1: 6539
Bralco Metal Industries   Vol 2: 7626
Brandeis University   Vol 1: 6542
Brandeis University - Rosenstiel Basic Medical Sciences Research Center   Vol 1: 6544
Brandon University   Vol 1: 6546
Brasserie Lipp   Vol 2: 6164
Bratislova City Hall   Vol 2: 1829

Braunschweig City Cultural Office   Vol 2: 6572
Brazil - Office of the President   Vol 2: 1409
Brazilian Academy of Letters   Vol 2: 1419, 10253
Brazilian-American Chamber of Commerce   Vol 1: 6548
Brazilian Association for the Advancement of Science   Vol 2: 1427
Brazilian Institute of Art and Culture   Vol 2: 1429
Brazilian Organization for Agricultural Research   Vol 2: 1446
Brazilian PEN Club   Vol 2: 1449
Brazilian Society of Cultural and Artistic Promotions   Vol 2: 1452
Brechner Center for Freedom of Information; Joseph L.   Vol 1: 6550
Brel Foundation; International Jacques   Vol 2: 1195
Bremen City Council   Vol 2: 6577
Brian Halford Productions Ltd.   Vol 2: 7785
Brick Development Association   Vol 2: 2214
Brick Institute of America   Vol 1: 2521
Bride's and Your New Home   Vol 1: 6552
Bride's Magazine   Vol 1: 6552
Bridge Publications   Vol 1: 6554
Bridgestone   Vol 1: 11106
Bridport Arts Centre   Vol 2: 2217
Brigham Young University   Vol 1: 6556
Brignetti Literary Award; Isle of Elba - Raffaello   Vol 2: 8322
Brisbane City Council   Vol 2: 292
Brisbane Warana Festival Ltd.   Vol 2: 291
Bristol-Myers   Vol 1: 6558, 15639, 15640
Bristol-Myers Squibb   Vol 1: 701, 704, 3058
Bristol-Myers Squibb Company   Vol 1: 3373
Bristol-Myers Squibb Foundation   Vol 1: 6558, 14341
British Academy   Vol 2: 2220
British Academy of Film and Television Arts   Vol 2: 2231
British Actors' Equity Association   Vol 2: 2235
British Aerospace   Vol 2: 2739
British Agricultural and Garden Machinery Association   Vol 2: 2237
British Airways   Vol 2: 4505
British Appaloosa Society   Vol 2: 2239
British Archaeological Association   Vol 2: 2242
British Archaeological Awards   Vol 2: 2244
British Association for Applied Linguistics   Vol 2: 12152
British Association for the Advancement of Science   Vol 2: 2253
British Association of Aesthetic Plastic Surgeons   Vol 2: 2257
British Association of Barbershop Singers   Vol 2: 2260
British Association of Dermatologists   Vol 2: 2263
British Association of Industrial Editors   Vol 2: 2265
British Association of Landscape Industries   Vol 2: 2268
British Association of Paediatric Surgeons   Vol 2: 10515
British Association of Rheumatology and Rehabilitation   Vol 2: 2518
British Association of Urological Surgeons   Vol 2: 2270
British Association of Women Entrepreneurs   Vol 2: 2279
British Association of Women Executives   Vol 2: 2279
British Astronomical Association   Vol 2: 2284

British Balneological and Climatological Society   Vol 2: 4254
British Birds   Vol 2: 2289
British Broadcasting Corporation   Vol 2: 2294
British Broadcasting Corporation - BBC Educational Radio   Vol 2: 10517
British Broadcasting Corporation and Welsh National Opera   Vol 2: 12154
British Broadcasting Corporation Television   Vol 2: 2296
British Business Press   Vol 2: 3773
British Canadian Holstein Society   Vol 2: 2392
British Canoe Union   Vol 2: 2298
British Cartographic Society   Vol 2: 2303
British Chess Federation   Vol 2: 2310
British Coatings Federation   Vol 2: 2314
British Columbia Historical Federation   Vol 1: 6567
British Comparative Literature Association   Vol 2: 2317
British Computer Society   Vol 2: 2320
British Council   Vol 1: 15402
British Cycle Speedway Council   Vol 2: 2324
British Cycle Speedway Federation   Vol 2: 2324
British Cycling Federation   Vol 2: 2326
British Deaf Association   Vol 2: 2328
British Direct Marketing Association Ltd.   Vol 2: 2330
British Ecological Society   Vol 2: 2332
British Embassy Players   Vol 1: 6570
British Fantasy Society   Vol 2: 2335
British Fashion Council   Vol 2: 2337
British Federation of Film Societies   Vol 2: 2339
British Film Institute   Vol 2: 2340, 2342
British Fire Services Association   Vol 2: 2350
British Gas   Vol 2: 2162, 2562
British Glass Manufacturers Confederation   Vol 2: 2353
British Government   Vol 2: 2355
British Grassland Society   Vol 2: 2388
British Hang Gliding Association   Vol 2: 12156
British Helicopter Advisory Board   Vol 2: 3002
British Herdsmens' Club   Vol 2: 2390
British Holstein Society   Vol 2: 2392
British Horse and Pony Society   Vol 2: 2543
British Industrial and Scientific Association   Vol 2: 3502
British Institute of Architectural Technicians   Vol 2: 2394
British Institute of Non-Destructive Testing   Vol 2: 2398
British Institute of Radiology   Vol 2: 2403
British International Print Exhibition   Vol 2: 2419
British Interplanetary Society   Vol 2: 2421
British Iris Society   Vol 1: 2704
British Italian Society   Vol 2: 4396
British Lichen Society   Vol 2: 2425
British Medical Association   Vol 2: 2427
British Mexican Society   Vol 2: 2456
British Music Society   Vol 2: 2458
British Nuclear Energy Society   Vol 2: 2460
British Numismatic Society   Vol 2: 12161
British Ornithologists' Union   Vol 2: 2463
British Overseas Trade Board   Vol 2: 3649
British Paper and Board Industry Federation   Vol 2: 2467
British Paper and Board Makers' Association   Vol 2: 2467
British Pelargonium and Geranium Society   Vol 2: 2469

British Petroleum   Vol 2: 2032, 3704, 10638, 12155
British Philatelic Federation   Vol 2: 2471
British Phonographic Industry   Vol 2: 2477
British Poultry Meat Federation   Vol 2: 2479
British Printing Industries Federation   Vol 2: 2481
British Psychological Society   Vol 2: 2485
British Quarter Horse Association   Vol 2: 2492
British Reserve Insurance   Vol 2: 10591, 10592
British Resorts Association   Vol 2: 3659
British School at Rome   Vol 2: 8175
British Science Fiction Association   Vol 2: 2495, 4337
British Short Film Institute   Vol 2: 2497
British Show Pony Society   Vol 2: 2499
British Slot Car Racing Association   Vol 2: 2504
British Small Animal Veterinary Association   Vol 2: 2506
British Society for Antimicrobial Chemotherapy   Vol 2: 2514
British Society for Research on Ageing   Vol 2: 2516
British Society for Rheumatology   Vol 2: 2518
British Society for the History of Science   Vol 2: 2522
British Society for the Study of Orthodontics   Vol 2: 2524
British Society of Animal Production   Vol 2: 10519
British Society of Rheology   Vol 2: 2527
British Society of Scientific Glassblowers   Vol 2: 2532
British Society of Soil Science   Vol 2: 2541
British Spotted Pony Society   Vol 2: 2543
British Telecom Inc.   Vol 2: 2888
British Theatre Association   Vol 2: 2546
British Tourist Authority   Vol 2: 2548
British Trout and Salmon Marketing Union   Vol 2: 2895
British Trust for Ornithology   Vol 2: 2550
British Union for the Abolition of Vivisection   Vol 2: 3544
British Veterinary Association   Vol 2: 2553
Britten-Pears Foundation   Vol 2: 2555
Brno; Ceskoslovensky Rozhlas,   Vol 2: 1847
Broadcast Cable Financial Management Association   Vol 1: 6572
Broadcast Designers Association   Vol 1: 6574
Broadcast Education Association   Vol 1: 12970
Broadcast Financial Management Association   Vol 1: 6572
Broadcast Music, Inc.   Vol 1: 6576
Broadcast Pioneers   Vol 1: 6578
Broadcast Promotion and Marketing Executives   Vol 1: 6581
Broadcasters Promotion Association   Vol 1: 6581
Broken Hill Proprietary Company   Vol 2: 295
Bromsgrove Festival Young Musicians' Platform   Vol 2: 2557
Bronfman Family Foundation; Samuel and Saidye   Vol 1: 6583
Brookhaven Women in Science   Vol 1: 6585
Broquette-Gonin; Fondation   Vol 2: 5803, 5806, 5833
Bross Foundation   Vol 1: 6587
Brotherhood of the Knights of the Vine   Vol 1: 6589
Brown & Williamson Tobacco Corporation   Vol 1: 6591
Brown Foundation; Hermione and Louis   Vol 1: 13567

Brown Foundation; James Barrett   Vol 1: 1135
Brown University   Vol 1: 6593
Brun World Arts and Academic Annual Awards   Vol 1: 6596
Bruner Foundation   Vol 1: 6598
Brussels International Fantasy Film Festival   Vol 2: 1090
Bryan Family Foundation   Vol 1: 15503
BT   Vol 2: 4641, 10673
BT plc   Vol 2: 4640
Bucchi; Fondazione Valentino   Vol 2: 8262
Buchhandlung Ziemann & Ziemann, Buxtehude   Vol 2: 7093
Buck Enterprises; H. Werner   Vol 1: 11367
Buck Foundation; Pearl S.   Vol 1: 6600
Buckeye Children's Book Award Council   Vol 1: 6602
Budapest City Council   Vol 2: 7297
Budapest Spring Festival   Vol 2: 7365
Budget Rent a Car   Vol 1: 11754
Budweiser   Vol 1: 2188
Bueller UK Ltd.   Vol 2: 3142
Buenos Aires Municipality   Vol 2: 34
Buhrmann-Ubbens Papierprijs   Vol 2: 9341
Builder   Vol 1: 6604
Builders Advertising Journal   Vol 1: 16456
Building Design & New Barbicon Motel   Vol 2: 2395
Building Employers Confederation - National Contractors Group   Vol 2: 2559
Building Officials and Code Administrators International   Vol 1: 6606
Building Owners and Managers Association International   Vol 1: 6610
Building Stone Institute   Vol 1: 6613
Bulgaria - Office of the President   Vol 2: 1503
Bulgarian Academy of Sciences   Vol 2: 1511
Bulgarian Association for Recreation and Tourism   Vol 2: 1535
Bulgarian Cinematography Corporation   Vol 2: 1520
Bulgarian Ministry of Culture   Vol 2: 1520
Bulgarian National Front   Vol 1: 6615
Bulgarian Photography Union   Vol 2: 1523
Bulgarian Society of Violin Makers   Vol 2: 1515
Bulgarian Television and Radio   Vol 2: 1517
Bulgarska Televiziya i Radio   Vol 2: 1517
The Bulletin   Vol 2: 297
Bund Deutscher Innenarchitekten   Vol 2: 6808
Bundesarztekammer   Vol 2: 6813
Bundesministerium des Innern   Vol 2: 6523
Bundesrepublik Deutschland - Bundesminister fur das Post- und Fernmeldewesen   Vol 2: 6747
Bundesvereinigung Deutscher Apothekerverbande   Vol 2: 6584
Bundeszahnarzte-kammer   Vol 2: 6795
Bunge y Born Foundation   Vol 2: 39
Bungei Shunju Ltd.   Vol 2: 8525, 8750, 8753
Bungei Shunju Publishing Company   Vol 2: 8749
Buning-Brongers Organization; Johan and Titia   Vol 2: 9343
Buning-Brongers Stichting; Johan en Titia   Vol 2: 9343
Buning-Brongers Stichting; Titia   Vol 2: 9343
BUPA   Vol 2: 4387
Burbank Fine Arts Federation   Vol 1: 6617
Bureau canadien de l'education internationale   Vol 1: 6825
Bureau de Controle Technique pour la Construction   Vol 2: 1361
Bureau International de la Recuperation   Vol 2: 1092
Bureau Issues Association   Vol 1: 6619

Bureau Laitier du Canada   Vol 1: 8499
Bureau of Florida Folklife Programs   Vol 1: 6625
Bureau of Land Management   Vol 1: 6627
Bureau of Security Control of Construction   Vol 2: 1361
Burlesque Historical Society   Vol 1: 9026
Burns Foods Endowment Fund   Vol 1: 19810
Burroughs Association; John   Vol 1: 6629
Burroughs Bibliophiles   Vol 1: 6632
Burroughs Wellcome Fund   Vol 1: 3718, 6635, 18070
Bush Foundation   Vol 1: 6640
Business and Industry Commitment to the Environment   Vol 2: 2561
Business and Professional Women's Foundation   Vol 1: 6642
Business Archives Council   Vol 2: 2563
Business Committee for the Arts   Vol 1: 6644
Business Contact Group   Vol 1: 6648
Business Enterprise Trust   Vol 1: 6650
Business Forms Management Association   Vol 1: 6652
Business History Conference   Vol 1: 6658
Business Marketing Association   Vol 1: 6660
Business/Professional Advertising Association   Vol 1: 6660
Business Publications   Vol 1: 9200
Business Roundtable   Vol 1: 19336
Business Week   Vol 1: 6663, 10158
Busoni International Piano Competition   Vol 2: 8180
Butler Company; John O.   Vol 1: 692
Butsuri-Tansa Gakkai   Vol 2: 8755
Bydale Foundation   Vol 1: 8004
Bynner Foundation for Poetry; Witter   Vol 1: 503
C. R. Bard, Inc.   Vol 1: 4132
Cable Television Administration Marketing Society   Vol 1: 6665
Cable Vision   Vol 1: 6666
Cabletelevision Advertising Bureau   Vol 1: 6667
Cadillac   Vol 1: 2188
Cadillac Convertible Owners of America   Vol 1: 6670
CADW - Wales   Vol 2: 2247
Cafe des Deux Magots   Vol 2: 5001
Caisse d'Epargne Rhone-Alpes Lyon   Vol 2: 5175
Caisses Populaires Desjardins   Vol 1: 7496
Caja Agraria   Vol 2: 1601
Caja de Ahorros de Ronda, Cadiz, Almeria, Malaga y Antequera   Vol 2: 11199
Caldwell AMROP Partners International   Vol 1: 9208
Caledonian Research Foundation   Vol 2: 10641
Calenberg-Grubenhagenschen-Landschaft   Vol 2: 6910
California Academy of Sciences   Vol 1: 6672
California Association of Teachers of English   Vol 1: 6679
California Avocado Society   Vol 1: 6674
California Emergency Services Training Academy   Vol 1: 13088
California Institute of the Arts   Vol 1: 6676
California Library Association   Vol 1: 6679
California Media and Library Educators Association   Vol 1: 6679
California National Watercolor Society   Vol 1: 14990
California Notary Association   Vol 1: 14398
California Reading Association   Vol 1: 6678
CALLERLAB - The International Association of Square Dance Callers   Vol 1: 6680
Camara Argentina del Libro   Vol 2: 25

Camara Municipal de Coimbra   Vol 2: 10223
Camara Municipal de Lisboa   Vol 2: 10263
Camara Municipal de Santarem   Vol 2: 10236
Camara Nacional de la Ciudad de Mexico   Vol 2: 8936
Camara Nacional de la Industria Quimico Farmaceutica   Vol 2: 8938
Cambridge Center for Behavioral Studies   Vol 1: 6682
Cambridge Ltd.   Vol 2: 2307
Cambridge Philosophical Society   Vol 2: 2565
Cambridge University Press   Vol 1: 20572
Camcorder User   Vol 2: 4603
Camera Club Liegeois   Vol 2: 1094
Camerata Musicale Barese   Vol 2: 8182
Cameron University - McMahon Foundation; Louise D.   Vol 1: 6684
Camp Fire   Vol 1: 6686
Camp Fire Boys and Girls   Vol 1: 6686
Campaign for the Protection of Rural Wales   Vol 2: 12163
Campaign for United Nations Reform   Vol 1: 6689
Campert Foundation; Jan   Vol 2: 9345
Campertstichting; Jan-   Vol 2: 9345
Campiello Foundation   Vol 2: 8184
Campus Outreach Opportunity League   Vol 1: 6691
Canada - The Chancellery   Vol 1: 6693
Canada - Department of Foreign Affairs and International Trade   Vol 1: 6716
Canada - Health Canada   Vol 1: 6718
Canada - Treasury Board of Canada Secretariat   Vol 1: 6721
Canada Council   Vol 1: 6724
Canada Packers Limited   Vol 1: 7144
Canada Packers Shurgain Ltd.   Vol 1: 7155
Canada Safety Council   Vol 1: 6754
Canada's Sports Hall of Fame   Vol 1: 6759
Canadian Academy of Recording Arts & Sciences   Vol 1: 6761
Canadian Aeronautics and Space Institute   Vol 1: 6763
Canadian Architect   Vol 1: 6770
Canadian Association for Studies on the Baha'i Faith   Vol 1: 5446
Canadian Association of Animal Breeders   Vol 1: 7156
Canadian Association of Broadcasters   Vol 1: 6772
Canadian Association of Gastroenterologists   Vol 1: 8462
Canadian Association of Geographers   Vol 1: 6779
Canadian Association of Medical Radiation Technologists   Vol 1: 6782
Canadian Association of Pathologists   Vol 1: 6792
Canadian Association of Petroleum Producers   Vol 1: 6796
Canadian Association of Physicists   Vol 1: 6800
Canadian Association of Public Libraries   Vol 1: 7003, 7004
Canadian Astronomical Society   Vol 1: 16930
Canadian Authors Association   Vol 1: 6739, 6804
Canadian Aviation Historical Society   Vol 1: 6811
Canadian Bar Foundation   Vol 1: 6813
Canadian Baseball Hall of Fame and Museum   Vol 1: 6815
Canadian Booksellers Association   Vol 1: 6818, 15705
Canadian Broadcasting Corporation   Vol 1: 6741, 6820

Canadian Bureau for International Education   Vol 1: 6825
Canadian Club of New York   Vol 1: 6828
Canadian Co-operative Wool Growers Limited   Vol 1: 6830
Canadian Commission for Unesco   Vol 1: 6745
Canadian Commission for UNESCO   Vol 1: 6833
Canadian Committee on Women's History   Vol 1: 6909
Canadian Community Newspapers Association   Vol 1: 6835
Canadian Conference of the Arts   Vol 1: 6837, 8309, 9205
Canadian Council for European Affairs   Vol 1: 6841
Canadian Council of Professional Engineers   Vol 1: 6843
Canadian Country Music Association   Vol 1: 6847
Canadian Daily Newspaper Association   Vol 1: 6850
Canadian Daily Newspaper Publishers Association   Vol 1: 6850
Canadian Dermatological Association   Vol 1: 6852
Canadian Dermatology Association   Vol 1: 6852
Canadian Economics Association   Vol 1: 6854
Canadian Education Association   Vol 1: 6856
Canadian Family Physician   Vol 1: 7920
Canadian Federation of Culinary Chefs   Vol 1: 6859
Canadian Federation of Humane Societies   Vol 1: 6861
Canadian Federation of University Women   Vol 1: 7042
Canadian Fiction Magazine   Vol 1: 6863
Canadian Film and Television Association   Vol 1: 6865
Canadian Film and Television Production Association   Vol 1: 6865
Canadian Folk Music Society   Vol 1: 7140
Canadian Football Council   Vol 1: 6869
Canadian Football League   Vol 1: 6869
Canadian Forestry Association   Vol 1: 6887
Canadian Foundation for Ileitis and Colitis   Vol 1: 8460
Canadian Geotechnical Society   Vol 1: 6891
Canadian Gospel Music Association   Vol 1: 6900
Canadian Guild of Crafts (Ontario)   Vol 1: 15707
Canadian Historical Association   Vol 1: 2285, 6902
Canadian Home Economics Association   Vol 1: 6910
Canadian Hospital Association   Vol 1: 6920
Canadian Imperial Bank of Commerce   Vol 1: 7693, 17064
Canadian Institute of Forestry   Vol 1: 6922
Canadian Institute of Mining and Metallurgy   Vol 1: 6926
Canadian Institute of Surveying   Vol 2: 8554
Canadian International Amateur Film Festival   Vol 1: 6958
Canadian International Annual Film Festival   Vol 1: 6958
Canadian Interuniversity Athletic Union   Vol 1: 6960
Canadian Library Association   Vol 1: 6997
Canadian Library Association - Canadian Association of Children's Librarians   Vol 1: 7002

Canadian Library Association - Canadian Association of College and University Libraries   Vol 1: 7005
Canadian Library Association - Canadian Association of Public Libraries   Vol 1: 7008
Canadian Library Association - Canadian Association of Special Libraries and Information Services   Vol 1: 7011
Canadian Library Association - Canadian Library Trustees' Association   Vol 1: 7015
Canadian Library Association - Canadian School Library Association   Vol 1: 7018
Canadian Mental Health Association   Vol 1: 7028
Canadian Museum of Nature   Vol 1: 7037
Canadian Museums Association   Vol 1: 7039
Canadian Music Centre   Vol 1: 6741, 7041
Canadian Music Competitions   Vol 1: 7043
Canadian Music Council   Vol 1: 7045
Canadian National Institute for the Blind   Vol 1: 7057
Canadian Nature Federation   Vol 1: 7065
Canadian Nautical Research Society   Vol 1: 7069
Canadian Nurses Association   Vol 1: 7071
Canadian Nurses Foundation   Vol 1: 7073
Canadian Opera Company   Vol 1: 7076
Canadian Paediatric Society   Vol 1: 7078
Canadian Parks and Wilderness Society   Vol 1: 7081
Canadian Parks/Recreation Association   Vol 1: 7083
Canadian Pest Management Society   Vol 1: 7089
Canadian Pharmaceutical Association   Vol 1: 7091
Canadian Phytopathological Society   Vol 1: 7093
Canadian Polar Commission   Vol 1: 7100
Canadian Post Corporation   Vol 1: 5329
Canadian Psychological Association   Vol 1: 7102
Canadian Public Health Association   Vol 1: 7105
Canadian Public Relations Society   Vol 1: 7111
Canadian Rehabilitation Council for the Disabled   Vol 1: 7115
Canadian Rugby Union   Vol 1: 7244
The Canadian School Executive   Vol 1: 7022
Canadian Science Writers' Association   Vol 1: 7125
Canadian Seed Growers' Association   Vol 1: 7127
Canadian Society for Chemical Engineering   Vol 1: 7139, 7539
Canadian Society for Chemical Technology   Vol 1: 7539
Canadian Society for Chemistry   Vol 1: 7539
Canadian Society for Electrical & Computer Engineering   Vol 1: 7131
Canadian Society for Electrical Engineering   Vol 1: 7131
Canadian Society for Mechanical Engineering   Vol 1: 7133, 7562
Canadian Society for Musical Traditions   Vol 1: 7140
Canadian Society for Nutritional Sciences   Vol 1: 7142
Canadian Society of Agricultural Engineering   Vol 1: 7145
Canadian Society of Animal Science   Vol 1: 7153
Canadian Society of Biochemistry and Nuclear Biology   Vol 1: 7162
Canadian Society of Children's Authors, Illustrators, and Performers   Vol 1: 7165

Canadian Society of Civil Engineering   Vol 1: 7167
Canadian Society of Hospital Pharmacists   Vol 1: 7180
Canadian Society of Laboratory Technologists   Vol 1: 7196
Canadian Society of Microbiologists   Vol 1: 7214
Canadian Society of Petroleum Geologists   Vol 1: 7219
Canadian Society of Zoologists   Vol 1: 7231
Canadian Soft Drink Association   Vol 1: 6916
Canadian Sport Aeroplane Association   Vol 1: 7237
Canadian Sport Council   Vol 1: 7239
Canadian Sport Parachuting Association   Vol 1: 7248
Canadian Theatre Critics Association   Vol 1: 7252
Canadian University Music Society   Vol 1: 7254
Canadian Veterinary Medical Association   Vol 1: 7257
Canadian Weekly Newspapers Association   Vol 1: 6835
Canadian Wildlife Federation   Vol 1: 7268
Canadian Wood Council   Vol 1: 5742
Canals International Music Competition, Barcelona; Maria   Vol 2: 11167
Canberra Times   Vol 2: 301
Cancer Association of South Africa   Vol 2: 10825
Cancer Control Society   Vol 1: 7274
Cancer Federation   Vol 1: 7276
Cancer Research Foundation   Vol 1: 7279
Cancer Research Foundation of America   Vol 1: 7281
Cancer Research Fund of the Damon Runyon - Walter Winchell Foundation   Vol 1: 7283
Cancer Society of Finland   Vol 2: 4672
C&G Software Systems, Inc.   Vol 1: 14817
Cannes International Film Festival   Vol 2: 5003
Cannon Seller   Vol 2: 8675
Canola Council of Canada   Vol 1: 7285
Canon Law Society of America   Vol 1: 7287
Canon USA   Vol 1: 14525, 16425, 19844
Canongate Publishing Ltd.   Vol 2: 10518
Canterbury Historical Association   Vol 2: 9708
Canterbury Press   Vol 1: 7289
Cape Cod Art Association   Vol 1: 7291
Cape Cod Museum of Natural History   Vol 1: 7293
Cape; Jonathan   Vol 2: 2568
Cape Tercentenary Foundation   Vol 2: 10827
Capezio/Ballet Makers Dance Foundation   Vol 1: 7295
Capezio Foundation   Vol 1: 7296
Capote Literary Trust; Truman   Vol 1: 18462, 19804
Capranica Foundation   Vol 1: 7297
Car and Driver   Vol 1: 7299
Carafax Publishing Company   Vol 2: 2760
Cardiac Society of Australia and New Zealand   Vol 2: 304
Career College Assoc.   Vol 1: 7301
Career Communications Group   Vol 1: 7303
Career Planning and Adult Development Network   Vol 1: 7306
Cargill   Vol 1: 3313
Caribbean Conference of Churches   Vol 2: 939
Caribbean Hotel Association   Vol 1: 7308
Caribbean Hotel Council of the Caribbean Travel Association   Vol 1: 7308
Caribbean Studies Association   Vol 1: 7310
The Caring Institute   Vol 1: 7313

Carlsberg Laboratorium   Vol 2: 1903
Carlsberg Laboratory   Vol 2: 1903
Carmel Music Society   Vol 1: 7315
Carnation Company   Vol 1: 7317
Carnegie Corporation of New York   Vol 1: 2859
Carnegie Foundation   Vol 2: 9352
Carnegie Fund; Andrew   Vol 1: 2936, 2937
Carnegie Hero Fund Commission   Vol 1: 7319
Carnegie Mellon University   Vol 1: 7321
Carnegie Mellon University - Graduate School of Industrial Administration   Vol 1: 2981
Carnegie Museum of Art   Vol 1: 7323
Carnegie Stichting   Vol 2: 9352
Carolina Biological Supply Company   Vol 1: 5631, 5633
Carrier Corporation   Vol 1: 4576
Carter - Menil Human Rights Foundation   Vol 1: 7326
Carter Center of Emory University   Vol 1: 7325
Cary Charitable Trust; Mary Flagler   Vol 1: 16866
Casa de Cultura in Campeche   Vol 2: 9232
Casadesus Society; Robert   Vol 1: 7840
Casagrande; Concorso Pianistico Internazionale Alessandro   Vol 2: 8206
Casco Northern Bank   Vol 1: 16327
Case IH   Vol 1: 4370
Case Western Reserve University   Vol 1: 7327
Case Western Reserve University - Case Institute of Technology and Western Reserve College   Vol 1: 7329
Case Western Reserve University - Department of Theater Arts   Vol 1: 7331
Cassa di Risparmio di Parma   Vol 2: 8169
Cassa di Risparmio di Perugia   Vol 2: 8409
Cassa di Risparmio di Torino   Vol 2: 8187
Cassa di Risparmio di Verona - Vicenza e Belluno   Vol 2: 8197
Castelbar International Song Contest   Vol 2: 7763
Casualty Actuarial Society   Vol 1: 7333
Catalan Board of Cinema   Vol 2: 11155
Catalonia - Department of Agriculture, Stock Farm and Fishing   Vol 2: 11169
Catalonia - Department of Youth   Vol 2: 11171
Catalonia - Office of the President   Vol 2: 11174
Catalonia Institute of Technology of Construction   Vol 2: 11191
Catalonian Council of Books for Young People   Vol 2: 11193
Catalysis Society Newsletter   Vol 1: 7340
Catalyst   Vol 1: 7345
Catboat Association   Vol 1: 7347
Catepillar Foundation   Vol 1: 8672
Caterer Hotelkeeper   Vol 2: 2570
Cathedral Arts   Vol 1: 7351
Catholic Book Club   Vol 1: 7353
Catholic Broadcasting Association   Vol 1: 18860
Catholic Campus Ministry Association   Vol 1: 7355
Catholic Church Extension Society   Vol 1: 7358
Catholic Health Association of Canada   Vol 1: 7360
Catholic Health Association of the United States   Vol 1: 7362
Catholic Hospital Association of Canada   Vol 1: 7360
Catholic Interracial Council of New York   Vol 1: 7364
Catholic Kolping Society of America   Vol 1: 7367

Catholic League for Religious and Civil Rights   Vol 1: 7370
Catholic Library Association   Vol 1: 7373
Catholic Press Association   Vol 1: 7382
Catholic Theological Society of America   Vol 1: 7386
Catholic University of America - Institute for Communications Law Studies   Vol 1: 7388
Catholic University of America Alumni Association   Vol 1: 7390
Catholic War Veterans of the United States of America   Vol 1: 7397
Catholic Youth Organization of the Archdiocese of New York   Vol 1: 7404
Catskill Center for Photography   Vol 1: 7446
Caucus for Producers, Writers and Directors   Vol 1: 7409
Caudill Young Readers' Book Award Committee (Illinois); Rebecca   Vol 1: 7413
CAUSE   Vol 1: 7415
Cavallo Foundation   Vol 1: 7419
Cavour Prize Association; Grinzane   Vol 2: 8186
Cazes; Prix   Vol 2: 6163
CD-ROM Professional   Vol 1: 15678
CDS International   Vol 1: 7421
Cefilm   Vol 2: 5005
Ceilings and Interior Systems Construction Association   Vol 1: 7423
Ceilings and Interior Systems Contractors Association   Vol 1: 7423
Celanese Mexicana S.A.   Vol 2: 8940
Celette (Industrial Housings) Ltd.   Vol 2: 3318
Cell Kinetics Society   Vol 1: 7425
Celtic Film and Television Association   Vol 2: 10521
Cement and Concrete Association of New Zealand   Vol 2: 9732
Center for Advanced Study in the Behavioral Sciences   Vol 1: 7427
Center for Children's and Young People's Film   Vol 2: 6590
Center for Chinese Studies   Vol 2: 11991
Center for Contemporary Opera   Vol 1: 7429
Center for Creative Leadership   Vol 1: 7431
Center for Democratic Policy   Vol 1: 7442
Center for Entrepreneurial Studies   Vol 1: 7433
Center for International Food and Agricultural Policy   Vol 1: 7435
Center for Judiac Studies   Vol 1: 7438
Center for Judicial Studies   Vol 1: 7440
Center for National Policy   Vol 1: 7442
Center for Philosophy, Law Citizenship   Vol 1: 7444
Center for Photography at Woodstock   Vol 1: 7446
Center for Population Options (California)   Vol 1: 7448
Center for Population Options (Washington, D.C.)   Vol 1: 7450
Center for Public Representation   Vol 1: 7453
Center for Public Resources   Vol 1: 7456
Center for Science and Industry   Vol 2: 5008
Center for Science in the Public Interest   Vol 1: 7458
Center for Studies in American Culture   Vol 1: 7460
Center for Sutton Movement Writing   Vol 1: 7462
Center for the Study of Comparative Folklore and Mythology   Vol 1: 7464
Center for the Study of Science Fiction   Vol 1: 7466
Center for the Study of Sport in Society   Vol 1: 7469

Center for the Study of the Presidency   Vol 1: 7472
Center for War, Peace and the News Media   Vol 1: 7474
Center of International Studies   Vol 2: 1591
Center of Tourist Initiatives   Vol 2: 11195
Center pour les Droits de l'Homme   Vol 2: 11952
Centers for Disease Control - United States Department of Health and Human Services   Vol 1: 14546
Centers for Disease Control and Prevention   Vol 1: 13059
Central Association of Obstetricians and Gynecologists   Vol 1: 7476
Central Council of Scientific-Technical Unions   Vol 2: 1530
Central Engineering Consultancy Bureau of Sri Lanka   Vol 2: 11409
Central Hidroelectrica de Betania   Vol 2: 1593
Central Missouri State University - Art Center Gallery   Vol 1: 7479
Central Neuropsychiatric Association   Vol 1: 7481
Central News Agency Ltd.   Vol 2: 10829
Central Pennsylvania Festival of the Arts   Vol 1: 7483
Central School Library - Coolidge Unified School District 21   Vol 1: 7488
Centrale Volksbank   Vol 2: 9379
Centre Africain de Recherche Appliquee et de Formation en Matiere de Developpement Social   Vol 2: 8850
Centre Belge de Documentation Musicale   Vol 2: 1054
Centre Culturel de Royan   Vol 2: 6214
Centre de Ballet Contemporain   Vol 2: 11671
Centre de Cooperation pour les Recherches Scientifiques relatives au Tabac (CORESTA)   Vol 2: 5081
Centre d'Etudes et des Recherches sur l'Orient Chretien   Vol 2: 5010
Centre d'etudes politique et Social   Vol 2: 5012
Centre du Cinema Grec   Vol 2: 7216
Centre Europeen pour la Communication sur l'Environment   Vol 2: 5115
Centre for Latin American Monetary Studies   Vol 2: 8943
Centre for Management Development   Vol 2: 9857
Centre for Political and Society Studies   Vol 2: 5012
Centre for World Development Education   Vol 2: 4634
Centre Francais de Droit Compare   Vol 2: 5254
Centre francophone Canadien du PEN International   Vol 1: 7490
Centre International de Creation Video, Montbeliard   Vol 2: 6069
Centre International de Criminologie Comparee   Vol 1: 10832
Centre International de l'Enfance   Vol 2: 5981
Centre International de Recherche sur le Cancer - Organisation Mondiale de la Sante   Vol 2: 6484
Centre International des Civilisations Bantu   Vol 2: 6506
Centre International d'Etudes et de Recherches en Socio-Economie de la Sante   Vol 2: 6021
Centre International Humanae Vitae   Vol 2: 5014
Centre Lyrique d'Auvergne   Vol 2: 4980
Centre National de la Cinematographie   Vol 2: 5175, 5248

Centre National de la Recherche Scientifique   Vol 2: 5016
Centre national de la Recherche Scientifique et Technologique   Vol 2: 8909
Centre of Art and Communication   Vol 2: 41
Centre quebecois du PEN International   Vol 1: 7490
Centre Regional Africain de Technologie   Vol 2: 10692
Centre Universitaire du Film Scientifique   Vol 2: 1096
Centro de Arte y Communicacion   Vol 2: 41
Centro de Estudios Internacionales   Vol 2: 1591
Centro de Estudios Monetarios Latinoamericanos (CEMLA)   Vol 2: 8943
Centro de Iniciativas Turisticas   Vol 2: 11195
Centro de Medios Audiovisuales   Vol 2: 11198
Centro del Libro y de la Lectura   Vol 2: 11383, 11384
Centro Euroarabe para las Comunicaciones Audiovisuales   Vol 2: 11225
Centro Impulsor de Educacion Profesional   Vol 2: 1394
Centro Insular de Cultura   Vol 2: 11256
Centro Meridionale di Educazione Ambientale   Vol 2: 8434
Centro Mexicano para los Derechos de la Infancia   Vol 2: 8945
Centro Regional de Sismologia para America del Sur   Vol 2: 10017
Centro Regional Para la Ensenanza de la Informatica   Vol 2: 11200
Centro Studi Nuovo Mezzogiorno   Vol 2: 8148
Century Productions   Vol 1: 9221
Cercle d'Etudes Numismatiques   Vol 2: 1099
Cercle Interallie   Vol 2: 5021
Cercles des Jeunes Naturalistes   Vol 1: 7492
Certamen Internacional de Cine Amateur Ciutat d'Igualada   Vol 2: 11202
Certamen Internacional de Cine para la Infancia y la Juventud de Gijon   Vol 2: 11251
Certamen Internacional de Films Cortos, Ciudad de Huesca   Vol 2: 11235
Ceskoslovenske houslarske souteze   Vol 2: 1849
Ceskoslovensky Rozhlas, Brno   Vol 2: 1847
Ceskoslovensky Svaz Bojovniku za Svobodu a Proti Fasismu   Vol 2: 1845
Cesky Rozhlas, Praga   Vol 2: 1837
Cetus Corporation   Vol 1: 15641
Ceylon Development Engineering Company, Ltd.   Vol 2: 11402
Ceylon Electricity Board   Vol 2: 11409
CFTO-TV Limited   Vol 1: 5329
CH2M Hill   Vol 1: 3973, 4103
Chaine des Rotisseurs   Vol 2: 5023
Chaine des Rotisseurs - Ordre Mondial des Gourmets Degustateurs   Vol 2: 5025
Chainlink Fence Manufacturers Institute   Vol 1: 7497
Challenger Society   Vol 2: 2575
Challenger Society for Marine Science   Vol 2: 2575
Chamber Music America   Vol 1: 4523, 7499
Chamber Music Chicago   Vol 1: 7504
Chamber Music in Yellow Springs   Vol 1: 7506
Chamber Music Society of Lincoln Center   Vol 1: 7508
Chamber Music Society of the Monterey Peninsula   Vol 1: 7510
Chamber of Geological Engineers of Turkey   Vol 2: 12045
Chamber of Mines of South Africa   Vol 2: 10831

Chamber Week Coordinating Committee   Vol 2: 925
Chambre Europeenne pour le Developpement du Commerce, de l'Industrie, et des Finances   Vol 2: 1124
Champagne d'Argent Federation   Vol 1: 7512
Championshiop Auto Racing Teams - CART   Vol 1: 7515
Championship Auto Racing Teams, Inc. - Indy Car   Vol 1: 7515
Chamrousse International Festival of Comedy Film   Vol 2: 5027
Chancery of Netherlands Orders   Vol 2: 9354
Channel 4 Television   Vol 2: 3764
Channel Four Television Corporation   Vol 2: 2693
Chapin Foundation; Harry   Vol 1: 20494
Chapman & Hall Scientific Data Division   Vol 2: 4219
Chapman E. Hall Journals Division   Vol 2: 4219
Charcot-Marie-Tooth Association   Vol 1: 7518
Charities Aid Foundation   Vol 2: 3081
Charity Forum   Vol 2: 3081
Charles River Canada   Vol 1: 7258
Charlotte Repertory Theatre   Vol 1: 7520
Charta 77 Foundation   Vol 2: 11448
Charter Medical Corporation   Vol 1: 533
Chartered Association of Certified Accountants   Vol 2: 2578
Chartered Institute of Building   Vol 2: 2580
Chartered Institute of Journalists   Vol 2: 2583
Chartered Institute of Transport   Vol 2: 2585
Chartered Institute of Transport in Australia   Vol 2: 307
Chartered Institution of Building Services Engineers   Vol 2: 2589
Chartered Insurance Institute   Vol 2: 2600
Chartered Society of Designers   Vol 2: 2606
Chatham College   Vol 1: 7522
Chattahoochee Valley Art Museum   Vol 1: 7524
Chautauqua Art Association   Vol 1: 7527
Chefs & Cooks Circle   Vol 2: 2610
Chelsea   Vol 1: 7530
Cheltenham Festival of Literature   Vol 2: 2612
The Chemical Bank   Vol 1: 7532
Chemical Engineering   Vol 1: 7534
Chemical Industry Institute of Toxicology   Vol 1: 7537
Chemical Institute of Canada   Vol 1: 7539
Chemical Management & Resources Association   Vol 1: 7567
Chemical Manufacturers Association   Vol 1: 7571
Chemical Marketing Research Association   Vol 1: 7567
Chemical Society   Vol 2: 4182
Chemical Society of Japan   Vol 2: 8511
Chemical Society of Mexico   Vol 2: 8947
Chemical Specialties Manufacturers Association   Vol 1: 7573
Cherokee National Historical Society   Vol 1: 7576
Chesapeake and Ohio Historical Society   Vol 1: 7578
Chesapeake Bay Foundation   Vol 1: 7583
Chess Journalists of America   Vol 1: 7585
Chevron Chemical Company   Vol 1: 13026
Chevron Corporation   Vol 1: 7587
Chevron Research & Technology Company   Vol 1: 2580
Chevron USA   Vol 1: 7587
Chia Hsin Cement Corporation   Vol 2: 11994
Chia Hsin Foundation   Vol 2: 11993
Chian Federation of America   Vol 1: 7589
Chibret Laboratories   Vol 2: 6036

Chibuku Breweries   Vol 2: 12220
Chicago Athenaeum   Vol 1: 7591
Chicago Book Clinic   Vol 1: 7593
Chicago Community Trust   Vol 1: 7598
Chicago Film Critics Award   Vol 1: 7603
Chicago International Children's Film Festival   Vol 1: 7605
Chicago International Festival of Children's Films   Vol 1: 7605
Chicago Tribune   Vol 1: 7607, 7608
Chihuahuan Desert Research Institute   Vol 1: 7610
Child Study Children's Book Committee   Vol 1: 7612
Children as Teachers of Peace   Vol 1: 7614
Children as the Peacemakers Foundation   Vol 1: 7614
Children's Book Bulletin   Vol 2: 2614
Children's Book Council   Vol 1: 7616
Children's Book Council of Australia   Vol 2: 309
Children's Book Council of Australia - New South Wales Branch   Vol 2: 314
Children's Book Council of Iran   Vol 2: 7734
Children's Book Foundation   Vol 2: 2616
Children's Broadcast Institute   Vol 1: 320
Children's Cultural Foundation   Vol 1: 7619
Children's Express Foundation   Vol 1: 7619
Children's Film and Television Center of America   Vol 1: 7621
Children's Literature Association   Vol 1: 7623
Children's Literature Research Collections   Vol 1: 7628
Children's Reading Round Table of Chicago   Vol 1: 7630
Children's Rights Workshop   Vol 2: 2614
Children's Wish Foundation International   Vol 1: 7632
Childs Memorial Fund for Medical Research; Jane Coffin   Vol 1: 7634
Chile - Ministerio de Educacion   Vol 2: 1544
Chilean Academy of Language   Vol 2: 1550
Chilean Society of Dermatology and Venereology   Vol 2: 1554
Chilean Society of History and Geography   Vol 2: 1556
China Stamp Society   Vol 1: 7636
Chinese Acupuncture Science Research Foundation   Vol 2: 11995
Chinese American Librarians Association   Vol 1: 7639
Chinese American Medical Society   Vol 1: 7641
Chinese Chemical Society   Vol 2: 1571
Chiropractic Association of South Africa   Vol 2: 10833
Chiropraktiese Vereninging van Suid-Afrika   Vol 2: 10833
Choate, Hall & Stewart   Vol 1: 7643
Choice   Vol 1: 7645
Chomhairle Ealaion   Vol 2: 7754
Chopin Association   Vol 1: 7647
Chopin Foundation of the United States   Vol 1: 7649
Chopin-Gesellschaft in der Bundesrepublik Deutschland Darmstadt   Vol 2: 6593
Chopin Singing Society of Buffalo, New York   Vol 1: 7652
Chopin Society, Czechoslovakia   Vol 2: 1832
Chopin Society; Frederic   Vol 2: 10065
Chopin Society Young Pianist's Competition   Vol 1: 7651
Chorus America - Association of Professional Vocal Ensembles   Vol 1: 7653
Chorus America Awards   Vol 1: 7654
Chow Chow Club   Vol 1: 7658
Chretiens-Medias   Vol 2: 5029

Christchurch International Amateur Film Festival   Vol 2: 9710
CHRISTIAN HANSEN   Vol 2: 9714
Christian Holiness Association   Vol 1: 7660
Christian Management Association   Vol 1: 7663
Christian Ministries Management Association   Vol 1: 7663
Christian Pharmacists Fellowship International   Vol 1: 7666
Christie, Manson & Woods   Vol 1: 2877
Christophers   Vol 1: 7668
The Chronicle of Higher Education   Vol 1: 8297
Chroniqueurs de la Vie au Grand Air du Canada   Vol 1: 15865
Chrysler 300 Club International   Vol 1: 7670
Chrysler Canada   Vol 1: 2316
Chrysler Motors Corporation   Vol 1: 7680, 18814
Chung Nip Hwe Gwan   Vol 2: 8819
Chungshan Cultural Foundation   Vol 2: 11997
Chuokoron-sha, Inc.   Vol 2: 8519
Church & Dwight Company   Vol 1: 10620
Church and Synagogue Library Association   Vol 1: 7672
Church Commissioners for England   Vol 2: 2618
Churchill Downs   Vol 1: 7679
Churchill Foundation of the United States; Winston   Vol 1: 7681
Churchill Study Unit   Vol 1: 10839
Cia de Seguros Bolivar   Vol 2: 1595
Ciani Teatro alla Scala International Competition for Young Pianists; Dino   Vol 2: 8188
Ciani Teatro alla Scala; Premio Dino   Vol 2: 8188
CIBA   Vol 2: 4219
CIBA-GEIGY Corporation   Vol 1: 536, 620, 622, 3520, 4233, 7683, 8923, 14698
CIBA-GEIGY ILAR Rheumatology Prize   Vol 2: 11673
CIBA Plant Protection   Vol 1: 7683
CIBC National Music Festival   Vol 1: 7691
CIBSE   Vol 2: 2597
Ciclo Internacional de Cine Submarino   Vol 2: 11352
Cigarrera la Moderna   Vol 2: 8949, 9211
CIGNA Corporation   Vol 1: 7457
CILQ-FM (Q107 Radio)   Vol 1: 7694
CINANIMA - Festival Internacional de Cinema de Animacao   Vol 2: 10225
CINANIMA - International Animated Film Festival   Vol 2: 10225
Cincinnati Museum of Natural History   Vol 1: 7696
Cincinnati Opera Association   Vol 1: 7698
Cincinnati Scholarship Association   Vol 1: 3163
Cineistes Independent de Badalona   Vol 2: 11204
Cinema/Chicago   Vol 1: 7700
Cinema du Reel   Vol 2: 5031
Cinema Femmes Montreal   Vol 1: 7703
Cinema Novo   Vol 2: 1101
Cinemateque   Vol 2: 7903
Cinematheque Royale   Vol 2: 1351
Cinerent Ltd.   Vol 2: 7265
Cineteca Nacional   Vol 2: 8951
Cintas Foundation, Inc.   Vol 1: 10377
Circle of Children's Book Friends in Slovakia   Vol 2: 1842
Circle of Dutch Theatre Critics   Vol 2: 9359
Circle of the Greek Children's Book   Vol 2: 7187
Circumnavigators Club   Vol 1: 7705
Circus Historical Society   Vol 1: 7707

Cirrus Research Limited   Vol 2: 3052
Cite des Sciences et de l'Industrie (La Villette)   Vol 2: 5008
Citizen Exchange Corps   Vol 1: 7709
Citizen Exchange Council   Vol 1: 7709
Citizens Budget Commission   Vol 1: 7711
Citizens Committee for New York City   Vol 1: 7713
Citizens Energy Council   Vol 1: 7715
Citizens Freedom Foundation   Vol 1: 8483
Citizens Union of the City of New York   Vol 1: 7718
City and Guilds of London Institute   Vol 2: 2620
City & Regional Magazine Association   Vol 1: 7720
City Club of New York   Vol 1: 7722
City Council of Dresden   Vol 2: 6921
City Council of Groningen   Vol 2: 9361
City of Ancona   Vol 2: 8190
City of Beverly Hills   Vol 1: 7726
City of Clermont-Ferrand   Vol 2: 4981
City of Cologne   Vol 2: 6595
City of Darmstadt   Vol 2: 6598
City of Hagen   Vol 2: 7068
City of Independence, Missouri   Vol 1: 7728
City of Lenexa   Vol 1: 7730
City of London Carl Flesch International Violin Competition   Vol 2: 2629
City of London Walther Gruner International Lieder Competition   Vol 2: 2631
City of Mesa - Parks, Recreation & Cultural Division Mesa Arts Center   Vol 1: 7732
City of New York - Department of Business Services   Vol 1: 7734
City of New York - Department of Cultural Affairs   Vol 1: 7736
City of New York - Mayor's Office of Special Projects and Events   Vol 1: 7738
City of Ottawa   Vol 1: 7741
City of Paris   Vol 2: 6431
City of Paris International Competitions   Vol 2: 5033
City of Perpignan   Vol 2: 5253
City of Philadelphia - Board of Directors of Trusts   Vol 1: 7749
City of Philadelphia - City Representative's Office   Vol 1: 7751
City of Philadelphia - Greater Philadelphia First Corporation   Vol 1: 9714
City of Springvale   Vol 2: 316
City of Sydney Cultural Council   Vol 2: 318
City of Sydney Eisteddfod   Vol 2: 318
City of Toronto   Vol 1: 7753, 18747
City of Turin   Vol 2: 8317
City of Vienna Magistrate   Vol 2: 788
City of Westminster Arts Council   Vol 2: 2633
CITY-TV   Vol 1: 18747
City University Business School   Vol 2: 2890
City University of New York - The City College   Vol 1: 7764
City University of New York - Doctoral Theater Students Association   Vol 1: 7771
Civic Trust   Vol 2: 2635
Civil Air Patrol   Vol 1: 19220
Civil Aviation Medical Association   Vol 1: 175
Civil War Press Corps   Vol 1: 7773
Civil War Round Table of New York   Vol 1: 7775
Civil War Society   Vol 1: 7780
Civil War Token Society   Vol 1: 7782
Civitan International   Vol 1: 7784
Cladan Cultural Exchange Institute of Australia   Vol 2: 324
Clairol, Inc.   Vol 1: 13785
Clarinet International   Vol 1: 10858
Clarinetwork International   Vol 1: 10858

Clarke College   Vol 1: 7798
Classic Car Club of America   Vol 1: 7801
Classical America   Vol 1: 7811
Classification and Compensation Society   Vol 1: 7814
Clay Minerals Society   Vol 1: 7827
Cleft Palate Foundation   Vol 1: 7831
Clemens & Associates Insurance Agency   Vol 1: 12260
Clemson Architectural Foundation   Vol 1: 7835
Clemson University - College of Architecture   Vol 1: 7834
Cleveland Foundation   Vol 1: 7836
Cleveland Institute of Music   Vol 1: 7838
Cleveland State University Poetry Center   Vol 1: 7841
Cleveland (UK) International Drawing Biennale   Vol 2: 2637
Cliburn Foundation; Van   Vol 1: 7843
Clifford Chance Solicitors   Vol 2: 2890
Clinical Immunology Society   Vol 1: 7845
Clinical Sociology Association   Vol 1: 18108
Clothing and Footwear Institute   Vol 2: 4513
Clowes Fund   Vol 1: 1749
CLSI, Inc.   Vol 1: 2909, 2932
Club Daguerre   Vol 2: 6604
Club de Periodistas   Vol 2: 9078
Club Europeen de la Sante   Vol 2: 5035
Club International d'Implants Oculaires   Vol 2: 3437
Club Partir   Vol 2: 5037
Club Tenco   Vol 2: 8192
Clubcentrum Usti-nad-Orlici   Vol 2: 1834
Clydesdale Bank PLC   Vol 2: 10531
CNA Casualty Company   Vol 1: 19028
Co-Ette Club   Vol 1: 7847
Co-op Subscriptions   Vol 2: 243
Coal Preparation Society   Vol 2: 3652
Coalition for Alternatives in Jewish Education   Vol 1: 7852
Coalition for Indian Education   Vol 1: 7849
Coalition for the Advancement of Jewish Education   Vol 1: 7852
Coalition on Government Information   Vol 1: 7854
Coastal Emergency Services   Vol 1: 8901
Coblentz Society   Vol 1: 7856, 15752, 17417
Coca-Cola USA   Vol 1: 5123
Coccia; Ente Musicale Novarese Carlo   Vol 2: 8219
Codazzi; Instituto Geografico Agustin   Vol 2: 1717
Coe Manufacturing Company   Vol 1: 9334
COGEDIM   Vol 2: 5039
Cohen Memorial Fund; Sophie and Shirley   Vol 1: 17633
Coindreau; Societe des Amis de Maurice Edgar   Vol 2: 6245
Colby College   Vol 1: 7859
Coldwater Community Theater   Vol 1: 7861
Colegio de Arquitectos de Honduras   Vol 2: 7259
Colegio de Arquitectos de Venezuela   Vol 2: 12141
Colegio de Arquitectos del Peru   Vol 2: 10013
Colegio de Contadores Publicos de Mexico   Vol 2: 8953
Colegio de Posgraduados   Vol 2: 8955
Colegio Ibero-Latino-mericano de Dermatologia   Vol 2: 1461
Colegio Medico Veterinario de Chile   Vol 2: 1559
Coleman Chamber Music Association   Vol 1: 7863
Coleopterists' Society   Vol 1: 7865

Colgate-Palmolive Company   Vol 1: 10621, 18071
Colilegi d'Aparelladors i Arquitectes Tecnics de Barcelona   Vol 2: 11206
Collaborative Testing Services, Inc.   Vol 1: 4865
Collective Promotion of the Netherlands Book   Vol 2: 9364
Collectors Club   Vol 1: 7867
Collectors of Religion on Stamps   Vol 1: 7873
College and University Personnel Association   Vol 1: 7875
College and University Systems Exchange   Vol 1: 7415
College Art Association of America   Vol 1: 7882
College English Association   Vol 1: 7892
College Football Association   Vol 1: 7898
College Language Association   Vol 1: 7901
College Media Advisers   Vol 1: 7903
College of Chaplains, Inc.   Vol 1: 7914
College of Chaplains of the American Protestant Health Association   Vol 1: 7914
College of Chemical Engineers   Vol 2: 487
College of Family Physicians of Canada   Vol 1: 7919
College of Mount Saint Joseph   Vol 1: 7928
College of Mount Saint Joseph on the Ohio   Vol 1: 7928
College of Optometrists in Vision Development   Vol 1: 7931
College of Physicians of Philadelphia - Section on Dermatology   Vol 1: 7934
College of Piping   Vol 2: 10523
College of Psychologists of British Columbia   Vol 1: 7936
College of Technical Architects and Buildings Foremen of Barcelona   Vol 2: 11206
College of William and Mary   Vol 1: 10255
College Ouest Africaine des Chirurgiens   Vol 2: 9868
College Royal des Medecins et Chirurgiens du Canada   Vol 1: 16937
College Sports Information Directors of America   Vol 1: 7939
College Swimming Coaches Association   Vol 1: 14248
College Swimming Coaches Association of America   Vol 1: 7945
Collegiate Hall of Fame   Vol 1: 7950
Collegium Internationale Chirurgiae Digestivae   Vol 2: 8194
Collegium Internationale Neuro-Psychopharmacologicum   Vol 2: 10526
Collins/Angus & Robertson Publishers Pty Ltd.   Vol 2: 327
Collins Publishers   Vol 2: 2639
Colmar International Competition for Chamber Music Ensembles   Vol 2: 5041
Cologne International Pianoforte Competition - Foundation Tomassoni   Vol 2: 6606
Cologne International Violin Competition   Vol 2: 6608
Colombia - Administrative Department of Civil Aeronautics   Vol 2: 1597
Colombia - Departemento Administrativo de Aeronoutica Civil   Vol 2: 1597
Colombia - Ministerio de Agricultura   Vol 2: 1599
Colombia - Ministerio de Asuntos Exteriores   Vol 2: 1617
Colombia - Ministerio de Comunicaciones   Vol 2: 1603
Colombia - Ministerio de Defensa Nacional   Vol 2: 1633
Colombia - Ministerio de Economico Desarrollo   Vol 2: 1607

Colombia - Ministerio de Educacion Nacional   Vol 2: 1650
Colombia - Ministerio de Interno Asuntos   Vol 2: 1622
Colombia - Ministerio de Justicia   Vol 2: 1624
Colombia - Ministerio de Obras Publicas y Transporte   Vol 2: 1668
Colombia - Ministerio de Salud   Vol 2: 1666
Colombia - Ministerio de Trabajo y Seguridad Social   Vol 2: 1631
Colombia - Ministry of Agriculture   Vol 2: 1599
Colombia - Ministry of Communications   Vol 2: 1603
Colombia - Ministry of Economic Development   Vol 2: 1607
Colombia - Ministry of Foreign Affairs   Vol 2: 1617
Colombia - Ministry of Government (Interior)   Vol 2: 1622
Colombia - Ministry of Justice   Vol 2: 1624
Colombia - Ministry of Labor and Social Security   Vol 2: 1631
Colombia - Ministry of National Defence   Vol 2: 1633
Colombia - Ministry of National Education   Vol 2: 1650
Colombia - Ministry of Public Health   Vol 2: 1666
Colombia - Ministry of Public Works and Transportation   Vol 2: 1668
Colombia - National Police   Vol 2: 1670
Colombia - Policia Nacional   Vol 2: 1670
Colombian Academy of Language   Vol 2: 1678
Colombian Association for the Advancement of Science   Vol 2: 1680
Colombian Association of Disabled People   Vol 2: 1683
Colombian Association of Librarians   Vol 2: 1685
Colombian Fund for Scientific Investigation and Special Projects Francisco Jose de Caldas (COLCIENCIAS)   Vol 2: 1687
Colombian Oceanographic Commission   Vol 2: 1689
Colombian Pediatric Society   Vol 2: 1691
Colombian Society of Economists   Vol 2: 1590
Colonial Players, Inc.   Vol 1: 7952
Colonial Williamsburg Foundation   Vol 1: 10255
Colophon Society   Vol 2: 330
Colorado Ranger Horse Association   Vol 1: 7954
Columbia: A Magazine of Poetry and Prose   Vol 1: 7958
Columbia College Chicago   Vol 1: 7960
Columbia College Chicago - Theater/Music Center   Vol 1: 7962
Columbia Engineering School Alumni Association   Vol 1: 7964
Columbia Historical Society   Vol 1: 9936
Columbia Pictures Television   Vol 1: 1756
Columbia Scholastic Press Association   Vol 1: 7967
Columbia University   Vol 1: 7970, 11485
Columbia University - Freedom Forum Media Studies Center   Vol 1: 7989
Columbia University - Gannett Center for Media Studies   Vol 1: 7989
Columbia University - Graduate School of Journalism   Vol 1: 4655, 7991
Columbia University - The Harriman Institute   Vol 1: 892
Columbia University - Keene Center of Japanese Culture; Donald   Vol 1: 7998

Columbia University - Office of Public Information   Vol 1: 8000
Columbia University - School of the Arts   Vol 1: 8003
Columbia University - Translation Center   Vol 1: 8005
Columbia University - Wien Prize in Corporate Social Responsibility; Lawrence A.   Vol 1: 8008
Columbian Squires   Vol 1: 8010
Columbus Bureau of Medical Economics   Vol 1: 12164
Columbus: Countdown 1992   Vol 1: 8014
Colworth Laboratory   Vol 2: 4354
Combined Organizations of Numismatic Error Collectors of America   Vol 1: 8018
Combustion Institute   Vol 1: 8020
Comhaltas Ceoltoiri Eireann   Vol 2: 7849
Comision Colombiana de Oceanografia   Vol 2: 1689
Comision Federal de Electricidad   Vol 2: 9033
Comision "Justicia y Paz" de Espana   Vol 2: 11208
Comision Nacional Bancaria   Vol 2: 8957
Comision para la Defensa de los Derechos Humanos en Centroamerica   Vol 2: 1758
Comision Premio Ames a la Investigacion en el Laboratorio Clinico   Vol 2: 1580
Comissao Nacional de Energia Nuclear   Vol 2: 2026
Comite Cesar Franck Orgel Concours   Vol 2: 9431
Comite d'Action de la Resistance   Vol 2: 5043
Comite d'action pour le solaire   Vol 2: 5045
Comite des Associations Europeennes de Fonderie   Vol 2: 5059
Comite d'Organisation de l'Anneau d'Or   Vol 2: 11737
Comite du Rayonnement Francais   Vol 2: 5047
Comite Europeen de Rink Hockey   Vol 2: 5117
Comite Francais de l'Association Mondiale Veterinaire   Vol 2: 5055
Comite Francais d'Histoire de l'Art   Vol 2: 5057
Comite International de la Croix-Rouge   Vol 2: 11770
Comite International de l'Organisation Mondiale de la Presse Periodique   Vol 2: 1103
Comite International de Medecine Militaire   Vol 2: 1180
Comite International des Sports des Sourds   Vol 2: 1959
Comite International Olympique   Vol 2: 11813
Comite International pour la Diffusion des Arts et des Lettres par le Cinema - CIDALC   Vol 2: 5990
Comite International pour la Diffusion des Arts et des Lettres par le Cinema - CIDALC   Vol 2: 5248
Comite International pour la Sauvegarde de la Langue Bretonne   Vol 2: 1178
Comite International pour le Fair Play   Vol 2: 5988
Comite International pour le Soutien de la Charte 77 en Tchecoslovaquie   Vol 2: 5992
Comite Mondial pour la Recherche Spatiale   Vol 2: 5061
Commercial Development Association   Vol 1: 8025
Commercial Finance Association   Vol 1: 8027
Commission canadienne pour l'UNESCO   Vol 1: 6833
Commission for the Defense of Human Rights in Central America   Vol 2: 1758

Commission Geographical Education   Vol 2: 6959
Commission Internationale de Psychologie Religieuse Scientifique   Vol 2: 1174
Commission Internationale du Genie Rural   Vol 2: 1176
Commission of the European Communities   Vol 2: 5096
Commission on Pastoral Research   Vol 1: 8029
Commission Permanente de la Croix-Rouge et du Croissant-Rouge   Vol 2: 11914
Commission Permanente de la Croix-Rouge Internationale   Vol 2: 11914
Commission Sericicole Internationale   Vol 2: 6045
Commissioner of Baseball   Vol 1: 8031
Committee for the Liberation of Vladimir Danchev   Vol 2: 6003
Committee of European Foundry Associations   Vol 2: 5059
Committee of Presidents of Statistical Societies   Vol 1: 8034
Committee on Classification Research of the Federation Internationale d'Information et de Documentation, The Hague   Vol 1: 8039
Committee on Continuing Education for School Personnel   Vol 1: 8041
Committee on Space Research   Vol 2: 5061
Common Boundary   Vol 1: 8044
Common Cause   Vol 1: 8046
The Common Good   Vol 1: 8048
Commonwealth Association of Architects   Vol 2: 2643
Commonwealth Association of Science and Mathematics Educators   Vol 2: 2645
Commonwealth Association of Science, Technology and Mathematics Educators   Vol 2: 2645
Commonwealth Association of Surveying and Land Economy   Vol 2: 2647
Commonwealth Athletic Club   Vol 1: 8050
Commonwealth Athletic Club of Kentucky   Vol 1: 12569
Commonwealth Bank of Australia   Vol 2: 141, 262
Commonwealth Chess Association   Vol 1: 8052
Commonwealth Club of California   Vol 1: 8054
Commonwealth Council for Educational Administration   Vol 2: 332
Commonwealth Forestry Association   Vol 2: 2649
Commonwealth Foundation   Vol 2: 2646, 2653
Commonwealth Games Federation   Vol 2: 2660
Commonwealth Institute   Vol 2: 2662
Commonwealth Institute of London   Vol 2: 2657
Commonwealth Magistrates' and Judges' Association   Vol 2: 2665
Commonwealth Magistrates' Association   Vol 2: 2665
Commonwealth Press Union   Vol 2: 2667
Commonwealth Weightlifting Federation   Vol 2: 12165
Commonwealth Youth Programme   Vol 2: 2670
Communaute des Radios Publiques de Langue Francaise - Maison de Radio France   Vol 2: 5069
Communaute Radiophonique des Programmes de Langue Francaise   Vol 2: 5069
Commune di Caltanissetta   Vol 2: 8107
Commune di Enna   Vol 2: 8204
Communication Arts   Vol 1: 8056

Communication   **Awards, Honors & Prizes, 1995-96**

Communication Association of the Pacific Vol 1: 20480
Communications Concepts, Inc. Vol 1: 8061
Community Action Network Vol 1: 8063
Community Children's Theatre of Kansas City Vol 1: 8065
Community College Association for Instruction and Technology Vol 1: 8067
Community College Humanities Association Vol 1: 8069
Community Colleges for International Development Vol 1: 8071
Compania Nacional de Navegacion - NAVENAL Vol 2: 1731
Compass Publications Inc. Vol 1: 12087, 14403
Compassionate Friends Vol 1: 8073
Composers & Songwriters International Vol 1: 8075
Composers, Authors and Publishers Association of Canada Vol 1: 17819
Composers Guild Vol 1: 8075
Composite Industry Monthly Vol 1: 18044
Composite Market Reports Vol 1: 18045
Composites Institute Vol 1: 18044
Composites Manufacturing Association of SME Vol 1: 17878
Computer and Automated Systems Association of the Society of Manufacturing Engineers Vol 1: 8077
Computer Press Association Vol 1: 8080
Computing to Assist Persons with Disabilities Vol 1: 8082
Comune di Ancona Vol 2: 8190
Comune di Sanguinetto Vol 2: 8196
Comune di Sondrio Mostra Internazionale dei Documentari sui Parchi Vol 2: 8432
Conamus Foundation Vol 2: 9370
Conamus; Stichting Vol 2: 9370
Concert Artists Guild Vol 1: 8084
Concord Press Board of Trustees Vol 2: 9860
Concordia: A Chamber Symphony Vol 1: 8086
Concordia Historical Institute Vol 1: 8088
Concorso Ettore Pozzoli Vol 2: 8198
Concorso Internationale d'Execuzione Musicale - Genevra Vol 2: 11773
Concorso Internazionale di Chitarra Classica Citta di Alessandria Vol 2: 8200
Concorso Internazionale di Composizione Organistica Oliver Messiaen Vol 2: 8202
Concorso Internazionale di Violino Nicolo Paganini Vol 2: 8394
Concorso Internazionale Michelangelo Abbado per Violinisti Vol 2: 7998
Concorso Internazionale Musicale Francesco Paolo Neglia Vol 2: 8204
Concorso Internazionale per Voci Verdiane Vol 2: 8292
Concorso Pianistico Internazionale Alessandro Casagrande Vol 2: 8206
Concorso Pianistico Internazionale Citta di Senigallia Vol 2: 8418
Concorso Pianistico Internazionale F. Busoni Vol 2: 8180
Concours de musique du Canada Vol 1: 7043
Concours Geza Anda Vol 2: 11675
Concours International d'Alto Maurice Vieux Vol 2: 6468
Concours International de Ballet, Varna Vol 2: 1538
Concours International de Chant de la Ville de Toulouse Vol 2: 6047
Concours International de Chant de Verviers Vol 2: 1214
Concours International de Chant Offenbach Vol 2: 5071

Concours International de Composition Musicale Opera et Ballet Geneve Vol 2: 11677
Concours International de Harpe en Israel Vol 2: 7898
Concours International de Musique de Chambre pour Ensembles d'Instruments a Vent Vol 2: 11679
Concours International de Musique de Montreal Vol 1: 12426
Concours International de Piano d'Epinal Vol 2: 5073
Concours International de Violoncelle Rostropovitch Vol 2: 6200
Concours International d'Ensembles de Musique de Chambre de Colmar Vol 2: 5041
Concours International d'Execution Musicale - Geneve Vol 2: 11773
Concours International du Festival de Musique de Toulon Vol 2: 5075
Concours International J. S. Bach Vol 2: 6935
Concours International Printemps de la Guitare Vol 2: 1105
Concours International Robert Schumann Vol 2: 6977
Concours Internationaux de la Ville de Paris Vol 2: 5033
Concours Musical International Reine Elisabeth de Belgique Vol 2: 1244
Concours National Feminin de Musique du Lyceum de Suisse Vol 2: 11681
Concours Seymour Cray France Vol 2: 5077
Concours Suisse de l'orgue Vol 2: 11944
Concrete Reinforcing Steel Institute Vol 1: 2522, 8091
Concrete Sawing and Drilling Association Vol 1: 8093
Concrete Sealants (U.S.) Vol 1: 288
Concrete Society Vol 2: 2672
Concrete Society of Southern Africa Vol 2: 10835
Concurs Internacional de Cant Francesc Vinas Vol 2: 11393
Concurs Internacional Maria Canals de Barcelona Vol 2: 11167
Concurso Internacional de Canto de Bilbao Vol 2: 11274
Concurso Internacional de Ejecucion Musical Dr. Luis Sigall Vol 2: 1569
Concurso Internacional de Piano Ciudad de Montevideo Vol 2: 12089
Concurso Internacional de Piano de Santander Vol 2: 11354
Concurso Internacional de Piano Pilar Bayona Vol 2: 11272
Concurso Internacional de Piano Premio Jaen Vol 2: 11280
Concurso Internacional Vianna da Motta Piano e Violino Vol 2: 10227
Conductors' Guild Vol 1: 8095
Confederacion Espanola de Cajas de Ahorros Vol 2: 11210
Confederate Air Force Flying Museum Vol 1: 8098
Confederate Memorial Literary Society Vol 1: 8103
Confederate Stamp Alliance Vol 1: 8106
Confederation Europeenne de Baseball Amateur Vol 2: 1115
Confederation Europeenne de l'Agriculture Vol 2: 1126
Confederation Europeenne de Roller Skating Vol 2: 5118
Confederation Europeenne des Relations Publiques Vol 2: 5121

Confederation Interalliee des Officiers de Reserve Vol 2: 1163
Confederation Internationale des Accordeonistes Vol 2: 813
Confederation Internationale des Negociants en Oeuvres d'Art Vol 2: 3390
Confederation Internationale des Societes d'Auteurs et Compositeurs Vol 2: 5994
Confederation of American Indians Vol 1: 8115
Confederation of British Industry Vol 2: 2674
Confederation of French Industries and Services Vol 2: 5126
Confederation of Nordic Bank Employees' Unions Vol 2: 11451
Confedertion Internationale d'Analyse Thermique Vol 2: 3387
Conference Canadienne des Arts Vol 1: 6837
Conference Internationale de la Mutualite et des Assurances Sociales Vol 2: 11836
Conference Internationale du Goudron Vol 2: 6053
Conference of Biological Editors Vol 1: 8346
Conference of Educational Administrators Serving the Deaf Vol 1: 8117
Conference of Executives of American Schools for the Deaf Vol 1: 8117
Conference of Federal Environmental Engineers Vol 1: 8122
Conference of Funeral Service Examining Boards Vol 1: 8124
Conference of Public Health Laboratorians Vol 1: 8126
Conference of Public Health Laboratory Directors Vol 1: 8126
Conference of Public Health Veterinarians Vol 1: 8128
Conference on British Studies Vol 1: 15401
Conference on Christianity and Literature Vol 1: 8130
Conference on College Composition and Communication Vol 1: 8132, 13763
Conference on English Education Vol 1: 13764, 13765
Conference on Latin American History Vol 1: 8137
Congregational Christian Historical Society Vol 1: 8144
Congress for Jewish Culture Vol 1: 8146
Congress of Neurological Surgeons Vol 1: 8148
Congress of Racial Equality - CORE Vol 1: 8153
Congressional Arts Caucus Vol 1: 8155
The Congressional Award Foundation Vol 1: 8157
Congressional Black Caucus Foundation Vol 1: 8159
Congressional Hispanic Caucus Institute Vol 1: 8166
Congressional Information Service Vol 1: 2895
Congressional Medal of Honor Society, United States of America Vol 1: 8169
Congressional Quarterly Vol 1: 8172
Connecticut River Watershed Council Vol 1: 8174
Connecticut Writer Vol 1: 8177
Conrad Society of America; Joseph Vol 1: 8179
Conseil Canadien de la Musique Vol 1: 7045
Conseil Canadien de la Securite Vol 1: 6754
Conseil de la Communaute francaise de Belgique Vol 2: 1109
Conseil de la Vie Francaise en Amerique Vol 1: 8181
Conseil de l'Europe Vol 2: 5086, 5188

Conseil de recherches en sciences naturelles et en genie du Canada Vol 1: 15074
Conseil de recherches medicales du Canada Vol 1: 12184
Conseil des Arts de la Communaute Urbaine de Montreal Vol 1: 12433
Conseil des arts de l'Ontario Vol 1: 15690
Conseil des Arts du Canada Vol 1: 6724
Conseil Europeen des Federations de l'Industrie Chimique Vol 2: 1128
Conseil Europeen des Services Communautaires Juifs Vol 2: 5123
Conseil General des Hauts de Seine Vol 2: 6102
Conseil International de la Chasse et de la Conservation du Gibier Vol 2: 5996
Conseil International de la Langue Francaise Vol 2: 5998
Conseil International d'education des adultes Vol 1: 10870
Conseil International des Infirmieres Vol 2: 11777
Conseil International des Radios - Televisions d'Expression Francaise Vol 2: 11775
Conseil International des Sciences Sociales Vol 2: 6049
Conseil International du Batiment Vol 2: 9481
Conseil International du Droit de l'Environnement Vol 2: 6939
Conseil Mondial de la Paix Vol 2: 4766
Conseil Mondial des Clubs d'Entraide de Jeunes Gens Vol 2: 9853
Conseil Mondiale de Management Vol 2: 8907
Consejo Consultivo de la Ciudad de Mexico Vol 2: 8959
Consejo Consultivo del Programa de Solidaridad Vol 2: 8962
Consejo Cultural Mundial Vol 2: 9305
Consejo de Fundaciones Americanas de Desarrollo, Solidarios Vol 2: 2014
Consejo Interamericano de Escultismo Vol 2: 1780
Consejo Interamericano de Seguridad Vol 1: 10512
Consejo Internacional de Buena Vecindad Vol 2: 9074
Consejo Internacional de Los Frutos Secos Vol 2: 11270
Consejo Mexicano de Fotografia Vol 2: 9243
Consejo Mundial de Boxeo Vol 2: 9303
Consejo Nacional de Ciencia y Tecnologia Vol 2: 8964, 9033
Consejo Nacional de Investigaciones Cientificas y Tecnologicas - CONICIT Vol 2: 12125
Consejo Nacional de la Cultura Vol 2: 12115
Consejo Nacional de la Cultura y las Artes Vol 2: 8966
Consejo Nacional de Poblacion Vol 2: 8968
Consejo Nacional para la Cultura y las Artes Vol 2: 9259
Consejo Nacional para la Ensenanza y la Investigacion de las Ciencias de la Comunicacion Vol 2: 8970
Consell Catala del Llibre per a Infants Vol 2: 11193
Conservation and Research Foundation Vol 1: 6488, 8184
Conservation Council of Ontario Vol 1: 8186
Conservation Foundation (France) Vol 2: 5079
Conservation Foundation (UK) Vol 2: 2676
Conservatorio di Musica A. Boito di Parma Vol 2: 8167

Conservatorio Profesional de Musica i Danza Les Illes Baleares Vol 2: 11212
Conservatory of Runic Parma - Sant'Agostino Cultural Centre Crema Vol 2: 8168
Consider the Alternatives Productions Vol 1: 8188
Consolidated Edison Vol 1: 16626
Consortium of College and University Media Centers Vol 1: 8190
Consortium of University Film Centers Vol 1: 8190
Constable & Co. Ltd. Vol 2: 2197, 2679
Construction Education Foundation Vol 1: 8192
Construction Industry Computing Association Vol 2: 2681
Construction Specifications Institute Vol 1: 8194
Construction Writers Association Vol 1: 8215
Consulting Psychologists Press Vol 1: 3707, 3800
Consumer Credit Insurance Association Vol 1: 8219
Consumer Electronics Group Vol 1: 8881
Consumer Federation of America Vol 1: 8222
Consumers for World Trade Vol 1: 8226
Contact Lens Manufacturers Association Vol 1: 8228
Containerization and Intermodal Institute Vol 1: 8230
Contemporary A Capella Society of America Vol 1: 8232
Contemporary Arts Center Vol 1: 8234
Contemporary Record Society Vol 1: 8237
Continental Basketball Association Vol 1: 8241
Continental Confederation of Adopted Indians Vol 1: 8249
Contract Magazine Vol 1: 10248
Convention Liaison Council Vol 1: 8251
Convention of American Instructors of the Deaf Vol 1: 8119
Conventual Franciscan Friars Vol 1: 9365
Conway Data Vol 1: 10160, 10161
Cook Europe; William Vol 2: 2274
Cook; Thomas Vol 2: 3649
Cook Travel; Thomas Vol 2: 2683
Cookson Group plc. Vol 2: 4219
Cooper-Biomedical Vol 1: 928
Cooper *Deloitte* Vol 2: 2734
Cooper Memorial Prize Fund; Duff Vol 2: 2685
Cooper Ohioana Library Association; Martha Kinney Vol 1: 15597
Cooper Ornithological Society Vol 1: 8253
Cooper Prize; Duff Vol 2: 2685
Cooper Union for the Advancement of Science and Art Vol 1: 8260
Cooperation Center for Scientific Research Relative to Tobacco (CORESTA) Vol 2: 5081
Cooperative Communicators Association Vol 1: 8265
Cooperative Education Association Vol 1: 8268
The Cooperative Foundation Vol 1: 5726
Cooperative International de Recherche et d'Action en Matiere de Communication Vol 2: 1107
Cooperative Work Experience Education Association Vol 1: 8272
Coopers Agropharm Inc. Vol 1: 7260
Coopers & Lybrand, Toronto Vol 1: 9210
Coopers Hill Society Vol 2: 3233
Coordinating Committee for International Voluntary Service Vol 2: 5084

Coordinating Committee on Women in the Historical Profession - Conference Group on Women's History Vol 1: 8275
Coordinating Council of Literary Magazines Vol 1: 8368
Coors "Man in the Can" Vol 1: 16511
Copley Society of Boston Vol 1: 20574
Copper Development Association Vol 2: 3147
Cordero; Fundacion Jorge Sanchez Vol 2: 8986
Coregis Group Vol 1: 16582
Cork International Choral Festival Vol 2: 7765
Cork International Film Festival Vol 2: 7768
Cornell Laboratory of Ornithology Vol 1: 11748
Cornell University Vol 1: 8971
Corning Glass Works Vol 1: 15760
Corporacion Nacional de Turismo Vol 2: 1693
Corporation for National and Community Service Vol 1: 16300
Corporation for Public Broadcasting Vol 1: 8277, 8627
Corporation on Disabilities and Telecommunication Vol 1: 8283
Corporation Professionnelle des Psychologues du Quebec Vol 1: 8285
Corpus Christi Young Artists' Competition Vol 1: 8289
Costa Rica - Ministerio de Cultura, Juventud y Deportes Vol 2: 1760
Costa Rica - Ministry of Culture, Youth and Sport Vol 2: 1760
Cote d'Ivoire - Presidency of the Republic Vol 2: 1786
Cotton Foundation; Dr. M. Aylwin Vol 2: 2687
Council for Advancement and Support of Education Vol 1: 9, 8291
Council for Art Education Vol 1: 8303
Council for Awards of Royal Agricultural Societies Vol 2: 2690
Council for Basic Education Vol 1: 8305
Council for British Archaeology/BUFVC AV Media Working Party Vol 2: 2692
Council for Business and the Arts in Canada Vol 1: 8307
Council for Chemical Research Vol 1: 8310
Council for Education in World Citizenship Vol 2: 2694
Council for Exceptional Children Vol 1: 8312
Council for Exceptional Children - Mental Retardation Division Vol 1: 8320
Council for Health and Human Service Ministries - United Chruch of Christ Vol 1: 8326
Council for International Exchange of Scholars Vol 1: 8328
Council for Learning Disabilities Vol 1: 8330
Council for National Academic Awards Vol 2: 2696
Council for National Cooperation in Aquatics Vol 1: 8333
Council for the Advancement of Science Writing Vol 1: 8335
Council for the Arts in Ottawa Vol 1: 7746
Council for the Order of Australia Vol 2: 334
Council for the Protection of Rural Wales Vol 2: 12163
Council for Wisconsin Writers Vol 1: 8337
Council of Administrators of Special Education Vol 1: 8340
Council of American Development Foundations, Solidarios Vol 2: 2014
Council of Authors and Journalists Vol 1: 8344
Council of Biology Editors Vol 1: 8346

Council of Chief State School Officers   Vol 1: 8349
Council of Commercial Plant Breeders   Vol 1: 8470
Council of Educational Facility Planners, International   Vol 1: 8352
Council of Engineering Deans of the Historically Black Colleges and Universities   Vol 1: 7304
Council of Europe   Vol 2: 5086, 11793
Council of European Industrial Federations   Vol 2: 2702
Council of Fashion Designers of America   Vol 1: 8354
Council of Film Organizations   Vol 1: 8357
Council of Graduate Schools   Vol 1: 8359
Council of Graduate Schools in the United States   Vol 1: 8359
Council of Jewish Federations   Vol 1: 8361
Council of Jewish Federations and Welfare Funds, Inc.   Vol 1: 8361
Council of Literary Magazines and Presses   Vol 1: 8368
Council of Logistics Management   Vol 1: 8373
Council of Natural Waters   Vol 1: 10810
Council of Nordic Academies of Music   Vol 2: 1905
Council of Sales Promotion Agencies   Vol 1: 8377
Council of Scientific Soceity Presidents   Vol 1: 8379
Council of State Education Communicators (Public Relations)   Vol 1: 8382
Council of the City of Frankfurt   Vol 2: 6610
Council of the French Community of Belgium   Vol 2: 1109
Council on Arteriosclerosis   Vol 1: 2239
Council on Basic Science   Vol 1: 2234
Council on Cardiopulmonary and Critical Care   Vol 1: 2243
Council on Cardiovascular Nursing   Vol 1: 2226, 2235, 2238
Council on Circulation   Vol 1: 2242
Council on Clinical Cardiology   Vol 1: 2236
Council on Economic Priorities   Vol 1: 8384
Council on Environmental Quality   Vol 1: 19336
Council on Fine Art Photography   Vol 1: 8386
Council on Foreign Relations   Vol 1: 8388
Council on Foundations   Vol 1: 8390
Council on Governmental Ethics Laws   Vol 1: 8394
Council on Hotel, Restaurant and Institutional Education   Vol 1: 8396
Council on International and Public Affairs   Vol 1: 8405
Council on International Nontheatrical Events   Vol 1: 8407
Council on Library Resources   Vol 2: 9496
Council on Technology Teacher Education   Vol 1: 8410
Council on Thrombosis   Vol 1: 2244
Count Dracula Society   Vol 1: 8412
Country Landowners Association   Vol 2: 2704
Country Markets Ltd.   Vol 2: 7835
Country Music Association   Vol 1: 8419, 10954
Country Music Showcase International   Vol 1: 8422
Courage Foundation   Vol 1: 8425
Courage Quotidien   Vol 2: 5097
Courtaulds plc.   Vol 2: 4219
Coventry Centre for the Performing Arts   Vol 2: 2706
Coventry General Charities   Vol 2: 2706
Cowles Business Media   Vol 1: 8427
Cox Newspapers   Vol 1: 18634

CQ, The Radio Amateur's Journal   Vol 1: 8429
CRABs (Children Raving About Books)   Vol 1: 8441
Cracow International Festival of Short Films   Vol 2: 10068
Craft Concepts   Vol 1: 8443
Crain Communications, Inc.   Vol 1: 6661
Cram Company; George   Vol 1: 13714
Crane Duplicating Service, Inc.   Vol 1: 20231
Cranial Academy   Vol 1: 8445
Crate and Barrel   Vol 1: 7920
Cravenne Conseil; Georges   Vol 2: 5100
Crawford & Company   Vol 1: 4782
Crawford Productions   Vol 2: 281
Cray Research France   Vol 2: 11705
Creative Dimensions   Vol 1: 14702
Creative Glass Center of America   Vol 1: 8449
Creative Hall of Fame   Vol 1: 15671
Creative Standards International   Vol 1: 10590
Creative Writing Program   Vol 1: 8451
Creativity Centre   Vol 2: 350
Credit Communal de Belgique   Vol 2: 1060
Credit Cooperatif   Vol 2: 5103
Credit Research Foundation   Vol 1: 9201
Credit Suisse   Vol 2: 11683
Creo Society   Vol 1: 8453
Crime Writers' Association   Vol 2: 2708
Crime Writers of Canada   Vol 1: 8456
Critikon   Vol 1: 1061
Croatian Library Association   Vol 2: 1798
Croatian Music Institute   Vol 2: 1800
Croatian National Theatre Split   Vol 2: 1802
Croatian Pharmaceutical Society   Vol 2: 1804
Croatian Philatelic Society   Vol 1: 8458
Crohn's and Colitis Foundation of Canada   Vol 1: 8460
Croix-Rouge et du Croissant-Rouge; Commission Permanente de la   Vol 2: 11914
Croix-Rouge Internationale; Commission Permanente de la   Vol 2: 11914
Cromwell Association   Vol 2: 2719
Cronkite Endowment for Journalism and Telecommunication; Walter   Vol 1: 8463
Crop Science Society of America   Vol 1: 8465
Cross-Canada Writers' Quarterly   Vol 1: 16063
Crossroad   Vol 1: 8474
Crossword Club   Vol 2: 2721
Crouch Foundation; George E.   Vol 1: 3467
Crown Princess Sonja International Music Competition   Vol 2: 9962
Crustacean Society   Vol 1: 8477
Cryogenic Engineering Conference   Vol 1: 8481
C.U.B.   Vol 2: 534
Cuban Book Institute   Vol 2: 1817
Cuban Film Institute   Vol 2: 1828
Cuban Government   Vol 2: 6411
Cuban Society of Mathematics   Vol 2: 1822
Cuban Society of Mathematics and Computer Science   Vol 2: 1822
Cult Awareness Network   Vol 1: 8483
Cultural Association Rodolfo Lipizer   Vol 2: 8208
Cultural Center of the Philippines   Vol 2: 10029
Cultural Department of the Municipality of Spittal and the Singkreis Porcia   Vol 2: 796
Cumann Leabharlann na hEireann   Vol 2: 7813
Cumann Leadoige na h-Eireann   Vol 2: 7799
Cumhuriyet Matbaacilik ve Gazetecilik T.A.S.   Vol 2: 12048
Cumhuriyet Newspaper   Vol 2: 12048

Curci Foundation; Alberto   Vol 2: 8210
Curriculum and Instruction Department of Northern Illinois University   Vol 1: 7414
Currie, Coopers and Lybrand   Vol 1: 6948
Curtins Consulting Engineers   Vol 2: 3235
Cushman Foundation for Foraminiferal Research   Vol 1: 8486
Cutty Sark Maritime Trust   Vol 2: 3632
Cymdeithas Amaethyddol Frenhinol Cymru   Vol 2: 12187
Cymdeithas Gelfyddydau Gogledd Cymru   Vol 2: 12180
Cyngor Celfyddydau Cymru   Vol 2: 12149
Cyngor Llyfrau Cymraeg   Vol 2: 12195
Cyprus American Archaeological Research Institute   Vol 1: 4016
Cyprus Foote Mineral Company   Vol 1: 14313
Cystic Fibrosis Foundation   Vol 1: 8488
Cystic Fibrosis Research Trust   Vol 2: 2723
Cytogen Corporation   Vol 1: 15656
Czech and Slovak Music Fund   Vol 2: 1848
Czech Music Fund Prague   Vol 2: 1858
Czech Radio, Prague   Vol 2: 1837
Czech Section of the International Board on Books for Young People   Vol 2: 1839
Czech Television   Vol 2: 1843
Czechoslovak Association of Anti-fascist Fighters   Vol 2: 1845
Czechoslovak Association of Liberty and Anti-Fascist Fighters   Vol 2: 1845
Czechoslovak Musical Instruments - Industrial Group   Vol 2: 1850
Czechoslovak Radio, Brno   Vol 2: 1847
Czechoslovak Society of Arts and Sciences   Vol 1: 8493
Czechoslovak Television, Prague   Vol 2: 1843
Czechoslovak Violin Makers Competitions   Vol 2: 1849
Czechoslovakia - Ministerstvo obchodu a cestovniho ruchu   Vol 2: 1851
Czechoslovakia - Ministry of Commerce and Tourism   Vol 2: 1851
Czechoslovakia - Ministry of Culture, Czech   Vol 2: 1853
Czechoslovakia - Office of the President   Vol 2: 1855
Czechoslovakia Music Fund   Vol 2: 1893
da Motta International Piano and Violin Competition; Vianna   Vol 2: 10227
Dada Research Center   Vol 2: 7046
Dagens Nyheter   Vol 2: 1989
Dahl's Cultural Library; Thorleif   Vol 2: 9925
Daily Gleaner   Vol 1: 10511
Daily Mail   Vol 2: 2725
Daily Mail Trophy   Vol 2: 3067
Daily Racing Form   Vol 1: 18706, 18707
Dairy and Food Industries Supply Association   Vol 1: 4360, 8495
Dairy Barn Southeastern Ohio Cultural Arts Center   Vol 1: 8497
Dairy Bureau of Canada   Vol 1: 8499
Dairy Industry Association of New Zealand   Vol 2: 9712
Dairy Shrine   Vol 1: 8501
Dairy Technology Society (New Zealand)   Vol 2: 9712
Daiwa Anglo-Japanese Foundation   Vol 2: 2729
Dalgety Australia Limited   Vol 2: 352
Dalgety Farmers Limited   Vol 2: 352
Dallas Advertising League   Vol 1: 18633
Dallas Market Center   Vol 1: 8505
Dallas Museum of Art   Vol 1: 8507
Dalmatian Club of America   Vol 1: 8511
Damien - Dutton Society for Leprosy Aid   Vol 1: 8513
Damm & Son A.S; N. W.   Vol 2: 9879

Dana Foundation Vol 1: 12697
Dana Foundation; Charles A. Vol 1: 8515
Danas-Vjesnik Vol 2: 1803
Dance Division Vol 1: 13841
Dance Educators of America Vol 1: 8517
Dance Films Association, Inc. Vol 1: 8519
Dance Magazine Vol 1: 8521
Dance Masters of America Vol 1: 8523
Dance Notation Bureau Vol 1: 8526
Dance Perspectives Foundation Vol 1: 8529
Dance Theater Workshop Vol 1: 8531
Dance/USA Vol 1: 8533
Danchev; Committee for the Liberation of Vladimir Vol 2: 6003
Daniels Pharmaceuticals Vol 1: 4909
Danish Academy Vol 2: 1908
Danish Academy of Technical Sciences Vol 2: 1910
Danish Jazz Center Vol 2: 1912
Danish Library Association Vol 2: 1914
Danish Packaging and Transportation Research Institute Vol 2: 1933
Danish Packaging Research Institute Vol 2: 1933
Danish Publishers Association Vol 2: 1917
Danish School Librarian Association Vol 2: 1919
Danish Timber Information Council Vol 2: 1921
Danish Writers' Association Vol 2: 1923
Danish Writers' Union Vol 2: 1937
Danmarks Biblioteksforening Vol 2: 1914
Danmarks Radio Vol 2: 1982, 1990
Danmarks Skolebibliotekarforening Vol 2: 1919
d'Annunzio Provincial Library; Gabriele Vol 2: 8212
Dansk Forfatterforening Vol 2: 1923
Dansk Geologisk Forening Vol 2: 1949
Dansk Husflidsselskab Vol 2: 1931
Dansk Teknologisk Institut Vol 2: 1933
Danske Akademi Vol 2: 1908
Danske Arkitekters Landsforbund/Akademisk Arkitektforening Vol 2: 1945
(Danske Forlaeggerforening) Vol 2: 1917
Danske Jazzcenter Vol 2: 1912
Danube Prize Vol 2: 10780
d'Arezzo Foundation; Guido Vol 2: 8214
Darussafaka Association Vol 2: 12050
Darussafaka Cemiyeti Vol 2: 12050
Data Processing Management Association Vol 1: 8723
DATABASE Vol 1: 15678
Dautrebande Physiopathology Foundation; Professor Lucien Vol 2: 1111
David; Pierre - Weill Foundation Vol 2: 5375
Davies Memorial Fund; Ryan Vol 2: 12167
Davis & Geck Vol 1: 1708
Davis & Kuelthau Vol 1: 14859
Davis Publications Vol 1: 20524
Davis Wound Care and Hyperbaric Medical Center; Jefferson C. Vol 1: 165
Davison Chemical Division Vol 1: 7342
Dawood Foundation Vol 2: 10005
Dayton Playhouse Vol 1: 8535
Dayton Repertory Theatre Vol 1: 8535
Daytona International Speedway Vol 1: 8537
D.C. Commission on the Arts and Humanities Vol 1: 8543
De Beers Industrial Diamond Division Vol 2: 11071
De Beers Industrial Diamond Division (Pty) Ltd. Vol 2: 11077
de Canarias; Gobierno Autonomo Vol 2: 11232
de Menil Trust Foundation; John and Dominique Vol 1: 16909

Deadline Club Vol 1: 8546
Deaf Accord Vol 2: 2731
Deaf and Hard of Hearing Entrepreneurs Council Vol 1: 8548
Deafness Research Foundation Vol 1: 8550
Dealers Safety and Mobility Council Vol 1: 9920
DeBakey International Surgical Society; Michael E. Vol 1: 8554
Debs Foundation; Eugene V. Vol 1: 8556
Decalogue Society of Lawyers Vol 1: 8560
Decathlon Athletic Club Vol 1: 8563
DECHEMA Vol 2: 4408, 6711
DECHEMA, Deutsche Gesellschaft fur Chemisches Apparatewesen, Chemische Technik und Biotechnologie e.V. Vol 2: 6613
Decision Sciences Institute, Alpha Iota Delta, and Boyd and Fraser Southwestern Publishing Company Vol 1: 8565
Decorative Lighting Association Vol 2: 3577
Deep South Writers Conference Vol 1: 8567
Deere and Company Vol 1: 19429
Defense Intelligence Agency Vol 1: 19483
DeKalb Genetics Corporation Vol 1: 19798
Del Mar Fair Vol 1: 8569
Delacorte Press Vol 1: 8572
Delegation Regionale a la Musique en Ile-de-France Vol 2: 6469
Delhi Management Association Vol 2: 7490
Delius Association of Northern Florida Vol 1: 8575
Deloitte Haskins & Sells Vol 2: 2733
Delphinium Society Vol 2: 2735
Delta Air Lines Vol 1: 12748
Delta Dental Plans Association Vol 1: 8577
Delta Education Vol 1: 5632
Delta Kappa Epsilon Fraternity Vol 1: 8579
Delta Kappa Gamma Society International Vol 1: 8582
Delta Nu Alpha Transportation Fraternity Vol 1: 8584
Delta Omega National Honorary Society Vol 1: 8586
Delta Omicron Vol 1: 8588
Delta Phi Epsilon, Professional Foreign Service Fraternity Vol 1: 8590
Delta Pi Epsilon Vol 1: 8592
Delta Psi Kappa Vol 1: 8594
Delta Publications (Nigeria) Vol 2: 9862
Delta Publications (Nigeria) Limited Vol 2: 9862
Delta Society Vol 1: 4983, 8596
Delta Tau Alpha, National Agricultural Honor Society Vol 1: 13008
DEMCO Vol 1: 10079
Demeure Historique Vol 2: 5105
Deming Memorial Fund; Money for Women/Barbara Vol 1: 12413
Denmark - Ministry of Cultural Affairs Vol 2: 1926, 1935
Denmark - Ordenskapitlet Vol 2: 1940
Dental Association of South Africa Vol 2: 10838
Dentists Association of Argentina Vol 2: 43
Dentsply International Vol 1: 10618
Dentsu Vol 2: 8523
Denver International Film Society Vol 1: 8605
Denver Public Library - Western History Department Vol 1: 8607
Deo Gloria Trust Vol 2: 2198
Department of Canadian Heritage - Parks Canada Vol 1: 8609
Department of National Health and Welfare Vol 1: 6718
Department of Trade and Industry Vol 2: 3773

Department of Veterans Affairs Leadership/Volunteer of the Year Award Vol 1: 5143
DePaul University School of Music Vol 1: 8611
Dermatology Foundation Vol 1: 8613
'Descant' Vol 1: 8618
Deschamps: Maison Henri Vol 2: 7257
Design Council Vol 2: 2737
Design Council - Scotland Vol 2: 10529
Design for Arts in Education Vol 1: 5321
Design Office Consortium Vol 2: 2681
Designers Institute of New Zealand Vol 2: 9719
Destino Publishing House Vol 2: 11214
Detroit Free Press Vol 1: 8620
Detroit Renaissance Vol 1: 8622
Deutsche Akademie der Naturforscher Leopoldina Vol 2: 6620
Deutsche Akademie fur Sprache und Dichtung Vol 2: 6764
Deutsche Bunsen-Gesellschaft fur Physikalische Chemie Vol 2: 6627
Deutsche Elektrochemische Gesellschaft Vol 2: 6627
Deutsche Forschungs fur Luft - und Raumfahrt E.V. Vol 2: 6771
Deutsche Gemmologische Gesellschaft Vol 2: 6762
Deutsche Gesellschaft fur Chirurgie Vol 2: 6873
Deutsche Gesellschaft fur Dokumentation Vol 2: 6835
Deutsche Gesellschaft fur Endokrinologie Vol 2: 6843
Deutsche Gesellschaft fur Ernahrung Vol 2: 6855
Deutsche Gesellschaft fur Fettwissenschaft Vol 2: 6837
Deutsche Gesellschaft fur Kinderheilkunde Vol 2: 6819
Deutsche Gesellschaft fur Mineralolwissenschaft und Kohlechemie eV Vol 2: 6860
Deutsche Gesellschaft fur Moor-und Torfkunde Vol 2: 6632
Deutsche Gesellschaft fur Parasitologie Vol 2: 6635
Deutsche Gesellschaft fur Physikalische Medizin und Rehabilitation Vol 2: 6863
Deutsche Gesellschaft fur Plastische und Wiederherstellungschirurgie Vol 2: 6867
Deutsche Gesellschaft fur Wehrmedizin und Wehrpharmazie e.V. Vol 2: 6852
Deutsche Gesellschaft fur Zerstorungsfreie Prufung e.V. Vol 2: 6841
Deutsche Glastechnische Gesellschaft Vol 2: 6637
Deutsche Landwirtschafts-Gesellschaft Vol 2: 6773
Deutsche Meteorologische Gesellschaft Vol 2: 6641
Deutsche Mineralogische Gesellschaft Vol 2: 6646
Deutsche Ornithologen-Gesellschaft Vol 2: 6650
Deutsche Pharmazeutische Gesellschaft Vol 2: 6822
Deutsche Physikalische Gesellschaft Vol 2: 6655
Deutsche Phytomedizinische Gesellschaft Vol 2: 6666
Deutsche Rontgengesellschaft Vol 2: 6827
Deutsche Veterinarmedizinische Gesellschaft Vol 2: 6886
Deutscher Literaturfonds Vol 2: 6670
Deutscher Memorial Prize; Isaac Vol 2: 2743

Deutscher Verband fur Fotografie DVF, Vol 2: 6756
Deutscher Zentralausschuss fur Chemie Vol 2: 6658
Deutsches Institut fur Normung Vol 2: 6806
Deutsches Institut fur Puppenspiel Vol 2: 6673
Deutsches Rontgen-Museum Vol 2: 6677
Deutsches Zentralkomitee zur Bekampfung der Tuberkulose Vol 2: 6679
Deutschsprachige Mykologische Gesellschaft Vol 2: 6871
Development Exchange Vol 1: 8625
DeVilliers Foundation Vol 1: 11834
Devon Industries Vol 1: 5579
Dewan Film Nasional Indonesia Vol 2: 7732
Dexter Chemical Corporation Vol 1: 1491, 17616
di Donatello; Ente David Vol 2: 8217
Dialogue: A Journal of Mormon Thought Vol 1: 8630
Dialogue Publications Vol 1: 8632
Diamond Council of America Vol 1: 8634
Dickens Society Vol 1: 8640
Dickinson College Vol 1: 8642
Dierkundige Vereniging Van Suidelike Afrika Vol 2: 11130
Difco Laboratories Vol 2: 3166, 3168
Digital Equipment Company Vol 2: 2745
Digital Equipment Corporation Vol 1: 1518
Digital Equipment Corporation Europe Vol 2: 11705
Diputacion Foral de Bizkaia Vol 2: 11275
Diputacion Foral de Vizcaya Vol 2: 11275
Diputacion Provincial de Valencia Vol 2: 11218
Direct Mail/Marketing Educational Foundation Vol 1: 8653
Direct Marketing Association Vol 1: 8646
Direct Marketing Creative Guild Vol 1: 8649
Direct Marketing Educational Foundation Vol 1: 8653
Direct Selling Association Vol 1: 8656
Direction du Livre Vol 2: 4991
Directorate for Cultural Relations with Iberoamerica Vol 1: 19824
Directors Guild of America Vol 1: 8660
Directors of Dental Hygiene Schools Vol 1: 17263
Dirksen Congressional Leadership Research Center; Everett McKinley Vol 1: 8671
Disabled American Veterans Vol 1: 8675, 16388, 16389
Disabled Peoples' Finance Trust of Kenya Vol 2: 8800
Disciples Peace Fellowship Vol 1: 8681
Disclosure, Inc. Vol 1: 2948
Discover America Travel Organizations Vol 1: 18796
The Dispatch Vol 1: 15299
DISTA Products Co. Vol 1: 17791
Distribution Vol 1: 12579
District of Columbia Public Library Vol 1: 8683
Dixie Council of Authors and Journalists Vol 1: 8344
Doberman Pinscher Club of America Vol 1: 8685
Documentary Film Festival - Amsterdam Vol 2: 9375
Documentation Research and Training Centre Vol 2: 7492
Dodge Foundation; Geraldine Vol 1: 8831
Dodge Foundation; Geraldine Rockefeller Vol 1: 14038

Doerenkamp and Gerhard Zbinden Foundation for Realistic Animal Protection in Bio-Medical Research; Hildegard Vol 2: 11745
Doerenkamp/Gerhard Zbinden Stiftung fur realistisch en Tierschutz; Hildegard Vol 2: 11745
Dofasco Limited Vol 1: 6940
Dog Writers' Association of America Vol 1: 8687
Dohne Merino Breeder's Society of South Africa Vol 2: 10842
Dole Foundation for Employment of People with Disabilities Vol 1: 8689
Doll Artisan Guild Vol 1: 8691
Dominion Council of Canada Vol 1: 6843
Dominion Salt Limited Vol 2: 9744
Donnelley and Sons Company; R. R. Vol 1: 1811
Donner Canadian Foundation Vol 1: 6730
Donner Foundation; William H. Vol 1: 20312
Donovan Memorial Foundation; William J. Vol 1: 20021
Door and Hardware Institute Vol 1: 8696
D'Orgue Europeen de Beauvais Vol 2: 5107
Dorset Natural History Vol 2: 2748
Dorset Natural History and Archaeological Society Vol 2: 2748
Doubleday Vol 1: 8706
Douglas-Home Memorial Trust; Charles Vol 2: 2750
Dow Chemical Canada, Inc Vol 1: 7554
Dow Chemical Company Vol 1: 1490, 1495, 1548, 2572, 2604, 4085
Dow Chemical Company Foundation Vol 1: 1483, 1538
Dow Corning Corporation Vol 1: 1565
Dow Jones News/Retrieval Vol 1: 8708
Dow Jones Newspaper Fund Vol 1: 8710
Downtown Athletic Club of New York City Vol 1: 8712
Downtown Jaycees of Washington, D.C. Vol 1: 8716
Downtown Research and Development Center Vol 1: 8719
Dozenal Society of America Vol 1: 8721
DPMA, Association of Information Systems Professionals Vol 1: 8723
Dracula Society Vol 2: 2752
Dragoco Inc. Vol 1: 17830
Drama Vol 2: 2547
Drama Association of Wales Vol 2: 12169
Drama Desk Vol 1: 8726
Drama League of New York Vol 1: 8728
Dramatic Festival Vol 2: 10704
Dramatists Guild Vol 1: 8736
Drexel University Vol 1: 8738, 15322
Dreyfus Foundation; Camille and Henry Vol 1: 1524, 1525, 8740
Driving School Association of the Americas Vol 1: 8748
Drum Major Magazine. Vol 1: 5128
Drummoyne Municipal Art Society Vol 2: 354
Drustvo na Pisatelite na SR Makedonija Vol 2: 8875
Drustvo Slovenskih Pisateljev Vol 2: 10800
Drysdales Western Wear Vol 1: 15917
du Pont de Nemours and Company; E. I. Vol 1: 1482, 1507, 1543, 1563, 2570, 2597, 2601, 11039, 12676
Du Pont KEVLAR Vol 1: 10701
Du Pont Prize Vol 2: 593
Dubuque Fine Arts Players Vol 1: 8751
Dubuque Fine Arts Society Vol 1: 8752
Ductile Iron Society Vol 1: 8753
Dudley International Piano Competition Vol 2: 2754

Dudley National Piano Competition Vol 2: 2754
Dudley Observatory Vol 1: 8755
Duke University Vol 1: 8759
Duke University - Center for Documentary Studies Vol 1: 8761
Duluth Art Institute Vol 1: 8763
Dumas; Societe des Amis d'Alexandre Vol 2: 6243
Dumbarton Oaks Vol 1: 8765
Duncan Lawrie Vol 2: 2103
Dungannon Foundation Vol 1: 8768
Dunn Technology Vol 1: 8770
Duodecimal Society of America Vol 1: 8721
DuPont Company Vol 1: 5743
DuPont Merck Pharmaceutical Company Vol 1: 3387
Dupont Pharmaceuticals Vol 1: 1618
DuPont Pharmaceuticals Vol 1: 1619
Durban Camera Club Vol 2: 10844
Durban International Film Festival Vol 2: 10846
Dusseldorf City Cultural Office Vol 2: 6681
Dutch Centre of IAIA Vol 2: 9378
Dutch Copyright Association Vol 2: 9380
Dutch Film Days Foundation Vol 2: 9382
Dutch Online Users Organization Vol 2: 9384
Dutch Section of the International Board on Books for Young People Vol 2: 9386
Dutch Society of Sciences Vol 2: 9388
Dutch Theatre Institute Vol 2: 9616
Dutton Children's Books Vol 1: 8772
Dutton Society for Leprosy Aid; Damien - Vol 1: 8513
Dykes Medal Vol 1: 12160
E. I. du Pont de Nemours and Company, Inc. Vol 1: 1554
E.A.F.O.R.D. - International Secretariat Vol 2: 11685
Eagle Forum Vol 1: 8774
Eaglehawk Dahlia and Arts Festival Vol 2: 356
Earnshaw Publications Vol 1: 8776
EARTHWATCH Vol 1: 8778
East & West Artists Vol 1: 8780
East Texas Historical Association Vol 1: 8782
Eastern Association of Mosquito Control Workers Vol 1: 3128
Eastern Association of Rowing Colleges Vol 1: 8784
Eastern Coast Breweriana Association Vol 1: 8786
Eastern College Athletic Conference Vol 1: 8789
Eastern College Athletic Conference Sports Information Directors Association Vol 1: 8792
Eastern Economic Association Vol 1: 8795
Eastern Music Festival Vol 1: 8797
Eastman Kodak Company Vol 1: 1497, 2074, 8713, 8831, 10831, 12564, 12944, 16166, 16496, 16498, 19465, 19844, 20263
Eastman Kodak Company - Office Imaging Division Vol 1: 8801
Eastman Kodak Company - Photographic Products Division Vol 1: 8803
Eastman Kodak Company Aerial Systems Division Vol 1: 4241
Eastman School of Music Vol 1: 8805
Eaton Literary Associates Vol 1: 8807
Ebel Watch Vol 2: 11688
EBSCO Subscription Services Vol 1: 2815
EBU/UER Vol 2: 7074
Ecole Superieure de Commerce de Paris Vol 2: 5318
Ecological Society of America Vol 1: 8809
Ecology Institute Vol 2: 6687

Econo-Clad Books   Vol 1: 2854, 2960
Econometric Society   Vol 1: 8819
Econometric Theory   Vol 1: 20572
Economic History Association   Vol 1: 8821
Economic History Society of Australia and New Zealand   Vol 2: 358
Economic Promotion Institute of the Austrian Federal Economic Chamber   Vol 2: 776, 777
ECRI   Vol 1: 8826
Ecuador - Casa de la Cultura Ecuatoriana   Vol 2: 2016
Ecuador - Department of Culture   Vol 2: 2016
EDGES Group   Vol 1: 8828
Ediciones Castillo   Vol 2: 8972
Ediciones Destino, S.A.   Vol 2: 11214
Ediciones Rialp, S.A.   Vol 2: 11326
Edinburgh Architectural Association   Vol 2: 10532
Edinburgh Festival Fringe   Vol 2: 10534
Edinburgh International Film Festival   Vol 2: 10540
Edison Electric Institute   Vol 1: 4105
Edison Fund; Charles   Vol 1: 8831, 17617
Edison Media Arts Consortium   Vol 1: 8830
Edison National Historic Site   Vol 1: 8831
Editions vwa   Vol 2: 11687
Editor & Publisher   Vol 1: 8832
Editorial Andres Bello   Vol 2: 1563
Editorial Costa Rica   Vol 2: 1767
Editorial Diana   Vol 2: 8974
Editorial *El Porvenir*   Vol 2: 8976
Editorial Los Amigos del Libro   Vol 2: 1396
Editorial Planeta   Vol 2: 11220
Editorial Planeta Mexicana, B.A. de C.V.   Vol 2: 8979
Editorial Universitaria Centroamericana   Vol 2: 1771
Editors Association   Vol 2: 9943
Edmonton Journal   Vol 1: 8837
EDO Corporation   Vol 1: 6185
EDP Auditors Association and the EDP Auditors Foundation   Vol 1: 8839
Education   Vol 2: 2756
Education Commission of the States   Vol 1: 8845
Education Film Library Association   Vol 1: 2044
Education Writers Association   Vol 1: 8847
Educational Foundation of the National Restaurant Association   Vol 1: 8850
Educational Paperback Association   Vol 1: 8854
Educational Press Association of America   Vol 1: 8856
Educational Publishers Council   Vol 2: 4549
Educational Television Association   Vol 2: 2759
Educational Testing Service   Vol 1: 8864, 14038
Educational Trust Fund   Vol 2: 3345
EDUCOM   Vol 1: 8866
EDVOTEK   Vol 1: 12952
EFE News Agency   Vol 2: 11361
EG&G Princeton Applied Research   Vol 1: 1484
Egypt Exploration Society   Vol 2: 2761
Egyptian Red Crescent Society   Vol 2: 2020
Ehrlich Foundation; Paul   Vol 2: 6690
Eichendorff-Institut   Vol 2: 6692
Eidgenossische Technische Hochschule Zurich   Vol 2: 11927
Eighteen-twenty Foundation   Vol 2: 10848
Einstein International Academy Foundation; Albert   Vol 1: 8868
Einstein Peace Prize Foundation; Albert   Vol 1: 8870
EIRE Philatelic Association   Vol 1: 8872

Eisteddfod Genedlaethol Frenhinol Cymr   Vol 2: 12184
Ekibiina Ekiyamba Abantu Abayiga Empola   Vol 2: 12085
El Comercio   Vol 1: 10511
El Mercurio   Vol 1: 10511
El Nacional   Vol 1: 10511
El Salvador - Ministerio de Salud Publica y Asistencia Social   Vol 2: 2024
El Tiempo   Vol 1: 10511
Elanco-Eli Lilly Division   Vol 1: 7157
Electric Car Racing Association   Vol 2: 2504
Electric Power Society of the German Association of Electrical Engineers   Vol 2: 6695
Electrical Generating Systems Association   Vol 1: 8875
Electrical Women's Round Table   Vol 1: 8877
Electricorp Production   Vol 2: 9740
Electrochemical Society of India   Vol 2: 7494
Electronic Associates, Inc.   Vol 1: 4086
Electronic Industries Association   Vol 1: 8880
Electronic Media Arts (Australia) Ltd.   Vol 2: 360
Electronics Industry Hall of Fame, Inc.   Vol 1: 8886
Electronics Technicians Association, International   Vol 1: 8888
Elf Petroleum UK   Vol 2: 2034
Eli Lilly and Company   Vol 1: 4812, 9093
Elizondo; Fundacion Luis   Vol 2: 8988
Elle   Vol 2: 5109
Ellen La Forge Memorial Poetry Foundation   Vol 1: 11735
Ellermann Foundation; Mogens and Wilhelm   Vol 2: 11943
Elsevier Science Publishers   Vol 1: 10959, 10960
Elsevier Scientific Publishing Company   Vol 1: 2129
Emballage & Transportinstituttet   Vol 2: 1933
Embassy of Spain   Vol 1: 8891
EmCare, Inc.   Vol 1: 8897
Emece Editores S.A.   Vol 2: 46
Emergency Department Nurses Association   Vol 1: 8902
Emergency Librarian   Vol 1: 2830
Emergency Medicine Residents Association   Vol 1: 8896
Emergency Nurses Association   Vol 1: 8902
Emilia-Romagna Region   Vol 2: 8293
Emphemera Society   Vol 2: 2763
Employment Department: National Training Awards Office   Vol 2: 2765
Employment Management Association   Vol 1: 8913
Empresa Brasileira de Pesquisa Agropecuaria   Vol 2: 1446
Emprise Bank of Wichita   Vol 1: 11649
EMS Concepts   Vol 1: 13088
EMSA Limited Partnership   Vol 1: 8900
Encyclopaedia Britannica Company   Vol 1: 2834, 8351, 8917
Encyclopaedia Universalis   Vol 2: 5111, 5190
Endocrine Society   Vol 1: 8919
Energiagazdelkodasi Tudomanyos Egyesulet   Vol 2: 7377
Energietechnische Gesellschaft im VDE   Vol 2: 6695
Engelhard   Vol 2: 4219
Engelhard Corporation   Vol 1: 11171
Engineering and Science Hall of Fame   Vol 1: 8927
Engineering College Magazines Associated   Vol 1: 8929
Engineering Council   Vol 2: 2768
Engineering Industries Association   Vol 2: 2772

Engineering Institute of Canada   Vol 1: 7172, 7174, 8931
Engineering News-Record   Vol 1: 8940
Engineering Research Council   Vol 1: 4101
Engineering Science   Vol 1: 5781
Engineers' Council for Professional Development   Vol 1: 90
English Academy of Southern Africa   Vol 2: 10850
English American Institute - University of Vienna   Vol 2: 798
English Association   Vol 2: 10854
English Association/Sydney Branch   Vol 2: 362
English Basket Ball Association   Vol 2: 2774
English Centre of International PEN   Vol 2: 2781
English China Clays   Vol 2: 2919
English Draughts Association   Vol 2: 2785
English Folk Dance and Song Society   Vol 2: 2788
English Heritage   Vol 2: 2247
English Speaking Board (International)   Vol 2: 2790
English-Speaking Union of the United States   Vol 1: 8938
English Stage Company at Royal Court Theatre   Vol 2: 2793
English Vineyards Association   Vol 2: 2795
Enna; Commune di   Vol 2: 8204
ENR   Vol 1: 8940
Ente Autonomo Fiere Internazionali di Bologna   Vol 2: 8170
Ente David di Donatello   Vol 2: 8217
Ente Musicale Novarese Carlo Coccia   Vol 2: 8219
Ente Teatro Comunale Treviso   Vol 2: 8221
Ente Triennale Internazionalele Degli Strumenti ad Arco   Vol 2: 8320
Entidades Oficiales del Gobierno Vasco   Vol 2: 11353
Entomological Society of America   Vol 1: 7687, 8943
Entomological Society of Canada   Vol 1: 8953
Environment Canada   Vol 1: 8609, 8956
Environmental Awards Council   Vol 1: 16787
Environmental Design Research Association   Vol 1: 8958
Environmental Mutagen Society   Vol 1: 8962
Environmental Systems Research Institute   Vol 1: 4249
Environmental Tectonics Corporation   Vol 1: 174
EOLAS/Irish Science and Technology Agency   Vol 2: 7770
Epilepsy Foundation of America   Vol 1: 8966
Episcopal Communicators   Vol 1: 8968
Epitestudomanyi Egyesulet   Vol 2: 7448
EPOCH   Vol 1: 8971
Epsilon Nu Eta Honor Society   Vol 1: 8973
Epsilon Pi Tau   Vol 1: 8976
Epsilon Sigma Phi   Vol 1: 8978
Epstein Awards; Lawrence S.   Vol 1: 8985
Epstein Performing Arts Awards; Lawrence S.   Vol 1: 8985
Equipment Maintenance Council   Vol 1: 8988
Erasmus Prize Foundation   Vol 2: 9395
Erba Foundation; Carlo   Vol 2: 8224
ERDAS   Vol 1: 4248, 4249
Ergonomics Society   Vol 2: 2797
Erhard-Stiftung; Ludwig-   Vol 2: 6698
Ericsson   Vol 2: 8982
Erie Art Center   Vol 1: 8992
Erie Art Museum   Vol 1: 8992
Ernst & Young   Vol 1: 8994
Ernst & Young, Inc. Magazine   Vol 1: 8995
Erol Simavi Hurriyet Vakfi   Vol 2: 12052

Errors, Freaks, Oddities Collectors Association   Vol 1: 8996
Errors, Freaks, Oddities Collectors Club   Vol 1: 8996
ESB Electricity Supply Board   Vol 2: 7795
Esperantista Go-Ligo Internacia   Vol 2: 8548
Esperantlingva Verkista Asocio   Vol 2: 9397
Esperanto Writers' Association   Vol 2: 9397
Esperia Foundation   Vol 1: 17054
ESPN Inc.   Vol 1: 8998
Essex Chronicle Newspaper Group   Vol 2: 3735, 3736
Essex Salon Office   Vol 2: 2809
Esso Brasileira de Petroleo S.A.   Vol 2: 1455
Esso Exploration and Production UK Limited   Vol 2: 2940
Esso Petroleum Company Ltd.   Vol 2: 4219
Estonian Music Center, U.S.A.   Vol 1: 9000
Eta Kappa Nu   Vol 1: 9002
Eta Verde   Vol 2: 8226
Eternit   Vol 2: 1113
Ethical Culture School   Vol 1: 9010
Ethicon   Vol 1: 18200, 18203
Ethics and Public Policy Center   Vol 1: 9012
Ethnic Affairs Commission of New South Wales   Vol 2: 686
Ethyl Corporation   Vol 1: 1551
Etudes Tsiganes; Les   Vol 2: 6114
EURALEX - European Association for Lexicography   Vol 2: 1943
Euroarabe-Audiovisuals Communications Center   Vol 2: 11225
Euroavia - Association of European Aeronautical and Astronautical Students   Vol 2: 9399
Euromoney Publications Limited   Vol 2: 2811
Europa Nostra   Vol 2: 9401
Europa Nostra/IBI   Vol 2: 9403
Europabevegelsen i Norge   Vol 2: 9881
Europaische Foderation Korrosion   Vol 2: 6709
Europaische Kernenergie-Gesellschaft   Vol 2: 11701
Europaische Schausteller Union   Vol 2: 8863
Europaische Vereinigung Bildender Kunstler aus Eifel und Ardennen   Vol 2: 6722
Europaische Vereinigung fur Gewasserreinhaltung   Vol 2: 6732
Europaischer Filmpreis   Vol 2: 6712
Europalia   Vol 2: 1153
European Academy of Anaesthesiology   Vol 2: 6700
European Amateur Baseball Confederation   Vol 2: 1115
European and Mediterranean Plant Protection Organization   Vol 2: 5113
European Aquaculture Society   Vol 2: 1118
European Association for Animal Production   Vol 2: 8228
European Association for Cancer Research   Vol 2: 2818
European Association for Signal Processing   Vol 2: 11689
European Association for the Promotion of Poetry   Vol 2: 1120
European Association for the Science of Air Pollution   Vol 2: 2821
European Association for the Study of Diabetes   Vol 2: 6702
European Association of Exploration Geophysicists   Vol 2: 9405
European Association of Programmes in Health Services Studies   Vol 2: 7774
European Association of Radiology   Vol 2: 1122
European Bridge League   Vol 2: 7874
European Broadcasting Union   Vol 2: 11691, 11738

European Centre for Environmental Communication   Vol 2: 5115
European Chamber for the Development of Trade, Industry, and Finances   Vol 2: 1124
European Chemical Marketing Research Association   Vol 2: 2823
European Cinema Society   Vol 2: 6713
European Commission, Dublin Office   Vol 2: 7769
European Committee for Rink Hockey   Vol 2: 5117
European Committee for Young Farmers and 4H Clubs   Vol 2: 10542
European Committee of the International Ozone Association   Vol 2: 5119
European Community Commission   Vol 2: 6008
European Confederation of Agriculture   Vol 2: 1126
European Confederation of Public Relations   Vol 2: 5121
European Coordinating Committee for Artificial Intelligence   Vol 2: 11694
European Council of Chemical Manufacturers Federations   Vol 2: 1128
European Council of International Schools   Vol 2: 2825
European Council of Jewish Community Services   Vol 2: 5123
European Council Panavision   Vol 2: 8472
European Cultural Foundation   Vol 2: 5096
European Direct Marketing Association   Vol 2: 1130
European Disposables and Nonwovens Association   Vol 2: 1132
European Environmental Mutagen Society   Vol 2: 11696
European Federation of Corrosion   Vol 2: 6709, 8464
European Federation of Societies for Ultrasound in Medicine and Biology   Vol 2: 2828
European Festival of Corporate Image   Vol 2: 5125
European Film Awards   Vol 2: 6712
European Football Commentators Association Television   Vol 2: 7772
European Free Trade Association   Vol 2: 11699
European General Galvanizers Association   Vol 2: 2830
European Geophysical Society   Vol 2: 6714
European Group of Artists of the Ardennes and the Eifel   Vol 2: 6722
European Healthcare Management Association   Vol 2: 7774
European Human Rights   Vol 2: 11453
European Information Industry Association   Vol 2: 8857
European Institute of Public Administration   Vol 2: 9409
European Investment Bank   Vol 2: 8859
European Mariculture Society   Vol 2: 1118
European Merit Foundation   Vol 2: 8861
European Molecular Biology Organization   Vol 2: 6726
European Movement in Norway   Vol 2: 9881
European Nuclear Society   Vol 2: 11701
European Ophthalmological Society   Vol 2: 1134
European Options Exchange   Vol 2: 9337
European Options Exchange Amsterdam   Vol 2: 9338
European Organization for Caries Research   Vol 2: 2834
European Organization for Testing New Flower Seeds   Vol 2: 9427
European Orthodontic Society   Vol 2: 2836

European Packaging Federation   Vol 2: 9411
European Parliament   Vol 2: 2839, 5096
European Physical Society   Vol 2: 11703
European Piano Teachers Association   Vol 2: 2842
European Rhinologic Society   Vol 2: 9413
European Showmen's Union   Vol 2: 8863
European Society for Ballistocardiography and Cardiovascular Dynamics   Vol 2: 10787
European Society for Cardiovascular Surgery   Vol 2: 5127
European Society for Clinical Investigation   Vol 2: 9415
European Society for Comparative Physiology and Biochemistry   Vol 2: 1137
European Society for Microcirculation   Vol 2: 2844
European Society for Neurochemistry   Vol 2: 11455
European Society for Noninvasive Cardiovascular Dynamics   Vol 2: 10787
European Society for Opinion and Marketing Research   Vol 2: 9417
European Society for Therapeutic Radiology and Oncology   Vol 2: 1139
European Society of Biomechanics   Vol 2: 6728
European Society of Culture   Vol 2: 8232
European Society of Paediatric Radiology   Vol 2: 5129
European Society of Regional Anaesthesia   Vol 2: 1141
European Society of Toxicology   Vol 2: 11708
European Sports Press Union   Vol 2: 1143
European Surfing Federation   Vol 2: 12172
European Table Tennis Union   Vol 2: 2848
European Thyroid Association   Vol 2: 11706
European Union of Geosciences   Vol 2: 5131
European Union of Jewish Students   Vol 2: 1145
European Union of Public Relations   Vol 2: 8234
European Water Pollution Control Association   Vol 2: 6732
European Weed Research Society   Vol 2: 6734
EUROTOX   Vol 2: 11708
Eutectic Castolin Corporation   Vol 1: 5096
Evaluation Network   Vol 1: 2004
Evaluation Research Society   Vol 1: 2004
Evangelical Christian Publishers Association   Vol 1: 9014
Events Analysis, Inc.   Vol 1: 18564
Everest and Jennings   Vol 1: 14047
Everett McKinley Dirksen Endowment Fund   Vol 1: 8672
Everhart Fan Club; Bob   Vol 1: 9017
Evidence Photographers International Council   Vol 1: 9019
Ewart-Biggs Memorial Award   Vol 2: 2850
Executive Communications Group   Vol 1: 9021
Executive Travel   Vol 2: 2852
Exhibit Designers and Producers Association   Vol 1: 9023
Exotic Dancers League of America   Vol 1: 9025
Expanded Entertainment   Vol 1: 5170
Experimental Natural Philosophy Society   Vol 2: 9419
Experimental Psychology Society   Vol 2: 2855
Explorers Club   Vol 1: 9027
Extrel FTMS, Millipore Corporation   Vol 1: 1555
Exxon/Arts Endowment Conductors Program   Vol 1: 184

Exxon Chemical Company   Vol 1: 1513, 1560, 1567
Exxon Company, U.S.A.   Vol 1: 11107, 11108
Exxon Research and Engineering Company   Vol 1: 1560, 1567, 1573, 2591
Eye Bank Association of America   Vol 1: 9030
Eye-Bank for Sight Restoration   Vol 1: 9034
Faber and Faber Limited   Vol 2: 2858
Faber-Castell (Aust) Pty. Ltd.; A. W.   Vol 2: 364
Facts On File, Inc.   Vol 1: 2941
Faculte Polytechnique de Mons   Vol 2: 1147
Faculty of Building   Vol 2: 2861
Falconbridge Limited   Vol 1: 6943
Family Service America   Vol 1: 9036
Family Service Association of America   Vol 1: 9036
Fan Circle International   Vol 2: 2863
Farabi Cinema Foundation   Vol 2: 7739
Farber Foundation   Vol 1: 614
Fargo-Moorhead Community Theatre   Vol 1: 9040
Fargo-Moorhead Symphony Orchestral Association   Vol 1: 9042
Farm and Industrial Equipment Institute   Vol 1: 13028
Farm Animal Reform Movement   Vol 1: 9044
Farmaceutsko drustvo Hrvatske   Vol 2: 1804
Farrel Corporation   Vol 1: 1486
Farrer Memorial Trust   Vol 2: 366
The Fashion Association of America   Vol 1: 9046
Father's Day Council   Vol 1: 9049
Fauchard Academy; Pierre   Vol 1: 9051
Faulding and Company, Ltd.; F. H.   Vol 2: 605
Fauna and Flora Preservation Society   Vol 2: 2188, 2865
Fauske & Associates   Vol 1: 2584
Fawcett Society   Vol 2: 2867
Federacion de Mujeres Profesionales y de Negocios de Costa Rica   Vol 2: 1782
Federacion Latinoamericana de Termalismo   Vol 2: 56
Federacion Nacional de Cafeteros de Colombia   Vol 2: 1733
Federacion Nacional de Cultivadores de Cereales   Vol 2: 1696
Federacion Panamericana de Asociaciones de Arquitectos   Vol 2: 12093
Federacion Panamericana de Asociaciones de Facultades (Escuelas) de Medicina   Vol 2: 12133
Federal Aviation Administration   Vol 1: 9056, 19220
Federal Bar Association - District of Columbia Chapter   Vol 1: 9065
Federal Bar Council   Vol 1: 9072
Federal Board of Austrian Pharmacists   Vol 2: 800
Federal Chamber of Pharmacists   Vol 2: 6587
Federal City Club   Vol 1: 9076
Federal Committee for Environment   Vol 2: 1862
Federal Executive Institute Alumni Association   Vol 1: 9080
Federal Ministry for Youth, Family Affairs, Women and Health   Vol 2: 6983
Federal Ministry of Education and Arts   Vol 2: 797
Federal Republic of Germany - Ministry of Defence   Vol 2: 6736
Federal Republic of Germany - Ministry of Foreign Affairs   Vol 2: 6738
Federal Republic of Germany - Ministry of Interior   Vol 2: 6740
Federal Republic of Germany - Ministry of Posts and Telecommunications   Vol 2: 6747

Federally Employed Women   Vol 1: 9082
Federally Employed Women - Legal & Education Fund   Vol 1: 9084
Federasie van Afrikaanse Kultuurvereniginge   Vol 2: 10856
Federatie Cultureel Jongeren Paspoort   Vol 2: 9421
Federation Aeronautique Internationale   Vol 2: 5136
Federation Canadienne de La Faune   Vol 1: 7268
Federation Dentaire Internationale   Vol 2: 3399
Federation des Jeux du Commonwealth   Vol 2: 2660
Federation du Saumon de l'Atlantique   Vol 1: 6118
Federation Equestre Internationale - FEI   Vol 2: 11779
Federation Europeenne de la Corrosion   Vol 2: 6709
Federation Europeenne de l'Emballage   Vol 2: 9411
Federation Europeenne de Zootechnie   Vol 2: 8228
Federation Europeenne des Associations Aerosols   Vol 2: 1149
Federation Francaise de Tennis   Vol 2: 5258
Federation francaise de vol a voile   Vol 2: 5170
Federation francaise des syndicats de libraires   Vol 2: 5256
Federation Halterophile du Commonwealth   Vol 2: 12165
Federation Internationale Balint   Vol 2: 11764
Federation Internationale d'Athletisme Amateur   Vol 2: 9313
Federation Internationale de Associations Vescillogiques   Vol 1: 10968
Federation Internationale de Boules   Vol 2: 1476
Federation Internationale de Canoe   Vol 2: 8283
Federation Internationale de Football Association   Vol 2: 11711
Federation Internationale de Judo   Vol 2: 6963
Federation Internationale de Korfbal   Vol 2: 9512
Federation Internationale de la Presse Cinematographique (FIPRESCI)   Vol 2: 6943
Federation Internationale de Lancer-Sport   Vol 1: 10824
Federation Internationale de l'Approvisionnement et l'Achat   Vol 2: 9503
Federation Internationale de l'Art Photographique   Vol 2: 6756, 8865
Federation Internationale de l'Art Photographique - Prix Kodak   Vol 2: 1188
Federation Internationale de l'Automobile   Vol 2: 5973
Federation Internationale de Luge de Course   Vol 2: 839
Federation Internationale de Natation Amateur   Vol 2: 11752
Federation Internationale de Rugby Amateur   Vol 2: 5951
Federation Internationale de Sauvetage Aquatique   Vol 2: 6750
Federation Internationale de Ski   Vol 2: 11832
Federation Internationale de Stenographie et de Dactylographie-INTERSTENO   Vol 2: 6951
Federation Internationale de Tennis   Vol 2: 3482
Federation Internationale des Architectes d'Interieur   Vol 2: 9488

Federation Internationale des Architectes Paysagistes   Vol 2: 6004
Federation Internationale des Associations d'Apiculture   Vol 2: 8298
Federation Internationale des Associations de Bibliothecaires et des Bibliotheques   Vol 2: 9490
Federation Internationale des Associations Medicales Catholiques   Vol 2: 12095
Federation Internationale des Auberges de la Jeunesse   Vol 2: 3509
Federation Internationale des Chasseurs de Son   Vol 2: 9532
Federation Internationale des Droits de l'Homme   Vol 2: 6002
Federation Internationale des Echecs (FIDE)   Vol 2: 7223
Federation Internationale des Editeurs de Journaux   Vol 2: 6006
Federation Internationale des Fabricants et Transformateurs d'Adhesifs et Thermocollants sur Papiers et Autres Supports   Vol 2: 9497
Federation Internationale des Jeux en Fauteuil Roulant   Vol 2: 3480
Federation Internationale des Journalistes et Ecrivains du Tourisme   Vol 2: 6478
Federation Internationale des Mutiles des Invalides du Travail et des Invalides Civils   Vol 2: 6945
Federation Internationale des Organisateurs de Festivals   Vol 1: 10961
Federation Internationale des Organisations de Sciences Sociales   Vol 2: 1859
Federation Internationale des Quillieurs   Vol 2: 4724
Federation Internationale des Societes Aerophilateliques   Vol 2: 11786
Federation Internationale des Societes de Recherche Operationnelle   Vol 2: 6009
Federation Internationale des Societes des Chimistes Cosmeticiens   Vol 2: 3420
Federation Internationale des Traducteurs   Vol 2: 821
Federation Internationale d'Escrime   Vol 2: 6011
Federation Internationale du Diabete   Vol 2: 1182
Federation Internationale Motocycliste   Vol 2: 11808
Federation Internationale Pharmaceutique   Vol 2: 9515
Federation Internationale pour la Recherche Theatrale   Vol 2: 3406
Federation Internationale pour l'Habitation, l'Urbanisme et l'Amernagement des Territoires   Vol 2: 9485
Federation Mondiale des Combattants, des Resistants et des Deportes Juifs   Vol 2: 7990
Federation Mondiale des Societes pour la Culture de la Rose   Vol 2: 108
Federation Mondiale des Sourds   Vol 2: 4764
Federation nationale des Entrepreneurs routiers   Vol 2: 6158
Federation Naturiste Internationale   Vol 2: 1197
Federation of Afrikaans Cultural Societies   Vol 2: 10856
Federation of Alberta Naturalists   Vol 1: 9086
Federation of American Health Systems   Vol 1: 9088
Federation of American Hospitals   Vol 1: 9088
Federation of American Societies for Experimental Biology   Vol 1: 9091

Federation of Analytical Chemistry and Spectroscopy Societies   Vol 1: 9094
Federation of Arab Scientific Councils   Vol 2: 7746
Federation of British Artists   Vol 2: 2869
Federation of British Columbia Writers   Vol 1: 9097
Federation of British Tape Recordists   Vol 2: 2871
Federation of Canadian Music Festivals   Vol 1: 7691, 17064
Federation of Children's Book Groups   Vol 2: 2873, 10514
Federation of Danish Architects   Vol 2: 1945
Federation of European Aerosol Associations   Vol 2: 1149
Federation of European Societies of Plant Physiology   Vol 2: 9423
Federation of Fly Fishers   Vol 1: 9099
Federation of Genealogical Societies   Vol 1: 9120
Federation of Historical Bottle Clubs   Vol 1: 9127
Federation of Historical Bottle Collectors   Vol 1: 9127
Federation of Hungarian Medical Societies   Vol 2: 7307
Federation of Insurance and Corporate Counsel   Vol 1: 9134
Federation of Insurance Counsel   Vol 1: 9134
Federation of Jewish Men's Club   Vol 1: 9136
Federation of Materials Societies   Vol 1: 9140
Federation of Norwegian Industries   Vol 2: 9885
Federation of Nova Scotia Heritage   Vol 1: 9142
Federation of Nova Scotia Historical and Heritage Societies   Vol 1: 9142
Federation of Old Cornwall Societies   Vol 2: 2875
Federation of Ontario Naturalists   Vol 1: 9145
Federation of Petanque U.S.A.   Vol 1: 9156
Federation of Reconstructionist Congregations and Havurot   Vol 1: 9158
Federation of Small Businesses   Vol 2: 2877
Federation of State Humanities Councils   Vol 1: 9160
Federation of Veterans' Associations of the People's Liberation War of Yugoslavia   Vol 2: 10706
Federation pour le planning des naissances du Canada   Vol 1: 16235
Federazione Ordini Farmacisti Italiani   Vol 2: 8236
The Fell Pony Society   Vol 2: 10544
Fellows of the American Bar Foundation   Vol 1: 9162
Fellowship of Australian Writers - New South Wales   Vol 2: 368
Fellowship of Australian Writers - Queensland   Vol 2: 370
Fellowship of Australian Writers - South Australia   Vol 2: 372
Fellowship of Australian Writers - Western Australia   Vol 2: 374
Fellowship of Australian Writers (VIC) Inc.   Vol 2: 377
Fellowship of Engineering   Vol 2: 3874
Fellowship of Reconciliation   Vol 1: 9165
Feminist Monthly   Vol 2: 9425
Feneon; Fondation   Vol 2: 5202
Feris Foundation of America   Vol 1: 9168
Fermi; Associazione Nazionale Enrico   Vol 2: 8143
Ferret Fanciers Club   Vol 1: 9170
Ferst Foundation of Atlanta   Vol 1: 17271
Fertiliser Association of India   Vol 2: 7498

Fertilizer Society of South Africa   Vol 2: 10858
Festival Bach   Vol 2: 8984
Festival Cinema d'Ales   Vol 2: 4885
Festival de Cine Cientifico   Vol 2: 11165
Festival de Cine de Alcala de Henares   Vol 2: 11227
Festival de Cinema de Barcelona, Films i Directors   Vol 2: 11154
Festival de Musique Sacree de Fribourg   Vol 2: 11735
Festival de Rouen du Livre Enfants-Jeunesse   Vol 2: 6202
Festival de Television de Monte Carlo   Vol 2: 9320
Festival dei Popoli - International Review of Social Documentary Film   Vol 2: 8238
Festival dei Popoli - Rassegna Internazionale del Film di Documentazione Sociale   Vol 2: 8238
Festival del Cine Nacional   Vol 2: 12108
Festival der Nationen   Vol 2: 802
Festival des Films du Monde - Montreal   Vol 1: 12435
Festival du Court Metrage en Plein Air   Vol 2: 5172
Festival du Film Court de Villeurbanne   Vol 2: 5174
Festival Estival de Paris   Vol 2: 5176
Festival Europeen de l'Image de l'entreprise   Vol 2: 5125
Festival Internacional Cortometrajes de las Palmas Gran Canaria   Vol 2: 11256
Festival Internacional de Cine Arte   Vol 2: 11229
Festival Internacional de Cine de Bilbao Documental y Cortometraje   Vol 2: 11266
Festival Internacional de Cine de San Sebastian   Vol 2: 11350
Festival Internacional de Cine Ecologico y de la Naturaleza   Vol 2: 11231
Festival Internacional de Cine Iberoamericano   Vol 2: 11260
Festival Internacional de Cine Imaginario y de Ciencia Ficcion de la Villa de Madrid   Vol 2: 11262
Festival Internacional de Cine para la Juventud de Gijon   Vol 2: 11251
Festival Internacional de Cinema da Costa do Estoril   Vol 2: 10237
Festival Internacional de Cinema da Figueira da Foz   Vol 2: 10233
Festival Internacional de Cinema de Santarem   Vol 2: 10235
Festival Internacional de Cinema do Algarve   Vol 2: 10229
Festival Internacional de Cinema do Porto-Fantasporto   Vol 2: 10290
Festival Internacional de Cinema Fantastic de Sitges   Vol 2: 11358
Festival Internacional de Cinema para a Infancia e Juventude - Tomar   Vol 2: 10231
Festival Internacional del Nuevo Cine Latinoamericano   Vol 2: 1827
Festival Internacional del Nuevo Cine Super 8 y Video   Vol 2: 12113
Festival International de Danse de Paris   Vol 2: 5178
Festival International de Films de Femmes   Vol 2: 1383
Festival International de Films de Femmes de Creteil et du Val de Marne   Vol 2: 6071
Festival International de Films et Video Amateurs a Hiroshima   Vol 2: 8532
Festival International de Jazz de Montreal   Vol 1: 9172
Festival International de l'Image   Vol 2: 6015

Festival International de Musique de Besancon et de Franche-Comte   Vol 2: 5180
Festival International de Paris du Film Fantastique et de Science-Fiction   Vol 2: 6148
Festival International du Cinema d'Animation - Annecy   Vol 2: 5956
Festival International du Court Metrage et de la Video   Vol 2: 6476
Festival International du Film Alpin Les Diablerets, Suisse   Vol 2: 11790
Festival International du Film Amateur   Vol 2: 12041
Festival International du Film, Cannes   Vol 2: 5003
Festival International du Film d'Amiens   Vol 2: 4889
Festival International du Film d'Architecture d'Urbanisme et d'Environnement Urbain de Bordeaux   Vol 2: 6017
Festival International du Film d'Architecture et d'Urbanisme de Lausanne   Vol 2: 11792
Festival International du Film de Berlin   Vol 2: 6563
Festival International du Film de Voile de La Rochelle   Vol 2: 6043
Festival International du Film de Vol Libre   Vol 2: 5183
Festival International du film d'Humour de Chamrousse   Vol 2: 5027
Festival International du Film Economique et de Formation   Vol 2: 1190
Festival International du Film et des Medias de Tourisme de Tarbes/Pyrenees   Vol 2: 6055
Festival International du Film Fantastique d'Avoriaz   Vol 2: 4982
Festival International du Film Historique   Vol 2: 5185
Festival International du Film Maritime et d'Exploration   Vol 2: 6013
Festival International du Film Medical de Mauriac   Vol 2: 6111
Festival International du Film sur l'Art Montreal   Vol 1: 12422
Festival International du Film sur l'Energie Lausanne   Vol 2: 11796
Festival International du Nouveau Cinema et de la Video Montreal   Vol 1: 12424
Festival Internationale del Cinema di Salerno   Vol 2: 8416
Festival Internazionale Cinema Giovani   Vol 2: 8461
Festival Internazionale del Film Locarno   Vol 2: 11874
Festival Internazionale del Film Turistico   Vol 2: 8318
Festival Internazionale di Cinema Sportivo   Vol 2: 8316
Festival La Plaine-Atlantique   Vol 2: 5187
Festival Mondial de l'Image de Montagne   Vol 2: 6480
Festival Mondial de l'Image Sous-Marine   Vol 2: 6482
Festival Mondial du Cinema de Court Metrages de Huy   Vol 2: 1159
Festival National de la Chanson de Granby   Vol 1: 9174
Festival of Contemporary Theatre   Vol 2: 10324
Festival of Kerry, Ltd.   Vol 2: 7826, 7827
Festival of Nations, Ebensee   Vol 2: 802
Festival of Southern Theatre Playwriting Competition   Vol 2: 9176
Festival Pan Africain du Cinema   Vol 2: 10690
Festival Panafricain du Cinema de Ouagadougou   Vol 2: 1540

Festival Turolense de Cine Superocho y Video   Vol 2: 11233
Festival van Mechelen   Vol 2: 1223
Festival van Vlaanderen - Brugge   Vol 2: 1151
Festivalul de Teatru Contemporan   Vol 2: 10324
Festspillene I Bergen   Vol 2: 9873
FIAJI   Vol 2: 5190
FIAT   Vol 2: 8247
Fiber Society   Vol 1: 9178
Fiction Collective Two   Vol 1: 9180
Fideicomiso   Vol 2: 9249
FIDIA Research Foundation   Vol 1: 12685
Fidia S.p.a.   Vol 2: 11456
Field Naturalists Club of Victoria   Vol 2: 401
Fiera del Libro per Ragazzi Bologna   Vol 2: 8170
FIFEL Foundation   Vol 2: 11797
Filharmonia Narodowa w Warszawie   Vol 2: 10213
Filipinas Shell Foundation   Vol 2: 10058
Film Advisory Board   Vol 1: 9182
Film and Television Institute (W.A.)   Vol 2: 403
Film and Video Press Group   Vol 2: 2879
Film and Video Producers Association   Vol 2: 7785
Film Council of Greater Columbus   Vol 1: 9184
Film Festival of Huesca   Vol 2: 11235
Film Safety Awards Committee   Vol 1: 14656
Film Society of Lincoln Center   Vol 1: 9193
Film Victoria   Vol 2: 525
Filmclub Volkermarkt   Vol 2: 897
Films de Femmes; Festival International de   Vol 2: 1383
Films de L'Atalante; Les   Vol 2: 5189
Films Incorporated   Vol 1: 2047
Filmtidskriften Chaplin   Vol 2: 11457
Filtration Society   Vol 2: 2881
Financial Analysts Federation   Vol 1: 5548
Financial Institutions Marketing Association   Vol 1: 9195
Financial Management Association   Vol 1: 9198
Financial Post   Vol 1: 8309
The *Financial Post*   Vol 1: 9203
Financial Times   Vol 2: 2885
Financial Times of Canada   Vol 1: 9209
Financial World   Vol 1: 9211
Fine Arts Association of Finland   Vol 2: 4675
Fine Arts Club of Arkansas   Vol 1: 5253
Fine Arts Work Center in Provincetown   Vol 1: 9214
Fingerprint Society   Vol 2: 2891
Finland - Ministry of Defense   Vol 2: 4677
Finnish Academy of Technology   Vol 2: 4681
Finnish Board of Literature   Vol 2: 4685
Finnish Broadcasting Company   Vol 2: 4690
Finnish Chemical Society   Vol 2: 4671
Finnish Cultural Foundation   Vol 2: 4692
Finnish Dramatists' Society   Vol 2: 4695
Finnish Foundation for Cancer Research   Vol 2: 4674
Finnish Historical Society   Vol 2: 4697
Finnish Library Association   Vol 2: 4699
Finnish Museums Association   Vol 2: 4701
Finnish Section of the International Board on Books for Young People   Vol 2: 4703
Finnish Society of Philosophy of Law   Vol 2: 4705
Finnish Society of Sciences and Letters   Vol 2: 4707
Finska Vetenskaps-Societeten   Vol 2: 4707
Fireball International   Vol 2: 2893
Firestone   Vol 1: 11109

First District Dental Society   Vol 1: 9216
First Marine Aviation Force Veterans' Association   Vol 1: 12053
First Special Service Force Association   Vol 1: 9219
Fischer and Porter Company   Vol 1: 4023
Fischer Stiftung Luzern; Edwin   Vol 2: 11718
Fischoff Chamber Music Association   Vol 1: 9221
Fish Farmers' Specialist Branch   Vol 2: 2895
Fisher Artist Program; Avery   Vol 1: 9223
Fisher Scientific (Canada) Ltd.   Vol 1: 7217
Fisher Scientific Company, Ltd.   Vol 1: 1531, 7202
Fisher Scientific Company Ltd.   Vol 1: 7549
Fisons plc Pharmaceutical Division   Vol 2: 4219
Fiterman Foundation; Miles and Shirley   Vol 1: 2133
Flag Plaza Foundation   Vol 1: 13972
Flanders Festival Bruges   Vol 2: 1151
Flat Earth Research Society International   Vol 1: 9225
Fleet Owner   Vol 1: 9229
Fleischner Society   Vol 1: 9231
Fletcher Challenge International Exhibition and Competition   Vol 2: 9721
Fleuroselect   Vol 2: 9427
Flexible Packaging Association   Vol 1: 9233
Flight Safety Foundation   Vol 1: 9237, 16437
Flint Institute of Music   Vol 1: 16994
Florence Times Daily   Vol 1: 15298
Florida Arts Council   Vol 1: 9245
Florida Audubon Society   Vol 1: 9249
Florida Craftsmen   Vol 1: 9261
Florida Education Fund   Vol 1: 9263
Florida Endowment Fund   Vol 1: 9263
Florida Federation of Music Clubs   Vol 1: 9265, 9266
Florida Freedom of Information Clearinghouse   Vol 1: 6550
Florida Nurserymen and Growers Association   Vol 1: 9267
Florida Park Service   Vol 1: 9266
Florida Space Coast Writers Conference   Vol 1: 18250
Florida State University   Vol 1: 9269
Florilege Vocal de Tours   Vol 2: 5191
Fluckiger Foundation   Vol 2: 6586
Fluid Power Society   Vol 1: 9271
Fluke Inc.; John   Vol 1: 4089
Fluor Daniel, Inc.   Vol 1: 2565
Flygtekniska Foreningen   Vol 2: 11647
Flying Fifteen International   Vol 2: 2897
Flying Physicians Association   Vol 1: 9277
Folger Shakespeare Library   Vol 1: 9281
Folio   Vol 1: 9284
Folio Educational Trust - c/o Hanson Publishing Group   Vol 1: 8427
Folkestone Menuhin International Violin Competition   Vol 2: 2899
Folklore Society   Vol 2: 2901
Follett Software Company   Vol 1: 2833
Fondation Agathon De Potter   Vol 1: 1007
Fondation Amon Ra   Vol 2: 5194
Fondation Andre et Berthe Nouffard   Vol 2: 5199
Fondation Armleder   Vol 2: 11720
Fondation Broquette-Gonin   Vol 2: 5803, 5806, 5833
Fondation C. F. Ramuz   Vol 2: 11722
Fondation Charles Veillon   Vol 2: 11966
Fondation Cousin de Mandet   Vol 2: 5909
Fondation David Kupfermann   Vol 2: 6073
Fondation de France   Vol 2: 5196
Fondation de la Maison de la Chimie   Vol 2: 5200

Fondation de la Vocation   Vol 2: 5211
Fondation des infirmieres et infirmiers du Canada   Vol 1: 7073
Fondation des Prix Michener   Vol 1: 12248
Fondation du Festival des Films du Monde   Vol 1: 12437
Fondation du Merite Europeen   Vol 2: 8861
Fondation Emile Blemont   Vol 2: 6103
Fondation Emile-Nelligan   Vol 1: 18879, 18880
Fondation en faveur de l'Art Choregraphique   Vol 2: 11724
Fondation E.W.R. Steacie   Vol 1: 18473
Fondation Feneon   Vol 2: 5202
Fondation France-Libertes   Vol 2: 5205
Fondation Franco-Americaine   Vol 2: 5207
Fondation Francqui   Vol 2: 1155
Fondation International   Vol 2: 5800
Fondation Internationale Jacques Brel   Vol 2: 1195
Fondation Islamique pour la Science, la Technologie et le Developpement   Vol 2: 10489
Fondation le Metais-Larlviere Fils   Vol 2: 5801
Fondation Lionel - Groulx   Vol 1: 10208
Fondation Louis Jeantet de Medecine   Vol 2: 11726
Fondation Louise Charpentier   Vol 2: 5209
Fondation Marcel Bleustein-Blanchet pour la Vocation   Vol 2: 5211
Fondation Mumm   Vol 2: 5101
Fondation Napoleon   Vol 2: 5213
Fondation Nature et Patrimoine Prix Ford France   Vol 2: 5079
Fondation Nessim Habif   Vol 2: 1287
Fondation Nestle   Vol 2: 11882
Fondation Paul Guggenheim   Vol 2: 11741
Fondation Paul Morand   Vol 2: 5802
Fondation Pierre Bearn Mandat des Poetes   Vol 2: 6107
Fondation pour la Liberte de la Presse   Vol 2: 5215
Fondation pour la Recherche Medicale   Vol 2: 5261
Fondation pour l'Enfance Anne-Aymone Giscard d'Estaing   Vol 2: 5221
Fondation pour les Etudes de Defense Nationale   Vol 2: 5229
Fondation Prince Pierre de Monaco   Vol 2: 9309
Fondation Roi Baudouin   Vol 2: 1216
Fondation Roucoules   Vol 2: 5804
Fondation Schiller Suisse   Vol 2: 11728
Fondation Simone et Cino del Duca   Vol 2: 5223
Fondation Singer-Polignac   Vol 2: 5225
Fondation Universitaire   Vol 2: 1377
Fondation Yves Rocher   Vol 2: 4800
Fondazione Alberto Curci   Vol 2: 8210
Fondazione Anna Pane   Vol 2: 8240
Fondazione Carlo Erba   Vol 2: 8224
Fondazione Francesco Somaini   Vol 2: 8242
Fondazione Franco Michele Napolitano   Vol 2: 8244
Fondazione Giacomo Puccini   Vol 2: 8410
Fondazione Giovanni Agnelli   Vol 2: 8246
Fondazione Guido d'Arezzo   Vol 2: 8214
Fondazione II Campiello   Vol 2: 8184
Fondazione Internazionale Balzan   Vol 2: 8279
Fondazione Maria Mezzanzana   Vol 2: 8293
Fondazione Pezcoller   Vol 2: 8396
Fondazione Pietro Caliceti   Vol 2: 8248
Fondazione Premio Internazionale Galileo Galilei dei Rotary Italiani   Vol 2: 8302
Fondazione Premio Laura Orvieto   Vol 2: 8250
Fondazione Premio Napoli   Vol 2: 8252

Fondazione Prof. Domenico Ganassini Vol 2: 8258
Fondazione Russolo-Pratella Vol 2: 8260
Fondazione Valentino Bucchi Vol 2: 8262
Fondazione Venezia Nostra Vol 2: 8264
Fondazione W. Stauffer Vol 2: 8321
Fondo Colombiano de Investigaciones Cientificas y Proyectos Especiales Francisco Jose de Caldas Vol 2: 1687
Fondo de Cultura Economica Vol 2: 9259
Food and Agriculture Organization of the United Nations Vol 2: 7569, 8266
Food and Drug Law Institute Vol 1: 9286
Food and Wines From France Vol 1: 9289
Food and Wines from France/SOPEXA Vol 2: 5227
Food Distribution Research Society Vol 1: 9291
Food Industry Association Executives Vol 1: 9293
Food Marketing Institute Vol 1: 9295
Foodservice & Packaging Institute Vol 1: 9300
Football Writers Association of America Vol 1: 9302
Football Writers Association of New York Vol 1: 12238
Foothills Art Center Vol 1: 9309
Forbes Vol 1: 6646
FORBES Vol 1: 6647
Ford Foundation Vol 1: 8389
Ford Foundation and Harvard University Vol 1: 9312
Ford Foundation; Gerald R. Vol 1: 9315
Ford Memorial Institute; A. Ward Vol 1: 4183
Ford Motor Company Vol 1: 3458
Ford Motor Company Fund Vol 1: 8292, 8295, 8296, 8300
Ford Motor Company Limited Vol 2: 2677
Ford New Holland Vol 1: 19798
Forderkreis Deutscher Schriftsteller in Baden-Wurttemberg Vol 2: 6753
Fordham University - Graduate School of Business Vol 1: 9765
Fordham University - McGannon Communication Research Center; Donald Vol 1: 9318
Fordham University - School of Law Vol 1: 9320
Ford's Theater Vol 1: 9322
Foreign Language Learning Today Vol 1: 1873
Foreign Policy Research Institute Vol 1: 9324
Foreign Services Research Institute Vol 1: 9326
Foreningen for Vattenhygien Vol 2: 11616
Foreningen Svensk Form Vol 2: 11650
Foreningen til Ski-Idrettens Fremme Vol 2: 9870
Forensic Science Society Vol 2: 2904
Forest History Society Vol 1: 9329
Forest Pharmaceuticals Vol 1: 4910
Forest Press, Inc.; OCLC/ Vol 1: 2814
Forest Products Agency Vol 1: 15505
Forest Products Research Society Vol 1: 9332
Formed by merger of: British Glass Industry Research Association; Glass Manufacturers Federation. Vol 2: 2353
Forschungsgesellschaft fur das Weltfluchtlingsproblem Vol 2: 8103
Forster; Pannell Kerr Vol 1: 9335
Forsyth County Defense League Vol 1: 15062
Fort Collins Symphony Association Vol 1: 9337
Fort Scott Community College Vol 1: 9339
Forte Vol 2: 3818

FORTH Dimensions Interest Group Vol 1: 9341
Forum Atomique Europeen Vol 2: 2124
The Fossils Vol 1: 9343
Foto-Cine Clube Bandeirante Vol 2: 1457
FOTODYNE Vol 1: 12956
Fotogruppe Burghausen Vol 2: 6755
Foundation Dr. A. Hedri-Stiftung, Zurich Vol 2: 11731
Foundation Europalia International Vol 2: 1153
Foundation for Australian Literary Studies Vol 2: 405
Foundation for Cultural Cooperation - Sticusa Vol 2: 9429
Foundation for Field Research Vol 2: 7233
Foundation for German Science Vol 2: 6903
Foundation for Global Community Vol 1: 9346
Foundation for Hospice and Home Care Vol 1: 9348
Foundation for Microbiology Vol 1: 12692
Foundation for National Defense Studies Vol 2: 5229
Foundation for Nutrition Research Vol 2: 4671
Foundation for Philosophy of Creativity Vol 1: 9350
Foundation for the Advancement of Canadian Letters Vol 1: 9352
Foundation for the Establishment of an International Criminal Court Vol 1: 9354
Foundation for the Peoples of the South Pacific Vol 1: 9356
Foundation for the Promotion of Finnish Music Vol 2: 4709
Foundation for the Promotion of Science and Technology under the Patronage of H.M. the King Vol 2: 12024
Foundation for the Promotion of Science of the State of Sao Paulo Vol 2: 1459
Foundation for the Promotion of the Translation of Dutch Literary Works Vol 1: 8006
Foundation of Lower Saxony Vol 2: 6757
Foundation of Socio-Cultural Services Vol 2: 11399
Foundation of the Dramatists Guild Vol 1: 12292
Foundation of the Dramitist Guild Vol 1: 20617
Foundation of the Wall and Ceiling Industry Vol 1: 6009
Foundation South Australia Vol 2: 675
Foundry Educational Foundation Vol 1: 15418
Four Freedoms Foundation Vol 1: 16895
Four Juries Prize Vol 2: 5231
Fournier Productions; J. M. Vol 2: 5233
Fragrance Foundation and Fragrance Research Fund Vol 1: 9359
Fragrance Foundation and Olfactory Research Fund Vol 1: 9359
France - Grande Chancellerie de la Legion d'Honneur Vol 2: 5235
France - Ministere de la Culture et de la Communication Vol 2: 5272
France - Ministere de la Defense Vol 2: 5242
France - Ministere de la Jeunesse et des Sports Vol 2: 5247
France - Ministere de l'Agriculture et Foret Vol 2: 5239
France - Ministry of Agriculture and Forestry Vol 2: 5239
France - Ministry of Culture and Communication Vol 2: 5072, 5175, 6085, 6431, 6469
France - Ministry of Defense Vol 2: 5242
France - Ministry of Health Vol 2: 6112

France - Ministry of Youth and Sports Vol 2: 5247
France - Office of the Prime Minister Vol 2: 5250
France Challenges Grundig Vol 2: 6044
France; La Vol 2: 5252
France Ministry of Culture and Communication Vol 2: 5188
France Telecom Vol 2: 4981
Francescatti; Association Zino Vol 2: 4971
Franciscan Retreat Center Vol 1: 9364
Franciscan University of Steubenville Vol 1: 9366
Franck Organ Competition Committee; Cesar Vol 2: 9431
Franco-British Society Vol 2: 2906
Francqui Foundation Vol 2: 1155
Frank-Fonds; Anne Vol 2: 11733
Frankfort-Elberta National Soaring Hall of Fame Vol 1: 9369
Franklin Institute Vol 1: 9371
Franklin J. Matchette Foundation Vol 1: 3423
Franklin National Memorial; Benjamin Vol 1: 9373
Franklin Pierce Law Center Vol 1: 16557
Fredkin Foundation Vol 1: 11054
Free Market Foundation of Southern Africa Vol 2: 10864
Free Press Association Vol 1: 9391
Freedom Forum World Center Vol 1: 9393
Freedom From Religion Foundation Vol 1: 9396
Freedom House Vol 1: 9398
Freedom to Read Foundation Vol 1: 9400
Freedoms Foundation at Valley Forge Vol 1: 9402
French-American Chamber of Commerce in the United States Vol 1: 9406
French Association of Conchology Prize Vol 2: 6483
French Center of Comparative Law Vol 2: 5254
French Embassy Vol 2: 9433
French Federation of Booksellers Vol 2: 5256
French Federation of Tennis Vol 2: 5258
French Foundation for Medical Research Vol 2: 5261
French, Inc.; Samuel Vol 1: 1759
French-Language Cultural and Technical Union Vol 2: 5266
French League for Animal Rights Vol 2: 5270
French Ministry of Culture and Communication Vol 2: 5272
French Society for Medical Hydrology and Climatology Vol 2: 5296
Freundeskreis zur internationalen Forderung literarischer und wissenschaflicher Ubersetzungen Vol 2: 6759
Fribourg Festival of Sacred Music Vol 2: 11735
Friday Morning Music Club Foundation Vol 1: 20112
Friday Woodmere Music Club Young Artists Competition Vol 1: 9408
Friedheim Foundation; Eric Vol 1: 11671
Friedrich-Ebert-Stiftung Vol 2: 8890
Friends of Algonquin Park Vol 1: 9410
Friends of American Writers Vol 1: 9412
Friends of Children and Literature Vol 1: 9414
Friends of Children's Books Vol 2: 10764
Friends of Free China Vol 1: 9416
Friends of Libraries U.S.A. - American Library Association Vol 1: 9418
Friends of Old-Time Radio Vol 1: 9422
Friends of Patrick Henry Vol 1: 9424
Friends of Photography Vol 1: 9426

Friends of Sadler's Wells Vol 2: 2910
Friends of the Atlanta-Fulton Public Library Vol 1: 9431
Friends of the Chicago Public Library Vol 1: 9433
Friends of the Dutch National Ballet Vol 2: 9435
Friends of the Earth Vol 2: 2912
Friends of the Princeton University Library Vol 1: 9435
Friestelsvereniging van Suid-Afrika Vol 2: 10967
Front de l'Independence Vol 2: 1157
Frozen Food Association of New England Vol 1: 9437
Fuchs Memorial Scholarship Fund Auditions; Viktor Vol 1: 20028
Fujihara Foundation of Science Vol 2: 8526
Fujisankei Communications International Vol 2: 6085
Fulcrum Vol 1: 9441
Fuller Fund; Anna Vol 1: 9443
Fund for Modern Courts Vol 1: 9445
Fund for Renewable Energy & Environment Vol 1: 16786
Fund for the Advancement of Social Studies Education Board Vol 1: 13715
Fund for the City of New York Vol 1: 9448
Fund for UFO Research Vol 1: 9450
Fundacao de Amparo a Pesquisa do Estado de S. Paulo Vol 2: 1459
Fundacao Moinho Santista Vol 2: 1495
Fundacio Enciclopedia Catalana Vol 2: 11237
Fundacion Alejandro Angel Escobar Vol 2: 1582
Fundacion Ames Pro Investigacion en Ciencias de la Salud ''Fundames'' Vol 2: 1580
Fundacion Antonio Machado Vol 2: 1722
Fundacion Bunge y Born Vol 2: 39
Fundacion Jacinto e Inocencio Guerrero Vol 2: 11240
Fundacion Jorge Sanchez Cordero Vol 2: 8986
Fundacion Luis Elizondo Vol 2: 8988
Fundacion Mariano Ospina Perez Vol 2: 1698
Fundacion Miguel Aleman Vol 2: 8991
Fundacion nexos Vol 2: 8993
Fundacion Pablo Neruda Vol 2: 1565
Fundacion Pedro Barrie de la Maza, Conde de Fenosa Vol 2: 11244
Fundacion Principado de Asturias Vol 2: 11247
Fundacion Quinquela Martin para la Investigacion y Docencia en Medicina Vol 2: 48
FUNDALECTURA - Fundacion para el fomento de la Lectura Vol 2: 1700
Fusion/Biennale Internationale de Limoges - Arts Du Feu Vol 2: 5298
Fusion Power Associates Vol 1: 9452
Future Business Leaders of America - Phi Beta Lambda Vol 1: 9455
Future of Freedom Conference Committee Vol 1: 16668
Fyssen Foundation Vol 2: 5300
G. W. Blunt White Library Vol 1: 12552
Gabrovo International Biennial of Humour and Satire in the Arts Vol 1: 1521
Gaines Dog Care Center Vol 1: 9459
Gaines Dog Research Center Vol 1: 9459, 15328
Gairdner Foundation Vol 1: 9465
Gale Researc, Inc. Vol 1: 2942
Gale Research Inc Vol 1: 2887
Gale Research Inc. Vol 1: 2816, 2837, 2943
Galerie Cailleux Vol 2: 5058

Galerie de la Renommee et le Musee Nautiques du Canada Vol 1: 5203
Galesburg Civic Art Center Vol 1: 9469
Galilei Prize Foundation of the Rotary Club of Italy; International Galileo Vol 2: 8302
Gallaher Business Challenge Vol 2: 7858
Galley Club Vol 2: 408
Galpin Society Vol 2: 2914
Gamma Biologicals Vol 1: 923
Gamma Sigma Delta Vol 1: 9471
Gamma Sigma Sigma National Service Sorority Vol 1: 9473
Ganassini; Fondazione Prof. Domenico Vol 2: 8258
Gandhi Memorial Trust; Indira Vol 2: 7501
Gandhi Peace Centre Vol 1: 9480
Gannett Center for Media Studies - Columbia University Vol 1: 7989
Gannett Foundation Vol 1: 9393
Garden Centers of America Vol 1: 9482
Garden Club of America Vol 1: 9485
Garden Writers Association of America Vol 1: 9488
The Gardners of America, Inc./Men's Garden Clubs of America Vol 1: 9492
Gas Processors Association Vol 1: 9503
Gathering of Nations Vol 1: 9508
Gaudeamus Foundation Vol 2: 9437
Gautier et Andree Gautier; Association des Amis de Jacques Vol 2: 4913
Gay and Lesbian Press Association Vol 1: 9510
Gaylord Brothers, Inc. Vol 1: 2908
GEAC Inc. Vol 1: 2932
Geary 18 International Yacht Racing Association Vol 1: 9512
Geijutsu-in Vol 2: 8596
Gelber Foundation; Lionel Vol 1: 9767
Gemeente Groningen Vol 2: 9361
Gemeinschaft zur Forderung der Kunst Vol 2: 7085
Gemini Industries, Inc. Vol 1: 11173
Gemmological Association and Gem Testing Laboratory of Great Britain Vol 2: 2916
Gemmological Association of Germany Vol 2: 6762
Gemmological Association of Great Britain Vol 2: 2916
Genealogical Association of Nova Scotia Vol 1: 9514
Genealogical Publishing Company Vol 1: 2944
General Agents and Managers Conference of the National Association of Life Underwriters Vol 1: 9516
General Arab Women Federation Vol 2: 7748
General Aviation Manufacturers Association Vol 1: 9521
General Commission on Archives and History of the United Methodist Church Vol 1: 9523
General Electric Company Vol 1: 4091, 16764
General Electric Foundation Vol 1: 1566, 3456, 3461, 4106, 10139
General Mills Vol 1: 9526
General Monitors Vol 1: 17284
General Motors Cancer Research Foundation Vol 1: 9528
General Society of Spanish Authors Vol 2: 11249
Generalitat de Catalunya - Department d'Agricultura, Ramaderia i Pesca Vol 2: 11169
Generalitat de Catalunya - Department de la Presidencia Vol 2: 11174
Generalitat de Catalunya - Direccio General de Joventut Vol 2: 11171
Genetics Society of America Vol 1: 9533

Genetics Society of Canada Vol 1: 9536
Genetics Society of Japan Vol 2: 8528
Geneva Association Vol 2: 11761
Genootschap Ter Bevordering van Natuurgenees-en Heelkunde Vol 2: 9555
Genootschap van Nederlandstalige Misdaadauteuurs Vol 2: 9440
Geochemical Society Vol 1: 9540
Geodetic and Cartographic Society Vol 2: 7309
Geodeziai es Kartografiai Egyesulet Vol 2: 7309
Geografsko drustvo Bosne i Hercegovine Vol 2: 1399
Geographic Society of Chicago Vol 1: 9544
Geographic Society of Lima Vol 2: 10015
Geographical Society of Bosnia and Hercegovina Vol 2: 1399
Geographical Society of Finland Vol 2: 4711
Geographical Society of India Vol 2: 7503
Geographical Society of Philadelphia Vol 1: 9550
Geological Society Vol 2: 2918
Geological Society of America Vol 1: 9554
Geological Society of Denmark Vol 2: 1949
Geological Society of Finland Vol 2: 4715
Geological Society of France Vol 2: 5302
Geological Society of South Africa Vol 2: 10866
Geological Society of Sweden Vol 2: 11459
Geological Society of Turkey Vol 2: 12045
Geologiese Vereniging van Suid-Afrika Vol 2: 10866
Geologiska Foreningen Vol 2: 11459
Geologiska Foreningen i Stockholm Vol 2: 11459
George Washington University Vol 1: 1648
Georgetown University Vol 1: 5691
Georgetown University - Institute for the Study of Diplomacy Vol 1: 9569
Georgia Agricultural Commodity Commission for Peanuts Vol 1: 9571
Georgia Peanut Commission Vol 1: 9571
Gepipari Tudomanyos Egyesulet Vol 2: 7454
Geranium Society Vol 2: 2469
German Academy of Language and Poetry Vol 2: 6764
German Aerospace Research Establishment Vol 2: 6771
German Agricultural Society Vol 2: 6773
German Booksellers and Publishers Association Vol 2: 6775
German Booksellers Association Vol 2: 6775
German Chemical Society Vol 2: 6777
German Dental Association Vol 2: 6795
German Design Council Vol 2: 6802
German Forestry Association Vol 1: 2098
German Institute of Standards Vol 2: 6806
German Interior Architects Association Vol 2: 6808
German Iron and Steel Institute Vol 2: 6811
German Marshall Fund of the United States Vol 1: 9578
German Medical Association Vol 2: 6813
German Ministry of Economic Affairs Vol 2: 6804
German Nutrition Foundation Vol 2: 6859
German Pediatric Association Vol 2: 6819
German Pharmaceutical Society Vol 2: 6822
German Physical Society Vol 2: 3184
German Rontgen Society Vol 2: 6827
German Section of the International Board on Books for Young People Vol 2: 6832
German Society for Documentation Vol 2: 6835
German Society for Fat Science Vol 2: 6837

German Society for Medicinal Plant Research   Vol 2: 7081
German Society for Non-Destructive Testing   Vol 2: 6841
German Society of Endocrinology   Vol 2: 6843
German Society of Metallurgical and Mining Engineers   Vol 2: 6848
German Society of Military Medicine and Military Pharmacology   Vol 2: 6852
German Society of Nutrition   Vol 2: 6855
German Society of Petroleum Sciences and Coal Chemistry   Vol 2: 6860
German Society of Physical Medicine and Rehabilitation   Vol 2: 6863
German Society of Plastic and Reconstructive Surgery   Vol 2: 6867
German Society of School Music Educators   Vol 2: 6869
German-Speaking Mycological Society   Vol 2: 6871
German Surgical Society   Vol 2: 6873
German Veterinary Medical Association   Vol 2: 6886
Germans from Russia Heritage Society   Vol 1: 9580
Germany Philatelic Society   Vol 1: 9582
Gerontological Society for America   Vol 1: 9585
Gesellschaft der Musikfreunde in Wien   Vol 2: 883
Gesellschaft Deutscher Chemiker   Vol 2: 6629, 6777
Gesellschaft Deutscher Naturforscher und Arzte   Vol 2: 6889
Gesellschaft fur Arzneipflanzenforschung   Vol 2: 7081
Gesellschaft fur Biologische Chemie   Vol 2: 6891
Gesellschaft fur deutsche Sprache   Vol 2: 6893
Gesellschaft fur Naturkunde in Wurttemberg   Vol 2: 6896
Gesellschaft fur Versuchstierkunde - GV SOLAS   Vol 2: 11907
Gesellschaft fur Wirbelsaulenforschung   Vol 2: 7083
Gesellschaft Karl-Richter-Orgelwettbewerb   Vol 2: 6898
Gesellschaft zur Forderung des Instituts fur Weltwirtschaft   Vol 2: 7007
Getty Grant Program   Vol 1: 9595
Gettysburg College - Lincoln and Soldiers Institute   Vol 1: 9599
Geyer - McAllister Publications   Vol 1: 9601
Ghana Institution of Engineers   Vol 2: 7174
Giant Schnauzer Club of America   Vol 1: 9605
Gichner Systems Group   Vol 1: 12069
Gijon; Festival Internacional de Cine para la Juventud de   Vol 2: 11251
Gijon International Film Festival for Young People   Vol 2: 11251
Gilpin County Arts Association   Vol 1: 9610
Girls' Brigade International Council   Vol 2: 2931
Girls Friday of Show Business   Vol 1: 20399
Giscard d'Estaing; Fondation pour l'Enfance Anne-Aymone   Vol 2: 5221
Givaudan-Roure   Vol 1: 1558
Glamour   Vol 1: 9612
Glasgow Development Agency   Vol 2: 10653
The Glasgow Herald   Vol 2: 10546
Glaxo   Vol 1: 3379
Glaxo/Association of British Science Writers   Vol 2: 2935
Glaxo Group Research Ltd.   Vol 2: 4219

Glaxo, Inc.   Vol 1: 622, 15954
Gleeson Library Associates   Vol 1: 9614
Glencoe   Vol 1: 2338
Glencoe - McGraw-Hill   Vol 1: 9616
Glenn Foundation for Medical Research   Vol 1: 9589
Glenn Gould Foundation   Vol 1: 6738
Gloag and Son Ltd.; Matthew   Vol 2: 3004
Global Futures Network   Vol 2: 7505
Global Tomorrow Coalition   Vol 1: 9620
Globe and Horn Book, Inc.   Vol 1: 6464
The Globe and Mail   Vol 1: 10511
Gluskin Sheff & Associates   Vol 1: 5329
Glyndebourne Festival Opera   Vol 2: 2937
Go Kart Club of America   Vol 1: 11061
Gobernacion - Cartagena-Bolivar   Vol 2: 1704
Gobernacion Del Estado Tachira - Venezuela   Vol 2: 12110
Gobierno Autonomo de Canarias   Vol 2: 11232
Gobierno del Estado de Baja California Sur   Vol 2: 8995
Gobierno del Estado de Jalisco   Vol 2: 9259
Gobierno del Estado de Mexico   Vol 2: 9007
Gobierno del Estado de Morelos   Vol 2: 8997
Gobierno del Estado de Puebla   Vol 2: 8999
Gobierno del Estado de Sinaloa   Vol 2: 9011
Gobierno del Estado de Tlaxcala   Vol 2: 9003
Gobierno del Estado de Veracruz-Llave   Vol 2: 9005
Godwin Memorial Trust; Tony   Vol 1: 9622
Goethe Institut   Vol 2: 6900
Goethe Institute   Vol 1: 1215
Golden Archer Awards Program   Vol 1: 9624
Golden Gate Audubon Society   Vol 1: 9627
Golden Gloves Association of America   Vol 1: 9630
Golden Ring Organizing Committee   Vol 2: 11737
Goldman Environmental Foundation   Vol 1: 9632
Goldsmith Awards Program - Joan Shorenstein Barone Center on the Press, Politics and Public Policy   Vol 1: 9634
Goldsmith Foundation; Horace W.   Vol 1: 8389
Goldsmith-Greenfield Foundation   Vol 1: 9636
Goldsmiths' Company   Vol 2: 2944
Golf Course Superintendents Association of America   Vol 1: 9638
Golf Digest   Vol 1: 9643
Golf Manufacturers and Distributors Association   Vol 1: 16474
Golf Writers Association of America   Vol 1: 9650
Gonzalez; Hospital General Dr. Manuel Gea   Vol 2: 9023
Goodwill Industries International Inc.   Vol 1: 9654
Goodyear Tire and Rubber Company   Vol 1: 13030
Gorgas Memorial Institute   Vol 1: 4816
Gorsedd Board   Vol 2: 12185
Goshen College   Vol 1: 9668
Gospel Music Association   Vol 1: 9670
Goto Optics   Vol 2: 8509
Government Computer News   Vol 1: 9673
Government Employees Insurance Company   Vol 1: 9675
Government Executive   Vol 1: 9677
Government Finance Officers Association of the United States & Canada   Vol 1: 9679
Government Management Information Sciences   Vol 1: 9683
Government of India   Vol 2: 7573

Government of Malaysia - Language and Literary Agency   Vol 2: 8900
Government of Navarra   Vol 2: 11253
Government of the State of Mexico   Vol 2: 9007
Government of the State of Sinaloa   Vol 2: 9011
Governmental Research Association   Vol 1: 9685
Governor Baxter School for the Deaf   Vol 1: 9687
Governors of Dromkeen   Vol 2: 410
GPA Book Award   Vol 2: 7776
GPA Dublin International Piano Competition   Vol 2: 7778
Grace and Company; W. R.   Vol 1: 7342, 7343
GRAFIA - Association of Finnish Graphic Design   Vol 2: 4717
Grafia - Graafisen Suunnittelun Jarjesto   Vol 2: 4717
Graham Foundation   Vol 1: 9692
Gran Canaria International Short Film Festival   Vol 2: 11256
Granada Television Limited   Vol 2: 2946
Grand Ole Opry   Vol 1: 10954
Grand Prix de la Publicite   Vol 2: 5318
Grande Chancellerie   Vol 2: 8877
Grandes Compagnies de l'Est Parisien; Les   Vol 2: 5320
Grant & Sons; William   Vol 2: 2948
Grant Foundation; William T.   Vol 1: 9694
Graphic Arts Technical Foundation   Vol 1: 9696
Graphic Design: USA   Vol 1: 9705
Graphics: Awards   Vol 1: 9704
Grassland Society of Southern Africa   Vol 2: 10873
Graviner, Ltd.   Vol 1: 9244
Graz School of Music and Dramatic Art   Vol 2: 804
Great Grimsby International Competition for Singers   Vol 2: 2950
Great Lakes Carbon Corporation   Vol 1: 1418
Great Lakes Colleges Association   Vol 1: 9706
Great Lakes Commission   Vol 1: 9708
Greater Haverhill Arts Association   Vol 1: 9710
Greater Lynn Camera Club   Vol 1: 9712
Greater Montreal Council of Arts   Vol 1: 12433
Greater New York Fund/United Way   Vol 1: 19701
Greater Philadelphia First   Vol 1: 9714
Greater Pittsburgh Council   Vol 1: 13974
Greater St. Louis Amateur Baseball Hall of Fame   Vol 1: 9716
Greek Ministry of Culture - Section for Theatre and Dance   Vol 2: 7191
Greek National Bank Foundation   Vol 2: 7194
Greek National Tourist Organization   Vol 2: 7197
Greek Radio Corporation   Vol 2: 7199
Green Meadow Foundation   Vol 2: 11739
Greenburger Foundation; Francis J.   Vol 1: 9719
Greenland Society   Vol 2: 1951
The Greensboro Review   Vol 1: 9721
Greeting Card Association   Vol 1: 9723
Grenfell Henry Lawson Festival of Arts   Vol 2: 413
Greyhound Charities   Vol 1: 11649
Griffes American Music Competition; Charles Tomlinson   Vol 1: 9725
Griffis Fund for Zoological Research; Nixon   Vol 1: 9727

Griffith Show Appreciation Society; Andy   Vol 1: 9729
Grody/Tellem Communications   Vol 1: 16915
Grolier   Vol 1: 2817, 14550
Grolier Educational Corporation   Vol 1: 2962
Grolier Poetry Book Shop, Inc.   Vol 1: 11735
Gronlandske Selskab   Vol 2: 1951
Group for Advanced Analytical Methods   Vol 2: 5323
Group for Design in Business   Vol 1: 9206
Group for the Use of Psychology in History   Vol 1: 9731
Group W Satellite Communications   Vol 1: 9733
Groupe Consultatif International de Recherche sur le Colza   Vol 2: 5325
Groupe de Musique Experimentale de Bourges   Vol 2: 4998
Groupe pour l'Avancement des Science Analytiques   Vol 2: 5323
Groupement des Allergologistes et Immunologistes de Langues Latines   Vol 2: 10221, 10242
Groupement des Ecrivains Medecins   Vol 2: 6500
Groupement Europeen, des artistes des Ardennes et de l'Eifel   Vol 2: 6722
Groupement Latin et Mediterraneen de Medecine du Sport   Vol 2: 6076
Groupement pour l'Avancement des Methodes Spectroscofiques et Physico-chimiques d'Anolyte   Vol 2: 5323
Groupement Regional d'Action Cinematographique   Vol 2: 5175
Grumbacher   Vol 1: 18640
Grumbacher Company; M.   Vol 1: 12611
Grumman Corporation   Vol 1: 12074
Grune & Statton   Vol 1: 4596
Gruner International Lieder Competition; City of London Walther   Vol 2: 2631
Grupo Aluminio, S.A. de C.V.   Vol 2: 9017
Grupo Fotocinematografico Fonmina   Vol 2: 11303
Gruppo Corale Vallecorsa   Vol 2: 8467
Guadalupe Cultural Arts Center   Vol 1: 9736
The Guardian   Vol 2: 2952
Guardian Anti Corrosives (PVT)   Vol 2: 7495
Guggenheim; Fondation Paul   Vol 2: 11741
Guggenheim Foundation; Paul   Vol 2: 11741
Guggenheim Memorial Foundation; John Simon   Vol 1: 9738
Guild Hall of East Hampton   Vol 1: 9740
Guild of Agricultural Journalists of Great Britain   Vol 2: 2958
Guild of Agricultural Journalists of the United Kingdom   Vol 2: 3777
Guild of British Butlers   Vol 2: 2960
Guild of Carilloneurs in North America   Vol 1: 9743
Guild of Hairdressers   Vol 2: 2962
Guild of Incorporated Surveyors   Vol 2: 2968
Guild of Motoring Writers   Vol 2: 2970
Guild of Picture Editors   Vol 2: 2888
Guild of Professional Toastmasters   Vol 2: 2974
Guild of Surveyors   Vol 2: 2968
Guild of Taxidermists   Vol 2: 10548
Guild of Television Cameramen   Vol 2: 2976
Guild of Yachting Writers   Vol 2: 4639
Guilde Europeenne du Raid   Vol 2: 5327
Guildhall School of Music and Drama   Vol 2: 2978
Guitar Foundation of America   Vol 1: 9745
Gujarat Vidyapith   Vol 2: 7507
Gulbenkian Foundation; Calouste   Vol 2: 10234, 10303

Gulbenkian Foundation (Lisbon); Calouste   Vol 2: 2980
Gulf Coast Association of Geological Societies   Vol 1: 1103
Gutenberg-Gesellschaft   Vol 2: 6911
Gutenberg Society   Vol 2: 6911, 6912
Guyana - Office of the President   Vol 2: 7242
Gyldendalske Boghandel   Vol 2: 1953
Gym Master   Vol 1: 13002
Haagudah Lezechuyot Haezrach Beyisrael   Vol 2: 7862
Haarlem Boekenstad   Vol 2: 9442
Hacker Instruments, Inc.   Vol 1: 14749
Hadassah Magazine   Vol 1: 9747
Hadassah, The Women's Zionist Organization of America   Vol 1: 9749
Haddonfield Symphony   Vol 1: 9751
Hague Academy of International Law   Vol 2: 9444
Haifa Municipality   Vol 2: 7876
Haiku Society of America, Inc.   Vol 1: 9753
Hall and Company; G. K.   Vol 1: 2818
Hall of Fame for Great Americans   Vol 1: 9760
Halsmuseum; Frans   Vol 2: 9446
Hamdard Foundation Pakistan   Vol 2: 9974
Hamdard National Foundation   Vol 2: 9974
Hammer Prize Foundation   Vol 1: 9762
Hampstead Theatre   Vol 2: 10536
Hancock Mutual Life Insurance Company; John   Vol 1: 9764
Harare African Traditional Dance Association   Vol 2: 12219
Harbinger   Vol 1: 10249
Harbourfront Reading Series   Vol 1: 9766
Harcourt Brace & Company   Vol 1: 9769
Harcourt Brace Jovanovich   Vol 1: 1876, 9769
Harcros Chemical Group   Vol 2: 4219
Hardwood Research Council   Vol 1: 9771
Hardy Society; Thomas   Vol 2: 2982
Harian Creative Press - Books   Vol 1: 9773
Harkness Fellowships of the Commonwealth Fund of New York   Vol 2: 2984
Harlequin Enterprises Ltd.   Vol 1: 6805
Harlow Foundation; Bryce   Vol 1: 9775
Harmony, Inc.   Vol 1: 9777
Harness Tracks of America   Vol 1: 9792
Harp Renaissance Society   Vol 1: 6306
Harper Collins   Vol 2: 2293
Harper Collins Publishers   Vol 1: 12954
Harris County Public Library   Vol 1: 9796
Harrogate International Festival   Vol 2: 2986
Hart; Horace   Vol 1: 9798
Hartley Fund; Marcellus   Vol 1: 12686
Harvard Alumni Association   Vol 1: 9800
Harvard Business Review   Vol 1: 9803
Harvard Lampoon   Vol 1: 9806
Harvard University   Vol 1: 15321
Harvard University - Graduate School of Business Administration   Vol 1: 15326
Harvard University - Graduate School of Design   Vol 1: 9812
Harvard University - Nieman Foundation   Vol 1: 9814
Harvard University Center for Italian Renaissance Studies   Vol 2: 8473
Harvard University Press   Vol 1: 9817
Harvard University Ukrainian Research Institute   Vol 1: 9821
Harveian Society   Vol 2: 2989
Harvey Foundation; Lena P.   Vol 2: 7945
Harvey W. Watt & Co.   Vol 1: 166
Harveys Leeds International Pianoforte Competition   Vol 2: 2993
Haryana Sahitya Akademi   Vol 2: 7509
Haskil Association; Clara   Vol 2: 11743
Hastings Writer's Group   Vol 2: 2995

Hasty Pudding Theatricals   Vol 1: 9823
HAUM Publishers   Vol 2: 11060
Hawaii Association of School Librarians   Vol 1: 9826
Hawaii International Film Festival   Vol 1: 9828
Hawaii Literary Arts Council   Vol 1: 9832
Hawaii Society - American Institute of Architects   Vol 1: 9833
Hawaii State Foundation on Culture and the Arts   Vol 1: 9830
Hawaii Visitors Bureau   Vol 1: 9834
Hawk Migration Association of North America   Vol 1: 9836
Hawk Mountain Sanctuary Association   Vol 1: 9838
Hawthornden Literary Institute   Vol 2: 10550
Hayesod; United Israel Appeal - Keren   Vol 2: 7972
Head Sports   Vol 1: 10549
Headliners Club   Vol 1: 9840
Headliners Foundation   Vol 1: 9840
Health Care Exhibitors Association   Vol 1: 9858
Health Education Division   Vol 1: 5610
Health Industry Distributors Association   Vol 1: 9842
Health Physics Society   Vol 1: 9845
Health Sciences Communications Association   Vol 1: 9847
Healthcare Convention & Exhibitors Association   Vol 1: 9858
Healthcare Financial Management Association   Vol 1: 9862
Healthcare Information and Management Systems Society   Vol 1: 9867
Hear Center   Vol 1: 9870
Hear Foundation   Vol 1: 9870
Hearst Corporation   Vol 1: 19336
Hearst Foundation; William Randolph   Vol 1: 9872, 11797, 14547
Hearst Newspapers   Vol 1: 9874
Heat Transfer Research, Inc.   Vol 1: 2590
Heavy Specialized Carriers Conference   Vol 1: 18290
Heberden Society   Vol 2: 2518
Hebrew Immigrant Aid Society   Vol 1: 9876
Hebrew Union College - Jewish Institute of Religion   Vol 1: 9880
Hebrew University - Hadassah Medical School   Vol 2: 7887
Hebrew Writers Association in Israel   Vol 2: 7889
Heidelberg Repatriation Hospital - Department of Veterans' Affairs   Vol 2: 416
Heineken Foundation   Vol 2: 9450, 9600
Heineken Stichting   Vol 2: 9450
Heineman Foundation for Research, Educational, Charitable, and Scientific Purposes   Vol 1: 1268, 3457
Heineman-Stiftung; Minna-James-   Vol 2: 6908
Heiser Program for Research in Leprosy and Tuberculosis   Vol 1: 9882
Helicopter Association International   Vol 1: 9884
Helicopter Association of America   Vol 1: 9884
Helicopter Club of Great Britain   Vol 2: 2998
Helliniki Radiophonia   Vol 2: 7199
Helm Publishers; Christopher   Vol 2: 2293
Helmholtz Fonds   Vol 2: 6913
Helsingfors Festspel   Vol 2: 4719
Helsingin Juhlaviikot   Vol 2: 4719
Helsinki Festival   Vol 2: 4719
Helvetica Chimica Acta   Vol 2: 11884
Henley - Management College   Vol 2: 4163

Heraldo de Mexico; El Vol 2: 9019
Herb Society of America Vol 1: 9903
Herb Thomas Memorial Trust Vol 2: 390
Herff Jones Vol 1: 13311, 13747
Heritage Canada Foundation Vol 1: 9909
Heritage Center Vol 1: 9913
Hermes Vol 1: 2188
Herpetologists' League Vol 1: 9915
Hewlett-Packard Company Vol 1: 4121, 9917
Hickok Manufacturing Company Vol 1: 18569
HiFi/Stereo Review Vol 1: 18486
Highway Research Board Vol 1: 18777
Highway Users Federation for Safety and Mobility Vol 1: 9919
Hildegard Doerenkamp and Gerhard Zbinden Foundation for Realistic Animal Protection in Bio-Medical Research Vol 2: 11745
Hill and Knowlton Ireland Vol 2: 7780
Hill Organization; William Vol 2: 3009
Hill-Rom Vol 1: 1661
Hillman Foundation; Sidney Vol 1: 9921
Hill's Pet Products Vol 1: 4983, 7263, 8597
Hippokrates Verlag Vol 2: 6915
Hippopotamus Press Vol 2: 3011
Hiradastechnikai Tudomanyos Egyesulet Vol 2: 7451
Hiroshima Festival Office Vol 2: 8530
Hiroshima International Amateur Film and Video Festival Vol 2: 8532
Histadruth Ivrith of America Vol 1: 9925
Histochemical Society Vol 1: 9927
Histology Control Systems Vol 1: 14745
Historian Ystavain Liitto Vol 2: 4755
Historic - Scotland Vol 2: 2247
Historic American Buildings Survey Vol 1: 17746
Historic Churches Preservation Trust and Incorporated Church Building Society Vol 2: 3014
Historic New Orleans Collection - Williams Prizes Committee Vol 1: 9930
Historical and Ethnological Society of Greece Vol 2: 7201
Historical Association Vol 2: 3016
Historical Branch Advisory Committee Vol 2: 9723
Historical Commission of the Southern Baptist Convention Vol 1: 9932
Historical Metallurgy Society Vol 2: 12174
Historical Society of Washington, D.C. Vol 1: 9936
History of Dermatology Society Vol 1: 9938
History of Economics Society Vol 1: 9942
History of Education Society Vol 1: 9944
History of Science Society Vol 1: 9948
Hitachi Ltd. Vol 1: 7900
Hobby Industry of America Vol 1: 12322
Hochschule fur Grafik und Buchkunst Leipzig Vol 2: 7032
Hochschule fur Musik Vol 2: 6918
Hochschule fur Musik Carl Maria von Weber Vol 2: 6920
Hochschule fur Musik und Darstellende Kunst, Graz Vol 2: 804
Hochschule fur Musik und darstellende Kunst Mozarteum, Salzburg Vol 2: 871
Hochschule fur Musik und Darstellende Kunst, Wien Vol 2: 917
Hockey Hall of Fame Vol 1: 9955
Hockey Hall of Fame and Museum Vol 1: 9955
The Hockey News Vol 1: 9959
Hodder and Stoughton Ltd. Vol 2: 3018
Hodges International Piano Competition; Joanna Vol 1: 9961
Hodson Corporation Vol 1: 18081
Hoffman-La Roche Vol 1: 4232, 4392

Hoffmann-LaRoche Vol 1: 622
Hogg National Young Artist Audition; Ima Vol 1: 9963
Hoken Kaikan Foundation Vol 2: 8502
Holiday Inn Vol 1: 20491
Holland Animation Film Festival Vol 2: 9453
Holland Society of New York Vol 1: 9966
Hollandsche Maatschappij der Wetenschappen Vol 2: 9388
Holly Society of America Vol 1: 9968
Hollywood Chapter of the National Academy of Television Arts and Sciences Vol 1: 85
Hollywood Foreign Press Association Vol 1: 9972
Hollywood Radio and Television Society Vol 1: 9975
Hollywood Women's Press Club Vol 1: 9978
Home Orchard Society Vol 1: 9983
HomeStyles Publishing Vol 1: 2556
Honda Foundation Vol 2: 8534
Honda Motor Company. Vol 1: 4707
Honens International Piano Competition Foundation; Esther Vol 1: 9985
Hong Kong Film Awards Association Ltd. Vol 2: 7263
Hong Kong International Film Festival Vol 2: 7263
Hong Kong Study Circle Vol 2: 3020
Honolulu Publishing Company Vol 1: 9987
Honor Society of Phi Kappa Phi Vol 1: 9989
Honorable Society of King's Inns Vol 2: 7782
Honourable Society of Cymmrodorion Vol 2: 3022
Hood's Texas Brigade Association Vol 1: 17285
Hoover Presidential Library Association; Herbert Vol 1: 9993
Horizons Theatre Vol 1: 9995
Horsley Marketing and Communications Vol 2: 3024
Hosei Daigaku Kokusaikouryu Center Vol 2: 8536
Hosei University - International Center Vol 2: 8536
Hospital Financial Management Association Vol 1: 9862
Hospital General Dr. Manuel Gea Gonzalez Vol 2: 9023
Hospital Management Systems Society Vol 1: 9867
Hospital Militar Central Vol 2: 1706
Hospitality Sales and Marketing Association International Vol 1: 9997
Hostelling International - American Youth Hostels Vol 1: 10005
Hotel Rotorua Vol 2: 9765
Hotel Sales and Marketing Association International Vol 1: 9997
Hotel Sales Management Association Vol 1: 9997
Houghton Mifflin Company Vol 1: 10015, 11194
House & Garden Vol 2: 3026
House of Culture of Aguascalientes Vol 2: 9236
House of Humour and Satire Vol 2: 1519
Houston Advanced Research Center - Center for Global Studies Vol 1: 10017
Houston Grand Opera Vol 1: 10020, 10021
Houston International Film Festival Vol 1: 20537
Houston Opera Studio Vol 1: 10019
Houston Symphony Orchestra Vol 1: 9964
Houston Underwater Club Vol 1: 10022
Howard Foundation; George A. and Eliza Gardner Vol 1: 10024

Howard University Center for Sickle Cell Disease Vol 1: 10026
Hoyres Pressebyra Vol 2: 9911
Hoyt Institute of Fine Arts Vol 1: 10029
H.R. and E.J. Hay Charitable Trust Fund Vol 1: 5744
Hradec nad Moravici Castles Administration Vol 2: 1857
Hrvatski Glazbeni Zavod Vol 2: 1800
Hrvatsko Bibliotekarsko Drustvo Vol 2: 1798
Hrvatsko Farmaceutsko drustvo Vol 2: 1804
Hrvatsko narodno kazaliste Split Vol 2: 1802
HTV Cymru/Wales Vol 2: 12181
Hubbard Museum Vol 1: 10031
Huddersfield Contemporary Music Festival Vol 2: 3028
The Hudson Review Vol 1: 10033
Hughes Aircraft Vol 1: 12073
Hughes Medical Institute; Howard Vol 1: 10035
Human and Ergonomics Factors Society Vol 1: 10037
Human Factors Society Vol 1: 10037
Human Family Educational and Cultural Institute Vol 1: 10045
Human Rights Campaign Fund Vol 1: 10047
Humane Slaughter Association Vol 2: 3030
Humane Society of the United States Vol 1: 10051
Humboldt State University - Theatre Arts Department Vol 1: 10055
Hungarian Academy of Sciences Vol 2: 7311
Hungarian Association of Non-professional Film and Videomakers Vol 2: 7313
Hungarian Astronautical Society Vol 2: 7318
Hungarian Chemical Society Vol 2: 7321
Hungarian Electrotechnical Association Vol 2: 7325
Hungarian Forestry Association Vol 2: 7343
Hungarian Hydrological Society Vol 2: 7347
Hungarian Mining and Metallurgical Society Vol 2: 7352
Hungarian Music Council Vol 2: 7364
Hungarian PEN Centre Vol 2: 7366
Hungarian Pharmaceutical Society Vol 2: 7368
Hungarian Publishers and Booksellers Association Vol 2: 7370
Hungarian Radio Vol 2: 7416
Hungarian Scientific Society for Food Industry Vol 2: 7372
Hungarian Scientific Society of Energetics Vol 2: 7377
Hungarian Society for Food Industry Vol 2: 7372
Hungarian Society for Human Settlements Vol 2: 7382
Hungarian Society of Textile Technology and Science Vol 2: 7384
Hungarian Writers' Union Vol 2: 7388
Hungary - Council of Ministers Vol 2: 7391
Hungary - Ministry of Agriculture Vol 2: 7393
Hungary - Ministry of Culture and Education Vol 2: 7396
Hungary - Office of the Prime Minister Vol 2: 7409
The Hunger Project Vol 1: 10057
Hunt Institute for Botanical Documentation Vol 1: 6486
Hunter Charitable Foundation; K. M. Vol 1: 5329
Hunter Society; William Vol 1: 10059
Hunterdon Art Center Vol 1: 10061
Hunterian Society Vol 2: 3032
Hunting Group Vol 2: 3760
Hunting Retriever Club Vol 1: 18929
Huntington Galleries Vol 1: 10063

Organization Index
Volume 2: International and Foreign

Huntington Museum of Art Vol 1: 10063
Hurriyet Foundation Vol 2: 12052
Hurriyet Vakfi Vol 2: 12052
Hustinx Foundation; Edmond Vol 2: 9681
Hutchins Library Vol 1: 6331
Huy - World Festival of Movies of Short Films Vol 2: 1159
Huysmans Stichting; Camille Vol 2: 1055
Hyatt Foundation Vol 1: 16422
Hydro-Quebec Vol 1: 7491, 16433
Hydrographic Society Vol 2: 3034
Hymn Society in the United States and Canada Vol 1: 10065
Hymn Society of America Vol 1: 10065
Hyphenate Lobby Vol 1: 7409
IADR Dental Materials Group Vol 1: 10625
IAMANEH Vol 2: 11880
IBC Award Vol 2: 3383
Ibero-American Institute of Aeronautic and Space Law Vol 2: 11258
Ibero-Latin-American College of Dermatology Vol 2: 1461
Iberoamerican Film Festival Vol 2: 11260
IBM Vol 2: 2732, 6373, 6376
IBM Corporation Vol 1: 1544, 10262, 10284
IBM France Vol 2: 5329
Ibsen Society of America Vol 1: 10067
ICD - International Center for the Disabled Vol 1: 10069
Ice Skating Institute of America Vol 1: 10071
Iceland - Office of the President Vol 2: 7463
Icelandic Horse Trekkers Vol 1: 10074
Icelandic Pony Trekkers Vol 1: 10074
ICI plc Vol 2: 4219
ICONA Vol 2: 11232
Iditarod Trail Committee Vol 1: 10076
IEEE Vol 1: 4119
IEEE Aerospace and Electronic Systems Society Vol 1: 10287
IEEE Industry Applications Society Vol 1: 10277
IFA International Aviation Scholarship Vol 2: 3412
IFMA Foundation Vol 1: 12024
IFPA Film and Video Communicators Vol 1: 6001
Ikatan Dokter Indonesia Vol 2: 7726
Ilford Vol 2: 11854
Illinois Arts Council Vol 1: 6365
Illinois Association of Teachers of English Vol 1: 7414
Illinois Ethnic Consultation Vol 1: 1870
Illinois Foreign Language Teachers Association Vol 1: 1870
Illinois Library Association Vol 1: 10078
Illinois Reading Council Vol 1: 7414
Illinois School Library Media Association Vol 1: 7414
Illinois Society for Microbiology Vol 1: 10082
Illuminating Engineering Society of North America Vol 1: 10084
The Illustrated London News Vol 2: 3037
ILSI-North America Vol 1: 2654
Ilustre Municipalidad de Santiago Vol 2: 1567
Image Film/Video Center Vol 1: 10091
IMAGFIC Festival Internacional de Cine de Madrid Vol 2: 11262
IMAGFIC International Film Festival of Madrid Vol 2: 11262
Imagin'Art, Brussels International Art and Archaeology Film FestivaL Vol 2: 1161
Imagin'Art, Festival International du Film d'Art et d'Archeologie de Bruxelles Vol 2: 1161
IMAGINE - Canadian Centre for Philanthropy Vol 1: 10094
Immigration History Society Vol 1: 10096

Immucor Vol 1: 925
Imperial Chemical Industries Vol 2: 4210
Imperial Oil Vol 1: 6839
Imperial Tobacco Company Vol 2: 3006
Importers and Exporters Association of Taipei Vol 2: 11999
In-Plant Management Association Vol 1: 10098
In-Plant Printing Management Association Vol 1: 10098
In-Plant Reproductions Vol 1: 10102
Inamori Foundation Vol 2: 8538
INCAST Vol 1: 10106
Incentive Manufacturers Representatives Association Vol 1: 10111
Inco Europe Ltd. Vol 2: 4219
Incorporated Guild of Hairdressers, Wigmakers and Perfumers Vol 2: 2962
Incorporated Society of Musicians Vol 2: 3040
The Independent Vol 2: 3043, 10536
Independent Bakers Association Vol 1: 10113
Independent Colleges and Universities of Florida Vol 1: 10115
Independent Free Papers of America Vol 1: 10118
Independent Insurance Agents of America Vol 1: 10120
Independent Retailer Organisation Vol 2: 3045
Independent Sector Vol 1: 10138
India - Indian Law Institute Vol 2: 7515
India - Lalit Kala Akademi Vol 2: 7533
India - Ministry of Human Resource Development, Dept. of Youth Affairs & Sports Vol 2: 7517
India - Ministry of Human Resource Development, Directorate of Adult Education Vol 2: 7526
India - Ministry of Information and Broadcasting Vol 2: 7528, 7689
India - Ministry of Science and Technology Vol 2: 7531
India - National Academy of Art Vol 2: 7533
India - National Academy of Letters Vol 2: 7536
India - National Academy of Music, Dance and Drama Vol 2: 7540
India - Office of the Prime Minister Vol 2: 7546
India - Sahitya Akademi Vol 2: 7536
India - Sangeet Natak Akademi Vol 2: 7540
India Study Circle for Philately Vol 1: 10140
Indian Adult Education Association Vol 2: 7565
Indian Arts and Crafts Association Vol 1: 10142
Indian Association for the Advancement of Science Vol 2: 7568
Indian Books Centre Vol 2: 7570
Indian Council for Cultural Relations Vol 2: 7572
Indian Council of Agricultural Research Vol 2: 7574
Indian Council of Medical Research Vol 2: 7576
Indian Cryogenics Council Vol 2: 7469, 7470, 7471, 7472
Indian Dairy Association Vol 2: 7615
Indian Hospital Association Vol 2: 7619
Indian Institute of Metals Vol 2: 7621
Indian National Science Academy Vol 2: 7635
Indian Physics Association Vol 2: 7680
Indian Science Congress Association Vol 2: 7682

Indian Society for Afro-Asian Studies Vol 2: 7686
Indian Space Research Organization Vol 2: 5067
Indiana Black Expo Vol 1: 10144
Indiana Directions Vol 1: 10153
Indiana Mental Health Memorial Foundation Vol 1: 14358
Indiana Opera Theatre Vol 1: 10148
Indiana State University Vol 1: 11961
Indiana University - Purdue University at Indianapolis Vol 1: 10150
Indianapolis Art League Vol 1: 10152
Indianapolis Motor Speedway Vol 1: 10154
Indice - O Banco de Dados Vol 2: 1463
Indonesian Medical Association Vol 2: 7726
Industrial Designers Society of America Vol 1: 10157
Industrial Development Corporation of SA Ltd. Vol 2: 11077
Industrial Development Research Council Vol 1: 10159
Industrial Fabrics Association International Vol 1: 10162
Industrial Management Club Vol 1: 11097
Industrial Research and Development Vol 1: 16793
Industrial Research Institute Vol 1: 10164
Industrie Canada Vol 1: 10168
Industry Canada Vol 1: 10168
Infant Formula Council Vol 1: 664
Infectious Diseases Society of America Vol 1: 10170
Information Access Company Vol 1: 15675, 15676
Information Council of the Americas Vol 1: 10174
Information Industry Association Vol 1: 10182
Information Management Vol 1: 10252
Information Science and Technology Association, Japan Vol 2: 8540
Informationstechnische Gesellschaft im Verband Deutscher Elektrotechn iker Vol 2: 6529
InfoText Magazine Vol 1: 10188
Ing. Castaldi Illuminazione Vol 2: 8273
Ingenjorsvetenskapsakademien Vol 2: 11522
Ingersoll Foundation Vol 1: 8775, 10190
Ingersoll Milling Machine Company Vol 1: 10191, 10192
Ingram Book Company Vol 1: 18181
Initiative LiBeraturpreis im Okumenischen Zentrum Christuskirche Vol 2: 6922
Inland Bird Banding Association Vol 1: 10193
Inland Press Association Vol 1: 10197
Inland Steel - Ryerson Foundation Vol 1: 10204
Inner Swiss Cultural Foundation Vol 2: 11747
Innerschweizerische Kulturstiftung Vol 2: 11747
Institut Belge des Sciences Administratives Vol 2: 1058
Institut Canadien des Ingenieurs Vol 1: 8931
Institut Catala, d'Estudis Mediterranis Vol 2: 11175
Institut Culturel Africain et Mauricien Vol 2: 10686
Institut de Biologie Physicochimique Vol 2: 5331
Institut de Chimie du Canada Vol 1: 7539
Institut de Droit International Vol 2: 11750
Institut de France Vol 2: 5333
Institut de France - Academie des Beaux Arts Vol 2: 5350
Institut de France - Academie des Inscriptions et Belle-Lettres Vol 2: 5430

Institut de France - Academie des Sciences Vol 2: 5476
Institut de France - Academie des Sciences Morales et Politiques Vol 2: 5706
Institut de France - Academie Francaise Vol 2: 5798
Institut de la Vie Vol 2: 5932
Institut de Paleontologie Humaine Vol 2: 5934
Institut de Tecnologia de la Construccio de Catalunya (ITEC) Vol 2: 11191
Institut del Teatre de la Diputacio de Barcelona Vol 2: 11156
Institut des Sciences de la Sante Vol 2: 5936
Institut d'Histoire de l'Amerique Francaise Vol 1: 10206
Institut et Hopital Neurologiques de Montreal Vol 1: 12428
Institut Europeen d'Administration Publique Vol 2: 9409
Institut fur Anglistik und Amerikanistik der Universitat Wien Vol 2: 798
Institut fur Chemische Pflanzen Physiologie der Universitat Tubingen Vol 2: 6568
Institut fur Deutsch als Fremdsprache der Universitat Munchen Vol 2: 6553
Institut fur Weltwirtschaft an der Universitat Kiel Vol 2: 7006
Institut International de Droit Humanitaire Vol 2: 8306
Institut International de la Potasse Vol 2: 11819
Institut International de la Soudure Vol 2: 3431
Institut International de Promotion et de Prestige Vol 2: 11804
Institut International des Caisses d'Epargne Vol 2: 11826
Institut International du Froid Vol 2: 6027
Institut Internazionale di Diritto Umanitario Vol 2: 8306
Institut Mondial du Phosphate Vol 2: 9323
Institut National Canadien pour les Aveugles Vol 1: 7057
Institut National de la Sante et de la Recherche Medicale Vol 2: 5941
Institut National du Logement Vol 2: 1225
Institut Pierre Mendes France Vol 2: 6117
Institut Royal d'Architecture du Canada Vol 1: 16917
Institut Valencia de la Juventut Vol 1: 8894
Institute for Advanced Studies in the Theatre Arts Vol 1: 15528
Institute for Briquetting and Agglomeration Vol 1: 10211
Institute for Complementary Medicine Vol 2: 3047
Institute for Court Management of the National Center for State Courts Vol 1: 10214
Institute for Education by Radio-Television Vol 1: 10216
Institute for Financial Crime Prevention Vol 1: 10218
Institute for Intercultural Studies Vol 1: 10220
Institute for International Economics Vol 2: 8814
Institute for Latin American Cooperation Vol 2: 11325
Institute for Latin American Integration Vol 2: 50
Institute for Mediation and Conflict Resolution Vol 1: 10222
Institute for Policy Studies Vol 1: 10224
Institute for Productivity of Labor and Production Vol 1: 7891
Institute for Public Relations Research and Education Vol 1: 10226

Institute for Quantitative Research in Finance Vol 1: 10229
Institute for Research in Hypnosis and Psycho-therapy Vol 1: 10231
Institute for Scientific Information Vol 1: 2867, 2873, 4169, 4172, 12180, 12678, 17602
Institute for Social Inventions Vol 2: 3049
Institute for Socioeconomic Studies Vol 1: 10233
Institute for Southern Studies Vol 1: 10236
Institute for Telecommunication Sciences Vol 1: 19113
Institute for the Achievement of Human Potential Vol 1: 10238
Institute for the Advancement of Engineering Vol 1: 10240
Institute for the Study of American Cultures Vol 1: 10242
Institute for University Cooperation Vol 2: 8275
Institute Forestier du Canada Vol 1: 6922
Institute of Acoustics Vol 2: 3051
Institute of Actuaries Vol 2: 3057
Institute of Administrative Accountants Vol 2: 3099
Institute of Administrative Management Vol 2: 3061
Institute of Advanced Legal Studies Vol 2: 3063
Institute of Advanced Philosophic Research Vol 1: 10244
Institute of Advertising Practitioners in Ireland Vol 2: 7785
Institute of African Studies Vol 2: 7176
Institute of Amateur Cinematographers Vol 2: 3066
Institute of Archaeology Vol 2: 2242
Institute of British Foundrymen Vol 2: 3068
Institute of Business Designers Vol 1: 10246, 10570
Institute of Ceramics Vol 2: 3077
Institute of Certified Financial Planners Vol 1: 10250
Institute of Certified Management Accountants Vol 1: 10383
Institute of Certified Records Managers - ARMA Vol 1: 10252
Institute of Chartered Accountants in England and Wales Vol 2: 3079
Institute of Chartered Accountants in Ireland Vol 2: 3080
Institute of Chartered Accountants of Scotland Vol 2: 3080, 10552
Institute of Chartered Financial Analysts Vol 1: 5548
Institute of Civil Defence and Disaster Studies Vol 2: 3083
Institute of Contemporary History and Wiener Library Vol 2: 3085
Institute of Early American History and Culture Vol 1: 10254
Institute of Electrical and Electronics Engineers Vol 1: 4458, 4468, 4681, 10256, 17619, 17775, 20227
Institute of Electrical and Electronics Engineers - Computer Society Vol 1: 10293
Institute of Electrical and Electronics Engineers - Computer Society, West Coast Publications Office Vol 1: 10306
Institute of Electrical and Electronics Engineers - Laser and Electro-optics Society Vol 1: 15760
Institute of Electrical and Electronics Engineers - Power Engineering Society Vol 1: 10308
Institute of Electrical and Electronics Engineers, Inc. Vol 1: 18914

Institute of Energy Vol 2: 3087
Institute of Engineers and Technicians Vol 2: 3089
Institute of Environmental Sciences Vol 1: 10322
Institute of Export Vol 2: 3097
Institute of Financial Accountants Vol 2: 3099
Institute of Food Science and Technology (UK) Vol 2: 3101
Institute of Food Technologists Vol 1: 10339
Institute of Heraldic and Genealogical Studies Vol 2: 3103
Institute of Hispanic Culture Vol 2: 52
Institute of Home Office Underwriters Vol 1: 10351
Institute of Hygiene Vol 2: 4082
Institute of Industrial Engineers Vol 1: 10353
Institute of Information Scientists Vol 2: 3105
Institute of Internal Auditors Vol 1: 10367
Institute of International Education/Arts International Program Vol 1: 10376
Institute of International Law Vol 2: 11750
Institute of Jamaica Vol 2: 8481
Institute of Jazz Studies Vol 1: 10379
Institute of Journalists Vol 2: 2583
Institute of Management Vol 2: 3107
Institute of Management Accountants, Inc. Vol 1: 10382
Institute of Management Sciences Vol 1: 10401, 15737
Institute of Manufacturing Vol 2: 3112
Institute of Marine Engineers Vol 2: 3114
Institute of Marketing Vol 2: 3122
Institute of Marketing Management Vol 2: 10875
Institute of Materials Vol 2: 3124, 4187
Institute of Mathematical Statistics Vol 1: 8036, 10404
Institute of Measurement and Control Vol 2: 3156
Institute of Mechanical Engineering Vol 2: 4307
Institute of Mechanical Engineers Vol 2: 3236, 4312
Institute of Medical Laboratory Sciences Vol 2: 3165
Institute of Metals and Materials Australasia Vol 2: 418
Institute of Motor Industry Vol 2: 3176
Institute of Navigation Vol 2: 4074
Institute of Noetic Sciences Vol 1: 10417
Institute of Nuclear Materials Management Vol 1: 10420
Institute of Packaging Professionals Vol 1: 10424
Institute of Patentees and Investors Vol 2: 3178
Institute of Petroleum Vol 2: 3180
Institute of Physics Vol 2: 3183, 6372
Institute of Practitioners in Advertising Vol 2: 3199
Institute of Professional Investigators Vol 2: 3201
Institute of Public Administration of Canada Vol 1: 10429
Institute of Public Relations Vol 2: 3203
Institute of Quarrying Vol 2: 3205
Institute of Real Estate Management Vol 1: 10432
Institute of Road Transport Engineers Vol 2: 3207
Institute of South African Architects Vol 2: 10879
Institute of Statisticians Vol 2: 3209
Institute of Store Planners Vol 1: 10444
Institute of Technology and Higher Studies of Monterrey Vol 2: 9025

Institute of the Furniture Warehousing and Removing Industry Vol 2: 3211
Institute of Traffic Officers of Southern Africa Vol 2: 10884
Institute of Transportation Engineers Vol 1: 10447
Institute of Turkish Studies Vol 1: 10466
Institute of Water Engineers (Great Britain) Vol 1: 5021
Institute of Youth Vol 2: 10226
Institute on Religion and Democracy Vol 1: 10468
Institution of Chemical Engineers Vol 2: 431, 432, 487, 3213
Institution of Civil Engineers Vol 2: 3226, 3272
Institution of Diagnostic Engineers Vol 2: 3265
Institution of Electrical Engineers Vol 2: 3236, 3267, 3383
Institution of Engineers, Australia Vol 2: 420
Institution of Engineers, Bangladesh Vol 2: 935
Institution of Engineers, Pakistan Vol 2: 9976
Institution of Engineers, Sri Lanka Vol 2: 11401
Institution of Environmental Sciences Vol 2: 3313
Institution of Gas Engineers Vol 2: 3315
Institution of Mechanical Engineers Vol 2: 3332
Institution of Mining and Metallurgy Vol 2: 3335, 12205
Institution of Nuclear Engineers Vol 2: 3344
Institution of Plant Engineers Vol 2: 3355
Institution of Professional Engineers New Zealand Vol 2: 9726
Institution of Structural Engineers Vol 2: 3358
Institutional and Municipal Parking Congress Vol 1: 10470
Institutional Investor Vol 1: 10472
Instituto Brasil - Estados Unidos Vol 2: 1465
Instituto Brasileiro de Arte e Cultura Vol 2: 1429
Instituto Caro y Cuervo Vol 2: 1710
Instituto Colombiano de Cultura Vol 2: 1712
Instituto Cubano del Libro Vol 2: 1817
Instituto Cultural Domecq, A.C. Vol 2: 9028
Instituto de Cultura Hispana Vol 2: 52
Instituto de Cultura Puertorriquena Vol 1: 10475
Instituto de Investigaciones Electricas Vol 2: 9032
Instituto de Investigaciones Technologicas Vol 2: 1715
Instituto de la Juventud del Ministerio de Cultura Vol 2: 11232
Instituto Geografico Agustin Codazzi Vol 2: 1717
Instituto Guatemalteco Americano Vol 2: 7239
Instituto Iberoamericano de Derecho Aeronautico y del Espacio Vol 2: 11258
Instituto Interamericano de Cooperacion para la Agricultura Vol 2: 1773
Instituto Interamericano de Derechos Humanos Vol 2: 1778
Instituto Mexicano de Contadores Publicos Vol 2: 9034
Instituto Mexicano de Ejecutivos de Finanzas Vol 2: 9037
Instituto Mexicano de Ingenieros Quimicos Vol 2: 9104
Instituto Mexicano de Recursos Naturales Renovables Vol 2: 9039

Instituto Mexicano del Mercado de Capitales Vol 2: 9041
Instituto Mexicano del Seguro Social Vol 2: 9043
Instituto Mexiquense de Cultura Vol 2: 9045
Instituto Nacional de Administracion Publica Vol 2: 9050
Instituto Nacional de Antropologia e Historia Vol 2: 9052
Instituto Nacional de Bellas Artes Vol 2: 9205
Instituto Nacional de Investigaciones en Geociencias-Mineria y Quimica Vol 2: 1735
Instituto Nacional de Neurologia y Neurocirugia Vol 2: 9064
Instituto Nacional do Ambiente Vol 2: 10288
Instituto Nacional do Livro Vol 2: 1468
Instituto Nacional Indigenista Vol 2: 9066
Instituto Nami Jafet para o Progreso da Ciencia e Cultura Vol 2: 1487
Instituto Para la Integracion de America Latina Vol 2: 50
Instituto Politecnico Nacional Vol 2: 9068
Instituto Syntex Vol 2: 9070
Instituto Technologico y de Estudios Superiores de Monterrey Vol 2: 9025
Instituto Torcuato di Tella Vol 2: 54
Instituut van Bemarkingsbestuur Vol 2: 10875
Instituut van Verkeersbeamptes van Suider-Africa Vol 2: 10884
Instituut voor Epilepsiebestrijding Vol 2: 6924
Instructional Telecommunications Council - AACC Vol 1: 10477
Instrument Society of America Vol 1: 10479
Instrumentation Laboratory Vol 1: 850, 4191, 14747
Instytut Historii Vol 2: 10128
Instytut Wydawniczy Paz Vol 2: 10084
Insulation Contractors Association of America Vol 1: 10497
Insulators of Maryland Vol 1: 10497
Insurance Institute of America Vol 1: 14794
Intellectual Property Owners Vol 1: 10499
Inter-American Association of Sanitary Engineering and Environmental Sciences Vol 1: 10501
Inter-American Bar Foundation Vol 1: 10506
Inter-American Institute for Cooperation on Agriculture Vol 2: 1773
Inter-American Institute of Human Rights Vol 2: 1778
Inter-American Music Council Vol 1: 15834
Inter-American Music Friends Vol 1: 15834
Inter-American Organization for Higher Education Vol 1: 10508
Inter-American Press Association Vol 1: 10510
Inter-American Safety Council Vol 1: 10512
Inter-American Scout Committee Vol 2: 1780
Inter-Collegiate Yacht Racing Association of North America Vol 1: 10518
Inter Nationes Vol 2: 6926
Inter-Society Color Council Vol 1: 10522
Interactive Services Vol 1: 10526
Interagency Committee for Women in Science and Engineering Vol 1: 20395
Interallied Confederation of Reserve Officers Vol 2: 1163
Interamerican Accounting Association Vol 1: 10531
Interamerican Society of Cardiology Vol 2: 9072
Interart Festivalcenter Vol 2: 7413
Interart Festivalkozpont Vol 2: 7413
Interatom Vol 2: 11705

Intercollegiate Men's Chorus, A National Association of Male Choruses Vol 1: 10533
Intercollegiate Musical Council Vol 1: 10533
Intercollegiate Rowing Association Vol 1: 10535
Intercollegiate Soccer Association of America Vol 1: 10537
Intercollegiate Studies Institute Vol 1: 10546
Intercollegiate Tennis Association Vol 1: 10548
Interconcert Festival Bureau Vol 2: 7413
Interdata Publishing Vol 1: 16739
Interfaith Movement Vol 1: 10563
Interfilm Festival Vol 2: 10790
Interfilm - The International Interchurch Film Centre Vol 2: 9455
InterFuture Vol 1: 10565
Interior Design Vol 1: 10247, 10249, 10568
Interior Design Magazine Vol 1: 4623
Interior Design Society Vol 1: 10573
Internacia Asocio de Bibliistoj kaj Orientalistoj Vol 2: 8277
Internacia Ligo de Esperantistaj Radioamatoroj Vol 2: 7424
Internationaal Filmgebeuren van Vlaanderen - Gent Vol 2: 1192
Internationaal Vocalisten Concours 's-Hertogenbosch Vol 2: 9538
International 210 Association Vol 1: 10578
International Academy for Child Brain Development Vol 1: 10581
International Academy of Astronautics Vol 2: 5943
International Academy of Cytology Vol 2: 6928
International Academy of Medicine and Psychology Vol 2: 497
International Academy of Nutrition and Preventive Medicine Vol 1: 10583
International Academy of the History of Science Vol 2: 5948
International Academy of Trial Lawyers Vol 1: 10587
International Advertising Association Vol 1: 10589
International Advertising Festival Vol 2: 3361
International Advertising Festival of Ireland Vol 2: 7784
International Agency for Research on Cancer Vol 2: 5962
International Agency for the Prevention of Blindness Vol 2: 3365
International Air Transport Association Vol 1: 20464
The International Alliance, An Association of Executive and Professional Women Vol 1: 10594
International Amateur Athletic Federation Vol 2: 9313
International Amateur Rugby Federation Vol 2: 5951
International Amateur Swimming Federation Vol 2: 11752
International American Albino Association and White Horse Ranch National Foundation Vol 1: 10596
International ANDY Awards Vol 1: 10601
International Animated Film Association Vol 2: 9888
International Animated Film Centre Vol 2: 5956
International Animated Film Society, ASIFA—Hollywood - ASIFA—Hollywood Vol 1: 10603
International Association for Bridge and Structural Engineering Vol 2: 11754
International Association for Cereal Science and Technology Vol 2: 806

International Association for Computer Information Systems   Vol 1: 10610
International Association for Dental Research   Vol 1: 10613
International Association for Dental Research - Craniofacial Biology Group   Vol 1: 10627
International Association for Energy Economics   Vol 1: 10629
International Association for Exposition Management   Vol 1: 10634
International Association for Great Lakes Research   Vol 1: 10638
International Association for Hydraulic Research   Vol 2: 9457
International Association for Identification   Vol 1: 10644
International Association for Impact Assessment   Vol 1: 10646
International Association for Insurance Law - Portuguesa Section   Vol 2: 10321
International Association for Maternal and Neonatal Health - IAMANEH   Vol 2: 11880
International Association for Mathematical Geology   Vol 1: 10648
International Association for Non-Violent Sport   Vol 2: 9316
International Association for Orthodontics   Vol 1: 10651
International Association for Physical Education in Higher Education   Vol 2: 1165
International Association for Plant Taxonomy   Vol 2: 6931
International Association for Religious Freedom   Vol 2: 3367
International Association for Research in Income and Wealth   Vol 1: 10653
International Association for Shell and Spatial Structures   Vol 2: 11264
International Association for Structural Mechanics in Reactor Technology   Vol 2: 8542
International Association for Suicide Prevention   Vol 2: 810
International Association for the Defense of Religious Liberty   Vol 2: 11758
International Association for the Evaluation of Educational Achievement   Vol 2: 9464
International Association for the Exchange of Students for Technical Experience   Vol 2: 5958
International Association for the Prevention of Blindness   Vol 2: 3365
International Association for the Protection of Monuments and Restoration of Buildings   Vol 2: 6933
International Association for the Scientific Study of Mental Deficiency   Vol 2: 5960
International Association for the Study of Insurance Economics (Geneva Association)   Vol 2: 11760
International Association for the Study of Lung Cancer   Vol 2: 1955
International Association for the Study of Pain   Vol 1: 10655
International Association of Assessing Officers   Vol 1: 10659
International Association of Biblicists and Orientalists   Vol 2: 8277
International Association of Bryologists   Vol 1: 10676
International Association of Business Communicators   Vol 1: 10681
International Association of Campus Law Enforcement Administrators   Vol 1: 10686
International Association of Cancer Registries   Vol 2: 5962
International Association of Cancer Victims and Friends   Vol 1: 10688

International Association of Cancer Victims and Friends   Vol 1: 10688
International Association of Chiefs of Police   Vol 1: 10694
International Association of Clothing Designers   Vol 1: 10702
International Association of Cooking Professionals   Vol 1: 10710
International Association of Correctional Officers   Vol 1: 10704
International Association of Crime Writers   Vol 2: 1824
International Association of Crime Writers - North American Branch   Vol 1: 10706
International Association of Culinary Professionals   Vol 1: 10710
International Association of Defense Counsel   Vol 1: 10712
International Association of Dentistry for Children   Vol 2: 3369
International Association of Educators for World Peace   Vol 1: 10715
International Association of Energy Economists   Vol 1: 10629
International Association of Engineering Geology   Vol 2: 5964
International Association of Ethicists   Vol 1: 10721
International Association of Fire Chiefs   Vol 1: 10728
International Association of Fire Fighters, AFL-CIO-CLC   Vol 1: 10731
International Association of Fish and Wildlife Agencies   Vol 1: 10733
International Association of Geodesy   Vol 2: 5966
International Association of Gerontology   Vol 2: 7417
International Association of Horticultural Producers   Vol 2: 1067, 9466
International Association of Hospital Central Service Materials Management   Vol 1: 10738
International Association of Hungarian Studies   Vol 2: 7419
International Association of Hydrological Sciences   Vol 2: 9468
International Association of Industrial Accident Boards and Commissions   Vol 1: 10746
International Association of Insurance Counsel   Vol 1: 10712
International Association of Jazz Educators   Vol 1: 10750
International Association of Justice Volunteerism   Vol 1: 10752
International Association of Lighting Designers   Vol 1: 10757
International Association of Logopedics and Phoniatrics   Vol 2: 11461
International Association of Medical Laboratory Technologists   Vol 2: 11463
International Association of Milk, Food and Environmental Sanitarians   Vol 1: 10759
International Association of Motion Picture and Television Producers   Vol 1: 10768
International Association of Museums of Arms and Military History   Vol 2: 11469
International Association of Music Libraries - United Kingdom Branch   Vol 2: 10572
International Association of Official Human Rights Agencies   Vol 1: 10770
International Association of Paediatric Dentistry   Vol 2: 3369
International Association of Penal Law   Vol 2: 5968
International Association of Personnel in Employment Security   Vol 1: 10772

International Association of Personnel in Employment Services   Vol 1: 10772
International Association of Pet Cemeteries   Vol 1: 10775
International Association of Political Consultants   Vol 1: 10778
International Association of Ports and Harbors   Vol 2: 8544
International Association of Professional Bureaucrats   Vol 1: 10780
International Association of Professional Numismatists   Vol 2: 11762
International Association of School Librarianship   Vol 1: 10785
International Association of Sedimentologists   Vol 2: 1957
International Association of Sports Museums and Halls of Fame   Vol 1: 10787
International Association of Teachers of German   Vol 2: 10070
International Association of Teachers of Russian Language and Literature   Vol 2: 10450
International Association of Technological University Libraries   Vol 2: 10574
International Association of Theoretical and Applied Limnology   Vol 1: 10789
International Association of Traffic and Safety Sciences   Vol 2: 8546
International Association of University Presidents   Vol 2: 12026
International Association of Volcanology and Chemistry of the Earth's Interior   Vol 2: 499
International Association of Wall and Ceiling Contractors   Vol 1: 6007
International Association of Women Police   Vol 1: 10791
International Association on the Political Use of Psychiatry   Vol 2: 9471
International Association on Water Pollution Research and Control   Vol 2: 3371, 11553
International Association on Water Quality   Vol 2: 3371
International Astronautical Federation   Vol 2: 5970, 6030
International Atlantic Salmon Federation   Vol 1: 6118
International Audiovisual Society   Vol 1: 10793
International Automobile Federation   Vol 2: 5973
International Bach Competition   Vol 2: 6935
International Badminton Federation   Vol 2: 3376
International Balint Society   Vol 2: 11764
International Balzan Foundation   Vol 2: 8279
International Banana Club (R)   Vol 1: 10795
International Bandy Federation   Vol 2: 9890
International Bantu Civilization Centre   Vol 2: 6506
International Bar Association   Vol 2: 3381
International Beefalo Association   Vol 1: 1332
International Biennial Exhibition of Humour in Art, Tolentino   Vol 2: 8281
International Biennial of Lace-Making - D.B.K. asbl.   Vol 2: 1167
International Biennials of Poetry   Vol 2: 1169
International Black Writers   Vol 1: 10797
International Blade Collectors Association and The Blade Magazine   Vol 1: 10799
International Bluegrass Music Association   Vol 1: 10802
International Board on Books for Young People   Vol 2: 11766
International Board on Books for Young People (IBBY) - Canada   Vol 1: 10804

International Board on Books for Young People (IBBY) - Canadian Section   Vol 1: 10804
International Bocce Federation   Vol 2: 1476
International Border Fancy Canary Club   Vol 1: 10808
International Bottled Water Association   Vol 1: 10810
International Braille Chess Association   Vol 2: 11471
International Brain Research Organization   Vol 2: 5979
International Bridge Academy   Vol 2: 9473
International Broadcasting Convention   Vol 2: 3383
International Buckskin Horse Association   Vol 1: 10812
International Builders Exchange Executives, Inc.   Vol 1: 10814
International Bulb Society   Vol 1: 10816
International Business Communications Council of Japan   Vol 2: 4335
International Business Council MidAmerica   Vol 1: 1870
International Business Machines Corporation   Vol 1: 12679
International Camaro Club   Vol 1: 10818
International Canoe Federation   Vol 2: 8283
International Carbohydrate Organization   Vol 2: 3385
International Casting Federation   Vol 1: 10824
International Castles Institute   Vol 2: 9403
The International Cat Association   Vol 1: 10826
International Catholic Organization for Cinema and Audiovisual   Vol 2: 1171
International Center for Peace in the Middle East   Vol 2: 7893
International Center for the Study of the Preservation and the Restoration of Cultural Property   Vol 2: 8285
International Center in New York   Vol 1: 10828
International Center of Photography   Vol 1: 10830
International Centre for Comparative Criminology   Vol 1: 10832
International Centre for Heat and Mass Transfer   Vol 2: 10709
International Centre for Theoretical Physics   Vol 2: 8287, 8449, 8456
International Centre of Graphic Arts   Vol 2: 10793
International Centre of Insect Physiology and Ecology   Vol 2: 8802
International Children's Centre   Vol 2: 5981
International Chiropractors Association   Vol 1: 10834
International Choir Festival   Vol 2: 9476
International Churchill Society   Vol 1: 10839
International Cinema Festival of Algarve   Vol 2: 10229
International Cinema Week   Vol 2: 8290
International Circulation Managers Association   Vol 1: 8835, 10843, 15354
International City Management Association   Vol 1: 10845
International Civil Aviation Organization   Vol 1: 10856
International Clarinet Association   Vol 1: 10858
International Clarinet Society   Vol 1: 10858
International Colour Association   Vol 2: 9479
International Commission for Optics   Vol 2: 5983, 11485
International Commission for Scientific Religious Psychology   Vol 2: 1174
International Commission for the Eriksson Prize Fund   Vol 2: 11474
International Commission for the Preservation of Islamic Cultural Heritage (ICPICH)   Vol 2: 12054
International Commission of Agricultural Engineering   Vol 2: 1176
International Commission on Physics Education   Vol 2: 11486
International Commission on Radiation Units and Measurements   Vol 1: 10860
International Committee for Amateur-Built Aircraft   Vol 2: 5986
International Committee for Fair Play   Vol 2: 5988
International Committee for Shell Structures   Vol 2: 11264
International Committee for the Defense of the Breton Language   Vol 2: 1178
International Committee for the Diffusion of Arts and Literature Through the Cinema   Vol 2: 5990
International Committee for the Support of Charter 77 in Czechoslovakia   Vol 2: 5992
International Committee of Military Medicine   Vol 2: 1180
International Committee of Military Medicine and Pharmacy   Vol 2: 1180
International Committee of Sports for the Deaf   Vol 2: 1959
International Committee of the Red Cross   Vol 2: 1528, 11770
International Committee on Systematic Bacteriology   Vol 2: 6066
International Communication Association   Vol 1: 10862
International Communications Industries Association   Vol 1: 10864
International Competition for Musical Performers - Geneva   Vol 2: 11773
International Competition for Verdian Voices   Vol 2: 8292
International Competition for Young Opera Singers - Sofia   Vol 2: 1524
International Competition of Maritime Film-TV   Vol 2: 8294
International Confederation for Thermal Analysis   Vol 2: 3387
International Confederation of Art Dealers   Vol 2: 3390
International Confederation of Societies of Authors and Composers   Vol 2: 5994
International Conference of Building Officials   Vol 1: 10866
International Congress of Americanists   Vol 2: 3392
International Consumer Credit Association   Vol 1: 10887
International Council for Adult Education   Vol 1: 10870
International Council for Bird Preservation   Vol 2: 2187
International Council for Bird Preservation - United States Section   Vol 1: 10874
International Council for Building Research, Studies and Documentation   Vol 2: 9481
International Council for Game and Wildlife Conservation   Vol 2: 5996
International Council for Small Business   Vol 1: 10876
International Council for the Improvement of Reading   Vol 1: 11183
International Council of Ballroom Dancing   Vol 2: 4623
International Council of Christians and Jews   Vol 2: 6937
International Council of Environmental Law   Vol 2: 6939
International Council of French-Speaking Radio and Television   Vol 2: 11775
International Council of Graphic Design Associations   Vol 2: 3394
International Council of Nurses   Vol 2: 11777
International Council of Ophthalmology   Vol 2: 9483
International Council of Shopping Centers   Vol 1: 10879
International Council of Societies of Industrial Design   Vol 2: 6461
International Council of Sport and Physical Education   Vol 2: 4721
International Council of Sport Science and Physical Education   Vol 2: 4721
International Council of the French Language   Vol 2: 5998
The International Council of the National Academy of Television Arts and Sciences   Vol 1: 10883
International Council on Education for Teaching   Vol 1: 10885
International Council on Management of Population Programmes   Vol 2: 8905
International Council on Monuments and Sites   Vol 2: 6000
International Credit Association   Vol 1: 10887
International Cryogenic Engineering Committee   Vol 2: 6941
International Cryogenic Materials Conference   Vol 1: 10897
International Customer Service Association   Vol 1: 10899
International Dairy Foods Association   Vol 1: 1912, 10901
International Dance Teachers' Association   Vol 2: 3397
International Dancing Masters Association   Vol 2: 3397
International Database Management Association   Vol 1: 10903
International Dental Federation   Vol 2: 3399
International Desalination Association   Vol 1: 10905
International Design   Vol 1: 10908
International Diabetes Federation   Vol 2: 1182
International Dmitri Shostakovich Competition of String Quartets   Vol 2: 10452
International Documentary and Short Film Festival of Bilbao   Vol 2: 11266
International Documentary Association   Vol 1: 10910
International Double Reed Society   Vol 1: 10912
International Downtown Association   Vol 1: 10915
International Downtown Executive Association   Vol 1: 10915
International Dull Folks, Unlimited   Vol 1: 10917
International Economy   Vol 1: 10920
International Egg Commission   Vol 2: 3404
InterNational Electrical Testing Association   Vol 1: 10922
International Electronics Packaging Society   Vol 1: 10924
International Embryo Transfer Society   Vol 1: 10926
International Energy Agency   Vol 2: 11797
International Equestrian Federation   Vol 2: 11779
International Esperantist League for Go   Vol 2: 8548
International Evangelism Crusades   Vol 1: 10929

International Exhibition Logistics Associates   Vol 2: 11781
International Exhibition of Author Films   Vol 2: 8296
International Exhibitors Association   Vol 1: 10932
International Facility Management Association   Vol 1: 10934
International Family Recreation Association   Vol 1: 10949
International Fan Club Organization   Vol 1: 10951
International Federation for Housing and Planning   Vol 2: 9485
International Federation for Information Processing   Vol 2: 11783
International Federation for Medical and Biological Engineering   Vol 2: 2186
International Federation for the Rights of Man   Vol 2: 6002
International Federation for Theatre Research   Vol 2: 3406
International Federation of Accordionists   Vol 2: 813
International Federation of Aero-Philatelic Societies   Vol 2: 11786
International Federation of Air Line Pilots Associations   Vol 2: 3408
International Federation of Airworthiness   Vol 2: 3412
International Federation of Asian and Western Pacific Contractors' Associations   Vol 2: 10035
International Federation of Automatic Control   Vol 2: 815
International Federation of Beekeepers' Associations   Vol 2: 8298
International Federation of Bowlers   Vol 2: 4724
International Federation of Business and Professional Women   Vol 2: 1782
International Federation of Catholic Medical Associations   Vol 2: 12095
International Federation of Children's Choirs   Vol 1: 10955
International Federation of Cinematographic Press   Vol 2: 6943
International Federation of Clinical Chemistry   Vol 2: 7895
International Federation of Clinical Neurophysiology   Vol 1: 10958
International Federation of Disabled Workers and Civilian Handicapped   Vol 2: 6945
International Federation of Essential Oils and Aroma Trades   Vol 2: 3414
International Federation of Festival Organizations   Vol 1: 10961
International Federation of Interior Architects/Interior Designers   Vol 2: 9488
International Federation of Landscape Architects   Vol 2: 6004, 6424
International Federation of Leather Guilds   Vol 1: 10964
International Federation of Library Associations and Institutions   Vol 2: 9490
International Federation of Manufacturers and Converters of Pressure-Sensitive and Heatseals on Paper and Other Base Materials   Vol 2: 9497
International Federation of Multiple Sclerosis Societies   Vol 2: 3416
International Federation of Netball Associations   Vol 2: 502
International Federation of Newspaper Publishers   Vol 2: 6006
International Federation of Operational Research Societies   Vol 2: 6009

International Federation of Ophthalmological Societies   Vol 2: 9499
International Federation of Oto-Rhino-Laryngological Societies   Vol 2: 1184
International Federation of Photographic Art - Kodak Award   Vol 2: 1188
International Federation of Popular Sports   Vol 2: 6947
International Federation of Postcard Dealers   Vol 1: 10966
International Federation of Psychoanalytic Societies   Vol 2: 4726
International Federation of Purchasing and Materials Management   Vol 2: 9503
International Federation of Roofing Contractors   Vol 2: 6949
International Federation of Shorthand and Typewriting   Vol 2: 6951
International Federation of Social Science Organizations   Vol 2: 1859
International Federation of Societies for Electroencephalography and Clinical Neurophysiology   Vol 1: 10958
International Federation of Societies of Cosmetic Chemists   Vol 2: 3420
International Federation of Sports Medicine   Vol 2: 1478
International Federation of Translators   Vol 2: 821
International Federation of University Women   Vol 2: 11788
International Federation of Vexillological Associations   Vol 1: 10968
International Federation of Women's Travel Organizations   Vol 1: 10971
International Fencing Federation   Vol 2: 6011
International Festival of Alpine Films Les Diablerets, Switzerland   Vol 2: 11790
International Festival of Cinema for Children and Youth - Tomar   Vol 2: 10231
International Festival of Economics and Training Films   Vol 2: 1190
International Festival of Film, Television and Video of Rio de Janeiro   Vol 2: 1481
International Festival of Films and Television Programs on Environmental Problems - Ekofilm   Vol 2: 1861
International Festival of Films for TV   Vol 1: 6260
International Festival of Films on Architecture and Town-planning of Lausanne   Vol 2: 11792
International Festival of Films on Art   Vol 2: 11794
International Festival of Films on Energy Lausanne   Vol 2: 11796
International Festival of Maritime and Exploration Films   Vol 2: 6013
International Festival of New Latin American Cinema   Vol 2: 1827
International Festival of Red Cross and Health Films   Vol 2: 1527
International Festival of the Image   Vol 2: 6015
International Festival of the New Super 8 Cinema and Video   Vol 2: 12113
International Festival of Urban Architecture, Town Planning and Urban Environment Films of Bordeaux   Vol 2: 6017
International Filariasis Association   Vol 2: 3423
International Film and Student Directors Festival   Vol 2: 6019
International Film Festival Mannheim   Vol 2: 6953
International Film Festival of Figueira da Foz   Vol 2: 10233

International Film Festival of India   Vol 2: 7688
International Film Festival of Santarem   Vol 2: 10235
International Film Festival of the Estoril Coast   Vol 2: 10237
International Film Festival Rassegna - Nature, Man and His Environment   Vol 2: 8300
International Film Festivals Foundation   Vol 2: 1194
International Filmwochenende Wurzburg   Vol 2: 6955
International Finn Association   Vol 2: 9506
International Fire Buff Associates   Vol 1: 10974
International Fire Photographers Association   Vol 1: 10977
International Fire Service Training Association   Vol 1: 10981
International Fiscal Association   Vol 2: 9510
International Flanders Film Festival - Ghent   Vol 2: 1192
International Flat Earth Research Society   Vol 1: 9225
International Flavors and Fragrances, Inc.   Vol 1: 17830
International Flight Attendants Association   Vol 1: 10983
International Folklore Association   Vol 1: 19765
International Food, Wine and Travel Writers Association   Vol 1: 10985
International Foodservice Manufacturers Association   Vol 1: 10987
International Formalwear Association   Vol 1: 10989
International Foundation Mozarteum   Vol 2: 825
International Foundation of Employee Benefit Plans   Vol 1: 10991
International Franchise Association   Vol 1: 10995
International Frisbee Disc Association   Vol 1: 20252
International Furnishings and Design Association   Vol 1: 11000
International Furnishings and Design Association Educational Foundation   Vol 1: 11004
International Galileo Galilei Prize Foundation of the Rotary Club of Italy   Vol 2: 8302
International Game Fish Association   Vol 1: 11006
International Gas Turbine Institute   Vol 1: 4706
International Geographic Information Foundation   Vol 1: 4244, 4255
International Geographical Union   Vol 2: 6957
International Geographical Union - Commission Geographical Education   Vol 2: 6959
International Glaciological Society   Vol 2: 3425
International Glaucoma Congress-American Society for Contemporary Ophthalmology   Vol 1: 4536
International Good Neighbor Council   Vol 2: 9074
International Graphic Information Foundation   Vol 1: 4254
International Graphics   Vol 1: 11008
International Graphoanalysis Society   Vol 1: 11010
International Guild of Artists   Vol 2: 3427
International Guild of Candle Artisans   Vol 1: 11012
International Guild of Professional Electrologists   Vol 1: 11017

International Gustav Mahler Society   Vol 2: 831
International Hall of Fame   Vol 1: 19660
International Handball Federation   Vol 2: 11798
International Harp Contest in Israel   Vol 2: 7898
International Health Centre of Socio-Economics Researches and Studies   Vol 2: 6021
International Henri Langlois Encounters   Vol 2: 6023
International Henryk Wieniawski Competitions   Vol 2: 10072
International Home and Private Poker Players Association   Vol 1: 11024
International Horn Society   Vol 1: 11026
International Hot Rod Association   Vol 1: 11029
International House of Poetry   Vol 2: 1170
International House - World Trade Center   Vol 1: 20527
International Hugo Wolf Society   Vol 2: 833
International Human Assistance Programs   Vol 1: 11036
International Human Powered Vehicle Association   Vol 1: 11038
International Human Rights Law Group   Vol 1: 11040
International Hydrofoil Society   Vol 2: 3429
International Hydrographic Organization   Vol 2: 9318
International Ice Hockey Federation   Vol 2: 11802
International Information Management Congress   Vol 1: 11043
International Institute for Applied Systems Analysis   Vol 2: 835
International Institute for Promotion and Prestige   Vol 2: 11804
International Institute for the Science of Sintering   Vol 2: 10712
International Institute of Human Rights   Vol 2: 6025
International Institute of Humanitarian Law   Vol 2: 8306
International Institute of Islamic Thought   Vol 1: 11049
International Institute of Refrigeration   Vol 2: 6027
International Institute of Space Law   Vol 2: 6030
International Institute of Welding   Vol 2: 3431
International Interactive Communications Society   Vol 1: 11051
International Intra-ocular Implant Club   Vol 2: 3437
International Jacques Brel Foundation   Vol 2: 1195
International Jazz Federation   Vol 2: 6756
International Jean Sibelius Violin Competition   Vol 2: 4728
International Joint Conference on Artificial Intelligence   Vol 1: 11053
International Joseph A. Schumpeter Society   Vol 2: 6961
International Judges Association   Vol 1: 19570
International Judo Federation   Vol 2: 6963
International Jugglers Association   Vol 1: 11055
International Juvenile Officer's Association   Vol 1: 11057
International Kart Federation   Vol 1: 11061
International Kodaly Society   Vol 2: 7422
International Korfestival   Vol 2: 9476
International Korfball Federation   Vol 2: 9512

International Kuhlau Competition for Flautists   Vol 2: 6965
International Labor Communications Association, AFL-CIO, CLC   Vol 1: 11063
International Labor Press Association   Vol 1: 11063
International Labour Organization   Vol 2: 11806
International Lactation Consultant Association   Vol 1: 11066
International Law Students Association   Vol 1: 4630
International League Against Epilepsy   Vol 2: 6967
International League Against Rheumatism   Vol 1: 11069
International League for Animal Rights   Vol 2: 8870
International League for Human Rights   Vol 1: 11071
International League of Antiquarian Booksellers   Vol 2: 6969
International League of Esperantist Radioamateurs   Vol 2: 7424
International League of Women Composers   Vol 1: 11074
International Legal Fraternity Phi Delta Phi   Vol 1: 11076
International Life Sciences Institute - Nutrition Foundation   Vol 1: 10341, 11081
International Lightning Class Association   Vol 1: 11083
International Lilac Society   Vol 1: 11086
International Ludwig Spohr Violin Competition   Vol 2: 6971
International Luge Federation   Vol 2: 839
International Magnesium Association   Vol 1: 11091
International Management Council of the YMCA   Vol 1: 11097
International Manifestations of Ceramic Arts   Vol 2: 8308
International Map Collectors' Society   Vol 2: 3439
International Martial Arts Federation   Vol 2: 3441
International Mathematical Union   Vol 2: 4730
International MC Class Sailboat Racing Association   Vol 1: 11100
International Measurement Confederation   Vol 2: 7427
International Medical Film and Health Education Week   Vol 2: 11268
International Metallographic Society   Vol 1: 5361
International Motor Press Association   Vol 1: 11102
International Motor Sports Association   Vol 1: 11104
International Motorcycle Federation   Vol 2: 11808
International Motorsports Hall of Fame   Vol 1: 11111
International Movement of Catholic Lawyers   Vol 2: 6033
International Music Center   Vol 2: 841
International Music Competition of the Broadcasting Stations of the Federal Republic of Germany   Vol 2: 6973
International Music Council   Vol 2: 6421, 10784
International Music Institute of the City of Darmstadt   Vol 2: 6975
International Musical Contest Dr. Luis Sigall Competition   Vol 2: 1569
International Mystery Film Festival   Vol 2: 8387

International Narcotic Enforcement Officers Association   Vol 1: 11113
International Naturist Federation   Vol 2: 1197
International New Music Composers Competition   Vol 1: 11120
International Newspaper Marketing Association   Vol 1: 8836, 11122
International Newspaper Promotion Association   Vol 1: 11122
International Nickel Company of Canada   Vol 1: 7547
International Nickel Company of Canada, Limited   Vol 1: 6945
International Nut Council   Vol 2: 11270
International Oceanographic Foundation   Vol 1: 11124
International Odense Film Festival   Vol 2: 1962
International Old Lacers   Vol 1: 11126
International Olympic Committee   Vol 2: 4723, 11738, 11813
International Optometric and Optical League   Vol 2: 3443
International Organ Competition, Odense   Vol 2: 1964
International Organ Festival Society   Vol 2: 3447
International Organisation for the Elimination of All Forms of Racial Discrimination.   Vol 2: 11685
International Organization Against Trachoma   Vol 2: 6035
International Organization for Chemical Sciences in Development   Vol 2: 9076
International Organization for Mycoplasmology   Vol 1: 11128
International Organization for Succulent Plant Study   Vol 2: 3451
International Organization of Good Templars   Vol 2: 9893
International Organization of Journalists   Vol 2: 1863
International Organization of Plant Biosystematists   Vol 2: 8550
International Organization of Supreme Audit Institutions   Vol 2: 845
International Orienteering Federation   Vol 2: 11476
International Paper Company Foundation   Vol 1: 13800
International Peace Academy   Vol 1: 11134
International Pediatric Association   Vol 2: 6037
International PEN - Philippines   Vol 2: 10039
International PEN - Scotland   Vol 2: 10577
International PEN - Sydney Centre   Vol 2: 505
International Personnel Management Association   Vol 1: 11136
International Pharmaceutical Federation   Vol 2: 9515
International Pharmaceutical Students' Federation   Vol 2: 7900
International Pharmaceutical Zambon   Vol 2: 1199
International Philatelic Press Club   Vol 1: 11140
International Photobiology Association   Vol 2: 11817
International Phycological Society   Vol 2: 3453
International Piano Composition Contest   Vol 2: 6039
International Pilar Bayona Piano Competition   Vol 2: 11272
International Planned Parenthood Federation   Vol 1: 11142

International Platform Association Vol 1: 11144
International Police Association Vol 2: 3455
International Political Science Association Vol 2: 9895
International Polka Association Vol 1: 11166
International Potash Institute Vol 2: 11819
International Powerlifting Federation Vol 2: 11478
International Precious Metals Institute Vol 1: 11170
International Primary Aluminum Institute Vol 2: 3457
International Print Biennale Vol 2: 10076
International Print Triennial Vol 2: 10076
International Prize for the First Novel Vol 2: 6041
International Professional Security Association Vol 2: 3459
International Professional Surfers Vol 1: 5971
International Psychohistorical Association Vol 1: 11174
International Public Relations Association Vol 2: 11821
International Radiation Protection Association Vol 2: 9523
International Radio and Television Organization Vol 2: 1866
International Radio and Television Society Vol 1: 11180
International Reading Association Vol 1: 11183
International Recreation Association Vol 1: 20499
International Reference Organization in Forensic Medicine and Sciences Vol 1: 11199
International Rescue Committee Vol 1: 11203
International Research Group on Wood Preservation Vol 2: 11481
International Road Federation Vol 1: 11205
International Road Transport Union Vol 2: 11824
International Robert Schumann Competition Vol 2: 6977
International Rock 'n' Roll Music Association Vol 1: 11207
International Sailing Film Festival in La Rochelle Vol 2: 6043
International Salon of Cartoons Vol 1: 11209
International Save The Pun Foundation Vol 1: 11211
International Savings Banks Institute Vol 2: 11826
International Science Policy Foundation Vol 2: 3461, 4337
International Scientific and Technical Gliding Organisation Vol 2: 6980
International Scientific Film Association Vol 2: 11199
International Seaweed Association Vol 2: 1483
International Security and Detective Alliance Vol 1: 11213
International Sericultural Commission Vol 2: 6045
International Sheep Dog Society Vol 2: 3463
International Short Film Festival, Oberhausen Vol 2: 6982
International Show Car Association Vol 1: 11320
International Shuffleboard Association Vol 1: 11215
International Side-Saddle Organization Vol 1: 11217
International Silo Association Vol 1: 11219

International Singing Competition of Bilbao Vol 2: 11274
International Singing Competition of Toulouse Vol 2: 6047
International Skating Union Vol 2: 11828
International Ski Federation Vol 2: 11832
International Ski Film Festival Vol 1: 11222
International Ski Writers Association Vol 2: 11834
International Soap Box Derby Vol 1: 11224
International Social Science Council Vol 2: 6049
International Social Security Association Vol 2: 11836
International Society for Animal Rights Vol 1: 11226
International Society for Astrological Research Vol 1: 11228
International Society for Augmentative and Alternative Communication Vol 1: 11230
International Society for Burn Injuries and International Burn Foundation Vol 1: 11234
International Society for Clinical Enzymology Vol 1: 11236
International Society for Clinical Laboratory Technology Vol 1: 11238
International Society for Contemporary Music Vol 2: 9525
International Society for Developmental Psychobiology Vol 1: 11244
International Society for Education Through Art Vol 2: 3466
International Society for Engineering Education Vol 2: 848
International Society for General Systems Research Vol 1: 11272
International Society for Heart and Lung Transplantation Vol 1: 11247
International Society for Heart Research Vol 2: 3468
International Society for Heart Transplantation Vol 1: 11247
International Society for Human and Animal Mycology Vol 2: 1201
International Society for Hybrid Microelectronics Vol 1: 11252
International Society for Individual Liberty Vol 1: 11257
International Society for Medical and Psychological Hypnosis Vol 2: 8310
International Society for Military Law and Law of War Vol 2: 1203
International Society for Neurochemistry Vol 2: 1966
International Society for Philosophical Enquiry Vol 1: 11259
International Society for Photogrammetry and Remote Sensing Vol 2: 8552
International Society for Plant Pathology - Bacteria Section Vol 2: 6051
International Society for Research on Civilization Diseases and Environment Vol 2: 1205
International Society for Rock Mechanics Vol 2: 10239
International Society for Soil Mechanics and Foundation Engineering Vol 2: 3472
International Society for the Arts, Sciences and Technology Vol 1: 11265
International Society for the History of Pharmacy Vol 2: 6985
International Society for the Study of European Ideas Vol 2: 3474
International Society for the Study of Human Ideas on Ultimate Reality and Meaning Vol 1: 11269
International Society for the Systems Sciences Vol 1: 11272

International Society of Air Safety Investigators Vol 1: 11274
International Society of Biometeorology Vol 1: 11276
International Society of Blood Transfusion Vol 2: 3476
International Society of Certified Electronics Technicians Vol 1: 11280
International Society of Chemotherapy Vol 2: 9897
International Society of Dermatology: Tropical, Geographic and Ecologic Vol 2: 1720
International Society of Electrochemistry Vol 2: 11839
International Society of Hypertension Vol 2: 1969
International Society of Literature Vol 2: 3478
International Society of Paediatric Oncology Vol 2: 9527
International Society of Parametric Analysts Vol 1: 11284
International Society of Pharmaceutical Engineers Vol 1: 11290
International Society of Phonetic Sciences Vol 1: 11295
International Society of Postmasters Vol 1: 11299
International Society of Psychoneuroendocrinology Vol 2: 1207
International Society of Radiology Vol 2: 11841
International Society of Reliabilty Engineers Vol 1: 18023
International Society of Sugar Cane Technologists Vol 2: 1485
International Society of Surgery (ISS/SIC) Vol 2: 11843
International Society of Tropical Dermatology Vol 2: 1720
International Society of Tropical Ecology Vol 2: 7690
International Society of Violin and Bow Makers Vol 2: 9530
International Society of Weekly Newspaper Editors Vol 1: 11302
International Society of Weighing and Measurement Vol 1: 11305
International Society on Electrocardiology Vol 2: 10579
International Society on Toxinology Vol 2: 6988
International Sociological Association Vol 2: 11276
International Softball Congress Vol 1: 11312
International Softball League Vol 1: 11312
International Solar Energy Society Vol 2: 507
International Songwriters' Association Vol 2: 7786
International Sound Hunters Federation Vol 2: 9532
International Space Hall of Fame Vol 1: 11318
International Specialty Car Association Vol 1: 11320
International Spectrum Vol 1: 10904
International Sport Film Festival of Palermo Vol 2: 8312
International Sport Press Association Vol 2: 8314
International Sports Film Festival Vol 2: 8316
International Sports Film Festival of Hungary Vol 2: 7430
International Statistical Institute Vol 2: 9534, 9547
International Steel Guitar Convention Vol 1: 11322

International Stoke Mandeville Games Federation   Vol 2: 3480
International Stoke Mandeville Wheelchair Sports Federation   Vol 2: 3480
International Student Film Festival   Vol 2: 7902
International Studies Association   Vol 1: 11324
International Swimming Hall of Fame   Vol 1: 11328
International Tape/Disc Association   Vol 1: 11482
International Tar Conference   Vol 2: 6053
International Tchaikovsky Competition   Vol 2: 10454
International Technology Education Association   Vol 1: 11331
International Technology Institute   Vol 1: 11339
International Telecommunications Union   Vol 2: 11847
International Teleconferencing Association   Vol 1: 11342
International Telephone and Telegraph Corporation   Vol 1: 10271
International Teleproduction Society   Vol 1: 11345
International Television Association   Vol 2: 3501
International Television Festival of Monte Carlo   Vol 2: 1376, 9320
International Television Symposium and Technical Exhibition - Montreux   Vol 2: 11850
International Tennis Federation   Vol 2: 3482
International Tennis Hall of Fame   Vol 1: 11349
International Theatre Institute   Vol 2: 4733
International THEOS Foundation   Vol 1: 11356
International Thermal Conductivity Conference   Vol 1: 11358
International Thespian Society   Vol 1: 11360
International Tourist Film and Video Festival of Tarbes/Pyrenees   Vol 2: 6055
International Tourist Film Festival   Vol 2: 8318
International Trade Mart   Vol 1: 20527
International Transactional Analysis Association   Vol 1: 11364
International Travel Film and Video Festival   Vol 1: 11366
International Travel Film Festival   Vol 1: 11366
International Triennial Exhibition of Photography   Vol 2: 11853
International Triennial of Stringed Instruments   Vol 2: 8320
International Trombone Association   Vol 1: 11368
International Trumpet Guild   Vol 1: 11370
International Tube Association   Vol 2: 3486
International Unicycling Federation   Vol 1: 11376
International Union Against Cancer   Vol 2: 11855
International Union for Quaternary Research   Vol 2: 3488
International Union for Surface Finishing   Vol 2: 3490
International Union for the Modern Pentathlon and Biathlon   Vol 2: 6990
International Union for Vacuum Science, Technique, and Applications   Vol 2: 3492
International Union of Air Pollution Prevention Associations   Vol 2: 3494
International Union of Amateur Cinema   Vol 2: 9536

International Union of Architects   Vol 2: 6057, 6423
International Union of Crystallography   Vol 2: 3497
International Union of Forestry Research Organizations   Vol 2: 850
International Union of Master Painters   Vol 2: 6992
International Union of Microbiological Societies   Vol 2: 6063
International Union of Pure and Applied Chemistry   Vol 2: 3499
International Union of Pure and Applied Physics   Vol 2: 11483
International Union of Radio Science   Vol 2: 1209
International Union of Students   Vol 2: 1868
International Union of Testing and Research Laboratories for Materials and Structures   Vol 2: 6067
International Union of Vacuum Science, Technique and Applications   Vol 1: 11378
International Veteran Boxers Association   Vol 1: 11380
International Video Creation Center, Montbeliard   Vol 2: 6069
International Video Week of Geneva   Vol 2: 11864
International Visual Communications Association   Vol 2: 2702, 3501
International Vocal Competition 's-Hertogenbosch   Vol 2: 9538
International Voice Competition of Verviers   Vol 2: 1214
International Water Supply Association   Vol 2: 3503, 11553
International Week of Sea and Marine Cinema - Cartagena   Vol 2: 11278
International Weightlifting Federation   Vol 2: 7432
International Wheat Gluten Association   Vol 1: 11391
International Wild Waterfowl Association   Vol 1: 11393
International Wildlife Film Festival   Vol 1: 11401
International Wine and Food Society   Vol 2: 3505
International Wire and Machinery Association   Vol 2: 3507
International Wizard of Oz Club   Vol 1: 11403
International Women's Film Festival, Creteil   Vol 2: 6071
International Women's Media Foundation   Vol 1: 11405
International World Games Association   Vol 2: 9540
International Yacht Racing Union   Vol 1: 19532
International Young Instrumentalist of the Year   Vol 2: 12177
International Young Singer of the Year   Vol 2: 12177
International Youth Hostel Federation   Vol 2: 3509
International Youth Library   Vol 2: 6994
Internationale Alpenlandische Film- und Autorenakademie   Vol 2: 720
Internationale Carl Nielsen Violin Konkurrence   Vol 2: 1983
Internationale Deutschlehrerverband   Vol 2: 10070
Internationale Filmfestspiele Berlin   Vol 2: 6563
Internationale Filmwoche Mannheim   Vol 2: 6953

Internationale Foderation des Dachdeckerchandwerks   Vol 2: 6949
Internationale Gesellschaft fur Felsmechanik   Vol 2: 10239
Internationale Gesellschaft fur Getreidewissenschaft und technologie   Vol 2: 806
Internationale Gesellschaft fur Ingenieurpadagogik   Vol 2: 848
Internationale Gustav Mahler Gesellschaft   Vol 2: 831
Internationale Hugo Wolf-Gesellschaft   Vol 2: 833
Internationale Joseph A. Schumpeter Gesellschaft   Vol 2: 6961
Internationale Jugendbibliothek   Vol 2: 6994
Internationale Kurzfilmtage Oberhausen   Vol 2: 6982
Internationale Messtechnische Konfoderation   Vol 2: 7427
Internationale Orientierungslauf Foderation   Vol 2: 11476
Internationale Stiftung Mozarteum   Vol 2: 825
Internationale Vereinigung fur Bruckenbau und Hochbau   Vol 2: 11754
Internationalen Robert-Schumann-Wettbewerbes   Vol 2: 6977
Internationaler Draht-und Maschinenverband   Vol 2: 3507
Internationaler Johann-Sebastien-Bach-Wettbewerb   Vol 2: 6935
Internationaler Kuhlau-Wettbewerb fur Flotisten   Vol 2: 6965
Internationaler Musikwettbewerb der Rundfunkanstalten der Bundesrepublik Deutschland   Vol 2: 6973
Internationaler Pianistenwettbewerb Busoni   Vol 2: 8180
Internationaler Rohrverband   Vol 2: 3486
Internationaler Verband Forstlicher Forschungsanstalten   Vol 2: 850
Internationaler Violinwettbewerb Koln   Vol 2: 6608
Internationaler Violinwettbewerb Ludwig Spohr   Vol 2: 6971
Internationaler Volkssportverband   Vol 2: 6947
Internationales Festival der Filmhochschulen Munchen   Vol 2: 7058
Internationales Kuratorium fur das Jugendbuch   Vol 2: 11766
Internationales Musikinstitut Darmstadt   Vol 2: 6975
Internationales Musikzentrum Wien   Vol 2: 841
Internationales Trickfilm Festival Stuttgart   Vol 2: 7141
Internationella Bandyforbundet   Vol 2: 9890
INTERPHIL   Vol 2: 11866
Interpretation Competition   Vol 2: 1870
Interstate Mining Compact Commission   Vol 1: 11407
Interstate Printers and Publishers   Vol 1: 13010
Intertel Foundation   Vol 1: 11409
Intravenous Nurses Society   Vol 1: 11411
Inventors Clubs of America - International Hall of Fame   Vol 1: 11415
Inventors Workshop International Education Foundation   Vol 1: 11422
Invest-In-America Foundation   Vol 1: 11424
Investigative Reporters and Editors   Vol 1: 11427
Investment Casting Institute   Vol 1: 10106
Investment Company Institute   Vol 1: 4947
Investment Education Institute   Vol 1: 11430
IODE - Municipal Chapter of Toronto   Vol 1: 11432

Iota Sigma Pi   Vol 1: 11434
Iowa Arts Council   Vol 1: 11440
Iowa Educational Media Association   Vol 1: 11442
Iowa School of Letters   Vol 1: 11445
Iowa Writers Workshop   Vol 1: 19803
Iqbal Academy Pakistan   Vol 2: 9978
Iranian Research Organization for Science and Technology   Vol 2: 7736
Ireland - Department of Defence   Vol 2: 7788
IREM Foundation   Vol 1: 10440
Irino Prize Foundation   Vol 2: 8558
Irish Academy of Letters   Vol 2: 7791
Irish American Cultural Institute   Vol 2: 7835
Irish-American Cultural Institute   Vol 1: 11449
Irish Dairy Board   Vol 2: 7834
Irish Farm Centre   Vol 2: 7794
Irish Hotels Federation   Vol 2: 7797
Irish Lawn Tennis Association   Vol 2: 7799
Irish Life Assurance   Vol 2: 7801
Irish Life Dublin Theatre Festival   Vol 2: 7805
Irish Master Farriers Association   Vol 2: 7834
The Irish Times   Vol 2: 7809
Irish Youth Film & Arts Company   Vol 2: 7811
Iron and Steel Institute   Vol 2: 3127
Iron and Steel Institute of Japan   Vol 2: 8560
Iron and Steel Society   Vol 1: 11456
Iron and Steel Society of the American Institute of Mining, Metallurgical and Petroleum Engineers   Vol 1: 11456
Ironbridge Gorge Museum Trust   Vol 2: 2248
Irrigation Association   Vol 1: 11473
Irwin Company; Richard D.   Vol 1: 2983
Isfahan International Festival of Films for Children and Young Adults   Vol 2: 7738
Isfahan Mayorality   Vol 2: 7739
Iskowitz Foundation; Gershon   Vol 1: 11478
Islamic Capitals Organization   Vol 2: 10501
Islamic Development Bank   Vol 2: 10487
Islamic Foundation for Science, Technology and Development   Vol 2: 10489
Islamic Republic of Iran - Ministry of Education   Vol 2: 7740
Islamic Research and Training Institute   Vol 2: 10487
Islamic States Broadcasting Services Organization   Vol 2: 10491
Island Resources Foundation   Vol 1: 11480
Isle of Elba - Raffaello Brignetti Literary Award   Vol 2: 8322
Israel - Ministry of Education and Culture   Vol 2: 7904
Israel - Ministry of Labour and Social Affairs, Unit for Volunteer Services   Vol 2: 7910
Israel Archives Association   Vol 2: 7912
Israel Biochemical Society   Vol 2: 7914
Israel Broadcasting Authority - The Voice of Israel - Jerusalem   Vol 2: 7916
Israel Museum   Vol 2: 7919
Istanbul Foundation for Culture and Arts   Vol 2: 12059
Istanbul Kultur ve Sanat Vakfi   Vol 2: 12059
Istel Ltd   Vol 1: 3839
Istituto Internazionale delle Comunicazioni   Vol 2: 8324
Istituto Italiano della Saldatura   Vol 2: 8355
Istituto Italiano di Cultura di Tokyo   Vol 2: 8569
Istituto Italo-Latino Americano   Vol 2: 8327
Istituto Nazionale di Studi Romani   Vol 2: 8329
Istituto Nazionale di Studi Verdiani - Rotary Club di Parma   Vol 2: 8385
Istituto Papirologico Girolamo Vitelli   Vol 2: 8331
Istituto per la Cooperazione Universitaria   Vol 2: 8275

ITA   Vol 1: 11482
Italia Nostra-Association Nazionale per la Tutela del Patrimonio Storico Artistico e Naturale della Nazione   Vol 2: 8360
Italia Sul Mare - Rassegna Internazionale dei Documentari Cine - TV Marinari   Vol 2: 8294
Italian and Romansh PEN Centre of PEN International   Vol 2: 11868
Italian Association for Cancer Research   Vol 2: 2819
Italian Association for Metallurgy   Vol 2: 8333
Italian Chemical Society   Vol 2: 8335
Italian Council of Ministers   Vol 2: 8341
Italian Cultural Institute of New York   Vol 1: 11484
Italian Electrical and Electronics Association   Vol 2: 8344
Italian Institute of Culture   Vol 2: 8569
Italian Institute of Culture for the United Kingdom   Vol 2: 4396
Italian Institute of Welding   Vol 2: 8355
Italian Mathematical Union   Vol 2: 8357
Italian Nostra-National Association for the Preservation of the Historical, Artistic and Natural Heritage of the Nation   Vol 2: 8360
Italian PEN Club   Vol 2: 8362
Italo American National Union   Vol 1: 11486
Italy   Vol 2: 8368
Italy - Ministero del turismo e dello spettacolo   Vol 2: 8370
Italy - Ministero della pubblica istruzione   Vol 2: 8366
Italy - Ministero per i beni culturali e ambientali   Vol 2: 8364
Italy - Ministry for Culture and the Environment   Vol 2: 8364
Italy - Ministry for Tourism and Performing Arts   Vol 2: 8392, 8393
Italy - Ministry of Education   Vol 2: 8181, 8366
Italy - Ministry of the Interior   Vol 2: 8368
Italy - Ministry of Tourism and Performing Arts   Vol 2: 8370
Italy - Office of the President of the Council of Ministers   Vol 2: 8372
Italy - Presidenza del consiglio dei ministri   Vol 2: 8372
Italy - the President of the Council of Ministers   Vol 2: 8181
ITC-Foundation   Vol 2: 8557
ITI International Ballet Competition, Helsinki   Vol 2: 4733
ITI/The Strauman Company   Vol 1: 1086
IUPAP Commission C2: Sun Amco   Vol 2: 11488
Ives Center for the Arts; Charles   Vol 1: 11492
Ivy Society; Robert H.   Vol 1: 4760
Iwatani Naoji Foundation   Vol 2: 8572
Iwatani Naoji Kinen Zaidan   Vol 2: 8572
Ix-Xirka   Vol 2: 8914
Jabotinsky Foundation   Vol 1: 11494
Jackson Book Company Ltd.; Holt   Vol 2: 3570
Jackson Foundation; Henry M.   Vol 1: 11496
Jacksonville University - Theatre Arts Department   Vol 1: 11501
Jaen International Piano Competition, Jaen Prize   Vol 2: 11280
Jafet Institute for the Advancement of Science and Culture; Nami   Vol 2: 1487
Jahnsson Foundation; Yrjo   Vol 2: 4735
Jahnssonin Saatio; Yrjo   Vol 2: 4735
Jahres Humanitaere Stiftelse; Anders   Vol 2: 9899
Jamaica - Chancery of the Orders of the Societies of Honour   Vol 2: 8483

James Fine Arts Committee; Lucile   Vol 1: 9340
Jamestown-Yorktown Foundation   Vol 1: 10255
Jamnalal Bajaj Foundation   Vol 2: 7692
Janssen Foundation; Hans   Vol 2: 6909
Janssen Pharmaceutica   Vol 1: 14043
Japan - Ministry of Education, Science and Culture   Vol 2: 8574
Japan - Office of the Prime Minister   Vol 2: 8581
Japan - Science and Technology Agency   Vol 2: 8590
Japan Academy   Vol 2: 8592
Japan Art Academy   Vol 2: 8596
Japan Art Association   Vol 2: 8598
Japan Association of Cultural Film Producers   Vol 2: 8774
Japan Broadcasting Corporation   Vol 2: 8600, 8727
Japan Design Foundation   Vol 2: 8604
Japan External Trade Organisation   Vol 2: 4335
Japan Federation of Musicians   Vol 2: 8607
Japan Federation of Printing Industries   Vol 2: 8609
Japan Foundation   Vol 2: 8611, 8727
Japan Golf Association   Vol 2: 8616
Japan Information Center of Science and Technology   Vol 2: 8619
Japan International Film - Video Festival of Adventure and Sports in Hakuba   Vol 2: 8621
Japan International League of Artists   Vol 2: 8623
Japan National Committee for UICC   Vol 2: 11863
Japan Newspaper Publishers and Editors Association   Vol 2: 8625
Japan Poets' Association   Vol 2: 8630
Japan Printers' Association   Vol 2: 8609
Japan Prize Preparatory Foundation   Vol 2: 8735
Japan P.T.A. Association   Vol 2: 8675
Japan Society for Analytical Chemistry   Vol 2: 8633
Japan Society for the Promotion of Science   Vol 2: 7157, 8635
Japan Society for Translators   Vol 2: 8637
Japan Society of Human Genetics   Vol 2: 8640
Japan Society of Lubrication Engineers   Vol 2: 8668
Japan Society of Mechanical Engineers   Vol 2: 8642
Japan Welding Society   Vol 2: 8644
Japanese American Citizens League   Vol 1: 11503
Japanese Biochemical Society   Vol 2: 8649
Japanese Society for Tuberculosis   Vol 2: 8651
Japanese Society of Applied Entomology and Zoology   Vol 2: 8653
Japanese Society of Hematology   Vol 2: 8655
Japanese Society of Sericultural Science   Vol 2: 8658
Japanese Society of Snow and Ice   Vol 2: 8661
Japanese Society of Soil Science and Plant Nutrition   Vol 2: 8665
Japanese Society of Tribologists   Vol 2: 8668
Japanese Society of Veterinary Science   Vol 2: 8670
Japanese Society of Zootechnical Science   Vol 2: 8672
Jardin Exotique   Vol 2: 3452
Jardin zoologique du Quebec   Vol 1: 16623

Javelin Class Association   Vol 1: 11507
Jazz World Database   Vol 1: 11513
J.C. Penney Company   Vol 1: 2789
JCC Association   Vol 1: 11515
JCC of Metropolitan New Jersey   Vol 1: 11521
Jeantet de Medecine; Fondation Louis   Vol 2: 11726
Jebsen & Company   Vol 2: 7275
Jefferson Memorial Foundation; Thomas   Vol 1: 11523
Jellinek Memorial Fund   Vol 1: 11526
Jeppesen Sanderson, Inc.   Vol 1: 12764
Jerome Foundation   Vol 1: 16056, 16250
Jersey City State College   Vol 1: 8831
Jerusalem International Book Fair - Municipality of Jerusalem   Vol 2: 7932
Jerusalem Municipality   Vol 2: 7934, 7935
Jerwood Award   Vol 2: 3512
Jerwood Foundation   Vol 2: 3513
The Jerwood Foundation   Vol 2: 3671
Jeunesses Musicales de Suisse   Vol 2: 11736
Jeunesses Musicales Hungary   Vol 2: 7416
Jeunesses Musicales of Austria   Vol 2: 774
Jeunesses Musicales of Serbia   Vol 2: 10716
Jewish Book Council   Vol 1: 11528
Jewish Book Council/JWB (Jewish Welfare Board)   Vol 1: 11528
Jewish Community Center Theater of Cleveland   Vol 1: 11542
Jewish Educators Assembly   Vol 1: 11544
Jewish Federation of Metropolitan Detroit   Vol 1: 11546
Jewish Foundation for Christian Reseverts/ADL   Vol 1: 5177
Jewish Historical Society of England   Vol 2: 3514
Jewish Institute for National Security Affairs   Vol 1: 11548
Jewish Labor Committee   Vol 1: 11550
Jewish Museum   Vol 1: 11552
Jewish National Fund   Vol 1: 11554
Jewish Peace Fellowship   Vol 1: 11560
Jewish Reconstructionist Foundation   Vol 1: 9158
Jewish Teachers Association   Vol 1: 11562
Jewish Theological Seminary of America   Vol 1: 11566
Jewish War Veterans of the U.S.A.   Vol 1: 11572
Jewish Welfare Federation of Metropolitan Detroit   Vol 1: 11546
Jobber News   Vol 1: 11576
Jobber Topics   Vol 1: 11578
Jobst Company   Vol 1: 18201
Jockey Club of Canada   Vol 1: 11580
John Coutts Library Services   Vol 1: 7000
John Deere & Co.   Vol 1: 4369
John F. Kennedy Center for Performing Arts   Vol 1: 17214
John Sloan Dickey Center for International Understanding - Dartmouth College   Vol 1: 11582
John Sloan Dickey Endowment for International Understanding   Vol 1: 11582
Johns Hopkins Center on Aging   Vol 1: 334
Johns Hopkins University   Vol 1: 11584
Johnson & Higgins   Vol 1: 4785
Johnson & Johnson   Vol 1: 667, 694, 10616
JOHNSON & JOHNSON Consumer Products, Inc.   Vol 1: 1943
Johnson & Johnson Medical   Vol 1: 5575
Johnson Foundation; Lyndon Baines   Vol 1: 11586
Johnson Foundation; Robert Wood   Vol 1: 12698, 12699
Johnson Foundation; Stanley Thomas   Vol 1: 11913

Johnson Matthey plc, Materials Technology Division   Vol 2: 4219
Johnson Music Foundation; Edward   Vol 1: 11589
Johnson Publishing Company   Vol 1: 11593
Johnson Smith & Knisely Accord   Vol 1: 11596
Joint Action in Community Service   Vol 1: 11598
Joint Baltic American National Committee   Vol 1: 11602
Joint Council on Economic Education   Vol 1: 13799
Joint Council on Research in Pastoral Care and Counseling   Vol 1: 8029
Joint Financial Management Improvement Program   Vol 1: 11604
Jones Foundation; Chester H.   Vol 1: 11606
Jordan - Ministry of Education   Vol 2: 8798
Jordan - Wizarat-At-Tarbiya Wat Ta'lim   Vol 2: 8798
Jornadas Internacionales de Cine Medico de San Sebastian   Vol 2: 11282
Joseph Foundation   Vol 1: 9881
Jostens Company   Vol 1: 11608
Journal of Consumer Research   Vol 1: 11610
Journal of Healthcare Materiel Management   Vol 1: 10743
Journal of Industrial Economics   Vol 2: 3516
Journal of International Economic Integration   Vol 2: 8815
Journal of the American Planning Association   Vol 1: 3533
Journal of the APMA   Vol 1: 3545
Journalism Education Association   Vol 1: 11612
Journalists' Club   Vol 2: 9078
Journees Cinematographique de Carthage   Vol 2: 12041
Jowett Car Club   Vol 2: 3518
Joy in Singing   Vol 1: 11619
Jugend musiziert   Vol 2: 852
Jujamcyn Theaters   Vol 1: 11621
Jump Memorial Foundation; William A.   Vol 1: 11623
Junior Achievement   Vol 1: 11625
Junior Achievement of Canada   Vol 1: 11627
Junior Engineering Technical Society   Vol 1: 11629
Junior Philatelic Society of America   Vol 1: 11631
Junior Philatelists of America   Vol 1: 11631
Junior Wireless Club   Vol 1: 16639
Juniper Prize   Vol 1: 11635
Jurzykowski Foundation; Alfred   Vol 1: 11637
Juselius Foundation; Sigrid   Vol 2: 4738
Justus-Liebig-Universitat-Giessen   Vol 2: 6996
Jutland Archaeological Society   Vol 2: 1977
Juvenile Diabetes Foundation International   Vol 1: 11639
Juventudes Musicales de Espana   Vol 2: 11284
JWB   Vol 1: 11515
Jysk Arkaeologisk Selskab   Vol 2: 1977
K. G. Saur   Vol 1: 2878
Kabushiki Kaisha Dentsu   Vol 2: 8523
Kadokawa Bunka Shinko Zaidan   Vol 2: 8674
Kadokawa Culture Promotion Foundation   Vol 2: 8674
Kadokawa Shoten   Vol 2: 8675
Kairali Childrens Book Trust   Vol 2: 7695
Kal Kan   Vol 1: 8604
Kaleidoscope, Immigrant Filmmakers Association   Vol 2: 11489
Kaleidoscope, Ivandrar Filmarnas forening   Vol 2: 11489
Kamloops Symphony Society   Vol 1: 11641

Kansas Arts Commission   Vol 1: 11646, 11649
Kansas City Sports Commission   Vol 1: 6363
Kansas Magazine   Vol 1: 11645
Kansas Pastel Society   Vol 1: 11643
Kansas Quarterly   Vol 1: 11645
Kansas Watercolor Society   Vol 1: 11648
Kanselarij der Nederlandse Orden   Vol 2: 9354
Kaplun Foundation; Morris J. and Betty   Vol 1: 329
Kappa Alpha Theta Foundation   Vol 1: 13830
Kappa Tau Alpha   Vol 1: 11650
Karanegala Maha Sahitya Sangamaya   Vol 2: 11399
Karger-Gedaechtnis-Stiftung; Heinz   Vol 2: 11870
Karger Memorial Foundation; Heinz   Vol 2: 11870
Katanning Shire Council   Vol 2: 510
Kaufmann-Ruud Foundation; Minna   Vol 1: 7523
Kaula Endowment for Library and Information Science; Professor   Vol 2: 7697
Kaustinen Folk Music Festival   Vol 2: 4740
Kaustisen Kansanmusiikkijuhlat   Vol 2: 4740
Kay Jewelers   Vol 1: 13582
Kearney, Inc.; A. T.   Vol 1: 8376
Keats - Shelley Association of America   Vol 1: 11652
Keene State College   Vol 1: 11655
Keep America Beautiful   Vol 1: 11657
Keimer Foundation for Comparative Research in Archaeology and Ethnology; Ludwig   Vol 2: 11872
Keller International; Helen   Vol 1: 11662
Kellogg   Vol 2: 6857
Kellogg Foundation; W. K.   Vol 1: 11665
Kelly Associates; Michael   Vol 2: 10581
Kelly's UK Exports   Vol 2: 3649
Keltic Society and the College of Druidism   Vol 2: 10583
Ken-L Ration   Vol 1: 11667
Kennedy Center Education Department   Vol 1: 19998
Kennedy Center for the Performing Arts; John F.   Vol 1: 1753, 11669
Kennedy Center for the Performing Arts; John F. - Education Program/Alliance for Arts Education   Vol 1: 11673
Kennedy, Jr. Foundation; Joseph P.   Vol 1: 11677
Kennedy Library Foundation; John F.   Vol 1: 11679
Kennedy Memorial; Robert F.   Vol 1: 11681
Kennedy School of Government; John F.   Vol 1: 9314
Kentucky Arts Council   Vol 1: 11685
Kentucky Watercolor Society   Vol 1: 11687
Kenya National Academy of Sciences - Ministry of Research, Science & Technology   Vol 2: 8804
Kenya Publishers Association   Vol 2: 8809
Kenyon Hill Publications   Vol 1: 15135
Kerajaan Malaysia - Dewan Bahasa dan Pustaka   Vol 2: 8900
Kerala Sahitya Akademi   Vol 2: 7700
Keren Wolf   Vol 2: 7986
Keuffel and Esser Ltd.   Vol 2: 2306
Kevock Choir Midlothian Scotland   Vol 2: 10585
Keyboard Teachers Association International   Vol 1: 14820
KF Ltd. - Agrofilm   Vol 2: 1872
Kidde-Graviner, Ltd.   Vol 1: 9244
Kiekhaefer Aero-marine   Vol 1: 6439
Kiel Institute of World Economics   Vol 2: 7006

Kihara Memorial Yokohama Foundation for the Advancement of Life Sciences   Vol 2: 8529
Kilby Awards Foundation   Vol 1: 11689
Kiln Trust; Robert   Vol 2: 2250
Kimberly-Clark   Vol 2: 4170
Kinder-und Jugendfilmzentrum in der Bundesrepublik Deutschland   Vol 2: 6590
King Abdul Aziz Research Centre   Vol 2: 10493
King Baudouin Foundation   Vol 2: 1216
King County Bar Association   Vol 1: 11691
King Faisal International Prize General Secretariat   Vol 2: 10495
King George's Fund for Sailors   Vol 2: 3520
King, Jr. Center for Nonviolent Social Change; Martin Luther   Vol 1: 11696
King, Jr. Center for Social Change; Martin Luther   Vol 1: 11696
King Memorial Prize; Martin Luther   Vol 2: 3522
Kingcrafts   Vol 1: 15714
King's School   Vol 2: 3524
Kingsbury   Vol 1: 15535
Kingsmoor Publications Ltd.   Vol 2: 2415
Kingsport Symphony Orchestra   Vol 1: 11701
Kinokuniya Company   Vol 2: 8680
Kinsey Institute for Research in Sex, Gender, and Reproduction   Vol 1: 11703
Kirkus Reviews   Vol 1: 11705
Kiwanis International Foundation   Vol 1: 11707
Klasina Smelik Stichting   Vol 2: 9387
Klein Foundation; Roger   Vol 1: 16589
Klingler-Stiftung; Karl   Vol 2: 7008
Klubcentrum Usti-nad-Orlici   Vol 2: 1834
Knight Fellowships; John S.   Vol 1: 11709
Knights Boxing Team International   Vol 1: 11711
Knights of Columbus   Vol 1: 8013
Kobe International Flute Competition   Vol 2: 8682
Kobenhavns Universitet   Vol 2: 2010
Kodak   Vol 2: 5190, 11854
Kodak Canada   Vol 1: 6868
Kodak Ltd. (Far East)   Vol 2: 7265
Kodak (UK) Ltd.   Vol 2: 2880
Kodak UK Professional Photography Division   Vol 2: 2132
Kodaly Society of Japan   Vol 2: 7423
Kodansha Ltd.   Vol 2: 8684
Kohler; Stichting Charlotte   Vol 2: 9687
Kokusai Gejutsu Renmei   Vol 2: 8623
Kokusai Koryu Kikin   Vol 2: 8611
Kol Yisrael - Yerushalayim; Rashut Hashidur -   Vol 2: 7916
Komen Breast Cancer Foundation; Susan G.   Vol 1: 11716
Komitet Kinematografii - Warszawa   Vol 2: 10144
Komitet Nagrod Panstwowych   Vol 2: 10203
Kone Instruments   Vol 2: 2118
Kongelige Danske Geografiske Selskab   Vol 2: 1996
Kongelige Norske Videnskabers Selskab   Vol 2: 9967
Kongelige Teater og Kapel   Vol 2: 2002
Koning Boudewijstichting   Vol 2: 1216
Koninklijk Belgisch Filmarchief   Vol 2: 1351
Koninklijk Nederlands Aardrijkskundig Genootschap   Vol 2: 9585
Koninklijk Nederlands Geologisch Mijnbouwkundig Genootschap   Vol 2: 9587
Koninklijke Academie Voor Geneeskunde Van Belgie   Vol 2: 1308
Koninklijke Academie Voor Nederlandse Taal-en Letterkunde   Vol 2: 1263
Koninklijke Academie voor Wetenschappen, Letteren en Schone Kunsten Van Belgie   Vol 2: 1248
Koninklijke Beiaardschool Jef Denijn   Vol 2: 1346
Koninklijke Nederlandse Akademie van Wetenschappen   Vol 2: 9592
Koninklijke Nederlandse Chemische Vereniging   Vol 2: 9608
Koninklijke Nederlandse Toonkunstenoorsvereniging   Vol 2: 9606
Konzertagentur Fahrenholtz   Vol 2: 7010
Korber-Stiftung   Vol 2: 7012
Kordelin Foundation   Vol 2: 4743
Korea Broadcasting System   Vol 2: 8818
Korea Design and Packaging Center   Vol 2: 8816
Korea Polio Association   Vol 2: 8819
Korean Culture and Arts Foundation   Vol 2: 8821
Korean PEN Centre   Vol 2: 8824
Kortfilmfestivalen; Stiftelsen   Vol 2: 9947
Kosciuszko Foundation   Vol 1: 11722
Koussevitzky Music Foundation in the Library of Congress; Serge   Vol 1: 11727
Koussevitzky Music Foundation; Serge   Vol 1: 11729
Kozponti Asztronautikai Szakosztaly   Vol 2: 7318
KPMG Peat Marwick Thorne   Vol 1: 29
Kraft General Foods   Vol 1: 1917
Kraszna-Krausz Foundation   Vol 2: 3526
Krause Publications   Vol 1: 11731
Kreditanstalt fur Wiederaufbau   Vol 2: 6999
Kreisler International Competition; Fritz   Vol 2: 854
Kring van Nederlandse Theatercritici   Vol 2: 9359
Kudelski, S.S.A.   Vol 2: 8472
Kulturamt der Stadt Monchengladbach   Vol 2: 7014
Kulturamt der Stadt Uberlingen   Vol 2: 7145
Kulturamt Spittal und Singkreis Porcia   Vol 2: 796
Kulturni stredisko zamek Hradec   Vol 2: 1857
Kungl. Akademien for de Fria Konsterna   Vol 2: 11510
Kungl. Vetenskapsakademien   Vol 2: 11531
Kungliga Fysiografiska Sallskapet i Lund   Vol 2: 11512
Kungnip Kugagwon   Vol 2: 8833
Kunstlergilde   Vol 2: 6522
Kupfermann Foundation; David   Vol 2: 6073
Kuratorium fur die Verleihung des Heinrich-Wieland Preises   Vol 2: 7016
Kuwait Foundation for the Advancement of Sciences   Vol 2: 8841
Kuwait National Council for Arts, Letters, and Humanities   Vol 2: 8842
La Forge Memorial Poetry Foundation; Ellen   Vol 1: 11734
La Leche League International   Vol 1: 11736
La Salle College   Vol 1: 11743
La Salle University   Vol 1: 11743
La Stampa Publishing Group   Vol 2: 8291
Labatt's Brewery   Vol 1: 18744
Labologists Society   Vol 2: 3528
Labor Research Association   Vol 1: 11746
Laboratoires DEBAT   Vol 2: 6238
Laboratory of Ornithology   Vol 1: 11748
Lacrosse Foundation and Hall of Fame Museum   Vol 1: 11750
Ladies Association of British Barbershop Singers   Vol 1: 9786
Ladies' Golf Union   Vol 2: 10587
Ladies Professional Golf Association   Vol 1: 11752
Laerdal Medical Corporation   Vol 1: 13094
Lahti Organ Festival   Vol 2: 4745
Laing PLC; John   Vol 2: 3530
Lake Michigan Federation   Vol 1: 11768
Lalit Kala Akademi - India   Vol 2: 7533
Lambda Book Report   Vol 1: 11770
Lambda Kappa Sigma   Vol 1: 11772
Lancia Motor Club Limited   Vol 2: 3532
Land Improvement Contractors of America   Vol 1: 11775
Land-Rover Register 1947-1951   Vol 2: 3535
Landeshauptstadt Dusseldorf   Vol 2: 6681
Landeshauptstadt Munchen   Vol 2: 7018
Landeshauptstadt Stuttgart   Vol 2: 7134
Landesregierung Nordrhein-Westfalen   Vol 2: 7025
Landscape Architecture Foundation   Vol 1: 11777
Landschaftsverband Westfalen - Lippe Kulturpflegeabteilung   Vol 2: 7027
Lane Foundation; Allen   Vol 2: 3651
Langerhuizen Lambertuszoon-fonds; Pieter   Vol 2: 9391
Langlois Encounters; International Henri   Vol 2: 6023
Lanka Electricity Company   Vol 2: 11404
Lanka Mahila Samiti   Vol 2: 11411
Lannan Foundation   Vol 1: 11781
LaPorte Amateur Radio Club   Vol 1: 3886
Lappeenrannan Kaupunki   Vol 2: 4747
Lappeenranta City   Vol 2: 4747
Larbaud; Bibliotheque Municipale Valery   Vol 2: 4986
Laser Institute of America   Vol 1: 11783
Laser Scan Laboratories   Vol 2: 2307
Laser Technology, Inc.   Vol 1: 18321
Lasers in Graphics/Electronic Design in Print   Vol 1: 8771
Lasker Foundation; Albert and Mary   Vol 1: 11785
Lasserson Memorial Trust; Sascha   Vol 2: 3537
Latin American Association of Freight and Transport Agents   Vol 2: 10011
Latin American Federation of Thermalism and Climatism   Vol 2: 56
Latin and Mediterranean Group for Sport Medicine   Vol 2: 6076
Latin Languages Allergists and Immunologists Group   Vol 2: 10242
Lautenberg Center for General and Tumor Immunology   Vol 2: 7887
Law and Society Association   Vol 1: 11790
Lawn Tennis Association   Vol 2: 3539
Lawrence Foundation   Vol 1: 16361
Lawson Festival of Arts; Grenfell Henry   Vol 2: 413
Lawton Philharmonic Society   Vol 1: 6685
Laymen's National Bible Association   Vol 1: 11793
Laymen's National Bible Committee   Vol 1: 11793
LDA Publishers   Vol 1: 11800
Le Croy Corporation   Vol 2: 11705
Le Giornate del Cinema Muto   Vol 2: 8399
Le Manuscript de Vercorin   Vol 2: 8471
Leacock Associates; Stephen   Vol 1: 11802
Leadership Conference on Civil Rights   Vol 1: 11805
League Against Cruel Sports   Vol 2: 3542
League for Industrial Democracy   Vol 1: 11807
League of American Theatres and Producers   Vol 1: 4902, 11809
League of Canadian Poets   Vol 1: 11811
League of Composers - International Society of Contemporary Music   Vol 1: 11815

Organization Index
Volume 2: International and Foreign

League of Families   Vol 2: 1218
League of Historic American Theatres   Vol 1: 11817
League of New Hampshire Craftsmen   Vol 1: 20574
League of New York Theatres and Producers, Inc.   Vol 1: 11809
League of Off Broadway Theatres and Producers   Vol 1: 11941
Leahy Archives   Vol 1: 10253
Leakey Foundation for Research Related to Human Origins, Behavior and Survival; L. S. B.   Vol 1: 11820
Learning About Learning Education Foundation   Vol 1: 12299
Leatherneck Magazine   Vol 1: 12080
Leche Trustees   Vol 2: 2939
Leco Corporation   Vol 1: 17418
Lederle Laboratories   Vol 1: 2651, 4537, 15644
Lee Foundation; Clifford E.   Vol 1: 6259
Lee Gallery; Rudolph E.   Vol 1: 7835
Leeds and Northrup Foundation   Vol 1: 10280
Leeds International Pianoforte Competition   Vol 2: 2993
Leeds Philosophical and Literary Society   Vol 2: 3547
Leek Arts Festival   Vol 2: 3549
Lefthanders International   Vol 1: 11822
Legatbestyrelsen for Ellen og Niels Bjerrum's Kemikerpris   Vol 2: 1979
Legion of Valor of the United States of America   Vol 1: 11824
Lehmbruck-Museum Duisburg; Wilhelm-   Vol 2: 7030
Lehrerinnen und Lehrer Schweiz   Vol 2: 11946
Leica   Vol 1: 4520
Leica Canada Inc.   Vol 1: 6794
Leipzig College of Graphic Arts and Book Design   Vol 2: 7032
Leipziger Dok-Filmwoche GmbH   Vol 2: 7034
Leland Community Development Fellowship Program; Mickey - African Governance Program   Vol 1: 11827
Lemelson Medical, Education & Research Foundation, Ltd.   Vol 1: 12114
Lenoir News-Topic   Vol 1: 15299
Lentz Peace Research Association   Vol 1: 11829
Leopoldina Academy of Researchers in Natural Sciences   Vol 2: 7104
Lepidopterists' Society   Vol 1: 11831
LEPRA   Vol 2: 3551
Leukemia Society of America   Vol 1: 11834
Leven Prize for Poetry Trust; Grace   Vol 2: 512
Leventritt Foundation; Edgar M.   Vol 1: 11839
Lever Rexona   Vol 2: 9797
Leverhulme Trust   Vol 2: 3553, 4152
Levine School of Music   Vol 1: 11841
Levy Economics Institute of Bard College; Jerome   Vol 1: 11843
Levy Hill Laboratories   Vol 2: 2411
Lewis and Clark Trail Heritage Foundation   Vol 1: 11845
Lewis Medical Limited   Vol 2: 2275
Leyster Stichting; Judith   Vol 2: 9542
LGesellschaft Deutscher Metallhutten und Bergleute   Vol 2: 6848
Liberal International   Vol 2: 3556
Liberian Association of Writers   Vol 2: 8848
Libertarian Alliance   Vol 2: 3558
Libertarian Center Netherlands   Vol 2: 1221
Libertarian Futurist Society   Vol 1: 11850
Libertarian International   Vol 1: 11257
Libertarisch Centrum   Vol 2: 1221

Liberty Seated Collectors Club   Vol 1: 11853
Librairie Cosmos 2000   Vol 2: 6078
Librairie le Pont Traverse   Vol 2: 6080
Library Administration and Management Association   Vol 1: 2869, 2906
Library Administration and Management Association; Public Relations Section of the   Vol 1: 2905
Library and Information Research Group   Vol 2: 3560
Library and Information Service of Western Australia   Vol 2: 514
Library and Information Technology Association   Vol 1: 2869, 2909
Library Association   Vol 2: 3562
The Library Association   Vol 2: 4448
Library Association of Australia   Vol 2: 236
Library Association of Ireland   Vol 2: 7813
Library Association of Slovenia   Vol 2: 10796
Library Directory Associates Publishers   Vol 1: 11800
Library of Congress   Vol 1: 11855
Library Public Relations Council   Vol 1: 11860
Lichfield District Council   Vol 2: 3575
Lidhja e Shkrimtareve dhe Artisteve te Shqiperise   Vol 2: 1
Liederkranz Foundation   Vol 1: 11863
Life Communicators Association   Vol 1: 11865
Life Insurance Advertisers Association   Vol 1: 11865
Life Insurance Marketing and Research Association   Vol 1: 13197
Life Office Management Association   Vol 1: 11868
Life Technologies   Vol 1: 12958
Lifefleet   Vol 1: 13098
Liga Argentina Contra la Tuberculosis   Vol 2: 58
Liga de Economistas Revolucionarios   Vol 2: 9094
Lighter Than Air Society   Vol 1: 11872
Lighting Association   Vol 2: 3577
Lighting Industry Federation   Vol 2: 3579
Ligue des Familles   Vol 2: 1218
Ligue des Femmes Abstinentes   Vol 2: 715
Ligue Europeenne de Bridge   Vol 2: 7874
Ligue Francaise de l'Enseignement et de l'Education Permanente   Vol 2: 6082
Ligue Francaise des Droits de l'Animal   Vol 2: 5270
Ligue Internationale de la Librairie Ancienne   Vol 2: 6969
Ligue Internationale des Droits de l'Animal   Vol 2: 8870
Lilly and Company; Eli   Vol 1: 1502, 4231, 4401
Lilly & Company; Eli   Vol 1: 17791
Lilly Company; Eli   Vol 1: 14042
Lilly Research Centre Ltd.   Vol 2: 4219
Limnological Society of America   Vol 1: 4651
Lincoln Arc Welding Foundation; James F.   Vol 1: 11874
Lincoln Association; Abraham   Vol 1: 11878
Lincoln Center for the Performing Arts   Vol 1: 11883
Lincoln College   Vol 1: 11889
Lincoln Electric Company   Vol 1: 5080, 5097
Lincoln University of Missouri - Dept. of Communications   Vol 1: 11891
Lindapter International Ltd.   Vol 2: 3249
Lindbergh Fund; Charles A.   Vol 1: 11893
Linguistic Association of Canada and the United States   Vol 1: 11895
Link Foundation   Vol 1: 11897
Linnean Society of London   Vol 2: 3583
Linzer Veranstaltungsgesellschaft   Vol 2: 856

Lions Club International Foundation   Vol 1: 1953
Lipizer; Cultural Association Rodolfo   Vol 2: 8208
Lisbon Academy of Sciences   Vol 2: 1423, 10244
Listen for Pleasure Tapes/Audio Language Studies Read Along Division   Vol 1: 7016
Liszt Ferenc Tarsasag   Vol 2: 7437
Liszt Society   Vol 2: 3591
Liszt Society; Ferenc   Vol 2: 7437
Literacy Volunteers of America   Vol 1: 11899
Literary Translators' Association of Canada   Vol 1: 11905
Lithuanian Catholic Women   Vol 1: 11907
Little Big Horn Associates, Inc.   Vol 1: 11909
Little, Brown and Company   Vol 1: 11912
Little Chapter of All Nations   Vol 1: 5247
Little, Inc.; A. D.   Vol 1: 2592
Little Theatre of Alexandria   Vol 1: 11914
Litton Data Systems   Vol 1: 12064
Litton Itek Optical Systems   Vol 1: 18322
Live Free   Vol 1: 11916
Liverpool School of Tropical Medicine   Vol 2: 3593
Livestock Marketing Association   Vol 1: 15059
Livestock Publications Council   Vol 1: 11918
Livewire UK   Vol 2: 3595
Livingston and Doughty Company Ltd   Vol 2: 3007
Llangollen International Musical Eisteddfod   Vol 2: 12176
Lloyds Bank   Vol 2: 2233, 2234, 2297
Lloyd's of London Press   Vol 2: 3597
Locarno Internationale Film Festival   Vol 2: 11874
Lockheed Aeronautical Systems, Inc.   Vol 1: 12063
Lockheed Corporation   Vol 1: 172, 12090
Lockheed-Georgia   Vol 1: 12065
Lockheed Sciences and Engineering Company   Vol 1: 171
Lockwood, Kessler, and Bartlett   Vol 1: 4243
Locus Publications   Vol 1: 11922
Loeb Foundation, Inc.; G. and R.   Vol 1: 19752
The Loft, a place for writing and literature   Vol 1: 11924
Logical Designs   Vol 2: 11125
Login Brothers Book Company   Vol 1: 12170
Logos Agvet   Vol 2: 10843
London Club   Vol 1: 11930
London College of Printing   Vol 2: 2483
The London Evening Standard   Vol 2: 3599
London International Piano Competition   Vol 2: 3603
London International String Quartet Competition   Vol 2: 3605
London Mathematical Society   Vol 2: 3607
London School of Hygiene and Tropical Medicine   Vol 2: 4279
London Stock Exchange   Vol 2: 3080
London Symphony Orchestra   Vol 2: 3617
London Women's Suffrage Society   Vol 2: 2867
Londres; Association du Prix Albert   Vol 2: 4939
Long and Jacques Thibaud International Competition; Marguerite   Vol 2: 6084
Long Island University - Journalism Department   Vol 1: 11932
Long - Jacques Thibaud; Concours International Marguerite   Vol 2: 6084
LoonWatch   Vol 1: 11935
Loral Fairchild Systems   Vol 1: 18327
Lord & Taylor   Vol 1: 11937
Lortel Theatre; Lucille   Vol 1: 11940

Los Angeles Advertising Women   Vol 1: 11942
Los Angeles Athletic Club   Vol 1: 11944, 12571
Los Angeles Film Critics Association   Vol 1: 11946
Los Angeles Times Book Review   Vol 1: 11948
Loteria Nacional para las Asistencia Publica   Vol 2: 9259
Lothian and Edinburgh Enterprise Limited   Vol 2: 10653
Louisiana Association of School Librarians   Vol 1: 11954
Louisiana Historical Association   Vol 1: 9931
Louisiana Library Association   Vol 1: 11950
Louisiana Pacific Corporation   Vol 1: 5742
Louisiana State University Press   Vol 1: 11958
Louisville Orchestra   Vol 1: 11960
Love Creek Production   Vol 1: 11962
Love Creek Productions   Vol 1: 11964
Lower Austria Cultural Department   Vol 2: 858
Lowin Trust; Paul   Vol 2: 516
Loyola University Chicago   Vol 1: 11967
LTV Aerospace and Defense Corporation   Vol 1: 12061
Lubeck Hanseatic City Cultural Office   Vol 2: 7036
Lubelskie Towarzystwo Naukowe   Vol 2: 10078
Lublin Scientific Society   Vol 2: 10078
Luis Herrera de la Fuente   Vol 2: 8985
lundesrepublik Deutschland - Bundesminister des Innern   Vol 2: 6740
Luovan Saveltaiteen edistamissaatio   Vol 2: 4709
Luster Products   Vol 1: 5153
Lutheran Education Association   Vol 1: 11976
Lutheran Historical Conference   Vol 1: 11979
Lynam; Lynn E.   Vol 1: 13216
The Lyric   Vol 1: 11981
Maatschappij Arti et Amicitiae   Vol 2: 9544
Maatschappij der Nederlandse Letterkunde   Vol 2: 9624
MacArthur Foundation; John D. and Catherine T.   Vol 1: 8389, 8849, 11985
MacDowell Colony   Vol 1: 11989
MacGregor Golf Japan   Vol 2: 8618
Machado Foundation; Antonio   Vol 2: 1722
Machine Vision Association of the Society of Manufacturing Engineers   Vol 1: 11991
Maclean Hunter Limited   Vol 1: 5329
Macmillan   Vol 1: 2338
Macmillan Children's Books   Vol 2: 3756
Macmillan Publishing Company   Vol 1: 17411
Macra na Feirme   Vol 2: 7794
Macworld   Vol 1: 15999
Madeira, Regional Secretary of Tourism, Culture and Emigration   Vol 2: 10260
Madeira, Secretaria Regional do Turismo, Cultura e Emigracao   Vol 2: 10260
Mademoiselle   Vol 1: 11993
Madison Square Garden Television Productions   Vol 1: 12350
Madrid - Departamento de Auditorios y Centros Culturales   Vol 2: 11286
Magazine and Bookseller   Vol 1: 11995
Magazine Publishers Association   Vol 1: 11998
Magazine Publishers of America   Vol 1: 11998
Magistrat der Landeshauptstadt Salzburg   Vol 2: 863
Magistrat der Stadt Frankfurt am Main   Vol 2: 6610

Magistrat der Stadt Wien   Vol 2: 788
Magistrat der Universitatsstadt Giessen   Vol 2: 7039
Magnes Museum; Judah L.   Vol 1: 12001
Magnolia Society   Vol 1: 12003
Magsaysay Award Foundation; Ramon   Vol 2: 10041
Magyar Amatorfilm es Video Szovetseg   Vol 2: 7313
Magyar Amatorfilm Szovetseg   Vol 2: 7439
Magyar Asztronautikai Tarsasag   Vol 2: 7318
Magyar Elektrotechnikai Egyesulet   Vol 2: 7325
Magyar Elelmezesipari Tudomanyos Egyesulet   Vol 2: 7372
Magyar Geofizikusok Egyesulete   Vol 2: 7284
Magyar Gyogyszereszeti Tarsasag   Vol 2: 7368
Magyar Hidrologiai Tarsasag   Vol 2: 7347
Magyar Iroszovetseg   Vol 2: 7388
Magyar Kemikusok Egyesulete   Vol 2: 7321
Magyar Konyvkiadokes Konyvterjesztok Egyesulese   Vol 2: 7370
Magyar Konyvtarosok Egyesulete   Vol 2: 7293
Magyar Nemzetkozi Sportfilm Fesztival   Vol 2: 7430
Magyar Orvostudomanyi Tarsasagok es Egyesuletek Szovetsege   Vol 2: 7307
Magyar PEN Centre   Vol 2: 7366
Magyar Szakszervezetek Orszagos Szovetsege   Vol 2: 7441
Magyar Szakszervezetek Orszagos Tanacsa/SZOT   Vol 2: 7441
Magyar Tudomanyos Akademia   Vol 2: 7311
Magyar Ujsagirok Orszagos Szovetsege   Vol 2: 7291
Magyar Urbanisztikai Tarsasag   Vol 2: 7382
Magyarorszag - Foldugyi es Terkepeszeti Fooosztaly   Vol 2: 7393
Mahler Society; International Gustav   Vol 2: 831
Mail Advertising Service Association   Vol 1: 12005
Mail and Guardian Newspaper   Vol 2: 11125
The Mail on Sunday   Vol 2: 2201
Mail Systems Management Association   Vol 1: 12013
Mainichi Newspaper   Vol 2: 8727
Mairie de Palaiseau   Vol 2: 6086
Mairie de Paris - Direction des Affaires Culturelles   Vol 2: 6088
Mairies de France   Vol 2: 6098
Maison de Chateaubriand   Vol 2: 6101
Maison de la Culture de Rennes   Vol 2: 5248
Maison de Poesie   Vol 2: 6103
Maisons de la Presse   Vol 2: 6105
Maitrise des Rotisseurs   Vol 2: 5023
Malacological Society of London   Vol 2: 3619
Malaga International Week of Author Films   Vol 2: 11302
Malagasy - Ministry of Revolutionary Culture and Art   Vol 2: 8880
Malagasy Academy   Vol 2: 8885
Malahat Review   Vol 1: 12017
Malayan Banking Berhad   Vol 2: 8903
Malko International Competition for Young Conductors; Nicolai   Vol 2: 1981
Mallinckrodt Canada   Vol 1: 6787
Mallinckrodt Specialty Chemicals Company, Inc.   Vol 1: 1523
Mallinson-Denny   Vol 2: 3622
Malta Amateur Cine Circle   Vol 2: 8911
Maltese-American Benevolent Society   Vol 1: 12019
Maltsters Association of Great Britain   Vol 2: 3624

Malvern & Caufield Youth Accomodation Services, Inc.   Vol 2: 395
Mamaroneck Artists Guild   Vol 1: 12021
Man For Mankind   Vol 2: 937
Management Professionals Association   Vol 2: 7709
Managing Office Technology   Vol 1: 12023
Mananan Festival Trust   Vol 2: 3626
Mandat des Poetes   Vol 2: 6107
Manhattan College   Vol 1: 12025
Manhattan Institute for Policy Research   Vol 1: 12030
Manifestazioni Internazionali della Ceramica   Vol 2: 8308
Mann League of the U.S.A.; Horace   Vol 1: 12033
Manning Awards Foundation; Ernest C.   Vol 1: 12035
Manning, Selvage and Lee   Vol 1: 12037
Manomet Bird Observatory   Vol 1: 12039
Manpower Services Commission   Vol 2: 2765
Manpower Society   Vol 2: 3628
Manufacturers Association of Nigeria   Vol 2: 9865
Manufacturing Chemists Association   Vol 1: 7571
Manufacturing Excellence Center   Vol 1: 12041
Manulife Bank of Canada   Vol 1: 11804
Manuscripts International   Vol 1: 12043
Marcel Stanley Novice Award   Vol 2: 9789
Marconi International Fellowship Council   Vol 1: 12045
Marcophily Prize   Vol 2: 9789
Marcus Group, Secaucus & Trenton   Vol 1: 15190
Margarine Institute for Health Nutrition   Vol 2: 7017
Marian Library   Vol 1: 19783
Marigold Society of America   Vol 1: 12047
Marimolin   Vol 1: 12049
Marin Self Publishers Association   Vol 1: 12051
Marin Small Publishers Association   Vol 1: 12051
Marine Biological Association of the United Kingdom   Vol 2: 3630
Marine Corps Aviation Association   Vol 1: 12053
Marine Corps Historical Foundation   Vol 1: 12079
Marine Corps Parachute Rigger's Association   Vol 1: 12062
Marine Section of the National Safety Council   Vol 1: 2628
Marine Technology Society   Vol 1: 12086
Mariological Society of America   Vol 1: 12092
Marion Laboratories   Vol 1: 1378, 1384
Marion Merrell Dow, Inc.   Vol 1: 3391
Marion Merrell Dow Inc.   Vol 1: 14044
Marion Merrell Dow, Inc.   Vol 1: 15572
The Maritime Trust   Vol 2: 3632
Marketing Bestsellers   Vol 1: 11995
Marketing Communications Executives International   Vol 1: 12094
Marketing Science Institute   Vol 1: 12096
Marlowe Society of America   Vol 1: 12098
Marquette University - Department of Journalism   Vol 1: 12100
Marquis de Amodio   Vol 2: 6109
Marriott   Vol 1: 8398
Marriott Corporation   Vol 1: 599
Mars   Vol 2: 4630, 4631
Marschall Products-Rhone-Poulenc, Inc.   Vol 1: 1915
Marsh & McLennan Insurance Brokers   Vol 1: 4786

Martin Humanitarian Award; C.F. Vol 1: 6848
Mary Jane Company Vol 1: 11742
Maryborough Golden Wattle Festival Association Vol 2: 519
Maryland Casualty Company Vol 1: 4781
Maryland Jockey Club - Pimlico Race Course Vol 1: 12103
Mascot Chemical Works Vol 2: 7496
Masquers Club Vol 1: 12109
Massachusetts Cultural Council Vol 1: 9215
Massachusetts Historical Society Vol 1: 12111
Massachusetts Institute of Technology - Sloan School of Management Vol 1: 12113
Massey-Ferguson (UK) Ltd. Vol 2: 3634
Massey Foundation Vol 1: 16936
Masson Editores Vol 2: 9188
Master Lock Vol 1: 13450
Master of Professional Writing Program Vol 1: 12115
Masterplayers International Music Academy Vol 2: 11876
Master's Men Department - National Association of Free Will Baptist Vol 1: 12117
Mastiff Club of America Vol 1: 12119
Materials Research Society Vol 1: 12121
Mathematical Association of America Vol 1: 12126
Mathematical Programming Society Vol 2: 9547
Mathematical Society of Japan Vol 2: 8695
Mathematical Society of the Philippines Vol 2: 10059
Mature Market Resource Center Vol 1: 12140
Mauriac International Medical Film Festival Vol 2: 6111
Maurier Arts Limited; du Vol 1: 5329
Maximoff; Mateo Vol 2: 6113
May and Baker Ltd. Vol 2: 4215
Maynard Scientific Vol 1: 7204
McClatchy Newspapers Vol 1: 10511
McClelland & Stewart, Inc. Vol 1: 12142
McDonald Children's Charities; Ronald Vol 1: 12144
McDonnell/Douglas Corporation Vol 1: 12070, 12077
McGovern Fund for the Behavioral Sciences Vol 1: 889
McGraw Foundation; Max Vol 1: 14692
McGraw-Hill Vol 1: 2338, 12148
McGraw-Hill Book Company Vol 1: 4100
MC! Vol 1: 11761
MCI Communications Corporation Vol 1: 8083
McKee (Australia); Davy Vol 2: 432
McKinsey Foundation for Management Research Vol 1: 9804
McKnight Foundation Vol 1: 16251
McKnight Foundation Arts Funding Plan Vol 1: 16252
McKnight Programs in Higher Education Vol 1: 9263
McLaughlin Foundation; R. Samuel Vol 1: 16958
McNally Company; Rand Vol 1: 1811
McNeil Consumer Products Company Vol 1: 671
MD Magazine Vol 1: 12150
Mead Johnson and Company Vol 1: 541, 1684, 2653, 17395
Mead Johnson Pharmaceutical Vol 1: 1686
Meade Instruments Vol 1: 6090
Meadows Foundation, Inc. Vol 1: 18229
Mechelen Festival Vol 2: 1223
Meckauer Kreis; Walter Vol 2: 7041
Meckler Corporation Vol 1: 2812, 6998, 18269
Med-Chem Laboratories Vol 1: 7207

Media Alliance Vol 1: 12152
Media and Methods Vol 1: 12154
Media Arts Vol 1: 14406
Media Entertainment and Arts Alliance Vol 2: 522
Media Messages Vol 2: 6115
Mediacom Vol 1: 12156
Median Iris Society Vol 1: 12159
Medical Academy of Sao Paulo Vol 2: 1489
Medical Association of South Africa Vol 2: 10886
Medical Correctional Society Vol 1: 1037
Medical-Dental-Hospital Bureaus of America Vol 1: 12161
Medical Library Association Vol 1: 12165
Medical Mycological Society of the Americas Vol 1: 12181
Medical Research Council of Canada Vol 1: 12184
Medical Society of London Vol 2: 3636
Medical Society of the State of New York Vol 1: 12194
Medical Women's International Association Vol 2: 7043
Mediese Vereniging van Suid-Afrika Vol 2: 10886
Medieval Academy of America Vol 1: 12198
Medikinale International Parma Vol 2: 8374
Medique Products, Inc. Vol 1: 1350
Mednarodni Graficni Likovni Center Vol 2: 10793
Medunarodni Festival Naucnog Filma Beograd Vol 2: 10698
Meeting Planners International Vol 1: 12202
Meetings and Conventions Vol 1: 12206
Meiji Jingu Homotsuden Vol 2: 8697
Meiji Shrine Treasure Museum Vol 2: 8697
Melbourne 8mm Movie Club Vol 2: 526
Melbourne International Film Festival Vol 2: 524
Melchior Heldentenor Foundation; Lauritz Vol 1: 12208
Mellett Fund for a Free and Responsible Press Vol 1: 16054
Mellon Foundation; Andrew W. Vol 1: 8389, 12235
Mellon Fund; Andrew W. Vol 1: 12234
Melpomene Institute for Women's Health Research Vol 1: 12210
Melun-Senart; Syndicat d'Agglomeration Nouvelle de Vol 2: 6469
MEMC Vol 2: 526
Memorial Foundation for Jewish Culture Vol 1: 12212
Memphis State Review Vol 1: 16852
Mendelssohn Choir Foundation; Toronto Vol 1: 6744
Mendes France Institute; Pierre Vol 2: 6117
Menil Human Rights Foundation - Carter Vol 1: 7326
Men's Fashion Association of America Vol 1: 9046
Men's International Professional Tennis Council Vol 1: 12215
Mensa International Vol 2: 3639
Merch Sharp and Dohme Vol 1: 2180
Merchandise Mart Properties Vol 1: 12217
Merck Vol 1: 2578
Merck and Company Vol 1: 941, 942, 4039, 4394, 18807
Merck & Co.,Inc. Vol 1: 1916
Merck Frosst Centre for Therapeutic Research Vol 1: 7555
Merck Human Health Division Vol 1: 4208
Merck Ltd. Vol 2: 4219
Merck Pharmaceutical Company; DuPont Vol 1: 3387

Merck Research Laboratories Vol 1: 1561
Merck Sharp & Dohme Vol 1: 5578
Merck Sharp & Dohme Research Laboratories Vol 1: 624, 1561
Mercury Books Vol 2: 3641
Mercury Communications Vol 2: 4487
Meridien des Quatres Jurys; Prix Vol 2: 5231
Merit Shop Foundation Vol 1: 8192
Merkaz Zalman Shazar Le'Historia Yehudit/Ha'Hevra Ha'Historit Ha 'Israelit Vol 2: 7939
Merkur Vol 2: 1852
Merrill Lynch Vol 1: 8995
Messiaen; Concorso Internazionale di Composizione Organistica Oliver Vol 2: 8202
Metal Construction Association Vol 1: 12219
Metal Fabricating Institute Vol 1: 12221
Metal Powder Industries Federation Vol 1: 12223
Metallurgical and Engineering Consultants (India) Limited Vol 2: 7631
Metallurgical Society Vol 1: 12306
Metcalf Foundation; George C. Vol 1: 6808
Meteoritical Society Vol 2: 3643
Metro Athletic Conference Vol 1: 12230
Metro Conference Vol 1: 12230
Metropolitan Life Vol 1: 14727
Metropolitan Life Foundation Vol 1: 18678
Metropolitan Museum of Art Vol 1: 12233
Metropolitan New York Football Writers Association Vol 1: 12238
Metropolitan Opera Vol 2: 571
Metropolitan Opera Association Vol 1: 12243
Metropolitan Opera Guild Vol 1: 12246
Metropolitan Owners' Club Vol 2: 3646
Mexican Academy of Cinematographic Arts and Sciences Vol 2: 9096
Mexican Academy of Dermatology Vol 2: 9098
Mexican Academy of Surgery Vol 2: 9100
Mexican-American Engineering Society Vol 1: 17894
Mexican Institute of Chemical Engineers Vol 2: 9104
Mexican National Academy of Medicine Vol 2: 9111
Mexican Pharmaceutical Association Vol 2: 9117
Mexican Section of the International Board on Books for Young People Vol 2: 9119
Mexican Society for the History of Science and Technology Vol 2: 9121
Mexico - Camara de Diputados Vol 2: 9123
Mexico - Camara de Senadores Vol 2: 9142
Mexico - Chamber of Deputies Vol 2: 9123
Mexico - Consejo de Salubridad General Vol 2: 9125
Mexico - Council of General Health Vol 2: 9125
Mexico - Ministry of Foreign Affairs Vol 2: 9132
Mexico - Ministry of Health and Welfare Vol 2: 9134
Mexico - Ministry of Labor and Social Security Vol 2: 9136
Mexico - Ministry of the Interior Vol 2: 9138
Mexico - Secretaria de Gobernacion Internal Vol 2: 9138
Mexico - Secretaria de Relaciones Exteriores Vol 2: 9132
Mexico - Secretaria de Salud Vol 2: 9134
Mexico - Secretaria de Trabajo y Prevision Social Vol 2: 9136
Mexico - Senate of the Republic Vol 2: 9142
Mexico Ministry of Public Education Vol 2: 9144
Mexinox, S. A. de C. V. Vol 2: 9157

Mezinarodni   **Awards, Honors & Prizes, 1995-96**

Mezinarodni festival filmu a televiznich poradu o zivotnim prostredi - Ekofilm Vol 2: 1861
Mezinarodni hudebni festival Prazske jaro Vol 2: 1879
Mezinarodni organizace novinaru Vol 2: 1863
Mezzanzana; Fondazione Maria Vol 2: 8293
The Miami Herald Vol 1: 10511
Michener Awards Foundation Vol 1: 12248
Michigan Council Vol 1: 14302
Michigan Outdoor Writers Association Vol 1: 12251
Michigan United Conservation Clubs Vol 1: 12253
Micro Hall Art Center - LITERATURIUM Vol 2: 7046
Mid-America Publishers Association (MAPA) Vol 1: 12255
Mid-West Truckers Association Vol 1: 12257
Middle Atlantic Placement Association Vol 1: 12261
Midland Bank Vol 2: 3648, 4163
Midland-Odessa Symphony & Chorale Vol 1: 12263
Midwest Archives Conference Vol 1: 12265
Miedzynarodowe Konkursy Im. Henryka Wieniawskiego Vol 2: 10072
Miedzynarodowe Triennale Grafiki Vol 2: 10076
Miescher Institute of CIBA-GEIGY; Friedrich Vol 2: 11923
Mikes of America Vol 1: 12269
Miles Diagnostics Division Vol 1: 14747, 14748
Miles Inc. Vol 1: 848, 851, 14158
Miles Laboratories, Inc Vol 2: 7897
Miles Pharmaceuticals Vol 1: 4198
Military Chaplains Association of the U.S.A. Vol 1: 12271
Military Educators & Counselors Association Vol 1: 12274
Military Operations Research Society Vol 1: 12277
Military Order of the Foreign Wars of the United States Vol 1: 12281
Military Order of the World Wars Vol 1: 12283
Milk Industry Foundation Vol 1: 1917
Milkweed Chronicle Vol 1: 12286
Milkweed Editions Vol 1: 12286
Mill Mountain Theatre Vol 1: 12289
Millard Memorial Fund; Gregory Vol 1: 12291
Miller Clock Company; Howard Vol 1: 12294
Miller Fellowship Fund; John William Vol 1: 12296
Miller Harness Saddlery Vol 1: 2188
Miller Lite Vol 1: 14002
Millipore Corporation Vol 1: 15955
Milliyet Vol 2: 12061
Milton Bradley Company Vol 1: 14710
MIND (National Association for Mental Health) Vol 2: 3650
Mind Science Foundation Vol 1: 12298
Mine Safety and Health Administration Vol 1: 3117
Mine Safety Appliances Company Vol 1: 2438
Mineralogical Society of America Vol 1: 12300
Minerals Engineering Society Vol 2: 3652
Minerals, Metals, and Materials Society Vol 1: 12306
Mini-America's Cup Association Vol 1: 12320
Mini Caire Vol 2: 8985
Mining and Metallurgical Society of America Vol 1: 12325

Ministarstvo Znanosti Vol 2: 1806
Minister of Energy, Mines and Resources Canada Vol 1: 6934
Ministeres des Affaires Internationales Vol 1: 12328
Ministerium fur Familie, Frauen, Weiterbildung und Kunst - Baden-Wurttemberg Vol 2: 7053
Ministerium fur Familie, Frauen, Weiterbildung und Kunst Baden-Wurttemberg Vol 2: 6754
Ministerium fur Wissenschaft und Kunst Baden-Wurttemberg Vol 2: 6761
Ministero del Tourismo e dello Spettacolo Vol 2: 8409
Ministero Del'interno Vol 2: 8368
Ministry of International Trade and Industry Vol 2: 8605, 8606
Minit/*European Management Journal* Vol 2: 3656
Minnesota Advocates for Human Rights Vol 1: 12330
Minnesota Association for Vocational Special Needs Personnel Vol 1: 12914
Minnesota Historical Society Vol 1: 12332
Minnesota Ink Vol 1: 12335
Minnesota State Arts Board Vol 1: 12339
Minnesota State Legislature Vol 1: 12340
Minot State University - Northwest Art Center Vol 1: 12343
Mirror Group Newspapers Vol 2: 3658
Miss America Foundation Vol 1: 12347
Miss America Organization Vol 1: 12345
Miss America Pageant Vol 1: 12345
Miss Galaxy International Pageant Vol 1: 12348
Miss Universe Inc. Vol 1: 12350
Mississippi Children's Book Award Committee Vol 1: 12354
Mississippi Historical Society Vol 1: 12356
Mississippi Valley Historical Association Vol 1: 15810
Missouri Archaeological Society Vol 1: 12363
Missouri Arts Council Vol 1: 7480, 18433
Missouri Association of School Librarians Vol 1: 12367
Missouri Botanical Garden Vol 1: 6485
Missouri Southern State College Vol 1: 12369
Misstofvereniging van Suid-Afrika Vol 2: 10858
MIT Press Vol 1: 5465
Mita Society for Library and Information Science Vol 2: 8699
Mita Toshakan Joho Gakkai Vol 2: 8699
Mitchell Energy & Development Corp. Vol 1: 10018
Mitchell Foundation Vol 1: 12371
Mixed Blood Theatre Company Vol 1: 12373
Mlada Fronta Publishing House Vol 2: 1887
Mlade Leta Publishing House Vol 2: 10766
Mlade leta, slovenske vydavatel'stvo knih pre mladez Vol 2: 10785
Mladinska Knjiga Vol 2: 10806
MMI of Detroit Vol 1: 12375
Mobil Vol 1: 7305
Mobil Chemical Company Vol 1: 1540
Mobil Oil Australia Limited Vol 2: 528
Mobil Oil Company Limited Vol 2: 4004
Mobil Oil Corporation Vol 1: 7304, 12377
Mobil Research and Development Corporation Vol 1: 2607
Mobil Sekiyu Kabushiki Kaisha Vol 2: 8701
Mobile Industrial Caterers Association Vol 1: 12380
Mobile Opera Guild Vol 1: 12382
Model A Restorers Club Vol 1: 12384

Model Missiles Association Vol 1: 13290
Model News and Models & Talent International Network Vol 1: 12388
Model T Ford Club of America Vol 1: 12390
Modern Language Association of America Vol 1: 12392
Modern Language Association of Poland Vol 2: 10080
The Modern Language Journal Vol 1: 1873, 1874
Modern Medicine Vol 1: 12406
Modern Plastics Vol 1: 12408, 18045
Modern Poetry Association Vol 1: 16262
Modern Railroads Vol 1: 12410
Modern Railroads/Rail Transit Magazine Vol 1: 12410
Modern Salon Vol 1: 6304
Moet & Chandon Vol 2: 4505, 6119, 6121
Mogens and Wilhelm Ellermann Foundation Vol 2: 11943
Mokslu Akademija Vol 2: 8854
Molins plc Vol 2: 2739
Molson Brewery Vol 1: 6027
Molson Family Foundation Vol 1: 6728
Monadhamat Al-Modon Al-Arabiyah Vol 2: 8839
Monde de la Mer Vol 2: 6483
Monde; Le Vol 2: 4883
Money for Women/Barbara Deming Memorial Fund Vol 1: 12413
Monika Foundation; Anna- Vol 2: 7056
Monika Stiftung; Anna- Vol 2: 7056
Monk Institute of Jazz; Thelonious Vol 1: 12415
Monsanto Vol 2: 4219
Monsanto Agricultural Products Company Vol 1: 4749
Monsanto Company Vol 1: 1537, 2605, 4788, 12417, 12684
Montana Arts Council Vol 1: 12420
Monte Carlo Television Festival Vol 2: 9320
Monthly Labor Review Vol 1: 19263
Montreal International Festival of Films on Art Vol 1: 12422
Montreal International Festival of New Cinema and Video Vol 1: 12424
Montreal International Music Competition Vol 1: 12426
Montreal Neurological Institute and Hospital Vol 1: 12428
Montreal Symphony Orchestra Vol 1: 12431
Montreal Urban Community Arts Council Vol 1: 12433
Montreal World Film Festival Vol 1: 12435
Montres Rolex Vol 2: 11898
Montreux Detroit JAZZ Festival Vol 1: 12517
Montreux International Choral Festival Vol 2: 11878
Moore Fund for Writers; Jenny McKean Vol 1: 12438
Moose Jaw Kinsmen International Band & Choral Festival Vol 1: 12440
Morand; Fondation Paul Vol 2: 5802
Morgan 4/4 Club Vol 2: 3660
Morgan Guaranty Trust Company Vol 1: 8532
Morgan Sports Car Club, Ltd. Vol 2: 3660
Morris Agency; William Vol 1: 1759
Morse Poetry Prize Committee Vol 1: 12442
Mortar Board Vol 1: 12444
Mortgage Bankers Association of America Vol 1: 12448
Mosby Lifelines Vol 1: 13096
Mosby Publishing Company; C.V. Vol 1: 12959
Moscow International Ballet Competition Vol 2: 10456
Moss-Thorns Gallery of Art Vol 1: 12451

Mostra Cinematografica Internazionale - La Natura, l'Uomo e il suo Ambiente   Vol 2: 8300
Mostra de Valencia, Cinema del Mediterrani   Vol 2: 11304
Mostra Internacional de Cinema Em Sao Paulo   Vol 2: 1498
Mostra Internazionale del Cinema; Biennale di Venezia -   Vol 2: 8469
Mostra Internazionale del Film d'Autore - Sanremo   Vol 2: 8296
Mother and Child International   Vol 2: 11880
Mother Lode Art Association   Vol 1: 12453
Motor Boating & Sailing   Vol 1: 14334
Motor Marketing International   Vol 1: 12455
Motor Trend   Vol 1: 12457
Motorcycle Safety Foundation   Vol 1: 12461
Motorhome Travelers Association   Vol 1: 12463
Motorola   Vol 1: 10700
Motorola Corporation   Vol 1: 10730
Mountain West Center for Regional Studies   Vol 1: 12466
Mountaineers   Vol 1: 12468
Mountainfilm   Vol 1: 12470
Mountainside Publishing Company   Vol 1: 2872
Mouvement Contre le Racisme et pour l'Amitie Entre les Peuples   Vol 2: 6123
Mouvement International Juristes Catholiques   Vol 2: 6033
Movement Against Racism and for Friendship Between Peoples   Vol 2: 6123
Movement Shorthand Society   Vol 1: 7462
Movies on a Shoestring   Vol 1: 16869
Movies on a Shoestring, Inc.   Vol 1: 16870
Mozart Association of Czechoslovakia   Vol 2: 1875
Mozart Gemeinde Wien   Vol 2: 912
Mozarteum Academy of Music and Performing Arts in Salzburg   Vol 2: 871
Mr. Blackwell   Vol 1: 12472
MTM Association for Standards and Research   Vol 1: 12475
MTV   Vol 1: 12478
Mu Phi Epsilon   Vol 1: 12480
Mu Phi Epsilon Foundation   Vol 1: 12482
Muir Medical Center; John   Vol 1: 55
Multi-Color Exhibitors Association   Vol 2: 10043
Munich International Filmschool Festival   Vol 2: 7058
Municipal Art Society of New York   Vol 1: 12484
Municipal Council of Budapest   Vol 2: 7414
Municipal Finance Officers and Association of the United States and Canada   Vol 1: 9679
Municipal Treasurers Association of the United States and Canada   Vol 1: 12493
Municipality of Bolzano   Vol 2: 8181
Municipality of Lisbon   Vol 2: 10263
Municipality of Monterrey   Vol 2: 9159
Municipality of Rueil-Malmaison   Vol 2: 6125
Municipality of San Juan del Rio   Vol 2: 9161
Municipality of Sofia   Vol 2: 1533
Municipality of Tampico   Vol 2: 9163
Municipality of Terni   Vol 2: 8207
Muscatine Art Center   Vol 1: 12496
Muscular Dystrophy Association   Vol 1: 12498
Museo Angel Orensanz y Artes de Serrablo   Vol 2: 11306
Museu de Arte Moderna de Sao Paulo   Vol 2: 1491
Museu Villa-Lobos   Vol 2: 1500
Museum Association of the American Frontier   Vol 1: 12500
Museum in the Community   Vol 1: 12502

Museum of Art, Carnegie Institute   Vol 1: 7323
Museum of Fine Arts   Vol 1: 5253
Museum of Modern Art of Sao Paulo   Vol 2: 1491
Museum of New Mexico   Vol 1: 12504
Museum of Science, Boston   Vol 1: 12507
Museum of the City of New York   Vol 1: 12510
Museums Association of Australia   Vol 2: 530
Mushroom Growers Association   Vol 2: 3663
Music & Opera Singers Trust Unlimited   Vol 2: 261
Music Center of Los Angeles County   Vol 1: 12512
The Music City News   Vol 1: 9735
Music Distributors Association   Vol 1: 12514
Music Hall   Vol 1: 12516
Music Operators Association   Vol 1: 5138
Music Teacher   Vol 2: 3666
Music Teachers National Association   Vol 1: 12518
MUSICA SACRA   Vol 1: 12526
Musical America Publishing   Vol 1: 12528
Musical Club of Hartford   Vol 1. 12530
Musicians Benevolent Fund   Vol 2: 3668
Musicians Club of New York   Vol 1: 12533
Musicians Emergency Fund   Vol 1: 12536
Musikschule der Stadt Ettlingen   Vol 2: 7060
Mutual Assistance of Latin American State Owned Companies   Vol 2: 12091
Mutual of Omaha Insurance Company   Vol 1: 12538
Muzicka Omaladina Srbije   Vol 2: 10716
Mycological Society of America   Vol 1: 12540
MYSON Group   Vol 2: 2597
Mystery Writers of America   Vol 1: 12547
Mystfest   Vol 2: 8387
Mystic Seaport Museum   Vol 1: 12551
Mystic Valley Railway Society   Vol 1: 12553
Mythic Society   Vol 2: 7712
Mythopoeic Society   Vol 1: 12555
Naantali Music Festival   Vol 2: 4749
Naantalin Musiikkijuhlat   Vol 2: 4749
Nabisco Brands   Vol 1: 2649
Nacion; La   Vol 1: 10511
Nacional; El   Vol 2: 9166
NACME   Vol 1: 12558
NAHB Research Center   Vol 1: 16454
NAHRO International Committee   Vol 1: 13144
NAHRO Manufacturers and Suppliers Council   Vol 1: 13145
Naismith Memorial Basketball Hall of Fame   Vol 1: 12560
Naito Foundation   Vol 2: 8704
NAMBA International (North American Model Boating Association)   Vol 1: 12572
Namibian Arts Association   Vol 2: 9325
Napoleon; Fondation   Vol 2: 5213
Napolitano; Fondazione Franco Michele   Vol 2: 8244
Narishige Scientific Instrument Laboratory   Vol 2: 8797
Narodny vybor hlavneho mesta SSR Bratislavy   Vol 2: 10768
Narvesen Ltd.   Vol 2: 9944
NASCENTE - Cooperative Society with Cultural Purposes   Vol 2: 10226
Nasco   Vol 1: 10760
Nase Vojsko, nakladatelstvi   Vol 2: 1877
Nash Car Club of America   Vol 1: 12574
Nashville Songwriters Association International   Vol 1: 12576
NASSTRAC   Vol 1: 12578
Nathan Trust; George Jean   Vol 1: 12580
Nat.Inst. of Sericultural and Entomological Science   Vol 2: 8658

National Academic Advising Association   Vol 1: 12582
National Academy of Arts   Vol 2: 8828
National Academy of Cable Programming   Vol 1: 12589
National Academy of Design   Vol 1: 12592
National Academy of Education   Vol 1: 12636
National Academy of Engineering   Vol 1: 12638
National Academy of Fine Arts   Vol 2: 10283
National Academy of Medicine   Vol 2: 61, 1724
National Academy of Neuro-psychology   Vol 1: 12643
National Academy of Opticianry   Vol 1: 12645
National Academy of Popular Music   Vol 1: 12648
National Academy of Public Administration   Vol 1: 4271, 12650
National Academy of Recording Arts and Sciences   Vol 1: 12654
National Academy of Sciences   Vol 2: 5705
National Academy of Sciences - Institute of Medicine   Vol 1: 12696
National Academy of Sciences known as the Forty   Vol 2: 8376
National Academy of Songwriters   Vol 1: 12700
National Academy of Sports   Vol 1: 12706
National Academy of Television Arts and Sciences   Vol 1: 12708
National Academy of Television Arts and Sciences; Hollywood Chapter of the   Vol 1: 85
National Academy of Western Art   Vol 1: 13837
National Account Management Association   Vol 1: 12715
National Accreditation Council for Agencies Serving the Blind and Visually Handicapped   Vol 1: 12717
National Aeronautic Association of the U.S.A.   Vol 1: 12721
National Aeronautics and Space Administration   Vol 1: 12728, 19220, 19247, 19620
National Agricultural Aviation Association   Vol 1: 12745
National Agricultural Center and Hall of Fame   Vol 1: 12756
National Agricultural Marketing Officials   Vol 1: 12759
The National Air Transportation Association (NATA)   Vol 1: 12761
National Alliance for Research on Schizophrenia and Depression   Vol 1: 12767
National Alliance of Business   Vol 1: 12771
National Alliance of Businessmen   Vol 1: 12771
National Alliance of Supermarket Shoppers   Vol 1: 12773
National Alumni Board of Directors of the Notre Dame Alumni Association   Vol 1: 19852
National Alumni Board of the Notre Dame Alumni Association   Vol 1: 19853
National Amateur Cycle Speedway Association   Vol 2: 2324
National American Legion Press Association   Vol 1: 12775
National Amputee Golf Association   Vol 1: 12779
National and Provincial Parks Association of Canada   Vol 1: 7081
National Animal Control Association   Vol 1: 12783
National Anxiety Center   Vol 1: 12785
National Arbor Day Foundation   Vol 1: 12787
National Arborist Association   Vol 1: 12789

National Archery Association of the United States Vol 1: 12791
National Art Collections Fund Vol 2: 3670
National Art Education Association Vol 1: 12795
National Art Gallery of Namibia Vol 2: 9325
National Art Library at the Victoria and Albert Museum Vol 2: 4595
National Art Library of the Victoria and Albert Museum. Vol 2: 4344
National Art Materials Trade Association Vol 1: 12812
National Arts Centre Orchestra Vol 1: 12816
National Arts Club Vol 1: 12818
National Arts Council of Zimbabwe Vol 2: 12206, 12219
National Asphalt Pavement Association Vol 1: 12831
National Association for Campus Activities Vol 1: 12837
National Association for Clean Air Vol 2: 10898
National Association for Corporate Speaker Activities Vol 1: 12849
National Association for Creative Children and Adults Vol 1: 12851
National Association for Crime Victims Rights Vol 1: 12854
National Association for Environmental Education Vol 1: 15393
National Association for Equal Opportunity in Higher Education Vol 1: 12856
National Association for Ethnic Studies Vol 1: 12860
National Association for Gifted Children Vol 1: 12863
National Association for Girls and Women in Sport Vol 1: 12868
National Association for Holocaust Education Vol 1: 12870
National Association for Hospital Development Vol 1: 5527
National Association for Humane and Environmental Education Vol 1: 12872
National Association for Industry-Education Cooperation Vol 1: 12874
National Association for Music Therapy Vol 1: 12877
National Association for Outlaw and Lawman History Vol 1: 12879
National Association for Professional Saleswomen Vol 1: 12881
National Association for Public Continuing and Adult Education Vol 1: 825
National Association for Puerto Rican Civil Rights Vol 1: 12883
National Association for Pupil Transportation Vol 1: 12885
National Association for Remedial Teaching Vol 1: 11183
National Association for Research in Science Teaching Vol 1: 12887
National Association for Search and Rescue Vol 1: 12893
National Association for Sport and Physical Education Vol 1: 12899, 13747
National Association for Stock Car Auto Racing (NASCAR) Vol 1: 12901
National Association for the Advancement of Colored People Vol 1: 12903
National Association for the Advancement of Humane Education Vol 1: 12872
National Association for the Specialty Food Trade Vol 1: 12908
National Association for Vocational Education Special Needs Personnel Vol 1: 12911

National Association for Women Deans, Administrators, and Counselors Vol 1: 12915
National Association of Academic Advisors for Athletics Vol 1: 12918
National Association of Academies of Science Vol 1: 12920
National Association of Accountants Vol 1: 10382
National Association of Accredited Cosmetology Schools Vol 1: 5670
National Association of Activity Professionals Vol 1: 12922
National Association of Advertising Publishers Vol 1: 5808
National Association of Agricultural Journalists Vol 1: 12928
National Association of Amateur Oarsmen Vol 1: 19513
National Association of American Composers and Conductors Vol 1: 13018
National Association of Animal Breeders Vol 1: 12931
National Association of Anorexia Nervosa and Associated Disorders; ANAD - Vol 1: 5148
National Association of Assessing Officers Vol 1: 10659
National Association of Attorneys General Vol 1: 12935
National Association of Auto Trim Shops Vol 1: 12938
National Association of Barber Schools Vol 1: 12940
National Association of Barber Styling Schools Vol 1: 12940
National Association of Basketball Coaches Vol 1: 12942
National Association of Biblical Instructors Vol 1: 713
National Association of Biology Teachers Vol 1: 12951
National Association of Black Journalists Vol 1: 12960, 19806
National Association of Black Women Attorneys Vol 1: 12962
National Association of Boards of Education/ NCEA Vol 1: 13542, 13547, 13549
National Association of Boards of Pharmacy Vol 1: 12966
National Association of Broadcasters Vol 1: 12968
National Association of Catholic Chaplains Vol 1: 12982
National Association of College and University Business Officers Vol 1: 12985
National Association of College and University Food Services Vol 1: 12987
National Association of College Auxiliary Services Vol 1: 12992
National Association of College Broadcasters Vol 1: 12994
National Association of College Gymnastics Coaches (Men) Vol 1: 12996
National Association of College Stores Vol 1: 13004
National Association of Colleges and Teachers of Agriculture Vol 1: 13006
National Association of Community Health Centers Vol 1: 13014
National Association of Competitive Mounted Orienteering Vol 1: 13016
National Association of Composers, USA Vol 1: 13018
National Association of Conservation Districts Vol 1: 13023, 13029
National Association of Consumer Agency Administrators Vol 1: 13036

National Association of Corrosion Engineers Vol 1: 13038
National Association of Counties Vol 1: 13046, 13061
National Association of County Agricultural Agents Vol 1: 7688, 13049
National Association of County and Prosecuting Attorneys Vol 1: 13858
National Association of County Engineers Vol 1: 13052
National Association of County Health Officials Vol 1: 13055
National Association of County Information Officers Vol 1: 13061
National Association of Credit Management Vol 1: 13063
National Association of Criminal Defense Lawyers Vol 1: 13065
National Association of Development Organizations Vol 1: 13068
National Association of Diocesan Ecumenical Officers Vol 1: 13071
National Association of Display Industries Vol 1: 13073
National Association of Dramatic and Speech Arts Vol 1: 13077
National Association of Elementary School Principals Vol 1: 13083, 16698, 19224
National Association of Emergency Medical Technicians Vol 1: 13086
National Association of Environmental Professionals Vol 1: 13100
National Association of Evangelicals Vol 1: 20522
National Association of Farm Broadcasters Vol 1: 7689
National Association of Federal Credit Unions Vol 1: 13102
National Association of Federal Veterinarians Vol 1: 13106
National Association of Federally Licensed Firearms Dealers Vol 1: 13108
National Association of Fire Investigators Vol 1: 13110
National Association of First Responders Vol 1: 13112
National Association of Fleet Administrators Vol 1: 13114
National Association of Foreign Trade Zones Vol 1: 13116
National Association of Geology Teachers Vol 1: 13118
National Association of Government Communicators Vol 1: 13122
National Association of Greeting Card Publishers Vol 1: 9723
National Association of Health and Welfare Ministries of the United Methodist Church Vol 1: 18930
National Association of Health Underwriters Vol 1: 13126
National Association of Hispanic Journalists Vol 1: 13129
National Association of Home and Workshop Writers Vol 1: 13132
National Association of Home Builders Vol 1: 2099, 13134, 16451
National Association of Hospital Hospitality Houses Vol 1: 13140
National Association of Housing and Development Officials Vol 1: 13142
National Association of Independent Fee Appraisers Vol 1: 13150
National Association of Independent Publishers Vol 1: 13152
National Association of Independent Record Distributors and Manufacturers Vol 1: 13154

National Association of Independent Resurfacers   Vol 1: 13156
National Association of Industrial and Office Parks   Vol 1: 13158
National Association of Intercollegiate Athletics   Vol 1: 13163, 13990, 13995
National Association of Interpretation   Vol 1: 13177
National Association of Investors Corporation   Vol 1: 5930, 11430
National Association of Jazz Educators   Vol 1: 10750
National Association of Jewelry Appraisers   Vol 1: 13182
National Association of Journalism Directors   Vol 1: 11612
National Association of Juvenile Correctional Agencies   Vol 1: 13186
National Association of Left-Handed Golfers - NAIG   Vol 1: 13188
National Association of Legal Investigators, Inc.   Vol 1: 13192
National Association of Life Underwriters   Vol 1: 13194
National Association of Manufacturers   Vol 1: 19352
National Association of Metal Finishers   Vol 1: 13202
National Association of Musical Merchandise Wholesalers   Vol 1: 12514
National Association of Negro Business and Professional Women's Club   Vol 1: 13208
National Association of Neonatal Nurses   Vol 1: 13215
National Association of Norwegian Architects   Vol 2: 9901
National Association of Nuclear Engineering   Vol 2: 8383
National Association of Orthopaedic Nurses   Vol 1: 13217
National Association of OTC Companies   Vol 1: 5929
National Association of Pastoral Musicians   Vol 1: 13219
National Association of Pediatric Nurse Associates and Practitioners   Vol 1: 13221
National Association of Personal Financial Advisors   Vol 1: 13224
National Association of Pet Cemeteries   Vol 1: 10775
National Association of Photo Equipment Technicians   Vol 1: 13226
National Association of Physical Therapists   Vol 1: 13228
National Association of Pipe Coating Applicators - Commercial National Bank Bldg.   Vol 1: 13234
National Association of Printing Ink Manufacturers   Vol 1: 13236
National Association of Private Psychiatric Hospitals   Vol 1: 13253
National Association of Private Residential Resources   Vol 1: 3188
National Association of Produce Market Managers   Vol 1: 13240
National Association of Professional Baseball Leagues   Vol 1: 13242
National Association of Professional Gardeners   Vol 1: 16483
National Association of Professional Insurance Agents   Vol 1: 13246
National Association of Professional Organizers   Vol 1: 13251
National Association of Psychiatric Health Systems   Vol 1: 13253
National Association of Public Golf Courses   Vol 2: 3672

National Association of Purchasing Management   Vol 1: 13258
National Association of Quick Printers   Vol 1: 13260
National Association of Railroad Passengers   Vol 1: 13268
National Association of Real Estate Editors   Vol 1: 13271
National Association of Realtors   Vol 1: 13273
National Association of Recording Merchandisers   Vol 1: 13278
National Association of Rehabilitation Facilities   Vol 1: 3932
National Association of Relay Manufacturers   Vol 1: 13288
National Association of Rocketry   Vol 1: 13290
National Association of Sanitarians   Vol 1: 13904
National Association of Scholars   Vol 1: 13292
National Association of School Nurses   Vol 1: 13294
National Association of School Psychologists   Vol 1: 3784
National Association of Schools of Art and Design   Vol 1: 5322, 5323
National Association of Schools of Dance   Vol 1: 5322, 5323
National Association of Schools of Music   Vol 1: 5322, 5323
National Association of Schools of Public Affairs and Administration   Vol 1: 13299
National Association of Schools of Theatre   Vol 1: 5322, 5323
National Association of Science Writers   Vol 1: 13304
National Association of Scientific Materials Managers   Vol 1: 13306
National Association of Secondary School Principals   Vol 1: 13308, 16698, 19224
National Association of Shopfitters   Vol 2: 3675
National Association of Social Workers   Vol 1: 13313
National Association of State Directors of Vocational Technical Education   Vol 1: 14976
National Association of State Education Department Information Officers   Vol 1: 8382
National Association of State Information Resource Executives   Vol 1: 13318
National Association of State Purchasing Officials   Vol 1: 13320
National Association of State Units on Aging   Vol 1: 13322
National Association of Store Fixture Manufacturers   Vol 1: 13324
National Association of Student Personnel Administrators   Vol 1: 13326
National Association of Summer Sessions   Vol 1: 15395
National Association of Swedish Architects   Vol 2: 11491
National Association of Swine Test Stations   Vol 1: 14875
National Association of Teachers of Singing   Vol 1: 13335
National Association of Television Program Executives   Vol 1: 13337
National Association of Television Program Executives International   Vol 1: 13337
National Association of Temporary Services   Vol 1: 13343
National Association of the Bureau of Animal Industry Veterinarians   Vol 1: 13106
National Association of the Holy Name Society   Vol 1: 13348

National Association of the Physically Handicapped   Vol 1: 13353
National Association of the Remodeling Industry   Vol 1: 13356
National Association of Theatre Owners   Vol 1: 13369
National Association of Towns and Townships   Vol 1: 13371
National Association of Towns and Townships - National Center for Small Communities   Vol 1: 13373
National Association of Trade and Technical Schools   Vol 1: 7301
National Association of Underwater Instructors   Vol 1: 13375
National Association of University Women   Vol 1: 13379
National Association of Wholesale Independent Distributors   Vol 1: 13381
National Association of Women Artists   Vol 1: 13383
National Association of Women Judges   Vol 1: 13385
National Association of Writing Instrument Distributors   Vol 1: 13381
National Association of Youth Orchestras   Vol 2: 10590
National Association on Volunteers in Criminal Justice   Vol 1: 10752
National Athletic Trainers' Association   Vol 1: 13387
National Auctioneers Association   Vol 1: 13390
National Audio-Visual Association   Vol 1: 10864
National Audubon Society   Vol 1: 1000, 13394
National Auto Auction Association   Vol 1: 13397
National Auto Racing Historical Society   Vol 1: 13399
National Automobile Dealers Association   Vol 1: 9920, 18712
National Automotive Dealers Association   Vol 1: 16632
National Autonomous University of Mexico   Vol 2: 9168
National Aviation Club   Vol 1: 13401
National Aviation Hall of Fame   Vol 1: 13403
National Avionics Society   Vol 1: 13408
National Back Pain Association   Vol 2: 3677
National Backgammon Players Society (of Great Britain)   Vol 2: 3679
National Ballet of Canada   Vol 1: 13410
National Band & Choral Directors Hall of Fame - College Division   Vol 1: 13412
National Band & Choral Directors Hall of Fame - Grade/Middle School Division   Vol 1: 13417
National Band & Choral Directors Hall of Fame - High School Division   Vol 1: 13419
National Band Association   Vol 1: 13424
National Bank   Vol 2: 1493
National Bank of Canada   Vol 1: 5435
National Bank of Mexico   Vol 2: 9201
National Bank of Pakistan   Vol 2: 10007
National Bar Association   Vol 1: 13434
National Baseball Hall of Fame and Museum   Vol 1: 13438
National Basketball Association   Vol 1: 13442
National Black Lung Association   Vol 1: 6394
National Black Police Association   Vol 1: 13458
National Black Programming Consortium   Vol 1: 13463
National Board for Certification in Hearing Instrument Sciences   Vol 1: 14116

National Board for Science and Technology Vol 2: 7770
National Board of Review of Motion Pictures Vol 1: 13465
National Book Council Vol 2: 533
National Book Council of Pakistan Vol 2: 9980
National Book Critics Circle Vol 1: 13467
National Book Development Council of Singapore Vol 2: 10733
National Book Foundation Vol 1: 13469
National Book League (England) Vol 2: 2193
National Book League (Scotland) Vol 2: 10513
National Book Service Vol 1: 7026
National Bowling Hall of Fame and Museum Vol 1: 13471
National Broadcast Editorial Association Vol 1: 13473, 19806
National Broiler Council Vol 1: 16345
National Buffalo Association Vol 1: 13477
National Building Museum Vol 1: 13480
National Bureau of Standards Vol 1: 19099
National Bureau of Standards - United States Department of Commerce Vol 1: 19109
National Burglar and Fire Alarm Association Vol 1: 13482
National Burglar and Fire Alarm Association - National Training School (NTS) Vol 1: 13488
National Burglar and Fire Alarm Association - Public Safety Comitee Vol 1: 13491
National Business Aircraft Association Vol 1: 13494
National Business Education Association Vol 1: 13501
National Business Forms Association Vol 1: 13507
National Cable Television Association Vol 1: 13511
National Carousel Association Vol 1: 13521
National Cartoonists Society Vol 1: 13523
National CASA Association Vol 1: 13828
National Catalog Managers Association Vol 1: 13529
National Catholic Band Association Vol 1: 13531
National Catholic Bandmasters' Association Vol 1: 13531
National Catholic Development Conference Vol 1: 13538
National Catholic Educational Association Vol 1: 13541
National Catholic Pharmacists Guild of The United States Vol 1: 13556
National Catholic Stewardship Council Vol 1: 13562
National Caucus and Center on Black Aged Vol 1: 13565
National Center for Business & Economic Communication Vol 1: 4946
National Center for Clinical Infant Programs. Vol 1: 20635
National Center for Preventive Law Vol 1: 13567
National Center for Public Policy Research Vol 1: 13569
National Center for State Courts Vol 1: 13571
National Centre of Films for Children and Young People Vol 2: 7714
National Chamber of Commerce for Women Vol 1: 13575
National Child Labor Committee Vol 1: 13578
National Christian College Athletic Association Vol 1: 13580
National Citizens' Coalition Vol 1: 13591
National Civic League Vol 1: 13593
National Classical Music Institute Vol 2: 8833

National Classification Management Society Vol 1: 13595
National Coalition for Consumer Education Vol 1: 13597
National Coalition for Marine Conservation Vol 1: 13599
National Coalition of 100 Black Women Vol 1: 13601
National Coffee Service Association Vol 1: 13603
National College of District Attorneys Vol 1: 13605
National Collegiate Athletic Association Vol 1: 13608, 13986, 13992, 13997, 19345
National Collegiate Athletic Association - Division 1 Track Coaches Association Vol 1: 13614
National Collegiate Football Association Vol 1: 13621
National Collegiate Lettermens Association Vol 1: 13624
National Commercial Finance Association Vol 1: 8027
National Commission on Correctional Health Care Vol 1: 13626
National Commission on Culture and the Arts Vol 2: 10045
National Commission on Working Women Vol 1: 20280
National Committee, Arts for the Handicapped Vol 1: 19992
National Committee for Adoption Vol 1: 13681
National Committee for Bulk Materials Handling Vol 2: 484
National Committee for Recording for the Blind Vol 1: 16716
National Committee for Responsible Patriotism Vol 1: 13628
National Committee for the Observance of Mother's Day Vol 1: 14371
National Committee of the Capital of Slovakia Bratislava Vol 2: 10768
National Committee on American Foreign Policy Vol 1: 13630
National Committee on Bulk Materials Handling Vol 2: 429
National Committee on Coastal and Ocean Engineering Vol 2: 488
National Committee on Water Engineering Vol 2: 422
National Community Mental Healthcare Council Vol 1: 13632
National Company of Navigation - NAVENAL Vol 2: 1731
National Composition and Prepress Association Vol 1: 13634
National Composition Association Vol 1: 13634
National Computer Graphics Association Vol 1: 13637
National Concrete Masonry Association Vol 1: 2541
National Confectionery Sales Association of America Vol 1: 13640
National Confederation of Hungarian Trade Unions Vol 2: 7441
National Conference of Christians and Jews Vol 1: 13642
National Conference of Diocesan Directors of Religious Education - CDD Vol 1: 13646
National Conference of Editorial Writers Vol 1: 19806
National Conference of Governmental Industrial Hygienists Vol 1: 1797
National Conference of Puerto Rican Women, Inc. Vol 1: 13648

National Conference of Religious Vocation Directors Vol 1: 14612
National Conference of Women's Bar Associations Vol 1: 13650
National Conference on Peacemaking and Conflict Resolution Vol 1: 13652
National Conference on Soviet Jewry Vol 1: 13654
National Congress of Jewish Deaf Vol 1: 13656
National Consumers League Vol 1: 13662
National Coordinating Board of Family Planning Vol 2: 7731
National Coordinating Council on Emergency Management Vol 1: 13664
National Corn Growers Association Vol 1: 13669
National Corvette Restorers Society Vol 1: 13671
National Cosmetology Association Vol 1: 13674
National Costumers Association Vol 1: 13678
National Council for Adoption Vol 1: 13681
National Council for Black Studies Vol 1: 13683
National Council for Children's Rights Vol 1: 13685
National Council for Community Relations Vol 1: 13703
National Council for Culture Vol 2: 12115
National Council for Culture of Venezuela Vol 1: 15832
National Council for GeoCosmic Research Vol 1: 13689
National Council for Geographic Education Vol 1: 13691
National Council for Interior Design Qualification Vol 1: 13697
National Council for International Health Vol 1: 13699
National Council for Marketing and Public Relations Vol 1: 13703
National Council for Scientific and Technological Research Vol 2: 12125
National Council for Small Business Management Development Vol 1: 10876
National Council for the Social Studies Vol 1: 13708
National Council of Administrative Women in Education Vol 1: 13722
National Council of College Publications Advisers Vol 1: 7903
National Council of Commercial Plant Breeders Vol 1: 13724
National Council of Education for the Ceramic Arts Vol 1: 13728
National Council of Engineering Examiners Vol 1: 13731
National Council of Examiners for Engineering and Surveying Vol 1: 13731
National Council of Farmer Cooperatives Vol 1: 13734
National Council of Juvenile and Family Court Judges Vol 1: 13738
National Council of La Raza Vol 1: 13740
National Council of Patent Law Associations Vol 1: 19120
National Council of Physical Distribution Management Vol 1: 8373
National Council of Science and Technology Vol 2: 9122
National Council of Secondary School Athletic Directors Vol 1: 13746
National Council of Senior Citizens Vol 1: 13748
National Council of Social Security Management Associations Vol 1: 13754

National Council of Supervisors of Mathematics Vol 1: 13758
National Council of Teachers of English Vol 1: 8132, 8133, 13760
National Council of Teachers of English - Assembly on Literature for Adolescents Vol 1: 13782
National Council of Women of the United States Vol 1: 13784
National Council on Alcoholism Vol 1: 13787
National Council on Alcoholism and Drug Dependence Vol 1: 13787
National Council on Community Services and Continuing Education Vol 1: 13795
National Council on Community Services for Community and Junior Colleges Vol 1: 13795
National Council on Economic Education Vol 1: 13799
National Council on Education for the Ceramic Arts Vol 1: 13801
National Council on Family Relations Vol 1: 13803
National Council on Intellectual Disability Vol 2: 535
National Council on Public History Vol 1: 13811
National Council on Radiation Protection and Measurements Vol 1: 13813
National Council on Religion and Public Education Vol 1: 13815
National Council on Schoolhouse Construction Vol 1: 8352
National Council on the Aging Vol 1: 13817
National Council on the Aging - National Voluntary Organizations for Independent Living for the Aging Vol 1: 13820
National Council on U.S. - Arab Relations Vol 1: 13823
National Court Appointed Special Advocates Association Vol 1: 13827
National Court Reporters Association Vol 1: 13831
National Cowboy Hall of Fame and Western Heritage Center Vol 1: 13836
National Cutting Horse Association Vol 1: 13839
National Cyclists Union Vol 2: 2326
National Dairy Council Vol 1: 4053
National Dance Association Vol 1: 13841
National Deaf Children's Society Vol 2: 3681
National Defense Transportation Association Vol 1: 13847
National Democratic Institute for International Affairs Vol 1: 13852
National Derby Rallies Vol 1: 13854
National DeSoto Club Vol 1: 13856
National District Attorneys Association Vol 1: 13858
National Duckpin Bowling Congress Vol 1: 13862
National Easter Seal Society Vol 1: 13864
National Easter Seal Society for Crippled Children and Adults Vol 1: 13864
National Economic Association Vol 1: 13879
National Education Association Vol 1: 16698
National Education Association - Department of School Nurses Vol 1: 13294
National Educational Film & Video Festival Vol 1: 13881
National Electric Sign Association Vol 1: 13883
National Electrical Manufacturers Representatives Association Vol 1: 13885
National Electrical Testing Association Vol 1: 10922

National Electronics Sales and Service Dealers Association Vol 1: 13887
National Electronics Service Dealers Association Vol 1: 13887
National EMS Pilot Association Vol 1: 5674
National Endowment for the Arts Vol 1: 23, 185, 6365, 8236, 8831, 9215, 9813, 12340, 13889, 15084, 17288, 20231, 20340
National Endowment for the Arts Literature Program Vol 1: 18545
National Endowment for the Humanities Vol 1: 13895
National Energy Resources Organization Vol 1: 13899
National Environmental Health Association Vol 1: 13904, 14663
National Environmental Training Association Vol 1: 13915
National Ethnic Coalition of Organizations Vol 1: 13920
National Euchre Players Association Vol 1: 13922
National Executive Housekeepers Association Vol 1: 13924
National Farm-City Council Vol 1: 13926
National Father's Day Committee Vol 1: 13928
National Federation Interscholastic Officials Association Vol 1: 13954
National Federation of Abstracting and Information Services Vol 1: 13930
National Federation of Building Trades Employers Vol 2: 2559
National Federation of Business and Professional Women in Finland Vol 2: 4751
National Federation of Coffee Growers of Colombia Vol 2: 1733
National Federation of Community Broadcasters Vol 1: 13933
National Federation of Democratic Women Vol 1: 13935
National Federation of Jewish Men's Clubs Vol 1: 9136
National Federation of Local Cable Programmers Vol 1: 324
National Federation of Music Clubs Vol 1: 8096, 13939
National Federation of Music Societies Vol 2: 3683, 3770
National Federation of Parents for Drug-Free Youth Vol 1: 13941
National Federation of Plastering Contractors Vol 2: 3685
National Federation of Press Women Vol 1: 13943
National Federation of Self Employed and Small Business Vol 2: 2877
National Federation of State High School Associations Vol 1: 13948
National Federation of State High School Associations - National Federation Interscholastic Coaches Association Vol 1: 13954
National Federation of State High School Associations - National Interscholastic Athletic Administrators Association Vol 1: 13959
National Federation of State High School Athletic Associations Vol 1: 13948
National Federation of State Humanities Councils Vol 1: 9160
National Federation of State Poetry Societies Vol 1: 13962
National Federation of the Blind Vol 1: 13964
National Federation of Women's Institutes Vol 2: 3687
National Field Archery Association Vol 1: 13968

National Film Board of Canada Vol 1: 18746
National Film Carriers Vol 1: 14319
National Film Council of Indonesia Vol 2: 7732
National Fisheries Institute Vol 1: 17153
National Fishing Lure Collectors Club Vol 1: 13970
National Flag Foundation Vol 1: 13972
National Flexible Packaging Association Vol 1: 9233
National Flight Nurses Association Vol 1: 5675
National Flight Paramedics Association Vol 1: 5675
National Fluid Power Association Vol 1: 13978
National Flute Association Vol 1: 13981
National Football Foundation and Hall of Fame Vol 1: 13985
National Football League Vol 1: 13998
National Football League Players Association Vol 1: 14006
National Foreign Trade Council Vol 1: 14010
National Forensic Association Vol 1: 14012
National Forensic League Vol 1: 14014
National Forest Products Assocation Vol 1: 2093
National Forest Products Association Vol 1: 476, 5742, 14027
National Forum for Black Public Administrators Vol 1: 14032
National Forum of Greek Orthodox Church Musicians Vol 1: 14035
National Foundation for Advancement in the Arts Vol 1: 14037, 19226
National Foundation for Infectious Diseases Vol 1: 14040
National Foundation for Peroneal Muscular Atrophy Vol 1: 7518
National Foundation of Wheelchair Tennis Vol 1: 14046
National Friends of Public Broadcasting Vol 1: 14049
National Frozen Food Association Vol 1: 14054
National Fund for Literature and Art Vol 2: 12001
National Funeral Directors Association Vol 1: 14056
National Garden Bureau Vol 1: 14058
National Genealogical Society Vol 1: 14060
National Geographic Society Vol 2: 2308
National Geriatrics Society Vol 1: 14078
National Glass Association Vol 1: 14081
National Golf Foundation Vol 1: 14084
National Governors' Association Vol 1: 14088
National Grange Vol 1: 14090
National Grocers Association Vol 1: 14092
National Guard Association of the United States Vol 1: 14095
National Guild of Community Schools of the Arts Vol 1: 14098
National Guild of Piano Teachers Vol 1: 1677
National Gymnastics Judges Association Vol 1: 14101
National Hacky Sack Footbag Players Association Vol 1: 20490, 20491
National Hairdressers and Cosmetologists Association Vol 1: 13674
National Hamiltonian Party Vol 1: 14103
National Head Injury Foundation Vol 1: 14105
National Headache Foundation Vol 1: 14108
National Headliner Club Vol 1: 14113
National Health and Medical Research Council Vol 2: 537
National Hearing Aid Society Vol 1: 14115

National Hearing Conservation Association   Vol 1: 14118
National Hemophilia Foundation   Vol 1: 14123
National Hereford Hog Record Association   Vol 1: 14139
National High Blood Pressure Education Program   Vol 1: 3058
National High School Athletic Coaches Association   Vol 1: 14146
National High School Rodeo Association   Vol 1: 14149
National Highway Traffic Safety Administration   Vol 1: 10696, 10697, 14551, 14552
National Historical Society   Vol 1: 14151
National History Day   Vol 1: 14154
National Hockey League   Vol 1: 14156
National Hockey League Broadcasters' Association   Vol 1: 14157
National Hockey League Players' Association   Vol 1: 14174
National Home Center News   Vol 1: 14184
National Home Fashions League   Vol 1: 11000
National Home Improvement Council   Vol 1: 13356
National Horseshoe Pitchers Association   Vol 1: 14186
National Hot Rod Association   Vol 1: 14193
National Housing Conference   Vol 1: 14196
National Housing Institute   Vol 2: 1225
National Humanities Center   Vol 1: 14200
National Hypertension Association   Vol 1: 14202
National Independent Automobile Dealers Association   Vol 1: 14204
National Indian Health Board   Vol 1: 14206
National Indian Social Workers Association   Vol 1: 14208
National Industries for the Blind   Vol 1: 14211
National Institute for Architectural Education   Vol 1: 14214
National Institute for Music Theater   Vol 1: 14219
National Institute for the Environment   Vol 2: 10288
National Institute for the Foodservice Industry   Vol 1: 8850
National Institute for Trial Advocacy   Vol 1: 14222
National Institute for Urban Wildlife   Vol 1: 14224
National Institute for Women of Color   Vol 1: 14226
National Institute of American Doll Artists   Vol 1: 14228
National Institute of Ceramic Engineers   Vol 1: 1459, 1462, 1475
National Institute of Fine Arts   Vol 2: 9205
National Institute of Folk and Traditional Heritage   Vol 2: 9984
National Institute of Genetics   Vol 2: 8528
National Institute of Geosciences, Mining and Chemistry Research (INGEOMINAS)   Vol 2: 1735
National Institute of Governmental Purchasing   Vol 1: 14231
National Institute of Mental Health   Vol 1: 1692, 3655
National Institute of Real Estate Brokers   Vol 1: 16708
National Institute of Social Sciences   Vol 1: 14239
National Institute of Standards and Technology   Vol 1: 19110
National Institute of Verdi Studies - Rotary Club of Parma   Vol 2: 8385

National Institute on Alcohol Abuse and Alcoholism   Vol 1: 1693
National Instituut voor de Huisvesting   Vol 2: 1225
National Intelligence Study Center   Vol 1: 14241
National Intercollegiate Soccer Officials Association   Vol 1: 14243
National Interfraternity Conference, Inc.   Vol 1: 14245
National Interscholastic Swimming Coaches Association of America   Vol 1: 14247
National Intramural-Recreational Sports Association   Vol 1: 14251
National Intravenous Therapy Association   Vol 1: 11411
National Jewish Girl Scout Committee - Synagogue Council of America   Vol 1: 14254
National Junior College Athletic Association   Vol 1: 14256
National Kidney Foundation   Vol 1: 14268
National Kiswahili Council   Vol 2: 12012
National Landscape Association   Vol 1: 14279
National Lawyers Wives   Vol 1: 2788
National League for Nursing   Vol 1: 14282
National League of American Pen Women   Vol 1: 14293
National Legal Aid and Defender Association   Vol 1: 14295
National Legislative Council for the Handicapped   Vol 1: 14301
National Lesbian and Gay Journalists Association   Vol 1: 14303
National Library for the Handicapped Child - Reach Resource Centre   Vol 2: 3690
National Library of Australia   Vol 2: 547
National Library of Medicine   Vol 1: 12172
National Library of Mexico   Vol 2: 9248
The National Library of Poetry   Vol 1: 14305
National Lighting Bureau   Vol 1: 14307
National Liquor Stores Association   Vol 1: 15349
National Literacy Coalition   Vol 1: 14309
National LP-Gas Association   Vol 1: 14533
National Lubricating Grease Institute   Vol 1: 14311
National Magazine & Film Carriers   Vol 1: 14319
National Magazine Awards Foundation (Canada)   Vol 1: 14321
National Male Nurses Association   Vol 1: 815
National Management Association   Vol 1: 14323
National Marine Educators' Association   Vol 1: 14327
National Marine Manufacturers Association   Vol 1: 14333, 19529
National Marine Representatives Association   Vol 1: 14336
National Maritime Museum   Vol 2: 3692
National Medical Fellowships   Vol 1: 14340
National Mental Health Association   Vol 1: 14354
National Micrographics Association   Vol 1: 5538
National Migraine Foundation   Vol 1: 14108
National Military Fish and Wildlife Association   Vol 1: 14364
National Military Intelligence Association   Vol 1: 14366
National Milk Producers Federation   Vol 1: 1919
National Minority Supplier Development Council, Inc.   Vol 1: 14369
National Mother's Day Committee   Vol 1: 14371

National Motorsports Press Association   Vol 1: 14373
National Moving and Storage Technical Foundation   Vol 1: 14375
National Multiple Sclerosis Society   Vol 1: 14377
National Municipal League   Vol 1: 13593
National Museum of Nature   Vol 1: 7037
National Museum of Racing and Hall of Fame   Vol 1: 14386
National Music Council   Vol 1: 14388
National Network of Women in Sales   Vol 1: 14390
National Newspaper Association   Vol 1: 14392
National Newspaper Publishers Association   Vol 1: 14396
National Notary Association   Vol 1: 14398
National Nuclear Energy Commission   Vol 2: 2026
National Ocean Industries Association   Vol 1: 14401
National Ocean Service   Vol 1: 19116
National Opera Association   Vol 1: 14404
National Opera Institute   Vol 1: 14219
National Operatic and Dramatic Association   Vol 2: 3694
National Organization for Men   Vol 1: 14410
National Organization for Rare Disorders   Vol 1: 14412
National Organization for Victim Assistance   Vol 1: 14414
National Organization for Women Foundation   Vol 1: 15543
National Organization of Human Service Education   Vol 1: 14424
National Organization of Human Service Educators   Vol 1: 14424
National Organization on Disabilities   Vol 1: 1157
National Organization on Disability   Vol 1: 2882, 14430
National Organization Taunting Safety and Fairness Everywhere (NOT-SAFE)   Vol 1: 14432
National Orientation Directors Association   Vol 1: 14434
National Paint and Coatings Association   Vol 1: 14436
National Paperbox and Packaging Association   Vol 1: 14444
National Paperbox Association   Vol 1: 14444
National Park Academy of the Arts   Vol 1: 14446
National Parkinson Foundation   Vol 1: 14448
National Parks and Conservation Association   Vol 1: 14451
National Parks Association   Vol 1: 14451
National Peace Foundation   Vol 1: 14456
National Peace Institute Foundation   Vol 1: 14456
National Peace Prize of Sri Lanka   Vol 2: 11439
National Peach Council   Vol 1: 14458
National Peanut Council   Vol 1: 14461
National Pest Control Association   Vol 1: 14463
National Pigeon Association   Vol 1: 14467
National Pizza and Pasta Association   Vol 1: 14472
National Planning Association   Vol 1: 14474
National Playwrights Conference   Vol 1: 14476
National Pocket Billiard Association   Vol 1: 14478
National Poetry Association   Vol 1: 14481
National Poetry Foundation   Vol 2: 3696

National Poetry Series Vol 1: 14483
National Police Officers Association of America Vol 1: 14485
National Pony Society Vol 2: 3700
National Portrait Gallery - London Vol 2: 3703
National Power PLC Vol 2: 3604
National Power World Piano Competition London Vol 2: 3603
National Premium Sales Executives Vol 1: 5828
National Press Club Vol 1: 14495
National Press Foundation Vol 1: 14502, 14504
National Press Photographers Association Vol 1: 14511, 19844
National Propane Gas Association Vol 1: 14533
National Property Management Association Vol 1: 14540
National Psychological Consultants to Mnagement Vol 1: 3702
National PTA Vol 1: 14544
National Railroad Construction and Maintenance Association Vol 1: 14553
National Rebel Class Association Vol 1: 14556
National Recreation and Park Association Vol 1: 14558
National Recreation and Park Association - National Therapeutic Recreation Society Vol 1: 14570
National Recycling Coalition Vol 1: 14577
National Rehabilitation Association Vol 1: 14581
National Rehabilitation Association - Vocational Evaluation and Work Adjustment Association Vol 1: 14589
National Rehabilitation Counseling Association Vol 1: 14593
National Rehabilitation Hospital Vol 1: 14599
National Religious Broadcasters Vol 1: 14601
National Religious Vocation Conference Vol 1: 14612
National Remodeling Association Vol 1: 13356
National Repertory Theatre Foundation Vol 1: 14615
National Republican Heritage Groups (Nationalities) Council Vol 1: 14617
National Research Council Vol 2: 7465
National Research Council of Canada Vol 1: 15074
National Restaurant Association Vol 1: 14622
National Restaurant Association Foundation Vol 1: 14627
National Retail Merchants Association Vol 1: 14630
National Reye's Syndrome Foundation Vol 1: 14637
National Rifle Association Vol 2: 3705
National Rifle Association of America Vol 1: 14641
National Right to Work Committee Vol 1: 14646
National Rural Health Association Vol 1: 14648
National Rural Health Care Association Vol 1: 14648
National RV Owners Club Vol 1: 14654
National Safety Council Vol 1: 14656
National Sanitation Foundation International Vol 1: 14662
National Scale Men's Association Vol 1: 11305
National Scholastic Press Association Vol 1: 14665

National Scholastic Press Association/Associated Collegiate Press Vol 1: 18506
National School Boards Association Vol 1: 11675
National School Orchestra Association Vol 1: 14667
National School Public Relations Association Vol 1: 14669
National School Transportation Association Vol 1: 14674
National Schools Committee for Economic Education Vol 1: 14678
National Science Board Vol 1: 14682
The National Science Foundation Vol 1: 8083
National Science Foundation Vol 1: 14680, 19499
National Science Foundation - Directorate for Science & Engineering Education Vol 1: 14689
National Science Supervisors Association Vol 1: 14691
National Science Teachers Association Vol 1: 14695
National Scrabble Association Vol 1: 14709, 14710
National Sculpture Society Vol 1: 14711
National Secretaries Association Vol 1: 16514
National Security Agency Vol 1: 19483
National Security Council Vol 1: 14716
National Security Industrial Association Vol 1: 14718
National Sheep Association Vol 2: 3707
National Shellfisheries Association Vol 1: 14720
National Sheriffs' Association Vol 1: 10696
National Shorthand Reporters Association Vol 1: 13831
National Silo Association Vol 1: 11219
National Sisters Vocation Conference Vol 1: 14612
National Skeet Shooting Association Vol 1: 14723
National Small-Bore Rifle Association Vol 2: 3709
National Small Shipments Traffic Conference Vol 1: 12578
National Soccer Coaches Association of America Vol 1: 14725
National Society - Daughters of the American Revolution Vol 1: 14730
National Society - Sons of the American Revolution Vol 1: 14733
National Society for Art Education Vol 2: 3711
National Society for Education in Art and Design Vol 2: 3711
National Society for Histotechnology Vol 1: 14744
National Society for Park Resources Vol 1: 14756
National Society for Performance and Instruction Vol 1: 14759
National Society of Artists Vol 1: 14772
National Society of Arts and Letters Vol 1: 14774
National Society of Biomedical Equipment Technicians Vol 1: 14776
National Society of Daughters of Founders and Patriots of America Vol 1: 14778
National Society of Film Critics Vol 1: 14780
National Society of Fingerprint Officers Vol 2: 2891
National Society of Fund Raising Executives Vol 1: 14782
National Society of Insurance Premium Auditors Vol 1: 14793

National Society of Interior Design Vol 1: 4620
National Society of Newspaper Columnists Vol 1: 14796
National Society of Painters in Casein and Acrylic Vol 1: 14798
National Society of Professional Engineers Vol 1: 14800, 20227
National Society of Professional Surveyors Vol 1: 14813
National Society of Student Keyboardists Vol 1: 14819
National Society of Tole and Decorative Painters Vol 1: 14821
National Softball Congress Vol 1: 11312
National Sojourners Vol 1: 14825
National Spa and Pool Institute Vol 1: 14827
National Space Club Vol 1: 14829
National Speakers Association Vol 1: 14842
National Speleological Society Vol 1: 14845
National Spinal Cord Injury Association Vol 1: 14855
National Sports Law Institute Vol 1: 14857
National Sportscasters and Sportswriters Association Vol 1: 14860
National Spotted Saddle Horse Association Vol 1: 14864
National Staff Leasing Association Vol 1: 14867
National Steeplechase and Hunt Association Vol 1: 14869
National Stereoscopic Association Vol 1: 14871
National Stroke Association Vol 1: 14873
National Swimming Pool Institute Vol 1: 14827
National Swine Improvement Federation Vol 1: 14875
National Symphony Orchestra Vol 1: 14877
National Tattoo Association Vol 1: 14879
National Tattoo Club of the World Vol 1: 14879
National Taxpayers Union Vol 1: 14881
National Telemedia Council Vol 1: 14883
National Telephone Cooperative Association Vol 1: 14886
National Textbook Company Vol 1: 1875
National Theatre Conference Vol 1: 14895
National Thespian Society Vol 1: 11360
National Threshers Association Vol 1: 14897
National Torch Tip Company Vol 1: 5087
The National Tourism Awareness Week Award Vol 1: 18768
National Tractor Pullers Association Vol 1: 14899
National Traditional Country Music Association Vol 1: 14912
National Traditionalist Caucus Vol 1: 14917
National Transportation Week Vol 1: 14919
National Trappers Association Vol 1: 14924
National Trust for Historic Preservation Vol 1: 14933
National Turf Writers Association Vol 1: 14938, 18706, 18707
National Turkey Federation Vol 1: 14942
National University Continuing Education Association Vol 1: 14944
National University Extension Association Vol 1: 14944
National Urban Coalition Vol 1: 14956
National Urban Indian Council Vol 1: 14968
National Urban League Vol 1: 14970
National Vaccine and Serum Institute Beijing Vol 2: 1573
National Vocational Agricultural Teachers' Association Vol 1: 15061

National Vocational Technical Educational Foundation   Vol 1: 14975
National Water Resources Association   Vol 1: 14977
National Water Safety Congress   Vol 1: 14980
National Waterbed Retailers Association   Vol 1: 14985
National Watercolor Society   Vol 1: 14990
National Westminster Bank plc   Vol 2: 4512
National Wheelchair Athletic Association   Vol 1: 14993
National Wheelchair Basketball Association   Vol 1: 14998
National Whistleblower Center   Vol 1: 15517
National Wild Turkey Federation   Vol 1: 15002
National Wildlife   Vol 1: 15005
National Wildlife Federation   Vol 1: 15007
National Wildlife Rehabilitation Association   Vol 1: 15012
National Woman's Party   Vol 1: 15016
National Women's Economic Alliance   Vol 1: 15019
National Women's Economic Alliance Foundation   Vol 1: 15019
National Women's Hall of Fame   Vol 1: 15022
National Women's Political Caucus   Vol 1: 15025
National Women's Studies Association   Vol 1: 15029
National Wood Flooring Association   Vol 1: 15037
National Woodland Owners Association   Vol 1: 15039
National Wool Growers' Association   Vol 2: 10900
National Wrestling Coaches Association   Vol 1: 15046
National Wrestling Hall of Fame & Museum   Vol 1: 15049
National Writers Club   Vol 1: 15053
National Young Farmer Educational Association   Vol 1: 15058
Nationalekonomiska Foreningen   Vol 2: 11620
Nationalist Movement   Vol 1: 15062
Nation's Restaurant News   Vol 1: 15064
NationsBank of Texas N.A.   Vol 1: 168, 170
Nationwide Building Society   Vol 2: 2249
Nativelle Foundation for Art and Medicine; Claude-Adolphe   Vol 2: 6127
Natural Food Associates   Vol 1: 15069
Natural Resources Defense Council   Vol 1: 15072
Natural Resources Foundation; Renewable   Vol 1: 16788
Natural Sciences and Engineering Research Council of Canada   Vol 1: 15074
Natural World   Vol 2: 3713
Nature Conservancy   Vol 1: 15078
Nature's Window Art Gallery   Vol 1: 7269
Natuurlewevereniging van Suidelike Afrika   Vol 2: 11126
Naumburg Foundation; Walter W.   Vol 1: 15083
Nautical Institute   Vol 2: 3715
Naval Enlisted Reserve Association   Vol 1: 15086
Naval Submarine League   Vol 1: 15088
NCEA Parents Office   Vol 1: 13553, 13555
NCR Ltd.   Vol 2: 2138
NCTE Research Foundation   Vol 1: 13770, 13780
NDT Cevenini Company   Vol 2: 8356
Near East/South Asia Council of Overseas Schools   Vol 2: 7203
Neave Trust; Airey   Vol 2: 3717
Nebraska Library Association   Vol 1: 15098

Nebraska Library Association - School, Children's Young Peoples Section   Vol 1: 15102
The Nebraska Review   Vol 1: 15105
NEC America   Vol 1: 18626
NEC America and NEC Information Systems (USA)   Vol 1: 10278
NEC Corp   Vol 2: 11822
Nedeljne Informativne Novine   Vol 2: 10718
Nederlandse Bridge Bond   Vol 2: 9473
Nederlandse Taalunie   Vol 2: 9551
Nederlandse Vereniging Voor Amateurtheater   Vol 2: 9378
Nederlandse Vereniging voor Internationaal Recht   Vol 2: 9553
Nederlandse Vereniging voor Psychiatrie   Vol 2: 9561
Neglia; Concorso Internazionale Musicale Francesco Paolo   Vol 2: 8204
Nelligan; Fondation Emile-   Vol 1: 18879, 18880
Nematological Society of Southern Africa   Vol 2: 10902
Nemzetkozi Kodaly Tarsasag   Vol 2: 7422
Nemzetkozi Magyar Filologiai Tarsasag   Vol 2: 7419
Neon Limited; Claude   Vol 1: 12156
Nestle Enterprises   Vol 1: 6917
Nestle Foundation   Vol 2: 11882
Nestle Rowntree   Vol 2: 2206
Netherlands - Ministry of Culture   Vol 2: 9333
Netherlands Association for the Advancement of Natural, Medical and Surgical Sciences   Vol 2: 9555
Netherlands Film Institute   Vol 2: 9375, 9455
Netherlands Psychiatric Association   Vol 2: 9561
Netherlands Society of Photogrammetry   Vol 2: 8555
Network for Continuing Medical Education   Vol 1: 9852
Neue Schweizerische Chemische Gesellschaft   Vol 2: 11884
Neue Schweizerischer Chemische Gesellschaft   Vol 2: 11889
New Balance Shoe   Vol 1: 14726
New Brunswick Institute of Agrologists   Vol 1: 15107
New Clio Awards Inc.   Vol 1: 15111
New Delta Review   Vol 1: 15113
New Dramatists   Vol 1: 15115
New England Council   Vol 1: 15117
New England Lyric Operetta   Vol 1: 15119
New England Poetry Club   Vol 1: 15121
New England Press Association   Vol 1: 15133
New England Review/Bread Loaf Quarterly   Vol 1: 15135
New England Roentgen Ray Society   Vol 1: 15137
New England Theatre Conference   Vol 1: 15139
New England Water Works Association   Vol 1: 15148
New England Wildflower Preservation Society   Vol 1: 15159
New England Wildflower Society   Vol 1: 15159
New Foundation A Blomme   Vol 2: 1230
New Hampshire Library Association/CHILIS (Children's Librarians of New Hampshire)   Vol 1: 15166
New Haven Symphony Orchestra   Vol 1: 15168
New Hope Foundation   Vol 1: 15171
New Hope Foundation/*The Nation*   Vol 1: 15170
New Jersey Bell   Vol 1: 15191
New Jersey Center for Visual Arts   Vol 1: 15173

New Jersey Health Products Council   Vol 1: 15192
New Jersey Historical Commission   Vol 1: 15176
New Jersey Institute of Technology   Vol 1: 15179, 15312
New Jersey Jazz Society   Vol 1: 10380
New Jersey Library Association   Vol 1: 15181
New Jersey Literary Hall of Fame   Vol 1: 15185
New Jersey Patent Law Association   Vol 1: 15187
New Jersey Press Association   Vol 1: 15189
New Jersey Public Serivice Electric & Gas   Vol 1: 8831
New Jersey State Council on the Arts   Vol 1: 8831
New Jersey Symphony Orchestra   Vol 1: 15193
New Law Journal   Vol 2: 2715
New Letters   Vol 1: 15195
New Mexico Art League   Vol 1: 15197
New Music for Young Ensembles   Vol 1: 15199
New Options   Vol 1: 15201
New Orleans Institute for the Performing Arts   Vol 1: 15203
New Rivers Press   Vol 1: 15205
New School for Social Research - Graduate School of Management and Urban Policy   Vol 1: 15207
New South Wales Film & TV Office   Vol 2: 550
New Statesman   Vol 2: 3719
New Swiss Chemical Society   Vol 2: 11884
New Swiss Chemical Society Symposia   Vol 2: 11889
New Voices   Vol 1: 15209
New World Symphony   Vol 1: 15211
New York Academy of Sciences   Vol 1: 15213
New York Arthritis Foundation   Vol 1: 15220
New York Board of Trade   Vol 1: 15222
New York Book Show   Vol 1: 15225
New York Botanical Garden   Vol 1: 6484
New York Business Press Editors   Vol 1: 15227
New York Civil Liberties Union   Vol 1: 15229
New York Community Trust   Vol 1: 9883, 15232
New York Drama Critics' Circle   Vol 1: 15234
New York Festivals   Vol 1: 15236
New York Financial Writers' Association   Vol 1: 15240
New York Flute Club   Vol 1: 15242
New York Foundation for the Arts   Vol 1: 15244
New York International Ballet Competition   Vol 1: 15247
New York Metropolitan Section   Vol 1: 1472
New York Press Club   Vol 1: 15249
New York Public Library   Vol 1: 15260, 16091
New York Racing Association   Vol 1: 15266
New York Road Runners Club   Vol 1: 15268
New York Society for Ethical Culture   Vol 1: 15271
New York Society of Architects   Vol 1: 15273
New York State Association of Criminal Defense Lawyers   Vol 1: 15278
New York State Association of Foreign Language Teachers   Vol 1: 1869
New York State Association of Library Boards   Vol 1: 15280
New York State Bar Association   Vol 1: 15282
New York State Council on the Arts   Vol 1: 15284
New York State Historical Association   Vol 1: 15286

Organization Index
Volume 2: International and Foreign — North

New York State Society of CPAs   Vol 1: 15290
New York State Writers Institute of the State University of New York   Vol 1: 15292
The New York Times   Vol 1: 15295
The New York Times Regional Newspaper Group   Vol 1: 15297
New York University   Vol 1: 15301
New York University - Department for University Development   Vol 1: 15306
New York University Stern School of Business   Vol 1: 7434
New York Urban League   Vol 1: 15308
New York Yankees   Vol 1: 15310
New Zealand - Department of Internal Affairs   Vol 2: 9747
New Zealand Academy of Fine Arts   Vol 2: 9749
New Zealand Association of Scientists   Vol 2: 9751
New Zealand Book Publishers Association   Vol 2: 9704
New Zealand Concrete Society   Vol 2: 9732
New Zealand Corrosion Association   Vol 2: 138
New Zealand Council for Educational Research   Vol 2: 9756
New Zealand Dental Association   Vol 2: 9758
New Zealand Department of Internal Affairs   Vol 2: 9724
New Zealand Institute of Refrigeration Heating and Air Conditioning Engineers   Vol 2: 9729
New Zealand Library Association   Vol 2: 9760
New Zealand Maori Arts and Crafts Institute   Vol 2: 9764
New Zealand National Society for Earthquake Engineering   Vol 2: 9766
New Zealand Society of Designers   Vol 2: 9719
New Zealand Society of Industrial Design   Vol 2: 9719
New Zealand Theatre Federation   Vol 2: 9768
New Zealand Tourist Industry Federation and New Zealand Tourism Department   Vol 2: 9771
New Zealand Women Writers' Society   Vol 2: 9773
Newark Black Film Festival   Vol 1: 15311
Newark Museum   Vol 1: 15312
Newark Public Library   Vol 1: 15312
Newark Symphony Hall   Vol 1: 15312
Newberry Library   Vol 1: 15313
Newbury House   Vol 1: 18592, 18594
Newcomen Society in North America   Vol 1: 15320
Newcomen Society of the United States   Vol 1: 15320
Newfoundland Club of America   Vol 1: 15327
Newman Center; Scott   Vol 1: 15329
Newman Foundation; Scott   Vol 1: 15329
Newpaper Association of America   Vol 1: 15331
Newport International Competition for Young Pianists Committee   Vol 2: 12178
Newport Pianoforte Competition   Vol 2: 12178
Newsbank, Inc.   Vol 1: 2844
Newsday   Vol 1: 15338
Newsletter Association   Vol 1: 14502, 15343
Newsletter Clearinghouse   Vol 1: 15340
Newsletter Publishers Association   Vol 1: 15343
Newspaper Advertising Bureau   Vol 1: 15345
Newspaper Association of America   Vol 1: 15345
Newspaper Association of America Foundation   Vol 1: 15352
Newspaper Comics Council   Vol 1: 15362

Newspaper Enterprise Association   Vol 1: 15358
Newspaper Farm Editors of America   Vol 1: 12928
Newspaper Features Council   Vol 1: 15362
Newspaper Fund   Vol 1: 8710
The Newspaper Guild   Vol 1: 15364
Newspaper Guild of New York   Vol 1: 15366
Newspaper Personnel Relations Association   Vol 1: 15368
Newspaper Purchasing Management Association   Vol 1: 15370
Newspaper Research Council   Vol 1: 15337
Newsweek   Vol 1: 8296, 8297
Newswomen's Club of New York   Vol 1: 15372
NHFL Educational Foundation   Vol 1: 11004
Niagara University   Vol 1: 15375
Nicol Scales, Inc.   Vol 1: 11306
Nicolai Malko Foundation   Vol 2: 1982
Nielsen International Violin Competition; Carl   Vol 2: 1983
Nigar Weekly   Vol 2: 9986
Nigerian Academy of Science   Vol 2: 9864
Nihon Bunsekikagaku-Kai   Vol 2: 8633
Nihon Enso Renmei   Vol 2: 8607
Nihon Gakujutsu Shinko-Kai   Vol 2: 8635
Nihon Hon'yakukka Kyokai   Vol 2: 8637
Nihon Iden Gakkai   Vol 2: 8528
Nihon Insatsu Sangyo Rengokai   Vol 2: 8609
Nihon Jinrui Iden Gakkai   Vol 2: 8640
Nihon Ju-i Gakkai   Vol 2: 8670
Nihon Junkatsu Gakkai   Vol 2: 8668
Nihon Kagaku-Gijyutsu Joho Sentah   Vol 2: 8619
Nihon Kagaku Gijyutsu Renmi   Vol 2: 8775
Nihon Keizai Shimbun   Vol 2: 8706
Nihon Kikai Gakkai   Vol 2: 8642
Nihon Sanshi Gakkai   Vol 2: 8658
Nihon Seppyo Gakkai   Vol 2: 8661
Nihon Shinbun Kyokai   Vol 2: 8625
Nihon Sugakukai   Vol 2: 8695
Nihon Tenmon Gakkai   Vol 2: 8506
Nihon Yakugakkai   Vol 2: 8714
Nijhoff International; Martinus   Vol 1: 2875
Nikkei Economic Journal   Vol 2: 8706
Nikon, Inc.   Vol 1: 4517, 17333
NIMROD - Arts & Humanities Council of Tulsa   Vol 1: 15381
Nine Lives Associates   Vol 1: 15384
Ninety-Nines   Vol 1: 15386
The Ninety-Nines, Inc.   Vol 1: 12727
Nippon Chikusan Gakkai   Vol 2: 8672
Nippon Dobutsu Gakkai   Vol 2: 8796
Nippon Dojohiryo Gakkai   Vol 2: 8665
Nippon Gakushiin   Vol 2: 8592
Nippon Hoso Kyokai   Vol 2: 8600
Nippon Kagakukai   Vol 2: 8511
Nippon Kekkaku-byo Gakkai   Vol 2: 8651
Nippon Ketsueki Gakkai   Vol 2: 8655
Nippon Oyo Dobutsu Konchu Gakkai   Vol 2: 8653
Nippon Shokubutsu-Byori Gakkai   Vol 2: 8723
Nippon Tekko Kyokai   Vol 2: 8560
The Nissan FOCUS Awards   Vol 1: 15389
Nissen   Vol 1: 13002
Niwano Heiwa Zaidan   Vol 2: 8708
Niwano Peace Foundation   Vol 2: 8708
Nixon Newspapers, Inc   Vol 1: 6230
Nobel Foundation   Vol 2: 11493
Nobelstiftelsen   Vol 2: 11493
Noir International Festival   Vol 2: 8387
NOMUS - Nordic Music Committee   Vol 2: 11500
NOMUS - Nordisk Musikkomite   Vol 2: 11500
Noranda   Vol 1: 7557
Noranda Mines Limited   Vol 1: 6927

Nordic Council   Vol 2: 11501
Nordic Council (Sweden)   Vol 2: 11502
Nordisk orkesterdirigentkonkurrence   Vol 2: 1905
Nordiska Bankmannaunionen   Vol 2: 11451
Nordiska Radet - Sweden   Vol 2: 11502
Nordiska Samarbetsradet for Kriminologi   Vol 2: 11563
Nordiska Samfundet Mot Plagsamma Dourfarsak   Vol 2: 11638
Nordkapp Culture Office - the North Cape Festival   Vol 2: 9909
Nordkapp Kulturkontor - Nordkapp Festivalen   Vol 2: 9909
Nordmanns-Forbundet   Vol 2: 9913
Norges Forskningsraad   Vol 2: 9964
Norges Industriforbund   Vol 2: 9885
Norpress - Norsk Pressebyra   Vol 2: 9911
Norsemen's Federation   Vol 2: 9913
Norsk Kjemisk Selskap   Vol 2: 9931
Norsk Komponistforening   Vol 2: 9969
Norsk Kulturrad   Vol 2: 9933
Norsk Malermestrenes Landsforbund   Vol 2: 9939
Norsk Oversetterforening   Vol 2: 9956
Norsk Presseforbund   Vol 2: 9941
Norske Akademi for Sprog og Litteratur   Vol 2: 9924
Norske Arkitekters Landsforbund   Vol 2: 9901
Norske Filmfestivalen   Vol 2: 9937
Norske Forfatterforening   Vol 2: 9928
Norske Sivilingeniorers Forening   Vol 2: 9951
Norske Videnskaps-Akademi   Vol 2: 9926
North American Academy of Liturgy   Vol 1: 15391
North American Association for Environmental Education   Vol 1: 15393
North American Association of Summer Sessions   Vol 1: 15395
North American Association of Wardens and Superintendents   Vol 1: 15397
North American Bluebird Society   Vol 1: 15399
North American Conference on British Studies   Vol 1: 15401
North American Council on Adoptable Children   Vol 1: 15407
North American Die Casting Association   Vol 1: 15411
North American Fruit Explorers   Vol 1: 15424
North American Gladiolus Council   Vol 1: 15426
North American Lily Society   Vol 1: 15428
North American Loon Fund   Vol 1: 15431
North American Mustang Association and Registry   Vol 1: 15433
North American Mycological Association   Vol 1: 15435
North American Patristic Society   Vol 1: 15438
North American Publishing Co.   Vol 1: 11995
North American Ski Journalists Association   Vol 1: 15440
North American Society for Oceanic History   Vol 1: 15446
North American Society for Sport History   Vol 1: 15448
North American Society for Sport Management   Vol 1: 15450
North American Society for the Psychology of Sport and Physical Activity   Vol 1: 15452
North American Society of Pacing and Electrophysiology   Vol 1: 15456
North American South Devon Association   Vol 1: 15464
North American Trail Ride Conference   Vol 1: 15466

North American Vexillological Association   Vol 1: 15484
North American Warmblood Association   Vol 1: 15488
North Atlantic Treaty Alliance - Brussels   Vol 2: 1232
North Carolina Arts Council - Dept. of Cultural Resources   Vol 1: 15490
North Carolina Literary and Historical Association   Vol 1: 15493
North Carolina Symphony   Vol 1: 15502
North Dallas Chamber of Commerce   Vol 1: 11689
North Wales Arts Association   Vol 2: 12180
Northampton Borough Council   Vol 2: 3721
Northeast Asia Council   Vol 1: 5444
Northeast Modern Language Association   Vol 1: 15595
Northeast Ohio Balloon Pilots Association   Vol 1: 6240
Northeastern Bird-Banding Association   Vol 1: 5796
Northeastern Loggers' Association   Vol 1: 15504
Northeastern Lumber Manufacturers Association   Vol 1: 15506
Northern Arts   Vol 2: 2638, 3724
Northern Cross Society   Vol 1: 15508
Northern Kentucky University   Vol 1: 15511
Northern Kentucky University - Department of Fine Arts   Vol 1: 15513
Northern Territory Literary Awards Committee   Vol 2: 552
Northern Territory University   Vol 2: 556
Northland Insurance Company   Vol 1: 12260
Northport/B. J. Spoke Gallery   Vol 1: 15515
Northport Galleries   Vol 1: 15515
Northrop Corporation   Vol 1: 12059
Northwest Environmental Advocates - National Whistleblower Center   Vol 1: 15517
Northwest Farm Managers Association   Vol 1: 15519
Northwest Film Center   Vol 1: 15521
Northwest Film Study Center   Vol 1: 15521
Northwest Watercolor Society and Bellevue Art Museum   Vol 1: 15525
Northwood University   Vol 1: 15527
Norton Company   Vol 1: 17523
Norwalk Symphony Society   Vol 1: 15534
Norway - Ministry of Cultural and Scientific Affairs   Vol 2: 9915
Norway - Ministry of Foreign Affairs   Vol 2: 9917
Norwegian Academy for Language and Literature   Vol 2: 9924
Norwegian Academy of Science and Letters   Vol 2: 9926
Norwegian-American Museum   Vol 1: 15536
Norwegian Authors' Union   Vol 2: 9928
Norwegian Broadcasting Corporation   Vol 2: 9943
Norwegian Chemical Society   Vol 2: 9931
Norwegian Cultural Council   Vol 2: 9933
Norwegian Directorate for Public & School Libraries   Vol 2: 9915
Norwegian Film Festival   Vol 2: 9937
Norwegian Master-Painter Organization   Vol 2: 9939
Norwegian Newspaper Publishers Association   Vol 2: 9943
Norwegian Nobel Committee   Vol 2: 11495
Norwegian Press Agency   Vol 2: 9912
Norwegian Press Association   Vol 2: 9941
Norwegian Section of the International Board on Books for Young People   Vol 2: 9945
Norwegian Short Film Festival   Vol 2: 9947

Norwegian Society of Chartered Engineers   Vol 2: 9951
Norwegian Translators' Association   Vol 2: 9956
Norwegian Union of Journalists   Vol 2: 9943
Nouveau Prix Populiste   Vol 2: 6129
Nouvelle Societe Suisse De Chimie   Vol 2: 11889
Nova Petrochemicals, Inc.   Vol 1: 1516
Nova University Programs for Higher Education   Vol 1: 15541
Novacor Chemical Ltd.   Vol 1: 7553, 7558
Novedades   Vol 2: 9250
Novell, Inc.   Vol 1: 7416
Novo Nordisk Foundation   Vol 2: 1985
NOW Foundation   Vol 1: 15543
NOW Legal Defense and Education Fund   Vol 1: 15545
NTC Publishing Group   Vol 1: 2934
Nuclear Age Peace Foundation   Vol 1: 15551
Numerical Control Society   Vol 1: 15554
Numerical Control Society/Association for Integrated Manufacturing Technology   Vol 1: 15554
Numismatic News   Vol 1: 11733
Numismatic Services   Vol 1: 15558
Nuovi Spazi Sonori; Associazione   Vol 2: 8132
Nutley Symphony Society of Northern New Jersey   Vol 1: 15562
Nutrition Foundation; International Life Sciences Institute -   Vol 1: 11081
Nutrition Foundation of the Philippines   Vol 2: 10050
Nutrition Professionals   Vol 1: 1920
Nycomed (UK) Ltd.   Vol 2: 2414
Nynex   Vol 1: 10831
Nyon International Documentary Film Festival   Vol 2: 11891
Nypels Stichting; Charles   Vol 2: 9563
O Estado de S. Paulo   Vol 1: 10511
Oak Ridge Associated Universities   Vol 1: 15565
Oakton Community College   Vol 1: 15567
Obec architektu   Vol 2: 1881
Oboe International   Vol 1: 15569
Obra Cultural of the Montes de Piedad   Vol 2: 11199
The Observer   Vol 2: 3727
Occidental Petroleum Corporation   Vol 1: 1546, 12682
Oceania Basketball Confederation   Vol 2: 558
Oceania Philatelic Society   Vol 1: 17747
Oceania Weightlifting Federation   Vol 2: 560
Ochsner Medical Foundation; Alton   Vol 1: 15571
OCLC/Forest Press, Inc.   Vol 1: 2814
Octopus Publishing Group   Vol 2: 9802
Odense kommune   Vol 2: 1962
Odyssey Institute Corporation   Vol 1: 15573
Offender Aid and Restoration/USA   Vol 1: 15575
Office Municipal du Tourisme d'Anglet   Vol 2: 6131
Office National des Debouches Agricoles et Horticoles   Vol 2: 1066
Office National Hellenique du Tourisme   Vol 2: 7197
Office of Naval Research   Vol 1: 3454
Office of the Mayor of Zurich   Vol 2: 11893
Official Publications, Inc.   Vol 1: 1894
Oglebay Institute   Vol 1: 15578
O'Hara Institute for Rural Ministry Education; Edwin Vincent   Vol 1: 16969
Ohaus Scale Corporation   Vol 1: 14703, 14704
Ohio Academy of History   Vol 1: 15580
Ohio Arts Council   Vol 1: 15584

Ohio Federation of Music Clubs   Vol 1: 8096
Ohio State University - Mershon Center   Vol 1: 15586
Ohio State University Press   Vol 1: 15588
Ohio University - Scripps School of Journalism; E. W.   Vol 1: 15590
Ohio University Press   Vol 1: 15593
Ohioana Library Association   Vol 1: 15597
Oil and Color Chemists' Association   Vol 2: 3729
Oita International Wheelchair Marathon   Vol 2: 8710
Oklahoma Association of School Library Media Specialists   Vol 1: 15606
Oklahoma City Orchestra League   Vol 1: 15608
Oklahoma Interscholastic Press Association   Vol 1: 15611
Oklahoma Library Association - Sequoyah Children's Book Award Committee   Vol 1: 15613
OKOMEDIA Institut   Vol 2: 7062
Old Bottle Club of Great Britain/B.B.R. Publishing   Vol 2: 3732
Old Sturbridge Village Research Library Society   Vol 1: 15616
Olin Corporation   Vol 1: 1556
Olin Fine Arts Center Gallery   Vol 1: 15618
Olivetti Society   Vol 2: 8389
Olsten Temporary Services   Vol 1: 17486
Olympus Optical Company   Vol 2: 11863
Omaha Symphony Guild   Vol 1: 15620
Omega Society   Vol 2: 562
O'Melveny and Myers   Vol 1: 15622
Omicron Chi Epsilon   Vol 1: 15624
Omicron Delta Epsilon   Vol 1: 15624
Omicron Delta Gamma   Vol 1: 15624
Omicron Delta Kappa   Vol 1: 15627
Omicron Kappa Upsilon   Vol 1: 15634
Omnium Cultural   Vol 2: 11239, 11308
OMV   Vol 2: 911
Onassis Public Benefit Foundation; Alexander S.   Vol 2: 7205
Oncology Nursing Society   Vol 2: 11860
One Club for Art & Copy   Vol 1: 15670
One Reel   Vol 1: 15672
One Step Beyond Adventure Group   Vol 1: 6256
O'Neill Memorial Theatre Center; Eugene   Vol 1: 14476
Ongar Music Club   Vol 2: 3734
ONLINE   Vol 1: 15678
Online, Inc.   Vol 1: 15674
Ontario   Vol 1: 15679
Ontario - Ministry of Culture Tourism & Recreation   Vol 1: 15685
Ontario - Ministry of Natural Resources   Vol 1: 15687
Ontario Arts Council   Vol 1: 15690
Ontario Choral Federation   Vol 1: 15691
Ontario Craft Foundation   Vol 1: 15707
Ontario Crafts Council   Vol 1: 15707
Ontario Federation of Agriculture   Vol 1: 15720
Ontario Psychological Association   Vol 1: 15723
Openbare Skakelinstituut van Suidelike Afrika   Vol 2: 10911
Opera/Columbus   Vol 1: 15726
Opera Foundation Australia   Vol 2: 564
Opera Foundation Victoria   Vol 2: 568
Opera Guild of San Antonio   Vol 1: 15728
Operations Management Education and Research Foundation   Vol 1: 15730
Operations Research Society of America   Vol 1: 15732

Ophthalmic Photographers' Society   Vol 1: 15738
Ophthalmological Society of Egypt   Vol 2: 2022
Oporto Internacional Film Festival - Fantasporto   Vol 2: 10290
Oppenheim John Downes Memorial Trust   Vol 2: 3737
Optical, Acoustical and Filmtechnical Society   Vol 2: 7443
Optical Data Corporation   Vol 1: 14708
Optical Publishing Association   Vol 1: 15740
Optical Research Associates   Vol 1: 18318
Optical Society of America   Vol 1: 15743, 17417
Optikai, Akusztikai Es Filmtechnikai Egyesulet   Vol 2: 7443
Optimist International   Vol 1: 15762
Optometric Editors Association   Vol 1: 15764
Opzy/Feministisch Maanblad   Vol 2: 9425
Oral-B Laboratories   Vol 1: 10615, 10628
Oratorio Society of New York   Vol 1: 15766
Orchard Lake Schools   Vol 1: 15768
Orchestra Sinfonica dell'Emilia-Romagna Arturo Toscanini   Vol 2: 8391
Orchestre de Melun-Senart   Vol 2: 6469
Orchestre Symphonique de Montreal   Vol 1: 12431
Orchid Society of Great Britain   Vol 2: 3739
Order of Daedalians   Vol 1: 15770
Order of Lafayette   Vol 1: 15789
Order of St. John/St. John Ambulance   Vol 2: 3741
Order of the Coif   Vol 1: 15791
Order of the Founders and Patriots of America   Vol 1: 15793
Order Sons of Italy in America   Vol 1: 15797
Ordre Souverain d'Occident   Vol 2: 1369
Oregon Newspaper Publishers Association   Vol 1: 15799
Orensanz y Artes de Serrablo; Museo Angel   Vol 2: 11306
ORF   Vol 2: 774, 843
Organ Historical Society   Vol 1: 15801
Organic Reactions, Inc.   Vol 1: 1545
Organic Syntheses, Inc.   Vol 1: 1545
Organisation Catholique Internationale du Cinema et de l'Audiovisuel   Vol 2: 1171
Organisation de l'aviation civile internationale   Vol 1: 10856
Organisation des Assurances Africaines   Vol 2: 1542
Organisation des Nations Unies pour l'alimentation et l'agriculture   Vol 2: 8266
Organisation des Radiodiffusions des Etats Islamiques   Vol 2: 10491
Organisation du Traite de l'Atlantique Nord - Bruxelles   Vol 2: 1232
Organisation Europeenne et Mediterraneenne pour la Protection des Plantes   Vol 2: 5113
Organisation for Economic Co-operation and Development   Vol 2: 11797
Organisation Internationale Contre le Trachome   Vol 2: 6035
Organisation Internationale de Biosystematiciens Vege taux   Vol 2: 8550
Organisation Internationale de Radiodiffusion et Television   Vol 2: 1866
Organisation Internationale de Recherche sur le Cerveau   Vol 2: 5979
Organisation Internationale des Femmes Sionistes   Vol 2: 7988
Organisation Internationale des Journalistes   Vol 2: 1863
Organisation Internationale des Sciences Chimiques pour la Developpement   Vol 2: 9076

Organisation Meteorologique Mondiale   Vol 2: 11977
Organisation Mondiale de la Sante   Vol 2: 11972
Organisation Mondiale de la Sante - Centre International de Recherche sur le Cancer   Vol 2: 6484
Organisation Mondiale des Anciens et Anciennes Eleves de l'Enseignement Catholique   Vol 2: 8475
Organisation Mondiale pour la Systemique et la Cybernetique   Vol 2: 6487
Organisation of Commonwealth Associations   Vol 2: 3746
Organisation Recherche de la Carie   Vol 2: 2834
Organisation Scientifique et Technique Internationale du Vol a Voile   Vol 2: 6980
Organizacion de Estados Iberoamericanos Para la Educacion, la Ciencia y la Cultura   Vol 2: 11311
Organizacion de los Estados Unidos   Vol 1: 15831
Organizacion Espanola para el Libro Infantil y Juvenil   Vol 2: 11382
Organizacion Estereo Mundo   Vol 2: 9254
Organizacion Internacional de las Ciencias Quimicas para el Desarrollo   Vol 2: 9076
Organizacion Internactional para el Libro Juvenil   Vol 2: 11766
Organizacion para Estudios Tropicales   Vol 2: 1784
Organization Development Institute   Vol 1: 15806
Organization for the Phyto-Taxonomic Investigation of the Mediterranean Area   Vol 2: 7064
Organization for Tropical Studies   Vol 2: 1784
Organization Mondiale Contre Le Cecite   Vol 2: 3365
Organization of American Historians   Vol 1: 14155, 15810
Organization of American States - Inter-American Council for Education, Science and Culture   Vol 1: 15826
Organization of American States - Inter-American Music Council   Vol 1: 15831
Organization of Arab Petroleum Exporting Countries   Vol 2: 8846
Organization of Ibero-American States for Education, Science and Culture   Vol 2: 11311
Organization of Islamic Capitals and Cities (OICC)   Vol 2: 10501
Organization of Professional Employees of the United States Department of Agriculture   Vol 1: 15835
Organizing Committee for the Winter Universiade   Vol 2: 8712
Organizing Committee of the Shanghai Television Festival   Vol 2: 1575
Oriental Ceramic Society   Vol 2: 3748
Original Theatre Works   Vol 1: 15838
Orion Publishing Group   Vol 2: 3576
Orr and Associates; Ken   Vol 1: 15840
Orszagos Erdeszeti Egyesulet   Vol 2: 7343
Orszagos Magyar Banyaszati Es Kohaszati Egyesulet   Vol 2: 7352
Ortho Diagnostic Systems   Vol 1: 930, 4195, 7212, 7213
Ortho Diagnostic Systems, Inc.   Vol 1: 4518
Ortho Diagnostic Systems Limited   Vol 2: 3174
Ortho-McNeil (Canada) Ltd.   Vol 1: 7921, 7922, 7923
Ortho Pharmaceutical (Canada) Ltd.   Vol 1: 16237
Ortho Pharmaceutical Inc.   Vol 1: 4772

Orthopaedic Nurses' Association   Vol 1: 13217
Orthopaedic Research Society   Vol 1: 15842
Orton Dyslexia Society   Vol 1: 15845
Orvieto; Fondazione Premio Laura   Vol 2: 8250
Orwell Memorial Fund; George   Vol 2: 3750
Osaka Chamber of Commerce and Industry   Vol 2: 8605, 8606
Oslo Kommune   Vol 2: 9958
Oslo University   Vol 2: 9960
Osterreichische Apothekerkammer   Vol 2: 800
Osterreichische Film Tage   Vol 2: 873
Osterreichische Geographische Gesellschaft   Vol 2: 778
Osterreichische Gesellschaft fur Filmwissenschaft   Vol 2: 745
Osterreichische Gesellschaft fur Filmwissenschaft Kommunikations-und Medienforschung   Vol 2: 783
Osterreichische Gesellschaft fur Klinische Chemie   Vol 2: 875
Osterreichische Statistische Gesellschaft   Vol 2: 786
Osterreichische Werbewissenschaftliche   Vol 2: 754
Osterreichischer Komponistenbund   Vol 2: 773
Osterreichischer Rundfunk - Landesstudio Oberosterreich   Vol 2: 771
Osterreichisches Institut fur Formgebung   Vol 2: 775
Osthaus-Museum; Karl Ernst   Vol 2: 7067
Ottawa Field-Naturalists' Club   Vol 1: 15847
Ottawa Little Theater   Vol 1: 15854
Oulu International Children's Film Festival   Vol 2: 4753
Our Army Publishing House   Vol 2: 1877
Outdoor Advertising Association of America   Vol 1: 15856
Outdoor Writers Association of America   Vol 1: 15859
Outdoor Writers of Canada   Vol 1: 15865
Outer Critics Circle   Vol 1: 15868
Outokumpu Company   Vol 2: 4716
Ovarian Cancer Prevention and Early Detection Foundation   Vol 1: 15870
Overseas Academy of Sciences   Vol 2: 6133
Overseas Education Fund International   Vol 1: 15872
Overseas Press and Media Association   Vol 2: 3752
Overseas Press Club of America   Vol 1: 15874
Owens-Corning Corporation   Vol 1: 18044
OX5 Aviation Pioneers   Vol 1: 15876
Oxford Preservation Trust   Vol 2: 3754
Oxoid Ltd.   Vol 2: 4348
Oy. Yleisradio Ab.   Vol 2: 4690
Ozark Society   Vol 1: 15879
Pacific Area Newspaper Publishers Association   Vol 2: 573
Pacific Area Travel Association   Vol 1: 15881
Pacific Arts Association   Vol 2: 576
Pacific Asia Travel Association   Vol 1: 15881
Pacific Coast Council on Latin American Studies   Vol 1: 15883
Pacific Cultural Foundation   Vol 2: 12004
Pacific Northwest Library Association   Vol 1: 15885
Pacific Northwest Writers Conference   Vol 1: 15887
Pacific Public Radio   Vol 1: 8626
Pacific Science Association   Vol 1: 15889
Pacific Sociological Association   Vol 1: 15893

Pacific Stars and Stripes Alumni Association, Inc.   Vol 1: 15898
Pacific Telesis Foundation   Vol 1: 12513
Packaging Education Forum   Vol 1: 15900
Packer Engineering Associates   Vol 1: 4373
Paganini; Concorso Internazionale di Violino Nicolo   Vol 2: 8394
Paganini International Violin Competition; Nicolo   Vol 2: 8394
Paine National Histroical Association; Thomas   Vol 1: 15903
Painting and Decorating Contractors of America   Vol 1: 15905
Paintmakers Association of Great Britain Limited   Vol 2: 2314
Pakistan - Ministry of Education   Vol 2: 9979, 9983, 9989
Pakistan Academy of Sciences   Vol 2: 9992
Pakistan Government - Cabinet Division   Vol 2: 9994
Pakistan Television Corporation   Vol 2: 9998
Pakistan Writers' Guild   Vol 2: 10003
Palanca Foundation and La Tondena, Inc.; Carlos   Vol 2: 10052
Palaontologische Gesellschaft   Vol 2: 6532
Paleontological Society   Vol 1: 15907
Pall Corporation   Vol 1: 15954
Pall Mall Export Stichting   Vol 2: 9565
Palm Springs International Film Festival   Vol 1: 15911
Palme Memorial Fund for International Understanding and Common Security; Olof   Vol 2: 11505
Palo Alto Film Festival   Vol 1: 15913
Palomino Horse Breeders of America   Vol 1: 15915
Palynological Society of India   Vol 2: 7716
Pan American Federation of Engineering Societies   Vol 2: 12131
Pan American Health and Education Foundation   Vol 1: 15922
Pan American Society of the United States   Vol 1: 5124
Pan Macmillan Children's Books   Vol 2: 3756
Panafrican Film and Television of Ouagadougou Festival   Vol 2: 1540
Panama-America   Vol 1: 10511
Panamerican Federation of Architects' Associations   Vol 2: 12093
Panamerican Federation of Associations of Medical Schools   Vol 2: 12133
Panasonic Broadcast Europe   Vol 2: 2760
Panasonic Company   Vol 1: 19995
Pane; Fondazione Anna   Vol 2: 8240
Panel of Chefs of Ireland   Vol 2: 7816
Paneuropa-Union   Vol 2: 7069
Paneuropean Union   Vol 2: 7069
Panorama Sound   Vol 2: 11125
Panstwowa Filharmonia Slaska   Vol 2: 10211
Pansy Ellen Products   Vol 1: 11742
Pantone Color Institute   Vol 1: 15927
Paperboard Packaging Council   Vol 1: 15929
PARADE   Vol 1: 10699
Parade   Vol 1: 15931
Paralyzed Veterans of America   Vol 1: 15933, 16389
Parapsychology Institute of America   Vol 1: 15943
Paratore, Jr. Memorial Foundation; Philip G.   Vol 1: 14773
Parent Co-operative Preschools International   Vol 1: 15946
Parenteral Drug Association Foundation for Pharmaceutical Sciences   Vol 1: 15951
Parents' Choice Foundation   Vol 1: 15956
Parents Helping Parents   Vol 1: 15958
Parents Without Partners   Vol 1: 15960

Parents Without Partners International, Inc.   Vol 1: 15960
Paris Audiovisuel   Vol 2: 6145
Paris International Science-Fiction and Fantasy Films Festival   Vol 2: 6148
The Paris Review   Vol 1: 15967
Paris Transport Authority   Vol 2: 6150
Park kultury a oddechu, Olomouc   Vol 2: 1892
Parke-Davis   Vol 1: 622, 4908
Parke-Davis Division   Vol 1: 15954
Parker Harris and Company   Vol 2: 3759
Parker Pen   Vol 1: 9988
Parkinson Memorial Trust; Dorothy   Vol 2: 2987
Parkinson's Disease Foundation   Vol 1: 15971
Parks Canada   Vol 1: 8609
Parks Council   Vol 1: 15973
Parnassos Society   Vol 2: 7211
Partitioning & Interiors Association   Vol 2: 3761
Partitioning Industry Association   Vol 2: 3761
Partnership for Service-Learning   Vol 1: 15977
Pascall Foundation; Geraldine   Vol 2: 579
Passano Foundation   Vol 1: 15980
Pastel Society of America   Vol 1: 15982
Patriotic Order Sons of America   Vol 1: 15987
Patronato de la Feria de San Marcos   Vol 2: 9211
Patrons of New Art   Vol 2: 3763
Patterson Foundation; Alicia   Vol 1: 15993
Paulist Catholic Evangelization Association   Vol 1: 15995
Paulo Cello Competition   Vol 2: 4749
Paulo Foundation   Vol 2: 4750
Pax Association   Vol 2: 10083
Pax Christi International   Vol 2: 1234
Pax Mundi, Diplomatic Academy of Peace   Vol 2: 1236
Pays Protestante   Vol 2: 6152
Paz y Cooperacion   Vol 2: 11313
PBS   Vol 1: 16564
PC World   Vol 1: 16000
PCR Inc.   Vol 1: 1521
PCW Communications   Vol 1: 15997
Peabody Conservatory of Music   Vol 1: 16002
The Peabody Institute of the City of Baltimore   Vol 1: 16001
Peabody Institute of The Johns Hopkins University   Vol 1: 16001
Peace and Cooperation   Vol 2: 11313
Peace Development Fund and the Pacific Peace Fund   Vol 1: 16003
Peace Research Laboratory   Vol 1: 11829
Pearce - Kirklees Trust; J. W.   Vol 2: 3765
Pearson Peace Park; Lester B.   Vol 1: 16005
Pedal Steel Guitar Association   Vol 1: 16007
Peirce Society; Charles S.   Vol 1: 16009
Pelham Historical Association; John   Vol 1: 16011
PEN American Center   Vol 1: 16013
PEN Club della Svizzera Italiana e Retoromancia   Vol 2: 11868
PEN Club Francais   Vol 2: 6154
PEN Club Italiano   Vol 2: 8362
PEN Club Liechtenstein   Vol 2: 8852
PEN Clube do Brasil   Vol 2: 1449
PEN Clube Portugues   Vol 2: 10292
PEN/Faulkner Foundation   Vol 1: 16038
PEN New Zealand, Inc.   Vol 2: 9777
Pena Fotografica Rosarina   Vol 2: 104
Penn State University   Vol 1: 1758
Penney Company, Inc.; JC   Vol 1: 2882
Penney Company; JC   Vol 1: 19843
Pennsylvania Association of Environmental Professionals   Vol 1: 16041

Pennsylvania Council on the Arts   Vol 1: 16043
Pennsylvania Library Association   Vol 1: 16045
Pennsylvania Newspaper Publishers' Association   Vol 1: 16047
Pennsylvania School Librarians Association   Vol 1: 16051
Pennsylvania Society of Newspaper Editors   Vol 1: 16050
Pennsylvania State University - School of Communications   Vol 1: 16053
Pentax Corporation   Vol 1: 14815
Penumbra Theatre Company   Vol 1: 16055
People for the American Way   Vol 1: 16057
People for the Ethical Treatment of Animals   Vol 1: 16059
People to People International   Vol 1: 16061
People's Poetry Award   Vol 1: 16063
Percussive Arts Society   Vol 1: 16066
Perfins Club   Vol 1: 16068
Performers of Connecticut   Vol 1: 16070
Performing Arts Publicists' Association, Edmonton & Northern Alberta   Vol 1: 16072
Performing Right Society   Vol 2: 3767
Performing Rights Organization of Canada   Vol 1: 17819
Pergamon Press   Vol 2: 1208
Pergamon Press Ltd.   Vol 2: 4219
Periodical Marketers of Canada   Vol 1: 9352
Periodical Publishers Association   Vol 2: 3771
Periodistas Cinematograficos de Mexico   Vol 2: 9256
Perkin-Elmer Corporation   Vol 1: 1485
Perkin-Elmer Ltd.   Vol 2: 4219
Perkins Engines Limited   Vol 2: 3776
Permanent International Altaistic Conference   Vol 1: 16074
Permanent International Association of Navigation Congresses   Vol 2: 1238
Permanent International Association of Navigation Congresses - U.S. Section   Vol 1: 16076
Permanent International Association of Road Congresses   Vol 2: 6157
Perpetual Trustee Company   Vol 2: 124, 512, 516, 707
Perskor Publishers   Vol 2: 10905
Perten Foundation; Harald   Vol 2: 808
Peruvian Paso Horse Registry of North America   Vol 1: 16078
PETA   Vol 1: 16060
Peters Corporation; C. F.   Vol 1: 508
Peters Library Service Ltd.   Vol 2: 3566, 3568
Petersen Publishing Company   Vol 1: 12457
Petro-Canada   Vol 1: 6747
Petrocanada   Vol 2: 12092
Petroleos Mexicanos   Vol 2: 9259
Petroleum Society   Vol 1: 6952
Pettinos Foundation; Charles E. and Joy C.   Vol 1: 1420
Pevecko - hudebni spolek Zerotin   Vol 2: 1892
Pew Charitable Trusts   Vol 1: 8389
Peymey Diffusion   Vol 2: 1240
Pezcoller Foundation   Vol 2: 8396
Pfizer Agricultural Division   Vol 1: 19798
Pfizer and Company; Charles   Vol 1: 4396
Pfizer Animal Health   Vol 1: 4986
Pfizer, Inc.   Vol 1: 1506
Pfizer Limited   Vol 2: 3778
Pfizer Ltd.   Vol 2: 4213
Pfizer Pharmaceuticals   Vol 1: 1018
Pfizer/Roerig   Vol 1: 702
Pharmaceutical Institute of the University of Bern   Vol 2: 6586

Pharmaceutical Institute of the University of Strasburg   Vol 2: 6586
Pharmaceutical Manufacturers Association   Vol 1: 16085
Pharmaceutical Manufacturers Association of Canada   Vol 1: 16087
Pharmaceutical Society of Ghana   Vol 2: 7178
Pharmaceutical Society of Japan   Vol 2: 8714
Pharmaceutical Society of Nigeria   Vol 2: 9866
Pharmaceutical Society of Slovenia   Vol 2: 10802
Pharmacia (Canada)   Vol 1: 7164
Pharmacia Deltec   Vol 1: 15646, 15647
Pharmacy Adria   Vol 1: 15658
Pharmacy Guild of Australia   Vol 2: 581
Pharmazeutische Industrie; Die   Vol 2: 7071
Phelps-Stokes Fund   Vol 1: 16089
Phi Alpha Theta   Vol 1: 16092
Phi Beta Kappa   Vol 1: 16098
Phi Chi Pharmacy Fraternity   Vol 1: 16105
Phi Delta Chi Pharmacy Fraternity   Vol 1: 16105
Phi Lambda Upsilon, National Honorary Chemical Society   Vol 1: 16107
Phi Tau Sigma   Vol 1: 10344
Phi Theta Kappa Honors Society   Vol 1: 16110
Phi Upsilon Omicron   Vol 1: 16117
Philadelphia Art Alliance Press   Vol 1: 16124
Philadelphia Award   Vol 1: 16128
Philadelphia/Pavarotti Competition   Vol 1: 16130
Philalethes Society   Vol 1: 16132
Philanthropic Service for Institutions   Vol 1: 16137
Philatelic Foundation   Vol 1: 16140
Philatelic Music Circle   Vol 1: 16142
Philatelic Traders' Society   Vol 2: 3780
Philip Morris; Association pour le Prix Scientifique   Vol 2: 4963
Philip Morris France   Vol 2: 5234
Philippine Numismatic and Antiquarian Society   Vol 2: 10054
Philippines - Department of Education, Culture and Sports   Vol 2: 10058
Philippines - Department of Education, Culture, and Sports   Vol 2: 10061
Philippines - Department of Science and Technology   Vol 2: 10056, 10061
Philips   Vol 2: 11705
Philips Electronics   Vol 1: 6789
Philips Electronics;   Vol 1: 10283
Phillips Business Information, Inc.   Vol 1: 16144
Phillips Petroleum Company   Vol 1: 1532, 19628
Phillips Publishing   Vol 1: 16144
Phoenix House Foundation   Vol 1: 16147
Phoenix Theatre   Vol 1: 16149
Photo Electronic Imaging   Vol 1: 16496
Photo Express   Vol 2: 281
Photogrammetric Society   Vol 2: 3782
Photographic Art and Science Foundation   Vol 1: 16151
Photographic Historical Society of New York   Vol 1: 3439
Photographic Manufacturers and Distributors Association   Vol 1: 16153
Photographic Salon Exhibitors Association   Vol 2: 7266
Photographic Society HKUSU   Vol 2: 7274
Photographic Society of America   Vol 1: 3135, 16158, 16230
Photographic Society of Ireland   Vol 2: 7818
Photographic Society of Japan   Vol 2: 8721
Photographic Society of Poznan   Vol 2: 10085

Photographic Society of Southern Africa   Vol 2: 10910
Phycological Society of America   Vol 1: 16171
Physical Culture and Tourism Agency   Vol 2: 10090
Physical Education Association of Ireland   Vol 2: 7821
Physical Society   Vol 2: 3190
Physical Society de Londres   Vol 2: 6372
Phytopathological Society of Japan   Vol 2: 8723
PI Gamma Mu   Vol 1: 16175
Pi Kappa Alpha Education Foundation   Vol 1: 16177
Pi Kappa Alpha Memorial Foundation   Vol 1: 16177
Pi Kappa Phi   Vol 1: 16183
Pi Lambda Theta   Vol 1: 16189
Pi Tau Sigma   Vol 1: 4686, 4698, 4703
Piano Technicians Guild   Vol 1: 16198
PICA   Vol 1: 3545
Pickle Packers International   Vol 1: 16203
Pierce-Arrow Society   Vol 1: 16206
Pierian Press   Vol 1: 2910
Pigskin Club of Washington   Vol 1: 16211
Pijls Foundation; Catharina   Vol 2: 9683
Pillsbury Company   Vol 1: 16216
The Pilot   Vol 1: 16218
Pilot Club International   Vol 1: 16220
Pilot International   Vol 1: 16220
Pilsudski Institute of America for Research in the Modern History of Poland; Jozef   Vol 1: 16222
PIMS International, PLC   Vol 2: 3204
Pioneer Hi-Bred International   Vol 1: 1922
Pioneer Hi-Bred International, Inc.   Vol 1: 13029
Pipe Collectors Club of America   Vol 1: 16225
Pipe Collectors International   Vol 1: 16225
Pittsburgh New Music Ensemble   Vol 1: 16227
Placer Camera Club   Vol 1: 16229
Plain English Campaign   Vol 2: 3785
Planned Parenthood - World Population   Vol 1: 16231
Planned Parenthood Federation of America   Vol 1: 16231
Planned Parenthood Federation of Canada   Vol 1: 16235
Plastics Academy   Vol 1: 16238
Plastics Compounding   Vol 1: 18045
Plastics World   Vol 1: 18045
Playboy   Vol 1: 16242
Playboy Foundation   Vol 1: 16245
Player Piano Group   Vol 2: 3787
Playhouse on the Square/Circuit Playhouse   Vol 1: 16247
Playmarket   Vol 2: 9783
Playwrights' Center   Vol 1: 16249
Please Touch Museum for Children   Vol 1: 16254
Plumsock Fund   Vol 1: 20039
PMNETwork   Vol 1: 16528
P.O.B. Publishing Company   Vol 1: 14818
Podiatry Management   Vol 1: 16257
Poet Lore   Vol 1: 16259
Poetry   Vol 1: 16262
The Poetry Center   Vol 1: 16270
Poetry Committee of the Greater Washington DC Area   Vol 1: 16272
Poetry Film Workshop   Vol 1: 14482
Poetry International Foundation   Vol 2: 9567
Poetry Magazine   Vol 1: 19757
The Poetry Society   Vol 2: 3789
Poetry Society of America   Vol 1: 16274
Poets International Organization   Vol 2: 7719
Point-of-Purchase Advertising Institute   Vol 1: 16296

The Points of Light Foundation   Vol 1: 16298
Points of Light Volunteer Organization   Vol 1: 16298
Poland - Kancelaria Prezydenta   Vol 2: 10096
Poland - Ministerstwo Kultury i Sztuki   Vol 2: 10087
Poland - Ministry of Culture and Art   Vol 2: 10087
Poland - Ministry of Culture and Arts   Vol 2: 10067
Poland - Ministry of National Defense Publishing House   Vol 2: 10092
Poland - Office of the President   Vol 2: 10096
Poland - Office of the Prime Minister   Vol 2: 10125
Poland - Urzad RADY Ministrow   Vol 2: 10125
Poland - Wydawnictwo Ministerstwa Obrony Narodowej   Vol 2: 10092
Polaroid   Vol 2: 11854
Polaroid Foundation   Vol 1: 15751
Policy Studies Organization   Vol 1: 16301
Polish Academy of Sciences   Vol 2: 10127, 10151
Polish American Historical Association   Vol 1: 16310
Polish Artistic Agency PAGART   Vol 2: 10129
Polish Association of Pediatric Surgeons   Vol 2: 10131
Polish Chemical Society   Vol 2: 10133
Polish Composers Union   Vol 2: 10140
Polish Film Festival   Vol 2: 10143
Polish Geographical Society   Vol 2: 10145
Polish Geological Society   Vol 2: 10149
Polish Institute and Sikorski Museum   Vol 2: 3794
Polish Librarians Association   Vol 2: 10152
Polish Mathematical Society   Vol 2: 10155
Polish Medical Society of Radiology   Vol 2: 10160
Polish Musicians Association   Vol 2: 10163
Polish Nurses Association   Vol 2: 10165
Polish PEN Club   Vol 2: 10167
Polish Phonetic Association   Vol 2: 10169
Polish Physical Society   Vol 2: 10171
Polish Psychological Association   Vol 2: 10173
Polish Rheumatological Society   Vol 2: 10176
Polish Section of the International Board on Books for Young People   Vol 2: 10178
Polish Society for Commodity Science   Vol 2: 10180
Polish Society for Contemporary Music   Vol 2: 10182
Polish Society of Endocrinology   Vol 2: 10184
Polish Society of Epidemiologists and Infectionists   Vol 2: 10186
Polish Society of Hygiene   Vol 2: 10189
Polish Society of Veterinary Science   Vol 2: 10196
Polish Sociological Association   Vol 2: 10198
Polish Theological Association in Cracow   Vol 2: 10201
Political Studies Association of the United Kingdom   Vol 2: 7860
Politiken   Vol 2: 1988
Pollock-Krasner Foundation   Vol 1: 16314
Polshi PEN Club   Vol 2: 10167
Polska Akademia Nauk   Vol 2: 10127
Polska Sekcja IBBY   Vol 2: 10178
Polskie Lekarskie Towarzystwo Radiologiczne   Vol 2: 10160
Polskie Towarzystwo Chemiczne   Vol 2: 10133
Polskie Towarzystwo Chirurgow Dzieciecych   Vol 2: 10131
Polskie Towarzystwo Endokrynologiczne   Vol 2: 10184

Polskie Towarzystwo Epidemiologow i Lekarzy Chorob Zakaznych Vol 2: 10186
Polskie Towarzystwo Fizyczne Vol 2: 10171
Polskie Towarzystwo Fonetyczne Vol 2: 10169
Polskie Towarzystwo Geograficzne Vol 2: 10145
Polskie Towarzystwo Geologiczne Vol 2: 10149
Polskie Towarzystwo Higieniczne Vol 2: 10189
Polskie Towarzystwo Mathematyczne Vol 2: 10155
Polskie towarzystwo Nauk Weterynaryjnych Vol 2: 10196
Polskie Towarzystwo Neofilologiczne Vol 2: 10080
Polskie Towarzystwo Pielegniarskie Vol 2: 10165
Polskie Towarzystwo Psychologiczne Vol 2: 10173
Polskie Towarzystwo Reumatologiczne Vol 2: 10176
Polskie Towarzystwo Socjologiczne Vol 2: 10198
Polskie Towarzystwo Teologiczne w Krakowie Vol 2: 10201
Polskie Towarzystwo Towaroznawcze Vol 2: 10180
Polynesian Society Incorporated Vol 2: 9785
Polysar Rubber Corporation Vol 1: 7545, 7546
Polytechnic Institute of New York Vol 1: 1898
Ponselle Charitable Foundation, Inc.; Rosa Vol 1: 16316
Pontifical Academy of Sciences Vol 2: 12097
Pontificia Academia Scientiarum Vol 2: 12097
Pontificia Universidad Javeriana Vol 2: 1739
Pony Club of Great Britain Vol 2: 3796
Population Institute Vol 1: 16319
Population Reference Bureau Vol 1: 16321
Pordenone Silent Film Festival Vol 2: 8399
Porter and Zwickel Vol 1: 13002
Portland Art Museum Vol 1: 15521
Portland Opera Vol 1: 16323
Portland Symphony Orchestra Vol 1: 16325
Portugal - Ministerio da Educacao y Cultura Vol 2: 10294
Portugal - Ministry of Education and Culture Vol 2: 10294
Portugal - State Secretariat of Culture Vol 2: 10296
Portuguese Academy of History Vol 2: 10299
Portuguese Association of Writers Vol 2: 10307
Portuguese Continental Union of the United States Vol 1: 16328
Portuguese League Against Cancer Vol 2: 10314
The Post Office Vol 2: 2232
Postal History Society Vol 1: 16330
Postal History Society of Canada Vol 1: 16334
Postal History Society of New Zealand Vol 2: 9788
Potamkin Foundation Vol 1: 621
The Potato Board Vol 1: 16337
Pott Inland Waterways Library; Herman T. Vol 1: 16339
Poultry Science Association Vol 1: 3599, 16341
Pound-American Trial Lawyers Foundation; Roscoe Vol 1: 16355
Pound Foundation; Roscoe Vol 1: 16355
Poznanskie Towarzystwo Fotograficzne Vol 2: 10085

Pozzoli; Concorso Ettore Vol 2: 8198
PPG Industries Vol 1: 7517
Practical Builder Vol 1: 16450
Prague Spring International Music Competition Vol 2: 1879
Prairie Schooner Vol 1: 16359
Prasidialabteilung der Stadt Zurich Vol 2: 11893
Pratella; Fondazione Russolo- Vol 2: 8260
Pratt Free Library; Enoch Vol 1: 6249
Pratt Institute Vol 1: 16367
Praxair Inc. Vol 1: 2586
Precast/Prestressed Concrete Institute Vol 1: 16369
Precision Metalforming Association Vol 1: 16377
Prehistoric Society Vol 2: 3798
Prehistoric Society of East Anglia Vol 2: 3798
Premio Bancarella Vol 2: 8161
Premio Dino Ciani Teatro alla Scala Vol 2: 8188
Premio Letterario Isola d'Elba - Raffaello Brignetti Vol 2: 8322
Premio Musicale Citta di Trieste Vol 2: 8401
Premio Riccione Ater Vol 2: 8403
Premio Tomassoni Internationaler Klavier-Wettbewerb of Musikhochschule Koln Vol 2: 6606
Premio Viareggio Vol 2: 8406
Premium Industry Club Vol 1: 16532
Prensa Espanola Vol 2: 11315
Prensa; La Vol 2: 106
Prensa Nueva Vol 2: 1742
Prentice-Hall Vol 1: 5466, 12957, 14693
Prentice-Hall Publishing Company Vol 1: 1129
Preseren Fund - Cultural Community of Slovenia Vol 2: 10798
Presernov Sklad Vol 2: 10798
President's Committee on Employment of People with Disabilities Vol 1: 16381, 18797
President's Committee on the Arts and the Humanities Vol 1: 11670
President's Council on Physical Fitness and Sports Vol 1: 16393, 19428
President's Council on Youth Fitness Vol 1: 16393
Presidenza del Consiglio dei Ministri Vol 2: 8341
Presidium of the Supreme Soviet of the USSR Vol 2: 10458
Presidium of the Supreme Soviet of the USSR - Committee on Lenin and USSR State Prizes in the Fields of Science and Technology Vol 2: 10468
Presidium of the Supreme Soviet of the USSR - International Lenin Peace Prize Committee Vol 2: 10471
Press Association of Thailand Vol 2: 12014
Pretoria International Exhibition of Photography Vol 2: 10909
Priateia detskaj knihy Vol 2: 10764
Price Waterhouse Vol 2: 3649, 10530
Prince Bernhard Foundation Vol 2: 9570
Prince Bernhard Fund Vol 2: 9390
Prince Manufacturing Vol 1: 10550, 10561
Prince of Wales' Committee Vol 2: 12182
Princess Grace Foundation - USA Vol 1: 16398
Princeton Applied Research; EG&G Vol 1: 1484
Princeton University - Wilson School of Public and International Affairs; Woodrow Vol 1: 16402
Princeton University Alumni Council Vol 1: 16404

Princeton University Press Vol 1: 16407
Prins Bernhard Fonds Vol 2: 9570
Print Club Vol 1: 16409
Printing Industries of America Vol 1: 16411
Printing Industries of America - International Thermographers Association Vol 1: 16414
Printing Industries of America - Master Printers of America Vol 1: 16416
Printing Industries of America - Non-Heatset Web Section Vol 1: 16419
PRINTPAC-UEB Vol 2: 9714
PRISA Vol 2: 11320
Pritzker Architecture Prize Vol 1: 16421
Prix Adolf Bentinck Vol 2: 6159
Prix Aujourd'hui Vol 2: 6161
Prix Cazes Vol 2: 6163
Prix de Composition Musicale Reine Marie-Jose Vol 2: 11895
Prix du Meilleur Livre Etranger Vol 2: 6179
Prix du Palais Litteraire Vol 2: 6165
Prix *Femina* Vol 2: 6167
Prix Futura Berlin/SFB Vol 2: 7073
Prix Georges Sadoul Vol 2: 6169
Prix Guillaume Apollinaire Vol 2: 6171
Prix Jeunesse Foundation Vol 2: 7075
Prix Medicis Vol 2: 6173
Prix Meridien des Quatres Jurys Vol 2: 5231
Prix Theophraste Renaudot Vol 2: 6177
Prize for the Best Foreign Book Vol 2: 6179
Pro Basketball Writers Association of America Vol 1: 13446
PRO Dogs National Charity Vol 2: 3801
Pro Femina Theatre Vol 1: 9995
Pro Football Hall of Fame Vol 1: 16423
Pro Loco Tourist Association of Corciano Vol 2: 8408
Pro Musicis Foundation Vol 1: 16426
Procrastinators' Club of America Vol 1: 16428
Procter & Gamble Company Vol 1: 690, 696, 1508, 1535, 10626, 12351, 12352, 12353
Procter & Gamble Pharmaceuticals Vol 1: 3392
Procter & Gamble Productions Vol 1: 16430
Proctor and Gamble Denture Care Vol 1: 10622
Productions Scenat Vol 1: 16432
Productoras e Importadoras de Papel Vol 2: 9259
Professional Aviation Maintenance Association Vol 1: 16434
Professional Basketball Writers Association of America Vol 1: 16442
Professional Bowlers Association of America Vol 1: 13472, 16444
Professional Builder Vol 1: 16450
Professional Construction Estimators Association Vol 1: 16457
Professional Cycling Association Vol 2: 3803
Professional Disposables Vol 1: 929
Professional Engineers Ontario Vol 1: 16459
Professional Fraternity Association Vol 1: 16464
Professional Golfers' Association Vol 2: 3807
Professional Golfers' Association of America Vol 1: 16466
Professional Grounds Management Society Vol 1: 16483
Professional Hockey Writers' Association Vol 1: 14171
Professional Institute of the Public Service of Canada Vol 1: 16489
Professional Insurance Mass-Marketing Association Vol 1: 16492
Professional Interfraternity Conference Vol 1: 16464

Professional Panhellenic Association   Vol 1: 16464
Professional Photographers of America   Vol 1: 16494
Professional Picture Framers Association   Vol 1: 16499
Professional Putters Association   Vol 1: 16505
Professional Rehabilitation Workers With the Adult Deaf   Vol 1: 1935
Professional Rodeo Cowboys Association   Vol 1: 16507
Professional Secretaries International   Vol 1: 16514
Professional Services Management Association   Vol 1: 16516
Program to Assist Foreign Sinologist Carry Out Research in the R.O.C.   Vol 2: 11991
Programme des Nations Unies pour l'Environnement   Vol 2: 8811
Progressive Architecture   Vol 1: 16518
Project Censored   Vol 1: 16522
Project Management Institute   Vol 1: 16524
Promoting Enduring Peace   Vol 1: 16530
Promotion Industry Club   Vol 1: 16532
Promotion Marketing Association of America, Inc.   Vol 1: 16534
Promotional Products Association International   Vol 1: 16536
Prorodeo Sports News   Vol 1: 16509
Prospectors and Developers Association of Canada   Vol 1: 16538
Prosvjta Publishing House   Vol 2: 10721
Proust Prize; Marcel   Vol 2: 6181
Province of Antwerp/Eugene Baie Foundation   Vol 2: 1242
Provincia di Sondrio   Vol 2: 7998
Provincia di Trento   Vol 2: 8465
Provinciebestuur van Antwerpen/Eugene Baiecomite   Vol 2: 1242
Provinzialverband Westfalen   Vol 2: 7027
Proxmire; Senator William   Vol 1: 16542
Prudential Awards for the Arts   Vol 2: 3825
Prudential Corporation   Vol 2: 3826
Psi Chi   Vol 1: 3673
Psi Chi, The National Honor Society in Psychology   Vol 1: 16544
Psychological Assessment Resources, Inc.   Vol 1: 3706
Psychological Association of Manitoba   Vol 1: 16548
Psychological Dimensions of Peacework Fund   Vol 1: 16552
Psychologists for Social Responsibility   Vol 1: 16550
Psychologists for the Ethical Treatment of Animals   Vol 1: 16555
PTC Research Foundation   Vol 1: 16557
PTN Publishing Company   Vol 1: 16561
Public Broadcasting Service   Vol 1: 16563
Public Choice Society   Vol 1: 16565
Public Employees Roundtable   Vol 1: 16567
Public Relations Consultants Association   Vol 2: 3827
Public Relations Institute of South Africa   Vol 2: 10911
Public Relations Institute of Southern Africa   Vol 2: 10911
Public Relations Section of the Library Administration and Management Association   Vol 1: 2905
Public Relations Society of America   Vol 1: 16572
Public Relations Society of America - Health Academy   Vol 1: 16578
Public Risk Insurance Management Association   Vol 1: 16580

Public Risk Management Association   Vol 1: 16580
Public Utilities Communicators Association   Vol 1: 19970
Public Voice for Food and Health Policy   Vol 1: 16583
Publishers Association for Cultural Exchange   Vol 2: 8726
Publishers Marketing Association   Vol 1: 16585
Publishers Weekly   Vol 1: 16587
Puccini Foundation; Giacomo   Vol 2: 8410
Puppeteers of America   Vol 1: 16590
Purchasing Management Association of Canada-(PMAC)   Vol 2: 9505
Purdue Frederick   Vol 1: 15648
Purebred Hanoverian Association of American Owners and Breeders   Vol 1: 16594
Purina Mills   Vol 1: 4399
Pushcart Press   Vol 1: 16597
Putnam and Grosset Book Group   Vol 1: 2863
Putnam Honor Fund; Herbert W.   Vol 1: 2822
Putt-Putt Golf Courses of America   Vol 1: 16506
Pwyllgor Tywysog Cymru   Vol 2: 12182
Pyrotechnics Guild International   Vol 1: 16600
QRL Poetry Series   Vol 1: 16602
Quadrant   Vol 2: 586
Quaid-i-Azam Academy   Vol 2: 10009
Quality Digest   Vol 1: 16604
Quality Paperback Book Club   Vol 1: 16606
Quarterly Review of Literature   Vol 1: 16602
Quarterly West   Vol 1: 16608
Quebec - Ministere de la Culture et des Communications   Vol 1: 16610
Quebec - Ministere de l'Education, de l'Enseignement Superieur et de la Science   Vol 1: 16616
Quebec Film Critics Association   Vol 1: 12425
Quebec Society for the Promotion of English Language Literature (QSPELL)   Vol 1: 16621
Quebec Zoological Gardens   Vol 1: 16623
Queen Elisabeth International Music Competition of Belgium   Vol 2: 1244
Queen Elizabeth II Arts Council of New Zealand   Vol 2: 153, 9707, 9790
Queen Elizabeth II Arts Council of New Zealand - Literature Programme   Vol 2: 9795
Queen Juliana Foundation   Vol 2: 9612
Queen Marie Jose International Musical Composition Prize   Vol 2: 11895
The Queen Sonja International Music Competition   Vol 2: 9962
Queen's Awards Office   Vol 2: 3829
Queens Opera Association   Vol 1: 16625
Queretaro State Government   Vol 2: 9235
Quick Printing   Vol 1: 16627
Quotidien du Medecin; Le   Vol 2: 6502
R & R Promotions International   Vol 1: 12323
Racegoers Club   Vol 2: 3833
Radcliffe College - Bunting Institute; Mary Ingraham   Vol 1: 16629
Radical Libertarian Alliance   Vol 2: 3558
Radio Advertising Bureau   Vol 1: 16631
Radio and Television News Directors Association   Vol 1: 16634
Radio Club of America   Vol 1: 16639
Radio Creative Fund   Vol 1: 16633
Radio Denmark   Vol 2: 1990
Radio Exterior de Espana   Vol 2: 11322
Radio France   Vol 2: 5177
Radio France and the City of Tarbes   Vol 2: 6183
Radio Industries Club   Vol 2: 4506
Radio Research Board   Vol 2: 271
Radio Suisse Romande   Vol 2: 11736

Radio Technical Commission for Aeronautics   Vol 1: 16652
Radio Telefis Eireann   Vol 2: 7785, 7823
Radio-Television News Directors Association   Vol 1: 16654
Radio Television Sarajevo   Vol 2: 1401
Radio-Television Suisse Romande   Vol 2: 11678
Radio-Televizija Sarajevo   Vol 2: 1401
Radiodifuziunea Romana   Vol 2: 10326
Radiological Society of North America   Vol 1: 1740, 16658
RAI - Radiotelevisione Italiana   Vol 2: 8412
Railway Tie Association   Vol 1: 16660
Rainbird, Inc.   Vol 1: 4363
Raintree Publishers   Vol 1: 16663
Ralston Purina Company   Vol 1: 9294
Ralston Purina International   Vol 1: 1913
Rampart Institute   Vol 1: 16666
Ramsay Memorial Fellowships Trust   Vol 2: 3836
Ramuz; Fondation C. F.   Vol 2: 11722
Rand Institute; Ayn   Vol 1: 16669
Rand McNally & Company   Vol 1: 1427
Randolph Institute; A. Philip   Vol 1: 16672
Rannsoknarad Rikisins   Vol 2: 7465
Raoul Wallenberg Committee of the United States   Vol 1: 16677
Rapeseed Association of Canada   Vol 1: 7285
Raptor Research Foundation   Vol 1: 16681
Rare Earth Research Conference   Vol 1: 16685
Rashut Hashidur - Kol Yisrael - Yerushalayim   Vol 2: 7916
Rassegna di Palermo/International Sportfilmfestiva   Vol 2: 8312
Rassegna Internazionale dei Documentari Cine - TV Marinari; Italia Sul Mare -   Vol 2: 8294
Rassegna Internazionale del Film di Documentazione Sociale; Festival dei Popoli -   Vol 2: 8238
Rat fur Formgebung   Vol 2: 6802
Rationalisation Group Packaging within the German Management and Productivity Centre   Vol 2: 7077
Rationalisierungs-Gemeinschaft Verpackung im RKW   Vol 2: 7077
Rawlings Sporting Goods Company   Vol 1: 16687
Rawson Academy of Aquatic Science   Vol 1: 16692
Raytheon Company   Vol 1: 16695
Raytheon Corporation   Vol 1: 12060
Reader's Digest Association   Vol 1: 16697
Reader's Digest Foundation   Vol 1: 6536, 17291
Readex Corporation   Vol 1: 2896
Real Academia de Farmacia   Vol 2: 11330
Real Academia Espanola   Vol 2: 11344
Real Estate Educators Association   Vol 1: 16699
Realtors National Marketing Institute - Residential Sales Council   Vol 1: 16708
Reason Foundation   Vol 1: 16714
Recording for the Blind   Vol 1: 16716
Recording Industry Association of America   Vol 1: 16719
Recreation Vehicle Industry Association   Vol 1: 16725
Red Cross; Australian   Vol 2: 11915
Red Cross; International Committee of the   Vol 2: 1528, 11770
Redbook, The Hearst Corporation   Vol 1: 16733
Redd Center for Western Studies; Charles   Vol 1: 16736

Redditch Music Society   Vol 2: 3838
Redheads International and New Style Communications   Vol 1: 16738
Redland Roof Tiles   Vol 2: 3840
Redshaw Ltd.; James   Vol 2: 3576
Reebok International Ltd. - Reebok Human Rights Program   Vol 1: 16743
Reed Methuen Publishers   Vol 2: 9802
Reed Publishing (NZ) Ltd.   Vol 2: 9802
Reference Service Press   Vol 1: 2949
Reference Sources Committee   Vol 1: 2947
REFORMA: National Association to Promote Library Services to the Spanish Speaking   Vol 1: 16745
Refractories Institute   Vol 1: 16747
Regie Autonome des Transports Parisiens   Vol 2: 6150
Region Languedoc Roussilon   Vol 2: 6186
Regional Centre for Seismology for South America   Vol 2: 10017
Regional Council of Auvergne   Vol 2: 6112
Regional Exhibition   Vol 1: 10153
Regional Government of Carinthia   Vol 2: 797
Regional Government of Emilia-Romagna   Vol 2: 8393
Regional Plan Association   Vol 1: 16749
Regione Lombardia   Vol 2: 8166
Regular Veterans Association   Vol 1: 16751
Rehabilitation International   Vol 1: 16755
Reinforced Concrete Research Council   Vol 1: 16759
Religion in American Life   Vol 1: 16761
Religion Newswriters Association   Vol 1: 16765
Religious Heritage of America   Vol 1: 16770
Religious Public Relations Council   Vol 1: 16780
Religious Speech Communication Association   Vol 1: 16782
Remodeling   Vol 1: 13139
Remote Sensing Society   Vol 2: 3842
Renaissance Society of America   Vol 1: 16784
Rencontres chorales internationales de Montreux   Vol 2: 11878
Rencontres Internationales de Chant Choral de Tours   Vol 2: 5191
Rencontres Internationales de la Photographie   Vol 2: 6188
Rencontres Internationales Henri Langlois   Vol 2: 6023
Rencontres Musicales d'Evian   Vol 2: 6191
Renew America   Vol 1: 16786
Renewable Natural Resources Foundation   Vol 1: 16788
Renshaw-Heilman and Associates   Vol 1: 14777
Renton Foundation   Vol 2: 4483
REO Club of America   Vol 1: 16791
Replacement Parts Industrie   Vol 1: 14777
Replacement Parts Industries, Inc.   Vol 1: 5628
Repubblika ta' Malta   Vol 2: 8913
Republic Committee for Science, Technology and Informatics   Vol 2: 1806
Republic of China Motion Picture Development Foundation   Vol 2: 12009
Republic of Croatia - Ministry of Science, Technology and Informatics   Vol 2: 1806
Republic of South Africa - Department of Foreign Affairs   Vol 2: 10913
Republic of South Africa - Department of National Education   Vol 2: 10915
Republic of South Africa - South African Defense Force   Vol 2: 10918
Republic of South Africa - South African Railways Police   Vol 2: 10949

Republic of South Africa - State President's Office   Vol 2: 10957
Republica de Venezuela - Despacho del Presidente   Vol 2: 12135
Republika Hrvatska   Vol 2: 1806
Research & Development   Vol 1: 16793
Research and Development Associates for Military Food and Packaging Systems   Vol 1: 16799
Research and Theory Division of the Association for Educational Communications and Technology   Vol 1: 5516
Research Center for Religion and Human Rights in Closed Societies   Vol 1: 16802
Research Centre for Islamic History, Art and Culture   Vol 2: 12054
Research Corporation   Vol 1: 3446
Research Council of Norway   Vol 2: 9964
Research Foundation for Pharmaceutical Sciences   Vol 2: 8715, 8716, 8719, 8720
Research Institute of Scripps Clinic   Vol 1: 16804
Resistance Welder Manufacturers' Association   Vol 1: 5095
Resistol   Vol 1: 16513
Resort and Commercial Recreation Association   Vol 1: 16806
Resort Condominiums International   Vol 1: 16150
Resource and Information Center for Chinese Studies   Vol 2: 11991
Resources Council Inc.   Vol 1: 10572
Resources for the Future   Vol 1: 16808
Resources Foundation; Renewable Natural   Vol 1: 16788
Restaurant Hospitality   Vol 1: 16811
Retail Advertising Conference   Vol 1: 16813
Retail Council   Vol 1: 15336
Reticuloendothelial Society   Vol 1: 17547
Retirement Research Foundation   Vol 1: 16816
Reunion Internationale des Laboratoires d'Essais et de Recherches sur les Materiaux et les Constructions   Vol 2: 6067
Reunion of Professional Entertainers   Vol 1: 16819
Reuter Foundation   Vol 2: 3849
The Review of Income and Wealth   Vol 2: 3852
Review of Social Economy   Vol 1: 5600
Reynolds Metals Company   Vol 1: 2543
Rheims; Fondation   Vol 2: 5682
Rhode Island Medical Society   Vol 1: 16821
Rhode Island Philharmonic Orchestra   Vol 1: 16823
Rhodes 19 Class Association   Vol 1: 16825
Rhodes College   Vol 1: 16827
Rhyme Time Poetry Newsletter   Vol 1: 16829
Rhythm and Blues Foundation   Vol 1: 16831
Rialp Publishing House   Vol 2: 11326
Ricardo Graph, plc.   Vol 2: 3880
Richard III Society   Vol 1: 16833
Richards Free Library   Vol 1: 16835
Richardson Gold Medal Trust   Vol 2: 3179
RID - USA   Vol 1: 16837
Rielo Foundation; Fernando   Vol 2: 11328
Right Livelihood Awards Foundation   Vol 2: 11508
Rijksakademie van Beeldende Kunsten   Vol 2: 9577
Rijksuniversiteit Limburg   Vol 2: 9680
Riksforbundet Sveriges Amatororkestrar   Vol 2: 11443
Riminicinema International Film Festival   Vol 2: 8414
Riminicinema Mostra Internazionale   Vol 2: 8414

Rinehart Fund; Mary Roberts   Vol 1: 16840
The Ring   Vol 1: 16842
Ringier France SA   Vol 2: 6193
Ripon Society   Vol 1: 16848
Risc - Sauve Qui Peut le Court Metrage   Vol 2: 6195
Rittenhouse Medical Book Store   Vol 1: 12179
Ritz Hotel   Vol 2: 6198
River City   Vol 1: 16852
Road Racing Drivers Club   Vol 1: 18393
Roberts Theatre; Forest   Vol 1: 16855
Robinson Foundation; Jackie   Vol 1: 16857
Robot Institute of America   Vol 1: 16860
Robotic Industries Association   Vol 1: 16860
Roche   Vol 1: 15660
Roche Diagnostic Systems   Vol 1: 852
Roche Laboratories   Vol 1: 3652
Roche Products Ltd.   Vol 2: 4219
Rochester Association for the United Nations   Vol 1: 16862
Rochester Institute of Technology - School of Printing Management and Sciences   Vol 1: 16864
Rochester International Amateur Film Festival   Vol 1: 16868
Rochester International Independent Film Festival   Vol 1: 16868
Rock and Roll Hall of Fame and Museum   Vol 1: 16871
Rockefeller Foundation   Vol 1: 2289, 3424, 8236, 14100
Rockford College   Vol 1: 16873
Rockwell International   Vol 1: 4069, 10411, 13291
Rocky Mountain Book Publishers Association   Vol 1: 16875
Rodeo Cowboys Association   Vol 1: 16507
Rodeo Historical Society   Vol 1: 16877
Roderick Foundation for the Prevention of Inadvertent Nuclear War; Hilliard   Vol 1: 879
Roethke Memorial Foundation; Theodore   Vol 1: 16880
Rohm and Haas Company   Vol 1: 339, 1542
Rohrer, Hibler and Replogle   Vol 1: 3703
Rolex Awards for Enterprise   Vol 2: 11897
Rolex Watch U.S.A.   Vol 1: 10552, 11764
Roll Call Inc.   Vol 1: 16882
Rolling Stone   Vol 1: 16886
Rolls-Royce   Vol 1: 12056
Rolls-Royce Enthusiasts Club   Vol 2: 3854
Romance Writers of America   Vol 1: 16889
Romanian Academy   Vol 2: 10328
Romanian Fine Arts Union   Vol 2: 10393
Romanian Union of Composers and Musicologists   Vol 2: 10405
Romantic Novelists' Association   Vol 2: 3856
Romich Company; Prentke   Vol 1: 11231
Roosevelt Association; Theodore   Vol 1: 16893
Roosevelt Institute; Franklin and Eleanor   Vol 1: 16895
Roosevelt Memorial Association   Vol 1: 16893
Rorer Company; William H.   Vol 1: 8924
Rosary College   Vol 1: 16897
Rose Hybridizers Association   Vol 1: 16900
Rose of Tralee International Festival   Vol 2: 7825
Rosenthal Foundation; Richard and Hinda   Vol 1: 517, 1722
Roshd International Film Festival   Vol 2: 7742
Ross Laboratories   Vol 1: 472, 15661
Ross Trust; Dr. William Baird   Vol 2: 10594
Rossel & Cie; S. A. - Journal *Le Soir*   Vol 2: 1246
Rostropovitch International Cello Competition   Vol 2: 6200

Rotary Club of Houston Foundation   Vol 1: 16903
Rotary International   Vol 1: 16905
Rothko Chapel   Vol 1: 16908
Rotorua Maori Arts and Crafts Institute   Vol 2: 9764
Rotterdam Arts Council   Vol 2: 9579
Rotterdam Arts Foundation   Vol 2: 9438
Rotterdam Maaskant Foundation   Vol 2: 9582
Rotterdamse Kunststichting   Vol 2: 9579
Roucoules; Fondation   Vol 2: 5804
Rouen Festival of Books for the Young   Vol 2: 6202
ROUNDALAB   Vol 1: 16911
Roussel-Uclaf   Vol 2: 6204
Routledge   Vol 2: 3859
Rowland Company   Vol 1: 16915
Royal Academy for Sciences, Letters and Fine Arts of Belgium   Vol 2: 1248
Royal Academy of Arts   Vol 2: 3862
Royal Academy of Dancing   Vol 2: 3866
Royal Academy of Dramatic Art   Vol 2: 3872
Royal Academy of Dutch Language and Literature   Vol 2: 1263
Royal Academy of Engineering   Vol 2: 3874
Royal Academy of Fine Arts   Vol 2: 11510
Royal Academy of French Language and Literature   Vol 2: 1281
Royal Academy of Medicine   Vol 2: 1308
Royal Academy of Medicine - Health Research Board   Vol 2: 7831
Royal Academy of Medicine in Ireland   Vol 2: 7828
Royal Academy of Medicine of Belgium   Vol 2: 1322
Royal Academy of Music   Vol 2: 3876
Royal Academy of Pharmacy   Vol 2: 11330
Royal Aeronautical Society   Vol 2: 3879
Royal Agricultural Society of England   Vol 2: 3916
Royal Agriculture Society of England   Vol 2: 2691
Royal Amateur Orchestral Society   Vol 2: 4114
Royal and Ancient Golf Club of St. Andrews   Vol 2: 10596
Royal Anthropological Institute of Great Britain and Ireland   Vol 2: 3925
Royal Architectural Institute of Canada   Vol 1: 16917
Royal Asiatic Society   Vol 2: 3932
Royal Asiatic Society of Sri Lanka   Vol 2: 11413
Royal Association for Disability and Rehabilitation   Vol 2: 2037
Royal Astronomical Society   Vol 2: 3936
Royal Astronomical Society of Canada   Vol 1: 16925
Royal Australasian College of Dental Surgeons   Vol 2: 588
Royal Australasian College of Radiologists   Vol 2: 591
Royal Australasian College of Surgeons   Vol 2: 594
Royal Australian Chemical Institute   Vol 2: 431, 596
Royal Australian College of General Practitioners   Vol 2: 604
Royal Australian Historical Society   Vol 2: 606
Royal Australian Institute of Architects   Vol 2: 608
Royal Australian Institute of Public Administration   Vol 2: 142
Royal Automobile Club   Vol 2: 3943
Royal Bank of Canada   Vol 1: 16932, 18750

Royal Bath and West of England Society   Vol 2: 3945
Royal Belgian Numismatic Society   Vol 2: 1344
Royal Blind Society of New South Wales   Vol 2: 611
Royal Canadian Geographical Society   Vol 1: 16934
Royal Canadian Legion   Vol 1: 7075
Royal Carillon School Jef Denyn   Vol 2: 1346
Royal College of General Practitioners   Vol 2: 7283
Royal College of Obstetricians and Gynaecologists   Vol 2: 3948
Royal College of Pathologists of Australasia   Vol 2: 613
Royal College of Physicians and Surgeons of Canada   Vol 1: 16937
Royal College of Physicians and Surgeons of Glasgow   Vol 2: 10598
Royal College of Psychiatrists   Vol 2: 3958
Royal College of Radiologists   Vol 2: 3971
Royal College of Surgeons of Edinburgh   Vol 2: 10605
Royal College of Surgeons of England   Vol 2: 3973
Royal College of Veterinary Surgeons   Vol 2: 3982
Royal Commonwealth Society   Vol 2: 3996
Royal Court Theatre   Vol 2: 2859
Royal Danish Geographical Society   Vol 2: 1996
Royal Danish Theatre   Vol 2: 2002
Royal Dublin Society   Vol 2: 7795, 7833
Royal Dutch Geographical Society   Vol 2: 9585
Royal Dutch Shell Company   Vol 2: 9392
Royal Economic Society   Vol 2: 3999
Royal Entomological Society of Belgium   Vol 2: 1349
Royal Entomological Society of London   Vol 2: 4001
Royal Exchange Theatre Company Manchester   Vol 2: 4003
Royal Film Archive of Belgium   Vol 2: 1351
Royal Geographical Society   Vol 2: 4005
Royal Geographical Society of Queensland   Vol 2: 615
Royal Geological and Mining Society of the Netherlands   Vol 2: 9587
Royal Hibernian Academy of Arts   Vol 2: 7836
Royal Highland and Agricultural Society of Scotland   Vol 2: 2691, 10624
Royal Historical Society   Vol 2: 4018
Royal Horticultural Society   Vol 2: 4022
Royal Humane Society   Vol 2: 4065
Royal Incorporation of Architects in Scotland   Vol 2: 10609
Royal Institute   Vol 2: 12028
Royal Institute of British Architects   Vol 2: 2886, 3686, 4067
Royal Institute of British Architects and The Times   Vol 2: 4072
Royal Institute of Dutch Architects   Vol 2: 9589
Royal Institute of Navigation   Vol 2: 4074
Royal Institute of Public Administration   Vol 2: 4080
Royal Institute of Public Health   Vol 2: 4082
Royal Institute of Public Health and Hygiene   Vol 2: 4082
Royal Institution of Chartered Surveyors   Vol 2: 4084
Royal Institution of Great Britain   Vol 2: 4086
Royal Institution of Naval Architects   Vol 2: 3236, 4088
Royal Irish Academy   Vol 2: 7838

Royal Life Saving Society U.K.   Vol 2: 4099
Royal Mail Streamline   Vol 2: 2331
Royal Melbourne Institute of Technology   Vol 2: 618
Royal Meteorological Society   Vol 2: 4102
Royal Musical Association   Vol 2: 4106
Royal National Eisteddfod of Wales   Vol 2: 12184
Royal National Rose Society   Vol 2: 4108
Royal Neighbors of America   Vol 1: 16942
Royal Netherlands Academy of Arts and Sciences   Vol 2: 9592
Royal Netherlands Association of Musicians   Vol 2: 9606
Royal Netherlands Chemical Society   Vol 2: 9608
Royal New Zealand Aero Club   Vol 2: 9806
Royal Northern College of Music   Vol 2: 4110
Royal Norwegian Society of Sciences and Letters   Vol 2: 9967
Royal Nova Scotia Historical Society   Vol 1: 16945
Royal N.S. Historical Society - Genealogical Committee   Vol 1: 9514
Royal Orchestral Society for Amateur Musicians   Vol 2: 4114
Royal Over-Seas League   Vol 2: 4116
Royal Palace Foundation, Amsterdam   Vol 2: 9611
Royal Philatelic Society, London   Vol 2: 4118
Royal Philharmonic Society   Vol 2: 4124
Royal Photographic Society of Great Britain   Vol 2: 4129
Royal Physiographical Society of Lund   Vol 2: 11512
Royal School of Church Music   Vol 2: 4138
Royal Scottish Academy of Painting, Sculpture and Architecture   Vol 2: 10618
Royal Scottish Automobile Club   Vol 2: 10620
Royal Scottish Forestry Society   Vol 2: 10622
Royal Scottish Geographical Society   Vol 2: 10627
Royal Society   Vol 2: 1210, 3236, 3555, 4140
Royal Society for Nature Conservation   Vol 2: 4160
Royal Society for the Mentally Handicapped Children and Adults   Vol 2: 4162
Royal Society for the Prevention of Accidents   Vol 2: 4164
Royal Society for the Protection of Birds   Vol 2: 4174, 4650
Royal Society, London   Vol 2: 5065
Royal Society of British Artists   Vol 2: 4176
Royal Society of British Sculptors   Vol 2: 4179
Royal Society of Canada   Vol 1: 16947
Royal Society of Chemistry   Vol 2: 4182
Royal Society of Edinburgh   Vol 2: 10636
Royal Society of Health   Vol 2: 4225
Royal Society of Literature   Vol 2: 4230
Royal Society of London   Vol 1: 16968
Royal Society of Medicine   Vol 2: 4234
Royal Society of New South Wales   Vol 2: 621
Royal Society of New Zealand   Vol 2: 9834
Royal Society of South Africa   Vol 2: 10964
Royal Society of South Australia   Vol 2: 631
Royal Society of Tasmania   Vol 2: 633
Royal Society of Tropical Medicine and Hygiene   Vol 2: 4275
Royal Society of Victoria   Vol 2: 637
Royal Society of Western Australia   Vol 2: 639
Royal South Australian Society of Arts   Vol 2: 641
Royal Spanish Academy   Vol 2: 11344
Royal Swedish Academy of Engineering Sciences   Vol 2: 11522

Royal Swedish Academy of Music   Vol 2: 11529
Royal Swedish Academy of Sciences   Vol 2: 11475, 11496, 11498, 11531
Royal Television Society   Vol 2: 4282
Royal Town Planning Institute   Vol 2: 4289, 10653
Royal Ulster Agricultural Society   Vol 2: 2691
Royal United Services Institute for Defence Studies   Vol 2: 4293
Royal Watercolour Society   Vol 2: 4296
Royal Welsh Agricultural Society   Vol 2: 2691, 12187
Royal Western Australian Historical Society   Vol 2: 643
Royal Western Yacht Club   Vol 1: 18331
Royal Yachting Association   Vol 2: 4298
Royal Zoological Society of New South Wales   Vol 2: 645
Royce Memorial Foundation; Sir Henry   Vol 2: 3303, 4300
R.R. Bowker   Vol 1: 7000
RSA   Vol 2: 4317
RSA Advertising   Vol 2: 7785
RTL/Poesie 1   Vol 2: 6206
RTZ Corporation   Vol 2: 4326
Rubinstein International Music Society; Arthur   Vol 2: 7937
Ruigrok Foundation; J. C.   Vol 2: 9393
Rulfo Latin American and Caribbean Prize for Literature; Juan   Vol 2: 9258
Runyon - Walter Winchell Cancer Fund; Damon   Vol 1: 7283
Runyon - Walter Winchell Foundation; Cancer Research Fund of the Damon   Vol 1: 7283
Rural Ministry Institute   Vol 1: 16969
Rural Sociological Society   Vol 1: 16971
Russell Society; Bertrand   Vol 1: 16977
Russian Academy of Sciences   Vol 2: 7115
Russian Association in International Co-operation and Development   Vol 2: 4352
Russian PEN Club   Vol 2: 7120
Russolo-Pratella; Fondazione   Vol 2: 8260
Rutgers, The State University, Newark Campus   Vol 1: 15312
Ruttenberg Arts Foundation   Vol 1: 9430
Ryan Foundation; Irene   Vol 1: 1760
SA Bibliographic and Information Network   Vol 2: 11061
SA Holstein Friesland Society   Vol 2: 10967
Saatchi & Saatchi Advertising   Vol 2: 7785
SABAM   Vol 2: 1170
SACEM   Vol 2: 5175
Sadoul; Prix Georges   Vol 2: 6169
SAE Aerospace Council   Vol 1: 17779
The Safety Society   Vol 1: 16981
Sahabdeen Trust Foundation; Abdul Majeed Mohamed   Vol 2: 11415
Sahitya Akademi - India   Vol 2: 7536
Sail America   Vol 1: 5120
St. Bonaventure University - Department of Mass Communication   Vol 1: 16986
St. Cecilia Society   Vol 1: 16993
Saint Joan's International Alliance   Vol 2: 1354
St. Joan's International Alliance U.S. Section   Vol 1: 16995
St. John's College   Vol 2: 4328
St. John's University   Vol 1: 12565, 16626
St. Kilda Film Festival   Vol 2: 647
Saint Louis Conservatory of Music   Vol 1: 16997
Saint Louis University   Vol 1: 16999
Sakura Finetek U.S.A. Inc.   Vol 1: 14755
SALALM   Vol 1: 17193
Salem State College   Vol 1: 17006

Salerno International Film Festival   Vol 2: 8416
Sales and Marketing Executives of Greater New York   Vol 1: 17008
Sales Association of the Chemical Industry   Vol 1: 17013
Sales Executives Club of New York   Vol 1: 17008
Salesmen's Association of the American Chemical Industry   Vol 1: 17013
Salmon Unlimited   Vol 1: 17015
Salon du Laboratoire   Vol 2: 6208
Salon DV Livre De Montreal   Vol 1: 17017
Salon Films (HK) Ltd.   Vol 2: 7265
Salters' Institute of Industrial Chemistry   Vol 2: 4331
Saltire Society   Vol 2: 10650
Samahang Pisika ng Pilipinas   Vol 2: 10060
Samiti; Lanka Mahila   Vol 2: 11411
San Angelo Symphony Orchestra   Vol 1: 17021
San Antonio International Keyboard Competition   Vol 1: 17023
San Diego Art Institute   Vol 1: 17025
San Francisco Art Institute International Film & Video Festival   Vol 1: 17028
San Francisco Foundation   Vol 1: 17030
San Francisco International Film Festival   Vol 1: 17038
San Francisco State University - Broadcast Industry Conference   Vol 1: 17040
San Jose State University   Vol 1: 17044
San Jose Studies   Vol 1: 17046
San Juan 21 Class Association   Vol 1: 17049
San Remo Municipality   Vol 2: 8193
San Sebastian International Film Festival   Vol 2: 11350
San Sebastian Underwater Film Cycle   Vol 2: 11352
Sander's Associates   Vol 1: 12067
Sandoz Corporation   Vol 1: 17051
Sandoz Crop Protection   Vol 1: 8944
Sandoz Forschungsinstitut   Vol 2: 877
Sandoz, Inc.   Vol 1: 622
Sandoz Ltd.   Vol 2: 7418
Sandoz Research Institute   Vol 2: 877
Sangeet Natak Akademi - India   Vol 2: 7540
Sankei Shimbun   Vol 2: 8728
Sankei Shinbun-Sha   Vol 2: 8728
Sanremo; Mostra Internazionale del Film d'Autore -   Vol 2: 8296
Santa Barbara Symphony   Vol 1: 17053
Santander International Piano Competition   Vol 2: 11354
Santista Foundation; Moinho   Vol 2: 1495
Sao Paulo International Film Festival   Vol 2: 1498
Sapporo Sports Promotion Corporation   Vol 2: 8730
Sara Lee Corporation   Vol 1: 17055
Sara Lee Foundation   Vol 1: 17057
Sargeson Trust   Vol 2: 9843
Sarnoff Research Center; David   Vol 1: 10288
Sarton Comite van de Rijksuniversiteit Gent   Vol 2: 1356
Sarton Committee of the University of Ghent   Vol 2: 1356
SAS Institute   Vol 1: 17058
Saskatchewan Library Association   Vol 1: 17061
Saskatchewan Music Festival Association   Vol 1: 17063
Saskatchewan Natural History Society   Vol 1: 17066
Saskatchewan Parks, Recreation and Culture   Vol 1: 17070
Saskatchewan Writers Guild   Vol 1: 17072

Saunders Company; W. B.   Vol 1: 3507
Savage Memorial Trust Fund; Leonard J.   Vol 1: 17074
Save and Prosper Educational Trust   Vol 2: 2874, 2913
Save Our Strays   Vol 1: 17076
Save the Children - Canada   Vol 1: 17078
Savez Udruzenja Boraca Narodnooslobodilackog Rata Jugoslavije   Vol 2: 10706
Savings Institutions Marketing Society of America   Vol 1: 9195
SBA Consulting Group   Vol 2: 8732
Scale Dealers Association   Vol 1: 11307
Scan Newsletter   Vol 1: 6162
Scandinavian Collectors Club   Vol 1: 17082
The Scandinavian Journal of Economics   Vol 2: 11561
Scandinavian Packaging Association   Vol 2: 2004
Scandinavian Research Council for Criminology   Vol 2: 11563
Scandinavian Society for Plant Physiology   Vol 2: 11565
Scandinavian Tobacco Company   Vol 2: 1913
Scarecrow Press   Vol 1: 5564
Scarecrow Press, Inc.   Vol 1: 2811
Schenectady Museum and Planetarium   Vol 1: 17089
Schering   Vol 1: 7924
Schering Corporation   Vol 1: 15663, 15664
Schering-Plough Corporation   Vol 1: 1559, 15952
Scheveningen Internationaal Muziek Concours   Vol 2: 9613
Scheveningen International Music Competition   Vol 2: 9613
Schlatter Productions; George   Vol 1: 17091
Schmidheiny Foundation; Max   Vol 2: 11899
Schmidheiny Stiftung; Max   Vol 2: 11899
Schmidt Society; Franz   Vol 2: 879
Schoharie County Arts Council   Vol 1: 17093
Scholastic   Vol 1: 13717
Scholastic   Vol 1: 14550
Scholastic Inc.   Vol 1: 2835
Schomburg Center for Research in Black Culture   Vol 1: 16091
Schonstedt Instrument Company   Vol 1: 1819
School for Cabaret Music and Contemporary Music Theater   Vol 2: 9615
School Library Journal   Vol 1: 2958
School Library Media Specialists of Southeastern New York   Vol 1: 17095
School Management Study Group   Vol 1: 17098
School of American Ballet   Vol 1: 17101
School of American Research   Vol 1: 17103
School of Oriental and African Studies   Vol 2: 4333
School of the Arts Institute of Chicago   Vol 1: 17105
Schot Foundation; Aleida   Vol 2: 9617
Schot Stichting; Aleida   Vol 2: 9617
Schubert Gesellschaft Wien-Lichtental   Vol 2: 881
Schumann Competition; International Robert   Vol 2: 6977
Schumpeter Gesellschaft; Internationale Joseph A.   Vol 2: 6961
Schumpeter Society; International Joseph A.   Vol 2: 6961
Schwartz Foundation; Ruth   Vol 1: 15705
Schweizer Musikedition   Vol 2: 11940
Schweizerische Akademie der Medizinischen Wissenschaften   Vol 2: 11916
Schweizerische Bankgesellschaft   Vol 2: 11950

Schweizerische Gesellschaft fur Biochemie   Vol 2: 11922
Schweizerische Gesellschaft fur Innere Medizin   Vol 2: 11901
Schweizerische Gesellschaft fur Theaterkultur   Vol 2: 11920
Schweizerische Neurologische Gesellschaft   Vol 2: 11942
Schweizerische Schillerstiftung   Vol 2: 11728
Schweizerische Stiftung fur Parapsychologie, Brugg/Biel   Vol 2: 11938
Schweizerischer Lehrerverein   Vol 2: 11946
Schweizerischer Tonkunstlerverein   Vol 2: 11657
Science and Technology Foundation of Japan (JSTF)   Vol 2: 8735
Science Council of British Columbia   Vol 1: 17107
Science Council of Japan   Vol 1: 15891
Science Education Institute   Vol 2: 10056, 10059, 10060
Science Fiction and Fantasy Writers of America, Inc.   Vol 1: 17112
Science Fiction Foundation   Vol 2: 4336
Science Fiction Poetry Association   Vol 1: 17114
Science Fiction Research Association   Vol 1: 17116
Science Fiction Writers of America   Vol 1: 17112
Science Fiction Writers of Earth   Vol 1: 17118
Science Museum, London   Vol 2: 4157
Science Service   Vol 1: 17120
Scientific American, Inc.   Vol 1: 3438
Scientific and Technical Research Council of Turkey (Tubitak)   Vol 2: 12064
Scientific Committee of the Tytgat Prize   Vol 2: 1359
Scientific Group for Space Research   Vol 2: 7214
Scientific Research Society of America   Vol 1: 17270
Scientific Society for Building   Vol 2: 7448
Scientific Society for Telecommunications   Vol 2: 7451
Scientific Society of Mechanical Engineers   Vol 2: 7454
The Scotsman   Vol 2: 10658
Scott Arboretum of Swarthmore College   Vol 1: 17123
Scott, Foresman and Company   Vol 1: 11184
Scott Horticultural Foundation   Vol 1: 17123
Scottish Arts Council   Vol 2: 10659, 10685
Scottish Association of the Institution of Civil Engineers   Vol 2: 10652
Scottish Bowling Association   Vol 2: 10662
Scottish Canoe Association   Vol 2: 10664
Scottish Centre   Vol 2: 3281
Scottish Daily Express   Vol 2: 10539
Scottish Enterprise   Vol 2: 10613
Scottish Football Association   Vol 2: 10667
Scottish Industrial and Trade Exhibitions   Vol 2: 10670
Scottish International Piano Competition   Vol 2: 10672
Scottish Libraries Association   Vol 2: 10518
Scottish Opera   Vol 2: 10674
Scottish Photographic Federation   Vol 2: 10676
Scottish Power PLC   Vol 2: 10663
Scottish Society for the Prevention of Vivisection   Vol 2: 3544
Scottish Tartans Society   Vol 2: 10678
Scrabble Players   Vol 1: 14709
Screen Actors Guild   Vol 1: 17125
Screen Printing Association International   Vol 1: 17127

Scribes   Vol 1: 17134
Scribner's Sons; Charles   Vol 1: 17138
Scripps Howard Foundation   Vol 1: 17142
SCT Corporation   Vol 1: 7417
Sea Grant Association   Vol 1: 17151
Seagram & Sons; Joseph E.   Vol 1: 10711
Seagram's Distillers Company   Vol 1: 17154
Seagram's Distillers Company - Chivas Regal   Vol 1: 17156
Seaplane Pilots Association   Vol 1: 17158
Seastrom Manufacturing Company   Vol 1: 16380
Seattle Art Museum   Vol 1: 17161
Seattle Group Theatre Company   Vol 1: 17163
Seattle International Film Festival   Vol 1: 17165
SECO Technical Control Bureau for Construction   Vol 2: 1361
Second Street Gallery   Vol 1: 17168
Secondary School Admission Test Board   Vol 1: 17170
Secretaria de Comercio y Fomento Industrial   Vol 2: 9260
Secretaria de Desarrollo Urbano y Ecologia   Vol 2: 9262
Secretaria de Education Publica   Vol 2: 9144
Secretariat of the Committee of State Prizes   Vol 2: 10203
Security Equipment Industry Association   Vol 1: 17172
Security Industry Association   Vol 1: 17172
Sekcija Za Spekulativno Umetnost   Vol 2: 10804
Self Help for Hard of Hearing People   Vol 1: 17174
Self-Service Storage Association   Vol 1: 17187
Self Storage Association   Vol 1: 17187
Seliger-Gemeinde   Vol 2: 7079
Selskabet for Naturlarens Udbredelse   Vol 2: 2006
Semaine Internationale de Video de Geneve   Vol 2: 11864
Semaine Internationale du Cinema Naval et de la Mer   Vol 2: 11278
Semaine Nationale des Transports   Vol 1: 14919
Semana Internacional de Cine de Autor   Vol 2: 11302, 11356
Semana Internacional de Cine de Valladolid   Vol 2: 11391
Semana Internacional de Cine Medico y de Educacion Sanitaria   Vol 2: 11268
Semana Internacional de Cine Naval y del Mar   Vol 2: 11278
Semiconductor Equipment and Materials Institute   Vol 1: 17190
Semiconductor Equipment and Materials International   Vol 1: 17190
Seminar on the Acquisition of Latin American Library Materials (SALALM)   Vol 1: 17192
Sempervivium Society   Vol 2: 4338
Senat der Hansestadt Lubeck   Vol 2: 7036
Senate of Berlin   Vol 2: 5096
Sender Freies Berlin   Vol 2: 7073, 7074
Sender Freies Berlin-ARD   Vol 2: 5096
Senigallia International Competition for Pianists   Vol 2: 8418
Senior Executives Association - Professional Development League   Vol 1: 17194
SEPIA   Vol 2: 6210
Serbian Academy of Sciences and Arts   Vol 2: 10723
Serbian PEN Centre   Vol 2: 10725
Serrablo; Museo Angel Orensanz y Artes de   Vol 2: 11306
Sertoma International   Vol 1: 17196

Servicio Cultural de la Caja de Ahorros de la Immaculata   Vol 2: 11166
Sestri Levante Municipality   Vol 2: 8421
Setmana Internacional de Cinema de Barcelona   Vol 2: 11154
Seventeen   Vol 1: 17199
Seventh Day Baptist Historical Society   Vol 1: 17201
Sewanee Review   Vol 1: 17204
SGD Swiss Graphic Designers   Vol 2: 11903
Shakespeare Globe Centre   Vol 1: 17206
Shakespeare Theatre   Vol 1: 17208
Shakespeare Theatre at the Folger   Vol 1: 17208
Shallway Foundation   Vol 1: 17210
Shandon Inc.   Vol 1: 14755
Shandon-Johns Scientific   Vol 1: 7211
Shandon-Lipshaw   Vol 1: 4546
Shandon/Lipshaw   Vol 1: 14750
Sharp Corporation   Vol 1: 17533
Shaw Mudge & Co.   Vol 1: 17830
Shawmut First Bank   Vol 1: 12566
Shazar Center for Jewish History; Zalman - Historical Society of Israel   Vol 2: 7939
Sheldon Laboratory Systems   Vol 1: 14706
Shell Company of Australia   Vol 2: 572
Shell Oil Company Foundation   Vol 1: 13312
Shell Research Ltd.   Vol 2: 4219
Shell South Africa   Vol 2: 10877
Shell UK Ltd.   Vol 2: 3596, 3618, 4219
Shenan Arts   Vol 1: 17212
Shenandoah Playwrights Retreat   Vol 1: 17212
Sherbrooke Art Society   Vol 2: 649
Sherwin-Williams Company   Vol 1: 1510
Shibusawa Foundation for Ethnological Studies   Vol 2: 8737
Shibusawa Memorial Foundation for Ethnology; K.   Vol 2: 8737
Shin Jinbutsu Oraisha Company   Vol 2: 8739
Shin-Norinsha Company Limited of Japan   Vol 2: 4367
Shincho-Sha Publishing Company   Vol 2: 8741
Shinsho Corporation   Vol 1: 5083
Shiras Institute   Vol 1: 16856
Shogakukan   Vol 2: 8746
Shoppers Drug Mart   Vol 1: 7092
Shoraye Ketabe Koudak   Vol 2: 7734
Shreveport Civic Opera   Vol 1: 17217
Shreveport Opera Company   Vol 1: 17217
Shreveport Parks and Recreation/Shreveport Regional Arts Council   Vol 1: 17219
Shuppan Bunka Kokusai Koryukai   Vol 2: 8726
Siam Cement Company   Vol 2: 12025
Sibelius Society of Finland   Vol 2: 4729
Sibelius Viikot (Sibelius Weeks)   Vol 2: 4719
Sibelius Violin Competition; International Jean   Vol 2: 4728
Siegel Houston and Associates, Inc.   Vol 1: 2583
Siemens A.G.   Vol 2: 6665
Siemens AG   Vol 2: 11705
Siena College - Dept. of Fine Arts   Vol 1: 17221
Sierra Club   Vol 1: 17223
Sierra Repertory Theatre   Vol 1: 17248
Sigall Competition; International Musical Contest Dr. Luis   Vol 2: 1569
Sigma Alpha Iota Foundation   Vol 1: 17251
Sigma Alpha Iota Philanthropies   Vol 1: 17251
Sigma Delta Epsilon - Graduate Women in Science   Vol 1: 17253
Sigma Gamma Tau   Vol 1: 17257
Sigma Iota Epsilon   Vol 1: 17259
Sigma Phi Alpha   Vol 1: 17261

Sigma Phi Epsilon Fraternity   Vol 1: 17264
Sigma Pi Sigma Trust Fund   Vol 1: 2666
Sigma Theta Tau International   Vol 1: 17266
Sigma Xi   Vol 1: 17270
Sigma Xi, The Scientific Research Society   Vol 1: 17270
Sigma Zeta   Vol 1: 17274
Sikkens Foundation   Vol 2: 9619
Sikorsky Aircraft   Vol 1: 9900, 12072
Silver Burdett and Ginn, Inc.   Vol 1: 11193
Silver Wings Fraternity   Vol 1: 17276
Silverfish Review   Vol 1: 17278
Silvermine Guild Arts Center   Vol 1: 17280
Simon Fraser University   Vol 1: 17283
Simon Memorial Fund; Andre   Vol 2: 4341
Simpson Hill College Confederate Research Center; H. B.   Vol 1: 17285
Simulation Sciences Inc.   Vol 1: 2572
Sindicato de Trabajadores de Produccion Cinematografica   Vol 2: 9264
Singapore - Office of the Prime Minister   Vol 2: 10735
Singapore Chefs Association   Vol 2: 10751
Singapore Press   Vol 2: 10734
Singermuseum   Vol 2: 9622
Singkreis Porcia-Spittal an der Drau   Vol 2: 797
Single Service Institute   Vol 1: 9300
Sinking Creek Film/Video Festival   Vol 1: 17287
S.I.N.U.S. Association   Vol 2: 6212
Sir Patrick Geddes Memorial Trust   Vol 2: 10653
Sire   Vol 2: 8097
SIRP   Vol 2: 6214
Sister Cities International   Vol 1: 17289
Sister Kenny Institute   Vol 1: 17292
Sitges International Fantasy Film Festival   Vol 2: 11358
Sixteenth Century Studies Conference   Vol 1: 17295
Sjostrands Forlag   Vol 2: 11567
SKF   Vol 2: 12216
Ski Industries America   Vol 1: 17303
Ski Racing   Vol 1: 17305
Slipstream   Vol 1: 17307
Sloan Foundation; Alfred P.   Vol 1: 9449
Slocum Society; Joshua   Vol 1: 17309
Slovak Fund of Creative Arts   Vol 2: 10765
Slovak Literary Fund   Vol 2: 10767
Slovak Music Fund   Vol 2: 10770
Slovak Radio, Bratislava   Vol 2: 10777
Slovak Studies Association   Vol 1: 17319
Slovak Television, Bratislava   Vol 2: 10779
Slovakia - Ministry of Culture, Slovak   Vol 2: 10781
Slovenia Writers Association   Vol 2: 10800
Slovenian Research Center of America and Kent State University Foundation   Vol 1: 17321
Slovenska televizia, Bratislava   Vol 2: 10779
Slovensko Farmacevtsko Drustvo   Vol 2: 10802
Slovensky hudobny fond   Vol 2: 10770
Slovensky Rozhlas, Bratislava   Vol 2: 10777
Slovkoncert, Czechoslovakia Artists Agency   Vol 2: 10783
Slovkoncert, Slovak Artist Management   Vol 2: 10783
Small Business Administration   Vol 1: 6202
Small Business Council of America   Vol 1: 17323
Small Business Foundation of America   Vol 1: 17327
Small Motor Manufacturers Association   Vol 1: 5517

Small Press Writers and Artists Organization   Vol 1: 17329
Smith and Son; W. H.   Vol 2: 4343, 4595, 4649
Smith Breeden Associates   Vol 1: 2055
Smith Corona   Vol 1: 16887
Smith, Kline & French   Vol 1: 15665
Smith Kline Corporation   Vol 1: 4236
Smith Memorial Fund; W. Eugene   Vol 1: 17332
SmithKline Beecham   Vol 2: 1342
SmithKline Beecham Clinical Laboratories   Vol 1: 4548
SmithKline Beecham Corporation   Vol 1: 1550
SmithKline Beecham Pharmaceuticals   Vol 1: 169, 2134
Smithsonian Institution   Vol 1: 17334
Smithsonian Institution - Smithson Society; James   Vol 1: 17347
Smithsonian Women's Committee   Vol 1: 17350
SMM Instruments (Pty) Ltd.   Vol 2: 11075, 11076
Snipe Class International Racing Association   Vol 1: 17352
Soap Opera Digest   Vol 1: 17354
Soaring Society of America   Vol 1: 17356
Soccer Association for Youth   Vol 1: 17371
Soccer Industry Council of America   Vol 1: 17374
Social Issues Resources   Vol 1: 13710
Social Issues Resources Series   Vol 1: 2828, 2832, 2899, 2955, 10786, 11955, 18616
Social Science Research Council   Vol 1: 17376
Social Studies School Service   Vol 1: 13720
Socialist Republic of Croatia   Vol 2: 1806
Sociedad Alfonsina Internacional   Vol 2: 9266
Sociedad Chilena de Dermatologia y Venereologia   Vol 2: 1554
Sociedad Chilena de Historia y Geografia   Vol 2: 1556
Sociedad Colombiana de Ingenieros   Vol 2: 1744
Sociedad Colombiana de Pediatria   Vol 2: 1691
Sociedad Cubana de Matematica y Computacion   Vol 2: 1822
Sociedad de Autores y Compositores de Musica   Vol 2: 9269
Sociedad de Cosmetologos de Mexico   Vol 2: 9271
Sociedad de Turismo de Antioquia S.A. Turantioquia   Vol 2: 1585
Sociedad General de Autores de Espana   Vol 2: 11249
Sociedad General de Autores de la Argentina   Vol 2: 29
Sociedad General de Autores Espanoles   Vol 2: 11140
Sociedad General de Escritores de Mexico   Vol 2: 9273
Sociedad Geografica de Lima   Vol 2: 10015
Sociedad Interamericana de Cardiologia   Vol 2: 9072
Sociedad Interamericana de Prensa   Vol 1: 10510
Sociedad Mexicana de Cardiologia   Vol 2: 9275
Sociedad Mexicana de Historia de La Ciencia y de La Tecnologia   Vol 2: 9121
Sociedad Mexicana de Matematicas   Vol 2: 9281
Sociedad para la Preservacion de la Fauna y Flora   Vol 2: 2865
Sociedad Quimica de Mexico   Vol 2: 8947
Sociedad Venezolana de Geologos   Vol 2: 12143

Sociedad Venezolana de Ingenieros Civiles   Vol 2: 12147
Sociedade Brasileira de Realizacoes Artistico-Culturais   Vol 2: 1452
Sociedade Brasileira para o Progresso da ciencia   Vol 2: 1427
Sociedade de Geografia de Lisboa   Vol 2: 10316
Sociedade Portuguese de Autores   Vol 2: 10318
Societa Arcantorie   Vol 1: 7592
Societa Chimica Italiana   Vol 2: 8335
Societa del Quartetto   Vol 2: 8424
Societa Editrice Internazionale   Vol 2: 8187
Societa Geologica Italiana   Vol 2: 8426
Societa Incremento Toristico Alberghiero Valdostano   Vol 2: 8428
Societa Italiana delle Scienze   Vol 2: 8376
Societa Italiana di Nipiologia   Vol 2: 8430
Societa Olivetti   Vol 2: 8389
Societas Biochemica, Biophysica Microbiologica Fenniae   Vol 2: 4670
Societas Internationalis Limnologiae   Vol 1: 10789
Societas Ophthalmologica Europaea   Vol 2: 1134
Societas Physiologiae Plantarum Scandinavica   Vol 2: 11565
Societe Astronomique de France   Vol 2: 6216
Societe Belge des Auteurs, Compositeurs et Editeurs   Vol 2: 1070
Societe Beneluxienne de Phlebologie   Vol 2: 1088
Societe Botanique de France   Vol 2: 4992
Societe canadienne de genie mecanique   Vol 1: 7133
Societe Canadienne de Genie Rural   Vol 1: 7145
Societe Canadienne de Geotechnique   Vol 1: 6891
Societe Canadienne de Pediatrie   Vol 1: 7078
Societe canadienne des auteurs, compositeurs, et editeurs de musique   Vol 1: 17819
Societe Canadienne des Microbiologistes   Vol 1: 7214
Societe canadienne des relations publiques   Vol 1: 7111
Societe Canadienne pour la Recherche Nautique   Vol 1: 7069
Societe Canadienne pour les Traditions Musicales   Vol 1: 7140
Societe Celine   Vol 2: 6231
Societe Chimique de Belgique   Vol 2: 1364
Societe d'Anthropologie de Paris   Vol 2: 4895
Societe de Chimie Biologique   Vol 2: 6233
Societe de Chimie Industrielle   Vol 2: 6356
Societe de Chimie Therapeutique   Vol 2: 6237
Societe de Geographie de Geneve   Vol 2: 11905
Societe de musique des universites canadiennes   Vol 1: 7254
Societe de Numismatique de Belgique   Vol 2: 1344
Societe de Pathologie Exotique   Vol 2: 6240
Societe des Amis d'Alexandre Dumas   Vol 2: 6243
Societe des Amis de Maurice Edgar Coindreau   Vol 2: 6245
Societe des Amis d'Honore de Balzac   Vol 2: 6247
Societe des Auteurs, Compositeurs, Editeurs de Musique   Vol 2: 6249
Societe des Auteurs et Compositeurs Dramatiques   Vol 2: 6394
Societe des Gens de Lettres de France   Vol 2: 6246, 6259

Societe des Poetes et Artistes de France Vol 2: 6301
Societe des Poetes Francais Vol 2: 6303
Societe d'Etude du XVII Siecle Vol 2: 6345
Societe du Comte Dracula Vol 2: 2752
Societe du Tour de France Ltd. Vol 2: 6347
Societe Europeene de Radiologie-Pediatrie Vol 2: 5129
Societe Europeenne de Chirurgie Cardiovasculaire Vol 2: 5127
Societe Europeenne de Culture Vol 2: 8232
Societe Francaise D'Acoustique Vol 2: 6349
Societe Francaise de Chimie Vol 2: 6355
Societe Francaise de Numismatique Vol 2: 6360
Societe Francaise de Physique Vol 2: 6363, 6372, 6660
Societe Francaise des Traducteurs Vol 2: 6278
Societe Generale Vol 2: 6382
Societe Geologique de Belgique Vol 2: 1056
Societe Geologique de France Vol 2: 5302
Societe historique du Canada Vol 1: 6902
Societe Internationale de chimiotherapie Vol 2: 9897
Societe Internationale de Chirurgie Vol 2: 11843
Societe Internationale de Droit Penal Militaire et de Droit de la Guerre Vol 2: 1203
Societe Internationale de Mecanique des Roches Vol 2: 10239
Societe Internationale de Neurochimie Vol 2: 1966
Societe Internationale de Transfusion Sanguine Vol 2: 3476
Societe Internationale d'Electrochimie Vol 2: 11839
Societe Internationale d'Enzymologie Clinique Vol 1: 11236
Societe Internationale des Filarioses Vol 2: 3423
Societe Internationale d'Oncologie Pediatrique Vol 2: 9527
Societe Internationale pour la Recherche sur les Maladies de Civilisation et l'Environnement Vol 2: 1205
Societe Internationale pour l'Education Artistique Vol 2: 3466
Societe Internationale Pour les Hydroglisseurs Vol 2: 3429
Societe Protex Vol 2: 6385
Societe quebecoise pour la promotion de la litterature de langue anglaise Vol 1: 16621
Societe Royale Belge d'Entomologie Vol 2: 1349
Societe Royale de Chimie Vol 2: 1364
Societe Royale des Sciences de Liege Vol 2: 1367
Societe royale du Canada Vol 1: 16947
Societe Saint-Jean-Baptiste de la Mauricie Vol 1: 17378
Societe Saint-Jean-Baptiste de Montreal Vol 1: 17381
Societe Shering Vol 2: 5241
Societe Suisse de Radiodiffusion et Television et la Ville de Montreux Vol 2: 11924
Societes de Statistique de Paris et de France Vol 2: 6387
Society for Adolescent Medicine Vol 1: 17394
Society for Advancement of Management Vol 1: 17399
Society for Advancement of the Handicapped Vol 1: 89
Society for American Baseball Research Vol 1: 17408
Society for Animal Rights Vol 1: 11226
Society for Applied Anthropology Vol 1: 797

Society for Applied Bacteriology Vol 2: 4347
Society for Applied Spectroscopy Vol 1: 15752, 17413
Society for Army Historical Research Vol 2: 4349
Society for Behavioral Pediatrics Vol 1: 17422
Society for Biomaterials Vol 1: 17424
Society for Cinema Studies Vol 1: 17428
Society for Clinical and Experimental Hypnosis Vol 1: 17431
Society for Co-operation in Russian and Soviet Studies Vol 2: 4351
Society for Collegiate Journalists Vol 1: 17440
Society for Cultural Relations with the USSR Vol 2: 4351
Society for Diagnostic Medical Sonographers Vol 1: 17444
Society for Drug Research Vol 2: 4359
Society for Economic Botany Vol 1: 17447
Society for Educational Reconstruction Vol 1: 17450
Society for Environmental Graphic Design Vol 1: 17452
Society for Epidemiologic Research Vol 1: 17454
Society for Ethnomusicology Vol 1: 17456
Society for Film Art in Tampere Vol 2: 4757
Society for French Historical Studies Vol 1: 17460
Society for General Microbiology Vol 2: 4353
Society for Health and Human Values Vol 1: 17462
Society for Historians of American Foreign Relations Vol 1: 17464
Society for Historians of the Early American Republic Vol 1: 17470
Society for History in the Federal Government Vol 1: 17473
Society for Human Resource Management Vol 1: 17479
Society for Humanistic Anthropology Vol 1: 17492
Society for Humanistic Judaism Vol 1: 17494
Society for Imaging Science and Technology Vol 1: 15751, 17496
Society for Industrial and Applied Mathematics Vol 1: 3003, 3011, 17509
Society for Industrial Archeology Vol 1: 17522
Society for Industrial Microbiology Vol 1: 17524
Society for Information Display Vol 1: 17529
Society for International Numismatics Vol 1: 17538
Society for Investigative Dermatology Vol 1: 17541
Society for Italian Historical Studies Vol 1: 2297, 17543
Society for Italic Handwriting Vol 2: 4357
Society for Leukocyte Biology Vol 1: 17547
Society for Medicinal Plant Research Vol 2: 7081
Society for Medicines Research Vol 2: 4359
Society for Medieval Archaeology Vol 2: 4361
Society for Military History Vol 1: 17553
Society for Mining, Metallurgy, and Exploration Vol 1: 17558
Society for Nautical Research Vol 2: 4365
Society for Nondestructive Testing Vol 1: 4213
Society for Pediatric Dermatology Vol 1: 17582
Society for Range Management Vol 1: 17585

Society for Research into Higher Education Vol 2: 4367
Society for Research into Hydrocephalus and Spina Bifida Vol 2: 4369
Society for Sedimentary Geology Vol 1: 17589
Society for Sex Therapy and Research Vol 1: 17599
Society for Social Studies of Science Vol 1: 17601
Society for Spanish and Portuguese Historical Studies Vol 1: 17605
Society for Spinal Research Vol 2: 7083
Society for Technical Communication Vol 1: 17607
Society for the Advancement of Anaesthesia in Dentistry Vol 2: 4371
Society for the Advancement of the Arts and Film Vol 1: 20327, 20329
Society for the Dissemination of Natural Science Vol 2: 2006
Society for the Family of Man Vol 1: 17611
Society for the History of Alchemy and Chemistry Vol 2: 4373
Society for the History of Technology Vol 1: 17614
Society for the Preservation of American Business History Vol 1: 20073
Society for the Preservation of Bluegrass Music of America Vol 1: 17622
Society for the Preservation of Film Music Vol 1: 17624
Society for the Preservation of Old Mills Vol 1: 17626
Society for the Promotion of African, Asian and Latin American Literature Vol 2: 6923
Society for the Promotion of Art and the City of Karlsruhe Vol 2: 7085
Society for the Promotion of Japanese Literature Vol 2: 8749
Society for the Promotion of New Music Vol 2: 4375
Society for the Psychological Study of Ethnic Minority Issues Vol 1: 17628
Society for the Psychological Study of Social Issues Vol 1: 17630
Society for the Scientific Study of Sex Vol 1: 17634
Society for the Study of Amphibians and Reptiles Vol 1: 17637
Society for the Study of Evolution Vol 1: 17639
Society for the Study of Inborn Errors of Metabolism Vol 2: 4377
Society for the Study of Social Problems Vol 1: 17641
Society for the Study of Southern Literature Vol 1: 17644
Society for the Study of Symbolic Interaction, SSSI Vol 1: 17647
Society for Theatre Research Vol 2: 4379
Society for Traumatic Stress Studies Vol 1: 17651
Society for Utopian Studies Vol 1: 17653
Society for Women in Philosophy Vol 1: 17656
Society of Actuaries Vol 1: 17658
Society of Allied Weight Engineers, Inc. Vol 1: 17662
Society of American Archivists Vol 1: 17668
Society of American Florists Vol 1: 17679
Society of American Foresters Vol 1: 17682
Society of American Graphic Artists Vol 1: 17692
Society of American Historians Vol 1: 17694
Society of American Law Teachers Vol 1: 17698

Society of American Military Engineers   Vol 1: 17700
Society of American Registered Architects   Vol 1: 17722
Society of American Travel Writers   Vol 1: 17733
Society of American Travel Writers Foundation   Vol 1: 17735, 17736
Society of Antiquaries of London   Vol 2: 4382
Society of Antiquaries of Scotland   Vol 2: 10680
Society of Applied Botany   Vol 2: 7087
Society of Architects   Vol 2: 8760
Society of Architects in Wales   Vol 2: 12189
Society of Architectural and Associated Technicians   Vol 2: 2394
Society of Architectural Historians   Vol 1: 17737
Society of Australasian Specialists   Vol 1: 17747
Society of Australasian Specialists/Oceania   Vol 1: 17747
Society of Australian Film and Television Arts and Sciences   Vol 2: 652
Society of Authors   Vol 2: 4385, 4396, 4397, 4398
Society of Authors - Translators Association   Vol 2: 4395
Society of Authors, Composers and Music Publishers in Israel   Vol 2: 7941
Society of Authors (ZAiKS)   Vol 2: 10205
Society of Automotive Engineers   Vol 1: 18915
Society of Automotive Engineers - Australasia   Vol 2: 654
Society of Automotive Engineers, Inc.   Vol 1: 17749
Society of Automotive Historians   Vol 1: 17781
Society of Biological Psychiatry   Vol 1: 17788
Society of Cable Television Engineers   Vol 1: 17794
Society of Canadian Ornithologists   Vol 1: 17797
Society of Cardiovascular Anesthesiologists   Vol 1: 17799
Society of Certified Credit Executives   Vol 1: 10896
Society of Chemical Industry   Vol 2: 4186, 4399
Society of Chemical Industry - American Section   Vol 1: 17801
Society of Chemical Industry - Canadian Section   Vol 1: 17804
Society of Children's Book Writers   Vol 1: 17810
Society of Clinical Ecology   Vol 1: 559
Society of Colonial Wars   Vol 1: 17814
Society of Commercial Seed Technologists   Vol 1: 17816
Society of Community Medicine   Vol 2: 4459
Society of Company Meeting Planners   Vol 1: 17822
Society of Composers, Authors and Music Publishers of Canada   Vol 1: 17819
Society of Corporate Meeting Professionals   Vol 1: 17822
Society of Cosmetic Chemists   Vol 1: 17825
Society of Czech Architects   Vol 2: 1881
Society of Designer-Craftsmen   Vol 2: 4428
Society of Die Casting Engineers   Vol 1: 15411
Society of Dramatic Authors and Composers   Vol 2: 6394
Society of Dyers and Colourists   Vol 2: 4431
Society of Economic Geologists   Vol 1: 17831
Society of Economic Paleontologists and Mineralogists   Vol 1: 17589
Society of Engineering Illustrators   Vol 1: 17833
Society of Engineers   Vol 2: 4440
Society of Environmental Graphic Designers   Vol 1: 17452
Society of Experimental Test Pilots   Vol 1: 17835
Society of Exploration Geophysicists   Vol 1: 17840
Society of Exploration Geophysicists of Japan   Vol 2: 8755
Society of Film and Television Arts   Vol 2: 2231
Society of Fire Protection Engineers   Vol 1: 17850
Society of Flight Test Engineers   Vol 1: 17854
Society of Forensic Toxicologists   Vol 1: 17857
Society of Friends of Music - Vienna   Vol 2: 883
Society of Friends of the Polish Language   Vol 2: 10209
Society of German Cooks   Vol 2: 7089
Society of Illinois Bacteriologists   Vol 1: 10082
Society of Illustrators   Vol 1: 17859
Society of Indexers   Vol 2: 3574, 4446
Society of Industrial and Applied Mathematics   Vol 2: 9548
Society of Industrial Artists and Designers   Vol 2: 2606
Society of Insurance Research   Vol 1: 17861
Society of Laboratory Animal Science   Vol 2: 11907
Society of Logistics Engineers   Vol 1: 17864
Society of Magazine Writers   Vol 1: 4632
Society of Manufacturing Engineers   Vol 1: 17875
Society of Medical Dental Management Consultants   Vol 1: 17890
Society of Medical Friends of Wine   Vol 1: 17892
Society of Medical Laboratory Technologists of South Africa   Vol 2: 10969
Society of Metaphysicians   Vol 2: 4449
Society of Mexican-American Engineers and Scientists   Vol 1: 17894
Society of Midland Authors   Vol 1: 17896
Society of Motion Picture and Television Engineers   Vol 1: 17898
Society of Municipal Arborists   Vol 1: 17914
Society of National Association Publications   Vol 1: 17917
Society of Naval Architects and Marine Engineers   Vol 1: 17775, 17919
Society of Nematologists   Vol 1: 17932
Society of Netherlands Literature   Vol 2: 9624
Society of Newspaper Design   Vol 1: 17939
Society of Newspaper Designers   Vol 1: 17939
Society of Norwegian Composers   Vol 2: 9969
Society of Nuclear Medicine   Vol 1: 17941
Society of Ornamental Turners   Vol 2: 4451
Society of Packaging and Handling Engineers   Vol 1: 10424
Society of Petroleum Engineers   Vol 1: 17958
Society of Petroleum Engineers of the American Institute of Mining, Metallurgical and Petroleum Engineers   Vol 1: 17958
Society of Philatelists and Numismatists   Vol 1: 17977
Society of Photographic Scientists and Engineers   Vol 1: 17496
Society of Physics Students   Vol 1: 2657, 2663, 2666
Society of Plastics Engineers   Vol 1: 17981
Society of Professional Investigators   Vol 1: 17992
Society of Professional Journalists   Vol 1: 8546, 8547, 17994
Society of Professional Journalists First Amendment Center   Vol 1: 18004
Society of Professional Well Log Analysts   Vol 1: 18006
Society of Public Health   Vol 2: 4459
Society of Publication Designers   Vol 1: 18013
Society of Ration Token Collectors   Vol 1: 18016
Society of Real Estate Appraisers   Vol 1: 5189
Society of Recreation Executives   Vol 1: 18021
Society of Reliability Engineers   Vol 1: 18023
Society of Research Administrators   Vol 1: 18027
Society of Rheology   Vol 1: 18032
Society of Southwest Archivists   Vol 1: 17674
Society of Surgical Oncology   Vol 1: 18034
Society of Swiss Cuisiniers   Vol 2: 11910
Society of Systematic Biologists   Vol 1: 18039
Society of Systematic Zoology   Vol 1: 18039
Society of Technical Writers and Publishers   Vol 1: 17607
Society of the Cincinnati   Vol 1: 18041
Society of the Friends of History   Vol 2: 4755
Society of the Plastics Industry   Vol 1: 12409, 18043
Society of the Silurians   Vol 1: 18064
Society of Toxicology   Vol 1: 6638, 18067
Society of Tribologists and Lubrication Engineers   Vol 1: 18078
Society of United States Air Force Flight Surgeons   Vol 1: 18086
Society of USAF Flight Surgeons of the Aerospace Medical Association   Vol 1: 177
Society of Vertebrate Paleontology   Vol 1: 18089
Society of West End Theatre   Vol 2: 4465
Society of Wildlife Artists   Vol 2: 4467
Society of Woman Geographers   Vol 1: 18095
Society of Women Engineers   Vol 1: 18098
Society of Women Writers Australia   Vol 2: 661
Society of Wood Science and Technology   Vol 1: 18105
Society of Writers of Macedonia   Vol 2: 8875
Sociological Practice Association   Vol 1: 18108
Sofia International Film Festival on Organization and Automation of Production and Management   Vol 2: 1529
Software Maintenance Association   Vol 1: 18110
Software Management Association   Vol 1: 18110
Software Publishers Association   Vol 1: 15998, 18114
Soho Poly Theatre   Vol 2: 4469
Soil and Water Conservation Society   Vol 1: 18121
Soil Association   Vol 2: 4471
Soil Conservation Society of America   Vol 1: 18121
Soil Science Society of America   Vol 1: 18129
Solar Energy Industries Association   Vol 1: 18138
Solothurner Filmtage   Vol 2: 11912
Solvay Duphar   Vol 1: 3717
Somaini; Fondazione Francesco   Vol 2: 8242
Sondrio; Provincia di   Vol 2: 7998

Sondrio Town Council International Festival of Documentary Films on Parks   Vol 2: 8432
Songwriters Guild of America   Vol 1: 18141
Songwriters' Resources and Services   Vol 1: 12700
Sonic Arts Network   Vol 2: 4474
Sonning Foundation   Vol 2: 2010
Sonning Music Foundation; Leonie   Vol 2: 2008
Sonnings Musikfond; Leonie   Vol 2: 2008
Sonora Review   Vol 1: 18143
Sons of the Republic of Texas   Vol 1: 18146
Sons of the Revolution in the State of New York   Vol 1: 18149
Sony Broadcast   Vol 2: 4476
Sony Corporation   Vol 2: 8758
Sony Corporation of America   Vol 1: 2053, 10270
Sony Foundation of Science Education   Vol 2: 8757
Sony Industrial   Vol 2: 9670
Soroptimist International of the Americas   Vol 1: 18151
Soroptimist International of the South West Pacific   Vol 2: 667
Soros Foundation   Vol 2: 7416
Soul Train Music Awards   Vol 1: 18154
Sounds Australian - Australian Music Centre Ltd.   Vol 2: 669
Source Theatre Company   Vol 1: 18156
Sousa Foundation; John Philip   Vol 1: 18159
South African Academy of Science and Arts   Vol 2: 10984
South African Association for Learning and Educational Disabilities   Vol 2: 11014
South African Association for the Advancement of Science   Vol 2: 11016
South African Association of Botanists   Vol 2: 11021
South African Association of Consulting Engineers   Vol 2: 11025
South African Association of Occupational Therapists   Vol 2: 11027
South African Association of University Women   Vol 2: 11029
South African Biological Society   Vol 2: 11031
South African Broadcasting Corporation   Vol 2: 11036
South African Chemical Institute   Vol 2: 11044
South African Geographical Society   Vol 2: 11052
South African Institute for Librarianship and Information Science   Vol 2: 11056
South African Institute of Civil Engineering Technicians and Technologists   Vol 2: 11065
South African Institute of Civil Engineers   Vol 2: 11065
South African Institute of Electrical Engineers   Vol 2: 11067
South African Institute of Physics   Vol 2: 11069
South African National Committee on Illumination   Vol 2: 11078
South African National Council for the Blind   Vol 2: 11081
South African Optical Society   Vol 2: 11083
South African Society for Plant Pathology   Vol 2: 11102
South African Society for Plant Pathology and Microbiology   Vol 2: 11102
South African Society of Dairy Technology   Vol 2: 11085
South African Society of Music Teachers   Vol 2: 11087
South African Sugar Technologists' Association   Vol 2: 11089

South African Veterinary Association   Vol 2: 11091
South Asia Council   Vol 1: 5442
South Atlantic Modern Language Association   Vol 1: 18169
South Australia - Ministry for the Arts and Cultural Heritage   Vol 2: 672
South Australian Council for Children's Films and Television   Vol 2: 675
South Australian Film and Video Centre   Vol 2: 674
South Australian Photographic Federation   Vol 2: 676
South Carolina Arts Commission   Vol 1: 18172
South Carolina Association of School Librarians   Vol 1: 18174
South Carolina Department of Parks, Recreation and Tourism   Vol 1: 18176
South Dakota Library Association   Vol 1: 18178
South East Asia Iron and Steel Institute   Vol 2: 10062
South Publications (UK)   Vol 2: 4478
Southam Foundation   Vol 1: 19882
Southdown Press - *TV Week*   Vol 2: 678
Southeast A. Arkansas Arts & Science Center   Vol 1: 5319
Southeast Asian Ministers of Education Organization   Vol 2: 12030
Southeast Booksellers Association   Vol 1: 18180
Southeastern American Society for Eighteenth-Century Studies   Vol 1: 18182
Southeastern Center for Contemporary Art   Vol 1: 18184
Southeastern Composers' League   Vol 1: 18186
Southeastern Conference   Vol 1: 18189
Southeastern Library Association   Vol 1: 18191
Southeastern Surgical Congress   Vol 1: 18199
Southeastern Surgical Nurses Association   Vol 1: 18202
Southeastern Theatre Conference   Vol 1: 18204
Southern Africa Road Federation   Vol 2: 11094
Southern African Association of Industrial Editors   Vol 2: 11096
Southern African Institute of Forestry   Vol 2: 11098
Southern African Ornithological Society   Vol 2: 11100
Southern African Society for Plant Pathology   Vol 2: 11102
Southern Anthropological Society   Vol 1: 18207
Southern Arts Association   Vol 2: 4480
Southern Arts Board   Vol 2: 4480
Southern California Council on Literature for Children and Young People   Vol 1: 18209
Southern Center for Environmental Education   Vol 2: 8434
Southern Economic Association   Vol 1: 18211
Southern Forest Products Association   Vol 1: 5742
Southern Historical Association   Vol 1: 18213
Southern Home Furnishings Association   Vol 1: 18219
Southern Illinois University   Vol 1: 6365
Southern Illinois University at Carbondale - School of Journalism   Vol 1: 18221
Southern Methodist University - De Golyer Institute for American Studies; Everette Lee and Nell   Vol 1: 18226

Southern Methodist University - Meadows School of the Arts   Vol 1: 18228
Southern Poetry Review   Vol 1: 18230
Southern Pulp and Paper Magazine   Vol 1: 18234, 18235
Southern Pulp and Paper Safety Association   Vol 1: 18232
Southern Regional Council   Vol 1: 18236
The Southern Review - Louisiana State University   Vol 1: 18238
Southwest Review   Vol 1: 18240
Southwestern Association of Naturalists   Vol 1: 18243
Southwestern Booksellers Association - *The Dallas Times Herald*   Vol 1: 18248
Sovereign Western Order   Vol 2: 1369
Soviet Land   Vol 2: 7721
Sovinterfest   Vol 2: 10473
Space Coast Writers Guild   Vol 1: 18250
Space Foundation   Vol 1: 18252
Space Research Institute, Moscow   Vol 2: 5068
Spain - Ministerio de Industria, Comercio y Turismo   Vol 2: 11365
Spain - Ministry of Culture   Vol 2: 11355
Spain - Ministry of Foreign Affairs   Vol 2: 11360
Spain - Ministry of Industry, Trade and Tourism   Vol 2: 11365
Spain - Ministry of Public Works   Vol 2: 11265
Spain Ministerio de Cultura   Vol 2: 11367
Spain Ministry of Culture   Vol 2: 11367
Spain's '92 Foundation   Vol 1: 19824
Spanish Association of Painters and Sculptors   Vol 2: 11380
Spanish Cultural Institute   Vol 2: 7856
Spanish Ministry of Culture   Vol 2: 11285
Spanish Mustang Registry   Vol 1: 18255
Spanish Organization for Children's and Juvenile Literature   Vol 2: 11382
Spar Aerospace Limited   Vol 1: 18258
Sparkasse Ettlingen   Vol 2: 7061
Sparrowgrass Poetry Forum   Vol 1: 18260
Special Libraries Association   Vol 1: 18263
Special Libraries Association - Museums, Arts and Humanities Division   Vol 1: 18276
Special Libraries Association - News Division   Vol 1: 18279
Special Libraries Association - Transportation Division   Vol 1: 18284
Special Olympics   Vol 1: 18286
Special Recreation, Inc.   Vol 1: 18288
Specialized Carriers and Rigging Association   Vol 1: 18290
Specialty Equipment Market Association   Vol 1: 18300
The Spectator   Vol 2: 4482
Spectroscopy Society of Pittsburgh   Vol 1: 17415
Spectrum Emergency Care   Vol 1: 8898
Speculative Arts Association   Vol 2: 10804
Speech Association of America   Vol 1: 18302
Speech Communication Association   Vol 1: 18302
Speed Equipment Market Association   Vol 1: 18300
Spero Communications   Vol 2: 4486
SPIE - The International Society for Optical Engineers   Vol 1: 18317
Spill Control Association of America   Vol 1: 18328
Spinks Scale Company   Vol 1: 11310
Spinoy Foundation; A.   Vol 2: 1371
Spirit of Los Angeles Committee   Vol 1: 18330
Spirit of Place - Sendai Planning Committee   Vol 2: 8759

Spitball, the Literary Baseball Magazine   Vol 1: 18332
Spohr Violin Competition; International Ludwig   Vol 2: 6971
Spoke Gallery; Northport/B. J.   Vol 1: 15515
Spolak slovenskych spisovatelov   Vol 2: 10753
Spolecnost Fryderyka Chopina v CSSR   Vol 2: 1832
Sport Australia Hall of Fame   Vol 2: 680
Sport Fishing Institute   Vol 1: 18334
Sporting Goods Agents Association   Vol 1: 18336
The Sporting News   Vol 1: 18340
Sports Car Club of America   Vol 1: 18388
Sports Car Collectors Society of America   Vol 1: 18420
Sports Federation of Canada   Vol 1: 7239
Sports Foundation   Vol 1: 18422
Sports Illustrated   Vol 1: 18426
The Sports Network   Vol 1: 6972
Sports Philatelists International   Vol 1: 18430
Sprava zamku Hradce nad Moravici a Radune   Vol 2: 1857
Springfield Art Museum   Vol 1: 18432
Sprinkler Irrigation Association   Vol 1: 11473
Squibb Canada   Vol 1: 18434
Squibb Diagnostic Canada   Vol 1: 6790
Sri Kapila Humanitarian Society   Vol 2: 11419
Sri Lanka - Ministry of Cultural Affairs   Vol 2: 11421
Sri Lanka - Office of the President   Vol 2: 11428
Srpska Akademij Naukai Umetnosti   Vol 2: 10723
Stadt Aachen   Vol 2: 7091
Stadt Braunschweig-Kulturamt   Vol 2: 6572
Stadt Buxtehude   Vol 2: 7093
Stadt Darmstadt   Vol 2: 6598
Stadt Dortmund   Vol 2: 7095
Stadt Koln   Vol 2: 6595
Stadt Mannheim   Vol 2: 7097
Stadt Pforzheim, Kulturamt   Vol 2: 7101
Stadt Schweinfurt   Vol 2: 7103
Stadt Villach   Vol 2: 886
Stadtmagistrat Innsbruck   Vol 2: 889
Stage Directors and Choreographers Foundation   Vol 1: 18440
Stamford Community Arts Council   Vol 1: 18444
Stand Magazine   Vol 2: 4491
Standard Bank Investment Corporation   Vol 2: 10849
Standard Electrica Portuguesa   Vol 2: 10248
Standard Quarter Horse Association   Vol 1: 18447
Standards Engineering Society   Vol 1: 6076, 18449
Standing Commission of the Red Cross and Red Crescent   Vol 2: 11914
Standing Committee of Correspondents   Vol 1: 18458
Stanford University - Creative Writing Program   Vol 1: 18461
Stanford University Center for Russian and East European Studies   Vol 1: 893
Stanley Publishing Company   Vol 1: 6171
Starfleet   Vol 1: 18463
Starr Foundation   Vol 1: 8389
State Bar of California   Vol 1: 18465
State Bar of Michigan   Vol 1: 18469
State Department and Construction Corporation   Vol 2: 11408
State Foundation for the National Youth Orchestra of Venezuela   Vol 1: 15832
State Library of New South Wales   Vol 2: 682

State Silesian Philharmonic Orchestra   Vol 2: 10211
State University College at Buffalo   Vol 1: 7652
Statistical Society of Canada   Vol 1: 8036
Status of Women Canada   Vol 1: 18471
Stauffer; Fondazione W.   Vol 2: 8321
Steacie Memorial Fund; E. W. R.   Vol 1: 18473
Steber Foundation; Eleanor   Vol 1: 15727
Stedman Art Gallery   Vol 1: 18475
Steel Authority of India, Ltd.   Vol 2: 7632
Steel Founders' Society of America   Vol 1: 18477
Stein Collectors International   Vol 1: 18481
Stellenbosch Farmers' Winery   Vol 2: 11106
Stephens College   Vol 1: 18484
Stereo Review   Vol 1: 18486
Sterijino pozorje   Vol 2: 10704
Sterling National Bank & Trust Company of New York   Vol 1: 18488
Stern School of Business; Leonard N.   Vol 1: 7433
Stern School of Business; New York University   Vol 1: 7434
Stichting A. Spinoy   Vol 2: 1371
Stichting Aanmoedigingsfonds voor de Kunsten   Vol 2: 9334
Stichting AKO Literatuur Prijs   Vol 2: 9632
Stichting Amsterdams Fonds voor de Kunst   Vol 2: 9634
Stichting Charlotte Kohler   Vol 2: 9687
Stichting Collectieve Propaganda van het Nederlandse Boek   Vol 2: 9364
Stichting Conamus   Vol 2: 9370
Stichting de Vlaamse Gids   Vol 2: 1373
Stichting Dramaastricht   Vol 2: 9655
Stichting Edmond Hustinx   Vol 2: 9654
Stichting Fonds Kunst en Educatie   Vol 2: 9332
Stichting Fonds voor de Geld - en Effectenhandel   Vol 2: 9394
Stichting Frans Erensprijs   Vol 2: 9656
Stichting Gaudeamus   Vol 2: 9437
Stichting Internationaal Orgelconcours   Vol 2: 9658
Stichting Kijkhuis/World Wide Video Festival   Vol 2: 9669
Stichting Koningin Wilhelmina Fonds   Vol 2: 9660
Stichting Koninklijk Paleis te Amsterdam   Vol 2: 9611
Stichting Liszt Concours   Vol 2: 9662
Stichting Nederlandse Filmdagen   Vol 2: 9382
Stichting P.C. Hooftprijs voor Letterkunde   Vol 2: 9664
Stichting Poetry International   Vol 2: 9567
Stichting Praemium Erasmianum   Vol 2: 9395
Stichting Rotterdam-Maaskant   Vol 2: 9582
Stichting Sikkens   Vol 2: 9619
Stichting Studiefonds Oskar Back   Vol 2: 9336
Stichting voor Culturele Samenwerking - Sticusa   Vol 2: 9429
Stichting Vrienden van het Nationale Ballet   Vol 2: 9435
Stichting Wereld Muziek Concours Kerkrade   Vol 2: 9693
Stichting Wonen   Vol 2: 9667
Stichting World Wide Video Centre   Vol 2: 9669
Stichting Woutertje Pieterse Prijs   Vol 2: 9671
Stiftelsen Kortfilmfestivalen   Vol 2: 9947
Stiftelsen Litteraturframjandet   Vol 2: 11641
Stiftung der Sparkasse Bochum zur Forderung von Kultur und Wissenschaft   Vol 2: 6675
Stiftung F.V.S.   Vol 2: 7106

Stiftung im Gruene   Vol 2: 11739
Stiftung Niedersachsen   Vol 2: 6757
Stiftung zur Forderung der DGE   Vol 2: 6858
Stigting Simon Van der Stel   Vol 2: 11118
Stoessl-Stiftung; Otto   Vol 2: 892
Stone Center for Children's Books; George G.   Vol 1: 18490
Stone Foundation; W. Clement and Jessie V.   Vol 1: 18492
Stowarzyszenie Autorow (ZAiKS)   Vol 2: 10205
Stowarzyszenie Bibliotekarzy Polskich   Vol 2: 10152
Stowarzyszenie Pax   Vol 2: 10083
Stowarzyszenie Polskich Artystow Muzykow   Vol 2: 10163
Strat X S.A.   Vol 2: 6401
Strategic Planning Society   Vol 2: 4493
Strathin Enterprises Ltd.   Vol 2: 7847
Strauman Company; ITI/The   Vol 1: 1086
Stravinsky Awards   Vol 1: 18494
Strega Alberti Benevento   Vol 2: 8438
Streisand Center for Jewish Cultural Arts at UCLA Hillel   Vol 1: 18497
Stroud and District Festival   Vol 2: 4496
Structural Chemistry - Kratos Group plc.   Vol 2: 4219
Studebaker Drivers Club   Vol 1: 18500
Student Council for Exceptional Children   Vol 1: 8313
Student Press Law Center   Vol 1: 18505
Studio Museum in Harlem   Vol 1: 18507
Stulberg Auditions; Julius   Vol 1: 18510
Stuttgart City Council   Vol 2: 7134
Stuttgart International Animation Film Festival   Vol 2: 7141
Substance Abuse and Mental Health Services Administration   Vol 1: 530
Suburban Cablevision   Vol 1: 8831
Suburban Newspapers of America   Vol 1: 18512
Successful Meetings Magazine   Vol 1: 18515
Sudler Foundation of Chicago; Louis   Vol 1: 18165, 18166, 18167, 18168
Sudwestfunk   Vol 2: 7143
Sugar Industry Technologists   Vol 1: 18520
Suid-Afrikaanse Akademie vir Wetenskap en Kuns   Vol 2: 10984
Suid-Afrikaanse Biologiese Vereniging   Vol 2: 11031
Suid-Afrikaanse Chemiese Instituut   Vol 2: 11044
Suid-Afrikaanse Instituut var Siviele Ingenieurs   Vol 2: 11065
Suid-Afrikaanse Instituut vir Biblioteek-en Inligtingwese   Vol 2: 11056
Suid-Afrikaanse Instituut vir Fisika   Vol 2: 11069
Suid-Afrikaanse Nasionale Komitee vir Verlingting   Vol 2: 11078
Suid Afrikaanse Vereniging van Arbeidsterapeute   Vol 2: 11027
Suid-Afrikaanse Vereniging van Musiekonderwysers   Vol 2: 11087
Suid-Afrikaanse Vereniging van Raadgewende Ingenieurs   Vol 2: 11025
Suider-Afrikaanse Instituut van Boswese   Vol 2: 11098
Suider-Afrikaanse Vereniging vir Bedryfsredakteurs   Vol 2: 11096
Suissimage   Vol 2: 8472
Sulphur Institute U.S.A.   Vol 2: 7500
Sumi-e Society of America   Vol 1: 18523
Summer and Casual Furniture Manufacturers Association   Vol 1: 18525
Summit Art Center   Vol 1: 15173
Summit Brass   Vol 1: 18527

Sun Life Assurance Society - *Amateur Photographer*   Vol 2: 4498
Sunday Express   Vol 2: 4500
Sunday Telegraph   Vol 2: 4163
Sunday Times   Vol 2: 4502
The Sunday Times   Vol 2: 4503
Sunday Times   Vol 2: 4504
The Sunday Times   Vol 2: 9784
Sunday Times Business Times   Vol 2: 11108
Sunset Center   Vol 1: 18529
Sunset Magazine   Vol 1: 18531
Suntory Foundation   Vol 2: 8761
Suntory Limited of Japan   Vol 2: 8525
Suomen Arvostelijain Liitto Finlands Kritikerforbund ry   Vol 2: 4759
Suomen Geologinen Seura-Geologiska Sal-Iskapet i Finland   Vol 2: 4715
Suomen Historiallinen Seura   Vol 2: 4697
Suomen Kirjasaatio   Vol 2: 4685
(Suomen Kirjastoseura)   Vol 2: 4699
Suomen Kulttuurirahasto   Vol 2: 4692
Suomen Liike- ja Virkanaisten Liitto - Finlands Yrkeskvinnors Forbund   Vol 2: 4751
Suomen Maantieteellinen Seura   Vol 2: 4711
Suomen museoliitto ry   Vol 2: 4701
Suomen Naytelmakirjailijaliitto   Vol 2: 4695
Suomen Nuorisokirjailijatry   Vol 2: 4666
Suomen Nuortenkirjaneuvosto   Vol 2: 4703
Suomen Oikeusfilosofinen yhdistys   Vol 2: 4705
Suomen Taideyhdistys-Finska Konstforeningen   Vol 2: 4675
Suomen Taiteilijaseura/Konstnarsgiller i Finland   Vol 2: 4664
SUPELCO   Vol 1: 1534
Support Systems International   Vol 1: 1379
Surface Design Journal   Vol 1: 18533
Surgipath Medical Industries Inc.   Vol 1: 14751
Sutherland Committee; Zena   Vol 1: 18537
Svaz ceskychspisovatelu   Vol 2: 1885
Svenska Akademien   Vol 2: 11581
Svenska Arkitekters Riksforbund   Vol 2: 11491
Svenska Dagbladet   Vol 2: 11569
Svenska Filminstitutet   Vol 2: 11624
Svenska Forsakringsforeningen   Vol 2: 11628
Svenska Matematikersamfundet   Vol 2: 11634
Sveriges Allmanna Biblioteksforening   Vol 2: 11630
Sveriges Film- och Videoamatorer   Vol 2: 11622
Sveriges Forfattarfond   Vol 2: 11618
Svjetlost Publishing House   Vol 2: 1403
Svjetski Festival Animiranih Filmova, Zagreb   Vol 2: 1815
Swarovski International   Vol 2: 565
Swarowsky International Conducting Competition; Hans   Vol 2: 894
Swarowsky Internationale Dirigenten Wettbewerb; Hans   Vol 2: 894
Sweden - Chancery of the Royal Orders   Vol 2: 11577
Sweden - Utrikesdepartementet   Vol 2: 11577
Swedish Academy   Vol 2: 11581
Swedish Academy of Pharmaceutical Sciences   Vol 2: 11614
Swedish Association for Water Hygiene   Vol 2: 11616
Swedish Authors' Fund   Vol 2: 11618
Swedish Council of America   Vol 1: 18539
Swedish Economic Association   Vol 2: 11620
Swedish Federation of Film and Video Amateurs   Vol 2: 11622
Swedish Film Institute   Vol 2: 11490, 11624
Swedish Insurance Society   Vol 2: 11628
Swedish Library Association   Vol 2: 11630

Swedish Mathematical Society   Vol 2: 11634
Swedish Section of the International Board on Books for Young People   Vol 2: 11636
Swedish Society Against Painful Experiments on Animals   Vol 2: 11638
Swedish Society for Promotion of Literature   Vol 2: 11641
Swedish Society of Aeronautics and Astronautics   Vol 2: 11647
Swedish Society of Crafts and Design   Vol 2: 11650
Swiss Academy of Medical Sciences   Vol 2: 11916
Swiss Association for the Scientific Films   Vol 2: 11793
Swiss Association for Theatre Studies   Vol 2: 11920
Swiss Association of Chemists   Vol 2: 11884, 11889
Swiss Biochemical Society   Vol 2: 11922
Swiss Broadcasting Corporation   Vol 2: 11738
Swiss Broadcasting Corporation and the City of Montreux   Vol 2: 11924
Swiss Chemical Society   Vol 2: 11884
Swiss Cooperative Society   Vol 2: 11963
Swiss Federal Institute of Technology   Vol 2: 11793
Swiss Federal Institute of Technology Zurich   Vol 2: 11927
Swiss Foundation for Parapsychology   Vol 2: 11938
Swiss Foundation Pro Helvetia   Vol 1: 6733
Swiss Music - Edition   Vol 2: 11940
Swiss Neurological Society   Vol 2: 11942
Swiss Organ Competition   Vol 2: 11944
Swiss Pharmaceutical Association   Vol 2: 6586
Swiss Teachers' Association   Vol 2: 11946
Swope Art Museum; Sheldon   Vol 1: 18542
Sydney Conservatorium of Music   Vol 2: 326
Sydney Film Festival   Vol 2: 684
Symposium International et Exposition technique de Television - Montreux   Vol 2: 11850
Syndicat d'Agglomeration Nouvelle de Melun-Senart   Vol 2: 6469
Syndicate of Professional Drama and Music Critics   Vol 2: 6404
Syndicate Professionnel de la Critique Dramatique et Musicale   Vol 2: 6404
Syndicated Fiction Project   Vol 1: 18544
Syntex Corporation   Vol 1: 15952
Syntex Research (Canada)   Vol 1: 7565
Syntex (U.S.A.)   Vol 1: 18546
Synthetic Organic Chemical Manufacturers Association   Vol 1: 18548
Syracuse University - Newhouse School of Public Communications; S. I.   Vol 1: 18550
Syracuse University Press   Vol 1: 18553
System Safety Society   Vol 1: 18555
Systems & Computer Technology Corporation (SCT)   Vol 1: 7418
Szent-Gyorgyi Albert Orvostudomanyi Egyetem Szeged   Vol 2: 7457
Szent-Gyorgyi Medical University; Albert   Vol 2: 7457
Tackle and Shooting Sports Agents Association   Vol 1: 18565
Tackle Representatives Association International   Vol 1: 18565
Tafelberg Publishers Ltd.   Vol 2: 11112
Taft Institute of Government; Robert A.   Vol 1: 18567
Tai Fung & Co.   Vol 2: 7265
Taipei City Symphony Orchestra   Vol 2: 12006
Taipei Golden Horse Film Festival   Vol 2: 12008

Taipei International Film Exhibition   Vol 2: 12008
Taiwan - Ministry of Education   Vol 2: 12010
Tampere Film Festival   Vol 2: 4757
Tampereen elokuvajuhlat   Vol 2: 4757
Tandheelkundige Vereniging van Suid-Afrika   Vol 2: 10838
Tandy Brand Accessories, Inc.   Vol 1: 18569
Tandy Corporation   Vol 1: 18572
Tandy Technology Scholars   Vol 1: 18571
Tate and Lyle   Vol 2: 4192
Tau Beta Pi Association   Vol 1: 18573
Tau Beta Sigma   Vol 1: 18576
Tau Sigma Delta   Vol 1: 18580
Tax Foundation   Vol 1: 18584
TBS Britannica Company   Vol 2: 8762
Tchaikovsky Competition; International   Vol 2: 10454
Teacher & Sons Limited; William   Vol 2: 4489
Teachers of English to Speakers of Other Languages   Vol 1: 18586
Teachers USA   Vol 1: 18595
Teatro Comunale di Firenze   Vol 2: 8440
Teatro Municipale Valli   Vol 2: 8443
Technical Association of the Australian and New Zealand Pulp and Paper Industry   Vol 2: 688
Technical Association of the Graphic Arts   Vol 1: 18597
Technical Association of the Pulp and Paper Industry - TAPPI   Vol 1: 18599
Technical Divisions/Societies of CIM   Vol 1: 6957
Technical Services Interest Group   Vol 1: 7012
Technikon Witwatersrand   Vol 2: 11116
Technion - Israel Institute of Technology   Vol 2: 7944
Technion - Machon Technologi le'Israel   Vol 2: 7944
Technology Student Association   Vol 1: 18603
Teen Association of Model Railroaders   Vol 1: 18607
Teen International Entomology Group   Vol 1: 20604
Tel Aviv Municipality   Vol 2: 7946
Tel Aviv Museum of Art   Vol 2: 7964
Tel Aviv University   Vol 2: 7903
Telcipro   Vol 2: 5190
Telebec   Vol 1: 16433
Teleconfronto - International TV Drama Series Festival   Vol 2: 8445
Teleconfronto - Mostra Internazionale del Telefilm   Vol 2: 8445
Teledyne McKay   Vol 1: 5084
Teledyne Ryan Electronics   Vol 1: 12071
Teleglobe Canada   Vol 1: 6745
Television and Radio Industries Club   Vol 2: 4506
Television Society of Australia   Vol 2: 690
Telly Awards   Vol 1: 18609
Telocator Network of America   Vol 1: 18611
Temple de la Renommee des Sports du Canada   Vol 1: 6759
Temple de la Renommee du Baseball Canadien et Musee   Vol 1: 6815
Templeton Foundation   Vol 2: 927
Tempo; II   Vol 2: 8447
Tennessee Arts Commission   Vol 1: 17288
Tennessee Library Association   Vol 1: 18613
Tennis   Vol 1: 10552, 10561, 18618
Tennis Week   Vol 1: 18625
Tercuman   Vol 2: 12069
Terumo Corporation   Vol 1: 922
Test and Cricket Board   Vol 2: 4511
Texas Armadillo Association   Vol 1: 18627

Texas Association of Business and the Center for Private Enterprise Vol 1: 18629
Texas Daily Newspaper Association Vol 1: 18631
Texas Fine Arts Association Vol 1: 18639
Texas Institute of Letters Vol 1: 18641
Texas Instruments Foundation Vol 1: 18655
Texas Library Association Vol 1: 18657
Texas Medical Association Vol 1: 18659
Texas Tech University Vol 1: 18662
Texas Western Press - University of Texas at El Paso Vol 1: 18666
Texas Woman's University Vol 1: 18668
Textile Institute Vol 2: 4513
Textilipari Muszaki es Tudomanyos Egyesulet Vol 2: 7384
Textron Lycoming Vol 1: 6194
Teyte Prize Fund; Maggie Vol 2: 4529
Thalben-Ball Memorial Trust; Sir George Vol 2: 4531
Thames Television Limited Vol 2: 4533
Theater Hall of Fame Vol 1: 18670
Theatre Americana Vol 1: 18672
Theatre Americana - Altadena's Community Theatre Vol 1: 18672
Theatre Communications Group Vol 1: 18674
Theatre Historical Society of America Vol 1: 18684
Theatre Library Association Vol 1: 18686
Theatre Memphis Vol 1: 18689
Theatre World Vol 1: 18691
Theatreworks Vol 1: 18693
Thermal Syndicate, Ltd Vol 2: 2539
THESE-PAC Association Vol 2: 9698
Thessaloniki Film Festival Vol 2: 7216
Theta Alpha Phi Vol 1: 18695
Theta Sigma Phi Vol 1: 20373
Thibaud; Concours International Marguerite Long - Jacques Vol 2: 6084
Thibaud International Competition; Marguerite Long and Jacques Vol 2: 6084
Thieme Publishers; Georg Vol 2: 9424
Thimble Press Vol 2: 4536
Third Street Music School Settlement Vol 1: 18697
Third World Academy of Sciences Vol 2: 8449, 8457, 8458, 8805, 8806, 8808, 8910, 8918
Third World Foundation for Social and Economic Studies Vol 2: 4538
Third World Network of Scientific Organizations Vol 2: 8456
Thistle Class Association Vol 1: 18700
Thomson Foundation Vol 2: 12191
Thomson Tubes Electroniques Vol 2: 11705
Thorntree Press Vol 1: 18703
Thoroughbred Racing Associations of North America Vol 1: 18705
Thorpe Smith Vol 1: 1817
Three M Data Products Vol 1: 8081
Tidy Britain Group Vol 2: 4540
Tilburg University - Faculty of Letters Vol 2: 9673
Tile Contractors' Association of America Vol 1: 18708
Time Incorporated Vol 1: 8299, 8302
Time Inc. Vol 1: 18710
Time Out Group Ltd. Vol 2: 4543
The Times; ABSA/Arthur Andersen Awards in Association with Vol 2: 2029
The Times Educational Supplement Vol 2: 4547
Times-News Vol 1: 15299
The *Times/PM* Environment Award Vol 2: 4550
Tioxide Group Ltd. Vol 2: 4219
Tirreno Gruppo Editoriale Vol 2: 11948
Tissue Culture Association, Inc. Vol 1: 18714

Titanium Development Association Vol 1: 18722
Tmmob Jeoloji Muhendisleri Oiasi Vol 2: 12045
TNT (UK) Ltd. Vol 2: 2587, 2588
Toastmasters International Vol 1: 18724
Tokens and Medals Society Vol 1: 2713
Tokyo Broadcasting System Vol 2: 8772
Tokyo Geographical Society Vol 2: 8765
Tokyo International Film Festival Vol 2: 8767
Tokyo International Music Competition Vol 2: 8769
Tokyo Music Festival Foundation Vol 2: 8771
Tokyo Popular Music Promotion Association Vol 2: 8771
Toledo Bird Association, Zebra Finch Club of America Vol 1: 18726
Tolkien Society of America Vol 1: 12555
Tollit & Harvey Ltd. Vol 2: 2878
Tomar; Festival Internacional de Cinema para a Infancia e Juventude - Vol 2: 10231
Tonga and Tin Can Mail Study Circle Vol 1: 18728
Toonder Stichting; Marten Vol 2: 9675
Top Blacks in Law Enforcement Vol 1: 6399
Topps Chewing Gum Vol 1: 18732
Topps Company, Inc. Vol 1: 18732
Torello Excursionist Center Vol 2: 11385
Torello Film Festival Vol 2: 11385
Toronto Historical Board Vol 1: 18741
Toronto International Film Festival, Inc. Vol 1: 18743
Toronto Mendelssohn Choir Foundation Vol 1: 6744
Toronto Press Club Vol 1: 18748
Torrey Botanical Club Vol 1: 18751
Toshiba America Foundation Vol 1: 14707
Toshiba America Group Vol 1: 14707
Toshiba Corp. Vol 1: 14707
Touchdown Club of Memphis Vol 1: 7899
Touchdown Club of Washington, D.C. Vol 1: 18755
Touche, Ross and Company Vol 1: 10383
Tourism Industry Association of Canada Vol 1: 18766
Touristik-Verband Klopeiner See/Turnersee Vol 2: 896
Towarzystwo im. Fryderyka Chopina w Warszawie Vol 2: 10065
Towarzystwo Milosnikow Jezyka Polskiego Vol 2: 10209
Towing and Recovery Association of America Vol 1: 18769
Town and Country Vol 1: 18772
Town and Country Planning Association Vol 2: 4552
Town Council of Busseto Vol 2: 8293
Townsville Foundation for Australian Literary Studies Vol 2: 405
Towson State University Vol 1: 18775
Trading Stamp Institute of America Vol 1: 5940
Traditional Irish Singing and Dancing Society Vol 2: 7849
Traebranchens Oplysningsraad Vol 2: 1921
Traffic Institute Vol 1: 10697
Traffic Management Vol 1: 12579
Trama Visual Vol 2: 9284
Transport Canada Vol 1: 20553
Transport Insurance Company Vol 1: 4930
Transportation Research Board Vol 1: 18777
Transportation Research Forum Vol 1: 18785
Travel and Tourism Research Association Vol 1: 18787
Travel Holiday Vol 1: 18794
Travel Industry Association of America Vol 1: 18796

Travel Research Association Vol 1: 18787
Travers-Borgstroem Foundation Vol 2: 11965
Treasurer to the Queen Vol 2: 4554
Trees for Tomorrow Vol 1: 18801
Trento Filmfestival Internazionale Montagna Esplorazione Vol 2: 8459
Trento International Film Festival of Mountains and Exploration Vol 2: 8459
Trial Advocacy Institute Vol 1: 14222
Trial Lawyers for Public Justice Vol 1: 18804
Triangle Coalition for Science and Technology Education Vol 1: 18806
Triathlon Federation Vol 1: 18808
Tribune Entertainment Vol 1: 18154
Triennale internationale de la photographie Vol 2: 11853
Trimestre Economico; El Vol 2: 9286
Trinidad and Tobago Government - Prime Minister's Office Vol 2: 12032
Triple Crown Productions, Inc. Vol 1: 18813
Triptyque; Le Vol 2: 6407
Trophy Dealers of America Vol 1: 6203
Trotting Horse Museum Vol 1: 19381
Trout Unlimited Vol 1: 18816
Truck Renting and Leasing Association Vol 1: 18820
Truman Good Neighbor Award Foundation; Harry S. Vol 1: 18822
Truman Library Institute for National and International Affairs; Harry S Vol 1: 18826
Trustees Executors and Agency Company of New Zealand Vol 2: 9845
Trustees Savings Bank Vol 2: 10643
TRW Vol 1: 3469, 10286
Tucker Music Foundation; Richard Vol 1: 18828
Tugac Foundation; Husamettin Vol 2: 12068
Tulsa City - County Library System Vol 1: 18834
Tulsa Library Trust Vol 1: 18835, 18836
Tunbridge Wells International Young Concert Artists Competition Vol 2: 4556
Turikiye Bilimsel ve Teknik Arastirna Kurumu Vol 2: 12064
Turin International Film Festival Vol 2: 8461
Turk dil Karumu Vol 2: 12074
Turk Plastik Cerrahi Dernegi Vol 2: 12081
Turk Tarih Kurumu Vol 2: 12071
Turkish Historical Society Vol 2: 12071
Turkish Language Institute Vol 2: 12074
Turkish Society of Plastic Surgeons Vol 2: 12081
Turkiye Radyo Televizyon Kurumu Vol 2: 12083
Turner Broadcasting System Vol 1: 18837
The Tuscaloosa News Vol 1: 15298
Tusquets Editores S.A. Vol 2: 11387
Tutmonda Esperantista Kuracista Asocio Vol 2: 8777
TVR Car Club North America Vol 1: 18839
TVR Car Club of England Vol 1: 18839
Tweed River Regional Art Gallery Vol 2: 692
Twentieth Century Spanish Association of America Vol 1: 18841
Two/Ten Foundation Vol 1: 18843
Two/Ten International Footwear Foundation Vol 1: 18843
Type Directors Club Vol 1: 18846
U. The National College Newspaper Vol 1: 7905
Uberlingen City Cultural Office Vol 2: 7145
Uclaf; Roussel Vol 1: 4400
Ucross Foundation Vol 1: 18848
UDC Society of Japan, Japan Documentation Society Vol 2: 8540
Uelzen Vol 2: 6966

Organization Index
Volume 2: International and Foreign

Uganda Association for the Mentally Handicapped   Vol 2: 12085
Uglies Unlimited   Vol 1: 18850
UK - Department of Trade & Industry   Vol 2: 4558
UK Committee for the Thouron Awards   Vol 2: 10682
UK Press Gazette   Vol 2: 4560
Ukrainian National Association   Vol 1: 5993
Ukrainian Philatelic and Numismatic Society   Vol 1: 18852
Ullensaker Cykleklub   Vol 2: 9972
UMI/Data Courier   Vol 1: 18857
UNAPEL   Vol 2: 5030
Unda Association Catholique Internationale pour la Radio et la Television   Vol 2: 1375
Unda International Catholic Association for Radio and Television   Vol 2: 1375
Unda-USA, the National Catholic Association of Broadcasters and Communicators   Vol 1: 18860
Undersea and Hyperbaric Medical Society   Vol 1: 18862
Undersea Medical Society, Inc.   Vol 1: 18862
Underwater Society of America   Vol 1: 18867
UNESCO   Vol 2: 824, 5084, 6034, 6409, 9469, 10784
UNESCO - International Book Committee   Vol 2: 898
Uniao dos Escritores Angolanos   Vol 2: 3
Unicam Ltd.   Vol 2: 4219
Unicycling Society of America   Vol 1: 18872
UniJapan Film   Vol 2: 8773
Unileve Research and Engineering   Vol 2: 4219
Unilever   Vol 1: 19452
Unilever New Zealand   Vol 2: 9707
Unilever Research   Vol 2: 4219, 4354
Unilever Research Laboratory   Vol 2: 2171
UNIMA-USA   Vol 1: 18874
Union Bank of Switzerland   Vol 2: 11950
Union Carbide Canada Limited   Vol 1: 7566
Union Carbide Corporation   Vol 1: 1496, 1571, 2596
Union Culturelle et Technique de Langue Francaise   Vol 2: 5266
Union de Banques Suisses   Vol 2: 11950
Union des Annonceurs   Vol 2: 6428
Union des Ecrivaines et Ecrivains Quebecois   Vol 1: 18877
Union des Femmes Artistes et Musiciennes   Vol 2: 6430
Union des Foires Internationales   Vol 2: 6456
Union des Journaux et Journalistes d'Entreprise de France   Vol 2: 6433
Union Europeene de Radio-Television   Vol 2: 11691
Union Europeene des Etudiants Juifs   Vol 2: 1145
Union Europeenne de la Presse Sportive   Vol 2: 1143
Union Fidelity Trustee Company of Australia   Vol 2: 371
Union Film Laboratory Ltd.   Vol 2: 7265
Union for the International Language IDO   Vol 2: 4562
Union Geofisica Mexicana   Vol 2: 9288
Union Geographique Internationale   Vol 2: 6957
Union International pour les livres de jeuness - Canada   Vol 1: 10804
Union Internationale Contre le Cancer   Vol 2: 11855
Union Internationale de Pentathlon Moderne et Biathlon   Vol 2: 6990
Union Internationale de Physique Pure et Appliquee   Vol 2: 11483

Union Internationale des Architectes   Vol 2: 6057
Union Internationale des Association de Prevention de la Pollution Atmospherique   Vol 2: 3494
Union Internationale des Associations Techniques Cinematographiques   Vol 2: 6435
Union Internationale des Entrepreneurs de Peinture   Vol 2: 3061, 6992
Union Internationale des Etudiants   Vol 2: 1868
Union Internationale des Instituts de Recherches Forestieres   Vol 2: 850
Union Internationale des Telecommunications   Vol 2: 11847
Union Internationale des Transports Routiers   Vol 2: 11824
Union Internationale du Cinema Non Professionel - UNICA   Vol 2: 9536
Union Internationale pour la Science, la Technique et les Applications   Vol 2: 3492
Union Internationale pour les Livres de Jeunesse   Vol 2: 11766
Union Laique de Muret   Vol 2: 6437
Union Litteraire et Artistique de France   Vol 2: 6440
Union Mundial para la Naturaleza   Vol 2: 11968
Union of Arab Football Associations   Vol 2: 10503
Union of Architects of Romania   Vol 2: 10407
Union of Architects of the SRR   Vol 2: 10407
Union of Artists   Vol 2: 1
Union of Bulgarian Artists   Vol 2: 1531
Union of Bulgarian Motorists   Vol 2: 1534
Union of Bulgarian Writers   Vol 2: 1536
Union of Councils for Soviet Jews   Vol 1: 18882
Union of Czech Architects   Vol 2: 1881
Union of Czech Writers   Vol 2: 1885
Union of Finnish Critics   Vol 2: 4759
Union of International Fairs   Vol 2: 6456
Union of Japanese Scientists and Engineers   Vol 2: 8775
Union of Soviet Architects   Vol 2: 10475
Union of Soviet Friendship Societies   Vol 2: 4352
Union of Soviet Journalists   Vol 2: 10477
Union of Writers   Vol 2: 1
Union of Writers and Artists of Albania   Vol 2: 1
Union Pan-American de Asociaciones de Igenieros   Vol 2: 12131
Union Postale Universelle   Vol 2: 11956
Union Radio Scientifique Internationale   Vol 2: 1209, 4141
Union Rationaliste   Vol 2: 6458
Union Saint-Jean Baptiste   Vol 1: 18884
Unione Matematica Italiana   Vol 2: 8357
Uniono por la Linguo Internaciona IDO   Vol 2: 4562
Unipath   Vol 2: 4348
Uniroyal Chemical Company   Vol 1: 1504
Unisys Corporation   Vol 1: 5469, 9715
Unitarian Universalist Association   Vol 1: 18886
United Airlines   Vol 1: 19723
United Astrology Congress   Vol 1: 18897
United Biscuits (Holdings) PLC   Vol 2: 10582
United Catalysts   Vol 1: 7344
United Cerebral Palsy Associations   Vol 1: 18899
United Church of Christ Coordinating Center for Women in Church and Society   Vol 1: 18909
United Daughters of the Confederacy   Vol 1: 18911

U.S.

United Engineering Trustees   Vol 1: 18913
United Hellenic Voters of America   Vol 1: 18916
United HIAS Service   Vol 1: 9876
United Israel Appeal - Keren Hayesod   Vol 2: 7972
United Jewish Appeal - Federation of Jewish Philanthropies of New York   Vol 1: 18918
United Kennel Club   Vol 1: 18927
United Methodist Association of Health and Welfare Ministries   Vol 1: 18930
United Methodist Church, Board of Global Ministries - Health and Welfare Ministries Division   Vol 1: 18939
United Mirror Class Association   Vol 1: 18945
United Nations - Centre for Human Rights   Vol 2: 11952
United Nations - High Commission for Refugees   Vol 2: 11954
United Nations - Sri Chinmoy: The Peace Meditation at the United Nations   Vol 1: 18947
United Nations - United Nation's Children's Fund - UNICEF   Vol 1: 18949
United Nations Association of Sri Lanka   Vol 2: 11438
United Nations Association of the U.S.A.   Vol 1: 18954
United Nations Association - UK   Vol 2: 4564
United Nations Environment Program   Vol 2: 8811
United Nations Population Fund   Vol 1: 18956
United Nations Society of Writers   Vol 1: 18958
United New Conservationists   Vol 1: 18960
United Ostomy Association   Vol 1: 18963
United Parents and Teachers Association of Jewish Schools   Vol 1: 18965
United Press International   Vol 1: 18968
United Scleroderma Foundation   Vol 1: 18972
United Seamen's Service   Vol 1: 18974
United Service Organizations   Vol 1: 18979
United Ski Industries Association   Vol 1: 17303
U.S. Agency for International Development   Vol 1: 18986
United States Air Force   Vol 1: 14625
United States Air Force Academy   Vol 1: 12282, 18988
United States Amateur Boxing   Vol 1: 18990
United States Amateur Confederation of Roller Skating   Vol 1: 18997
U.S. Aquatic Sports   Vol 1: 18999
United States Arms Control and Disarmament Agency   Vol 1: 19002
United States Army, Corps of Engineers, Headquarters   Vol 1: 19005
United States Association for Blind Athletes   Vol 1: 19007
United States Association of Former Members of Congress   Vol 1: 19012
United States Auto Club   Vol 1: 19014
United States Badminton Association   Vol 1: 19033
United States BASE Association   Vol 1: 19040
U.S. Bicycling Hall of Fame   Vol 1: 19042
United States Billiard Association   Vol 1: 19044
United States Boomerangs   Vol 1: 19046
U.S. Bureau of Mines and Explosives Engineers   Vol 1: 3117
U.S. Cancellation Club   Vol 1: 19049
U.S. Catholic   Vol 1: 19051
United States Catholic Historical Society   Vol 1: 19053
U.S. Chamber of Commerce   Vol 1: 19055
U.S. Chess Federation   Vol 1: 19057

881

United States Civil Defense Council   Vol 1: 13664
United States Civil Service Commission   Vol 1: 19479
United States Coast Guard Academy   Vol 1: 12282, 15323
United States Committee of the International Council on Monuments and Sites   Vol 1: 19059
United States Conference of Mayors   Vol 1: 19061
United States Congress   Vol 1: 19480
United States Congress - Committee on Banking, Finance, and Urban Affairs   Vol 1: 19068
United States Council for International Business   Vol 1: 19070
United States Council for IYDP   Vol 1: 14430
U.S. Council of Energy Awareness   Vol 1: 19072
United States Council of the International Chamber of Commerce   Vol 1: 19070
U.S. Curling Association   Vol 1: 19076
United States Cycling Federation   Vol 1: 19079
United States Department of Agriculture - Foreign Agricultural Service   Vol 1: 19081
United States Department of Agriculture - Forest Service   Vol 1: 19083
United States Department of Army - Civilian Marksmanship Program   Vol 1: 19086
United States Department of Commerce   Vol 1: 19088
United States Department of Commerce - Bureau of the Census   Vol 1: 19092
United States Department of Commerce - International Trade Administration   Vol 1: 19094
United States Department of Commerce - International Trade Administration, Office of Foreign Operations   Vol 1: 19097
United States Department of Commerce - National Bureau of Standards   Vol 1: 19109
United States Department of Commerce - National Institute of Standards and Technology   Vol 1: 19099
United States Department of Commerce - National Institute of Standards and Technology, Baldrige Award   Vol 1: 19109
United States Department of Commerce - National Marine Fisheries Service   Vol 1: 19111
United States Department of Commerce - National Telecommunications and Information Administration   Vol 1: 19113
United States Department of Commerce - NOAA   Vol 1: 19115
United States Department of Commerce - Patent and Trademark Office   Vol 1: 19119
United States Department of Commerce - Technology Administration   Vol 1: 19121
United States Department of Defense   Vol 1: 19123
United States Department of Defense - Armed Forces Decorations and Awards   Vol 1: 19127
United States Department of Defense - Armed Forces Decorations and Awards, Civilian   Vol 1: 19196
United States Department of Defense - Defense Investigative Service   Vol 1: 19211
United States Department of Defense - Defense Logistics Agency   Vol 1: 19213
United States Department of Defense - Defense Nuclear Agency   Vol 1: 19215
United States Department of Defense - Department of the Air Force   Vol 1: 19217

United States Department of Defense - Office of the Secretary of Defense   Vol 1: 19221
United States Department of Education   Vol 1: 19223
United States Department of Education - White House Commission on Presidential Scholars   Vol 1: 19225
United States Department of Energy   Vol 1: 19227, 19499
United States Department of Energy - Office of Environmental Restoration and Waste Management   Vol 1: 15566
United States Department of Energy - Office of Fossil Energy   Vol 1: 19232
United States Department of Health and Human Services   Vol 1: 19234
United States Department of Health and Human Services - National Institutes of Health   Vol 1: 19238
United States Department of Health and Human Services, Public Health Service - Centers for Disease Control and Prevention (CDC)   Vol 1: 19240
United States Department of Interior - Federal Duck Stamp Program   Vol 1: 19243
United States Department of Interior - Office of the Director of Personnel   Vol 1: 19245
United States Department of Justice   Vol 1: 19483
United States Department of Justice - Federal Bureau of Investigation   Vol 1: 19249
United States Department of Justice - Office of Justice Programs   Vol 1: 19251
United States Department of Labor   Vol 1: 19254
United States Department of Labor - Bureau of Labor Statistics   Vol 1: 19262
United States Department of Labor - Employment and Training Administration   Vol 1: 19264
United States Department of Labor - Office of Job Corps, Employment and Training Administration   Vol 1: 19266
United States Department of Navy - U.S. Naval Observatory   Vol 1: 19271
United States Department of State   Vol 1: 19275, 19483
United States Department of the Treasury - Financial Management Service   Vol 1: 19309
United States Department of Transportation - Federal Highway Administration   Vol 1: 19311
United States Department of Veterans Affairs   Vol 1: 19313
United States Diving   Vol 1: 19315
United States Dressage Federation   Vol 1: 19322
United States Environmental Protection Agency   Vol 1: 19330
United States Executive Office of the President   Vol 1: 12730, 13893, 13894, 14686, 19069, 19096, 19122, 19222, 19226, 19252, 19253, 19331, 19332, 19483, 19484, 19485
United States Federation for Culture Collections   Vol 1: 19339
United States Fencing Coaches Association   Vol 1: 19342
United States Festivals Association   Vol 1: 19350
United States Figure Skating Association   Vol 1: 19353
United States General Services Administration   Vol 1: 19356
United States Golf Association   Vol 1: 19358
United States Handball Association   Vol 1: 19364

United States Hang Gliding Association   Vol 1: 19366
United States Harness Writers Association   Vol 1: 19372
U.S. Hispanic Engineer   Vol 1: 7305
United States Hockey Hall of Fame   Vol 1: 19393
U.S. Holocaust Memorial Council   Vol 1: 19395
United States Information Agency   Vol 1: 8329
United States Information Agency - Artistic Ambassador Program   Vol 1: 19398
United States Institute for Theatre Technology   Vol 1: 19400
United States Institute of Peace   Vol 1: 19402
United States Intercollegiate Lacrosse Association   Vol 1: 19407
U.S. International Fireball Association   Vol 1: 19423
U.S. - Israel Binational Science Foundation   Vol 2: 7974
United States Jaycees   Vol 1: 19427
United States Junior Chamber of Commerce   Vol 1: 16394, 19427
United States Lawn Tennis Association   Vol 1: 19642
United States Lighthouse Society   Vol 1: 19431
U.S. Maimed Soldiers League   Vol 1: 16751
United States Marine Corps Combat Correspondents Association   Vol 1: 19433
United States Masters Swimming   Vol 1: 19439
U.S. Metric Association   Vol 1: 19444
U.S. - Mexico Border Health Association   Vol 1: 19446
United States Military Academy   Vol 1: 5827, 12282
United States Military Academy Association of Graduates   Vol 1: 19448
United States Military Sports Association   Vol 1: 19450
U.S. Modern Pentathlon Association   Vol 1: 19454
United States National Commission on Libraries and Information Science   Vol 1: 19456
United States Naval Academy   Vol 1: 10521, 12282, 15094
United States Naval Institute   Vol 1: 15096, 19458
United States Navy   Vol 1: 2162
United States of America Amateur Boxing Federation   Vol 1: 18990
United States of America Rugby Football Union Limited   Vol 1: 19467
United States Office of Personnel Management   Vol 1: 19479
United States Office of Personnel Management - President's Commission on White House Fellowships   Vol 1: 19486
United States Olympic Committee   Vol 1: 19488
U.S. Orienteering Federation   Vol 1: 19495
U.S. Particle Accelerator School   Vol 1: 19498
United States Pilots Association   Vol 1: 19500
United States Police Canine Association   Vol 1: 19502
United States Powerlifting Federation   Vol 1: 19505
United States Powerlifting Federation of the AAU   Vol 1: 19505
United States Professional Tennis Association   Vol 1: 19507, 19668
United States Rowing Association (USRowing)   Vol 1: 19513

U.S. Sailing Association (U.S. SAILING)   Vol 1: 19525
United States Ski Association   Vol 1: 19547
United States Ski Writers Association   Vol 1: 15440
U.S. Skiing   Vol 1: 19547
U.S. Small Business Administration   Vol 1: 19597
United States Soccer Federation   Vol 1: 19605
United States Space Education Association   Vol 1: 19611
United States Space Foundation   Vol 1: 19618
U.S. Sports Acrobatics Federation   Vol 1: 19621
United States Swimming   Vol 1: 19623
United States Synchronized Swimming, Inc.   Vol 1: 19633
U.S. Table Tennis Association   Vol 1: 19640
United States Tennis Association   Vol 1: 19642
U.S. Trivia Association   Vol 1: 19672
United States Trotting Association   Vol 1: 19674
United States Water Polo   Vol 1: 19679
United States Women's Curling Association   Vol 1: 19686
U.S. Wrestling Foundation   Vol 1: 454
U.S. Yacht Racing Union   Vol 1: 19525
United States Youth Soccer Association   Vol 1: 19689
United Technologies Corporation   Vol 1: 2259, 6190
United Technologies Research Center   Vol 1: 15746
United Way of America   Vol 1: 19698
United Way of New York City   Vol 1: 19701
United Workers' Club Usti-nad-Orlici   Vol 2: 1834
UNITER   Vol 2: 10325
Uniunea Arhitectilor din Romania   Vol 2: 10407
Uniunea Artistilor Plastici din Romania   Vol 2: 10393
Uniunea Compozitorilor si Musicologilor din Romania   Vol 2: 10405
Uniunea Scriitorilor din Romania   Vol 2: 10409
Universal Esperanto Association   Vol 2: 9677
Universal Laboratory Ltd.   Vol 2: 7265
Universal Medical Esperanto Association   Vol 2: 8777
Universal Pantheist Society   Vol 1: 19703
Universal Postal Union   Vol 2: 11956
Universal Ship Cancellation Society   Vol 1: 19705
Universala Esperanto-Asocio   Vol 2: 9677
Universala Medicina Esperanto Asocio   Vol 2: 8777
Universidad Autonoma de Ciudad Juarez   Vol 2: 9291
Universidad Autonoma de Queretaro   Vol 2: 9293
Universidad Autonoma Metropolitana   Vol 2: 9122, 9296
Universidad de Colima, Rectoria   Vol 2: 9299
Universidad de Guadalajara   Vol 2: 9259
Universidad de Medellin   Vol 2: 1750
Universidad del Valle   Vol 2: 1753
Universidad Externado de Colombia   Vol 2: 1755
Universidad Nacional Autonoma de Mexico   Vol 2: 9122, 9168
Universidade de Lisboa   Vol 2: 10320
Universita degli Studi di Bologna   Vol 2: 8173
Universita di Ferrara - Centro di Studi sulla Corrosione   Vol 2: 8463

Universita di Padova - Premio Europeo di Letteratura Giovanile P. P. Vergerio   Vol 2: 8465
Universitat Basel   Vol 2: 11961
Universitat Karlsruhe (Technische Hochschule)   Vol 2: 7147
Universite de Geneve   Vol 2: 11958
Universite de technologie de Compiegne   Vol 2: 6460
Universite Libre de Bruxelles   Vol 2: 6940
Universitetet I Oslo   Vol 2: 9960
Universities Athletic Union   Vol 2: 4566
Universities Federation for Animal Welfare   Vol 2: 4570
University Aviation Association   Vol 1: 19720
University Council for Educational Administration   Vol 1: 19724
University Foundation   Vol 2: 1377
The University Museum   Vol 1: 19727
University of Alabama at Birmingham   Vol 1: 19731
University of Arizona - Department of Journalism   Vol 1: 19733
University of Arizona - Department of Radio and Television   Vol 1: 19735
University of Basel   Vol 2: 11961
University of Berne   Vol 2: 11964
University of British Columbia   Vol 1: 19737
University of California - Office of the President   Vol 1: 19739
University of California, Los Angeles - Alumni Association   Vol 1: 19741
University of California, Los Angeles - Anderson Graduate School of Management; John E.   Vol 1: 19751
University of Canterbury   Vol 2: 9847
University of Chicago   Vol 2: 6929
University of Chicago - Department of Germanic Languages and Literatures   Vol 1: 19764
University of Chicago Alumni Association   Vol 1: 19766
University of Chicago Medical Alumni Association   Vol 1: 19774
University of Chicago Medical and Biological Sciences Alumni Association   Vol 1: 19774
University of Chicago Press   Vol 1: 19778
University of Cincinnati - College Conservatory of Music   Vol 1: 19780
University of Colorado   Vol 1: 18693
University of Colorado at Boulder   Vol 1: 9181
University of Copenhagen   Vol 2: 2010
University of Dayton   Vol 1: 19782
University of Denver - College of Business Administration   Vol 1: 19785
University of Edinburgh   Vol 2: 10684
University of Georgia - College of Education   Vol 1: 19787
University of Georgia - College of Journalism and Mass Communication   Vol 1: 19791
University of Georgia Press   Vol 1: 19794
University of Hawaii   Vol 1: 5496
University of Houston   Vol 1: 10020
University of Illinois   Vol 1: 19797
University of Illinois - College of Fine & Applied Arts   Vol 1: 19799
University of Illinois - Graduate School of Library and Information Science   Vol 1: 19801
University of Illinois Press   Vol 1: 15031
University of Iowa - Iowa Writers Workshop   Vol 1: 19803
University of Kansas - White School of Journalism and Mass Communication; William Allen   Vol 1: 19805
University of Kentucky - Department of History   Vol 1: 19807

University of Lethbridge - Faculty of Management & Accounting Education Resource Centre   Vol 1: 19809
University of Limburg   Vol 2: 9680
University of Liverpool   Vol 2: 4573
University of London   Vol 2: 4577
University of London - Institute of Commonwealth Studies   Vol 2: 4580
University of Louisville - Department of Political Science   Vol 1: 19811
University of Louisville - Louisville Presbyterian Theological Seminary   Vol 1: 19813
University of Louisville - School of Education   Vol 1: 19815
University of Louisville - School of Music   Vol 1: 19817
University of Maryland - College of Library and Information Services   Vol 1: 19819
University of Maryland International Music Competitions   Vol 1: 19821
University of Melbourne - Faculty of Arts   Vol 2: 694
University of Melbourne - Faculty of Science   Vol 2: 696
University of Miami - Graduate School of International Studies   Vol 1: 19823
University of Miami - Theatre Arts Department   Vol 1: 19825
University of Michigan   Vol 1: 19827
University of Michigan - Graduate School of Business Administration   Vol 1: 19830
University of Michigan Press   Vol 1: 19832
University of Minnesota   Vol 1: 19835
University of Missouri-Columbia - School of Journalism   Vol 1: 14525, 19838
University of Missouri Press   Vol 1: 19846
University of New South Wales   Vol 2: 698
University of Newcastle   Vol 2: 703
University of North Carolina Press   Vol 1: 10255
University of Notre Dame - Alumni Association   Vol 1: 19848
University of Notre Dame - Dept. of P.R. and Information   Vol 1: 19860
University of Oklahoma   Vol 1: 20502
University of Oklahoma School of Journalism   Vol 1: 14529
University of Otago   Vol 2: 9849
University of Oxford   Vol 2: 4582
University of Padua - Vergerio European Prize for Children's Literature; P. P.   Vol 2: 8465
University of Peradeniya, Sri Lanka   Vol 2: 11406
University of Pittsburgh Press   Vol 1: 19863
University of Rochester   Vol 1: 19866
University of Sheffield   Vol 2: 4584
University of Southern California   Vol 1: 19868
University of Southern California - School of Journalism   Vol 1: 19870
University of Southern Mississippi - School of Library Science   Vol 1: 19872
University of Southwestern Louisiana   Vol 1: 8568
University of Sussex Library   Vol 2: 4586
University of Technology of Compiegne   Vol 2: 6460
University of Texas - M. D. Anderson Cancer Center   Vol 1: 19874
University of Toronto   Vol 1: 19880
University of Toronto - Faculty of Law   Vol 1: 19883
University of Toronto - University College   Vol 1: 19885
University of Toronto Law Alumni Association   Vol 1: 19884

University of Utah - Eccles Health Sciences Library Vol 1: 19887
University of Wisconsin Press Vol 1: 19889
University Photographers' Association of America Vol 1: 19891
University Productions Vol 1: 19895
Unlimited Potential Vol 1: 13587
UNOCAL 76 Corporation Vol 1: 11112
The Unterberg Poetry Center of the 92nd Street Y Vol 1: 19897
UNYSIS Corporation Vol 1: 12054
UOP Vol 1: 2582
UOP Incorporated Vol 1: 10496
Upjohn Vol 1: 1691, 4393, 7924, 15667
Upper Austria State Government Vol 2: 900
Uppsala Film Festival Vol 2: 11653
Upsilon Pi Epsilon Association Vol 1: 19899
Uranium Institute Vol 2: 4588
Urban Affairs Association Vol 1: 19901
Urban Council Public Libraries Office Vol 2: 7276
Urban Land Institute Vol 1: 19903
Urzad Miasta - Gdynia Vol 2: 10144
Urzad Wojewodzki - Gdansk Vol 2: 10144
US-Asia Institute Vol 1: 19905
US Black Engineer Vol 1: 7304
USA Baseball Vol 1: 19908
USA Film Festival Vol 1: 19918
USA Hockey Vol 1: 19921
USA International Ballet Competition, Jackson Vol 1: 19923
USA International Harp Competition Vol 1: 19926
U.S.A. - Korean Karate Association Vol 1: 19928
USA Track and Field Vol 1: 19930
USO of Metropolitan New York Vol 1: 19965
USSA Eastern Alpine Official's Committee Vol 1: 19556
USSR Council of Ministers Vol 2: 10483
USSR Council of Ministers and the Central Committee of the Communist Party of the Soviet Union Vol 2: 10485
Ustredni Reditelstvi Ceskoslovenskeho Filmu Vol 2: 1889
USX Foundation Vol 1: 12986
Utah Arts Council - Literary Program Vol 1: 19968
Utell International Vol 2: 2854
Utility Communicators International Vol 1: 19970
Utley Memorial Fund; T. E. Vol 2: 4590
UVESCO Vol 1: 7746
Val de Marne; Festival International de Films de Femmes de Creteil et du Vol 2: 6071
Valencia County Council Vol 2: 11219
Valic Vol 1: 13085
Valladolid International Film Festival Vol 2: 11391
Vallecorsa Choral Group Vol 2: 8467
Valley Players Vol 1: 19972
Van der Stel Foundation; Simon Vol 2: 11118
van Duyl-Schwartze Foundation; Therese Vol 2: 9684
van Duyl-Schwartze Stichting; Therese Vol 2: 9684
Van Nostrand Reinhold Vol 1: 8403
Vance Publishing Corporation Vol 1: 6304
Vancouver International Film Festival Vol 1: 19974
Vancouver Professional Theatre Alliance Vol 1: 19976
Vanderbilt University Vol 1: 17288
Vanderbilt University Press Vol 1: 19978
Varian Associates Vol 1: 4966
Varian NMR Division Vol 2: 4219
Varian Prize Vol 2: 593
Variety Clubs International Vol 1: 19980
Varna International Ballet Competition Vol 2: 1538
Vatel-Club Luxembourg Vol 2: 8872
The Vatican Vol 2: 12099
Vector Laboratories Vol 1: 4212
Veillon Foundation; Charles Vol 2: 11966
Venezuela - Office of the President Vol 2: 12135
Venezuelan Architectural Association Vol 2: 12141
Venezuelan Geological Society Vol 2: 12143
Venezuelan Section of the International Board on Books for Young People Vol 2: 12145
Venezuelan Society of Civil Engineers Vol 2: 12147
Venice International Film Festival Vol 2: 8469
Ventura County Symphony Association Vol 1: 19984
VER Poets Vol 2: 4592
Verband der Sparkassen Vol 2: 784
Verband Deutscher Elektrotechniker Vol 2: 6527
Verband Deutscher Schulmusiker Vol 2: 6869
Verbandder Koche Deutschlands Vol 2: 7089
Verbatim, The Language Quarterly Vol 2: 1944
The Vercorin Manuscript Vol 2: 8471
Verein der Zellstoff- und Papier-Chemiker und -Ingenieure Vol 2: 6536
Verein Deutscher Eisenhuttenleute Vol 2: 6811
Verein fur Volkskunde Vol 2: 907
Verein von Altertumsfreunden im Regierungs- Bezirk Darmstadt Vol 2: 7149
Verein zur Forderung von Berufsmusikerin- nen Vol 2: 11665
Vereinigung fur Angewandte Botanik Vol 2: 7087
Vereinigung Osterreichischer Bi- bliothekarinnen Bibiothekare Vol 2: 737
Vereinigung Osterreichischer Indus- trieller Vol 2: 735
Vereniging van Letterkundigen Vol 2: 9686
Vereniging van Schouwburg - en Con- certgebouwdirecties in Nederland Vol 2: 9689
Vereniging van Suid-Afrikaanse Bourekenaars Vol 2: 10817
Vereniging voor Auteursrecht Vol 2: 9380
Verlag Junge Welt Vol 2: 7151
Verlanger; Jean Pierre Vol 2: 6462
Vermont Congress of Parents and Teachers and Vermont Department of Libraries Vol 1: 19986
Vermont Historical Society Vol 1: 19988
Very Special Arts Vol 1: 19992
Veteran Wireless Operators Association Vol 1: 19999
Veterans of Foreign Wars Ladies Auxil- iary Vol 1: 20003
Veterans of Foreign Wars of the U.S.A. Vol 1: 20008
Veterans of Safety Vol 1: 4787
Veterans of the Office of Strategic Services in World War II Vol 1: 20020
Viare Publishing Corporation Vol 1: 20022
Victor Company of Japan Vol 2: 8779
Victoria and Albert Museum Vol 2: 4594
Victoria and Albert Museum; National Art Li- brary at the Vol 2: 4595
Victorian Military Society Vol 2: 4596
Video Danse Vol 2: 6464
Video Software Dealers Association Vol 1: 20025
Videotex Industry Association Vol 1: 10526
Vieilles Maisons Francaises Vol 2: 6466
Vienna Chamber Opera Vol 2: 910
Vienna Mozart Society Vol 2: 912
Vienna University of Music and Dramatic Arts Vol 2: 917
Viennese Culture Club Vol 1: 20028, 20029
Vietheer Memorial Trust; Erich Vol 2: 2943
Vietnam Combat Veterans LTD. Vol 1: 20030
Vietnam Veterans of America Vol 1: 20032
Vieux International Alto Competition; Mau- rice Vol 2: 6468
Viking Penguin Vol 1: 20036
Viking Society for Northern Research Vol 2: 4598
Villa I Tatti - Harvard University Center for Italian Renaissance Studies Vol 2: 8473
Villa-Lobos Museum Vol 2: 1500
The Village Voice Vol 1: 20038
Ville de Grenoble Vol 2: 6470
Ville de Lyon Vol 2: 6472
Ville de Perpignan Vol 2: 6187
Ville de Rennes Vol 2: 5248
Ville de Wattrelos Vol 2: 6477
Vinas International Singing Competition; Fran- cisco Vol 2: 11393
Vincent Owners Club Vol 2: 4600
Vinifera Wine Growers Association Vol 1: 20040
Vintage Sailplane Association Vol 1: 20044
Vintage Thunderbird Club International Vol 1: 20049
Vintage Thunderbird Club of America Vol 1: 20049
Vinyl Window and Door Institute Vol 1: 18046
Violin Society of America Vol 1: 20051
Virchow-Pirquet Medical Society Vol 1: 20053
Virgin Group Vol 2: 2252
Virginia Beach Arts Center Vol 1: 20056
Virginia Beach Center for the Arts Vol 1: 20056
Virginia Beach Orchestral Association Vol 1: 20059
Virginia Beach Pops Orchestra Vol 1: 20058
Virginia Commission for the Arts Vol 1: 17216, 20060
Virginia Film Office Vol 1: 20063, 20064
Virginia Poultry Breeders Club Vol 1: 20065
Virginia Quarterly Review Vol 1: 20068
Virginia Recreation and Park Society Vol 1: 20070
Virginia Tech Foundation Vol 1: 2340
Visa U.S.A. Vol 1: 2391, 2392, 2393, 2394, 2395
VisAbility Vol 1: 8628, 8629
Vitelli; Istituto Papirologico Girolamo Vol 2: 8331
Vitromex Vol 2: 9301
Vlaamse Wetenschappeliike Stichting Vol 2: 1381
VM & SD Vol 1: 10446
VMI Cadet Investment Group Vol 1: 20072
Vocational Industrial Clubs of America Vol 1: 20074
Vogin - Nederlandse Vereniging van Gebruik- ers van Online Informatie Systerem Vol 2: 9384
Voice Foundation Vol 1: 20078
Voice of Youth Advocates Vol 1: 2959
Voluntary Health Association of India Vol 2: 7620
Volvo North American Corporation Vol 1: 10558, 10559, 10560, 10561
Volvo Tennis Vol 1: 10549
von Humboldt Foundation; Alexander Vol 1: 6730, 16948
von Humboldt Foundation of New York; Alex- ander Vol 1: 11585

von Humboldt-Stiftung; Alexander   Vol 2: 7153
Von Siemens Foundation; Ernst   Vol 2: 7162
Von Siemens-Stiftung; Ernst   Vol 2: 7162
von Weber; Hochschule fur Musik Carl Maria   Vol 2: 6920
W. V. Publications   Vol 2: 4602
WACC/Europe and Unda/Europe   Vol 2: 7164
Wagner College   Vol 1: 20080
Wagner Society   Vol 2: 567
Wagonlit Travel   Vol 2: 2853
WAIF   Vol 1: 20082
Walkaloosa Horse Association   Vol 1: 20084
Walking Horse Trainers Association   Vol 1: 20086
Wall Colmonoy Corporation   Vol 1: 5088
The Wall Street Journal   Vol 1: 8915
Wallace Reader's Digest Fund; Lila   Vol 1: 20088
Wallant Book Award; Edward Lewis   Vol 1: 20090
Wallenbergs Stiftelse   Vol 2: 11635
Walton League of America; Izaak   Vol 1: 20092
WAMSO Young Artist Competition   Vol 1: 20101
WAQT Productions   Vol 1: 6278
Ward Memorial Fund, Inc.; Winifred   Vol 1: 779
Warman International   Vol 2: 493
Warner-Lambert Company   Vol 1: 1944, 10617, 10619
Warner-Lambert Foundation   Vol 1: 15954
Warner-Lambert/Parke-Davis   Vol 1: 4234
Warringah Shire Council   Vol 2: 705
Warsaw Ministry of Culture and the Arts   Vol 2: 10212
Warsaw Philharmonic   Vol 2: 10213
Warszawskie Towarzystwo Higieniczne   Vol 2: 10189
Waseda Daigaku   Vol 2: 8782
Waseda University   Vol 2: 8782
Washington Academy of Sciences   Vol 1: 20103
Washington-Baltimore Newspaper Guild   Vol 1: 20105
Washington College   Vol 1: 20107
Washington Craft Show   Vol 1: 17350
Washington Independent Writers   Vol 1: 20109
Washington International Competition   Vol 1: 20111
Washington Journalism Center   Vol 1: 20113
Washington Journalism Review   Vol 1: 2754
The Washington Monthly   Vol 1: 20115
Washington Opera Guild   Vol 1: 20118
The Washington Pilgrimage   Vol 1: 16770
The Washington Post - Children's Book Guild of Washington, D.C.   Vol 1: 20120
The Washington Post Company Educational Foundation   Vol 1: 20122
Washington Square Sculpture Program   Vol 1: 20125
Washington State Bar Association - World Peace Through Law Section   Vol 1: 20127
Washington State Library - Washington Authors Collection   Vol 1: 20129
Washington Theatre Awards Society   Vol 1: 20132
Washington Writers' Publishing House   Vol 1: 20134
Washingtonian Magazine   Vol 1: 20136
Watchdogs of the Treasury, Inc.   Vol 1: 20138
Water Environment Federation   Vol 1: 20140
Water Institute of Southern Africa   Vol 2: 11120

Water Instituut van Suidelike Africa   Vol 2: 11120
Water Pollution Control Federation   Vol 1: 20157
Waterbed Manufacturers Association   Vol 1: 20166
Waterbed Retailers Association   Vol 1: 14985
Waterford Glass   Vol 1: 16805
Waterstone and Company   Vol 2: 2051
Wattrelos Short Film and Video Festival   Vol 2: 6476
WAYSEE 2000   Vol 2: 4615
Weatherby Health Care   Vol 1: 8899
Weavers' Company   Vol 2: 4528
Wedding Photographers International   Vol 1: 20173
Wedding Photographers of America   Vol 1: 20173
Wedekind Foundation   Vol 2: 6906
Wedgewood Group   Vol 2: 2251
Weekly Mail & Guardian Film Festival   Vol 2: 11124
Weekly Reader   Vol 1: 13716, 13718
Weekly Reader Corporation   Vol 1: 11191
Weidigsvereniging van Suidelike Afrika   Vol 2: 10873
Weizmann Institute of Science   Vol 2: 7977
Welch Foundation; Robert A.   Vol 1: 20175
Wellberry Books   Vol 1: 20177
Wellcome Trust   Vol 2: 3931
Wellmark Diagnostics   Vol 1: 7208
Welsh Academy   Vol 2: 12193
Welsh Arts Council   Vol 2: 12149
Welsh Books Council   Vol 2: 12195
Welsh National Agricultural Society   Vol 2: 12187
Welsh National Centre for Children's Literature   Vol 2: 12195
Welsh Pony and Cob Society of America   Vol 1: 20179
Welsh Pony Society of America   Vol 1: 20179
Welsh Society   Vol 1: 20181
Welsh Society of Philadelphia   Vol 1: 20181
Welsh Water   Vol 2: 12183
West African College of Surgeons   Vol 2: 9868
West Agro   Vol 1: 1925
West Coast Book Prize Society   Vol 1: 20183
West Indian Tobacco Company   Vol 2: 12037
West London Synagogue   Vol 2: 3515
West Virginia Children's Book Award   Vol 1: 20190
West Virginia Geological Survey   Vol 1: 10648
Westchester Library Association   Vol 1: 20192
Westerby-fondet; Erik   Vol 2: 2012
Westerby Foundation; Erik   Vol 2: 2012
Western and English Manufacturers Association   Vol 1: 20194
Western Associated Modelers   Vol 1: 20197
Western Association of Map Libraries   Vol 1: 20199
Western Electronic Manufacturers Association   Vol 1: 1981
Western Forestry and Conservation Association   Vol 1: 20202
Western Governmental Research Association   Vol 1: 20205
Western Interpretation Association   Vol 1: 13177
Western Magazine Awards Foundation   Vol 1: 20207
Western Political Science Association   Vol 1: 20209
Western Publishing Company   Vol 1: 20211
Western Red Cedar Lumber Association   Vol 1: 2545

Western Reserve Historical Society   Vol 1: 20213
Western Society of Engineers   Vol 1: 20221, 20227
Western States Advertising Agencies Association   Vol 1: 20228
Western States Arts Federation   Vol 1: 20230
Western Wood Products Association   Vol 1: 5742
Western World Pet Supply Association   Vol 1: 20232
Western Writers of America   Vol 1: 20234
Westerners International   Vol 1: 20238
Westinghouse Educational Foundation   Vol 1: 887
Westinghouse Electric Corporation   Vol 1: 10265, 14431, 17122
Westinghouse Foundation   Vol 1: 10279
Westminster Kennel Club   Vol 1: 20243
Westpac Banking Corporation   Vol 2: 317
Wexner Center for the Arts   Vol 1: 20248
Wexner Foundation   Vol 1: 20250
Weyerhaeuser Company Foundation   Vol 1: 5742
Weyerhauser Company Foundation   Vol 1: 15673
Wham-O   Vol 1: 20252, 20491
WHAT Video   Vol 2: 4603
Whatman Scientific Ltd.   Vol 2: 4219
Wheatland Foundation   Vol 1: 20254
Whirlpool Corporation   Vol 1: 12141
Whirly-Girls   Vol 1: 20256
Whitaker Foundation   Vol 1: 6379
White Foundation; William Allen   Vol 1: 10202, 20259
White Horse Ranch Foundation   Vol 1: 10600
White House Commission on Presidential Scholars   Vol 1: 19225
White House News Photographers' Association   Vol 1: 20262
White Library; William Allen   Vol 1: 20264
White Literary Award Trust; Patrick   Vol 2: 707
White-Willis Theatre   Vol 1: 20266
Whitechapel Art Gallery   Vol 2: 4604
Whitesides Company; George   Vol 1: 11220
Whiting Foundation; Mrs. Giles   Vol 1: 20268
Whitman Center for the Arts and Humanities; Walt   Vol 1: 20271
Whitman Cultural Arts Center; Walt   Vol 1: 20271
Whitney; James Lyman   Vol 1: 2937
Wholesale Florists and Florist Suppliers of America   Vol 1: 20273
Wholesale Nursery Growers of America   Vol 1: 14280
Wholesale Stationers' Association   Vol 1: 20275
Whooping Crane Conservation Association   Vol 1: 20278
Wichita Art Museum   Vol 1: 11649
Wider Opportunities for Women   Vol 1: 20280
Wiener Kammeroper   Vol 2: 910
Wieniawski Competitions; International Henryk   Vol 2: 10072
Wiesel Foundation for Humanity; Elie   Vol 1: 20282
Wiesenthal Center; Simon   Vol 1: 20285
Wihuri Foundation for International Prizes   Vol 2: 4761
Wihurin kansainvalisten palkintojen rahasto   Vol 2: 4761
Wilcher Fund; Denny and Ida   Vol 1: 17247
Wild Heerbrugg Instruments   Vol 1: 1821
Wilderness Medical Society   Vol 1: 20288
Wilderness Society   Vol 1: 20291

Wildlife Conservation Society of Zambia   Vol 2: 12202
Wildlife Diseases Association   Vol 1: 20295
Wildlife Society   Vol 1: 20299
Wildlife Society of Southern Africa   Vol 2: 11126
Wildlife Society of Zimbabwe   Vol 2: 12208
Wiley & Sons; John   Vol 1: 2849, 8404
Wiley & Sons Publishing Company; John   Vol 1: 4102
Wilkinson Sword   Vol 2: 2325
Willamette Industries, Incorporated   Vol 1: 5742
Williams Real Estate Company   Vol 1: 12490
Williamson-White Medal   Vol 1: 12160
Willow Bee Publishing House   Vol 1: 20307
Wilmington Star-News   Vol 1: 15299
Wilson Company; H. W.   Vol 1: 2823, 2824, 2905, 4619, 18275
Wilson International Center for Scholars; Woodrow   Vol 1: 20310
Wilson National Fellowship Foundation; Woodrow   Vol 1: 20313
Wilson Ornithological Society   Vol 1: 20317
Wilson Sporting Goods Company   Vol 1: 1322, 10562
Winchell Cancer Fund; Damon Runyon - Walter   Vol 1: 7283
Winchell Foundation; Cancer Research Fund of the Damon Runyon - Walter   Vol 1: 7283
Winchester Press   Vol 1: 20324
Wine Country Film Festival   Vol 1: 20326
The Wine Spectator   Vol 1: 20330
Wingfoot Lighter than Air Society   Vol 1: 11872
Wings Club   Vol 1: 20333
Wings Inc.   Vol 1: 1343
Winnebago Software Company   Vol 1: 5251
Winton Tourist Promotion Association   Vol 2: 709
Wire Association International   Vol 1: 20335
Wisconsin Arts Board   Vol 1: 20339
Wisconsin Cheese Makers' Association   Vol 1: 20341
Wisconsin Library Association   Vol 1: 20344
Wissenschaftlich-Technischer Arbeitskreis fur Denkmalpflege und Bauwerksanierung   Vol 2: 6933
Wissenschaftlicher Verein fur Bauwesen   Vol 2: 7448
Witter Bynner Foundation for Poetry   Vol 1: 20231
Wloclawek Scientific Society   Vol 2: 10215
Wloclawskie Towarzystwo Naukowe   Vol 2: 10215
WMX Technologies, Inc. (Waste Management, Inc.)   Vol 1: 19064
Wo/Man's Showcase   Vol 1: 20266
Wolf Foundation   Vol 2: 7986
Wolf Society; International Hugo   Vol 2: 833
Wolfe Art Club; Catharine Lorillard   Vol 1: 20347
Wolfe Pack   Vol 1: 20349
Wolfe Society; Thomas   Vol 1: 20351
Wolfson Foundation   Vol 2: 4607
Woman in the Moon Press   Vol 1: 15034
Woman's Building   Vol 1: 20355
Woman's Day   Vol 2: 9297
Woman's Journal   Vol 2: 4609
Women Band Directors National Association   Vol 1: 20357
Women Business Owners of New York   Vol 1: 20368
Women in Communications, Inc.   Vol 1: 20373
Women in Communications, New York Chapter   Vol 1: 20377
Women in Community Service   Vol 1: 20379

Women in Film   Vol 1: 20381
Women in Film and Video/New England   Vol 1: 20387
Women in Government Relations   Vol 1: 20389
Women in Management   Vol 1: 20391
Women in Sales Association   Vol 1: 20393
Women in Science and Engineering   Vol 1: 20395
Women in Show Business   Vol 1: 20399
Women in the Arts Foundation   Vol 1: 20402
Women Marines Association   Vol 1: 20404
Women's Action for New Directions Education Fund   Vol 1: 20406
Women's Bar Association of the District of Columbia   Vol 1: 20409
Women's Campaign for Soviet Jewry   Vol 2: 4611
Women's Caucus   Vol 2: 142
Women's Caucus for Art   Vol 1: 20411
Women's Equity Action League   Vol 1: 20413
Women's Institute   Vol 1: 4945
Women's International Bowling Congress   Vol 1: 13472, 20417
Women's International Film Festival   Vol 2: 1383
Women's International League for Peace and Freedom   Vol 1: 133
Women's International Zionist Organization   Vol 2: 7988
Women's Literary Society   Vol 2: 7218
Women's National Book Association   Vol 1: 20420
Women's Sports Foundation   Vol 1: 20423
Women's Symphony Committee of Kingsport   Vol 1: 11702
Women's Transportation Seminar - National   Vol 1: 20438
Women's Veterinary Medical Association   Vol 1: 5662
Wonder Woman Foundation   Vol 1: 20442
Woodson Art Museum; Leigh Yawkey   Vol 1: 20444
Woodstock School of Art   Vol 1: 20447
Wool Bureau   Vol 1: 20450
Woolknit Associates   Vol 1: 20452
Wootton; Jones Lang   Vol 2: 204
Word Works Washington Prize   Vol 1: 20454
Workers Defense League   Vol 1: 20456
Working Press Association of New Jersey   Vol 1: 20458
Workshop Library on World Humour   Vol 1: 20460
World Academy of Art and Science   Vol 2: 919
World Affairs Council of Northern California   Vol 1: 20462
World Airlines Clubs Association   Vol 1: 20464
The World Almanac   Vol 1: 15359, 15360, 15361
World Anti-Communist League   Vol 2: 8835
World Artifex Society   Vol 1: 20467
World Assembly of Small and Medium Enterprises   Vol 2: 7723
World Association for Celebrating Year 2000 - WAYSEE 2000   Vol 2: 4615
World Association for Public Opinion Research   Vol 1: 20469
World-Association for the History of Veterinary Medicine   Vol 2: 9691
World Association of Christian Radio Amateurs and Listeners   Vol 2: 4617
World Association of Inventors and Researchers   Vol 2: 1385
World Association of Sarcoidosis & Other Granulomatous Disorders   Vol 2: 4619

World Association of Societies of Pathology (Anatomic and Clinical)   Vol 2: 8787
World Association of Veterinary Anatomists   Vol 1: 20471
World Bank   Vol 1: 20473
World Beefalo Association   Vol 1: 1332
World Book   Vol 1: 7381, 14545, 14550
World Book, Inc.   Vol 1: 2825
World Bowling Writers   Vol 1: 20475
World Boxing Council   Vol 2: 9303
World Chess Federation   Vol 2: 7223
World Coin News   Vol 1: 11732
World Communication Association   Vol 1: 20480
World Confederation for Physical Therapy   Vol 2: 4621
World Conservation Union   Vol 2: 11968
World Council of Management (CIOS)   Vol 2: 8907
World Council of Young Men's Service Clubs   Vol 2: 9853
World Cultural Council   Vol 2: 9305
World Dance & Dance Sport Council   Vol 2: 4623
World Environment Center   Vol 1: 20482
World Federation for Culture Collections   Vol 2: 711
World Federation of Bergen-Belsen Associations   Vol 1: 20484
World Federation of Hungarian Freedom Fighters   Vol 1: 20486
World Federation of Jewish Fighters, Partisans and Camp Inmates   Vol 2: 7990
World Federation of Personnel Management Associations   Vol 2: 713
World Federation of Rose Societies   Vol 2: 108
World Federation of the Deaf   Vol 2: 4764
World Federation of Travel Journalists and Writers   Vol 2: 6478
World Festival of Mountain Pictures   Vol 2: 6480
World Festival of Underwater Pictures   Vol 2: 6482
The World Food Prize Foundation   Vol 1: 20488
World Footbag Association   Vol 1: 20490
World Golf Village   Vol 1: 16476
World Health Organization   Vol 2: 1528, 6112, 11972
World Health Organization - International Agency for Research on Cancer   Vol 2: 6484
World Hunger Year   Vol 1: 20492
World Institute of Black Communications   Vol 1: 20495
World International Nail and Beauty Association   Vol 1: 20497
World League for Freedom and Democracy   Vol 2: 8835
World Leisure and Recreation Association   Vol 1: 20499
World Literature Today   Vol 1: 20501
World Meteorological Organization   Vol 2: 9469, 11977
World Methodist Council   Vol 1: 20503
World Millennial Association   Vol 2: 4615
World Modeling Association   Vol 1: 20505
World Music Contest Foundation, Kerkrade   Vol 2: 9693
World Ocean and Cruise Liner Society   Vol 1: 20513
World of Poetry   Vol 1: 20515
World Organisation of General Systems and Cybernetics   Vol 2: 6487
World Organisation of Systems and Cybernetics   Vol 2: 6487

World Organization of Former Pupils of Catholic Education   Vol 2: 8475
World Organization of Gastroenterology   Vol 2: 7166
World Organization of Jewish Deaf   Vol 2: 7992
World Organization of National Colleges, Academies and Academic Associations of General Practitioners/Family Physicians   Vol 2: 7280
World Organization of the Scout Movement   Vol 2: 11981
World Packaging Organisation   Vol 2: 6489
World Peace Council   Vol 2: 4766
World Philatelic Congress of Holy Land and Israel   Vol 1: 20517
World Phosphate Institute   Vol 2: 9323
World Phosphate Rock Institute   Vol 2: 9323
World Ploughing Organisation   Vol 2: 4625
World Press Photo Foundation   Vol 2: 9696
World Press Review   Vol 1: 20519
World Relief Commission   Vol 1: 20521
World Relief Corporation   Vol 1: 20521
World Science Fiction Society   Vol 1: 20523
World SF   Vol 2: 6491
World Ship Trust   Vol 2: 4627
World Small Animal Veterinary Association   Vol 2: 4629
World Society for the Protection of Animals   Vol 2: 4632
World Taekwondo Federation   Vol 2: 8837
World Tennis   Vol 1: 20525
World Trade Center of New Orleans   Vol 1: 20527
World Union of Karate-do Organizations   Vol 2: 6496
World University Service of Canada   Vol 1: 20532
World Veterans Federation   Vol 2: 6498
World Veterinary Association   Vol 2: 11395
World Veterinary Poultry Association   Vol 2: 7170, 7171
World Wildlife Fund   Vol 2: 11985
Worldaware   Vol 2: 4634
Worlddidac Foundation   Vol 2: 11983
WORLDFEST - Houston International Film and Video Festival   Vol 1: 20537
Worldradio   Vol 1: 20540
World's Poultry Science Association   Vol 2: 7172
World's Woman's Christian Temperance Union   Vol 2: 715
Worldwide Fund for nature   Vol 2: 11553
Worshipful Company of Carmen   Vol 2: 4310
Worshipful Company of Carpenters   Vol 2: 3623
Worshipful Company of Constructors   Vol 2: 3230
Worshipful Company of Ironmongers   Vol 2: 3076
Worshipful Company of Musicians   Vol 2: 2938
Worshipful Company of Plaisterers   Vol 2: 3686
Worshipful Society of Apothecaries of London   Vol 2: 4636
Worthington Pump, Inc.   Vol 1: 4715
Worthington Pump International   Vol 2: 8477
WOSU Stations   Vol 1: 20542
WPC Club   Vol 1: 20544
Wrangler Jeans World Champion Bullfighter   Vol 1: 16511
Wright State University   Vol 1: 16552

Wrigley, Jr. Company; William   Vol 1: 10623
Writers' Development Trust   Vol 1: 20547, 20552
Writer's Digest   Vol 1: 20549
Writers' Federation of Nova Scotia   Vol 1: 20551
Writers Guild of Alberta   Vol 1: 20554
Writers Guild of America, west   Vol 1: 20556
Writer's Union of the SRR   Vol 2: 10409
Writers Workshop   Vol 1: 20563
Writing Doctors Association   Vol 2: 6500
Wroclaw International Triennial of Drawing   Vol 2: 10217
Wroclaw Scientific Society   Vol 2: 10219
Wroclawskie Towarzystwo Naukowe   Vol 2: 10219
Wurlitzer Foundation; Farny R.   Vol 1: 12524
WWF World Wide Fund for Nature   Vol 2: 11985
Wyeth-Ayerst Laboratories   Vol 1: 15650, 17398
Xavier University   Vol 1: 20565
Xerox Corporation   Vol 1: 185, 3465, 4075, 15761, 17498, 19066
Xerox Foundation   Vol 1: 16863, 20231
Yachting Journalists' Association   Vol 2: 4639
Yad Vashem   Vol 2: 7994
Yale Series of Younger Poets   Vol 1: 20567
Yale University - Beinecke Library   Vol 1: 20569
Yale University - Cowles Foundation for Research in Economics   Vol 1: 20571
Yamaha Corporation of America   Vol 1: 18528
Yamaha Music Corporation of America   Vol 1: 12525
Yankee Magazine   Vol 1: 20573
Yeats Club   Vol 2: 4642
Yediot Ahronot   Vol 2: 7996
Yellow Springs Institute   Vol 1: 20575
Yellow Springs Institute for Contemporary Studies and the Arts   Vol 1: 20575
Yeshiva University   Vol 1: 20577
Yeshiva University - Einstein College of Medicine; Albert   Vol 1: 20589
YM-YWHA of Metropolitan New Jersey   Vol 1: 11521
Ymgyrch Diogelu Cymru Wledig   Vol 2: 12163
Yomiuri Shimbun   Vol 2: 8790
Yorkshire Post   Vol 2: 4644
Yorkshire Terrier Club of America   Vol 1: 20591
Yorkton International Short Film & Video Festival 1981   Vol 1: 20596
Yorkton Short Film & Video Festival   Vol 1: 20596
Yosetsu Gakkai   Vol 2: 8644
Young Adult Services Interest Group   Vol 1: 7001
Young American Bowling Alliance   Vol 1: 20598
Young Australians Best Book Award Council   Vol 2: 718
Young Concert Artists   Vol 1: 20602
Young Concert Artists Trust   Vol 2: 4648
Young Entomologists' Society   Vol 1: 20604
Young Men's Christian Association   Vol 1: 20607
Young Men's Christian Association of Greater New York   Vol 1: 20609
Young Menswear Association   Vol 1: 20613
Young Menswear Association of the Men's Apparel Industry   Vol 1: 20613
Young Ornithologists' Club   Vol 2: 4650

Young Patronesses of the Opera   Vol 1: 20615
Young Playwrights Inc.   Vol 1: 20617
Young Printing Executives Club   Vol 1: 20619
Young Women's Christian Association Council of Zimbabwe   Vol 2: 12210
Young Years Publishing House   Vol 2: 10785
Youth Book Publishing House   Vol 2: 10806
YR Academi Gymreig   Vol 2: 12198
Y's Men International   Vol 2: 11989
YTV Canada   Vol 1: 20621
Yuchi Indian Tribe   Vol 1: 10243
Yuchi Tribal Organization   Vol 1: 10243
Yugoslav Theatre Festival   Vol 2: 10704
YWCA of Houston   Vol 1: 20623
YWCA of New York   Vol 1: 20626
Zachary Society for the Performing Arts; Loren L.   Vol 1: 20629
Zagreb World Festival of Animated Films   Vol 2: 1815
Zaidan-hojin Tokyo Ongakusai Kyokai   Vol 2: 8771
Zalozba Mladinska Knjiga   Vol 2: 10806
Zaragoza Fair   Vol 2: 11397
Zaragoza Institution for Fairs and Exhibitions   Vol 2: 11397
Zbinden Foundation for Realistic Animal Protection in Bio-Medical Research; Hildegard Doerenkamp and Gerhard   Vol 2: 11745
Zbinden Stiftung fur realistisch en Tierschutz; Hildegard Doerenkamp/Gerhard   Vol 2: 11745
Zeiss Foundation; Carl   Vol 2: 6640
Zeiss Optical; Carl   Vol 1: 9839
Zeitschrift fur Allgemeinmedizin   Vol 2: 6917
Zen-Do Kai Martial Arts Association   Vol 1: 20631
Zeneca Pharmaceuticals Group   Vol 1: 176, 703, 3059
ZERO TO THREE: National Center for Clinical Infant Programs   Vol 1: 20635
Zerotin Singing Choir   Vol 2: 1892
Zeta Beta Tau   Vol 1: 20637
Zijlstra Foundation; Adama   Vol 2: 9614
Zimbabwe Institution of Engineers   Vol 2: 12212
Zimbabwe Literature Bureau   Vol 2: 12217
Zimbabwe National Traditional Dance Association   Vol 2: 12219
Zimbabwe Scientific Association   Vol 2: 12221
Zimbabwe Teachers Association   Vol 2: 12224
Zinc Development Association   Vol 2: 4653
Zionist Organization of America   Vol 1: 20641
Zisking-Somerfeld Research Foundation   Vol 1: 17793
ZOE-CON Corporation   Vol 2: 5083
Zonta Club di Napoli - Italia   Vol 2: 8479
Zonta International Foundation   Vol 1: 20643
Zonta International, Naples Area - Italy   Vol 2: 8479
Zoological Society of Japan   Vol 2: 8796
Zoological Society of London   Vol 2: 4655
Zoological Society of Southern Africa   Vol 2: 11130
Zurich Opera   Vol 2: 11676
Zveza bibliotekarskih drustev Slovenije   Vol 2: 10796
Zweites Deutsches Fernseh   Vol 2: 7074
Zwiazek Kompozytorow Polskich   Vol 2: 10140

Award Index

The Award Index provides an alphabetical listing of all awards appearing in both volumes, as well as alternate-language, former, and popular award names. Identically named awards are followed by an indented alphabetical list of the organizations administering an award by that name. Each award name is followed by the volume in which it appears. The numbers following the volume references refer to award book entry numbers, not page numbers.

3M/JMRT Professional Development Grant Vol. 1: 2920
3M Life Sciences Award Vol. 1: 9092
3M Mayneord Memorial Lecture Vol. 2: 2404
3M/NMRT Professional Development Grant Vol. 1: 2920
3M Talking Book of the Year Vol. 2: 612
20th Century Prize Vol. 1: 12372
21st Century Award Vol. 1: 10595
$24 Citizenship Award Vol. 1: 12511
25th Anniversary Pioneer Award Vol. 1: 3933
"54" Founders Award Vol. 1: 20093
100-lecie czasopisma Zdrowie Vol. 2: 10194
The 100 Show Vol. 1: 1443
125th Anniversary Medals Vol. 1: 7765
369th Veterans' Association Service Award Vol. 1: 7
AA Life/M-NET Vita Film Awards Vol. 2: 10814
AA Life Vita Art Now Vol. 2: 10809
AA Life Vita Ballet and Opera Awards Vol. 2: 10810
AA Life Vita Contemporary Choreography and Dance Awards Vol. 2: 10811
AA Life Vita National Theatre Awards Vol. 2: 10812
AA Life Vita Regional Theatre Awards Vol. 2: 10813
AAA Championship Race Vol. 1: 7517
AAAE Outstanding Young Member Award Vol. 1: 833
AAAM Award of Merit Vol. 1: 5607
AAAM Service Award Vol. 1: 5608
AAAP Research Award Vol. 1: 912
AAAS Academy Research Grants Vol. 1: 878
AAAS Hilliard Roderick Prize in Science, Arms Control and International Security Vol. 1: 879
AAAS Mentor Award Vol. 1: 880
AAAS Newcomb Cleveland Prize Vol. 1: 881
AAAS Philip Hauge Abelson Prize Vol. 1: 882
AAAS Prize for Behavioral Science Research Vol. 1: 883
AAAS - Rosenstiel Award in Oceanographic Science Vol. 1: 884
AAAS Scientific Freedom and Responsibility Award Vol. 1: 885
AAAS - Socio-Psychological Prize Vol. 1: 883
AAAS Thousand Dollar Prize Vol. 1: 881
AAAS - Westinghouse Award for Public Understanding of Science and Technology Vol. 1: 886
AAAS - Westinghouse Science Journalism Awards Vol. 1: 887
AAASS Award for Distinguished Contributions to Slavic Studies Vol. 1: 891
AABB Scholarship Awards Vol. 1: 920

AABP Amstutz - Williams Award Vol. 1: 938
AABP Distinguished Service Award Vol. 1: 939
AACC Education Award Vol. 1: 2563
AACC International Fellowship Vol. 1: 846
AACC Past President's Award Vol. 1: 847
AACD/Carl D. Perkins Legislative Award Vol. 1: 1879
AACD Distinguished Professional Service Award Vol. 1: 1885
AACD Legislative Service Award Vol. 1: 1878
AACG Crystal Growth Award Vol. 1: 855
AACP Clinical Research Award Vol. 1: 541
AACS/TEC Teacher of the Year Vol. 1: 5671
AACT Corporate Award Vol. 1: 971
AACTP Award of Excellence for an Outstanding Correctional Training System Vol. 1: 980
AADA Alumni Achievement Award Vol. 1: 552
AAE School Administrator Awards Vol. 1: 11674
AAESA Outstanding Service Award Vol. 1: 1171
AAESA Special Recognition Award Vol. 1: 1172
AAF Best in the West Creative Competition Vol. 1: 743
AAFP Award of Merit Vol. 1: 577
AAFP President's Award Vol. 1: 578
AAHA Award Vol. 1: 784
AAHA Veterinary Awareness Gold Key Award Vol. 1: 785
AAHE Distinguished Service Award Vol. 1: 5611
AAHE Scholar Award Vol. 1: 5612
AAHS Trophy (American Aviation Historical Society) Vol. 2: 2041
AAIE Hall of Fame Vol. 1: 5617
AAII Doctoral Dissertation Grant Vol. 1: 9199
AALAS Animal Technician Award Vol. 1: 864
AALAS Research Award Vol. 1: 863
AALAS Technical Notes Award Vol. 1: 868
AAMC Award for Distinguished Research in the Biomedical Sciences Vol. 1: 5687
AAMI Annual Meeting Manuscript Awards Vol. 1: 5622
AAMI Foundation Awards Vol. 1: 5620
AAMI Foundation Prize
   Association for the Advancement of Medical Instrumentation Vol. 1: 5620
   Association for the Advancement of Medical Instrumentation Foundation Vol 1: 5623
AAMR Awards Vol. 1: 1250
AAN American Beautification Award Vol. 1: 1063
AAN Media Award Vol. 1: 627
AAN Nursery Extension Award Vol. 1: 1064

Aanmoedigingsprijs Vol. 2: 9636
Aanmoedigingsprijzen Vol. 2: 9635
AAOHN Clinical Session Awards Vol. 1: 1074
AAP Awards for Excellence in Pediatric Research Vol. 1: 661
AAP Distinguished Public Information Service Award Vol. 1: 662
AAP Excellence in Public Service Award Vol. 1: 663
AAP Nutrition Award Vol. 1: 664
AAPA Humanitarian Physician Assistant of the Year Vol. 1: 700
AAPA Inner City Physician Assistant of the Year Vol. 1: 701
AAPA Outstanding Physician Assistant of the Year Award Vol. 1: 702
AAPA PA Awareness Achievement Award Vol. 1: 703
AAPA Rural Physician Assistant of the Year Vol. 1: 704
AAPAA Media Awards (Jimmie Awards) Vol. 1: 5704
AAPL Distinguished Service Award Vol. 1: 709
AAPL Outstanding Service Award Vol. 1: 709
AAPOR Award Vol. 1: 870
AAPSC Outstanding Agency Award Vol. 1: 1142
AAPSC Outstanding Practitioner Award Vol. 1: 1143
Aarestrup Prize; Emil Vol. 2: 1924
AARP Disability Project Award Vol. 1: 1157
AARP Legacy Awards Vol. 1: 1158
AART Playwrighting Contest Vol. 1: 115
Aarvold Award for International Achievement; Carl Vol. 2: 3540
AARWBA All-America Auto Racing Teams Vol. 1: 1283
AARWBA Hall of Fame Award (Legends of Racing) Vol. 1: 1284
AAS - American Society for Eighteenth-Century Studies Fellowships Vol. 1: 799
AAS Distinguished Service Medallions Vol. 1: 5274
AAS Flight Achievement Award Vol. 1: 1252
AAS Honorary National Commander Vol. 1: 5275
AAS Individual Awards Vol. 1: 5276
AAS National Commander Awards Vol. 1: 5277
AAS National Medal and Ribbon Vol. 1: 5278
AAS Outstanding Area Advisor Vol. 1: 5279
AAS Outstanding Squadron Advisor Vol. 1: 5280
AAS Space Flight Award Vol. 1: 1253
AAS Squadron Awards Vol. 1: 5281
AASCU/Christa McAuliffe Showcase for Excellence Awards Vol. 1: 1197

889

AASCU Distinguished Alumnus Award Vol. 1: 1198
AASCU Showcase for Excellence Awards Vol. 1: 1197
AASECT Award Vol. 1: 1192
AASL ABC/CLIO Leadership Grant Vol. 1: 2827
AASL Distinguished School Administrators Award Vol. 1: 2828
AASL Distinguished Service Award Vol. 1: 2829
AASL/EB School Library Media Program of the Year Award Vol. 1: 2834
AASL Emergency Librarian Publication Award Vol. 1: 2830
AASL Frances Henne Award Vol. 1: 2831
AASL Intellectual Freedom Award Vol. 1: 2832
AASL Microcomputer in the Media Center Award Vol. 1: 2833
AASL National School Library Media Program of the Year Award Vol. 1: 2834
AASL President's Award Vol. 1: 2829
AASL/SIRS Intellectual Freedom Award Vol. 1: 2832
AATA Animal Welfare Award Vol. 1: 5164
AATE Distinguished Book Award Vol. 1: 766
AATE Research Award Vol. 1: 767
AATE Special Recognition Citations Vol. 1: 768
AAU Association Communications Award Vol. 1: 401
AAU James E. Sullivan Memorial Award Vol. 1: 402
AAU Jujitsu Service Award; Professor Regennitter Vol. 1: 447
AAU Media Award Vol. 1: 403
AAU Outstanding Wrestling Official of the Year Vol. 1: 404
AAU Promotions Award Vol. 1: 405
AAU Volunteer Hall of Fame Vol. 1: 406
AAU Wrestling Person of the Year Vol. 1: 407
AAUA Foundation Award; Dr. Donald A. Gatzke Vol. 1: 1227
AAUA Foundation Award; Dr. Leo and Margaret Goodman-Malamuth Vol. 1: 1227
AAUP Award for Excellence in Coverage of Higher Education Vol. 1: 1229
AAUP Design Show Vol. 1: 5697
AAUW Achievement Award Vol. 1: 1234
AAZPA Bean Award Vol. 1: 1243
ABA Ostwald Band Composition Award Vol. 1: 1293
ABB Transformatori and Telettra Vol. 2: 8346
Abbado for Violinists; International Competition M. Vol. 2: 7999
Abbe Award for Distinguished Service to Atmospheric Sciences by an Individual; Cleveland Vol. 1: 3070
Abbot Award; Charles Greeley Vol. 1: 4835
Abbott Award Vol. 1: 7181
Abbott Award; Mr. Vol. 1: 18441
Abbott Best Editorial Awards; Robert S. Vol. 1: 14397
Abbott Laboratories Award in Clinical and Diagnostic Immunology Vol. 1: 4197
Abbott Prize Vol. 2: 4387
ABBY Award Vol. 1: 1360
ABC Breed Promotion Vol. 1: 1327
ABC Certification Award Vol. 1: 5716
ABC Champion Performance Horse Vol. 1: 1328
ABC Champion Trail Horse Vol. 1: 1329
ABC-CLIO America: History and Life Award Vol. 1: 15811

ABC Concerts and Vocal Competition Vol. 2: 197
ABC Excellence in Construction Awards Vol. 1: 5393
ABC Hall of Fame Vol. 1: 1366
ABC Sports Award of the Year Vol. 2: 195
ABC Sportsman of the Year Vol. 2: 195
ABC Young Performers' Competition Vol. 2: 197
ABCA Coach of the Year Award Vol. 1: 1315
ABCA Hall of Fame Vol. 1: 1316
ABCA Honor Awards Vol. 1: 1317
ABCA Twenty-Five Year Awards Vol. 1: 1318
Abe Prize Vol. 2: 8602
Abel Award in Pharmacology; John J. Vol. 1: 4231
Abel Award; Paul Vol. 1: 16728
Abella; Prix Charles Vol. 2: 5352
Abella; Prix Francoise Vol. 2: 5391
Abello; Premio Juan Vol. 2: 11341
Abelson Prize; AAAS Philip Hauge Vol. 1: 882
Abendroth Award; Evelyn A. Vol. 1: 1390
Aberconway Medal Vol. 2: 2919
Abercrombie Prize; Sir Patrick Vol. 2: 6058
Aberdeen Memorial Trophy; Coach Stuart W. Vol. 1: 6961
Aberg Post Graduate Award; Ulf Vol. 2: 2798
ABET Fellow Vol. 1: 91
ABET Honor Roll Vol. 1: 92
ABI/BMA Trophy Vol. 2: 2430
Ability Fund Award Vol. 1: 7116
Abitibi-Temiscaminque International Film Festival Vol. 1: 16433
Able ALDAn Award Vol. 1: 5849
Ablett Prize Vol. 2: 3125
ABMM Professional Recognition Award Vol. 1: 4198
ABOA Foundation - National Scholastic Press Association Pacemaker Awards Vol. 1: 15355
ABP National Awards for Cooperation and Journalistic Excellence Vol. 1: 5417
ABPA/Andrew Fabinyi Award Vol. 2: 193
Abragam; Fondation Anatole et Suzanne Vol. 2: 5486
Abram Open Obedience Award Vol. 1: 3984
Abrams Award; V. Talbert Vol. 1: 4240
Abrams Medal; General Creighton W. Vol. 1: 5983
Abrams Scholarship Program; Charles Vol. 1: 3528
Abravanel Second Prize; Lucy Vol. 1: 6217
ABS Founders' Memorial Award Vol. 1: 5158
ABSA Business Awards Vol. 2: 2030
ABU Engineering Award Vol. 2: 8888
ABU Prize Competitions for Radio and Television Programmes Vol. 2: 8889
Abundy Service Award Vol. 1: 15
Abzug Memorial Award; Martin Vol. 1: 15026
ACA/Carl D. Perkins Government Relations Award Vol. 1: 1879
ACA Extended Research Award Vol. 1: 1880
ACA Gold Medal Award Vol. 1: 5720
ACA Honors Award Vol. 1: 1423
ACA Outstanding Achievement Award Vol. 1: 1424
ACA Professional Development Award Vol. 1: 1881
ACA Public Service Award Vol. 1: 1896
ACA Research Award Vol. 1: 1882
Academic Achievement Award
  Association of Medical Rehabilitation Administrators Vol. 1: 5862
  College Football Association Vol 1: 7899
Academic Achievement Awards Vol. 1: 5012

Academic Athletes of the Year (All Academic Team) Vol. 1: 13615
Academic Medicine Fellowship Program Vol. 1: 14341
Academic or Research Librarian of the Year Award Vol. 1: 2866
Academic Team-of-the-Year Vol. 1: 14257
Academic Year Grant Program Vol. 1: 10467
Academico Honorario Vol. 2: 7238
Academy Award Vol. 1: 611
Academy Award of Sports Vol. 1: 12707
Academy Awards
  American Academy of Arts and Letters Vol. 1: 494
  New Zealand Academy of Fine Arts Vol 2: 9750
Academy Awards of Merit (Oscar) Vol. 1: 57
Academy Awards Program Vol. 1: 2994
Academy Fellow
  Academy of Criminal Justice Sciences Vol. 1: 33
  Academy of Security Educators and Trainers Vol 1: 84
Academy Honorary Awards Vol. 1: 58
Academy-Institute Awards Vol. 1: 494
Academy Nikola Obreshkov Prize Vol. 2: 1513
Academy of Athens Medal Vol. 2: 7181
Academy of Athens Prize Vol. 2: 7182
Academy of Authors Vol. 1: 10433
Academy of Country Music Awards Vol. 1: 31
Academy of Distinguished Entrepreneurs Vol. 1: 6213
Academy of Fellows Vol. 1: 11332
Academy of Legends Vol. 1: 179
Academy of Management Book Award Vol. 1: 47
Academy of Natural Sciences Gold Medal for Distinction in Natural History Art Vol. 1: 68
Academy of Pharmaceutical Research and Science Fellow Vol. 1: 3371
Academy of Pharmacy Practice and Management Fellow Vol. 1: 3372
Academy of Research Honorary Member Vol. 1: 3295
Academy of Students of Pharmacy Chapter Achievement Award Vol. 1: 3373
Academy of Students of Pharmacy Chapter Membership Achievement Awards Vol. 1: 3374
Acanfora International Prize; Ermanno Vol. 2: 8435
ACB Foundation Award Vol. 2: 2114
Access Award Vol. 1: 7754
Accessible Design Award Vol. 1: 18900
ACCI Thesis/Dissertation Award Vol. 1: 1860
Accord Award Vol. 1: 9778
Accountancy Journalist of the Year Vol. 2: 2579
Accountants, Bankers and Factors Division Award Vol. 1: 2728
Accounting Case Writing Competition Vol. 1: 19810
ACCP/Alfred Soffer Research Awards Vol. 1: 1617
ACCP Critical Care Research Award; DuPont Pharmaceuticals/ Vol. 1: 1618
ACCP Young Investigator Awards; DuPont Pharmaceuticals/ Vol. 1: 1619
ACCU Prizes for Fully-Illustrated Literacy Follow-up Materials Vol. 2: 8498
ACE Award Vol. 1: 13524
Ace Award Vol. 1: 18516
ACE Awards (Awards for Cable Excellence) for Programming Vol. 1: 12590

Award Index
Volume 2: International and Foreign

ACE Distinguished Service Award for Lifetime Achievement   Vol. 1: 1866
ACE Eddie Award   Vol. 1: 1580
ACE Fellows Program   Vol. 1: 1867
ACEA Engineering Awards   Vol. 2: 135
Aceves; Premio Maestro Salvador   Vol. 2: 9279
ACF Public Service Award   Vol. 1: 5761
ACFAS/Northern Telecom Science Teaching Award   Vol. 1: 5430
ACHA Article Award   Vol. 1: 1656
Acha Award for Veterinary Public Health; Pedro   Vol. 1: 15923
ACHA World Champion Coonhound   Vol. 1: 1830
Achard; Prix Charles   Vol. 2: 4815
ACHEMA-Plakette in Titan   Vol. 2: 6614
ACHEMA Plaque in Titanium   Vol. 2: 6614
Achievement Award
   Alpha Omega Fraternity   Vol. 1: 366
   American Association of Managing General Agents   Vol 1: 1033
   American Association of Meat Processors   Vol 1: 1035
   American Equilibration Society   Vol 1: 1999
   American Foreign Law Association   Vol 1: 2083
   American Kinesiotherapy Association   Vol 1: 2766
   American Network of Community Options and Resources   Vol 1: 3189
   American Scientific Glassblowers Society   Vol 1: 4024
   American Trucking Associations - National Freight Claim and Security Council   Vol 1: 4936
   American Women in Radio and Television   Vol 1: 5109
   Association for Systems Management   Vol 1: 5602
   Deafness Research Foundation   Vol 1: 8551
   Lighter Than Air Society   Vol 1: 11873
   National Association of County Agricultural Agents   Vol 1: 13050
   National Black Police Association   Vol 1: 13459
   Society of Toxicology   Vol 1: 18068
   Society of Women Engineers   Vol 1: 18099
   USA Baseball   Vol 1: 19909
Achievement Award in Rehabilitation   Vol. 1: 2766
Achievement Awards   Vol. 1: 9848
Achievement Awards in Children's Television   Vol. 1: 111
Achievement Awards in Writing   Vol. 1: 13761
Achievement Citation Award   Vol. 1: 2842
Achievement in Ceramics Award   Vol. 1: 1446
Achievement in Children's Television Awards   Vol. 1: 111
Achievement in Communication   Vol. 1: 10682
Achievement in the Arts Award   Vol. 1: 15528
Achievement Medal: Air Force   Vol. 1: 19128
Achievement Medal: Army   Vol. 1: 19129
Achievement Medal: Coast Guard   Vol. 1: 19130
Achievement Medal: Navy - Marine Corps   Vol. 1: 19131
Achievement of Social Studies Education General Grant   Vol. 1: 13709
Achievement of the Year Award   Vol. 1: 5812
Achievement Through Action Award   Vol. 2: 508
Achiever of the Year   Vol. 1: 9655
Achievers' Circle   Vol. 1: 12882
Achieving Excellence Award   Vol. 1: 10902
ACI Construction Practice Award   Vol. 1: 1774
ACI Fellows   Vol. 1: 1775

ACI Structural Research Award   Vol. 1: 1776
Acker; Prix Ernest   Vol. 2: 958
Ackerley Prize; J. R.   Vol. 2: 2782
Ackerman Marketing Director of the Year; Raymond   Vol. 2: 10876
Ackermann Medal for Excellence in Water Management; William C.   Vol. 1: 4999
ACM Doctoral Dissertation Award   Vol. 1: 5465
ACM Karl V. Karlstrom Outstanding Educator Award   Vol. 1: 5466
ACMS Scientific Achievement Award   Vol. 1: 7642
A.C.N.O. Merit Award   Vol. 2: 4960
ACNP Travel Fellowship   Vol. 1: 1686
Acorn Awards   Vol. 2: 2571
Acorn Memorial People's Poetry Award; Milton   Vol. 1: 16064
ACRL Doctoral Dissertation Fellowship   Vol. 1: 2867
ACRL/EBSS Distinguished Education and Behavioral Sciences Librarian Award   Vol. 1: 2868
ACS Award for Computers in Chemistry   Vol. 1: 1518
ACS Award for Creative Advances in Environmental Science and Technology   Vol. 1: 1519
ACS Award for Creative Invention   Vol. 1: 1520
ACS Award for Creative Work in Fluorine Chemistry   Vol. 1: 1521
ACS Award for Creative Work in Synthetic Organic Chemistry   Vol. 1: 1522
ACS Award for Distinguished Service in the Advancement of Inorganic Chemistry   Vol. 1: 1523
ACS Award for Encouraging Disadvantaged Students into Careers in the Chemical Sciences   Vol. 1: 1524
ACS Award for Encouraging Women into Careers in the Chemical Sciences   Vol. 1: 1525
ACS Award for Nuclear Applications in Chemistry   Vol. 1: 1526
ACS Award for Nuclear Chemistry   Vol. 1: 1526
ACS Award for Outstanding Performance by Divisions   Vol. 1: 1527
ACS Award for Outstanding Performance by Local Sections   Vol. 1: 1528
ACS Award for Pollution Control   Vol. 1: 1529
ACS Award for Research at an Undergraduate Institution   Vol. 1: 1530
ACS Award in Analytical Chemistry   Vol. 1: 1531
ACS Award in Applied Polymer Science   Vol. 1: 1532
ACS Award in Chemical Education   Vol. 1: 1571
ACS Award in Chemical Instrumentation   Vol. 1: 1533
ACS Award in Chromatography   Vol. 1: 1534
ACS Award in Colloid or Surface Chemistry   Vol. 1: 1535
ACS Award in Industrial Chemistry   Vol. 1: 1536
ACS Award in Inorganic Chemistry   Vol. 1: 1537
ACS Award in Organometallic Chemistry   Vol. 1: 1538
ACS Award in Petroleum Chemistry   Vol. 1: 1539
ACS Award in Polymer Chemistry   Vol. 1: 1540
ACS Award in Pure Chemistry
   Alpha Chi Sigma   Vol. 1: 338

   American Chemical Society - Research, Grants, and Awards   Vol 1: 1541
ACS Award in Separations Science and Technology
   Alpha Chi Sigma   Vol. 1: 339
   American Chemical Society - Research, Grants, and Awards   Vol 1: 1542
ACS Award in the Chemistry of Materials   Vol. 1: 1543
ACS Award in Theoretical Chemistry   Vol. 1: 1544
ACS Medal of Honor   Vol. 1: 1410
ACSA/American Wood Council Student Competition   Vol. 1: 5742
ACSA Creative Achievement Award   Vol. 1: 5745
ACSA Distinguished Professor Award   Vol. 1: 5745
ACSA/DuPont Company Student Design Competition   Vol. 1: 5743
ACSA/Future Cities Student Design Competition   Vol. 1: 5744
ACSA Honorary Award   Vol. 1: 5745
ACSA Honors and Awards Program   Vol. 1: 5745
ACSA Merit Awards   Vol. 1: 1903
ACSA New Faculty Teaching Award; AIAS/   Vol. 1: 5745
ACSA Topaz Medallion for Lifetime Achievement in Architectural Education; AIA/   Vol. 1: 5745
ACSM Map Design Competition Awards   Vol. 1: 1811
ACT-NUCEA Innovations in Continuing Education Awards   Vol. 1: 14952
ACTA Australian Maritime Art Award   Vol. 2: 116
Acta Metallurgica et Materialia Outstanding Paper Award   Vol. 1: 106
Acta Metallurgica Gold Medal   Vol. 1: 107
Acta Metallurgica J. Herbert Hollomon Award   Vol. 1: 108
Acta Metallurgica Outstanding Paper Award   Vol. 1: 106
ACTA Special Medallion Award   Vol. 1: 271
ACTF Awards for Theatrical Design Excellence   Vol. 1: 1754
ACTF Musical Theatre Award   Vol. 1: 1755
ACTFL Anthony Papalia Award for Excellence in Teacher Education   Vol. 1: 1869
ACTFL Edwin Cudecki International Business Award   Vol. 1: 1870
ACTFL Florence Steiner Award for Leadership in Foreign Language Education, K-12   Vol. 1: 1871
ACTFL Florence Steiner Award for Leadership in Foreign Language Education, Postsecondary   Vol. 1: 1872
ACTFL - MLJ Emma Marie Birkmaier Award for Doctoral Dissertation Research in Foreign Language Education   Vol. 1: 1873
ACTFL - MLJ Paul Pimsleur Award for Research in Foreign Language Education   Vol. 1: 1874
ACTFL National Textbook Company Award for Building Community Interest in Foreign Language Education   Vol. 1: 1875
ACTFL Nelson Brooks Award for Excellence in the Teaching of Culture   Vol. 1: 1876
Action for Birds Award   Vol. 2: 4652
Actonian Prize   Vol. 2: 4087
Actor of the Year Award   Vol. 2: 2753
Actors' Fund Medal   Vol. 1: 124
ACTS Awards   Vol. 1: 128
ACTS Competition   Vol. 1: 1765
ACTS Scholarships   Vol. 1: 1764
ACUHO-I Award   Vol. 1: 5734

ACUM Medal for Performing and Distribution of Israeli Works, Music and Literature   Vol. 2: 7942
ACUM Prizes for Literature and Music   Vol. 2: 7943
Ad Adstra Decoration   Vol. 2: 10919
ADA Career Development Awards   Vol. 1: 1950
ADA Foundation Award for Excellence in the Practice of Clinical Nutrition   Vol. 1: 1957
ADA Foundation Awards for Excellence   Vol. 1: 1957
ADA Foundation Scholarships   Vol. 1: 1958
ADA Research Awards   Vol. 1: 1951
Adair Trophy; Norman R.   Vol. 1: 14645
Adam and Company/Spectator Art Award   Vol. 2: 4483
Adam-Even; Prix Paul   Vol. 2: 943
Adam Prize   Vol. 2: 9796
Adams Award; Dorothy Garrigus   Vol. 1: 17267
Adams Award for Conservation Photography; Ansel   Vol. 1: 17224
Adams Award in Organic Chemistry; Roger   Vol. 1: 1545
Adams Award; Jack   Vol. 1: 14157
Adams Conservation Award; Ansel   Vol. 1: 20292
Adams Lecture Award; Comfort A.   Vol. 1: 5070
Adams Memorial Membership Award   Vol. 1: 5071
Adams Memorial Trophy; Mrs. Charles Francis   Vol. 1: 19545
Adams Playwriting Competition; Maude   Vol. 1: 18485
Adams Prize; Henry   Vol. 1: 17474
Adams Prize; Herbert Baxter   Vol. 1: 2280
Adams SEASECS Article Prize; Percy G.   Vol. 1: 18183
Adams Short Story Contest; Nick   Vol. 1: 5399
Adams Trophy; Cato W.   Vol. 1: 16214
Adams Trophy; U.S. Women's Sailing Championship - Mrs. Charles Francis   Vol. 1: 19546
Adamson Award for Distinguished Service in the Advancement of Surface Chemistry; Arthur W.   Vol. 1: 1546
Adana Memorial Challenge Cup   Vol. 1: 3984
ADARN of the Year   Vol. 1: 1938
Addams Award; ASHRAE ASHAE - Homer   Vol. 1: 4568
Addams Award; Homer   Vol. 1: 4568
Addams Children's Book Award; Jane   Vol. 1: 133
Addams Medal; Jane   Vol. 1: 16874
Additional Honours   Vol. 1: 6694
ADDY Campaign Awards; National   Vol. 1: 739
ADE Francis Andrew March Award   Vol. 1: 5763
A'Deane Coke Medal; Major John Sacheverell   Vol. 2: 2920
Adelaide Festival of Arts   Vol. 2: 673
Adelaide International Exhibition of Photography; Interphot -   Vol. 2: 677
Adelskoldska Medaljen   Vol. 2: 11532
Adenauer-Forschungs-preis; Konrad-   Vol. 2: 7154
Adenauer Research Award; Konrad
  Royal Society of Canada   Vol. 1: 16948
  Alexander von Humboldt-Stiftung   Vol 2: 7154
Adhesion Society Award for Excellence in Adhesion Science   Vol. 1: 135
Adhesives Award   Vol. 1: 6032
adidas - Adi Dassler Memorial Award   Vol. 1: 10538

adidas - Female Goalkeeper of the Year   Vol. 1: 10539
adidas - Female Player of the Year   Vol. 1: 10540
adidas - Outstanding Senior Goalkeeper Award   Vol. 1: 10541
ADIRCAE Prizes   Vol. 2: 11140
Adirondack Wilderness Award   Vol. 1: 5331
Adirondacks National Exhibition of American Watercolors   Vol. 1: 5331
Adkins Instructor Membership Award; Howard E.   Vol. 1: 5072
Adler Lectureship Award in the Field of Materials Physics; David   Vol. 1: 3442
Administrative Committee Prize   Vol. 1: 2738
Administrative Division Executive Committee Award   Vol. 1: 2141
Administrative Psychiatry Award   Vol. 1: 3621
Administrative Visitors Fellowship Programme   Vol. 2: 1860
Administrator of the Year
  American Federation of School Administrators   Vol. 1: 2033
  International Association of Industrial Accident Boards and Commissions   Vol 1: 10749
  United Methodist Association of Health and Welfare Ministries   Vol 1: 18931
Administrator of the Year Award   Vol. 1: 1671
Administrators' Award   Vol. 1: 11361
Admiral of the Ocean Sea   Vol. 1: 18975
ADO National Champions   Vol. 1: 1933
ADO Points Champions   Vol. 1: 1934
Adolescent Health Award   Vol. 1: 671
Adopt-Action Service Award   Vol. 1: 15408
Adoption Activist Awards   Vol. 1: 15408
Adorno Award; Theodor W.   Vol. 2: 6611
Adorno-Preis; Theodor-W.-   Vol. 2: 6611
Adrian Advertising Awards   Vol. 1: 9998
Adult Advisor to Young Numismatists   Vol. 1: 3198
Adult Development and Aging Student Research Award   Vol. 1: 3678
Adult Volunteer of the Year   Vol. 1: 2212
Advancement in Medical Rehabilitation Award   Vol. 1: 3945
Advancement of Literacy Award   Vol. 1: 2928
Advertising Age Awards   Vol. 1: 150
Advertising and Marketing Awards Competition   Vol. 1: 17918
Advertising and Public Relations Awards Competition   Vol. 1: 13344
Advertising Award   Vol. 1: 1065
Advertising Awards   Vol. 1: 13391
Advertising Awards Competition   Vol. 1: 6263
Advertising Competiton   Vol. 1: 9196
Advertising Council Award for Public Service   Vol. 1: 154
Advertising Credit Executive of the Year   Vol. 1: 156
Advertising Design Club of Canada   Vol. 1: 152
Advertising Grand Prize   Vol. 2: 5319
Advertising Hall of Achievement   Vol. 1: 734
Advertising Hall of Fame   Vol. 1: 735
Advertising Leader of the Year Award   Vol. 1: 20229
Advertising Print Campaign of the Year   Vol 1: 9361
Advertising/Promotion Awards   Vol. 1: 18513
Advertising TV Campaign of the Year   Vol. 1: 9361
Advisor of the Year   Vol. 1: 343
Advisory Board Member of the Year   Vol. 1: 344
Advocacy for the Disabled Award   Vol. 1: 2789

Advocates for Children Award   Vol. 1: 14545
Adzija Award; Bozidar   Vol. 2: 1810
AE 50 Company Recognition Program   Vol. 1: 4353
Aebersold Award   Vol. 1: 17942
AECI Medal   Vol. 2: 11045
AECT Annual Achievement Award   Vol. 1: 5500
AECT Distinguished Service Award   Vol. 1: 5501
AECT/EBEC International Student Media Festival   Vol. 1: 5502
AECT International Student Media Festival   Vol. 1: 5502
AECT Leadership Development Grants   Vol. 1: 5506
AECT Memorial Scholarship Award   Vol. 1: 5507
AECT National Convention - Earl F. Shrobehn Internship Program   Vol. 1: 5508
AECT National Convention Internship Program   Vol. 1: 5508
AECT/SIRS Intellectual Freedom Award   Vol. 1: 5503
AECT Special Service Award   Vol. 1: 5504
AEDOS Agricultural Award   Vol. 2: 11135
AEEP Founders' Award   Vol. 1: 5778
AEEP Outstanding Paper Award   Vol. 1: 5779
AEG Publication Award   Vol. 1: 5771
AEJMC Ethics Prize; Carol Burnett/University of Hawaii/   Vol. 1: 5496
Aelod o Orsedd Beirdd Ynys Prydain   Vol. 2: 12185
AERA - American College Testing Program Award   Vol. 1: 1977
AERA Award for Distinguished Contributions Relating Research to Practice   Vol. 1: 1974
AERA - PDK Award for Distinguished Contributions Relating Research to Practice   Vol. 1: 1974
AERC Hall of Fame   Vol. 1: 1991
Aeresmedlem   Vol. 2: 2000
Aerespris   Vol. 2: 9965
AERF Practitioners Award   Vol. 1: 130
Aerial Achievement Medal   Vol. 1: 19132
Aero Club of America Trophy   Vol. 1: 12723
Aero Engine Services Trophy   Vol. 2: 9807
Aerobics Athlete of the Year   Vol. 1: 408
Aerobics Contributor of the Year   Vol. 1: 409
Aerobics Man and Woman of the Year   Vol. 1: 410
Aerobics Official of the Year   Vol. 1: 411
Aerophilatelic Class Award   Vol. 2: 3781
Aerosol Package Design Award   Vol. 1: 7574
Aerospace Division/AIAA Educational Achievement Award   Vol. 1: 4069
Aerospace Laureate   Vol. 1: 6198
AES Awards of Excellence   Vol. 1: 11
AES Man of the Year Award   Vol. 1: 12
AES Publications Award   Vol. 1: 6130
AESE Award for Outstanding Editorial or Publishing Contributions   Vol. 1: 5765
AESE Award for Outstanding Publication   Vol. 1: 5766
AESF Gold Medal   Vol. 1: 1984
AESF Industrial Achievement Award   Vol. 1: 1985
AESF Leadership Award   Vol. 1: 1986
AESF Scientific Achievement Award   Vol. 1: 1987
AESF Service Award   Vol. 1: 1988
AESF Silver Medal   Vol. 1: 1989
AF ROTC Cadet of the Year Award   Vol. 1: 227
AFA Air Force Reserve Troop Carrier Wing Trophy   Vol. 1: 251
AFA Newsletter Award   Vol. 1: 5804

Award Index
Volume 2: International and Foreign

AFAA Airmanship Award Vol. 1: 2039
AFAA Honorees Vol. 1: 2040
AFAEP Awards Vol. 2: 2131
AFAEP/Kodak Student Competition Vol. 2: 2132
AFAR Award of Distinction Vol. 1: 2023
AFBS Congressional Science Fellowship Vol. 1: 2553
AFCEAN of the Year Vol. 1: 5264
AFDCS Distinguished Service Award Vol. 1: 2057
Affair on the Square Art Festival Vol. 1: 7525
Affaire de Coeur Awards Vol. 1: 182
Affaire in the Gardens Vol. 1: 7727
Affiche d'Or Award; L' Vol. 1: 12157
Affiliate Artists Conductors Program Vol. 1: 184
Affiliate Artists' Xerox Pianists Program Vol. 1: 185
Affiliate Award Vol. 1: 7066
Affiliate Corporation Award Vol. 1: 10935
Affiliate of the Year Award Vol. 1: 13741
Affiliated Group Award Vol. 1: 1655
Affiliated Societies' Cup Vol. 2: 4023
Affirmative Action and Equal Employment Opportunity Award Vol. 1: 20214
Affirmative Action Award of the Year Vol. 1: 18940
AFI Honor Roll Vol. 1: 5787
AFIA Award Vol. 1: 4978
AFIPS Education Award Vol. 1: 2025
AFIPS Product of the Year Award Vol. 1: 2026
AFJ Awards Competition Vol. 1: 5802
AFMS Scholarship Foundation Honorary Award Vol. 1: 2031
AFN - AGFA Awards Vol. 2: 2127
AFRES Outstanding Unit Award Vol. 1: 228
Africa Prize for Leadership for the Sustainable End of Hunger Vol. 1: 10058
African Centre for Applied Research and Training in Social Development Awards Vol. 2: 8851
African Insurance Organization Awards Vol. 2: 1543
African Regional Centre for Technology Awards Vol. 2: 10693
Afro-Asia Club Championship Vol. 2: 8892
Afro-Asia Nations Cup Vol. 2: 8893
AFS Award for Excellence in Fisheries Education Vol. 1: 2061
AFS Award of Excellence Vol. 1: 2062
AFS Distinguished Service Awards Vol. 1: 2063
AFS Meritorious Service Award Vol. 1: 2064
AFTMA Award of Merit Vol. 1: 4848
AFUD/NKF Resident Fellowships Vol. 1: 2111
AFUD/Ph.D. Research Scholars Program Vol. 1: 2112
AFUD Research Scholars Vol. 1: 2113
AFUW - QLD Commemorative Fellowship Vol. 2: 214
AFUW - Queensland International Fellowship Vol. 2: 11789
AFUW - QLD Freda Bage Fellowship Vol. 2: 214
AFUW-SA Inc. Trust Fund Bursary Vol. 2: 216
AGA Advanced Research Training Awards Vol. 1: 2128
AGA/Elsevier Research Initiative Award Vol. 1: 2129
AGA Foundation/Merck Senior Fellow Research Awards Vol. 1: 2130
AGA/Industry Research Scholar Awards Vol. 1: 2131

AGA International Travel Fellowship Awards Vol. 1: 2132
Aga Khan Award for Architecture Vol. 2: 11656
Aga Khan Prize for Fiction Vol. 1: 15968
Aga Khan Trophy Vol. 2: 7834
AGA/Miles and Shirley Fiterman Foundation Awards for Clinical Research Vol. 1: 2133
AGA - NSTA Science Teaching Achievement Recognition (Star) Award Vol. 1: 14696
AGA Senior Fellow Research Awards Vol. 1: 2130
AGA/SmithKline Beecham Clinical Research Awards Vol. 1: 2134
AGA Student Abstract Prize Vol. 1: 2135
AGA Student Research Fellowships Vol. 1: 2136
AGA Student Summer Research Fellowships Vol. 1: 2136
Agan Scholarships; Tessie Vol. 1: 1020
Agassiz Medal; Alexander Vol. 1: 12662
AGBU Aram Khachaturian Music Competition Vol. 1: 5270
The Age Book of the Year Awards Vol. 2: 118
Age d'Or Prijs Vol. 2: 1352
Age Group Diving Coach of the Year Vol. 1: 19316
AGEC-Preis Vol. 2: 9477
Agency Management Hall of Fame Vol. 1: 9517
Agfa - Gevaert Gold Medal Award Vol. 1: 17899
AGGIE Award Vol. 1: 18142
Aggiornamento Award Vol. 1: 7374
Aggrey Medal Vol. 1: 16090
AGHE Award Vol. 1: 5524
Agnelli International Prize; Senator Giovanni Vol. 2: 8247
Agnon Gold Medal; S. Y. Vol. 1: 2117
Agopoff Award; Agop Vol. 1: 12593
Agopoff Memorial Prize; Agop Vol. 1: 14714
AGPAM National Recognition Award Vol. 1: 2199
Agricola Denkmunze; Georg Vol. 2: 6849
Agricola-Medaille; Georg- Vol. 2: 6647
Agricultural Engineering Award Vol. 2: 421
Agricultural Hall of Fame Vol. 1: 12757
Agricultural Initiative Award Vol. 1: 15108
Agricultural Leadership Award Vol. 1: 15109
Agricultural Organization of the Year Vol. 1: 15110
Agriculture Award Vol. 2: 10425
Agrinaut Award Vol. 1: 12746
Agrofilm International Short Film Festival Vol. 2: 1873
Agronomic Achievement Award - Crops Vol. 1: 4376
Agronomic Achievement Award - Soils Vol. 1: 4377
Agronomic Extension Education Award Vol. 1: 4378
Agronomic Research Award Vol. 1: 4379
Agronomic Resident Education Award Vol. 1: 4380
Agronomic Service Award Vol. 1: 4381
AGS Award for Outstanding Contributions to Gravestone Studies Vol. 1: 5526
Agusta International Helicopter Fellowship Award; Gruppo Vol. 1: 2246
Agway Young Scientist Award Vol. 1: 1905
AHA Hospital Awards for Volunteer Excellence Vol. 1: 2368
AHA National Homebrew Competition Awards Vol. 1: 2344
AHEA Commemorative Lecture Award Vol. 1: 2336

AHF Lifeline Award Vol. 1: 2217
Ahlstrom Prize; Walter Vol. 2: 4682
AHS Director's Award Vol. 1: 2247
AHS Public Service Award Vol. 1: 2272
AHSA Equestrian of the Year Vol. 1: 2346
AHSA Jumper Course Designer; Mr. and Mrs. William C. Cox Memorial Trophy - Vol. 1: 2348
AHSA National Horse of the Year Championships Vol. 1: 2347
Ahwash Literary Award; Kamal M. Vol. 1: 11854
AIA/ACSA Award for Architectural Education Vol. 1: 2518
AIA/ACSA Research Council - Otis Elevator International Student Design Competition Vol. 1: 5746
AIA/ACSA Topaz Medallion for Excellence in Architectural Education Vol. 1: 2518
AIA/ACSA Topaz Medallion for Lifetime Achievement in Architectural Education Vol. 1: 5745
AIA/ALA Library Buildings Award Vol. 1: 2519
AIA - American Association of Medical Clinics Awards Vol. 1: 2520
AIA Award for Fieldwork Vol. 2: 2105
AIA/BIA Brick in Architecture Awards of Excellence Vol. 1: 2521
AIA Concrete Reinforcing Steel Institute Design Award Vol. 1: 2522
AIA Conference Award Vol. 2: 2106
AIA - Naval Facilities Engineering Command Awards Vol. 1: 2523
AIA Twenty-Five Year Award Vol. 1: 2524
AIAA Abe M. Zarem Award for Distinguished Achievement Vol. 1: 2443
AIAA Aeroacoustics Award Vol. 1: 2444
AIAA Aerodynamic Decelerator Systems Award Vol. 1: 2445
AIAA Aerodynamics Award Vol. 1: 2446
AIAA Aerospace Communications Award Vol. 1: 2447
AIAA Aerospace Contribution to Society Award Vol. 1: 2448
AIAA Aerospace Design Engineering Award Vol. 1: 2449
AIAA Aerospace Maintenance Award Vol. 1: 2450
AIAA Aerospace Power Systems Award Vol. 1: 2451
AIAA Aerospace Software Engineering Award Vol. 1: 2452
AIAA Air Breathing Propulsion Award Vol. 1: 2453
AIAA Aircraft Design Award Vol. 1: 2454
AIAA Aircraft Operations Excellence Award Vol. 1: 2455
AIAA Certificate of Merit Awards Vol. 1: 2456
AIAA Chanute Flight Award Vol. 1: 2457
AIAA Command, Control, Communication & Intelligence Award Vol. 1: 2458
AIAA Computer-Aided Engineering and Manufacturing Award Vol. 1: 2459
AIAA De Florez Training Award for Flight Simulation Vol. 1: 2460
AIAA Digital Avionics Award Vol. 1: 2461
AIAA Distinguished Service Award Vol. 1: 2462
AIAA Dryden Lectureship in Research Vol. 1: 2463
AIAA Durand Lectureship for Public Service Vol. 1: 2464
AIAA Educational Achievement Award; Aerospace Division/ Vol. 1: 4069
AIAA Energy Systems Award Vol. 1: 2465

AIAA Awards, Honors & Prizes, 1995-96

AIAA Engineer of the Year Award   Vol. 1: 2466
AIAA F. E. Newbold V/STOL Award   Vol. 1: 2467
AIAA Fluid Dynamics Award   Vol. 1: 2468
AIAA George M. Low Space Transportation Award   Vol. 1: 2469
AIAA Goddard Astronautics Award   Vol. 1: 2470
AIAA Ground Testing Award   Vol. 1: 2471
AIAA Haley Space Flight Award   Vol. 1: 2472
AIAA History Manuscript Award   Vol. 1: 2473
AIAA Information Systems Award   Vol. 1: 2474
AIAA International Cooperation Award   Vol. 1: 2475
AIAA Jay Hollingsworth Speas Airport Award   Vol. 1: 2476
AIAA Jeffries Medical Research Award   Vol. 1: 2477
AIAA Lawrence Sperry Award   Vol. 1: 2478
AIAA Leadership in Quality Management   Vol. 1: 2479
AIAA Losey Atmospheric Science Award   Vol. 1: 2480
AIAA Mechanics and Control of Flight Award   Vol. 1: 2481
AIAA Membership Award   Vol. 1: 2482
AIAA Missile Systems Award   Vol. 1: 2483
AIAA Multidisciplinary Design Optimization Award   Vol. 1: 2484
AIAA National Faculty Advisor Award   Vol. 1: 2485
AIAA National Student Awards   Vol. 1: 2486
AIAA Newsletter Award   Vol. 1: 2487
AIAA Onward and Upward Certificate   Vol. 1: 2488
AIAA Otto C. Winzen Lifetime Achievement Award   Vol. 1: 2489
AIAA Pendray Aerospace Literature Award   Vol. 1: 2490
AIAA Piper General Aviation Award   Vol. 1: 2491
AIAA Plasmadynamics and Lasers Award   Vol. 1: 2492
AIAA Propellants and Combustion Award   Vol. 1: 2493
AIAA Public Policy Award   Vol. 1: 2494
AIAA Public Service Award   Vol. 1: 2495
AIAA Reed Aeronautics Award   Vol. 1: 2496
AIAA Service Special Citation   Vol. 1: 2497
AIAA Space Operations and Support Award   Vol. 1: 2498
AIAA Space Processing Award   Vol. 1: 2499
AIAA Space Science Award   Vol. 1: 2500
AIAA Space Systems Award   Vol. 1: 2501
AIAA Structures, Structural Dynamics and Materials Award   Vol. 1: 2502
AIAA Support Systems Award   Vol. 1: 2503
AIAA Survivability Award   Vol. 1: 2504
AIAA System Effectiveness and Safety Award   Vol. 1: 2505
AIAA Thermophysics Award   Vol. 1: 2506
AIAA Von Braun Award for Excellence in Space Program Management   Vol. 1: 2507
AIAA Von Karman Lectureship in Astronautics   Vol. 1: 2508
AIAA Walter J. and Angeline H. Crichlow Trust Prize   Vol. 1: 2509
AIAA William Littlewood Memorial Lecture   Vol. 1: 2510
AIAA Wright Brothers Lectureship in Aeronautics   Vol. 1: 2511
AIAA Wyld Propulsion Award   Vol. 1: 2512
AIAA Young Member Activity Award   Vol. 1: 2513

AIAS/ACSA New Faculty Teaching Award   Vol. 1: 5745
AIASA Recognition Awards   Vol. 1: 18605
AIBD National Design Competition   Vol. 1: 2556
AIBS-ASZ Congressional Science Fellowship   Vol. 1: 2553
AIBS Distinguished Service Award   Vol. 1: 2554
AIC Ethics Award   Vol. 1: 2610
AICP National Historic Planning Landmarks and Pioneers Program   Vol. 1: 3529
AICP Outstanding Student Project Award   Vol. 1: 3530
AICPA Medal of Honor   Vol. 1: 2558
Aid to Advertising Education Award   Vol. 1: 736
Aide a la diffusion de films de qualite en Belgique   Vol. 2: 1353
AIDIS Prize   Vol. 1: 10502
AIDS Education Award   Vol. 1: 14546
AIGA Design Leadership Award   Vol. 1: 2620
AIGA Medal   Vol. 1: 2621
Aigle d'Or   Vol. 2: 5186
AIIE Award for Excellence in Productivity Improvement   Vol. 1: 10362
AIIM Company of Fellows   Vol. 1: 5539
Aikat Oration Award; Professor B. K.   Vol. 2: 7577
Aiken Prize; William H.   Vol. 1: 18601
AIM Children's Book Awards
  Booksellers of New Zealand   Vol. 2: 9707
  Queen Elizabeth II Arts Council of New Zealand - Literature Programme   Vol 2: 9797
.Aim Quarterly Magazine Short Story Award   Vol. 1: 215
AIME Distinguished Service Award   Vol. 1: 2632
AIMR Distinguished Service Award   Vol. 1: 5549
AIMR Special Service Award   Vol. 1: 5550
AIP Science Writing Awards   Vol. 1: 2656
AIPE Fellow Award   Vol. 1: 2668
AIPEA Medals   Vol. 2: 1048
AIPH and Grand Prix d'Excellence; Grand Prix de l'   Vol. 2: 9467
Air Canada Award
  Academy of Canadian Cinema & Television   Vol. 1: 29
  Montreal World Film Festival   Vol 1: 12436
Air Canada Award; Canadian Authors Association/   Vol. 1: 6807
Air Canada Prize   Vol. 1: 8500
Air Command and Control Marine of the Year   Vol. 1: 12054
Air Force Association AFLC Logistics Executive Management Award   Vol. 1: 230
Air Force Association AFLC Logistics Junior Management Awards   Vol. 1: 229
Air Force Association AFLC Logistics Middle Management Award   Vol. 1: 231
Air Force Association AFMC Junior Management Award   Vol. 1: 229
Air Force Association AFMC Logistics Executive Management Award   Vol. 1: 230
Air Force Association AFMC Middle Management Award   Vol. 1: 231
Air Force Association AFSC Distinguished Award for Management   Vol. 1: 230
Air Force Association AFSC Junior Management Award   Vol. 1: 229
Air Force Association AFSC Management Awards   Vol. 1: 231
Air Force Association Special Presidential Citations   Vol. 1: 5282

Air Force Cross
  British Government   Vol. 2: 2356
  Republic of South Africa - South African Defense Force   Vol 2: 10920
  United States Department of Defense - Armed Forces Decorations and Awards   Vol 1: 19133
Air Force Medal   Vol. 2: 2357
Air Force Reserve Troop Carrier Wing Trophy; AFA   Vol. 1: 251
Air France/City of Paris Photography Award   Vol. 2: 6146
Air League Challenge Trophy   Vol. 2: 2044
Air League Founders' Medal   Vol. 2: 2045
Air Medal   Vol. 1: 19134
Air National Guard Outstanding Unit Award   Vol. 1: 232
Air New Zealand Award   Vol. 2: 9791
Air Reserve Forces Meritorious Service Medal - Air Force   Vol. 1: 19135
Air Service Training Blind Flying Trophy   Vol. 2: 9816
Air Transport World Awards   Vol. 1: 281
Airborne Regiment Trophy   Vol. 1: 7251
AIRCO Welding Award   Vol. 1: 5073
Aircraft Safety Prize   Vol. 2: 4103
Airey Award; H. T.   Vol. 1: 6927
Airline of the Year   Vol. 2: 2853
Airman of the Year   Vol. 1: 9278
Airman's Medal   Vol. 1: 19136
Airone   Vol. 2: 8319
Airport Commissioners Roundtable Congressional Leadership Award   Vol. 1: 287
Airport Crash/Fire/Rescue/Medical Preparedness Award   Vol. 1: 6182
Airtour Sword   Vol. 2: 2999
Airways Corporation Trophy   Vol. 2: 9808
Airwork Cup   Vol. 2: 9809
Aitken Memorial Award; Irene   Vol. 2: 10970
Aizstrauts Team Sportsmanship; Arnie   Vol. 1: 412
Akashvani Annual Awards   Vol. 2: 7480
Akashvani Annual Awards for Technical Excellence   Vol. 2: 7481
AKC Canine Research Award   Vol. 1: 4986
Akermarks stipendium; Carl   Vol. 2: 11582
Akiva Club Award   Vol. 1: 5915
Akiyama Prize   Vol. 2: 8545
AKO Literatuur Prijs   Vol. 2: 9633
Akutagawa Prize   Vol. 2: 8750
Akzo prijs   Vol. 2: 9389
AL and NL Baseball Player Comeback of the Year   Vol. 1: 18341
AL and NL Comeback Players of the Year   Vol. 1: 18341
AL and NL Hillerich and Bradsby/The Sporting News Silver Slugger Awards   Vol. 1: 18342
AL and NL Manager of the Year   Vol. 1: 18343
AL and NL Pitchers of the Year   Vol. 1: 18344
AL and NL Relief Pitcher of the Year   Vol. 1: 18345
AL and NL Rookie Pitchers of the Year   Vol. 1: 18346
ALA Award; CIS/GODORT/   Vol. 1: 2895
ALA Equality Award   Vol. 1: 2811
ALA Goal Awards; World Book -   Vol. 1: 2825
ALA Library Buildings Award; AIA/   Vol. 1: 2519
ALA/Meckler Library of the Future Award   Vol. 1: 2812
Alabama Authors Award   Vol. 1: 291
Alabama Prize   Vol. 1: 15298
Alabama Sportswriters Hall of Fame   Vol. 1: 11112
AlaHoSo Bowl   Vol. 1: 2377

Award Index
Volume 2: International and Foreign

ALAN Award Vol. 1: 13783
Alaska Cup Award Vol. 1: 19548
Alaux; Fondation Jean-Paul Vol. 2: 5388
Albano Memorial Award; John Vol. 1: 20106
Albena Zlatni Piassatsi Sliven Vol. 2: 1535
Albers Award; William H. Vol. 1: 9296
Albers-Schonberg Medaille; Heinrich-E.- Vol. 2: 6828
Albert Award; Henry J. Vol. 1: 11171
Albert Lectureship; Adrien Vol. 2: 4183
Albert Medal
  British Government Vol. 2: 2358
  RSA Vol 2: 4318
Albert; Prix Jos Vol. 2: 961
Alberta Awards Vol. 1: 6445
Alberta Culture Poetry Award Vol. 1: 293
Alberta New Fiction Competition Vol. 1: 294
Alberta Non-Fiction Award Vol. 1: 295
Alberta Writing for Youth Competition Vol. 1: 296
Albrand Award for Nonfiction; PEN/Martha Vol. 1: 16023
Albright Award; Fuller Vol. 1: 4045
ALCA Safety Award Contests Vol. 1: 5405
Alcan Award Vol. 1: 6928
Alcan du court metrage; Prix Vol. 1: 6024
Alcan Jazz Prize Vol. 1: 9173
Alcan Lecture Award Vol. 1: 7540
Alcanes/Muestra Cinematografica de Atlantico Vol. 2: 11138
Alcuin Citations for Book Design Vol. 1: 304
Alcuin Society Award Vol. 1: 305
ALDA Angel Award Vol. 1: 5850
Aldeburgh Poetry Festival Prize Vol. 2: 2051
Aldo Awards for Fashion Journalism Vol. 1: 9047
Aldre Linnemadeljen i guld Vol. 2: 11533
Aldrich Award; C. Anderson Vol. 1: 665
Aldrich Service Award; Robert B. Vol. 1: 8661
AIEA III International Composition Prize Vol. 1: 6471
Aleph Award Vol. 1: 6524
Alert Youth Award Vol. 1: 13247
Ales Film Festival Vol. 2: 4886
Alexander Award; J. Allen Vol. 1: 4022
Alexander Award; Mary Vol. 1: 7594
Alexander Graham Bell Volta Award Vol. 1: 6318
Alexander Medal; G.N. Vol. 2: 422
Alexander Prize Vol. 2: 4019
Alexander, Sr., NAACP State Conference President's Award; Kelly M. Vol. 1: 12904
Alexander Shield Vol. 2: 2786
Alexander Trophy; Viscount Vol. 1: 7240
Alexopoulos Award Vol. 1: 12541
Alfa Laval Agri Dairy Extension Award Vol. 1: 1906
Alfano; Premio F. Vol. 2: 8480
Alger Awards; Horatio Vol. 1: 307
Algren Awards for Short Fiction; Nelson Vol. 1: 7608
Algren Fiction Award; PEN/Nelson Vol. 1: 16025
Alice Award Vol. 2: 662
ALISE Award for Professional Contribution to Library and Information Science Education Vol. 1: 5558
ALISE Award for Teaching Excellence in the Field of Library and Information Science Education Vol. 1: 5559
ALISE Doctoral Dissertation Competition Vol. 1: 5560
ALISE Research Grant Awards Vol. 1: 5561
ALISE Research Paper Competition Vol. 1: 5562
ALISE Service Award Vol. 1: 5563

Alison Award; John R. Vol. 1: 233
Alka-Seltzer Plus Award Vol. 1: 14158
All-America Awards Vol. 1: 14726
All-America Basketball Team Vol. 1: 18347
All-America City Award Program Vol. 1: 13594
All-America Football Team Vol. 1: 18348
All-America Rose Selections Award of Excellence Vol. 1: 315
All-America Rose Selections Certificate of Merit Vol. 1: 316
All America Team Vol. 1: 9303
All America Teams Vol. 1: 1319
All-American Association Award Vol. 1: 413
All American Awards Vol. 1: 13616
All-American Awards Vol. 1: 14258
All American Dive Team Vol. 1: 18868
All American Inter-Collegiate Sailor Vol. 1: 10519
All-American Soap Box Derby Vol. 1: 11225
All Americans - Football Vol. 1: 13622
All-Around Amateur Golden Horse Vol. 1: 15916
All-Around Golden Horse Award Vol. 1: 15917
All Around NAMAR Mustang Vol. 1: 15434
All-Breeds Awards Vol. 1: 19323
All Conference - Football Vol. 1: 13623
All-Defensive Team Vol. 1: 13443
All India Competition for Radio Playwrights Vol. 2: 7482
All-Ireland Horseshoe Pitching Championship Vol. 2: 7834
All Japan Description Contest from A Pocket Book Reading Vol. 2: 8675
All-NBA Team Vol. 1: 13444
All Party Parliamentary Award for Soviet Jewry Vol. 2: 4612
All Sonatina, All Sonata, All Bach Programs Vol. 1: 1678
All Sport Insurance Marketing Ltd. Volunteer of the Year Award Vol. 1: 7241
All-Star Game Most Valuable Player Vol. 1: 8242
Allan Award; Florence Vol. 1: 7511
Allan Memorial Award; William Vol. 1: 4611
Allan Memorial Cup; D. M. Vol. 2: 9810
Allard Silver Medal; Peter Vol. 2: 3880
Allderdice Jr., Award; Charles Vol. 1: 7575
Allee Best Student Paper Award of the Animal Behavior Society; Warder Clyde Vol. 1: 5159
Allemand de Gunche Prize; Elena Vol. 2: 62
Allen & Hanburys Pulmonary Fellowship Vol. 1: 1621
Allen Award; Alfred Vol. 1: 5488
Allen Award; Alfred W. Vol. 1: 1447
Allen Award; Arthur A. Vol. 1: 11749
Allen Award; Edward B. Vol. 1: 2174
Allen Award; Ruth Vol. 1: 3517
Allen Awards; Virginia French Vol. 1: 18587
Allen Distinguished Service Award; Harvey Stuart Vol. 1: 1378
Allen Fellowships; Frances C. Vol. 1: 15315
Allen - Heath Memorial Director-in-Residence Vol. 1: 17249
Allen Leadership and Achievement Award; George Vol. 1: 18760
Allen Memorial Fellowship; A. D. and P. A. Vol. 2: 2084
Allen of Hurtwood Trust Award; Lady Vol. 2: 2055
Allen Prize Vol. 1: 15744
Allen Prize; Cath Vol. 2: 2576
Allen Prize; Derek Vol. 2: 2221
Allen Scholarship; Dr. J. Frances Vol. 1: 2065

Allendoerfer Awards; Carl B. Vol. 1: 12127
Alliance Award Vol. 1: 769
Allied Corporation Award Vol. 1: 10936
Allied Industry Individual Award Vol. 1: 12747
Allied Member Award Vol. 1: 4806
Allied Professional Award Vol. 1: 14415
Allied-Signal Awards Vol. 1: 2657
Allied-Signal Outstanding Student Branch Award Vol. 1: 17750
AlliedSignal Achievement Awards in Aging Vol. 1: 334
Allin Prize; Russell Vol. 2: 3227
Allis Chalmers Conservation District Awards; NACD Deutz/ Vol. 1: 13031
Allis Chalmers Conservation Teacher Awards; NACD - Vol. 1: 13032
Allison Award; American Center for Children's Television - Fran Vol. 1: 1440
Alliss and Roy Beckett Crystal Rose Bowl; Peter Vol. 2: 3673
Allorge; Fondation Valentine Vol. 2: 5675
Allorge; Prix Pierre Vol. 2: 5675
Allport Intergroup Relations Prize; Gordon Vol. 1: 3813
Allstate Good Hands Award Vol. 1: 13445
Almond Award; Gabriel Vol. 1: 3567
Alpar Erem Vol. 2: 7449
Alpar Medal Vol. 2: 7449
Alpe Adria Prize Vol. 2: 8402
Alpenlandischer Volksmusikwettbewerb Vol. 2: 726
Alpha Awards Vol. 1: 1441
Alpha Beta Kappa Award Vol. 1: 8635
Alpha Chi Sigma Award in Chemical Engineering Research Vol. 1: 2564
Alpha Chi Sigma Scholarship Award Vol. 1: 340
Alpha Kappa Psi - Spangler Award Vol. 1: 3961
Alpha Omega Alpha Distinguished Teacher Awards
  Alpha Omega Alpha Honor Medical Society Vol. 1: 362
  Association of American Medical Colleges Vol 1: 5688
Alpha Omega Alpha Student Essay Award Vol. 1: 363
Alpha Omega Alpha Student Research Fellowships Vol. 1: 364
Alpha Sigma Nu National Book Award Vol. 1: 5838
Alpine Coaches of the Year Vol. 1: 19549
Alpine World Cup Champions Vol. 2: 11833
Alport Memorial Prize; Simon Vol. 2: 3052
Alsberg - Schoch Memorial Lecture Vol. 1: 945
ALSC/Book Wholesalers Summer Reading Program Grant Vol. 1: 2853
ALSC/Econo-Clad Literature Program Award Vol. 1: 2854
Alsop Award Vol. 1: 2800
Alston Award; Ralph E. Vol. 1: 6473
Alston Medal; R. P. Vol. 2: 3881
ALTA/Gale Outstanding Trustee Conference Grant Vol. 1: 2837
ALTA Literacy Award Vol. 1: 2838
ALTA Major Benefactor Honor Award Vol. 1: 2839
ALTA Outstanding Translations of the Year Vol. 1: 2966
Altamarino Medal; Ignacio Manuel Vol. 2: 9145
Altamirano Prize for Novel; Ignacio Manuel Vol. 2: 9046
Alter Cup; National Multihull Championship - Vol. 1: 19530

Alternative Nobel Prize   Vol. 2: 11509
Altman (Figure) Prize; Benjamin   Vol. 1: 12594
Altman (Landscape) Prize; Benjamin   Vol. 1: 12595
Altmeier-Medaille Europamunze der EVBK   Vol. 2: 6723
Alumni Achievement Award   Vol. 1: 552
Alumni Achievement Awards   Vol. 1: 7391
Alumni Administration   Vol. 1: 8292
Alumni Medal   Vol. 1: 19767
Alumni Merit Award   Vol. 1: 17000
Alumni Research Grant   Vol. 1: 16118
Alumni Service Award Medal   Vol. 1: 386
Alumni Service Citations   Vol. 1: 19768
Alumnus-of-the-Decade   Vol. 1: 8261
Alumnus of the Year   Vol. 1: 8261
Alumnus of the Year Award   Vol. 1: 16987
Alvarez Memorial Award; Walter C.   Vol. 1: 3056
Alvarez Prize; Geronimo H.   Vol. 2: 63
Alvarez Prize; Premio Dr. Jose Aguilar   Vol. 2: 9102
Alves de Carvalho Fernandes; Premio Antonio   Vol. 2: 10248
Alzate Distinction; Jose Maria   Vol. 2: 9008
Alzate Prize; Jose Antonio   Vol. 2: 9079
AMA Distinguished Service Award   Vol. 1: 3017
AMA - ERF Award for Health Education   Vol. 1: 3018
AMA/Irwin Distinguished Marketing Educator Award   Vol. 1: 2983
AMA Marketing Scholar of the Year; George Hay Brown/   Vol. 1: 2984
AMA Medal of Valor   Vol. 1: 3019
AMADE-UNESCO; Prix   Vol. 2: 9322
Amadeus Trophy   Vol. 2: 3606
Amado de Encenacao Teatral; Premio Municipal Fernando   Vol. 2: 10268
Amanda Award for Television and Cinematographic Merit   Vol. 2: 9938
Amanda Film - OG Fjernsynspris   Vol. 2: 9938
Amantakul Prize; Isara   Vol. 2: 12015
Amateur Achievement Award   Vol. 1: 6093
Amateur Astronomers Medal   Vol. 1: 394
Amateur Baseball Hall of Fame   Vol. 1: 9717
Amateur Music Family of the Year   Vol. 1: 3161
Amateur PSA/VMPD American International Film and Video Festival   Vol. 1: 16159
Ambassador Award
　American Council of the Blind   Vol. 1: 1852
　Educational Foundation of the National Restaurant Association   Vol 1: 8851
　Federation of Fly Fishers   Vol 1: 9100
Ambassador Award of Hospitality   Vol. 1: 14628
Ambassador Book Awards   Vol. 1: 8939
Ambassador of Honor Book Awards   Vol. 1: 8939
Amber Nightingale   Vol. 2: 10130
Amber Record   Vol. 2: 10130
Ambiente na Literatura Infantil   Vol. 2: 10289
AMC Van Operator Lifetime Achievement Award   Vol. 1: 3149
AMCA Plaque for Best Mosquito Slide   Vol. 1: 3129
AMCA Plaque for Best Slide by an AMCA Member   Vol. 1: 3130
AMCS President's Medal   Vol. 1: 5872
Ameghino; Premio Florentino   Vol. 2: 28
Amelia Annual Awards   Vol. 1: 474
Amer Award; Mohamed   Vol. 1: 7935
Amerbach-Preis   Vol. 2: 11962

America/Israel Friendship Award   Vol. 1: 5132
American Academy Award for Humanistic Studies   Vol. 1: 523
American Academy of Arts and Letters Rome Fellowship in Literature   Vol. 1: 495
American Academy of Periodontology Student Award   Vol. 1: 688
American Accordionists' Association Contest and Festival   Vol. 1: 730
American Action Fund Scholarship   Vol. 1: 13965
American Agri-Women Awards   Vol. 1: 745
American Association for Geodetic Surveying Graduate Fellowship Award   Vol. 1: 858
American Association of Collegiate Registrars and Admissions Officers - Division of Psychopharmacology and Substance Abuse   Vol. 1: 378
American Association of Community Theatre Festival Award   Vol. 1: 972
American Association of University Women Award in Juvenile Literature   Vol. 1: 15494
American Ballet Competition   Vol. 1: 1291
American Bar Association Medal   Vol. 1: 1306
American Beefalo World Registry's National Beefalo Show & Sale   Vol. 1: 1333
American Beefalo World Registry's Regional Beefalo Shows   Vol. 1: 1334
American Black Achievement Awards   Vol. 1: 11594
American Board for Occupational Health Nurses, Inc.   Vol. 1: 1351
American Board for Occupational Health Services   Vol. 1: 1075
American Book Awards   Vol. 1: 6310
American Bureau of Shipping - Captain Joseph H. Linnard Prize   Vol. 1: 17920
American Cancer Society Award for Excellence in Cancer Epidemiology and Prevention   Vol. 1: 840
American Cancer Society Eleanor Roosevelt International Cancer Fellowships   Vol. 2: 11856
American Cancer Society International Cancer Research Fellowships   Vol. 2: 11856
American Cartographic Association Scholarship Award   Vol. 1: 1425
American Center for Children's Television - Fran Allison Award   Vol. 1: 1440
American Center for Children's Television - Ollie Awards   Vol. 1: 1441
American Children's Television Festival - Fran Allison Award   Vol. 1: 1440
American Citizenship Award   Vol. 1: 15988
American College of Physicians Award   Vol. 1: 1713
American College of Physicians Distinguished Teacher Award   Vol. 1: 1714
American College of Psychiatrists Distinguished Service Award   Vol. 1: 1730
American College of Sports Medicine Citation Awards   Vol. 1: 1742
American College of Sports Medicine Honor Award   Vol. 1: 1743
American College of Sports Medicine International Scholars Program   Vol. 1: 1744
American College of Sports Medicine New Investigator Award   Vol. 1: 1745
American College of Sports Medicine Visiting Scholar Award   Vol. 1: 1746
American College of Surgeons Faculty Fellowship   Vol. 1: 1748
American College Testing Program Award; AERA -   Vol. 1: 1977

American Collegiate Talent Showcase   Vol. 1: 1765
American Comedy Awards   Vol. 1: 17092
American Community Leadership Award   Vol. 1: 13372
American Composers Competition   Vol. 1: 16824
American Concrete Pipe Association Award of Excellence   Vol. 1: 1793
American Continental Championship   Vol. 1: 18389
American Council of Learned Societies Fellowships   Vol. 1: 1846
American Craft Council Fellows   Vol. 1: 1889
American Craft Council Honorary Fellow   Vol. 1: 1889
American Crossword Puzzle Champion   Vol. 1: 1894
American Cyanamid - American Association of Bovine Practitioners Award for Excellence   Vol. 1: 940
American Cyanamid Company Award   Vol. 1: 1907
American Dade/Canlab Award in Hematology   Vol. 1: 7197
American Dance Guild Award
　American Dance Guild   Vol. 1: 1931
　Congressional Medal of Honor Society, United States of America   Vol 1: 8171
American Dance Guild Award for Outstanding Achievement in Dance   Vol. 1: 1931
American Dewar Trophy   Vol. 1: 14645
American Eagle Award
　Invest-In-America Foundation   Vol. 1: 11425
　National Music Council   Vol 1: 14389
American Education Award   Vol. 1: 1173
American Egg Board Research Award   Vol. 1: 16342
American Exemplar Medal   Vol. 1: 9405
American Express Award for Best Musical   Vol. 2: 4466
American Express - IACP Police Science Award   Vol. 1: 10695
American Express New Zealand Tourism Awards   Vol. 2: 9772
American Express Short Story Award   Vol. 2: 9701
American Express Tribute   Vol. 1: 20133
American Family Therapy Academy Awards   Vol. 1: 2017
American Family Therapy Association   Vol. 1: 2017
American Family Therapy Association Awards   Vol. 1: 2017
American Farm Bureau Federation's Award for Distinguished Service   Vol. 1: 2021
American Feed Industry Association Award
　American Dairy Science Association   Vol. 1: 1908
　American Society of Animal Science   Vol 1: 4391
　Poultry Science Association   Vol 1: 16343
American Feed Manufacturers Association Award   Vol. 1: 1908
American Fiction Awards   Vol. 1: 2037
American Film and Video Festival Awards   Vol. 1: 2045
American Film Festival Awards   Vol. 1: 2045
American Film Institute Award for Independent Film and Video Artists   Vol. 1: 2051
American Fishing Tackle Manufacturers Association   Vol. 1: 4848
American Friendship Medal   Vol. 1: 9405
American Fund for Alternatives to Animal Research Award   Vol. 1: 2126
American Heritage Award   Vol. 1: 14913

American Heritage Biographical Prizes   Vol. 1: 2269
American Heroes in Education Awards; Reader's Digest   Vol. 1: 16698
American Hiking Society Award   Vol. 1: 2273
American Honorary Members   Vol. 1: 496
American Image Awards   Vol. 1: 9048
American Image Enhancement Award   Vol. 1: 13675
American Independent Animator Award   Vol. 1: 5171
American Initiative for Creativity, Invention and Entrepreneurship   Vol. 1: 11423
American Institute of Musical Studies Award   Vol. 2: 565
American International Film/Video Festival   Vol. 1: 3143
American International Music Award   Vol. 1: 12534
American Iris Society Distinguished Service Award   Vol. 1: 2701
American Iris Society Gold Medal   Vol. 1: 2702
American Iris Society Hybridizer's Medal   Vol. 1: 2703
American Iron and Steel Institute Medal   Vol. 1: 2708
American Jazz Masters Fellowship Awards   Vol. 1: 13890
American Kennel Club Career Achievement Award in Canine Research   Vol. 1: 4979
American Laryngological Association Award   Vol. 1: 2780
American League All-Star Team   Vol. 1: 18349
American League Most Valuable Player   Vol. 1: 6280
American League Player of the Year   Vol. 1: 18350
American League Rookie of the Year   Vol. 1: 18351
American Legion Fourth Estate Award   Vol. 1: 2804
American Legion Mercury Award   Vol. 1: 2804
American Liberties Medallion   Vol. 1: 2722
American Library Association Trustee Citation   Vol. 1: 2840
American Machinist   Vol. 1: 2977
American Manager of the Year   Vol. 1: 14324
American Music Awards   Vol. 1: 3157
American Musical Theater Festival Award for New Musicals   Vol. 1: 3170
American Needlepoint Guild Book Award   Vol. 1: 3187
American Needlepoint Guild Literary Award   Vol. 1: 3187
American Numismatic Society Graduate Fellowship   Vol. 1: 3274
American Occupational Therapy Foundation Awards   Vol. 1: 3308
American Patriots Medal   Vol. 1: 9405
American Peace Prize   Vol. 1: 8591
American Penal Press Contest   Vol. 1: 18222
American Pharmaceutical Association - Student Leadership Award   Vol. 1: 3394
American Physical Society Prize for Physics   Vol. 1: 3443
American Poetry Association Annual Poetry Contest   Vol. 1: 3547
American Poultry Historial Society Award   Vol. 1: 16344
American Preparedness Award   Vol. 1: 1582
American Revolution Round Table Book Award   Vol. 1: 3949
American Romanian Academy Awards   Vol. 1: 3976

American-Scandinavian Foundation/PEN Translation Prizes   Vol. 1: 16014
American School and University Annual Architectural Portfolio   Vol. 1: 3990
American Society for Microbiology Fellowships   Vol. 1: 4199
American Society of Cytology Award for Meritorious Achievement in Cytology   Vol. 1: 4551
American Society of Dentistry for Children Prize   Vol. 1: 4553
American Society of Mammalogists Award   Vol. 1: 4657
American Society of Pharmacognosy Awards and Grants   Vol. 1: 4744
American Society of Safety Engineers Fellow   Vol. 1: 4780
American Society of Swedish Engineers Award   Vol. 1: 4794
American Spirit Awards   Vol. 1: 8049
American Sportscasters Hall of Fame   Vol. 1: 4852
American Stars Awards   Vol. 1: 481
American Statesman Medal   Vol. 1: 9405
American-Swiss Friendship Award   Vol. 1: 6649
American Theatre Wing Design Awards   Vol. 1: 4901
American Therapeutic Recreation Association Awards   Vol. 1: 4904
American Tradition Award   Vol. 1: 13949
American Translators Association Award   Vol. 1: 4917
American Water Landmarks   Vol. 1: 5013
American Wine Competition   Vol. 1: 6348
American Winery of the Year   Vol. 1: 6348
American Woman of the Year   Vol. 1: 16996
Americanism News Media Award   Vol. 1: 7398
America's 2000 National Works on Paper Exhibition   Vol. 1: 12344
America's Best Awards   Vol. 1: 8049
America's Corporate Conscience Award   Vol. 1: 8385
America's Cup   Vol. 1: 5121
America's Democratic Legacy Award   Vol. 1: 5176
America's Junior Miss Pageant   Vol. 1: 5123
America's Ten Outstanding Young Men   Vol. 1: 19430
America's Young Woman of the Year   Vol. 1: 5123
AmeriStar Packaging Competition   Vol. 1: 10425
Ames Award; Rosemary   Vol. 1: 2400
Ames Histology Award   Vol. 2: 10971
Ames Medal and Award   Vol. 2: 2115
Ames Prize for Investigation in the field of Basic Health Sciences   Vol. 2: 1581
Amex Bank Review Awards   Vol. 2: 2078
AMF Head Arthur Ashe Sportsmanship Award   Vol. 1: 10549
AMGEN Award   Vol. 1: 7182
AMHA Man of the Year Award/AMHA Woman of the Year Award   Vol. 1: 3121
AMHA Medal Class Awards   Vol. 1: 3122
AMHA Open Competition Awards   Vol. 1: 3123
AMHA Trail Ride Award   Vol. 1: 3124
AMHA Woman of the Year Award; AMHA Man of the Year Award/   Vol. 1: 3121
AMHA Youth of the Year Award   Vol. 1: 3125
AMHA Youth Person of the Year Award   Vol. 1: 3126
AMHAY Horsemastership Awards   Vol. 1: 3127
AMI Literary Award   Vol. 1: 5857

AMI Salon Awards   Vol. 1: 5858
Amicus Award   Vol. 1: 710
Amiens International Film Festival   Vol. 2: 4890
Amir Chand Prize; Basanti Devi   Vol. 2: 7578
Amir Chand Prizes; Shakuntala   Vol. 2: 7579
Amirikian Memorial Maritime Welding Award; Arsham   Vol. 1: 5074
Amis d'Escoffier Society Awards   Vol. 1: 5130
Ammann Research Fellowship in Structural Engineering; O. H.   Vol. 1: 4431
AMOA Cigarette Vending Machine Promotion Award   Vol. 1: 5139
AMOA Games Awards   Vol. 1: 5140
AMOA Jukebox Awards   Vol. 1: 5141
Amoroso Award   Vol. 2: 2507
Amory Prize; Francis   Vol. 1: 524
Amos Award   Vol. 1: 14393
AMP W.G. Walkley Awards for Journalism   Vol. 2: 523
AMS 50 Dissertations Fellowships   Vol. 1: 3172
AMS Award for Achievements in and Contributions to Management   Vol. 1: 143
AMS Award for Achievements in Management and Outstanding Service to AMS   Vol. 1: 144
AMS/Industry Graduate Fellowships   Vol. 1: 3071
AMS/Industry Undergraduate Scholarships   Vol. 1: 3072
AMSA International Piano Competition   Vol. 1: 3164
AMSCO Scholarship   Vol. 1: 10739
Amsterdam Prize   Vol. 2: 9451
Amsterdam Prize for Art
  Heineken Foundation   Vol. 2: 9451
  Royal Netherlands Academy of Arts and Sciences   Vol 2: 9593
Amsterdam Prize for History   Vol. 2: 9594
Amsterdam Prize for Medicine
  Heineken Foundation   Vol. 2: 9451
  Royal Netherlands Academy of Arts and Sciences   Vol 2: 9595
Amsterdam Prize for the Environment   Vol. 2: 9596
AMSUS Award for Excellence in Clinical Pharmacy Practice   Vol. 1: 5874
AMSUS Medical Student Award   Vol. 1: 5875
AMTEC Media Festival   Vol. 1: 6857
AMT's Outstanding Medical Assistant Students   Vol. 1: 3036
AMT's Outstanding Students   Vol. 1: 3036
Amundson Student Presentation Award; Terry   Vol. 1: 20298
AMVETS National Awards Program   Vol. 1: 5143
AMVETS National Employer of the Year Award   Vol. 1: 5144
AMVETS Silver Helmet Awards   Vol. 1: 5145
AMWA Medical Book Awards   Vol. 1: 3057
Amy Award in Hematology; New Graduate Award - Harold   Vol. 1: 7210
AMY Awards   Vol. 1: 20614
Amy Writing Awards   Vol. 1: 5147
ANA Club Award to Outstanding Young Numismatist   Vol. 1: 3199
ANA Constituent Nurses' Associations Publications Awards   Vol. 1: 2751
ANA Literary Award for Paper Money Studies   Vol. 1: 3200
ANA Literary Prize   Vol. 2: 9856
ANA Numismatic Art Award for Excellence in Medallic Sculpture   Vol. 1: 3201
ANA - YN Exhibit Award   Vol. 1: 3202
ANAD Award   Vol. 1: 5149
ANAD Service Awards   Vol. 1: 5150
Analar Lectureship   Vol. 2: 4184

Anand Endowment Lecture; Dr. Nitya   Vol. 2: 7636
Ancel; Prix Louis   Vol. 2: 6379
Ancona International Music Composition Competition for Wind Instruments   Vol. 2: 8191
Anda International Piano Competition; Geza   Vol. 2: 11676
Andeoud; Prix Jules   Vol. 2: 5767
Andersen Award for the Business in the Arts Advisor of the Year; The Arthur   Vol. 2: 2031
Andersen Award; William C.   Vol. 1: 16682
Andersen Awards; Hans Christian   Vol. 2: 11767
Andersen Awards; International Hans Christian   Vol. 2: 11767
Andersen Ballet Award; H. C.   Vol. 2: 2003
Andersen Balletprisen; H. C.   Vol. 2: 2003
Andersen Honour Diploma; Hans Christian   Vol. 2: 11769
Andersen Memorial Scholarships; Hugh J.   Vol. 1: 14342
Andersen Prize   Vol. 2: 8422
Anderson Award; Arthur R.   Vol. 1: 1777
Anderson Award; Elda E.   Vol. 1: 9846
Anderson Award; F. Paul   Vol. 1: 4569
Anderson Award; H. C. L.   Vol. 2: 237
Anderson Award; Harlan J.   Vol. 1: 6033
Anderson Award; Jack   Vol. 1: 11145
Anderson Award; Kathleen S.   Vol. 1: 12040
Anderson Award; Marian   Vol. 1: 11493
Anderson Award; William   Vol. 1: 3568
Anderson Bank Prize   Vol. 2: 2917
Anderson-Berry Medal; David   Vol. 2: 10637
Anderson - Everett Award   Vol. 1: 10639
Anderson Lectureship; Glenn   Vol. 1: 7094
Anderson Medal   Vol. 2: 2917
Anderson Medal of Honor in Applied Geography; James R.   Vol. 1: 5682
Anderson Memorial Award; Ronald H.   Vol. 1: 4317
Anderson Merit Award; William G.   Vol. 1: 758
Anderson Outstanding Paper Award   Vol. 1: 34
Anderson Playwrights Series Prize; Maxwell   Vol. 1: 18445
Anderson Prize Essay   Vol. 2: 4366
Anderson Prize for Violin; Emily   Vol. 2: 2630
Anderson Safety Student of the Year Award; John E.   Vol. 1: 4781
Anderson Silver Medal; Sir Rowand   Vol. 2: 10610
Anderson Student Paper Award   Vol. 1: 35
Anderson Trophy; Samuel E.   Vol. 1: 5281
Anderson Vocal Arts Competition; Marian   Vol. 1: 19822
Anderson Young Writers Poetry Award; FAW Fedora   Vol. 2: 388
Andes National Award; Ammon S.   Vol. 1: 17258
Andre; Concours International de Trompette Maurice   Vol. 2: 5034
Andreescu Prize; Ion   Vol. 2: 10329
Andrew Award   Vol. 1: 18752
Andrew Common Grants; Thomas   Vol. 2: 3333
Andrews Bibliographic Award; Joseph L.   Vol. 1: 1027
Andrews Glass Award   Vol. 1: 4023
Andrews Memorial Essay Prize; P. W. S.   Vol. 2: 3517
Andrews Narrative Poetry Prize; John Williams   Vol. 1: 16260
Andrus Award   Vol. 1: 1159
Andry Award; Nicolas   Vol. 1: 5718
Anerkennungspreis des Landes Niederosterreich   Vol. 2: 860

Angel Award - Distinguished Hispanic-American Artist; El   Vol. 1: 6367
Angel Award - For Corporate Contribution to the Development of Hispanic-American Arts; El   Vol. 1: 6368
Angel Escobar Charity Prizes; Alejandro   Vol. 2: 1583
Angel Escobar Science Prize; Alejandro   Vol. 2: 1584
Angel Flight Silver Wings Individual Awards   Vol. 1: 5283
Angel Flight Unit Awards   Vol. 1: 5284
Angel Literary Award   Vol. 2: 2080
Angel of the Year   Vol. 1: 20400
Angelette Award   Vol. 1: 5283
Angeli Prize; Marguerite de   Vol. 1: 8573
Angler of the Year   Vol. 1: 6286
Anglo-Hellenic League's Runciman Award   Vol. 2: 2194
ANGOC Award for Rural Development   Vol. 2: 10020
Angus & Robertson Writers' Fellowship   Vol. 2: 328
Angus & Robertson Writers for the Young Fellowship   Vol. 2: 329
Angus Award   Vol. 2: 9727
Angus Medal; Robert W.   Vol. 1: 7134
Anhinga Poetry Prize   Vol. 1: 5155
Aniara Priset   Vol. 2: 11631
Aniara Prize   Vol. 2: 11631
Anik Award   Vol. 1: 18768
Animal Behavior Society Best Student Paper Award   Vol. 1: 5159
Animal Behavior Society Film Festival Awards   Vol. 1: 5160
Animal Control Employee of the Year Award   Vol. 1: 12784
Animal Growth and Development Award   Vol. 1: 4392
Animal Humanitarian of the Year   Vol. 1: 5162
Animal Industry Service Award   Vol. 1: 4393
Animal Management Award   Vol. 1: 4394
Animal Physiology and Endocrinology Award   Vol. 1: 4395
Animal Rights Writing Award   Vol. 1: 11227
Animal Technician Award; AALAS   Vol. 1: 864
Anisfield - Wolf Book Award in Race Relations   Vol. 1: 7837
Anisfield-Wolf Book Awards/Exploring Human Diversity and Prejudice   Vol. 1: 7837
Ann Arbor Film Festival   Vol. 1: 5174
Anneau d'Or - Concours International d'Emissions Sportives en Television   Vol. 2: 11738
Annecy Festival Prizes   Vol. 2: 5957
Annecy International Animated Film Festival   Vol. 2: 5957
Annenberg Foundation Prize   Vol. 1: 1264
Annett Award for Children's Literature; R. Ross   Vol. 1: 20555
Annie Award for Outstanding Achievement in an Animated Feature Production   Vol. 1: 10604
Annie Award for Outstanding Achievement in an Animated Television Program   Vol. 1: 10605
Annie Award for Outstanding Acievement in an Animated Television Commercial   Vol. 1: 10606
Annie Award for Outstanding Individual Achievement in the Field of Animation   Vol. 1: 10607
Annin Award; Douglas H.   Vol. 1: 10480
Anniversary of People's Poland Awards   Vol. 2: 10097

Annual Academy Lecturer   Vol. 1: 651
Annual Achievement Award   Vol. 1: 11879
Annual ACTRA Awards
 Academy of Canadian Cinema & Television   Vol. 1: 26
 Alliance of Canadian Cinema, Television and Radio Artists   Vol 1: 327
Annual Art Competition & Exhibition   Vol. 1: 18524
Annual Artist Award   Vol. 1: 19993
Annual Aviation Mechanic Safety Award   Vol. 1: 9057
Annual Award
 British Society of Rheology   Vol. 2: 2528
 League for Industrial Democracy   Vol 1: 11808
 Malacological Society of London   Vol 2: 3620
 Parks Council   Vol 1: 15974
Annual Award for Excellence in Writing on an Information Topic   Vol. 1: 15675
Annual Award for Outstanding Achievement in the Field of Information Science   Vol. 2: 3106
Annual Award for Planning Achievement   Vol. 2: 4290
Annual Award of CPPQ   Vol. 1: 8286
Annual Award of the Dozenal Society of America   Vol. 1: 8722
Annual Award of the S.A. Transport Services/Transnet   Vol. 2: 10985
Annual Award to Regular Columnists   Vol. 1: 15676
Annual Awards
 American Society of Contemporary Artists   Vol. 1: 4532
 British Quarter Horse Association   Vol 2: 2493
 Guild of Television Cameramen   Vol 2: 2977
Annual Awards Competition   Vol. 1: 8338
Annual Awards for Chapter Programming   Vol. 1: 15961
Annual Awards for Distinction in Financial Management   Vol. 1: 19310
Annual Awards in Teleconferencing   Vol. 1: 11343
Annual Central Prize Award and Certificate of Merit Award   Vol. 1: 7477
Annual Central Prize Award, President's Certificate of Merit Award, and Central Poster Award   Vol. 1: 7477
Annual Championship Prizes   Vol. 1: 9157
Annual Chapter Newsletter Award   Vol. 1: 2767
Annual Chapter Recognition Award   Vol. 1: 10740
Annual Chapter Volunteer Service Award   Vol. 1: 15935
Annual Chautauqua International Exhibition of Art   Vol. 1: 7528
Annual Chautauqua International Exhibition of American Art   Vol. 1: 7528
Annual Club Competition   Vol. 2: 9789
Annual Competition Awards   Vol. 2: 3479
Annual Competition - Grand Award   Vol. 1: 7868
Annual Conference and EXPO Awards   Vol. 1: 18044
Annual Conference Paper Awards   Vol. 1: 18045
Annual Contest
 Inter-American Safety Council   Vol. 1: 10513
 National Federation of State Poetry Societies   Vol 1: 13963

Award Index
Volume 2: International and Foreign

Annual Corrective Therapy Award   Vol. 1: 2768
Annual Design Awards   Vol. 1: 6575
Annual Display Award   Vol. 1: 13074
Annual Distinguished Student Paper Competition   Vol. 1: 15894
Annual Education Publications and Electronic Media Contest   Vol. 1: 14670
Annual Environmental Awards   Vol. 2: 3755
Annual Essay Contest   Vol. 1: 5447
Annual Excellence in Writing Competition   Vol. 1: 4411
Annual Exhibition
  Allied Artists of America   Vol. 1: 332
  Audubon Artists, Inc.   Vol 1: 6140
  National Watercolor Society   Vol 1: 14991
Annual Exhibition Awards   Vol. 1: 17860
Annual Exhibition of the Royal Scottish Academy   Vol. 2: 10619
Annual Exhibition of Weaving in the Norwegian Tradition   Vol. 1: 15537
Annual Exhibitions/National & International   Vol. 1: 5293
Annual Florida Space Coast Writers Conference Awards   Vol. 1: 18251
Annual Gold Leaf Awards   Vol. 1: 6762
Annual Graphics Competition   Vol. 1: 4412
Annual High Point Awards   Vol. 1: 16079
Annual Honor Roll   Vol. 1: 7716
Annual Juried Show   Vol. 1: 15174
Annual Kinesiotherapy Award   Vol. 1: 2768
Annual Lecturer Award   Vol. 1: 12542
Annual Legal Writing Competition   Vol. 1: 12963
Annual Literary Award   Vol. 2: 8849
Annual Literary Festival   Vol. 2: 782
Annual Manuscript Competition   Vol. 1: 5202
Annual Medal Design Award   Vol. 1: 2712
Annual Media & Corporate Awards   Vol. 1: 8064
Annual Meeting Paper Presentation Award   Vol. 1: 10448
Annual Multi-media Juried Art Exhibition   Vol. 1: 6618
Annual National Chief's Challenge   Vol. 1: 10696
Annual News Award   Vol. 1: 11195
Annual OCLC on the Front Line Award   Vol. 1: 15677
Annual One-Act Play Festival Award   Vol. 2: 9769
Annual Open Exhibition   Vol. 1: 20348
Annual Open Exhibition ''For Pastels Only''   Vol. 1: 15983
Annual Pacific Sociological Association Distinguished Scholarship Award   Vol. 1: 15895
Annual Photography Contest   Vol. 1: 19432
Annual Political Book Award   Vol. 1: 20116
Annual Prize   Vol. 1: 17659
Annual Prize for Best Restoration Program   Vol. 2: 5106
Annual Prize for Scientific Works   Vol. 2: 12126
Annual Prize in History in Honor of Samuel Eliot Morison   Vol. 2: 2270
Annual Prize of the Czech Musical Fund   Vol. 2: 1854
Annual Prize of the Society of Czech Architects   Vol. 2: 1882
Annual Professorship in Jerusalem   Vol. 1: 4009
Annual Promotional Activity Award   Vol. 2: 8858
Annual Report Award   Vol. 1: 3852
Annual Report Awards Competition   Vol. 1: 9212
Annual Report Contest Awards   Vol. 1: 5930

Annual RTNDA Awards   Vol. 1: 16635
Annual School and College Publications Contest   Vol. 1: 14670
Annual Sculpture Downtown Exhibition   Vol. 1: 7529
Annual Spring Show Award   Vol. 1: 8993
Annual Stimulus Subprize   Vol. 2: 64
Annual Tour Scholarship   Vol. 1: 17738
Annual Truman Capote Award for Literary Criticism in Memory of Newton Arvin   Vol. 1: 19804
Annual Writing Competition   Vol. 1: 8688
Annual Young Artists' Competition   Vol. 1: 11522
Anode Trophy   Vol. 2: 11079
Anonymous Prize   Vol. 1: 12596
ANPA Foundation - Associated Collegiate Press Pacemakers Awards   Vol. 1: 15353
ANPA Foundation - International Circulation Managerges Association C. K. Jefferson Award   Vol. 1: 15354
ANPA Foundation - Newspaper in Education Program Excellence Award   Vol. 1: 15356
Anslinger Award   Vol. 1: 11114
Anson Award; Jack L.   Vol. 1: 5805
Antarctic Medal   Vol. 2: 206
Antarctica Service Medal
  National Science Foundation   Vol. 1: 14681
  United States Department of Defense - Armed Forces Decorations and Awards   Vol 1: 19137
Antarjatik Beshamarik Sheba Sangstha Competitions   Vol. 2: 932
Antenne d'or Festival international du film et de la bande video sur les telecominictions et l'electronigue   Vol. 2: 11848
Anthem Essay Contest   Vol. 1: 16670
Anthes-Preis fur Archaologische Forschungen; Eduard-   Vol. 2: 7150
Anthropology in Media Award   Vol. 1: 793
Anti-Censorship Award   Vol. 1: 18005
Anti-Priset   Vol. 2: 11639
Anti-Prize   Vol. 2: 11639
Antipa Prize; Grigore   Vol. 2: 10330
Antoinette Perry Awards (Tony Awards)   Vol. 1: 4902
Antoniorrobles Award   Vol. 2: 9120
Antonov Aeromodelling Diploma   Vol. 2: 5137
Antwoorden Prijsvragen, Klasse der Letteren   Vol. 2: 1249
Antwoorden Prijsvragen, Klasse der Schone Kunsten   Vol. 2: 1250
Antwoorden Prijsvragen, Klasse der Wetenschappen   Vol. 2: 1251
Anugerah Sastera Negara   Vol. 2: 8901
Anuvrat Award for International Peace   Vol. 2: 7484
ANZAAS Medal   Vol. 2: 188
ANZAC Fellowships   Vol. 2: 9748
AOCS/Supelco Research Award   Vol. 1: 3310
AOJT Award   Vol. 1: 5915
AOPA Awards for Achievement & Endeavor in Light Aviation   Vol. 2: 2049
AORC Award   Vol. 1: 5911
AOS Show Certificate   Vol. 1: 3324
AOS Show Trophy   Vol. 1: 3325
AOTA COTA/OTR Partnership Award   Vol. 1: 3306
AOTOS Mariner's Plaque   Vol. 1: 18976
AP Collegiate Basketball Player of the Year   Vol. 1: 8051
APA Assembly Warren Williams Awards   Vol. 1: 3622
APA/Dista Products Resident Research Award   Vol. 1: 3623
APA Distinguished Career Award   Vol. 1: 469
APA Journalism Awards   Vol. 1: 3531

Application

APA/Pennwalt Resident Research Award   Vol. 1: 3623
APA Planning Fellowship   Vol. 1: 3532
APA Research Award   Vol. 1: 470
APA Teaching Award   Vol. 1: 471
APA/Wisniewski Young Psychiatrist Research Award   Vol. 1: 3624
APAA Annual Art Exhibit   Vol. 1: 3497
Apaczai Janos Csere Dij   Vol. 2: 7397
Apaczai Prize; Janos Csere   Vol. 2: 7397
APALA Distinguished Service Award   Vol. 1: 5347
Apathy Commemorative Medal; Istvan   Vol. 2: 7458
Apathy Istvan Emlekerem   Vol. 2: 7458
APB National Awards for Cooperative and Journalistic Excellence   Vol. 1: 5417
APB National Awards for Journalistic Excellence   Vol. 1: 5417
APBA Gold Cup   Vol. 1: 3602
APBA Honor Squadron   Vol. 1: 3603
A.P.C. - Diane D. Boehret Award   Vol. 1: 3400
APEX - Awards for Publication Excellence   Vol. 1: 8062
APF Gold Medal Award for Life Achievement in the Application of Psychology   Vol. 1: 3833
APF Gold Medal Award for Life Contribution by a Psychologist in the Public Interest   Vol. 1: 3833
APFC Man/Woman of the Year Award   Vol. 1: 5920
Apfelbaum Award   Vol. 1: 3411
Apgar Award; Virginia   Vol. 1: 666
APhA - Academy of Pharmacy Practice and Management Merit Awards   Vol. 1: 3375
APhA Academy of Students of Pharmacy Chapter Achievement Award   Vol. 1: 3395
APhA Academy of Students of Pharmacy Membership Achievement Award   Vol. 1: 3396
APHA Award for Excellence   Vol. 1: 3845
APHBA Amateur Register of Merit   Vol. 1: 15918
APIC New Investigator Research Award   Vol. 1: 5575
Apker Award; Leroy   Vol. 1: 3444
Aplan Award   Vol. 1: 9914
APO Award   Vol. 2: 8505
APO National Award   Vol. 2: 8504
APO Regional Award   Vol. 2: 8505
APO Special National Award   Vol. 2: 8504
Apollinaire; Prix Guillaume   Vol. 2: 6172
Apollo Award
  American Optometric Association   Vol. 1: 3320
  Arnold Air Society   Vol 1: 5281
  Eaglehawk Dahlia and Arts Festival   Vol 2: 357
  Summer and Casual Furniture Manufacturers Association   Vol 1: 18526
APPA Century Award   Vol. 1: 3853
APPA Honor Roll   Vol. 1: 3854
APPA Safety Contest Awards   Vol. 1: 3855
Appeal of Conscience Award   Vol. 1: 5188
Appel-Denkmunze; Otto-   Vol. 2: 6667
Appert Award; Nicholas   Vol. 1: 10340
Apple Awards   Vol. 1: 13882
Apple Tree Award   Vol. 2: 3691
Applebaum Award; William   Vol. 1: 9292
Appleseed Award; Johnny   Vol. 1: 9493
Appleton Prize
  International Union of Radio Science   Vol. 2: 1210
  Royal Society   Vol 2: 4141
Application Award   Vol. 1: 11092
Application to Practice Award   Vol. 1: 12307

Applications Award   Vol. 2: 2799
Applications Paper Prize   Vol. 2: 816
Applied Consumer Economics Award   Vol. 1: 1861
Applied Research Award   Vol. 1: 19100
Applied Research Medal   Vol. 2: 597
Applied Social Issues Internship Program   Vol. 1: 17631
Appreciation Award
   Lewis and Clark Trail Heritage Foundation   Vol. 1: 11846
   Pedal Steel Guitar Association   Vol 1: 16008
   Sporting Goods Agents Association   Vol 1: 18337
The Appreciation Award   Vol. 1: 14259
Appreciation Certificates for Service to NATRC   Vol. 1: 15467
APPROTECH ASIA Special Award   Vol. 2: 10058
Aprilia Trophy; Reuben Lovell Memorial   Vol. 2: 3533
APRS Annual Award   Vol. 2: 10506
APS Cadiovascular Section Awards   Vol. 1: 3499
APS Career Enhancement Awards   Vol. 1: 3500
APS Environmental and Exercise Physiology Section Awards   Vol. 1: 3501
APS Fellow   Vol. 1: 3518
APS Gastrointestinal Physiology Section Awards   Vol. 1: 3502
Apsey Playwriting Award; Ruby Lloyd   Vol. 1: 19732
Apuraha tai Palkinto   Vol. 2: 4710
APWA Distinguished Service Award   Vol. 1: 3872
Aqua Awards
   International Bottled Water Association   Vol. 1: 10811
   Waterbed Manufacturers Association   Vol 1: 20167
Aquatic Hall of Fame   Vol. 1: 5204
Aqueous Show   Vol. 1: 11688
Aquinas Medal   Vol. 1: 1437
ARA Awards for Contribution to the Cause of Freedom and Human Rights   Vol. 1: 3976
ARA Hall of Fame   Vol. 1: 6204
Arab Book Fair Prize   Vol. 2: 8842
Arab League Translation Awards   Vol. 1: 8006
Arab Sports Pressman Award   Vol. 2: 10504
Arabic Honor Student   Vol. 1: 1212
Arabic Translation Contest Award   Vol. 1: 1213
Arabization Prizes   Vol. 2: 7747
Arafura Short Story Award   Vol. 2: 553
Arango International Design Exhibition   Vol. 1: 5206
Aranha Prize; Graca   Vol. 2: 1450
Arany Szarvas   Vol. 2: 7314
Aranytoll   Vol. 2: 7292
Arata Award   Vol. 2: 3432
Arbeit Memorial Prizes; Arnold A.   Vol. 1: 14217
Arbeitsgemeinschaft Schweizer Grafiker Competitions   Vol. 2: 11904
Arbor Day Awards   Vol. 1: 12788
Arbor Day Celebration Awards   Vol. 1: 12788
Arboricultural Association Award   Vol. 2: 2089
Arbuse Gold Medals; Gussie and Samuel   Vol. 1: 15248
Arbuthnot Award   Vol. 1: 11184
ARC Distinguished Research Award   Vol. 1: 5214

ARC of Excellence Awards for Media   Vol. 1: 5213
ARCA Championship Hall of Fame   Vol. 1: 11112
Arce; Premio Julio G.   Vol. 2: 9016
Arch of Fame Award   Vol. 1: 4991
Archaeological Book Award   Vol. 2: 2245
Archaeological Fieldwork Grants   Vol. 2: 8176
Archaeological Geology Division Award   Vol. 1: 9566
Archambault Prize in Physical Sciences and Mathematics; Urgel   Vol. 1: 5431
Archenbaud; Prix Fraternite Gaby   Vol. 2: 6124
Archer Award; Ellinor   Vol. 2: 238
Archer Award; Harry   Vol. 1: 1703
Archer-Burton Poetry Competition; Kitty   Vol. 2: 663
Arches Papers Award   Vol. 1: 5035
Archibald Prize   Vol. 2: 124
Architectural Award   Vol. 2: 2215
Architectural Awards   Vol. 2: 8840
Architectural Awards Competition   Vol. 1: 13159
Architectural Awards of Excellence   Vol. 1: 2678
Architectural Critics and Writers Award   Vol. 2: 10880
Architectural Design Competition   Vol. 1: 7812
Architectural Exhibition Catalogue Award   Vol. 1: 17739
Architectural Technician of the Year Award   Vol. 2: 2395
Architecture Award   Vol. 2: 2886
Architecture Firm Award   Vol. 1: 2525
Arctic Institute of North America, Grant-in-Aid   Vol. 1: 5236
Arctowski Medal   Vol. 1: 12663
Arderne Medal and Prize; John   Vol. 2: 4235
Ardley Prize; Bimcam   Vol. 2: 3157
Area Community Service Awards   Vol. 1: 1160
Area Rating Award   Vol. 1: 10542
Arellano Cultural Merit Medal; Gerardo   Vol. 2: 1651
Arellano; Medalla al Merito Cultural de Gerardo   Vol. 2: 1651
Arenth Excellence in Cancer Nursing Administration Award; ONS/Roxane Laboratories Linda   Vol. 1: 15662
Arets Katt   Vol. 2: 11568
Arets pris i svensk forsakring   Vol. 2: 11629
Arets Verk   Vol. 2: 9970
Arfvidson; Prix Andre   Vol. 2: 5352
Arfvidson; Prix Paul   Vol. 2: 5352
Argentinian Association of Dermatology Awards   Vol. 2: 33
Argyll Postal History Salver   Vol. 2: 3781
Ari Medal of Merit; Carina   Vol. 2: 11442
Ari Medaljen; Carina   Vol. 2: 11442
Arid Lands Hydraulic Engineering Award   Vol. 1: 4432
Ariel Maritime UK Ltd. Prize   Vol. 2: 3098
Ariel Prizes for Cinematography   Vol. 2: 9097
Arima Award   Vol. 2: 6064
Arini de Masnatta Prize; Elsa E.   Vol. 2: 65
Arinos Prize; Afonso   Vol. 2: 1420
Arisawa Awards; Hiromi   Vol. 1: 5698
Arizona Author Award   Vol. 1: 5243
Arizona Authors' Association Annual National Literary Contest   Vol. 1: 5241
Arizona Young Readers Award   Vol. 1: 5244
Arjomaria/Arches/Rivers Award   Vol. 1: 5035
Arjuna Awards   Vol. 2: 7518
Arkitekturprisen   Vol. 2: 1948

Arlen Memorial Fund Award; Stephen   Vol. 2: 2096
ARLIS/NA Art Book Publishing Awards   Vol. 1: 5300
Arlt Award in the Humanities; Gustave O.   Vol. 1: 8360
ARM of the Year   Vol. 1: 10434
Armada Dish (Biffa Trophy)   Vol. 2: 2898
Armand; Fondation Louis   Vol. 2: 5621
Armed Forces Athletes of the Year   Vol. 1: 19451
Armed Forces Expeditionary Medal   Vol. 1: 19138
Armed Forces Military Association Patriotism Medal   Vol. 1: 5268
Armed Forces Reserve Medal   Vol. 1: 19139
Armed Services Award for Women's Athletic Excellence   Vol. 1: 20424
Armitage Medal   Vol. 1: 17865
Armourers & Brasiers' Award   Vol. 2: 4142
Armstrong Award; James   Vol. 1: 19849
Armstrong Award; Keith S.   Vol. 1: 7117
Armstrong Award; Robert H.   Vol. 1: 5190
Armstrong Awards; Major   Vol. 1: 5272
Armstrong-Ellington Best Entertainment Section   Vol. 1: 14397
Armstrong Industries Literary Award   Vol. 1: 13087
Armstrong Lecture   Vol. 2: 4400
Armstrong Lecture; George   Vol. 1: 472
Armstrong Medal   Vol. 1: 16640
Armstrong Siddeley Car Rally Prizes   Vol. 2: 2098
Armure Studio Award for Excellence in Weaving   Vol. 1: 15708
Armwrestler of the Year (Male and Female)   Vol. 1: 807
Armwrestling Championship Award; National   Vol. 1: 808
Army Cross   Vol. 2: 10921
Army of Occupation Medal - Army-Air Force   Vol. 1: 19140
Army Reserve Components Achievement Medal   Vol. 1: 19141
Arnau S.J. - Obra De San Lazaro Prize; Padre Fermin G.   Vol. 2: 66
Arnbergska Priset   Vol. 2: 11534
Arnold Air Letter Trophy   Vol. 1: 5276
Arnold Award; H. H.   Vol. 1: 234
Arnold Sabre; H. H.   Vol. 1: 5276
Arnow Award; Philip   Vol. 1: 19255
ARRL Herb S. Brier Instructor of the Year Award   Vol. 1: 3886
ARRL Professional Educator of the Year Award   Vol. 1: 3887
ARRL Professional Instructor of the Year Award   Vol. 1: 3888
ARRL Technical Merit Award   Vol. 1: 3895
Arrowhead Biennial Exhibition   Vol. 1: 8764
ARS Award for Distinction in the Field of Recorder   Vol. 1: 3906
ARSC Award for Excellence in Historical Sound Recorded Research   Vol. 1: 5589
Art and Craft in Architecture Award   Vol. 2: 10651
Art and Education Prize   Vol. 2: 9333
Art Award   Vol. 1: 16111
Art Centre Delft Prize   Vol. 2: 9670
Art Criticism Prize   Vol. 1: 12372
Art Director's Choice Award   Vol. 1: 16495
Art Directors Club Hall of Fame   Vol. 1: 5294
Art Directors Club of Toronto Awards and Show Presentation   Vol. 1: 152
Art in All Media Awards   Vol. 1: 8570
Art of Caring Award   Vol. 1: 10418
The Art of Listening Award   Vol. 1: 329

Art of Northeast USA Competition   Vol. 1: 17281
Art of Reporting Award   Vol. 1: 330
ART Radio Script Writing Competition   Vol. 1: 3897
Art Scholarship   Vol. 2: 3946
Art Song Festival   Vol. 1: 7839
ARTA Magazine Awards   Vol. 2: 10394
Artaud; Prix Antonin   Vol. 2: 4932
ARTBA Award   Vol. 1: 3966
Arte in Piazza International Competition   Vol. 2: 8098
Artes Awards   Vol. 2: 11037
Arthroscopy Research Grants   Vol. 1: 5307
Arthur A. Hitchcock Award for Distinguished Service   Vol. 1: 1885
Arthur Award; Rosemary   Vol. 2: 3697
Arthur, M.D. Award; Capt. Ransom J.   Vol. 1: 19440
Arthur Memorial Trophy; Jesse   Vol. 1: 3104
Article of the Year Award   Vol. 1: 1676
Artist Assistance Fellowship Grants   Vol. 1: 12340
Artist Award   Vol. 1: 18506
Artist Award for a Distinguished Body of Work, Exhibition, Presentation or Performance   Vol. 1: 7883
Artist Fellowships   Vol. 1: 15491
Artist of the Year
    Canadian Music Council   Vol. 1: 7046
    Indian Arts and Crafts Association   Vol 1: 10143
    Washington Opera Guild   Vol 1: 20119
Artist of the Year, Helsinki Festival   Vol. 2: 4720
Artist-Teacher Award   Vol. 1: 4867
Artiste Europeen Prize   Vol. 2: 1125
Artistic Ambassador Program   Vol. 1: 19399
Artistic Award   Vol. 2: 7298
Artistic Certificate (for Artistic Display of Orchids in Use)   Vol. 1: 3326
Artistiche Sculture del noto Maestro Enzo Assenza Rappresentante la X musa   Vol. 2: 8417
Artists Association of Finland Award   Vol. 2: 4665
Artists' Fellowship Program   Vol. 1: 15245
Artists Fund Prize   Vol. 1: 12597
Artists-in-Residence Program   Vol. 1: 18509
The Artist's Magazine All Media Competition   Vol. 1: 5318
The Artist's Magazine Annual Painting Competition   Vol. 1: 5318
The Artist's Magazine Award   Vol. 1: 5036
The Artist's Magazine Still Life Painting Competition   Vol. 1: 5318
Artists Workspace Fellowship Program   Vol. 1: 20448
Artot; Prix Paul   Vol. 2: 966
Arts Achievement Award   Vol. 2: 8575
Arts and Letters Award   Vol. 1: 6829
Arts and Letters Awards   Vol. 1: 494
Arts and Riverwoods Award   Vol. 1: 5297
Arts Council of Great Britain Schemes   Vol. 2: 2100
Arts Council of Northern Ireland Bursaries and Awards   Vol. 2: 7854
Arts Council of Wales Book of the Year Awards   Vol. 2: 12150
Arts Council Writing Grants   Vol. 2: 9798
Arts Festival Award   Vol. 2: 8576
Arts for the Parks Competition   Vol. 1: 14447
Arts Management Award for Arts Administrator of the Year   Vol. 1: 5333
Arts Management Award for Career Service   Vol. 1: 5334

Arts Management Special Award   Vol. 1: 5335
Arts Person of the Year Award   Vol. 1: 15175
Arts Prize - Meir Dizengoff Prize   Vol. 2: 7947
Arts Prize - Moshe Halevi Prize   Vol. 2: 7948
Arts Prize - Yoel Engel Prize   Vol. 2: 7949
Arts Recognition and Talent Search   Vol. 1: 19226
Arts Recognition and Talent Search (ARTS)   Vol. 1: 14038
Artz Distinguished Service Award; Curtis P.   Vol. 1: 1379
Arvon Foundation International Poetry Competition   Vol. 2: 2103
Aryabhata Medal   Vol. 2: 7637
Arzner International Film and Video Festival Award; Dorothy   Vol. 1: 20388
The ASA Award   Vol. 1: 4821
ASA Award for Outstanding Statistical Application   Vol. 1: 4860
ASA Business Awards   Vol. 1: 4822
ASA Leadership Award   Vol. 1: 4823
ASA Lure Challenge Trophy   Vol. 1: 3984
ASA Media Award   Vol. 1: 4861
ASA Media Awards   Vol. 1: 4824
ASA National Championships   Vol. 1: 462
ASA Perpetual Challenge Trophies   Vol. 1: 3984
ASA Senior Award   Vol. 1: 4825
ASAE Fellow   Vol. 1: 4408
ASAE Fellows   Vol. 1: 4354
ASAE Paper Awards   Vol. 1: 4355
ASAE Past Presidents Award   Vol. 1: 4356
ASAE Student Engineer of the Year   Vol. 1: 4357
ASAE Student Paper Awards   Vol. 1: 4358
Asahi Fellowship   Vol. 2: 8488
Asahi Forestry Culture Prize   Vol. 2: 8489
Asahi Kokusai Jido Tosho Fukyu Sho   Vol. 2: 8494
Asahi Kokusai Shorei Kin   Vol. 2: 8488
Asahi Nogyo Sho   Vol. 2: 8490
Asahi Physical Culture Prize   Vol. 2: 8493
Asahi Reading Promotion Award; IBBY -   Vol. 2: 11768
Asahi Shakai Fukushi Sho   Vol. 2: 8491
Asahi Shinrin Bunka Sho   Vol. 2: 8489
Asahi Sho   Vol. 2: 8492
Asahi Sports Prize   Vol. 2: 8493
Asahi Sports Sho   Vol. 2: 8493
ASAP - Gralnick Foundation Research Award   Vol. 1: 4030
ASAS Extension Award   Vol. 1: 4396
ASAS Fellow   Vol. 1: 4397
ASBC - Merck Award   Vol. 1: 4039
ASBMB - Angen Award   Vol. 1: 4038
ASBMB - Merck Award   Vol. 1: 4039
ASBMB - Schering Plough Young Investigator Award   Vol. 1: 4040
ASC Recognition Award   Vol. 1: 4061
ASCA Awards of Excellence   Vol. 1: 4881
ASCA Chapter Age Group Coaches of the Year   Vol. 1: 4882
ASCA Coaches Hall of Fame   Vol. 1: 4883
ASCA Contemporary Art Awards   Vol. 1: 4532
ASCAP Chamber Music Awards   Vol. 1: 4523
ASCAP/Chorus America Awards for Adventuresome Programming   Vol. 1: 7654
ASCAP - Deems Taylor Awards   Vol. 1: 4524
ASCAP Foundation College Musical Theatre Award   Vol. 1: 1755
ASCAP - Richard Rodgers Award   Vol. 1: 4525
ASCAP Triple Play Award   Vol. 1: 4526
ASCE News Correspondent Award   Vol. 1: 4433
ASCE Presidents' Award   Vol. 1: 4434

ASCE President's Medal   Vol. 1: 4435
ASCE State-of-the-Art of Civil Engineering Award   Vol. 1: 4436
ASCLA Exceptional Service Award   Vol. 1: 2880
ASCLA Leadership Achievement Award
    American Library Association - Association of Specialized and Cooperative Library Agencies   Vol. 1: 2881
    American Library Association - Association of Specialized and Cooperative Library Agencies   Vol 1: 2881
ASCLA/National Organization on Disability Award for Library Service for Persons with Disabilities   Vol. 1: 2882
ASCLA Professional Achievement Award   Vol. 1: 2883
ASCLA Service Award   Vol. 1: 2884
Ascona Prize for a Narrative Work in Literature   Vol. 2: 11869
ASCP - CAP Joint Annual Award   Vol. 1: 4514
ASCP - CAP Joint Distinguished Service Award   Vol. 1: 4514
ASCP Distinguished Pathology Educator Award Honoring H. P. Smith   Vol. 1: 4515
ASCP Distinguished Service to Clinical Pathology Award Honoring Ward Burdick   Vol. 1: 4516
ASCP Medical Photography Competition   Vol. 1: 4517
ASCP Outstanding Research Award Honoring Philip Levine   Vol. 1: 4518
ASDA Prize   Vol. 2: 4909
ASEA-Brown Boveri-Forschungspreis   Vol. 2: 11928
ASEAN Award for Literature   Vol. 2: 10030
ASEAN Award for the Performing Arts   Vol. 2: 10031
ASEAN Award for Visual Arts   Vol. 2: 10032
ASF Awards for Scandinavians   Vol. 1: 3986
ASF Grants and Fellowships   Vol. 1: 3987
ASF Translation Prize   Vol. 1: 3988
ASFD Life-Time Achievement Award   Vol. 1: 4562
ASFSA Thelme Fienegan Gold Award   Vol. 1: 3998
ASGE/C. R. Bard Outstanding Manuscript Prize Award   Vol. 1: 4132
Asgrow Award in Vegetable Crops   Vol. 1: 4153
ASH Scholar Awards   Vol. 1: 4593
ASHA Media Awards for Journalists   Vol. 1: 4839
Ashby Memorial Award; Robert H.   Vol. 1: 79
Ashe Award for Courage; Arthur   Vol. 1: 8999
Ashe Sportsmanship Award; AMF Head Arthur   Vol. 1: 10549
Asher Award; Eugene   Vol. 1: 8626
Ashford Medal; Bailey K.   Vol. 1: 4812
Ashmore Award for Service to CASE   Vol. 1: 8294
Ashok Chakra   Vol. 2: 7547
ASHP Research Award   Vol. 1: 4603
ASHRAE - Alco Medal for Distinguished Public Service   Vol. 1: 4570
ASHRAE ASHAE - Homer Addams Award   Vol. 1: 4568
ASHRAE Energy Awards   Vol. 1: 4591
ASHRAE Fellows   Vol. 1: 4571
ASHRAE Hall of Fame   Vol. 1: 4572
ASHRAE Journal Paper Award   Vol. 1: 4573
ASHRAE Symposium Paper Award   Vol. 1: 4574
ASHRAE Technical Paper Award   Vol. 1: 4575
ASHRAE - Willis H. Carrier Award   Vol. 1: 4576
Ashton Scholastic Award   Vol. 2: 193

Ashville Cinematique Awards Vol. 1: 17288
Ashworth Fellowship Vol. 1: 12485
Asia and the Pacific Photography Contest Vol. 2: 8499
ASIA Award Vol. 1: 4846
ASIA Young Executive of the Year Vol. 1: 6169
Asian Advertising Award Vol. 2: 4479
Asian American Journalists Association National Awards Vol. 1: 5341
Asian/Asian-American Award Vol. 1: 3625
Asian Champion Club Tournament Vol. 2: 8894
Asian Club Championship Vol. 2: 8894
Asian Cup Vol. 2: 8895
Asian Cup Winners Championship Vol. 2: 8896
Asian Cup Women's Football Championship Vol. 2: 8897
Asian Winter Games, Sapporo Vol. 2: 8713
Asian Youth Football Championship (Under 16) Vol. 2: 8898
Asian Youth Football Championship (Under 19) Vol. 2: 8899
Asiaweek Short Story Competition Vol. 2: 7262
ASID Designer of Distinction Award Vol. 1: 4621
ASID Fellowship Vol. 1: 4622
ASID Human Environment Award Vol. 1: 4626
ASID/*Interior Design* Neocon Showroom Competition Vol. 1: 10569
ASID Interior Design Project Awards Vol. 1: 4623
ASID Interior Design Specialty Awards Vol. 1: 4623
ASID Medalist Award Vol. 1: 4624
ASID Product Design Awards Vol. 1: 4625
ASIFA Special Award Vol. 2: 9889
ASIS Research Award Vol. 1: 4157
ASJA Outstanding Article Award Vol. 1: 4633
ASJA Outstanding Author Award Vol. 1: 4634
ASJMC Distinguished Service Award Vol. 1: 5953
ASJSA Citation of Merit Award Vol. 1: 5953
ASLA Medal Vol. 1: 4638
ASLA President's Medal Vol. 1: 4639
ASLP Professional Award Vol. 2: 10026
ASLP Service Award Vol. 2: 10027
ASLP Special Citizen Awards Vol. 2: 10028
ASM Award in Applied and Environmental and Microbiology Vol. 1: 4210
ASM Distinguished Service Award Vol. 1: 4200
ASM International and The Metallurgical Society Distinguished Lectureship in Materials and Society Vol. 1: 5349
ASM International and The Minerals, Metals and Materials Society Distinguished Lectureship in Materials and Society Vol. 1: 5349
ASME Medal Vol. 1: 4665
ASNT Fellows Vol. 1: 4214
ASNT Fellowship Award Vol. 1: 4215
ASNT Gold Medal Vol. 1: 4220
ASNT Meritorious Service Award Vol. 1: 4216
ASNT Technician of the Year Award Vol. 1: 4217
Asolo International Animation Festival Vol. 2: 8100
ASP World Champions Vol. 1: 5972
ASPA/NASPAA Distinguished Research Award Vol. 1: 13300
Aspen Filmfest Awards Vol. 1: 5368
Aspen Institute Corporate Award for Excellence in Leadership Vol. 1: 5370

Aspen Institute Public Service Award for Excellence in Leadership Vol. 1: 5371
ASPEN Research Scholar Award Vol. 1: 4227
ASPET Award for Experimental Therapeutics Vol. 1: 4232
Aspis Prize; Laura E. Vol. 1: 1575
ASPRS International Educational Literature Award Vol. 1: 4241
Asquith Award; Anthony Vol. 2: 2343
Asselin; Prix Olivar- Vol. 1: 17391
Assistant Secretary's Award for Excellence in Information Systems Management Vol. 1: 19276
Associate Member of the Year Vol. 1: 13508
Associate Member Section Distinguished Service Award Vol. 1: 4519
Associate of the Photographic Salon Exhibitors Association Vol. 2: 7267
Associate of the Year Vol. 1: 8989
Associate Remodeler of the Year Award Vol. 1: 13135
Associated American Artists Purchase Award Vol. 1: 17693
Associated Collegiate Press Pacemakers Awards; NAA Foundation - Vol. 1: 15353
Associated Member Distinguished Service Award Vol. 1: 4519
Associated Press Sports Awards Vol. 1: 5415
Associates Award Vol. 1: 13514
Associates of Honour Vol. 2: 4024
The Associateship of the City and Guilds of London Institute Vol. 2: 2621
Associateship of the Society Vol. 2: 10628
Association Achievement Award Vol. 1: 13195
Association Award Vol. 2: 7268
Association Awards Vol. 2: 2131
Association des Musees Canadiens - Americain Foundation de Affaire d e Coeur Societe Vol. 1: 378
Association Executive of the Year Vol. 1: 6030
Association for Civil Rights in Israel Awards Vol. 2: 7863
Association Internationale de la Presse Sportive Awards Vol. 2: 8315
Association of Finnish Graphic Design Awards Vol. 2: 4718
Association of Irish Choirs Trophy Vol. 2: 7766
Association of Jewish Libraries Reference Book Award Vol. 1: 5842
Association of Latin Languages Allergologists and Immunologists Award Vol. 2: 10222
Association of Orthodox Jewish Teachers Awards Vol. 1: 5915
Association of Photographers/Kodak Student Competition Vol. 2: 2132
Association of Psychologists of Nova Scotia President's Award Vol. 1: 5928
Association of Southeast Asian Institutions of Higher Learning Awards Vol. 2: 12019
Association of Swedish Amateur Orchestras Awards Vol. 2: 11444
Association of the United States Army Awards Vol. 1: 5983
Association of Track and Field Statisticians Honorary Member Vol. 2: 2134
Association Rakkasan of the Year Vol. 1: 2
Association Seal Vol. 2: 7269
Association Silver Pin Awards Vol. 1: 414
Association Wrestling Award Vol. 1: 415
Association Youth Sport Membership Award Vol. 1: 416
Association Youth Sport Programming Award Vol. 1: 417
Astar Award Vol. 1: 16814

Astin Measurement Science Award; Allen V. Vol. 1: 19101
Astin - Polk International Standards Medal Vol. 1: 3178
ASTM Award of Merit Vol. 1: 6034
ASTM Award to Executives Vol. 1: 6035
ASTM Memorial Award for Meritorious Service; Robert J. Painter SES/ Vol. 1: 18455
ASTM - Standards Engineers Society Outstanding Publication Award Vol. 1: 6036
Aston Award; Tilly Vol. 2: 287
Astor Award Vol. 2: 2668
Astor Award; Brooke Russell Vol. 1: 15261
Astor Memorial Leadership Essay Contest; Vincent Vol. 1: 19459
Astor Presidents Cup; Lady Vol. 2: 2470
ASTR Fellowship Vol. 1: 4297
ASTR Younger Scholars Prize Vol. 1: 4298
Astra Award Vol. 2: 1970
Astra Trophy Vol. 2: 10509
Astra USA, Inc. Postdoctoral Fellowship in Infectious Disease Training and Herpes Virus Research; NFID - Vol. 1: 14041
Astrological Association Awards Vol. 2: 2137
Astronautics Award Vol. 1: 2472
Astronautics Engineer Award Vol. 1: 14830
Astronautics Literature Award Vol. 1: 1257
Astronomical League Award Vol. 1: 6089
Astwood Lectureship; Edwin B. Vol. 1: 8920
ASU Commander's Cup Vol. 1: 5276
Asundi Memorial Lecture; Prof. R. K. Vol. 2: 7638
AT & T National Pro-Am Youth Award Vol. 1: 7511
At-Large Award Vol. 1: 1382
At the Forefront Vol. 1: 3934
ATA National Truck Driving Championships Vol. 1: 4925
ATA National Truck Roadeo Vol. 1: 4925
AT&T Foundation Awards Vol. 1: 4068
AT&T Istel Young Musicians Awards Vol. 2: 3839
ATAS Governors Award Vol. 1: 86
Ataturk International Peace Prize Vol. 2: 12044
Ataturk Uluslararasi Baris Odulu Vol. 2: 12044
ATCA Industrial Award Vol. 1: 272
ATELJE 212 on the Bitef Award Vol. 2: 10695
ATERB Medal Outstanding Young Investigator Telecommunications and Electronics Vol. 2: 272
Atesto di Merito Vol. 2: 4563
Athayde International Cancer Prize; Mucio Vol. 2: 11857
ATHE Career Achievement Award Vol. 1: 5646
ATHE Career Achievement Award - Academic Theater Vol. 1: 5647
ATHE Career Achievement Award - Professional Theater Vol. 1: 1707
ATHE Research Award for Outstanding Booklength Study Vol. 1: 5648
ATHE Research Award for Outstanding Journal Article Vol. 1: 5649
ATHE Teaching Award Vol. 1: 5650
Athena Arts Prize Vol. 2: 2141
ATHENA (Awards to Honor Excellent Newspaper Advertising) Awards Vol. 1: 15346
Athena Cup Vol. 1: 19690
Athenaeum Literary Award Vol. 1: 6100
Athlete of the Year
  American Athletic Association for the Deaf Vol. 1: 1280
  United States Synchronized Swimming, Inc. Vol 1: 19634
Athlete of the Year - Men, Vol. 1: 5415

Athlete of the Year - Women   Vol. 1: 5415
Athlete Service Award   Vol. 1: 19317
Athletes United for Peace Award   Vol. 1: 6105
Athletic Director of the Year Award   Vol. 1: 13747
Athletic Foundation Halls of Fame   Vol. 1: 396
Ati Vishisht Seva Medal   Vol. 2: 7548
Atiyah Prize   Vol. 2: 8289
Atkinson Memorial Award; Hugh C.
 American Library Association - Association of College and Research Libraries   Vol. 1: 2869
 Illinois Library Association   Vol 1: 10079
Atlanta Film and Video Festival   Vol. 1: 10092
Atlantic Award   Vol. 2: 1233
Atlantic Award for Excellence in Writing   Vol. 1: 6115
Atlantic Chrysler Cup   Vol. 1: 2316
Atlantic Film Festival   Vol. 1: 6113
Atlantic Offshore Fishermen's Association Annual Award   Vol. 1: 6117
Atlas Travel Marketing Campaign Awards   Vol. 1: 5989
Atlas Travel Marketing Executive Award   Vol. 1: 5990
Atmos Clock   Vol. 1: 9048
ATOM Awards   Vol. 2: 270
Atomic Energy of Canada Ltd. Award   Vol. 1: 7135
ATP Tennis Awards   Vol. 1: 6124
ATP Tour Doubles Team of the Year   Vol. 1: 6124
ATP Tour Humanitarian of the Year   Vol. 1: 6124
ATP Tour Most Improved Player   Vol. 1: 6124
ATP Tour Newcomer of the Year   Vol. 1: 6124
ATP Tour Player of the Year   Vol. 1: 6124
ATP Tour Sportsmanship Awards   Vol. 1: 6124
ATP Tour Tennis Awards   Vol. 1: 6124
ATP Tour Tournament of the Year   Vol. 1: 6124
Atrium Award   Vol. 1: 19792
Attack Squadron of the Year   Vol. 1: 12076
Attila Prize; Jozsef   Vol. 2: 7398
Atwood Award; J. Leland   Vol. 1: 2514
Atwood Award; John Leland   Vol. 1: 4069
AUA Health Science Award   Vol. 1: 4951
AUA Triennial Eugene Fuller Prostate Award   Vol. 1: 4952
AUA William P. Didusch Award   Vol. 1: 4953
Aubry Award; Claude   Vol. 1: 10805
Audelco Recognition Award   Vol. 1: 6128
Audio Engineering Society Medal Award   Vol. 1: 6131
Audio Visual Department of the Year Awards   Vol. 1: 6006
Audiotext Awards   Vol. 1: 10189
Audiovisual Competition   Vol. 1: 17610
Audiovisual Pioneer Award   Vol. 1: 10794
Audubon Medal   Vol. 1: 13395
Auerbach Trophy; NBA Coach of the Year - Red   Vol. 1: 13448
Auge-Laribe; Prix Michel-   Vol. 2: 5241
Augier; Prix Emile   Vol. 2: 5847
August Memorial Award; Helen   Vol. 1: 3401
Augusto; Premio Cesare   Vol. 2: 8090
Ault Award   Vol. 1: 13237
Aurelian Prize; Petre S.   Vol. 2: 10331
Austern Memorial; H. Thomas   Vol. 1: 9287
The Austin Chronicle Best of Austin   Vol. 1: 6154
The Austin Chronicle Readers' Poll Music Awards   Vol. 1: 6155
The Austin Chronicle Readers' Restaurant Poll   Vol. 1: 6156
Austin Hot Sauce Contest   Vol. 1: 6157

Austin-Matthews Award   Vol. 1: 6962
Austin Music Awards   Vol. 1: 6155
Austin Prize; Lord   Vol. 2: 3294
Australasian Corrosion Association Awards   Vol. 2: 139
Australasian Seabird Group Awards   Vol. 2: 9703
Australia-New Zealand Literary Exchange   Vol. 2: 153
Australian Active Service Medal   Vol. 2: 337
Australian Applied Health Sciences Fellowships   Vol. 2: 538
Australian Artists Creative Fellowships   Vol. 2: 160
Australian Arts Award   Vol. 2: 414
Australian Audio Book-of-the-Year   Vol. 2: 548
Australian Bicentennial Heritage Award   Vol. 2: 204
Australian Bird Call Championship   Vol. 2: 520
Australian Bravery Decorations   Vol. 2: 207
Australian Camellia Research Society Trophy   Vol. 1: 1391
Australian College of Education Medal   Vol. 2: 201
Australian Composer National Opera Awards   Vol. 2: 670
Australian Film Institute Awards   Vol. 2: 221
Australian Fire Service Medal   Vol. 2: 335
Australian Geomechanics Award - John Jaeger Memorial Award   Vol. 2: 423
Australian Gumleaf Playing Championship   Vol. 2: 521
Australian Heritage Award   Vol. 2: 204
Australian Institute of Energy Medal   Vol. 2: 225
Australian International Video Festival   Vol. 2: 361
Australian International Widescreen Festival   Vol. 2: 281
Australian Literature Society Gold Medal   Vol. 2: 130
Australian Mathematical Society Medal   Vol. 2: 253
Australian Musical Assoc. Prize   Vol. 2: 4117
Australian Musical Foundation in London Award   Vol. 2: 2147
Australian Natural History Medallion   Vol. 2: 402
Australian One-Act Opera Project   Vol. 2: 670
Australian Police Medal   Vol. 2: 336
Australian Post-Doctoral Fellowships   Vol. 2: 539
Australian Service Medals   Vol. 2: 337
Australian Society of Archivists Award   Vol. 2: 267
Australian Transport Industry Award   Vol. 2: 308
Australian Visual Arts Board Award for Illustration   Vol. 2: 161
Australian/Vogel Literary Award   Vol. 2: 120
Austrian Medal of Honor in the Arts and Sciences   Vol. 2: 756
Austrian National Book Award for Children's Literature   Vol. 2: 757
Austrian Operatic Award   Vol. 2: 566
Austrian State Encouragement Prizes   Vol. 2: 758
Austrian State Grand Prize   Vol. 2: 759
Austrian State Prize for Cultural Publications   Vol. 2: 760
Austrian State Prize for European Composers   Vol. 2: 761
Austrian State Prize for European Literature   Vol. 2: 762

Austrian State Prize for Literary Translators   Vol. 2: 763
Austrian State Prize for Poetry for Children   Vol. 2: 764
Austrian State Recognition Prizes   Vol. 2: 765
Austriaprijs; Maria   Vol. 2: 9636
Auszeichnung; Dr. Max-Luthi   Vol. 2: 11885
Auszeichnung fur wissenschaftliche Arbeiten zu der Geschichte der Justus-Liebig-Universitat   Vol. 2: 6997
Auteursrechtprijs   Vol. 2: 9381
Author of the Year Award   Vol. 1: 4634
Author's Award   Vol. 1: 5813
Authors Awards   Vol. 1: 9353
Authors' Club First Novel Award   Vol. 2: 2149
Auto-Alloys Precision Trophy   Vol. 2: 3000
Automated Imaging Achievement Award   Vol. 1: 6159
Automatica Prize Paper Awards   Vol. 2: 817
Autometric Award   Vol. 1: 4242
Automobilclub Von Deutschland Awards   Vol. 2: 6549
Automotive Achievement Award   Vol. 1: 12224
Automotive Aftermarket Education Award   Vol. 1: 15529
Automotive Dealer Education Award   Vol. 1: 15530
Automotive Hall of Fame   Vol. 1: 6164
Automotive Industry Leader of the Year   Vol. 1: 6165
Automotive Leader of the Year   Vol. 1: 6173
Automotive Man of the Year   Vol. 1: 6173
Automotive Replacement Management Award   Vol. 1: 15529
Automotive Training Awards   Vol. 1: 6171
Autosound Grand Prix Awards   Vol. 1: 6136
Autran Prize; Joseph   Vol. 2: 6304
Auxiliar de Enfermera Lucia Salcido   Vol. 2: 9126
AVA Prize for Undergraduates   Vol. 2: 274
AVA Service Award   Vol. 1: 5652
AVA Student Award   Vol. 2: 275
Avatar Award   Vol. 1: 6573
Avenatech Inc. Essay Award   Vol. 1: 10741
AVES Honorary Diploma   Vol. 1: 4972
Aviation Education Certificates of Merit   Vol. 1: 6175
Aviation Environment Award   Vol. 1: 9058
Aviation Hall of Fame and Museum of New Jersey   Vol. 1: 6178
Aviation Hall of Fame Award   Vol. 1: 13405
Aviation Hall of Fame Gold Medal of Honor and Achievement   Vol. 1: 13406
Aviation Hall of Fame Silver Medal of Outstanding Service   Vol. 1: 13407
Aviation Journalism Award   Vol. 1: 12762
Aviation Maintenance Department Safety Award   Vol. 1: 13495
Aviation Ordnance Technician of the Year   Vol. 1: 12055
Aviation Support Services Safety Award   Vol. 1: 13496
Aviation Week & Space Technology Distinguished Service Award   Vol. 1: 9238
AVMA Animal Welfare Award   Vol. 1: 4980
AVMA Award   Vol. 1: 4981
AVMA Humane Award   Vol. 1: 4982
Avodah Award   Vol. 1: 11563
Avogadro; Medaglia Amedeo   Vol. 2: 8378
Avon Flare Young Adult Novel Competition   Vol. 1: 6200
Avoriaz Film Awards   Vol. 2: 4983
AVS Student Prizes   Vol. 1: 4959
A.W. Farrall Young Educator Award   Vol. 1: 4362

AWA Distinguished Public Service Award   Vol. 1: 6184
AWA Earl D. Osborn Award   Vol. 1: 6185
AWA Harry Lever Award   Vol. 1: 6186
AWA Industry Communications Award   Vol. 1: 6187
AWA James J. Strebig Award   Vol. 1: 6188
AWA Journalism Awards   Vol. 1: 6189
AWA Lauren D. Lyman Award   Vol. 1: 6190
AWA Public Affairs Award   Vol. 1: 6191
AWA Public Relations Award   Vol. 1: 6192
AWA Robert S. Ball Memorial Award   Vol. 1: 6193
AWA Textron Helicopter Heroism Award   Vol. 1: 6194
AWAPA (Academy of Wind and Percussion Arts) Award   Vol. 1: 13425
Award Certificates   Vol. 1: 15944
Award Emeritus   Vol. 1: 16700
Award for Aboriginal and Torres Strait Islander Writers   Vol. 2: 554
Award for Academic Excellence in Global Awareness   Vol. 1: 5985
Award for Achievement   Vol. 2: 9799
Award for Achievement for Sustained Contributions to the Literature of Hospital Pharmacy   Vol. 1: 4604
Award for Achievement in Business Growth   Vol. 1: 8028
Award for Achievement in Engineering Enterprise   Vol. 2: 424
Award for Achievement in Technical Services   Vol. 1: 7012
Award for Achievement in the Professional Practice of Hospital Pharmacy   Vol. 1: 4605
Award for Achievement: Individual   Vol. 1: 14061
Award for Achievement: Organization   Vol. 1: 14062
Award for an Outstanding Publication   Vol. 1: 2304
Award for Best Unpublished Manuscript   Vol. 1: 17544
Award for Book Review in the Daily Press   Vol. 2: 7870
Award for Career Development in Honor of L.P. Cookingham   Vol. 1: 10848
Award for Children's Literature   Vol. 2: 7871
Award for Community Service   Vol. 1: 14082
Award for Composers 30 Years of Age and Over; SOCAN   Vol. 1: 17820
Award for Distinction in Islamic Science   Vol. 2: 12055
Award for Distinguished Achievement   Vol. 1: 7971
Award for Distinguished Achievement in Music   Vol. 1: 18698
Award for Distinguished Achievement in the Arts   Vol. 1: 18698
Award for Distinguished Archaeological Achievement   Vol. 1: 5225
Award for Distinguished College or University Teaching of Mathematics   Vol. 1: 12128
Award for Distinguished Cultural Service   Vol. 2: 8577
Award for Distinguished Public Service
  American Mathematical Society   Vol. 1: 3002
  United States Conference of Mayors   Vol 1: 19062
Award for Distinguished Service
  Federal Aviation Administration   Vol. 1: 9059
  Mathematical Association of America   Vol 1: 12133
Award for Distinguished Service to Children   Vol. 1: 13084

Award for Distinguished Service to Music   Vol. 1: 18699
Award for Distinguished Service to Sport   Vol. 2: 8783
Award for Distinguished Service to the Arts
  American Academy of Arts and Letters   Vol. 1: 497
  Third Street Music School Settlement   Vol 1: 18699
Award for Distinguished Services to Art   Vol. 2: 8784
Award for Drug Discovery   Vol. 2: 4360
Award for Educational Excellence   Vol. 1: 17480
Award for Entrepreneurial Excellence   Vol. 1: 15741
Award for Excellence
  American Liszt Society   Vol. 1: 2964
  American Society for Training and Development - Management Development Professional Practice Area   Vol 1: 4327
  National Association of Professional Organizers   Vol 1: 13252
  Order of the Founders and Patriots of America   Vol 1: 15796
  Rural Sociological Society   Vol 1: 16972
Award for Excellence: Genealogical Methods and Sources   Vol. 1: 14063
Award for Excellence: Genealogy and Family History   Vol. 1: 14064
Award for Excellence in Book Publication   Vol. 1: 714
Award for Excellence in Clinical Teaching   Vol. 1: 3478
Award for Excellence in Corporate Reporting   Vol. 1: 5551
Award for Excellence in Environmental Health   Vol. 1: 13056
Award for Excellence in Fusion Engineering   Vol. 1: 9453
Award for Excellence in Leadership   Vol. 1: 4332
Award for Excellence in Multicultural Health   Vol. 1: 13057
Award for Excellence in Plasma Physics Research   Vol. 1: 3445
Award for Excellence in Poetry for Children; NCTE   Vol. 1: 13772
Award for Excellence in Power Distribution Engineering   Vol. 1: 10309
Award for Excellence in Professional Writing   Vol. 1: 963
Award for Excellence in Religious Studies   Vol. 1: 714
Award for Excellence in Renal Research   Vol. 1: 3503
Award for Excellence in Science Teaching   Vol. 1: 18660
Award for Excellence in Teaching   Vol. 1: 1482
Award for Excellence in Teaching Geography   Vol. 1: 9545
Award for Excellence in Technical and Scientific Writing   Vol. 1: 13762
Award for Excellence: *National Genealogical Society Quarterly*   Vol. 1: 14065
Award for Executive Excellence   Vol. 1: 7568
Award for Exemplary State/University Collaboration   Vol. 1: 3626
Award for Extraordinary Scientific Achievement   Vol. 1: 3096
Award for Extraordinary Service   Vol. 1: 9060
Award for Heroism   Vol. 1: 19277
Award for Historical Works Pertaining to Justus-Liebig University   Vol. 2: 6997
Award for Human Rights in Europe   Vol. 2: 11454

Award for Innovative Approaches to the Employment of People with Disabilities   Vol. 1: 18797
Award for Life Service to Veterans   Vol. 1: 15934
Award for Lifetime Public Service   Vol. 1: 9922
Award for Literature   Vol. 2: 12075
Award for Local Government Education   Vol. 1: 10846
Award for Medical Students   Vol. 2: 11765
Award for Meritorious Public Service   Vol. 1: 9923
Award for Original Hebrew Novel   Vol. 2: 7872
Award for Original Hebrew Poetry   Vol. 2: 7873
Award for Oustanding Contribution to Psychology and the Arts   Vol. 1: 3768
Award for Outstanding Achievement   Vol. 1: 13865
Award for Outstanding Achievement in Acupuncture Research   Vol. 2: 11996
Award for Outstanding Achievement in Advertising on Cable Television   Vol. 1: 6668
Award for Outstanding Achievement in Bioclimatology   Vol. 1: 3073
Award for Outstanding Achievement in Biometeorology   Vol. 1: 3073
Award for Outstanding Achievement in Employee Involvement in the Workplace   Vol. 1: 4340
Award for Outstanding Achievement in International Business   Vol. 1: 20528
Award for Outstanding Achievement in Management   Vol. 1: 10354
Award for Outstanding Candidate   Vol. 1: 4798
Award for Outstanding Contribution to the Advance of Applied Meteorology   Vol. 1: 3074
Award for Outstanding Contribution to the Training and Development of Special Populations   Vol. 1: 4333
Award for Outstanding Contributions in Research and Education   Vol. 1: 1634
Award for Outstanding Contributions to the Promotion of Scholarship in the Third World   Vol. 1: 5986
Award for Outstanding Dissertation   Vol. 1: 3658
Award for Outstanding Forestry Legislation   Vol. 1: 15040
Award for Outstanding Forestry Magazine of an Affiliated State Woodland Owner Association   Vol. 1: 15041
Award for Outstanding Innovation/Invention   Vol. 1: 7742
Award for Outstanding Paper *The Energy Journal*   Vol. 1: 10630
Award for Outstanding Performance in Third World Studies   Vol. 1: 5987
Award for Outstanding Research   Vol. 1: 7095
Award for Outstanding Research Paper   Vol. 1: 4799
Award for Outstanding Service   Vol. 1: 13866
Award for Outstanding Service by a Broadcast Meteorologist   Vol. 1: 3075
Award for Outstanding Service by a Weather Forecaster   Vol. 1: 3076
Award for Outstanding Services to Meteorology by a Corporation   Vol. 1: 3077
Award for Outstanding Yes Group, Project, or Volunteer   Vol. 1: 13875
Award for Patient Advocacy   Vol. 1: 3627
Award for Professional Excellence
  Association for Investment Management and Research   Vol. 1: 5552

Iota Sigma Pi Vol 1: 11435
  Society for Human Resource Management Vol 1: 17481
Award for Programs for the Disadvantaged Vol. 1: 10851
Award for Research on Aging Vol. 1: 335
Award for Research on Automotive Lubricants Vol. 1: 17751
Award for Service To People Vol. 1: 4437
Award for Service to Society Vol. 1: 2565
Award for Service to the Society Vol. 1: 15160
Award for Skill in Intergovernmental Relations Vol. 1: 10847
Award for Software Process Achievement Vol. 1: 10294
Award for Special Librarianship in Canada Vol. 1: 7013
Award for Special Service to Hospital Dentistry Vol. 1: 1016
Award for Technical Excellence Vol. 1: 1504
Award for Technical Innovation in Industrial Engineering Vol. 1: 10355
Award for the Advancement and Preservation of Civilization Vol. 1: 14918
Award for the Promotion of Polish Entertainment Creativity Vol. 2: 10206
Award for the Promotion of University-Industry Relations Vol. 1: 8311
Award for Valor Vol. 1: 19278
Award for Valour Vol. 2: 2299
Award for Young Leadership and Excellence Vol. 1: 6166
Award in Chemical Engineering Practice Vol. 1: 2566
Award in Chemical Instrumentation Vol. 1: 1483
Award in Electrochemistry Vol. 1: 1484
Award in Science Vol. 1: 16102
Award in Spectrochemical Analysis Vol. 1: 1485
Award in the Chemistry of Plastics and Coatings Vol. 1: 1532
Award of Achievement Vol. 1: 14920
Award of Austrian Film Days Vol. 2: 874
Award of Commendation
  Association of Graduates Vol. 1: 5826
  Concordia Historical Institute Vol 1: 8089
Award of Distinction
  American Association for State and Local History Vol. 1: 873
  American Orchid Society Vol 1: 3327
  American Phytopathological Society Vol 1: 3519
  International Technology Education Association Vol 1: 11333
  Professional Picture Framers Association Vol 1: 16500
Award of Engineering Excellence; Technology Award/ Vol. 1: 4591
Award of Excellence
  Business Forms Management Association Vol. 1: 6653
  Film Advisory Board Vol 1: 9183
  Genetics Society of Canada Vol 1: 9537
  International Information Management Congress Vol 1: 11044
  National Transportation Week Vol 1: 14921
  Professional Aviation Maintenance Association Vol 1: 16435
  United Nations Society of Writers Vol 1: 18959
Award of Excellence for Distinguished Educators Vol. 1: 13832
Award of Excellence of the Pipeline Division Vol. 1: 4438
Award of Fellow Vol. 1: 3351

Award of Honor
  American Association of Homes for the Aging Vol. 1: 1006
  American Dairy Science Association Vol 1: 1909
  American Hospital Association Vol 1: 2369
  American Society of Hospital Pharmacists Vol 1: 4599
  California Avocado Society Vol 1: 6675
  National School Public Relations Association Vol 1: 14671
Award of Honour Vol. 2: 2300
Award of Hope and Courage Vol. 1: 14874
Award of Merit
  American Academy of Arts and Letters Vol. 1: 498
  American Association for State and Local History Vol 1: 874
  American Association of Botanical Gardens and Arboreta Vol 1: 933
  American Association of Cost Engineers Vol 1: 982
  American Bar Association Vol 1: 1307
  American College of Dentists Vol 1: 1629
  American Concrete Pipe Association Vol 1: 1794
  American Heart Association Vol 1: 2222
  American Occupational Therapy Association Vol 1: 3296
  American Oil Chemists' Society Vol 1: 3311
  American Orchid Society Vol 1: 3328
  American Osteopathic Healthcare Association and College of Osteopathic Healthcare Executives Vol 1: 3356
  American Otological Society Vol 1: 3359
  American Philological Association Vol 1: 3417
  American Public Works Association Vol 1: 3873
  American Revolution Round Table Vol 1: 3950
  American Society for Information Science Vol 1: 4158
  American Vocational Association Vol 1: 4992
  Associated Church Press Vol 1: 5395
  Association for Information and Image Management Vol 1: 5540
  Association of Records Managers and Administrators - ARMA International Vol 1: 5935
  B'nai B'rith Foundation (Canada) Vol 1: 6423
  British Canoe Union Vol 2: 2301
  British Philatelic Federation Vol 2: 2472
  Canadian Dermatology Association Vol 1: 6853
  Canadian Parks/Recreation Association Vol 1: 7084
  Canadian Society of Laboratory Technologists Vol 1: 7198
  Cape Tercentenary Foundation Vol 2: 10828
  City of Toronto Vol 1: 7755
  Conference of Educational Administrators Serving the Deaf Vol 1: 8118
  Deafness Research Foundation Vol 1: 8551
  Door and Hardware Institute Vol 1: 8697
  Federation of Genealogical Societies Vol 1: 9121
  International Association of Personnel in Employment Security Vol 1: 10773
  International Weightlifting Federation Vol 2: 7433
  Lambda Kappa Sigma Vol 1: 11773

  Military Order of the World Wars Vol 1: 12284
  National Association of Federally Licensed Firearms Dealers Vol 1: 13109
  National Association of Metal Finishers Vol 1: 13203
  National Commission on Correctional Health Care Vol 1: 13627
  National Congress of Jewish Deaf Vol 1: 13657
  National Federation of State High School Associations Vol 1: 13950
  National Federation of State High School Associations - National Interscholastic Athletic Administrators Association Vol 1: 13960
  National Genealogical Society Vol 1: 14066
  National Religious Broadcasters Vol 1: 14606
  National Religious Broadcasters Vol 1: 14607
  National Religious Broadcasters Vol 1: 14611
  National Transportation Week Vol 1: 14921
  New England Water Works Association Vol 1: 15149
  Philadelphia Art Alliance Press Vol 1: 16125
  Professional Aviation Maintenance Association Vol 1: 16436
  Society of Manufacturing Engineers Vol 1: 17876
Award of Merit Certificate Vol. 1: 13557
Award of Merit/Distinguished Service Award Vol. 1: 13749
Award of Merit - Earth Shelter and Architecture Vol. 1: 4940
Award of Merit for Outstanding Achievement Vol. 1: 43
Award of Merit in Broadcasting Vol. 1: 16781
Award of Merit in Journalism Vol. 1: 16781
Award of Merit - Life Member Vol. 1: 5101
Award of Merit - Planning and Development Vol. 1: 4941
Award of Merit Scheme Vol. 2: 4339
Award of Merit - Tunnels and Deep Space Vol. 1: 4942
Award of Meritorious Achievement Vol. 1: 11847
Award of Minarik Vol. 2: 10803
Award of Quality Vol. 1: 3329
Award of Recognition
  American Association of Cost Engineers Vol. 1: 988
  Conference of Funeral Service Examining Boards Vol 1: 8125
  Professional Picture Framers Association Vol 1: 16501
Award of Recognition: AACRAO Internships Vol. 1: 967
Award of Recognition: Outstanding AACRAO Annual Meeting Program Sessions Vol. 1: 966
Award of Recognition: Professional Development Grant Vol. 1: 967
Award of Recognition: State/Regional Professional Activity Vol. 1: 968
Award of Recognition: Workshop Grant Vol. 1: 969
Award of Special Merit Vol. 1: 1090
Award of the Circle of the Greek Children's Book Vol. 2: 7188
Award of the Year Vol. 1: 13338
Award of Valor
  National Collegiate Athletic Association Vol. 1: 13609
  National Transportation Week Vol 1: 14922

Award Program to Assist Foreign Scholars in Carrying Out Sinological Research in the R.O.C.   Vol. 2: 11992
Award to a Faculty Member for Research in an Undergraduate Institution   Vol. 1: 3446
Awards
  Asian Association of Occupational Health   Vol. 2: 10732
  Association for Cooperation in Banana Research in the Caribbean and Tropical America   Vol 2: 7236
  European Confederation of Agriculture   Vol 2: 1127
  European Football Commentators Association Television   Vol 2: 7773
  European Society for Clinical Investigation   Vol 2: 9416
  European Society for Therapeutic Radiology and Oncology   Vol 2: 1140
  Fondazione Anna Pane   Vol 2: 8241
  Global Futures Network   Vol 2: 7506
  International Association for the Scientific Study of Mental Deficiency   Vol 2: 5961
  International Association of Traffic and Safety Sciences   Vol 2: 8547
  International Committee for Amateur-Built Aircraft   Vol 2: 5987
  International Jacques Brel Foundation   Vol 2: 1196
  International Map Collectors' Society   Vol 2: 3440
  International Society for Education Through Art   Vol 2: 3467
  Near East/South Asia Council of Overseas Schools   Vol 2: 7204
  Oceania Weightlifting Federation   Vol 2: 561
  Polish Institute and Sikorski Museum   Vol 2: 3795
  Saint Joan's International Alliance   Vol 2: 1355
  Women's International Zionist Organization   Vol 2: 7989
  World League for Freedom and Democracy   Vol 2: 8836
Awards and Grants   Vol. 2: 1958
Awards at the AGM and the Concours   Vol. 2: 3533
Awards Competition   Vol. 1: 20459
Awards for Achievement in Arc Welded Design, and Engineering and Fabrication   Vol. 1: 11875
Awards for Achievement in Managing Information Technology   Vol. 1: 2981
Awards for Bravery   Vol. 2: 10832
Awards for Contributions in Banking   Vol. 2: 11827
Awards for Courage   Vol. 1: 15518
Awards for Distinguished Service in Environmental Planning   Vol. 1: 10160
Awards for Excellence
  American Society for Training and Development - Organization Development Professional Practice Area   Vol. 1: 4338
  American Vocational Association   Vol 1: 4993
  Government Finance Officers Association of the United States & Canada   Vol 1: 9680
  Susan G. Komen Breast Cancer Foundation   Vol 1: 11717
  Society for the Family of Man   Vol 1: 17612
Awards for Excellence in Business and Financial Journalism (Hancock Awards)   Vol. 1: 9765
Awards for Excellence in Cable Marketing and Advertising   Vol. 1: 6666

Awards for Excellence in Corporate Community Service   Vol. 1: 16299
Awards for Excellence in Teaching of the Classics   Vol. 1: 3416
Awards for Excellence in the Design and Construction of Arc Welded Short Span Bridges   Vol. 1: 11876
Awards for Excellence in the Teaching of Private Enterprise   Vol. 1: 18630
Awards for Exemplary Contributions to the Human Resource Management Field   Vol. 2: 714
Awards for Innovation   Vol. 2: 7771
Awards for Outstanding Achievements in Cartographic Design   Vol. 1: 1426
Awards for Outstanding Area Research   Vol. 1: 10161
Awards for Outstanding Consultancy Practice   Vol. 2: 3828
Awards for Outstanding Performance   Vol. 1: 18046
Awards for Program Excellence   Vol. 1: 10851
Awards for Publication Excellence; APEX -   Vol. 1: 8062
Awards for Published Accounts   Vol. 2: 3080
Awards for Regional Literature   Vol. 2: 10004
Awards for Research and Outstanding Publications in Agricultural Economics   Vol. 1: 749
Awards for Scientific Achievement   Vol. 1: 20104
Awards for the Best Produced Books in Hong Kong   Vol. 2: 7277
Awards for Work Displaying Engineering Excellence   Vol. 2: 425
Awards for Young Composers; SOCAN   Vol. 1: 17821
Awards in History   Vol. 2: 9724
Awards in Oral History   Vol. 2: 9725
Awards in Recognition of Excellence   Vol. 2: 9516
Awards in the Visual Arts   Vol. 1: 18185
Awards of Appreciation   Vol. 1: 1052
Awards of Distinction   Vol. 1: 1890
Awards of E.A. International Salon of Photography   Vol. 2: 7270
Awards of Excellence
  Agricultural Communicators in Education   Vol. 1: 200
  Alliance for Children and Television   Vol 1: 321
  Canada - Treasury Board of Canada Secretariat   Vol 1: 6722
  National Community Mental Healthcare Council   Vol 1: 13633
  Small Press Writers and Artists Organization   Vol 1: 17330
Awards of Merit
  American Association of Blood Banks   Vol. 1: 921
  National Park Academy of the Arts   Vol 1: 14447
Awards of Poetic Excellence   Vol. 1: 18261
Awards of Recognition   Vol. 1: 14618
Awards of Special Recognition   Vol. 1: 13204
Awards Program
  American Design Drafting Association   Vol. 1: 1948
  Association for Conservation Information   Vol 1: 5479
Awards to Younger Scholars   Vol. 1: 17606
Awgie Awards   Vol. 2: 283
AWIS Educational Foundation Predoctoral Award   Vol. 1: 5661
AWNY Advertising Woman of the Year   Vol. 1: 158

AWP Award Series   Vol. 1: 5419
AWRA Board of Directors Service Awards   Vol. 1: 5000
AWRA Outstanding State Section Award   Vol. 1: 5001
AWS Bronze Medal of Honor   Vol. 1: 5037
AWS Gold Medal of Honor   Vol. 1: 5038
AWS Silver Medal of Honor   Vol. 1: 5039
AWWA American/Canadian/Mexican Water Landmarks Award   Vol. 1: 5013
AWWA Distinguished Public Service Award   Vol. 1: 5014
AWWA Heroism Award   Vol. 1: 5015
AWWA Publications Award   Vol. 1: 5016
AWWA Research Award   Vol. 1: 5017
AWWA Safety Awards   Vol. 1: 5018
Ayer Distinguished Service Award; William Ward   Vol. 1: 14602
Ayers Award; A. Jean   Vol. 1: 3308
Ayerst Award
  Canadian Society of Biochemistry and Nuclear Biology   Vol. 1: 7164
  Endocrine Society   Vol 1: 8921
AYH Pioneer Leader Award   Vol. 1: 10006
Ayrton Premium   Vol. 2: 3273
Azcarraga Vidaurreta Prize; Emilio   Vol. 2: 9080
Azevedo Prize; Arthur   Vol. 2: 1421
AZO Achievement Medal   Vol. 1: 369
AZO Meritorious Award   Vol. 1: 370
AZO Undergraduate Award   Vol. 1: 371
BAAL Book Prize   Vol. 2: 12153
BAAPS Senior Registrar's Prize   Vol. 2: 2258
Babbage Premium; Charles   Vol. 2: 3268
Babbidge, Jr., Award; Homer D.   Vol. 1: 5642
Babcock and Wilcox Trophy   Vol. 2: 3001
Babcock-Hart Award   Vol. 1: 10341
Baber Research Grant; Carrol Preston   Vol. 1: 2926
Babes Prize; Victor   Vol. 2: 10332
Bablik Medal   Vol. 2: 2831
Babson Business Initiative Award   Vol. 1: 6213
Babut; Prix   Vol. 2: 6361
Bach & Handel Aria Competition   Vol. 1: 15563
Bach Competitions   Vol. 1: 6215
Bach Festival   Vol. 2: 8985
Bachauer International Piano Competition; Gina   Vol. 1: 6217
Bachmann Prize; Alois   Vol. 2: 67
Bacigalupi, Jr., Awards; Tadini   Vol. 1: 14416
Back Award   Vol. 2: 4006
Back Pain Association Medal   Vol. 2: 3678
Backer Memorial Scholarships; Bill   Vol. 1: 2835
Backmans stipendium; Ida   Vol. 2: 11583
Bacon Award; Paul   Vol. 1: 19550
Bacon Medal for Memorial Architecture; Henry   Vol. 1: 2526
Bacon Person of the Year Award; Clare E.   Vol. 1: 18047
Bacteria Section Awards   Vol. 2: 6052
Bacteriology Prize of the IMLS   Vol. 2: 3166
Bactlab Systems Gold Award   Vol. 2: 10972
Bactlab Systems Premier Award   Vol. 2: 10973
Badalona Short Film and Video Festival   Vol. 2: 11205
Baddams Bursary; Thenie   Vol. 2: 217
Baddy Award   Vol. 1: 163
Baden-Wurttemberg Schiller Memorial Prize   Vol. 2: 7055
Bader Award   Vol. 2: 4185
Bader Award in Bioinorganic or Bioorganic Chemistry; Alfred   Vol. 1: 1547

Bader Award in Organic Chemistry; Alfred Vol. 1: 7541
Badge for the Protection of Monuments Vol. 2: 10088
Badge of Honour Vol. 2: 9513
Badminton Hall of Fame Vol. 1: 19034
Badvertising Awards (Baddy Award) Vol. 1: 163
Baehelin; Prix de Litterature Regionaliste Henri Vol. 2: 6276
Baekeland Lecture Vol. 2: 4401
Baekelmans Prize; Lode Vol. 2: 1264
Baes; Prix Professeur Louis Vol. 2: 1036
Baethke - Eleanor J. Carlin Award for Excellence in Academic Teaching; Dorothy E. Vol. 1: 3475
Baethke - Eleanor J. Carlin Award for Teaching Excellence; Dorothy E. Vol. 1: 3475
BAFTA Scholarship Vol. 2: 2232
Bage Fellowship; AFUW - QLD Freda Vol. 2: 214
Baghdad Prize for Arab Culture Vol. 2: 6410
BAGMA Annual Awards Vol. 2: 2238
Baguley Award; R. M. Vol. 2: 3799
Bagutta Prize Vol. 2: 8160
BAIE Editing for Industry Awards Vol. 2: 2266
BAIE National House Journal Competition Vol. 2: 2266
Baier Technical Achievement Award; Edward J. Vol. 1: 2430
Bailey Award; Alton E. Vol. 1: 3312
Bailey Award; Dr. and Mrs. D. L. Vol. 1: 7096
Bailey Award; E. G. Vol. 1: 10481
Bailey Medal; Clyde H. Vol. 2: 807
Bailey Medal; Liberty Hyde Vol. 1: 2352
Bailey Memorial Award; Clement F. Vol. 1: 15559
Bailly; Prix Antoine-Nicolas Vol. 2: 5359
Bainton Book Prize; Roland Vol. 1: 17296
Baird Award; Audrey Vol. 1: 4891
Baird Excellence in Writing Awards in Clinical Practice and Nursing Research; ONS/Chiron Therapeutics Susan Vol. 1: 15655
Baird Memorial Competition for Young Composers; Tadeusz Vol. 2: 10141
Baker and Taylor Conference Grants Vol. 1: 2957
Baker Award; Bud Vol. 1: 12056
Baker Award; "Cannonball" Vol. 1: 8538
Baker Distinguished Research Award; Dr. David F. Vol. 1: 10356
Baker Highway Safety Award; J. Stannard Vol. 1: 10697
Baker, III - Howard Wilkins Award for Excellence in the Direction and Management of Overseas Missions; James A. Vol. 1: 19279
Baker Medal Vol. 2: 3228
Baker Memorial Award; Eugene Vol. 1: 5754
Baker Memorial Award; Hobey Vol. 1: 8564
Baker Memorial Fellowship for Radiologists; Thomas Vol. 2: 592
Baker Prize Award; W. R. G. Vol. 1: 10257
Baker Research Award; Philip Noel Vol. 2: 4722
Baker/W.E.B. DuBois Africana Students Competition; Ella Vol. 1: 13684
Bakjian Award; Andy Vol. 1: 19931
Balanzs Prize for Cinematography; Bela Vol. 2: 7399
Balasaraswati/Joy Ann Dewey Beinecke Chair for Distinguished Teaching Vol. 1: 1927
Balbuena; Medalla Bernardo Vol. 2: 9013
Balcescu Prize; Nicolae Vol. 2: 10333
Balch Prize; Emily Clark Vol. 1: 20069
Balcon Award; Michael Vol. 2: 2233
Bald is Beautiful Vol. 1: 6221

Baldrige National Quality Award; Malcolm Vol. 1: 19110
Baldwin Award; F. W. (Casey) Vol. 1: 6764
Baldwin Distinguished Service Award; A. Richard Vol. 1: 3313
Baldwin Junior High School Piano Award; MTNA- Vol. 1: 12520
Baldwin Medal of Liberty; Roger Vol. 1: 1585
Balfour Scholarship Vol. 1: 11077
Balfour Silver and Golden Anniversary Awards Vol. 1: 12943
BALI National Landscape Awards Vol. 2: 2269
Balint Society Prize Essay Vol. 2: 2156
Ball Local History Awards; Alan Vol. 2: 3563
Ball Memorial Award; AWA Robert S. Vol. 1: 6193
Ball Memorial Award; Clifford Vol. 1: 15877
Ball Memorial Award; James R. Vol. 1: 4343
Ballantine Medal; Stuart Vol. 1: 9372
Ballantyne Award; Harry M. Vol. 2: 11990
Balleroy; Prix
  Institut de France Vol. 2: 5338
  Institut de France - Academie des Beaux Arts Vol 2: 5362
Ballogie Cup Vol. 2: 10623
Ballot Medal; Buys Vol. 2: 9597
Balmis Prize; Dr. Francisco Javier Vol. 2: 9112
Balsdon Fellowship Vol. 2: 8177
Baltic American Freedom League Article Award Vol. 1: 6246
Baltic Freedom Award
  Baltic American Freedom League Vol. 1: 6247
  Joint Baltic American National Committee Vol 1: 11603
Baltimore Independent Film/Video Makers Competition Vol. 1: 6249
Baltimore Opera Guild Award Vol. 1: 6251
Baltimore Opera International Vocal Competition for Operatic Artists Vol. 1: 6251
Baltimore Opera Vocal Competition for North American Operatic Artists Vol. 1: 6251
Balvenie Medal Vol. 2: 10524
Balzan Prize; Eugenio Vol. 2: 8280
Banach Award Vol. 2: 10156
BANAMEX Economics Prize Vol. 2: 9202
BANAMEX Science and Technology Prize Vol. 2: 9203
Banana Club (R) Man/Woman of the Year Vol. 1: 10796
Bananister Award Vol. 1: 10796
Banbury Award; Fernley H. Vol. 1: 1486
Bancarella Sport Prize Vol. 2: 8162
Bancarellino Prize Vol. 2: 8163
Bancroft Award Vol. 1: 16949
Bancroft Gold Medal Vol. 2: 3873
Bancroft History Prize; Caroline Vol. 1: 8608
Bancroft - Mackerras Medal of the Australian Society for Parasitology Vol. 2: 264
Bancroft Prizes Vol. 1: 7972
Band Booster Award Vol. 1: 13426
Band WAZ Award Vol. 1: 8430
Bandeira Paulista Vol. 2: 1499
Bandeirante Trophy Vol. 2: 1458
Banff Centre for the Arts National Award Vol. 1: 6255
Banff Concours International de Quatuor A Cordes Vol. 1: 6257
Banff Festival of Mountain Films Vol. 1: 6256
Banff Festival of the Arts Vol. 1: 6259
Banff International String Quartet Competition Vol. 1: 6257
Banff Rockie Award Vol. 1: 6261
Banff Television Festival Vol. 1: 6261

Bang Scholarship in Marine Invertebrate Immunology; Frederick B. Vol. 1: 1023
Bangkok Bank Documentary Film Competition Prizes Vol. 2: 12021
Bangkok Bank Prize for Thai Literature Competition Vol. 2: 12022
Bangla Academy Literary Award Vol. 2: 934
Banjo Awards Vol. 2: 534
Bank of New Zealand Katharine Mansfield Award Vol. 2: 9774
Bank of New Zealand Novice Writers' Awards Vol. 2: 9775
Bank of New Zealand Young Writers' Award Vol. 2: 9776
Bank of Sweden Prize in Memory of Alfred Nobel Vol. 2: 11494
Bank Senior Silver Medal; Hermann Vol. 2: 6763
Banker of the Year Vol. 2: 2812
Bankers of the Year Vol. 1: 10473
Banki Award; Donat Vol. 2: 7455
Banki Donat Dij Vol. 2: 7455
Banks Composer Fellowship; Don Vol. 2: 158
Banks Fellowship; Don Vol. 2: 162
Banner Competition Vol. 1: 7484
Banta Awards Vol. 1: 20345
Bantug Award Vol. 2: 10055
Baoren's Award; Professor Wang Vol. 2: 1572
Bappu Memorial Award; INSA - Vainu Vol. 2: 7653
BAPS Annual Prize Vol. 2: 10516
Baptista Rosa de Video; Premio Municipal Joao Vol. 2: 10270
Barany Medal; Nandor Vol. 2: 7444
Baratz; Prix Leon Vol. 2: 4855
Barbagelata; Premio A. Vol. 2: 8345
Barbara Hanrahan Fellowship Vol. 2: 673
Barbato Award; Lewis Vol. 1: 1596
Barbed Wire Award Vol. 1: 2011
Barber Memorial Award; Gordon Vol. 1: 16275
Barber Saab Pro Series Vol. 1: 11110
Barbering Hall of Fame Vol. 1: 12941
Barbier; Prix Vol. 2: 5303
Barbier Prize; Dr. Karel Vol. 2: 1265
Barbour Award; Buchanan Vol. 2: 3882
Barbour Award; Laura Taber Vol. 1: 9239
Barcelona Film Festival Vol. 2: 11155
Barcelona International Week of Cinema in Color Awards Vol. 2: 11155
Barchi Prize; Richard H. Vol. 1: 12278
Barclay Medal Vol. 2: 2405
Barclay Prize Vol. 2: 2406
Barcs International Brass Chamber Music Competition Vol. 2: 7416
Bard Award Vol. 2: 2271
Bard Award; Al Vol. 1: 9999
Bard Awards for Excellence in Architecture and Urban Design Vol. 1: 7723
Bard Outstanding Manuscript Prize Award; ASGE/C. R. Vol. 1: 4132
Bard UTI Research Award Vol. 1: 5576
Barde; Prix Andre Vol. 2: 6396
Bardet; Prix Rene Vol. 2: 5914
Bare Knuckle Champions Vol. 1: 16847
Bargate Award; Verity Vol. 2: 4470
Baritiu Prize; Gheorghe Vol. 2: 10334
Barkan Memorial Award; Manuel Vol. 1: 12776
Barker Award; Kathleen Vol. 2: 4381
Barker Awards; Aubrey Vol. 2: 2648
Barker Distinguished Research Award; Roger Vol. 1: 3781
Barker Silver Medal Vol. 2: 2590
Barlow Award of Honor; Thomas E. Vol. 1: 18478

Barlow International Competition   Vol. 1: 6270
Barlow Memorial Medal   Vol. 1: 6929
Barnard Award; Bernard L.   Vol. 1: 10660
Barnard Medal   Vol. 1: 7973
Barnard Prize; Henry   Vol. 1: 9945
Barnato Trophy; Woolf   Vol. 1: 18390
Barner Theatre Arts Teacher of the Year Award; John C.   Vol. 1: 770
Barnes Award for Leadership in Chemical Research Management; Earle B.   Vol. 1: 1548
Barnes Award; Minnie   Vol. 1: 18501
Barnes Award; Rudolph John   Vol. 1: 16458
Barnes Life Membership Award; Charles Reid   Vol. 1: 4746
Barnes Publisher of the Year; John W.   Vol. 1: 1361
Barnes Student Paper Award; K.K.   Vol. 1: 4358
Barnes Trophy   Vol. 1: 19514
Barnett Prize; Helen Foster   Vol. 1: 12598
Barnouw Award; Erik   Vol. 1: 15812
Barnum Industry Award; Harold   Vol. 1: 10760
Barnutiu Prize; Simion   Vol. 2: 10335
Barometer Star Poll   Vol. 1: 6511
Baron Award in Fluid-Particle Systems; Thomas   Vol. 1: 2567
Baron de Courcel; Prix du
   Institut de France - Academie des Inscriptions et Belle-Lettres   Vol. 2: 5450
   Institut de France - Academie des Sciences Morales et Politiques   Vol 2: 5733
Baron de Joest; Prix du   Vol. 2: 5451
Baron; Premio Fundacion Rene   Vol. 2: 12
Baron; Premio Vilfred   Vol. 2: 15
Baron Travelling Scholarship in Obstetrics and Gynaecology; Bernhard   Vol. 2: 3949
Barondess/Lincoln Award   Vol. 1: 7776
Barr Award; Andy   Vol. 1: 5814
Barr Award; Jere. Hess   Vol. 1: 3402
Barr Award; Mel   Vol. 1: 14337
Barr Award; Myer   Vol. 1: 8636
Barr, Jr. Award; Alfred H.   Vol. 1: 7884
Barr Memorial Cup; Peter   Vol. 2: 4025
Barrabe; Prix   Vol. 2: 5304
Barraza Leadership Award; Maclovio   Vol. 1: 13742
Barre; Prix Andre
   Institut de France - Academie Francaise   Vol. 2: 5812
   Societe des Gens de Lettres de France   Vol 2: 6270
Barreda; Gabino   Vol. 2: 9000
Barrer Award   Vol. 2: 4186
Barrer Journalism Award; Myra E.   Vol. 1: 4945
Barrett Award; Roland   Vol. 1: 19892
Barrett-Colea Foundry Prize   Vol. 1: 14714
Barringer Medal
   American Association of Genito-Urinary Surgeons   Vol. 1: 1003
   Meteoritical Society   Vol 2: 3644
Barringer Memorial Trophy; Lewin B.   Vol. 1: 17357
Barrot; Prix Odilon   Vol. 2: 5784
Barrow Award; Dame Nita   Vol. 1: 10871
Barry Award   Vol. 1: 1435
Barry Award; Gerald   Vol. 2: 2947
Barry Award in Human Relations; Lillian and Henry   Vol. 1: 16190
Barry Award; Redmond   Vol. 2: 239
Barry Ohioana Award for Editorial Excellence; James P.   Vol. 1: 15598
Barstow Award for Strings - Coleman   Vol. 1: 7864
Bartels Leadership Recognition Award; Elmer C.   Vol. 1: 14856

Bartels Prize; William H.   Vol. 1: 5297
Bartelsmeyer Award   Vol. 1: 3967
Barter Award; Gwen   Vol. 2: 3543
Barth Service Award; Alan   Vol. 1: 1587
Barthel, Jr. Award; Christopher E.   Vol. 2: 3495
Bartholomew Award; Harland   Vol. 1: 4439
Bartholomew Award; John   Vol. 2: 2304
Bartholomew Award; Marshall   Vol. 1: 10534
Barthou; Prix Alice Louis   Vol. 2: 5810
Barthou; Prix Louis   Vol. 2: 5884
Barthou; Prix Max   Vol. 2: 5897
Bartle Playwriting Award; Margaret   Vol. 1: 8066
Bartlett 12-tone Poem Award; Elizabeth   Vol. 1: 6276
Bartlett Award   Vol. 1: 2527
Bartlett Award; Charlie   Vol. 1: 9651
Bartlett Award; Ford   Vol. 1: 4243
Bartlett Award; George S.   Vol. 1: 1201
Bartlett Lecture   Vol. 2: 2856
Bartlett Medal; Sir Frederic   Vol. 2: 2800
Bartlett Prize; Alice Hunt   Vol. 2: 3790
Bartok International Choir Contest; Bela   Vol. 2: 7296
Bartok Piano Competition - Liszt   Vol. 2: 7414
Bartolozzi; Premio   Vol. 2: 8358
Barton Fellowship; George A.   Vol. 1: 4010
Barton Medal; C.N.   Vol. 2: 445
Barton Top Debate Speaker Award; Phyllis Flory   Vol. 1: 14015
Bartow Award; Edward   Vol. 1: 1487
Bartow Memorial Award; Buzz
   Meeting Planners International   Vol. 1: 12204
   Meeting Planners International   Vol 1: 12205
Bartsch Award; Paul   Vol. 1: 6142
Bartter Award; Frederic C.   Vol. 1: 4046
Baruch Award; Ismar   Vol. 1: 7815
Baruch Essay Award; Bernard M.   Vol. 1: 1803
Baruch University Award; Mrs. Simon   Vol. 1: 18912
Baruk; Prix Henri   Vol. 2: 4843
Barwin Scholarship; Norman   Vol. 1: 16236
BASE Award   Vol. 1: 19041
Base Military Athlete of the Year Award   Vol. 1: 19452
Baseball Outstanding Volunteer Award   Vol. 1: 418
Baseball Weekly Award   Vol. 1: 17409
Basel Salon Culinaire Mondial   Vol. 2: 11911
Basic Research Prize   Vol. 1: 2223
Basketball Coach of the Year   Vol. 1: 6963
Basketball Hall of Fame Curt Gowdy Award   Vol. 1: 12561
Bass Arts Award   Vol. 2: 7855
Bass Ireland Arts Award   Vol. 2: 7855
Bass'n Gal National Champion   Vol. 1: 6287
Bastian-prisen   Vol. 2: 9957
Bastian Prize   Vol. 2: 9957
Bastien-Lepage; Prix   Vol. 2: 5363
Bastien Memorial Trophy; Aldege "Baz"   Vol. 1: 2317
Bastos e Antonio Silva de Interpretacao Teatral; Premios Municipais Palmira   Vol. 2: 10282
Batchelder Award; Mildred L.   Vol. 1: 2855
Batchelor Award; J. E.   Vol. 2: 655
Batcher Memorial Award; Ralph   Vol. 1: 16641
Batel-Rouvier; Prix Andre   Vol. 2: 4809
Bates Medal; Sir David   Vol. 2: 6715
Bates Memorial Award; P. H.   Vol. 1: 6037
Bates Short Story Competition; H. E.   Vol. 2: 3722

The Bathurst: Narrator of the Year   Vol. 2: 288
Baton Twirling Achievement   Vol. 1: 419
Battan Author's Award; Louis J.   Vol. 1: 3078
Batten Memorial Trophy; Jean   Vol. 2: 9811
Battisti Award; Eugenio   Vol. 1: 17654
Battle Award; Helen I.   Vol. 1: 7232
Bauer Founders Award; Louis H.   Vol. 1: 165
Bauer Memorial Exhibit Award; George   Vol. 1: 3203
Bauer Preis fur Chirurgische Tumorforschung; Karl Heinrich   Vol. 2: 6874
Bauer Prize; Evelyn   Vol. 1: 11175
Bauer Prize for Surgical Tumor Research; Karl Heinrich   Vol. 2: 6874
Bauer Special Award; K. Jack   Vol. 1: 15447
Baum Award; Albert H.   Vol. 1: 6607
Baum Memorial Award; L. Frank   Vol. 1: 11404
Bauman Award; Mary K.   Vol. 1: 5489
Baumann-Trophy; Hans-   Vol. 2: 11799
Baumgardt Memorial Lecture   Vol. 1: 3419
Baumont; Prix Fanny et Maurice   Vol. 2: 5744
BAUS Travelling Fellowship   Vol. 2: 2272
Bausch and Lomb Trophy   Vol. 1: 14645
Bavarian Academy of Science Competition Prize   Vol. 2: 6557
Bavarian Academy of Science Prize   Vol. 2: 6558
BAWE Businesswomen's Enterprise Award   Vol. 2: 2280
Baxter American Foundation Prize   Vol. 1: 6000
Baxter Award   Vol. 1: 7183
Baxter Award for Healthcare Management in Europe   Vol. 2: 7775
Baxter-Dade Award   Vol. 2: 11464
Baxter Diagnostics Award   Vol. 2: 11464
Baxter Diagnostics Microscan Young Investigator Award   Vol. 1: 4201
Baxter Foundation Health Services Research Prize   Vol. 1: 6000
Baxter Healthcare, Scientific Products Division Graduate Scholarship   Vol. 1: 4188
Baxter Prize; Samuel   Vol. 2: 4089
Bay Area Book Reviewers Associations Awards   Vol. 1: 6291
Bayer Diagnostics Award   Vol. 2: 10982
Bayfield Award; St. Clair   Vol. 1: 120
Bayle Prijs; Pierre   Vol. 2: 9580
Baynes Prize; Norman Hepburn   Vol. 2: 4578
Bayona Piano Competition; International Pilar   Vol. 2: 11273
Bayreuth Scholarship   Vol. 2: 567
Bazin; Fondation Henry   Vol. 2: 5580
BBC Award for Best Play   Vol. 2: 4466
BBC Newcomers Award   Vol. 2: 7074
BBC Television Young Musician of the Year   Vol. 2: 2297
BC Prize for Poetry   Vol. 1: 20188
BCA Founders Award   Vol. 1: 6645
BCA Leadership Award   Vol. 1: 6646
BCF Player of the Year   Vol. 2: 2311
BCL Award Lecture   Vol. 2: 2116
BCLA Translation Competition (EC Languages)   Vol. 2: 2318
BCLA Translation Competition (Non-EC Languages)   Vol. 2: 2319
BCPA International Salon of Colour Slides   Vol. 2: 7489
BCS Awards   Vol. 2: 2321
BDF Awards   Vol. 2: 2158
BDH Award In Analytical Biochemistry   Vol. 2: 2169
BDH Award in Cytology-Histology   Vol. 1: 7199
BDIA-Preis   Vol. 2: 6809

BDMA/Post Office Direct Marketing Awards   Vol. 2: 2331
The Beacon Award   Vol. 1: 1444
Beadleston Memorial Award; Sam   Vol. 1: 3105
Beale Memorial Award; John A.   Vol. 1: 17683
Beamish Award; Jim   Vol. 1: 7146
Bean Award; Dan   Vol. 1: 19551
Bean Award; Edward H.   Vol. 1: 1245
Bean Memorial Trophy; Gladys   Vol. 1: 6964
Beard Award; J. Howard   Vol. 1: 13058
Beard Awards for Electronic Media; James   Vol. 1: 6298
Beard Food & Beverage Book Awards; James   Vol. 1: 6299
Beard Humanitarian Award; James   Vol. 1: 6301
Beard Journalism Awards; James   Vol. 1: 6300
Beard Lifetime Achievement Award; James   Vol. 1: 6301
Beard Memorial Award; Ralph H.   Vol. 1: 8722
Beard/Perrier-Jouet Restaurant Awards; James   Vol. 1: 6301
Beard Who's Who of Food and Beverage in America; James   Vol. 1: 6302
Bearns Prizes in Music; Joseph H.   Vol. 1: 7974
Beatrice Pris   Vol. 2: 1909
Beattie Medal; Catherine   Vol. 1: 9486
Beaubien Award   Vol. 1: 5757
Beaudet Award; Jean-Marie   Vol. 1: 6725
Beaujour; Prix Felix de   Vol. 2: 5745
Beaumarchais; Medaille   Vol. 2: 6395
Beaumont Award in Medicine; Dr. William   Vol. 1: 3020
Beauperthuy; Fondation Louis-Daniel   Vol. 2: 5622
Beaver Award; Lister Boyd   Vol. 2: 2990
Beca Eugenia Gomez Sierra   Vol. 2: 1586
Becas de Creacion Artistica   Vol. 2: 11142
Becerra Duque Trophy; Gregorio   Vol. 2: 1587
Bech Prize; Joseph   Vol. 2: 7107
Bechtel Fellowship Award; Louise Seaman   Vol. 1: 2856
Bechtel, Jr. Energy Award; Stephen D.   Vol. 1: 4440
Bechtel Pipeline Engineering Award; Stephen D.   Vol. 1: 4441
Beck Award; Carl   Vol. 1: 11325
Beck Award; Frederick A.   Vol. 1: 12850
Beck International Award   Vol. 1: 19552
Beckenback Book Prize   Vol. 1: 12129
Becker Award; Joseph   Vol. 1: 11457
Beckes Award; Isaac K.   Vol. 1: 14283
Becket Memorial Trophy; DeMarco -   Vol. 1: 6874
Beckett Award; Samuel   Vol. 2: 2859
Beckett Crystal Rose Bowl; Peter Alliss and Roy   Vol. 2: 3673
Beckman Founder Award; Arnold O.   Vol. 1: 10482
Beclere; Prix Antoine et Claude   Vol. 2: 4810
Beclere Prize; Antoine   Vol. 2: 11842
Becquerel; Fondation Henri   Vol. 2: 5575
Becton Dickinson and Company Award in Clinical Microbiology   Vol. 1: 4202
Bedat Award; Andre   Vol. 2: 9517
Bedell Award   Vol. 1: 20151
Bedell Award; Arthur Sidney   Vol. 1: 20141
Bedells Bursary; The Phyllis   Vol. 2: 3867
Bedi-Makky Foundry Prize   Vol. 1: 14714
Bednall Award; Colin   Vol. 2: 691
Bedo Albert emlekerem   Vol. 2: 7344

Bedo Award; Albert   Vol. 2: 7344
Beebe Award; Frank Huntington   Vol. 1: 6308
Beeching Award for Arboricultural Contracts   Vol. 2: 2090
Beekler Award; Martin V.   Vol. 1: 9711
Beeman Award for Advancement Writing   Vol. 1: 8294
Beer Prize; George Louis   Vol. 1: 2281
Beernaert Prize; August   Vol. 2: 1266
Beernhaert Prize   Vol. 2: 1282
Beers Award; Clifford W.   Vol. 1: 14355
Beethovenova Hradce; Cena   Vol. 2: 1858
Beethoven's Hradec Music Competition   Vol. 2: 1858
Begay Memorial Award; Tony   Vol. 1: 9914
Behnke, Award; Albert R.   Vol. 1: 18863
Behring Diagnostics Award   Vol. 2: 10974
Beigel Research Award; Society for the Scientific Study of Sex Hugo G.   Vol. 1: 17635
Beijerinck Virology Medal; M. W.   Vol. 2: 9598
Beilby Medal and Prize   Vol. 2: 4187
Beilstein-Denkmunze; Gmelin-   Vol. 2: 6778
Beisswenger Memorial Award; Robert H.   Vol. 1: 13514
Beit Award; Otto   Vol. 2: 4180
Bejarano Civic Medal for Health and Welfare Merits; Jorge   Vol. 2: 1667
Bekesy Prize   Vol. 2: 7445
Belcher Memorial Lectureship; Ronald   Vol. 2: 4188
Belford Award; Elizabeth Russell   Vol. 1: 17267
Belgian American Educational Foundation Fellowships   Vol. 1: 6316
Belgian Film Archive Prizes for the Distribution of Quality Films   Vol. 2: 1353
Belgian Institute of Administrative Sciences Prize   Vol. 2: 1059
Belgium Prize   Vol. 2: 6158
Belgrade International Festival of Scientific Films   Vol. 2: 10699
Belgrand; Prix Docteur Albert   Vol. 2: 4829
Belinsky Prize   Vol. 2: 10421
Belkin Memorial Award; John N.   Vol. 1: 3131
Bell; Alexander Graham - OHIS Youth Achievement Award (Oral Hearing Impaired Section)   Vol. 1: 6319
Bell Award; Alexander Graham   Vol. 1: 6320
Bell Award; Elliott V.   Vol. 1: 15241
Bell Award; Grover E.   Vol. 1: 2248
Bell Canada Award in Video Art   Vol. 1: 6726
Bell Honors; Alexander Graham   Vol. 1: 6321
Bell, Jr. Visiting Scholars Program; Alfred D.   Vol. 1: 9330
Bell Laboratories) Horner Travel Award; DBL (David/   Vol. 1: 7188
Bell Lifetime Achievement Award; Campton   Vol. 1: 771
Bell Medal; Alexander Graham
  Institute of Electrical and Electronics Engineers   Vol. 1: 10258
  National Geographic Society   Vol 1: 14069
Bell Memorial Award; Benjamin   Vol. 1: 8857
Bell Memorial Award; Lawrence D.   Vol. 1: 9885
Bell Prize; Gordon   Vol. 1: 10307
Bell Ringer Award   Vol. 1: 1936
Bell Scholarship; Leslie   Vol. 1: 15691
Bell Trophy (NFL Rookie of the Year); Bert   Vol. 1: 15359
Bella Prize; Jan Levoslav   Vol. 2: 10771
Bellarmine Medal   Vol. 1: 6323
Beller Medal; Esther Hoffman   Vol. 1: 15745
Bellman/Bellwoman of the Year   Vol. 1: 2393

Bellman Control Heritage Award; Richard E.
  American Automatic Control Council   Vol. 1: 1286
  American Institute of Chemical Engineers   Vol 1: 2568
Bellmanpriset   Vol. 2: 11584
Bello Inter-American Education Prize; Andres   Vol. 1: 15827
Bello Medal; Andres   Vol. 2: 1652
Bello; Medalla Andres   Vol. 2: 1652
Bello; Order of Andres   Vol. 2: 12137
Bello; Premio de Novela Andres   Vol. 2: 1564
Bello; Prix Andres   Vol. 2: 11751
Bello Prize; Mario   Vol. 2: 8460
Bellonci Scholarship   Vol. 2: 3407
Belmondo; Prix Paul   Vol. 2: 5348
Belmont Medal   Vol. 1: 12247
Belmont Memorial Cup; August   Vol. 1: 15267
Belmont Stakes
  New York Racing Association   Vol. 1: 15267
  Triple Crown Productions, Inc.   Vol 1: 18815
Beltran de Historia de La Ciencia y La Tecnologia; Premio Dr. Enrique   Vol. 2: 9122
Beltran Prize of the History of Science and Technology; Dr. Enrique   Vol. 2: 9122
Belwin Student Composition; CPP/   Vol. 1: 12519
Bemis President's Trophy; F. Gregg   Vol. 1: 10579
Bemis Trophy; F. Gregg   Vol. 1: 19541
Ben David Award; Mordecai   Vol. 1: 20578
Ben-Haim Competition; Paul   Vol. 2: 7918
Benchmark Book Award   Vol. 1: 7441
Benda Prize; Harry J.   Vol. 1: 5441
Bendahan; Prix Blanche   Vol. 2: 6274
Bendix Automotive Electronics Engineering Award; Vincent   Vol. 1: 17752
Bendix Award; Vincent
  American Society for Engineering Education   Vol. 1: 4070
  American Society for Engineering Education   Vol 1: 4091
Bendix Minorities in Engineering Award; Vincent   Vol. 1: 4070
Benefactor Award   Vol. 1: 14925
Benella Award   Vol. 2: 289
Benelux Libertarian Award   Vol. 2: 1222
Benemerenti Medals
  Bavarian Academy of Science   Vol. 2: 6559
  The Vatican   Vol 2: 12100
Bengough Medal and Prize; Guy   Vol. 2: 3126
Benham Award; Rhoda   Vol. 1: 12182
Benjamin Award for Creative Publishing; Curtis G.   Vol. 1: 5693
Benjamin Medal; L. R.   Vol. 2: 689
Benjamin National Memorial Trophy; Henry   Vol. 2: 2064
Benjamin; Special Citation in Honor of Rudy and Hertha   Vol. 1: 3440
Benlliure; Premio Mariano   Vol. 2: 11297
Bennet Awards; John Z.   Vol. 1: 8568
Bennett Award   Vol. 1: 10034
Bennett Award; Cyril   Vol. 2: 4284
Bennett Award; Hugh Hammond   Vol. 1: 18122
Bennett Award; Robert M.   Vol. 1: 2050
Bennett Commonwealth Prize; R. B.   Vol. 2: 4319
Bennett Fellowship; Viscount   Vol. 1: 6814
Bennett High Point Award; Harry   Vol. 1: 1100
Bennett Memorial Award; Walter H.   Vol. 1: 10121
Bennett Prize; Mrs. Louis   Vol. 1: 14714
Bennett Research Awards; A. E.   Vol. 1: 17789

Bennett Travelling Fellowship; W. H.   Vol. 2: 3316
Bennion Essay Prize; Lowell L.   Vol. 1: 8631
Benoist Prize; Marcel   Vol. 2: 11668
Benoit Mid-Career Award; Anthony H.   Vol. 1: 11951
Benoit; Prix Pierre   Vol. 2: 5909
Benoliel de Fotografia; Premio Municipais Joshua   Vol. 2: 10264
Bensinger - Liddell Salmon Fellowship   Vol. 1: 6119
Benson and Hedges Awards   Vol. 2: 685
Benson and Hedges Fireworks Competition   Vol. 1: 6329
Benson and Hedges Media Awards   Vol. 2: 7781
Benson Medal   Vol. 2: 4231
Bensusan Memorial Fund Prize; Arthur   Vol. 2: 12205
Bentinck; Prix Adolf   Vol. 2: 6160
Benveniste; Prix de la Fondation Emile   Vol. 2: 5444
Benz Award; Carl   Vol. 1: 17782
Berakah Award   Vol. 1: 15392
Berber Memorial Award; Naomi   Vol. 1: 9697
Berdie Memorial Research Award; Ralph F.   Vol. 1: 1883
Berg Award; Patty   Vol. 1: 11753
Bergan Career Development Award; Judge   Vol. 1: 8756
Berger Award; Frederick J.   Vol. 1: 4071
Berger Award; Meyer   Vol. 1: 7992
Berger; Fondation Jean-Jacques   Vol. 2: 5597
Berger Memorial Award for Volunteer Service; Wiley -   Vol. 1: 2342
Berger Memorial Prize; Fred   Vol. 1: 3420
Berger; Prix J. J.   Vol. 2: 5404
Berger; Prix Jean Jacques
  Institut de France - Academie des Inscriptions et Belle-Lettres   Vol. 2: 5465
  Institut de France - Academie des Sciences Morales et Politiques   Vol. 2: 5761
Berger; Prix Jean-Jacques   Vol. 2: 5871
Berger Trophy   Vol. 2: 7764
Berghman; Prix Arvid   Vol. 2: 945
Bergman Plaquette; Ingmar   Vol. 2: 11625
Bergmann Memorial Award; Prof. E. D.   Vol. 2: 7975
Bergmann; Prix Anton   Vol. 2: 978
Bergmann Prize; Ernst David   Vol. 2: 7978
Bergmans; Prix Simone   Vol. 2: 949
Bergstrom Award; E. Alexander   Vol. 1: 5797
Bering Medaillen; Vitus   Vol. 2: 1997
Bering Medal; Vitus   Vol. 2: 1997
Berkeley Memorial Award; Maureen   Vol. 1: 4555
Berkner Award; Lloyd V.   Vol. 1: 1254
Berkowitz Memorial Award; Edward B.   Vol. 1: 14872
Berkshire Summer Fellowship   Vol. 1: 16630
Berlanda Preis; Emil   Vol. 2: 727
Berliawsky Award; Nathan and Lillian   Vol. 1: 499
Berlin Art Prizes   Vol. 2: 6509
Berlin International Film Festival   Vol. 2: 6564
Berliner Award; Emile   Vol. 1: 6134
Berliner Morgenpost; Readers Prize of the   Vol. 2: 6564
Berlyne Prize; Daniel E.   Vol. 1: 3769
Berman Award; Tom   Vol. 1: 5174
Bernabei Prize; Emilio   Vol. 1: 11176
Bernal Prize; John Desmond   Vol. 1: 17602
Bernard Award; Jessie   Vol. 1: 4827
Bernard Foundation Prize; Leon   Vol. 2: 11973
Bernard Lecturer; Claude   Vol. 2: 6703
Bernard; Prix Albert   Vol. 2: 6134

Bernard; Prix Tristan   Vol. 2: 6400
Bernard; Prix Victor   Vol. 2: 6343
Bernardo Trophy; Antonio   Vol. 2: 10230
Bernath Article Prize; Stuart L.   Vol. 1: 17465
Bernath Book Prize; Stuart L.   Vol. 1: 17466
Bernath Lecture Prize; Stuart L.   Vol. 1: 17467
Bernays Award; Edward L.   Vol. 1: 10002
Bernays Prize   Vol. 2: 4445
Berne Memorial Scientific Award; Eric   Vol. 1: 11365
Bernhard Fonds-Prijs; Prins   Vol. 2: 9390
Bernhard Fund Prize; Prince   Vol. 2: 9390
Bernhard-Harms-Medaille   Vol. 2: 7007
Bernhardt Distinguished Service Award; Homer I.   Vol. 1: 4072
Bernheim European Prizes; Emile   Vol. 2: 1378
Bernheimer, Jr. Award; Leo G. Bill   Vol. 1: 12006
Bernstein Award for Excellence in Journalism; Helen B.   Vol. 1: 15262
Bernstein Award; Leslie   Vol. 1: 564
Bernstein, M.D. Award; Albion O.   Vol. 1: 12195
Berntsen Scholarship in Surveying   Vol. 1: 1812
Berr Atochem; Prix Raymond   Vol. 2: 6359
Berry Fellowship; Rosann   Vol. 1: 17740
Berry Medal; Albert E.   Vol. 1: 7168
Berry Prize; David   Vol. 2: 4020
Berry Scholar Award for Excellence in Writing; Chester A.   Vol. 1: 5739
Berryman and James T. Berryman Award for Editorial Cartoonist; Clifford K.   Vol. 1: 14505
Berson-Yalow Award   Vol. 1: 17943
Bertelsen Prize; Paul and Margaret   Vol. 1: 12599
Bertelsmann-Preis; Carl   Vol. 2: 6566
Bertelsmann Prize; Carl   Vol. 2: 6566
Berthault; Prix Claude
  Institut de France - Academie des Beaux Arts   Vol. 2: 5371
  Institut de France - Academie des Sciences Morales et Politiques   Vol 2: 5726
Berthault; Prix de Madame Claude   Vol. 2: 5691
Berthe; Fondation Aime   Vol. 2: 5477
Berthold-Preis   Vol. 2: 6842
Bertholf Award for Chapter Efficiency; Lloyd M.   Vol. 1: 6334
Bertholf Award for Chapter Excellence; Lloyd M.   Vol. 1: 6334
Bertillon Prize   Vol. 2: 4896
Bertner Memorial Award; Ernst W.   Vol. 1: 19875
Bertrand; Fondation Paul   Vol. 2: 5643
Bertrand; Prix Leon   Vol. 2: 5312
Berwick Prize   Vol. 2: 3608
Berzeliusmedaljen i guld   Vol. 2: 11535
BES Fellowships and Grants   Vol. 2: 2333
Besancon International Competition for Young Conductors   Vol. 2: 5181
Beskow Plaketten; Elsa   Vol. 2: 11632
Beskow Plaque; Elsa   Vol. 2: 11632
Beskowska resestipendiet   Vol. 2: 11585
Bessaraboff Prize; Nicolas   Vol. 1: 3166
Bessemer Gold Medal   Vol. 2: 3127
Bessemer Prize   Vol. 2: 4445
Bessey Award; Charles Edwin   Vol. 1: 6474
Bessie Awards   Vol. 1: 8532
Best Academic Paper   Vol. 1: 16701
Best Annual Bird Report   Vol. 2: 2290
Best Annual Reports   Vol. 1: 10474
Best Apprentice Competition   Vol. 2: 5060
Best Article Award   Vol. 1: 6568

Best Article - *Journal of Parametrics* Award   Vol. 1: 11285
Best Bird Book of the Year   Vol. 2: 2291
Best Book Awards   Vol. 1: 3590
Best Books for Children Awards   Vol. 2: 12146
Best Booth Award   Vol. 1: 4627
Best Booth in Show   Vol. 1: 4976
Best Cars   Vol. 1: 3102
Best Chapter Event Award   Vol. 1: 4159
Best Chief Resident Paper   Vol. 2: 12082
Best Critic Prize   Vol. 2: 12070
Best Design Award   Vol. 1: 8867
Best Dissertation Award   Vol. 1: 3591
Best-Dressed Women   Vol. 1: 12473
Best Economic Nematology Paper Award   Vol. 1: 17933
Best Economic Paper Award   Vol. 1: 17933
Best Film Script in the Dutch Language   Vol. 2: 1077
Best First Presentation   Vol. 2: 7285
Best Food Photography   Vol. 1: 6299
Best Ideas Contest   Vol. 1: 4885
Best in American Living Award   Vol. 1: 13136
Best in American Living Awards   Vol. 1: 16451
Best in American Remodeling Awards   Vol. 1: 16452
Best in Class/Best of Show Awards   Vol. 1: 18421
Best in Media Awards   Vol. 1: 13686
Best in Show   Vol. 1: 20244
Best in the Business Awards   Vol. 1: 2755
Best in Topical Awards   Vol. 1: 4914
Best Indy 500 Camaro Award   Vol. 1: 10819
Best Information Science Book Award   Vol. 1: 4160
Best *JASIS* Paper Award   Vol. 1: 4161
Best Journalist Work of the Year   Vol. 2: 10478
Best Management Essay Award   Vol. 2: 9858
Best MBA Student Award   Vol. 2: 9859
Best Membership Training Award   Vol. 1: 5284
Best Memorial Award; Elmer S.   Vol. 1: 9052
Best Memorial Medal; Elsdon   Vol. 2: 9786
Best New Divisional Road Rally   Vol. 1: 18401
Best New Regional Road Rally Program   Vol. 1: 18401
Best of Breed   Vol. 1: 8512
Best of Breed or Best of Variety of Breed   Vol. 1: 20245
Best of Conference Paper Award   Vol. 1: 12409
Best of Europe - International Direct Marketing Awards   Vol. 2: 1131
Best of *Grist* Awards   Vol. 1: 14757
Best of Industry Annual Report Awards   Vol. 1: 9212
Best of LRTS Award   Vol. 1: 2846
Best of Saskatchewan Award   Vol. 1: 20597
Best of Show
  Florida Craftsmen   Vol. 1: 9262
  International Federation of Postcard Dealers   Vol 1: 10967
  Waterbed Manufacturers Association   Vol 1: 20168
Best of the Best Promotion Contest   Vol. 1: 12969
Best Original Article   Vol. 2: 9474
Best Paper Award
  Academy of Management   Vol. 1: 48
  Asian-Pacific Weed Science Society   Vol 2: 10022
  Association for Business Simulation and Experiential Learning   Vol 1: 5456

Canadian Institute of Mining and Metallurgy   Vol 1: 6930
Center for Entrepreneurial Studies   Vol 1: 7434
European Weed Research Society   Vol 2: 6735
Geological Society of America   Vol 1: 9558
Indian Dairy Association   Vol 2: 7616
International Cryogenic Materials Conference   Vol 1: 10898
International Wheat Gluten Association   Vol 1: 11392
Society of Professional Well Log Analysts   Vol 1: 18007
West African College of Surgeons   Vol 2: 9869
Best Paper Awards   Vol. 1: 18045
Best Paper in *Journal of Crustacean Biology*   Vol. 1: 8478
Best Paper of the Year Award   Vol. 1: 7569
Best Paper Presentation Award   Vol. 1: 18008
Best Paper Published in the *Canadian Journal of Chemical Engineering*   Vol. 1: 7542
Best Papers of the Year   Vol. 2: 7286
Best Project of the Year Prize   Vol. 2: 10484
Best Prospectus Award   Vol. 1: 9859
Best Publication by an ASIS Chapter   Vol. 1: 4162
Best Published Book Award (Publisher and Author)   Vol. 2: 9981
Best Radio Script for "Money Talks" Award   Vol. 1: 3204
Best Recycling Innovation   Vol. 1: 14578
Best Regional Program   Vol. 1: 14578
Best Research Lectures on Sarcoidosis   Vol. 2: 4620
Best Rural Program   Vol. 1: 14578
Best Safety Record Award   Vol. 1: 18233
Best Scientific or Technological Journal Prize   Vol. 2: 12127
Best SIG Publication Award   Vol. 1: 4163
Best Single Education Program   Vol. 1: 16702
Best Space Operations Crew Award   Vol. 1: 235
Best Sports Stories and Photos Competition   Vol. 1: 18352
Best Stock Z28 Award   Vol. 1: 10820
Best Student Paper   Vol. 1: 4818
Best Student Paper Award
  American Society for Information Science   Vol. 1: 4164
  Chemical Institute of Canada   Vol 1: 7543
  Crustacean Society   Vol 1: 8479
  Society of Nematologists   Vol 1: 17934
Best Subscriber Communication Program   Vol. 1: 14887
Best Television Commercial/Advertising Film of the Year   Vol. 2: 9999
Best Theoretical Paper on Hypnosis Award   Vol. 1: 17435
Best Trade Show Product and Best Booth Display   Vol. 1: 6205
Best UKRAINPEX Show Theme Exhibit   Vol. 1: 18853
Best Urban Program   Vol. 1: 14578
Best Use of Plant Material in a Private Home Award   Vol. 1: 14280
Best Written and Researched Article   Vol. 1: 8459
Besterman Medal   Vol. 2: 3564
Beta Phi Mu Award   Vol. 1: 2813
Beton - YN Exhibit Award; James L.   Vol. 1: 3205
Better Communications Contest   Vol. 1: 19971
Better Environment Awards for Industry   Vol. 2: 4321
Better Life Award   Vol. 1: 2213

Better Newspapers Competition   Vol. 1: 6836
Better World Award   Vol. 1: 20004
Better World Medals   Vol. 1: 6346
Bettineski Memorial Child Advocate Award; G. F.   Vol. 1: 13828
Bettis Fellowship Award; John   Vol. 1: 12701
Beule; Fondation de Mme. Veuve   Vol. 2: 5388
Beule; Prix Karl   Vol. 2: 5408
Beveridge Award; Albert J.   Vol. 1: 2282
Beveridge Editor of the Year Award; George   Vol. 1: 14506
Beverly Hills Theatre Guild - Julie Harris Playwright Award Competition   Vol. 1: 6350
Beville, Jr. Award; Hugh Malcolm   Vol. 1: 12970
Beyer Award; Bianca   Vol. 1: 7074
Beyer Award; Robert   Vol. 1: 10383
Beyond War Award   Vol. 1: 9347
BFA President's Award   Vol. 1: 6233
BFI Fellowships   Vol. 2: 2344
BFI Film Award   Vol. 2: 2345
BFI Special Awards   Vol. 2: 2346
BGRC Silver Jubilee Oration Award   Vol. 2: 7580
Bhabha Medal; Homi J.   Vol. 2: 7639
Bharat Ratna   Vol. 2: 7549
Bharati Prize; Vidy   Vol. 2: 7622
Bhatnagar Award   Vol. 2: 7532
Bhoruka Gold Medal   Vol. 2: 7623
BHP Awards for the Pursuit of Excellence   Vol. 2: 296
Bi-Monthly Dullness Awards   Vol. 1: 10919
BIA Brick in Architecture Awards of Excellence; AIA/   Vol. 1: 2521
Bialik Prize for Literature; Literary Prize -   Vol. 2: 7953
Bialik Prize for Research   Vol. 2: 7905
Bianco; Premio Umberto Zanotti   Vol. 2: 8361
Biancotto Diploma; Leon   Vol. 2: 5138
BIAT/Pugh Award   Vol. 2: 2396
BIAT Student Award   Vol. 2: 2397
Bibby Cup   Vol. 2: 2533
Bibliographical Society of America Fellowships   Vol. 1: 6352
Bibliotheconomy and Documentation National Award   Vol. 2: 1469
Bicentenary Medal
  Linnean Society of London   Vol. 2: 3584
  RSA   Vol 2: 4320
Bicentennial Awards   Vol. 1: 8262
Bicentennial Fellowship   Vol. 2: 7839
Bicentennial Fiction Award   Vol. 2: 196
Bick Ehrenmedaille; Dr. Josef   Vol. 2: 738
Bickel Award; John O.   Vol. 1: 4442
Bickersteth Memorial Medal; Julian   Vol. 2: 3104
Bicking Award; Lew   Vol. 1: 14846
Bicycle Action Awards   Vol. 1: 6354
Bidault de l'Isle; Prix G.   Vol. 2: 6223
Biedenbach Distinguished Service Award; Joseph M.   Vol. 1: 4073
Bienal de Cine y Video Cientifico   Vol. 2: 11166
Bienal de Fotografia   Vol. 2: 8967
Bienal de Iberoamericana de Arte   Vol. 2: 9029
Bienal de Pintores Rufino Tamayo   Vol. 2: 9206
Bienal Iberoamericana de Arte   Vol. 2: 9207
Bienal Internacional del Cartel en Mexico   Vol. 2: 9285
Bienal Nacional Diego Rivera for Drawings and Prints   Vol. 2: 9208
Bienek Preis fur Lyrik; Horst   Vol. 2: 6551
Biennale di Venezia - Mostra Internazionale del Cinema   Vol. 2: 8470

Biennale Europeenne du Film Sur l'Environnement   Vol. 2: 5116
Biennale Internationale de Gravure   Vol. 2: 10795
Biennale Internationale de Limoges   Vol. 2: 5299
Biennale Internationale du Cinema Humain Marcel Mignon   Vol. 2: 1095
Biennale Jonge Nederlandse Architecten   Vol. 2: 9668
Biennial AIDIS Prize   Vol. 1: 10503
Biennial Award   Vol. 1: 99
Biennial Communications Award   Vol. 1: 9037
Biennial Composers Competition   Vol. 1: 728
Biennial Exhibition Awards
  Museum of New Mexico   Vol. 1: 12505
  Museum of New Mexico   Vol 1: 12506
Biennial of Bantu Contemporary Art   Vol. 2: 6507
Biennial of Young Dutch Architects   Vol. 2: 9668
Bier Award; William C.   Vol. 1: 3765
Bietila Award; Paul   Vol. 1: 19553
Big Brother of the Year   Vol. 1: 6356
Big Brothers/Big Sisters of America Annual Journalism Award   Vol. 1: 6357
Big East Conference Academic Awards   Vol. 1: 6360
Big Eight Male/Female Athlete of the Year   Vol. 1: 6363
Big Muddy Film Festival Awards   Vol. 1: 6365
Big Sister of the Year   Vol. 1: 6358
Bigelow Traveling Fellowship; Wilfred G.   Vol. 1: 15457
Bigelow Trophy   Vol. 1: 7802
Biggs Fellowship; E. Power   Vol. 1: 15802
Biggs Memorial Award; Walter   Vol. 1: 12600
Bighorn Trophy   Vol. 1: 6628
Bigsby Medal   Vol. 2: 2921
Bijnsprijs; Anna   Vol. 2: 9340
Bijou Awards   Vol. 1: 26
Bikila Award; Abebe   Vol. 1: 15269
Bilac Prize; Olavo   Vol. 2: 1422
Bild Practitioner of the Year Award; Charles E.   Vol. 1: 786
Bilim Odulu   Vol. 2: 12065
Bilitch Fellowship in Cardiac Pacing and Electrophysiology; Michael   Vol. 1: 15458
Billboard Music Awards   Vol. 1: 6370
Billboard Radio Awards   Vol. 1: 6371
Billi Award   Vol. 1: 12158
Billiards and Snookers Awards   Vol. 2: 7519
Billington Book Award; Ray A.   Vol. 1: 20239
Billington Prize; Ray Allen   Vol. 1: 15813
Biltris Prize; Doctor Raoul   Vol. 2: 1309
BIMCO/Lloyd's List Maritime Book Prize   Vol. 2: 3598
Binani Gold Medal   Vol. 2: 7624
Bindesboll Medal; Thorvald   Vol. 2: 1896
Binet-Sangle; Prix Docteur   Vol. 2: 5840
Bing Award; Elisabeth   Vol. 1: 5379
Bing Award; Richard J.   Vol. 2: 3469
Bing Prize; Robert   Vol. 2: 11917
Bingham Medal   Vol. 1: 18033
Bingham Prize; Worth   Vol. 1: 6377
Binkhorst Medal Lecture   Vol. 1: 4414
Binkley - Stephenson Award   Vol. 1: 15814
Binneweg Trophy; Ed   Vol. 1: 19373
Binney Memorial Award   Vol. 2: 2945
Binnie Scholarship; Ruth   Vol. 1: 6911
Bintang Bakti Masharakat   Vol. 2: 10749
Bintang Temasek   Vol. 2: 10750
Bio-Serv Award in Experimental Animal Nutrition   Vol. 1: 2647
Biodeterioration Society Awards   Vol. 2: 2181
Biological Council Awards   Vol. 2: 2183

Biological Mineralization Research Award   Vol. 1: 10614
Biological Physics Prize   Vol. 1: 3447
Biomedical Instrumentation & Technology Awards   Vol. 1: 5624
Biomerieux Award   Vol. 2: 11465
BioMerieux Vitek Sonnenwirth Award   Vol. 1: 4203
Biometeorological Research Foundation Award   Vol. 1: 11277
Biotechnology Grants   Vol. 1: 15952
Biotechnology Teaching Award   Vol. 1: 12952
BIR Gold Medal   Vol. 2: 1093
BIR Travel Bursaries   Vol. 2: 2407
Birch Award; Carroll L.   Vol. 1: 3049
Bird Illustrator of the Year   Vol. 2: 2292
Bird Photograph of the Year   Vol. 2: 2293
Birdlife International/FFPS Conservation Expedition Competition   Vol. 2: 2188
Birds in Art Exhibition   Vol. 1: 20446
Birdsall Prize in European Military and Strategic History; Paul   Vol. 1: 2283
Birdseye Prize; Clarence   Vol. 2: 6029
Birkebeinerrennet Ski Race   Vol. 2: 9878
Birkenhead International Colour Salon   Vol. 2: 2190
Birkhoff Prize; George David   Vol. 1: 17510
Birkhoff Prize in Applied Mathematics; George David   Vol. 1: 3003
Birkmaier Award for Doctoral Dissertation Research in Foreign Language Education; ACTFL - MLJ Emma Marie   Vol. 1: 1873
Birla Award; R. D.   Vol. 2: 7681
Birla Memorial Gold Medal; G. D.   Vol. 2: 7625
Birmingham Medal   Vol. 2: 3317
Birmingham Opera Theater Vocal Competition   Vol. 1: 6386
BIS Bibliographic Instruction Publication of the Year Award   Vol. 1: 2870
Bischoff Award; Ernst   Vol. 1: 851
Bishop Award; Colonel James H.   Vol. 1: 19643
Bishop Award; Joan Fiss   Vol. 1: 4276
Bishop Award of Distinction; John and Peg   Vol. 1: 11105
Bishop, III Memorial Trophy; Louis F.   Vol. 1: 20246
Bisson Award; Edmond E.   Vol. 1: 18079
Bittner Extension Award in Horticulture; Carl S.   Vol. 1: 4148
Bittner Service Citation for Outstanding Service to NUCEA; Walton S.   Vol. 1: 14945
Bizet; Prix Georges
   Institut de France   Vol. 2: 5342
   Institut de France - Academie des Beaux Arts   Vol 2: 5394
Bjerrum Award for Chemists; Ellen and Niels   Vol. 2: 1980
Bjerrum's Kemikerpris; Ellen og Niels   Vol. 2: 1980
Blachowski Award; Professor Stefan   Vol. 2: 10174
Blachowskiego; Nagroda im. Profesora Stefana   Vol. 2: 10174
Black Award; Elliott -   Vol. 1: 2003
Black Award for Excellence in Children's Literature; Irma S. and James H.   Vol. 1: 6268
Black Award for Excellence in Children's Literature; Irma Simonton   Vol. 1: 6268
Black Bear Review Poetry Competition for Social Awareness   Vol. 1: 6390
Black Bear Review Poetry Contest   Vol. 1: 6390
Black Curtain Award   Vol. 2: 7047
Black Doctoral Fellowship Program; McKnight   Vol. 1: 9264

Black Engineer of the Year Awards   Vol. 1: 7304
Black Lung Association Award   Vol. 1: 6394
Black Memorial Prizes; James Tait   Vol. 2: 10685
Black Panel Malewitsch Medaille   Vol. 2: 6571
Black Panel World Foundation Awards   Vol. 2: 6571
Black Prize; Duncan   Vol. 1: 16566
Black Tie Award   Vol. 1: 10990
Black Travel Fellowship; Malcolm   Vol. 2: 3950
Blackall Machine Tool and Gage Award   Vol. 1: 4666
Blackburn Award; Donald G.   Vol. 1: 13187
Blackburn Prize; Susan Smith   Vol. 1: 6398
Blackstone Award; Harry   Vol. 1: 11146
Blackwell Medal; Elizabeth   Vol. 1: 3050
Blackwell Memorial Lecture; W. H. M.   Vol. 2: 9728
Blackwell North America Scholarship Award   Vol. 1: 2847
The Blade Magazine Manufacturers Awards   Vol. 1: 10800
Blagoev Prize; Dimiter   Vol. 2: 1513
Blaine Award   Vol. 2: 2508
Blair Award; G. W. Scott   Vol. 1: 946
Blair-Bell Medal   Vol. 2: 4236
Blair-Bell Memorial Fellowship; Florence and William   Vol. 2: 3951
Blair-Bell Memorial Lectureship in Obstetrics and Gynaecology; William   Vol. 2: 3952
Blair Eminent Naturalist Award; W. Frank   Vol. 1: 18244
Blair Memorial Award; W. Frank   Vol. 1: 7611
Blair Scholarship; Scott   Vol. 2: 2529
Blair Service Award; Lucy   Vol. 1: 3476
Blair Trophy; Hunter   Vol. 2: 10624
Blake Award for Distinguished Graduate Teaching; M. A.   Vol. 1: 4149
Blake Prize for Religious Art   Vol. 2: 285
Blakeley Lifetime Achievement Award; Dr. Phyllis R.   Vol. 1: 9143
Blaker Award for Best Restored Engine; LeRoy   Vol. 1: 14898
Blakey Memorial Prize; O. F.   Vol. 2: 426
Blanc; Prix Armand   Vol. 2: 1177
Blanc Prize; Armand   Vol. 2: 1177
Blanche; Prix Robert   Vol. 2: 5707
Blanco; Premio a la Actividad Cientifica Dr. Alvaro Blanco   Vol. 2: 1560
Blarney Trophy   Vol. 2: 7812
Blaskeslee Awards; Howard W.   Vol. 1: 2224
BIAT National Student Award   Vol. 2: 2397
BLAT Video Seal of Educational Value   Vol. 2: 2428
Blathy Award   Vol. 2: 7326
Blathy Dij   Vol. 2: 7326
Blatt Humanitarian Award; Burton   Vol. 1: 8321
Blaylock Medal; Selwyn G.   Vol. 1: 6931
Bledisloe Aviation Trophy   Vol. 2: 9812
Bledisloe Gold Medal for Landowners   Vol. 2: 3917
Bledisloe Veterinary Award   Vol. 2: 3918
Bledsoe Award; C. Warren   Vol. 1: 5490
Blegen Award; Julius   Vol. 1: 19554
Blegen Award; Theodore C.   Vol. 1: 12333
Bleininger Award; Albert Victor   Vol. 1: 1448
Blekinge County Council Culture Prize   Vol. 2: 11446
Blekinge County Council Environment Prize   Vol. 2: 11447
Blekinge lans landstings kulturpris   Vol. 2: 11446

Blekinge Lans landstings Miljovardspris   Vol. 2: 11447
Blenheim Award   Vol. 1: 10840
Bleriot Medal; Louis   Vol. 2: 5139
Blewett Playwright's Award; Jill   Vol. 2: 673
Bleyer Award   Vol. 1: 5495
Blick Merchandise Award; Dick   Vol. 1: 17693
Blignault Medal; Andries   Vol. 2: 10887
Bliss Editors' Award; A. Harry   Vol. 1: 13908
Bliss Medal   Vol. 1: 17701
Bliss Memorial Award; Gordon M.
   American Society for Training and Development   Vol. 1: 4300
   American Society for Training and Development - International Professional Practice Area   Vol 1: 4320
Bliss Prize Fellowship in Byzantine Studies   Vol. 1: 8766
BLITHE Video Seal of Educational Value   Vol. 2: 2428
Blitzstein Award; Marc   Vol. 1: 500
Blizil Memorial Literature Award; George A.   Vol. 1: 9583
Bloch Award; Herbert   Vol. 1: 4541
Bloch International Competition for Musical Composition; Ernest   Vol. 2: 11949
Bloem Distinguished Service Award; Delmar L.   Vol. 1: 1778
Blomska stipendiet   Vol. 2: 11586
Blomstrom Memorial Prize; Ake   Vol. 2: 7074
Blood Award; Frank R.   Vol. 1: 18069
Bloodless Medicine and Surgery Institute Man of the Year Award   Vol. 1: 604
Bloom Memorial Award; A. A.   Vol. 1: 18844
Bloomer Award; H. H.   Vol. 2: 3585
Bloomfield Award; John J.   Vol. 1: 1798
Blosser Dedicated Service Award; Ronald E.   Vol. 1: 6019
Blount Memorial Scholarship   Vol. 2: 2085
Blue Pencil Competition   Vol. 1: 13123
Blue Planet Prize   Vol. 2: 8486
Blue Ribbon Award   Vol. 1: 2045
Blue Ribbon Awards   Vol. 1: 6512
Bluebird Research Grants   Vol. 1: 15400
Bluegrass Music Awards   Vol. 1: 17623
Blues Hall of Fame   Vol. 1: 6415
Blues Music Awards (W. C. Handy Awards)   Vol. 1: 6416
Blum; Bourse Marcelle   Vol. 2: 5708
Blumenthal-Leviton-Blonder Prize   Vol. 1: 16263
Blumenthal Prize; Oscar   Vol. 1: 16263
Blumer Award; Herbert   Vol. 1: 17648
Blumgart Award   Vol. 1: 17944
Blumlein-Brown-Willans Premium Award   Vol. 2: 3269
Blundell Trust; K.   Vol. 2: 4386
Blunk Memorial Award; Jim   Vol. 1: 19015
Blutet; Fondation Paul Doistau - Emile   Vol. 2: 5644
Bly/Thomas D. Zumbo Cub Reporter Award; New York Press Club Nellie   Vol. 1: 15257
BMA Film and Video Competition   Vol. 2: 2429
BMA Hall of Fame   Vol. 1: 6661
BMA Medicine in the Media Award   Vol. 2: 2430
BMEC Donald Maxwell Award   Vol. 2: 3115
BMET of the Year Award; SBET/Replacement Parts Industries, Inc.   Vol. 1: 5628
BMI Awards to Student Composers   Vol. 1: 6577
BNA - Cube   Vol. 2: 9590
BNA - Kubus   Vol. 2: 9590
B'nai B'rith Gold Medallion for Humanitarianism   Vol. 1: 6426
Board Awards   Vol. 1: 5943

Board of Directors' Award
  American Gear Manufacturers Association   Vol. 1: 2142
  Healthcare Financial Management Association   Vol 1: 9863
  National Religious Broadcasters   Vol 1: 14603
Board of Directors Award of Recognition   Vol. 1: 5706
Board of Directors Distinguished Service Award for Senior ACS Administrators   Vol. 1: 1549
Board of Directors IMAX Award   Vol. 1: 9829
Board of Directors Student Paper Awards   Vol. 1: 8254
Board of Governors Award   Vol. 1: 6132
Board of Governors Trophy   Vol. 1: 13189
Board of Trade Medal for Life Saving at Sea   Vol. 2: 2386
Board of Trustees Hall of Fame Awards   Vol. 1: 13155
Boardman Tasker Memorial Award for Mountain Literature   Vol. 2: 2192
Boardwalk Art Show   Vol. 1: 20057
Boas Medal; Walter   Vol. 2: 233
Boase Award; Arthur J.   Vol. 1: 16760
Boase Award of the Reinforced Concrete Research Council; Arthur J.   Vol. 1: 4443
Boat Representative of the Year   Vol. 1: 14338
Boating Writers International Writing Contest   Vol. 1: 6438
Bob Gomulinski Community Service Award   Vol. 1: 5143
Bobbitt National Prize for Poetry; Rebekah Johnson   Vol. 1: 11856
Bobek Preis; Hans   Vol. 2: 779
Bobst Literary Awards; Elmer Holmes   Vol. 1: 15302
Bocher Memorial Prize   Vol. 1: 3004
Bochumer Textpreis fur Figurentheater   Vol. 2: 6674
Bock Prize; Frederick   Vol. 1: 16264
Bocking Award; Douglas   Vol. 1: 18438
Bockus Medal; H. L.   Vol. 2: 7167
Bode - Norman Holmes Pearson Prize; Carl   Vol. 1: 4872
Bodensee-Literaturpreis der Stadt Uberlingen   Vol. 2: 7146
Boehm Graduate Fellowship in the Fisheries Sciences; Andrew J.   Vol. 1: 4849
Boehm Medal   Vol. 2: 6864
Boehret Award; A.P.C. - Diane D.   Vol. 1: 3400
Boehringer Ingelheim Research and Training Fellowship   Vol. 1: 1621
Boehringer Mannheim Award   Vol. 2: 2116
Boehringer Mannheim Canada Prize   Vol. 1: 7163
Boehringer Mannheim GmbH Award   Vol. 2: 11466
Boehringer Mannheim Prize   Vol. 2: 10975
Boehringer Mannheim S.A. Award   Vol. 2: 10975
Boeing Student Research Award   Vol. 1: 18788
Boerma Award; A. H.   Vol. 2: 8267
Bogdanfy Medal; Odon   Vol. 2: 7348
Bogdanfy Odon Emlekerem   Vol. 2: 7348
Boger Award; Robert F.   Vol. 1: 8216
Bogg Memorial Award; Wm. G.   Vol. 1: 8109
Boggess Award; William R.   Vol. 1: 5002
Boggs Award; Fitzhugh W.   Vol. 1: 5208
Boggs Award; Larry   Vol. 1: 13513
Boggs Award; Lindy   Vol. 1: 3297
Boggs Award; Phil   Vol. 1: 19318

Boggs Service Award; Andrew T.   Vol. 1: 4577
Bogie Prize; The David J   Vol. 2: 10553
Bogin Memorial Award; George   Vol. 1: 16276
Bogle International Library Travel Fund   Vol. 1: 2902
Bogolubov Prize   Vol. 2: 8289
Bohlen Award; Avis   Vol. 1: 2085
Boisen Award; Anton T.   Vol. 1: 5870
Bok Award   Vol. 1: 16129
Bold Award; Harold C.   Vol. 1: 16172
Boldrewood Award; Rolf   Vol. 2: 357
Boldy Memorial Award; Julian   Vol. 1: 6932
Bolivar de Oro; Gran   Vol. 2: 1596
Bolivar; Gran Premio Libertador Simon   Vol. 2: 12109
Bolivar Lecture; Simon   Vol. 1: 3628
Bolivar Medal; Simon   Vol. 2: 1653
Bolivar; Medalla Simon   Vol. 2: 1653
Bolivar Prize; International Simon   Vol. 2: 6415
Bollingen Prize in Poetry   Vol. 1: 20570
Bollinger Humanitarian Award; Glen   Vol. 1: 9871
Bolton Memorial Prize; Herbert Eugene   Vol. 1: 8138
Boltzmann Medal   Vol. 2: 11484
BOMA International Awards Program   Vol. 1: 6611
Bombardier Prize in Technological Innovation; J. Armand   Vol. 1: 5432
Bombay International Film Festival   Vol. 2: 7529
Bomford Prize; Guy   Vol. 2: 5967
Bonatz Preis; Paul   Vol. 2: 7135
Bonazinga Award; Marie T.   Vol. 1: 17548
Bonchev Prize; Academician George   Vol. 2: 1513
Bond Award; Polly   Vol. 1: 8969
Bond Memorial Consumer Award; Ethel   Vol. 1: 13015
Bond Memorial Trophy; Sam   Vol. 1: 14645
Bonderman IUPUI Youth Theatre Playwriting Competition; Waldo M. and Grace C.   Vol. 1: 10151
Bonduelle; Prix Paul   Vol. 2: 967
Bonetti Grand Prize; Pascal   Vol. 2: 6305
Boni Prize; Vittorio   Vol. 2: 8446
Bonica Distinguished Lectureship; John J.   Vol. 1: 10656
Bonin Award; Wilbrod   Vol. 1: 18438
Bonn Mileata Calmachta; An   Vol. 2: 7790
Bonn Seirbhise Dearscna; An   Vol. 2: 7789
Bonner Prize in Nuclear Physics; Tom W.   Vol. 1: 3448
Bonnet; Fondation Andre C.   Vol. 2: 5488
Bonniers Pris; Gerard   Vol. 2: 11587
Bonorino Cuenca Prize; Juan   Vol. 2: 68
Bonorino Udaondo Prize; Carlos   Vol. 2: 69
Bonsai and Orchid Association Award   Vol. 1: 6443
Booby Prize
  Association for the Promotion of Humor in International Affairs   Vol. 2: 4944
  Association for the Promotion of Humor in International Affairs (APHIA)   Vol 1: 5639
Book Award
  British Psychological Society   Vol. 2: 2486
  Phi Alpha Theta   Vol 1: 16093
Book Awards
  National Book Development Council of Singapore   Vol. 2: 10734
  Organization of Islamic Capitals and Cities (OICC)   Vol 2: 10502
  Scottish Arts Council   Vol 2: 10660
Book Design Awards   Vol. 2: 193

Book of Fame Citation   Vol. 1: 7058
Book-of-the-Month Club Translation Prize; PEN   Vol. 1: 16020
Book of the Sea Award   Vol. 2: 3521
Book of the Year   Vol. 2: 7371
Book of the Year Award
  Academy of Parish Clergy   Vol. 1: 73
  Evangelical Christian Publishers Association   Vol 1: 9015
Book of the Year Award: Older Readers   Vol. 2: 310
Book of the Year Award: Younger Readers   Vol. 2: 311
Book of the Year for Children Award   Vol. 1: 7019
Book of the Year for Children Medal   Vol. 1: 7003
Book Printer Award   Vol. 2: 193
Book Prize   Vol. 1: 7154
Book Prizes of the Circle of the Greek Children's Book   Vol. 2: 7189
Book Publishers of Texas Children's/Young People's Award   Vol. 1: 18642
Book Show   Vol. 1: 2622
Bookbuilders West Book Show   Vol. 1: 6450
Booker McConnell Prize   Vol. 2: 2195
Booker Prize   Vol. 2: 2195
Booker Russian Novel Prize   Vol. 2: 2196
Bookland Piano Competition; Portland Symphony Orchestra/   Vol. 1: 16326
Bookman Media Excellence Award; Ron   Vol. 1: 6124
Books Abroad/Neustadt International Prize   Vol. 1: 20502
Books of the Year Awards   Vol. 1: 2752
BooksCity/Books in Canada Student Writing Awards   Vol. 1: 6453
Boone and Crockett Award   Vol. 1: 10734
Boone Award; Joel T.   Vol. 1: 5876
Boosey Award; Leslie   Vol. 2: 3768
Booster Award   Vol. 1: 1795
Booth Award; Edwin   Vol. 1: 7772
Booth Award; Taylor   Vol. 1: 10295
Boothby Award; Walter M.   Vol. 1: 166
Boothby - Edwards Award   Vol. 1: 166
Boothman Bursary; Harry   Vol. 1: 7085
Boots Romantic Novel of the Year   Vol. 2: 3858
Bora; Fondazione Ettore   Vol. 2: 8052
Borba Award   Vol. 2: 10703
Borciani; Premio Paolo   Vol. 2: 8444
Bordalo Pinheiro de Banda Desenhada, Cartoon e Caricaturista; Premio Municipal Rafael   Vol. 2: 10276
Borden Award
  American Dairy Science Association   Vol. 1: 1910
  American Home Economics Association Foundation   Vol 1: 2337
  American Industrial Hygiene Association   Vol 1: 2431
  Association of American Medical Colleges   Vol 1: 5687
Borden Award in Nutrition
  American Institute of Nutrition   Vol. 1: 2648
  Canadian Society for Nutritional Sciences   Vol 1: 7143
Borders P A Award   Vol. 1: 5284
Bordewijk Prize; F.   Vol. 2: 9346
Bordin; Prix   Vol. 2: 5364
Borduas; Prix Paul-Emile-   Vol. 1: 16615
Borgia; Fondazione Premio Dotte Giuseppe   Vol. 2: 8063
Boring Awards   Vol. 1: 6458
Borman Award; Alvah K.   Vol. 1: 4074
Born Award; Max   Vol. 1: 15746
Born Medal and Prize; Max   Vol. 2: 3184

Born-Preis; Max- Vol. 2: 6656
Borrower of the Year Vol. 2: 2813
Bosch Foundation Fellowships; Robert Vol. 1: 7422
Bosch Prize; Samuel M. Vol. 2: 70
Bose Medal; Satyendranath Vol. 2: 7640
Bose Memorial Award; Anil Kumar Vol. 2: 7641
Boskovic Awards; Rudjer Vol. 2: 1807
Boston Ballet Award for Choreography Vol. 1: 6462
Boston Globe - Horn Book Awards Vol. 1: 6464
Boston International Choreography Competition Vol. 1: 6462
Boston Marathon Vol. 1: 6460
Boswell Award Vol. 2: 11092
Botein Fellowships; Stephen Vol. 1: 799
Botelho da Costa Veiga Prize; Augusto Vol. 2: 10300
Botelho de Pintura; Premio Municipal Carlos Vol. 2: 10267
Botev International Prize for Revolutionary Poetry; Christo Vol. 2: 1504
Botiaux-Dulac; Prix Vol. 2: 5339
Bottaro Prize; Osvaldo L. Vol. 2: 71
Bottorf Award; Jim Vol. 1: 13
Bottorff Award; C. A. Vol. 1: 913
Bouchard; Fondations Bellion - Charles Vol. 2: 5678
Bouchard; Prix Charles Vol. 2: 5678
Bouillon Award; Lincoln Vol. 1: 4578
Boujassy; Prix Jeanne Vol. 2: 6286
Bouland; Prix Leclerc - Maria Vol. 2: 5411
Boulanger Award; Jean P. Vol. 1: 17723
Bound to Stay Bound Books Scholarship Vol. 1: 2857
Bourcart; Fondation Jacques Vol. 2: 5587
Bourcart; Prix Jacques Vol. 2: 5311
Bourgelat Award Vol. 2: 2509
Bourke Lectureship Vol. 2: 4189
Bourse Bancroft Vol. 1: 16949
Bourse Goncourt de la Nouvelle Vol. 2: 4797
Bourse Gonzague Mulliez Vol. 2: 4802
Bourse Harry Boothman Vol. 1: 7085
Bourse Marcelle Blum Vol. 2: 5708
Bourse Prince Rainier III de Monaco Vol. 2: 5935
Bourse Rene-Payot Vol. 2: 5070
Bourse Sir Arthur Sims Vol. 1: 16964
Bourse Veronique Dejouany Vol. 2: 4803
Bourses Commemoratives E. W. R. Steacie Vol. 1: 15077
Bourses de la Vocation Vol. 2: 5212
Bourses de quatre mois Vol. 1: 12250
Bourses Guy Levis Mano Vol. 2: 4954
Boury Prize; Karel Vol. 2: 1267
Bouscatel; Prix Jean Vol. 2: 5870
Bouvier-Parviliez Prize; Ernest Vol. 2: 1283
Bouwer Prize; Alba Vol. 2: 10986
Bouwhuis Memorial Scholarship; Rev. Andrew L. Vol. 1: 7375
Bovey Award; Edmund C. Vol. 1: 8308
Bovine Research Award Vol. 1: 4986
Bowditch Lecture; Henry R. Vol. 1: 3504
Bowen Medal; R. W. Vol. 2: 11082
Bowen Memorial Award; Betty Vol. 1: 17162
Bowen Public Relations Award; Harold S. Vol. 1: 10122
Bower Award and Prize for Achievement in Science Vol. 1: 9373
Bower Award for Business Leadership Vol. 1: 9374
Bower Memorial Award; Ros
  Australia Council - Community Cultural Development Board Vol. 2: 151
  Australia Council for the Arts - Visual Arts/Craft Board Vol 2: 163
Bowie Medal Vol. 2: 3108
Bowie Medal; William Vol. 1: 2160
Bowis Award Vol. 1: 1731
Bowis Award; E.B. Vol. 1: 1730
Bowker Award; Isadore Gilbert Mudge - R. R. Vol. 1: 2945
Bowker/Ulrich's Serials Librarianship Award Vol. 1: 2848
Bowler of the Month Vol. 1: 6500
Bowler of the Year Vol. 1: 6501
Bowles Cup Vol. 2: 4026
Bowling Magazine Writing Competition Vol. 1: 1367
Bowling National Mine Reclamation Awards; Kenes C. Vol. 1: 11408
Bowman Award; Raymond C. Vol. 1: 17497
Bowser Distinguished Network Service Award; John A. Vol. 1: 14957
Box Office Manager of the Year Vol. 1: 6506
Box Office of the Year Vol. 1: 6507
Boxer of the Year
  Knights Boxing Team International Vol. 1: 11712
  United States Amateur Boxing Vol 1: 18991
Boxing Hall of Fame Vol. 1: 11381
Boxing Hall of Fame Award Vol. 1: 16843
Boyd Award; Julian P. Vol. 1: 5483
Boyd Award; Robin Vol. 2: 609
Boyd Lectureship; William Vol. 1: 6793
Boyd Trophy; Lennox Vol. 2: 2049
Boyden Premium Vol. 1: 9375
Boydston Essay Prize Vol. 1: 5484
Boyer Award; Elizabeth Vol. 1: 20414
Boyer Lecture on Public Policy; Francis Vol. 1: 1997
Boyer Medal; Marian Angell Godfrey Vol. 1: 19728
Boyle Award; Hal Vol. 1: 15875
Boyle Award; Rosalie Vol. 1: 15122
Boyle Medal in Analytical Chemistry; Robert Vol. 2: 4190
Boyle Prize; Edward Vol. 2: 2994
Boynton Award; Melbourne W. Vol. 1: 1255
Boynton Award; Ruth E. Vol. 1: 1597
Boynton's Gala Artist Awards Vol. 1: 6529
Boys - A Rahman Lectureship; S. F. Vol. 2: 4191
Boys & Girls Club Medallion Vol. 1: 6531
Boys' Basketball Past Chair Recognition Vol. 1: 420
Boys' Basketball Vision Award Vol. 1: 421
Boys Cup; Sir Francis Vol. 2: 9813
Boys Medal and Prize; Charles Vernon Vol. 2: 3185
BP Arts Award Vol. 2: 2032
BP Arts Media Awards Vol. 2: 210
BP Award Vol. 2: 2246
BP Oil Award Vol. 2: 3356
BP Peter Pears Award Vol. 2: 2213
BP Portrait Award Vol. 2: 3704
BP Prize Lectureship in the Humanities Vol. 2: 10638
BPAA Special Award Vol. 1: 6498
B.P.E. Inter-Federation Award Vol. 2: 3781
BPW Career Advancement Scholarship Program Vol. 1: 6643
Brabender Award; Carl Wilhelm Vol. 1: 947
Brachet; Prix Albert Vol. 2: 1008
Brachetto Brian Prize; Domingo J. Vol. 2: 72
Brackenbury Award Vol. 2: 2431
Bracket World Finals Team Championship Vol. 1: 11030
Brackett Memorial Award; Dexter Vol. 1: 15150
Braddock Award; CCCC Richard Vol. 1: 13763
Braddock Award; Richard Vol. 1: 8133
Bradley Award Vol. 2: 1049
Bradley Award; Barbara Vol. 1: 15123
Bradley Distinguished Service Award; James J. Vol. 1: 17783
Brady Award; Ken Vol. 1: 12385
Brady Award; Mathew B. Vol. 1: 19839
Brady Memorial Awards; Gerald Vol. 1: 9754
Braem-Preis; Helmut M. Vol. 2: 6760
Bragg Gold Medal for Excellence in Physics Vol. 2: 234
Bragg Medal and Prize Vol. 2: 3186
Brahney Award; James M. Vol. 1: 10099
Braille and Talking Book Library Award Vol. 2: 290
Braille Book of the Year Vol. 2: 290
Brain Research Foundation Creativity Awards Vol. 1: 6540
Bralco Gold Medal Vol. 2: 7626
Bramah Scholarship Vol. 2: 3333
Brand Annual Art Competition Vol. 1: 5421
Brandeis University Creative Arts Awards Vol. 1: 6543
Branding Hammer Award Vol. 1: 16661
Brandt Volunteer Service Award; Sandy Vol. 1: 14356
Brannon Award; R. A. Vol. 1: 13039
Brasov Writers Association Award Vol. 2: 10410
Brass Balls Award Vol. 1: 9807
Brasted Memorial Lecture Vol. 1: 1488
Bratislava Literary Prize Vol. 2: 10754
Bratislava Radio Prize for Folklore Music Vol. 2: 10778
Braude Award for Light Verse; Michael Vol. 1: 501
Brauer Prize; Hamburg Max Vol. 2: 7108
Braun Award; E. Lucy Vol. 1: 8810
Braun Award; Fred Vol. 1: 19555
Braun Prize; Karl Ferdinand Vol. 1: 17530
Braunstein Memorial Award; Jules Vol. 1: 1103
Bravery Medal Vol. 2: 207
Bravo Award Vol. 1: 16898
Bravo Awards Vol. 1: 9996
Bray Award for Poetry; John Vol. 2: 673
Bray Award; Robert S. Vol. 1: 1848
Brazier Young Investigator Award; M. A. B. Vol. 1: 10959
Brazilian Association for the Advancement of Science Awards Vol. 2: 1428
Brazos Bookstore Short Story Award Vol. 1: 18643
Breach Award; Malcolm Vol. 2: 3167
Breakthrough Award Vol. 1: 20415
Breasted Prize; James Henry Vol. 1: 2284
Breaute; Prix Vol. 2: 5365
Brechner Freedom of Information Award; Joseph L. Vol. 1: 6551
Brecht-Denkmunze; Walter- Vol. 2: 6537
Breed Awards Vol. 1: 15468
Breed Challenge Shield Vol. 1: 3984
Breed Horse Show Awards Vol. 2: 2544
Bregger Essay Award Vol. 1: 3595
Breir Award; Nabila Vol. 2: 10872
Breithaupt Award; Chef Herman Vol. 1: 8397
Breitkreutz Leadership Award - Volleyball; Emil Vol. 1: 422
Bremen Literary Prize Vol. 2: 6578
Bremer Bildhauerpreis Vol. 2: 6582
Bremer Forderpreis fur Bildende Kunst Vol. 2: 6579
Bremer Forderpreis fur Kunsthandwerk Vol. 2: 6580
Bremner Awards; M. D. K. Vol. 1: 723

Brennan Award; FAW Christopher   Vol. 2: 386
Brennan Award; Thomas J.   Vol. 1: 6094
Brennan Award; William J.   Vol. 1: 15279
Brennan Awards; William J.   Vol. 1: 14223
Brennan Medal   Vol. 2: 3214
Brenner Prize   Vol. 2: 7890
Brent Inter-American Award; Theodore   Vol. 1: 20529
Bretnall Award; William B.   Vol. 1: 17171
Breuil; Fondation Jean du Hamel de   Vol. 2: 5596
Brevoort - Eickemeyer Prize   Vol. 1: 7975
Brewer Prize; Frank S. and Elizabeth D.   Vol. 1: 4425
Brewer Trophy; Frank G.   Vol. 1: 12722
Brewster Memorial Award; William   Vol. 1: 3345
Brice Outstanding Student Award; Leonard R.   Vol. 1: 17482
Brick Design Awards   Vol. 2: 2215
Bridge Book of the Year   Vol. 1: 1371
Bridgeport Prize   Vol. 2: 3270
Bridges Memorial (High Average Horsemanship Award); Polly   Vol. 1: 15469
Bridgestone Potenza Super Car Championship   Vol. 1: 11106
Bridgestone Supercar Championship   Vol. 1: 11106
The Bridport Prize   Vol. 2: 2218
Brier Instructor of the Year Award; ARRL Herb S.   Vol. 1: 3886
Brigestone Potenza Super Car Championship   Vol. 1: 11106
Briggs Award; Charles W.
    ASTM   Vol. 1: 6038
    Iron and Steel Society   Vol 1: 11458
Briggs Dissertation Award in Engineering Psychology; George E.   Vol. 1: 3684
Briggs Folklore Award; Katharine   Vol. 2: 2902
Briggs Memorial Scientific Inquiry Award; Dorothy   Vol. 1: 3477
Briggs Memorial Technical and Operating Medal; Charles W.   Vol. 1: 18479
Brigham Award; Reuben   Vol. 1: 201
Brigham Award; Richard and Grace   Vol. 1: 17784
Bright Idea Award   Vol. 1: 18632
Bright Memorial Award; Norman and Marion   Vol. 1: 7544
Brignetti Literary Award; Isle of Elba - Raffaello   Vol. 2: 8323
Brill Trophy; John   Vol. 1: 12120
Brillat-Savarin; Prix   Vol. 2: 4791
Brimdey Lecture; George W.   Vol. 1: 7828
Brin; Premio Irene   Vol. 2: 8004
Brine Awards; W. H.   Vol. 1: 19408
Brinell Medal   Vol. 2: 11523
Brink Award for Distinguished Service; Victor Z.   Vol. 1: 10368
Brinker Award; Maureen Connolly   Vol. 1: 19644
Brinker International Award for Breast Cancer Research   Vol. 1: 11718
Brinker Outstanding Junior Girl Award; Maureen Connolly   Vol. 1: 19644
Brinkhous Award; Dr. Kenneth   Vol. 1: 14124
Brinkley Award; Rawn   Vol. 1: 10384
Brisbane Prize; MakDougall-   Vol. 2: 10646
Brissett Award; Belva B.   Vol. 1: 12971
Bristol Award
    Canadian Society of Hospital Pharmacists   Vol. 1: 7184
    Infectious Diseases Society of America   Vol 1: 10171

Bristol-Myers Award for Distinguished Achievement in Cancer Research   Vol. 1: 6559
Bristol-Myers Award for Distinguished Achievement in Nutrition Research   Vol. 1: 6565
Bristol-Myers Company Unrestricted Medical Grants Program   Vol. 1: 6564
Bristol-Myers Oncology Division Community Health Research Grant; Oncology Nursing Foundation/   Vol. 1: 15639
Bristol-Myers Oncology Division Distinguished Researcher Award; ONS   Vol. 1: 15652
Bristol-Myers Oncology Division Research Grant; Oncology Nursing Foundation/   Vol. 1: 15640
Bristol-Myers Squibb Award   Vol. 1: 7184
Bristol-Myers Squibb Award for Distinguished Achievement in Cancer Research   Vol. 1: 6559
Bristol-Myers Squibb Award for Distinguished Achievement in Cardiovascular Research   Vol. 1: 6560
Bristol-Myers Squibb Award for Distinguished Achievement in Infectious Disease Research   Vol. 1: 6561
Bristol-Myers Squibb Award for Distinguished Achievement in Neuroscience Research   Vol. 1: 6562
Bristol-Myers Squibb Award for Distinguished Achievement in Pain Research   Vol. 1: 6563
Bristol-Myers Squibb Company Unrestricted Medical Grants Program   Vol. 1: 6564
Bristol-Myers Squibb/Mead Johnson Award for Distinguished Achievement in Nutrition Research   Vol. 1: 6565
Bristol-Myers Squibb/Zimmer Award for Distinguished Achievement in Orthopaedic Research   Vol. 1: 6566
BRIT Awards   Vol. 2: 2478
Britain in Bloom Awards   Vol. 2: 4541
Britannica Awards   Vol. 1: 8918
British Academy Fellowship   Vol. 2: 7840
British Academy of Film and Television Arts Awards - Film   Vol. 2: 2233
British Academy of Film and Television Arts Awards - Television   Vol. 2: 2234
British Academy Research Awards   Vol. 2: 2222
British Aerophilatelic Federation Award   Vol. 2: 3781
British Amateur Video Awards   Vol. 2: 4603
British-American Research Fellowship   Vol. 1: 2233
British Appaloosa Society National Champions   Vol. 2: 2240
British Association Film and Television Awards   Vol. 2: 2254
British Association Medal   Vol. 2: 11017
British Association of Dermatologists Awards   Vol. 2: 2264
British Association of Paediatric Surgeons Awards   Vol. 2: 10516
British Book Design and Production Awards   Vol. 2: 2482
British Bronze Medal   Vol. 2: 3883
British Caribbean Philatelic Study Group Award   Vol. 2: 3781
British Cartographic Society Design Award   Vol. 2: 2305
British Council Prize in the Humanities   Vol. 1: 15402
British Design Awards   Vol. 2: 2738
British Empire Medal   Vol. 2: 2359
British Fantasy Awards   Vol. 2: 2336
British Fashion Council Awards
    British Fashion Council   Vol. 2: 2338

British Fashion Council   Vol 2: 2338
British Federation Crosby Hall Fellowship   Vol. 2: 11789
British Foundry Medal and Prize   Vol. 2: 3069
British Gas Award   Vol. 2: 2163
British Glass Manufacturers Confederation Awards   Vol. 2: 2354
British Gold Medal   Vol. 2: 3884
British Grassland Society Award   Vol. 2: 2389
British Hang Gliding Association Trophy   Vol. 2: 12157
British Helicopter Advisory Board (BHAB) Trophy   Vol. 2: 3002
British International Print Exhibition   Vol. 2: 2420
British Journal of Urology Travelling Fellowship   Vol. 2: 2273
British Lichen Society Awards   Vol. 2: 2426
British Mexican Society Postgraduate Prize   Vol. 2: 2457
British Music Society Awards   Vol. 2: 2459
British National Carnation Society Award   Vol. 2: 2726
British Nuclear Energy Society Travelling Scholarships   Vol. 2: 2461
British Open Golf Champion   Vol. 2: 10597
British Open Golf Championship
    Professional Golfers' Association   Vol. 2: 3820
    Professional Golfers' Association   Vol 2: 3821
    Professional Golfers' Association   Vol 2: 3822
British Petroleum Build A Car Competition   Vol. 2: 4301
British Press Awards   Vol. 2: 4561
British Psychological Society Prize for ''A'' Level Psychology   Vol. 2: 2487
British Reserve Insurance Conducting Prize   Vol. 2: 10591
British Reserve Insurance Youth Orchestra Award   Vol. 2: 10592
British School at Rome Fellowship   Vol. 2: 7854
British Science Fiction Association Awards   Vol. 2: 2496
British Short Film Festival   Vol. 2: 2498
British Show Pony Society Rosettes   Vol. 2: 2500
British Silver Medal   Vol. 2: 3885
British Society of Magazine Editors Awards   Vol. 2: 3772
British Sociological Association/Council for National Academic Awards Annual Undergraduate Essay Prize in Sociology   Vol. 2: 2697
Brito Award; Gene   Vol. 1: 18756
Brito Golden Porpoise Award; Lou   Vol. 1: 4938
Britt Literary Award   Vol. 1: 5936
Brittain Award; Donald   Vol. 1: 26
Britten Composers' Competition; Benjamin   Vol. 2: 2556
Britten Prize; John   Vol. 2: 3886
Brittingham Prize in Poetry and Felix Pollak Prize in Poetry   Vol. 1: 19890
Britton Award for Inquiry within the English Language Arts; CEE James N.   Vol. 1: 13764
Brizard; Prix   Vol. 2: 5366
Brno Literary Prize   Vol. 2: 1886
Broad Axe Award
    Catboat Association   Vol. 1: 7348
    Railway Tie Association   Vol 1: 16662
Broadcast/Cable Journalism Awards - Jack R. Howard Awards   Vol. 1: 17143
Broadcast/Cable News Awards - Jack R. Howard Awards   Vol. 1: 17143

Broadcast Journalistic Excellence - Jack R. Howard Broadcast Awards   Vol. 1: 17143
Broadcast Media Awards   Vol. 1: 17041
Broadcast Media Awards for Radio and Television   Vol. 1: 11185
Broadcast Media Awards for Television   Vol. 1: 11185
Broadcast Pioneers' Hall of Fame   Vol. 1: 6579
Broadcast Preceptor Awards   Vol. 1: 17042
Broadcaster of the Year Award   Vol. 1: 11181
Broadcasting Hall of Fame   Vol. 1: 12972
Broca Prize   Vol. 2: 4897
Brock Gold Medal Award   Vol. 2: 8553
Brodie Award in Drug Metabolism; Bernard B.   Vol. 1: 4233
Brodie Medal; John A.   Vol. 2: 427
Brodman Award for the Academic Medical Librarian of the Year; Estelle   Vol. 1: 12166
Broedel Award; Max   Vol. 1: 5858
Brohee Medal   Vol. 2: 7168
Broida Prize in Atomic, Molecular, or Chemical Physics; Herbert P.   Vol. 1: 3449
Broiler Research Award   Vol. 1: 16345
Brokaw Memorial Trophy; Irving   Vol. 1: 19354
Bromsgrove Festival Young Musicians' Platform   Vol. 2: 2558
Bronfman Award for Excellence in the Crafts; Saidye   Vol. 1: 6584
Bronze Anvil Award   Vol. 1: 16573
The Bronze Baby   Vol. 1: 6965
Bronze Elephant Award   Vol. 2: 7715
Bronze Key Award   Vol. 1: 13788
Bronze Medal
  Association of Surgeons of South Africa   Vol. 2: 10820
  Australian Numismatic Society   Vol 2: 258
  International Federation of Sports Medicine   Vol 2: 1479
  Royal Institute of Navigation   Vol 2: 4075
  South African Geographical Society   Vol 2: 11053
  Tau Sigma Delta   Vol 1: 18581
Bronze Plaque Awards   Vol. 1: 9186
Bronze Star Medal   Vol. 1: 19142
Bronze Swagman Award   Vol. 2: 710
Bronze Wolf   Vol. 2: 11982
Brood Bitch Trophy   Vol. 1: 3984
Brooke Scholarship; John   Vol. 2: 7783
Brookes Memorial Fellowship; Dame Mabel   Vol. 2: 568
Brooks Award for Excellence in Student Research; Frank G.   Vol. 1: 6335
Brooks Award for Excellence in the Teaching of Culture; ACTFL Nelson   Vol. 1: 1876
Brooks Award for Outstanding Services to the Society; Charles Franklin   Vol. 1: 3079
Brooks Memorial Award; Charles E.   Vol. 1: 9101
Brooks' Memorial Award; John   Vol. 1: 9250
Brooks Undergraduate Essay Competition; F. G.   Vol. 1: 6335
Brophy AAO Distinguished Service Award; James E.   Vol. 1: 1091
Bross Prize   Vol. 1: 6588
Brosseau Memorial Award; Robert P.   Vol. 1: 8195
Brother Barnabas Award   Vol. 1: 8011
Brotherhood Award   Vol. 1: 13643
Brothers Grimm Prize   Vol. 2: 6561
Brothers St. Cyril and Methodius International Prize   Vol. 2: 1505
Brough Memorial Prize; Frederick   Vol. 2: 428
Broun Award; Heywood   Vol. 1: 15365
Broun Award; Maurice   Vol. 1: 9837

Brouwer Award; Dirk
  American Astronautical Society   Vol. 1: 1256
  American Astronomical Society   Vol 1: 1265
Brower Environmental Journalism Award; David R.   Vol. 1: 17225
Brower Prize; Mr. and Mrs. J. F.   Vol. 1: 5297
Brown/AMA Marketing Scholar of the Year; George Hay   Vol. 1: 2984
Brown Award and Medal; S. G.   Vol. 2: 4143
Brown Award; Antoinette   Vol. 1: 18910
Brown Award; Dublin Corporation Biennial Christy   Vol. 2: 7758
Brown Award for Meritorious Service; Lydia   Vol. 2: 2285
Brown Award; Gwilym   Vol. 1: 19932
Brown Award; James Barrett   Vol. 1: 1135
Brown Award; Ray E.   Vol. 1: 5877
Brown Award; Roger J. E.   Vol. 1: 6892
Brown Awards; Ham   Vol. 1: 15860
Brown Bear Award   Vol. 1: 5390
Brown Boettner Award for Outstanding Government Leadership; Beth   Vol. 1: 14578
Brown Boveri-Forschungspreis fur Energietechnik   Vol. 2: 11928
Brown Freedom Medal and Award; Colin M.   Vol. 1: 13592
Brown IV Annual Award of Excellence for Outstanding Community Service; James   Vol. 1: 7599
Brown, Jr. Root Cutter Award; Samuel W.   Vol. 1: 10243
Brown; Mary Louise   Vol. 1: 1351
Brown Medal; Frank P.   Vol. 1: 9376
Brown Medal; W.P.   Vol. 2: 452
Brown Memorial Award; Charlie   Vol. 1: 13376
Brown Memorial Award; J. Hammond   Vol. 1: 15860
Brown Memorial Grant; Leslie H.   Vol. 1: 16683
Brown Memorial Public Service Award; Aaron L.   Vol. 1: 13015
Brown Prize; John Nicholas   Vol. 1: 12199
Brown Prize; Sir Vernon   Vol. 2: 3887
Brown Public Service Award; the James Wright   Vol. 1: 8547
Brown Publication Award; James W.   Vol. 1: 5509
Brown Research Award; Mary Louise
  American Association of Occupational Health Nurses   Vol. 1: 1076
  American Association of Occupational Health Nurses   Vol 1: 1081
Brown Trophy; Jack   Vol. 1: 19526
Brown Voluntarism Award; H. Barksdale   Vol. 1: 9038
Browne Gold Medal; Denis   Vol. 2: 10516
Browne Medal for Original Research   Vol. 2: 4597
Browne Memorial Bowl; George H.   Vol. 1: 19354
Browne Prize Medal; Buckston   Vol. 2: 2991
Brownell Media Award; Emery A.   Vol. 1: 14296
Brownell Press Award; Emery A.   Vol. 1: 14296
Browning Award; Alice C.   Vol. 1: 10798
Browning Trophy; Cary Mark   Vol. 1: 14644
Brownlow Award; Louis   Vol. 1: 4263
Brownlow Book Award; Louis   Vol. 1: 12651
Brownlow Publications Award; Cecil   Vol. 1: 9240
Brubaker Memorial Award; John   Vol. 1: 7376
Bruce Award for Children's Literature; FAW Mary Grant   Vol. 2: 397

Bruce Medal; Catherine Wolfe   Vol. 1: 6095
Bruce Medal; W. S.   Vol. 2: 10639
Bruce Memorial Award; James D.   Vol. 1: 1715
Bruce Prize; Alexander Ninian   Vol. 2: 10640
Brudney Award; Ruth P.   Vol. 1: 14357
Bruel Noise Control and Acoustics Medal; Per   Vol. 1: 4667
Bruel; Prix Georges   Vol. 2: 6135
Bruemmer Award; Mary A.   Vol. 1: 17001
Brugnon; Coupe Jacques   Vol. 2: 5259
Bruhn Prize; Erik   Vol. 1: 13411
Brumbaugh Award   Vol. 1: 4280
Brumbaugh Medal   Vol. 1: 4280
Brun; Fondation Edmond   Vol. 2: 5549
Brun World Arts and Academic Annual Awards   Vol. 1: 6597
Brunel Medal   Vol. 2: 3229
Bruner Award for Excellence in the Urban Environment; Rudy   Vol. 1: 6599
Bruner Award; Jerome S.   Vol. 1: 16255
Bruner Science Writing Fellowship; Ray   Vol. 1: 3846
Brunet Memorial Trophy; Jean-Pierre   Vol. 1: 19354
Brunetti Award; Cledo   Vol. 1: 10259
Brunner Grant; Arnold W.   Vol. 1: 2549
Brunner Memorial Prize in Architecture; Arnold W.   Vol. 1: 502
Brunnstrom Award for Excellence in Clinical Teaching; Signe   Vol. 1: 3478
Brusiin Award; Otto   Vol. 2: 4706
Brusiin palkinto; Otto   Vol. 2: 4706
Brussels International Art and Archaeology Film Festival   Vol. 2: 1162
Brussels International Festival of Fantasy Thriller and Science- Fiction Films   Vol. 2: 1241
Brussels International Festival of Films on the Engineering Profession   Vol. 2: 1097
Brussels International Festival of Scientific and Technical Films   Vol. 2: 1098
Bryan Award; Kirk   Vol. 1: 9555
Bryan Donkin Awards   Vol. 2: 3333
Bryan International String   Vol. 1: 15503
Bryan, Jr. Scholarships; Joseph M.   Vol. 1: 8798
Bryan Young Artists Competition; Kathleen and Joseph M.   Vol. 1: 15503
Bryant Award; David C.   Vol. 1: 973
Bryant Coach of the Year; Paul "Bear"   Vol. 1: 9304
Bryant Gold Medal; Henry Grier   Vol. 1: 9551
BSA Merit Awards   Vol. 1: 6475
Bua-Luang Art Competition Prize   Vol. 2: 12023
Bublick Hebrew University Awards; Solomon   Vol. 1: 2118
Bucchi Prize of Rome Capital City; Valentino   Vol. 2: 8263
Buchanan Cup   Vol. 1: 17265
Buchanan Medal   Vol. 2: 4144
Buchanan Outstanding Chapter Award   Vol. 1: 17265
Buchanan Prize in Esperanto; John   Vol. 2: 4574
Buchannon Scholarship; Donald A.   Vol. 1: 19267
Bucharest Writers Association Award   Vol. 2: 10411
Bucher Medal; Walter H.   Vol. 1: 2161
Bucher Prize; Heinrich Hatt-   Vol. 2: 11929
Buchner Forschungsstiftung; DECHEMA Preis der Max   Vol. 2: 6617
Buchner-Preis; Georg-   Vol. 2: 6765
Buck Award; Solon J.   Vol. 1: 12334

Buck Memorial Award; H. Werner Vol. 1: 11367
Buck Woman's Award; Pearl S. Vol. 1: 6601
Buckendale Lecture; L. Ray Vol. 1: 17753
Buckeye Children's Book Award Vol. 1: 6603
Bucking Stock of the Year Vol. 1: 16508
Buckland Literary Award Vol. 2: 9846
Buckley Condensed-Matter Physics Prize; Oliver E. Vol. 1: 3450
Buckner Medal; Emory Vol. 1: 9073
Buckwell Memorial Scholarship; Arthur Vol. 1: 16918
Bud Light/NHL Man of the Year Vol. 1: 14159
Budapest International Composers' Competition Vol. 2: 7365
Budapest International Music Competition Vol. 2: 7414
Budapest Nemzetkozi Sportfilm Fesztival Vol. 2: 7431
Budapest Pro Urbe Prize Vol. 2: 7404
Buddingh Prize for New Dutch Poetry; C. Vol. 2: 9569
Budeanu Prize; Constantin Vol. 2: 10336
Budgen Award; John Vol. 2: 2122
Budget CAR Coaches Award (Coaches Advisory Roundtable); WSF - Vol. 1: 20437
Budget Service Award Vol. 1: 11754
Budo Koro Sho Vol. 2: 3442
Budweiser/NHL Man of the Year Vol. 1: 14159
Bueche Award; Arthur M. Vol. 1: 12639
Buell Award; Murray F. Vol. 1: 8811
Buenos Aires Drama Prize Vol. 2: 35
Buenos Aires Literary Prizes Vol. 2: 36
Buenos Aires Music Prize Vol. 2: 37
Buerger Award; Martin J. Vol. 1: 1897
Buffalo Hall of Fame Vol. 1: 13478
Bugnet Award for Fiction; Georges Vol. 1: 20555
Buhrmann-Ubbens Papierprijs Vol. 2: 9342
Build a Building Competition Vol. 2: 3230
Builder of the Year Vol. 1: 16453
Builders' Awards Vol. 2: 10036
Builder's Choice Awards for Excellence in Design and Planning Vol. 1: 6605
Builder's Choice Design and Planning Awards Vol. 1: 6605
Building Manager of the Year Awards Vol. 2: 2581
Bujkovsky Memorial Award); Education Award (Gustav J. Vol. 1: 11046
Bulgarian Academy of Science Honorary Badge - Marin Drinov Medal Vol. 2: 1512
Bulgarian Academy of Science - Kliment Ohridski University of Sofia Prizes Vol. 2: 1513
Bulk Materials Handling Award Vol. 2: 429
Bulkley Medal Vol. 1: 9486
Bullen Prize; John Vol. 1: 6903
Bulletin Award Vol. 2: 193
The Bulletin Black and White Artists' Awards Vol. 2: 298
The Bulletin/Compaq Young Executive of the Year Vol. 2: 299
Bulletin Contest Vol. 1: 9779
The Bulletin/Qantas Business Woman of the Year Vol. 2: 300
Bullock Memorial Dissertation Award; Donald American Society for Training and Development Vol. 1: 4301
 American Society for Training and Development - International Professional Practice Area Vol 1: 4321
Bullrich Prize; Rafael A. Vol. 2: 73
Bumbershoot, The Seattle Arts Festival Vol. 1: 15673

Bumbershoot/Weyerhaeuser Foundation Publication Award Vol. 1: 15673
Bunche Award; Ralph
 King County Bar Association Vol. 1: 11692
 Washington State Bar Association - World Peace Through Law Section Vol 1: 20128
Bunche Award; Ralph J. Vol. 1: 3569
Bunche Memorial Award; Ralph Vol. 1: 19742
Bundespreis fur Forderer des Designs Vol. 2: 6805
Bundespreis Gute Form Vol. 2: 6804
Bundespreis Produktdesign Vol. 2: 6804
Bungakukai Prize for New Writers Vol. 2: 8751
Bungakukai Shinjin Sho Vol. 2: 8751
Buning-Brongers Award; Titia Vol. 2: 9344
Buning-Brongers prys; Johan en Titia Vol. 2: 9344
Bunka Korosha Vol. 2: 8577
Bunka-Kunsho Vol. 2: 8579
Bunkamura Orchard Hall Award Vol. 2: 11774
Bunker Memorial Lecture Vol. 2: 2181
Bunn Award; John W. Vol. 1: 12562
Bunsen-Denkmunze Vol. 2: 6628
Bunsen Medal Vol. 2: 6628
Bunting Institute Fellowship Program Vol. 1: 16630
Bunuel; Premio Luis Vol. 2: 11295
Bunyan Award; Paul Vol. 1: 1592
BUPA Prizes for Medical Writing and Illustration Vol. 2: 4387
Burch Memorial Safety Award; Gary Vol. 1: 13269
Burchfield Award; Laverne Vol. 1: 4264
Burden Award; Ione Vol. 1: 8568
Burdett, Jr. Army Aviation Flight Safety Award; Lt. Gen. Allen M. Vol. 1: 15771
Burdette Pi Sigma Alpha Award; Franklin L. Vol. 1: 3570
Burdy; Prix Jeanne Vol. 2: 5345
Burfitt Medal and Prize; Walter Vol. 2: 622
Burger Award; Eric and Amy Vol. 1: 15875
Burger Award in Medicinal Chemistry; Alfred Vol. 1: 1550
Burger Award; Warren E.
 Institute for Court Management of the National Center for State Courts Vol. 1: 10215
 National Center for State Courts Vol 1: 13572
Burger Healer Awards; Chief Justice Warren E. Vol. 1: 13687
Burger Memorial Award Vol. 2: 10788
Burgess Award; E. W. Vol. 1: 13804
Burggraf Award; Fred Vol. 1: 18778
Burgheim Medaille; Hedwig- Vol. 2: 7040
Burgos; Palma Julia de Vol. 1: 5587
Burka Award Vol. 1: 10410
Burkan Memorial Competition; Nathan Vol. 1: 4527
Burke Essay Contest; Arleigh Vol. 1: 19460
Burke, Jr. Award; George W. Vol. 1: 20142
Burke Memorial Award; John "Sonny" Vol. 1: 19503
Burke Memorial Award; Tom Vol. 1: 18391
Burke Memorial Lecture; Donal Vol. 2: 7829
Burke Perpetual Challenge Trophy Vol. 2: 3919
Burke Trophy; Sir Roland Vol. 2: 3919
Burket Award; Lester Vol. 1: 645
Burkett-Dodge Award Vol. 1: 19556
Burkitt Medal for Biblical Studies Vol. 2: 2223
Burks Award; G. Edwin Vol. 1: 4117
Burleigh Prize; The J. C. Vol. 2: 10554

Burmah-Castrol Silver Medal Vol. 2: 3090
Burn Award; Harry T. Vol. 1: 6325
Burn Prevention Award Vol. 1: 1380
Burnet Lecture Vol. 2: 171
Burnet Memorial Award; Sir John Vol. 2: 10611
Burnett Award; Hallie and Whit Vol. 1: 15875
Burnett/University of Hawaii/AEJMC Ethics Prize; Carol Vol. 1: 5496
Burnham Manufacturing Management Award; David C. Vol. 1: 17877
Burnham Medal Vol. 2: 3109
Burns Award; Bernard J. Vol. 1: 10123
Burr Award; Franklin L. Vol. 1: 14070
Burrin Award; Esther V. Vol. 1: 5532
Burroughs List of Nature Books for Young Readers; John Vol. 1: 6630
Burroughs Medal; John Vol. 1: 6631
Burroughs Wellcome Award Vol. 1: 7185
Burroughs Wellcome Fund Scholar Award in Experimental Therapeutics Vol. 1: 6636
Burroughs Wellcome New Investigator Award Vol. 1: 6637
Burroughs Wellcome Scholar Award Vol. 1: 6637
Burroughs Wellcome Scholars in Molecular Parasitology Vol. 1: 6637
Burroughs Wellcome Scholars in Toxicology
 Burroughs Wellcome Fund Vol. 1: 6638
 Society of Toxicology Vol 1: 18070
Bursaries, Scholarships, and Travel Awards Vol. 2: 7755
Bursary Award; J. D. Stewart Vol. 2: 3565
Burton Memorial Medal Vol. 2: 3933
Burton Memorial Trophy; Gale Cotton Vol. 1: 19557
Burwell, Jr. Award; E. B. Vol. 1: 9556
Burwell Lectureship in Catalysis; Robert Vol. 1: 7341
Busch Grand National Vol. 1: 12902
Busch Prize; Thomas W. Vol. 1: 18601
Bush Artist Fellowships Vol. 1: 6641
Bush Award; Vannevar Vol. 1: 14682
Bush Foundation Fellowships for Artists Vol. 1: 6641
Bushkin Friend of the Foundation Award; Oncology Nursing Foundation Ellyn Vol. 1: 15642
Bushnell Trophy; Asa S. Vol. 1: 13986
Busignies Memorial Award Vol. 1: 16642
Business and Economic Reporting Contest Vol. 1: 7904
Business and Industry Commitment to the Environment Awards Vol. 2: 2562
Business and Industry Honor Award Vol. 1: 5666
Business and Professional Awards Vol. 1: 16771
Business Aviation Meritorious Award Vol. 1: 9241
Business Conservation Leadership Award Vol. 1: 13024
Business/Economic Writing Award Vol. 1: 7904
Business Enterprise Awards
 Business Enterprise Trust Vol. 1: 6651
 Royal Society for the Mentally Handicapped Children and Adults Vol 2: 4163
Business in the Arts Awards Vol. 1: 6647
Business in the Future Award Vol. 2: 2953
Business Leadership Award Vol. 1: 19831
Business Promotion Awards Competition Vol. 1: 17128
Business Reporting Awards Vol. 1: 15190
Business Speaks Award Vol. 1: 15223
Businessperson of the Year Vol. 2: 925
Busk Medal Vol. 2: 4007

Busk Prize Vol. 2: 3888
Busoni Prize; F. Vol. 2: 8181
Bussart Memorial Award; J. E. Vol. 1: 8944
Bustad Companion Animal Veterinarian Award
  American Veterinary Medical Association Vol. 1: 4983
  Delta Society Vol 1: 8597
Bustillo; Premio Jose Maria Vol. 2: 13
Busustow Award; The Grace Vol. 2: 3868
Buszek Memorial Award; Buz Vol. 1: 9102
Butler Literary Award Vol. 1: 11450
Butler Medal Vol. 1: 7976
Butlin Prize; S. J. Vol. 2: 359
Butsuri-Tansa Gakkai-sho Vol. 2: 8756
Butt Award in Hepatology or Nutrition; H. R. Vol. 1: 2133
Butterfield Award; Lyman H. Vol. 1: 5485
Butterfield Trophy; Jack A. Vol. 1: 2318
Butterley - F. Earle Hooper Award; H. M. Vol. 2: 363
Butterworth Memorial Trophy; James A. Vol. 1: 14644
Butterworth Prize Vol. 1: 3330
Buttgenbach; Prix Henri Vol. 2: 1024
Butts Award in Embroidery; Mary Diamond Vol. 1: 15709
Butts - Whiting Award Vol. 1: 5740
Butzel Memorial Award for Distinguished Community Service; Fred M. Vol. 1: 11547
Buxtehude Prize; Dietrich Vol. 2: 7037
Buxtehuder Bulle Vol. 2: 7094
"Buy Recycled" Campaign Awards Program Vol. 1: 19063
Buyer of the Year Award Vol. 1: 14232
BVA Achievement Award Vol. 1: 6408
By-Line Award Vol. 1: 12101
Byng Memorial Trophy; Lady Vol. 1: 14160
Bynner Prize for Poetry; Witter Vol. 1: 503
Byrd Young Artist Competition; William C. Vol. 1: 16994
Byrne Memorial Literary Award; Ray Vol. 1: 3206
C. A. D. Trophy Vol. 2: 9814
C SADF Commendation Medal Vol. 2: 10935
CA Advertising Annual Vol. 1: 8057
CA Design Annual Vol. 1: 8058
CAA Literary Awards Vol. 1: 6805
CAA National Awards Vol. 2: 2644
Caballero; Gran Medalla Augustin Nieto Vol. 2: 1654
Caballero Medal; Augustin Nieto Vol. 2: 1654
Cabanne; Premio Prof. Dr. Alejandro Vol. 2: 44
CableACE Awards Vol. 1: 12590
Cabot and Louis Delezenne/Prize of the LMGMS; Joachim Vol. 2: 6077
Cabot Award; Maria Moors Vol. 1: 7993
Cabot Prizes; Maria Moors Vol. 1: 7977
Caccioppoli; Premio Vol. 2: 8359
Cacique's Crown of Honor Vol. 2: 7243
Cacique's Crown of Valor Vol. 2: 7244
Cactus d'Or Vol. 2: 3452
Cadbury Award; William and Charlotte Vol. 1: 14343
Cadbury Medal; Christopher Vol. 2: 4161
Cade Memorial Fellowship; Lady Vol. 2: 10826
Cadman Memorial Medal Vol. 2: 3181
Cadmus Memorial Award; Bradford Vol. 1: 10369
Cady Award; Gilbert H. Vol. 1: 9557
Cady Award; Harrison Vol. 1: 5040
CAG Award for Scholarly Distinction in Geography Vol. 1: 6780
CAG Award for Service to the Profession of Geography Vol. 1: 6781

Cagigal Award in Physical Education; International Jose Maria Vol. 2: 1166
Cahn Memorial Poetry Prize; Cynthia Vol. 1: 5156
Cahours; Prix Vol. 2: 5508
Caille Memorial Medal; Pierre Francois Vol. 2: 822
Caille; Prix de Traduction Pierre-Francois Vol. 2: 6278
Cailleux; Prix Paul Vol. 2: 5058
Cain Memorial Award; B. F. Vol. 1: 841
CALAM/ACTAL - Charles River Award Vol. 1: 7258
Calcium Nutrition Education Award Vol. 1: 3051
Caldas Science Prize Vol. 2: 1688
Caldecott Medal; Randolph Vol. 1: 2858
Calder Bequest Vol. 2: 4090
Calder Cup (Playoff Champion) Vol. 1: 2319
Calder Memorial Trophy Vol. 1: 14161
Caldicott Leadership Award; Helen Vol. 1: 20407
Caledonian Research Foundation Prize Lecturehip Vol. 2: 10641
Calendario Azteca de Oro Vol. 2: 8926
CALGON/IAHCSMM Annual Representative to the Board Award Vol. 1: 10742
Calhoun Scholarship; Hermoine Grant Vol. 1: 13965
Caliceti; Premio Internazionale Pietro Vol. 2: 8249
California Condor Award (Golden Condor Award) Vol. 1: 8387
California Gold Medal Vol. 2: 7835
California Young Reader Medal Vol. 1: 6679
Call for Papers Awards Program Vol. 1: 1028
Callan Memorial Medal; Elizabeth Vol. 1: 5041
Callas Gold Medal; Maria Vol. 2: 7185
Callas Grand Prix for Pianists; Maria Vol. 2: 7185
Callas Grand Prix, Opera, Oratorio-Lied; Maria Vol. 2: 7186
Callas International Music Competitions; Maria
  Athenaeum International Cultural Center Vol. 2: 7185
  Athenaeum International Cultural Center Vol 2: 7186
Callas International Opera, Oratorio-Lied Competition; Maria Vol. 2: 7186
Callas International Piano Competition; Maria Vol. 2: 7185
Callaway Award; Joe A.
  Actors' Equity Foundation Vol. 1: 121
  Stage Directors and Choreographers Foundation Vol 1: 18442
Callaway Prize for the Defense of the Right to Privacy; Joe Vol. 1: 15230
Callebaut Prize; Octaaf Vol. 2: 1252
Callendar Medal Vol. 2: 3158
CALLERLAB Milestone Award Vol. 1: 6681
Callow Memorial Award; Russell S. Vol. 1: 8785
Calvino Award; Italo Vol. 1: 8006
Calvo; Premios Maria Guerrero y Ricardo Vol. 2: 11300
Calvo; Prix Carlos Vol. 2: 11751
Camara Award Vol. 2: 11257
Cambridge Instruments Photogrammetry and Remote Sensing Award Vol. 1: 4244
Camden Poetry Award Vol. 1: 20272
Cameli; Premio F. Vol. 2: 8352
CAMEO Vol. 1: 15333
Camera d'Or Vol. 2: 5004
Cameraman of the Year Vol. 1: 20263
Cameron Award; T. W. N. Vol. 1: 7233

Cameron Gold Medal; Donald Vol. 1: 6255
Camoes Prize Vol. 2: 10297
Camp Medal; Thomas R. Vol. 1: 20143
Camp Memorial Trophy; Mary C. Vol. 1: 14642
Camp of the Month Award Vol. 1: 16943
Camp Trophy; Mary C. Vol. 1: 14645
Campana Prize; Walter M. Vol. 1: 5297
Campana Translation Prize Vol. 1: 11485
Campbell Award; Donald Vol. 1: 16302
Campbell Award for Distinguished Research in Social Psychology; Donald T. Vol. 1: 3804
Campbell Award for Young Authors; A. B. Vol. 1: 13040
Campbell Award; Frank W. Vol. 1: 16335
Campbell Award of Merit; E. K. Vol. 1: 4579
Campbell Award; Richard G. Vol. 1: 8273
Campbell Bowl; Clarence S. Vol. 1: 14162
Campbell Citation; Francis Joseph Vol. 1: 2885
Campbell Memorial Award; Dr. Robert Vol. 1: 5165
Campbell Memorial Award; John W.
  Center for the Study of Science Fiction Vol. 1: 7467
  World Science Fiction Society Vol 1: 20524
Campbell Memorial Lecture; Edward DeMille Vol. 1: 5350
Campbell Memorial Travel Award; George Vol. 2: 7756
Campbell Memorial Travel Grant; George Vol. 2: 7856
Campbell Memorial Trophy; Sir George Vol. 2: 10625
Campbell Outstanding Public Broadcasting Award; Elizabeth Vol. 1: 14050
Campert Prize; Jan Vol. 2: 9347
Campiello Prize Vol. 2: 8185
Campion Award; Saint Edmund Vol. 1: 7354
Campionato Europeo Baseball Vol. 2: 1117
Campus Entertainer of the Year Award Vol. 1: 12838
Campus Entertainment Awards Vol. 1: 12838
Camus; Prix Gustave Vol. 2: 959
CAN-AM Amity Award Vol. 1: 7169
Can-AM Civil Engineering Amity Award Vol. 1: 4444
Canada-Australia Literary Award Vol. 2: 154
Canada - Australia Literary Prize Vol. 1: 6727
Canada Award Vol. 1: 27
Canada Awards for Business Excellence Vol. 1: 10169
Canada Council Molson Prizes Vol. 1: 6728
Canada Export Award Vol. 1: 6717
Canada - French Community of Belgium Literary Prize Vol. 1: 6729
Canada - Germany Research Award Vol. 1: 6730
Canada Gold Medal for Science and Engineering Vol. 1: 15075
Canada International Lecture Vol. 2: 4402
Canada - Italy Literary Prize Vol. 1: 6731
Canada - Japan Book Award Vol. 1: 6732
Canada Lecture and Medal Vol. 2: 4403
Canada Medal Award Lectures Vol. 1: 17805
Canada Packers' Medal Vol. 1: 7155
Canada Packers - Shurgain Award for Excellence in Nutrition and Meat Science Vol. 1: 7155
Canada - Switzerland Literary Prize Vol. 1: 6733
Canada Volunteer Award Vol. 1: 6719
Canada's Sports Hall of Fame Vol. 1: 6760
Canadian Agricultural Engineering of the Year Award. Vol. 1: 7152

Canadian Architect Magazine Awards of Excellence   Vol. 1: 6771
Canadian Architect Yearbook   Vol. 1: 6771
Canadian Association of Animal Breeders' Award for Excellence in Genetics and Physiology   Vol. 1: 7156
Canadian Author & Bookman Creative Writing Awards   Vol. 1: 6806
Canadian Author Creative Writing Awards   Vol. 1: 6806
Canadian Authors Association/Air Canada Award   Vol. 1: 6807
Canadian Award for Financial Reporting   Vol. 1: 9681
Canadian Business Hall of Fame   Vol. 1: 11628
Canadian Cardiovascular Society Research Achievement Award   Vol. 1: 18435
Canadian Country Music Association's Citation Awards   Vol. 1: 6848
Canadian Country Music Awards   Vol. 1: 6849
Canadian Education Association Achievement Award   Vol. 1: 6857
Canadian Engineers' Gold Medal Award   Vol. 1: 6844
Canadian Federation of Humane Societies Media Award   Vol. 1: 6862
Canadian Film Awards   Vol. 1: 28
Canadian Football Hall of Fame and Museum   Vol. 1: 6870
Canadian Forces Decoration   Vol. 1: 6695
Canadian Forestry Achievement Award   Vol. 1: 6923
Canadian Forestry Scientific Achievement Award   Vol. 1: 6924
Canadian Friends of Yeshiva University Bora Laskin Distinguished Service Award   Vol. 1: 20579
Canadian Geotechnical Colloquium   Vol. 1: 6893
Canadian Hospital Association Award of Excellence for Service and Leadership   Vol. 1: 6921
Canadian International Amateur Film Festival   Vol. 1: 6959
Canadian International Annual Film Festival   Vol. 1: 6959
Canadian International Medal Lecture   Vol. 2: 4402
Canadian Library Association Book of the Year for Children Award   Vol. 1: 7003
Canadian Mineral Processors Division of CIM Awards   Vol. 1: 6933
Canadian Music Competitions   Vol. 1: 7044
Canadian Music Council Medal   Vol. 1: 7047
Canadian Music Council Radio Awards   Vol. 1: 7048
Canadian Music Council Special Award   Vol. 1: 7049
Canadian Music Council Special Mention   Vol. 1: 7050
Canadian Music Council Television Awards   Vol. 1: 7051
Canadian National Playwriting Competition   Vol. 1: 15855
Canadian News Hall of Fame   Vol. 1: 18749
Canadian Outdoorsman of the Year Award   Vol. 1: 7269
Canadian Pacific Rail Engineering Medal   Vol. 1: 8932
Canadian Paediatric Society Award for Excellence   Vol. 1: 7079
Canadian Pest Management Society Graduate Student Award   Vol. 1: 7090
Canadian Player of the Year   Vol. 1: 6817
The Canadian Prize   Vol. 2: 10555

Canadian School Library Association Merit Award   Vol. 1: 7027
Canadian Society for Chemical Engineering Award in Industrial Practice   Vol. 1: 7545
Canadian Society of Microbiologists Award   Vol. 1: 7215
Canadian Women's Club of New York City Award   Vol. 1: 7430
Canals de Barcelona; Concours Internacional Maria   Vol. 2: 11168
Canals International Music Competition for Musical Performance, Barcelona; Maria   Vol. 2: 11168
Canberra Book of the Year Award   Vol. 2: 331
Canberra Times and Commonwealth Bank National Short Story of the Year   Vol. 2: 302
Canberra Times National Art Award   Vol. 2: 303
Cancer Campaign Medals of Merit   Vol. 2: 4673
Cancer Control Society Awards   Vol. 1: 7275
Cancer Research Campaign International Fellowships   Vol. 2: 11858
Candace Award   Vol. 1: 13602
Cande Memorial Trophy; Donald H.   Vol. 1: 3106
Candle Artisan of the Year   Vol. 1: 11013
Candy Hall of Fame   Vol. 1: 13641
Cane Award; Melville   Vol. 1: 16277
Cane Pace   Vol. 1: 19677
CANEBSCO School Library Media Award   Vol. 1: 7020
Canedo; Premio Gustavo D.   Vol. 2: 9016
Canham Scholarship; Robert A.   Vol. 1: 20144
Caniff Spirit of Flight Award; Milton   Vol. 1: 13404
Canine Frisbee World Championship   Vol. 1: 12038
Cann Plaque; Jack R. C.   Vol. 1: 12776
Canne d'Or   Vol. 2: 11661
Cannes International Film Festival
  Cannes International Film Festival   Vol. 2: 5004
  France - Ministry of Youth and Sports   Vol 2: 5249
Canning Travel Awards; R. G.   Vol. 1: 13855
Canning Trophy; Richard F.   Vol. 1: 2320
Cannizzaro; Fondazione Premio Stanislao   Vol. 2: 8064
Cannizzaro; Medaglia Stanislao   Vol. 2: 8340
Cannon Award in Astronomy; Annie Jump
  American Association of University Women Educational Foundation   Vol. 1: 1235
  American Astronomical Society   Vol 1: 1266
Cannon Prize   Vol. 1: 12601
Canoeist of the Year   Vol. 2: 10665
Canon Photo Essay Award   Vol. 1: 14525
Cansave Children Award   Vol. 1: 17080
Cantelli; Concorso Internazionale per giovani Direttori d'orchestgra Premio Guido   Vol. 2: 8158
Cantelli International Competition for Young Conductors; Guido   Vol. 2: 8158
Canton Prize; Eliseo   Vol. 2: 74
CAP Joint Annual Award; ASCP -   Vol. 1: 4514
CAP Medal for Achievement in Physics   Vol. 1: 6801
CAP Medal for Outstanding Achievement in Industrial and Applied Physics   Vol. 1: 6802
Capa Gold Medal; Robert   Vol. 1: 15875
Capanema Prize; Gustavo   Vol. 2: 1430
Capar Award; Wes   Vol. 1: 18854
Capdeville (De Beziers); Prix Auguste   Vol. 2: 5817

Cape Young Writers Prize; *The Times*/Jonathan   Vol. 2: 2569
Capezio Dance Award   Vol. 1: 7296
Capital Award   Vol. 1: 17483
CAPL Public Library Services Award   Vol. 1: 7009
Caples International Awards; John   Vol. 1: 8650
Caplet; Prix Andre   Vol. 2: 5358
Capote Award for Literary Criticism in Memory of Newton Arvin; Annual Truman   Vol. 1: 19804
Capote Award for Literary Criticism in Memory of Newton Arvin; Truman   Vol. 1: 18462
Cappon Essay Prize; Dorothy Churchill   Vol. 1: 15196
Capra Achievement Award; Frank   Vol. 1: 8662
Capranica Foundation Award in Neuroethology   Vol. 1: 7298
Captains of Achievement   Vol. 1: 487
Caraccio Purchase Award; Kathleen   Vol. 1: 17693
Caragiale Prize; Ion Luca   Vol. 2: 10337
Carbohydrate Chemistry Award   Vol. 2: 4192
Carbonell; Premi Josep M.   Vol. 2: 11159
Carborundum Golden Jubilee Trophy   Vol. 2: 2062
Carclew Fellowship   Vol. 2: 673
Card Award; George   Vol. 1: 1849
Cardiff Literature Festival   Vol. 2: 12194
Cardiff Singer of the World Competition   Vol. 2: 12155
Cardiovascular Young Investigator Award   Vol. 1: 17945
Cardozo School of Law Distinguished Public Service Award; Benjamin N.   Vol. 1: 20580
Carducci Prize; Giosue   Vol. 2: 8174
Career Achievement Award
  Professional Fraternity Association   Vol. 1: 16465
  Society for the Preservation of Film Music   Vol 1: 17625
Career Advancement of Visual Artists (CAVA)   Vol. 1: 14039
Career Contribution Award   Vol. 1: 9558
Career Development Award   Vol. 1: 9518
Career Development Award in Skin Research   Vol. 1: 8614
Career Development Awards   Vol. 1: 11640
Career Development Resource Award   Vol. 1: 7307
Career Grants   Vol. 1: 18829
Career of Distinguished Scholarship Award   Vol. 1: 4828
Career Opportunity Grants   Vol. 1: 12341
Carey Award   Vol. 2: 4447
Carey Distinguished District Chair Awards; Ralph E.   Vol. 1: 14016
Carey, Jr. Distinguished Service Award; W. N.   Vol. 1: 18779
Carey Lectureship; William D.   Vol. 1: 888
Carey - Thomas Awards   Vol. 1: 16588
Caribbean Hotel Association Awards   Vol. 1: 7309
Caribbean Prize for Peace Through the Pursuit of Justice   Vol. 2: 940
Carillon School Prize   Vol. 2: 1347
Caring Award   Vol. 1: 7314
Caring Company Award   Vol. 1: 10095
Caritas Medal   Vol. 1: 15376
Carl XVI Gustavs Medalj   Vol. 2: 11536
Carlin Award for Excellence in Academic Teaching; Dorothy E. Baethke - Eleanor J.   Vol. 1: 3475
Carlin Award for Teaching Excellence; Dorothy E. Baethke - Eleanor J.   Vol. 1: 3475

Carlin Service Award; John   Vol. 1: 19515
Carll Award; John Franklin   Vol. 1: 17959
Carlos Teixeira Prize   Vol. 2: 10245
Carlsberg Light People's Choice Award   Vol. 1: 18744
Carlsen Award; Emil and Dines   Vol. 1: 12602
Carlson Award; Chester F.   Vol. 1: 17498
Carlson Award for Innovation in Engineering Education; Chester F.   Vol. 1: 4075
Carlstrom Memorial Award; C. O.   Vol. 1: 13229
Carmel Chamber Music Competition   Vol. 1: 7511
Carmen Award; Bliss   Vol. 1: 6258
Carmen Teresa du Hurtado Machado Latin American Competition for Voice   Vol. 2: 12116
Carnation Award   Vol. 1: 788
Carnation Company Incentive Award   Vol. 1: 6917
Carnational Award   Vol. 1: 788
Carnegie International Exhibition   Vol. 1: 7324
Carnegie Medal
    Carnegie Hero Fund Commission   Vol. 1: 7320
    Library Association   Vol 2: 3566
Carnegie Medal; Andrew   Vol. 1: 2859
Carnegie Prize   Vol. 1: 7324
Carnegie Prize; Andrew   Vol. 1: 12603
Carnegie Reading List Awards   Vol. 1: 2936
Carnegie Research Fund; Andrew   Vol. 2: 3128
Carnot Award in Energy Conservation; Sadi   Vol. 1: 19228
Carnot; Prix Lazare   Vol. 2: 5699
Carnot Prize; Sadi   Vol. 2: 6029
Caro and Rufino Jose Cuervo National Order; Miguel Antonio   Vol. 2: 1711
Caro y Rufino Jose Cuervo; Orden Nacional de Miguel Antonio   Vol. 2: 1711
Carolina Prize   Vol. 1: 15299
Carolus Award; Clusius   Vol. 2: 7345
Carolus Clusius emlekerem   Vol. 2: 7345
Carothers Medal   Vol. 2: 4514
Carpenter Award; Leroy H.   Vol. 1: 8876
Carpenter Prize; Margaret Haley   Vol. 1: 11983
Carpenters Award   Vol. 2: 3623
Carr Award; Wilbur J.   Vol. 1: 19280
Carr Premium; Robert Alfred   Vol. 2: 3231
Carrel Prize; Alexis   Vol. 2: 6029
Carreno Competition for Composers; Inocente   Vol. 2: 12117
Carreno Latin American Competition for Piano; Teresa   Vol. 2: 12118
Carrier Award; ASHRAE - Willis H.   Vol. 1: 4576
Carriere; Prix Eugene   Vol. 2: 5850
Carriker, Jr. Memorial Award; Clyde   Vol. 1: 18729
Carringer Mental Health Journalism Award; Helen   Vol. 1: 14361
Carroll Advancement of Management Awards; Phil   Vol. 1: 17400
Carroll Foundation Award   Vol. 2: 2870
Carroll Literary Award; Little Big Horn Associates' John M.   Vol. 1: 11911
Carroll Prize; Mitchell B.   Vol. 2: 9511
Carron Award; I. Louis   Vol. 1: 18701
Carski Foundation Distinguished Teaching Award   Vol. 1: 4204
Carsoel; Prix Pierre   Vol. 2: 968
Carson Award; Ellis   Vol. 2: 2601
Carson Award; Rachel   Vol. 1: 11769
Carson Gold Memorial Short Story Competition Awards   Vol. 2: 371

Carson Outstanding Electrical Engineering Junior Award; Norman R.   Vol. 1: 9003
Carstensen Award in Agricultural History; Vernon   Vol. 1: 206
CART/PPG Indy Car World Series   Vol. 1: 12456
CART Series Special Awards   Vol. 1: 7516
Carta de Reconocimiento   Vol. 2: 10516
Cartan; Fondation Elie   Vol. 2: 5550
Carter Award; Amon G.   Vol. 1: 18644
Carter Award; Leona Lyons   Vol. 1: 3037
Carter Bronze Medal   Vol. 2: 2591
Carter - Menil Human Rights Prize   Vol. 1: 7326
Carter Supply Effectiveness Award; Maj. Gen. Warren R.   Vol. 1: 15772
Carter Trophy   Vol. 1: 10385
Cartianu Prize; George   Vol. 2: 10338
Cartwright Award; L. J.   Vol. 1: 6783
Cartwright Group Travelling Scholarship   Vol. 2: 2560
Cartwright Prize   Vol. 2: 3974
Carty Medal for the Advancement of Science; John J.   Vol. 1: 12664
Carus Lectures   Vol. 1: 3421
Carus-Medaille   Vol. 2: 6621
Carus Medal
    Deutsche Akademie der Naturforscher Leopoldina   Vol. 2: 6621
    Stadt Schweinfurt   Vol 2: 7104
Carus Preis   Vol. 2: 7104
Caruso International Jazz Trumpet Solo Competition; Carmine   Vol. 1: 11371
Caruthers Memorial Award; Jimmy   Vol. 1: 19016
Caruthers Memorial Championship Rookie Driver of the Year Award; Jimmy   Vol. 1: 19016
CASA/SME Industry LEAD Award   Vol. 1: 8078
CASA/SME University LEAD Award   Vol. 1: 8079
Casadesus International Piano Competition; Robert   Vol. 1: 7840
Casagrande International Piano Competition; Alessandro   Vol. 2: 8207
Casagrande Professional Development Award; Arthur   Vol. 1: 4445
Casals Violoncello Competition; Pablo   Vol. 2: 7414
Casasola Prize; Augustin   Vol. 2: 9081
Casati in Discipline Scientifiche; Premio di Laurea Luigi   Vol. 2: 8074
Casati in Discipline Uranistiche; Premio di Laurea Luigi   Vol. 2: 8075
Casavalle Prize; Carlos   Vol. 2: 26
CASE Achievement in Mobilizing Support (AIMS) Awards Program   Vol. 1: 8293
Case Medal; Cyrus Hall McCormick - Jerome Increase   Vol. 1: 4370
CASE Outstanding Administrator Award   Vol. 1: 8341
CASE Promising Leadership Award   Vol. 1: 8342
Casella International Piano Competition; Alfredo   Vol. 2: 8048
Casey Award   Vol. 1: 18333
Casey Award; Helen L.   Vol. 1: 6039
Casey Award in Letters; Bill   Vol. 1: 17047
Casey Minnesota Award; Ralph D.   Vol. 1: 10198
Casgrain Award; Therese   Vol. 1: 6720
Cash-In-A-Flash Award Program   Vol. 1: 19089
Cash Prize; Merrit H.   Vol. 1: 12196
Cash Prizes to Universities   Vol. 2: 7520
Casida Award; L. E.   Vol. 1: 4398

CASME Award   Vol. 2: 2646
Caso; Premio Alfonso   Vol. 2: 9053
Cass Correctional Achievement Award; E. R.   Vol. 1: 1832
Cassavetes Award; John   Vol. 1: 8606
Casselberry Award   Vol. 1: 2781
Cassels Memorial Award; Louis   Vol. 1: 16766
Cassin Competition; Rene   Vol. 2: 5092
Cassin; Prix Rene   Vol. 2: 5788
Castaneda; Premio Dr. Gonzalo   Vol. 2: 9101
Casteel Memorial Award; Marvin   Vol. 1: 11313
Castellani - Reiss Medal and Award   Vol. 2: 1721
Castello-Sanguinetto Prize   Vol. 2: 8197
Castelltort I Ferrer Trophy; Josep   Vol. 2: 11203
Castelo Branco Prize; Camilo   Vol. 2: 10319
Castex; Prix Amiral   Vol. 2: 5230
Castex; Prix Louis   Vol. 2: 5885
Castex Prize; Mariano R.   Vol. 2: 75
Castiau; Prix Adelson   Vol. 2: 977
Castiglioni Prize; AnnaMaria   Vol. 2: 8420
Castillejos; Premio Dr. Manuel J.   Vol. 2: 9103
Castle Corporation's Past President's Award   Vol. 1: 10743
Castle of Good Hope Decoration   Vol. 2: 10922
CASTME Awards   Vol. 2: 2646
Castner Lecture and Medal   Vol. 2: 4404
Castorena y Urzua; Juan Ignacio   Vol. 2: 9082
Castrol Award   Vol. 2: 3090
Castrol Gold Medal   Vol. 2: 3177
Catalan Biography Award   Vol. 2: 11136
Catalan; Prix Eugene   Vol. 2: 1020
Catalog of the Year Awards   Vol. 1: 13530
Catalonia Illustration Prize   Vol. 2: 11194
Catalonia International Award   Vol. 2: 11175
Catalonian Agriculture, Stock Farm, Forestry, Conservation of Nature and Fishing Awards   Vol. 2: 11170
Catalonian Certificate of Merit for Promotion of the Catalan Culture   Vol. 2: 11176
Catalonian Government Prize for Tourism   Vol. 2: 11177
Catalonian Government Prizes for Economic Energy Consumption and Diversification   Vol. 2: 11178
Catalonian Prize for Technical Application and Industrial Products   Vol. 2: 11179
Catalonian Prizes for Catalan Literature   Vol. 2: 11180
Catalonian Prizes for Cinematography   Vol. 2: 11181
Catalonian Prizes for Music   Vol. 2: 11182
Catalonian Prizes for Videography   Vol. 2: 11183
Catalunya; Gran Premio Generalitat de   Vol. 2: 11394
Catalunya Trophy; Generalitat de   Vol. 2: 11203
Catalyst Award   Vol. 1: 15369
Catalyst Awards   Vol. 1: 7572
Cate, Jr., Annual Research Fellowship; Weston A.   Vol. 1: 19989
Category A Fellowships   Vol. 2: 155
Category Awards   Vol. 1: 17048
Category B Fellowships   Vol. 2: 156
Catenacci; Prix   Vol. 2: 5367
Catenacci; Prix Hercule
    Institut de France   Vol. 2: 5343
    Institut de France - Academie des Sciences Morales et Politiques   Vol 2: 5757
    Institut de France - Academie Francaise   Vol 2: 5867

Award Index
Volume 2: International and Foreign — Certificate

Catey Awards Vol. 2: 2572
Catholic Book Awards Vol. 1: 7383
Catholic Pharmacist of the Year Vol. 1: 13558
Catlin Peace Pipe Award
  American Indian Lore Association Vol. 1: 2425
  Continental Confederation of Adopted Indians Vol 1: 8250
Cattell Cup Vol. 2: 4452
Cattell Early Career Award for Programmatic Research; Raymond B. Vol. 1: 1975
Cattell Memorial Award; McKeen Vol. 1: 1623
Catton Prize; Bruce Vol. 1: 17695
Catullus Prize Vol. 2: 4643
CATV Community Service Awards Vol. 1: 17043
Caty; Prix Charles Vol. 2: 953
Caudill Young Readers' Book Award; Rebecca Vol. 1: 7414
Caulfield, Jr. Medal for Exemplary Contributions to National Water Policy; Henry P. Vol. 1: 5003
CAUSE Award for Excellence in Campus Networking Vol. 1: 7416
CAUSE/EFFECT Contributor of the Year Award Vol. 1: 7417
CAUSE Exemplary Leadership and Information Technology Excellence Award (ELITE Award) Vol. 1: 7418
CAUSE Recognition Award for Excellence and Leadership Vol. 1: 7418
Cavaliere of the Order Star of Italian Solidarity Vol. 2: 8373
Cavallaro Medal
  European Federation of Corrosion Vol. 2: 6710
  Universita di Ferrara - Centro di Studi sulla Corrosione Vol 2: 8464
Cavallo Prize Vol. 1: 7420
Cavanaugh, C.S.C. Award; Rev. John J. Vol. 1: 19850
Cavanaugh Memorial Award; W. T. Vol. 1: 6040
Cavanaugh Memorial Prize; John Vol. 1: 14714
Cave Scholarship; Wilfrid Vol. 2: 3947
Cavender Award of Service; Maggie Vol. 1: 12577
Caveness, M.D. Memorial Award; William Fields Vol. 1: 14106
Caves Award; Philip K. Vol. 1: 11248
Cavett Award Vol. 1: 14843
Cavour Prize; Grinzane Vol. 2: 8187
Cawood Award; Harold Vol. 1: 1392
Cawood Japonica Award; Arminta Vol. 1: 1393
Cayeux; Fondation Lucien Vol. 2: 5624
CBC Honors Program Vol. 1: 7617
CBC Medal Vol. 1: 7712
CBC National Radio Competition for Young Composers Vol. 1: 6821
CBC Radio National Competition for Amateur Choirs Vol. 1: 6822
CBC Radio National Competition for Young Performers Vol. 1: 6823
CBC Radio/Saturday Night Magazine Literary Competition Vol. 1: 6824
CBC Radio Talent Competition Vol. 1: 6823
CBCF Lifetime Achievement Award Vol. 1: 8160
CBE Certificate of Appreciation Vol. 1: 8347
CBE Meritorious Award Vol. 1: 8348
CBI Award for Effective Communication Vol. 2: 3502
CBS - Pharmacia Award Vol. 1: 7164

CCA Excellence in Arts Journalism Vol. 1: 6839
CCB Award of Merit Vol. 1: 7059
CCCC Exemplar Award Vol. 1: 8134
CCCC Outstanding Book Award Vol. 1: 8135
CCCC Outstanding Dissertation Award Vol. 1: 8136
CCCC Richard Braddock Award Vol. 1: 13763
CCFC Book Prize Vol. 1: 8461
CCFC/CAG Student Research Award Vol. 1: 8462
CCIA Gavel Award Vol. 1: 8220
CCL Book of the Year Award Vol. 1: 8131
CCP Awards for Alternative Film and Video Vol. 2: 10046
CCP Awards for Radio Vol. 2: 10047
CCP Awards for Television Vol. 2: 10033
CCP Awards for the Arts Vol. 2: 10048
CCP Literary Awards Vol. 2: 10034
CDC Medal of Excellence Vol. 1: 19242
CEA Distinguished Service Award Vol. 1: 7893
CEA Honorary Life Membership Vol. 1: 7894
CEA Professional Achievement Award Vol. 1: 7895
CEA Whitworth Award Vol. 1: 6858
CEBA Awards (Communications Excellence to Black Audiences) Vol. 1: 20496
CEBA Honour List Vol. 2: 1116
Cecil Arthritis Medical Journalism Awards; Russell L. Vol. 1: 5302
Cecil Award; Lawrence K. Vol. 1: 2569
Cecil Writing Awards; Russell L. Vol. 1: 5302
CEE James N. Britton Award for Inquiry within the English Language Arts Vol. 1: 13764
CEE Richard Meade Award for Research in English Education Vol. 1: 13765
CEFIC Environment Award Vol. 2: 1129
CEIF Grand Prix Vol. 2: 2703
Celan-Preis; Paul Vol. 2: 6671
Celebrity of Tomorrow Vol. 1: 20506
Celette Prize Vol. 2: 3318
Cellier; Prix Alphonse Vol. 2: 5356
Cellular Pathology Prize Vol. 2: 3168
Cellular Toxicology Graduate Student Award Vol. 1: 18715
Celtic Cross Award Vol. 1: 7399
Cements Award Vol. 1: 1450
Cements Division Best Paper Award Vol. 1: 1449
Cena Beethovenova Hradce Vol. 2: 1858
Cena Chopinovy klavirni souteze Vol. 2: 1833
Cena Frana Kral'a Vol. 2: 10767
Cena Frantisek Kriegel Vol. 2: 11449
Cena Frica Kafendu Vol. 2: 10772
Cena Jana Levoslava Bellu Vol. 2: 10771
Cena Jaroslava Seiferta Vol. 2: 11450
Cena Josefa Havlicka Vol. 2: 1883
Cena L'dovita Fullu Vol. 2: 10765
Cena Narodneho vyboru hlavneho mesta Bratislavy Vol. 2: 10769
Cena Obce Architektu za Realizaci Roku Vol. 2: 1882
Cena Oskara Nedbala Vol. 2: 1850
Cena Pavla Orszagha Hviezdoslava Vol. 2: 10758
Cena Svazu ceskych architektu Vol. 2: 1884
Cena Trojruza Vol. 2: 10767
Cena Vilenica Vol. 2: 10755
Cena Vydavatel'stva Mlade leta Vol. 2: 10786
Cena Zvazu slovenskych spisovatelov Vol. 2: 10756
Cenafor Prize for a Monograph Vol. 2: 1431
Cendala Gomez; Premio al Merito Nacional Enfermera Isabel Vol. 2: 9128

Cenko Prize in Ukrainian Bibliography Vol. 1: 9822
Census Award of Excellence Vol. 1: 19093
Centenary Lectureship Vol. 2: 4193
Centenary Medal
  Royal Photographic Society of Great Britain Vol. 2: 4130
  Royal Scottish Geographical Society Vol 2: 10629
Centenary Medal and Lecture Vol. 2: 4405
Centennial Fellowship Vol. 1: 12185
Centennial Medal Vol. 1: 387
Center for Judaic Studies Post Doctoral Fellowships Vol. 1: 7439
Centorino Award; James Vol. 1: 14328
Central Banker of the Year Vol. 2: 2814
Central Poster Award Vol. 1: 7477
Centre of Art and Communication Awards Vol. 2: 42
Centres Premium Vol. 2: 3271
Centurion Award Vol. 1: 423
Century Awards Vol. 1: 17362
Century Club Award
  American Baseball Coaches Association Vol. 1: 1320
  American Numismatic Association Vol 1: 3207
CEO of the Year Vol. 1: 9213
Ceresis Award Vol. 2: 10018
CERT/Irish Life Souvenir of Ireland Challenge Vol. 2: 7802
Certamen Anual Nacional de Tesis de Ingenieria Vol. 2: 9033
Certamen Capitolinum Vol. 2: 8330
Certamen de video Elies Rogent de Rehabilitacio i Restauracio Vol. 2: 11207
Certamen Internacional de Cine Amateur Ciutat d'Igualada Vol. 2: 11203
Certamen Internacional de Curtmetratges i Video Vol. 2: 11205
Certamen Internacional de Guitarra Francisco Tarrega Vol. 2: 11153
Certamen Internacional de Masas Corales de Tolosa Vol. 2: 11197
Certamen Internacional de Video Vol. 2: 11234
Certamen International de Cine y Video Agrario Vol. 2: 11398
Certamen International de Films Cortos, Ciudad de Huesca Vol. 2: 11236
Certamen Nacional de Literatura *El Porvenir* Vol. 2: 8977
Certamen Nacional de Periodismo Rogelio Cantu Gomez Vol. 2: 8978
Certamen Nacional de Poesia, Alfonso Reyes Vol. 2: 9160
Certamen Nacional la Letra Impresa Vol. 2: 9251
Certamen National de Ensayos Sobre Politica Exterior Vol. 2: 1592
Certificado Especial Vol. 1: 10517
Certificate of Achievement
  Chesapeake and Ohio Historical Society Vol. 1: 7579
  Herb Society of America Vol 1: 9904
Certificate of Achievement of Focussed Studies Vol. 1: 74
Certificate of Advanced Pastoral Studies Vol. 1: 75
Certificate of Appreciation
  American Occupational Therapy Association Vol. 1: 3298
  American Police Hall of Fame Vol 1: 3549
  American Society of Artists Vol 1: 4405
  Arab Federation for Food Industries Vol 2: 7745

Certificate

Associated Exhibitors of the American Alliance for Health, Physical Education, Recreation and Dance   Vol 1: 5401
Blinded Veterans Association   Vol 1: 6404
Chesapeake and Ohio Historical Society   Vol 1: 7580
Construction Specifications Institute   Vol 1: 8201
Federal Aviation Administration   Vol 1: 9061
Federation of Genealogical Societies   Vol 1: 9122
The Gardners of America, Inc./Men's Garden Clubs of America   Vol 1: 9494
Herb Society of America   Vol 1: 9905
National Aeronautics and Space Administration   Vol 1: 12729
National Amputee Golf Association   Vol 1: 12780
National Carousel Association   Vol 1: 13522
National Police Officers Association of America   Vol 1: 14486
National Schools Committee for Economic Education   Vol 1: 14679
National Trappers Association   Vol 1: 14926
National Water Safety Congress   Vol 1: 14981
John Pelham Historical Association   Vol 1: 16012
Rural Sociological Society   Vol 1: 16973
Women Band Directors National Association   Vol 1: 20358
Certificate of Appreciation and Recognition   Vol. 1: 18280
Certificate of Appreciation for Meritorious Service   Vol. 1: 4245
Certificate of Botanical Recognition   Vol. 1: 3331
Certificate of Commendation
American Academy of Family Physicians   Vol. 1: 579
American Association for State and Local History   Vol 1: 875
American Institute of the History of Pharmacy   Vol 1: 2686
Federal Aviation Administration   Vol 1: 9062
The Gardners of America, Inc./Men's Garden Clubs of America   Vol 1: 9495
National Council on Family Relations   Vol 1: 13805
Royal Life Saving Society U.K.   Vol 2: 4100
Certificate of Conservation Awards   Vol. 1: 8175
Certificate of Craftsmanship   Vol. 1: 16417
Certificate of Cultural Merit   Vol. 1: 3332
Certificate of Honor
All-Union Leninist Young Communist League   Vol. 2: 10426
American Society for Advancement of Anesthesia in Dentistry   Vol 1: 4035
India - Office of the Prime Minister   Vol 2: 7550
International Institute of Space Law   Vol 2: 6031
Singapore - Office of the Prime Minister   Vol 2: 10736
Certificate of Honor - HSA   Vol. 1: 9971
Certificate of Honour   Vol. 2: 2057
Certificate of Horticultural Merit   Vol. 1: 3333
Certificate of Literature   Vol. 1: 16133
Certificate of Marriage Award   Vol. 1: 7106
Certificate of Merit
American Association of Teachers of German   Vol. 1: 1215

Awards, Honors & Prizes, 1995-96

American Equilibration Society   Vol 1: 2000
American Library Association - Armed Forces Libraries Round Table   Vol 1: 2843
American Red Cross   Vol 1: 3909
American Society for Engineering Education   Vol 1: 4076
American Society of International Law   Vol 1: 4629
Bookbuilders West   Vol 1: 6451
Canadian Public Health Association   Vol 1: 7107
Canadian Society of Animal Science   Vol 1: 7157
Catholic Library Association   Vol 1: 7377
Conference of Educational Administrators Serving the Deaf   Vol 1: 8119
Franklin Institute   Vol 1: 9377
Governor Baxter School for the Deaf   Vol 1: 9688
International Animated Film Society, ASIFA—Hollywood - ASIFA—Hollywood   Vol 1: 10608
International Tennis Hall of Fame   Vol 1: 11352
Knights Boxing Team International   Vol 1: 11713
Mathematical Association of America   Vol 1: 12130
National Association of the Physically Handicapped   Vol 1: 13354
National Environmental Health Association   Vol 1: 13905
National Police Officers Association of America   Vol 1: 14487
National Speleological Society   Vol 1: 14847
South African Association for the Advancement of Science   Vol 2: 11018
Union for the International Language IDO   Vol 2: 4563
United States Fencing Coaches Association   Vol 1: 19343
World Wildlife Fund   Vol 1: 20535
Zoological Society of Southern Africa   Vol 2: 11131
Certificate of Merit Award
National Geriatrics Society   Vol. 1: 14079
Precast/Prestressed Concrete Institute   Vol 1: 16370
Certificate of Merit - Commercial Wool Production in Canada   Vol. 1: 6831
Certificate of Merit for Marching Excellence   Vol. 1: 13427
Certificate of Merit for the Promotion of School Library Media Services   Vol. 1: 15607
Certificate of Merit for Zookeeper Education   Vol. 1: 1241
Certificate of Meritorious Arrangement   Vol. 1: 3334
Certificate of Meritorious Service   Vol. 1: 580
Certificate of Outstanding Work in the Field of Voluntary Service   Vol. 2: 5085
Certificate of Recognition
Florida Audubon Society   Vol. 1: 9251
The Gardners of America, Inc./Men's Garden Clubs of America   Vol 1: 9496
National Recreation and Park Association - National Therapeutic Recreation Society   Vol 1: 14571
Certificate of Victory   Vol. 1: 14096
Certificates of Appreciation, Citations, Commendations, First Class Skier Award   Vol. 1: 17226
Certificates of Honor and Appreciation   Vol. 1: 1737

Certificates of Merit
Football Writers Association of America   Vol. 1: 9305
Institute of Engineers and Technicians   Vol 2: 3091
National Academy of Design   Vol 1: 12604
Certificates of Merit Awards - Regional History   Vol. 1: 6904
Certificates of Merit for Excellence in Writing - *Journal of Allied Health*   Vol. 1: 5944
Certificates of Recognition   Vol. 1: 14946
Certificates of Recognition/Appreciation   Vol. 1: 3763
Certified Kapnismologist Award   Vol. 1: 16226
CERTIFIED PROPERTY MANAGER (CPM) of the Year Award   Vol. 1: 10435
Certified Remodeler (CR) "Superstar" Award   Vol. 1: 13357
Cervantes Prize for Literature; Miguel   Vol. 2: 11368
Cervi Award; Eugene   Vol. 1: 11303
Cesar Awards   Vol. 2: 4793
Cesar Machado de Jornalismo; Premio Municipal Julio   Vol. 2: 10273
Cesery Award   Vol. 1: 18709
Cetus Corporation Biotechnology Research Award   Vol. 1: 4205
Cetus Corporation Grant for Research Involving Biotherapy or Immunotherapy; Oncology Nursing Foundation/   Vol. 1: 15641
Cevenini; Premio Angela   Vol. 2: 8356
Cevenini Prize; Angela   Vol. 2: 8356
Ceylon Development Engineering Award   Vol. 2: 11402
CFA Distinguished Service Award   Vol. 1: 8223
CFA Scholar-Athlete Team Award; Hitachi/   Vol. 1: 7900
CFDA Fashion Awards   Vol. 1: 8355
CFIC Book Prize   Vol. 1: 8461
CFIC/CAG Student Research Award   Vol. 1: 8462
CFL Outstanding Player Awards   Vol. 1: 6871
CFM Award   Vol. 1: 5761
CFM Contributor's Prize   Vol. 1: 6864
CFP Research Award   Vol. 1: 7920
CFS Medal   Vol. 1: 5042
CFTPA Achievement Awards   Vol. 1: 6866
CFUW A. Vibert Douglas International Fellowship   Vol. 2: 11789
CGS Graduate Student Paper Award   Vol. 1: 6894
CGS Prize   Vol. 1: 6895
Ch2M-Hill/AEEP Doctoral Thesis Award   Vol. 1: 5780
Chabas; Prix Paul   Vol. 2: 5417
Chabon Award; Irwin   Vol. 1: 5380
Chabrol; Prix Etienne   Vol. 2: 4838
Chacko Award; I. C.   Vol. 2: 7701
Chaconia Medal of the Order of the Trinity   Vol. 2: 12033
Chadwick Educator's Award; L. C.   Vol. 1: 1066
Chai Award   Vol. 1: 6419
Chain and Simcha Tova Mizel Memorial Exhibit Award; Menachem   Vol. 1: 3208
Chainlink Fence Design Award   Vol. 1: 7498
Chair of Music   Vol. 1: 10956
Chairman of the Board Awards, Competition Division   Vol. 1: 6234
Chairman's Award
Aluminum Company of America   Vol. 1: 382
American Academy of Medical Administrators   Vol 1: 594
American Association of Engineering Societies   Vol 1: 998

American Chamber of Commerce Executives   Vol 1: 1480
   Goodwill Industries International Inc.   Vol 1: 9656
   International Society of Certified Electronics Technicians   Vol 1: 11281
   Literacy Volunteers of America   Vol 1: 11900
   Machine Vision Association of the Society of Manufacturing Engineers   Vol 1: 11992
   National Association of Television Program Executives International   Vol 1: 13339
   National Kidney Foundation   Vol 1: 14269
   National Religious Broadcasters   Vol 1: 14604
   Outdoor Advertising Association of America   Vol 1: 15857
   Society of Cable Television Engineers   Vol 1: 17795
Chairman's Awards   Vol. 1: 16568
Chairman's Citation of Merit Awards   Vol. 1: 273
Chairman's Safety Award   Vol. 1: 16748
Chairman's Special Award   Vol. 1: 19352
Chair's Citation   Vol. 1: 1007
Chakravarty Awards; Prof. Hira Lal   Vol. 2: 7683
Challenge for Road Safety   Vol. 2: 5974
Challenge of Excellence Award   Vol. 1: 13183
Challenge Shield   Vol. 2: 3661
Challenge Trophies   Vol. 1: 2019
Challenger Award   Vol. 1: 13520
Chalmers Award for Crafts; Jean A.   Vol. 1: 15692
Chalmers Award for Creativity in Dance; Jean A.   Vol. 1: 15693
Chalmers Award for Distinction in Choreography; Jean A.   Vol. 1: 15694
Chalmers Award for Visual Arts; Jean A.   Vol. 1: 15695
Chalmers Awards for Musical Composition; Jean A.   Vol. 1: 15696
Chalmers Canadian Children's Play Awards   Vol. 1: 15697
Chalmers Canadian Play Awards; Floyd S.   Vol. 1: 15698
Chalmers Choreographic Award; Jean A.   Vol. 1: 15699
Chalmers Memorial Medal   Vol. 2: 4276
Chalmers National Music Award; Jean A.   Vol. 1: 15700
Chalmers Performing Arts Training Grants   Vol. 1: 15701
Chamber Music America Commissioning Program   Vol. 1: 7500
Chamber Music Chicago Discovery Competition   Vol. 1: 7505
Chamber Music Society of the Monterey Peninsula Competition   Vol. 1: 7511
Chamber Music Yellow Springs Competition   Vol. 1: 7507
Chamber Opera Competition   Vol. 1: 14405
Chamberlain Award; C. K.   Vol. 1: 8783
Chambers Award; Frank A.   Vol. 1: 217
Chamois Top Obedience Award   Vol. 1: 3984
Champion Bird   Vol. 1: 20066
Champion of Champions   Vol. 1: 3412
Champion of the Arts Award   Vol. 1: 15246
Champion Outstanding Player of the Year   Vol. 1: 14266
Champion Player of the Year Award   Vol. 1: 12563
Champion Shots Medal   Vol. 2: 338
Championnats d'Europe de Rink-Hockey   Vol. 2: 5118
Championnats Internationaux de France   Vol. 2: 5259

Champions of Higher Independent Education in Florida (C.H.I.E.F.) Awards   Vol. 1: 10116
Championship Award   Vol. 1: 19706
Championship Awards   Vol. 1: 18256
Championship Director Awards, Competition Division   Vol. 1: 6235
Championship of Champions   Vol. 1: 19526
Championship Silver Challenge Trophy   Vol. 2: 3674
The Championships, Wimbledon   Vol. 2: 2053
Chamrousse International Festival of Comedy Films   Vol. 2: 5028
Chancellor's Medal   Vol. 1: 7766
Chandler Award; Paulette   Vol. 1: 8339
Chandler Medal; Charles Frederick   Vol. 1: 7978
Chandler - Misener Award   Vol. 1: 10640
Chandra Bose Medal; Jagdish   Vol. 2: 7642
Chang Award for Lipid or Flavor Science; Stephen S.   Vol. 1: 10342
Chang Award; Stephen S.   Vol. 1: 3314
Channel 4 Film Awards   Vol. 2: 2693
Chant Medal of the Royal Astronomical Society of Canada   Vol. 1: 16926
Chanute Award; Octave   Vol. 1: 2457
Chanute Medal; Octave   Vol. 1: 20222
Chapbook Award; Amelia   Vol. 1: 474
Chapin Award for Contributions to Humanity; Harry   Vol. 1: 12838
Chapin Award for Volunteers in the Arts; Elizabeth   Vol. 1: 7714
Chapin Award; Harold C.   Vol. 1: 1220
Chapin Humanitarian Award; Harry   Vol. 1: 13279
Chapin Media Awards; Harry   Vol. 1: 20493
Chapin Self-Reliance Award; Harry   Vol. 1: 20494
Chaplain Emeritus Award   Vol. 1: 7915
Chaplain of the Year   Vol. 1: 18932
Chaplin Award; Charles   Vol. 2: 10541
Chaplin Prize   Vol. 2: 11458
Chaplin Prize; Charlie   Vol. 2: 1520
Chapman-Franzmeier Memorial Award   Vol. 1: 922
Chapman Medal   Vol. 2: 3937
Chapman Medal; R. W.   Vol. 2: 430
Chapman Memorial Award; Charles F.   Vol. 1: 14334
Chapman Memorial Fund Award; Frank M.   Vol. 1: 3152
Chapman Memorial Prize; John H.   Vol. 1: 18259
Chapman Prize Essay   Vol. 2: 2525
Chapter Achievement Award   Vol. 1: 8698
Chapter Activities Award   Vol. 1: 1779
Chapter Activity Award Contest   Vol. 1: 9066
Chapter Award   Vol. 1: 17083
Chapter Award for Excellence in Educational Programming   Vol. 1: 10937
Chapter Award for Excellence in Membership Marketing   Vol. 1: 10938
Chapter Award for Excellence in Newsletter Publishing   Vol. 1: 10939
Chapter Award for Minority Enhancement   Vol. 1: 3479
Chapter Awards
   Society of Logistics Engineers   Vol. 1: 17866
   Tau Beta Pi Association   Vol 1: 18574
Chapter Competition   Vol. 1: 10386
Chapter Excellence   Vol. 1: 2200
Chapter Excellence Awards and Chapter of the Year Award   Vol. 1: 2985
Chapter History Award   Vol. 1: 6336
Chapter Hope Chest Award   Vol. 1: 14382
Chapter Member-of-The-Year Award   Vol. 1: 4165

Chapter Merit Award   Vol. 1: 17484
Chapter Merit Awards   Vol. 1: 13345
Chapter Merit Awards for Students   Vol. 1: 17485
Chapter of the Year
   Alpha Epsilon Rho - The National Broadcasting Society   Vol. 1: 345
   ASPO/Lamaze   Vol 1: 5381
   Association for Practitioners in Infection Control   Vol 1: 5577
   Association of Records Managers and Administrators - ARMA International   Vol 1: 5937
   Florida Audubon Society   Vol 1: 9252
   Hospitality Sales and Marketing Association International   Vol 1: 10000
   Meeting Planners International   Vol 1: 12203
   National Property Management Association   Vol 1: 14541
   System Safety Society   Vol 1: 18556
   United States Hang Gliding Association   Vol 1: 19367
Chapter of the Year Award
   American Society for Information Science   Vol. 1: 4166
   American Society of Certified Engineering Technicians   Vol 1: 4417
   International Facility Management Association   Vol 1: 10940
   Mail Systems Management Association   Vol 1: 12014
   Numerical Control Society/Association for Integrated Manufacturing Technology   Vol 1: 15555
Chapter of the Year - International and Regional   Vol. 1: 6654
Chapter or Unit Awards   Vol. 1: 1161
Chapter President of the Year   Vol. 1: 7664
Chapter Presidents Trophy Award   Vol. 1: 11412
Chapter Program of the Year   Vol. 1: 5382
Chapter Publications Contest   Vol. 1: 10370
Chapter Research Award   Vol. 1: 10371
Chapter Service Award   Vol. 1: 5815
Chapter Service Awards   Vol. 1: 7816
Chapter SHRM/Olsten Pinnacle Awards   Vol. 1: 17486
Chapter Sports and Recreation Award   Vol. 1: 15935
Chapter Technical Excellence Awards   Vol. 1: 8196
Chapter Volunteer of the Year   Vol. 1: 5383
Chapters Council Award   Vol. 1: 10310
Charamis Medal   Vol. 2: 1135
Charcot Award; J. B.   Vol. 1: 17310
Charcot Award; Jean-Martin   Vol. 2: 3417
Chard Decoration; John   Vol. 2: 10923
Chard Medal; John   Vol. 2: 10924
Charity Accounts Award   Vol. 2: 3081
Charles Lifetime Achievement Award; Ray   Vol. 1: 16832
Charles River Prize   Vol. 1: 4984
The Charlie Local and National Comedy Awards   Vol. 1: 5748
Charlier-Anciaux; Prix Alix   Vol. 2: 1291
Charlotte Festival/New Plays in America   Vol. 1: 7521
Charlson Award; Jim   Vol. 1: 5675
Charm Prize; Philip   Vol. 1: 6213
Charmian Medal   Vol. 2: 4219
Charney Award; Jule G.   Vol. 1: 3080
Charpentier; Concours International de Harpe Louise   Vol. 2: 5210
Chartered Institute of Journalists Gold Medal   Vol. 2: 2584

Chartered State Association Executive Director of the Year   Vol. 1: 13483
Chartered State Association of the Year   Vol. 1: 13484
Chartered State Association President of the Year   Vol. 1: 13485
Chartier; Prix   Vol. 2: 5369
Chartres International Organ Competition   Vol. 2: 4936
Chase Award for Physician Executive Excellence; John D.   Vol. 1: 5878
Chase Award; Joe   Vol. 1: 16437
Chase Award; Joe M.   Vol. 1: 9242
Chasko Distinguished Service Award; Lawrence J.   Vol. 1: 1017
Chasman Scholarship for Women; Renate W.   Vol. 1: 6586
Chassie Awards; RAB   Vol. 1: 16632
Chateauneuf-du-Pape Grand Prize   Vol. 2: 6306
Chatelain Award; Leon   Vol. 1: 13867
Chattanooga Research Award   Vol. 1: 3480
Chatterjee Memorial Lecture; Dr. G. P.   Vol. 2: 7643
Chatterjee Memorial Medal; A. N.   Vol. 2: 7469
Chaudesaigues; Prix   Vol. 2: 5370
Chauleur; Prix Pierre   Vol. 2: 6136
Chautauqua National Exhibition of American Art   Vol. 1: 7528
Chauveau Medal; Pierre   Vol. 1: 16950
Chauvenet Prize   Vol. 1: 12131
Chavee; Prix Honore   Vol. 2: 5464
Chavez; Premio Maestro Ignacio   Vol. 2: 9277
Chavez Prize; Ferreira   Vol. 2: 10301
Chavez Young Investigator Award; Professor Ignacio   Vol. 2: 9073
Chayefsky Laurel Award for Television; Paddy   Vol. 1: 20557
CHEA/ACEF Major Body of Research Accomplishments Award   Vol. 1: 6912
CHEA Honor Awards   Vol. 1: 6913
Chedanne; Fondation   Vol. 2: 5388
Chedoudi; Prix Jocelyn   Vol. 2: 4852
Cheek Exemplary Service Award; Willard L.   Vol. 1: 4077
Cheese Hunt Chase   Vol. 2: 7834
Chef Ireland
   Chefs & Cooks Circle   Vol. 2: 2611
   National Restaurant Association   Vol 1: 14623
   Panel of Chefs of Ireland   Vol 2: 7817
   Singapore Chefs Association   Vol 2: 10752
   Society of German Cooks   Vol 2: 7090
   Society of Swiss Cuisiniers   Vol 2: 11911
Cheiron Medal   Vol. 2: 9692
Chelsea Award   Vol. 1: 7531
Chemeca Medal   Vol. 2: 431
Chemeca Student Design Prize   Vol. 2: 432
The Chemical Bank Awards for Distinguished Newspaper Art Criticism   Vol. 1: 7533
Chemical Cleaning/Trigon Packaging Achievement Award   Vol. 2: 9713
Chemical Education Medal   Vol. 2: 11046
Chemical Health and Safety Award   Vol. 1: 1489
Chemical Industry Medal   Vol. 2: 4406
Chemical Industry Medal of the American Section   Vol. 1: 17802
Chemical Institute of Canada Awards for High School Chemistry Teachers   Vol. 1: 7546
Chemical Institute of Canada Medal   Vol. 1: 7547
Chemical Pioneer Awards   Vol. 1: 2611
Chemical Society of Japan Award   Vol. 2: 8512

Chemical Society of Japan Award for Chemical Education   Vol. 2: 8513
Chemical Society of Japan Award for Distinguished Technical Achievements   Vol. 2: 8514
Chemical Society of Japan Award for Technological Development   Vol. 2: 8515
Chemical Society of Japan Award for Young Chemists   Vol. 2: 8516
Chemical Society of Japan Award of Merits for Chemical Education   Vol. 2: 8517
Chemical Technology Award   Vol. 2: 8941
Cheney Award; Frances Neel   Vol. 1: 18614
Chennault Award; Lt. General Claire Lee   Vol. 1: 236
Chennault Trophy   Vol. 1: 5281
Chercheur; Prix Jeune   Vol. 2: 6352
Cherian Memorial Award; Dr. P. V.   Vol. 2: 7581
Cherokee National Hall of Fame   Vol. 1: 7577
Cherry Award for Great Teachers; Robert Foster   Vol. 1: 6295
Cherry Chair for Distinguished Teaching; Robert Foster   Vol. 1: 6296
Cherry Prize; Professor J.   Vol. 2: 3294
Cherry Student Prize; T. M.   Vol. 2: 122
Cherry Tree Marathon   Vol. 1: 15270
Chesneau; Prix Marc   Vol. 2: 6337
Chesney Memorial Gold Medal   Vol. 2: 4294
Chess Awards   Vol. 2: 7521
Chess Journalism Merit Awards Competition   Vol. 1: 7586
Chess Olympiad for the Blind   Vol. 2: 11472
Chess World Champions   Vol. 2: 7224
Chetwynd Award for Entrepreneurial Excellence   Vol. 1: 6867
Chevalier de l'Ordre de la Saint Croix de Jerusalem   Vol. 2: 8476
Chevalier; Fondation Auguste   Vol. 2: 5498
Chevallier; Prix Jean-Baptiste   Vol. 2: 5759
Chevassu; Prix Jeanne et Maurice   Vol. 2: 4851
Cheverus Medal   Vol. 1: 18885
Chevron Conservation Awards   Vol. 1: 7588
Chevron - Times Mirror Magazines Conservation Awards   Vol. 1: 7588
Chevron U.S.A. Marketing Award   Vol. 1: 14312
Chia Hsin Prize   Vol. 2: 11994
Chicago Film Critics Awards - Chicago Flame   Vol. 1: 7604
Chicago Folklore Prize   Vol. 1: 19765
Chicago International Children's Film Festival   Vol. 1: 7606
Chicago International Festival of Children's Films   Vol. 1: 7606
Chicago International Film Festival   Vol. 1: 7701
Chick Trophy; John   Vol. 1: 2321
Chicken Little Award   Vol. 1: 12786
Chief of Engineers Award of Excellence   Vol. 1: 19006
Chief of Engineers Design and Environmental Awards Program   Vol. 1: 19006
Chief of the South African Defense Force Commendation Medal   Vol. 2: 10935
Chiff Award   Vol. 2: 675
Chiiki Koryu Shinko Sho   Vol. 2: 8614
Child Advocate of the Year   Vol. 1: 15409
Child and Adolescent Service System Program Award   Vol. 1: 530
Child Award; Julia   Vol. 1: 10711
Child Cookbook Awards; Julia   Vol. 1: 10711
Child Study Children's Book Award   Vol. 1: 7613
Childers Award for Distinguished Graduate Teaching; Norman F.   Vol. 1: 4149

Childers, Jr., Award; Waco F.   Vol. 1: 2397
Children's Abby Award   Vol. 1: 1362
Children's Book Award
   Association of Jewish Libraries   Vol. 1: 5846
   Federation of Children's Book Groups   Vol 2: 2874
Children's Book Bridges   Vol. 1: 7618
Children's Book Council Award   Vol. 2: 7735
Children's Book Prize
   Swedish Society for Promotion of Literature   Vol. 2: 11642
   West Coast Book Prize Society   Vol 1: 20185
Children's Books Open Door Competition   Vol. 1: 13766
Children's Choice Election   Vol. 1: 9797
Children's Express Journalism Award   Vol. 1: 7620
Children's Literature Association Award for Literary Criticism   Vol. 1: 7624
Children's Literature Association Book Award   Vol. 1: 7625
Children's Literature Association Research Grants   Vol. 1: 7626
Children's Literature Festival Award   Vol. 1: 11656
Children's Novel Writing Competition   Vol. 2: 8902
Children's Reading Round Table Award   Vol. 1: 7631
Children's Story Prize   Vol. 2: 9047
Children's TV Hall of Fame   Vol. 1: 112
Children's Wish Foundation International Award   Vol. 1: 7633
Childs Award; James Bennett   Vol. 1: 2894
Childs Award; James Lawton   Vol. 1: 20094
Chilean Academy of Language Prize   Vol. 2: 1551
Chilean Society Awards for Scientific Works   Vol. 2: 1555
Chilmark Award by Lance   Vol. 1: 14714
Chilton Prize; Ken   Vol. 1: 16927
Chin Memorial Award; Robert   Vol. 1: 17632
China Service Medal - Navy, Marine Corps, Coast Guard   Vol. 1: 19143
China Stamp Society Special Award   Vol. 1: 7637
Chinard Prizes; Gilbert   Vol. 1: 17461
Chinese-American Librarians Association Distinguished Service Award   Vol. 1: 7640
Chinese American Medical Society Scientific Achievement Award   Vol. 1: 7642
Chinese Chemical Society Awards   Vol. 2: 1572
Chinese Martial Arts Leadership Award   Vol. 1: 424
Chinese Martial Arts Outstanding Service Award   Vol. 1: 425
Chipman Award; John   Vol. 1: 11459
Chipp Memorial Award; Rodney D.   Vol. 1: 18100
Chiron Corporation Biotechnology Research Award   Vol. 1: 4205
Chiron Therapeutics Award for Excellence of Scholarship and Consistency of Contribution to the Oncology Nursing Literature; ONS/   Vol. 1: 15653
Chiron Therapeutics Chapter Excellence Award; ONS/   Vol. 1: 15654
Chiron Therapeutics Susan Baird Excellence in Writing Awards in Clinical Practice and Nursing Research; ONS/   Vol. 1: 15655
Chiropractor of the Year
   Chiropractic Association of South Africa   Vol. 2: 10834

International Chiropractors Association Vol 1: 10835
Chisholm Award for Lifetime Contribution; Jack Vol. 1: 6868
Chivalry Cross of the Order of Polish State Renascence Vol. 2: 10166
Chivas Regal Young Entrepreneur Awards Vol. 1: 17157
Chivas Regal Young Entrepreneurs of the Year Vol. 1: 17157
ChLA Research Fellowships Vol. 1: 7626
Choco Magico Folklorico Vol. 2: 1658
Choice Outstanding Academic Books and Nonprint Materials Vol. 1: 7646
Choice's Outstanding Academic Books Vol. 1: 7646
Choku Prize Vol. 2: 8676
Cholmondeley Award for Poets Vol. 2: 4388
Chon'guk Kugak Kyongyon Tachoe Vol. 2: 8834
Chopin Competition; Warsaw Vol. 2: 6594
Chopin; Grand Prix du Disque Frederic Vol. 2: 10066
Chopin-Klavierwettbewerb; Europaischer Vol. 2: 6594
Chopin Piano Competition, Czechoslovakia Vol. 2: 1833
Chopin Prize Vol. 1: 7840
Chopin Society Young Pianist's Competition Vol. 1: 7652
Chopinovy klavirni souteze; Cena Vol. 2: 1833
Choppin Memorial Award; IEA - Bruce H. Vol. 2: 9465
Chopra Lecture; Bashambar Nath Vol. 2: 7644
Chorbachi Prizes; The Walid Vol. 2: 10556
Choreography and Flamenco Dance Competition Vol. 1: 8892
Choreography Fellowship Vol. 1: 1928
Chorpenning Playwright Award; Charlotte B. Vol. 1: 772
Chorus Prize Vol. 1: 6822
Chow Chow Club Annual Awards Vol. 1: 7659
Chree Medal and Prize; Charles Vol. 2: 3187
CHRIE Achievement Award Vol. 1: 8398
CHRIE Industry Recognition Award Vol. 1: 8399
Chris Statuette Vol. 1: 9186
Christchurch International Amateur Film Festival Awards Vol. 2: 9711
Christensen Memorial Exhibit Award; Henry Vol. 1: 3209
Christensen Memorial Prize; F. G. Vol. 2: 589
Christian Management Award Vol. 1: 7665
Christian Stewardship Award Vol. 1: 13563
Christian Values Writing Contest Vol. 1: 6557
Christie Award; John Vol. 2: 2938
Christman Award; Luther Vol. 1: 816
Christopher Awards Vol. 1: 7669
Christophers Medal; Sir Rickard Vol. 2: 4277
Christopherson Lectureship Award; E. H. Vol. 1: 667
Christus Magister Award Vol. 1: 11977
Chronicle of Komsomol Honor Vol. 2: 10427
Chrysler Corporation Cup Vol. 1: 20545
Chrysler Triple Crown Challenge Vol. 1: 18814
Chungshan Cultural Foundation Prizes Vol. 2: 11998
Church Medal; Edwin F. Vol. 1: 4668
Church Prose Memorial Prize; Hubert Vol. 2: 9778
Churchill Award; H. V. Vol. 1: 6041
Churchill Award; Harold E. Vol. 1: 18502

Churchill Award; Winston
  Winston Churchill Foundation of the United States Vol. 1: 7682
  International Platform Association Vol 1: 11147
Churchill Cup Vol. 1: 6966
Churchill Medal Vol. 2: 4441
Churchill Memorial Award; Winston Vol. 1: 13570
Churchman, Churchwoman of the Year Vol. 1: 16772
CIA Merit Awards Vol. 2: 814
Cianci; Premio Maria Vol. 2: 8304
Ciani International Competition for Young Pianists; Dino Vol. 2: 8189
Ciani; Premio Dino Vol. 2: 8189
Ciapetta Lectureship in Catalysis; F. G. Vol. 1: 7342
Ciardi; Fondazione Professor Giuseppe Vol. 2: 1204
C.I.A.U. Media Award Vol. 1: 6967
CIAU Player of the Year Vol. 1: 9960
CIB Developing Countries Fellowships Vol. 2: 9482
CIBA-GEIGY Award Vol. 1: 3520
CIBA-GEIGY Award for Best Controlled Clinical Trial Vol. 2: 6968
CIBA-GEIGY/Award in Agronomy Vol. 1: 4382
CIBA-GEIGY Corporation Vol. 1: 7684
CIBA-GEIGY Exemplary Elementary Science Teaching Award Vol. 1: 14697
CIBA-GEIGY Exemplary High School Science Teaching Award Vol. 1: 14698
CIBA-GEIGY Exemplary Middle/Junior High School Science Teaching Award Vol. 1: 14699
CIBA-GEIGY Exemplary Middle Level Science Teaching Award Vol. 1: 14699
CIBA-GEIGY ILAR Rheumatology Prize Vol. 2: 11674
CIBA-GEIGY Nematology Award Vol. 1: 17935
CIBA Medal and Prize Vol. 2: 2170
CIBA Plant Protection Agricultural Writing Award Vol. 1: 7684
CIBA Plant Protection American Phytopathological Society Award Vol. 1: 7685
CIBA Plant Protection Award in Agronomy Vol. 1: 7686
CIBA Plant Protection Entomological Society of America Award Vol. 1: 7687
CIBA Plant Protection NACAA Agricultural Award Vol. 1: 7688
CIBA Plant Protection NAFB Farm Broadcasting Award Vol. 1: 7689
CIBA Plant Protection Weed Science Society of America Award Vol. 1: 7690
CIBC National Music Festival
  CIBC National Music Festival Vol. 1: 7692
  Saskatchewan Music Festival Association Vol. 1: 17064
CIC Fellowship Vol. 1: 7548
CICAE Prize Vol. 2: 6564
Ciccoli Joint Operations Award Vol. 1: 5284
Cichan Award Vol. 1: 6476
Ciclo Internacional de Cine Submarino Vol. 2: 11353
CIDA Awards for Canadians Vol. 1: 6826
CIDA Awards for Professionals Vol. 1: 6827
CIDALC Prize Vol. 2: 7431
Cidermaker of the Year Vol. 1: 2344
CIERSES Awards Vol. 2: 6022
CIFEJ Prize Vol. 2: 6564
Cillie Award; C. G. Vol. 2: 11121
CIM/EMR Journalism Awards Vol. 1: 6934

CIM Fellowship Vol. 1: 6935
CINANIMA Vol. 2: 10226
Cincinnati Opera Outreach Program Vol. 1: 7699
Cinderella Stamp Club Trophy Vol. 2: 3781
CINDY Awards Vol. 1: 6002
CINE Eagle Award Vol. 1: 8408
CINE Golden Eagle Award Vol. 1: 8409
CINOA Art History Prize Vol. 1: 5289
CINOA Award Vol. 2: 3391
Cintas Foundation Fellowships Vol. 1: 10377
Cioffrese Prizes for Health Care; Cecilia Vol. 2: 8225
CIOS Gold Medal Vol. 2: 8908
Cipariu Prize; Timotei Vol. 2: 10339
Circulation Council Awards Vol. 1: 15332
Circus Hall of Fame Vol. 1: 7708
Cirrus Cup Vol. 1: 3984
CIS/ALA GODORT Documents to the People Award Vol. 1: 2895
CIS/GODORT/ALA Award Vol. 1: 2895
CISAC Prize Vol. 2: 5995
CISLB Awards Vol. 2: 1179
Cisneros Award; Rosa Vol. 1: 11143
CISS Medallions of Honor Vol. 2: 1960
Citation Vol. 1: 8197
Citation Award Vol. 1: 10761
Citation for Bravery Vol. 1: 14488
Citation for Distinguished Leadership and Service Vol. 1: 4868
Citation for Distinguished Service Vol. 1: 7803
Citation for Distinguished Service to Art and Artists and the Community Vol. 1: 4533
Citation for Excellence in Community Architecture Vol. 1: 2534
Citation for Excellence in Total Design Vol. 1: 15274
Citation for Exceptional Leadership and Merit Vol. 1: 4868
Citation for Felony Arrests Vol. 1: 14489
Citation for Leadership and Service
  Conference of Educational Administrators Serving the Deaf Vol. 1: 8120
  Governor Baxter School for the Deaf Vol 1: 9689
Citation for Meritorious Service
  American Hospital Association Vol. 1: 2370
  President's Committee on Employment of People with Disabilities Vol 1: 16382
Citation for Outstanding Achievement Vol. 1: 7086
Citation for Public Service Vol. 1: 3005
Citation of a Layman for Distinguished Service Vol. 1: 3021
Citation of Appreciation Vol. 1: 11794
Citation of Excellence Vol. 1: 13428
Citation of Excellence in Advertising Vol. 1: 20145
Citation of Honor
  Air Force Association Vol. 1: 237
  Associated Church Press Vol 1: 5396
  International Information Management Congress Vol 1: 11045
  National Association for Creative Children and Adults Vol 1: 12852
Citation of Merit
  International Association of Personnel in Employment Security Vol. 1: 10774
  Pacific Arts Association Vol 2: 577
Citation of Merit Award Vol. 1: 20359
Citation of Special Recognition Vol. 1: 5423
Citation to a Senior Scholar Vol. 1: 17545
Citations Vol. 1: 13019
Citations of Merit Vol. 1: 12819
Citations pour Service Eminent Vol. 1: 7086
Citibank Choral Awards Vol. 2: 319

Citicorp/Wriston Fellowship   Vol. 1: 12031
Citizen Awareness of the Law Award   Vol. 1: 2790
Citizen Exchange Council Award   Vol. 1: 7710
Citizen Involvement Program Excellence Award   Vol. 1: 10851
Citizen of the Year
  American Association of Dental Examiners   Vol. 1: 990
  Center for Philosophy, Law Citizenship   Vol 1: 7445
  Knights Boxing Team International   Vol 1: 11714
Citizen of the Year Award   Vol. 1: 7743
Citizen of the Year Conservation Award   Vol. 1: 2096
Citizens Europe Prize   Vol. 2: 5087
Citizens Savings Athletic Foundation Gymnastics Hall of Fame   Vol. 1: 12998
Citizenship Award
  The Arc   Vol. 1: 5209
  Towing and Recovery Association of America   Vol 1: 18770
Citizensip Education Program Excellence Award   Vol. 1: 10851
Citra Award   Vol. 2: 7733
City Livability Awards Program   Vol. 1: 19064
City Medallion   Vol. 1: 7739
City of Alessandria International Competition in Classical Guitar   Vol. 2: 8201
City of Brisbane Short Story Award   Vol. 2: 292
City of Cardiff International Poetry Competition   Vol. 2: 12194
City of Huy Prize   Vol. 2: 1160
City of Lisbon Literary Prize   Vol. 2: 10308
City of London Carl Flesch International Violin Competition   Vol. 2: 2630
City of London Walther Gruner International Lieder Competition   Vol. 2: 2632
City of Munich Prizes   Vol. 2: 7019
City of Paris Grand Prize   Vol. 2: 5034
City of Paris Photography Award; Air France/   Vol. 2: 6146
City of Sacile Prize   Vol. 2: 8094
City of Sondrio Gold Plaque   Vol. 2: 8433
City of Sondrio Invitational Award   Vol. 2: 8433
City of Sorrento Prize   Vol. 2: 8436
City of Springvale 21-26 Award   Vol. 2: 317
City of Springvale Open Award   Vol. 2: 317
City of Springvale Short Story Awards   Vol. 2: 317
City of Sydney Ballet Scholarship   Vol. 2: 320
City of Sydney Eisteddfod Pianoforte Scholarship   Vol. 2: 321
City of Sydney Piano Scholarship   Vol. 2: 321
City of Toronto Apprenticeship Screen Award   Vol. 1: 7756
City of Toronto Awards for Excellence in Fashion Design   Vol. 1: 7757
City of Toronto Book Awards   Vol. 1: 7758
City of Vienna Prizes for Art, Science, and Humanities   Vol. 2: 789
City of Vienna Prizes for Books for Children and Young People   Vol. 2: 790
City of Vienna Promotional Prizes   Vol. 2: 791
Ciutat d'Igualada Grand Prize   Vol. 2: 11203
Civic Award Citation   Vol. 1: 11968
Civic Leadership Award   Vol. 1: 7719
Civic Medal of Cartagena   Vol. 2: 1608
Civic Trust Awards   Vol. 2: 2636
Civil Aeronautics Cross of Merit   Vol. 2: 1598
Civil Air Patrol Aerospace Education Cadet of the Year   Vol. 1: 238
Civil Air Patrol Cadet of the Year   Vol. 1: 238
Civil Air Patrol Hall of Honor   Vol. 1: 19218

Civil Engineering Award   Vol. 2: 10652
Civil Engineering Division Best Paper Award   Vol. 1: 4078
Civil Engineering History and Heritage Award   Vol. 1: 4446
Civil Engineering Prizes for Students   Vol. 2: 3232
Civil Government Award   Vol. 1: 4447
Civil War Press Corps Award   Vol. 1: 7774
Civil War Round Table of New York Young Readers Award   Vol. 1: 7777
Civilian Awards   Vol. 1: 239
Civitan International Honor Keys   Vol. 1: 7785
CLA Award for Distinguished Contribution to Literary or Linguistic Scholarship   Vol. 1: 7902
CLA Membership Promotion Award   Vol. 1: 7378
Cladan Award   Vol. 2: 325
Claden Award; People's Choice Prize   Vol. 2: 326
Clagett Tro phy; U.S. Junior Women's Sailing Championship - Nancy Leiter   Vol. 1: 19542
Clagett Trophy; U.S. SAILING/Rolex Junior Women's Championship - Nancy Leiter   Vol. 1: 19542
Clair Memorial Award; John   Vol. 1: 19558
Clairol Mentor Program   Vol. 1: 15020
Clairol Scholarship Program   Vol. 1: 6643
Clamer Medal; Francis J.   Vol. 1: 9378
Clancy Memorial Award; King   Vol. 1: 9960
Clancy Memorial Trophy; King   Vol. 1: 14163
Clapham Prize in International Business; Sir Michael   Vol. 2: 2698
Clapp Award; Otis   Vol. 1: 1077
Clapp; Otis   Vol. 1: 1351
Clapp Research Award; Otis   Vol. 1: 1081
Clapper Memorial Awards; Raymond   Vol. 1: 18459
Clare Prize; John   Vol. 1: 20178
Clarion Awards   Vol. 1: 20374
Clark Award; Allen W.   Vol. 1: 14437
Clark Award; Daphne   Vol. 2: 3561
Clark Award; Evert   Vol. 1: 14507
Clark Award; John   Vol. 1: 7147
Clark Award; John C.   Vol. 1: 8873
Clark Award; John William   Vol. 2: 2432
Clark Award; Justice Tom C.   Vol. 1: 9067
Clark Award; Russell   Vol. 2: 9761
Clark Award; Septima Poinsette   Vol. 1: 358
Clark, Jr. Trophy; W. Van Alan   Vol. 1: 19527
Clark Medal; Grahame   Vol. 2: 2224
Clark Medal; John Bates   Vol. 1: 1967
Clark Medal; Walton   Vol. 1: 9379
Clark Memorial Award; F. Ambrose   Vol. 1: 14870
Clark National Memorial Trophy; G. Melville   Vol. 2: 2065
Clark New Playwright Contest; Bob   Vol. 1: 19826
Clark - Newman Award   Vol. 1: 7128
Clark Outdoor Writing Award; Greg   Vol. 1: 15688
Clark Prize; Grenville   Vol. 1: 11583
Clark Research Award; Kenneth E.   Vol. 1: 7432
Clark Travelling Fellowship   Vol. 2: 3319
Clark Trophy; Jim   Vol. 2: 10621
Clarke Award; Arthur C.   Vol. 2: 4337
Clarke Award; Ethel Palmer   Vol. 1: 17267
Clarke Award for Outstanding Creative Contribution to Television; Alan   Vol. 2: 2234
Clarke Conservation Award; Doug   Vol. 1: 7270
Clarke Cup; Stephenson R.   Vol. 2: 4027
Clarke Freedom Award; Mary Frances   Vol. 1: 7799

Clarke Medal   Vol. 2: 623
Clarke Medal; F. W.   Vol. 1: 9541
Clarke Memorial Lectureship   Vol. 2: 624
Clarke Memorial Prize; Broadus James   Vol. 1: 5297
Clarke Memorial Scholarship; Mary A.   Vol. 1: 6914
Clarke Memorial Trophy; Colonel Gillard H.   Vol. 1: 14645
Clarke Outstanding Educator Award; Robert B.   Vol. 1: 8654
Clarke Prize; Thomas B.   Vol. 1: 12605
Clarke Trophy; Robert W.   Vol. 1: 2322
Class Prizes in British Amateur Tape Recording Contest   Vol. 2: 2872
Classic Award   Vol. 1: 4640
Classic Television Hall of Fame   Vol. 1: 15112
Classical Fellowship   Vol. 1: 12234
Classified Council Awards   Vol. 1: 15333
Classifiers Column Awards   Vol. 1: 7817
Clauder Competition for Excellence in Playwriting   Vol. 1: 15210
Claudet Student's Prize; Arthur   Vol. 2: 3336
Clausse; Fondation Gustave   Vol. 2: 5388
Clavijero; Premio Francisco Javier   Vol. 2: 9055
Clay Award; Garland W.   Vol. 1: 636
Claypoole, Sr. Memorial Award; Ralph O.   Vol. 1: 1716
Clayton Award; Charles C.   Vol. 1: 18223
Clayton Doctoral Dissertation Proposal Award; Alden G.   Vol. 1: 12097
Clayton Grants   Vol. 2: 3333
Clayton Grants for Postgraduate Studies   Vol. 2: 3333
Claytor Memorial Award; Gertrude B.   Vol. 1: 16278
CLC Hall of Leaders   Vol. 1: 8252
Clean Machine Award   Vol. 1: 6671
Cleary Award; Edward J.   Vol. 1: 554
Cleese Comedy Award; John   Vol. 1: 6002
Clegg Award; Annie   Vol. 2: 2433
Cleland Cup   Vol. 2: 8898
Clemente Award; Roberto
  Commissioner of Baseball   Vol. 1: 8032
  National Association for Puerto Rican Civil Rights   Vol 1: 12884
Clemm-Denkmunze; Hans-   Vol. 2: 6538
Clemson Award   Vol. 1: 17425
Clemson National Print and Drawing Exhibition   Vol. 1: 7835
Clemy Award   Vol. 1: 15560
Clench Award; Harry K.   Vol. 1: 11832
Clendenin Award; David L.   Vol. 1: 20457
Clergyman of the Year   Vol. 1: 16773
Clermont-Ferrand International Short Film Festival   Vol. 2: 6196
Clermont-Ferrand National Short Film Festival   Vol. 2: 6197
Clermont-Ganneau; Prix Charles   Vol. 2: 5442
Cleveland International Drawing Biennale Prize   Vol. 2: 2638
Cleveland Prize; AAAS Newcomb   Vol. 1: 881
Cleveland Quartet Competition   Vol. 1: 8806
Cleveland State University Poetry Center Prize   Vol. 1: 7842
Cliburn International Piano Competition; Van   Vol. 1: 7844
Clifford Prize; James L.   Vol. 1: 4065
Clift Scholarship; David H.   Vol. 1: 2923
Climatics Award   Vol. 1: 10323
Cline Memorial Prize; Howard Francis   Vol. 1: 8139
Clinical Anesthesia Practitioner Award   Vol. 1: 1053
Clinical/Biomedical Engineering Achievement Award   Vol. 1: 5625

Award Index
Volume 2: International and Foreign — Collegiate

Clinical Engineering/Biomedical Engineering Achievement Award   Vol. 1: 5620
Clinical Instructor of the Year Award   Vol. 1: 1054
Clinical Medicine Research Award   Vol. 1: 9586
Clinical MRI Prize   Vol. 2: 2408
Clinical Nursing Excellence Award   Vol. 1: 5879
Clinical Research Award in Periodontology   Vol. 1: 689
Clinical Research Grants   Vol. 1: 1952
Clinical Scientist in Nephrology Award   Vol. 1: 2763
Clinical Teacher of the Year   Vol. 1: 18438
Clinician of the Year   Vol. 1: 1136
Clinician - Scientist Award   Vol. 1: 2225
Clinician-Scientist Program   Vol. 1: 12186
Clinton Trophy; Port   Vol. 1: 14645
Clio Awards   Vol. 1: 15112
Clore International Award; Gerald   Vol. 1: 9657
Clore Prize for Distinguished Service of Science to the Society; Sir Charles   Vol. 2: 7979
Clowes, Jr., M.D., F.A.C.S. Memorial Research Career Development Award; George H. A.   Vol. 1: 1749
Clowes Memorial Award; G. H. A   Vol. 1: 842
CLTA Achievement in Literacy Award   Vol. 1: 7016
CLTA Merit Award   Vol. 1: 7017
Club Achievement Awards Competition   Vol. 1: 737
Club of Champions Award   Vol. 1: 7405
Club of the Year   Vol. 2: 2312
Clubok Award; Miriam   Vol. 1: 14425
Cluj Writers Association Award   Vol. 2: 10412
Clusmann Prize; William and Bertha   Vol. 1: 5297
CMA/ASCAP Awards for Adventuresome Programming   Vol. 1: 7501
CMA Awards for Outstanding Achievement   Vol. 1: 7040
CNA Literary Award   Vol. 2: 10830
CNA Media Awards   Vol. 1: 7072
CNAA/RIPA Prize in Public Administration   Vol. 2: 2699
Co-founders Book Award   Vol. 1: 20239
Co-op Feeds Young Scientist's Award   Vol. 1: 7161
Coach of the Year
   American Football Coaches Association   Vol. 1: 2074
   College Swimming Coaches Association of America   Vol 1: 7946
   Continental Basketball Association   Vol 1: 8243
   English Basket Ball Association   Vol 2: 2775
   Ladies Professional Golf Association   Vol 1: 11755
   National Association of College Gymnastics Coaches (Men)   Vol 1: 12997
   United States Amateur Boxing   Vol 1: 18992
   United States Professional Tennis Association   Vol 1: 19508
   United States Synchronized Swimming, Inc.   Vol 1: 19635
Coach of the Year Award
   American Swimming Coaches Association   Vol. 1: 4884
   Football Writers Association of America   Vol 1: 9304
   National Association of Intercollegiate Athletics   Vol 1: 13164
   National Soccer Coaches Association of America   Vol 1: 14727
   National Wrestling Coaches Association   Vol 1: 15047
Coach of the Year Awards   Vol. 1: 16212
Coaches Hall of Fame   Vol. 1: 14017
Coal Award   Vol. 1: 6936
Coal Division Distinguished Service Award   Vol. 1: 17559
Coan, Sr. Award; Carl A.S.   Vol. 1: 14197
Coanda Prize; Henri   Vol. 2: 10340
Coast Guard Arctic Service Medal   Vol. 1: 19144
Coast Guard Essay Contest   Vol. 1: 19461
Coast Guard Exemplary Service Medal   Vol. 1: 6696
Coast Guard Medal   Vol. 1: 19145
Coast Guard Reserve Good Conduct Medal   Vol. 1: 19146
Cobalcescu Prize; Grigore   Vol. 2: 10341
Cobb, Jr. Award for Initiative and Success in Trade Development; Charles E.   Vol. 1: 19281
Cobb Memorial Award; Grover C.   Vol. 1: 12973
Cobb Memorial Trophy; James S.   Vol. 1: 14645
Cobb Young Investigator Award; W. A.   Vol. 1: 10960
Cobbing Travelling Fellowship (Psychiatry of Mental Handicap); Natalie   Vol. 2: 3959
Coblentz Award   Vol. 1: 7857
Coca-Cola Cup   Vol. 2: 11717
Coccia International Singing Competition; Carlo   Vol. 2: 8220
Cochrane Award; Vice Admiral E. L.   Vol. 1: 17921
Cockayne Memorial Lecture; Leonard   Vol. 2: 9835
Cockcroft Award; Ron   Vol. 2: 11482
Codazzi Medal; Agustin   Vol. 2: 1718
Codazzi Prize; Lorenzo   Vol. 2: 1745
Codes and Standards Medal   Vol. 1: 4669
Codies: SPA Excellence in Software Awards   Vol. 1: 18115
Codofil Award   Vol. 1: 8568
Cody Award; Fred   Vol. 1: 6291
Coelho; Premio Laranjo   Vol. 2: 10246
Coelho Prize; Laranjo   Vol. 2: 10246
Coffeetable Award   Vol. 1: 13153
Cogan Award   Vol. 1: 5591
Cogel Service Award   Vol. 1: 8395
Cogswell Outstanding Industrial Security Achievement Award; James S.   Vol. 1: 19212
Cohen Award; Harry and Martha   Vol. 1: 302
Cohen Award; Lord   Vol. 2: 4226
Cohen Award; Morton N.   Vol. 1: 12393
Cohen Award; Nathan   Vol. 1: 7253
Cohen Distinguished Career Award; Milton   Vol. 1: 3935
Cohen of Birkenhead Medal; Lord   Vol. 2: 2517
Cohen Purchase Award; Joan   Vol. 1: 17693
Coin of the Year Award   Vol. 1: 11732
Coindreau; Prix Maurice Edgar   Vol. 2: 6246
Coker Prize for Finding Aids; C.F.W.   Vol. 1: 17669
Colaco de Azulejaria; Premio Municipal Jorge   Vol. 2: 10271
Colamonico; Premio Carmelo   Vol. 2: 8073
Colas; Prix Eugene   Vol. 2: 5851
Colbert Medal   Vol. 1: 17702
Colburn Award for Excellence in Publications by a Young Member of the Institute; Allan P.   Vol. 1: 2570
Colby Award; William R.   Vol. 1: 17227
Colby Memorial Award; Dorothy   Vol. 1: 3403
Colclough Medal and Prize; Tom   Vol. 2: 3129
Cole Award; Art   Vol. 1: 974
Cole Award for Automotive Engineering Innovation; Edward N.   Vol. 1: 17754
Cole Grants-in-Aid; Arthur H.   Vol. 1: 8822
Cole Human Rights Award; Kitty   Vol. 1: 1884
Cole Prize; Arthur H.   Vol. 1: 8823
Cole Prizes in Algebra and Number Theory; Frank Nelson   Vol. 1: 3006
Coleman - Barstow Award for Strings   Vol. 1: 7864
Coleman Chamber Ensemble Competition   Vol. 1: 7864
Coleopterists Society Youth Award   Vol. 1: 7866
Coler - Maxwell Medal   Vol. 1: 11266
Colgate-Palmolive Post-Doctoral Fellowship Award in *In Vitro* Toxicology   Vol. 1: 18071
Colibri Diploma   Vol. 2: 5140
Colin-Prijs; Fernand   Vol. 2: 1379
Collacott Prize   Vol. 2: 3266
Collar of the Supreme Order of the Chrysanthemum   Vol. 2: 8582
Collection System Award   Vol. 1: 20146
Collectors Club Medal for Best Program Presented to the Collectors Club   Vol. 1: 7869
Collectors Club Medal for Devoted Service   Vol. 1: 7872
Collectors Club Medal for Outstanding Article with *The Collectors Club Philatelist*   Vol. 1: 7870
College All-America Baseball Team   Vol. 1: 18353
College Art Association/National Institute for Conservation Award   Vol. 1: 7885
College Athletics Top Ten   Vol. 1: 13610
College Athletics Top Twelve   Vol. 1: 13610
College Awards   Vol. 1: 1843
College Baseball Coach of the Year   Vol. 1: 18354
College Baseball Player of the Year   Vol. 1: 18355
College Basketball Coach of the Year   Vol. 1: 18356
College Basketball Player of the Year   Vol. 1: 18357
College Cartoonist - Charles M. Schulz Award   Vol. 1: 17144
College Conservatory of Music Play or Musical Awards   Vol. 1: 19781
College Fiction Competition   Vol. 1: 11994
College Football Coach of the Year   Vol. 1: 18358
College Football Defensive Player of the Year Trophy   Vol. 1: 9306
College Football Hall of Fame   Vol. 1: 13987
College Football Official Award   Vol. 1: 13988
College Football Player of the Year   Vol. 1: 18359
College Journalism Competition   Vol. 1: 16887
College Journalist of the Year   Vol. 1: 7905
College Media Adviser Hall of Fame   Vol. 1: 7906
College of Diplomates Award   Vol. 1: 8852
College of Diplomates Awards   Vol. 1: 14629
College of Electrical Engineers Student Prizes   Vol. 2: 433
College of Fellows Grants   Vol. 1: 2551
College Poetry Contest   Vol. 1: 11982
Collegiate Advisor Award   Vol. 1: 16119
Collegiate Award   Vol. 1: 19636
Collegiate Chamber Music Competition; MTNA-   Vol. 1: 12521
Collegiate Coach of the Year   Vol. 1: 19344
Collegiate Hall of Fame   Vol. 1: 13625

Collegiate-Scholastic Swimming Trophy   Vol. 1: 14248
Collier Award   Vol. 1: 9331
Collier Award for Juvenile Fiction; Julia   Vol. 1: 8568
Collier Award; Margaret   Vol. 1: 27
Collier Trophy; Robert J.   Vol. 1: 12723
Collingwood Prize   Vol. 1: 4448
Collins Australian English Dictionaries Award   Vol. 2: 193
Collins Award; Carr P.   Vol. 1: 18645
Collins Award for Community Service; George W.   Vol. 1: 8161
Collins Award; George R.   Vol. 1: 864
Collins Award; Joseph P.   Vol. 1: 13755
Collins Award; Samuel C.   Vol. 1: 8482
Collins Dictionaries/*The Times* Crossword Championship   Vol. 2: 2641
Collins Distinguished and Unusual Service Award; W. Leighton   Vol. 1: 4079
Collins, Jr. Research Promotion Award; William J.   Vol. 1: 4580
Collins Memorial Award; Norman   Vol. 2: 2534
Collins Poetry Award; Tom   Vol. 2: 375
Collins Religious Book Award   Vol. 2: 2640
Colman Award; Norman Jay   Vol. 1: 1067
Colmar International Competition for Chamber-Music Ensemble   Vol. 2: 5042
Colmont; Prix   Vol. 2: 5373
Cologne International Pianoforte Competition   Vol. 2: 6607
Cologne International Violin Competition/Foundation/Shiflung Georg Kulenkampff   Vol. 2: 6609
Colombe Unda   Vol. 2: 1376
Colombian Academy of Science Prize   Vol. 2: 1578
Colombian Academy of Science Third World Prize   Vol. 2: 1579
Colombian Composers Competition Prizes   Vol. 2: 1655
Colonna Prize; Antonina   Vol. 2: 8448
Color of Many Colors   Vol. 1: 10597
Color Slide Division Awards   Vol. 1: 16160
Color Television Advertising Award   Vol. 2: 4534
Colt Fund   Vol. 2: 4362
Columbia/Embassy Television Playwriting Award   Vol. 1: 1756
Columbia Journalism Award   Vol. 1: 7979
Columbia Pictures Television Playwriting Award   Vol. 1: 1756
Columbia University Prize in American Economic History in Honor of Allan Nevins   Vol. 1: 7980
Columbia University Prize in American Economic History in Honor of Allan Nevins   Vol. 1: 8824
Columbus Award; Christopher   Vol. 1: 9185
Columbus: Countdown 1992 Award   Vol. 1: 8015
Columbus International Film and Video Festival   Vol. 1: 9186
Columbus Prize   Vol. 2: 8325
Colvin Awards; Ruth J.   Vol. 1: 11901
Colwell Cooperative Engineering Medal; Arch T.   Vol. 1: 17755
Colwell Merit Award; Arch T.   Vol. 1: 17756
Colworth Medal   Vol. 2: 2171
Colworth Prize Lecture   Vol. 2: 4354
Colyer Gold Medal   Vol. 2: 3975
Colyer Prize   Vol. 2: 4237
Comas Award; Juan   Vol. 1: 1118
Comas; Premio Juan   Vol. 2: 9057
Combat Readiness Medal   Vol. 1: 19147
Come to Britain Trophy   Vol. 2: 2549

Comeback Player of the Year   Vol. 1: 18619
Comedy Artist Hall of Fame   Vol. 1: 5749
Come'N Get It Canine Film Festival   Vol. 1: 12038
Comer Awards   Vol. 1: 531
Comer Minority Research Fellowship for Medical Students; James   Vol. 1: 531
Comfort Memorial Award; A. C.   Vol. 2: 4238
Comiant; Prix Pol   Vol. 2: 5912
Comino Foundation Grant   Vol. 2: 2771
Command and Control Unit of the Year   Vol. 1: 12060
Commandant's Aviation Efficiency Award   Vol. 1: 12057
Commander-in-Chief's Annual Award for Installation Excellence   Vol. 1: 19222
Commandeur de l'Ordre de Saint Gregoire le Grand   Vol. 2: 8476
Commemorative Arts Awards   Vol. 1: 5327
Commemorative Award   Vol. 1: 15156
Commendation   Vol. 1: 8198
Commendation Award   Vol. 1: 18123
Commendation Awards
    American Women in Radio and Television   Vol. 1: 5110
    International Narcotic Enforcement Officers Association   Vol 1: 11115
Commendation by the Minister of State for Science and Technology   Vol. 2: 8591
Commendation for Brave Conduct   Vol. 2: 207
Commendation for Distinguished Service   Vol. 2: 341
Commendation for Gallantry   Vol. 2: 342
Commendation for Humane Services   Vol. 1: 17077
Commendation Medal: Air Force   Vol. 1: 19148
Commendation Medal: Army   Vol. 1: 19149
Commendation Medal: Coast Guard   Vol. 1: 19150
Commendation Medal (Military)   Vol. 2: 10737
Commendation Medal: Navy   Vol. 1: 19151
Commercial Award   Vol. 1: 2353
Commercial Design Award   Vol. 1: 10574
Commercial Director Award   Vol. 1: 8663
Commercial Member of the Year   Vol. 1: 12464
Commercial Transaction of the Year Award   Vol. 1: 16709
Commercial Wine Competition Awards   Vol. 1: 5102
Commission for the Defense of Human Rights in Central America Awards   Vol. 2: 1759
Commission Geographical Education Awards   Vol. 2: 6960
Commissioner's Award
    Canadian Football League   Vol. 1: 6872
    Ladies Professional Golf Association   Vol 1: 11756
Commissioners' Award   Vol. 1: 20281
Commissioner's Trophy Awards   Vol. 1: 6361
Commissions   Vol. 1: 11730
Commissions for New Musical Works   Vol. 1: 11728
Commitment to Chicago Award   Vol. 1: 7604
Committee Award   Vol. 1: 13261
Committee D-2 Award   Vol. 1: 6042
Committee D-12 Award   Vol. 1: 6043
Committee D-20 Award of Excellence   Vol. 1: 6044
Committee E-24 Best Student Paper Award   Vol. 1: 6045
Committee Man of the Year   Vol. 1: 1084
Committee of the Year Award   Vol. 1: 14464
Committee Person of the Year Award   Vol. 1: 14465
Commodore Cooper Trust   Vol. 2: 9319

Common Boundary Dissertation/Thesis Award   Vol. 1: 8045
Common Wealth Awards of Distinguished Service   Vol. 1: 6266
Commons Award; Veblen -   Vol. 1: 5522
Commonwealth Chess Championship   Vol. 1: 8053
Commonwealth Club of California Book Awards   Vol. 1: 8055
Commonwealth Essay Competition   Vol. 2: 3997
Commonwealth Fund Fellowships   Vol. 2: 2985
Commonwealth Fund Medical Fellowship Program   Vol. 1: 14341
Commonwealth Games Federation   Vol. 2: 2661
Commonwealth Industrial Training and Experience Programme   Vol. 2: 2656
Commonwealth Magistrates' Hall of Fame   Vol. 2: 2666
Commonwealth Poetry Prize   Vol. 2: 2663
Commonwealth Press Union Scholarships   Vol. 2: 2669
Commonwealth Professional Associations Awards for Innovation   Vol. 2: 3747
Commonwealth Secretariat's Fellowships and Training Programme   Vol. 2: 2656
Commonwealth Weightlifting Federation   Vol. 2: 12166
Commonwealth Writers Prize   Vol. 2: 2654
Commonwealth Youth Service Awards   Vol. 2: 2671
Communication and Marketing Awards   Vol. 1: 10436
Communication Policy Research Award   Vol. 1: 9319
Communications Award   Vol. 1: 2729
Communications Awards
    Goodwill Industries International Inc.   Vol. 1: 9658
    National Association of Conservation Districts   Vol 1: 13025
Communications Competition   Vol. 1: 9196
Communications Graphics   Vol. 1: 2623
Communications Group Trophy   Vol. 2: 11080
Communications Media Award   Vol. 1: 19981
Communications Program Awards   Vol. 1: 9294
Communicator of the Year
    British Association of Industrial Editors   Vol. 2: 2267
    National Association of Government Communicators   Vol 1: 13124
    National Council for Marketing and Public Relations   Vol 1: 13704
    National Council for Marketing and Public Relations   Vol 1: 13705
Communicator of the Year Award
    International Association of Business Communicators   Vol. 1: 10682
    Southern African Association of Industrial Editors   Vol 2: 11097
    University of Chicago Alumni Association   Vol 1: 19769
Communicator's Award   Vol. 1: 5210
Community Access Award   Vol. 1: 3936
Community and Junior College Design Awards   Vol. 1: 2528
Community Architecture Award   Vol. 2: 4073
Community Awards Program (Encore Awards)   Vol. 1: 16817
Community Awareness Award   Vol. 1: 5210
Community Children's Theater of Kansas City Annual Playwriting Contest   Vol. 1: 8066
Community College Learning Resources Library Achievement Awards   Vol. 1: 2871

Community Education Award   Vol. 1: 10889
Community Enterprise Award for New Business   Vol. 2: 4073
Community Enterprise Award for Training   Vol. 2: 4073
Community Enterprise Scheme   Vol. 2: 4073
Community, Environment, Art, and Design (CEAD) Award   Vol. 2: 164
Community Hospital Award   Vol. 1: 7478
Community Long-Term Care Award   Vol. 1: 14291
Community Museum of the Year   Vol. 2: 4490
Community of the Year Award   Vol. 1: 16762
Community Outreach Award   Vol. 1: 2571
Community Outreach Awards   Vol. 1: 17175
Community Partnership Awards Program   Vol. 1: 14431
Community Preventive Dentistry Award   Vol. 1: 1943
Community Projects Foundation Award for Partnership   Vol. 2: 4073
Community Radio Program Awards   Vol. 1: 13934
Community Relations Award (Labor)   Vol. 1: 2730
Community Service Award
　American Academy of Facial Plastic and Reconstructive Surgery   Vol. 1: 565
　American Public Power Association   Vol 1: 3856
　American Rehabilitation Association   Vol 1: 3936
　Helicopter Association International   Vol 1: 9886
　Inland Press Association   Vol 1: 10199
　Martin Luther King, Jr. Center for Nonviolent Social Change   Vol 1: 11697
　National Council of Social Security Management Associations   Vol 1: 13756
　National Grange   Vol 1: 14091
　Sierra Club   Vol 1: 17228
　University of California, Los Angeles - Alumni Association   Vol 1: 19743
　Waterbed Manufacturers Association   Vol 1: 20169
Community Service Awards   Vol. 1: 15975
Community Service Fellowship   Vol. 1: 7600
Community Service Recognition Program   Vol. 1: 17129
Compagna: Premio Francesco   Vol. 2: 8002
Companion   Vol. 2: 4111
Companion Membership   Vol. 2: 4515
Company Appreciation Award   Vol. 1: 16438
Company Award of Excellence   Vol. 1: 13248
Company of Fellows   Vol. 1: 5938
Company of World Traders Silver Salver   Vol. 2: 3098
Company Representative of the Year   Vol. 1: 13249
Company Safety Awards   Vol. 1: 15412
Compass Distinguished Achievement Award   Vol. 1: 12087
Compass Industrial Award   Vol. 1: 12088
Compass International Award   Vol. 1: 12089
Compassionate Friends Award   Vol. 1: 8074
Competitie de Impact van Muziek op Film   Vol. 2: 1193
Competition and Achievement Awards   Vol. 1: 4970
Competition for Children's Theater or Stories   Vol. 2: 9012
Competition for Composers   Vol. 2: 7015
Competition for Films and Videos on Japan   Vol. 2: 8774
Competition for Performing Artists   Vol. 1: 8238

Competition for Young Researchers   Vol. 2: 11820
Competition for Young Statisticians from Developing Countries   Vol. 2: 9535
Competition Honors   Vol. 1: 19047
Competition Internationale d'Oeuvres Video   Vol. 2: 6070
Competition of Composition for Choirs   Vol. 2: 11196
Competitions
　Association for the Study of the World Refugee Problem   Vol. 2: 8104
　International Society for Research on Civilization Diseases and Environment   Vol 2: 1206
　Latin American Association of Freight and Transport Agents   Vol 2: 10012
　Oceania Basketball Confederation   Vol 2: 559
　Pan American Federation of Engineering Societies   Vol 2: 12132
　World Taekwondo Federation   Vol 2: 8838
Competitions and Tournaments   Vol. 2: 9891
Competitive Extramural Grants Program
　American Nurses Foundation   Vol. 1: 3293
　American Nurses Foundation   Vol 1: 3293
Competitive Papers Award   Vol. 1: 9200
Composer of the Year
　Canadian Music Council   Vol. 1: 7052
　Musical America Publishing   Vol 1: 12529
Composer's Award for String Quartet   Vol. 1: 12503
Composers Guild Annual Composition Contest   Vol. 1: 8076
Composition Award   Vol. 1: 14820
Composition Competition, Tours   Vol. 2: 5192
Composition Competitions   Vol. 2: 4376
Composition Contest   Vol. 1: 11027
Composition of the Year   Vol. 2: 9970
Composition Prize   Vol. 2: 4125
Composition Prize for Young European Composers   Vol. 2: 9337
Compton Award; Karl Taylor   Vol. 1: 2658
Compton Award; Neil   Vol. 1: 15880
Comptroller's Award for Distinction in Public Finance   Vol. 1: 19282
Computer Educator of the Year   Vol. 1: 10611
Computer Entrepreneur Award   Vol. 1: 10296
Computer Graphics Achievement Award   Vol. 1: 5474
Computer Pioneer Award   Vol. 1: 10297
Computer Press Awards   Vol. 1: 8081
Computer Sciences Man of the Year   Vol. 1: 8724
Computing in Chemical Engineering Award   Vol. 1: 2572
Computing Practice Award   Vol. 1: 2573
Comstock Prize   Vol. 1: 12665
Comune di Sondrio Mostra Internazionale dei Documentari sui Parchi   Vol. 2: 8433
Conant Award in High School Chemistry Teaching; James Bryant   Vol. 1: 1551
Conant Award; James Bryant   Vol. 1: 8846
Concerned Broadcaster of the Year   Vol. 1: 350
Concerns of Children Media Awards Competition   Vol. 1: 15574
Concert Artists Guild New York Competition   Vol. 1: 8085
Concertino Prague International Radio Competition for Young Musicians   Vol. 2: 1838
Concerto Competition   Vol. 1: 15609
Concha de Oro   Vol. 2: 11351
Concha de Plata   Vol. 2: 11351
Concord Press Award for Academic Publishing   Vol. 2: 9861

Concordia Composer's Competition   Vol. 1: 8087
Concorso Coreografico Internazionale di Modern Jazz Dance   Vol. 2: 8110
Concorso Esercitazioni agrarie   Vol. 2: 8007
Concorso Internacional de Violao Villa-Lobos   Vol. 2: 1501
Concorso Internationale di Musica da Camera "Palma d'Oro" di Citta di Finale Lingure   Vol. 2: 8120
Concorso Internazionale della Ceramica d'Arte   Vol. 2: 8309
Concorso Internazionale di Canto Carlo Coccia   Vol. 2: 8220
Concorso Internazionale di Chitarra Classica Citta' di Alessandria   Vol. 2: 8201
Concorso internazionale di composizione   Vol. 2: 8133
Concorso Internazionale di Composizione Goffredo Petrassi   Vol. 2: 8392
Concorso Internazionale di Composizione Guido d'Arezzo   Vol. 2: 8215
Concorso Internazionale di Composizione Musicale per Strumenti a Fiato, Ancona   Vol. 2: 8191
Concorso Internazionale di Composizione Organistica Oliver Messiaen   Vol. 2: 8203
Concorso Internazionale di Composizione Originale per Banda   Vol. 2: 8409
Concorso Internazionale di Composizione Sinfonica, Trieste   Vol. 2: 8402
Concorso Internazionale di Direzione d'Orchestra Arturo Toscanini   Vol. 2: 8393
Concorso Internazionale di Direzione d'Orchestra Vittorio Gui   Vol. 2: 8441
Concorso Internazionale di Musica da Camera di Finale Ligure   Vol. 2: 8106
Concorso Internazionale di Musica e Danza G. B. Viotti   Vol. 2: 8425
Concorso Internazionale di Violino Alberto Curci   Vol. 2: 8211
Concorso Internazionale di Violino Nicolo Paganini   Vol. 2: 8395
Concorso Internazionale di Violino Premio Rodolfo Lipizer   Vol. 2: 8209
Concorso Internazionale di violoncello Gaspar Cassado   Vol. 2: 8442
Concorso Internazionale Luigi Russolo   Vol. 2: 8261
Concorso Internazionale Mauro Giuliani Duo di Chitarre   Vol. 2: 8183
Concorso Internazionale Michelangelo Abbado per Violinisti   Vol. 2: 7999
Concorso Internazionale Musicale Francesco Paolo Neglia   Vol. 2: 8205
Concorso Internazionale per Cantanti Toti Dal Monte   Vol. 2: 8222
Concorso Internazionale per Complessi da Camera, Citta di Firenze   Vol. 2: 8102
Concorso Internazionale per Contrabbasso Giovanni Bottesini   Vol. 2: 8168
Concorso Internazionale per giovani Direttori d'orchestra Premio Guido Cantelli   Vol. 2: 8158
Concorso Internazionale per la Conquista della Chitarra Classica   Vol. 2: 8018
Concorso Internazionale per Quartetto d'Archi   Vol. 2: 8444
Concorso Internazionale per Voci Verdiane   Vol. 2: 8293
Concorso Internazionale per Voci Verdiane Alessandro e Maria Ziliani   Vol. 2: 8293
Concorso Internazionale Pianistico Liszt - Premio Mario Zanfi   Vol. 2: 8169
Concorso Internazionale Vincenzo Bellini per Pianisti e Cantanti Lirici   Vol. 2: 8108

Concorso Nazionale di Canto Corale Sacro   Vol. 2: 8468
Concorso nazionale pianistico Premio Rendano   Vol. 2: 8138
Concorso Pianistico Internazionale Alessandro Casagrande   Vol. 2: 8207
Concorso Pianistico Internazionale Alfredo Casella   Vol. 2: 8048
Concorso Pianistico Internazionale Citta di Senigallia   Vol. 2: 8420
Concorso Pianistico Internazionale Ettore Pozzoli   Vol. 2: 8199
Concorso Pianistico Internazionale Rina Sala Gallo   Vol. 2: 8140
Concorso Polifonico Internazionale Guido d'Arezzo   Vol. 2: 8216
Concoulrs Reportage Seer le Japon   Vol. 2: 4907
Concours   Vol. 1: 7671
Concours Awards   Vol. 1: 20050
Concours Canadien de Journalisme   Vol. 1: 6851
Concours Clara Haskil   Vol. 2: 11744
Concours de Composition, Tours   Vol. 2: 5192
Concours de Jazz   Vol. 2: 5070
Concours de l'Union Litteraire et Artistique de France   Vol. 2: 6441
Concours de musique du Canada   Vol. 1: 7044
Concours de Nouvelles   Vol. 2: 6087
Concours de Sauvegarde Vieilles Maisons Francaises   Vol. 2: 6467
Concours des Antiquites de la France   Vol. 2: 5431
Concours des Prix de Journalisme Erit   Vol. 1: 6799
Concours des Prix Nationaux de Journalisme - Concours des Prix de Radiotelejournalisme   Vol. 1: 6797
Concours des Prix Nationaux de Journalisme sur l'Environnement   Vol. 1: 6798
Concours D'Orgue Europeen de Beauvais   Vol. 2: 5108
Concours du Meilleure Jeune Commis Rotisseur   Vol. 2: 5024
Concours et Seminaire International d'alto   Vol. 2: 3627
Concours Europeen de Piano   Vol. 2: 4916
Concours Geza Anda   Vol. 2: 11676
Concours Internacional Maria Canals de Barcelona   Vol. 2: 11168
Concours International d'Alto Maurice Vieux   Vol. 2: 6469
Concours International de Ballet, Varna   Vol. 2: 1539
Concours International de campagnes de Marketing Direct   Vol. 2: 1131
Concours International de Chant Choral de Tours   Vol. 2: 5193
Concours International de Chant de Paris   Vol. 2: 6431
Concours International de Chant de Rio de Janeiro   Vol. 2: 1454
Concoulrs International de Chant de Toulouse   Vol. 2: 6048
Concours International de Chant Francisco Vinas   Vol. 2: 11394
Concours International de Chant la Plaine-Atlantique   Vol. 2: 5188
Concours International de Chant Lyrique de Verviers   Vol. 2: 1215
Concours International de Chant Offenbach   Vol. 2: 5072
Concours International de Choregraphie du CBC, Nyon   Vol. 2: 11672
Concours International de Cinema de la Montagne Vila de Torello   Vol. 2: 11386

Concours International de Clavecin de Paris   Vol. 2: 5177
Concours International de Composition   Vol. 2: 6040
Concours international de composition Camillo Togni   Vol. 2: 8133
Concours International de Composition de Musique Sacree   Vol. 2: 11736
Concours International de Composition Musicale   Vol. 2: 5182
Concours International de Composition Musicale, Avray   Vol. 2: 4977
Concours International de Composition Musicale Opera et Ballet Geneve   Vol. 2: 11678
Concours International de Composition Vienne   Vol. 2: 774
Concours International de Danse de Paris   Vol. 2: 5179
Concours International de Flute Jean-Pierre Rampal   Vol. 2: 5034
Concours International de Guitare   Vol. 2: 6184
Concours International de Harpe en Israel   Vol. 2: 7899
Concours International de Harpe Louise Charpentier   Vol. 2: 5210
Concours International de Jeunes Chanteurs d'Opera   Vol. 2: 1525
Concours International de Jeunes Chefs d'Orchestre Besancon   Vol. 2: 5181
Concours International de l'Orgue a Lahti   Vol. 2: 4746
Concours International de Lutherie   Vol. 2: 1516
Concours International de Lutherie et d'Archeterie de la Ville de Paris   Vol. 2: 5034
Concours International de Musique de Chambre de Paris   Vol. 2: 6432
Concours International de Musique de Chambre pour Ensembles d'Instruments a Vent   Vol. 2: 11680
Concours international de musique de Montreal   Vol. 1: 12427
Concours International de Musique Electroacoustique Bourges   Vol. 2: 4999
Concours International de Piano de Senigallia   Vol. 2: 8420
Concours International de Piano, Epinal   Vol. 2: 5074
Concours International de Piano Jazz Martial Solal   Vol. 2: 5034
Concours International de Quatuor a Cordes d'Evian   Vol. 2: 6192
Concours International de Trompette Maurice Andre   Vol. 2: 5034
Concours International de Violon Tibor Varga   Vol. 2: 11664
Concours international de Violoncelle Paulo   Vol. 2: 4750
Concours International de Violoncelle Rostropovitch   Vol. 2: 6201
Concours International d'Emissions Sportives en Television; Anneau d'Or -   Vol. 2: 11738
Concours International d'Ensembles de Musique de Chambre de Colmar   Vol. 2: 5042
Concours International des Jeunesses Musicales - Belgrade   Vol. 2: 10717
Concours International d'Execution Musicale - Geneve   Vol. 2: 11774
Concours International d'Oratorio et de Lied   Vol. 2: 4981
Concours International d'Orgue de Chartres   Vol. 2: 4936
Concours International du Festival de Musique de Toulon   Vol. 2: 5076

Concours International Printemps de la Guitare   Vol. 2: 1106
Concours International Trisannuel de Carillon - la Reine Fabiola   Vol. 2: 1348
Concours Lepine   Vol. 2: 4938
Concours Max-Pol Fouchet   Vol. 2: 4974
Concours National Feminin de Musique du Lyceum de Suisse   Vol. 2: 11682
Concours OSM   Vol. 1: 12432
Concours Pour Pianistes Accompagnateurs   Vol. 2: 1453
Concours Promethee   Vol. 2: 4975
Concours Seymour Cray France   Vol. 2: 5078
Concours Suisse de l'orgue   Vol. 2: 11945
Concours Technique International du Film de l'UNIATEC   Vol. 2: 6436
Concourt Fellowship   Vol. 2: 4797
Concrete Element Prize   Vol. 2: 9902
Concrete Man of the Year   Vol. 2: 10836
Concrete Society Award   Vol. 2: 2673
Concrete Structure Plaque   Vol. 2: 9903
Concurs Internacional de Cant Francesc Vinas   Vol. 2: 11394
Concurso Anual   Vol. 1: 10513
Concurso Anual de Literatura Premios Franz Tamayo   Vol. 2: 1388
Concurso Anual de Tesis Profesionales   Vol. 2: 8937
Concurso Carmen Lyra   Vol. 2: 1768
Concurso de anto Beca Francsco Araiza   Vol. 2: 9169
Concurso de Caricatura Periodistica   Vol. 2: 9167
Concurso de Cine   Vol. 2: 9265
Concurso de Composicion Vasca Para Masas Corales   Vol. 2: 11196
Concurso de Compositores de Colombia   Vol. 2: 1655
Concurso de Cuento de Ciencia Ficcion   Vol. 2: 9170
Concurso de cuento y de Teatro Infantil   Vol. 2: 9012
Concurso de Ecologia Cacique Chuira   Vol. 2: 1594
Concurso de Ilustraciones   Vol. 2: 11383
Concurso de Jovenes Solistas   Vol. 2: 9171
Concurso de Resena Teatral   Vol. 2: 9172
Concurso Internacional de Canto de Bilbao   Vol. 2: 11275
Concurso Internacional de Canto do Rio de Janeiro   Vol. 2: 1454
Concurso Internacional de Canto Julian Gayarre   Vol. 2: 11254
Concurso Internacional de la Escultura en Madera   Vol. 2: 9009
Concurso Internacional de Piano Ciudad de Montevideo   Vol. 2: 12090
Concurso Internacional de Piano de Santander   Vol. 2: 11355
Concurso Internacional de Piano Frederic Chopin   Vol. 2: 11213
Concurso Internacional de Piano Jose Iturbi   Vol. 2: 11219
Concurso Internacional de Piano Pilar Bayona   Vol. 2: 11273
Concurso Internacional de Piano Villa-Lobos   Vol. 2: 1502
Concurso Internacional de Violin Pablo Sarasate   Vol. 2: 11255
Concurso Internacional para Pianistas Acompanhadores   Vol. 2: 1453
Concurso Internacional Vianna da Motta   Vol. 2: 10228
Concurso Internazionale per Cantanti Lirici Citta di Ercolano   Vol. 2: 8480
Concurso Joven Creacion   Vol. 2: 1769

Concurso la Mejor Tesis sobre la Mujer in la UNAM   Vol. 2: 9173
Concurso Latinoamericano de Cuento   Vol. 2: 9209
Concurso Literario Premio Emece   Vol. 2: 47
Concurso Nacional Carta a mi Hijo   Vol. 2: 9252
Concurso Nacional de Acuarela acera de Temas Turisticos del Estado de Mexico   Vol. 2: 9010
Concurso Nacional de Artes Plasticas - Grafica (Mini Estampa)   Vol. 2: 9210
Concurso Nacional de Biografias Hector Cossio Salinas   Vol. 2: 1397
Concurso Nacional de Cuartetos de Cuerdas   Vol. 2: 9174
Concurso Nacional de Cuento Periodico Prensa Nueva   Vol. 2: 1743
Concurso Nacional de Diseno para Uso y aplicacon del Aluminio   Vol. 2: 9018
Concurso Nacional de Ensino de Redacao   Vol. 2: 1437
Concurso Nacional de Escritores de Teatro   Vol. 2: 9274
Concurso Nacional de Fotografia   Vol. 2: 1756
Concurso Nacional de Fotografia Cientifica   Vol. 2: 9175
Concurso Nacional de Novela Erich Guttentag   Vol. 2: 1398
Concurso Nacional de Obras Medicas   Vol. 2: 1725
Concurso Nacional de Tecnologie   Vol. 2: 8950
Concurso Nacional de Violin   Vol. 2: 9176
Concurso Nacional del Cuento   Vol. 2: 1757
Concurso Nacional para Estudiantes de Artes Plasticas en Aguascalientes   Vol. 2: 9211
Concurso Permanente De Jovenes Interpretes   Vol. 2: 11285
Concurso Univeritario de Cuento   Vol. 2: 9177
Concurso Universitario de Artes Plasticas   Vol. 2: 9178
Concurso Universitario de Fotografia   Vol. 2: 9179
Condecoracion al Merito Social   Vol. 2: 9013
Condecoracion al Merito Turistico   Vol. 2: 1610
Condecoracion del Merito Universitario   Vol. 2: 1751
Condecoracion Dr. Eduardo Liceaga   Vol. 2: 9127
Condecoracion Servicios Distinguidos en Guerra Exterior   Vol. 2: 1634
Condliffe Memorial Prize; Margaret   Vol. 2: 9848
Condon Award; Edward Uhler   Vol. 1: 19102
Condor of the Andes   Vol. 2: 1393
Conductor of the Year   Vol. 1: 12529
Confederate Air Force Cross   Vol. 1: 8099
Confederate Air Force Distinguished Flying Medal   Vol. 1: 8100
Confederation Award   Vol. 1: 18768
Conference Chairman Award   Vol. 1: 2769
Conference Chairperson of the Year   Vol. 1: 18941
Conference Coordinator Award   Vol. 1: 11018
Conference Division Chairman Award   Vol. 1: 18941
Conference Medallion   Vol. 1: 12231
Conference on Latin American History Prize   Vol. 1: 8140
Conference Speaker Award and Best Workshop Speaker Awards   Vol. 1: 11286
Congress Medal   Vol. 2: 2473
Congress Prizes   Vol. 2: 3393
Congressional Arts Caucus Award   Vol. 1: 8156

Congressional Award
  American College of Medical Practice Executives   Vol. 1: 1672
  Small Business Council of America   Vol 1: 17324
The Congressional Award   Vol. 1: 8158
Congressional Award for Exemplary Service to the Public   Vol. 1: 19480
Congressional Fellowship   Vol. 1: 3571
Congressional Gold Medal   Vol. 1: 19069
Congressional Medal of Honor   Vol. 1: 19169
Congressional Merit Award   Vol. 1: 16883
Congressional Research Grant Program   Vol. 1: 8672
Congressional Science Fellowship   Vol. 1: 4199
Congressional Space Medal of Honor   Vol. 1: 12730
Congressman Leo J. Ryan Commemorative Award   Vol. 1: 8484
Congressman of the Year   Vol. 1: 14378
Congressperson of the Year   Vol. 1: 5816
CONI Prize   Vol. 2: 8460
Conkling Memorial Award; Robert J.   Vol. 1: 5075
Conley Award; Dean   Vol. 1: 1656
Conley Award in Plastics Engineering and Technology; Fred O.   Vol. 1: 17982
Connare Award for Distinguished Service; Bishop William G.   Vol. 1: 13564
Connecticut Association Membership Award   Vol. 1: 10124
Connecticut River Watershed Council Conservation Award   Vol. 1: 8176
Connecticut Writer Award   Vol. 1: 8178
Connell Award; Edward P.   Vol. 1: 2143
Connell Award; W.F.   Vol. 1: 18438
Connelly Heroism Award; Robert P.   Vol. 1: 11708
Connelly, Jr. Mentorship Award; H. Walton   Vol. 1: 4140
Conner Memorial Scholarship; Paul W.   Vol. 1: 10566
Conners Prize for Poetry; Bernard F.   Vol. 1: 15969
Connie Award   Vol. 1: 8231
Connor Award; Robert D. W.   Vol. 1: 15495
Conquest of the Classical Guitar International Competition   Vol. 2: 8018
Conrad Memorial Lecture; Miles   Vol. 1: 13931
Conrad Poetry Award; Joseph   Vol. 1: 8180
Conrady Award; A. E.   Vol. 1: 18318
Conscience In Media Award   Vol. 1: 4635
Conseil Interamericain de Musique   Vol. 1: 15834
Consejo Interamericano de Music   Vol. 1: 15834
Conselho Interamericano de Musica   Vol. 1: 15834
Conservation Award
  American Association of Zoological Parks and Aquariums   Vol. 1: 1246
  International Wild Waterfowl Association   Vol 1: 11394
  National Speleological Society   Vol 1: 14848
  New England Wildflower Society   Vol 1: 15161
  Ottawa Field-Naturalists' Club   Vol 1: 15848
  Saskatchewan Natural History Society   Vol 1: 17067
Conservation Education Award   Vol. 1: 20300
Conservation Film/Video Award Program   Vol. 1: 15861
Conservation Medal   Vol. 1: 15161
Conservation News Award   Vol. 1: 18128

Conservation Service Awards   Vol. 1: 19246
Conservation Tillage Awards   Vol. 1: 13026
Conservationist of the Year
  Adirondack Council   Vol. 1: 137
  American Forestry Association   Vol 1: 2096
  Chesapeake Bay Foundation   Vol 1: 7584
  Florida Audubon Society   Vol 1: 9253
  Wildlife Society of Southern Africa   Vol 2: 11127
Considine Award; Bob
  Overseas Press Club of America   Vol. 1: 15875
  St. Bonaventure University - Department of Mass Communication   Vol 1: 16988
Consolidated Gold Fields Gold Medal   Vol. 2: 3337
Conspicuous Gallantry Medal
  British Government   Vol. 2: 2360
  Singapore - Office of the Prime Minister   Vol 2: 10738
Conspicuous Service Cross (CSC)   Vol. 2: 339
Conspicuous Service Decorations   Vol. 2: 339
Conspicuous Service Medal (CSM)   Vol. 2: 339
Constable Trophy
  Book Trust (England)   Vol. 2: 2197
  Constable & Co. Ltd.   Vol 2: 2680
Constellation Assurance Company Award   Vol. 1: 7121
Construction Industry Computing Association Awards   Vol. 2: 2682
Construction Industry Service Award   Vol. 1: 8941
Construction Management Award   Vol. 1: 4449
Construction's Man of the Year   Vol. 1: 8942
Construmat Award   Vol. 2: 11192
Consular Service Award   Vol. 1: 19283
Consumer Action Award   Vol. 1: 1162
Consumer Education Award   Vol. 1: 16703
Consumer Education Materials Contest   Vol. 1: 13598
Consumer Journalism Award   Vol. 1: 14496
Consumer Participation Award   Vol. 1: 7029
Consumer Research Award   Vol. 1: 11611
Conta Prize; Vasile   Vol. 2: 10342
Contact Vamp Trophee   Vol. 2: 9400
Contemporary A Cappella Recording Awards ("CARAs")   Vol. 1: 8233
Contemporary Music Festival   Vol. 1: 11961
Contemporary Poetry Series   Vol. 1: 19795
Contender's Award   Vol. 1: 1844
Contest for Piano Accompanists   Vol. 2: 1453
Continental Casualty Award   Vol. 1: 19028
Continental Grain Company Poultry Products Research Award   Vol. 1: 16346
Continuare Protessus Articulatus Excellare   Vol. 1: 14844
Continuous Service Award   Vol. 1: 1593
Continuum Women's Studies Award   Vol. 1: 8475
Contractor of the Year
  Land Improvement Contractors of America   Vol. 1: 11776
  National Railroad Construction and Maintenance Association   Vol 1: 14554
Contractor of the Year Award   Vol. 1: 3874
Contractor of the Year Awards (CotY Award)   Vol. 1: 13358
Contractors' Award   Vol. 2: 3762
Contributions to Agriculture Award   Vol. 1: 5424
Control Engineering Textbook Prize   Vol. 2: 818
Control Heritage Award   Vol. 1: 1286
Control Systems Award   Vol. 1: 10260

Convention Exhibitor Awards   Vol. 1: 8199
Convention Medal and Convention Certificate   Vol. 2: 936
Convention Scholarship Award   Vol. 1: 14745
Convention Scholarship for the Disabled   Vol. 1: 14745
Convention Service Manager of the Year   Vol. 1: 18517
Converse Coach of the Year Awards   Vol. 1: 14266
Conway Lecture   Vol. 2: 7830
Conway Medal; O'Reilly -   Vol. 1: 16219
Coogler Award; J. Gordon   Vol. 1: 4837
Cook - Douglas Medal   Vol. 1: 12160
Cook Medal; James   Vol. 2: 625
Cook Memorial Trophy; Jim   Vol. 1: 18419
Cook Prize   Vol. 2: 3130
Cook Prize; Gladys Emerson   Vol. 1: 12606
Cook Travel and Guide Book Awards; Thomas   Vol. 2: 2684
Cook Travelling Fellowship; William   Vol. 2: 2274
Cookbook Hall of Fame   Vol. 1: 6299
Cookbook of the Year   Vol. 1: 6299
Cookingham; Award for Career Development in Memory of L.P.   Vol. 1: 10848
Cookson Cup; Catherine   Vol. 2: 2996
Cookson Paleobotanical Award; Isabel C.   Vol. 1: 6477
Cooley Award; Charles Horton   Vol. 1: 17649
Cooley Award; George R.
   American Society of Plant Taxonomists   Vol. 1: 4753
   Botanical Society of America   Vol 1: 6478
Cooley Memorial Award; Emily   Vol. 1: 923
Cooley Memorial Lectureship; Emily   Vol. 1: 923
Coolidge Award; Edgar D.   Vol. 1: 994
Coolidge Essay Contest; Calvin   Vol. 1: 14741
Coomaraswamy Book Prize; Anada Kentish   Vol. 1: 5442
Coombes Medal; L.P.   Vol. 2: 434
Coonley Medal; Howard   Vol. 1: 3179
Coons Achievement Award   Vol. 1: 7804
Coons Award; Steven A.   Vol. 1: 5475
Cooper Architecture Award; Shirley   Vol. 1: 1174
Cooper Award; Mario   Vol. 1: 5043
Cooper Award; W. S.   Vol. 1: 8812
Cooper Medal; Commodore A. H.   Vol. 2: 9319
Cooper Medal; Dale Meyers   Vol. 1: 5331
Cooper Memorial Lecturer; Lenna F.   Vol. 1: 1959
Cooper Memorial Medal and Prize; E. R.   Vol. 2: 9836
Cooper Memorial Meridian Award; Billy H.   Vol. 1: 12183
Cooper Memorial Prize; Duff   Vol. 2: 2686
Cooper Prize; Duff   Vol. 2: 2686
Cooper Prize; J. R.   Vol. 2: 3889
Cooper Trophy; Alice Allgood   Vol. 1: 14645
Cooperation Award   Vol. 1: 8200
Cooperative Marketing and Sales Council Awards   Vol. 1: 15334
Cooperative Month Awards   Vol. 1: 13735
Cooperative Prize   Vol. 2: 11963
Cooperative Professor of the Year Award   Vol. 1: 1175
Coopers Deloitte Bookcover Award   Vol. 2: 2734
Coopers Hill War Memorial Prize   Vol. 2: 3233
Coopers Hill War Memorial Prize and Medal   Vol. 2: 3272
Coordinating Council of Lilterart Nagazubes   Vol. 1: 8369

Coote-Lake Medal for Folklore Research   Vol. 2: 2903
Cope Award; Arthur C.   Vol. 1: 1552
Cope Fund Grant; Arthur C.   Vol. 1: 1552
Cope Scholar Award; Arthur C.   Vol. 1: 1553
Cope Travel Grant; Arthur C.   Vol. 1: 1553
Copeland Award   Vol. 1: 1450
Copeland Award; Arthur E.   Vol. 1: 19008
Copeland Award; Edith Moore   Vol. 1: 17267
Copeland Scholarship; Arthur E.   Vol. 1: 19009
Copeland Scholarship; Helen   Vol. 1: 19010
Coplen Roll of Honor Award; Ron   Vol. 1: 18277
Copley Medal   Vol. 2: 4145
Copova Diploma   Vol. 2: 10797
Copp Award; Nan   Vol. 1: 6968
Coppa Mussolini   Vol. 2: 8470
Coppens Prize; J.   Vol. 2: 1253
Copper Club Award/Committee B-5 Award   Vol. 1: 6046
Copying Assistance Program   Vol. 1: 3159
Copyright Prize   Vol. 2: 9381
Corbeil; Prix Giles -   Vol. 1: 18880
Corbett Medal; Arthur   Vol. 2: 459
Corbetta Concrete Constructor Award; Roger H.   Vol. 1: 1780
Corbin Cool Hand Luke Award; Paul   Vol. 1: 9077
Corby, C.S.C. Award; Rev. William   Vol. 1: 19851
Corcoran Award   Vol. 1: 15371
Corcoran Award; W.   Vol. 1: 4080
Corday-Morgan Medal and Prize   Vol. 2: 4194
Cordero; Premio Juridico Mtro. Jorge Sanchez   Vol. 2: 8987
Cordoba; Orden del Merito Jose Maria   Vol. 2: 1644
Coremans; Premio Paul   Vol. 2: 9062
CORESTA Prize   Vol. 2: 5082
Corey Award; Albert B.   Vol. 1: 876
Corey Prize in Canadian-American Relations; Albert B.
   American Historical Association   Vol. 1: 2285
   Canadian Historical Association   Vol 1: 6905
Corinth-Preis; Lovis-   Vol. 2: 6523
Cork International Choral and Folk Dance Festival   Vol. 2: 7766
Cork International Choral Festival   Vol. 2: 7766
Cork International Film Festival   Vol. 2: 7769
Cork Youth International Video and Film Festival   Vol. 2: 7812
Corlette Medal; J.M.C.   Vol. 2: 460
Cornerstone Competition: A National Playwrighting Competition   Vol. 1: 16056
Cornette Prize; Arthur H.   Vol. 2: 1268
Cornevin; Prix Robert   Vol. 2: 6137
Cornforth Medal   Vol. 2: 598
Corning Award   Vol. 2: 2117
Corning Cup   Vol. 2: 2533
COROS Ribbon   Vol. 1: 7874
Corpas Prize; Juan N.   Vol. 2: 1726
Corporate Achievement Award   Vol. 1: 11253
Corporate and Professional Firm Leadership Award   Vol. 1: 7346
Corporate Award
   Canadian Sport Council   Vol. 1: 7242
   Ecological Society of America   Vol 1: 8813
   Florida Audubon Society   Vol 1: 9254
Corporate Awards   Vol. 1: 20369
Corporate Citizenship Award   Vol. 1: 7744
Corporate/Commercial Business Flying Safety Award   Vol. 1: 13497

Corporate Conservation Council's Environmental Achievement Award   Vol. 1: 15008
Corporate Executive of the Year   Vol. 1: 19910
Corporate Leadership Award
   National Hemophilia Foundation   Vol. 1: 14125
   Western Reserve Historical Society   Vol 1: 20215
Corporate Recognition Award   Vol. 1: 11253
Corporate Technical Achievement Award   Vol. 1: 1451
Corporation of the Year   Vol. 1: 16794
Corporation Professionelle des Psychologues du Quebec Merite Annuel   Vol. 1: 8287
Corps d'Elite Award   Vol. 1: 8012
Corpsmember Leadership Award   Vol. 1: 19268
Corpus Christi Young Artists' Competition   Vol. 1: 8290
Correctional Officer of the Year   Vol. 1: 10705
Corrections Exemplary Service Medal   Vol. 1: 6697
Corrections Film Festival   Vol. 1: 1833
Correspondent Membership   Vol. 2: 4698
Corresponding Members
   Botanical Society of America   Vol. 1: 6479
   German Society of Physical Medicine and Rehabilitation   Vol 2: 6865
Corson Medal; Bolton L.   Vol. 1: 9380
Corstorphine Medal   Vol. 2: 10867
Corwin Award; Edward S.   Vol. 1: 3572
Corwin Award; Sherrill C.   Vol. 1: 13370
Cory Cup   Vol. 2: 4028
Cory Memorial Cup; Reginald   Vol. 2: 4028
Cory - Wright Cup   Vol. 2: 9815
CoSIDA Backbone Award   Vol. 1: 7940
COSPAR Award   Vol. 2: 5062
COSPAR Distinguished Service Medal   Vol. 2: 5063
Cost Reduction Incentive Awards   Vol. 1: 12986
Costa Award; Joseph   Vol. 1: 14512
Costa Courtroom Photography Award; Joseph   Vol. 1: 6223
Costanzi; Premio Elio   Vol. 2: 8001
Coste; Prix Jean-Francois   Vol. 2: 4849
Coster Prize; Laurens Janszoon   Vol. 2: 9443
COTA Award of Excellence   Vol. 1: 3299
Cothenius-Medaille   Vol. 2: 6622
Cothenius Medal   Vol. 2: 6622
Cottle Honor Award; Dr. Maurice H.   Vol. 1: 3952
Cotton Foundation Fellowship Awards; Dr. M. Aylwin   Vol. 2: 2688
Cotton Foundation Publication Grants; Dr. M. Aylwin   Vol. 2: 2689
Cotton; Prix Aime   Vol. 2: 6366
CotY Award   Vol. 1: 13358
Cotzias Lecture; George   Vol. 1: 613
Coudenhove-Kalergi Award   Vol. 2: 7070
Coues Award; Elliott   Vol. 1: 3346
Coulter Memorial Lecturer; John Stanley   Vol. 1: 1804
Council Award of Excellence   Vol. 1: 9103
Council for Chemical Research Mac Pruitt Award   Vol. 1: 8311
Council Medal   Vol. 2: 3215
Council Meritorious Service Award   Vol. 1: 1635
Council of Catalonia Prize for Export   Vol. 2: 11184
Council of Europe Museum Prize   Vol. 2: 5088
Council of Film Organizations Film Awards   Vol. 1: 8358

Council of Logistics Management Scholarship   Vol. 1: 8374
Council of Reus Award for Excellence   Vol. 1: 14844
Council of the City of Sydney Prize   Vol. 2: 326
Council of the Year Award   Vol. 1: 10941
Council on Cardiovascular Nursing New Investigator Awards   Vol. 1: 2226
Counselor Educator of the Year   Vol. 1: 3064
Counselor of the Year   Vol. 1: 3065
Counselor of the Year Award   Vol. 1: 14594
Counsilman Creative Coaching Awards   Vol. 1: 4885
Counson Prize; Albert   Vol. 2: 1284
Count of Cartagena Prizes   Vol. 2: 11348
Counterpoise Grand Design Award   Vol. 1: 18044
Counting Coup Award   Vol. 1: 2420
Country Music Association Awards   Vol. 1: 8420
Country Music Hall of Fame   Vol. 1: 8421
Country of the Year Award   Vol. 1: 17978
Coupe des Mousquetaires   Vol. 2: 5259
Coupe d'Europe de Jeux d'Histoire   Vol. 2: 5321
Coupe Olympique   Vol. 2: 11814
Coupe Sazerac   Vol. 2: 6467
Coupes Merites Aux Individus   Vol. 1: 7493
Courage Award
   American Cancer Society   Vol. 1: 1411
   Courage Foundation   Vol 1: 8426
Courage in Journalism Award   Vol. 1: 11406
Courage to Care Award   Vol. 1: 5177
Courrier; Fondation Janine   Vol. 2: 5590
Course Rally Rookie of the Year   Vol. 1: 18392
Coursing Shield   Vol. 1: 3984
Courtis Prize; Baudilio   Vol. 2: 76
Courtois; Prix Gustave   Vol. 2: 5396
Cousin; Prix Victor   Vol. 2: 5794
Cousins National Chapter Award; Psi Chi/Ruth Hubbard   Vol. 1: 16547
Coutinho Prize; Admiral Gago   Vol. 2: 10317
Covarrubias; Premio Miguel   Vol. 2: 9059
Covello Award; Leonard   Vol. 1: 2715
Covenant Awards   Vol. 1: 6901
Covert Award; Cathy   Vol. 1: 5497
Cowart Plaque   Vol. 1: 17703
Cowen Award; Sir Zelman   Vol. 2: 609
Cowie Prize; The James M.   Vol. 2: 10557
Cowley Prize; Malcolm   Vol. 1: 20037
Cox Award; Morgan   Vol. 1: 20558
Cox Award; Norman W.   Vol. 1: 9933
Cox Bequest; Bertram   Vol. 2: 4131
Cox Memorial Prize; Jennifer   Vol. 2: 435
Cox Memorial Trophy - AHSA Jumper Course Designer; Mr. and Mrs. William C.   Vol. 1: 2348
CP Writers Award   Vol. 1: 8107
CPB Local Radio Development Awards
   Corporation for Public Broadcasting   Vol. 1: 8278
   Development Exchange   Vol 1: 8627
CPB Public Radio Program Awards   Vol. 1: 8279
CPB Public Television Local Program Awards   Vol. 1: 8280
CPC International Award   Vol. 1: 16347
CPhA Centennial Award   Vol. 1: 7092
CPP/Belwin Student Composition   Vol. 1: 12519
CPPQ Professional Award   Vol. 1: 8288
CPR Legal Program Awards for Excellence and Innovation in Alternative Dispute Resolution   Vol. 1: 7457
CPRS Award of Attainment   Vol. 1: 7113

CPRS Awards of Excellence Program   Vol. 1: 7112
CPRS Lamp of Service   Vol. 1: 7113
CPRS Lectern   Vol. 1: 7113
CPRS Major Awards Program   Vol. 1: 7113
CPRS Shield of Public Service   Vol. 1: 7113
CPRS Societal Award   Vol. 1: 7113
CQ DX Awards   Vol. 1: 8431
CQ DX Honor Roll   Vol. 1: 8432
CQ Novice Century Club   Vol. 1: 8433
CQ Press Award   Vol. 1: 8173
CRA Award   Vol. 2: 436
Crab Apple Cup   Vol. 2: 2393
CRAbbery Award   Vol. 1: 8442
Cracow International Festival of Short Films   Vol. 2: 10069
Crafoord Prize   Vol. 2: 11537
Craft Concepts - Jury Awards and Purchase Prizes   Vol. 1: 8444
Crafts Council of Ireland Purchase Award   Vol. 2: 7835
Craftsman's Award   Vol. 2: 4683
Craftsmen's Choice Award   Vol. 1: 17351
Craigie Award; Andrew   Vol. 1: 5880
Craik Award; Kenneth   Vol. 2: 4329
Crain Award for Distinguished Editorial Careers in the Business Press   Vol. 1: 1387
Crain Award; G. D.   Vol. 1: 6661
Craine Award; Zur   Vol. 1: 11220
Cramer Award; W. E.   Vol. 1: 1452
Cramer Zone Flower Arrangement Award; Barbara Spaulding   Vol. 1: 9486
Cramphorn Theater Scholarship; Rex   Vol. 2: 146
Crampton Prize   Vol. 2: 3234
Crane Distinguished Service Award; Fred C.   Vol. 1: 10357
Craniofacial Biology Group Distinguished Scientist Award   Vol. 1: 10615
Craniofacial Biology Research Award
   International Association for Dental Research   Vol. 1: 10615
   International Association for Dental Research - Craniofacial Biology Group   Vol 1: 10628
Cranko Memorial Award; John   Vol. 2: 9729
Cranston Awards; FAW Di   Vol. 2: 387
Crasilneck Award; Sherry K. and Harold B.   Vol. 1: 17432
Crate and Barrel Israeli Product Design Award for the Home and its Surroundings   Vol. 2: 7920
Cravath Memorial Award (MEF Auditions)   Vol. 1: 12537
Craven Award; Avery O.   Vol. 1: 15815
Craven Award; Richard C.   Vol. 1: 2398
Cravenne Prize; Engineering Prize - Avraham   Vol. 2: 7950
Crawferd Young Professional Award; Robert   Vol. 1: 14559
Crawford & Company Student Section Scholarship Award   Vol. 1: 4782
Crawford Award; Dorothy   Vol. 2: 283
Crawford Award; Hector   Vol. 2: 283
Crawford Award; J. G.   Vol. 2: 256
Crawford Medal
   Australian Academy of the Humanities   Vol. 2: 183
   Royal Philatelic Society, London   Vol 2: 4119
Crawford Meritorious Service Award; Frederick C.   Vol. 1: 20216
Crawley Plaque   Vol. 2: 2261
Crawshay Prize for English Literature; Rose Mary   Vol. 2: 2225
CRCD Award   Vol. 1: 7118
Creanga Prize; Ion   Vol. 2: 10343

Creasey Memorial Award; CWA John   Vol. 2: 2713
Creative and Innovative Awards   Vol. 1: 15396
Creative Arts Award
   Canadian Music Centre   Vol. 1: 7042
   Inventors Clubs of America - International Hall of Fame   Vol 1: 11416
Creative Design Award   Vol. 1: 11938
Creative Drama for Human Awareness Award   Vol. 1: 773
Creative Jewellery Design in Metal   Vol. 1: 15710
Creative Justice Program   Vol. 1: 10753
Creative Polymer Chemistry Award   Vol. 1: 1490
Creative Program of the Year   Vol. 1: 10753
Creative Writing Competition   Vol. 2: 2218
Creative Writing Junior Competition   Vol. 2: 2219
Creativity Achievement Award   Vol. 1: 7876
Creativity Centre Inc. Poetry Prize   Vol. 2: 351
Creativity Show   Vol. 1: 5291
Credit Executive of the Year   Vol. 1: 13064
Credit Research Foundation Award   Vol. 1: 9201
Credit Suisse Design Prize for Technical and Industrial Innovation in Geneva   Vol. 2: 11684
Cressey Memorial Award; Donald R.   Vol. 1: 10219
Cressman Award; Reginald J.   Vol. 1: 5727
Cresson Medal; Elliott   Vol. 1: 9381
Cresta Awards   Vol. 1: 10590
Cretsos Leadership Award; James M.   Vol. 1: 4167
Creu de Sant Jordi   Vol. 2: 11185
Crew Chief of the Year Award   Vol. 1: 240
Crew of the Year Award   Vol. 1: 9887
CRFA Fellowship Grants   Vol. 1: 7282
Crichlow Trust Prize; AIAA Walter J. and Angeline H.   Vol. 1: 2509
Crighton Trophy; Hec   Vol. 1: 6969
Crile Award; George   Vol. 1: 11148
Criminal Investigation Award   Vol. 1: 3550
Crimson Glory Award; Colonel A. T. Reid   Vol. 1: 5283
Crisp Medal   Vol. 2: 141
Criss Award   Vol. 1: 12539
Critical Writing Awards Competition   Vol. 1: 18535
Critici in Erba Prize   Vol. 2: 8171
Critics' and Readers' Pick   Vol. 1: 16888
Critic's Award   Vol. 1: 8664
Critics Prize   Vol. 2: 10298
Crittenden Award; Eugene Casson   Vol. 1: 19103
Crittenden Memorial Award; Christopher   Vol. 1: 15496
Crittenden Memorial Award; John and Jessie   Vol. 1: 6208
Croatian Socialist Republic Prizes   Vol. 2: 1808
Crocodile d'Or   Vol. 2: 6020
Croes Medal; J. James R.   Vol. 1: 4450
Croiset; Prix Alfred   Vol. 2: 5434
Croix de Guerre   Vol. 2: 5243
Cromer Greek Awards   Vol. 2: 2226
Crompton Premium   Vol. 2: 3273
Cromwell Association Award   Vol. 2: 2720
Cronin Award; Joe   Vol. 1: 2798
Cronin Club Award   Vol. 1: 13321
Cronkite Award for Excellence in Journalism and Telecommunication; Walter   Vol. 1: 8464
Croom Helm Nursing Prize   Vol. 2: 3860
Crop Science Award   Vol. 1: 8466

Crop Science International Activity Award   Vol. 1: 8467
Crosfield Cup   Vol. 2: 4029
Cross-Commodity Publication Award   Vol. 1: 4144
Cross Country Coaches of the Year   Vol. 1: 19559
Cross Country Merit Award   Vol. 1: 19933
Cross for Military Action of the Polish Armed Forces in the West   Vol. 2: 10098
Cross for Participation in the War of 1918-1921   Vol. 2: 10099
Cross of Auschwitz   Vol. 2: 10100
Cross of Mannerheim   Vol. 2: 4678
Cross of Merit   Vol. 2: 10101
Cross of Merit for Bravery   Vol. 2: 10102
Cross of Merit for Moral and Civic Education   Vol. 2: 1432
Cross of Merit with Swords   Vol. 2: 10103
Cross of Mourning   Vol. 2: 4678
Cross of the Battle of Lenino   Vol. 2: 10104
Cross of the Warsaw Uprising   Vol. 2: 10105
Cross of Valour
   Australian Decorations Advisory Committee - Australian Bravery Decorations   Vol. 2: 207
   Canada - The Chancellery   Vol 1: 6698
   Poland - Office of the President   Vol 2: 10106
Cross Pen Awards for Professional Sales Achievement   Vol. 1: 12882
Crossfield Aerospace Education Teacher of the Year Award; A. Scott   Vol. 1: 19219
Crossroad Women's Studies Award   Vol. 1: 8476
Crossroads Market/NLGJA Prize   Vol. 1: 14304
Crossword Champion   Vol. 2: 2641
Crossword Club Competitions   Vol. 2: 2722
Crouch Fellowship; John Mitchell   Vol. 2: 595
Crouch Medal; Herbert   Vol. 2: 130
Crowe, M.D. Memorial Exhibit Award; Charles W.   Vol. 1: 3210
Crowe Memorial Award; Norton H.   Vol. 1: 7243
Crowe Star of Tomorrow; Alberta E.
   Women's International Bowling Congress   Vol. 1: 20418
   Young American Bowling Alliance   Vol 1: 20599
Crowley Scholarship; Francis X.   Vol. 1: 15151
Crown Awards   Vol. 1: 7968
Crown Princess Sonja International Music Competition   Vol. 2: 9963
CRPLF Awards   Vol. 2: 5070
CRS (Certified Residential Specialist Designation)   Vol. 1: 16710
CRS National Festival for the Performing Arts Competition   Vol. 1: 8239
CRSI Design Awards Program   Vol. 1: 8092
Cruce Trophy; Marion C.   Vol. 1: 17358
Cruess Award; William V.   Vol. 1: 10343
Cruickshank Award; Dr. James W.   Vol. 1: 605
Cruickshank Memorial Award; Allan D.   Vol. 1: 9255
Cruikshank Award; Nelson   Vol. 1: 13750
Cruising Story Award   Vol. 1: 11508
Crum Award; Roy W.   Vol. 1: 18780
Crumbine Consumer Protection Award; Samuel J.
   Foodservice & Packaging Institute   Vol. 1: 9301
   International Association of Milk, Food and Environmental Sanitarians   Vol 1: 10762
Crump Trophy; Jack   Vol. 2: 2062

Cruz de Boyaca   Vol. 2: 1618
Cruz Medal of Merit; Oswaldo   Vol. 2: 1410
Cruz Prize; Oswaldo   Vol. 2: 1411
Crymes Fellowships to the TESOL Summer Institute; Ruth   Vol. 1: 18588
Crystal Apple   Vol. 1: 8351
Crystal Award
   National Association of Negro Business and Professional Women's Club   Vol. 1: 13209
   Sugar Industry Technologists   Vol 1: 18521
Crystal Awards
   National Association of Broadcasters   Vol. 1: 12974
   Women in Film   Vol 1: 20382
Crystal Prism Award   Vol. 1: 159
Crystallography Research Award   Vol. 1: 12301
Crystie Awards   Vol. 1: 15742
CSA Trophy   Vol. 1: 8108
CSAE/CSSBI Award   Vol. 1: 7151
CSAE Fellow   Vol. 1: 7148
CSAE Maple Leaf Award   Vol. 1: 7149
Csaki Award   Vol. 2: 7327
Csaki Dij   Vol. 2: 7327
CSC Jazz Award; Reverend George C. Wiskirchen/   Vol. 1: 13537
CSD Medal   Vol. 2: 2607
CSM Graduate Scholarship   Vol. 1: 7216
CSME Student Design Competition   Vol. 1: 7135
CSME Student Gold Medals   Vol. 1: 7136
CSPA Awards of Excellence   Vol. 1: 8378
CSPA Service Award   Vol. 1: 7249
CSPG Graduate Students Thesis Awards   Vol. 1: 7220
CSPG Undergraduate Scholarship; Norcen/   Vol. 1: 7226
CSRT Essay Award   Vol. 1: 6783
CSSBI Award; CSAE/   Vol. 1: 7151
Cubitt Award   Vol. 2: 3797
Cuchulainn Trophy   Vol. 2: 7812
Cudecki International Business Award; ACTFL Edwin   Vol. 1: 1870
Cuervo National Order; Miguel Antonio Caro and Rufino Jose   Vol. 2: 1711
Cuervo; Orden Nacional de Miguel Antonio Caro y Rufino Jose   Vol. 2: 1711
Cuesta National Poetry Prize; Jorge   Vol. 2: 9006
Cuesta; Premio Nacional de Poesia Jorge   Vol. 2: 9006
Cugnot Award   Vol. 1: 17782
Cugnot Award; Nicholas-Joseph   Vol. 1: 17785
Culbertson Award; Jack A.   Vol. 1: 19725
Culbertson Outstanding Volunteer Service Award; Charles V.   Vol. 1: 4783
Culinary Arts Salon
   Canadian Federation of Culinary Chefs   Vol. 1: 6860
   Chefs & Cooks Circle   Vol 2: 2611
   National Restaurant Association   Vol 1: 14623
   Panel of Chefs of Ireland   Vol 2: 7817
   Singapore Chefs Association   Vol 2: 10752
   Society of German Cooks   Vol 2: 7090
   Society of Swiss Cuisiniers   Vol 2: 11911
Culinary Masters
   Chefs & Cooks Circle   Vol 2: 2611
   National Restaurant Association   Vol 1: 14623
   Panel of Chefs of Ireland   Vol 2: 7817
   Singapore Chefs Association   Vol 2: 10752
   Society of German Cooks   Vol 2: 7090
   Society of Swiss Cuisiniers   Vol 2: 11911
Culinary Masters Competition   Vol. 1: 6860
Culinary Military Cup   Vol. 2: 8873

Culinary Olympics
   Canadian Federation of Culinary Chefs   Vol. 1: 6860
   Chefs & Cooks Circle   Vol 2: 2611
   Panel of Chefs of Ireland   Vol 2: 7817
   Singapore Chefs Association   Vol 2: 10752
   Society of German Cooks   Vol 2: 7090
   Society of Swiss Cuisiniers   Vol 2: 11911
Culinary World Cup
   Canadian Federation of Culinary Chefs   Vol. 1: 6860
   Chefs & Cooks Circle   Vol 2: 2611
   National Restaurant Association   Vol 1: 14623
   Panel of Chefs of Ireland   Vol 2: 7817
   Singapore Chefs Association   Vol 2: 10752
   Society of German Cooks   Vol 2: 7090
   Society of Swiss Cuisiniers   Vol 2: 11911
   Vatel-Club Luxembourg   Vol 2: 8874
Cullis Grants; Winifred   Vol. 2: 11789
Cullum Geographical Medal   Vol. 2: 2151
Cultural Achievement Award   Vol. 1: 2731
Cultural Cooperation Award   Vol. 1: 8893
Cultural Diversity Outreach Award   Vol. 1: 3910
Cultural Merit Award   Vol. 2: 10089
Cultural Pluralism Award   Vol. 1: 5945
Culture Prize
   European Movement in Norway   Vol. 2: 9882
   Norwegian Cultural Council   Vol 2: 9934
   Oslo Kommune   Vol 2: 9959
Culver Award; Byron G.   Vol. 1: 16865
Culver Distinguished Service Award; Essae M.   Vol. 1: 11952
Culver Gold Medal; Helen   Vol. 1: 9546
Cummings Memorial Award; Donald E.   Vol. 1: 2432
Cumont; Prix Franz   Vol. 2: 988
Cumulative Mileage Awards   Vol. 1: 15470
Cunha Award; Octacilio   Vol. 2: 2027
Cunha; Premio Octacilio   Vol. 2: 2027
Cunningham Agricultural Journalist of the Year; Glenn   Vol. 1: 12929
Cunningham Award; Glenn   Vol. 1: 19934
Cunningham Award (Marine Aviator of the Year); Alfred A.   Vol. 1: 12058
Cunningham Award; Robinson/   Vol. 1: 537
Cunningham Award; Thomas F.   Vol. 1: 20530
Cunningham Inter-American Award; Thomas F.   Vol. 1: 20530
Cunningham International Cinema Award; Dr. Frank H.   Vol. 1: 8413
Cunningham Memorial Award; Ed   Vol. 1: 15875
Cunningham Memorial International Fellowship   Vol. 1: 12167
Cunningham Plaque (Most Valuable Player); Les   Vol. 1: 2323
Cunningham-Steward Memorial Award   Vol. 2: 199
Cup of Cups   Vol. 2: 1117
Curci; Concorso Internazionale di Violino Alberto   Vol. 2: 8211
Curci International Violin Competition; Alberto   Vol. 2: 8211
Cured Meats Hall of Fame   Vol. 1: 1036
Curie Award; Marie   Vol. 1: 905
Curl Award; Earl   Vol. 1: 11306
Curl Bequest Prize   Vol. 2: 3926
Curren Award   Vol. 1: 19680
Currey Memorial Fellowship; C. H.   Vol. 2: 683
Currie Award; Margaret   Vol. 1: 1078
Curti Award; Merle   Vol. 1: 15816
Curtin Medal; Bill   Vol. 2: 3235
Curtin Plaque   Vol. 1: 17704

Curtis Cup Vol. 1: 19359
Curtis European Award; Leonard Vol. 2: 3843
Curtis Lecture Award; John A. Vol. 1: 4081
Curtis Medal; J.H. Vol. 2: 450
Curtis Memorial Prize; Edmund Vol. 2: 7841
Cushman Award; Joseph A. Vol. 1: 8487
Customer Service Enhancement Competition Award Vol. 1: 1040
Cutler Award; Lady Vol. 2: 315
Cutlery Hall of Fame Vol. 1: 10801
Cutting Edge Gemstone Competition Vol. 1: 2148
Cutty Sark Medal Vol. 2: 3633
Cutty Sark Men's Fashion Awards Vol. 1: 20451
Cuvillier; Fondation Jean Vol. 2: 5593
CVB Amateur Theatre Award Vol. 2: 9379
CVB Amateurtheater Prijs Vol. 2: 9379
CVMA Award Vol. 1: 7259
CVMA Humane Award Vol. 1: 7260
CVMA Plaque Vol. 1: 7261
CVMA President's Award Vol. 1: 7262
CWA '92 Award Vol. 2: 2709
CWA/Cartier Diamond Dagger Award Vol. 2: 2710
CWA Gold Dagger Award Vol. 2: 2711
CWA Gold Dagger Award for Non-Fiction Vol. 2: 2712
CWA John Creasey Memorial Award Vol. 2: 2713
CWA Last Laugh Award Vol. 2: 2714
CWA Rumpole Award Vol. 2: 2715
CWA Short Story Competition Vol. 2: 2716
CWI of the Year Award Vol. 1: 5077
Cycle Award
   American Animal Hospital Association Vol. 1: 787
   American Veterinary Medical Association Vol 1: 4985
Cycle Fido Award Vol. 1: 9460
Cycle Obedience Award Vol. 1: 9461
Cycle Obedience Person of the Year Vol. 1: 9462
Cymmrodorion Medal Vol. 2: 3023
Cyr Gold Reel Award; Helen Vol. 1: 6249
Cyril and Methodius Prize Vol. 2: 1514
Cytogen Corporation Excellence in Cancer Nursing Administration Award; ONS/ Vol. 1: 15656
Cytotechnologist Award for Outstanding Achievement Vol. 1: 4546
Cytotechnologist Award of the American Society of Cytology Vol. 1: 4547
Cytotechnologist of the Year Award Vol. 1: 4546
Cytotechnologist Scientific Presentation Award Vol. 1: 4547
Czechoslovak Association of Liberty and Anti-Fascist Fighters Awards Vol. 2: 1846
Czechoslovak National Artist Vol. 2: 1856
Czerny Preis; Adalbert Vol. 2: 6820
Czlonek Honorowy
   Polish Association of Pediatric Surgeons Vol. 2: 10132
   Polish Sociological Association Vol 2: 10199
Czlonek honorowy dozywotni Vol. 2: 10202
Czlonkostwo Honorowe
   Modern Language Association of Poland Vol. 2: 10081
   Polish Geographical Society Vol 2: 10147
   Polish Society of Endocrinology Vol 2: 10185
   Society of Friends of the Polish Language Vol 2: 10210

da Conceicao Silva de Espacos Interiores abertos ao publico; Premio Municipal Francisco Vol. 2: 10269
Da Gama Machado; Fondation Vol. 2: 5527
da Motta International Competition; Vianna Vol. 2: 10228
da Vinci Award; The Leonardo Vol. 1: 10239
Da Vinci Diploma; Leonardo Vol. 2: 5141
Da Vinci Medal; Leonardo Vol. 1: 17615
Da Vinci World Award of Arts; Leonardo Vol. 2: 9306
d'Abbadie; Fondation Antoine Vol. 2: 5493
DAC Trophy Vol. 1: 8714
Dacco Award; Aldo Vol. 2: 8126
Dach InVEST Award Vol. 1: 10125
Daedalian Award Vol. 1: 15775
Daedalian Civilian Air Safety Award Vol. 1: 15779
Daedalian Distinguished Achievement Award Vol. 1: 15773
Daedalian Scholarship Awards Vol. 1: 15774
Daedalian Supply Effectiveness Award Vol. 1: 15772
Daedalian Trophy
   Order of Daedalians Vol. 1: 15771
   Order of Daedalians Vol 1: 15772
   Order of Daedalians Vol 1: 15776
   Order of Daedalians Vol 1: 15777
   Order of Daedalians Vol 1: 15778
   Order of Daedalians Vol 1: 15779
   Order of Daedalians Vol 1: 15781
   Order of Daedalians Vol 1: 15782
   Order of Daedalians Vol 1: 15783
   Order of Daedalians Vol 1: 15784
   Order of Daedalians Vol 1: 15786
   Order of Daedalians Vol 1: 15787
Daedalian Weapon System Award Vol. 1: 15775
Daeyang Prize in Economics Vol. 2: 8815
Dagenais Award; Camille A. Vol. 1: 7170
Daggs Award; Ray G. Vol. 1: 3505
Dagnan-Bouveret; Fondation Jean Vol. 2: 5594
Dagnan-Bouveret; Prix
   Institut de France - Academie des Beaux Arts Vol. 2: 5374
   Institut de France - Academie des Sciences Morales et Politiques Vol 2: 5709
Dagra Prize Vol. 2: 10243
Daguerre-Preis Vol. 2: 6605
Dahlberg Peace Award; Edwin T. Vol. 1: 1295
The *Daily Mail* Awards of Excellence Vol. 2: 2727
Daily Point of Light Vol. 1: 19333
Daily Reporter Award for Civil Liberties Journalism Vol. 1: 7454
The *Daily Telegraph* Award Vol. 2: 2033
Dain Library History Dissertation Award; Phyllis Vol. 1: 2913
Dairy Industry Quality Performance Awards Vol. 2: 9714
Dairy Progressive Breeder Awards Vol. 1: 3107
Dairy Technology Awards Vol. 2: 11086
Daiwa Scholarships Vol. 2: 2730
Dakotsu Prize Vol. 2: 8677
Dalby Prize Vol. 2: 4239
Dale Award; Edgar
   Association for Indiana Media Educators Vol. 1: 5533
   Film Council of Greater Columbus Vol 1: 9187
Dale Fellowships; Chester Vol. 1: 12234
Dalgety Farmers Limited Awards for Excellence in Rural Journalism Vol. 2: 353
Dalgety Study Award Vol. 2: 353

Dallas Advertising League Award Vol. 1: 18633
Dall'Onda Borghese Prize; Fondazione Contessa Caterina Pasolini Vol. 2: 8050
Dallos Award; Joseph Vol. 1: 8229
d'Alviella; Prix Goblet Vol. 2: 989
Daly Award; Sgt. Maj. Dan Vol. 1: 12080
Daly Medal; Charles P. Vol. 1: 2152
d'Alzon Medal; Emmanuel Vol. 1: 6150
Dama del Paraigues (Lady with the Umbrella) Vol. 2: 11155
D'Amato; Fondazione Luigi Vol. 2: 8061
D'Ambrisi Award; Richard H. Vol. 1: 5909
Damele Memorial Award; Peter L. Vol. 1: 1330
Damen Award Vol. 1: 11969
Dameshek Prize Vol. 1: 4594
Damien - Dutton Award Vol. 1: 8514
Damm-prisen Vol. 2: 9880
Damm prize Vol. 2: 9880
D'Amour Award; O'Neil Vol. 1: 13542
Dana Award; Eleanor Naylor Vol. 1: 2218
Dana Award; Margaret Vol. 1: 6047
Dana Award; SLA John Cotton Vol. 1: 18268
Dana Awards for Pioneering Achievements in Health; Charles A. Vol. 1: 12697
Dana Awards for Pioneering Achievements in Higher Education; Charles A. Vol. 1: 8516
Dana Library Public Relations Awards; John Cotton Vol. 1: 2905
Dana Publicity Award; John Cotton Vol. 1: 2905
Dance Educator of the Year Vol. 1: 13842
Dance Grants Vol. 1: 16399
Dance Magazine Annual Awards Vol. 1: 8522
Dance on Camera Festival Vol. 1: 8520
Dance Screen Award Vol. 2: 842
Dance/USA National Honors Vol. 1: 8534
Dando Memorial Conference Chairman Award; Harry B. Vol. 1: 2769
D'Andria Memorial Trophy; Edmund P. Vol. 1: 3119
Dandurand Trophy; Leo Vol. 1: 6873
DANDY Awards Vol. 1: 15347
Danielopolu Prize; Daniel Vol. 2: 10344
Daniels Award; Farrington Vol. 2: 509
Daniels Award; H. G. Vol. 1: 17026
Danielson Best Paper Awards; Philip A. Vol. 1: 20240
Danis Prize; Robert Vol. 2: 11844
Danish Academy Prize for Literature Vol. 2: 1909
Danish Authors Lyric Prize Vol. 2: 1925
Danish Prize for Children's Literature Vol. 2: 1936
Danmarks Radio TV Award Vol. 2: 1991
Danmarks Skolebibliotekarforenings Bornebogspris Vol. 2: 1920
d'Annunzio; Premio G. Vol. 2: 8213
Dansk Oversaetterforbunds Aerespris
   Danish Writers' Association Vol. 2: 1926
   Denmark - Ministry of Cultural Affairs Vol 2: 1937
Danstar Vol. 2: 1934
Danstrom Award; Charlotte Vol. 1: 20392
Dantas; Premio General Casimiro Vol. 2: 10247
Dantas Prize; General Casimiro Vol. 2: 10247
Dantzig Prize Vol. 2: 9548
Dantzig Prize; George B. Vol. 1: 17511
Danzig Award; Sarah Palfrey Vol. 1: 19645
Danzig Goodguy Award; Allison Vol. 1: 12239
Darbaker Prize Vol. 1: 6480
Darby Award for Inspirational Leadership; Rear Admiral Jack N. Vol. 1: 15089

Dare Award   Vol. 1: 11715
d'Arezzo; International Composition Contest Guido   Vol. 2: 8215
d'Arezzo; International Polyphonic Contest Guido   Vol. 2: 8216
Darjah Utama Bakti Chemerlang   Vol. 2: 10739
Darjah Utama Nila Utama   Vol. 2: 10744
Darjah Utama Temasek   Vol. 2: 10745
Darling Foundation Prize   Vol. 2: 11974
Darling Medal - Conservationist of the Year; Jay N. "Ding"   Vol. 1: 15009
Darling Medal for Distinguished Achievement in Collection Development in the Health Sciences; Louise   Vol. 1: 12168
Darmstaedter Preis; Paul Ehrlich - und Ludwig   Vol. 2: 6691
Darne Memorial Award; Frances Rice   Vol. 1: 17531
Darolles; Prix Docteur   Vol. 2: 4830
Darracq; Fondation Alexandre   Vol. 2: 5480
Darracq; Fondation Louise   Vol. 2: 5623
Darrow Award; Clarence   Vol. 1: 11149
Darrow Award for Excellence in Viticulture and Small Fruits; George M.   Vol. 1: 4145
Dartmouth Medal   Vol. 1: 2939
Darwin International Medal for Science and Environment; Sir Charles   Vol. 2: 7717
Darwin Medal   Vol. 2: 4146
Darwin-Plakette   Vol. 2: 6623
Darwin Plaque   Vol. 2: 6623
Darwin - Wallace Medals   Vol. 2: 3586
Das Jaigopal Memorial Award; Chaturvedi Ghanshyam   Vol. 2: 7582
Das Memorial Award; Chaturvedi Kalawati Jagmohan   Vol. 2: 7583
d'Aschen-Presles; Prix   Vol. 2: 5340
Dasher Best Paper Award; Benjamin J.   Vol. 1: 4082
Daskalov Prize; Academician Hristo   Vol. 2: 1513
Dassler Memorial Award; adidas - Adi   Vol. 1: 10538
Data Courier Award   Vol. 1: 18858
Data Courier Award; UMI/   Vol. 1: 15675
Data Processing Professional of the Year Award   Vol. 1: 9684
Datta Memorial Oration Award; Dr. Dharamvir   Vol. 2: 7584
Dauberville; Prix Henri   Vol. 2: 5400
Daubney Research Fellowship in Virology and Helminthology; Robert   Vol. 2: 3983
d'Aumale; Prix   Vol. 2: 5341
Daumet; Fondation   Vol. 2: 5388
Dauphin Trophies   Vol. 2: 5006
Dautrebande Physiopathology Foundation Prize   Vol. 2: 1112
Dauzat Prize; Albert   Vol. 2: 6307
Davenport Exhibit Award; John S.   Vol. 1: 3211
David Awards   Vol. 1: 11487
David Film Awards   Vol. 2: 8218
David - Gerald Award   Vol. 1: 18840
David Library of the American Revolution Award for Playwriting on American Freedom   Vol. 1: 1757
David Medal; Edgeworth   Vol. 2: 626
David; Prix Athanase-   Vol. 1: 16612
David; Prix Maxime   Vol. 2: 5413
David - Weill; Prix de Dessin Pierre   Vol. 2: 5375
Davidoff Award; National Planning Awards - Paul   Vol. 1: 3543
Davids Award; Bob   Vol. 1: 17410
Davidson ASPRS President's Award for Practical Papers; John I.   Vol. 1: 4246
Davidson Award; Park O.   Vol. 1: 7937

Davidson Lecture; Mackenzie   Vol. 2: 2409
Davidson Lectureship and Award; Murray   Vol. 1: 668
Davidson Medal   Vol. 1: 17922
Davidson Medal; George   Vol. 1: 2153
Davidson Memorial Award for Sportsmanship; Kenneth R.   Vol. 1: 19035
Davidson Memorial Award; Gustav   Vol. 1: 16279
Davidson Memorial Trophy; Sam   Vol. 1: 6970
Davidson Prize in Economics; David   Vol. 2: 11562
Davies Award; Mary Carolyn   Vol. 1: 16280
Davies Award; Valentine   Vol. 1: 20559
Davies Awards; Ryan   Vol. 2: 12168
Davies Memorial Award for Playwriting; D. T.   Vol. 2: 12170
Davignon; Prix Henri   Vol. 2: 1301
Davila Award of Merit; Robert R.   Vol. 1: 9690
Davis Award; Arthur Vining   Vol. 1: 383
Davis Award; Earl R.   Vol. 1: 17286
Davis Award; Henry B.   Vol. 1: 4790
Davis Award; Jefferson   Vol. 2: 8104
Davis Award; John Eisele   Vol. 2: 2770
Davis Award; John P.   Vol. 1: 4717
Davis Award; Shelby Cullom   Vol. 1: 9013
Davis Award; W. Allison and Elizabeth Stubbs   Vol. 1: 12486
Davis Award; Watson   Vol. 1: 4168
Davis Awards; Nathan   Vol. 1: 3022
Davis Awards of Excellence; Graham L.   Vol. 1: 9864
Davis Cup   Vol. 1: 19646
Davis Fund Awards; Henry and Lily   Vol. 2: 3669
Davis Graduate Scholarship Award; Keith   Vol. 1: 17260
Davis, Jr. Award; Sammy   Vol. 1: 18155
Davis Lecture Series; Raymond E.   Vol. 1: 1781
Davis Medal; George E.   Vol. 2: 3216
Davis Memorial Award; Charles   Vol. 1: 9409
Davis Memorial Award; Suzanne M.   Vol. 1: 18205
Davis Memorial Award; Tad   Vol. 1: 19453
Davis Memorial Award; William J.   Vol. 1: 19726
Davis Memorial Lecture; E. H.   Vol. 2: 437
Davis Prize in Old Age Psychiatry; Philip   Vol. 2: 3960
Davis Prize; Watson   Vol. 1: 9949
Davis Silver Medal Award; A. F.   Vol. 1: 5076
Davis Trampoline Coach of the Year; Milton B.   Vol. 1: 426
Davison Award; FAW Frank Dalby   Vol. 2: 389
Davisson-Germer Prize in Atomic or Surface Physics   Vol. 1: 3451
Davy Medal   Vol. 2: 4147
Dawdon Trophy   Vol. 2: 2066
Dawood Prize for Literature   Vol. 2: 10005
Dawson Achievement Awards   Vol. 1: 5917
Dawson Award for Legislative Development; William L.   Vol. 1: 8162
Dawson Award; Sir John William   Vol. 1: 16951
Day Cup; Colonel George E.   Vol. 1: 5276
Day Medal; Arthur L.   Vol. 1: 9559
Day Memorial Award; Richard Hopper   Vol. 1: 69
Day Prize and Lectureship; Arthur L.   Vol. 1: 12666
Dayton Playhouse Future Fest   Vol. 1: 8536
Dayton Playhouse National Playwriting Competition   Vol. 1: 8536
Daytona 500 NASCAR Stock Car Race   Vol. 1: 8539

DBL (David Bell Laboratories) Horner Travel Award   Vol. 1: 7188
de Amodio Prize; Anne   Vol. 2: 6110
De Angelis Award; George   Vol. 1: 12386
de Araujo Pereira de Design; Premio Municipal Roberto   Vol. 2: 10277
De Backer Prize; Paul   Vol. 2: 1310
de-Bary-Medaille; Anton-   Vol. 2: 6668
de Beaufort-prijs; Henriette   Vol. 2: 9625
de Beauregard; Prix Georges   Vol. 2: 4962
de Beauregard Prize; Georges   Vol. 2: 4962
De Beers Gold Medal Award; SAIP -   Vol. 2: 11071
de Caen; Fondation   Vol. 2: 5388
de Carli Award; Felice   Vol. 2: 8127
de Carvalho Fernandes Prize; Antonio Alves   Vol. 2: 10248
de Castilho de Olisipografia; Premio Municipal Julio   Vol. 2: 10274
de Cavia; Premio Mariano   Vol. 2: 11318
de Cervantes; Premio Miguel   Vol. 2: 11368
de Clercq; Prix de la Fondation Louis   Vol. 2: 5446
De Clercq Prize; C.   Vol. 2: 1254
de Conway Little Medal of Honor; Helen   Vol. 1: 9906
de Coubertin; Trophee International du Fair Play Pierre   Vol. 2: 5989
de Dios Batiz; Medalla Juan   Vol. 2: 9069
de Donder; Prix Theophile   Vol. 2: 1037
de Ercilla Award; Alonso   Vol. 2: 1552
de Ercilla; Premio Alonso   Vol. 2: 1552
de Falloise Quinquennial Prize; Arthur   Vol. 2: 1065
de Ferranti Premium; Sebastian Z.   Vol. 2: 3273
de Ferrari Doria; Fondation Jules et Louis Jeanbernat et Barthelemy   Vol. 2: 5604
de Ferrari Doria; Prix Jules et Louis Jeanbernat et Barthelemy
   Institut de France   Vol. 2: 5346
   Institut de France - Academie des Beaux Arts   Vol 2: 5407
   Institut de France - Academie des Inscriptions et Belle-Lettres   Vol 2: 5467
   Institut de France - Academie des Sciences Morales et Politiques   Vol 2: 5768
   Institut de France - Academie Francaise   Vol 2: 5874
de Figueiredo Prize; Jose   Vol. 2: 10284
de Florez Flight Safety Award; Admiral Luis   Vol. 1: 9243
De Florez Training Award   Vol. 1: 2460
De Florez Training Award for Flight Simulation; AIAA   Vol. 1: 2460
De Forest Audion Award   Vol. 1: 20000
De Francis Award; Vincent   Vol. 1: 2399
de Give de Muache; Prix du Docteur Louis   Vol. 2: 1332
De Golyer Institute for American Studies Prize   Vol. 1: 18227
de Gonzalya Foundation Prize; Deldebat   Vol. 2: 6308
de Goote Memorial Chamber Music Award; Steven   Vol. 1: 7844
de Goya; Premio Francisco   Vol. 2: 11290
De Graaff Medal; Reynier   Vol. 2: 9556
De Greef; Prix Arthur   Vol. 2: 951
de Gunzburg Prize; Minda   Vol. 2: 4910
de Hauteroche; Prix Allier   Vol. 2: 5436
de Hevia; Orden Francisco Javier Garcia   Vol. 2: 12111
de Horion; Prix Constant   Vol. 2: 1041
de Joest; Prix du Baron   Vol. 2: 5383
de Jouvenal; Prix Roland   Vol. 2: 5917
De Keyn; Prix Joseph   Vol. 2: 992

de la Cabada; Premio Nacional de Cuento para Ninos Juan   Vol. 2: 9232
De la Court Prize   Vol. 2: 9599
de la Cruz; Premio Martin   Vol. 2: 9130
de la Maza; Premio Francisco   Vol. 2: 9054
de la Serna; Premio Juan   Vol. 2: 11342
De la Torre Bueno Prize   Vol. 1: 8530
De La Vaulx Medal   Vol. 2: 5142
de Lamothe; Prix   Vol. 2: 5305
de Lara "Tono" de Humor Grafico; Premio Antonio   Vol. 2: 11287
de las Casas; Premio Bartolome   Vol. 2: 11362
De Laszlo Medal   Vol. 2: 4177
De Lavalforelasning   Vol. 2: 11524
de Laveleye; Prix Emile   Vol. 2: 985
de Leon; Premio Nacional de Poesia Joven Francisco Gonzalez   Vol. 2: 9237
de Lera Hispanism Prize for Literature; Angel Maria   Vol. 1: 18842
de-Maisonneuve; Prix Chomedey-   Vol. 1: 17385
De Marquez, Santiago Perez, and Antonio Ricaurte Prizes; Jose Ignacio   Vol. 2: 1625
de Martens; Prix Frederic   Vol. 2: 11751
De Mellis; Premio Cavolini -   Vol. 2: 8087
de Menasce Memorial Trust; George   Vol. 2: 3749
de Mendizabal; Premio Miguel Othon   Vol. 2: 9060
de Menezes Veiga; Premio Frederico   Vol. 2: 1447
de Menezes Veiga Prize; Frederico   Vol. 2: 1447
de Meyer; Fondation Jean   Vol. 2: 1002
De Mille Award; Cecil B.   Vol. 1: 9973
de Miranda; Order of Francisco   Vol. 2: 12138
de Monaco; Fondation Albert I   Vol. 2: 5479
de Montequin Fellowship in Iberian and Latin American Architecture; Edilia   Vol. 1: 17741
De Morgan Medal   Vol. 2: 3609
de Morogues; Fondation Bigot   Vol. 2: 5503
de Morogues; Prix Bigot   Vol. 2: 5718
de Neuville et Sanford Saltus; Prix Alphonse   Vol. 2: 5357
de Paepe; Prix Polydore   Vol. 2: 996
de Parville; Fondation Henri   Vol. 2: 5576
de Pessemier; Prix Paul   Vol. 2: 1053
de Piauhy; Prix Alvarenga   Vol. 2: 1325
De Pimodan Foundation Prize   Vol. 2: 6309
de Poesie; Prix Annuel   Vol. 2: 5814
de Pontecoulant; Fondation G.   Vol. 2: 5562
De Potter; Prix Agathon   Vol. 2: 1007
de Quevado; Premio Francisco   Vol. 2: 11291
de Regnier; Prix Pierre   Vol. 2: 5910
de Rothschild Cup; Lionel   Vol. 2: 4030
de Rufz de La Vison; Fondation Jean   Vol. 2: 5595
De Ruyck Prize; Dr. Roland   Vol. 2: 1311
de Sagarra; Premi Josep Maria   Vol. 2: 11160
de Sahagun; Premio Fray Bernardino   Vol. 2: 9056
de Saint Rat Award; Louis   Vol. 2: 7373
de Saridakis; Fondation Laura Mounier   Vol. 2: 5613
de Sousa Prego Freedom Prize; Visconde   Vol. 2: 10295
de Sousa Prize; Luisa Claudio   Vol. 2: 1451
de Soussay; Prix   Vol. 2: 5379
de Souza Award; Antonio   Vol. 1: 10984
de Tena; Premio Luca   Vol. 2: 11317
de Tiere Prize; Nestor   Vol. 2: 1269
de Tocqueville Prize; Alexis   Vol. 2: 9410
de Tocqueville Prize in United States History; Alexis   Vol. 1: 2286
de Varona Award; Donna   Vol. 1: 20431
de Vattel; Prix Emer   Vol. 2: 11751

de Vega; Premio Lope   Vol. 2: 11294
de Vernon; Prix Frederic et Jean   Vol. 2: 5392
de Vries Award; Hendrik   Vol. 2: 9362
de Vries prijs; Hendrik   Vol. 2: 9362
de Vries Stipend; Hendrik   Vol. 2: 9363
de Vries Stipendium; Hendrik   Vol. 2: 9363
De Waal Gedenktoekenning; Jan   Vol. 2: 10859
De Waal Memorial Award; Jan   Vol. 2: 10859
de Wegmann; Prix Vega et Lods   Vol. 2: 5928
De Wet Decoration   Vol. 2: 10925
De Wet Medal   Vol. 2: 10926
de Wever; Prix Franz   Vol. 2: 1297
de Wiart; Prix Carton   Vol. 2: 1294
de Wolmar; Prix Valentine   Vol. 2: 5927
DEA Award   Vol. 1: 8518
Deadline Club Awards   Vol. 1: 8547
Deaf/Hard of Hearing Entrepreneur of the Year   Vol. 1: 8549
Deafness Research Foundation Otological Research Fellowship for Medical Students   Vol. 1: 8552
Deak Award; Francis O.   Vol. 1: 4630
Deakin Award; Charles   Vol. 2: 7175
Dealer and Exhibit Awards   Vol. 1: 8109
Dealer Awards   Vol. 1: 6206
Dealer Education Award   Vol. 1: 15530
Dealer Member of the Year   Vol. 1: 6207
Dealer of the Year Award   Vol. 1: 3212
Dealers' Hall of Fame   Vol. 1: 6204
Dean Memorial Award; H. Trendley   Vol. 1: 10616
Dean Research Award   Vol. 1: 1732
Deane Award; Hamilton   Vol. 2: 2753
Deauville - Trouville; Prix Alexandre Dumas   Vol. 2: 6244
Deaver Award; Sally   Vol. 1: 19560
DeBakey Award; Michael E.   Vol. 1: 8555
Debenedetti; Prix Medecin General Inspecteur Raymond   Vol. 2: 4862
Deborah Award   Vol. 1: 2732
Debreczeni Medal; Marton   Vol. 2: 7353
Debs Award; Eugene V.   Vol. 1: 8557
Debs Foundation Bryant Spann Memorial Prize; Eugene V.   Vol. 1: 8558
Debye Award in Physical Chemistry; Peter   Vol. 1: 1554
Debye Prize; Peter   Vol. 2: 9681
DeCelle Award; Robert E.   Vol. 1: 19935
Dechelle; Fondation Ernest   Vol. 2: 5553
DECHEMA Ehrenmitgliedschaft   Vol. 2: 6615
DECHEMA Honorary Membership   Vol. 2: 6615
DECHEMA-Medaille   Vol. 2: 6616
DECHEMA Medal   Vol. 2: 6616
DECHEMA Preis der Max Buchner Forschungsstiftung   Vol. 2: 6617
Decker Memorial Outreach Award; Bea   Vol. 1: 11357
Decoration for Distinguished Service in the South African Railways Police Force   Vol. 2: 10950
Decoration for Exceptional Public Service   Vol. 1: 19216
Decoration for Meritorious Service   Vol. 2: 10958
Decorations   Vol. 2: 6946
Decorations and Medals   Vol. 2: 8578
Decorative Arts Collection Awards   Vol. 1: 14822
Dedicated Service Award
    American Society of Mechanical Engineers   Vol. 1: 4670
    National Society of Tole and Decorative Painters   Vol 1: 14823
Dedrick, Jr. Award; Dewey R.   Vol. 1: 4791
Deep South Writers Conference   Vol. 1: 8568

Deere Awards; NACTA John   Vol. 1: 13011
Deere Medal; John   Vol. 1: 4359
Defant-Medaille; Albert   Vol. 2: 6642
Defence Force Service Awards   Vol. 2: 340
Defence Force Service Medal   Vol. 2: 340
Defender of Jerusalem Award   Vol. 1: 11495
Defenders of Justice   Vol. 2: 1626
Defense Distinguished Service Medal   Vol. 1: 19152
Defense Industry Award for Defense Preparedness   Vol. 1: 1941
Defense Meritorious Service Medal   Vol. 1: 19153
Defense of Academic Freedom Award   Vol. 1: 13710
Defense Superior Service Medal   Vol. 1: 19154
Defensores de la Justicia   Vol. 2: 1626
Deflandre et Marthe Deflandre-Rigaud; Fondation Georges   Vol. 2: 5567
Deflandre-Rigaud; Fondation Georges Deflandre et Marthe   Vol. 2: 5567
DeForest Award; Lee   Vol. 1: 16643
Defresne Prize   Vol. 2: 9607
Defries Award; R. D.   Vol. 1: 7108
Degelleke Award   Vol. 1: 7424
DeGolyer Distinguished Service Medal   Vol. 1: 17960
DeGolyer Memorial Fund Award; Clare Hart   Vol. 1: 8508
Deguchi Prize   Vol. 2: 9678
Dehem; Prix Louise   Vol. 2: 965
Dehio-Preis; Georg-   Vol. 2: 6524
Dejouany; Bourse Veronique   Vol. 2: 4803
DeKalb-Pfizer Crop Science Distinguished Career Award   Vol. 1: 8468
deKieffer International Fellowship Award; Robert   Vol. 1: 5510
Del Gaudio Award of the New York Society of Architects for Excellence in Total Design; Matthew W.   Vol. 1: 15274
del Serrablo International Sculpture Award; Museo Angel Orensanz and Artes   Vol. 2: 11307
del Toro; Premio Carlos Perez   Vol. 2: 8954
Delacorte Press Prize for a First Young Adult Novel   Vol. 1: 8574
Delacour Medal   Vol. 2: 10875
Delacroix; Prix Eve   Vol. 2: 5853
Delannoy-Robbe; Prix Emile   Vol. 2: 4837
Delano Award; Jane A.   Vol. 1: 3911
DeLaval Dairy Extension Award
    American Dairy Science Association   Vol. 1: 1906
    American Dairy Science Association   Vol 1: 1906
Delavan Award   Vol. 1: 2086
Delavignette; Prix Robert   Vol. 2: 6138
Delbos; Prix Victor   Vol. 2: 5795
Delcros, Houllevigue, Saintour, Jules Mahyer; Fondations Estrade   Vol. 2: 5679
Delcros; Prix Estrade   Vol. 2: 5679
Delcros; Prix Estrade-   Vol. 2: 5457
Delezenne/Prize of the LMGMS; Joachim Cabot and Louis   Vol. 2: 6077
Delius Composition Contest   Vol. 1: 8576
Delius Medal; Christoph Traugott   Vol. 2: 7354
Dellinger Gold Medal; John Howard   Vol. 2: 1211
Delphinium Society Awards   Vol. 2: 2736
Delta Air Lines Puffer Award   Vol. 1: 12748
Delta Art Exhibition   Vol. 1: 5254
Delta Fiction Award   Vol. 2: 9863
Delta; Penelope   Vol. 2: 7190
Delta Pi Epsilon Research Award   Vol. 1: 8593

Delta Psi Kappa Research Award   Vol. 1: 8595
Delta Sigma Rho - Tau Kappa Alpha Trophy   Vol. 1: 14020
Delta Society/American Animal Hospital Association Assistance Animal Award   Vol. 1: 8598
Delta Society/Awards to Service and Therapy Animals   Vol. 1: 8598
Delta Society Community Human-Animal Project Grant   Vol. 1: 8599
Delta Society Distinguished Service Awards   Vol. 1: 8600
Delta Society Media Award - Print   Vol. 1: 8601
Delta Society Media Awards - Television, Radio, Film   Vol. 1: 8602
Delta Society Model Program Awards   Vol. 1: 8603
Delta Tau Alpha Teacher-Advisor Award; NACTA   Vol. 1: 13008
DeMarco - Becket Memorial Trophy   Vol. 1: 6874
Deming Application Prize   Vol. 2: 8776
Deming Memorial Fund Grants; Money for Women/Barbara   Vol. 1: 12414
Deming Prize   Vol. 2: 8776
Deming Prize for Individual Person   Vol. 2: 8776
Demingu Sho   Vol. 2: 8776
Deminne et sa femme nee Anne Fabry; Prix du Docteur Jules   Vol. 2: 1331
Demolon; Fondation de Madame Albert   Vol. 2: 5533
Dempster Travelling Fellowship   Vol. 2: 3320
Demuth Grant for Research in the Field of Parenteral Nutrition; Nina Dale   Vol. 1: 15953
Demuth Medical Foundation; Young Investigator Awards of the Dr. C. and F.   Vol. 2: 1976
Den Store Journalistprisen   Vol. 2: 9943
Denali Press Award   Vol. 1: 2940
Denayer; Prix Felix   Vol. 2: 1285
Denayer Prize; Felix   Vol. 2: 1285
Dendy Awards for Australian Short Films   Vol. 2: 685
Denig Distinguished Service Award; Brig. Gen. Robert L.   Vol. 1: 19434
Denk Congressional Award; Horst G.   Vol. 1: 10114
Denman Cup   Vol. 2: 3688
Denmark National Faculty Advisor Award; Psi Chi/Florence L.   Vol. 1: 16546
Denning Award; Anthony   Vol. 2: 4381
Dennis Award; FAW C. J.   Vol. 2: 383
Dennis Award for Prospector of the Year; Bill   Vol. 1: 16539
Dennis Prize for Poetry; C. J.   Vol. 2: 149
Denny Gold Medal   Vol. 2: 3116
Denny Poetry Award; Billee Murray   Vol. 1: 11890
Densmore Prize; Frances   Vol. 1: 3167
Dent Medal   Vol. 2: 4107
Dental Fellowships   Vol. 1: 12187
Dentist Citizen of the Year   Vol. 1: 990
Dentsu Advertising Awards   Vol. 2: 8524
Denver International Film Festival   Vol. 1: 8606
Denyn Prize; Jef   Vol. 2: 1347
Deo Gloria Award   Vol. 2: 2198
Department Crime Prevention Award   Vol. 1: 3551
Department of Defense Distinguished Civilian Service Award   Vol. 1: 19197
Department of Trade and Industry Prizes   Vol. 2: 3098

Department of Transportation Award for Heroism   Vol. 1: 9063
Department of Veteran's Affairs Employee of the Year Award   Vol. 1: 241
Department Traffic Safety Award   Vol. 1: 3552
Deputy Secretary's Award for Excellence in Labor Diplomacy   Vol. 1: 19284
Deren Award; Maya   Vol. 1: 2051
Deri Award   Vol. 2: 7328
Deri Dij   Vol. 2: 7328
Derleth Fantasy Award; August   Vol. 2: 2336
deRoaldes Award   Vol. 1: 2782
Deruyts; Prix Francois   Vol. 2: 1021
Deruyts; Prix Jacques   Vol. 2: 1025
Derwent Award (British); Clarence   Vol. 2: 2236
Derwent Award; Clarence   Vol. 1: 122
Derwood Award; Oscar Williams and Gene   Vol. 1: 15233
des Vosges; Prix Blaise   Vol. 2: 5719
Desbordes-Valmore; Prix Marceline   Vol. 2: 6339
Descamps; Prix L.-Pierre   Vol. 2: 1051
Deschamps Literary Prize; Henri   Vol. 2: 7258
Desert Palm Achievement Award   Vol. 1: 15912
Desguin International Prize; Arthur   Vol. 2: 1104
Desguin; Premio Internacional Arthur   Vol. 2: 1104
Deshabandu   Vol. 2: 11429
Deshamanya   Vol. 2: 11430
DESI Awards   Vol. 1: 9705
Design and Application Award
  International Magnesium Association   Vol. 1: 11092
  International Magnesium Association   Vol 1: 11093
Design and Engineering Exhibition Award   Vol. 1: 8881
Design & Light Competition   Vol. 2: 8274
Design Award
  Interactive Services   Vol. 1: 10527
  International Magnesium Association   Vol 1: 11093
Design Awards   Vol. 1: 16520
Design Council Awards   Vol. 2: 2738
Design Council British Aerospace Engineering Design Prizes   Vol. 2: 2739
Design Council GKN Production Engineer's Design Prize   Vol. 2: 2740
Design Council Molins Design Prize   Vol. 2: 2739
Design/Development Awards Program   Vol. 1: 13159
Design Fellowship Competition   Vol. 1: 11005
Design for Arts in Education   Vol. 1: 5322
Design for Excellence Residential Award   Vol. 1: 10575
Design for Humanity Award   Vol. 1: 4626
Design Management Prize
  Svenska Dagbladet   Vol. 2: 11570
  Swedish Society of Crafts and Design   Vol 2: 11652
Desmond Memorial Award, Competition Division; Albert   Vol. 1: 6236
Desnuelle; Fondation Pierre   Vol. 2: 5652
DeSoto Award; Hernando   Vol. 1: 13857
Detroit Grand Prix   Vol. 1: 12456
Deutsch Award; Karl   Vol. 1: 11326
Deutsch Memorial Award; Wilbur   Vol. 1: 18080
Deutsch Memorial Trophy   Vol. 1: 7805
Deutsche Meteorologische Gesellschaft Ehrenmitgliedschaft   Vol. 2: 6643
Deutsche Meteorologische Gesellschaft e.V. Forderpreis   Vol. 2: 6644

Deutsche Meteorologische Gesellschaft e.V. Jugendpreis   Vol. 2: 6644
Deutscher Filmpreis   Vol. 2: 6741
Deutscher Jugend-Video-Preis   Vol. 2: 6591
Deutscher Jugendliteratur Preis   Vol. 2: 6833
Deutscher Memorial Prize; Isaac   Vol. 2: 2744
Deutscher Verpackungs-Wettbewerb   Vol. 2: 7078
Deutz/Allis Chalmers Conservation District Awards; NACD   Vol. 1: 13031
Deutz-Allis National Student Design Competition   Vol. 1: 4372
Deux Magots Prize   Vol. 2: 5002
Developer of the Year Award   Vol. 1: 16540
Developing Scientist Awards   Vol. 1: 10763
Development Grants   Vol. 2: 9518
Developmental Psychology Awards   Vol. 1: 3711
Devereux II Memorial Sportsmanship Trophy; Walter Bourchier   Vol. 1: 2349
DeVilliers Award   Vol. 1: 11835
Devine Award; George   Vol. 2: 2794
Devine Memorial Award; Edward A.   Vol. 1: 19409
Devins Award for Poetry   Vol. 1: 19847
Devlin Award; Jones F.   Vol. 1: 2627
Devlin Memorial Award for Poetry; Denis   Vol. 2: 7757
Devonshire Trophy   Vol. 2: 4031
Dew Award for Journalistic Achievement; G. Richard   Vol. 1: 16048
Dewey Humanist Award; John   Vol. 1: 2409
Dewey Medal; Melvil   Vol. 1: 2814
DeWolf Award; L. Harold   Vol. 1: 15576
Dexter Award in the History of Chemistry   Vol. 1: 1491
Dexter Prize   Vol. 1: 17616
DFAP National One-Act Playwriting Contest   Vol. 1: 8752
DFISA-ASAE Food Engineering Award   Vol. 1: 8496
DFISA-FPEI Food Engineering Award   Vol. 1: 4360
DFPA ROTC Award   Vol. 1: 14779
Dharmaraja - King of Dharma   Vol. 1: 10716
Dhere; Fondation Charles   Vol. 2: 5514
Di Castagnola Award; Alice Fay   Vol. 1: 16281
Di Guglielmo; Fondazione Giovanni   Vol. 2: 8057
di Nola; Premio Mario   Vol. 2: 8078
Diabetes Australia Alan Marshall Prize for Children's Literature   Vol. 2: 149
Diables d'Or   Vol. 2: 11791
Dial Award   Vol. 1: 18757
Dialogue-Silver Foundation Awards   Vol. 1: 8631
Dialogue Writing Awards   Vol. 1: 8631
Diamond Coach   Vol. 1: 14018
Diamond Cover Merit Award   Vol. 1: 14746
Diamond ECHO Award   Vol. 1: 8648
Diamond Key Award   Vol. 1: 14018
Diamond Memorial Award; Harry   Vol. 1: 10261
Diamond Memorial Prize; A. S.   Vol. 2: 3515
Diamond Pin Service Award   Vol. 1: 646
Diaz del Castillo Prize; Bernal   Vol. 2: 9083
Diaz International Competition for Guitar; Alirio   Vol. 2: 12119
Dibello Memorial Exhibit Award; Gaston   Vol. 1: 3213
Dibner Award for Excellence in Exhibits   Vol. 1: 17617
Dick Medal of Merit; Charles   Vol. 1: 14096
Dickason Award; Donald E.   Vol. 1: 7877
Dickerson, III, Award; Ben F.   Vol. 1: 17560
Dickinson Award; Emily   Vol. 1: 16282

Award Index
Volume 2: International and Foreign — Distinguished

Dickinson Award in Clinical Microbiology; Becton   Vol. 1: 7200
Dickinson Career Achievement Award; Becton Association for the Advancement of Medical Instrumentation   Vol. 1: 5620
Association for the Advancement of Medical Instrumentation Foundation   Vol 1: 5626
Dickinson College Arts Award   Vol. 1: 8643
Dickinson Teacher Award; John   Vol. 1: 566
Dickson Alumnus of the Year Achievement Award; Edward A.   Vol. 1: 19744
Dickson Award; J. Frank   Vol. 1: 4933
Dickson Memorial Award; Donald L.   Vol. 1: 19435
Dickson Memorial Award; Dorothy Stredicke   Vol. 1: 3608
Dickson Scholarship; Alec   Vol. 1: 15978
Dicus Award; Robert G.   Vol. 1: 3495
Didactic Instructor of the Year Award   Vol. 1: 1055
Didusch Award; AUA William P.   Vol. 1: 4953
Die Weissen Raben   Vol. 2: 6995
Dieckman Distinguished Educational Award of Honor; The John   Vol. 1: 14638
Diederich Award   Vol. 1: 9914
Diefenbaker Award; John G.   Vol. 1: 6734
Diehl; Prix Charles and Marguerite   Vol. 2: 5441
Diener Award; Irving   Vol. 1: 6405
Dienes Award; Louis   Vol. 1: 11129
Diesel and Gas Engine Power Award   Vol. 1: 4682
Dieterichs/Maclay Memorial Prize   Vol. 2: 3321
Dieterichs Memorial Prize; William   Vol. 2: 3321
Dietrich Trophy   Vol. 1: 7806
Dietsch Sculpture Prize; C. Percival   Vol. 1: 14714
Dietz Award; August   Vol. 1: 8110
Diez Mejores Libros para Ninos   Vol. 2: 12146
Digital Dance Awards   Vol. 2: 2746
Digital Premier Award   Vol. 2: 2746
Digital Schneider Trophy   Vol. 2: 2747
Dillard Award; Harrison   Vol. 1: 19936
Dilling Award; Dick   Vol. 1: 6161
Dillon Medal for Research in Polymer Physics; John H.   Vol. 1: 3452
DiMascio Lecture Series; Albert   Vol. 1: 1687
Dimbleby Award; Richard   Vol. 2: 2234
Dimitrije Tucovic Nonfiction Award   Vol. 2: 10719
Dimock Award; Hedley S.   Vol. 1: 1403
Dimock Award; Marshall E.   Vol. 1: 4265
Dinerman Award; Helen S.   Vol. 1: 20470
Dinerman Memorial Prize; Helen S.   Vol. 1: 871
Dingley Memorial Award; Dr. H. B.   Vol. 2: 7585
Dingley Oration Award; Smt. Swaran Kanta   Vol. 2: 7586
Dining Idea Exchange Contest   Vol. 1: 12988
Dinsdale Award; Walter   Vol. 1: 7119
diNunzio Special Award; Michael A.   Vol. 1: 19066
Diploma al Merito Educativo   Vol. 2: 1656
Diploma al Merito Universitario   Vol. 2: 9180
Diploma de Reconeixements de Merits en favor del Patronomi Cultural de la Generalitat de Catalunya   Vol. 2: 11176
Diploma for Outstanding Airmanship   Vol. 2: 5143
Diploma of Honour and Medal   Vol. 2: 3456
Diploma Trade Prize   Vol. 2: 2917
Diplomate Award   Vol. 1: 12983

Diplomate of the American Board of Psychological Hypnosis   Vol. 1: 1358
Diplomatic Courier Award   Vol. 1: 19285
Diplome d'honneur   Vol. 1: 6838
Diplomes de Medailles   Vol. 2: 4769
DiPrima Prize; Richard C.   Vol. 1: 17512
Dirac Medal
 International Centre for Theoretical Physics   Vol. 2: 8288
 University of New South Wales   Vol 2: 699
Dirac Medal and Prize; Paul   Vol. 2: 3188
Direct Vocational Special Needs Support Person of the Year   Vol. 1: 12912
Director General of the Foreign Service and the Director of Personnel's Award for Excellence in Personnel Management   Vol. 1: 19286
Director General's Award for Reporting   Vol. 1: 19287
Director of the University Museum Prize   Vol. 1: 19729
Director of the Year
 International Association of Pet Cemeteries   Vol. 1: 10776
 National Trappers Association   Vol 1: 14927
Directorate Award   Vol. 1: 10884
Directors Apprenticeship Program   Vol. 1: 8729
Director's Award
 American Alliance for Theatre & Education   Vol. 1: 780
 Federation of Genealogical Societies   Vol 1: 9123
 SPIE - The International Society for Optical Engineers   Vol 1: 18319
Directors Award
 Friends of Algonquin Park   Vol. 1: 9411
 Society of Flight Test Engineers   Vol 1: 17855
Directors' Choice Awards   Vol. 1: 15021
Directors Emeriti Award   Vol. 1: 11884
Directors Project   Vol. 1: 8729
Dirksen Award for Distinguished Reporting of Congress; Everett McKinley   Vol. 1: 8673
Dirksen Center Award for Meritorious Service   Vol. 1: 8674
Disability Award   Vol. 2: 8801
Disability Awareness Award   Vol. 1: 15941
Disabled Athletes of the Year   Vol. 1: 19011
Disabled Professional Woman of the Year   Vol. 1: 16221
Discailles; Prix Ernest   Vol. 2: 986
Disciplined Services Medal for Long Service and Good Conduct   Vol. 2: 7245
Disciplined Services Medal for Meritorious Service   Vol. 2: 7246
Disciplined Services Star for Distinguished Service   Vol. 2: 7247
Disclosure Student Travel Award; RASD/ BRASS   Vol. 1: 2948
Discover America National Travel Marketing Awards   Vol. 1: 18799
Discover Award   Vol. 1: 6272
Discoverers Awards   Vol. 1: 16086
Discovery Artist Award   Vol. 1: 19985
"Discovery" Award   Vol. 1: 19898
Discovery Award   Vol. 1: 9188
Discovery of New Celestial Bodies Award   Vol. 2: 8507
Discovery of the Year   Vol. 1: 9979
"Discovery"/The Nation: The Joan Leiman Jacobson Prizes   Vol. 1: 19898
Dissertation Award
 American Psychological Association - Evaluation, Measurement, and Statistics Division   Vol. 1: 3724

American Sociological Association   Vol 1: 4829
 Association of Black Nursing Faculty in Higher Education   Vol 1: 5710
Dissertation Award in Nuclear Physics   Vol. 1: 3453
Dissertation Awards   Vol. 1: 18303
Dissertation Honors   Vol. 2: 6998
Dissertation of the Year Award   Vol. 1: 5644
Dissertation Prize   Vol. 2: 5255
Dissertation Prize in Economics   Vol. 2: 4736
Dissertation Prize in Environmental and Resource Economics   Vol. 1: 16809
Dista Products Resident Research Award; APA/   Vol. 1: 3623
Distance Award and Best-Conditioned & Trail Class Award   Vol. 1: 10075
Distant Accords Awards   Vol. 1: 10962
Distincion Felix Restrepo   Vol. 2: 1740
Distincion Universidad Nacional para Jovenes Academicos   Vol. 2: 9181
Distinction for Distinguished Services   Vol. 2: 1627
Distinction for Time of Service   Vol. 2: 1628
Distinguished 50-Year Member Award   Vol. 1: 4581
Distinguished Achievement Award
 American Gastroenterological Association Foundation   Vol. 1: 2137
 American Society for Healthcare Education and Training   Vol. 1: 4141
 American Society of Contemporary Medicine, Surgery and Ophthalmology   Vol. 1: 4535
 AMIT Women   Vol 1: 5133
 Association of Records Managers and Administrators - ARMA International   Vol 1: 5939
 Instrument Society of America   Vol 1: 10492
 International Franchise Association   Vol 1: 10996
 Pi Kappa Alpha Education Foundation   Vol 1: 16178
 Society of Exploration Geophysicists   Vol 1: 17841
 Wings Club   Vol 1: 20334
Distinguished Achievement Award for Community Service   Vol. 1: 10199
Distinguished Achievement Award for News Pictures   Vol. 1: 10200
Distinguished Achievement Award for Petroleum Engineering Faculty   Vol. 1: 17961
Distinguished Achievement Award to Fluid Power Educator   Vol. 1: 9272
Distinguished Achievement Awards
 American Association of Colleges for Teacher Education   Vol. 1: 959
 American Medical Technologists   Vol 1: 3038
Distinguished Achievement Awards for Local Public Affairs   Vol. 1: 10201
Distinguished Achievement in Basic or Applied Fiber Science   Vol. 1: 9179
Distinguished Achievement in Occupational Safety and Health Award   Vol. 1: 14660
Distinguished Achievement in RV Journalism Award   Vol. 1: 16726
Distinguished Achievement in RV Standards Award   Vol. 1: 16727
Distinguished Administrator Award   Vol. 1: 1643
Distinguished Adviser Award   Vol. 1: 7907
Distinguished Affiliate   Vol. 1: 3716
Distinguished Alumni Citation of the Year   Vol. 1: 12857
Distinguished Alumnus Award   Vol. 1: 19820

Distinguished American Award Vol. 1: 13989
Distinguished American Woman Award Vol. 1: 7929
Distinguished Artist Award for Lifetime Achievement Vol. 1: 7886
Distinguished Assessment Jurisdiction Award Vol. 1: 10661
Distinguished Author Award Vol. 1: 10942
Distinguished Book Award Vol. 1: 17554
Distinguished Budget Presentation Award Vol. 1: 9682
Distinguished Building Award Vol. 1: 17724
Distinguished Career Award
  American Rehabilitation Association Vol. 1: 3935
  Real Estate Educators Association Vol 1: 16704
  Southeastern Theatre Conference Vol 1: 18206
Distinguished Career Award for the Practice of Sociology Vol. 1: 4830
Distinguished Career Contribution to Education and Training in Psychology Vol. 1: 3659
Distinguished Career in Clinical Sociology Vol. 1: 18109
Distinguished Career Research in Social Studies Award Vol. 1: 13711
Distinguished Career Service Awards Vol. 1: 19256
Distinguished Ceramist Award Vol. 1: 1453
Distinguished Chapter Award Vol. 1: 6008
Distinguished Citizen Award
  Congressional Medal of Honor Society, United States of America Vol. 1: 8170
  National Consumers League Vol 1: 13663
Distinguished Citizens Awards Vol. 2: 925
Distinguished Civilian Service Award - Navy/Marine Corps Vol. 1: 19198
Distinguished Clinical Chemist Award Vol. 2: 7896
Distinguished Clinical Neuropsychologist Vol. 1: 12644
Distinguished Clinician Award Vol. 1: 900
Distinguished Communicator Award Vol. 1: 16992
Distinguished Community Service Award
  The Arc Vol. 1: 5211
  National Urban Coalition Vol. 1: 14958
Distinguished Conduct Medal Vol. 2: 2361
Distinguished Consultant Vol. 1: 17652
Distinguished Contribution Award
  American Psychological Association - Adult Development and Aging Division Vol. 1: 3679
  Project Management Institute Vol 1: 16525
Distinguished Contribution for Child Advocacy Vol. 1: 3687
Distinguished Contribution for Peace Vol. 1: 16551
Distinguished Contribution to Education and Training in Psychology Vol. 1: 3660
Distinguished Contribution to Ethnic Minority Issues Award Vol. 1: 3807
Distinguished Contribution to Ethnic Minority Psychology Award Vol. 1: 17629
Distinguished Contribution to Human Resource Development Award
  American Society for Training and Development Vol. 1: 4302
  American Society for Training and Development - International Professional Practice Area Vol 1: 4322
Distinguished Contribution to Nursing Science Award Vol. 1: 3291
Distinguished Contribution to Practice in Community Psychology Award Vol. 1: 3787

Distinguished Contribution to Professional Psychology Vol. 1: 1356
Distinguished Contribution to Psychology and Law Vol. 1: 3681
Distinguished Contribution to Psychology and the Media Vol. 1: 3740
Distinguished Contribution to Psychology in the Public Interest Vol. 1: 3661
Distinguished Contribution to Research Administration Award Vol. 1: 18028
Distinguished Contribution to Scholarship Award Vol. 1: 4832
Distinguished Contribution to Theory and Research in Community Psychology Award Vol. 1: 3788
Distinguished Contributions Award Vol. 1: 12888
Distinguished Contributions to Applied Psychology as a Professional Practice Vol. 1: 3662
Distinguished Contributions to Asian Studies Vol. 1: 5443
Distinguished Contributions to Canadian Psychology as a Profession Vol. 1: 7103
Distinguished Contributions to Canadian Psychology as a Science Vol. 1: 7104
Distinguished Contributions to Journalism Vol. 1: 14508
Distinguished Contributions to Non-aversive Behavioral Intervention Vol. 1: 5568
Distinguished Contributions to Research in Public Policy Vol. 1: 3663
Distinguished Contributions to Teaching Award Vol. 1: 4831
Distinguished Contributions to the International Advancement of Psychology Vol. 1: 3664
Distinguished Corporate Leadership Award Vol. 1: 14959
Distinguished Corporate Urban Affairs Award Vol. 1: 14960
Distinguished Creative Contribution to Gerontology Award Vol. 1: 9587
Distinguished Dairy Cattle Breeder Award Vol. 1: 8502
Distinguished Designer Award Vol. 1: 4563
Distinguished Diplomatic Award Vol. 1: 9078
Distinguished Dissertation Award in Higher Education Vol. 1: 5644
Distinguished Dissertation in Teacher Education Vol. 1: 5979
Distinguished Drinking Water Public Involvement Award Vol. 1: 15152
Distinguished Eagle Scout Award Vol. 1: 6514
Distinguished Economic Botanist Vol. 1: 17448
Distinguished Educational Contribution Award Vol. 1: 3808
Distinguished Educator Award Vol. 1: 738
Distinguished EEA - SHIP Member Award Vol. 1: 11334
Distinguished Engineering Educator Award Vol. 1: 18101
Distinguished Extended Family/Community Integration Award Vol. 1: 5569
Distinguished Extension Programs Vol. 1: 750
Distinguished Faculty Award Vol. 1: 13606
Distinguished Fellow
  American College of Cardiology Vol. 1: 1610
  American Economic Association Vol 1: 1968
  American Park and Recreation Society Vol 1: 3362

  Royal College of Pathologists of Australasia Vol 2: 614
Distinguished Fellow Award
  American College of Neuropsychiatrists Vol. 1: 1680
  History of Economics Society Vol 1: 9943
  International Council on Education for Teaching Vol 1: 10886
  Society of Toxicology Vol 1: 18072
Distinguished Fellows Award
  American Council on Consumer Interests Vol. 1: 1862
  National Association of Pediatric Nurse Associates and Practitioners Vol 1: 13222
Distinguished Flying Cross
  British Government Vol. 2: 2362
  United States Department of Defense - Armed Forces Decorations and Awards Vol 1: 19155
Distinguished Flying Medal Vol. 2: 2363
Distinguished Flying Unit Plaques Vol. 1: 14096
Distinguished Foreign Cartoonists Award Vol. 1: 5679
Distinguished Foreign Colleague Award Vol. 1: 10038
Distinguished Graduate Award in Premium Auditing Vol. 1: 14794
Distinguished Graduate Student Award Vol. 1: 19852
Distinguished Grant Maker Award Vol. 1: 8391
Distinguished Grasslander Award Vol. 1: 2078
Distinguished Honor Award Vol. 1: 19288
Distinguished Humanitarian Award Vol. 1: 19775
Distinguished Humanities Educator Vol. 1: 8070
Distinguished Individual of Foreign Birth Award Vol. 1: 10829
Distinguished Information Sciences Award Vol. 1: 8724
Distinguished International Cooperation, Peace and Security Award Vol. 1: 9355
Distinguished International Criminal Law Award Vol. 1: 9355
Distinguished International Services Award Vol. 2: 7897
Distinguished Investigator Award Vol. 1: 1624
Distinguished Labor Leadership Vol. 1: 14961
Distinguished Lecture Award Vol. 1: 794
Distinguished Lecture Program Award Vol. 1: 12839
Distinguished Lecturers Vol. 1: 6937
Distinguished Life Member
  ASM International Vol. 1: 5351
  North American Die Casting Association Vol 1: 15413
Distinguished Life Member Award Vol. 1: 1454
Distinguished Mayor Award Vol. 1: 14962
Distinguished Member Vol. 1: 17962
Distinguished Member Award
  American Medical Record Association Vol. 1: 3031
  Clay Minerals Society Vol 1: 7829
  International Facility Management Association Vol 1: 10943
  Iron and Steel Society Vol 1: 11460
  Society for Mining, Metallurgy, and Exploration Vol 1: 17561
  Women in Government Relations Vol 1: 20390

Distinguished Member Service Award   Vol. 1: 1805
Distinguished Membership Award   Vol. 1: 3280
Distinguished Merit Award   Vol. 1: 975
Distinguished Musician Award   Vol. 2: 3041
Distinguished Mycologist Award   Vol. 1: 12543
Distinguished National Leadership Award   Vol. 1: 14963
Distinguished National Service Award   Vol. 1: 2227
Distinguished New Engineer Award   Vol. 1: 18102
Distinguished New Yorker Award   Vol. 1: 7724
Distinguished Officer of the Year   Vol. 1: 6400
Distinguished Osteopathic Surgeon Award   Vol. 1: 1708
Distinguished Paper in Psychology Award   Vol. 1: 6481
Distinguished Parent Award   Vol. 1: 5570
Distinguished Peace Leadership Award   Vol. 1: 15552
Distinguished Peacekeeper Award   Vol. 1: 11135
Distinguished Performance Award   Vol. 1: 12772
Distinguished Performance Awards   Vol. 1: 19436
Distinguished Performance in Software Management Award   Vol. 1: 18111
Distinguished Philatelist   Vol. 2: 2474
Distinguished Pi Lambda Thetan Award   Vol. 1: 16191
Distinguished Play Awards   Vol. 1: 774
Distinguished Poet Awards   Vol. 1: 18262
Distinguished Policy Contribution   Vol. 1: 751
Distinguished Popular Scientific Publishing of Plant Physiology   Vol. 2: 11566
Distinguished Presidential Citation   Vol. 1: 17725
Distinguished Principal Founding Member   Vol. 2: 836
Distinguished Professional Contribution Award
  American Psychological Association - Clinical Psychology Division   Vol. 1: 3690
  American Psychological Association - Society for Consumer Psychology Division   Vol. 1: 3793
  American Psychological Association - Society for Psychological Study of Lesbian and Gay Issues Division   Vol. 1: 3809
  Kenya National Academy of Sciences - Ministry of Research, Science & Technology   Vol. 2: 8805
Distinguished Professional Contributions Award   Vol. 1: 3796
Distinguished Professional Contributions to Clinical Psychology   Vol. 1: 3691
Distinguished Professional Contributions to Knowledge   Vol. 1: 3665
Distinguished Professional Contributions to Public Service   Vol. 1: 3666
Distinguished Programs in Teacher Education   Vol. 1: 5980
Distinguished Psychological Contributions to Asian Americans   Vol. 1: 5343
Distinguished Psychologist Award for Contributions to Psychology and Psychotherapy   Vol. 1: 3777
Distinguished Psychologist of the Year   Vol. 1: 3713
Distinguished Public Service Award
  American Forensic Association   Vol. 1: 2092

Center for National Policy   Vol 1: 7443
  Ford Foundation and Harvard University   Vol 1: 9313
  Tax Foundation   Vol 1: 18585
Distinguished Public Service Awards   Vol. 1: 14683
Distinguished Public Service Medal
  Mineralogical Society of America   Vol. 1: 12302
  National Aeronautics and Space Administration   Vol 1: 12731
Distinguished Publication Award   Vol. 1: 4832
Distinguished Publication Awards/Distinguished Career Award   Vol. 1: 5658
Distinguished Recognition Award   Vol. 1: 11087
Distinguished Regulatory Entomology Award   Vol. 1: 1068
Distinguished Research and Development Award   Vol. 1: 10662
Distinguished Research Award
  American Society for Public Administration - Section for Women in Public Administration   Vol. 1: 4277
  National Council of Teachers of English   Vol 1: 13779
Distinguished Research in Teacher Education   Vol. 1: 5981
Distinguished Resident Award   Vol. 1: 906
Distinguished Resident Award in Radiation Oncology   Vol. 1: 907
Distinguished Rural Sociologists   Vol. 1: 16974
Distinguished Scholar Award
  Keats - Shelley Association of America   Vol. 1: 11653
  National Association for Gifted Children   Vol 1: 12864
  North American Society for the Psychology of Sport and Physical Activity   Vol 1: 15453
Distinguished Scholar Program   Vol. 1: 3292
Distinguished Scientific Award for an Early Career Contribution to Psychology   Vol. 1: 3667
Distinguished Scientific Award for the Applications of Psychology   Vol. 1: 3668
Distinguished Scientific Contribution Award
  American Psychological Association   Vol. 1: 3669
  American Psychological Association - Society for Consumer Psychology Division   Vol 1: 3794
  American Psychological Association - Society for Psychological Study of Lesbian and Gay Issues Division   Vol 1: 3810
Distinguished Scientific Contribution to Clinical Psychology   Vol. 1: 3692
Distinguished Scientific Contributions Award   Vol. 1: 3797
Distinguished Scientist   Vol. 1: 1611
Distinguished Scientist Award
  American Psychological Association - Clinical Psychology Division   Vol. 1: 3693
  North American Society of Pacing and Electrophysiology   Vol 1: 15459
Distinguished Service   Vol. 1: 1612
Distinguished Service/Achievement Awards   Vol. 1: 17229
Distinguished Service Award
  Alpine Club of Canada   Vol. 1: 374
  American Academy of Medical Administrators   Vol 1: 595
  American Academy of Otolaryngology - Head and Neck Surgery   Vol 1: 655
  American Anthropological Association   Vol 1: 795

American Arbitration Association   Vol 1: 801
American Association for Agricultural Education   Vol 1: 834
American Association of Blood Banks   Vol 1: 924
American Association of Homes for the Aging   Vol 1: 1008
American Association of Housing Educators   Vol 1: 1021
American Association of Motor Vehicle Administrators   Vol 1: 1041
American Association of Museums   Vol 1: 1044
American Association of Oral and Maxillofacial Surgeons   Vol 1: 1085
American Association of Petroleum Geologists   Vol 1: 1104
American Association of Public Health Physicians   Vol 1: 1155
American Association of School Administrators   Vol 1: 1176
American Association of Teachers of Spanish and Portuguese   Vol 1: 1218
American Association of University Administrators   Vol 1: 1224
American Camping Association   Vol 1: 1404
American Cancer Society   Vol 1: 1412
American Chemical Society - Divisional Activities   Vol 1: 1492
American Chemical Society - Divisional Activities   Vol 1: 1493
American College of Clinical Pharmacology   Vol 1: 1625
American College of Dentists   Vol 1: 1630
American College of Neuropsychiatrists   Vol 1: 1681
American College of Preventive Medicine   Vol 1: 1726
American Council for Polish Culture   Vol 1: 1841
American Dairy Science Association   Vol 1: 1911
American Forestry Association   Vol 1: 2097
American Hospital Association   Vol 1: 2371
American Jersey Cattle Club   Vol 1: 2717
American Library Association - Association for Library Service to Children   Vol 1: 2860
American Mining Congress   Vol 1: 3116
American Optometric Association   Vol 1: 3321
American Osteopathic Healthcare Association and College of Osteopathic Healthcare Executives   Vol 1: 3357
American Phytopathological Society   Vol 1: 3521
American Police Hall of Fame   Vol 1: 3553
American Psychiatric Association   Vol 1: 3629
American Psychological Association - Clinical Psychology Division   Vol 1: 3694
American Psychological Association - Society for Industrial and Organizational Psychology   Vol 1: 3798
American Public Gas Association   Vol 1: 3842
American Public Power Association   Vol 1: 3861
American Railway Development Association   Vol 1: 3904
American Society for Adolescent Psychiatry   Vol 1: 4031
American Society for Engineering Education   Vol 1: 4083

American Society for Gastrointestinal Endoscopy   Vol 1: 4133
American Society for Healthcare Education and Training   Vol 1: 4142
American Society of Abdominal Surgery   Vol 1: 4350
American Society of Heating, Refrigerating and Air-Conditioning Engineers   Vol 1: 4582
American Society of Plastic and Reconstructive Surgeons - Plastic Surgery Educational Foundation   Vol 1: 4766
American String Teachers Association   Vol 1: 4869
American Thyroid Association   Vol 1: 4906
Americans for Constitutional Action   Vol 1: 5117
AMIT Women   Vol 1: 5134
Arizona State Library Association   Vol 1: 5245
ASPO/Lamaze   Vol 1: 5379
Associates of National Agricultural Library   Vol 1: 5425
Association for Asian Studies   Vol 1: 5443
Association for Bridge Construction and Design   Vol 1: 5449
Association for Computing Machinery   Vol 1: 5467
Association for Documentary Editing   Vol 1: 5486
Association for Systems Management   Vol 1: 5603
Association for Women Veterinarians   Vol 1: 5663
Association of Fraternity Advisors, Inc.   Vol 1: 5806
Association of Free Community Papers   Vol 1: 5809
Association of Schools of Allied Health Professions   Vol 1: 5946
Association of University Architects   Vol 1: 5997
Ayrshire Breeders' Association   Vol 1: 6211
Better Roads and Transportation Council   Vol 1: 6343
Caribbean Studies Association   Vol 1: 7311
Catholic Kolping Society of America   Vol 1: 7368
Catholic University of America Alumni Association   Vol 1: 7392
Caucus for Producers, Writers and Directors   Vol 1: 7410
Chemical Management & Resources Association   Vol 1: 7570
Chicago Book Clinic   Vol 1: 7595
Christian Holiness Association   Vol 1: 7661
Citizens Union of the City of New York   Vol 1: 7719
College and University Personnel Association   Vol 1: 7878
College of Chaplains, Inc.   Vol 1: 7916
Concordia Historical Institute   Vol 1: 8090
Conference on Latin American History   Vol 1: 8141
Congress of Neurological Surgeons   Vol 1: 8149
Congressional Hispanic Caucus Institute   Vol 1: 8167
Construction Specifications Institute   Vol 1: 8201
Council of Chief State School Officers   Vol 1: 8350
Council of Logistics Management   Vol 1: 8375
Cranial Academy   Vol 1: 8446
Cult Awareness Network   Vol 1: 8485

Dairy Industry Association of New Zealand   Vol 2: 9715
Dance Notation Bureau   Vol 1: 8527
Electronic Industries Association   Vol 1: 8882
Epsilon Nu Eta Honor Society   Vol 1: 8974
Eta Kappa Nu   Vol 1: 9004
European Association for Animal Production   Vol 2: 8229
Federation of Genealogical Societies   Vol 1: 9124
Federation of Jewish Men's Club   Vol 1: 9137
Flying Physicians Association   Vol 1: 9279
Gamma Sigma Sigma National Service Sorority   Vol 1: 9474
Geographic Society of Chicago   Vol 1: 9547
Georgia Agricultural Commodity Commission for Peanuts   Vol 1: 9572
Golf Course Superintendents Association of America   Vol 1: 9639
Healthcare Convention & Exhibitors Association   Vol 1: 9860
Historical Commission of the Southern Baptist Convention   Vol 1: 9934
Illuminating Engineering Society of North America   Vol 1: 10085
Independent Free Papers of America   Vol 1: 10119
Institute of Certified Financial Planners   Vol 1: 10251
Institute of Nuclear Materials Management   Vol 1: 10421
Interactive Services   Vol 1: 10528
International Association for Exposition Management   Vol 1: 10635
International Association of Cancer Victors and Friends   Vol 1: 10689
International Association of Justice Volunteerism   Vol 1: 10754
International Badminton Federation   Vol 2: 3377
International Management Council of the YMCA   Vol 1: 11098
International Measurement Confederation   Vol 2: 7428
Lewis and Clark Trail Heritage Foundation   Vol 1: 11848
Lutheran Historical Conference   Vol 1: 11980
Military Order of the World Wars   Vol 1: 12285
National Accreditation Council for Agencies Serving the Blind and Visually Handicapped   Vol 1: 12718
The National Air Transportation Association (NATA)   Vol 1: 12763
National Association for Gifted Children   Vol 1: 12865
National Association of Academies of Science   Vol 1: 12921
National Association of Animal Breeders   Vol 1: 12932
National Association of Biology Teachers   Vol 1: 12953
National Association of Boards of Pharmacy   Vol 1: 12967
National Association of Broadcasters   Vol 1: 12975
National Association of Catholic Chaplains   Vol 1: 12983
National Association of Conservation Districts   Vol 1: 13027
National Association of County Agricultural Agents   Vol 1: 13051
National Association of Elementary School Principals   Vol 1: 13084

National Association of Environmental Professionals   Vol 1: 13101
National Association of Fleet Administrators   Vol 1: 13115
National Association of Personal Financial Advisors   Vol 1: 13225
National Association of Realtors   Vol 1: 13274
National Catholic Development Conference   Vol 1: 13539
National Center for State Courts   Vol 1: 13573
National Composition and Prepress Association   Vol 1: 13635
National Council for Geographic Education   Vol 1: 13692
National Council of Examiners for Engineering and Surveying   Vol 1: 13732
National Council of Teachers of English   Vol 1: 13767
National Court Reporters Association   Vol 1: 13833
National Easter Seal Society   Vol 1: 13868
National Energy Resources Organization   Vol 1: 13900
National Federation of State High School Associations - National Federation Interscholastic Coaches Association   Vol 1: 13955
National Institute of Governmental Purchasing   Vol 1: 14233
National Kidney Foundation   Vol 1: 14270
National Moving and Storage Technical Foundation   Vol 1: 14376
National Parkinson Foundation   Vol 1: 14449
National Propane Gas Association   Vol 1: 14534
National Recreation and Park Association - National Therapeutic Recreation Society   Vol 1: 14572
National School Transportation Association   Vol 1: 14675
National Society of Professional Engineers   Vol 1: 14801
North American Association for Environmental Education   Vol 1: 15394
Ohio Academy of History   Vol 1: 15581
Optical Society of America   Vol 1: 15747
Organ Historical Society   Vol 1: 15803
Organization Development Institute   Vol 1: 15807
President's Committee on Employment of People with Disabilities   Vol 1: 16383
Professional Golfers' Association of America   Vol 1: 16467
Prospectors and Developers Association of Canada   Vol 1: 16541
Radio and Television News Directors Association   Vol 1: 16636
ROUNDALAB   Vol 1: 16912
The Safety Society   Vol 1: 16982
St. Bonaventure University - Department of Mass Communication   Vol 1: 16989
Society for Applied Spectroscopy   Vol 1: 17414
Society for Sedimentary Geology   Vol 1: 17590
Society of American Archivists   Vol 1: 17670
Society of Logistics Engineers   Vol 1: 17867
Society of Naval Architects and Marine Engineers   Vol 1: 17923
Society of Petroleum Engineers   Vol 1: 17963

Award Index
Volume 2: International and Foreign — Divisional

Society of Professional Well Log Analysts Vol 1: 18009
Society of Research Administrators Vol 1: 18030
Society of Wood Science and Technology Vol 1: 18106
Standards Engineering Society Vol 1: 18450
Towing and Recovery Association of America Vol 1: 18771
Trout Unlimited Vol 1: 18817
United Kennel Club Vol 1: 18928
United States Association of Former Members of Congress Vol 1: 19013
Waterbed Manufacturers Association Vol 1: 20170
Wildlife Diseases Association Vol 1: 20296
The Wine Spectator Vol 1: 20331
World Communication Association Vol 1: 20481
Young Printing Executives Club Vol 1: 20620
Distinguished Service Award by Ortho Vol. 1: 7186
Distinguished Service Award by Ortho-McNeil Vol. 1: 7186
Distinguished Service Award (Coaching) Vol. 1: 13956
Distinguished Service Award for School Administrators Vol. 1: 7021
Distinguished Service Award for School Executives Vol. 1: 7022
Distinguished Service Award in Investment Education Vol. 1: 11431
Distinguished Service Award of the Archaeological Institute of America Vol. 1: 5226
Distinguished Service Award (Officiating) Vol. 1: 13956
Distinguished Service Awards
  American Catholic Historical Society Vol. 1: 1435
  American School Health Association Vol 1: 4003
  American Speech-Language-Hearing Association Vol 1: 4840
  Council for Advancement and Support of Education Vol 1: 8294
  International Credit Association Vol 1: 10888
  Military Chaplains Association of the U.S.A. Vol 1: 12272
  National Federation of State High School Associations - National Interscholastic Athletic Administrators Association Vol 1: 13961
  National Governors' Association Vol 1: 14089
  Royal Society for the Prevention of Accidents Vol 2: 4165
  University of Chicago Medical and Biological Sciences Alumni Association Vol 1: 19776
Distinguished Service Certificate
  National Council of Examiners for Engineering and Surveying Vol. 1: 13732
  Pharmacy Guild of Australia Vol 2: 582
Distinguished Service Citation
  Acoustical Society of America Vol. 1: 95
  American Association of Physics Teachers Vol 1: 1125
  American Society for Engineering Education Vol 1: 4084
  Association for Information and Image Management Vol 1: 5541
  Automotive Hall of Fame Vol 1: 6167
  Ecological Society of America Vol 1: 8814
  Lambda Kappa Sigma Vol 1: 11774

National Science Teachers Association Vol 1: 14700
Distinguished Service Cross
  British Government Vol. 2: 2364
  United States Department of Defense - Armed Forces Decorations and Awards Vol 1: 19156
Distinguished Service Cross (DSC) Vol. 2: 341
Distinguished Service Decorations Vol. 2: 341
Distinguished Service in Aging Award Vol. 1: 1009
Distinguished Service in Journalism Award Vol. 1: 17441
Distinguished Service in the Cause of Open and Competitive World Trade Award Vol. 1: 8227
Distinguished Service Key
  National Forensic League Vol. 1: 14019
  Omicron Delta Kappa Vol 1: 15628
Distinguished Service Medal
  American Legion Vol. 1: 2805
  British Government Vol 2: 2365
  Canadian Institute of Mining and Metallurgy Vol 1: 6938
  Ireland - Department of Defence Vol 2: 7789
  Museum Association of the American Frontier Vol 1: 12501
  National Police Officers Association of America Vol 1: 14490
  Pharmacy Guild of Australia Vol 2: 583
Distinguished Service Medal: Air Force Vol. 1: 19157
Distinguished Service Medal: Army Vol. 1: 19158
Distinguished Service Medal Awards Vol. 1: 18551
Distinguished Service Medal: Coast Guard Vol. 1: 19159
Distinguished Service Medal (DSM) Vol. 2: 341
Distinguished Service Medal (NASA Medal) Vol. 1: 12732
Distinguished Service Medal: Navy - Marine Corps Vol. 1: 19160
Distinguished Service Medals Vol. 1: 6179
Distinguished Service Order
  British Government Vol. 2: 2366
  Singapore - Office of the Prime Minister Vol 2: 10739
Distinguished Service to Agriculture Vol. 1: 4557
Distinguished Service to Agriculture Award Vol. 1: 9472
Distinguished Service to Children Award Vol. 1: 15962
Distinguished Service to Families Award Vol. 1: 13806
Distinguished Service to Powder Metallurgy Award Vol. 1: 12225
Distinguished Service to Rural Life Vol. 1: 16975
Distinguished Service to Safety Education Vol. 1: 16982
Distinguished Service to the Cause of Liberal Religion Vol. 1: 18887
Distinguished Service to the Cause of Unitarian Universalism Vol. 1: 18887
Distinguished Service to the RV Industry Award Vol. 1: 16728
Distinguished Society Service Award Vol. 1: 10483
Distinguished Speaker Award Vol. 1: 1455
Distinguished State Leadership in Higher Education Award Vol. 1: 1199

Distinguished Student Award Vol. 1: 19853
Distinguished Student Development Award Vol. 1: 12840
Distinguished Student Service Award Vol. 1: 7908
Distinguished Teacher Award Vol. 1: 4399
Distinguished Teacher in Journalism Vol. 1: 17995
Distinguished Teaching Achievement Award Vol. 1: 13693
Distinguished Teaching Award
  National Science Teachers Association Vol. 1: 14701
  University of California, Los Angeles - Alumni Association Vol 1: 19745
Distinguished Teaching in Psychology Vol. 1: 3831
Distinguished Teaching of Art Award Vol. 1: 7887
Distinguished Teaching of Art History Award Vol. 1: 7888
Distinguished Technical Achievement Award Vol. 1: 18010
Distinguished Topical Philatelist Award Vol. 1: 4915
Distinguished Transportation Research Award Vol. 1: 18786
Distinguished Undergraduate Teaching Awards Vol. 1: 752
Distinguished Urban Journalism Award Vol. 1: 14964
Distinguished Wildlife Artist Vol. 1: 20445
Distinguished Women of Northwood Institute Vol. 1: 15531
Distinguished Writing Award Vol. 1: 16049
Distinguished Writing Awards Competition Vol. 1: 4739
Distinguished Younger Member Award Vol. 1: 17757
Distintivo al Merito Canino Vol. 2: 1671
Distintivo al Merito Docente Gabriel Gonzales Vol. 2: 1672
Distintivo de Antiguedad; El Vol. 2: 1628
Distintivo de Servicios Distinguidos; El Vol. 2: 1627
Distributor of the Year Award Vol. 1: 13359
District Award Vol. 1: 15947
District Award of Merit Vol. 1: 6515
District Bulletin Award Vol. 1: 7786
District Coach of the Year Vol. 1: 13617
District Distinguished Service Awards Vol. 1: 6939
District Newsletter Contest Vol. 1: 13028
District Representatives Award Vol. 1: 11019
District/Section Newsletter Award Vol. 1: 10449
Ditson Conductor's Award; Alice M. Vol. 1: 7981
Dittrich-Ehrenring; Franz- Vol. 2: 801
DivCHAS College Health and Safety Award Vol. 1: 1494
Diven Memorial Medal; John M. Vol. 1: 5026
Divine Award; Thomas F. Vol. 1: 5598
Division Awards (American Water Works Association) Vol. 1: 5019
Division of Independent Practice Distinguished Public Service Award Vol. 1: 3714
Division of Peace Psychology Presidential Award for Outstanding Contribution to Peace Psychology Vol. 1: 3750
Division of Polymer Chemistry Award Vol. 1: 1495
Division of the Year Vol. 1: 19509
Divisional Award of the Chemical Society of Japan Vol. 2: 8518
Divisional Premium Vol. 2: 3273

Divisional   Awards, Honors & Prizes, 1995-96

Divisional PRO Rally of the Year Vol. 1: 18401
Divisional PRO Rally Program of the Year Vol. 1: 18401
Divisional Team Championships Vol. 2: 4567
Divisions Safety Professional of the Year Vol. 1: 4788
Dix Award; Walter S. Vol. 1: 1813
Dix Leadership Award; Marion Quin Vol. 1: 12797
Dixon Award; Russell A. Vol. 1: 1863
Dixon, DDS Leadership Award; F. Gene Vol. 1: 8578
Dixon Lecture; W. E. Vol. 2: 4240
Dixon Medal; John W. Vol. 1: 5983
Dixon Trophy Vol. 2: 2898
Dizengoff Prize; Arts Prize - Meir Vol. 2: 7947
DMA Annual Award Vol. 1: 8524
DMA Hall of Fame Vol. 1: 8647
DMA/Royal Mail Direct Marketing Awards Vol. 2: 2331
DMAS Annual Art Awards Vol. 2: 355
DML/ICDDS Annual Award for Academic Research into Disaster Management Vol. 2: 3084
do Piaui (Brasil) Prize; Alvarenga Vol. 2: 10249
do Piaui; Premio Alvarenga Vol. 2: 10249
do Rego Prize; Abilio Lopes Vol. 2: 10250
Doane Award; D. Howard Vol. 1: 4558
Dobbs Award; Ella Victoria Vol. 1: 16192
Doberman Pinscher Club of America Awards Program Vol. 1: 8686
Dobie-Paisano Writing Fellowships Vol. 1: 18646
Dobinson Award Vol. 2: 2695
Doblin Prize; Alfred Vol. 2: 6510
Doblougska priset Vol. 2: 11588
Dobo Prize; Laszlo Vol. 2: 7378
Dobrolyubov Prize; N. A. Vol. 2: 10422
Dobson Lecture Vol. 2: 9730
Dobzhansky Memorial Award; Thomas Vol. 1: 6312
Dobzhansky Prize; Theodosius Vol. 1: 17640
Docent of Orbital Arts Vol. 2: 6571
d'Octon; Prix Paul Vigne Vol. 2: 5787
Dr. Max Luthi Preis Vol. 2: 11890
Doctor of Philosophical Enquiry (D.Ph.E.), Honoris Causa Vol. 1: 11260
Doctoral Awards Program Vol. 1: 1227
Doctoral Dissertation Award Vol. 1: 8376
Doctoral Dissertation Grants in Women's Studies Vol. 1: 20314
Doctoral Research Fellowships Vol. 1: 2625
Documentary Film Festival - Amsterdam Vol. 2: 9376
Documentary of the Year Vol. 2: 10000
Documentary Prize of the South German Broadcasting Company Vol. 2: 6954
Documents to the People Award Vol. 1: 2895
DOD Distinguished Service Award Vol. 1: 13848
DOD Medal for Distinguished Public Service Vol. 1: 19124
DOD Meritorious Award Vol. 1: 19125
Dodge Award Vol. 1: 20610
Dodge Award; Harold F. Vol. 1: 6048
Dodge Performance of the Year Vol. 1: 14164
Dodge Performer of the Year Award Vol. 1: 14165
Dodge Ram Tough Award Vol. 1: 14166
Doe Lectureship; Janet Vol. 1: 12169
Doebber Industrial Traffic Management Specialty Award; Frederick A. Vol. 1: 4800
Doehler Award Vol. 1: 15414

Doerfer Engineering Concept of the Year Award Vol. 1: 4363
Dofasco Award Vol. 1: 6940
Dog Gone Memorial Award Vol. 1: 12038
Dog of the Year Award Vol. 1: 3984
Dohrenwend Lecture in Social and Community Epidemiology; Barbara Vol. 1: 3789
Doistau - Emile Blutet; Fondation Paul Vol. 2: 5644
Dole Award; Gertrude Vol. 1: 9711
Dole Foundation Annual Leadership Award Vol. 1: 8690
Doll Award; Edgar A. Vol. 1: 3744
Dollar Award Vol. 1: 14011
Dollinger Award; National Leader's Award - Moe Vol. 1: 8750
Dolphin Award Vol. 1: 7349
Dolphin Fellowship Vol. 1: 5044
Dolphin Medal Vol. 1: 5044
Domac Medal; Julije Vol. 2: 1805
Domac; Medalja Julije Vol. 2: 1805
Dombo Communications Award Vol. 1: 11836
Dominguez Medal of Honor; Belisario Vol. 2: 9143
Dominguez; Premio IMIQ, Victor Marquez Vol. 2: 9109
The Dominion Sunday Times Bruce Mason Playwrights Award Vol. 2: 9784
Domtar Awards of the Chemical Institute of Canada for High School Chemistry Teachers Vol. 1: 7546
Donald Award; National Planning Awards - Diana Vol. 1: 3536
Donald Medal Vol. 2: 3217
Donaldson Award; Dale Vol. 1: 17331
Donath Medal Vol. 1: 9568
Donato; Premio Magda Vol. 2: 8930
Donato Prize; Magda Vol. 2: 8930
Dondero Award; John A. Vol. 1: 10645
Donegani; Fondazione Guido Vol. 2: 8059
Donehoo Essay Award Vol. 1: 10663
Donlan Memorial Exhibit Award; William Vol. 1: 3214
Donne Essay Prize on the Anthropology of Art; J. B. Vol. 2: 3927
Donnellan Award; J. Edward Vol. 1: 20336
Donnelley & Sons Co. Awards; R.R. Vol. 1: 1811
Donnelley & Sons Co. Exhibit Award; R.R. Vol. 1: 3215
Donnelley Award for Outstanding Service to the Developmentally Disabled; Naomi Williams Vol. 1: 7601
Donner Medal in Canadian Studies Vol. 1: 5459
Donohue Award; Mark Vol. 1: 18393
Donovan Award; William J. Vol. 1: 20021
Donovan Individual Achievement Award; James D. Vol. 1: 3857
Dooley Award; Dr. Thomas Vol. 1: 19854
Doolitte Award; Arthur K. Vol. 1: 1496
Doolittle Award; J. H. Vol. 1: 17836
Dorcus Award; Roy M. Vol. 1: 17433
Dori Prize; Ya'acov Vol. 2: 7877
Dornstein Memorial Creative Writing Contest for Young Adult Writers; David Vol. 1: 7853
D'oro; Premio Atomo Vol. 2: 8090
Dorot Research Professorship Vol. 1: 4011
Dorothea Award for Conservation Vol. 2: 2107
Dorros Award; Donna and Sidney Vol. 1: 15972
Dorweiler Prize Vol. 1: 7334
dos Santos Prize; Dr. Joao Vol. 2: 10234
Dosogne Memorial Scholarship; Rene Vol. 1: 13220

Dott, Sr., Memorial Award; Robert H. Vol. 1: 1105
Doubleday Lectureship Vol. 2: 4241
Doublespeak Award Vol. 1: 13768
Dougherty Award; John L. Vol. 1: 5410
Douglas Award; Marjory Stoneman Vol. 1: 14452
Douglas Award; William O. Vol. 1: 17230
Douglas Entrepreneurial Prizes Vol. 1: 6213
Douglas Gold Medal; James Vol. 1: 2633
Douglas-Home Memorial Award; Charles Vol. 2: 2751
Douglas International Fellowship; CFUW A. Vibert Vol. 2: 11789
Douglas Lecture; George Vol. 2: 4432
Douglas Medal - Cook Vol. 1: 12160
Douglas Memorial Medal; R. J. W. Vol. 1: 7221
Douglass Award; Frederick Vol. 1: 15309
Douglass Prize; Jane Dempsey Vol. 1: 4426
DOUMENG Trophy Vol. 1: 19384
Dove Awards Vol. 1: 9671
Dow Award for Excellence in Composites Research Vol. 1: 18048
Dow Corning Award of Merit Vol. 1: 4757
Dow Creativity Center Summer Residency Fellowships; Alden B. Vol. 1: 15532
Dow Geriatrics Clinician of the Year; AGS/ Marion Merrell Vol. 1: 2175
Dow Jones Award Vol. 1: 820
Dow Jones News/Retrieval Essay Contest Vol. 1: 8709
Dow Outstanding Young Faculty Award Vol. 1: 4085
Dowding Medal and Prize Vol. 2: 3131
Dower Prize Vol. 2: 3048
Dowling Lectureships Vol. 2: 4242
Down Award; Vera Vol. 2: 2434
Downes Jr. Memorial Award; William E. Vol. 1: 288
Downing Award; Antoinette Forrester Vol. 1: 17742
Downing Award; Glenn Vol. 1: 7150
Downs Award; Robert B. Vol. 1: 19802
Downs Travelling Scholarship Vol. 2: 4243
Downtown Development Award Vol. 1: 8720
Downtown Jaycees Teachers Grant Awards Vol. 1: 8717
Doyle Award; William H. Vol. 1: 2574
Dozier Travel Grant; Otis and Velma Davis Vol. 1: 8509
DPI-ACOPIM Journalism Award Vol. 2: 1684
DRAC d'Argent Vol. 2: 11155
Dracea Prize; Marin Vol. 2: 10345
Dracup Scholarship Award; Joseph F. Vol. 1: 859
Draddy Fellowship Vol. 1: 13996
Drainie Award for Distinguished Contribution to Broadcasting; John Vol. 1: 327
Drainie Award; John Vol. 1: 27
Drake Award; Russell Vol. 1: 5858
Drake Memorial Award; Howard Vol. 2: 3064
Drama Award Vol. 1: 18888
Drama Critics Prizes Vol. 2: 6405
Drama Desk Awards Vol. 1: 8727
Drama Festival (Jashan-E-Tamseel) Awards Vol. 2: 10001
Drama League's Delia Austrian Medal for Distinguished Performance Vol. 1: 8730
Drama League's Distinguished Performance Award Vol. 1: 8730
Drama League's Musical Achievement Award Vol. 1: 8731
Drama League's Playwrights Award Vol. 1: 8732
Drama League's Unique Contribution Award Vol. 1: 8733

Drama Magazine Awards   Vol. 2: 2547
Dramatic Arts Creativity Special Encouragement Award   Vol. 2: 8575
Draper Award; Charles Stark   Vol. 2: 5971
Draper Medal; Henry   Vol. 1: 12667
Draper Memorial Medal   Vol. 1: 10868
Draper Prize; Charles Stark   Vol. 1: 12640
Drechsel Achievement Award; Helmet   Vol. 1: 4024
Drew Award; Charles R.   Vol. 1: 3912
Drew Trophy; Charles Richard   Vol. 1: 16214
Drewitt Award; Gerald   Vol. 2: 3084
Drexel Citation   Vol. 1: 8739
Drexel Medal; Lucy Wharton   Vol. 1: 19730
Dreyfus Faculty Start-up Grants for Undergraduate Institutions; Camille and Henry   Vol. 1: 8741
Dreyfus New Faculty Awards Program; Camille and Henry   Vol. 1: 8742
Dreyfus Scholar/Fellow Program for Undergraduate Institutions; Camille and Henry   Vol. 1: 8743
Dreyfus Special Grant Program in the Chemical Sciences; Camille and Henry   Vol. 1: 8744
Dreyfus Teacher-Scholar Awards Program; Camille   Vol. 1: 8745
Dreyfus Teacher-Scholar Awards Program; Camille and Henry   Vol. 1: 8746
Dreyfus Teacher-Scholar Awards Program; Henry   Vol. 1: 8747
Driejaarlijkse Internationale Beiaardwedstrijd Koningin Fabiola   Vol. 2: 1348
Drilling Engineering Award   Vol. 1: 17964
Drinov Medal; Marin   Vol. 2: 1512
Driscoll Fellowship; Governor Alfred E.   Vol. 1: 15177
Driscoll Publication Prize; Alfred E.   Vol. 1: 15177
Driskill National Football Foundation Fellowship; Walter   Vol. 1: 13996
Driver Award; Captain William   Vol. 1: 13973
Driver Award; William   Vol. 1: 15485
Driver Memorial Trophy; Marvin D.   Vol. 1: 14644
Driver of the Year
   Austin Ten Drivers Club Ltd.   Vol. 2: 2145
   International Motor Sports Association   Vol 1: 11107
   Truck Renting and Leasing Association   Vol 1: 18821
Driver of the Year Award
   American Trucking Association   Vol. 1: 4926
   Guild of Motoring Writers   Vol 2: 2971
Droin; Prix Alfred   Vol. 2: 6269
Dromkeen Librarian's Award   Vol. 2: 411
Dromkeen Medal   Vol. 2: 412
Dronacharya Award   Vol. 2: 7522
Drossos Award; Erani P.   Vol. 1: 3404
Drotman Memorial Award; Jay S.   Vol. 1: 3847
Drouin; Prix Edmond   Vol. 2: 5455
Drug Therapy Research Award   Vol. 1: 4606
Drummond-Jackson Prize   Vol. 2: 4372
Dryburgh Memorial Trophy; Dave   Vol. 1: 6875
Dryden Lectureship in Research; AIAA   Vol. 1: 2463
Dryden Memorial Science Fellowship; Dr. Hugh L.   Vol. 1: 14831
Dryerre Prize Lecture; Henry   Vol. 2: 10642
Dryfoos Prize; Nancy   Vol. 1: 14715

Du Bois Award; William E. B.   Vol. 1: 5962
Du Bois Medal; William Edward Burghardt   Vol. 1: 12905

du Breuil; Prix Andre Jullien   Vol. 2: 5813
du Cayla-Martin; Prix E.   Vol. 2: 955
du Fay; Fondation Arthur   Vol. 2: 5497
Du Perron Award; E.   Vol. 2: 9674
Du Perron-Prijs; E.   Vol. 2: 9674
du Pont Crowninshield Award; Louise   Vol. 1: 14934
du Pont Gold Medal Award; E. I.   Vol. 1: 17906
Du Pont Human Powered Watercraft Speed Prizes   Vol. 1: 11039
du Pont Trophy; Richard C.   Vol. 1: 17359
du Pre Award; Jacqueline   Vol. 2: 3418
du Teil; Prix Joseph   Vol. 2: 5763
du Toit Malherbe Prize for Genealogical Research; D. F.   Vol. 2: 10987
du Toit Medal; Frans   Vol. 2: 10988
Du Toit Memorial Lecturer; Alex L.   Vol. 2: 10869
du Veuzit; Prix Max   Vol. 2: 6291
Duais Bhonn De Hide   Vol. 2: 7759
Duais don bhFiliocht i nGaelige; An   Vol. 2: 7761
Dubin Award; Sam   Vol. 1: 18964
Dublin Award; Louis I.
   American Association of Suicidology   Vol. 1: 1207
   National Association of Life Underwriters   Vol 1: 13196
Dublin Corporation Arts Scholarship   Vol. 2: 7758
Dublin Corporation Biennial Christy Brown Award   Vol. 2: 7758
Dublin Horse Show   Vol. 2: 7834
Duboff Award; Samuel J.   Vol. 1: 9446
DuBois Africana Students Competition; Ella Baker/W.E.B.   Vol. 1: 13684
DuBois - Johnson - Frazier Award   Vol. 1: 4833
Duc de Loubat; Prix du   Vol. 2: 5453
Duckham Research Award; Arthur   Vol. 2: 3322
Ductile Iron Society Annual Award   Vol. 1: 8754
Duculot; Prix Jules   Vol. 2: 994
Duddell Medal and Prize   Vol. 2: 3189
Duddell Premium   Vol. 2: 3273
Duden Preis der Stadt Mannheim; Konrad   Vol. 2: 7098
Dudley Award for Bibliographic Instruction; Miriam   Vol. 1: 2872
Dudley International Piano Competition   Vol. 2: 2755
Dudley Medal; Charles B.   Vol. 1: 6049
Dudley National Piano Competition   Vol. 2: 2755
Dudrick Research Scholar Award; Stanley J.   Vol. 1: 4227
Duer Scholarship Award; A. O.   Vol. 1: 13165
Duffy Award   Vol. 1: 11062
Dufrenoy; Prix Jean   Vol. 2: 4771
Dufresne Award; A. O.   Vol. 1: 6941
Dufton Silver Medal Award   Vol. 2: 2592
Duggan Medal; G. H.   Vol. 1: 7137
Duisberg-Gedachtnispreis; Carl-   Vol. 2: 6779
Duisberg-Plakette; Carl-   Vol. 2: 6780
Dujarric de la Riviere; Fondation Rene   Vol. 2: 5659
Dukaatti Prizes   Vol. 2: 4676
Duke and Duchess of York Prize in Photography   Vol. 1: 6735
Duke-Elder Glaucoma Award; Sir Stewart   Vol. 1: 4536
Duke Lifeline Earthquake Engineering Award; Charles Martin   Vol. 1: 4451
Duke of Buccleuch Memorial Trophy   Vol. 2: 10626

Duke of Edinburgh Prize   Vol. 2: 8593
Duke of Edinburgh Prize for the Japan Academy   Vol. 2: 8593
Duke of Edinburgh's Designer's Prize   Vol. 2: 2742
Dulac; Fondation   Vol. 2: 5351
Dull Brain Award   Vol. 1: 10919
Dumas; Fondation Jean-Baptiste   Vol. 2: 5592
Dumas Medal; Russell   Vol. 2: 466
Dumbarton Oaks Fellowships   Vol. 1: 8767
Dumesnil; Prix Rene   Vol. 2: 5421
Dumfries Octocentenary Trophy   Vol. 2: 10677
DuMont Citation; Allen B.   Vol. 1: 16644
Dumont Medal; Andre H.   Vol. 2: 1057
Dunbar Award   Vol. 2: 6733
Dunbar Memorial Award; Walter   Vol. 1: 3615
Duncan Prize Lectureship; Henry   Vol. 2: 10643
Dunedin Award for Architectural Photography; RIAS/   Vol. 2: 10616
Dunham Award for Excellence in Teaching; Meneve   Vol. 1: 7800
Dunkin Award   Vol. 2: 2510
Dunlap Lecture Award   Vol. 1: 7553
Dunleavy Award   Vol. 1: 15377
Dunlop Memorial Award; Jerry   Vol. 1: 9780
Dunlop Open Golf Championship   Vol. 2: 8617
Dunn Award for Excellence; James Clement   Vol. 1: 19289
Dunn Award; Gano   Vol. 1: 8263
Dunn Trophy; Eleanor   Vol. 1: 14645
Dunning Award; H. A. B.   Vol. 1: 3376
Dunning Award; John and Harriet   Vol. 1: 15079
Dunning Prize in United States History; John H.   Vol. 1: 2287
Dunsford Memorial Award; Ivor   Vol. 1: 925
Duo-Piano Competition   Vol. 1: 12531
Dupau; Prix Georges   Vol. 2: 5858
DUPHAR Award   Vol. 2: 3984
Dupin; Prix Charles
   Institut de France - Academie des Sciences Morales et Politiques   Vol. 2: 5722
   Institut de France - Academie des Sciences   Vol 2: 5596
DuPont Award; ICTA   Vol. 2: 3388
duPont - Columbia Univerity Awards; Alfred I.   Vol. 1: 7994
Dupont; Fondation Octave   Vol. 2: 1005
DuPont Pharma/Society of Nuclear Medicine Research Fellowship Program for Cardiovascular Nuclear Medicine   Vol. 1: 17946
DuPont Pharmaceuticals/ACCP Critical Care Research Award   Vol. 1: 1618
DuPont Pharmaceuticals/ACCP Young Investigator Awards   Vol. 1: 1619
Dupont; Prix Lucien   Vol. 2: 5778
Dupont Prize; O.   Vol. 2: 1255
Dupuis; Fondation Eugene et Amelie   Vol. 2: 5554
DuQuesne Award   Vol. 2: 4643
Durand-Claye; Fondation Alfred   Vol. 2: 5482
Durand et Edouard Ordonneau; Prix Auguste   Vol. 2: 5361
Durand Lectureship for Public Service; AIAA   Vol. 1: 2464
Durand; Prix Jacques   Vol. 2: 5405
Durban International Exhibition of Photography   Vol. 2: 10845
Durban International Film Festival Awards   Vol. 2: 10847
Durban Medal   Vol. 2: 11019
Durenberger Grassroots Government Leadership Award; Dave   Vol. 1: 13372
Dury Award; Ralph E.   Vol. 1: 7697
Duseigneur; Prix Raoul   Vol. 2: 5470

Dusek Competition of Musical Youth   Vol. 2: 1876
Duskova Soutez Hudebni Mla'deze   Vol. 2: 1876
Dusmet World Championship Cup; Edith Oliver   Vol. 1: 11084
Dussich Founder's Award; John J. P.   Vol. 1: 14417
Dustin; Prix Albert-Pierre-Jean   Vol. 2: 1323
Dutens; Fondation Alfred   Vol. 2: 5483
Dutens; Prix Alfred   Vol. 2: 5435
Dutens; Prix Joseph   Vol. 2: 5764
Duterme; Prix Robert   Vol. 2: 1305
Duthie Booksellers' Choice; Bill   Vol. 1: 20184
Dutton Award; Damien -   Vol. 1: 8514
Dutton Children's Books Picture Book Competition   Vol. 1: 8773
Duttweiler Prize; Gottlieb   Vol. 2: 11740
Duvand; Prix Adrien   Vol. 2: 5713
Duvernay; Prix Ludger-   Vol. 1: 17389
Duvivier; Prix Charles   Vol. 2: 980
Dwiggins Award; William A.   Vol. 1: 6447
Dwyer Memorial Medal; Francis Patrick   Vol. 2: 700
Dwyer Scholarships; Peter   Vol. 1: 6736
DX Hall of Fame   Vol. 1: 8434
Dyckman Award for Service; Herbert P.   Vol. 1: 1337
Dye Award; Thomas R.   Vol. 1: 16303
Dyer Aviation Education Award; Janice Marie   Vol. 1: 6176
Dykes Medal Award for America   Vol. 1: 2704
Dymond Public Service Environmental Award; J. R.   Vol. 1: 9146
Dyplom Honorowy   Vol. 2: 10216
E. H. Trophy   Vol. 2: 4032
EAA Award for Architecture   Vol. 2: 10533
EAAP Annual Meeting Awards   Vol. 2: 8230
EACR Italian Fellowship Program   Vol. 2: 2819
EACR Travel Fellowships   Vol. 2: 2820
Eadie Medal; Thomas W.   Vol. 1: 16952
Eager Scholarship; John P.   Vol. 1: 5542
Eagle Award   Vol. 1: 15989
Eagle Manned Mission Success Award   Vol. 1: 14832
Eagle Scout   Vol. 1: 6516
Eagle Scout Scholarship   Vol. 1: 14741
Eagle Star Award for Keyboard   Vol. 2: 4117
Eagle Star Award for Strings   Vol. 2: 4117
Eagle Star Training Award   Vol. 2: 4166
Eagle Trophy   Vol. 1: 5281
EAI Award   Vol. 1: 4086
Ealing Strings Prize   Vol. 2: 3627
Ear of Wheat Trophies   Vol. 2: 6519
Earhart Medal; Amelia   Vol. 1: 15388
Earhart Memorial Scholarship Award; Amelia   Vol. 1: 15387
Earl Award (Daytona 500); Harley   Vol. 1: 8539
Earle Award; Wilton R.   Vol. 1: 18716
Earle Memorial Award; Clarence E.   Vol. 1: 14313
Earle Trophy; Sir George   Vol. 2: 4167
Early Award; Joseph D.   Vol. 1: 14126
Early Career Distinguished Scholar Award   Vol. 1: 15454
Early Career Research Award   Vol. 1: 12889
Early Career Scientist/Practitioner Award   Vol. 1: 3705
Early Contributions Award   Vol. 1: 3720
Early Leader Award   Vol. 1: 12866
Early Music Festival - Bruges   Vol. 2: 1152
Early Scholar Award   Vol. 1: 12867
Earnie Awards   Vol. 1: 8777
Earthcare Award   Vol. 1: 17231
EARTHWATCH Film Awards   Vol. 1: 8779

EARTHWORM Children's Book Award   Vol. 2: 2913
East & West Artists Prize for New York Debut   Vol. 1: 8781
East Anglian Trophy   Vol. 2: 3662
East Asia Journalism Program Awards   Vol. 1: 7995
East European Support Award   Vol. 2: 6716
East Medal; L.R.   Vol. 2: 457
East Prize; Ben   Vol. 1: 12254
East-West Award   Vol. 1: 9829
East-West Center Award   Vol. 1: 9829
Easter Seals Award   Vol. 1: 7120
Eastern National Champion/Western National Champion   Vol. 1: 17050
Eastman Award
   Downtown Athletic Club of New York City   Vol. 1: 8713
   Naismith Memorial Basketball Hall of Fame   Vol 1: 12564
   National Association of Basketball Coaches   Vol 1: 12944
Eastman Kodak Award for Excellence in Cinematography   Vol. 1: 9829
Eastman Kodak Company Award for Cooperative Research in Polymer Science and Engineering   Vol. 1: 1497
Eastman Kodak Gold Medal Award   Vol. 1: 17900 Literary Awards Program   Vol. 1: 8808
Eaton Memorial Trophy; Warren E.   Vol. 1: 17360
Eaton Prize; Max A.   Vol. 1: 3081
Eavenson Award; Howard N.   Vol. 1: 17562
EBEC International Student Media Festival; AECT/   Vol. 1: 5502
Ebel Memorial Award; Max and Greta   Vol. 1: 7166
Ebert Award; Carl   Vol. 2: 2939
Ebert Prize   Vol. 1: 3377
EBONY Lifetime Achievement Award   Vol. 1: 11594
Ebright Service Award; Harry E.   Vol. 1: 1456
EBSCO ALA Conference Sponsorship   Vol. 1: 2815
Eby Memorial Award for the Art of Teaching; Harvey L.   Vol. 1: 19745
ECAC Distinguished Achievement Award   Vol. 1: 8790
ECAC Merit Medal   Vol. 1: 8791
ECAC Service Bureau Award   Vol. 1: 8793
ECAC - SIDA Media Award   Vol. 1: 8792
Eccles Medal   Vol. 1: 17868
Echeverria Prize; Aquileo J.   Vol. 2: 1761
ECHO Awards; Leonard J. Raymond Collegiate   Vol. 1: 8648
ECIS Award For International Understanding   Vol. 2: 2826
ECIS Awards   Vol. 2: 2827
Eckersberg Medal   Vol. 2: 1897
Eckert - Mauchly Award
   Association for Computing Machinery   Vol. 1: 5468
   Institute of Electrical and Electronics Engineers - Computer Society   Vol 1: 10298
Eckert Sr. Memorial Award; William   Vol. 1: 11200
Eckhardt-Gramatte National Competition for the Performance of Canadian Music   Vol. 1: 6547
Eckman Award; Donald P.   Vol. 1: 1287
Eckman Education Award; Donald P.   Vol. 1: 10484
Eckstein Memorial Prize; Otto   Vol. 1: 8796
Eclipse Awards   Vol. 1: 18706
Eclipse Awards for Media   Vol. 1: 18707
ECMA Awards   Vol. 1: 8930

Ecological Section Award   Vol. 1: 6482
Ecology Institute Prize   Vol. 2: 6688
Economic Award   Vol. 1: 11177
Economic Equity Award (Big WEAL)   Vol. 1: 20416
Economics and Evaluation Award   Vol. 1: 17965
Economics Prize   Vol. 2: 1226
ECRI Medical Technology Media Awards Program   Vol. 1: 8827
Ecroyd Award; Donald H.   Vol. 1: 18304
Ecumenical Prize   Vol. 2: 1172
Eddington Medal   Vol. 2: 3938
Edds Memorial Lecture in Developmental Biology; Mac V.   Vol. 1: 6594
Eddy Medal; Harrison Prescott   Vol. 1: 20147
Edeiken Award   Vol. 1: 2778
Edelman Award for Excellence in Continuing Jewish Education; Lily   Vol. 1: 6431
Edelman Award for Management Science Achievement; Franz   Vol. 1: 10402
Eden Travelling Fellowship in Obstetrics and Gynaecology   Vol. 2: 3953
Edenburn Trophy; Eddie   Vol. 1: 19017
Edgar Research Fellowship   Vol. 2: 3954
Edgars   Vol. 1: 12550
Edgerton Award; Harold E.   Vol. 1: 18320
Edgerton Civil Liberties Award; Henry W.   Vol. 1: 1588
Edholm Award; Otto   Vol. 2: 2801
EDI Award for Corporate Leadership   Vol. 1: 13869
EDI Awards (Equality/Dignity/Independence)   Vol. 1: 13870
Edinburgh Fellowship   Vol. 1: 3422
Edinburgh International Film Festival   Vol. 2: 10541
Edison Awards   Vol. 1: 2986
Edison Black Maria Film and Video Festival; Thomas A.   Vol. 1: 8831
Edison/Max McGraw Scholarship; Thomas   Vol. 1: 14692
Edison Medal   Vol. 1: 10262
Edition International Film Festival   Vol. 1: 8894
Editions Barenreiter, Basle & Kassel Prize   Vol. 2: 11879
Editor & Publisher/ANCAM Promotion Awards   Vol. 1: 8833
Editor & Publisher/ANPA Technical Awards   Vol. 1: 8834
Editor & Publisher/ICMA Award   Vol. 1: 8835
Editor & Publisher INMA Promotion Awards   Vol. 1: 8836
Editor of the Year Award   Vol. 1: 14513
Editor-Publisher Award   Vol. 1: 13193
Editorial and Cartoon Strip Contest   Vol. 1: 7909
Editorial and Graphics Awards Competition   Vol. 1: 17918
Editorial Award Winner   Vol. 1: 16243
Editorial Awards
   Association of Area Business Publications   Vol. 1: 5702
   Photographic Society of America   Vol 1: 16161
   Suburban Newspapers of America   Vol 1: 18514
Editorial Cartoon Contest   Vol. 1: 17328
Editorial Costa Rica Literary Prize   Vol. 2: 1770
Editorial Excellence Award
   Inland Press Association   Vol. 1: 10202
   National Broadcast Editorial Association   Vol 1: 13474
Editorial Fellowship Program   Vol. 2: 7933

Editorial Planeta - Joaquin Mortiz International Prize for Novel   Vol. 2: 8980
Editorial Writing - Walker Stone Award   Vol. 1: 17145
Editor's Award
   American Meteorological Society   Vol. 1: 3082
   International Association for Great Lakes Research   Vol 1: 10641
Editor's Award - *Journal of Allied Health*   Vol. 1: 5947
Editors' Book Award   Vol. 1: 16598
Editor's Editor of the Year   Vol. 2: 3772
Editor's Grants   Vol. 1: 8369
Editors of the Year   Vol. 2: 3772
Editors' Prize for Poetry and Short Fiction   Vol. 1: 16065
Edlundska Priset   Vol. 2: 11538
Edmonds Playwriting Award; S. Randolph   Vol. 1: 13078
Edmonds Young Scholars Competition; Randolph   Vol. 1: 6396
Edmonton Journal Literary Award   Vol. 1: 8838
EDPAA Best Newsletter Awards   Vol. 1: 8840
EdPress Distinguished Achievement Awards for Excellence in Educational Journalism   Vol. 1: 8858
EdPress Honor Awards - Best Newsletter   Vol. 1: 8859
EdPress Honor Awards - Golden Lamp Award   Vol. 1: 8860
EdPress Honor Awards - Golden Shoestring   Vol. 1: 8861
EdPress Honor Awards - Most Improved Publication   Vol. 1: 8862
EDRA Career Award   Vol. 1: 8959
EDRA Student Award   Vol. 1: 8960
EDRA Student Design Competition   Vol. 1: 8961
Edstrom Medal   Vol. 2: 3433
Education and Research Award   Vol. 1: 3946
Education and Training Awards   Vol. 1: 5817
Education Award
   American Association of Occupational Health Nurses   Vol. 1: 1079
   American Association of Zoological Parks and Aquariums   Vol 1: 1247
   American Automatic Control Council   Vol 1: 1288
   American College of Health Care Administrators   Vol 1: 1644
   American Water Works Association   Vol 1: 5020
   Association of Surgical Technologists   Vol 1: 5974
   New England Wildflower Society   Vol 1: 15162
   Self Help for Hard of Hearing People   Vol 1: 17176
Education Award (Gustav J. Bujkovsky Memorial Award)   Vol. 1: 11046
Education Awards   Vol. 1: 10889
Education Commendation   Vol. 1: 8202
Education Council/GATF Individual Award   Vol. 1: 9699
Education Council of the Graphic Arts Industry; Horace Hart Award of the   Vol. 1: 9799
Education Medal   Vol. 2: 8799
Education Partnership Award   Vol. 1: 19619
Education School Design Award   Vol. 2: 2757
Education Writing Awards   Vol. 1: 8848
Educational Advancement Award   Vol. 1: 5578
Educational Aids Competition Blue Ribbon Awards   Vol. 1: 4361
Educational Exhibit   Vol. 1: 3335

Educational Foundation Award   Vol. 1: 13340
Educational Foundation Grant   Vol. 2: 1183
Educational Interiors Showcase   Vol. 1: 3991
Educational Merit Diploma   Vol. 2: 1656
Educational Program Award   Vol. 1: 5728
Educational Psychology Dissertation Award   Vol. 1: 3721
Educational Research Award   Vol. 1: 17858
Educational Scholarships   Vol. 1: 14747
Educational Sponsorship Award   Vol. 1: 12875
Educational Television Awards Scheme   Vol. 2: 2760
Educator Award
   International Association of Milk, Food and Environmental Sanitarians   Vol. 1: 10764
   International Facility Management Association   Vol 1: 10944
   Minerals, Metals, and Materials Society   Vol 1: 12308
Educator-Industry Award
   International Association of Milk, Food and Environmental Sanitarians   Vol. 1: 10760
   International Association of Milk, Food and Environmental Sanitarians   Vol 1: 10764
Educator of the Year   Vol. 1: 18557
Educator of the Year Award   Vol. 1: 5215
Educator's Award   Vol. 1: 8583
EDUCOM Higher Education Software Awards   Vol. 1: 8867
EDUCOM/NCRIPTAL Higher Education Software Awards   Vol. 1: 8867
Edward Award; Derrick   Vol. 1: 11130
Edward Medal   Vol. 2: 2367
Edwards Award; Boothby -   Vol. 1: 166
Edwards Award; Charlie
   Radio and Television News Directors Association   Vol. 1: 16635
   Radio and Television News Directors Association   Vol 1: 16637
Edwards Award; Douglas   Vol. 1: 16990
Edwards Award; Howard K.   Vol. 1: 166
Edwards Award; Margaret A.   Vol. 1: 2958
Edwards Industry Advancement Award; Harry H.   Vol. 1: 16371
Edwards Medal   Vol. 1: 4281
Edwards Medal; Margaret Hay   Vol. 1: 837
Edwards Memorial Award; Everett Eugene   Vol. 1: 207
Edwards Memorial Medal; J. T.   Vol. 2: 3985
Edwards Prize   Vol. 1: 20318
Edwards Prize; Alan   Vol. 2: 4244
Eeckhout Prize; Joris   Vol. 2: 1270
EEMS Award   Vol. 2: 11697
EEMS Award to Young Scientists   Vol. 2: 11698
Eenhoornprijs   Vol. 2: 9676
Efficiency Medal
   Guyana - Office of the President   Vol. 2: 7248
   Singapore - Office of the Prime Minister   Vol 2: 10740
Efficiency of Labor Award   Vol. 2: 10428
Effie Awards   Vol. 1: 2998
Efron Research Award; Daniel H.   Vol. 1: 1688
EFTA Awards   Vol. 2: 11700
Egan Memorial Trophy; Raymond   Vol. 2: 7800
Egede Medaillen   Vol. 2: 1998
Egede Medal   Vol. 2: 1998
Egerton Medal; Sir Alfred   Vol. 1: 8021
EGGA Pin   Vol. 2: 2832
Egging Memorial Award; Mary   Vol. 1: 3138
Eggleston Award for Nonfiction; Wilfrid   Vol. 1: 20555
Egleston Medal   Vol. 1: 7965

Egoff Children's Prize; Sheila A.   Vol. 1: 20185
EGS Badge Award   Vol. 2: 6717
Egyed Laszlo emlekerem   Vol. 2: 7287
Egyed Memorial Award; Laszlo   Vol. 2: 7287
Egypt Exploration Society Centenary Studentship   Vol. 2: 2762
Egyptian Red Crescent Society Competitions   Vol. 2: 2021
Ehninger Distinguished Rhetorical Scholar Award; Douglas   Vol. 1: 18305
Ehrenburgerbrief   Vol. 2: 864
Ehrenmitglied
   Association of Palaeontology   Vol. 2: 6533
   Society of Laboratory Animal Science   Vol 2: 11909
Ehrenmitgliedschaft   Vol. 2: 787
Ehrenmitgliedschaft im IDV   Vol. 2: 10071
Ehrennadel der Deutschen Apotheker   Vol. 2: 6585
Ehrennadel fur Verdienste um die Osterreichische Volkskunde Huterstern   Vol. 2: 908
Ehrenring der ehemaligen Forschungsstelle Papiergeschichte   Vol. 2: 6539
Ehrenring der Stadt Salzburg   Vol. 2: 865
Ehrentafel   Vol. 2: 840
Ehrenzeichen   Vol. 2: 6946
Ehrenzeichen der Bundeswehr   Vol. 2: 6737
Ehrenzeichen der deutschen Arzteschaft   Vol. 2: 6815
Ehrlich - und Ludwig Darmstaedter Preis; Paul   Vol. 2: 6691
EIB Prize   Vol. 2: 8860
Eichendorff Medal   Vol. 2: 6693
Eichendorff Plakette   Vol. 2: 6742
Einhorn Prize; Science Prize - Dr. Moshe   Vol. 2: 7960
Einstein Award   Vol. 1: 1341
Einstein Award; Alfred   Vol. 1: 3173
Einstein Award for Research in Psychiatry and Related Disciplines; Albert   Vol. 1: 20590
Einstein Award; Hans Albert   Vol. 1: 4452
Einstein Commemorative Award; Albert   Vol. 1: 20581
Einstein Medal; Albert   Vol. 1: 8869
Einstein Peace Prize; Albert   Vol. 1: 8871
Einstein World Award of Science; Albert   Vol. 2: 9307
Eisendrath Prize; Joseph N.   Vol. 1: 5297
Eisenhower Award   Vol. 1: 1941
Eisenhower Award; Dwight D.   Vol. 1: 14618
Eisenhower Distinguished Service Award; VFW Dwight David   Vol. 1: 20013
Eisenhower Liberation Medal   Vol. 1: 19396
Eisenhower Medallion   Vol. 1: 16062
Eisenhower Trophy; Dwight D.   Vol. 1: 13990
Eisenman Award; William Hunt
   ASM International   Vol. 1: 5352
   International Association for Exposition Management   Vol 1: 10636
Eisenstein Award; Laura   Vol. 1: 5661
Eisner Award for Young Playwrights; Helen   Vol. 1: 18498
Ekblad-Eldhs pris; Signe   Vol. 2: 11589
Eklund Prize   Vol. 2: 8289
Ekofilm Awards   Vol. 1: 1862
Elaut Prize; Prof. Leon   Vol. 2: 1271
Elder Intenational Medal; Duke   Vol. 2: 9484
Elder International Medal; Sir Stewart Duke   Vol. 2: 9500
Elder Poetry Award; FAW Anne   Vol. 2: 380
Elder Statesman of Aviation Award   Vol. 1: 12724
Eldredge Award; Marie H.   Vol. 1: 3630

Eleazar and Rose Tartakow Levinson Prize; Samuel   Vol. 1: 17618
Electric Furnace Honorable Mention   Vol. 1: 11461
Electronic Imaging Management Award   Vol. 1: 5543
Electronic Innovation Commendation   Vol. 1: 8203
Electronic Media Book of the Year Award   Vol. 1: 12976
Electronic Media Presentations   Vol. 1: 8295
Electronic Office Design Competition   Vol. 1: 12024
Electronic Prepress Pioneer Award   Vol. 1: 8771
Electronic Systems News Premium   Vol. 2: 3275
Electronics and Communication Engineering Journal Premium   Vol. 2: 3274
Electronics Division Award   Vol. 1: 1457
Electronics Education Premium   Vol. 2: 3275
Electronics Industry Hall of Fame Awards   Vol. 1: 8887
Electronics Innovation Award   Vol. 2: 8326
Electronics Letters Premium Awards   Vol. 2: 3276
Electrotechnical Award   Vol. 2: 7329
Electrotechnical Dij   Vol. 2: 7329
Elegant Work Prize   Vol. 2: 3132
Elementary, Middle, and Secondary School Physical Education Teacher of the Year   Vol. 1: 12900
Elf Arts Award   Vol. 2: 2034
Eli Lilly Fellowship in Infectious Diseases; NFID -   Vol. 1: 14042
Eliot Award for Creative Writing; Ingersoll Prize - T. S.   Vol. 1: 10192
Eliot Award; Martha May   Vol. 1: 3848
Eliot Prize; Ida and George   Vol. 1: 12170
ELITE Award   Vol. 1: 7418
Elizalde Prize; Pedro I.   Vol. 2: 77
Elizondo - Premio Cientifico y Technologico; Premio Luis   Vol. 2: 8989
Elizondo - Premio Humanitario; Premio Luis   Vol. 2: 8990
Elizondo Prize; Jose F.   Vol. 2: 9084
Elkes International Award; Joel   Vol. 1: 1689
Elle; Grand Prix des Lectrices de   Vol. 2: 5110
Elle Literary Prize   Vol. 2: 5110
Ellery Memorial Plaque; James H.   Vol. 1: 2324
Ellet Award; Charles   Vol. 1: 20223
Ellinger-Gardonyi Award   Vol. 2: 3730
Elliot Medal; Daniel Giraud   Vol. 1: 12668
Elliot Prize; Van Courtlandt   Vol. 1: 12200
Elliott - Black Award   Vol. 1: 2003
Elliott Distinguished Service Award; Henry W.   Vol. 1: 4056
Elliott Memorial Award; F. J.   Vol. 1: 7201
Elliott Memorial Award; John   Vol. 1: 926
Ellis Award; Arthur   Vol. 1: 8457
Ellis Award; Perry   Vol. 1: 8355
Ellis Island Medal of Honor   Vol. 1: 13921
Ellis Jr. Award; Lewis C.   Vol. 1: 5283
Ellis Memorial Award; David James   Vol. 1: 18673
Ellis Memorial Trophy; Dick   Vol. 1: 7244
Ellis Prize; Vivian   Vol. 2: 3769
Ellison-Cliffe Medal and Lecture   Vol. 2: 4245
Ells Award for Program Excellence; Eleanor P.   Vol. 1: 1405
Elmer Award
   Harvard Lampoon   Vol. 1: 9808
   Medical-Dental-Hospital Bureaus of America   Vol 1: 12162
Elmer Award; S. Lewis   Vol. 1: 2194

Elmore Fellowships; Stanley   Vol. 2: 3338
Elovitz Prize; Rose and Michael David   Vol. 1: 11178
Elsa Knight Thompson Award for Special Achievement   Vol. 1: 12153
Elsey Award for Outstanding Involvement of Youth; George M.   Vol. 1: 3913
Elson Award for International Achievement in Physical Therapy; Mildred   Vol. 2: 4622
Eltiste Memorial Breeders Shield; William   Vol. 1: 3984
Elvehjem Award for Public Service in Nutrition; Conrad A.   Vol. 1: 2649
Elver Mineral Economics Award; Robert   Vol. 1: 6942
Ely Award; Jerome H.   Vol. 1: 10039
Ely Lecture; Richard T.   Vol. 1: 1969
EMA Achievement Award   Vol. 1: 8916
EMA Advertising Excellence Awards   Vol. 1: 8914
EMA Foundation School/Business Partnership Award   Vol. 1: 8915
EMA National Service Award   Vol. 1: 8916
EMA Special Award   Vol. 1: 8916
EMAS/Performing Right Society Prize   Vol. 2: 4475
Emberson Award; Richard M.   Vol. 1: 10263
EMBO Medal   Vol. 2: 6727
Emden; Fondation Fanny   Vol. 2: 5555
Emens Award for Support of a Free Student Press; John R.   Vol. 1: 6224
Emergent Entrepreneur Award   Vol. 2: 10877
Emeritus Award
   Association for the Education of Teachers in Science   Vol. 1: 5630
   Wildlife Diseases Association   Vol 1: 20297
Emeritus Membership   Vol. 1: 12266
Emerson Award; Ralph Waldo
   International Platform Association   Vol. 1: 11150
   Phi Beta Kappa   Vol 1: 16099
Emerson Medal; Charles Alvin   Vol. 1: 20148
Emerson Scholarship; Gladys Anderson   Vol. 1: 11439
Emerson - Thoreau Medal   Vol. 1: 525
Emery Edge Award   Vol. 1: 14167
EMIERT/Gale Research Multicultural Award   Vol. 1: 2887
Emil Memorial Award; Allan D.   Vol. 2: 5972
Emily Award
   American Film and Video Association   Vol. 1: 2046
   National Women's Hall of Fame   Vol 1: 15023
Eminent Activist Medal   Vol. 2: 7379
Eminent Ecologist   Vol. 1: 8815
Eminent Members   Vol. 1: 9005
Eminent Service Award   Vol. 1: 637
Eminescu Prize; Mihail   Vol. 2: 10346
Emley Award; Edward   Vol. 2: 3133
EMMA Awards   Vol. 1: 15027
Emmaus Award   Vol. 1: 14613
Emme Astronautical Literature Award; Eugene M.   Vol. 1: 1257
Emmett Award in Fundamental Catalysis; Paul H.   Vol. 1: 7343
Emmons Award; W. J.   Vol. 1: 5707
Emmy Awards (1949-1976)   Vol. 1: 12709
Emmy Awards for Daytime Programming   Vol. 1: 12710
Emmy Awards for Primetime Programming   Vol. 1: 86
Empain; Prix Scientifiques Louis   Vol. 2: 1380
Employee for Tomorrow Award   Vol. 1: 3945
Employer of the Month Award   Vol. 1: 4418

Employer of the Year Award
   American Society of Certified Engineering Technicians   Vol. 1: 4419
   The Arc   Vol 1: 5212
   Blinded Veterans Association   Vol 1: 6407
   President's Committee on Employment of People with Disabilities   Vol 1: 16384
   United Cerebral Palsy Associations   Vol 1: 18901
Employer of the Year Awards Business/Industry and Government   Vol. 1: 5212
Employer's Merit Award   Vol. 1: 16385
Employers of the Year   Vol. 1: 9659
Empress Elizabeth National Champion   Vol. 1: 11218
EMRA Academic Excellence Award   Vol. 1: 8897
EMRA Award for Excellence in Teaching   Vol. 1: 8898
EMRA Clinical Excellence Award   Vol. 1: 8899
EMRA Leadership Award   Vol. 1: 8900
EMS Administrator of the Year Award   Vol. 1: 13088
EMS Award   Vol. 1: 8963
EMS Environmental Mutagenesis Recognition Award   Vol. 1: 8964
EMS Instructor Coordinator of the Year Award   Vol. 1: 13099
EMT - Paramedic of the Year   Vol. 1: 13113
EMT-Paramedic Emergency Medical Service of the Year Award   Vol. 1: 13089
En iYi Bas Asistan Tebligi   Vol. 2: 12082
ENA Micromedex Best Original Research Award   Vol. 1: 8903
Encore Awards   Vol. 1: 16817
Encouragement Award   Vol. 2: 12067
Encuentro Nacional de Arte Joven   Vol. 2: 9212
Encyclopaedia Britannica Canadian School Library Awards   Vol. 1: 7023
Endoscopic Outcomes and Effectiveness Developmental Research Awards   Vol. 1: 4134
Endoscopic Research Awards   Vol. 1: 4135
Endowment Achievement Awards   Vol. 1: 8362
Endowment for Biblical Research, Summer Research and Travel Grants   Vol. 1: 4012
Energy Conservation Award   Vol. 1: 13901
Energy Innovator Award   Vol. 1: 3858
Energy Leadership Award   Vol. 1: 5119
Energy Management in Lighting Awards Scheme   Vol. 2: 3580
Energy Managers' Hall of Fame   Vol. 1: 5768
Energy Prize   Vol. 2: 6383
Enersen Award; Lawrence   Vol. 1: 12788
Enesco International Composition Competition; Georges   Vol. 2: 11949
Enescu Prize; George   Vol. 2: 10347
Engel Award; Al J.   Vol. 1: 20217
Engel Award; Marian
   Harbourfront Reading Series   Vol. 1: 9768
   Writers' Development Trust   Vol 1: 20548
Engel Prize; Arts Prize - Yoel   Vol. 2: 7949
Engelberger Awards; Joseph F.   Vol. 1: 16861
Engelberger Robotics Awards; Joseph F.   Vol. 1: 16861
Engelhard Medallion; Charles W.   Vol. 1: 18601
Engelman Prize; Camille   Vol. 2: 1286
Engestromska medaljen for tillampad naturvetenskap   Vol. 2: 11513
Engineer of the Year   Vol. 1: 18558
Engineer of the Year in Southern California   Vol. 1: 10241
Engineering 2000 Awards   Vol. 2: 438

Engineering Achievement Award
American Institute of Mining, Metallurgical and Petroleum Engineers Vol. 1: 2638
National Association of Broadcasters Vol 1: 12977
Zimbabwe Institution of Engineers Vol 2: 12213
Engineering Achievement Awards Program Vol. 1: 4362
Engineering Achievement in Radio Vol. 1: 12977
Engineering Achievement in Television Vol. 1: 12977
Engineering and Construction Contracting Division Award Vol. 1: 2575
Engineering and Science Hall of Fame Vol. 1: 8928
Engineering Award
Association for Information and Image Management Vol. 1: 5544
National Association of Broadcasters Vol 1: 12977
Engineering Award of Excellence Vol. 1: 8883
Engineering Concept of the Year Award Vol. 1: 4363
Engineering Council Young Engineer for Britain Competition Vol. 2: 4302
Engineering Development Award Vol. 1: 12711
Engineering Excellence Awards Vol. 1: 15748
Engineering Excellence Awards Competition Vol. 1: 1825
Engineering Journals Premia Vol. 2: 3277
Engineering Management Achievement Awards Vol. 1: 13053
Engineering Materials Achievement Award Vol. 1: 5353
Engineering Medal Vol. 1: 16460
Engineering Meetings Board Outstanding Oral Presentation Award; SAE Vol. 1: 17771
Engineering Prize - Avraham Cravenne Prize Vol. 2: 7950
Engineering Prize - Dov Hoz Prize Vol. 2: 7951
Engineering Prize - Israel Rokach Prize Vol. 2: 7952
Engineering Science/AEEP Doctoral Thesis Award Vol. 1: 5781
Engle Fellowship; James A. Michener - Paul Vol. 1: 11447
Engle Trophy Vol. 1: 14645
Engleheart Cup Vol. 2: 4033
Engler Gold Medal Vol. 2: 6932
Engler Medal; Carl Vol. 2: 6861
English Academy Medal Vol. 2: 10851
English Association Literary Competition Vol. 2: 10855
English Badminton Award Vol. 2: 2153
English Journal Writing Awards Vol. 1: 13769
English Wine of the Year Competition Vol. 2: 2796
Englund Prize; Carl-Emil Vol. 2: 11643
Engstrom Award; Emmett Vol. 1: 3190
Enlisted Aviation Safety Award Vol. 1: 12062
Enlisted Leadership Award Vol. 1: 12073
Enners Award; Lt. Raymond J. Vol. 1: 19410
Ennor Manufacturing Technology Award; William T. Vol. 1: 4671
Ensemble Company of Cincinnati Opera (ECCO) Vol. 1: 7699
Ensemble of the Year Vol. 1: 7053
Ensminger-Interstate Distinguished Teacher Award; NACTA Vol. 1: 13010
Enstrommedalj; Axel F. Vol. 2: 11525
Entente Florale Vol. 2: 1067
Enterprise Computing Award Vol. 1: 17059

Enterprise Information Group Special Prize Vol. 2: 2703
Enterprise Reporting Awards Vol. 1: 15191
Entomological Society of Canada Gold Medal Award Vol. 1: 8954
Entomology Writing Competition Award Vol. 1: 20605
Entrepreneur Award Vol. 1: 10183
Entrepreneur Awards Vol. 1: 20370
Entrepreneur of the Year
Ernst & Young Vol. 1: 8995
International Franchise Association Vol 1: 10997
Entrepreneur of the Year Award Vol. 1: 3937
Entrepreneurial Success Award Vol. 1: 19598
Entrepreneurs Workshop International Vol. 1: 11423
Entry Films Competition Vol. 1: 6365
Entwicklungslanderpreises der Justus-Liebig-Universitat Giessen Vol. 2: 6999
The Environment Award for Engineers Vol. 2: 2769
Environment in Children's Literature Award Vol. 2: 10289
Environment Medal Vol. 2: 4407
Environmental Achievement Awards Vol. 1: 8957
Environmental and Conservation Award Vol. 1: 9501
Environmental and Energy Achievement Awards Program Vol. 1: 476
Environmental and Safety Distinguished Achievement Award Vol. 1: 17966
Environmental Award
Institute of Packaging Professionals Vol. 1: 10425
Institution of Professional Engineers New Zealand Vol 2: 9731
Environmental Conservation Distinguished Service Award Vol. 1: 2634
Environmental Division Service Award Vol. 1: 2576
Environmental Education Award Vol. 1: 13916
Environmental Improvement Awards Program Vol. 1: 5406
Environmental Innovations Award Vol. 1: 3945
Environmental Journalism - Edward J. Meeman Awards Vol. 1: 17146
Environmental Management Awards Vol. 2: 4321
Environmental Protection Award Vol. 2: 10429
Environmental Quality Achievement Awards Vol. 1: 2391
Environmental Quality Research Award Vol. 1: 4383
Environmental Restoration/Waste Management Distinguished Young Faculty Award Program Vol. 1: 15566
Environmental Science Award Vol. 1: 168
Environmentalist of the Year Vol. 1: 18961
EOSAT Award for Application of Digital Landsat TM Data Vol. 1: 4247
Eotvos Memorial Medal; Lorand Vol. 2: 7288
Epilepsy Foundation of America Awards Vol. 1: 8967
Epilepsy Research Award for Outstanding Contributions to the Pharmacology of Antiepileptic Drugs Vol. 1: 4234
Epitoipar Kivalo Munkaert Vol. 2: 7330
Epstein Choreography Award; Lawrence S. Vol. 1: 8986
Epstein Foundation Awards; Norma Vol. 1: 19886

Epstein Playwriting Award; Lawrence S. Vol. 1: 8987
Equal Employment Opportunity Award
United States Department of Commerce - National Institute of Standards and Technology Vol. 1: 19104
United States Department of State Vol 1: 19290
Equal Employment Opportunity Awards Vol. 1: 19257
Equal Employment Opportunity Medal Vol. 1: 12733
Equal Justice Award Vol. 1: 13435
Equal Opportunity/Affirmative Action Exemplary Practices Award Vol. 1: 4266
Equal Opportunity Award Vol. 1: 15546
Equal Opportunity Day Award Vol. 1: 14971
Equine Research Award Vol. 1: 4986
Erasmus Prijs Vol. 2: 9396
Erasmus Prize Vol. 2: 9396
ERB Life Achievement Award Vol. 1: 6633
Erb; Prix of Marie-Joseph Vol. 2: 5042
ERDAS Award for Best Scientific Paper in Remote Sensing Vol. 1: 4248
Erdtman International Award for Palynology; Professor Gunnar Vol. 2: 7718
Erdtman International Medal; Gunnar Vol. 2: 7718
Ereskalejdoskop Vol. 2: 1946
Ergonomics Society Special Award Vol. 2: 2802
Ergonomics Society's Meritorious Service Award Vol. 2: 2803
Erhard-Preis fur Wirtschaftspublizistik; Ludwig- Vol. 2: 6699
Erickson Award; Bonnie Vol. 1: 9914
Ericson's Award for Outstanding Doll Sculpture; Rolf Vol. 1: 8692
Ericsson Award in Renewable Energy; John Vol. 1: 19229
Ericsson Medal Award; John Vol. 1: 4795
Ericsson National Science and Technology Prize Vol. 2: 8983
Eriksson Prize; Jakob Vol. 2: 11539
Eriksson Prize Medal; Jakob Vol. 2: 11475
Erikssons Pris; Hilda och Alfred Vol. 2: 11540
Erikssons stipendium; Lydia och Herman Vol. 2: 11590
Erkel - Kodaly Singing Competition Vol. 2: 7414
Erkel Prize for Musical Composition; Ferenc Vol. 2: 7400
Erlanger Foundation Prize Vol. 2: 6310
Ernst & Young Award for Singers Vol. 2: 4117
Ernst Award in Art; Jimmy Vol. 1: 504
Errera; Prix Leo Vol. 2: 1029
Erskine Outstanding Achievement Award; Addine Vol. 1: 11239
Erwin Literary Achievement Awards; Robert C. Vol. 1: 1709
Erwin Memorial Trophy; Franklin Vol. 1: 19707
ESA Distinguished Achievement Award in Extension Vol. 1: 8945
ESA Distinguished Achievement Award in Regulatory Entomology Vol. 1: 8946
ESA Distinguished Achievement Award in Teaching Vol. 1: 8947
ESA Founder's Memorial Award Vol. 1: 8948
ESA Recognition Award in Entomology Vol. 1: 8949
Esau Award; Katherine Vol. 1: 6483
ESB Clinical Biomechanics Award Vol. 2: 6729

ESB Community Enterprise Award   Vol. 2: 7795
ESB Poster Award   Vol. 2: 6730
ESB Research Award in Biomechanics   Vol. 2: 6731
Escalante Prize; Constantino   Vol. 2: 9085
Escalle; Prix Jean   Vol. 2: 4847
Escorts Book Award   Vol. 2: 7491
ESCPB Young Scientists Awards   Vol. 2: 1138
Eseman Award; Eugene (Butch)   Vol. 1: 12104
Esguerra Prize; Carlos   Vol. 2: 1727
Eskola Medal   Vol. 2: 4716
Eskola-Mitali   Vol. 2: 4716
Eskow Scholarship; Seymour   Vol. 1: 15979
ESM Career Development Award   Vol. 2: 2845
ESOMAR Awards   Vol. 2: 9418
Espejo National Prize for Culture; Eugenio   Vol. 2: 2017
Espejo; Premio Nacional de Cultura de Ecuador Eugenio   Vol. 2: 2017
Espenschade Award; Park W.   Vol. 1: 10324
Esperantista Go-Ligo Internacia Competitions   Vol. 2: 8549
Esperanto   Vol. 2: 8778
Esperanto Diploma   Vol. 2: 7425
ESPY Awards   Vol. 1: 8999
ESRI Award for Best Scientific Paper in Geographic Information Systems   Vol. 1: 4249
Essay Award   Vol. 1: 16112
Essay Competition
    Jane Austen Society of North America   Vol. 1: 6152
    Indian Hospital Association   Vol 2: 7620
Essay Contest   Vol. 1: 13816
Essay Contest Award   Vol. 1: 15544
Essay Contest for Professionals in Rehabilitation   Vol. 1: 1806
Essay Prize   Vol. 2: 11759
The Essex Chronicle Awards for the Essex Schools Musician of the Year   Vol. 2: 3735
Essex International Salon of Photography   Vol. 2: 2810
Essig Award; Otto   Vol. 1: 19937
Essman Awards; Pansy Ellen   Vol. 1: 11742
Esso Award   Vol. 2: 439
Esso Energy Award and Medal   Vol. 2: 4148
Esso - Glyndebourne Touring Opera Singers' Award   Vol. 2: 2940
Esson Prize for Drama; Louis   Vol. 2: 149
Established Chapter of the Year   Vol. 1: 13262
Established Investigator Award   Vol. 1: 2228
Established Investigator Awards   Vol. 1: 12768
Estes Memorial Pioneer Jujitsu Award; Bud   Vol. 1: 427
Estrada; Premio Genaro   Vol. 2: 9016
Estrelicia Dourada   Vol. 2: 10261
Estrella de la Policia   Vol. 2: 1673
Estridge, Jr. Award; Capt. W. W.   Vol. 1: 19721
Etancelin; Fondation Leon-Alexandre   Vol. 2: 5616
ETE Erdemerem   Vol. 2: 7450
ETE Merit Medal   Vol. 2: 7450
Eternal Light Medal   Vol. 1: 11567
Ethical Culture School Book Award   Vol. 1: 9011
Ethical Humanist Award   Vol. 1: 15272
Ethicon Fellowship   Vol. 2: 10599
Ethicon Film Award   Vol. 1: 18200
Ethicon Laureate Awards   Vol. 1: 18203
Ethics Award   Vol. 1: 8904

Ethnic Affairs Commission of New South Wales Award   Vol. 2: 686
Ethnic and Cultural Pluralism Award   Vol. 1: 3569
Etienne; Prix Eugene   Vol. 2: 6139
Etiennette Avares Correa Competition   Vol. 2: 9338
ETR&D Young Scholar Award   Vol. 1: 5511
ETS Award for Distinguished Service to Measurement   Vol. 1: 8865
Ettl Award for Sculpture; Alex   Vol. 1: 12607
Ettl Grant; Alex J.   Vol. 1: 14712
Ettlingen International Competition for Young Pianists   Vol. 2: 7061
Eubank Morale, Welfare and Recreation Award; Maj. Gen. Eugene L.   Vol. 1: 15776
Eulau Award; Heinz   Vol. 1: 3573
Euro Best Awards   Vol. 2: 3362
EURO Golden Medal   Vol. 2: 6010
Euroarabe and Television Festival   Vol. 2: 11226
Euromusica Competition   Vol. 2: 11323
Europa Award   Vol. 2: 11155
Europa Medal   Vol. 2: 7779
Europa Nostra Awards   Vol. 2: 9402
Europa Preis fur Denkmalpflege   Vol. 2: 7110
Europa Prize   Vol. 2: 2840
Europaischer Chopin-Klavierwettbewerb   Vol. 2: 6594
Europaischer Designpreis   Vol. 2: 6803
Europaischer Filmpreis   Vol. 2: 6713
Europalia Literary Prize of the European Community   Vol. 2: 1154
Europe Prize   Vol. 2: 5089
Europe Prize - Flag of Honor   Vol. 2: 5090
Europe Prize - Plaque of Honor   Vol. 2: 5091
European Association for Signal Processing Awards   Vol. 2: 11690
European Awards Program   Vol. 1: 10880
European Baseball Championships   Vol. 2: 1117
European Baseball Cup   Vol. 2: 1117
European Bridge Champion   Vol. 2: 7875
European Businesswoman of the Year   Vol. 2: 2281
European Chopin Piano Competition   Vol. 2: 6594
European Committee for Young Farmers and 4H Clubs Awards   Vol. 2: 10543
European Community Design Prize   Vol. 2: 6803
European Competitions   Vol. 2: 2849
European Coordinating Committee for Artificial Intelligence Awards   Vol. 2: 11695
European Cup Competitions   Vol. 2: 11800
European Cup for Diaporama Epinal   Vol. 2: 6016
European Cup of Wargame   Vol. 2: 5321
European Disposables and Nonwovens Association Awards   Vol. 2: 1133
European Environmental Film Festival   Vol. 2: 5116
European Federation of Corrosion Medal   Vol. 2: 6711
European Film Awards (Felix Awards)   Vol. 2: 6713
European Finn Seniors Championship   Vol. 2: 9507
European Geophysical Society Honorary Membership   Vol. 2: 6718
European Grand Prix of Corporate Image   Vol. 2: 5006
European Human Rights Competition (Rene Cassin Competition)   Vol. 2: 5092
European Human Rights Prize   Vol. 2: 5093
European Junior Finn Championship   Vol. 2: 9508

European Markstrat Competition   Vol. 2: 6402
European Merit Award   Vol. 2: 8862
European Music and Poetry Competitions   Vol. 2: 1121
European Nature Conservation Diploma   Vol. 2: 5094
European Nuclear Society Awards   Vol. 2: 11702
European Packaging Competition   Vol. 2: 9412
European Parliament Sakharov Prize for Freedom of Thought   Vol. 2: 2841
European Piano Competition   Vol. 2: 4916
European Poetry Translation Prize   Vol. 2: 3791
European Prize   Vol. 1: 6842
European Prize for Statesmanship   Vol. 2: 7109
European Prize for the Preservation of Historic Monuments   Vol. 2: 7110
European Prizes for Folk Art   Vol. 2: 7111
European Rhinologic Society Prizes   Vol. 2: 9414
European Short Film Award   Vol. 2: 7769
European Showmen's Union Awards   Vol. 2: 8864
European Sportsman and Sportswoman of the Year   Vol. 2: 1144
European Surfing Championships - Open Champion   Vol. 2: 12173
European Theatre Prize   Vol. 2: 5095
European Thyroid Association Awards   Vol. 2: 11707
European Young Jazz Artists   Vol. 1: 11514
Eurosense Award   Vol. 2: 3843
EUROSON Young Persons Award   Vol. 2: 2829
Eurostar Awards for Packaging   Vol. 2: 9412
EUROTOX Young Scientist's Poster Award   Vol. 2: 11709
Eurovision Song Contest   Vol. 2: 11692
Eustis Award; James Biddle   Vol. 1: 20531
Evans Award; John K.   Vol. 1: 10631
Evans Biography Award; David Woolley and Beatrice Cannon   Vol. 1: 12467
Evans Memorial Lecture; Everett Idris   Vol. 1: 1381
Evans Nonfiction Prize; Hubert   Vol. 1: 20186
Evans Trophy; Edward S.   Vol. 1: 17359
Eva's Choice Award   Vol. 1: 8693
Evening Standard Ballet Award   Vol. 2: 3600
Evening Standard Drama Awards   Vol. 2: 3601
Events of the Year   Vol. 1: 18809
Everard Trophy   Vol. 2: 3003
Everest and Jennings Player of the Year   Vol. 1: 14047
Everett Award; Anderson -   Vol. 1: 10639
Everett Award; Woody   Vol. 1: 4087
Everychild Conference Honors Program   Vol. 1: 7617
Evian International String Quartet Competition   Vol. 2: 6192
Ewald Prize   Vol. 2: 3498
Ewald Prize; Johannes   Vol. 2: 1927
Ewart-Biggs Memorial Prize; Christopher   Vol. 2: 2851
Ewing Layman's Award; James   Vol. 1: 18035
Ewing Lecturer; James   Vol. 1: 18036
Ewing Medal; James Alfred   Vol. 2: 3236
Ewing Medal; Maurice
    American Geophysical Union   Vol. 1: 2162
    Society of Exploration Geophysicists   Vol 1: 17842
Excel Awards   Vol. 1: 17918
Excellence Award   Vol. 1: 18029

Excellence Award for Network Programs and Activities
　American Society for Training and Development - Council of Networks Vol. 1: 4313
　American Society for Training and Development - Multicultural Network Vol 1: 4334
Excellence Award for Outstanding Service Vol. 1: 4335
Excellence Awards Vol. 2: 3395
Excellence in Administration Award Vol. 1: 19357
Excellence in Advanced Neonatal Nursing Award Vol. 1: 13216
Excellence in Advertising Awards Vol. 1: 13360
Excellence in Aerospace Education Vol. 2: 7474
Excellence in City Financial Management Award Vol. 1: 19065
Excellence in College Store Management Vol. 1: 13005
Excellence in Communication Award Vol. 1: 12813
Excellence in Communication Leadership Vol. 1: 10682
Excellence in Communications Award Vol. 1: 9888
Excellence in Corporate Advertising Vol. 1: 6664
Excellence in Craft Award Vol. 1: 15862
Excellence in Documentation Award Vol. 1: 10485
Excellence in Education Vol. 1: 16193
Excellence in Education Award Vol. 1: 11869
Excellence in Environmental Engineering Vol. 1: 555
Excellence in Financial Journalism Vol. 1: 15291
Excellence in Highway Design Awards Vol. 1: 19312
Excellence in Human Resource Development Award Vol. 1: 4323
Excellence in Human Resource Development Awards Vol. 1: 4303
Excellence in Human Resource Management Award Vol. 1: 7879
Excellence in In-Plant Promotion Award Vol. 1: 10100
Excellence in Leadership Award
　American Society for Training and Development - Council of Industry Groups Vol. 1: 4311
　American Society for Training and Development - Instructional Technology Professional Practice Area Vol 1: 4318
Excellence in Military Scholarship Vol. 1: 14367
Excellence in Outstanding Service Award Vol. 1: 4329
Excellence in Pilot Training Award Vol. 1: 12764
Excellence in Professional Journalism Vol. 1: 14814
Excellence in Programming Awards Vol. 1: 12841
Excellence in Research Vol. 1: 8480
Excellence in Research Awards
　American Orthopaedic Society for Sports Medicine Vol. 1: 3348
　American Veterinary Medical Association Vol. 1: 4986
Excellence in Sports Journalism Award Vol. 1: 7470
Excellence in Swedish Design Prize Vol. 2: 11651
Excellence in the Arts Award Vol. 1: 20033
Excellence in the Media Award Vol. 1: 20034

Excellence in Zookeeping Award Vol. 1: 1242
Excellence of Presentation Award Vol. 1: 17591
Excellent Swedish Design Prize Vol. 2: 11651
Excelsior Endurance Award Vol. 2: 2165
Exceptional Achievement Award Vol. 1: 12059
Exceptional Achievement Medal Vol. 1: 12734
Exceptional Bravery Medal Vol. 1: 12735
Exceptional Civilian Service Award - Air Force Vol. 1: 19199
Exceptional Civilian Service Award - Army Vol. 1: 19200
Exceptional Engineering Achievement Medal Vol. 1: 12736
Exceptional Leadership Award Vol. 1: 5667
Exceptional Merit Awards Vol. 1: 3039
Exceptional Merit Media Award Vol. 1: 15027
Exceptional Scientific Achievement Medal Vol. 1: 12737
Exceptional Service Vol. 1: 19368
Exceptional Service Award Vol. 1: 8446
Exceptional Service Medal Vol. 1: 12738
Exchange Fellowships Vol. 2: 7842
Exchange of the Year Award Vol. 1: 16711
Excursions and Journeys in Greece Award Vol. 2: 7219
Executive Board Merit of Exhibit Award Vol. 1: 18017
Executive Committee Award Vol. 1: 20200
Executive Excellence Awards Vol. 1: 17195
Executive Housekeeper of the Year Vol. 1: 13925
Executive of the Year
　Caucus for Producers, Writers and Directors Vol. 1: 7411
　Continental Basketball Association Vol 1: 8244
　Federal Executive Institute Alumni Association Vol 1: 9081
　National Management Association Vol 1: 14325
　Research & Development Vol 1: 16795
Exemplar of Humanics Award Vol. 1: 2407
Exemplary Achievement Vol. 1: 10747
Exemplary Board of Education Vol. 1: 17099
Exemplary Dissertation in Social Studies Education Award Vol. 1: 13712
Exemplary Journalism Award Vol. 1: 14059
Exemplary Leadership Award Vol. 1: 4315
Exemplary Preparation Award Vol. 1: 1177
Exemplary Rehabilitation Program Award Vol. 1: 3945
Exemplary Research in Social Studies Education Award Vol. 1: 13713
Exemplary Service Award Vol. 1: 3216
Exemplary Teacher Vol. 1: 17100
Exercise and Sport Psychology Outstanding Dissertation Award Vol. 1: 3726
Exhibit and Poster Award Vol. 1: 656
Exhibit Award Vol. 1: 1248
Exhibit Awards Vol. 1: 18044
Exhibit Design Award Vol. 1: 4627
Exhibit Focus Awards Vol. 1: 10933
Exhibition 280 - Award of Excellence Vol. 1: 10064
Exhibition by Artists of Chicago and Vicinity Vol. 1: 5297
Exhibition Catalogue Awards; RBMS Vol. 1: 2874
Exhibition of Hooked Rugs Vol. 1: 15538
Exhibition of Woodcarving in the Norwegian Tradition Vol. 1: 15539
Exhibitors Competition Vol. 1: 16502
Exil-Preis; Internationaler Vol. 2: 6555

Experimental Pathologist-in-Training Award Vol. 1: 4178
Experimental Psychology Society Prize Vol. 2: 2857
ExploraVision Awards; Toshiba/NSTA Vol. 1: 14707
Explore Canada Awards Vol. 1: 18768
Explorers Medal Vol. 1: 9028
Expo Vol. 1: 15516
Export Awards for Small Businesses Vol. 2: 3649
Export Prize Vol. 2: 9371
Exporters Medal Vol. 2: 1609
Extended Neuroscience Research Award Vol. 1: 618
Extension Award Vol. 1: 3522
Extraction & Processing Lecture Award Vol. 1: 12309
Extraction & Processing Science Award Vol. 1: 12310
Extraction & Processing Technology Award Vol. 1: 12311
Extractive Metallurgy Division Best Paper Award
　Minerals, Metals, and Materials Society Vol. 1: 12310
　Minerals, Metals, and Materials Society Vol 1: 12311
Extraordinary Plaque Vol. 1: 10514
Exxon Awards Vol. 1: 821
Exxon Solid State Chemistry Fellowship Award Vol. 1: 1498
Exxon Supreme GT Vol. 1: 11107
Exxon World Sports Car Championship Vol. 1: 11108
Eyck Award; Charlotte Vol. 2: 2435
Eyck Memorial Trophy; Jim Ten Vol. 1: 10536
Eyebright Award Vol. 2: 10507
Eyster Prize Vol. 1: 15114
Faber-Castell Award for Drawing Vol. 2: 365
Faber Memorial Prize; Geoffrey Vol. 2: 2860
Fabinyi Award; ABPA/Andrew Vol. 2: 193
Fabre Seaplane Pilots Association Award; Henri Vol. 1: 17159
Fabregas; Premi Xavier Vol. 2: 11164
Fabri Prize; Ralph Vol. 1: 12608
Fabricator of the Year Vol. 1: 12222
Fabulous Fashion Independents Vol. 1: 12473
Face in the Crowd Vol. 1: 18427
"Faces of China" Speech Contest Vol. 1: 9417
Facilities Management Excellence Awards (FAME Awards) Vol. 1: 2669
Facility Excellence Award Vol. 1: 7087
Facility Management Achievement Award Vol. 1: 10945
Facility of the Year Vol. 1: 17188
Facilty Psychiatric Technician of the Year Vol. 1: 1148
FACSS Student Award Vol. 1: 9095
Facts On File Award Vol. 1: 2941
Facts On File Current Affairs Grant Vol. 1: 2941
Faculty Advisor Award Vol. 1: 4672
Faculty Publication of the Year Vol. 1: 596
Fagan Distinguished Service Award; Edna F. Vol. 1: 5388
Fagley Awards Competition Vol. 1: 8145
Fagnan; Fondation Edmond Vol. 2: 973
Faguet; Prix Emile Vol. 2: 5848
FAI Aeromodelling Gold Medal Vol. 2: 5144
FAI Airsport Medal Vol. 2: 5145
FAI Bronze Medal Vol. 2: 5146
FAI Gold Air Medal Vol. 2: 5147
FAI Gold Parachuting Medal Vol. 2: 5148

FAI Gold Rotorcraft Medal   Vol. 2: 5149
FAI Silver Jubilee Award   Vol. 2: 7499
Faik Odulu; Sait   Vol. 2: 12051
Faik Prize; Sait   Vol. 2: 12051
Failor Award; Clarence W.   Vol. 1: 1881
Fain, Jr. Award; P. Kemp   Vol. 1: 10251
Fair Medal; Gordon Maskew   Vol. 1: 20149
Fair Memorial Award; Gordon Maskew   Vol. 1: 556
Fair Play Award   Vol. 2: 2776
Fairbank Prize in East Asian History; John K.   Vol. 1: 2288
Fairchild Education Achievement Award; Gen. Muir S.   Vol. 1: 15777
Fairless Award; Benjamin F.
   American Institute of Mining, Metallurgical and Petroleum Engineers   Vol. 1: 2635
   Iron and Steel Society   Vol 1: 11462
Fairless Memorial Award; Benjamin F.   Vol. 1: 2709
Fairley Fellowships; Neil Hamilton   Vol. 2: 540
Faith and Freedom Awards   Vol. 1: 16774
Falcon Golden Spike Award; George   Vol. 1: 13270
Falconbridge Innovation Award   Vol. 1: 6943
Falder Award; Bob   Vol. 2: 2238
Faletti-Nosari; Premio Maria   Vol. 2: 8354
Falkaordan   Vol. 2: 7464
Fall Award   Vol. 1: 20178
Fallgatter Distinguished Service Award; Florence   Vol. 1: 16120
Fallot-Jeremine; Fondation Paul   Vol. 2: 5645
Fallot Literary Award   Vol. 1: 13153
Family International Talent Awards Program   Vol. 1: 15963
Family Involvement Award   Vol. 1: 17177
Family of Man Award   Vol. 1: 17613
Family Physician of the Year   Vol. 1: 7921
Family Planning Volunteer Award   Vol. 1: 16237
Family Psychologist of the Year   Vol. 1: 3730
Family Psychology Certificates of Appreciation   Vol. 1: 3731
Family Psychology Student Research Award   Vol. 1: 3732
Famous Grouse Trophy   Vol. 2: 3004
Fankuchen Memorial Award in X-Ray Crystallography   Vol. 1: 1898
Fann Memorial Challenge Trophy; J. W.   Vol. 1: 14866
Fanny Award   Vol. 1: 9026
Fano/Weekly Mail Short Film Competition   Vol. 2: 11125
Fantasy & Science Fiction Award   Vol. 1: 8568
Fantasy Film Awards   Vol. 2: 1091
Fantus, M.D., Medal; Bernard   Vol. 1: 927
Fantz Memorial Fund Award; Robert L.   Vol. 1: 3832
FAO Technical Assistance Fellowship   Vol. 2: 8268
Faraday Award; Michael   Vol. 2: 4149
Faraday House Commemorative Prize   Vol. 2: 3278
Faraday Medal   Vol. 2: 3279
Faraday Medal and Lectureship   Vol. 2: 4195
Faraday Prize; Michael   Vol. 2: 2771
Farber Award; Anne and Jason   Vol. 1: 614
Farber First Book Award; Norma   Vol. 1: 16283
Farber Prize; Norma   Vol. 1: 15124
Farberware Millennium Chef of the Year   Vol. 1: 6301
Farjeon Award; Eleanor   Vol. 2: 2617
Farm & Ranch Management Award   Vol. 1: 15059

Farm Buildings Award Scheme   Vol. 2: 2705
Farm-City Award   Vol. 1: 13927
Farm Management Conservation Award   Vol. 1: 13029
Farmer Appreciation Award   Vol. 1: 6237
Farmer Award; Prudence   Vol. 2: 3720
Farmer International Business Dissertation Award; Richard N.   Vol. 1: 45
Faro Award; R. Vale   Vol. 1: 16207
Farquhar Award; Francis P.   Vol. 1: 17232
Farquhar Mountaineering Award; Francis   Vol. 1: 17232
Farr Medal; Bertrand   Vol. 1: 2263
Farrant Award; Arthur   Vol. 2: 137
Farrell Award for Distinguished Teaching in the Catholic Elementary School; Miriam Joseph   Vol. 1: 13543
Farrer Memorial Medal   Vol. 2: 367
Farrer Trophy   Vol. 2: 4034
Farriery Competitions   Vol. 2: 7834
Farries Public Relations and Publicity Awards; T. C.   Vol. 2: 3567
Farrington Award of Excellence; J. D.   Vol. 1: 13090
Fasching Antal Emlekplakett   Vol. 2: 7394
Fasching Commemorative Plaque; Anthony   Vol. 2: 7394
FASEB Excellence in Science Award   Vol. 1: 9093
Fashion Awards   Vol. 2: 8235
Fashion Fiasco of the Year   Vol. 1: 12474
Father of the Year
   Father's Day Council   Vol. 1: 9050
   National Father's Day Committee   Vol 1: 13929
Father Washington Award   Vol. 1: 7400
Fauchard Academy Bronze Service Citation; Pierre   Vol. 1: 9053
Fauchard Gold Medal   Vol. 1: 9054
Faucher; Prix Leon   Vol. 2: 5773
Fauconnier; Prix Henry   Vol. 2: 1335
Faulding Memorial Fellowship; Francis Hardy   Vol. 2: 605
Faulkes Award; W. F.   Vol. 1: 14582
Faulkner Award for Excellence in Writing; Virginia   Vol. 1: 16360
Faulkner Award for Fiction; PEN/   Vol. 1: 16039
Faulstich Grand Award; Edith M.   Vol. 1: 16331
Fauna and Flora Preservation Society Grants   Vol. 2: 2866
Fauria Award; Mrs. Inez M.   Vol. 1: 8414
Favart Trophy; Jacques   Vol. 2: 11829
Favre; Prix Jules   Vol. 2: 5875
FAW Adele Shelton-Smith Award for Play, Radio or Other Scripts for Young Writers   Vol. 2: 378
FAW Alan Marshall Award   Vol. 2: 379
FAW Anne Elder Poetry Award   Vol. 2: 380
FAW Australian Native's Association Literature Award   Vol. 2: 381
FAW Australian Unity Award   Vol. 2: 381
FAW Barbara Ramsden Award   Vol. 2: 382
FAW C. J. Dennis Award   Vol. 2: 383
FAW Caltex-Bendigo Advertiser Award   Vol. 2: 384
FAW Christina Stead Award   Vol. 2: 385
FAW Christopher Brennan Award   Vol. 2: 386
FAW Di Cranston Awards   Vol. 2: 387
FAW Fedora Anderson Young Writers Poetry Award   Vol. 2: 388
FAW Frank Dalby Davison Award   Vol. 2: 389
FAW Herb Thomas Literary Award   Vol. 2: 390
FAW John Morrison Short Story Award   Vol. 2: 391

FAW John Shaw Neilson Award   Vol. 2: 392
FAW Judah Waten Collection of Creative Writing (Young Writers)   Vol. 2: 393
FAW K and M Teychenne Short Story Awards   Vol. 2: 394
FAW Kate Tracy Memorial Young Writers Award   Vol. 2: 395
FAW Local History Award   Vol. 2: 396
FAW Mary Grant Bruce Award for Children's Literature   Vol. 2: 397
FAW Patricia Weickhardt Award   Vol. 2: 398
FAW Warana Writers' Award   Vol. 2: 399
FAW Wilke Literary Award   Vol. 2: 400
Fawcett Award; James Waldo   Vol. 1: 3405
Fawcett Book Prize   Vol. 2: 2868
Fay Award; Edward Allen
   Conference of Educational Administrators Serving the Deaf   Vol. 1: 8121
   Governor Baxter School for the Deaf   Vol 1: 9691
FBI Honorary Medals   Vol. 1: 19250
FBI Medal for Meritorious Achievement   Vol. 1: 19250
FBI Medal of Valor   Vol. 1: 19250
FBI Memorial Star   Vol. 1: 19250
FBI Shield of Bravery   Vol. 1: 19250
FBI Star   Vol. 1: 19250
FCI Competition Essay   Vol. 2: 2864
Feasibility Grants   Vol. 1: 1951
Fedden Award; Sir Roy   Vol. 2: 3890
Federacion Nacional de Cultivadores de Cereales Competitions   Vol. 2: 1697
Federacion Panamericans de Asociaciones de Arquitectos Premios   Vol. 2: 12094
Federal City Club Award for Very Distinguished Public Service   Vol. 1: 9079
Federal Credit Union of the Year   Vol. 1: 13103
Federal Design Achievement Awards   Vol. 1: 13894
Federal Engineer of the Year Award   Vol. 1: 14802
Federal Environmental Engineer of the Year   Vol. 1: 8123
Federal Health Care Executive Special Achievement Award   Vol. 1: 2372
Federal Librarians Achievement Award   Vol. 1: 2891
Federal Migratory Bird Hunting and Conservatory Stamp Contest   Vol. 1: 19244
Federal Nursing Service Award   Vol. 1: 5881
Federal Property Person of the Year   Vol. 1: 14542
Federation Equestre Internationale Awards   Vol. 2: 11780
Federation Internationale de Canoe   Vol. 2: 8284
Federation of Afrikaans Cultural Societies Awards   Vol. 2: 10857
Federation of British Artists Prizes and Awards   Vol. 2: 2870
Federation of Insurance and Corporate Counsel Annual Award   Vol. 1: 9135
Federation of Insurance Counsel Award   Vol. 1: 9135
Federation of Norwegian Industries Environment Prize   Vol. 2: 9887
Federation of Norwegian Industries Prize   Vol. 2: 9886
Federation of Ontario Naturalists' Camp Scholarship   Vol. 1: 9147
Fehr Memorial; John   Vol. 1: 7513
Fehring Award of Merit; William P. "Dutch"   Vol. 1: 19911
Fein Fellowship; Ruth B.   Vol. 1: 2739
Feinberg Award; Frederick L.   Vol. 1: 2249
Feinbloom Award; William   Vol. 1: 638

Award Index
Volume 2: International and Foreign — Fellowship

Feis Award for Nonacademically-Affiliated Historians; Herbert Vol. 1: 2289
Feis Award; Herbert Vol. 1: 2289
Feldblit de Garfunkel Prize; Rosalia Vol. 2: 78
Feldman Memorial Award Vol. 1: 4036
Feldman Memorial Exhibit Award; Aaron Vol. 1: 3217
Felheim Award; Marvin Vol. 1: 5174
Felix Awards Vol. 2: 6713
Felix Awards, Artistic Vol. 1: 139
Felix Awards, Industrial Vol. 1: 140
Felix Awards, Music Vol. 1: 141
Felix; Fondation Clement Vol. 2: 5523
Felix Memorial Award; John R. Vol. 1: 19681
Fell Pony Society Ridden Championship Vol. 2: 10545
Fell Student Award; Honor B. Vol. 1: 18717
Fellers Award; Carl R. Vol. 1: 10344
Fellipe Medal; Carneiro Vol. 2: 2028
Fellipe; Medalha Carneiro Vol. 2: 2028
Fellow
  Academy of Dentistry for the Handicapped Vol. 1: 40
  Agricultural Institute of Canada Vol 1: 210
  American Academy of Child and Adolescent Psychiatry Vol 1: 532
  American Academy of Periodontology Vol 1: 690
  American Academy of Safety Education Vol 1: 716
  American Academy of Somnology Vol 1: 721
  American Agricultural Economics Association Vol 1: 753
  American Association for the Study of Headache Vol 1: 899
  American Association of Cost Engineers Vol 1: 983
  American Camellia Society Vol 1: 1394
  American Ceramic Society Vol 1: 1458
  American Council on Alcoholism Vol 1: 1854
  American Geophysical Union Vol 1: 2163
  American Helicopter Society Vol 1: 2250
  American Institute of Nutrition Vol 1: 2650
  American Meteorological Society Vol 1: 3083
  American Osteopathic College of Pathologists Vol 1: 3354
  American Psychological Association - Society of Experimental Psychologists Vol 1: 3817
  American Society for Adolescent Psychiatry Vol 1: 4032
  American Society for Photogrammetry and Remote Sensing Vol 1: 4250
  American Society of Sanitary Engineering Vol 1: 4792
  ASM International Vol 1: 5354
  Australian Library and Information Association Vol 2: 240
  British Academy Vol 2: 2227
  Canadian Phytopathological Society Vol 1: 7097
  Canadian Society of Civil Engineering Vol 1: 7171
  Center for Advanced Study in the Behavioral Sciences Vol 1: 7428
  Commonwealth Council for Educational Administration Vol 2: 333
  Engineering Institute of Canada Vol 1: 8933
  Entomological Society of America Vol 1: 8950
  Garden Writers Association of America Vol 1: 9489
  Hymn Society in the United States and Canada Vol 1: 10066
  Institute of Environmental Sciences Vol 1: 10325
  Institute of Packaging Professionals Vol 1: 10426
  Museums Association of Australia Vol 2: 531
  National Council of Education for the Ceramic Arts Vol 1: 13729
  Pharmaceutical Society of Ghana Vol 2: 7179
  Philalethes Society Vol 1: 16134
  Project Management Institute Vol 1: 16526
  Radio Club of America Vol 1: 16645
  Royal Geographical Society of Queensland Vol 2: 616
  Royal Institute of Navigation Vol 2: 4076
  Royal Northern College of Music Vol 2: 4112
  Royal Nova Scotia Historical Society Vol 1: 16946
  Royal South Australian Society of Arts Vol 2: 642
  Society for Advancement of Management Vol 1: 17401
  Society for Imaging Science and Technology Vol 1: 17499
  Society for Industrial Microbiology Vol 1: 17525
  Society for Range Management Vol 1: 17586
  Society of Allied Weight Engineers, Inc. Vol 1: 17663
  Society of Logistics Engineers Vol 1: 17869
  Society of Nematologists Vol 1: 17936
  Society of Plastics Engineers Vol 1: 17983
  Soil and Water Conservation Society Vol 1: 18124
  Soil Science Society of America Vol 1: 18130
  South African Geographical Society Vol 2: 11054
  Southern African Society for Plant Pathology Vol 2: 11103
  Woodrow Wilson International Center for Scholars Vol 1: 20311
  World Organization of National Colleges, Academies and Academic Associations of General Practitioners/Family Physicians Vol 2: 7281
  Zimbabwe Scientific Association Vol 2: 12222
Fellow Award
  American College of General Practitioners in Osteopathic Medicine and Surgery Vol. 1: 1640
  American Kinesiotherapy Association Vol 1: 2771
  Institute of Industrial Engineers Vol 1: 10358
  MTM Association for Standards and Research Vol 1: 12476
  National Association of Interpretation Vol 1: 13178
  Standards Engineering Society Vol 1: 18451
Fellow Designation
  American Association for Agricultural Education Vol. 1: 835
  Illuminating Engineering Society of North America Vol 1: 10086
Fellow Emeritus Status Vol. 1: 1645
Fellow for Research in Esoteric Areas of Knowledge Vol. 1: 5222
Fellow Grade Membership Vol. 1: 4088
Fellow Grade of Membership Vol. 1: 218
Fellow Member Vol. 1: 5004
Fellow of IMC Vol. 1: 11047
Fellow of Merit Vol. 1: 11048
Fellow of the Academy of Parish Clergy Vol. 1: 76
Fellow of the Academy of Professional Reporters Vol. 1: 13834
Fellow of the American Society of Agronomy Vol. 1: 4384
Fellow of the American Statistical Association Vol. 1: 4862
Fellow of The Athenaeum Vol. 1: 6101
Fellow of the Crop Science Society of America Vol. 1: 8469
Fellow of the Metallurgical Society. Vol. 1: 12312
Fellow of the Minerals, Metals, & Materials Society (TMS) Vol. 1: 12312
Fellow of the Photographic Salon Exhibitors Association Vol. 2: 7271
Fellow of the Society
  International Society for Hybrid Microelectronics Vol. 1: 11254
  National Speleological Society Vol 1: 14849
Fellow of the Special Libraries Association Vol. 1: 18264
Fellow Recognition Vol. 1: 11001
Fellows
  American Society for Quality Control Vol. 1: 4282
  Association for Business Simulation and Experiential Learning Vol 1: 5457
Fellows and Associates of Royal Agricultural Societies Vol. 2: 2691
Fellows and Honor Awards Vol. 1: 13802
Fellows Award
  American Association of Cereal Chemists Vol. 1: 948
  East Texas Historical Association Vol 1: 8783
  Virginia Recreation and Park Society Vol 1: 20071
Fellows Award of Merit Vol. 1: 1826
Fellows Medal Vol. 1: 4641
Fellows' Medal Vol. 1: 6673
Fellows of the American Association of Community Theatre Vol. 1: 976
Fellows of the Association Vol. 1: 4841
Fellows of the Metallurgical Society of AIME Vol. 1: 12312
Fellows of the Society Vol. 1: 17996
Fellows Program Award Vol. 1: 5948
Fellowship
  American Institute of Architects Vol. 1: 2529
  Construction Specifications Institute Vol 1: 8204
  Creative Glass Center of America Vol 1: 8450
  National Humanities Center Vol 1: 14201
Fellowship and Grant Award Program Vol. 1: 8615
Fellowship Award
  Pharmaceutical Society of Nigeria Vol. 2: 9867
  University Photographers' Association of America Vol 1: 19893
Fellowship Awards of the Jane Coffin Childs Memorial Fund for Medical Research Vol. 1: 7635
Fellowship for a Chinese Student or Visiting Scholar Vol. 1: 15030
Fellowship for Poets of Proven Merit Vol. 1: 19
Fellowship in AACT Vol. 1: 543

Fellowship

Fellowship in Aviation History   Vol. 1: 268
Fellowship in the Association   Vol. 1: 2192
Fellowship of the Augustan Society   Vol. 1: 6148
Fellowship of the Australian College of Education   Vol. 2: 202
Fellowship of the City and Guilds of London Institute   Vol. 2: 2622
Fellowship of the Scottish Tartans Society   Vol. 2: 10679
Fellowship Program
   American Association of University Women Educational Foundation   Vol. 1: 1236
   Pennsylvania Council on the Arts   Vol 1: 16044
Fellowship Scheme to Promote Commonwealth Understanding   Vol. 2: 2655
Fellowships
   American Society of Hospital Pharmacists Research and Education Foundation   Vol. 1: 4607
   Medical Research Council of Canada   Vol 1: 12188
Fellowships and Awards   Vol. 1: 4873
Fellowships and Scholarships   Vol. 2: 146
Fellowships and Training Programmes   Vol. 2: 2656
Fellowships for Art History Research   Vol. 1: 12234
Fellowships for Biological and Biomedical Sciences   Vol. 1: 10036
Fellowships for Independent Study in the Humanities   Vol. 1: 8306
Fellowships for Playwrights   Vol. 1: 17213
Fellowships for Scholars from Central/Eastern Europe   Vol. 1: 9596
Fellowships for Study in Conservation   Vol. 1: 12235
Fellowships in Arts and Crafts   Vol. 2: 2657
Feltrinelli; Premi Antonio   Vol. 2: 8069
Female Athlete of the Year   Vol. 1: 19516
Female Style Maker of the Year   Vol. 1: 13676
Female Writers Literary Award   Vol. 2: 8520
Femoyer Trophy; Robert E.   Vol. 1: 5281
Fencer of the Year (Men and Women)   Vol. 1: 19345
Fenderbosch Award For Exceptional Service; Henry   Vol. 1: 13361
Fenelon Research Grant; Pauline   Vol. 1: 13298
Feneon; Prix Felix   Vol. 2: 5203
Fennell Award; Earle J.   Vol. 1: 1814
Fennell International Young Conductor Competition; Frederick   Vol. 1: 18160
Fennia Gold Medal   Vol. 2: 4712
Fennia Silver Medal   Vol. 2: 4713
Fenno, Jr. Prize; Richard F.   Vol. 1: 3588
FENS European Nutrition Award   Vol. 2: 11883
Fenton Accessory Design Awards; Richard   Vol. 1: 10576
Fenton Medal   Vol. 2: 4132
Fentress Memorial Award; H. M.   Vol. 1: 18634
Fenwick Medal   Vol. 1: 9486
Ferber Award for Consumer Research; Robert   Vol. 1: 11611
Ferguson Award   Vol. 1: 9427
Ferguson Award; Virginia   Vol. 1: 17233
Ferguson Lecture Series; Phil M.   Vol. 1: 1781
Ferguson Medal; Cedric K.   Vol. 1: 17967
Ferguson Memorial Award; Elmer   Vol. 1: 9956
Ferguson Prize; Wallace K.   Vol. 1: 6906
Fermi Award; Enrico   Vol. 1: 19230

Awards, Honors & Prizes, 1995-96

Fermi; Premio Enrico   Vol. 2: 8145
Fermoy Memorial Prize; Ruth   Vol. 2: 3627
Fern Award; Harold   Vol. 2: 2067
Fern National Trophy; Harold   Vol. 2: 2068
Fernandez de Lizaldi Prize; Jose Joaquin   Vol. 2: 9086
Fernandez Madrid; Orden del Merito Sanitario Jose   Vol. 2: 1647
Fernandez Trophy; Anthony   Vol. 1: 19708
Fernbach Award; Sidney   Vol. 1: 10299
Fernow Award; Bernhard Eduard   Vol. 1: 2098
Fernow Award in International Forestry   Vol. 1: 2098
Fernschopernpreis der Stadt Salzburg   Vol. 2: 870
Ferraris; Premio AEI Galileo   Vol. 2: 8347
Ferraro Award; Barbara V.   Vol. 1: 9475
Ferrez Photography Award; Marc   Vol. 2: 1433
Ferrier; Prix Gabriel   Vol. 2: 5393
Ferris Bowl; William   Vol. 2: 3781
Ferris Championship Trophy; Daniel J.   Vol. 1: 19938
Ferroguard Award in Electrochemical Technology   Vol. 2: 7495
Ferst Award; Monie A.   Vol. 1: 17271
FES Award   Vol. 2: 8890
Feser Award; Leo   Vol. 1: 9640
FESPP Award   Vol. 2: 9424
Fessenden Award; Reginald   Vol. 1: 17843
Festival Awards   Vol. 2: 3038
Festival Awards for Literature   Vol. 2: 673
Festival da Torneira Poetica   Vol. 2: 1406
Festival de Biarritz du Film Iberique et Latino-Americain   Vol. 2: 4968
Festival de Cine Cientifico   Vol. 2: 11166
Festival de Cine de Alcala de Henares   Vol. 2: 11228
Festival de Cine y TV Euroarabe   Vol. 2: 11226
Festival de la Harpe d'Or   Vol. 2: 7824
Festival dei Popoli   Vol. 2: 8239
Festival del Cine Nacional   Vol. 2: 12109
Festival der Nationen   Vol. 2: 803
Festival du Court-Metrage en Plein Air   Vol. 2: 5173
Festival du Film Court de Villeurbanne   Vol. 2: 5175
Festival du Film de Fin d'Etudes Cinematographiques   Vol. 2: 6024
Festival du Film de l'Atlantique   Vol. 1: 6113
Festival du Film Sportif Lille   Vol. 2: 5038
Festival Europeen de l'Image de l'Entreprise   Vol. 2: 5006
Festival Film Indonesia   Vol. 2: 7733
Festival Filmu pro Deti Gottwaldov   Vol. 2: 1890
Festival Internacional Cortometrajes de las Palmas Gran Canaria   Vol. 2: 11257
Festival Internacional de Cine Arte   Vol. 2: 11230
Festival Internacional de Cine de Bilbao Documental y Cortometraje   Vol. 2: 11267
Festival Internacional de Cine de San Sebastian   Vol. 2: 11351
Festival Internacional de Cine Ecologico y de la Naturaleza   Vol. 2: 11232
Festival Internacional de Cine Iberoamericano   Vol. 2: 11261
Festival Internacional de Cine para la Juventud de Gijon   Vol. 2: 11252
Festival Internacional de Cine Realizado por Mujeres   Vol. 2: 11149
Festival Internacional de Cinema da Costa do Estoril   Vol. 2: 10238

Festival Internacional de Cinema de Muntanya, Vila de Torello   Vol. 2: 11386
Festival Internacional de Cinema de Santarem   Vol. 2: 10236
Festival Internacional de Cinema do Algarve   Vol. 2: 10230
Festival Internacional de Cinema do Porto - Fantasporto   Vol. 2: 10291
Festival Internacional de Cinema para a Infancia e Juventude - Tomar   Vol. 2: 10232
Festival Internacional del Nuevo Cine Super 8 y Video   Vol. 2: 12114
Festival International de Diaporamas   Vol. 2: 1224
Festival International de Films de Femmes   Vol. 2: 1384
Festival International de Films de Femmes de Creteil et du Val de Marne   Vol. 2: 6072
Festival International de l'Image   Vol. 2: 6016
Festival International de Paris du Film Fantastique et de Science-Fiction   Vol. 2: 6149
Festival International de Television de Monte Carlo   Vol. 2: 9322
Festival International de Television Prague d'Or   Vol. 2: 1844
Festival International des Programmes Audiovisuels   Vol. 2: 5274
Festival International du Cinema d'Animation Annecy   Vol. 2: 5957
Festival International du Court Metrage de Clermont-Ferrand   Vol. 2: 6196
Festival International du Court Metrage et de la Video   Vol. 2: 6477
Festival International du Dessin Humoristique   Vol. 2: 6132
Festival International du Film Alpin Les Diablerets, Suisse   Vol. 2: 11791
Festival International du Film Amateur   Vol. 2: 12042
Festival International du Film, Cannes   Vol. 2: 5004
Festival International du Film Consacre au Metier d'Ingenieur   Vol. 2: 1097
Festival International du Film d'Amiens   Vol. 2: 4890
Festival International du Film d'Architecture d'Urbanisme et d'Environement Urbain de Bordeaux   Vol. 2: 6018
Festival International du Film d'Architecture et d'Urbanisme de Lausanne   Vol. 2: 11793
Festival International du Film d'Art et d'Archeologie de Bruxelles   Vol. 2: 1162
Festival International du Film de Berlin   Vol. 2: 6564
Festival International du Film de Comedie de Vevey   Vol. 2: 11661
Festival International du Film de Voile de La Rochelle   Vol. 2: 6044
Festival International du Film de Vol Libre   Vol. 2: 5184
Festival International du Film d'Histoire   Vol. 2: 5186
Festival International du Film d'Humour de Chamrousse   Vol. 2: 5028
Festival International du Film et des Medias de Tourisme   Vol. 2: 6056
Festival International du Film et des Realisateurs des Ecoles de Cinema   Vol. 2: 6020
Festival International du Film Ethnographique et Sociologique Cinema du Reel   Vol. 2: 5032
Festival International du Film Fantastique, de Science-Fiction, et Th riller de Bruxelles   Vol. 2: 1241
Festival International du Film Maritime et d'Exploration   Vol. 2: 6014

Festival International du Film Medical de Mauriac   Vol. 2: 6112
Festival International du Film Scientifique et Technique, Bruxelles   Vol. 2: 1098
Festival International du Film Sportif   Vol. 2: 5248
Festival International du Film sur l'Art Montreal   Vol. 1: 12423
Festival International du Film sur l'Energie Lausanne   Vol. 2: 11797
Festival Internationl du Film d'Aventure de la Plagne (La Plagne International Real Life Adventure Film Festival)   Vol. 2: 5328
Festival Internazionale Cinema Giovani   Vol. 2: 8462
Festival Internazionale de Film Locarno   Vol. 2: 11875
Festival Internazionale di Cinema Sportivo   Vol. 2: 8317
Festival Mondial de l'Image de Montagne   Vol. 2: 6481
Festival Mondial de l'Image Sous-Marine   Vol. 2: 6483
Festival National de la Chanson de Granby   Vol. 1: 9175
Festival National de l'Audiovisuel d'Entreprise   Vol. 2: 5007
Festival National et International du Court Metrage de Clermont-Ferrand   Vol. 2: 6197
Festival of Agricultural and Enviromental Short Films   Vol. 2: 10236
Festival of American Community Theatre   Vol. 1: 972
Festival of Contemporary Theatre   Vol. 2: 10325
Festival of Firsts Playwriting Competition   Vol. 1: 18530
Festival of Nations   Vol. 2: 803
Festival of Southern Theatre Playwriting Competition   Vol. 1: 9177
Festival of the Americas   Vol. 1: 20539
Festival Panafrican du Cinema de Ouagadougou   Vol. 2: 1541
Festivalul de Teatru Contemporan   Vol. 2: 10325
FEW Distinguished Service Award   Vol. 1: 9083
FFC Award of Recognition   Vol. 1: 9171
FFF Conservation Award   Vol. 1: 9104
FIA F3000 International Champion   Vol. 2: 5975
FIA Formula 1 World Champion   Vol. 2: 5976
FIA World Rally Champion   Vol. 2: 5977
FIA World Sports Prototype Champion   Vol. 2: 5978
FIAP Awards   Vol. 2: 8866
FIAP Gold Medal   Vol. 2: 7489
FIAP Gold Medals   Vol. 2: 10677
FIAP Kodak Award   Vol. 2: 1189
FIAP Kodak Award; International   Vol. 2: 1189
FIAP Medals
  Federation Internationale de l'Art Photographique   Vol. 2: 8867
  Greater Lynn Camera Club   Vol 1: 9713
FIAP Service Awards   Vol. 2: 8868
FIAP World Cups   Vol. 2: 8869
Fiction Contest   Vol. 1: 12336
Fiction Writers Contest   Vol. 1: 11994
FIDE Master   Vol. 2: 7225
Fidelitas Medal   Vol. 1: 15769
Fidler Award; Kathleen   Vol. 2: 10514
Fiducia Award; Freddie   Vol. 1: 11382
Field and Joe L. Franklin Award for Outstanding Achievement in Mass Spectrometry; Frank H.   Vol. 1: 1555
Field Award; Carolyn W.   Vol. 1: 16046
Field Award; Crosby   Vol. 1: 4583

Field Award; Thomas E.   Vol. 1: 8874
Field Awards   Vol. 1: 17870
Field of the Year/Groundskeeper of the Year   Vol. 1: 1321
Fieldgate Trophy; Norm   Vol. 1: 6876
Fields Medal   Vol. 2: 4731
Fienegan Gold Award; ASFSA Thelme   Vol. 1: 3998
Fies Award; John   Vol. 1: 10867
FIFA Five-a-Side (Indoor Football) World Championship   Vol. 2: 11712
FIFA Futsal (Indoor Football) World Championship   Vol. 2: 11712
FIFA U-17 World Championship   Vol. 2: 11713
FIFA U-17 World Tournament   Vol. 2: 11713
FIFA Women's World Football Championship   Vol. 2: 11714
FIFA World Cup Trophy   Vol. 2: 11715
FIFI Awards   Vol. 1: 9361
Fifth Sense Commendation   Vol. 1: 9360
Fiftieth Anniversary Scholarship   Vol. 1: 6915
Fifty Books of the Year   Vol. 1: 2622
Fifty-Year Award   Vol. 1: 9163
Fifty-Year Club   Vol. 1: 6944
Fifty Year Club Member Certificate   Vol. 1: 3218
Fifty Year Membership Medal and Pin   Vol. 1: 3219
FIGGIE   Vol. 1: 9342
Fighter/Attack Squadron of the Year   Vol. 1: 12061
Fighter of the Year   Vol. 1: 11383
Figueroa Nogueron Prize; Gilberto   Vol. 2: 8998
Filho Prize; Hermilio Borba   Vol. 2: 1439
Filipovic Awards; Ivan   Vol. 2: 1809
Filley Memorial Awards for Excellence in Respiratory Physiology and Medicine; Giles F.   Vol. 1: 3506
Fillmore Award; Anna M.   Vol. 1: 14284
Film Company of the Year Award   Vol. 1: 20327
Film Competition   Vol. 2: 9265
Film Grants   Vol. 1: 16400
Film Society of the Year Award   Vol. 2: 2340
Filmotheque of the Youth   Vol. 2: 6983
Filmpreis   Vol. 2: 6875
Filmpreis der Bundesarztekammer   Vol. 2: 6814
FIM Fair Play Trophy   Vol. 2: 11809
FINA Prize   Vol. 2: 11753
FINA Prize Eminence   Vol. 2: 11753
Finale Ligure International Chamber Music Competition   Vol. 2: 8106
Finance Minister of the Year   Vol. 2: 2815
Financial Management Improvement Award   Vol. 1: 11605
Financial Planner of the Year   Vol. 1: 13225
Financial Post Annual Report Awards   Vol. 1: 9204
Financial Post Awards for Business in the Arts
  Council for Business and the Arts in Canada   Vol. 1: 8309
  The *Financial Post*   Vol 1: 9205
Financial Post Design Effectiveness Awards   Vol. 1: 9206
Financial Post Environment Awards for Business   Vol. 1: 9207
Financial Post Outstanding CEO of the Year Award   Vol. 1: 9208
Financial Security Nest Egg Award   Vol. 1: 11866
Financial Times/London Business School Design Management Award   Vol. 2: 2887
Finch Law Day U.S.A. Speech Award; Judge Edward R.   Vol. 1: 1308

Findlay Plaque   Vol. 1: 9781
Fine Arts Association of Finland Awards   Vol. 2: 4676
Fine Arts Prize   Vol. 2: 8829
Fine Arts Union Prize   Vol. 2: 10395
Fine Arts Work Center Fellowships   Vol. 1: 9215
Fine Awards; Benjamin   Vol. 1: 13309
Fine Dining Hall of Fame   Vol. 1: 15065
Fine Printing Awards   Vol. 1: 10102
Finegan Standards Medal   Vol. 1: 3180
Fink Prize Award; Donald G.   Vol. 1: 10264
Finlaison Medal   Vol. 2: 3058
Finland Award in Infectious Diseases; Maxwell   Vol. 1: 10172
Finlandia Award   Vol. 1: 19561
Finlandia-palkinto   Vol. 2: 4686
Finlandia Prize   Vol. 2: 4686
Finlay Prize; Carlos J.   Vol. 2: 6411
Finley Medal; John H.   Vol. 1: 388
Finn Gold Cup   Vol. 2: 9509
Finneburgh EHF Award of Excellence; M. L.   Vol. 1: 13888
Finnerud Award; Clark W.   Vol. 1: 8616
Finnish Cultural Foundation's Prize   Vol. 2: 4693
Finnish Library Association Awards   Vol. 2: 4700
Finnish Museums Association 50th Anniversary Medal   Vol. 2: 4702
Finnish picturebook prize   Vol. 2: 4669
Finocchiaro Award for Excellence in the Development of Pedagogical Materials; Mary   Vol. 1: 18589
Finochietto Prize; Enrique   Vol. 2: 79
Finot; Prix Jean   Vol. 2: 5760
Finsen Prize   Vol. 2: 11818
FIP Fellowships   Vol. 2: 9519
FIP International Travel Scholarships   Vol. 2: 9520
FIP Lifetime Achievement in the Pharmaceutical Sciences Award   Vol. 2: 9516
FIP Lifetime Achievement in the Practice of Pharmacy Award   Vol. 2: 9516
FIP Pharmaceutical Scientist of the Year Award   Vol. 2: 9516
FIP Practitioner of the Year Award   Vol. 2: 9516
FIPRESCI Diploma   Vol. 2: 10069
FIPRESCI Jury Prize   Vol. 1: 12436
FIPRESCI Prize
  International Federation of Cinematographic Press   Vol. 2: 6944
  Turin International Film Festival   Vol 2: 8462
FIPRESCI-Prizes   Vol. 2: 6564
FIRA Championship Awards   Vol. 2: 5952
Fire Explorer Post Award   Vol. 1: 10729
Fire Fighter of the Year   Vol. 1: 13492
Fire Investigator of the Year   Vol. 1: 13111
Fire Management Award   Vol. 1: 19084
Fire Protection Man/Woman of the Year   Vol. 1: 17851
Fire Safety Award   Vol. 2: 2109
Fire Safety Awards   Vol. 1: 10126
Fire Services Exemplary Service Medal   Vol. 1: 6699
Firehouse Magazine Heroism and Community Service Award   Vol. 1: 16562
Fireman of the Year   Vol. 1: 10975
Fireman of the Year (Relief Pitcher)   Vol. 1: 18345
Firestone Firehawk Endurance Championship   Vol. 1: 11109
Firm of the Year   Vol. 1: 7054
First Amendment Awards   Vol. 1: 17997

First Amendment Defender Award   Vol. 1: 7389
First Amendment Journalism Awards   Vol. 1: 16058
First Book Award   Vol. 1: 16094
First Book Prize
  Argentina - Ministry of Education and Justice   Vol. 2: 21
  Mitchell Foundation   Vol 1: 12372
First Breeding Award   Vol. 1: 11395
First Class Certificate   Vol. 1: 3336
First Class Order of the Rising Sun Paulownia Flowers   Vol. 2: 8583
First Interstate Athletic Foundation Gymnastics Hall of Fame Award   Vol. 1: 12998
First Responder Award   Vol. 1: 13113
First Step Award   Vol. 1: 2849
First Step Award - Wiley Professional Development Grant   Vol. 1: 2849
FIS Medal of Merit   Vol. 2: 6751
FISA Medal   Vol. 2: 11787
Fischer Award; Kermit   Vol. 1: 4023
Fischer Environmental Award; Kermit   Vol. 1: 10486
Fischer - Gedenkpreis; Edwin   Vol. 2: 11719
Fischer-Medaille; Emil-   Vol. 2: 6781
Fischer-Medaille; Hellmuth   Vol. 2: 6618
Fischer Medal; Helen Field   Vol. 1: 2264
Fischer Memorial Cup; Donn   Vol. 1: 2267
Fischer Memorial Prize; Edwin   Vol. 2: 11719
Fischer-Preis; Georg A.   Vol. 2: 11930
Fischetti Editorial Cartoon Competition; John   Vol. 1: 7961
Fischoff National Chamber Music Competition   Vol. 1: 9222
Fish Memorial Award; Robert L.   Vol. 1: 12548
Fisher Article Award; Irving   Vol. 1: 15625
Fisher Artist Program; Avery   Vol. 1: 9224
Fisher Award; Elaine R. "Boots"   Vol. 1: 9068
Fisher Award; Eunice   Vol. 1: 2378
Fisher Award for Distinguished Service to Education   Vol. 1: 8294
Fisher Award; Mr. and Mrs. Kenneth R.   Vol. 1: 15526
Fisher Award - Publisher of the Year; Henry Johnson   Vol. 1: 11999
Fisher Award; R. A.   Vol. 1: 8035
Fisher Career Grant; Avery   Vol. 1: 9224
Fisher Career Grants; Avery   Vol. 1: 11885
Fisher Children's Book Award; Dorothy Canfield   Vol. 1: 19987
Fisher Dissertation Awards; Joseph L.   Vol. 1: 16809
Fisher Distinguished Writing Award; M. K.   Vol. 1: 6300
Fisher Fellowship; Gordon N.   Vol. 1: 19881
Fisher Memorial Lecture   Vol. 1: 10405
Fisher Prize   Vol. 1: 6122
Fisher Prize; Avery
  Avery Fisher Artist Program   Vol. 1: 9224
  Lincoln Center for the Performing Arts   Vol 1: 11886
Fisher Scientific Award   Vol. 1: 7217
Fisher Scientific Award in Clinical Chemistry   Vol. 1: 7202
Fisher Scientific Company Award for Applied and Environmental Microbiology   Vol. 1: 4210
Fisher Scientific Company Undergraduate Scholarship   Vol. 1: 4191
Fisher Scientific Lecture Award   Vol. 1: 7549
Fisherman of the Year   Vol. 1: 17016
Fishleder Photography Award; Jack   Vol. 1: 14702
Fishman Memorial Award; Miles D.   Vol. 1: 11307

FISITA Travelling Fellowship   Vol. 2: 656
Fiske Fund Prize Essay; Caleb   Vol. 1: 16822
FIT Astrid Lindgren Translation Prize   Vol. 2: 823
FIT C. B. Nathhorst Translation Prize
  International Federation of Translators   Vol. 2: 824
  International Federation of Translators   Vol 2: 824
FIT - UNESCO Translation Prize   Vol. 2: 824
Fitelberg Competition for Conductors in Katowice; International Grzegorz   Vol. 2: 10212
Fiterman Foundation Awards for Clinical Research; AGA/Miles and Shirley   Vol. 1: 2133
Fitts Award; Paul M.   Vol. 1: 10040
Fitz Award; Mr.   Vol. 1: 14939
Fitzgerald Award for Ecumenism; James   Vol. 1: 13072
Fitzgerald Award; James   Vol. 1: 13072
Fitzgerald Award; Thomas H.   Vol. 1: 8841
Fitzgerald Coke Medal; Major Edward D'Ewes   Vol. 2: 2922
Fitzgerald Rookie of the Year; Jim   Vol. 1: 18394
Fitzpatrick Award; Percy   Vol. 2: 11057
Five State Exhibition   Vol. 1: 11649
Flach; Prix Jacques   Vol. 2: 5758
Flach; Prix Marcel   Vol. 2: 5781
Flack Memorial Trophy; David   Vol. 2: 2535
Flagg Multicultural Award; Ann   Vol. 1: 775
Flags of America Award   Vol. 1: 13974
Flaherty Documentary Award   Vol. 2: 2234
Flaiano; Premio Internazionale Enno   Vol. 2: 8114
Flammarion; Plaquette du Centenaire de Camille   Vol. 2: 6219
Flammarion; Prix Gabrielle et Camille   Vol. 2: 6224
Flanagan Youth Art Month Grand Award; Clare   Vol. 1: 8304
Flandrin/Michon Life Achievement Award   Vol. 1: 2209
Flashes of Brilliance Competition   Vol. 1: 2995
Flat Earth Scientist Award   Vol. 1: 9226
Flat; Prix Paul   Vol. 2: 5904
Flattie International Yacht Racing Association Championship   Vol. 1: 9513
Flavelle Medal   Vol. 1: 16953
Fleck Prize; Ludwik   Vol. 1: 17603
Fleet Owners's Vehicle Graphic Design Awards   Vol. 1: 9230
Fleet Safety Award   Vol. 1: 4931
Fleischner Society Memorial Award   Vol. 1: 9232
Fleming Award   Vol. 2: 4355
Fleming Award for Young Composers; Robert   Vol. 1: 7055
Fleming Award; John Adam   Vol. 1: 2164
Fleming Award; Rodney R.   Vol. 1: 3875
Fleming Premium; Ambrose   Vol. 2: 3273
Flemming Award; Arthur S.   Vol. 1: 8718
Fletcher Award; Eric   Vol. 2: 4362
Fletcher Challenge International Ceramics Award   Vol. 2: 9722
Fletcher Memorial Lecture; Ernest   Vol. 2: 4246
Fletcher Memorial Prize Lecture; Alexander   Vol. 2: 10600
Fletcher Prize Trust; Sir Banister   Vol. 2: 2150
Fleur-de-Lis Awards   Vol. 2: 2974
Fleur-de-Lis Medal   Vol. 1: 17002
Fleuroselect Gold Medal   Vol. 2: 9428
Fleury-Mesplet Literary Prizes   Vol. 1: 17018
Fleury Prize; Ernest   Vol. 2: 6311

Flexner Award for Distinguished Service to Medical Education; Abraham   Vol. 1: 5689
Flight Instructor of the Year Award Program   Vol. 1: 9064
Flight Nurse of the Year Award   Vol. 1: 167
Flight Simulation Silver Medal   Vol. 2: 3891
Flinders Lecture; Matthew   Vol. 2: 172
Flintoff Medal and Prize   Vol. 2: 4196
Flipper trophies   Vol. 2: 6483
Flisser; Premio Lola e Igo   Vol. 2: 9182
FLMI Insurance Education Award   Vol. 1: 11870
Floor of the Year Contest   Vol. 1: 15038
Florales Prize of San Juan del Rio, Queretaro; Juegos   Vol. 2: 9162
Florian Prize; Mircea   Vol. 2: 10348
Floricultural Hall of Fame   Vol. 1: 17680
Florida Artists Hall of Fame   Vol. 1: 9246
Florida Arts Recognition Awards   Vol. 1: 9247
Florida Audubon Society's Latin American Award for Conservation   Vol. 1: 9256
Florida Folk Heritage Awards   Vol. 1: 6626
Florida Prize   Vol. 1: 15300
Florio Prize; John   Vol. 2: 4396
Flormanska Belöningen   Vol. 2: 11541
Flotation Image Award   Vol. 1: 20167
Fluckiger Medaille   Vol. 2: 6586
Flude Memorial Prize   Vol. 2: 2410
Fluegelman Award; Andrew   Vol. 1: 15998
Fluid and Plasmadynamics Award   Vol. 1: 2468
Fluid Dynamics Prize   Vol. 1: 3454
Fluid Power Achievement Award   Vol. 1: 13979
Fluidized Processes Recognition Award   Vol. 1: 2577
Fluids Engineering Award   Vol. 1: 4673
Fluke Award for Excellence in Laboratory Instruction; John   Vol. 1: 4089
Fluman Awards; Lon   Vol. 1: 16113
Fluvanna Prize   Vol. 1: 11983
Fly Neighborly Award   Vol. 1: 9886
Flying Fifteen World Championship   Vol. 2: 2898
FMCT Playwrights Competition   Vol. 1: 9041
FMI - *Woman's Day* Advertising Merit Awards   Vol. 1: 9297
FOCAL Award   Vol. 1: 9415
Foch; Prix Marechal   Vol. 2: 5892
Foederpreis Vogelschutz   Vol. 2: 6651
Foer Memorial Award; Melvin B.   Vol. 1: 8637
Foerderungspreise des Bundesministeriums fur Unterricht und Kunst   Vol. 2: 758
Fogelman Memorial Trophy; Harry   Vol. 1: 19647
Fogelson Cultural and Creative Arts Program; Gertrude   Vol. 1: 3139
Fogerty Public Personnel Award; James E.   Vol. 1: 16392
Fogle Award; J. Roy   Vol. 1: 13069
Folch; Premio Fundacion Rafael   Vol. 2: 11339
Foldes Award; Ferenc   Vol. 2: 7299
Folger Shakespeare Library Fellowships and National Endowment for the Humanities Senior Fellowships   Vol. 1: 9282
Foliage Hall of Fame   Vol. 1: 9268
Folio Poetry and Fiction Awards   Vol. 1: 9285
Folk Arts Apprenticeship Grants   Vol. 1: 12342
Folk Heritage Awards   Vol. 1: 15492
Folk Music Festival - Plaketti   Vol. 2: 4741
Folkestone Menuhin International Violin Competition   Vol. 2: 2900
Follereau; Prix Raoul   Vol. 2: 5913
Foltz Award; Clara Shortridge   Vol. 1: 14297

Award Index
Volume 2: International and Foreign — Fondation

FOLUSA/Baker & Taylor Books Award   Vol. 1: 9419
Folz Memorial Award; Sam   Vol. 1: 13672
FON Achievement Certificates   Vol. 1: 9154
FON Conservation Award   Vol. 1: 9152
FON Conservation Trophy   Vol. 1: 9150
FON Corporate Award   Vol. 1: 9148
FON Distinguished Service Award   Vol. 1: 9146
Fond; Operasangerinnen Fanny Elstas   Vol. 2: 9875
Fonda Senior Citizens Playwrights Award; Henry   Vol. 1: 19996
Fonda Young Playwrights Project; Henry   Vol. 1: 19997
Fondation Aime Berthe   Vol. 2: 5477
Fondation Aime Laussedat   Vol. 2: 5478
Fondation Albert I de Monaco   Vol. 2: 5479
Fondation Alexandre Darracq   Vol. 2: 5480
Fondation Alexandre Joannides   Vol. 2: 5481
Fondation Alfred Durand-Claye   Vol. 2: 5482
Fondation Alfred Dutens   Vol. 2: 5483
Fondation Alhumbert   Vol. 2: 5484
Fondation Alphonse Laveran   Vol. 2: 5485
Fondation Anatole et Suzanne Abragam   Vol. 2: 5486
Fondation Ancel   Vol. 2: 5487
Fondation Andre C. Bonnet   Vol. 2: 5488
Fondation Andre Lallemand   Vol. 2: 5489
Fondation Andre Policard-Lacassagne   Vol. 2: 5490
Fondation Andre-Romain Prevot   Vol. 2: 5491
Fondation Aniuta Winter-Klein   Vol. 2: 5492
Fondation Antoine d'Abbadie   Vol. 2: 5493
Fondation Antoinette Janssen   Vol. 2: 5494
Fondation Arago   Vol. 2: 5495
Fondation Argut   Vol. 2: 5496
Fondation Arthur du Fay   Vol. 2: 5497
Fondation Auguste Chevalier   Vol. 2: 5498
Fondation Ayme Poirson   Vol. 2: 5499
Fondation Barbier   Vol. 2: 5500
Fondation Bariot-Faynot   Vol. 2: 5501
Fondation Berthelot   Vol. 2: 5502
Fondation Bigot de Morogues   Vol. 2: 5503
Fondation Binoux   Vol. 2: 5504
Fondation Boileau   Vol. 2: 5505
Fondation Bordin   Vol. 2: 5506
Fondation Breant   Vol. 2: 5507
Fondation Cahours, Houzeau   Vol. 2: 5508
Fondation Camere   Vol. 2: 5509
Fondation Camille Liegeois
  Academie Royale de Belgique - Classe des Lettres et des Sciences Morales et Politiques   Vol. 2: 972
  Academie Royale de Belgique - Classe des Sciences   Vol 2: 1001
Fondation Carre-Bessault   Vol. 2: 5510
Fondation Carriere de Mathematiques   Vol. 2: 5511
Fondation Carriere de Mineralogie   Vol. 2: 5512
Fondation Charles-Adam Girard   Vol. 2: 5513
Fondation Charles Dhere   Vol. 2: 5514
Fondation Charles Eugene Guye   Vol. 2: 5515
Fondation Charles Fremont   Vol. 2: 5516
Fondation Charles Jacob   Vol. 2: 5517
Fondation Charles-Leopold Mayer   Vol. 2: 5518
Fondation Charles-Louis de Saulses de Freycinet   Vol. 2: 5519
Fondation Chaussier   Vol. 2: 5520
Fondation Chedanne   Vol. 2: 5388
Fondation Claude Lallemand   Vol. 2: 5521
Fondation Clavel   Vol. 2: 5522
Fondation Clement Felix   Vol. 2: 5523
Fondation Coron-Thevenet   Vol. 2: 5524
Fondation Costantino Gorini   Vol. 2: 5525

Fondation Cuvier   Vol. 2: 5526
Fondation Da Gama Machado   Vol. 2: 5527
Fondation Damoiseau   Vol. 2: 5528
Fondation Dandrimont-Benicourt   Vol. 2: 5529
Fondation Danton   Vol. 2: 5530
Fondation Daumet   Vol. 2: 5388
Fondation de Caen   Vol. 2: 5388
Fondation de Coincy   Vol. 2: 5531
Fondation de la Fons-Melicocq   Vol. 2: 5532
Fondation de Madame Albert Demolon   Vol. 2: 5533
Fondation de Madame Edmond Hamel   Vol. 2: 5534
Fondation de Madame Victor Noury   Vol. 2: 5535
Fondation de Mme. Veuve Beule   Vol. 2: 5388
Fondation Delalande-Guerineau   Vol. 2: 5536
Fondation Delesse   Vol. 2: 5537
Fondation Demolombe   Vol. 2: 5538
Fondation Deslandres   Vol. 2: 5539
Fondation Desmazieres   Vol. 2: 5540
Fondation du Baron de Joest   Vol. 2: 5541
Fondation du Baron Larrey   Vol. 2: 5542
Fondation du Docteur et de Madame Henri Labbe   Vol. 2: 5543
Fondation du Docteur et de Madame Peyre   Vol. 2: 5544
Fondation du Docteur Jean Toy   Vol. 2: 5545
Fondation du General Ferrie   Vol. 2: 5546
Fondation du General Muteau   Vol. 2: 5547
Fondation Dulac   Vol. 2: 5351
Fondation Dusgate   Vol. 2: 5548
Fondation Edmond Brun   Vol. 2: 5549
Fondation Edmond Fagnan   Vol. 2: 973
Fondation Elie Cartan   Vol. 2: 5550
Fondation Emil Picard   Vol. 2: 5551
Fondation Emile Jungfleisch   Vol. 2: 5552
Fondation Emile Waxweiler   Vol. 2: 974
Fondation Ernest Dechelle   Vol. 2: 5553
Fondation Ernest Mahaim   Vol. 2: 975
Fondation Eugene et Amelie Dupuis   Vol. 2: 5554
Fondation Fanny Emden   Vol. 2: 5555
Fondation Fernand Holweck   Vol. 2: 5556
Fondation Fontannes   Vol. 2: 5557
Fondation Foulon   Vol. 2: 5558
Fondation Fourneyron   Vol. 2: 5559
Fondation Francoeur   Vol. 2: 5560
Fondation Frederic Forthuny   Vol. 2: 5561
Fondation G. de Pontecoulant   Vol. 2: 5562
Fondation Gabrielle Sand   Vol. 2: 5563
Fondation Gaston Rousseau   Vol. 2: 5564
Fondation Gay   Vol. 2: 5565
Fondation Gegner   Vol. 2: 5566
Fondation General Muteau   Vol. 2: 5799
Fondation Georges Deflandre et Marthe Deflandre-Rigaud   Vol. 2: 5567
Fondation Georges Millot   Vol. 2: 5568
Fondation Godard   Vol. 2: 5569
Fondation Grammatickakis-Neuman   Vol. 2: 5570
Fondation Gustave Clausse   Vol. 2: 5388
Fondation Gustave Germain   Vol. 2: 5388
Fondation Gustave Ribaud   Vol. 2: 5571
Fondation Gustave Roussy   Vol. 2: 5572
Fondation Gustave Roux   Vol. 2: 5573
Fondation Helene Helbronner-Fould   Vol. 2: 5574
Fondation Henri Becquerel   Vol. 2: 5575
Fondation Henri de Parville   Vol. 2: 5576
Fondation Henri Mondor   Vol. 2: 5577
Fondation Henri Pirenne   Vol. 2: 976
Fondation Henri Poincare   Vol. 2: 5578
Fondation Henriette Regnier   Vol. 2: 5579
Fondation Henry Bazin   Vol. 2: 5580
Fondation Henry Giffard   Vol. 2: 5581
Fondation Henry Le Chatelier   Vol. 2: 5582

Fondation Henry Wilde   Vol. 2: 5583
Fondation Hirn   Vol. 2: 5584
Fondation Hughes   Vol. 2: 5585
Fondation Ivan Peyches   Vol. 2: 5586
Fondation Jacques Bourcart   Vol. 2: 5587
Fondation Jaffe   Vol. 2: 5334
Fondation Jaffe   Vol. 2: 5588
Fondation James Hall   Vol. 2: 5589
Fondation Janine Courrier   Vol. 2: 5590
Fondation Janssen   Vol. 2: 5591
Fondation Jean-Baptiste Dumas   Vol. 2: 5592
Fondation Jean Cuvillier   Vol. 2: 5593
Fondation Jean Dagnan-Bouveret   Vol. 2: 5594
Fondation Jean de Meyer   Vol. 2: 1002
Fondation Jean de Rufz de La Vison   Vol. 2: 5595
Fondation Jean du Hamel de Breuil   Vol. 2: 5596
Fondation Jean-Jacques Berger   Vol. 2: 5597
Fondation Jean Lebrun   Vol. 2: 1003
Fondation Jean-Marie Le Goff   Vol. 2: 5598
Fondation Jean-Paul Alaux   Vol. 2: 5388
Fondation Jean Reynaud   Vol. 2: 5599
Fondation Jean Thore   Vol. 2: 5600
Fondation Jecker   Vol. 2: 5601
Fondation Jerome Ponti   Vol. 2: 5602
Fondation Joseph Labbe   Vol. 2: 5603
Fondation Jules et Louis Jeanbernat et Barthelemy de Ferrari Doria   Vol. 2: 5604
Fondation Kastner-Boursault   Vol. 2: 5605
Fondation Kodak-Pathe-Landucci   Vol. 2: 5606
Fondation L. La Caze   Vol. 2: 5607
Fondation La Caille   Vol. 2: 5608
Fondation Lamb   Vol. 2: 5609
Fondation Langevin   Vol. 2: 5610
Fondation Lannelongue   Vol. 2: 5611
Fondation Laplace   Vol. 2: 5612
Fondation Laura Mounier de Saridakis   Vol. 2: 5613
Fondation Lavoisier   Vol. 2: 5614
Fondation Le Conte   Vol. 2: 5615
Fondation Leon-Alexandre Etancelin   Vol. 2: 5616
Fondation Leon Grelaud   Vol. 2: 5617
Fondation Leon Lutaud   Vol. 2: 5618
Fondation Leon Velluz   Vol. 2: 5619
Fondation Lonchampt   Vol. 2: 5620
Fondation Louis Armand   Vol. 2: 5621
Fondation Louis-Daniel Beauperthuy   Vol. 2: 5622
Fondation Louise Darracq   Vol. 2: 5623
Fondation Lucien Cayeux   Vol. 2: 5624
Fondation Marc Poll   Vol. 2: 1004
Fondation Marie Guido Triossi   Vol. 2: 5625
Fondation Marie Leon-Houry   Vol. 2: 5626
Fondation Marmottan   Vol. 2: 5388
Fondation Marquet   Vol. 2: 5627
Fondation Martin-Damourette   Vol. 2: 5628
Fondation Maujean   Vol. 2: 5629
Fondation Max-Fernand Jayle   Vol. 2: 5630
Fondation Mege   Vol. 2: 5631
Fondation Memain-Pelletier   Vol. 2: 5335
Fondation Memain-Pelletier   Vol. 2: 5632
Fondation Mergier-Bourdeix   Vol. 2: 5633
Fondation Millet-Ronssin   Vol. 2: 5634
Fondation Montagne   Vol. 2: 5635
Fondation Montyon de Medicine et Chirugie   Vol. 2: 5636
Fondation Montyon de Physiologie   Vol. 2: 5637
Fondation Montyon des Arts Insalubres   Vol. 2: 5638
Fondation Montyon des Statistiques   Vol. 2: 5639
Fondation Nicolas Zvorikine   Vol. 2: 5640
Fondation Octave Dupont   Vol. 2: 1005

Fondation Odette Lemenon Vol. 2: 5641
Fondation Parkin Vol. 2: 5642
Fondation Paul Bertrand Vol. 2: 5643
Fondation Paul Doistau - Emile Blutet Vol. 2: 5644
Fondation Paul Fallot-Jeremine Vol. 2: 5645
Fondation Paul Gallet Vol. 2: 5646
Fondation Paul Marguerite de la Charlonie Vol. 2: 5647
Fondation Paul Pascal Vol. 2: 5648
Fondation Petit d'Ormoy Vol. 2: 5649
Fondation Philipeaux Vol. 2: 5650
Fondation Philippe A. Guye Vol. 2: 5651
Fondation Pierre Desnuelle Vol. 2: 5652
Fondation Pierre Lafitte Vol. 2: 5653
Fondation Pierson-Perrin Vol. 2: 5654
Fondation Pinette Vol. 2: 5388
Fondation Plumey Vol. 2: 5655
Fondation Poncelet Vol. 2: 5656
Fondation Pouchard Vol. 2: 5657
Fondation Pourat Vol. 2: 5658
Fondation Redon Vol. 2: 5388
Fondation Rene Dujarric de la Riviere Vol. 2: 5659
Fondation Roberge Vol. 2: 5660
Fondation Rochat-Juliard Vol. 2: 5661
Fondation Rogissart-Sarazin-Vandevyere Vol. 2: 5662
Fondation Roy-Vaucouloux Vol. 2: 5663
Fondation Salman A. Waksman Vol. 2: 5664
Fondation Savigny Vol. 2: 5665
Fondation Schutzenberger Vol. 2: 5666
Fondation Serres Vol. 2: 5667
Fondation Servant Vol. 2: 5668
Fondation Tchihatchef Vol. 2: 5669
Fondation Theurlot Vol. 2: 5670
Fondation Thorlet
    Institut de France - Academie des Sciences Vol. 2: 5671
    Institut de France - Academie des Sciences Morales et Politiques Vol 2: 5710
Fondation Tregouboff Vol. 2: 5672
Fondation Tremont Vol. 2: 5673
Fondation Vaillant Vol. 2: 5674
Fondation Valentine Allorge Vol. 2: 5675
Fondation Victor Raulin Vol. 2: 5676
Fondation Victor Thebault Vol. 2: 5677
Fondations Bellion - Charles Bouchard Vol. 2: 5678
Fondations Estrade Delcros, Houllevigue, Saintour, Jules Mahyer Vol. 2: 5679
Fondations Gaston Plante, Francois Hebert-Paul Jousselin Vol. 2: 5680
Fondations Lalande - Benjamin Valz Vol. 2: 5681
Fondazione Angiolo Silvio e Jacopo Novaro Vol. 2: 8051
Fondazione Ettore Bora Vol. 2: 8052
Fondazione Eugenio Morelli Vol. 2: 8053
Fondazione Francesco Sarerio Nitti Prize Vol. 2: 8054
Fondazione Giorgio Maria Sangiorgi Vol. 2: 8055
Fondazione Giovanna Jucci Vol. 2: 8056
Fondazione Giovanni Di Guglielmo Vol. 2: 8057
Fondazione Giuseppe Lugli Vol. 2: 8058
Fondazione Guido Donegani Vol. 2: 8059
Fondazione Guido Lenghi e Flaviano Magrassi Vol. 2: 8060
Fondazione Luigi D'Amato Vol. 2: 8061
Fondazione Premio Battista Grassi Vol. 2: 8062
Fondazione Premio Dotte Giuseppe Borgia Vol. 2: 8063
Fondazione Premio Stanislao Cannizzaro Vol. 2: 8064

Fondazione Professor Giuseppe Ciardi Vol. 2: 1204
Fondazione Valeria Vincenzo Landi Vol. 2: 8065
Fondazione Wilhelm Conrad Rontgen Vol. 2: 8066
Fondiller Prize; Woodward - Vol. 1: 7339
Fones Award; Alfred C. Vol. 1: 1946
Fono Albert Erem Vol. 2: 7319
Fono Award Vol. 2: 7319
Fonseca Prize; Fernando Vol. 2: 10315
Fontaine Trophy; Frank Vol. 1: 2331
Fontane Prize Vol. 2: 6509
Fontannes; Prix Vol. 2: 5307
Fonyo Medal of Courage; Steven Vol. 1: 7759
Food and Agricultural Policy Article Competition Vol. 1: 7436
Food and Drug Law Institute Scholarship Vol. 1: 9288
Food & Hotel Asia Competition
    Canadian Federation of Culinary Chefs Vol. 1: 6860
    Chefs & Cooks Circle Vol 2: 2611
    National Restaurant Association Vol 1: 14623
    Panel of Chefs of Ireland Vol 2: 7817
    Society of German Cooks Vol 2: 7090
    Society of Swiss Cuisiniers Vol 2: 11911
Food Industry Award Vol. 1: 13906
Food, Pharmaceutical and Bioengineering Division Award in Chemical Engineering Vol. 1: 2578
Food Service and Retail Awards Vol. 1: 9438
Food Service Awards Vol. 1: 9438
Food Technology Industrial Achievement Award Vol. 1: 10345
Foodservice Awards Vol. 1: 8500
Foodservice Operator of the Year Vol. 1: 10988
Foote Award; Lucy B. Vol. 1: 11953
For Budapest Award Vol. 2: 7300
For Church and Profession (of Pharmacy) Award Vol. 1: 13559
For New York Award Vol. 1: 7725
Forand Award; Aime J. Vol. 1: 13751
FORATOM Award Vol. 2: 2125
Forbes Award; Harriette Merrifield Vol. 1: 5526
Forbes Magazine Vol. 1: 15875
Forbes Magazine Award Vol. 1: 11151
Forbes Memorial Award; Carrol Vol. 1: 11314
Ford Award; Fred Vol. 1: 18049
Ford Award of Excellence; Henry Vol. 1: 12387
Ford Awards; Betty Vol. 1: 11719
Ford Awards; Lester R. Vol. 1: 12132
Ford European Conservation Awards Vol. 2: 2677
Ford/Farmer's Journal Riding Club Jumping Chase Vol. 2: 7834
Ford Foundation Postdoctoral Fellowships for Minorities Vol. 1: 14620
Ford II Distinguished Award for Excellence in Automotive Engineering; Henry Vol. 1: 17758
Ford Memorial Award; Consuelo Vol. 1: 16284
Ford Memorial Award; Henry Vol. 1: 17759
Ford Motor Company Fund Vol. 1: 8294
Ford New Holland Young Researcher Award Vol. 1: 4362
Ford Prize for Distinguished Reporting on National Defense; Gerald R. Vol. 1: 9316
Ford Prize for Distinguished Reporting on the Presidency; Gerald R. Vol. 1: 9317

Ford Trophy; Leonard Guy "Lenny" Vol. 1: 16214
Forder Lectureship Vol. 2: 3610
Forderpreis der Eichendorff - Gesellschaft Vol. 2: 6694
Forderpreis der ITG Vol. 2: 6530
Forderpreis des Landes Nordrhein-Westfalen fur junge Kunstlerinnen und Kunstler Vol. 2: 7026
Forderpreis fur bildende Kunst der Landeshauptstadt Dusseldorf Vol. 2: 6682
Forderpreis fur hervorragende Diplomarbeiten auf dem Gebiet der Innenarchitektur Vol. 2: 6810
Forderpreis fur Literatur der Landeshauptstadt Dusseldorf Vol. 2: 6683
Forderpreis fur Musik der Landeshauptstadt Dusseldorf Vol. 2: 6684
Forderpreis fur Wissenschaften Vol. 2: 6685
Forderungspreis der Osterreichische Gesellschaft fur Klinische Chemie Vol. 2: 876
Forderungspreis des Landes Niederosterreich Vol. 2: 859
Forderungspreise der Stadt Wien Vol. 2: 791
Fordham - Stein Prize Vol. 1: 9321
Foreign Affairs Award for Public Service Vol. 1: 19291
Foreign Honorary Fellow Vol. 2: 5132
Foreign Honorary Member Vol. 1: 1970
Foreign Honorary Members Vol. 1: 505
Foreign Language Book and Foreign Language Article Prize Vol. 1: 15817
Foreign Service National of the Year Award Vol. 1: 19292
Foremarke Cup Vol. 2: 4035
Forensic Science Society Awards Vol. 2: 2905
Forero Prize; Manuel Vol. 2: 1728
Forest Industry Leader Award Vol. 1: 14028
Forest Press Award; John Ames Humphry/ Vol. 1: 2903
Forest Products Division Award in Chemical Engineering Vol. 1: 2579
Forest Runes Award Vol. 1: 5331
Forest Stewardship State of the Year Vol. 1: 15042
Forestry Capital of Canada Award Vol. 1: 6888
Forestry Department Accreditation Vol. 1: 17915
"Forintos"-Prize Vol. 2: 7389
Forkosch Prize; Morris D. Vol. 1: 2290
Forman Award; Jonathan Vol. 1: 560
Formation Evaluation Award Vol. 1: 17968
Forms and Brochures Contest Awards Vol. 1: 10436
Forrest Medal; James Vol. 2: 3237
Forrestal III, Leadership Award for Professional Ethics and Standards of Investment Practice; Daniel J. Vol. 1: 5553
Forrestal Memorial Award; James Vol. 1: 14719
Forster Award; E. M. Vol. 1: 506
Forster Memorial Lecture; Theodor Vol. 2: 6629
Forster's Financial Writing Achievement Award; Pannell Kerr Vol. 1: 9336
Forsyth Award; Charles Vol. 1: 7356
Fort Adams/MACA Cup Vol. 1: 12321
Fortescue Fellowship; Charles LeGeyt Vol. 1: 10265
Forthuny; Fondation Frederic Vol. 2: 5561
Fortuny; Prix Pascal Vol. 2: 5903
Forty Year Membership Pin Vol. 1: 3220
Forty Year Plaque Vol. 1: 7767
Forum Award Vol. 1: 19073

Forum Award for Promoting Public Understanding of the Relation of Physics to Society   Vol. 1: 3455
Foss Award   Vol. 1: 2041
Foss Award; Hal   Vol. 1: 12894
Foster Accompanist's Prize; Megan   Vol. 2: 4530
Foster Award; Eugene   Vol. 1: 2267
Foster Award; Harvey G.   Vol. 1: 19855
Foster Fellows Visiting Scholars Program; William C.   Vol. 1: 19003
Fothergillian Gold Medal   Vol. 2: 3637
Fothergillian Medal   Vol. 2: 3637
Fould; Prix Louis   Vol. 2: 5469
Fould-Stirbey; Prix Achille   Vol. 2: 5353
Foulley; Prix Yvonne   Vol. 2: 4878
Foulois Memorial Award; Maj. Gen. Benjamin D.   Vol. 1: 15778
Foundation Award to the Technician of the Year in the Rolls-Royce Dealer Network Chosen by a Craft Competition   Vol. 2: 4303
Foundation for Gifted and Talented Children   Vol. 1: 11423
Foundation of ACHCA Long-Term Care Research Award   Vol. 1: 1646
Foundation of ACHCA Quality Nursing in Long-Term Care Scholarships   Vol. 1: 1647
Foundation of Socio-Cultural Services Competitions   Vol. 2: 11400
Foundation Prestige Lectures   Vol. 2: 4304
Foundation Prize Awards   Vol. 1: 2206
Foundation Research Grants   Vol. 1: 15954
Foundations Fund Prize for Research in Psychiatry   Vol. 1: 3631
Founder and First President Award   Vol. 1: 11020
Founder Award   Vol. 1: 4922
Founder's Award
   Academy of Criminal Justice Sciences   Vol. 1: 36
   American Academy of Neurology   Vol 1: 615
   American Alliance for Theatre & Education   Vol 1: 780
   Civitan International   Vol 1: 7787
   National Academy of Songwriters   Vol 1: 12702
   Pratt Institute   Vol 1: 16368
   Society for Biomaterials   Vol 1: 17426
   Society of Architectural Historians   Vol 1: 17743
Founders Award
   American College of Utilization Review Physicians   Vol. 1: 1751
   American Hockey Coaches Association   Vol 1: 2309
   American Institute of Chemical Engineers   Vol 1: 2580
   Confederate Memorial Literary Society   Vol 1: 8105
   Indiana Black Expo   Vol 1: 10145
   The International Council of the National Academy of Television Arts and Sciences   Vol 1: 10884
   Marigold Society of America   Vol 1: 12048
   National Academy of Engineering   Vol 1: 12641
   National Association for Campus Activities   Vol 1: 12842
   National Association of Display Industries   Vol 1: 13075
   National Head Injury Foundation   Vol 1: 14107
   New York Arthritis Foundation   Vol 1: 15221
   Niagara University   Vol 1: 15378
   ROUNDALAB   Vol 1: 16913

Founders' Award
   Arthritis Foundation   Vol. 1: 5303
   Chemical Industry Institute of Toxicology   Vol 1: 7538
   International Thespian Society   Vol 1: 11362
The Founders Award   Vol. 1: 6208
Founder's Award for Humane Excellence   Vol. 1: 4295
Founders' Award for Public Service   Vol. 1: 14783
Founders Award Program   Vol. 1: 14758
Founders' Awards   Vol. 1: 17267
Founder's Day Alumni/Alumnae Citations   Vol. 1: 11970
Founders Day Award for Distinguished Government Service   Vol. 1: 16558
Founders' Day Project Award   Vol. 1: 17178
Founders' Graduate Service Award   Vol. 1: 358
Founder's Medal
   Association of Military Surgeons of the United States   Vol. 1: 5882
   Royal Geographical Society   Vol 2: 4008
Founders Medal
   Institute of Electrical and Electronics Engineers   Vol. 1: 10266
   National Academy of Engineering   Vol 1: 12641
   Society of Logistics Engineers   Vol 1: 17871
Founders' Memorial Award   Vol. 1: 8699
Founders' Prize   Vol. 1: 18656
Founder's Trophy   Vol. 1: 19528
Founders' Undergraduate Service Award   Vol. 1: 358
Founding Societies' Centenary Award   Vol. 2: 3082
Foundry Industry Award   Vol. 2: 3070
Fountain of Universal Peace Award   Vol. 1: 10717
The Fountainhead Essay Competition   Vol. 1: 16671
Four Masters Award   Vol. 1: 11451
Four Seasons Critics Awards   Vol. 1: 18745
Four Wheel Drive Truck Puller of the Year   Vol. 1: 14900
Four-Year College Section Teaching Award   Vol. 1: 12954
Fouraignan Foundation Prize   Vol. 2: 6312
Fourmarier; Prix Paul   Vol. 2: 1034
Fournier Prize; Pierre   Vol. 2: 6201
Fourth Estate Award   Vol. 1: 14497
Fourth of July Prize   Vol. 2: 10707
Fowler Award; Raymond D.   Vol. 1: 3670
Fox Award for Communications Leadership Toward a Just Society; Muriel   Vol. 1: 15547
Fox Award; Ruth Berrien   Vol. 1: 15125
Fox Award; Terry   Vol. 1: 20622
Fox Founder's Award; A. Roger   Vol. 1: 13091
Fox Gold Medal; E. J.   Vol. 2: 3071
Fox Lifetime Achievement Award; Daniel W.   Vol. 1: 16239
Fox of Poster for Books for the Young   Vol. 2: 6203
Fox Trophy; UFFA   Vol. 2: 2898
The Foxy   Vol. 1: 15547
Fraenkel Prize in Contemporary History   Vol. 2: 3086
Fragrance Foundation Hall of Fame   Vol. 1: 9361
Fragrance Foundation Recognition Awards (FIFI Awards)   Vol. 1: 9361
Fragrance Packaging Introduction of the Year   Vol. 1: 9361
Frame Award; Boy   Vol. 1: 4047

Framstaende Popularvetenskapug Publicering I Vaxtfyscologi   Vol. 2: 11566
France-Canada Lectureship   Vol. 1: 16954
Francescatti; International Violin Competition Zino   Vol. 2: 4972
Franciscan International Award   Vol. 1: 9365
Francisco Award; Peter   Vol. 1: 16329
Franck Award   Vol. 2: 6054
Franck Organ Competition; Cesar   Vol. 2: 9432
Franck Orgelconcours; Cesar   Vol. 2: 9432
Francke Medal; Donald E.   Vol. 1: 4600
Francken-prijs; Dr. Wijnaendts   Vol. 2: 9626
Franco-British Landscape Gardening Award   Vol. 2: 2907
Franco Prize; Roberto   Vol. 2: 1729
Francoeur; Prix Albert-Emile   Vol. 1: 18439
Francois Medal; Jules
   International Council of Ophthalmology   Vol. 2: 9484
   International Federation of Ophthalmological Societies   Vol 2: 9501
Francoisprijs   Vol. 2: 9554
Francou Legacy; Andre   Vol. 1: 16919
Francqui Prize   Vol. 2: 1156
Frandson Award for Literature; Phillip E.   Vol. 1: 14947
Frank Award; Eugene M.   Vol. 1: 8842
Frank H. Armstrong Prize   Vol. 1: 5297
Frank Literary Award; Anne   Vol. 2: 11734
Frank-Literaturpreis; Anne   Vol. 2: 11734
Frankel Prize; Charles   Vol. 1: 13896
Frankenstein Travel Awards   Vol. 1: 9022
Frankfurter Guckkastenmennchen   Vol. 2: 6592
Frankland Fellowship; Sir Edward   Vol. 2: 4197
Frankland Prize Lectureship; Sir Edward   Vol. 2: 4198
Franklin Award; Ben   Vol. 1: 9189
Franklin Award for Distinguished Public Service; Benjamin   Vol. 1: 3430
Franklin Award for Outstanding Achievement in Mass Spectrometry; Frank H. Field and Joe L.   Vol. 1: 1555
Franklin Awards; Benjamin   Vol. 1: 16586
Franklin Literary Award; Miles   Vol. 2: 127
Franklin Medal
   American Philosophical Society   Vol. 1: 3431
   Franklin Institute   Vol 1: 9382
Franklin Medal; Benjamin   Vol. 2: 4322
Franklin Medal; Ned   Vol. 2: 3218
Franklin Mint Exhibit Award   Vol. 1: 3221
Franklin Publication Prize; John Hope   Vol. 1: 4874
Franklin Service Award; Jack   Vol. 1: 19517
Franny Award   Vol. 1: 10996
Frans Erensprijs   Vol. 2: 9657
Franz; Prix Henry   Vol. 2: 6283
Franzmeier Memorial Award; Chapman-   Vol. 1: 922
Frappier; Prix Armand   Vol. 1: 16617
Frary Award; Francis C.   Vol. 1: 384
Fraser Award; Soeurette Diehl   Vol. 1: 18647
Fraser Landscape Heritage Fund Award; Grace and Robert   Vol. 1: 11778
Fraser Memorial Award; Ian Shenstone   Vol. 1: 9149
Fraunces Tavern Museum Book Award   Vol. 1: 18150
Fraunhofer Award; Joseph   Vol. 1: 15749
Frederick Award; Major General Robert T.   Vol. 1: 9220
Frederick Research Grant; Oncology Nursing Foundation/Purdue   Vol. 1: 15648
Fredericq; Prix Leon et Henri   Vol. 2: 1030

Fredkin Foundation Prize for Computer Chess   Vol. 1: 11054
Free Enterprise Award   Vol. 1: 10998
Free Enterprise Writer of the Year   Vol. 1: 14326
Free Market Award   Vol. 2: 10865
Free Spirit Award   Vol. 1: 9394
Freedley Memorial Award; George   Vol. 1: 18687
Freedman Foundation Patent Award   Vol. 1: 2612
Freedom Award
 American Ex-Prisoners of War   Vol. 1: 2012
 Freedom House   Vol 1: 9399
 Indiana Black Expo   Vol 1: 10146
 International Rescue Committee   Vol 1: 11204
 National Committee for Responsible Patriotism   Vol 1: 13629
 Order of Lafayette   Vol 1: 15790
 World Federation of Hungarian Freedom Fighters   Vol 1: 20487
Freedom Forum Journalism Scholarships   Vol. 1: 9395
Freedom Leadership Medal   Vol. 1: 9405
Freedom Medal   Vol. 1: 16896
Freedom Medal of the City of Philadelphia   Vol. 1: 7752
Freedom of Information Award   Vol. 1: 5411
Freedom of the Human Spirit Award   Vol. 1: 10070
Freedom of the Press Awards   Vol. 1: 14498
Freedom Prize
 Politiken   Vol. 2: 1989
 Max Schmidheiny Foundation   Vol 2: 11900
Freedom to Read Roll of Honor   Vol. 1: 9401
Freedom to Write Awards; PEN   Vol. 1: 16021
Freedom Torch   Vol. 1: 11258
Freeman Article Award; Ned E.   Vol. 1: 1850
Freeman Fellowship   Vol. 1: 4453
Freeman Lectureship in Geriatrics   Vol. 1: 9588
Freeman Memorial Grant-in-Aid; Don   Vol. 1: 17813
Freeman Music Competition   Vol. 1: 6677
Freeman Scholar Award   Vol. 1: 4674
Freer Medal; Charles Lang   Vol. 1: 17335
Freese Environmental Engineering Award and Lecture; Simon W.   Vol. 1: 4454
Freethinker   Vol. 1: 9397
FREEZE Peace Award; SANE/   Vol. 1: 8189
Freiburg Ecological Film Festival   Vol. 2: 7063
Freiheitspreis   Vol. 2: 11900
Freiman Award; Frank   Vol. 1: 11287
Freire Prize; Luciano   Vol. 2: 10302
Fremont; Fondation Charles   Vol. 2: 5516
French-American Chamber of Commerce Person of the Year Award   Vol. 1: 9407
French Booksellers Prize   Vol. 2: 5257
French Most Valuable Player Award; William   Vol. 1: 14266
French Open   Vol. 2: 5259
French Society for Medical Hydrology and Climatology Prize   Vol. 2: 5297
French Tastemaker Awards; R. T.   Vol. 1: 6299
French Wine and Spirits Sommelier Competition
 Food and Wines From France   Vol. 1: 9290
 Food and Wines from France/SOPEXA   Vol 2: 5228
Frend Medal   Vol. 2: 4383
Frenkel Prize   Vol. 1: 10713
Fresenius-Preis   Vol. 2: 6782
Freshley Award; Marylene   Vol. 1: 14116
Freud Award; Sigmund   Vol. 1: 4776

Freud-Preis; Sigmund-   Vol. 2: 6766
Freudenthal Medal; Alfred M.   Vol. 1: 4455
Freund Award; Clement J.   Vol. 1: 4090
Freville; Prix Edmond   Vol. 2: 5738
Frew Fellowship; Geoffrey   Vol. 2: 173
Frew National Leadership Award; Stephen A.   Vol. 1: 13092
Frey Memorial Award; Hey   Vol. 1: 15711
Frey Preis; E. K.   Vol. 2: 6876
Freyssinet Award   Vol. 2: 9732
Frick Award; Ford C.   Vol. 1: 13439
Friedberg Lecture   Vol. 1: 1459
Friedenpreis des Deutschen Buchhandels   Vol. 2: 6776
Friedenwald Medal; Julius   Vol. 1: 2138
Friedenwald Memorial Award   Vol. 1: 5592
Friedenwald Memorial Award; Jonas S.   Vol. 1: 5592
Friedman Award; Abraham   Vol. 1: 9926
Friedman Award Medal; Lee Max   Vol. 1: 2740
Friedman Distinguished Clinician/Researcher Award; Arnold   Vol. 1: 900
Friedman Essay Contest; Milton   Vol. 1: 5113
Friedman Medal; Sue Tyler   Vol. 2: 2923
Friedman Memorial Award; Harold   Vol. 1: 9877
Friedman Professional Recognition Award; Edmund   Vol. 1: 4456
Friedman Young Engineer Award for Professional Achievement; Edmund   Vol. 1: 4457
Friel Memorial Lecture; Ernest Sheldon   Vol. 2: 2837
Friend of Adoption   Vol. 1: 13682
Friend of ASP   Vol. 1: 3397
Friend of Automotive History Award   Vol. 1: 17786
Friend of Children Award   Vol. 1: 15410
Friend of Libraries U.S.A. Award (Friend of the Year)   Vol. 1: 9420
Friend of the Academy of Students of Pharmacy Award   Vol. 1: 3378
Friend of the American Indian   Vol. 1: 2417
Friend of the APhA Academy of Students of Pharmacy ("Friend of ASP") Award   Vol. 1: 3397
Friend of the Rottweiler   Vol. 1: 3980
"Friend of the Satellite Dealer" Award; Pat Porter Memorial Award -   Vol. 1: 8889
Friend of the South Pacific Award   Vol. 1: 9357
Friend of the Year   Vol. 1: 9420
Friends of Libraries U.S.A. Award   Vol. 1: 9419
Friends of Libraries U.S.A. Public Service Award   Vol. 1: 9421
Friends of Old-Time Radio Award   Vol. 1: 9423
Friends of Patrick Henry Awards   Vol. 1: 9425
Friends of SEAISI Award   Vol. 2: 10063
Friends of the Dallas Public Library Award   Vol. 1: 18648
Friendship Cup   Vol. 2: 4453
Friendship Medal
 All-Union Leninist Young Communist League   Vol. 2: 10430
 American Water Works Association   Vol 1: 5021
Friendship Trophy   Vol. 2: 4626
Frihedspris   Vol. 2: 1989
Friman Best in Show; Elmer   Vol. 1: 9857
Frink Medal for British Zoologists   Vol. 2: 4656
Fris Award (Command and Control Unit of the Year); Edward S.   Vol. 1: 12060
Frisbee Disc Championships; U.S. Open   Vol. 1: 20253

Frisch Medal Award   Vol. 1: 8820
Frishmuth Memorial Award; Harriet W.   Vol. 1: 20348
Friskies PetCare Award   Vol. 1: 788
Frite Award   Vol. 1: 1590
Fritz Award   Vol. 1: 1590
Fritz Medal; John
 American Society of Civil Engineers   Vol. 1: 4458
 United Engineering Trustees   Vol 1: 18914
Frohlich Two-Year Fellowship in Conservation; L. W.   Vol. 1: 12235
Front de l'Independance Awards   Vol. 2: 1158
Front Page Award   Vol. 1: 10203
Front Page Awards
 Newswomen's Club of New York   Vol. 1: 15373
 Washington-Baltimore Newspaper Guild   Vol 1: 20106
Frontrunner Award   Vol. 1: 17056
Frost Award; Little Big Horn Associates' Dr. Lawrence A.   Vol. 1: 11910
Frost Award; Robert   Vol. 2: 386
Frost Medal   Vol. 1: 16285
Froude Medal; William   Vol. 2: 4091
Froude Research Scholarship in Naval Architecture   Vol. 2: 4092
Fruit Publication Award   Vol. 1: 4145
Fry Award; Margery   Vol. 1: 14418
Fry Lecture Award; Glenn A.   Vol. 1: 639
Fry Medal   Vol. 1: 7234
Fry Memorial Lecture; William J.   Vol. 1: 2690
FSSA Gold Medal   Vol. 2: 10860
FSSA Silver Medal (Extension)   Vol. 2: 10861
FSSA Silver Medal (Research)   Vol. 2: 10862
FSSA Silver Medal (Research and Extension)   Vol. 2: 10863
Fuchs Memorial Scholarship Award; Viktor   Vol. 1: 20029
Fucik Honorary Medal; Julius   Vol. 2: 1864
Fudpucker Award; Elmer   Vol. 1: 11369
Fuels and Petrochemical Division Annual Award   Vol. 1: 2581
Fuentes Fiction Award; Carlos   Vol. 1: 7959
Fuerison; Prix Irene   Vol. 2: 960
Fuertes Award; Louis Agassiz   Vol. 1: 20319
Fuji Gold Medal Award   Vol. 1: 17901
Fujihara Award   Vol. 2: 8527
Fulbright Awards - American Program   Vol. 2: 185
Fulbright Awards - Australian Program   Vol. 2: 186
Fulbright Scholar Program   Vol. 1: 8329
Fulbright Senior Scholar Awards   Vol. 1: 8329
Fulcrum American Writing Award   Vol. 1: 9442
Fulkerson Fund; Delbert Ray   Vol. 1: 3007
Fulkerson Prize   Vol. 2: 9549
Fulla Prize; L'udovit   Vol. 2: 10765
Fuller Award; Anna   Vol. 1: 9444
Fuller Award; Oliver Torry   Vol. 1: 5584
Fuller Award; Solomon Carter   Vol. 1: 3632
Fuller Memorial Awards; George Warren   Vol. 1: 5022
Fuller Prostate Award; AUA Triennial Eugene   Vol. 1: 4952
Fullerton Award; Jim   Vol. 1: 2307
Fulling Award; Edmund H.   Vol. 1: 17449
Fulltime Homemaker Awards   Vol. 1: 8775
Fullum Award; Ernest F.   Vol. 1: 8757
Fulrath Award; Richard M.   Vol. 1: 1460
Fulton Awards   Vol. 2: 10837
Fulton-Downer Award   Vol. 2: 9733
Fulton Toekenning   Vol. 2: 10837
Fund Dr. en Mevr. Schamelhout-Koetlitz   Vol. 2: 1312
Fund for New American Plays   Vol. 1: 11670

Fundacion del Premio Fastenrath   Vol. 2: 11345
Funderburg Research Scholar Awards in Gastric Cancer Biology; R. Robert & Sally D.   Vol. 1: 2139
Funk, Sr. Memorial Scholarship; Virgil C.   Vol. 1: 13220
Furkert Award   Vol. 2: 9734
Furniss, Jr. National Security Book Award; Edgar S.   Vol. 1: 15587
Furon; Prix Raymond et Madeleine   Vol. 2: 5314
Furtherance of Justice Award   Vol. 1: 13859
Furuseth Award; Andrew   Vol. 1: 18976
Future Captain of Industry   Vol. 1: 20073
Future Leader Awards   Vol. 1: 11082
Future of Freedom Award   Vol. 1: 16667
FVH Award   Vol. 2: 11617
FVH-priset   Vol. 2: 11617
Gabor Award; Dennis   Vol. 1: 18321
Gabor Medal   Vol. 2: 4150
Gabor Prize; Andor   Vol. 2: 7404
Gabreski Award   Vol. 1: 2042
Gabriel Award   Vol. 1: 18861
Gabriel Award for Personal Achievement   Vol. 1: 18861
Gabriel Dissertation Prize; Ralph Henry   Vol. 1: 4875
Gaede - Langmuir Award   Vol. 1: 4960
Gagarin Gold Medal; Yuri A.   Vol. 2: 5150
Gagne Instructional Development Research Award; Robert M.   Vol. 1: 5512
Gahan Scholarship or Development Grant; Muriel   Vol. 2: 7835
Gaige Fund Award   Vol. 1: 4613
Gain; Prix du Roman Emil Zola - Raoul   Vol. 2: 6279
Gain Program Awards   Vol. 1: 3108
Gaines Award   Vol. 1: 787
Gaines Fido Award   Vol. 1: 9460
Gaines Medal for Good Sportsmanship   Vol. 1: 15328
Gaines Obedience Person of the Year   Vol. 1: 9462
Gaines Obedience Award   Vol. 1: 9461
Gairdner Foundation International Award of Merit   Vol. 1: 9466
Gairdner Foundation International Awards   Vol. 1: 9467
Gairdner Foundation Wightman Award   Vol. 1: 9468
Gairn E.E.C. Medal   Vol. 2: 4442
Gakujutsu-sho   Vol. 2: 8663
GALA Film Award   Vol. 1: 20328
Galantiere Literary Translation Prize; Lewis   Vol. 1: 4918
Galardon Estado de Mexico   Vol. 2: 9008
Galardones SGAE   Vol. 2: 11250
Galathea Medaillen   Vol. 2: 1999
Galathea Medal   Vol. 2: 1999
Galatti Award   Vol. 1: 196
Galbraith Award   Vol. 1: 8150
Gale Research Award for Excellence in Business Librarianship   Vol. 1: 2942
Gale Research Award for Excellence in Reference and Adult Services   Vol. 1: 2943
Gale Research Inc. Financial Development Award   Vol. 1: 2816
Gale Research Multicultural Award; EMIERT/   Vol. 1: 2887
Galen Medal   Vol. 2: 4637
Galeria Mesa Awards   Vol. 1: 7733
Galerie d'Essai; La   Vol. 2: 6189
Galex 28 Awards   Vol. 1: 9470
Galilei International Prize of the Rotary Club of Italy; Galileo   Vol. 2: 8303

Galileo Galilei International Prize of the Rotary Club of Italy   Vol. 2: 8303
Galkin Award; Harry   Vol. 1: 10664
Gallagher Award; Mike   Vol. 1: 19562
Gallagher Distinguished Service Award; Marian Gould   Vol. 1: 1029
Gallaher Business Challenge   Vol. 2: 7859
Gallantry Award   Vol. 1: 13876
Gallantry Decorations   Vol. 2: 342
Gallantry Medal   Vol. 2: 2351
Gallatin Fellowship in International Affairs; Albert   Vol. 1: 9169
Gallatin Medal; Albert   Vol. 1: 15307
Galleghan Encouragement Award; Lady   Vol. 2: 569
Galleghan Prize; Lady   Vol. 2: 571
Gallegos Novel Prize; Romulo   Vol. 2: 12120
Gallet; Fondation Paul   Vol. 2: 5646
Galley Club Award for Excellence   Vol. 2: 409
Gallo; Concorso Pianistico Internazionale Rina Sala   Vol. 2: 8140
Gallo International Piano Competition; Rina Sala   Vol. 2: 8140
Galloway Spacemodeling Service Award; H.   Vol. 1: 13291
Galvani Prize; Luigi   Vol. 2: 6569
GAMA Learn to Fly Award for Excellence in Aviation Education   Vol. 1: 9522
Gamble Award; Clarence James   Vol. 2: 920
Gamble Award; Sam G.   Vol. 2: 8554
Gamble Research Prize; Norman   Vol. 2: 4247
Gamgee Medal   Vol. 2: 11396
Gamma Sigma Sigma Woman of the Year Award   Vol. 1: 9476
GAMNI-SMAI; Prix Blaise Pascal du   Vol. 2: 5685
GAMS Prize   Vol. 2: 5324
Gamzu Prize; Dr. Haim   Vol. 2: 7965
Ganassini; Premio Europeo Prof. D.   Vol. 2: 8259
Gandhi Prize for Peace, Disarmament and Development; Indira   Vol. 2: 7502
Gandhi Prize for Popularization of Science; Indira   Vol. 2: 7645
Gantrelle; Prix Joseph   Vol. 2: 993
Gantt Medal; Henry Laurence   Vol. 1: 2979
Garant Awards; Serge   Vol. 1: 17821
Garavito; Orden al Merito Julio   Vol. 2: 1669
Garcia Monge Prize; Joaquin   Vol. 2: 1762
Garcia Prize; Manuel   Vol. 2: 11462
Gard Superior Citizen Volunteer Award; Robert E.   Vol. 1: 977
Garde Nationale Trophy   Vol. 1: 14096
Garden Center Award   Vol. 1: 9483
Garden Club of America Medals and Awards   Vol. 1: 9486
Garden Club of America National Medals   Vol. 1: 9487
Garden Club of America Small Flower Show Award   Vol. 1: 9486
Garden Communicator's Award   Vol. 1: 1069
Garden Machinery Annual Awards   Vol. 2: 2238
Garden State Children's Book Awards   Vol. 1: 15182
Garden Trophy; Oscar   Vol. 2: 9816
Gardening From the Heart Award   Vol. 1: 9497
Gardner Award; Henry A.   Vol. 1: 6050
Gardner Leadership Award; John W.   Vol. 1: 10139
Gardner Memorial Youth Award; Charles B.   Vol. 1: 9128
Gardner Trophy   Vol. 1: 19545
Garg Memorial Award; K. L.   Vol. 2: 7470

Garibay Kintana Prize for Literary Essay; Angel Maria   Vol. 2: 9048
Garland Award; Robert C.   Vol. 1: 17760
Garland Educator Award; Robin F.   Vol. 1: 14514
Garland Refrigeration Award; Milton W.   Vol. 1: 4584
Garneau Medal; Francois-Xavier   Vol. 1: 6907
Garner-Themoin Medal   Vol. 2: 9504
Garnir; Prix George   Vol. 2: 1299
Garnsey Trainers Award; Glen   Vol. 1: 19374
Garoglio; Premio P. G.   Vol. 2: 8044
Garrett Memorial Trophy (Outstanding Rookie Player); Dudley (Red)   Vol. 2: 2325
Garrett Turbomachinery Engineering Award; Cliff   Vol. 1: 17761
Garrison Prize; E.   Vol. 1: 5297
Garrod Medal   Vol. 2: 2515
Garrud Fellowship; T. V.   Vol. 2: 3323
Garvan - John M. Olin Medal; Francis P.   Vol. 1: 1556
Garvan Medal   Vol. 1: 1556
Garvey Award; Joseph J.   Vol. 1: 865
Gary Medal   Vol. 1: 2710
Gas Balloon Championships   Vol. 1: 6238
Gas Turbine Award
   American Society of Mechanical Engineers   Vol. 1: 4675
   American Society of Mechanical Engineers - International Gas Turbine Institute   Vol 1: 4718
   Society of Automotive Engineers - Australasia   Vol 2: 657
Gascoigne Medal; George Bradley   Vol. 1: 20150
Gascoigne Prize Essay Competition; Trench   Vol. 2: 4295
Gaskell Medal and Prize   Vol. 2: 3961
Gaskellprijs; Sonia   Vol. 2: 9637
Gasset; Premio Ortega y   Vol. 2: 11299
Gassner Award; John   Vol. 1: 15869
Gassner Memorial Playwriting Award; John   Vol. 1: 15140
Gaster Bronze Medal; Leon   Vol. 2: 2593
Gaston Writing Award   Vol. 1: 12878
Gates Memorial Award; Roy   Vol. 1: 18018
GATF Award of Excellence in Education for an Association   Vol. 1: 9698
GATF Award of Excellence in Education for an Individual in Industry and in Education   Vol. 1: 9699
Gatorade Rookie of the Year   Vol. 1: 11757
Gatto; Premio Internazionale Paolo   Vol. 2: 8076
Gatzke AAUA Foundation Award; Dr. Donald A.   Vol. 1: 1227
Gaucho; Medal El   Vol. 2: 105
Gaudeamus Prize   Vol. 2: 9439
Gaudin Award; Antoine M.   Vol. 1: 17563
Gaudry; Prix   Vol. 2: 5308
Gaul Composition Contest; Harvey   Vol. 1: 16228
Gaus Lecture; John   Vol. 1: 3574
Gauss Award; Christian   Vol. 1: 16100
Gautier; Prix Jacque   Vol. 2: 4914
Gavel Award   Vol. 1: 802
Gavel Awards   Vol. 1: 1309
Gawad AGKATEK (Agham, Kapaligiran at Teknolohiya)   Vol. 2: 10057
Gawad CCP Para sa Alternatibong Pelikula at Video   Vol. 2: 10046
Gawad CCP Para sa Radyo   Vol. 2: 10047
Gawad CCP Para sa Sining   Vol. 2: 10048
Gawad CCP Sa Panitikan   Vol. 2: 10034
Gay and Lesbian Press Association Awards   Vol. 1: 9511
Gay Book Award   Vol. 1: 2953

Gay/Lesbian Book Award Vol. 1: 2953
Gay Press Association Awards Vol. 1: 9511
Gay Teddy Bear Vol. 2: 6564
Gayarre; Concurso Internacional de Canto Julian Vol. 2: 11254
Gayarre International Singing Competition; Julian Vol. 2: 11254
Gaydar Award Vol. 2: 10431
Gaylord Award for Achievement in Library and Information Technology; LITA/ Vol. 1: 2908
Gayner Perpetual Trophy; Arthur Vol. 2: 2810
Gazzola Prize Vol. 2: 6001
GCN Agency Awards Vol. 1: 9674
GCN Government Executive of the Year Vol. 1: 9674
GCN Industry Executive of the Year Vol. 1: 9674
Gdansk Golden Lions Vol. 2: 10144
GEAC-CLSI Scholarship in Library and Information Technology; LITA/ Vol. 1: 2909
Geach Memorial Award; Portia Vol. 2: 128
Geary 18 International Yacht Racing Association Championship Regatta Vol. 1: 9513
Geddes Memorial Award; William F. Vol. 1: 949
Geddes Planning Award; Patrick Vol. 2: 10653
Geesink Prize; Joop Vol. 2: 9454
Geeta Award Vol. 2: 7510
Gehrt Memorial Award; Jack Vol. 1: 7807
GEICO Public Service Awards Vol. 1: 9676
Geiger Award Vol. 1: 12081
Geihutsu Korosha Vol. 2: 8784
Geijsbeek Award; Samuel Vol. 1: 1461
Geijutsu-in Sho Vol. 2: 8597
Geijutsu Sensho Vol. 2: 8575
Geijutsusai Sho Vol. 2: 8576
Geils Memorial Award; G. Ruth Vol. 1: 9782
Geisness Outstanding Lawyer or Non-Lawyer; Helen M. Vol. 1: 11693
Gelber Foundation Award; Sylva Vol. 1: 6737
Gelber Prize; Lionel Vol. 1: 9767
Gelsted pris; Otto Vol. 2: 1909
Gelsthorpe Cup Vol. 2: 2787
GEM Award Vol. 1: 17564
Gem of Mexico City Vol. 2: 8960
Gemant Award; Andrew Vol. 1: 2659
Gemeaux Awards Vol. 1: 25
Gemell Cup; David Vol. 2: 2997
Gemenis Award; Maria Vol. 2: 241
Gemini Awards Vol. 1: 26
Gemini Awards - Special Awards Vol. 1: 27
Genee Award; Adeline Vol. 2: 3869
General Aviation Award Vol. 1: 2491
General Aviation Service Technician Award Vol. 1: 12765
General Award Vol. 2: 8806
General Commendation Vol. 1: 3554
General Commendation Certificate Vol. 1: 14491
General Diagnostics Lectureship in Clinical Chemistry Vol. 1: 848
General Electric Foundation Awards for Younger Writers Vol. 1: 8370
General Electric Senior Research Award Vol. 1: 4091
General Federation of Women's Clubs/KAB Community Improvement Awards Vol. 1: 11660
General Practitioner of the Year Vol. 1: 1641
General Service Medal Vol. 2: 10927
General Services Achievement Award Vol. 1: 19293
Generalitat de Catalunya Trophy Vol. 2: 11203
Generous American Award Vol. 1: 18773

Genetics and Plant Breeding Award for Academia; NCCPB Vol. 1: 13726
Genetics and Plant Breeding Award for Industry Vol. 1: 8470
Genetics and Plant Breeding Award for Industry; NCCPB Vol. 1: 13727
Genetics and Plant Breeding Awards Vol. 1: 13725
Genetics Society of America Medal Vol. 1: 9534
Geneva-Europe Prizes for Television Writing Vol. 2: 11693
Genie Awards
  Academy of Canadian Cinema & Television Vol. 1: 28
  City of Toronto Vol 1: 7756
Genie Awards - Special Awards Vol. 1: 29
Genootschapsmedaille Vol. 2: 9557
Genossenschaftspreis Vol. 2: 11963
Gentilli Prize; Edgar Vol. 2: 3955
Geochimie; Prix de Vol. 2: 5568
Geography Grant Vol. 1: 13714
Geologiska Foreningens Medaljfondsstipendium Vol. 2: 11460
Georg Award; ISHAM Lucille K. Vol. 2: 1202
George Award; Judy Vol. 1: 20616
George Civilian Airmanship Award; Lt. Gen. Harold L. Vol. 1: 15779
George Cross Vol. 2: 2368
George Daedalian Fellowship Award; Lt. Gen. Harold L. Vol. 1: 15780
George London Grants for Singers Vol. 1: 14220
George Medal Vol. 2: 2369
George Prize; C. Oswald Vol. 2: 3210
Georgescu-Roegen Prize in Economics Vol. 1: 18212
Georgia Author of the Year Vol. 1: 8345
Georgia Children's Book Award Vol. 1: 19788
Georgia Children's Picture Storybook Award Vol. 1: 19789
Georgia Media Award Vol. 1: 9573
Georgia Peanut Export Award Vol. 1: 9574
Georgia Peanut Hall of Fame Vol. 1: 9575
Georgia Peanut Research and Education Award Vol. 1: 9576
Georgiev Prize; Academician Vladimir Vol. 2: 1513
Geotechnical Research Medal Vol. 2: 3238
Gerard; Prix Auguste Vol. 2: 5716
Gerber Prize for Excellence in Pediatrics Vol. 1: 14344
Gerhold Award in Chemical Separations Technology; Clarence (Larry) G. Vol. 1: 2582
Geriatric Dental Health Care Award Vol. 1: 1944
Gerin; Prix Leon- Vol. 1: 16618
Gerke Music Education Award; Madge C. Vol. 1: 12481
Gerlach-Medaille; Stern- Vol. 2: 6657
Gerlach-Preis fur Physik; Stern- Vol. 2: 6657
Germain; Fondation Gustave Vol. 2: 5388
German Chemical Society Prize for Journalists and Authors Vol. 2: 6788
German Design Prize Vol. 2: 6804
German Marshall Fund of the United States Fellowships and Awards Vol. 1: 9579
German Nutrition Foundation Travel Scholarship Vol. 2: 6856
German Operatic Award Vol. 2: 570
German Prize for Design Promoters Vol. 2: 6805
German Youth Literature Prize Vol. 2: 6833
Geographical Award Vol. 2: 4009
Gerrard Award; Louise B. Vol. 1: 13323

Gerrish Trophy; Ebby Vol. 2: 3781
Gerrity Award; Thomas P. Vol. 1: 242
Gerry Award Vol. 1: 14080
Gerry Fellowship; Eloise Vol. 1: 17254
Gerschenkron Prize; Alexander Vol. 1: 8825
Gershkoff Memorial Award; Aaron Vol. 1: 589
Gershoy Award; Leo Vol. 1: 2291
Gerstaecker-Preis; Friedrich- Vol. 2: 6573
Gervais Award; Arthur J. Vol. 1: 18395
Gervasi Award; Leonilda S. Vol. 1: 12609
Getman Award; G. N. Vol. 1: 7932
Getty Postdoctoral Fellowships in the History of Art and the Humanities; J. Paul Vol. 1: 9597
Getty Wildlife Conservation Prize; J. Paul Vol. 1: 20536
Getz Award; Oscar and Emmy Vol. 1: 7701
Getz World Peace Award Vol. 1: 7701
Gevaert Award; Lieven - Vol. 1: 17500
Geyer's Office Dealer Merchandising Achievement Awards Vol. 1: 9602
Gezelle Prize; Guido Vol. 2: 1272
GGAS Service Awards Vol. 1: 9628
Ghandi Peace Award Vol. 1: 16531
Ghatage Award; Dr. V. M. Vol. 2: 7475
Gheorghiu Prize; Stefan Vol. 2: 10349
Ghigi; Premio Maria Teresa e Allessandro Vol. 2: 8021
Ghirshman; Prix Roman et Tania Vol. 2: 5471
Ghiselli Award for Research Design; Edwin E. Vol. 1: 3799
Ghosh Memorial Award; Tapati Vol. 2: 7504
Giant of the Year (The Gaines Award) Vol. 1: 9606
Giant Schnauzer of the Year, Dog Vol. 1: 9607
Giant Steps Award Vol. 1: 7471
Gibb Award; Jack Vol. 1: 15808
Gibbons Cup; Stanley Vol. 2: 3781
Gibbons Medal; Cardinal Vol. 1: 7393
Gibbs Brothers Medal Vol. 1: 12669
Gibbs, Jr. Memorial Award for Excellence in Systematic Ichthyology; Robert H. Vol. 1: 4614
Gibson Award Vol. 1: 10612
Gibson Award; Milo Vol. 1: 15425
Gibson Research Scholarship for Medical Women; William Vol. 2: 4248
Gibson Trophy; Frank M. Vol. 1: 6877
Giegengack Award; Robert Vol. 1: 19939
Gieh ir-Repubblika Honor Society Vol. 2: 8914
Gierows pris for hangiven bildningsverksamhet; Karin Vol. 2: 11591
Gierows pris for kunskapsformedlande framstallningskonst; Karin Vol. 2: 11592
Gies Award; William John Vol. 1: 1631
Gies Foundation Award in Memory of Arthur Hastings Merritt; William J. Vol. 1: 691
Giese Structures and Environment Award; Henry Vol. 1: 4364
Giffard; Fondation Henry Vol. 2: 5581
Giffuni Brothers Award for Exceptional Merit Vol. 1: 15983
Gift of Music Best Seller Awards Vol. 1: 13282
Gift of Sight Award Vol. 1: 9031
Gifted Teacher Vol. 1: 1613
Gifts and Decorative Accessories Merchandising Achievement Awards Vol. 1: 9603
Gijon International Film Festival for Young People Vol. 2: 11252
Gilbert Award; G. K. Vol. 1: 9560
Gilbert Award; Glenn Vol. 1: 13759
Gilbert Award; John Vol. 1: 13015
Gilbert Media Award; Doug Vol. 1: 7245

Gilbert Memorial Award; Glen A. Vol. 1: 274
Gilbert Memorial Trustee Award; Gloria F. "Mike" Vol. 1: 4189
Gilbreth Industrial Engineering Award; Frank and Lillian Vol. 1: 10359
Gilbreth Medal Vol. 1: 17402
Gildas; Prix Hubert Vol. 2: 6284
Giles Award; Annie T. Vol. 1: 2267
Giles Minority Scholarship; Louise Vol. 1: 2924
Giles; Prix Herbert Allen Vol. 2: 5463
Gill Medal Vol. 2: 10822
Gill Memorial Vol. 2: 4010
Gill Memorial Award; Tom Vol. 2: 2650
Gill Memorial Medal Vol. 2: 11101
Gill Prize; Brendan Vol. 1: 12487
Gill Prize; Roma Vol. 1: 12099
Gillet Performance Competition; Fernand Vol. 1: 10913
Gillet Young Artist Performance Competition; Fernand Vol. 1: 10913
Gillette Cup Vol. 2: 4512
Gilliams Prize; Maurice Vol. 2: 1273
Gillies Award; Sir Harold Delf Vol. 1: 567
Gillies Memorial Trophy; John Wallace Vol. 1: 14645
Gillis Prize; J. Vol. 2: 1256
Gilliss Award for Outstanding Service; Captain James M. Vol. 1: 19272
Gilman Award in Drug Receptor Pharmacology; Goodman and Vol. 1: 4236
Gilmore Award; Mary Vol. 2: 131
Gilmore - Behind the Scenes Award; Diana Fell Vol. 1: 19018
Gilmore Bursary; Jean Vol. 2: 218
Gilmore Championship - Rookie Mechanic of the Year Award Vol. 1: 19019
Gilpin County Arts Association Annual Exhibition Vol. 1: 9611
Gilruth Prize Vol. 2: 276
Gilson; Grands Prix Paul- Vol. 2: 5070
Giltner Memorial Trophy; Joe Vol. 1: 17361
Gimmicks and Gadgets Award Vol. 1: 5023
Ginestie; Prix Jean-Francois Vol. 2: 4850
Gingles Award; Violet B. Vol. 1: 5259
Gingrich Memorial Award; Arnold Vol. 1: 9105
Gintzig Commemorative Student Award; Leon I. Vol. 1: 1648
Ginwala Gold Medal; Sir Padamji Vol. 2: 7627
Giolitti Steel Medal; Federico Vol. 2: 8128
Girard; Fondation Charles-Adam Vol. 2: 5513
Girard; Prix Antoine Vol. 2: 5815
Girard; Prix Edmond Vol. 2: 6222
Girard; Prix Maurice-Louis Vol. 2: 4861
Girardeau; Prix Emile Vol. 2: 5739
Girls' Basketball National Volunteer of the Year Vol. 1: 428
Gish Award; Lillian Vol. 1: 20383
Gitelson Memorial Essay Awards; Moses Leo Vol. 1: 7473
Gitlin Literary Prize; Zelda Vol. 1: 20352
Giuliani Duo di Chitarre; Concorso Internazionale Mauro Vol. 2: 8183
Givry; Prix Alexandre Vol. 2: 5534
Gjesdals pris; Tor Vol. 2: 9942
Gjesdals Prize; Tor Vol. 2: 9942
Glabb Memorial Trophy; Joseph P. Vol. 1: 14645
Gladiolia Society Award Vol. 2: 2728
Glaser Distinguished Service Award; Jerome Vol. 1: 669
Glasgow Certificate Award; Janet M. Vol. 1: 3052
The Glasgow Herald Science Fiction Short Story Competition Vol. 2: 10547

Glass Dealer of the Year Vol. 1: 14083
Glass Globe Vol. 2: 9586
Glass Prize Vol. 2: 9904
Glass Professional of the Year Vol. 1: 14083
Glassco Translation Prize; John Vol. 1: 11906
Glauber Rocha Award Vol. 2: 1482
Glauber Rocha Prize Vol. 2: 10234
Glaxo Award Vol. 1: 7187
Glaxo Prize for Medical Writing Vol. 2: 4387
Glaxo Science Writers Awards Vol. 2: 2936
Glazebrook Medal and Prize Vol. 2: 3190
Glazen Globe Vol. 2: 9586
Gleason Award; Henry Allan Vol. 1: 6484
Gleason Award of Excellence; Doug Vol. 1: 18566
Gleason Music Book Awards; Ralph J. Vol. 1: 15303
Glen Award; Esther Vol. 2: 9762
Glenfiddich Awards Vol. 2: 2949
Glenfiddich Trophy Vol. 2: 10525
Glenn Award; R. A. Vol. 1: 6051
Glenn Foundation Award Vol. 1: 9589
Glickson Annual Research Prize; Mordechai (Momma) Vol. 2: 7980
Global Equity Awards Vol. 2: 2816
Global Media Awards for Excellence in Population Reporting Vol. 1: 16320
Global Releaf for New Communities Vol. 1: 2099
Global Statesman Award Vol. 1: 6690
Globe of Leadership Award Vol. 1: 5931
Glogau Award; Otto Vol. 2: 9767
Gloria Medal Vol. 1: 14715
Gloucester Navigation Trophy Vol. 2: 9817
Glueck Award; Sellin - Vol. 1: 4542
Gluge; Prix Theophile Vol. 2: 1038
Glushien Award; Ann Williams Vol. 1: 5045
Glyndebourne Peter Stuyvesant Award Vol. 2: 2941
Godbey Award; William D. Vol. 1: 5834
Goddard Astronautics Award; AIAA Vol. 1: 2470
Goddard Award Vol. 1: 2470
Goddard Award; George W. Vol. 1: 18322
Goddard Historical Essay Award; Dr. Robert H. Vol. 1: 14833
Goddard Medal Vol. 1: 17705
Goddard Memorial Trophy; Dr. Robert H. Vol. 1: 14834
Goddard Scholarship; Dr. Robert H. Vol. 1: 14835
Gode Medal; Alexander Vol. 1: 4919
Godeaux; Prix Lucien Vol. 2: 1368
Godlove Award Vol. 1: 10523
Godman-Salvin Medal Vol. 2: 2464
GODORT/ALA Award; CIS/ Vol. 1: 2895
GODORT/ALA Catharine J. Reynolds Grant; Readex/ Vol. 1: 2896
Godwin Award; Tony Vol. 1: 9623
Goeppert-Mayer Award; Maria Vol. 1: 3456
Goethals Medal; George W. Vol. 1: 17706
Goethe House - PEN Translation Prize Vol. 1: 16015
Goethe Medaille Vol. 2: 6901
Goethe Prize; Hanseatic Vol. 2: 7112
Goethepreis Vol. 2: 6612
Gold Anchor Vol. 2: 6014
Gold and Platinum Video Awards Vol. 1: 11483
Gold Anvil Award Vol. 1: 16574
Gold Award
  American Healthcare Radiology Administrators Vol. 1: 2220
  Polish Geographical Society Vol 2: 10146
Gold Award for Coordinated Sales Promotion Vol. 1: 14631

Gold Award; Harry Vol. 1: 4235
Gold Badge Vol. 2: 2789
Gold Badge of Honour Vol. 2: 2327
Gold Ball Award Vol. 1: 17372
Gold Baton Award
  American Symphony Orchestra League Vol. 1: 4892
  Columbia University - Graduate School of Journalism Vol 1: 7994
Gold Book Vol. 2: 1395
Gold Caduces Vol. 1: 13230
Gold Camera Award Vol. 1: 19352
Gold Certificate Vol. 1: 3337
Gold Composing Stick Award Vol. 1: 9344
Gold Conch Vol. 2: 7529
Gold Crown Awards Vol. 1: 7968
Gold Cystoscope Award Vol. 1: 4954
Gold Diploma of Honor Vol. 2: 7226
Gold Edelweiss Vol. 2: 11386
Gold Gentian Vol. 2: 8460
Gold Headed Cane
  Seventh Day Baptist Historical Society Vol. 1: 17202
  World Association of Societies of Pathology (Anatomic and Clinical) Vol 2: 8788
Gold Headed Cane Award Vol. 1: 4179
Gold Heart Award Vol. 1: 2229
Gold Honor Medal Vol. 1: 3978
Gold Key Award
  American Congress of Rehabilitation Medicine Vol. 1: 1807
  Columbia Scholastic Press Association Vol 1: 7969
  Incentive Manufacturers Representatives Association Vol 1: 10112
  Meetings and Conventions Vol 1: 12207
  National Council on Alcoholism and Drug Dependence Vol 1: 13789
Gold Key Awards
  Society of Professional Journalists Vol. 1: 18001
  University of Chicago Medical and Biological Sciences Alumni Association Vol 1: 19777
Gold Key Laureates Vol. 1: 16145
Gold Key Public Relations Achievement Awards Vol. 1: 2392
Gold Level Achievement Awards Vol. 1: 18604
Gold Lifesaving Medal Vol. 1: 19161
Gold Lion
  International Advertising Festival Vol. 2: 3363
  Venice International Film Festival Vol 2: 8470
Gold Mailbox Award Vol. 1: 8648
Gold Medal
  Acoustical Society of America Vol. 1: 96
  American Academy of Arts and Letters Vol 1: 507
  American College of Radiology Vol 1: 1738
  American Craft Council Vol 1: 1891
  American Institute of Architects Vol 1: 2530
  American Institute of Chemists Vol 1: 2613
  American Irish Historical Society Vol 1: 2706
  American Rhododendron Society Vol 1: 3956
  ASM International Vol 1: 5355
  Australian Numismatic Society Vol 2: 259
  Bahrain Contemporary Art Association Vol 2: 930
  British Society of Rheology Vol 2: 2530
  Chilean Society of History and Geography Vol 2: 1557

European and Mediterranean Plant Protection Organization   Vol 2: 5114
Filtration Society   Vol 2: 2882
The Gardners of America, Inc./Men's Garden Clubs of America   Vol 1: 9498
Geographic Society of Chicago   Vol 1: 9548
Guildhall School of Music and Drama   Vol 2: 2979
Institute of Actuaries   Vol 2: 3059
Institute of Chartered Accountants of Scotland   Vol 2: 10558
Institute of Management   Vol 2: 3110
Institute of South African Architects   Vol 2: 10881
Institution of Engineers, Pakistan   Vol 2: 9977
Institution of Structural Engineers   Vol 2: 3359
Inter-American Safety Council   Vol 1: 10515
International Federation of Sports Medicine   Vol 2: 1480
National Football Foundation and Hall of Fame   Vol 1: 13991
National Institute of Social Sciences   Vol 1: 14240
North American Gladiolus Council   Vol 1: 15427
Alexander S. Onassis Public Benefit Foundation   Vol 2: 7206
Ophthalmological Society of Egypt   Vol 2: 2023
Pakistan Academy of Sciences   Vol 2: 9993
Poetry Society of America   Vol 1: 16286
Professional Institute of the Public Service of Canada   Vol 1: 16490
Radiological Society of North America   Vol 1: 16659
Royal Asiatic Society   Vol 2: 3934
Royal Astronomical Society   Vol 2: 3939
Royal Canadian Geographical Society   Vol 1: 16935
Royal Institute of Navigation   Vol 2: 4077
Royal Philharmonic Society   Vol 2: 4126
Royal Scottish Geographical Society   Vol 2: 10635
Royal Society of Health   Vol 2: 4227
Royal Town Planning Institute   Vol 2: 4291
SA Holstein Friesland Society   Vol 2: 10968
Scientific Group for Space Research   Vol 2: 7215
Society of American Registered Architects   Vol 1: 17726
Society of Antiquaries of London   Vol 2: 4384
South African Chemical Institute   Vol 2: 11047
South African Geographical Society   Vol 2: 11055
South African Sugar Technologists' Association   Vol 2: 11090
Svenska Dagbladet   Vol 2: 11571
Tau Sigma Delta   Vol 1: 18582
Uranium Institute   Vol 2: 4589
Wildlife Society of Southern Africa   Vol 2: 11128
WWF World Wide Fund for Nature   Vol 2: 11986
Zimbabwe Scientific Association   Vol 2: 12223
Zoological Society of Southern Africa   Vol 2: 11132
Gold Medal Award
  American Academy of Periodontology   Vol. 1: 692
  American College of Healthcare Executives   Vol 1: 1657
  American Society of Naval Engineers   Vol 1: 4729
  Audio Engineering Society   Vol 1: 6133
  Canadian Society of Laboratory Technologists   Vol 1: 7203
  Dairy Industry Association of New Zealand   Vol 2: 9716
  International Radio and Television Society   Vol 1: 11182
  Mining and Metallurgical Society of America   Vol 1: 12326
  National Planning Association   Vol 1: 14475
  National Retail Merchants Association   Vol 1: 14632
  Professional Grounds Management Society   Vol 1: 16484
  Religious Heritage of America   Vol 1: 16775
  Society of Biological Psychiatry   Vol 1: 17790
  Society of Woman Geographers   Vol 1: 18096
Gold Medal Award for Distinguished Service   Vol. 1: 19966
Gold Medal Award for Life Achievement in Psychological Science   Vol. 1: 3833
Gold Medal Award for Outstanding Leadership in Rural Development   Vol. 2: 12017
Gold Medal Award for Technical Achievement   Vol. 1: 18011
Gold Medal Award for Water Pollution Control   Vol. 1: 18423
Gold Medal Awards
  American Psychological Foundation   Vol. 1: 3833
  Science Council of British Columbia   Vol 1: 17108
Gold Medal Conanti Award   Vol. 2: 1898
Gold Medal for Achievement in Science and Technology   Vol. 2: 10989
Gold Medal for Craft Excellence   Vol. 2: 2623
Gold Medal for Development of the Technological Environment   Vol. 2: 9952
Gold Medal for Distinguished Achievement
  American Petroleum Institute   Vol. 1: 3369
  Holland Society of New York   Vol 1: 9967
Gold Medal for Distinguished Merit   Vol. 2: 2436
Gold Medal for Distinguished Service
  American Institute of Certified Public Accountants   Vol. 1: 2559
  Society of American Military Engineers   Vol 1: 17707
Gold Medal for Distinguished Services to Agriculture   Vol. 2: 3920
Gold Medal for Engineering   Vol. 1: 5265
Gold Medal for Outstanding Architectural Achievement   Vol. 2: 6059
Gold Medal Forum   Vol. 1: 18201
Gold Medal of Achievement   Vol. 1: 3338
Gold Medal of Honor for Dance   Vol. 1: 12820
Gold Medal of Honor for Design   Vol. 1: 12821
Gold Medal of Honor for Education   Vol. 1: 12822
Gold Medal of Honor for Film/Video   Vol. 1: 12823
Gold Medal of Honor for Literature   Vol. 1: 12824
Gold Medal of Honor for Music   Vol. 1: 12825
Gold Medal of Honor for Photography   Vol. 1: 12826
Gold Medal of Honor for Theater/Drama   Vol. 1: 12827
Gold Medal of Honor for Visual Arts   Vol. 1: 12828
Gold Medal of Honour   Vol. 2: 10818
Gold Medal of Merit   Vol. 1: 11573
Gold Medal of the Academy of Greece   Vol. 2: 7202
Gold Medal of the FIM   Vol. 2: 11810
Gold Medal of the Royal Order of the Polar Star   Vol. 2: 11578
Gold Medal of the Royal Society of Medicine   Vol. 2: 4249
Gold Medal of the Society   Vol. 1: 18323
Gold Medallion   Vol. 1: 6532
Gold Medallion Book Awards   Vol. 1: 9016
Gold Nibs Award   Vol. 1: 2210
Gold Paintbrush   Vol. 2: 9365
Gold Pencil   Vol. 2: 9366
Gold Plaque   Vol. 2: 11526
Gold Plate Award recipient   Vol. 1: 10988
Gold Plate of ANDIN   Vol. 2: 8384
Gold Quill   Vol. 1: 10683
Gold Quill Award   Vol. 1: 4559
Gold Ribbon   Vol. 2: 1840
Gold Ribbon for Broadcast Excellence   Vol. 1: 6773
Gold Ribbon for Canadian Talent Development   Vol. 1: 6774
Gold Ribbon for Community Service   Vol. 1: 6775
Gold Ribbon for Distinguished Service   Vol. 1: 6773
Gold Ribbon for Engineering Achievement   Vol. 1: 6776
Gold Ribbon for News   Vol. 1: 6777
Gold Ribbon for Public Affairs and Documentaries   Vol. 1: 6778
Gold Screen Competition   Vol. 1: 13125
Gold Seal Award   Vol. 1: 6755
Gold Sesterce   Vol. 2: 11892
Gold Shell   Vol. 2: 11351
Gold, Silver, Bronze and Merit Awards   Vol. 2: 4168
Gold Space Medal   Vol. 2: 5151
Gold Star Award   Vol. 1: 14438
Gold Star Medal   Vol. 2: 10459
Gold Trout Award   Vol. 1: 18818
Gold Vine Award   Vol. 1: 6590
Gold Water Drop Award   Vol. 1: 5024
Goldberg Award; Rube   Vol. 1: 13527
Goldberg Prize for Manuscripts in the Humanities; Norman L. and Roselea J.   Vol. 1: 19979
Goldberger Award in Clinical Nutrition; Joseph B.   Vol. 1: 3023
Goldblatt Cytology Award; Maurice   Vol. 2: 6929
Golden ACE Award   Vol. 1: 12591
Golden Achievement Award   Vol. 1: 10487
Golden Achievement Awards   Vol. 1: 14672
Golden Aesop Prize   Vol. 2: 1521
Golden Anniversary Monograph Awards   Vol. 1: 18306
Golden Antenna - International Film/Video Festival on Telecommunications and Electronics   Vol. 2: 11848
Golden Apple
  Slovakia - Ministry of Culture, Slovak   Vol. 2: 10782
  World Federation of Travel Journalists and Writers   Vol 2: 6479
Golden Apple Award   Vol. 1: 711
Golden Apple - Star of the Year   Vol. 1: 9980
Golden Archer Award   Vol. 1: 9625
Golden Arrow of Achievement   Vol. 2: 7249
Golden Arrow of Courage   Vol. 2: 7250
Golden Award of the Micro Hall Art Center   Vol. 2: 7048
Golden Aztec Calendar Prize   Vol. 2: 8926
Golden Berlin Bear   Vol. 2: 6564
Golden Bobbin   Vol. 2: 1168

Golden Book Prize   Vol. 2: 8342
Golden Bowl   Vol. 2: 1694
Golden Brain Award   Vol. 1: 6541
Golden Bug Statuette   Vol. 2: 11626
Golden Bulldog Award   Vol. 1: 20139
Golden Bunch   Vol. 2: 10236
Golden Butterfly   Vol. 2: 7739
Golden Cable Award   Vol. 1: 18291
Golden Cactus   Vol. 2: 3452
Golden Carnation Awards for Excellence of Nutrition Coverage by Daily Newspaper Food Editors   Vol. 1: 7318
Golden Carrot Award   Vol. 1: 16584
Golden Cat Award   Vol. 2: 11568
Golden Chest International Television Festival   Vol. 2: 1518
Golden Chili Pepper Award   Vol. 1: 4844
Golden Choice Award   Vol. 1: 16890
Golden Circles Award   Vol. 1: 10946
Golden Coin Award   Vol. 1: 6264
Golden Crane Award   Vol. 1: 18292
Golden Crocodile   Vol. 2: 6020
Golden Deer   Vol. 2: 7314
Golden Diamond Awards   Vol. 1: 19912
Golden Diana   Vol. 2: 897
Golden Dozen   Vol. 1: 11304
Golden Dragon   Vol. 2: 10069
Golden Ear   Vol. 2: 6519
Golden Echo Prize   Vol. 2: 8371
Golden Elephant Award   Vol. 2: 7715
Golden Eye Trophy   Vol. 2: 9697
Golden Field Award   Vol. 1: 19913
Golden Fleece Award   Vol. 1: 16543
Golden Flower Award   Vol. 2: 1852
Golden Forceps Award   Vol. 1: 14748
Golden Fork Awards   Vol. 1: 10986
Golden Freight Car Awards Competition   Vol. 1: 12411
Golden Gate Awards   Vol. 1: 17039
Golden Gavel Award   Vol. 1: 18725
Golden Gazelle Awards   Vol. 1: 15548
Golden Globe Awards   Vol. 1: 9974
Golden Gloves National Champions   Vol. 1: 9631
Golden Hammer Award   Vol. 1: 16199
Golden Hammer Awards   Vol. 1: 14185
Golden Harp   Vol. 2: 9372
Golden Harp Television Festival   Vol. 2: 7824
Golden Head Mirror Honor Award   Vol. 1: 3953
Golden Heart Award   Vol. 1: 16891
Golden Horse Awards   Vol. 2: 12009
Golden Jubilee Commemoration Medal for Biology   Vol. 2: 7646
Golden Jubilee Commemoration Medal for Chemistry   Vol. 2: 7647
Golden Key Award   Vol. 1: 1178
Golden Kite Awards   Vol. 1: 17811
Golden Knight International Amateur Film and Video Festival   Vol. 2: 8912
Golden Knight International Amateur Film Festival   Vol. 2: 8912
Golden Lamp Award; EdPress Honor Awards -   Vol. 1: 8860
Golden Link Award   Vol. 1: 18293
Golden Lion Award   Vol. 1: 6634
Golden Lulu Achievement Award   Vol. 1: 11943
Golden Medallion Media Awards   Vol. 1: 18466
Golden Merit Award   Vol. 1: 14676
Golden Mike Award   Vol. 1: 10175
Golden Mike Awards   Vol. 1: 2807
Golden Nica   Vol. 2: 772
Golden Nut Award   Vol. 2: 11271
Golden Paladino   Vol. 2: 8313
Golden Palm   Vol. 2: 8106

Golden Peanut Research and Education Award   Vol. 1: 14462
Golden Pen
  Affaire de Coeur   Vol. 1: 182
  Association of Hungarian Journalists   Vol 2: 7292
  Eastern Coast Breweriana Association   Vol 1: 8787
  European Movement in Norway   Vol 2: 9883
Golden Pen Award   Vol. 1: 3481
Golden Pen of Freedom   Vol. 2: 6007
Golden Pen Prize   Vol. 2: 8343
Golden Penguin Awards   Vol. 1: 14055
Golden Phone Awards   Vol. 1: 10189
Golden Plate Awards   Vol. 1: 487
Golden Plough Trophy   Vol. 2: 4626
Golden Poet-Tree Award   Vol. 2: 7049
Golden Press Awards   Vol. 1: 2807
Golden Pyramid Competition Award   Vol. 1: 16537
Golden Quill Award
  International Society of Weekly Newspaper Editors   Vol. 1: 11304
  North American Ski Journalists Association   Vol 1: 15441
Golden R   Vol. 2: 8415
Golden Ram Award   Vol. 2: 10901
Golden Raster Award   Vol. 1: 9849
Golden Reel Award
  Academy of Canadian Cinema & Television   Vol. 1: 29
  International Television Association   Vol 1: 11348
Golden Ring - International Contest of Televised Sports, Lausanne   Vol. 2: 11738
Golden ROPE Awards   Vol. 1: 16820
Golden Rose   Vol. 1: 15126
Golden Rose of Montreux Award   Vol. 2: 11925
Golden Saddleman Award   Vol. 1: 20235
Golden Sands Rally   Vol. 2: 1535
Golden Score Award   Vol. 1: 4722
Golden Scroll Award
  Academy of Science Fiction, Fantasy and Horror Films   Vol. 1: 82
  American Academy of Achievement   Vol 1: 487
Golden Sheaf Awards   Vol. 1: 20597
Golden Sheaf Craft Awards   Vol. 1: 20597
Golden Ship Grand Prix of the President of the Bulgarian Red Cross   Vol. 2: 1528
Golden Shoestring; EdPress Honor Awards -   Vol. 1: 8861
Golden Shopping Cart Awards   Vol. 1: 12774
Golden Skier Award   Vol. 2: 11835
Golden Sower Award   Vol. 1: 15103
Golden Sower Young Adult Award   Vol. 1: 15104
Golden Space Needle Awards   Vol. 1: 17166
Golden Spike   Vol. 2: 11392
Golden Spike Advertising Award   Vol. 1: 5933
Golden Spikes Award   Vol. 1: 19914
Golden Spur Awards   Vol. 1: 20236
Golden Squeegee Awards Competition   Vol. 1: 17130
Golden Squirrel   Vol. 2: 9377
Golden Star Award   Vol. 1: 19612
Golden Swordfish   Vol. 1: 13600
Golden Toad Award   Vol. 1: 10918
Golden Toucan   Vol. 2: 1482
Golden Triangle Award   Vol. 1: 10007
Golden Trident   Vol. 1: 18854
Golden Tulip Award   Vol. 2: 12060
Golden Unicorn
  Alpine Countries International Filmmaking and Writing Academy   Vol. 2: 721

Amiens International Film Festival   Vol 2: 4890
Golden Werner-Medaille   Vol. 2: 11888
Golden Wheel Award   Vol. 1: 18294
Golden Wheel Society Awards   Vol. 1: 3968
Golden World of Travel Trophy   Vol. 1: 11367
Golden Youth Awards   Vol. 1: 6533
Goldene Gehlhoff-Ring   Vol. 2: 6638
Goldene Mozart-Medaille   Vol. 2: 826
Goldene Mozart-Nadel   Vol. 2: 827
Goldene Vereinsnadel   Vol. 2: 6540
Goldhill Award for Sculpture; Jack   Vol. 2: 3863
Goldman Environmental Prize   Vol. 1: 9633
Goldschmidt-Clermont Prize   Vol. 2: 3434
Goldschmidt Medal; V. M.   Vol. 1: 9542
Goldschmidt Preis; Viktor-Moritz-   Vol. 2: 6648
Goldsmith Award; Emily   Vol. 1: 5046
Goldsmith Book Prize   Vol. 1: 9635
Goldsmith Cup; Tony   Vol. 2: 3280
Goldsmith Prize in Investigative Journalism   Vol. 1: 9636
Goldsmith Research Awards   Vol. 1: 9637
Goldstein Award for Regional Reporters; Robin   Vol. 1: 14499
Goldstein Foundation Purchase Award; Ben and Beatrice   Vol. 1: 17693
Goldstein Memorial Award; Rose Zeitlin   Vol. 1: 18919
Goldwater Scholarship   Vol. 1: 3889
Goldy Award   Vol. 1: 8147
Golf Digest - LPGA Founders Cup
  Golf Digest   Vol. 1: 9644
  Ladies Professional Golf Association   Vol 1: 11758
Golf Writers Award   Vol. 1: 9641
Golfer of the Year   Vol. 2: 2129
Golgi Lecture   Vol. 2: 6707
Golgi; Premio Camillo   Vol. 2: 8072
Golmick Scholarship; Paul   Vol. 2: 2602
Gomez Award; Lefty   Vol. 1: 1322
Gomez de la Serna; Prenio Ramon   Vol. 2: 11301
Gomez Prize; Rodrigo   Vol. 2: 8944
Gompers American Red Cross National Labor Award; Samuel   Vol. 1: 3914
Goncourt Prize   Vol. 2: 4798
Gondos Memorial Service Award; Victor   Vol. 1: 17555
Gonin Medal
  International Council of Ophthalmology   Vol. 2: 9484
  International Federation of Ophthalmological Societies   Vol 2: 9502
Gonzales; Distintivo al Merito Docente Gabriel   Vol. 2: 1672
Gonzalez Camarena; Guillermo   Vol. 2: 9087
Gonzalez Ochoa Award; Dr. Antonio   Vol. 2: 9099
Gonzalez - PUIC; Premio Gea   Vol. 2: 9024
Good Conduct Medal   Vol. 1: 19162
Good Design Selection   Vol. 2: 8817
Good Government Pharmacist of the Year Award   Vol. 1: 3379
Good Guys Awards   Vol. 1: 15028
Good Memorial Award; Harry M.   Vol. 1: 10300
Good Neighbor Award
  American Red Cross   Vol. 1: 3915
  International Good Neighbor Council   Vol 2: 9075
  Royal Neighbors of America   Vol. 1: 16944
Good Samaritan Award
  American Police Hall of Fame   Vol. 1: 3555
  National Catholic Development Conference   Vol 1: 13540

Good Sportsmanship Award Vol. 1: 3981
Good Steward Award Vol. 1: 12788
Goodacre Medal and Gift; Walter Vol. 2: 2286
Goodall Award; Charles Vol. 1: 8363
Goode Memorial Award; Harry Vol. 1: 2027
Goodfellowship Award Vol. 1: 3222
Goodman and Gilman Award in Drug Receptor Pharmacology Vol. 1: 4236
Goodman Award; Arnold Vol. 1: 18955
Goodman Fielder Wattie Book Award Vol. 2: 9705
Goodman-Malamuth AAUA Foundation Award; Dr. Leo and Margaret Vol. 1: 1227
Goodnight Award for Outstanding Performance as a Dean; Scott Vol. 1: 13327
Goodwill Ambassadors for UNICEF Vol. 1: 18950
Goodwill Industries Volunteer Services (GIVS) Volunteer Group of the Year Vol. 1: 9660
Goodwill Industries Volunteer Services (GIVS) Volunteer of the Year Vol. 1: 9661
Goodwin Award of Merit; Charles J. Vol. 1: 3417
Goodyear Award; Charles Vol. 1: 1499
Goodyear Conservation Awards Vol. 1: 13030
Goodys Dash Series Vol. 1: 12902
Gorder Award; Zenno A. Vol. 1: 5027
Gordon Award; Alan Vol. 1: 6003
Gordon Award; Eva L. Vol. 1: 3185
Gordon Award for Children's Science Literature; Eva L. Vol. 1: 3185
Gordon Award for Excellence in the Field of Advising; NACADA Virginia N. Vol. 1: 12585
Gordon Award; Seth Vol. 1: 10735
Gordon Award; Winston Vol. 1: 7060
Gordon-Lennox Cup Vol. 2: 4036
Gordon Memorial Award; Alan Vol. 1: 4251
Gordon Memorial Award - Health Insurance Industry Man of the Year; Harold R. Vol. 1: 13127
Gore-Browne Trophy Vol. 2: 2796
Gorgas Medal Vol. 1: 5883
Gorin Award for Outstanding Achievement in Rural Health Care; Louis Vol. 1: 14649
Gorin Award; Susan Phillips Vol. 1: 8313
Gorini; Fondation Costantino Vol. 2: 5525
Gorman Memorial Award; Tom Vol. 1: 9718
Gorman Trophy; Peter Vol. 1: 6971
Gorterprijs; Herman Vol. 2: 9638
Gorthy Award; Willis C. Vol. 1: 3938
Gospel Music Hall of Fame Vol. 1: 9672
Gosselet; Prix Vol. 2: 5310
Gosset Award; George R. Vol. 1: 4155
Gotshal World Trade Arbitration Medal; Sylvan Vol. 1: 803
Gottesfeld Award Vol. 1: 17445
Gottheil Award; Richard J. H. Vol. 1: 20638
Gottheil Memorial Bone Marrow Transplant Career Development Awards; Oncology Nursing Foundation/Josh Vol. 1: 15643
Gottingen Academy of Sciences Prize Vol. 2: 6903
Gottingen Academy of Sciences Prize for Biology Vol. 2: 6904
Gottingen Academy of Sciences Prize for Chemistry Vol. 2: 6905
Gottingen Academy of Sciences Prize for German History Vol. 2: 6906
Gottingen Academy of Sciences Prize for Physics Vol. 2: 6907
Gottlieb Award Vol. 1: 55
Gottlieb Memorial Award; Jeffrey A. Vol. 1: 19876
Gottlieb Prize; Murray Vol. 1: 12171

Gottlieb Trophy; NBA Rookie of the Year - Eddie Vol. 1: 13454
Gottschalk Medal Vol. 2: 174
Gottschalk Prize; Louis Vol. 1: 4066
Gottwaldov Festival of Children's Films Vol. 2: 1890
Gouancz Prize; Sir Israel Vol. 2: 2228
Gouden Eekhoorn Vol. 2: 9377
Gouden Griffel Vol. 2: 9366
Gouden Penseel Vol. 2: 9365
Gouden Strop Vol. 2: 9441
Goudy Distinguished Lecture; Frederic W. Vol. 1: 16866
Goueram-Toekenning Vol. 2: 10901
Gould Memorial Award; Maurice M. Vol. 1: 15561
Gould Memorial Literary Award Vol. 1: 3223
Gould; Prix de la Fondation Florence Vol. 2: 5376
Gould Prize; Benjamin Apthorp Vol. 1: 12670
Gould Prize; Glenn Vol. 1: 6738
Goulden Memorial Award; Loran L. Vol. 1: 9087
Gourley Award in Pomology; Joseph Harvey Vol. 1: 4145
Goveia Prize; Elsa Vol. 1: 5723
Governing Board's Award for the Best Paper Vol. 1: 19902
Government Achievement Award Vol. 1: 14127
Government Affairs Award
  American Society of Heating, Refrigerating and Air-Conditioning Engineers Vol. 1: 4585
  National Association of the Remodeling Industry Vol 1: 13362
Government Civil Engineer of the Year Award Vol. 1: 4459
Government Computer News Awards Program Vol. 1: 9674
Government Executive Leadership Award Vol. 1: 9678
Government of Canada Award Vol. 1: 20533
Governmental Affairs and Public Service Award Vol. 1: 14583
Governor General Art Award Vol. 2: 9750
Governor General's Awards for Architecture Vol. 1: 16920
Governor General's Awards in Commemoration of the Persons Case Vol. 1: 18472
Governor General's Conservation Awards Vol. 1: 18767
Governor General's Literary Awards Vol. 1: 6739
Governor General's Literary Awards for Children's Literature Vol. 1: 6739
Governor General's Literary Awards for Translation Vol. 1: 6739
Governor of the Year Vol. 1: 14379
Governor's Award
  International Society of Certified Electronics Technicians Vol. 1: 11282
  SPIE - The International Society for Optical Engineers Vol 1: 18319
  Western Society of Engineers Vol 1: 20224
Governors Award Vol. 1: 12591
Governor's Award for Distinguished Achievement in Culture, the Arts and Humanities Vol. 1: 9831
Governor's Awards for the Arts Vol. 1: 9247
Governor's Cup Vol. 1: 8538
Governor's Green Survival Award Vol. 1: 1063
Governor's National Leadership Award Vol. 1: 13092
Governor's Screenwriting Competition Vol. 1: 20064

Governor's Writers Award Vol. 1: 20130
Gowdy Award; Basketball Hall of Fame Curt Vol. 1: 12561
Goyau; Prix Georges Vol. 2: 5859
GPA Book Award Vol. 2: 7777
GPA Citation for Service Vol. 1: 9504
GPA Dublin International Piano Competition Vol. 2: 7779
GPA Recognition Award Vol. 1: 9505
GRA Annual Awards Vol. 1: 9686
Graduate Award Vol. 2: 3345
Graduate Awards Vol. 1: 13736
Graduate Fellowships Vol. 1: 9990
Graduate Fellowships in Mycology Vol. 1: 12544
Graduate Grants for Research Vol. 1: 10992
Graduate of the Year Vol. 1: 9662
Graduate of the Year Award Vol. 1: 7204
Graduate Prizes Vol. 2: 4332
Graduate Research Prizes Vol. 1: 12545
Graduate Student Award
  Canadian Society of Microbiologists Vol. 1: 7218
  Coordinating Committee on Women in the Historical Profession - Conference Group on Women's History Vol 1: 8276
  Materials Research Society Vol 1: 12122
  United States Federation for Culture Collections Vol 1: 19340
Graduate Student Competition Awards Vol. 1: 7158
Graduate Student Paper Award Vol. 1: 16976
Graduate Student Research Award Vol. 1: 4754
Graduate Student Research Competition in Population and Environmental Psychology Vol. 1: 3754
Graduate Study Fellowship Vol. 1: 7437
Graduateship of the City and Guilds of London Institute Vol. 2: 2624
Grady Award for Interpreting Chemistry for the Public; James T. Vol. 1: 1557
Grady - James H. Stack Award for Interpreting Chemistry for the Public; James T. Vol. 1: 1557
Graef Memorial Scholarship; Irving Vol. 1: 14345
Graffin Lectureship Award Vol. 1: 1417
Graffis Award; The Vol. 1: 14085
Graffis Award; Herb Vol. 1: 14085
Graffis Award; Joe Vol. 1: 14085
Graffis Cup; Herb Vol. 1: 16468
Graffis Fund for Zoological Research Grants; Nixon Vol. 1: 9728
Graham and Dodd Award Vol. 1: 5554
Graham Award; Duncan Vol. 1: 16938
Graham Award of Merit; James H. Vol. 1: 16939
Graham Book Prize; Edgar Vol. 2: 4334
Graham Foundation Grant Vol. 1: 9693
Graham Memorial Prize; Edgar Vol. 2: 4334
Graham Senior Clinician Award; John Vol. 1: 901
Grain d'Or Vol. 2: 11791
Gralnick Award; Dr. Alexander Vol. 1: 1144
Gralnick Foundation-High Point Hospital Award Vol. 1: 3834
Gramatky Memorial Award; Hardie Vol. 1: 5047
Grammy Awards Vol. 1: 12655
Grammy Living Legends Award Vol. 1: 12656
Gran Bolivar de Oro Vol. 2: 1596
Gran Canaria International Short Film Festival Vol. 2: 11257
Gran Cruz Vol. 2: 1705
Gran Cruz de la Universidad del Valle Vol. 2: 1754

Gran Premio de Cine Espanol Vol. 2: 11267
Gran Premio de Cine Vasco Vol. 2: 11267
Gran Premio de Honor Argentores Vol. 2: 30
Gran Premio del Festival de Bilbao Vol. 2: 11267
Gran Premio Generalitat de Catalunya Vol. 2: 11394
Gran Premio Libertador Simon Bolivar Vol. 2: 12109
Gran Premio Nacional de Medicina Vol. 2: 12088
Gran Trofeo Golfo di Salerno Vol. 2: 8417
Granberg Award; Mickey Vol. 1: 13280
Grand Award
  American First Day Cover Society Vol. 1: 2058
  CIBC National Music Festival Vol 1: 7693
  Mediacom Vol 1: 12158
  The Wine Spectator Vol 1: 20332
Grand Award for Outstanding Support of Traffic Safety Vol. 1: 9920
Grand Champion and Reserve Grand Champion Boar and Gilt Vol. 1: 14140
Grand Collier Vol. 2: 1787
Grand Conceptor Award Vol. 1: 1825
Grand Cordon of the Supreme Order of the Chrysanthemum Vol. 2: 8584
Grand Effie Vol. 1: 2998
Grand International Trophy for Excellence of Design and Fabric Vol. 1: 13679
Grand Journalism Prize Vol. 2: 9943
Grand Master Award Vol. 1: 17113
Grand National Exhibition Vol. 1: 812
Grand National Medal General Francisco de Paula Santander Vol. 2: 1657
Grand National Pulling Circuit Rookie of the Year Vol. 1: 14901
Grand Prior's Trophies Vol. 2: 3742
Grand Prix Vol. 2: 4902
Grand Prix Amon Ra Vol. 2: 5195
Grand Prix C. F. Ramuz Vol. 2: 11723
Grand Prix Chimie Industrielle Vol. 2: 6356
Grand Prix d'Architecture de l'Academie des Beaux-Arts Vol. 2: 5352
Grand Prix de Composition de Ville d'Avray Vol. 2: 4977
Grand Prix de la Bibliotheque Nationale Vol. 2: 4989
Grand Prix de la Chanson Francaise Vol. 2: 6250
Grand Prix de la Critique Litteraire Vol. 2: 4956
Grand Prix de la Fondation pour la Recherche Medicale Vol. 2: 5262
Grand Prix de la Francophonie Vol. 2: 5800
Grand Prix de la Litterature Vol. 2: 6260
Grand Prix de la Maison de Poesie Vol. 2: 6104
Grand Prix de la Melodie Francaise Vol. 2: 6408
Grand Prix de la Mer Vol. 2: 4918
Grand Prix de la Musique Francaise d'Aujourd'hui Vol. 2: 6256
Grand Prix de la Musique Symphonique Vol. 2: 6251
Grand Prix de la Photographie de la Ville de Paris Vol. 2: 6089
Grand Prix de la Poesie
  Societe des Auteurs, Compositeurs, Editeurs de Musique Vol. 2: 6255
  Societe des Gens de Lettres de France Vol 2: 6261
Grand Prix de la Publicite Vol. 2: 5319
Grand Prix de la Societe de Chimie Vol. 2: 6356
Grand Prix de la Societe des Gens de Lettres Vol. 2: 6262

Grand Prix de la Technique de la Ville de Paris Vol. 2: 6090
Grand Prix de la Ville de Paris
  City of Paris International Competitions Vol. 2: 5034
  Rostropovitch International Cello Competition Vol 2: 6201
Grand Prix de la Ville de Tours Vol. 2: 5193
Grand Prix de la Ville de Villeurbanne Vol. 2: 5175
Grand Prix de la Ville de Wattrelos Vol. 2: 6477
Grand Prix de l'Academie des Sciences Morales et Politiques Vol. 2: 5711
Grand Prix de l'AIPH and Grand Prix d'Excellence Vol. 2: 9467
Grand Prix de l'Architecture de la Ville de Paris Vol. 2: 6091
Grand Prix de l'Audiovisuel Vol. 2: 6254
Grand Prix de l'Edition Musicale Vol. 2: 6252
Grand Prix de l'Histoire - Moet-Hennessy Vol. 2: 6120
Grand Prix de l'Humour Vol. 2: 6253
Grand Prix de Litterature Vol. 2: 5801
Grand Prix de Litterature Francaise hors de France Vol. 2: 1287
Grand Prix de Litterature Paul Morand Vol. 2: 5802
Grand Prix de l'Oeuvre Musicale Audiovisuelle Vol. 2: 6254
Grand Prix de Philosophie Vol. 2: 5803
Grand Prix de Physique Jean Ricard Vol. 2: 6364
Grand Prix de Poesie Vol. 2: 5804
Grand Prix de Poesie Albert Mockel Vol. 2: 1289
Grand Prix de S. A. S. Le Prince Rainier III Vol. 2: 9310
Grand Prix de Vitesse en Planeur a Luchon Vol. 2: 5171
Grand Prix des Arts de la Ville de Paris Vol. 2: 6092
Grand Prix des Biennales Internationales de Poesie Vol. 2: 1170
Grand Prix des Lectrices de *Elle* Vol. 2: 5110
Grand Prix des Metiers d'Art Vol. 2: 6473
Grand Prix des Poetes Vol. 2: 6255
Grand Prix des Sciences Chimiques et Naturelles Vol. 2: 5695
Grand Prix des Sciences Mathematiques et Physiques Vol. 2: 5695
Grand Prix des Treize Vol. 2: 5030
Grand Prix d'Histoire Vol. 2: 6102
Grand Prix d'Histoire de la Vallee aux Loups Vol. 2: 6102
Grand Prix d'Histoire Nationale Maurice Payard Vol. 2: 4881
Grand Prix d'Honneur Vol. 2: 11825
Grand Prix d'Interpretation de la Musique Francaise d'Aujourd'hui Vol. 2: 6256
Grand Prix du Brazil Trophy Vol. 1: 14644
Grand Prix du disque (Canada) Vol. 1: 7056
Grand Prix du Disque Frederic Chopin Vol. 2: 10066
Grand Prix du Festival Europeen Vol. 2: 5126
Grand Prix du FIFAL Vol. 2: 11793
Grand Prix du Jazz Vol. 2: 6257
Grand Prix du Journal d'Entreprise Vol. 2: 6434
Grand Prix du Journalisme Radiophonique Vol. 2: 5070
Grand Prix du Jury Vol. 2: 5004
Grand Prix du Livre de Montreal Vol. 1: 17019
Grand Prix du Rayonnement de la Langue Francaise Vol. 2: 5805
Grand Prix du Roman Vol. 2: 5806

Grand Prix du Romantisme Vol. 2: 6102
Grand Prix du Souvenir Napoleonien Vol. 2: 5214
Grand Prix Europeen Vol. 2: 5080
Grand Prix FIFART Vol. 2: 11795
Grand Prix Hydro-Quebec Vol. 1: 16433
Grand Prix ICA Vol. 2: 10691
Grand Prix ICA - Prix de la Meilleure Chanson en Langue Traditionnelle Vol. 2: 10687
Grand Prix ICA - Prix de la Recherche Scientifique Vol. 2: 10688
Grand Prix ICA - Prix de Sculpture Vol. 2: 10689
Grand Prix ICA - Prix du Meilleur Film Documentaire Vol. 2: 10690
Grand Prix International d'Arts et Lettres Notre-Dame et la Mer Vol. 2: 4958
Grand Prix International de Poesie de la Ville de Grenoble Vol. 2: 6302
Grand Prix International Video Danse Vol. 2: 6465
Grand Prix Ivo Pogorelich Vol. 1: 18495
Grand Prix Litteraire de la Femme Vol. 2: 4997
Grand Prix litteraire de la Societe Saint-Jean-Baptiste de la Mauricie Vol. 1: 17379
Grand Prix Litteraire de la Ville de Lyon Vol. 2: 6474
Grand Prix Litteraire de l'Afrique Noire Vol. 2: 4919
Grand Prix Litteraire de l'Oceanie Vol. 2: 4920
Grand Prix Litteraire de Madagascar Vol. 2: 4921
Grand Prix Litteraire Sola-Cabiati Vol. 2: 6097
Grand Prix Magdeleine Cluzel Vol. 2: 6263
Grand Prix Marcel Mignon Vol. 2: 1095
Grand Prix Montreal - Brive du livre pour l'adolescence Vol. 1: 17020
Grand Prix Musical de la Ville de Paris Vol. 2: 6093
Grand Prix National de la Chanson Vol. 2: 5273
Grand Prix National de la Creation Audiovisuelle Vol. 2: 5274
Grand Prix National de la Creation Industrielle Vol. 2: 5275
Grand Prix National de la Danse Vol. 2: 5276
Grand Prix National de la Museographie Vol. 2: 5277
Grand Prix National de la Musique Vol. 2: 5278
Grand Prix National de la Peinture Vol. 2: 5279
Grand Prix National de la Photographie Vol. 2: 5280
Grand Prix National de la Poesie Vol. 2: 5281
Grand Prix National de la Sculpture Vol. 2: 5282
Grand Prix National de la Traduction Vol. 2: 5283
Grand Prix National de l'Archeologie Vol. 2: 5284
Grand Prix National de l'Architecture Vol. 2: 5285
Grand Prix National de l'Entreprise Culturelle Vol. 2: 5286
Grand Prix National des Arts
  French Ministry of Culture and Communication Vol. 2: 5279
  French Ministry of Culture and Communication Vol 2: 5282
  French Ministry of Culture and Communication Vol 2: 5287

Grand Prix National des Arts Graphique   Vol. 2: 5287
Grand Prix National des Lettres   Vol. 2: 5288
Grand Prix National des Metiers d'Art   Vol. 2: 5289
Grand Prix National d'Histoire   Vol. 2: 5290
Grand Prix National du Cinema   Vol. 2: 5291
Grand Prix National du Cirque   Vol. 2: 5292
Grand Prix National du Patrimoine   Vol. 2: 5293
Grand Prix National du Theatre   Vol. 2: 5294
Grand Prix of Honour for a Yugoslav Artist   Vol. 2: 10794
Grand Prix of Sofia   Vol. 2: 1525
Grand Prix of the Americas   Vol. 1: 12436
Grand Prix of the Dutch Film Golden Calf   Vol. 2: 9383
Grand Prix of the European Festival   Vol. 2: 5126
Grand Prix of the Film Festival Mannheim   Vol. 2: 6954
Grand Prix of the League of Red Cross and Red Crescent Societies   Vol. 2: 1528
Grand Prix of the Town of Varna   Vol. 2: 1532
Grand Prix Paul Feval de Litterature Populaire de la Societe des Gens de Lettres   Vol. 2: 6264
Grand Prix Poncetton de la Societe des Gens de Lettres   Vol. 2: 6265
Grand Prix Quinquennal de l'Etat   Vol. 2: 1087
Grand Prix RTL/Poesie 1   Vol. 2: 6207
Grand Prix SACD   Vol. 2: 6395
Grand Prix Scientifique de la Ville de Paris   Vol. 2: 6094
Grand Prix SOPEXA du Sommelier   Vol. 2: 5228
Grand Prix Suisse de la Photographie - Jeunesse en Suisse   Vol. 2: 11951
Grand Prix Technique   Vol. 2: 5004
Grand Prix Thyde Monnier   Vol. 2: 6266
Grand Prix/Virginia Slims Tournament of the Year   Vol. 2: 3540
Grand Prize
   Ambiente-Incontri   Vol. 2: 8095
   Brussels International Fantasy Film Festival   Vol. 2: 1091
   Carmel Music Society   Vol 1: 7316
   Montreal Urban Community Arts Council   Vol 1: 12434
Grand Prize for a Novel   Vol. 2: 11644
Grand Prize for Literature   Vol. 2: 11645
Grand Prize for Press Freedom   Vol. 1: 10511
Grand Prize of AIPM/Grand Prize of Excellence   Vol. 2: 9467
Grand Prize of French Poets   Vol. 2: 6313
Grand Prize of the National Festival of Hungarian Non-professional Film and Videomakers   Vol. 2: 7315
Grand Slam Award   Vol. 1: 11056
Grand Slam of Tennis   Vol. 2: 3483
Grande Premio de Romance e Novela da Associacao Portuguesa de Escritores   Vol. 2: 10309
Grandmaison; Prix Antoine   Vol. 2: 4892
Grandmaster   Vol. 2: 7227
Grandmaster Award   Vol. 1: 12549
Grands Prix de la Fondation Napoleon   Vol. 2: 5214
Grands Prix du *Journal de Montreal*   Vol. 1: 18878
Grands Prix Litteraire de la Ville de Paris   Vol. 2: 6095
Grands Prix Paul-Gilson   Vol. 2: 5070
Graney Award (Media Award); Jack   Vol. 1: 6816
Granjon Prize   Vol. 2: 3435

Grant Award; Eugene L.
   American Society for Engineering Education   Vol. 1: 4092
   American Society for Quality Control   Vol 1: 4283
Grant Faculty Scholars; William T.   Vol. 1: 9695
Grant Memorial Award; Peter J.   Vol. 1: 1343
Grant Memorial Prize; John   Vol. 2: 10516
Grant or Prize   Vol. 2: 4710
Grant Program   Vol. 1: 19403
Grant/Stan Getz Award; Felix   Vol. 1: 6412
Grants   Vol. 1: 13770
Grants for Astrological Research   Vol. 1: 11229
Grants for Field Research   Vol. 2: 7234
Grants for Research Projects   Vol. 1: 8553
Grants-in-Aid of Research   Vol. 1: 17272
Grants-in-Aid Program
   Lyndon Baines Johnson Foundation   Vol. 1: 11587
   Society for the Psychological Study of Social Issues   Vol 1: 17633
Grants Program   Vol. 1: 11497
Grants to Young Composers   Vol. 1: 4528
Graphic Arts Awards Competition   Vol. 1: 16412
Graphic Arts Awards Competition for Non-Heatset Printers   Vol. 1: 16420
Graphics Prize Fiera di Bologna for Children and Young Adults   Vol. 2: 8172
Grasselli Medal   Vol. 1: 17802
Grassi; Fondazione Premio Battista   Vol. 2: 8062
Grassi Prize   Vol. 2: 8195
Grassland Society of Southern Africa Awards   Vol. 2: 10874
Grassroots Government Leadership Award   Vol. 1: 13372
Grauer Award; Ben   Vol. 1: 15875
Grauls Prize; Noordstarfonds - Dr. Jan   Vol. 2: 1275
Graves Lecture   Vol. 2: 7831
Graves Prize; Robert
   Hungarian Writers' Union   Vol. 2: 7390
   Hungary - Ministry of Culture and Education   Vol 2: 7404
Gravesande Prize; G. H.'s -   Vol. 2: 9348
Gray Award; Asa   Vol. 1: 4755
Gray Award; Eva Kenworthy   Vol. 1: 1338
Gray Award; Henry   Vol. 1: 909
Gray Award; Stanley   Vol. 2: 3117
Gray Awards for Excellence in the Teaching of Private Enterprise; L. W. (Bill)   Vol. 1: 18630
Gray Citation of Merit; William S.   Vol. 1: 11186
Gray Fellowships; Stanley   Vol. 2: 3118
Gray Medal; ICRU -   Vol. 1: 10861
Graznak Award; Michael   Vol. 1: 8266
Grealis Special Achievement Award; Walt   Vol. 1: 6762
Great American Artificer Award   Vol. 1: 13975
Great American Award   Vol. 1: 18980
Great American Family Recognition Program   Vol. 1: 2015
Great American Home Awards   Vol. 1: 14935
Great Gold Medal   Vol. 2: 11527
Great Heart Award   Vol. 1: 19982
Great Idea Contest   Vol. 1: 11423
Great Lakes - Skakel Award   Vol. 1: 1418
Great Menu Award   Vol. 1: 14624
Great Stone Face Book Award   Vol. 1: 15167
Great Stone Face Hall of Fame   Vol. 1: 15167
Great Swedish Heritage Award   Vol. 1: 18540
Great Teachers Award   Vol. 1: 391

Greater Haverhill Arts Association Annual Exhibition   Vol. 1: 9711
Greater Lynn International Color Slide Salon   Vol. 1: 9713
Greater Midwest International Exhibition   Vol. 1: 7480
Greater Union Awards   Vol. 2: 685
Greathouse Distinguished Leadership Award; Frank   Vol. 1: 5818
Greathouse Medal; Walser S.   Vol. 1: 5048
Greaves-Walker Award; Albert Frederick   Vol. 1: 1462
Greek National Tourist Organization Awards   Vol. 2: 7198
Greeley Award; Horace   Vol. 1: 15134
Greeley Award; Samuel Arnold   Vol. 1: 4460
Greeley Award; William B.   Vol. 1: 2100
Greeley Local Government Service Award; Samuel A.   Vol. 1: 3876
Green-Armytage and Spackman Travelling Scholarship   Vol. 2: 3956
Green Audio Excellence Award; Rose Layos   Vol. 1: 6002
Green Award; Daniel H.   Vol. 1: 6052
Green Award; Fletcher M.   Vol. 1: 18214
Green Award for Entrepreneurial Science; Cecil   Vol. 1: 17109
Green Award; Gordon J.   Vol. 1: 7098
Green Globe Award   Vol. 1: 9234
Green Journalism Awards; Charles E.   Vol. 1: 9841
Green - Ramsdell Award   Vol. 1: 18214
Green Round Hill Trophy; Colonel   Vol. 1: 3604
Green Section Award   Vol. 1: 19360
Green Survival Award; Governor's   Vol. 1: 1063
Green Thumb of the Year   Vol. 1: 18962
Greenaway Medal; Kate   Vol. 2: 3568
Greenberg Award; Noah   Vol. 1: 3174
Greenburger Award; Francis J.   Vol. 1: 9720
Greene Award in Bryology; Stanley   Vol. 1: 10677
Greene Homeland Defense Award; Lorne   Vol. 1: 1583
Greene, Jr., Award; General Wallace M.   Vol. 1: 12082
Greene Medal; Arnold   Vol. 2: 3219
Greene Memorial Award; Jerry   Vol. 1: 13520
Greene Memorial United States Numismatics - YN Exhibit Award; Gordon Z.   Vol. 1: 3224
Greene Trophy; W. Henry "Stud"   Vol. 1: 16214
Greenman Award; Jesse M.   Vol. 1: 6485
The Greensboro Review Literary Awards   Vol. 1: 9722
Greenstone Diving Safety Award; Leonard   Vol. 1: 13377
Greenwich Prize; Royal Naval College,   Vol. 2: 3350
Greer Prize; Dessie   Vol. 1: 12610
Gregg Award; Dr. Randy   Vol. 1: 6972
Gregg Award in Business Education; John Robert   Vol. 1: 9617
Gregor Scholarship; Helen Frances   Vol. 1: 15712
Gregori Aminoffs Pris   Vol. 2: 11542
Gregory Award; Joseph T.   Vol. 1: 18090
Gregory Awards; Eric   Vol. 2: 4389
Gregory Medal; Eric   Vol. 2: 7792
Gregory Medal; Herbert E.   Vol. 1: 15890
Gregson's Founder Award   Vol. 1: 17727
Greig Scholarship; Walter T.   Vol. 2: 2603
Greim Award; Willard   Vol. 1: 429
Grelaud; Fondation Leon   Vol. 2: 5617
Grenfell Henry Lawson Festival of Arts Awards   Vol. 2: 415

Grenzebach Awards for Outstanding Research in Philanthropy for Education; John   Vol. 1: 9
Gresham Award; D. Todd   Vol. 1: 12004
Greshoff Prize; J.   Vol. 2: 9349
Greve Award; Bell   Vol. 1: 14584
Grey Award; Earle   Vol. 1: 27
Grey Award for Best Acting Performance in Television in a Leading Role; Earle   Vol. 1: 327
Grey Cup   Vol. 1: 6878
Grice Award; Winthrop W.   Vol. 1: 10001
Grierson Award   Vol. 2: 2347
Grierson Award; John   Vol. 1: 2047
Grierson International Gold Medal Award; John   Vol. 1: 17902
Griffen Award; Walter Burley   Vol. 2: 609
Griffes American Music Composers Competition; Charles Tomlinson   Vol. 1: 9726
Griffin Award; Charles A.   Vol. 1: 866
Griffin Press Award   Vol. 2: 193
Griffin Press Literary Award   Vol. 2: 400
Griffin Rolex Award; Ellen   Vol. 1: 11759
Griffith Award; D. W.   Vol. 1: 8665
Griffith Award; Ruby   Vol. 1: 6571
Griffith Awards; David Wark   Vol. 1: 13466
Griffith Medal and Prize; A. A.   Vol. 2: 3134
Griffith Memorial Award; Clark C.   Vol. 1: 18758
Grillparzer Prize; Franz   Vol. 2: 7113
Grillparzerringe   Vol. 2: 766
Grimley Award; Horace   Vol. 2: 3519
Grimm Prize; Harold J.   Vol. 1: 17297
Grimwade Medal; John   Vol. 2: 2399
Grindley Medal   Vol. 1: 211
Grinter Distinguished Service Award; Linton E.   Vol. 1: 93
Griscom Award; Ludlow   Vol. 1: 1344
Griswold Award; S. Smith   Vol. 1: 219
Griswold Prize in American Law and Society; Littleton -   Vol. 1: 2296
Grocers Care Awards   Vol. 1: 14093
Grohmann Award; H. Victor   Vol. 1: 9998
Grohmann Prize; Will   Vol. 2: 6511
Grolier Award for Research in School Librarianship   Vol. 1: 7024
Grolier Foundation Award   Vol. 1: 2817
Grolier National Library Week Grant   Vol. 1: 2962
Grolier Poetry Prize   Vol. 1: 11735
Groot Fellowship; Jennifer C.   Vol. 1: 4013
Gross Animation Award; Yoram   Vol. 2: 685
Gross Restoration Award; Frank   Vol. 1: 20045
Grosse Literaturstipendien des Landes Tirol   Vol. 2: 728
Grosser Fotopreis der Schweiz - Jugend in der Schweiz   Vol. 2: 11951
Grosser Literaturpreis der Bayerische Akademie der Schonen Kunste   Vol. 2: 6552
Grosser Oesterreichischer Staatspreis   Vol. 2: 759
Grosser Schillerpreis   Vol. 2: 11729
Grossinger Award for Humanitarian Endeavor; Paul   Vol. 1: 89
Grossman Award; Louis I.   Vol. 1: 995
Grossmann Young Author Award; Marcus A.   Vol. 1: 5356
Grosvenor Medal   Vol. 1: 14071
Grote Prijs van de Nederlandse Film Gouden Kalf   Vol. 2: 9383
Grote Prys Alfons Blomme   Vol. 2: 1231
Grotius; Prix   Vol. 2: 11751
Grounds Maintenance Awards   Vol. 1: 16485
Grounds Manager of the Year   Vol. 1: 16486

Group Achievement Award
   National Aeronautics and Space Administration   Vol. 1: 12739
   Wildlife Society   Vol 1: 20301
Group Citation for Bravery   Vol. 2: 207
Group Trophies   Vol. 1: 20246
Group Volunteer of the Year Award   Vol. 1: 2214
Grove-Rasmussen Memorial Award; Morten   Vol. 1: 928
Groves Fund; Donald   Vol. 1: 3275
Grow Award; Malcolm C.   Vol. 1: 18087
Growth and Promotion Award   Vol. 1: 18702
Grubenwehrehrenzeichen   Vol. 2: 740
Gruber Award and Heidi Castleman Award for Excellence in Chamber Music Teaching   Vol. 1: 7502
Gruber Award for Excellence in Chamber Music Teaching   Vol. 1: 7502
Gruber Fund Award of the AAD; Lila   Vol. 1: 549
Gruber Memorial Cancer Research Award and Lectureship; Lila   Vol. 1: 548
Gruber Scholarship Program; Kathern F.   Vol. 1: 6406
Grulee Award; Clifford G.   Vol. 1: 670
Grumbacher Art Award and Gold Medal   Vol. 1: 12611
Grumbacher Corporation Award   Vol. 1: 10030
Grumbacher Gold Medal   Vol. 1: 15619
Grumbacher Gold Medallion Award   Vol. 1: 9711
Grumbacher Golden Award   Vol. 1: 17026
Grumbacher Silver Medallion; M.   Vol. 1: 20348
Grumbridge Pacific Island Trophy; Jack   Vol. 2: 3781
Gruner International Lieder Competition; City of London Walther   Vol. 2: 2632
Gruner International Lieder Competition; Walther   Vol. 2: 2632
Grunfeld Memorial Award and Medal; Dr. Paul   Vol. 2: 3135
Grunfeld-Preis; Paul   Vol. 2: 6850
Grunfeld Prize; Paul   Vol. 2: 6850
Gryphius-Preis; Andreas-   Vol. 2: 6525
GSA Distinguished Service Award   Vol. 1: 9561
GTE Academic All-America Hall of Fame   Vol. 1: 7941
GTE Academic All-American of the Year   Vol. 1: 7942
Guaccero Prize; Domenico   Vol. 2: 8191
Guadelupe Posada Prize; Jose   Vol. 2: 9088
Gual; Premi Adria   Vol. 2: 11157
Guardia Memorial Trophy; Ed   Vol. 1: 19370
Guardian Award   Vol. 1: 12034
The Guardian Children's Fiction Award   Vol. 2: 2954
The Guardian Fiction Prize   Vol. 2: 2955
Guardian Student Drama Award   Vol. 2: 10535
Guardians of the Seas Award   Vol. 1: 19709
Guardons de l'Agricultura, Ramaderia, Forest, Conservacio de la Natura i Pesca Catalana   Vol. 2: 11170
Gude, Jr. Award; Adolph E.   Vol. 1: 4747
Guelph Spring Festival   Vol. 1: 11590
Guenther Award in the Chemistry of Essential Oils and Related Products; Ernest   Vol. 1: 1558
Guenther Award in the Chemistry of Natural Products; Ernest   Vol. 1: 1558
Guenther Award; Louis   Vol. 1: 9212
Guerin; Prix Andre-   Vol. 1: 17383
Guerin; Prix Marcelin   Vol. 2: 5890

Guerrero a la Labor Teatral; Premio Maria   Vol. 2: 11363
Guest Lectureship Award on Basic Cell Research in Cytology   Vol. 1: 4548
Guest of Honor   Vol. 1: 629
Guest of Honor Award   Vol. 1: 8503
Guggenheim International Astronautics Award; Daniel and Florence   Vol. 2: 5944
Guggenheim Medal; Daniel
   Society of Automotive Engineers, Inc.   Vol. 1: 17762
   United Engineering Trustees   Vol 1: 18915
Guggenheim Memorial Foundation Fellowships; John Simon   Vol. 1: 9739
Guggenheim; Prix Paul   Vol. 2: 11742
Guggenheim Prize; Paul   Vol. 2: 11742
Guha Memorial Lecture; Bires Chandra   Vol. 2: 7648
Gui; Premio Vittorio   Vol. 2: 8102
Guild Blowstyling Award   Vol. 2: 2965
Guild-CAT National Open Presentation Trophy   Vol. 2: 2963
Guild College Fantasy Championship   Vol. 2: 2964
Guild of Professional Toastmasters Best After Dinner Speaker of the Year   Vol. 2: 2975
Guild Silver Medal   Vol. 2: 2969
Guild under "18" Styling Award   Vol. 2: 2965
Guilday Prize; Peter   Vol. 1: 1431
Guildhall Helping Hand Awards   Vol. 2: 2878
Guilhermina Suggia Gift for the Cello   Vol. 2: 3669
Guillaumet; Prix Anick Campion-Guillaumet et Bernard   Vol. 2: 6323
Guinier; Prix Daniel   Vol. 2: 6367
Guise Medal; Arthur B.   Vol. 1: 17852
Guitar Foundation of America Solo Guitar Competition   Vol. 1: 9746
Guiteras Award; Ramon   Vol. 1: 4955
Gulbenkian Award for Community Centres   Vol. 2: 4073
Gulbenkian Award for Workplaces   Vol. 2: 4073
Gulbenkian Foundation Grants; Calouste   Vol. 2: 2981
Gulbenkian - PEN Translation Prize; Calouste   Vol. 1: 16016
Gulbenkian Prize; Calouste   Vol. 2: 7899
Gulbenkian Prizes for History; Calouste   Vol. 2: 10303
Gulbenkian Translation Prize; Calouste   Vol. 2: 10251
Guldbaggar   Vol. 2: 11626
Guldberg and Waage's Law of Mass Action Memorial Medal   Vol. 2: 9932
Gulf of Salerno Grand Trophy   Vol. 2: 8417
Gulick Award; Luther Halsey   Vol. 1: 759
Gulliver Award   Vol. 2: 11637
Gullmedalje for Utvikling av det Teknologiske Miljo   Vol. 2: 9952
Gullo and Treiber Award   Vol. 1: 15415
Gullpennen   Vol. 2: 9883
Gun och Olof Engqvists stipendium   Vol. 2: 11593
Gundolf-Preis fur die Vermittlung deutscher Kultur im Ausland; Friedrich-   Vol. 2: 6767
Gung and Dr. Charles Y. Hu Award for Distinguished Service to Mathematics; Yueh-Gin   Vol. 1: 12133
Gunlogson Countryside Engineering Award; G. B.   Vol. 1: 4365
Gunlogson Medal; G. B.   Vol. 1: 2354
Gunn Award for Individual Achievement in Conservation; W. W. H.   Vol. 1: 9150
Gunn International Fellowship; Neil   Vol. 2: 10661
Gunnarson Award; Arthur B.   Vol. 1: 10387

Gunnerus Medal; J. E. Vol. 2: 9968
Gunnerusmedaljen Vol. 2: 9968
Gunning Victoria Jubilee Prize Lectureship Vol. 2: 10644
Gunton Award; T. P. Vol. 2: 2437
Gunzo Fiction Prize Vol. 2: 8685
Gusti Prize; Dimitrie Vol. 2: 10350
Gutenberg Award Vol. 2: 6912
Gutenberg-Preis Vol. 2: 6912
Gutenberg Prize; Johann Vol. 1: 17532
Guth Memorial Awards; Edwin F. Vol. 1: 10088
Guthrie Award; RSA Vol. 2: 10619
Guthrie Medal and Prize Vol. 2: 3191
Guthrie Medal; Faldt Vol. 2: 456
The Guthrie Prize Vol. 2: 10559
Gutierrez Award; Pablo Elias Vol. 2: 1707
Gutierrez Prize; Avelino Vol. 2: 80
Guttentag Award; Marcia Vol. 1: 2005
Guttentag; Concurso Nacional de Novela Erich Vol. 2: 1398
Guttentag Fellowship; Marcia Vol. 1: 2005
Guttmacher Award; Manfred S. Vol. 1: 3633
Guye; Fondation Charles Eugene Vol. 2: 5515
Guye; Fondation Philippe A. Vol. 2: 5651
Guyot Memorial Award; Arnold Vol. 1: 14072
Guyton Physiology Teacher of the Year Award; Arthur C. Vol. 1: 3507
Guze Award; Henry Vol. 1: 17434
GV-SOLAS Competition Vol. 2: 11908
GV-SOLAS Preisausschreiben Vol. 2: 11908
GWAA Hall of Fame Vol. 1: 9490
GWAA Honorary Member Vol. 1: 9491
Gwobr Goffa Alun Llywelyn-Williams Vol. 2: 12181
Gwobr Goffa Griffith John Williams Vol. 2: 12199
Gwobr Goffa Sir Bryner Jones Vol. 2: 12188
Gwobrau Cynllunwaith Tai yng Nghymru Vol. 2: 12190
Gwobrau Tir na n-og Vol. 2: 12196
Gwobrau Tywysog Cymru Vol. 2: 12183
Gyldendal Prisen; Soren Vol. 2: 1954
Gyllenbergs pris; Fabian Vol. 2: 11514
Gymnastics National Volunteer of the Year Vol. 1: 430
Gyngell Critics Award; Bruce Vol. 2: 691
Gzowski Medal Vol. 1: 7172
Haas Award; Walter H. Vol. 1: 5853
Haber Award; William Vol. 1: 6428
Haberlandt Medal; Michael Vol. 2: 909
Habib Bank Prize for Literature Vol. 2: 10006
Habif; Prix Mondial Nessim Vol. 2: 11960
Habif Prize; Nessim Vol. 2: 6412
Hachemeister Prize; Charles A. Vol. 1: 7335
Hacke Scholar-Teacher Award; Robert Vol. 1: 7896
Hacker Award; William J. Vol. 1: 14749
Hackett Award; James K. Vol. 1: 7768
Hackett Memorial Prize Vol. 2: 2259
Hackney Award; Mike Vol. 1: 17664
Hackney Literary Awards Vol. 1: 6388
Haddings pris; Assar Vol. 2: 11515
Haddonfield Symphony Solo Competition Vol. 1: 9752
Haddonfield Symphony Solo Competition for Young Instrumentalists Vol. 1: 9752
Haddow Lecture; Alexander Vol. 2: 4250
Hadfield Medal and Prize; Sir Robert Vol. 2: 3136
Hadia Cerpen Malayan Banking - DBP Vol. 2: 8903
Hadiah Cerpen Maybank - DBP Vol. 2: 8903
Hadiah Sastera Malaysia Vol. 2: 8904
Hadley Medal; Henry Vol. 1: 13020

Hadley Memorial Achievement Award; Ross Vol. 1: 19020
Hadow/Donald Stuart Short Story Award; Lyndall Vol. 2: 376
Haendle Affiliate of the Year Award (Community-based Affiliates); Connie Vol. 1: 11902
Hafner VTOL Prize Vol. 2: 3892
Hagan Trophy Vol. 1: 5281
Hagedoorn Award Vol. 2: 9406
Hague Academy of International Law Scholarships Vol. 2: 9445
Hague Award; John L. Vol. 1: 6053
Hahn-Preis fur Chemie und Physik; Otto-Deutsche Physikalische Gesellschaft Vol. 2: 6658
German Chemical Society Vol 2: 6783
HAI Safety Award Vol. 1: 9889
Haifa Prize Vol. 2: 7878
Haig-Brown Award; Roderick
  Canadian Wildlife Federation Vol. 1: 7271
  Federation of Fly Fishers Vol 1: 9106
Haig-Brown Regional Prize Vol. 1: 20187
Haight Award; Walter Vol. 1: 14940
Haim Award; Ben Vol. 2: 7918
Haiman Award for Distinguished Scholarship in Freedom of Speech; Franklyn S. Vol. 1: 18307
Haiman Award; Miecislas Vol. 1: 16311
Hair Designer of the Year Vol. 1: 5408
Hajek Prize; Louise Vol. 1: 11983
Hakanson Award; R. C. Vol. 1: 9020
Hake Award; Don Vol. 1: 3728
Hake - Brandly Award Vol. 1: 13923
Hakluyt Award Vol. 1: 17311
Halas Trophy; George S. Vol. 1: 13999
Halas Trophy (NFL Top Defensive Player); George Vol. 1: 15360
Halbouty Human Needs Award; Michel T. Vol. 1: 1106
Halcrow Premium Vol. 2: 3239
Haldane Essay Competition Medal Vol. 2: 4081
Hale Award; Sarah Josepha Vol. 1: 16836
Hale Prize; George Ellery Vol. 1: 1267
Halecki Award; Oscar Vol. 1: 16312
Hales Prize; Stephen Vol. 1: 4748
Halevi Prize; Arts Prize - Moshe Vol. 2: 7948
Haley Space Flight Award; AIAA Vol. 1: 2472
Hali Award Vol. 2: 7511
Hall Award for Library Literature; G. K. Vol. 1: 2818
Hall Award; G. Stanley Vol. 1: 3711
Hall Award; Rosa O. Vol. 1: 1296
Hall Book Prize; John Whitney Vol. 1: 5444
Hall Composites Manufacturing Award; J. H. "Jud" Vol. 1: 17878
Hall; Fondation James Vol. 2: 5589
Hall Freedom Cup; George Robert Vol. 1: 5281
Hall Medal for Research into Animal Diseases; G. Norman Vol. 2: 3986
Hall Memorial Award; Albert H. Vol. 1: 14234
Hall Memorial Medal; David Vol. 1: 2267
Hall of Barry, Glamorgan, Prize; R. W. Vol. 2: 3987
Hall of Champions Vol. 1: 3605
Hall of Distinguished Americans Vol. 1: 15050
Hall of Fame
  Amateur Speedskating Union of the United States Vol. 1: 467
  American Association of Owners and Breeders of Peruvian Paso Horses Vol 1: 1101
  American Athletic Association for the Deaf Vol 1: 1281

  American Indian Lore Association Vol 1: 2426
  American Theatre Organ Society Vol 1: 4897
  Asphalt Emulsion Manufacturers Association Vol 1: 5373
  Billiard Congress of America Vol 1: 6375
  Council for Health and Human Service Ministries - United Chruch of Christ Vol 1: 8327
  Country Music Showcase International Vol 1: 8423
  Libertarian Futurist Society Vol 1: 11851
  Management Professionals Association Vol 2: 7710
  National Association of Auto Trim Shops Vol 1: 12939
  National Association of Black Women Attorneys Vol 1: 12964
  National Association of Display Industries Vol 1: 13076
  National Association of Left-Handed Golfers - NAIG Vol 1: 13190
  National Auto Auction Association Vol 1: 13398
  National Cutting Horse Association Vol 1: 13840
  National Motorsports Press Association Vol 1: 14374
  National Museum of Racing and Hall of Fame Vol 1: 14387
  National Pigeon Association Vol 1: 14468
  National Pocket Billiard Association Vol 1: 14479
  National Sportscasters and Sportswriters Association Vol 1: 14861
  National Staff Leasing Association Vol 1: 14868
  Piano Technicians Guild Vol 1: 16200
  Pickle Packers International Vol 1: 16204
  U.S. Curling Association Vol 1: 19077
  United States Synchronized Swimming, Inc. Vol 1: 19637
  United States Water Polo Vol 1: 19682
  Zen-Do Kai Martial Arts Association Vol 1: 20632
Hall of Fame Award
  Association for Electric Motors, Their Control, and Application Vol. 1: 5518
  Catholic University of America Alumni Association Vol 1: 7394
  Direct Selling Association Vol 1: 8657
  International Federation of Leather Guilds Vol 1: 10965
  Livestock Publications Council Vol 1: 11919
  National Forum for Black Public Administrators Vol 1: 14033
  National School Transportation Association Vol 1: 14677
Hall of Fame for Engineering, Science and Technology Vol. 1: 11340
Hall of Fame for Great Americans Vol. 1: 9761
Hall of Fame in Philanthropy
  United Methodist Association of Health and Welfare Ministries Vol. 1: 18933
  United Methodist Church, Board of Global Ministries - Health and Welfare Ministries Division Vol 1: 18942
Hall of Fame Meritorious Award (soccer) Vol. 1: 19606
Hall of Fame - NARM Vol. 1: 13289
Hall of Fame of Distinguished Band Conductors Vol. 1: 13429
Hall of Foam Vol. 1: 8788
Hall of Honor Vol. 1: 6849

Hall of Outstanding Americans Vol. 1: 15050
Hall of Victory Vol. 1: 14600
Hall Prize; R. T. Vol. 2: 305
Hall Star of Tomorrow; Chuck Vol. 1: 20600
Hall Trophy; Sylvester R. "Sal" Vol. 1: 16214
Halladay Awards; Henry G. Vol. 1: 14346
Halle Research Award; Herman L. Vol. 1: 9584
Hallgarten Prizes; Julius Vol. 1: 12612
Hallinan Award; Archbishop Paul Vol. 1: 7357
Hallock Card Award Vol. 1: 16069
Halmstad Prize Vol. 1: 131
Halperin Electric Transmission and Distribution Award; Herman Vol. 1: 10267
Halsell Prize; Willie D. Vol. 1: 12357
Halsprijs voor Tentoonstellingsvormgeving; Frans Vol. 2: 9447
Ham-Wasserman Lecture Vol. 1: 4595
Hamburger; Prix Fondation Bernard Vol. 2: 4788
Hamdard Foundation Pakistan Awards Vol. 2: 9975
Hamel; Fondation de Madame Edmond Vol. 2: 5534
Hamel; Prix Joseph Vol. 2: 5765
Hamer and Elizabeth Hamer Kegan Award; Philip M. Vol. 1: 17671
Hamilton Award; Constance E. Vol. 1: 7760
Hamilton Award; James A. Vol. 1: 1658
Hamilton Award; Jimmie Vol. 1: 4730
Hamilton Award; Mary Ellen Vol. 1: 14298
Hamilton Award; Scott Vol. 1: 19940
Hamilton Award; Stevenson - Vol. 2: 11133
Hamilton Hospital Administrators' Book Award; James A. Vol. 1: 1658
Hamilton Memorial Award for Government Service; T. J. Vol. 1: 2583
Hamilton Memorial CWI of the Year Award; Dalton E. Vol. 1: 5077
Hamilton Memorial Prize Vol. 2: 9837
Hamilton Memorial Prize; Max Vol. 2: 10527
Hamilton Prize; Alice and Edith Vol. 1: 19833
Hamilton Volunteer of the Year Award; Katherine Vol. 1: 14358
Hamlin Award; Ann Vol. 1: 7430
Hamman, M.D. Award; J. Shue Vol. 1: 1751
Hammer and Sickle Gold Medal Vol. 2: 10460
Hammer Cancer Prize Vol. 1: 9763
Hammerman Award; Harold Vol. 1: 13363
Hammerschlag Trust Award; Alice Berger Vol. 2: 7857
Hammett Award Vol. 2: 1825
Hammett Prize Vol. 1: 10707
Hamming Medal; Richard W. Vol. 1: 10268
Hammond Memorial Prize; Sir John Vol. 2: 10520
Hammond Prize; Dr. George P. Vol. 1: 16096
Hampel Award; Leslie A. Vol. 1: 2201
Hancock Awards Vol. 1: 9765
Hancock Brick and Tile Soil and Water Engineering Award Vol. 1: 4366
Hancor Award Vol. 1: 13910
Hancor Soil and Water Engineering Award Vol. 1: 4366
Hand Award for Academic Achievement in Folklore and Mythology Studies; Wayland D. Vol. 1: 7465
Hand Award; Judge Learned Vol. 1: 2723
Hand Medal; Learned Vol. 1: 9074
H&CP Service Video Achievement Awards Vol. 1: 3634
Handel Medallion Vol. 1: 7740
Handicapped Professional Woman of the Year Vol. 1: 16221
Hands in Applause Award Vol. 1: 17009

Handy Awards; W. C. Vol. 1: 6416
Hanes Natural History Award; Anne Vol. 1: 15849
Hanford Sr. Distinguished Faculty Award; Lloyd D. Vol. 1: 10437
Hang Gliding Diploma Vol. 2: 5152
Hank IBA Defensive Player of the Year Vol. 1: 12945
Hanks, Jr., Scholarship in Meteorology; Howard H. Vol. 1: 3084
Hanks Memorial Award for Professional Excellence; Nancy Vol. 1: 1045
Hanlon Award Vol. 1: 9506
Hann Award; Elmer L. Vol. 1: 17924
Hannah Medal; Jason A. Vol. 1: 16955
Hannigan Research Award; Jane Anne Vol. 1: 5564
Hanover International Violin Competition Vol. 2: 6758
Hanover Memorial Recognition Award; Philip Vol. 1: 13658
Hansberry Playwriting Award; Lorraine Vol. 1: 1758
Hansell Publication Award; Dorothy E. Vol. 1: 934
Hansen Award; Ann Vol. 1: 19563
Hansen Fondets Pris for Mikrobiologisk Forskning; Emil Christian Vol. 2: 1904
Hansen Foundation for Microbiological Research Award; Emil Christian Vol. 2: 1904
Hansen Medal; C. F. Vol. 2: 1899
Hansen Memorial Award; Isabel Vol. 1: 15526
Hansen Memorial Award; Polly Vol. 1: 16869
Hansen; Premio Profesor Dr. Ricardo Vol. 2: 60
Hansen Publication Award; Kathryn G. Vol. 1: 7880
Hansens Bibliotekspris; R. Lysholt Vol. 2: 1915
Hanson Award (Fighter/Attack Squadron of the Year); Robert M. Vol. 1: 12061
Hanson Awards Program; Abel Vol. 1: 14784
Hanson Medal Vol. 2: 3220
Hanson Medal; Carl Vol. 2: 4408
Harabaszewski Medal; Jan Vol. 2: 10134
Haraucourt Prize; Edmond Vol. 2: 6314
Harbourfront Festival Prize Vol. 1: 9768
Hardee Dissertation of the Year Award; Melvene D. Vol. 1: 13328
Hardeman Prize; D. B. Vol. 1: 11588
Harden Medal Vol. 2: 2174
Harden-Simons Prize Vol. 1: 4093
Hardesty Award; Shortridge Vol. 1: 4461
Harding Award Vol. 2: 2037
Harding Management Award Vol. 1: 13475
Hardinge Award; Hal Williams
  American Institute of Mining, Metallurgical and Petroleum Engineers Vol. 1: 2636
  Society for Mining, Metallurgy, and Exploration Vol 1: 17565
Hardison Award; J. Brown Vol. 1: 16726
Hardison Jr. Poetry Prize; O. B. Vol. 1: 9283
Hardwick Award; Gordon Vol. 1: 12262
Hardy Award; Samuel
  International Tennis Hall of Fame Vol. 1: 11350
  United States Tennis Association Vol 1: 19648
Hardy Awards; W. J. Vol. 1: 3109
Hardy Keynote Address; R. M. Vol. 1: 6896
Hardy Lectureship Vol. 2: 3611
Hardy Medal Award; Robert Lansing Vol. 1: 12313
Hardy Prize; William Bate Vol. 2: 2566
Hardy Society Book Prize; Thomas Vol. 2: 2983

Hare Award; "Jimmy" Vol. 1: 19840
Haret Prize; Spiru Vol. 2: 10351
Harger Memorial Award; Don Vol. 1: 9107
Hargrove Award; Bill Vol. 1: 19941
Harian Creative Awards Vol. 1: 9774
Haring Prize; Clarence H. Vol. 1: 2292
Harishchandra Award; Bharatendu Vol. 2: 7530
Harkin Conservation Award; J. B. Vol. 1: 7082
Harkin Medal; J. B. Vol. 1: 7082
Harkness Fellowships Vol. 2: 2985
Harley Award; Herbert Vol. 1: 2757
Harlow Business-Government Relations Award; Bryce Vol. 1: 9776
Harman Award; Katherine Bishop Vol. 2: 2438
Harman Award; Nathaniel Bishop Vol. 2: 2439
Harmers Diamond Jubilee Trophy Vol. 2: 3781
Harmon Award; Lt. Gens. Millard F. and Hubert R. Vol. 1: 15781
Harmony Queens Vol. 1: 9783
Harms-Preis; Bernhard- Vol. 2: 7007
Harness Horse of the Year Vol. 1: 19675
Harness Track of America's Art Competition Vol. 1: 9793
Harp of King David Vol. 2: 7997
Harper Bursary; Alan Vol. 2: 2888
Harpsichord and Fortepiano Competitions Vol. 2: 1152
Harrelson Service Award; Major Vol. 1: 13680
Harrevold Memorial Award; Van Vol. 1: 3508
Harries Award; Katrine Vol. 2: 11058
Harriestoekenning; Katrine Vol. 2: 11058
Harriman Award for Distinguished Volunteer Service Vol. 1: 3916
Harriman Award; W. Averell Vol. 1: 2087
Harriman Democracy Award; W. Averell Vol. 1: 13853
Harriman Memorial Trophy Horse of the Year - Headliner Award; E. Roland Vol. 1: 19375
Harrington Jr. Award; Dr. Joseph Vol. 1: 15556
Harrington-Lux Creative Design Award; Holly Vol. 1: 9857
Harris Award; Albert J. Vol. 1: 11187
Harris Award; Hayden - Vol. 1: 724
Harris Award; Peter Vol. 2: 3470
Harris Hybrid Award Vol. 1: 1395
Harris Literature Award; Albert H. Vol. 2: 3781
Harris Medal; JPA H. E. Vol. 1: 11633
Harris Medal; Townsend Vol. 1: 389
Harris Playwright Award Competition; Beverly Hills Theatre Guild - Julie Vol. 1: 6350
Harris State Leadership Award; Jeffrey S. Vol. 1: 13093
Harris Trophy; Urch Vol. 2: 3781
Harrison Award; Harry Vol. 2: 6492
Harrison Award of Merit; Bernard P. Vol. 1: 13627
Harrison Memorial Prize Vol. 2: 4199
Harrison Prize Vol. 1: 16956
Harrison Prize (Laryngological Section); W. J. Vol. 2: 4251
Harshbarger Landscape Design Plaque Vol. 1: 2379
Hart Award; Horace Vol. 1: 9799
Hart Award of the Education Council of the Graphic Arts Industry; Horace Vol. 1: 9799
Hart Cup Vol. 1: 19564
Hart Distinguished Consumer Service Award; Philip Vol. 1: 8223
Hart Memorial Award; Moss Vol. 1: 15141

Hart Memorial Trophy   Vol. 1: 14168
Hart Public Service Award; Philip   Vol. 1: 8224
Hart Trophy; Nelson C.   Vol. 1: 6973
Hartford-Nicholsen Award   Vol. 1: 18030
Hartley Medal; Sir Harold   Vol. 2: 3159
Hartman Excellence in Sportswriting Award; Fred   Vol. 1: 18635
Hartnett Award   Vol. 2: 658
Hartranft Award; Joseph B.   Vol. 1: 283
Hartree Premium   Vol. 2: 3273
Hartshorne Trophies   Vol. 1: 19354
Hartwig Sculpture Award; Cleo   Vol. 1: 12613
Harvard Alumni Association Award   Vol. 1: 9801
Harvard Medal   Vol. 1: 9802
Harvard - Newcomen Postdoctoral Fellowship in Business History   Vol. 1: 15321
Harvard University Press Faculty Prize   Vol. 1: 9818
Harvest Award   Vol. 1: 14614
Harvey Award; Ethel   Vol. 1: 8568
Harvey Awards for Excellence; William   Vol. 1: 3058
Harvey Awards for Writing on Hypertension; William   Vol. 1: 3058
Harvey Cup   Vol. 2: 2062
Harvey Essay Prize   Vol. 2: 2992
Harvey Memorial Lecture; Samuel C.   Vol. 1: 838
Harvey Prize   Vol. 2: 7945
Harveys Leeds International Pianoforte Competition   Vol. 2: 2994
Harwick Award; Harry J.   Vol. 1: 1673
Haryana Sahitya Award   Vol. 2: 7512
Hasdeu Prize; Bogdan Petriceicu   Vol. 2: 10352
Haseltine Memorial Fellowship in Science Writing; Nate   Vol. 1: 8336
Haskell Silver Medal; Frank   Vol. 2: 3092
Haskil Competition; Clara   Vol. 2: 11744
Haskins Medal   Vol. 1: 12201
Haslam Award for Excellence in Bookselling; Charles S.   Vol. 1: 18181
Haslam International Scholarship; Charley   Vol. 1: 1363
Hasler Award; Maurice F.   Vol. 1: 17415
Hasler Medal; Georg   Vol. 2: 11830
Hasluck Short Story Competition; Dame Alexandra   Vol. 2: 664
Hassan II des Quatre Jurys   Vol. 2: 5232
Hasse Prize; Merten   Vol. 1: 12134
Hastings Award; Sir Charles   Vol. 2: 2440
Hasty Pudding Man of the Year   Vol. 1: 9824
Hasty Pudding Woman of the Year   Vol. 1: 9825
Haswell Memorial Award; W. S.   Vol. 1: 8700
Hatai Medal; Shinkishi   Vol. 1: 15891
Hatchett Award; Charles   Vol. 2: 3137
Hatfield Award; W. Wilbur   Vol. 1: 13767
Hatfield Award; William D.   Vol. 1: 20151
Hatfield Scholar; Mark O.   Vol. 1: 16849
Hathaway Prize; Baxter   Vol. 1: 8972
Hatieganu Prize; Iuliu   Vol. 2: 10353
Hatikvah Award   Vol. 1: 11555
Hatton Awards Competition for Junior Investigators; Edward H.   Vol. 1: 10617
Hattori Prize   Vol. 2: 8561
Hattori Prize; S.   Vol. 1: 10678
Haub Prize; Elizabeth   Vol. 2: 6940
Hauer Spelean History Award; Peter M.   Vol. 1: 14850
Haueter Memorial Award; Paul E.   Vol. 1: 2251
Haughton Good Guy Award; Bill   Vol. 1: 19376
Hauling Job of the Year Award   Vol. 1: 18295

Haurwitz Memorial Lecturer; Bernhard   Vol. 1: 3085
Hausman Volunteer of the Year Award; Ethel   Vol. 1: 18902
Havenga Prize for Science and Technology   Vol. 2: 10990
Haverhill Library Award   Vol. 1: 9711
Havez-Planque; Prix Marie   Vol. 2: 5894
Haviland Award; P. H.   Vol. 2: 12214
Havlicek Prize; Josef   Vol. 2: 1883
Hawaii Award for Literature   Vol. 1: 9832
Hawaii Filmmakers Award   Vol. 1: 9829
Hawaii International Film Festival   Vol. 1: 9829
Hawaiian Architectural Arts Award   Vol. 1: 9833
Hawk Mountain - Zeiss Research Award   Vol. 1: 9839
Hawk Trophy; One Ton Championship -   Vol. 1: 19533
Hawkins Award; Ann T.   Vol. 1: 5284
Hawkins Award; R. R.   Vol. 1: 5695
Hawley Fearless Leader Award; Bob   Vol. 1: 5851
Haworth Memorial Lectureship and Medal   Vol. 2: 4200
Hawthornden Prize   Vol. 2: 10551
Hawthorne Award; Charles Oliver   Vol. 2: 2441
Hay Medal; Logan   Vol. 1: 11880
Hayden Fellowship; Alice H.   Vol. 1: 5571
Hayden -Harris Award   Vol. 1: 724
Hayden Memorial Geological Award   Vol. 1: 70
Hayes Award; Sheldon G.   Vol. 1: 12836
Hayes Awards; Helen   Vol. 1: 20133
Hayes Student Prize Paper Award; T. Burke   Vol. 1: 10311
Hayhow Award; Edgar C.   Vol. 1: 1659
Hayling Island SC Trophy   Vol. 2: 2898
Hayman Award for Distinguished Staff Service; Harry   Vol. 1: 10301
Hayman Trophy; Lew   Vol. 1: 6879
Haynes Awards; Elizabeth Sterling   Vol. 1: 16073
Hays Award   Vol. 1: 10411
Hays Exhibit Industry Award; Hazel   Vol. 1: 9024
Haythorntwaite Cup   Vol. 2: 4454
Hayward Trophy   Vol. 1: 17353
Hazbarah Award   Vol. 1: 11564
Hazen Art Essay Award for 20th Century Art Literature; Joseph H.   Vol. 2: 7921
Head Arthur Ashe Sportsmanship Award   Vol. 1: 10549
Head Memorial Award; Florence Roberts   Vol. 1: 15599
Head/*Tennis* College Player of the Year   Vol. 1: 10561
Headberg Prize; Virginia K.   Vol. 1: 5297
Headliner Award
  Livestock Publications Council   Vol. 1: 11920
  United States Harness Writers Association   Vol 1: 19377
  Women in Communications, Inc.   Vol 1: 20375
Headliner Awards   Vol. 1: 11892
Heads Up Award   Vol. 1: 20241
Health Achievement in Industry Award   Vol. 1: 1697
Health Achievement in Occupational Medicine Award   Vol. 1: 1697
Health Advancement Award   Vol. 1: 14271
Health Advocate Award   Vol. 1: 3300
Health Advocate of the Year   Vol. 1: 15871

Health and Disability Insurance Sales Achievement   Vol. 1: 13128
Health and Safety Award   Vol. 1: 3917
Health Care Executive of the Year Award   Vol. 1: 597
Health Care Professional Award   Vol. 1: 16386
Health Education Professional of the Year Awards   Vol. 1: 5613
Health Journalism Awards   Vol. 1: 1578
Health Management Research Award   Vol. 1: 1660
Healthy American Fitness Leaders Award
  President's Council on Physical Fitness and Sports   Vol. 1: 16394
  United States Junior Chamber of Commerce   Vol 1: 19428
Healy Award; Gus   Vol. 2: 7769
Heaps Prize; Norman   Vol. 2: 2577
Hearn Cup; George   Vol. 2: 2069
Hearst Educator of the Year Award   Vol. 1: 14547
Hearst Memorial Trophy; John Randolph   Vol. 1: 9875
Hearst Newspapers Writing and Photography Contests   Vol. 1: 9875
Heart and Torch Award   Vol. 1: 2230
Heart of America   Vol. 1: 2807
Heart of the Program Award   Vol. 1: 3994
Heart of the Year Award   Vol. 1: 2231
Heartland Prizes   Vol. 1: 7609
Heat Transfer and Energy Conversion Division Award   Vol. 1: 2584
Heat Transfer Memorial Award   Vol. 1: 4676
Heath Award; Edward   Vol. 2: 4011
Heath Literary Award   Vol. 1: 3225
Heath Memorial Award   Vol. 1: 19877
Heaviside Premium   Vol. 2: 3273
Hebb Award; D. O.   Vol. 1: 3752
Hebel-Preis; Johann-Peter-   Vol. 2: 7054
Hebert; Prix Louis-Phillipe-   Vol. 1: 17388
Hebrew Radio Play Prize   Vol. 2: 7917
Hecht Award; Max   Vol. 1: 6054
Heck Prize; Mathilda   Vol. 1: 20102
Heckel Award; George Baugh   Vol. 1: 14439
Hector Memorial Medal and Prize   Vol. 2: 9838
Hedley Award; George   Vol. 2: 3708
Hedri-Preis; Dr. A.   Vol. 2: 11732
Hedrick Awards; U. P.   Vol. 1: 3595
Hedrick Lectureship   Vol. 1: 12135
Hedwig Medal   Vol. 1: 10679
Heeney Memorial Award; Robert C.   Vol. 1: 13066
Hefley Educator of the Year Award; Sue   Vol. 1: 11954
Hefner First Amendment Award; Hugh M.   Vol. 1: 16246
Hegarty Prize   Vol. 2: 574
Hegel-Preis der Landeshauptstadt Stuttgart   Vol. 2: 7136
Hei Tiki Trophy   Vol. 2: 9711
Heideman Award   Vol. 1: 126
Heidsieck Award; RPS Charles   Vol. 2: 4128
Heilprin Literary Award Medal; Angelo   Vol. 1: 9552
Heiman Impact Award for Excellence in Educational Support; John C.   Vol. 1: 2585
Heimann Service Award; Jack   Vol. 1: 18482
Heine Prize; Heinrich   Vol. 2: 6686
Heineken Prijs; Dr. H. P.   Vol. 2: 9452
Heineken Prize; Dr. H. P.
  Heineken Foundation   Vol. 2: 9452
  Royal Netherlands Academy of Arts and Sciences   Vol 2: 9600
Heineman Prize; Dannie   Vol. 2: 6908

Heineman Prize for Astrophysics; Dannie N.
American Astronomical Society Vol. 1: 1268
American Institute of Physics Vol 1: 2660
Heineman Prize for Mathematical Physics; Dannie N.
American Institute of Physics Vol. 1: 2661
American Physical Society Vol 1: 3457
Heineman Trophy Vol. 1: 16814
Heinemann Memorial Trustee Award for Educational Development; Ruth I. Vol. 1: 4190
Heinemann/Reed Fiction Award Vol. 2: 9803
Heinl, Jr., Memorial Award in Marine Corps History; Colonel Robert D. Vol. 1: 12083
Heinse-Medaille; Wilhelm- Vol. 2: 6514
Heinz Award; John H. Vol. 1: 14419
Heinz Literature Prize; Drue Vol. 1: 19864
Heinzerling Trophy Vol. 1: 17353
Heise Award; Leonard Vol. 1: 9032
Heisenberg Prize Vol. 2: 8289
Heiser Program for Research in Leprosy and Tuberculosis Vol. 1: 9883
Heiskell Awards; Andrew Vol. 1: 18711
Heisman Memorial Trophy Vol. 1: 8714
Heizer Prize; Robert F. Vol. 1: 4129
Helbronner-Fould; Fondation Helene Vol. 2: 5574
Helicopter Airframe Technician Award Vol. 1: 9890
Helicopter Avionics Technician Award Vol. 1: 9891
Helicopter Club of Great Britain Championship Trophy Vol. 2: 3005
Helicopter Electrical/Electronics Technician Award Vol. 1: 9892
Helicopter Maintenance Award Vol. 1: 9893
Helicopter Powerplant Technician Award Vol. 1: 9894
Helicopter Squadron of the Year Vol. 1: 12072
Helin International Singing Competition; Mirjam Vol. 2: 4694
Heller Award; Florence G. Vol. 1: 11516
Hellinger Award; Mark Vol. 1: 16991
Hellings Award; Susan R. Vol. 1: 13581
Hellman Research Award; Milo Vol. 1: 1092
Hellrung Award; Robert T. Vol. 1: 12163
Hellthaler International GmbH Award Vol. 2: 7142
Helm Award; McKay - Vol. 1: 5084
Helmerich Distinguished Author Award; Peggy V. Vol. 1: 18835
Helmholtz Medal Vol. 2: 1136
Helmholtz-Preise Vol. 2: 6914
Helmholtz Prizes Vol. 2: 6914
Helms Award; Edgar J. Vol. 1: 9663
Helpern Memorial Award; Milton Vol. 1: 11201
Helping Hands Award Vol. 1: 20522
Helpmann Scholarship; Robert Vol. 2: 146
Helsingin Juhlaviikkojen Vuoden taiteilija Vol. 2: 4720
Helsinki International Ballet Competition Vol. 2: 4734
Helvetia Trophy; H.L. Katcher Vol. 2: 3781
Hemans Prize for Lyrical Poetry; Felicia Vol. 2: 4575
Hemingway Award; Ritz Paris Vol. 2: 6199
Hemingway Foundation Award; Ernest Vol. 1: 16017
Hemisphere Award Vol. 1: 10504
Hemley Memorial Award; Cecil Vol. 1: 16287
Hemley Poetry Prize; Cecil Vol. 1: 15594
Hemphill Award; Bernice Vol. 1: 929
Hemschemeyer Award; Hattie Vol. 1: 1695
Hench Award; Philip Vol. 1: 5884
Hendershott Award; Robert Vol. 1: 3226

Henderson Alumni Award; William M. Vol. 1: 8580
Henderson Award; Alexander Vol. 2: 227
Henderson Award for Achievement; National Aviation Club - Cliff Vol. 1: 13402
Henderson Exhibit Award; William C. Vol. 1: 3227
Henderson Lecture Award; Edward Vol. 1: 2176
Henderson Medal; George R. Vol. 1: 9383
Henderson Memorial Award; Harold G. Vol. 1: 9755
Henderson Memorial Prize; Ian Vol. 2: 440
Henderson Memorial Student Award; Edward Vol. 1: 2177
Henderson Service to the Section Award; Julia Vol. 1: 4278
Henderson Trophy Vol. 1: 13402
Henderson Trophy; Edwin Bancroft Vol. 1: 16214
Hendy Memorial Award; James C. Vol. 1: 2326
Henebry Roll of Honor Award; Agnes Vol. 1: 18281
Heneman Personnel Creative Application Award; Yoder- Vol. 1: 17490
Heneman Personnel Creative Application Awards; Yoder- Vol. 1: 17490
Heneman Personnel Research Award; Yoder- Vol. 1: 17491
Henley Media Award; Vernon Vol. 1: 1851
Henne Award; AASL Frances Vol. 1: 2831
Henne Research Grant; Frances Vol. 1: 2959
Henne YASD/VOYA (Voice of Youth Advocates) Research Grant; Frances Vol. 1: 2959
Hennequin; Prix Albert Vol. 2: 6268
Hennessy Awards Vol. 1: 14625
Hennessy Trophy; John L. Vol. 1: 14625
Henniker Premium; Harry Vol. 2: 3281
Henry Award; Charles D. Vol. 1: 760
Henry Award; O. Vol. 1: 18649
Henry Citation; Patrick Vol. 1: 14096
Henry Medal Vol. 1: 17336
Henry Student Research Award; Ted Vol. 1: 17487
Henry Volunteer of the Year Award; Robert Lee Vol. 1: 14128
Hensel Award; Catherine "Cathy" Vol. 1: 8749
Henshall Award; James A. Vol. 1: 4850
Henshall; Dr. James Vol. 1: 9108
Henshel Award; Colonel Harry D. Vol. 1: 431
Hensler Award; Bill and Sue Vol. 1: 9914
Hepites Prize; Stefan Vol. 2: 10354
Heraldic Ring Vol. 2: 865
Heraldo Music Prizes; El Vol. 2: 9020
Heraldo Prizes; El Vol. 2: 9021
Heraldo Sport Prizes; El Vol. 2: 9022
Heran Violoncello Competition Vol. 2: 1835
Herb S. Brier Instructor of the Year Award Vol. 1: 3886
Herb Society of America Grant Vol. 1: 9907
Herbert Error/Variety - YN Exhibit Award; Alan Vol. 1: 3228
Herbert Medal Vol. 1: 10817
Herbert Pharmaceutical Dermatology Award Vol. 1: 4772
Hercules Award Vol. 2: 11357
Herds Competition Vol. 2: 2393
Herdsman of the Year Vol. 2: 2391
Hereford Airport Communication Excellence Award; Peggy Vol. 1: 289
Hereford Excellence in Communications Award; Peggy Vol. 1: 289
Hering Medal; Henry Vol. 1: 14713
Hering Medal; Rudolph Vol. 1: 4462

Heritage APA Service Award Vol. 1: 3771
Heritage Art Awards Vol. 2: 322
Heritage Award
American Public Works Association Vol. 1: 3877
Department of Canadian Heritage - Parks Canada Vol 1: 8610
Irish-American Cultural Institute Vol 1: 11452
National Dance Association Vol 1: 13843
Heritage Award; Doris Vol. 1: 19942
Heritage Award for Outstanding Career Achievement Vol. 1: 18155
Heritage Canada Achievement Awards Vol. 1: 9910
Heritage in Britain Award Vol. 2: 2247
Heritage Practice Award Vol. 1: 3771
Heritage Public Policy Award Vol. 1: 3771
Heritage Publications Award Vol. 1: 3771
Heritage Research Award Vol. 1: 3771
Herlitzka per la Fisiologia; Premio Internazionale Amedeo e Frances Vol. 2: 8023
Herman Award; Robert H. Vol. 1: 4052
Herman Memorial Award; M. Justin Vol. 1: 13143
Hermann Award Vol. 1: 10538
Hermann Memorial Award; Fred Vol. 1: 10326
Hernandez Award; Francisco Vol. 2: 12134
Herndon National Legislative Award; Maurice G. Vol. 1: 10127
Hero of Socialist Labor Vol. 2: 10460
Hero of the Year Vol. 1: 4853
Heroism Award
Flight Safety Foundation Vol. 1: 9244
National Telephone Cooperative Association Vol 1: 14888
Herpetologists' League Award for Graduate Research Vol. 1: 9916
Herpetologists' League Student Prize Vol. 1: 9916
Herrera al Merito en Ecologia y Conservacion; Medalla Alfonso L. Vol. 2: 9040
Herrera Vegas Prize; Marcellino Vol. 2: 81
Herreshoff Trophy; Nathaniel G. Vol. 1: 19529
Herrick Award; C. Judson Vol. 1: 910
Herrick Award; James B. Vol. 1: 2232
Herring Memorial Awards; Hubert B. Vol. 1: 15884
Herring Memorial Prize; Sir Edward Vol. 2: 144
Herriot Award; James Vol. 1: 10052
Herrman Founder's Award; Margaret S. Vol. 1: 13653
Herrndorf Media Arts Award; Peter Vol. 1: 5329
Herschel Medal Vol. 2: 3940
Herschel Medal; John F. W. Vol. 2: 10965
Herschfus Memorial Award Vol. 1: 647
Hersey Award; Mayo D. Vol. 1: 4677
Hershberg Award for Important Discoveries in Medicinally Active Substances; E. B. Vol. 1: 1559
Hershey Player of the Year Vol. 1: 12946
Hersholt Humanitarian Award; Jean Vol. 1: 59
Herskovits Award Vol. 1: 191
Herter Award; Christian A. Vol. 1: 2088
Hertert Memorial Award; Lucien Dean Vol. 1: 918
Herty, Jr., Award; Charles W. Vol. 1: 11463
Hertz Medal; Heinrich Vol. 1: 10269
Hertz Preis; Heinrich Vol. 2: 7148
Hertz-Preis (Physik-Preis); Gustav- Vol. 2: 6659

Hertz; Prix Henri   Vol. 2: 5204
Hertzog Prize   Vol. 2: 10991
Hervey and Broadcasters Awards; John   Vol. 1: 19676
Hervey Journalism Award; John   Vol. 1: 19676
Hervey - Torrey Botanical Club Award; Annette   Vol. 1: 18753
Hervieu; Prix Paul   Vol. 2: 5905
Herzberg Medal   Vol. 1: 6803
Herzl Award; Theodore   Vol. 1: 20642
Herzog; Premio Anual de Investigacion Economica Jesus Silva   Vol. 2: 9184
Hesburgh, C.S.C., Award; Rev. Theodore M.   Vol. 1: 5725
HeSCA/Gilbert Altschul Film Festival   Vol. 1: 9850
HeSCA JBC Literary Award   Vol. 1: 9851
HeSCA/Marion Laboratories Print Media Festival   Vol. 1: 9854
HeSCA/NCME Award   Vol. 1: 9852
HeSCA/NCME Post Graduate Physician Continuing Medical Education Award   Vol. 1: 9857
HeSCA/NCME Video Festivals   Vol. 1: 9852
HeSCA/Pfizer Interactive Materials Festival   Vol. 1: 9853
HeSCA Print Media Festival   Vol. 1: 9854
HeSCA/Ralston Purina Excellence in Veterinary Medicine Award   Vol. 1: 9857
HeSCA/SmithKline Beecham Still Media Festival   Vol. 1: 9855
Heschel Award; Martin Luther King, Jr. - Abraham Joshua   Vol. 1: 6434
Heschel Peace Award; Abraham Joshua   Vol. 1: 11561
Hess Award; Henry   Vol. 1: 4678
Hess Medal; Harry H.   Vol. 1: 2165
Hesse Prize; Hermann   Vol. 2: 7086
Hesselroth Leadership Award; Frank   Vol. 1: 13166
Heston Award for Outstanding Scholarship in Interpretation and Performance Studies; Lilla A.   Vol. 1: 18308
Hestrin Prize   Vol. 2: 7915
Hetherington Award   Vol. 1: 592
Hetzel Memorial Fund Prize; Kurt   Vol. 1: 9327
Heubner Preis; Otto   Vol. 2: 6821
Heuer Timing Road Rally Rookie   Vol. 1: 18392
Heux; Prix Gaston et Mariette   Vol. 2: 1298
Hevesy Nuclear Medicine Pioneer Award   Vol. 1: 17947
Hewitt Award; C. Gordon   Vol. 1: 8955
Hewitt Award for Excellence in Sports Broadcasting; Foster   Vol. 1: 327
Hewitt Award; Richard   Vol. 2: 4252
Hewitt Memorial Award; Foster   Vol. 1: 9957
Hewko - Gallagher Memorial Award   Vol. 1: 13231
Hewlett-Packard Europhysics Prize   Vol. 2: 11704
Hewlett-Packard Medical Fellowship Awards   Vol. 1: 9918
Hexagono de Oro   Vol. 2: 10014
Hexter Prize; Margaret   Vol. 1: 14714
Hexter Prize; Maurice B.   Vol. 1: 14714
Heymans; Prijs Jan-Frans   Vol. 2: 1313
HG 100 EJ Esperanto Radio Amateur Station Award   Vol. 2: 7426
HHS Distinguished Public Service Award   Vol. 1: 19235
Hi-Fi Grand Prix Awards   Vol. 1: 6137
HIA U.S. Trials Silver Bucket   Vol. 1: 12322
Hibbs Award; Samuel G.   Vol. 1: 3635
Hickinbottom Fellowship   Vol. 2: 4201

Hickman Medal; Henry Hill   Vol. 2: 4253
Hickok Golden Link Award   Vol. 1: 18570
Hicks Award; C. M.   Vol. 1: 7030
Hickson Trophy   Vol. 2: 10589
HIFF Documentary Award   Vol. 1: 9829
Higdon Distinguished Educator Award; Archie   Vol. 1: 4094
Higenbottam Memorial Prize; Frank   Vol. 2: 3104
Higgins Lectureship Award; T. R.   Vol. 1: 2679
Higgins Redesign Award   Vol. 1: 16378
Higgs and Hill Bursary   Vol. 2: 4178
High Energy and Particle Physics Prize   Vol. 2: 11705
High Point Horse   Vol. 1: 15471
High Point Horsemenship   Vol. 1: 15472
High Point Performance Horse Awards   Vol. 1: 16080
High-Polymer Physics Prize   Vol. 1: 3458
High Quality of Work Award   Vol. 2: 10432
High School All Star Award   Vol. 1: 20425
High School Hall of Fame   Vol. 1: 13957
High School Jazz Musician Award   Vol. 1: 13430
High School - Randolph Award   Vol. 1: 14965
High School Soloist Competition   Vol. 1: 13982
High Winds Medal   Vol. 1: 5049
Higham Prize for Fiction; David   Vol. 2: 2199
Higher Education Writers Award   Vol. 1: 1229
Highet Award; Allan   Vol. 2: 9792
Highland Park Parliamentarian of the Year Awards; Spectator/   Vol. 2: 4485
Highly Commended Certificate   Vol. 1: 3339
Highway Research Board Distinguished Service Award   Vol. 1: 18780
Highway Safety Awards   Vol. 1: 10128
Higuchi Research Prize; Takeru   Vol. 1: 3380
Hild Janos Emlekerem   Vol. 2: 7383
Hild Medal; Janos   Vol. 2: 7383
Hildebrand Award in the Theoretical and Experimental Chemistry of Liquids; Joel Henry   Vol. 1: 1560
Hilditch Lecture   Vol. 2: 4409
Hildreth Award; Harold M.   Vol. 1: 3762
Hilendarski Prize; Paisiy   Vol. 2: 1513
Hilgard and Josephine R. Hilgard Award; Ernest R.   Vol. 1: 17435
Hilgard Dissertation Award   Vol. 1: 3756
Hilgard Hydraulic Prize; Karl Emil   Vol. 1: 4463
Hill Award and William O. Russell Lectureship in Anatomical Pathology; Joanne Vandenberge   Vol. 1: 19878
Hill Award; Reuben   Vol. 1: 13807
Hill Community Development Awards; Charlotte   Vol. 1: 14052
Hill Fellowship; Lister   Vol. 1: 4813
Hill, Jr. Award; Nicholas S.   Vol. 1: 5027
Hill Memorial Award; Bill   Vol. 1: 14535
Hill Memorial Prize; L. Ronald   Vol. 1: 17660
Hill Memorial Scholarship Program; George   Vol. 1: 14347
Hill-Rom Management Essay Competition in Healthcare Administration   Vol. 1: 1661
Hill Sports Book of the Year; William   Vol. 2: 3010
Hill Trophy; Talmadge L. "Marse"   Vol. 1: 16214
Hill Volunteers in Fund-Raising Award; Charlotte   Vol. 1: 14051
Hillbilly Heart Award   Vol. 1: 9018
Hillier Award; Doris   Vol. 2: 2442
Hillis Achievement Award for Choral Excellence; Margaret   Vol. 1: 7655

Hillman Foundation Prize Awards; Sidney   Vol. 1: 9924
Hill's Public Relations Award   Vol. 1: 7263
Hilti-Preis fur Innovative Forschung   Vol. 2: 11931
Hime Memorial Trophies; Alan   Vol. 2: 2070
Hinchley Medal; John William   Vol. 2: 3221
Hinderstein Award; Jeanette Robinson   Vol. 1: 12006
Hinds Award; Julian   Vol. 1: 4464
Hine Awards; NCLC Lewis   Vol. 1: 13579
Hinman Trophy; U.S. Team Race Championship - George R.   Vol. 1: 19544
Hinrichsen Award; Walter
    American Academy of Arts and Letters   Vol. 1: 508
    Columbia University   Vol 1: 7982
Hinton Medal   Vol. 2: 3346
Hinzelin; Prix Emile   Vol. 2: 5849
Hippocrates Medal   Vol. 2: 6916
Hippocratic Oath Award   Vol. 1: 10690
Hirata Award; Dr.   Vol. 2: 8662
Hirata-sho   Vol. 2: 8662
Hiroshima International Amateur Film and Video Festival   Vol. 2: 8533
Hirsch Award for Excellence in Broadcasting; Harold S.   Vol. 1: 15442
Hirsch Award for Excellence in Ski Photography; Harold S.   Vol. 1: 15443
Hirsch Award; Harold S.   Vol. 1: 15444
Hirsch Award; John   Vol. 1: 15702
Hirschfeld Scholar Award   Vol. 1: 9096
Hirschmann Award in Peptide Chemistry; Ralph F.   Vol. 1: 1561
Hirschs pris; Axel   Vol. 2: 11594
Hirsh Award for Outstanding Student Papers on Legal Medicine   Vol. 1: 1667
Hirst Premium; Lord   Vol. 2: 3273
Hirt Prize; Victor   Vol. 2: 10510
Hislop Award; David   Vol. 2: 3240
Hislop Award for Outstanding Contributions to Professional Literature; Helen J.   Vol. 1: 3482
Hispanic Culture Gold Medal   Vol. 2: 53
Hispanic Engineer of the Year Awards   Vol. 1: 7305
Historian Ystavain Liiton Palkinto   Vol. 2: 4756
Historic Novel Award   Vol. 2: 7220
Historic Preservation Award   Vol. 1: 3599
Historic Theatre Preservation Award   Vol. 1: 11818
Historical Achievement Award
    Ohio Academy of History   Vol. 1: 15581
    Ohio Academy of History   Vol 1: 15582
Historical Literature Award   Vol. 2: 8740
Historical Metallurgy Society Grants   Vol. 2: 12175
History Book Contest   Vol. 1: 9784
History of Education Society Award   Vol. 1: 9946
History of Geology Award   Vol. 1: 9562
History of Psychology Student Paper Award   Vol. 1: 3738
History of Women in Science Prize   Vol. 1: 9950
History Prize   Vol. 2: 1061
History Section Genealogical Publishing Company Award   Vol. 1: 2944
Histotechnologist of the Year Award   Vol. 1: 14750
Hit of the season   Vol. 2: 1402
Hitachi/CFA Scholar-Athlete Team Award   Vol. 1: 7900
Hitar Petar/Artful Peter/Grand Prize for Humor and Satire in Literature   Vol. 2: 1522
Hitchcock Award; Edward   Vol. 1: 1598

Hitchcock Book Award; Alice Davis   Vol. 1: 17744
Hitchcock Distinguished Professional Service Award; Arthur A.   Vol. 1: 1885
Hitchcock Landscape in Sunlight Prize; George   Vol. 1: 12614
Hizmet Odulu   Vol. 2: 12066
Hlushko Memorial Award to Young Co-operative Educators; William   Vol. 1: 5729
HMS Sultan Prize   Vol. 2: 3347
Hoagland Award; Dennis Robert   Vol. 1: 4749
Hoar Award   Vol. 1: 7235
Hobart Memorial Medal Award; W. H.   Vol. 1: 5078
Hobbs Award; Nicholas   Vol. 1: 3688
Hoberman Award; Solomon   Vol. 1: 8274
Hobson Bequest; G. Vernon   Vol. 2: 3339
Hocart Prize; Arthur Maurice   Vol. 2: 3928
Hoch Distinguished Award; Paul   Vol. 1: 1690
Hoch; Paul H.   Vol. 1: 3839
Hochwalt Award; Charles A. Thomas and Carroll A.   Vol. 1: 12419
Hockey Hall of Fame and Museum   Vol. 1: 14169
Hockey Hall of Fame and Museum Honored Member   Vol. 1: 9958
The Hockey News Awards   Vol. 1: 9960
Hodder Cup   Vol. 1: 19546
Hodges International Piano Competition; Joanna   Vol. 1: 9962
Hodgins Award for Outstanding Accomplishment; Agatha   Vol. 1: 1056
Hodgkins Medal and Prize   Vol. 1: 17337
Hodgson - Distinguished Service Award; Kenneth O.   Vol. 1: 15153
Hodgson Prize   Vol. 2: 3893
Hodson Junior Award; Walter D.   Vol. 1: 18081
Hoduski Founders Award; Bernadine Abbott   Vol. 1: 2892
Hoechst Prize para Investigacion Medica   Vol. 2: 9113
Hoechst-Roussel Award   Vol. 1: 4206
Hoepfner Award; Theodore Christian   Vol. 1: 6126
Hoexter Award; Dr. Werner   Vol. 1: 20518
Hoey Award for Interracial Justice; James J. and Jane   Vol. 1: 7365
Hoffman Award for Outstanding Achievement in Graduate Research; Anna Louise   Vol. 1: 11436
Hoffman Award; Paul R.   Vol. 1: 14590
Hoffman Award; Phillip R.   Vol. 1: 4465
Hoffman Memorial Award; Cecile Pollack   Vol. 1: 10691
Hoffman Memorial Award; Craig   Vol. 1: 18864
Hoffman Prize; Edward Fenno   Vol. 1: 14715
Hoffman Prize for Distinguished Publication on Christopher Marlowe; Calvin and Rose G.   Vol. 2: 3525
Hofhaimer Prize of the Tyrolian Capital City Innsbruck; Paul   Vol. 2: 890
Hofhaimer - Wettbewerb der Landeshauptstadt Innsbruck; Paul   Vol. 2: 890
Hofheimer Prize Award   Vol. 1: 3631
Hofmann Award; Adele Dellenbaugh   Vol. 1: 671
Hofmeyr Prize; W. A.   Vol. 2: 11113
Hofmeyr-prys; W. A.   Vol. 2: 11113
Hog Promoter of the Year   Vol. 1: 14141
Hogan Award; Ben   Vol. 1: 9652
Hogan Distinguished Service Award; John S.   Vol. 1: 16655
Hogan Environmental Law Essay Contest; Roscoe   Vol. 1: 16356

Hogan Memorial Award; John R.   Vol. 1: 16167
Hogentogler Award; C. A.   Vol. 1: 6055
Hogg Medal   Vol. 2: 4039
Hogg National Young Artist Audition; Ima   Vol. 1: 9964
Hogg Prize; Francis   Vol. 2: 3988
Hoggard Performance Medallion; Lara   Vol. 1: 12264
Hogsflesh Trophy; George   Vol. 2: 2062
Hohenberg Award   Vol. 1: 16853
Hoke Award; Henry   Vol. 1: 8648
Hoke, Sr. Award; Henry   Vol. 1: 12007
Hokin Prize; Bess   Vol. 1: 16265
Holberg Medal   Vol. 2: 1928
Holbrook Alumni Award; Frances Morton   Vol. 1: 16121
Holden Award; David   Vol. 2: 4561
Holden Medal   Vol. 2: 4516
Holden Wood Scholarship; Hildreth G.   Vol. 1: 15713
Holdredge Award; Claire P.   Vol. 1: 5772
Holford Medal   Vol. 2: 4037
Holgersson Plaketten; Nils   Vol. 2: 11633
Holgersson Plaque; Nils   Vol. 2: 11633
Holiness Exponent of the Year   Vol. 1: 7662
Holladay Distinguished Fellow Award; Louise and Bill   Vol. 1: 4586
Hollaender Award; Alexander   Vol. 1: 8965
Holland Animation Film Festival Awards   Vol. 2: 9454
Holland Award for Outstanding Achievement in Career and Personality Research; John   Vol. 1: 3706
Holland Award; Maurice   Vol. 1: 10165
Holley Medal   Vol. 1: 4679
Holliday Prize; Leslie   Vol. 2: 3138
Hollingsworth Award; Mark   Vol. 1: 18601
Hollingworth Award   Vol. 1: 11410
Hollister Award; Jean   Vol. 1: 8901
Hollmann Award; Frank   Vol. 1: 14469
Hollomon Award; Acta Metallurgica J. Herbert   Vol. 1: 108
Holloway Best Editorial Cartoon; Wilbert L.   Vol. 1: 14397
Holloway Medal; Tienie   Vol. 2: 10992
Holly Memorial Award; T. Kenyon   Vol. 1: 18845
Holly Prize; Jan   Vol. 2: 10757
Holman Award for Literary Scholarship; C. Hugh   Vol. 1: 17645
Holmenkoll Medal   Vol. 2: 9871
Holmenkollen Ski Festival   Vol. 2: 9872
Holmenkollmedaljen   Vol. 2: 9871
Holmes Award; James S.   Vol. 1: 8006
Holmes Award; John   Vol. 1: 15127
Holmes Award; Oliver Wendell   Vol. 1: 17672
Holmes Bill of Rights Award; Oliver Wendell   Vol. 1: 1588
Holmes Lecture   Vol. 2: 10728
Holmes Lectureship; George W.   Vol. 1: 15138
Holmes Medal; Arthur-   Vol. 2: 5133
Holmes Memorial Trophy (Outstanding Goaltender); Harry (Hap)   Vol. 1: 2327
Holmes Pioneer Award; Joseph H.   Vol. 1: 2691
Holmes Scholars; William Cartwright   Vol. 2: 3331
Holmes - Weatherly Award   Vol. 1: 18889
Holroyd Prize; Margaret   Vol. 2: 2519
Holst Medal; Gilles   Vol. 2: 9601
Holst-prijs; Henriette Roland   Vol. 2: 9627
Holt Award; Charlotte   Vol. 1: 5858
Holt Award; Geoffrey   Vol. 2: 2443
Holtby Memorial Prize; Winifred   Vol. 2: 4232

Holte Literary Prize; Clarence L.   Vol. 1: 16091
Holter Memorial Prize; Casey   Vol. 2: 4370
Holthusen-Ring; Hermann-   Vol. 2: 6829
Holtkamp/AGO Award in Organ Composition   Vol. 1: 2195
Holweck; Fondation Fernand   Vol. 2: 5556
Holweck Medal and Prize   Vol. 2: 3192
Holzman Distinguished Educator Award; Albert G.   Vol. 1: 10360
Home Army Cross   Vol. 2: 10107
Home Economics Teacher of the Year Award   Vol. 1: 2338
Home Orchard Society Awards   Vol. 1: 9984
Homebrew Club of the Year   Vol. 1: 2344
Homebrewer of the Year   Vol. 1: 2344
Homeric Award   Vol. 1: 7590
Homes for Better Living Award   Vol. 1: 2531
Homes of Distinction Awards   Vol. 1: 18061
Hometown USA Video Festival   Vol. 1: 325
Homewood Honorary Award; Lee -   Vol. 1: 5636
Honda Prize   Vol. 2: 8535
Honegger de Composition Musicale; Prix International Arthur   Vol. 2: 5197
Honens International Piano Competition; Esther   Vol. 1: 9986
Honeywell International Medal   Vol. 2: 3160
Honeywell Prize   Vol. 2: 3161
Hong Kong Biennial Awards for Chinese Literature   Vol. 2: 7278
Hong Kong Film Awards   Vol. 2: 7264
Hong Kong Independent Short Film Competition/Urban Council Short Film Awards   Vol. 2: 7265
Hong Kong International Film Festival   Vol. 2: 7264
HONOLULU Magazine/Parker Pen Company Fiction Contest   Vol. 1: 9988
Honor al Merito   Vol. 2: 1783
Honor Award
    American Alliance for Health, Physical Education, Recreation, and Dance   Vol. 1: 761
    American Camping Association   Vol 1: 1406
    American Society for Photogrammetry and Remote Sensing   Vol 1: 4252
    Association of Indians in America   Vol 1: 5832
    Commercial Development Association   Vol 1: 8026
    Council for National Cooperation in Aquatics   Vol 1: 8334
    National Building Museum   Vol 1: 13481
    National Intramural-Recreational Sports Association   Vol 1: 14252
    National Soccer Coaches Association of America   Vol 1: 14728
    Ohio University - E. W. Scripps School of Journalism   Vol 1: 15591
    Sigma Zeta   Vol 1: 17275
    Soil and Water Conservation Society   Vol 1: 18125
    Tennessee Library Association   Vol 1: 18615
    Whooping Crane Conservation Association   Vol 1: 20279
Honor Award and Senior Honor Award   Vol. 1: 630
Honor Awards
    American Academy of Otolaryngology - Head and Neck Surgery   Vol. 1: 657
    Information Council of the Americas   Vol 1: 10176
    University Photographers' Association of America   Vol 1: 19894
Honor Awards for Architecture   Vol. 1: 2532

Honor Awards for Interiors   Vol. 1: 2533
Honor Awards for Program Excellence   Vol. 1: 6534
Honor Awards for Urban Design   Vol. 1: 2534
Honor Awards Program   Vol. 1: 19090
Honor Certificate   Vol. 1: 953
Honor Club of Distinction   Vol. 1: 7788
Honor Club of Distinction Award   Vol. 1: 7788
Honor Coach Award   Vol. 1: 12999
Honor Coach Certificate   Vol. 1: 13000
Honor et Veritas Award   Vol. 1: 7401
Honor Legion   Vol. 1: 14492
Honor Medal with Crossed Palms   Vol. 1: 6517
Honor Roll   Vol. 1: 10813
Honor Roll Adviser Award   Vol. 1: 7910
Honor Roll of Housing   Vol. 1: 14198
Honorable Mention   Vol. 2: 6815
Honorary Affiliate Membership   Vol. 1: 7205
Honorary Alumni of the Hebrew University   Vol. 1: 2119
Honorary Alumnus Award   Vol. 1: 19746
Honorary and Life Fellowships   Vol. 1: 640
Honorary Award
  American Society of Plastic and Reconstructive Surgeons   Vol. 1: 4758
  Association for the History of Chiropractic   Vol 1: 5636
  Research Council of Norway   Vol 2: 9965
Honorary Award of the American Association of Plastic Surgeons   Vol. 1: 1137
Honorary Awards to Private Citizens and Organizations   Vol. 1: 19214
Honorary Citation   Vol. 1: 4759
Honorary Citations   Vol. 1: 13665
Honorary Citizen of the City of Salzburg   Vol. 2: 864
"Honorary Citizen" Title   Vol. 2: 7301
Honorary Companion   Vol. 2: 3905
Honorary Degree of Fellows   Vol. 1: 1096
Honorary Diploma   Vol. 2: 10216
Honorary Distinguished Physicians Award   Vol. 1: 1682
Honorary Distinguished Service Award   Vol. 1: 1683
Honorary Doctor of Divinity Degree   Vol. 1: 10930
Honorary Doctor of Hobbit Letters (DhL)   Vol. 1: 4912
Honorary Doctor of Philosophy in Science (Neurological - Orthopaedic)   Vol. 1: 606
Honorary Emeritus Membership   Vol. 1: 5630
Honorary Fellow
  Acoustical Society of America   Vol. 1: 97
  American Academy of Oral Medicine   Vol 1: 648
  American College of Cardiology   Vol 1: 1614
  American College of Clinical Pharmacology   Vol 1: 1626
  American College of Physicians   Vol 1: 1717
  American College of Radiology   Vol 1: 1739
  American Helicopter Society   Vol 1: 2252
  American Society of Civil Engineers   Vol 1: 4466
  Association for Social Anthropology in Oceania   Vol 1: 5596
  British Interplanetary Society   Vol 2: 2422
  British Psychological Society   Vol 2: 2488
  Chartered Society of Designers   Vol 2: 2608
  Chemical Institute of Canada   Vol 1: 7550
  Ergonomics Society   Vol 2: 2804
  Geological Society of America   Vol 1: 9563
  Institute of Environmental Sciences   Vol 1: 10327
  Institute of Food Science and Technology (UK)   Vol 2: 3102
  Institute of Medical Laboratory Sciences   Vol 2: 3169
  International Federation of Library Associations and Institutions   Vol 2: 9491
  Israel Museum   Vol 2: 7922
  Kenya National Academy of Sciences - Ministry of Research, Science & Technology   Vol 2: 8807
  Library Association of Ireland   Vol 2: 7814
  National Federation of Abstracting and Information Services   Vol 1: 13932
  Photographic Salon Exhibitors Association   Vol 2: 7272
  Royal Agricultural Society of England   Vol 2: 3921
  Royal Asiatic Society   Vol 2: 3935
  Royal College of Surgeons of Edinburgh   Vol 2: 10606
  Royal Horticultural Society   Vol 2: 4038
  Royal Scottish Geographical Society   Vol 2: 10630
  Royal Society of Tropical Medicine and Hygiene   Vol 2: 4278
  Society of Allied Weight Engineers, Inc.   Vol 1: 17665
  Society of Antiquaries of Scotland   Vol 2: 10681
  Society of Dyers and Colourists   Vol 2: 4433
  Society of Experimental Test Pilots   Vol 1: 17837
  Textile Institute   Vol 2: 4517
Honorary Fellow Award
  American Institute of Chemists   Vol. 1: 2614
  American Institute of Ultrasound in Medicine   Vol 1: 2692
Honorary Fellowship
  American College of Dentists   Vol. 1: 1632
  American College of Healthcare Executives   Vol 1: 1662
  American College of Preventive Medicine   Vol 1: 1728
  American Institute of Architects   Vol 1: 2535
  Institution of Nuclear Engineers   Vol 2: 3348
  Royal Photographic Society of Great Britain   Vol 2: 4133
Honorary Fellowship Award   Vol. 1: 1649
Honorary Fellowships   Vol. 1: 598
Honorary Founder of the Guild   Vol. 1: 13560
Honorary Gold Pin   Vol. 2: 6796
Honorary Group Diploma   Vol. 2: 5153
Honorary Human Rights Award   Vol. 1: 3281
Honorary Knights of the Golden Fleece   Vol. 1: 6832
Honorary Life Award   Vol. 1: 15948
Honorary Life Direct Member   Vol. 2: 7282
Honorary Life Fellow
  Pacific Science Association   Vol. 1: 15892
  Standards Engineering Society   Vol 1: 18452
Honorary Life Member
  American Art Therapy Association   Vol. 1: 810
  American Association of Botanical Gardens and Arboreta   Vol 1: 935
  American Association of Cost Engineers   Vol 1: 984
  American Council on Alcoholism   Vol 1: 1855
  American Helvetia Philatelic Society   Vol 1: 2261
  Association for Volunteer Administration   Vol 1: 5653
  British Psychological Society   Vol 2: 2489
  Canadian Parks/Recreation Association   Vol 1: 7088
  Canadian Public Health Association   Vol 1: 7109
  Canadian Seed Growers' Association   Vol 1: 7129
  Canadian Society for Musical Traditions   Vol 1: 7141
  Church and Synagogue Library Association   Vol 1: 7673
  Confederate Stamp Alliance   Vol 1: 8111
  Cranial Academy   Vol 1: 8447
  Directors Guild of America   Vol 1: 8666
  European Union of Jewish Students   Vol 2: 1146
  Federation of Ontario Naturalists   Vol 1: 9151
  International Double Reed Society   Vol 1: 10914
  International Pharmaceutical Students' Federation   Vol 2: 7901
  Northeastern Lumber Manufacturers Association   Vol 1: 15507
  Pharmacy Guild of Australia   Vol 2: 584
  Polish Theological Association in Cracow   Vol 2: 10202
  Sierra Club   Vol 1: 17234
  Society for Leukocyte Biology   Vol 1: 17549
  Society for the Preservation of Old Mills   Vol 1: 17627
  Textile Institute   Vol 2: 4518
Honorary Life Members
  American Wine Society   Vol. 1: 5103
  European Aquaculture Society   Vol 2: 1119
Honorary Life Membership
  American Association of State Climatologists   Vol. 1: 1194
  American Hosta Society   Vol. 1: 2380
  Canadian Society of Animal Science   Vol 1: 7159
  International Organization for Mycoplasmology   Vol 1: 11131
  Mathematical Association of America   Vol 1: 12136
  Newspaper Association of America   Vol 1: 15348
Honorary Life Membership Award   Vol. 1: 10765
Honorary Life Vice-Presidents   Vol. 2: 3378
Honorary Lifetime Member   Vol. 1: 13263
Honorary Lifetime Membership
  American Adoption Congress   Vol. 1: 732
  National Auto Racing Historical Society   Vol 1: 13400
  Western Association of Map Libraries   Vol 1: 20201
Honorary Long Service Award   Vol. 2: 10668
Honorary Member
  Agricultural Economics Society   Vol. 2: 7852
  Agricultural Institute of Canada   Vol 1: 212
  Air and Waste Management Association   Vol 1: 220
  American Academy of Environmental Engineers   Vol 1: 557
  American Academy of Family Physicians   Vol 1: 581
  American Academy of Periodontology   Vol 1: 693
  American Association of Cereal Chemists   Vol 1: 950
  American Association of Nurse Anesthetists   Vol 1: 1057

Award Index
Volume 2: International and Foreign — Honorary

American Association of Petroleum Geologists   Vol 1: 1107
American Astronomical Society   Vol 1: 1269
American Bridge Teacher's Association   Vol 1: 1372
American Bugatti Club   Vol 1: 1374
American Ceramic Society   Vol 1: 1463
American Concrete Institute   Vol 1: 1782
American Congress on Surveying and Mapping   Vol 1: 1815
American Hospital Association   Vol 1: 2373
American Industrial Hygiene Association   Vol 1: 2433
American Institute of Architects   Vol 1: 2536
American Institute of Professional Geologists   Vol 1: 2671
American Library Association   Vol 1: 2819
American Otological Society   Vol 1: 3360
American Pharmaceutical Association   Vol 1: 3381
American Physical Therapy Association   Vol 1: 3483
American Public Works Association   Vol 1: 3878
American Society for Engineering Education   Vol 1: 4095
American Society for Microbiology   Vol 1: 4207
American Society for Photogrammetry and Remote Sensing   Vol 1: 4253
American Society for Quality Control   Vol 1: 4284
American Society of Agronomy   Vol 1: 4385
American Society of Artists   Vol 1: 4406
American Society of Civil Engineers   Vol 1: 4467
American Society of Furniture Designers   Vol 1: 4564
American Society of Heating, Refrigerating and Air-Conditioning Engineers   Vol 1: 4587
American Society of Landscape Architects   Vol 1: 4642
American Society of Mechanical Engineers   Vol 1: 4680
American Society of Safety Engineers   Vol 1: 4784
American Society of Swedish Engineers   Vol 1: 4796
American Society of Zoologists   Vol 1: 4819
American Theatre Organ Society   Vol 1: 4898
American Vacuum Society   Vol 1: 4961
American Water Resources Association   Vol 1: 5005
American Water Works Association   Vol 1: 5025
American Watercolor Society   Vol 1: 5050
American Welding Society   Vol 1: 5079
Archival Association   Vol 2: 4663
Arnold Air Society   Vol 1: 5285
ASM International   Vol 1: 5357
Association in Scotland to Research Into Astronautics   Vol 2: 10511
Association of Asphalt Paving Technologists   Vol 1: 5708
Association of Black Nursing Faculty in Higher Education   Vol 1: 5711
Association of Development Financing Institutions in Asia and the Pacific   Vol 2: 10024
Association of Medical Rehabilitation Administrators   Vol 1: 5863
Association of Pulp and Paper Chemists and Engineers   Vol 2: 6541

Association of University Architects   Vol 1: 5998
Australian Society of Archivists   Vol 2: 268
Austrian Statistical Society   Vol 2: 787
Beta Beta Beta Biological Society   Vol 1: 6337
Biochemical Society   Vol 2: 2172
British Philatelic Federation   Vol 2: 2475
Business Forms Management Association   Vol 1: 6655
Canadian Phytopathological Society   Vol 1: 7099
Canadian Society of Laboratory Technologists   Vol 1: 7206
Canadian Society of Petroleum Geologists   Vol 1: 7222
Canadian Veterinary Medical Association   Vol 1: 7264
Chesapeake and Ohio Historical Society   Vol 1: 7581
Chicago Book Clinic   Vol 1: 7596
Chilean Society of History and Geography   Vol 2: 1558
Czechoslovak Society of Arts and Sciences   Vol 1: 8494
Deutsche Bunsen-Gesellschaft fur Physikalische Chemie   Vol 2: 6630
Deutsche Gesellschaft fur Moor-und Torfkunde   Vol 2: 6633
Ecological Society of America   Vol 1: 8816
Engineering Institute of Canada   Vol 1: 8934
Epsilon Nu Eta Honor Society   Vol 1: 8975
European General Galvanizers Association   Vol 2: 2833
Pierre Fauchard Academy   Vol 1: 9055
Flat Earth Research Society International   Vol 1: 9227
Flying Physicians Association   Vol 1: 9280
Geographical Society of Bosnia and Hercegovina   Vol 2: 1400
Geological Society of South Africa   Vol 2: 10870
German Dental Association   Vol 2: 6797
German Society of Physical Medicine and Rehabilitation   Vol 2: 6866
Guild of Carilloneurs in North America   Vol 1: 9744
Ibsen Society of America   Vol 1: 10068
Incorporated Society of Musicians   Vol 2: 3042
Indian Institute of Metals   Vol 2: 7628
Institute of British Foundrymen   Vol 2: 3072
Institute of Industrial Engineers   Vol 1: 10361
Institute of Packaging Professionals   Vol 1: 10427
Instrument Society of America   Vol 1: 10488
International Association for Exposition Management   Vol 1: 10637
International Association for Hydraulic Research   Vol 2: 9458
International Association of Cancer Registries   Vol 2: 5963
International Association of Museums of Arms and Military History   Vol 2: 11470
International Association of Penal Law   Vol 2: 5969
International Association on Water Quality   Vol 2: 3372
International Churchill Society   Vol 1: 10841
International Korfball Federation   Vol 2: 9514
International Magnesium Association   Vol 1: 11094

International Primary Aluminum Institute   Vol 2: 3458
International Silo Association   Vol 1: 11221
International Society for Contemporary Music   Vol 2: 9526
International Society for Philosophical Enquiry   Vol 1: 11261
International Society of Biometeorology   Vol 1: 11278
International Union for Quaternary Research   Vol 2: 3489
Iron and Steel Institute of Japan   Vol 2: 8562
Lublin Scientific Society   Vol 2: 10079
Medical Women's International Association   Vol 2: 7044
Missouri Archaeological Society   Vol 1: 12364
Modern Language Association of Poland   Vol 2: 10081
National Association of Biology Teachers   Vol 1: 12955
National Association of Interpretation   Vol 1: 13179
National Association of Metal Finishers   Vol 1: 13205
National Avionics Society   Vol 1: 13409
National Council of Education for the Ceramic Arts   Vol 1: 13730
National Environmental Health Association   Vol 1: 13907
National Federation of Press Women   Vol 1: 13944
National Fishing Lure Collectors Club   Vol 1: 13971
National Marine Educators' Association   Vol 1: 14329
National Speleological Society   Vol 1: 14851
New England Water Works Association   Vol 1: 15154
North American Vexillological Association   Vol 1: 15486
Organ Historical Society   Vol 1: 15804
Ottawa Field-Naturalists' Club   Vol 1: 15850
Pastel Society of America   Vol 1: 15984
Pharmacy Guild of Australia   Vol 2: 585
Phi Lambda Upsilon, National Honorary Chemical Society   Vol 1: 16108
Photographic Salon Exhibitors Association   Vol 2: 7273
Photographic Society of America   Vol 1: 16162
Physical Education Association of Ireland   Vol 2: 7822
Piano Technicians Guild   Vol 1: 16201
Polish Association of Pediatric Surgeons   Vol 2: 10132
Polish Geographical Society   Vol 2: 10147
Polish Medical Society of Radiology   Vol 2: 10161
Polish Society for Commodity Science   Vol 2: 10181
Polish Society of Endocrinology   Vol 2: 10185
Polish Society of Hygiene   Vol 2: 10190
Polish Sociological Association   Vol 2: 10199
Royal Academy of Music   Vol 2: 3877
Royal Astronomical Society of Canada   Vol 1: 16928
Royal Danish Geographical Society   Vol 2: 2000
Royal Institute of Navigation   Vol 2: 4078
Royal Northern College of Music   Vol 2: 4113
Scandinavian Collectors Club   Vol 1: 17084

Franz Schmidt Society Vol 2: 880
Sigma Delta Epsilon - Graduate Women in Science Vol 1: 17255
Sigma Phi Alpha Vol 1: 17262
Society for Applied Spectroscopy Vol 1: 17416
Society for Imaging Science and Technology Vol 1: 17501
Society of American Foresters Vol 1: 17684
Society of Applied Botany Vol 2: 7088
Society of Commercial Seed Technologists Vol 1: 17817
Society of Dyers and Colourists Vol 2: 4434
Society of Exploration Geophysicists Vol 1: 17844
Society of Friends of the Polish Language Vol 2: 10210
Society of Laboratory Animal Science Vol 2: 11909
Society of Manufacturing Engineers Vol 1: 17879
Society of Motion Picture and Television Engineers Vol 1: 17903
Society of Nematologists Vol 1: 17937
Society of Petroleum Engineers Vol 1: 17969
Southern African Society for Plant Pathology Vol 2: 11104
Surface Design Journal Vol 1: 18534
Texas Armadillo Association Vol 1: 18628
United Mirror Class Association Vol 1: 18946
United States Harness Writers Association Vol 1: 19378
Water Environment Federation Vol 1: 20152
Wildlife Society Vol 1: 20302
World Conservation Union Vol 2: 11969
Wroclaw Scientific Society Vol 2: 10220
Honorary Member and Honorary Associate Vol. 2: 3788
Honorary Member Award Vol. 1: 17312
Honorary Member, Foreign Honorary Member, and Fellow Vol. 1: 526
Honorary Membership
 American Kinesiotherapy Association Vol. 1: 2776
 Association of Hungarian Geophysicists Vol 2: 7289
 Construction Specifications Institute Vol 1: 8205
 Polish Chemical Society Vol 2: 10135
 Royal Photographic Society of Great Britain Vol 2: 4134
Honorary Membership Award
 American Nurses' Association Vol. 1: 3280
 National Athletic Trainers' Association Vol 1: 13388
 Southeastern Library Association Vol 1: 18192
Honorary Membership (Outstanding Contributors) Vol. 1: 13618
Honorary Nurse Practitioner Award Vol. 1: 3282
Honorary Nursing Practice Award Vol. 1: 3282
Honorary Plaque Vol. 2: 6798
Honorary President
 American Pharmaceutical Association Vol. 1: 3382
 International Federation of Library Associations and Institutions Vol 2: 9492
Honorary President, Honorary Member Vol. 1: 20472

Honorary President of the Guild Vol. 1: 13561
Honorary Recognition Vol. 1: 11002
Honorary Recognition Award Vol. 1: 3283
Honorary Recognition Awards Vol. 1: 11372
Honorary Research Lecture Vol. 1: 4126
Honorary Ring Vol. 2: 6528
Honorary Rings of the City of Salzburg Vol. 2: 865
Honorary Scholar Vol. 2: 837
Honorary Senior Stick Award Vol. 1: 18438
Honorary Title of Inventor Vol. 1: 11417
Honorary Titles of the USSR Vol. 2: 10461
Honored Guest Vol. 1: 20067
Honored Student Award Vol. 1: 3315
Honoree of the Year Award Vol. 1: 13386
Honoree of the Year (Women's Long Distance Running) Vol. 1: 19963
Honoris Crux Vol. 2: 10928
Honoris Crux Diamond Vol. 2: 10929
Honoris Crux Gold Vol. 2: 10930
Honoris Crux Silver Vol. 2: 10931
Honors and Achievement Award Vol. 1: 11088
Honors Award
 American Library Association - Map and Geography Round Table Vol. 1: 2918
 Association of American Geographers Vol 1: 5683
Honors Chorus Vol. 1: 10957
Honors for Meritorious Contributions Vol. 1: 5683
Honors for Outstanding Achievement Vol. 1: 5683
Honors for Outstanding Achievement and for Meritorious Contributions Vol. 1: 5683
Honors of the Association
 American Speech-Language-Hearing Association Vol. 1: 4842
 International Society of Phonetic Sciences Vol 1: 11296
Honour Distinctions Vol. 2: 10166
Honour Roll Vol. 2: 840
Honourably Mentioned in Despatches Vol. 2: 10932
Honourary Member Vol. 1: 375
Honours Award Vol. 2: 10871
Hood Award; E. I. Vol. 1: 6784
Hood Award for Diplomatic Correspondence; Edwin M. Vol. 1: 14500
Hood Medal Vol. 2: 4135
Hooft Prize; Pieter Cornelisz Vol. 2: 9665
Hoogendijk Prijs; Steven Vol. 2: 9420
Hoogenhouttoekenning; C.P. Vol. 2: 11059
Hook Memorial Award; Sidney
 National Association of Scholars Vol. 1: 13293
 Phi Beta Kappa Vol 1: 16101
Hooker of the Year Vol. 1: 14902
Hooper Fellowship in International Relations; Thornton D. Vol. 1: 9325
Hoover Award; VFW J. Edgar Vol. 1: 20016
Hoover Book Award; Herbert Vol. 1: 9994
Hoover Humanitarian Award; Herbert Vol. 1: 6535
Hoover Medal
 American Society of Civil Engineers Vol. 1: 4468
 American Society of Mechanical Engineers Vol 1: 4681
Hoover Memorial Award; Herbert Vol. 1: 6535
Hoover Police Service Award; John Edgar Vol. 1: 3556
Hoover Trophy Vol. 1: 3556
Hopeinen Fennia-mitali Vol. 2: 4713
Hopkins Lecture Vol. 2: 9735

Hopkins Memorial Lecture; Sir Frederick Gowland Vol. 2: 2173
Hopkins Prize; William Vol. 2: 2567
Hopkinson Literature Award; Walter W. Vol. 1: 6620
Hopkinson Memorial Trophy; Walter W. Vol. 1: 6621
Hopkinson Premium; John Vol. 2: 3273
Hopper Award; Grace Murray Vol. 1: 5469
Hopps Award; Hope E. Vol. 1: 18718
Hora Medal; Chandrakala Vol. 2: 7649
Horn Memorial Scholarship; Frank Walton Vol. 1: 13965
Horne Lecture; Robert Vol. 2: 4410
Horne Memorial Award; John Robert Vol. 1: 12749
Horne Student Calendar Awards; Robert Vol. 2: 2483
Horner Award; B. Elizabeth Vol. 1: 4658
Horner Award; Wesley W. Vol. 1: 4469
Horner Travel Award Vol. 1: 7188
Horning Memorial Award; Harry L. Vol. 1: 17763
Horonjeff Award of the Air Transport Division; Robert Vol. 1: 4470
Horowitz Memorial Prize; David Vol. 2: 7868
Horse of the Year
 American Grandprix Association Vol. 1: 2186
 National Spotted Saddle Horse Association Vol 1: 14865
 Thoroughbred Racing Associations of North America Vol 1: 18706
Horse of the Year - Headliner Award Vol. 1: 19375
Horse of the Year Awards Vol. 1: 19324
Horseback Hours Award Vol. 1: 2421
Horseback Miles Award Vol. 1: 2422
Horseshoe Hall of Fame Vol. 1: 14187
Horta; Prix Baron Vol. 2: 952
Horticultural Communication Award Vol. 1: 2355
Horticultural Therapy Award Vol. 1: 2356
Horticultural Writing Citation Vol. 1: 2357
Horton Award; Dutch Vol. 1: 5799
Horton Award; Robert E. Vol. 1: 2166
Horton Lecturer in Hydrology; Robert E. Vol. 1: 3086
Horton Medal; Robert E. Vol. 1: 2167
Horton Trophy; Tim Vol. 1: 2328
Horwitz Award for Inter-American Health; Abraham Vol. 1: 15924
Horwitz Prize; Louisa Gross Vol. 1: 7983
Hosei International Fund Foreign Scholars Fellowship Vol. 2: 8537
Hosking Award; Eric Vol. 2: 2162
Hoso Bunka Foundation Prize Vol. 2: 8602
Hospital and Community Psychiatry Achievement Awards Vol. 1: 3636
Host-Madsen Medal Vol. 2: 9521
Host Service Award Vol. 1: 936
Hot Mix Asphalt Hall of Fame Vol. 1: 12832
Hotel of the Year Awards Vol. 2: 2854
Hotelier of the Year Award Vol. 2: 2573
Hotelympia
 Canadian Federation of Culinary Chefs Vol. 1: 6860
 National Restaurant Association Vol 1: 14623
 Panel of Chefs of Ireland Vol 2: 7817
 Singapore Chefs Association Vol 2: 10752
 Society of German Cooks Vol 2: 7090
 Society of Swiss Cuisiniers Vol 2: 11911
Hotelympia Competition Vol. 2: 2611
Hottenroth-Denkmunze; Valentin- Vol. 2: 6542
Houdry Award in Applied Catalysis; Eugene J. Vol. 1: 7344

Hougenhout Award; C. P. Vol. 2: 11059
Hough-Grassby Memorial Award; Alec Vol. 2: 3162
Houghton Award Vol. 2: 3544
Houghton Award; Firman Vol. 1: 15128
Houghton Award; Henry G. Vol. 1: 3087
Houghton Mifflin Literary Fellowship Vol. 1: 10016
Houle World Award for Literature in Adult Education; Cyril O. Vol. 1: 826
Houllevigue; Prix Vol. 2: 5679
Houphouet-Boigny Peace Prize; Felix Vol. 2: 6413
Hourglass Award Vol. 1: 12295
House & Garden/IDDA Decorex Young Designer of the Year Vol. 2: 3027
House of the Year Vol. 1: 13136
Houseparents Length of Service Awards Vol. 1: 10008
Housing Associations Charitable Trust Award for Housing Vol. 2: 4073
Housing Design Award Vol. 2: 10654
Housing Design Awards Vol. 2: 4068
Houssa; Prix Nicole Vol. 2: 1304
Houssay Inter-American Science Prize; Bernardo A. Vol. 1: 15828
Houston Award; Charles S. Vol. 1: 20289
Houston Opera Studio Career Award Vol. 1: 10021
Houston Opera Studio Member Vol. 1: 10020
Houston Research Awards; W. J. B. Vol. 2: 2838
Houston State University Award; Sam Vol. 1: 3616
Houston Symphony Student Auditions Vol. 1: 9965
Houzeau; Prix Vol. 2: 5508
Howard Award; Ernest E. Vol. 1: 4471
Howard Award for Horticulture; Nancy Putnam Vol. 1: 9908
Howard Awards; Broadcast/Cable Journalism Awards - Jack R. Vol. 1: 17143
Howard Awards; Public Service Reporting - Roy W. Vol. 1: 17149
Howard Broadcast Award; Roy Vol. 1: 17143
Howard Broadcast Awards; Broadcast Journalistic Excellence - Jack R. Vol. 1: 17143
Howard Citation of Musical Excellence for Military Band; Colonel George S. Vol. 1: 18161
Howard Fellows Vol. 1: 10025
Howard-Gibbon Illustrator's Award; Amelia Frances
  Canadian Library Association - Canadian Association of Children's Librarians Vol. 1: 7004
  Canadian Library Association - Canadian School Library Association Vol 1: 7025
Howard, Mackie Awards Vol. 1: 6974
Howard Medal Vol. 2: 3241
Howard Memorial Medal; Ebenezer Vol. 2: 4553
Howard Public Service Awards; Roy W. Vol. 1: 17149
Howard Quinquennial Prize Vol. 2: 3241
Howard World Book Encyclopedia - ALA Goal Awards; J. Morris Jones and Bailey K. Vol. 1: 2825
Howe Award; C. D. Vol. 1: 6765
Howe Award; William A. Vol. 1: 4004
Howe Cup Vol. 2: 4455
Howe Medal Vol. 1: 3318
Howe Medal; Henry Marion Vol. 1: 5358
Howe Memorial Lecturer Vol. 1: 11464
Howe Memorial Trophy; Henry Wainwright Vol. 1: 19354
Howe Prize; Lucien Vol. 1: 12197
Howell Award; A. Brazier Vol. 1: 8255

Howell Award; Brazier Vol. 1: 4659
Howells Medal Vol. 1: 509
Howland Award; John Vol. 1: 3367
Howley, Sr. Prize for Research in Arthritis; Lee C. Vol. 1: 5304
Hoyen Medal; N. L. Vol. 2: 1900
Hoyres Pressebyra Press Prize Vol. 2: 9912
Hoyt Award; National Milk Producers Federation - Richard M. Vol. 1: 1919
Hoyt National Art Show Vol. 1: 10030
Hoyt National Drawing and Painting Show Vol. 1: 10030
Hoz Prize; Engineering Prize - Dov Vol. 2: 7951
Hrdlicka Award; Ales Vol. 1: 1119
Hrinemann Prize; Butterworth Vol. 2: 2185
HRLSD Exceptional Service Award Vol. 1: 2880
Hsieh Award; T. K. Vol. 2: 3242
HSMA Advertising Awards Vol. 1: 9998
HSMAI Golden Bell Public Relations Awards Vol. 1: 10002
HSMAI Hall of Fame Vol. 1: 10003
HSMAI Public Relations Competition Vol. 1: 10002
Hubbard Art Award of Excellence Vol. 1: 10032
Hubbard Award; Prevost Vol. 1: 6056
Hubbard Lemon Award; Harlan Page Vol. 1: 7459
Hubbard Medal Vol. 1: 14073
Hubbard Race Relations Award; William P. Vol. 1: 7761
Hubbard's Writers of the Future Contest; L. Ron Vol. 1: 6555
Hubele National Graduate Student Award; Glen E. Vol. 1: 1886
Huber Civil Engineering Research Prizes; Walter L. Vol. 1: 4472
Huber; Prix Michel Vol. 2: 6393
Hubley Award; John and Faith Vol. 1: 17288
Huch-Preis; Ricarda- Vol. 2: 6599
Huchel-Preis fur Lyrik; Peter- Vol. 2: 7144
Hudgens Memorial Award - Young Healthcare Executive of the Year; Robert S. Vol. 1: 1663
Hudgens Memorial Award - Young Hospital Administrator of the Year; Robert S. Vol. 1: 1663
Hudiburg Award; Everett E. Vol. 1: 10982
Hudson Award in Carbohydrate Chemistry; Claude S. Vol. 1: 1562
Hudson Award; Sir William Vol. 2: 476
Hudson Medal; Manley O. Vol. 1: 4631
Huerta National Prize for Short Story and Poetry; Efrain Vol. 2: 9164
Huetprijs; Busken Vol. 2: 9639
Hug Teacher of the Year Award; Clarissa Vol. 1: 8314
Huggins-Quarles Award Vol. 1: 15818
Hugh Last Award Vol. 2: 8178
Hugh Terry Prize Vol. 2: 3736
Hughes Award; Howard Vol. 1: 2253
Hughes Gold Medal Award; Charles Evans Vol. 1: 13644
Hughes, Jr., Memorial Award; Daniel C. Vol. 1: 11255
Hughes Law Enforcement Award Vol. 1: 9896
Hughes Medal Vol. 2: 4151
Hugo Awards Vol. 1: 7702
Hugo Memorial Book Prize; Old Sturbridge Village Research Library Society - E. Harold Vol. 1: 15617
Hugues Prize; Clovis Vol. 2: 6315
Huh Kyun Literary Award Vol. 2: 8825
Huk Memorial Trophy; Dr. Wolodymir Vol. 1: 5992

Hulbert Memorial Trophy; Ruth and Jim Vol. 2: 2060
Hull Award; T. J. Vol. 1: 13041
Hull - Kate Warriner Award; Elizabeth Vol. 1: 8737
Hull Memorial Plaque; Bill Vol. 1: 9501
Hult Medal; Ragnar Vol. 2: 4714
Hult-mitali; Ragnar Vol. 2: 4714
Hulubei Prize; Horia Vol. 2: 10355
Human Interest Reporting - Ernie Pyle Award Vol. 1: 17147
Human Needs Award Vol. 1: 1106
Human Relations Award Vol. 1: 17403
Human Rights Award
  American Federation of Teachers, AFL-CIO Vol. 1: 2035
  American Psychiatric Association Vol 1: 3637
  Human Rights Campaign Fund Vol 1: 10048
  International Association of Official Human Rights Agencies Vol 1: 10771
  International League for Human Rights Vol 1: 11072
Human Rights in Media Award Vol. 1: 11073
Human Rights Medal Vol. 2: 6026
Human Rights Prize Vol. 2: 11953
Humana Festival of New American Plays Vol. 1: 126
Humane Award Vol. 1: 2400
Humane Innovator of the Year Vol. 1: 16556
Humane Services Recognition Award Vol. 1: 17077
Humanist Arts Award Vol. 1: 2410
Humanist Contributions to Science Award Vol. 1: 2411
Humanist Distinguished Service Award Vol. 1: 2412
Humanist Fellow Award Vol. 1: 2412
Humanist Heroine Award Vol. 1: 2413
Humanist of the Year Award Vol. 1: 2414
Humanist Pioneer Award Vol. 1: 2415
Humanitarian Award
  American Cancer Society Vol. 1: 1413
  American College of Oral and Maxillofacial Surgeons, Inc. Vol 1: 1704
  American Sportscasters Association Vol 1: 4854
  AMIT Women Vol 1: 5135
  B'nai B'rith Foundation (Canada) Vol 1: 6424
  Council for Exceptional Children - Mental Retardation Division Vol 1: 8321
  International Association of Cancer Victors and Friends Vol 1: 10692
  International Society for Clinical Laboratory Technology Vol 1: 11240
  International Veteran Boxers Association Vol 1: 11384
  Inventors Clubs of America - International Hall of Fame Vol 1: 11418
  National Association of Recording Merchandisers Vol 1: 13279
  National Council on Alcoholism and Drug Dependence Vol 1: 13790
  National Hemophilia Foundation Vol 1: 14129
  National Parkinson Foundation Vol 1: 14450
  National Press Photographers Association Vol 1: 14515
  People for the Ethical Treatment of Animals Vol 1: 16060
  Variety Clubs International Vol 1: 19983
  Elie Wiesel Foundation for Humanity Vol 1: 20283

Humanitarian Award for Human Rights and Social Justice Vol. 1: 8163
Humanitarian of the Year Vol. 1: 5462
Humanitarian of the Year Award Vol. 1: 3939
Humanitarian Service Medal Vol. 1: 19163
Humanitas Prize Vol. 1: 10046
Humanities Award Vol. 1: 16157
Humboldt International Film and Video Festival Vol. 1: 10056
Humboldt Research Awards to Foreign Scholars Vol. 2: 7155
Humboldt Research Fellowships Vol. 2: 7156
Hume Award; Paul Vol. 1: 11842
Hume Memorial Award; David M. Vol. 1: 14272
Hume-Rothery Award; William Vol. 1: 12314
Hume-Rothery Prize Vol. 2: 3139
Huml International Violin Competition; Vaclav Vol. 2: 1801
Hummingbird Medal of the Order of the Trinity Vol. 2: 12034
Humphrey Award; Hubert Vol. 1: 16304
Humphrey Award; Hubert H.
  American Pharmaceutical Association Vol. 1: 3383
  American Political Science Association Vol 1: 3575
Humphrey Award; Touchdown Club Hubert H. Vol. 1: 18762
Humphrey Civil Rights Award; Hubert H. Vol. 1: 11806
Humphrey Doctoral Fellowships in Arms Control and Disarmament; Hubert H. Vol. 1: 19004
Humphrey First Amendment Freedoms Prize; Hubert H. Vol. 1: 5178
Humphrey Humanitarian Award; Hubert H. Vol. 1: 14966
Humphrey/OCLC/Forest Press Award; John Ames Vol. 1: 2903
Humphrey Research Grant; Hubert Vol. 1: 3995
Humphry/Forest Press Award; John Ames Vol. 1: 2903
Hungarian Academy of Sciences Gold Medal Vol. 2: 7312
Hungarian PEN Club Medal Vol. 2: 7367
Hunkins Award; Ruth E. Vol. 1: 9711
Hunt Award for Administrative Excellence; Leamon Vol. 1: 19294
Hunt Award; Robert W. Vol. 1: 11465
Hunt Memorial Award; Captain Alfred E. Vol. 1: 18082
Hunt Memorial Medal; Charles Vol. 2: 3324
Hunt Memorial Prize; Renee Redfern Vol. 2: 3243
Hunt Memorial Trophy; Fred T. Vol. 1: 2329
Hunt Postdoctoral Research Fellowship; Frederick V. Vol. 1: 98
Hunt Trophy; Jo Vol. 1: 14644
Hunt Trophy; Lamar Vol. 1: 14000
Hunter, Jr. Award Thesis; Charles A. Vol. 1: 2206
Hunter Medal and Triennial Prize; John Vol. 2: 3976
Hunter Memorial Award in Therapeutics of the ASCPT; Oscar B. Vol. 1: 4057
Hunter Memorial Award; J. Norman Vol. 1: 8206
Hunter Prize; Richard S. Vol. 1: 18601
Hunter Visiting Professorship; William Vol. 1: 10060
Hunterdon Art Center National Print Exhibition Purchase Awards Vol. 1: 10062
Hunterdon Art Center Prizes Vol. 1: 10062
Hunterian Medal Vol. 2: 3033
Hunterian Oration Vol. 2: 3977

Hunterian Oration and Festival Vol. 2: 3977
Hunting Group Art Prizes Vol. 2: 3760
Hunting/*Observer* Art Prizes Vol. 2: 3760
Hunting Retriever Champion Vol. 1: 18929
Huntington Bronze Medals; Anna Hyatt Vol. 1: 20348
Huntington Medal Award; Archer M. Vol. 1: 3276
Hurd Award; James A. Vol. 1: 5735
Hurmuzachi Prize; Eudoxiu Vol. 2: 10356
Hurmuzescu Prize; Dragomir Vol. 2: 10357
Hurowitz Award Vol. 1: 18920
Hurst Prize Vol. 1: 11791
Hurter Lecture Vol. 2: 4411
Husain Prize for Young Scientists; Javed Vol. 2: 6414
Husodo Award; Wahidin Sudiro Vol. 2: 7727
Hustinx Prize for Science; Edmond Vol. 2: 9682
Hustinxprijs; Edmond Vol. 2: 9655
Hutchins Award; Lee M. Vol. 1: 3523
Hutchinson Award; G. Evelyn Vol. 1: 4652
Hutchison Medal Vol. 2: 3222
Hutton Memorial Award; Brig. Gen. Carl I. Vol. 1: 15782
Hutton Memorial Medal and Prize Vol. 2: 9839
Huxley Award; Thomas Henry Vol. 2: 4657
Huxley Memorial Medal and Lecture Vol. 2: 3929
Huy - World Festival of Movies of Short Films Awards Vol. 2: 1160
Huygens Prize; Constantijn Vol. 2: 9350
Huysmans; Prix Quadriennal de Composition Musicale Camille Vol. 2: 1055
Huysmans; Vierjaarlijkse prijs voor muziekcompositie Camille Vol. 2: 1055
Hvatningarverdlaun Rannsoknarads Vol. 2: 7466
Hviezdoslav Prize; Pavol Orszagh Vol. 2: 10758
Hyatt Award; John W. Vol. 1: 17984
Hyde Award; Donald F. Vol. 1: 9436
Hyde Gold Medal; Douglas Vol. 2: 7759
Hyde Memorial Lecture; Samuel Vol. 2: 4254
Hyde Trophy; Walter Vol. 2: 3625
Hydraulic Structures Medal Vol. 1: 4473
Hydrolab/IAGLR Best Student Paper Competition Vol. 1: 10642
Hyman Award; Women's Sports Foundation Flo Vol. 1: 20435
Hyman Fellowship in Cardiac Pacing; Albert S. Vol. 1: 15458
Hyman Memorial Golden Gazelle; Flo Vol. 1: 15548
I Care Awards Vol. 1: 1179
IAA Public Service Advertising Award Vol. 1: 10591
IAA Value of Advertising Award Vol. 1: 10592
IAAF/Mobil Grand Prix Final Vol. 2: 9314
IAAF/Reebok World Cup of Race Walking Vol. 2: 9314
IAAF/Snickers World Cross Country Championships Vol. 2: 9314
IAAF World Athletic Series Vol. 2: 9314
IAAF World Championships Vol. 2: 9315
IAAF World Cup in Athletics Vol. 2: 9314
IAAF World Half Marathon Championships Vol. 2: 9314
IAAF World Indoor Championships Vol. 2: 9314
IAAF World Junior Championships Vol. 2: 9314
IAAF World Marathon Cup Vol. 2: 9314
IAAF World Road Relay Championships Vol. 2: 9314

IAAO Global Award Vol. 1: 10665
IAAO Journalism Citation Vol. 1: 10666
IABC Chairman's Award Vol. 1: 10684
IABC Fellow Vol. 1: 10685
IABO Awards Vol. 2: 8278
IABSE Prize Vol. 2: 11755
IAC American Cup Vol. 2: 3067
IAC International Film and Video Competition Vol. 2: 3067
IACP Cookbook Awards Vol. 1: 10711
IAE Distinguished Member or Fellow Vol. 1: 10722
IAE Honorary Member or Fellow Vol. 1: 10723
IAE International Graduate Student Award Vol. 1: 10724
IAE Professional Service Award Vol. 1: 10725
IAE Research Award Vol. 1: 10726
IAEE Journalism Award Vol. 1: 10631
IAESTE Award Certificate Vol. 2: 5959
IAEWP Diploma of Honour Vol. 1: 10718
IAEWP Membership in Good Standing Vol. 1: 10719
IAFF International Media Awards Vol. 1: 10732
IAGLR Scholarship Vol. 1: 10643
IAHCSMM Annual Representative to the Board Award; CALGON/ Vol. 1: 10742
IAHCSMM's Past President Award Vol. 1: 10743
IAHR-APD Award Vol. 2: 9459
IAHR Lecturer Award Vol. 2: 9460
IAIA - Rose Hulman Award Vol. 1: 10647
IAJE Hall of Fame Vol. 1: 10751
IALD Lighting Design Awards Vol. 1: 10758
IAMANEH Award Vol. 2: 11881
IAMP Awards Vol. 2: 498
IANU Award Vol. 1: 11488
IAPA - Bartolome Mitre Award Vol. 1: 10511
IAPA - Commentary Award Vol. 1: 10511
IAPA - *The Globe and Mail* Award Vol. 1: 10511
IAPA - Harmodio Arias Award Vol. 1: 10511
IAPA - McClatchy Newspapers Award Vol. 1: 10511
IAPA - Pedor Joaquin Chamorro Award Vol. 1: 10511
IAPA - Quesada Award; Jose Antonio Miro Vol. 1: 10511
IAPA - Tom Wallace Award Vol. 1: 10511
IAPA Journalism Awards Vol. 1: 10511
IAPB Awards Vol. 2: 3366
IAPH Essay Contest Vol. 2: 8545
IASL/SIRS International Commendation Award Vol. 1: 10786
IASP Research Prize Vol. 1: 10657
IATUL Essay Prize Vol. 2: 10575
IAWPRC Pergamon Publications Medal Vol. 2: 3373
IAWQ Pergamon Publications Medal Vol. 2: 3373
Ibarguengoitia; Premio de Narrativa Jorge Vol. 2: 9217
IBBY - Asahi Reading Promotion Award Vol. 2: 11768
IBBY-Asahi Reading Promotion Award Vol. 2: 8494
IBBY Honour List Vol. 2: 11769
IBC Award Vol. 2: 3384
IBC John Tucker Award Vol. 2: 3384
IBD/*Interior Design* Magazine Contract Design Competition Vol. 1: 10570
IBD Magazine Contract Design Competition Vol. 1: 10247
IBD Product Design Competition Vol. 1: 10248

Award Index
Volume 2: International and Foreign — Imperial

IBD Will Ching, FIBD Design Competition Vol. 1: 10249
Iben Award; Icko Vol. 1: 5006
Iberoamerican Film Festival Vol. 2: 11261
IBEU Theater Prize Vol. 2: 1466
IBEU Visual Arts Award Vol. 2: 1467
IBF Distinguished Service Award Vol. 1: 19036
IBF Gold Medal Vol. 2: 9892
IBF Meritorious Service Award Vol. 1: 19037
IBFCC Award Vol. 1: 10809
IBM MEng Project Prize Vol. 2: 3294
IBMA Certificate of Merit Vol. 1: 10803
IBRO/UNESCO Fellowship Programme Vol. 2: 5980
Ibuka Consumer Electronics Award; Masaru Vol. 1: 10270
ICA Fellow Vol. 1: 10863
ICA Technique Award Vol. 1: 10836
ICAAC Young Investigator Awards Vol. 1: 4208
Icarus Award Vol. 2: 2336
ICCJ - Sternberg Award Vol. 2: 6938
ICCROM Award Vol. 2: 8286
Ice Skating Hall of Fame Vol. 1: 10072
Ice Skating Man and Woman of the Year Vol. 1: 10073
ICHMT Fellows Awards Vol. 2: 10710
ICI Award Vol. 2: 441
ICI Prize Vol. 2: 3163
ICI Research Scholarship Vol. 2: 6701
ICI Traveling Lectureship Vol. 1: 18073
ICIA Achievement Awards Vol. 1: 10865
ICMA Newspaper Carrier Hall of Fame Vol. 1: 10844
ICMR Prize for Biomedical Research Conducted in Underdeveloped Areas Vol. 2: 7587
ICMR Prize for Biomedical Research for Scientists belonging to Under-privileged Communities Vol. 2: 7588
ICO Galileo Galilei Medal Vol. 2: 5984
ICO Prize
  International Commission for Optics Vol. 2: 5985
  International Union of Pure and Applied Physics Vol 2: 11485
ICOMP Population Award
  International Council on Management of Population Programmes Vol. 2: 8906
  International Council on Management of Population Programmes Vol 2: 8906
ICOMP Population Programmes Management Award Vol. 2: 8906
ICPE Medal for Physics Teaching Vol. 2: 11486
ICRU - Gray Medal Vol. 1: 10861
ICSA Award of Excellence Vol. 1: 10900
ICSC Annual Awards Vol. 1: 10881
ICSC International Design and Development Awards Vol. 1: 10881
ICSID/Compiegne Industrial Design Award Vol. 2: 6461
ICTA DuPont Award Vol. 2: 3388
ICTA Young Scientist Award Vol. 2: 3389
ICTP Prize Vol. 2: 8289
ID Annual Design Review Vol. 1: 10909
IDA Achievement Awards Vol. 1: 10916
IDA Prizes Vol. 1: 10703
Ideal Corporation - USAC National Championship Crew Chief Award Vol. 1: 19021
Idepris Vol. 2: 9966
Iditarod Trail International Sled Dog Race Vol. 1: 10077
IEA - Bruce H. Choppin Memorial Award Vol. 2: 9465

IEC Promotion and Marketing Award Vol. 2: 3405
IEE Achievement Medal Vol. 2: 3282
IEE Benefactors Prize Vol. 2: 3283
IEE Measurement Prize Vol. 2: 3284
IEE Prize Vol. 2: 3285
IEE Prize for Helping Disabled People Vol. 2: 3286
IEE Prize for Innovation Vol. 2: 3287
IEE Rayleigh Book Award Vol. 2: 3288
IEE Scotland North Premium Vol. 2: 3289
IEEE Award in International Communication Vol. 1: 10271
IEEE Corporate Innovation Recogniton Award Vol. 1: 10272
IEEE Education Medal Vol. 1: 10273
IEEE Engineering Leadership Recognition Vol. 1: 10274
IEEE Life Members' Prize in Electrical History Vol. 1: 17619
IEEE Medal for Engineering Excellence Vol. 1: 10275
IEEE Medal of Honor Vol. 1: 10276
IERE Benefactors Premium Vol. 2: 3290
IES Gold Medal Vol. 1: 10087
IES Medal Vol. 1: 10087
IESL Award Vol. 2: 11403
IET Woman's Engineer Award Vol. 2: 3093
IFA Hall of Fame Award Vol. 1: 10999
IFA International Aviation Scholarship Vol. 2: 3413
IFA Len Gore Scholarship Vol. 2: 3413
IFALPA Scroll of Merit Vol. 2: 3409
IFAWPCA-CHOI Fieldman Award Vol. 2: 10037
IFAWPCA-PCA Foundation Research Award Vol. 2: 10038
IFCO Booth Competition Awards Vol. 1: 10952
IFCO Tex Ritter Award Vol. 1: 10953
IFDA-Student Design Competition Vol. 1: 11005
IFEAT Distinguished Service Medal Vol. 2: 3415
IFHP International Film/Video Competition Vol. 2: 9486
IFHP International Student Competition Vol. 2: 9487
IFI Award Vol. 2: 9489
IFLA Competitions Vol. 2: 6005
IFLA Medal Vol. 2: 9493
IFOS Golden Award Vol. 2: 1185
IFOS Thanking Award Vol. 2: 1186
IFPA Award Vol. 1: 6004
IFSCC Award and IFSCC Honorary Mention Vol. 2: 3421
IFSCC Poster Prize Vol. 2: 3422
IFT Food Science Journalism Awards Vol. 1: 10346
IFT International Award Vol. 1: 10347
IFUW Awards Competition Vol. 2: 11789
IFUW Ida Smedley MacLean International Fellowship Vol. 2: 11789
IFWTO Berger - Sullivan Award Vol. 1: 10972
IGI Art Competition Vol. 1: 11009
IGIP Award Vol. 2: 849
IGIP-Preis Vol. 2: 849
Iglesia de Llano Prize; Angela Vol. 2: 82
Iglesias; Premi Ignasi Vol. 2: 11158
Iguchi Award; Motonari Vol. 2: 8608
IHRA Pro Alcohol Funny Car World Champion Vol. 1: 11031
IHRA Pro Modified World Champion Vol. 1: 11032
IHRA Pro Nitro Dragster World Champion Vol. 1: 11035

IHRA Pro Nitro Funny Car World Champion Vol. 1: 11033
IHRA Pro Stock World Championship Vol. 1: 11034
IHRA Pro Top Fuel Dragster World Champion Vol. 1: 11035
IIAA Publications Award Vol. 1: 10129
IICS Mark of Excellence Awards Vol. 1: 11052
IIE Award for Excellence in Productivity Improvement Vol. 1: 10362
IIE Distinguished Educator Award Vol. 1: 10360
IIE Doctoral Dissertation Award Vol. 1: 10363
IIE - Joint Publishers Book of the Year Award Vol. 1: 10364
IIE Transactions Development and Applications Paper Award Vol. 1: 10365
IIIT Dissertation Award Vol. 1: 11050
IIM Platinum Medal Vol. 2: 7629
IIM Rolling Trophy Vol. 2: 7630
Ikarus Medaille Vol. 2: 7050
Ikarusmedaille Vol. 2: 6571
ILAR CIBA-GEIGY Prize Vol. 1: 11070
Ilavsky Memorial Scholarship; Jan Vol. 1: 6219
ILCA Film and Broadcast Competition Vol. 1: 11064
ILCA Journalistic Awards Contest Vol. 1: 11065
Iler Award in the Chemistry of Colloidal Materials; Ralph K. Vol. 1: 1563
Illges Seedling Japonica Award Vol. 1: 1396
Illinois - NWSA Manuscript Award Vol. 1: 15031
Illinois Opera Guild Auditions of the Air Vol. 1: 8612
Illustration Annual Vol. 1: 8059
Illustration Award Vol. 2: 11383
Illustratorprisen Vol. 2: 1938
Image Award Vol. 1: 13364
Image Awards Vol. 1: 12906
Images Competition Vol. 1: 7485
IMAGFIC Festival Internacional de Cine de Madrid Vol. 2: 11263
IMAGFIC International Film Festival of Madrid Vol. 2: 11263
Imagineer Awards Vol. 1: 12299
Imamura Memorial Prize Vol. 2: 8652
Imbrie Humanitarian Award; Frank Vol. 1: 14986
IMEF National Prize for Financial Research Vol. 2: 9038
Imhoff - Pierre Koch Medal; Karl Vol. 2: 3374
IMM Gold Medal Vol. 2: 3340
IMM Honorary Fellow Vol. 2: 3341
Immermann Preis Vol. 2: 6683
Immroth Memorial Award for Intellectual Freedom; John Phillip Vol. 1: 2898
IMMY Awards (Information Industry Marketing Achievement Awards) Vol. 1: 10184
Impact of Music on Film Competition Vol. 2: 1193
Impact Through Applied Photography Vol. 1: 16496
IMPC Award for Excellence in Parking Design Vol. 1: 10471
IMPC Award for Excellence in Parking Design and Program Innovation Vol. 1: 10471
Imperial Oil Award for Excellence in Arts Journalism Vol. 1: 6839
Imperial Prize
  Japan Academy Vol. 2: 8594
  Japan Art Academy Vol 2: 8597
Imperial Service Order Vol. 2: 2370
Imperial Tobacco Awards Vol. 2: 4477
Imperial Tobacco Portrait Award Vol. 2: 3704

Imperial Tobacco Trophy   Vol. 2: 3006
Implications of Research for Educational Practice   Vol. 1: 5631
Importers and Exporters Association of Taipei Competitions   Vol. 2: 12000
IMTEC Innovation Award   Vol. 1: 13275
In-Plant Management Award   Vol. 1: 10101
In-Print Award   Vol. 1: 10102
In the Tradition of the American Cowboy Award   Vol. 1: 20195
In the Tradition of the American West Award   Vol. 1: 20195
INATAPROBU Rejection Scroll   Vol. 1: 10781
INATAPROBU Spirometric Citation   Vol. 1: 10782
Inaugural Red Ochre Award   Vol. 2: 165
INCA Communicator Awards   Vol. 1: 10177
INCA Meritor Awards   Vol. 1: 10178
INCA Sustainer Awards   Vol. 1: 10179
Incentive for Publications of Articles in International Journals   Vol. 2: 9982
Incentive Showcase Awards   Vol. 1: 5829
Inco Medal   Vol. 1: 6945
Incoming President Award   Vol. 1: 3229
Incontro Internazionale Giovani Pianisti Citta di Senigallia   Vol. 2: 8419
Independent Bakers Association Congressional Award   Vol. 1: 10114
The Independent Foreign Fiction Award   Vol. 2: 3044
Independent Retailer of the Year Award   Vol. 1: 14633
Independent Retailer Organisation Awards   Vol. 2: 3046
Independent Theatre Award   Vol. 2: 10536
India Study Circle Award   Vol. 1: 10141
Indian Achievement Award   Vol. 1: 14969
Indian Books Centre Oriental Studies Award   Vol. 2: 7571
Indian Documentary Producers Association Award   Vol. 2: 7529
Indian Educator of the Year   Vol. 1: 7850
Indian Horse Hall of Fame Award   Vol. 1: 2423
Indian Social Worker of the Year Award   Vol. 1: 14209
Indian Student of the Year   Vol. 1: 7851
Indiana Journalism Award   Vol. 1: 6225
Indiana Scholastic Journalism Award   Vol. 1: 6226
Indiana State Senator Carolyn Mosby Above and Beyond Award   Vol. 1: 10147
Indiana University Prize for Altaic Studies   Vol. 1: 16075
Indianapolis 500 Mile Race   Vol. 1: 10155
Indianapolis Art League Exhibitions   Vol. 1: 10153
Indianapolis Motor Speedway Hall of Fame   Vol. 1: 10156
Indie Awards; NAIRD   Vol. 1: 13155
Indirect Providers of Major Support Services and Contributions to the Field of Special Vocational Needs Education Award   Vol. 1: 12913
Individual Artist Fellowship
    Montana Arts Council   Vol. 1: 12421
    Ohio Arts Council   Vol 1: 15585
Individual Award   Vol. 1: 3612
Individual Championships   Vol. 2: 4568
Individual Citation   Vol. 1: 14573
Individual of the Year Award   Vol. 1: 9089
Individual Outstanding Service Award   Vol. 1: 3937
Indonesian Film Festival   Vol. 2: 7733
Indradipta Memorial Medal   Vol. 2: 7471
Industrial Appreciation Award   Vol. 1: 985

Industrial Arts Teacher Educator of the Year   Vol. 1: 8411
Industrial Chemistry Medal   Vol. 2: 11048
Industrial Design Excellence Awards (IDEA)   Vol. 1: 10158
Industrial Leadership Award   Vol. 1: 1258
Industrial Lectureship   Vol. 2: 4202
Industrial Minerals Young Scientist Award   Vol. 1: 17566
Industrial Photographer of the Year   Vol. 2: 2889
Industrial Research Institute Achievement Award   Vol. 1: 10166
Industrial Research Institute Medal   Vol. 1: 10167
Industrial Safety Contest   Vol. 1: 4927
Industrial Scientist Award   Vol. 1: 10348
Industrial Wastes Medal   Vol. 1: 20160
Industriepreis fur technisch-wissenschaftliche Arbeiten   Vol. 2: 6639
Industriforbundets Miljovernpris   Vol. 2: 9887
Industry Achievement Award   Vol. 1: 11474
Industry Achievement Awards
    National Paint and Coatings Association   Vol. 1: 14440
    Plastics Academy   Vol 1: 16240
Industry Advancement Award   Vol. 1: 3013
Industry Award   Vol. 1: 10422
Industry Award of Distinction
    Health Industry Distributors Association   Vol. 1: 9843
    National Association of Quick Printers   Vol 1: 13264
Industry Awards of Excellence   Vol. 1: 6553
Industry Division Transportation Service Award   Vol. 1: 10450
Industry Information Technology Awards   Vol. 1: 9674
Industry Innovation Award   Vol. 1: 8658
Industry Leadership Award   Vol. 1: 12515
Industry Recognition Award   Vol. 1: 12833
Industry Service Award   Vol. 1: 6373
Industry Statesman Awards   Vol. 1: 14441
Indy 500 Hall of Fame   Vol. 1: 10156
Indy Car World Series; CART/PPG   Vol. 1: 12456
INEOA Medal of Valor   Vol. 1: 11116
INF-Press Prize   Vol. 2: 1198
INF-Presse Preis   Vol. 2: 1198
Infection Control Research Grant   Vol. 1: 5579
Infinity Awards   Vol. 1: 10831
INFORFILM Award   Vol. 1: 19352
Information Industry Hall of Fame Award   Vol. 1: 10185
Information Industry Marketing Achievement Awards   Vol. 1: 10184
Information Processing Public Service Award   Vol. 1: 8725
Information Product of the Year Award   Vol. 1: 15678
Information Resources Management Hall of Fame   Vol. 1: 9674
INFOSTA Award   Vol. 2: 8541
INGAA - University of Missouri Awards   Vol. 1: 19841
Ingbar Distinguished Lectureship; Sidney H.   Vol. 1: 4907
Ingberg Award; S. H.   Vol. 1: 6057
Ingersoll Award; E. P.   Vol. 1: 17787
Ingersoll Prize - Richard M. Weaver Award for Scholarly Letters   Vol. 1: 10191
Ingersoll Prize - T. S. Eliot Award for Creative Writing   Vol. 1: 10192
Ingersoll Rand - Triple Crown Chief Mechanic's Award   Vol. 1: 19022
Ingle Service Award; Robert   Vol. 1: 2006

Inglehart First Amendment Award; Louis E.   Vol. 1: 7911
Inglis Award; Rewey Belle   Vol. 1: 13771
Ingold-Albert Lectureship   Vol. 2: 4203
Ingold Lectureship   Vol. 2: 4203
Ingram Trophy; Syd   Vol. 2: 2810
Initiative in the Newly Independent States of the Former Soviet Union: Research and Writing Grants   Vol. 1: 11986
Injalbert; Prix
    Institut de France   Vol. 2: 5344
    Institut de France - Academie des Beaux Arts   Vol 2: 5388
Inklings   Vol. 1: 12556
Inner Swiss Culture Award   Vol. 2: 11748
Inner Swiss Literature Award   Vol. 2: 11749
Innerschweizerischer Kulturpreis   Vol. 2: 11748
Innerschweizerischer Literaturpreis   Vol. 2: 11749
Innis - Gerin Medal   Vol. 1: 16957
Innovation Achievement Award   Vol. 1: 7006
Innovation Award
    American Assembly of Collegiate Schools of Business   Vol. 1: 822
    Direct Selling Association   Vol 1: 8658
    Interactive Services   Vol 1: 10529
Innovation in Civil Engineering Award   Vol. 1: 4474
Innovation in Teaching Science Teachers   Vol. 1: 5632
Innovation of the Year Awards   Vol. 1: 1010
Innovation Writer of the Year   Vol. 2: 3773
Innovations in State and Local Government Awards Program   Vol. 1: 9314
Innovative Intermodal Solutions for Urban Transportation Award   Vol. 1: 10451
Innovative Products and Services Awards   Vol. 1: 3940
Innovative Teaching of Secondary School Physics Award   Vol. 1: 1126
Innovator Award
    American Society of Cataract and Refractive Surgery   Vol. 1: 4415
    Paralyzed Veterans of America   Vol 1: 15936
Innsbruck Radio Prize for Early Music   Vol. 2: 843
Innsbrucker Radiopreis fur Alter Musik   Vol. 2: 843
INSA Medal for Young Scientists   Vol. 2: 7650
INSA Prize for Material Sciences   Vol. 2: 7651
INSA - T. S. Tirumurti Memorial Lecture   Vol. 2: 7652
INSA - Vainu Bappu Memorial Award   Vol. 2: 7653
Insatsu Bunka Sho   Vol. 2: 8610
Insignia for Mention in Dispatches   Vol. 1: 6700
Insole Award   Vol. 2: 2444
Inspecteur Honoraire de la Federation Internationale de Sauvetage Aquatique   Vol. 2: 6752
Institut Francais de Washington   Vol. 1: 17461
Institute Award for Excellence in Industrial Gases Technology   Vol. 1: 2586
Institute for Latin American Integration Award   Vol. 2: 51
Institute for Reading Research Fellowship   Vol. 1: 11188
Institute for University Cooperation Awards   Vol. 2: 8276
Institute Honors   Vol. 1: 2537
Institute Lecture   Vol. 1: 2587
Institute Manuscript Award   Vol. 1: 10255
Institute Medal   Vol. 2: 4519

Institute of Administrative Accountants Awards Vol. 2: 3100
Institute of Administrative Management Competitions Vol. 2: 3062
Institute of Ceramics Awards Vol. 2: 3078
Institute of Civil Defence and Disaster Studies Competitions Vol. 2: 3084
Institute of Energy Award Vol. 2: 3088
Institute of Export Prizes Vol. 2: 3098
Institute of Financial Accountants Awards Vol. 2: 3100
Institute of Manufacturing Awards Vol. 2: 3113
Institute of Marketing Awards Vol. 2: 3123
Institute of Metals Division Award Vol. 1: 12318
Institute of Metals Lecture and Robert Franklin Mehl Award Vol. 1: 12315
Institute of Professional Investigators Awards Vol. 2: 3202
Institute of Quarrying Awards Vol. 2: 3206
Institute of the Furniture Warehousing and Removing Industry Awards Vol. 2: 3212
Institute of Traffic Officers of Southern Africa Awards Vol. 2: 10885
Institute Service Awards Vol. 1: 16491
Institute Silver Medal Vol. 2: 3119
Institution Bronze Medal Vol. 2: 3325
Institution Gold Medal
  Institution of Civil Engineers Vol. 2: 3244
  Institution of Gas Engineers Vol 2: 3326
Institution Medal and Premium (Local Associations) Competition Vol. 2: 3245
Institution Medal and Premium (London Universities) Competition Vol. 2: 3246
Institution Medal and Premium (Universities) Competition Vol. 2: 3246
Institution of Engineers, Australia Award - Australian Maritime College Vol. 2: 442
Institution of Engineers, Australia Award - Ballarat University College Vol. 2: 443
Institution of Engineers, Australia Award - Curtin University of Technology Vol. 2: 444
Institution of Engineers, Australia Award - James Cook University of North Queensland Vol. 2: 445
Institution of Engineers, Australia Award - LaTrobe University College of Northern Victoria Vol. 2: 446
Institution of Engineers, Australia Award - Monash University Vol. 2: 447
Institution of Engineers, Australia Award - Monash University - Caulfield Campus Vol. 2: 448
Institution of Engineers, Australia Award - Monash University Gippsland Vol. 2: 449
Institution of Engineers, Australia Award - Queensland University of Technology Vol. 2: 450
Institution of Engineers, Australia Award - Royal Melbourne Institute of Technology Vol. 2: 451
Institution of Engineers, Australia Award - Swinburne Institute of Technology Vol. 2: 452
Institution of Engineers, Australia Award - University College of Southern Queensland Vol. 2: 453
Institution of Engineers, Australia Award - University of Adelaide Vol. 2: 454
Institution of Engineers, Australia Award - University of Canberra Vol. 2: 455
Institution of Engineers, Australia Award - University of College of Central Queensland Vol. 2: 456
Institution of Engineers, Australia Award - University of Melbourne Vol. 2: 457

Institution of Engineers, Australia Award - University of New South Wales Vol. 2: 458
Institution of Engineers, Australia Award - University of New South Wales - Australian Defence Force Academy Vol. 2: 459
Institution of Engineers, Australia Award - University of Newcastle Vol. 2: 460
Institution of Engineers, Australia Award - University of Queensland Vol. 2: 461
Institution of Engineers, Australia Award - University of South Australia Vol. 2: 462
Institution of Engineers, Australia Award - University of Sydney Vol. 2: 463
Institution of Engineers, Australia Award - University of Tasmania Vol. 2: 464
Institution of Engineers, Australia Award - University of Technology, Sydney Vol. 2: 465
Institution of Engineers, Australia Award - University of Western Australia Vol. 2: 466
Institution of Engineers, Australia Award - University of Wollongong Vol. 2: 467
Institution of Engineers, Australia Award - Victoria University of Technology - Footscray Campus Vol. 2: 468
Institution of Engineers Medal Vol. 2: 469
Institution of Environmental Sciences Awards Vol. 2: 3314
Institution of Mechanical Engineers Awards Vol. 2: 3333
Institution of the Year Vol. 1: 18943
Institution or Organization Citation Vol. 1: 14574
Institution Premium Vol. 2: 3291
Institution Silver Medal Vol. 2: 3327
Institutional Award Vol. 1: 3613
Institutional Long Term Care Award Vol. 1: 14292
Institutional Relations Awards Vol. 1: 8296
Institutionalist Prize Vol. 1: 5521
Instituto de Bellas Artes Concurso de Becas Literarias Vol. 2: 9213
Instructional Innovation Award Vol. 1: 8566
Instructional Telecommunications Council Awards Vol. 1: 10478
Instructor of the Year
  American Riding Instructor Certification Program Vol. 1: 3959
  National Burglar and Fire Alarm Association - National Training School (NTS) Vol 1: 13489
  U.S.A. - Korean Karate Association Vol 1: 19929
  Zen-Do Kai Martial Arts Association Vol 1: 20633
Instrumental and Vocal Competition Vol. 2: 197
Instrumentalist of the Year Vol. 1: 12529
Instrumentation Laboratory Undergraduate Scholarship Vol. 1: 4191
Instrumentaton Laboratory Educational Scholarship Vol. 1: 14747
Insurance Law Prize Vol. 2: 10321
Integrated Young Playwrights Project Vol. 1: 19997
Intellectual Freedom Award
  Illinois Library Association Vol. 1: 10080
  Louisiana Library Association Vol 1: 11955
Intellectual Freedom Round Table State and Regional Achievement Award Vol. 1: 2899
Intellectual Freedom Round Table State Program Award Vol. 1: 2899
Inter-American Agricultural Award for Young Professionals Vol. 2: 1774
Inter-American Agricultural Development Award Vol. 2: 1775

Inter-American Agricultural Medal Vol. 2: 1776
Inter-American Award for the Participation of Women in Rural Development Vol. 2: 1777
Inter-American Course for Young Orchestra Conductors Vol. 1: 15832
Inter-American Institute of Human Rights Awards Vol. 2: 1779
Inter-American Music Awards Vol. 1: 17252
Inter-Collegiate Sailing Hall of Fame Vol. 1: 10520
Inter-Collegiate Sailor of the Year Vol. 1: 10521
Inter Nationes - Kulturpreis Vol. 2: 6927
Inter Nationes - Preis fur Werke der Literatur und bildenden Kunst Vol. 2: 6927
Inter Nations Culture Prize Vol. 2: 6927
Interamerica Prize Vol. 1: 10509
Intercollegiate All-Star Team Vol. 1: 10552
Intercollegiate Polo Awards Vol. 1: 18774
Intercollegiate Rifle Trophy Vol. 1: 14643
INTERCOM - The Industrial Film Festival (Hugo Awards) Vol. 1: 7702
Interfaith Award Vol. 1: 10564
Interfilm Award Vol. 2: 9456
Interior Architecture Awards of Excellence Vol. 1: 2533
Interior Design Hall of Fame Vol. 1: 10571
Internal Combustion Engine Award Vol. 1: 4682
Internationaal Franz Liszt Pianoconcours Vol. 2: 9663
International Academy of Astronautics Book Awards Vol. 2: 5945
International Academy of Astronautics Section Awards Vol. 2: 5946
International Achievement Awards Competition Vol. 1: 10163
International Activities Award Vol. 1: 4588
International Activities Service Award Vol. 1: 20153
International Adult Talent Awards Vol. 1: 15963
International Advertising Association Award Vol. 1: 10593
International Advertising Award Vol. 2: 3753
International Advertising Festival, Cannes Vol. 2: 3363
International Advertising Festival of Ireland Vol. 2: 7785
International Advertising Festival of New York
  New York Festivals Vol. 1: 15237
  New York Festivals Vol 1: 15237
International Advertising Press & Poster Festival Vol. 2: 3364
International Affairs Committee Foreign Scholarship Award Vol. 1: 616
International Affairs Fellowship Program Vol. 1: 8389
International Aluminum Extrusion Design Competition Vol. 1: 380
International Amateur Film Festival, Golden Diana Vol. 2: 897
International ANDY Awards Vol. 1: 10602
International Animal Agriculture Award Vol. 1: 4400
International Animation Festival Vol. 1: 5172
International Animation Festival in Japan, Hiroshima Vol. 2: 8531
International Arbiter Vol. 2: 7228
International Art Book Prize Vol. 2: 7923
International Art Photography Exhibition "Foto Expo" Vol. 2: 10086
International Arts Award Vol. 1: 8016
International Association for the Protection of Monuments and Restoration of Buildings Awards Vol. 2: 6934

International Association for the Study of Lung Cancer Awards   Vol. 2: 1956
International Association of Engineering Geology Awards   Vol. 2: 5965
International Association of Jazz Educators Scholarship   Vol. 1: 12517
International Association of Machinists and Aerospace Workers - Nati onal Champion Chief Mechanic's Award   Vol. 1: 19023
International Association of University Presidents Awards   Vol. 2: 12027
International Auctioneer Championship   Vol. 1: 13392
International Award
   American String Teachers Association   Vol. 1: 4870
   Animal Transportation Association   Vol 1: 5166
   Girls' Brigade International Council   Vol 2: 2932
   North American Die Casting Association   Vol 1: 15416
   Parent Co-operative Preschools International   Vol 1: 15949
   Society of Plastics Engineers   Vol 1: 17985
   System Safety Society   Vol 1: 18559
   Women in Film   Vol 1: 20384
International Award for Distinguished Contributions to Natural History   Vol. 1: 17338
International Award for Outstanding Achievement in Business Management   Vol. 1: 17986
International Award for Outstanding Achievement in Plastics Research   Vol. 1: 17987
International Award for the Furtherance of Human Understanding   Vol. 2: 11686
International Award Lectures   Vol. 1: 17806
International Award of Excellence   Vol. 1: 13341
International Award of Merit in Structural Engineering   Vol. 2: 11756
International Awards   Vol. 1: 5769
International Awards for Excellence in Arc Welded Design, Engineering & Fabrication   Vol. 1: 11877
International Beethoven Piano Competition   Vol. 2: 918
International Belvedere Competition for Opera Singers   Vol. 2: 911
International Benjamin Franklin Fire Service Award   Vol. 1: 10730
International Bidding Contest   Vol. 2: 9475
International Biennial Exhibition of Humour in Art   Vol. 2: 8282
International Biennial of Graphic Art   Vol. 2: 10795
International Biennial of Illustrations Bratislava   Vol. 2: 10782
International Biomedical Science Journalism Prizes   Vol. 1: 9529
International Bocce Federation Competitions   Vol. 2: 1477
International Book Award   Vol. 2: 899
International Braille Chess Association Awards   Vol. 2: 11473
International Broadcasting Awards   Vol. 1: 9976
International Bulwer-Lytton Fiction Contest   Vol. 1: 17045
International Business Dissertation Award   Vol. 1: 45
International Calligraphy Competition   Vol. 2: 12056
International Cancer Research Technology Transfer Project   Vol. 2: 11859
International Carl Maria von Weber Competition, Dresden   Vol. 2: 6921

International Casting Federation Awards   Vol. 1: 10825
International Center for Peace in the Middle East Awards   Vol. 2: 7894
International Centre of Insect Physiology and Ecology Awards   Vol. 2: 8803
International Ceramic Art Competition   Vol. 2: 8309
International Certificate of Appreciation   Vol. 1: 3918
International Championship Chorus   Vol. 1: 9785
International Charlemagne Prize of Aachen   Vol. 2: 7092
International Children's Film and Television Festival, Los Angeles   Vol. 1: 7622
International Children's Film and Video Festival   Vol. 2: 675
International Children's Film Festival of India   Vol. 2: 7715
International Children's Peace Prize   Vol. 1: 7615
International Chili Cook-off   Vol. 1: 4844
International Choir Festival   Vol. 2: 9478
International Choral Competition of Tolosa   Vol. 2: 11197
International Choral Competition, Tours   Vol. 2: 5193
International Christian Television Week   Vol. 2: 7165
International Cinema Festival of Algarve   Vol. 2: 10230
International Circulation Managers Association C. K. Jefferson Award; NAA Foundation -   Vol. 1: 15354
International Citation of Merit   Vol. 1: 11189
International Classified Advertising Week   Vol. 1: 5902
International Coastal Engineering Award   Vol. 1: 4475
International Committee for Studies of Bauxites and Aluminum-Oxides-Hydroxides Medal   Vol. 2: 7355
International Competition   Vol. 1: 11840
International Competition for Chamber Music Ensembles   Vol. 2: 8102
International Competition for Choirs   Vol. 2: 797
International Competition for Composers Mozart   Vol. 2: 884
International Competition for Musical Performers - Geneva   Vol. 2: 11774
International Competition for Original Composition for Band   Vol. 2: 8409
International Competition for Symphonic Composition, Trieste   Vol. 2: 8402
International Competition for Verdian Voices   Vol. 2: 8293
International Competition for Violin and Viola Makers   Vol. 2: 1516
International Competition for Young Opera Singers - Sofia   Vol. 2: 1525
International Competition in Composition of Sacred Music   Vol. 2: 11736
International Competition M. Abbado for Violinists   Vol. 2: 7999
International Competition of Franz Schubert and Twentieth Century Music   Vol. 2: 805
International Competition of Music Composition   Vol. 2: 5182
International Competition of Video Works   Vol. 2: 6070
International Competition, Opera and Bel Canto   Vol. 2: 1069
International Competitions for New Instruments and Bows   Vol. 1: 20052

International Composers Competition   Vol. 2: 8559
International Composers Competition Kazimierz Serocki   Vol. 2: 10183
International Composition Contest Guido d'Arezzo   Vol. 2: 8215
International Composition Prize   Vol. 2: 4977
International Computer Animation Competition   Vol. 1: 13638
International Conceptual Furniture Competition   Vol. 1: 16519
International Conductors' Competition   Vol. 2: 9694
International Conductors Competition of the Hungarian Television   Vol. 2: 7415
International Conservation Roll of Honour   Vol. 2: 11987
International Contest for Carillon Composition   Vol. 2: 1347
International Contest of Agrarian Cinema and Video   Vol. 2: 11398
International Contest of Short Films, City of Huesca   Vol. 2: 11236
International Cooperation Medal   Vol. 2: 5064
International Council for Game and Wildlife Conservation Awards   Vol. 2: 5997
International Council of Ophthalmology Awards   Vol. 2: 9484
International Council of the French Language Competitions   Vol. 2: 5999
International Council Outstanding Service Award   Vol. 1: 9664
International Critics Award   Vol. 1: 18745
International Crystal Growth Award   Vol. 1: 855
International Cytotechnology Award of the IAC   Vol. 2: 6930
International Dag Hammarskjold Award   Vol. 2: 1237
International Dairy Foods Association Research Award   Vol. 1: 1912
International Dairy Production Award   Vol. 1: 1913
International Democracy Award   Vol. 1: 10779
International Design Award, Osaka   Vol. 2: 8605
International Design Competition, Osaka   Vol. 2: 8606
International Designer Awards   Vol. 1: 10703
International Diaporama Festival   Vol. 2: 1224
International Director's Award   Vol. 1: 11363
International DLG Prize   Vol. 2: 6774
International Dmitri Shostakovich Competition of String Quartets   Vol. 2: 10453
International Doctoral Scholarship for Studies Specializing in Jewish Fields   Vol. 1: 12213
International Documentary and Short Film Festival of Bilbao   Vol. 2: 11267
International Documentary Association Awards   Vol. 1: 10911
International Double Bass Competition Giovanni Bottesini   Vol. 2: 8168
International DXer of the Year   Vol. 1: 5905
International ECHO Awards Competition   Vol. 1: 8648
International Editor of the Year   Vol. 1: 20520
International Egg Marketing Award   Vol. 2: 3405
International Electroacoustic Music Competition Bourges   Vol. 2: 4999
International Emmy Award   Vol. 1: 10884
International Essay Award in Applied Ethics   Vol. 1: 10727
International Exhibit for Pastels Only   Vol. 1: 11644
International Exhibition Logistics Associates Awards   Vol. 2: 11782

International Exhibition of Photography   Vol. 1: 8571
International Exhibition of Professional Photography   Vol. 1: 16497
International Fan Club Organization Display Competition Award   Vol. 1: 10954
International Fashion Model   Vol. 1: 20507
International Federation of Beekeepers' Associations Awards   Vol. 2: 8299
International Federation of Bowlers Awards   Vol. 2: 4725
International Federation of Netball Associations Awards   Vol. 2: 503
International Federation of Netball Associations Service Awards   Vol. 2: 504
International Federation of Shorthand and Typewriting Competitions   Vol. 2: 6952
International Fellowship of Certified Collectors   Vol. 1: 1594
International Fellowships   Vol. 1: 2339
International Fellowships in Jewish Studies   Vol. 1: 12214
International Fencing Federation Awards   Vol. 2: 6012
International Festival of Alpine Films Les Diablerets, Switzerland   Vol. 2: 11791
International Festival of Authors   Vol. 1: 9768
International Festival of Cinema for Children and Youth   Vol. 2: 10232
International Festival of Ecological Film Events   Vol. 2: 10791
International Festival of Economics and Training Films   Vol. 2: 1191
International Festival of Film and Television in the Celtic Countries   Vol. 2: 10522
International Festival of Films Directed by Women   Vol. 2: 11149
International Festival of Films on Architecture and Town-planning of Lausanne   Vol. 2: 11793
International Festival of Films on Energy Lausanne   Vol. 2: 11797
International Festival of Historic Films, Rueil-Malmaison   Vol. 2: 5186
International Festival of Maritime and Exploration Films   Vol. 2: 6014
International Festival of Mountain Films, Vila de Torello   Vol. 2: 11386
International Festival of Red Cross and Health Films   Vol. 2: 1528
International Festival of Sport Films   Vol. 2: 5248
International Festival of Sports and Tourist Films   Vol. 2: 10792
International Festival of the Image   Vol. 2: 6016
International Festival of the New Super 8 Cinema and Video   Vol. 2: 12114
International Festival of Tourist Films - Tourfilm   Vol. 2: 1852
International Festival on General Health, the Red Cross and Environmental Protection Amateur Films   Vol. 2: 7440
International FIAP Kodak Award   Vol. 2: 1189
International Film and Student Directors Festival   Vol. 2: 6020
International Film and Television Festival of New York   Vol. 1: 15239
International Film Competition at the Green Week Berlin   Vol. 2: 6519
International Film Festival Bludenz   Vol. 2: 721
International Film Festival for Young Australians   Vol. 2: 675
International Film Festival - Nature, Man and His Environment   Vol. 2: 8301

International Film Festival of Figueira da Foz   Vol. 2: 10234
International Film Festival of India   Vol. 2: 7689
International Film Festival of Santarem   Vol. 2: 10236
International Film Festival of the Estoril Coast   Vol. 2: 10238
International Film Festival of Visual Anthropology and Social Documentation   Vol. 2: 5032
International Film/Video Festival on Telecommunications and Electronics; Golden Antenna -   Vol. 2: 11848
International Filmfestival des nichtprofessionell en Films, Goldene Diana   Vol. 2: 897
International Filmfestival Mannheim/Heidelberg   Vol. 2: 6954
International Fireball Worlds Trophy   Vol. 2: 2894
International Floral Decoration Competition   Vol. 2: 1067
International Forestry Achievement Award   Vol. 1: 6925
International Franz Liszt Piano Competition   Vol. 2: 9663
International Franz Schubert Male Choir Contest - Vienna   Vol. 2: 882
International Frederic Chopin Piano Competition   Vol. 2: 10067
International Freedom Festival Freedom Award   Vol. 1: 8623
International Furniture Competition   Vol. 1: 16519
International Game Fish Association Awards   Vol. 1: 11007
International Gas Turbine Institute Scholar Award   Vol. 1: 4719
International Gaudeamus Interpreters Competition   Vol. 2: 9438
International Gaudeamus Musicweek for Young Composers Award   Vol. 2: 9439
International Geological L. A. Spendiarov Prize of the USSR Academy of Sciences   Vol. 2: 10418
International Gold Medallion Awards   Vol. 1: 6582
International Golden Rose Award   Vol. 1: 20360
International Good Neighbor Award   Vol. 1: 18824
International Graduate Student Paper Contest   Vol. 1: 5359
International Grand Champion   Vol. 1: 11321
International Grand Prix for Liszt Records   Vol. 2: 7438
International Graphoanalyst of the Year   Vol. 1: 11011
International Greeting Card Awards (Louie Awards)   Vol. 1: 9724
International Grzegorz Fitelberg Competition for Conductors in Katowice   Vol. 2: 10212
International Guitar Competition   Vol. 2: 6184
International Guitar Contest   Vol. 2: 11241
International Guitar Makers Competition   Vol. 2: 6185
International Hall of Fame of Sportscasters   Vol. 1: 4855
International Hall of Fame World Award   Vol. 1: 11419
International Hans Christian Andersen Awards   Vol. 2: 11767
International Harp Contest in Israel   Vol. 2: 7899
International Health and Medical Film Festival   Vol. 1: 55

International Health Leadership Award   Vol. 1: 13700
International Health Service Award for Individuals   Vol. 1: 13701
International Health Service Award for Organizations   Vol. 1: 13702
International Henryk Wieniawski Composers Competition   Vol. 2: 10073
International Henryk Wieniawski Violin Competition   Vol. 2: 10074
International Henryk Wieniawski Violinmakers Competition   Vol. 2: 10075
International Honor Awards   Vol. 1: 17880
International Human Rights Law Award   Vol. 1: 11041
International Humanitarian Award
    American Radio Relay League   Vol. 1: 3890
    American Red Magen David for Israel   Vol 1: 3931
International Humanitarian Service Award   Vol. 1: 3919
International Hydrology Prize   Vol. 2: 9469
International Ice Hockey Federation Competition   Vol. 2: 11803
International Illumination Design Awards Program   Vol. 1: 10088
International Imitation Hemingway Competition   Vol. 1: 16916
International Industrial Film and Video Awards   Vol. 2: 2703
International Industrial Film Festival Awards   Vol. 2: 2703
International Inn of the Year   Vol. 1: 11078
International Institute for Promotion and Prestige Awards   Vol. 2: 11805
International Institute of Humanitarian Law Prize   Vol. 2: 8307
International Institute of Refrigeration Prize   Vol. 2: 6028
International J. S. Bach Competition   Vol. 2: 6936
International Jean Sibelius Violin Competition   Vol. 2: 4729
International Jeunesses Musicales Competition - Belgrade   Vol. 2: 10717
International Jose Maria Cagigal Award in Physical Education   Vol. 2: 1166
International Journalism Prize   Vol. 2: 1865
International Judo Federation   Vol. 2: 6964
International Karl Richter Organ Competition   Vol. 2: 6899
International Kuhlau Competition for Flautists   Vol. 2: 6966
International Leadership Award   Vol. 1: 19071
International Legal Aid Award   Vol. 2: 3382
International Leipzig Documentary and Animation Film Festival   Vol. 2: 7035
International Lenin Peace Prize   Vol. 2: 10472
International Letter-Writing Competition for Young People   Vol. 2: 11957
International Librarian of the Year   Vol. 2: 3569
International Lieder Competition   Vol. 2: 885
International Literary Award Vilenica   Vol. 2: 10801
International Literary Awards   Vol. 1: 12044
International Ludwig Spohr Violin Competition   Vol. 2: 6972
International Markstrat Competition   Vol. 2: 6403
International Master   Vol. 2: 7229
International Medal   Vol. 1: 14634
International Mediation Medal   Vol. 1: 804
International Medical and Health Education Film Week   Vol. 2: 11269
International Medical Scientific Film Festival   Vol. 2: 8375

International Mercedes-Benz Sponsorship Award for the Animated Film   Vol. 2: 7142
International Meteorological Organization Prize   Vol. 2: 11978
International Miller Prize   Vol. 2: 3400
International Monitor Awards   Vol. 1: 11346
International Motorsports Hall of Fame   Vol. 1: 11112
International Mozart Competition   Vol. 2: 872
International Multimedia Science Film Festival   Vol. 2: 8375
International Music Competition of Japan   Vol. 2: 8608
International Music Council Prize   Vol. 2: 6421
International Musical Contest Dr. Luis Sigall Competition   Vol. 2: 1570
International Nathalie Masse Prize   Vol. 2: 5982
International Navies Essay Contest   Vol. 1: 19462
International Navies Photo Contest   Vol. 1: 19463
International New Music Competition   Vol. 1: 15621
International New Music Composers Competition   Vol. 1: 11121
International Odense Film Festival   Vol. 2: 1963
International Offenbach Singing Competition   Vol. 2: 5072
International Old Lacers Contest   Vol. 1: 11127
International Olympic Committee; Prize of the   Vol. 2: 7431
International Oncology Nursing Fellowships   Vol. 2: 11860
International Opera Singers Competition   Vol. 1: 7430
International Optometrist of the Year   Vol. 2: 3444
International Oratorio and Lied Competition   Vol. 2: 4981
International Organ Competition, Odense   Vol. 2: 1965
International Organ Competitions   Vol. 2: 1152
International Organ Festival   Vol. 2: 3448
International Organization for Chemical Sciences in Development Awards   Vol. 2: 9077
International Paulo Cello Competition   Vol. 2: 4750
International Peace and Tourism Award   Vol. 1: 4807
International PEN - Philippines Awards   Vol. 2: 10040
International Photographic Competition to Commemorate Islamic Heritage   Vol. 2: 12057
International Photographic Research Show   Vol. 2: 6215
International Photography Hall of Fame and Museum   Vol. 1: 16152
International Piano Competition Liszt - Mario Zanfi Prize   Vol. 2: 8169
International Piano Composition Contest   Vol. 2: 6040
International Pilar Bayona Piano Competition   Vol. 2: 11273
International Platform Association Award   Vol. 1: 11152
International Polka Festival   Vol. 1: 11169
International Polyphonic Contest Guido d'Arezzo   Vol. 2: 8216
International Popular Sports Achievement Award   Vol. 2: 6948

International Powerlifting Federation Awards   Vol. 2: 11479
International Premium Awards   Vol. 2: 3292
International Prevention of Blindness Award   Vol. 1: 631
International Print Biennal - Varna   Vol. 2: 1532
International Print Biennale   Vol. 2: 10077
International Print Triennial   Vol. 2: 10077
International Prints Competition   Vol. 1: 17282
International Prize   Vol. 2: 5301
International Prize for Architecture   Vol. 2: 1114
International Prize for Architecture of the National Housing Institute   Vol. 2: 1227
International Prize for Biology   Vol. 2: 8636
International Prize for New Materials   Vol. 1: 3459
International Prize for the First Novel   Vol. 2: 6042
International Prize Paladino D'Oro   Vol. 2: 8313
International Pro-Comm Awards Competition   Vol. 1: 6662
International Property Tax Achievement Award   Vol. 1: 10667
International Protestant Film Jury Prize   Vol. 2: 6564
International Publications Cultural Award   Vol. 2: 8727
International Radio and Television Festivals and Competitions   Vol. 2: 1867
International Radio Festival of New York   Vol. 1: 15238
International Reading Association Prize   Vol. 2: 6422
International Record Critics Award   Vol. 2: 11663
International Research Fellowship   Vol. 1: 2233
International Residential Product Design Award   Vol. 1: 4625
International Robert Schumann Choir Competition   Vol. 2: 6978
International Robert Schumann Competition   Vol. 2: 6979
International Rostrum of Young Performers/ UNESCO   Vol. 2: 10784
International Sailing Film Festival in La Rochelle   Vol. 2: 6044
International Salon of Cartoons Awards   Vol. 1: 11210
International Scholarship Program   Vol. 1: 8799
International Science and Engineering Fair
    American Intellectual Property Law Association   Vol. 1: 2695
    Science Service   Vol 1: 17121
International Scientific and Technical Gliding Organisation Awards   Vol. 2: 6981
International Sculpture Competition in Madera   Vol. 2: 9009
International Seaweed Association Awards   Vol. 2: 1484
International Secretary of the Year   Vol. 1: 16515
International Service Award
    Association for Worksite Health Promotion   Vol. 1: 5668
    Epsilon Sigma Phi   Vol 1: 8979
    Helen Keller International   Vol 1: 11663
International Service Award to a Foreign Woman   Vol. 1: 358
International Service in Agronomy Award   Vol. 1: 4386
International Short Film Festival, Oberhausen   Vol. 2: 6984

International Short Film Prize   Vol. 2: 6954
International Show and Sale   Vol. 1: 3196
International Simavi Cartoon Competition   Vol. 2: 12053
International Simon Bolivar Prize   Vol. 2: 6415
International Singing Competition of Toulouse   Vol. 2: 6048
International Singing Contest of Rio de Janeiro   Vol. 2: 1454
International Ski Film Festival   Vol. 1: 11223
International Social Security Association Medal   Vol. 2: 11837
International Society for Medical and Psychological Hypnosis Awards   Vol. 2: 8311
International Society of Electrochemistry Awards   Vol. 2: 11840
International Society of Violin and Bow Makers Competitions   Vol. 2: 9531
International Soil Science Award   Vol. 1: 18131
International Songwriters' Association Awards   Vol. 2: 7787
International Space Hall of Fame   Vol. 1: 11319
International Special Librarians Day/National Library Week Award   Vol. 1: 18265
International Sports Film Festival   Vol. 2: 8317
International Sports Film Festival in Budapest   Vol. 2: 7431
International Stepping-Stone Scholarships   Vol. 1: 7044
International Store Interior Design Competition   Vol. 1: 10446
International String Quartet Competition   Vol. 2: 8444
International Student Award   Vol. 1: 5580
International Student Film Festival   Vol. 2: 7903
International Student Paper Contest   Vol. 1: 5360
International Student Salon of Photography   Vol. 2: 7275
International Superintendent of the Year   Vol. 1: 5618
International Swimming Hall of Fame Gold Medallion Award   Vol. 1: 11329
International Swimming Hall of Fame Honoree   Vol. 1: 11330
International Tabletop Award   Vol. 1: 8506
International Tchaikovsky Competition   Vol. 2: 10455
International Technical Art Competition   Vol. 1: 17608
International Technical Publications Competition   Vol. 1: 17609
International Television Festival Golden Prague   Vol. 2: 1844
International Television Festival of Monte Carlo   Vol. 2: 9322
International Tennis Hall of Fame   Vol. 1: 11351
International Thermal Conductivity Award   Vol. 1: 11359
International Thermographers Association Product Excellence Contest   Vol. 1: 16415
International Thermographers Product Excellence Contest   Vol. 1: 16415
International Travel Film and Video Festival   Vol. 1: 11367
International Travel Grant Award   Vol. 1: 489
International Triennial Exhibition of Photography Prizes   Vol. 2: 11854
International Triennial of Stringed Instruments   Vol. 2: 8321

International Trophy Competition
  Cork International Choral Festival Vol. 2: 7766
  Cork International Choral Festival Vol 2: 7767
International Trumpet Guild Composition Contest Vol. 1: 11373
International Union for Surface Finishing Awards Vol. 2: 3491
International Union of Master Painters Competitions Vol. 2: 6993
International Vaptsarov Prize Vol. 2: 1537
International Vasco Vilalva Prize Vol. 2: 10252
International Video Competition Vol. 1: 17610
International Video Contest Vol. 2: 11234
International Video Dance Grand Prix Vol. 2: 6465
International Video Week of Geneva Vol. 2: 11865
International Villa-Lobos Guitar Competition Vol. 2: 1501
International Villa-Lobos Piano Contest Vol. 2: 1502
International Violin Competition of Indianapolis Vol. 1: 7352
International Violin Competition Rodolfo Lipizer Prize Vol. 2: 8209
International Violin Competition Zino Francescatti Vol. 2: 4972
International Visual Communications Association Awards Vol. 2: 3502
International Vocal Competition 's-Hertogenbosch Vol. 2: 9539
International Vocalisten Concours 's-Hertogenbosch Vol. 2: 9539
International Voice Competition la Plaine-Atlantique Vol. 2: 5188
International Voice Competition of Bilbao Vol. 2: 11275
International Want Ad Week Award Vol. 1: 5902
International Warsaw Autumn Festival of Contemporary Music Vol. 2: 10164
International Week of Scientific Films Vol. 2: 11199
International Week of Sea and Marine Cinema - Cartagena Vol. 2: 11279
International West German Short Film Festival, Oberhausen Vol. 2: 6984
International Wildlife Film Festival Vol. 1: 11402
International Women-Composer's Competition Vol. 2: 11666
International Women's Film Festival, Creteil Vol. 2: 6072
International Women's Sports Hall of Fame Vol. 1: 20426
International Youth Award Vol. 2: 7687
International Youth Exbibit Awards Vol. 1: 15963
Internationale Carl Nielsen Violin Konkurrence Vol. 2: 1984
Internationale Eugene Baieprijs Vol. 2: 1243
Internationale Filmfestspiele Berlin Vol. 2: 6564
Internationale Filmwoche Mannheim Vol. 2: 6954
Internationale Kompositiewedstrijd voor Beiaard Vol. 2: 1347
Internationale Kurtzfilmtage Oberhausen Vol. 2: 6984
Internationale Leipziger Dokumetar- und Kurzfilmwoche fur Kino und Fernsehen Vol. 2: 7035
Internationale Muziekdagen - Brugge Vol. 2: 1152
Internationale Prijs voor Architectuur Eternit Vol. 2: 1114
  National Housing Institute Vol 2: 1227
Internationalen Carl-Maria-von-Weber-Wettbewerb, Dresden Vol. 2: 6921
Internationalen Karlpreis der Stadt Aachen Vol. 2: 7092
Internationalen Klavierwettbewerb Koln Vol. 2: 6607
Internationalen Robert-Schumann-Wettbewerbes Vol. 2: 6979
Internationaler Anton-Bruckner-Orgelwettbewerb Linz Vol. 2: 857
Internationaler Beethoven Klavierwettbewerb Vol. 2: 918
Internationaler Belvedere Wettbewerb fur Opernsanger Wien Vol. 2: 911
Internationaler Chorbewerb Vol. 2: 797
Internationaler Direct Marketing Wettbewerb Vol. 2: 1131
Internationaler DLG-Preis Vol. 2: 6774
Internationaler Exil-Preis Vol. 2: 6555
Internationaler Filmwettbewerb zur Grunen Woche Berlin Vol. 2: 6519
Internationaler Fotosalon Vol. 2: 6756
Internationaler Karl Richter Orgelwettbewerb Vol. 2: 6899
Internationaler Karlspreis zu Aachen Vol. 2: 7092
Internationaler Kompositionswettbewerb Vol. 2: 4977
Internationaler Kompositionswettbewerb Geistlicher Musik Vol. 2: 11736
Internationaler Kompositionswettbewerb Mozart Vol. 2: 884
Internationaler Kompositionswettbewerb Wien Vol. 2: 774
Internationaler Kuhlau-Wettbewerb fur Flotisten Vol. 2: 6966
Internationaler Mannerchor Wettbewerb Franz Schubert - Wien Vol. 2: 882
Internationaler Mercedes-Benz Forderpreis fur the Animaionsfilm Vol. 2: 7142
Internationaler Mozart Wettbewerb Vol. 2: 872
Internationaler Musikwettbewerb der ARD Vol. 2: 6974
Internationaler Musikwettbewerb Tokyo Vol. 2: 8770
Internationaler Plakatpreis fur Figurentheater Vol. 2: 6675
Internationaler Violin-Wettbewerb Hannover Vol. 2: 6758
Internationaler Violinwettbewerb Koln Vol. 2: 6609
Internationaler Violinwettbewerb Ludwig Spohr Vol. 2: 6972
Internationaler Wettbewerb Franz Schubert und Musik des 20 Jahrhundes Vol. 2: 805
Internationaler Wettbewerb fur Junge Pianisten Ettlingen Vol. 2: 7061
Internationaler Wettbewerb fur Liedgesang Vol. 2: 885
Internationaler Wettbewerb fur Streichquartett Karl Klinger Preis Vol. 2: 7009
Internationaler Wettbewerb und Seminar fur Bratsche Vol. 2: 3627
Internationales Festival der Filmhochschulen Munchen Vol. 2: 7059
Internationales Trickfilm Festival Stuttgart Vol. 2: 7142
Internationales Volkssportabzeichen Vol. 2: 6948
Interphot - Adelaide International Exhibition of Photography Vol. 2: 677
Interpret America Award Vol. 1: 10009
Interpretation Competition Vol. 2: 3448
Interpreters Competition of Slovak Republic Vol. 2: 1871
Intertech Technology Awards Vol. 1: 9700
Intra-Society Merit Award Vol. 1: 8561
Introductory Undergraduate Award Vol. 1: 1127
Invacare Award Vol. 1: 11153
Invent Magazine Vol. 1: 11423
Inventiveness Prize Vol. 2: 9966
Inventor of the Year Award Vol. 1: 16559
InVEST Award Vol. 1: 10130
Investigator Development Award Vol. 1: 568
Investigator of the Year Vol. 1: 5788
IOF Gold Medal Award Vol. 1: 11125
IOF Pins of Honour Vol. 2: 11477
IOGT International August Forell Award Vol. 2: 9894
ION Navigation Award (California Maritime Academy) Vol. 1: 10412
ION Navigation Award (U.S. Air Force Academy) Vol. 1: 10413
Ionescu de la Brad Prize; Ion Vol. 2: 10358
Ionescu-Sisesti Prize; Gheorge Vol. 2: 10359
IOOL Emeritus Vol. 2: 3445
IOOL Medal Vol. 2: 3446
Iorga Prize; Nicolae Vol. 2: 10360
Iowa Children's Choice Award Vol. 1: 11443
Iowa Country Music Hall of Fame Vol. 1: 14914
Iowa Literary Awards Vol. 1: 11441
Iowa School of Letters Award for Short Fiction Vol. 1: 11446
Iowa Short Fiction Award Vol. 1: 11446
Iowa Teen Award Vol. 1: 11444
IPA Advertising Effectiveness Awards Vol. 2: 3200
IPA Medal Vol. 2: 6038
IPA silver bowl Vol. 1: 11165
IPA Top Discovery in the Field of Humor Vol. 1: 11154
IPAC Award for Innovative Management Vol. 1: 10430
Ipar Kivalo Munkaert Vol. 2: 7331
Ipatieff Prize Vol. 1: 1564
IPDC - UNESCO Prize for Rural Communication Vol. 2: 6416
IPENZ Craven Post-Graduate Research Scholarship Vol. 2: 9736
IPENZ Structural Award Vol. 2: 9737
IPF Hall of Fame Vol. 2: 11480
IPMA Award for Excellence Vol. 1: 11137
IPMA Educational Award Vol. 1: 10099
IPMA Fellow Member Vol. 1: 10103
IPMA Honorary Life Membership Vol. 1: 11138
IPMA International Vendor/Associate Member of the Year Award Vol. 1: 10104
IPMI Distinguished Achievement Award Vol. 1: 11172
IPMI Graduate Student Award Vol. 1: 11173
IPMI Student Award Vol. 1: 11173
Ippen Award; Arthur Thomas Vol. 2: 9461
IPRA Golden World Awards for Excellence Vol. 2: 11822
IPRA President's Award Vol. 2: 11823
Iqbal Award Vol. 2: 9979
IR-100 Competition Vol. 1: 16797
IRA Children's Book Award Vol. 1: 11190
Irby Distinguished Service Award; Charles C. Vol. 1: 12861
IRE Awards Vol. 1: 11428
Ireland Special Award; Philip W. Vol. 1: 7638
IREM Foundation Minority Scholarship Award Vol. 1: 10438
Irino Prize Vol. 2: 8559
Iris Award Vol. 1: 6553
Iris Awards Vol. 1: 13342

Irish Advertising Awards Festival   Vol. 2: 7785
Irish Federation of Musicians & Associated Professions Trophy   Vol. 2: 7766
Irish Life Business Awareness Awards   Vol. 2: 7803
Irish Life Drama Award   Vol. 2: 7804
Irish Life Festival Choice Awards   Vol. 2: 7805
Irish Life Manager of the Month   Vol. 2: 7806
Irish Life Manager of the Year   Vol. 2: 7806
Irish Life Pensioner of the Year Awards   Vol. 2: 7807
Irish Life Souvenir of Ireland Challenge; CERT/   Vol. 2: 7802
Irish Pony Club Mounted Games   Vol. 2: 7834
Irish Research Funds   Vol. 1: 11453
The Irish Times Literature Prizes   Vol. 2: 7810
Irish Trophy   Vol. 2: 7834
IRMA Award   Vol. 1: 11208
Iron and Steel Development Award   Vol. 2: 8563
Iron Eyes Cody Award   Vol. 1: 11658
Iron Grandma Award   Vol. 2: 2393
Ironbridge Award   Vol. 2: 2248
IRPE Prize (International Recognition of Professional Excellence)   Vol. 2: 6689
Irrgang Memorial Award; William   Vol. 1: 5080
Irving Children's Book Choice Award; Washington   Vol. 1: 20193
Irwin Award for Scholarly Contributions to Management; Richard D.   Vol. 1: 49
Irwin Award; Robert B.   Vol. 1: 14212
Irwin Medal; George R.   Vol. 1: 6058
ISA Fellow   Vol. 1: 10489
ISA Technology Award   Vol. 1: 10496
ISAA Award   Vol. 1: 14266
ISAAC Consumer Lecture Award; WORDS+   Vol. 1: 11232
ISAAC Consumer Scholarship Award; WORDS+   Vol. 1: 11233
ISAAC Scholarship; Prentke Romich -   Vol. 1: 11231
Isaacs Awards for Outstanding Newsletter; Marx   Vol. 1: 2588
Isaacs Lifetime Achievement Award   Vol. 1: 11795
Isadore Gilbert Mudge - R. R. Bowker Award   Vol. 1: 2945
Isakson Prize for Optical Effects in Solids; Frank   Vol. 1: 3460
Isbrandt Automotive Safety Engineering Award; Ralph H.   Vol. 1: 17764
ISC All-World Awards   Vol. 1: 11316
ISC Hall of Fame   Vol. 1: 11315
ISC World Championship Trophy   Vol. 1: 11314
ISC World Tournament   Vol. 1: 11314
ISCA Young Scientists' Awards   Vol. 2: 7684
ISCC Service Award   Vol. 1: 10525
ISDA Special Commendation   Vol. 1: 11214
ISDP Dissertation Prize   Vol. 1: 11245
ISHAM Lucille K. Georg Award   Vol. 2: 1202
Ishikawa Medal   Vol. 1: 4285
ISI Information Science Doctoral Dissertation Scholarship   Vol. 1: 4169
Isidor Memorial Medal; Joseph S.   Vol. 1: 12615
ISIJ Award for Service   Vol. 2: 8566
Isker Award; Colonel Rohland A.   Vol. 1: 16800
Iskowitz Prize; Gershon   Vol. 1: 11479
Islamic Countries Festival for Radio Production   Vol. 2: 10492

Islamic Development Bank Prizes in Islamic Economics and Islamic Banking   Vol. 2: 10488
Islamic Foundation Awards   Vol. 2: 10490
The Islamic Organization for Medical Sciences Prizes   Vol. 2: 8843
Isle of Elba - Raffaello Brignetti Literary Award   Vol. 2: 8323
ISN Medal   Vol. 2: 1967
ISP Student Competition   Vol. 1: 10445
ISP/*VM & SD* International Design Competition   Vol. 1: 10446
ISPA Service Award   Vol. 1: 11288
ISPE Distinguished Achievement Award   Vol. 1: 11291
ISPE Engineer of The Year   Vol. 1: 11291
Israel Archives Association Awards   Vol. 2: 7913
Israel Discount Bank Prize   Vol. 2: 7924
Israel Prize   Vol. 2: 7906
Israeli Discount Bank Prize   Vol. 2: 7966
Issaccs Trophy   Vol. 1: 17353
Isserlis Scholarship; Julius   Vol. 2: 4127
Istanbul International Film Festival   Vol. 2: 12060
ISU Speed and Figure Skating Championships   Vol. 2: 11831
ISWM Woody Woodland Memorial Award   Vol. 1: 11308
ITA Award   Vol. 1: 11369
ITA Golden Videocassette Awards   Vol. 1: 11483
Italia Sul Mare Prize   Vol. 2: 8295
Italian Association for Metallurgy Awards   Vol. 2: 8334
Italian Minister for Culture and the Environment Prizes   Vol. 2: 8365
Italian PEN Prize   Vol. 2: 8363
ITCA All America   Vol. 1: 10557
ITCA Graduate Scholarships   Vol. 1: 10550
ITCA Hall of Fame   Vol. 1: 11344
ITCA Scholar Athletes   Vol. 1: 10559
Itek Award   Vol. 1: 17502
ITF Award for Services to the Game   Vol. 2: 3484
ITG Student Performance Competitions   Vol. 1: 11374
ITS Technology Transfer and Commercialization Award   Vol. 1: 19114
Itschner Plaques   Vol. 1: 17708
Ittleson Research in Child Psychiatry Award; Blanche F.   Vol. 1: 3638
ITU Centenary Prize   Vol. 2: 11849
Iturbi International Piano Competition; Jose   Vol. 2: 11219
ITVA Video Festival   Vol. 1: 11348
IUPUI National Children's Theatre Playwriting Competition   Vol. 1: 10151
Iuventus Mundi Cantat Competition   Vol. 2: 1893
Ivanausko premija; Tadas   Vol. 2: 8855
Ivens Film Prize; Joris   Vol. 2: 9376
Ivens; Prix Joris   Vol. 2: 5032
Ives Awards; Charles   Vol. 1: 510
Ives Journal Award (Engineering); Charles E.   Vol. 1: 17503
Ives Medal; Frederic   Vol. 1: 15750
IVOMEC Award for Effective Sheep Breeding   Vol. 1: 10843
Ivy Society Award; Robert H.   Vol. 1: 4760
Iwatani Naoji Memorial Prize   Vol. 2: 8573
IWEM Award   Vol. 1: 15158
IWES Award   Vol. 1: 15158
IWF International Awards   Vol. 2: 7434
IWF National Awarwd   Vol. 2: 7435
IWLA Conservation Award   Vol. 1: 20095
IWLA Hall of Fame Award   Vol. 1: 20096

IWLA Honor Roll Award   Vol. 1: 20097
Iyengar Memorial Award; Dr. M. O. T.   Vol. 2: 7589
Iyer Oration Award; Dr. C. G. S.   Vol. 2: 7590
IYHF Certificate of Merit   Vol. 2: 3510
IYHF Roll of Honour   Vol. 2: 3511
J-M Renaitour Prize   Vol. 2: 6314
Jaag-Gewasserschutz-Preis; Otto   Vol. 2: 11932
Jabach Medaille   Vol. 2: 6596
Jabach Medal   Vol. 2: 6596
Jabotinsky Prize   Vol. 1: 11495
Jabuti Prize   Vol. 2: 1470
Jack Murphy Appreciation Award   Vol. 1: 13963
Jackling Award; Daniel C.   Vol. 1: 17567
Jacks Memorial Award; Robert L.   Vol. 1: 2589
Jackson Aerospace Award; Nelson P.   Vol. 1: 14836
Jackson Award; Anna M.   Vol. 1: 4660
Jackson Award for Distinguished Public Service; Henry M.   Vol. 1: 11498
Jackson Award; Hartley H. T.   Vol. 1: 4661
Jackson Award; Joseph Henry   Vol. 1: 17031
Jackson Award; Nel   Vol. 1: 8628
Jackson Award; Percy   Vol. 2: 3120
Jackson Award; William E.   Vol. 1: 16653
Jackson Awards; C. C.   Vol. 1: 19943
Jackson Best Column Writing; Emory O.   Vol. 1: 14397
Jackson C.B.E. Cup; Jim   Vol. 2: 2393
Jackson Community Initiative Award; Holt   Vol. 2: 3570
Jackson Diesel Engine Award; Percy   Vol. 2: 3120
Jackson Distinguished Service Award; Henry M.   Vol. 1: 11549
Jackson Lecture and Medal; Hughlings   Vol. 2: 4255
Jackson Memorial Award; Sara E.   Vol. 1: 13486
Jackson Memorial Cup; C. N.   Vol. 2: 2062
Jackson Memorial Graduate Assistant Grant; Nell   Vol. 1: 19944
Jackson Memorial Lecture Award; Edward   Vol. 1: 632
Jackson Memorial Lectures; Henry M.   Vol. 1: 11499
Jackson Mid-Career Scientist Award; Marion L. and Chrystie M.   Vol. 1: 7830
Jackson (nee Gwilt) Gift and Medal; Hannah   Vol. 2: 3941
Jackson Prize; John Brinckerhoff   Vol. 1: 5684
Jackson Silver Medal   Vol. 2: 3094
Jackson Social Responsibility Award; Hobart   Vol. 1: 1011
Jacksonian Prize   Vol. 2: 3978
Jacksonville University Playwriting Contest   Vol. 1: 11502
JACL'er of the Biennium   Vol. 1: 11504
Jacob; Fondation Charles   Vol. 2: 5517
Jacob Poetry Prize; Max   Vol. 2: 6081
Jacob Trophy; Bruno E.   Vol. 1: 14020
Jacobi Award; Abraham   Vol. 1: 672
Jacobs Award; Alvin H.   Vol. 1: 673
Jacobsen Award; Earl Grant   Vol. 1: 17085
Jacobson Award; Richard S.   Vol. 1: 16357
Jacobson Prizes; "Discovery"/*The Nation*: The Joan Leiman   Vol. 1: 19898
Jacobson Study Grants; Robert M.   Vol. 1: 18830
Jacobus Award; Donald Lines   Vol. 1: 4566
Jacquard Memorial Award; Joseph Marie   Vol. 1: 15557
Jacquemetton; Prix Marius   Vol. 2: 6229

Award Index
Volume 2: International and Foreign

Jacquet Gold Medal and the Francis F. Lucas Award for Excellence in Metallography; Pierre   Vol. 1: 5361
Jacquet-Lucas Award for Excellence in Metallography; IMS and AMS   Vol. 1: 5361
JACS Scholarship Award   Vol. 1: 11599
Jade of Chiefs   Vol. 1: 15863
Jaeger Memorial Award; Australian Geomechanics Award - John   Vol. 2: 423
Jaeger Prize; Thomas A.   Vol. 2: 8543
Jaen Prize   Vol. 2: 11281
Jaezat Al Malik Faisal Al Alamiyyah Li Khidmt Al Islam   Vol. 2: 10498
Jaezat Al Malik Faisal Al Alamiyyah Lil Adab Al Arabi   Vol. 2: 10496
Jaezat Al Malik Faisal Al Alamiyyah Lil Derasat Al Islamiyyah   Vol. 2: 10497
Jaezat Al Malik Faisal Al Alamiyyah Lil Tib   Vol. 2: 10499
Jaezat Al Malik Faisal Al Alamiyyah Lil Ulum   Vol. 2: 10500
Jafet Prize; Nami   Vol. 2: 1488
Jaffe; Fondation   Vol. 2: 5334
Jahnsson Award in Economics; Yrjo   Vol. 2: 4737
Jahre Prize for Contributions to Norwegian Culture; Anders   Vol. 2: 9900
Jahre Prize in Medicine; Anders   Vol. 2: 9961
Jakob Klaesi-Preis   Vol. 2: 11918
Jakob Memorial Award; Max   Vol. 1: 4683
JAKS Awards   Vol. 1: 6124
Jaksch-Gedachtnis-Preis; Wenzel-   Vol. 2: 7080
JALMA Trust Fund Oration Award In The Field Of Leprosy   Vol. 2: 7591
James Award; William   Vol. 1: 3766
James Beard/Seagram Restaurant Awards   Vol. 1: 6301
James Book Award; William   Vol. 1: 3734
James Clinical Research Award; Lucy Wortham   Vol. 1: 18037
James Fellowship; T. V.   Vol. 2: 2445
James H. Wilson Full-Length Play Awards   Vol. 1: 8568
James Lynah Memorial Award   Vol. 1: 8790
James Memorial Trophy; Eddie   Vol. 1: 6880
Jameson Archival Advocacy Award; J. Franklin   Vol. 1: 17673
Jameson Fellowship in American History; J. Franklin   Vol. 1: 11857
Jameson Prize for Editorial Achievement; J. Franklin   Vol. 1: 2293
Jamestown Foundation Award   Vol. 1: 10255
Jamestown Prize   Vol. 1: 10255
Jamieson Fellowship; Donald   Vol. 1: 7173
Jamnalal Bajaj Foundation Awards   Vol. 2: 7693
Jamnalal Bajaj International Award for Promoting Gandhian Values Outside India   Vol. 2: 7694
Jancso Commemorative Medal; Miklos   Vol. 2: 7459
Jancso Miklos emlekerem es jutalomdij   Vol. 2: 7459
Jandoli Award of Execellence   Vol. 1: 16992
Jane Memorial Lecture Award; R. S.   Vol. 1: 7551
Janeway Medal   Vol. 1: 3900
Janin; Prix Jules   Vol. 2: 5876
Janssen; Fondation Antoinette   Vol. 2: 5494
Janssen Pharmaceutica Postdoctoral Fellowship in Medical Mycology; NFID -   Vol. 1: 14043
Janssen; Prix Paul   Vol. 2: 1365
Janssen Prize; Hans   Vol. 2: 6909
Janssens; Prix Rene   Vol. 2: 969

Janus Awards for Outstanding Economic and Financial News Broadcasting   Vol. 1: 12449
Janus Awards for Real Estate Reporting   Vol. 1: 12450
Japan Academy Prize   Vol. 2: 8595
Japan Art Academy Prize   Vol. 2: 8597
Japan Art Award   Vol. 2: 8742
Japan Association for Education Broadcasting Prize   Vol. 2: 8602
Japan Broadcasting Corporation Prize   Vol. 2: 8727
Japan Foundation Award   Vol. 2: 8612
Japan Foundation Grant Programs   Vol. 2: 8613
Japan Foundation Prize   Vol. 2: 8727
Japan Foundation Prize for the Promotion of Community-Based Cultural Exchange   Vol. 2: 8614
Japan Foundation Special Prizes   Vol. 2: 8615
Japan Golf Championships   Vol. 2: 8617
Japan International Film - Video Festival of Adventure and Sports in Hakuba   Vol. 2: 8622
Japan Prize   Vol. 2: 8736
Japan Society for Analytical Chemistry Award   Vol. 2: 8634
Japan Society for the Promotion of Science Research Fellowships Science and Technology   Vol. 2: 7157
Japan Society of Human Genetics Award   Vol. 2: 8641
Japan Sports Prize   Vol. 2: 8791
Japan Translation Culture Prize   Vol. 2: 8638
Japan Translation Prize for Publishers   Vol. 2: 8639
Japan-U.S. Friendship Commission Prize for the Translation of Japanese Literature   Vol. 1: 7999
Japan Welding Society Award   Vol. 2: 8645
Japanese American of the Biennium   Vol. 1: 11505
Japanese Biochemical Society's Shorei-Sho Awards   Vol. 2: 8650
Japanese Non-Fiction Prize   Vol. 2: 8678
Japanese Society of Sericultural Science Award   Vol. 2: 8659
Japanese Society of Soil Science and Plant Nutrition Award   Vol. 2: 8666
Japanese Society of Veterinary Science Award   Vol. 2: 8671
Japanese Society of Zootechnical Science Award   Vol. 2: 8673
Jarabak Memorial International Teachers and Research Award; Louise Ada   Vol. 1: 1093
Jashnvare Beynolmelale e Filmhaye Amouzeshi Tarbeyati Roshd   Vol. 2: 7741
Jassy Writers Association Award   Vol. 2: 10413
Jaszai Prize; Mari   Vol. 2: 7401
Javits Award for Public Service   Vol. 1: 7714
Javits Excellence in Public Service Award; Jacob K.   Vol. 1: 16850
Javits Public Service Award; Jacob   Vol. 1: 3639
Jayezeye Shoraye Ketabe Koudak   Vol. 2: 7735
Jayle; Fondation Max-Fernand   Vol. 2: 5630
Jazz Band Director of the Year   Vol. 1: 13420
Jazz Contribution Awards   Vol. 1: 6413
Jazz Educators Award   Vol. 1: 13431
Jazz Hall of Fame   Vol. 1: 10380
Jazz Master Award   Vol. 1: 5337
Jazz Prize   Vol. 1: 9173
Jazzpar Prize   Vol. 2: 1913
JCC Biennial Communications Awards Competition   Vol. 1: 11517
JCC Program Awards   Vol. 1: 11518

JEA Research and Development Fund Award   Vol. 1: 11545
Jean-Christophe Prizes   Vol. 2: 6316
Jeanbernat et Barthelemy de Ferrari Doria; Fondation Jules et Louis   Vol. 2: 5604
Jeanbernat et Barthelemy de Ferrari Doria; Prix Jules et Louis
   Institut de France   Vol. 2: 5346
   Institut de France - Academie des Beaux Arts   Vol 2: 5407
   Institut de France - Academie des Inscriptions et Belle-Lettres   Vol 2: 5467
   Institut de France - Academie des Sciences Morales et Politiques   Vol 2: 5768
   Institut de France - Academie Francaise   Vol 2: 5874
"Jeanie" Musical Scholarship Winner   Vol. 1: 9266
Jeantet Prize for Medicine; Louis   Vol. 2: 11727
Jeevan Raksha Padak   Vol. 2: 7551
Jefferson Award; NAA Foundation - International Circulation Managers Association C. K.   Vol. 1: 15354
Jefferson Award; Thomas   Vol. 1: 18663
Jefferson Awards   Vol. 1: 2440
Jefferson Awards for Public Architecture; Thomas   Vol. 1: 2538
Jefferson Awards/*Weekly Reader*   Vol. 1: 2441
Jefferson Center for International Dermatology Resident/Student Contest   Vol. 1: 9939
Jefferson Freedom Award; Thomas   Vol. 1: 2809
Jefferson Grape-wine Loving Cup Trophy   Vol. 1: 20042
Jefferson Lecture in the Humanities   Vol. 1: 13897
Jefferson Medal   Vol. 1: 15188
Jefferson Medal; Thomas   Vol. 1: 3432
Jefferson Memorial Foundation Award in Law; Thomas   Vol. 1: 11524
Jefferson Memorial Foundation Medal in Architecture; Thomas   Vol. 1: 11525
Jefferson Prize; Thomas   Vol. 1: 17475
Jeffery Award; Thomas B.   Vol. 1: 12575
Jeffords, Jr. Trophy; Walter M.   Vol. 1: 20246
Jeffrey Award; Bill   Vol. 1: 10543
Jeffries Award; John   Vol. 1: 2477
Jeffries Medical Research Award; AIAA   Vol. 1: 2477
Jeffries Trophy; Three-quarter Ton Championship - J. Amory   Vol. 1: 19536
Jehlinger Award; Charles   Vol. 1: 551
Jellinek Memorial Award; E. M.   Vol. 1: 11527
Jendrosezek Gold Medal; Alfred   Vol. 2: 7489
Jenkins Medal; Samuel H.   Vol. 2: 3375
Jenkins Memorial Prize; Robert Rice   Vol. 1: 5297
Jenner Medal   Vol. 2: 4256
Jenner Medal; Annie Burr   Vol. 1: 9486
Jennings Memorial Award; Charles H.   Vol. 1: 5081
Jennings Trophy; William M.   Vol. 1: 14170
Jeno Kvassay Prize   Vol. 2: 7349
Jensen Award; Harry T.   Vol. 1: 2254
Jeoloji Muhendisleri Odasi Emek Odulu   Vol. 2: 12047
Jephcott Lectures   Vol. 2: 4257
Jeppson Medal; John   Vol. 1: 1464
Jerard Fund Award; PEN/   Vol. 1: 16022
Jeremiah Memorial Award (College Division); Edward   Vol. 1: 2308
Jerome Playwright-in-Residence Fellowship   Vol. 1: 16250
Jerusalem Municipality Awards   Vol. 2: 7936

Jerusalem Prize for the Freedom of the Individual in Society   Vol. 2: 7934
Jerwood Award   Vol. 2: 3513
Jesselson Prize for Contemporary Judaica Design   Vol. 2: 7925
Jessen Fellowship in Children's Dentistry   Vol. 2: 3401
Jessie T. MacKnight Award   Vol. 1: 18439
Jessies   Vol. 1: 19977
Jester Award   Vol. 1: 15363
Jeter Award; Frank   Vol. 1: 202
Jetfonden   Vol. 2: 11648
Jetfoundation   Vol. 2: 11648
Jeton de Vermeil   Vol. 2: 6362
JETS National TEAMS Awards   Vol. 1: 11630
Jewett Memorial Award; Lew   Vol. 1: 9109
Jewish Colonization in the Argentine Republic Prize   Vol. 2: 83
Jewish Community Center Theater of Cleveland Playwriting Competition   Vol. 1: 11543
Jewish Heritage Award for Excellence in Literature   Vol. 1: 6432
Jewish Historical Society of New York Fellowships   Vol. 1: 2741
Jewish Humanist Leadership Award   Vol. 1: 17495
Jeyes Lectureship; John   Vol. 2: 4204
Jimmie Awards   Vol. 1: 5704
Jnanpith Award   Vol. 2: 7486
Joannides; Fondation Alexandre   Vol. 2: 5481
Job Corps Fine Arts and Crafts Contest   Vol. 1: 19269
Job Corps Hall of Fame   Vol. 1: 19270
Jobber of the Year   Vol. 1: 11577
Jobst Foundation Award; Annual Conrad   Vol. 1: 1808
Jobst Research Award; Conrad   Vol. 1: 18201
Joest; Fondation du Baron de   Vol. 2: 5541
Joffrey Award of Merit; Robert   Vol. 1: 19925
Johinke Medal; K.   Vol. 2: 462
John Paul II Award   Vol. 1: 14614
John Paul II Religious Freedom Award   Vol. 1: 7371
John T. Galey, Sr. Memorial Public Service Award   Vol. 1: 2672
John W. Cox Award   Vol. 1: 17409
Johnckheere sur l'Historie de la Medecine; Prix du Docteur Frans   Vol. 2: 1330
Johns Hopkins National Search for Computing to Assist Persons with Disabilities   Vol. 1: 8083
Johnson Achievement Award; Alfred E.   Vol. 1: 1202
Johnson & Higgins Scrivener Award   Vol. 1: 4785
Johnson and Johnson Award   Vol. 2: 10976
Johnson & Johnson Preventive Dentistry Awards   Vol. 2: 3402
Johnson Annual Prize; Walter J.   Vol. 1: 9770
Johnson Annual Scholarship Winners; Edward   Vol. 1: 11590
Johnson Award; Charles A.   Vol. 1: 6059
Johnson Award; Eleanor M.   Vol. 1: 11191
Johnson Award; Kelly   Vol. 1: 17856
Johnson Award; Lady Bird   Vol. 1: 12788
Johnson Award; Laurence B.   Vol. 1: 8863
Johnson Award; Lawrence J.   Vol. 1: 19000
Johnson Award; Mrs. Lyndon B.   Vol. 1: 11659
Johnson Award; Orinne   Vol. 1: 16122
Johnson Award; Pyke   Vol. 1: 18781
Johnson Award; Robert B.   Vol. 1: 10010
Johnson Award; Stanley Thomas   Vol. 2: 11913
Johnson Award; Thomas W.   Vol. 1: 582
Johnson Forderpreis/Prix Cinegramm; Stanley Thomas   Vol. 2: 11913

Johnson Health Policy Fellowships; Robert Wood   Vol. 1: 12698
Johnson Honorary Member Award; Philip D.   Vol. 1: 4218
Johnson Journal Award; G. Wesley   Vol. 1: 13812
Johnson, Jr., Award; J. E.   Vol. 1: 11466
Johnson Lecture; Axel Ax:son   Vol. 2: 11528
Johnson Memorial Award; Palmer O.   Vol. 1: 1976
Johnson Memorial Awards; James P.   Vol. 1: 10381
Johnson Memorial; Michael   Vol. 2: 4593
Johnson Memorial Trophy; Joe   Vol. 1: 6975
Johnson Music Competition; Edward   Vol. 1: 11590
Johnson Prize; Harry G.   Vol. 1: 6855
Johnson, Smith, and Kinsely Award for New Perspectives on Executive Leadership   Vol. 1: 11597
Johnson Smith & Knisely Accord Executive Leadership Award   Vol. 1: 11597
Johnson Woman in Action Award; Gertrude   Vol. 1: 13210
Johnston Award for Excellence in Position Classification; David C.   Vol. 1: 7818
Johnston Award; William M.   Vol. 1: 19649
Johnston Memorial Medal; R. M.   Vol. 2: 634
Johnston Service Award; Floyd T.   Vol. 1: 5773
Johnstone Award   Vol. 1: 17404
Johnstone Award; Fraser   Vol. 1: 1500
Johnstone III Trophy (Singlehanded); Robert L.   Vol. 1: 19532
Joint Service Achievement Medal   Vol. 1: 19164
Joint Service Commendation Medal   Vol. 1: 19165
Jokun Hosho   Vol. 2: 8578
Joliet-Curie Gold Medal for Peace   Vol. 2: 4767
Jonckheere; Prix Tobie   Vol. 2: 998
Jones and Bailey K. Howard World Book Encyclopedia - ALA Goal Awards; J. Morris   Vol. 1: 2825
Jones & Shipman Prize   Vol. 2: 3294
Jones Award; Anson   Vol. 1: 18661
Jones Award; Bob   Vol. 1: 19361
Jones Award for Executive Leadership; Roger W.   Vol. 1: 4949
Jones Award; Jesse H.   Vol. 1: 18650
Jones Award; Mary Vaughan   Vol. 2: 12197
Jones Award - Most Miles Stallion Award; Jim   Vol. 1: 1992
Jones Award; Rufus   Vol. 2: 921
Jones Award; Tom   Vol. 1: 5858
Jones-Bateman Cup   Vol. 2: 4039
Jones Community Service Award; Edward C.   Vol. 1: 3014
Jones Distinguished Service Award; Reginald H.   Vol. 1: 12559
Jones Fiction Award; Margaret   Vol. 1: 6392
Jones Fleet Engineer Award; Claude A.   Vol. 1: 4731
Jones; Gwobr Goffa Sir Bryner   Vol. 2: 12188
Jones International Brass Chamber Music Competition, Barcs; Philip   Vol. 2: 7416
Jones London Medal; H. E.   Vol. 2: 3328
Jones Memorial Award; Peter   Vol. 2: 2896
Jones Perpetual Memorial Award; Sir Bryner   Vol. 2: 12188
Jones Playwrighting Competition; Margo   Vol. 1: 18669
Jonssons pris; Bengt   Vol. 2: 11516
Jordaanprijs; L. J.   Vol. 2: 9640
Jordan Achievement Award; Harry E.   Vol. 1: 5014

Jordan Award   Vol. 2: 3731
Jordan Medal; Karl   Vol. 1: 11833
Jordan Memorial Challenge Trophy; Lynn   Vol. 1: 14866
Jorge Prize; Jose M.   Vol. 2: 84
Jory Copying Assistance Program; Margaret Fairbank   Vol. 1: 3159
Joryu Bungaku Award   Vol. 2: 8520
Joseph Award; Stephen   Vol. 2: 4381
Joseph Award; Thomas L.   Vol. 1: 11467
Joseph Prize   Vol. 2: 10977
Joseph Prize for Human Rights   Vol. 1: 5179
Joseph Prize; Roger E.   Vol. 1: 9881
Joseph W. Rosenbluth Memorial Award   Vol. 1: 4809
Joseph W. Rosenbluth Memorial Travel Agent of the Year Award   Vol. 1: 4809
Joshua Trophy   Vol. 1: 17313
Josten's Most Improved National Midget Championship Series Driver Award   Vol. 1: 19024
Joule Medal; James Prescott   Vol. 2: 3247
Joule Prize; James   Vol. 2: 6029
Journal Award
  National Council on Public History   Vol. 1: 13812
  Society for Applied Spectroscopy   Vol 1: 17418
  Society of Motion Picture and Television Engineers   Vol 1: 17904
Journal Award (Science)   Vol. 1: 17504
Journal Contributor Awards   Vol. 1: 5104
Journal Editor's Award   Vol. 1: 13908
Journal of Allied Health Award   Vol. 1: 5950
Journal of Geography Awards   Vol. 1: 13694
Journal of Property Management Article of the Year Awards   Vol. 1: 10439
Journal of Risk and Insurance Awards   Vol. 1: 3962
Journal of the American Planning Association Award   Vol. 1: 3533
Journal of the American Society for Information Science Referees 5-Year Citation   Vol. 1: 4170
Journalism Alumni Award   Vol. 1: 6227
Journalism Award
  American Association of Petroleum Geologists   Vol 1: 1108
  American College of Health Care Administrators   Vol 1: 1650
  American Society of Abdominal Surgery   Vol 1: 4351
Journalism Awards
  Catholic Press Association   Vol. 1: 7384
  Leukemia Society of America   Vol 1: 11837
Journalism Awards Contest   Vol. 1: 15765
Journalism Awards for Excellence in Personal Finance Reporting   Vol. 1: 4947
Journalism Awards of Excellence
  American Academy of Facial Plastic and Reconstructive Surgery   Vol. 1: 569
  American College of Emergency Physicians   Vol 1: 1636
Journalism Awards Program   Vol. 1: 9873
Journalism Citation   Vol. 1: 10668
Journalism Competition Prizes   Vol. 2: 12121
Journalism Hall of Fame   Vol. 1: 6228
Journalism Prize
  Belgian Municipal Credit Institution   Vol. 2: 1062
  International Federation for the Rights of Man   Vol 2: 6003
Journalist of the Year Award   Vol. 1: 12961
Journalist Prize of the DGE   Vol. 2: 6857
Journalistenpreis of the DGE   Vol. 2: 6857
Journey Prize
  Harbourfront Reading Series   Vol. 1: 9768

McClelland & Stewart, Inc. Vol 1: 12143
Jousselin; Fondations Gaston Plante, Francois Hebert-Paul Vol. 2: 5680
Jousselin; Prix Henri Vol. 2: 5865
Jowett Medal Vol. 2: 4456
Joy In Singing Award Recital Vol. 1: 11620
Joyce Award Vol. 2: 2282
Jozwiak Memorial Special Achievement Award; Joseph Vol. 1: 11167
JPA Blue Ribbon and Certificate Vol. 1: 11632
JPA H. E. Harris Medal Vol. 1: 11633
JPA Research Award Vol. 1: 11634
JRST Award Vol. 1: 12890
JSLE Best Paper Award Vol. 2: 8669
JSME Medal Vol. 2: 8643
JTPA Awards for Excellence Vol. 1: 13047
JTPA Presidential Awards Vol. 1: 19265
Jubilaumspreis Vol. 2: 6877
Jubilee Lecture and Harden Medal Vol. 2: 2174
Jubilee Medal
  British Trust for Ornithology Vol. 2: 2551
  Geological Society of South Africa Vol 2: 10872
Jubilee Prize Vol. 2: 2542
Jubilee Trophy Vol. 2: 9818
Jucci; Fondazione Giovanna Vol. 2: 8056
Judd AIC Award Vol. 2: 9480
Judeen Memorial Award; Erik Vol. 1: 19565
Judge of the Year Vol. 1: 10827
Judge of the Year Award Vol. 1: 13386
Judges Appreciation Award Vol. 1: 3230
Judges Choice Award Vol. 1: 11014
Judges' Commendation Vol. 1: 3340
Judiciary Award Vol. 1: 5789
Jugend musiziert Preis Vol. 2: 853
Jujamcyn Theaters Award Vol. 1: 11622
Jujitsu Outstanding Competitor Vol. 1: 432
Julien; Prix Stanislas Vol. 2: 5473
Julius Medal; George Vol. 2: 470
Julliard Prize; Jean Vol. 2: 3477
Jump Award; William A. Vol. 1: 11624
Jumping/Nordic Combined Coaches of the Year Vol. 1: 19566
Jungfleisch; Fondation Emile Vol. 2: 5552
Junior Achievement National Business Hall of Fame Vol. 1: 11626
Junior Award Vol. 1: 4678
Junior Berwick Prize Vol. 2: 3612
Junior Captain Scott Commemorative Medal Vol. 2: 10993
Junior European Baseball Champion Vol. 2: 1117
Junior Golf Leader Vol. 1: 16469
Junior Grand Champion Vol. 1: 15473
Junior Handler Award Vol. 1: 3984
Junior High Average Horsemanship Vol. 1: 15474
Junior Inventor of the Year Vol. 2: 11404
Junior Investigators Award Vol. 1: 1024
Junior Javelin Championship Vol. 1: 11509
Junior Member and Travel Awards Vol. 2: 593
Junior Moulton Medal Vol. 2: 3223
Junior National Championship Vol. 1: 15475
Junior National Championships Vol. 1: 19080
Junior Paper Award Vol. 1: 17928
Junior Player of the Year Vol. 1: 9960
Junior Players of the Year Vol. 1: 18620
Junior Research Fellowship Vol. 2: 7508
Junior Showmanship Vol. 1: 14142
Junior Triathletes of the Year Vol. 1: 18811
Junior Whitehead Prize Vol. 2: 3613
Junior/Young Rider Awards Vol. 1: 19325
Juniper Prize Vol. 1: 11636
Juno Awards Vol. 1: 6762

Juno Hall of Fame Vol. 1: 6762
Jupiter Award Vol. 1: 6329
Jurdant Prize in Environmental Science; Michel Vol. 1: 5433
Juried Crafts Exhibition Vol. 1: 7486
Juror's Choice Awards - Annual Jury Show Vol. 1: 12497
Juror's Choice Awards - Biennial Jury Show Vol. 1: 12497
Jury Award Vol. 2: 8096
Jury's Special Award Vol. 2: 3449
Jurzykowski Foundation Awards; Alfred Vol. 1: 11638
Justice and Peace Prize for Human Values Vol. 2: 11209
Justice Award Vol. 1: 2758
Justice Award/Fund for Religious Liberty Award Vol. 1: 2733
Justice Volunteer of the Year Vol. 1: 10755
Jutra Award; Claude Vol. 1: 29
Juvenile Court Judge of the Year Vol. 1: 13829
Juvenile Stake Challenge Trophy Vol. 1: 14866
Juventud de las Americas Vol. 2: 1781
JVC President Award Vol. 2: 8780
JVST Shop Note Award Vol. 1: 4962
JWS Citation Award for Papers of the Year Vol. 2: 8646
K-9 Dog Award Vol. 1: 3557
Kaan Award; Karoly Vol. 2: 7346
Kaan Karoly emlekerem Vol. 2: 7346
Kabarett Award; LITERATURIUMS Vol. 2: 7051
Kable Electrification Award; George W. Vol. 1: 4371
Kade Collaborative Works Fellowships Vol. 1: 10378
Kadokawa Prize; Genyoshi Vol. 2: 8679
Kafenda Prize; Frico Vol. 2: 10772
Kafka Prize; Janet Vol. 1: 19867
Kafka Prize; Janet Heidinger Vol. 1: 19867
Kagy Education Award of Excellence; Frederick D. Vol. 1: 9701
Kahn Award; Noah A. Vol. 1: 6060
Kahn Award; Sanders A. Vol. 1: 5191
Kaiko Award; Takeshi Vol. 2: 8762
Kainz-Medaille der Stadt Wien; Josef Vol. 2: 792
Kaiser Educational Award; L. U. "Luke" Vol. 1: 12008
Kaitz Award for Outstanding Contribution Through a State or Regional Association; Walter Vol. 1: 13519
Kaitz Award; Idell Vol. 1: 13513
Kal Kan Award Vol. 1: 791
Kal Kan Volunteer of the Year Vol. 1: 2401
Kala Bhushana Honours Vol. 2: 11422
Kala Prapoorna in Dance; Bharta Vol. 2: 7541
Kala Prapoorna in Drama; Nataka Vol. 2: 7542
Kala Prapoorna in Music; Gana Vol. 2: 7543
Kala Praveena Award Vol. 2: 7544
Kalakirthi Vol. 2: 11431
Kalashoori Vol. 2: 11432
Kalbache and Zahara Ben Mamou Award; Azar Vol. 1: 11179
Kaleidoscope Immigrantfilmfestival Vol. 2: 11490
Kaleidoscope of Honor Vol. 2: 1946
Kaletta Award; Father Paul Vol. 1: 13563
Kalikow Award for Exceptional Merit; Mrs. S. Vol. 1: 15983
Kalinga Prize Vol. 2: 6417
Kalish Innovative Publication Award; Richard Vol. 1: 9590

Kallebergerstipendiet Vol. 2: 11595
Kallen Award; Horace M. Vol. 1: 2734
Kalmus Gold Medal Award; Technicolor/Herbert T. Vol. 1: 17912
Kalokerinos Foundation Prize Vol. 2: 7212
Kalven Prize Vol. 1: 11792
Kamani Gold Medal Vol. 2: 7632
Kamei Katsuichiro Prize Vol. 2: 8686
Kaminitz Research Awards; Armando Vol. 2: 7981
Kammer Merit in Authorship Award; Adoph G. Vol. 1: 1698
Kammerer Award; Gladys M. Vol. 1: 3576
Kanakasree Award Vol. 2: 7702
Kandhari Award; Lala Ram Chand Vol. 2: 7592
Kando Award; Kalman Vol. 2: 7332
Kando Kalman Dijasok Vol. 2: 7332
Kandutsch Preis; Jorg Vol. 2: 846
Kane Award; Robert J. Vol. 1: 19489
Kane Medal; Elisha Kent Vol. 1: 9553
Kanev Memorial Award; Sydney M. Vol. 1: 1684
Kaniel Prize; Yehoshua Vol. 2: 7879
Kanin Playwriting Award Program); National Student Playwriting Award (Michael Vol. 1: 1759
Kanin Playwriting Awards Program; Michael
  American College Theatre Festival Vol. 1: 1755
  American College Theatre Festival Vol 1: 1759
Kansainvalinen Mirjam Helin laulukilpailu Vol. 2: 4694
Kansainvalinen Paulon Sellokilpailu Vol. 2: 4750
Kansas National Small Painting, Drawing and Print Exhibition Vol. 1: 12452
Kansas News Enterprise Award Vol. 1: 20260
Kansas Quarterly/Kansas Arts Commission Awards Vol. 1: 11646
Kansas Quarterly Seaton Awards Vol. 1: 11647
Kant Prize; Immanuel Vol. 2: 7114
Kapell Piano Competition; University of Maryland International Piano Festival and William Vol. 1: 19822
Kapell Piano Competition; William Vol. 1: 19822
Kapitan Award; Josef S. Vol. 1: 11468
Kapitza Prize; Peter Vol. 2: 6029
Kaplan Medal Vol. 1: 9159
Kaplan Prize Vol. 2: 7892
Kaplan Sportsmanship Award; Bobby Vol. 1: 19650
Kapp Foundation Engineering Award; Martin S. Vol. 1: 4476
Kappa Alpha Theta Program Director of the Year Vol. 1: 13830
Kappe Award; Stanley E. Vol. 1: 558
Kapur Oration; Dr. B. L. Vol. 2: 7620
Karacan Prize Vol. 2: 12062
Karant Award for Excellence in Aviation Journalism; Max Vol. 1: 284
Karel Award Vol. 2: 6493
Karger Memorial Foundation Annual Award; Heinz Vol. 2: 11871
Kari Medal Vol. 2: 9946
Karibu Vol. 2: 1102
Karlsson Award; Hans Vol. 1: 10302
Karlstrom Outstanding Educator Award; ACM Karl V. Vol. 1: 5466
Karmel Award; Marjorie Vol. 1: 5384
Karo Plaque Vol. 1: 17709
Karpinskij Prizes; Alexander Petrowitsch Vol. 2: 7115

Karsh Award; Solange   Vol. 1: 15855
Kasden Award; Lawrence   Vol. 1: 5174
Kasic Award; Bartol   Vol. 2: 1810
Kaskela Award for the Best ASIS Chapter or Special Interest Group Newsletter; Elaine D.   Vol. 1: 4171
Kastler Prize   Vol. 2: 8289
Kastler-Prize; Gentner-   Vol. 2: 6660
Katanning Art Prize   Vol. 2: 511
Kates Award; W. A.   Vol. 1: 10490
Katz Award; Donald L.   Vol. 1: 9507
Katz Award in Composition; Erich   Vol. 1: 3907
Katz Basic Science Research Prize for Young Investigators; Louis N.   Vol. 1: 2234
Katz Memorial Award; Fred Michael   Vol. 1: 5566
Katz Memorial Prizes; Sidney L.   Vol. 1: 14216
Kauffman Gold Medal; Virgil   Vol. 1: 17845
Kaufman Prize for First Fiction; Sue   Vol. 1: 511
Kaufmann Award; Richard Harold   Vol. 1: 10277
Kaufmann Memorial Lecture   Vol. 2: 6838
Kaufmann-Preis; H. P.   Vol. 2: 6839
Kaula Gold Medal; Professor   Vol. 2: 7698
Kaula - Ranganathan Gold Medal   Vol. 2: 7699
Kautz Merit Award; Sena   Vol. 1: 5534
Kavlin Photography Grant; Enrique   Vol. 2: 7926
Kawai Prize   Vol. 2: 326
Kay Elemetrics Award for Research in Phonetics   Vol. 1: 11297
Kay Jeweler's/J. B. Robinson Award   Vol. 1: 13582
Kazanjian Foundation Awards Program for the Teaching of Economics   Vol. 1: 13800
Kazdin Memorial Fund Award; S. Edwin   Vol. 1: 5192
Keane; Award for Excellence in Honor of Mark E.   Vol. 1: 10849
Keane Award for Excellence; Mark E.   Vol. 1: 10849
Keane Distinguished Service Award; Charles V.   Vol. 1: 986
Kearney Award for Outstanding Research in General Management; A. T.   Vol. 1: 50
Kearton Award   Vol. 2: 4169
Kearton Medal and Award; Cherry   Vol. 2: 4012
Keats/Kerlan Collection Fellowship; Ezra Jack   Vol. 1: 19836
Keats Memorial Fellowship; Ezra Jack   Vol. 1: 19836
Keats - Shelley Association Annual Prize   Vol. 1: 11654
Keefer/CFI Award; Eugene C.   Vol. 1: 6005
Keefer Medal   Vol. 1: 7174
Keeling Dissertation Award; William B.   Vol. 1: 18789
Keep America Beautiful National Awards Program   Vol. 1: 11660
Keep America Beautiful National Recycling Awards   Vol. 1: 11661
Keepers Preservation Education Fund Fellowship   Vol. 1: 17745
Keeping the Blues Alive Awards   Vol. 1: 6417
Kegan Award; Philip M. Hamer and Elizabeth Hamer   Vol. 1: 17671
Kehoe Award of Merit; Robert A.   Vol. 1: 1699
Kehoe Memorial Award; Fr. George   Vol. 1: 6976
Kehrlein Award; Oliver   Vol. 1: 17235
Keilin Memorial Lecture   Vol. 2: 2175

Keimer Foundation Prizes; Ludwig   Vol. 2: 11873
Keith Award; Nathaniel S.   Vol. 1: 14199
Keith Medal   Vol. 2: 10645
Kell Fellowship Program; James H.   Vol. 1: 10452
Kelleher Award; Judith C.   Vol. 1: 8905
Kellendonk-prijs; Frans   Vol. 2: 9628
Keller Award; James   Vol. 1: 7669
Keller International Award; Helen   Vol. 1: 11664
Keller Prize; Gottfried   Vol. 2: 11670
Keller Trophy   Vol. 1: 10388
Kellett Island Trophy   Vol. 2: 2898
Kelley Memorial Award; Frank   Vol. 1: 1116
Kellgrenpriset   Vol. 2: 11596
Kelliher Student of Honour; Sir Henry   Vol. 2: 9765
Kellogg Award   Vol. 1: 1590
Kellogg Award; Charles Flint   Vol. 1: 5784
Kellogg National Fellowship Program   Vol. 1: 11666
Kelly Award   Vol. 1: 5836
Kelly Award; Jack   Vol. 1: 19518
Kelly Award; Joe W.   Vol. 1: 1783
Kelly Award of Excellence; Billy   Vol. 2: 7798
Kelly Award; Stephen E.   Vol. 1: 12000
Kelly Fair Play Award; Jack   Vol. 1: 19490
Kelly - Founder's Award; John Snooks   Vol. 1: 2309
Kelly Memorial Award; John B.   Vol. 1: 19624
Kelly Memorial Prize in Women's History; Joan   Vol. 1: 2294
Kelly Trophy; C. Markland   Vol. 1: 19411
Kelpie for the Nineties; A   Vol. 2: 10518
Kelsey Award; Guy   Vol. 1: 3969
Keltic Society Awards   Vol. 2: 10584
Kelvin Medal   Vol. 2: 3248
Kelvin Premium   Vol. 2: 3273
Kemal Award; Orhan   Vol. 2: 12072
Kemp Award; James Furman   Vol. 1: 7984
Kemper Award; Edward C.   Vol. 1: 2539
Kempf Fund Award for Research Development in Psychobiological Psychiatry   Vol. 1: 3640
Ken-L Ration Dog Hero of the Year   Vol. 1: 11668
Kendall and Florence P. Kendall Award for Outstanding Achievement in Clinical Practice; Henry O.   Vol. 1: 3484
Kendall Oration and Medal   Vol. 2: 277
Kendrick Prize; John W.   Vol. 2: 3853
Kenko Yuryo Gakko Hyosho   Vol. 2: 8495
Kennan Award; George F.   Vol. 1: 7710
Kennedy Astronautics Award; John F.   Vol. 1: 1259
Kennedy Award for Humanitarianism and Excellence; John Fitzgerald   Vol. 1: 7848
Kennedy Award; Frank L.   Vol. 1: 1823
Kennedy Award; Henry L.   Vol. 1: 1784
Kennedy Award of the Massachusetts Historical Society; John F.   Vol. 1: 12112
Kennedy Award; William M.   Vol. 1: 17925
Kennedy Book Awards; Robert F.   Vol. 1: 11682
Kennedy Center Friedheim Awards for New Music   Vol. 1: 11671
Kennedy Center Honors   Vol. 1: 11672
Kennedy Center/National School Boards Association Award   Vol. 1: 11675
Kennedy Center Teacher Fellows   Vol. 1: 11676
Kennedy Citizenship Award; J. Walter
 National Basketball Association   Vol. 1: 13446
 Professional Basketball Writers Association of America   Vol 1: 16443

Kennedy-Clerk Maxwell Award; Joe   Vol. 1: 16166
Kennedy Foundation International Awards in Mental Retardation   Vol. 1: 11678
Kennedy Human Rights Award; Robert F.   Vol. 1: 11683
Kennedy Journalism Awards; Robert F.   Vol. 1: 11684
Kennedy Medal; Sir John   Vol. 1: 8935
Kennedy Memorial Prize; Byron   Vol. 2: 222
Kennedy Prize; Dr. M.   Vol. 2: 326
Kennedy Profile in Courage Award; John F.   Vol. 1: 11680
Kennedy Student Paper Competition; John F.   Vol. 2: 9462
Kennedy Trophy; John F.   Vol. 1: 13992
Kenneth D. Naden Award   Vol. 1: 13736
Kent Award; Donald P.   Vol. 1: 9591
Kent Conservation Book Prize; Sir Peter   Vol. 2: 2200
Kent Prize; George   Vol. 1: 16266
Kentucky Artists Fellowships   Vol. 1: 11686
Kentucky Bluegrass Award   Vol. 1: 15512
Kentucky Derby
 Churchill Downs   Vol. 1: 7680
 Triple Crown Productions, Inc.   Vol 1: 18815
Kenyatta Prize for Literature; Jomo   Vol. 2: 8810
Kenyon Medal for Classical Studies   Vol. 2: 2229
Keogh Award for Distinguished Public Service; Eugene J.   Vol. 1: 392
Kerala Sahitya Akademi Awards   Vol. 2: 7703
Kerkrade World Music Contest   Vol. 2: 9695
Kerlan Award   Vol. 1: 19837
Kerlan Award of the University of Minnesota   Vol. 1: 7629
Kern Award; Donald Q.   Vol. 1: 2590
Kern Award; Jim   Vol. 1: 2274
Kern Lecture Award; Richard A.   Vol. 1: 5885
Kernow Goth Trophy   Vol. 2: 2876
Kerpely Medal; Antal   Vol. 2: 7356
Kerr High School Scholars Program in Arab and Islamic Studies; Malcolm H.   Vol. 1: 13824
Kerr History Prize   Vol. 1: 15287
Kerr Prize; Sophie   Vol. 1: 20108
Kerr Scholars Program; Malcolm H.   Vol. 1: 13824
Kershaw Award; John   Vol. 2: 4460
Kerwin, Jr. Readiness Award; Walter T.   Vol. 1: 14096
Kesselring Fund Award; Joseph   Vol. 1: 12829
Kesselring Prize   Vol. 1: 12829
Kessler Awards; Henry H.   Vol. 1: 16756
Kessler Awards in International Rehabilitation; Henry and Estelle   Vol. 1: 16756
Kestenberg Medal; Leo   Vol. 2: 6870
Kesteven Medal   Vol. 2: 278
Kesteven Poetry Prize; Harold   Vol. 2: 351
Kestler Humanitarian Award; Doctor Otto   Vol. 1: 607
Ketcham Memorial Award; Albert H.   Vol. 1: 1353
Ketterer Picture; Yves   Vol. 2: 3533
Kettering Award; Charles F.
 American Society of Plant Physiologists   Vol. 1: 4750
 Cooperative Education Association   Vol 1: 8269
 PTC Research Foundation   Vol 1: 16560
Kettering Medal; Charles F.   Vol. 1: 9530
Keuffel and Esser Awards   Vol. 2: 2306

Kevock Choir and Bank of Scotland Scottish Folk Song Arrangement Competition   Vol. 2: 10586
Key Award   Vol. 1: 4409
Key Employee Award   Vol. 1: 14889
Keyes Award; Marjorie Hiscott   Vol. 1: 7031
Keyes Medal   Vol. 1: 1004
Keyhoe UFO Journalism Award; Donald E.   Vol. 1: 9451
Keystone Award   Vol. 1: 17179
Keystone Press Awards Contest   Vol. 1: 16050
The Kharazmi Prize   Vol. 2: 7737
Kheel Award of the Institute for Mediation and Conflict Resolution; Theodore W.   Vol. 1: 10223
Kho Liang Ie-prijs   Vol. 2: 9641
Kibbee Award for Public Service and Achievement; Robert J.   Vol. 1: 7769
Kibler Memorial Award; Robert J.   Vol. 1: 18309
Kidd Award; J. Roby   Vol. 1: 10873
Kidd Subdivision Award; John W.   Vol. 1: 8322
Kidder Award; Alfred Vincent   Vol. 1: 796
KidFilm Festival   Vol. 1: 19919
Kiene Fellowship; Julia   Vol. 1: 8878
Kievman Leadership Award; NNWS Beverly   Vol. 1: 14391
Kihara Award   Vol. 2: 8529
Kihara Sho   Vol. 2: 8529
Kikuchi Prize   Vol. 2: 8752
Kikundo Tanaka Memorial Award   Vol. 2: 8647
Kilby Awards   Vol. 1: 11690
Kilby Awards of Excellence; Jack St. Clair   Vol. 1: 11690
Kilgore Freedom of Information Internship; Barney   Vol. 1: 17998
Killam Fellowships; Izaak Walton   Vol. 1: 12429
Killam Memorial Prize; Izaak Walton   Vol. 1: 6740
Killam Research Fellowships; Izaak Walton   Vol. 1: 6740
Killam Scholarship; Elson T.   Vol. 1: 15155
Kilmer Award; Joyce   Vol. 1: 12788
Kilmer Prize   Vol. 1: 3384
Kilpatrick Award; James   Vol. 1: 11155
Kilrea Trophy; Wally   Vol. 1: 2334
Kimball Award; Justin Ford   Vol. 1: 2374
Kimball Medal; George E.   Vol. 1: 15733
Kimball Medallion; Miles   Vol. 1: 12009
Kimberly-Clark Special Award   Vol. 2: 4170
Kimberly Cup   Vol. 1: 18396
Kimble Methodology Award   Vol. 1: 8127
Kimbrough Fund Award; Anne Giles   Vol. 1: 8510
Kimbrough Fund Award; Arch and Anne Giles   Vol. 1: 8510
Kimbrough Medal Award   Vol. 1: 2680
Kincheloe Award; Iven C.   Vol. 1: 17838
Kind-Preis der ETG; Herbert-   Vol. 2: 6696
Kinder- und Jugendbuchpreis der Stadt Wien   Vol. 2: 790
King Abdul Aziz Prize   Vol. 2: 10494
King Award   Vol. 1: 19054
King Award; Dr. Lyndon   Vol. 1: 8019
King Award; Martin Luther   Vol. 1: 11933
King Baudouin International Development Prize   Vol. 1: 1217
King Book Award; Coretta Scott   Vol. 1: 2954
King Contest   Vol. 1: 14143
King Contribution Award; Billie Jean   Vol. 1: 20427
King Excalibur Award; Ruth Allen   Vol. 1: 8829

King Fahd Awards for Design and Research in Islamic Architecture   Vol. 2: 12058
King Faisal International Prize for Arabic Literature   Vol. 2: 10496
King Faisal International Prize for Islamic Studies   Vol. 2: 10497
King Faisal International Prize for the Service of Islam   Vol. 2: 10498
King Faisal International Prize in Medicine   Vol. 2: 10499
King Faisal International Prize in Science   Vol. 2: 10500
King Faisal Prize   Vol. 2: 10494
King, Jr. - Abraham Joshua Heschel Award; Martin Luther   Vol. 1: 6434
King, Jr. Achievement Award; Martin Luther   Vol. 1: 8154
King, Jr. Award; Martin Luther   Vol. 1: 9166
King, Jr. Humanitarian Award; Martin Luther   Vol. 1: 11698
King, Jr. Leadership Awards; Martin Luther   Vol. 1: 8684
King, Jr. Medal; Martin Luther   Vol. 1: 7770
King, Jr. Nonviolent Peace Prize; Martin Luther   Vol. 1: 11699
King, Jr., Prize for Research in African American History; Martin Luther   Vol. 1: 19808
King, Jr. Scholarship Award; Martin Luther   Vol. 1: 1834
King Leadership Award; Helen   Vol. 1: 12703
King Lucille Award; B. B.   Vol. 1: 6415
King Memorial Award; Donald   Vol. 1: 7241
King Memorial Award.; Donald   Vol. 1: 7241
King Memorial Award; Robert W.   Vol. 1: 5819
King Memorial Certificate; Milton W.   Vol. 1: 14878
King Memorial Prize; Martin Luther   Vol. 2: 3523
King of Prussia's Gold Medal   Vol. 2: 3015
King of Spain Journalism Prizes   Vol. 2: 11361
King Outstanding Management Award; Kenneth K.   Vol. 1: 9665
King Prize; Earl   Vol. 2: 3170
King Sejong Literacy Prize   Vol. 2: 6422
King's Cross for Distinguished Service   Vol. 2: 9918
King's Medal for Distinguished Service   Vol. 2: 9918
King's Prize   Vol. 2: 3706
Kingslake Medal and Prize; Rudolf   Vol. 1: 18324
Kingsley Medal; Mary   Vol. 2: 3594
Kini Family Award   Vol. 2: 7472
Kinias Service Award; George A.   Vol. 1: 13917
Kinkeldey Award; Otto   Vol. 1: 3175
Kinley Memorial Fellowship; Kate Neal   Vol. 1: 19800
Kinnard, Jr. Academic Award; Dr. William   Vol. 1: 5193
Kinokuniya Theatre Awards   Vol. 2: 8681
Kinor David   Vol. 2: 7997
Kinsale Yacht Club Trophy   Vol. 2: 2898
Kinsey Institute Dissertation Award   Vol. 1: 11704
Kinsley Memorial Trophy; Charles A.
  Photographic Society of America   Vol. 1: 16159
  Photographic Society of America   Vol. 1: 16160
  Photographic Society of America   Vol. 1: 16163
  Photographic Society of America   Vol. 1: 16164

  Photographic Society of America   Vol 1: 16165
  Photographic Society of America   Vol 1: 16166
  Photographic Society of America   Vol 1: 16167
  Photographic Society of America   Vol 1: 16170
Kintner Award for Distinguished Service; Earl   Vol. 1: 9069
Kintzele Distinguished Service Award; Leland T.   Vol. 1: 20274
Kipping Award in Organosilicon Chemistry; Frederic Stanley   Vol. 1: 1565
Kiputh Award   Vol. 1: 19625
Kirjeenvaihtajajasenyys   Vol. 2: 4698
Kirk Award for Outstanding Graduate Student Research; Barbara A.   Vol. 1: 3707
Kirklees Young Musician of the Year   Vol. 2: 3766
Kirklin M.D. Award for Professional Excellence; John W.   Vol. 1: 1210
Kirkpatrick Chemical Engineering Achievement Award   Vol. 1: 7535
Kirkpatrick Memorial Award; James R.   Vol. 1: 1180
Kirkus Literacy Award   Vol. 1: 11706
Kirkwood Award; Robert C.   Vol. 1: 17032
Kirsch Award; Robert   Vol. 1: 11949
Kirsner Award in Gastroenterology; J. B.   Vol. 1: 2133
Kirti Chakra   Vol. 2: 7552
Kishida International Award   Vol. 1: 4367
Kiskadden Lecturer   Vol. 1: 1138
Kisz KB Aranykoszorus Kisz Jelveny   Vol. 2: 7333
Kivalo Egyesuleti Munkaert Erem   Vol. 2: 7385
Kivalo Nevelo   Vol. 2: 7460
Kiwanis International Award   Vol. 2: 1106
Kjeld Abell Pris   Vol. 2: 1909
Klaesi Awards; Jakob   Vol. 2: 11918
Klausmeyer Service Award; Otto   Vol. 1: 16208
Kleemeier Award; Robert W.   Vol. 1: 9592
Klein Award; Abraham   Vol. 2: 7918
Klein Award for Children's Fiction; PEN/Norma   Vol. 1: 16027
Klein Award for Editing; PEN/Roger   Vol. 1: 16589
Klein Award; Lawrence R.   Vol. 1: 19263
Klein Award; PW/Roger   Vol. 1: 16589
Klein Playwriting Award; Marc A.   Vol. 1: 7332
Klein Research Award; Eugene   Vol. 1: 3406
Kleiner Memorial Awards; Joseph J.   Vol. 1: 4192
Kleitman Distinguished Service Award; Nathaniel   Vol. 1: 4028
Klemin Award; Dr. Alexander   Vol. 1: 2255
Klemm-Preis; Wilhelm-   Vol. 2: 6784
Klerner Lecture Series; Gerald   Vol. 1: 1691
Kliass Fifth Prize; Joseph and Lydia   Vol. 1: 6217
Klieneberger Nobel Award; Emmy   Vol. 1: 11132
Klinefelter Award; H. E.   Vol. 1: 8267
Klinger Preis; Internationaler Wettbewerb fur Streichquartett Karl   Vol. 2: 7009
Klinker Award; Mary T.   Vol. 1: 167
Klopsteg Memorial Lecture   Vol. 1: 1128
Klose Prize; Hans   Vol. 2: 7116
Klumpke - Isaac Roberts; Prix Dorothea   Vol. 2: 6221
Klumpke-Roberts Award   Vol. 1: 6096
KNCV Gold Medal   Vol. 2: 9609
Knight-Bagehot Fellowships   Vol. 1: 7996

Knight Fellowship; John S.   Vol. 1: 11710
Knight Medal; Allen   Vol. 2: 464
Knight NACTA Journal Award; E. B.   Vol. 1: 13007
Knight of African Agriculture   Vol. 2: 2019
Knighton Service Award; Harry and Elsie   Vol. 1: 15436
Knights of Justice Award   Vol. 1: 3558
Knouff Line Officer of the Year Award; Scotia   Vol. 1: 3617
Knowledge Industry Publications, Inc. Award for Library Literature   Vol. 1: 2818
Knowlton Medal   Vol. 1: 12160
Knox Memorial Fellowship - Harvard University; Frank   Vol. 1: 5995
Knox Reticulata Award; Charlotte C.   Vol. 1: 1397
Knudsen Award   Vol. 1: 1700
Knuth Award; Karl F.   Vol. 1: 6439
Kobayashi Computers and Communications Award; Koji   Vol. 1: 10278
Kobe International Flute Competition   Vol. 2: 8683
Kober Medal; George M.   Vol. 1: 5691
Kobs; Prix Jean   Vol. 2: 1302
Koch Award; Erwin T.   Vol. 1: 12365
Koch Award; Fred Conrad   Vol. 1: 8922
Koch Memorial Medal Award; Carel C.   Vol. 1: 641
Kocian Violin Competition   Vol. 2: 1836
Kodak All-American Team   Vol. 1: 14266
Kodak Award for Photographic Excellence   Vol. 1: 17610
Kodak Award; International FIAP   Vol. 2: 1189
Kodak Coach of the Year   Vol. 1: 12947
Kodak Community Award   Vol. 2: 2341
Kodak Excellence in Colour Reproduction Award   Vol. 2: 2483
Kodak Gold Star Quality Award   Vol. 1: 8802
Kodak International Newspaper Snapshot Awards   Vol. 1: 8804
Kodak Student Competition; Association of Photographers/   Vol. 2: 2132
Kodak/WHNPA Achievement Award   Vol. 1: 20263
Kodaly Singing Competition - Erkel   Vol. 2: 7414
Kodansha Prize   Vol. 2: 8687
Kodansha Prize for Cartoon Book   Vol. 2: 8688
Kodiat Award; M.   Vol. 2: 7728
Koehl Award; Albert E.   Vol. 1: 10004
Koffler Prize; Sam and Blanche   Vol. 1: 5297
Koga Gold Medal; Issac   Vol. 2: 1212
Kogalniceau Prize; Mihail   Vol. 2: 10361
Kohl Memorial Exhibit Award; Melvin and Leona   Vol. 1: 3231
Kohler Challenge Trophy; Charlotte M.   Vol. 1: 20592
Kohler Prijs; Charlotte   Vol. 2: 9571
Kohlerprijs; Charlotte   Vol. 2: 9687
Kohlstedt Exhibit Award   Vol. 1: 2889
Kohn Memorial Trophy; David   Vol. 1: 8109
Kohnstamm Prize; M. V.   Vol. 1: 5297
Kohrtz' stipendium; Ilona   Vol. 2: 11597
Koivu - palkinto; Rudolf   Vol. 2: 4687
Koivu Prize; Rudolf   Vol. 2: 4687
Kokoku Dentus Sho   Vol. 2: 8524
Kokusai Koryu Kikin Sho   Vol. 2: 8612
Kokusai Koryu Shorei Sho   Vol. 2: 8615
Kokusai Seibutsugaku-sho   Vol. 2: 8636
Kolb Prize; Eugene   Vol. 2: 7967
Kolk Air Transportation Progress Award; Franklin W.   Vol. 1: 17765
Koller Gold Medal; Karl   Vol. 2: 1142
Kolliner Award for a Young Israeli Artist; Beatrice S.   Vol. 2: 7927

Kolovakos Award; Gregory   Vol. 1: 16018
Kolping Award   Vol. 1: 7369
Kolstad Junior Soaring Awards   Vol. 1: 17362
Kolthoff Gold Medal Award in Analytical Chemistry   Vol. 1: 3385
Komarov Diploma; V. M.   Vol. 2: 5154
Komen Award of Scientific Distinction   Vol. 1: 11720
Komponistenpreis des STV   Vol. 2: 11658
Kompositionspreis der Landeshauptstadt Stuttgart   Vol. 2: 7138
Kompositionswettbewerb   Vol. 2: 7015
Komsomol Medal   Vol. 2: 10433
Komsomol Propagandist Award   Vol. 2: 10434
Komsomol Special Award for Science and Technology   Vol. 2: 10435
Komsomol Work Award   Vol. 2: 10436
Komura Prize   Vol. 2: 8564
Kondic Medal; Voya   Vol. 2: 3073
Kondracki Award; Alojzy and Elizabeth   Vol. 1: 16223
Kone Award   Vol. 2: 2118
Konheim Award; Beatrice G.   Vol. 1: 1230
Konig-Gedenkmunze; Joseph-   Vol. 2: 6785
Koninklijke/Shell prijs   Vol. 2: 9392
Koninklijke Subsidie voor de Vrije Schilderkunst   Vol. 2: 9612
Konkurs Mlodych Kompozytorow im. Tadeusza Bairda   Vol. 2: 10141
Konnik Order; Madarski   Vol. 2: 1506
Koob Award; C. Albert   Vol. 1: 13544
Kook Prize; Literary Prize - Rav   Vol. 2: 7957
KOOL Achiever Awards   Vol. 1: 6592
Koontz Memorial Award; Louis Knott   Vol. 1: 2301
Koopal Bursary for Literature   Vol. 2: 1078
Koopmans Econometric Theory Prize; Tjalling C.   Vol. 1: 20572
Kopf Humanitarian Award; Edward H.   Vol. 1: 608
Korczak Humanitarian Award; Janusz   Vol. 1: 12871
Korczak Literary Award; Janusz   Vol. 2: 10179
Korczak Literary Competition; Janusz   Vol. 1: 5180
Kordelin Prize   Vol. 2: 4744
Korea Good-Packaging Exhibition   Vol. 2: 8818
Korea Polio Association Awards   Vol. 2: 8820
Korea Translation Award   Vol. 2: 8826
Korean Composition Award   Vol. 2: 8822
Korean National Literary Award   Vol. 2: 8823
Korean Service Medal   Vol. 1: 19166
Korey Award; Saul R.   Vol. 1: 618
Korf Playwriting Award; Lee   Vol. 1: 15839
Korn Award; Martin P.   Vol. 1: 16372
Korn Corporate Recognition Award; The Michael   Vol. 1: 7656
Korn Honorary Citation; The Micheal   Vol. 1: 7657
Korolev Diploma   Vol. 2: 5155
Korrespondierendes Mitglied   Vol. 2: 6534
Korsts Memorial Award; Voldemars   Vol. 1: 14618
Korte Medaille; Werner   Vol. 2: 6878
Kortweg Pall Mallprijs   Vol. 2: 9566
Koryagin Award; Anatoly   Vol. 2: 9472
Kosar Award; William F.   Vol. 1: 9969
Kosar Memorial Award   Vol. 1: 17505
Kosciuszko Foundation Doctoral Dissertation Award   Vol. 1: 11723
Kosciuszko Foundation Exchange Program with Poland   Vol. 1: 11724
Koseki-sho   Vol. 2: 8664
Kosoff Memorial Literary Award; Abe   Vol. 1: 3232

Kossler Award; Captain William J.   Vol. 1: 2256
Kossuth Prize   Vol. 2: 7410
Kostanecki Medal; Stanislaw   Vol. 2: 10136
Kostov Prize; Academician Doncho   Vol. 2: 1513
Kostrzewski Award; Professor Jozef   Vol. 2: 10187
Kosutany Memorial Medal; Tamas   Vol. 2: 7374
Kotler Award; Philip   Vol. 1: 2996
Kotyk Award; Eugene   Vol. 1: 18855
Koussevitzky Commissions   Vol. 1: 11858
Koussevitzky International Recording Award   Vol. 1: 12534
Koussevitzky; Prix International du Disque Serge et Olga   Vol. 2: 11663
Koussevitzky Young Artists Awards; Olga   Vol. 1: 12535
Kovacs Prize; Katherine Singer   Vol. 1: 12394
Kovacs Prize; Richard   Vol. 2: 4258
Kovalenko Medal; Jessie Stevenson   Vol. 1: 12671
Kowalski; Prix de Poesie Roger   Vol. 2: 6475
Koyre Medal; Alexander   Vol. 2: 5949
Kozik Award for Environmental Reporting; Robert L.   Vol. 1: 14501
KPMG Peat Marwick Award   Vol. 1: 20133
Kraft Award; Jack A.   Vol. 1: 10041
Krains; Prix Hubert   Vol. 2: 1043
Kral Prize; Frano   Vol. 2: 10786
Kramer Award of Excellence; William S.   Vol. 1: 15635
Kramer - John Preston Personal Service Award; Harold   Vol. 1: 3859
Kramer Scarlet Quill Award; Murray   Vol. 1: 6467
Kranichsteiner Musikpreis   Vol. 2: 6976
Krasner Award; Jack D.   Vol. 1: 3778
Kraszna-Krausz Award   Vol. 2: 3527
Kraus Award; Francis L. (Babe)   Vol. 1: 19412
Krayer Award in Pharmacology; Otto   Vol. 1: 4237
Krebs Memorial Scholarship   Vol. 2: 2176
Krebs-Preis; Hans Adolf   Vol. 2: 6858
Kreisher Award; Peter   Vol. 1: 17748
Kreisler International Competition Prizes; Fritz   Vol. 2: 855
Kremers Award; Edward   Vol. 1: 2687
Krenek-Preis der Stadt Wien; Ernst   Vol. 2: 793
Kresanek Prize; Jozef   Vol. 2: 10773
Kress Foundation Fellowship; Samuel H.   Vol. 1: 4014
Kriegel Prize; Dr. Frantisek   Vol. 2: 11449
Krieger Award; Richard   Vol. 1: 8109
Krieghbaum Under-40 Award   Vol. 1: 5498
Kris Prize; Ernst   Vol. 1: 4778
Krishnan Memorial Lecture; K. S.   Vol. 2: 7654
Kriskie Memorial Award; George W.   Vol. 1: 275
Krisna Cup   Vol. 1: 3984
Kritiikin kannukset   Vol. 2: 4760
Krogh Lecture and Award; August   Vol. 2: 1986
Kroll Medal and Prize   Vol. 2: 3140
Krommert Award   Vol. 2: 9690
Kroonorde   Vol. 2: 1074
Krooss Prize   Vol. 1: 6659
Krout Ohioana Poetry Award; Helen and Laura   Vol. 1: 15600
Krueger Paper Money - YN Exhibit Award; Kurt   Vol. 1: 3233
Krumbein Medal; William Christian   Vol. 1: 10649

Kruszynski Achievement Award; Edward A.   Vol. 1: 15417
Krutch Medal; Joseph Wood   Vol. 1: 10053
Kruyskamp-prijs   Vol. 2: 9629
Kryger Prize   Vol. 2: 1992
Krygerprisen   Vol. 2: 1992
Kryski Canadian Heritage Award; Antoinette (Nettie)   Vol. 1: 20597
Krzyz Armii Krajowej   Vol. 2: 10107
Krzyz Batalonow Chlopskich   Vol. 2: 10121
Krzyz Bitwy pod Lenino   Vol. 2: 10104
Krzyz Czynu Bojowego Polskich Sil Zbrojnych na Zachodzie   Vol. 2: 10098
Krzyz Narodowego Czynu Zbrojnego   Vol. 2: 10116
Krzyz Oswiecimski   Vol. 2: 10100
Krzyz Partyzancki   Vol. 2: 10120
Krzyz Walecznych   Vol. 2: 10106
Krzyz Za Udzial w Wojnie 1918-1921   Vol. 2: 10099
Krzyz Zaslugi   Vol. 2: 10101
Krzyz Zaslugi z Mieczami   Vol. 2: 10103
Krzyz Zaslugi za Dzielnosc   Vol. 2: 10102
Kshanika Oration Award to a Woman Scientist for Research in the Field of Biomedical Sciences   Vol. 2: 7593
KSO Young People's Concerto Competition Award   Vol. 1: 11702
Ku Meritorious Award; P.M.   Vol. 1: 18083
Kubsch Award for Achievement in International Education; Dr. Werner   Vol. 1: 8072
Kucera Memorial Award; L. A.   Vol. 1: 9964
Kucharski Young Investigator Award for Research in Developmental Psychobiology; David   Vol. 1: 11246
Kuchler-Killian Memorial Scholarship   Vol. 1: 13965
Kucyna International Composition Prize   Vol. 1: 6471
Kuczynski Diploma; G. C.   Vol. 2: 10714
Kuebler Award; John R.   Vol. 1: 341
Kuehl Prize; Warren F.   Vol. 1: 17468
Kuhn Award; Dr. L. Michael   Vol. 1: 14130
Kuhn-Medaille; Richard-   Vol. 2: 6786
Kuhn-Preis; Julius-   Vol. 2: 6669
Kuiper Prize; Gerard P.   Vol. 1: 1270
Kukuljevic Charter   Vol. 2: 1799
Kukuljeviceva povelja   Vol. 2: 1799
Kulenkampff; Cologne International Violin Competition/Foundation/Shiflung Georg   Vol. 2: 6609
Kulp Memorial Award; Clarence Arthur   Vol. 1: 3963
Kultainen Fennia-mitali   Vol. 2: 4712
Kultureller Ehrenpreis   Vol. 2: 7020
Kulturministeriets Bornebogspris   Vol. 2: 1936
Kulturpreis   Vol. 2: 862
Kulturpreis der Stadt Dortmund - Nelly-Sachs-Preis   Vol. 2: 7096
Kulturpreis der Stadt Villach   Vol. 2: 887
Kulturprisen   Vol. 2: 9882
Kumar Award; C. B.   Vol. 2: 7704
Kumar Memorial Award; Prof. L. S. S.   Vol. 2: 7655
Kungliga priset   Vol. 2: 11598
Kunitz Poetry Award; Stanley   Vol. 1: 7959
Kunst Prize; Jaap   Vol. 1: 17457
Kunst-und Kulturpreis des Groupement   Vol. 2: 6724
Kunstpreis der Stadt Darmstadt   Vol. 2: 6600
Kunstpreis der Stadt Zurich   Vol. 2: 11894
Kunstpreis des Landes Bremen   Vol. 2: 6581
Kuntz '07 Award; Frank A.   Vol. 1: 7395
Kupferman Award   Vol. 1: 11796
Kupfmuller-Preis der ITG; Karl-   Vol. 2: 6531
Kupfmuller Prize; Karl   Vol. 2: 6531

Kurien Award; Dr.   Vol. 2: 7617
Kushner Award for Writing Achievement in the Field of Breast Cancer; Rose   Vol. 1: 3059
Kusnetz Award   Vol. 1: 2434
Kusworm Award; Sidney G.   Vol. 1: 6420
Kutambula   Vol. 2: 12086
Kutschenreuter Scholarship; Paul H.   Vol. 1: 3088
Kutter-Preis; Fritz   Vol. 2: 11933
Kuttippuzha Award   Vol. 2: 7705
Kuttna Award; Mari   Vol. 2: 2348
Kuwait Prize   Vol. 2: 8844
Kvassay Jeno dij   Vol. 2: 7349
Kwapil Memorial Award; Joseph F.   Vol. 1: 18282
Kyle Prize; Bruce   Vol. 2: 4494
KYLIX Awards   Vol. 1: 15349
Kyoto Prizes   Vol. 2: 8539
L/M Award   Vol. 1: 1590
"L. PeRCy" Awards   Vol. 1: 11861
La Caze; Fondation L.   Vol. 2: 5607
La Gorce Medal; John Oliver   Vol. 1: 14074
La Guardia Award; Fiorello H.   Vol. 1: 15208
La Raza Award   Vol. 1: 13743
La Salle Collegian Award   Vol. 1: 11744
Labatt Classic Film Award; John   Vol. 1: 18744
Labatt's Award for the Most Popular Film   Vol. 1: 18744
Labbe; Fondation du Docteur et de Madame Henri   Vol. 2: 5543
Labbe; Fondation Joseph   Vol. 2: 5603
Labbe-Vauquelin; Prix Paul   Vol. 2: 5906
LABBS Trophy   Vol. 1: 9786
Label of the Year Competition   Vol. 2: 3529
Labor Affairs Award   Vol. 1: 14972
Labor Courage Award   Vol. 2: 10437
Labor Human Rights Award   Vol. 1: 11551
Labor, Management, Government Social Responsibility Awards   Vol. 1: 11700
Labor Participation Citation for Services   Vol. 1: 3920
Labor Press Journalistic Awards Contest   Vol. 1: 11065
Labor Social Responsibility Award   Vol. 1: 11700
Laboratory Analyst Excellence Award   Vol. 1: 20154
Laboratory of the Year Award   Vol. 1: 16796
Labrow Grant   Vol. 2: 3333
Lack Studentship; David   Vol. 2: 2465
LaCorbeau Grand Prix   Vol. 2: 1241
Lacquet; Fund Professor Doctor A.   Vol. 2: 1314
Lacrosse Hall of Fame   Vol. 1: 11751
Lacroze de Fortabat Annual Music Fellowship; Amalia   Vol. 1: 15833
Ladd Award; William E.   Vol. 1: 674
Ladies' British Open Amateur Championship   Vol. 1: 10588
Ladougne; Prix Bernard   Vol. 2: 4812
LaDue Safety Awards; Wendall R.   Vol. 1: 5018
Lady and Gentleman of the Year Award   Vol. 1: 12020
Lady Canoeist of the Year   Vol. 2: 10666
Lady Flavelle Award   Vol. 1: 15714
Lady Members Group   Vol. 2: 10560
Lady of the Year Award   Vol. 1: 11309
Lady Riders Challenge Trophy   Vol. 1: 14866
Laerdal Award for Excellence (EMT-Paramedic of the Year); Asmund S.   Vol. 1: 13094
Laetare Medal   Vol. 1: 19861
LAF Alfred B. LaGasse Medal   Vol. 1: 4643
LaFarge Memorial Award for Interracial Justice; John   Vol. 1: 7366

Lafenestre Foundation Prize; Georges   Vol. 2: 6317
Lafferty Memorial Trophy; Terry   Vol. 1: 7251
Lafitte; Fondation Pierre   Vol. 2: 5653
LaGasse Medal   Vol. 1: 11779
LaGrange National   Vol. 1: 7526
Lagrange; Prix Charles   Vol. 2: 1011
Lahden Kansainvalinen Urkukilpailu   Vol. 2: 4746
Lahm Memorial Award for Flight Safety; Brig. Gen. Frank P.   Vol. 1: 15783
Lahti International Organ Competition   Vol. 2: 4746
Laidlaw Award; Ron
  Radio and Television News Directors Association   Vol. 1: 16635
  Radio and Television News Directors Association   Vol 1: 16637
Laine Memorial Scholarship Program; David   Vol. 1: 15418
Laing Collection Art Competition   Vol. 2: 3531
Laing Prize; Gordon J.   Vol. 1: 19779
Lake Constance Literary Prize   Vol. 2: 7146
Lake Memorial Award; Ruth   Vol. 1: 16288
Lallemand; Fondation Andre   Vol. 2: 5489
Lallemand; Fondation Claude   Vol. 2: 5521
Lamare; Prix Lise   Vol. 2: 6287
Lamb Memorial Trophy; Charles   Vol. 1: 14866
Lamb Outstanding Educator Award; Helen   Vol. 1: 1058
Lambacher Trophy   Vol. 1: 11873
Lambda Literary Awards   Vol. 1: 11771
Lambert; Prix Charles   Vol. 2: 5723
Lamberton Award for Teaching High School Science; Bernice G.   Vol. 1: 20104
Lambort Award   Vol. 1: 3499
Lameere; Prix Eugene   Vol. 2: 987
LaMer Award; Victor K.   Vol. 1: 1501
Lamke Award; Orah Ashley   Vol. 1: 12481
Lamme Award; Benjamin Garver   Vol. 1: 4096
Lamme Medal   Vol. 1: 10279
Lamont Poetry Selection   Vol. 1: 20
Lampert Memorial Award; Gerald   Vol. 1: 11812
Lampitt Medal   Vol. 2: 4412
Lampl Hugo Dij   Vol. 2: 7350
Lampl; Hugo   Vol. 2: 7350
Lancaster Award   Vol. 1: 954
Lancaster Award; E. Jack   Vol. 1: 4286
Lanchester Prize; Frederick W.   Vol. 1: 15734
Lancia Motor Club Trophies   Vol. 2: 3534
Land Medal; Edwin H.   Vol. 1: 15751
"Land of Freedom" Essay Contest and "I Speak for Freedom" Speech Contest   Vol. 1: 9417
Land-Rover Register Shield   Vol. 2: 3536
Landa Music Scholarship for Pianists; David Paul   Vol. 2: 146
Landberg Award for Excellence in Applied Climatology; Helmut   Vol. 1: 1195
Landen ARTBA Annual Highway Safety Award; John C. "Jake"   Vol. 1: 3970
Landesgirokasse Stuttgart Award   Vol. 2: 7142
Landeshaupstadt Munchen Preise   Vol. 2: 7019
Landeskreditbank Baden-Wurttemberg (L-Bank) Award   Vol. 2: 7142
Landeskulturpreis fur Architektur   Vol. 2: 906
Landeskulturpreis fur Bildende Kunst   Vol. 2: 902
Landeskulturpreis fur Film und Video   Vol. 2: 901
Landeskulturpreis fur Literatur   Vol. 2: 903
Landeskulturpreis fur Musik   Vol. 2: 904

Landeskulturpreis fur Wissenschaft   Vol. 2: 905
Landi; Fondazione Valeria Vincenzo   Vol. 2: 8065
Landis Award (Most Valuable Player); Kenesaw M.   Vol. 1: 6280
Landis Medal; James N.   Vol. 1: 4684
Landon Translation Award; Harold Morton   Vol. 1: 21
Landry Award; Jules F.
   Louisiana State University Press   Vol. 1: 11959
   Louisiana State University Press   Vol 1: 11959
Landscape Architecture Award of Excellence   Vol. 1: 4644
Landscape Design Award   Vol. 1: 2358
Landscape Manager of the Year   Vol. 1: 16486
Landsteiner Memorial Award; Karl   Vol. 1: 930
Lane Award; Ben B.   Vol. 1: 19990
Lane Award; Bishop Loris   Vol. 1: 13545
Lane Award; Kenneth S.   Vol. 1: 4943
Lane Award; Richard   Vol. 2: 283
Lane Award; Sister M. Claude   Vol. 1: 17674
Lane Industrial Award; Frank E.   Vol. 1: 1985
Lane Memorial Award; Diane   Vol. 1: 12784
Lang Medal   Vol. 2: 4263
Lang Memorial Award for Health Care Administration; John C.   Vol. 1: 4193
Lang Memorial Trustee Award for Administration and Management; John C.   Vol. 1: 4193
Lang Prize Paper Award; Warren R.   Vol. 1: 4549
Lang Resident Physician Award; Warren R.   Vol. 1: 4549
Lange International Award; John D.   Vol. 1: 13144
Lange - Paul Taylor Prize; Dorotea   Vol. 1: 8762
Langenhoven Prize; C. J.   Vol. 2: 10994
Langer Award; Esther   Vol. 1: 19754
Langer Award; William L.   Vol. 1: 9732
Langer Nuclear Codes and Standards Award; Bernard F.   Vol. 1: 4685
Langerhuizen Bate; Pieter   Vol. 2: 9391
Langerhuizen Prijs; Pieter   Vol. 2: 9391
Langlands Medal; Ian   Vol. 2: 447
Langley Gold Medal   Vol. 1: 17339
Langmuir Award in Chemical Physics; Irving   Vol. 1: 1566
Langmuir Prize in Chemical Physics; Irving   Vol. 1: 3461
Langsam Educational Reconstruction Award; Gertrude   Vol. 1: 17451
Lanka Sikkhamani   Vol. 2: 11433
Lankester Investigatorship; Ray   Vol. 2: 3631
Lannan Literary Awards   Vol. 1: 11782
Lantz Prize; Walter and Michael   Vol. 1: 14715
Lapchick Award; Joe   Vol. 1: 12565
Lapeenranta National Singing Competition Awards   Vol. 2: 4748
Laporte Award for Research in Fluid Dynamics; Otto   Vol. 1: 3462
Lappeenrannan Valtakunnalliset Laulukilpailut   Vol. 2: 4748
Larbaud; Prix Valery   Vol. 2: 4987
Larragoiti; Premio   Vol. 2: 10253
Larragoiti Prize; Antonio
   Brazilian Academy of Letters   Vol. 2: 1423
   Lisbon Academy of Sciences   Vol 2: 10253
Larrey; Fondation du Baron   Vol. 2: 5542
Larsen - Miller Community Service Award   Vol. 1: 12750
Larson Award; Gustus L.   Vol. 1: 4686

Lascoff Memorial Award; J. Leon   Vol. 1: 1607
Laser Institute of America Honored Speaker Award   Vol. 1: 11784
Laser Scan Award in Digital Cartography   Vol. 2: 2307
Lashley Award; Karl Spencer   Vol. 1: 3433
Lasker Award; Albert D.   Vol. 1: 2240
Lasker Basic Medical Research Award; Albert   Vol. 1: 11786
Lasker Civil Liberties Award; Florina   Vol. 1: 15231
Lasker Clinical Medical Research Award; Albert   Vol. 1: 11787
Lasker Public Service Award; Albert   Vol. 1: 11788
Lasker Special Public Health Award; Albert   Vol. 1: 11789
Laskine Award; Lily   Vol. 1: 6306
Lasky Humanitarian Service Award; Elaine J.   Vol. 1: 14639
LASL Educator's Award   Vol. 1: 11954
Lasserson Memorial Trust Prize; Sascha   Vol. 2: 3538
Lasswell Award; Harold   Vol. 1: 16305
Lasswell Award; Harold D.   Vol. 1: 3577
Lasswell Award; Harold Dwight   Vol. 2: 922
Last Award; Hugh   Vol. 2: 8178
Latham Memorial Grants; Barbara Aronofsky   Vol. 1: 17106
Latham Sportsman Service Award; Roger M.   Vol. 1: 15003
Latin American Center for Graduate Studies in Music Fellowships   Vol. 1: 15833
Latin American Federation of Thermalism and Climatism Awards   Vol. 2: 57
Latsis-Preis   Vol. 2: 11934
Lauer Traffic Safety Award; A. R.   Vol. 1: 10042
Laufer; Prix Docteur Rene-Joseph   Vol. 2: 5712
Laughlin Award (American)   Vol. 1: 1734
Laughlin Award (International)   Vol. 1: 1735
Laughlin Prize   Vol. 2: 3962
Launoy; Prix Leon   Vol. 2: 4856
Laureat d'Honneur of the International Geographical Union   Vol. 2: 6958
Laureat Musician   Vol. 1: 9001
Laureate   Vol. 1: 10969
Laureate of the Triennial of the Realistic Painting   Vol. 2: 1533
Laurel Award for Screen   Vol. 1: 20560
Laurel Crowned Circle Award   Vol. 1: 15629
Laurel Leaf Award   Vol. 1: 1772
Laurels Awards   Vol. 1: 6198
Laurendeau Prize in Humanities; Andre   Vol. 1: 5434
Laurent; Prix Emile   Vol. 2: 1019
Laurent; Prix Marie   Vol. 2: 5782
Laurie Award in Floriculture and Ornamental Horticulture; Alex   Vol. 1: 4147
Laurie Prize; James   Vol. 1: 4477
Lauriers de la FM   Vol. 2: 6116
Laursen Award; Capt. V. L.   Vol. 1: 19722
Laussedat; Fondation Aime   Vol. 2: 5478
Lavachery; Prix Henri   Vol. 2: 990
Lavallee; Prix Calixa-   Vol. 1: 17384
Lavan Younger Poet Awards; Peter I. B.   Vol. 1: 22
Laveran; Fondation Alphonse   Vol. 2: 5485
Lavin Recognition Award; Tom   Vol. 1: 15070
Lavington Prize; R. J.   Vol. 2: 3171
Lavry Prize; Marc   Vol. 2: 7880
Law Alumni Association's Distinguished Alumnus Award   Vol. 1: 19884
Law and Economics Prize   Vol. 1: 1063
Law Award; Frank G.   Vol. 1: 4732

Law Books in Hindu Prize   Vol. 2: 7516
Law Day U.S.A. Public Service Awards   Vol. 1: 1310
Law Day/Week Award   Vol. 1: 2791
Law Enforcement Award   Vol. 1: 13460
Law Enforcement Leadership Award   Vol. 1: 5790
Law Library Journal Article of the Year Award   Vol. 1: 1030
Law Library Publication Award   Vol. 1: 1031
Law Prize   Vol. 2: 1228
Law-Related Education Teacher of the Year Award   Vol. 1: 2792
Lawn Tennis Association National Awards   Vol. 2: 3540
Lawrence and Harriet Chappell Owsley Award; Frank   Vol. 1: 18215
Lawrence Foundation Award   Vol. 1: 16361
Lawrence Medal   Vol. 2: 4040
Lawrence Memorial Award
   Botanical Society of America   Vol. 1: 6486
   Carnegie Mellon University   Vol 1: 7322
Lawrence Memorial Award; Ernest Orlando   Vol. 1: 19231
Lawrence; Prix Alfred-Joseph   Vol. 1: 18439
Lawrie Factor Ltd. Prize; Alex   Vol. 2: 3098
Lawson Festival of Arts Awards; Grenfell Henry   Vol. 2: 415
Lawton Boating Safety Award; Captain Fred E.   Vol. 1: 16696
Lay Award; Herman   Vol. 1: 5923
Laycock Fourth Prize; Roxanne   Vol. 1: 6217
Layman, Jr., Award; Paul Nash   Vol. 1: 19567
Layman of the Year   Vol. 1: 12118
Layman Support Award   Vol. 1: 14109
Laymen's National Bible Association - Color Slide Competition   Vol. 1: 11798
Layperson's Award   Vol. 1: 10837
Lazar Deak Emlekerem
   Geodetic and Cartographic Society   Vol. 2: 7310
   Hungary - Ministry of Agriculture   Vol 2: 7395
Lazar Memorial Medal; Deak   Vol. 2: 7310
Lazar Prize; Gheorghe   Vol. 2: 10362
Lazarillo Prize   Vol. 2: 11384
Lazarsfeld Award for Evaluation Theory   Vol. 1: 2007
Lazarsfeld Award for Research   Vol. 1: 2007
Lazarus Commemorative Medal; Diaconus   Vol. 2: 7395
Lazerow Fellowship for Research in Acquisitions or Technical Services; Samuel   Vol. 1: 2873
LBJ Cup   Vol. 1: 5281
LCP National Poetry Contest   Vol. 1: 11813
LDA Award for Excellence in Library Achievement   Vol. 1: 11801
Le Caine Awards; Hugh   Vol. 1: 17821
Le Chatelier; Fondation Henry   Vol. 2: 5582
Le Coq-Joli   Vol. 2: 1160
Le Cristal du CNRS   Vol. 2: 5017
Le Cwerneu d'Or   Vol. 2: 1160
Le Goff; Fondation Jean-Marie   Vol. 2: 5598
Le Mans 24-hour Grand Prix d'Endurance   Vol. 2: 4979
Le Mouel Foundation Prize; Eugene   Vol. 2: 6318
Le Pegase Prize of the Audience   Vol. 2: 1241
Le Prix de Poesie Charles Vildrac   Vol. 2: 6267
Le-Roy; Prix Eugene-   Vol. 2: 5241
Le Sueur Award; Herbert   Vol. 2: 3894
Le Sueur Lecture   Vol. 2: 4413
LEA Award   Vol. 2: 4696
LEA-palkinto   Vol. 2: 4696

Leab and Daniel J. Leab *American Book Prices Current* Exhibition Catalogue Awards; Katharine Kyes   Vol. 1: 2874
Leach Medal; Digby   Vol. 2: 444
Leacock Medal for Humour; Stephen   Vol. 1: 11803
Leadership and Distinguished Service Awards   Vol. 1: 10186
Leadership and Service Awards   Vol. 1: 5736
Leadership Award
  American Society for Hospital Materials Management   Vol. 1: 4155
  American Society for Training and Development - Quality of Work Life/Employee Involvement Network   Vol 1: 4341
  Association of Surgical Technologists   Vol 1: 5975
  Cooperative Work Experience Education Association   Vol 1: 8274
  International Association of Cancer Victors and Friends   Vol 1: 10693
  Minerals, Metals, and Materials Society   Vol 1: 12316
  National Association for Equal Opportunity in Higher Education   Vol 1: 12858
  National Council of Administrative Women in Education   Vol 1: 13723
  National Trappers Association   Vol 1: 14928
  Women's Sports Foundation   Vol 1: 20428
Leadership Award for Residents   Vol. 1: 533
Leadership Award for Women   Vol. 1: 19651
Leadership Awards
  Fusion Power Associates   Vol 1: 9454
  Literacy Volunteers of America   Vol 1: 11903
Leadership Citation   Vol. 1: 3671
Leadership Development Awards   Vol. 1: 11519
Leadership for Learning Award   Vol. 1: 1181
Leadership in Human Services Award   Vol. 1: 3866
Leading Chapter Award   Vol. 1: 14021
League Executive of the Year Awards   Vol. 1: 13243
League Leaders - COOL Community Service Awards   Vol. 1: 6692
Leahy Award; Emmett   Vol. 1: 10253
Leakey Foundation Prize for Multidisciplinary Research on Ape and Human Evolution; L. S. B.   Vol. 1: 11821
Lean Award for Best Achievement in Direction; David   Vol. 2: 2233
Lear Award for Achievement in Comedy Playwriting; Norman   Vol. 1: 1756
Learning Through Listening Awards   Vol. 1: 16717
Leary Award; Dick   Vol. 1: 10011
Least Cooperative to the Press   Vol. 1: 9982
Leaven Award   Vol. 1: 746
Leavey Awards for Excellence in Private Enterprise Education   Vol. 1: 9403
Leavin Prize; William H.   Vol. 1: 12616
Leavitt Memorial Lecture Award; Milo D.   Vol. 1: 2178
LeBair Memorial Trophy; Harold A.   Vol. 1: 19652
Lebrun; Fondation Jean   Vol. 2: 1003
LeCaine-NACO Prize   Vol. 1: 12817
Leche International Award of Achievement; La   Vol. 1: 11737
Leche League International Award of Appreciation; La   Vol. 1: 11738
Leche League International Award of Excellence; La   Vol. 1: 11739
Leche League International Award of Recognition; La   Vol. 1: 11740

Leche League International Founders' Award; La   Vol. 1: 11741
Leche League International Teen - Parent Program Awards; La   Vol. 1: 11742
Leclere; Prix Achille   Vol. 2: 5354
Leclerc; Prix Leon   Vol. 2: 995
Leconte Foundation Prize; Sebastien-Charles   Vol. 2: 6319
Lecturer of Merit   Vol. 1: 13607
Lectureship Award   Vol. 1: 4097
Lederer Award; Jerome F.   Vol. 1: 11275
Lederle Award in Human Nutrition   Vol. 1: 2651
Lederle International Citation   Vol. 1: 4537
Lederle Laboratories Research Grant; Oncology Nursing Foundation/   Vol. 1: 15644
Lederman Memorial Award; Ben   Vol. 1: 14131
Lederman Memorial Lectures; Leah   Vol. 2: 4259
Lee Award; Carlton   Vol. 1: 561
Lee Award for Television; Larry   Vol. 1: 12153
Lee Award; Mabel   Vol. 1: 762
Lee Award; Walker S.   Vol. 1: 6608
Lee Award; Wellington   Vol. 1: 16166
Lee Choreography Award; Clifford E.   Vol. 1: 6259
Lee Consumer Education Award; Stewart M.   Vol. 1: 1864
Lee - Founders Award   Vol. 1: 17642
Lee Grand Prize; Norman H.   Vol. 1: 2058
Lee - Homewood Honorary Award   Vol. 1: 5636
Lee International Award; R.A.G.   Vol. 2: 3781
Lee Memorial Award; James W.   Vol. 1: 19683
Lee Memorial Trophy; Penny West   Vol. 1: 14866
Lee Prize; Jesse   Vol. 1: 9524
Lee Scholarship Award; Ed   Vol. 1: 19468
Lee Trophy; Mike   Vol. 1: 19379
Leeds Award; Morris E.   Vol. 1: 10280
Leeds Philosophical and Literary Society Medal   Vol. 2: 3548
Leedy Urban Wildlife Conservation Award; Daniel L.   Vol. 1: 14225
Leek Arts Festival International Poetry Competition   Vol. 2: 3550
Leeser Memorial; Werner M.   Vol. 1: 8701
Leet Grants; Dorothy   Vol. 2: 11789
Lefcowitz Prizes; Rose   Vol. 1: 16261
Lefebvre Memorial Award; Jacques   Vol. 2: 5130
Lefkowitz Award   Vol. 1: 15248
Lefort; Prix Jules   Vol. 2: 5769
Lefranc Scholarships; Maurice   Vol. 2: 1148
Lefthanders of the Year Awards   Vol. 1: 11823
Lefuel; Prix Hector   Vol. 2: 5399
Legal & General Silver Trowel Award   Vol. 2: 2249
Legal Award   Vol. 1: 5791
Legal Writing Contest   Vol. 1: 10713
Legends of Racing   Vol. 1: 1284
Leger Medal; Gabrielle   Vol. 1: 9911
Leger Prize for New Chamber Music; Jules   Vol. 1: 6741
Legget Award; R. F.   Vol. 1: 6897
Legion d'Honneur; Ordre de   Vol. 2: 5237
Legion of Honor
  American Police Hall of Fame   Vol. 1: 3559
  Jewish National Fund   Vol. 1: 11556
Legion of Honour Award   Vol. 2: 7724
Legion of Merit
  National Pocket Billiard Association   Vol. 1: 14480

United States Department of Defense - Armed Forces Decorations and Awards   Vol 1: 19167
Legion of Valor Bronze Cross for Achievement   Vol. 1: 11825
Legion of Valor Silver Cross for Valor   Vol. 1: 11826
Legislation Award   Vol. 1: 5976
Legislative Accomplishment Award   Vol. 1: 3943
Legislative Advocacy Award   Vol. 1: 18903
Legislative Award
  Association of Federal Investigators   Vol. 1: 5792
  Council for Exceptional Children - Mental Retardation Division   Vol 1: 8323
Legislative Awards   Vol. 1: 10890
Legislative Excellence Award
  Classification and Compensation Society   Vol. 1: 7819
  Florida Audubon Society   Vol 1: 9257
Legislative Service Award; NRA   Vol. 1: 14583
Legislator of the Year
  United Hellenic Voters of America   Vol. 1: 18917
  Vietnam Veterans of America   Vol 1: 20035
Legjobb nemzeti kollekcio dija   Vol. 2: 7316
Lehman Award; Arnold J.   Vol. 1: 18074
Lehman Awards; Naomi and Howard   Vol. 1: 18921
Lehman Ethics Award; Herbert H.   Vol. 1: 11568
Lehman Human Relations Award; Herbert H.   Vol. 1: 2724
Lehman Memorial Award; Bill   Vol. 1: 12784
Lehmann-Medaille; Lilli-   Vol. 2: 828
Lehmann; Prix Henri   Vol. 2: 5401
Lehmbruck Prize; Wilhelm   Vol. 2: 7031
Lehr Ferenc Textilipari Ifjusagi Erem   Vol. 2: 7386
Leica Canada Scientific Award   Vol. 1: 6794
Leica Photogrammetric Fellowship Award   Vol. 1: 4254
Leica Scientific Award   Vol. 1: 6794
Leica Surveying Scholarships   Vol. 1: 1816
Leidy Award; Joseph   Vol. 1: 71
Leighton Memorial Medal   Vol. 2: 599
Leipholz Medal   Vol. 1: 7175
Leipoldt Memorial Medal; Louis   Vol. 2: 10888
Leipzig Book Fair   Vol. 2: 7152
Leitch Memorial Prize   Vol. 1: 11983
Leiter Lectureship; Joseph   Vol. 1: 12172
Leitman Memorial Award; Samuel   Vol. 1: 5051
Lejins Research Award; Peter P.   Vol. 1: 1835
Leland Award for International Health Service; Mickey   Vol. 1: 13701
Leland Community Development Fellowship Program; Mickey   Vol. 1: 11828
Leland Humanitarian Award; George Thomas "Mickey"   Vol. 1: 8163
Leland Memorial Prize; Waldo Gifford   Vol. 1: 17675
Leland Prize; Waldo G.   Vol. 1: 2295
Leland Prize; Waldo Gifford   Vol. 1: 17675
Lemaire; Prix Charles   Vol. 2: 1012
Lemaitre; Prix Troyon et Edouard   Vol. 2: 5429
LeMay Bomber Aircrew Award; General Curtis E.   Vol. 1: 243
LeMay Morale, Welfare, and Recreation Award; Gen. Curtis E.   Vol. 1: 15784
Lemay-Ohio Award   Vol. 1: 5281
LeMay Strategic Aircrew Award; General Curtis E.   Vol. 1: 243

997

LeMay Trophy; General Curtis E. Vol. 1: 14644
Lemberg Travelling Fellowship; Rudi Vol. 2: 175
Lembright Award; Katharine A. Vol. 1: 2235
Lemburg Award for Distinguished Service; Wayne A. Vol. 1: 2987
The Lemelson-MIT Prize for Invention and Innovation Vol. 1: 12114
Lemen Fellowship; J. Winton Vol. 1: 14516
Lemenon; Fondation Odette Vol. 2: 5641
Lemieux Award for Organic Chemistry; R. U. Vol. 1: 7552
Lemieux Memorial Award; Fabian Vol. 1: 15703
Lemieux Prize; Jacqueline Vol. 1: 6742
Lemkin Medal Vol. 2: 4520
Lemonon; Prix Ernest Vol. 2: 5740
Lemos; Premio Aboim Sande Vol. 2: 10254
Lemos Prize; Aboim Sande Vol. 2: 10254
Lenaerts Prize; R. Vol. 2: 1257
Lendholt-Denkmunze; Eugen- Vol. 2: 6543
Lenexa's National 3-Dimensional Art Show Vol. 1: 7731
Lenexa's National Art Show Vol. 1: 7731
Lenghi e Flaviano Magrassi; Fondazione Guido Vol. 2: 8060
Lenglen; Coupe Suzanne Vol. 2: 5259
Lenin Prize Vol. 2: 10469
Lenington All-American Award Vol. 1: 2267
Lenne-Preis des Landes Berlin; Peter Joseph Vol. 2: 6562
Lenne Prize; Peter Joseph Vol. 2: 6562
Lenoir; Prix Yvonne Vol. 2: 6300
LeNoire Award; Rosetta Vol. 1: 117
Lentz International Peace Research Award Vol. 1: 11830
Leo Lee Award for Radio Vol. 1: 12153
Leon-Houry; Fondation Marie Vol. 2: 5626
Leon; Premio Nicolas Vol. 2: 9061
Leonard Award; Richard M. Vol. 1: 17236
Leonard Medal Vol. 2: 3645
Leonardo Medal for Excellence Vol. 1: 11266
Leonardslee Bowl Vol. 2: 4041
Leone Award; Lucile Petry Vol. 1: 14285
Leonide Moguy CIDALC Prize Vol. 2: 5991
Leonor Magro de Radio; Premio Municipal Maria Vol. 2: 10275
Leopold Memorial Award; Aldo Vol. 1: 20303
Leopold Prize; Richard W. Vol. 1: 15819
Leopoldsorde Vol. 2: 1073
Lepoix; Prix Joseph Vol. 2: 1336
LEPRA Essay Competition Vol. 2: 3552
LePrince Medal; Joseph Augustin Vol. 1: 4814
Lequeux; Prix Andre
  Institut de France Vol. 2: 5337
  Institut de France - Academie des Sciences Morales et Politiques Vol 2: 5714
Lerche Forschungspreis; Martin Vol. 2: 6887
Leriche Prize; Rene Vol. 2: 11845
Lerner-Gray Fund for Marine Research Award Vol. 1: 3153
Lerner Memorial Medal; Victor Vol. 1: 6496
Lerner - Scott Prize Vol. 1: 15820
Leroy-Beaulieu; Prix Paul Vol. 2: 5785
Leroy Fellowship; A. M. Vol. 2: 8231
Leroy Prize; Andre Vol. 2: 3436
Les Ecrans De L'Aventure International Festival of Adventure Documentaries Vol. 2: 5328
Lesinsky Award; Adam P. Vol. 1: 13532
Leslie Awards; Ian Murray Vol. 2: 2582
Lesmuller-Medaille Vol. 2: 6587
Lessing Memorial Medal Vol. 2: 3653
Lester Award; Elmer Vol. 1: 9129
Lester Honor Lecture Vol. 1: 4219

LeSueur Memorial Lectures Vol. 1: 17807
Letelier - Moffitt Memorial Human Rights Awards Vol. 1: 10225
Letourneau Award for Outstanding Student Papers on Legal Medicine Vol. 1: 1668
Letourneau Student Research Paper of the Year Award; Marriott Corporation Health Care Services Charles U. Vol. 1: 599
Letras de Oro Literary Prizes Vol. 1: 19824
Letter of Citizenship of the City of Salzburg Vol. 2: 866
Letter of Commendation Vol. 1: 14729
Letter of Recognition
  Australian Library and Information Association Vol. 2: 242
  Inter-American Safety Council Vol 1: 10516
Letterstedtska Forfattarpriset Vol. 2: 11543
Letterstedtska Medaljen i guld Vol. 2: 11544
Letterstedtska Priset for Oversattningar Vol. 2: 11545
Lettsomian Medal Vol. 2: 3638
Leuver Exhibit Award; Robert J. Vol. 1: 3234
Leven Prize for Poetry; Grace Vol. 2: 513
Levenson Prizes in Chinese Studies; Joseph Vol. 1: 5445
Leventritt Artists Series Vol. 1: 11840
Leveque; Prix Charles Vol. 2: 5724
Lever Award; AWA Harry Vol. 1: 6186
Leverett, Jr. Environmental Science Award; Sidney D. Vol. 1: 168
Leverhulme Lecture Vol. 2: 4414
Leverhulme Medal Vol. 2: 4152
Leverhulme Memorial Lecture Vol. 2: 3554
Leverhulme Tercentenary Medal Vol. 2: 3555
Levi-Strauss - Women's Sports Foundation Contribution Award Vol. 1: 20429
Levin Prize; Harry Vol. 1: 1769
Levine Memorial Award for Excellence in Public Service; Charles E. Vol. 1: 4267
Levine Young Clinical Investigator Awards; Samuel A. Vol. 1: 2236
Levins Festspillfond; Robert Vol. 2: 9874
Levinson Award; Harry
  American Psychological Association - Consulting Psychology Division Vol. 1: 3701
  American Psychological Foundation Vol 1: 3835
Levinson Prize Vol. 1: 16267
Levinson Prizes; Morris L. Vol. 2: 7982
Levinstein Memorial Lecture; Ivan Vol. 2: 4415
Leviton Award; Robert Vol. 1: 3089
Levitt Memorial Award; Lou Vol. 1: 19380
Levorsen Memorial Award; A. I. Vol. 1: 1109
Levstik Prize; Fran Vol. 2: 10807
Levy Art Encouragement Fund Prizes; Jacob and Bessie Vol. 1: 5297
Levy Citizen's Award; Commodore Uriah P. Vol. 1: 11574
Levy Medal Stipend; Louis E. Vol. 1: 9384
Levy Memorial Prize; Leonard Vol. 2: 2411
Levy Prize for a Young Photographer; Gerard Vol. 2: 7928
Lew Award; Isiah Vol. 1: 590
Lewin Award; Elizabeth Vol. 1: 13576
Lewin Memorial Award; Kurt Vol. 1: 3814
Lewis Award; Arthur O. Vol. 1: 17655
Lewis Award for Contributions in Chemical Engineering Educacation; Warren K. Vol. 1: 2591
Lewis Award for Research; Harold E. Vol. 2: 2446
Lewis Award; John F. Vol. 1: 3434
Lewis Award; Ralph Vol. 1: 4587
Lewis Fellowships in American History; Lloyd Vol. 1: 15314
Lewis Medal; Bernard Vol. 1: 8022

Lewis Medical Travelling Scholarship Vol. 2: 2275
Lewis Memorial Award; Richard B. Vol. 1: 5513
Lewis Memorial Executive of the Year Award Vol. 1: 16413
Lewkowitsch Memorial Lecture; Julius Vol. 2: 4416
Lexer Preis; Erich Vol. 2: 6879
Leysterprijs; Judith
  Frans Halsmuseum Vol. 2: 9448
  Judith Leyster Stichting Vol 2: 9543
LHAT Award Vol. 1: 11819
Lhermite; Prix Pierre et Celine Vol. 2: 4871
Li Award; K. C. Vol. 1: 7985
Liang Memorial Award; Ta Vol. 1: 4255
Liard; Prix Louis Vol. 2: 5775
LiBerature Prize Vol. 2: 6923
LiBeraturpreis Vol. 2: 6923
Libertarian Alliance Awards Vol. 2: 3559
Liberty Award Vol. 1: 9878
Liberty Awards Vol. 1: 10180
Liberty Bell Award Vol. 1: 10117
Librarian of the Year
  Arizona State Library Association Vol. 1: 5246
  Illinois Library Association Vol 1: 10081
Libraries Prize Vol. 2: 8153
Library Buildings Award Program Vol. 1: 2906
Library Contest Awards Vol. 2: 8154
Library Hi Tech Award; LITA/ Vol. 1: 2910
Library Manager of the Year Vol. 2: 243
Library Public Relations Council Award Vol. 1: 11861
Library Research and Development Committee Research Grants Vol. 1: 7014
Library Research Round Table Research Award Vol. 1: 2916
Library Service Award Vol. 1: 15183
Library Technician of the Year Vol. 2: 244
Library Video Award Vol. 1: 2929
Libris Woutertje Pieterse Prijs Vol. 2: 9672
Libro de Oro Vol. 2: 1395
Liceaga; Condecoracion Dr. Eduardo Vol. 2: 9127
Liceaga; Premio Dr. Eduardo Vol. 2: 9114
Licentiateship of the City and Guilds of London Institute Vol. 2: 2625
Licette Scholarship; Miriam Vol. 2: 3669
Lichfield Prize Vol. 2: 3576
Lichten Award; Robert L. Vol. 1: 2257
Lichtenfelt Award; Richard Vol. 1: 12989
Lichtenstein Medal; Alfred F. Vol. 1: 7871
Lichtwitz; Prix Andre Vol. 2: 5942
Lidwill Travelling Fellowships; Mark C. Vol. 1: 15460
Lieber Awards for Young Singers; Eleanor Vol. 1: 16324
Lieber; Prix Francis Vol. 2: 11751
Lieber Prize Vol. 1: 12769
Lieber Purchase Award; Judith Vol. 1: 17693
Lieberman Student Poetry Award; Elias Vol. 1: 16289
Lieberson Fellowships; Goddard Vol. 1: 512
Liebig-Denkmunze Vol. 2: 6787
Liebig Prizes; Justus von Vol. 2: 7127
Liebmann Award; Morris N. Vol. 1: 10281
Liebmann Book Award; Fred L. Vol. 1: 15275
Liebstoeckl; Prix Frederic Vol. 2: 5042
Liechtenstein-Preis zur Forderung junger Lyriker Vol. 2: 8853
Liederkranz Scholarship Awards Competitions Vol. 1: 11864

Liegeois; Fondation Camille
  Academie Royale de Belgique - Classe des Lettres et des Sciences Morales et Politiques   Vol. 2: 972
  Academie Royale de Belgique - Classe des Sciences   Vol 2: 1001
Liegeois; Prix du Camera Club   Vol. 2: 1095
Lienhard Award; Gustav O.   Vol. 1: 12699
Lieutenant Governor's Conservation Award   Vol. 1: 8187
Lieutenant-Governor's Medal   Vol. 1: 9912
Lieutenant-Governor's Medal for Historical Writing   Vol. 1: 6569
Life Achievement Award
  American Film Institute   Vol. 1: 2052
  American Radio Theatre   Vol 1: 3898
  National Telephone Cooperative Association   Vol 1: 14890
  Republic of Croatia - Ministry of Science, Technology and Informatics   Vol 2: 1811
Life Achievement Award in Sports   Vol. 1: 8667
Life and Freedom Award   Vol. 1: 11917
Life Member   Vol. 1: 13206
Life Membership
  Committee on Continuing Education for School Personnel   Vol. 1: 8042
  Genealogical Association of Nova Scotia   Vol 1: 9515
  Institute for Briquetting and Agglomeration   Vol 1: 10212
  International Organization of Plant Biosystematists   Vol 2: 8551
  Society of Exploration Geophysicists   Vol 1: 17846
Life Membership Award
  American Road & Transportation Builders Association   Vol. 1: 3971
  Association of Medical Rehabilitation Administrators   Vol 1: 5864
Life Membership Awards   Vol. 1: 2772
Life Membership of IMLS   Vol. 2: 3172
Life-Saving Honorary Medal   Vol. 2: 7402
Life-Saving Medal of the Order   Vol. 2: 3743
Life-Time Membership Award   Vol. 1: 8424
Lifesaving and Meritorious Action Awards of the National Court of Honor   Vol. 1: 6517
Lifesaving or Merit Award   Vol. 1: 13113
Lifestyle Award   Vol. 1: 6719
Lifetime Achievement
  Box Office Management International   Vol. 1: 6508
  National Association of Social Workers   Vol 1: 13314
Lifetime Achievement Award
  Alliance for Children and Television   Vol. 1: 322
  American Association of Physical Anthropologists   Vol 1: 1120
  American Numismatic Association   Vol 1: 3235
  AMIT Women   Vol 1: 5136
  Association of Medical Illustrators   Vol 1: 5859
  Council of Fashion Designers of America   Vol 1: 8356
  Foundation for Hospice and Home Care   Vol 1: 9349
  International Institute of Space Law   Vol 2: 6032
  Journalism Education Association   Vol 1: 11613
  National Academy of Popular Music   Vol 1: 12649
  National Academy of Songwriters   Vol 1: 12704
  National Association of Black Journalists   Vol 1: 12961
  National Wildlife Rehabilitation Association   Vol 1: 15013
  New York Society of Architects   Vol 1: 15276
  Podiatry Management   Vol 1: 16258
Lifetime Achievement Awards
  Guild Hall of East Hampton   Vol. 1: 9741
  National Academy of Recording Arts and Sciences   Vol 1: 12657
Lifetime Achievement in Education and Research Award   Vol. 1: 5712
Lifetime Achievement in Energy Award   Vol. 1: 13900
Lifetime Membership Award   Vol. 1: 12843
Lifetime of Service to Aviculture Award   Vol. 1: 11396
Lifetime Sales Achievement Award   Vol. 1: 18338
Light Metals Award   Vol. 1: 12317
Lighting Award   Vol. 2: 2594
Lighting Design Awards   Vol. 2: 3581
Lilienfeld Prize; Julius Edgar   Vol. 1: 3463
Lilienthal Medal   Vol. 2: 5156
Lilje Prize; Hanns   Vol. 2: 6910
Liljencrantz Award; Eric   Vol. 1: 169
Lill Awards for Essex Young Musician of the Year; John   Vol. 2: 3736
Lill Awards for the Essex Schools Musician of the Year; John   Vol. 2: 3735
Lille Sport Film Festival   Vol. 2: 5038
Lillegren Award; Austin T.   Vol. 1: 15419
Lillie Award; Ralph D.   Vol. 1: 9928
Lillie Memorial Award; Howard   Vol. 1: 1465
Lilly and Company Research Award in Microbiology and Immunology; Eli   Vol. 1: 4209
Lilly Award in Biological Chemistry; Eli   Vol. 1: 1502
Lilly/EASD Research Fellowship in Diabetes & Metabolism; Eli   Vol. 2: 6704
Lilly Pilot Research Award for Junior Faculty and Child Psychiatry Fellows; Eli   Vol. 1: 534
Lilly Poetry Fellowship; Ruth   Vol. 1: 16268
Lilly Psychiatric Research Fellowship   Vol. 1: 3641
Lilly Travelling Fellowships   Vol. 2: 3963
Limerick Competition Awards   Vol. 1: 7290
Limon; Premio Nacional de Danza INBA-Sinaloa Jose   Vol. 2: 9233
Lin Award; T. Y.   Vol. 1: 4478
Linacre Lecture and Award   Vol. 2: 4330
Lincoln Arc Welding Design and Engineering Awards Program; James F.   Vol. 1: 11875
Lincoln Award; Barondess/   Vol. 1: 7776
Lincoln Center Award; Beverly Sills -   Vol. 1: 11888
Lincoln-Douglas Debate   Vol. 1: 14024
Lincoln Food Service Research Grant   Vol. 1: 3996
Lincoln Gold Medal Award; James F.   Vol. 1: 5082
Lincoln Lawyer Award   Vol. 1: 11881
Lincoln Medal   Vol. 1: 9323
Lincoln Prize   Vol. 1: 9600
Lind Award; Erv   Vol. 1: 463
Lind Award; Wilbur H.   Vol. 1: 6609
Lindapter Award   Vol. 2: 3249
Lindau Award; Alfred E.   Vol. 1: 1785
Lindberg Award; Robert A.   Vol. 1: 1382
Lindberg Diploma; Charles   Vol. 2: 5157
Lindbergh Grant   Vol. 1: 11894
Lindbomska Beloningen   Vol. 2: 11546
Lindeman Award; R.   Vol. 1: 4653
Linderman Award   Vol. 1: 16509
Lindquist Award; E. F.   Vol. 1: 1977
Lindren Award   Vol. 1: 17832
Lindsay Award for Distinguished Research in Teacher Education; Margaret   Vol. 1: 960
Lindsay Award; Hilarie   Vol. 2: 665
Lindsay Award; R. Bruce   Vol. 1: 99
Line Manager's Excellence in Classification and Position Management Award   Vol. 1: 7820
Lingeman Award; Marie Hippenstell   Vol. 1: 17267
Lingle Community Resources Award; Kendall I.   Vol. 1: 13739
Link Award   Vol. 1: 7223
Link Award; Fred M.   Vol. 1: 16646
Link Foundation Energy Fellowship Program   Vol. 1: 11898
Link House Thematic Trophy   Vol. 2: 3781
Link Land Mobile Award   Vol. 1: 16646
Link Prize; Arthur S.   Vol. 1: 17469
Linnard Prize; American Bureau of Shipping - Captain Joseph H.   Vol. 1: 17920
Linnean Medal   Vol. 2: 3587
Linnemedaljen for botanik   Vol. 2: 11517
Linneprisen   Vol. 2: 11518
Linnert Honorary Award; Fritz   Vol. 2: 6799
Linon Prize; Michel   Vol. 2: 5122
Linton Award; Margaret M.   Vol. 1: 9477
Linville's R. H. Wright Award in Olfactory Research; Frank Allison   Vol. 1: 17284
Linz International Anton Bruckner Organ Competition   Vol. 2: 857
Lion Trophy   Vol. 1: 8581
Lions Club International Clinical Research Program in Diabetic Eye Disease   Vol. 1: 1953
Lions of the Performing Arts   Vol. 1: 15263
Lions SightFirst Diabetic Retinopathy Research Program   Vol. 1: 1953
Lipizer Prize; International Violin Competition Rodolfo   Vol. 2: 8209
Lipmann Lectureship; Fritz   Vol. 1: 4041
Lippert Memorial Award; George R.   Vol. 1: 17173
Lipphard Award for Distinguished Service to Religious Journalism; William B.   Vol. 1: 5397
Lippincott Award; Ellis R.
  Optical Society of America   Vol. 1: 15752
  Society for Applied Spectroscopy   Vol 1: 17417
Lippincott Award in Political Theory; Benjamin Evans   Vol. 1: 3578
Lippincott Award; Joseph W.   Vol. 1: 2820
Lippitt Memorial Award   Vol. 1: 4338
Lipshaw Student Scholarship; Shandon/   Vol. 1: 14755
Lipton Award; Benjamin H.   Vol. 1: 14994
Lipton Mixed Doubles Amateur Champions   Vol. 1: 18621
Liquid Tide Trans-Am Tour   Vol. 1: 18416
Lira Poetry Prize; Miguel N.   Vol. 2: 9004
Liscombe Trophy; Carl   Vol. 1: 2334
Liska Award; Jozsef   Vol. 2: 7334
Liska Jozsef Dijasok   Vol. 2: 7334
Liskin Foundation Award; Joyce and Elliot   Vol. 1: 14714
Lisnyk Professional Achievement Award; Dr. James A.   Vol. 1: 5955
Lissner Award; H. R.   Vol. 1: 4687
List Purchase Award; Vera   Vol. 1: 17693
Listar Memorial Lecture   Vol. 2: 4417
Lister Memorial Medal   Vol. 2: 3979
Lister Memorial Trophy; C. B.   Vol. 1: 14645
Lister Professorship   Vol. 2: 10607
Liston Award; Emil S.   Vol. 1: 13167
Liszt - Bartok Piano Competition   Vol. 2: 7414
Liszt Medal   Vol. 1: 2964

Liszt Prize; Franz Vol. 2: 7403
Liszt Society Prize Vol. 2: 3592
LITA Award for Achievement in Library and Information Technology Vol. 1: 2908
LITA/Gaylord Award for Achievement in Library and Information Technology Vol. 1: 2908
LITA/GEAC-CLSI Scholarship in Library and Information Technology Vol. 1: 2909
LITA/Library Hi Tech Award Vol. 1: 2910
LITA/OCLC Minority Scholarship in Library and Information Technology Vol. 1: 2911
Litchfield Award; Jessie Vol. 2: 557
Litehiser Memorial Award; Robert R. Vol. 1: 6061
Literacy - Charles E. Scripps Awards Vol. 1: 17148
Literarischer Marz Vol. 2: 6601
Literary Award
　American Medical Record Association Vol. 1: 3032
　Germans from Russia Heritage Society Vol 1: 9581
　Svenska Dagbladet Vol 2: 11572
Literary Awards
　Academie de Gastronomie Brillat-Savarin Vol. 2: 4791
　Chaine des Rotisseurs - Ordre Mondial des Gourmets Degustateurs Vol 2: 5026
　Friends of American Writers Vol 1: 9413
　Hungary - Ministry of Culture and Education Vol 2: 7404
Literary Awards and Prizes for Sinhalese Literature Vol. 2: 11423
Literary Competition
　Eaglehawk Dahlia and Arts Festival Vol. 2: 357
　Zimbabwe Literature Bureau Vol 2: 12218
Literary Competition (Regina Award) Vol. 1: 17073
Literary Fund Writing Grants Vol. 2: 9798
Literary Lions Vol. 1: 15264
Literary Prize
　National Academy of Arts Vol. 2: 8830
　South African Academy of Science and Arts Vol 2: 10995
Literary Prize - Bialik Prize for Literature Vol. 2: 7953
Literary Prize - Education and Instruction Prize Vol. 2: 7954
Literary Prize for Translation Vol. 2: 10996
Literary Prize - Mendele Prize Vol. 2: 7955
Literary Prize - Nachum Sokolov Prize Vol. 2: 7956
Literary Prize of PLA Vol. 2: 10153
Literary Prize of the Resistance Vol. 2: 5044
Literary Prize - Rav Kook Prize Vol. 2: 7957
Literary Prize - Tchernichowsky Prize Vol. 2: 7958
Literary Prizes
　British Society of Scientific Glassblowers Vol. 2: 2536
　Greek Ministry of Culture - Section for Theatre and Dance Vol 2: 7192
Literary Prizes for Tamil Literature Vol. 2: 11424
Literary Publishers Marketing Development Program Vol. 1: 8371
Literary Writers Competition Vol. 1: 9098
Literature and Art Awards Vol. 2: 12011
Literature and Belief Writing Contest Vol. 1: 6557
Literature, Art, Journalism, and Architecture Awards Vol. 2: 10438
Literature Award
　Healthcare Information and Management Systems Society Vol. 1: 9868
　Society of Cosmetic Chemists Vol 1: 17826
Literature Awards for Children and Young People Vol. 2: 9916
Literature Board's Emeritus Fellowship Awards Vol. 2: 166
Literature of the Year Awards Vol. 1: 13162
Literature Paper Prize Vol. 1: 17298
Literature Prize Vol. 2: 12075
Literature Program Innovation Award Vol. 1: 19790
LITERATURIUMS Kabarett Award Vol. 2: 7051
LITERATURIUMS Kabarett-Preis Vol. 2: 7051
Literaturpreis der Bayerische Akademie der Schonen Kunste Vol. 2: 6552
Literaturpreis der Bundesarztekammer Vol. 2: 6816
Literaturpreis der ETG Vol. 2: 6697
Literaturpreis der Freien Hansestadt Bremen Vol. 2: 6578
Literaturpreis der Landeshauptstadt Stuttgart Vol. 2: 7139
Literaturpreis des Kranichs mit dem Stein Vol. 2: 6672
Literavision Preis Vol. 2: 7021
Lithuanian Catholic Women. Vol. 1: 11908
Litsky, Ph.D. Educator of the Year Award; Bertha Yanis Vol. 1: 10744
Litt Medal; Mary S. Vol. 1: 5052
Litteraire Prijs Sticusa Vol. 2: 9430
Little Archer Award Vol. 1: 9626
Little Award; Arthur Dehon Vol. 1: 2592
Little Award; Bud and Mary Vol. 1: 19568
Little Big Horn Associates' Dr. Lawrence A. Frost Award Vol. 1: 11910
Little Big Horn Associates' John M. Carroll Literary Award Vol. 1: 11911
Little Brown Jug Vol. 1: 19677
Little General Vol. 1: 5287
Little Theatre of Alexandria National One-Act Playwriting Competition Vol. 1: 11915
Littleton - Griswold Prize in American Law and Society Vol. 1: 2296
Littlewood Memorial Lecture; AIAA William Vol. 1: 2510
Littlewood Memorial Lecture; William Vol. 1: 17766
Littre Prize Vol. 2: 6501
Liversidge Lectureship Vol. 2: 4205
Liversidge Memorial Lectureship Vol. 2: 627
Livesay Poetry Prize; Dorothy Vol. 1: 20188
Livesey Medal Vol. 2: 3989
Livesey Research Fellowship Vol. 2: 2086
Livewire Start-up Awards Vol. 2: 3596
Livewire UK Awards Vol. 2: 3596
Living Hall of Fame Vol. 1: 19381
Living Legacy Award Vol. 1: 13566
Living Legends Award Vol. 1: 14973
Livingston and Doughty Trophy Vol. 2: 3007
Livingston Awards for Young Journalists Vol. 1: 19828
Livingstone Centenary Medal; David Vol. 1: 2154
Livingstone Gold Medal Vol. 2: 10631
Llangollen International Musical Eisteddfod Vol. 2: 12177
Llewellyn Award; Allan Vol. 2: 357
Lloyd Conservation Award; Stanley Vol. 1: 9110
Lloyd Prize; David D. Vol. 1: 18827
Lloyds Bank British Fashion Awards Vol. 2: 2338
Lluch Prize; Jordi Vol. 2: 11186
Lluesma Award; Jorge Vol. 2: 11263
Llywelyn-Williams; Gwobr Goffa Alun Vol. 2: 12181
Llywelyn-Williams Memorial Award; Alun Vol. 2: 12181
LMP Awards Vol. 1: 6494
LNBA Lifetime Achievement Award Vol. 1: 11795
Lobato Prize; Monteiro Vol. 2: 1424
Local Association Achievement Award Vol. 1: 13365
Local Association Community Project Award Vol. 1: 13366
Local Association Public Relations Contest Vol. 1: 1368
Local Association Publications Contest Vol. 1: 1368
Local Association Service Award Vol. 1: 1369
Local Chapter President Award Vol. 1: 13367
Local Committee Appreciation Vol. 1: 3236
Local Council Community Service Award Vol. 1: 11192
Local Government Engineering Medal Vol. 2: 471
Local Horticulture Award Vol. 1: 2359
Local Interest Numismatic Material Exhibit Award Vol. 1: 3237
Local Society Awards Vol. 1: 19991
Locarno International Film Festival Vol. 2: 11875
Locher Award; John Vol. 1: 5680
Lochner Medaille; Stephan Vol. 2: 6597
Lochner Medal; Stephan Vol. 2: 6597
Lock Endowment Awards; Ottis Vol. 1: 8783
Lockem; Prix Georges Vol. 2: 1300
Lockette Humanitarian Award; Rutherford B. Vol. 1: 11335
Lockheed Award for Ocean Science and Engineering Vol. 1: 12090
Lockheed Ocean Engineering Award Vol. 1: 12090
Lockwood Award; Admiral Vol. 1: 19710
Lockwood Award for Submarine Professional Excellence; Charles A. Vol. 1: 15090
Loctite - USAC Mechanic of the Year Reliability Award - Frank DelRoy Memorial Vol. 1: 19025
Locus Awards Vol. 1: 11923
Locy Award; Francis E. Vol. 1: 19711
Loder Cup Vol. 2: 4042
Loder Rhododendron Cup Vol. 2: 4043
Lodge Premium; Oliver Vol. 2: 3273
Loeb Awards; Gerald Vol. 1: 19752
Loeb Fellowship Vol. 1: 9813
Loebner Prize (Turing Test Award) Vol. 1: 6683
Loew Jr. Crystal Vision Award; Arthur Vol. 1: 5800
Lofler Foundation Prize; Paul Vol. 2: 6320
Loft Children's Literature Prizes Vol. 1: 11925
Loft Creative Nonfiction Award Vol. 1: 11926
Loft-McKnight Award Vol. 1: 11927
Loft-McKnight Awards of Distinction Vol. 1: 11928
Loft-McKnight Fellows Vol. 1: 11927
Loft Mentor Series Award Vol. 1: 11929
Log of Mystic Seaport Prize Article Contest Vol. 1: 12552
Logan Art Institute Medal and Prizes; Mr. and Mrs. Frank G. Vol. 1: 5297
Loggie Prize; Helen M. Vol. 1: 12617
Lohann Prize; Carl Vol. 2: 11060
Lohse Information Technology Medal; Edward Vol. 1: 3181
Loines Award for Poetry Vol. 1: 513
Loiseau; Prix Yvan Vol. 2: 5931
Lojek Award; Jerzy Vol. 1: 16224

Lomax - Irving T. Marsh Trophy; Stan   Vol. 1: 12240
Lomb Medal; Adolph   Vol. 1: 15753
Lombardi Award   Vol. 1: 16904
Lombardi Award; Rotary   Vol. 1: 16904
Lombardi Trophy; Vince   Vol. 1: 14005
Lomonosov Gold Medal   Vol. 2: 10419
London Administration Award; Louis M.   Vol. 1: 13232
London Award   Vol. 2: 11487
London Awards   Vol. 2: 3038
London Club Award   Vol. 1: 11931
The London Evening Standard Ballet and Opera Awards   Vol. 2: 3600
The London Evening Standard Drama Awards   Vol. 2: 3601
London International String Quartet Competition   Vol. 2: 3606
London Memorial Award; Fritz   Vol. 1: 8760
Londres; Prix Albert   Vol. 2: 4940
Loney Trophy; Don   Vol. 1: 6977
Long and Jacques Thibaud International Competition; Marguerite   Vol. 2: 6085
Long Distance Running Merit Award   Vol. 1: 19945
Long Employment Award; Wilburn H.   Vol. 1: 6407
Long et Jacques Thibaud; Concours International Marguerite   Vol. 2: 6085
Long Memorial Prize; Birch Burdette   Vol. 1: 5230
Long Poem Prize   Vol. 1: 12018
The Long Range Planning Award   Vol. 2: 4495
Long-Service Medal   Vol. 2: 4044
Longacre Award; Raymond F.   Vol. 1: 170
Longfellow Award   Vol. 1: 1796
Longford Award; Raymond   Vol. 2: 223
Longo Prize; David W.   Vol. 1: 11983
Longstaff Medal   Vol. 2: 4206
Longstreth Medal; Edward   Vol. 1: 9385
Lopes do Rego; Premio Abilio   Vol. 2: 10250
Lopes Medal; Pepe   Vol. 2: 5158
Lopes of Ameida Prize; Julia   Vol. 2: 1425
Lopez Award; Coronel Medico Jorge Esguerra   Vol. 2: 1708
Lopez Community Service Award in New York; Diego   Vol. 1: 10049
Lopez; Premio Ricardo Monge   Vol. 2: 9289
Lopez Prize; Lucio V.   Vol. 2: 85
Loraine Award for Nature Conservation   Vol. 2: 4472
Lorax Award   Vol. 1: 9621
Lord - Chaim Essay Contest Award   Vol. 1: 9217
Lord Derby's Knowsley Safari Park Tournament   Vol. 2: 3808
Lord Kings Norton Prize in Economics   Vol. 2: 2700
Lord Memorial Medal; Clive   Vol. 2: 635
Lord Prize; Walter Frewen   Vol. 2: 3998
Lorentz Medal   Vol. 2: 9602
Lorenz Memorial Medal; Frederick A.   Vol. 1: 18480
Lorenz Research Award; Walter   Vol. 1: 1705
Lorgna; Premio Anton Mario   Vol. 2: 8380
Lorimer Memorial Award; Sir Robert   Vol. 2: 10612
Lortel Award; Lucille   Vol. 1: 11941
Lortie; Prix Leon-   Vol. 1: 17387
Los Angeles Dramatists Award   Vol. 1: 14616
Los Angeles Film Critics Achievement Awards   Vol. 1: 11947
Los Angeles International Animation Celebration   Vol. 1: 5171
Los Angeles Times Book Prizes   Vol. 1: 11949

Losana Gold Medal; Luigi   Vol. 2: 8129
Loschimidt Prize; Josepf   Vol. 2: 4207
Losey Atmospheric Science Award; AIAA   Vol. 1: 2480
Losey Award; Robert M.   Vol. 1: 2480
Lothar-Preis; Kaiser-   Vol. 2: 6725
Lotus Decoration   Vol. 2: 7554
Lotz Commemorative Medal; John   Vol. 2: 7420
Lotz Janos Emlekerem   Vol. 2: 7420
Louie Awards   Vol. 1: 9724
Louis Award; Joe   Vol. 1: 18428
Louis E. Levy Medal and Lionel F. Levy Stipend   Vol. 1: 9384
Louisiana Literary Award   Vol. 1: 11956
Louisiana State University Short Fiction Award; *The Southern Review*/   Vol. 1: 18239
Louisville Grawemeyer Award in Religion   Vol. 1: 19814
Lounsbery Award; Richard   Vol. 1: 12672
Lounsbery; Prix Fondation Richard   Vol. 2: 4789
Lounsbery; Prix Richard   Vol. 2: 5705
Loup de Bronze   Vol. 2: 11982
Love Creek Mini Festival   Vol. 1: 11965
Love Creek Short Play Festival   Vol. 1: 11966
Love Prize in History; Walter D.   Vol. 1: 15403
Love Token Society Exhibit Award   Vol. 1: 3238
Lovejoy Award; Elijah Parish
 Colby College   Vol. 1: 7860
 Southern Illinois University at Carbondale - School of Journalism   Vol 1: 18224
Lovelace Award; Augusta Ada   Vol. 1: 5656
Lovelace II Award; W. Randolph   Vol. 1: 1260
Loveland Memorial Award; Edward R.   Vol. 1: 1718
Lovell Memorial Aprilia Trophy; Reuben   Vol. 2: 3533
Lovenmedaljen   Vol. 2: 11547
Low and Moderate Income Housing Awards Program   Vol. 1: 2540
Low Memorial Engineering Fellowship; Dr. George M.   Vol. 1: 14837
Low Space Transportation Award; AIAA George M.   Vol. 1: 2469
Low Trophy; George M.   Vol. 1: 12740
Lowe Memorial Award; Emily   Vol. 1: 5053
Lowell Award; Ralph   Vol. 1: 8281
Lowell Poetry Travelling Scholarship; Amy   Vol. 1: 7644
Lowell Prize; James Russell   Vol. 1: 12395
Lowenfeld Award   Vol. 1: 12798
Lowenheim Memorial Award; Frederick A.   Vol. 1: 6062
Lower Austria Prize for the Advancement of Fine Arts and Literature   Vol. 2: 859
Lower Austria Prize of Honor   Vol. 2: 862
Lower Austria Recognition Prize in Arts and Sciences   Vol. 2: 860
Lowery Memorial Award; Louis R.   Vol. 1: 19437
Lowi Award; Theodore   Vol. 1: 16306
Lowin Compostition Awards; Paul   Vol. 2: 146
Lowin Orchestral Prize; Paul   Vol. 2: 517
Lowin Song Cycle Prize; Paul   Vol. 2: 518
Lowman Award; Edward W.   Vol. 1: 1809
Lowry Award; SCN Elizabeth   Vol. 1: 20597
Lowry Memorial Award in Fossil Energy; Homer H.   Vol. 1: 19233
Lowry; Premio Internacional de Ensayo Literario Malcolm   Vol. 2: 9226
Lowther Memorial Award; Pat   Vol. 1: 11814
Loyalty Award
 National Republican Heritage Groups (Nationalities) Council   Vol. 1: 14618

 Pi Kappa Alpha Education Foundation   Vol 1: 16179
Loyalty Cup Award   Vol. 1: 14260
Loyola Camellia   Vol. 1: 11971
LPGA Hall of Fame   Vol. 1: 11760
LRA Labor Award   Vol. 1: 11747
LTA Colours and Badges   Vol. 2: 3541
LTA International Award   Vol. 2: 3541
Lubalin Award; Herb   Vol. 1: 18014
Lubatti Award; Eugenio   Vol. 2: 8130
Lubberhuizen prijs; Geertjan   Vol. 2: 9676
Lubell Memorial Award; Jeannette and Samuel L.   Vol. 2: 7983
Luby Senior Distinguished Service Award; Mort   Vol. 1: 6502
Lucarelli International Competition for Solo Oboe Players   Vol. 1: 15570
Lucas Automotive Electronic Engineering Award; Oliver   Vol. 2: 3293
Lucas Gold Medal; Anthony F.
 American Institute of Mining, Metallurgical and Petroleum Engineers   Vol. 1: 2637
 Society of Petroleum Engineers   Vol 1: 17970
Lucas Landscape Award; Homer   Vol. 1: 15163
Lucas Memorial Award; Tad   Vol. 1: 16878
Lucas Trophy   Vol. 1: 14645
Lucille Award; B. B. King   Vol. 1: 6415
Luck and Pluck Award   Vol. 1: 309
Luck Award; James Murray   Vol. 1: 12678
Ludington Memorial Award; Jeremiah   Vol. 1: 8855
Lueg Commemoration Medal; Carl   Vol. 2: 6812
Lueg-Denkmunze; Carl-   Vol. 2: 6812
Lueshen Harris' Sparrow Endowment; Willetta   Vol. 1: 10194
Lueshen Student Membership Award; Willetta   Vol. 1: 10195
Luff Awards   Vol. 1: 3413
Lugli; Fondazione Giuseppe   Vol. 2: 8058
Luikov Medal   Vol. 2: 10711
Luke Award; Hugh J.   Vol. 1: 16362
Lulu Awards   Vol. 1: 9047
Lum Award; Louise and Y. T.   Vol. 1: 5194
Lum Award; Louise L. and Y. T.   Vol. 1: 10440
Lumen Award Program   Vol. 1: 10089
Lumen Christi Award   Vol. 1: 7359
Luminas Awards   Vol. 1: 20385
Luna Foreign Scholarship; Lee G.   Vol. 1: 14751
Lund Award; A. J. (Jack)   Vol. 1: 10868
Lund Public Service Award; PRSA Paul M.   Vol. 1: 16575
Lundell-Bright Memorial Award   Vol. 1: 6063
Lupi Prize   Vol. 2: 10304
Lush Award; J. L.   Vol. 1: 1914
Lush Biomedical Postgraduate Scholarships; Dora   Vol. 2: 541
Lutaud; Fondation Leon   Vol. 2: 5618
Lutheran Educator of the Year   Vol. 1: 11977
Lutoslawski International Composers Competition; Witold   Vol. 2: 10214
Lutzeier Memorial Award (Founders Award); Paul   Vol. 1: 8624
Lyautey; Prix Marechal   Vol. 2: 6140
Lybrand Medal Awards   Vol. 1: 10389
Lydecken - palkinto   Vol. 2: 4667
Lydecken prize   Vol. 2: 4667
Lyell Medal   Vol. 2: 2924
Lyle Medal; Thomas Ranken   Vol. 2: 176
Lyman Award; AWA Lauren D.   Vol. 1: 6190
Lyman Award; Robert J.   Vol. 1: 16373
Lyman Book Awards; John   Vol. 1: 15447

Lynch-Staunton Awards; Victor Martyn   Vol. 1: 6743
Lynen Research Fellowships; Feodor   Vol. 2: 7158
Lyon-Caen; Prix Charles   Vol. 2: 5725
Lyon Memorial Award; James P.   Vol. 1: 8794
Lyons Award; Louis M.   Vol. 1: 9815
Lyons Award; Sir William   Vol. 2: 2972
Lyons Memorial Award; Ronald D.   Vol. 1: 19438
Lyr; Prix Rene   Vol. 2: 1044
Lyra Literary Prize; Carmen   Vol. 2: 1768
The Lyric Annual Awards   Vol. 1: 11983
The Lyric Memorial Prize   Vol. 1: 11983
Lysakowski Scientific Prize; Adam   Vol. 2: 10154
Lyster Award; Theodore C.   Vol. 1: 171
Lyttel Lily Cup   Vol. 2: 4045
Lyttel Trophy   Vol. 2: 2058
M. E. R. Prize   Vol. 2: 11114
M. E. R.-prys   Vol. 2: 11114
M-Net Vita Film Award   Vol. 2: 10814
MAA Activities Award   Vol. 1: 12137
Maas Achievement Award; Major General Melvin J.   Vol. 1: 6408
Maberley Memorial Scholarships; Charles Thomas Astley   Vol. 2: 11129
Mabingwa wa Kiswahili   Vol. 2: 12013
"Mac Tools" SCCA Mechanic of the Year   Vol. 1: 18406
MACA Cup; Fort Adams/   Vol. 1: 12321
MacAllister Awards for Opera Singers   Vol. 1: 10149
MacArthur Award for Outstanding New Play; Charles   Vol. 1: 20133
MacArthur Award; Robert H.   Vol. 1: 8817
MacArthur Bowl Award   Vol. 1: 13993
MacArthur Fellows   Vol. 1: 11987
MacArthur Fellowship; Charles   Vol. 1: 14477
MacArthur Prize Fellows   Vol. 1: 11987
Macaulay Fellowship   Vol. 2: 7760
Macbeth Award   Vol. 1: 10524
MacBride Award; Van Dyk   Vol. 1: 8109
Maccabee Award   Vol. 1: 6525
MacColl Award; Hugh   Vol. 2: 2400
Macdonald; Le Prix Sir John   Vol. 1: 6908
Macdonald Medal; George   Vol. 2: 4279
MacDonald Memorial Award; Thomas H.   Vol. 1: 1203
MacDonald Outstanding Young Electrical Engineering Professor Award; C. Holmes   Vol. 1: 9006
Macdonald Prize; Sir John A.   Vol. 1: 6908
Macdougall Medal   Vol. 2: 7173
MacDowell Medal; Edward   Vol. 1: 11990
Mace; Prix Jean   Vol. 2: 6083
MacEachern Awards   Vol. 1: 16579
Macelwane Annual Awards in Meteorology; Father James B.   Vol. 1: 3090
Macelwane Medal; James B.   Vol. 1: 2168
MacFarland Award; Douglas   Vol. 1: 5491
Machado Award; Angie   Vol. 1: 7511
Machado de Assis Prize   Vol. 2: 1426
Machado Prize for Essay; Antonio   Vol. 2: 1723
Machine Design Award   Vol. 1: 4688
Machinery Award Scheme   Vol. 2: 3922
Macinnis Award; John   Vol. 1: 2310
MacIntosh Award   Vol. 1: 9787
Mackay Award; Roland P.   Vol. 1: 618
Mackay Medal; Donald   Vol. 2: 4280
Mackay Memorial Prize; Jessie   Vol. 2: 9780
Mackay Trophy   Vol. 1: 12725
MacKellar Award   Vol. 2: 3990
MacKeller Award; Lillian   Vol. 1: 19638
MacKenzie Award; Agnes Mure   Vol. 2: 10655

MacKenzie Award for Investigative Journalism; Angus   Vol. 1: 12153
MacKenzie Book Prize; W. J. M.   Vol. 2: 7861
Mackenzie Junner Rose-Bowl Trophy   Vol. 2: 3208
Mackie Awards; Howard,   Vol. 1: 6974
Mackie Medal   Vol. 2: 189
Maclaren Travelling Fellowship; RIAS/John   Vol. 1: 10615
Maclay Memorial Prize; James Archibald   Vol. 2: 3321
MacLean Award; Angus H.   Vol. 1: 18890
MacLean Citation   Vol. 2: 9738
MacLean International Fellowship; IFUW Ida Smedley   Vol. 2: 11789
MacLeod prijs   Vol. 2: 1258
MacMillan Awards; Sir Ernest   Vol. 1: 17821
MacMillan Memorial Prize in Choral Conducting; Sir Ernest   Vol. 1: 6744
Macmillan Prize for a Children's Picture Book   Vol. 2: 3757
Macmillan - SABR Baseball Research Awards   Vol. 1: 17411
Macmillan Silver Pen Award for Fiction   Vol. 2: 2783
Macnab Medal   Vol. 2: 3224
Macoun Conservationist Award; John   Vol. 1: 7038
MacPhail Trophy; Larry   Vol. 1: 13244
MacQuarie Award; Lachlan   Vol. 2: 609
MacRobert Award   Vol. 2: 3875
Macromolecular Science and Engineering Lecture Award   Vol. 1: 7553
Macuilxochitl Prize   Vol. 2: 8926
MacVicar Outstanding Nurse Executive Award; Jean   Vol. 1: 14286
Macworld World Class Awards   Vol. 1: 15999
Madarali Prize; Fikret   Vol. 2: 12073
Maddison Prize   Vol. 2: 4461
"Made in Colorado" Excellence Award   Vol. 1: 12042
Madersperger; Tiroler Erfinderpreis Josef   Vol. 2: 731
Madgearu Prize; Virgil   Vol. 2: 10363
Madigan Award; John J.   Vol. 1: 6064
Madison Award; Dolley   Vol. 1: 20636
Madison Award for Distinguished Public Service; James   Vol. 1: 5099
Madison Award; James
   American Political Science Association   Vol. 1: 3579
   Coalition on Government Information   Vol 1: 7855
   National Broadcast Editorial Association   Vol 1: 13476
Madison Constitution Heritage Award; James   Vol. 1: 14936
Madison Medal; James   Vol. 1: 16405
Madison Prize; James   Vol. 1: 17476
Madsen Medal; John   Vol. 2: 472
Madzsar Award; Jozsef   Vol. 2: 7302
Maeda Prize   Vol. 2: 8602
Maerskline UK Prize   Vol. 2: 3098
Maganini Award in Composition; Quinto   Vol. 1: 15535
Magazine and Bookseller Best Book Cover   Vol. 1: 11996
Magazine and Bookseller Best Newsstand Covers   Vol. 1: 11997
Magazine Merit Awards   Vol. 1: 17812
Magazine Photographer of the Year
   National Press Photographers Association   Vol. 1: 14525
   University of Missouri-Columbia - School of Journalism   Vol 1: 19844
Magazine Picture Editing Award   Vol. 1: 19844

Magazine Suppliers' Man of the Year; *Quick Printing*   Vol. 1: 16628
MAGB Malting Diploma   Vol. 2: 3625
Magellanic Premium Award   Vol. 1: 3435
Magen Ha'sar   Vol. 2: 7911
Magge Award   Vol. 1: 8694
Maggid Award   Vol. 1: 2749
Magical Folklore of Choco Prize   Vol. 2: 1658
Magill Distinguished Service Award; Arthur Napier   Vol. 1: 7061
Magna Charta Day Award   Vol. 1: 6274
Magnani; Premio Anna   Vol. 2: 8122
Magnel Prize   Vol. 2: 1362
Magnes Award; Judah L.   Vol. 1: 2120
Magnolia Prize   Vol. 2: 1576
Magnussen Award; Ann   Vol. 1: 3921
Magnusson Memorial Prize; Bengt   Vol. 2: 3370
Magny; Prix Adrien Constantin de   Vol. 2: 5682
Magon National Prize of Culture   Vol. 2: 1763
Magrassi; Fondazione Guido Lenghi e Flaviano   Vol. 2: 8060
Magruder Award for Museology (Museum Displays)   Vol. 1: 12084
Magsaysay Awards; Ramon   Vol. 2: 10042
Maguire Award (Enlisted Aviation Safety Award); James   Vol. 1: 12062
Magyar Elektrotechnikai Egyesulet Mtezs   Vol. 2: 7335
Magyar Konyvtarosok Egyesuleteert Emlekerem   Vol. 2: 7294
Magyar Televizio Nemzetkozi Karmesterversenye   Vol. 2: 7415
Maha Vir Chakra   Vol. 2: 7553
Mahaim; Fondation Ernest   Vol. 2: 975
Mahalanobis Medal; P. C.   Vol. 2: 7656
Maharam Theatrical Design Awards   Vol. 1: 4901
Maheshwari Memorial Lecture Award; Prof. Panchanan   Vol. 2: 7657
Mahler Medaille; Gustav   Vol. 2: 832
Mahler Medal; Gustav   Vol. 2: 832
Mahnke Film Production Award; Carl F. and Viola V.   Vol. 1: 5514
Mahoney Award; Mary   Vol. 1: 3284
Mahyer; Prix Jules   Vol. 2: 5679
Mai Service Award; Ludwig   Vol. 1: 5599
The Mail on Sunday - John Llewellyn Rhys Prize   Vol. 2: 2201
Mail System Management Hall of Fame   Vol. 1: 12016
Mailing Industry Ingenuity Award   Vol. 1: 12010
Mailly; Prix Edouard   Vol. 2: 1018
Maimonides Award   Vol. 1: 5181
Main Awards; Charles T.   Vol. 1: 4689
Mainichi Newspaper Prize   Vol. 2: 8727
Maintenance/Avionics Technician Safety Award   Vol. 1: 13498
Maiquez; Premio Isidoro   Vol. 2: 11279
Maisons solaires, maisons d'aujourd'hui   Vol. 2: 5046
Majerova Award; Marie   Vol. 2: 1841
Majewska Medal; Pelagia   Vol. 2: 5159
Major Awgie Award   Vol. 2: 283
Major League All-Star Team   Vol. 1: 18349
Major League Baseball Player of the Year   Vol. 1: 18360
Major League Executive of the Year   Vol. 1: 18361
Major League Manager of the Year   Vol. 1: 18362
Major League Pennant Winner   Vol. 1: 8033
Major Victory Award   Vol. 1: 14029
Majorana Prize   Vol. 2: 8289
MakDougall-Brisbane Prize   Vol. 2: 10646

Make-Up Competition   Vol. 1: 180
Makeup and Design Award   Vol. 1: 10203
Making the Difference   Vol. 2: 536
Makki Al Juma International Cancer Prize; Hussain   Vol. 2: 11861
Maksymczuk Award; Julian   Vol. 1: 18856
Malaga International Week of Author Films   Vol. 2: 11303
Malamud Memorial Award; PEN/   Vol. 1: 16040
Malan Medal; D. F.   Vol. 2: 10997
Malan Prize; Recht   Vol. 2: 11115
Malan-prys; Recht   Vol. 2: 11115
Malaysian Literary Prize   Vol. 2: 8904
Malcuzynski Award; Karol   Vol. 2: 10207
Male Athlete of the Year   Vol. 1: 19519
Male Style Maker of the Year   Vol. 1: 13677
Malewitsch Medaille; Black Panel   Vol. 2: 6571
Malheiros; Premio Artur   Vol. 2: 10255
Malheiros; Premio Ricardo   Vol. 2: 10256
Malheiros Prize; Artur   Vol. 2: 10255
Malheiros Prize; Ricardo   Vol. 2: 10256
Malina - *Leonardo* Prize; Frank J.   Vol. 1: 11267
Malkin Prize; Harold   Vol. 2: 3957
Malko International Competition for Young Conductors; Nicolai   Vol. 2: 1982
Mallett Award for Best Acting Performance in Radio; Jane   Vol. 1: 327
Mallett - Lamp of Knowledge Award; Dr. Marshall   Vol. 1: 6785
Mallett Student Plaque; Dr. M.   Vol. 1: 6786
Mallinckrodt Award of Excellence   Vol. 1: 6787
Mallinckrodt Research and Development Fellowship   Vol. 1: 17948
Mallory Cup; U.S. Men's Sailing Championship - Clifford D.   Vol. 1: 19539
Mallory/Volunteer of the Year Award; James L. and Lavon Madden   Vol. 1: 13871
Malloy Award; Margaret   Vol. 1: 15526
Malone Faculty Fellows Program in Arab and Islamic Studies; Joseph J.   Vol. 1: 13825
Malone Memorial Diving Award; Mike   Vol. 1: 19319
Malone Post-Doctoral Fellows Program; Joseph J.   Vol. 1: 13825
Malpertuis Prize   Vol. 2: 1288
Malpighi Prize   Vol. 2: 2846
Maltby Trophy; John   Vol. 2: 3534
Malusardi; Premio F.   Vol. 2: 8353
MAMA Awards   Vol. 1: 12153
Mamaroneck Artists Guild National Open Juried Exhibition   Vol. 1: 12022
Mambembe Trophy   Vol. 2: 1434
Mamer Fellowship; Lyle   Vol. 1: 8879
Mamou Award; Azar Kalbache and Zahara Ben   Vol. 1: 11179
Mamoulian Award; Rouben   Vol. 2: 687
Man for Mankind Awards   Vol. 2: 938
MAN National Science Prize   Vol. 2: 9865
Man of the Year
    Federation of Fly Fishers   Vol. 1: 9111
    Financial World   Vol 1: 9213
    The Hockey News   Vol 1: 9960
    InterNational Electrical Testing Association   Vol 1: 10923
    International Fire Photographers Association   Vol 1: 10978
    International Road Federation   Vol 1: 11206
    Society of the Plastics Industry   Vol 1: 18050
    United Hellenic Voters of America   Vol 1: 18917

Man of the Year Award
    Brazilian-American Chamber of Commerce   Vol. 1: 6549
    Frozen Food Association of New England   Vol 1: 9439
    National Association of Jewelry Appraisers   Vol 1: 13184
    Society of Philatelists and Numismatists   Vol 1: 17979
Man of the Year in Law Enforcement   Vol. 1: 17993
Man of the Year in Travel   Vol. 1: 18800
Man of the Year Peace Award   Vol. 1: 16006
Man or Woman of the Year
    Association for Children with Retarded Mental Development   Vol. 1: 5463
    Cancer Federation   Vol 1: 7277
    Hollywood Radio and Television Society   Vol 1: 9977
Man or Woman of the Year Award in Advertising   Vol. 1: 9977
Man Sing Prize   Vol. 2: 3627
Man/Woman of the Year   Vol. 1: 7717
Man/Woman of Vision   Vol. 1: 9035
Management Achievement Award
    American College of Medical Practice Executives   Vol. 1: 1671
    Association of Retail Marketing Services   Vol 1: 5941
    National Telephone Cooperative Association   Vol 1: 14891
    Professional Services Management Association   Vol 1: 16517
Management Award   Vol. 1: 5295
Management Effectiveness Awards   Vol. 1: 3992
Management Expert   Vol. 2: 7711
Management Innovation Award
    American College of Medical Practice Executives   Vol. 1: 1674
    International City Management Association   Vol. 1: 10851
Management Innovation Poster Session Award   Vol. 1: 1664
Manager Award   Vol. 1: 8906
Manager of the Year
    International Veteran Boxers Association   Vol. 1: 11385
    Self Storage Association   Vol 1: 17189
    System Safety Society   Vol 1: 18560
Manager of the Year Award
    Baseball Writers Association of America   Vol. 1: 6281
    Mail Systems Management Association   Vol 1: 12015
Manby Premium   Vol. 2: 3250
Mancini; Prix   Vol. 2: 11751
Mandat des Poetes   Vol. 2: 6108
Mande; Prix Aimee et Raymond   Vol. 2: 4807
Manenti Prize; Bruno   Vol. 2: 8168
Mangold Award; Walter S.   Vol. 1: 13909
Manhattan College De La Salle Medal   Vol. 1: 12026
Manhattan College Pacem in Terris Medal   Vol. 1: 12027
Manhattan Institute Fellowships   Vol. 1: 12032
Manifestation Internationale de Video et de Television de Montbeliard   Vol. 2: 6070
Manila International Exhibition of Photography   Vol. 2: 10044
Manly Memorial Medal; Charles M.   Vol. 1: 17767
Mann Citation; Margaret   Vol. 1: 2850
Mann Founder's Award; Marty   Vol. 1: 13791
Mann Guardian Award; Horace   Vol. 1: 12034
Mann Prize; The John   Vol. 2: 10561
Mann Prize; Thomas   Vol. 2: 7038

Mannheim Award; Herman   Vol. 1: 10833
Mannheim International Filmweek   Vol. 2: 6954
Mannich Medal; Carl   Vol. 2: 6823
Manning Award; Robert E.   Vol. 1: 8997
Manning Awards   Vol. 1: 12036
Mano; Bourses Guy Levis   Vol. 2: 4954
Manpower Society Essay Competition   Vol. 2: 3629
Mansel-Pleydell and Cecil Trusts   Vol. 2: 2749
Mansfield and Bank of New Zealand Short Story Award; Katherine   Vol. 2: 9774
Mansfield Award; Bank of New Zealand Katharine   Vol. 2: 9774
Mansfield Memorial Fellowship; Katherine   Vol. 2: 9800
Manson Medal   Vol. 2: 4281
Manton Prize; Irene   Vol. 2: 3588
Manu Daula Frigate Bird Award   Vol. 2: 578
Manufacturer Member of the Year
    Awards and Recognition Association   Vol. 1: 6209
    National Business Forms Association   Vol 1: 13508
Manufacturer of the Year
    International Society of Pharmaceutical Engineers   Vol. 1: 11292
    Wholesale Stationers' Association   Vol 1: 20276
Manufacturers' Hall of Fame   Vol. 1: 6204
Manufacturers Hanover Art/World Awards for Distinguished Newspaper Art Criticism   Vol. 1: 7533
Manufacturing Prize   Vol. 2: 3294
Manulife Bank of Canada Cash Award   Vol. 1: 11803
Manuscript Award
    International Lactation Consultant Association   Vol. 1: 11067
    Abraham Lincoln Association   Vol 1: 11882
    Phi Alpha Theta   Vol 1: 16095
Manzelli Prize; Art   Vol. 2: 5083
Manzullo; Premio Fundacion   Vol. 2: 11
Maple Leaf Award
    International Federation of Purchasing and Materials Management   Vol. 2: 9505
    Tourism Industry Association of Canada   Vol 1: 18768
Maple/Longman Memorial Travel Grant; Robert   Vol. 1: 18590
Mara Memorial CYO Sportsman of the Year Award; John V.   Vol. 1: 7406
Marais Prize; Eugene   Vol. 2: 10998
Marcel; Prix Amelie   Vol. 2: 4808
Marcel; Prix Jean-Etienne   Vol. 2: 4848
Marceneiro de Fado; Premio Municipal Alfredo   Vol. 2: 10265
Marchal; Prix Joseph-Edmond   Vol. 2: 962
Marchig Animal Welfare Award   Vol. 2: 4633
Marciano Memorial Award; Rocky   Vol. 1: 8715
Marckwardt Travel Grants; Albert H.   Vol. 1: 18591
Marconi Award; Guglielmo   Vol. 1: 15798
Marconi International Fellowship   Vol. 1: 12046
Marconi Memorial Gold Medal of Service   Vol. 1: 20001
Marconi Memorial Scroll of Honor   Vol. 1: 20002
Marconi; Premio AEI Guglielmo   Vol. 2: 8348
Marconi; Premio Guillermo   Vol. 2: 11292
Marconi Premium   Vol. 2: 3273
Marconi Radio Awards   Vol. 1: 12978

Marcorelles; Prix Louis   Vol. 2: 5032
Marcorelli; Premio Cesare   Vol. 2: 8282
Marcus Award; Colonel Mickey   Vol. 1: 11575
Marcus Award for Book Design; Stanley   Vol. 1: 18651
Mardel Prize; Julio   Vol. 2: 10305
Mares; Premio Nacional de Literatura Jose Fuentes   Vol. 2: 9292
Marescalchi; Premio A.   Vol. 2: 8042
Marett Award; H. B.   Vol. 1: 13168
Margaret P. Esmond Memorial Scholarship   Vol. 1: 7626
Margolin Prizes for Distinguished Business Reporting; Morton   Vol. 1: 19786
Marguerite de la Charlonie; Fondation Paul   Vol. 2: 5647
Mari; Premio Luigi   Vol. 2: 8282
Mari; Premio Maria Teresa Messori Roncaglia and Eugenio   Vol. 2: 8077
Maria; Premio Especial Antonio   Vol. 2: 1471
Maria Special Award; Antonio   Vol. 2: 1471
Marian Library Award   Vol. 1: 19783
Marian Prize; Simion Florea   Vol. 2: 10364
Marianist Award   Vol. 1: 19784
Marianne d'Or   Vol. 2: 6099
Marie Antoinette Award for Community Consciousness   Vol. 1: 9481
Marigold City USA   Vol. 1: 12048
Marimo; Prix Zerilli   Vol. 2: 5797
Marimolin Composition Contest   Vol. 1: 12050
Marin; Prix de M. et Mme. Louis   Vol. 2: 5837
Marin; Prix de Monsieur et Madame Louis   Vol. 2: 6141
Marin; Prix Louis   Vol. 2: 5776
Marine Accessory Representative of the Year   Vol. 1: 14339
Marine Aerial Refueler Squadron of the Year (Henry Wildfang Award)   Vol. 1: 12063
Marine Air Command and Control Officer of the Year   Vol. 1: 12064
Marine Aircrewman (Fixed-Wing) of the Year   Vol. 1: 12065
Marine Aircrewman (Helicopter) of the Year   Vol. 1: 12066
Marine Aviation Electronic Technician of the Year   Vol. 1: 12067
Marine Aviation Ground Officer of the Year   Vol. 1: 12068
Marine Aviation Logistics Squadron of the Year   Vol. 1: 12069
Marine Aviator of the Year   Vol. 1: 12058
Marine Corps Essay Contest   Vol. 1: 19464
Marine Corps Expeditionary Medal   Vol. 1: 19168
Marine Education Award   Vol. 1: 14330
Marine Flight Officer of the Year   Vol. 1: 12074
Marine Plane Captain of the Year   Vol. 1: 12070
Marine Wing Support Squadron of the Year   Vol. 1: 12071
Mariner's Rosette   Vol. 1: 18977
Marinescu Prize; Gheorghe   Vol. 2: 10365
Mariological Award   Vol. 1: 12093
Marion Laboratories Print Media Festival; HeSCA/   Vol. 1: 9854
Marion Merrell Dow, Inc. Postdoctoral Fellowship in Nosocomial/Gram Positive Infection Research and Training; NFID -   Vol. 1: 14044
Marion; Prix Seraphin-   Vol. 1: 17392
Maritime Heritage Award Medal   Vol. 2: 4628
Mariucci Award; John   Vol. 1: 2311
Mark Award; William B.   Vol. 1: 4183
Mark Boxer Award   Vol. 2: 3772
Mark Memorial Award; Peter   Vol. 1: 4963
Mark of Excellence Awards   Vol. 1: 17999

Market Development and Promotion Council Awards   Vol. 1: 15335
Market Manager of the Year   Vol. 1: 13241
Marketer of the Year
   American Marketing Association   Vol. 1: 2988
   Biomedical Marketing Association   Vol 1: 6384
Marketing Achievement   Vol. 1: 14892
Marketing Achievement Awards   Vol. 1: 14536
Marketing Award
   American Kinesiotherapy Association   Vol. 1: 2773
   National Cable Television Association   Vol 1: 13515
Marketing Bestsellers Annual Magazine Cover Awards   Vol. 1: 11997
Marketing Competition   Vol. 1: 9197
Marketing Division Hall of Fame Award   Vol. 1: 2593
Marketing Excellence Awards   Vol. 1: 12095
Marketing Executive of the Year   Vol. 1: 12716
Marketing Man of the Year   Vol. 1: 12716
Marketing Man/Woman of the Year Award   Vol. 2: 10878
Marketing Methods Competition   Vol. 1: 16493
Marketing Motivation Awards   Vol. 1: 5829
Marketing Person of the Year and Marketing Firm of the Year   Vol. 1: 2989
Marketing Services Award of Excellence   Vol. 1: 8884
Marketing Statesman of the Year Award   Vol. 1: 17010
Markham Memorial Prize; Arthur   Vol. 2: 4585
Markham Poetry Prize; Edwin   Vol. 1: 8559
Markon Prize; Robert   Vol. 1: 11591
Markowe Public Education Prize; Morris   Vol. 2: 3964
Marks Award; Louis B.   Vol. 1: 10090
Marks of Excellence Award   Vol. 1: 14034
Markwardt Award; L. J.   Vol. 1: 6065
Markwardt Wood Engineering Award; L. J.   Vol. 1: 9333
Marlboro Million   Vol. 1: 7516
Marlow Medal and Prize   Vol. 2: 4208
Marlowe Award   Vol. 2: 4429
Marlowe Award; Donald E.   Vol. 1: 4098
Marmier; Prix Xavier   Vol. 2: 5930
Marmottan; Fondation   Vol. 2: 5388
Marmottan; Prix Paul   Vol. 2: 5419
Marotta; Medagila Domenico   Vol. 2: 8336
Marotta; Premio Domenico   Vol. 2: 8381
Marquee Award   Vol. 1: 18685
Marquis Memorial Award; John E.   Vol. 1: 1466
Marra Award; George G.   Vol. 1: 18107
Marraro Prize; Helen and Howard R.   Vol. 1: 17546
Marraro Prize; Howard R.
   American Catholic Historical Association   Vol. 1: 1432
   Modern Language Association of America   Vol 1: 12396
Marraro Prizes in Italian History; Helen and Howard R.   Vol. 1: 2297
Marriott Corporation Health Care Services Charles U. Letourneau Student Research Paper of the Year Award   Vol. 1: 599
Marriott President's Award; Phyllis B.   Vol. 1: 3140
Marrs Plaques; Lieutenant Theodore C.   Vol. 1: 5286
Marsalis Scholarship; Wynton   Vol. 1: 8800

Marschall - Rhone - Poulenc International Dairy Science Award   Vol. 1: 1915
Marsden Award; Charles P.   Vol. 1: 6066
Marsden Medal for Outstanding Service to Science; Sir Ernest   Vol. 2: 9752
Marsden Professional Award; T.B.   Vol. 2: 3141
Marsh & McLennan Student Paper Awards   Vol. 1: 4786
Marsh Award; Alan   Vol. 2: 3895
Marsh Distinguished Service Award; Burton W.   Vol. 1: 10453
Marsh Graduate Fellowship; Burton W.   Vol. 1: 10454
Marsh Medal; Alan   Vol. 2: 3896
Marsh Memorial Award; Irving T.   Vol. 1: 8793
Marsh Memorial Prize; James R.   Vol. 1: 10062
Marsh Safety Award; William O.   Vol. 1: 12751
Marsh Trophy; Stan Lomax - Irving T.   Vol. 1: 12240
Marshall Award; FAW Alan   Vol. 2: 379
Marshall Award in Musical Theatre; David B.   Vol. 1: 19896
Marshall Award; Louis   Vol. 1: 11569
Marshall Award; Robert   Vol. 1: 20293
Marshall Black Education Fund Educational Achievement Award; Thurgood   Vol. 1: 11594
Marshall Medal; George Catlett   Vol. 1: 5983
Marshall Prize for Children's Literature; Diabetes Australia Alan   Vol. 2: 149
Marshall/*The Nation* Prize for Poetry; Lenore   Vol. 1: 15171
Marshall Trophy; C. Herbert   Vol. 1: 16214
Marsteller Memorial Scholarship; Robert   Vol. 1: 11369
Marti-Ibanez Book Prize; Felix   Vol. 1: 12151
Martin Award; Allie Beth   Vol. 1: 2930
Martin Award; J. J.   Vol. 1: 4099
Martin Fellowships; C. J.   Vol. 2: 542
Martin Foundation Prize; Quinquela   Vol. 2: 49
Martin Medal; Orel F.   Vol. 1: 1710
Martin Medallion Recipient; E. O.   Vol. 1: 1097
Martin Memorial Award; Eric W.   Vol. 1: 3060
Martin Memorial Foundation Faculty Fellowship; Franklin H.   Vol. 1: 1748
Martin Memorial Scholarship; George C.   Vol. 2: 10903
Martin Outstanding Younger Member Award; John   Vol. 1: 10328
Martin; Prix Marie-Eugene Simon Henri   Vol. 2: 5893
Martin - Scofield Award   Vol. 1: 13141
Martin Short Story Award; Willie Lee   Vol. 1: 474
Martin Trophy; Dr. Beattie   Vol. 1: 6881
Martin Trophy; Harold Douglass   Vol. 1: 16214
Martinez-Marquez Journalism Award; Guillermo   Vol. 1: 13130
Martino Award; John O.   Vol. 1: 6503
Martonik Prize; Ladislav   Vol. 2: 10774
Martorell; Premi Artur   Vol. 2: 11172
Marvin Award; C. Raymond   Vol. 1: 12936
Marvin Grant; Walter Rumsey
   Ohioana Library Association   Vol. 1: 15601
   Thomas Wolfe Society   Vol 1: 20353
Marvin Kansas News Enterprise Award; Burton W.   Vol. 1: 20260
Marwah Award; Prof. Surindar Mohan   Vol. 2: 7594

Marx Memorial Scholarship; Ellie Vol. 2: 11088
Maryland Cup Vol. 1: 5281
Marzocco d'Ora Vol. 2: 8239
MASA President's Plaque Vol. 1: 12011
Maschler Award; Emil Kurt Vol. 2: 2202
Maschler Award; Kurt Vol. 2: 2202
Mascot National Award Vol. 2: 7496
Masefield Memorial Award; John Vol. 1: 16290
Mashtots Award; Mesrop Vol. 2: 112
Masliansky Award; Zvi Hirsch Vol. 1: 9879
Mason Award; Jack Vol. 1: 12052
Mason Memorial Award; Karl Vol. 1: 16042
Mason Playwrights Award; *The Dominion Sunday Times* Bruce Vol. 2: 9784
Mason Playwrights' Award; *The Sunday Times* Bruce Vol. 2: 9784
Mason Prize; Michael Vol. 2: 2520
Mason Reference Award; Harold Vol. 1: 5842
Masonry Prize Vol. 2: 9905
Masotto Cup; Patricia L. Vol. 1: 19691
Maspero; Prix Gaston Vol. 2: 5459
Mass Communications Hall of Fame Vol. 1: 18664
Mass Communications Outstanding Alumni Awards Vol. 1: 18665
Massa Award; Richard Vol. 1: 817
Massachusetts Bay Trophy Vol. 1: 19541
Massachusetts Children's Book Award Vol. 1: 17007
Massey Award Vol. 2: 5065
Massey - Ferguson Medal Vol. 1: 4368
Massey Ferguson National Agricultural Award Vol. 2: 3635
Massey-Ferguson National Award for Services to United Kingdom Agriculture Vol. 2: 3635
Massey Medal Vol. 1: 16936
Massey Medals for Architecture Vol. 1: 16920
Massie Medal and Prize; Harrie Vol. 2: 3193
Massie Medal; Harrie Vol. 2: 235
Massine Prize for the Art of the Dance; Leonida Vol. 2: 8156
Master Agency Award Vol. 1: 9519
Master Agency Builder Vol. 1: 9519
Master Breeder Award
  American Jersey Cattle Club Vol. 1: 2718
  National Pigeon Association Vol 1: 14470
Master Clinician Award Vol. 1: 694
Master Fire Photographer Vol. 1: 10979
Master - Gold Hands Award Vol. 2: 10439
Master of Ceremonies - ANA Banquet Vol. 1: 3239
Master of Philosophical Enquiry (M.Ph.E.), Honoris Causa Vol. 1: 11262
Master of the Game Award Vol. 1: 14858
Master Pastelist Vol. 1: 15985
Master Steinologist Vol. 1: 18483
Master Triathletes of the Year Vol. 1: 18811
Master Wildlife Artist Vol. 1: 20446
Mastercard Outstanding Service Award Vol. 1: 6301
Mastermind Award Vol. 2: 2295
Masterplayers International Music and Conductors Competition Vol. 2: 11877
Masterplayers Prize Vol. 2: 11877
Masters Vol. 1: 1719
Masters Administrator of the Year Vol. 1: 19946
Masters and Johnson SSTAR Award Vol. 1: 17600
Masters Athlete of the Year Vol. 1: 19639
Masters Award Vol. 1: 19639
Masters Golf Tournament Vol. 1: 6146

Masters Long Distance Running Awards Vol. 1: 19947
Masters Race Walking Award Vol. 1: 19948
Master's Thesis Award Vol. 1: 10227
Masters Transportation Engineering Award; Frank M. Vol. 1: 4479
Masterson Memorial Trophy; Bill Vol. 1: 14171
Masterson Memorial Trophy; Glenn R. Vol. 1: 7250
Masubuchi/Shinsho Corporation Award; Professor Vol. 1: 5083
Masursky Meritorious Service Award; Harold Vol. 1: 1271
Matchette Award Vol. 1: 1438
Matchette Prize; Franklin J. Vol. 1: 3423
Materials Handling Award Vol. 1: 17405
Mathematical Contest in Modeling Vol. 1: 17513
Mathematics Excellence Award Vol. 1: 3000
Mather Award; Frank Jewett Vol. 1: 7889
Mather Award; John Vol. 1: 15715
Mather Award; Stephen Tyng Vol. 1: 14453
Mather Premium Vol. 2: 3273
Mathewson Gold Medal Award; Champion H. Vol. 1: 12318
Mathiasen Award; Geneva Vol. 1: 13818
Mathieu; Prix Paul Vol. 2: 4869
Mathy & Opera Awards Vol. 2: 262
Mathy Scholarship; Marianne Vol. 2: 262
Matrix Award Vol. 1: 20378
Matson Memorial Award; George C. Vol. 1: 1110
Matson Memorial Award; Theodore M. Vol. 1: 10455
Matsunaga Medal of Peace; Spark M. Vol. 1: 19404
Mattara Poetry Prize Vol. 2: 704
Matteucci; Medaglia Vol. 2: 8377
Matteucci Medal Vol. 2: 8377
Matthew Award; Robert Vol. 2: 2644
Matthew Prize; Sir Robert Vol. 2: 6060
Matthews Award; Austin- Vol. 1: 6962
Matthews Outstanding Chapter Award; R.C. Vol. 1: 18574
Matthews Physician/Scientist Award; Leroy Vol. 1: 8489
Matthews Prize; Keith Vol. 1: 7070
Mature Women Scholarship Grant Vol. 1: 14294
Mauchly Award; Eckert -
  Association for Computing Machinery Vol. 1: 5468
  Institute of Electrical and Electronics Engineers - Computer Society Vol 1: 10298
Mauck Award; Stanley R. Vol. 1: 12164
Maugham Awards; Somerset Vol. 2: 4390
Mauguin; Prix Georges Vol. 2: 5750
Maulana Abul Kalam Azad Trophy Vol. 2: 7523
Maura; Premio Antonio Vol. 2: 11288
Mauri Memorial Trophy; Carlo Vol. 2: 8460
Mauriac International Medical Film Festival Vol. 2: 6112
Maury Medal; Matthew Fontaine Vol. 1: 17340
Maury; Prix Joseph-Antoine Vol. 2: 4853
Mauss; Premio Marcos y Celia Vol. 2: 9194
Mawson Lecture Vol. 2: 177
MAXI Awards Program Vol. 1: 10882
Maxim Gold Medal; Hiram Percy Vol. 1: 3891
Maxim Memorial Award; Hiram Percy Vol. 1: 3891
Maxine; Prix Vol. 1: 6022
Maxwell Award; Bertha Vol. 1: 13684
Maxwell Award; BMEC Donald Vol. 2: 3115

Maxwell Award; Joe Kennedy-Clerk Vol. 1: 16166
Maxwell Medal and Prize Vol. 2: 3194
Maxwell Premium Vol. 2: 3273
Maxwell Prize for Plasma Physics; James Clerk Vol. 1: 3464
Maxwell Prizes Vol. 2: 3475
May and Baker Lectureship Vol. 2: 4215
May Award; Arthur A. Vol. 1: 5195
May Award; John R. Vol. 1: 17033
May Foundation Scholarship; New South Wales Government and Frederick Vol. 2: 146
May Research Award Program; S. C. Vol. 1: 20206
Mayberry Achievement Award Vol. 1: 9730
Mayborn Award for Community Leadership Vol. 1: 18636
Mayden Award in Informatics; Priscilla M. Vol. 1: 19888
Mayden Award; Priscilla M. Vol. 1: 19888
Mayer Award for Educational Leadership; Edward N. Vol. 1: 8655
Mayer; Fondation Charles-Leopold Vol. 2: 5518
Mayer Memorial Trophy; Lady Dorothy Vol. 2: 7766
Mayer Research Award; Cecile Lehman Vol. 1: 1620
Mayer Research Fellowship; Andre Vol. 2: 8269
Mayfield Award Vol. 1: 8151
Mayfield Cotton Engineering Award Vol. 1: 4369
Mayflower Award Vol. 1: 15497
Maynard Award; Harold H. Vol. 1: 2990
Maynard Book of the Year Award; H. B. Vol. 1: 10364
Maynard Cup Vol. 2: 12171
Maynard Memorial Medal; Hamilton Vol. 2: 10889
Maynard Prize; Isaac N. Vol. 1: 12618
Mayoral Awards of Honor for Art and Culture Vol. 1: 7737
Mayor's Arts Awards Vol. 1: 8544
Mayor's Award Vol. 1: 9190
Mayor's Award of Honor for Science and Technology Vol. 1: 7735
Mayors' Awards Program Vol. 1: 19066
Mayors' Financial Leadership Award Vol. 1: 19065
Mayr Student Award; Ernst Vol. 1: 18040
Mays Award; Captain "Willie" Vol. 1: 5281
Mazurkiewicz Award Vol. 2: 10157
MBB Golden Hour Award Vol. 1: 9895
Mc Connell Award Vol. 2: 7751
MC National Championship Regatta Vol. 1: 11101
MCA Annual Merit Awards Program Vol. 1: 12220
McAlear Memorial Award; Robert A. Vol. 1: 5721
McAlpin, Jr. Mental Health Research Achievement Award; William R. Vol. 1: 14359
McAnsh Award; James Vol. 1: 7286
McArthur Award; Dan
  Radio and Television News Directors Association Vol. 1: 16635
  Radio and Television News Directors Association Vol. 1: 16637
McArthur Prize; The Robert Vol. 2: 10562
McAulay Award; John H. Vol. 1: 5492
McAuliffe Award; Christa Vol. 1: 13715
McAuliffe Memorial Award; Christa Vol. 1: 266
McAuliffe Showcase for Excellence Awards; AASCU/Christa Vol. 1: 1197

McBryde Medal; W. A. E.   Vol. 1: 7554
McCaffree Award; Charles   Vol. 1: 7947
McCaffrey Trophy; James P.   Vol. 1: 6882
McCall Life Pattern Fund (Training Award)   Vol. 1: 18152
McCallam Award; James A.   Vol. 1: 5886
McCampbell Award   Vol. 1: 2043
McCandless Award; Boyd R.   Vol. 1: 3711
McCanse Award; Jessie   Vol. 1: 14884
McCarren Award   Vol. 1: 10669
McCarthy Good Guy Award; Clem   Vol. 1: 19376
McCay Award; Windsor   Vol. 1: 10609
McClatchy Newspapers Award - IAPA   Vol. 1: 10511
McCloskey Award; Mike   Vol. 1: 17237
McCloy Award; John J.   Vol. 1: 9447
McClung Award   Vol. 1: 6338
McClure Award for Outstanding Environmental and Community Leadersip; Tim   Vol. 1: 14578
McClure Award; Timothy P.   Vol. 1: 19569
McClure One-Act Play Award; Frank   Vol. 1: 474
McCluskey Award of Excellence; Roger   Vol. 1: 19026
McClusky Research Award; Dean and Sybil   Vol. 1: 5515
McCollum Award; E. V.   Vol. 1: 4053
McCollum International Lectureship in Nutrition; E. V.   Vol. 1: 2652
McCollum Young Artist Awards; Eleanor   Vol. 1: 10021
McColvin Medal   Vol. 2: 3571
McConnell Award; Micky   Vol. 1: 1323
McConnell Award; Robert Earll   Vol. 1: 2638
McCord Education Award; L. P.   Vol. 1: 10131
McCormack Award   Vol. 1: 5966
McCormick Award for Distinguished Early Career Contributions; Ernest J.   Vol. 1: 3800
McCormick - Jerome Increase Case Medal; Cyrus Hall   Vol. 1: 4370
McCormick, M.D. Award; J. B.   Vol. 1: 14752
McCormick Medal; Cyrus Hall   Vol. 1: 4370
McCormick Prize for Scholarly Publication; Richard P.   Vol. 1: 15178
McCoy Award; Walter R.   Vol. 1: 3407
McCredie; Kenneth B.   Vol. 1: 11838
McCree, Jr. Awards for the Advancement of Justice; Wade H.   Vol. 1: 18470
McCreight Award for Distinguished Service to the Humanities   Vol. 1: 9161
McCulloch Award; Warren Sturgis   Vol. 1: 4062
McCulloch Memorial Lecture and Award; Michael J.   Vol. 1: 8604
McCullough Award; Dr. Robert D.   Vol. 1: 10584
McCune Award for Collaborative Efforts in Adult Education; Donald A.   Vol. 1: 827
McCurdy Award   Vol. 1: 6766
McCutcheon Award (Helicopter Squadron of the Year); Keith B.   Vol. 1: 12072
McDaniel Ambassador Award; Durward K.   Vol. 1: 1852
McDonald Achievement Award; Touchdown Club Arch   Vol. 1: 18761
McDonald Award; Gerald   Vol. 2: 3618
McDonald Children's Charities Awards of Excellence; Ronald   Vol. 1: 12145
McDonald Children's Charities Grants Program; Ronald   Vol. 1: 12146
McDonald Outstanding Chapter Award; Edward E.   Vol. 1: 17442
McDonald's City of Sydney Performing Arts Challenge   Vol. 2: 320
McDonald's Operatic Aria   Vol. 2: 323

McDonnell Douglas Law Enforcement Award   Vol. 1: 9896
McDonough Award; Jim   Vol. 1: 20304
McDowell Award; W. Wallace   Vol. 1: 10303
McElligott Medallion   Vol. 1: 5855
McElreath Memorial Awards; James   Vol. 1: 19027
McEwan Memorial Award (Masters Athlete of the Year); May   Vol. 1: 19639
McFarland Award Program; Forest R.   Vol. 1: 17768
McFarlane Environmental Award; Euan P.   Vol. 1: 11481
McFeely Award; W. M.   Vol. 1: 11099
McGan Silver Antenna Award; Philip J.   Vol. 1: 3892
McGavin Award; Agnes Purcell   Vol. 1: 3642
McGee Service Award; George   Vol. 1: 15851
McGee Trophy; Francis J.   Vol. 1: 14642
McGee Trophy; W. P.   Vol. 1: 6978
McGibbon Award; Pauline   Vol. 1: 15704
McGill Award; John   Vol. 1: 18397
McGill Music Scholarship; Jack   Vol. 2: 9793
McGillen Award; Pete   Vol. 1: 15866
McGinnis Memorial Award; John H.   Vol. 1: 18241
McGivern Challenge Bowl   Vol. 1: 20246
McGovern Award
  Association of Newspaper Classified Advertising Managers   Vol. 1: 5903
  Newpaper Association of America   Vol 1: 15333
McGovern Award in the Behavioral Sciences; John B.   Vol. 1: 889
McGovern Award; John P.   Vol. 1: 3061
McGovern Award Lectureship; John P.   Vol. 1: 12173
McGovern Umpires' Award; John T.   Vol. 1: 19653
McGraw Award in Engineering Technology Education; James H.   Vol. 1: 9618
McGraw Award; James H.   Vol. 1: 4100
McGraw, Jr. Prize in Education; Harold W.   Vol. 1: 12149
McGraw Research Award; Curtis W.   Vol. 1: 4101
McGraw Scholarship; Thomas Edison/ Max   Vol. 1: 14692
McGuigan Research Fund; F. J.   Vol. 1: 3836
McGuire Cup; James P.   Vol. 1: 19692
McHenry Award; Earle Willard   Vol. 1: 7144
McHenry Award; Lawrence C.   Vol. 1: 617
MCI Streak Award   Vol. 1: 11761
McIntire Community Theatre Service Awards; Ruth   Vol. 1: 15142
McIntyre Award   Vol. 2: 10823
McIver Public Health Nurse Award; Pearl   Vol. 1: 3285
McKay - Helm Award   Vol. 1: 5084
McKean Award; Arch   Vol. 1: 11089
McKee Award; Harley J.   Vol. 1: 5585
McKee Trophy   Vol. 1: 6767
McKenna Award; Father   Vol. 1: 13349
McKenzie Award; Dorothy C.   Vol. 1: 18210
McKenzie Award; Ken   Vol. 1: 2330
McKenzie Award; R. Tait   Vol. 1: 763
McKenzie Cup   Vol. 1: 9112
McKenzie Plaque   Vol. 1: 9112
McKenzie Senior Fellowship in Educational Research; J. R.   Vol. 2: 9757
McKinney Award   Vol. 1: 14394
McKinney Award; William M.   Vol. 1: 4736
McKinnon Award; Marthe T.   Vol. 1: 5054
McKinsey Article Awards   Vol. 1: 9804
McKinsey Award   Vol. 1: 19755
McKinsey Book Awards   Vol. 1: 9805
McKnight Advancement Grants   Vol. 1: 16251

McKnight Black Doctoral Fellowship Program   Vol. 1: 9264
McKnight Doctoral Fellowship Program in Arts and Sciences, Mathematics, Business and Engineering   Vol. 1: 9264
McKnight Fellowships   Vol. 1: 16252
McKune Memorial Award; Frank B.   Vol. 1: 11469
McLaren Award; Post Office   Vol. 2: 10541
McLaren Cup   Vol. 2: 4046
McLaughlin Award of Merit; Kenneth P.   Vol. 1: 14517
McLaughlin, Jr. Memorial Award; Lt. Donald   Vol. 1: 19413
McLaughlin Medal   Vol. 1: 16958
McLaughry Award; Tuss   Vol. 1: 2075
McLean Award; Franklin C.   Vol. 1: 14348
McLemore Prize   Vol. 1: 12358
McLeod Literary Prize; Enid   Vol. 2: 2908
McLeod Society Trophy; Stuart Cameron   Vol. 1: 10390
McLintock Prize; The Sir William   Vol. 2: 10563
McLuhan Teleglobe Canada Award
  Canada Council   Vol. 1: 6745
  Canadian Commission for UNESCO   Vol 1: 6834
McMahon International Music Competition; Louise D.   Vol. 1: 6685
McMaster Award; Albert   Vol. 2: 2447
McMaster Gold Medal; Robert C.   Vol. 1: 4220
McMicken Award; Alfred   Vol. 2: 251
McMillan; Dean   Vol. 1: 20046
McMillan Lecture Award; Mary   Vol. 1: 3485
McMillan Scholarship; Mary   Vol. 1: 3486
McMullen Weapon System Maintenance Award; Maj. Gen. Clements   Vol. 1: 15785
McNally Award; Andrew   Vol. 1: 1427
McNally Awards; Rand   Vol. 1: 1811
McNally Memorial Prize; Nic   Vol. 2: 2412
McNamara Fellowships Program; Robert S.   Vol. 1: 20474
McNamee Award; Graham   Vol. 1: 4856
McNeer Award; Lenore   Vol. 1: 14426
McNeill Memorial Fund Award; Harry V.   Vol. 1: 3837
McNeir Ring Award; Nancy   Vol. 1: 17003
McNickle Center for the History of the American Indian Fellowships; D'Arcy   Vol. 1: 15315
McNicol Prize; J. N.   Vol. 2: 619
McNulty Award; J. D.   Vol. 1: 6009
McParland Memorial Medal; Donald J.   Vol. 1: 6946
McQuade Memorial Fund Award; Gerard   Vol. 1: 11397
McRae Russell Award; Walter   Vol. 2: 132
McTLC Award   Vol. 1: 12147
McVitie's Prize for the Scottish Writer of the Year   Vol. 2: 10582
McWhirter Foundation Awards; Ross   Vol. 2: 4613
McWilliams Award; Carey   Vol. 1: 3580
MDT Castle Educator of the Year Award   Vol. 1: 10744
Meacham Award; Monte   Vol. 1: 776
Mead Award; George Herbert   Vol. 1: 17650
Mead Award; In the Spirit of Margaret   Vol. 1: 10221
Mead Award; Margaret   Vol. 1: 797
Mead Johnson Award   Vol. 1: 2653
Mead Johnson Young Investigator Award   Vol. 1: 17395
Mead Prize; Sidney E.   Vol. 1: 4427
Mead Prizes; Daniel W.   Vol. 1: 4480

Meade Award for Research in English Education; CEE Richard   Vol. 1: 13765
Meade Award; George and Eleanore   Vol. 1: 18522
Meadmaker of the Year   Vol. 1: 2344
Meadows Award for Excellence in the Arts   Vol. 1: 18229
Meadows Memorial Award; C. F. "Buzz"   Vol. 1: 13145
Meat Research Award   Vol. 1: 4401
MEC Art Prizes   Vol. 2: 1442
Mechaelis Memorial Prize   Vol. 2: 9850
Mechanic of the Year   Vol. 1: 8990
Mechanic of the Year Award   Vol. 1: 16441
Mechanic of the Year; "Mac Tools" SCCA   Vol. 1: 18406
Mechanical Engineering Prize   Vol. 2: 470
Mechelen Prize; Stad   Vol. 2: 1347
Meckauer-Plakette; Walter-   Vol. 2: 7042
Meckler Award for Innovation Through Information Technology   Vol. 2: 3572
Meckler Award for Innovations in Technology; SLA   Vol. 1: 18269
Meckler Award for Innovative Technology; CLA/   Vol. 1: 6998
Meckler Library of the Future Award; ALA/   Vol. 1: 2812
MECON Award   Vol. 2: 7631
Medaglia Domenico Marotta   Vol. 2: 8336
Medaglia Amedeo Avogadro   Vol. 2: 8378
Medaglia d'Acciaio Federico Giolitte   Vol. 2: 8128
Medaglia dell'Accademia Nazionale dei XL   Vol. 2: 8379
Medaglia d'Oro Aim ai Soci Fondtori   Vol. 2: 8131
Medaglia d'Oro Icilio Guareschi   Vol. 2: 8237
Medaglia d'oro Luigi Losana   Vol. 2: 8129
Medaglia d'Oro Pio XI   Vol. 2: 12098
Medaglia Emanuele Paterno   Vol. 2: 8337
Medaglia Giulio Natta   Vol. 2: 8338
Medaglia Matteucci   Vol. 2: 8377
Medaglia Raffaele Piria   Vol. 2: 8339
Medaglia Stanislao Cannizzaro   Vol. 2: 8340
Medaille Abbott   Vol. 2: 4947
Medaille Beaumarchais   Vol. 2: 6395
Medaille Bene Merenti de Patria   Vol. 1: 17382
Medaille Boris Rajewsky   Vol. 2: 1123
Medaille Bourdin   Vol. 2: 6388
Medaille Cavallaro   Vol. 2: 8464
Medaille d'Archeologie   Vol. 2: 4773
Medaille d'Architecture Fondation le Soufache   Vol. 2: 4774
Medaille d'Architecture Prix Dejean ou Prix Delarue   Vol. 2: 4775
Medaille d'Argent du CNRS   Vol. 2: 5018
Medaille de Bronze du CNRS   Vol. 2: 5019
Medaille de la FISA   Vol. 2: 11787
Medaille de la Jurisprudence   Vol. 2: 4776
Medaille de la Recherche et de la Technique   Vol. 2: 4777
Medaille de la Restauration   Vol. 2: 4778
Medaille de l'Academie d'Architecture   Vol. 2: 4779
Medaille de l'ACP pour Contribution Exceptionnelle a la Physique   Vol. 1: 6801
Medaille de l'AISS   Vol. 2: 11837
Medaille de l'Analyse Architecturale   Vol. 2: 4780
Medaille de l'Architecture d'Accompagnement   Vol. 2: 4781
Medaille de l'Histoire de l'Art   Vol. 2: 4782
Medaille de l'Urbanisme   Vol. 2: 4783
Medaille der Mozartstadt Salzburg   Vol. 2: 867
Medaille des Anciens Presidents   Vol. 2: 6217

Medaille des Arts Plastiques   Vol. 2: 4784
Medaille des Publications   Vol. 2: 4785
Medaille des Soixante Ans et Fondation Manley-Bendall   Vol. 2: 6218
Medaille d'honneur   Vol. 2: 6991
Medaille d'Honneur de la Police   Vol. 2: 1788
Medaille d'Honneur de l'Academie d'Architecture   Vol. 2: 4786
Medaille d'Honneur des Douanes   Vol. 2: 1789
Medaille d'Honneur du Comite Francais de l'AMV   Vol. 2: 5056
Medaille d'Honneur du Merite Europeen   Vol. 2: 8862
Medaille d'Honneur du Travail   Vol. 2: 1790
Medaille d'Or
  European and Mediterranean Plant Protection Organization   Vol. 2: 5114
  Societe de Geographie de Geneve   Vol 2: 11906
Medaille d'Or de la Communication Musicale   Vol. 2: 6258
Medaille d'Or de l'Academie d'Architecture   Vol. 2: 4787
Medaille d'Or du CNRS   Vol. 2: 5020
Medaille d'Or du Trachome   Vol. 2: 6036
Medaille d'Or Laveran   Vol. 2: 6241
Medaille d'Or Pie XI   Vol. 2: 12098
Medaille du Lieutenant-Gouverneur   Vol. 1: 9912
Medaille Flavelle   Vol. 1: 16953
Medaille fur Naturwissenschaftliche Publizistik   Vol. 2: 6661
Medaille Gabrielle Leger   Vol. 1: 9911
Medaille Georges Perrot   Vol. 2: 5432
Medaille Henry Dunant   Vol. 2: 11915
Medaille Henry Marshall Tory   Vol. 1: 16966
Medaille Innis - Gerin   Vol. 1: 16957
Medaille Jason A. Hannah   Vol. 1: 16955
Medaille Jean Thevenot   Vol. 2: 9533
Medaille Lorne Pierce   Vol. 1: 16961
Medaille McLaughlin   Vol. 1: 16958
Medaille Militaire   Vol. 2: 5244
Medaille Pierre Chauveau   Vol. 1: 16950
Medaille Pierre Francois Caille   Vol. 2: 822
Medaille Rammal   Vol. 2: 6365
Medaille Thomas W. Eadie   Vol. 1: 16952
Medaille Tisserand   Vol. 2: 4769
Medaille Willet G. Miller   Vol. 1: 16959
Medailles Commemoratives Rutherford   Vol. 1: 16963
Medailles d'Argent de la SFA   Vol. 2: 6350
Medailles de la FIRA   Vol. 2: 5953
Medailles D'Honneur   Vol. 2: 9404
Medailles du Merite   Vol. 2: 5954
Medailles et Diplomes Olympique   Vol. 2: 11815
Medal: 80 lat PTH   Vol. 2: 10191
Medal: 80 Years of the Polish Society of Hygiene   Vol. 2: 10191
Medal Award   Vol. 1: 17827
Medal Awards   Vol. 1: 1348
Medal El Gaucho   Vol. 2: 105
Medal Federacion Espanola de Montanismo   Vol. 2: 11386
Medal for a Noble Deed   Vol. 2: 9919
Medal for Armed Forces in the Service of the Fatherland   Vol. 2: 10093
Medal for Brave Performance in Mining   Vol. 2: 740
Medal for Bravery
  Canadian Institute of Mining and Metallurgy   Vol. 1: 6947
  Colombia - Ministry of Justice   Vol 2: 1629
  Republic of South Africa - South African Railways Police   Vol 2: 10951
Medal for Civic Virtue   Vol. 2: 9920

Medal for Courage   Vol. 2: 8915
Medal for Distinguished Conduct and Loyal Service   Vol. 2: 10933
Medal for Distinguished Philanthropy   Vol. 1: 1046
Medal for Distinguished Service to Tropical Ecology   Vol. 2: 7691
Medal for Gallantry (MG)   Vol. 2: 342
Medal for Good Speech on the Stage   Vol. 1: 514
Medal for Long Marital Life   Vol. 2: 10108
Medal for Merit in Action   Vol. 2: 10109
Medal for Outstanding Service to AWWA   Vol. 1: 5026
Medal for Outstanding Sports Achievements   Vol. 2: 10090
Medal for Participation in the Battle for Berlin   Vol. 2: 10094
Medal for Participation in the War of 1939   Vol. 2: 10110
Medal for Peace and Friendship through Music and Arts   Vol. 1: 10963
Medal for Postal Merit   Vol. 2: 1604
Medal for Self-Sacrifice and Courage   Vol. 2: 10111
Medal for Service to the Republic   Vol. 2: 8916
Medal for Services to Bibliography   Vol. 2: 2167
Medal for Serving the Association of Hungarian Librarians   Vol. 2: 7294
Medal for Spoken Language   Vol. 1: 514
Medal for the Advancement of Research   Vol. 1: 5362
Medal for the Odra, Nysa and Baltic Sea   Vol. 2: 10115
Medal for the Services to the Country's Defense   Vol. 2: 10112
Medal for Valour   Vol. 2: 10741
Medal for Warsaw   Vol. 2: 10115
Medal for Your Freedom and Ours   Vol. 2: 10113
Medal im. prof. Ludwika Zabrockiego   Vol. 2: 10082
Medal Jubilee: One Hundred Years of the PSH   Vol. 2: 10192
Medal Jubileuszowy: 90 Lat PTH   Vol. 2: 10193
Medal Jubileuszowy: 100 lat PTH   Vol. 2: 10192
Medal Komisji Edukacji Narodowej   Vol. 2: 10114
Medal Mariana Smoluchowskiego   Vol. 2: 10172
Medal of Achievement
  American Electronics Association   Vol. 1: 1982
  Philadelphia Art Alliance Press   Vol 1: 16126
Medal of Bravery   Vol. 1: 6701
Medal of Commission of National Education   Vol. 2: 10114
Medal of Distinction
  General Arab Women Federation   Vol. 2: 7749
  Institute of South African Architects   Vol 2: 10882
Medal of Freedom   Vol. 1: 19335
Medal of Honor
  Electronic Industries Association   Vol. 1: 8885
  Federation of Danish Architects   Vol 2: 1947
  Fragrance Foundation and Olfactory Research Fund   Vol 1: 9362
  Herb Society of America   Vol 1: 9906

Medal

International Association of Professional Numismatists Vol 2: 11763
Niagara University Vol 1: 15379
Singapore - Office of the Prime Minister Vol 2: 10742
South African Academy of Science and Arts Vol 2: 10999
Medal of Honor Award
  American Mosquito Control Association Vol. 1: 3132
  Precast/Prestressed Concrete Institute Vol 1: 16374
Medal of Honor (Congressional Medal of Honor) Vol. 1: 19169
Medal of Honor for Career Service Vol. 1: 18012
Medal of Honor for Promotion of a Scientific Field Vol. 2: 11000
Medal of Honor of the Physical Sciences and Technique Vol. 2: 11001
Medal of Honour
  British Deaf Association Vol. 2: 2329
  International Union for the Modern Pentathalon and Biathlon Vol 2: 6991
  Pharmaceutical Manufacturers Association of Canada Vol 1: 16088
Medal of Liberty Vol. 1: 1585
Medal of Merit
  American Numismatic Association Vol. 1: 3240
  Canadian Society of Petroleum Geologists Vol 1: 7224
  Deutsche Akademie der Naturforscher Leopoldina Vol 2: 6624
  Finnish Academy of Technology Vol 2: 4684
  Journalism Education Association Vol 1: 11614
Medal of Merit for Tourism Vol. 2: 1695
Medal of Merit for Valor Vol. 1: 14493
Medal of Merit in Tourism Vol. 2: 1610
Medal of Military Valour Vol. 1: 6702
Medal of Service Vol. 2: 7251
Medal of the Endocrine Society Vol. 1: 8922
Medal of the French Resistance Vol. 2: 5245
Medal of the Mozart City of Salzburg Vol. 2: 867
Medal of the Polish Geographical Society Vol. 2: 10148
Medal of the Tokyo Geographical Society Vol. 2: 8766
Medal of Valor
  American Correctional Association Vol. 1: 1836
  National Police Officers Association of America Vol 1: 14493
  Regular Veterans Association Vol 1: 16752
Medal Polski Ludowej Vol. 2: 10097
Medal Polskiego Towarzystwa Geograficznego Vol. 2: 10148
Medal Za Dlugoletnie Pozycie Malzenskie Vol. 2: 10108
Medal Za Ofiarnosc i Odwage Vol. 2: 10111
Medal Za Udzial w Walkach o Berlin Vol. 2: 10094
Medal Za Udzial w Wojnie Obronnej 1939 Vol. 2: 10110
Medal Za Wasza Wolnosc i Nasza Vol. 2: 10113
Medal Za Wybitne Osiagniecia Sportowe Vol. 2: 10090
Medal Zasluzonym na Polu Chwaly Vol. 2: 10109
Medalha Carneiro Fellipe Vol. 2: 2028
Medalha de Merito Turistico Vol. 2. 10262
Medalja Julije Domac Vol. 2: 1805

Medalje til minne om Guldberg og Waages Massevirkningslov Vol. 2: 9932
Medalla Agricola Interamericano Vol. 2: 1776
Medalla Agustin Ramirez Vol. 2: 9013
Medalla al Marito Civico de la Ciudad de Mexico Vol. 2: 8961
Medalla al Merito Cafetero Manuel Mejia Vol. 2: 1734
Medalla al Merito Cultural de Gerardo Arellano Vol. 2: 1651
Medalla al Merito Logisgtico y Administrativo Contralmirante Rafael Tono Vol. 2: 1635
Medalla al Merito Postal Vol. 2: 1604
Medalla al Merito Turistico en Investigacion Vol. 2: 1616
Medalla al Valor
  Colombia - Ministry of Justice Vol. 2: 1629
  Colombia - National Police Vol 2: 1674
Medalla Alfonso L. Herrera al Merito en Ecologia y Conservacion Vol. 2: 9040
Medalla Antonio Rosales Vol. 2: 9013
Medalla Bernardo Balbuena Vol. 2: 9013
Medalla Carmen y Aguiles Serdan Vol. 2: 9001
Medalla Ciudad de Rosario Vol. 2: 105
Medalla Civica de Cartagena Vol. 2: 1608
Medalla Civica del Merito Asistencial y Sanitario Jorge Bejarano Vol. 2: 1667
Medalla de Honor Belisario Dominguez Vol. 2: 9143
Medalla de la Generalitat de Catalunya Vol. 2: 11187
Medalla de l'Esport de la Generalitat de Catalunya Vol. 2: 11190
Medalla de Oro
  Chilean Society of History and Geography Vol. 2: 1557
  Inter-American Safety Council Vol 1: 10515
Medalla de Oro and Padrino/Madrina Awards Vol. 1: 17895
Medalla de Plata Vol. 1: 17895
Medalla de Servicios Distinguidos Vol. 2: 1716
Medalla del Exportador Vol. 2: 1609
Medalla Eduardo Neri Vol. 2: 9124
Medalla Gabin Barreda Vol. 2: 9000
Medalla General Santander Vol. 2: 1676
Medalla i Placa Narcis Monturiol al merit cientific i technologic Vol. 2: 11188
Medalla Ignacio Manuel Altamarino Vol. 2: 9145
Medalla Ing. Salvador Toscano Vol. 2: 8952
Medalla Instituto Colombiano de Cultura Vol. 2: 1713
Medalla Juan de Dios Batiz Vol. 2: 9069
Medalla Lazaro Cardenas del Rio Vol. 2: 9300
Medalla Merito de las Comunicaciones Manuel Murillo Toro Vol. 2: 1605
Medalla Militar Francisco Jose de Caldas Vol. 2: 1636
Medalla Militar Soldado Juan Bautista Solarte Obando Vol. 2: 1637
Medalla Rafael Ramirez Vol. 2: 9155
Medalla Servicios Distinguidos a la Aviacion Naval Vol. 2: 1638
Medalla Servicios Distinguidos en Orden Publico Vol. 2: 1639
Medalla Servicios Distinguidos Infanteria de Marinia Vol. 2: 1640
Medalla Servicios Distinguidos la Fuerza de Superficie Vol. 2: 1641
Medalla Tiempo de Servicio Vol. 2: 1642
Medallas de Geografia Fisica, Humana, Economica Vol. 2: 10016

Medallion Award
  American Forage and Grassland Council Vol. 1: 2079
  Realtors National Marketing Institute - Residential Sales Council Vol 1: 16712
Medallion De Bronce Vol. 1: 16081
Medallion for Entrepreneurship Vol. 1: 6340
Medallion of Honor
  All-America Selections Vol. 1: 319
  Theta Alpha Phi Vol 1: 18696
Medallion of Merit Vol. 1: 3040
Medallions of Excellence Vol. 1: 8167
Medallon de Oro Vol. 1: 16082
Medallon de Plata Vol. 1: 16083
Medallos de los Servicios Vol. 2: 1675
Medals for Acts of Distinction Vol. 2: 8369
Medals for Excellence Vol. 2: 2626
Medals of Commendation Vol. 1: 60
Medals of Honor Vol. 2: 8585
Medals of Honour Vol. 2: 9404
Medals of the National Academy of Science Vol. 2: 8379
Medals of the Society of Dyers and Colourists Vol. 2: 4435
Medbery Nature Landscape/Seascape Award; Lorena Vol. 1: 16163
Medellin University Prize Vol. 2: 1752
Medi-Physics Research Fellowship for Therapeutic Nuclear Medicine; Society of Nuclear Medicine/ Vol. 1: 17956
Media Alliance Meritorious Achievement Awards (MAMA Awards) Vol. 1: 12153
Media and Methods Awards Portfolio Vol. 1: 12155
Media and Methods Maxi Awards Vol. 1: 12155
Media Award
  American Psychological Association - Media Psychology Vol. 1: 3742
  American School Food Service Association Vol 1: 3997
  Emergency Nurses Association Vol 1: 8907
  National Space Club Vol 1: 14838
  President's Committee on Employment of People with Disabilities Vol 1: 16387
  USA Baseball Vol 1: 19915
Media Award; James W. Byers Vol. 1: 13739
Media Awards
  The Association for Persons with Severe Handicaps (TASH) Vol. 1: 5572
  Canadian Sport Council Vol 1: 7245
  National Coordinating Council on Emergency Management Vol 1: 13666
  National Retail Merchants Association Vol 1: 14635
Media Awards Competition
  National Council on Family Relations Vol. 1: 13808
  New York State Bar Association Vol 1: 15283
Media Citation Vol. 1: 11615
Media Commendation Vol. 1: 8602
Media Excellence Awards Vol. 1: 5213
Media-Field Award Vol. 1: 200
Media Peace Prize Vol. 2: 4565
Media Psychology Graduate Student Research Award Vol. 1: 3741
Media Support Award Vol. 1: 14110
Median Iris Awards Vol. 1: 12160
Medical Academy of Sao Paulo Prize Vol. 2: 1490
Medical Association of South Africa Awards for Excellence in Medical Reporting (Press, Radio, Television) Vol. 2: 10890
Medical Association of South Africa Branch Award for Meritorious Service Vol. 2: 10891

Medical Association of South Africa Bronze Medal Award   Vol. 2: 10892
Medical Association of South Africa Gold Medal Award   Vol. 2: 10893
Medical Association of South Africa Group Award for Meritorious Service   Vol. 2: 10894
Medical Association of South Africa Pro Meritis Award   Vol. 2: 10895
Medical Association of South Africa Silver Medal Award   Vol. 2: 10896
Medical Education Awards   Vol. 1: 675
Medical Electives Bursaries   Vol. 2: 2658
Medical Executive Award   Vol. 1: 1675
Medical Instrumentation Award   Vol. 1: 5627
Medical Journalism Awards
    American Medical Association   Vol. 1: 3024
    Sandoz Corporation   Vol 1: 17052
Medical Postgraduate Research Scholarships and Dental Postgraduate Research Scholarships   Vol. 2: 543
Medical Research Grants   Vol. 2: 4739
Medical Sciences Award   Vol. 2: 10323
Medical Services Cross   Vol. 2: 10934
Medical Student Award   Vol. 1: 706
Medical Student Diabetes Research Fellowship Program   Vol. 1: 1954
Medical Student Essay Awards   Vol. 1: 618
Medical Students' Prize   Vol. 2: 10897
Medical Technologist of the Year   Vol. 1: 4521
Medicinal Chemistry Award   Vol. 1: 1503
Medicine Pipe Bearer's Award   Vol. 1: 20236
Medienpreis fur Sprachkultur   Vol. 2: 6894
Medieval Archaeology Research Fund   Vol. 2: 4363
Medique Leadership Awards   Vol. 1: 1350
Medlicott Medal; Norton   Vol. 2: 3017
Medunarodni Festival Naucnog Filma Beograd   Vol. 2: 10699
Medunarodno violinisticko natjecanje Vaclav Huml   Vol. 2: 1801
Medwick Memorial Award; Lucille   Vol. 1: 16291
Medwick Memorial Award; Lucille J.   Vol. 1: 16019
Medzinarodna tribuna mladych interpretov/UNESCO   Vol. 2: 10784
MEE Award   Vol. 2: 7336
MEE Kivalo Dij   Vol. 2: 7336
Meek Award; Howard B.   Vol. 1: 8400
Meeker Award; Donald   Vol. 1: 19570
Meeking Award for Poetry; Charles   Vol. 2: 666
Meeman Awards; Environmental Journalism - Edward J.   Vol. 1: 17146
Meeman Conservation Awards; Edward J.   Vol. 1: 17146
Mees Medal; C. E .K.   Vol. 1: 15754
Meesterschap; Prijs voor   Vol. 2: 9630
Meeting Planner of the Year   Vol. 1: 5481
(MEF Auditions); Cravath Memorial Award   Vol. 1: 12537
Megaw Memorial Prize; Eric   Vol. 2: 3295
Meggers Award; William F.
    Optical Society of America   Vol. 1: 15755
    Society for Applied Spectroscopy   Vol 1: 17418
Meggers Project Award; William F. and Edith R.   Vol. 1: 2662
Meghnad Saha Medal   Vol. 2: 7658
Mehedinti Prize; Simion   Vol. 2: 10366
Mehl Award; Institute of Metals Lecture and Robert Franklin   Vol. 1: 12315
Mehl Award; Robert Franklin   Vol. 1: 12315
Mehl Honor Lecture   Vol. 1: 4221
Meijimura Prize   Vol. 2: 8698
Meiklejohn Award; Alexander   Vol. 1: 1231

Meillet; Prix Antoine   Vol. 2: 5438
Meinzer Award; O. E.   Vol. 1: 9564
Meiselman Prize; Leonard J.   Vol. 1: 14714
Meisinger Award   Vol. 1: 3091
Meisner Foundry Award; Joel   Vol. 1: 14714
Meissner Prize; Leo   Vol. 1: 12619
Mejia Medal of Merit in the Coffee Industry; Manuel   Vol. 2: 1734
Melamed Award; Leo   Vol. 1: 19756
Melbourne International Film Festival Shorts Awards   Vol. 2: 525
Melcher Book Award; Frederic G.   Vol. 1: 18891
Melcher Scholarship; Frederic G.   Vol. 1: 2861
Melchers Memorial Medal; Gari   Vol. 1: 5312
Melchior Prize   Vol. 2: 12209
Meldola Medal and Prize   Vol. 2: 4209
Mellett Award for Improving Journalism Through Critical Evaluation; Lowell   Vol. 1: 16054
Mellon Award; Richard Beatty   Vol. 1: 221
Mellon Fellowship; Andrew W.   Vol. 1: 485
Mellon Fellowships; Andrew W.   Vol. 1: 12234
Mellon Fellowships in Conservation; Andrew W.   Vol. 1: 12235
Mellon Fellowships in Humanistic Studies; Andrew W.   Vol. 1: 20315
Mellor Award; Sam   Vol. 1: 14518
Mellor Lecture in Chemical Education; David   Vol. 2: 701
Melpomene Outstanding Achievement Award   Vol. 1: 12211
Melrose Memorial Trust; D. R.   Vol. 2: 3991
Melsens; Prix Louis   Vol. 2: 1031
Melton Award   Vol. 2: 2511
Melville Award; Stanley   Vol. 2: 2413
Melville Junior Stamp Competition   Vol. 2: 2476
Melville Medal   Vol. 1: 4690
Memain-Pelletier; Fondation   Vol. 2: 5335
Member   Vol. 2: 4468
Member Association Safety Award   Vol. 1: 20155
Member Booster Award   Vol. 1: 3241
Member Director Award   Vol. 1: 12933
Member of Honour   Vol. 2: 7045
Member of Note   Vol. 1: 16202
Member of the National Academy of Sciences   Vol. 1: 12673
Member of the Year
    Alpha Epsilon Rho - The National Broadcasting Society   Vol. 1: 346
    Caucus for Producers, Writers and Directors   Vol 1: 7412
    Institute of Packaging Professionals   Vol 1: 10428
    International Society of Pharmaceutical Engineers   Vol 1: 11293
    Motorhome Travelers Association   Vol 1: 12465
    National Business Forms Association   Vol 1: 13509
    National Recreation and Park Association - National Therapeutic Recreation Society   Vol 1: 14575
    Numerical Control Society/Association for Integrated Manufacturing Technology   Vol 1: 15556
    Ottawa Field-Naturalists' Club   Vol 1: 15852
    Society of Cable Television Engineers   Vol 1: 17796
    Society of Corporate Meeting Professionals   Vol 1: 17823
    United States Space Education Association   Vol 1: 19613

Member of the Year Award
    American Society of Certified Engineering Technicians   Vol. 1: 4420
    Dance Masters of America   Vol 1: 8525
    In-Plant Management Association   Vol 1: 10105
    International Association of Assessing Officers   Vol 1: 10670
    International Camaro Club   Vol 1: 10821
    International Family Recreation Association   Vol 1: 10950
    Intravenous Nurses Society   Vol 1: 11413
    National RV Owners Club   Vol 1: 14655
    Omega Society   Vol 2: 563
    Society of Recreation Executives   Vol 1: 18022
Member of the Year - Regional   Vol. 1: 6656
Member Organization of the Year   Vol. 1: 19654
Member Recognition for Excellence in Public Relations   Vol. 1: 18273
Member Service Award   Vol. 1: 16439
Members and Fellows Lecture Award   Vol. 1: 2615
Members Award   Vol. 1: 6948
Members Choice Award   Vol. 1: 11015
Members of Honour   Vol. 2: 11988
Members Prize   Vol. 2: 3357
Membership Achievement Award   Vol. 1: 7113
Membership Award   Vol. 1: 12275
Membership Awards
    American Association of Occupational Health Nurses   Vol. 1: 1080
    American Water Works Association   Vol 1: 5027
    International Credit Association   Vol 1: 10891
    National PTA   Vol 1: 14548
Membership Contest   Vol. 1: 9130
Membership Enrichment Award   Vol. 1: 15420
Membership in Omicron Kappa Upsilon   Vol. 1: 15636
Membership in Retirement   Vol. 2: 3173
Membership of the City and Guilds of London Institute   Vol. 2: 2627
Membership of the Gorsedd of Bards of Great Britain   Vol. 2: 12185
Membership Promotion Award   Vol. 1: 14030
Membership Recruiter of the Year   Vol. 1: 6509
Membership Service Award   Vol. 1: 10132
Membership's Choice Award   Vol. 1: 19614
Membre d'honneur   Vol. 2: 4951
Membres Honoraires a Vie   Vol. 1: 7088
Memorial Award   Vol. 1: 7568
Memorial Awards   Vol. 1: 14948
Memorial Hall of Fame Award   Vol. 1: 2693
Memorial Lecturer Award and Honoree(s)   Vol. 1: 3133
Memorial Life Membership Award   Vol. 1: 9113
Memorial Scholarship   Vol. 1: 20257
Menapace Fellowship in Urban Land Use Law; Ralph C.   Vol. 1: 12488
Mencion IMIQ   Vol. 2: 9105
Mencken Awards   Vol. 1: 9392
Mencken Writing Award; H. L.   Vol. 1: 6253
Mendel Award; Osborne and   Vol. 1: 2654
Mendel-Medaille   Vol. 2: 6625
Mendel Medal   Vol. 2: 6625
Mendel; Prix Gustave   Vol. 2: 5461
Mendele Prize; Literary Prize -   Vol. 2: 7955
Mendelson Memorial Awards; Robin H.   Vol. 1: 4194
Mendelssohn Award   Vol. 2: 6942
Mendes Awards; Chico   Vol. 1: 17238

Mendes France Prize; Pierre   Vol. 2: 6118
Mendes Prize; Odorico   Vol. 2: 1435
Mendoza; Premio Vicente T.   Vol. 2: 9063
Menefee Memorial Combined Horse and Horsemanship Award; Jim   Vol. 1: 15476
Menil Human Rights Prize; Carter -   Vol. 1: 7326
Menninger Award; William C.   Vol. 1: 7482
Menninger Memorial Award; William C.   Vol. 1: 1720
Menon Medical Research Award; Dr. Kamala   Vol. 2: 7595
Men's Amateur Cup (soccer)   Vol. 1: 19607
Men's Fragrance of the Year - Broad Introductions   Vol. 1: 9361
Men's Fragrance of the Year - Exclusive Distribution   Vol. 1: 9361
Men's Fragrance of the Year - Limited Distribution   Vol. 1: 9361
Men's Fragrance of the Year - Mass Introductions   Vol. 1: 9361
Men's National Championship Cup Finals   Vol. 2: 2777
Men's National Young Hairstyling Championship   Vol. 2: 2966
Men's Open Cup (soccer)   Vol. 1: 19608
Mensa International Competitions   Vol. 2: 3640
Mensforth International Gold Medal   Vol. 2: 3296
Mental Health Employer of the Year   Vol. 1: 14360
Mental Health Media Awards   Vol. 1: 14361
Mentor   Vol. 1: 11263
Mentor-Based Postdoctoral Fellowships   Vol. 1: 1955
Menu Idea Exchange Award   Vol. 1: 14624
Menuhin Memorial Scholarship; Hephzibah   Vol. 2: 326
Menuhin Prize   Vol. 2: 3606
Menuhin Prize for Young Composers   Vol. 2: 2634
Menzel Award; Margaret   Vol. 1: 6487
Mercer Award; George   Vol. 1: 8818
Mercer Award; Johnny   Vol. 1: 12649
Mercer Award; Mabel   Vol. 1: 18487
Mercet; Prix Emile   Vol. 2: 6392
Merchandise Mart Hall of Fame   Vol. 1: 12218
Merchandiser of the Year Award   Vol. 1: 13286
Merchant Manufacturing Medal; M. Eugene   Vol. 1: 4691
Merck AgVet Dairy Management Research Award   Vol. 1: 1916
Merck Award   Vol. 2: 10978
Merck Award for Achievement in Poultry Science   Vol. 1: 16348
Merck Ehrung; Johann-Heinrich-   Vol. 2: 6602
Merck Frosst Award   Vol. 1: 7189
Merck Frosst Centre for Therapeutic Research Lecture Award   Vol. 1: 7555
Merck Preis; Johann-Heinrich-   Vol. 2: 6768
Merck Sharp & Dohme   Vol. 1: 1711
Merck, Sharp and Dohme International Award   Vol. 2: 1971
Merck Sharp & Dohme Lecture Award   Vol. 1: 7555
Mercure Awards; Pierre   Vol. 1: 17821
Mercure d'Argent   Vol. 2: 1191
Mercury Business Book Award   Vol. 2: 3642
Mercury Communications Award for the Prince's Trust   Vol. 2: 4487
Mercury Gold Award   Vol. 1: 16633
Mercury Silver Award   Vol. 1: 16633
Meredith Perpetual Memorial Award; Ruth O'Keefe   Vol. 1: 2350
Merghelynck Prize; Arthur   Vol. 2: 1274

Meriam/Wiley Distinguished Author Award   Vol. 1: 4102
Merit Award
   American Baptist Homes and Hospitals Association   Vol. 1: 1304
   American Council for Polish Culture   Vol 1: 1841
   American Society for Enology and Viticulture   Vol 1: 4127
   American Society for Photogrammetry and Remote Sensing   Vol 1: 4256
   Association for Indiana Media Educators   Vol 1: 5534
   Association for Systems Management   Vol 1: 5604
   Association of Official Seed Analysts   Vol 1: 5913
   Decalogue Society of Lawyers   Vol 1: 8562
   German Dental Association   Vol 2: 6800
   International Credit Association   Vol 1: 10892
   North American Die Casting Association   Vol 1: 15421
   Society of Cosmetic Chemists   Vol 1: 17828
   Society of Toxicology   Vol 1: 18075
   Soil and Water Conservation Society   Vol 1: 18126
   United Parents and Teachers Association of Jewish Schools   Vol 1: 18966
Merit Award for Excellent Arrest   Vol. 1: 3560
Merit Awards
   American Academy of Safety Education   Vol. 1: 717
   National Newspaper Publishers Association   Vol 1: 14397
Merit Book Awards   Vol. 1: 9756
Merit Certificate   Vol. 1: 2080
Merit Citation   Vol. 1: 16184
MERIT Competition   Vol. 2: 3251
MERIT Game   Vol. 2: 3251
Merit Medal   Vol. 1: 17539
Merit of Breeding Award   Vol. 1: 1961
Merit of Exhibits   Vol. 1: 3242
Merit of Polish Culture Badge   Vol. 2: 10091
Merit Plaque Award   Vol. 2: 7260
Meritas Award   Vol. 1: 11300
Meritorious Accountant of the Americas   Vol. 1: 10532
Meritorious Achievement Award
   American Association of Zoo Keepers   Vol. 1: 1243
   American Conference of Government Industrial Hygienists   Vol 1: 1799
Meritorious Achievement Award - Coast Guard   Vol. 1: 19201
Meritorious Award   Vol. 1: 17818
Meritorious Civilian Service Award - Air Force   Vol. 1: 19202
Meritorious Civilian Service Award - Army   Vol. 1: 19203
Meritorious Civilian Service Award - Navy/Marine Corps   Vol. 1: 19204
Meritorious Contributions to Psychology on the Part of Nonpsychologists   Vol. 1: 3742
Meritorious Honor Award   Vol. 1: 19295
Meritorious Public Service Awards   Vol. 1: 14684
Meritorious Research Award   Vol. 1: 6916
Meritorious Service Award
   Alpha Omega Fraternity   Vol. 1: 367
   American Association of Homes for the Aging   Vol 1: 1012
   American Baseball Coaches Association   Vol 1: 1324
   American College of Occupational and Environmental Medicine   Vol 1: 1701
   American Horticultural Society   Vol 1: 2360

   American Mosquito Control Association   Vol 1: 3134
   American National Standards Institute   Vol 1: 3182
   American Park and Recreation Society   Vol 1: 3363
   American Public Works Association   Vol 1: 3879
   Australian Veterinary Association   Vol 2: 279
   Caribbean Studies Association   Vol 1: 7312
   Cranial Academy   Vol 1: 8447
   Institute of Electrical and Electronics Engineers - Power Engineering Society   Vol 1: 10312
   Institute of Nuclear Materials Management   Vol 1: 10423
   International Badminton Federation   Vol 2: 3379
   International Technology Education Association   Vol 1: 11336
   Life Communicators Association   Vol 1: 11867
   National Association of Interpretation   Vol 1: 13180
   National Christian College Athletic Association   Vol 1: 13584
   National Council of Examiners for Engineering and Surveying   Vol 1: 13733
   Society of Nematologists   Vol 1: 17938
Meritorious Service Awards   Vol. 1: 6845
Meritorious Service Certificate   Vol. 1: 15630
Meritorious Service Cross - Civil Division   Vol. 1: 6703
Meritorious Service Cross - Military Division   Vol. 1: 6704
Meritorious Service Decoration   Vol. 2: 2352
Meritorious Service in Communications Award   Vol. 1: 4560
Meritorious Service Medal
   Singapore - Office of the Prime Minister   Vol. 2: 10743
   United States Department of Defense - Armed Forces Decorations and Awards   Vol 1: 19170
Meritorious Service Medal - Civil Division   Vol. 1: 6705
Meritorious Service Medal - Military Division   Vol. 1: 6706
Meritorious Service Trophy   Vol. 1: 14314
Meritorious Services Medal   Vol. 2: 3074
Meritorious Unit Citation   Vol. 2: 347
Merkelbachprijs   Vol. 2: 9642
Merlin Medal and Gift   Vol. 2: 2287
Merlinge Prize   Vol. 2: 11896
Mermod Award; Camille   Vol. 1: 3053
Merola International Prize; Aldo   Vol. 2: 8437
Meroney/Mayberry Achievement Award; John   Vol. 1: 9730
Merrell Dow - American Academy of Allergy and Immunology Scholar in Allergy Award   Vol. 1: 490
Merriam Award; C. Hart   Vol. 1: 4662
Merrill Award; George P.   Vol. 1: 12674
Merrill Memorial Award; George P.   Vol. 1: 8702
Merrill Nordic Award; Al   Vol. 1: 19571
Merryfield Design Award; Fred   Vol. 1: 4103
Mertz Trophy; Allegra Knapp   Vol. 1: 19545
Merwin Award for Distinguished Service; Richard E.   Vol. 1: 10304
Merz and Dade Award   Vol. 2: 11464
Mesopotamian Fellowship   Vol. 1: 4015
Mesple; Prix Mady   Vol. 2: 5188
Messel Medal and Lecture   Vol. 2: 4418
Messenger and Brown Prize   Vol. 2: 3060
Messenger Stake   Vol. 1: 19677

Messiaen; Concorso Internazionale di Composizione Organistica Oliver   Vol. 2: 8203
Messing, Jr. Award; Wilma and Roswell   Vol. 1: 5428
Mestaripelimanni, Mestarikansanlaulaja   Vol. 2: 4742
Mestres Prize; Apel Les   Vol. 2: 11215
Metal Building Manufacturers Association Award   Vol. 1: 4364
Metal Mining Division Award for Mining Engineering Achievement   Vol. 1: 6949
The Metallurgical Society   Vol. 1: 12319
Metaserv Awards   Vol. 2: 3142
Metcalf Body of Work and Short Story Awards; Vicky   Vol. 1: 6808
Metcalfe Medallion   Vol. 2: 245
Meteorology Prize   Vol. 2: 4104
Metras Trophy; J. P.   Vol. 1: 6979
Metropolitan Award   Vol. 1: 12948
Metropolitan Life Foundation Award Program for Academic Excellence in Medicine   Vol. 1: 14349
Metropolitan Opera Auditions - Australian Regional Finals   Vol. 2: 571
Mewaldt-King Student Research Award   Vol. 1: 8256
Mexican Order of the Aztec Eagle   Vol. 2: 9133
Mexico City Medal of Civic Merit   Vol. 2: 8961
Mexinox Prize   Vol. 2: 9158
Meyer Gold Headed Cane Award; K. F.   Vol. 1: 4973
Meyer Lectureship; Adolf   Vol. 1: 3643
Meyer Medaille; Hans   Vol. 2: 6588
Meyer Memorial Award; Irving   Vol. 1: 3110
Meyer Memorial Medal; Frank N.   Vol. 1: 8471
Meyer Outstanding Teacher Awards; Agnes   Vol. 1: 20123
Meyer Prize; Carl S.   Vol. 1: 17299
Meyer Prize; Ernst   Vol. 2: 11761
Meyer-Schutzmeister Memorial Award; Luise   Vol. 1: 5661
Meyerhof Award; Geofrey G.   Vol. 1: 6898
Meyers Award; John Francis   Vol. 1: 13546
Mezinarodni Festival Filmu Cestovniho Ruchu - Tourfilm   Vol. 2: 1852
Mezinarodni hudebni soutez Prazske jaro   Vol. 2: 1880
Mezinarodni rozhlasova soutez Mladych hudebniku Concertino Praga   Vol. 2: 1838
Mezinarodni Televizni Festival Zlata Praha   Vol. 2: 1844
MGCA Beautification Certificate   Vol. 1: 9499
MGCA Golden Quill Award   Vol. 1: 9500
The Michael   Vol. 1: 15186
Michael Award   Vol. 2: 6925
Michael Award for Outstanding Emerging Director; Ray   Vol. 1: 19977
Michael Preis   Vol. 2: 6925
Michaut; Prix Narcisse   Vol. 2: 5901
Micheaux Award; The Oscar   Vol. 1: 13464
Michel Award; Dr.   Vol. 1: 11021
Michel; Prix Edmond   Vol. 2: 6391
Michel Prize; Louis   Vol. 2: 5013
Michelangelo Award   Vol. 1: 11488
Michelbacher Prize   Vol. 1: 7336
Michell Medal; A. G. M.   Vol. 2: 473
Michels New Investigator Award; Eugene   Vol. 1: 3487
Michelson Award; Albert A.   Vol. 1: 7330
Michelson Medal; Albert A.   Vol. 1: 9386
Michelson - Morley Award   Vol. 1: 7330
Michener Award   Vol. 1: 12249
Michener Conservation Award; Roland   Vol. 1: 7272
Michener de Journalism; Prix   Vol. 1: 12249

Michener Four-Month Fellowships   Vol. 1: 12250
Michener - Paul Engle Fellowship; James A.   Vol. 1: 11447
Michigan Industrial Hygiene Society Award for Authorship   Vol. 1: 2435
Michot; Prix Auguste   Vol. 2: 1293
Mickle Award; D. Grant   Vol. 1: 18782
Microbiology Prize   Vol. 2: 3166
Micromedex/ENA Emergency Nursing Research Award   Vol. 1: 8903
Miculescu Prize; Constantin   Vol. 2: 10367
Mid-America Country Music Hall of Fame   Vol. 1: 14914
Mid-America Old-Time Fiddlers Hall of Fame   Vol. 1: 14915
Mid-America Publishers Association (MAPA) Awards Program   Vol. 1: 12256
Mid South Playwrights Competition   Vol. 1: 16248
Midalja ghall-Qadi tar-Repubblika   Vol. 2: 8916
Midalja ghall-Qlubija   Vol. 2: 8915
Middlebrooks Award; Thomas A.   Vol. 1: 4481
Middlemore Award   Vol. 2: 2448
Middleton Award; William S.   Vol. 1: 19314
Middleton Shaw Fellowshipq; J.C.   Vol. 2: 10839
Midland Assurance Trophy   Vol. 2: 4166
Midland Bank Prize   Vol. 2: 3098
Midland Bank Travel Award   Vol. 2: 3098
Midwest Award   Vol. 1: 7631
Miedzynarodowe Triennale Grafiki   Vol. 2: 10077
Miedzynarodowe Triennale Rysunku - Wroclaw   Vol. 2: 10218
Miedzynarodowy Konkurs Dyrygentow im. Grzegorza Fitelberga   Vol. 2: 10212
Miedzynarodowy Konkurs Kompozytorski im-Witolda Lutoslawskiego   Vol. 2: 10214
Miembro de Honor   Vol. 2: 11259
Miembro Honorario   Vol. 2: 12144
Miescher Prize; Friedrich   Vol. 2: 11923
Migel Medal for Outstanding Service to Blind Persons   Vol. 1: 2108
Mignet Diploma; Henry   Vol. 2: 5160
Mignon; Grand Prix Marcel   Vol. 2: 1095
Mike Award, Broadcasters Foundation, Inc.   Vol. 1: 6580
Mike of the Year Award   Vol. 1: 12270
Mikeldi de Oro   Vol. 2: 11267
Mikeldi Plata   Vol. 2: 11267
Mikoviny Medal; Samuel   Vol. 2: 7357
Milan International Competition on Maritime Film - TV Documentaries   Vol. 2: 8295
Milan Prize; Fust   Vol. 2: 7404
Milankovitch Medal; Milutin   Vol. 2: 6719
Milburn Award; C. H.   Vol. 2: 2449
Mildenberger Prize; Kenneth W.   Vol. 1: 12397
Mildon Award; James R.   Vol. 1: 10329
Miles Educational Scholarship   Vol. 1: 14747
Miles - Marschall International Award   Vol. 1: 1915
Milione Memorial Award; Louis G.   Vol. 1: 11426
Militaire Willems-Orde   Vol. 2: 9355
Military Astronautics Award   Vol. 1: 1261
Military Awards   Vol. 2: 10440
Military Cross   Vol. 2: 2371
Military Decorations   Vol. 2: 10115
Military Journalist of the Year   Vol. 1: 15899
Military Medal   Vol. 2: 2372
Military Medal for Gallantry   Vol. 2: 7790
Military Merit Medal   Vol. 2: 10935
Military Order of Purple Heart   Vol. 1: 961
Military Order of William   Vol. 2: 9355

Military Photographers of the Year   Vol. 1: 14519
Military Psychology Award   Vol. 1: 3746
Military Psychology Student Paper Award   Vol. 1: 3747
Military Service Medal   Vol. 2: 7252
Military Service Star   Vol. 2: 7253
Miljovernpris   Vol. 2: 9955
Milk Industry Foundation and Kraft General Foods Teaching Award in Dairy Science   Vol. 1: 1917
Milkweed National Fiction Prize   Vol. 1: 12287
Milkweed Prize for Children's Literature   Vol. 1: 12288
Mill Man of the Year Award   Vol. 1: 6933
Mill Mountain Theatre New Play Competition   Vol. 1: 12290
Millar Award
  Chartered Institution of Building Services Engineers   Vol. 2: 2599
  Chartered Institution of Building Services Engineers   Vol. 2: 2599
Millar Award for Innovative Approaches to Adolescent Health Care; Hilary E. C.   Vol. 1: 17396
Millard Awards for Young Playwrights; Gregory   Vol. 1: 12292
Millard Fellowship; Gregory   Vol. 1: 12293
Miller Award
  Cooper Ornithological Society   Vol. 1: 8257
  Deep South Writers Conference   Vol 1: 8568
Miller Award; Banner I.   Vol. 1: 3092
Miller Award; Carroll R.
  American Society for Horticultural Science   Vol. 1: 4145
  National Peach Council   Vol 1: 14459
Miller Award; Elizabeth McWilliams   Vol. 1: 17267
Miller Award for Excellence in Cold Planing; John A.   Vol. 1: 5377
Miller Award; Merl K.   Vol. 1: 4104
Miller Award; Muriel McLatchie   Vol. 1: 5858
Miller Award; Norton H. Walton/Russell L.   Vol. 1: 2606
Miller Award; Susan   Vol. 1: 17239
Miller Biomedical Award; John J.   Vol. 1: 10585
Miller Cartographic Medal; O. M.   Vol. 1: 2155
Miller Essay Prize; John William   Vol. 1: 12297
Miller Legal Services Award; Loren   Vol. 1: 18467
Miller Lite Women's Sports Journalism Awards   Vol. 1: 20430
Miller Medal; Willet G.   Vol. 1: 16959
Miller Memorial Award; Barse   Vol. 1: 5055
Miller Memorial Award; Monte   Vol. 2: 283
Miller Memorial Lecture Award; Samuel Charles   Vol. 1: 649
Miller Memorial Medal Award; Samuel Wylie   Vol. 1: 5085
Miller Memorial Prize; Robert A.   Vol. 1: 7897
Miller; Prix Louis P.   Vol. 2: 5886
Miller Prizes   Vol. 2: 3252
Milli Award   Vol. 2: 199
Millie Award   Vol. 1: 8695
Millier; Prix Marcelle   Vol. 2: 5891
Millikan Medal; Robert A.   Vol. 1: 1129
Million Mile Club Award   Vol. 1: 14657
Millot; Fondation Georges   Vol. 2: 5568
Millot; Prix Georges   Vol. 2: 5309
Mills Award; C. Wright   Vol. 1: 17643
Mills Award for Meritorious Service   Vol. 1: 1637
Mills Award; Miriam   Vol. 1: 16307

Mills Outstanding Contribution to Emergency Medicine; James D. Vol. 1: 1637
Mills Scholarship; J. Clawson Vol. 1: 12234
Millson Award for Invention; Henry E. Vol. 1: 1221
Millwright Job of the Year Vol. 1: 18296
Milne Memorial Award; Jack Vol. 1: 433
Milner Award Vol. 1: 9432
Mimografieprijs Amsterdam Vol. 2: 9643
Minah Distinguished Award; Theodore Vol. 1: 12990
Minarikovo Odlicje Vol. 2: 10803
Minasian Award; George T. Vol. 1: 222
MIND Book of the Year - Allen Lane Award Vol. 2: 3651
Miner Award; Neil A. Vol. 1: 13119
Mineral Economics Award Vol. 1: 2639
Mineral Industry Education Award Vol. 1: 2640
Mineral Resources Student Prize Paper Contest Vol. 1: 12327
Mineralogical Society of America Award Vol. 1: 12303
Mineralogy/Petrology Research Grant Vol. 1: 12304
Minerva Awards
 Chartered Society of Designers Vol. 2: 2609
 New York Public Library Vol 1: 15265
Mini-America's Cup Vol. 1: 12323
Mini Rod Puller of the Year Vol. 1: 14903
Mini Sled of the Year Vol. 1: 14904
Mining and Exploration Division Distinguished Service Award Vol. 1: 17568
Minister of National Defense Prize Vol. 2: 10095
Minister of the Year Vol. 1: 10931
Ministere des Affaires etrangeres et du Commerce international Vol. 1: 6717
Ministry of Defence Medal Vol. 2: 4305
Ministry of National Education Medal Vol. 2: 1659
Minit/EMJ Trophy Vol. 2: 3657
Minkowski Prize Vol. 2: 6705
Minks Award; Nancy Vol. 1: 2381
Minnesmedaljen i guld Vol. 2: 11519
Minnesota Award Vol. 1: 12914
Minnesota Blue Award Vol. 1: 2382
Minnesota Gold Award Vol. 1: 2383
Minnesota International Human Rights Award Vol. 1: 12331
Minnesota Voices Project Vol. 1: 15206
Minns Award; Francis Vol. 2: 2203
Minor Hockey Player of the Year Vol. 1: 9960
Minor League Executive of the Year Vol. 1: 18363
Minor League Manager of the Year Vol. 1: 18364
Minor League Player of the Year Vol. 1: 18365
Minor Pro Coach of the Year Vol. 1: 9960
Minor Pro Player of the Year Vol. 1: 9960
Minority Achievement Award Vol. 1: 3488
Minority Business Leadership Awards Vol. 1: 14370
Minority Initiatives Award Vol. 1: 3489
Minority Issues Award Vol. 1: 8547
Minority Network Trainer of the Year Award Vol. 1: 4336
Minority Scientist Development Award Vol. 1: 2237
Minority Student Awards Vol. 1: 17676
Minority Travel Fellowship Award Vol. 1: 1692
Minshall Award; Lewis Vol. 2: 2892
Mintz Award; Morton Vol. 1: 20106
Minville; Prix Esdras- Vol. 1: 17386

Mirkin Service Award; A. J. Vol. 1: 5608
Mirlo Poetry Prize; Josue Vol. 2: 9049
Mirror of Spain Prize Vol. 2: 11221
Misener Award; Chandler - Vol. 1: 10640
Mishima Award; Yukio Vol. 2: 8743
Miss America Vol. 1: 12346
Miss America Women's Achievement Award Vol. 1: 12347
Miss Black America Vol. 1: 5153
Miss Dance of Great Britain Vol. 2: 3398
Miss Exotic World Contest Vol. 1: 9026
Miss Galaxy International Pageant Vol. 1: 12349
Miss Indian World Vol. 1: 9509
Miss Majorette of America Vol. 1: 5128
Miss Redheads International (State) Queen Vol. 1: 16739
Miss Teen USA Vol. 1: 12351
Miss Teen USA Pageant Vol. 1: 12351
Miss Universe Vol. 1: 12352
Miss Universe Pageant Vol. 1: 12352
Miss USA Vol. 1: 12353
Miss USA Pageant Vol. 1: 12353
Missarel; Prix Nicolas Vol. 2: 5902
Mission Accomplished Creative Commercial Production Awards Vol. 1: 6669
Mission Support Trophy Vol. 1: 14096
Mississippi Children's Book Award Vol. 1: 12355
Missouri Honor Awards Vol. 1: 19842
Missouri Southern International Piano Competition Vol. 1: 12370
Mistral Inter-American Culture Prize; Gabriela Vol. 1: 15829
MIT Prize for Invention and Innovation; The Lemelson- Vol. 1: 12114
MIT Trophy Vol. 1: 14643
Mita Society for Library and Information Science Prize Vol. 2: 8700
Mita Toshokan Joho Gakkai-Sho Vol. 2: 8700
Mitchell Award; Bob Vol. 2: 298
Mitchell Award; Charles L. Vol. 1: 3076
Mitchell Award for C4 Excellence; General Bill Vol. 1: 244
Mitchell Award; Gen. Billy Vol. 1: 244
Mitchell Award; H. L. Vol. 1: 18216
Mitchell Award; James G. Vol. 1: 14852
Mitchell Award; S. Weir Vol. 1: 619
Mitchell Community Development Award; Jan Vol. 1: 14052
Mitchell International Prize for Sustainable Development; George and Cynthia Vol. 1: 10018
Mitchell Memorial Fund; Prof. W. M. Vol. 2: 3992
Mitchell National Debate Trophy; Harland B. Vol. 1: 14022
Mitchell Prize; Eric Vol. 1: 12372
Mitchell Prize for the History of Art Vol. 1: 12372
Mitchell Prize; Lillias Vol. 2: 7835
Mitchell Young Extension Worker Award; Nolan Vol. 1: 4362
Mitjavile; Prix Henry et Mary Jane Vol. 2: 4845
Mitra Memorial Lecture; Sisir Kumar Vol. 2: 7659
Mitropoulos International Music Competition; Dimitri Vol. 1: 18922
Mitry Award; Jean Vol. 2: 8400
Mitscherlich-Denkmunze; Alexander- Vol. 2: 6544
Mittasch-Medaille; Alwin Vol. 2: 6619
Mittelstadt Ski Jumping Officials Award Vol. 1: 19572
Mixed Blood versus America Vol. 1: 12374

MLA Award for Distinguished Public Service Vol. 1: 12174
MLA Research, Development and Demonstration Projects Awards Vol. 1: 12175
MLA Scholarship for Minority Students Vol. 1: 12176
MLA Scholarships and Fellowships Vol. 1: 12176
Mlada Fronta Award Vol. 2: 1887
Mlade leta Prize Vol. 2: 10786
Mobil Business in the Arts Awards Vol. 2: 529
Mobil Children's Culture Award Vol. 2: 8702
Mobil Cup Vol. 1: 19949
Mobil Design Award for Small Firms Vol. 2: 2741
Mobil Fellowship in Arts Administration Vol. 2: 529
Mobil Grand Prix Final; IAAF/ Vol. 2: 9314
Mobil Music Award Vol. 2: 8703
Mobil Playwriting Competition for the Royal Exchange Theatre, Manchester Vol. 2: 4004
Mobil Travel Guide Five-Star Award Vol. 1: 12378
Mobius Advertising Awards Vol. 1: 19351
Mobius Broadcasting Awards Vol. 1: 19351
Mobral Journalism Prize Vol. 2: 1412
MOC Cup Vol. 2: 3647
Mockel Grand Prize for Poetry; Albert Vol. 2: 1289
Modeling Awards Vol. 1: 20508
Models Hall of Fame Vol. 1: 12389
Modern Language Association Prize for a First Book Vol. 1: 12398
Modern Language Association Prize for Independent Scholars Vol. 1: 12399
Modern Maturity Awards for Creativity in Advertising Depicting Older Americans Vol. 1: 1163
Modern Medicine Award for Distinguished Achievement Vol. 1: 12407
Modern Office Technology/IFMA Foundation Award for Excellence in Facility Vol. 1: 12024
Modern Poet Prize Vol. 2: 8631
Modern Railroad Man of the Year Vol. 1: 12412
Modisette Award Vol. 1: 11957
Mody-Unichem Prize for Research in Cardiology, Neurology and Gastroenterology; Amrut Vol. 2: 7596
Mody-Unichem Prize for Research in Maternal and Child Health and Chest Diseases; Amrut Vol. 2: 7597
Moe Prize for a Catalogue of Distinction in the Arts; Henry Allen Vol. 1: 15288
Moe Prize in the Humanities; Henry Allen Vol. 1: 3436
Moffat - Frank E. Nichol Harbor and Coastal Engineering Award; John G. Vol. 1: 4482
Moffitt Memorial Human Rights Awards; Letelier - Vol. 1: 10225
Mogens and Wilhelm Ellermann Foundation Prize Vol. 2: 11943
Mohawk-Hudson Regional Art Exhibition Award Vol. 1: 17090
Mohr Medal; William Vol. 1: 5238
Moisseiff Award Vol. 1: 4483
Mold Makers Division Distinguished Service Award Vol. 1: 18051
Molesworth Award; Jack Vol. 1: 8109
Molfenter-Preis der Landeshauptstadt Stuttgart/Galerie; Hans- Vol. 2: 7137
Molieres; Les Vol. 2: 4970
Molins Award; Desmond Vol. 2: 2739
Moll Memorial Award; Dale C. Vol. 1: 8207

Mollegaard BB RAT Travel Fellowship   Vol. 2: 6706
Moller/AGO Award in Choral Composition   Vol. 1: 2196
Molodovsky Award; Nicholas   Vol. 1: 5555
Mols Award; Herbert Joseph   Vol. 1: 434
Molster Fonds Prijs   Vol. 2: 9385
Molster Foundation; Prize of the   Vol. 2: 9385
Molt Trophy; Alice D.   Vol. 1: 14645
Mompezat; Prix Jacqueline   Vol. 2: 6335
Mompezat; Prix Marcel   Vol. 2: 6338
Monash Medal; John   Vol. 2: 474
Moncado Prizes for Best Article   Vol. 1: 17556
Moncrieff Prize; Scott   Vol. 2: 4397
Mond Lectureship; Ludwig   Vol. 2: 4210
Mondor; Fondation Henri   Vol. 2: 5577
Mondor; Prix Henri
   Academie Nationale de Medecine   Vol. 2: 4844
   Institut de France - Academie Francaise   Vol 2: 5866
Mondragon Medal; Magdalena   Vol. 2: 8922
Mondriaan Lecture; Piet   Vol. 2: 9620
Monell Medal and the Ambrose Monell Prize for Distinguished Service in Mineral Technology; Ambrose   Vol. 1: 7986
Money for Women/Barbara Deming Memorial Fund Grants   Vol. 1: 12414
Monika Foundation Prize; Anna   Vol. 2: 7057
Monika Stiftung Preis; Anna-   Vol. 2: 7057
Monitor Awards   Vol. 1: 11346
Monk International Jazz Competition; Thelonious   Vol. 1: 12416
Monk International Jazz Piano Competition; Thelonious   Vol. 1: 12416
Monnier; Grand Prix Thyde   Vol. 2: 6266
Monnier; Prix Thyde   Vol. 2: 6298
Monod; Prix Gabriel   Vol. 2: 5746
Monpetit; Prix Michel   Vol. 2: 5701
Monro Memorial Cup; George   Vol. 2: 4047
Monroe Library Adult Services Award; Margaret E.   Vol. 1: 2946
Monroe Poetry Award; Harriet   Vol. 1: 19757
Montaigne Prize   Vol. 2: 7117
Montald; Prix Constant   Vol. 2: 954
Montalte; Prix de Poesie Louis   Vol. 2: 6277
Montana Book Awards   Vol. 2: 9705
Montana Memorial Prize; Pietro and Alfrieda   Vol. 1: 14714
Monte Carlo International Forum for New Images Imagina   Vol. 2: 9321
Monte Carlo International Prize of Contemporary Art   Vol. 2: 9310
Montefiore Foundation Prize; George   Vol. 2: 1046
Montefiore; Prix de la Fondation George   Vol. 2: 1046
Monteiro; Premio Manuel Alves   Vol. 2: 10257
Monteiro Prize; Manuel Alves   Vol. 2: 10257
Montes de Oca Prize; Juan Jose   Vol. 2: 86
Montgolfier Diploma   Vol. 2: 5161
Montgolfier Trophy   Vol. 1: 11873
Montgomery Consulting Engineers/AEEP Master's Thesis Awards; James M.   Vol. 1: 5782
Montgomery Distinguished Service Award; Reid   Vol. 1: 7912
Month of Photography Awards   Vol. 2: 6147
Monticello College Foundation Fellowship for Women   Vol. 1: 15316
Montreal International Festival of Films and Videos by Women   Vol. 1: 7704
Montreal International Festival of Films on Art   Vol. 1: 12423
Montreal International Festival of New Cinema and Video   Vol. 1: 12425

Montreal International Music Competition   Vol. 1: 12427
Montreal Medal   Vol. 1: 7556
Montreal World Film Festival   Vol. 1: 12436
Montreux Achievement Gold Medal   Vol. 2: 11851
Montreux International Choral Festival   Vol. 2: 11879
Montreux International Electronic Cinema Festival   Vol. 2: 11852
Monturiol Medal and Plaque for Science and Technology; Narcis   Vol. 2: 11188
MOOFW Award   Vol. 1: 12282
Moomba International Amateur Film Festival   Vol. 2: 527
Moon Fish Award   Vol. 2: 7052
Mooney Award; James   Vol. 1: 18208
Mooney Distinguished Technology Award; Melvin   Vol. 1: 1504
Moonsnail Award   Vol. 1: 6113
Moore Alumni Award; Mary   Vol. 1: 5284
Moore Award   Vol. 1: 1048
Moore Award; Bessie Boehm   Vol. 1: 2821
Moore Award; Clarence H.   Vol. 1: 15925
Moore Award for Outstanding New Academic Faculty Member; Margaret L.   Vol. 1: 3490
Moore Award; Michael   Vol. 1: 5174
Moore Award; Roy E.   Vol. 1: 435
Moore Award; Velma K.   Vol. 1: 15281
Moore Award; Virginia P.   Vol. 1: 6746
Moore Career Development Awards; Oncology Nursing Foundation/Pearl   Vol. 1: 15645
Moore Medal   Vol. 1: 17592
Moore Medal for Excellence in Paleontology; Raymond C.   Vol. 1: 17592
Moore Medal; George   Vol. 2: 4048
Moore Medal; Leo B.   Vol. 1: 18453
Moore Memorial Award; Barrington   Vol. 1: 17685
Moore Memorial Award; Lucy B.   Vol. 1: 5056
Moore Prize; Glover   Vol. 1: 12359
Moore Trophy; W. Max   Vol. 1: 16713
Moore Writer-in-Washington; Jenny McKean   Vol. 1: 12439
Moortidevi Sahitya Puraskar   Vol. 2: 7487
Moose Jaw Kinsmen International Band and Choral Festival   Vol. 1: 12441
Mora Distinction; Jose Maria Luis   Vol. 2: 9008
Mora Memorial Medal; Ferenc   Vol. 2: 7405
Moragas; Premi Ricard   Vol. 2: 11163
Moral Leadership Award   Vol. 1: 14267
Morales First Prize for Popular Music; Jose A.   Vol. 2: 1655
Morales Prize; Enrique   Vol. 2: 1746
Moran Memorial Research Award; James D.   Vol. 1: 2340
Moran Portraiture Prize; Douglas J.   Vol. 2: 693
Morand; Grand Prix de Litterature Paul   Vol. 2: 5802
Morando Lifetime Achievement Award; Rocco V.   Vol. 1: 13095
Mordica Memorial Award   Vol. 1: 20337
More Medal for Book Collecting; Sir Thomas   Vol. 1: 9615
Moreell Medal   Vol. 1: 17710
Morelli; Fondazione Eugenio   Vol. 2: 8053
Morey Award; George W.   Vol. 1: 1467
Morey Book Award; Charles Rufus   Vol. 1: 7890
Morgan Award; Frederick C.   Vol. 1: 9865
Morgan Award; Joseph F.   Vol. 1: 18719
Morgan Individual Achievement Award; Frederick C.   Vol. 1: 9865
Morgan Medal; Philip F.   Vol. 1: 20156
Morgan Medal; Thomas Hunt   Vol. 1: 9535

Morgan Research Award; Agnes Faye   Vol. 1: 11437
Morgan Scholarship Award; Hazel B.   Vol. 1: 12481
Morgan Silver Cup; John E.   Vol. 2: 3095
Morgan Trophy; Daniel   Vol. 1: 14645
Morgenthau Award; Hans J.   Vol. 1: 13631
Morgenthau Memorial Award; Hans J.   Vol. 1: 13631
Morgotch Award; Larry   Vol. 1: 17068
Morikawa Evangelism Award; Jitsuo   Vol. 1: 1297
Morim Award   Vol. 1: 11565
Morin; Prix Victor-   Vol. 1: 17393
Morishita Prize   Vol. 2: 8502
Morishita Sho   Vol. 2: 8502
Morison Prize; Samuel Eliot   Vol. 1: 17557
Morlan Faculty Secretary Award; Robert L.   Vol. 1: 15631
Morley Award; Colonel Bill   Vol. 1: 5284
Morley Award; Elise   Vol. 1: 5283
Morley Outstanding Programmer Award; Patsy   Vol. 1: 12844
Morneault Piano Competition; Portland Symphony Orchestra/Priscilla   Vol. 1: 16326
Morrell Memorial Award; David   Vol. 1: 18398
Morris Award; Arthur J.   Vol. 1: 8221
Morris Award; Old Tom   Vol. 1: 9642
Morris Award; Robert   Vol. 1: 20182
Morris Jr. Journalism Internship Program in the Arab World; Joe Alex   Vol. 1: 13826
Morris Memorial Prize; Lindsay   Vol. 1: 14714
Morris Prize Article Contest; Gerald E.   Vol. 1: 12552
Morris Sustaining Member of the Year Award; J. W.   Vol. 1: 17711
Morris Trophy; Ted   Vol. 1: 6980
Morrison Award   Vol. 1: 4402
Morrison Award; Francis   Vol. 1: 17062
Morrison Communicator Award; Thomas   Vol. 1: 19296
Morrison Playwriting Fellowship; Jack   Vol. 1: 17214
Morrison Short Story Award; FAW John   Vol. 2: 391
Morrison Trophy; W. A.   Vol. 2: 9819
Morrisset; Prix Gerard-   Vol. 1: 16614
Morrow Award; Elizabeth Cutter   Vol. 1: 20627
MORS Prize   Vol. 1: 12279
Morse Lectureship   Vol. 1: 15735
Morse Medal; Samuel Finley Breese   Vol. 1: 2156
Morse Poetry Prize; Samuel French   Vol. 1: 12443
Morse Writer's Award; Robert T.   Vol. 1: 3644
Mortar Board Chapter Citation Award   Vol. 1: 12445
Mortar Board Honorary Member   Vol. 1: 12446
Mortimer Memorial Silver Plated Trophy; James   Vol. 1: 20247
Mortiz International Prize for Novel; Editorial Planeta - Joaquin   Vol. 2: 8980
Mortiz; Premio Internacional para Novela Planeta - Joaquin   Vol. 2: 8980
Morton Award; Harry   Vol. 1: 11133
Morton Award; J. Sterling   Vol. 1: 12788
Morton Award; Jack A.   Vol. 1: 10282
Morton Lecture   Vol. 2: 2177
Mosby Award; Henry S.   Vol. 1: 15004
Moscow International Ballet Competition   Vol. 2: 10457
Moscow International Film Festival   Vol. 2: 10474
Moseley Award; Harry G.   Vol. 1: 172

Moseley Jr. Award in Radiation Protection in Medicine; Robert D.   Vol. 1: 13814
Moser Memorial Trophy; Mike   Vol. 1: 6981
Mosher and Frederick C. Mosher Award; William E.   Vol. 1: 4268
Most Active Woman Award   Vol. 1: 12752
Most Ancient and Most Noble Order of the Thistle   Vol. 2: 2373
Most Beautiful and the Best Children's Book of spring, summer, autumn, winter in Slovakia   Vol. 2: 10760
Most Beautiful Books of Austria   Vol. 2: 741
Most Beautiful House in the World Competition   Vol. 1: 7592
Most Colorful Walkaloosa   Vol. 1: 20085
Most Cooperative to the Press   Vol. 1: 9980
Most Distinguished Greek American   Vol. 1: 18917
Most Distinguished Order of St. Michael and St. George   Vol. 2: 2374
Most Excellent Order of the British Empire   Vol. 2: 2375
Most Honourable Order of the Bath   Vol. 2: 2376
Most Improved Associations of the Year   Vol. 1: 19950
Most Improved Award   Vol. 1: 18234
Most Improved Chapter of the Year   Vol. 1: 347
Most Improved Driver
　International Motor Sports Association   Vol. 1: 11107
　International Motor Sports Association   Vol 1: 11108
Most Improved Golfer   Vol. 1: 12781
Most Improved Golfer Men/Women Pros   Vol. 1: 9645
Most Improved Players   Vol. 1: 18622
Most Innovative Advanced Composite Application Award   Vol. 1: 18044
Most Innovative Local Market Development Award   Vol. 1: 14578
Most Interesting Surveying Project of the Year Award   Vol. 1: 14815
Most Noble Order of the Garter   Vol. 2: 2377
Most Outstanding Catholic War Veteran   Vol. 1: 7402
Most Outstanding Educational Program   Vol. 1: 16705
Most Outstanding Lithuanian Woman   Vol. 1: 11908
Most Outstanding Member   Vol. 1: 19501
Most Outstanding Post of the Year Award   Vol. 1: 7403
Most Popular Convention Award   Vol. 1: 3100
Most Registrations   Vol. 1: 14144
Most Significant Player of the Past 30 Years   Vol. 1: 20526
Most Valuable Member Award   Vol. 1: 10671
Most Valuable Player   Vol. 1: 8245
Most Valuable Player in the Rose Bowl   Vol. 1: 397
Most Valuable Player; Super Bowl   Vol. 1: 14003
Most Versatile Horse Award   Vol. 1: 7955
Mostacci Prize; Antonino   Vol. 2: 8420
Mostra Cinematografica Internazionale - La Natura, l'Uomo e il suo Ambiente   Vol. 2: 8301
Mostra de Valencia, Palmero de Oro   Vol. 2: 11305
Mostra Internazionale del Cinema; Biennale di Venezia -   Vol. 2: 8470
Mostra Internazionale del Film d'Autore Gran Premio   Vol. 2: 8297
Moten Award; Ollie B.   Vol. 1: 1599
MOTESZ-Dij   Vol. 2: 7308

MOTESZ Prize   Vol. 2: 7308
Mother and Child International Award   Vol. 2: 11881
Mother/Father of the Year Award   Vol. 1: 14380
Mother Goose Award   Vol. 2: 2209
Mother Lode International Color Slide Exhibition and Travel Photo Exhibition   Vol. 1: 16230
Mother Lode National Art Exhibition   Vol. 1: 12454
Mother Lode Western Region Art Exhibition   Vol. 1: 12454
Mother of the Year   Vol. 1: 3141
Motivator of the Year   Vol. 1: 5830
Motley EMT (Emergency Medical Technician) of the Year Award; Robert E.   Vol. 1: 13096
Motor Trend Car of the Year   Vol. 1: 12458
Motor Trend Import Car of the Year   Vol. 1: 12459
Motor Trend Truck of the Year   Vol. 1: 12460
Motorcycle Safety Foundation Awards Program   Vol. 1: 12462
Motorsports Hall of Fame   Vol. 1: 12376
Motru prize; Constantin Radulescu   Vol. 2: 10368
Mott Conservationist of the Year; William Penn   Vol. 1: 14454
Mott, Jr. Awards Program; William Penn   Vol. 1: 14758
Mott - Kappa Tau Alpha Research/Book Award; Frank Luther   Vol. 1: 11651
Mott Medal; Charles S.   Vol. 1: 9531
Mott Scholarship; Gerald O.   Vol. 1: 8472
Mouezy-Eon; Prix Andre   Vol. 2: 6397
Mount Scopus Citation   Vol. 1: 2121
Mountainfilm Festival in Telluride   Vol. 1: 12471
Mountbatten Medal   Vol. 2: 4101
Mountbatten Premium   Vol. 2: 3273
Mounte Carlo Television Festival   Vol. 2: 9322
Movie Worsts Awards   Vol. 1: 9809
Mowbray Ecumenical Award; Luke   Vol. 1: 1298
Moye; Prix Marcel   Vol. 2: 6228
Moyer Resident Award; Carl A.   Vol. 1: 1383
Mozart Concerto Prize   Vol. 2: 326
Mozart Festival Competition for Young Artists   Vol. 2: 6919
Mozart Interpretation-Preis   Vol. 2: 914
Mozart Medal
　Instituto Cultural Domecq, A.C.   Vol. 2: 9030
　Vienna Mozart Society   Vol 2: 913
Mozart Opera Prize   Vol. 2: 911
Mozart Prize   Vol. 1: 7840
Mozart-Prize   Vol. 2: 11676
Mozartfest Wettbewerb   Vol. 2: 6919
Mozartfest-Wettbewerb Wurzburg fur Gesang/Oper   Vol. 2: 6919
MPA Kelly Award   Vol. 1: 12000
MPI Planner of the Year   Vol. 1: 12204
MPI Supplier of the Year   Vol. 1: 12205
Mr. and Ms. Future Business Executive   Vol. 1: 9456
Mr. and Ms. Future Business Leaders of America   Vol. 1: 9457
Mr. and Ms. Future Business Teacher   Vol. 1: 9458
Mr. Blackwell's Hall of Fame   Vol. 1: 12474
Mr. H's Prize   Vol. 2: 8632
Mr. OX5   Vol. 1: 15877
Mrazec Prize; Ludovic   Vol. 2: 10369
Mrazik-Cleaver Canadian Picture Book Award; Elizabeth   Vol. 1: 10806
MRC Scientists   Vol. 1: 12189

Mrost Prize; Mischa   Vol. 2: 11049
Mrozowski Award; Stanislaw W.   Vol. 1: 1419
MRS Medalist Program   Vol. 1: 12123
MS Achievement Award   Vol. 1: 14381
MS Hope Award   Vol. 1: 14382
MS Patient Achievement Award   Vol. 1: 14381
Ms Photogenic Contest   Vol. 1: 16498
MS Public Education Awards   Vol. 1: 14383
MSD AGVET AABP Award for Excellence in Preventive Veterinary Medicine - Beef Cattle   Vol. 1: 941
MSD AGVET AABP Award for Excellence in Preventive Veterinary Medicine - Dairy Cattle   Vol. 1: 942
MSD AGVET Dairy Management Research Award   Vol. 1: 1916
MSI Annual Doctoral Dissertation Proposal Award   Vol. 1: 12097
MSMA Distinguished Service Award   Vol. 1: 12016
MTNA-Baldwin Junior High School Piano Award   Vol. 1: 12520
MTNA-Collegiate Chamber Music Competition   Vol. 1: 12521
MTNA National Student Composition Contest   Vol. 1: 12519
MTNA-Selmer Junior High School Instrumental Competitions   Vol. 1: 12522
MTNA-Shepherd Distinguished Composer of the Year Award   Vol. 1: 12523
MTNA-Wurlitzer Collegiate Artist Competition   Vol. 1: 12524
MTNA-Yamaha High School Auditions   Vol. 1: 12525
MTS Special Commendation   Vol. 1: 12091
MTV Station I.D. Competition   Vol. 1: 5172
MTV Video Music Awards   Vol. 1: 12479
Mu Phi Epsilon Annual Awards and Contests   Vol. 1: 12481
Mu Phi Epsilon International Competition   Vol. 1: 12483
Mudd Award; Stuart   Vol. 2: 6065
Mudge Citation; Isadore Gilbert   Vol. 1: 2945
Mudge - R. R. Bowker Award; Isadore Gilbert   Vol. 1: 2945
Muehsam Memorial Award; Gerd   Vol. 1: 5299
Muellen Whirly-Girls Scholarship; Doris   Vol. 1: 20258
Mueller Lecture Award; James I.   Vol. 1: 1468
Mueller Medal   Vol. 2: 190
MUFSO Golden Chain Award   Vol. 1: 15066
MUFSO Pioneer of the Year   Vol. 1: 15067
Muhlmann Prize; Maria and Eric   Vol. 1: 6097
Muir Award; John   Vol. 1: 17240
Muir Medical Film Festival; John   Vol. 1: 55
Mullard Award and Medal   Vol. 2: 4153
Mullen National Arts and Humanities Award; Dorothy   Vol. 1: 14560
Muller Award   Vol. 2: 10240
Muller Lectureship; Hugo   Vol. 2: 4211
Muller Prize; Dr. Erich   Vol. 2: 6801
Mulliez; Bourse Gonzague   Vol. 2: 4802
Mullins Award; Nicholas   Vol. 1: 17604
Multatuliprijs   Vol. 2: 9644
Multi-Cultural Playwrights' Festival   Vol. 1: 17164
Multi-Cultural Theatre Works Series   Vol. 1: 17164
Multi-Event Outstanding Women Award   Vol. 1: 19962
Multi-Unit Food Service Operator of the Year   Vol. 1: 15068
Multicultural Programs Awards   Vol. 1: 12845
Multinational Force and Observers Medal   Vol. 1: 19171
Mumford Prize; Erika   Vol. 1: 15129

Munasinghe Memorial Award; T. P. de S. Vol. 2: 11405
Mundt Trophy; Senator Karl E. Vol. 1: 14023
Munford Research Fellowship; Ulverscroft Vol. 2: 3573
Mungo Park Medal Vol. 2: 10632
Munich International Filmschool Festival Vol. 2: 7059
Munich International Music Competition of the Broadcasting Stations of the Federal Republic of Germany (ARD) Vol. 2: 6974
Municipal Art League Prize Vol. 1: 5297
Municipal Art Society of New York Annual Awards Vol. 1: 12489
Municipal Chapter of Toronto IODE Book Award Vol. 1: 11433
Munk Poetry Award; Margaret Rampton Vol. 1: 8631
Munkacsy Prize for Visual and Applied Arts; Michaly Vol. 2: 7406
Munro Oration; C. H. Vol. 2: 475
Munson Award; Ida Vol. 1: 2267
Muntendamprijs; Prof. Dr. P. Vol. 2: 9661
Murchison Award Vol. 2: 4013
Murchison Medal Vol. 2: 2925
Murdie Memorial Awards; Ian Vol. 2: 373
Murdoch Award; Connie Vol. 1: 17325
Murgoci Prize; Gheorghe Vol. 2: 10370
Murie Award; Olaus and Margaret Vol. 1: 20294
Murillo Annual Salon of Visual Arts Prizes; Pedro Domingo Vol. 2: 1389
Murillo Toro Medal for Postal Merit; Manuel Vol. 2: 1605
Murnaghan Memorial Prize; James Vol. 2: 7783
Murphree Award in Industrial and Engineering Chemistry; E. V. Vol. 1: 1567
Murphy Award for Excellence in Copy Editing; John Vol. 1: 18637
Murphy Award; Glenn Vol. 1: 4105
Murphy Award; John Killam Vol. 1: 7350
Murphy Community Service Awards; Carl Vol. 1: 14397
Murphy Excellence in Teaching Award; Mother Evelyn Vol. 1: 16899
Murphy Prize; The Forbes
   Institute of Chartered Accountants of Scotland Vol. 2: 10564
   Institute of Chartered Accountants of Scotland Vol 2: 10565
Murray Award; Henry A. Vol. 1: 3805
Murray Award; John Courtney Vol. 1: 7387
Murray - Green Award Vol. 1: 2029
Murray - Green - Meany Award for Community Service Vol. 1: 2029
Murray Prize Competition; Roger F. Vol. 1: 10230
Murrell Award; Hywel Vol. 2: 2805
Murrow Award; Edward R.
   American Film and Video Association Vol. 1: 2048
   Corporation for Public Broadcasting Vol 1: 8282
   Overseas Press Club of America Vol 1: 15875
Murrow Awards; Edward R. Vol. 1: 16656
Murtagh Memorial Prize; Lillian Vol. 1: 2197
MUSA Silwer Medalje (Navorsing en Voorligting) Vol. 2: 10863
MUSA Silwer Medalje (Voorligting) Vol. 2: 10861
Museo Angel Orensanz and Artes del Serrablo International Sculpture Award Vol. 2: 11307
Museum of Haiku Literature Awards Vol. 1: 9757

Museum of the Year Award Vol. 2: 3039
Museum of the Year Awards Vol. 2: 532
Musgrave Medal Vol. 2: 8482
Music Award Vol. 1: 16114
Music Campers Citation Vol. 1: 13432
Music Center Spotlight Awards Vol. 1: 12513
Music City News Country Awards Vol. 1: 9735
Music City News Country Songwriters Awards Vol. 1: 9734
Music Critics Prizes Vol. 2: 6406
Music Prize Vol. 2: 8831
Music Teacher Awards Vol. 2: 3667
Musica Antiqua Competition Bruges Vol. 2: 1152
MUSICA SACRA Bach Vocal Competition Vol. 1: 12527
Musical Freestyle Awards Vol. 1: 19326
Musician of the Year
   Incorporated Society of Musicians Vol. 2: 3041
   Musical America Publishing Vol 1: 12529
   Society of Norwegian Composers Vol 2: 9971
Musicians Benevolent Fund Awards Vol. 2: 3669
Musicians Emergency Fund's Vocal Awards Vol. 1: 12537
Musikwissenschaftspreis Vol. 2: 915
Muskett Award; Netta Vol. 2: 3857
Musselman Award; Dawn Vol. 1: 19441
Musselman Memorial Award; Don S. Vol. 1: 14557
Mussolini; Coppa Vol. 2: 8470
Muteau; Prix General Vol. 2: 5749
MVP of the Playoffs Vol. 1: 9960
MVSA Goue Medalje Vol. 2: 10860
MVSA Silwer Medalje (Navorsing) Vol. 2: 10862
MWSP Meritorious Award Vol. 1: 11470
My Country - USSR Award
   All-Union Leninist Young Communist League Vol. 2: 10441
   All-Union Leninist Young Communist League Vol 2: 10442
Myer Award; Haydn Vol. 1: 8112
Myers Award in Materials Engineering; Sir Rupert H. Vol. 2: 702
Myers Award; Paul W. Vol. 1: 245
Myers Brother Award Vol. 1: 14374
Myers Man of the Year Award; Howdy Vol. 1: 19414
Myers Nelson Achievement Awards; Beverly Vol. 1: 12646
Myers Nelson Student Awards; Beverly Vol. 1: 12647
Myers Writers Award; Cordelia Vol. 1: 3301
Myhre Awards; Paul Vol. 1: 19843
Myrdal Award for Evaluation Practice Vol. 1: 2008
Myrdal Award for Government Service Vol. 1: 2009
Myrdal Award for Science Vol. 1: 2007
Myrdal Human Service Delivery Award; Gunnar Vol. 1: 2008
Myrdal Prize; Gunnar Vol. 2: 11621
Myrdals och sparbankernas pris for basta artikel; Gunnar Vol. 2: 11621
Myrto's Book Award Vol. 2: 7221
Mystery Prize Vol. 2: 8388
Mystery Time Short Story Contest; Rhyme Time Poetry Contest/Story Time Fiction Contest/ Vol. 1: 16830
Mythic Society Scholar Vol. 2: 7713
Mythopoeic Fantasy Award Vol. 1: 12556
Mythopoeic Scholarship Award Vol. 1: 12557

N4A National Academic Achievement Award Vol. 1: 12919
NAA Foundation - Associated Collegiate Press Pacemakers Awards Vol. 1: 15353
NAA Foundation - International Circulation Managers Association C. K. Jefferson Award Vol. 1: 15354
NAA Foundation - National Scholastic Press Association Pacemaker Awards Vol. 1: 15355
NAA Foundation - Newspaper in Education Program Excellence Award Vol. 1: 15356
NAAA Falcon Club Vol. 1: 12753
NAAB Research Award Vol. 1: 12934
NAAP Activity Professional Award for Excellence Vol. 1: 12923
NAAP Activity Volunteer of the Year Award Vol. 1: 12924
NAAP Administrator of the Year Vol. 1: 12925
NAAP Distinguished Merit Award Vol. 1: 12926
NAAP Distinguished Service Award Vol. 1: 12927
NABE Board Member of the Year Vol. 1: 13547
NABE Executive Officer of the Year Vol. 1: 13548
NABE Honor Roll of Outstanding Members Vol. 1: 13549
Nabisco Masters "Master of Tennis" Award Vol. 1: 12216
NABT Molecular Biology Teaching Award Vol. 1: 12956
NAC Award Vol. 1: 12719
NACA Clean Air Award Vol. 2: 10899
NACA Hall of Fame Award Vol. 1: 12846
NACA Service Award Vol. 1: 12784
NACAA Annual Consumer Education Awards Vol. 1: 13037
NACADA Award for Service to the Organization Vol. 1: 12583
NACADA Student Research Award Vol. 1: 12584
NACADA Virginia N. Gordon Award for Excellence in the Field of Advising Vol. 1: 12585
NACBS/Huntington Library Fellowship Vol. 1: 15404
NACCA Hall of Fame Vol. 1: 12853
NACD - Allis Chalmers Conservation Teacher Awards Vol. 1: 13032
NACD Deutz/Allis Chalmers Conservation District Awards Vol. 1: 13031
NACD - ICI Americas Conservation District Awards Vol. 1: 13031
NACD - ICI Americas Conservation Teacher Awards Vol. 1: 13032
NACE Distinguished Service Award Vol. 1: 13042
NACE Technical Achievement Award Vol. 1: 13043
NACHO Achievement Award Vol. 1: 13058
NACIO Awards of Excellence Vol. 1: 13062
NACO Prize; LeCaine- Vol. 1: 12817
NACTA Delta Tau Alpha Teacher-Advisor Award Vol. 1: 13008
NACTA Distinguished Educator Award Vol. 1: 13009
NACTA Ensminger-Interstate Distinguished Teacher Award Vol. 1: 13010
NACTA John Deere Awards Vol. 1: 13011
NACTA Regional Outstanding Teacher Award Vol. 1: 13012
NACTA Teacher Fellow Vol. 1: 13012
NACTA Tressler - VNR/AVI Teacher Award Vol. 1: 13013
Nadai Award Vol. 1: 4692

Nadal Prize Vol. 2: 11216
Nadebaum Distinguished Service Award; Oertel Vol. 2: 689
NADEO Annual Award for Ecumenism Vol. 1: 13072
Nadi Prize; Yunus Vol. 2: 12049
Nadi Yarismasi; Yunus Vol. 2: 12049
NADSA Outstanding Service Award Vol. 1: 13079
NADSA Research Award Vol. 1: 13080
NADSA Scholar Award Vol. 1: 13081
NADSA Special Recognition Vol. 1: 13082
Nadzhakov Prize; Academician Georgi Vol. 2: 1513
NAEA Art Educator of the Year Vol. 1: 12799
NAEA Distinguished Service Award (Outside the Profession) Vol. 1: 12800
NAEA Distinguished Service Award (Within the Profession) Vol. 1: 12801
NAEA Presidential Citation Award Vol. 1: 12802
NAEA Program Standards Award Vol. 1: 12803
NAEA State/Province Association Newsletter Award Vol. 1: 12804
NAEA State/Province Newsletter Editor Award Vol. 1: 12804
NAEA Student Art Achievement Award Vol. 1: 12805
NAEA Student Chapter Sponsor Award of Excellence Vol. 1: 12806
Naegeli-Preis; Theodor- Vol. 2: 6880
Naegeli Prize; Theodor Vol. 2: 6880
NAFCU Awards Program Vol. 1: 13103
NAFCU Hall of Fame Vol. 1: 13104
NAFI Man of the Year Vol. 1: 13111
Naftali Prize; Science Prize - Peretz Vol. 2: 7962
Nagel Most Improved Chapter Award; R.H. Vol. 1: 18574
Nagrada Saveta Fonda SO SUBNOR Cetvrti jul Vol. 2: 10707
Nagroda im. Bohdana Zawadzkiego Vol. 2: 10175
Nagroda im. Henryka Swidzinskiego Vol. 2: 10150
Nagroda im. Jozefa Kostrzewskiego Vol. 2: 10187
Nagroda im. Ludwika Zejsznera Vol. 2: 10151
Nagroda im. Profesora Stefana Blachowskiego Vol. 2: 10174
Nagroda im. Professor Feliksa Przesmyckiego Vol. 2: 10188
Nagroda im. Stanislawa Ossowskiego Vol. 2: 10200
Nagroda imienia Karola Malcuzynskiego Vol. 2: 10207
Nagroda literacka im. Janusza Korczaka Vol. 2: 10179
Nagroda Literacka SBP Vol. 2: 10153
Nagroda Ministra Obrony Narodowej Vol. 2: 10095
Nagroda Muzyczna Zwiazku Kompozytorow Polskich Vol. 2: 10142
Nagroda Naukowa im. Adama Lysakowskiego Vol. 2: 10154
Nagroda naukowa w dziedzinie radiologii Vol. 2: 10162
Nagroda Panstwowa Vol. 2: 10204
Nagroda Polskiego Towarzystwa Fonetycznego Vol. 2: 10170
Nagroda Polskiego Towarzystwa Reumatologicznego Vol. 2: 10177
Nagroda Sekretarza Naukowego Polskiej Akademii Nauk Vol. 2: 10128

Nagroda za popularyzacje polskiej tworczosci rozrywkowej Vol. 2: 10206
Nagrody im. S. Banacha Vol. 2: 10156
Nagrody im. S. Mazurkiewicza Vol. 2: 10157
Nagrody im. S. Zaremby Vol. 2: 10159
Nagrody im. W. Sierpinskiego Vol. 2: 10158
Nagy Award Vol. 2: 7320
Nagy Erno Erem Vol. 2: 7320
NAHRO Agency Awards of Excellence in Housing and Community Development Vol. 1: 13146
NAHRO Agency Awards of Merit in Housing and Community Development Vol. 1: 13147
NAHWW/Stanley Awards (Stanleys) Vol. 1: 13133
NAIA Academic All-America Awards Vol. 1: 13170
NAIA All-America Awards Vol. 1: 13169
NAIA All-America Scholar-Athlete Awards Vol. 1: 13170
NAIA All-Tournament Teams/Outstanding Athlete Award Vol. 1: 13171
NAIA Awards of Merit Vol. 1: 13172
NAIA Distinguished Alumnus Award Vol. 1: 13173
NAIA Hall of Fame Program Vol. 1: 13174
NAIA - SIDA All-Sports Championship Awards Vol. 1: 13175
NAIFA Appraiser of the Year Award Vol. 1: 13151
NAIOP Chapter of the Year Vol. 1: 13160
NAIOP Developer of the Year Vol. 1: 13161
NAIOP Literature and Video Awards Vol. 1: 13162
NAIOP Man of the Year Award Vol. 1: 13161
NAIP Book Awards Vol. 1: 13153
Naipaul Memorial Prize; Shiva Vol. 2: 4484
NAIRD Founder Awards Vol. 1: 13155
NAIRD Indie Awards Vol. 1: 13155
Naismith College Coach of the Year Vol. 1: 6107
Naismith College Officials of the Year Vol. 1: 6108
Naismith Collegiate Awards (Naismith Trophy) Vol. 1: 6109
Naismith Hall of Fame Award (Men and Women); Frances Pomeroy Vol. 1: 12566
Naismith High School Awards Vol. 1: 6110
Naismith Memorial Basketball Hall of Fame Vol. 1: 12567
Naismith Outstanding Contribution to Basketball Award Vol. 1: 6111
Naismith Player of the Year Vol. 1: 6109
Naismith Prep Player of the Year Vol. 1: 6110
Naismith Trophy Vol. 1: 6109
Naismith Trophy (Men and Women) Vol. 1: 12568
Naito Foundation Research Prize Vol. 2: 8705
Naito Kinen Kagaku Shinko Sho Vol. 2: 8705
The NAJCA Award Vol. 1: 13187
Najkrajsia a najlepsia detska kniha jari, leta, jesene a zimy na Slovensku Vol. 2: 10760
NALPA Best Publication Award Vol. 1: 12777
NALPA Past President Award Vol. 1: 12778
NAMA Award for Contributions to Amateur Mycology Vol. 1: 15437
NAMBA Hall of Fame Vol. 1: 12573
Namboodiri Award; K. R. Vol. 2: 7706
NAMO Marketing Award Vol. 1: 12760
NAMTA Hall of Fame Award Vol. 1: 12814
Nandino; Premio de Poesia Joven de Mexico Elias Vol. 2: 9223
Nansen Award; Fridtjof Vol. 2: 9927
Nansen Medal Vol. 2: 11955
Naoki Prize Vol. 2: 8753

NAPA Brochure Competition Vol. 1: 12834
NAPA Ecological Award Vol. 1: 12835
NAPA Pavement Awards Vol. 1: 12836
NAPA Quality Paving Vol. 1: 12836
NAPET La Croix Award Vol. 1: 13227
NAPH Medallion Vol. 1: 13355
Napier Sailing Club Trophy Vol. 2: 2898
Napier - Shaw Bronze Medal Vol. 2: 2595
Naples Prize for Literature Vol. 2: 8253
Naples Prize for the Study of Southern and Northern Countries in the World Vol. 2: 8254
Napoleon; Grands Prix de la Fondation Vol. 2: 5214
Napoleonien; Grand Prix du Souvenir Vol. 2: 5214
Napolitano Student History Award; Ernest G. Vol. 1: 5637
NAPT Award Vol. 1: 13233
NAPT Distinguished Service Award Vol. 1: 12886
Nardini Award; Dr. John Vol. 1: 2013
NARI Professionalism Award Vol. 1: 13368
Narino; Orden del Merito Militar Antonio Vol. 2: 1645
NARM Advertising Award Vol. 1: 13281
NARM Best Seller Awards Vol. 1: 13282
NARM Display Contest Vol. 1: 13283
NARM Independent Distributors Best Seller Awards - Indie Best Sellers Vol. 1: 13284
NARM Presidential Award Vol. 1: 13285
Narrative Screenwriting Award Vol. 1: 9192
NARST Award Vol. 1: 12891
Narvesen-prisen Vol. 2: 9944
Narvesen Prize Vol. 2: 9944
NAS Design Prize Vol. 2: 3676
NASA Medal Vol. 1: 12732
NASA Outstanding Leadership Medal Vol. 1: 12741
NASA Service Award Pin Vol. 1: 18464
NASAR Bob Wright National Youth Leadership Award Vol. 1: 12895
NASAR Service Award Vol. 1: 12896
NASAR Valor Award Vol. 1: 12897
NASCAR Championships Vol. 1: 12902
NASCAR Grand National Championship Vol. 1: 8542
NASCAR Mechanics Hall of Fame; Western Auto Vol. 1: 11112
NASCAR Stock Car Race; Daytona 500 Vol. 1: 8539
Nascher/Manning Lecture Award Vol. 1: 2179
NASDVTE - Outstanding Business, Industry, Organization, or Individual Contribution Award Vol. 1: 14976
Nase Vojsko Prizes Vol. 2: 1878
NASEDIO Awards for Excellence in Educational Communications Vol. 1: 8383
Nash Award; Ruth Lopin Vol. 1: 15767
Nash Gold Medal; Kevin Vol. 2: 3473
Nashville Songwriters Association International Awards Vol. 1: 12577
NASPAA Annual Dissertation Award Vol. 1: 13301
NASPAA/ASPA Distinguished Research Award Vol. 1: 4269
NASPAA Award for Excellence in Teaching Vol. 1: 13302
NASPE Fellowship in Cardiac Pacing and Electrophysiology Vol. 1: 15461
NASSH Book Award Vol. 1: 15449
NASSTRAC Awards Program Vol. 1: 12579
NATA Twenty-five Year Award Vol. 1: 13389
Natakavedi (Bombay) Award Vol. 2: 7707
Nathan Award for Dramatic Criticism; George Jean Vol. 1: 12581

Award Index
Volume 2: International and Foreign

Nathhorst Translation Prize; FIT C. B. International Federation of Translators Vol. 2: 824
  International Federation of Translators Vol 2: 824
National Academy of Design Gold Medal Vol. 1: 12620
National Academy of Medicine Prize Vol. 2: 87
National Academy of Recording Arts and Sciences Hall of Fame Vol. 1: 12658
National Academy of Sciences Award for Behavioral Research Relevant to the Prevention of Nuclear War Vol. 1: 12675
National Academy of Sciences Award for Chemistry in Service to Society Vol. 1: 12676
National Academy of Sciences Award for Initiatives in Research Vol. 1: 12677
National Academy of Sciences Award for Scientific Reviewing Vol. 1: 12678
National Academy of Sciences Award for the Industrial Application of Science Vol. 1: 12679
National Academy of Sciences Award in Aeronautical Engineering Vol. 1: 12680
National Academy of Sciences Award in Applied Mathematics and Numerical Analysis Vol. 1: 12681
National Academy of Sciences Award in Chemical Sciences Vol. 1: 12682
National Academy of Sciences Award in Mathematics Vol. 1: 12683
National Academy of Sciences Award in Microbiology Vol. 1: 12692
National Academy of Sciences Award in Molecular Biology Vol. 1: 12684
National Academy of Sciences Award in the Neurosciences Vol. 1: 12685
National Academy of Sciences Public Welfare Medal Vol. 1: 12686
National Academy of Western Art Exhibition Vol. 1: 13837
National Achievement Award Vol. 1: 13211
National Achievement Awards Vol. 1: 358
National Achievement Citation Vol. 1: 2931
National ADDY Awards Vol. 1: 739
National ADDY Campaign Awards Vol. 1: 739
National Aeronautical Prize Vol. 2: 7476
National Affairs Award
  American Society for Training and Development Vol. 1: 4304
  American Society for Training and Development - International Professional Practice Area Vol 1: 4324
National Air and Space Museum Trophy Vol. 1: 17341
National Akademi Award Vol. 2: 7534
National Amateur Wine Competition Awards Vol. 1: 5105
National Amputee Golf Champion Vol. 1: 12782
National and International High Points Competition Vol. 1: 10598
National Annual Exhibition of Fine Arts Vol. 2: 1436
National Appreciation Award Vol. 1: 13212
National Aquarell Contest Vol. 2: 9010
National Aquatic Servic e, Inc. - Annual Service Recognition Award Vol. 1: 14266
National Arborist Association Award of Merit Vol. 1: 12790
National Architecture Awards Vol. 2: 609
National Armed Act Cross Vol. 2: 10116
National Armstrong Daily Award Vol. 1: 19382
National Art Collections Awards Vol. 2: 3671

National Art Honor Society Sponsor Award Vol. 1: 12807
National Artist Award/International Artist Award Vol. 2: 10049
National Arts Centre Orchestra Association Award Vol. 1: 12817
National Arts Centre Orchestra Bursary Competition Vol. 1: 12817
National Arts Club Award for Exceptional Merit Vol. 1: 15983
National Arts Council of Zimbabwe Competitions Vol. 2: 12207
National Association for Outlaw and Lawman History Hall of Fame Vol. 1: 12880
National Association of Black Journalists Salute to Excellence Awards Vol. 1: 12961
National Association of Community Health Centers Awards Vol. 1: 13015
National Association of Counties Achievement Awards Vol. 1: 13048
National Association of First Responders Awards Vol. 1: 13113
National Association of Foreign Trade Zones Person of the Year Vol. 1: 13117
National Association of Jazz Educators Scholarship Vol. 1: 12517
National Association of Pipe Coating Applicators Hall of Fame Award Vol. 1: 13235
National Association of Teachers of Singing Artist Awards Vol. 1: 13336
National Association of University Women National Fellowship Vol. 1: 13380
National Athletic Director of the Year Vol. 1: 13747
National Auctioneers Association Hall of Fame Award Vol. 1: 13393
National Audio Book of the Year Award Vol. 2: 548
National Aviation Club - Cliff Henderson Award for Achievement Vol. 1: 13402
National Aviation Hall of Fame Award Vol. 1: 13405
National Aviation Hall of Fame Gold Medal of Honor and Achievement Vol. 1: 13406
National Aviation Hall of Fame Silver Medal of Outstanding Service Vol. 1: 13407
National Award
  American Cancer Society Vol. 1: 1410
  American College Theatre Festival Vol 1: 1759
  National Water Safety Congress Vol 1: 14982
  Parent Co-operative Preschools International Vol 1: 15950
  Scandinavian Collectors Club Vol 1: 17086
National Award for Community Service Vol. 1: 12712
National Award for Literature and Arts Vol. 2: 12002
National Award for Media Excellence Vol. 1: 14561
National Award for Painting and Graphics Vol. 2: 9990
National Award for Sports Vol. 1: 12713
National Awards Vol. 1: 14024
National Awards Competition Vol. 1: 12788
National Awards Contest Vol. 1: 20374
National Awards for Education Reporting Vol. 1: 8848
National Awards for Teaching Economics Vol. 1: 13800
National Awards Program
  Freedoms Foundation at Valley Forge Vol. 1: 9404
  OX5 Aviation Pioneers Vol 1: 15877
National Back Pain Association Medal Vol. 2: 3678

National Ballet Achievement Award Vol. 1: 19924
National Bank Art Award Vol. 2: 9750
National Bank of Pakistan Prize for Literature Vol. 2: 10007
National Banking Commission Prize Vol. 2: 8958
National Baseball Hall of Fame Vol. 1: 13440
National Beethoven Fellowship Piano Auditions Vol. 1: 3526
National Better Newspaper Contest Awards Vol. 1: 14395
National Bible Week Editorial Contest Vol. 1: 11797
National Book Awards Vol. 1: 13470
National Book Critics Circle Awards Vol. 1: 13468
National Book Institute Juvenile Literature Award Vol. 2: 1472
National Book Service Teacher-Librarian of the Year Award Vol. 1: 7026
National Book Week Vol. 1: 13470
National Bottle Show Champion Vol. 2: 3733
National Bowling Hall of Fame Vol. 1: 13472
National Boy of the Year Vol. 1: 6536
National Breeders Trophy Vol. 1: 19383
National Business and Industry Award Vol. 1: 13872
National Business Book Award Vol. 1: 9210
National Business Calendar Awards Vol. 2: 2483
National Business Writing Awards Vol. 1: 18750
National Cadet Bisley Grand Champion Medal Vol. 2: 10936
National Camellia Hall of Fame Vol. 1: 1398
National Cartoonists Society Category Awards Vol. 1: 13525
National Catholic Book Awards Vol. 1: 7383
National Champion Vol. 1: 19622
National Champion Challenge Cup Vol. 2: 2241
National Champion Donkey, National Champion Mule Vol. 1: 1962
National Championship
  American International Checkers Society Vol. 1: 2699
  American Motorcyclist Association Vol 1: 3146
  Rhodes 19 Class Association Vol 1: 16826
  U.S. International Fireball Association Vol 1: 19424
National Championship and Scholarship Program Vol. 1: 1325
National Championship Cup Finals Vol. 2: 2777
National Championship Regatta Vol. 1: 10536
National Championships
  Canadian Sport Parachuting Association Vol. 1: 7251
  Scottish Bowling Association Vol 2: 10663
  United States Badminton Association Vol 1: 19038
  U.S. Curling Association Vol 1: 19078
  United States Cycling Federation Vol 1: 19080
National Chief of Protocol Vol. 1: 5287
National Children's Play Award Vol. 2: 4073
National Chopin Piano Competition
  Chopin Foundation of the United States Vol. 1: 7650
  Kosciuszko Foundation Vol 1: 11725
National Citation Vol. 1: 12447
National Citation Award of the William Allen White Foundation Vol. 1: 20261
National Citations Vol. 1: 14595
National Citizen of the Year Vol. 1: 12273

National City Challenge to Stop Drunk Driving Vol. 1: 19067
National Classical Music Contest Vol. 2: 8834
National Club Championship Award (Men) Vol. 1: 19469
National Club Championship Award (Women) Vol. 1: 19470
National Club Sevens Championship Award (Men) Vol. 1: 19471
National Coach of the Year
  National Association of College Gymnastics Coaches (Men) Vol. 1: 12997
  National Collegiate Athletic Association - Division 1 Track Coaches Association Vol 1: 13619
National Coin Week Vol. 1: 3243
National College Band and Choral Directors Hall of Fame Band of the Year Vol. 1: 13413
National College Band Director of the Year Vol. 1: 13414
National College Championship Award Vol. 1: 19472
National College Championship Award (Women) Vol. 1: 19473
National College Choral Director of the Year Vol. 1: 13415
National College Choral Directors Hall of Fame Choir of the Year Vol. 1: 13416
National College Football Champions
  Associated Press - Sports Department Vol. 1: 5415
  National Collegiate Athletic Association Vol 1: 13611
National College Radio and TV Awards Vol. 1: 12995
National Collegiate All Conference Championships Award Vol. 1: 19474
National Collegiate and Scholastic Swimming Trophy Vol. 1: 7948
National Comedy Award Vol. 1: 5750
National Committee for Biochemistry Award Vol. 2: 7843
National Community Service Award
  Jewish Theological Seminary of America Vol. 1: 11570
  National Association of Negro Business and Professional Women's Club Vol 1: 13213
National Community Service Prize Vol. 2: 9135
National Competition for Composers Recording Vol. 1: 8240
National Competition in Teaching of Journalism Prize Vol. 2: 1437
National Composers' Competition Vol. 1: 11816
National Concrete Masonry Awards for Design Excellence Vol. 1: 2541
National Conference of Puerto Rican Women Award Vol. 1: 13649
National Congress on Aerospace Education Crown Circle Award Vol. 1: 19220
National Congressional Award Vol. 1: 14562
National Conservation Achievement Awards Program Vol. 1: 15010
National Construction Photography Awards Vol. 1: 5403
National Contest for Opera Singers Vol. 2: 1438
National Contest of Medical Research Works Vol. 2: 1725
National Contractors Travelling Scholarship Vol. 2: 2560
National Convention Awards Program Vol. 1: 7514
National Corporate Humanitarian Award Vol. 1: 14563

National Council Awards Vol. 1: 15336
National Council of Juvenile and Family Court Judges Awards Vol. 1: 13739
National Course Rally Manufacturer Champion Vol. 1: 18401
National Court Reporters Foundation Scholarships Vol. 1: 13835
National Credit Education Week Public Relations Award Vol. 1: 10893
National Cross Country Trophy Vol. 2: 12158
National Cultural Awards Vol. 2: 1413
National Cup Boys Under 18 (Boys National Championship) Vol. 1: 19693
National Cup Girls Under 18 (Girls National Championship) Vol. 1: 19694
National Dairy Council Award for Excellence in Medical/Dental Nutrition Education Vol. 1: 4054
National Dance Association Scholar Vol. 1: 13844
National Dealer Safety Awards Vol. 1: 9920
National Defense Service Medal Vol. 1: 19172
National Design Competition for the Use of Aluminum Vol. 2: 9018
National Distinction of the Environment Vol. 2: 1600
National Distinguished Principal Award Vol. 1: 13085
National Distinguished Professional Award Vol. 1: 14564
National Distinguished Research Award Vol. 1: 5214
National Distinguished Service Award Vol. 1: 14596
National Distinguished Service Awards
  Canadian Mental Health Association Vol. 1: 7032
  National High School Athletic Coaches Association Vol 1: 14147
National Distinguished Service Ruby Award Vol. 1: 8980
National Division Art Educator of the Year Vol. 1: 12808
National Divisional Award Vol. 1: 1414
National Doctoral Fellowship Program in Business and Management Vol. 1: 823
National Dog Week Editorial Award Vol. 1: 9463
National Drama Contest Vol. 2: 1439
National Economics Prize Vol. 2: 9095
National Editors Award Vol. 1: 2202
National Educational Film & Video Festival Vol. 1: 13882
National Endowment for the Arts Programs Vol. 1: 13891
National Endowment for the Humanities Fellowships Vol. 1: 799
National Endowment for the Humanities Post Doctoral Fellowships, Nicosia Vol. 1: 4016
National Endowment for the Humanities Programs Vol. 1: 13898
National Engineering Award Vol. 1: 999
National Engineering Excellence Awards Vol. 2: 476
National Engineering Prize Vol. 2: 1747
National Environmental Achievement Award - Searching for Success Pro gram Vol. 1: 16787
National Equal Employment/Affirmative Action Exemplary Practices Award Vol. 1: 4266
National Essay Contest Vol. 1: 10234
National Essay Contest on Colombian Foreign Policy Vol. 2: 1592
National Essay Contest on Public Health as Social Justice Vol. 1: 8587

National Essay Contest on "The Role of Public Health in Healthcare Reform" Vol. 1: 8587
National Excellence Awards for Engineering Journalism Vol. 2: 477
National Federation Citations Vol. 1: 13951
National Federation Interscholastic Coaches Association Annual Awards Vol. 1: 13957
National Federation Interscholastic Officials Association Vol. 1: 13957
National Federation of Music Clubs Awards and Scholarships Vol. 1: 13940
National Federation of the Blind Educator of Tomorrow Award Vol. 1: 13965
National Federation of the Blind Humanities Scholarship Vol. 1: 13965
National Federation of the Blind Scholarship Program Vol. 1: 13965
National Fellowships Vol. 1: 2341
National Fellowships in Education Reporting Vol. 1: 8849
National Field Archery Championship Vol. 1: 13969
National Film Board Award for Best Short Film Vol. 1: 18746
National Film Board Kathleen Shannon Award Vol. 1: 20597
National Film Board of Canada Prize for Creativity Vol. 1: 12423
National Food and Energy Council Electrification Award Vol. 1: 4371
National Food Processors Association Award in Raw Products Research Vol. 1: 4146
National Footbag Championships Vol. 1: 20491
National Football League Players Association Parade of Champions Vol. 1: 14007
National Forensic Association Awards Vol. 1: 14013
National Fresenius Award Vol. 1: 16109
National Friend of Extension Award Vol. 1: 8981
National Genealogical Society Youth Award in Honor of Milton Rubinc am Vol. 1: 14067
National Geographic Society Award
  American Cartographic Association Vol. 1: 1428
  British Cartographic Society Vol 2: 2308
National Geographic Society Centennial Award Vol. 1: 14075
National Geology Award Vol. 2: 1736
National Gold Medal Awards Vol. 1: 18424
National Gold Pin Awards Vol. 1: 436
National Golf Foundation's Jack Nicklaus Golf Family of the Year Award Vol. 1: 14086
National Goodwill Worker of the Year Vol. 1: 9655
National Grade/Middle School Band and Choral Directors Hall of Fame Vol. 1: 13418
National Graphics Competition Vol. 1: 12847
National Guard Association of the United States Awards Program Vol. 1: 14096
National Handicapped Awareness Award Vol. 1: 13873
National Headache Foundation Lectureship Award Vol. 1: 14111
National Headliner Awards Vol. 1: 14114
National Heritage Fellowships Vol. 1: 13892
National High Point, Team Vol. 1: 13017
National High School Ad & Coaches of the Year Vol. 1: 14148
National High School Band Director of the Year Vol. 1: 13420
National High School Band Directors Hall of Fame and Band of the Year Award Vol. 1: 13421

National High School Championships Award   Vol. 1: 19475
National High School Choral Director of the Year   Vol. 1: 13422
National High School Choral Directors Hall of Fame Choir of the Year   Vol. 1: 13423
National High School Journalism Teacher of the Year   Vol. 1: 8711
National High School Rodeo Finals   Vol. 1: 14150
National High School Sports Hall of Fame Awards   Vol. 1: 13952
National High Score Awards   Vol. 1: 20180
National History Day Awards   Vol. 1: 14155
National Home Center Industry Advertising Awards   Vol. 1: 14185
National Honor Society Scholarship Program   Vol. 1: 13310
National Honorary Member   Vol. 1: 11438
National Honorees   Vol. 1: 6341
National Hotel Receptionist Award   Vol. 2: 2574
National House Journal Competition   Vol. 2: 11097
National Housing Hall of Fame   Vol. 1: 13137
National Housing Quality Award   Vol. 1: 16454
National Human Relations Award   Vol. 1: 2725
National Humane Education Teacher of the Year   Vol. 1: 12873
National Humanitarian Award
  National Recreation and Park Association   Vol. 1: 14565
  WAIF   Vol 1: 20083
National Hunt Champion Award   Vol. 2: 3834
National Hypertension Association Recognition Award   Vol. 1: 14203
National Indian Health Board   Vol. 1: 14207
National Institute of Folk and Traditional Heritage Awards   Vol. 2: 9985
National Institute of Insurance International Prizes   Vol. 2: 8067
National Inventor of the Year   Vol. 1: 10500
National Inventor's Hall of Fame   Vol. 1: 19120
National Jersey Youth Achievement Award   Vol. 1: 2719
National Jewish Book Award - Autobiography/Memoir   Vol. 1: 11529
National Jewish Book Award - Children's Literature   Vol. 1: 11530
National Jewish Book Award - Children's Picture Book   Vol. 1: 11531
National Jewish Book Award - Contemporary Jewish Life   Vol. 1: 11532
National Jewish Book Award - Fiction   Vol. 1: 11533
National Jewish Book Award - Holocaust   Vol. 1: 11534
National Jewish Book Award - Israel   Vol. 1: 11535
National Jewish Book Award - Jewish History   Vol. 1: 11536
National Jewish Book Award - Jewish Thought   Vol. 1: 11537
National Jewish Book Award - Scholarship   Vol. 1: 11538
National Jewish Book Award - Sephardic Studies   Vol. 1: 11539
National Jewish Book Award - Visual Arts   Vol. 1: 11540
National Jewish Book Award - Yiddish Literature   Vol. 1: 11541
National Jockeys Hall of Fame   Vol. 1: 12105
National Journal Award   Vol. 1: 2203
National Journalism Award   Vol. 1: 6230

National Journalism Awards - Broadcast Awards Competition   Vol. 1: 6797
National Journalism Awards - Environmental Awards Competition   Vol. 1: 6798
National Journalism Awards - Print Awards Competition   Vol. 1: 6799
National Journalism Scholarship Program   Vol. 1: 16388
National Junior Art Honor Society Sponsor Award   Vol. 1: 12809
National Junior Leader of the Year   Vol. 1: 20601
National Juried Exhibition   Vol. 1: 17026
National Labor Prize   Vol. 2: 9137
National Landscape Award   Vol. 1: 1070
National Landscape Design Awards   Vol. 1: 14281
National Law and Social Justice Leadership Award   Vol. 1: 194
National Law Enforcement Saved by the Belt/Air Bag Awards Program   Vol. 1: 10698
National Leader's Award - Moe Dollinger Award   Vol. 1: 8750
National Leadership   Vol. 1: 20286
National Leadership Award
  Irish Farm Centre   Vol. 2: 7796
  National Council on Community Services and Continuing Education   Vol 1: 13796
National League All-Star Team   Vol. 1: 18366
National League Most Valuable Player   Vol. 1: 6280
National League Player of the Year
  English Basket Ball Association   Vol. 2: 2778
  The Sporting News   Vol 1: 18367
National League Rookie of the Year   Vol. 1: 18368
National Lecture Competition   Vol. 2: 3143
National Lectureship Award   Vol. 1: 848
National Legislative Award   Vol. 1: 16729
National Library of Colombia Prize   Vol. 2: 1714
National Lifesaving Leadership Award   Vol. 1: 16838
National Lighting Awards   Vol. 2: 3582
National Lighting Awards Program   Vol. 1: 14308
National Literacy Honors   Vol. 1: 14310
National Literary Award   Vol. 1: 14566
National Literature Award   Vol. 2: 4
National Lupus Hall of Fame   Vol. 1: 2975
National Magazine Awards   Vol. 1: 4655
National Magazine Awards (Canada)   Vol. 1: 14322
National Man/Woman of the Year   Vol. 1: 17277
National Management Award   Vol. 1: 9520
National Marine Science Prize   Vol. 2: 1690
National Maritime Museum Ship Model Competition   Vol. 2: 3693
National Mass Media Award   Vol. 1: 2726
National Mass Media Awards   Vol. 1: 13645
National Materials Advancement Award   Vol. 1: 9141
National Mature Media Awards Program   Vol. 1: 12141
National Medal   Vol. 2: 208
National Medal of Arts   Vol. 1: 13893
National Medal of Technology   Vol. 1: 19122
National Media Award   Vol. 1: 7033
National Media Awards   Vol. 1: 1603
National Media Owl Awards   Vol. 1: 16818
National Mental Health Association Film Festival   Vol. 1: 14362
National Meritorious Award   Vol. 1: 5086
National Military Championships Award   Vol. 1: 19476

National Milk Producers Federation Graduate Student Paper Presentation Contest   Vol. 1: 1918
National Milk Producers Federation - Richard M. Hoyt Award   Vol. 1: 1919
National Model Car Racing Champion   Vol. 2: 2505
National Most Colorful Contest   Vol. 1: 20085
National Multihull Championship - Alter Cup   Vol. 1: 19530
National Music Award   Vol. 2: 1440
National Music Awards   Vol. 1: 3162
National Music Theater Awards   Vol. 1: 14221
National Newsletter Awards Competition   Vol. 1: 15341
National Newspaper Association - Quill and Scroll Award   Vol. 1: 15357
National Newspaper Awards   Vol. 1: 6851
National Notary Association Achievement Award   Vol. 1: 14399
National Ocean Service Employee of the Year Award   Vol. 1: 19116
National Officials Outstanding Service Award   Vol. 1: 19931
National Offshore Championship - Lloyd Phoenix Trophy   Vol. 1: 19531
National One-Act Play Contest   Vol. 1: 126
National Open Tournament Championship Flight   Vol. 1: 2786
National Opera Association Vocal Competition   Vol. 1: 14406
National Operatic and Dramatic Association Awards   Vol. 2: 3695
National Order of Education   Vol. 2: 1414
National Order of Merit   Vol. 2: 5236
National Order of the Legion of Honor   Vol. 2: 5237
National Order of the Liberation   Vol. 2: 5238
National Order of the Southern Cross   Vol. 2: 1415
National Organization for Rare Disorders Awards   Vol. 1: 14413
National Peace Essay Contest   Vol. 1: 19405
National Person of the Year Award   Vol. 1: 13796
National Philatelic Society Queen Elizabeth II Silver Jubilee Trophy   Vol. 2: 3781
National Philharmonic Award   Vol. 2: 10067
National Photography Competition   Vol. 2: 1756
National Physical Fitness Award   Vol. 1: 16395
National Piano Competition   Vol. 1: 20059
National Piano Fellowship Auditions   Vol. 1: 3526
National Planning Awards - Chapter Improvement Award   Vol. 1: 3534
National Planning Awards - Current Topic Award   Vol. 1: 3535
National Planning Awards - Diana Donald Award   Vol. 1: 3536
National Planning Awards - Distinguished Leadership Award   Vol. 1: 3537
National Planning Awards - Distinguished Service Award   Vol. 1: 3538
National Planning Awards - Division Achievement Award   Vol 1: 3539
National Planning Awards - Division Improvement Award   Vol. 1: 3540
National Planning Awards - Karen B. Smith Chapter Achievement Awards   Vol. 1: 3541
National Planning Awards - Outstanding Planning Awards   Vol. 1: 3542
National Planning Awards - Paul Davidoff Award   Vol. 1: 3543
National Plastic Arts Prize   Vol. 2: 11369
National Play Award   Vol. 1: 14616

National Playwrights Conference and New Drama for Media Project   Vol. 1: 14477
National Playwrights Conference and New Drama for Television Project   Vol. 1: 14477
National Poetry Competition
  Chester H. Jones Foundation   Vol. 1: 11607
  The Poetry Society   Vol 2: 3792
National Poetry Foundation   Vol. 2: 3698
National Poetry Series Open Competition   Vol. 1: 14484
National Point Leader Award, Competition Division   Vol. 1: 6239
National Police Award for Traffic Safety   Vol. 1: 6756
National Police Shooting Championship Trophies   Vol. 1: 14642
National Postal Museum Medal   Vol. 2: 3781
National Poster Contest   Vol. 1: 19599
National Poster Contest Award   Vol. 1: 6889
National Poster Scholarship Program   Vol. 1: 16389
National Power World Piano Competition London   Vol. 2: 3604
National President's Award   Vol. 1: 2204
National President's Trophy - Man of the Year   Vol. 1: 20639
National Print and Drawing Exhibition   Vol. 1: 12344
National Print Exhibition   Vol. 1: 17693
National Prize Competition for Literature for Neo-Literates   Vol. 2: 7527
National Prize for Agriculture   Vol. 2: 1601
National Prize for Anthropology   Vol. 2: 1623
National Prize for Architecture   Vol. 2: 12142
National Prize for Arts   Vol. 2: 1660
National Prize for Chemistry   Vol. 2: 1737
National Prize for Civic Merit   Vol. 2: 9139
National Prize for Consulting   Vol. 2: 742
National Prize for Fine Arts   Vol. 2: 9146
National Prize for Good Building   Vol. 2: 9906
National Prize for History   Vol. 2: 1661
National Prize for History, Social Sciences and Philosophy   Vol. 2: 9147
National Prize for Illustration of Literature for Children and Young People   Vol. 2: 11370
National Prize for Industrial and Commercial Building   Vol. 2: 743
National Prize for Jewelry   Vol. 2: 744
National Prize for Journalism and Information   Vol. 2: 9140
National Prize for Journalism for Young People   Vol. 2: 8946
National Prize for Linguistics and Literature   Vol. 2: 9148
National Prize for Literature
  Argentina - Ministry of Education and Justice   Vol. 2: 22
  Colombia - Ministry of National Education   Vol 2: 1662
  National Council for Culture   Vol 2: 12122
National Prize for Music Maestro Sojo   Vol. 2: 12123
National Prize for Physics, Mathematics and Natural Sciences   Vol. 2: 9149
National Prize for Quality   Vol. 2: 9261
National Prize for Sciences   Vol. 2: 1663
National Prize for Sports   Vol. 2: 9150
National Prize for Technical Development/Colombia   Vol. 2: 12128
National Prize for Technology and Design   Vol. 2: 9151
National Prize for Theatre Juana Sujo   Vol. 2: 12124
National Prize in Science and Art   Vol. 2: 9152
National Prize of Quality   Vol. 2: 1611

National Prize of the President of the Republic   Vol. 2: 8068
National Prizes for Culture   Vol. 2: 1391
National Pro-Am Championship   Vol. 2: 3809
National PRO Rally of the Year   Vol. 1: 18401
National Professional Responsibility Exemplary Practices Award   Vol. 1: 4270
National Professional Young Engineer of the Year
  Institution of Engineers, Australia   Vol. 2: 478
  Institution of Engineers, Australia   Vol 2: 481
National Psychiatric Technician of the Year   Vol. 1: 1149
National Psychological Consultants to Management Award   Vol. 1: 3702
National Psychology Awards for Excellence in the Media   Vol. 1: 3672
National Public Citizen of the Year   Vol. 1: 13315
National Public Relations Achievement Award   Vol. 1: 6229
National Public Service Awards
  American Society for Public Administration   Vol. 1: 4271
  National Academy of Public Administration   Vol 1: 12652
National Public Service Media Awards   Vol. 1: 1164
National PVA Membership Development Award   Vol. 1: 15935
National Quality Award   Vol. 1: 13197
National Radio Award   Vol. 1: 12979
National Ranking Award   Vol. 1: 13863
National Recognition Medal   Vol. 1: 9405
National Record Award   Vol. 2: 1416
National Recycling Coalition Annual Awards   Vol. 1: 14578
National Research Awards   Vol. 1: 5305
National Research Council   Vol. 1: 10036
National Research Council Canada, Division of Mechanical Engineering Award   Vol. 1: 7135
National Research Council Research Associateship Programs   Vol. 1: 14621
National Research Council Stimulation Prize   Vol. 2: 7466
National Restaurant Association Ice Carving Classic   Vol. 1: 14626
National Rifle and Pistol Championship Trophy Match   Vol. 1: 19087
National Rosemaling Exhibition   Vol. 1: 15540
National Safety Council's National Fleet Safety Contests   Vol. 1: 14658
National Safety Council's Safe Driver Award Program   Vol. 1: 14659
National Sales Achievement Award   Vol. 1: 13198
National Sales Hall of Fame   Vol. 1: 17011
National Salon of Fine Arts Prizes   Vol. 2: 1441
National Scholastic Journalism Hall of Fame   Vol. 1: 15612
National Scholastic Press Association Pacemaker Awards; NAA Foundation -   Vol. 1: 15355
National Science Foundation Young Investigator Award   Vol. 1: 14685
National Science, Literature and Art Prize   Vol. 2: 7183
National Science Prize   Vol. 2: 12129
National Scots Song Competition   Vol. 2: 10656
National Scrabble Championship   Vol. 1: 14710

National Sculpture Society Annual Exhibition Awards   Vol. 1: 14714
National Security Award   Vol. 1: 13667
National Security Medal   Vol. 1: 14717
National Senior Champion   Vol. 1: 1993
National Service Award
  Chamber Music America   Vol. 1: 7503
  Institute for Socioeconomic Studies   Vol 1: 10235
  Recreation Vehicle Industry Association   Vol 1: 16730
National Service Medal   Vol. 1: 9405
National Short Film and Video Competition   Vol. 1: 19920
National Short Story Competition   Vol. 2: 1757
National Ski Hall of Fame   Vol. 1: 19573
National Small Business Person of the Year   Vol. 1: 19600
National Small Painting Exhibition   Vol. 1: 15198
National Small Works Exhibition   Vol. 1: 17094
National Smokey Bear Awards   Vol. 1: 19085
National Soaring Hall of Fame   Vol. 1: 9370
National Soccer Hall of Fame Award   Vol. 1: 19609
National Social Worker of the Year   Vol. 1: 13316
National Society of Artists Awards   Vol. 1: 14773
National Society of Arts and Letters Gold Medal of Merit Award   Vol. 1: 14775
National Society of Film Critics Awards   Vol. 1: 14781
National Society of Newspaper Columnists Awards   Vol. 1: 14797
National Society of Painters in Casein and Acrylic Awards   Vol. 1: 14799
National Softball Hall of Fame   Vol. 1: 464
National Sojourners ROTC Award for Americanism   Vol. 1: 14826
National Sportscaster and Sportswriter of Year   Vol. 1: 14862
National Sportscaster of the Year   Vol. 1: 4857
National Sportscasters and Sportswriters Award   Vol. 1: 14863
National Student Advertising Competition   Vol. 1: 740
National Student Competition   Vol. 1: 4645
National Student Design Competition   Vol. 1: 4372
National Student Playwriting Award (Michael Kanin Playwriting Award Program)   Vol. 1: 1759
National Student Production Awards Competition   Vol. 1: 348
National Target Champions   Vol. 1: 12792
National Tattoo Association Awards   Vol. 1: 14880
National Teacher of the Year   Vol. 1: 8351
National Technology Competition   Vol. 2: 8950
National Ten-Minute Play Contest   Vol. 1: 126
National Territorial Union Championship Award   Vol. 1: 19477
National Theatre Awards   Vol. 2: 9991
National Touring Rally Manufacturer Champion   Vol. 1: 18401
National Touring Rally of the Year   Vol. 1: 18401
National Track and Field Hall of Fame   Vol. 1: 19951
National Traditional Music Performer Award   Vol. 1: 14916
National Training Award for Individual Achievement   Vol. 2: 2766

National Training Awards   Vol. 2: 2767
National Translation Award   Vol. 2: 1473
National Transportation Award   Vol. 1: 13849
National Travel Marketing Awards   Vol. 1: 18799
National Treasure Award   Vol. 1: 20608
National Tree Planting Award   Vol. 1: 2101
National Trivia Hall of Fame   Vol. 1: 19673
National Trophy   Vol. 1: 13863
National Trophy (Men and Women)   Vol. 2: 2779
National Turkey Federation Research Award
   National Turkey Federation   Vol. 1: 14943
   Poultry Science Association   Vol 1: 16349
National Unicycle Meet Top Point Winners   Vol. 1: 18873
National Vaccine and Serum Institute Award   Vol. 2: 1574
National Violin Competition
   Oskar Back Scholarship Foundation   Vol. 2: 9337
   Oskar Back Scholarship Foundation   Vol 2: 9338
National Vocal Competition   Vol. 1: 11592
National Vocal Competition for Young Opera Singers   Vol. 1: 20630
National Voluntary Service Award   Vol. 1: 14567
National Volunteer Disaster Services Award   Vol. 1: 3922
National Volunteer Leadership Award   Vol. 1: 1415
National Volunteer of the Year
   The Arc   Vol. 1: 5219
   Joint Action in Community Service   Vol 1: 11600
National Water and Energy Conservation Award   Vol. 1: 11475
National Watercolor Society Arts and Humanities Award   Vol. 1: 14992
National Westminster Bank Prize   Vol. 2: 3098
National Westminster Bank Trophy   Vol. 2: 4512
National Wildlife Photo Contest   Vol. 1: 15006
National Wildlife Rehabilitation Association Grants Program   Vol. 1: 15014
National Wohelo Order Award   Vol. 1: 6688
National Women's Hall of Fame   Vol. 1: 15024
National Woodland Owners Award of Merit   Vol. 1: 15043
National Work & Well-being Award   Vol. 1: 7034
National Works on Paper Exhibition   Vol. 1: 12344
National Wrestling Hall of Fame Distinguished Member   Vol. 1: 15051
National Young Artist Competition   Vol. 1: 12264
National Young Artists Competition in Organ Performance   Vol. 1: 2197
National Young Farmer Spokesperson for Agriculture   Vol. 1: 15060
National Young Hairstyling Championship   Vol. 2: 2967
National Youth Award   Vol. 1: 13214
National Youth Awards   Vol. 2: 7524
National Youth Cup Boys   Vol. 1: 19695
National Youth of the Year Award   Vol. 1: 6536
National Youth Prize   Vol. 2: 9153
National Zoological Park Medal   Vol. 1: 17342
Nationwide Silver Trowel Award   Vol. 2: 2249
Nativelle Prize for Medicine; Claude-Adolphe   Vol. 2: 6128
NATO Awards   Vol. 1: 13370
NATO Fellowship Programmes   Vol. 1: 16960

NATO Stars of the Year   Vol. 1: 13370
NATRC Honorary Lifetime Membership   Vol. 1: 15477
NATRC National Champions   Vol. 1: 15478
NATRC Ride Awards   Vol. 1: 15479
NATRC's Oldest Rider   Vol. 1: 15480
NATS Leadership Award   Vol. 1: 13346
Natta; Medaglia Giulio   Vol. 2: 8338
NATTCO National Welding and Cutting Award   Vol. 1: 5087
NATTS Hall of Fame   Vol. 1: 7302
Natural Food Associates Hall of Fame   Vol. 1: 15071
Natural World Book of the Year Award   Vol. 2: 3714
Naturalistes de l'Annee   Vol. 1: 7494
Nature Division Awards   Vol. 1: 16163
Naturskyddsmedaljen   Vol. 2: 11548
NatWest Bank Engineering Marketing Award   Vol. 2: 2773
Naude Medal; Meiring   Vol. 2: 10966
Naumann - August Thienemann Medal; Einar   Vol. 1: 10790
Naumburg Chamber Music Award   Vol. 1: 15084
Naumburg International Competition   Vol. 1: 15085
Nautica/U.S. SAILING Youth Championship   Vol. 1: 19532
Nautical Institute Competitions   Vol. 2: 3716
Naval and Maritime Photo Contest   Vol. 1: 19465
Naval Reserve Medal   Vol. 1: 19173
Naval Reserve Meritorious Service Medal   Vol. 1: 19174
Naval Submarine League Active Duty Essay Contest   Vol. 1: 15091
Naval Submarine League Literary Honorarium Award   Vol. 1: 15092
Naval Submarine League NROTC Essay Contest   Vol. 1: 15093
Naval Submarine League/USNA Essay Contest   Vol. 1: 15094
Navarro Prize; Juan Carlos   Vol. 2: 88
Navy and Marine Corps Medal   Vol. 1: 19175
Navy Cross
   Republic of South Africa - South African Defense Force   Vol. 2: 10937
   United States Department of Defense - Armed Forces Decorations and Awards   Vol 1: 19176
Navy Expeditionary Medal   Vol. 1: 19177
Navy Occupation Service Medal - Navy-Marine Corps-Coast Guard   Vol. 1: 19178
NAWA Annual Exhibition Awards   Vol. 1: 13384
Nax Trophy   Vol. 1: 3341
Nayacakalou Medal   Vol. 2: 9787
Nayla Jabor Prize   Vol. 2: 1454
Naylor Distinguished Member Service Award; Harriet   Vol. 1: 5654
Naylor Prize in Applied Mathematics   Vol. 2: 3614
Nazor Awards; Vladimir   Vol. 2: 1812
NBA All-Rookie Team   Vol. 1: 13447
NBA All-Star Team   Vol. 1: 18369
NBA Coach of the Year   Vol. 1: 18370
NBA Coach of the Year - Red Auerbach Trophy   Vol. 1: 13448
NBA Coaches All-America Team   Vol. 1: 13449
NBA Defensive Player of the Year   Vol. 1: 13450
NBA Executive of the Year
   National Basketball Association   Vol. 1: 13451
   The Sporting News   Vol 1: 18371

NBA Most Improved Player   Vol. 1: 13452
NBA Most Valuable Player Award - Maurice Podoloff Trophy   Vol. 1: 13453
NBA Player of the Year   Vol. 1: 18372
NBA Rookie of the Year   Vol. 1: 18373
NBA Rookie of the Year - Eddie Gottlieb Trophy   Vol. 1: 13454
NBA Sixth Man Award   Vol. 1: 13455
NBA World Championship - Larry O'Brien Trophy   Vol. 1: 13456
NBAA Award for Meritorious Service to Aviation   Vol. 1: 13499
NBCC Citation for Excellence in Reviewing   Vol. 1: 13468
NBEA Collegiate Teacher of the Year   Vol. 1: 13502
NBEA Distinguished Service Award (Administrator)   Vol. 1: 13503
NBEA Distinguished Service Award (Organization)   Vol. 1: 13504
NBEA Postsecondary Teacher of the Year   Vol. 1: 13505
NBEA Secondary Teacher of the Year   Vol. 1: 13506
NBST Excellence in Technology Award   Vol. 2: 7771
NBST New Product Development Award   Vol. 2: 7771
NBST Scientist of the Year Award   Vol. 2: 7771
NBU Scholarship   Vol. 2: 11452
NCAA National Championships   Vol. 1: 13612
NCADD Leadership Award   Vol. 1: 13792
NCBA Service Award   Vol. 1: 13533
NCCPB Genetics and Plant Breeding Award for Academia   Vol. 1: 13726
NCCPB Genetics and Plant Breeding Award for Industry   Vol. 1: 13727
NCEA Elementary Departmental Award in Recognition of Commitment to Catholic Elementary Education   Vol. 1: 13550
NCEA Merit Award   Vol. 1: 13544
NCEA Presidential Award   Vol. 1: 13551
NCEA Secondary Department Award   Vol. 1: 13552
NCGA Corn Yield Contest   Vol. 1: 13670
NCGA Honor Awards   Vol. 1: 13639
NCJD Hall of Fame   Vol. 1: 13659
NCLC Lewis Hine Awards   Vol. 1: 13579
NCLIS Recognition Awards   Vol. 1: 19457
NCME Post Graduate Physician Continuing Medical Education Award; HeSCA/   Vol. 1: 9857
NCPDM Scholarship   Vol. 1: 8374
NCR Book Award   Vol. 2: 2139
NCRIPTAL Higher Education Software Awards; EDUCOM/   Vol. 1: 8867
NCRS - Duntov Mark of Excellence Award   Vol. 1: 13673
NCS Silver T-Square   Vol. 1: 13526
NCSC Community Service Award/Certificate of Merit   Vol. 1: 13752
NCTE Award for Excellence in Poetry for Children   Vol. 1: 13772
NCTE Executive Committee Award   Vol. 1: 13773
NDCS Scholarship   Vol. 2: 3682
NDR Championship Awards   Vol. 1: 13855
NDTA Distinguished Service Award   Vol. 1: 13850
NDTA Presidents Award   Vol. 1: 13851
Neal Editorial Achievement Award; Jesse H.   Vol. 1: 1388
Neal Writers' Award; Larry   Vol. 1: 8545
Neatby en Histoire des Femmes; Le Prix Hilda   Vol. 1: 6909
Neatby Prize; Hild   Vol. 1: 6909

Neave Research Award; Airey Vol. 2: 3718
Neave Scholarship; Airey Vol. 2: 3718
Nebenzahl Prize Vol. 1: 15317
Nebraska Library Association Meritorious Service Award Vol. 1: 15099
Nebraska Library Association Trustee Award Vol. 1: 15100
NECCC Medal Vol. 1: 9713
Nedbal Award; Oskar Vol. 2: 1850
Nederburg Opera and Ballet Award Vol. 2: 11107
Nederlandse Grafiekprijs Vol. 2: 9623
Nee; Prix Alfred Vol. 2: 5808
Neech Prize Vol. 2: 4462
Neese Prize; E.H. Vol. 1: 18601
Neglia; Concorso Internazionale Musicale Francesco Paolo Vol. 2: 8205
Nehru Award for International Understanding; Jawaharlal Vol. 2: 7573
Nehru Birth Centenary Lectures; Jawaharlal Vol. 2: 7660
Nehru Birth Centenary Medal; Jawaharlal Vol. 2: 7661
Nehru Birth Centenary Visiting Fellowship; Jawaharlal Vol. 2: 7662
Nehru Literacy Award Vol. 2: 7566
Neill Medal Vol. 2: 10647
Neill Memorial Prize in Music; Philip Vol. 2: 9851
Neilson Award; FAW John Shaw Vol. 2: 392
Neinken Medal; Mortimer L. Vol. 1: 16141
Nelissenprijs; Jan Vol. 2: 9645
Nellie Award Vol. 1: 27
Nelligan; Prix Emile- Vol. 1: 18879
Nelod; Prix Gilles Vol. 2: 1042
Nelson Award; Byron Vol. 1: 9646
Nelson Award for Diagnosis of Yield Limiting Factors; Werner L. Vol. 1: 4387
Nelson Award; Mrs. James Vol. 2: 716
Nelson Award; Ruth and Bill Vol. 1: 10012
Nelson Award; Thurlow C. Vol. 1: 14721
Nelson Hurst & Marsh Biography Award Vol. 2: 2151
Nelson Prize; William Vol. 1: 16785
Nelson Service Award; Harold E. Vol. 1: 17853
Nemet Award Vol. 2: 2401
NEMRA Manufacturer of the Year Vol. 1: 13886
NEMRA Manufacturer of the Year - Thomas F. Preston Award Vol. 1: 13886
Nemzetkozi Eneklo Ifjusag, Kodaly Zoltan Korusverseny Vol. 2: 7423
Nemzetkozi Liszt Hanglemez Nagydij Vol. 2: 7438
Nene Award Vol. 1: 9827
Nenitescu Prize; C. D. Vol. 2: 10371
Neometaphysical Merit Award Vol. 2: 4450
Ner Tamid Award Vol. 1: 6526
Neri; Medalla Eduardo Vol. 2: 9124
Nerken Award; Albert Vol. 1: 4964
Nernst - Haber - Bodenstein-Preis Vol. 2: 6631
Neruda Prize for Poetry; Pablo Vol. 1: 15382
Nesburn Award; Dr. Henry and Lilian Vol. 1: 6350
NESDA Awards Vol. 1: 13888
Neshamwari Traditional Music and Dance Festival Vol. 2: 12220
Ness Award; Mrs. Patrick Vol. 2: 4014
Ness Book Award; Frederic W. Vol. 1: 5677
NESS Communications Award Vol. 1: 13870
Ness Memorial Seminary Award; John Harrison Vol. 1: 9525
Nestle Enterprises Award Vol. 1: 6917
Nestroy-Ring der Stadt Wien Vol. 2: 794
NETA Special Service Award Vol. 1: 13917

NETC Annual Award for Outstanding Creative Achievement in the American Theatre Vol. 1: 15143
NETC Host Awards Vol. 1: 15144
NETC Regional Citation Vol. 1: 15145
NETC Special Award Vol. 1: 15146
Netcast Aerospace Award Vol. 1: 10107
Netcast Award of the Year Vol. 1: 10108
Netcast Commercial Award Vol. 1: 10109
Netcast Non-ferrous Award Vol. 1: 10110
Netherlands Fund for Chemistry Prize Vol. 2: 9603
Netherthorpe Award Vol. 2: 2959
Netter Lecture Vol. 1: 620
Netter; Prix du Docteur Robert Vol. 2: 4833
Network Awards Vol. 1: 16637
Neubacher Award; James Vol. 1: 8621
Neuberg Medal; Carl Vol. 1: 20054
Neue Stimmen - Europaischer Sangerwettstreit Vol. 2: 6567
Neufeld Memorial Research Grant; Prof. Henry Vol. 2: 7976
Neuhausen Foundation Award Vol. 2: 1901
Neuman Award; William F. Vol. 1: 4048
Neumann Prize; Bernhard H. Vol. 2: 254
Neumueller Award in Optics; Julius F. Vol. 1: 642
Neustadt International Prize for Literature Vol. 1: 20502
Neva Corporation of Alberta Award for Chemistry Teaching in Community and Technical Colleges Vol. 1: 7558
Nevanlinna Prize; Rolf Vol. 2: 4732
Nevelson Award in Art; Louise Vol. 1: 515
Nevins; Columbia University Prize in American Economic History in Honor of Allan Vol. 1: 7980
Nevins Physiology and Human Environment Award; Ralph G. Vol. 1: 4589
Nevins Prize; Allan Vol. 1: 17696
New Administrator Award Vol. 1: 1651
New American Talent Show Vol. 1: 18640
New and Creative Framing Competition Vol. 1: 16503
New and Creative Ideas Framing Competition Vol. 1: 16503
New Celebrity Competition Vol. 1: 11642
New Chapter of the Year Vol. 1: 13265
New Clio Awards Vol. 1: 15112
New Concept Award Vol. 1: 51
New Constellation Award Vol. 1: 13976
New Designers Vol. 2: 3027
New Director's New Works Award Vol. 1: 8734
New Director's Prize Vol. 1: 20329
New Directors Showcase Vol. 1: 17167
New Engineering Educator Excellence Award Vol. 1: 4106
New England Award for Literary Excellence; Shaeffer - PEN/ Vol. 1: 16037
New England Book Show Juried Selection Vol. 1: 6448
New England Exhibit Awards Vol. 1: 7292
New England Film and Video Festival Vol. 1: 5325
New England Lyric Operetta National Vocal Competition Vol. 1: 15120
New England Prize Vol. 1: 11983
New England Railroading Calendar Photo Contest Vol. 1: 12554
New Englander of the Year Vol. 1: 15118
New Focus Student Travel Grants Vol. 1: 15756
New Frontiers in Cytology Award Vol. 1: 4550
New Graduate Award - Clinical Chemistry Vol. 1: 7207

New Graduate Award - Clinical Microbiology Vol. 1: 7208
New Graduate Award - Cytotechnology Vol. 1: 7209
New Graduate Award - Harold Amy Award in Hematology Vol. 1: 7210
New Graduate Award - Histotechnology Vol. 1: 7211
New Graduate Award - Immunohematology Vol. 1: 7212
New Horizons Award Vol. 1: 11268
New Investigator Award Competition Vol. 1: 2238
New Investigator Awards Vol. 1: 2180
New Jersey Author Citation Vol. 1: 15180
New Leaders Travel Grant Vol. 1: 2932
New Letters Literary Awards Vol. 1: 15196
New Mexico Fine Arts Competition Vol. 1: 12505
New Model USA Showcase Vol. 1: 16740
New Music Competition Vol. 1: 11961
New Music for Young Ensembles Composition Prize Vol. 1: 15200
New Options Political Book Award Vol. 1: 15202
New Orleans International Piano Competition Vol. 1: 15204
New Play Competition Vol. 1: 8235
New Playwrights Competition and Festival Vol. 1: 20267
New Product Achievement Awards Vol. 1: 10187
New Product Award Vol. 1: 11420
New Product Awards Vol. 1: 14803
New Professional Award Vol. 1: 1013
New South Wales Film and Television Office Rouben Mamoulian Award Vol. 2: 687
New South Wales Premier's Literary Awards Vol. 2: 147
New South Wales State Literary Awards Vol. 2: 147
New Swiss Chemical Society Prizes Vol. 2: 11890
New Voice Award Vol. 1: 16607
New Voices - European Singing Contest Vol. 2: 6567
"New Voices, New World" Multicultural Fiction Contest Vol. 1: 11913
New Writers Awards Vol. 1: 9707
New York Academy of Sciences Award in Recognition of Services in Behalf of the Human Rights of Scientists Vol. 1: 15214
New York Academy of Sciences Award Supported by Boris Pregel Vol. 1: 15215
New York Book Show Vol. 1: 15226
New York Chopin Competition Vol. 1: 7648
New York City Marathon Vol. 1: 15270
New York Dance and Performance Awards (Bessie Awards) Vol. 1: 8532
New York Debut and Distinguished Artists Award Auditions Vol. 1: 5316
New York Drama Critics' Circle Awards Vol. 1: 15235
New York Fellowship Vol. 2: 7854
New York Festivals (Print Advertising Competition) Vol. 1: 15237
New York Festivals (Radio Competitions) Vol. 1: 15238
New York Festivals (Television Advertising, Programming and Non-Broadcast Competitions) Vol. 1: 15239
New York Flute Club Competition Vol. 1: 15243
New York International Ballet Competition Vol. 1: 15248
New York International Competition for Solo Oboists Vol. 1: 15570

New York Life Foundation Scholarship Program for Women in the Health Professions Vol. 1: 6643
New York Preservation Awards Vol. 1: 12490
New York Press Club Art Award Vol. 1: 15250
New York Press Club Byline Awards Vol. 1: 15251
New York Press Club Feature Awards Vol. 1: 15252
New York Press Club Feature Photo Award Vol. 1: 15253
New York Press Club Feature Video Photo Award Vol. 1: 15254
New York Press Club Gold Typewriter Award Vol. 1: 15255
New York Press Club Heart of New York Awards Vol. 1: 15256
New York Press Club Nellie Bly Cub Reporter of the Year Award Vol. 1: 15257
New York Press Club Nellie Bly/Thomas D. Zumbo Cub Reporter Award Vol. 1: 15257
New York Press Club Spot News Video Photo Award Vol. 1: 15258
New York Press Club/Thommy Weber Spot News Photo Award Vol. 1: 15259
New York State Governor's Arts Award Vol. 1: 15285
New York State Historical Association Manuscript Award Vol. 1: 15289
New York - Tidewater Chapters History of Military Medicine Essay Award Vol. 1: 5887
The New York Times Choice of the Best Illustrated Children's Books of the Year Vol. 1: 15296
New Yorker for New York Awards Vol. 1: 7714
New Zealand Association of Scientists Certificate for Science Journalism Vol. 2: 9753
New Zealand Association of Scientists Prize for Science Communication Vol. 2: 9754
New Zealand Book Awards Vol. 2: 9801
New Zealand Dental Association Awards Vol. 2: 9759
New Zealand Herald Challenge Trophy Vol. 2: 9820
New Zealand Library Association Non-Fiction for Young People Award Vol. 2: 9763
New Zealand Science and Technology Post-Doctoral Fellowship Vol. 2: 9840
New Zealand Society of Designers Awards
  Designers Institute of New Zealand Vol. 2: 9720
  Designers Institute of New Zealand Vol 2: 9720
"New Zealand Wings" Trophy Vol. 2: 9821
Newark Black Film Festival Vol. 1: 15312
Newberry Library National Endowment for the Humanities Fellowships Vol. 1: 15318
Newbery Medal; John Vol. 1: 2862
Newbigin Prize Vol. 2: 10633
Newbold V/STOL Award; AIAA F. E. Vol. 1: 2467
Newbury House Award for Excellence in Teaching; TESOL/ Vol. 1: 18592
Newby Trophy Vol. 2: 2393
Newcastle Award; Lena Vol. 1: 5057
Newcomb Award for Research Achievement; Simon Vol. 1: 19273
Newcomb Award; James E. Vol. 1: 2783
Newcomb Award; Simon Vol. 1: 16929
Newcombe Doctoral Dissertation Fellowship; Charlotte W. Vol. 1: 20316
Newcomen Award for Notable Proficiency in Mathematics, Physics and Chemistry Vol. 1: 15322

Newcomen Award in Applied Science Vol. 1: 15323
Newcomen Award in Material History Vol. 1: 15324
Newcomen Awards in Business History; Thomas Vol. 1: 15325
Newcomen Book Award in Business History; Thomas Vol. 1: 15326
Newcomer Award - Health Care Executive of the Year; William Vol. 1: 597
Newcomer Award - Medical Administrator of the Year Vol. 1: 597
Newcomer of the Year Vol. 1: 8246
Newcomers Award Vol. 2: 3804
Newell Award; William S. Vol. 1: 18978
Newell Prize; W. W. Vol. 1: 2071
Newhouse Citation Vol. 1: 18552
Newington Prize Vol. 1: 812
Newkirk Award; Burt L. Vol. 1: 4693
Newman Award; Clark - Vol. 1: 7128
Newman Award for Excellence in Research; Edwin B. Vol. 1: 3673
Newman Award; Sir Jack Vol. 2: 9772
Newman Cup Vol. 2: 9822
Newman Drug Abuse Prevention Award; Scott Vol. 1: 15330
Newman Graduate Research Award; Psi Chi/ Edwin B. Vol. 1: 16545
Newman International Memorial Award; Tom Vol. 2: 2480
Newman Iron Ore Award; Mt. Vol. 2: 10064
Newman Medal Vol. 1: 17712
Newman Prize; Ewell L. Vol. 1: 2305
Newman's Own First Amendment Award; PEN/ Vol. 1: 16026
Newmark Medal; Nathan M. Vol. 1: 4484
Newnham Memorial Lecture; W. L. Vol. 2: 9739
Newport International Competition for Young Pianists Vol. 2: 12179
Newport Mayor's Cup Vol. 1: 12324
News and Documentary Award Vol. 1: 12714
News Media Award for Community Service Vol. 1: 3561
News Pictures of the Year Vol. 1: 14530
Newsbank Scholarship Award Vol. 1: 2844
Newsboy Award Vol. 1: 310
Newsfilm Cameramen of the Year Vol. 1: 14529
Newsletter Association Journalism Awards Vol. 1: 15344
Newsletter Award
  American Lawyers Auxiliary Vol. 1: 2793
  Catholic Library Association Vol 1: 7379
  Institute of Environmental Sciences Vol 1: 10330
Newsletter Awards Vol. 1: 5820
Newsletter Competition Vol. 1: 10391
Newsletter Contest Vol. 1: 9131
Newsletter Journalism Awards Vol. 1: 14502
Newsletter of the Year
  United States Hang Gliding Association Vol. 1: 19369
  United States Professional Tennis Association Vol 1: 19510
Newsletter of the Year Award
  American Society for Photogrammetry and Remote Sensing Vol. 1: 4257
  National Society for Histotechnology Vol 1: 14753
Newsletter Promotion Awards Competition Vol. 1: 15342
Newsletter Publishers Association Journalism Awards Vol. 1: 15344
Newsmaker of the Year Award Vol. 1: 18112
Newson Award; John Vol. 2: 2911
Newspaper Advertising Prize Vol. 2: 8626

Newspaper Award Vol. 1: 372
Newspaper Cartoon Competition Vol. 2: 9167
Newspaper Culture Award Vol. 2: 8627
Newspaper in Education Program Excellence Award; NAA Foundation - Vol. 1: 15356
Newspaper Language Prize Vol. 2: 12076
Newspaper Photographer of the Year
  National Press Photographers Association Vol. 1: 14525
  University of Missouri-Columbia - School of Journalism Vol 1: 19844
Newspaper Picture Editing Award Vol. 1: 19844
Newth Memorial Prize; Arthur Vol. 2: 4463
Newton Memorial Award for Outstanding Achievment in Human Development; Niles Vol. 1: 11068
Nex Prize; Martin Andersen Vol. 2: 1929
Neyman Lecture Vol. 1: 10406
NFA Orchestral Audition Vol. 1: 13983
NFA Young Artist Competition Vol. 1: 13984
NFDW Humanitarian Award Vol. 1: 13936
NFICA Certificates for Each State Vol. 1: 13958
NFICA Contributor Awards Vol. 1: 13958
NFID - Astra USA, Inc. Postdoctoral Fellowship in Infectious Disease Training and Herpes Virus Research Vol. 1: 14041
NFID - Burroughs Welcome Fund Young Investigator Awards Vol. 1: 14045
NFID - Eli Lilly Fellowship in Infectious Diseases Vol. 1: 14042
NFID - Janssen Pharmaceutica Postdoctoral Fellowship in Medical Mycology Vol. 1: 14043
NFID - Marion Merrell Dow, Inc. Postdoctoral Fellowship in Nosocomial/Gram Positive Infection Research and Training Vol. 1: 14044
NFID - Young Investigator Matching Grants Vol. 1: 14045
NFL All-Star Team Vol. 1: 18374
NFL Coach of the Year Vol. 1: 18375
NFL Executive of the Year Vol. 1: 18376
NFL Man of the Year Vol. 1: 14001
NFL Most Valuable Player Vol. 1: 15361
NFL Offensive and Defensive Linemen of the Year Vol. 1: 14002
NFL Player of the Year; The Sporting News Vol. 1: 18385
NFL Rookie of the Year Vol. 1: 15359
NFL Rookie of the Year; The Sporting News/ Marlboro Vol. 1: 18384
NFL Top Defensive Player Vol. 1: 15360
NFMS/ESSO Young Concert Artists Vol. 2: 3684
NFP National Recognition Award Vol. 1: 13942
NFPA Award
  American Society for Horticultural Science Vol. 1: 4145
  American Society for Horticultural Science Vol 1: 4153
NFPA Member of the Year Vol. 1: 14031
NFPW President's Award Vol. 1: 13945
NFSPS Award Vol. 1: 13963
NFSPS Past President's Award Vol. 1: 13963
NFWI Design Award Vol. 2: 3689
NFWT Service Award Vol. 1: 14048
NGJA Hall of Fame Vol. 1: 14102
NHCA Media Award Vol. 1: 14119
NHK Broadcast Cultural Award Vol. 2: 8601
NHK Broadcasting Culture Prize Vol. 2: 8601
NHK Japan Prize Contest Vol. 2: 8602
NHK Prize Vol. 2: 8727
NHL All Star Team Vol. 1: 9960
NHL All-Star Team Vol. 1: 18377

NHL — Awards, Honors & Prizes, 1995-96

NHL Coach of the Year
 The Hockey News Vol. 1: 9960
 The Sporting News Vol 1: 18378
NHL Executive of the Year
 The Hockey News Vol. 1: 9960
 The Sporting News Vol 1: 18379
NHL Goalie Vol. 1: 9960
NHL Man of the Year; Bud Light/ Vol. 1: 14159
NHL Player of the Year
 The Hockey News Vol. 1: 9960
 The Sporting News Vol 1: 18380
NHL Player of the Year Award; Pro Set Vol. 1: 14177
NHL Rookie of the Year
 The Hockey News Vol. 1: 9960
 The Sporting News Vol 1: 18381
NHPA Achievement Award Vol. 1: 14188
NHRA Media Award Vol. 1: 14194
NHRA Public Relations Award Vol. 1: 14195
NHS Book Prize Vol. 1: 14152
NIADA National Quality Dealer Award Vol. 1: 14205
NIAE/ATBCB Student Design Competition Vol. 1: 14215
NIAE International Student Design Competition Vol. 1: 14216
NIC Gold or Silver Medal Vol. 1: 14246
Nice Award; Margaret Morse Vol. 1: 20320
Nicholl Screenwriting Fellowship; Don and Gee Vol. 1: 61
Nicholls Award; Percy Vol. 1: 4694
Nicholls Award; Percy W. Vol. 1: 17569
Nichols Award; Charles Walter Vol. 1: 3880
Nichols Award; Christopher D. Vol. 1: 5276
Nichols Challenge Trophy; Marguerite S. Vol. 1: 20593
Nichols Fellowship Vol. 2: 4260
Nicholson Award (Enlisted Leadership Award); James E. Vol. 1: 12073
Nicholson Award; J. Lee Vol. 1: 10392
Nicholson Award; Joyce Vol. 2: 193
Nicholson Awards Program Vol. 1: 5930
Nicholson Gold Medal Award; Gunnar Vol. 1: 18600
Nicholson, Jr., Memorial Award; George E. Vol. 1: 15736
Nicholson Prize; Edgardo Vol. 2: 89
Nickerson-ISCC Award; Dorothy Vol. 1: 10525
Nicklaus Best Junior Golfer; Jack Vol. 2: 8618
Nicklaus Family Award; Jack Vol. 1: 14086
Nicklaus Golf Family of the Year Award; National Golf Foundation's Jack Vol. 1: 14086
Nicklin Memorial Trophy; Jeff Vol. 1: 6883
Nicloux; Prix Maurice Vol. 2: 6236
Nicol Trophy; William A. Vol. 2: 4166
Nicolau Prize; Stefan S. Vol. 2: 10372
Nicolini Prize; Raul Vol. 2: 90
NIDDK Travel Fellowships for Minority Physiologists Vol. 1: 3509
Niedermair Award; John C. Vol. 1: 5956
Niederman Award; Allan and Joyce Vol. 1: 9914
Niels Nielsen Prisen Vol. 2: 2001
Nielsen Award; Niels Vol. 2: 2001
Nielsen International Violin Competition; Carl Vol. 2: 1984
Nielsen Violin Konkurrence; Internationale Carl Vol. 2: 1984
Nielubowicz Award; Mary J. Vol. 1: 5888
Nieman Fellowships for Journalists Vol. 1: 9816
Nigar Public Film Awards Vol. 2: 9987
Nigar Weekly Public Film Awards Vol. 2: 9987

Nigar Weekly Song Award Vol. 2: 9988
Nightingale; Medaille Florence Vol. 2: 11771
Nightingale Medal; Florence Vol. 2: 11771
Nightingale Prize Vol. 2: 2186
NIGP Chapter of the Year Awards Vol. 1: 14235
NIGP Fellow Award Vol. 1: 14234
Nihon Honyaku Bunkasho Vol. 2: 8638
Nihon Honyaku Shuppan Bunkasho Vol. 2: 8639
Nihon Jinrui Iden Gakkai Sho Vol. 2: 8641
Nihon Ketsueki Gakkai Shorei Sho Vol. 2: 8657
Nihon Kokusai Ongaku Konkuru Vol. 2: 8608
Nihon Shinbun Kyokai Awards Vol. 2: 8628
Nihon Sugakukai Iyanaga Sho Vol. 2: 8696
Nihon Tenmon Gakki Kenkyu Soreisho Vol. 2: 8508
Nihon Yakugakkai Gakkaisho Vol. 2: 8715
Nihon Yakugakkai Gakujutsukokensho Vol. 2: 8717
Nihon Yakugakkai Gijutsusho Vol. 2: 8718
Nihon Yakugakkai Korosho Vol. 2: 8716
Nihon Yakugakkai Kyoikusho Vol. 2: 8719
Nihon Yakugakkai Shoreisho Vol. 2: 8720
Nijhoff International West European Specialist Study Grant; Martinus Vol. 1: 2875
Nijhoff Prijs voor Vertalingen; Martinus Vol. 2: 9572
Nijhoff Study Grant; Martinus Vol. 2: 9494
Nike Cup Vol. 1: 14266
Nikkei Advertising Awards Vol. 2: 8707
Nikolsky Honorary Lectureship; Alexander A. Vol. 1: 2258
Nile Gold Medal Vol. 2: 5162
Niles Award; Colonel Elliott A. Vol. 1: 6421
Nilon Excellence in Minority Fiction Award; Charles H. and N. Mildred Vol. 1: 9181
Nimmo Medal; W.H.R. Vol. 2: 461
Nimmo Premium; Henry Vol. 2: 3297
NINDS Javits Neuroscience Investigator Award Vol. 1: 19239
Ninety-Nines NIFA Achievement Award Vol. 1: 15388
Ninkasi Award Vol. 1: 2344
Niotis Cup; D. J. Vol. 1: 19695
NIPDOK Award Vol. 2: 8541
Nippon Chikusan Gakkai Sho Vol. 2: 8673
Nippon Dojohiryo Gakkai Sho Vol. 2: 8666
Nippon Dojohiryo Gakkai Shorei Sho Vol. 2: 8667
Nippon Gakushiin Ejinbara-ko Sho Vol. 2: 8593
Nippon Gakushiin Sho Vol. 2: 8595
Nippon Oyo Dobutsu Konchu Gakkai Sho Vol. 2: 8654
NISCA 25 Year Awards Vol. 1: 14250
NISCA Appreciation Awards Vol. 1: 14250
NISCA Hall of Fame Award Vol. 1: 14249
NISCA Outstanding Service Award Vol. 1: 14250
NISCA Special Service Awards Vol. 1: 14250
Nisei of the Biennium Vol. 1: 11505
Nishan-i-Haider Vol. 2: 9996
Nishan-i-Imtiaz Vol. 2: 9996
Nishan-i-Shujaat Vol. 2: 9996
Nishiyama Medal Vol. 2: 8565
NISOA Honor Award Vol. 1: 14244
Nissan - Fitzgerald Vol. 1: 18394
Nissan FOCUS Awards Competition Vol. 1: 15390
Nissen Award Vol. 1: 13001
Nissim Award; Rudolf Vol. 1: 4529
NISWA International Indian Child Conference Outstanding Leadership Awards Vol. 1: 14210
Nitti; Premio Federico Vol. 2: 8382

Nitti Prize; Fondazione Francesco Sarerio Vol. 2: 8054
Niven Award; Frederick Vol. 2: 10578
Nivo Award Vol. 2: 7337
Nivo Dij Vol. 2: 7337
Niwa Prize Vol. 2: 8620
Niwano Peace Prize Vol. 2: 8709
Nixon National Journalism Writing Award Vol. 1: 6230
NJCAA Achievement Award Vol. 1: 14261
NJCAA All-American Baseball Team Vol. 1: 14266
NJCAA Coaches Association Awards Vol. 1: 14262
NJCAA Merit Award Vol. 1: 14263
NJCAA Outstanding Male & Female Athletes-of-the-Year Vol. 1: 14264
NJCAA Service Award Vol. 1: 14265
Nkruma Prize in African Studies; Kwame Vol. 2: 7177
NLA Award for Outstanding Achievement Vol. 1: 15385
NLA Garden Awards Vol. 1: 1071
NLA Residential Landscape Award Program Vol. 1: 1071
NLGI Authors' Award Vol. 1: 14315
NLGI Award for Achievement Vol. 1: 14316
NLGI Fellows Award Vol. 1: 14317
NLGI Honorary Membership Vol. 1: 14318
NLGJA Prize; Crossroads Market/ Vol. 1: 14304
NLN Distinguished Service Award Vol. 1: 14287
NMA Merit Scholarships Vol. 1: 14350
NMFS Publication of the Year Award Vol. 1: 19112
NMIA Academic Excellence Awards - Defense Intelligence College Vol. 1: 14367
NMIA Military Intelligence Professionalism Awards Vol. 1: 14368
NMMA Director's Award Vol. 1: 14335
NMRT Mid-Career Award Vol. 1: 11951
NMRT Professional Development Grant; 3M/ Vol. 1: 2920
NNWS Beverly Kievman Leadership Award Vol. 1: 14391
NOAA Administrator's Award Vol. 1: 19117
NOAA Technology Transfer Award Vol. 1: 19118
Noah Awards Vol. 1: 89
Noah Bee Award Vol. 1: 2746
Nobel Laureate Signature Award for a Graduate Student in Chemistry Vol. 1: 1568
Nobel Laureate Signature Award for Graduate Education in Chemistry Vol. 1: 1568
Nobel Peace Prize Vol. 2: 11495
Nobel Prize for Chemistry Vol. 2: 11496
Nobel Prize for Literature Vol. 2: 11497
Nobel Prize for Physics Vol. 2: 11498
Nobel Prize for Physiology or Medicine Vol. 2: 11499
Nobel Prizes Vol. 2: 11549
Noble Bursary; John Vol. 2: 10675
Noble Prize
 Association for the Promotion of Humor in International Affairs Vol. 2: 4945
 Association for the Promotion of Humor in International Affairs (APHIA) Vol 1: 5640
Noble Prize; Alfred
 American Society of Civil Engineers Vol. 1: 4485
 Western Society of Engineers Vol 1: 20224
Noceti and Atilio Tiscornia Prize; Adolfo Vol. 2: 91
NODA Scholarship Vol. 1: 14435
Noel-des-Vergers; Prix Adolphe Vol. 2: 5433
NOGI Awards Vol. 1: 18869

NOIA Award for Excellence in Environmental Conservation Vol. 1: 14402
Nolan One-Act Play Awards; Paul T. Vol. 1: 8568
Nolan Service Award; William G. Vol. 1: 10980
Nolte Award for Extraordinary Leadership; Julius M. Vol. 1: 14949
Nolting; International Award in Honor of Orin F. Vol. 1: 10850
Noma Award for Publishing in Africa Vol. 2: 2039
Noma Concours for Picture Book Illustrations Vol. 2: 8500
Noma Illustration Prizes Vol. 2: 8689
Noma Prize Vol. 2: 6422
Noma Prize for Juvenile Novel Vol. 2: 8690
Noma Prize for Literature Vol. 2: 8691
Noma Prize for Translation Vol. 2: 8692
Non-Clinical Bursary Vol. 2: 2521
Non-Heatset Web Printing Awards Competition Vol. 1: 16420
Non-Performing-Business Award Vol. 1: 16820
Nonnenmacher Industrial Service Award; Tom Vol. 1: 13157
Noordstarfonds - Dr. Jan Grauls Prize Vol. 2: 1275
Noranda Lecture Award Vol. 1: 7557
Norcen/CSPG Undergraduate Scholarship Vol. 1: 7226
Nordberg Medal Vol. 2: 5066
Nordic Award
 International Association of Medical Laboratory Technologists Vol. 2: 11467
 U.S. Skiing Vol 1: 19574
Nordic Biennial for Young Soloists Vol. 2: 1906
Nordic Competition for Young Orchestra Conductors Vol. 2: 1907
Nordic Council Literature Prize Vol. 2: 11503
Nordic Council Music Prize
 NOMUS - Nordic Music Committee Vol. 2: 11501
 Nordic Council (Sweden) Vol 2: 11504
Nordic World Cup Leaders Vol. 2: 11833
Nordisk Rads Musikpris Vol. 2: 11501
Nordiska Radets Litteraturpris Vol. 2: 11503
Nordmanns-Forbundet oversetterstotte Vol. 2: 9914
Nordrhein-Westfalen Prize for the Advancement of Young Artists Vol. 2: 7026
Noria de Bustamente Prize; Carlos Vol. 2: 9089
Noriega Morales Science and Technology Prizes; Manuel Vol. 1: 15830
Noriega Prize; Alfonso Sordo Vol. 2: 9090
NORMA Award Vol. 1: 15350
Norman Medal Vol. 1: 4486
Normand; Prix Jacques Vol. 2: 6285
Normann-Medaille; W. Vol. 2: 6840
Noro Prize Vol. 2: 8566
Norpress Press Prize Vol. 2: 9912
Norris Award in Physical Organic Chemistry; James Flack Vol. 1: 1569
Norris Memorial Trophy; James Vol. 1: 14172
Norsemen's Federation Translation Grant Vol. 2: 9914
Norsk kulturrads oversettespris Vol. 2: 9936
Norsk kulturrads pris for kulturjournalistikk Vol. 2: 9935
Norske Akademis Pris Til Minne om Thorleif Dahl Vol. 2: 9925
Norske Sivilingeniorers Forenings Teknologipris Vol. 2: 9955

North American Bluebird Society Grants Vol. 1: 15400
North American Bridge Championships Vol. 1: 1828
North American Championship Vol. 1: 19425
North American Championship Trophy Vol. 1: 11085
North American Conference Dissertation Fellowship Vol. 1: 15405
North American Hairstyling Awards Vol. 1: 6304
North American Loon Fund Grants Vol. 1: 15432
North American Mixing Award Vol. 1: 2594
North American Open Poetry Contest Vol. 1: 14306
North American Patristic Foundation Award for Best First Article in Patristics Vol. 1: 15439
North American Sculpture Exhibition Awards Vol. 1: 9310
North American Shortwave Broadcast DXer of the Year Vol. 1: 5906
North American South Devon Association Hall of Fame Award Vol. 1: 15465
North American Warmblood Association Awards Vol. 1: 15489
North Carolina Awards for Literature Vol. 1: 15498
North Carolina Prize Vol. 1: 15299
North of Scotland Sub Centre Premium Vol. 2: 3289
North Shore Trophy Vol. 2: 9823
Northcroft Memorial Lecture Vol. 2: 2526
Northeastern Loggers' Association Awards Program Vol. 1: 15505
Northern Arts Literary Fellowship Vol. 2: 3725
Northern Arts Writers' Awards Vol. 2: 3726
Northern California Athlete of the Year Vol. 1: 398
Northern Cross Book Award Vol. 1: 15509
Northern Cross Survivor Award Vol. 1: 15510
Northern Light Award Vol. 1: 17314
Northern New England Playwrights Award Vol. 1: 19973
Northern Rockies Sustainable Agriculture Award Vol. 1: 378
Northern Science Award Vol. 1: 7101
Northern Telecom Arts Europe Vol. 2: 4488
Northup Lecturer Award; Thomas L. Vol. 1: 651
Northwest Film and Video Festival Vol. 1: 15522
Northwest Watercolor Society Awards Vol. 1: 15526
Norton Award; Margaret Cross Vol. 1: 12267
Norton Distinguished Ceramist Award; F. H. Vol. 1: 1469
Norton Memorial Scholarship Award for Women; Mary R. Vol. 1: 6067
Norton Prize Vol. 1: 17523
Norwegian Master-Painter Organization Awards Vol. 2: 9940
Norwhich Eaton Student Leadership Award Vol. 1: 3394
Norwich Eaton Student Leadership Award Vol. 1: 3394
Nossack Academy Writers Award Vol. 2: 6515
Nossack-Akademiepreises fur Dichter und ihre Ubersetzer Vol. 2: 6515
Notable Wisconsin Authors Vol. 1: 20346
Notary of the Year Award Vol. 1: 14400
Notre Dame Award Vol. 1: 19862
Noufflard; Prix de Peinture Andre et Berthe Vol. 2: 5199

Nourse Award; Edwin G. Vol. 1: 13736
Noury; Fondation de Madame Victor Vol. 2: 5535
Noury; Prix Michel Vol. 2: 4865
Nouveau Prix Populiste Vol. 2: 6130
Nova Awards Vol. 1: 9794
NOVA Program of Distinction Awards Vol. 1: 14416
Novacor Chemical Ltd. Award for Chemistry Teaching in Community and Technical Colleges Vol. 1: 7558
Novaro; Fondazione Angiolo Silvio e Jacopo Vol. 2: 8051
Novel of the Year Award Vol. 2: 10720
Novella Award Vol. 1: 16609
Novello Youth Orchestra Award Vol. 2: 10593
November 17th Medal Vol. 2: 1869
Nover Memorial Awards; Barnet Vol. 1: 18460
Novice Award Vol. 1: 19712
Novikoff Memorial Award; Philip A. Vol. 1: 7114
Novo Nordisk Prize Vol. 2: 1987
Novopharm Award Vol. 1: 7190
NOW LDEF Equal Opportunity Award Vol. 1: 15549
Noyes Award; Marcia C. Vol. 1: 12177
NPA Outstanding Service Award Vol. 1: 14471
NPC Achievement Award Vol. 1: 14460
NPM Scholarship Vol. 1: 13220
NPPA Association Fellowship Award Vol. 1: 14520
NPPA Award of Excellence Vol. 1: 14473
NPPA Citations Vol. 1: 14521
NPPA Special Citations Vol. 1: 14522
NPS Medal of Honour Vol. 2: 3701
NPS Stud Assistant's Certificate Vol. 2: 3702
NRA Gold Medal Vol. 2: 3706
NRA Intercollegiate Championship Trophies Vol. 1: 14643
NRA International Championship Trophies Vol. 1: 14644
NRA Legislative Service Award Vol. 1: 14583
NRA Meritorious Service Award Vol. 1: 14585
NRA National Championship Trophies Vol. 1: 14645
NRA Organizational Award Vol. 1: 14586
NRB Milestone Award Vol. 1: 14605
NRCA Fellow Vol. 1: 14597
NRDC Environmental Award Vol. 1: 15073
NSC Marine Section Safety Awards Vol. 1: 2628
NSEAD/Berol Curriculum Development Award for Art and Design Teachers Vol. 2: 3712
NSERC Doctoral Prizes Vol. 1: 15076
NSFRE National Chairman's Award for Distinguished Service Vol. 1: 14785
NSIF Awards Program Vol. 1: 14876
NSIF Continuing Service Award Vol. 1: 14876
NSIF Graduate Student Award Vol. 1: 14876
NSIPA Distinguished Service Award Vol. 1: 14795
NSOA Orchestra Composition Contest Vol. 1: 14668
NSPE Award Vol. 1: 14804
NSPI International Pool, Spa and Tub Design Awards Vol. 1: 14828
NSPRA Gold Medallion Awards Competition Vol. 1: 14673
NSPS Scholarship Vol. 1: 14816
NSRA Heritage Foundation Scholarships Fund Vol. 1: 13835
NSSA/Prentice-Hall Outstanding Science Supervisor Vol. 1: 14693
NSSA Presidential Awards Vol. 1: 14694

NSTA ExploraVision Awards; Toshiba/ Vol. 1: 14707
NTC Citation   Vol. 1: 14896
NUCEA Distinguished Service Key and Certificate   Vol. 1: 14950
NUCEA Divisional Awards   Vol. 1: 14951
NUCEA Innovations in Continuing Education Awards   Vol. 1: 14952
NUCEA Outstanding Nontraditional Student Award for Degree Candidates   Vol. 1: 14953
Nuclear Medicine Technologist Award   Vol. 1: 17949
Nuclear Physics Postgraduate Student Awards   Vol. 2: 11070
Nuclear Ships Trophy   Vol. 1: 19713
Nuffield Lecture   Vol. 2: 4261
Nuffield Silver Medal   Vol. 2: 3298
Numismatic Ambassador Award   Vol. 1: 11733
Numismatic Error Collectors Exhibit Award   Vol. 1: 3244
Nunn Media Award for Environmental Communication; Carl   Vol. 1: 9152
Nursery Extension Award for Distinguished Service to the Nursery Industry   Vol. 1: 4148
Nurserymen's Hall of Fame   Vol. 1: 1072
Nursey Prize   Vol. 2: 4445
Nursing Education Award   Vol. 1: 8908
Nursing Practice Award   Vol. 1: 8909
Nursing Professionalism Award   Vol. 1: 8910
Nursing Research Award
  Emergency Nurses Association   Vol. 1: 8911
  International Society for Heart and Lung Transplantation   Vol 1: 11249
Nursing Research Grants Program   Vol. 1: 3293
Nursing Service Cross   Vol. 2: 343
Nutley Symphony Young Artist Competition   Vol. 1: 15564
Nutrition Professionals, Inc. Applied Dairy Nutrition Award   Vol. 1: 1920
Nutting Award; Mary Adelaide   Vol. 1: 14288
NWAA Athletes of the Year   Vol. 1: 14995
NWAA Hall of Fame   Vol. 1: 14996
NWBA Hall of Fame   Vol. 1: 14999
NWBA Most Valuable Player   Vol. 1: 15000
NWC Article/Essay Contest   Vol. 1: 15054
NWC Novel Manuscript Award   Vol. 1: 15055
NWC Poetry Award   Vol. 1: 15056
NWC Short Story Award   Vol. 1: 15057
NWRA Distinguished Service Award   Vol. 1: 14978
NWRA Manufacturer of the Year   Vol. 1: 14987
NWRA Retailer of the Year Award   Vol. 1: 14988
NWRA Woman of the Year   Vol. 1: 19523
NWSA Graduate Scholarship in Lesbian Studies   Vol. 1: 15032
NWSA Pre K-12 Fellowship   Vol. 1: 15033
NYBPE Annual Editorial Awards Competition   Vol. 1: 15228
Nycomed Prize   Vol. 2: 9528
Nycomed Scandinavian Scholarships   Vol. 2: 2414
Nyholm Lectureship   Vol. 2: 4212
Nymph Awards   Vol. 2: 9322
Nyon International Documentary Film Festival   Vol. 2: 11892
Nypels Prijs; Charles   Vol. 2: 9564
NYSBA John Peter Zenger Media Award   Vol. 1: 15283
Nyselius Award   Vol. 1: 15422
Nystrom Award; J. Warren   Vol. 1: 5685
Nystroms pris; Professor E. J.   Vol. 2: 4708
Nystroms Prize; Professor E. J.   Vol. 2: 4708

NZFUW/Wellington Suffrage Fellowship   Vol. 2: 11789
NZNFFA Trophy   Vol. 2: 2898
NZNSEE Award   Vol. 2: 9767
Oaboos Prize for Environmental Preservation; Sultan   Vol. 2: 6418
Oak Leaf Award   Vol. 1: 15080
OAPEC Award for Scientific Research   Vol. 2: 8847
Obee Small Player Award; V. C. "Bub"   Vol. 1: 14266
Oberle Award for Outstanding Teaching in Grades K-12; Marcella E.   Vol. 1: 18310
Oberly Award for Bibliography in the Agricultural Sciences   Vol. 1: 2876
Oberly Memorial Award; Eunice Rockwell   Vol. 1: 2876
Oberst Award; Byron B.   Vol. 1: 676
OBIE Awards   Vol. 1: 20039
Oboler Memorial Award; Eli M.   Vol. 1: 2900
Obreshkov Prize; Academy Nikola   Vol. 2: 1513
O'Brien Award; Robert F.   Vol. 1: 13534
O'Brien; Patrick   Vol. 2: 10566
O'Brien Trophy; NBA World Championship - Larry   Vol. 1: 13456
Obrig Prize; Adolph and Clara   Vol. 1: 12621
Obrig Prize for Painting in Oil; Adolph and Clara   Vol. 1: 12622
Observer Award for Outstanding Achievement   Vol. 2: 4466
O'Byrne Award; Father Patrick   Vol. 1: 19941
Ocampo Lecture   Vol. 2: 10729
Ocampo Prize; Angelica   Vol. 2: 92
Ocaranza; Premio Dr. Fernando   Vol. 2: 9115
OCC Scholarships   Vol. 1: 15716
Occupational Safety and Health Achievement Award   Vol. 1: 6757
Occupational Safety/Health Award Program   Vol. 1: 14660
Occupational Safety/Health Contests   Vol. 1: 14661
Ocean Crew and Great Lakes Awards of Merit   Vol. 1: 3068
Ocean Sciences Award   Vol. 1: 2169
Oceaneering International Award   Vol. 1: 18865
Ochsner Award Relating Smoking and Health; Alton   Vol. 1: 15572
OCIC-Prize
  Berlin International Film Festival   Vol. 2: 6564
  International Catholic Organization for Cinema and Audiovisual   Vol 2: 1173
OCLC Minority Scholarship in Library and Information Technology; LITA/   Vol. 1: 2911
O'Connor Award   Vol. 2: 3424
O'Connor Award for Short Fiction; Flannery   Vol. 1: 19796
O'Connor Memorial Award; Frank   Vol. 1: 8619
October Prizes of the City of Belgrade   Vol. 2: 10696
October Show Awards   Vol. 2: 10697
Odaka Prize   Vol. 2: 8603
ODAS Youth Achievement Award   Vol. 1: 6319
O'Day Trophy Javelin National Champion   Vol. 1: 11510
O'Day Trophy; U.S. Singlehanded Sailing Championship - George D.   Vol. 1: 19543
Odd Fellows Book Award   Vol. 2: 2204
O'Dell Award for Historical Fiction; Scott   Vol. 1: 18538
O'Dell Award; William   Vol. 1: 2991
Odesser Judaic Literary Award; Ben and Sylvia   Vol. 1: 2713

ODK Leader of the Year Award   Vol. 1: 15632
Odlum Award; Doris   Vol. 2: 2450
O'Donoghue Sports Injury Research Award   Vol. 1: 3349
Odontological Commemorative Lecture   Vol. 2: 4262
Odyssey Diploma   Vol. 2: 5163
Odyssey Institute of Connecticut Media Awards   Vol. 1: 15574
Oecuminical Jury Prize   Vol. 1: 12436
Oed GmbH Award for the Film and Media Exchange; TC-Studios Fred   Vol. 2: 7142
Oed GmbH fur die Film-und Medienborse; Preis der TC-Gruppe Fred   Vol. 2: 7142
Oehlenschlager Prize; Adam   Vol. 2: 1930
OEI Gold Medal   Vol. 2: 11312
OEI Medalla de Oro   Vol. 2: 11312
Oenslager Scholastic Achievement Awards; Mary P.   Vol. 1: 16718
Oersted Medal   Vol. 1: 1130
Oesterreichischer Auslandskulturpreis   Vol. 2: 767
Oesterreichischer Kinderlyrik-Staatspreis   Vol. 2: 764
Oesterreichischer Kinderund Juyendbuchpreis   Vol. 2: 757
Oesterreichischer Staatspreis fur Europaeische Komponisten   Vol. 2: 761
Oesterreichischer Staatspreis fur Europaeische Literatur   Vol. 2: 762
Oesterreichischer Staatspreis fur Kulturpublizistik   Vol. 2: 760
Oesterreichischer Staatspreis fur literarische Ubersetzer   Vol. 2: 763
Oesterreichischer Wuerdigungspreis fur Kinder-und Jugendliteratur   Vol. 2: 769
Oesterreichisches Ehrenzeichen fur Wissenschaft und Kunst   Vol. 2: 756
OFA Hall of Fame   Vol. 1: 15721
OFA Media Award   Vol. 1: 15722
Off-Off-Broadway Original Short Play Festival Award   Vol. 1: 11963
Offenbach Singing Competition; International   Vol. 2: 5072
Officers Medallion   Vol. 1: 11022
Official of the Year   Vol. 1: 18993
Official of the Year Award   Vol. 1: 18810
Official UNESCO Award for Distinguished Services to Physical Education and Sport   Vol. 2: 6419
Offshore Technology Conference Distinguished Service Awards   Vol. 1: 2595
O'Flaherty Service Award; Fred   Vol. 1: 2801
Ofsthun Award; SRE Stan   Vol. 1: 18026
Ogden Award; H. R. "Russ"   Vol. 1: 6068
Ogle Literary Awards; Lucille E.   Vol. 1: 20212
O'Hagan Award for Short Fiction; Howard   Vol. 1: 20555
O'Hair Memorial Award; Robert C.   Vol. 1: 20098
O'Hana Prize; Jacques and Eugenie   Vol. 2: 7968
O'Hara Award; Cardinal   Vol. 1: 19856
O'Hara Award; Edwin Vincent   Vol. 1: 16970
Ohaus - NSTA Award for College Science Teachers; Gustav   Vol. 1: 14703
Ohaus - NSTA Award for Elementary and Secondary Science Teachers; Gustav   Vol. 1: 14704
O'Hearn/SBS Bookshow Prize for Literary Translation; Dinny   Vol. 2: 149
O'Henry Awards   Vol. 1: 8707
Ohio State Awards
  Institute for Education by Radio-Television   Vol. 1: 10217
  WOSU Stations   Vol 1: 20543

Ohio State University Press/*The Journal* Award in Poetry Vol. 1: 15589
Ohio University Press - NEMLA Book Award Vol. 1: 15595
Ohioana Award for Editorial Excellence Vol. 1: 15598
Ohioana Book Award Vol. 1: 15602
Ohioana Career Medal Vol. 1: 15603
Ohioana Citation Vol. 1: 15604
Ohioana Pegasus Award Vol. 1: 15605
Oils and Fats Group International Lecture Vol. 2: 4419
Oita International Wheelchair Marathon Vol. 2: 8711
Okanagan Short Fiction Award Vol. 1: 6809
Oke Trophy; F. G. (Teddy) Vol. 1: 2331
Oken Medaille; Lorenz Vol. 2: 6890
Okes Award; Imogene Vol. 1: 828
OKOMEDIA International Ecological Film Festival Vol. 2: 7063
OKOMEDIA Internationale Tage des Okologischen Films Vol. 2: 7063
Okuma Academic Commemorative Prize Vol. 2: 8785
Okuma Academic Encouragement Prize Vol. 2: 8786
Okuma Gakujutsu Kinensho Vol. 2: 8785
Okuma Gakujutsu Shoreisho Vol. 2: 8786
O'Laoghaire Memorial Trophy; Pilib Vol. 2: 7766
Old Forge Hardware Prize Vol. 1: 5331
Old Guard Prizes Vol. 1: 4695
Old Hilltop Award Vol. 1: 12106
Old Masters Award Vol. 2: 3428
Old Sturbridge Village Research Library Society - E. Harold Hugo Memorial Book Prize Vol. 1: 15617
Old Tackle Makers Vol. 1: 13971
Oldenburger Medal; Rufus Vol. 1: 4696
Oldendorf Award; William H. Vol. 1: 4737
Oldfield Cup (Premier Award); Lucy Vol. 2: 2537
Oldman Prize; C. B. Vol. 2: 10573
O'Leary Award; Morgan Vol. 1: 19829
Olfactory Research Fund Sense of Smell Award Vol. 1: 9363
Olimpiada de Matematicas Mexicana Vol. 2: 9282
Olin Award; John M. Vol. 1: 20325
Olin Fellowships Vol. 1: 6120
Olin Medal; Francis P. Garvan - John M. Vol. 1: 1556
Olive Branch Awards Vol. 1: 7475
Oliveira; Prix Helena Vol. 2: 5188
Oliver Prize in the Psychiatry of Learning Disabilities; Brian Vol. 2: 3965
Oliver Scholarship; William C. Vol. 1: 13835
Olivier Awards; Laurence Vol. 2: 4466
Olle Prize; Archibald D. Vol. 2: 628
Ollie Awards; American Center for Children's Television - Vol. 1: 1441
Olman Publishers Award; Abe Vol. 1: 12649
Olmstead Medal; Frederick Law Vol. 1: 4646
Olmsted Award; George Vol. 1: 477
Olmsted Liberal Education Award for Innovation Vol. 1: 4107
Olney Medal Vol. 1: 1222
Olofson Memorial Award; Shirley Vol. 1: 2921
Olson Award; Harris Vol. 1: 2267
Olson Common Loon Research Award; Sigurd T. Vol. 1: 11936
Olsten Pinnacle Awards; Chapter SHRM/ Vol. 1: 17486
Olympia International Composition Prize Vol. 2: 7200
Olympic Cup Vol. 2: 11814

Olympic Football Tournaments (Men and Women) Vol. 2: 11716
Olympic Medals and Diplomas Vol. 2: 11815
Olympic Order Vol. 2: 11816
Olympic Spirit Award Vol. 1: 19491
Olympique; Ordre Vol. 2: 11816
O'Mahony Bursary; Eoin Vol. 2: 7844
O'Malley Art Award Vol. 1: 11454
O'Malley Award; Diane Vol. 1: 5283
O'Malley Award; General Jerome F. Vol. 1: 246
O'Malley Memorial Award (Angel of the Year); Diane Vol. 1: 247
O'Melveny and Myers Annual Centennial Grant Vol. 1: 15623
Omicron Delta Kappa Scholarships Vol. 1: 15633
On Behalf of Youth Award Vol. 1: 6687
On Site Waste Management Award Vol. 1: 13910
On-the-Spot Awards Vol. 1: 19091
Onassis Competition for the Letters, the Sciences and the Arts Vol. 2: 7207
Onassis Prize for Culture, Arts and Humanities Vol. 2: 7208
Onassis Prize for International Understanding and for Social Achievement Vol. 2: 7209
Onassis Prize for Man and Culture - Olympia Vol. 2: 7208
Onassis Prize for Man and His Environment - Delphi Vol. 2: 7210
Onassis Prize for Man and Mankind - Athinai Vol. 2: 7207
Onassis Prize for Man and Society - Aristotelis Vol. 2: 7207
Onassis Prize for the Environment Vol. 2: 7210
Onciul Prize; Dimitrie Vol. 2: 10373
Oncology Certified Nurse of the Year Award Vol. 1: 15638
Oncology Nursing Foundation/Bristol-Myers Oncology Division Community Health Research Grant Vol. 1: 15639
Oncology Nursing Foundation/Bristol-Myers Oncology Division Research Grant Vol. 1: 15640
Oncology Nursing Foundation/Cetus Corporation Grant for Research Involving Biotherapy or Immunotherapy Vol. 1: 15641
Oncology Nursing Foundation Ellyn Bushkin Friend of the Foundation Award Vol. 1: 15642
Oncology Nursing Foundation/Josh Gottheil Memorial Bone Marrow Transplant Career Development Awards Vol. 1: 15643
Oncology Nursing Foundation/Lederle Laboratories Research Grant Vol. 1: 15644
Oncology Nursing Foundation/Pearl Moore Career Development Awards Vol. 1: 15645
Oncology Nursing Foundation/Pharmacia Deltec Ambulatory Infusion Pump Research Grant Vol. 1: 15646
Oncology Nursing Foundation/Pharmacia Deltec Vascular Access Device Research Grant Vol. 1: 15647
Oncology Nursing Foundation/Purdue Frederick Research Grant Vol. 1: 15648
Oncology Nursing Foundation Research Grants Vol. 1: 15649
Oncology Nursing Foundation/Wyeth-Ayerst Laboratories New Investigators Research Grants Vol. 1: 15650
One Hundred Years of the Periodical *Health* Medal Vol. 2: 10194
One Show Awards Vol. 1: 15671
One Ton Championship - Hawk Trophy Vol. 1: 19533

O'Neal Safety Award; Jack Vol. 1: 19028
O'Neill Award (Canadian Player of the Year); James "Tip" Vol. 1: 6817
O'Neill Award; Joseph E. Vol. 1: 14859
Ong Memorial Award; William A. Vol. 1: 12766
Ongoing Public Relations Award Vol. 1: 10894
ONS/AMGEN Inc. Excellence in Patient/Public Education Award Vol. 1: 15651
ONS Bristol-Myers Oncology Division Distinguished Researcher Award Vol. 1: 15652
ONS/Chiron Therapeutics Award for Excellence of Scholarship and Consistency of Contribution to the Oncology Nursing Literature Vol. 1: 15653
ONS/Chiron Therapeutics Chapter Excellence Award Vol. 1: 15654
ONS/Chiron Therapeutics Susan Baird Excellence in Writing Awards in Clinical Practice and Nursing Research Vol. 1: 15655
ONS/Cytogen Corporation Excellence in Cancer Nursing Administration Award Vol. 1: 15656
ONS Honorary Membership Vol. 1: 15657
ONS/Pharmacy Adria Excellence in Oncology Nursing Private Practice Award Vol. 1: 15658
ONS Public Service Award Vol. 1: 15659
ONS/Roche Distinguished Service Award Vol. 1: 15660
ONS/Ross Excellence in Cancer Nursing Education Award Vol. 1: 15661
ONS/Roxane Laboratories Linda Arenth Excellence in Cancer Nursing Administration Award Vol. 1: 15662
ONS/Schering Excellence in Biotherapy Nursing Award Vol. 1: 15663
ONS/Schering Excellence in Cancer Nursing Research Award Vol. 1: 15664
ONS/Smith, Kline & French Research Grant Vol. 1: 15665
ONS/SmithKline Beecham Research Grant Vol. 1: 15666
ONS/Upjohn Quality of Life Award Vol. 1: 15667
ONS/Varian Excellence in Radiation Therapy Nursing Award Vol. 1: 15668
ONS/Zeneca Pharmaceuticals/Komen Foundation Excellence in Breast Cancer Education Award Vol. 1: 15669
Onshi Sho Vol. 2: 8594
Ontario Bicentennial Medal Vol. 1: 15680
Ontario Conservationist of the Month Vol. 1: 15689
Ontario Crafts Council Design Awards Vol. 1: 15717
Ontario Medal for Firefighters Bravery Vol. 1: 15681
Ontario Medal for Good Citizenship Vol. 1: 15682
Ontario Medal for Police Bravery Vol. 1: 15683
Ontario Psychological Association Applied Division Award Vol. 1: 15724
Ontario Psychological Association Award of Merit Vol. 1: 15725
Open Bible Award Vol. 1: 15990
Open Book Awards Vol. 1: 4636
Open de la Ville de Paris Vol. 2: 5260
Open Division Overall Vol. 1: 5010
Open Door Award Vol. 1: 10013
Open Exhibition Vol. 2: 4605
Open Water Swimmer of the Year Vol. 1: 19626

Opera Company of Philadelphia/Luciano Pavarotti International Voice Competition Vol. 1: 16131
Opera Prize Vol. 2: 11573
Opera Production Competition Vol. 1: 14407
Opera Screen Award Vol. 2: 844
Opera Talent Search Competition Vol. 1: 15729
Operasangerinnen Fanny Elstas Fond Vol. 2: 9875
Operations-Services Awards Vol. 1: 9666
Operator's Contest Award Vol. 1: 12381
Operator's Meritorious Service Award Vol. 1: 5028
Opernwelt Prize Vol. 2: 911
OpFlow Publication Award Vol. 1: 5029
Ophthalmology Fund Prizes and Lectures Vol. 2: 4263
Opie Prize; Peter and Iona Vol. 1: 2072
Oporto International Film Festival - Fantasporto Vol. 2: 10291
Oppenheim John Downes Memorial Trust Vol. 2: 3738
Oppenheimer Award Vol. 1: 4108
Oppenheimer Memorial Award; Ernst Vol. 1: 8923
Oppenheimer/*Newsday* Playwriting Award; George Vol. 1: 15339
Oppy Award Vol. 1: 15339
Oprescu Prize; George Vol. 2: 10374
OPTIMA Gold Medal Vol. 2: 7065
OPTIMA Silver Medal Vol. 2: 7066
Optimist International Awards Vol. 1: 15763
Optometrist of the Year Award Vol. 1: 3322
Optometry Outstanding Service and Recognition Award Vol. 1: 5889
OPUS Prizes Vol. 2: 7240
Ora Award Vol. 1: 14255
Oral and Maxillofacial Surgery Resident Scientific Presentation Awards Vol. 1: 1086
Oral Science Research Award Vol. 1: 10626
Orators Hall of Fame Vol. 1: 11156
Orban Prize; Balint Vol. 1: 695
Orbis Pictus Award for Outstanding Nonfiction for Children Vol. 1: 13774
Orbit Award of the ANZAAS International Scientific Film Exhibition and Competition Vol. 2: 191
Orbitalorden Vol. 2: 6571
ORCA Rolex Prize Vol. 2: 2835
Orchard-Hays Prize Vol. 2: 9550
Orchard Medal; William J. Vol. 1: 20157
Orchestral Direction Competition Vol. 2: 11774
Orde van Leopold II Vol. 2: 1075
Orde van Oranje-Nassau Vol. 2: 9356
Orden al Merito Industrial Vol. 2: 1732
Orden al Merito Julio Garavito Vol. 2: 1669
Orden al Merito Turistico Vol. 2: 11366
Orden de la Cruz del Merito Aeronautico Civil Vol. 2: 1598
Orden del Merito Aeronautico Antonio Ricaurte Vol. 2: 1643
Orden del Merito Agricola Vol. 2: 1602
Orden del Merito Comercial Vol. 2: 1613
Orden del Merito Industrial Vol. 2: 1614
Orden del Merito Jose Maria Cordoba Vol. 2: 1644
Orden del Merito Militar Antonio Narino Vol. 2: 1645
Orden del Merito Naval Almirante Padilla Vol. 2: 1646
Orden del Merito Penitenciario Vol. 2: 1630
Orden del Merito Sanitario Jose Fernandez Madrid Vol. 2: 1647
Orden del Trabajo Vol. 2: 1632
Orden Departmental de Bolivar Vol. 2: 1612

Orden Francisco Hernandez Vol. 2: 12134
Orden Francisco Javier Garcia de Hevia Vol. 2: 12111
Orden Manuel Felipe Rugeles Vol. 2: 12112
Orden Mexicana del Aguila Azteca Vol. 2: 9133
Orden Militar San Mateo Vol. 2: 1648
Orden Nacional al Merito Vol. 2: 1619
Orden Pour le merite fur Wissenschaften und Kunste Vol. 2: 6743
Orden Rafael Nunez Vol. 2: 1705
Orden Rodrigo Correa Palacio Vol. 2: 1588
Orden Universidad Javeriana Vol. 2: 1741
Order for Industrial Merit Vol. 2: 1732
Order for Merit in Work Vol. 2: 12136
Order for Meritorious Service Vol. 2: 10958
Order Ingenio et Arti Vol. 2: 1939
Order Krzyza Grunwaldu Vol. 2: 10118
Order Odrodzenia Polski Vol. 2: 10119
Order of Andres Bello Vol. 2: 12137
Order of Australia Vol. 2: 344
Order of Canada Vol. 1: 6707
Order of Cultural Merit Vol. 2: 8579
Order of Culture Vol. 2: 8586
Order of Dionysus Vol. 1: 978
Order of Distinction Vol. 2: 8484
Order of Excellence of Guyana Vol. 2: 7254
Order of Francisco de Miranda Vol. 2: 12138
Order of Friendship of Peoples Vol. 2: 10462
Order of Good Hope
  Republic of South Africa - Department of Foreign Affairs Vol. 2: 10914
  Republic of South Africa - State President's Office Vol 2: 10959
Order of Imtiaz Vol. 2: 9995
Order of Jamaica Vol. 2: 8484
Order of James Smithson Vol. 1: 17343
Order of Khidmat Vol. 2: 9995
Order of Labor Vol. 2: 1632
Order of Lenin Vol. 2: 10463
Order of Leopold Vol. 2: 1073
Order of Magellan Vol. 1: 7706
Order of Mariposa Vol. 1: 11804
Order of Merit
  British Government Vol. 2: 2378
  Jamaica - Chancery of the Orders of the Societies of Honour Vol 2: 8484
  National Wrestling Hall of Fame & Museum Vol 1: 15052
Order of Merit in Agriculture Vol. 2: 1602
Order of Merit in Commerce Vol. 2: 1613
Order of Merit in Industry Vol. 2: 1614
Order of Merit in the Sciences and Arts Vol. 2: 6743
Order of Merit of the Republic of Poland Vol. 2: 10117
Order of Military Merit Vol. 1: 6708
Order of National Hero Vol. 2: 8484
Order of Nature Award Vol. 2: 8871
Order of Nila Utama Vol. 2: 10744
Order of Ontario Vol. 1: 15684
Order of Orange-Nassau Vol. 2: 9356
Order of Pakistan Vol. 2: 9995
Order of Pius IX Vol. 2: 12101
Order of Quaid-i-Azam Vol. 2: 9995
Order of Red Triangle Vol. 1: 20611
Order of Rio Branco Vol. 2: 1417
Order of Roraima of Guyana Vol. 2: 7255
Order of St. Gregory the Great Vol. 2: 12102
Order of St. John Vol. 2: 3744
Order of St. John of Jerusalem Vol. 1: 6694
Order of St. Sylvester Vol. 2: 12103
Order of San Carlos Vol. 2: 1620
Order of Santa Barbara Vol. 1: 6950
Order of Shujaat Vol. 2: 9995
Order of Temasek Vol. 2: 10745
Order of the 27th of June Vol. 2: 12139

Order of the Academic Palms Vol. 2: 5295
Order of the Bird Vol. 1: 10783
Order of the Companions of Honour Vol. 2: 2379
Order of the Compassionate Heart Vol. 1: 16753
Order of the Cross of Grunwald Vol. 2: 10118
Order of the Cross of Liberty Vol. 2: 4678
Order of the Crown Vol. 2: 1074
Order of the Dannebrog Vol. 2: 1941
Order of the Egg Vol. 1: 10784
Order of the Elephant Vol. 2: 1942
Order of the Falcon Vol. 2: 7464
Order of the Glory of Labor Vol. 2: 10464
Order of the Golden Ark Vol. 2: 9357
Order of the Golden Eagle Vol. 1: 16754
Order of the Golden Microscope Vol. 1: 3041
Order of the Golden Rose Vol. 2: 7826
Order of the Golden Spur (Golden Militia) Vol. 2: 12104
Order of the Lapis Lazuli Vol. 1: 9114
Order of the Liberator Vol. 2: 12140
Order of the Lion of Finland Vol. 2: 4679
Order of the Nation Vol. 2: 8484
Order of the Netherlands Lion Vol. 2: 9358
Order of the October Revolution Vol. 2: 10465
Order of the Rebirth of Poland Vol. 2: 10119
Order of the Red Banner Vol. 2: 10466
Order of the Red Banner of Labor Vol. 2: 10467
Order of the Rose Vol. 2: 1507
Order of the Southern Cross Vol. 2: 10960
Order of the Star of South Africa (Military) Vol. 2: 10961
Order of the Star of South Africa (Non-Military) Vol. 2: 10962
Order of the White Rose of Finland Vol. 2: 4680
Order of West Range Vol. 1: 16180
Order Wojenny Virtuti Militari Vol. 2: 10123
Order Zaslugi Rzeczypospolitej Polskiej Vol. 2: 10117
Orders of the Precious Crown Vol. 2: 8587
Orders of the Rising Sun Vol. 2: 8588
Orders of the Sacred Treasure Vol. 2: 8589
Orders of the U.S. Air Force Vol. 1: 19179
Orders of the U.S. Army Vol. 1: 19180
Orders of the U.S. Coast Guard Vol. 1: 19181
Orders of the U.S. Marine Corps Vol. 1: 19182
Orders of the U.S. Navy Vol. 1: 19183
Ordonneau; Prix Auguste Durand et Edouard Vol. 2: 5361
Ordre de la Couronne Vol. 2: 1074
Ordre de la Fidelite Francaise Vol. 1: 8182
Ordre de la Liberation Vol. 2: 5238
Ordre de la Saint Croix de Jerusalem; Chevalier de l' Vol. 2: 8476
Ordre de la Sante Publique Vol. 2: 1791
Ordre de l'Education Nationale Vol. 2: 1792
Ordre de Legion d'Honneur Vol. 2: 5237
Ordre de Leopold Vol. 2: 1073
Ordre de Leopold II Vol. 2: 1075
Ordre de Merit de Madagascar Vol. 2: 8878
Ordre de Saint Gregoire le Grand; Commandeur de l' Vol. 2: 8476
Ordre du Merite Agricole
  Cote d'Ivoire - Presidency of the Republic Vol. 2: 1793
  France - Ministry of Agriculture and Forestry Vol 2: 5240
Ordre du Merite des P. et T. Vol. 2: 1794
Ordre du Merite Ivoirien Vol. 2: 1795
Ordre du Merite Sportif Vol. 2: 1796
Ordre Merite Vol. 2: 5236
Ordre Nacional de Madagascar Vol. 2: 8879

Ordre National Vol. 2: 1797
Ordre Olympique Vol. 2: 11816
Ordre Souverain d'Occident Vol. 2: 1370
O'Reilly - Conway Medal Vol. 1: 16219
Oren Medal Vol. 1: 17713
Orensanz and Artes del Serrablo International Sculpture Award; Museo Angel Vol. 2: 11307
Orenstein Memorial Fund; Doris Vol. 1: 5843
Organ Historical Society Archival Fellowship Vol. 1: 15805
Organization Development Consultant of the Year Award Vol. 1: 15809
Organization Distinguished Service Award Vol. 1: 3936
Organization for Tropical Studies Awards Vol. 2: 1785
Organization of the Year Vol. 1: 18934
Organizational Award Vol. 1: 4307
Organizational Certificate of Appreciation Vol. 1: 8208
Organizational Meritorious Award Vol. 1: 13461
Organon Award Vol. 1: 7191
Original Doll Artist Competition Vol. 1: 5339
Original Short Play Festival Award Vol. 1: 11963
Oringer Award for Excellence in Dental Electrosurgery; Maurice J. Vol. 1: 546
Orlando Award; Babe Vol. 1: 11386
Ormes Trophy; Sam Vol. 1: 18759
Ormond Medal; Francis Vol. 2: 620
Ornamentals Publication Award Vol. 1: 4147
Ornish Award; Natalie Vol. 1: 18652
Ornithologen-Preis Vol. 2: 6652
O'Rourke Scholarship; Margaret Vol. 2: 2933
Orpheus Award Vol. 2: 10164
Orr Award; Joan Vol. 1: 248
Orr Award; Verne Vol. 1: 249
ORSA/TIMS von Neumann Prize Vol. 1: 15737
Orsted Medal; H. C. Vol. 2: 2007
Orsted Medaljen; H. C. Vol. 2: 2007
Orszagos Amatorfilm Fesztival Nagydija Vol. 2: 7315
Ortega y Gasset Award for Journalism Vol. 2: 11321
Ortega y Gasset; Premio Vol. 2: 11299
Orth Memorial Trophy; Franklin L. Vol. 1: 14644
Ortho Award
   Canadian Public Health Association Vol. 1: 7110
   Canadian Society of Hospital Pharmacists Vol. 1: 7186
Ortho Award in Immunohematology Vol. 1: 7213
Ortho Biotech Faculty Fellowship Vol. 1: 1748
Ortho Diagnosis Systems Educational Award Vol. 2: 11468
Ortho Diagnostic Systems Scholarship in Immunohematology Vol. 1: 4195
Ortho French Literary Award Vol. 1: 7922
Ortho Literary Award Vol. 1: 7923
Orthodiagnostic Prizes Vol. 2: 10979
Orton Award; Samuel T. Vol. 1: 15846
Orton, Jr., Memorial Lecture Award; Edward Vol. 1: 1470
Orvieto Prize; Laura Vol. 2: 8251
Orville Scholarship in Meteorology; Howard T. Vol. 1: 3093
Orwell Award for Distinguished Contributions to Honesty and Clarity in Public Language; George Vol. 1: 13775
Orwell Memorial Fund Prize; George Vol. 2: 3751

Oryx Press Award; Louis Shores - Vol. 1: 2951
Osaragi Jiro Prize Vol. 2: 8496
Osas Festspillfond; Sigbjorn Bernhoft Vol. 2: 9876
Osborn Award; AWA Earl D. Vol. 1: 6185
Osborn Award; E. B. Vol. 1: 13911
Osborne and Mendel Award Vol. 1: 2654
Osborne Award; Ernest G. Vol. 1: 13809
Osborne Medal; Thomas Burr Vol. 1: 951
Oscar Vol. 1: 57
Oscar la Villette du Jeu et Jouet a Caractere Scientifique et Technique Vol. 2: 5009
Oscars in Agriculture Vol. 1: 19798
Oselle Vol. 2: 8470
O'Shannessy Award Vol. 2: 659
O'Shaughnessy Award for Poetry; Lawrence and Elizabeth Vol. 1: 11455
Osiris Award Vol. 2: 8270
Osiris; Prix Vol. 2: 5347
Osler Award Vol. 1: 18438
Osler Medal; William Vol. 1: 895
Oslo Bys Kulturpris Vol. 2: 9959
Ospina Perez Award; Mariano Vol. 2: 1699
Ossian Prize Vol. 2: 7118
Ossowski Award; Stanislaw Vol. 2: 10200
Ossowskiego; Nagroda im. Stanislawa Vol. 2: 10200
Ostermeier Memorial Award; Rosemary and Donald Vol. 1: 14754
Osterreichischer Filmhistorikerpreis Vol. 2: 785
Osterreichischer Graphikwettbewerb Vol. 2: 729
Osterreichischer Staatspreis fur den Werbefilm
   Austria - Ministry of Economic Affairs Vol. 2: 745
   Austrian Society of Film Sciences, Communications and Media Research Vol 2: 784
Osterreichischer Staatspreis fur Innovation Vol. 2: 752
Osterreichischer Theaterpreis Vol. 2: 768
Osthaus-Preis; Karl Ernst Vol. 2: 7068
Osthaus Prize; Karl Ernst Vol. 2: 7068
Ostrander Award; Ron Vol. 1: 10331
Osuna Sportsmanship Award Vol. 1: 10551
Ot ACUM Baad Bizua Vehafaza Shel Hayezira Ha Israelit Vol. 2: 7942
Otaka Prize Vol. 2: 8603
OTAN de Bourses de Recherche; Programme Vol. 1: 16960
Otero; Premio Miguel Vol. 2: 9131
The Other Award Vol. 2: 2615
OTM Prize Vol. 2: 11879
Otology Politzer Society Award Vol. 2: 1187
Ott Award for Outstanding Contribution to Children's Literature; Helen Keating Vol. 1: 7674
Ott Prize; Theodore Vol. 2: 11919
Ousley Special Service Award; Robert Vol. 1: 4886
Oustanding Academic Librarian Award Vol. 1: 7007
Oustanding Community Service Award Vol. 1: 18904
Outdoor Writing Awards Vol. 1: 15867
Outgoing Governor Award Vol. 1: 3245
Outgoing Officer Award Vol. 1: 11023
Outgoing President Award Vol. 1: 3246
Outhwaite Trophy; Philip Vol. 2: 2393
Outland Trophy Vol. 1: 9307
Outler Prize in Ecumenical Church History; Albert C. Vol. 1: 4428
Outpost's Poetry Competition Vol. 2: 3012
Outreach Services Award Vol. 1: 5247

Outstanding Academy of Students of Pharmacy Chapter Advisor Award Vol. 1: 3386
Outstanding Accomplishments as an Executive of a State or Provincial Psychological Association Award
   American Psychological Association - State Psychological Association Affairs Division Vol. 1: 3820
   American Psychological Association - State Psychological Association Affairs Division Vol 1: 3821
Outstanding Accounting Educator Award Vol. 1: 2560
Outstanding Achievement Award
   Alliance for Children and Television Vol. 1: 323
   American Historic Inns, Inc. Vol 1: 2278
   American Institute of Professional Geologists Vol 1: 2673
   American Public Welfare Association Vol 1: 3869
   Canada - Treasury Board of Canada Secretariat Vol 1: 6723
   Dairy Industry Association of New Zealand Vol 2: 9717
   Interactive Services Vol 1: 10530
   Renewable Natural Resources Foundation Vol 1: 16789
   Society for Range Management Vol 1: 17587
   Society of Woman Geographers Vol 1: 18097
   United States Amateur Boxing Vol 1: 18994
Outstanding Achievement Award - Coast Guard Vol. 1: 19205
Outstanding Achievement Awards
   American Psychological Association Vol. 1: 3674
   Association of Ukrainian Sports Clubs in North America Vol 1: 5993
   International Wild Waterfowl Association Vol 1: 11398
Outstanding Achievement in Water Pollution Control Award Vol. 1: 20158
Outstanding Administrator Award Vol. 1: 929
Outstanding Advising Program Awards Vol. 1: 12586
Outstanding Advisor Awards Vol. 1: 12587
Outstanding Advocate Award Vol. 1: 13874
Outstanding Affiliate Award Vol. 1: 15011
Outstanding Alpine Athlete Award Vol. 1: 19575
Outstanding Alumnus Award Vol. 1: 17443
Outstanding American Indian Awards Vol. 1: 2418
Outstanding Animal Control Agency Award Vol. 1: 12784
Outstanding APhA Academy of Students of Pharmacy Chapter Advisor Award Vol. 1: 3398
Outstanding Area Chapter Vol. 1: 16194
Outstanding Arrest Citation Vol. 1: 14489
Outstanding Article Award Vol. 1: 1937
Outstanding Article in *American Journal of Agricultural Economics* Award Vol. 1: 754
Outstanding Artist of Hungary Vol. 2: 7411
Outstanding Associate Business Member of the Year Vol. 1: 12258
Outstanding Association Executive Award Vol. 1: 6010
Outstanding Aviation Maintenance Technology Instructor Vol. 1: 6196
Outstanding Band Musician Award Vol. 1: 13433
Outstanding Biology Teacher Award Vol. 1: 12957

Outstanding Biomedical Engineering Educator Award   Vol. 1: 4109
Outstanding Book Award
   Academy of Criminal Justice Sciences   Vol. 1: 37
   American Educational Research Association   Vol 1: 1978
   History of Education Society   Vol 1: 9947
Outstanding Booth Awards   Vol. 1: 12815
Outstanding Business Leaders Award   Vol. 1: 15533
Outstanding Campus Chapter   Vol. 1: 16195
Outstanding Certified Flight Instructor Award   Vol. 1: 9897
Outstanding Chapter Award
   Eta Kappa Nu   Vol. 1: 9007
   Fluid Power Society   Vol 1: 9273
   Institute of Electrical and Electronics Engineers - Power Engineering Society   Vol 1: 10313
   International Association of Assessing Officers   Vol 1: 10672
Outstanding Chapter Awards   Vol. 1: 677
Outstanding Chapter Leadership Award   Vol. 1: 14132
Outstanding Chapter Newsletter Award   Vol. 1: 14133
Outstanding Civil Engineering Achievement   Vol. 1: 4487
Outstanding Civilian Career Service Award - Air Force   Vol. 1: 19206
Outstanding Civitan Awareness   Vol. 1: 7789
Outstanding Civitan Awareness Project   Vol. 1: 7790
Outstanding Club Bulletin   Vol. 1: 7791
Outstanding Club Publication   Vol. 1: 3247
Outstanding Club Representative   Vol. 1: 3248
Outstanding Colleague Award   Vol. 1: 12984
Outstanding Collegiate Athlete Award   Vol. 1: 7951
Outstanding Committee Chairman Award   Vol. 1: 6011
Outstanding Community Service   Vol. 1: 7792
Outstanding Community Service Project   Vol. 1: 7793
Outstanding Company   Vol. 1: 11294
Outstanding Competition Management Awards   Vol. 1: 19327
Outstanding Congregational Librarian   Vol. 1: 7675
Outstanding Congregational Library   Vol. 1: 7676
Outstanding Congressional Service Award   Vol. 1: 13860
Outstanding Consumer Media Service Award   Vol. 1: 8225
Outstanding Continuing Education Student Awards   Vol. 1: 14953
Outstanding Contribution Award   Vol. 1: 13185
Outstanding Contribution by a Psychologist to the Development of Psychology in the States and Provinces   Vol. 1: 3822
Outstanding Contribution to ACM Award   Vol. 1: 5470
Outstanding Contribution to Amateur Football   Vol. 1: 13994
Outstanding Contribution to Co-operative Education and Training   Vol. 1: 5730
Outstanding Contribution to Congregational Libraries   Vol. 1: 7677
Outstanding Contribution to Higher Education Award   Vol. 1: 13329
Outstanding Contribution to Literature or Research Award   Vol. 1: 13330

Outstanding Contribution to Ophthalmic Photography   Vol. 1: 15739
Outstanding Contribution to Rehabilitation Award   Vol. 1: 3782
Outstanding Contribution to Rural Life Award   Vol. 1: 16975
Outstanding Contribution to the Titanium Industry   Vol. 1: 18723
Outstanding Contributions in Education   Vol. 1: 849
Outstanding Contributions Through Service to the Profession of Clinical Chemistry   Vol. 1: 850
Outstanding Contributions to Clinical Chemistry   Vol. 1: 851
Outstanding Contributions to Clinical Chemistry in a Selected Area of Research   Vol. 1: 852
Outstanding Contributions to Health Psychology   Vol. 1: 3736
Outstanding Contributions to the Field of Hearing Conservation   Vol. 1: 14120
Outstanding Contributions to the IAEE   Vol. 1: 10632
Outstanding Contributions to the Profession Award   Vol. 1: 10633
Outstanding Contributor Award   Vol. 1: 8315
Outstanding Contributor Awards   Vol. 1: 10372
Outstanding Contributor to Justice Volunteerism   Vol. 1: 10756
Outstanding Corporation Award   Vol. 1: 14786
Outstanding Cross Country Athlete Award   Vol. 1: 19576
Outstanding Dance Students   Vol. 1: 13845
Outstanding Decision Maker Award   Vol. 1: 5248
Outstanding Directorial Achievement Award for Feature Films   Vol. 1: 8668
Outstanding Directorial Achievement Award for Television   Vol. 1: 8669
Outstanding Disabled Alpine Athlete Award   Vol. 1: 19577
Outstanding Disabled Athlete of the Year   Vol. 1: 19952
Outstanding Disabled Cross Country Athlete Award   Vol. 1: 19578
Outstanding Disabled Veteran of the Year   Vol. 1: 8676
Outstanding Disabled Veteran Outreach Coordinator   Vol. 1: 8677
Outstanding Dissertation Award
   American Association of Colleges for Teacher Education   Vol. 1: 962
   American Psychological Association - Clinical Psychology Division   Vol 1: 3695
   National Association for Research in Science Teaching   Vol 1: 12892
Outstanding Dissertation of the Year Award   Vol. 1: 11193
Outstanding District Delegate   Vol. 1: 3249
Outstanding Division Award   Vol. 1: 10491
Outstanding Doctoral Dissertation Award   Vol. 1: 9
Outstanding Doctoral Thesis Award   Vol. 1: 755
Outstanding Donor Recruiter Award   Vol. 1: 922
Outstanding Earth Science Teacher Award   Vol. 1: 13120
Outstanding Educator Award
   Academy of Management   Vol. 1: 52
   American Ceramic Society   Vol 1: 1471
   Public Relations Society of America   Vol 1: 16576
   Religious Heritage of America   Vol 1: 16776

   Very Special Arts   Vol 1: 19994
Outstanding Elected Democratic Woman Holding Public Office   Vol. 1: 13937
Outstanding Elementary Social Studies Teacher of the Year   Vol. 1: 13716
Outstanding Engineering Achievement Awards   Vol. 1: 14805
Outstanding Ethnic Man of the Year Award   Vol. 1: 14618
Outstanding Ethnic Woman of the Year Award   Vol. 1: 14618
Outstanding Extension Educator Award   Vol. 1: 4148
Outstanding Faculty Adviser   Vol. 1: 16196
Outstanding Federal Services Health Administrator Award   Vol. 1: 5890
Outstanding Field Chapter   Vol. 1: 16194
Outstanding Financial Executive Award   Vol. 1: 9202
Outstanding Financial Manager   Vol. 1: 5276
Outstanding Flight Commander   Vol. 1: 5283
Outstanding Fluid Power Educator   Vol. 1: 9272
Outstanding Forestry Extension Publication Award   Vol. 1: 15044
Outstanding Forestry Extension Video Award   Vol. 1: 15045
Outstanding Foundation Award   Vol. 1: 14787
Outstanding Freestyle Athlete Award   Vol. 1: 19579
Outstanding Fund Raising Executive Award   Vol. 1: 14788
Outstanding German Educator Award   Vol. 1: 1216
Outstanding Giant Schnauzer Award   Vol. 1: 9608
Outstanding Government Service Award
   American Bar Association   Vol. 1: 1311
   American Numismatic Association   Vol 1: 3250
Outstanding Graduate Educator Award   Vol. 1: 4149
Outstanding Graduate Student Award   Vol. 1: 19747
Outstanding Grassland Farmer or Rancher Award   Vol. 1: 2081
Outstanding Health Worker   Vol. 1: 19447
Outstanding High School Teacher Awards   Vol. 1: 10205
Outstanding Historical Publication Award   Vol. 1: 15582
Outstanding Human Performance System Award   Vol. 1: 14760
Outstanding Human Service Student   Vol. 1: 14427
Outstanding Humanitarian Service Award   Vol. 1: 633
Outstanding Industry Leader   Vol. 1: 9274
Outstanding Industry Scientist Award   Vol. 1: 4150
Outstanding Information Science Teacher Award   Vol. 1: 4172
Outstanding Institutional Chaplain   Vol. 1: 1299
Outstanding Instructional Communication Award   Vol. 1: 14761
Outstanding Instructional Product   Vol. 1: 14762
Outstanding Instructional Product or Intervention Award   Vol. 1: 14762
Outstanding Instructor   Vol. 2: 7460
Outstanding International Travel Agent of the Year   Vol. 1: 5752
Outstanding Journalism Award   Vol. 1: 17443
Outstanding Journalism Educator-Administrator   Vol. 1: 18225
Outstanding Journalist Award   Vol. 1: 9258

Outstanding Judge Vol. 1: 11694
Outstanding Junior Member Contest Vol. 1: 14731
Outstanding Junior Shorthorn Breeder Award Vol. 1: 2761
Outstanding Kiswahili Scholars Vol. 2: 12013
Outstanding Large and Small Employer Award Vol. 1: 8678
Outstanding Law Enforcement Achievement Award Vol. 1: 10736
Outstanding Lawyer or Non-Lawyer Vol. 1: 11695
Outstanding Lay Individual Vol. 1: 1145
Outstanding Lay Organization Vol. 1: 1146
Outstanding Leadership and Service to NHCA Vol. 1: 14122
Outstanding Leadership Award
　Africa Travel Association Vol. 1: 187
　Great Lakes Commission Vol 1: 9709
Outstanding Lecture Award Vol. 1: 14121
Outstanding Library Board Vol. 1: 5249
Outstanding Local Veterans' Employment Representative Vol. 1: 8679
Outstanding Lodging Employee of the Year Vol. 1: 2393
Outstanding Male and Female Athlete of the Year Vol. 1: 13620
Outstanding Management Innovator Award Vol. 1: 10849
Outstanding Manager Award Vol. 1: 13005
Outstanding Master's Thesis Award Vol. 1: 756
Outstanding Media Arts Productions Award Vol. 2: 8575
Outstanding Media Coverage Vol. 1: 19615
Outstanding Member Vol. 1: 5106
Outstanding Member Award
　Association for Bridge Construction and Design Vol. 1: 5450
　Association of Schools of Allied Health Professions Vol 1: 5949
Outstanding Member of the Year Vol. 1: 12259
Outstanding Merchandising Achievement Award Vol. 1: 16297
Outstanding Middle Level Social Studies Teacher of the Year Vol. 1: 13717
Outstanding Military Chaplain Vol. 1: 1300
Outstanding Mother Award Vol. 1: 14372
Outstanding National Guard Unit Award Vol. 1: 15794
Outstanding Nationality Federation of the Year Vol. 1: 14618
Outstanding New Biology Teacher Award Vol. 1: 12958
Outstanding New Major Structure Vol. 1: 5451
Outstanding New Member Vol. 1: 19616
Outstanding New Multiple Span Structure Vol. 1: 5452
Outstanding New Professional Award Vol. 1: 3033
Outstanding New Single Span Structure Vol. 1: 5453
Outstanding New Systematic Application Award Vol. 1: 14763
Outstanding New Systematic Approach Vol. 1: 14763
Outstanding Newsletter Award
　Amateur Athletic Union of the United States Vol. 1: 437
　National Press Photographers Association Vol 1: 14523
Outstanding Newsletter Recognitions Vol. 1: 17180
Outstanding NFDW Member of the Year Vol. 1: 13938

Outstanding Nontraditional Student Award for Non-Degree Students Vol. 1: 14953
Outstanding Nordic Combined Athlete Award Vol. 1: 19580
Outstanding NSPI Chapter Award Vol. 1: 14764
Outstanding NSPI Chapter Publication Award Vol. 1: 14765
Outstanding NSPI Member Award Vol. 1: 14766
Outstanding Nurse Award Vol. 1: 14134
Outstanding Offensive and Defensive Linemen of the Year Awards Vol. 1: 14008
Outstanding Offensive and Defensive Player Awards Vol. 1: 10544
Outstanding Offensive and Defensive Player in the Senior Bowl Vol. 1: 10545
Outstanding Organization Vol. 1: 14428
Outstanding Organization Award Vol. 1: 14767
Outstanding Orthopaedic Nurse Award Vol. 1: 13218
Outstanding OTC Geophysical Paper Award Vol. 1: 17847
Outstanding Paper Award
　American Society for Engineering Education Vol. 1: 4110
　International Association for Bridge and Structural Engineering Vol 2: 11757
Outstanding Paper Awards
　American Society for Nondestructive Testing Vol. 1: 4222
　Council on Hotel, Restaurant and Institutional Education Vol 1: 8401
Outstanding Paper in Surveying Vol. 1: 1817
Outstanding Paper Presented at Convention Vol. 1: 17591
Outstanding Paper(s) in Geophysics Vol. 1: 17848
Outstanding Pastoral Counselor Vol. 1: 1301
Outstanding Pennsylvania Author or Illustrator Vol. 1: 16052
Outstanding Performance Aid Award Vol. 1: 14768
Outstanding *Performance & Instruction* Article Award Vol. 1: 14769
Outstanding Performance Award Vol. 1: 11414
Outstanding *Performance Improvement Quarterly* Article Award Vol. 1: 14770
Outstanding Ph.D. Dissertation Award Vol. 1: 5781
Outstanding Philanthropic Organization Award Vol. 1: 14789
Outstanding Philanthropist Award Vol. 1: 14790
Outstanding Plant Engineering Program Awards Vol. 1: 2669
Outstanding Power Engineering Educator Award Vol. 1: 10314
Outstanding Presentation Award Vol. 1: 17849
Outstanding Professional Vol. 1: 5840
Outstanding Professional Designee Vol. 1: 10673
Outstanding Project Award for Biomedical Research in Aging Vol. 1: 336
Outstanding Promoter Vol. 1: 14866
Outstanding Promotional Service Award Vol. 1: 188
Outstanding Public Affairs Award Vol. 1: 5281
Outstanding Public Media Award Vol. 1: 1856
Outstanding Public Service Award Vol. 1: 8316

Outstanding Publication Award
　Institute of Industrial Engineers Vol. 1: 10365
　National Press Photographers Association Vol 1: 14523
Outstanding Published Scholarship Award Vol. 1: 9
Outstanding Reference Sources Vol. 1: 2947
Outstanding Region Advisor Vol. 1: 5283
Outstanding Region Commander Vol. 1: 5283
Outstanding Regional Chairman Award Vol. 1: 6012
Outstanding Regional Coordinator Vol. 1: 3251
Outstanding Regional Director Vol. 1: 8703
Outstanding Rehabilitated Bridge Vol. 1: 5454
Outstanding Research Award
　Council for Learning Disabilities Vol. 1: 8331
　Hardwood Research Council Vol 1: 9772
Outstanding Research Awards
　American Association of School Administrators Vol. 1: 1182
　International Society for Heart Research Vol 2: 3471
Outstanding Researcher Award Vol. 1: 4151
Outstanding ROTC Cadet Award Vol. 1: 15795
Outstanding ROTC Unit Award Vol. 1: 15796
Outstanding Rural Health Program Vol. 1: 14650
Outstanding Rural Practice Vol. 1: 14651
Outstanding School Health Educator Award Vol. 1: 4005
Outstanding School Nurse of the Year Award Vol. 1: 4006
Outstanding School Psychological Services in Public Schools Award Vol. 1: 3784
Outstanding Science Educator of the Year Vol. 1: 5633
Outstanding Scientific Achievements by a Young Investigator Vol. 1: 853
Outstanding Scientific Materials Managers Award Vol. 1: 13307
Outstanding Scientist Award Vol. 2: 12025
Outstanding Secondary Social Studies Teacher of the Year Vol. 1: 13718
Outstanding Section and Region Award Vol. 1: 987
Outstanding Section Award Vol. 1: 17769
Outstanding Section Awards Vol. 1: 2515
Outstanding Section Campus Representative Award Vol. 1: 4111
Outstanding Section Member Award Vol. 1: 18454
Outstanding Senior Award Vol. 1: 13695
Outstanding Service Award
　Africa Travel Association Vol. 1: 189
　American Assembly for Men in Nursing Vol 1: 818
　American Council on Alcoholism Vol 1: 1857
　American Physical Therapy Association - Private Practice Sector Vol 1: 3495
　American Society for Photogrammetry and Remote Sensing Vol 1: 4258
　American Vocational Association Vol 1: 4994
　Association of Medical Illustrators Vol 1: 5860
　Association of Scientists and Engineers of the Naval Sea Systems Command Vol 1: 5957
　Association of Southern Baptist Campus Ministries Vol 1: 5964
　Blinded Veterans Association Vol 1: 6409

Chicago Book Clinic   Vol 1: 7594
Chicago Book Clinic   Vol 1: 7594
Committee on Continuing Education for School Personnel   Vol 1: 8043
International Federation for Information Processing   Vol 2: 11784
National Association of College Auxiliary Services   Vol 1: 12993
Soil and Water Conservation Society   Vol 1: 18127
Outstanding Service Award for Military Pediatrics   Vol. 1: 678
Outstanding Service Award - Karate   Vol. 1: 438
Outstanding Service Awards
  National Agricultural Aviation Association   Vol. 1: 12754
  National Federation of State High School Associations   Vol 1: 13953
Outstanding Service Citation   Vol. 1: 17905
Outstanding Service Desk Set Trophy   Vol. 1: 19445
Outstanding Service in Fire Management Award   Vol. 1: 19084
Outstanding Service to Budapest Award   Vol. 2: 7303
Outstanding Service to Librarianship Award   Vol. 1: 6999
Outstanding Service to the Mentally and/or Physically Handicapped   Vol. 1: 7794
Outstanding Service to the Public Health Award   Vol. 1: 14413
Outstanding Ski Jumping Athlete Award   Vol. 1: 19581
Outstanding Small Businessman of the Year   Vol. 1: 10877
Outstanding Society Awards   Vol. 1: 11871
Outstanding Southeastern Author Award   Vol. 1: 18193
Outstanding Southeastern Library Program Award   Vol. 1: 18194
Outstanding Speed Skiing Athlete Award   Vol. 1: 19582
Outstanding Sportsman Award   Vol. 2: 7881
Outstanding SPS Chapter Advisor Award   Vol. 1: 2663
Outstanding State Association Award   Vol. 1: 3934
Outstanding State Chapter Activity Award   Vol. 1: 3941
Outstanding State Chapter Award   Vol. 1: 3941
Outstanding State Council of the Year   Vol. 1: 14618
Outstanding State Leader Award   Vol. 1: 7917
Outstanding Student CEC Member of the Year Award   Vol. 1: 8317
Outstanding Student Chapter Award
  American Water Resources Association   Vol. 1: 5007
  Society for Mining, Metallurgy, and Exploration   Vol 1: 17570
Outstanding Student Chapter Counselor Award   Vol. 1: 2596
Outstanding Teacher Award
  Council for Learning Disabilities   Vol. 1: 8332
  National Marine Educators' Association   Vol 1: 14331
Outstanding Teacher Educator in Reading Award   Vol. 1: 11194
Outstanding Teacher of American History   Vol. 1: 14732
Outstanding Teaching Award   Vol. 1: 15583
Outstanding Technical Paper Award
  International Society for Clinical Laboratory Technology   Vol. 1: 11241

Metal Powder Industries Federation   Vol 1: 12226
Outstanding Total Service to the Mentally and/or Physically Handicapped   Vol. 1: 7795
Outstanding Total Youth   Vol. 1: 7796
Outstanding Undergraduate Educator Award   Vol. 1: 4152
Outstanding Veterinary Public Health Student   Vol. 1: 8129
Outstanding Vocational Classroom Teacher Award   Vol. 1: 4997
Outstanding Vocational Educator   Vol. 1: 4995
Outstanding Vocational Educators   Vol. 1: 20075
Outstanding Volunteer Fund Raiser Award   Vol. 1: 14791
Outstanding Volunteer of the Year   Vol. 1: 14618
Outstanding Volunteer Service Award
  Canadian Mental Health Association   Vol. 1: 7035
  National Multiple Sclerosis Society   Vol 1: 14384
Outstanding Wine Service Award   Vol. 1: 6301
Outstanding Woman Veterinarian Award   Vol. 1: 5664
Outstanding Women in Music Award   Vol. 1: 18577
Outstanding Women of Color   Vol. 1: 14227
Outstanding Women's Award   Vol. 1: 20624
Outstanding Wrestler in NCAA Championships   Vol. 1: 15048
Outstanding Writing Award   Vol. 1: 963
Outstanding YES Service Award   Vol. 1: 13875
Outstanding Young Agents Committee Award   Vol. 1: 10133
Outstanding Young Citizen Award   Vol. 2: 7882
Outstanding Young Electrical Engineer Award   Vol. 1: 9008
Outstanding Young Farmer Advisor   Vol. 1: 15061
Outstanding Young Farmer Awards   Vol. 1: 19429
Outstanding Young Industrial Engineer Award   Vol. 1: 10366
Outstanding Young Investigator Award   Vol. 1: 12124
Outstanding Young Manufacturing Engineer Award   Vol. 1: 17881
Outstanding Young Numismatist   Vol. 1: 3252
Outstanding Young Scientist Award   Vol. 2: 5134
The Outstanding Young Scientists (TOYS)   Vol. 2: 10058
Outstanding Young Working Women Award   Vol. 1: 9613
Outstanding Younger Member Award   Vol. 1: 17770
Outstanding Youth Leadership   Vol. 1: 16777
Outstanding Youth Project   Vol. 1: 7797
The Outstanding Youth Science Researchers   Vol. 2: 10058
Outstanding Zone Campus Activity Coordinator Award   Vol. 1: 4112
Outstanding Zone Campus Representative Award   Vol. 1: 4112
Overall Control Line Flyers Champion   Vol. 1: 20198
Overall Point Trophy   Vol. 1: 19496
Overall Triathletes of the Year   Vol. 1: 18811
Overly Scholarship; Helene   Vol. 1: 20439
Overseas Premium   Vol. 2: 3253
Overseas Press Club of America Annual Awards Competition   Vol. 1: 15875

Overseas Prize   Vol. 2: 4117
Overseas Student Medallion
  Institution of Electrical Engineers   Vol. 2: 3299
  Institution of Electrical Engineers   Vol 2: 3305
Overseas Study Bursaries and Flatman Grants   Vol. 2: 3333
Overstterprisen   Vol. 2: 1909
OWA Award in Wood   Vol. 1: 15718
OWAA Photography Awards   Vol. 1: 15864
O'Ware Prize; Harris   Vol. 1: 18601
OWC Annual Outdoor Writing Award   Vol. 1: 15867
Owen Medal; Morgan   Vol. 2: 2604
Owen Memorial Scholarship; Melva T.   Vol. 1: 13965
Owen Memorial Trophy   Vol. 1: 19354
Owen National Prize for Literature; Gilbert   Vol. 2: 9014
Owen Poetry Prize; Guy   Vol. 1: 18231
Owen; Premio Nacional de Literatura Gilberto   Vol. 2: 9014
Owens Award; Jesse   Vol. 1: 19953
Owe's Prisbelonningsfond; Generaldirektor Aage W.   Vol. 2: 9953
Owsley Award; Frank Lawrence and Harriet Chappell   Vol. 1: 18215
OX5 Aviation Pioneers Hall of Fame   Vol. 1: 15878
OX5; Mr.   Vol. 1: 15877
Oxley Trophy; Lawrence Augustus   Vol. 1: 16214
Oya Soichi Non-Fiction Prize   Vol. 2: 8754
P/A Awards   Vol. 1: 16520
P/A Awards for Architectural Research   Vol. 1: 16521
P & O Containers Prize   Vol. 2: 3098
P1-prisen   Vol. 2: 1993
P1-Prize   Vol. 2: 1993
Paaskynen palkinto   Vol. 2: 4668
Pablos Editorial Merit Prize; Juan   Vol. 2: 9154
Pace Award   Vol. 1: 439
Pacesetter Award
  National Academic Advising Association   Vol. 1: 12588
  National Council for Marketing and Public Relations   Vol 1: 13705
Pacific Coast Branch Award   Vol. 1: 2302
Pacific Cultural Foundation Awards   Vol. 2: 12005
Pacific Islander of the Year Award   Vol. 1: 9358
Pacific Man of the Year Award   Vol. 1: 9358
Pacific Sociological Association Award for Distinguished Contribution to teaching   Vol. 1: 15896
Pacific Sociological Association Distinguished Contributions to Teaching   Vol. 1: 15897
Pacific Southwest Section Outstanding Community College Educator Award   Vol. 1: 4113
Pacing Triple Crown   Vol. 1: 19677
Packaging Awards Competition (Top Packaging Awards)   Vol. 1: 9235
Packaging Competition Awards   Vol. 1: 14445
Packaging Engineer of the Year   Vol. 1: 10925
Packaging Leaders of the Year   Vol. 1: 15901
Packaging Man of the Year   Vol. 1: 15901
Packard International Parks Merit Award/Commission on Parks and Protected Areas; Fred M.   Vol. 2: 11970
Packard Outstanding Educator Award; Robert L.   Vol. 1: 18245
Packer Engineering Safety Award   Vol. 1: 4373

Padilla; Orden del Merito Naval Almirante   Vol. 2: 1646
Padivy Prize; Karol   Vol. 2: 10775
Padma Bhushan   Vol. 2: 7554
Padma Shri   Vol. 2: 7555
Padma Vibhushan   Vol. 2: 7556
Paganini; Concorso Internazionale di Violino Nicolo   Vol. 2: 8395
Paganini International Violin Competition; Nicolo   Vol. 2: 8395
Paganini Prize   Vol. 2: 8395
Page Award for Young Investigators; Irvine H.   Vol. 1: 2239
Page Award; Handley   Vol. 2: 3897
Page One Awards in Journalism   Vol. 1: 15367
Page Prize in Adolescent Psychiatry; Gillian   Vol. 2: 3966
Pagels Human Rights of Scientists Award of the New York Academy of Sciences; Heinz R.   Vol. 1: 15216
Pahlsons pris; Margit   Vol. 2: 11599
Paine Award; Thomas   Vol. 1: 15904
Paine Prize; Robert Troup   Vol. 1: 9819
Painter SES/ASTM Memorial Award for Meritorious Service; Robert J.   Vol. 1: 18455
Painton Award; Harry R.   Vol. 1: 8258
Pake Prize; George E.   Vol. 1: 3465
Pakenham Memorial Award; Catherine   Vol. 2: 3602
Pakistan Civil Awards   Vol. 2: 9995
Pakistan Military Awards   Vol. 2: 9996
Pal Memorial Award; George   Vol. 1: 81
Palach Prize; Jan   Vol. 2: 5993
Palanca Memorial Awards for Literature; Don Carlos   Vol. 2: 10053
Palazzeschi; Premio Aldo   Vol. 2: 8241
Paleontological Society Medal   Vol. 1: 15908
Palestrina Prize   Vol. 1: 6822
Paletou Award; J. Wallace   Vol. 1: 10441
Pall Mall Export Swing Award   Vol. 2: 9566
Palladium Medal   Vol. 1: 1000
Palma Julia de Burgos   Vol. 1: 5587
Palmai-Tenser Scholarship Awards; Rose   Vol. 1: 12383
Palme d'Or
 Cannes International Film Festival   Vol. 2: 5004
 International Advertising Festival   Vol 2: 3363
 International Advertising Festival of Ireland   Vol 2: 7785
Palme Memorial Fund Scholarships; Olof   Vol. 2: 11506
Palme Prize; Olof   Vol. 2: 11507
Palmer Award; Joe   Vol. 1: 14941
Palmer Memorial Prize; Edwin   Vol. 1: 12623
Palmer Prize for Fiction; Vance   Vol. 2: 149
Palmer Prize for Non-fiction; Nettie   Vol. 2: 149
Palmer Prize; Frederick   Vol. 2: 3254
Palmer Prize; Pauline   Vol. 1: 5297
Palmes Academiques   Vol. 2: 5295
Palo Alto Film Festival   Vol. 1: 15914
Pam Fellowship; Edgar   Vol. 2: 3342
PAMA/ATP Award   Vol. 1: 16440
Pamir Hizmet Odulu; Hamit Nafiz   Vol. 2: 12046
Pamplin Distinguished Awards   Vol. 1: 9405
Pan American Gold Insigne of the Americas Society   Vol. 1: 5125
Pan American Gold Medal of the Americas Society   Vol. 1: 5126
Pan Macmillan School Library Award   Vol. 2: 3758
Panafrican Film and Television Festival of Ouagadougou   Vol. 2: 1541

Panasonic Young Soloists Award   Vol. 1: 19995
Panchaud Medallions; John   Vol. 2: 2724
Panetti International Prize with Gold Medal; Professor Modesto   Vol. 2: 8024
Panetti; Premio Internazionale con Medaglia d'oro, Professor Modesto   Vol. 2: 8024
Pani; Premio de Composicion Arquitectonica Alberto J.   Vol. 2: 9189
Pannell Award; Lucile Micheels   Vol. 1: 20421
Panofsky Prize; W. K. H.   Vol. 1: 3466
Panorama de Arte Atual Brasileira   Vol. 2: 1492
Panorama of Actual Brasilian Art   Vol. 2: 1492
Panowski Playwriting Award; Mildred & Albert   Vol. 1: 16856
PANPA Newspaper Awards   Vol. 2: 575
Pantheon of Philanthropy Hall of Fame   Vol. 1: 14792
Pantone Color Award   Vol. 1: 15928
Papalia Award for Excellence in Teacher Education; ACTFL Anthony   Vol. 1: 1869
Papanicolaou Award of the American Society of Cytology   Vol. 1: 4551
Papentuss Poster Award; George F.   Vol. 2: 3454
Paper Industry Gold Medal   Vol. 2: 2468
Paper Prize Award   Vol. 1: 16096
Paperboard Packaging Competition   Vol. 1: 15930
Papers and Publications Committee Prizes   Vol. 2: 3654
Par Excellence Award   Vol. 1: 10748
Paracelsus Medaille   Vol. 2: 6817
Paracelsus Preis   Vol. 2: 11890
Paracelsus-Preis   Vol. 2: 11886
Paracelsus Ring   Vol. 2: 865
Paracelsusring der Stadt Villach   Vol. 2: 888
Parade - IACP Police Service Award   Vol. 1: 10699
Parade/Kodak Photography Contest   Vol. 1: 15932
Paragon Awards   Vol. 1: 13706
Param Vir Chakra   Vol. 2: 7557
Param Vishisht Seva Medal   Vol. 2: 7558
Parametrician of the Year   Vol. 1: 11289
Parandowski Prize; Jan   Vol. 2: 10168
Paraprofessional of the Year Award   Vol. 1: 5250
Parapsychology Hall of Fame   Vol. 1: 15945
Paratore, Jr. Memorial Medallion Awards; Philip G.   Vol. 1: 14773
Parbo Medal; Sir Arvi   Vol. 2: 454
Parcel - Leif J. Sverdrup Civil Engineering Management Award; John I.   Vol. 1: 4488
Pardoe Space Award   Vol. 2: 3898
Parent Education Grant   Vol. 1: 14549
Parent Involvement Award   Vol. 1: 17181
Parent Organization Recognition Awards   Vol. 1: 13553
Parent-Patient Leadership Award   Vol. 1: 7832
Parenteau Memorial Award; William A.   Vol. 1: 276
Parenting Awards   Vol. 1: 13688
Parents' Choice Awards   Vol. 1: 15957
Parents' Choice Classic Award   Vol. 1: 15957
Parents Magazine Best Book for Babies Award   Vol. 2: 2205
Parhon; Constantin I.   Vol. 2: 10375
Paris Open   Vol. 2: 5260
Paris Prize Architectural Design Competition   Vol. 1: 14217
Parish Pastor of the Year   Vol. 1: 77
Parish Volunteer Award   Vol. 1: 7407
Parizeau Prize in Biology; Leo   Vol. 1: 5435

Park Award in Critical Writing; Betty   Vol. 1: 18535
Parke-Davis Award
 American Society for Investigative Pathology   Vol. 1: 4181
 Canadian Society of Hospital Pharmacists   Vol 1: 7192
Parke-Davis Distinguished Lectureship   Vol. 1: 4908
Parker Award; Ely ("Eli") S.   Vol. 1: 2428
Parker Award; R. Hunt   Vol. 1: 15499
Parker Awards for Spoken Business Japanese; Sir Peter   Vol. 2: 4335
Parker Memorial Award; Jim   Vol. 1: 13059
Parker Memorial Medal; Ben H.   Vol. 1: 2674
Parker Poetry Award; Pat   Vol. 1: 15034
Parker Trophy; Jackie   Vol. 1: 6884
Parkinson Award for Young British Musicians; Dorothy   Vol. 2: 2987
Parkman Medal   Vol. 2: 3255
Parkman Medal for Special Achievement; Francis   Vol. 1: 17697
Parkman Prize; Francis   Vol. 1: 17697
Parks Award; Edd Winfield   Vol. 1: 17646
Parks Award; Orville   Vol. 1: 5858
Parks Award; Rosa   Vol. 1: 20380
Parks Commemorative Photography Competition; Gordon   Vol. 1: 9340
Parlin Award   Vol. 1: 2992
Parma Rotary Club International Prize "Giuseppe Verdi"   Vol. 2: 8386
Parmele Award; Howard   Vol. 1: 17131
Parnassos Foundation Prize   Vol. 2: 7213
Parr Award; Geoffrey   Vol. 2: 4287
Parr; Royal Television Society Technology Awards in Memory of Geoffrey   Vol. 2: 4287
Parran Award; Thomas   Vol. 1: 5115
Parrondo Prize; Gil   Vol. 2: 11252
Parry Award; Evan   Vol. 2: 9740
Parsonage Design Award   Vol. 2: 2619
Parsons Award; Charles Lathrop   Vol. 1: 1570
Parsons Award; Frank   Vol. 2: 283
Parsons Award; Louella O.   Vol. 1: 9981
Parsons Memorial Prize; R. W.   Vol. 2: 479
Parsons Memorial Trophy; Frank   Vol. 1: 14645
Parsons Prize; Elsie Clews   Vol. 1: 7461
Parsons Prize for Social Science; Talcott   Vol. 1: 527
Participant Physical Fitness Award   Vol. 1: 16396
Particle Technology Award   Vol. 1: 2597
Partington Prize   Vol. 2: 4374
Partisans' Cross   Vol. 2: 10120
Partlow Prize   Vol. 1: 8641
Partnership Award   Vol. 1: 3923
Parvan Prize; Vasile   Vol. 2: 10376
Pascal du GAMNI-SMAI; Prix Blaise   Vol. 2: 5685
Pascal; Fondation Paul   Vol. 2: 5648
Pascal Medal   Vol. 1: 9275
Pascall Prize   Vol. 2: 580
Pascatti Rotary Prize; Antonio   Vol. 2: 8460
Pasja Dlaka, Slovenian/Universal Science Fiction Award   Vol. 2: 10805
Pasja Dlaka, Slovenska/Svetovna Znanstvenofantasticna Nagrada   Vol. 2: 10805
Pask - Coffeen - Rigterink Award   Vol. 1: 1472
Pasquier; Prix Alex   Vol. 2: 1040
Passano Foundation Award   Vol. 1: 15981
Past President's Award   Vol. 1: 18436
Past Presidents Award   Vol. 1: 5865
Past Presidents' Award
 National Environmental Health Association   Vol. 1: 13912

New England Water Works Association   Vol 1: 15156
Past-President's Award   Vol. 1: 11242
Past Presidents' Award for Merit in Transportation   Vol. 1: 10456
Past President's Best Practices Award   Vol. 1: 14591
Past Presidents' Canadian Legislator Award   Vol. 1: 7273
Past-President's Certificate   Vol. 1: 7160
Past Presidents' Memorial Medal   Vol. 1: 6951
Pastel Society of America Hall of Fame   Vol. 1: 15986
Pasteur Award   Vol. 1: 10083
Pasteur Medal; Louis   Vol. 2: 5491
Pasteur; Prix Louis   Vol. 2: 6046
Pasteur Prize; Louis   Vol. 2: 6046
PATA Gold Awards   Vol. 1: 15882
Pate Memorial Award; Maurice   Vol. 1: 18951
Paterno; Medaglia Emanuele   Vol. 2: 8337
Paterson Medal and Prize   Vol. 2: 3195
Pathfinder Award   Vol. 1: 10228
Paton, M.D., Award; R. Townley   Vol. 1: 9033
Paton Prize; William A.   Vol. 1: 12624
Patrick Award; Dan   Vol. 1: 10815
Patrick Trophy; Lester   Vol. 1: 14173
Patriot Award   Vol. 1: 8171
Patriot of the Nation   Vol. 1: 15063
Patriot's Award   Vol. 1: 15991
Patriots Award   Vol. 1: 3562
Patron Honor Award   Vol. 1: 14229
Patron of Architecture Award   Vol. 2: 10883
Patron of the American Community Theatre Association   Vol. 1: 976
Patron of the Arts Award   Vol. 1: 12649
Patrons and Fellows   Vol. 2: 7618
Patron's Medal   Vol. 2: 4015
Patrons of AAS   Vol. 1: 1272
Patsy Awards - Top Performing Animal in Television and Motion Pictures   Vol. 1: 2402
Pattantyus Abraham Geza Dij   Vol. 2: 7456
Pattantyus Award; Abraham Geza   Vol. 2: 7456
Patterson Award; A. L.   Vol. 1: 1899
Patterson Foundation Fellowship Program for Journalists; Alicia   Vol. 1: 15994
Patterson Prize; Bryan   Vol. 1: 18091
Patton, Jr. Memorial Trophy; General George S.   Vol. 1: 19455
Patwardhan Prize in Nutritional Sciences; Dr. V. N.   Vol. 2: 7598
Paul Award; Alice   Vol. 1: 15017
Paul Award for the Promotion of Science & Technology Policy; Swraj   Vol. 2: 3462
Paul Duffy Trophy   Vol. 1: 16214
Pauling Prize   Vol. 1: 1900
Paulist Fathers' Award for Catholic Lay Evangelization   Vol. 1: 15996
Paumgartner-Medaille; Bernhard-   Vol. 2: 829
Pavarotti International Voice Competition; Opera Company of Philadelphia/Luciano   Vol. 1: 16131
Pavie; Prix Auguste   Vol. 2: 6142
Pawsey Medal   Vol. 2: 178
Pax Publishing Institute   Vol. 2: 10084
Paxton Memorial Award for Service to Amateur Journalism; Russel L.   Vol. 1: 9345
Payen Award; Anselme   Vol. 1: 1505
Payne Award; Ed   Vol. 1: 17666
Payot; Bourse Rene-   Vol. 2: 5070
Paz; Premio Ramos   Vol. 2: 10258
Paz Prize; Ramos   Vol. 2: 10258
PBA Bowler of the Year   Vol. 1: 16445
PBA Hall of Fame   Vol. 1: 16446
PBA Player of the Year   Vol. 1: 16447
PBA Rookie of the Year   Vol. 1: 16448

PBA Senior Player of the Year   Vol. 1: 16449
PBS Advertising and Promotion Awards   Vol. 1: 16564
PC World World Class Awards   Vol. 1: 16000
PDF Grassroots Peace Award   Vol. 1: 16004
PDF/PPF Peace Prize   Vol. 1: 16004
Peabody Broadcasting Awards; George Foster   Vol. 1: 19793
Peabody Medal; George   Vol. 1: 16002
Peace and Cooperation School Award   Vol. 2: 11314
Peace Award   Vol. 2: 1235
Peace Fellowship   Vol. 1: 16630
Peace Play Contest   Vol. 1: 9669
Peace Prize of the German Book Trade   Vol. 2: 6776
Peace Quilt Awards   Vol. 1: 6441
PEACE Trophy   Vol. 2: 7766
Peacemaker Award   Vol. 1: 14457
Pean; Prix Berthe   Vol. 2: 4813
Peanut Research and Education Award   Vol. 1: 14462
Pearce Award; William T.   Vol. 1: 6069
Pearce - Kirklees Prize; J. W.   Vol. 2: 3766
Pearl Award; Minnie   Vol. 1: 9735
Pearson Award   Vol. 1: 2394
Pearson Award; Drew   Vol. 1: 11157
Pearson Award; Ike   Vol. 1: 13176
Pearson Award; L. B. "Mike"   Vol. 1: 6982
Pearson Award; Lester B.   Vol. 1: 14174
Peasantry Batallion Cross   Vol. 2: 10121
Pease Award; Theodore Calvin   Vol. 1: 17677
Peaslee Brazing Award; Robert L.   Vol. 1: 5088
Peat Marwick Award; KPMG   Vol. 1: 20133
Peccei; Premio Aurelio   Vol. 2: 8227
Peccei Prize; Aurelio   Vol. 2: 8227
Peccei Scholar   Vol. 2: 838
Pech Medal; Antal   Vol. 2: 7358
Peck Award; Walter D.   Vol. 1: 16727
Pecora Award; William T.   Vol. 1: 19247
Pedagogy Award   Vol. 2: 10443
Pedersens Bibliotekfonds Forfatterpris; Edvard   Vol. 2: 1916
Pederson, CTC Award; Melva C.   Vol. 1: 4808
Pediatric Resident Research Award   Vol. 1: 679
Pediatric Urology Medal   Vol. 1: 680
Pedler Lectureship and Medal   Vol. 2: 4213
Pedrick Memorial Literary Award; Don   Vol. 2: 11425
Pedroli Prize; Castelli   Vol. 2: 6707
Pedrotti International Competition for Orchestra Conductors; Antonio   Vol. 2: 8112
Pedrotti; Premio Internazionale di Direzione d'Orchestra Antonio   Vol. 2: 8112
Peek Award; Cuthbert   Vol. 2: 4016
Peele Memorial Award; Robert   Vol. 1: 17571
Peer Awards in Creative Photography: Distinguished Career in Photography   Vol. 1: 9428
Peer Awards in Creative Photography: Photographer of the Year   Vol. 1: 9429
Peer Sasanqua Award   Vol. 1: 1399
Peet Travelling Prize; Thomas Eric   Vol. 2: 4576
PEF Packaging Hall of Fame   Vol. 1: 15902
Pegasus Prize for Literature   Vol. 1: 12379
Pegasus Trophy
    Mobil Sekiyu Kabushiki Kaisha   Vol. 2: 8702
    Mobil Sekiyu Kabushiki Kaisha   Vol 2: 8703
PEI Distinguished Service Award   Vol. 1: 14806
Peirce Essay Contest Award; C. S.   Vol. 1: 16010
Pekar Memorial Scholarship; Anne   Vol. 1: 13965

Pelander Award; Carl E.   Vol. 1: 17087
Peleg Prize; Frank   Vol. 2: 7883
Pelles Prize   Vol. 2: 7865
Pelletier; Prix Denise-   Vol. 1: 16613
Peltier Award; Leslie C.   Vol. 1: 6090
Peltier Plaque   Vol. 1: 17714
Pelton Award; Jeanette Siron
    Botanical Society of America   Vol. 1: 6488
    Conservation and Research Foundation   Vol 1: 8185
Pelzer Memorial Award; Louis   Vol. 1: 15821
Pemberton Trophy   Vol. 2: 2973
PEN Best First Book of Fiction Award   Vol. 2: 9778
PEN Best First Book of Non-fiction Award   Vol. 2: 9779
PEN Best First Book of Poetry Award   Vol. 2: 9780
PEN Book-of-the-Month Club Translation Prize   Vol. 1: 16020
PEN Emlekerem   Vol. 2: 7367
PEN/Faulkner Award for Fiction   Vol. 1: 16039
PEN Freedom to Write Awards   Vol. 1: 16021
PEN/Jerard Fund Award   Vol. 1: 16022
PEN Literary Award   Vol. 2: 8827
PEN/Malamud Memorial Award   Vol. 1: 16040
PEN/Martha Albrand Award for Nonfiction   Vol. 1: 16023
PEN Medal for Translation   Vol. 1: 16024
PEN/Nelson Algren Fiction Award   Vol. 1: 16025
PEN/New England Award for Literary Excellence; Shaeffer -   Vol. 1: 16037
PEN/Newman's Own First Amendment Award   Vol. 1: 16026
PEN/Norma Klein Award for Children's Fiction   Vol. 1: 16027
PEN Prizes (Poetry, Essay, Novel)   Vol. 2: 10293
PEN Publisher Citation   Vol. 1: 16028
PEN/Revson Foundation Fellowships   Vol. 1: 16029
PEN/Roger Klein Award for Editing   Vol. 1: 16589
PEN/Spielvogel-Diamonstein Award   Vol. 1: 16030
PEN Translation Prize; Calouste Gulbenkian -   Vol. 1: 16016
PEN Translation Prize; Goethe House -   Vol. 1: 16015
PEN Translation Prizes; American-Scandinavian Foundation/   Vol. 1: 16014
PEN/Voelcker Award for Poetry   Vol. 1: 16031
PEN/West Rediscovery Award   Vol. 1: 16032
PEN/West Small Press Publishers Award   Vol. 1: 16033
PEN Writing Awards for Prisoners   Vol. 1: 16034
PEN Young Writers' Incentive Awards   Vol. 2: 9781
Pena; Premio Enrique   Vol. 2: 18
Penaud Diploma; Alphonse   Vol. 2: 5164
Pendleton Award; S. Alden   Vol. 1: 10393
Pendray Award; G. Edward   Vol. 1: 2490
Penfield; Prix Wilder-   Vol. 1: 16620
Penguin Award   Vol. 2: 193
Penguin Awards   Vol. 2: 691
Penitentiary Order of Merit   Vol. 2: 1630
Penner Prize; Donald W.   Vol. 1: 6795
Penney - University of Missouri Awards in Lifestyle Journalism; JC   Vol. 1: 19843
Penney - University of Missouri Newspaper Awards; JC   Vol. 1: 19843
Penney - University of Missouri Television Awards for Community Leadership; JC   Vol. 1: 19845

Award Index
Volume 2: International and Foreign — Pharmacy

Pennsylvania Diving Association Award   Vol. 1: 19316
Pennwalt Resident Research Award; APA/   Vol. 1: 3623
Penrose Award (University Division); Spencer   Vol. 1: 2312
Penrose Medal Award   Vol. 1: 9565
People's Choice Award   Vol. 1: 3253
People's Choice Awards   Vol. 1: 16431
People's Choice Prize Claden Award   Vol. 2: 326
Peplau Award; Hildegard   Vol. 1: 3286
Pepler International Award; George   Vol. 2: 4292
PEPP Award   Vol. 1: 14807
PEPP Chairman's Award   Vol. 1: 14808
PEPP Merit Award   Vol. 1: 14809
PEPP QBS Award   Vol. 1: 14810
Peppe Award; Mike   Vol. 1: 19320
Pepper Award; Claude   Vol. 1: 13753
Pepper Trophy; W. J.   Vol. 2: 2062
Pepsi-Cola Award   Vol. 2: 2062
Pepys Medal; Samuel   Vol. 2: 2764
Per Ludos Fraternitas   Vol. 2: 9317
Peral; Premio Isaac   Vol. 2: 11279
Peralta Award; Lope Carvajal   Vol. 2: 1709
Peralta Ramos Prize; Alberto   Vol. 2: 93
Percival Award; Don   Vol. 1: 6162
Percussive Arts Hall of Fame   Vol. 1: 16067
Perdrizet; Prix Maise Ploquin-Caunan et Docteur Jacques   Vol. 2: 5889
Pereira Award; Professor E. O. E.   Vol. 2: 11406
The Perennial Success Award   Vol. 1: 9361
Perera Memorial; Aylet Lilly   Vol. 2: 11407
Pereyra Prize; Carlos   Vol. 2: 8994
Perez Ortiz Prize; Ruben   Vol. 2: 1686
Performance Awards
   Javelin Class Association   Vol. 1: 11511
   Outer Critics Circle   Vol 1: 15869
   Purebred Hanoverian Association of American Owners and Breeders   Vol 1: 16595
Performance Citation Award   Vol. 1: 7361
Performance Scholarship   Vol. 1: 11028
Performance Test Codes Medal   Vol. 1: 4697
Performing Arts Program Achievement Award   Vol. 1: 12848
Performing Awards   Vol. 1: 20509
Performing Right Society Award   Vol. 2: 4117
Pergamon Electrochimie Gold Medal   Vol. 2: 11840
Pergamon - NWSA Graduate Scholarships in Women's Studies   Vol. 1: 15035
Pergamon Scott Blair Biorheology Scholarship   Vol. 2: 2531
Pericles Awards   Vol. 1: 8916
Periodical Awards   Vol. 1: 8297
Perkin Medal
   Society of Chemical Industry   Vol. 2: 4420
   Society of Dyers and Colourists   Vol 2: 4436
Perkin Medal of the American Section   Vol. 1: 17803
Perkins Award; Dudley   Vol. 1: 3147
Perkins Award; Marlin   Vol. 1: 1242
Perkins Government Relations Award; ACA/ Carl D.   Vol. 1: 1879
Perkins Humanitarian Award; Carl   Vol. 1: 4996
Perkins, Jr. Memorial Fellowship; John F.   Vol. 1: 3510
Perkins Legislative Award; AACD/Carl D.   Vol. 1: 1879
Perkins Memorial Scholarship Awards; John J.   Vol. 1: 5581
Perkins Power Award   Vol. 2: 3777

Perkins Prize for a First Novel; Maxwell   Vol. 1: 17139
Perlemuter Piano Scholarship; Vlado   Vol. 2: 2909
Perlman Award for Human Advancement   Vol. 1: 6436
Perlman Award; Itzhak   Vol. 1: 19995
Perlman Gallery Cash Award; Miriam   Vol. 1: 17693
Perloff President's Prize   Vol. 1: 2005
Permanent Force Good Service Medal   Vol. 2: 10944
Perpetual Trophy Awards   Vol. 2: 2494
Perpetual World Championship Trophies   Vol. 2: 2898
Perreau; Prix Jules   Vol. 2: 4854
Perret; Prix Paul-Michel   Vol. 2: 5786
Perret Prize; Auguste   Vol. 2: 6061
Perrier Award   Vol. 2: 10537
Perrier-Jouet Rising Star Chef of the Year   Vol. 1: 6301
Perrier Pick of the Fringe Season   Vol. 2: 10537
Perrier Restaurant of the Year   Vol. 1: 6301
Perrin; Prix Jean   Vol. 2: 6374
Perrot; Medaille Georges   Vol. 2: 5432
Perry Award; Newel   Vol. 1: 13966
Perry Awards (Tony Awards); Antoinette   Vol. 1: 11810
Perry Distinguished Authors Award; J. Warren   Vol. 1: 5950
Perry Fly Tyer's Assistance Award; Virginia Buszek   Vol. 1: 9115
Perseverance Award   Vol. 1: 11512
Pershing Plaque   Vol. 1: 14096
Perskor Prize for Leisure Reading   Vol. 2: 10906
Perskor Prize for Literature   Vol. 2: 10907
Perskor Prize for Youth Literature   Vol. 2: 10908
Person of the Year Award
   Brazilian-American Chamber of Commerce   Vol. 1: 6549
   Irrigation Association   Vol 1: 11476
   Project Management Institute   Vol 1: 16527
   United Service Organizations   Vol 1: 18981
Personal Achievement Award   Vol. 1: 13876
Personal Achievement in Chemical Engineering Awards   Vol. 1: 7536
Personal Recognition Awards in Education   Vol. 2: 8367
Personal Service Award   Vol. 1: 3843
Persons Awards   Vol. 1: 18472
Persoon Medal; Christiaan Hendrik   Vol. 2: 11105
Perspektiefprys   Vol. 2: 9335
Perten Award; Harald   Vol. 2: 808
PES Prize Paper Award   Vol. 1: 10315
Pessimist of the Year   Vol. 1: 6327
Peterford Trophy   Vol. 1: 19384
Peters' Cartridge Company Trophy   Vol. 1: 14645
Peterson Award; Everette   Vol. 1: 11157
Peterson Christian Sportsmanship Award; Ben   Vol. 1: 13585
Peterson Consumer Service Award; Esther   Vol. 1: 9298
Peterson Distinguished Service Award; Elaine   Vol. 1: 14053
Peterson Fellows; Charles E.   Vol. 1: 6102
Peterson Fellowships/Internships; Charles E.   Vol. 1: 6102
Peterson Fellowships; Kate B. and Hall J.   Vol. 1: 799
Peterson Foundation Awards; William F.   Vol. 1: 11279
Petiet; Prix Rene   Vol. 2: 5915

Petrassi; Concorso Internazionale di Composizione Goffredo   Vol. 2: 8392
Petrassi International Competition for Composers; Goffredo   Vol. 2: 8392
Petrie Memorial Award; Dr.   Vol. 1: 6788
Petrizzo Career Service Award; D. Richard   Vol. 1: 13707
Petro-Canada Award   Vol. 1: 6747
Petroleum Society of CIM Distinguished Service Award   Vol. 1: 6952
Petronius Award; Gaius   Vol. 1: 14104
Petrovici Prize; Ion   Vol. 2: 10377
Pettigrew Award; Kenneth J.   Vol. 1: 19627
Pettinos Foundation Award   Vol. 1: 1420
Petzval Medal; Jozsef   Vol. 2: 7446
Peurifoy Construction Research Award   Vol. 1: 4489
Peyches; Fondation Ivan   Vol. 2: 5586
Peyre; Fondation du Docteur et de Madame   Vol. 2: 5544
Peyton Award for Cold Regions Engineering; Harold R.   Vol. 1: 4490
Pezcoller Prize   Vol. 2: 8397
Pezcoller Recognition for Dedication to Oncology   Vol. 2: 8398
Pezzuto Award; Albert M.   Vol. 1: 18325
Pfeffer Peace Prize   Vol. 1: 9167
Pfeifer Medal; Ignac   Vol. 2: 7322
Pfeiffer Service Award; Peggy Leach   Vol. 1: 5535
Pfeil Medal and Prize   Vol. 2: 3144
Pfeil Prize; Wilhelm Leopold   Vol. 2: 7119
Pfister Award; Oskar   Vol. 1: 3645
Pfizer Academic Awards   Vol. 2: 3779
Pfizer/AG Postdoctoral Fellowship Award   Vol. 1: 2181
Pfizer Award
   American Dairy Science Association   Vol. 1: 1921
   History of Science Society   Vol 1: 9951
Pfizer Award Fellowship   Vol. 2: 1972
Pfizer Award in Enzyme Chemistry   Vol. 1: 1506
Pfizer Extension Teaching Award   Vol. 1: 16350
PGA Championship   Vol. 1: 16470
PGA Club Professional Championship   Vol. 2: 3810
PGA Club Professional Player of the Year   Vol. 1: 16471
PGA Cup   Vol. 2: 3811
PGA Fourball Championship   Vol. 2: 3812
PGA Golf Professional of the Year   Vol. 1: 16472
PGA Junior Championship   Vol. 2: 3813
PGA Leading Money Winner   Vol. 1: 16473
PGA Merchandisers of the Year   Vol. 1: 16474
PGA National Assistants' Championship   Vol. 2: 3814
PGA Player of the Year   Vol. 1: 16475
PGA Pro-Am Matchplay Championship   Vol. 2: 3815
PGA Pro-Captain Challenge   Vol. 2: 3816
PGA Regional Team Championship   Vol. 2: 3817
PGA Seniors' Championship   Vol. 2: 3818
PGA/World Golf Hall of Fame   Vol. 1: 16476
PGMS Scholarships   Vol. 1: 16487
Pharmacia Deltec Ambulatory Infusion Pump Research Grant; Oncology Nursing Foundation/   Vol. 1: 15646
Pharmacia Deltec Vascular Access Device Research Grant; Oncology Nursing Foundation/   Vol. 1: 15647
Pharmacy Practice Research Award   Vol. 1: 4608

PHBA Amateur Superior Award   Vol. 1: 15918
PHBA Amateur Supreme Champion   Vol. 1: 15918
PHBA Hall of Fame   Vol. 1: 15919
PHBA National Youth Congress Horse Show High Point Youth   Vol. 1: 15921
PHBA Supreme Champion   Vol. 1: 15920
PHBA Youth World Championship Horse Show High Point Youth   Vol. 1: 15921
Phelan Art Awards; James D.   Vol. 1: 17034
Phelan Award; Joseph G.   Vol. 1: 11058
Phelan Awards in Literature; James D.   Vol. 1: 17035
Phelan Memorial Award; Paul F.   Vol. 1: 3972
Phenix - U.D.A.   Vol. 2: 6429
Phenixprijs   Vol. 2: 9581
Phi Alpha Theta Westerners International Doctoral Dissertation in Western History Award   Vol. 1: 16097
Phi Beta Kappa Award in Science   Vol. 1: 16102
Phi Epsilon Pi Fraternity International Service Award   Vol. 1: 20640
Phi Kappa Phi Artist Award   Vol. 1: 9991
Phi Kappa Phi Scholar Award   Vol. 1: 9992
Phi Theta Kappa Hall of Honor   Vol. 1: 16115
Philadelphia Award   Vol. 1: 16129
Philadelphia International Film Festival (Philafilm Awards)   Vol. 1: 10769
Philadelphia Liberty Medal   Vol. 1: 9715
Philafilm Awards   Vol. 1: 10769
Philalethes Lecture   Vol. 1: 16135
Philatelic Foundation Medal   Vol. 1: 16141
Philatelic Hall of Fame   Vol. 1: 3414
Philatelic Press Club Award   Vol. 1: 11141
Philip Morris International Prize   Vol. 2: 5082
Philip Morris; Prix Scientifique   Vol. 2: 4964
Philipp Prize; Robert and Rochelle   Vol. 1: 12625
Philippine Mathematical Olympiad   Vol. 2: 10059
Philippine Physics Olympiad   Vol. 2: 10060
Philips Award; Frederik   Vol. 1: 10283
Philips Award; Henry M.   Vol. 1: 3437
Philips Memorial Award; Irving   Vol. 1: 535
Philips Prize for Australian Studies; A. A.   Vol. 2: 149
Philips Rose Bowl   Vol. 1: 6789
Philips Trophy   Vol. 2: 2062
Phillips Award; A. A.   Vol. 2: 133
Phillips Award; Dr. Jackson R. E.   Vol. 1: 12494
Phillips Award; Mary   Vol. 1: 19977
Phillips Award; Melba Newell   Vol. 1: 1131
Phillips Award; Rutherford T.   Vol. 1: 2403
Phillips Award; Sarah Thorniley   Vol. 1: 16123
Phillips Memorial Award; John   Vol. 1: 1721
Phillips Memorial Medal; John C.   Vol. 2: 11971
Phillips Performance Award
  United States Diving   Vol. 1: 19321
  United States Swimming   Vol 1: 19628
Phillips Petroleum Company ISC All-World Awards   Vol. 1: 11316
Phillips Petroleum Performance Award   Vol. 1: 14025
Phillips Poetry Prize; Turnbull Fox   Vol. 2: 534
Phillips Trophy, P.T.S. Trophy   Vol. 2: 3781
Philos Award - Philanthropist of the Year   Vol. 1: 3924
Phoenix Award   Vol. 1: 7627
Phoenix Awards   Vol. 1: 17734
Phoenix Diploma   Vol. 2: 5165
Phoenix House Award for Public Service   Vol. 1: 16148

Phoenix Trophy; National Offshore Championship - Lloyd   Vol. 1: 19531
Photo-Jokes Competition   Vol. 2: 1523
Photo-Journalism Division Awards   Vol. 1: 16164
Photo-Journalism Slide Exhibition for National Bible Week   Vol. 1: 11798
Photo-Sonics Achievement Award   Vol. 1: 17906
Photo-Travel Division Awards   Vol. 1: 16165
Photogrammetric (Fairchild) Award   Vol. 1: 4259
Photographers Fund   Vol. 1: 7447
Photographic Society of America Best of Show Award   Vol. 1: 3135
Photographic Society of Japan Awards   Vol. 2: 8722
Photography Annual   Vol. 1: 8060
Photography Awards   Vol. 1: 2265
Photojournalism Award   Vol. 1: 13131
Physician Assistant Award   Vol. 1: 5891
Physician Executive Award   Vol. 1: 1675
Physician of the Year
  American Association of Osteopathic Specialists   Vol. 1: 1098
  United States Amateur Boxing   Vol 1: 18996
Physician Scientist Award   Vol. 1: 1621
Physics Division Distinguished Educator and Service Award   Vol. 1: 4114
Physiological Section Award   Vol. 1: 6489
Physiology in Perspective Lecture   Vol. 1: 3511
Phytopathological Society of Japan Prize   Vol. 2: 8724
Phytopathological Society of Japan Scientific Research Promotion Award   Vol. 2: 8725
Pi Gamma Mu Scholarship   Vol. 1: 16176
Pi Kapp Scholar   Vol. 1: 16185
Pi Kappa Alpha Chapter and Alumni Awards   Vol. 1: 16181
Pi Kappa Phi Hall of Fame   Vol. 1: 16186
Pi Kappa Phi; Mr.   Vol. 1: 16187
Pi Kappa Phi Student of the Year   Vol. 1: 16188
Pi-Prijs; Professor   Vol. 2: 9646
Pi Tau Sigma Gold Medal   Vol. 1: 4698
PIA Foundation for Hospital Psychiatry Research Fellowship   Vol. 1: 3646
Piafsky Young Investigator Award of the Canadian Society for Clinical Pharmacology; K. M.   Vol. 1: 18437
PIC of the Year Award   Vol. 1: 16533
Picard; Fondation Emil   Vol. 2: 5551
Piccard; Prix Eugene   Vol. 2: 5852
Pickell Award; Mark   Vol. 1: 11310
Pickering Award for Playwrighting Excellence; Robert J.   Vol. 1: 7862
Pico della Mirandola Prize   Vol. 2: 8570
Picot; Prix Georges   Vol. 2: 5751
Pictorial Print Color Division Awards   Vol. 1: 16166
Pictorial Print Monochrome Division Awards   Vol. 1: 16167
Picture Book of the Year Award   Vol. 2: 312
Picture Editor of the Year   Vol. 1: 14524
"Picture It Painted Professionally" Contractor Contest   Vol. 1: 15906
Picture of the Year Competition   Vol. 1: 19844
Pictures of the Year Competition   Vol. 1: 14525
Pidal; Premio Menendez   Vol. 2: 11347
Pidal Prize; Menendez   Vol. 2: 11347
Pied Piper Award   Vol. 1: 4530
Piel Award for Service to Science in the Cause of Man; Gerard   Vol. 1: 3438
Piepenbrink Award; Harold C.   Vol. 1: 5868

Pierce Award; Janette   Vol. 1: 8970
Pierce Master Achievement Award; Don   Vol. 1: 16820
Pierce Medal; Lorne   Vol. 1: 16961
Pierce Memorial Prize; W. H.   Vol. 2: 4348
Pierce Prize in Astronomy; Newton Lacy   Vol. 1: 1273
Piercy Award; Esther J.   Vol. 1: 2851
Pieri Memorial Award: Louis A. R.   Vol. 1: 2332
Pierre de Coubertin International Trophy for Fair Play   Vol. 2: 5989
Pierron; Prix Sander   Vol. 2: 1306
Pietro Caliceti International Prize   Vol. 2: 8249
Pietrzak Award   Vol. 2: 10084
Pietsch Preis; Erich   Vol. 2: 6836
Pigskin Club Honor Roll   Vol. 1: 16213
Pigskin Club of Washington Trophies   Vol. 1: 16214
Pijls Prize; Catharine   Vol. 2: 9683
Pijlsprijs; Catharina   Vol. 2: 9683
Pike Memorial Prize; John   Vol. 1: 12626
Pike Prize for Service to People with Disabilities   Vol. 1: 6469
Pike Prize for the Handicapped   Vol. 1: 6469
Pilcher-Usborne   Vol. 2: 3899
Pilgrim Award   Vol. 1: 17117
Pillsbury BAKE-OFF (R) Contest   Vol. 1: 16217
Pilot of the Year   Vol. 1: 17160
Pilot of the Year Award   Vol. 1: 9898
Pilot Safety Award   Vol. 1: 13500
Pimentel Award in Chemical Education; George C.   Vol. 1: 1571
Pimlott Conservation Award; Douglas H.   Vol. 1: 7067
Pimsleur Award for Research in Foreign Language Education; ACTFL - MLJ Paul   Vol. 1: 1874
Pin of Honour   Vol. 2: 6950
Pinchot Medal; Gifford   Vol. 1: 17686
Pinette; Fondation   Vol. 2: 5388
Pingat Bakti Masharakat   Vol. 2: 10748
Pingat Berkebolehan   Vol. 2: 10740
Pingat Gagah Perkasa   Vol. 2: 10738
Pingat Jasa Gemilang   Vol. 2: 10743
Pingat Keberanian   Vol. 2: 10741
Pingat Kehormatan   Vol. 2: 10742
Pingat Kepujian (Tentera)   Vol. 2: 10737
Pingat Pentadbiran Awam   Vol. 2: 10747
Pingat Polis Keberanian   Vol. 2: 10746
Pinkard Leader in Federal Equity Award; Mary D.   Vol. 1: 9085
Pinkerton Award   Vol. 2: 3349
Pinnacle Award
  Association of Wall and Ceiling Industries - International   Vol. 1: 6013
  International Credit Association   Vol 1: 10895
Pinnacle Awards   Vol. 1: 17918
Pinnacle Awards for Convention and Visitor Bureaus   Vol. 1: 18518
Pinnacle Awards for Hotels/Resorts   Vol. 1: 18519
Pinschof Scholarship; Carl Ludwig   Vol. 2: 9794
Pinsker Merit Award; Leon J.   Vol. 1: 10652
Pinski Prize; David   Vol. 2: 7884
Pinto Prize; Roquette   Vol. 2: 1418
Pioneer Achiever Award   Vol. 1: 15018
Pioneer Award
  Agricultural Communicators in Education   Vol. 1: 202
  American Institute of Ultrasound in Medicine   Vol 1: 2691

Award Index
Volume 2: International and Foreign
Polka

Association for Information and Image Management   Vol 1: 5545
Audience Development Committee (AUDELCO)   Vol 1: 6128
Dairy Shrine   Vol 1: 8504
National Scholastic Press Association   Vol 1: 14666
Science Fiction Research Association   Vol 1: 17117
Women Business Owners of New York   Vol 1: 20371
Pioneer Award for Milestones   Vol. 1: 10927
Pioneer Awards   Vol. 1: 16832
Pioneer Citation   Vol. 1: 16647
Pioneer Hi-Bred Forage Award   Vol. 1: 1922
Pioneer in Clay Science Lecture   Vol. 1: 7830
Pioneer Man-of-the-Year Chinese Martial Arts Award   Vol. 1: 440
Pioneer of Fitness Hall of Fame   Vol. 1: 5921
Pioneer of the Year Award   Vol. 1: 15520
Pioneer Women of the Podium   Vol. 1: 20361
Pioneers of Discovery   Vol. 1: 14075
Pioneers of Underwater Acoustics Medal   Vol. 1: 100
Piore Award; Emanuel R.   Vol. 1: 10284
Piot; Prix Eugene   Vol. 2: 5389
Piper Prize; C. S.   Vol. 2: 600
Pirenne; Fondation Henri   Vol. 2: 976
Piria; Medaglia Raffaele   Vol. 2: 8339
Pirovano Prize; Ignacio   Vol. 2: 94
Pisk Prize; Paul A.   Vol. 1: 3176
Pistolese; Premio Francesco   Vol. 2: 8003
Pisuisse Prijs   Vol. 2: 9616
Pisuisse Prize   Vol. 2: 9616
Pitcher Patriot Award; Molly   Vol. 1: 13977
Piteau Outstanding Young Member Award; Douglas R.   Vol. 1: 5774
Pitou Foundation Prize; Charles   Vol. 2: 6321
Pitou; Prix de Fondation Charles   Vol. 2: 6321
Pitt-Rivers Award   Vol. 2: 2250
Pittaway Memorial Award; Gordon   Vol. 2: 357
Pittman, Sr. Exhibit Award; John Jay   Vol. 1: 3254
Pius IX; Order of   Vol. 2: 12101
Pius XI Gold Medal   Vol. 2: 12098
PJC Award for Individual Merit   Vol. 2: 2292
PLA/CLSI International Study Grant   Vol. 1: 2933
Pla; Premi Josep   Vol. 2: 11217
Pla Prize; Josep   Vol. 2: 11217
Placa de Honor al Merito   Vol. 2: 7260
Placa Extraordinaria   Vol. 1: 10514
Placa i Medalla President Macia   Vol. 2: 11189
Plain English Award   Vol. 2: 3786
Plaisterers Trophy Competition   Vol. 2: 3686
Plaketa Ludmily Podjavorinskej   Vol. 2: 10766
Planck-Medaille; Max-   Vol. 2: 6662
Planck Research Awards; Max   Vol. 2: 7159
Planeta Prize   Vol. 2: 11222
Planned Parenthood Federation of America Maggie Awards   Vol. 1: 16232
Planned Parenthood Federation of America Margaret Sanger Award   Vol. 1: 16233
Planner of the Year   Vol. 1: 8353
Plante, Francois Hebert-Paul Jousselin; Fondations Gaston   Vol. 2: 5680
Plants Award for Special Events; Helen L.   Vol. 1: 4115
Plapinger Endowment Award; Henry and Anna   Vol. 1: 13660
Plaques   Vol. 2: 10195
Plaques of SUBNOR   Vol. 2: 10708
Plaquette du Centenaire de Camille Flammarion   Vol. 2: 6219
Plaskett Medal   Vol. 1: 16930

Plass Award; William T.   Vol. 1: 4290
Plastics Hall of Fame   Vol. 1: 16241
Plateau Audience Award; Joseph   Vol. 2: 1194
Plateau Life Achievement Award; Joseph   Vol. 2: 1194
Plateau Music Award; Joseph   Vol. 2: 1194
Plateau Prize; Joseph   Vol. 2: 1194
Plateauprijzen; Joseph   Vol. 2: 1194
Platinum Medal   Vol. 2: 3145
Platt Corning Medal; Elizabeth   Vol. 1: 9486
Plaut Community Leadership Award; Johanna Cooke   Vol. 1: 13877
Playboy College Fiction Contest   Vol. 1: 16244
Player of the Year   Vol. 1: 19511
Player of the Year (Men and Women)   Vol. 2: 2780
Player Portrait Award; John   Vol. 2: 3704
Players Appreciation Award   Vol. 1: 19039
Players Appreciation Cup   Vol. 1: 19039
Playhouse on the Square New Play Competition   Vol. 1: 16248
Playlabs   Vol. 1: 16253
Playoff Most Valuable Player   Vol. 1: 8247
Playthings Merchandising Achievement Awards   Vol. 1: 9604
Playwright Award Competition   Vol. 1: 6350
Playwrights' Forum Awards   Vol. 1: 18694
Playwrights USA Awards   Vol. 1: 18675
Pleasant Inter-Religious Award; Earle B.   Vol. 1: 16763
Please Touch Museum Book Award   Vol. 1: 16256
Pleissner Memorial Award; Mary   Vol. 1: 5058
Pleissner Memorial Award; Ogden   Vol. 1: 5059
Pleissner Memorial Award; Ogden M.   Vol. 1: 12627
Pless International Graduate of the Year; J. Will   Vol. 1: 11079
Ploquin-Caunan et Docteur Jacques Perdrizet; Prix Maise   Vol. 2: 6288
Plouf Consistently Very Fragrant Award; L. Ernest   Vol. 1: 2267
Plowden Prize   Vol. 2: 2462
Plowman Business Logistics Management Specialty Award; E. Grosvenor   Vol. 1: 4801
Pluma de Oro   Vol. 1: 19824
Plume d'Or de la Liberte   Vol. 2: 6007
Plummer Memorial Educational Lecture Award   Vol. 1: 5089
Plyler Prize; Earle K.   Vol. 1: 3467
PMDA Celebrity Photographer Award   Vol. 1: 16155
PMDA Man of the Year Award   Vol. 1: 16154
PMDA Professional Photographer Award   Vol. 1: 16155
PMDA Scientific or Technical Achievement Award   Vol. 1: 16156
PMDA Special Award   Vol. 1: 16157
PNWC Literary Awards   Vol. 1: 15888
Pocasni Clan   Vol. 2: 1400
Podjavorinska Plaque; Ludmila
  Bibiana, International House of Art for Children   Vol. 2: 10761
  Friends of Children's Books   Vol 2: 10766
Podjavorinskej; Plaketa Ludmily   Vol. 2: 10766
Podoloff Trophy; NBA Most Valuable Player Award - Maurice   Vol. 1: 13453
Poe Awards (Edgars); Edgar Allan   Vol. 1: 12550
Poe; Prix Lugne   Vol. 2: 6398
Poehlman Award; William J.   Vol. 1: 17419
Poel Memorial Festival; William   Vol. 2: 4380

Poet Laureate, Consultant in Poetry   Vol. 1: 11859
Poet Laureate of Ottawa   Vol. 1: 7745
Poetic Prose Prize   Vol. 2: 6322
Poetker Award; Frances Jones   Vol. 1: 2361
Poetry and Fiction Contest   Vol. 1: 7959
Poetry Award   Vol. 1: 18704
Poetry Books Award   Vol. 1: 20135
The Poetry Center Book Award   Vol. 1: 16271
Poetry Committee Book Award   Vol. 1: 16273
Poetry Contest   Vol. 1: 12337
Poetry Film Festival   Vol. 1: 14482
Poetry Film/Video Festival   Vol. 1: 14482
Poetry International Award
  Poetry International Foundation   Vol. 2: 9568
  Poetry International Foundation   Vol 2: 9569
Poetry International Eregeld   Vol. 2: 9568
Poetry International Festival   Vol. 2: 9568
Poetry International/Poetry on the Road Festival   Vol. 2: 9569
Poetry, Short Story or Drama Award   Vol. 1: 16116
Poetry Society of Texas Award   Vol. 1: 13963
Poets International Organization Awards   Vol. 2: 7720
Poggendorff Memorial Lecture   Vol. 2: 629
Poggioli Translation Award; Renato   Vol. 1: 16035
Pohl-Preis; Robert-Wichard-   Vol. 2: 6663
Poiley Memorial Award; Sarah L.   Vol. 1: 15217
Poincare; Fondation Henri   Vol. 2: 5578
Poincare; Prix Henri   Vol. 2: 5515
Poirson; Fondation Ayme   Vol. 2: 5499
Polak Prize; Emil   Vol. 2: 1290
Polakoff Award; Joseph   Vol. 1: 2745
Polanyi Lecture Award; John C.   Vol. 1: 7559
Polar Medal   Vol. 2: 2380
Polar Music Prize   Vol. 2: 11530
Polaris Award   Vol. 2: 3410
Polayes National Young Violinist Competition; Marcia   Vol. 1: 15169
Policard-Lacassagne; Fondation Andre   Vol. 2: 5490
Police Exemplary Service Medal   Vol. 1: 6709
Police Medal for Valour   Vol. 2: 10746
Police Medal of Honor   Vol. 1: 3563
Police Officer of the Year
  American Police Hall of Fame   Vol. 1: 3564
  National Burglar and Fire Alarm Association - Public Safety Committee   Vol 1: 13493
Police Officer of the Year Award   Vol. 1: 10699
Police Overseas Service Medal   Vol. 2: 345
Police Review Board   Vol. 2: 2717
Policymaker of the Year   Vol. 1: 10921
Polish Chemical Society Medal   Vol. 2: 10137
Polish Composers Union Prize   Vol. 2: 10142
Polish PEN Centre Prizes   Vol. 2: 10168
Polish Phonetic Association Award   Vol. 2: 10170
Polish Prime Minister Award for Literature for Children and Youth   Vol. 2: 10126
Polish Radio Award   Vol. 2: 10067
Polish Rheumatological Society Award   Vol. 2: 10177
Polish Society of Veterinary Science Awards   Vol. 2: 10197
Politis Composition Prize   Vol. 1: 6471
Politzer Society Award; Otology   Vol. 2: 1187
Polk Awards; George   Vol. 1: 11934
Polk Memorial Awards; George   Vol. 1: 11934
Polka Music Awards   Vol. 1: 11168
Polka Music Hall of Fame   Vol. 1: 11169

Poll; Fondation Marc   Vol. 2: 1004
Pollack Award; Maxwell A.   Vol. 1: 9593
Pollack Distinguished Achievement Award; Seymour   Vol. 1: 712
Pollak Fellowship; Hansi   Vol. 2: 11030
Pollak Prize in Poetry; Brittingham Prize in Poetry and Felix   Vol. 1: 19890
Pollak-Virag Award   Vol. 2: 7452
Pollie Awards   Vol. 1: 1140
Pollock Award; Herbert C.   Vol. 1: 8758
Pollock-Krasner Foundation Grants   Vol. 1: 16315
Pollution Prevention Award   Vol. 1: 14442
Polo; Premio Marco   Vol. 2: 8571
Polo Prize; Marco   Vol. 2: 8571
Polya Award; George   Vol. 1: 12138
Polya Prize   Vol. 2: 3615
Polya Prize; George   Vol. 1: 17514
Polymer Education Award   Vol. 1: 1507
Polysar Awards for Chemistry Teaching in Community and Technical Colleges   Vol. 1: 7558
Polyurethane Division Awards   Vol. 1: 18052
Polyurethane Division Hall of Fame Awards   Vol. 1: 18053
Pomerance Award of the Archaeological Institute of America for Scientific Contributions to Archaeology   Vol. 1: 5227
Pomeroy Award; Edward C.   Vol. 1: 964
Pomme d'Or   Vol. 2: 6479
Pon Memorial Award; Ernest M.   Vol. 1: 12862
Ponce de Leon Prize; Manuel   Vol. 2: 1748
Pond's Fellowship and Other Awards in Dentistry; Elida   Vol. 2: 10840
Poniatoff Gold Medal Award; Alexander M.   Vol. 1: 17907
Pons Goldaracena Prize; Jorge E.   Vol. 2: 95
Ponselle All Marylanders Competition; Rosa   Vol. 1: 16317
Ponselle International Competition for the Vocal Arts; Rosa   Vol. 1: 16318
Ponti; Fondation Jerome   Vol. 2: 5602
Poodles, Sr. Award; Joe   Vol. 1: 11387
Pool Memorial Award; Judith G.   Vol. 1: 5661
Pool Postgraduate Research Fellowships in Hemophilia; Judith Graham   Vol. 1: 14135
Poort-Prize   Vol. 2: 10995
Pope Award; E. P.   Vol. 1: 1239
Pope John XIII Peace Prize   Vol. 2: 12105
Pope John XXI Prize   Vol. 2: 12096
Popenoe Award; Wilson   Vol. 1: 4145
Poporo de Oro   Vol. 2: 1694
Poppe Prize   Vol. 2: 11574
Poppele Broadcast Award; Jack   Vol. 1: 16648
Popper Memorial Prize; Jan   Vol. 2: 2135
Porcellati Award   Vol. 2: 11456
Poretsky Prize in Photography; Rita   Vol. 2: 7969
Porges; Prix Helene   Vol. 2: 5864
Porraz International Coastal Engineering Award; Mauricio   Vol. 1: 4475
Porter Award; Charles   Vol. 1: 17526
Porter Award; Frank C.   Vol. 1: 20106
Porter Award; J. Roger   Vol. 1: 19341
Porter Award; USFCC/J. Roger   Vol. 1: 4211
Porter Lecture Award; William C.   Vol. 1: 5892
Porter Medal   Vol. 2: 3500
Porter Memorial Award - "Friend of the Satellite Dealer" Award; Pat   Vol. 1: 8889
Porter Prize; Arthur Kingsley   Vol. 1: 7891
Porter Prize for Fiction; Katherine Anne   Vol. 1: 15383
Porter Trophy; Irvine C.   Vol. 1: 14645

Portland International Film Festival   Vol. 1: 15523
The Portland Opera Lieber Awards   Vol. 1: 16324
Portland Symphony Orchestra/Bookland Piano Competition   Vol. 1: 16326
Portland Symphony Orchestra/Priscilla Morneault Piano Competition   Vol. 1: 16326
Portland Symphony Orchestra Young Artist Competition   Vol. 1: 16327
Porumbescu Prize; Ciprian   Vol. 2: 10378
Poseidon Trophy   Vol. 1: 13377
Posey Trophy; John W.   Vol. 1: 16214
Positiva Priset   Vol. 2: 11640
Positive Prize   Vol. 2: 11640
Post Award in Floriculature and Ornamental Horticulture; Kenneth   Vol. 1: 4147
Post Office Best Documentary Award   Vol. 2: 3502
Post Office Direct Marketing Awards; BDMA/   Vol. 2: 2331
Post Office McLaren Award   Vol. 2: 10541
Post Office Trophy   Vol. 2: 3781
Postal History Award   Vol. 2: 3781
Postal History Journal Awards   Vol. 1: 16332
Postal History Society Medal   Vol. 1: 16333
Postdoctoral Fellowship Program   Vol. 1: 3154
Postdoctoral Grants for Research   Vol. 1: 10993
Postdoctoral Research Fellowships for Basic and Physician Scientists   Vol. 1: 7284
Poster Award   Vol. 1: 11250
Poster Paper Prize   Vol. 2: 3844
Poster Presentation Award   Vol. 1: 902
Poster Presentation Competition   Vol. 2: 3146
Poster Prize   Vol. 2: 2576
Poster Session Awards   Vol. 1: 2436
Postgiro Grand Prix   Vol. 2: 9973
Postgiro Norway   Vol. 2: 9973
Postgraduate Scholarship   Vol. 1: 12232
Postgraduate Study Awards   Vol. 1: 7924
Postlethwait Award; Samuel Noel   Vol. 1: 6490
Potamkin Prize for Alzheimer's Disease Research   Vol. 1: 621
Potier-Boes; Prix Diane   Vol. 2: 5839
Potorff Professional Designee of the Year Award; Verne W.   Vol. 1: 10673
Pott Memorial Award; Anthony   Vol. 2: 2092
Potter Award of Special Recognition; Helen   Vol. 1: 5600
Potter Award; Stuart G.   Vol. 1: 6176
Potter Gold Medal; James Harry   Vol. 1: 4699
Potts Medal; Howard N.   Vol. 1: 9387
Potts Memorial Award; John H.   Vol. 1: 6133
Potts Memorial Fellowship Award; Ralph H.   Vol. 1: 3316
Poulsen Gold Medal; Valdemar   Vol. 2: 1911
Poultry Industry Hall of Fame   Vol. 1: 3600
Poultry Science Association, Inc. Fellows   Vol. 1: 16351
Poultry Science Association Research Award   Vol. 1: 16352
Poultry Welfare Research Award   Vol. 1: 16353
Pound Award for Excellence in Teaching Trial Advocacy   Vol. 1: 16358
Poverello Medal   Vol. 1: 9367
Powder Metallurgy Landmark Award   Vol. 1: 12227
Powder Metallurgy Part-of-the-Year Design Competition   Vol. 1: 12228
Powder Metallurgy Pioneer Award   Vol. 1: 12229
Powell Award for Black Political Empowerment; Adam Clayton   Vol. 1: 8164

Powell Award; John Wesley   Vol. 1: 17477
Powell Award; Michael   Vol. 2: 10541
Powell Award; William and Mousie   Vol. 1: 11762
Powell Book Award; Michael   Vol. 2: 2349
Powell Joint Warfighting Essay Contest; Colin L.   Vol. 1: 19466
Power Missile Crew Award; General Thomas S.   Vol. 1: 250
Power of Life Award   Vol. 1: 10316
Power Strategic Combat Missle Crew Award; General Thomas S.   Vol. 1: 250
Powerlifting National Hall of Fame   Vol. 1: 19506
Powers Award
   Heritage Center   Vol. 1: 9914
   Pi Kappa Alpha Education Foundation   Vol 1: 16182
Powers Memorial Medal Award; Sidney   Vol. 1: 1111
Powers Research Achievement Award in Pharmaceutical Analysis; Justin L.   Vol. 1: 3389
Pownall Award: Information Books; Eve   Vol. 2: 313
Pozzoli International Piano Competition; Ettore   Vol. 2: 8199
PPA Magazines Awards for Editorial and Publishing Excellence   Vol. 2: 3774
PPA National Putting Champion   Vol. 1: 16506
PPA Subscription Awards   Vol. 2: 3775
PPFA Hall of Fame
   Professional Picture Framers Association   Vol. 1: 16503
   Professional Picture Framers Association   Vol 1: 16504
PPG Cup   Vol. 1: 7517
PPG Indy Car World Series - CART Champions   Vol. 1: 7517
PR Professional of the Year   Vol. 1: 16146
PR-Staatspreis   Vol. 2: 746
Praad Memorial Oration Award; Dr. D. N.   Vol. 2: 7599
Practice Excellence Award   Vol. 1: 3387
Practicing Urologist Research Awards   Vol. 1: 2114
Practitioner of the Year   Vol. 1: 13704
Practitioner of the Year Award
   American Society of Podiatric Medicine   Vol. 1: 4774
   Dermatology Foundation   Vol 1: 8617
Practitioner Presentation Award   Vol. 1: 8324
Practitioner Research Award
   American Academy of Pediatrics   Vol. 1: 681
   American Veterinary Medical Association   Vol 1: 4987
Practitioners Hall of Fame   Vol. 1: 15542
Praemium Erasmianum   Vol. 2: 9396
Praemium Imperiale   Vol. 2: 8599
Praga; Prix Andre   Vol. 2: 1292
Prague Literary Prize   Vol. 2: 1888
Prague Spring International Music Competition   Vol. 2: 1880
Prain Medal and Prize   Vol. 2: 3147
Prairie Schooner Readers' Choice Awards   Vol. 1: 16363
Prairie Schooner Strousse Award   Vol. 1: 16364
Pramie fur die Beantwortung einer Literarischen oder Philologischen Frage   Vol. 2: 6769
Pras Harvey   Vol. 2: 7945
Pras Hestrin   Vol. 2: 7915
Pras l'Bikoret Sifrutit   Vol. 2: 7870
Pras Leib Yaffe   Vol. 2: 7973
Pras l'Roman Ivri Mekori   Vol. 2: 7872

Award Index
Volume 2: International and Foreign — Premio

Pras l'Sefer Shira Ivri Mekori Vol. 2: 7873
Pras l'Sifrut Yeladim Vol. 2: 7871
Pras Zalman Shazar Le'heker Toldot Am Israel Vol. 2: 7940
Prasad Award; Dr. Rajendra Vol. 2: 7575
Prasad Memorial Lecture Award; Prof. M. R. N. Vol. 2: 7663
Prasey ACUM Lesifruth Vemusika Vol. 2: 7943
Prather Award; Victor A. Vol. 1: 1262
Pratley Award; P. L. Vol. 1: 7176
Pratt and Whitney Canada Grand Prize Vol. 1: 12423
Pratt Award; Fletcher Vol. 1: 7778
Pratt Award; Haraden Vol. 1: 10285
Pratt Memorial Award; Wallace E.
  American Association of Petroleum Geologists Vol. 1: 1105
  American Association of Petroleum Geologists Vol 1: 1112
PRB Award for Outstanding Contributions in the Field of Population Vol. 1: 16322
PRCA World Champion/All-Around Cowboys Vol. 1: 16510
PRCA World Champions Vol. 1: 16510
Pre-College Award Vol. 1: 1132
Preakness Stakes
  Maryland Jockey Club - Pimlico Race Course Vol. 1: 12107
  Triple Crown Productions, Inc. Vol 1: 18815
Precision Timing Trophy Vol. 2: 3008
Predoctoral Minority Fellowship Vol. 1: 4199
Preedy Post-Graduate Bursary; Winifred E. Vol. 2: 219
Prehm Student Presentation Award; Herbert J. Vol. 1: 8325
Preis der Deutschen Physikalische Gesellschaft Vol. 2: 6659
Preis der DVG zur Forderung von Nachwuchswissenschaftlern Vol. 2: 6888
Preis der Gesellschaft Deutscher Chemiker fur Journalisten und Schriftsteller Vol. 2: 6788
Preis der Justus-Liebig-Universitat Giessen Vol. 2: 7000
Preis der Landes Baden-Wurttemberg Vol. 2: 7142
Preis der Landeshauptstadt Innsbruck fur Kunstlerisches Schaffen Vol. 2: 891
Preis der Landeshauptstadt Stuttgart Vol. 2: 7142
Preis der Mogens und Wilhelm Ellermann-Stiftung Vol. 2: 11943
Preis der Neuen Darmstadter Sezession fur Junge Kunstler Vol. 2: 6603
Preis der Osterreichischen Film Tage Vol. 2: 874
Preis der Schweizerischen Gesellschaft fur Innere Medizin Vol. 2: 11902
Preis der Schweizerischen Schillerstiftung Vol. 2: 11730
Preis der Stadt Mannheim fur junge Kunstler Vol. 2: 7099
Preis der Stiftung Kunststoff-Technik Vol. 2: 11935
Preis der TC-Gruppe Fred Oed GmbH fur die Film-und Medienborse Vol. 2: 7142
Preis des Suddeutschen Rundfunks Vol. 2: 7142
Preis fur Film und Fernsehforschung Vol. 2: 785
Preis fur Nachwuchswissenschaftler Vol. 2: 6517
Preis fur Pharma-Technik Vol. 2: 7072
Preis fur Poster - Ausstellungen Vol. 2: 6881

Preis fur Wissenschaftliche Ausstellungen Vol. 2: 6882
Preis of the Pfluger-Stiftung Freiburg Vol. 2: 6972
Preise der Stadt Wien fur Kunst, Wissenschaft und Volksbildung Vol. 2: 789
Preise fur herausragende wissenschaftliche Leistungen Vol. 2: 6772
Preller Prize; Gustav Vol. 2: 11002
Preller Prize Lectureship; Bruce- Vol. 2: 10648
Premi
  Accademia di Medicina di Torino Vol. 2: 8026
  Accademia di Scienze, Lettere e Arti di Palermo Vol 2: 8030
  Accademia di Studi Storici Aldo Moro Vol 2: 8032
  Accademia Internazionale della Tavola Rotonda Vol 2: 8036
  Associazione Napoletana Amici di Malta Vol 2: 8142
Premi a l'Aplicado de la Tecnologia al Proceso o al Producto Industrial de la Generalitat de Catalunya Vol. 2: 11179
Premi Adria Gual Vol. 2: 11157
Premi Anita Vecchi Vol. 2: 8020
Premi Antonio Feltrinelli Vol. 2: 8069
Premi Apel Les Mestres Vol. 2: 11215
Premi Artur Martorell Vol. 2: 11172
Premi Catalonia d'illustracio Vol. 2: 11194
Premi Cecilia Cioffrese Nel Settore Della Cura Della Salute Vol. 2: 8225
Premi Concorsi Letterari Vol. 2: 8012
Premi culturali Vol. 2: 8038
Premi David di Donatello per la Cinematografia Internazionale Vol. 2: 8218
Premi David Speciali Vol. 2: 8218
Premi de la Generalitat de Catalunya al Foment de l'Exportacio Vol. 2: 11184
Premi de Poesia Carles Riba Vol. 2: 11238
Premi del Ministro per i Beni Culturali e Ambientali Vol. 2: 8070
Premi d'Honor de les Lletres Catalanes Vol. 2: 11310
Premi e Concorsi il Compasso d'oro Vol. 2: 8147
Premi Festival Internacional de Cinema Fantastic de Sitges Vol. 2: 11359
Premi Giosue Carducci Vol. 2: 8174
Premi Ignasi Iglesias Vol. 2: 11158
Premi Internacional Catalunya Vol. 2: 11175
Premi internazionali vitivinicoli Vol. 2: 8092
Premi Jordi Lluch i de Andres Vol. 2: 11186
Premi Josep M. Carbonell Vol. 2: 11159
Premi Josep Maria de Sagarra Vol. 2: 11160
Premi Josep Pla Vol. 2: 11217
Premi Joventut Vol. 2: 11173
Premi Ministeriali Vol. 2: 8071
Premi Nacional d'Activitats Teatrals Vol. 2: 11161
Premi Nacional d'Arts Esceniques Vol. 2: 11161
Premi Nacional d'Interpretacio Teatral i de Dansa Vol. 2: 11162
Premi Nazionali Paestum Vol. 2: 8028
Premi Ricard Moragas Vol. 2: 11163
Premi Sant Jordi Vol. 2: 11309
Premi Xavier Fabregas Vol. 2: 11164
Premie for barne-og ungdomslitteratur Vol. 2: 9916
Premier Award
  CIBC National Music Festival Vol. 1: 7693
  Eternit Vol 2: 1114
Premier Awards Vol. 1: 6189
Premier Breeder at the North American International Livestock Exposition Vol. 1: 1838

Premier Prix Vol. 2: 6074
Premier Prix Mondial de l'Automatisation Postale Vol. 2: 1386
Premier Prospectus Award Vol. 1: 9861
Premier Technology Shandon Award Vol. 2: 10980
Premier's Literary Awards Vol. 2: 149
Premier's Poetry Award Vol. 2: 293
Premies voor de verspreiding van de betere film in Belgie Vol. 2: 1353
Premio A. Barbagelata Vol. 2: 8345
Premio a la Actividad Cientifica Dr. Alvaro Blanco Blanco Vol. 2: 1560
Premio a la Actividad Gremial Dr. Roberto Tapia Alarcon Vol. 2: 1561
Premio a la Actividad Profesional Dr. Hugo K. Sievers Wicke Vol. 2: 1562
Premio a la Innovacion Tecnologica Vol. 2: 1682
Premio a la Mejor Labor de Promocion de Lectura Vol. 2: 1701
Premio a la Mejor Revista Cientifica o Tecnologica Vol. 2: 12127
Premio a las Mejores Obras Cientificas o Tecnicas Publicadas en el Ano Vol. 2: 1818
Premio A. Marescalchi Vol. 2: 8042
Premio ABB Vol. 2: 8346
Premio Abilio Lopes do Rego Vol. 2: 10250
Premio Aboim Sande Lemos Vol. 2: 10254
Premio Academia Chilena de la Lengua Vol. 2: 1551
Premio Academia Colombiana de Ciencias Vol. 2: 1578
Premio Academia de Ciencias del Tercer Mundo Vol. 2: 1579
Premio Academia de Medicina de Sao Paulo Vol. 2: 1490
Premio Academia Nacional de Agronomia y Veterinaria Vol. 2: 6
Premio Academia Nacional de la Historia Vol. 2: 17
Premio Adonais de Poesia Vol. 2: 11327
Premio AEI Galileo Ferraris Vol. 2: 8347
Premio AEI Guglielmo Marconi Vol. 2: 8348
Premio AEI - Milano Section Vol. 2: 8349
Premio AEI Ricerche Vol. 2: 8348
Premio Agricola AEDOS Vol. 2: 11135
Premio Agricola Interamericano para Profesionales Jovenes Vol. 2: 1774
Premio Agustin Yanez para Primera Novela Vol. 2: 8981
Premio al Deportista Universitario Vol. 2: 9183
Premio al Mejor Libro Infantil y Juvenil Colombiano Vol. 2: 1702
Premio Al Merito Cientifico Vol. 2: 1681
Premio al Merito Nacional Enfermera Isabel Cendala Gomez Vol. 2: 9128
Premio Alberdi - Sarmiento Vol. 2: 107
Premio Alberto Comenge Vol. 2: 11331
Premio Aldo Palazzeschi Vol. 2: 8241
Premio Alejandro Silva de la Fuente Vol. 2: 1553
Premio Alejandro Zazuete Vol. 2: 9016
Premio Alfonso Caso Vol. 2: 9053
Premio Alfonso X de Traduccion Literaria Vol. 2: 9214
Premio Alonso de Ercilla Vol. 2: 1552
Premio Alter Vol. 2: 11332
Premio Alvarenga do Piaui Vol. 2: 10249
Premio Alvarez Quintero Vol. 2: 11346
Premio Ames a la Investigacion en Ciencias Basicas de la Salud Vol. 2: 1581
Premio Ames a la Investigacion en el Laboratorio Clinico Vol. 2: 1581
Premio Angela Cevenini Vol. 2: 8356
Premio Anna Magnani Vol. 2: 8122

Premio   **Awards, Honors & Prizes, 1995-96**

Premio Antibioticos   Vol. 2: 11333
Premio Anton Mario Lorgna   Vol. 2: 8380
Premio Antonio Alves de Carvalho Fernandes   Vol. 2: 10248
Premio Antonio de Lara "Tono" de Humor Grafico   Vol. 2: 11287
Premio Antonio Maura   Vol. 2: 11288
Premio Antoniorrobles   Vol. 2: 9120
Premio Anual de Aquisicao   Vol. 2: 10285
Premio Anual de Investigacao   Vol. 2: 10286
Premio Anual de Investigacion Economica Jesus Silva Herzog   Vol. 2: 9184
Premio Anual de Investigacion en Epilpsia   Vol. 2: 9065
Premio Anual de Investigacion Medica Dr. Jorge Rosenkranz   Vol. 2: 9071
Premio Anual de Servicio Social Gustavo Baz Prada   Vol. 2: 9185
Premio Aquilino Ribeiro   Vol. 2: 10259
Premio Argentores   Vol. 2: 31
Premio Ariel de Cinematografia   Vol. 2: 9097
Premio Artur Malheiros   Vol. 2: 10255
Premio Ateneo de Valladolid de Novela Corta   Vol. 2: 11147
Premio Atomo D'oro   Vol. 2: 8090
Premio Aurelio Peccei   Vol. 2: 8227
Premio Balzan   Vol. 2: 8280
Premio BANAMEX Atanasio G. Saravia de Historia Regional Mexicana   Vol. 2: 9204
Premio BANAMEX de Ciencia y Tecnologia   Vol. 2: 9203
Premio BANAMEX de Economia   Vol. 2: 9202
Premio Bancarella   Vol. 2: 8164
Premio Banco de la Republica   Vol. 2: 1590
Premio Bartolome de las Casas   Vol. 2: 11362
Premio Bartolozzi   Vol. 2: 8358
Premio Bayer en Ciencias Veterinarias   Vol. 2: 7
Premio Beato Egidio da Taranto   Vol. 2: 8241
Premio Beca Nacional de Diseno Industrial Clara Porset   Vol. 2: 9186
Premio Biella   Vol. 2: 8010
Premio Blanco y Negro de Pintura   Vol. 2: 11316
Premio Bolsa de Cereales de Buenos Aires   Vol. 2: 8
Premio Bonazzi   Vol. 2: 8350
Premio Bottani   Vol. 2: 8351
Premio Caccioppoli   Vol. 2: 8359
Premio Cacho Pallerocici   Vol. 2: 11236
Premio Caldas de Ciencias   Vol. 2: 1688
Premio Calixto Torres Umana   Vol. 2: 1692
Premio Camillo Golgi   Vol. 2: 8072
Premio Campiello   Vol. 2: 8185
Premio Carabela Ciudad de Cartagena   Vol. 2: 11279
Premio Caracola de Mar   Vol. 2: 11279
Premio Carlos Mateo Sanchez   Vol. 2: 9016
Premio Carlos Perez del Toro   Vol. 2: 8954
Premio Carlos Teixeira   Vol. 2: 10245
Premio Carlotta Strampelli   Vol. 2: 8008
Premio Carmelo Colamonico   Vol. 2: 8073
Premio Castello   Vol. 2: 8197
Premio Cavolini - De Mellis   Vol. 2: 8087
Premio Cenafor de Monografica   Vol. 2: 1431
Premio Ceppo Proposte Nicola Lisi   Vol. 2: 8084
Premio Ceresis   Vol. 2: 10018
Premio Cesare Augusto   Vol. 2: 8090
Premio Cesare Augusto   Vol. 2: 8090
Premio Cesare Marcorelli   Vol. 2: 8282
Premio Cidade de Lisboa   Vol. 2: 10308
Premio Ciencia e Informacao   Vol. 2: 1448
Premio Cientifico   Vol. 2: 1738
Premio Cinema d'Essai - Targa AIACE   Vol. 2: 8124

Premio Citta di Ercolano   Vol. 2: 8480
Premio Citta Eterna   Vol. 2: 8241
Premio Comillas de Biografia, Autobiografia y Memorias   Vol. 2: 11388
Premio Comision Nacional Bancaria   Vol. 2: 8958
Premio Comunicacao   Vol. 2: 1408
Premio Condumex   Vol. 2: 9187
Premio Consagracion Rodolfo A. Vaccarezza   Vol. 2: 59
Premio CORAL   Vol. 2: 1828
Premio Corazon de Oro   Vol. 2: 9270
Premio CREI de Informatica   Vol. 2: 11201
Premio Critici in Erba   Vol. 2: 8171
Premio da critica   Vol. 2: 10298
Premio Dagra   Vol. 2: 10243
Premio Daniel Zuloaga   Vol. 2: 11289
Premio de Biblioteconomia e Documentacao   Vol. 2: 1469
Premio de Biografia   Vol. 2: 9215
Premio de Biografia Catalana AEDOS   Vol. 2: 11136
Premio de Ciencas Morfologicas Dr. Enrique Acosta Vidrio   Vol. 2: 9188
Premio de Ciencias Alejandro Angel Escobar   Vol. 2: 1584
Premio de Composicion Arquitectonica Alberto J. Pani   Vol. 2: 9189
Premio de Critica de Arte Luis Cardoza y Aragon   Vol. 2: 9216
Premio de Cuento para Ninos   Vol. 2: 9047
Premio de Cuentos Hucha de Oro   Vol. 2: 11211
Premio de Ecologia   Vol. 2: 9263
Premio de Ensayo Literario Angel Maria Garibay Kintana   Vol. 2: 9048
Premio de Escultura Villa de Madrid   Vol. 2: 11297
Premio de Investigacion Ahciet   Vol. 2: 11144
Premio de la Compania Espanola de Penicilina y Antibioticos   Vol. 2: 11334
Premio de la Critica a los Mejores Libros Publicados   Vol. 2: 1819
Premio de la Real Academia de Farmacia   Vol. 2: 11335
Premio de Musica de la Generalitat de Catalunya   Vol. 2: 11182
Premio de Narrativa Jorge Ibarguengoitia   Vol. 2: 9217
Premio de Novela Andres Bello   Vol. 2: 1564
Premio de Novela Ateneo de Sevilla   Vol. 2: 11223
Premio de Novela Ignacio Manuel Altamirano   Vol. 2: 9046
Premio de Novela Jose Ruben Romero   Vol. 2: 9218
Premio de Obra de Teatro   Vol. 2: 9219
Premio de Obra de Teatro para Ninos   Vol. 2: 9220
Premio de Periodismo Cultural   Vol. 2: 9221
Premio de Periodismo Rosario Castellanos   Vol. 2: 8928
Premio de Pesquisa Estudantil Instituto Nacional do Livro   Vol. 2: 1443
Premio de Poesia Carlos Pellicer   Vol. 2: 9222
Premio de Poesia Josue Mirlo   Vol. 2: 9049
Premio de Poesia Joven de Mexico Elias Nandino   Vol. 2: 9223
Premio de Poesia Miguel N. Lira   Vol. 2: 9004
Premio de Radio Villa de Madrid   Vol. 2: 11292
Premio de Revelacao de Ensaio   Vol. 2: 10311
Premio de Revelacao de Ficcao   Vol. 2: 10312

Premio de Revelacao de Poesia   Vol. 2: 10313
Premio de Tecnologia Quimica   Vol. 2: 8941
Premio de Tecnologia Textil   Vol. 2: 8942
Premio de Testimonio   Vol. 2: 9224
Premio de Traducao Calouste Gulbenkian   Vol. 2: 10251
Premio de Traduccion de Poesia   Vol. 2: 9225
Premio Deguci   Vol. 2: 9678
Premio del Certamen Literario Latinoamericano   Vol. 2: 1772
Premio del Colegio Oficial de Farmaceuticos   Vol. 2: 11336
Premio del Consejo General de Colegios Oficiales de Farmaceuticos de Espana   Vol. 2: 11337
Premio del Instituto Nacional de Administracion Publica   Vol. 2: 9051
Premio del Rey Prize   Vol. 1: 2298
Premio del Seminario de Economia Agricola del Tercer Mundo   Vol. 2: 9190
Premio Derechos Humanos   Vol. 2: 9191
Premio di laurea   Vol. 2: 8135
Premio di Laurea Luigi Casati in Discipline Scientifiche   Vol. 2: 8074
Premio di Laurea Luigi Casati in Discipline Uranistiche   Vol. 2: 8075
Premio di Natale piccolo formato   Vol. 2: 8241
Premio Dino Ciani   Vol. 2: 8189
Premio Direito dos Seguros   Vol. 2: 10321
Premio Dr. Eduardo Liceaga   Vol. 2: 9114
Premio Dr. Enrique Beltran de Historia de La Ciencia y La Tecnologia   Vol. 2: 9122
Premio Dr. Fernando Ocaranza   Vol. 2: 9115
Premio Dr. Francisco C. Rosenbusch   Vol. 2: 9
Premio Dr. Gonzalo Castaneda   Vol. 2: 9101
Premio Dr. Jose Aguilar Alvarez Prize   Vol. 2: 9102
Premio Dr. Manuel J. Castillejos   Vol. 2: 9103
Premio Domenico Marotta   Vol. 2: 8381
Premio dos Culturas en Origen   Vol. 2: 8969
Premio Editorial Costa Rica   Vol. 2: 1770
Premio Efraim Hernandez Xolocotzi   Vol. 2: 8956
Premio el Professor Distinguido   Vol. 2: 9035
Premio Elio Costanzi   Vol. 2: 8001
Premio en Desarrollo Agricola Interamericano   Vol. 2: 1775
Premio en Favor del Foment del Turisme   Vol. 2: 11177
Premio Enrico Fermi   Vol. 2: 8145
Premio Enrique Pena   Vol. 2: 18
Premio Escolar Paz y Cooperacion   Vol. 2: 11314
Premio Especial Antonio Maria   Vol. 2: 1471
Premio Espejo de Espana   Vol. 2: 11221
Premio Esso de Jornalismo   Vol. 2: 1456
Premio Europeo di Letteratura Giovanile "Pier Paolo Vergerio"   Vol. 2: 8466
Premio Europeo Prof. D. Ganassini   Vol. 2: 8259
Premio F. Alfano   Vol. 2: 8480
Premio F. Busoni   Vol. 2: 8181
Premio F. Cameli   Vol. 2: 8352
Premio F. Malusardi   Vol. 2: 8353
Premio Fabrica Espanola de Productos Quimicos y Farmaceuticos   Vol. 2: 11338
Premio Facultad de Derecho a la Mejor Tesis   Vol. 2: 9192
Premio Faro Cabo de Palos   Vol. 2: 11279
Premio Federico Nitti   Vol. 2: 8382
Premio Felipe Tena Ramirez   Vol. 2: 9193
Premio Florentino Ameghino   Vol. 2: 28
Premio Francesco Compagna   Vol. 2: 8002
Premio Francesco Pistolese   Vol. 2: 8003

Premio Francisco de Goya   Vol. 2: 11290
Premio Francisco de la Maza   Vol. 2: 9054
Premio Francisco de Quevado   Vol. 2: 11291
Premio Francisco Javier Clavijero   Vol. 2: 9055
Premio Fray Bernardino de Sahagun   Vol. 2: 9056
Premio Frederico de Menezes Veiga   Vol. 2: 1447
Premio Fundacion Celulosa Argentina   Vol. 2: 10
Premio Fundacion Eli Lilly   Vol. 2: 9116
Premio Fundacion Manzullo   Vol. 2: 11
Premio Fundacion Quinquela Martin   Vol. 2: 49
Premio Fundacion Rafael Folch   Vol. 2: 11339
Premio Fundacion Rene Baron   Vol. 2: 12
Premio FUNDALECTURA de Literatura Infantil y Juvenil Colombiana   Vol. 2: 1703
Premio G. d'Annunzio   Vol. 2: 8213
Premio G. Vitelli   Vol. 2: 8332
Premio Gea Gonzalez - PUIC   Vol. 2: 9024
Premio Genaro Estrada   Vol. 2: 9016
Premio General Casimiro Dantas   Vol. 2: 10247
Premio Gerardo Varela   Vol. 2: 9129
Premio Gilberto Figueroa Nogueron   Vol. 2: 8998
Premio Giorgio Dal Piaz   Vol. 2: 8427
Premio Gleb Wataghin   Vol. 2: 1460
Premio grafico Fiera di Bologna per l'infanzia e la gioventu   Vol. 2: 8172
Premio Grinzane Cavour   Vol. 2: 8187
Premio Guillermo Marconi   Vol. 2: 11292
Premio Guillermo Tena   Vol. 2: 11340
Premio Gustavo D. Canedo   Vol. 2: 9016
Premio Hispanoamericano Xavier Villaurrutia   Vol. 2: 9267
Premio Iberoamericano de Primeras Novelas   Vol. 2: 1564
Premio IBEU de Artes Plasticas   Vol. 2: 1467
Premio IBEU de Teatro   Vol. 2: 1466
Premio Iglesias   Vol. 2: 8118
Premio Il Ceppo   Vol. 2: 8085
Premio IMIQ   Vol. 2: 9106
Premio IMIQ-CONACYT   Vol. 2: 9107
Premio IMIQ, ING. Estanislao Ramirez   Vol. 2: 9108
Premio IMIQ, Victor Marquez Dominguez   Vol. 2: 9109
Premio Innovazione Elettronica   Vol. 2: 8326
Premio Instituto Nacional do Livro de Literatura Infantil   Vol. 2: 1472
Premio Interamericano a la Participacion de la Mujer en el Desarrollo Rural   Vol. 2: 1777
Premio Internacional Alfonso Reyes   Vol. 2: 9268
Premio Internacional Almirante Gago Coutinho   Vol. 2: 10317
Premio Internacional Arthur Desguin   Vol. 2: 1104
Premio Internacional Daniel Cosio Villegas   Vol. 2: 9287
Premio Internacional de Canto Fundacion Guerrero   Vol. 2: 11242
Premio Internacional de Educacion Fisica Jose Maria Cagigal   Vol. 2: 1166
Premio Internacional de Ensayo Literario Malcolm Lowry   Vol. 2: 9226
Premio Internacional de Guitarra S.A.R. La Infanta Dona Christina   Vol. 2: 11241
Premio Internacional de Novela, Nuevo Leon   Vol. 2: 8973
Premio Internacional de Piano Fundacion Guerrero   Vol. 2: 11243
Premio Internacional para Novela Planeta - Joaquin Mortiz   Vol. 2: 8980

Premio Internacional Vasco Vilvalva   Vol. 2: 10252
Premio International de Ensayo Antonio Machado   Vol. 2: 1723
Premio Internazionale Accademia Musicale Chigiana Siena   Vol. 2: 8046
Premio Internazionale Aldo Merola   Vol. 2: 8437
Premio Internazionale Amedeo e Frances Herlitzka per la Fisiologia   Vol. 2: 8023
Premio Internazionale Citta di Sorrento   Vol. 2: 8436
Premio Internazionale con Medaglia d'oro, Professor Modesto Panetti   Vol. 2: 8024
Premio Internazionale di Direzione d'Orchestra Antonio Pedrotti   Vol. 2: 8112
Premio Internazionale di Meridionalistica Guido Dorso   Vol. 2: 8149
Premio Internazionale di Viticoltura G. Dalmasso   Vol. 2: 8043
Premio Internazionale Enno Flaiano   Vol. 2: 8114
Premio Internazionale Ermanno Acanfora   Vol. 2: 8435
Premio Internazionale Galileo Galilei dei Rotary italiani   Vol. 2: 8303
Premio Internazionale Paladino D'Oro   Vol. 2: 8313
Premio Internazionale Paolo Gatto   Vol. 2: 8076
Premio Internazionale per la Zootecnia Uovo d'Oro   Vol. 2: 8151
Premio Internazionale per un Articolo o Studio Scientifico o Tecnico   Vol. 2: 8265
Premio Internazionale Pietro Caliceti   Vol. 2: 8249
(Premio internazionale Rotary Club di Parma "Giuseppe Verdi")   Vol. 2: 8386
Premio Internazionali dell' Instituto Nazionale delle Assicurazioni   Vol. 2: 8067
Premio Irene Brin   Vol. 2: 8004
Premio Isaac Peral   Vol. 2: 11279
Premio Isidoro Maiquez   Vol. 2: 11279
Premio Istituto Italo-Latino Americano   Vol. 2: 8328
Premio Jabuti   Vol. 2: 1470
Premio Jaen   Vol. 2: 11281
Premio Jean Mitry   Vol. 2: 8400
Premio Jinete Iberico   Vol. 2: 11236
Premio Jose Cayetano Valdez   Vol. 2: 9016
Premio Jose Maria Bustillo   Vol. 2: 13
Premio Josefina Vicens para Novela Breve   Vol. 2: 9227
Premio Joven Investigador Profesor Ignacio Chavez   Vol. 2: 9073
Premio Juan Abello   Vol. 2: 11341
Premio Juan Comas   Vol. 2: 9057
Premio Juan de la Serna   Vol. 2: 11342
Premio Juan Pablos al Merito Editorial   Vol. 2: 9154
Premio Juan Rulfo Para Primera Novela   Vol. 2: 9228
Premio Juegos Florales de San Juan del Rio, Queretaro   Vol. 2: 9162
Premio Julio G. Arce   Vol. 2: 9016
Premio Juridico Mtro. Jorge Sanchez Cordero   Vol. 2: 8987
Premio Justicia y Paz a los Valores Humanos   Vol. 2: 11209
Premio Kaulak   Vol. 2: 11293
Premio La Ceramica n la Arquitectura   Vol. 2: 9302
Premio La Sonrisa Vertical   Vol. 2: 11390
Premio Laranjo Coelho   Vol. 2: 10246
Premio Larragoiti   Vol. 2: 10253
Premio Latinoamericano de Cuento   Vol. 2: 9229

Premio Latinoamericano de Narrativa, Colima   Vol. 2: 9230
Premio Laura Orvieto   Vol. 2: 8251
Premio Lazarillo   Vol. 2: 11384
Premio Letterario del Frignano Riccio d'Oro   Vol. 2: 8016
Premio Letterario Isola d'Elba   Vol. 2: 8323
Premio Letterario Isola d'Elba - Raffaello Brignetti   Vol. 2: 8323
Premio Letterario Racconti di Carnevale   Vol. 2: 8116
Premio Libro d'Oro   Vol. 2: 8342
Premio Linceo   Vol. 2: 8080
Premio Literario Internacional *Novedades* y Diana Editorial Diana   Vol. 2: 8975
Novedades   Vol 2: 9253
Premio Literario Miguel Torga - Cidade de Coimbra   Vol. 2: 10224
Premio Literario Netzahualcoyotl   Vol. 2: 9031
Premio Literario Ramon Llull   Vol. 2: 11224
Premio Litterario Viareggio   Vol. 2: 8407
Premio Liverdade-Visconde de Sousa Prego   Vol. 2: 10295
Premio Lope de Vega   Vol. 2: 11294
Premio Luca de Tena   Vol. 2: 11317
Premio Luchino Visconti   Vol. 2: 8218
Premio Luigi Mari   Vol. 2: 8282
Premio Luigi Prete   Vol. 2: 8040
Premio Luis Bunuel   Vol. 2: 11295
Premio Luis de Camoes   Vol. 2: 10297
Premio Luis Elizondo - Premio Cientifico y Technologico   Vol. 2: 8989
Premio Luis Elizondo - Premio Humanitario   Vol. 2: 8990
Premio Luis Zambrano a la Inventiva Tecnologica Nacional   Vol. 2: 12130
Premio Maestro Arturo Rosenblueth   Vol. 2: 9276
Premio Maestro Ignacio Chavez   Vol. 2: 9277
Premio Maestro Manuel Vaquero   Vol. 2: 9278
Premio Maestro Salvador Aceves   Vol. 2: 9279
Premio Maestro Villa   Vol. 2: 11296
Premio Magda Donato   Vol. 2: 8930
Premio Manuel Alves Monteiro   Vol. 2: 10257
Premio Manuel Buendia   Vol. 2: 9294
Premio Manuel Toussaint   Vol. 2: 9058
Premio Mar Menor   Vol. 2: 11279
Premio Marcos y Celia Mauss   Vol. 2: 9194
Premio Maria Cianci   Vol. 2: 8304
Premio Maria Faletti-Nosari   Vol. 2: 8354
Premio Maria Guerrero a la Labor Teatral   Vol. 2: 11363
Premio Maria Teresa e Allessandro Ghigi   Vol. 2: 8021
Premio Maria Teresa Messori Roncaglia and Eugenio Mari   Vol. 2: 8077
Premio Mariano Benlliure   Vol. 2: 11297
Premio Mariano de Cavia   Vol. 2: 11318
Premio Mariano Ospina Perez   Vol. 2: 1699
Premio Mario di Nola   Vol. 2: 8078
Premio Martin de la Cruz   Vol. 2: 9130
Premio Massey Ferguson   Vol. 2: 14
Premio MEC de Arte   Vol. 2: 1442
Premio Menendez Pidal   Vol. 2: 11347
Premio Mesonero Romanos   Vol. 2: 11298
Premio Mesquite   Vol. 1: 9737
Premio Mexinox   Vol. 2: 9158
Premio Miguel Covarrubias   Vol. 2: 9059
Premio Miguel Hidalgo   Vol. 2: 9141
Premio Miguel Otero   Vol. 2: 9131
Premio Miguel Othon de Mendizabal   Vol. 2: 9060
Premio Mingote   Vol. 2: 11319
Premio Mixcoatl   Vol. 2: 9255

Premio   **Awards, Honors & Prizes, 1995-96**

Premio Mondo e Cultura   Vol. 2: 8005
Premio Municipais Joshua Benoliel de Fotografia   Vol. 2: 10264
Premio Municipal Alfredo Marceneiro de Fado   Vol. 2: 10265
Premio Municipal Augusto Vieira da Silva de Investigacao   Vol. 2: 10266
Premio Municipal Carlos Botelho de Pintura   Vol. 2: 10267
Premio Municipal de Literatura   Vol. 2: 1568
Premio Municipal Fernando Amado de Encenacao Teatral   Vol. 2: 10268
Premio Municipal Francisco da Conceicao Silva de Espacos Interiores abertos ao publico   Vol. 2: 10269
Premio Municipal Joao Baptista Rosa de Video   Vol. 2: 10270
Premio Municipal Jorge Colaco de Azulejaria   Vol. 2: 10271
Premio Municipal Jose Simoes de Almeida de Escultura   Vol. 2: 10272
Premio Municipal Julio Cesar Machado de Jornalismo   Vol. 2: 10273
Premio Municipal Julio de Castilho de Olisipografia   Vol. 2: 10274
Premio Municipal Maria Leonor Magro de Radio   Vol. 2: 10275
Premio Municipal Rafael Bordalo Pinheiro de Banda Desenhada, Cartoon e Caricaturista   Vol. 2: 10276
Premio Municipal Roberto de Araujo Pereira de Design   Vol. 2: 10277
Premio Municipal Trabalho e Estudo   Vol. 2: 10278
Premio Nacional a Desarollo Tecnologico   Vol. 2: 12128
Premio Nacional de Agriculture   Vol. 2: 1601
Premio Nacional de Arte   Vol. 2: 1545
Premio Nacional de Artes   Vol. 2: 1660
Premio Nacional de Artes Plasticas   Vol. 2: 11369
Premio Nacional de Bellas Artes   Vol. 2: 9146
Premio Nacional de Biblioteconomia e Documentacao   Vol. 2: 1469
Premio Nacional de Calidad   Vol. 2: 9261
Premio Nacional de Ciencia   Vol. 2: 12129
Premio Nacional de Ciencia y Technologia Ericsson   Vol. 2: 8983
Premio Nacional de Ciencia y Tecnologia de Alimentos   Vol. 2: 8965
Premio Nacional de Ciencias
   Chile - Ministerio de Educacion   Vol. 2: 1546
   Colombia - Ministry of National Education   Vol 2: 1663
Premio Nacional de Ciencias del Mar   Vol. 2: 1690
Premio Nacional de Ciencias Fisico - Matematicas y Naturales   Vol. 2: 9149
Premio nacional de Ciencias y Artes   Vol. 2: 9152
Premio Nacional de Ciencias y Tecnologia Clodomiro Picado Twight   Vol. 2: 1764
Premio Nacional de Cinematografia   Vol. 2: 11371
Premio Nacional de Critica Literaria Mirta Aguirre   Vol. 2: 1820
Premio Nacional de Cuento   Vol. 2: 9231
Premio Nacional de Cuento para Ninos Juan de la Cabada   Vol. 2: 9232
Premio Nacional de Cultura de Ecuador Eugenio Espejo   Vol. 2: 2017
Premio Nacional de Danza   Vol. 2: 11372
Premio Nacional de Danza Clasica Contemporanea   Vol. 2: 9297
Premio Nacional de Danza Etnocoreografica   Vol. 2: 9298

Premio Nacional de Danza INBA-Sinaloa Jose Limon   Vol. 2: 9233
Premio Nacional de Deportes   Vol. 2: 9150
Premio Nacional de Desarrollo Quimico Cosmetico   Vol. 2: 9272
Premio Nacional de Economia   Vol. 2: 9095
Premio Nacional de Educaccion   Vol. 2: 923
Premio Nacional de Ensayo Literario Jose Revueltas   Vol. 2: 9234
Premio Nacional de Geologia   Vol. 2: 1736
Premio Nacional de Historia
   Chile - Ministerio de Educacion   Vol. 2: 1547
   Colombia - Ministry of National Education   Vol 2: 1661
Premio Nacional de Historia, Ciencias Sociales y Filosofia   Vol. 2: 9147
Premio Nacional de Historia de Espana   Vol. 2: 11373
Premio Nacional de Illustracion de Libros Infantiles y Juveniles   Vol. 2: 11370
Premio Nacional de Ingenieria   Vol. 2: 1747
Premio Nacional de Integracion Latinoamericana   Vol. 2: 8934
Premio Nacional de Investigacion Financiera IMEE   Vol. 2: 9038
Premio Nacional de la Calidad   Vol. 2: 1611
Premio Nacional de la Contaduria Publica   Vol. 2: 9036
Premio Nacional de la Cultura   Vol. 1: 10476
Premio Nacional de la Juventud   Vol. 2: 9153
Premio Nacional de las Letras Espanolas   Vol. 2: 11374
Premio Nacional de Linguistica y Literatura   Vol. 2: 9148
Premio Nacional de Literatura
   Angolan Writers Union   Vol. 2: 4
   Chile - Ministerio de Educacion   Vol 2: 1548
   Colombia - Ministry of National Education   Vol 2: 1662
   Cuban Book Institute   Vol 2: 1821
   Spain Ministry of Culture   Vol 2: 11375
Premio Nacional de Literatura Gilberto Owen   Vol. 2: 9014
Premio Nacional de Literatura Jose Fuentes Mares   Vol. 2: 9292
Premio Nacional de Literatura Paula Allende   Vol. 2: 9295
Premio Nacional de Medicina, Dr. Luis Edmundo Vasquez   Vol. 2: 2025
Premio Nacional de Merito Civico   Vol. 2: 9139
Premio Nacional de Novela   Vol. 2: 9235
Premio Nacional de Periodismo   Vol. 2: 1549
Premio Nacional de Periodismo Pio Viquez   Vol. 2: 1765
Premio Nacional de Periodismo y de Informacion   Vol. 2: 9140
Premio Nacional de Poesia   Vol. 2: 9236
Premio Nacional de Poesia Ciudad de la Paz   Vol. 2: 8996
Premio Nacional de Poesia Jorge Cuesta   Vol. 2: 9006
Premio Nacional de Poesia Joven Francisco Gonzalez de Leon   Vol. 2: 9237
Premio Nacional de Quimica   Vol. 2: 1737
Premio Nacional de Servicios a la Comunidad   Vol. 2: 9135
Premio Nacional de Teatro
   Costa Rica - Ministry of Culture, Youth and Sport   Vol. 2: 1766
   Spain Ministry of Culture   Vol 2: 11376
Premio Nacional de Tecnologia y Diseno   Vol. 2: 9151
Premio Nacional de Television Simon Bolivar   Vol. 2: 1596

Premio Nacional de Trabajo   Vol. 2: 9137
Premio Nacional de Trabajos Recepcionales escritos en Comunicacion   Vol. 2: 8971
Premio Nacional de Traducao   Vol. 2: 1473
Premio Nacional de Traduccion   Vol. 2: 11377
Premio Nacional del Mercado de Valores   Vol. 2: 9042
Premio Nacional Periodismo porla Infancia   Vol. 2: 8946
Premio Nacional Serfin, sobre Medio Ambiente   Vol. 2: 8935
Premio Nacional Teponaxtli de Malinalco   Vol. 2: 8932
Premio Nacionales de Musica   Vol. 2: 11378
Premio Nadal   Vol. 2: 11216
Premio Napoli di Giornalismo   Vol. 2: 8255
Premio Napoli di Narrativa   Vol. 2: 8253
Premio Napoli di Saggistica - Il Rapporto Nord-Sud nel Mondo   Vol. 2: 8254
Premio Napoli - Mezzogiorno   Vol. 2: 8256
Premio Napolitain Illustri   Vol. 2: 8257
Premio Nazionale Composizione   Vol. 2: 8245
Premio Nazionale del Presidente della Repubblica   Vol. 2: 8068
Premio Nazionale di Narrativa   Vol. 2: 8144
Premio Nazionale di Poesie   Vol. 2: 8145
Premio Nicolas Leon   Vol. 2: 9061
Premio Nicoletta Quinto   Vol. 2: 8305
Premio Nipiol-Buitoni   Vol. 2: 8431
Premio Norma Padilla   Vol. 2: 7241
Premio Norman Sverdlin   Vol. 2: 9195
Premio Octacilio Cunha   Vol. 2: 2027
Premio Omeyocan   Vol. 2: 9196
Premio Ortega y Gasset   Vol. 2: 11299
Premio Ospitalita Citta di Sondrio   Vol. 2: 8433
Premio P. G. Garoglio   Vol. 2: 8044
Premio Pablo Neruda   Vol. 2: 1566
Premio Pablo Villavicencio   Vol. 2: 9016
Premio Paolo Borciani   Vol. 2: 8444
Premio para el Estimulo de Docencia e Investigacion en Ingenieria Quimica   Vol. 2: 9110
Premio Paul Coremans   Vol. 2: 9062
Premio Penna d'Oro   Vol. 2: 8343
Premio Periodismo Cultural   Vol. 2: 9238
Premio Periodistico   Vol. 2: 1553
Premio Petrocanada   Vol. 2: 12092
Premio Pezcoller   Vol. 2: 8397
Premio Pico della Mirandola   Vol. 2: 8570
Premio Planeta de Novela   Vol. 2: 11222
Premio Poesia y Narrativa   Vol. 2: 1772
Premio Positano Leonida Massine per l'Arte della Danza   Vol. 2: 8156
Premio Prof. Dr. Alejandro Cabanne   Vol. 2: 44
Premio Profesor Dr. Ricardo Hansen   Vol. 2: 60
Premio Puma   Vol. 2: 9197
Premio Rafael Heliodoro Valle   Vol. 2: 9249
Premio Ramos Paz   Vol. 2: 10258
Premio Regional de Pintura   Vol. 2: 9165
Premio Reina Sofia de Investigacion sobre prevencion de la subnormalidad   Vol. 2: 11246
Premio Republica Argentina   Vol. 2: 19
Premio Revista Ahciet   Vol. 2: 11145
Premio Revista Punto de Partida   Vol. 2: 9198
Premio Ricardo Malheiros   Vol. 2: 10256
Premio Ricardo Monge Lopez   Vol. 2: 9289
Premio Riccione - ATER: per un teatro d'autore   Vol. 2: 8404
Premio Rodrigo Gomez   Vol. 2: 8944
Premio Romulo Garza para Investigacion   Vol. 2: 9026
Premio Romulo Garza para Publicaciones   Vol. 2: 9027

Premio Santa Rosa   Vol. 2: 1475
Premio Santoro   Vol. 2: 8079
Premio scientifico-technico   Vol. 2: 8136
Premio Sinaloa de Ciencias y Artes   Vol. 2: 9015
Premio Sinaloa de Periodismo   Vol. 2: 9016
Premio Sirena   Vol. 2: 11279
Premio Solidaridad   Vol. 2: 8963
Premio Solidarios con el Desarrollo de America Latina y del Caribe   Vol. 2: 2015
Premio Sor Maria del Roble   Vol. 2: 9280
Premio Sotero Prieto a la Mejor Tesis de Licenciatura en Matematicas   Vol. 2: 9283
Premio Teatral Tirso de Molina   Vol. 2: 11364
Premio Tenco   Vol. 2: 8193
Premio Tenore   Vol. 2: 8088
Premio Teofilo Patni - Castel di Sangro   Vol. 2: 8241
Premio Tetradramma d'oro   Vol. 2: 8034
Premio Trienal Instituto Torcuato di Tella Mozarteum Argentina   Vol. 2: 55
Premio Triennale per la Fisica Francesco Somaini   Vol. 2: 8243
Premio Tusquets Editores de Novela   Vol. 2: 11389
Premio TWAS (Third World Academy of Sciences)   Vol. 2: 8918
Premio Umberto Zanotti Bianco   Vol. 2: 8361
Premio Union Geofisca Mexicana   Vol. 2: 9290
Premio Universidad Nacional   Vol. 2: 9199
Premio Valentino Bucchi di Roma Capitale   Vol. 2: 8263
Premio Valmor e Municipal de Arquitectura   Vol. 2: 10279
Premio Vicente T. Mendoza   Vol. 2: 9063
Premio Vilfred Baron   Vol. 2: 15
Premio Visconde de Cairu   Vol. 2: 1464
Premio Vittorio Gui   Vol. 2: 8102
Premio Zamenhof por Internacia Komprenigo   Vol. 2: 9679
Premio Zonta   Vol. 2: 8480
Premios a la Investigacion Medica   Vol. 2: 9044
Premios ADIRCAE   Vol. 2: 11140
Premios Anuales a los Mejores Trabajos Cientificos   Vol. 2: 12126
Premios Asociacion de Reporteros Graficos   Vol. 2: 8924
Premios CANIFARMA   Vol. 2: 8939
Premios de Beneficencia Alejandro Angel Escobar   Vol. 2: 1583
Premios de Cinematografia de la Generalitat de Catalunya   Vol. 2: 11181
Premios de Investigacion Cientifica   Vol. 2: 8919
Premios de la Cooperativa Farmaceutica Espanola   Vol. 2: 11343
Premios de la Fundacion Conde de Cartagena   Vol. 2: 11348
Premios de Literatura Catalana de la Generalitat de Catalunya   Vol. 2: 11180
Premios de Salao Nacional de Artes Plasticas   Vol. 2: 1441
Premios de Videografia de la Generalitat de Catalunya   Vol. 2: 11183
Premios Diosa de Plata   Vol. 2: 9257
Premios INI   Vol. 2: 9067
Premios Literarios Nacionais   Vol. 2: 1474
Premios Maria Guerrero y Ricardo Calvo   Vol. 2: 11300
Premios Municipais Eca de Queiroz de Literatura   Vol. 2: 10280
Premios Municipais Joly Braga Santos de Musica   Vol. 2: 10281
Premios Municipais Palmira Bastos e Antonio Silva de Interpretacao Teatral   Vol. 2: 10282

Premios Nacionales de Cultura   Vol. 2: 1391
Premios Nacionales de Literatura Infantil y Juvenil   Vol. 2: 11379
Premios PEN   Vol. 2: 10293
Premios Principe de Asturias   Vol. 2: 11248
Premios Rey de Espan a de Periodismo   Vol. 2: 11361
Premios Vitalicios   Vol. 2: 11245
Premios Weizmann de la Academia de la Investigacion Cientifica   Vol. 2: 8920
Premis Construmat   Vol. 2: 11192
Prenio Ramon Gomez de la Serna   Vol. 2: 11301
Prentice Award in Animal Breeding and Genetics; Rockefeller   Vol. 1: 4403
Prentice Hall Regents Fellowship for Graduate Study; TESOL/   Vol. 1: 18593
Prentice Medal; Charles F.   Vol. 1: 643
Prentice Memorial Award; Justus A.   Vol. 1: 1183
Prescott Award; Gerald W.   Vol. 1: 16173
Prescott Award; Samuel Cate   Vol. 1: 10349
Prescott Scholarship; Raymond Coleman   Vol. 2: 3333
Presea Ignacio Zaragosa   Vol. 2: 9002
Preseren Award   Vol. 2: 10799
Presernova Nagrada   Vol. 2: 10799
Preservation Honor Awards   Vol. 1: 14937
Preservation Publication Award   Vol. 1: 17678
President Award   Vol. 1: 15937
President Macia Plaque and Medal   Vol. 2: 11189
Presidential Academic Fitness Awards   Vol. 1: 19224
Presidential Award
    American Academy of Periodontology   Vol. 1: 696
    American Association of Blood Banks   Vol 1: 931
    American Association of Mental Health Professionals in Corrections   Vol 1: 1038
    American Society of Plastic and Reconstructive Surgeons   Vol 1: 4761
    International Camaro Club   Vol 1: 10822
    National Association of the Holy Name Society   Vol 1: 13350
    Society for Leukocyte Biology   Vol 1: 17550
Presidential Award for Leadership in Psychiatry   Vol. 1: 13254
Presidential Award for Mental Health Administration   Vol. 1: 13255
Presidential Award for Psychiatric Research   Vol. 1: 13256
Presidential Award for Volunteer Trustee   Vol. 1: 13257
Presidential Award of the New York Academy of Sciences   Vol. 1: 15218
Presidential Award of the New York Academy of Sciences Supported by A. Cressy Morrison   Vol. 1: 15218
Presidential Award of the RES - Annie R. Beasley Memorial Award   Vol. 1: 17550
Presidential Award on Best Book on Quaid-i-Azam and Pakistan   Vol. 2: 10010
Presidential Award (Presidential Citation)   Vol. 1: 4762
Presidential Awards for Design Excellence   Vol. 1: 13894
Presidential Awards for Excellence in Science and Mathematics Teaching   Vol. 1: 14690
Presidential Awards for Outstanding Federal Employees with Disabilities   Vol. 1: 19481
Presidential Certificates of Merit   Vol. 1: 2675
Presidential Citation
    American Academy of Otolaryngology - Head and Neck Surgery   Vol. 1: 658

    American College of Cardiology   Vol 1: 1615
    American Kinesiotherapy Association   Vol 1: 2774
    American Mosquito Control Association   Vol 1: 3136
    Association for the Advancement of Health Education   Vol 1: 5614
    Genetics Society of Canada   Vol 1: 9538
    National Coordinating Council on Emergency Management   Vol 1: 13668
    National Environmental Health Association   Vol 1: 13913
    Society of American Registered Architects   Vol 1: 17728
    United States Hang Gliding Association   Vol 1: 19370
Presidential Citation for Excellence in Standard Purchasing Procedures   Vol. 1: 14236
Presidential Citation of Merit   Vol. 1: 2616
Presidential Citations and Awards   Vol. 1: 14576
Presidential Citations for Exceptional Service   Vol. 1: 1818
Presidential Citations for Meritorious Service   Vol. 1: 4260
Presidential Citizens Medal   Vol. 1: 19334
Presidential Commendation
    British Canoe Union   Vol. 2: 2302
    National Association of Criminal Defense Lawyers   Vol 1: 13067
    United States Executive Office of the President   Vol 1: 19337
Presidential Commendations   Vol. 1: 3647
Presidential Design Awards   Vol. 1: 13894
Presidential End Hunger Awards   Vol. 1: 18987
Presidential Faculty Fellows Program   Vol. 1: 14686
Presidential Medal of Freedom   Vol. 1: 19335
Presidential Physical Fitness Award   Vol. 1: 16396
Presidential Proclamation   Vol. 1: 17908
Presidential Public Safety Communication Award   Vol. 1: 19337
Presidential Quality and Management Improvement Award   Vol. 1: 19482
Presidential Rank Awards   Vol. 1: 19483
Presidential Rank Awards for the Drug Enforcement Agency   Vol. 1: 19483
Presidential Rank Awards for the Federal Bureau of Investigation   Vol. 1: 19483
Presidential Rank Awards for the Senior Cryptologic Executive Service   Vol. 1: 19483
Presidential Rank Awards for the Senior Foreign Service   Vol. 1: 19483
Presidential Recognition Awards   Vol. 1: 764
Presidential Scholar Award   Vol. 1: 536
Presidential Sports Award   Vol. 1: 16397
Presidential Sword   Vol. 2: 3900
Presidential World Without Hunger Award   Vol. 1: 18987
Presidential Young Investigator Award
    National Science Foundation   Vol. 1: 14685
    National Science Foundation   Vol 1: 14686
President's Academic Effort Award   Vol. 1: 19224
President's Achievement Award   Vol. 1: 9090
Presidents Achievement Award   Vol. 1: 18561
President's Appreciative Award   Vol. 1: 3352
President's Award
    Advertising Women of New York   Vol. 1: 160
    American Association of Petroleum Geologists   Vol 1: 1105
    American Association of Petroleum Geologists   Vol 1: 1112

American Forestry Association   Vol 1: 2102
American Humane Association   Vol 1: 2404
American Lung Association   Vol 1: 2970
American Medical Technologists   Vol 1: 3042
American Probation and Parole Association   Vol 1: 3618
American Public Welfare Association   Vol 1: 3867
American Rehabilitation Association   Vol 1: 3939
American Society for Nondestructive Testing   Vol 1: 4223
American Society of Music Arrangers   Vol 1: 4723
American Society of Naturalists   Vol 1: 4725
American Society of Plastic and Reconstructive Surgeons - Plastic Surgery Educational Foundation   Vol 1: 4767
Asphalt Recycling and Reclaiming Association   Vol 1: 5376
Association for Electric Motors, Their Control, and Application   Vol 1: 5519
Association for Information and Image Management   Vol 1: 5546
Association of Conservation Engineers   Vol 1: 5755
Association of Schools of Allied Health Professions   Vol 1: 5951
Australian Institute of Genealogical Studies   Vol 2: 227
Bureau Issues Association   Vol 1: 6622
Canadian Booksellers Association   Vol 1: 6819
Canadian Society of Petroleum Geologists   Vol 1: 7225
Classification and Compensation Society   Vol 1: 7821
Film Council of Greater Columbus   Vol 1: 9191
Flexible Packaging Association   Vol 1: 9236
Fluid Power Society   Vol 1: 9273
Institute of Environmental Sciences   Vol 1: 10332
Institution of Professional Engineers New Zealand   Vol 2: 9741
International Association of Business Communicators   Vol 1: 10684
International Association of Industrial Accident Boards and Commissions   Vol 1: 10749
International Association of Pet Cemeteries   Vol 1: 10777
International Lilac Society   Vol 1: 11090
International Society for Heart and Lung Transplantation   Vol 1: 11251
International Thespian Society   Vol 1: 11363
Library Association of Ireland   Vol 2: 7815
Literacy Volunteers of America   Vol 1: 11900
Machine Vision Association of the Society of Manufacturing Engineers   Vol 1: 11992
Medical Library Association   Vol 1: 12178
Military Educators & Counselors Association   Vol 1: 12276
MTM Association for Standards and Research   Vol 1: 12477
National Association of Social Workers   Vol 1: 13317
National Association of Student Personnel Administrators   Vol 1: 13331
National Association of Television Program Executives International   Vol 1: 13339
National Business Forms Association   Vol 1: 13510
National Cable Television Association   Vol 1: 13512
National Catholic Band Association   Vol 1: 13535
National Council of La Raza   Vol 1: 13744
National District Attorneys Association   Vol 1: 13861
National Kidney Foundation   Vol 1: 14273
National Marine Educators' Association   Vol 1: 14332
National Organization of Human Service Education   Vol 1: 14429
National Rehabilitation Association   Vol 1: 14587
National Religious Broadcasters   Vol 1: 14604
National Religious Broadcasters   Vol 1: 14604
National Trappers Association   Vol 1: 14929
North American Society for the Psychology of Sport and Physical Activity   Vol 1: 15455
Paralyzed Veterans of America   Vol 1: 15935
President's Committee on Employment of People with Disabilities   Vol 1: 16390
Professional Grounds Management Society   Vol 1: 16488
Puppeteers of America   Vol 1: 16591
Radio and Television News Directors Association   Vol 1: 16638
Radio Club of America   Vol 1: 16649
Remote Sensing Society   Vol 2: 3845
Royal Scottish Geographical Society   Vol 2: 10634
Society of Cable Television Engineers   Vol 1: 17795
Society of Insurance Research   Vol 1: 17862
Southeastern Library Association   Vol 1: 18195
Specialized Carriers and Rigging Association   Vol 1: 18297
SPIE - The International Society for Optical Engineers   Vol 1: 18326
Stage Directors and Choreographers Foundation   Vol 1: 18443
United States Boomerangs   Vol 1: 19048
USA Track and Field   Vol 1: 19954
Women's Sports Foundation   Vol 1: 20431
WPC Club   Vol 1: 20546
Presidents Award
  American Society of Law and Medicine   Vol 1: 4650
  Building Owners and Managers Association International   Vol 1: 6612
  Midwest Archives Conference   Vol 1: 12268
Presidents' Award
  British Psychological Society   Vol 2: 2490
  Committee of Presidents of Statistical Societies   Vol 1: 8036
  Institute of Management Accountants, Inc.   Vol 1: 10394
  National Water Safety Congress   Vol 1: 14983
The President's Award   Vol. 2: 3870
President's Award for Association Excellence   Vol. 1: 18113
President's Award for Distinguished Federal Civilian Service   Vol. 1: 19484
President's Award for Educational Excellence   Vol. 1: 19224
President's Award for Exceptional Service   Vol. 1: 19485
President's Award for Merit   Vol. 1: 17872
President's Award for Outstanding Performance   Vol. 1: 8843
President's Award for Outstanding Service   Vol. 1: 5008
President's Award for Pride of Performance   Vol. 2: 9995
President's Award for Services to Chess   Vol. 2: 2313
Presidents' Award for the AFRES   Vol. 1: 251
President's Award for the Outstanding Conference Paper   Vol. 1: 13918
President's Award (Israel)   Vol. 2: 4614
President's Award of Excellence, Honor and Merit   Vol. 1: 4647
Presidents Award of Merit   Vol. 1: 5969
President's Award to Outstanding Member Clubs   Vol. 1: 15011
President's Awards
  Horatio Alger Society   Vol. 1: 311
  American School Food Service Association   Vol 1: 3998
  Association of Government Accountants   Vol 1: 5821
  Chesapeake and Ohio Historical Society   Vol 1: 7582
  Federation of Nova Scotia Heritage   Vol 1: 9144
  Geological Society   Vol 2: 2926
  United States Harness Writers Association   Vol 1: 19385
President's Certificate of Merit Award   Vol. 1: 7477
President's Chris Award   Vol. 1: 9191
President's Citation
  Aerospace Medical Association   Vol. 1: 173
  American Association of Homes for the Aging   Vol 1: 1007
  Manhattan College   Vol 1: 12028
  Society for Imaging Science and Technology   Vol 1: 17506
  Society for Mining, Metallurgy, and Exploration   Vol 1: 17572
President's Citation for Service to the Public   Vol. 1: 3025
President's Club   Vol. 1: 20225
President's Commendation for Brave Conduct   Vol. 2: 7256
President's Committee Book Award   Vol. 1: 16391
President's Conservation Achievement Award   Vol. 1: 15081
President's Continuing Education Grant   Vol. 1: 1384
President's Council Award of Distinction   Vol. 1: 15351
President's Cup
  English Vineyards Association   Vol. 2: 2796
  Society of Ornamental Turners   Vol 2: 4457
  Society of Plastics Engineers   Vol 1: 17988
  Sports Car Club of America   Vol 1: 18399
President's Cup (National Sweepstakes Champion)   Vol. 1: 15481
President's Diploma of Honour   Vol. 2: 7436
President's Distinguished Service Award   Vol. 1: 20277
President's "E" Award for Exports Program   Vol. 1: 19095
President's "E Star" Award   Vol. 1: 19096
President's Environment and Conservation Challenge Awards   Vol. 1: 19336
President's Environmental Merit Awards Program   Vol. 1: 19331
President's Environmental Youth Awards   Vol. 1: 19331
President's Essay Prize   Vol. 2: 3967
President's Exhibit Award   Vol. 1: 18019
President's Exhibitor Trophy   Vol. 1: 2384

President's Fellowship Vol. 1: 4199
President's Fellowship Program Vol. 1: 19740
President's Gold Medal Vol. 2: 7559
President's Grant-In-Aid Award Vol. 1: 491
President's Honors Awards Vol. 1: 17004
President's International Trophy Vol. 2: 4109
President's Leadership Award
  National Association of Emergency Medical Technicians Vol. 1: 13097
  National Council on Community Services and Continuing Education Vol 1: 13797
President's Medal
  Bowling Proprietors' Association of America Vol. 1: 6497
  British Ecological Society Vol 2: 2334
  Ergonomics Society Vol 2: 2806
  Municipal Art Society of New York Vol 1: 12491
  National Press Photographers Association Vol 1: 14526
  Niagara University Vol 1: 15380
  Photogrammetric Society Vol 2: 3783
  Society of Chemical Industry Vol 2: 4421
  Society of Engineers Vol 2: 4443
President's Medal for Merit Vol. 1: 7872
President's Medallion Vol. 1: 11972
President's Merit Awards Vol. 1: 12659
President's Modal Awards Vol. 1: 1204
President's National Leadership Vol. 1: 441
President's National Medal of Science Vol. 1: 14687
President's New Researcher's Award Vol. 1: 5439
Presidents Paper Trophy Award Vol. 2: 3508
President's Pin Award Vol. 1: 9116
President's Plaque Vol. 1: 16477
President's Plaques Vol. 1: 8209
President's Points Award Vol. 1: 4223
President's Postdoctoral Fellowship Program Vol. 1: 19740
President's Prize
  Chartered Institution of Building Services Engineers Vol. 2: 2596
  Hydrographic Society Vol 2: 3035
  Institution of Engineers, Australia Vol 2: 480
  Ottawa Field-Naturalists' Club Vol 1: 15853
  Photogrammetric Society Vol 2: 3784
Presidents' Prize Vol. 1: 11896
President's Prize of the International Association for Mathematical Geology Vol. 1: 10650
President's Pro Bono Service Award Vol. 1: 18468
President's Public Service Award Vol. 1: 15081
President's Shield Vol. 1: 7242
President's Special Achievement Award Vol. 1: 14579
President's Stewardship Award Vol. 1: 15082
President's Team Award Vol. 1: 17824
President's Trophy
  American Trucking Association Vol. 1: 4928
  British Hang Gliding Association Vol 2: 12159
  Canadian Interuniversity Athletic Union Vol 1: 6983
  Confederate Stamp Alliance Vol 1: 8113
  International 210 Association Vol 1: 10579
  International Council of Graphic Design Associations Vol 2: 3396
  National Association of Professional Baseball Leagues Vol 1: 13245
Presidents' Trophy Vol. 1: 14175
President's Trophy - Papers Award Vol. 2: 3487

President's Volunteer Action Awards Vol. 1: 16300
Presiding Bishop's Award for Distinguished Service Vol. 1: 5785
Presidio La Bahia Award Vol. 1: 18147
Press Language Prize Vol. 2: 12076
Press Prize Vol. 2: 9884
Press Prize for Broadcasters Vol. 2: 11926
Pressman Award; Jeffrey Vol. 1: 16308
Pressure Vessel and Piping Award Vol. 1: 4700
Presteel Award Vol. 1: 16379
Preston Award; NEMRA Manufacturer of the Year - Thomas F. Vol. 1: 13886
Preston Personal Service Award; Harold Kramer - John Vol. 1: 3859
Prestwich Medal Vol. 2: 2927
Prestwich; Prix Vol. 2: 5313
Prete; Premio Luigi Vol. 2: 8040
Pretoria International Exhibition of Photography Vol. 2: 10910
Preventive Law Prize Award Vol. 1: 13568
Prevot; Fondation Andre-Romain Vol. 2: 5491
Price Annual Chapter Award; John M. Vol. 1: 15935
Price Award; Derek Vol. 1: 9952
Price Award; Edward B. Vol. 1: 20233
Price Chapter Award; John M. Vol. 1: 15938
Price Medal Vol. 2: 3942
Price Oration; Joseph Vol. 1: 2207
Priddle Medal; R.A. Vol. 2: 463
Priestley Award; Joseph Vol. 1: 8644
Priestley Medal Vol. 1: 1572
Priestley Memorial Medal; H. T. Vol. 2: 407
Prijs A. Spinoy Vol. 2: 1372
Prijs de Vlaamse Gids Vol. 2: 1374
Prijs der Nederlandse Letteren Vol. 2: 9552
Prijs Kunst en Educatie Vol. 2: 9333
Prijs Simone Bergmans Vol. 2: 949
Prijs van de Kritiek Vol. 2: 9360
Prijs van de Nederlandse Kinderjury Vol. 2: 9367
Prijs voor Meesterschap Vol. 2: 9630
Prijs voor wetenschappelijk Werk van de Stad Lier Vol. 2: 1382
Primary Care Award Vol. 1: 13060
PRIMA's Risk Management Achievement Awards Vol. 1: 16581
Prime Contractor of the Year Vol. 1: 19601
Prime Minister's Prize Vol. 2: 7907
Prime Minister's Prize for Composition Vol. 2: 7908
Prime Movers Committee Award Vol. 1: 4701
Primo Scolastico di Raccordo Vol. 2: 8014
Prince Albert Ier de Monaco; Prix Vol. 2: 4872
Prince Award; Morton Vol. 1: 17436
Prince, M.D. Award; Morton Vol. 1: 10232
Prince of Asturias Prizes Vol. 2: 11248
Prince of Wales Award for Industrial Innovation and Production Vol. 2: 2770
Prince of Wales' Awards Vol. 2: 12183
Prince of Wales Bowl; U.S. Match Racing Championship - Vol. 1: 19538
Prince of Wales Trophy Vol. 1: 14176
Prince Peter Award; H.R.H. Vol. 2: 1164
Prince Philip Medal Vol. 2: 2628
Prince Philip Prize Vol. 2: 4658
Prince Philip Prize for the Designer of the Year Vol. 2: 2742
Prince Rainier III; Grand Prix de S. A. S. Le Vol. 2: 9310
Prince Takamado Award Vol. 2: 8608
Princeps Cantorum Vol. 2: 12177
Princesse Grace; Prix Fondation Vol. 2: 9310
Princeton Series of Contemporary Poets Vol. 1: 16408

Principado de Asturias Prize Vol. 2: 11252
Principal's Leadership Award Vol. 1: 13311
Pringle Award; Thomas Vol. 2: 10852
Prins Bernhard Fonds Monumenten Prijs Vol. 2: 9573
Prins Bernhard Fonds Museum Prijs Vol. 2: 9574
Print Club Annual International Competition Vol. 1: 16410
Print Framing Competition Vol. 1: 16504
Print Media Award Vol. 1: 11195
Printing Culture Prize Vol. 2: 8610
Printing Ink Pioneer Vol. 1: 13238
Printmaker in Residence Fellowship Vol. 2: 7854
Prints and the Paper Vol. 1: 17027
Prints, Drawings and Photographs Exhibition Vol. 1: 5255
Prinz Wilhelm Obedience Award (The Willie Award) Vol. 1: 9609
Prisbelonning - Eydes Pris Vol. 2: 9954
Prisoner of War Medal Vol. 1: 19184
Pritzker Architecture Prize Vol. 1: 16422
Private Company Recognition Award Vol. 1: 3942
Private Enterprise Essay Contest for College Students Vol. 1: 5113
Private Enterprise Exemplar Medal Vol. 1: 9405
Private Enterprise Recognition Award Vol. 1: 3942
Private Sector Partnership Award Vol. 1: 3942
Prix 2000 SG Vol. 2: 6384
Prix a l'Etudiant Medaille d'Or de l'Internat Vol. 2: 4804
Prix a un Etudiant de l'Ecole Dentaire Vol. 2: 4805
Prix a un Etudiant en Chirurgie Vol. 2: 4806
Prix Achille Fould-Stirbey Vol. 2: 5353
Prix Achille Leclere Vol. 2: 5354
Prix Adelson Castiau Vol. 2: 977
Prix Adolf Bentinck Vol. 2: 6160
Prix Adolphe Crevecoeur Vol. 2: 1350
Prix Adolphe Noel-des-Vergers Vol. 2: 5433
Prix Adolphe Wetrems Vol. 2: 1006
Prix Adrien Constantin de Magny Vol. 2: 5682
Prix Adrien Duvand Vol. 2: 5713
Prix Agathon De Potter Vol. 2: 1007
Prix Aime Cotton Vol. 2: 6366
Prix Aimee et Raymond Mande Vol. 2: 4807
Prix Air France/Ville de Paris Vol. 2: 6146
Prix Alberic Rocheron Vol. 2: 5807
Prix Albert Brachet Vol. 2: 1008
Prix Albert Counson Vol. 2: 1284
Prix Albert-Emile Francoeur Vol. 1: 18439
Prix Albert Hennequin Vol. 2: 6268
Prix Albert Londres Vol. 2: 4940
Prix Albert-Pierre-Jean Dustin Vol. 2: 1323
Prix Albert-Tessier Vol. 1: 16611
Prix Alcan du court metrage Vol. 1: 6024
Prix Alcan du long metrage Vol. 1: 6024
Prix Alex Pasquier Vol. 2: 1040
Prix Alexander Straetmans Vol. 2: 1324
Prix Alexandre Dumas Deauville - Trouville Vol. 2: 6244
Prix Alfred Croiset Vol. 2: 5434
Prix Alfred Droin Vol. 2: 6269
Prix Alfred Dutens Vol. 2: 5435
Prix Alfred-Joseph Lawrence Vol. 1: 18439
Prix Alfred Kastler Vol. 2: 5271
Prix Alfred Nee Vol. 2: 5808
Prix Alfred Verdaguer
  Institut de France Vol. 2: 5336
  Institut de France - Academie des Beaux Arts Vol 2: 5355

Institut de France - Academie des Sciences Vol 2: 5683
Institut de France - Academie Francaise Vol 2: 5809
Prix Alice Louis Barthou Vol. 2: 5810
Prix Alioune Diop pour les Lettres Africaine Vol. 2: 10691
Prix Alix Charlier-Anciaux Vol. 2: 1291
Prix Allier de Hauteroche Vol. 2: 5436
Prix ALPHA de la Nouvelle Vol. 2: 4900
Prix Alphonse Cellier Vol. 2: 5356
Prix Alphonse de Neuville et Sanford Saltus Vol. 2: 5357
Prix Alvarenga de Piauhy Vol. 2: 1325
Prix Alvine-Belisle Vol. 1: 6021
Prix AMADE-UNESCO Vol. 2: 9322
Prix Ambatielos Vol. 2: 5437
Prix Amelie Marcel Vol. 2: 4808
Prix Amerlinck Vol. 2: 944
Prix Amiral Castex Vol. 2: 5230
Prix Ampere d'Electricite de France Vol. 2: 5684
Prix Anais Segalas Vol. 2: 5811
Prix Andre Arfvidson Vol. 2: 5352
Prix Andre Barde Vol. 2: 6396
Prix Andre Barre
 Institut de France - Academie Francaise Vol. 2: 5812
 Societe des Gens de Lettres de France Vol 2: 6270
Prix Andre Batel-Rouvier Vol. 2: 4809
Prix Andre Caplet Vol. 2: 5358
Prix Andre-Guerin Vol. 1: 17383
Prix Andre Jullien du Breuil Vol. 2: 5813
Prix Andre Lequeux
 Institut de France Vol. 2: 5337
 Institut de France - Academie des Sciences Morales et Politiques Vol 2: 5714
Prix Andre Leroux Vol. 1: 6025
Prix Andre Lichtwitz Vol. 2: 5942
Prix Andre Mouezy-Eon Vol. 2: 6397
Prix Andre Praga Vol. 2: 1292
Prix Andres Bello Vol. 2: 11751
Prix Anick Campion-Guillaumet et Bernard Guillaumet Vol. 2: 6323
Prix Anime Vol. 1: 16433
Prix Anne de Amodio Vol. 2: 6110
Prix Annuel de Poesie Vol. 2: 5814
Prix Anonyme Vol. 2: 1326
Prix Antoine et Claude Beclere Vol. 2: 4810
Prix Antoine Girard Vol. 2: 5815
Prix Antoine Grandmaison Vol. 2: 4892
Prix Antoine Meillet Vol. 2: 5438
Prix Antoine-Nicolas Bailly Vol. 2: 5359
Prix Anton Bergmann Vol. 2: 978
Prix Antonin Artaud Vol. 2: 4932
Prix Antony Valabregue Vol. 2: 5816
Prix Aram Sayabalian Vol. 2: 6271
Prix Armand Blanc Vol. 2: 1177
Prix Armand Frappier Vol. 1: 16617
Prix Ars Electronica Vol. 2: 772
Prix Art Manzelli Vol. 2: 5083
Prix Arthur De Greef Vol. 2: 951
Prix Artois - Baillet Latour de la Sante Vol. 2: 1327
Prix Arvid Berghman Vol. 2: 945
Prix Ary Scheffer Vol. 2: 5360
Prix Athanase-David Vol. 1: 16612
Prix Atlantique Vol. 2: 1233
Prix au Merite Motocycliste Vol. 2: 11811
Prix Audiffred Vol. 2: 5715
Prix Auguste Beernaert Vol. 2: 1282
Prix Auguste Capdeville (De Beziers) Vol. 2: 5817
Prix Auguste Durand et Edouard Ordonneau Vol. 2: 5361
Prix Auguste Gerard Vol. 2: 5716

Prix Auguste Michot Vol. 2: 1293
Prix Auguste Sacre Vol. 2: 1009
Prix Auguste Secretan Vol. 2: 4811
Prix Auguste Teirlinck Vol. 2: 979
Prix Aujourd'hui Vol. 2: 6162
Prix Auvergne Vol. 2: 6442
Prix Bagdad de la Culture Arabe Vol. 2: 6410
Prix Balleroy
 Institut de France Vol. 2: 5338
 Institut de France - Academie des Beaux Arts Vol 2: 5362
Prix Balleroy Vol. 2: 5818
Prix Balzac Vol. 2: 6248
Prix Barbier Vol. 2: 5303
Prix Baron Horta Vol. 2: 952
Prix Baron Van Ertborn Vol. 2: 1010
Prix Barrabe Vol. 2: 5304
Prix Bastien-Lepage Vol. 2: 5363
Prix Baudelaire Vol. 2: 6272
Prix Beaubien Vol. 1: 5757
Prix Bellion Vol. 2: 5678
Prix Benevolat Canada Vol. 1: 6719
Prix Benjamin Sulte Vol. 1: 17380
Prix Benjamin Valz Vol. 2: 5681
Prix Bernard Ladougne Vol. 2: 4812
Prix Bernard Versele Vol. 2: 1219
Prix Berriat Saint-Prix Vol. 2: 5717
Prix Berthe Pean Vol. 2: 4813
Prix biennal Marcel Thiebaut Vol. 2: 6273
Prix Bigot de Morogues Vol. 2: 5718
Prix Biguet Vol. 2: 5819
Prix Blaise des Vosges Vol. 2: 5719
Prix Blaise Pascal du GAMNI-SMAI Vol. 2: 5685
Prix Blanche Bendahan Vol. 2: 6274
Prix Bordin Vol. 2: 5364
Prix Bordin
 Institut de France - Academie des Inscriptions et Belle-Lettres Vol. 2: 5439
 Institut de France - Academie des Sciences Morales et Politiques Vol 2: 5720
 Institut de France - Academie Francaise Vol 2: 5820
Prix Botiaux-Dulac Vol. 2: 5339
Prix Botta Vol. 2: 5821
Prix Boudenoot Vol. 2: 5822
Prix Breaute Vol. 2: 5365
Prix Brieux Vol. 2: 5823
Prix Brillat-Savarin Vol. 2: 4791
Prix Brizard Vol. 2: 5366
Prix Broquette-Gonin Vol. 2: 5824
Prix Brunet Vol. 2: 5440
Prix C. Douglas Taylor Vol. 1: 7123
Prix Calixa-Lavallee Vol. 1: 17384
Prix Calmann-Levy Vol. 2: 5825
Prix Campion - Guillaumet Vol. 2: 6275
Prix Canada pour l'excellence en affaires Vol. 1: 10169
Prix Canal Vol. 2: 5175
Prix Cancer Vol. 2: 4814
Prix Capuran Vol. 2: 5826
Prix Cardinal Grente Vol. 2: 5827
Prix Carlier Vol. 2: 5721
Prix Carlos Calvo Vol. 2: 11751
Prix Carton de Wiart Vol. 2: 1294
Prix Catenacci Vol. 2: 5367
Prix Cazes-Brasserie Lipp Vol. 2: 6164
Prix CCRH Vol. 1: 7118
Prix Celine Vol. 2: 6232
Prix Ch. M. Tornov-Loeffler Vol. 2: 5368
Prix Champlain Vol. 1: 8183
Prix Charles Abella Vol. 2: 5352
Prix Charles Achard Vol. 2: 4815
Prix Charles and Marguerite Diehl Vol. 2: 5441
Prix Charles Blanc Vol. 2: 5828

Prix Charles Bouchard Vol. 2: 5678
Prix Charles Caty Vol. 2: 953
Prix Charles Clermont-Ganneau Vol. 2: 5442
Prix Charles Dupin Vol. 2: 5722
Prix Charles Duvivier Vol. 2: 980
Prix Charles Lagrange Vol. 2: 1011
Prix Charles Lambert Vol. 2: 5723
Prix Charles Lemaire Vol. 2: 1012
Prix Charles Leveque Vol. 2: 5724
Prix Charles Lyon-Caen Vol. 2: 5725
Prix Charles Zwickert Vol. 2: 5042
Prix Chartier Vol. 2: 5369
Prix Chateaubriand Vol. 2: 5048
Prix Chaudesaigues Vol. 2: 5370
Prix Chavasse de la SFA Vol. 2: 6351
Prix Chavasse - GALF Vol. 2: 6351
Prix Chimie Vol. 2: 4816
Prix Chomedey-de-Maisonneuve Vol. 1: 17385
Prix Chretiente d'Orient Vol. 2: 5011
Prix Christie's Vol. 2: 6467
Prix CIBA-GEIGY Vol. 2: 4817
Prix Cinema du Reel Vol. 2: 5032
Prix CINOA Vol. 2: 3391
Prix CIRTEF de Corealisation Vol. 2: 11776
Prix Cites T.V. Vol. 2: 5175
Prix Ciudad de Huesca Vol. 2: 11236
Prix Claire Virenque Vol. 2: 5829
Prix Claude - Rostand Vol. 2: 6406
Prix Claude Aubry Vol. 1: 10805
Prix Claude Berthault
 Institut de France - Academie des Beaux Arts Vol. 2: 5371
 Institut de France - Academie des Sciences Morales et Politiques Vol 2: 5726
Prix Claude Raphael-Leygues Vol. 2: 5372
Prix Claude Sernet Vol. 2: 4933
Prix Clement Marot de Poesie Vol. 2: 6502
Prix COGEDIM Vol. 2: 5040
Prix Colette Vol. 2: 11721
Prix Colmont Vol. 2: 5373
Prix Comite Albert Roussel Vol. 2: 5188
Prix Constant Dauguet Vol. 2: 5830
Prix Constant de Horion Vol. 2: 1041
Prix Constant Montald Vol. 2: 954
Prix Corbay Vol. 2: 5727
Prix Cordier Vol. 2: 4818
Prix CORESTA Vol. 2: 5082
Prix Cornelis - Lebegue Vol. 2: 1328
Prix Cosmos 2000 Vol. 2: 6079
Prix Coste Vol. 2: 6389
Prix Courage Quotidien Vol. 2: 5098
Prix C.P.S. Vol. 2: 9699
Prix Credit Suisse de la Creation technique, et industrielle a Geneve Vol. 2: 11684
Prix Crouzet Vol. 2: 5728
Prix d'Aeronautique Vol. 2: 4903
Prix Dagnan-Bouveret Vol. 2: 5374
Prix Daniel Guinier Vol. 2: 6367
Prix Danube Festival, Bratislava Vol. 2: 10780
Prix d'Aschen-Presles Vol. 2: 5340
Prix d'Astronautique Vol. 2: 4904
Prix d'Aumale Vol. 2: 5341
Prix d'Aumale
 Institut de France - Academie des Sciences Vol. 2: 5686
 Institut de France - Academie des Sciences Morales et Politiques Vol 2: 5729
Prix de Biologie Alfred Kastler Vol. 2: 5271
Prix de Boelpaepe Vol. 2: 1013
Prix de Bruxelles Vol. 2: 1089
Prix de Centre International Humanae Vitae Vol. 2: 5015
Prix de Chenier Vol. 2: 5443
Prix de Coincy Vol. 2: 4993
Prix de Compositeur de l'AMS Vol. 2: 11658

Prix de Composition Musicale   Vol. 2: 9311
Prix de Composition Musicale Reine Marie Jose   Vol. 2: 11896
Prix de Dessin Pierre David - Weill   Vol. 2: 5375
Prix de Fondation Charles Pitou   Vol. 2: 6321
Prix de Fondation Duchesse de Rohan   Vol. 2: 6324
Prix de Fondation Erlanger   Vol. 2: 6310
Prix de Fondation Eugene Le Mouel   Vol. 2: 6318
Prix de Fondation Fouraignan   Vol. 2: 6312
Prix de Fondation Georges Lafenestre   Vol. 2: 6317
Prix de Fondation Labbe-Vauquelin   Vol. 2: 6325
Prix de Gravure Lacouriere   Vol. 2: 5198
Prix de Grenoble   Vol. 2: 6302
Prix de Jazz Alcan   Vol. 1: 9173
Prix de Joest
   Institut de France - Academie des Sciences Morales et Politiques   Vol. 2: 5730
   Institut de France - Academie Francaise   Vol 2: 5831
Prix de Journalisme Scientifique   Vol. 1: 7126
Prix de Jouy   Vol. 2: 5832
Prix de la Banque Royale   Vol. 1: 16933
Prix de la Belgica   Vol. 2: 1014
Prix de la Belgique   Vol. 2: 6158
Prix de la Biographie   Vol. 2: 5833
Prix de la Caisse d'Epargne   Vol. 2: 5175
Prix de la Caisse Nationale des Monuments Historiques   Vol. 2: 6467
Prix de la Compagnie d'assurances la Constellation   Vol. 1: 7121
Prix de la CPPQ   Vol. 1: 8286
Prix de la Critique
   Association Quebecoise des Critiques de Cinema   Vol. 1: 6027
   Institut de France - Academie Francaise   Vol 2: 5834
Prix de la Critique Internationale   Vol. 2: 6944
Prix de la critique internationale   Vol. 1: 6026
Prix de la Critique Poetique   Vol. 2: 6326
Prix de la Fonction Publique du Canada pour Services Insignes   Vol. 1: 6723
Prix de la Fondation Athena   Vol. 2: 5687
Prix de la Fondation de la Maison de la Chimie   Vol. 2: 5201
Prix de la Fondation du 150e anniversaire de la Societe royale des Sciences de Liege   Vol. 2: 1368
Prix de la Fondation Emile Benveniste   Vol. 2: 5444
Prix de la Fondation Emile Senart   Vol. 2: 5445
Prix de la Fondation Florence Gould   Vol. 2: 5376
Prix de la Fondation Fyssen   Vol. 2: 5301
Prix de la Fondation George Montefiore   Vol. 2: 1046
Prix de la Fondation Jean-Bernard Verlot   Vol. 2: 4949
Prix de la Fondation Louis de Clercq   Vol. 2: 5446
Prix de la Fondation Mumm pour la Presse Ecrite   Vol. 2: 5101
Prix de la Fondation Paul Cailleux   Vol. 2: 5058
Prix de la Fondation pour la Recherche Medicale   Vol. 2: 5263
Prix de la Fondation Xavier - Bernard   Vol. 2: 4770
Prix de La Fons-Melicocq   Vol. 2: 5447
Prix de la Fraternite   Vol. 2: 6124
Prix de La Grange   Vol. 2: 5448
Prix de la Jeunesse   Vol. 2: 5249

Prix de la Liberte   Vol. 2: 6155
Prix de la Meilleure Initiative Franco-Americaine   Vol. 2: 5208
Prix de la Meilleure Nouvelle Francophone   Vol. 2: 4883
Prix de la Meilleure une Journalistique - Les Libertes d'Or   Vol. 2: 5216
Prix de la Memoire   Vol. 2: 5206
Prix de la Mutualite Interprofessionnelle   Vol. 2: 4819
Prix de la Nouvelle
   Institut de France - Academie Francaise   Vol. 2: 5835
   Union Litteraire et Artistique de France   Vol 2: 6443
   Writing Doctors Association   Vol 2: 6505
Prix de la Nouvelle de la France   Vol. 2: 5253
Prix de la Press Poetique   Vol. 2: 6327
Prix de la Presse des radiodiffuseurs   Vol. 2: 11926
Prix de la Presse Libre - Les Libertes d'Or   Vol. 2: 5217
Prix de la Promotion Cinematographique   Vol. 2: 6328
Prix de la Promotion Poetique   Vol. 2: 6329
Prix de la Promotion Radiophonique de la Poesie   Vol. 2: 6330
Prix de la Promotion Televisuelle de la Poesie   Vol. 2: 6331
Prix de la Prose Poetique   Vol. 2: 6322
Prix de la Prudentielle d'Angleterre, Compagnie d'Assurance   Vol. 1: 7121
Prix de la Resistance   Vol. 2: 5044
Prix de la Scam   Vol. 2: 5032
Prix de la Societe des Eaux Minerales d'Evian-des-Bains   Vol. 2: 4820
Prix de la Societe Francaise de Gravure   Vol. 2: 5377
Prix de la Ville de Lausanne   Vol. 2: 11793
Prix de la Ville de Paris   Vol. 2: 4821
Prix de l'Academie des Sciences, Arts et Belles Lettres de Dijon   Vol. 2: 4795
Prix de l'Academie des Sciences du Tiers Monde   Vol. 2: 8910
Prix de l'Academie Mallarme   Vol. 2: 4800
Prix de l'Academie Nationale de Medecine   Vol. 2: 4822
Prix de l'adjudant Hubert Lefebvre   Vol. 2: 1015
Prix de l'Afrique Mediterraneenne/Maghreb   Vol. 2: 4922
Prix de l'Age d'Or   Vol. 2: 1352
Prix de l'American Women's Group in Paris   Vol. 2: 6467
Prix de Lamothe   Vol. 2: 5305
Prix de l'APERR   Vol. 2: 4966
Prix de L'Associati on Suisse Pour le Film Scientifique   Vol. 2: 11793
Prix de l'Association des Musiciens de Geneve   Vol. 2: 11774
Prix de Lausanne   Vol. 2: 11725
Prix de l'Ecole Centrale   Vol. 2: 5688
Prix de l'Education Alfred Weichselbaum   Vol. 2: 5124
Prix de l'enseignement   Vol. 2: 6329
Prix de L'EPFL   Vol. 2: 11793
Prix de l'Essai   Vol. 2: 5836
Prix de l'Histoire Vecue   Vol. 2: 6503
Prix de l'Illustration des Arts   Vol. 2: 5049
Prix de l'Information Scientifique   Vol. 2: 5689
Prix de l'Institut Francais du Petrole   Vol. 2: 5690
Prix de Litterature des Alpes et du Jura   Vol. 2: 4923
Prix de Litterature Regionaliste Henri Baehelin   Vol. 2: 6276

Prix de l'Union Nationale des Caisses Chirurgicales Mutualistes   Vol. 2: 4823
Prix de M. et Mme. Louis Marin   Vol. 2: 5837
Prix de Madame Claude Berthault   Vol. 2: 5691
Prix de Merite   Vol. 1: 7084
Prix de Musique Folklorique de Radio Bratislava   Vol. 2: 10778
Prix de Musique International Arthur Honegger   Vol. 2: 5197
Prix de Pays Protestants   Vol. 2: 6153
Prix de Peinture Andre et Berthe Noufflard   Vol. 2: 5199
Prix de Poesie   Vol. 2: 5212
Prix de Poesie Louis Montalte   Vol. 2: 6277
Prix de Poesie Max d'Arthez   Vol. 2: 6444
Prix de Poesie Roger Kowalski   Vol. 2: 6475
Prix de poesie Rutebeuf   Vol. 2: 6075
Prix de Poesie SEPIA   Vol. 2: 6211
Prix de Portrait Paul-Louis Weiller   Vol. 2: 5378
Prix de Presse FNI   Vol. 2: 1198
Prix de Promotion Internationale   Vol. 2: 11805
Prix de Psychologie   Vol. 2: 981
Prix de Rome   Vol. 2: 9578
Prix de Rome in Architecture   Vol. 1: 6748
Prix de Saint-Genois   Vol. 2: 982
Prix de Sciences Humaines Esdras-Minville   Vol. 1: 17386
Prix de Soliste de l'AMS   Vol. 2: 11659
Prix de Soussay   Vol. 2: 5379
Prix de Soussay   Vol. 2: 5838
Prix de Stassart   Vol. 2: 983
Prix de Stassart pour Histoire Nationale   Vol. 2: 984
Prix de These   Vol. 2: 5255
Prix de Traduction de Litterature Enfantine   Vol. 2: 4991
Prix de Traduction Pierre-Francois Caille   Vol. 2: 6278
Prix de West   Vol. 1: 13837
Prix Decouverte du Japon   Vol. 2: 4907
Prix Delahautemaison   Vol. 2: 5264
Prix Delalande-Guerineau   Vol. 2: 5449
Prix Demeures et Chateaux du Soleil   Vol. 2: 6467
Prix Demolombe   Vol. 2: 5731
Prix d'Encouragement a la recherche en Chimie Therapeutique   Vol. 2: 6238
Prix Denis Thienpont   Vol. 2: 1329
Prix Denise-Pelletier   Vol. 1: 16613
Prix Dermatologie Immunologie   Vol. 2: 4824
Prix Dermatologie Syphiligraphie   Vol. 2: 4825
Prix des Ambassadeurs   Vol. 2: 9434
Prix des Bibliotheques   Vol. 2: 5032
Prix des Cathedrales   Vol. 2: 5380
Prix des Chants Perdus   Vol. 2: 6332
Prix des Dames   Vol. 2: 6220
Prix des Delegues   Vol. 2: 6467
Prix des Deux-Magots   Vol. 2: 5002
Prix des droits de l'homme   Vol. 2: 5251
Prix des Fondations Oulmont, Zaval, Dreyfous   Vol. 2: 4826
Prix des Jeunes   Vol. 2: 4905
Prix des Libraires   Vol. 2: 5257
Prix des Maisons de la Presse Prize   Vol. 2: 6106
Prix des Montreal   Vol. 1: 12437
Prix des Producteurs de Cinema Francais   Vol. 2: 5175
Prix des Sciences Biologiques et Medicales   Vol. 2: 5050
Prix des Sciences de la Mer   Vol. 2: 5692
Prix des Sciences Economiques et Sociales   Vol. 2: 5051

Prix des Sciences Physiques et Mathematiques   Vol. 2: 5052
Prix des Timbres de Paques   Vol. 1: 7120
Prix Deschiens   Vol. 2: 4827
Prix Desprez   Vol. 2: 5381
Prix Devouement   Vol. 2: 4828
Prix d'Excellence d'Heritage   Vol. 1: 9910
Prix d'Excellence Environnementale   Vol. 1: 8957
Prix d'excellence Pedagogique   Vol. 1: 18438
Prix d'Excellence pour les Installations   Vol. 1: 7087
Prix d'excellence YTV   Vol. 1: 20622
Prix d'Histoire de la Vallee aux Loups   Vol. 2: 6102
Prix d'Honneur Courage Quotidien   Vol. 2: 5099
Prix Diane Potier-Boes   Vol. 2: 5839
Prix Diderot Universalis   Vol. 2: 5112
Prix Dina Surdin   Vol. 2: 6234
Prix Docteur Albert Belgrand   Vol. 2: 4829
Prix Docteur Binet-Sangle   Vol. 2: 5840
Prix Docteur Darolles   Vol. 2: 4830
Prix Dr. Max-Luthi   Vol. 2: 11885
Prix Dodo   Vol. 2: 5841
Prix Dorothea Klumpke - Isaac Roberts   Vol. 2: 6221
Prix Doublemard   Vol. 2: 5382
Prix Drieu-Cholet   Vol. 2: 4831
Prix Drouyn de Lhuys   Vol. 2: 5732
Prix du Baron de Courcel
  Institut de France - Academie des Inscriptions et Belle-Lettres   Vol. 2: 5450
  Institut de France - Academie des Sciences Morales et Politiques   Vol 2: 5733
Prix du Baron de Courcel   Vol. 2: 5842
Prix du Baron de Joest   Vol. 2: 5383
Prix du Baron de Joest   Vol. 2: 5451
Prix du Budget
  Institut de France - Academie des Inscriptions et Belle-Lettres   Vol. 2: 5452
  Institut de France - Academie des Sciences Morales et Politiques   Vol 2: 5734
Prix du Camera Club Liegeois   Vol. 2: 1095
Prix du Canton de Vaud   Vol. 2: 11793
Prix du Centre de Recherches Cliniques et Biologiques sur la Nutritiotion de l'Homme   Vol. 2: 4832
Prix du Chanoine Delpeuch   Vol. 2: 5735
Prix du Cinema Europeen   Vol. 2: 6713
Prix du Cinema - Prix Jean Leduc   Vol. 2: 5843
Prix du Comite Albert Roussel   Vol. 2: 5074
Prix du Commisariat a l'Energie Atomique   Vol. 2: 5693
Prix du Conseil de la Societe   Vol. 2: 4994
Prix du Conte de Noel   Vol. 2: 6445
Prix du court et moyen metrage
  Association Quebecoise des Critiques de Cinema   Vol. 1: 6025
  Association Quebecoise des Critiques de Cinema   Vol 1: 6028
Prix du Court Metrage   Vol. 2: 5032
Prix du Docteur Frans Johnckheere sur l'Historie de la Medecine   Vol. 2: 1330
Prix du Docteur Jules Deminne et sa femme nee Anne Fabry   Vol. 2: 1331
Prix du Docteur Louis de Give de Muache   Vol. 2: 1332
Prix du Docteur Robert Netter   Vol. 2: 4833
Prix du Duc de Loubat   Vol. 2: 5453
Prix du Fonds de Readaptation   Vol. 1: 7116
Prix du GAMS   Vol. 2: 5324
Prix du Gaz de France   Vol. 2: 5694
Prix du Gouverneur General en Conservation   Vol. 1: 18767

Prix du Groupe d'Etudes et de Recherches sur les Lipides et les Lipoproteines   Vol. 2: 6235
Prix du Jeune Conteur ou Nouvelliste   Vol. 2: 6446
Prix du Jeune Ecrivain "BNP" avec Le Monde   Vol. 2: 6438
Prix du Jeune Ecrivain Francophone   Vol. 2: 6439
Prix du Journalism   Vol. 2: 1062
Prix du Journalisme d'Investigation - Les Libertes d'Or   Vol. 2: 5218
Prix du Libraire   Vol. 2: 6329
Prix du Livre de Photographies   Vol. 2: 6190
Prix du Livre Historique d'Investigation - Les Libertes d'Or   Vol. 2: 5219
Prix du Livre Media ou du Livre d'Investigation - Les Libertes d'Or   Vol. 2: 5220
Prix du l'Union Rationaliste   Vol. 2: 6459
Prix du Meilleur Livre Etranger   Vol. 2: 6180
Prix du Ministere de la Jeunesse et des Sports   Vol. 2: 4834
Prix du Mois de la Photo   Vol. 2: 6147
Prix du Palais Litteraire   Vol. 2: 6166
Prix du Patrimoine   Vol. 2: 5032
Prix du PEN Club   Vol. 2: 6156
Prix du Poeme Breton   Vol. 2: 6447
Prix du Poeme Regionaliste   Vol. 2: 6448
Prix du Public   Vol. 2: 5193
Prix du Public du Meilleur Court-Metrage Europeen   Vol. 2: 1241
Prix du Quebec   Vol. 1:
Prix du Reportage Touristique   Vol. 2:
Prix du Roman Emil Zola - Raoul Gain   Vol. 2: 6279
Prix du Salon du Laboratoire   Vol. 2: 6209
Prix du Sonnet de la Pensee Francaise   Vol. 2: 6450
Prix du Statisticien d'Expression Francaise   Vol. 2: 6390
Prix du Syndicat de la Critique Dramatique et Musicale   Vol. 2: 6405
Prix du Theatre   Vol. 2: 5844
Prix du Troisieme Cycle   Vol. 2: 4952
Prix Dubois - Debauney   Vol. 2: 1016
Prix Duc   Vol. 2: 5384
Prix Duchalais   Vol. 2: 5454
Prix Dulac
  Institut de France - Academie des Beaux Arts   Vol. 2: 5385
  Institut de France - Academie des Sciences Morales et Politiques   Vol 2: 5736
Prix Dumas-Millier
  Institut de France - Academie des Beaux Arts   Vol. 2: 5386
  Institut de France - Academie Francaise   Vol 2: 5845
Prix Dupin Aine   Vol. 2: 5737
Prix Durchon-Louvet   Vol. 2: 5846
Prix d'Urologie   Vol. 2: 4835
Prix E. du Cayla-Martin   Vol. 2: 955
Prix Edmond de Selys Longchamps   Vol. 2: 1017
Prix Edmond Drouin   Vol. 2: 5455
Prix Edmond Freville   Vol. 2: 5738
Prix Edmond Girard   Vol. 2: 6222
Prix Edmond Michel   Vol. 2: 6391
Prix Edouard Mailly   Vol. 2: 1018
Prix Edouard Van Beneden   Vol. 2: 1368
Prix Egide Rombaux   Vol. 2: 956
Prix Electrotherapie   Vol. 2: 4836
Prix Elie Faure   Vol. 2: 4985
Prix Elizabeth Mrazik Cleaver pour le meilleur livre d'images canadien   Vol. 1: 10806
Prix Emer de Vattel   Vol. 2: 11751
Prix Emile Augier   Vol. 2: 5847

Prix Emile de Laveleye   Vol. 2: 985
Prix Emile Delannoy-Robbe   Vol. 2: 4837
Prix Emile Faguet   Vol. 2: 5848
Prix Emile Girardeau   Vol. 2: 5739
Prix Emile Hinzelin   Vol. 2: 5849
Prix Emile Laurent   Vol. 2: 1019
Prix Emile Le Senne   Vol. 2: 5456
Prix Emile Mercet   Vol. 2: 6392
Prix Emile-Nelligan   Vol. 1: 18879
Prix Emile Polak   Vol. 2: 1290
Prix Emile Sacre   Vol. 2: 957
Prix Emmanuel Vossaert   Vol. 2: 1295
Prix Enzymologia   Vol. 2: 5525
Prix Ernest Acker   Vol. 2: 958
Prix Ernest Bouvier-Parviliez   Vol. 2: 1283
Prix Ernest Discailles   Vol. 2: 986
Prix Ernest Lemonon   Vol. 2: 5740
Prix Ernest Thorel   Vol. 2: 5741
Prix Ernst Meyer   Vol. 2: 11761
Prix Esclangon   Vol. 2: 6368
Prix Esdras-Minville   Vol. 1: 17386
Prix Estrade Delcros   Vol. 2: 5679
Prix Estrade-Delcros   Vol. 2: 5387
Prix Estrade-Delcros   Vol. 2: 5457
Prix Estrade-Delcros   Vol. 2: 5742
Prix et Fondations Concernant l'Academie de France a Rome   Vol. 2: 5388
Prix Etienne Chabrol   Vol. 2: 4838
Prix Eugene Carriere   Vol. 2: 5850
Prix Eugene Catalan   Vol. 2: 1020
Prix Eugene Colas   Vol. 2: 5851
Prix Eugene Lameere   Vol. 2: 987
Prix Eugene-Le-Roy   Vol. 2: 5241
Prix Eugene Piccard   Vol. 2: 5852
Prix Eugene Piot   Vol. 2: 5389
Prix Eugene Salvan   Vol. 2: 5743
Prix Eugene Schmits   Vol. 2: 1296
Prix Europa   Vol. 2: 5096
Prix Europe et Medecine   Vol. 2: 5937
Prix Europeen de l'ADELF   Vol. 2: 4924
Prix Europeen de l'Essai Charles Veillon   Vol. 2: 11967
Prix Europeens Emile Bernheim   Vol. 2: 1378
Prix Eve Delacroix   Vol. 2: 5853
Prix Exceptionnel du Centenaire Leon Dubois du Rayonnement Francais   Vol. 2: 5053
Prix Fabien   Vol. 2: 5854
Prix Fanny et Maurice Baumont   Vol. 2: 5744
Prix Fauconnier   Vol. 2: 4839
Prix Federation Mondiale des Sourds   Vol. 2: 4765
Prix Felix de Beaujour   Vol. 2: 5745
Prix Felix Denayer   Vol. 2: 1285
Prix Felix Feneon   Vol. 2: 5203
Prix Felix Robin   Vol. 2: 6369
Prix *Femina*   Vol. 2: 6168
Prix Femina Etranger   Vol. 2: 6168
Prix Femina Vacaresco   Vol. 2: 6168
Prix Fernand Mery-Prix Animalier   Vol. 2: 6504
Prix Feydau de Brou   Vol. 2: 5855
Prix FIT de la Traduction Astrid Lindgren   Vol. 2: 823
Prix FIT - UNESCO de la Traduction   Vol. 2: 824
Prix Florent Schmitt   Vol. 2: 5390
Prix Fondation Bernard Hamburger   Vol. 2: 4788
Prix Fondation Pierre Pruvost   Vol. 2: 5306
Prix Fondation Princesse Grace   Vol. 2: 9310
Prix Fondation Richard Lounsbery   Vol. 2: 4789
Prix Fonde par l'Etat   Vol. 2: 5695
Prix Fontannes   Vol. 2: 5307
Prix Foucault   Vol. 2: 6370
Prix Foulon de Vaulx   Vol. 2: 6280
Prix FR3   Vol. 2: 5175

Prix France-Acadie   Vol. 2: 4894
Prix France - Belgique   Vol. 2: 4925
Prix France - Liban   Vol. 2: 4926
Prix France Telecom   Vol. 2: 5696
Prix Frances E. Russell   Vol. 1: 10807
Prix Francis Lieber   Vol. 2: 11751
Prix Franco-Britannique de l'Academie des Sciences   Vol. 2: 5697
Prix Francois Coppee   Vol. 2: 5856
Prix Francois Deruyts   Vol. 2: 1021
Prix Francoise Abella   Vol. 2: 5391
Prix Francqui   Vol. 2: 1156
Prix Franz Cumont   Vol. 2: 988
Prix Franz de Wever   Vol. 2: 1297
Prix Fraternite Gaby Archenbaud   Vol. 2: 6124
Prix Frederic de Martens   Vol. 2: 11751
Prix Frederic et Jean de Vernon   Vol. 2: 5392
Prix Frederic Liebstoeckl   Vol. 2: 5042
Prix Frederic Swarts   Vol. 2: 1022
Prix Friends of VMF   Vol. 2: 6467
Prix Fuji   Vol. 2: 5175
Prix Furtado (de Bayonne)   Vol. 2: 5857
Prix Futura Berlin   Vol. 2: 7074
Prix Futuriste   Vol. 2: 6451
Prix G. Bidault de l'Isle   Vol. 2: 6223
Prix G. Rolin-Jaequemyns   Vol. 2: 11751
Prix G. Zambon   Vol. 2: 1200
Prix Gabriel-Auguste Prost   Vol. 2: 5458
Prix Gabriel Ferrier   Vol. 2: 5393
Prix Gabriel Monod   Vol. 2: 5746
Prix Gabrielle et Camille Flammarion   Vol. 2: 6224
Prix Gallet   Vol. 2: 5747
Prix Gallet et Breton   Vol. 2: 4840
Prix Gandoger   Vol. 2: 4995
Prix Gaston et Mariette Heux   Vol. 2: 1298
Prix Gaston Maspero   Vol. 2: 5459
Prix Gaudry   Vol. 2: 5308
Prix Gazzola   Vol. 2: 6001
Prix Gegner   Vol. 2: 5748
Prix Gemeaux   Vol. 1: 25
Prix Gemini   Vol. 1: 26
Prix General Muteau   Vol. 2: 5749
Prix Genie   Vol. 1: 28
Prix Gentner-Kastler   Vol. 2: 6371
Prix George Garnir   Vol. 2: 1299
Prix Georges Bizet
    Institut de France   Vol. 2: 5342
    Institut de France - Academie des Beaux Arts   Vol 2: 5394
Prix Georges de Beauregard   Vol. 2: 4962
Prix Georges Dupau   Vol. 2: 5858
Prix Georges Goyau   Vol. 2: 5859
Prix Georges Lockem   Vol. 2: 1300
Prix Georges Mauguin   Vol. 2: 5750
Prix Georges Millot   Vol. 2: 5309
Prix Georges Picot   Vol. 2: 5751
Prix Georges Sadoul   Vol. 2: 6170
Prix Georges Vanderlinden   Vol. 2: 1023
Prix Georges Vaxelaire   Vol. 2: 1307
Prix Georges Wildenstein   Vol. 2: 5395
Prix Gerard de Nerval   Vol. 2: 6281
Prix Gerard-Morrisset   Vol. 1: 16614
Prix Gerard Philipe de la Ville de Paris   Vol. 2: 6096
Prix Giles - Corbeil   Vol. 1: 18880
Prix Gilles Nelod   Vol. 2: 1042
Prix Glassco de Traduction   Vol. 1: 11906
Prix GLM   Vol. 2: 4954
Prix Gobert
    Institut de France - Academie des Inscriptions et Belle-Lettres   Vol. 2: 5460
    Institut de France - Academie Francaise   Vol 2: 5860
Prix Goblet d'Alviella   Vol. 2: 989
Prix Goncourt   Vol. 2: 4798

Prix Gosselet   Vol. 2: 5310
Prix Grammaticakis-Neuman   Vol. 2: 5752
Prix Griffuel   Vol. 2: 4942
Prix Grotius   Vol. 2: 11751
Prix Guillaume Apollinaire   Vol. 2: 6172
Prix Guizot   Vol. 2: 5861
Prix Gustave Camus   Vol. 2: 959
Prix Gustave Chaix d'Est Ange   Vol. 2: 5753
Prix Gustave Courtois   Vol. 2: 5396
Prix Gustave-Francois Redon   Vol. 2: 5397
Prix Gustave Le Metais Lariviere Fils (Prix d'Academie)   Vol. 2: 5862
Prix Gustave Mendel   Vol. 2: 5461
Prix Gustave Roussy   Vol. 2: 4841
Prix Gustave Schlumberger   Vol. 2: 5462
Prix Guy-Fregault   Vol. 1: 10207
Prix Halperine-Kaminsky/Societe de Gens de Lettres de France   Vol. 2: 6282
Prix Halphen
    Institut de France - Academie des Sciences Morales et Politiques   Vol. 2: 5754
    Institut de France - Academie Francaise   Vol 2: 5863
Prix Hamoir   Vol. 2: 1333
Prix Harrison   Vol. 1: 16956
Prix Haumont   Vol. 2: 5398
Prix Hector Lefuel   Vol. 2: 5399
Prix Helena Oliveira   Vol. 2: 5188
Prix Helene Porges   Vol. 2: 5864
Prix Helene Rubillard   Vol. 2: 4842
Prix Helene Seguin   Vol. 2: 6333
Prix Henri Baruk   Vol. 2: 4843
Prix Henri Buttgenbach   Vol. 2: 1024
Prix Henri Dauberville   Vol. 2: 5400
Prix Henri Davignon   Vol. 2: 1301
Prix Henri Hertz   Vol. 2: 5204
Prix Henri Jousselin   Vol. 2: 5865
Prix Henri Lavachery   Vol. 2: 990
Prix Henri Lehmann   Vol. 2: 5401
Prix Henri Mondor
    Academie Nationale de Medecine   Vol. 2: 4844
    Institut de France - Academie Francaise   Vol 2: 5866
Prix Henri Rey   Vol. 2: 6225
Prix Henri Texier   Vol. 2: 5755
Prix Henri Texier II   Vol. 2: 5756
Prix Henri Wheaton   Vol. 2: 11751
Prix Henriette Renie   Vol. 2: 5402
Prix Henriette Simont   Vol. 2: 1334
Prix Henry et Mary Jane Mitjavile   Vol. 2: 4845
Prix Henry Fauconnier   Vol. 2: 1335
Prix Henry Franz   Vol. 2: 6283
Prix Herbert Allen Giles   Vol. 2: 5463
Prix Hercule Catenacci
    Institut de France   Vol. 2: 5343
    Institut de France - Academie des Sciences Morales et Politiques   Vol 2: 5757
    Institut de France - Academie Francaise   Vol 2: 5867
Prix Heredia   Vol. 2: 5868
Prix Herman Schoolmeesters   Vol. 2: 991
Prix Holweck   Vol. 2: 6372
Prix Honore Chavee   Vol. 2: 5464
Prix Houllevigue   Vol. 2: 5403
Prix Houllevigue   Vol. 2: 5679
Prix Hubert Gildas   Vol. 2: 6284
Prix Hubert Krains   Vol. 2: 1043
Prix Humoristique Max d'Arthez   Vol. 2: 6452
Prix IBM   Vol. 2: 6373
Prix Ilarie Voronca   Vol. 2: 4934
Prix Injalbert
    Institut de France   Vol. 2: 5344
    Institut de France - Academie des Beaux Arts   Vol 2: 5388
Prix Interallie   Vol. 2: 5022

Prix International Architecture de l'Institut National du Logement   Vol. 2: 1227
Prix International d'Architecture   Vol. 2: 1114
Prix international de la paix (PEN - Quebec)   Vol. 1: 7491
Prix International de la Societe Europeenne de Culture   Vol. 2: 8233
Prix International des Amities Francaises   Vol. 2: 6334
Prix International des Critiques de Disques   Vol. 2: 11663
Prix International du Disque Serge et Olga Koussevitzky   Vol. 2: 11663
Prix International Nathalie Masse   Vol. 2: 5982
Prix Internationaux Dag Hammarskjold   Vol. 2: 1237
Prix Irene Fuerison   Vol. 2: 960
Prix Italia   Vol. 2: 8413
Prix J. J. Berger   Vol. 2: 5404
Prix J. J. Weiss   Vol. 2: 5869
Prix Jack Sarney   Vol. 1: 7122
Prix Jacquard   Vol. 2: 5175
Prix Jacque Gautier   Vol. 2: 4914
Prix Jacqueline Mompezat   Vol. 2: 6335
Prix Jacques Bourcart   Vol. 2: 5311
Prix Jacques Deruyts   Vol. 2: 1025
Prix Jacques Durand   Vol. 2: 5405
Prix Jacques Flach   Vol. 2: 5758
Prix Jacques Lefebvre   Vol. 2: 5130
Prix Jacques Normand   Vol. 2: 6285
Prix Jacques Raphael-Leygues   Vol. 2: 6336
Prix Jansen   Vol. 2: 4846
Prix Janssen   Vol. 2: 6226
Prix Japon - Concours International de Programmes Educatifs   Vol. 2: 8602
Prix Jean-Baptiste Chevallier   Vol. 2: 5759
Prix Jean Bouscatel   Vol. 2: 5870
Prix Jean Dufrenoy   Vol. 2: 4771
Prix Jean Escalle   Vol. 2: 4847
Prix Jean-Etienne Marcel   Vol. 2: 4848
Prix Jean Finot   Vol. 2: 5760
Prix Jean-Francois Coste   Vol. 2: 4849
Prix Jean-Francois Ginestie   Vol. 2: 4850
Prix Jean Jacques Berger
    Institut de France - Academie des Inscriptions et Belle-Lettres   Vol. 2: 5465
    Institut de France - Academie des Sciences Morales et Politiques   Vol 2: 5761
Prix Jean-Jacques Berger   Vol. 2: 5871
Prix Jean Kobs   Vol. 2: 1302
Prix Jean Mace   Vol. 2: 6083
Prix Jean Mermoz   Vol. 2: 5267
Prix Jean Perrin   Vol. 2: 6374
Prix Jean Reynaud
    Institut de France - Academie des Beaux Arts   Vol. 2: 5406
    Institut de France - Academie des Inscriptions et Belle-Lettres   Vol 2: 5466
    Institut de France - Academie des Sciences Morales et Politiques   Vol 2: 5762
    Institut de France - Academie Francaise   Vol 2: 5872
Prix Jean Ricard   Vol. 2: 6375
Prix Jean-Servais Stas   Vol. 2: 1026
Prix Jean Vigo   Vol. 2: 5190
Prix Jeanne Boujassy   Vol. 2: 6286
Prix Jeanne Burdy   Vol. 2: 5345
Prix Jeanne et Maurice Chevassu   Vol. 2: 4851
Prix Jeanne Scialtel   Vol. 2: 5873
Prix Jeune Chercheur   Vol. 2: 6352
Prix Jeune Chercheur IBM   Vol. 2: 6376
Prix Jeunesse International Munchen   Vol. 2: 7076
Prix Joachim Cabot et Louis Delezenne/Prix du GLMMS   Vol. 2: 6077

Prix Jocelyn Chedoudi Vol. 2: 4852
Prix John L. Synge Vol. 1: 16965
Prix John Westlake Vol. 2: 11751
Prix Joliot-Curie Vol. 2: 6377
Prix Jos Albert Vol. 2: 961
Prix Joseph-Antoine Maury Vol. 2: 4853
Prix Joseph De Keyn Vol. 2: 992
Prix Joseph du Teil Vol. 2: 5763
Prix Joseph Dutens Vol. 2: 5764
Prix Joseph-Edmond Marchal Vol. 2: 962
Prix Joseph Gantrelle Vol. 2: 993
Prix Joseph Hamel Vol. 2: 5765
Prix Joseph Lepoix Vol. 2: 1336
Prix Joseph Rey Vol. 2: 5042
Prix Joseph Saillet Vol. 2: 5766
Prix Joseph Schepkens Vol. 2: 1027
Prix Jules Andeoud Vol. 2: 5767
Prix Jules Duculot Vol. 2: 994
Prix Jules et Louis Jeanbernat et Barthelemy de Ferrari Doria
   Institut de France Vol. 2: 5346
   Institut de France - Academie des Beaux Arts Vol 2: 5407
   Institut de France - Academie des Inscriptions et Belle-Lettres Vol 2: 5467
   Institut de France - Academie des Sciences Morales et Politiques Vol 2: 5768
   Institut de France - Academie Francaise Vol 2: 5874
Prix Jules Favre Vol. 2: 5875
Prix Jules Janin Vol. 2: 5876
Prix Jules Lefort Vol. 2: 5769
Prix Jules Mahyer Vol. 2: 5679
Prix Jules Perreau Vol. 2: 4854
Prix Jules Raeymaekers Vol. 2: 963
Prix Jules Voncken Vol. 2: 1181
Prix Julia Verlanger Vol. 2: 6463
Prix Julien Saget Vol. 2: 6227
Prix Juteau-Duvigneaux Vol. 2: 5877
Prix Karl Beule Vol. 2: 5408
Prix Kastner-Boursault
   Institut de France - Academie des Beaux Arts Vol. 2: 5409
   Institut de France - Academie Francaise Vol 2: 5878
Prix Keith S. Armstrong Vol. 1: 7117
Prix Koenigswarter Vol. 2: 5770
Prix L.-E. Ouimet - Molson Vol. 1: 6027
Prix L. E. Rivot Vol. 2: 5698
Prix L.-Pierre Descamps Vol. 2: 1051
Prix Lac Vol. 2: 5525
Prix Lafontaine Vol. 2: 5879
Prix Lalande Vol. 2: 5681
Prix Lamarck Vol. 2: 1028
Prix Lambert Vol. 2: 5880
Prix Lange Vol. 2: 5881
Prix Langevin Vol. 2: 6378
Prix Langlois Vol. 2: 5882
Prix Latsis Vol. 2: 11959
Prix Lavalleye-Coppens Vol. 2: 964
Prix Lazare Carnot Vol. 2: 5699
Prix Le Bel Vol. 2: 6357
Prix Le Dissez de Penanrun Vol. 2: 5771
Prix Le Fevre-Deumier (de Pons)
   Institut de France - Academie des Inscriptions et Belle-Lettres Vol. 2: 5468
   Institut de France - Academie Francaise Vol 2: 5883
Prix Le Guay-Lebrun Vol. 2: 5410
Prix Leclerc - Maria Bouland Vol. 2: 5411
Prix Lecouteaux Vol. 2: 5241
Prix Lefevre-Deumier de Pons Vol. 2: 5772
Prix Leo Errera Vol. 2: 1029
Prix Leo Wildmann Vol. 2: 11838
Prix Leon Baratz Vol. 2: 4855
Prix Leon Bertrand Vol. 2: 5312
Prix Leon et Henri Fredericq Vol. 2: 1030

Prix Leon Faucher Vol. 2: 5773
Prix Leon-Gerin Vol. 1: 16618
Prix Leon Launoy Vol. 2: 4856
Prix Leon Leclere Vol. 2: 995
Prix Leon-Lortie Vol. 1: 17387
Prix Leonardo Vol. 2: 8375
Prix Leopold Rosy Vol. 2: 1303
Prix Leopold Sedar Senghor Vol. 2: 5268
Prix les Transports, l'Homme et la Ville Vol. 2: 6151
Prix Lespiau Vol. 2: 5522
Prix Lian Vol. 2: 4857
Prix Liberte Litteraire Vol. 2: 11721
Prix Limantour Vol. 2: 5774
Prix Lionel-Groulx Vol. 1: 10208
Prix Lionel - Groulx - les Cooperants Vol. 1: 10208
Prix Lise Lamare Vol. 2: 6287
Prix litteraire de la Ville de La Chaux-de-Fonds et de la revue vwa Vol. 2: 11688
Prix Litteraire de la Vocation Vol. 2: 5212
Prix Litteraire de l'Asie Vol. 2: 4927
Prix Litteraire des Caraibes Vol. 2: 4928
Prix Litteraire des Mascareignes, des Seychelles et des Comores Vol. 2: 4929
Prix Litteraire du Conseil de la Communaute Francaise de Belgique Vol. 2: 1110
Prix Litteraire France - Quebec/Jean Hamelin Vol. 2: 4930
Prix Litteraire Henri Deschamps Vol. 2: 7258
Prix Litteraire International Charles-Helou Vol. 2: 4884
Prix Litteraire Prince Pierre-de-Monaco Vol. 2: 9312
Prix Litteraires
   Academie de Gastronomie Brillat-Savarin Vol. 2: 4791
   Chaine des Rotisseurs - Ordre Mondial des Gourmets Degustateurs Vol 2: 5026
Prix Littre Vol. 2: 6501
Prix Louis Ancel Vol. 2: 6379
Prix Louis Barthou Vol. 2: 5884
Prix Louis Castex Vol. 2: 5885
Prix Louis d'Or Vol. 2: 1368
Prix Louis Fould Vol. 2: 5469
Prix Louis Jeantet de Medecine Vol. 2: 11727
Prix Louis Liard Vol. 2: 5775
Prix Louis Marin Vol. 2: 5776
Prix Louis Melsens Vol. 2: 1031
Prix Louis P. Miller Vol. 2: 5886
Prix Louis-Phillipe-Hebert Vol. 1: 17388
Prix Louis Renault Vol. 2: 11751
Prix Louise Dehem Vol. 2: 965
Prix Lucien de Reinach Vol. 2: 5777
Prix Lucien Dupont Vol. 2: 5778
Prix Lucien Godeaux Vol. 2: 1368
Prix Lucien Malpertuis Vol. 2: 1288
Prix Lucien Tisserand Vol. 1: 5887
Prix Ludger-Duvernay Vol. 1: 17389
Prix Lugne Poe Vol. 2: 6398
Prix Lutte Contre L'Alcoolisme Vol. 2: 4858
Prix Lutte Contre le Tabagisme Vol. 2: 4859
Prix Mady Mesple Vol. 2: 5188
Prix Maille-Latour-Landry Vol. 2: 5888
Prix Maise Ploquin-Caunan et Docteur Jacques Perdrizet Vol. 2: 5889
Prix Maise Ploquin-Caunan et Docteur Jacques Perdrizet Vol. 2: 6288
Prix Maisondieu Vol. 2: 5779
Prix Maladies Mentales Vol. 2: 4860
Prix Malouet Vol. 2: 5780
Prix Mancini Vol. 2: 11751
Prix Marc Chesneau Vol. 2: 6337
Prix Marcel Flach Vol. 2: 5781
Prix Marcel Mompezat Vol. 2: 6338
Prix Marcel Moye Vol. 2: 6228
Prix Marcelin Guerin Vol. 2: 5890

Prix Marceline Desbordes-Valmore Vol. 2: 6339
Prix Marcelle Millier Vol. 2: 5891
Prix Marechal Foch Vol. 2: 5892
Prix Maria Star. Adrienne Cambry Vol. 2: 6289
Prix Marie-Claire-Daveluy Vol. 1: 6022
Prix Marie-Eugene Simon Henri Martin Vol. 2: 5893
Prix Marie Havez-Planque Vol. 2: 5894
Prix Marie Laurent Vol. 2: 5782
Prix Marie-Victorin Vol. 1: 16619
Prix Marius Jacquemetton Vol. 2: 6229
Prix Marthe Ripert-Sarrut Vol. 2: 6340
Prix Master Foods des Demeures Historiques Vol. 2: 1052
Prix Maujean Vol. 2: 5895
Prix Maurice Edgar Coindreau Vol. 2: 6246
Prix Maurice-Edgar Coindreau Vol. 2: 6290
Prix Maurice-Louis Girard Vol. 2: 4861
Prix Maurice Nicloux Vol. 2: 6236
Prix Maurice R... D... Vol. 2: 5412
Prix Maurice-Richard Vol. 1: 17390
Prix Maurice Travers Vol. 2: 5783
Prix Maurice Trubert Vol. 2: 5896
Prix Max Barthou Vol. 2: 5897
Prix Max du Veuzit Vol. 2: 6291
Prix Max Jacob de Poesie Vol. 2: 6081
Prix Maxime David Vol. 2: 5413
Prix Maxime-Raymond Vol. 1: 10209
Prix Maxine Vol. 1: 6022
Prix McLuhan Teleglobe Canada Vol. 1: 6834
Prix Medecin General Inspecteur Raymond Debenedetti Vol. 2: 4862
Prix Medecine Vol. 2: 4863
Prix Medecine et Culture Vol. 2: 5938
Prix Medecine Veterinaire Vol. 2: 4864
Prix Medicis Vol. 2: 6174
Prix Medicis de l'Essai Vol. 2: 6175
Prix Medicis Etranger Vol. 2: 6176
Prix Mediterranee Vol. 2: 6187
Prix Melsens Vol. 2: 1337
Prix Mentzer des Rencontres de Chemie Therapeutique Vol. 2: 6239
Prix Mesucora Vol. 2: 5700
Prix Meurand Vol. 2: 5414
Prix Michel-Auge-Laribe Vol. 2: 5241
Prix Michel-Brunet Vol. 1: 10210
Prix Michel Huber Vol. 2: 6393
Prix Michel Monpetit Vol. 2: 5701
Prix Michel Noury Vol. 2: 4865
Prix Michener de Journalism Vol. 1: 12249
Prix Minda de Gunzburg Vol. 2: 4910
Prix Moet-Hennessy Louis-Vuitton Vol. 2: 5933
Prix Molson de l'Academie Canadienne-Francaise Vol. 1: 18881
Prix Monbinne Vol. 2: 5415
Prix Mondial Cino del Duca Vol. 2: 5224
Prix Mondial Nessim Habif Vol. 2: 11960
Prix Monseigneur Marcel Vol. 2: 5898
Prix Montyon Vol. 2: 5899
Prix Montyon de Mecanique Vol. 2: 5702
Prix Mottart Vol. 2: 5900
Prix Mounet-Sully Vol. 2: 6341
Prix Mumm Kleber-Haedens Vol. 2: 5102
Prix Musical de Radio Brno Vol. 2: 1848
Prix Narcisse Michaut Vol. 2: 5901
Prix Nature et Patrimoine Vol. 2: 5080
Prix Neurologie Vol. 2: 4866
Prix Nicolas Missarel Vol. 2: 5902
Prix Nicole Houssa Vol. 2: 1304
Prix Nicolo Vol. 2: 5416
Prix Nine Choucroun Vol. 2: 5332
Prix Normande-Juneau Vol. 1: 6028
Prix Noury-Lemarie Vol. 2: 6242
Prix Nouvelle-Caledonia Vol. 2: 9699

Prix Obstetrique Vol. 2: 4867
Prix Odilon Barrot Vol. 2: 5784
Prix of Marie-Joseph Erb Vol. 2: 5042
Prix Olivar-Asselin Vol. 1: 17391
Prix O.R.L. Vol. 2: 4868
Prix Osiris Vol. 2: 5347
Prix Osiris Vol. 2: 5703
Prix P. J. et Edouard Van Beneden Vol. 2: 1032
Prix Paris Chapter Friends of VMF Vol. 2: 6467
Prix Pascal Fortuny Vol. 2: 5903
Prix Paul and Marie Stroobant Vol. 2: 1033
Prix Paul Arfvidson Vol. 2: 5352
Prix Paul Artot Vol. 2: 966
Prix Paul Belmondo Vol. 2: 5348
Prix Paul Bonduelle Vol. 2: 967
Prix Paul Cailleux Vol. 2: 5058
Prix Paul Chabas Vol. 2: 5417
Prix Paul de Pessemier Vol. 2: 1053
Prix Paul-Emile-Borduas Vol. 1: 16615
Prix Paul Flat Vol. 2: 5904
Prix Paul Fourmarier Vol. 2: 1034
Prix Paul Guggenheim Vol. 2: 11742
Prix Paul Hervieu Vol. 2: 5905
Prix Paul Janssen Vol. 2: 1365
Prix Paul Labbe-Vauquelin Vol. 2: 5906
Prix Paul Leroy-Beaulieu Vol. 2: 5785
Prix Paul-Louis Weiller Vol. 2: 5418
Prix Paul Marmottan Vol. 2: 5419
Prix Paul Mathieu Vol. 2: 4869
Prix Paul-Michel Perret Vol. 2: 5786
Prix Paul Streit Vol. 2: 11774
Prix Paul Teissonniere Vol. 2: 5907
Prix Paul Verlaine Vol. 2: 5908
Prix Paul Vigne d'Octon Vol. 2: 5787
Prix Pechiney Vol. 2: 5704
Prix Pfizer Vol. 2: 1338
Prix Pharmacie Vol. 2: 4870
Prix Philips Vol. 2: 6353
Prix Philips - France Vol. 2: 6353
Prix Pierre Benoit Vol. 2: 5909
Prix Pierre Carsoel Vol. 2: 968
Prix Pierre de Regnier Vol. 2: 5910
Prix Pierre et Celine Lhermite Vol. 2: 4871
Prix Pierre Mendes France Vol. 2: 6118
Prix Pierre Sue Vol. 2: 6358
Prix Pierre Villey Vol. 2: 5911
Prix Pinet Vol. 2: 5420
Prix Plasma Vol. 2: 6380
Prix Poetique Francais Vol. 2: 6453
Prix Pol and Christiane Swings Vol. 2: 1035
Prix Pol Comiant Vol. 2: 5912
Prix Pol Swings Vol. 2: 1368
Prix Polydore de Paepe Vol. 2: 996
Prix pour jeunes diplomes Vol. 2: 6029
Prix pour les Droits de l'Homme Vol. 2: 11953
Prix Prestwich Vol. 2: 5313
Prix Prince Albert Ier de Monaco Vol. 2: 4872
Prix Professeur Louis Baes Vol. 2: 1036
Prix Professionel Vol. 1: 8288
Prix Prosper Veil Vol. 2: 4873
Prix Protex Vol. 2: 6386
Prix Pyral Vol. 2: 5175
Prix Quadriennal de Composition Musicale Camille Huysmans Vol. 2: 1055
Prix Quebec-Paris Vol. 1: 12329
Prix Quinquennal de Numismatique Vol. 2: 1100
Prix Quinquennal de Psychologie Religieuse Scientifique Vol. 2: 1175
Prix Quinquennal des Sciences Pharmaceutiques et Therapeutiques Vol. 2: 1339
Prix Quinquennal Docteur Albert Dubois pour la Pathologie tropicale Vol. 2: 1340

Prix Quinquennaux des Sciences Medicales du Gouvernement Vol. 2: 1341
Prix Radio Bassinia Vol. 2: 1160
Prix Raoul Duseigneur Vol. 2: 5470
Prix Raoul Follereau Vol. 2: 5913
Prix Raymond Berr Atochem Vol. 2: 6359
Prix Raymond et Madeleine Furon Vol. 2: 5314
Prix Reader's Digest Vol. 1: 7124
Prix Recherche et Medecine Vol. 2: 5939
Prix Regner de gravure Vol. 2: 4912
Prix Renaudot Vol. 2: 6178
Prix Rene Bardet Vol. 2: 5914
Prix Rene Cassin Vol. 2: 5788
Prix Rene Dumesnil Vol. 2: 5421
Prix Rene Janssens Vol. 2: 969
Prix Rene Lyr Vol. 2: 1044
Prix Rene Petiet Vol. 2: 5915
Prix Richard Lounsbery Vol. 2: 5705
Prix Richelieu Vol. 2: 6126
Prix Richtenberger Vol. 2: 5422
Prix Ringier Vol. 2: 6194
Prix Riquer Vol. 2: 946
Prix Roberge Vol. 2: 5916
Prix Robert Duterme Vol. 2: 1305
Prix Roger Nimier Vol. 2: 6121
Prix Roland de Jouvenal Vol. 2: 5917
Prix Roman et Tania Ghirshman Vol. 2: 5471
Prix Romanes International Vol. 2: 6114
Prix Rosen de Cancerologie Vol. 2: 5265
Prix Rossi Vol. 2: 5789
Prix Rossini Vol. 2: 5423
Prix Roussel Vol. 2: 6205
Prix Rouyer Vol. 2: 5424
Prix Ruhlman Vol. 2: 5425
Prix Sabine Sicaud Vol. 2: 6342
Prix SACEM Vol. 2: 5175
Prix Saint-Cricq-Theis Vol. 2: 5918
Prix Saintour Vol. 2: 5472
Prix Saintour Vol. 2: 5679
Prix Saintour
   Institut de France - Academie des Sciences Morales et Politiques Vol. 2: 5790
   Institut de France - Academie Francaise Vol 2: 5919
Prix Samuel Pufendorf Vol. 2: 11751
Prix Samuel - Rousseau Vol. 2: 5426
Prix Sander Pierron Vol. 2: 1306
Prix Sandmeyer Vol. 2: 11887
Prix Sante et Entreprise Vol. 2: 5036
Prix Sante Publique Vol. 2: 5940
Prix Sao Payo Vol. 2: 947
Prix Schreyer Vol. 1: 5759
Prix Science et Defense Vol. 2: 5246
Prix Science pour l'Art - Moet-Hennessy - Louis Vuitton Vol. 2: 6122
Prix Scientifique IBM France Vol. 2: 5330
Prix Scientifique Philip Morris Vol. 2: 4964
Prix Scientifique/Prix Encouragements/Prix Artistique Vol. 2: 5222
Prix Scientifique/Prix Innovante/Prix Media Vol. 2: 5222
Prix Scientifiques Louis Empain Vol. 2: 1380
Prix Seraphin-Marion Vol. 1: 17392
Prix SGDL de la Nouvelle Vol. 2: 6292
Prix SGDL de l'Essai Vol. 2: 6293
Prix SGDL des Arts Vol. 2: 6294
Prix SGDL du Livre d'Histoire Vol. 2: 6295
Prix SGDL du Livre Jeunesse Vol. 2: 6296
Prix SGDL du Roman Vol. 2: 6297
Prix Simone Bergmans Vol. 2: 949
Prix S.I.N.U.S. Vol. 2: 6213
Prix Sir John William Dawson Vol. 1: 16951
Prix Sivet Vol. 2: 5920
Prix SmithKline Beecham Vol. 2: 1342
Prix Sobrier-Arnould Vol. 2: 5921
Prix Socio-economie de la Sante Vol. 2: 5940

Prix Sola-Cabiati Vol. 2: 6097
Prix Specia Vol. 2: 4874
Prix Special Albert Roussel Vol. 2: 6432
Prix Special ASIFA Vol. 2: 9889
Prix Special du Jury Vol. 2: 11793
Prix Special Jeunes Chercheurs Vol. 2: 5078
Prix Specialities Chirurgicales Vol. 2: 4875
Prix Stanislas Julien Vol. 2: 5473
Prix Stassart Vol. 2: 5791
Prix Steacie Vol. 1: 18474
Prix Stendhal de la Nouvelle Vol. 2: 6471
Prix Stephania de Poesie Vol. 2: 6454
Prix Suisse Vol. 2: 11774
Prix Sully-Olivier-de-Serres Vol. 2: 5241
Prix Susse Freres Vol. 2: 5427
Prix Suzanne Tassier Vol. 2: 997
Prix Talents Nouveau Vol. 2: 6399
Prix Tanesse Vol. 2: 5792
Prix Teilhard/Londres Vol. 1: 9328
Prix Telebec Vol. 1: 16433
Prix Territoria Vol. 2: 6100
Prix Theodore Ott Vol. 2: 11919
Prix Theophile de Donder Vol. 2: 1037
Prix Theophile Gluge Vol. 2: 1038
Prix Therouanne Vol. 2: 5922
Prix Thiers Vol. 2: 5923
Prix Thomson Sintra Vol. 2: 6354
Prix Thorlet Vol. 2: 5428
Prix Thyde Monnier Vol. 2: 6298
Prix Tobie Jonckheere Vol. 2: 998
Prix Toirac Vol. 2: 5924
Prix Total du Rayonnement Francais dans le Tiers Monde Vol. 2: 5054
Prix Toutain Vol. 2: 5925
Prix Toutain-Blanchet Vol. 2: 5474
Prix triennal de Bibliographie Vol. 2: 6970
Prix Triennal de la Societe Royale de Chimie Vol. 2: 1366
Prix Triennal Professeur Pierre Rijlant pour l'Electrophysiologie Cardiaque Vol. 2: 1343
Prix Trillium Vol. 1: 15686
Prix Tristan Bernard Vol. 2: 6400
Prix Tristan Tzara de Traduction (Franco-Hongrois) Vol. 2: 6299
Prix Troyon et Edouard Lemaitre Vol. 2: 5429
Prix Tuberculose Vol. 2: 4876
Prix Ugo Papi - Gaston Leduc Vol. 2: 5793
Prix UNDA Vol. 2: 11925
Prix UNESCO d'Architecture Vol. 2: 6423
Prix UNESCO Droits de l'Homme Vol. 2: 6034
Prix Valentine Abraham Verlain Vol. 2: 5926
Prix Valentine de Wolmar Vol. 2: 5927
Prix Valery Larbaud Vol. 2: 4987
Prix Van Der Beeken Vol. 2: 1220
Prix Vega et Lods de Wegmann Vol. 2: 5928
Prix Victor Bernard Vol. 2: 6343
Prix Victor Cousin Vol. 2: 5794
Prix Victor Delbos Vol. 2: 5795
Prix Victor et Clara Soriano Vol. 2: 4877
Prix Victor-Morin Vol. 1: 17393
Prix Victor Rossel Vol. 2: 1247
Prix Victor Tourneur
   Academie Royale de Belgique - Classe des Beaux-Arts Vol. 2: 970
   Academie Royale de Belgique - Classe des Lettres et des Sciences Morales et Politiques Vol. 2: 999
Prix Vieilles Maisons Francaises Vol. 2: 6467
Prix Viennet-Damien Vol. 2: 6230
Prix Viquesnel Vol. 2: 5315
Prix Vitet Vol. 2: 5929
Prix Vitoria Vol. 2: 11751
Prix Vocation Japon Vol. 2: 8734
Prix Volney Vol. 2: 5349
Prix Volney Vol. 2: 5475
Prix Walter Dinsdale Vol. 1: 7119
Prix Wegmann Vol. 2: 5316

Prix Whipper Watson   Vol. 1: 7124
Prix Wilder-Penfield   Vol. 1: 16620
Prix Wolowski   Vol. 2: 5796
Prix Xavier Marmier   Vol. 2: 5930
Prix XVII Siecle   Vol. 2: 6346
Prix Yvan Loiseau   Vol. 2: 5931
Prix Yves-Le-Kervadec   Vol. 2: 6455
Prix Yves Rocard   Vol. 2: 6381
Prix Yvonne Foulley   Vol. 2: 4878
Prix Yvonne Lenoir   Vol. 2: 6300
Prix Zerilli Marimo   Vol. 2: 5797
Prize   Vol. 2: 5120
Prize Bridge Award   Vol. 1: 2681
Prize Dissertation in Opera   Vol. 1: 14408
Prize for a Flemish Short Film   Vol. 2: 1079
Prize for Achievement in Accelerator Physics and Technology   Vol. 1: 19499
Prize for Art Critique   Vol. 2: 10396
Prize for Better Work   Vol. 2: 8886
Prize for Colored Musicians   Vol. 2: 11038
Prize for Composers and Performers of Afrikaans Folk Musik   Vol. 2: 11039
Prize for Decorative Arts   Vol. 2: 10397
Prize for Design   Vol. 2: 10398
Prize for Distinguished Leadership   Vol. 1: 2122
Prize for Fabrication of Traditional Musical Instrument   Vol. 2: 8881
Prize for Freedom   Vol. 2: 3557
Prize for Graphic Arts   Vol. 2: 10399
Prize for Industrial Applications of Physics   Vol. 1: 2664
Prize for Innovative Applied Physicss of the Division of Industrial and Applied Physics.   Vol. 1: 6802
Prize for Journalism on Arts and Culture   Vol. 2: 9935
Prize for Junior Scientists   Vol. 2: 6517
Prize for Literature of the Council of the French Community of Belgium   Vol. 2: 1110
Prize for Meritorious Achievement   Vol. 1: 19499
Prize for Monumental Art   Vol. 2: 10400
Prize for Mozart Interpretation   Vol. 2: 914
Prize for Musicology   Vol. 2: 915
Prize for Narrative Poetry   Vol. 1: 15136
Prize for Novel   Vol. 2: 7793
Prize for Optics   Vol. 2: 11084
Prize for Painting   Vol. 2: 10401
Prize for Performance of Israeli Works   Vol. 2: 7909
Prize for Performers of Classical Music   Vol. 2: 11040
Prize for Poetry in Irish   Vol. 2: 7761
Prize for Research and Studies of the Repercussions of the Iraqi Invasion of Kuwait   Vol. 2: 8845
Prize for Research in Education of the National Institute of the Book   Vol. 2: 1443
Prize for Revolutionary Song   Vol. 2: 8882
Prize for Scenography   Vol. 2: 10402
Prize for Sculpture   Vol. 2: 10403
Prize for Social Sciences and Humanities   Vol. 2: 12077
Prize for the Best Foreign Book   Vol. 2: 6180
Prize for Theatre or Cinema   Vol. 2: 8832
Prize for Young Historians of Science   Vol. 2: 5950
Prize in Economic Sciences in Memory of Alfred Nobel   Vol. 2: 11549
Prize Mission Special Japan   Vol. 2: 8733
Prize Objective Japan   Vol. 2: 8734
Prize Objective Japan - Students   Vol. 2: 8734
Prize of Architecture   Vol. 2: 1948
Prize of Honor for Catalan Letters   Vol. 2: 11310
Prize of INTERFILM   Vol. 2: 6984

Prize of National Committee of the Capital of Slovakia Bratislava   Vol. 2: 10769
Prize of the Audience
　Brussels International Fantasy Film Festival   Vol. 2: 1091
　International Filmwochenende Wurzburg   Vol 2: 6956
Prize of the Berlin Children's Jury   Vol. 2: 6564
Prize of the Best National Collection   Vol. 2: 7316
Prize of the Capital of Slovakia Bratislava   Vol. 2: 1830
Prize of the City of Fribourg   Vol. 2: 11736
Prize of the City of The Hague   Vol. 2: 9670
Prize of the FIPRESCI   Vol. 2: 6984
Prize of the German Art Film Theatre Association   Vol. 2: 6564
Prize of the Hungarian Trade Union   Vol. 2: 7404
Prize of the International Olympic Committee   Vol. 2: 7431
Prize of the Mayor of the City of Bratislava   Vol. 2: 1831
Prize of the Molster Foundation   Vol. 2: 9385
Prize of the Photo Book   Vol. 2: 6190
Prize of the Societe Internationale de Chirurgie   Vol. 2: 11846
Prize of UNICEF   Vol. 2: 6564
Prize to Stimulate Teaching and Research in Chemical Engineering   Vol. 2: 9110
Prized Pieces Competition   Vol. 1: 13464
Prizes for a Theatrical Play   Vol. 2: 8883
Prizes for Answering a Literary or Philogical Question   Vol. 2: 6769
Prizes for Excellence in the Study of International Affairs   Vol. 2: 229
Prizes for Literature   Vol. 2: 8884
Prizes for Manuscripts for Juveniles   Vol. 2: 10008
Prizes for Theatrical Works   Vol. 2: 7193
Prizes to Young Graduates   Vol. 2: 6029
Pro Bono Publico Awards   Vol. 1: 1312
Pro Bono Service Award   Vol. 1: 11042
PRO Dogs National Charity Open Creative Writing & Photographic Competition   Vol. 2: 3802
Pro Ecclesia et Pontifice Medal   Vol. 2: 12106
Pro Ecclesia et Professione (Pharmaciae)   Vol. 1: 13559
Pro Ecelesia et Pontifice   Vol. 2: 8476
Pro Football Hall of Fame   Vol. 1: 16424
Pro Football Hall of Fame Photo Contest   Vol. 1: 16425
PRO-GRAMME Award   Vol. 1: 10904
Pro Merito Decoration   Vol. 2: 10938
Pro Merito Medal   Vol. 2: 10939
Pro Musica Medal   Vol. 2: 6744
Pro Musicis International Award   Vol. 1: 16427
Pro Patria Medal   Vol. 2: 10940
PRO Rally Region of the Year   Vol. 1: 18401
Pro Rodeo Clown of the Year   Vol. 1: 16511
Pro Rodeo Hall of Fame   Vol. 1: 16512
Pro Set NHL Player of the Year Award   Vol. 1: 14177
Pro Silentio   Vol. 2: 7447
Pro Stock Puller of the Year   Vol. 1: 14905
Pro Universitate Emlekerem   Vol. 2: 7462
Pro Urbe Budapest Award   Vol. 2: 7304
Pro Urbe Prize   Vol. 2: 7305
Pro Virtute Decoration   Vol. 2: 10941
Pro Virtute Medal   Vol. 2: 10942
Process Award   Vol. 1: 11095
Procopiu Prize; Stefan   Vol. 2: 10379
Procrastinator of the Year Award   Vol. 1: 16429

Procter & Gamble Award in Physical Chemistry   Vol. 1: 1508
Procter & Gamble Professional Opportunity Awards   Vol. 1: 3512
Procter Prize; William   Vol. 1: 17273
Proctor and Gamble Award in Applied and Environmental Microbiology   Vol. 1: 4210
Proctor Medal   Vol. 1: 5593
Proctor Memorial Leadership Award; Charles Henry   Vol. 1: 1986
Proctor Prize; George   Vol. 1: 7255
Proctor Prize; Thomas R.   Vol. 1: 12628
Proctor Research Medal Award; Francis I.   Vol. 1: 5593
Procurement Award   Vol. 1: 14578
Procurement Awards   Vol. 1: 19601
Product Division Executive Committee Award   Vol. 1: 2141
Product of the Year   Vol. 2: 4507
Production Engineering Award   Vol. 1: 17971
Products Design Award   Vol. 1: 9276
Professional Achievement Award
　American Medical Record Association   Vol. 1: 3034
　Associates of National Agricultural Library   Vol 1: 5426
　Association of Medical Rehabilitation Administrators   Vol 1: 5866
　Association of Scientists and Engineers of the Naval Sea Systems Command   Vol 1: 5958
　Institute of Real Estate Management   Vol 1: 10442
　Special Libraries Association - Transportation Division   Vol 1: 18285
Professional Achievement Awards
　Professional Builder   Vol. 1: 16455
　University of California, Los Angeles - Alumni Association   Vol 1: 19748
Professional Achievement Citations   Vol. 1: 19770
Professional Agent of the Year   Vol. 1: 13250
Professional Alarm Technician of the Year   Vol. 1: 13490
Professional and Scholarly Publishing Division Annual Awards Program   Vol. 1: 5695
Professional Assistance Awards   Vol. 1: 11686
Professional Award
　Agricultural Communicators in Education   Vol. 1: 203
　American Horticultural Society   Vol 1: 2362
Professional Awards Program   Vol. 1: 4647
Professional Chapter Buyer of the Year Award   Vol. 1: 14232
Professional Chapter Purchasing Manager of the Year Award   Vol. 1: 14237
Professional Commitment Award   Vol. 2: 9742
Professional Contribution Award   Vol. 1: 4344
Professional Contribution by ACE Member   Vol. 1: 5731
Professional Design Award   Vol. 1: 17729
Professional Development Award   Vol. 1: 18562
Professional Development Awards   Vol. 1: 14811
Professional Development Coordinator of the Year   Vol. 1: 349
Professional Development Leadership Award   Vol. 1: 4348
Professional Development Program Awards   Vol. 1: 20076
Professional Education Award   Vol. 1: 10889
Professional Engineer of the Year
　Institution of Engineers, Australia   Vol. 2: 478

Institution of Engineers, Australia   Vol 2: 481
Professional Engineers Citizenship Award   Vol. 1: 16461
Professional Engineers Gold Medal   Vol. 1: 16462
Professional Engineers Ontario - Order of Honour   Vol. 1: 16463
Professional Excellence Award   Vol. 1: 7822
Professional Excellence in Religious Communication Award   Vol. 1: 12102
Professional Fund-raiser of the Year Award   Vol. 1: 3925
Professional Growth Award   Vol. 1: 3999
Professional Manager   Vol. 1: 17406
Professional Member   Vol. 2: 10549
Professional Member of the Year   Vol. 1: 350
Professional of the Year
  Association of Jewish Center Professionals   Vol. 1: 5840
  Ladies Professional Golf Association   Vol 1: 11763
  Organization of Professional Employees of the United States Department of Agriculture   Vol 1: 15836
  Professional Cycling Association   Vol 2: 3805
  United States Professional Tennis Association   Vol 1: 19512
Professional-of-the-Year   Vol. 1: 17014
Professional of the Year Award   Vol. 1: 5215
Professional Preparation Award   Vol. 1: 5669
Professional Progress Award for Outstanding Progress in Chemical Engineering   Vol. 1: 2598
Professional Recognition/Appreciation Award   Vol. 1: 5530
Professional Safety Paper Awards   Vol. 1: 4787
Professional Service Award
  Association for the Advancement of Health Education   Vol. 1: 5615
  College of Chaplains, Inc.   Vol 1: 7918
  National Association of Conservation Districts   Vol 1: 13033
Professional Service to Safety Education   Vol. 1: 16985
Professional Support Award   Vol. 1: 14112
Professional Teacher of the Year Award   Vol. 1: 3887
Professor of the Year   Vol. 1: 8298
Progetto & Luce   Vol. 2: 8274
Prognosticator of the Year   Vol. 1: 18759
Program Director of the Year Award   Vol. 1: 1059
Program Excellence Award for Innovations in Local Government Management   Vol. 1: 10851
Program Excellence Awards
  International City Management Association   Vol. 1: 10851
  National Association of Television Program Executives International   Vol 1: 13342
Program of the Year Award   Vol. 1: 18905
Program on Peace and International Cooperation Research and Writing Grants   Vol. 1: 11988
Program to Assist Foreign Sinologists Carry Out Research in the R.O.C.   Vol. 2: 11992
Program to Recognize Excellence in Student Literary Magazines   Vol. 1: 13776
Programme OTAN de Bourses de Recherche   Vol. 1: 16960
Programming Systems and Languages Paper Award   Vol. 1: 5471

Progress Award
  Amateur Athletic Union of the United States   Vol. 1: 442
  Photographic Society of America   Vol 1: 16168
Progress Award of Japanese Society of Soil Science and Plant Nutrition   Vol. 2: 8667
Progress Medal   Vol. 2: 4136
Progress Medal Award   Vol. 1: 17909
Progressive School Library Media Award   Vol. 1: 5251
Project of the Year   Vol. 1: 16528
Project on African Agriculture   Vol. 1: 17377
Projects With Industry Outstanding Employee Awards   Vol. 1: 17293
Prometheus Award   Vol. 1: 11852
Promises of Hope Award   Vol. 1: 17079
Promising Personality   Vol. 1: 18692
Promising Playwright Award   Vol. 1: 7953
Promising Researcher Awards   Vol. 1: 13777
Promising Young Writers Program   Vol. 1: 13778
Promoter of the Year   Vol. 1: 19029
Promotional Achievement Awards   Vol. 1: 11579
Promotional Prizes   Vol. 2: 7022
Propane Gallery of Architectural Design Competition Awards   Vol. 1: 14537
Property Person of the Year   Vol. 1: 14543
Propes Prize; Aharon Tzvi & Mara   Vol. 2: 7899
Prosceniumprijs   Vol. 2: 9690
Proskauer Prize; Edith H. and Richmond   Vol. 1: 14714
Prost; Prix Gabriel-Auguste   Vol. 2: 5458
Prosvjeta Prize   Vol. 2: 10722
Protective Coatings Award   Vol. 1: 7560
Protege Awards   Vol. 1: 5328
Protein Awards   Vol. 1: 3111
Proust Prize; Marcel   Vol. 2: 6182
Provasoli Award; Luigi   Vol. 1: 16174
Provincial Police Award   Vol. 2: 2112
Proximity Achievement Award   Vol. 1: 19386
PRS Awards for Choral Enterprise   Vol. 2: 3770
PRS Enterprise Awards   Vol. 2: 3770
Prudential Awards for the Arts   Vol. 2: 3826
Prudential Group Assurance Company of England (Canada) Award   Vol. 1: 7121
Pruitt Award; Council for Chemical Research Mac   Vol. 1: 8311
Pruszynski Prize; Ksawery   Vol. 2: 10168
Pruvost; Prix Fondation Pierre   Vol. 2: 5306
Pruzansky Memorial Fund for Maternal and Child Health Nursing; Donna   Vol. 1: 7833
Pryne Memorial Award, Competition Division; Annie   Vol. 1: 6240
Pryor Award; Nancy Blankenship   Vol. 1: 20131
Pryor Award; Susy   Vol. 1: 5262
Pryor Memorial Award; Bill   Vol. 1: 20106
Przesmycki Award; Professor Feliks   Vol. 2: 10188
PSA Contemporary Medal   Vol. 2: 9713
PSA Gold Medal
  Bombay Creative Photographers Association   Vol. 2: 7489
  Placer Camera Club   Vol 1: 16230
PSA Gold Medals   Vol. 2: 10677
PSA Medal
  Greater Lynn Camera Club   Vol. 1: 9713
  Laymen's National Bible Association   Vol 1: 11798
PSA Yankee Medal   Vol. 1: 9713
Psi Chi/Edwin B. Newman Graduate Research Award   Vol. 1: 16545

Psi Chi/Florence L. Denmark National Faculty Advisor Award   Vol. 1: 16546
Psi Chi/Ruth Hubbard Cousins National Chapter Award   Vol. 1: 16547
PSI Creative Communication Awards Program   Vol. 1: 16138
PSI Gold Medals   Vol. 2: 7819
PSI Medals   Vol. 2: 7820
PSJ Award   Vol. 2: 8715
PSJ Award for Distinguished Service   Vol. 2: 8716
PSJ Award for Divisional Scientific Contributions   Vol. 2: 8717
PSJ Award for Drug Research and Development   Vol. 2: 8718
PSJ Award for Educational Services   Vol. 2: 8719
PSJ Award for Young Scientists   Vol. 2: 8720
Psychoanalysis Doctoral Award   Vol. 1: 3828
Psychoanalysis Post-Doctoral Award   Vol. 1: 3829
Psychological Dimensions of Peacework Award   Vol. 1: 16552
Psychological Hypnosis Best Clinical Paper   Vol. 1: 3757
Psychological Hypnosis Best First Non-Student Paper   Vol. 1: 3758
Psychological Hypnosis Best Theoretical Paper   Vol. 1: 3759
Psychological Hypnosis Graduate Student Award   Vol. 1: 3760
Psychological Research on Women Award   Vol. 1: 5659
Psychologist of the Year   Vol. 1: 16556
Psychology and Law Dissertation Award   Vol. 1: 3682
Psychology of Women Heritage Awards   Vol. 1: 3771
Psychology of Women Student Research Prize   Vol. 1: 3772
Psychotherapy Division Graduate Student Awards   Vol. 1: 3779
PTV Annual Award   Vol. 2: 10002
Public Administration Medal   Vol. 2: 10747
Public Advocate Award   Vol. 1: 20171
Public Affairs Competition   Vol. 1: 1042
Public Affairs Network Awards   Vol. 1: 3648
Public Awareness Award   Vol. 1: 5793
Public Communications Award   Vol. 1: 18076
Public Education Award
  National Energy Resources Organization   Vol. 1: 13902
  National Recycling Coalition   Vol 1: 14578
  Water Environment Federation   Vol 1: 20159
Public Education Award for Excellence in Plastic Surgery Journalism   Vol. 1: 4763
Public Education Prize   Vol. 2: 1730
Public Employer Award   Vol. 1: 16392
Public Golf Achievement Award   Vol. 1: 14087
Public Health Award   Vol. 2: 4464
Public Health Travelling Fellowships   Vol. 2: 544
Public Information Program Award   Vol. 1: 10674
Public Interest Awards   Vol. 1: 7455
Public Media Award   Vol. 1: 3191
Public Recreation Department of the Year   Vol. 1: 443
Public Recreation Man and Woman of the Year   Vol. 1: 444
Public Recreation Volunteer of the Year Award   Vol. 1: 445
Public Relations Achievement   Vol. 1: 14893
Public Relations Award
  Amateur Athletic Union of the United States   Vol. 1: 446

Association of Surgical Technologists   Vol 1: 5977
Canadian Library Association - Canadian Association of Public Libraries   Vol 1: 7010
National Association of Life Underwriters   Vol 1: 13199
Society of Medical Laboratory Technologists of South Africa   Vol 2: 10981
United Methodist Association of Health and Welfare Ministries   Vol 1: 18935
Public Relations Awards   Vol 1: 15964
Public Relations Competition
  Council of Jewish Federations   Vol 1: 8364
  Institute of Management Accountants, Inc.   Vol 1: 10395
Public Relations Coordinator of the Year   Vol. 2: 351
Public Relations/Development/Marketing Award   Vol 1: 18935
Public Relations Flim/Video Competition   Vol. 1: 16573
Public Relations' Hall of Fame   Vol 1: 16146
Public Relations Institute of Southern Africa Awards   Vol 2: 10912
Public Relations Recognition Award   Vol. 1: 1060
Public Relations Regional Achievement Award   Vol 1: 18400
Public Relations State Emblem   Vol 2: 746
Public Risk Manager of the Year Award   Vol. 1: 16582
Public Rose Garden Achievement Award   Vol 1: 317
Public Safety Program Excellence Award   Vol. 1: 10851
Public Service Achievement Awards   Vol 1: 8047
Public Service Award
  American Academy of Ophthalmology   Vol. 1: 634
  American Association of Petroleum Geologists   Vol 1: 1113
  American College of Health Care Administrators   Vol 1: 1652
  American Institute of Professional Geologists   Vol 1: 2672
  American Public Power Association   Vol 1: 3860
  American Veterinary Medical Association   Vol 1: 4988
  Animal Transportation Association   Vol 1: 5167
  Associated Press - Managing Editors Association   Vol 1: 5412
  Association of Consulting Engineers of Canada   Vol 1: 5758
  Association of Federal Investigators   Vol 1: 5794
  International Foundation of Employee Benefit Plans   Vol 1: 10994
  National Conference of Women's Bar Associations   Vol 1: 13651
  National Kidney Foundation   Vol 1: 14274
  National Legislative Council for the Handicapped   Vol 1: 14302
  National Police Officers Association of America   Vol 1: 14494
  Sigma Theta Tau International   Vol 1: 17268
  Society of Petroleum Engineers   Vol 1: 17972
Public Service Awards
  Fund for the City of New York   Vol. 1: 9449
  United States Department of Interior - Office of the Director of Personnel   Vol 1: 19248
  University of California, Los Angeles - Alumni Association   Vol 1: 19749
Public Service Citations   Vol. 1: 19771
Public Service Excellence Awards   Vol. 1: 16569
Public Service Excellence Awards for Retirees   Vol. 1: 16570
Public Service Group Achievement Award   Vol. 1: 12742
Public Service Medal
  Council for the Order of Australia   Vol. 2: 346
  National Aeronautics and Space Administration   Vol 1: 12743
  Singapore - Office of the Prime Minister   Vol 2: 10748
Public Service Medal of Merit of the Order of the Trinity   Vol. 2: 12035
Public Service Reporting - Roy W. Howard Awards   Vol 1: 17149
Public Service Star   Vol. 2: 10749
Public Service to Human Resource Development in National Affairs Award   Vol. 1: 4304
Public Services Award   Vol. 1: 1025
Public Understanding of Science Award   Vol. 1: 8380
Publication Award
  Geographic Society of Chicago   Vol. 1: 9549
  National Council for Geographic Education   Vol 1: 13696
  Philadelphia Art Alliance Press   Vol 1: 16127
  Religious Speech Communication Association   Vol 1: 16783
Publication Design Award   Vol. 1: 18015
Publications Award
  American Association of Cost Engineers   Vol 1: 987
  Flight Safety Foundation   Vol 1: 9240
  United Cerebral Palsy Associations   Vol 1: 18906
Publications Awards   Vol. 1: 8299
Publications Board's Newsletter Competition   Vol. 1: 9070
Publications Commendation   Vol. 1: 8210
Publieksprijs voor het Nederlandse Boek   Vol. 2: 9368
Publish-A-Book Contest   Vol. 1: 16664
Publisher of the Year   Vol. 1: 5810
Publishers Prize   Vol. 2: 1918
Publisher's Prizes   Vol. 2: 9522
Publishing Division Honor Roll   Vol. 1: 18277
Publishing Division Roll of Honor Award   Vol. 1: 18277
Publishing Hall of Fame   Vol. 1: 8428
Puccini Prize; Giacomo   Vol. 2: 8411
Puckett Creativity Award; Harriet Dewaele   Vol. 1: 9486
Puckey Prize; Sir Walter   Vol. 2: 3294
Pufendorf; Prix Samuel   Vol. 2: 11751
Puget Sound Group of Northwest Painters Award   Vol. 1: 15526
Puhlev Prize; Academician Aleksi   Vol. 2: 1513
Pulitzer Fellowships   Vol. 1: 8001
Pulitzer Prizes   Vol. 1: 8002
Pull of the Year   Vol. 1: 14906
Puller of the Year   Vol. 1: 14911
Pulliam Fellowship for Editorial Writers; Eugene C.   Vol. 1: 18000
Pulling Family of the Year   Vol. 1: 14907
Pulling Hall of Fame   Vol. 1: 14908
Pulp Biology Research Award   Vol. 1: 10618
Pulp Press International Three-Day Novel Competition   Vol. 1: 5184
Pundik Fund; Mendel   Vol. 2: 7970

Punster of the Year   Vol. 1: 11212
Pupin Medal   Vol. 1: 7966
Puppeteers of America Award   Vol. 1: 16592
Purchasing Manager of the Year Award   Vol. 1: 14237
Purdue Cup   Vol. 1: 5284
Purdue Frederick Research Grant; Oncology Nursing Foundation/   Vol. 1: 15648
Purdy Award; Ken W.   Vol. 1: 11103
Purdy Award; Ross Coffin   Vol. 1: 1473
Purina Mills, Inc. Teaching Award   Vol. 1: 1923
Purina Teaching Award   Vol. 1: 16354
Purkey, Jr. Memorial Outstanding Pitcher Award; Robert   Vol. 1: 14266
Purple Heart   Vol. 1: 19185
Purse Doctoral Fellowship; Ross C.   Vol. 1: 7062
Pursuit of Excellence Award   Vol. 1: 14057
Pursuit Trophy   Vol. 2: 3481
Purvis Lecture; Arthur B.   Vol. 2: 4422
Purvis Memorial Lectures   Vol. 1: 17808
Puschkin Prize; Alexander   Vol. 2: 7120
Pushcart Prize: Best of the Small Presses   Vol. 1: 16599
Pushkin Institute Scholarship, Moscow   Vol. 2: 4352
Pushkin Prize; Alexander Sergeovich   Vol. 2: 10423
Pushkin's Medal; A. S.   Vol. 2: 10451
Puskas Tivadar Award   Vol. 2: 7453
Putman Memorial Trophy; Byron E.   Vol. 1: 14644
Putnam & Grosset Group Award   Vol. 1: 2863
Putnam Honor Award; Herbert W.   Vol. 1: 2822
Putnam Publishing Group Award   Vol. 1: 2863
Putnam Service Award; Allan Ray   Vol. 1: 5363
Puy of Electroacoustic Music Competition   Vol. 2: 5000
PVA Donor Recognition Award   Vol. 1: 15939
PVA Patriot Award   Vol. 1: 15939
PVA "Speedy" Award   Vol. 1: 15940
PW/Roger Klein Award   Vol. 1: 16589
Pyle Award; Human Interest Reporting - Ernie   Vol. 1: 17147
Pyrotechnics Guild International Awards   Vol. 1: 16601
Pyser-SGI Award   Vol. 2: 2309
Q107 Homegrown Contest   Vol. 1: 7695
Qoboza Award for Foreign Journalists; Percy   Vol. 1: 12961
QRL Poetry Series Awards   Vol. 1: 16603
QSPELL Awards   Vol. 1: 16622
QST Cover Plaque Award   Vol. 1: 3893
Quadrennial Prize of the Royal Belgian Numismatic Society   Vol. 2: 1345
Quaid-i-Azam Police Medal for Gallantry   Vol. 2: 9997
Quality Brickwork Award   Vol. 2: 2216
Quality Digest Award   Vol. 1: 16605
Quality of Work Life Network National Award for Outstanding Achievement in Employee Involvement in the Workplace   Vol. 1: 4340
Quarter-Century Honor Roll   Vol. 1: 13105
Quarter Century News Achievement Award   Vol. 1: 18065
Quarter Midgets of America Hall of Fame   Vol. 1: 11112
Quarterly Awards   Vol. 1: 11984
Quazza Medal; Giorgio   Vol. 2: 819
Queen Award; Ellery   Vol. 1: 12550
Queen Contest   Vol. 1: 14145
Queen Elisabeth International Music Competition of Belgium Prizes   Vol. 2: 1245

Queen Elizabeth II Coronation Award   Vol. 2: 3871
Queen Fabiola Prize   Vol. 2: 1168
Queen Fabiola; Triennial International Carillon Competition -   Vol. 2: 1348
Queen Marie Jose International Musical Composition Prize   Vol. 2: 11896
Queen Mother's Birthday Awards   Vol. 2: 4542
Queen Sofia Award for Research into Mental Retardation   Vol. 2: 11246
Queen's Award   Vol. 2: 2934
Queen's Award for Forestry   Vol. 2: 2651
Queen's Awards for Environmental Achievement   Vol. 2: 3830
Queen's Awards for Export Achievement   Vol. 2: 3831
Queen's Awards for Technological Achievement   Vol. 2: 3832
Queen's Commendation for Excellence   Vol. 2: 3878
Queen's Fire Service Medal for Gallantry   Vol. 2: 2381
Queen's Gallantry Medal   Vol. 2: 2382
Queen's Gold Medal for Poetry   Vol. 2: 4555
Queen's Medal for Champion Shots   Vol. 1: 6710
Queens Opera Association Annual Vocal Competition   Vol. 1: 16626
Queen's Police Medal for Gallantry   Vol. 2: 2383
Queen's Prize NRA Gold Medal   Vol. 2: 3706
Queen's Silver Jubilee Competition   Vol. 2: 4306
Queensland Division Chemical Branch Award   Vol. 2: 482
Queensland International Fellowship - AFUW   Vol. 2: 11789
Queeny Award; Edgar M.   Vol. 1: 12418
Queeny Safety Professional of the Year Award; Edgar Monsanto   Vol. 1: 4788
Queirolo Prize; Pilade   Vol. 2: 8423
Queneau Award (Palladium Medal); Joan Hodges   Vol. 1: 1000
Queneau Palladium Medal; Joan Hodges   Vol. 1: 13396
Quesada Award; General E. R.   Vol. 1: 277
Quest for a Kelpie; A   Vol. 2: 10518
Quick Printer of the Year   Vol. 1: 13266
Quick Printing Magazine Man/Woman of the Year   Vol. 1: 16628
Quick Printing Magazine Suppliers' Man of the Year   Vol. 1: 16628
Quill and Scroll Award; National Newspaper Association -   Vol. 1: 15357
Quill Award   Vol. 1: 13382
Quilt National Awards   Vol. 1: 8498
Quinn Award; Dave   Vol. 1: 19583
Quinquennial Award in the Psychology of Religion   Vol. 2: 1175
Quintero; Premio Alvarez   Vol. 2: 11346
Quinto Prize; Nicoletta   Vol. 2: 8305
Quiroga Prize; Marcial V.   Vol. 2: 96
Quixote Prize; Don   Vol. 2: 5957
R & D 100 Awards   Vol. 1: 16797
R D'Oro   Vol. 2: 8415
R38 Memorial Prize   Vol. 2: 3901
Raabe-Preis; Wilhelm-   Vol. 2: 6574
RAB Chassie Awards   Vol. 1: 16632
Rabassa Prize for Translation of Fiction; Gregory   Vol. 1: 2967
Rabb Award; Sidney R.   Vol. 1: 9299
Rabbinical Awards   Vol. 1: 8365
Rabi Prize; I. I.   Vol. 1: 3468
Rabone Award   Vol. 2: 9743
RAC Awards   Vol. 1: 16814
RAC Hall of Fame   Vol. 1: 16815

Race Organizer of the Year   Vol. 1: 19029
Race Prize; R. R.   Vol. 2: 3174
Racehorse of the Year Award   Vol. 2: 3835
Rackoff Humanitarian Award; Bella   Vol. 1: 20401
Racovita Prize; Emil   Vol. 2: 10380
RAD Magazine Best Poster Prize   Vol. 2: 2415
Radcliffe Awards; Mrs. Ann   Vol. 1: 8415
Radcliffe Travelling Fellowship; Frank   Vol. 2: 3902
Raddall Atlantic Fiction Award; Thomas   Vol. 1: 20552
Radde - Educator of the Year Award; Leon R.   Vol. 1: 10373
Radin Distinguished Service Award; Alex   Vol. 1: 3861
Radin Memorial Award; Jacqueline Z.   Vol. 1: 15374
Radio and Television Language Prize   Vol. 2: 12078
Radio Bantu Prize for Works Written for the Radio   Vol. 2: 11041
Radio Broadcasting Hall of Fame   Vol. 1: 12972
Radio Denmark Language Award   Vol. 2: 1994
Radio Exterior de Espana Prize   Vol. 2: 11324
Radio Mercury Awards   Vol. 1: 16633
Radio Mercury Gold Award   Vol. 1: 16633
Radio Mercury Public Service Award   Vol. 1: 16633
Radio Program Producer of the Year   Vol. 1: 14606
Radio Station of the Year   Vol. 1: 14607
Radio Times Drama & Comedy Awards   Vol. 2: 2160
Radiology News Awards Competition   Vol. 1: 1740
Radius-Prijs; Alexandra   Vol. 2: 9436
Radius Prize; Alexandra   Vol. 2: 9436
Radix Pin; Harry E.   Vol. 1: 19354
Radix Trophy   Vol. 1: 19354
Radix Trophy; Henry E.   Vol. 1: 16482
Raeymaekers; Prix Jules   Vol. 2: 963
RAF Apprentice Engineering Technician Prize   Vol. 2: 3300
Rafaelsen Fellowship Award   Vol. 2: 10528
Rafaty Memorial Award; F. Mark   Vol. 1: 570
Raffles Award; Stamford   Vol. 2: 4659
Raginsky Award; Bernard B.   Vol. 1: 17437
Rahman Gold Cup   Vol. 2: 8899
RAIA Gold Medal   Vol. 2: 610
RAIC Allied Arts Medal   Vol. 1: 16921
RAIC Gold Medal   Vol. 1: 16922
RAIC Student Medal   Vol. 1: 16923
Raikes Medal   Vol. 2: 11050
Rail Transportation Award   Vol. 1: 4702
Railroad Construction Award   Vol. 2: 10444
Railway Engineering Award   Vol. 2: 483
Raimondi Prize; Alejandro A.   Vol. 2: 97
Raimundring   Vol. 2: 766
Raine Award; Noel   Vol. 2: 4378
Rainier III de Monaco; Bourse Prince   Vol. 2: 5935
Raise Your Sites Award   Vol. 1: 9886
Rajchman Prize; Jan   Vol. 1: 17533
Raju Oration Award; Dr. P. N.   Vol. 2: 7600
Rakkasan NCO of the Year   Vol. 1: 3
Rakkasan of the Year   Vol. 1: 4
Rakkasan Soldier of the Year   Vol. 1: 4
Raleigh Award; Sir Walter   Vol. 1: 15500
Rally Awards   Vol. 1: 18401
Ralph W. Westcott Award   Vol. 1: 19670
Ralston Purina Company Teaching Award in Dairy Science   Vol. 1: 1923

Ralston Purina Excellence in Veterinary Medicine Award; HeSCA/   Vol. 1: 9857
Ramachandran 60th Birthday Commemoration Medal Award; Prof. G. N.   Vol. 2: 7664
Ramachar Award in Electrochemical Science   Vol. 2: 7497
Ramaermedaille   Vol. 2: 9562
Ramage Award; Lillian Harlan   Vol. 1: 12481
Raman Medal; Chandrasekhara Venkata   Vol. 2: 7665
Raman Prize   Vol. 2: 8289
Ramanathan Medal; K. R.   Vol. 2: 7666
Ramirez Medal; Rafael   Vol. 2: 9155
Ramirez; Medalla Agustin   Vol. 2: 9013
Ramirez; Premio Felipe Tena   Vol. 2: 9193
Ramirez; Premio IMIQ, ING. Estanislao   Vol. 2: 9108
Ramirez Prize; Ignacio   Vol. 2: 9091
Ramo Award; Simon   Vol. 1: 3469
Ramo Medal; Simon   Vol. 1: 10286
Ramos Prize; Doctor Gustavo Cordeiro   Vol. 2: 10287
Rampal; Concours International de Flute Jean-Pierre   Vol. 2: 5034
Ramsaur Travel Writing Award; Ned   Vol. 1: 18177
Ramsay Medal; Erskine
  American Institute of Mining, Metallurgical and Petroleum Engineers   Vol. 1: 2641
  Society for Mining, Metallurgy, and Exploration   Vol 1: 17573
Ramsay Memorial Fellowship for Chemical Research   Vol. 2: 3837
Ramsdell Award; Charles   Vol. 1: 18214
Ramsdell Award; Green -   Vol. 1: 18214
Ramsden Award; FAW Barbara   Vol. 2: 382
Ramsey National Football Foundation Graduate Fellowship; Frank   Vol. 1: 13996
Ramuz; Grand Prix C. F.   Vol. 2: 11723
Rancho Gabriel Novice Obedience Award   Vol. 1: 3984
Rand Memorial Gold Medal; Charles F.   Vol. 1: 2642
Rand Trophy; Remington   Vol. 1: 10396
Randall Award; Ollie A.   Vol. 1: 13819
R&B Foundation Awards   Vol. 1: 16832
Randolph Achievement Award; A. Philip   Vol. 1: 16673
Randolph/Bayard Rustin Freedom Award; A. Philip   Vol. 1: 16674
Randolph Freedom Award; A. Philip   Vol. 1: 16674
Randolph Program for International Peace; Jennings   Vol. 1: 19406
Raney Fund Award   Vol. 1: 4615
Ranganathan Award for Classification Research
  Committee on Classification Research of the Federation Internationale d'Information et de Documentation, The Hague   Vol. 1: 8040
  Documentation Research and Training Centre   Vol 2: 7493
Ranganathan Gold Medal; Kaula -   Vol. 2: 7699
Ransom Memorial Medals; James   Vol. 2: 3329
Rao Award; Dr. T. Ramachandra   Vol. 2: 7601
Rao Award; Tilak Venkoba   Vol. 2: 7602
Rao Memorial Lecture; Prof. K. Rangadhama   Vol. 2: 7667
Rao Oration Award in Microbiology; Dr. Y. S. Narayana   Vol. 2: 7603
Raphael-Leygues; Prix Claude   Vol. 2: 5372
Raphael-Leygues; Prix Jacques   Vol. 2: 6336
Raphel Memorial Award; Arnold L.   Vol. 1: 19297

Rare Books and Manuscripts Librarianship Award   Vol. 1: 2877
RASD/BRASS Disclosure Student Travel Award   Vol. 1: 2948
Rask Award; Dr. Michael R.   Vol. 1: 609
Rassegna Internazionale dei Documentari Cine-TV Marinari   Vol. 2: 8295
Raster Award   Vol. 1: 9849
Ratcliff Trophy; Tom   Vol. 2: 2898
Ratner Award; Bret   Vol. 1: 682
Raulin; Fondation Victor   Vol. 2: 5676
Rauriser Literaturpreis   Vol. 2: 723
Raven Award   Vol. 1: 12550
Raven Lecturer   Vol. 2: 1967
Ravenswood Prize   Vol. 1: 20178
Rawley Prize; James A.   Vol. 1: 15822
Rawlings Award for Energy Conservation (Manager and Tehcnician); General Edwin W.   Vol. 1: 252
Rawlings Award for Environmental Achievement (Manager and Technician); General Edwin W.   Vol. 1: 252
Rawlings Big Stick Award
    National Junior College Athletic Association   Vol. 1: 14266
    Rawlings Sporting Goods Company   Vol 1: 16688
Rawlings Bronze Glove Award   Vol. 1: 16689
Rawlings Gold Glove Award
    Rawlings Sporting Goods Company   Vol. 1: 16690
    The Sporting News   Vol 1: 18382
Rawlings Player of the Year   Vol. 1: 12949
Rawlings Silver Glove Award   Vol. 1: 16691
Rawls - Palmer Award and Lectureship   Vol. 1: 4058
Rawson Academy Award for Excellence   Vol. 1: 16693
Rawson Academy Touring Lectureship   Vol. 1: 16694
Ray Award in Memory of Margaret Sutermeister; Isaac   Vol. 1: 3649
Rayleigh Book Award; IEE   Vol. 2: 3288
Rayleigh Medal   Vol. 2: 3053
Raymond Collegiate ECHO Awards; Leonard J.   Vol. 1: 8648
Raymond Literary Award; Wayte and Olga   Vol. 1: 3255
Raymond Memorial Award; Rossiter W.   Vol. 1: 2643
Razorback Award   Vol. 1: 5284
RBMS Exhibition Catalogue Awards   Vol. 1: 2874
Rea Award for the Short Story   Vol. 1: 8769
Reader Prize; Ralph   Vol. 2: 306
Readers' and Critics' Poll   Vol. 1: 16888
Reader's Digest American Heroes in Education Awards   Vol. 1: 16698
Reader's Digest Award   Vol. 1: 7124
Reader's Digest Young Designer Award   Vol. 2: 193
Readers Prize of the *Berliner Morgenpost*   Vol. 2: 6564
Readex/GODORT/ALA Catharine J. Reynolds Grant   Vol. 1: 2896
Reading Award   Vol. 1: 14550
Real Estate Educator of the Year   Vol. 1: 16706
Real Estate Journalism Competition
    National Association of Real Estate Editors   Vol. 1: 13272
    National Association of Realtors   Vol 1: 13276
Real Estate Regulator of the Year   Vol. 1: 16707
Reale Mamorial Award; Nicholas   Vol. 1: 5060

Realia Honors   Vol. 1: 10245
Realtor of the Year   Vol. 1: 13277
Reardon Award; Paul C.   Vol. 1: 13574
Reason Memorial Cup; George   Vol. 1: 6790
Recent American Works on Paper: A National Juried Exhibition   Vol. 1: 17169
Rechter Award; Zeev   Vol. 2: 7866
Reckord Trophy; Major General Milton A.   Vol. 1: 14644
Reckord Trophy; Milton A.   Vol. 1: 14096
Reclamation Researcher of the Year   Vol. 1: 4291
Reclamationist of the Year   Vol. 1: 4292
Recognition Award
    Agricultural Institute of Canada   Vol. 1: 213
    American Lupus Society   Vol 1: 2975
    Association for Systems Management   Vol 1: 5605
    Association for the Education of Teachers in Science   Vol 1: 5634
    International Association of Campus Law Enforcement Administrators   Vol 1: 10687
    National Association of School Nurses   Vol 1: 13295
Recognition Award for Outstanding Achievement in Adolescent Medicine   Vol. 1: 17397
Recognition Award for Young Scholars   Vol. 1: 1237
Recognition Awards   Vol. 1: 8300
Recognition Medal   Vol. 1: 17540
Recognition of Achievement Award   Vol. 1: 5374
Recognition of Advertising Merit   Vol. 1: 14466
Recognition of Long Service to the Society   Vol. 2: 10824
Recognition of Professional Service Award   Vol. 1: 7918
Recognition of Service   Vol. 1: 7762
Recognition of Service and Involvement   Vol. 1: 8704
Recognition of Services to the International Softball Congress   Vol. 1: 11317
Recognition Plaque   Vol. 1: 10027
Recognition Prize for Children's and Youth's Literature   Vol. 2: 769
Record Houses of the Year   Vol. 1: 5233
Record Interiors of the Year   Vol. 1: 5234
Record of the Year Prize   Vol. 2: 4691
Rector's Medal   Vol. 2: 11117
Recycler of the Year   Vol. 1: 14578
Recycling Hall of Fame   Vol. 1: 14580
Red Award for ANG Aerospace Maintenance; Chief Master Sergeant Dick   Vol. 1: 253
Red Cloud Indian Art Show   Vol. 1: 9914
Red Earth Poetry Award   Vol. 2: 555
Red Ribbon Award   Vol. 1: 2045
Redbook Children's Book Awards   Vol. 1: 16735
Redbook's Short Story Contest   Vol. 1: 16734
Redbook's Top Ten Picture Books of the Year   Vol. 1: 16735
Redd Center Manuscript Competition; Charles   Vol. 1: 16737
Redeker Preis; Franz   Vol. 2: 6680
Reden Plakette   Vol. 2: 6851
Redfield Trophy   Vol. 1: 14643
Redford Memorial Award; Polly   Vol. 1: 9259
Redhead Superstar Contest Award   Vol. 1: 16741
Redi Award   Vol. 2: 6989
Redland Pitched Roof Awards   Vol. 2: 3841
Redmond Award for Nursing; Juanita   Vol. 1: 254
Redon; Fondation   Vol. 2: 5388
Redon; Prix Gustave-Francois   Vol. 2: 5397
Redshaw Memorial Award; Alec   Vol. 2: 2951

Redwood Lectureship; Theophilus   Vol. 2: 4214
Redwood Medal   Vol. 2: 3182
Reebok Human Rights Award   Vol. 1: 16744
Reebok World Cup of Race Walking; IAAF/   Vol. 2: 9314
Reed and Mallik Medal   Vol. 2: 3256
Reed Award   Vol. 1: 82
Reed Award; President Dr. Donald A.   Vol. 1: 8416
Reed Award; Roger J.   Vol. 1: 2066
Reed Award; Sylvanus Albert   Vol. 1: 2496
Reed Fiction Award   Vol. 2: 9803
Reed Fiction Award; Heinemann/   Vol. 2: 9803
Reed Medal; Walter   Vol. 1: 4815
Reed Memorial Award; Dave   Vol. 1: 14930
Reed Memorial Award; Paul   Vol. 1: 8857
Reed Memorial Book Award; A. W.   Vol. 2: 9804
Reed Memorial Children's Book Award; A. W.   Vol. 2: 9805
Reed Technology Medal; Robert F.   Vol. 1: 9702
Reese Memorial Prize; Trevor   Vol. 2: 4581
Reese Research Prize; Raymond C.   Vol. 1: 4491
Reese Structural Research Award; Raymond C.   Vol. 1: 1776
Reeves Award; Roberta Wright   Vol. 1: 2400
Reeves Premium; A. H.   Vol. 2: 3301
Reference Service Press Award   Vol. 1: 2949
REFORMA Scholarship Program   Vol. 1: 16746
Regeneration of Scotland Design Award   Vol. 2: 10613
Regennitter AAU Jujitsu Service Award; Professor   Vol. 1: 447
Regents Publishing Company Fellowship; TESOL/   Vol. 1: 18593
Reger Memorial Award   Vol. 1: 14598
Reggiani Prize; Stefano   Vol. 2: 8291
Reggie Awards   Vol. 1: 16535
Regina Award   Vol. 1: 17073
Regina Medal   Vol. 1: 7380
Region 14 Sequence Award   Vol. 1: 2265
Region of the Year   Vol. 1: 352
Region of the Year Award   Vol. 1: 4261
Regional Achievement Award   Vol. 1: 18402
Regional Artists Projects   Vol. 1: 8236
Regional Auditions   Vol. 1: 12244
Regional Award   Vol. 1: 14984
Regional Awards   Vol. 1: 13332
Regional Clubs of the Year   Vol. 1: 20465
Regional Coach of the Year   Vol. 1: 19346
Regional Cultural Commendation   Vol. 2: 8580
Regional Director of the Year   Vol. 1: 14189
Regional Director of the Year Award   Vol. 1: 600
Regional Directors Award   Vol. 1: 6241
Regional Distinguished Service Award   Vol. 1: 8982
Regional Diver of the Year Award   Vol. 1: 18870
Regional Division Art Educator of the Year   Vol. 1: 12810
Regional Ecumenism Award   Vol. 2: 941
Regional Graduate Scholarships   Vol. 1: 7226
Regional Horse Awards   Vol. 1: 15482
Regional Leadership Award   Vol. 1: 13798
Regional Medallions   Vol. 1: 16084
Regional Media Awards   Vol. 1: 17269
Regional Mid-Career Award   Vol. 1: 8983
Regional Outstanding Practitioner Award   Vol. 1: 789

Regional Outstanding Service Award   Vol. 1: 790
Regional Person of the Year Award   Vol. 1: 13798
Regional Plan Association Award   Vol. 1: 16750
Regional Presidents Award   Vol. 1: 12991
Regional Production Prizes   Vol. 2: 23
Regional Psychiatric Technician of the Year   Vol. 1: 1150
Regional Publication Awards   Vol. 1: 18403
Regional Radio and Television Awards   Vol. 2: 1108
Regional Representative of the Year   Vol. 1: 353
Regional Safety Professional of the Year   Vol. 1: 4788
Regional Team Award   Vol. 1: 8984
Regional Television Photographers of the Year   Vol. 1: 14527
Regional Volunteer of the Year   Vol. 1: 11601
Register of Merit Award   Vol. 1: 1963
Registrar's Prize   Vol. 2: 4265
Regnier; Fondation Henriette   Vol. 2: 5579
Regnone Service Award; Debbie   Vol. 1: 16807
Regulus Awards   Vol. 1: 18898
Rehabilitation 2000 Congressional Leadership Award   Vol. 1: 3943
Rehabilitation Awareness Award   Vol. 1: 3944
Rehabilitation Discovery Awards   Vol. 1: 3945
Rehabilitation Facility Recognition Award   Vol. 1: 3945
Rehabilitation International Presidential Award   Vol. 1: 16757
Rehabilitation Outcomes Award   Vol. 1: 3946
Reichart Award; Stuart   Vol. 1: 255
Reichelderfer Award; Francis W.   Vol. 1: 3076
Reid Award; Helen Dwight   Vol. 1: 3581
Reid Memorial Award; Crawford   Vol. 1: 11477
Reid Prize; W.T. and Sdaba   Vol. 1: 17515
Reimann Prize; Christiane   Vol. 2: 11778
Reinhart Award; Frank W.   Vol. 1: 6070
Reinhart Ring; Hans   Vol. 2: 11921
Reinhold Award for Innovation in Teaching; Van Nostrand   Vol. 1: 8402
Reinman, Jr. Award; Alfred E.   Vol. 1: 5196
Reis Medal; Philipp   Vol. 2: 6748
Reisinger Trophy; Curt H.   Vol. 1: 1828
Reisner-Pennycuik Concerto Prize   Vol. 2: 326
Reiss Memorial Judaica Library Awards; Joseph   Vol. 1: 18923
Reitman Memorial Award; Stanley S.   Vol. 1: 11243
Reitter Award; Ferenc   Vol. 2: 7306
Rekishi Bungaku Sho   Vol. 2: 8740
Related Industry Award   Vol. 1: 12755
Relating Research to Practice Awards   Vol. 1: 1979
Reliability Test and Evaluation Award   Vol. 1: 10333
Relief Pitcher   Vol. 1: 18345
Religious Art and Architecture Design Awards   Vol. 1: 2542
Religious Broadcasting Hall of Fame   Vol. 1: 14608
Religious Freedom Award - Human Rights Award   Vol. 1: 16803
Religious Liberty Award   Vol. 1: 10469
Remembrance Award   Vol. 1: 20485
Remi Award
 WORLDFEST - Houston International Film and Video Festival   Vol. 1: 20538
 WORLDFEST - Houston International Film and Video Festival   Vol 1: 20539

Remington Honor Medal   Vol. 1: 3388
Remmey AWS Memorial Award; Paul B.   Vol. 1: 5061
Remodeler of the Month/Year Awards   Vol. 1: 13138
Remote Sensing Lecturer   Vol. 1: 3094
Remote Sensing Society Medal   Vol. 2: 3846
Remote Sensing Society Student Awards   Vol. 2: 3847
Renaissance Award   Vol. 1: 11489
Renaissance Awards   Vol. 1: 13139
Renaitour Prize; J-M   Vol. 2: 6314
Renards de l'affiche du livre de jeunesse   Vol. 2: 6203
Renault; Prix Louis   Vol. 2: 11751
Renchard Prize for Historic Preservation   Vol. 1: 9937
Rencontre Internationale des Jeunes Pianistes Senigallia   Vol. 2: 8419
Rencontres chorales internationales de Montreux   Vol. 2: 11879
Rencontres Internationales des Maitres Guitariers   Vol. 2: 6185
Rendano; Concorso nazionale pianistico Premio   Vol. 2: 8138
Renie; Prix Henriette   Vol. 2: 5402
Renku Competition   Vol. 1: 9758
Renner Award; Frederick G.   Vol. 1: 17588
Renner Crime Reporting Award; Tom   Vol. 1: 11429
Renner Memorial Award; J.   Vol. 2: 7290
Renner Preis; Karl   Vol. 2: 795
Rennie Memorial Medal   Vol. 2: 601
Renold Fellowship; Albert   Vol. 2: 6708
Repaci Prize; Leonida   Vol. 2: 8407
Repligen Corporation Award in Chemistry of Biological Processes   Vol. 1: 1509
Replogle Award for Management Improvement; Luther I.   Vol. 1: 19298
Reporter of the Year Award   Vol. 1: 1796
Republic of Vietnam Campaign Medal   Vol. 1: 19186
Republican of the Year   Vol. 1: 16851
Research Achievement Award
 American Heart Association   Vol. 1: 2240
 National Association for Equal Opportunity in Higher Education   Vol 1: 12859
Research Achievement Award in Economic, Social and Administrative Sciences   Vol. 1: 3389
Research Achievement Award in Natural Products   Vol. 1: 3389
Research Achievement Award in Pharmaceutical and Medicinal Chemistry   Vol. 1: 3389
Research Achievement Award in Pharmacodynamics   Vol. 1: 3389
Research Achievement Awards   Vol. 1: 3389
Research and Development Award
 American Diabetes Association   Vol. 1: 1950
 National Energy Resources Organization   Vol 1: 13903
Research and Education Excellence Award   Vol. 1: 14652
Research and Special Libraries Award   Vol. 1: 5842
Research Award
 American Institute of Aeronautics and Astronautics   Vol. 1: 2463
 ASPO/Lamaze   Vol 1: 5385
 Astronomical Society of Japan   Vol 2: 8508
 Commission on Pastoral Research   Vol 1: 8030
 Consortium of College and University Media Centers   Vol 1: 8191
 Council for Exceptional Children   Vol 1: 8318

 Ergonomics Society   Vol 2: 2807
 Fellows of the American Bar Foundation   Vol 1: 9164
 National Association of College Gymnastics Coaches (Men)   Vol 1: 13002
 Society of Insurance Research   Vol 1: 17863
Research Award Competition   Vol. 1: 1860
Research Award for Amateurs   Vol. 2: 8509
Research Award for Junior Astronomers   Vol. 2: 8510
Research Award in Teacher Education   Vol. 1: 5981
Research Award of Merit   Vol. 1: 15337
Research Award on Psychotherapy with Women   Vol. 1: 3773
Research Awards
 American Association of Occupational Health Nurses   Vol. 1: 1081
 American Board for Occupational Health Nurses, Inc.   Vol 1: 1351
 American College Health Association   Vol 1: 1600
 American College of Chest Physicians   Vol 1: 1621
 Association of Government Accountants   Vol 1: 5822
 Burroughs Wellcome Fund   Vol 1: 6639
 Psychologists for Social Responsibility   Vol 1: 16553
 Society for Theatre Research   Vol 2: 4381
Research Awards in Otolaryngology   Vol. 1: 659
Research Council Award   Vol. 1: 4007
Research Council Awards   Vol. 1: 15337
Research Fellowship   Vol. 1: 1087
Research Fellowship Awards   Vol. 1: 622
Research Fellowship Grants   Vol. 1: 4768
Research Fellowships   Vol. 1: 11721
Research Gallery   Vol. 2: 6189
Research Grant
 Galpin Society   Vol. 2: 2915
 Society for Pediatric Dermatology   Vol 1: 17583
Research Grant Award   Vol. 1: 14640
Research Grants
 American Society of Plastic and Reconstructive Surgeons - Plastic Surgery Educational Foundation   Vol. 1: 4769
 British School at Rome   Vol 2: 8179
Research in Action Award   Vol. 1: 1061
Research in Dental Caries Award   Vol. 1: 10619
Research in Oral Biology Award   Vol. 1: 10620
Research in Periodontal Disease Award   Vol. 1: 10621
Research in Prosthodontics and Implants Award   Vol. 1: 10622
Research in Prosthodontics Award   Vol. 1: 10622
Research Interest Section/Newbury House Distinguished Research Award; TESOL   Vol. 1: 18594
Research Medal
 New Zealand Association of Scientists   Vol. 2: 9755
 Royal Scottish Geographical Society   Vol 2: 10629
Research Medal for Research Work of Benefit to Agriculture   Vol. 2: 3923
Research Prize and Bronze Medal   Vol. 2: 3968
Research Program Grants   Vol. 2: 545
Research Programs in Cystic Fibrosis   Vol. 1: 8490
Research Project Grants   Vol. 2: 546

Research Recognition Award   Vol. 1: 1088
Research Scientist Award   Vol. 1: 726
Research Training Fellowship   Vol. 2: 6485
Researcher of the Year   Vol. 1: 3066
Reserve Force Decoration (RFD)   Vol. 2: 340
Reserve Force Medal   Vol. 2: 340
Reserve Grand Award   Vol. 1: 19714
Reserve Rakkasan of the Year   Vol. 1: 5
Reservoir Engineering Award   Vol. 1: 17973
Residency Fellowships for Artists and Ensembles Developing New Works   Vol. 1: 20576
Resident Achievement Awards   Vol. 1: 1711
Resident and Fellow Injury Prevention Achievement Awards   Vol. 1: 683
Resident Award
   Congress of Neurological Surgeons   Vol. 1: 8152
   Society for Pediatric Dermatology   Vol 1: 17584
   Society of Surgical Oncology   Vol 1: 18038
Resident Awards   Vol. 1: 1086
Resident Case of the Year Award   Vol. 1: 3954
Resident Essay Award   Vol. 1: 3901
Resident Essay Contest   Vol. 1: 861
Resident Physician's Prize Paper Award   Vol. 1: 4549
Resident Research Award   Vol. 1: 3954
Resident Research Awards
   American Academy of Facial Plastic and Reconstructive Surgery   Vol. 1: 571
   Jerome Levy Economics Institute of Bard College   Vol 1: 11844
Resident Research Competition   Vol. 1: 17800
Residential Fellowships   Vol. 1: 7990
Residential Landscape Design Awards   Vol. 1: 14281
Residential Services Award   Vol. 1: 3192
Residents' Award   Vol. 1: 707
Resident's - Fellow Essay Award   Vol. 1: 5308
Resistol Rookie of the Year   Vol. 1: 16513
Resnik Award; Judith A.   Vol. 1: 10287
Resnik Challenger Medal   Vol. 1: 18103
Resolution for Meritorious Service   Vol. 1: 13878
Resolution in Appreciation of Dedicated Leadership   Vol. 1: 13878
Resopal Award   Vol. 2: 1114
Resort Condominiums International (RCI) Festival of Emerging American Theatre Competition   Vol. 1: 16150
Resources Council Annual Product Design Awards Program   Vol. 1: 10572
Restaurant Award of Excellence   Vol. 1: 13479
Reston Prize   Vol. 1: 5322
Restrepo Prize for Philology; Felix   Vol. 2: 1679
Retail Awards   Vol. 1: 9440
Retail Nurseryman Award - Jack F. Schneider Award   Vol. 1: 9484
Retail Store Award   Vol. 1: 10577
Retailer of the Year Award   Vol. 1: 13286
Retailers of the Year   Vol. 1: 9361
Retreat Alumni Fellowship   Vol. 1: 17215
Rettie Memorial Trophy   Vol. 1: 2786
Reuben Award (Rube Goldberg Award)   Vol. 1: 13527
Reuchlinpreis der Stadt Pforzheim   Vol. 2: 7102
Reumer Prijs; Wanda   Vol. 2: 9328
Reuter Foundation Fellowship   Vol. 2: 3850
Reuter Prize; Fritz   Vol. 2: 7121
Reuter Prize; Paul   Vol. 2: 11772
Revelation Prize for Children's Literature   Vol. 2: 10310

Revelation Prize for Essay   Vol. 2: 10311
Revelation Prize for Fiction   Vol. 2: 10312
Revelation Prize for Poetry   Vol. 2: 10313
Reves Award; Emery   Vol. 1: 10842
Review of Research Award   Vol. 1: 1980
Revson Foundation Fellowships; PEN/   Vol. 1: 16029
Revueltas; Premio Nacional de Ensayo Literario Jose   Vol. 2: 9234
Reward for Excellence in Writing on Intelligence   Vol. 1: 14242
Rey; Prix Henri   Vol. 2: 6225
Rey; Prix Joseph   Vol. 2: 5042
Reyes; Premio Internacional Alfonso   Vol. 2: 9268
Reyes Prize; Alfonso   Vol. 2: 9156
Reynaud; Fondation Jean   Vol. 2: 5599
Reynaud; Prix Jean
   Institut de France - Academie des Beaux Arts   Vol. 2: 5406
   Institut de France - Academie des Inscriptions et Belle-Lettres   Vol 2: 5466
   Institut de France - Academie des Sciences Morales et Politiques   Vol 2: 5762
   Institut de France - Academie Francaise   Vol 2: 5872
Reynolds Award; Orr E.   Vol. 1: 3513
Reynolds Award; William D.   Vol. 1: 19857
Reynolds Grant; Readex/GODORT/ALA Catharine J.   Vol. 1: 2896
Reynolds Medal; Osborne   Vol. 2: 3219
Reynolds Media Awards; Nancy Susan   Vol. 1: 7449
Reynolds Memorial Award; R. S.   Vol. 1: 2543
RHA Best Seedling Award   Vol. 1: 16901
Rhatigan Award; Frank M.   Vol. 1: 9844
Rhoades Award; Edward H.   Vol. 1: 1302
Rhoads Lecture; Jonathan E.   Vol. 1: 4228
Rhoads Memorial Award; C. P.   Vol. 1: 843
Rhodes Best Original Advertising; E. Washington   Vol. 1: 14397
Rhomberg Preis; Alexander   Vol. 2: 6895
Rhondda Award; Margaret   Vol. 2: 4391
Rhone - Poulenc Lectureship   Vol. 2: 4215
RHS Vegetable Cup   Vol. 2: 4049
Rhyme Time Poetry Contest/Story Time Fiction Contest/Mystery Time Short Story Contest   Vol. 1: 16830
Rhys Memorial Prize; John Llewellyn   Vol. 2: 2201
Rhys Prize; *The Mail on Sunday* - John Llewellyn   Vol. 2: 2201
Rhysling Award   Vol. 1: 17115
Rhythm and Blues Award Show   Vol. 1: 6278
RIAA Cultural Award   Vol. 1: 16720
RIAA Gold Music Video Award   Vol. 1: 16721
RIAA Gold Record Award   Vol. 1: 16722
RIAA Platinum Music Video Award   Vol. 1: 16723
RIAA Platinum Record Award   Vol. 1: 16724
Riada Memorial Trophy; Sean O.   Vol. 2: 7766
RIAS/Acanthus Award for Measured Drawing   Vol. 2: 10614
RIAS/Alastair Hunter Award for Architectural Photography   Vol. 2: 10616
RIAS Award for Measured Drawing   Vol. 2: 10614
RIAS/Dunedin Award for Architectural Photography   Vol. 2: 10616
RIAS/John Maclaren Travelling Fellowship   Vol. 2: 10615
RIAS/Whitehouse Studio Award for Architectural Photography   Vol. 2: 10616
RIBA Architecture Awards   Vol. 2: 4069
Riba Poetry Prize; Carles   Vol. 2: 11238
RIBA Student Competition   Vol. 2: 4070

Ribalow Prize; Harold U.   Vol. 1: 9748
Ribaud; Fondation Gustave   Vol. 2: 5571
Ribeiro Literary Prize; Aquilino   Vol. 2: 10259
Ribeiro; Premio Aquilino   Vol. 2: 10259
Ricard; Grand Prix de Physique Jean   Vol. 2: 6364
Ricard Grand Prize for Physics; Jean   Vol. 2: 6364
Ricard; Prix Jean   Vol. 2: 6375
Riccione TTVV - Teatro Televisione Video   Vol. 2: 8405
Rice Award; Neal   Vol. 1: 10213
Rice - Drama Desk Awards; Vernon   Vol. 1: 8727
Rice Merit Award; D. I.   Vol. 1: 7925
Rice National Championship Trophy; Grantland   Vol. 1: 9308
Rich Competition; Wilmer Shields   Vol. 1: 8392
Rich Memorial Award; Margaret Elden   Vol. 1: 9039
Rich Moot Court Competition; Giles Sutherland   Vol. 1: 2696
Richard III Society/William Schallek Memorial Graduate Study Fellowship   Vol. 1: 16834
Richard Memorial Prize; Therese and Edwin H.   Vol. 1: 14714
Richard; Prix Maurice-   Vol. 1: 17390
Richards Alumni Award; Loretta   Vol. 1: 7930
Richards Award; Robert H.
   American Institute of Mining, Metallurgical and Petroleum Engineers   Vol. 1: 2644
   Society for Mining, Metallurgy, and Exploration   Vol 1: 17574
Richards Award; Tudor   Vol. 1: 6144
Richards Awards; Linda   Vol. 1: 14289
Richards Career Grant; Ruth   Vol. 1: 18831
Richards Memorial Award; Charles Russ   Vol. 1: 4703
Richards Natural History Education Award   Vol. 1: 9153
Richardson Award; Richard   Vol. 2: 2292
Richardson Award; Sally   Vol. 1: 2067
Richardson Award; William D.   Vol. 1: 9653
Richardson Gold Medal   Vol. 2: 3179
Richardson Medal; David   Vol. 1: 15757
Richardson Memorial Literary Trust; Evelyn   Vol. 1: 20553
Richardson Research Grant; Henry and Sylvia   Vol. 1: 8951
Richardson Theatre Awards (Jessies); Jessie   Vol. 1: 19977
Richardson Trophy   Vol. 2: 4050
Richart Award; Frank E.   Vol. 1: 6071
Richmond Cerebral Palsy Center Award   Vol. 1: 483
Richner, Jr. Scholarship Award; Cedric A.   Vol. 1: 13347
Richter Awards for Art Critics   Vol. 2: 4676
Richter Orgelwettbewerb; Internationaler Karl   Vol. 2: 6899
Richter Prize; Johan C.F.C.   Vol. 1: 18601
Richter Prize; Kurt P.   Vol. 1: 1208
Richtmyer Memorial Lecture   Vol. 1: 1133
Rickard Scholarship; Howard Brown   Vol. 1: 13965
Ricketts Award Fund; Howard T.   Vol. 1: 19758
Rickey Medal   Vol. 1: 4492
Ricks Award; Earl T.   Vol. 1: 256
Ricky's Red Rose Challenge Trophy   Vol. 1: 14866
Ricompense al Valor Civile e Merito Civile   Vol. 2: 8369
RICS Awards   Vol. 2: 4085
RID National Humanitarian Award   Vol. 1: 16839

Award Index
Volume 2: International and Foreign

Riddell Trophy for Vegetables   Vol. 2: 4051
Ridder Award; Walter T.   Vol. 1: 17182
Riddet Award   Vol. 2: 9718
Rideal Memorial Lecture   Vol. 2: 4423
Rider Award Program   Vol. 1: 19328
Rider of the Year   Vol. 1: 2187
Ridges Memorial Award; Robert V.   Vol. 1: 18404
Ridgway Student Chapter Award; Robert   Vol. 1: 4493
Riding Hours and Riding Miles Awards   Vol. 1: 1964
Ridley; In-Service Training Award in Memory of Clarence E.   Vol. 1: 10852
Ridley Medal   Vol. 2: 3438
Ridout Awards; Godfrey   Vol. 1: 17821
Rieder-Medaille; Hermann-   Vol. 2: 6830
Riegelman Research Achievement Award in Pharmaceutics; Sidney   Vol. 1: 3389
Rielo World Prize for Mystical Poetry; Fernando   Vol. 2: 11329
Rietz Lecture   Vol. 1: 10407
Rifbjerg; Klaus   Vol. 2: 1909
Rigdon Conservation Writer and Broadcaster Awards; Heath Cooper   Vol. 1: 18128
Rigging Job of the Year   Vol. 1: 18298
Right Livelihood Award   Vol. 2: 11509
Righteous Among the Nations   Vol. 2: 7995
Riha Prize; Bohumil   Vol. 2: 1842
Rijlant pour l'Electrophysiologie Cardiaque; Prix Triennal Professeur Pierre   Vol. 2: 1343
RILEM Award   Vol. 2: 6068
Riley Prize; Franklin L.   Vol. 1: 12360
Rimbaud Prize; Arthur   Vol. 2: 6104
Rimet Cup; Jules   Vol. 2: 11715
RINA Gold, Silver and Bronze Medals   Vol. 2: 4093
RINA Small Craft Group Medal   Vol. 2: 4094
Rinascimento 2000 - Certificate of Recognition; II   Vol. 1: 11490
Rinehart Grant; Mary Roberts   Vol. 1: 16841
Ring Award for Investigative Reporting; Selden   Vol. 1: 19871
Ring Championship Belt   Vol. 1: 16847
Ring Fighter of the Year   Vol. 1: 16844
The Ring Magazine Merit Award   Vol. 1: 16845
The Ring Progress Award   Vol. 1: 16846
Ringier Prize   Vol. 2: 6194
Ringwood Award for Drama; Gwen Pharis   Vol. 1: 20555
Rink Medaillen   Vol. 2: 1952
Rink Medal   Vol. 2: 1952
Rinkel Award; Herbert J.   Vol. 1: 562
Rio de La Loza Prize; Dr.   Vol. 2: 9118
Rio National Prize in Chemistry; Andres Manuel del   Vol. 2: 8948
Rio; Premio Nacional de Quimica Andres Manuel del   Vol. 2: 8948
Rip Rapp Archaeological Geology Award   Vol. 1: 9566
Ripert-Sarrut; Prix Marthe   Vol. 2: 6340
Ripperton Award; Lyman A.   Vol. 1: 223
Rising Award; James S.   Vol. 1: 4116
Rising Star Award
 British Association of Women Entrepreneurs   Vol. 2: 2283
 United States Harness Writers Association   Vol 1: 19387
Rising Sun Prize
 Asahi Shimbun Publishing Company   Vol. 2: 8494
 International Board on Books for Young People   Vol 2: 11768
Rispens Research Award; Dr. Bart   Vol. 2: 7171
Rist Prize; David   Vol. 1: 12279

RITA Award   Vol. 1: 16892
Rittenhouse Award   Vol. 1: 12179
Ritter Award; Max   Vol. 1: 19001
Rittle, Sr. Memorial Scholarship Award; Paul H.   Vol. 1: 10443
Ritz Paris Hemingway Award   Vol. 2: 6199
Rivadavia Prize; Bernandino   Vol. 2: 98
Rivadeneira Prizes   Vol. 2: 11349
Rivenes Award - Taekwondo; David G.   Vol. 1: 448
River Award; CALAM/ACTAL - Charles   Vol. 1: 7258
River City Writing Awards in Fiction   Vol. 1: 16854
Rivers International Scholarship; Tom and Ruth   Vol. 1: 20500
Rivet; Prix Paul   Vol. 2: 6143
Rivis Prize; Mrs. F. E.   Vol. 2: 4052
Rivkin Award; William R.   Vol. 1: 2089
Rivot; Prix L. E.   Vol. 2: 5698
Rizal Medal; Jose   Vol. 2: 10730
RMA of the Year   Vol. 1: 3043
RMBPA Design Competition   Vol. 1: 16876
Roanoke - Chowan Award   Vol. 1: 15501
Roback Scholarship; Herbert   Vol. 1: 12653
Robb Research Award; D. M.   Vol. 1: 7926
Robbins Award; Harold   Vol. 1: 4837
Robbins Award; William J.   Vol. 1: 18754
Robe of Achievement   Vol. 1: 17203
Robert Fleming Prize   Vol. 1: 6749
Robert M. Burley Prize   Vol. 1: 15749
Roberts Award; A.W.   Vol. 2: 484
Roberts Award; Frances   Vol. 1: 8259
Robert's Award; Margaret Christie   Vol. 1: 8290
Roberts Award; Phil   Vol. 1: 10869
Roberts Award; Summerfield G.   Vol. 1: 18148
Roberts Award; Tom   Vol. 2: 650
Roberts Lecture in Interdisciplinary Sciences; Walter Orr   Vol. 1: 3095
Roberts Lecture; Lloyds   Vol. 2: 4264
Roberts Memorial Prize   Vol. 1: 11983
Roberts Playwriting Award; Forest A.   Vol. 1: 16856
Roberts Scholarship; W. Towyn   Vol. 2: 12186
Robertson Associate   Vol. 1: 7130
Robertson Memorial Lecture of the National Academy of Sciences   Vol. 1: 12687
Robertson Memorial Prize; James Alexander   Vol. 1: 8142
Robertson Memorial Trophy; C. P.   Vol. 2: 2047
Robertson Memorial Trophy; Heaton R.   Vol. 1: 19354
Robertson Professional Continuing Educator Award; Adelle F.   Vol. 1: 14954
Robertson Textile Award; Mary   Vol. 1: 15719
Robeson Award; Paul   Vol. 1: 118
Robeson Awards; Paul   Vol. 1: 15312
Robichaux Award; Joseph   Vol. 1: 19955
Robie Award for Achievement in Industry   Vol. 1: 16858
Robie Award for Humanitarianism   Vol. 1: 16859
Robin Hood Multifoods Limited Award   Vol. 1: 6918
Robin Hood Plaquette   Vol. 2: 11627
Robin Memorial Award; Andrew E.   Vol. 1: 9810
Robinson Award; C. S.   Vol. 1: 1190
Robinson Award for Athletics; Jackie   Vol. 1: 11594
Robinson Award; J. Franklin   Vol. 1: 537
Robinson Award; James H.   Vol. 1: 192
Robinson Award (Marine Flight Officer of the Year); Robert Guy   Vol. 1: 12074

Robinson Award; Renault   Vol. 1: 13462
Robinson Awards; Robert L.   Vol. 1: 3650
Robinson/Cunningham Award   Vol. 1: 537
Robinson Lectureship; Robert   Vol. 2: 4216
Robinson, M.D. Memorial Prizes in Surgery; James H.   Vol. 1: 14351
Robinson Memorial Lectureship; R. A.   Vol. 2: 4217
Robinson Memorial Medal for Begonia Hybrid; Alfred D.   Vol. 1: 1339
Robinson Periodontal Regeneration Award; R. Earl   Vol. 1: 697
Robinson Prize; James Harvey   Vol. 1: 2299
Robinson Prize; Joan Cahalin   Vol. 1: 17620
Robinson Rookie of the Year; Jackie   Vol. 1: 6282
Robinson Scholarship/Award in Conducting; Thelma A.   Vol. 1: 8096
Robinson Sports Award; Jackie   Vol. 1: 12906
Robson Award; Clifford J.   Vol. 1: 16549
Rocard; Prix Yves   Vol. 2: 6381
Rocha Medal; Manuel   Vol. 2: 10241
Roche Award   Vol. 1: 7193
Roche Distinguished Service Award; ONS/   Vol. 1: 15660
Rocheron; Prix Alberic   Vol. 2: 5807
Rochester International Independent Film Festival   Vol. 1: 16870
Rock and Roll Hall of Fame   Vol. 1: 16872
Rock Mechanics Award   Vol. 1: 17575
Rockefeller 3rd Award; John D.   Vol. 1: 5345
Rockefeller Prize   Vol. 1: 3424
Rockefeller Public Service Award   Vol. 1: 16403
Rockefeller Trophy; William A.   Vol. 1: 20246
Rockower Awards for Excellence in Jewish Journalism; Simon   Vol. 1: 2746
Rockwell Award; Martha   Vol. 1: 19584
Rockwell, Jr. Medal; Willard F.   Vol. 1: 11341
Rocky Mountain National Watermedia Exhibition Awards   Vol. 1: 9311
Rodale National Environmental Achievement Award - Searching for Success Program; Robert   Vol. 1: 16787
Rodda Award   Vol. 2: 660
Rodeo Hall of Fame   Vol. 1: 16879
Roderick Lectures; Collin   Vol. 2: 406
Roderick Prize in Science, Arms Control and International Security; AAAS Hilliard   Vol. 1: 879
Rodermund Service Award; Matthew   Vol. 1: 7337
Rodgers Achievement Award; Samuel U.   Vol. 1: 13015
Rodgers Production Award; Richard   Vol. 1: 516
Rodman Medal   Vol. 2: 4137
Rodney P. Savoy, Jr. Trophy   Vol. 1: 16214
Rodriguez Memorial Award; Pedro   Vol. 1: 8540
Rodrugues Prize; Nelson   Vol. 2: 1439
Roe Award; John Orlando   Vol. 1: 572
Roe Award; Kenneth Andrew   Vol. 1: 1001
Roe Award; Ralph Coats   Vol. 1: 4117
Roe Medal; Ralph Coats   Vol. 1: 4704
Roebling Award   Vol. 1: 4494
Roebling Medal   Vol. 1: 12305
Roebuck Cup   Vol. 2: 2340
Roelker Award   Vol. 1: 4934
Roelker Prize; Nancy Lyman   Vol. 1: 17300
Roell Prijs; David   Vol. 2: 9575
Roemer Conservation Awards; Elsie   Vol. 1: 9629
Roentgen-Preis   Vol. 2: 7001
Roerig Fellow in Hospital Dental Practice   Vol. 1: 1018

Roeske Certificate of Recognition for Excellence in Medical Student Education; Nancy C. A.   Vol. 1: 3651
Roethke Memorial Foundation Poetry Prize; Theodore   Vol. 1: 16881
Rogent Video Competition on Rehabilitation and Restoration; Elies   Vol. 2: 11207
Rogers Award; Dave   Vol. 1: 16635
Rogers Award for Citizenship; Leon   Vol. 1: 12855
Rogers Award; John Jacob   Vol. 1: 19299
Rogers Award; Martha E.   Vol. 1: 14290
Rogers Award; William   Vol. 1: 5391
Rogers Collaborative Research Award; Lina   Vol. 1: 13296
Rogers Communications Inc. Media Award   Vol. 1: 6840
Rogers Exhibit Award; Lelan G.   Vol. 1: 3256
Rogers Information Advancement Award; Frank Bradway   Vol. 1: 12180
Rogers Prize
  University of London   Vol. 2: 4579
  Worshipful Society of Apothecaries of London   Vol. 2: 4638
Rohrer Consulting Psychology Practice Award; Perry L.   Vol. 1: 3703
Rojas Prize; Ricardo   Vol. 2: 38
Rokach Prize; Engineering Prize - Israel   Vol. 2: 7952
Rokkan Fellowship; Stein   Vol. 2: 9896
Rokkan Prize in Comparative Research; Stein   Vol. 2: 6050
Rolandpreis fur Kunst im offentlichen Raum   Vol. 2: 6582
Role Model Award   Vol. 1: 8168
Role of Law Award   Vol. 1: 7288
Rolex Awards for Enterprise   Vol. 2: 11898
Rolex Collegiate All-Star Team   Vol. 1: 10552
Rolex Cup   Vol. 1: 8540
Rolex International Women's Keelboat Championship   Vol. 1: 19534
Rolex Junior Championships; U.S. SAILING/   Vol. 1: 19541
Rolex Junior Women's Championship - Nancy Leiter Clagett Trophy; U.S. SAILING/   Vol. 1: 19542
Rolex Player of the Year   Vol. 1: 11764
Rolex Player to Watch   Vol. 1: 10553
Rolex Rookie of the Year Men/Women Pros   Vol. 1: 9647
Rolex Rookies of the Year   Vol. 1: 18623
Rolin-Jaequemyns; Prix G.   Vol. 2: 11751
Roll Call Congressional Baseball Award   Vol. 1: 16884
Roll Call Congressional Staff Award   Vol. 1: 16885
Roll of Honor   Vol. 2: 3460
Rolls-Royce Enthusiasts Awards   Vol. 2: 3855
Rolls Royce Jubilee Award   Vol. 2: 3302
Romanell Lecture   Vol. 1: 3425
Romanell - Phi Beta Kappa Professorship in Philosophy   Vol. 1: 16103
Romanian Radio and Television Award   Vol. 2: 10327
Romanian Union of Composers Prizes   Vol. 2: 10406
Romanian Writers' Union Prizes   Vol. 2: 10414
Romanos; Premio Mesonero   Vol. 2: 11298
Romanowski Medal; Miroslaw   Vol. 1: 16962
Romantic Novel of the Year   Vol. 2: 3858
Rombaux; Prix Egide   Vol. 2: 956
Rome Memorial Award; Sidney R.   Vol. 1: 372
Rome Memorial Award; Stuart   Vol. 1: 6249
Rome Prize Fellowships   Vol. 1: 485
Romein Prys; Annie   Vol. 2: 9426

Romer Prize; Alfred Sherwood   Vol. 1: 18092
Romer - Simpson Medal   Vol. 1: 18093
Romero Award; Rothko Chapel Oscar   Vol. 1: 16910
Romero Folklore Prize; Silvio   Vol. 2: 1444
Romero Medal; Pedro   Vol. 2: 1615
Romero; Premio de Novela Jose Ruben   Vol. 2: 9218
Romich Communication Technology Award; Prentke   Vol. 1: 18907
Romich - ISAAC Scholarship; Prentke   Vol. 1: 11231
Roms Guldmedalje; N. C.   Vol. 2: 1932
Roncaglia and Eugenio Mari; Premio Maria Teresa Messori   Vol. 2: 8077
Rontgen; Fondazione Wilhelm Conrad   Vol. 2: 8066
Rontgen Plakette   Vol. 2: 6678
Rontgen-Preis; Wilhelm Conrad   Vol. 2: 6831
Rontgen Prize   Vol. 2: 2416
Roof Award; Maynard   Vol. 1: 17870
Rookie Businessperson of the Year   Vol. 2: 926
Rookie Chapter of the Year   Vol. 1: 354
Rookie Mechanic of the Year Award; Gilmore Championship -   Vol. 1: 19019
Rookie Member of the Year   Vol. 1: 355
Rookie Newsletter Award   Vol. 1: 449
Rookie of the Year
  American Grandprix Association   Vol. 1: 2188
  Balloon Federation of America   Vol 1: 6242
  Baseball Writers Association of America   Vol 1: 6282
  Bass'n Gal   Vol 1: 6288
  Continental Basketball Association   Vol 1: 8248
Rookie of the Year; SCCA Road Rally   Vol. 1: 18392
Rookies of the Meet Award   Vol. 1: 19629
Roomkeeper of the Year   Vol. 1: 2395
Rooney Prize for Irish Literature   Vol. 2: 7848
Roosevelt Award; Eleanor   Vol. 1: 11158
Roosevelt Award for Excellence in Recreation and Park Research; Theodore and Franklin   Vol. 1: 14568
Roosevelt Award; Theodore
  International Platform Association   Vol. 1: 11159
  National Collegiate Athletic Association   Vol 1: 13613
Roosevelt Distinguished Service Medal; Theodore   Vol. 1: 16894
Roosevelt Four Freedoms Awards; Franklin D.   Vol. 1: 16896
Roosevelt Medallion of Honor; Anna Eleanor   Vol. 1: 358
Roosevelt Memorial Fund Award; Theodore   Vol. 1: 3155
Roosevelt Prize; Franklin Delano   Vol. 1: 17478
Roosevelt Trophy; Theodore   Vol. 1: 13995
Roosevelt Woman of Courage Award; Eleanor   Vol. 1: 20443
Root Memorial Award; Charles D.   Vol. 1: 19050
Roozeboom Medal; Bakhuis   Vol. 2: 9604
ROPE Awards   Vol. 1: 16820
Roquemore Memorial Award; A. D.   Vol. 1: 2265
Rorer Award; William H.   Vol. 1: 8924
Rorer Pharmaceuticals Award; Van Meter/   Vol. 1: 4910
Rosa Award; Edward Bennett   Vol. 1: 19105
Rosa Camuna   Vol. 2: 8166
Rosales; Medalla Antonio   Vol. 2: 9013

Rosario International Photographic Salon   Vol. 2: 105
ROSCOE Awards   Vol. 1: 10572
Roscoe Fellowship; H. C.   Vol. 2: 2451
Rose Award   Vol. 1: 11939
Rose Award in Biochemisty; William C.   Vol. 1: 4042
Rose Award; Rod   Vol. 1: 18031
Rose Bowl Player in the Game   Vol. 1: 397
Rose Cello Competition; Leonard   Vol. 1: 19822
Rose des Poetes   Vol. 2: 6344
Rose Education Award   Vol. 1: 13200
Rose Gold Medal   Vol. 2: 109
Rose of French Poets Prize   Vol. 2: 6344
Rose of Lidice Prize   Vol. 2: 1891
Rose of Tralee   Vol. 2: 7827
Rose Pin   Vol. 2: 110
Rosen Fellowship in Cardiac Pacing and Electrophysiology; Kenneth M.   Vol. 1: 15462
Rosenau Silver Medallion; Ruth   Vol. 1: 5331
Rosenbaum Memorial Award; Colonel Samuel   Vol. 1: 14099
Rosenberg Annual Poetry Award; Dorothy   Vol. 1: 18892
Rosenberg Award; Bill   Vol. 1: 9045
Rosenberg Award for Poems on the Jewish Experience; Anna Davidson   Vol. 1: 12002
Rosenberg Memorial Award; Adeline   Vol. 1: 9338
Rosenberger Medal   Vol. 1: 19759
Rosenbloom Prize   Vol. 2: 7899
Rosenblueth; Premio Maestro Arturo   Vol. 2: 9276
Rosenbusch; Premio Dr. Francisco C.   Vol. 2: 9
Rosenhain Medal and Prize   Vol. 2: 3148
Rosenhaus Lectureship Award; Matthew B.   Vol. 1: 3849
Rosenkjaer Prize   Vol. 2: 1995
Rosenkjaerprisen   Vol. 2: 1995
Rosenkranz; Premio Anual de Investigacion Medica Dr. Jorge   Vol. 2: 9071
Rosenstiel Award for Distinguished Work in Basic Medical Research; Lewis S.   Vol. 1: 6545
Rosenstiel Award in Oceanographic Science; AAAS -   Vol. 1: 884
Rosenthal Award; Walter   Vol. 1: 12391
Rosenthal Foundation Award; Richard and Hinda   Vol. 1: 844
Rosenthal Foundation Awards; Richard and Hinda
  American Academy of Arts and Letters   Vol. 1: 517
  American College of Physicians   Vol 1: 1722
Rosenzweig Award   Vol. 1: 5252
Rosenzweig National Bennial Competition and Exhibition; Irene   Vol. 1: 5320
Rosette Awards   Vol. 2: 4340
Roshd International Educational Film Festival   Vol. 2: 7741
Roshd International Film Festival Awards   Vol. 2: 7743
Rosica, Jr. Memorial Award; Albert E.   Vol. 1: 1608
Rosolino Jazz Award; Frank   Vol. 1: 11369
Ross Award   Vol. 1: 7080
Ross Award; Harland   Vol. 1: 20047
Ross Award; Madeline Dane   Vol. 1: 15875
Ross Award; Sam   Vol. 1: 16635
Ross Award; Thomas   Vol. 2: 10617
Ross Awards; Arthur   Vol. 1: 7813
Ross Education Awards   Vol. 1: 675
Ross Excellence in Cancer Nursing Education Award; ONS/   Vol. 1: 15661

Ross Laboratories Award for Distinguished Service to ACHCA   Vol. 1: 1653
Ross Laboratories Community Long-Term Care Award   Vol. 1: 14291
Ross Laboratories Institutional Long-Term Care Award   Vol. 1: 14292
Ross Medal; R. A.   Vol. 1: 7132
Ross Medal; Will   Vol. 1: 2971
Ross Prize; The John Munn   Vol. 2: 10567
Ross Safety Award; Pete   Vol. 1: 12075
Ross Trophy; Art   Vol. 1: 14178
Ross Trust Competition; Dr. William Baird   Vol. 2: 10595
Rossby Award for Extraordinary Scientific Achievement; Carl-Gustaf   Vol. 1: 3096
Rossby Research Medal; Carl-Gustaf   Vol. 1: 3096
Rosse Cup   Vol. 2: 4053
Rossel; Prix Victor   Vol. 2: 1247
Rossi Prize; Bruno   Vol. 1: 1274
Rostand - Prix Claude   Vol. 2: 6406
Roster of Fellows   Vol. 1: 3302
Roster of Honor   Vol. 1: 3303
Rostkowski Award; Nicolaus   Vol. 1: 9914
Rostropovitch; Concours International de Violoncelle   Vol. 2: 6201
Rostropovitch International Cello Competition   Vol. 2: 6201
Rosy; Prix Leopold   Vol. 2: 1303
Rotary Award for World Understanding   Vol. 1: 16906
Rotary Club of Palma Giuseppe Verdi Prize   Vol. 2: 8386
Rotary Lombardi Award   Vol. 1: 16904
Roth/Saaled Bursary; Irma   Vol. 2: 11015
Rotheim Medal; Erik   Vol. 2: 1150
Rothko Chapel Awards for Commitment to Truth and Freedom   Vol. 1: 16909
Rothko Chapel Oscar Romero Award   Vol. 1: 16910
Rothman Memorial Award; Stephen   Vol. 1: 17542
Rothmans Foundation Ballet Scholarship   Vol. 2: 320
Rothrock Award   Vol. 1: 18196
Rothschild Challenge Cup   Vol. 2: 4054
Rotorua Trophy   Vol. 2: 9824
Rotterdam-Maaskant Award   Vol. 2: 9583
Rotterdam Maaskant Award for Young Architects   Vol. 2: 9584
Rotterdam-Maaskantprijs   Vol. 2: 9583
Rotterdam-Maaskantprijs voor Yonge Architekten   Vol. 2: 9584
Round Table Award   Vol. 1: 10374
Roundup USA   Vol. 1: 10599
Rourke Prize; Constance   Vol. 1: 4876
Rous-Whipple Award   Vol. 1: 4180
Rouse Gold Medallion   Vol. 1: 5331
Rouse Hydraulic Engineering Lecture; Hunter   Vol. 1: 4495
Rousseau Fellowship; Theodore   Vol. 1: 12236
Rousseau Fellowships; Theodore   Vol. 1: 12234
Rousseau; Fondation Gaston   Vol. 2: 5564
Rousseau Prize in Interdisciplinarity; Jacques   Vol. 1: 5436
Roussel; Prix Comite Albert   Vol. 2: 5188
Roussel; Prix du Comite Albert   Vol. 2: 5074
Roussel; Prix Special Albert   Vol. 2: 6432
Roussy; Fondation Gustave   Vol. 2: 5572
Roussy; Prix Gustave   Vol. 2: 4841
Routledge Ancient History Prize   Vol. 2: 3861
Roux; Fondation Gustave   Vol. 2: 5573
Rover Midlander Open Design Award   Vol. 2: 4307

Rowe & John O. Rowe Citizen of the Year Award; Lillian B. Wood   Vol. 1: 3112
Rowe Medals; N. E.   Vol. 2: 3903
Rowing Hall of Fame   Vol. 1: 19520
Rowland Award; Dunbar   Vol. 1: 12361
Rowland Prevention Award; Lela   Vol. 1: 14363
Rowland Prize; Thomas Fitch   Vol. 1: 4496
Roxane Laboratories Linda Arenth Excellence in Cancer Nursing Administration Award; ONS/   Vol. 1: 15662
Roy Award; Thomas   Vol. 1: 6899
Roy Space Science and Design Award; Dr. Biren   Vol. 2: 7477
Roy Trust Award; Dr. Biren   Vol. 2: 7478
Royal Academy Summer Exhibition   Vol. 2: 3864
Royal Aeronautical Society Bronze Medal   Vol. 2: 3904
Royal Aeronautical Society Companion   Vol. 2: 3905
Royal Aeronautical Society Gold Medal   Vol. 2: 3906
Royal Aeronautical Society Honorary Fellow   Vol. 2: 3907
Royal Aeronautical Society Silver Medal   Vol. 2: 3908
Royal Asiatic Society Medal   Vol. 2: 11414
Royal Australian Historical Society Competitions   Vol. 2: 607
Royal Bank Award   Vol. 1: 16933
Royal Bath and West Scholarship Awards (World and European)   Vol. 2: 3947
Royal Canadian Legion Fellowships in Gerontological Nursing   Vol. 1: 7075
Royal Canadian Mounted Police Long Service Medal   Vol. 1: 6711
Royal Charter Prize   Vol. 2: 3149
Royal College of Physicians of Canada Medal in Medicine   Vol. 1: 16940
Royal College of Radiologists Award   Vol. 2: 3972
Royal College of Surgeons of Canada Medal in Surgery   Vol. 1: 16941
Royal College of Surgeons of England Honorary Medal   Vol. 2: 3980
Royal Companies Award   Vol. 2: 11109
Royal Designers for Industry   Vol. 2: 4323
Royal Dublin Society Crafts Competition   Vol. 2: 7835
Royal Dutch Shell Prize   Vol. 2: 9392
Royal Economic Society Prize   Vol. 2: 4000
Royal Gold Medal for Architecture   Vol. 2: 4071
Royal Hibernian Academy of Arts Awards   Vol. 2: 7837
Royal Horticultural Society of Ireland Flower Show   Vol. 2: 7834
Royal Humane Society Awards   Vol. 2: 4066
Royal Institute of Public Health and Hygiene Awards   Vol. 2: 4083
Royal Medals   Vol. 2: 4154
Royal Naval College, Greenwich Prize   Vol. 2: 3350
Royal Norwegian Order of Merit   Vol. 2: 9921
Royal Norwegian Order of St. Olav   Vol. 2: 9922
Royal Orchestral Society Medal   Vol. 2: 4115
Royal Order of the Polar Star   Vol. 2: 11579
Royal Order of the Seraphim   Vol. 2: 11580
Royal Over-Seas League Music Competition   Vol. 2: 4117
Royal Philatelic Society, London Exhibition Medal   Vol. 2: 4120
Royal Philatelic Society, London Medal   Vol. 2: 4121
Royal Red Cross   Vol. 2: 2384

Royal Society Fellowship/Study Visit   Vol. 2: 7845
Royal Society Grants   Vol. 2: 4155
Royal Society of Literature Award   Vol. 2: 4233
Royal Society of Tasmania Medal   Vol. 2: 636
Royal Society of Victoria Medal   Vol. 2: 638
Royal Society of Western Australia Medal   Vol. 2: 640
Royal Subsidy for Modern Painting   Vol. 2: 9612
Royal Television Society Gold Medal   Vol. 2: 4283
Royal Television Society Programme Awards   Vol. 2: 4284
Royal Television Society Silver Medal   Vol. 2: 4285
Royal Television Society Student Director Award   Vol. 2: 4286
Royal Television Society Technology Awards in Memory of Geoffrey Parr   Vol. 2: 4287
Royal Television Society Television Journalism Awards   Vol. 2: 4288
Royal Victorian Order
 British Government   Vol. 2: 2385
 Canada - The Chancellery   Vol 1: 6694
Royal Watercolour Society Award   Vol. 2: 4297
Royce Award for Achievement; IIE Sir Henry   Vol. 2: 4308
Royce Award; Sir Henry   Vol. 2: 3303
Royce Initiative Award; Sir Henry   Vol. 2: 4309
Royce, Jr., M.D. Memorial Award; Stephen W.   Vol. 1: 3029
Royce Lectures in the Philosophy of the Mind   Vol. 1: 3426
Royce Memorial Award of the Worshipful Company of Carmen; Sir Henry   Vol. 2: 4310
Royce Memorial Award; Sir Henry   Vol. 2: 4311
Royce Memorial Lecture; Sir Henry
 Sir Henry Royce Memorial Foundation   Vol. 2: 4312
 Sir Henry Royce Memorial Foundation   Vol 2: 4313
Royce Prestige Lecture on the Institution of Incorporated Engineers; Sir Henry   Vol. 2: 4314
Royce Pupil Prize; Sir Henry   Vol. 2: 4315
Royce Trophy for the Pursuit of Excellence; Sir Henry   Vol. 2: 4316
Rozanas Memorial Tumbling Coach of the Year; James A.   Vol. 1: 450
Rozelle Trophy; Pete   Vol. 1: 14003
Rozsa Prize; Ferenc   Vol. 2: 7407
RPS Music Awards   Vol. 2: 4128
RSA Benno Schotz Prize   Vol. 2: 10619
RSA Guthrie Award   Vol. 2: 10619
RSA Medal for Architecture   Vol. 2: 10619
RSA Music Scholarships   Vol. 2: 4324
RSC Interdisciplinary Awards   Vol. 2: 4218
RSC Sponsored Awards   Vol. 2: 4219
RSM May and Baker Pharmaceuticals Prizes   Vol. 2: 4265
RSPB Medal   Vol. 2: 4175
Rubens-Alcais Challenge   Vol. 2: 1961
Rubillard; Prix Helene   Vol. 2: 4842
Rubinc am; National Genealogical Society Youth Award in Honor of Milton   Vol. 1: 14067
Rubinstein Award   Vol. 1: 1049
Rubinstein International Piano Master Competition; Arthur   Vol. 2: 7938
Rubinstein Memorial Prize; Arthur   Vol. 2: 3627

Rubloff Memorial Award; Arthur   Vol. 1: 18908
Rubner-Preis; Max   Vol. 2: 6859
Ruby Honorarium; Mike   Vol. 1: 7956
Ruckert Preis; Friedrich   Vol. 2: 7105
Rudd Award; Steele   Vol. 2: 294
Rudolfs Award; Willem   Vol. 1: 20160
Rudolphi-Medaille; Carl-Asmund-   Vol. 2: 6636
Rudolphi Medal; Carl Asmund   Vol. 2: 6636
Rudwick Prize; Elliott   Vol. 1: 15823
Rugby World Juniors Championship Awards   Vol. 2: 5955
Rugeles; Orden Manuel Felipe   Vol. 2: 12112
Ruger World Team Trophy; William B.   Vol. 1: 14642
Ruggles Right to Work Scholarship; William B.   Vol. 1: 14647
Ruggles Travel Awards; Nancy   Vol. 1: 10654
Ruigrok-Prijs; Johannes Cornelis   Vol. 2: 9393
Rulfo Latin American and Caribbean Prize for Literature; Juan   Vol. 2: 9259
Rulfo Para Primera Novela; Premio Juan   Vol. 2: 9228
Rumbaugh Oration Contest; Joseph S.   Vol. 1: 14741
Rumford Medal
  American Academy of Arts and Sciences   Vol. 1: 528
  Royal Society   Vol 2: 4156
Runner of the Year   Vol. 1: 19956
Runyon - Walter Winchell Cancer Fund Fellowships; Damon   Vol. 1: 7284
Rupp Trophy; Adolph F.
  Commonwealth Athletic Club   Vol. 1: 8051
  Naismith Memorial Basketball Hall of Fame   Vol 1: 12569
Ruppert Award; David P.   Vol. 1: 10498
Ruppin Prize; Dr. Arthur   Vol. 2: 7885
Rural County Engineer of the Year   Vol. 1: 13053
Rural Health Practitioner of the Year   Vol. 1: 14653
Rural Wales Award   Vol. 2: 12164
Rush Award; Benjamin   Vol. 1: 8645
Rush Award for Citizenship and Community Service; Benjamin   Vol. 1: 3026
Rush Award; Gertrude E.   Vol. 1: 13436
Rush Bicentennial Award; Benjamin   Vol. 1: 3026
Rush Lectureship Award; Benjamin   Vol. 1: 3652
Russel Memorial Trophy; Jeff   Vol. 1: 6885
Russell and Burch Award   Vol. 1: 10054
Russell Award   Vol. 1: 7864
Russell Award for Distinguished Research in the Teaching of English; David H.   Vol. 1: 13779
Russell Award; Frances E.   Vol. 1: 10807
Russell Award; T. Randolph   Vol. 1: 8217
Russell Awards; Helen Crocker   Vol. 1: 17036
Russell, Jr. Award; Emmett   Vol. 1: 10352
Russell, Jr., Memorial Award; Louis B.   Vol. 1: 2241
Russell Lectureship; Henry Norris   Vol. 1: 1275
Russell Lectureship in Anatomical Pathology; Joanne Vandenberge Hill Award and William O.   Vol. 1: 19878
Russell Memorial Award; J. S.   Vol. 1: 12930
Russell Memorial Award; John Newton   Vol. 1: 13201
Russell Memorial Medal; Peter Nicol   Vol. 2: 485
Russell Memorial Merit Award; Howard L.   Vol. 1: 3868

Russell Naval Aviation Flight Safety Award; Adm. James S.   Vol. 1: 15786
Russell Scholarship; Norman K.   Vol. 1: 14435
Russell Society Award; Bertrand   Vol. 1: 16978
Russell Society Book Award; Bertrand   Vol. 1: 16979
Russell Society Lifetime Achievement Award; Bertrand   Vol. 1: 16980
Russell Transportation Service Award; T. Randolph   Vol. 1: 6344
Russell Trophy; Alvin   Vol. 2: 12160
Russolo; Concorso Internazionale Luigi   Vol. 2: 8261
Russwurm Trophy; John B.   Vol. 1: 14397
Rustin Freedom Award; A. Philip Randolph/Bayard   Vol. 1: 16674
Rustin Humanitarian Award; Bayard   Vol. 1: 16675
Rutebeuf Poetry Prize   Vol. 2: 6075
Rutgers National/Works on and of Paper Competition   Vol. 1: 18476
Rutherford Lecture; UK-Canada   Vol. 1: 16968
Rutherford Medal and Prize   Vol. 2: 3196
Rutherford Memorial Lecture   Vol. 2: 3196
Rutherford Memorial Medals   Vol. 1: 16963
Ruttenberg Fellowship   Vol. 1: 9430
Rutter Gold Medal and Prize   Vol. 2: 2605
Ruud Scholarship   Vol. 1: 7523
Ruzicka-Preis   Vol. 2: 11936
Ruzicka-Prize   Vol. 2: 11936
RV Automotive Achievement Award   Vol. 1: 16731
RYA Award   Vol. 2: 4299
Ryan Award; Cornelius   Vol. 1: 15875
Ryan Award; Robert G.   Vol. 1: 8705
Ryan Canada Trophies; John T.   Vol. 1: 6953
Ryan Commemorative Award; Congressman Leo J.   Vol. 1: 8484
Ryan Winners Circle Acting Awards; Irene   Vol. 1: 1760
Ryan Winners Circle Evening of Scenes; Irene   Vol. 1: 1760
Ryder Cup
  Professional Golfers' Association   Vol. 2: 3819
  Professional Golfers' Association of America   Vol 1: 16478
Ryle Memorial Medal   Vol. 2: 3820
SAAB Junior Medal for Botany   Vol. 2: 11022
SAAB Senior Medal for Botany   Vol. 2: 11023
SAACE/SA Construction World Awards for Excellence in Engineering   Vol. 2: 11026
Saaled Bursary   Vol. 2: 11015
Sabater Prize; Rosa   Vol. 2: 11281
SABC Prize for Television and Radio   Vol. 2: 11003
Sabine Medal; Wallace Clement   Vol. 1: 101
SABINET Prize   Vol. 2: 11061
SABINET-Prys   Vol. 2: 11061
SABR Salutes Award   Vol. 1: 17412
SAC Gold Medal   Vol. 2: 4220
SAC Silver Medal   Vol. 2: 4221
Sachs Award; Curt   Vol. 1: 3168
Sachs Memorial Award; Somach -   Vol. 2: 7985
Sackheim Award; Maxwell   Vol. 1: 8651
Sackter Award; Bill   Vol. 1: 5216
Sacre; Prix Auguste   Vol. 2: 1009
Sacre; Prix Emile   Vol. 2: 957
Sacred Choral Chant National Competition   Vol. 2: 8468
Sadasivan Lecture Award; Prof. T. S.   Vol. 2: 7668
Saddleman Award   Vol. 1: 20235
Sadoul; Prix Georges   Vol. 2: 6170

SAE Distinguished Speaker Award   Vol. 1: 17771
SAE Engineering Meetings Board Outstanding Oral Presentation Award   Vol. 1: 17771
SAE Fellow Grade of Membership   Vol. 1: 17772
SAE Medal of Honor   Vol. 1: 17773
Safe and Courteous Driver of the Year   Vol. 1: 12260
Safe Driving Award   Vol. 1: 19300
Safe Worker Award   Vol. 1: 4929
Safety and Health Awards   Vol. 1: 19258
Safety Award
  Helicopter Association International   Vol. 1: 9899
  National Propane Gas Association   Vol 1: 14538
Safety Award for Superior Accomplishment   Vol. 1: 19106
Safety Award Program   Vol. 1: 18054
Safety Awards
  British Printing Industries Federation   Vol. 2: 2484
  National Paint and Coatings Association   Vol 1: 14443
Safety Codes and Standards Medal   Vol. 1: 4705
Safety Contest   Vol. 1: 18299
Safety Director of the Year Award   Vol. 1: 4930
Safety Engineer of the Year   Vol. 1: 18558
Safety Excellence Award   Vol. 1: 18235
Safety in Construction Medal   Vol. 2: 3257
Safety in Seas Award   Vol. 1: 14403
Safety Manager of the Year   Vol. 1: 18560
Safety Officer of the Year   Vol. 2: 4171
Safety Society Presidential Citation   Vol. 1: 16983
Sagar Award; Dr. Vidya   Vol. 2: 7604
Sagendorph Memorial Prize for Art; Robb   Vol. 1: 20574
Saget; Prix Julien   Vol. 2: 6227
Sahabdeen Award for International Understanding; Mohamed   Vol. 2: 11416
Sahabdeen Award for Literature; Mohamed   Vol. 2: 11417
Sahabdeen Award for Science; Mohamed   Vol. 2: 11418
Sahitya Akademi Awards   Vol. 2: 7537
Sahitya Akademi Fellowship   Vol. 2: 7538
Sahitya Akademi Prize for Translation   Vol. 2: 7539
Sahitya Award; Bala   Vol. 2: 7696
Sail Gold Medal   Vol. 2: 7632
SAILIS Bibliografiese Toekenning   Vol. 2: 11062
SAILIS Bibliographic Award   Vol. 2: 11062
SAILIS Research Award   Vol. 2: 11063
SAILIS Research Certificate   Vol. 2: 11064
Saillet; Prix Joseph   Vol. 2: 5766
St. Anthony Medallion   Vol. 1: 11491
St. Francis de Sales Award   Vol. 1: 7385
St. Francis International Masters Regatta   Vol. 1: 19528
St. Gaudens Medal; Augustus   Vol. 1: 8264
St. Gregory the Great; Order of   Vol. 2: 12102
St. Hubert's Giralda Trophy   Vol. 1: 20246
St. James Literary Award; Ian   Vol. 2: 2642
St. Kilda Film Festival   Vol. 2: 648
Saint La Salle Medal   Vol. 1: 12026
St. Lawrence Section Outstanding Educator Award   Vol. 1: 4118
Saint Louis Literary Award   Vol. 1: 5428
St. Louis Refractories Award   Vol. 1: 1474
St. Luke's Lecture   Vol. 2: 7832
St. Matthew Award   Vol. 1: 14613

St. Michael Religious Freedom Award   Vol. 1: 7372
St. Olav Medal   Vol. 2: 9923
St. Petersburg Yacht Club Trophy   Vol. 1: 19535
Saint-Prix; Prix Berriat   Vol. 2: 5717
St. Romanos the Melodist Medallion   Vol. 1: 14036
St. Sylvester; Order of   Vol. 2: 12103
Saint-Vincent International Prize for Journalism   Vol. 2: 8429
Saintour; Prix   Vol. 2: 5679
SAIP - De Beers Gold Medal Award   Vol. 2: 11071
SAIP Science Olympiad Medal   Vol. 2: 11072
SAIP - Silver Jubilee Medal Award   Vol. 2: 11073
Saito Award; Hideo   Vol. 2: 8770
Sajous Achievement Award; Edward T.   Vol. 1: 12909
Sakemaker of the Year   Vol. 1: 2344
Sakharov Memorial Lectureship; Andrei   Vol. 1: 11500
Sakura Finetek Student Scholarship   Vol. 1: 14755
Sakurai Prize for Theoretical Particle Physics; J. J.   Vol. 1: 3470
Salao Nacional de Artes Plasticas   Vol. 2: 1436
Salazar Award for Communications; Ruben   Vol. 1: 13745
Salazar Award; Nick   Vol. 1: 13070
Salcedo, Jr. Memorial Lecturer; Dr. Juan   Vol. 2: 10051
Salcedo Jr. Science Education Award; Dr. Juan S.   Vol. 2: 10061
Salcido; Auxiliar de Enfermera Lucia   Vol. 2: 9126
Sales Leader of the Year Award   Vol. 1: 20394
Sales Literature and Promotional Materials Competition   Vol. 1: 1972
Saligny Prize; Anghel   Vol. 2: 10381
Salin Prize; Kasper   Vol. 2: 11492
Salinas; Concurso Nacional de Biografias Hector Cossio   Vol. 2: 1397
Salinpriset; Kasper   Vol. 2: 11492
Salivary Research Award   Vol. 1: 10623
Sallie Mae First Year Teacher Awards   Vol. 1: 1184
Sallie Mae Teacher Tribute Awards   Vol. 1: 1185
Salmagundi Medal of Honor   Vol. 1: 5313
Salmon Award - Blind Worker of the Year; Peter J.   Vol. 1: 14213
Salmon Award; Dr. Daniel E.   Vol. 1: 13107
Salmon Memorial Lecture   Vol. 1: 1186
Salon Anual de Artes Plasticas Premios Pedro Domingo Murillo   Vol. 2: 1389
Salon Culinaire Mondial
   Canadian Federation of Culinary Chefs   Vol 1: 6860
   Chefs & Cooks Circle   Vol 2: 2611
   National Restaurant Association   Vol 1: 14623
   Panel of Chefs of Ireland   Vol 2: 7817
   Singapore Chefs Association   Vol 2: 10752
   Society of German Cooks   Vol 2: 7090
Salon International de la Recherche Photographique   Vol. 2: 6215
Salon International de l'Invention de Paris   Vol. 2: 4938
Salon International diapositives d'Auvergne   Vol. 2: 4888
Salon International Fotografico de Rosario   Vol. 2: 105

Salon Nacional de Artes Plasticas - Ceramica   Vol. 2: 9239
Salon Nacional de Artes Plasticas - Dibujo   Vol. 2: 9240
Salon Nacional de Artes Plasticas - Escultura   Vol. 2: 9241
Salon Nacional de Artes Plasticas - Espacios Alternativos   Vol. 2: 9242
Salon Nacional de Artes Plasticas - Fotografia   Vol. 2: 9243
Salon Nacional de Artes Plasticas - Graphic Art   Vol. 2: 9244
Salon Nacional de Artes Plasticas - Graphica (Interpretation del Quijo te de la Mancha)   Vol. 2: 9245
Salon Nacional de Artes Plasticas - Pintura   Vol. 2: 9246
Salon Nacional de Artes Plasticas - Tapiz y Arte Textil   Vol. 2: 9247
Saloutos Book Prize; Theodore   Vol. 1: 10097
Saloutos Memorial Book Award; Theodore   Vol. 1: 208
SALT Award   Vol. 1: 17699
Salter Award; Janet & Hon. Maxwell   Vol. 1: 6350
Saltire Society and The Royal Bank of Scotland - Scottish Science Award   Vol. 2: 10657
Saltire Society Scottish Literary Awards   Vol. 2: 10658
Saltus Medal Award; J. Sanford   Vol. 1: 3277
Saltus Medal for Merit; J. Sanford   Vol. 1: 12629
Saltus Medal; Sanford   Vol. 2: 12162
Saltus; Prix Alphonse de Neuville et Sanford   Vol. 2: 5357
Salute to Excellence Awards   Vol. 1: 14629
Salvan; Prix Eugene   Vol. 2: 5743
Salzburg Heraldic Medal   Vol. 2: 868
Salzburg Prize for the Promotion of the Arts, Science and Literature   Vol. 2: 869
Salzman Award for Excellence in International Economic Performance; Herbert   Vol. 1: 19301
Samaritan Award   Vol. 1: 11765
SAMES Postgraduate Student Award   Vol. 2: 11074
Samford Chess Fellowship   Vol. 1: 1576
Samiti Awards; Lanka Mahila   Vol. 2: 11412
SAMLA Book Award   Vol. 1: 18170
SAMLA Prize for an Outstanding Article in the South Atlantic Review   Vol. 1: 18171
Sammy Awards   Vol. 2: 653
Sample Student Excellence Award; W. Frederick   Vol. 1: 17446
Sampson Award; Donald K.   Vol. 1: 7938
Samsonov Prize   Vol. 2: 10715
Samu Award; Charles   Vol. 1: 19920
San Antonio Cine Festival   Vol. 1: 9737
San Antonio International Keyboard Competition   Vol. 1: 17024
San Francisco Art Institute International Film & Video Festival   Vol. 1: 17029
San Francisco Foundation Award   Vol. 1: 17037
San Sebastian Underwater Film Cycle   Vol. 2: 11353
Sanchez Memorial Award; George I.   Vol. 1: 16746
Sanchez; Premio Carlos Mateo   Vol. 2: 9016
Sanchez Prize; Diodoro   Vol. 2: 1749
Sand; Fondation Gabrielle   Vol. 2: 5563
Sand Volunteer of the Year Award; Rebecca   Vol. 1: 7519
Sandberg Grant for Research and/or Development   Vol. 2: 7929
Sandberg Prize for Israeli Art   Vol. 2: 7930
Sandbergprijs   Vol. 2: 9647

Sandburg Award; Carl   Vol. 1: 11160
Sandburg Literary Arts Award; Carl   Vol. 1: 9434
Sanderson Award; A. B.   Vol. 1: 7177
Sanderson Award (Attack Squadron of the Year); Lawson H. M.   Vol. 1: 12076
Sandles Award; Arthur   Vol. 2: 4561
The Sandlot Kid   Vol. 1: 18360
Sandmeyer Preis   Vol. 2: 11890
Sandmeyer-Preis   Vol. 2: 11887
Sandoz Award   Vol. 1: 7194
Sandoz Award; Mari   Vol. 1: 15101
Sandoz Oration Award for Research in Cancer   Vol. 2: 7605
Sandoz Preis   Vol. 2: 878
Sandoz Prize for Gerontological Research   Vol. 2: 7418
Sandrof/Board Award; Ivan   Vol. 1: 13468
SANE Education Fund/Consider the Alternatives Peace Award   Vol. 1: 8189
SANE/FREEZE Peace Award   Vol. 1: 8189
Sanger Award; Planned Parenthood Federation of America Margaret   Vol. 1: 16233
Sangiorgi; Fondazione Giorgio Maria   Vol. 2: 8055
Sangster Memorial Award; Allan   Vol. 1: 6810
Sanitarian's Award   Vol. 1: 10766
Sankei Jidoh Bunka Shuppan Shoh   Vol. 2: 8729
Sanshigaku Shinpo Sho   Vol. 2: 8660
Sanshigaku Sho   Vol. 2: 8659
Sansone Award; Michael   Vol. 1: 7763
Sansum Medal; W.E.   Vol. 2: 455
Sant Jordi   Vol. 2: 11239
Santa Cecilia Academy Competition for Orchestral Conductors Prize   Vol. 2: 8082
Santa Rosa Award   Vol. 2: 1475
Santa Rosa; Premio   Vol. 2: 1475
Santander Athenaeum Novel Award   Vol. 2: 11151
Santander; Grand National Medal General Francisco de Paula   Vol. 2: 1657
Santander International Piano Competition   Vol. 2: 11355
Santander Medal; General   Vol. 2: 1676
Santander; Medalla General   Vol. 2: 1676
Santarelli Award; Donald E.   Vol. 1: 14420
Santista Juventude; Premios Moinho   Vol. 2: 1496
Santista; Premio Moinho   Vol. 2: 1497
Santista Prizes for Young People; Moinho   Vol. 2: 1496
Santista Prizes; Moinho   Vol. 2: 1497
Santos Prize; Dos   Vol. 2: 5128
Sao Paulo International Film Festival   Vol. 2: 1499
Saouma Award; Edouard   Vol. 2: 8271
Sapop Memorial Award; Arnold   Vol. 1: 18187
Sapporo International Ski Marathon   Vol. 2: 8731
Sara Lee Foundation Leadership Award   Vol. 1: 17057
Sarabhai Medal; Vikram   Vol. 2: 5067
Sarasate International Violin Competition; Pablo   Vol. 2: 11255
Sarbadhikari Gold Medal   Vol. 2: 7681
Sarber Fellowship; Raymond W.   Vol. 1: 4199
Sarby Trophy; Richard   Vol. 2: 9507
SARF Bursary   Vol. 2: 11095
Sargeet Natak Akademi Fellowships   Vol. 2: 7545
Sargent Award   Vol. 1: 552
Sargent, Jr. Award; Lowrie B.   Vol. 1: 6072
Sargent Medal   Vol. 1: 17715
Sargent Medal; M. A.   Vol. 2: 486

Sargent Progress Award; SME Albert M.   Vol. 1: 17883
Sargeson Writer's Fellowship   Vol. 2: 9844
Sarney Award; Jack   Vol. 1: 7122
Sarnoff Award; David
   Armed Forces Communications and Electronics Association   Vol. 1: 5266
   Institute of Electrical and Electronics Engineers   Vol 1: 10288
Sarnoff Award for Outstanding Achievement in Radio and Television; David   Vol. 1: 19736
Sarnoff Citation   Vol. 1: 16650
Sarnoff Medal Award; David   Vol. 1: 17910
Sarton Award; May   Vol. 1: 15130
Sarton Chair   Vol. 2: 1357
Sarton Leersoel   Vol. 2: 1357
Sarton Medaille   Vol. 2: 1358
Sarton Medal
   History of Science Society   Vol. 1: 9953
   Sarton Committee of the University of Ghent   Vol 2: 1358
Sarvotten Jeevan Raksha Padak   Vol. 2: 7560
Sasakawa Health Prize   Vol. 2: 11975
Sasaki Memorial Award   Vol. 2: 8648
Saskatchewan Talent Program - Scholarships   Vol. 1: 17071
Sass Medal; Hans and Jacob   Vol. 1: 12160
Satbir Award; Smt. Kamal   Vol. 2: 7606
Satter Prize in Mathematics; Ruth Lyttle   Vol. 1: 3008
Saturn Awards   Vol. 1: 81
SAUK Prys vir Televisie en Radio   Vol. 2: 11003
Saulses de Freycinet; Fondation Charles-Louis de   Vol. 2: 5519
Saunders Award for Natural History Achievement; W. E.   Vol. 1: 9154
Saunders Award; Harold E.   Vol. 1: 4733
Saunders Gold Medal; William Lawrence
   American Institute of Mining, Metallurgical and Petroleum Engineers   Vol. 1: 2645
   Society for Mining, Metallurgy, and Exploration   Vol 1: 17576
Saunders Sr. Award; Harris   Vol. 1: 4923
Saunderson Award   Vol. 1: 7864
Saur Award for Best Article in *College and Research Libraries*; K. G.   Vol. 1: 2878
Sauveur Achievement Award; Albert   Vol. 1: 5364
SAVA Gold Medal   Vol. 2: 11093
Savage Award; Warren F.   Vol. 1: 5090
Savage "Miles From Nowhere" Memorial Award; Barbara   Vol. 1: 12469
Savage Thesis Award; Leonard J.   Vol. 1: 17075
Savago New Voice Award; Joe   Vol. 1: 16607
Savard Award; Felix Antoine   Vol. 1: 8006
Save Our Streams Award   Vol. 1: 20099
Save the Children Canada Award   Vol. 1: 17080
Savory Award for Science Communication; Eve   Vol. 1: 17110
Savory Shield Award   Vol. 1: 2385
Savulescu Prize; Traian   Vol. 2: 10382
Sawyer Award; Gordon E.   Vol. 1: 62
Sawyer Award; R. Tom
   American Society of Mechanical Engineers   Vol. 1: 4706
   American Society of Mechanical Engineers - International Gas Turbine Institute   Vol 1: 4720
Sawyer Prize; Leila Gardin   Vol. 1: 12630
Saxen Medal; Erkki   Vol. 2: 4674
Saxton Memorial Exhibit Award; Burton   Vol. 1: 3257
Sayabalian; Prix Aram   Vol. 2: 6271

Sayen Award; Clarence N.   Vol. 2: 3411
Sayers Humanitarian Citation; Gale   Vol. 1: 14004
SBET/Renshaw-Heilman BMET of the Year Award   Vol. 1: 14777
SBET/Replacement Parts Industries, Inc. BMET of the Year   Vol. 1: 5620
SBET/Replacement Parts Industries, Inc. BMET of the Year Award   Vol. 1: 5628
SBP Lectureship in Developmental and Behavioral Pediatrics   Vol. 1: 17423
SBS Bookshow Prize for Literary Translation; Dinny O'Hearn/   Vol. 2: 149
SCA Distinguished Service Award   Vol. 1: 18311
SCA Golden Anniversary Book Award   Vol. 1: 18306
SCA Golden Anniversary Fund Awards   Vol. 1: 18306
SCA Public Service Announcement Contest   Vol. 1: 18312
Scaglione Prize for Comparative Literary Studies; Aldo and Jeanne   Vol. 1: 12400
Scaglione Prize for French and Francophone Studies; Aldo and Jeanne   Vol. 1: 12401
Scaglione Prize for Literary Translation; Aldo and Jeanne   Vol. 1: 12402
Scaglione Prize for Studies in Germanic Languages and Literatures; Aldo and Jeanne   Vol. 1: 12403
Scaglione Prize for Studies in Slavic Languages and Literatures; Aldo and Jeanne   Vol. 1: 12404
Scaife Award; J. D.   Vol. 2: 3304
Scandinavian Design Prize   Vol. 2: 11652
Scandinavian Research Council for Criminology Awards   Vol. 2: 11564
Scanstar Packaging Competiton   Vol. 2: 2005
Scantlebury Memorial Award; Donald L.   Vol. 1: 11605
Scarpette d'Argente   Vol. 2: 8156
Scattergood System Achievement Award; E. F.   Vol. 1: 3862
SCC Award Medals   Vol. 1: 17088
SCC Chapter Awards   Vol. 1: 17829
SCCA/CASCT North American Rally Cup   Vol. 1: 18405
SCCA Mechanic of the Year   Vol. 1: 18406
SCCA Pro Rally Cup   Vol. 1: 18407
SCCA Pro Rally Manufacturer's Award   Vol. 1: 18408
SCCA Road Rally Rookie of the Year   Vol. 1: 18392
Scechenyi Prize   Vol. 2: 7412
Schaad Award; W. Frederick   Vol. 1: 7511
Schaar Biennium Playwright Award; Ruby Yoshino   Vol. 1: 11506
Schachern Memorial Award; Harold J.   Vol. 1: 16767
Schaefer Award; Hugo H.   Vol. 1: 3390
Schaeffer Environmental Award; William Dwight   Vol. 1: 9703
Schaeffler Award; Willy   Vol. 1: 19585
Schafarzik Ferenc Emlekerem   Vol. 2: 7351
Schafarzik Medal; Ferenc   Vol. 2: 7351
Schaff Prize; Philip   Vol. 1: 4429
Schaffner Achievement Award; Franklin J.   Vol. 1: 8670
Schalekamp Award; Maarten   Vol. 2: 3504
Schall-Preis; Walter   Vol. 1: 6897
Schaller Scholarship Award; Jerome D.   Vol. 1: 11599
Schamelhout-Koettlitz; Fund Dr. en Mevr.   Vol. 2: 1312
Scharansky Freedom Award; Anatoly   Vol. 1: 18883
Schary Awards; Dore   Vol. 1: 5182

Schattschneider Award; E.E.   Vol. 1: 3582
Schatz Award; Jack   Vol. 1: 451
Schaufus Grant in the Field of Parenteral Processing; Charles P.   Vol. 1: 15955
Schawlow Award; Arthur L.   Vol. 1: 11784
Schechter Medal; Solomon   Vol. 1: 11571
Scheel-Preis; Karl-   Vol. 2: 6664
Scheele Award   Vol. 2: 11615
Scheele Medal; Herbert   Vol. 2: 2154
Scheele Plakette   Vol. 2: 6589
Scheele-priset   Vol. 2: 11615
Scheele Trophy; Herbert   Vol. 2: 3380
Scheepers Prize   Vol. 2: 11004
Scheffer; Prix Ary   Vol. 2: 5360
Scheleen Award for Excellence; Joseph C.   Vol. 1: 4802
Schelenz Plaque   Vol. 2: 6986
Schenck Award; Carl Alwin   Vol. 1: 17687
Schenley Award - Most Outstanding Player   Vol. 1: 6871
Schepens Award; Charles   Vol. 1: 4538
Schepkens; Prix Joseph   Vol. 2: 1027
Schering A. G. Berlin Study Grants   Vol. 2: 593
Schering Award   Vol. 1: 7195
Schering Excellence in Biotherapy Nursing Award; ONS/   Vol. 1: 15663
Schering Excellence in Cancer Nursing Research Award; ONS/   Vol. 1: 15664
Schering Plough International Award Fellowship   Vol. 2: 1973
Schering Veterinary Award   Vol. 1: 7265
Schermerhorn Award   Vol. 2: 8555
Scheveningen International Music Competition   Vol. 2: 9614
Schick Pivotal Player Award   Vol. 1: 13457
Schidlof Prize; Peter   Vol. 2: 3627
Schiefer Hall of Fame; SEMA/Paul   Vol. 1: 18301
Schiffer Memorial Award; Louis   Vol. 1: 7426
Schiller-Gedachtnispreis des Land Baden-Wurttemberg   Vol. 2: 7055
Schiller Preis der Stadt Mannheim   Vol. 2: 7100
Schimmel Award for Distinguished Contribution to Archaeology in Israel; Percia   Vol. 2: 7931
Schimmel Fellowship for Mediterranean Art and Archaeology; Norbert   Vol. 1: 12234
Schindler Award; Rudolf   Vol. 1: 4136
Schlack Award; Carl A.   Vol. 1: 5893
Schlafman Award; Sophie   Vol. 1: 9711
Schlegel - Tieck Prize   Vol. 2: 4398
Schleiden-Medaille   Vol. 2: 6626
Schleiden Medal   Vol. 2: 6626
Schlemmer Medal; Ferdinand   Vol. 2: 6824
Schlenz Medal; Harry E.   Vol. 1: 20161
Schlich Memorial Award; Sir William   Vol. 1: 17688
Schlich Memorial Trust Award   Vol. 2: 2652
Schloss Memorial Scholarship Fund; Harold W.   Vol. 1: 7338
Schlottmann Prize; Federico Guillermo   Vol. 2: 99
Schlueter Stroke Awards National Winners   Vol. 1: 4887
Schlumberger Award; Conrad   Vol. 2: 9407
Schlumberger; Prix Gustave   Vol. 2: 5462
Schlumpf Award; Mildred   Vol. 1: 2265
Schmeisser Memorial Trophy; William   Vol. 1: 19415
Schmidheiny Prize for Free Enterprise and Political Liberty; Max   Vol. 2: 11900
Schmidt Memorial Prize; Gerhard M. J.   Vol. 2: 7984
Schmidt Prize; Annie M. G.   Vol. 2: 9373
Schmits; Prix Eugene   Vol. 2: 1296

Award Index
Volume 2: International and Foreign

Schmitt Award for Outstanding Corporate Leadership; Fred Vol. 1: 14578
Schmitt; Prix Florent Vol. 2: 5390
Schmitthoff Commercial Law Prize; Clive Vol. 2: 3098
Schmitthoff Prize; Clive and Twinkie Vol. 2: 3098
Schmitz Award for Outstanding Contributions to the Frontiers in Education Conference; Ronald J. Vol. 1: 4119
Schmitz Silver Spoon Award; Ronald C. Vol. 1: 12910
Schmorl-Preis; Georg- Vol. 2: 7084
Schmutz Award; George L. Vol. 1: 5197
Schneck Award; Shirley Vol. 1: 17438
Schneider Award; Dean Herman Vol. 1: 8270
Schneider Award; Jack F. Vol. 1: 9484
Schneider Director Award; Alan Vol. 1: 18676
Schoch Memorial Lecture; Alsberg - Vol. 1: 945
Schoeller-Junkmann-Preis Vol. 2: 6844
Schoemaker Award; Harold Jan Vol. 2: 9463
Schoenberg International Award and Lecture in Neuroepidemiology; Bruce S. Vol. 1: 623
Schoenlein-Plakette Vol. 2: 6872
Scholander Award Vol. 1: 3514
Scholar-Athlete Awards Vol. 1: 13996
Scholarly Paper Competition Vol. 1: 14409
Scholarly Studies Prize Vol. 2: 12079
Scholarship Award
    National Association of Black Women Attorneys Vol. 1: 12965
    New England Water Works Association Vol 1: 15157
    Recreation Vehicle Industry Association Vol 1: 16732
Scholarship Awards to Postdoctoral Trainees Vol. 1: 5582
Scholarship Contest Vol. 1: 4770
Scholarship in Jewish Women's Studies Vol. 1: 15036
Scholarship of Rentes Genevoise Vol. 2: 11774
Scholarship Prizes Vol. 2: 6512
Scholarships
    Medical Research Council of Canada Vol. 1: 12190
    Harry S. Truman Good Neighbor Award Foundation Vol 1: 18823
Scholarships and Research Grants for Women Doing Behavioral Studies Vol. 1: 13577
Scholarships of the City of Munich Vol. 2: 7023
Scholastic Achievement Awards Vol. 1: 16718
Scholastic Award Vol. 2: 8808
Scholastic Press Freedom Award Vol. 1: 18506
Scholdstroms pris; Birger Vol. 2: 11600
Scholl-Preis; Geschwister- Vol. 2: 7024
Schonfeld Award (Honorary Members); William A. Vol. 1: 4033
Schonstedt Scholarship in Surveying Vol. 1: 1819
School Administrators Distinguished Library Service Award Vol. 1: 2828
School Nurse of the Year Vol. 1: 13297
School of Medicine Award Vol. 1: 18438
Schooley World Team Trophy; John M. Vol. 1: 14642
Schoolmeesters; Prix Herman Vol. 2: 991
Schools Curriculum Award Vol. 2: 2758
Schot Award; Aleida Vol. 2: 9618
Schot-Prijs; Aleida Vol. 2: 9618
Schott Denkmunze; Otto Vol. 2: 6640

Schottky-Preis fur Festkorperforschung; Walter- Vol. 2: 6665
Schotz Prize; RSA Benno Vol. 2: 10619
Schoutedenprijs; H. Vol. 2: 1259
Schreder 15-Meter Class Trophy Vol. 1: 17363
Schreiber Award; Frederick C. Vol. 1: 1938
Schreiber Awards; Ida Vol. 1: 13370
Schreiner Prize; Olive Vol. 2: 10853
Schreyer Award for Consulting Engineering Vol. 1: 5759
Schrieffer Prize; J. Robert Vol. 2: 8289
Schroeder Distinguished Service Award; Bill Vol. 1: 10788
Schroepfer Medal; George J. Vol. 1: 20162
Schubert and Twentieth Century Music; International Competition of Franz Vol. 2: 805
Schubert Award for Teaching College Science; Leo Vol. 1: 20104
Schuchert Award; Charles Vol. 1: 15909
Schuck Award; O. Hugo Vol. 1: 2599
Schuck Award; Victoria Vol. 1: 3583
Schuck Best Paper Award; O. Hugo Vol. 1: 1289
Schuckska priset Vol. 2: 11601
Schultz Lecture Vol. 1: 3427
Schultz Perpetual Memorial Trophy; Jack Vol. 1: 19388
Schultz Prize; Bruno Vol. 1: 16036
Schulz Award; College Cartoonist - Charles M. Vol. 1: 17144
Schulz Literary Prize; Bruno Vol. 1: 2106
Schumacher Memorial Award; Max Vol. 1: 9886
Schumacher Prizes; Fritz Vol. 2: 7122
Schuman Award; William Vol. 1: 8004
Schuman Prize; Henry and Ida Vol. 1: 9954
Schumann Choir Competition; International Robert Vol. 2: 6978
Schumann Competition; International Robert Vol. 2: 6979
Schumann Prize; Robert Vol. 2: 7123
Schumann-Wettbewerbes; Internationalen Robert- Vol. 2: 6979
Schumpeter-Preis Vol. 2: 6962
Schumpeter Prize Vol. 2: 6962
Schunk-Preis fur Medizin; Ludwig Vol. 2: 7003
Schunk-Preis fur Veterinarmedizin; Ludwig Vol. 2: 7004
Schunk-Preis fur Wirtschaftswissenschaften Vol. 2: 7002
Schunk Prize for Medicine; Ludwig Vol. 2: 7003
Schunk Prize for Veterinary Medicine; Ludwig Vol. 2: 7004
Schurmann-Medaille; Paul Vol. 2: 6853
Schurmann-Preis; Paul Vol. 2: 6854
Schutt Silver Cup Vol. 1: 2386
Schutz Perpetual Trophy Vol. 2: 7766
Schwab Award for Outstanding Achievement in Plastics Education; International Fred E. Vol. 1: 17989
Schwartz Award for Children's Literature; Ruth Vol. 1: 15705
Schwartz Award for Outstanding Student Papers on Legal Medicine Vol. 1: 1669
Schwartz Emergency Medical Service of the Year Award; Leo R. Vol. 1: 13098
Schwartz Fellowship; Frances M. Vol. 1: 3278
Schwartz Memorial Award; Paul Vol. 1: 5062
Schwartz Memorial Poetry Award; Delmore Vol. 1: 15304
Schwartzwalder - PACE Award Vol. 1: 1475
Schwarzenberger Prize in International Law; Georg Vol. 2: 3065

Scientific

Schweikert, Jr. Disability Awareness Award; Harry A. Vol. 1: 15941
Schweisguth Prize Vol. 2: 9529
Schweitzer Award; Albert Vol. 2: 3368
Schweitzer Medal; Albert Vol. 1: 5169
Schweitzer Medal; Friedrich Vol. 2: 809
Schweitzer Music Award; Albert Vol. 1: 8454
Schweitzer Prize for Humanitarianism; Albert Vol. 1: 11585
Schweitzer Prize; William P. and Gertrude Vol. 1: 12631
Schweizer Musikedition Vol. 2: 11941
Schweizer-Preis fur Parapsychologie Vol. 2: 11939
Schweizerischer Jugendbuchpreis Vol. 2: 11947
Schwidder Award; Werner Vol. 2: 4727
Schwidefsky Medal Vol. 2: 8556
Schwiglhofer Trophy; Oscar Vol. 2: 10512
SCI International Medal Vol. 2: 4424
Scialtel; Prix Jeanne Vol. 2: 5873
Science and Information Prize Vol. 2: 1448
Science and Technology Media Fellowships Vol. 2: 2255
Science Award
    Cancer Federation Vol. 1: 7278
    Japanese Society of Snow and Ice Vol 2: 8663
    National Space Club Vol 1: 14839
    Scientific and Technical Research Council of Turkey (Tubitak) Vol 2: 12065
Science Book Prizes Vol. 2: 4157
Science Council Chairman's Award for Career Achievement Vol. 1: 17111
Science Directorate Dissertation Research Awards Vol. 1: 3675
Science Fiction Achievement Awards (Hugo Awards) Vol. 1: 20524
Science Fiction/Fantasy Short Story Contest Vol. 1: 17119
Science-in-Society Journalism Awards Vol. 1: 13305
Science Journalism Awards Vol. 1: 7126
Science/Medical Writing Awards Vol. 1: 15192
Science Prize Vol. 2: 8080
Science Prize - Dr. Chaim Weizman Prize Vol. 2: 7959
Science Prize - Dr. Moshe Einhorn Prize Vol. 2: 7960
Science Prize - Henrietta Szold Prize Vol. 2: 7961
Science Prize - Peretz Naftali Prize Vol. 2: 7962
Science Recognition Award for New Investigators Vol. 1: 7846
Science Screen Report Vol. 1: 14705
Science Service ISEF Grand Awards Vol. 1: 17121
Scientific Achievement Award
    American Medical Association Vol. 1: 3027
    International Union of Forestry Research Organizations Vol 2: 851
Scientific Award
    American Horticultural Society Vol. 1: 2363
    Hildegard Doerenkamp and Gerhard Zbinden Foundation for Realistic Animal Protection in Bio-Medical Research Vol 2: 11746
Scientific Award in the Field of Radiology Vol. 2: 10162
Scientific/Engineering Award Vol. 2: 10816
Scientific Exhibit Awards Vol. 1: 17950
Scientific Investigation and Research Award Vol. 1: 2001
Scientific Medal Vol. 2: 4660
Scientific Merit Award Vol. 2: 1681

Scientific or Technical Awards   Vol. 1: 63
Scientific Prize   Vol. 2: 1738
Scientific Research and Development Award   Vol. 1: 18563
Scientific Research Prizes   Vol. 2: 8919
Scientific Researcher of the Year   Vol. 1: 10838
Scientific Secretary of the Polish Academy of Sciences Award   Vol. 2: 10128
Scientist of the Year and Best Author   Vol. 2: 9983
Scientist of the Year Award   Vol. 1: 16798
SCN Elizabeth Lowry Award   Vol. 1: 20597
Scobee Lecturer   Vol. 1: 955
Scobie Memorial Award for Preliminary Ph.D. Research; James R.   Vol. 1: 8143
Scopus Award   Vol. 1: 2123
Scotsman Fringe First Awards   Vol. 2: 10538
Scott Award; Arnold H.   Vol. 1: 6073
Scott Award; Elizabeth L.   Vol. 1: 8037
Scott Award; Jessie M.   Vol. 1: 3287
Scott Award; John   Vol. 1: 7750
Scott Award of Merit; Margaret B.   Vol. 1: 7027
Scott Education Award; Russell and Mary Hugh   Vol. 1: 4956
Scott Garden and Horticulture Award; Arthur Hoyt   Vol. 1: 17124
Scott, II Best Circulation Promotion; W.A.   Vol. 1: 14397
Scott Memorial Award; Bob   Vol. 1: 11512
Scott Memorial Medal; Junior Captain   Vol. 2: 11032
Scott Memorial Medal; Senior Captain   Vol. 2: 11033
Scott Memorial Scholarship; Peter   Vol. 2: 3969
Scott Memorial Trophy (Doublehanded); Manton D.   Vol. 1: 19532
Scott Prize Lectureship; James   Vol. 2: 10649
Scott Prizes; James Brown   Vol. 2: 11751
Scott Quartette Service Award; Chris   Vol. 1: 9788
Scott Student Research Fellowship; David B.   Vol. 1: 10624
Scotti Prize; Alexander S.   Vol. 2: 6984
Scottish Annual Report Prize   Vol. 2: 10530
Scottish Book of the Year   Vol. 2: 10658
Scottish Book of the Year Award   Vol. 2: 10658
Scottish Daily Express New Names Awards   Vol. 2: 10539
Scottish Designer of the Year Award   Vol. 2: 10531
Scottish First Book of the Year   Vol. 2: 10658
Scottish Geographical Medal   Vol. 2: 10635
Scottish International Piano Competition   Vol. 2: 10673
Scottish Marketing Awards   Vol. 2: 10671
Scottish Salon of Photography   Vol. 2: 10677
Scourby Narrator of the Year Award; Alexander   Vol. 2: 2109
Scout Leader Award   Vol. 2: 10445
Screen Actors Guild Lifetime Achievement Award   Vol. 1: 17126
Screen Awards   Vol. 1: 20561
Screenwriter's Contest Award and Promotion   Vol. 1: 20564
Scribes Annual Notes and Comments Competition   Vol. 1: 17135
Scribes Book Award   Vol. 1: 17136
Scribes Brief-Writing Competition   Vol. 1: 17137
Scribner Award; B. F.   Vol. 1: 6074
Scribner Crime Novel Award   Vol. 1: 17140
Scribner Science Writing Prize   Vol. 1: 17141

Scripps/American Dance Festival Award; Samuel H.   Vol. 1: 1929
Scripps Award; Service to the First Amendment - Edward Willis   Vol. 1: 17150
Scripps Awards; Literacy - Charles E.   Vol. 1: 17148
Scripta Metallurgica et Materialia Outstanding Paper Award   Vol. 1: 109
Scripta Metallurgica Outstanding Paper Award   Vol. 1: 109
Scrivener Editorial Award   Vol. 1: 4785
Scrivner Award; Robert W.   Vol. 1: 8393
Scroggie, M.D. Memorial Award; Val D.   Vol. 1: 18409
Scroll of Excellence   Vol. 1: 20362
Scroll of Honor   Vol. 1: 18578
SCS Dissertation Award   Vol. 1: 17429
SDC Concours Awards   Vol. 1: 18503
SDC Publication Committee Awards   Vol. 1: 18504
Sea Gallantry Medal   Vol. 2: 2386
Sea Grant Award   Vol. 1: 17152
Seaborg Award; Glenn   Vol. 1: 11161
Seaborg Award; Glenn T.   Vol. 1: 2275
Seagram's Seven Crowns of Sports   Vol. 1: 17155
Seal Memorial Trophy Award; George H.   Vol. 1: 8680
Seal of the German Surgical Society   Vol. 2: 6883
Sealants Hall of Fame Award   Vol. 1: 6075
Seaman Prize; Major Louis Livingston   Vol. 1: 5894
SEAMEO Testimonial for the Southeast Asian Ministers of Education Council (SEAMEC) President   Vol. 2: 12031
Search for New Music   Vol. 1: 11075
Search for Outstanding Contributions to Science Education   Vol. 2: 10061
Searching for Success Program   Vol. 1: 16787
Searle Award   Vol. 1: 9592
Searle Scholars   Vol. 1: 7602
Sears Cup   Vol. 1: 19541
SEASECS Article Prize   Vol. 1: 18183
SEASECS Article Prize; Percy G. Adams   Vol. 1: 18183
Seaspace Underwater Photographic Competition   Vol. 1: 10023
Seastrom Safety Award   Vol. 1: 16380
Seaver/National Endowment for the Arts Conductors Awards   Vol. 1: 15212
Seavey Quality in Law Enforcement Award Program; Webber   Vol. 1: 10700
Second Half Century Award   Vol. 1: 3080
Second Intellectual List of Leaders Yearbook   Vol. 1: 5223
Secretan; Prix Auguste   Vol. 2: 4811
Secretary of Defense Award for Outstanding Public Service   Vol. 1: 19126
Secretary of Defense Meritorious Civilian Service Medal   Vol. 1: 19207
Secretary of State's Distinguished Service Award   Vol. 1: 19302
Secretary of the Year Awards   Vol. 1: 19303
Secretary's Award   Vol. 1: 19304
Secretary's Distinguished Volunteer Service Award   Vol. 1: 19236
Secretary's Exceptional Achievement Awards   Vol. 1: 19259
Secretary's Exceptional Service Gold Medal Awards   Vol. 1: 17344
Section Awards   Vol. 2: 4521
Section Education Award   Vol. 1: 5030
Section Special Event Awards   Vol. 1: 2516
Section Technical Award   Vol. 1: 10457
Sector Awards   Vol. 2: 4172

Security Engineering Officer of the Year Award   Vol. 1: 19305
Security Officer of the Year Award   Vol. 1: 19306
Seddon Award; Richard   Vol. 1: 312
Sedgwick Memorial Medal   Vol. 1: 3850
Seed Grants   Vol. 1: 8372
Seedstock Breeder of the Year   Vol. 1: 14876
Seeger Prize; Charles   Vol. 1: 17458
Seeker for Truth   Vol. 1: 9228
Seeker of the Truth   Vol. 1: 9227
Segal Award; Martin E.   Vol. 1: 11887
Segalas; Prix Anais   Vol. 2: 5811
Segar Award   Vol. 1: 13528
SEGD Design Awards Competition   Vol. 1: 17453
Segner Prize; Janos Andras   Vol. 2: 7380
Segrave Trophy   Vol. 2: 3944
Seguin; Prix Helene   Vol. 2: 6333
Seidel Award; Harris F.   Vol. 1: 5716
Seidlin Preis; Oskar   Vol. 2: 6694
Seidman Distinguished Award in Political Economy; Frank E.   Vol. 1: 16828
Seifert Prize; Jaroslav   Vol. 2: 11450
Sejong Literacy Prize; King   Vol. 2: 6422
Selby Fellowship   Vol. 2: 179
Seldin Award; Donald W.   Vol. 1: 14275
Seldin Peace Award; Joel R.   Vol. 1: 16554
Selected Marine Corps Reserve Medal   Vol. 1: 19187
Selenick - CASE Distinguished Service Award; Harrie M.   Vol. 1: 8343
Self-Adhesive Labelling Awards   Vol. 2: 9498
Selfe Medal; Norman   Vol. 2: 442
Selig Award; Robert W.   Vol. 1: 13370
Seligman Award; Monroe   Vol. 1: 10334
Seligman Crystal   Vol. 2: 3426
Seligman Lecture; Richard   Vol. 2: 4425
Selke Trophy; Frank J.   Vol. 1: 14179
Sellin - Glueck Award   Vol. 1: 4542
Sells Awards; Elijah Watt   Vol. 1: 2561
Selmer Junior High School Instrumental Competitions; MTNA-   Vol. 1: 12522
Selskabets pris   Vol. 2: 1909
Selye Award; Hans   Vol. 1: 2684
SEMA Hall of Fame   Vol. 1: 18301
SEMA/Paul Schiefer Hall of Fame   Vol. 1: 18301
Semaine Internationale de Television Chretienne   Vol. 2: 7165
Semaine Internationale de Video de Geneve   Vol. 2: 11865
Semaine Internationale du Cinema Maritime Carthagene   Vol. 2: 11279
Semana Internacional de Cine Cientifico   Vol. 2: 11199
Semana Internacional de Cine de Autor   Vol. 2: 11357
Semana Internacional de Cine de Autor de Malaga   Vol. 2: 11303
Semana Internacional de Cine Medico y de Educacion Sanitaria   Vol. 2: 11269
Semana Internacional de Cine Naval y del Mar - Cartagena   Vol. 2: 11279
Sembrich Scholarship in Voice; Marcella   Vol. 1: 11726
SEMI Awards   Vol. 1: 17191
Seminary Award   Vol. 1: 9525
Sen Award; B. R.   Vol. 2: 8272
Sen Oration Award for Practice of Medicine; M. N.   Vol. 2: 7607
Senart; Prix de la Fondation Emile   Vol. 2: 5445
Sendai International Design Competition   Vol. 2: 8760
Sengstacke General Excellence; John H.   Vol. 1: 14397

Senigallia International Meeting of Young Pianists   Vol. 2: 8419
Senigallia International Piano Competition   Vol. 2: 8420
Senior Captain Scott Commemoration Medal   Vol. 2: 11005
Senior Dental and Dental Hygiene Student Awards   Vol. 1: 41
Senior Fellow   Vol. 1: 12642
Senior Ladies Bonspiel   Vol. 1: 19687
Senior Member   Vol. 1: 17507
Senior Memorial Award for Deserving Writers/Artists; Willoughby F.   Vol. 1: 20308
Senior Moulton Medal   Vol. 2: 3225
Senior Recognition Award for Distinguished Contributors to the Counseling Psychology Division   Vol. 1: 3708
Senior Research Grants   Vol. 1: 9598
Senior Service Award   Vol. 1: 5959
Senior Visiting Fellowship   Vol. 2: 7846
Senior Whitehead Prize   Vol. 2: 3616
Seniors Division - Highest Point Car over 900 Points   Vol. 1: 7671
Seniors' Service Award   Vol. 1: 19655
Senn Lectureship and Award; Milton J. E.   Vol. 1: 684
Senne; Prix Emile Le   Vol. 2: 5456
Sense of Smell Award   Vol. 1: 9363
Sensenbaugh Award; J. Deane   Vol. 1: 224
Sentential of the Seas   Vol. 1: 18871
Sentinels of Safety   Vol. 1: 3117
SEPM Best Paper Award in *Palaios*   Vol. 1: 17593
SEPM Best Paper Award in the *Journal of Paleontology*   Vol. 1: 17594
SEPM Best Paper Award in the *Journal of Sedimentary Petrology*   Vol. 1: 17595
SEPM Honorary Member   Vol. 1: 17596
Sequoyah Award   Vol. 1: 8116
Sequoyah Children's Book Award   Vol. 1: 15614
Sequoyah Young Adult Book Award   Vol. 1: 15615
Serbian Academy of Sciences and Arts Awards   Vol. 2: 10724
Serdan Prize; Carmen and Aguiles   Vol. 2: 9001
Serena Medal for Italian Studies   Vol. 2: 2230
Sergeant Memorial Award; Howard   Vol. 2: 3013
Sergel Prize   Vol. 2: 11511
Sergelpriset   Vol. 2: 11511
Sericultural Science Advancement Award   Vol. 2: 8660
Sernet; Prix Claude   Vol. 2: 4933
Serono Symposia USA Research Award   Vol. 1: 13298
Serra Award of the Americas   Vol. 1: 17
Sertoma International Humanitarian Award   Vol. 1: 17197
Serturner Medal   Vol. 2: 6825
Service Award
 Agricultural Communicators in Education   Vol. 1: 204
 American Camping Association   Vol 1: 1407
 American Occupational Therapy Association   Vol 1: 3304
 American Philatelic Congress   Vol 1: 3408
 Association for Indiana Media Educators   Vol 1: 5535
 Civil War Token Society   Vol 1: 7783
 College Swimming Coaches Association of America   Vol 1: 7949
 Japanese Society of Snow and Ice   Vol 2: 8664
 National Accreditation Council for Agencies Serving the Blind and Visually Handicapped   Vol 1: 12720
 National Intramural-Recreational Sports Association   Vol 1: 14253
 Scientific and Technical Research Council of Turkey (Tubitak)   Vol 2: 12066
 Society for Imaging Science and Technology   Vol 1: 17508
Service Award for the Promotion and Teaching of Football   Vol. 2: 10669
Service Award Medal of the Royal Astronomical Society of Canada   Vol. 1: 16931
Service Award of Chamber of Geological Engineers   Vol. 2: 12047
Service Award of the American College of Utilization Review Physicians   Vol. 1: 1752
Service Awards
 Canadian Society of Petroleum Geologists   Vol. 1: 7227
 Health Sciences Communications Association   Vol 1: 9856
 Municipal Treasurers Association of the United States and Canada   Vol 1: 12495
 National Association of Underwater Instructors   Vol 1: 13378
 USA Baseball   Vol 1: 19916
 Western Society of Engineers   Vol 1: 20226
Service Badge   Vol 1: 374
Service Bowl Award   Vol. 1: 19656
Service Medal   Vol. 2: 4522
Service Medal of the Order   Vol. 2: 3745
Service Orders of West Germany   Vol. 2: 6739
Service to Children Television Awards   Vol. 1: 12980
Service to Democracy Award   Vol. 1: 814
Service to the First Amendment - Edward Willis Scripps Award   Vol. 1: 17150
Service to the Water Industry Award   Vol. 1: 5031
Service to Youth Award
 Boys & Girls Clubs of America   Vol. 1: 6537
 Young Men's Christian Association of Greater New York   Vol 1: 20612
Servicios Distinguidos
 Colombia - National Police   Vol. 2: 1677
 Venezuelan Geological Society   Vol 2: 12144
Servicios Distinguidos a la Fuerza Submarina   Vol. 2: 1649
Serviscope Trophy   Vol. 2: 4507
SES - ASTM Robert J. Painter Memorial Award   Vol. 1: 6076
SES Award for Outstanding Paper   Vol. 1: 18456
Seshadri Prize in the Field of Practice of Community Medicine; Dr. M. K.   Vol. 2: 7608
Seshadri Seventieth Birthday Commemoration Medal; Professor T. R.   Vol. 2: 7669
Sesher Sportsmanship Award; Charles   Vol. 1: 14266
Sessions Memorial Award; John   Vol. 1: 2950
Seton Award; Ernest Thompson   Vol. 1: 10737
Seton Award; NCEA Elizabeth Ann   Vol. 1: 13554
Seton Award; Saint Elizabeth Ann   Vol. 1: 13555
Seton Distinguished Volunteer Award; Fenmore R.   Vol. 1: 16758
Setterfield Memorial Scholarship; Ellen   Vol. 1: 13965
Seven Hats Award   Vol. 1: 3863
Sevensma Prize; T. P.   Vol. 2: 9495
Seventeen Magazine Fiction Contest   Vol. 1: 17200
Seventeen Magazine/Smith Corona Fiction Contest   Vol. 1: 17200
Seventeen Seventy-Six Award ("1776 Award")   Vol. 1: 15087
Seventy-Five Year Club Member Certificate   Vol. 1: 3258
Severinghaus Award; Aura E.   Vol. 1: 14352
Sevigne Award; Frank   Vol. 1: 19957
Sewell Medal   Vol. 2: 4055
Sewell Mutant Award   Vol. 1: 1400
Seyffert Memorial Award; Richard   Vol. 1: 12830
Seymour Award   Vol. 1: 5528
Seymour Award; Whitney North   Vol. 1: 9075
Seymour, Sr. Award; Whitney North   Vol. 1: 805
Sforza Award in Philanthropy   Vol. 2: 11867
SFWA Nebula Awards   Vol. 1: 17113
SFWoE Author of the Eighties   Vol. 1: 17119
Sgambati/Cansave Media Award; Fred   Vol. 1: 17081
SGD Swiss Graphic Designers   Vol. 2: 11904
Shaara Outstanding Writer Award; Michael   Vol. 1: 18251
Shackman Travelling Fellowship   Vol. 2: 2276
Shacknai Memorial Prize and Lectureship; Rabbi Shai   Vol. 2: 7888
Shadle Fellowship; Albert R. and Alma   Vol. 1: 4663
Shadrack Coursing Continuum   Vol. 1: 3984
Shaeffer - PEN/New England Award for Literary Excellence   Vol. 1: 16037
Shafer Award; George E.   Vol. 1: 18088
Shafer Award; Stephen   Vol. 1: 14421
Shaffer Award for Academic Excellence as a Graduate Faculty Member; Robert H.   Vol. 1: 13333
Shaffer Award; Robert H.   Vol. 1: 5807
Shahin Trophy   Vol. 1: 3984
Shakespeare Award for Classical Theatre (Will Award); William   Vol. 1: 17209
Shakespeare Globe Award   Vol. 1: 17207
Shakespeare Library Fellowships and National Endowment for the Humanities Senior Fellowships; Folger   Vol. 1: 9282
Shakespeare Prize   Vol. 2: 7124
Shaler Company's Rislone Most Improved Championship Driver Award   Vol. 1: 19030
Shalom Peace Award   Vol. 1: 11557
Shandon/Lipshaw Student Scholarship   Vol. 1: 14755
Shands Award; A. R.   Vol. 1: 15843
Shanghai Television Festival   Vol. 2: 1576
Shannon Award; National Film Board Kathleen   Vol. 1: 20597
Shanti Swarup Bhatnagar Medal   Vol. 2: 7670
Shantz Award; Stan   Vol. 1: 16336
Shapira Prize; Francois   Vol. 2: 7971
Shapiro Award; Arthur   Vol. 1: 17439
Share-Jones Lectureship in Veterinary Anatomy   Vol. 2: 3993
Share the Wealth Packets   Vol. 1: 11862
Sharp Award; A.J.   Vol. 1: 6491
Sharp Memorial Prize; Frank Chapman   Vol. 1: 3428
Sharpe Prize; Roy   Vol. 2: 2402
Sharples Perpetual Award; Laurence P.   Vol. 1: 285
Shatalov Award; Mikhail and Ekateryna   Vol. 1: 12632
Shattuck Award; Charles B.   Vol. 1: 5198
Shaughnessy Prize; Mina P.   Vol. 1: 12405
Shaumian Prize; Stephan   Vol. 2: 113
Shaurya Chakra   Vol. 2: 7561
Shaw Award; Cliff   Vol. 1: 17069
Shaw Award; Nathan   Vol. 1: 8629

Shazar Award for Research in Jewish History; Zalman   Vol. 2: 7940
Shea Award; James H.   Vol. 1: 13121
Shea Prize; John Gilmary   Vol. 1: 1433
Sheaffer Pen Prize for First Fiction   Vol. 2: 149
Sheahan Award; John Drury   Vol. 1: 8375
SHEAR Article Prize   Vol. 1: 17471
SHEAR Book Prize   Vol. 1: 17472
Sheard - Sanford Medical Student Award   Vol. 1: 4520
Shedden Pacific Medal and Prize   Vol. 2: 487
Sheehan Memorial Award; Joseph M.   Vol. 1: 12241
Sheehan Memorial Educational Scholarship; Dezna C.   Vol. 1: 14747
Sheeline Award for Excellence in Public Relations; Randall D.   Vol. 1: 2600
Shelburne Award; Tilton E.   Vol. 1: 6077
Sheldon Audio-Visual Award; M. Vernon   Vol. 1: 3259
Sheldon Exemplary Equipment and Facilities Award   Vol. 1: 14706
Shell Century III Leaders Program   Vol. 1: 13312
Shell - LSO Music Scholarship   Vol. 2: 3618
Shell Playwrights Award   Vol. 2: 9770
Shell, Royal Opera House, Covent Garden Scholarship   Vol. 2: 572
Shell Sponsorship Award   Vol. 2: 4490
Shelley Memorial Award   Vol. 1: 16292
Shelton Award; Robert M.   Vol. 1: 9866
Shelton-Smith Award for Play, Radio or Other Scripts for Young Writers; FAW Adele   Vol. 2: 378
Shenandoah Playwrights Retreat
  Shenandoah Playwrights Retreat   Vol. 1: 17213
  Shenandoah Playwrights Retreat   Vol 1: 17214
  Shenandoah Playwrights Retreat   Vol 1: 17215
  Shenandoah Playwrights Retreat   Vol 1: 17216
Shenk Award   Vol. 1: 12793
Shepard Award; Glenn   Vol. 1: 14898
Shepard Award of Distinction; Earl E.   Vol. 1: 1354
Shepard Award of Distinction; Earl E. and Wilma S.   Vol. 1: 1354
Shepard Award; Paul   Vol. 1: 3596
Shepard Medal   Vol. 1: 17597
Shepard Medal for Excellence in Marine Geology; Francis P.   Vol. 1: 17597
Shepard Science Award; Charles C.   Vol. 1: 19241
Shephard Award; Will   Vol. 1: 5858
Shepheard Award for Achievement in Merchant Marine Safety; Rear Admiral Halert C.   Vol. 1: 1376
Shepheard Award; Halert C.   Vol. 1: 2629
Shepherd Distinguished Composer of the Year Award; MTNA-   Vol. 1: 12523
Sheppard Award; C. Stewart   Vol. 1: 5556
Sheppard Award; Eugenia   Vol. 1: 8355
Sheppard Memorial Lecture; John   Vol. 2: 7753
Shera Award for Research; Jesse H.   Vol. 1: 2916
Shercliff Prize; University of Cambridge Arthur   Vol. 2: 3352
Sherif Memorial Lectureship; Carolyn Wood   Vol. 1: 3774
Sherman Award   Vol. 1: 8853
Sherman Leadership Award; Simon   Vol. 1: 17375
Sherrard Awards; J. M.   Vol. 2: 9709

Sherrington Memorial Lecture   Vol. 2: 4266
Sherritt Hydrometallurgy Award   Vol. 1: 6954
Shertz Essay Award; Harold S.   Vol. 1: 14320
Sherwin International Award; Raymond J.   Vol. 1: 17241
Sherwin-Williams Student Award in Applied Polymer Science   Vol. 1: 1510
Shetland People Hall of Fame   Vol. 1: 4026
Shewhart Medal   Vol. 1: 4287
Shibusawa Memorial Prize   Vol. 2: 8738
Shiebler Award; George L.   Vol. 1: 8794
Shield Award   Vol. 1: 15992
Shield of Blessed Gregory X   Vol. 1: 13351
Shield of the Minister of Labour and Social Affairs   Vol. 2: 7911
Shields Medal   Vol. 1: 17716
Shields Memorial Award for Twin Research; James   Vol. 1: 6313
Shields-Trauger Award   Vol. 1: 6243
Shilling Award; Charles W.   Vol. 1: 18866
Shilling Award; David C.   Vol. 1: 257
Shimbun Bunka Sho   Vol. 2: 8627
Shimbun Kokoku Sho   Vol. 2: 8626
Shinbum Kyokai Sho   Vol. 2: 8628
Shincho Art and Science Award   Vol. 2: 8744
Shinsho Corporation Award; Professor Masubuchi/   Vol. 1: 5083
Ship of the Year   Vol. 1: 20514
Ship Safety Achievement Awards   Vol. 1: 2630
Shipley Award; Robert M.   Vol. 1: 2146
Shipman Gold Medal; J.   Vol. 1: 13259
Shipper/Carrier Partnership of the Year   Vol. 1: 4803
Shiras Institute/Mildred & Albert Panowski Playwriting Award   Vol. 1: 16856
Shiu-Ying Hu Award   Vol. 1: 9970
Shneidman Award; Edwin   Vol. 1: 1208
Shock Compression Science Award   Vol. 1: 3471
Shock New Investigator Award; Nathan   Vol. 1: 9594
Shoemaker Award of Merit; Ralph J.   Vol. 1: 18283
Shofar Award (Ram's Horn)   Vol. 1: 6527
Shogakukan Bungaku-Sho   Vol. 2: 8747
Shogakukan Jido-Bunka-Sho
  Shogakukan   Vol. 2: 8747
  Shogakukan   Vol. 2: 8748
Shogakukan Kaiga-Sho   Vol. 2: 8748
Shogren Award   Vol. 1: 10767
Shore Composition Award; Bernard   Vol. 2: 4117
Shore Plaque (Outstanding Defenseman); Eddie   Vol. 1: 2333
Shores - Oryx Press Award; Louis   Vol. 1: 2951
Short Film Festival Prize   Vol. 2: 9948
Short Play Awards Program   Vol. 1: 1761
Short Stories for Small Children Award   Vol. 2: 7222
Short Story Award   Vol. 2: 6505
Short Story Contest   Vol. 1: 12338
Shostakovich Competition of String Quartets; International Dmitri   Vol. 2: 10453
Shotwell Memorial Award; Ambrose M.   Vol. 1: 5493
Shousha Foundation Prize; Dr. A. T.   Vol. 2: 11976
Show Flyer/Poster Contest   Vol. 1: 9132
Show Hunter Ponies Awards   Vol. 2: 2501
Show Ponies Awards   Vol. 2: 2502
Showcase Study Award   Vol. 1: 53
ShoWester Award   Vol. 1: 13370
Shreveport Opera Singer of the Year   Vol. 1: 17218
Shri Dhanwantari Prize   Vol. 2: 7671

SHRM Book Award   Vol. 1: 17488
SHRM Outstanding Graduate Student Award   Vol. 1: 17489
Shrobehn Internship Program; AECT National Convention - Earl F.   Vol. 1: 5508
Shroder Awards; William J.   Vol. 1: 8366
Shryock Medal; Richard H.   Vol. 1: 896
Shulitz Cancer Prize and Lectureship; Simon M.   Vol. 1: 19760
Shull Award; Charles Albert   Vol. 1: 4751
Shulman Book Prize; Marshall   Vol. 1: 892
Shumavon Award; Leo   Vol. 1: 13888
Shuster Memorial Award; Ben   Vol. 1: 573
Shute Award; Gladys G.   Vol. 1: 15568
Shwachman Clinical Investigator Award; Harry   Vol. 1: 8491
Shy Award; G. Milton   Vol. 1: 618
SIA Service Award   Vol. 1: 17173
SIAD Medal   Vol. 2: 2607
SIAM Activity Group on Linear Algebra Prize   Vol. 1: 17516
SIAM Prize for Distinguished Service to the Profession   Vol. 1: 17517
SIAM Prize in Numerical Analysis and Scientific Computing   Vol. 1: 17521
Sibelius palkinto; Wihurin   Vol. 2: 4763
Sibelius Violin Competition; International Jean   Vol. 2: 4729
Sibley Fellowship; Mary Isabel   Vol. 1: 16104
Sibley Magazine of the Year; Robert   Vol. 1: 8297
Sicaud; Prix Sabine   Vol. 2: 6342
Sicher First Research Essay Award; Harry   Vol. 1: 1094
Sickle Cell Center Research Award   Vol. 1: 10028
SID Award (Store Interior Design Award)   Vol. 1: 13325
Sidewalk Sale and Exhibition   Vol. 1: 7487
Sidey Medal and Prize; T. K.   Vol. 2: 9841
Sidley Memorial Award; Dorothy   Vol. 2: 3031
Sidmar Prize   Vol. 2: 1315
Siedenburg Award   Vol. 1: 11973
Siegel Award; Robt.   Vol. 1: 8109
Siegel der Deutschen Gesellschaft fur Chirurgie   Vol. 2: 6883
Siegel Memorial Award; Joseph A.   Vol. 1: 17882
Siegel Service Award; Joseph A.   Vol. 1: 17882
Siemens Elema Young Investigators Award   Vol. 2: 10580
Siena College Playwrights' Competition   Vol. 1: 17222
Sierpinski Award   Vol. 2: 10158
Sierra Club Literary Prize   Vol. 1: 17242
Siesel Award for Community Service; E. Hank   Vol. 1: 14082
Sievers Wicke; Premio a la Actividad Profesional Dr. Hugo K.   Vol. 2: 1562
Sievert Award   Vol. 2: 9524
SIG Member-of-The-Year Award   Vol. 1: 4173
SIG-of-the-Year Award   Vol. 1: 4174
SIGCOMM Award   Vol. 1: 5477
Sigma Delta Chi Awards   Vol. 1: 18001
Sigma Delta Epsilon Fellowships   Vol. 1: 17256
Sigma Gamma Tau Honors Undergraduate Award   Vol. 1: 17258
Sigma Iota Epsilon Scholarship Awards   Vol. 1: 17260
Sigma Phi Alpha Dental Hygiene Honor Society   Vol. 1: 17263
Sigmond Memorial Medal; Elek   Vol. 2: 7375
Sign Design Competition   Vol. 1: 13884
Signal Poetry Award   Vol. 2: 4537
Signature of Excellence Award   Vol. 1: 14955

Significant Achievement Award
　National Wildlife Rehabilitation Association　Vol. 1: 15015
　Rotary International　Vol 1: 16907
Significant Contributions to the Engineering Illustrating Profession Award　Vol. 1: 17834
Significant Research Contribution Award in Pediatric Psychology　Vol. 1: 3696
Signum Fidei Medal　Vol. 1: 11745
Signy Foreign Fellowship; Gordon　Vol. 2: 8789
Sijil Kemuliaan　Vol. 2: 10736
Sikkensprijs　Vol. 2: 9621
Sikorsky Award for Humanitarian Service; Igor I.　Vol. 1: 9900
Sikorsky International Trophy; Igor I.　Vol. 1: 2259
Silbert Annual Economic Forecasting Award; Theodore H.　Vol. 1: 18489
Silesian Insurrectionary Cross　Vol. 2: 10122
Silky Award; Fran　Vol. 1: 16792
Silliman Anthem Award; Vincent Brown　Vol. 1: 18893
Sills - Lincoln Center Award; Beverly　Vol. 1: 11888
Silurian Excellence in Journalism Awards　Vol. 1: 18066
Silva de Interpretacao Teatral; Premios Municipais Palmira Bastos e Antonio　Vol. 2: 10282
Silva de la Fuente Award; Alejandro　Vol. 2: 1553
Silva Service Award　Vol. 1: 19497
Silver and Golden Scroll Awards　Vol. 1: 82
Silver Anniversary Top Six　Vol. 1: 13610
Silver Antelope　Vol. 1: 6518
Silver Anvil Awards　Vol. 1: 16577
Silver Ball Award　Vol. 1: 17373
Silver Baton Award　Vol. 1: 20363
Silver Beaver　Vol. 1: 6519
Silver Buffalo Award　Vol. 1: 6520
Silver Carnation　Vol. 2: 9576
Silver Chalice Award　Vol. 1: 1858
Silver Circle Award　Vol. 1: 16913
Silver Combustion Medal　Vol. 1: 8023
Silver Core Award　Vol. 2: 11785
Silver Crown Awards　Vol. 1: 7968
Silver Dart Aviation History Award　Vol. 1: 6812
Silver Edelweiss　Vol. 2: 11386
Silver Elephant Award　Vol. 2: 7715
Silver Fawn Award　Vol. 1: 6521
Silver Gentian　Vol. 2: 8460
Silver-gilt Medal for Bibliography　Vol. 2: 2167
Silver Halo Award　Vol. 1: 16914
Silver Hardhat Award　Vol. 1: 8218
Silver Harp　Vol. 2: 9374
Silver Hawk Award　Vol. 1: 12077
Silver Jubilee Award　Vol. 2: 2542
Silver Jubilee Commemoration Medal　Vol. 2: 7672
Silver Jubilee Medal Award; SAIP -　Vol. 2: 11073
Silver Jubilee Scholarship　Vol. 1: 6919
Silver Key Award　Vol. 1: 13793
Silver Lifesaving Medal　Vol. 1: 19188
Silver Magnolia Blossom　Vol. 1: 8101
Silver Mailcoach　Vol. 2: 3781
Silver Medal
　Acoustical Society of America　Vol. 1: 102
　American Rhododenron Society　Vol 1: 3957
　Australian Numismatic Society　Vol 2: 260
　British Coatings Federation　Vol 2: 2315
　The Gardners of America, Inc./Men's Garden Clubs of America　Vol 1: 9501
　Institute of Actuaries　Vol 2: 3058
　Institute of Metals and Materials Australasia　Vol 2: 419
　Royal Institute of Navigation　Vol 2: 4079
　Royal Society of British Sculptors　Vol 2: 4181
　Tau Sigma Delta　Vol 1: 18583
　Zoological Society of London　Vol 2: 4661
Silver Medal Award
　Advertising Women of New York　Vol. 1: 161
　Association of Scientists and Engineers of the Naval Sea Systems Command　Vol 1: 5960
　Audio Engineering Society　Vol 1: 6134
　Canadian Institute of Mining and Metallurgy　Vol 1: 6955
Silver Medal Award Program　Vol. 1: 741
Silver Medal of Merit　Vol. 1: 3342
Silver Medallion　Vol. 1: 6538
Silver Medallion Award　Vol. 1: 5137
Silver Memorial Award; Henry K.　Vol. 1: 13223
Silver Page Award　Vol. 1: 4559
Silver Palette Award　Vol. 1: 14824
Silver Pen Award
　English Centre of International PEN　Vol. 2: 2783
　English Centre of International PEN　Vol 2: 2784
Silver Plaque　Vol. 2: 2423
Silver Plaque Awards　Vol. 1: 14636
Silver Playwriting Competition; Dorothy　Vol. 1: 11543
Silver Quill Editorial Achievement Award　Vol. 1: 5091
Silver Rope for Leadership　Vol. 1: 376
Silver Rose Bowl　Vol. 2: 4626
Silver Satellite Award　Vol. 1: 5111
Silver Screen Award　Vol. 1: 19352
Silver Seal Certificate　Vol. 1: 6758
Silver Service/Silver Cup Awards　Vol. 1: 13604
Silver Shadow Award　Vol. 1: 16205
Silver Shovel Award　Vol. 1: 11123
Silver Slugger Team　Vol. 1: 18383
Silver Snail Award　Vol. 1: 15550
Silver Spike　Vol. 2: 11392
Silver Star: Army　Vol. 1: 19189
Silver Star for Bravery　Vol. 1: 3565
Silver Star: Navy　Vol. 1: 19190
Silver Tray of RHA　Vol. 1: 16902
Silver Turnbuckle　Vol. 2: 3909
Silver World Award　Vol. 1: 6522
Silver Wrench Award　Vol. 1: 8991
Silverfish Review Poetry Chapbook Award　Vol. 1: 17279
Silverman Award; Irving　Vol. 1: 11388
Silvio e Jacopo Novaro; Fondazione Angiolo　Vol. 2: 8051
Sily Zbrojne w Sluzbie Ojczyzny　Vol. 2: 10093
Simkins Award; Francis Butler　Vol. 1: 18217
Simmonds Medal　Vol. 2: 4056
Simmons First National Bank Grand Purchase Award　Vol. 1: 5320
Simmons Short Fiction Award; John　Vol. 1: 11448
Simms Medal　Vol. 2: 4444
Simms Prize　Vol. 2: 3910
Simoes de Almeida de Escultura; Premio Municipal Jose　Vol. 2: 10272
Simon Award　Vol. 2: 2512
Simon Award; Fannie　Vol. 1: 18278
Simon Award; George　Vol. 1: 9232
Simon Children's Book Award; Charlie May　Vol. 1: 5257
Simon Fund Book Awards; Andre　Vol. 2: 4342
Simon Medal; Andre　Vol. 2: 3506
Simon Memorial Prize　Vol. 2: 3197
Simon Memorial Scholarship; Dr. May K.　Vol. 1: 5844
Simon Sherman Industry Service Award　Vol. 1: 17375
Simons Medal; Fitz　Vol. 2: 11034
Simons Prize; Harden-　Vol. 1: 4093
Simonsen Lectureship　Vol. 2: 4222
Simont; Prix Henriette　Vol. 2: 1334
Simpers Award; Lucille　Vol. 1: 2387
Simpla Research Prize　Vol. 2: 2277
Simpson Memorial Award; W. Arthur　Vol. 1: 3113
Simpson Technical Editor's Award; Maurice　Vol. 1: 10335
Sims Award; Arthur　Vol. 2: 2123
Sims Scholarship; Sir Arthur　Vol. 1: 16964
Simulation and Ground Testing Award　Vol. 1: 2471
Sinclair Award; David　Vol. 1: 830
Sinclair Award for Excellence in Broadcast Journalism; Gordon　Vol. 1: 327
Sinclair Award; Gordon　Vol. 1: 26
Sinclaire Award; Matilda W.　Vol. 1: 2090
Sinden Award　Vol. 2: 3664
Singapore Food and Hotel Asia Competition　Vol. 2: 10752
Singer Award; Colonel Merton　Vol. 1: 16801
Singer-Polignac Grants　Vol. 2: 5226
Singer Prize　Vol. 2: 2523
Singh Award; Bhai Santokh　Vol. 2: 7513
Singh of Kalsia Memorial Cancer Research Award; Raja Ravi Sher　Vol. 2: 7609
Singing Youth International, Zoltan Kodaly Choral Competition　Vol. 2: 7423
Single Parent of the Year Award　Vol. 1: 15965
Sinhala Drama Awards　Vol. 2: 11426
Sinking Creek Film Festival　Vol. 1: 17288
Sinkula Award; Christina　Vol. 1: 1082
Sintra; Prix Thomson　Vol. 2: 6354
S.I.N.U.S. Association Prize　Vol. 2: 6213
Siphers Memorial Scholarship; Kathryn　Vol. 1: 20364
SIRS Intellectual Freedom Award; AECT/　Vol. 1: 5503
SIRS/Peace Award　Vol. 1: 2955
Sister Cities Expressions of Peace Youth Art Contest　Vol. 1: 17290
Sister Cities Impressions of Freedom Young Artist Awards　Vol. 1: 17290
Sister Cities International Awards　Vol. 1: 17291
Sister Cities Youth Program Awards　Vol. 1: 17291
Sister Kenny Institute International Art Show by Artists with Disabilities　Vol. 1: 17294
Sisyphus Award　Vol. 1: 13690
Sitges International Fantasy Film Festival Awards　Vol. 2: 11359
SITPRO Prize　Vol. 2: 3098
Sivickio premija; P.　Vol. 2: 8856
Sixteenth Century Journal Literature Prize　Vol. 1: 17301
Sixteenth Century Studies Conference Medal　Vol. 1: 17302
Sixty Year Membership Medal　Vol. 1: 3260
Skakel Award; Great Lakes -　Vol. 1: 1418
Skeffington Award; A. M.　Vol. 1: 7933
Skellerup Award　Vol. 2: 9744
Ski Magazine Cup　Vol. 1: 19586
Ski Retailer of the Year Awards　Vol. 1: 17304

Skier of the Year
  International Ski Federation   Vol. 2: 11833
  Ski Racing   Vol 1: 17306
Skiing Magazine Development Cup   Vol. 1: 19587
Skinner Award   Vol. 1: 18094
Skinner Award; Clarence R.   Vol. 1: 18894
Skinner Award; Constance Lindsay   Vol. 1: 20422
Skinner Memorial Fund Award   Vol. 1: 2068
Skoda Ring; Albin   Vol. 2: 770
Skolnik Award; Herman   Vol. 1: 1511
SLA Hall of Fame   Vol. 1: 18266
SLA Honorary Member   Vol. 1: 18267
SLA John Cotton Dana Award   Vol. 1: 18268
SLA Meckler Award for Innovations in Technology   Vol. 1: 18269
SLA Media Award   Vol. 1: 18270
SLA Presidents Award   Vol. 1: 18271
SLA Professional Award   Vol. 1: 18272
SLA Public Relations Member Achievement Award   Vol. 1: 18273
SLA Research Grant   Vol. 1: 18274
Slack Awards for Medical Journalism   Vol. 1: 14353
Slager sezone   Vol. 2: 1402
Slagle Lectureship; Eleanor Clarke   Vol. 1: 3305
Slaski Krzyz Powstanczy   Vol. 2: 10122
Slate - MacDaniels Award   Vol. 1: 15429
Slates Memorial Award; Philip   Vol. 1: 18188
Slattery Marketing Awards; J. Desmond   Vol. 1: 18790
Slaughter Research Award; Robert E.   Vol. 1: 9619
Sledz - Lou Wener Community Service Award in Washington, DC; Carroll   Vol. 1: 10050
Sleeks Prize; Ary   Vol. 2: 1276
Slessor Prize; Kenneth   Vol. 2: 147
Slichter Award; William P.   Vol. 1: 19107
Sliffe Awards for Distinguished High School Mathematics Teaching; Edyth May   Vol. 1: 12139
Slim-Jim All-Pro Series   Vol. 1: 12902
Slipper Gold Medal; Stanley   Vol. 1: 7228
Slipstream's Annual Chapbook Contest   Vol. 1: 17308
SLMSSENY Annual Children's Literature Award   Vol. 1: 17096
SLMSSENY Author Award   Vol. 1: 17097
Sloan, Jr. Medal; Alfred P.   Vol. 1: 9532
Sloan Public Service Awards of the Fund for the City of New York   Vol. 1: 9449
Slobe Memorial Prize; Laura   Vol. 1: 5297
Slocum Medal   Vol. 1: 17315
Slote Award; Bernice   Vol. 1: 16365
Slovak Studies Association Prize   Vol. 1: 17320
Slovenian Studies Award   Vol. 1: 17322
Small Animal Practitioner Award   Vol. 1: 7266
Small Business Advocates of the Year   Vol. 1: 19602
Small Business Exporter of the Year   Vol. 1: 19603
Small Business Person of the Year   Vol. 1: 17326
Small Firms Merit Awards for Research & Technology   Vol. 2: 4559
Small Memorial Award; Ben John   Vol. 1: 8211
Small Print Division Awards   Vol. 1: 16169
Small Project Grants   Vol. 2: 4571
Small Town America Hall of Fame   Vol. 1: 13374
Smallwood Jr. Award of Merit; Grahame Thomas   Vol. 1: 5926

Smart Anthem Competition; Harold   Vol. 2: 4139
SMART (Small Firms Merit Awards for Research & Technology)   Vol. 2: 4559
Smarties Book Prize   Vol. 2: 2206
Smarties Prize fro Children's Books   Vol. 2: 2206
SMD President's Award   Vol. 1: 17891
SME Albert M. Sargent Progress Award   Vol. 1: 17883
SME Distinguished Contributions Award   Vol. 1: 17884
SME Education Award   Vol. 1: 17885
SME Engineering Citation   Vol. 1: 17886
SME Frederick W. Taylor Research Medal   Vol. 1: 17887
SME Gold Medal   Vol. 1: 17888
SME Industry LEAD Award; CASA/   Vol. 1: 8078
SME Interprofessional Cooperation Award   Vol. 1: 17884
SME Progress Award   Vol. 1: 17883
SME Research Medal   Vol. 1: 17887
SME University LEAD Award; CASA/   Vol. 1: 8079
Smedley Memorial Award; Glenn   Vol. 1: 3261
Smelik/IBBY Prize; Jenny   Vol. 2: 9387
Smelik-Kiggenprijs; Jenny   Vol. 2: 9387
Smetana Piano Competition   Vol. 2: 1894
Smetanovska klavirni souteze   Vol. 2: 1894
SMFA Concerto Competition   Vol. 1: 17065
Smiley Memorial Award; Gordon   Vol. 1: 18410
Smissman-Bristol-Meyers-Squibb Award   Vol. 1: 1512
Smith Affiliate of the Year Award (Agency-based Affiliates); Eleanor Touey   Vol. 1: 11904
Smith and Miss Aleen Cust Research Fellowships of the RCVS; Sir Frederick   Vol. 2: 3994
Smith and Wesson Trophy   Vol. 1: 14645
Smith Arts Programme; W.H.   Vol. 2: 4344
Smith Award; Adam   Vol. 1: 5924
Smith Award; Bob   Vol. 2: 3800
Smith Award; Daniel B.   Vol. 1: 3391
Smith Award for National Distinguished Service; Franklin   Vol. 1: 5217
Smith Award for Submarine Support Achievement; Levering   Vol. 1: 15095
Smith Award; Georgina   Vol. 1: 1232
Smith Award; Horton   Vol. 1: 16479
Smith Award; I.   Vol. 1: 7138
Smith Award; Isabel and Monroe   Vol. 1: 10014
Smith Award; Job Lewis   Vol. 1: 685
Smith Award; Lilian Ida   Vol. 2: 9782
Smith Award; Nila Banton   Vol. 1: 11196
Smith Award; O. P.   Vol. 1: 2190
Smith Award; Reginald Heber   Vol. 1: 14299
Smith Award; W. W. "Red"   Vol. 1: 9795
Smith Award; Wilbur S.   Vol. 1: 4497
Smith Book Awards; Lillian   Vol. 1: 18237
Smith/*Books in Canada* First Novel Award; W. H.   Vol. 1: 6454
Smith Breeden Prizes   Vol. 1: 2055
Smith Center for the History of Cartography Fellowships; Hermon Dunlap   Vol. 1: 15319
Smith Chapter Achievement Awards; National Planning Awards - Karen B.   Vol. 1: 3541
Smith Corona Fiction Contest; *Seventeen Magazine*/   Vol. 1: 17200
Smith Distinguished Educator Award; Wilbur S.   Vol. 1: 10458
Smith Distinguished Service Award; Robert M.   Vol. 1: 686

Smith Fellowships; Al   Vol. 1: 11686
Smith Fiction Awards; Reed   Vol. 1: 474
Smith Grant in Humanistic Photography; W. Eugene   Vol. 1: 17333
Smith Hydraulic Fellowship; J. Waldo   Vol. 1: 4498
Smith Illustration Award; W. H.   Vol. 2: 4595
Smith Illustration Awards; W. H.   Vol. 2: 4344
Smith, Kline and French Prize   Vol. 1: 3502
Smith, Kline & French Research Grant; ONS/   Vol. 1: 15665
Smith Literary Award; W. H.   Vol. 2: 4345
Smith Medal; Blakely   Vol. 1: 17926
Smith Medal; Gilbert Morgan   Vol. 1: 12688
Smith Medal; H. G.   Vol. 2: 602
Smith Medal in Anthropology; Percy   Vol. 2: 9852
Smith Medal; J. Lawrence   Vol. 1: 12689
Smith Medal; Julian C.   Vol. 1: 8936
Smith Medal; Waldo E.   Vol. 1: 2170
Smith Medal; William   Vol. 2: 2928
Smith Memorial   Vol. 1: 11298
Smith Memorial Award; H. Ward   Vol. 1: 11202
Smith Memorial Award; Howard DeWitt   Vol. 1: 6078
Smith Memorial Exhibit Award; Sidney W.   Vol. 1: 3262
Smith Memorial Medal; S. G.   Vol. 2: 4523
Smith Memorial Scholarship; Frank   Vol. 1: 11369
Smith National Award; Sidney O.   Vol. 1: 10134
Smith Prize for the Most Distinguished American Review of Canadian Studies; Rufus Z.   Vol. 1: 5460
Smith Sr. Award; Bruce   Vol. 1: 38
Smith Solo Performance Competition; Ellsworth   Vol. 1: 11375
Smith Trophy; General   Vol. 1: 14645
Smith Trust Fund; Posworth   Vol. 2: 3343
Smith - U.S. Water Award; James R. "Jimmy"   Vol. 1: 19684
Smith Young Writers' Competition; W. H.   Vol. 2: 4346
Smithbooks/*Books in Canada* First Novel Award   Vol. 1: 6454
Smithers Award; R. Brinkley   Vol. 1: 13794
SmithKline Beecham Pharmaceuticals Young Investigator   Vol. 2: 1974
SmithKline Beecham; Prix   Vol. 2: 1342
Smithson Medal   Vol. 1: 17345
Smithson; Order of James   Vol. 1: 17343
Smithson Society Founder Medal; James   Vol. 1: 17348
Smithson Society Grants; James   Vol. 1: 17349
Smithsonian Craft Show   Vol. 1: 17351
Smithsonian Research Fellowships   Vol. 1: 17346
SMM Postgraduate Student Award   Vol. 2: 11075
SMM Prize   Vol. 2: 11076
Smokies of the Seas Award   Vol. 1: 19709
Smolar Award for Excellence in North American Jewish Journalism; Boris   Vol. 1: 2747
Smoluchowski Medal; Marian   Vol. 2: 10172
Smyth Salver   Vol. 2: 10589
Smyth Statesman Award; Henry DeWolf   Vol. 1: 19074
Smythe International Service Citation; Hugh H. and Mable M.   Vol. 1: 10567
Smythe Trophy; Conn   Vol. 1: 14180
Smythe Trophy; D. Verner   Vol. 1: 19541
Smythies Award; Jill   Vol. 2: 3589
SNA Affirmative Action Award   Vol. 1: 3288
SNC Plant Design Competition   Vol. 1: 7561

Snedecor Award for the Best Publication in Biometry; George W. Vol. 1: 4863
Snedecor Award; George W. Vol. 1: 8038
Snell Premium Vol. 2: 3273
Snellius Medal Vol. 2: 9558
Sniadecki Medal; Jedrzej Vol. 2: 10138
Snickers World Cross Country Championships; IAAF/ Vol. 2: 9314
SNM Distinguished Educator Award Vol. 1: 17951
SNM Distinguished Service Award Vol. 1: 17952
SNM Honorary Member Vol. 1: 17953
SNM Named Lectureships Vol. 1: 17954
SNM Presidential Distinguished Service Award Vol. 1: 17955
Snodgrass Memorial Research Grant Vol. 1: 8952
Snoekprijs; Hans Vol. 2: 9690
Snoeyenbos New Investigator Award; Glenn Vol. 1: 914
Snow Foundation Prize; John Ben Vol. 1: 15406
Snow Prize; John Ben Vol. 1: 18554
Snowy Owl Conservation Award Vol. 1: 16624
Snyder Award; Anne D. Vol. 1: 7781
Snyder Award; Walter F. Vol. 1: 14663
Soap Opera Awards Vol. 1: 17355
Soapies Vol. 1: 17355
Soares Dos Reis Prize Vol. 2: 10306
Soaring Hall of Fame Vol. 1: 17364
Sober Memorial Lectureship; Herbert Vol. 1: 4043
Sobotta Preis Vol. 2: 6521
SOCAN Award for Composers 30 Years of Age and Over Vol. 1: 17820
SOCAN Awards for Young Composers Vol. 1: 17821
Soccer Coach of the Year Vol. 1: 6984
Soccer Outstanding Service Award Vol. 1: 452
Social Inventions Prizes Vol. 2: 3050
Social Issues Dissertation Award Vol. 1: 3815
Social Justice Award Vol. 1: 20218
Social Policy Association Essay Prize Vol. 2: 2701
Social Responsibility in Advertising Awards Vol. 1: 12029
Social Science Prize of the American Academy Vol. 1: 527
Social Studies Programs of Excellence Vol. 1: 13719
Sociedad Cubana de Matematica y Computacion "Pablo Miguel" Awards Vol. 2: 1823
Societas Pharmaceutica Hungarica, and Kazay Endre Award Vol. 2: 7369
Society Award Vol. 1: 17463
Society Awards Vol. 1: 7830
Society Awards for Journal Articles Vol. 2: 3036
Society for Biomaterials Student Awards for Outstanding Research Vol. 1: 17427
Society for Cinema Studies Student Award for Scholarly Writing Vol. 1: 17430
Society for Community Research and Action: Division of Community Psychology Dissertation Award Vol. 1: 3790
Society for Community Research and Action: Division of Community Psychology Special Award Vol. 1: 3791
Society for Information Display Fellow Vol. 1: 17534
Society for Italic Handwriting Award Vol. 2: 4358

Society for Research into Higher Education Awards Vol. 2: 4368
Society for the Psychological Study of Lesbian and Gay Issues Distinguished Student Award Vol. 1: 3811
Society for the Scientific Study of Sex Hugo G. Beigel Research Award Vol. 1: 17635
Society for the Scientific Study of Sex Student Research Grant Vol. 1: 17636
Society for the Study of Amphibians and Reptiles (SSAR) Grants-in-Herpetology Vol. 1: 17638
Society Lecturer Vol. 2: 2808
Society Medal
  Royal Society of New South Wales Vol. 2: 630
  Society for Leukocyte Biology Vol 1: 17551
Society of Australasian Specialists/Oceania Medals Vol. 1: 17748
Society of Biological Psychiatry/DISTA Fellowship Awards Vol. 1: 17791
Society of Certified Credit Executives Outstanding Fellow Award Vol. 1: 10896
Society of Children's Book Writers Grants Vol. 1: 17813
Society of Colonial Wars Annual Award Vol. 1: 17815
Society of Colonial Wars Distinguished Book Award Vol. 1: 17815
Society of Cosmetic Chemists Awards Vol. 1: 17830
Society of Exploration Geophysicists of Japan Award Vol. 2: 8756
Society of Midland Authors Award Vol. 1: 17897
Society of Municipal Arborists Awards Vol. 1: 17916
Society of Newspaper Design Awards Competition Vol. 1: 17940
Society of Newspaper Design Best of Newspaper Design Competition Vol. 1: 17940
Society of Nuclear Medicine/Medi-Physics Research Fellowship for Therapeutic Nuclear Medicine Vol. 1: 17956
Society of Nuclear Medicine Research Fellowship Program for Cardiovascular Nuclear Medicine; DuPont Pharma/ Vol. 1: 17946
Society of Petroleum Engineers of AIME Distinguished Service Award Vol. 1: 17963
Society of Ration Token Collectors (SRTC) National Merit of Exhibit Award Vol. 1: 18020
Society of Shipping Executives Education Trust Prize Vol. 2: 3098
Society of the Cincinnati Prize Vol. 1: 18042
Society of the Friends of History Award Vol. 2: 4756
Society of Women Musicians Prize Vol. 2: 4117
Society of Writers of Macedonia Awards Vol. 2: 8876
Society's Medal and Lecture Vol. 2: 4426
Society's Prizes Vol. 2: 4445
Socio Colabrador Vol. 2: 45
Socio-Psychological Prize; AAAS - Vol. 1: 883
Sociology Prize Vol. 2: 1229
SOCMA Gold Medal for Outstanding Achievement in Environmental Chemistry Vol. 1: 18549
Soderbergs Pris Vol. 2: 11550
Soderstrom Gold Medal Vol. 2: 11551
Soderstrom Memorial Award; Deborah Vol. 1: 9964
Soderstromska Medaljen i guld Vol. 2: 11551
Soffer Research Awards; ACCP/Alfred Vol. 1: 1617

Sofia de Investigacion sobre prevencion de la subnormalidad; Premio Reina Vol. 2: 11246
Sofia International Film Festival on Organization and Automation of Production and Management Awards Vol. 2: 1530
Software Maintenance Association Vol. 1: 18111
Software System Award Vol. 1: 5471
Soichiro Honda Medal Vol. 1: 4707
Soil Association Awards for Organic Food Products Vol. 2: 4473
Soil Science Applied Research Award Vol. 1: 18132
Soil Science Award Vol. 1: 4388
Soil Science Distinguished Service Award Vol. 1: 18133
Soil Science Education Award Vol. 1: 18134
Soil Science Professional Service Award Vol. 1: 18135
Soil Science Research Award (Soil Science Award) Vol. 1: 18136
Sokhey Award; Maj. Gen. Saheb Singh Vol. 2: 7610
Sokolov Prize; Literary Prize - Nachum Vol. 2: 7956
Solal; Concours International de Piano Jazz Martial Vol. 2: 5034
Solar Congressman of the Year, Solar Salute Vol. 1: 18139
Solar Man of the Year, Solar Salute Vol. 1: 18139
Solar Senator of the Year, Solar Salute Vol. 1: 18140
Solberg Award Vol. 1: 4734
Soldier's Medal Vol. 1: 19191
Solid-State Circuits Award Vol. 1: 10289
Solid State Physics and Materials Science Essay Prize Vol. 2: 11077
Solidarios Award to Latinoamerican and Caribbean Development Vol. 2: 2015
Solidarity Prize Vol. 2: 8963
Solistenpreis des STV Vol. 2: 11659
Sollenberger Trophy (Leading Scorer); John B. Vol. 1: 2334
Sollmann Award in Pharmacology; Torald Vol. 1: 4238
Solo Competition Vol. 1: 15767
Solo II Cup Vol. 1: 18411
Solo II Driver of Eminence Award Vol. 1: 18412
Solo II Driver of the Year Vol. 1: 18412
Solo II Rookie of the Year Vol. 1: 18413
Solomon Award; King Vol. 1: 479
Soltz Medal; Vilmos Vol. 2: 7359
Solvay Duphar Award Vol. 1: 3717
Somach - Sachs Memorial Award Vol. 2: 7985
Somaini; Premio Triennale per la Fisica Francesco Vol. 2: 8243
Something Special in the Air Award Vol. 1: 19588
Sommer/A. J. Viehman, Jr. Scholarship; MPA Donald E. Vol. 1: 16418
Sommer Award; Ralph F. Vol. 1: 996
Sommers Award; Ben Vol. 1: 8528
Sommerville Prize; Helen Vol. 2: 10568
Sonderpreis Vol. 2: 6834
Sondrio Town Council International Festival of Documentary Films on Parks Vol. 2: 8433
Song Foundation Award for Plant Tissue Culture; John S. Vol. 1: 18720
Songsearch Vol. 1: 12705
Songwriter/Composer Award Vol. 1: 16820
Songwriter of the Year Vol. 1: 12577
Songwriters Hall of Fame Vol. 1: 12649
Songwriting Merit Award Vol. 1: 1766

Sonnenwirth Award; BioMerieux Vitek   Vol. 1: 4203
Sonnenwirth Memorial Award   Vol. 1: 4203
Sonnichsen Book Award; C. L.   Vol. 1: 18667
Sonning Music Award; Leonie   Vol. 2: 2009
Sonning Prize   Vol. 2: 2011
Sonnings Musikpris; Leonie   Vol. 2: 2009
Sonntag Award; Al   Vol. 1: 18084
Sonora Review Poetry Award   Vol. 1: 18144
Sonora Review Short Story Award   Vol. 1: 18145
Sons of Martha Medal   Vol. 1: 16463
Sons of Norway Junior Jumping Trophy   Vol. 1: 19589
Sons of the American Revolution Bronze Good Citizenship Medal   Vol. 1: 14734
Sons of the American Revolution Gold Good Citizenship Medal   Vol. 1: 14735
Sons of the American Revolution Law Enforcement Commendation Medal   Vol. 1: 14736
Sons of the American Revolution Martha Washington Award Medal   Vol. 1: 14737
Sons of the American Revolution Medal of Appreciation   Vol. 1: 14738
Sons of the American Revolution Minuteman Award Medal   Vol. 1: 14739
Sons of the American Revolution Patriot Medal   Vol. 1: 14740
Sons of the American Revolution Scholarship Contests   Vol. 1: 14741
Sons of the American Revolution Silver Good Citizenship Medal   Vol. 1: 14742
Sons of the American Revolution War Service Medal   Vol. 1: 14743
Sontheime Award   Vol. 1: 4925
Sony Industrial Award   Vol. 2: 9670
Sony Radio Awards   Vol. 2: 4477
Sony Science Education Promotion Fund   Vol. 2: 8758
Soper Award; Fred L.   Vol. 1: 15926
Soper Award; Lord   Vol. 2: 3545
Soper Lecture; Fred L.   Vol. 1: 4816
Sopot International Song Festival   Vol. 2: 10130
Sorantin Award for Young Artists; Hemphill-Wells   Vol. 1: 17022
Sorantin Young Artist Award   Vol. 1: 17022
Soriano; Prix Victor et Clara   Vol. 2: 4877
Sorin Award; Edward Frederic   Vol. 1: 19858
Sorokin Lecture   Vol. 1: 4832
Soroptimist International of the South West Pacific Awards   Vol. 2: 668
Soroptimist Training Awards Program   Vol. 1: 18152
Soroptimist Youth Citizenship Awards   Vol. 1: 18153
Sorum Award; William   Vol. 1: 3653
Sosman Memorial Lecture Award   Vol. 1: 1476
Soteriological Award   Vol. 1: 13647
Souder Award; Wilmer   Vol. 1: 10625
Soul Train Music Awards   Vol. 1: 18155
Sounds Australian Awards   Vol. 2: 671
Sounds Australian Music Awards   Vol. 2: 671
Sounds Australian Presenter Awards   Vol. 2: 671
Sour Apple Award   Vol. 1: 9982
Source Awards   Vol. 1: 18157
South Africa Medal   Vol. 2: 11020
South African Association of Occupational Therapists Awards   Vol. 2: 11028
South African Broadcasting Corporation Prize   Vol. 2: 11042
South African Defence Force Champion Shot Medal   Vol. 2: 10943

South African Defence Force Good Service Medal   Vol. 2: 10944
South African Institute of Civil Engineering Technicians and Technologists Awards   Vol. 2: 11066
South African Institute of Electrical Engineers Awards   Vol. 2: 11068
South African Medal for Botany   Vol. 2: 11024
South African Police Cross for Valour   Vol. 2: 10952
South African Railways Police Medal for Combating Terrorism   Vol. 2: 10953
South African Railways Police Star for Distinguished Leadership   Vol. 2: 10954
South African Railways Police Star for Distinguished Service   Vol. 2: 10955
South African Sports Merit Award   Vol. 2: 10916
South Carolina Children's Book Award   Vol. 1: 18175
South Carolina Junior Book Award   Vol. 1: 18175
South Carolina Young Adult Book Award   Vol. 1: 18175
South Dakota Prairie Pasque Children's Book Award   Vol. 1: 18179
Southam Fellowships for Journalists   Vol. 1: 19882
Southeastern Conference Scholar-Athlete Award   Vol. 1: 18190
Southeastern Librarian Wilson Award   Vol. 1: 18197
Southeastern Screenwriting Competition   Vol. 1: 10093
Southend-on-Sea Borough Council Trophy   Vol. 2: 2810
Southern Africa Medal   Vol. 2: 10945
Southern African Institute of Forestry Award   Vol. 2: 11099
Southern Arts Literature Prize   Vol. 2: 4481
Southern Books Competition   Vol. 1: 18198
Southern California Athlete of the Year   Vol. 1: 398
Southern California Council on Literature for Children and Young People Awards   Vol. 1: 18210
Southern Cross Decoration   Vol. 2: 10946
Southern Cross Medal   Vol. 2: 10947
Southern Journalism Award   Vol. 1: 10237
The Southern Review/Louisiana State University Short Fiction Award   Vol. 1: 18239
Southgate Memorial Trophy; Hugh M.   Vol. 1: 6623
Southwest Asia Service Medal   Vol. 1: 19192
Southwest Fine Arts Competition   Vol. 1: 12506
Southwest Regional Beefalo Show   Vol. 1: 1335
Southwick Memorial Award in Aviculture; Justin A.   Vol. 1: 11399
Sovereign Award   Vol. 1: 11581
Sovereign Western Order   Vol. 2: 1370
Soviet Jewry Freedom Awards   Vol. 1: 13655
Soviet Journalists Media Prize   Vol. 2: 10479
Soviet Land Nehru Award   Vol. 2: 7722
SPA Certification Awards   Vol. 1: 18116
SPA Community Service Citation   Vol. 1: 18117
SPA Critics' Choice Awards   Vol. 1: 18118
SPA Journalism Recognition Awards   Vol. 1: 18119
SPA Lifetime Achievement Award   Vol. 1: 18120
Spaatz Trophy   Vol. 1: 14096
Space Achievement Medal   Vol. 2: 2424
Space Coast Writers Conference Awards   Vol. 1: 18251

Space Development Strategies Award   Vol. 1: 18253
Space Educator Award   Vol. 1: 14840
Space Flight Medal   Vol. 1: 12744
Space Industrialization Fellowship   Vol. 1: 18254
Space Simulation Award   Vol. 1: 10336
Space Technology Hall of Fame   Vol. 1: 19620
Spacecraft Design Award   Vol. 1: 2501
Spacelabs/AAMI Annual Meeting Research-Manuscript Award   Vol. 1: 5622
Spacu Prize; Gheorghe   Vol. 2: 10383
Spaeth Award   Vol. 1: 9742
Spain and America in the Quincentennial of the Discovery Prize   Vol. 1: 8895
Spalding Player of the Year   Vol. 1: 12949
Spangler Award; Lew   Vol. 1: 14238
Spanish Association of Painters and Sculptors Prizes   Vol. 2: 11381
Spanish Mustang Registry Awards Program   Vol. 1: 18257
Spanjian Memorial Foundation Award; Sarkis   Vol. 1: 6456
SPAR National Art Exhibition   Vol. 1: 17220
Sparks Medal; Ben C.   Vol. 1: 4708
Sparks-Thomas Award   Vol. 1: 1513
Sparlin Award; Ezra M   Vol. 1: 10135
Sparreska Priset   Vol. 2: 11552
SPE Distinguished Lecturers   Vol. 1: 17974
Speaker of the Year   Vol. 2: 2791
Spearman Medal   Vol. 2: 2491
Speas Airport Award; AIAA Jay Hollingsworth   Vol. 1: 2476
Special Achievement   Vol. 1: 14894
Special Achievement Award
  American Society of Plastic and Reconstructive Surgeons   Vol. 1: 4764
  Association of Government Accountants   Vol 1: 5823
  Philalethes Society   Vol 1: 16136
  Sierra Club   Vol 1: 17243
Special Achievement Awards
  Academy of Motion Picture Arts and Sciences   Vol. 1: 64
  American Psychological Association - Psychologists in Public Service Division   Vol 1: 3763
  Association of Federal Investigators   Vol 1: 5795
  National Council of Social Security Management Associations   Vol 1: 13757
Special Act Award   Vol. 1: 14365
Special Act Awards   Vol. 1: 19307
Special Agency Awards   Vol. 1: 11117
Special Award
  American Society for Information Science   Vol. 1: 4175
  American Society for Surface Mining & Reclamation   Vol 1: 4293
  Association for Information and Image Management   Vol 1: 5547
  International Magnesium Association   Vol 1: 11096
  International Veteran Boxers Association   Vol 1: 11389
  National Association of Interpretation   Vol 1: 13181
  National Legal Aid and Defender Association   Vol 1: 14298
  National Urban Coalition   Vol 1: 14967
Special Award - ACHA   Vol. 1: 1601
Special Award for Contributions to Urban Political Theory   Vol. 1: 3592
Special Award for Dedicated Service   Vol. 1: 12583

Special Awards
  Association of Engineering Geologists   Vol. 1: 5775
  Commonwealth Foundation   Vol 2: 2659
  Georgia Agricultural Commodity Commission for Peanuts   Vol 1: 9577
  Health Sciences Communications Association   Vol 1: 9857
  Institution of Structural Engineers   Vol 2: 3360
  Journalism Education Association   Vol 1: 11616
  National Hemophilia Foundation   Vol 1: 14136
  Religious Heritage of America   Vol 1: 16778
  United States Harness Writers Association   Vol 1: 19389
Special Awards and Citations   Vol. 1: 3097
Special Awards Established by the President   Vol. 1: 19337
Special Awards of Honor   Vol. 1: 11118
Special Awards to Winners of International Sports Events   Vol. 2: 7525
Special Board Recognition Award   Vol. 1: 8912
Special Certificate   Vol. 1: 10517
Special Citation
  Helicopter Association International   Vol. 1: 9901
  International Tennis Hall of Fame   Vol 1: 11352
  Pigskin Club of Washington   Vol 1: 16215
Special Citation Award   Vol. 1: 2682
Special Citation in Honor of Rudy and Hertha Benjamin   Vol. 1: 3440
Special Citation in Journalism   Vol. 1: 6231
Special Citations   Vol. 1: 698
Special Commendation Award
  American College of Preventive Medicine   Vol. 1: 1727
  Florida Audubon Society   Vol 1: 9260
Special Commendation Awards   Vol. 1: 17911
Special Contribution by an Organization   Vol. 1: 5732
Special Distinguished Service Award   Vol. 1: 9351
Special District Awards   Vol. 1: 8301
Special Edgar   Vol. 1: 12550
Special Educational Merit Award for Women   Vol. 1: 11355
Special EST Prize   Vol. 2: 11710
Special Eternit Prize   Vol. 2: 1114
Special Focus Awards   Vol. 1: 6605
Special Friend of Hearing Impaired People Award   Vol. 1: 17183
Special Gold Medal   Vol. 1: 14074
Special Grand Prix of the Jury   Vol. 1: 12436
Special Innovation Award   Vol. 1: 10397
Special Interest Residency Scholarships   Vol. 1: 8735
Special Lectures   Vol. 2: 2256
Special Legend Awards   Vol. 1: 14973
Special Merit Citation   Vol. 1: 2759
Special National Geographic Society Award   Vol. 1: 14076
Special NJCAA Awards   Vol. 1: 14266
Special Olympics Sports Awards for Distinguished Service to Individuals with Mental Retardation Through Sports   Vol. 1: 18287
Special President's Award   Vol. 2: 6494
Special President's Award of Merit   Vol. 1: 1205
Special Prize of the Jury   Vol. 2: 1091
Special Program Awards   Vol. 1: 1165
Special Projects Award   Vol. 1: 17184

Special Recognition and Presidential Awards   Vol. 1: 14190
Special Recognition Award
  American Association of Retired Persons   Vol. 1: 1166
  American Camping Association   Vol 1: 1408
  American College of Preventive Medicine   Vol 1: 1728
  Asphalt Recycling and Reclaiming Association   Vol 1: 5377
  ASPO/Lamaze   Vol 1: 5386
  Canadian Mental Health Association   Vol 1: 7036
  Classification and Compensation Society   Vol 1: 7823
  Inventors Clubs of America - International Hall of Fame   Vol 1: 11421
  National Association of Conservation Districts   Vol 1: 13034
  Standards Engineering Society   Vol 1: 18457
  Western and English Manufacturers Association   Vol 1: 20196
  World Assembly of Small and Medium Enterprises   Vol 2: 7725
Special Recognition Awards   Vol. 1: 17535
Special Recognition Citation   Vol. 1: 11337
Special Recognition for Excellence in Public Relations   Vol. 1: 18265
Special Recognition in the Arts and Humanities Award   Vol. 1: 8017
Special Recognition Service Award   Vol. 1: 20305
Special Recreation Awards
  Special Recreation, Inc.   Vol. 1: 18289
  Sports Foundation   Vol 1: 18425
Special Recreation for Disabled Awards   Vol. 1: 18289
Special Recreation for People with Disabilities Awards   Vol. 1: 18289
Special Service/Achievement Awards   Vol. 1: 17244
Special Service Award
  American Association of Avian Pathologists   Vol. 1: 915
  Classification and Compensation Society   Vol 1: 7824
  International Reading Association   Vol 1: 11197
  National Association of Conservation Districts   Vol 1: 13035
  North American Die Casting Association   Vol 1: 15423
Special Service Awards
  Information Council of the Americas   Vol. 1: 10181
  National Association of County Engineers   Vol 1: 13054
  National Small-Bore Rifle Association   Vol 2: 3710
Special Service Awards (Citations)   Vol. 1: 17730
Special Service Citation   Vol. 1: 18450
Special Service Medal   Vol. 1: 6712
Special Services Award
  National Association of College Gymnastics Coaches (Men)   Vol. 1: 13003
  Radio Club of America   Vol 1: 16651
Special Services Citation   Vol. 1: 18450
Specialty Band DXer of the Year   Vol. 1: 5907
Specifications Competition   Vol. 1: 8212
Spectator/Highland Park Parliamentarian of the Year Awards   Vol. 2: 4485
Spector Award; Beryl   Vol. 1: 16564
Spectrum Awards Design Competition   Vol. 1: 2149

Spedding Award; Frank H.   Vol. 1: 16686
Speirs Award; Doris Huestis   Vol. 1: 17798
Speiss Award; Ray H.   Vol. 1: 4120
Speller Award; Frank Newman   Vol. 1: 13044
Speller Award; Thomas H.   Vol. 1: 17774
Spellman Award; Cardinal   Vol. 1: 7387
Spelvin Award; George   Vol. 1: 12110
Spenadel Award; Henry   Vol. 1: 9218
Spence Trophy; G. M.   Vol. 2: 9825
Spencer Artistic Achievement Award; Sara   Vol. 1: 777
Spencer Award; William I.   Vol. 1: 20628
Spencer Post-Doctoral Fellows   Vol. 1: 12637
Spencer Top Butler of the Year Award; Ivor   Vol. 2: 2961
Sperry Award; AIAA Lawrence   Vol. 1: 2478
Sperry Award; Elmer A.   Vol. 1: 17775
Sperry Founder Award; Albert F.   Vol. 1: 10492
Sperry Young Achievement Award; Lawrence   Vol. 1: 2478
Spes Hominum Award   Vol. 1: 14664
Speyer Memorial Prize; Ellin P.   Vol. 1: 12633
SPHE International Packaging and Handling Design Competition   Vol. 1: 10425
SPHE Packaging Competition   Vol. 1: 10425
SPI Eastern Section Annual Achievement Award   Vol. 1: 18055
SPI Midwest Section Founder's Award   Vol. 1: 18056
SPI New England Section Recognition Award   Vol. 1: 18057
SPI Structural Foam Division Annual Recognition Award   Vol. 1: 18058
SPI Structural Plastics Division Annual Recognition   Vol. 1: 18058
SPIE Technology Achievement Award   Vol. 1: 18327
Spielvogel-Diamonstein Award; PEN/   Vol. 1: 16030
Spiers Memorial Lectureship   Vol. 2: 4223
Spies Memorial Award; Tom   Vol. 1: 10586
Spingarn Medal   Vol. 1: 12907
Spink Award; J. G. Taylor   Vol. 1: 13441
Spink Memorial Award; J. G. Taylor   Vol. 1: 6283
Spinoy Award; A.   Vol. 2: 1372
Spinoza Award   Vol. 1: 19704
Spirit Award
  Amateur Athletic Union of the United States   Vol. 1: 453
  International Federation of Women's Travel Organizations   Vol 1: 10973
Spirit Awards for Communications   Vol. 1: 7363
Spirit of America Award
  National Council for the Social Studies   Vol. 1: 13720
  National Grocers Association   Vol 1: 14094
Spirit of America Awards   Vol. 1: 19699
Spirit of Broadcasting Award   Vol. 1: 12981
Spirit of Fighting Awards   Vol. 2: 3442
Spirit of Flight Award   Vol. 1: 13404
Spirit of Saint Louis Award   Vol. 1: 17005
Spirit of St. Louis Medal   Vol. 1: 4709
Spirit of SHHH Award   Vol. 1: 17185
Spivack Volunteer Service Award; Martin   Vol. 1: 14107
Split Summer Festival   Vol. 2: 1803
Splitsko Ljeto   Vol. 2: 1803
Spohr; Internationaler Violinwettbewerb Ludwig   Vol. 2: 6972
Spohr-Preis; Ludwig-   Vol. 2: 6575
Spohr Violin Competition; International Ludwig   Vol. 2: 6972
Sponsor Recognition Awards   Vol. 1: 14885
Sponsorship Award   Vol. 2: 2251

Sport Australia Hall of Fame   Vol. 2: 681
Sport Fishery Research Program   Vol. 1: 18335
Sport Medal of Catalonia   Vol. 2: 11190
Sport Science Award of the IOC President   Vol. 2: 4723
Sporting Goods Agents Hall of Fame   Vol. 1: 18339
The Sporting News Man of the Year   Vol. 1: 18386
The Sporting News/Marlboro NFL Rookie of the Year   Vol. 1: 18384
The Sporting News NFL Player of the Year   Vol. 1: 18385
The Sporting News Sportsman of the Year   Vol. 1: 18386
Sportive et Sportif Europeen de l'Annee   Vol. 2: 1144
Sportplakete des Bundespraesidenten   Vol. 2: 6745
Sports Award   Vol. 2: 10446
Sports Hall of Fame   Vol. 2: 12038
Sports Illustrated Sportsman/Sportswoman of the Year   Vol. 1: 18429
Sports Korosha   Vol. 2: 8783
Sports Ministries Award   Vol. 1: 13586
Sports Personality of the Year Award   Vol. 1: 4858
Sports Philatelists International Awards   Vol. 1: 18431
SportsCar Awards   Vol. 1: 18414
SportsMan and SportsWoman of the Year   Vol. 1: 19492
Sportsman of the Year Award
  Milliyet   Vol. 2: 12063
  Sales and Marketing Executives of Greater New York   Vol 1: 17012
Sportswomen of the Year Awards   Vol. 1: 20432
Spowers Marketing Award; Gale M.   Vol. 1: 16375
Sprague Memorial Award; Joseph A.   Vol. 1: 14528
Spraragen Memorial Membership Award; William   Vol. 1: 5092
Spray Trophy   Vol. 1: 17316
Sprent Prize; John Frederick Adrian   Vol. 2: 265
Spring Art Founder Award; John   Vol. 1: 14714
Spring Meeting Paper Award   Vol. 1: 17927
Springbok Radio Sarie Awards   Vol. 2: 11043
Springer Award; Fred   Vol. 1: 3365
Springer Award; LT GEN. Robert D.   Vol. 1: 5283
Springer Award; Russell S.   Vol. 1: 17776
Springer Silver Wings Award; Bonnie J.   Vol. 1: 5283
Springold Trophy; Nathan B.   Vol. 1: 1828
Springstead Memorial Trophy; Velma   Vol. 1: 7246
Sprogprisen   Vol. 2: 1994
Sproule Memorial Award; J. C. "CAM"   Vol. 1: 1114
Sproule Memorial Plaque; J. C.   Vol. 1: 6956
Sprout Award; Harold and Margaret   Vol. 1: 11327
Spruance Safety Award; William W.   Vol. 1: 14096
Spruce Award; Richard   Vol. 1: 10680
Spuddy   Vol. 1: 16338
Spur Awards   Vol. 1: 20236
Spurrier Memorial Lecture; Henry   Vol. 2: 2586
Spurs of Criticism   Vol. 2: 4760
Squibb Award   Vol. 1: 10173

Squibb Award for Excellence in Medical Teaching   Vol. 1: 18438
Squibb Award for Excellence in Pharmaceutical Teaching   Vol. 1: 18439
Squibb Pan American Award; Doctor   Vol. 1: 18436
SRE Certificate of Excellence   Vol. 1: 18024
SRE Certificate of Recognition   Vol. 1: 18025
SRE Stan Ofsthun Award   Vol. 1: 18026
Sree Padmanabha Swari Prize   Vol. 2: 7708
Sri Kapila Humanitarian Society Competitions   Vol. 2: 11420
Sri Lanka Abhimanya   Vol. 2: 11434
Sri Lankatillaka   Vol. 2: 11435
Srinivasa Ramanujan Medal   Vol. 2: 7673
Sriramachari Award; Smt. Pushpa   Vol. 2: 7611
Srivastav Award in the Field of Virology; Dr. J. B.   Vol. 2: 7612
Srivastava Foundation Award; Prof. B. C.   Vol. 2: 7613
SSA Certificate of Appreciation   Vol. 1: 17365
SSA Exceptional Achievement Award   Vol. 1: 17366
SSA Exceptional Service Award   Vol. 1: 17367
SSIEM Award   Vol. 2: 4378
STA Travel Award   Vol. 2: 685
Staats Award; Elmer   Vol. 1: 5824
Staats International Journal Award; Elmer B.   Vol. 2: 847
Staats Public Service Career Awards; Elmer B.   Vol. 1: 13303
Staatspreis fur Consulting   Vol. 2: 742
Staatspreis fur Design   Vol. 2: 777
Staatspreis fur die Schonsten Bucher Osterreichs   Vol. 2: 741
Staatspreis fur gepruffte Qualitat   Vol. 2: 747
Staatspreis fur gestaltendes Handwerk   Vol. 2: 748
Staatspreis fur getaltendes Handwerk   Vol. 2: 776
Staatspreis fur gewerbliche und industrielle Bauten   Vol. 2: 743
Staatspreis fur Gute Form   Vol. 2: 753
Staatspreis fur gute Form   Vol. 2: 777
Staatspreis fur Gutes Design   Vol. 2: 753
Staatspreis fur Mobel   Vol. 2: 751
Staatspreis fur Radiowerbung   Vol. 2: 749
Staatspreis fur Schmuck aus Edelmetall   Vol. 2: 744
Staatspreis fur Vorbildliche Verpackung   Vol. 2: 750
Staatspreise fur Wirtschaftswerbung (Inland/Export) und Werbung fur gesellschaftliche Anliegen   Vol. 2: 754
Staatsprijs ter Bekroning Van een Schrijverscarriere   Vol. 2: 1080
Staatsprijs voor Jeugdliteratuur   Vol. 2: 1081
Staatsprijs voor Kritiek en Essay   Vol. 2: 1082
Staatsprijs voor Poezie   Vol. 2: 1083
Staatsprijs voor Romans en Verhalend Proza   Vol. 2: 1084
Staatsprijs voor Toneelletterkunde   Vol. 2: 1085
Staatsprijs Voor Vertaling Van Nederlandse Letterkunde   Vol. 2: 1086
Stachiewicz Medal; Jules
  Canadian Society for Mechanical Engineering   Vol. 1: 7139
  Chemical Institute of Canada   Vol 1: 7562
Stack Award for Interpreting Chemistry for the Public; James T. Grady - James H.   Vol. 1: 1557
Staf Nees Prize   Vol. 2: 1347
Stagg Award; Amos Alonzo   Vol. 1: 2076
Stagg Trophy; Amos Alonzo   Vol. 1: 13997

Stahl Award; Egon   Vol. 2: 7082
Stahl Preis; Egon   Vol. 2: 7082
Stahr Award; Jack   Vol. 1: 19657
Stainer Preis; Jakob   Vol. 2: 730
Staley Prize; J. I.   Vol. 1: 17104
Stalker Award; John   Vol. 1: 4000
Stall Memorial Award; Pat   Vol. 1: 14230
Stals Prize for the Humanities   Vol. 2: 11006
Stamford Radio Theater Competition   Vol. 1: 18446
Stamitz-Preis; Johann-Wenzel-   Vol. 2: 6526
Stampex Exhibition Awards   Vol. 2: 3781
Stamprijs; Mark   Vol. 2: 9648
Stand International Short Story Competition   Vol. 2: 4492
Standard Bank Namibia Biennale   Vol. 2: 9326
Standard Bank Young Artists' Awards   Vol. 2: 10849
Standard Chartered Commonwealth Photography Award   Vol. 2: 2664
Standard Class Trophy   Vol. 1: 17368
Standard Quarter Horse Association Awards   Vol. 1: 18448
Standards and Practices Award   Vol. 1: 10493
Standards Development Awards   Vol. 1: 13980
Standards Medal   Vol. 1: 3180
Standish Award; Myles   Vol. 1: 15857
Stanfield Distinguished Service Award; Howard E.   Vol. 1: 18329
Stanfield Trophy; Robert L.   Vol. 1: 6985
Stanford Poetry Prize; Ann   Vol. 1: 12116
Stanford Prize; Winifred Mary   Vol. 2: 3019
Stangler Gedachtnispreis fur Erwachsenenbildung; Franz   Vol. 2: 861
Stangler Memorial Prize for Adult Education; Franz   Vol. 2: 861
Stanhope Gold Medal   Vol. 2: 4066
Stanley Award   Vol. 1: 7463
Stanley Award; Edward   Vol. 1: 16366
Stanley Award; Robert   Vol. 1: 20048
Stanley Awards (Stanleys); NAHWW/   Vol. 1: 13133
Stanley Cup   Vol. 1: 14181
Stanley Drama Award   Vol. 1: 20081
Stanley, Sr., Best Feature Story Awards; Frank L.   Vol. 1: 14397
Stanleys   Vol. 1: 13133
Stanswa Biennale   Vol. 2: 9326
Stapp Award; John Paul   Vol. 1: 174
Star. Adrienne Cambry; Prix Maria   Vol. 2: 6289
Star Boy Award   Vol. 2: 4754
Star for Merit in the South African Railways Police Force   Vol. 2: 10956
Star of Courage
  Australian Decorations Advisory Committee - Australian Bravery Decorations   Vol. 2: 207
  Canada - The Chancellery   Vol 1: 6713
Star of Gallantry (SG)   Vol. 2: 342
Star of Military Valour   Vol. 1: 6714
Star of Temasek   Vol. 2: 10750
Stara Planina Order   Vol. 2: 1508
Stark Award   Vol. 1: 4145
Stark Memorial Award; Kevin   Vol. 2: 488
Starkey Award; John William   Vol. 2: 4228
Starr Award; Paul   Vol. 1: 4909
Starr Award; Walter   Vol. 1: 17245
Starr Fellowship   Vol. 1: 12235
Starr Fellowships in Asian Conservation   Vol. 1: 12237
Starrett Poetry Prize Competition; Agnes Lynch   Vol. 1: 19865
Stas; Prix Jean-Servais   Vol. 2: 1026
State Achievement Awards   Vol. 1: 13319

State Awards
  New England Wildflower Society   Vol. 1: 15164
  Sounds Australian - Australian Music Centre Ltd.   Vol 2: 671
State/Canadian Province SAR Award   Vol. 1: 12898
State Capital Stuttgart Award   Vol. 2: 7142
State Coordinator   Vol. 1: 356
State Development and Construction Corporation Award   Vol. 2: 11408
State Director of the Year Award
  American Academy of Medical Administrators   Vol. 1: 601
  National Propane Gas Association   Vol 1: 14539
State Emblem for Adequate Packaging   Vol. 2: 750
State Emblem for Furniture   Vol. 2: 751
State Emblem for Innovation   Vol. 2: 752
State Emblem for Outstanding Design   Vol. 2: 753
State Emblems for Economic Advertising (Domestic/Foreign) and Advertising for Social Matters   Vol. 2: 754
State Grand Prize for Literature   Vol. 2: 1087
State of Baden-Wurttemberg Award   Vol. 2: 7142
State of Florida Fellowship   Vol. 1: 9248
State of Hawaii Order of Distinction for Cultural Leadership   Vol. 1: 9831
State of the Art Award   Vol. 1: 16376
State President's Sport Award   Vol. 2: 10917
State Prize
  Hungary - Office of the Prime Minister   Vol. 2: 7412
  Secretariat of the Committee of State Prizes   Vol 2: 10204
State Prize for Arts and Crafts   Vol. 2: 776
State Prize for Design   Vol. 2: 777
State Prize for Literature   Vol. 2: 9665
State Prize in Science and Technology   Vol. 2: 10470
State/Province Art Educator of the Year   Vol. 1: 12811
State Psychiatric Technician of the Year   Vol. 1: 1151
State Public Official Award for Significant Legislative Achievement   Vol. 1: 1167
State/Regional Association Award   Vol. 1: 13519
State Society Publications Awards   Vol. 1: 3044
State Travel Director of the Year   Vol. 1: 18798
State Writing Competition   Vol. 1: 2753
States Student Award; John D.   Vol. 1: 5609
Statesman of the Year   Vol. 1: 602
Statton Lecture; Henry M   Vol. 1: 4596
Statue of Freedom Award   Vol. 1: 6624
The Statuette with Pedestal   Vol. 1: 10582
Staudinger-Preis; Hermann-   Vol. 2: 6789
Stauffer Prizes; Joseph S.   Vol. 1: 6750
Stavros Gold Medal; George   Vol. 2: 7195
Stavros Silver Medal; George   Vol. 2: 7196
Staz Scholarship for Dental Research; Julius   Vol. 2: 10841
Steacie Award in Chemistry; E. W. R.   Vol. 1: 7563
Steacie Memorial Fellowships; E. W. R.   Vol. 1: 15077
Steacie Prize   Vol. 1: 18474
Stead Award; FAW Christina   Vol. 2: 385
Stead Prize; Christina   Vol. 2: 147
Steavenson Memorial Award   Vol. 2: 2288
Stebbins, Jr. Distinguished Service Award; H. Grady   Vol. 1: 5199

Stebbins Trophy; James F.   Vol. 1: 20246
Steber Foundation Award for Musical Excellence; Eleanor   Vol. 1: 15727
Steber Music Foundation Award; Eleanor   Vol. 1: 13336
Steck - Vaughn Award   Vol. 1: 18642
Steel and Tube Travelling Scholarship   Vol. 2: 9745
Steel Distributor of the Year Award   Vol. 1: 5970
Steel Eighties Award   Vol. 2: 7633
Steel Guitar Hall of Fame   Vol. 1: 11323
Steel Memorial Medal; John Henry   Vol. 2: 3995
Steele Award; James H.   Vol. 1: 4974
Steele-Bodger Memorial Scholarship; Harry   Vol. 2: 2554
Steele Prizes; Leroy P.   Vol. 1: 3009
Steelmaking Conference Award   Vol. 1: 11471
Steen Award; Ralph W.   Vol. 1: 8783
Steer Clear Video Competiton   Vol. 1: 14551
Steere History Essay Competition; Lee   Vol. 2: 644
Stefanko Best Paper Award   Vol. 1: 17577
Steffens Award; Lincoln   Vol. 1: 11145
Steffens Prize; Henrik   Vol. 2: 7125
Stegner Fellowships in Creative Writing; Wallace E.   Vol. 1: 8452
Steiger Award; William   Vol. 1: 1800
Stein Award; Jean   Vol. 1: 518
Stein Make-up Award; Jack   Vol. 1: 15147
Stein Prize; Fordham -   Vol. 1: 9321
Steinberg Award; S. S.   Vol. 1: 3973
Steinbock Award; Max   Vol. 1: 11065
Steindler Award; Arthur   Vol. 1: 15844
Steiner Award for Leadership in Foreign Language Education, K-12; ACTFL Florence   Vol. 1: 1871
Steiner Award for Leadership in Foreign Language Education, Postsecondary; ACTFL Florence   Vol. 1: 1872
Steiner Trophy   Vol. 1: 7808
Steinmetz Award; Charles Proteus   Vol. 1: 10290
Stendhal; Prix   Vol. 2: 6008
Stenersen Prize; Rolf   Vol. 2: 9929
Stengel Memorial Award; Alfred   Vol. 1: 1723
Stengel Research Award   Vol. 2: 811
Stengel Service Award   Vol. 2: 812
Stennis Student Congress Awards; John C.   Vol. 1: 14026
Steno Medal   Vol. 2: 1950
Steno Medaljen   Vol. 2: 1950
Stephannson Award for Poetry; Stephan G.   Vol. 1: 20555
Stephens Lecture   Vol. 2: 3054
Stephens Memorial Award; George Findlay   Vol. 1: 6921
Stephenson Medal; George   Vol. 2: 3258
Stephenson Memorial Lecture; Marjory   Vol. 2: 4356
Stephenson Outstanding Service Award; William J.   Vol. 1: 14853
Stephenson Prize Lecture; Marjory   Vol. 2: 4356
Stereo Division Awards   Vol. 1: 16170
Sterija Award   Vol. 2: 10705
Sterijina Nagrada   Vol. 2: 10705
Sterling Medal; John B.   Vol. 1: 8937
Sterling Staff Competition   Vol. 1: 12483
Stern Award; Philip M.   Vol. 1: 20110
Stern-Gerlach-Preis fur Physik   Vol. 2: 6657
Sternberg Chamber Music Prize; Edward   Vol. 2: 326
Stevens Article of the Year Award; Edward B.   Vol. 1: 1676
Stevens Award; J. C.   Vol. 1: 4499

Stevens Award; K. G.   Vol. 2: 12215
Stevens Award; Senator   Vol. 1: 20433
Stevens Memorial Award; Don C.   Vol. 1: 2267
Stevenson Cup; Roza   Vol. 2: 4057
Stevenson - Hamilton Award   Vol. 2: 11133
Stevenson History of Latin-American Music and Musicology Award; Robert   Vol. 1: 15834
Stevenson Trophy   Vol. 1: 10398
Stewart Award; Bill   Vol. 2: 3502
Stewart Award for Alumni Service   Vol. 1: 8294
Stewart Award; Paul A.   Vol. 1: 20321
Stewart Awards National Operatic Voice Competition   Vol. 1: 15610
Stewart Distinguished Achievement Award; Jerry   Vol. 1: 5939
Stewart Endowment; Paul   Vol. 1: 10196
Stewart Engineering-Humanities Award; Robert E.   Vol. 1: 4374
Stewart Prize; Douglas   Vol. 2: 147
Steyn Prize for Achievement in Science and Technology; M. T.   Vol. 2: 11007
Stichting Internationaal Orgelconcours   Vol. 2: 9659
Stichting Sikkensprijs   Vol. 2: 9621
Stickel Awards; William J.   Vol. 1: 3545
Sticusa Literature Prize   Vol. 2: 9430
Stiftelsen Kortfilmfestivalen   Vol. 2: 9948
Stiftelsen Natur och Kulturs oversattarpris   Vol. 2: 11602
Stigting Simon Van der Stel Medalje   Vol. 2: 11119
Stiles Medal; Guillermo Lee   Vol. 2: 1606
Stiles Memorial Award; William C.   Vol. 1: 19416
Still Medallion of Honor; Andrew Taylor   Vol. 1: 652
Stillman Award; William O.   Vol. 1: 2405
Stine Award in Materials Engineering and Science; Charles M. A.   Vol. 1: 2601
Stipendien an Autoren/Autorinnen   Vol. 2: 6583
Stipendium ur Lena Vendelfelts minnesfond   Vol. 2: 11603
Stir The Pot Award   Vol. 1: 14433
Stitt Award   Vol. 1: 5895
Stitt Lecture Award; Edward Rhodes   Vol. 1: 5895
STLE National Award   Vol. 1: 18085
Stock-Gedachtnispreis; Alfred-   Vol. 2: 6790
Stock of the Year   Vol. 1: 16508
Stockberger Achievement Award; Warner W.   Vol. 1: 11139
Stockholm Prize   Vol. 2: 11575
Stockholm Water Prize   Vol. 2: 11553
Stoeger Composer's Chair; Elise L.   Vol. 1: 7509
Stoeger Prize; Elise L.   Vol. 1: 7509
Stoessl-Preis; Otto   Vol. 2: 893
Stohr Medal; A.E.   Vol. 2: 443
Stoilov Prize; Simon   Vol. 2: 10384
Stokdyk Award; E. A.   Vol. 1: 13736
Stokes Award; Thomas L.
  National Press Foundation   Vol. 1: 14509
  Washington Journalism Center   Vol 1: 20114
Stokes Memorial Award   Vol. 1: 14191
Stokinger Award; Herbert E.   Vol. 1: 1801
Stokinger Award Lecture   Vol. 1: 1801
Stokowiec Medal and Prize   Vol. 2: 3150
Stokowski Conducting Competition; Leopold   Vol. 1: 4889
Stollmeyer Memorial Award; Jeffrey   Vol. 2: 12039

Stolz Trophy for Music Philately; Robert   Vol. 1: 16143
Stone Award; Donald C.
    American Public Works Association   Vol. 1: 3881
    American Society for Public Administration   Vol 1: 4272
Stone Award; Editorial Writing - Walker   Vol. 1: 17145
Stone Award; Howard E. (Rocky)   Vol. 1: 17186
Stone Award; Peter   Vol. 2: 2110
Stone Center for Children's Books Recognition of Merit; George G.   Vol. 1: 18491
Stone "Endow A Dream" Award; W. Clement   Vol. 1: 18493
Stone Graduate Research Award; Ralph W.   Vol. 1: 14854
Stone Memorial Award; Walter   Vol. 2: 369
Stone Memorial Award; Wilson S.   Vol. 1: 19879
Stone Prize   Vol. 2: 9907
Stone Prize for Student Journalism; *The Nation*/I. F.   Vol. 1: 15172
STOP, LOOK & LISTEN Awards   Vol. 1: 113
Stora Linnemedaljen i guld   Vol. 2: 11554
Stora priset   Vol. 2: 11604
Storch Award in Fuel Chemistry; Henry H.   Vol. 1: 1573
Store Interior Design Award   Vol. 1: 13325
Store of the Year   Vol. 1: 10446
Storer Awards   Vol. 1: 4616
Storey Leadership Award; Walter   Vol. 1: 4308
Storey Medal; John   Vol. 2: 231
Storey Professional Award; Walter   Vol. 1: 4309
Stork Fellow; Charles Wharton   Vol. 1: 6103
Storke International Journalism Awards; Thomas More   Vol. 1: 20463
Storm Award; Paul   Vol. 1: 8638
Storrs Memorial Piano Scholarships; Evelyn Bonar   Vol. 1: 12532
Story Time Fiction Contest/Mystery Time Short Story Contest; Rhyme Time Poetry Contest/   Vol. 1: 16830
Storywriting and Art Project
    Australia - Department of Veterans' Affairs, Public Relations Dept.   Vol. 2: 144
    Heidelberg Repatriation Hospital - Department of Veterans' Affairs   Vol 2: 417
Stouffer Award   Vol. 1: 4828
Stoughton Award for Young Teachers; Bradley   Vol. 1: 5365
Stoughton Award for Young Teachers of Metallurgy; Bradley   Vol. 1: 5365
Stout Medal   Vol. 1: 2267
Stover Memorial Award; Elizabeth Matchett   Vol. 1: 18242
Stowe Award; Allen B.   Vol. 1: 19666
Stoye Awards   Vol. 1: 4617
STP Most Improved Championship Driver Award   Vol. 1: 19030
Strachauer Medal; Ehrma   Vol. 1: 20102
Strader Memorial Award; Noel Ross   Vol. 1: 7913
Stradford Award; C. Francis   Vol. 1: 13437
Straelen; Prix van   Vol. 2: 5317
Straetmans; Prix Alexander   Vol. 2: 1324
Strampelli; Premio Carlotta   Vol. 2: 8008
Stranahan Award; Jason G. (Stranny)   Vol. 1: 19417
Strang Research Award; Ruth   Vol. 1: 12916
Strasbourg Prizes and Gold Medal   Vol. 2: 7126
Strasser Award; Jani   Vol. 2: 2942

Strategic Communications Award   Vol. 1: 16564
Strathglass Trophy   Vol. 1: 20246
Strathmore Paper Company Award   Vol. 1: 15526
Strating Prize; Albert   Vol. 2: 11008
Stratton Award; Samuel Wesley   Vol. 1: 19108
Stratton-Jaffe Hematology Scholar Award   Vol. 1: 4593
Stratton Medal; Henry M.   Vol. 1: 4596
Straub Award; Sandor   Vol. 2: 7338
Straub Sandor Dijasok   Vol. 2: 7338
Straus Award; Ralph I.   Vol. 1: 14385
Strausbaugh Club Relations Award; Bill   Vol. 1: 16480
Strauss Award; Leo   Vol. 1: 3584
Strauss Award; Sidney L.   Vol. 1: 15277
Strauss Livings; Mildred and Harold   Vol. 1: 519
Stravinsky Awards International Piano Competition and Festival   Vol. 1: 18496
Strebig Award; AWA James J.   Vol. 1: 6188
Streeton Award; Sir Arthur   Vol. 2: 651
Strega Prize   Vol. 2: 8439
Streisand Recognition Awards   Vol. 1: 18499
Stresemann-Preis; Erwin-   Vol. 2: 6653
Striker Junior Paper Award; Gyorgy   Vol. 2: 7429
Strimple Award   Vol. 1: 15910
Stritch Medal   Vol. 1: 11974
Strive and Succeed Award   Vol. 1: 313
Strock Award; Lester W.   Vol. 1: 17420
Strom Award; Ken   Vol. 1: 11301
Stromer-Ferrnerska Belöningen   Vol. 2: 11555
Stroobant; Prix Paul and Marie   Vol. 2: 1033
Stroud and District Festival   Vol. 2: 4497
Stroud Festival International Composers Competition   Vol. 2: 4497
Stroud Festival International Poetry Competition   Vol. 2: 4497
Stroud Memorial Award; Clara   Vol. 1: 5063
Stroud Memorial Award; Ida Wells   Vol. 1: 5064
Stroukoff Memorial Trophy; Larissa   Vol. 1: 17369
Struck Prize; Prof. Hermann   Vol. 2: 7886
Structural Foam Division Awards   Vol. 1: 18059
Structural Plastics Division Awards   Vol. 1: 18059
Struggle for Liberation of Bulgaria Award   Vol. 1: 6616
Stryja Special Memorial Prize; Professor Karol   Vol. 2: 1984
Strzelecki Prize; Jan   Vol. 2: 10168
Stuart Award; Herbert Akroyd   Vol. 2: 3121
Stuart Memorial Lectureship; Charles A.   Vol. 1: 6595
Stuart Prize; Akroyd   Vol. 2: 3911
Stubbs Gold Medal; Oliver   Vol. 2: 3075
Stuckey Memorial Award; Bill   Vol. 1: 1994
Stud Dog Trophy   Vol. 1: 3984
Student Academy Awards   Vol. 1: 65
Student Achievement Award   Vol. 1: 10947
Student Advocacy Award   Vol. 1: 10588
Student Article Contest   Vol. 1: 7000
Student Award
    American Society of Heating, Refrigerating and Air-Conditioning Engineers   Vol. 1: 4590
    American Society of Hospital Pharmacists Research and Education Foundation   Vol 1: 4609
    Canadian Society of Microbiologists   Vol 1: 7218
    Livestock Publications Council   Vol 1: 11921

    National Council on Family Relations   Vol 1: 13810
    Society for Applied Spectroscopy   Vol 1: 17421
    Society of Allied Weight Engineers, Inc.   Vol 1: 17667
Student Award of Excellence   Vol. 1: 18536
Student Award - Postgraduate Division   Vol. 2: 2798
Student Award - Undergraduate Division   Vol. 2: 2805
Student Awards
    American Institute of Chemical Engineers   Vol. 1: 2602
    Sea Grant Association   Vol 1: 17153
    Wildlife Diseases Association   Vol 1: 20298
Student Chapter Award   Vol. 1: 10459
Student Chapter Awards   Vol. 1: 1665
Student Chapter of the Year   Vol. 1: 13914
Student Chapter of the Year Award
    American Society for Information Science   Vol. 1: 4176
    American Society of Certified Engineering Technicians   Vol 1: 4421
    International Facility Management Association   Vol 1: 10948
Student Chapters Merit Award   Vol. 1: 7564
Student Competition   Vol. 1: 10928
Student Design Awards   Vol. 1: 17731
Student Essay Competition   Vol. 1: 6957
Student Film Award   Vol. 1: 65
Student Film Awards   Vol. 1: 65
Student Leadership Award   Vol. 1: 3392
Student Liaison Award   Vol. 1: 8213
Student Lighting Design Awards   Vol. 2: 3578
Student Literary Award   Vol. 1: 13846
Student Medallion Award   Vol. 2: 3305
Student Media Awards   Vol. 2: 2956
Student Merit Award   Vol. 1: 17809
Student Merit Award for Outstanding Achievement in Community Dentistry   Vol. 1: 1153
Student Paper Award
    Human and Ergonomics Factors Society   Vol. 1: 10043
    Institute of Transportation Engineers   Vol 1: 10460
    Project Management Institute   Vol 1: 16529
Student Paper Award for Four and Five Year Students   Vol. 1: 10494
Student Paper Award for Two and Three Year Students   Vol. 1: 10495
Student Paper Awards   Vol. 1: 17928
Student Paper Competition
    American Association for Public Opinion Research   Vol. 1: 871
    Water Environment Federation   Vol 1: 20163
Student Paper Contest   Vol. 1: 17578
Student Performance Competition   Vol. 1: 7256
Student Poster Award   Vol. 1: 1121
Student Presentation Award   Vol. 1: 8325
Student Prize Paper   Vol. 1: 17455
Student Professional Paper   Vol. 1: 5776
Student Project Competition   Vol. 1: 4590
Student Project of the Year Award   Vol. 1: 14817
Student Public Service Scholarships   Vol. 1: 16571
Student Publication Contest   Vol. 1: 17689
Student Recruitment Marketing Awards   Vol. 1: 8302
Student Research Award
    American Geriatrics Society   Vol. 1: 2182
    National Society for Performance and Instruction   Vol 1: 14771

Student Research Award for Clinical Child Psychology Vol. 1: 3697
Student Research Award for the Society of Pediatric Psychology Vol. 1: 3698
Student Research Grant Vol. 1: 3699
Student/Resident Award Vol. 1: 992
Student Scholarships Vol. 1: 14755
Student Translation Award Vol. 1: 4920
Student Travel Awards Vol. 1: 3676
Student Writing Awards Vol. 1: 3045
Students Aid Fund Vol. 2: 3333
Studentship Vol. 1: 12191
Study Grant Awards Vol. 2: 246
Stukus Trophy - Coach of the Year; Annis Vol. 1: 6886
Stulberg Auditions; Julius Vol. 1: 18511
Sturdivant Awards; B. V. "Sturdy" Vol. 1: 13370
Sture Centerwalls Pris Vol. 2: 11556
Sturgeon Memorial Award; Theodore Vol. 1: 7468
Sturgis Medal Vol. 1: 17717
Stuttgart City Prize for Young Composers Vol. 2: 7138
Stuttgart International Festival of Animated Film Vol. 2: 7142
Stuttgart Literary Prize Vol. 2: 7139
Stuyvesant Award; Glyndebourne Peter Vol. 2: 2941
Subcontractor of the Year Vol. 1: 19601
Subdivision Award Vol. 1: 8322
Sublette Award of Excellence; Louise Vol. 1: 4001
Submarine/ASW Writing Award Vol. 1: 15096
Suburban Journalist of the Year Vol. 1: 18514
Subvention de l'Academie Nationale de Medecine Vol. 2: 4879
Successful Projects Initiative Awards Vol. 1: 3869
Sudden Opportunity Grants Vol. 1: 12341
Suddeutscher Rundfunk Award Vol. 2: 7142
Suden Professional Opportunity Awards; Caroline tum Vol. 1: 3515
Sudjono Djuned Poesponegoro Award Vol. 2: 7729
Sudler Cup Vol. 1: 18162
Sudler Flag of Honor Vol. 1: 18163
Sudler International High School Marching Band Championship Video Competition Vol. 1: 18167
Sudler International Wind Band Composition Competition; Louis Vol. 1: 18164
Sudler Order of Merit of the Sousa Foundation Vol. 1: 18165
Sudler Scroll Vol. 1: 18166
Sudler Shield Vol. 1: 18167
Sudler Trophy Vol. 1: 18168
Sudrey's Fund Vol. 2: 4364
Sugahara Awards; Kay Vol. 1: 19906
Sugg Heritage Award Vol. 2: 3330
Suggester of the Year Award Vol. 1: 19237
Suider-Afrikaanse Instituut van Boswese Toekenning Vol. 2: 11099
Sullivan Award for Architecture; Louis Vol. 1: 2544
Sullivan Fishery Conservation Award; Carl R. Vol. 1: 2069
Sullivan Memorial Award; AAU James E. Vol. 1: 402
Sullivan Trophy; Senator Joseph A. Vol. 1: 6986
Sulman Prize Vol. 2: 125
Sulphur Institute Award Vol. 2: 7500
Sultan Prize; HMS Vol. 2: 3347
Sulzberger Award; Mayer Vol. 1: 11553

Sulzberger Memorial Award and Lectureship; Marion B. Vol. 1: 549
Summer Fellowships in Allergy and Immunology for Medical Students Vol. 1: 492
Summer Student Fellowships Vol. 1: 2115
Summers Distinguished Merit Award; Alex J. Vol. 1: 2388
Summers Distinguished Merit Hosta; Alex J. Vol. 1: 2389
Summers Memorial Award; Rev. Dr. Montague Vol. 1: 8417
Summit Award Vol. 1: 17897
Summit Awards Vol. 1: 19700
Summit Brass International Brass Ensemble Competition Vol. 1: 18528
Summit of Excellence Award Vol. 1: 6256
Sun Alliance Trophy Vol. 2: 4173
Sun Life/Amateur Photographer Monochrome Awards Vol. 2: 4499
SunAmco Medal Vol. 2: 11488
SunBank 24 At Daytona Vol. 1: 8540
Sunday Express Book of the Year Award Vol. 2: 4501
Sunday Express Magazine - Veuve Clicquot Short Story Competition Vol. 2: 2718
Sunday Independent/Irish Life Arts Awards Vol. 2: 7808
Sunday People Tattersall Trophy Vol. 2: 3659
The Sunday Times Bruce Mason Playwrights' Award Vol. 2: 9784
Sunday Times Small Publishers Award Vol. 2: 4504
The Sunday Times Sportswomen of the Year Award Vol. 2: 4505
Sunder Lal Hora Medal Vol. 2: 7674
Sunkel Stiftung; Werner Vol. 2: 6654
Sunkist Young Designer Award Vol. 1: 4362
Sunshine Award Vol. 1: 18002
Suntory Awards for Mystery Fiction Vol. 2: 8525
Suntory Prize for Community Cultural Activities Vol. 2: 8763
Suntory Prize for Social Sciences and Humanities Vol. 2: 8764
Suomalainen kuvakirja palkinto Vol. 2: 4669
Suomen museoliiton 50-vuotisjuhlamitali Vol. 2: 4702
Suomen Taiteilijaseuran tunnustusapuaraha Vol. 2: 4665
Super Bowl Vol. 1: 14005
Super Bowl Most Valuable Player Vol. 1: 14003
Super Ecran Prize Vol. 1: 12436
Super Picker Award Vol. 1: 16820
Super Senior Service Award Vol. 1: 19658
Super Stock Puller of the Year Vol. 1: 14909
Super Van Operator of the Year Vol. 1: 3150
Superchannel Award Vol. 1: 20597
Superfest Vol. 1: 8284
Superintendent of the Year Award Vol. 1: 1187
Superintendent's Award for Distinguished Service Vol. 1: 19274
Superior Achievement Award Vol. 1: 10414
Superior Civilian Service Award - Army Vol. 1: 19208
Superior Civilian Service Award - Navy/Marine Corps Vol. 1: 19209
Superior Honor Award Vol. 1: 19308
Superior Scientist Award Vol. 2: 5326
Supple Memorial Award; James O. Vol. 1: 16768
Supplier Member of the Year Award Vol. 1: 6014
Supplier of the Year
International Society of Pharmaceutical Engineers Vol. 1: 11294

National Association of Quick Printers Vol 1: 13267
National Railroad Construction and Maintenance Association Vol 1: 14555
Supplier Who Contributed Most to ISPE Vol. 1: 11294
Support of Science Award Vol. 1: 8381
Supreme Champion Vol. 2: 3464
Supreme Champion Awards Vol. 2: 2545
Supreme Knights Special Service Citation Award Vol. 1: 8013
Supreme Order of Christ (Militia of Our Lord Jesus Christ) Vol. 2: 12107
Sur Award Vol. 2: 7514
Surdin; Prix Dina Vol. 2: 6234
Surgan Award; Edith Vol. 1: 14422
Surgitek Prize Vol. 2: 2278
Surrency Prize; Erwin C. Vol. 1: 4185
Survey and General Instrument Company Award Vol. 2: 2309
Surveying and Mapping Award Vol. 1: 4500
Surveying Excellence Award Vol. 1: 14818
Survivors' Club Vol. 1: 10701
Susman Prize; Gene Wise - Warren Vol. 1: 4877
Sustained Achievement Award Vol. 1: 16790
Sustained Ad Campaign Vol. 1: 20164
Sustained Contributions to the Classification and Compensation Society Vol. 1: 7825
Sustained Professional Accomplishment Award Vol. 1: 7826
Sustained Superior Performance Award Vol. 1: 454
Sustaining Fund Awards Vol. 1: 7927
Sustaining Member Recognition Award Vol. 1: 20606
Sustaining Members Twenty-Year Awards Vol. 1: 1820
Sustaining Membership Award Vol. 1: 5896
Sustaining Membership Lecture Award Vol. 1: 5896
Sutherland Award; Edwin H. Vol. 1: 4543
Sutherland Memorial Lecture Vol. 1: 8448
Sutherland Prize; Donald M. Vol. 1: 4186
Sutherland Prize; Kenneth J. G. Vol. 2: 590
Sutherland Trophy Vol. 2: 2345
Suttle Award; H. K. Vol. 2: 2883
Sutton Award; George Miksch Vol. 1: 20322
Sutton Trophy; Major General W. J. Vol. 1: 14645
Svante Arrhenius Medaljen Vol. 2: 11557
Svenska Akademiens Finlandspris Vol. 2: 11605
Svenska Akademiens nordiska pris Vol. 2: 11606
Svenska Akademiens oversattarpris Vol. 2: 11607
Svenska Akademiens sprakvardspris Vol. 2: 11608
Svenska Akademiens svensklararpris Vol. 2: 11609
Svenska Akademiens teaterpris Vol. 2: 11610
Svenska Akademiens tolkningspris Vol. 2: 11611
Sverdlin; Premio Norman Vol. 2: 9195
Sverdrup Civil Engineering Management Award; John I. Parcel - Leif J. Vol. 1: 4488
Sverdrup Gold Medal Vol. 1: 3098
Sverdrup Medal Vol. 1: 17718
Svjetlost Prizes Vol. 2: 1404
Svjetski Festival Animiranih Filmova, Zagreb Vol. 2: 1816
Swackhamer Prize Student Essay Contest Vol. 1: 15553
Swaffer National Press Awards; Hannen Vol. 2: 4561
Swallow Prize Vol. 2: 4668

Swammerdam Medal; Jan   Vol. 2: 9559
Swan Premium   Vol. 2: 3273
Swan Prize; Anni   Vol. 2: 4704
Swanberg Distinguished Service Award; Harold   Vol. 1: 3062
Swanin Mitali; Anni   Vol. 2: 4704
Swanson Award; Lynn D.   Vol. 1: 11059
Swarowsky International Conducting Competition; Hans   Vol. 2: 895
Swarts; Prix Frederic   Vol. 2: 1022
Swarup Memorial Lecture; Dr. Har   Vol. 2: 7675
Swastek Award; Rev. Joseph V.   Vol. 1: 16313
Swearingen Award; Harry S.   Vol. 1: 3882
Swearingen Award; Noble G.   Vol. 1: 5967
Swecker Award; Herbert N.   Vol. 1: 7957
Swedish Authors' Fund Awards   Vol. 2: 11619
Swedish Mathematical Society Fellowship   Vol. 2: 11635
Sweeney; Academic Award in Memory of Stephen B.   Vol. 1: 10853
Sweeney Award; Catherine H.   Vol. 1: 2364
Sweeney Award; Craig   Vol. 1: 19478
Sweeney Medal; Edward C.   Vol. 1: 9029
Sweepstakes Trophy   Vol. 1: 14025
Sweepstakes Winner   Vol. 1: 13946
Sweet Award; Ralph   Vol. 1: 5858
Sweet Fellowship; Georgina   Vol. 2: 212
Swenson Leadership Award; Reed K.   Vol. 1: 14267
SWG Literary Awards   Vol. 1: 17073
Swidzinski Award; Henryk   Vol. 2: 10150
Swidzinskiego; Nagroda im. Henryka   Vol. 2: 10150
Swimmer of the Year Award   Vol. 1: 19630
Swimming Coach of the Year   Vol. 1: 6987
Swimming Enterprises Trophy for Synchronised Swimmer of the Year   Vol. 2: 2071
The Swimming Times Water Polo Award   Vol. 2: 2072
Swiney Prize for a Work on Jurisprudence   Vol. 2: 4325
Swings; Prix Pol   Vol. 2: 1368
Swings; Prix Pol and Christiane   Vol. 2: 1035
Swiss Association of Chemists Prizes   Vol. 2: 11890
Swiss Children's Book Prize   Vol. 2: 11947
Swiss Grand Prize Photo Competition - Youth in Switzerland   Vol. 2: 11951
Swiss Music - Edition   Vol. 2: 11941
Swiss Organ Competition   Vol. 2: 11945
Swiss Organ Festival   Vol. 2: 11945
Swiss Prize for Parapsychology   Vol. 2: 11939
Swiss Society for Internal Medicine Prize   Vol. 2: 11902
Swissair/Crossair Special Prize   Vol. 2: 11875
Sword of Excellence Awards   Vol. 2: 3204
Sword of Ignatius Loyola Award   Vol. 1: 17005
Sword of Loyola   Vol. 1: 11975
Swormstedt Memorial Award; David   Vol. 1: 17132
Sydney International Piano Competition of Australia   Vol. 2: 326
Sydney PEN Short Story Award   Vol. 2: 506
Sydney Sun Aria Contest   Vol. 2: 323
Sydnor Award; Charles S.   Vol. 1: 18218
Sylvester Medal   Vol. 2: 4158
Sylvia Cup Award   Vol. 1: 17681
Syme Professorship   Vol. 2: 10608
Syme Research Prize; David   Vol. 2: 697
Symington Award; W. Stuart   Vol. 1: 258
Symmes Municipal Environmental Award; Lee   Vol. 1: 9155
Symons Memorial Medal   Vol. 2: 4105
Syndicated Fiction Prizes   Vol. 1: 18545

Synergy Award   Vol. 1: 17732
Synge Award; John L.   Vol. 1: 16965
Syntex Animal Health - Bovine Practitioner of the Year Award   Vol. 1: 943
Syntex Award   Vol. 1: 7565
Syntex Award in Physical Organic Chemistry   Vol. 1: 7565
Syntex Scholars Program   Vol. 1: 18547
System Safety Technology Innovation Award   Vol. 1: 18564
Szabo Medal; Ervin   Vol. 2: 7408
Szakszervezeti Muveszeti Kulturalis Dij   Vol. 2: 7442
Szczesny Prize; Commander Kazimierz   Vol. 2: 10168
Szent-Gyorgyi Albert Emlekerem   Vol. 2: 7461
Szent-Gyorgyi Commemorative Medal; Albert   Vol. 2: 7461
Szentkiralyi Medal; Zsigmond   Vol. 2: 7360
Szikla Prize; Geza   Vol. 2: 7381
Szilard Award for Physics in the Public Interest; Leo   Vol. 1: 3472
Szirmai Endre dij   Vol. 2: 7421
Szirmai Prize; Endre   Vol. 2: 7421
Szocialista Kulturaert   Vol. 2: 7339
Szold Award; Henrietta   Vol. 1: 9750
Szold Prize; Science Prize - Henrietta   Vol. 2: 7961
SZOT Prize   Vol. 2: 7442
Szymanski Award; Walter A.   Vol. 1: 18044
T & R (Insurance Services) Limited Prize   Vol. 2: 3098
Tableau d'honneur   Vol. 2: 840
Tabler Memorial Award; Pat   Vol. 1: 7678
TAC Heptathlon Award   Vol. 1: 19962
Tachau Pre-Collegiate Teaching Award; Mary K. Bonsteel   Vol. 1: 15824
Tacussel; Prix Jacques   Vol. 2: 11840
Taff Transportation and Logistics Educational Service Award; Charles A.   Vol. 1: 4804
Taft Accolades for Excellent Teachers   Vol. 1: 18568
TAGA Honors Award   Vol. 1: 18598
Taggart Award; Arthur F.   Vol. 1: 17579
Taggart Award; Pat   Vol. 1: 18638
Tagore Literacy Award   Vol. 2: 7567
Taguchi Award   Vol. 1: 4879
Taipei International Music Competition   Vol. 2: 12007
Taishoff Award for Excellence in Broadcast Journalism; Sol   Vol. 1: 14510
Tait Trophy   Vol. 1: 9789
Tajima Prize   Vol. 2: 11840
Takamado Award; Prince   Vol. 2: 8608
Take Pride in America/Keep America Beautiful Public Lands Day Joint Award   Vol. 1: 11660
Talbert Junior Sportsmanship Award; Bill   Vol. 1: 11353
Talbert Junior Sportsmanship Awards; Bill   Vol. 1: 19659
Talbot Prize for African Anthropology; Amaury   Vol. 2: 3930
Talking Book of the Year   Vol. 1: 7063
Tall Man Water Freezer Award   Vol. 1: 9811
Talley EMS Educator of the Year Award; Mary Ann   Vol. 1: 13099
Tallix Foundry Prize   Vol. 1: 14714
Tallmadge Award for Contributions to Coating Technology; John A.   Vol. 1: 2603
Tallone Prize; C. Augusto   Vol. 2: 8106
Talvela Prize; Martti   Vol. 2: 4694
Tamayo Annual Competition for Literature Prizes; Franz   Vol. 1: 1388
Tamil Drama Award   Vol. 2: 11427
Tamisiea Award; John A.   Vol. 1: 175

Tampere International Short Film Festival   Vol. 2: 4758
Tampereen Kansainvaliset lyhytelokuvajuhlat Grand Prix   Vol. 2: 4758
TAMR Award   Vol. 1: 18608
Tanasescu Prize; Tudor   Vol. 2: 10385
Tandy Technology Scholars Awards   Vol. 1: 18572
Tanizaki Award; Junichiro   Vol. 2: 8521
Tanner Award   Vol. 2: 2597
Tanner Award; Martin W.   Vol. 1: 18415
Tanner Trophy; Elaine   Vol. 1: 7247
Tanner - Vandeput Boswick Prize for Burn Research   Vol. 1: 11235
Tanner - Vandeput Prize for Burn Research   Vol. 1: 11235
Tanneyhill Award; Ann   Vol. 1: 14974
Tantramar Trophy   Vol. 1: 6988
Taormina Memorial Award; Silvio C.   Vol. 1: 13207
Tapia Alarcon; Premio a la Actividad Gremial Dr. Roberto   Vol. 2: 1561
Tapling Medal   Vol. 2: 4122
TAPPI Distinguished Service Award   Vol. 1: 18601
TAPPI Fellow Award   Vol. 1: 18602
TAPPI Gold Medal   Vol. 1: 18600
Tarbut Award   Vol. 1: 11558
Targa d'Oro ANDIN   Vol. 2: 8384
Targa d'Oro Citta di Sondrio   Vol. 2: 8433
Target Awards for Excellence in Builder Advertising   Vol. 1: 16456
Targhe d'Oro per l'Ecologia   Vol. 2: 8301
Tarjan Memorial Award; George   Vol. 1: 538
Tarnopol Trophy   Vol. 1: 7809
Tarrega; Certamen Internacional de Guitarra Francisco   Vol. 2: 11153
Tarrega International Guitar Competition; Francisco   Vol. 2: 11153
Taruna Cup   Vol. 1: 3984
TASH Collaboration Award   Vol. 1: 5573
Tasmania Division Award of Merit   Vol. 2: 489
Tassier; Prix Suzanne   Vol. 2: 997
Tastemaker Awards; R. T. French   Vol. 1: 6299
Tata Gold Medal   Vol. 2: 7634
Tate and Lyle Award for Sustainable Development   Vol. 2: 4635
Tate International Award; John T.   Vol. 1: 2665
Tattersall Trophy   Vol. 2: 3659
Tau Beta Pi Laureate   Vol. 1: 18575
Tauber Prize; Richard   Vol. 2: 2082
Tausk-Preis; Marius-   Vol. 2: 6845
Taussig Article Award; Frank W.   Vol. 1: 15626
Tawara Gold Medal   Vol. 2: 8567
Taxpayer's Best Friend/Taxpayer's Friend/Big Spender   Vol. 1: 14882
Taylor and Francis Best Letter Award   Vol. 2: 3848
Taylor Architecture Award; Walter   Vol. 1: 1188
Taylor Award; Alan   Vol. 2: 2322
Taylor Award; C. Douglas   Vol. 1: 7123
Taylor Award; E. N. "Mully"   Vol. 1: 18802
Taylor Award; Fannie   Vol. 1: 5918
Taylor Award for Modern American Poetry; Aiken   Vol. 1: 17205
Taylor Award for Private Gardens; Kathryn S.   Vol. 1: 15165
Taylor Award for Voluntary Service; Dwain   Vol. 1: 15942
Taylor Award; Franklin V.   Vol. 1: 3685
Taylor Body of Work Award; Sydney   Vol. 1: 5845

Taylor Children's Book Awards; Sydney   Vol. 1: 5846
Taylor Essay Prize; Reginald   Vol. 2: 2243
Taylor Key Award   Vol. 1: 17407
Taylor Manuscript Competition; Sydney   Vol. 1: 5847
Taylor Medal; David W.   Vol. 1: 17929
Taylor Medal; J. Hall   Vol. 1: 4710
Taylor Memorial Medal; Braid   Vol. 2: 3821
Taylor (of Australia) Prize; George   Vol. 2: 3912
Taylor Playwriting Award; Marvin   Vol. 1: 17250
Taylor; Prix C. Douglas   Vol. 1: 7123
Taylor Prize; Dorotea Lange - Paul   Vol. 1: 8762
Taylor Research Medal; SME Frederick W.   Vol. 1: 17887
Taylor Spink Minor League Player-of-the-Year; Topps - J. G.   Vol. 1: 18733
TC-Studios Fred Oed GmbH Award for the Film and Media Exchange   Vol. 2: 7142
TCG Affiliated Artist Observerships   Vol. 1: 18677
TCG Hispanic Translation Commission   Vol. 1: 18682
TCG/Metropolitan Life Foundation Extended Collaboration Grants for Aritsts   Vol. 1: 18678
TCG/NEA Designer Fellows   Vol. 1: 18679
TCG/NEA Director Fellows   Vol. 1: 18680
TCG Rehearsal Observerships   Vol. 1: 18681
TCG Translation/Adaptation Commission   Vol. 1: 18682
Tchaikovsky Competition; International   Vol. 2: 10455
Tchernichowsky Prize; Literary Prize -   Vol. 2: 7958
TDMA Hall of Fame   Vol. 1: 6204
Teacher Award for Community Service   Vol. 1: 18807
Teacher of the Year
  Association of Accredited Cosmetology Schools   Vol. 1: 5671
  Ladies Professional Golf Association   Vol 1: 11766
Teacher of the Year Award
  The Arc   Vol. 1: 5218
  Professional Golfers' Association of America   Vol 1: 16481
Teacher Recognition Awards   Vol. 1: 11338
Teacher-Researcher Grants   Vol. 1: 13780
Teachers as Writers   Vol. 1: 18596
Teachers Scramble   Vol. 2: 4489
Teaching Award
  American Horticultural Society   Vol. 1: 2365
  American Phytopathological Society   Vol 1: 3524
Teaching Awards Program   Vol. 1: 3824
Teaching Excellence Award   Vol. 1: 7881
Teague Memorial Trophy; Marshall   Vol. 1: 8541
Teague Space Award; Olin E.   Vol. 1: 1259
Team Awards   Vol. 1: 11216
Team Champions   Vol. 2: 3806
Team Championship Award   Vol. 1: 19958
Team Championships (non-divisional)   Vol. 2: 4569
Teatro-Konkurso   Vol. 2: 9398
Techfilm International Film Festival   Vol. 2: 1874
Technical Achievement Award
  Institute of Electrical and Electronics Engineers - Computer Society   Vol. 1: 10305
  International Society for Hybrid Microelectronics   Vol 1: 11256

National Association of Printing Ink Manufacturers   Vol 1: 13239
Technical Achievement in Broadcasting Award   Vol. 1: 14609
Technical and Feature Writing Awards   Vol. 1: 3046
Technical Association of the Australian and New Zealand Pulp and Paper Industry Awards   Vol. 2: 689
Technical Commendation   Vol. 1: 8214
Technical Committee Prize Paper Award   Vol. 1: 10317
Technical Council Award   Vol. 1: 10461
Technical Council Distinguished Individual Service Award   Vol. 1: 10318
Technical Division Executive Committee Award   Vol. 1: 2144
Technical Excellence Award
  American Radio Relay League   Vol. 1: 3894
  International Society of Weighing and Measurement   Vol 1: 11311
Technical Merit Award   Vol. 1: 3895
Technical Paper Award   Vol. 1: 9868
Technical Publication Award   Vol. 1: 9869
Technical Standards Board Certificate of Appreciation   Vol. 1: 17777
Technical Writing Awards   Vol. 1: 278
Technician of the Month Award   Vol. 1: 4422
Technician of the Year
  Electronics Technicians Association, International   Vol. 1: 8890
  International Motor Sports Association   Vol 1: 11107
  International Motor Sports Association   Vol 1: 11108
Technician of the Year Award
  American Association for Laboratory Animal Science   Vol. 1: 867
  American Society of Certified Engineering Technicians   Vol 1: 4423
  Institute of Materials   Vol 2: 3151
  International Society of Certified Electronics Technicians   Vol 1: 11283
  Professional Aviation Maintenance Association   Vol 1: 16436
  Professional Aviation Maintenance Association   Vol 1: 16441
Technician Publication Award   Vol. 1: 868
Technician Recognition Award   Vol. 1: 867
Technicolor/Herbert T. Kalmus Gold Medal Award   Vol. 1: 17912
Technicon 50th Anniversary Award (Bayer Diagnostics Award)   Vol. 2: 10982
Technological Innovation Award   Vol. 2: 1682
Technologist of the Year
  American Medical Technologists   Vol. 1: 3047
  American Society of Clinical Pathologists   Vol 1: 4521
Technology Award   Vol. 2: 3924
Technology Award/Award of Engineering Excellence   Vol. 1: 4591
Technology Prize   Vol. 2: 9955
Technology Teacher Educator of the Year   Vol. 1: 8411
Technology Transfer and Extension Award   Vol. 1: 17690
Teclu Prize; Nicolae   Vol. 2: 10386
Teddy Award   Vol. 1: 13613
Teen Health Leadership Award   Vol. 1: 7451
Teen Health Leadership Awards   Vol. 1: 7452
Teen Model and Talent Pageant   Vol. 1: 20510
Teen Volunteer of the Year   Vol. 1: 2215
Teenage Youth Award   Vol. 1: 7408
Teer, Jr. Award; Nello L.   Vol. 1: 3974

Teetor Educational Award; Ralph R.   Vol. 1: 17778
Teirlinck; Prix Auguste   Vol. 2: 979
Teissonniere; Prix Paul   Vol. 2: 5907
Teixeira; Premio Carlos   Vol. 2: 10245
Teixeira Prize; Carlos   Vol. 2: 10245
Tekakwitha Award   Vol. 1: 6402
Teleconfronto   Vol. 2: 8446
Televised Opera Prize of the City of Salzburg   Vol. 2: 870
Televisio de Catalunya (TV3) Award   Vol. 2: 11203
Television Journalism Prize   Vol. 2: 40
Television News Photographers of the Year   Vol. 1: 14529
Television News Station of the Year   Vol. 1: 14530
Television Newsfilm Awards   Vol. 1: 14531
Television Program Producer of the Year   Vol. 1: 14610
Television-Radio Awards   Vol. 1: 20562
Television Station of the Year   Vol. 1: 14611
Telford Medal   Vol. 2: 3259
Telford Premium   Vol. 2: 3260
Telford Prize; Sir Robert   Vol. 2: 3294
Tellez-Giron; Premio Dr. Alfredo   Vol. 2: 8939
Telly Awards   Vol. 1: 18610
TELO Award   Vol. 1: 4895
Telocator Marketing Awards   Vol. 1: 18612
Temasek; Darjah Utama   Vol. 2: 10745
Temple Award for Creative Altruism   Vol. 1: 10419
Templer Medal   Vol. 2: 4350
Templeton Foundations Honor Roll Award   Vol. 1: 16715
Templeton Prize for Progress in Religion   Vol. 2: 928
Templeton Reporter of the Year Award; John   Vol. 1: 16769
Templin Award; Richard L.   Vol. 1: 6079
Ten Best Amateur Films   Vol. 1: 16159
Ten Best Cars   Vol. 1: 7300
Ten Best Censored Stories of the Year   Vol. 1: 16523
Ten Best of the West Film Festival   Vol. 1: 3144
Ten Dullest Americans   Vol. 1: 10919
Ten Outstanding Young Americans   Vol. 1: 19430
Tena; Premio Guillermo   Vol. 2: 11340
tenBroek Award; Jacobus   Vol. 1: 13967
Tenenbaum Award; Michael   Vol. 1: 11472
Tenhoff Award; Ray E.   Vol. 1: 17839
Tennant Memorial Lecture; Charles   Vol. 2: 4427
Tenneco Student Section Scholarship Award   Vol. 1: 4782
Tennessee Big "I" Advertising Award   Vol. 1: 10136
Tennis Educational Merit Award   Vol. 1: 11354
Tennis Educational Merit Award for Men   Vol. 1: 11354
Tennis Educational Merit Award for Women   Vol. 1: 11355
Tennis Educational Merit Awards for Men and Women   Vol. 1: 19660
Tennis Facility Awards   Vol. 1: 19661
Tennis Magazine /ITA College Players of the Year   Vol. 1: 18624
Tennis Week Great American Tennis Writing Awards   Vol. 1: 18626
Tennis World Champions   Vol. 2: 3485
Tentai Hakkensho   Vol. 2: 8507
Teodorescu Prize; Emanoil   Vol. 2: 10387
Teodorov-Balan Prize; Academician Aleksandar   Vol. 2: 1513

Teresa e Allessandro Ghigi; Premio Maria   Vol. 2: 8021
Terman Award; Frederick Emmons   Vol. 1: 4121
Terry Brittell COTA/OTR Partnership Award   Vol. 1: 3306
Terry, Jr., Memorial Merit Award; W. S.   Vol. 1: 3870
Terry Preservation Awards; Lucille   Vol. 1: 8783
Tertis Award; Lillian   Vol. 2: 3627
Tertis International Viola Competition and Workshop; Lionel   Vol. 2: 3627
Terzaghi Award; Karl   Vol. 1: 4501
Terzaghi Lecture; Karl   Vol. 1: 4502
TES Information Book Awards   Vol. 2: 4548
TES Schoolbook Award   Vol. 2: 4549
Tesla Award; Nikola
 Belgrade International Festival of Scientific Films   Vol. 2: 10699
 Institute of Electrical and Electronics Engineers   Vol 1: 10291
Tesla Awards; Nikola   Vol. 2: 1813
TESOL/Newbury House Award for Excellence in Teaching   Vol. 1: 18592
TESOL/Prentice Hall Regents Fellowship for Graduate Study   Vol. 1: 18593
TESOL/Regents Publishing Company Fellowship   Vol. 1: 18593
TESOL Research Interest Section/Newbury House Distinguished Research Award   Vol. 1: 18594
Tess Award in Coatings; Roy W.   Vol. 1: 1514
Tessenow Gold Medal; Henirich   Vol. 2: 7122
Tessier; Prix Albert-   Vol. 1: 16611
Testimonial Awards   Vol. 1: 4288
Testimonial Prize   Vol. 2: 11646
Tesvik Odulu   Vol. 2: 12067
Tetalman Award   Vol. 1: 17957
TETYC Best Article of the Year Award   Vol. 1: 13781
Texas Award   Vol. 1: 19920
Texas Bluebonnet Award   Vol. 1: 18658
Texas Collector's Institute Award   Vol. 1: 18651
Texas Literary Award   Vol. 1: 18249
Texas Star Award   Vol. 1: 20625
Texier II; Prix Henri   Vol. 2: 5756
Texier; Prix Henri   Vol. 2: 5755
Textile Institute Design Medal   Vol. 2: 4524
Textile Institute Development Award   Vol. 2: 4525
Textile Institute Jubilee Award   Vol. 2: 4526
Textile Section Award   Vol. 1: 15224
Textile Technology Award   Vol. 2: 8942
A Textilipar Fejleszteseert Erem   Vol. 2: 7387
Teyte Prize Competition; Maggie   Vol. 2: 4530
Thalben-Ball Memorial Scholarships; Sir George   Vol. 2: 4532
Thalberg Memorial Award; Irving G.   Vol. 1: 66
Thalia Prize   Vol. 2: 11576
Thames Television Award   Vol. 2: 2251
Thames Television Playwright Scheme   Vol. 2: 4535
Thames Valley Award   Vol. 2: 2538
Than Medal; Karoly   Vol. 2: 7323
Thanksgiving Award   Vol. 1: 7799
Thant Peace Award; U   Vol. 1: 18948
Thayer Award; Sylvanus
 Association of Graduates   Vol. 1: 5827
 United States Military Academy Association of Graduates   Vol 1: 19449
Theater Hall of Fame   Vol. 1: 18671
Theatre Award   Vol. 2: 9398
Theatre for Young Audiences Juried Awards   Vol. 1: 19977

Theatre Grants   Vol. 1: 16401
Theatre In Our Schools Month Award   Vol. 1: 778
Theatre Library Association Award   Vol. 1: 18688
Theatre Memphis New Play Competition   Vol. 1: 18690
Theatre Organist of the Year   Vol. 1: 4899
Theatre Prize   Vol. 2: 7963
Theatre Production Prize   Vol. 2: 24
Theatre World Award   Vol. 1: 18692
Thebault; Fondation Victor   Vol. 2: 5677
Theiler Memorial Medal   Vol. 2: 11035
Thelin Award; Dr. Murray   Vol. 1: 14137
Thelonius Monk International Jazz Instrumental Competition   Vol. 1: 12416
Theobald Trophy; Brenard   Vol. 2: 2796
Theoretical and Philosophical Psychology Student Paper Award   Vol. 1: 3826
Thermoforming Institute National Awards   Vol. 1: 18060
Theron Medal; Danie   Vol. 2: 10948
THESE-PAC Awards   Vol. 2: 9699
Thessaloniki Film Festival   Vol. 2: 7217
Thevenot Medal; Jean   Vol. 2: 9533
Thew Fund Awards; H.A.   Vol. 2: 3669
Thewlis Award; Malford W.   Vol. 1: 2183
Thibaud; Concours International Marguerite Long et Jacques   Vol. 2: 6085
Thibaud International Competition; Marguerite Long and Jacques   Vol. 2: 6085
Thiebaut; Prix biennal Marcel   Vol. 2: 6273
Thiele-Denkmunze; Dr. Edmund-   Vol. 2: 6545
Thienemann Medal; Einar Naumann - August   Vol. 1: 10790
Thienes Memorial Lecture; Clinton H.   Vol. 1: 544
Thienpont; Prix Denis   Vol. 2: 1329
Thienpont Prize; Denis   Vol. 2: 1316
Thiethnis Diagonismos Moussikis Synthessis   Vol. 2: 7200
Thijssenprijs; Theo   Vol. 2: 9666
Third Grade LRE Teacher Recognition Award   Vol. 1: 2794
Third World Academy of Science Prize   Vol. 2: 8910
Third World Prize   Vol. 2: 4539
Thirteen Centuries of Bulgaria Order   Vol. 2: 1509
Thom Award; Charles   Vol. 1: 17527
Thom Award for Early Design Achievement; Ronald J.   Vol. 1: 6751
Thomas and Carroll A. Hochwalt Award; Charles A.   Vol. 1: 12419
Thomas Award; Dylan   Vol. 2: 3793
Thomas Award for Communication; Lewis   Vol. 1: 1724
Thomas Award; Isaiah   Vol. 1: 16867
Thomas Award; Lowell
 International Platform Association   Vol. 1: 11162
 Overseas Press Club of America   Vol 1: 15875
Thomas Award; Moyer D.   Vol. 1: 6080
Thomas Award; Theodore   Vol. 1: 8097
Thomas, Jr. International Lecture Award; R. D.   Vol. 1: 5093
Thomas Lecture and Prize; E. Donnall   Vol. 1: 4597
Thomas Literary Award; FAW Herb   Vol. 2: 390
Thomas Medal and Prize; Sidney Gilchrist   Vol. 2: 3152
Thomas Memorial Award; Jesse Burgess   Vol. 1: 19715
Thomas Memorial Award; R. D.   Vol. 1: 5094

Thomas National Memorial Trophy; Norma   Vol. 2: 2073
Thomas Newspaper Preservation Prizes; Isaiah   Vol. 1: 4740
Thomas Sportsmanship Award; Homa S.   Vol. 1: 14266
Thomas Travel Journalism Awards; Lowell   Vol. 1: 17736
Thomas Travel Journalist; Lowell   Vol. 1: 17736
Thomas Trophy; Barbara   Vol. 1: 14644
Thomas Unipresser Award; Helen   Vol. 1: 18969
Thomason, Jr. Award; Colonel John W.   Vol. 1: 12085
Thompson Award for Distinguished Service; George N.   Vol. 1: 17792
Thompson Award; Helen M.   Vol. 1: 4893
Thompson Award in Vegetable Crops; Homer C.   Vol. 1: 4153
Thompson Award; S. Earl   Vol. 1: 5737
Thompson Award; Sanford E.   Vol. 1: 6081
Thompson Award; W. F.   Vol. 1: 2618
Thompson Award; Willard O.   Vol. 1: 2184
Thompson Brothers Memorial Cup   Vol. 1: 10600
Thompson Composition Competition; Sigvald   Vol. 1: 9043
Thompson Foundation Gold Medal; J. P.   Vol. 2: 617
Thompson Medal; Mary Clark   Vol. 1: 12690
Thompson Medal of Honor   Vol. 1: 12794
Thompson Memorial Award; Arthur R.   Vol. 1: 20100
Thompson Memorial Award; Robert D.   Vol. 1: 6082
Thompson Memorial Award; W. Robert   Vol. 1: 6314
Thompson Memorial Lecture; Silvanus   Vol. 2: 2417
Thompson Memorial Prize Award; Browder J.   Vol. 1: 10292
Thompson Premium; J. Langham   Vol. 2: 3306
Thoms Medal; Hermann   Vol. 2: 6826
Thomson Foundation Fellowships   Vol. 2: 12192
Thomson Gold Medal; Sir George   Vol. 2: 3164
Thomson Medal   Vol. 2: 9842
Thomson Medal; J. J.   Vol. 2: 3307
Thomson Medal; J. P.   Vol. 2: 617
Thomson Premium; J. J.   Vol. 2: 3273
Thomson Resistance Welding Award; Elihu   Vol. 1: 5095
Thorarinsson Medal   Vol. 2: 500
Thore; Fondation Jean   Vol. 2: 5600
Thoreau Award   Vol. 1: 7294
Thoreau Medal; Emerson -   Vol. 1: 525
Thorel; Prix Ernest   Vol. 2: 5741
Thornburgh Award; Bill   Vol. 1: 1995
Thorndike Award; Edward L.   Vol. 1: 3722
Thornton Award; John   Vol. 2: 2062
Thornton Gold Challenge Award; Mark   Vol. 2: 3430
Thornton Memorial Award and Lecture; John A.   Vol. 1: 4965
Thorpe Award; D. W.   Vol. 2: 193
Thorpe Award; Jim   Vol. 1: 19959
Thorpe Trophy (NFL Most Valuable Player); Jim   Vol. 1: 15361
Thorvaldsen Medal   Vol. 2: 1902
Thouron Fellowship   Vol. 2: 10683
A Thousand Points of Light   Vol. 1: 19333
Threadgill Award for Outstanding Service to NHCA; Michael Beall   Vol. 1: 14122
Three-Day Novel Competition   Vol. 1: 5184

Three-quarter Ton Championship - J. Amory Jeffries Trophy   Vol. 1: 19536
Throlson Scholarship Award; Dr. Ken   Vol. 1: 1346
Thulinmedaljen   Vol. 2: 11649
Thunbergmedaljen   Vol. 2: 11520
Thunderbird Award   Vol. 1: 5284
Thunderbird Foundation Scholarship/Award   Vol. 1: 9914
Thunen Gold Medal; Johann Heinrich von   Vol. 2: 7127
Thurlow Award   Vol. 1: 10415
Thurston Award; John B.   Vol. 1: 10375
Thurston Grand President's Award; Emory W.   Vol. 1: 16106
TIAC Media Awards   Vol. 1: 18768
Tibbitts Award; Clark   Vol. 1: 5524
Tibbitts Grand Champion Award (High Average Horse Award); Bev   Vol. 1: 15483
Tibble Poetry Competition; Anne   Vol. 2: 3723
Tickey Award; Bertha   Vol. 1: 465
Tiemann Award; Walter   Vol. 2: 7033
Tieto-Finlandia-palkinto   Vol. 2: 4688
Tieto-Finlandia Prize   Vol. 2: 4688
Tiffany Awards for Employee Excellence   Vol. 1: 3926
Tilak Lecture Award; Prof. B. D.   Vol. 2: 7676
Tilanus Medal   Vol. 2: 9560
Tilden Award for Interpreter of the Year; Freeman   Vol. 1: 14455
Tilden Lectureship   Vol. 2: 4224
Tilleard Medal   Vol. 2: 4123
Tillman Sease Award   Vol. 1: 16214
Tillmanns-Skolnik Award   Vol. 1: 1515
Tillyer Medal; Edgar D.   Vol. 1: 15758
Tilton Memorial Award; Randy   Vol. 1: 3606
Time-Life Silver Pen Award for Non-Fiction   Vol. 2: 2784
Time Magazine Award for Outstanding Map Design on Current Events   Vol. 1: 1429
Time Magazine Quality Dealer Award   Vol. 1: 18712
Time Man of the Year   Vol. 1: 18713
Time Out/01 - for London Awards   Vol. 2: 4545
Time Out Eating and Drinking Awards   Vol. 2: 4544
Time Out Theatre, Dance and Comedy Awards   Vol. 2: 4545
Time Out Travel Writer and Photographer of the Year   Vol. 2: 4546
The Times Critics' Award   Vol. 2: 2035
The Times Crossword Championship; Collins Dictionaries/   Vol. 2: 2641
The Times Environment Award   Vol. 2: 4073
The Times Higher Educational Supplement Award   Vol. 2: 2739
The Times/Jonathan Cape Young Writers Prize   Vol. 2: 2569
The Times/PM Environment Award   Vol. 2: 4551
Times - Shell Museums Year Award   Vol. 2: 4490
Timisoara Writers Association Award   Vol. 2: 10415
Timmie Awards   Vol. 1: 18760
Timmins Fellowships; Jeanne   Vol. 1: 12430
Timoshenko Medal   Vol. 1: 4711
TIMS Distinguished Service Award   Vol. 1: 10403
Tindall Trophy; Frank   Vol. 1: 6989
Tinkle Award; Lon   Vol. 1: 18653
Tinkle Research Excellence Award; Donald W.   Vol. 1: 18246
Tinsley Prize; Beatrice M.   Vol. 1: 1276
Tintera, M.D. Memorial Award; John W.   Vol. 1: 148

Tipping Bronze Apprentice Medal   Vol. 2: 3096
Tipton Award; Royce J.   Vol. 1: 4503
Tir Na N-Og Awards   Vol. 2: 12196
Tirgu Mures Writers Association Award   Vol. 2: 10416
Tiroler Erfinderpreis Josef Madersperger   Vol. 2: 731
Tiroler Landespreis fur Kunst   Vol. 2: 732
Tiroler Landespreis fur Wissenschaft   Vol. 2: 733
Tirumurti Memorial Lecture; INSA - T. S.   Vol. 2: 7652
Tison Award   Vol. 2: 9470
Tissandier Diploma; Paul   Vol. 2: 5166
Tisserand; Prix Lucien   Vol. 2: 5887
Tissue Culture Association Student Travel Awards   Vol. 1: 18716
Titan All America Hockey Squad (East and West) for Colleges   Vol. 1: 2313
Titan All-America Hockey Squad (East and West) for Universities   Vol. 1: 2314
Titeica Prize; Gheorghe   Vol. 2: 10388
Titulescu Prize; Nicholae   Vol. 2: 10389
Titus Award; Shirley   Vol. 1: 3289
Titus Memorial Trophy Award; Jerry   Vol. 1: 1283
Tjokronegoro Award; Sutomo   Vol. 2: 7730
TLA/SIRS Freedom of Information Award   Vol. 1: 18616
TLS/Cheltenham Literature Festival Poetry Competition   Vol. 2: 2613
TMS/ASM Joint Distinguished Lectureship in Materials and Society   Vol. 1: 12319
TNN *Music City News* Country Awards   Vol. 1: 9735
TNN Viewers' Choice Awards   Vol. 1: 9735
TNR Awards in Fiction and Poetry   Vol. 1: 15106
To Peace and Commerce Award   Vol. 1: 19098
Tobenkin Memorial Award; Paul   Vol. 1: 7997
Tobias, M.D. Award; Richard B.   Vol. 1: 1751
Tobin Award; Mrs. Edgar   Vol. 1: 12244
TOBY Awards   Vol. 1: 6611
Tocze Memorial Trophy; Emile   Vol. 1: 20466
Today's Top Six   Vol. 1: 13610
Todds Bursary; Walter   Vol. 2: 2297
Togni International Composers Competition; Camillo   Vol. 2: 8133
Tokle Memorial Award; Torger   Vol. 1: 19590
Tokyo International Competition for Chamber Music   Vol. 2: 8624
Tokyo International Competition for Guitar Composition   Vol. 2: 8624
Tokyo International Film Festival   Vol. 2: 8768
Tokyo International Music Competition   Vol. 2: 8770
Tokyo Interntational Competition for Guitar COmpositions   Vol. 2: 8624
Tokyo Music Festival   Vol. 2: 8772
Tokyo Video Festival   Vol. 2: 8780
Toledo Glass and Ceramic Award   Vol. 1: 1477
Tolgesy Arts Award; Victor   Vol. 1: 7746
Tollefsen Award; Lois   Vol. 1: 11016
Tolstoi Award; Alexei   Vol. 2: 1826
Tolstoy Award; Count Alexei   Vol. 2: 10708
Tom-Gallon Trust   Vol. 2: 4392
Tomes Award; Gilbert   Vol. 2: 3351
Tomforde Student Auditions; Josie   Vol. 1: 9965
Tomkinson Award; Helen   Vol. 2: 2452
Tommy Awards   Vol. 1: 3610
Tompkins Fellowship; Sally Kress   Vol. 1: 17746
Toncitch Prize; Voya   Vol. 2: 6040

Toner, Jr. Memorial Award; Arthur Carling   Vol. 1: 455
Tong Oration; Dr. James S.   Vol. 2: 7620
Tonga and Tin Can Mail Study Circle Award   Vol. 1: 18730
Tonkovic Prize; Pavol   Vol. 2: 10776
Tony Awards
  American Theatre Wing   Vol. 1: 4902
  League of American Theatres and Producers   Vol 1: 11810
Toonder Award; Marten   Vol. 2: 7762
Tooting Bec Cup   Vol. 2: 3822
Top 100 Companies Award   Vol. 2: 11110
Top Arcite   Vol. 1: 3982
Top Case of the Year   Vol. 1: 19504
Top Female Pilot   Vol. 1: 15388
Top Five Businessmen Award   Vol. 2: 11111
Top Honor Books, Chicago Book Clinic Annual Exhibit   Vol. 1: 7597
Top Job Award   Vol. 1: 8094
Top of the Table Award   Vol. 1: 16812
Top Performance Awards   Vol. 1: 5413
Top-Producing Dogs   Vol. 1: 20594
Top Ranking Cotswold Breeder's Young Flock at the Illinois State Fair   Vol. 1: 1839
Top Ten Female Style Makers of the Year   Vol. 1: 13676
Top Ten Public Works Leaders of the Year   Vol. 1: 3883
Top-Winning Yorkshire Terrier in the United States Award   Vol. 1: 20595
Topelius-palkinto   Vol. 2: 4689
Topelius Prize   Vol. 2: 4689
Topps All-Star Scout Award   Vol. 1: 18734
Topps Major League Rookie All-Star Team   Vol. 1: 18735
Topps Minor League Player-of-the-Month   Vol. 1: 18736
Topps National Association All-Star Teams   Vol. 1: 18737
Topps Organization Trophy   Vol. 1: 18738
Topps Scout-of-the-Month Awards   Vol. 1: 18739
Toradash Prize; Daniel   Vol. 2: 11252
Toramanian Prize; Toros   Vol. 2: 114
Torch Award
  American Society for Training and Development   Vol. 1: 4305
  American Society for Training and Development - International Professional Practice Area   Vol 1: 4325
  Federation of Jewish Men's Club   Vol 1: 9138
Torch of Learning Award   Vol. 1: 2124
Torchbearer Award   Vol. 1: 2764
Torga - Cidade de Coimbra; Premio Literario Miguel   Vol. 2: 10224
Torgi Talking Book of the Year   Vol. 1: 7063
Toribio Medina Awards; Jose   Vol. 1: 17193
Torico Trophy   Vol. 2: 11234
Torino Award   Vol. 1: 3534
Tornov-Loeffler; Prix Ch. M.   Vol. 2: 5368
Tornu Prize; Enrique   Vol. 2: 100
Toro Industry Advancement Award   Vol. 1: 11780
Torok Memorial Medal; Gabor   Vol. 2: 7376
Toronto Arts Awards   Vol. 1: 5329
Toronto-City Award for Best Canadian Feature Film   Vol. 1: 18747
Toronto City Award for Excellence in Canadian Production   Vol. 1: 18747
Toronto Historical Board Award of Merit   Vol. 1: 18742
Toronto Press Club National Newspaper Awards   Vol. 1: 6851
Torrens Award; Richard R.   Vol. 1: 4504
Torreon de Igueldo   Vol. 2: 11283

Torres Civic Medal; Camilio Vol. 2: 1664
Torres Umana Award; Calixto Vol. 2: 1692
Torroja Medal; Eduardo Vol. 2: 11265
Tory; Medaille Henry Marshall Vol. 1: 16966
Tory Medal; Henry Marshall Vol. 1: 16966
Toscanini; Concorso Internazionale di Direzione d'Orchestra Arturo Vol. 2: 8393
Toscanini International Competition for Conductors; Arturo Vol. 2: 8393
Toscano Medal; Salvador Vol. 2: 8952
Toscano; Medalla Ing. Salvador Vol. 2: 8952
Toscano Prize; Ing. Salvador Vol. 2: 9092
Toshiba/NSTA ExploraVision Awards Vol. 1: 14707
Toshiba Year of Invention Awards Vol. 2: 2675
Tosney AAUA Award for Excellence in the Practice of Higher Education Administration; Eileen M. Vol. 1: 1225
Totally Transparent Show Award Vol. 1: 11688
Toti Dal Monte International Singing Competition Vol. 2: 8222
Totius Prize for Theology and the Original Languages of the Bible Vol. 2: 11009
Touchdown Club Arch McDonald Achievement Award Vol. 1: 18761
Touchdown Club Hubert H. Humphrey Award Vol. 1: 18762
Touchdown Club Local Personality Makes Good Award Vol. 1: 18763
Touchdown Club Mr. Sam Award Vol. 1: 18764
Touchdown Club's Board of Governors Award Vol. 1: 18765
Touchstone Award; F. Morris Vol. 1: 19418
Touchstone Awards Vol. 1: 4138
Toulmin Medals Vol. 1: 17719
Tour Award; Sam Vol. 1: 6083
Tour de France Vol. 2: 6348
Tourism Research Prize and Medal of Merit Vol. 2: 1616
Tournament Royalty Point Winners - Top Ten Vol. 1: 11025
Tournemire Prize Vol. 2: 3450
Tourneur; Prix Victor
  Academie Royale de Belgique - Classe des Beaux-Arts Vol. 2: 970
  Academie Royale de Belgique - Classe des Lettres et des Sciences Morales et Politiques Vol 2: 999
Tournoi de Paris de Jeux d'Histoire Antico - medieval Vol. 2: 5322
Toussaint; Premio Manuel Vol. 2: 9058
Tovey Memorial Prize; Donald Vol. 2: 4583
Tower and Carillon Prize Vol. 2: 1347
Tower Trophy Vol. 1: 19354
Towers Flight Safety Award; Adm. John H. Vol. 1: 15787
Towley Award; Carl Vol. 1: 11617
Townes Award; Charles Hard Vol. 1: 15759
Towngate Theatre Playwriting Contest Vol. 1: 15579
Townsend Award; E. Vol. 2: 2453
Townsend Award; Oliver Vol. 1: 19075
Townsend Social Issues Award; Robert Vol. 1: 6002
Townshend Award; B. W. O. Vol. 2: 3913
Townsville Foundation for Australian Literary Studies Award Vol. 2: 407
Towson State University Prize for Literature Vol. 1: 18776
Toxicology Education Award Vol. 1: 18077
Toy and Game Inventors of America Vol. 1: 11423
Toy; Fondation du Docteur Jean Vol. 2: 5545

Toynbee Memorial Lectureship; Joseph Vol. 2: 4267
TQM-Rehabilitation Award Vol. 1: 3947
Trabajador del Ano en Salud Vol. 1: 19447
Tracey Memorial Award; Anna Vol. 1: 16197
Trachoma Gold Medal Vol. 2: 6036
Track & Field News Award Vol. 1: 19960
Tracks Award Vol. 1: 7229
Tracy Memorial Young Writers Award; FAW Kate Vol. 2: 395
Trade Union's Art and Cultural Prize Vol. 2: 7442
Traditional Irish Singing and Dancing Society Awards Vol. 2: 7850
Trail - Crisp Award Vol. 2: 3590
Trailblazer Award Vol. 1: 11003
Trailblazer in Philanthropy Award Vol. 1: 16139
Train Humor Prize; John Vol. 1: 15970
Trainer of the Year
  American Society for Training and Development - Multicultural Network Vol. 1: 4336
  International Veteran Boxers Association Vol 1: 11390
  Walking Horse Trainers Association Vol 1: 20087
Trainer of the Year Award
  American Society for Training and Development - Mind/Brain Network Vol. 1: 4330
  American Society for Training and Development - Technical and Skills Training Professional Practice Area Vol 1: 4346
  National Environmental Training Association Vol 1: 13919
Training Award Vol. 2: 10447
Training Programs in Cystic Fibrosis Vol. 1: 8492
Trakl Preis fur Lyrik; Georg Vol. 2: 724
Trakl Prize for Poetry; Georg Vol. 2: 724
Trampoline and Tumbling National Leadership Award Vol. 1: 456
Trans-Am Tour Vol. 1: 18416
Trans-American Sedan Championship Vol. 1: 18416
Trans Atlantic Reciprocal Award Vol. 1: 15158
Translation Awards Vol. 2: 12003
Translation Center Awards Vol. 1: 8006
Translation Prize Vol. 2: 9936
Transport Engineering Medal Vol. 2: 490
Transport Journalist of the Year Vol. 2: 2587
Transport, Man and Town Vol. 2: 6151
Transport Photographer of the Year Vol. 2: 2588
Transportation Achievement Award Vol. 1: 10462
Transportation Administrator of the Year Vol. 1: 12886
Transportation Energy & Environmental Award in Memory of Frederick A. Wagner Vol. 1: 10463
Transportation Man of the Year Vol. 1: 8585
Transportation Person of the Year Vol. 1: 14923
Transportation Research Board Distinguished Service Award Vol. 1: 18779
Transtel-Jury Prize Vol. 2: 7074
Trapper/Conservationist Award Vol. 1: 14931
Trapper of the Year Vol. 1: 14932
Trask Award; Betty Vol. 2: 4393
Trautman Minor League Player-of-the-Year; Topps - George M. Vol. 1: 18740
Travel Agent of the Year Award Vol. 1: 4809
Travel and Study Abroad Vol. 2: 2884
Travel Award Vol. 2: 3655
Travel Awards Vol. 2: 2847
Travel Fund Vol. 2: 2178

Travel Grants and Best Student Paper Award Vol. 1: 17536
Travel Hall of Fame Vol. 1: 4810
Travel Holiday Fine Dining Awards Vol. 1: 18795
Travel Holiday Good Value Dining Awards Vol. 1: 18795
Travel Industry Awards for Excellence Vol. 1: 18799
Travel Industry Hall of Leaders Vol. 1: 18800
Travel Journalism Award Vol. 1: 9835
Travel Prize Vol. 2: 12086
Travel Research Contest Vol. 1: 18788
Traveling Fellowship Award Vol. 1: 1385
Traveling Fellowship Award in Movement Disorders Vol. 1: 624
Traveling Fellowships in Architectural Design and Technology Vol. 1: 14218
Traveling Show Appreciation Award Vol. 1: 5065
Travelling Fellowship and Research Grants Vol. 2: 10576
Travelling Fellowships Vol. 2: 10601
Travelling Scholarships Vol. 2: 4394
Travers; Prix Maurice Vol. 2: 5783
Tree of Life Award Vol. 1: 11559
Trees and People Award Vol. 1: 6890
Trees for Tomorrow Award Vol. 1: 18803
Tregre Award; Louis S. Vol. 1: 13698
Treibs Award; Alfred E. Vol. 1: 9543
Trent - Crede Medal Vol. 1: 103
Trento Filmfestival Internazionale Montagna Esplorazione Vol. 2: 8460
Trento International Film Festival of Mountain and Exploration Vol. 2: 8460
Tresley Research Award; Ira Vol. 1: 574
Tressler - VNR/AVI Teacher Award; NACTA Vol. 1: 13013
Trevethan Award; P. J. Vol. 1: 9667
Treviso Lyric Prize Vol. 2: 8223
Trevithick Premium Vol. 2: 3261
Trevor Award Vol. 1: 18840
Tri-Color Trophy Vol. 1: 2266
Triad Vol. 1: 15731
Trial Lawyer of the Year Award Vol. 1: 18805
Trianti Grand Prix; Alexandra Vol. 2: 7186
Triathletes of the Year Vol. 1: 18811
Triathlon Federation/USA Appreciation Award Vol. 1: 18812
Tribute of the Film Society of Lincoln Center Vol. 1: 9194
TRIC Annual Celebrity Awards Vol. 2: 4508
TRIC/Electrical Retailing Advertising Awards Vol. 2: 4509
Trico Goaltender Award Vol. 1: 14182
Triennale-India Award of Lalit Kala Akademi Vol. 2: 7535
Triennale Internazionale le Degli Strumenti ad Arco Vol. 2: 8321
Triennial Challenge Cup Vol. 2: 1486
Triennial Coif Book Award Vol. 1: 15792
Triennial Composition Competition Vol. 1: 8589
Triennial International Carillon Competition - Queen Fabiola Vol. 2: 1348
Triennial Prize Vol. 1: 17661
Triennial Prize of Bibliography Vol. 2: 6970
Trieschman Award; Albert E. Vol. 1: 957
Trigon Packaging Achievement Award; Chemical Cleaning/ Vol. 2: 9713
Trillium Book Award Vol. 1: 15686
Trimble Memorial Award; Robert E. Vol. 1: 9902
Trimmer Merit Shop Teaching Award of Excellence; John Vol. 1: 8193
Trinity Cross of the Order of the Trinity Vol. 2: 12036

Trio basso International Competition for Composers   Vol. 2: 7011
Trio basso Internationaler Kompositions-Wettbewerb   Vol. 2: 7011
Triossi; Fondation Marie Guido   Vol. 2: 5625
Triple Crown Champion
  Churchill Downs   Vol. 1: 7680
  New York Racing Association   Vol 1: 15267
Triple Crown Trophy   Vol. 1: 18815
Triple Rose Prize
  Bibiana, International House of Art for Children   Vol. 2: 10762
  Friends of Children's Books   Vol 2: 10767
Troland Research Award   Vol. 1: 12691
Troll-Preis; Thaddaus-   Vol. 2: 6754
Trollope Medal; D. H.   Vol. 2: 491
Trondheim City Council Prize   Vol. 2: 9949
Trondheim Kommunes Pris   Vol. 2: 9949
Trophee du Fairplay FIM   Vol. 2: 11809
Trophee Environnement   Vol. 1: 7495
Trophee International   Vol. 2: 11805
Trophee International de la Reliure D'Art   Vol. 2: 4892
Trophee International du Fair Play Pierre de Coubertin   Vol. 2: 5989
Trophee Poirier   Vol. 2: 5260
Trophees de l'Initiative   Vol. 2: 5104
Trophees Desjardins   Vol. 1: 7496
Trophy   Vol. 1: 18727
Trotter Award; Mildred   Vol. 1: 1122
Trotting Triple Crown   Vol. 1: 19678
Troubadour de la SABAM   Vol. 2: 1071
Trout Conservationist of the Year   Vol. 1: 18819
Trubert; Prix Maurice   Vol. 2: 5896
Truck Puller of the Year   Vol. 1: 14900
Truck Safety Contest   Vol. 1: 4931
Trudeau Award   Vol. 1: 2972
Truman Award; Harry S.   Vol. 1: 14097
Truman Book Award; Harry S   Vol. 1: 18827
Truman Good Neighbor Award; Harry S.   Vol. 1: 18824
Truman Memorial Trophy; Jim   Vol. 1: 7516
Truman Prize; S. J. Wallace   Vol. 1: 12634
Truman Public Service Award; Harry S.   Vol. 1: 7729
Truman Silver Veteran's Medal   Vol. 1: 18825
Trump; Mary and Fred   Vol. 1: 15983
Trumpeter Award   Vol. 1: 13663
Trumpler Award; Robert J.   Vol. 1: 6098
Truog Soil Science Award; Emil   Vol. 1: 18137
Truran, Jr., Medical Materiel and Logistics Management Award; Paul F.   Vol. 1: 5897
Trusler Prize   Vol. 2: 4095
Trustee Award   Vol. 1: 18617
Trustee Awards   Vol. 1: 12660
Trustee Citations   Vol. 1: 2840
Trustee of the Year
  United Methodist Association of Health and Welfare Ministries   Vol. 1: 18936
  United Methodist Church, Board of Global Ministries - Health and Welfare Ministries Division   Vol 1: 18944
Trustee of the Year Award
  American Association of Homes for the Aging   Vol. 1: 1014
  New Jersey Library Association   Vol 1: 15184
Trustees Award
  Academy of Medical Films   Vol. 1: 55
  American Hospital Association   Vol 1: 2375
Trustees' Award
  National Kidney Foundation   Vol. 1: 14276
  Puppeteers of America   Vol 1: 16593
Trustees Trophy   Vol. 1: 8114
TryWorks Award   Vol. 1: 18895

TSA Recognition Awards   Vol. 1: 18605
TSA Technology Honor Society   Vol. 1: 18606
TSB Award   Vol. 2: 4430
Tschumi Prize; Jean   Vol. 2: 6062
TSL Trophy   Vol. 2: 2539
TSS Scholar Award   Vol. 1: 16984
Tsutsui Distinguished Graduate Research Award in Science; Minoru and Ethel   Vol. 1: 15219
TTRA Achievement Award   Vol. 1: 18791
TTRA Chapter of the Year Awards   Vol. 1: 18792
TTRA Travel Research Award   Vol. 1: 18793
Tubb Humanitarian Award; Ernest   Vol. 1: 16820
Tubiana Award   Vol. 2: 2418
TUBITAK Husamettin Tugac Award   Vol. 2: 12068
TUBITAK Husamettin Tugac Odulu   Vol. 2: 12068
Tucan Award; Fran   Vol. 2: 1814
Tucano de Ouro   Vol. 2: 1482
Tucker Architectural Awards Competition   Vol. 1: 6614
Tucker Award; Gabriel F.   Vol. 1: 2784
Tucker Award; IBC John   Vol. 2: 3384
Tucker Award; Richard   Vol. 1: 18832
Tucker Award; Rosina   Vol. 1: 16676
Tucker Distinguished Service Award; Sara   Vol. 1: 18833
Tucker Medal; Bernard   Vol. 2: 2552
Tudor Medal; Ralph A.   Vol. 1: 17720
Tully Medal   Vol. 2: 2917
Tully Memorial Grant; Stephen R.   Vol. 1: 16684
Tulsa Library Trust Award for Young Readers' Literature   Vol. 1: 18836
Tunbridge Wells International Young Concert Artist Competition   Vol. 2: 4557
Tunner Aircrew Award; Lt. General William H.   Vol. 1: 259
Tuntland Memorial Award; Paul E.   Vol. 1: 17370
Tupolev Diploma; Andrei   Vol. 2: 5167
Tupolev Medal; Andrei   Vol. 2: 5168
Turcotte Memorial Award; Robert   Vol. 1: 9790
Turin International Festival of Young Cinema   Vol. 2: 8462
Turing Award; A. M.   Vol. 1: 5472
Turing Test Award   Vol. 1: 6683
Turkish Language Prize   Vol. 2: 12080
Turkish Radio and Television Culture, Art and Science Prizes   Vol. 2: 12084
Turnbull Award; John   Vol. 1: 7151
Turnbull Lecture Award; W. Rupert   Vol. 1: 6768
Turnbull Trophy; Jack   Vol. 1: 19419
Turner Award; Alfred H.   Vol. 2: 2074
Turner Award for Outstanding Service to NASPA; Fred   Vol. 1: 13334
Turner Award; Frederick Jackson   Vol. 1: 15825
Turner Award; Peter   Vol. 2: 2760
Turner Award; Wava   Vol. 1: 18579
Turner Lecture   Vol. 2: 9746
Turner Lecture; Francis C.   Vol. 1: 4505
Turner Medal; Henry C.   Vol. 1: 1786
Turner Prize   Vol. 2: 3764
Turner Prize; Dr. Lynn W.   Vol. 1: 16096
Turner Prize in Ethnographic Writing; Victor   Vol. 1: 17493
Turner - Scholefield Award   Vol. 2: 4437
Turner Tomorrow Award   Vol. 1: 18838
Turner Trophy; Joe   Vol. 2: 2062
Turnquist Trophy   Vol. 1: 7810
Tutin Award; Dorothy   Vol. 2: 3699

Tutorial Citation Award   Vol. 1: 4224
Tutt Award; Wm. Thayer   Vol. 1: 19922
Tuttle Award; Arnold D.   Vol. 1: 176
TV Channel Canalt Prize   Vol. 2: 6024
TV Hall of Fame   Vol. 1: 87
TV Week Logie Awards   Vol. 2: 679
Twain Award; Mark
  International Platform Association   Vol. 1: 11163
  Missouri Association of School Librarians   Vol 1: 12368
TWAS Award in Basic Medical Sciences   Vol. 2: 8450
TWAS Award in Biology   Vol. 2: 8451
TWAS Award in Chemistry   Vol. 2: 8452
TWAS Award in Mathematics   Vol. 2: 8453
TWAS Award in Physics   Vol. 2: 8454
TWAS History of Science Prize   Vol. 2: 8455
Tweddle Medal   Vol. 2: 4458
Tweed Award; Harrison   Vol. 1: 1313
Twelfth International Veterinary Congress Prize   Vol. 1: 4989
Twenhofel Medal   Vol. 1: 17598
Twenty-Five Year Club Member Certificate   Vol. 1: 3263
Twenty-Five Year Membership Medals   Vol. 1: 3264
Twenty-four Dollar Award   Vol. 1: 12511
Twining Trophy; General   Vol. 1: 14645
TWNSO Award in Agriculture   Vol. 2: 8457
TWNSO Award in Technology   Vol. 2: 8458
Two-Handed Transatlantic Race   Vol. 1: 18331
Two-Sisters Humanitarian Award   Vol. 1: 146
Two Wheel Drive Puller of the Year   Vol. 1: 14910
Two-Year College Biology Teaching Award   Vol. 1: 12959
Tyler Award; Dr. Ralph W.   Vol. 1: 8271
Tyler Award; Leona   Vol. 1: 3709
Tyler Ecology Award   Vol. 1: 19869
Tyler, Jr. Miniature Award; John A.   Vol. 1: 1401
Tyler Prize for Environmental Achievement   Vol. 1: 19869
Tylman Research Grant Program; Stanley D.   Vol. 1: 585
Tylman Student Essay Award; Stanley D.   Vol. 1: 585
Tyndall Award; John   Vol. 1: 15760
Tyndall Medal   Vol. 2: 3055
Tyneside Trophy   Vol. 2: 2262
Typographic Excellence and Electronic Composition Competition   Vol. 1: 13636
Typographic Excellence Award   Vol. 1: 18847
Tyrrell Historical Medal; J. B.   Vol. 1: 16967
Tyson Trophy; James Guy "Pete"   Vol. 1: 16214
Tytgat Prize; Alexandre and Gaston   Vol. 2: 1360
Tzedakah Award   Vol. 1: 18924
Tzvi & Mara Propes Prize; Aharon   Vol. 2: 7899
U-20 World Youth Championship for the FIFA/Coca-Cola Cup   Vol. 2: 11717
Uballes Prize; Eufemio   Vol. 2: 101
UBC Medal for Popular Biography   Vol. 1: 19738
Ucross Foundation Artists-in-Residence Program   Vol. 1: 18849
UCTF Awards   Vol. 2: 5269
L'udovit Fulla Prize   Vol. 2: 10763
Ueberroth - U.S. Water Polo Award; Peter V.   Vol. 1: 19684
Ugly Stick   Vol. 1: 18851
UHVA Awards   Vol. 1: 18917
UICC Award   Vol. 2: 11862

UJA - Federation Distinguished Communal Service Award   Vol. 1: 18925
UK-Canada Rutherford Lecture   Vol. 1: 16968
UK Computer Press Awards   Vol. 2: 3025
UK Cup   Vol. 2: 3680
UK Technology Press Awards   Vol. 2: 3025
ULI Award for Excellence   Vol. 1: 19904
Ulianova Prize   Vol. 2: 10480
Ulmann Peace Prize; Liv   Vol. 1: 7606
Ulrich's Serials Librarianship Award; Bowker/   Vol. 1: 2848
Ulster Award   Vol. 2: 717
Ultra-Distance Athlete-of-the-Year   Vol. 1: 19961
Uluslararasi Istanbul Sinema Gunleri   Vol. 2: 12060
Uluslarasi Simavi Karikatur Yarismasi   Vol. 2: 12053
UMEA-Premio (Esperanto)   Vol. 2: 8778
UMEA-Shinoda-Premio   Vol. 2: 8778
Umezawa Prize for Chemotherapy; Hamao   Vol. 2: 9898
Umgeni Award   Vol. 2: 11122
UMI/Data Courier Award   Vol. 1: 15675
UMI/Data Courier Excellence in Writing Award UMI/Data Courier   Vol. 1: 18858
UMI/Data Courier   Vol 1: 18859
UMI/Data Courier Library Technology Award   Vol. 1: 18859
UMI Excellence in Writing Award   Vol. 1: 18858
UMI Library Technology Award   Vol. 1: 18859
Umpire Award   Vol. 1: 19917
Umweltpreis der Landeshauptstadt Stuttgart   Vol. 2: 7140
UN/INEOA Law Enforcement Medal   Vol. 1: 11119
UNA Awards   Vol. 2: 11439
UNA Study Circles Challenge Trophys   Vol. 2: 11440
Unda Dove   Vol. 2: 1376
Undergraduate Award for Excellence in Chemistry   Vol. 1: 11439
Undergraduate Awards   Vol. 1: 13737
Undergraduate Student Paper Competition   Vol. 1: 360
Underwater Athletes of the Year   Vol. 1: 18868
UNEP Sasakawa Environment Prize   Vol. 2: 8812
UNESCO Award for Distinguished Services to Physical Education and Sport; Official   Vol. 2: 6419
UNESCO Crafts Prize   Vol. 2: 6420
UNESCO Fellowship Programme; IBRO/   Vol. 2: 5980
UNESCO Human Rights Prize   Vol. 2: 6034
UNESCO - International Music Council Music Prize   Vol. 2: 6421
UNESCO Literacy Prizes   Vol. 2: 6422
UNESCO Prize for Architecture   Vol. 2: 6423
UNESCO Prize for Landscape Architecture   Vol. 2: 6424
UNESCO Prize for Peace Education   Vol. 2: 6425
UNESCO Prize for Rural Communication; IPDC -   Vol. 2: 6416
UNESCO Prize for the Teaching of Human Rights   Vol. 2: 6426
UNESCO Science Prize   Vol. 2: 6427
Unger Award for Conducting; Heinz   Vol. 1: 15706
UNICA Awards   Vol. 2: 9537
UNICA - MAFSZ Nemzetek dija   Vol. 2: 7317
UNICA Medal   Vol. 2: 11623
UNICA-medaljen   Vol. 2: 11623

UNICA Prize for the Best National Collection   Vol. 2: 7317
UNICEF Award for Distinguished Service   Vol. 1: 18952
UNICEF Award for Films   Vol. 1: 18953
UNICEF Prize   Vol. 2: 8602
UNICEF; Prize of   Vol. 2: 6564
UNIMA Citation for Excellence in the Art of Puppetry   Vol. 1: 18875
UNIMA-USA Scholarships   Vol. 1: 18876
Union Carbide Award for Chemical Education   Vol. 1: 7566
Union League Civic and Arts Foundation Poetry Prize   Vol. 1: 16269
Union Medal   Vol. 2: 2466
Union of Architects of Romania Prize   Vol. 2: 10408
Union of Architects of the SRR Prize   Vol. 2: 10408
Union of Czech Architects - Annual Prize   Vol. 2: 1884
Union of International Fairs Awards   Vol. 2: 6457
Union of Soviet Architects Prizes   Vol. 2: 10476
Union of the Year Award   Vol. 1: 6410
Union of Writers and Artists of Albania Competitions   Vol. 2: 2
Union Prize for Publicistic (Publishers)   Vol. 2: 10481
Unique and Useful Consumer Plastics Product Award   Vol. 1: 17990
Unique and Useful Industrial Plastics Product Award   Vol. 1: 17991
Unit Citation for Gallantry   Vol. 2: 347
Unit Citations   Vol. 2: 347
United Methodist Association Award of Distinguished Service   Vol. 1: 18937
United National Medals   Vol. 1: 6694
United Nations Environment Program Awards - Global 500 Roll of Honour   Vol. 2: 8813
United Nations Medal   Vol. 1: 19193
United Nations Population Award   Vol. 1: 18957
United Nations Service Medal (Korea)   Vol. 1: 19194
United Press International College Broadcast Awards   Vol. 1: 18970
United Press International National Broadcast Awards   Vol. 1: 18971
United States Air Force Twelve Outstanding Airmen of the Year   Vol. 1: 260
U.S. Art Magazine Award   Vol. 1: 14447
U.S. Auto Club Champions   Vol. 1: 7517
U.S. Bicycling Hall of Fame   Vol. 1: 19043
United States Boxing Hall of Fame   Vol. 1: 18995
U.S. Catholic Award   Vol. 1: 19052
U.S. Chamber Salutes   Vol. 1: 19056
United States Champion Cheese Maker   Vol. 1: 20342
U.S. Chess Championship   Vol. 1: 19058
U.S. College Player of the Year   Vol. 1: 9960
United States Executive Office of the President Awards   Vol. 1: 19338
United States Figure Skating Champions   Vol. 1: 19354
U.S. Fireball Championship   Vol. 1: 19426
United States Hang Gliding Association Commendation   Vol. 1: 19371
United States Hockey Hall of Fame   Vol. 1: 19394
U.S. Independence Cup   Vol. 1: 19537
U.S. Industrial Film & Video Festival   Vol. 1: 19352
U.S. Industrial Film and Video Festival   Vol. 1: 19352

U.S. International Film and Video Festival   Vol. 1: 19352
U.S. Junior Sailing Championships   Vol. 1: 19541
U.S. Junior Women's Sailing Championship - Nancy Leiter Clagett Trophy   Vol. 1: 19542
United States Lawn Bowls Championships   Vol. 1: 2787
U.S. Match Racing Championship - Prince of Wales Bowl   Vol. 1: 19538
U.S. Medal of Remembrance   Vol. 1: 19397
U.S. Men's Sailing Championship - Clifford D. Mallory Cup   Vol. 1: 19539
U.S. National Hot Air Balloon Champion   Vol. 1: 6244
United States National Roller Skating Championships   Vol. 1: 18998
United States of America Counties Award   Vol. 1: 8435
U.S. Olympic Hall of Fame   Vol. 1: 19493
U.S. Open Flying Disc Championships   Vol. 1: 20253
U.S. Open Frisbee Disc Championships   Vol. 1: 20253
United States Open Table Tennis Championships   Vol. 1: 19641
United States Open Tennis Championships   Vol. 1: 19662
U.S. Outdoor Travel Film Festival   Vol. 1: 12252
United States Presidential Scholars Program   Vol. 1: 19226
U.S. SAILING One-Design Awards   Vol. 1: 19540
U.S. SAILING/Rolex Junior Championships   Vol. 1: 19541
U.S. SAILING/Rolex Junior Women's Championship - Nancy Leiter Clagett Trophy   Vol. 1: 19542
United States Senate Productivity Award   Vol. 1: 11609
U.S. Singlehanded Sailing Championship - George D. O'Day Trophy   Vol. 1: 19543
United States Skill Olympics   Vol. 1: 20077
United States Steel Foundation Award in Molecular Biology   Vol. 1: 12684
United States Swimming Award   Vol. 1: 19631
United States Swimming Life Members   Vol. 1: 19632
U.S. Team Race Championship - George R. Hinman Trophy   Vol. 1: 19544
U.S. Television & Radio Commercials Festival   Vol. 1: 19351
United States Water Polo Award   Vol. 1: 19685
U.S. Women's Open Championships   Vol. 1: 19545
U.S. Women's Sailing Championship - Mrs. Charles Francis Adams Trophy   Vol. 1: 19546
U.S. Youth Sailing Championship   Vol. 1: 19532
United States Youth Soccer Association Coach of the Year for Boys and Girls   Vol. 1: 19696
United States Youth Soccer Association Youth Referee of the Year   Vol. 1: 19697
Unity Awards in Media   Vol. 1: 11892
University Alumni Service Medal   Vol. 1: 19772
University Biological Prize Award   Vol. 2: 12203
University Commemorative Medal   Vol. 2: 7462
University Cup   Vol. 1: 6990
University Founders Award   Vol. 1: 9368

University Medal
  Case Western Reserve University   Vol. 1: 7328
  New York University   Vol 1: 15305
University Medal for Excellence   Vol. 1: 7987
University of Alberta National Award   Vol. 1: 6255
University of Berne Prizes   Vol. 2: 11965
University of British Columbia Medal for Canadian Biography   Vol. 1: 19738
University of Cambridge Arthur Shercliff Prize   Vol. 2: 3352
University of Chicago Awards for Distinguished Performance at Argonne National Laboratory   Vol. 1: 19761
University of Chicago Medal   Vol. 1: 19762
University of Cincinnati Award   Vol. 1: 3619
University of Louisville Grawemeyer Award for Ideas Improving World Order   Vol. 1: 19812
University of Louisville Grawemeyer Award for Music Composition   Vol. 1: 19818
University of Louisville Grawemeyer Award in Education   Vol. 1: 19816
University of Manchester Prize   Vol. 2: 3353
University of Maryland International Music Competitions   Vol. 1: 19822
University of Maryland International Piano Festival and William Kapell Piano Competition   Vol. 1: 19822
University of Michigan Press Book Award   Vol. 1: 19834
University of Missouri Awards in Lifestyle Journalism; JCPenney -   Vol. 1: 19843
University of Missouri Television Awards for Community Leadership   Vol. 1: 19845
University of Missouri Television Awards for Community Leadership; JC Penney -   Vol. 1: 19845
University of North Texas Cup   Vol. 1: 5284
University of Queensland Press Award   Vol. 2: 193
University of Southern Mississippi Medallion   Vol. 1: 19873
University of Tasmania - Launceston Award   Vol. 2: 492
University Press Award   Vol. 1: 15596
University Service Awards   Vol. 1: 19750
Unlimited Modified Puller of the Year   Vol. 1: 14911
Unlimited Potential's Outstanding Christian Leadership Award   Vol. 1: 13587
Uno Lamm HVDC Award   Vol. 1: 10319
Unsung Hero Award   Vol. 1: 6015
Unsung Heroine Award   Vol. 1: 20005
Unsung Player of the Year   Vol. 1: 10554
Unsung Unitarian Universalist Award   Vol. 1: 18896
UOP Technology Award   Vol. 1: 10496
Up and Coming Award
  Women Business Owners of New York   Vol. 1: 20372
  Women's Sports Foundation   Vol 1: 20434
UPE Scholarship Awards   Vol. 1: 19900
UPI "One Up" College Broadcast Awards   Vol. 1: 18970
Upjohn Achievement Award   Vol. 1: 916
Upjohn Minority Summer Fellowship Awards   Vol. 1: 1693
Upjohn Physiology Award   Vol. 1: 1924
Upjohn Quality of Life Award; ONS/   Vol. 1: 15667
Upper Austria Culture Prize for Film   Vol. 2: 901
Upper Austria Culture Prize for Fine Arts   Vol. 2: 902

Upper Austria Culture Prize for Literature   Vol. 2: 903
Upper Austria Culture Prize for Music   Vol. 2: 904
Upper Austria Culture Prize for Science   Vol. 2: 905
Upper Austria Prize for Architecture   Vol. 2: 906
Uppsala Filmkaja   Vol. 2: 11654
UPS Ltd. Prize   Vol. 2: 3098
Upward Mobility Award   Vol. 1: 18104
URAM Award for Excellence in Creative Endeavors for Research and Scholarship   Vol. 1: 11270
URAM Award for Excellence in Creative Scholarly Writing   Vol. 1: 11271
Urban Beautification Award   Vol. 1: 2366
Urban Council Awards for Creative Writing in Chinese   Vol. 2: 7279
Urban Council Short Film Awards   Vol. 2: 7265
Urban County Engineer of the Year   Vol. 1: 13053
Urban Design Awards   Vol. 1: 7747
Urban Design Awards for Excellence   Vol. 1: 2534
Urban Forestry Awards   Vol. 1: 2103
Urban Politics and Policy Career Achievement Award   Vol. 1: 3593
Urban Traffic Engineering Achievement Awards   Vol. 1: 10464
Urbanek Award; Janos   Vol. 2: 7340
Urbanek Janos Dijasok   Vol. 2: 7340
Urdang Medal; George   Vol. 1: 2688
Ure Award for Sportsmanship; Captain James S.   Vol. 1: 15001
Uren Award; Lester C.   Vol. 1: 17975
Urethane Medal   Vol. 2: 3153
Urey Prize; Harold C.   Vol. 1: 1277
Uriarte Y Pineiro Prize; Leopoldo   Vol. 2: 102
US-Asia Institute Achievement Awards   Vol. 1: 19907
US/ICOMOS Fellows   Vol. 1: 19060
USA-CA Award   Vol. 1: 8435
USA International Ballet Competition, Jackson   Vol. 1: 19925
USA International Harp Competition   Vol. 1: 19927
USA Petites   Vol. 1: 16742
USAC Special Recognition Awards   Vol. 1: 19031
USAF Personnel Manager of the Year (Citation of Honor)   Vol. 1: 261
USATF Heptathlon Award   Vol. 1: 19962
USDA/PER "Unsung Hero" Award   Vol. 1: 15837
USDF/All-Breeds Awards   Vol. 1: 16596
User Feedback Award   Vol. 1: 17060
USF Grant Awards   Vol. 1: 18973
USFCA All-America Certificates (Men)   Vol. 1: 19347
USFCA All-America Certificates (Women)   Vol. 1: 19348
USFCA Honorable Mention (Men)   Vol. 1: 19349
USFCC/J. Roger Porter Award   Vol. 1: 4211
USFL Awards   Vol. 1: 18387
USGA Championships   Vol. 1: 19362
USHA National Championships   Vol. 1: 19365
Usher Prize; Abbott Payson   Vol. 1: 17621
USHWA Trophy   Vol. 1: 19390
USHWAn-of-the-Year   Vol. 1: 19391
USIA Fellowships   Vol. 1: 4017
USIA Fellowships, AIAR, Jerusalem   Vol. 1: 4018
USIA/NMERTP Post-doctoral Fellowships   Vol. 1: 4019

USIA/NMERTP Pre-doctoral Fellowships   Vol. 1: 4020
USILA Awards   Vol. 1: 19420
USILA Trophy   Vol. 1: 19421
USITT Award   Vol. 1: 19401
USMS Coach of the Year Award   Vol. 1: 19442
USO Annual Award   Vol. 1: 18982
USO Board of Governors Distinguished Service Award   Vol. 1: 18983
USO Christmas Award   Vol. 1: 18984
USO International Service Award   Vol. 1: 18985
USO Woman of the Year   Vol. 1: 19967
USOC Sports Equipment Student Design Contest   Vol. 1: 19494
USOP Essay Contest   Vol. 1: 8406
USSA Outstanding Alpine Masters Award   Vol. 1: 19591
USSEA Honorary Member   Vol. 1: 19617
USSR State Prize for Architecture   Vol. 2: 10486
USSWA Outstanding Competitor Award   Vol. 1: 15445
USTA Community Service Award   Vol. 1: 19663
USTA Girls' 18 National Championship Sportsmanship Award   Vol. 1: 19664
USTA Girls' Sportsmanship Award   Vol. 1: 19665
USTA Junior and Boys' Sportsmanship Award   Vol. 1: 19666
USTA National Junior Tennis League Chapter of the Year Award   Vol. 1: 19667
USTA/USPTA Public Service Award   Vol. 1: 19668
USTA Volunteer Service Award   Vol. 1: 19669
USTWA Collegiate Tennis Awards   Vol. 1: 10555
Usui Foundation for Hematological Research   Vol. 2: 8656
Usui Ketsuekigaku Kenkyu-Kikin   Vol. 2: 8656
USWCA Senior Ladies Trophy   Vol. 1: 19687
USX Foundation Award in Molecular Biology   Vol. 1: 12684
Utah Music Teachers Association Sixth Prize   Vol. 1: 6217
Utah Original Writing Competition   Vol. 1: 19969
Utility Design Awards   Vol. 1: 3858
Utilization Award   Vol. 1: 12876
Utley Memorial Award; T. E.   Vol. 2: 4591
Utmarkt Svensk Form   Vol. 2: 11651
Uttam Jeevan Raksha Padak   Vol. 2: 7562
V/STOL (Fixed-Wing) Squadron of the Year   Vol. 1: 12078
VA Wapensky Award   Vol. 1: 6498
Vacarezza Prize; Roberto A.   Vol. 2: 103
Vaccarezza; Premio Consagracion Rodolfo A.   Vol. 2: 59
Vachon Award; Romeo   Vol. 1: 6769
Vahue Memorial Award; L. Ray   Vol. 1: 15858
Vaisala Award; Prof. Dr. Vilho   Vol. 2: 11979
Valabregue; Prix Antony   Vol. 2: 5816
Valdata Prize; Achille   Vol. 2: 8462
Valdes; Premio Miguel Aleman   Vol. 2: 8992
Valdez; Premio Jose Cayetano   Vol. 2: 9016
Valencia Film Festival, Golden Palm Award   Vol. 2: 11305
Valencia Prize for Hispanic Culture; Guillermo   Vol. 2: 1621
Valente Producers Award; Renee   Vol. 1: 15390
Valladolid International Film Festival   Vol. 2: 11392
Vallance Award; William Roy   Vol. 1: 10507
Vallarta Prize   Vol. 2: 8289

Valley Forge Certificate Vol. 1: 14096
Valley Forge Cross for Heroism Vol. 1: 14096
Valley of the Hearts Award Vol. 1: 15959
Vallois Prize Vol. 2: 4898
Valor Award Vol. 2: 11970
Valor Award - Coast Guard Vol. 1: 19210
Valor Awards Vol. 1: 19260
Valvoline Trophy Vol. 1: 12456
Valz; Fondations Lalande - Benjamin Vol. 2: 5681
Valz; Prix Benjamin Vol. 2: 5681
Van Alen Fellowship; William Vol. 1: 14216
van Ameringen Award in Psychiatric Rehabilitation; Arnold L. Vol. 1: 3654
Van Anda Award; Carr Vol. 1: 15592
Van Antwerpen Award for Service to the Institute; F. J. and Dorothy Vol. 1: 2604
Van Beneden; Prix Edouard Vol. 2: 1368
Van Beneden; Prix P. J. et Edouard Vol. 2: 1032
Van Bercken Award; Lode Vol. 1: 8639
van Buren Structural Engineering Award; Maurice P. Vol. 1: 1787
Van Cleef Memorial Medal Vol. 1: 2157
Van Collen Prize; Willink Vol. 2: 9545
Van Couvering Memorial Award; Martin C. Vol. 1: 2676
Van Dalsumprijs; Albert Vol. 2: 9649
van de Kritiek; Prijs Vol. 2: 9360
van de Woestijne Prize; Karel Vol. 2: 1277
Van Den Bosch Award Vol. 1: 5700
Van Den Heever Prize for Jurisprudence; Toon Vol. 2: 11010
Van Der Beeken; Prix Vol. 2: 1220
van der Gracht-Penning; Van Waterschoot Vol. 2: 9588
van der Gracht Plaque; Van Waterschoot Vol. 2: 9588
Van der Hoogt-prijs; Lucy B. and C. W. Vol. 2: 9631
van der Linde Memorial Award; W. J. Vol. 2: 10904
van der Mueren Prize; Floris Vol. 2: 1260
van der Pol Gold Medal; Balthasar Vol. 2: 1213
Van der Stel Foundation Medal; Simon Vol. 2: 11119
van der Viesprijs; H. G. Vol. 2: 9688
Van Doren Book Award; Irita Vol. 1: 1364
van Drimmelen Medal; Rev. Pieter Vol. 2: 11011
van Duyl-Schwartze Portrait Award; Therese Vol. 2: 9685
van Duyl-Schwartze Portretprijs; Therese Vol. 2: 9685
Van Dyck; Prijs Albert Vol. 2: 1317
Van Eck Medal; Hendrik Vol. 2: 11051
Van Eck Prijs; A. J. Vol. 2: 9591
Van Eck Prize; A. J. Vol. 2: 9591
Van Elven Fund Prize; Paul Tetar Vol. 2: 9546
Van Ertborn; Prix Baron Vol. 2: 1010
Van Ginderachter Prize; Jozef Vol. 2: 1278
Van Goidsenhoven; Prijs Franz Vol. 2: 1318
Van Grover - YN Exhibit Award; Melissa Vol. 1: 3265
Van Helmont; Prijs J. B. Vol. 2: 1319
van Hichtum Prize; Nienke Vol. 2: 9351
Van Hook Service Award; Martin Vol. 1: 3193
Van Hoosen Award; Bertha Vol. 1: 3054
Van Leersumprijs; Emmy Vol. 2: 9650
Van Leeuwenhoek Medal Vol. 2: 9605
van Looyprijs; Jacobus Vol. 2: 9449
Van Marum Medaille Vol. 2: 9610
Van Marum Medal Vol. 2: 9610
Van Meter Award Vol. 1: 4910

Van Meter/Rorer Pharmaceuticals Award Vol. 1: 4910
Van Niel Prize Vol. 2: 6066
Van Nostrand Memorial Award; John Vol. 1: 10556
Van Nostrand Reinhold Research Award Vol. 1: 8403
Van Orman Trophy Vol. 1: 11873
van Oyeprijs; Paul Vol. 2: 1261
Van Sant Memorial Award; Gene and Mary Vol. 1: 14189
Van Tienhoven Prize Vol. 2: 7128
Van Vliet Trophy; M. L. Vol. 1: 6991
Van Weelden Award Vol. 2: 9408
Van Winkle Award; Rip Vol. 1: 6504
van Wyk Louw Prize; N. P. Vol. 2: 11012
Van Zandt Citizenship Award; VFW James E. Vol. 1: 20017
Van Zanten Memorial Medal; Ann Vol. 1: 17743
Vance Award; James A. Vol. 1: 7178
Vance Award; John C. Vol. 1: 18783
Vancouver International Film Festival Vol. 1: 19975
Vancouver Professional Theatre Alliance Award Vol. 1: 19977
Vandenberg Award; Hoyt S. Vol. 1: 262
Vanderbilt Cup; Harold S. Vol. 1: 1828
Vanderlinden; Prix Georges Vol. 2: 1023
Vanderlinden Prize; H. L. Vol. 2: 1262
Vanderlinden Public Official Award; Spence Vol. 1: 3864
Vanderveer Trophy
  Pierce-Arrow Society Vol. 1: 16209
  Pierce-Arrow Society Vol 1: 16210
Vandiver Award; Willard T. (Billy) Vol. 1: 457
Vanguard Award Vol. 1: 20376
Vanguard Award - Distinguished Vanguard Awards for Leadership Vol. 1: 13513
Vanguard Award for Associates Vol. 1: 13514
Vanguard Award for Marketing Vol. 1: 13515
Vanguard Award for Programmers Vol. 1: 13516
Vanguard Award for Public Relations Vol. 1: 13517
Vanguard Award for Science & Technology Vol. 1: 13518
Vanguard Award for State/Regional Association Leadership Vol. 1: 13519
Vanguard Award for Young Leadership Vol. 1: 13520
Vanier Cup Vol. 1: 6992
Vanier Medal Vol. 1: 10431
Vann Best Typography and Make-up; Robert L. Vol. 1: 14397
Vaptsarov International Prize; N. Vol. 2: 1510
Vaquero; Premio Maestro Manuel Vol. 2: 9278
Vardon Trophy Vol. 1: 16482
Vardon Trophy; Harry Vol. 2: 3823
Vare Trophy Vol. 1: 11767
Varela; Premio Gerardo Vol. 2: 9129
Varga International Competition for Violin; Tibor Vol. 2: 11664
Varian Excellence in Radiation Therapy Nursing Award; ONS/ Vol. 1: 15668
Varian Fellowship; Russell and Sigurd Vol. 1: 4966
Varietal Awards Vol. 1: 2267
Varna International Ballet Competition Vol. 2: 1539
Varoujan Award; Daniel Vol. 1: 15131
Vars Award; Harry M. Vol. 1: 4229
Vary International Film Festival; Karlovy Vol. 1: 1891
Vasarhelyi Prize; Pal Vol. 2: 7349

Vasconcelos World Award of Education; Jose Vol. 2: 9308
Vasquez; Premio Nacional de Medicina, Dr. Luis Edmundo Vol. 2: 2025
Vaughn Award; Steck - Vol. 1: 18642
Vaughn Concerto Competition; Elizabeth Harper Vol. 1: 11702
Vaughn Prize Vol. 2: 8629
Vaughn - Ueda Prize Vol. 2: 8629
Vaughn - Ueda Sho Vol. 2: 8629
Vaxelaire; Prix Georges Vol. 2: 1307
Vaxelaire Prize; Georges Vol. 2: 1307
VCC Fuchs Opera Award Vol. 1: 20029
Veale Prize; Sir Alan Vol. 2: 3294
Veblen - Commons Award Vol. 1: 5522
Veblen Prize in Geometry; Oswald Vol. 1: 3010
Vecchi; Premi Anita Vol. 2: 8020
Vector Award Vol. 1: 9929
Vector Young Investigator Award Vol. 1: 9929
Veegens-Prijs; Dirk Jacob Vol. 2: 9394
Vegetable Publication Award Vol. 1: 4153
Veiga Prize; Pedro Vol. 2: 1439
Veillon European Essay Prize; Charles Vol. 2: 11967
Veillon; Prix Europeen de l'Essai Charles Vol. 2: 11967
Veitch Memorial Medal Vol. 2: 4058
Velika Castna Nagrada za Jugoslovanskega Umetnika Vol. 2: 10794
Velluz; Fondation Leon Vol. 2: 5619
Venables Award Vol. 2: 2316
Venezuelan Society of Civil Engineers Award Vol. 2: 12148
Venice International Film Festival Vol. 2: 8470
Ventris Memorial Award; Michael Vol. 2: 2093
Venus de Badalona Vol. 2: 11205
Venz Kinder Boeken Prijs Vol. 2: 9369
Venzie Award; E. F. Vol. 1: 6013
VER Poets Open Competition Vol. 2: 4593
Verband Ehrenring Vol. 2: 6528
Verbatim Award Vol. 2: 1944
Vercelli Medal Vol. 1: 13352
Verco Medal; Sir Joseph Vol. 2: 632
The Vercorin Manuscript Writing Award Vol. 2: 8472
Vercoullie Prize; Jozef Vol. 2: 1279
Verdaguer; Prix Alfred
  Institut de France Vol. 2: 5336
  Institut de France - Academie des Beaux Arts Vol 2: 5355
  Institut de France - Academie des Sciences Vol 2: 5683
  Institut de France - Academie Francaise Vol 2: 5809
Verdeyen Prize for Soil Mechanics Vol. 2: 1363
Verdi Medal of Achievement Vol. 1: 12245
Verdienstmedaille Vol. 2: 6624
Verdienstorden der Bundesrepublik Deutschland Vol. 2: 6739
Verdonk; Fund Professor Doctor G. Vol. 2: 1320
Verebely Award; Laslo Vol. 2: 7341
Verebely Laszlo Dijasok Vol. 2: 7341
Vergara y Vergara Prize; Jose Maria Vol. 2: 1665
Vergerio European Prize for Children's Literature; Pier Paolo Vol. 2: 8466
Verissimo Prize; Jose Vol. 2: 1445
Veritas Award Vol. 1: 747
Verlagspreis zur Forderung popularwissenschaftlicher Literatur fur das jungere Lesealter Vol. 2: 7152

Verlain; Prix Valentine Abraham   Vol. 2: 5926
Verlaine; Prix Paul   Vol. 2: 5908
Verlanger; Prix Julia   Vol. 2: 6463
Verleysen Prize; Dr. Karel   Vol. 2: 1321
Verlot; Prix de la Fondation Jean-Bernard   Vol. 2: 4949
Vermeulenprijs; Matthijs   Vol. 2: 9651
Vermilye Medal; William M.   Vol. 1: 9388
Vermont Playwrights Award   Vol. 1: 19973
Verner Awards; Elizabeth O'Neill   Vol. 1: 18173
Verner von Heidenstams Guldmedalj   Vol. 2: 11558
Vernon, Jr. Achievement Award; Weston   Vol. 1: 8867
Vernon Memorial Lecture Award; Dr. Robert O.   Vol. 1: 10906
Versatility Hall of Fame   Vol. 1: 1965
Versele; Prix Bernard   Vol. 2: 1219
Vertical Smile   Vol. 2: 11390
Verulam Medal   Vol. 2: 3111
Verulam Medal and Prize   Vol. 2: 3154
Very Special Arts Senior Citizens Playwrights Project   Vol. 1: 19996
Very Special Arts Young Playwrights Program   Vol. 1: 19997
Very Special Arts Young Soloist Award   Vol. 1: 19998
Vesaas Debutant Prize; Tarjei   Vol. 2: 9930
Vesper Cup   Vol. 1: 19521
Vesta Award
  American Meat Institute   Vol. 1: 3015
  Woman's Building   Vol 1: 20356
Vestermark Award; Seymour   Vol. 1: 3655
Veteran's Administration Employee of the Year Award   Vol. 1: 241
Veterans Award   Vol. 1: 458
Veteran's Community Service Award   Vol. 1: 20031
Veterans Employment Awards   Vol. 1: 19261
Veterinarian of the Year   Vol. 1: 9464
Vetlesen Prize   Vol. 1: 7988
VEWAA Service Award   Vol. 1: 14592
The Vexillon   Vol. 1: 10970
Vezina Trophy   Vol. 1: 14183
VFW Americanism Award   Vol. 1: 20009
VFW Armed Forces Award   Vol. 1: 20010
VFW Aviation and Space Award   Vol. 1: 20011
VFW Congressional Award   Vol. 1: 20012
VFW Dwight David Eisenhower Distinguished Service Award   Vol. 1: 20013
VFW Emergency Services Award   Vol. 1: 20014
VFW Hall of Fame Award   Vol. 1: 20015
VFW J. Edgar Hoover Award   Vol. 1: 20016
VFW James E. Van Zandt Citizenship Award   Vol. 1: 20017
VFW News Media Award   Vol. 1: 20018
VFW Outstanding Firefighter Award   Vol. 1: 20014
VFW Outstanding Post Service Officer Award   Vol. 1: 20019
VGP Award   Vol. 1: 2171
Viareggio - Versilia International Prize   Vol. 2: 8407
Viareggio Prize   Vol. 2: 8390
Vice Admiral "Jerry" L. and Medal   Vol. 1: 17930
Vice Presidents' Award   Vol. 1: 10399
Vice-President's Trophy   Vol. 1: 10580
Vicens para Novela Breve; Premio Josefina   Vol. 2: 9227
Vick Outstanding Province President Award; A. Frank   Vol. 1: 11080
Vickers Award   Vol. 2: 2119
Vickers Award; Sir Geoffrey   Vol. 1: 11273

Vickrey Award; James "Tick"   Vol. 1: 5673
Vicoy Reuter Fellowship; Willie   Vol. 2: 3851
Victor Memorial Prize; Mildred   Vol. 1: 14714
Victoria Cross
  British Government   Vol. 2: 2387
  Canada - The Chancellery   Vol 1: 6715
Victoria Cross for Australia   Vol. 2: 348
Victoria Medal   Vol. 2: 4017
Victoria Medal of Honour in Horticulture - V.M.H.   Vol. 2: 4059
Victoria Prize   Vol. 2: 7783
Victorin Memorial Award; James F.   Vol. 1: 8633
Victorin; Prix Marie-   Vol. 1: 16619
Victory Awards   Vol. 1: 14600
Victory of the Human Spirit   Vol. 1: 14600
Video Competition   Vol. 1: 8068
Video Festival on Environment and Agriculture   Vol. 2: 10236
Video Free Show   Vol. 2: 10236
Video Grand Prix   Vol. 2: 8780
Video Grand Prix Awards   Vol. 1: 6138
Video Opera Prize   Vol. 2: 844
Video Production Merit Award   Vol. 1: 1767
Video Review Shootoff   Vol. 1: 20023
Videodisc Awards   Vol. 1: 14708
Videotex Design Award   Vol. 1: 10527
Videotex Innovation Award   Vol. 1: 10529
Vidrio; Premio de Ciencas Morfologicas Dr. Enrique Acosta   Vol. 2: 9188
Vidyajothi   Vol. 2: 11436
Vidyanidhi   Vol. 2: 11437
Viehman, Jr. Scholarship; MPA Donald E. Sommer/A. J.   Vol. 1: 16418
Vieira da Silva de Investigacao; Premio Municipal Augusto   Vol. 2: 10266
Vielehr Award   Vol. 1: 5297
Viener Prize; Saul   Vol. 1: 2742
Vienna International Composition Contest   Vol. 2: 774
Vierjaarlijkse prijs voor muziekcompositie Camille Huysmans   Vol. 2: 1055
Vietheer Memorial Award; Erich   Vol. 2: 2943
Vietnam Medal   Vol. 2: 349
Vietnam Service Medal   Vol. 1: 19195
Vieux; Concours International d'Alto Maurice   Vol. 2: 6469
Vieux International Alto Competition; Maurice   Vol. 2: 6469
Viewer's Choice Award   Vol. 1: 12479
Viewers' Choice Awards; TNN   Vol. 1: 9735
Vigen-Prisen; Terje   Vol. 2: 9950
Vigen Prize; Terje   Vol. 2: 9950
Vigness Memorial Award; Dr. Irwin   Vol. 1: 10337
Vigo; Prix Jean   Vol. 2: 5190
Vijverberg Prize   Vol. 2: 9346
Viking Society for Northern Research Awards   Vol. 2: 4599
Vilalva Prize; International Vasco   Vol. 2: 10252
Vilanova Prize; Xavier   Vol. 2: 1462
Vilas Literary Award; Carl H.   Vol. 1: 17317
Vildrac; Le Prix de Poesie Charles   Vol. 2: 6267
Vilella Award; Joseph R.   Vol. 1: 6084
Viljoen Medal for Journalism; Markus   Vol. 2: 11013
Villa I Tatti Fellowships   Vol. 2: 8474
Villa-Lobos Prize   Vol. 2: 1454
Villa; Premio Maestro   Vol. 2: 11296
Villain Prize; Georges   Vol. 2: 3403
Villaurrutia; Premio Hispanoamericano Xavier   Vol. 2: 9267
Villavicencio; Premio Pablo   Vol. 2: 9016
Villey; Prix Pierre   Vol. 2: 5911

Vilvalva; Premio Internacional Vasco   Vol. 2: 10252
Vinas; Concours International de Chant Francisco   Vol. 2: 11394
Vinas; Concurs Internacional de Cant Francesc   Vol. 2: 11394
Vinas International Singing Competition; Francisco   Vol. 2: 11394
Vincent Owners Club Awards   Vol. 2: 4601
Vincent Prize in Human Sciences; Marcel   Vol. 1: 5437
Vinifera Perpetual Monteith Trophy Award   Vol. 1: 20041
Vinsant Flight Nurse of the Year Award; Dolly   Vol. 1: 8102
Vinson Award; H. B.   Vol. 1: 8750
Vintage Cup Awards   Vol. 1: 19329
Vinyl Siding Institute Awards of Distinction   Vol. 1: 18061
Vinyl Window and Door Institute Awards for Outstanding Performance   Vol. 1: 18062
Viotti; Concorso Internazionale di Musica e Danza G. B.   Vol. 2: 8425
Viotti International Music and Dance Competition; G. B.   Vol. 2: 8425
Viquesnel; Prix   Vol. 2: 5315
Vir Chakra   Vol. 2: 7563
ViRA Awards   Vol. 1: 20024
Virchow Medal; Rudolf   Vol. 1: 20055
Virgilio Memorial Haiku Competition for High School Students; Nicholas A.   Vol. 1: 9759
Virgin Group Award   Vol. 2: 2252
Virginia Festival of American Film   Vol. 1: 20064
Virginia Playwriting Fellowship   Vol. 1: 17216
Virginia Prize   Vol. 1: 11983
Virginia Prize for Playwriting   Vol. 1: 20061
Virginia Prizes for Literature   Vol. 1: 20062
Virginia Slims Tournament of the Year; Grand Prix/   Vol. 1: 3540
Virginia Theaterworks   Vol. 1: 17216
Virginia Wine Competition   Vol. 1: 20042
Virginia Wine-Grape Productivity Trophy   Vol. 1: 20043
Virtanen - Award; A. I.   Vol. 2: 4671
Visconti; Premio Luchino   Vol. 2: 8218
Vishisht Seva Medal   Vol. 2: 7564
Vishwakarma Medal   Vol. 2: 7677
Vision for Tomorrow Award   Vol. 1: 8659
Visions of U.S. Video Contest   Vol. 1: 2053
Visiting Professorships   Vol. 1: 12192
Visiting Research Fellowships   Vol. 1: 799
Visiting Scientist Award   Vol. 2: 6486
Visiting Scientists   Vol. 1: 12193
Visser-Nederlandia dramaprijzen   Vol. 2: 9330
Visser-Neerlandiaprijs   Vol. 2: 9331
Vista (Rising Star) Award   Vol. 1: 6849
Visual Arts/Craft Board Emeritus Award   Vol. 2: 167
Visual Arts/Craft Board Emeritus Medal   Vol. 2: 168
Visual Arts/Craft Board's Emeritus Fellowships and Medals   Vol. 2: 169
Visual Communicators Department of the Year Awards   Vol. 1: 6006
Vita Film Awards; AA Life/M-NET   Vol. 2: 10814
Vitali Prize; Vincenzo   Vol. 2: 8048
Vitelli Prize; G.   Vol. 2: 8332
Vitoria; Prix   Vol. 2: 11751
Vladiguerov International Competition for Pianists; Pancho   Vol. 2: 1526
Vlaicu; Prix; Aurel   Vol. 2: 10390
VM i Linestampkasting   Vol. 2: 9910

Vocalist of the Year Vol. 1: 12529
Vocational Initiative and Club Achievement Program Awards Vol. 1: 20076
Vocational Teacher of the Year Award Vol. 1: 4997
Voelcker Award for Poetry; PEN/ Vol. 1: 16031
Vogel Memorial Life Membership Award; Julian Vol. 1: 2775
Vogels, Jr. Award; David S. Vol. 1: 9125
Vogelsang Memorial Manuscript Award; Frederic M. Vol. 1: 13148
Vogt-Preise; Franz Vol. 2: 7005
Vohra Award; Pran Vol. 2: 7685
Voice of Democracy Scholarship Program Vol. 1: 20006
Volhard Award; Franz Vol. 2: 1975
Volkein Memorial Scholarship; Virginia Vol. 1: 20365
Volkskrant Trophy Vol. 2: 9697
Volleyball Coach of the Year Vol. 1: 6993
Vollmer Award; August Vol. 1: 4544
Volney; Prix Vol. 2: 5349
Volpi Cup Vol. 2: 8470
Voluntarism in Action for the Aging Award Vol. 1: 13821
Volunteer Award
  Canadian Nature Federation Vol. 1: 7068
  National Organization for Victim Assistance Vol 1: 14423
Volunteer Awards Vol. 1: 7230
Volunteer Committee Scholarship Vol. 1: 15716
Volunteer Fund Raiser of the Year Vol. 1: 3927
Volunteer of Distinction Award Vol. 1: 9478
Volunteer of the Year
  American Health Care Association Vol. 1: 2212
  The Arc Vol 1: 5219
  International Human Assistance Programs Vol 1: 11037
  United Methodist Association of Health and Welfare Ministries Vol 1: 18938
Volunteer of the Year Award
  National Hemophilia Foundation Vol. 1: 14128
  National Multiple Sclerosis Society Vol 1: 14384
Volunteer of the Year Recognition Award Vol. 1: 2795
Volunteer Service Award
  American Lawyers Auxiliary Vol. 1: 2796
  National Kidney Foundation Vol 1: 14277
Volunteers in Fund Raising Awards Vol. 1: 14051
Volvo College Players of the Year Vol. 1: 18624
Volvo Tennis/Academic All-Americans Vol. 1: 10559
Volvo Tennis/All America Vol. 1: 10557
Volvo Tennis/Rookie Player of the Year Vol. 1: 10558
Volvo Tennis/Scholar Athletes Vol. 1: 10559
Volvo Tennis/Senior Player of the Year Vol. 1: 10560
Volvo Tennis/*Tennis* College Player of the Year Vol. 1: 10561
von-Baeyer-Denkmunze; Adolf- Vol. 2: 6791
Von Basedow Prize for Research into the Thyroid Gland Vol. 2: 6846
von Bekesy Medal Vol. 1: 104
Von Bergmann Gedenkmunze; Ernst Vol. 2: 6884
von Bergmann Plakette; Ernst Vol. 2: 6818
Von Braun Award for Excellence in Space Program Management; AIAA Vol. 1: 2507

von Briesen Award; Arthur Vol. 1: 14300
von-Chamisso-Preis; Adelbert- Vol. 2: 6553
von Ditfurth Prize; Hoimar Vol. 2: 7063
von-Droste-Hulshoff-Preis; Annette- Vol. 2: 7028
Von Graefe Award; Albrecht Vol. 1: 4539
von Gruber Award; Otto Vol. 2: 8557
von Hauer Medaille; Franz Vol. 2: 780
Von Herder Prizes; Gottfried Vol. 2: 7129
Von Hippel Award Vol. 1: 12125
von-Hofmann-Denkmunze; August-Wilhelm- Vol. 2: 6792
von Humboldt Award for Scientific Cooperation; Alexander Vol. 2: 7160
Von Humboldt Medal; Alexander Vol. 2: 7130
Von Karman Award Vol. 2: 5947
von Karman Award; Theodore Vol. 1: 263
Von Karman Lecture Vol. 1: 2508
Von Karman Lectureship in Astronautics; AIAA Vol. 1: 2508
von Karman Medal; Theodore Vol. 1: 4506
von Karman Prize; Theodore Vol. 1: 17518
Von Langenbeck Preis Vol. 2: 6885
Von Liebig Prize; Justus Vol. 2: 7131
von Linde Prize; Carl Vol. 2: 6029
Von Mises Merit of Honor Award, Ludwig Vol. 1: 16668
von Neumann Lecture; John Vol. 1: 17519
Von-Recklinghausen-Preis Vol. 2: 6847
von Sckell Ehrenring; Friedrich Ludwig Vol. 2: 6554
von Seemen Preis; Hans Vol. 2: 6868
von Seibold Award; Philipp Franz Vol. 2: 7161
Von Siemens Music Prize; Ernst Vol. 2: 7163
Von Siemens-Musikpreis; Ernst Vol. 2: 7163
von-Soest-Preis; Konrad- Vol. 2: 7029
von Spee Chapter Award; Graf Vol. 1: 19716
Von Stein Prize; Freiherr Vol. 2: 7132
von Stephan Medal; Heinrich Vol. 2: 6749
von Weber Competition, Dresden; International Carl Maria Vol. 2: 6921
von Zittel Medaille; Karl Alfred Vol. 2: 6535
Voncken; Prix Jules Vol. 2: 1181
Vondel Prizes; Joost van den Vol. 2: 7133
Vontobel-Fonds; Hans Vol. 2: 11937
Voorhies Award; Amos E. Vol. 1: 15800
Voronca; Prix Ilarie Vol. 2: 4934
Vorovsky Prizes Vol. 2: 10482
Vosper IFLA Fellows Program; Robert Vol. 2: 9496
Voss Award Vol. 1: 17318
Voss Award; Walter C. Vol. 1: 6085
Voss-Preis fur Ubersetzung; Johann-Heinrich- Vol. 2: 6770
Vossaert; Prix Emmanuel Vol. 2: 1295
Vouras Medal; Paul P. Vol. 1: 2158
Vravio tou Kyklou tou Ellinikou Paidikou Vivliou Vol. 2: 7188
VSDA Most Popular Video Awards Vol. 1: 20026
VSDA Presidential Award Vol. 1: 20027
Vucinich Prize; Wayne S. Vol. 1: 893
Vuia Prize; Traian Vol. 2: 10391
Vuoden Nainen Vol. 2: 4752
Vursell Memorial Award; Harold D. Vol. 1: 520
Vyrocni cena nakladatelstvi Nase vojsko Vol. 2: 1878
W. A. Film and Video Festival Vol. 2: 404
W & J National Painting Show Vol. 1: 15619
WA Special Librarian Award Vol. 2: 247
Wabash Valley Exhibition Vol. 1: 18543
Wachsmann Prize; Klaus Vol. 1: 17459
WACRAL Award Certificate Vol. 2: 4618
Waddams Award; Lawrie Vol. 2: 2824

"Waddy" Young Award; Walter R. Vol. 1: 5284
Wade Fiction Prize; Cassie Vol. 1: 474
Wade Memorial Award and Honorary Membership; Jake Vol. 1: 7943
Wade Trophy Vol. 1: 12869
Wade Trophy; Margaret Vol. 1: 12570
Wadham Memorial Award; E. J. and A. E. Vol. 1: 11577
Wadia Medal; D. N. Vol. 2: 7678
Wadlin Distinguished Service Award; George K. Vol. 1: 4122
Wadsworth Award; Milton E. Vol. 1: 17580
Wadsworth Prize for Business History Vol. 2: 2564
WAFFA Salver Vol. 2: 2898
Wager Prize; L. R. Vol. 2: 501
Wagner Award; C. Corwith Vol. 1: 3409
Wagner Award for Efficient Agriculture; Robert E. Vol. 1: 4389
Wagner Award; Percy and Betty Vol. 1: 5200
Wagner Memorial Award; Celia B. Vol. 1: 16293
Wagner Memorial Award; Martin Vol. 1: 14278
Wagner Narrative Screenwriting Award; Robert W. Vol. 1: 9192
Wagner Sanitarian Award; Davis Calvin Vol. 1: 719
Wagner; Transportation Energy & Environmental Award in Memory of Frederick A. Vol. 1: 10463
Wahi Award for Cytology and Preventive Oncology; Dr. Prem Nath Vol. 2: 7614
Wahlbergska Minnesmedaljen i guld Vol. 2: 11559
Wahlner Medal; Aladar Vol. 2: 7361
Wailes Award; B. L. C. Vol. 1: 12362
Waitemata Aero Club Cup Vol. 2: 9826
Wakefield Gold Medal Vol. 2: 3914
Wakeham Prize Vol. 2: 4096
Waksman Award in Microbiology; Selman A. Vol. 1: 12692
Waksman; Fondation Salman A. Vol. 2: 5664
Waksman SIM Outstanding Teaching Award Vol. 1: 17528
Walcott Medal; Charles Doolittle Vol. 1: 12693
Wald Award; Lillian Vol. 1: 13298
Wald Memorial Lecture Vol. 1: 10408
Waldo Award; Dwight Vol. 1: 4273
Waldschmidt Award; Ellen Vol. 1: 11978
Waley Medal; A. J. Vol. 2: 4060
Walker Award for Excellence in Contributions to Chemical Engineering Literature; William H. Vol. 1: 2605
Walker Award; Jack Vol. 1: 3491
Walker Award; R. V. L. Vol. 1: 7267
Walker Cup Vol. 1: 19363
Walker Journalism Award; Stanley Vol. 1: 18654
Walker Jr. Award; Philip L. Vol. 1: 1421
Walker Most Valuable Player Award; Preston Vol. 1: 14266
Walker Prize
  Museum of Science, Boston Vol. 1: 12508
  Royal College of Surgeons of England Vol 2: 3981
Walkley Awards for Journalism; AMP W.G. Vol. 2: 523
Wall of Honors Vol. 1: 12758
Wall Young Investigator Award; Patrick D. Vol. 1: 10658
Wallace Award; David Vol. 1: 14722
Wallace Competitor of the Year Award; Bill Vol. 1: 20634

Wallace Dissertation Award; S. Rains   Vol. 1: 3801
Wallace Essay Prize; Hugh   Vol. 2: 4268
Wallace Memorial Award; Karl R.   Vol. 1: 18313
Wallace-Reader's Digest Writers' Awards; Lila   Vol. 1: 20089
Wallace's Registrars' Prize; Hugh   Vol. 2: 4269
Wallach-Plakette; Otto-   Vol. 2: 6793
Wallant Book Award; Edward Lewis   Vol. 1: 20091
Wallant Memorial Award; Edward Lewis   Vol. 1: 20091
Wallder Award; Vic and Jessie   Vol. 1: 18417
Wallenberg Award; Raoul   Vol. 1: 16678
Wallenberg Civil Courage Award; Raoul   Vol. 1: 16679
Wallenberg Hero for Our Time Award; Raoul   Vol. 1: 16680
Wallenberg Humanitarian Award; Raoul   Vol. 1: 18541
Wallenberg World of Heroes Award; Raoul   Vol. 1: 16680
Wallenbergstipendiet   Vol. 2: 11635
Wallin Education of Handicapped Children Award; J. E. Wallace   Vol. 1: 8319
Wallis Lecture; C. E.   Vol. 2: 4270
Wallmarkska Priset   Vol. 2: 11560
Wallston Award; Barbara Strudler   Vol. 1: 3775
Walmap Prize   Vol. 2: 1494
Walpole Gold Medal; Horace   Vol. 1: 8418
Walsh Award; Edith   Vol. 2: 2454
Walsh Award; John G.   Vol. 1: 583
Walsh Award; Rudolfo   Vol. 1: 10709
Walsh - Weston Bronze Award   Vol. 2: 2598
Walter Ahlstromin palkinto   Vol. 2: 4682
Waltham Award   Vol. 1: 791
Walther-Preis; Carl-   Vol. 2: 6807
Waltke Trophy   Vol. 1: 13191
Walton/Russell L. Miller Award; Norton H.   Vol. 1: 2606
WAMSO Young Artist Competition   Vol. 1: 20102
WAND Family Award   Vol. 1: 20408
Wander Lecture; Albert   Vol. 2: 4271
Wanganui Trophy   Vol. 2: 9827
Wanner Award; Vance R.   Vol. 1: 12280
Wanzer, FPSA, Award; Douglas H.   Vol. 1: 16160
Wappenmedaille   Vol. 2: 868
War Order Virtuti Militari   Vol. 2: 10123
Warburg-Medaille; Otto-   Vol. 2: 6892
Warburg-Preis der Atlantik-Brucke; Eric-M.   Vol. 2: 6547
Warburg Prize of Atlantic Bridge; Eric M.   Vol. 2: 6547
Ward, Jr. Medal; Philip H.   Vol. 1: 9389
Ward, Jr. Memorial Award; Philip H.   Vol. 1: 2059
Ward Medal; Henry Baldwin   Vol. 1: 4742
Ward Memorial Award; Arch   Vol. 1: 7944
Ward Memorial Award; Earl F.   Vol. 1: 279
Ward Memorial Award; Julian E.   Vol. 1: 177
Ward Memorial Film Award; Jack   Vol. 1: 5160
Ward Memorial Posthumous Award; R. D. "Bob"   Vol. 1: 12784
Ward Memorial Salver; Jack   Vol. 2: 2796
Ward Prize for Outstanding New Children's Theatre Company; Zeta Phi Eta Winifred   Vol. 1: 782
Ward Prize for Playwriting; Theodore   Vol. 1: 7963
Ward Prize; Lynd   Vol. 1: 10062

Ward Prize; Zeta Phi Eta - Winifred   Vol. 1: 782
Ward Scholar; Winifred   Vol. 1: 779
Warden of the Year   Vol. 1: 15398
Warder Award for Outstanding Achievement; Frederick B.   Vol. 1: 15097
Warder Medal; John Aston   Vol. 1: 2104
Wardle Award; R. A.   Vol. 1: 7236
Ware Award for Distinguished (Undergrduate) Teaching; L. M.   Vol. 1: 4152
Wark Medal and Lecture; Ian William   Vol. 2: 180
Warm Water Fisheries Management   Vol. 1: 9117
Warman International Students Design Award Competition   Vol. 2: 493
Warmington Trophy; Ivon   Vol. 2: 9828
Warner Award; Edward   Vol. 1: 10857
Warner Award; Jo   Vol. 1: 6657
Warner Awards Program; William E.   Vol. 1: 8977
Warner Brothers Writers Award   Vol. 1: 1762
Warner-Lambert/Parke-Davis Award   Vol. 1: 4181
Warner Medal; Worcester Reed   Vol. 1: 4712
Warner Memorial Medal   Vol. 2: 4527
Warner Memorial Medal Award; Samuel L.   Vol. 1: 17913
Warner Prize for Astronomy; Helen B.   Vol. 1: 1278
Warner Third Prize; Ned   Vol. 1: 6217
Warner Trophy   Vol. 1: 10400
Warnier Prize for Information Science; J. D.   Vol. 1: 15841
Warren Award; Gretchen   Vol. 1: 15132
Warren Award; Hugh T.   Vol. 1: 18063
Warren Diffraction Physics Award; Bertram Eugene   Vol. 1: 1901
Warren Fellowship; Lloyd   Vol. 1: 14217
Warren Medal; Howard Crosby   Vol. 1: 3818
Warren Medal; W. H.   Vol. 2: 494
Warren Memorial Trophy; Ken   Vol. 2: 2143
Warren Prize; G. K.   Vol. 1: 12694
Warren R. Lang Prize Paper Award   Vol. 1: 4549
Warriner Award; Elizabeth Hull - Kate   Vol. 1: 8737
Warringah Art Prize   Vol. 2: 706
Warsaw Chopin Competition   Vol. 2: 6594
Warshawsky Award; Celia   Vol. 1: 13661
Warszawski Krzyz Powstanczy   Vol. 2: 10105
Wartenburg Lecture   Vol. 1: 625
Wartha Medal; Vince   Vol. 2: 7324
Washburn Award; Bradford   Vol. 1: 12509
Washburn Award; Sherwood L.   Vol. 1: 1123
Washington Award
  American Society of Civil Engineers   Vol. 1: 4507
  Western Society of Engineers   Vol 1: 20227
Washington Award for Excellence in Coalition Building; Harold   Vol. 1: 8165
Washington Award; George   Vol. 1: 10241
Washington Best Special Edition; Leon H.   Vol. 1: 14397
Washington Correspondence Awards   Vol. 1: 14503
Washington Craft Show   Vol. 1: 17351
Washington Honor Medal; George   Vol. 1: 9404
Washington International Competition   Vol. 1: 20112
The Washington Monthly Journalism Award   Vol. 1: 20117
The Washington Post Award for Distinguished Community Service   Vol. 1: 20133
The Washington Post/Children's Book Guild Nonfiction Award   Vol. 1: 20121

The Washington Post Distinguished Educational Leadership Awards   Vol. 1: 20124
Washington Prize   Vol. 1: 20455
Washington Square Sculpture Awards   Vol. 1: 20126
Washington Theatre Festival Awards   Vol. 1: 18158
Washingtonians of the Year   Vol. 1: 20137
Wasito Award; R.   Vol. 2: 7731
Wason Medal for Materials Research   Vol. 1: 1788
Wason Medal for the Most Meritorious Paper   Vol. 1: 1789
Wasserman Award; Prof. Dr. Rene D.   Vol. 1: 5096
Wasserman Foundation Prizes; Leo   Vol. 1: 2743
Waste Management Award   Vol. 1: 225
Wataghin Award; Gleb   Vol. 2: 1460
Watanabe Medal; G.   Vol. 2: 8568
Wateler Peace Prize   Vol. 2: 9353
Wateler-Vredesprijs   Vol. 2: 9353
Waten Collection of Creative Writing (Young Writers); FAW Judah   Vol. 2: 393
Water Industry Hall of Fame   Vol. 1: 5032
Water Quality Improvement Man of the Year Award   Vol. 1: 10907
Water Solutions Unlimited Most Improved Sprint Car Driver Award   Vol. 1: 19032
Water Statesman of the Year   Vol. 1: 14979
Water Utility Hall of Fame   Vol. 1: 5032
Water Wheel Awards   Vol. 1: 300
Water Widget Medal   Vol. 1: 9811
Waterbed Hall of Fame   Vol. 1: 14989
Watercolor U.S.A.   Vol. 1: 18433
Waterfall Award; Wallace   Vol. 1: 6086
Waterford Bio-Medical Science Award   Vol. 1: 16805
Waterfowl Breeders Hall of Fame   Vol. 1: 11400
Waterman Award; Alan T.   Vol. 1: 14688
Watkins Award; J. B. C.   Vol. 1: 6752
Watrous Gold Medal; Elizabeth N.   Vol. 1: 12635
Watson Award; Leland A.   Vol. 1: 14117
Watson Award; Robert C.   Vol. 1: 2697
Watson Award; Whipper   Vol. 1: 7124
Watson Essay Award; George   Vol. 2: 587
Watson Grants; Neil   Vol. 2: 3333
Watson, Jr.; Assistant Excellence in Leadership Award in Memory of Buford M.   Vol. 1: 10854
Watson, Jr. Medal of Excellence; William C.   Vol. 1: 19242
Watson Medal; Garth   Vol. 2: 3262
Watson Medal; James Craig   Vol. 1: 12695
Watson Prize; The Albert J   Vol. 2: 10569
Watson Prize Lecture   Vol. 2: 10602
Watt Award; Gladys Cameron   Vol. 1: 15855
Watt International Medal; James   Vol. 2: 3334
Watt Medal; James   Vol. 2: 3263
Watt Memorial Prize; David   Vol. 2: 4327
Wattrelos Short Film and Video Festival   Vol. 2: 6477
Watts Prize   Vol. 2: 4097
Wauwatosa Event   Vol. 1: 19688
Wauwatosa Trophy   Vol. 1: 19688
Waxweiler; Fondation Emile   Vol. 2: 974
Wayburn Award; Edgar   Vol. 1: 17246
Wayne Award; John   Vol. 1: 11164
Wayne Valley National Football Foundation Graduate Fellowship   Vol. 1: 13996
WBDNA Achievement Award   Vol. 1: 20366
WBDNA Performing Artists Award   Vol. 1: 20367
WBW Bowlers of the Year   Vol. 1: 20476

WBW Distinguished Service Award   Vol. 1: 20477
WBW Gosta Zellen Golden Quill Award   Vol. 1: 20478
WBW International Bowling Hall of Fame   Vol. 1: 20479
WCA Honors   Vol. 1: 20412
Weatherford Award Competition; W. D.   Vol. 1: 6331
Weatherly Award; Earl   Vol. 1: 8109
Weaver Award; Dean Myron   Vol. 1: 18438
Weaver Award for Scholarly Letters; Ingersoll Prize - Richard M.   Vol. 1: 10191
Weaver Broadcast Journalism Awards; Pat   Vol. 1: 12499
Weaver Fellowship; Richard M.   Vol. 1: 10547
Weaver Service Award; Warren   Vol. 1: 7667
Weaver's Company Medal and Prize   Vol. 2: 4528
Webb Award; Aileen Osborn   Vol. 1: 1892
Webb Award; James E.   Vol. 1: 4274
Webb Excellence in a Newsletter Award; Bob   Vol. 1: 15935
Webb Medal; William H.   Vol. 1: 17931
Webb Memorial Trophy; Francis   Vol. 2: 3781
Webb Prize   Vol. 2: 3264
Webb Service Award; Aileen Osborn   Vol. 1: 1892
Webb Space Administration Fellowship; James E.   Vol. 1: 14841
Webb Studentship; Bernard   Vol. 2: 2094
Weber Awards for Excellence in Management; Joseph   Vol. 1: 19702
Weber Medaille; C. A.   Vol. 2: 6634
Weber Spot News Photo Award; New York Press Club/Thommy   Vol. 1: 15259
Webster Award; Daniel   Vol. 1: 11165
Webster Memorial Trophy; John C.   Vol. 1: 7238
Webster Mentor Award; Robert L.   Vol. 1: 17133
WEC Gold Medal for International Corporate Environmental Achievement   Vol. 1: 20483
Wedeen Awards; Nathan   Vol. 1: 8085
Wedel Award; Cynthia   Vol. 1: 3928
Weekly Mail and Guardian Short Film Competition   Vol. 2: 11125
Weems Award   Vol. 1: 10416
Wegener-Medaille; Alfred   Vol. 2: 6645
Wegener Medal; Alfred-   Vol. 2: 5135
Wegmann; Prix   Vol. 2: 5316
Wehran Aviation Industrial Achievement Award; Fred L.   Vol. 1: 6180
Weichmann-Preis; Herbert   Vol. 2: 7013
Weichselbaum Education Prize; Alfred   Vol. 2: 5124
Weichselbaum; Prix de l'Education Alfred   Vol. 2: 5124
Weickhardt Award; Con   Vol. 2: 390
Weickhardt Award; FAW Patricia   Vol. 2: 398
Weil Award   Vol. 1: 1050
Weil Awards; Frank L.   Vol. 1: 11520
Weill Award; Raymond and Roger   Vol. 1: 8109
Weiller; Prix de Portrait Paul-Louis   Vol. 2: 5378
Weiller; Prix Paul-Louis   Vol. 2: 5418
Weinberg Memorial Award for Geriatric Psychiatry; Jack   Vol. 1: 3656
Weinberg Prize   Vol. 2: 8289
Weindling Prize; Rosalind G.   Vol. 2: 7899
Weiner String Quartet Competition; Leo   Vol. 2: 7414
Weinstock Award; Morris F.   Vol. 1: 13487
Weintal Prize for Diplomatic Reporting; Edward   Vol. 1: 9570

Weinzirl Award (Enthusiast of the Year); Elizabeth   Vol. 1: 14880
Weir Prize; The C. J.   Vol. 2: 10570
Weis Trophy; Bernard J.   Vol. 1: 16210
Weisbrod One-Act Competition   Vol. 1: 11915
Weisenfeld Award for Excellence in Ophthalmology; Mildred   Vol. 1: 5594
Weisinger Award; Mort   Vol. 1: 4633
Weiss Award; Harold   Vol. 1: 8844
Weiss; Premio Aida   Vol. 2: 9200
Weiss; Prix J. J.   Vol. 2: 5869
Weissberger Playwriting Award; Arnold   Vol. 1: 15116
Weissen Raben; Die   Vol. 2: 6995
Weisskopf Prize; V.F.   Vol. 2: 8289
Weissman Fund Fellowships; Polaire   Vol. 1: 12234
Weitzman Award; Richard E.   Vol. 1: 8925
Weizman Prize; Science Prize - Dr. Chaim   Vol. 2: 7959
Weizmann Prizes of the Academy of Scientific Research   Vol. 2: 8920
Welch Award in Chemistry; Robert A.   Vol. 1: 20176
Welch Award in Vacuum Science; Medard W.   Vol. 1: 4967
Welch Foundation Scholarship
    International Union for Vacuum Science, Technique, and Applications   Vol. 2: 3493
    International Union of Vacuum Science, Technique and Applications   Vol 1: 11379
Welch Medal; William H.   Vol. 1: 897
Welch Memorial Lecturer   Vol. 1: 6791
Weldon International Award   Vol. 2: 193
Wellberry Books Prizes   Vol. 1: 20178
Wellberry Prize   Vol. 1: 20178
Wellcome Diagnostics Student Award   Vol. 2: 10983
Wellcome Foundation Prize and Lecture   Vol. 2: 4159
Wellcome Medal and Prize; Sir Henry   Vol. 1: 5898
Wellcome Medal for Anthropological Research as applied to Medical Problems   Vol. 2: 3931
Wellcome Prize   Vol. 2: 2120
Wellcome Trust Award for Research in Biochemistry Related to Medicine   Vol. 2: 2179
Wellek Prize; Rene   Vol. 1: 1770
Wellington Prize; Arthur M.   Vol. 1: 4508
Wells Appreciation Award; Cliff   Vol. 1: 12950
Wells Award; Ida B.   Vol. 1: 19806
Wells Memorial Award; Elizabeth   Vol. 1: 13149
Wells Memorial Award; John   Vol. 1: 20172
Wells Memorial Key   Vol. 1: 18003
Welsh Arts Council Drama Prize   Vol. 2: 12151
Welsh Arts Council Prizes   Vol. 2: 12150
Welsh Housing Design Awards   Vol. 2: 12190
Welsh National Eisteddfod   Vol. 2: 12151
Welsh Society Medallion   Vol. 1: 20182
Weltmeister im Pflugen   Vol. 2: 4626
Wereld Muziek Concours Kerkrade   Vol. 2: 9695
Werkmanprijs; H. N.   Vol. 2: 9652
Werner Award; Louis S.   Vol. 1: 3266
Werner Award; Wallace "Bud"   Vol. 1: 19592
Werner Host Club Award; Louis S.   Vol. 1: 3267
Werner Medaille; Abraham-Gottlob-   Vol. 2: 6649
Werner-Medaille; Golden   Vol. 2: 11888
Werner Preis   Vol. 2: 11890
Werner-Preis   Vol. 2: 11888
Wertheimer Multilingual Award; Leonard   Vol. 1: 2934

Wessely Prize; Laszlo   Vol. 2: 7404
Wesson Memorial Physician of the Year Award; Dr. Ray   Vol. 1: 18996
West Agro, Inc. Award   Vol. 1: 1925
West Australian Young Readers' Book Award   Vol. 2: 249
West Award; Constance   Vol. 2: 4430
West Indian Tobacco Sports Foundation Award   Vol. 2: 12040
West Memorial Medal; Benjamin   Vol. 1: 5314
West Virginia Children's Book Award   Vol. 1: 20191
Westbrook Local History Award; Lucille   Vol. 1: 5260
Westcott USTA Family of the Year Award; Ralph W.   Vol. 1: 19670
Westerby-prisen; Erik   Vol. 2: 2013
Westerby Prize; Erik   Vol. 2: 2013
Westerfield Award; Samuel Z.   Vol. 1: 13880
Western Australia Week Literary Awards   Vol. 2: 515
Western Australian Premier's Book Awards   Vol. 2: 515
Western Australian School of Mines Award   Vol. 2: 495
Western Auto NASCAR Mechanics Hall of Fame   Vol. 1: 11112
Western Conference Trophy   Vol. 1: 6876
Western Electric Fund Award
    American Assembly of Collegiate Schools of Business   Vol. 1: 824
    American Society for Engineering Education   Vol 1: 4068
Western Forestry Award for Current Achievement   Vol. 1: 20203
Western Forestry Award for Lifetime Service   Vol. 1: 20204
Western Heritage Awards (Wrangler Award)   Vol. 1: 13838
Western Home Awards   Vol. 1: 18532
Western Magazine Awards   Vol. 1: 20208
Western Political Science Association Awards   Vol. 1: 20210
Western Reserve Aviation Hall of Fame   Vol. 1: 20219
Western States Book Awards   Vol. 1: 20231
Westinghouse Award for Public Understanding of Science and Technology; AAAS -   Vol. 1: 886
Westinghouse Award; George   Vol. 1: 4123
Westinghouse Medals; George   Vol. 1: 4713
Westinghouse Science Journalism Awards; AAAS -   Vol. 1: 887
Westinghouse Science Talent Search Scholarships   Vol. 1: 17122
Westlake; Prix John   Vol. 2: 11751
Weston Award for Teaching Excellence; William H.   Vol. 1: 12546
Weston Prize; Roy F.   Vol. 1: 18601
Westonbirt Orchid Medal   Vol. 2: 4061
Westpac Under 21 Award   Vol. 2: 317
Westrups beloning; Wilhelm   Vol. 2: 11521
Wetherill Medal; John Price   Vol. 1: 9390
Wetrems; Prix Adolphe   Vol. 2: 1006
Wettbewerb "Jugend musiziert"   Vol. 2: 734
Wexner Graduate Fellows   Vol. 1: 20251
Wexner Prize   Vol. 1: 20249
Weyerhaeuser Foundation Publication Award; Bumbershoot/   Vol. 1: 15673
Weyhe Gallery Purchase Award; E.   Vol. 1: 17693
WFCC Skerman Award for Taxonomy   Vol. 2: 712
Wham Leadership Medal; George S.   Vol. 1: 3183
Wharton Citation of Merit for Fiction Writers (State Author); Edith   Vol. 1: 15293

What the Papers Say Award   Vol. 2: 2947
Wheaties Champions Award   Vol. 1: 9527
Wheatland Prize   Vol. 1: 20255
Wheatley Award; William A.   Vol. 1: 19723
Wheatley Medal
   Library Association   Vol. 2: 3574
   Society of Indexers   Vol 2: 4448
Wheaton; Prix Henri   Vol. 2: 11751
Wheeler Award; Clifford   Vol. 2: 2880
Wheeler Cross Country Award   Vol. 1: 13588
Wheeler Medal   Vol. 1: 17721
Wheeler Track and Field Awards   Vol. 1: 13589
Wheeler-Voegelin Prize; Erminie   Vol. 1: 4130
Wheland Award; George W.   Vol. 1: 19763
Wheldon Award; Hu.   Vol. 2: 2234
Wherry Award; Edgar T.   Vol. 1: 6492
Wherry Award; Elizabeth   Vol. 2: 2455
Wherry Award; Robert J.   Vol. 1: 3802
Whetnall Lectureship; Edith   Vol. 2: 4272
Whetten Award; Nellie Yeoh   Vol. 1: 4968
Whipper Gold Award; Leigh   Vol. 1: 10769
Whistler Award; Roy L.   Vol. 2: 3386
Whitaker Distinguished Lectureship   Vol. 1: 6379
Whitaker Graduate Student Awards   Vol. 1: 6380
Whitaker International Competition; Mae M.   Vol. 1: 16998
Whitaker Senior Student Bioengineering Design Awards   Vol. 1: 6381
Whitaker Young Investigator Award   Vol. 1: 6382
Whitbread Book of the Year   Vol. 2: 2211
Whitbread Literary Awards   Vol. 2: 2211
Whitby Award for Distinguished Teaching and Academic Research; George Stafford   Vol. 1: 1516
Whitby Award; Kenneth   Vol. 1: 831
Whitcombe-Cox Trophy   Vol. 2: 3824
White Award; Dorothy   Vol. 1: 15855
White Award; John M.   Vol. 1: 2437
White Award; Leonard D.   Vol. 1: 3585
White Award Master List   Vol. 1: 20265
White Award; Paul Dudley   Vol. 1: 5899
White Award; Ryan   Vol. 1: 14138
White Awards   Vol. 1: 7721
White Awards; Marsh W.   Vol. 1: 2666
White Buffalo Award   Vol. 1: 9914
White Children's Book Award; William Allen   Vol. 1: 20265
White Distinguished Teacher Award; Albert Easton   Vol. 1: 5366
White Fellow; Wilford L.   Vol. 1: 10878
White Fellowship; Harold   Vol. 2: 549
White House Fellows   Vol. 1: 19487
White House News Photographers' Association Awards   Vol. 1: 20263
White Humanitarian Award; Byron "Whizzer"   Vol. 1: 14009
White Literary Award; Patrick   Vol. 2: 708
White Medal; Clarence G.   Vol. 1: 5239
White Medal for Design   Vol. 1: 7721
White Medal for Writing   Vol. 1: 7721
White Membership Award; Sandi   Vol. 1: 9791
White Memorial Award for Electronic Journalism; Paul   Vol. 1: 16657
White Memorial Award; Philip R.   Vol. 1: 18721
White National Defense Award; Thomas D.   Vol. 1: 18989
White National Memorial Trophy; Belle   Vol. 2: 2075
White Post-Graduate Scholarship in Naval Architecture; Sir William   Vol. 2: 4098
White Postdoctoral Fellowship Program; Gilbert F.   Vol. 1: 16810

White Prize; Frederick   Vol. 2: 181
White Prize Lecture; T. C.   Vol. 2: 10603
White Ravens   Vol. 2: 6995
White Space Trophy   Vol. 1: 14077
White Stag Award
   U.S. Skiing   Vol. 1: 19551
   U.S. Skiing   Vol 1: 19593
White Travelling Fellowship; T. C.   Vol. 2: 10604
Whitechapel Artists Award   Vol. 2: 4606
Whitehouse Studio Award for Architectural Photography; RIAS/   Vol. 2: 10616
Whitelaw Trophy; Robert (Scotty)   Vol. 1: 12242
White's Educational Foundation Music Scholarship; Sir Thomas   Vol. 2: 2707
White's Music Scholarship; Sir Thomas   Vol. 2: 2707
Whitfield Award; Willis J.   Vol. 1: 10338
Whitfield Prize   Vol. 2: 4021
Whiting Award; Butts -   Vol. 1: 5740
Whiting Award; John   Vol. 2: 2101
Whiting Fellowship in the Humanities   Vol. 1: 20269
Whiting Memorial Fund of ISPE Award   Vol. 1: 11264
Whiting Writers' Award   Vol. 1: 20270
Whitley Awards   Vol. 2: 646
Whitlock Award; Marvin   Vol. 1: 17779
Whitman Award; Walt   Vol. 1: 23
Whitman Citation of Merit Award for Poets (State Poet); Walt   Vol. 1: 15294
Whitmore Award; Lenore K.   Vol. 1: 10153
Whitney Award   Vol. 1: 15487
Whitney Award; Edgar A.   Vol. 1: 5066
Whitney Award; Harvey A. K.   Vol. 1: 4601
Whitney Award; Willis Rodney   Vol. 1: 13045
Whitney - Carnegie Awards   Vol. 1: 2937
Whitney Fellowships; Jane and Morgan   Vol. 1: 12234
Whitney Medal; Charles S.   Vol. 1: 1790
Whitney Memorial Award; Eli   Vol. 1: 17889
Whitney Productivity Award; Eli   Vol. 1: 17889
Whitten Medal; Charles A.   Vol. 1: 2172
Whitten Silver Medallion Award; E.B.   Vol. 1: 14588
Wholesaler of the Year Award   Vol. 1: 13287
Whyte Memorial Essay Prize; John   Vol. 1: 297
Wibautprijs   Vol. 2: 9653
WIBC Hall of Fame   Vol. 1: 20419
Wickard Award; Albert O.   Vol. 1: 19717
Wickenden Award; William Elgin   Vol. 1: 4124
Widowed Persons Service Award   Vol. 1: 1168
Wiebrecht Award   Vol. 1: 587
Wiegenstein Award for Meritorious Service   Vol. 1: 1638
Wiegenstein Leadership Award; John G.   Vol. 1: 1638
Wieland-Preis; Christoph-Martin-   Vol. 2: 6761
Wieland Preis; Heinrich-   Vol. 2: 7017
Wielkopolska Insurrectionary Cross   Vol. 2: 10124
Wielkopolski Krzyz Powstanczy   Vol. 2: 10124
Wien Awards; Mae L.   Vol. 1: 17102
Wien Prize in Corporate Social Responsibility; Lawrence A.   Vol. 1: 8009
Wiener Flotenuhr   Vol. 2: 916
Wiener Medal; Norbert   Vol. 1: 4063
Wiener Memorial Gold Medal; Norbert   Vol. 2: 6488
Wiener Prize in Applied Mathematics; Norbert   Vol. 1: 3011
Wiener Prize; Norbert   Vol. 1: 17520
Wiesel Award for Jewish Art and Culture; Elie   Vol. 1: 6429

Wiesel Prize in Ethics; Elie   Vol. 1: 20284
Wiesenthal Center Humanitarian Award; Simon   Vol. 1: 20287
Wigan Cup   Vol. 2: 4062
Wiggers Award; Carl J.   Vol. 1: 3499
Wigglesworth Medal   Vol. 2: 4002
Wigram Cup   Vol. 2: 9829
Wigram Cup (Sub-Competition) - Instrument Flying   Vol. 2: 9830
Wigram Cup (Sub-Competition) - Junior Landing   Vol. 2: 9831
Wigram Cup (Sub-Competition) - Non-instrument Circuits   Vol. 2: 9832
Wigram Cup (Sub-Competition) - Senior Landing   Vol. 2: 9833
Wihuri International Prize   Vol. 2: 4762
Wihuri Sibelius Prize   Vol. 2: 4763
Wihurin kansainvalinen palkinto   Vol. 2: 4762
Wihurin Sibelius palkinto   Vol. 2: 4763
Wilbur Awards   Vol. 1: 16781
Wilbur Prize for Translation of Poetry; Richard   Vol. 1: 2968
Wilbur Spotlight Award   Vol. 1: 16781
Wilby Memorial Scholarship; Ernest   Vol. 1: 16924
Wilcher Award; Denny and Ida   Vol. 1: 17247
Wilches Award; Belisario Ruiz   Vol. 2: 1719
Wilcox Award; Bill   Vol. 1: 2276
Wild Heerbrugg Geodetic Fellowship   Vol. 1: 1821
Wild Heerbrugg Surveying Scholarships   Vol. 1: 1816
Wild Leitz Photogrammetric Fellowship Award   Vol. 1: 4254
Wild-Leitz Scientific Award   Vol. 1: 6794
Wild-Leitz Surveying Scholarships   Vol. 1: 1816
Wild Places   Vol. 2: 4651
Wild Prize; Emilie L.   Vol. 1: 5297
Wildavsky Award; Aaron   Vol. 1: 16309
Wilde Award; Peter   Vol. 1: 5174
Wilde Cup and Webb Cup   Vol. 2: 3021
Wilde; Fondation Henry   Vol. 2: 5583
Wildenstein; Prix Georges   Vol. 2: 5395
Wilder Award; Laura Ingalls   Vol. 1: 2864
Wilder Medal   Vol. 1: 3597
Wilder Memorial Award; Russell   Vol. 1: 19594
Wilder Prize; Thornton Niven   Vol. 1: 8007
Wildfang Award; Henry   Vol. 1: 12063
Wildgans-Preis   Vol. 2: 736
Wildgans Prize of Austrian Industry; Anton   Vol. 2: 736
Wildlife Action Award   Vol. 2: 4652
Wildlife Photographer of the Year Competition   Vol. 2: 2162
Wildlife Publication Award   Vol. 1: 20306
Wildlife Society of Zimbabwe Competitions   Vol. 2: 12209
Wildmann; Prix Leo   Vol. 2: 11838
Wildmann Prize; Leo   Vol. 2: 11838
Wile Award; Simon   Vol. 1: 539
Wiley & Sons Award; John   Vol. 1: 8404
Wiley Award; Bell I.   Vol. 1: 7779
Wiley Award for Excellence in Engineering Technology Education   Vol. 1: 4071
Wiley Award; Harvey W.   Vol. 1: 5186
Wiley - Berger Memorial Award for Volunteer Service   Vol. 1: 2342
Wiley Distinguished Author Award; Meriam/   Vol. 1: 4102
Wiley Prize; Bell I.   Vol. 1: 14153
Wiley Professional Development Grant; First Step Award -   Vol. 1: 2849
Wilhelm Award in Chemical Reaction Engineering; R. H.   Vol. 1: 2607

Wilhelmi-Haskell Stewardship Award   Vol. 1: 13590
Wilke Literary Award; FAW   Vol. 2: 400
Wilke Memorial Award; Louis G.   Vol. 1: 459
Wilke-Preis; Rudolf-   Vol. 2: 6576
Wilkes Award   Vol. 2: 2323
Wilkins Award for Excellence in the Direction and Management of Overseas Missions; James A. Baker, III - Howard   Vol. 1: 19279
Wilkinson Award; John Henry   Vol. 1: 11237
Wilkinson Outstanding Young Electrical Engineer Award; Roger I.   Vol. 1: 9008
Wilkinson Prize in Numerical Analysis and Scientific Computing; James H.   Vol. 1: 17521
Wilkinson Sword Award of Merit   Vol. 2: 2325
Wilks Award   Vol. 1: 18247
Wilks Memorial Medal Award; Samuel S.   Vol. 1: 4864
Will Award   Vol. 1: 17209
Willan Grand Prize; Canada Council Healey   Vol. 1: 6822
Willan Prize; Heale   Vol. 1: 6753
Willans Premium   Vol. 2: 3308
Willauer Cup Award   Vol. 1: 19595
Willems Award (U.S. Section); Gustave   Vol. 1: 16077
Willems-Orde; Militaire   Vol. 2: 9355
Willems Prize; Gustave   Vol. 2: 1239
Willems Prize; Leonard   Vol. 2: 1280
Willen Award; Janet Younker   Vol. 1: 18926
Willensky Fund; Elliot   Vol. 1: 12492
Willey Distinguished Service Award; Calvert L.   Vol. 1: 10350
William Prize; Gwynne   Vol. 2: 12177
Williams and Gene Derwood Award; Oscar   Vol. 1: 15233
Williams Award; Boyce R.   Vol. 1: 1939
Williams Award; Burt   Vol. 1: 14532
Williams Award for Research in Physical Therapy; Marian   Vol. 1: 3492
Williams Award; George E.   Vol. 1: 9126
Williams Award; William Carlos   Vol. 1: 16294
Williams Awards; APA Assembly Warren   Vol. 1: 3622
Williams Distinguished Leadership Award; Robert H.   Vol. 1: 8926
Williams, Jr., Award; Alexander C.   Vol. 1: 10044
Williams Lecture; Michael   Vol. 2: 4273
Williams Medal; Bradford   Vol. 1: 4648
Williams Memorial Award; Edwin   Vol. 2: 2862
Williams Memorial Medal
   Royal Horticultural Society   Vol. 2: 4052
   Royal Horticultural Society   Vol 2: 4063
Williams Memorial Prize; Griffith John   Vol. 2: 12199
Williams Premium; F. C.   Vol. 2: 3273
Williams Prize   Vol. 2: 3155
Williams Prize; Francis   Vol. 2: 4595
Williams Prize; Roger T.   Vol. 1: 14715
Williams Prizes in Louisiana History; General L. Kemper   Vol. 1: 9931
Williams Space Medal   Vol. 1: 17873
Williams Trophy; George   Vol. 2: 2777
Williams - Wright Award   Vol. 1: 7858
Williams Writing Contest; Gertrude Johnson   Vol. 1: 11595
Williamson Neometaphysical Award   Vol. 2: 4450
Williamson Prize; The Ronald   Vol. 2: 10571
The Williamson Tea Award for Social Progress   Vol. 2: 4635
Willie Award   Vol. 1: 9609
Willis Award; George E.   Vol. 1: 5097
Willis Award of Merit   Vol. 1: 18220

Williston Medal; Arthur L.   Vol. 1: 4714
Williston Medal Contest; Arthur L.   Vol. 1: 4689
Willow Bee Publishing House Award for Literature   Vol. 1: 20309
Willson Award; Cedric   Vol. 1: 1791
Wilmoth Medal; G.R.   Vol. 2: 453
Wilson Award   Vol. 2: 11123
Wilson Award; E. H.   Vol. 1: 15430
Wilson Award for Young Musicians; Clive   Vol. 2: 2988
Wilson Award; Gill Robb   Vol. 1: 264
Wilson Award in Nuclear Chemical Engineering; Robert E.   Vol. 1: 2608
Wilson Award; Joseph C.   Vol. 1: 16863
Wilson Award; Peter   Vol. 2: 3546
Wilson Award; Ralph C.   Vol. 1: 14569
Wilson Award; Thomas J.   Vol. 1: 9820
Wilson Award; W. W.   Vol. 1: 3343
Wilson Award; Woodrow   Vol. 1: 3929
Wilson Center Media Studies Essay Competition   Vol. 1: 20312
Wilson Coach of the Year Award   Vol. 1: 10562
Wilson Company Award; H. W.   Vol. 1: 18275
Wilson Company Indexing Award; H. W.   Vol. 1: 4619
Wilson Fiction Prize; Ethel   Vol. 1: 20189
Wilson Foundation Book Award; Woodrow   Vol. 1: 3586
Wilson Foundation; Marie C. and Joseph C.   Vol. 1: 16863
Wilson Library Periodical Award; H. W.   Vol. 1: 2823
Wilson Library Staff Development Grant; H. W.   Vol. 1: 2824
Wilson Medal; E. B.   Vol. 1: 4050
Wilson Memorial Award; Charles E.   Vol. 1: 16764
Wilson Memorial Award; Hewitt   Vol. 1: 1478
Wilson Memorial Lecture Award; John Arthur   Vol. 1: 2802
Wilson Memorial Vase; Guy   Vol. 2: 4064
Wilson National High School Coaches - Ad of the Year   Vol. 1: 14148
Wilson Prize; Alexander   Vol. 1: 20323
Wilson Prize for Achievement in the Physics of Particle Accelerators; Robert R.   Vol. 1: 3473
Wilson Prize; Woodrow   Vol. 1: 16406
Wilson - Toekenning   Vol. 2: 11123
Wilwers Fire Buff of the Year; Henry N.   Vol. 1: 10976
Wimalasurendra Memorial Award; D. J.   Vol. 2: 11409
Wimberly Cup   Vol. 1: 18418
Wimps, Grumblers, and Grousers Award   Vol. 1: 14411
Win with Project Graduation Award   Vol. 1: 14552
Winans/Herbert A. Wichelns Memorial Award for Distinguished Scholarship; James A.   Vol. 1: 18314
WINBA Championship Title   Vol. 1: 20498
Winchell Cancer Fund Fellowships; Damon Runyon - Walter   Vol. 1: 7284
Wine & Spirits Professional of the Year   Vol. 1: 6301
Wine Label Competition   Vol. 1: 5107
Wine Research Award   Vol. 1: 17893
Wingate Awards; H. H.   Vol. 2: 2207
Wingate Trophy; Wilson   Vol. 1: 19422
Wingquist Award   Vol. 2: 12216
Wings of Gold Award   Vol. 1: 19718
Winking Award; Charles R.   Vol. 1: 13536
Winkler Plaque; Ludwig   Vol. 2: 6987
Winner Award; Beatrice   Vol. 1: 17537

Winner Memorial Award; Robert H.   Vol. 1: 16295
Winner Takes All Award   Vol. 1: 20263
Winners Circle Award   Vol. 1: 20511
Winner's Circle National Winners   Vol. 1: 12387
Winning Spirit Award   Vol. 1: 6016
Winsbury-White Lecture   Vol. 2: 4274
Winship Award; Laurence L.   Vol. 1: 6465
Winship Secondary School Theatre Award; F. Loren   Vol. 1: 780
Winslow Landscape Design Award; Philip N.   Vol. 1: 15976
Winsor and Newton Award   Vol. 1: 5067
Winsor Prize Essay; Justin   Vol. 1: 2914
Winston Cup
   Daytona International Speedway   Vol. 1: 8542
   National Association for Stock Car Auto Racing (NASCAR)   Vol 1: 12902
Winston Founder's Award; Ellen B.   Vol. 1: 13822
Winter Award; George   Vol. 1: 4509
Winter-Klein; Fondation Aniuta   Vol. 2: 5492
WinterFest Spotlight Award   Vol. 1: 12513
Winzen Lifetime Achievement Award; AIAA Otto C.   Vol. 1: 2489
Wippman Scientific Research Award; Arthur and Edith   Vol. 1: 16234
Wire Association Annual Medal Awards   Vol. 1: 20338
Wisam Al-Muallim (Al-Tarbiya)   Vol. 2: 8799
Wisconsin Arts Board Fellowships   Vol. 1: 20340
Wise Award   Vol. 2: 2771
WISE Award for Engineering Achievement   Vol. 1: 20396
WISE Award for Scientific Achievement   Vol. 1: 20397
Wise Award; Louise Waterman   Vol. 1: 2735
Wise Award; Stephen S.   Vol. 1: 2736
WISE Lifetime Achievement Award   Vol. 1: 20398
Wise - Warren Susman Prize; Gene   Vol. 1: 4877
Wisely American Civil Engineer Award; William H.   Vol. 1: 4510
Wiseman Book Award; James R.   Vol. 1: 5228
Wiskirchen/CSC Jazz Award; Reverend George C.   Vol. 1: 13537
Wisniewski Young Psychiatrist Research Award; APA/   Vol. 1: 3624
Wissenschaftlicher Wettbewerb der ZFA   Vol. 2: 6917
Wister Award; Owen   Vol. 1: 20237
Witherspoon Memorial Chaplain's Award   Vol. 1: 11799
Wittenborn Memorial Award; George
   Art Libraries Society of North America   Vol. 1: 5299
   Art Libraries Society of North America   Vol 1: 5300
Wittkamper Peace Award; Will   Vol. 1: 8682
Wittmer Award; Lightner   Vol. 1: 3785
Witty Short Story Award; Paul A.   Vol. 1: 11198
WKI Award   Vol. 1: 9914
WMA National Service Award   Vol. 1: 20405
WMO Research Award for Young Scientists   Vol. 2: 11980
WMS Research Award   Vol. 1: 20290
WNZ Award   Vol. 1: 8436
Wohelo Order   Vol. 1: 6688
Wolf Award; C. R.   Vol. 1: 9971
Wolf Book Award in Race Relations; Anisfield -   Vol. 1: 7837

Wolf Chamber Music Award; Andrew   Vol. 1: 6293
Wolf-Fenton Award   Vol. 1: 9971
Wolf Foundation Prizes   Vol. 2: 7987
Wolf-Medaille; Hugo   Vol. 2: 834
Wolf Officiating Award; Julian   Vol. 1: 19522
Wolfe Award; Nero   Vol. 1: 20350
Wolfe - Best of Show - YN Exhibit Award; Charles H.   Vol. 1: 3268
Wolfe Medal of Honor; Catharine Lorillard   Vol. 1: 20348
Wolfe Medieval and Ancient - YN Exhibit Award; Charles H.   Vol. 1: 3269
Wolfe Memorial Trophy; Colonel Franklin C.   Vol. 1: 15775
Wolfe Society Literary Prize; Thomas   Vol. 1: 20354
Wolfensohn Award; James D.   Vol. 2: 3419
Wolff Lecture Award; Harold G.   Vol. 1: 903
Wolfman Scholarship Prize; Mary   Vol. 1: 13336
Wolfskehl Preis fur Exilliteratur; Karl
   Bavarian Academy of Fine Arts   Vol. 2: 6555
   Bavarian Academy of Fine Arts   Vol 2: 6555
Wolfson Foundation Literary Awards for History   Vol. 2: 4608
Wollaston Award; Charles   Vol. 2: 3865
Wollaston Medal   Vol. 2: 2929
Wolman Award; Abel
   American Public Works Association   Vol. 1: 3884
   Inter-American Association of Sanitary Engineering and Environmental Sciences   Vol 1: 10505
Wolman Award of Excellence; Abel   Vol. 1: 5033
Wolper Student Documentary Achievement Award; David L.   Vol. 1: 10911
Wolskel Industrial Chemistry Essay Award   Vol. 2: 603
Woltemade Cross for Bravery   Vol. 2: 10963
Woltemade Decoration for Bravery   Vol. 2: 10963
Woman FIDE Master   Vol. 2: 7230
Woman Grandmaster   Vol. 2: 7231
Woman International Master   Vol. 2: 7232
Woman Lawyer of the Year   Vol. 1: 20410
Woman of Achievement Award   Vol. 1: 13947
Woman of the Year
   American Legion Auxiliary   Vol. 1: 2807
   Federation of Fly Fishers   Vol 1: 9118
   International Federation of Women's Travel Organizations   Vol 1: 10973
   National Chamber of Commerce for Women   Vol 1: 13577
   La Sertoma International   Vol 1: 17198
   United States Department of Agriculture - Foreign Agricultural Service   Vol 1: 19082
   USA Track and Field   Vol 1: 19963
Woman of the Year Award
   Society for Women in Philosophy   Vol. 1: 17657
   Society of Philatelists and Numismatists   Vol 1: 17980
Woman of the Year in Finland   Vol. 2: 4752
Woman of the Year in Travel   Vol. 1: 18800
Woman Officer of the Year   Vol. 1: 10792
Woman's Journal British Fashion Award   Vol. 2: 4610
Women and Politics Prize   Vol. 2: 142
Women at Work Awards   Vol. 1: 20281
Women Helping Women Awards   Vol. 1: 5151
Women in Development Award   Vol. 1: 15873
Women in Film Festival   Vol. 1: 20383

Women in Film Foundation Award   Vol. 1: 15390
Women in the Arts Award   Vol. 1: 20403
Women in the Arts Crown Award   Vol. 1: 20403
Women of Conscience Award   Vol. 1: 13785
Women of Enterprise Awards   Vol. 1: 6202
Women of the Year   Vol. 1: 19523
Women's Action for Nuclear Disarmament Education Fund   Vol. 1: 20407
The Women's All Event Trophy   Vol. 1: 19524
Women's British Open Championship   Vol. 2: 10589
Women's Field Hockey Championship Trophy   Vol. 1: 6994
Women's Field Hockey Coach of the Year   Vol. 1: 6995
Women's Fragrance of the Year - Broad Introductions   Vol. 1: 9361
Women's Fragrance of the Year - Exclusive Distribution   Vol. 1: 9361
Women's Fragrance of the Year - Limited Distribution   Vol. 1: 9361
Women's Fragrance of the Year - Mass Introductions   Vol. 1: 9361
Women's National Book Association Award   Vol. 1: 20422
Women's National Championship Cup Finals   Vol. 2: 2777
Women's National Collegiate Awards   Vol. 1: 19671
Women's Open Cup (soccer)   Vol. 1: 19610
Women's Research Award   Vol. 1: 12917
Women's Sailing Championship - Nancy Leiter Clagett Tro phy; U.S. Junior   Vol. 1: 19542
Women's Sports Foundation Flo Hyman Award   Vol. 1: 20435
Women's Sports Foundation's Team Spirit Award   Vol. 1: 20436
Women's World Championship   Vol. 1: 6289
WONCA Foundation Award   Vol. 2: 7283
Wonder Woman Awards   Vol. 1: 20443
Wood Award   Vol. 1: 9334
Wood Award; Coke   Vol. 1: 20242
Wood Cup; A. D.   Vol. 2: 2540
Wood Design Award   Vol. 1: 2094
Wood Medal and Prize; A. B.   Vol. 2: 3056
Wood Memorial Exhibit Award - Best of Show; Howland   Vol. 1: 3270
Wood Memorial Trophy; W. C.   Vol. 1: 3114
Wood Prize
   Danish Timber Information Council   Vol. 2: 1922
   National Association of Norwegian Architects   Vol 2: 9908
Wood Prize; R. W.   Vol. 1: 15761
Woodall, and William Cartwright Holmes Postgraduate Award; Corbet and Henry   Vol. 2: 3331
Woodall Scholarship; Corbet and Henry   Vol. 2: 3331
Woodard Award; M. L.   Vol. 1: 9914
Woodbridge Award; Donald B.   Vol. 1: 13596
Woodbury Award in Raw Products Research; Charles G.   Vol. 1: 4146
Wooden Award; John R.
   Los Angeles Athletic Club   Vol. 1: 11945
   Naismith Memorial Basketball Hall of Fame   Vol 1: 12571
Wooden Most Valuable High School Player Award; John R.   Vol. 1: 11945
Wooden Spoon Award   Vol. 2: 2817
Woodford-Williams Prize   Vol. 2: 3970
Woodhead Medal; Sims   Vol. 2: 3175
Woodrow Award   Vol. 2: 2513
Woods Award; K. B.   Vol. 1: 18784

Woods Memorial Award; David F.   Vol. 1: 12108
Woodson Award; Carter G.   Vol. 1: 6332
Woodson Book Award; Carter G.   Vol. 1: 13721
Woodson Memorial Award; Grace   Vol. 1: 9964
Woodstock National Exhibition   Vol. 1: 20449
Woodward Award; Julian   Vol. 1: 870
Woodward - Fondiller Prize   Vol. 1: 7339
Woodworth Memorial Award   Vol. 1: 10137
Woody Award; Brice L.   Vol. 1: 11060
Woolbert Research Award; Charles H.   Vol. 1: 18315
Wooldridge Farm Livestock Research Fellowship   Vol. 2: 2087
Woolknit Design Awards   Vol. 1: 20453
Woollard Award; George P.   Vol. 1: 9567
Woolley and Beatrice Cannon Evans Biography Award; David   Vol. 1: 12467
Woolley Award; Davis C.   Vol. 1: 9935
Woolmark Awards   Vol. 1: 20451
WORDS+ ISAAC Consumer Lecture Award   Vol. 1: 11232
WORDS+ ISAAC Consumer Scholarship Award   Vol. 1: 11233
Work-in-Progress Grants   Vol. 1: 17813
Worked 100 Nations Award   Vol. 1: 20541
Worked All Zones Award   Vol. 1: 8437
Worker Equity Business Partnerships Award   Vol. 1: 1169
Workers' Education Fellowships   Vol. 2: 11807
Workhorses of the Fleet Award   Vol. 1: 19719
Working Group Recognition Award   Vol. 1: 10320
Working Hunter Ponies Awards   Vol. 2: 2503
Workplace Diversity Professional Development Award   Vol. 1: 10855
World Artifex Society Award   Vol. 1: 20468
World Association for Celebrating Year 2000 Awards   Vol. 2: 4616
World Book - ALA Goal Awards   Vol. 1: 2825
World Book Award   Vol. 1: 7381
World Book Encyclopedia - ALA Goal Awards; J. Morris Jones and Bailey K. Howard   Vol. 1: 2825
World Book Prize of Mountain Pictures   Vol. 2: 6481
World Book Prize of Underwater Pictures   Vol. 2: 6483
World Boxing Council Awards   Vol. 2: 9304
World Challenge   Vol. 1: 18419
World Champion Trolling Fisherline Bucket   Vol. 2: 9910
World Championship   Vol. 2: 9509
World Championships   Vol. 2: 11801
World Championships in Ballroom and Latin Dancing   Vol. 2: 4624
World Clean Air Congress Award   Vol. 2: 3496
World Council of Young Men's Service Clubs Awards   Vol. 2: 9854
World Development Awards for Business Challenger Society for Marine Science   Vol. 2: 2577
   Worldaware   Vol 2: 4635
World Development Awards for Business.   Vol. 2: 4635
World Federation of Jewish Fighters, Partisans, and Camp Inmates Award   Vol. 2: 7991
World Festival of Mountain Pictures   Vol. 2: 6481
World Festival of Underwater Pictures   Vol. 2: 6483

World Figure Skating Hall of Fame   Vol. 1: 19355
World Film Festival of ORL Scientific Films and Videotapes   Vol. 2: 1187
World First Postal Automatization Award   Vol. 2: 1386
World Food Day Award   Vol. 2: 7569
World Food Policy Award   Vol. 1: 198
The World Food Prize   Vol. 1: 20489
World Footbag Championships   Vol. 1: 20491
World Games Competitions   Vol. 2: 9541
World Golf Hall of Fame   Vol. 1: 16476
World Heavyweight Champions   Vol. 1: 16847
World Horseshoe Pitching Champions   Vol. 1: 14192
World Humour Award   Vol. 1: 20461
World Hunger Media Awards   Vol. 1: 20493
World Karting Hall of Fame   Vol. 1: 11112
World Marathon Cup   Vol. 2: 9315
World Methodist Peace Award   Vol. 1: 20504
World Model Awards   Vol. 1: 20512
World Motorcycle Championships   Vol. 2: 11812
World Music Masters   Vol. 2: 5234
World of Poetry's Free Poetry Contest   Vol. 1: 20516
World of Wedding Photography Awards of Excellence   Vol. 1: 20174
World Open Three Cushion Billiard Championships   Vol. 1: 19045
World Organization of Jewish Deaf Competitions   Vol. 2: 7993
World Packaging Competition   Vol. 2: 6490
World Peace Academy Diploma   Vol. 1: 10720
World Peace Council Awards   Vol. 2: 4767
World Phosphate Institute Awards   Vol. 2: 9324
World Piano Competition   Vol. 1: 3164
World Player of the Year   Vol. 1: 9648
World Ploughing Championship Awards   Vol. 2: 4626
World Press Photo Children's Award   Vol. 2: 9697
World Press Photo Contest   Vol. 2: 9697
World Press Photo of the Year   Vol. 2: 9697
World Record for Game Fish Award   Vol. 1: 11007
World Series   Vol. 1: 8033
World Series Most Valuable Player   Vol. 1: 8033
World SF President's Award   Vol. 2: 6495
World Skeet Shooting Championships   Vol. 1: 14724
World Trophy   Vol. 1: 399
World Unicycling Championships   Vol. 1: 11377
World Union of Karatedo Organizations Championships   Vol. 2: 6497
World Wheelchair Weightlifting Championships   Vol. 1: 14997
World Wide Video Festival   Vol. 2: 9670
World Youth Sailing Championship   Vol. 1: 19532
Worldaware Business Awards   Vol. 2: 4635
Worlddidac Award   Vol. 2: 11984
WORLDFEST - Charleston International Film Festival   Vol. 1: 20538
WORLDFEST - Houston International Film and Video Festival   Vol. 1: 20539
World's Best Short Short Story Contest   Vol. 1: 9270
World's Champion Cheese Maker   Vol. 1: 20343
World's Paper Trade Review Medal   Vol. 2: 2468
Worldstars for Packaging   Vol. 2: 6490
Worldwide Awards Competition   Vol. 1: 8648
Worldwide Competition for Young Sociologists   Vol. 2: 11277
Worrall Public Official Award; Jay   Vol. 1: 15577
Worsaae Medal; J.J.A.   Vol. 2: 1978
Worshipful Company of Dyers Awards for Woodwind/Brass   Vol. 2: 4117
Worshipful Company of Dyers Research Medal   Vol. 2: 4438
Worshipful Company of Feltmakers Research Medal   Vol. 2: 4439
Worshipful Company of Ironmongers Jubilee Award   Vol. 2: 3076
Worst-Dressed Women   Vol. 1: 12474
Worst Finance Minister of the Year   Vol. 2: 2817
Wortelmann-Preis der Stadt Bochum fur das Amateur-Figurentheater; Fritz   Vol. 2: 6676
Wortelmann Preis of the City of Bochum for Amateur Puppetry; Fritz   Vol. 2: 6676
Worth Prize; John Edward   Vol. 2: 4229
Worth Prize; R. H.   Vol. 2: 2930
Worthingham Fellows of APTA; Catherine   Vol. 1: 3493
Worthington Medal; Henry R.   Vol. 1: 4715
Worthington Technical Award; Henry R.   Vol. 2: 8478
Worts Staff Service Award; Grace   Vol. 1: 7064
Woursell Prize; Abraham   Vol. 2: 799
WPX Award   Vol. 1: 8438
WPX Award of Excellence   Vol. 1: 8439
WPX Honor Roll   Vol. 1: 8440
Wran Award for Excellence; Nevill   Vol. 2: 551
Wrangler   Vol. 1: 13838
WRc Travel Fellowship   Vol. 1: 20165
WRCLA/AIA Cedar Design "Naturally" Awards   Vol. 1: 2545
Wren Prize; Dr. Peter   Vol. 2: 3104
Wrench Scholarship; Jesse   Vol. 1: 12366
Wrenn Award for A Humanitarian and Caring Person; Gilbert and Kathleen   Vol. 1: 1887
Wrestling Coach of the Year   Vol. 1: 6996
Wright Achievement Award; Orville   Vol. 1: 15788
Wright Al Service Award; Bob   Vol. 1: 6091
Wright Award; Captain Donald T.   Vol. 1: 16340
Wright Award; E. Whitman   Vol. 1: 7179
Wright Award; Elizur   Vol. 1: 3964
Wright Award in Olfactory Research; R. H.   Vol. 1: 17284
Wright Award; Mary Tolle   Vol. 1: 17267
Wright Award; Mickey   Vol. 1: 9649
Wright Award of Distinction; Irving S.   Vol. 1: 2023
Wright Award; Sewall   Vol. 1: 4726
Wright Award; William   Vol. 1: 575
Wright Award; Williams -   Vol. 1: 7858
Wright Brothers Lecture   Vol. 1: 2511
Wright Brothers Medal   Vol. 1: 17780
Wright Brothers Memorial Trophy   Vol. 1: 12726
Wright Creativity Award; Frank Lloyd   Vol. 1: 8455
Wright Cup; John Howie   Vol. 1: 12012
Wright Honorary Award; Asa   Vol. 2: 7467
Wright Mariological Award; Cardinal John J.   Vol. 1: 12093
Wright Memorial Award; Katharine   Vol. 1: 12727
Wright Memorial Exhibit Award; B.P.   Vol. 1: 3271
Wright Memorial Lecture; Wilbur and Orville   Vol. 2: 3915
Wright Memorial Trophy; Lee O.   Vol. 1: 14645
Wright National Youth Leadership Award; NASAR Bob   Vol. 1: 12895
Wright Prize for Poetry; Wesley Michel   Vol. 2: 695
Write For Radio Competition   Vol. 1: 298
Writer's Contest   Vol. 1: 18731
Writers Contest   Vol. 1: 9133
Writers Corner Hall of Fame   Vol. 1: 19392
Writer's Digest Writing Competition   Vol. 1: 20550
Writers' Fellowships   Vol. 2: 155
Writers Guild of Alberta Awards for Excellence   Vol. 1: 20555
Writer's Trophy   Vol. 2: 2042
Writing Awards   Vol. 1: 269
Writing Competition on the Teaching of Buddhism for Children   Vol. 2: 12029
Wroclaw International Triennale of Drawing   Vol. 2: 10218
WSAVA International Prize for Scientific Achievement   Vol. 2: 4630
WSAVA International Prize for Service to the Profession   Vol. 2: 4631
WSF - Budget CAR Coaches Award (Coaches Advisory Roundtable)   Vol. 1: 20437
WTS National Member of the Year   Vol. 1: 20440
WTS National Woman of the Year   Vol. 1: 20441
Wuerdigungspreise des BMUK   Vol. 2: 765
Wulff Award; Lee   Vol. 1: 9119
Wunderman Award; Irving   Vol. 1: 8652
Wurdigungspreis   Vol. 2: 862
Wurdigungspreis des Landes Tirol fur Literatur, Musik etc.   Vol. 2: 732
Wurlitzer Collegiate Artist Competition; MTNA-   Vol. 1: 12524
Wurzweiler School of Social Work Community Service Award   Vol. 1: 20582
Wurzweiler School of Social Work Distinguished Professor Award   Vol. 1: 20583
WVF Rehabilitation Prize   Vol. 2: 6499
Wyeth Award in Clinical Microbiology   Vol. 1: 4202
Wyeth-Ayerst Laboratories New Investigators Research Grants; Oncology Nursing Foundation/   Vol. 1: 15650
Wyeth-Ayerst Outstanding Chapter Awards   Vol. 1: 677
Wyeth-Ayerst Visiting Professor Award   Vol. 1: 17398
Wyld Propulsion Award; James H.   Vol. 1: 2512
Wyman Memorial Award   Vol. 1: 12937
Wyman Memorial Award; L. L.   Vol. 1: 6087
Wyman Memorial Trophy; Frank L.   Vol. 1: 14645
Xavier Medal; St. Francis   Vol. 1: 20566
Xenopol Prize; Alexandru   Vol. 2: 10392
Xirgu Radio Drama Prize; Margarita   Vol. 2: 11325
Xolocotzi; Premio Efraim Hernandez   Vol. 2: 8956
Yachtsman of the Year Award   Vol. 2: 4640
Yaffe; Pras Leib   Vol. 2: 7973
Yaffe Prize; Leib   Vol. 2: 7973
Yale Series of Younger Poets   Vol. 1: 20568
YALSA/Econo-Clad Award for Outstanding Young Adult Reading or Literature Program   Vol. 1: 2960
Yamagiwa-Yoshida Memorial International Cancer Study Grants   Vol. 2: 11863
Yamaha High School Auditions; MTNA-   Vol. 1: 12525

Yamaha International Brass Ensemble Competition   Vol. 1: 18528
Yamaha Prize   Vol. 1: 7840
Yamamoto Award; Shugoro   Vol. 2: 8745
Yancey Memorial Award   Vol. 1: 10714
Yanez First Novel Prize; Agustin   Vol. 2: 8981
Yanez para Primera Novela; Premio Agustin   Vol. 2: 8981
Yankee Awards   Vol. 1: 20574
Yant Award; William B.   Vol. 1: 2438
Yarnell Award; Bruce   Vol. 1: 20079
YASD/*School Library Journal* Author Achievement Award   Vol. 1: 2958
YASD/*School Library Journal* Young Adult Author Award   Vol. 1: 2958
Yaxley Memorial Scholarship; Don   Vol. 1: 11369
Ybl Miklos Dij   Vol. 2: 7392
Ybl Prize for Architecture; Miklos   Vol. 2: 7392
Yeadon Memorial Trophy; T. M.   Vol. 2: 2076
Year End Series New Play Festival   Vol. 1: 15514
Yearbook Dedication Award   Vol. 1: 653
Yeats Club Open Poetry Competition   Vol. 2: 4643
Yenko Memorial Award; Don   Vol. 1: 10823
Yennenga Stallion Trophy   Vol. 2: 1541
Yerkes Award   Vol. 1: 3748
Yeshiva University Award   Vol. 1: 20584
Yeshiva University Citation   Vol. 1: 20585
Yeshiva University Distinguished Service Award   Vol. 1: 20586
Yeshiva University Heritage Award   Vol. 1: 20587
Yeshiva University Sephardic Heritage Award   Vol. 1: 20588
YMCA Men, Women and Youth of the Year   Vol. 1: 20612
Yoder-Heneman Human Resource Creative Application Awards   Vol. 1: 17490
Yoder-Heneman Human Resource Management Research Award   Vol. 1: 17491
Yoder-Heneman Personnel Creative Application Award   Vol. 1: 17490
Yoder-Heneman Personnel Creative Application Awards   Vol. 1: 17490
Yoder-Heneman Personnel Research Award   Vol. 1: 17491
Yoder-Heneman Personnel Research Award   Vol. 1: 17491
Yomiuiri International Cooperation Prize   Vol. 2: 8781
Yomiuri Bungaku Sho   Vol. 2: 8795
Yomiuri Education Prize   Vol. 2: 8792
Yomiuri Human Document Prize   Vol. 2: 8793
Yomiuri Human Document Taisho   Vol. 2: 8793
Yomiuri International Cartoon Contest   Vol. 2: 8794
Yomiuri Kokusai Kyoryoku Sho   Vol. 2: 8781
Yomiuri Kokusai Manga Taisho   Vol. 2: 8794
Yomiuri Literature Prize   Vol. 2: 8795
Yonge Award; Sir Charles Maurice   Vol. 2: 3621
Yorkshire & Humberside Arts Young Composers Awards   Vol. 2: 3029
Yorkshire Arts Young Composers Competition   Vol. 2: 3029
Yorkshire Post Art and Music Award   Vol. 2: 4645
Yorkshire Post Best First Work Award   Vol. 2: 4646
Yorkshire Post Book of the Year Award   Vol. 2: 4647
Yorzyk Memorial Award; David   Vol. 1: 19443
Yoshikawa Eiji Bungaku Sho   Vol. 2: 8693

Yoshikawa Eiji Literary Prize   Vol. 2: 8693
Yoshikawa Elji Prize   Vol. 2: 8694
Yoshino Award; Sakuzo   Vol. 2: 8522
Yost Professional Service Award; Charles Peter   Vol. 1: 16985
You; Prix Emmanuel-Andre   Vol. 2: 6144
Youden Award in Interlaboratory Testing; W. J.   Vol. 1: 4865
Young Achievers Award   Vol. 1: 13786
Young Actors Award   Vol. 2: 221
Young Adult Canadian Book Award   Vol. 1: 7001
Young Agricultural Engineer of the Year Award   Vol. 1: 7152
Young Alumni Award   Vol. 1: 19859
Young Alumni Merit Award   Vol. 1: 7396
Young Alumni Service Citations   Vol. 1: 19773
Young America Photography Contest   Vol. 1: 15932
Young American Medal for Bravery   Vol. 1: 19252
Young American Medal for Service   Vol. 1: 19253
Young American Patriotic Art Competition   Vol. 1: 20007
Young Architects Citation   Vol. 1: 2546
Young Architects Forum   Vol. 1: 5231
Young Artist Award   Vol. 1: 19985
Young Artist Competition   Vol. 1: 9338
Young Artists and Distinguished Artists Award Auditions   Vol. 1: 5316
Young Artists Auditions - Awards for Excellence   Vol. 1: 15194
Young Artists Competition   Vol. 1: 10859
Young Artists' Competition   Vol. 1: 17054
Young Artists' Competition of Kol Israel   Vol. 2: 7918
Young Artists Competitions   Vol. 1: 16071
Young Artists Debut Award   Vol. 1: 5310
Young Artists Prize   Vol. 2: 10404
Young Australians Best Book Award   Vol. 2: 719
Young Author Award   Vol. 1: 856
Young Author Prize   Vol. 2: 820
Young Award; Cy   Vol. 1: 6284
Young Award; Hugh Hampton   Vol. 1: 4957
Young Business Writer   Vol. 2: 2890
Young Businessman of the Year Award   Vol. 2: 2957
Young Canadian Mozart Singers' Competition   Vol. 1: 7077
Young Chemists Award   Vol. 2: 1572
Young Cinema Festival   Vol. 2: 8768
Young Composers Awards   Vol. 1: 14100
Young Composers' Competition   Vol. 1: 13021
Young Concert Artists International Auditions   Vol. 1: 20603
Young Concert Artists Trust Award   Vol. 2: 4649
Young Consultants Award   Vol. 1: 10465
Young Contributor's Award   Vol. 1: 1208
Young Creators Literary Prize   Vol. 2: 1769
Young Crop Scientist Award   Vol. 1: 8473
Young Deaf Achiever   Vol. 2: 2732
Young Engineer Achievement Award   Vol. 1: 6846
Young Engineer Award   Vol. 1: 17581
Young Engineer Award; Walter Fee   Vol. 1: 10321
Young Engineer of the Year
   Institution of Electrical Engineers   Vol. 2: 3309
   Institution of Engineers, Sri Lanka   Vol 2: 11410
Young Engineer of the Year Award   Vol. 1: 14812
Young Engineers for Britain   Vol. 2: 2771

Young Engineers Speaking Competition   Vol. 2: 496
Young Enterprise Award   Vol. 2: 3310
Young Entrepreneur Award   Vol. 1: 19604
Young FAI Artists Contest   Vol. 2: 5169
Young Federal Health Care Administrator Award   Vol. 1: 5900
Young Filmmakers Festival   Vol. 1: 15524
Young Forester Leadership Award   Vol. 1: 17691
Young Government Civil Engineer of the Year Award   Vol. 1: 4511
Young Handler Award   Vol. 2: 3465
Young Healthcare Executive of the Year; Robert S. Hudgens Memorial Award -   Vol. 1: 1663
Young Hoosier Book Award   Vol. 1: 5536
Young Hoosier Picture Book Award   Vol. 1: 5537
Young Hospital Administrator of the Year; Robert S. Hudgens Memorial Award -   Vol. 1: 1663
Young - Hunter Memorial Award; John   Vol. 1: 5068
Young Investigator Award
   American Association of Electrodiagnostic Medicine   Vol. 1: 992
   American College of Clinical Pharmacology   Vol 1: 1627
   American Physiological Society   Vol 1: 3501
   Japanese Society of Hematology   Vol 2: 8657
   Squibb Canada   Vol 1: 18437
   World Organization of Gastroenterology   Vol 2: 7169
Young Investigator Award in Research   Vol. 1: 17552
Young Investigator Award of the ASCPT   Vol. 1: 4059
Young Investigator Award - Vector Laboratories   Vol. 1: 4212
Young Investigator Awards
   Cancer Research Foundation   Vol. 1: 7280
   National Alliance for Research on Schizophrenia and Depression   Vol 1: 12770
   North American Society of Pacing and Electrophysiology   Vol 1: 15463
Young Investigator Awards in Cardiovascular Integrated Physiology; Melvin L. Marcus   Vol. 1: 2242
Young Investigator Awards of the Dr. C. and F. Demuth Medical Foundation   Vol. 2: 1976
Young Investigator Matching Grants; NFID -   Vol. 1: 14045
Young Investigator Prizes in Cardiopulmonary and Critical Care; Cournand and Comroe   Vol. 1: 2243
Young Investigator Prizes in Thrombosis   Vol. 1: 2244
Young Investigators Award
   American College of Angiology   Vol. 1: 1605
   International Association for Dental Research   Vol 1: 10626
Young Investigators' Prizes   Vol. 1: 4727
Young Jersey Dairyman Award   Vol. 1: 2720
Young, Jr., Citation; Whitney M.   Vol. 1: 2547
Young, Jr. Memorial Football Classic Award; Whitney M.   Vol. 1: 15310
Young Leadership Awards   Vol. 1: 8367
Young Lighters of the Year   Vol. 2: 2599
Young Logistician Award   Vol. 1: 17874
Young Medal and Prize; Thomas   Vol. 2: 3198
Young Member Achievement Award   Vol. 1: 6017

Young Member Outstanding Service Award   Vol. 1: 17976
Young Musicians and Distinguished Artists Award Auditions   Vol. 1: 5316
Young NDT Professional Award   Vol. 1: 4225
Young Observer Fiction Prize   Vol. 2: 3728
Young Observer Teenage Fiction Prize   Vol. 2: 3728
Young Oncologist Essay Awards   Vol. 1: 3901
Young Oncologist Travel Grants   Vol. 1: 3902
Young Oration; Thomas   Vol. 2: 3198
Young Ornithologist of the Year   Vol. 2: 4651
Young People and Adult Supervisors Award   Vol. 2: 10448
Young People's Film and Video Festival   Vol. 1: 15524
Young Performers Award   Vol. 2: 197
Young Performers' Competition   Vol. 1: 13022
Young Performers Hall of Fame   Vol. 1: 17211
Young Pianists Yearly Award   Vol. 2: 2843
Young Playwrights Festival   Vol. 1: 20618
Young Poets Prize   Vol. 2: 6104
Young Psychopharmacologist Award   Vol. 1: 3718
Young Publish-a-Book   Vol. 1: 16665
Young Publisher Award   Vol. 1: 5713
Young Readers' Choice Award   Vol. 1: 15886
Young Researcher Award
  Association for Educational Communications and Technology and the ECT Foundation   Vol. 1: 5516
  Association of Black Nursing Faculty in Higher Education   Vol 1: 5714
Young Sailor of the Year Award   Vol. 2: 4641
Young Scholars Competition   Vol. 1: 6396
Young Scientist Award
  American Association for Crystal Growth   Vol. 1: 856
  European Association for the Science of Air Pollution   Vol 2: 2822
  EUROTOX   Vol 2: 11709
  Genetics Society of Canada   Vol 1: 9539
  International Society for Neurochemistry   Vol 2: 1968
Young Scientist Award (Donath Medal)   Vol. 1: 9568
Young Scientist Award in Noninvasive Cardiovascular Dynamics   Vol. 2: 10789
Young Scientist or Grower of the Year Award   Vol. 2: 3665
Young Scientist's Award   Vol. 1: 7161
Young Scientists for Rainforests   Vol. 2: 2678
Young Scientists Publication Awards   Vol. 2: 6720
Young Scientists Travel Awards   Vol. 2: 6721
Young Sculptor Awards Competition   Vol. 1: 14715
Young Service Award; Carl Haven   Vol. 1: 2776
Young Soloists Competition   Vol. 1: 14878
Young Speaker of the Year   Vol. 2: 2792
Young Teacher's Award   Vol. 2: 10449
Young Technician of the Year   Vol. 2: 4510
Young Teens Children's Literature Award   Vol. 1: 7489
Young Trophy; Eric   Vol. 2: 3740
Young Trophy; John L.   Vol. 1: 16214
Young Wildlife Photographer of the Year Competition   Vol. 2: 2163
Young Women's Christian Association Council of Zimbabwe Competitions   Vol. 2: 12211
Young Writers' Award   Vol. 1: 5323
Younger Federal Lawyer Award   Vol. 1: 9071
Younger Member Group Award   Vol. 1: 4512
Younger Members' Premiums Awards   Vol. 2: 3311
Youngman Award; Bruce   Vol. 2: 3354

Youth Achievement Award   Vol. 1: 11849
Youth Athletics Outstanding Association Award   Vol. 1: 19941
Youth Athletics Outstanding Individual Award   Vol. 1: 19957
Youth Award
  American Bashkir Curly Registry   Vol. 1: 1331
  France - Ministry of Youth and Sports   Vol 2: 5249
Youth Gardening Award   Vol. 1: 9502
Youth in the Community Journalism Award   Vol. 1: 11618
Youth Leader   Vol. 1: 16779
Youth Leader of the Year   Vol. 1: 20601
Youth Leadership Award   Vol. 1: 20220
Youth Medallion   Vol. 1: 9139
Youth of the Americas   Vol. 2: 1781
Youth of the Year   Vol. 1: 15966
Youth of the Year Award   Vol. 1: 7748
Youth Softball Volunteer of the Year   Vol. 1: 460
Youth Studies Prize   Vol. 2: 11173
Youth Theatre Director of the Year Award   Vol. 1: 781
Ysgoloriaeth W. Towyn Roberts   Vol. 2: 12186
YTV Achievement Awards   Vol. 1: 20622
Yugoslav Documentary and Short Films Festival Awards   Vol. 2: 10701
Yugoslav PEN Club Award   Vol. 2: 10726
Yukawa Prize   Vol. 2: 8289
Yunus Nadi Gift   Vol. 2: 12049
Za Zaslugi dla Obronnosci Kraju   Vol. 2: 10112
Zabel Award; Morton Dauwen   Vol. 1: 521
Zabrocki Medal; Prof. Ludwik   Vol. 2: 10082
Zabrockiego; Medal im. prof. Ludwika   Vol. 2: 10082
Zaccarelli Scholarship Award; Brother Herman E.   Vol. 1: 10745
Zachary Auditions   Vol. 1: 20630
Zagreb World Festival of Animated Films   Vol. 2: 1816
Zaheer Medal; S. H.   Vol. 2: 7679
ZAiKS Awards for Translators   Vol. 2: 10208
ZAiKS Literary Award for Translation's Output   Vol. 2: 10208
Zakon Lectureship; Samuel J.   Vol. 1: 9940
Zakon Prize; Samuel J.   Vol. 1: 9941
Zambrano National Prize for Inventive Technology; Luis   Vol. 2: 12130
Zamenhof Award for International Understanding   Vol. 2: 9679
Zanfi Prize; Mario   Vol. 2: 8169
Zangerle Award   Vol. 1: 10675
Zaragosa Jewel; Ignacio   Vol. 2: 9002
Zaragosa; Presea Ignacio   Vol. 2: 9002
Zarco Prize; Francisco   Vol. 2: 9093
Zarem Award for Distinguished Achievement; AIAA Abe M.   Vol. 1: 2443
Zaremba Award   Vol. 2: 10159
Zaremby; Nagrody im. S.   Vol. 2: 10159
Zarky Humanitarian Award; Norma   Vol. 1: 20386
Zarrow Award for Young Readers' Literature; Anne V.   Vol. 1: 18836
Zarwell Award; Gerald   Vol. 1: 15337
Zasluzony Dzialacz Kultury   Vol. 2: 10089
Zauberfloten-Medaille   Vol. 2: 830
Zawadzki Award; Prof. Bohdan   Vol. 2: 10175
Zawadzkiego; Nagroda im. Bohdana   Vol. 2: 10175
Zawidzki Medal; Jan   Vol. 2: 10139
Zazuete; Premio Alejandro   Vol. 2: 9016
Zeigler Distinguished Lecturer; Earle F.   Vol. 1: 15451
Zeisler Award   Vol. 1: 18683

Zeiss Research Award; Hawk Mountain -   Vol. 1: 9839
Zeitlin-Ver Brugge Prize   Vol. 1: 9952
Zejszner Prize; Ludwik   Vol. 2: 10151
Zejsznera; Nagroda im. Ludwika   Vol. 2: 10151
Zeldovich Gold Medal   Vol. 1: 8024
Zeldovich Medals   Vol. 2: 5068
Zellen Golden Quill Award; WBW Gosta   Vol. 1: 20478
Zelter Medal   Vol. 2: 6746
Zeneca Pharmaceuticals/Komen Foundation Excellence in Breast Cancer Education Award; ONS/   Vol. 1: 15669
Zenger Freedom of Information Award; John Peter   Vol. 1: 19734
Zenger Media Award; NYSBA John Peter   Vol. 1: 15283
Zerbe Award; Farran   Vol. 1: 3272
Zerbe Prize; Carl   Vol. 2: 6862
Zerby Outstanding Student (Electrical Engineering) Award; Alton B.   Vol. 1: 9009
Zerex Saab Pro Series   Vol. 1: 11110
Zeta Phi Eta Award   Vol. 1: 18316
Zeta Phi Eta - Winifred Ward Prize   Vol. 1: 782
Zeta Phi Eta Winifred Ward Prize for Outstanding New Children's Theatre Company   Vol. 1: 782
Zibetska priset   Vol. 2: 11612
Ziegler-Preis; Karl-   Vol. 2: 6794
Ziliani; Concorso Internazionale per Voci Verdiane Alessandro e Maria   Vol. 2: 8293
Zilveren Anjers   Vol. 2: 9576
Zilveren CJP   Vol. 2: 9422
Zimbabwe Teachers Association Awards   Vol. 2: 12225
Zimmerman Award; Margaret H.   Vol. 1: 9479
Zimmerman Founder's Award; O. T.   Vol. 1: 988
Zinc Castings 86   Vol. 2: 4654
Zinn Memorial Awards; Captain Ron   Vol. 1: 19964
Zipernowsky Dij   Vol. 2: 7342
Zipernowsky Prize   Vol. 2: 7342
Ziring Award for Distinguished Services; Mr. and Mrs. Alex   Vol. 1: 5220
Ziskind-Somerfeld Research Award   Vol. 1: 17793
Zlatarov Prize; Professor Dr. Asen   Vol. 2: 1513
Zlatarski Prize; Professor Vasil   Vol. 2: 1513
Zlatko Grgic Award   Vol. 2: 1816
Zlatnata Rakla   Vol. 2: 1518
Zlota Odznaka   Vol. 2: 10146
Zlote Lwy Gdanskie   Vol. 2: 10144
Zneimer Memorial Award; Leonard   Vol. 1: 3194
Zola - Raoul Gain; Prix du Roman Emil   Vol. 2: 6279
Zollman Award; Charles C.   Vol. 1: 16376
Zonta Amelia Earhart Fellowship Awards   Vol. 1: 20644
Zoo Animal Welfare Award   Vol. 2: 4572
Zoological Science Award   Vol. 2: 8797
Zorkoczy Medal; Samu Z.   Vol. 2: 7362
Zornska priset   Vol. 2: 11613
Zsigmondy Medal; Vilmos   Vol. 2: 7363
Zubin Award; Joseph   Vol. 1: 3840
Zue Memorial Award; Dick   Vol. 1: 19596
Zuloaga; Premio Daniel   Vol. 2: 11289
Zumbo Cub Reporter Award; New York Press Club Nellie Bly/Thomas D.   Vol. 1: 15257
Zvorikine; Fondation Nicolas   Vol. 2: 5640
Zweig Prize; Samuel   Vol. 1: 18601
Zwickert; Prix Charles   Vol. 2: 5042
Zworykin Premium; Dr. V. K.   Vol. 2: 3312

REF AS 8:A9 1995/96 v. 2

REF AS 8:A9 1995/96 v. 2